Federal Estate & Gift Taxes

Code & Regulations

Including Related Income Tax Provisions

As of March 1, 2023

Wolters Kluwer Editorial Staff Publication

Wolters Kluwer

Wolters Kluwer Editorial Staff Publication

Production Coordinator .... Govardhan L

Editors .... Alicia Ernst, Karen Notaro

ISBN: 978-0-8080-5926-4

2700 Lake Cook Road
Riverwoods, IL 60015
800 344 3734
CCHCPELink.com

Printed in the United States of America

Preface

This edition of *Federal Estate & Gift Taxes—Code & Regulations* reproduces, in Code section order, the full text of the estate, gift, and generation-skipping transfer (GST) tax provisions of the Internal Revenue Code and the corresponding official regulations, as of March 1, 2023. In addition to reproducing the Code and regulation sections of Subchapter J (governing the income taxation of estates, trusts, beneficiaries, and decedents), this edition provides coverage of income tax Code and regulation sections that closely relate to estate and gift taxes. Selected procedural Code sections and corresponding regulations are also reproduced.

Final and temporary regulations appear in Code section order. The income tax regulations relating to estates and trusts are designated as Part 1 of Title 26 of the Code of Federal Regulations, the estate tax regulations are designated as Part 20, the gift tax regulations as Part 25, the GST tax regulations as Part 26, and the procedure and administration regulations as Part 301. The proposed regulations complete the regulatory coverage and are preceded by a table of contents to aid the user in locating a particular proposal.

The unified transfer tax rates and the income tax rates applicable to estates and trusts are presented in tabular form for quick reference. Combined Code and regulation topical indexes make it possible to approach the contents by subject.

This edition reflects the Internal Revenue Code and federal tax regulations, as of March 1, 2023.

For more information on federal estate, gift, and GST taxes, see CCH© AnswerConnect, CCH's online research product. For more information on CCH© AnswerConnect, call 800-344-3734.

March 2023

Table of Contents

ESTATE AND GIFT TAXES

Legislative Changes

Changes to the transfer tax system that had been enacted by the Economic Growth and Tax Relief Reconciliation Act of 2001 (P.L. 107-16) (2001 Act) and the Tax Relief, Unemployment Insurance Reauthorization, and Job Creation Act of 2010 (P.L. 111-312) (2010 Act) were made permanent by the American Taxpayer Relief Act of 2012 (P.L. 112-240) (2012 Act). In addition, the 2012 Act increased the maximum transfer tax rate to 40 percent, rather than 35 percent as it had been under the 2010 Act. The Tax Cuts and Jobs Act (P.L. 115-97) (TCJA) made further changes to the transfer tax law by doubling the basic exclusion amount for purposes of federal estate and gift taxes and the exemption amount for purposes of the generation-skipping transfer (GST) tax, for the estates of decedents dying and gifts and generation-skipping transfers made after 2017 and before 2026.

Computation of Taxes

Estate Taxes. Estate taxes for decedents dying after 1976 are computed by applying the unified transfer tax rate schedule (with a maximum rate of 40 percent for decedents dying after December 31, 2012) to the aggregate of cumulative lifetime transfers and transfers at death and subtracting the gift taxes payable on the lifetime transfers.

Gift Taxes. Gift taxes for gifts made after 1976 are computed by applying the unified transfer tax rate schedule (with a maximum rate of 40 percent for decedents dying after December 31, 2012) to cumulative lifetime taxable transfers and subtracting the taxes paid for prior taxable periods.

Generation-Skipping Transfer (GST) Taxes. GST taxes are computed by multiplying the taxable amount of a taxable distribution, taxable termination, or direct skip by the applicable rate. For generation-skipping transfers made in years other than 2010, the applicable rate is the product of the maximum federal estate tax rate (40 percent for decedents dying after December 31, 2012) and the inclusion ratio with respect to the transfer.

Applicable Credit Amount

The 2010 Act increased the estate tax exclusion amount to $5 million for decedents dying after December 31, 2009, and increased the gift tax applicable exclusion amount for taxable gifts made after December 31, 2010, to $5 million. Beginning in 2012, these amounts are adjusted for inflation. The TCJA doubled the basic exclusion amount for purposes of federal estate and gift taxes from $5 million to $10 million, before adjustment for inflation, for the estates of decdents dying and gifts made after 2017 and before 2026. The $10 million amount is adjusted annually for inflation in the case of any decedent dying in a calendar year after 2017 using the Chained Consumer Price Index for All Urban Consumers (C-CPI-U) in the cost-of-living adjustment.

Estate Tax Applicable Credit Amount

Year	*Applicable Credit Amount*	*Applicable Exclusion Amount*
1987 through 1997	$192,800	$600,000
1998	202,050	625,000
1999	211,300	650,000
2000 and 2001	220,550	675,000
2002 and 2003	345,800	1,000,000
2004 and 2005	555,800	1,500,000

Year	*Applicable Credit Amount*	*Applicable Exclusion Amount*
2006 through 2008	780,800	2,000,000
2009	1,455,800	3,500,000
2010[1]	1,730,800	5,000,000
2011[2]	1,730,800	5,000,000
2012[3]	1,772,800	5,120,000
2013	2,045,800	5,250,000
2014	2,081,800	5,340,000
2015	2,117,800	5,430,000
2016	2,125,800	5,450,000
2017	2,141,800	5,490,000
2018	4,417,800	11,180,000
2019	4,505,800	11,400,000
2020	4,577,800	11,580,000
2021	4,625,800	11,700,000
2022	4,769,800	12,060,000
2023	5,113,800	12,920,000

Gift Tax Applicable Credit Amount

Year	*Applicable Credit Amount*	*Applicable Exclusion Amount*
1987 through 1997	$192,800	$600,000
1998	202,050	625,000
1999	211,300	650,000
2000 and 2001	220,550	675,000
2001 through 2009	345,800	1,000,000
2010[4]	330,800	1,000,000
2011	1,730,800	5,000,000
2012[5]	1,772,800	5,120,000
2013	2,045,800	5,250,000
2014	2,081,800	5,340,000
2015	2,117,800	5,430,000
2016	2,125,800	5,450,000
2017	2,141,800	5,490,000
2018	4,417,800	11,180,000
2019	4,505,800	11,400,000
2020	4,577,800	11,580,000
2021	4,625,800	11,700,000
2022	4,769,800	12,060,000
2023	5,113,800	12,920,000

[1] The 2010 Act set aside both the scheduled repeal of the estate tax and the imposition of the carryover basis rules for the estates of decedents dying in 2010. However, executors of the estates of decedents dying in 2010 could have elected to be bound by pre-2010 Act law (the carryover basis rules applied, but the estate tax did not).

[2] Beginning in 2011, the term "applicable exclusion amount" is the sum of the "basic exclusion amount" and the "deceased spousal unused exclusion amount." The applicable credit amount shown is computed using the basic exclusion amount.

[3] The applicable exclusion amount is adjusted for inflation for decedents dying after 2011.

[4] The gift tax applicable credit amount dropped to $330,000 for 2010 (even though the applicable exclusion amount stayed the same, at $1 million) because the maximum gift tax rate that applied to transfers made in 2010 was 35%.

[5] The applicable exclusion amount is adjusted for inflation for gifts made after 2011.

Unified Transfer Tax Rate Schedule

The unified rate schedule for decedents dying and gifts made after 2012 is as follows.

Column A	Column B	Column C	Column D
Taxable amount over	*Taxable amount not over*	*Tax on amount in column A*	*Rate of tax on excess over amount in column A*
			Percent
$ 0	$ 10,000	$ 0	18
10,000	20,000	1,800	20
20,000	40,000	3,800	22
40,000	60,000	8,200	24
60,000	80,000	13,000	26
80,000	100,000	18,200	28
100,000	150,000	23,800	30
150,000	250,000	38,800	32
250,000	500,000	70,800	34
500,000	750,000	155,800	37
750,000	1,000,000	248,300	39
1,000,000	....	345,800	40

Nonresident Aliens

For the estates of decedents dying after November 10, 1988, the estate and gift tax rates presently applicable to U.S. citizens are applicable to the estates of nonresident aliens.

Where permitted by treaty, the estate of a nonresident alien is allowed the unified credit available to a U.S. citizen multiplied by the percentage of the decedent's gross estate situated in the United States. In other cases, a unified credit of $13,000 is allowed. The estate of a resident of a U.S. possession is entitled to a unified credit equal to the greater of (1) $13,000 or (2) $46,800 multiplied by the percentage of the decedent's gross estate situated in the United States.

Credit for State Death Taxes

The credit for state death taxes was repealed in 2005 and replaced with a deduction from the gross estate for the amount of any state estate, inheritance, legacy, or succession taxes actually paid.

2023 AMOUNTS FOR INFLATION-ADJUSTED TAX ITEMS

The 2023 inflation-adjusted amounts applicable to estate, gift, and generation-skipping transfer (GST) taxes are listed below. Rev. Proc. 2022-38, I.R.B. 2022-45, 445 applies to any of the following transactions or events occurring in calendar year 2023. The Tax Cuts and Jobs Act requires that certain inflation-adjusted amounts be computed using the Chained Consumer Price Index for All Urban Consumers (C-CPI-U).

Estate and Gift Tax Unified Credit

For decedents dying after 2017 and before 2026, the Code Sec. 2010 basic exclusion amount is doubled from $5 million to $10 million, as adjusted for inflation. For decedents dying in 2023, the basic exclusion amount, as adjusted for inflation using C-CPI-U, is $12,920,000 ($12,060,000 in 2022). As a result, the unified credit is $5,113,800 ($4,769,800 in 2022).

Special Use Valuation

If the estate of a decedent who dies in 2023 elects to use the Code Sec. 2032A special use valuation method for qualified real property, the aggregate decrease in the property's value may not exceed $1,310,000, up from $1,230,000 in 2022.

Annual Exclusion for Gifts

The Code Sec. 2503 annual gift exclusion is $17,000 for 2023 ($16,000 in 2022). In addition, the first $175,000 of gifts (other than gifts of future interests in property) to a noncitizen spouse in 2023 are not included in the year's total amount of taxable gifts under Code Sec. 2503 and Code Sec. 2523(i)(2), up from $164,000 in 2022.

Generation-Skipping Transfer Tax Exemption

Because the exemption from the generation-skipping transfer (GST) tax is computed by reference to the basic exclusion amount used for estate and gift tax purposes, the GST exemption amount for GSTs occurring in 2023 is also $10 million ($12,920,000, as adjusted for inflation using C-CPI-U, up from $12,060,000 in 2022).

Interest on Estate Tax Installment Payments

For decedents dying in calendar year 2023, the dollar amount used to determine the two-percent portion (for purposes of calculating interest under Code Sec. 6601(j)) of the estate tax payable in installments under Code Sec. 6166 has increased to $1,750,000 from $1,640,000 in 2022.

Attorney Fee Awards

The attorney-fee award limitation under Code Sec. 7430(c)(1)(B)(iii) is $230 per hour for fees incurred in 2023, up from $220 per hour in 2022.

Estates and Trusts—Income Tax Rates

The Tax Rate Schedule below is to be used by an estate or a trust to compute the amount of its income tax.

• *2023 Tax Rates*

ESTATES AND TRUSTS
FOR TAX YEARS BEGINNING IN 2023

If taxable income is:		*The tax is:*	
Over—	*but not over—*		*of the amount over—*
$ 0	$2,900	10%	$ 0
2,900	10,550	$290 + 24%	2,900
10,550	14,450	2,126 + 35%	10,550
14,450	. . . .	3,491 + 37%	14,450

• *2022 Tax Rates*

ESTATES AND TRUSTS
FOR TAX YEARS BEGINNING IN 2022

If taxable income is:		*The tax is:*	
Over—	*but not over—*		*of the amount over—*
$ 0	$2,750	10%	$ 0
2,750	9,850	$275 + 24%	2,750
9,850	13,450	1,979 + 35%	9,850
13,450	. . . .	3,239 + 37%	13,450

How to Locate Specific Regulations

This volume contains all of the finally adopted (as of March 1, 2023) estate, gift, and generation-skipping transfer tax and related income tax Regulations under the 1986 Code. The Regulations are arranged in Code sequence. To locate a particular Regulation, always keep the Code section number in mind. This Code section number follows the decimal point in the Regulation section number.

The Regulations are further keyed by an introductory number preceding the decimal point. The income tax Regulation section numbers all contain the number 1 before the decimal point. The estate tax Regulations and the gift tax Regulations are introduced by the numbers 20 and 25, respectively. Generation-skipping transfer tax Regulations begin with the number 26.

> ***Example 1:*** Reg. § 1.641(a)-1 is an income tax Regulation that explains or interprets Code Sec. 641(a).
>
> ***Example 2:*** Reg. § 20.2056(b)-1 is an estate tax Regulation that explains or interprets Code Sec. 2056(b).
>
> ***Example 3:*** Reg. § 25.2515-1 is a gift tax Regulation that interprets or explains Code Sec. 2515.

Related income tax Regulations begin on page 779. The estate tax Regulations start on page 1179. The gift tax Regulations begin on page 1429. The generation-skipping transfer tax Regulations begin on page 1521. The special valuation Regulations begin on page 1575. The procedural and administrative Regulations begin on page 1617.

Proposed Regulations dealing with related income tax matters and the estate, gift, and generation-skipping transfer taxes begin on page 1869.

For a list of irregularly numbered regulations that appear in this book, see page 14.

Irregularly Numbered Regulations

There are a few exceptions to the standard method of numbering regulations described on page 13. The following table indicates the page on which the text of the irregularly numbered regulation begins and the subject of the regulation.

Irregularly Numbered Reg. §	*Subject*	*Page on Which Reg. § Begins*
8.1	Charitable remainder trusts	939
20.0-1	Introduction	1179
20.0-2	General description of tax	1180
22.0	Certain elections under the Economic Recovery Tax Act of 1981	1297
25.0-1	Introduction	1429

Law Changes Not Yet in the Regulations

There is a lapse of time between amendments to the Code and a corresponding change in the Regulations. This table shows those Regulations that do not yet reflect changes made in the Code as of this printing. For a list of the designated or popular titles of Public Laws noted below, see the table on page 19.

Once the Treasury Department finalizes a Regulation, it is reflected in this book. The reader, however, should always check this table to make sure that a particular Regulation has been amended to reflect the latest change in the law.

Regulations Section	Public Law Making Changes Not Reflected
1.112-1	104-117
1.213-1	97-248, 98-369, 99-514, 100-647, 101-508, 103-66, 104-191
1.303-2	94-455, 97-34
1.641(a)-0	95-600
1.641(a)-0(c)	98-369, 99-514, 100-647
1.641(a)-1	95-30, 104-188
1.641(a)-2	94-455, 99-514, 104-188, 110-28
1.641(b)-3	104-188, 110-28
1.642(a)(3)-1—1.642(a)(3)-2	99-514
1.642(b)-1	107-134
1.642(c)-5	98-369, 99-514, 100-647
1.642(c)-7	100-647
1.642(e)-1	97-34
1.642(f)-1	97-34
1.642(g)-1	94-455, 101-239
1.642(h)-1	91-172, 99-514
1.643(a)-1	97-248
1.643(a)-3	99-514, 105-34
1.643(a)-6	94-455, 99-514, 101-239, 104-188
1.643(a)-7	99-514
1.643(d)-1	94-455, 98-369, 99-514, 100-647, 104-188
1.643(d)-2	99-514, 105-34
1.652(b)-2	99-514
1.652(b)-3	99-514
1.652(c)-1	99-514, 105-34
1.652(c)-2	99-514, 105-34
1.652(c)-4	99-514, 105-34
1.661(a)-2(f)	98-369
1.661(c)-1	99-514
1.661(c)-2	99-514
1.662(b)-2	99-514
1.662(c)-1	99-514
1.662(c)-4	99-514
1.663(b)-1	105-34
1.663(b)-2	105-34
1.664-1	99-514, 105-34
1.664-1(f)	93-483, 94-455, 98-369, 100-647
8.1	95-600, 96-222, 96-605, 98-369, 100-647
1.664-2	105-34
1.664-2(a)(5)	98-369, 109-280
1.664-3	105-34
1.664-3(a)(5)	98-369, 109-280
1.665(a)-0A—1.665(b)-1A	94-455, 95-600, 105-34
1.665(b)-2A	94-455, 95-600
1.665(c)-1A, 1.665(d)-1A	94-455, 95-600, 104-188, 105-34
1.665(e)-1A, 1.665(g)-2A	94-455, 95-600, 105-34
1.666(a)-1A	94-455, 95-600, 105-34
1.666(b)-1A	94-455, 95-600, 105-34
1.666(c)-1A	94-455, 95-600, 105-34
1.666(c)-2A	94-455, 95-600, 105-34
1.666(d)-1A	94-455, 95-600, 105-34
1.667(b)-1A	94-455, 95-600, 99-514, 105-34
1.671-2	99-514, 100-647
1.672(a)-1	99-514, 100-647, 101-508
1.672(c)-1	99-514, 100-647, 104-188
1.672(d)-1	99-514, 100-647
1.673(a)-1	99-514, 100-647
1.673(d)-1	99-514, 100-647
1.674(a)-1	99-514, 100-647, 105-34
1.674(b)-1	99-514, 100-647, 105-34
1.674(c)-1—1.674(d)-2	99-514, 100-647
1.675-1	99-514, 100-647
1.676(a)-1	99-514, 100-647
1.676(b)-1	99-514, 100-647
1.677(a)-1	99-514, 100-647
1.677(b)-1	94-455, 99-514, 100-647
1.678(a)-1	99-514, 100-647
1.683-1—1.683-3	94-455

Regulations Section	Public Law Making Changes Not Reflected
1.691(a)-1—1.691(a)-3	94-455, 95-600, 96-222, 96-471, 99-514, 100-203, 100-647
1.691(a)-5	94-455, 95-600, 96-222, 96-471, 99-514, 100-203, 100-647
1.691(c)-1	94-455, 95-600, 96-222, 96-471, 99-514, 100-203, 100-647, 104-188, 105-34, 107-16, 111-312
1.691(c)-2	94-455, 95-600, 96-222, 96-471, 99-514, 100-203, 100-647, 105-34, 104-188, 107-16, 111-312.
1.691(e)-1	94-455
1.692-1	98-259, 98-369, 99-514, 107-134
1.1014-6	97-34
1.1014-8	97–34, 107-16, 111-312
1.1015-1	98-369
1.1221-1	94-455, 97-34, 107-16, 109-222, 109-432, 111-312
20.0-1	107-16, 111-312, 112-240
20.0-2	107-16, 111-312, 112-240
20.2001-1	107-16, 111-312, 112-240, 115-97
20.2011-1	94-455, 107-16, 107-134, 111-312, 112-240, 113-295
20.2011-2	94-455, 107-16, 107-134, 111-312, 112-240, 113-295
20.2012-1	107-16, 111-312, 112-240
20.2013-1	107-16, 111-312, 112-240
20.2013-2	94-455, 107-16, 111-312, 112-240
20.2013-3, 20.2013-4	107-16, 111-312, 112-240
20.2013-5, 20.2013-6	107-16, 111-312
20.2014-1—20.2014-7	107-16, 111-312, 112-240
20.2015-1	107-16, 111-312, 112-240
20.2016-1	107-16, 111-312, 112-240
20.2031-1(a), (b)	94-455, 95-600, 97-34, 97-448, 98-369, 99-514, 100-647, 101-508, 105-34, 105-206, 107-16, 111-312
20.2032A-3	97-34, 97-448, 98-369, 99-514, 100-647, 101-508, 105-34
20.2032A-4	97-34, 97-448, 98-369, 99-514, 100-647, 101-508, 105-34
20.2032A-8	97-34, 97-448, 98-369, 99-514, 100-647, 101-508, 105-34
20.2036-1	94-455, 95-600, 101-508
20.2038-1	94-455
20.2039-1(a)	93-406, 94-455
20.2039-2	97-34, 97-248, 97-448, 98-369, 99-514
20.2039-4, 20.2039-5	97-34, 97-248, 97-448, 98-369, 99-514
20.2040-1	94-455, 95-600, 96-222, 97-34
20.2053-10	107-16
20.2055-1, 20.2055-2	105-34
20.2055-3	107-16
20.2056(b)-1	105-34
20.2056(b)-7	105-34
20.2056(b)-8	105-34
20.2056A-2	105-34
20.2056A-5—20.2056A-6	107-16, 111-312
20.2056A-7	107-16
20.2101-1	107-16, 107-147, 111-312, 112-240
20.2102-1	104-188, 105-34, 107-16, 111-312, 112-240
20.2104-1(a)(3)	94-455
20.2105-1	100-647, 103-66, 105-34, 108-357
20.2105-1(i) and (m)	94-455
20.2106-1, 20.2106-2	107-16, 111-312, 112-240
20.2107-1	94-455, 104-191, 105-34, 107-16, 108-357, 111-312, 112-240
20.2207A-1	105-34
20.2207A-2	105-34
25.0-1	107-16, 111-312
25.2501-1	104-191, 105-34, 107-16, 108-357, 111-312, 114-113
25.2503-2	105-34, 107-16, 111-312, 115-97
25.2503-3	95-600, 97-34
25.2504-1, 25.2504-2	107-16, 111-312
25.2511-1	107-16, 107-147, 111-312
25.2511-2, 25.2511-3	107-16, 107-147
25.2512-1	94-455
25.2515-1—25.2515-4	94-455, 95-600
25.2516-1	98-369
26.2642-1—26.2642-5	107-16, 110-312, 112-240
26.2654-1	105-206
25.2701-1—25.2701-6	104-188
25.2702-1	104-188
1.6012-3	96-589, 105-34
20.6018-1	94-455, 97-34, 98-369, 105-34, 107-16, 111-312
20.6018-3	94-455, 107-16, 111-312
25.6019-1—25.6019-2	105-34
1.6034-1, 301.6034-1	109-280

Regulations Section	Public Law Making Changes Not Reflected
20.6065-1(b)	94-455
25.6065-1(b)	94-455
1.6071-1	105-206
20.6075-1	107-16, 111-312
25.6075-1	107-16, 111-312, 112-240
20.6151-1(c)	92-5 (repealed Code Sec. 6312)
20.6161-1(a)	94-455
20.6161-2	94-455
20.6163-1	94-455
20.6166-1	97-34, 105-34, 105-206, 107-16, 111-312, 112-240

Regulations Section	Public Law Making Changes Not Reflected
20.6166A-1	97-34 (repealed Code Sec. 6166A)
301.6601-1	99-514, 105-34, 105-206
301.6601-1(e)	97-248, 105-34
301.6621-1	99-514, 101-239, 101-508, 103-465, 105-206
1.6662-4(g)	105-34
1.6662-5	103-66
301.6721-1	114-27
301.6722-1	114-27
301.7701-9	94-455

Table Of Public Laws By Number and Title

Following is a list of the Public Laws referred to in "Law Changes Not Yet in the Regulations" (beginning on page 15) that have designated titles:

Public Law	Title and Enactment Date
91-172	Tax Reform Act of 1969 (Dec. 30, 1969)
93-406	Employee Retirement Income Security Act of 1974 (ERISA) (Sept. 2, 1974)
94-455	Tax Reform Act of 1976 (Oct. 4, 1976)
95-30	Tax Reduction and Simplification Act of 1977 (May 23, 1977)
95-600	Revenue Act of 1978 (Nov. 6, 1978)
96-222	Technical Corrections Act of 1979 (April 1, 1980)
96-471	Installment Sales Revision Act of 1980 (Oct. 19, 1980)
96-589	Bankruptcy Tax Act of 1980 (Nov. 24, 1980)
96-605	Miscellaneous Revenue Act of 1980 (Dec. 28, 1980)
97-34	Economic Recovery Tax Act of 1981 (ERTA) (Aug. 13, 1981)
97-248	Tax Equity and Fiscal Responsibility Act of 1982 (TEFRA) (Sept. 3, 1982)
97-448	Technical Corrections Act of 1982 (Jan. 12, 1983)
98-369	Tax Reform Act of 1984 (July 18, 1984)
99-514	Tax Reform Act of 1986 (Oct. 22, 1986)
100-203	Revenue Act of 1987 (Dec. 22, 1987)
100-647	Technical and Miscellaneous Revenue Act of 1988 (Nov. 10, 1988)
101-239	Omnibus Budget Reconciliation Act of 1989 (Dec. 19, 1989)
101-508	Omnibus Budget Reconciliation Act of 1990 (Nov. 5, 1990)
103-66	Omnibus Budget Reconciliation Act of 1993 (Aug. 10, 1993)
103-465	Uruguay Round Agreements Act (Dec. 8, 1994)
104-188	Small Business Job Protection Act of 1996 (Aug. 20, 1996)
104-191	Health Insurance Portability and Accountability Act of 1996 (Aug. 21, 1996)
105-34	Taxpayer Relief Act of 1997 (Aug. 5, 1997)
105-206	Internal Revenue Service Restructuring and Reform Act of 1998 (July 22, 1998)
107-16	Economic Growth and Tax Relief Reconciliation Act of 2001 (June 7, 2001)
107-134	Victims of Terrorism Tax Relief Act of 2001 (January 23, 2002)
107-147	Job Creation and Worker Assistance Act of 2002 (March 9, 2002)
108-357	American Jobs Creation Act of 2004 (October 22, 2004)
109-222	Tax Increase Prevention and Reconciliation Act of 2005 (May 17, 2006)
109-280	Pension Protection Act of 2006 (August 17, 2006)
109-432	Tax Relief and Health Care Act of 2006 (December 20, 2006)
110-28	Small Business Work Opportunity Act of 2007 (May 25, 2007)
111-312	Tax Relief, Unemployment Insurance Reauthorization, and Job Creation Act of 2010
112-240	American Taxpayer Relief Act of 2012 (January 2, 2013)
113-295	Tax Increase Prevention Act of 2014 (December 19, 2014)
113-295	Tax Technical Corrections Act of 2014 (December 19, 2014)

Public Law	Title and Enactment Date
113-295	Stephen Beck, Jr., Achieving a Better Life Experience Act of 2014 (December 19, 2014)
114-27	Trade Preferences Extension Aft of 2015 (June 29, 2015)
114-27	Trade Adjustment Assistance Reauthorization Act of 2015 (June 29, 2015)
114-113	Consolidated Appropriations Act, 2016 (December 18, 2015)
115-97	Tax Cuts and Jobs Act (December 22, 2017)

RELATED INCOME TAX PROVISIONS

TABLE OF CONTENTS

SUBTITLE A—INCOME TAXES

Chapter 1—Normal Taxes and Surtaxes

SUBCHAPTER B. COMPUTATION OF TAXABLE INCOME

PART I—DEFINITION OF GROSS INCOME, ADJUSTED GROSS INCOME, TAXABLE INCOME, ETC.

PART III—ITEMS SPECIFICALLY EXCLUDED FROM GROSS INCOME

PART VI—ITEMIZED DEDUCTIONS FOR INDIVIDUALS AND CORPORATIONS

PART VII—ADDITIONAL ITEMIZED DEDUCTIONS FOR INDIVIDUALS

SUBCHAPTER C. CORPORATE DISTRIBUTIONS AND ADJUSTMENTS

PART I—DISTRIBUTIONS BY CORPORATIONS

Subpart A—Effects on Recipients

SUBCHAPTER F. EXEMPT ORGANIZATIONS

PART VIII—HIGHER EDUCATION SAVINGS ENTITIES

SUBCHAPTER J. ESTATES, TRUSTS, BENEFICIARIES, AND DECEDENTS

PART I—ESTATES, TRUSTS, AND BENEFICIARIES

Subpart A—General Rules for Taxation of Estates and Trusts

Subpart B—Trusts Which Distribute Current Income Only

Subpart C—Estates and Trusts Which May Accumulate Income or Which Distribute Corpus

SUBTITLE A—INCOME TAXES

* * *

CHAPTER 1—NORMAL TAXES AND SURTAXES

* * *

Subchapter B—Computation of Taxable Income

* * *

PART I—DEFINITION OF GROSS INCOME, ADJUSTED GROSS INCOME, TAXABLE INCOME, ETC.

* * *

[Sec. 61]

GROSS INCOME DEFINED.

[Sec. 61(a)]

(a) GENERAL DEFINITION.—Except as otherwise provided in this subtitle, gross income means all income from whatever source derived, including (but not limited to) the following items:

(1) Compensation for services, including fees, commissions, fringe benefits, and similar items;

(2) Gross income derived from business;

(3) Gains derived from dealings in property;

(4) Interest;

(5) Rents;

(6) Royalties;

(7) Dividends;

(8) Annuities;

(9) Income from life insurance and endowment contracts;

(10) Pensions;

(11) Income from discharge of indebtedness;

(12) Distributive share of partnership gross income;

(13) Income in respect of a decedent; and

(14) Income from an interest in an estate or trust.

Amendments

• 2021, American Rescue Plan Act of 2021 (P.L. 117-2)

P.L. 117-2, § 5003(a) and (c), provides:

SEC. 5003. SUPPORT FOR RESTAURANTS.

(a) DEFINITIONS.—In this section:

(1) ADMINISTRATOR.—The term "Administrator" means the Administrator of the Small Business Administration.

(2) AFFILIATED BUSINESS.—The term "affiliated business" means a business in which an eligible entity has an equity or right to profit distributions of not less than 50 percent, or in which an eligible entity has the contractual authority to control the direction of the business, provided that such affiliation shall be determined as of any arrangements or agreements in existence as of March 13, 2020.

(3) COVERED PERIOD.—The term "covered period" means the period—

(A) beginning on February 15, 2020; and

(B) ending on December 31, 2021, or a date to be determined by the Administrator that is not later than 2 years after the date of enactment of this section.

(4) ELIGIBLE ENTITY.—The term "eligible entity"—

(A) means a restaurant, food stand, food truck, food cart, caterer, saloon, inn, tavern, bar, lounge, brewpub, tasting room, taproom, licensed facility or premise of a beverage alcohol producer where the public may taste, sample, or purchase products, or other similar place of business in which the public or patrons assemble for the primary purpose of being served food or drink;

(B) includes an entity described in subparagraph (A) that is located in an airport terminal or that is a Tribally-owned concern; and

(C) does not include—

(i) an entity described in subparagraph (A) that—

(I) is a State or local government-operated business;

(II) as of March 13, 2020, owns or operates (together with any affiliated business) more than 20 locations, regardless of whether those locations do business under the same or multiple names; or

(III) has a pending application for or has received a grant under section 324 of the Economic Aid to Hard-Hit Small Businesses, Nonprofits, and Venues Act (title III of division N of Public Law 116–260); or

(ii) a publicly-traded company.

(5) EXCHANGE; ISSUER; SECURITY.—The terms "exchange", "issuer", and "security" have the meanings given those terms in section 3(a) of the Securities Exchange Act of 1934 (15 U.S.C. 78c(a)).

(6) FUND.—The term "Fund" means the Restaurant Revitalization Fund established under subsection (b).

(7) PANDEMIC-RELATED REVENUE LOSS.—The term "pandemic-related revenue loss" means, with respect to an eligible entity—

(A) except as provided in subparagraphs (B), (C), and (D), the gross receipts, as established using such verification documentation as the Administrator may require, of the eligible entity during 2020 subtracted from the gross receipts of the eligible entity in 2019, if such sum is greater than zero;

(B) if the eligible entity was not in operation for the entirety of 2019—

(i) the difference between—

(I) the product obtained by multiplying the average monthly gross receipts of the eligible entity in 2019 by 12; and

(II) the product obtained by multiplying the average monthly gross receipts of the eligible entity in 2020 by 12; or

(ii) an amount based on a formula determined by the Administrator;

(C) if the eligible entity opened during the period beginning on January 1, 2020, and ending on the day before the date of enactment of this section—

(i) the expenses described in subsection (c)(5)(A) that were incurred by the eligible entity minus any gross receipts received; or

(ii) an amount based on a formula determined by the Administrator; or

(D) if the eligible entity has not yet opened as of the date of application for a grant under subsection (c), but has incurred expenses described in subsection (c)(5)(A) as of the date of enactment of this section—

(i) the amount of those expenses; or

(ii) an amount based on a formula determined by the Administrator.

For purposes of this paragraph, the pandemic-related revenue losses for an eligible entity shall be reduced by any amounts received from a covered loan made under paragraph (36) or (37) of section 7(a) of the Small Business Act (15 U.S.C. 636(a)) in 2020 or 2021.

(8) PAYROLL COSTS.—The term "payroll costs" has the meaning given the term in section 7(a)(36)(A) of the Small Business Act (15 U.S.C. 636(a)(36)(A)), except that such term shall not include—

(A) qualified wages (as defined in subsection (c)(3) of section 2301 of the CARES Act) taken into account in determining the credit allowed under such section 2301; or

(B) premiums taken into account in determining the credit allowed under section 6432 of the Internal Revenue Code of 1986.

(9) PUBLICLY-TRADED COMPANY.—The term "publicly-traded company" means an entity that is majority owned or controlled by an entity that is an issuer, the securities of which are listed on a national securities exchange under section 6 of the Securities Exchange Act of 1934 (15 U.S.C. 78f).

(10) TRIBALLY-OWNED CONCERN.—The term "Tribally-owned concern" has the meaning given the term in section 124.3 of title 13, Code of Federal Regulations, or any successor regulation.

* * *

(c) RESTAURANT REVITALIZATION GRANTS.—

(1) IN GENERAL.—Except as provided in subsection (b) and paragraph (3), the Administrator shall award grants to eligible entities in the order in which applications are received by the Administrator.

(2) APPLICATION.—

(A) CERTIFICATION.—An eligible entity applying for a grant under this subsection shall make a good faith certification that—

(i) the uncertainty of current economic conditions makes necessary the grant request to support the ongoing operations of the eligible entity; and

(ii) the eligible entity has not applied for or received a grant under section 324 of the Economic Aid to Hard-Hit Small Businesses, Nonprofits, and Venues Act (title III of division N of Public Law 116–260).

(B) BUSINESS IDENTIFIERS.—In accepting applications for grants under this subsection, the Administrator shall prioritize the ability of each applicant to use their existing business identifiers over requiring other forms of registration or identification that may not be common to their industry and imposing additional burdens on applicants.

(3) PRIORITY IN AWARDING GRANTS.—

(A) IN GENERAL.—During the initial 21-day period in which the Administrator awards grants under this subsection, the Administrator shall prioritize awarding grants to eligible entities that are small business concerns owned and controlled by women (as defined in section 3(n) of the Small Business Act (15 U.S.C. 632(n))), small business concerns owned and controlled by veterans (as defined in section 3(q) of such Act (15 U.S.C. 632(q))), or socially and economically disadvantaged small business concerns (as defined in section 8(a)(4)(A) of the Small Business Act (15 U.S.C. 637(a)(4)(A))). The Administrator may take such steps as necessary to ensure that eligible entities described in this subparagraph have access to grant funding under this section after the end of such 21-day period.

(B) CERTIFICATION.—For purposes of establishing priority under subparagraph (A), an applicant shall submit a self-certification of eligibility for priority with the grant application.

(4) GRANT AMOUNT.—

(A) AGGREGATE MAXIMUM AMOUNT.—The aggregate amount of grants made to an eligible entity and any affiliated businesses of the eligible entity under this subsection—

(i) shall not exceed $10,000,000; and

(ii) shall be limited to $5,000,000 per physical location of the eligible entity.

(B) DETERMINATION OF GRANT AMOUNT.—

(i) IN GENERAL.—Except as provided in this paragraph, the amount of a grant made to an eligible entity under this subsection shall be equal to the pandemic-related revenue loss of the eligible entity.

(ii) RETURN TO TREASURY.—Any amount of a grant made under this subsection to an eligible entity based on estimated receipts that is greater than the actual gross receipts of the eligible entity in 2020 shall be returned to the Treasury.

(5) USE OF FUNDS.—During the covered period, an eligible entity that receives a grant under this subsection may use the grant funds for the following expenses incurred as a direct result of, or during, the COVID–19 pandemic:

(A) Payroll costs.

(B) Payments of principal or interest on any mortgage obligation (which shall not include any prepayment of principal on a mortgage obligation).

(C) Rent payments, including rent under a lease agreement (which shall not include any prepayment of rent).

(D) Utilities.

(E) Maintenance expenses, including—

(i) construction to accommodate outdoor seating; and

(ii) walls, floors, deck surfaces, furniture, fixtures, and equipment.

(F) Supplies, including protective equipment and cleaning materials.

(G) Food and beverage expenses that are within the scope of the normal business practice of the eligible entity before the covered period.

(H) Covered supplier costs, as defined in section 7A(a) of the Small Business Act (as redesignated, transferred, and amended by section 304(b) of the Economic Aid to Hard-Hit Small Businesses, Nonprofits, and Venues Act (Public Law 116–260)).

(I) Operational expenses.

(J) Paid sick leave.

(K) Any other expenses that the Administrator determines to be essential to maintaining the eligible entity.

(6) RETURNING FUNDS.—If an eligible entity that receives a grant under this subsection fails to use all grant funds or permanently ceases operations on or before the last day of the covered period, the eligible entity shall return to the Treasury any funds that the eligible entity did not use for the allowable expenses under paragraph (5).

P.L. 117-2, § 9672, provides:

SEC. 9672. TAX TREATMENT OF TARGETED EIDL ADVANCES.

For purposes of the Internal Revenue Code of 1986—

(1) amounts received from the Administrator of the Small Business Administration in the form of a targeted EIDL advance under section 331 of the Economic Aid to Hard-Hit Small Businesses, Nonprofits, and Venues Act (title III of division N of Public Law 116–260) shall not be included in the gross income of the person that receives such amounts,

(2) no deduction shall be denied, no tax attribute shall be reduced, and no basis increase shall be denied, by reason of the exclusion from gross income provided by paragraph (1), and

(3) in the case of a partnership or S corporation that receives such amounts—

(A) any amount excluded from income by reason of paragraph (1) shall be treated as tax exempt income for purposes of sections 705 and 1366 of the Internal Revenue Code of 1986, and

(B) the Secretary of the Treasury (or the Secretary's delegate) shall prescribe rules for determining a partner's distributive share of any amount described in subparagraph (A) for purposes of section 705 of the Internal Revenue Code of 1986.

P.L. 117-2, §9673, provides:

SEC. 9673. TAX TREATMENT OF RESTAURANT REVITALIZATION GRANTS.

For purposes of the Internal Revenue Code of 1986—

(1) amounts received from the Administrator of the Small Business Administration in the form of a restaurant revitalization grant under section 5003 shall not be included in the gross income of the person that receives such amounts,

(2) no deduction shall be denied, no tax attribute shall be reduced, and no basis increase shall be denied, by reason of the exclusion from gross income provided by paragraph (1), and

(3) in the case of a partnership or S corporation that receives such amounts—

(A) except as otherwise provided by the Secretary of the Treasury (or the Secretary's delegate), any amount excluded from income by reason of paragraph (1) shall be treated as tax exempt income for purposes of sections 705 and 1366 of the Internal Revenue Code of 1986, and

(B) the Secretary of the Treasury (or the Secretary's delegate) shall prescribe rules for determining a partner's distributive share of any amount described in subparagraph (A) for purposes of section 705 of the Internal Revenue Code of 1986.

• 2020, COVID-related Tax Relief Act of 2020 (P.L. 116-260)

P.L. 116-260, §276(b), Div. N, provides:

(b) SUBSEQUENT PAYCHECK PROTECTION PROGRAM LOANS.—For purposes of the Internal Revenue Code of 1986, in the case of any taxable year ending after the date of the enactment of this Act—

(1) no amount shall be included in the gross income of an eligible entity (within the meaning of subparagraph (J) of section 7(a)(37) of the Small Business Act) by reason of forgiveness of indebtedness described in clause (ii) of such subparagraph,

(2) no deduction shall be denied, no tax attribute shall be reduced, and no basis increase shall be denied, by reason of the exclusion from gross income provided by paragraph (1), and

(3) in the case of an eligible entity that is a partnership or S corporation—

(A) any amount excluded from income by reason of paragraph (1) shall be treated as tax exempt income for purposes of sections 705 and 1366 of the Internal Revenue Code of 1986, and

(B) except as provided by the Secretary of the Treasury (or the Secretary's delegate), any increase in the adjusted basis of a partner's interest in a partnership under section 705 of the Internal Revenue Code of 1986 with respect to any amount described in subparagraph (A) shall equal the partner's distributive share of deductions resulting from costs giving rise to the forgiveness of indebtedness referred to in paragraph (1).

P.L. 116-260, §277, Div. N, provides:

SEC. 277. EMERGENCY FINANCIAL AID GRANTS.

(a) IN GENERAL.—In the case of a student receiving a qualified emergency financial aid grant—

(1) such grant shall not be included in the gross income of such individual for purposes of the Internal Revenue Code of 1986, and

(2) such grant shall not be treated as described in subparagraph (A), (B), or (C) of section 25A(g)(2) of such Code.

(b) DEFINITIONS.—For purposes of this subsection, the term "qualified emergency financial aid grant" means—

(1) any emergency financial aid grant awarded by an institution of higher education under section 3504 of the CARES Act,

(2) any emergency financial aid grant from an institution of higher education made with funds made available under section 18004 of the CARES Act, and

(3) any other emergency financial aid grant made to a student from a Federal agency, a State, an Indian tribe, an institution of higher education, or a scholarship-granting organization (including a tribal organization, as defined in section 4 of the Indian Self-Determination and Education Assistance Act (25 U.S.C.5304)) for the purpose of providing financial relief to students enrolled at institutions of higher education in response to a qualifying emergency (as defined in section 3502(a)(4) of the CARES Act).

(c) LIMITATION.—This section shall not apply to that portion of any amount received which represents payment for teaching, research, or other services required as a condition for receiving the qualified emergency financial aid grant.

(d) EFFECTIVE DATE.—This section shall apply to qualified emergency financial aid grants made after March 26, 2020.

P.L. 116-260, §278, Div. N, provides:

SEC. 278. CLARIFICATION OF TAX TREATMENT OF CERTAIN LOAN FORGIVENESS AND OTHER BUSINESS FINANCIAL ASSISTANCE.

(a) UNITED STATES TREASURY PROGRAM MANAGEMENT AUTHORITY.—For purposes of the Internal Revenue Code of 1986—

(1) no amount shall be included in the gross income of a borrower by reason of forgiveness of indebtedness described in section 1109(d)(2)(D) of the CARES Act,

(2) no deduction shall be denied, no tax attribute shall be reduced, and no basis increase shall be denied, by reason of the exclusion from gross income provided by paragraph (1), and

(3) in the case of a borrower that is a partnership or S corporation—

(A) any amount excluded from income by reason of paragraph (1) shall be treated as tax exempt income for purposes of sections 705 and 1366 of the Internal Revenue Code of 1986, and

(B) except as provided by the Secretary of the Treasury (or the Secretary's delegate), any increase in the adjusted basis of a partner's interest in a partnership under section 705 of the Internal Revenue Code of 1986 with respect to any amount described in subparagraph (A) shall equal the partner's distributive share of deductions resulting from costs giving rise to forgiveness described in section 1109(d)(2)(D) of the CARES Act.

(b) EMERGENCY EIDL GRANTS AND TARGETED EIDL ADVANCES.—For purposes of the Internal Revenue Code of 1986—

(1) any advance described in section 1110(e) of the CARES Act or any funding under section 331 of the Economic Aid to Hard-Hit Small Businesses, Nonprofits, and Venues Act shall not be included in the gross income of the person that receives such advance or funding,

(2) no deduction shall be denied, no tax attribute shall be reduced, and no basis increase shall be denied, by reason of the exclusion from gross income provided by paragraph (1), and

(3) in the case of a partnership or S corporation that receives such advance or funding—

(A) any amount excluded from income by reason of paragraph (1) shall be treated as tax exempt income for purposes of sections 705 and 1366 of the Internal Revenue Code of 1986, and

(B) the Secretary of the Treasury (or the Secretary's delegate) shall prescribe rules for determining a partner's distributive share of any amount described in subparagraph (A) for purposes of section 705 of the Internal Revenue Code of 1986.

(c) SUBSIDY FOR CERTAIN LOAN PAYMENTS.—For purposes of the Internal Revenue Code of 1986—

(1) any payment described in section 1112(c) of the CARES Act shall not be included in the gross income of the person on whose behalf such payment is made,

(2) no deduction shall be denied, no tax attribute shall be reduced, and no basis increase shall be denied, by reason of the exclusion from gross income provided by paragraph (1), and

(3) in the case of a partnership or S corporation on whose behalf of a payment described in section 1112(c) of the CARES Act is made—

(A) any amount excluded from income by reason of paragraph (1) shall be treated as tax exempt income for purposes of sections 705 and 1366 of the Internal Revenue Code of 1986, and

(B) except as provided by the Secretary of the Treasury (or the Secretary's delegate), any increase in the adjusted basis of a partner's interest in a partnership under section 705 of the Internal Revenue Code of 1986 with respect to any amount described in subparagraph (A) shall equal the sum of the partner's distributive share of deductions resulting from interest and fees described in section 1112(c) of the CARES Act and the partner's share, as determined under section 752 of the Internal Revenue Code of 1986, of principal described in section 1112(c) of the CARES Act.

(d) GRANTS FOR SHUTTERED VENUE OPERATORS.—For purposes of the Internal Revenue Code of 1986—

(1) any grant made under section 324 of the Economic Aid to Hard-Hit Small Businesses, Nonprofits, and Venues Act shall not be included in the gross income of the person that receives such grant,

(2) no deduction shall be denied, no tax attribute shall be reduced, and no basis increase shall be denied, by reason of the exclusion from gross income provided by paragraph (1), and

(3) in the case of a partnership or S corporation that receives such grant—

(A) any amount excluded from income by reason of paragraph (1) shall be treated as tax exempt income for purposes of sections 705 and 1366 of the Internal Revenue Code of 1986, and

(B) the Secretary of the Treasury (or the Secretary's delegate) shall prescribe rules for determining a partner's distributive share of any amount described in subparagraph (A) for purposes of section 705 of the Internal Revenue Code of 1986.

(e) EFFECTIVE DATES.—

(1) IN GENERAL.—Except as otherwise provided in this subsection, subsections (a), (b), and (c) shall apply to taxable years ending after the date of the enactment of the CARES Act.

(2) GRANTS FOR SHUTTERED VENUE OPERATORS; TARGETED EIDL ADVANCES.—Subsection (d), and so much of subsection (b) as relates to funding under section 331 of the Economic Aid to Hard-Hit Small Businesses, Nonprofits, and Venues Act, shall apply to taxable years ending after the date of the enactment of this Act.

P.L. 116-260, §279, Div. N, provides:

SEC. 279. AUTHORITY TO WAIVE CERTAIN INFORMATION REPORTING REQUIREMENTS.

The Secretary of the Treasury (or the Secretary's delegate) may provide an exception from any requirement to file an information return otherwise required by chapter 61 of the Internal Revenue Code of 1986 with respect to any amount excluded from gross income by reason of section 7A(i) of the Small Business Act or section 276(b), 277, or 278 of this subtitle.

• 2017, Tax Cuts and Jobs Act (P.L. 115-97)

P.L. 115-97, §11051(b)(1)(A):

Amended Code Sec. 61(a) by striking paragraph (8) and by redesignating paragraphs (9) through (15) as paragraphs (8) through (14), respectively. For the **effective** date, see Act Sec. 11051(c)(1)-(2), below. Prior to being stricken, Code Sec. 61(a)(8) read as follows:

(8) Alimony and separate maintenance payments;

P.L. 115-97, §11051(c)(1)-(2), provides:

(c) EFFECTIVE DATE.—The amendments made by this section shall apply to—

(1) any divorce or separation instrument (as defined in section 71(b)(2) of the Internal Revenue Code of 1986 as in effect before the date of the enactment of this Act) executed after December 31, 2018, and

(2) any divorce or separation instrument (as so defined) executed on or before such date and modified after such date if the modification expressly provides that the amendments made by this section apply to such modification.

• 2015, Protecting Americans from Tax Hikes Act of 2015 (P.L. 114-113)

P.L. 114-113, §343, Div. Q, provides:

SEC. 343. EXCLUSION FROM GROSS INCOME OF CERTAIN CLEAN COAL POWER GRANTS TO NON-CORPORATE TAXPAYERS.

(a) GENERAL RULE.—In the case of an eligible taxpayer other than a corporation, gross income for purposes of the Internal Revenue Code of 1986 shall not include any amount received under section 402 of the Energy Policy Act of 2005.

(b) REDUCTION IN BASIS.—The basis of any property subject to the allowance for depreciation under the Internal Revenue Code of 1986 which is acquired with any amount to which subsection (a) applies during the 12-month period beginning on the day such amount is received shall be reduced by an amount equal to such amount. The excess (if any) of such amount over the amount of the reduction under the preceding sentence shall be applied to the reduction (as of the last day of the period specified in the preceding sentence) of the basis of any other property held by the taxpayer. The particular properties to which the reductions required by this subsection are allocated shall be determined by the Secretary of the Treasury (or the Secretary's delegate) under regulations similar to the regulations under section 362(c)(2) of such Code.

(c) LIMITATION TO AMOUNTS WHICH WOULD BE CONTRIBUTIONS TO CAPITAL.—Subsection (a) shall not apply to any amount unless such amount, if received by a corporation, would be excluded from gross income under section 118 of the Internal Revenue Code of 1986.

(d) ELIGIBLE TAXPAYER.—For purposes of this section, with respect to any amount received under section 402 of the Energy Policy Act of 2005, the term "eligible taxpayer" means a taxpayer that makes a payment to the Secretary of the Treasury (or the Secretary's delegate) equal to 1.18 percent of the amount so received. Such payment shall be made at such time and in such manner as such Secretary (or the Secretary's delegate) shall prescribe. In the case of a partnership, such Secretary (or the Secretary's delegate) shall prescribe regulations to determine the allocation of such payment amount among the partners.

(e) EFFECTIVE DATE.—This section shall apply to amounts received under section 402 of the Energy Policy Act of 2005 in taxable years beginning after December 31, 2011.

• 2010, Claims Resolution Act of 2010 (P.L. 111-291)

P.L. 111-291, §101(f)(1)(A)-(B), provides:

SEC. 101. INDIVIDUAL INDIAN MONEY ACCOUNT LITIGATION SETTLEMENT.

***

(f) TAXATION AND OTHER BENEFITS.—

(1) INTERNAL REVENUE CODE.—For purposes of the Internal Revenue Code of 1986, amounts received by an individual Indian as a lump sum or a periodic payment pursuant to the Settlement shall not be—

(A) included in gross income; or

(B) taken into consideration for purposes of applying any provision of the Internal Revenue Code that takes into account excludable income in computing adjusted gross income or modified adjusted gross income, including section 86 of that Code (relating to Social Security and tier 1 railroad retirement benefits).

• 2009, Supplemental Appropriations Act, 2009 (P.L. 111-32)

P.L. 111-32, §1302(h)(2), provides:

(2) FOR PURPOSES OF TAXATION.—A voucher issued under the program or any payment made for such a voucher pursuant to subsection (a)(3) shall not be considered as gross income of the purchaser of a vehicle for purposes of the Internal Revenue Code of 1986.

• 2007 (P.L. 110-141)

P.L. 110-141, §1, provides:

SECTION 1. EXCLUSION FROM INCOME FOR PAYMENTS FROM THE HOKIE SPIRIT MEMORIAL FUND.

For purposes of the Internal Revenue Code of 1986, gross income shall not include any amount received from the Virginia Polytechnic Institute & State University, out of amounts transferred from the Hokie Spirit Memorial Fund established by the Virginia Tech Foundation, an organization organized and operated as described in section 501(c)(3) of the Internal Revenue Code of 1986, if such amount is paid on account of the tragic event on April 16, 2007, at such university.

• 2006, Tax Relief and Health Care Act of 2006 (P.L. 109-432)

P.L. 109-432, Division C, §403(c) and (d)(2), provide:

(c) TAX INCENTIVE FOR SALE OF EXISTING MINERAL AND GEOTHERMAL RIGHTS TO TAX-EXEMPT ENTITIES.—

(1) EXCLUSION.—For purposes of the Internal Revenue Code of 1986, gross income shall not include 25 percent of the qualifying gain from a conservation sale of a qualifying mineral or geothermal interest.

(2) QUALIFYING GAIN.—For purposes of this subsection, the term "qualifying gain" means any gain which would be recognized as long-term capital gain under such Code.

(3) CONSERVATION SALE.—For purposes of this subsection, the term "conservation sale" means a sale which meets the following requirements:

(A) TRANSFEREE IS AN ELIGIBLE ENTITY.—The transferee of the qualifying mineral or geothermal interest is an eligible entity.

(B) QUALIFYING LETTER OF INTENT REQUIRED.—At the time of the sale, such transferee provides the taxpayer with a qualifying letter of intent.

(C) NONAPPLICATION TO CERTAIN SALES.—The sale is not made pursuant to an order of condemnation or eminent domain.

(4) QUALIFYING MINERAL OR GEOTHERMAL INTEREST.—For purposes of this subsection—

(A) IN GENERAL.—The term "qualifying mineral or geothermal interest" means an interest in any mineral or geothermal deposit located on eligible Federal land which constitutes a taxpayer's entire interest in such deposit.

(B) ENTIRE INTEREST.—For purposes of subparagraph (A)—

(i) an interest in any mineral or geothermal deposit is not a taxpayer's entire interest if such interest in such mineral or geothermal deposit was divided in order to avoid the requirements of such subparagraph or section 170(f)(3)(A) of such Code, and

(ii) a taxpayer's entire interest in such deposit does not fail to satisfy such subparagraph solely because the taxpayer has retained an interest in other deposits, even if the other deposits are contiguous with such certain deposit and were acquired by the taxpayer along with such certain deposit in a single conveyance.

(5) OTHER DEFINITIONS.—For purposes of this subsection—

(A) ELIGIBLE ENTITY.—The term "eligible entity" means—

(i) a governmental unit referred to in section 170(c)(1) of such Code, or an agency or department thereof operated primarily for 1 or more of the conservation purposes specified in clause (i), (ii), or (iii) of section 170(h)(4)(A) of such Code, or

(ii) an entity which is—

(I) described in section 170(b)(1)(A)(vi) or section 170(h)(3)(B) of such Code, and

(II) organized and at all times operated primarily for 1 or more of the conservation purposes specified in clause (i), (ii), or (iii) of section 170(h)(4)(A) of such Code.

(B) QUALIFYING LETTER OF INTENT.—The term "qualifying letter of intent" means a written letter of intent which includes the following statement: "The transferee's intent is that this acquisition will serve 1 or more of the conservation purposes specified in clause (i), (ii), or (iii) of section 170(h)(4)(A) of the Internal Revenue Code of 1986, that the transferee's use of the deposits so acquired will be consistent with section 170(h)(5) of such Code, and that the use of the deposits will continue to be consistent with such section, even if ownership or possession of such deposits is subsequently transferred to another person.".

(6) TAX ON SUBSEQUENT TRANSFERS.—

(A) IN GENERAL.—A tax is hereby imposed on any subsequent transfer by an eligible entity of ownership or possession, whether by sale, exchange, or lease, of an interest acquired directly or indirectly in—

(i) a conservation sale described in paragraph (1), or

(ii) a transfer described in clause (i), (ii), or (iii) of subparagraph (D).

(B) AMOUNT OF TAX.—The amount of tax imposed by subparagraph (A) on any transfer shall be equal to the sum of—

(i) 20 percent of the fair market value (determined at the time of the transfer) of the interest the ownership or possession of which is transferred, plus

(ii) the product of—

(I) the highest rate of tax specified in section 11 of such Code, times

(II) any gain or income realized by the transferor as a result of the transfer.

(C) LIABILITY.—The tax imposed by subparagraph (A) shall be paid by the transferor.

(D) RELIEF FROM LIABILITY.—The person (otherwise liable for any tax imposed by subparagraph (A)) shall be relieved of liability for the tax imposed by subparagraph (A) with respect to any transfer if—

(i) the transferee is an eligible entity which provides such person, at the time of transfer, a qualifying letter of intent,

(ii) in any case where the transferee is not an eligible entity, it is established to the satisfaction of the Secretary of the Treasury, that the transfer of ownership or possession, as the case may be, will be consistent with section 170(h)(5) of such Code, and the transferee provides such person, at the time of transfer, a qualifying letter of intent, or

(iii) tax has previously been paid under this paragraph as a result of a prior transfer of ownership or possession of the same interest.

(E) ADMINISTRATIVE PROVISIONS.—For purposes of subtitle F of such Code, the taxes imposed by this paragraph shall be treated as excise taxes with respect to which the deficiency procedures of such subtitle apply.

(7) REPORTING.—The Secretary of the Treasury may require such reporting as may be necessary or appropriate to further the purpose under this subsection that any conservation use be in perpetuity.

(d) EFFECTIVE DATES.—

* * *

(2) TAX INCENTIVE.—Subsection (c) shall apply to sales occurring on or after the date of the enactment of this Act.

• 2005, Katrina Emergency Tax Relief Act of 2005 (P.L. 109-73)

P.L. 109-73, §304 [but see P.L. 110-343, Division C, §702, in the amendment notes for Code Sec. 1400N(a)], provides:

SEC. 304. MILEAGE REIMBURSEMENTS TO CHARITABLE VOLUNTEERS EXCLUDED FROM GROSS INCOME.

(a) IN GENERAL.—For purposes of the Internal Revenue Code of 1986, gross income of an individual for taxable years ending on or after August 25, 2005, does not include amounts received, from an organization described in section 170(c) of such Code, as reimbursement of operating expenses with respect to use of a passenger automobile for the benefit of such organization in connection with providing relief relating to Hurricane Katrina during the period beginning on August 25, 2005, and ending on December 31, 2006. The preceding sentence shall apply only to the extent that the expenses which are reimbursed would be deductible under chapter 1 of such Code if section 274(d) of such Code were applied—

(1) by using the standard business mileage rate in effect under section 162(a) at the time of such use, and

(2) as if the individual were an employee of an organization not described in section 170(c) of such Code.

(b) APPLICATION TO VOLUNTEER SERVICES ONLY.— Subsection (a) shall not apply with respect to any expenses relating to the performance of services for compensation.

(c) NO DOUBLE BENEFIT.—No deduction or credit shall be allowed under any other provision of such Code with respect to the expenses excludable from gross income under subsection (a).

P.L. 109-73, §401 [but see P.L. 110-343, Division C, §702, in the amendment notes for Code Sec. 1400N(a)], provides:

SEC. 401. EXCLUSIONS OF CERTAIN CANCELLATIONS OF INDEBTEDNESS BY REASON OF HURRICANE KATRINA.

(a) IN GENERAL.—For purposes of the Internal Revenue Code of 1986, gross income shall not include any amount which (but for this section) would be includible in gross income by reason of the discharge (in whole or in part) of indebtedness of a natural person described in subsection (b) by an applicable entity (as defined in section 6050P(c)(1) of such Code).

(b) PERSONS DESCRIBED.—A natural person is described in this subsection if the principal place of abode of such person on August 25, 2005, was located—

(1) in the core disaster area, or

(2) in the Hurricane Katrina disaster area (but outside the core disaster area) and such person suffered economic loss by reason of Hurricane Katrina.

(c) EXCEPTIONS.—

(1) BUSINESS INDEBTEDNESS.—Subsection (a) shall not apply to any indebtedness incurred in connection with a trade or business.

(2) REAL PROPERTY OUTSIDE CORE DISASTER AREA.—Subsection (a) shall not apply to any discharge of indebtedness to the extent that real property constituting security for such indebtedness is located outside of the Hurricane Katrina disaster area.

(d) DENIAL OF DOUBLE BENEFIT.—For purposes of the Internal Revenue Code of 1986, the amount excluded from gross income under subsection (a) shall be treated in the same manner as an amount excluded under section 108(a) of such Code.

(e) EFFECTIVE DATE.—This section shall apply to discharges made on or after August 25, 2005, and before January 1, 2007.

• 2002, Victims of Terrorism Tax Relief Act of 2001 (P.L. 107-134)

P.L. 107-134, §105, provides:

SEC. 105. EXCLUSION OF CERTAIN CANCELLATIONS OF INDEBTEDNESS.

(a) IN GENERAL.—For purposes of the Internal Revenue Code of 1986—

(1) gross income shall not include any amount which (but for this section) would be includible in gross income by reason of the discharge (in whole or in part) of indebtedness of any taxpayer if the discharge is by reason of the death of an individual incurred as the result of the terrorist attacks against the United States on September 11, 2001, or as the result of illness incurred as a result of an attack involving anthrax occurring on or after September 11, 2001, and before January 1, 2002; and

(2) return requirements under section 6050P of such Code shall not apply to any discharge described in paragraph (1).

(b) EFFECTIVE DATE.—This section shall apply to discharges made on or after September 11, 2001, and before January 1, 2002.

• 1984, Deficit Reduction Act of 1984 (P.L. 98-369)

P.L. 98-369, §531(c):

Amended Code Sec. 61(a) by striking out "commissions, and similar items" and inserting in lieu thereof "commissions, fringe benefits, and similar items". **Effective** 1-1-85.

P.L. 98-369, §531(h), as amended by P.L. 99-272, §13207(d), provides:

(h) Moratorium on Issuance of Regulations Relating to Faculty Housing.—

(1) In General.—Any regulation providing for the inclusion in gross income under section 61 of the Internal Revenue Code of 1954 of the excess (if any) of the fair market value of qualified campus lodging over the greater of—

(A) the operating costs paid or incurred in furnishing such lodging, or

(B) the rent received for such lodging, shall not be issued before January 1, 1986.

(2) Qualified Campus Lodging.—For purposes of this subsection, the term "qualified campus lodging" means lodging which is—

(A) located on (or in close proximity to) a campus of an educational institution (described in section 170(b)(1)(A)(ii) of the Internal Revenue Code of 1954), and

(B) provided by such institution to an employee of such institution, or to a spouse or dependent (within the meaning of section 152 of such Code) of such employee.

(3) Application of Subsection.—This subsection shall apply with respect to lodging furnished after December 31, 1983, and before January 1, 1986.

P.L. 98-369, §1026, provides:

SEC. 1026. NO GAIN RECOGNIZED FROM NET GIFTS MADE BEFORE MARCH 4, 1981.

(a) IN GENERAL.—In the case of any transfer of property subject to gift tax made before March 4, 1981, for purposes of subtitle A of the Internal Revenue Code of 1954, gross income of the donor shall not include any amount attributable to the donee's payment of (or agreement to pay) any gift tax imposed with respect to such gift.

(b) GIFT TAX DEFINED.—For purposes of subsection (a), the term "gift tax" means—

(1) the tax imposed by chapter 12 of such Code, and

(2) any tax imposed by a State (or the District of Columbia) on transfers by gifts.

(c) STATUTE OF LIMITATIONS.—If refund or credit of any overpayment of tax resulting from subsection (a) is prevented on the date of the enactment of this Act (or at any time within 1 year after such date) by the operation of any law or rule of law (including res judicata), refund or credit of such overpayment (to the extent attributable to subsection (a)) may nevertheless be made or allowed if claim therefor is filed within 1 year after the date of the enactment of this Act.

P.L. 95-427, §1, as amended by P.L. 97-34, §801, and P.L. 96-167, §1, provides:

SEC. 1. FRINGE BENEFIT REGULATIONS.

(a) IN GENERAL.—No fringe benefit regulation shall be issued—

(1) in final form on or after May 1, 1978, and on or before December 31, 1983, or

(2) in proposed or final form on or after May 1, 1978, if such regulation has an effective date on or before December 31, 1983.

(b) DEFINITION OF FRINGE BENEFIT REGULATION.—For purposes of subsection (a), the term "fringe benefit regulation" means a regulation providing for the inclusion of any fringe benefit in gross income by reason of section 61 of the Internal Revenue Code of 1954.

* * *

[Sec. 67]

SEC. 67. 2-PERCENT FLOOR ON MISCELLANEOUS ITEMIZED DEDUCTIONS.

[Sec. 67(a)]

(a) GENERAL RULE.—In the case of an individual, the miscellaneous itemized deductions for any taxable year shall be allowed only to the extent that the aggregate of such deductions exceeds 2 percent of adjusted gross income.

[Sec. 67(b)]

(b) MISCELLANEOUS ITEMIZED DEDUCTIONS.—For purposes of this section, the term "miscellaneous itemized deductions" means the itemized deductions other than—

(1) the deduction under section 163 (relating to interest),

(2) the deduction under section 164 (relating to taxes),

(3) the deduction under section 165(a) for casualty or theft losses described in paragraph (2) or (3) of section 165(c) or for losses described in section 165(d),

(4) the deductions under section 170 (relating to charitable, etc., contributions and gifts) and section 642(c) (relating to deduction for amounts paid or permanently set aside for a charitable purpose),

(5) the deduction under section 213 (relating to medical, dental, etc., expenses),

(6) any deduction allowable for impairment-related work expenses,

(7) the deduction under section 691(c) (relating to deduction for estate tax in case of income in respect of the decedent),

(8) any deduction allowable in connection with personal property used in a short sale,

(9) the deduction under section 1341 (relating to computation of tax where taxpayer restores substantial amount held under claim of right),

(10) the deduction under section 72(b)(3) (relating to deduction where annuity payments cease before investment recovered),

(11) the deduction under section 171 (relating to deduction for amortizable bond premium), and

(12) the deduction under section 216 (relating to deductions in connection with cooperative housing corporations).

Amendments

• 1998, Tax and Trade Relief Extension Act of 1998 (P.L. 105-277)

P.L. 105-277, §4004(b)(1):

Amended Code Sec. 67(b)(3) by striking "for losses described in subsection (c)(3) or (d) of section 165" and inserting "for casualty or theft losses described in paragraph (2) or (3) of section 165(c) or for losses described in section 165(d)". **Effective** for tax years beginning after 12-31-86.

• 1993, Omnibus Budget Reconciliation Act of 1993 (P.L. 103-66)

P.L. 103-66, §13213(c)(2):

Amended Code Sec. 67(b) by striking paragraph (6) and redesignating paragraphs (7) through (13) as paragraphs (6) through (12). **Effective** for expenses incurred after 12-31-93. Prior to amendment, Code Sec. 67(b)(6) read as follows:

(6) the deduction under section 217 (relating to moving expenses).

• 1988, Technical and Miscellaneous Revenue Act of 1988 (P.L. 100-647)

P.L. 100-647, §1001(f)(2)(A)-(B):

Amended Code Sec. 67(b)(4) by striking out "deduction" and inserting in lieu thereof "deductions", and by inserting before the comma at the end thereof "and section 642(c) (relating to deduction for amounts paid or permanently set aside for a charitable purpose)". **Effective** as if included in the provision of P.L. 99-514 to which it relates.

* * *

[Sec. 67(e)]

(e) DETERMINATION OF ADJUSTED GROSS INCOME IN CASE OF ESTATES AND TRUSTS.—For purposes of this section, the adjusted gross income of an estate or trust shall be computed in the same manner as in the case of an individual, except that—

(1) the deductions for costs which are paid or incurred in connection with the administration of the estate or trust and which would not have been incurred if the property were not held in such trust or estate, and

(2) the deductions allowable under sections 642(b), 651, and 661,

shall be treated as allowable in arriving at adjusted gross income. Under regulations, appropriate adjustments shall be made in the application of part I of subchapter J of this chapter to take into account the provisions of this section.

Amendments

• 1988, Technical and Miscellaneous Revenue Act of 1988 (P.L. 100-647)

P.L. 100-647, §1001(f)(3):

Amended Code Sec. 67(e). **Effective** as if included in the provision of P.L. 99-514 to which it relates. Prior to amendment, Code Sec. 67(e) read as follows:

(e) DETERMINATION OF ADJUSTED GROSS INCOME IN CASE OF ESTATES AND TRUSTS.—For purposes of this section, the adjusted gross income of an estate or trust shall be computed in the same manner as in the case of an individual, except that the deductions for costs which are paid or incurred in connection with the administration of the estate or trust and would not have been incurred if the property were not held in such trust or estate shall be treated as allowable in arriving at adjusted gross income.

• 1986, Tax Reform Act of 1986 (P.L. 99-514)

P.L. 99-514, §132(a):

Amended part I of subchapter B of chapter 1 by adding at the end thereof new Code Sec. 67. **Effective** for tax years beginning after 12-31-86.

[Sec. 67(f)]

(f) COORDINATION WITH OTHER LIMITATION.—This section shall be applied before the application of the dollar limitation of the second sentence of section 162(a) (relating to trade or business expenses).

Amendments

• 2000, Community Renewal Tax Relief Act of 2000 (P.L. 106-554)

P.L. 106-554, §319(2):

Amended Code Sec. 67(f) by striking "the last sentence" and inserting "the second sentence". **Effective** 12-21-2000.

• 1988, Technical and Miscellaneous Revenue Act of 1988 (P.L. 100-647)

P.L. 100-647, §1001(f)(1):

Amended Code Sec. 67 by adding at the end thereof new subsection (f). **Effective** as if included in the provision of P.L. 99-514 to which it relates.

[Sec. 67(g)]

(g) SUSPENSION FOR TAXABLE YEARS 2018 THROUGH 2025.—Notwithstanding subsection (a), no miscellaneous itemized deduction shall be allowed for any taxable year beginning after December 31, 2017, and before January 1, 2026.

Amendments

• 2017, Tax Cuts and Jobs Act (P.L. 115-97)

P.L. 115-97, §11045(a):

Amended Code Sec. 67 by adding at the end a new subsection (g). **Effective** for tax years beginning after 12-31-2017.

* * *

PART III—ITEMS SPECIFICALLY EXCLUDED FROM GROSS INCOME

* * *

Sec. 102. Gifts and inheritances.

* * *

Sec. 112. Certain combat zone compensation of members of the Armed Forces.

* * *

[Sec. 102]

SEC. 102. GIFTS AND INHERITANCES.

[Sec. 102(a)]

(a) GENERAL RULE.—Gross income does not include the value of property acquired by gift, bequest, devise, or inheritance.

[Sec. 102(b)]

(b) INCOME.—Subsection (a) shall not exclude from gross income—

(1) the income from any property referred to in subsection (a); or

(2) where the gift, bequest, devise, or inheritance is of income from property, the amount of such income.

Where, under the terms of the gift, bequest, devise, or inheritance, the payment, crediting, or distribution thereof is to be made at intervals, then, to the extent that it is paid or credited or to be distributed out of income from property, it shall be treated for purposes of paragraph (2) as a gift, bequest, devise, or inheritance of income from property. Any amount included in the gross income of a beneficiary under subchapter J shall be treated for purposes of paragraph (2) as a gift, bequest, devise, or inheritance of income from property.

[Sec. 102(c)]

(c) EMPLOYEE GIFTS.—

(1) IN GENERAL.—Subsection (a) shall not exclude from gross income any amount transferred by or for an employer to, or for the benefit of, an employee.

(2) CROSS REFERENCES.—

For provisions excluding certain employee achievement awards from gross income, see section 74(c).

For provisions excluding certain de minimis fringes from gross income, see section 132(e).

Amendments

• 1986, Tax Reform Act of 1986 (P.L. 99-514)

P.L. 99-514, §122(b):

Amended Code Sec. 102 by adding at the end thereof new subsection (c). **Effective** for prizes and awards granted after 12-31-86.

* * *

[Sec. 112]

SEC. 112. CERTAIN COMBAT ZONE COMPENSATION OF MEMBERS OF THE ARMED FORCES.

* * *

[Sec. 112(c)]

(c) DEFINITIONS.—For purposes of this section—

(1) The term "commissioned officer" does not include a commissioned warrant officer.

(2) The term "combat zone" means any area which the President of the United States by Executive Order designates, for purposes of this section or corresponding provisions of prior income tax laws, as an area in which Armed Forces of the United States are or have engaged in combat.

(3) Service is performed in a combat zone only if performed on or after the date designated by the President by Executive Order as the date of the commencing of combatant activities in such zone, and on or before the date designated by the President by Executive Order as the date of the termination of combatant activities in such zone.

(4) The term "compensation" does not include pensions and retirement pay.

(5) The term "maximum enlisted amount" means, for any month, the sum of—

(A) the highest rate of basic pay payable for such month to any enlisted member of the Armed Forces of the United States at the highest pay grade applicable to enlisted members, and

(B) in the case of an officer entitled to special pay under section 310, or paragraph (1) or (3) of section 351(a), of title 37, United States Code, for such month, the amount of such special pay payable to such officer for such month.

Amendments

• 2017, Tax Cuts and Jobs Act (P.L. 115-97)

P.L. 115-97, §11026, provides:

SEC. 11026. TREATMENT OF CERTAIN INDIVIDUALS PERFORMING SERVICES IN THE SINAI PENINSULA OF EGYPT.

(a) IN GENERAL.—For purposes of the following provisions of the Internal Revenue Code of 1986, with respect to the applicable period, a qualified hazardous duty area shall be treated in the same manner as if it were a combat zone (as determined under section 112 of such Code):

(1) Section 2(a)(3) (relating to special rule where deceased spouse was in missing status).

(2) Section 112 (relating to the exclusion of certain combat pay of members of the Armed Forces).

(3) Section 692 (relating to income taxes of members of Armed Forces on death).

(4) Section 2201 (relating to members of the Armed Forces dying in combat zone or by reason of combat-zone-incurred wounds, etc.).

(5) Section 3401(a)(1) (defining wages relating to combat pay for members of the Armed Forces).

(6) Section 4253(d) (relating to the taxation of phone service originating from a combat zone from members of the Armed Forces).

(7) Section 6013(f)(1) (relating to joint return where individual is in missing status).

(8) Section 7508 (relating to time for performing certain acts postponed by reason of service in combat zone).

(b) QUALIFIED HAZARDOUS DUTY AREA.—For purposes of this section, the term "qualified hazardous duty area" means the Sinai Peninsula of Egypt, if as of the date of the enactment of this section any member of the Armed Forces of the United States is entitled to special pay under section 310 of title 37, United States Code (relating to special pay; duty subject to hostile fire or imminent danger), for services performed in such location. Such term includes such location only during the period such entitlement is in effect.

(c) APPLICABLE PERIOD.—

(1) IN GENERAL.—Except as provided in paragraph (2), the applicable period is—

(A) the portion of the first taxable year ending after June 9, 2015, which begins on such date, and

(B) any subsequent taxable year beginning before January 1, 2026.

(2) WITHHOLDING.—In the case of subsection (a)(5), the applicable period is—

(A) the portion of the first taxable year ending after the date of the enactment of this Act which begins on such date, and

(B) any subsequent taxable year beginning before January 1, 2026.

(d) EFFECTIVE DATE.—

(1) IN GENERAL.—Except as provided in paragraph (2), the provisions of this section shall take effect on June 9, 2015.

(2) WITHHOLDING.—Subsection (a)(5) shall apply to remuneration paid after the date of the enactment of this Act.

• 2016, National Defense Authorization Act for Fiscal Year 2017 (P.L. 114-328)

P.L. 114-328, §618(k):

Amended Code Sec. 112(c)(5)(B) by inserting ", or paragraph (1) or (3) of section 351(a)," after "section 310". **Effective** 12-23-2016.

• 2014, Tax Technical Corrections Act of 2014 (P.L. 113-295)

P.L. 113-295, §221(a)(18)(A)-(B), Division A:

Amended Code Sec. 112(c) by striking "(after June 24, 1950)" before "engaged in combat" in paragraph (2), and by striking "such zone;" and all that follows in paragraph (3) and inserting "such zone.". **Effective** generally 12-19-2014. For a special rule, see Act Sec. 221(b)(2), Division A, below. Prior to amendment, Code Sec. 112(c)(3) read as follows:

(3) Service is performed in a combat zone only if performed on or after the date designated by the President by Executive Order as the date of the commencing of combatant activities in such zone, and on or before the date designated by the President by Executive Order as the date of the termination of combatant activities in such zone; except that June 25, 1950, shall be considered the date of the commencing of combatant activities in the combat zone designated in Executive Order 10195.

P.L. 113-295, §221(b)(2), Division A, provides:

(2) SAVINGS PROVISION.—If—

(A) any provision amended or repealed by the amendments made by this section applied to—

(i) any transaction occurring before the date of the enactment of this Act,

(ii) any property acquired before such date of enactment, or

(iii) any item of income, loss, deduction, or credit taken into account before such date of enactment, and

(B) the treatment of such transaction, property, or item under such provision would (without regard to the amendments or repeals made by this section) affect the liability for tax for periods ending after date of enactment. nothing in the amendments or repeals made by this section shall be construed to affect the treatment of such transaction, property, or item for purposes of determining liability for tax for periods ending after such date of enactment.

• 2000 (P.L. 106-398)

P.L. 106-398, §1089, provides:

SEC. 1089. SENSE OF CONGRESS REGARDING TAX TREATMENT OF MEMBERS RECEIVING SPECIAL PAY FOR DUTY SUBJECT TO HOSTILE FIRE OR IMMINENT DANGER.

It is the sense of Congress that members of the Armed Forces who receive special pay under section 310 of title 37, United States Code, for duty subject to hostile fire or imminent danger should receive the same treatment under Federal income tax laws as members serving in combat zones.

• 2000 (P.L. 106-65)

P.L. 106-65, §677, provides:

SEC. 677. SENSE OF CONGRESS REGARDING TREATMENT UNDER INTERNAL REVENUE CODE OF MEMBERS RECEIVING HOSTILE FIRE OR IMMINENT DANGER SPECIAL PAY DURING CONTINGENCY OPERATIONS.

It is the sense of Congress that a member of the Armed Forces who is receiving special pay under section 310 of title 37, United States Code, while assigned to duty in support of a contingency operation should be treated under the Internal Revenue Code of 1986 in the same manner as a member of the Armed Forces serving in a combat zone (as defined in section 112 of the Internal Revenue Code of 1986).

• 1999 (P.L. 106-21)

P.L. 106-21, §1(a)(2), (b) and (d)(1), provide:

SECTION 1. AVAILABILITY OF CERTAIN TAX BENEFITS FOR SERVICES AS PART OF OPERATION ALLIED FORCE.

(a) GENERAL RULE.—For purposes of the following provisions of the Internal Revenue Code of 1986, a qualified hazardous duty area shall be treated in the same manner as if it were a combat zone (as determined under section 112 of such Code):

* * *

(2) Section 112 (relating to the exclusion of certain combat pay of members of the Armed Forces).

* * *

(b) QUALIFIED HAZARDOUS DUTY AREA.—For purposes of this section, the term "qualified hazardous duty area" means any area of the Federal Republic of Yugoslavia (Serbia/Montenegro), Albania, the Adriatic Sea, and the northern Ionian Sea (above the 39th parallel) during the period (which includes the date of the enactment of this Act) that any member of the Armed Forces of the United States is entitled to special pay under section 310 of title 37, United States Code (relating to special pay: duty subject to hostile fire or imminent danger) for services performed in such area.

* * *

(d) EFFECTIVE DATES.—

(1) IN GENERAL.—Except as provided in paragraph (2), this section shall take effect on March 24, 1999.

• 1996 (P.L. 104-117)

P.L. 104-117, §1(a)(2), (b) and (e)(1), provide:

SECTION 1. TREATMENT OF CERTAIN INDIVIDUALS PERFORMING SERVICES IN CERTAIN HAZARDOUS DUTY AREAS.

(a) GENERAL RULE.—For purposes of the following provisions of the Internal Revenue Code of 1986, a qualified hazardous duty area shall be treated in the same manner as if it were a combat zone (as determined under section 112 of such Code):

* * *

(2) Section 112 (relating to the exclusion of certain combat pay of members of the Armed Forces).

* * *

(b) QUALIFIED HAZARDOUS DUTY AREA.—For purposes of this section, the term "qualified hazardous duty area" means Bosnia and Herzegovina, Croatia, or Macedonia, if as of the date of the enactment of this section any member of the Armed Forces of the United States is entitled to special pay under section 310 of title 37, United States Code (relating to special pay; duty subject to hostile fire or imminent danger) for services performed in such country. Such term includes any such country only during the period such entitlement is in effect. Solely for purposes of applying section 7508 of the Internal Revenue Code of 1986, in the case of an individual who is performing services as part of Operation Joint Endeavor outside the United States while deployed away from such individual's permanent duty station, the term "qualified hazardous duty area" includes, during the period for which such entitlement is in effect, any area in which such services are performed.

* * *

(e) EFFECTIVE DATE.—

(1) IN GENERAL.—Except as provided in paragraph (2), the provisions of and amendments made by this section shall take effect on November 21, 1995.

P.L. 104-117, §1(d)(2):

Amended Code Sec. 112(c) by adding at the end a new paragraph (5). **Effective** 11-21-95.

• 1975 (P.L. 93-597)

P.L. 93-597, §2(a):

Amended Code Sec. 112(c) by deleting former paragraph (5). **Effective** 7-1-73. Former paragraph (5) read as follows:

"(5) The term 'induction period' means any period during which, under laws heretofore or hereafter enacted relating to the induction of individuals for training and service in the Armed Forces of the United States, individuals (other than individuals liable for induction by reason of a prior deferment) are liable for induction for such training and service."

* * *

PART VI—ITEMIZED DEDUCTIONS FOR INDIVIDUALS AND CORPORATIONS

* * *

[Sec. 170]

SEC. 170. CHARITABLE, ETC., CONTRIBUTIONS AND GIFTS.

* * *

[Sec. 170(b)]

(b) PERCENTAGE LIMITATIONS.—

(1) INDIVIDUALS.—In the case of an individual, the deduction provided in subsection (a) shall be limited as provided in the succeeding subparagraphs.

(A) GENERAL RULE.—Any charitable contribution to—

(i) a church or a convention or association of churches,

(ii) an educational organization which normally maintains a regular faculty and curriculum and normally has a regularly enrolled body of pupils or students in attendance at the place where its educational activities are regularly carried on,

(iii) an organization the principal purpose or functions of which are the providing of medical or hospital care or medical education or medical research, if the organization is a hospital, or if the organization is a medical research organization directly engaged in the continuous active conduct of medical research in conjunction with a hospital, and during the calendar year in which the contribution is made such organization is committed to spend such contributions for such research before January 1 of the fifth calendar year which begins after the date such contribution is made,

(iv) an organization which normally receives a substantial part of its support (exclusive of income received in the exercise or performance by such organization of its charitable, educational, or other purpose or function constituting the basis for its exemption under section 501(a)) from the United States or any State or political subdivision thereof or from direct or indirect contributions from the general public, and which is organized and operated exclusively to receive, hold, invest, and administer property and to make expenditures to or for the benefit of a college or university which is an organization referred to in clause (ii) of this subparagraph and which is an agency or instrumentality of a State or political subdivision thereof, or which is owned or operated by a State or political subdivision thereof or by an agency or instrumentality of one or more States or political subdivisions,

(v) a governmental unit referred to in subsection (c)(1),

(vi) an organization referred to in subsection (c)(2) which normally receives a substantial part of its support (exclusive of income received in the exercise or performance by such organization of its charitable, educational, or other purpose or function constituting the basis for its exemption under section 501(a)) from a governmental unit referred to in subsection (c)(1) or from direct or indirect contributions from the general public,

(vii) a private foundation described in subparagraph (F),

(viii) an organization described in section 509(a)(2) or (3), or

(ix) an agricultural research organization directly engaged in the continuous active conduct of agricultural research (as defined in section 1404 of the National Agricultural Research, Extension, and Teaching Policy Act of 1977) in conjunction with a land-grant college or university (as defined in such section) or a non-land grant college of agriculture (as defined in such section), and during the calendar year in which the contribution is made such organization is committed to spend such contribution for such research before January 1 of the fifth calendar year which begins after the date such contribution is made,

shall be allowed to the extent that the aggregate of such contributions does not exceed 50 percent of the taxpayer's contribution base for the taxable year.

(B) OTHER CONTRIBUTIONS.—Any charitable contribution other than a charitable contribution to which subparagraph (A) applies shall be allowed to the extent that the aggregate of such contributions does not exceed the lesser of—

(i) 30 percent of the taxpayer's contribution base for the taxable year, or

(ii) the excess of 50 percent of the taxpayer's contribution base for the taxable year over the amount of charitable contributions allowable under subparagraph (A) (determined without regard to subparagraph (C)).

If the aggregate of such contributions exceeds the limitation of the preceding sentence, such excess shall be treated (in a manner consistent with the rules of subsection (d)(1)) as a charitable contribution (to which subparagraph (A) does not apply) in each of the 5 succeeding taxable years in order of time.

(C) SPECIAL LIMITATION WITH RESPECT TO CONTRIBUTIONS DESCRIBED IN SUBPARAGRAPH (A) OF CERTAIN CAPITAL GAIN PROPERTY.—

(i) In the case of charitable contributions described in subparagraph (A) of capital gain property to which subsection (e)(1)(B) does not apply, the total amount of contributions of such property which may be taken into account under subsection (a) for any taxable year shall not exceed 30 percent of the taxpayer's contribution base for such year. For purposes of this subsection, contributions of capital gain property to which this subparagraph applies shall be taken into account after all other charitable contributions (other than charitable contributions to which subparagraph (D) applies).

(ii) If charitable contributions described in subparagraph (A) of capital gain property to which clause (i) applies exceeds 30 percent of the taxpayer's contribution base for any taxable year, such excess shall be treated, in a manner consistent with the rules of subsection (d)(1), as a charitable contribution of capital gain property to which clause (i) applies in each of the 5 succeeding taxable years in order of time.

(iii) At the election of the taxpayer (made at such time and in such manner as the Secretary prescribes by regulations), subsection (e)(1) shall apply to all contributions of capital gain property (to which subsection (e)(1)(B) does not otherwise apply) made by the taxpayer during the taxable year. If such an election is made, clauses (i) and (ii) shall not apply to contributions of capital gain property made during the taxable year, and, in applying subsection (d)(1) for such taxable year with respect to contributions of capital gain property made in any prior contribution year for which an election was not made under this clause, such contributions shall be reduced as if subsection (e)(1) had applied to such contributions in the year in which made.

(iv) For purposes of this paragraph, the term "capital gain property" means, with respect to any contribution, any capital asset the sale of which at its fair market value at the time of the contribution would have resulted in gain which would have been long-term capital gain. For purposes of the preceding sentence, any property which is property used in the trade or business (as defined in section 1231(b)) shall be treated as a capital asset.

(D) SPECIAL LIMITATION WITH RESPECT TO CONTRIBUTIONS OF CAPITAL GAIN PROPERTY TO ORGANIZATIONS NOT DESCRIBED IN SUBPARAGRAPH (A).—

(i) IN GENERAL.—In the case of charitable contributions (other than charitable contributions to which subparagraph (A) applies) of capital gain property, the total amount of such contributions of such property taken into account under subsection (a) for any taxable year shall not exceed the lesser of—

(I) 20 percent of the taxpayer's contribution base for the taxable year, or

(II) the excess of 30 percent of the taxpayer's contribution base for the taxable year over the amount of the contributions of capital gain property to which subparagraph (C) applies.

For purposes of this subsection, contributions of capital gain property to which this subparagraph applies shall be taken into account after all other charitable contributions.

(ii) CARRYOVER.—If the aggregate amount of contributions described in clause (i) exceeds the limitation of clause (i), such excess shall be treated (in a manner consistent with the rules of subsection (d)(1)) as a charitable contribution of capital gain property to which clause (i) applies in each of the 5 succeeding taxable years in order of time.

(E) CONTRIBUTIONS OF QUALIFIED CONSERVATION CONTRIBUTIONS.—

(i) IN GENERAL.—Any qualified conservation contribution (as defined in subsection (h)(1)) shall be allowed to the extent the aggregate of such contributions does not exceed the excess of 50 percent of the taxpayer's contribution base over the amount of all other charitable contributions allowable under this paragraph.

(ii) CARRYOVER.—If the aggregate amount of contributions described in clause (i) exceeds the limitation of clause (i), such excess shall be treated (in a manner consistent with the rules of subsection (d)(1)) as a charitable contribution to which clause (i) applies in each of the 15 succeeding years in order of time.

(iii) COORDINATION WITH OTHER SUBPARAGRAPHS.—For purposes of applying this subsection and subsection (d)(1), contributions described in clause (i) shall not be treated as described in subparagraph (A), (B), (C), or (D) and such subparagraphs shall apply without regard to such contributions.

(iv) SPECIAL RULE FOR CONTRIBUTION OF PROPERTY USED IN AGRICULTURE OR LIVESTOCK PRODUCTION.—

(I) IN GENERAL.—If the individual is a qualified farmer or rancher for the taxable year for which the contribution is made, clause (i) shall be applied by substituting "100 percent" for "50 percent".

(II) EXCEPTION.—Subclause (I) shall not apply to any contribution of property made after the date of the enactment of this subparagraph which is used in agriculture or livestock production (or available for such production) unless such contribution is subject to a restriction that such property remain available for such production. This subparagraph shall be applied separately with respect to property to which subclause (I) does not apply by reason of the preceding sentence prior to its application to property to which subclause (I) does apply.

(v) DEFINITION.—For purposes of clause (iv), the term "qualified farmer or rancher" means a taxpayer whose gross income from the trade or business of farming (within the meaning of section 2032A(e)(5)) is greater than 50 percent of the taxpayer's gross income for the taxable year.

(F) CERTAIN PRIVATE FOUNDATIONS.—The private foundations referred to in subparagraph (A)(vii) and subsection (e)(1)(B) are—

(i) a private operating foundation (as defined in section 4942(j)(3)),

(ii) any other private foundation (as defined in section 509(a)) which, not later than the 15th day of the third month after the close of the foundation's taxable year in which contributions are received, makes qualifying distributions (as defined in section 4942(g), without regard to paragraph (3) thereof), which are treated, after the application of section 4942(g)(3), as distributions out of corpus (in accordance with section 4942(h)) in an amount equal to 100 percent of such contributions, and with respect to which the taxpayer obtains adequate records or other sufficient evidence from the foundation showing that the foundation made such qualifying distributions, and

(iii) a private foundation all of the contributions to which are pooled in a common fund and which would be described in section 509(a)(3) but for the right of any substantial contributor (hereafter in this clause called "donor") or his spouse to designate annually the recipients, from among organizations described in paragraph (1) of section 509(a), of the income attributable to the donor's contribution to the fund and to direct (by deed or by will) the payment, to an organization described in such paragraph (1), of the corpus in the common fund attributable to the donor's contribution; but this clause shall apply only if all of the income of the common fund is required to be (and is) distributed to one or more organizations described in such paragraph (1) not later than the 15th day of the third month after the close of the taxable year in which the income is realized by the fund and only if all of the corpus attributable to any donor's contribution to the fund is required to be (and is) distributed to one or more of such organizations not later than one year after his death or after the death of his surviving spouse if she has the right to designate the recipients of such corpus.

(G) INCREASED LIMITATION FOR CASH CONTRIBUTIONS.—

(i) IN GENERAL.—In the case of any contribution of cash to an organization described in subparagraph (A), the total amount of such contributions which may be taken into account under subsection (a) for any taxable year beginning after December 31, 2017, and before January 1, 2026, shall not exceed 60 percent of the taxpayer's contribution base for such year.

(ii) CARRYOVER.—If the aggregate amount of contributions described in clause (i) exceeds the applicable limitation under clause (i) for any taxable year described in such clause, such excess shall be treated (in a manner consistent with the rules of subsection (d)(1)) as a charitable contribution to which clause (i) applies in each of the 5 succeeding years in order of time.

(iii) COORDINATION WITH SUBPARAGRAPHS (A) AND (B).—

(I) IN GENERAL.—Contributions taken into account under this subparagraph shall not be taken into account under subparagraph (A).

(II) LIMITATION REDUCTION.—For each taxable year described in clause (i), and each taxable year to which any contribution under this subparagraph is carried over under clause (ii), subparagraph (A) shall be applied by reducing (but not below zero) the contribution limitation allowed for the taxable year under such subparagraph by the aggregate contributions allowed under this subparagraph for such taxable year, and subparagraph (B) shall be applied by treating any reference to subparagraph (A) as a reference to both subparagraph (A) and this subparagraph.

(H) CONTRIBUTION BASE DEFINED.—For purposes of this section, the term "contribution base" means adjusted gross income (computed without regard to any net operating loss carryback to the taxable year under section 172).

(2) CORPORATIONS.—In the case of a corporation—

(A) IN GENERAL.—The total deductions under subsection (a) for any taxable year (other than for contributions to which subparagraph (B) or (C) applies) shall not exceed 10 percent of the taxpayer's taxable income.

(B) QUALIFIED CONSERVATION CONTRIBUTIONS BY CERTAIN CORPORATE FARMERS AND RANCHERS.—

(i) IN GENERAL.—Any qualified conservation contribution (as defined in subsection (h)(1))—

(I) which is made by a corporation which, for the taxable year during which the contribution is made, is a qualified farmer or rancher (as defined in paragraph (1)(E)(v)) and the stock of which is not readily tradable on an established securities market at any time during such year, and

(II) which, in the case of contributions made after the date of the enactment of this subparagraph, is a contribution of property which is used in agriculture or livestock production (or available for such production) and which is subject to a restriction that such property remain available for such production,

shall be allowed to the extent the aggregate of such contributions does not exceed the excess of the taxpayer's taxable income over the amount of charitable contributions allowable under subparagraph (A).

(ii) CARRYOVER.—If the aggregate amount of contributions described in clause (i) exceeds the limitation of clause (i), such excess shall be treated (in a manner consistent with the rules of subsection (d)(2)) as a charitable contribution to which clause (i) applies in each of the 15 succeeding taxable years in order of time.

(C) QUALIFIED CONSERVATION CONTRIBUTIONS BY CERTAIN NATIVE CORPORATIONS.—

(i) IN GENERAL.—Any qualified conservation contribution (as defined in subsection (h)(1)) which—

(I) is made by a Native Corporation, and

(II) is a contribution of property which was land conveyed under the Alaska Native Claims Settlement Act,

shall be allowed to the extent that the aggregate amount of such contributions does not exceed the excess of the taxpayer's taxable income over the amount of charitable contributions allowable under subparagraph (A).

(ii) CARRYOVER.—If the aggregate amount of contributions described in clause (i) exceeds the limitation of clause (i), such excess shall be treated (in a manner consistent with the rules of subsection (d)(2)) as a charitable contribution to which clause (i) applies in each of the 15 succeeding taxable years in order of time.

(iii) NATIVE CORPORATION.—For purposes of this subparagraph, the term "Native Corporation" has the meaning given such term by section 3(m) of the Alaska Native Claims Settlement Act.

(D) TAXABLE INCOME.—For purposes of this paragraph, taxable income shall be computed without regard to—

(i) this section,

(ii) part VIII (except section 248),

(iii) any net operating loss carryback to the taxable year under section 172,

(iv) any capital loss carryback to the taxable year under section 1212(a)(1)

(v) section 199A(g).

Amendments

• 2020, Taxpayer Certainty and Disaster Tax Relief Act of 2020 (P.L. 116-260)

P.L. 116-260, §§301 and 304(a), Div. EE, provides:

SEC. 301. DEFINITIONS.

For purposes of this title—

(1) QUALIFIED DISASTER AREA.—

(A) IN GENERAL.—The term "qualified disaster area" means any area with respect to which a major disaster was declared, during the period beginning on January 1, 2020, and ending on the date which is 60 days after the date of the enactment of this Act, by the President under section 401 of the Robert T. Stafford Disaster Relief and Emergency Assistance Act if the incident period of the disaster with respect to which such declaration is made begins on or after December 28, 2019, and on or before the date of the enactment of this Act.

(B) COVID-19 EXCEPTION.—Such term shall not include any area with respect to which such a major disaster has been so declared only by reason of COVID-19.

(2) QUALIFIED DISASTER ZONE.—The term "qualified disaster zone" means that portion of any qualified disaster area which was determined by the President, during the period beginning on January 1, 2020, and ending on the date which is 60 days after the date of the enactment of this Act, to warrant individual or individual and public assistance from the Federal Government under the Robert T. Stafford Disaster Relief and Emergency Assistance Act by reason of the qualified disaster with respect to such disaster area.

(3) QUALIFIED DISASTER.—The term "qualified disaster" means, with respect to any qualified disaster area, the disaster by reason of which a major disaster was declared with respect to such area.

(4) INCIDENT PERIOD.—The term "incident period" means, with respect to any qualified disaster, the period specified by the Federal Emergency Management Agency as the period during which such disaster occurred (except that for purposes of this title such period shall not be treated as ending after the date which is 30 days after the date of the enactment of this Act).

SEC. 304. OTHER DISASTER-RELATED TAX RELIEF PROVISIONS.

(a) SPECIAL RULES FOR QUALIFIED DISASTER RELIEF CONTRIBUTIONS.—

(1) IN GENERAL.—In the case of a qualified disaster relief contribution made by a corporation—

(A) section 2205(a)(2)(B) of the CARES Act shall be applied first to qualified contributions without regard to any qualified disaster relief contributions and then separately to such qualified disaster relief contribution, and

(B) in applying such section to such qualified disaster relief contributions, clause (i) thereof shall be applied—

(i) by substituting "100 percent" for "25 percent", and

(ii) by treating qualified contributions other than qualified disaster relief contributions as contributions allowed under section 170(b)(2) of the Internal Revenue Code of 1986.

(2) QUALIFIED DISASTER RELIEF CONTRIBUTION.—For purposes of this subsection, the term "qualified disaster relief contribution" means any qualified contribution (as defined in section 2205(a)(3) of the CARES Act) if—

(A) such contribution—

(i) is paid, during the period beginning on January 1, 2020, and ending on the date which is 60 days after the date of the enactment of this Act, and

(ii) is made for relief efforts in one or more qualified disaster areas,

(B) the taxpayer obtains from such organization contemporaneous written acknowledgment (within the meaning of section 170(f)(8) of such Code) that such contribution was used (or is to be used) for relief efforts described in subparagraph (A)(ii), and

(C) the taxpayer has elected the application of this subsection with respect to such contribution.

(3) CROSS-REFERENCE.—For the suspension of the limitation on qualified disaster relief contributions made by an individual during 2020, see section 2205(a) of the CARES Act.

• 2020, Coronavirus Aid, Relief, and Economic Security (CARES) Act (P.L. 116-136)

P.L. 116-136, §2205(a) (as amended by P.L. 116-260, §213(a), Div. EE) and (c), provides:

(a) TEMPORARY SUSPENSION OF LIMITATIONS ON CERTAIN CASH CONTRIBUTIONS.—

(1) IN GENERAL.—Except as otherwise provided in paragraph (2), qualified contributions shall be disregarded in applying subsections (b) and (d) of section 170 of the Internal Revenue Code of 1986.

(2) TREATMENT OF EXCESS CONTRIBUTIONS.—For purposes of section 170 of the Internal Revenue Code of 1986—

(A) INDIVIDUALS.—In the case of an individual—

(i) LIMITATION.—Any qualified contribution shall be allowed as a deduction only to the extent that the aggregate of such contributions does not exceed the excess of the taxpayer's contribution base (as defined in subparagraph (H) of section 170(b)(1) of such Code) over the amount of all other charitable contributions allowed under section 170(b)(1) of such Code.

(ii) CARRYOVER.—If the aggregate amount of qualified contributions made in the contribution year (within the meaning of section 170(d)(1) of such Code) exceeds the limitation of clause (i), such excess shall be added to the excess described in section 170(b)(1)(G)(ii).

(B) CORPORATIONS.—In the case of a corporation—

(i) LIMITATION.—Any qualified contribution shall be allowed as a deduction only to the extent that the aggregate of such contributions does not exceed the excess of 25 percent of the taxpayer's taxable income (as determined under paragraph (2) of section 170(b) of such Code) over the amount of all other charitable contributions allowed under such paragraph.

(ii) CARRYOVER.—If the aggregate amount of qualified contributions made in the contribution year (within the meaning of section 170(d)(2) of such Code) exceeds the limitation of clause (i), such excess shall be appropriately taken into account under section 170(d)(2) subject to the limitations thereof.

(3) QUALIFIED CONTRIBUTIONS.—

(A) IN GENERAL.—For purposes of this subsection, the term "qualified contribution" means any charitable contribution (as defined in section 170(c) of the Internal Revenue Code of 1986) if—

(i) such contribution is paid in cash during calendar year 2020 or 2021 to an organization described in section 170(b)(1)(A) of such Code, and

(ii) the taxpayer has elected the application of this section with respect to such contribution.

(B) EXCEPTION.—Such term shall not include a contribution by a donor if the contribution is—

(i) to an organization described in section 509(a)(3) of the Internal Revenue Code of 1986, or

(ii) for the establishment of a new, or maintenance of an existing, donor advised fund (as defined in section 4966(d)(2) of such Code).

(C) APPLICATION OF ELECTION TO PARTNERSHIPS AND S CORPORATIONS.—In the case of a partnership or S corporation, the election under subparagraph (A)(ii) shall be made separately by each partner or shareholder.

* * *

(c) EFFECTIVE DATE.—This section shall apply to taxable years ending after December 31, 2019.

• 2019, Virginia Beach Strong Act (P.L. 116-98)

P.L. 116-98, §2, provides:

SEC. 2. SPECIAL RULES FOR CONTRIBUTIONS FOR RELIEF OF THE FAMILIES OF THE MASS SHOOTING IN VIRGINIA BEACH.

(a) CLARIFICATION THAT CONTRIBUTION WILL NOT FAIL TO QUALIFY AS A CHARITABLE CONTRIBUTION.—A cash contribution made for the relief of the families of the dead or wounded victims of the mass shooting in Virginia Beach, Virginia, on May 31, 2019, shall not fail to be treated as a charitable contribution for purposes of section 170 of the Internal Revenue Code of 1986 merely because such contribution is for the exclusive benefit of such families. The preceding sentence shall apply to contributions made on or after May 31, 2019.

(b) CLARIFICATION THAT PAYMENTS BY CHARITABLE ORGANIZATIONS TO FAMILIES TREATED AS EXEMPT PAYMENTS.—For purposes of the Internal Revenue Code of 1986, payments made on or after May 31, 2019, and on or before June 1, 2021, to the spouse or any dependent (as defined in section 152 of such Code) of the dead or wounded victims of the mass shooting in Virginia Beach, Virginia, on May 31, 2019, by an organization which (determined without regard to any such payments) would be an organization exempt from tax under section 501(a) of such Code shall—

(1) be treated as related to the purpose or function constituting the basis for such organization's exemption under such section; and

(2) shall not be treated as inuring to the benefit of any private individual,

if such payments are made in good faith using a reasonable and objective formula which is consistently applied with respect to such victims.

• 2019, Taxpayer Certainty and Disaster Tax Relief Act of 2019 (P.L. 116-94)

P.L. 116-94, §204(a), Div. Q, provides:

For a special rule, see Act Sec. 204(a), Div. Q, in the amendment notes for Code Sec. 1400S.

• 2018, Tax Technical Corrections Act of 2018 (P.L. 115-141)

P.L. 115-141, §401(a)(52), Div. U:

Amended Code Sec. 170(b)(1)(A)(ix) by inserting "National" before "Agricultural". **Effective** 3-23-2018.

• 2018, Bipartisan Budget Act of 2018 (P.L. 115-123)

P.L. 115-123, §20104(a), Div. B, provides:

For a special rule, see Act Sec. 20104(a), Div. B, in the amendment notes for Code Sec. 1400S(a)

• 2017, Tax Cuts and Jobs Act (P.L. 115-97)

P.L. 115-97, §11011(d)(5):

Amended Code Sec. 170(b)(2)(D) by striking "and" in clause (iv), by striking the period at the end of clause (v), and by adding at the end a new clause (vi). **Effective** for tax years beginning after 12-31-2017.

P.L. 115-97, §11023(a):

Amended Code Sec. 170(b)(1) by redesignating subparagraph (G) as subparagraph (H) and by inserting after subparagraph (F) a new subparagraph (G). **Effective** for contributions in tax years beginning after 12-31-2017.

P.L. 115-97, §13305(b)(2):

Amended Code Sec. 170(b)(2)(D), as amended by subtitle A, by striking clause (iv) and by redesignating clauses (v) and (vi) as clauses (iv) and (v). **Effective** for tax years beginning after 12-31-2017. Prior to being stricken, Code Sec. 170(b)(2)(D)(iv) read as follows:

(iv) section 199

• 2017, Disaster Tax Relief and Airport and Airway Extension Act of 2017 (P.L. 115-63)

P.L. 115-63, §504(a), provides:

For a special rule, see Act Sec. 504(a) in the amendment notes for Code Sec. 1400S(a).

• 2015, Protecting Americans from Tax Hikes Act of 2015 (P.L. 114-113)

P.L. 114-113, §111(a)(1), Div. Q:

Amended Code Sec. 170(b)(1)(E) by striking clause (vi). **Effective** for contributions made in tax years beginning after 12-31-2014. Prior to being stricken, Code Sec. 170(b)(1)(E)(vi) read as follows:

(vi) TERMINATION.—This subparagraph shall not apply to any contribution made in taxable years beginning after December 31, 2014.

P.L. 114-113, §111(a)(2), Div. Q:

Amended Code Sec. 170(b)(2)(B) by striking clause (iii). **Effective** for contributions made in tax years beginning after 12-31-2014. Prior to being stricken, Code Sec. 170(b)(2)(B)(iii) read as follows:

(iii) TERMINATION.—This subparagraph shall not apply to any contribution made in taxable years beginning after December 31, 2014.

P.L. 114-113, §111(b)(1), Div. Q:

Amended Code Sec. 170(b)(2) by redesignating subparagraph (C) as subparagraph (D), and by inserting after subparagraph (B) a new subparagraph (C). **Effective** for contributions made in tax years beginning after 12-31-2015. For a special rule, see Act Sec. 111(b)(3), Div. Q, below.

P.L. 114-113, §111(b)(2)(A), Div. Q:

Amended Code Sec. 170(b)(2)(A) by striking "subparagraph (B) applies" and inserting "subparagraph (B) or (C) applies". **Effective** for contributions made in tax years beginning after 12-31-2015. For a special rule, see Act Sec. 111(b)(3), below.

P.L. 114-113, §111(b)(2)(B), Div. Q:

Amended Code Sec. 170(b)(2)(B)(ii) by striking "15 succeeding years" and inserting "15 succeeding taxable years". **Effective** for contributions made in tax years beginning after 12-31-2015. For a special rule, see Act Sec. 111(b)(3), below.

P.L. 114-113, §111(b)(3), Div. Q, provides:

(3) VALID EXISTING RIGHTS PRESERVED.—Nothing in this subsection (or any amendment made by this subsection) shall be construed to modify the existing property rights validly conveyed to Native Corporations (within the meaning of section 3(m) of the Alaska Native Claims Settlement Act) under such Act.

P.L. 114-113, §331(a), Div. Q:

Amended Code Sec. 170(b)(1)(A) by striking "or" at the end clause (vii), by striking the comma at the end of clause (viii) and inserting ", or", and by inserting after clause (viii) a new clause (ix). **Effective** for contributions made on and after 12-18-2015.

• 2015, Slain Officer Family Support Act of 2015 (P.L. 114-7)

P.L. 114-7, §2, provides:

SEC. 2. ACCELERATION OF INCOME TAX BENEFITS FOR CHARITABLE CASH CONTRIBUTIONS FOR RELIEF OF THE FAMILIES OF NEW YORK POLICE DEPARTMENT DETECTIVES WENJIAN LIU AND RAFAEL RAMOS.

(a) IN GENERAL.—For purposes of section 170 of the Internal Revenue Code of 1986 a taxpayer may treat any contribution described in subsection (b) made between January 1, 2015, and April 15, 2015, as if such contribution was made on December 31, 2014, and not in 2015.

(b) CONTRIBUTION DESCRIBED.—A contribution is described in this subsection if such contribution is a cash contribution made for the relief of the families of slain New York Police Department Detectives Wenjian Liu and Rafael Ramos, for which a charitable contribution deduction is allowable under section 170 of the Internal Revenue Code of 1986.

(c) RECORDKEEPING.—In the case of a contribution described in subsection (b), a telephone bill showing the name of the donee organization, the date of the contribution, and the amount of the contribution shall be treated as meeting the recordkeeping requirements of section 170(f)(17) of the Internal Revenue Code of 1986.

(d) CLARIFICATION THAT CONTRIBUTION WILL NOT FAIL TO QUALIFY AS A CHARITABLE CONTRIBUTION.—A cash contribution made for the relief of the families of slain New York Police Department Detectives Wenjian Liu and Rafael Ramos shall not fail to be treated as a charitable contribution for purposes of section 170 of the Internal Revenue Code of 1986 and subsection (b) of this section merely because such contribution is for the exclusive benefit of such families. The preceding sentence shall apply to contributions made on or after December 20, 2014.

(e) CLARIFICATION THAT PAYMENTS BY CHARITABLE ORGANIZATIONS TO FAMILIES TREATED AS EXEMPT PAYMENTS.—For purposes of the Internal Revenue Code of 1986, payments made on or after December 20, 2014, and on or before October 15, 2015, to the spouse or any dependent (as defined in section 152 of such Code) of slain New York Police Department Detectives Wenjian Liu or Rafael Ramos by an organization which (determined without regard to any such payments) would be an organization exempt from tax under section 501(a) of such Code shall—

(1) be treated as related to the purpose or function constituting the basis for such organization's exemption under such section; and

(2) shall not be treated as inuring to the benefit of any private individual,

if such payments are made in good faith using a reasonable and objective formula which is consistently applied with respect to such Detectives.

• 2014, Tax Increase Prevention Act of 2014 (P.L. 113-295)

P.L. 113-295, §106(a), Div. A:

Amended Code Sec. 170(b)(1)(E)(vi) by striking "December 31, 2013" and inserting "December 31, 2014". **Effective** for contributions made in tax years beginning after 12-31-2013.

P.L. 113-295, §106(b), Div. A:

Amended Code Sec. 170(b)(2)(B)(iii) by striking "December 31, 2013" and inserting "December 31, 2014". **Effective** for contributions made in tax years beginning after 12-31-2013.

• 2014, Tax Technical Corrections Act of 2014 (P.L. 113-295)

P.L. 113-295, §221(a)(28)(A), Div. A:

Amended Code Sec. 170(b) by striking paragraph (3). **Effective** generally 12-19-2014. For a special rule, see Act Sec. 221(b)(2), Div. A, below. Prior to being stricken, Code Sec. 170(b)(3) read as follows:

(3) TEMPORARY SUSPENSION OF LIMITATIONS ON CHARITABLE CONTRIBUTIONS.—In the case of a qualified farmer or rancher (as defined in paragraph (1)(E)(v)), any charitable contribution of food—

(A) to which subsection (e)(3)(C) applies (without regard to clause (ii) thereof), and

(B) which is made during the period beginning on the date of the enactment of this paragraph and before January 1, 2009,

shall be treated for purposes of paragraph (1)(E) or (2)(B), whichever is applicable, as if it were a qualified conservation contribution which is made by a qualified farmer or rancher and which otherwise meets the requirements of such paragraph.

P.L. 113-295, §221(b)(2), Div. A, provides:

(2) SAVINGS PROVISION.—If—

(A) any provision amended or repealed by the amendments made by this section applied to—

(i) any transaction occurring before the date of the enactment of this Act,

(ii) any property acquired before such date of enactment, or

(iii) any item of income, loss, deduction, or credit taken into account before such date of enactment, and

(B) the treatment of such transaction, property, or item under such provision would (without regard to the amendments or repeals made by this section) affect the liability for tax for periods ending after date of enactment, nothing in the amendments or repeals made by this section shall be construed to affect the treatment of such transaction, property, or item for purposes of determining liability for tax for periods ending after such date of enactment.

• 2014, Philippines Charitable Giving Assistance Act (P.L. 113-92)

P.L. 113-92, §2(a)-(c), provides:

SEC. 2. ACCELERATION OF INCOME TAX BENEFITS FOR CHARITABLE CASH CONTRIBUTIONS FOR RELIEF OF VICTIMS OF TYPHOON HAIYAN IN THE PHILIPPINES.

(a) IN GENERAL.—For purposes of section 170 of the Internal Revenue Code of 1986, a taxpayer may treat any contribution described in subsection (b) made after the date of the enactment of this Act, and before April 15, 2014, as if such contribution was made on December 31, 2013, and not in 2014.

(b) CONTRIBUTION DESCRIBED.—A contribution is described in this subsection if such contribution is a cash contribution made for the relief of victims in areas affected by Typhoon Haiyan, for which a charitable contribution deduction is allowable under section 170 of the Internal Revenue Code of 1986.

(c) RECORDKEEPING.—In the case of a contribution described in subsection (b), a telephone bill showing the name of the donee organization, the date of the contribution, and the amount of the contribution shall be treated as meeting the recordkeeping requirements of section 170(f)(17) of the Internal Revenue Code of 1986.

• 2013, American Taxpayer Relief Act of 2012 (P.L. 112-240)

P.L. 112-240, §206(a):

Amended Code Sec. 170(b)(1)(E)(vi) by striking "December 31, 2011" and inserting "December 31, 2013". **Effective** for contributions made in tax years beginning after 12-31-2011.

P.L. 112-240, §206(b):

Amended Code Sec. 170(b)(2)(B)(iii) by striking "December 31, 2011" and inserting "December 31, 2013". **Effective** for contributions made in tax years beginning after 12-31-2011.

• 2010, Tax Relief, Unemployment Insurance Reauthorization, and Job Creation Act of 2010 (P.L. 111-312)

P.L. 111-312, §723(a):

Amended Code Sec. 170(b)(1)(E)(vi) by striking "December 31, 2009" and inserting "December 31, 2011". **Effective** for contributions made in tax years beginning after 12-31-2009.

P.L. 111-312, §723(b):

Amended Code Sec. 170(b)(2)(B)(iii) by striking "December 31, 2009" and inserting "December 31, 2011". **Effective** for contributions made in tax years beginning after 12-31-2009.

• 2010, (P.L. 111-126)

P.L. 111-126, §1(a)-(c), provides:

SECTION 1. ACCELERATION OF INCOME TAX BENEFITS FOR CHARITABLE CASH CONTRIBUTIONS FOR RELIEF OF VICTIMS OF EARTHQUAKE IN HAITI.

(a) IN GENERAL.—For purposes of section 170 of the Internal Revenue Code of 1986, a taxpayer may treat any contribution described in subsection (b) made after January 11, 2010, and before March 1, 2010, as if such contribution was made on December 31, 2009, and not in 2010.

(b) CONTRIBUTION DESCRIBED.—A contribution is described in this subsection if such contribution is a cash contribution made for the relief of victims in areas affected by the earthquake in Haiti on January 12, 2010, for which a charitable contribution deduction is allowable under section 170 of the Internal Revenue Code of 1986.

(c) RECORDKEEPING.—In the case of a contribution described in subsection (b), a telephone bill showing the name of the donee organization, the date of the contribution, and the amount of the contribution shall be treated as meeting the recordkeeping requirements of section 170(f)(17) of the Internal Revenue Code of 1986.

• 2008, Tax Extenders and Alternative Minimum Tax Relief Act of 2008 (P.L. 110-343)

P.L. 110-343, Div. C, §323(b)(1):

Amended Code Sec. 170(b) by adding a new paragraph (3). **Effective** for tax years ending after 10-3-2008.

• 2008, Heartland, Habitat, Harvest, and Horticulture Act of 2008 (P.L. 110-246)

P.L. 110-246, §15302(a)(1):

Amended Code Sec. 170(b)(1)(E)(vi) by striking "December 31, 2007" and inserting "December 31, 2009". **Effective** for contributions made in tax years beginning after 12-31-2007.

P.L. 110-246, §15302(a)(2):

Amended Code Sec. 170(b)(2)(B)(iii) by striking "December 31, 2007" and inserting "December 31, 2009". **Effective** for contributions made in tax years beginning after 12-31-2007.

• 2007, Tax Technical Corrections Act of 2007 (P.L. 110-172)

P.L. 110-172, §11(a)(14)(A):

Amended Code Sec. 170(b)(1)(A)(vii) by striking "subparagraph (E)" and inserting "subparagraph (F)". **Effective** 12-29-2007.

• 2006, Pension Protection Act of 2006 (P.L. 109-280)

P.L. 109-280, §1206(a)(1):

Amended Code Sec. 170(b)(1) by redesignating subparagraphs (E) and (F) as subparagraphs (F) and (G), respectively, and by inserting after subparagraph (D) a new subparagraph (E). **Effective** for contributions made in tax years beginning after 12-31-2005.

P.L. 109-280, §1206(a)(2):

Amended Code Sec. 170(b)(2). **Effective** for contributions made in tax years beginning after 12-31-2005. Prior to amendment, Code Sec. 170(b)(2) read as follows:

(2) CORPORATIONS.—In the case of a corporation, the total deductions under subsection (a) for any taxable year shall not exceed 10 percent of the taxpayer's taxable income computed without regard to—

(A) this section,

(B) part VIII (except section 248),

(C) section 199,

(D) any net operating loss carryback to the taxable year under section 172, and

(E) any capital loss carryback to the taxable year under section 1212(a)(1).

• 2005, Gulf Opportunity Zone Act of 2005 (P.L. 109-135)

P.L. 109-135, §403(a)(16):

Amended Code Sec. 170(b)(2) by redesignating subparagraphs (C) and (D) as subparagraphs (D) and (E), respectively, and by inserting after subparagraph (B) a new subparagraph (C). **Effective** as if included in the provision of the American Jobs Creation Act of 2004 (P.L. 108-357) to which it relates [**effective** for tax years beginning after 12-31-2004.—CCH].

• 2005, Katrina Emergency Tax Relief Act of 2005 (P.L. 109-73)

P.L. 109-73, §301 [repealed by P.L. 109-135, §201(b)(4)(B)], provides:

SEC. 301. TEMPORARY SUSPENSION OF LIMITATIONS ON CHARITABLE CONTRIBUTIONS.

(a) IN GENERAL.—Except as otherwise provided in subsection (b), section 170(b) of the Internal Revenue Code of 1986 shall not apply to qualified contributions and such contributions shall not be taken into account for purposes of applying subsections (b) and (d) of section 170 of such Code to other contributions.

(b) TREATMENT OF EXCESS CONTRIBUTIONS.—For purposes of section 170 of such Code—

(1) INDIVIDUALS.—In the case of an individual—

(A) LIMITATION.—Any qualified contribution shall be allowed only to the extent that the aggregate of such contributions does not exceed the excess of the taxpayer's contribution base (as defined in subparagraph (F) of section 170(b)(1) of such Code) over the amount of all other charitable contributions allowed under such section 170(b)(1).

(B) CARRYOVER.—If the aggregate amount of qualified contributions made in the contribution year (within the meaning of section 170(d)(1) of such Code) exceeds the limitation of subparagraph (A), such excess shall be added to the excess described in the portion of subparagraph (A) of such section which precedes clause (i) thereof for purposes of applying such section.

(2) CORPORATIONS.—In the case of a corporation—

(A) LIMITATION.—Any qualified contribution shall be allowed only to the extent that the aggregate of such contributions does not exceed the excess of the taxpayer's taxable income (as determined under paragraph (2) of section 170(b) of such Code) over the amount of all other charitable contributions allowed under such paragraph.

(B) CARRYOVER.—Rules similar to the rules of paragraph (1)(B) shall apply for purposes of this paragraph.

(c) EXCEPTION TO OVERALL LIMITATION ON ITEMIZED DEDUCTIONS.—So much of any deduction allowed under section 170 of such Code as does not exceed the qualified contributions paid during the taxable year shall not be treated as an itemized deduction for purposes of section 68 of such Code.

(d) QUALIFIED CONTRIBUTIONS.—

(1) IN GENERAL.—For purposes of this section, the term "qualified contribution" means any charitable contribution (as defined in section 170(c) of such Code)—

(A) paid during the period beginning on August 28, 2005, and ending on December 31, 2005, in cash to an organization described in section 170(b)(1)(A) of such Code (other than an organization described in section 509(a)(3) of such Code),

(B) in the case of a contribution paid by a corporation, such contribution is for relief efforts related to Hurricane Katrina, and

(C) with respect to which the taxpayer has elected the application of this section.

(2) EXCEPTION.—Such term shall not include a contribution if the contribution is for establishment of a new, or maintenance in an existing, segregated fund or account with respect to which the donor (or any person appointed or designated by such donor) has, or reasonably expects to have, advisory privileges with respect to distributions or investments by reason of the donor's status as a donor.

(3) APPLICATION OF ELECTION TO PARTNERSHIPS AND S CORPORATIONS.—In the case of a partnership or S corporation, the election under paragraph (1)(C) shall be made separately by each partner or shareholder.

• 2005, (P.L. 109-1)

P.L. 109-1, §1, provides:

SECTION 1. ACCELERATION OF INCOME TAX BENEFITS FOR CHARITABLE CASH CONTRIBUTIONS FOR RELIEF OF INDIAN OCEAN TSUNAMI VICTIMS.

(a) IN GENERAL.—For purposes of section 170 of the Internal Revenue Code of 1986, a taxpayer may treat any contribution described in subsection (b) made in January 2005 as if such contribution was made on December 31, 2004, and not in January 2005.

(b) CONTRIBUTION DESCRIBED.—A contribution is described in this subsection if such contribution is a cash contribution made for the relief of victims in areas affected by the December 26, 2004, Indian Ocean tsunami for which a charitable contribution deduction is allowable under section 170 of the Internal Revenue Code of 1986.

• 1986, Tax Reform Act of 1986 (P.L. 99-514)

P.L. 99-514, §1831:

Amended Code Sec. 170(b)(1)(C)(iv) by striking out "this subparagraph" and inserting in lieu thereof "this paragraph". **Effective** as if included in the provision of P.L. 98-369 to which it relates.

P.L. 98-369, §301(a)(1), (2):

Amended Code Sec. 170(b)(1)(B)(i) by striking out "20 percent" and inserting in lieu thereof "30 percent" and by adding at the end thereof a new sentence. **Effective** for contributions made in tax years ending after 7-18-84.

P.L. 98-369, §301(c)(1)

Amended Code Sec. 170(b)(1) by redesignating subparagraphs (D) and (E) as subparagraphs (E) and (F), respectively, and by inserting after subparagraph (C) new subparagraph (D). **Effective** for contributions made in tax years ending after 7-18-84.

P.L. 98-369, §301(c)(2)(A):

Amended Code Sec. 170(b)(1)(A)(vii) by striking out "subparagraph (D)" and inserting in lieu thereof "subparagraph (E)". **Effective** for contributions made in tax years ending after 7-18-84.

P.L. 98-369, §301(c)(2)(B):

Amended the heading of Code Sec. 170(b)(1)(C) and clause (i). **Effective** for contributions made in tax years ending after 7-18-84. Prior to amendment, they read as follows:

(C) Special Limitation With Respect to Contributions of Certain Capital Gain Property.—

(i) In the case of charitable contributions of capital gain property to which subsection (e)(1)(B) does not apply, the total amount of contributions of such property which may be taken into account under subsection (a) for any taxable year shall not exceed 30 percent of the taxpayer's contribution base for such year. For purposes of this subsection, contributions of capital gain property to which this paragraph applies shall be taken into account after all other charitable contributions.

• 1981, Economic Recovery Tax Act of 1981 (P.L. 97-34)

P.L. 97-34, §263(a):

Amended Code Sec. 170(b)(2) by striking out "5 percent" and inserting in lieu thereof "10 percent". **Effective** for tax years beginning after 12-31-81.

• 1976, Tax Reform Act of 1976 (P.L. 94-455)

P.L. 94-455, §1052(c):

Amended Code Sec. 170(b)(2) by adding "and" at the end of subparagraph (C), repealing subparagraph (D), and redesignating subparagraph (E) as subparagraph (D). **Effective** for tax years beginning after 12-31-79. Prior to repeal, Code Sec. 170(b)(2)(D) read as follows:

(D) section 922 (special deduction for Western Hemisphere trade corporations), and

P.L. 94-455, §1901(a)(28):

Amended Code Sec. 170(b)(1)(A)(vii) to substitute "subparagraph (D)" for "subparagraph (E)", amended Code Sec. 170(b)(1)(B)(ii) to substitute "subparagraph (C)" for "subparagraph (D)", repealed Code Sec. 170(b)(1)(C), and redesignated Code Secs. 170(b)(1)(D), (E), and (F) as Code Secs. 170(b)(1)(C), (D), and (E). **Effective** for tax years beginning after 12-31-76. Prior to repeal, Code Sec. 170(b)(1)(C) read as follows:

(C) UNLIMITED DEDUCTION FOR CERTAIN INDIVIDUALS.—Subject to the provisions of subsections (f)(6) and (g), the limitations in subparagraphs (A), (B), and (D), and the provisions of subsection (e)(1)(B), shall not apply, in the case of an individual for a taxable year beginning before January 1, 1975, if in such taxable year and in 8 of the 10 preceding taxable years, the amount of the charitable contributions, plus the amount of income tax (determined without regard to chapter 2, relating to tax on self-employment income) paid during such year in respect of such year or preceding taxable years, exceeds the transitional deduction percentage (determined under subsection (f)(6)) of the taxpayer's taxable income for such year, computed without regard to—

(i) this section,

(ii) section 151 (allowance of deductions for personal exemption), and

(iii) any net operating loss carryback to the taxable year under section 172.

In lieu of the amount of income tax paid during any such year, there may be substituted for that year the amount of income tax paid in respect of such year, provided that any amount so included in the year in respect of which payment was made shall not be included in any other year. In the case of a separate return for the taxable year by a married individual who previously filed a joint return with a former deceased spouse for any of the 10 preceding taxable years, the amount of charitable contributions and taxes paid for any such preceding taxable year, for which a joint return was filed with the former deceased spouse, shall be determined in the same manner as if the taxpayer had not remarried after the death of such former spouse.

P.L. 94-455, §1906(b)(13)(A):

Amended 1954 Code by substituting "Secretary" for "Secretary or his delegate" each place it appeared. **Effective** 2-1-77.

• 1969, Tax Reform Act of 1969 (P.L. 91-172)

P.L. 91-172, §201(a)(1):

Amended Code Sec. 170(b). **Effective** for tax years beginning after 12-31-69. Prior to amendment, Code Sec. 170(b) read as follows:

"(b) Limitations.—

"(1) Individuals.—In the case of an individual the deduction provided in subsection (a) shall be limited as provided in subparagraphs (A), (B), (C), and (D).

"(A) Special rule.—Any charitable contribution to—

"(i) a church or a convention or association of churches,

"(ii) an educational organization referred to in section 503(b)(2),

"(iii) a hospital referred to in section 503(b)(5) or to a medical research organization (referred to in section 503(b)(5)) directly engaged in the continuous active conduct of medical research in conjunction with a hospital, if during the calendar year in which the contribution is made such organization is committed to spend such contributions for such research before January 1 of the fifth calendar year which begins after the date such contribution is made,

"(iv) an organization referred to in section 503(b)(3) organized and operated exclusively to receive, hold, invest, and administer property and to make expenditures to or for the benefit of a college or university which is an organization referred to in clause (ii) of this subparagraph and which is an agency or instrumentality of a State or political subdivision thereof, or which is owned or operated by a State or political subdivision thereof or by an agency or instrumentality of one or more States or political subdivisions,

"(v) a governmental unit referred to in subsection (c)(1), or

"(vi) an organization referred to in subsection (c)(2) which normally receives a substantial part of its support (exclusive of income received in the exercise or performance by such organization of its charitable, educational, or other purpose or function constituting the basis for its exemption under section 501(a)) from a governmental unit referred to in subsection (c)(1) or from direct or indirect contributions from the general public,

shall be allowed to the extent that the aggregate of such contributions does not exceed 10 percent of the taxpayer's adjusted gross income computed without regard to any net operating loss carryback to the taxable year under section 172.

"(B) General limitation.—The total deductions under subsection (a) for any taxable year shall not exceed 20 percent of the taxpayer's adjusted gross income computed without regard to any net operating loss carryback to the taxable year under section 172. For purposes of this subparagraph, the deduction under subsection (a) shall be computed without regard to any deduction allowed under subparagraph (A) but shall take into account any charitable contributions described in subparagraph (A) which are in excess of the amount allowable as a deduction under subparagraph (A).

"(C) Unlimited deduction for certain individuals.—The limitation in subparagraph (B) shall not apply in the case of an individual if, in the taxable year and in 8 of the 10 preceding taxable years, the amount of the charitable contributions, plus the amount of income tax (determined without regard to chapter 2, relating to tax on selfemployment income) paid during such year in respect of such year or preceding taxable years, exceeds 90 percent of the taxpayer's taxable income for such year, computed without regard to—

"(i) this section,

"(ii) section 151 (allowance of deductions for personal exemptions), and

"(iii) any net operating loss carryback to the taxable year under section 172.

In lieu of the amount of income tax paid during any such year, there may be substituted for that year the amount of income tax paid in respect of such year, provided that any amount so included in the year in respect of which payment was made shall not be included in any other year.

"(D) Denial of deduction in case of certain transfers in trust.—No deduction shall be allowed under this section for the value of any interest in property transferred after March 9, 1954, to a trust if—

"(i) the grantor has a reversionary interest in the corpus or income of that portion of the trust with respect to which a deduction would (but for this subparagraph) be allowable under this section; and

"(ii) at the time of the transfer the value of such reversionary interest exceeds 5 percent of the value of the property constituting such portion of the trust.

For purposes of this subparagraph, a power exercisable by the grantor or a nonadverse party (within the meaning of section 672(b)), or both, to revest in the grantor property or income therefrom shall be treated as a reversionary interest.

"(2) Corporations.—In the case of a corporation, the total deductions under subsection (a) for any taxable year shall not exceed 5 percent of the taxpayer's taxable income computed without regard to—

"(A) this section,

"(B) part VIII (except section 248),

"(C) any net operating loss carryback to the taxable year under section 172, and

"(D) section 922 (special deduction for Western Hemisphere trade corporations).

Any contribution made by a corporation in a taxable year (hereinafter in this sentence referred to as the 'contribution year') in excess of the amount deductible for such year under the preceding sentence shall be deductible for each of the 5 succeeding taxable years in order of time, but only to the extent of the lesser of the two following amounts: (i) the excess of the maximum amount deductible for such succeeding taxable year under the preceding sentence over the sum of the contributions made in such year plus the aggregate of the excess contributions which were made in taxable years before the contribution year and which are deductible under this sentence for such succeeding taxable year; or (ii) in the case of the first succeeding taxable year, the amount of such excess contribution, and in the case of the second, third, fourth, or fifth succeeding taxable year, the portion of such excess contribution not deductible under this sentence for any taxable year intervening between the contribution year and such succeeding taxable year.

"(3) Special rule for corporations having net operating loss carryovers.—In applying the second sentence of paragraph (2) of this subsection, the excess of—

"(A) the contributions made by a corporation in a taxable year to which this section applies, over

"(B) the amount deductible in such year under the limitation in the first sentence of such paragraph (2),

shall be reduced to the extent that such excess reduces taxable income (as computed for purposes of the second sentence of section 172(b)(2)) and increases a net operating loss carryover under section 172 to a succeeding taxable year.

"(4) Reduction for certain interest.—If, in connection with any charitable contribution, a liability is assumed by the recipient or by any other person, or if a charitable contribution is of property which is subject to a liability, then, to the extent necessary to avoid the duplication of amounts, the amount taken into account for purposes of this section as the amount of the charitable contribution—

"(A) shall be reduced for interest (i) which has been paid (or is to be paid) by the taxpayer, (ii) which is attributable to the liability, and (iii) which is attributable to any period after the making of the contribution, and

"(B) in the case of a bond, shall be further reduced for interest (i) which has been paid (or is to be paid) by the taxpayer on indebtedness incurred or continued to purchase or carry such bond, and (ii) which is attributable to any period before the making of the contribution.

The reduction pursuant to subparagraph (B) shall not exceed the interest (including interest equivalent) on the bond which is attributable to any period before the making of the contribution and which is not (under the taxpayer's method of accounting) includible in the gross income of the taxpayer for any taxable year. For purposes of this paragraph, the term 'bond' means any bond, debenture, note, or certificate or other evidence of indebtedness.

"(5) Carryover of certain excess contributions by individuals.—

"(A) In the case of an individual, if the amount of charitable contributions described in paragraph (1)(A) payment of which is made within a taxable year (hereinafter in this paragraph referred to as the 'contribution year') beginning after December 31, 1963, exceeds 30 percent of the taxpayer's adjusted gross income for such year (computed without regard to any net operating loss carryback to such year under section 172), such excess shall be treated as a charitable contribution described in paragraph (1)(A) paid in each of the 5 succeeding taxable years in order of time, but, with respect to any such succeeding taxable year, only to the extent of the lesser of the two following amounts:

"(i) the amount by which 30 percent of the taxpayer's adjusted gross income for such succeeding taxable year (computed without regard to any net operating loss carryback to such succeeding taxable year under section 172) exceeds the sum of the charitable contributions described in paragraph (1)(A) payment of which is made by the taxpayer within such succeeding taxable year (determined without regard to this subparagraph) and the charitable contributions described in paragraph (1)(A) payment of which was made in taxable years (beginning after December 31, 1963) before the contribution year which are treated under this subparagraph as having been paid in such succeeding taxable year; or

"(ii) in the case of the first succeeding taxable year, the amount of such excess, and in the case of the second, third, fourth, or fifth succeeding taxable year, the portion of such excess not treated under this subparagraph as a charitable contribution described in paragraph (1)(A) paid in any taxable year intervening between the contribution year and such succeeding taxable year.

"(B) In applying subparagraph (A), the excess determined under subparagraph (A) for the contribution year shall be reduced to the extent that such excess reduces taxable income (as computed for purposes of the second sentence of section 172(b)(2)) and increases the net operating loss deduction for a taxable year succeeding the contribution year."

P.L. 91-172, §201(h):

Amended Code Sec. 170(b) by adding the last sentence to Sec. 170(b)(1)(C). **Effective** for tax years beginning after 12-31-68.

• 1964, Revenue Act of 1964 (P.L. 88-272)

P.L. 88-272, §209(a):

Amended subparagraph (A) of subsection (b)(1) by adding clauses (v) and (vi). **Effective** with respect to contributions which are paid in tax years beginning after 12-31-63.

P.L. 88-272, §209(c)(1):

Amended subsection (b) by adding paragraph (5) thereto. **Effective** with respect to contributions which are paid in tax years beginning after 12-31-63.

P.L. 88-272, §209(d)(1):

Amended section 170(b)(2) by inserting a new sentence to follow subparagraph (D). **Effective** for tax years beginning after 12-31-63, for contributions which are paid (or treated as paid under section 170(a)(2)) in tax years beginning after 12-31-61. Prior to amendment, the sentence following subparagraph (D) read:

"Any contribution made by a corporation in a taxable year to which this section applies in excess of the amount deductible in such year under the foregoing limitation shall be deductible in each of the two succeeding taxable years in order of time, but only to the extent of the lesser of the two following amounts: (i) the excess of the maximum amount deductible for such succeeding taxable year under the foregoing limitation over the contributions made in such year; and (ii) in the case of the first succeeding taxable year the amount of such excess contribution, and in the case of the second succeeding taxable year the portion of such excess contribution not deductible in the first succeeding taxable year."

• 1962 (P.L. 87-858)

P.L. 87-858, §2(a), (b):

Amended Code Sec. 170(b)(1)(A) by deleting "or" at the end of clause (ii), by inserting "or" at the end of clause (iii), and by inserting new clause (iv). Amended Code Sec. 170(b)(1)(B) by substituting "any charitable contributions described in subparagraph (A)" for "any charitable contributions to the organizations described in clauses (i), (ii), and (iii)." **Effective** 1-1-61.

• 1958, Technical Amendments Act of 1958 (P.L. 85-866)

P.L. 85-866, §10(a):

Added the last sentence in Sec. 170(b)(1)(C). **Effective** 1-1-58.

P.L. 85-866, §11:

Added paragraph (3) to Sec. 170(b). **Effective** 1-1-54.

P.L. 85-866, §12:

Added paragraph (4) to Sec. 170(b). **Effective** for tax years ending after 12-31-57, but only with respect to charitable contributions made after that date.

• 1956 (P.L. 1022, 84th Cong.)

P.L. 1022, 84th Cong., §[1]:

Amended Code Sec. 170(b)(1)(A)(iii) by adding after the phrase "section 503(b)(5)" the words "or to medical research organization (referred to in section 503(b)(5)) directly engaged in the continuous active conduct of medical research in conjunction with a hospital, if during the calendar year in which the contribution is made such organization is committed to spend such contributions for such research before January 1 of the fifth calendar year which begins after the date such contribution is made,". **Effective** under Sec. 2 only to tax years beginning after 1955.

[Sec. 170(c)]

(c) CHARITABLE CONTRIBUTION DEFINED.—For purposes of this section, the term "charitable contribution" means a contribution or gift to or for the use of—

(1) A State, a possession of the United States, or any political subdivision of any of the foregoing, or the United States or the District of Columbia, but only if the contribution or gift is made for exclusively public purposes.

(2) A corporation, trust, or community chest, fund, or foundation—

(A) created or organized in the United States or in any possession thereof, or under the law of the United States, any State, the District of Columbia, or any possession of the United States;

(B) organized and operated exclusively for religious, charitable, scientific, literary, or educational purposes, or to foster national or international amateur sports competition (but only if no part of its activities involve the provision of athletic facilities or equipment), or for the prevention of cruelty to children or animals;

(C) no part of the net earnings of which inures to the benefit of any private shareholder or individual; and

(D) which is not disqualified for tax exemption under section 501(c)(3) by reason of attempting to influence legislation, and which does not participate in, or intervene in (including the publishing or distributing of statements), any political campaign on behalf of (or in opposition to) any candidate for public office.

A contribution or gift by a corporation to a trust, chest, fund, or foundation shall be deductible by reason of this paragraph only if it is to be used within the United States or any of its possessions exclusively for purposes specified in subparagraph (B). Rules similar to the rules of section 501(j) shall apply for purposes of this paragraph.

(3) A post or organization of war veterans, or an auxiliary unit or society of, or trust or foundation for, any such post or organization—

(A) organized in the United States or any of its possessions, and

(B) no part of the net earnings of which inures to the benefit of any private shareholder or individual.

(4) In the case of a contribution or gift by an individual, a domestic fraternal society, order, or association, operating under the lodge system, but only if such contribution or gift is to be used exclusively for religious, charitable, scientific, literary, or educational purposes, or for the prevention of cruelty to children or animals.

(5) A cemetery company owned and operated exclusively for the benefit of its members, or any corporation chartered solely for burial purposes as a cemetery corporation and not permitted by its charter to engage in any business not necessarily incident to that purpose, if such company

or corporation is not operated for profit and no part of the net earnings of such company or corporation inures to the benefit of any private shareholder or individual.

For purposes of this section, the term "charitable contribution" also means an amount treated under subsection (g) as paid for the use of an organization described in paragraph (2), (3), or (4).

Amendments

• 1987, Revenue Act of 1987 (P.L. 100-203)

P.L. 100-203, § 10711(a)(1):

Amended Code Sec. 170(c)(2)(D) by striking out "on behalf of any candidate" and inserting in lieu thereof "on behalf of (or in opposition to) any candidate". **Effective** with respect to activities after 12-22-87.

• 1982, Tax Equity and Fiscal Responsibility Act of 1982 (P.L. 97-248)

P.L. 97-248, § 286(b):

Amended Code Sec. 170(c) by adding at the end of paragraph (2) the following sentence: "Rules similar to the rules of section 501(j) shall apply for purposes of this paragraph." **Effective** retroactively, on 10-5-76.

• 1976, Tax Reform Act of 1976 (P.L. 94-455)

P.L. 94-455, § 1307(d):

Substituted "which is not disqualified for tax exemption under section 501(c)(3) by reason of attempting to influence legislation," for "no substantial part of the activities of which is carrying on propaganda, or otherwise attempting, to influence legislation" in Code Sec. 170(c)(2)(D). **Effective** for tax years beginning after 12-31-76.

P.L. 94-455, § 1313(b):

Added ", or to foster national or international amateur sports competition (but only if no part of its activities involve the provision of athletic facilities or equipment)," after "or educational purposes" in Code Sec. 170(c)(2)(B). **Effective** 10-5-76.

P.L. 94-455, § 1901(a)(28):

Substituted "subsection (g)" for "subsection (h)" in the last sentence of Code Sec. 170(c). **Effective** for tax years beginning after 12-31-76.

• 1969, Tax Reform Act of 1969 (P.L. 91-172)

P.L. 91-172, § 201(a)(1):

Amended Code Secs. 170(c)(1), 170(c)(2)(A) and 170(c)(2)(D). **Effective** for tax years beginning after 12-31-69. Prior to amendment, these read as follows:

(c) Charitable Contribution Defined.—For purposes of this section, the term "charitable contribution" means a contribution or gift to or for the use of—

(1) A State, a Territory, a possession of the United States, or any political subdivision of any of the foregoing, or the United States or the District of Columbia, but only if the contribution or gift is made for exclusively public purposes.

(2) A corporation, trust, or community chest, fund, or foundation—

(A) created or organized in the United States or in any possession thereof, or under the law of the United States, any State or Territory, the District of Columbia, or any possession of the United States;

* * *

(D) no substantial part of the activities of which is carrying on propaganda, or otherwise attempting, to influence legislation.

• 1960 (P.L. 86-779)

P.L. 86-779, § 7(a)(1):

Added the last sentence to Code Sec. 170(c). **Effective** for tax years beginning after 1959.

[Sec. 170(d)]

(d) CARRYOVERS OF EXCESS CONTRIBUTIONS.—

(1) INDIVIDUALS.—

(A) IN GENERAL.—In the case of an individual, if the amount of charitable contributions described in subsection (b)(1)(A) payment of which is made within a taxable year (hereinafter in this paragraph referred to as the "contribution year") exceeds 50 percent of the taxpayer's contribution base for such year, such excess shall be treated as a charitable contribution described in subsection (b)(1)(A) paid in each of the 5 succeeding taxable years in order of time, but, with respect to any such succeeding taxable year, only to the extent of the lesser of the two following amounts:

(i) the amount by which 50 percent of the taxpayer's contribution base for such succeeding taxable year exceeds the sum of the charitable contributions described in subsection (b)(1)(A) payment of which is made by the taxpayer within such succeeding taxable year (determined without regard to this subparagraph) and the charitable contributions described in subsection (b)(1)(A) payment of which was made in taxable years before the contribution year which are treated under this subparagraph as having been paid in such succeeding taxable year; or

(ii) in the case of the first succeeding taxable year, the amount of such excess, and in the case of the second, third, fourth, or fifth succeeding taxable year, the portion of such excess not treated under this subparagraph as a charitable contribution described in subsection (b)(1)(A) paid in any taxable year intervening between the contribution year and such succeeding taxable year.

(B) SPECIAL RULE FOR NET OPERATING LOSS CARRYOVERS.—In applying subparagraph (A), the excess determined under subparagraph (A) for the contribution year shall be reduced to the extent that such excess reduces taxable income (as computed for purposes of the second sentence of section 172(b)(2)) and increases the net operating loss deduction for a taxable year succeeding the contribution year.

(2) CORPORATIONS.—

(A) IN GENERAL.—Any contribution made by a corporation in a taxable year (hereinafter in this paragraph referred to as the "contribution year") in excess of the amount deductible for such year under subsection (b)(2)(A) shall be deductible for each of the 5 succeeding taxable years in order of time, but only to the extent of the lesser of the two following amounts: (i) the excess of the maximum amount deductible for such succeeding taxable year under subsection (b)(2)(A) over the sum of the contributions made in such year plus the aggregate of the excess contributions which were made in taxable years before the contribution year and which are deductible under this subparagraph for such succeeding taxable year; or (ii) in the case of the first succeeding taxable year, the amount of such excess contribution, and in the case of the second, third, fourth, or fifth succeeding taxable year, the portion of such excess contribution not deductible under this subparagraph for any taxable year intervening between the contribution year and such succeeding taxable year.

(B) SPECIAL RULE FOR NET OPERATING LOSS CARRYOVERS.—For purposes of subparagraph (A), the excess of—

(i) the contributions made by a corporation in a taxable year to which this section applies, over

(ii) the amount deductible in such year under the limitation in subsection (b)(2)(A),

shall be reduced to the extent that such excess reduces taxable income (as computed for purposes of the second sentence of section 172(b)(2)) and increases a net operating loss carryover under section 172 to a succeeding taxable year.

Amendments

• 2020, Taxpayer Certainty and Disaster Tax Relief Act of 2020 (P.L. 116-260)

P.L. 116-260, §§301 and 304(a), Div. EE, provides:

SEC. 301. DEFINITIONS.

For purposes of this title—

(1) QUALIFIED DISASTER AREA.—

(A) IN GENERAL.—The term "qualified disaster area" means any area with respect to which a major disaster was declared, during the period beginning on January 1, 2020, and ending on the date which is 60 days after the date of the enactment of this Act, by the President under section 401 of the Robert T. Stafford Disaster Relief and Emergency Assistance Act if the incident period of the disaster with respect to which such declaration is made begins on or after December 28, 2019, and on or before the date of the enactment of this Act.

(B) COVID-19 EXCEPTION.—Such term shall not include any area with respect to which such a major disaster has been so declared only by reason of COVID-19.

(2) QUALIFIED DISASTER ZONE.—The term "qualified disaster zone" means that portion of any qualified disaster area which was determined by the President, during the period beginning on January 1, 2020, and ending on the date which is 60 days after the date of the enactment of this Act, to warrant individual or individual and public assistance from the Federal Government under the Robert T. Stafford Disaster Relief and Emergency Assistance Act by reason of the qualified disaster with respect to such disaster area.

(3) QUALIFIED DISASTER.—The term "qualified disaster" means, with respect to any qualified disaster area, the disaster by reason of which a major disaster was declared with respect to such area.

(4) INCIDENT PERIOD.—The term "incident period" means, with respect to any qualified disaster, the period specified by the Federal Emergency Management Agency as the period during which such disaster occurred (except that for purposes of this title such period shall not be treated as ending after the date which is 30 days after the date of the enactment of this Act).

SEC. 304. OTHER DISASTER-RELATED TAX RELIEF PROVISIONS.

(a) SPECIAL RULES FOR QUALIFIED DISASTER RELIEF CONTRIBUTIONS.—

(1) IN GENERAL.—In the case of a qualified disaster relief contribution made by a corporation—

(A) section 2205(a)(2)(B) of the CARES Act shall be applied first to qualified contributions without regard to any qualified disaster relief contributions and then separately to such qualified disaster relief contribution, and

(B) in applying such section to such qualified disaster relief contributions, clause (i) thereof shall be applied—

(i) by substituting "100 percent" for "25 percent", and

(ii) by treating qualified contributions other than qualified disaster relief contributions as contributions allowed under section 170(b)(2) of the Internal Revenue Code of 1986.

(2) QUALIFIED DISASTER RELIEF CONTRIBUTION.—For purposes of this subsection, the term "qualified disaster relief contribution" means any qualified contribution (as defined in section 2205(a)(3) of the CARES Act) if—

(A) such contribution—

(i) is paid, during the period beginning on January 1, 2020, and ending on the date which is 60 days after the date of the enactment of this Act, and

(ii) is made for relief efforts in one or more qualified disaster areas,

(B) the taxpayer obtains from such organization contemporaneous written acknowledgment (within the meaning of section 170(f)(8) of such Code) that such contribution was used (or is to be used) for relief efforts described in subparagraph (A)(ii), and

(C) the taxpayer has elected the application of this subsection with respect to such contribution.

(3) CROSS-REFERENCE.—For the suspension of the limitation on qualified disaster relief contributions made by an individual during 2020, see section 2205(a) of the CARES Act.

• 2020, Coronavirus Aid, Relief, and Economic Security (CARES) Act (P.L. 116-136)

P.L. 116-136, §2205(a) (as amended by P.L. 116-260, §213(a), Div. EE) and (c), provides:

(a) TEMPORARY SUSPENSION OF LIMITATIONS ON CERTAIN CASH CONTRIBUTIONS.—

(1) IN GENERAL.—Except as otherwise provided in paragraph (2), qualified contributions shall be disregarded in applying subsections (b) and (d) of section 170 of the Internal Revenue Code of 1986.

(2) TREATMENT OF EXCESS CONTRIBUTIONS.—For purposes of section 170 of the Internal Revenue Code of 1986—

(A) INDIVIDUALS.—In the case of an individual—

(i) LIMITATION.—Any qualified contribution shall be allowed as a deduction only to the extent that the aggregate of such contributions does not exceed the excess of the taxpayer's contribution base (as defined in subparagraph (H) of section 170(b)(1) of such Code) over the amount of all other charitable contributions allowed under section 170(b)(1) of such Code.

(ii) CARRYOVER.—If the aggregate amount of qualified contributions made in the contribution year (within the meaning of section 170(d)(1) of such Code) exceeds the limitation of clause (i), such excess shall be added to the excess described in section 170(b)(1)(G)(ii).

(B) CORPORATIONS.—In the case of a corporation—

(i) LIMITATION.—Any qualified contribution shall be allowed as a deduction only to the extent that the aggregate of such contributions does not exceed the excess of 25 percent of the taxpayer's taxable income (as determined under paragraph (2) of section 170(b) of such Code) over the amount of all other charitable contributions allowed under such paragraph.

(ii) CARRYOVER.—If the aggregate amount of qualified contributions made in the contribution year (within the meaning of section 170(d)(2) of such Code) exceeds the limitation of clause (i), such excess shall be appropriately taken into account under section 170(d)(2) subject to the limitations thereof.

(3) QUALIFIED CONTRIBUTIONS.—

(A) IN GENERAL.—For purposes of this subsection, the term "qualified contribution" means any charitable contribution (as defined in section 170(c) of the Internal Revenue Code of 1986) if—

(i) such contribution is paid in cash during calendar year 2020 or 2021 to an organization described in section 170(b)(1)(A) of such Code, and

(ii) the taxpayer has elected the application of this section with respect to such contribution.

(B) EXCEPTION.—Such term shall not include a contribution by a donor if the contribution is—

(i) to an organization described in section 509(a)(3) of the Internal Revenue Code of 1986, or

(ii) for the establishment of a new, or maintenance of an existing, donor advised fund (as defined in section 4966(d)(2) of such Code).

(C) APPLICATION OF ELECTION TO PARTNERSHIPS AND S CORPORATIONS.—In the case of a partnership or S corporation, the election under subparagraph (A)(ii) shall be made separately by each partner or shareholder.

* * *

(c) EFFECTIVE DATE.—This section shall apply to taxable years ending after December 31, 2019.

• 2006, Pension Protection Act of 2006 (P.L. 109-280)

P.L. 109-280, §1206(b)(1):

Amended Code Sec. 170(d)(2) by striking "subsection (b)(2)" each place it appears and inserting "subsection (b)(2)(A)". **Effective** for contributions made in tax years beginning after 12-31-2005.

• 1976, Tax Reform Act of 1976 (P.L. 94-455)

P.L. 94-455, §1901(a)(28):

Amended Code Sec. 170(d)(1)(A) by striking out "(30 percent, in the case of a contribution year beginning before January 1, 1970)" after "50 percent". **Effective** for tax years beginning after 12-31-76.

• 1969, Tax Reform Act of 1969 (P.L. 91-172)

P.L. 91-172, §201(a)(1):

Redesignated old Sec. 170(d) as Sec. 170(h) and added new Sec. 170(d). For purposes of applying section 170(d) (as amended by subsection (a)) with respect to contributions paid in a taxable year beginning before 1-1-70, subsection (b)(1)(D), subsection (e), and paragraphs (1), (2), (3), and (4) of subsection (f) of section 170 of such Code shall not apply.

[Sec. 170(e)]

(e) CERTAIN CONTRIBUTIONS OF ORDINARY INCOME AND CAPITAL GAIN PROPERTY.—

(1) GENERAL RULE.—The amount of any charitable contribution of property otherwise taken into account under this section shall be reduced by the sum of—

(A) the amount of gain which would not have been long-term capital gain (determined without regard to section 1221(b)(3)) if the property contributed had been sold by the taxpayer at its fair market value (determined at the time of such contribution), and

(B) in the case of a charitable contribution—

(i) of tangible personal property—

(I) if the use by the donee is unrelated to the purpose or function constituting the basis for its exemption under section 501 (or, in the case of a governmental unit, to any purpose or function described in subsection (c)), or

(II) which is applicable property (as defined in paragraph (7)(C), but without regard to clause (ii) thereof) which is sold, exchanged, or otherwise disposed of by the donee before the last day of the taxable year in which the contribution was made and with respect to which the donee has not made a certification in accordance with paragraph (7)(D),

(ii) to or for the use of a private foundation (as defined in section 509(a)), other than a private foundation described in subsection (b)(1)(F),

(iii) of any patent, copyright (other than a copyright described in section 1221(a)(3) or 1231(b)(1)(C)), trademark, trade name, trade secret, know-how, software (other than software described in section 197(e)(3)(A)(i)), or similar property, or applications or registrations of such property, or

(iv) of any taxidermy property which is contributed by the person who prepared, stuffed, or mounted the property or by any person who paid or incurred the cost of such preparation, stuffing, or mounting,

the amount of gain which would have been long-term capital gain if the property contributed had been sold by the taxpayer at its fair market value (determined at the time of such contribution).

For purposes of applying this paragraph (other than in the case of gain to which section 617(d)(1), 1245(a), 1250(a), 1252(a), or 1254(a) applies), property which is property used in the trade or business (as defined in section 1231(b)) shall be treated as a capital asset. For purposes of applying this paragraph in the case of a charitable contribution of stock in an S corporation, rules similar to the rules of section 751 shall apply in determining whether gain on such stock would have been long-term capital gain if such stock were sold by the taxpayer.

(2) ALLOCATION OF BASIS.—For purposes of paragraph (1), in the case of a charitable contribution of less than the taxpayer's entire interest in the property contributed, the taxpayer's adjusted basis in such property shall be allocated between the interest contributed and any interest not contributed in accordance with regulations prescribed by the Secretary.

(3) SPECIAL RULE FOR CERTAIN CONTRIBUTIONS OF INVENTORY AND OTHER PROPERTY.—

(A) QUALIFIED CONTRIBUTIONS.—For purposes of this paragraph, a qualified contribution shall mean a charitable contribution of property described in paragraph (1) or (2) of section

1221(a), by a corporation (other than a corporation which is an S corporation) to an organization which is described in section 501(c)(3) and is exempt under section 501(a) (other than a private foundation, as defined in section 509(a), which is not an operating foundation, as defined in section 4942(j)(3)), but only if—

(i) the use of the property by the donee is related to the purpose or function constituting the basis for its exemption under section 501 and the property is to be used by the donee solely for the care of the ill, the needy, or infants;

(ii) the property is not transferred by the donee in exchange for money, other property, or services;

(iii) the taxpayer receives from the donee a written statement representing that its use and disposition of the property will be in accordance with the provisions of clauses (i) and (ii); and

(iv) in the case where the property is subject to regulation under the Federal Food, Drug, and Cosmetic Act, as amended, such property must fully satisfy the applicable requirements of such Act and regulations promulgated thereunder on the date of transfer and for one hundred and eighty days prior thereto.

(B) AMOUNT OF REDUCTION.—The reduction under paragraph (1)(A) for any qualified contribution (as defined in subparagraph (A)) shall be no greater than the sum of—

(i) one-half of the amount computed under paragraph (1)(A) (computed without regard to this paragraph), and

(ii) the amount (if any) by which the charitable contribution deduction under this section for any qualified contribution (computed by taking into account the amount determined in clause (i), but without regard to this clause) exceeds twice the basis of such property.

(C) SPECIAL RULE FOR CONTRIBUTIONS OF FOOD INVENTORY.—

(i) GENERAL RULE.—In the case of a charitable contribution of food from any trade or business of the taxpayer, this paragraph shall be applied—

(I) without regard to whether the contribution is made by a C corporation, and

(II) only to food that is apparently wholesome food.

(ii) LIMITATION.—The aggregate amount of such contributions for any taxable year which may be taken into account under this section shall not exceed—

(I) in the case of any taxpayer other than a C corporation, 15 percent of the taxpayer's aggregate net income for such taxable year from all trades or businesses from which such contributions were made for such year, computed without regard to this section, and

(II) in the case of a C corporation, 15 percent of taxable income (as defined in subsection (b)(2)(D)).

(iii) RULES RELATED TO LIMITATION.—

(I) CARRYOVER.—If such aggregate amount exceeds the limitation imposed under clause (ii), such excess shall be treated (in a manner consistent with the rules of subsection (d)) as a charitable contribution described in clause (i) in each of the 5 succeeding taxable years in order of time.

(II) COORDINATION WITH OVERALL CORPORATE LIMITATION.—In the case of any charitable contribution which is allowable after the application of clause (ii)(II), subsection (b)(2)(A) shall not apply to such contribution, but the limitation imposed by such subsection shall be reduced (but not below zero) by the aggregate amount of such contributions. For purposes of subsection (b)(2)(B), such contributions shall be treated as allowable under subsection (b)(2)(A).

(iv) DETERMINATION OF BASIS FOR CERTAIN TAXPAYERS.—If a taxpayer—

(I) does not account for inventories under section 471, and

(II) is not required to capitalize indirect costs under section 263A,

the taxpayer may elect, solely for purposes of subparagraph (B), to treat the basis of any apparently wholesome food as being equal to 25 percent of the fair market value of such food.

(v) DETERMINATION OF FAIR MARKET VALUE.—In the case of any such contribution of apparently wholesome food which cannot or will not be sold solely by reason of internal standards of the taxpayer, lack of market, or similar circumstances, or by reason of being produced by the taxpayer exclusively for the purposes of transferring the food to an organization described in subparagraph (A), the fair market value of such contribution shall be determined—

(I) without regard to such internal standards, such lack of market, such circumstances, or such exclusive purpose, and

(II) by taking into account the price at which the same or substantially the same food items (as to both type and quality) are sold by the taxpayer at the time of the contribution (or, if not so sold at such time, in the recent past).

(vi) APPARENTLY WHOLESOME FOOD.—For purposes of this subparagraph, the term "apparently wholesome food" has the meaning given to such term by section 22(b)(2) of the Bill Emerson Good Samaritan Food Donation Act (42 U.S.C. 1791(b)(2)), as in effect on the date of the enactment of this subparagraph.

(D) This paragraph shall not apply to so much of the amount of the gain described in paragraph (1)(A) which would be long-term capital gain but for the application of sections 617, 1245, 1250, or 1252.

(4) SPECIAL RULE FOR CONTRIBUTIONS OF SCIENTIFIC PROPERTY USED FOR RESEARCH.—

(A) LIMIT ON REDUCTION.—In the case of a qualified research contribution, the reduction under paragraph (1)(A) shall be no greater than the amount determined under paragraph (3)(B).

(B) QUALIFIED RESEARCH CONTRIBUTIONS.—For purposes of this paragraph, the term "qualified research contribution" means a charitable contribution by a corporation of tangible personal property described in paragraph (1) of section 1221(a), but only if—

(i) the contribution is to an organization described in subparagraph (A) or subparagraph (B) of section 41(e)(6),

(ii) the property is constructed or assembled by the taxpayer,

(iii) the contribution is made not later than 2 years after the date the construction or assembly of the property is substantially completed,

(iv) the original use of the property is by the donee,

(v) the property is scientific equipment or apparatus substantially all of the use of which by the donee is for research or experimentation (within the meaning of section 174), or for research training, in the United States in physical or biological sciences,

(vi) the property is not transferred by the donee in exchange for money, other property, or services, and

(vii) the taxpayer receives from the donee a written statement representing that its use and disposition of the property will be in accordance with the provisions of clauses (v) and (vi).

(C) CONSTRUCTION OF PROPERTY BY TAXPAYER.—For purposes of this paragraph, property shall be treated as constructed by the taxpayer only if the cost of the parts used in the construction of such property (other than parts manufactured by the taxpayer or a related person) do not exceed 50 percent of the taxpayer's basis in such property.

(D) CORPORATION.—For purposes of this paragraph, the term "corporation" shall not include—

(i) an S corporation,

(ii) a personal holding company (as defined in section 542), and

(iii) a service organization (as defined in section 414(m)(3)).

(5) SPECIAL RULE FOR CONTRIBUTIONS OF STOCK FOR WHICH MARKET QUOTATIONS ARE READILY AVAILABLE.—

(A) IN GENERAL.—Subparagraph (B)(ii) of paragraph (1) shall not apply to any contribution of qualified appreciated stock.

(B) QUALIFIED APPRECIATED STOCK.—Except as provided in subparagraph (C), for purposes of this paragraph, the term "qualified appreciated stock" means any stock of a corporation—

(i) for which (as of the date of the contribution) market quotations are readily available on an established securities market, and

(ii) which is capital gain property (as defined in subsection (b)(1)(C)(iv)).

(C) DONOR MAY NOT CONTRIBUTE MORE THAN 10 PERCENT OF STOCK OF CORPORATION.—

(i) IN GENERAL.—In the case of any donor, the term "qualified appreciated stock" shall not include any stock of a corporation contributed by the donor in a contribution to which paragraph (1)(B)(ii) applies (determined without regard to this paragraph) to the extent that the amount of the stock so contributed (when increased by the aggregate amount of all prior such contributions by the donor of stock in such corporation) exceeds 10 percent (in value) of all of the outstanding stock of such corporation.

(ii) SPECIAL RULE.—For purposes of clause (i), an individual shall be treated as making all contributions made by any member of his family (as defined in section 267(c)(4)).

(6) [Stricken.]

(7) RECAPTURE OF DEDUCTION ON CERTAIN DISPOSITIONS OF EXEMPT USE PROPERTY.—

(A) IN GENERAL.—In the case of an applicable disposition of applicable property, there shall be included in the income of the donor of such property for the taxable year of such donor in which the applicable disposition occurs an amount equal to the excess (if any) of—

(i) the amount of the deduction allowed to the donor under this section with respect to such property, over

(ii) the donor's basis in such property at the time such property was contributed.

(B) APPLICABLE DISPOSITION.—For purposes of this paragraph, the term "applicable disposition" means any sale, exchange, or other disposition by the donee of applicable property—

(i) after the last day of the taxable year of the donor in which such property was contributed, and

(ii) before the last day of the 3-year period beginning on the date of the contribution of such property,

unless the donee makes a certification in accordance with subparagraph (D).

(C) APPLICABLE PROPERTY.—For purposes of this paragraph, the term "applicable property" means charitable deduction property (as defined in section 6050L(a)(2)(A))—

(i) which is tangible personal property the use of which is identified by the donee as related to the purpose or function constituting the basis of the donee's exemption under section 501, and

(ii) for which a deduction in excess of the donor's basis is allowed.

(D) CERTIFICATION.—A certification meets the requirements of this subparagraph if it is a written statement which is signed under penalty of perjury by an officer of the donee organization and—

(i) which—

(I) certifies that the use of the property by the donee was substantial and related to the purpose or function constituting the basis for the donee's exemption under section 501, and

(II) describes how the property was used and how such use furthered such purpose or function, or

(ii) which—

(I) states the intended use of the property by the donee at the time of the contribution, and

(II) certifies that such intended use has become impossible or infeasible to implement.

Amendments

• 2020, Coronavirus Aid, Relief, and Economic Security (CARES) Act (P.L. 116-136)

P.L. 116-136, §2205(b) (as amended by P.L. 116-260, §213(a), Div. EE) and (c), provides:

(b) INCREASE IN LIMITS ON CONTRIBUTIONS OF FOOD INVENTORY.—In the case of any charitable contribution of food during 2020 or 2021 which section 170(e)(3)(C) of the Internal Revenue Code of 1986 applies, subclauses (I) and (II) of clause (ii) thereof shall each be applied by substituting "25 percent" for "15 percent."

(c) EFFECTIVE DATE.—This section shall apply to taxable years ending after December 31, 2019.

• 2018, Tax Technical Corrections Act of 2018 (P.L. 115-141)

P.L. 115-141, §401(b)(14), Div. U:

Amended Code Sec. 170(e)(3) by striking subparagraph (D) and redesignating subparagraph (E) as subparagraph (D). **Effective** 3-23-2018. For a special rule, see Act Sec. 401(e), Div. U, below. Prior to being stricken, Code Sec. 170(e)(3)(D) read as follows:

(D) SPECIAL RULE FOR CONTRIBUTIONS OF BOOK INVENTORY TO PUBLIC SCHOOLS.—

(i) CONTRIBUTIONS OF BOOK INVENTORY.—In determining whether a qualified book contribution is a qualified contribution, subparagraph (A) shall be applied without regard to whether the donee is an organization described in the matter preceding clause (i) of subparagraph (A).

(ii) QUALIFIED BOOK CONTRIBUTION.—For purposes of this paragraph, the term "qualified book contribution" means a charitable contribution of books to a public school which is an educational organization described in subsection (b)(1)(A)(ii) and which provides elementary education or secondary education (kindergarten through grade 12).

(iii) CERTIFICATION BY DONEE.—Subparagraph (A) shall not apply to any contribution of books unless (in addition to the certifications required by subparagraph (A) (as modified by this subparagraph))), the donee certifies in writing that—

(I) the books are suitable, in terms of currency, content, and quantity, for use in the donee's educational programs, and

(II) the donee will use the books in its educational programs.

(iv) TERMINATION.—This subparagraph shall not apply to contributions made after December 31, 2011.

P.L. 115-141, §401(e), Div. U, provides:

(e) GENERAL SAVINGS PROVISION WITH RESPECT TO DEADWOOD PROVISIONS.—If—

(1) any provision amended or repealed by the amendments made by subsection (b) or (d) applied to—

(A) any transaction occurring before the date of the enactment of this Act,

(B) any property acquired before such date of enactment, or

(C) any item of income, loss, deduction, or credit taken into account before such date of enactment, and

(2) the treatment of such transaction, property, or item under such provision would (without regard to the amendments or repeals made by such subsection) affect the liability for tax for periods ending after such date of enactment,

nothing in the amendments or repeals made by this section shall be construed to affect the treatment of such transaction, property, or item for purposes of determining liability for tax for periods ending after such date of enactment.

• 2015, Protecting Americans from Tax Hikes Act of 2015 (P.L. 114-113)

P.L. 114-113, §113(a), Div. Q:

Amended Code Sec. 170(e)(3)(C) by striking clause (iv). **Effective** for contributions made after 12-31-2014. Prior to being stricken, Code Sec. 170(e)(3)(C)(iv) read as follows:

(iv) TERMINATION.—This subparagraph shall not apply to contributions made after December 31, 2014.

P.L. 114-113, §113(b), Div. Q:

Amended Code Sec. 170(e)(3)(C), as amended by Act Sec. 113(a), by striking clause (ii), by redesignating clause (iii) as clause (vi), and by inserting after clause (i) new clauses (ii)-(v). **Effective** for tax years beginning after 12-31-2015. Prior to being stricken, Code Sec. 170(e)(3)(C)(ii) read as follows:

(ii) LIMITATION.—In the case of a taxpayer other than a C corporation, the aggregate amount of such contributions for any taxable year which may be taken into account under this section shall not exceed 10 percent of the taxpayer's aggregate net income for such taxable year from all trades or businesses from which such contributions were made for such year, computed without regard to this section.

• 2014, Tax Increase Prevention Act of 2014 (P.L. 113-295)

P.L. 113-295, §126(a), Div. A:

Amended Code Sec. 170(e)(3)(C)(iv) by striking "December 31, 2013" and inserting "December 31, 2014". **Effective** for contributions made after 12-31-2013.

• 2014, Tax Technical Corrections Act of 2014 (P.L. 113-295)

P.L. 113-295, §221(a)(28)(B), Div. A:

Amended Code Sec. 170(e) by striking paragraph (6). **Effective** generally 12-19-2014. For a special rule, see Act Sec. 221(b)(2), Div. A, below. Prior to being stricken, Code Sec. 170(e)(6) read as follows:

(6) SPECIAL RULE FOR CONTRIBUTIONS OF COMPUTER TECHNOLOGY AND EQUIPMENT FOR EDUCATIONAL PURPOSES.—

(A) LIMIT ON REDUCTION.—In the case of a qualified computer contribution, the reduction under paragraph (1)(A) shall be no greater than the amount determined under paragraph (3)(B).

(B) QUALIFIED COMPUTER CONTRIBUTION.—For purposes of this paragraph, the term "qualified computer contribution" means a charitable contribution by a corporation of any computer technology or equipment, but only if—

(i) the contribution is to—

(I) an educational organization described in subsection (b)(1)(A)(ii),

(II) an entity described in section 501(c)(3) and exempt from tax under section 501(a) (other than an entity described in subclause (I)) that is organized primarily for purposes of supporting elementary and secondary education, or

(III) a public library (within the meaning of section 213(2)(A) of the Library Services and Technology Act (20 U.S.C. 9122(2)(A)), as in effect on the date of the enactment of the Community Renewal Tax Relief Act of 2000), established and maintained by an entity described in subsection (c)(1),

(ii) the contribution is made not later than 3 years after the date the taxpayer acquired the property (or in the case of property constructed or assembled by the taxpayer, the date the construction or assembling of the property is substantially completed),

(iii) the original use of the property is by the donor or the donee,

(iv) substantially all of the use of the property by the donee is for use within the United States for educational purposes that are related to the purpose or function of the donee,

(v) the property is not transferred by the donee in exchange for money, other property, or services, except for shipping, installation and transfer costs,

(vi) the property will fit productively into the donee's education plan,

(vii) the donee's use and disposition of the property will be in accordance with the provisions of clauses (iv) and (v), and

(viii) the property meets such standards, if any, as the Secretary may prescribe by regulation to assure that the property meets minimum functionality and suitability standards for educational purposes.

(C) CONTRIBUTION TO PRIVATE FOUNDATION.—A contribution by a corporation of any computer technology or equipment to a private foundation (as defined in section 509) shall be treated as a qualified computer contribution for purposes of this paragraph if—

(i) the contribution to the private foundation satisfies the requirements of clauses (ii) and (v) of subparagraph (B), and

(ii) within 30 days after such contribution, the private foundation—

(I) contributes the property to a donee described in clause (i) of subparagraph (B) that satisfies the requirements of clauses (iv) through (vii) of subparagraph (B), and

(II) notifies the donor of such contribution.

(D) DONATIONS OF PROPERTY REACQUIRED BY MANUFACTURER.—In the case of property which is reacquired by the person who constructed or assembled the property—

(i) subparagraph (B)(ii) shall be applied to a contribution of such property by such person by taking into account the date that the original construction or assembly of the property was substantially completed, and

(ii) subparagraph (B)(iii) shall not apply to such contribution.

(E) SPECIAL RULE RELATING TO CONSTRUCTION OF PROPERTY.—For the purposes of this paragraph, the rules of paragraph (4)(C) shall apply.

(F) DEFINITIONS.—For the purposes of this paragraph—

(i) COMPUTER TECHNOLOGY OR EQUIPMENT.—The term "computer technology or equipment" means computer software (as defined by section 197(e)(3)(B)), computer or peripheral equipment (as defined by section 168(i)(2)(B)), and fiber optic cable related to computer use.

(ii) CORPORATION.—The term "corporation" has the meaning given to such term by paragraph (4)(D).

(G) TERMINATION.—This paragraph shall not apply to any contribution made during any taxable year beginning after December 31, 2011.

P.L. 113-295, §221(b)(2), Div. A, provides:

(2) SAVINGS PROVISION.—If—

(A) any provision amended or repealed by the amendments made by this section applied to—

(i) any transaction occurring before the date of the enactment of this Act,

(ii) any property acquired before such date of enactment, or

(iii) any item of income, loss, deduction, or credit taken into account before such date of enactment, and

(B) the treatment of such transaction, property, or item under such provision would (without regard to the amendments or repeals made by this section) affect the liability for tax for periods ending after date of enactment, nothing in the amendments or repeals made by this section shall be construed to affect the treatment of such transaction, property, or item for purposes of determining liability for tax for periods ending after such date of enactment.

• 2013, American Taxpayer Relief Act of 2012 (P.L. 112-240)

P.L. 112-240, §101(a)(1)-(3), provides:

SEC. 101. PERMANENT EXTENSION AND MODIFICATION OF 2001 TAX RELIEF.

(a) PERMANENT EXTENSION.—

(1) IN GENERAL.—The Economic Growth and Tax Relief Reconciliation Act of 2001 is amended by striking title IX.

(2) CONFORMING AMENDMENT.—The Tax Relief, Unemployment Insurance Reauthorization, and Job Creation Act of 2010 is amended by striking section 304.

(3) EFFECTIVE DATE.—The amendments made by this subsection shall apply to taxable, plan, or limitation years beginning after December 31, 2012, and estates of decedents dying, gifts made, or generation skipping transfers after December 31, 2012.

P.L. 112-240, §314(a):

Amended Code Sec. 170(e)(3)(C)(iv) by striking "December 31, 2011" and inserting "December 31, 2013". **Effective** for contributions made after 12-31-2011.

• 2010, Tax Relief, Unemployment Insurance Reauthorization, and Job Creation Act of 2010 (P.L. 111-312)

P.L. 111-312, §301(a):

Amended Code Sec. 170(e)(1) to read as such provision would read if subtitle E of title V of the Economic Growth and Tax Relief Reconciliation Act of 2001 (P.L. 107-16) had never been enacted. **Effective** for estates of decedents dying, and transfers made, after 12-31-2009. For a special rule, see Act Sec. 301(c), below. Prior to amendment by P.L. 111-312, the flush text following Code Sec. 170(e)(1) read as follows:

For purposes of applying this paragraph (other than in the case of gain to which section 617(d)(1), 1245(a), 1250(a), 1252(a), or 1254(a) applies), property which is property used in the trade or business (as defined in section 1231(b)) shall be treated as a capital asset. For purposes of applying this paragraph in the case of a charitable contribution of stock in an S corporation, rules similar to the rules of section 751 shall apply in determining whether gain on such stock would have been long-term capital gain if such stock were sold by the taxpayer. For purposes of this paragraph, the determination of whether property is a capital asset shall be made without regard to the exception contained in section 1221(a)(3)(C) for basis determined under section 1022.

P.L. 111-312, §301(c), provides:

(c) SPECIAL ELECTION WITH RESPECT TO ESTATES OF DECEDENTS DYING IN 2010.—Notwithstanding subsection (a), in the case of an estate of a decedent dying after December 31, 2009, and before January 1, 2011, the executor (within the meaning of section 2203 of the Internal Revenue Code of 1986) may elect to apply such Code as though the amendments made by subsection (a) do not apply with respect to chapter 11 of such Code and with respect to property acquired or passing from such decedent (within the meaning of section 1014(b) of such Code). Such election shall be made at such time and in such manner as the Secretary of the Treasury or the Secretary's delegate shall provide. Such an election once made shall be revocable only with the consent of the Secretary of the Treasury or the Secretary's delegate. For purposes of section 2652(a)(1) of such Code, the determination of whether any property is subject to the tax imposed by such chapter 11 shall be made without regard to any election made under this subsection.

P.L. 111-312, §304, provides [but see P.L. 112-240, §101(a)(2)-(3), above]:

SEC. 304. APPLICATION OF EGTRRA SUNSET TO THIS TITLE.

Section 901 of the Economic Growth and Tax Relief Reconciliation Act of 2001 shall apply to the amendments made by this title.

P.L. 111-312, §740(a):

Amended Code Sec. 170(e)(3)(C)(iv) by striking "December 31, 2009" and inserting "December 31, 2011". **Effective** for contributions made after 12-31-2009.

P.L. 111-312, §741(a):

Amended Code Sec. 170(e)(3)(D)(iv) by striking "December 31, 2009" and inserting "December 31, 2011". **Effective** for contributions made after 12-31-2009.

P.L. 111-312, §742(a):

Amended Code Sec. 170(e)(6)(G) by striking "December 31, 2009" and inserting "December 31, 2011". **Effective** for contributions made in tax years beginning after 12-31-2009.

• 2008, Tax Extenders and Alternative Minimum Tax Relief Act of 2008 (P.L. 110-343)

P.L. 110-343, Div. C, §321(a):

Amended Code Sec. 170(e)(6)(G) by striking "December 31, 2007" and inserting "December 31, 2009". **Effective** for contributions made during tax years beginning after 12-31-2007.

P.L. 110-343, Div. C, §323(a)(1):

Amended Code Sec. 170(e)(3)(C)(iv) by striking "December 31, 2007" and inserting "December 31, 2009". **Effective** for contributions made after 12-31-2007.

P.L. 110-343, Div. C, §324(a):

Amended Code Sec. 170(e)(3)(D)(iv) by striking "December 31, 2007" and inserting "December 31, 2009". **Effective** for contributions made after 12-31-2007.

P.L. 110-343, Div. C, §324(b):

Amended Code Sec. 170(e)(3)(D)(iii) by inserting "of books" after "to any contribution". **Effective** for contributions made after 12-31-2007.

• 2007, Tax Technical Corrections Act of 2007 (P.L. 110-172)

P.L. 110-172, §3(c):

Amended Code Sec. 170(e)(7)(D)(i)(I) by striking "related" and inserting "substantial and related". **Effective** as if included in the provision of the Pension Protection Act of 2006 (P.L. 109-280) to which it relates [**effective** for contributions after 9-1-2006.—CCH].

P.L. 110-172, §11(a)(14)(B):

Amended Code Sec. 170(e)(1)(B)(ii) by striking "subsection (b)(1)(E)" and inserting "subsection (b)(1)(F)". **Effective** 12-29-2007.

P.L. 110-172, §11(a)(15):

Amended Code Sec. 170(e)(1)(B)(i)(II) by inserting ", but without regard to clause (ii) thereof" after "paragraph (7)(C)". **Effective** 12-29-2007.

• 2006, Tax Relief and Health Care Act of 2006 (P.L. 109-432)

P.L. 109-432, Div. A, §116(a)(1):

Amended Code Sec. 170(e)(6)(G) by striking "2005" and inserting "2007". **Effective** for contributions made in tax years beginning after 12-31-2005.

P.L. 109-432, Div. A, §116(b)(1)(A):

Amended Code Sec. 170(e)(4)(B)(ii) by inserting "or assembled" after "constructed". **Effective** for tax years beginning after 12-31-2005.

P.L. 109-432, Div. A, §116(b)(1)(B):

Amended Code Sec. 170(e)(4)(B)(iii) by inserting "or assembly" after "construction". **Effective** for tax years beginning after 12-31-2005.

P.L. 109-432, Div. A, §116(b)(2)(A):

Amended Code Sec. 170(e)(6)(B)(ii) by inserting "or assembled" after "constructed" and "or assembling" after "construction". **Effective** for tax years beginning after 12-31-2005.

P.L. 109-432, Div. A, §116(b)(2)(B):

Amended Code Sec. 170(e)(6)(D) by inserting "or assembled" after "constructed" and "or assembly" after "construction". **Effective** for tax years beginning after 12-31-2005.

• 2006, Pension Protection Act of 2006 (P.L. 109-280)

P.L. 109-280, §1202(a):

Amended Code Sec. 170(e)(3)(C)(iv) by striking "2005" and inserting "2007". **Effective** for contributions made after 12-31-2005.

P.L. 109-280, §1204(a):

Amended Code Sec. 170(e)(3)(D)(iv) by striking "2005" and inserting "2007". **Effective** for contributions made after 12-31-2005.

P.L. 109-280, §1214(a):

Amended Code Sec. 170(e)(1)(B) by striking "or" at the end of clause (ii), by inserting "or" at the end of clause (iii), and by inserting after clause (iii) a new clause (iv). **Effective** for contributions made after 7-25-2006.

P.L. 109-280, §1215(a)(1):

Amended Code Sec. 170(e)(1)(B)(i). **Effective** for contributions after 9-1-2006. Prior to amendment, Code Sec. 170(e)(1)(B)(i) read as follows:

(i) of tangible personal property, if the use by the donee is unrelated to the purpose or function constituting the basis for its exemption under section 501 (or, in the case of a governmental unit, to any purpose or function described in subsection (c)),

P.L. 109-280, §1215(a)(2):

Amended Code Sec. 170(e) by adding at the end a new paragraph (7). **Effective** for contributions after 9-1-2006.

• 2006, Tax Increase Prevention and Reconciliation Act of 2005 (P.L. 109-222)

P.L. 109-222, §204(b):

Amended Code Sec. 170(e)(1)(A) by inserting "(determined without regard to section 1221(b)(3))" after "long-term capital gain". **Effective** for sales and exchanges in tax years beginning after 5-17-2006.

• 2005, Katrina Emergency Tax Relief Act of 2005 (P.L. 109-73)

P.L. 109-73, §305(a):

Amended Code Sec. 170(e)(3) by redesignating subparagraph (C) as subparagraph (D) and by inserting after subparagraph (B) a new subparagraph (C). **Effective** for contributions made on or after 8-28-2005, in tax years ending after such date.

P.L. 109-73, §306(a):

Amended Code Sec. 170(e)(3), as amended by Act Sec. 305, by redesignating subparagraph (D) as subparagraph (E) and by inserting after subparagraph (C) a new subparagraph (D). **Effective** for contributions made on or after 8-28-2005, in tax years ending after such date.

• 2004, American Jobs Creation Act of 2004 (P.L. 108-357)

P.L. 108-357, §882(a):

Amended Code Sec. 170(e)(1)(B) by striking "or" at the end of clause (i), by adding "or" at the end of clause (ii), and by inserting after clause (ii) a new clause (iii). **Effective** for contributions made after 6-3-2004.

• 2004, Working Families Tax Relief Act of 2004 (P.L. 108-311)

P.L. 108-311, §306(a):

Amended Code Sec. 170(e)(6)(G) by striking "2003" and inserting "2005". **Effective** for contributions made in tax years beginning after 12-31-2003.

• 2002, Job Creation and Worker Assistance Act of 2002 (P.L. 107-147)

P.L. 107-147, §417(7):

Amended Code Sec. 170(e)(6)(B)(i)(III) by striking "2000," and inserting"2000),". **Effective** 3-9-2002.

P.L. 107-147, §417(22), provides:

(22) The amendment to section 170(e)(6)(B)(iv) made by section 165(b)(1) of the Community Renewal Tax Relief Act of 2000 (114 Stat. 2763A-626) shall be applied as if it struck "in any of the grades K-12".

• 2001, Economic Growth and Tax Relief Reconciliation Act of 2001 (P.L. 107-16)

P.L. 107-16, §542(e)(2)(B):

Amended Code Sec. 170(e)(1) by adding at the end a new sentence. **Effective** for estates of decedents dying after 12-31-2009.

P.L. 107-16, §901(a)-(b) as amended by P.L. 111-312, §101(a)(1), provides [but see P.L. 112-240, §101(a)(1) and (3), above]:

SEC. 901. SUNSET OF PROVISIONS OF ACT.

(a) IN GENERAL.—All provisions of, and amendments made by, this Act shall not apply—

(1) to taxable, plan, or limitation years beginning after December 31, 2012, or

(2) in the case of title V, to estates of decedents dying, gifts made, or generation skipping transfers, after December 31, 2012.

(b) APPLICATION OF CERTAIN LAWS.—The Internal Revenue Code of 1986 and the Employee Retirement Income Security Act of 1974 shall be applied and administered to years, estates, gifts, and transfers described in subsection (a) as if the provisions and amendments described in subsection (a) had never been enacted.

• 2000, Community Renewal Tax Relief Act of 2000 (P.L. 106-554)

P.L. 106-554, §165(a)(1):

Amended Code Sec. 170(e)(6) by striking "qualified elementary or secondary educational contribution" each place it occurs in the headings and text and inserting "qualified computer contribution". **Effective** for contributions made after 12-31-2000.

P.L. 106-554, §165(a)(2):

Amended Code Sec. 170(e)(6)(B)(i) by striking "or" at the end of subclause (I), by adding "or" at the end of subclause (II), and by inserting after subclause (II) a new subclause (III). **Effective** for contributions made after 12-31-2000.

P.L. 106-554, §165(a)(3):

Amended Code Sec. 170(e)(6)(B)(ii) by striking "2 years" and inserting "3 years". **Effective** for contributions made after 12-31-2000.

P.L. 106-554, §165(b)(1):

Amended Code Sec. 170(e)(6)(B)(iv) by striking "in any grades of the K–12" following "educational purposes". **Effective** for contributions made after 12-31-2000. [But see P.L. 107-147, §417(22).—CCH.]

P.L. 106-554, §165(b)(2):

Amended the heading of Code Sec. 170(e)(6) by striking "ELEMENTARY OR SECONDARY SCHOOL PURPOSES" and inserting "EDUCATIONAL PURPOSES". **Effective** for contributions made after 12-31-2000.

P.L. 106-554, §165(c):

Amended Code Sec. 170(e)(6)(F) by striking "December 31, 2000" and inserting "December 31, 2003". **Effective** for contributions made after 12-31-2000.

P.L. 106-554, §165(d):

Amended Code Sec. 170(e)(6)(B) by striking "and" at the end of clause (vi), by striking the period at the end of clause (vii) and inserting ", and", and by adding at the end a new clause (viii). **Effective** for contributions made after 12-31-2000.

P.L. 106-554, §165(e):

Amended Code Sec. 170(e)(6) by redesignating subparagraphs (D), (E), and (F) as subparagraphs (E), (F), and (G), respectively, and by inserting after subparagraph (C) a new subparagraph (D). **Effective** for contributions made after 12-31-2000.

• 1999, Tax Relief Extension Act of 1999 (P.L. 106-170)

P.L. 106-170, §532(c)(1)(A):

Amended Code Sec. 170(e)(3)(A) by striking "section 1221" and inserting "section 1221(a)". **Effective** for any instrument held, acquired, or entered into, any transaction entered into, and supplies held or acquired on or after 12-17-99.

P.L. 106-170, §532(c)(1)(B):

Amended Code Sec. 170(e)(4)(B) by striking "section 1221" and inserting "section 1221(a)". **Effective** for any instrument held, acquired, or entered into, any transaction entered into, and supplies held or acquired on or after 12-17-99.

• 1998, Tax and Trade Relief Extension Act of 1998 (P.L. 105-277)

P.L. 105-277, §1004(a)(1):

Amended Code Sec. 170(e)(5) by striking subparagraph (D). **Effective** for contributions made after 6-30-98. Prior to amendment, Code Sec. 170(e)(5)(D) read as follows:

(D) TERMINATION.—This paragraph shall not apply to contributions made—

(i) after December 31, 1994, and before July 1, 1996, or

(ii) after June 30, 1998.

• 1998, IRS Restructuring and Reform Act of 1998 (P.L. 105-206)

P.L. 105-206, §6004(e)(1):

Amended Code Sec. 170(e)(6)(B)(vi) and (vii) by striking "entity's" and inserting "donee's". **Effective** as if included in the provision of P.L. 105-34 to which it relates [**effective** for tax years beginning after 12-31-97.—CCH].

P.L. 105-206, §6004(e)(2):

Amended Code Sec. 170(e)(6)(B)(iv) by striking "organization or entity" and inserting "donee". **Effective** as if included in the provision of P.L. 105-34 to which it relates [**effective** for tax years beginning after 12-31-97.—CCH].

P.L. 105-206, §6004(e)(3):

Amended Code Sec. 170(e)(6)(C)(ii)(I) by striking "an entity" and inserting "a donee". **Effective** as if included in the provision of P.L. 105-34 to which it relates [**effective** for tax years beginning after 12-31-97.—CCH].

P.L. 105-206, §6004(e)(4):

Amended Code Sec. 170(e)(6)(F) by striking "1999" and inserting "2000". **Effective** as if included in the provision of P.L. 105-34 to which it relates [**effective** for tax years beginning after 12-31-97.—CCH].

• 1997, Taxpayer Relief Act of 1997 (P.L. 105-34)

P.L. 105-34, §224(a):

Amended Code Sec. 170(e) by adding a new paragraph (6). **Effective** for tax years beginning after 12-31-97.

P.L. 105-34, §602(a):

Amended Code Sec. 170(e)(5)(D)(ii) by striking "May 31, 1997" and inserting "June 30, 1998". **Effective** for contributions made after 5-31-97.

• 1996, Small Business Job Protection Act of 1996 (P.L. 104-188)

P.L. 104-188, §1206(a):

Amended Code Sec. 170(e)(5)(D). **Effective** for contributions made after 6-30-96. Prior to amendment, Code Sec. 170(e)(5)(D) read as follows:

(D) TERMINATION.—This paragraph shall not apply to contributions made after December 31, 1994.

P.L. 104-188, §1316(b):

Amended Code Sec. 170(e)(1) by adding at the end a new sentence. **Effective** for tax years beginning after 12-31-97.

• 1986, Tax Reform Act of 1986 (P.L. 99-514)

P.L. 99-514, §231(f):

Amended Code Sec. 170(e)(4)(B)(i). **Effective** for tax years beginning after 12-31-85. Prior to amendment, Code Sec. 170(e)(4)(B)(i) read as follows:

(i) the contribution is to an educational organization which is described in subsection (b)(1)(A)(ii) of this section and which is an institution of higher education (as defined in section 3304(f)),

P.L. 99-514, §301(b)(2):

Amended Code Sec. 170(e)(1) by striking out "40 percent (28/46 in the case of a corporation) of". **Effective** for tax years beginning after 12-31-86. Prior to amendment, Code Sec. 170(e)(1) read as follows:

(1) GENERAL RULE.—The amount of any charitable contribution of property otherwise taken into account under this section shall be reduced by the sum of—

(A) the amount of gain which would not have been long-term capital gain if the property contributed had been sold by the taxpayer at its fair market value (determined at the time of such contribution), and

(B) in the case of a charitable contribution—

(i) of tangible personal property, if the use by the donee is unrelated to the purpose or function constituting the basis for its exemption under section 501 (or, in the case of a governmental unit, to any purpose or function described in subsection (c)), or

(ii) to or for the use of a private foundation (as defined in section 509(a)), other than a private foundation described in subsection (b)(1)(E),

40 percent (28/46 in the case of a corporation) of the amount of gain which would have been long-term capital gain if the property contributed had been sold by the taxpayer at its fair market value (determined at the time of such contribution).

For purposes of applying this paragraph (other than in the case of gain to which section 617(d)(1), 1245(a), 1250(a), 1252(a), or 1254(a) applies), property which is property used in the trade or business (as defined in section 1231(b)) shall be treated as a capital asset.

• 1984, Deficit Reduction Act of 1984 (P.L. 98-369)

P.L. 98-369, §301(b):

Amended Code Sec. 170(e) by adding new paragraph (5). **Effective** for contributions made after 7-18-84, in tax years ending after such date.

P.L. 98-369, §301(c)(2)(C):

Amended Code Sec. 170(e)(1)(B)(ii) by striking out "subsection (b)(1)(D)" and inserting in lieu thereof "subsection (b)(1)(E)". **Effective** for contributions made in tax years ending after 7-18-84.

P.L. 98-369, §492(b)(1)(A):

Amended the second sentence of Code Sec. 170(e)(1) by striking out "1251(c),". **Effective** for tax years beginning after 12-31-83.

P.L. 98-369, §492(b)(1)(B):

Amended Code Sec. 170(e)(3)(C) by striking out "1251,". **Effective** for tax years beginning after 12-31-83.

• 1982, Subchapter S Revision Act of 1982 (P.L. 97-354)

P.L. 97-354, §5(a)(21)(A):

Amended Code Sec. 170(e)(3)(A) by striking out "an electing small business corporation within the meaning of section 1371(b))" and inserting in lieu thereof "an S corporation)". **Effective** for tax years beginning after 12-31-82.

P.L. 97-354, §5(a)(21)(B):

Amended Code Sec. 170(e)(4)(D)(i). **Effective** for tax years beginning after 12-31-82. Prior to amendment, it read as follows:

"(i) an electing small business corporation (as defined in section 1371(b)),"

• 1981, Economic Recovery Tax Act of 1981 (P.L. 97-34)

P.L. 97-34, §222(a):

Added Code Sec. 170(e)(4). **Effective** for charitable contributions made after 8-13-81, in tax years ending after such date.

• 1978, Revenue Act of 1978 (P.L. 95-600)

P.L. 95-600, §402(b)(2):

Amended Code Sec. 170(e)(1)(B) by striking out "50 percent" and inserting in lieu thereof "40 percent". **Effective** for contributions made after 10-31-78.

P.L. 95-600, §403(c)(1):

Amended Code Sec. 170(e)(1)(B) by striking out "62½ percent" and inserting in lieu thereof "28/46". **Effective** for gifts made after 12-31-78.

• 1976, Tax Reform Act of 1976 (P.L. 94-455)

P.L. 94-455, §205(c):

Substituted "1252(a), or 1254(a)" for "or 1252(a)" in Code Sec. 170(e)(1). **Effective** for tax years ending after 12-31-75.

P.L. 94-455, §1901(a)(28):

Substituted "subsection (b)(1)(D)" for "subsection (b)(1)(E)" in Code Sec. 170(e)(1)(B)(ii). **Effective** for tax years ending after 12-31-76.

P.L. 94-455, §1906(b)(13)(A):

Amended 1954 Code by substituting "Secretary" for "Secretary or his delegate" each place it appeared. **Effective** 2-1-77.

P.L. 94-455, §2135(a):

Added Code Sec. 170(e)(3). **Effective** for charitable contributions made after 10-4-76, in tax years ending after 10-4-76.

• 1969, Tax Reform Act of 1969 (P.L. 91-172)

P.L. 91-172, §201(a)(1):

Amended Code Sec. 170(e). **Effective** for contributions paid after 12-31-69, except that, with respect to a letter or memorandum or similar property described in section 1221(3) of such Code (as amended by section 514 of P.L. 91-172), subsection (e) shall apply to contributions paid after 7-25-69. Prior to amendment, Code Sec. 170(e) read as follows:

"(e) Special Rule for Charitable Contributions of Certain Property.—The amount of any charitable contribution taken into account under this section shall be reduced by the amount which would have been treated as gain to which section 617(d)(1), 1245(a), or 1250(a) applies if the property contributed had been sold at its fair market value (determined at the time of such contribution)."

• 1966 (P.L. 89-570)

P.L. 89-570, §[1(b)]:

Amended Code Sec. 170(e) by substituting "section 617(d)(1), 1245(a)," for "section 1245(a)", **Effective** for tax years ending after 9-12-66, but only for expenditures paid or incurred after that date.

• 1964, Revenue Act of 1964 (P.L. 88-272)

P.L. 88-272, § 231(b)(1):

Amended Code Sec. 170(e) to substitute the heading "Certain Property" for "Section 1245 Property", and substituted "section 1245(a) or 1250(a)" for "section 1245(a)". **Effective** for dispositions after 12-31-63, in tax years ending after such date.

• 1962, Revenue Act of 1962 (P.L. 87-834)

P.L. 87-834, § 13(d):

Redesignated Code Sec. 170(e) and (f) as Code Sec. 170(f) and (g) and added new Code Sec. 170(e). **Effective** for tax years beginning after 12-31-62.

[Sec. 170(f)]

(f) DISALLOWANCE OF DEDUCTION IN CERTAIN CASES AND SPECIAL RULES.—

(1) IN GENERAL.—No deduction shall be allowed under this section for a contribution to or for the use of an organization or trust described in section 508(d) or 4948(c)(4) subject to the conditions specified in such sections.

(2) CONTRIBUTIONS OF PROPERTY PLACED IN TRUST.—

(A) REMAINDER INTEREST.—In the case of property transferred in trust, no deduction shall be allowed under this section for the value of a contribution of a remainder interest unless the trust is a charitable remainder annuity trust or a charitable remainder unitrust (described in section 664), or a pooled income fund (described in section 642(c)(5)).

(B) INCOME INTERESTS, ETC.—No deduction shall be allowed under this section for the value of any interest in property (other than a remainder interest) transferred in trust unless the interest is in the form of a guaranteed annuity or the trust instrument specifies that the interest is a fixed percentage distributed yearly of the fair market value of the trust property (to be determined yearly) and the grantor is treated as the owner of such interest for purposes of applying section 671. If the donor ceases to be treated as the owner of such an interest for purposes of applying section 671, at the time the donor ceases to be so treated, the donor shall for purposes of this chapter be considered as having received an amount of income equal to the amount of any deduction he received under this section for the contribution reduced by the discounted value of all amounts of income earned by the trust and taxable to him before the time at which he ceases to be treated as the owner of the interest. Such amounts of income shall be discounted to the date of the contribution. The Secretary shall prescribe such regulations as may be necessary to carry out the purposes of this subparagraph.

(C) DENIAL OF DEDUCTION IN CASE OF PAYMENTS BY CERTAIN TRUSTS.—In any case in which a deduction is allowed under this section for the value of an interest in property described in subparagraph (B), transferred in trust, no deduction shall be allowed under this section to the grantor or any other person for the amount of any contribution made by the trust with respect to such interest.

(D) EXCEPTION.—This paragraph shall not apply in a case in which the value of all interests in property transferred in trust are deductible under subsection (a).

(3) DENIAL OF DEDUCTION IN CASE OF CERTAIN CONTRIBUTIONS OF PARTIAL INTERESTS IN PROPERTY.—

(A) IN GENERAL.—In the case of a contribution (not made by a transfer in trust) of an interest in property which consists of less than the taxpayer's entire interest in such property, a deduction shall be allowed under this section only to the extent that the value of the interest contributed would be allowable as a deduction under this section if such interest had been transferred in trust. For purposes of this subparagraph, a contribution by a taxpayer of the right to use property shall be treated as a contribution of less than the taxpayer's entire interest in such property.

(B) EXCEPTIONS.—Subparagraph (A) shall not apply to—

(i) a contribution of a remainder interest in a personal residence or farm,

(ii) a contribution of an undivided portion of the taxpayer's entire interest in property, and

(iii) a qualified conservation contribution.

(4) VALUATION OF REMAINDER INTEREST IN REAL PROPERTY.—For purposes of this section, in determining the value of a remainder interest in real property, depreciation (computed on the straight line method) and depletion of such property shall be taken into account, and such value shall be discounted at a rate of 6 percent per annum, except that the Secretary may prescribe a different rate.

(5) REDUCTION FOR CERTAIN INTEREST.—If, in connection with any charitable contribution, a liability is assumed by the recipient or by any other person, or if a charitable contribution is of property which is subject to a liability, then, to the extent necessary to avoid the duplication of amounts, the amount taken into account for purposes of this section as the amount of the charitable contribution—

(A) shall be reduced for interest (i) which has been paid (or is to be paid) by the taxpayer, (ii) which is attributable to the liability, and (iii) which is attributable to any period after the making of the contribution, and

(B) in the case of a bond, shall be further reduced for interest (i) which has been paid (or is to be paid) by the taxpayer on indebtedness incurred or continued to purchase or carry such bond, and (ii) which is attributable to any period before the making of the contribution.

The reduction pursuant to subparagraph (B) shall not exceed the interest (including interest equivalent) on the bond which is attributable to any period before the making of the contribution and which is not (under the taxpayer's method of accounting) includible in the gross income of the taxpayer for any taxable year. For purposes of this paragraph, the term "bond" means any bond, debenture, note, or certificate or other evidence of indebtedness.

(6) DEDUCTIONS FOR OUT-OF-POCKET EXPENDITURES.—No deduction shall be allowed under this section for an out-of-pocket expenditure made by any person on behalf of an organization described in subsection (c) (other than an organization described in section 501(h)(5) (relating to churches, etc.)) if the expenditure is made for the purpose of influencing legislation (within the meaning of section 501(c)(3)).

(7) REFORMATIONS TO COMPLY WITH PARAGRAPH (2).—

(A) IN GENERAL.—A deduction shall be allowed under subsection (a) in respect of any qualified reformation (within the meaning of section 2055(e)(3)(B)).

(B) RULES SIMILAR TO SECTION 2055(e)(3) TO APPLY.—For purposes of this paragraph, rules similar to the rules of section 2055(e)(3) shall apply.

(8) SUBSTANTIATION REQUIREMENT FOR CERTAIN CONTRIBUTIONS.—

(A) GENERAL RULE.—No deduction shall be allowed under subsection (a) for any contribution of $250 or more unless the taxpayer substantiates the contribution by a contemporaneous written acknowledgment of the contribution by the donee organization that meets the requirements of subparagraph (B).

(B) CONTENT OF ACKNOWLEDGEMENT.—An acknowledgement meets the requirements of this subparagraph if it includes the following information:

(i) The amount of cash and a description (but not value) of any property other than cash contributed.

(ii) Whether the donee organization provided any goods or services in consideration, in whole or in part, for any property described in clause (i).

(iii) A description and good faith estimate of the value of any goods or services referred to in clause (ii) or, if such goods or services consist solely of intangible religious benefits, a statement to that effect.

For purposes of this subparagraph, the term "intangible religious benefit" means any intangible religious benefit which is provided by an organization organized exclusively for religious purposes and which generally is not sold in a commercial transaction outside the donative context.

(C) CONTEMPORANEOUS.—For purposes of subparagraph (A), an acknowledgment shall be considered to be contemporaneous if the taxpayer obtains the acknowledgment on or before the earlier of—

(i) the date on which the taxpayer files a return for the taxable year in which the contribution was made, or

(ii) the due date (including extensions) for filing such return.

(D) REGULATIONS.—The Secretary shall prescribe such regulations as may be necessary or appropriate to carry out the purposes of this paragraph, including regulations that may provide that some or all of the requirements of this paragraph do not apply in appropriate cases.

(9) DENIAL OF DEDUCTION WHERE CONTRIBUTION FOR LOBBYING ACTIVITIES.—No deduction shall be allowed under this section for a contribution to an organization which conducts activities to which section 162(e)(1) applies on matters of direct financial interest to the donor's trade or business, if a principal purpose of the contribution was to avoid Federal income tax by securing a deduction for such activities under this section which would be disallowed by reason of section 162(e) if the donor had conducted such activities directly. No deduction shall be allowed under section 162(a) for any amount for which a deduction is disallowed under the preceding sentence.

(10) SPLIT-DOLLAR LIFE INSURANCE, ANNUITY, AND ENDOWMENT CONTRACTS.—

(A) IN GENERAL.—Nothing in this section or in section 545(b)(2), 642(c), 2055, 2106(a)(2), or 2522 shall be construed to allow a deduction, and no deduction shall be allowed, for any transfer to or for the use of an organization described in subsection (c) if in connection with such transfer—

(i) the organization directly or indirectly pays, or has previously paid, any premium on any personal benefit contract with respect to the transferor, or

(ii) there is an understanding or expectation that any person will directly or indirectly pay any premium on any personal benefit contract with respect to the transferor.

(B) PERSONAL BENEFIT CONTRACT.—For purposes of subparagraph (A), the term "personal benefit contract" means, with respect to the transferor, any life insurance, annuity, or endowment contract if any direct or indirect beneficiary under such contract is the transferor, any member of the transferor's family, or any other person (other than an organization described in subsection (c)) designated by the transferor.

(C) APPLICATION TO CHARITABLE REMAINDER TRUSTS.—In the case of a transfer to a trust referred to in subparagraph (E), references in subparagraphs (A) and (F) to an organization described in subsection (c) shall be treated as a reference to such trust.

(D) EXCEPTION FOR CERTAIN ANNUITY CONTRACTS.—If, in connection with a transfer to or for the use of an organization described in subsection (c), such organization incurs an obligation to pay a charitable gift annuity (as defined in section 501(m)) and such organization purchases any annuity contract to fund such obligation, persons receiving payments under the charitable gift annuity shall not be treated for purposes of subparagraph (B) as indirect beneficiaries under such contract if—

(i) such organization possesses all of the incidents of ownership under such contract,

(ii) such organization is entitled to all the payments under such contract, and

(iii) the timing and amount of payments under such contract are substantially the same as the timing and amount of payments to each such person under such obligation (as such obligation is in effect at the time of such transfer).

(E) EXCEPTION FOR CERTAIN CONTRACTS HELD BY CHARITABLE REMAINDER TRUSTS.—A person shall not be treated for purposes of subparagraph (B) as an indirect beneficiary under any life insurance, annuity, or endowment contract held by a charitable remainder annuity trust or a charitable remainder unitrust (as defined in section 664(d)) solely by reason of being entitled to any payment referred to in paragraph (1)(A) or (2)(A) of section 664(d) if—

(i) such trust possesses all of the incidents of ownership under such contract, and

(ii) such trust is entitled to all the payments under such contract.

(F) EXCISE TAX ON PREMIUMS PAID.—

(i) IN GENERAL.—There is hereby imposed on any organization described in subsection (c) an excise tax equal to the premiums paid by such organization on any life insurance, annuity, or endowment contract if the payment of premiums on such contract is in connection with a transfer for which a deduction is not allowable under subparagraph (A), determined without regard to when such transfer is made.

(ii) PAYMENTS BY OTHER PERSONS.—For purposes of clause (i), payments made by any other person pursuant to an understanding or expectation referred to in subparagraph (A) shall be treated as made by the organization.

(iii) REPORTING.—Any organization on which tax is imposed by clause (i) with respect to any premium shall file an annual return which includes —

(I) the amount of such premiums paid during the year and the name and TIN of each beneficiary under the contract to which the premium relates, and

(II) such other information as the Secretary may require.

The penalties applicable to returns required under section 6033 shall apply to returns required under this clause. Returns required under this clause shall be furnished at such time and in such manner as the Secretary shall by forms or regulations require.

(iv) CERTAIN RULES TO APPLY.—The tax imposed by this subparagraph shall be treated as imposed by chapter 42 for purposes of this title other than subchapter B of chapter 42.

(G) SPECIAL RULE WHERE STATE REQUIRES SPECIFICATION OF CHARITABLE GIFT ANNUITANT IN CONTRACT.—In the case of an obligation to pay a charitable gift annuity referred to in subparagraph (D) which is entered into under the laws of a State which requires, in order for the charitable gift annuity to be exempt from insurance regulation by such State, that each beneficiary under the charitable gift annuity be named as a beneficiary under an annuity contract issued by an insurance company authorized to transact business in such State, the requirements of clauses (i) and (ii) of subparagraph (D) shall be treated as met if—

(i) such State law requirement was in effect on February 8, 1999,

(ii) each such beneficiary under the charitable gift annuity is a bona fide resident of such State at the time the obligation to pay a charitable gift annuity is entered into, and

(iii) the only persons entitled to payments under such contract are persons entitled to payments as beneficiaries under such obligation on the date such obligation is entered into.

(H) MEMEBER OF FAMILY.—For purposes of this paragraph, an individual's family consists of the individual's grandparents, the grandparents of such individual's spouse, the lineal descendants of such grandparents, and any spouse of such a lineal descendant.

(I) REGULATIONS.—The Secretary shall prescribe such regulations as may be necessary or appropriate to carry out the purposes of this paragraph, including regulations to prevent the avoidance of such purposes.

(11) QUALIFIED APPRAISAL AND OTHER DOCUMENTATION FOR CERTAIN CONTRIBUTIONS.—

(A) IN GENERAL.—

(i) DENIAL OF DEDUCTION.—In the case of an individual, partnership, or corporation, no deduction shall be allowed under subsection (a) for any contribution of property for which a deduction of more than $500 is claimed unless such person meets the requirements of subparagraphs (B), (C), and (D), as the case may be, with respect to such contribution.

(ii) EXCEPTIONS.—

(I) READILY VALUED PROPERTY.—Subparagraphs (C) and (D) shall not apply to cash, property described in subsection (e)(1)(B)(iii) or section 1221(a)(1), publicly traded securities (as defined in section 6050L(a)(2)(B)), and any qualified vehicle described in paragraph (12)(A)(ii) for which an acknowledgement under paragraph (12)(B)(iii) is provided.

(II) REASONABLE CAUSE.—Clause (i) shall not apply if it is shown that the failure to meet such requirements is due to reasonable cause and not to willful neglect.

(B) PROPERTY DESCRIPTION FOR CONTRIBUTIONS OF MORE THAN $500.—In the case of contributions of property for which a deduction of more than $500 is claimed, the requirements of this subparagraph are met if the individual, partnership or corporation includes with the return for the taxable year in which the contribution is made a description of such property and such other information as the Secretary may require. The requirements of this subparagraph shall not apply to a C corporation which is not a personal service corporation or a closely held C corporation.

(C) QUALIFIED APPRAISAL FOR CONTRIBUTIONS OF MORE THAN $5,000.—In the case of contributions of property for which a deduction of more than $5,000 is claimed, the requirements of this subparagraph are met if the individual, partnership, or corporation obtains a qualified appraisal of such property and attaches to the return for the taxable year in which such contribution is made such information regarding such property and such appraisal as the Secretary may require.

(D) SUBSTANTIATION FOR CONTRIBUTIONS OF MORE THAN $500,000.—In the case of contributions of property for which a deduction of more than $500,000 is claimed, the requirements of this subparagraph are met if the individual, partnership, or corporation attaches to the return for the taxable year a qualified appraisal of such property.

(E) QUALIFIED APPRAISAL AND APPRAISER.—For purposes of this paragraph—

(i) QUALIFIED APPRAISAL.—The term "qualified appraisal" means, with respect to any property, an appraisal of such property which—

(I) is treated for purposes of this paragraph as a qualified appraisal under regulations or other guidance prescribed by the Secretary, and

(II) is conducted by a qualified appraiser in accordance with generally accepted appraisal standards and any regulations or other guidance prescribed under subclause (I).

(ii) QUALIFIED APPRAISER.—Except as provided in clause (iii), the term "qualified appraiser" means an individual who—

(I) has earned an appraisal designation from a recognized professional appraiser organization or has otherwise met minimum education and experience requirements set forth in regulations prescribed by the Secretary,

(II) regularly performs appraisals for which the individual receives compensation, and

(III) meets such other requirements as may be prescribed by the Secretary in regulations or other guidance.

(iii) SPECIFIC APPRAISALS.—An individual shall not be treated as a qualified appraiser with respect to any specific appraisal unless—

(I) the individual demonstrates verifiable education and experience in valuing the type of property subject to the appraisal, and

(II) the individual has not been prohibited from practicing before the Internal Revenue Service by the Secretary under section 330(c) of title 31, United States Code, at any time during the 3-year period ending on the date of the appraisal.

(F) AGGREGATION OF SIMILAR ITEMS OF PROPERTY.—For purposes of determining thresholds under this paragraph, property and all similar items of property donated to 1 or more donees shall be treated as 1 property.

(G) SPECIAL RULE FOR PASS-THRU ENTITIES.—In the case of a partnership or S corporation, this paragraph shall be applied at the entity level, except that the deduction shall be denied at the partner or shareholder level.

(H) REGULATIONS.—The Secretary may prescribe such regulations as may be necessary or appropriate to carry out the purposes of this paragraph, including regulations that may provide that some or all of the requirements of this paragraph do not apply in appropriate cases.

(12) CONTRIBUTIONS OF USED MOTOR VEHICLES, BOATS, AND AIRPLANES.—

(A) IN GENERAL.—In the case of a contribution of a qualified vehicle the claimed value of which exceeds $500—

(i) paragraph (8) shall not apply and no deduction shall be allowed under subsection (a) for such contribution unless the taxpayer substantiates the contribution by a contemporaneous written acknowledgement of the contribution by the donee organization that meets the requirements of subparagraph (B) and includes the acknowledgement with the taxpayer's return of tax which includes the deduction, and

(ii) if the organization sells the vehicle without any significant intervening use or material improvement of such vehicle by the organization, the amount of the deduction allowed under subsection (a) shall not exceed the gross proceeds received from such sale.

(B) CONTENT OF ACKNOWLEDGEMENT.—An acknowledgement meets the requirements of this subparagraph if it includes the following information:

(i) The name and taxpayer identification number of the donor.

(ii) The vehicle identification number or similar number.

(iii) In the case of a qualified vehicle to which subparagraph (A)(ii) applies—

(I) a certification that the vehicle was sold in an arm's length transaction between unrelated parties,

(II) the gross proceeds from the sale, and

(III) a statement that the deductible amount may not exceed the amount of such gross proceeds.

(iv) In the case of a qualified vehicle to which subparagraph (A)(ii) does not apply—

(I) a certification of the intended use or material improvement of the vehicle and the intended duration of such use, and

(II) a certification that the vehicle would not be transferred in exchange for money, other property, or services before completion of such use or improvement.

(v) Whether the donee organization provided any goods or services in consideration, in whole or in part, for the qualified vehicle.

(vi) A description and good faith estimate of the value of any goods or services referred to in clause (v) or, if such goods or services consist solely of intangible religious benefits (as defined in paragraph (8)(B)), a statement to that effect.

(C) CONTEMPORANEOUS.—For purposes of subparagraph (A), an acknowledgement shall be considered to be contemporaneous if the donee organization provides it within 30 days of—

(i) the sale of the qualified vehicle, or

(ii) in the case of an acknowledgement including a certification described in subparagraph (B)(iv), the contribution of the qualified vehicle.

(D) INFORMATION TO SECRETARY.—A donee organization required to provide an acknowledgement under this paragraph shall provide to the Secretary the information contained in the acknowledgement. Such information shall be provided at such time and in such manner as the Secretary may prescribe.

(E) QUALIFIED VEHICLE.—For purposes of this paragraph, the term "qualified vehicle" means any—

(i) motor vehicle manufactured primarily for use on public streets, roads, and highways,

(ii) boat, or

(iii) airplane.

Such term shall not include any property which is described in section 1221(a)(1).

(F) REGULATIONS OR OTHER GUIDANCE.—The Secretary shall prescribe such regulations or other guidance as may be necessary to carry out the purposes of this paragraph. The Secretary may prescribe regulations or other guidance which exempts sales by the donee organization which are in direct furtherance of such organization's charitable purpose from the requirements of subparagraphs (A)(ii) and (B)(iv)(II).

(13) CONTRIBUTIONS OF CERTAIN INTERESTS IN BUILDINGS LOCATED IN REGISTERED HISTORIC DISTRICTS.—

(A) IN GENERAL.—No deduction shall be allowed with respect to any contribution described in subparagraph (B) unless the taxpayer includes with the return for the taxable year of the contribution a $500 filing fee.

(B) CONTRIBUTION DESCRIBED.—A contribution is described in this subparagraph if such contribution is a qualified conservation contribution (as defined in subsection (h)) which is a restriction with respect to the exterior of a building described in subsection (h)(4)(C)(ii) and for which a deduction is claimed in excess of $10,000.

(C) DEDICATION OF FEE.—Any fee collected under this paragraph shall be used for the enforcement of the provisions of subsection (h).

(14) REDUCTION FOR AMOUNTS ATTRIBUTABLE TO REHABILITATION CREDIT.—In the case of any qualified conservation contribution (as defined in subsection (h)), the amount of the deduction allowed under this section shall be reduced by an amount which bears the same ratio to the fair market value of the contribution as—

(A) the sum of the credits allowed to the taxpayer under section 47 for the 5 preceding taxable years with respect to any building which is a part of such contribution, bears to

(B) the fair market value of the building on the date of the contribution.

(15) SPECIAL RULE FOR TAXIDERMY PROPERTY.—

(A) BASIS.—For purposes of this section and notwithstanding section 1012, in the case of a charitable contribution of taxidermy property which is made by the person who prepared, stuffed, or mounted the property or by any person who paid or incurred the cost of such preparation, stuffing, or mounting, only the cost of the preparing, stuffing, or mounting shall be included in the basis of such property.

(B) TAXIDERMY PROPERTY.—For purposes of this section, the term "taxidermy property" means any work of art which—

(i) is the reproduction or preservation of an animal, in whole or in part,

(ii) is prepared, stuffed, or mounted for purposes of recreating one or more characteristics of such animal, and

(iii) contains a part of the body of the dead animal.

(16) CONTRIBUTIONS OF CLOTHING AND HOUSEHOLD ITEMS.—

(A) IN GENERAL.—In the case of an individual, partnership, or corporation, no deduction shall be allowed under subsection (a) for any contribution of clothing or a household item unless such clothing or household item is in good used condition or better.

(B) ITEMS OF MINIMAL VALUE.—Notwithstanding subparagraph (A), the Secretary may by regulation deny a deduction under subsection (a) for any contribution of clothing or a household item which has minimal monetary value.

(C) EXCEPTION FOR CERTAIN PROPERTY.—Subparagraphs (A) and (B) shall not apply to any contribution of a single item of clothing or a household item for which a deduction of more than $500 is claimed if the taxpayer includes with the taxpayer's return a qualified appraisal with respect to the property.

(D) HOUSEHOLD ITEMS.—For purposes of this paragraph—

(i) IN GENERAL.—The term "household items" includes furniture, furnishings, electronics, appliances, linens, and other similar items.

(ii) EXCLUDED ITEMS.—Such term does not include—

(I) food,

(II) paintings, antiques, and other objects of art,

(III) jewelry and gems, and

(IV) collections.

(E) SPECIAL RULE FOR PASS-THRU ENTITIES.—In the case of a partnership or S corporation, this paragraph shall be applied at the entity level, except that the deduction shall be denied at the partner or shareholder level.

(17) RECORDKEEPING.—No deduction shall be allowed under subsection (a) for any contribution of a cash, check, or other monetary gift unless the donor maintains as a record of such contribution a bank record or a written communication from the donee showing the name of the donee organization, the date of the contribution, and the amount of the contribution.

(18) CONTRIBUTIONS TO DONOR ADVISED FUNDS.—A deduction otherwise allowed under subsection (a) for any contribution to a donor advised fund (as defined in section 4966(d)(2)) shall only be allowed if—

(A) the sponsoring organization (as defined in section 4966(d)(1)) with respect to such donor advised fund is not—

(i) described in paragraph (3), (4), or (5) of subsection (c), or

(ii) a type III supporting organization (as defined in section 4943(f)(5)(A)) which is not a functionally integrated type III supporting organization (as defined in section 4943(f)(5)(B)), and

(B) the taxpayer obtains a contemporaneous written acknowledgment (determined under rules similar to the rules of paragraph (8)(C)) from the sponsoring organization (as so defined) of such donor advised fund that such organization has exclusive legal control over the assets contributed.

(19) CERTAIN QUALIFIED CONSERVATION CONTRIBUTIONS.—

(A) IN GENERAL.—In the case of a qualified conservation contribution to which this paragraph applies, no deduction shall be allowed under subsection (a) for such contribution unless the partnership making such contribution—

(i) includes on its return for the taxable year in which the contribution is made a statement that the partnership made such a contribution, and

(ii) provides such information about the contribution as the Secretary may require.

(B) CONTRIBUTIONS TO WHICH THIS PARAGRAPH APPLIES.—This paragraph shall apply to any qualified conservation contribution—

(i) the conservation purpose of which is the preservation of any building which is a certified historic structure (as defined in subsection (h)(4)(C)),

(ii) which is made by a partnership (whether directly or as a distributive share of a contribution of another partnership), and

(iii) the amount of which exceeds 2.5 times the sum of each partner's relevant basis (as defined in subsection (h)(7)) in the partnership making the contribution.

(C) APPLICATION TO OTHER PASS-THROUGH ENTITIES.—Except as may be otherwise provided by the Secretary, the rules of this paragraph shall apply to S corporations and other pass-through entities in the same manner as such rules apply to partnerships.

Amendments

• 2022, SECURE 2.0 Act of 2022 (P.L. 117-328)

P.L. 117-328, §605(b):

Amended Code Sec. 170(f) by adding at the end a new paragraph (19). **Effective** for contributions made after 12-29-2022. For a special rule, see Act Sec. 605(c)(2), below.

P.L. 117-328, §605(c)(2), provides:

(2) NO INFERENCE.—No inference is intended as to the appropriate treatment of contributions made in taxable years ending on or before the date specified in paragraph (1), or as to any contribution for which a deduction is not disallowed by reason of section 170(h)(7) of the Internal Revenue Code of 1986, as added by this section.

• 2017, Tax Cuts and Jobs Act (P.L. 115-97)

P.L. 115-97, §13705(a):

Amended Code Sec. 170(f)(8) by striking subparagraph (D) and by redesignating subparagraph (E) as subparagraph (D). **Effective** for contributions made in tax years beginning after 12-31-2016. Prior to being stricken, Code Sec. 170(f)(8)(D) read as follows:

(D) SUBSTANTIATION NOT REQUIRED FOR CONTRIBUTIONS REPORTED BY THE DONEE ORGANIZATION.—Subparagraph (A) shall not apply to a contribution if the donee organization files a return, on such form and in accordance with such regulations as the Secretary may prescribe, which includes the information described in subparagraph (B) with respect to the contribution.

• 2006, Pension Protection Act of 2006 (P.L. 109-280)

P.L. 109-280, §1213(c):

Amended Code Sec. 170(f) by adding at the end a new paragraph (13). **Effective** for contributions made 180 days after 8-17-2006.

P.L. 109-280, §1213(d):

Amended Code Sec. 170(f), as amended by Act Sec. 1213(c), by adding at the end a new paragraph (14). **Effective** for contributions made after 8-17-2006.

P.L. 109-280, §1214(b):

Amended Code Sec. 170(f), as amended by this Act, by adding at the end a new paragraph (15). **Effective** for contributions made after 7-25-2006.

P.L. 109-280, §1216(a):

Amended Code Sec. 170(f), as amended by this Act, by adding at the end a new paragraph (16). **Effective** for contributions made after 8-17-2006.

P.L. 109-280, §1217(a):

Amended Code Sec. 170(f), as amended by this Act, by adding at the end a new paragraph (17). **Effective** for contributions made in tax years beginning after 8-17-2006.

P.L. 109-280, §1219(c)(1):

Amended Code Sec. 170(f)(11)(E). **Effective** generally for appraisals prepared with respect to returns or submissions filed after 8-17-2006. Prior to amendment, Code Sec. 170(f)(11)(E) read as follows:

(E) QUALIFIED APPRAISAL.—For purposes of this paragraph, the term "qualified appraisal" means, with respect to any property, an appraisal of such property which is treated for purposes of this paragraph as a qualified appraisal under regulations or other guidance prescribed by the Secretary.

P.L. 109-280, §1234(a):

Amended Code Sec. 170(f), as amended by this Act, by adding at the end a new paragraph (18). **Effective** for contributions made after the date which is 180 days after 8-17-2006.

• 2005, Gulf Opportunity Zone Act of 2005 (P.L. 109-135)

P.L. 109-135, §403(gg):

Amended Code Sec. 170(f)(12)(B) by adding at the end new clauses (v) and (vi). **Effective** as if included in the provision of the American Jobs Creation Act of 2004 (P.L. 108-357) to which it relates [**effective** for contributions made after 12-31-2004.—CCH].

• 2005, Katrina Emergency Tax Relief Act of 2005 (P.L. 109-73)

P.L. 109-73, §303 [but see P.L. 110-343, Div. C, §702, in the amendment notes for Code Sec. 1400N(a)], provides:

SEC. 303. INCREASE IN STANDARD MILEAGE RATE FOR CHARITABLE USE OF VEHICLES.

Notwithstanding section 170(i) of the Internal Revenue Code of 1986, for purposes of computing the deduction under section 170 of such Code for use of a vehicle described in subsection (f)(12)(E)(i) of such section for provision of relief related to Hurricane Katrina during the period beginning on August 25, 2005, and ending on December 31, 2006, the standard mileage rate shall be 70 percent of the standard mileage rate in effect under section 162(a) of such Code at the time of such use. Any increase under this section shall be rounded to the next highest cent.

• 2004, American Jobs Creation Act of 2004 (P.L. 108-357)

P.L. 108-357, §413(c)(30):

Amended Code Sec. 170(f)(10)(A) by striking "556(b)(2)," immediately preceding "642(c)". **Effective** for tax years of foreign corporations beginning after 12-31-2004, and for tax years of United States shareholders with or within which such tax years of foreign corporations end.

P.L. 108-357, §882(d):

Amended Code Sec. 170(f)(11)(A)(ii)(I), as added by this Act, by inserting "subsection (e)(1)(B)(iii) or" before "section 1221(a)(1)". **Effective** for contributions made after 6-3-2004.

P.L. 108-357, § 883(a):

Amended Code Sec. 170(f) by adding after paragraph (10) a new paragraph (11). **Effective** for contributions made after 6-3-2004.

P.L. 108-357, § 884(a):

Amended Code Sec. 170(f), as amended by this Act, by inserting after paragraph (11) a new paragraph (12). **Effective** for contributions made after 12-31-2004.

• 1999, Tax Relief Extension Act of 1999 (P.L. 106-170)

P.L. 106-170, § 537(a):

Amended Code Sec. 170(f) by adding at the end a new paragraph (10). **Effective** for transfers made after 2-8-99. For exceptions, see Act Sec. 537(b)(2)-(3), below.

P.L. 106-170, § 537(b)(2)-(3), provides:

(2) EXCISE TAX.—Except as provided in paragraph (3) of this subsection, section 170(f)(10)(F) of the Internal Revenue Code of 1986 (as added by this section) shall apply to premiums paid after the date of the enactment of this Act.

(3) REPORTING.—Clause (iii) of such section 170(f)(10)(F) shall apply to premiums paid after February 8, 1999 (determined as if the tax imposed by such section applies to premiums paid after such date).

• 1993, Omnibus Budget Reconciliation Act of 1993 (P.L. 103-66)

P.L. 103-66, § 13172(a):

Amended Code Sec. 170(f) by adding at the end thereof new paragraph (8). **Effective** for contributions made on or after 1-1-94.

P.L. 103-66, § 13222(b):

Amended Code Sec. 170(f), as amended by Act Sec. 13172, by adding at the end thereof a new paragraph (9). **Effective** for amounts paid or incurred after 12-31-93.

• 1984, Deficit Reduction Act of 1984 (P.L. 98-369)

P.L. 98-369, § 1022(b):

Amended Code Sec. 170(f) by adding at the end thereof new paragraph (7). **Effective** for reformations after 12-31-78; except that it shall not apply to any reformation to which Code Sec. 2055(e)(3) (as in effect on 7-17-84) applies. For purposes of applying Code Sec. 2055(e)(C)(iii) (as amended), the 90th day described therein shall be treated as the 90th day after 7-18-84.

• 1980, Miscellaneous Revenue Act of 1980 (P.L. 96-605)

P.L. 96-605, § 301(b)(2):

Amended Act Sec. 514 of P.L. 95-600 as follows:

(b) EFFECTIVE DATE.—

(2) CHARITABLE LEAD TRUSTS AND CHARITABLE REMAINDER TRUSTS IN THE CASE OF INCOME AND GIFT TAXES.—Section 514(b) (and section 514(c) insofar as it relates to section 514(b)) of the Revenue Act of 1978 shall be applied as if the amendment made by subsection (a) had been included in the amendment made by section 514(a) of such Act. [This provision extends until December 31, 1981, the time to amend, or commence judicial proceedings to amend, instruments of both charitable lead trusts or charitable remainder trusts that were executed before December 31, 1978, in order to conform such instruments to the requirements of P.L. 91-172 for income and gift tax purposes. See amendment note under Code Sec. 2055(e).]

• 1980, Technical Corrections Act of 1979 (P.L. 96-222)

P.L. 96-222, § 105(a)(4)(B):

Amended Act Sec. 514 of P.L. 95-600 by adding paragraph (c) to read as below:

(c) EFFECTIVE DATES.—

* * *

(2) FOR SUBSECTION (b).—Subsection (b)—

(A) insofar as it relates to section 170 of the Internal Revenue Code of 1954 shall apply to transfers in trust and contributions made after July 31, 1969, and

(B) insofar as it relates to section 2522 of the Internal Revenue Code of 1954 shall apply to transfers made after December 31, 1969.

• 1978, Revenue Act of 1978 (P.L. 95-600)

P.L. 95-600, § 514(b), provides as follows:

"(b) CHARITABLE LEAD TRUSTS AND CHARITABLE REMAINDER TRUSTS IN THE CASE OF INCOME AND GIFT TAXES.—Under regulations prescribed by the Secretary of the Treasury or his delegate, in the case of trusts created before December 31, 1977, provisions comparable to section 2055(c)(3) of the Internal Revenue Code of 1954 (as amended by subsection (a) [P.L. 95-600, § 514(a) shall be deemed to be included in sections 170 and 2522 of the Internal Revenue Code of 1954."

• 1980 (P.L. 96-541)

P.L. 96-541, § 6(a):

Amended Code Sec. 170(f)(3) by striking out subparagraphs (B) and (C) and inserting in lieu thereof a new subparagraph (B). **Effective** for transfers made after 12-31-80, in tax years ending after that date. Prior to amendment, subparagraphs (B) and (C) provided:

"(B) EXCEPTIONS.—Subparagraph (A) shall not apply to a contribution of—

(i) a remainder interest in a personal residence or farm,

(ii) an undivided portion of the taxpayer's entire interest in property,

(iii) a lease on, option to purchase, or easement with respect to real property granted in perpetuity to an organization described in subsection (b)(1)(A) exclusively for conservation purposes, or

(iv) a remainder interest in real property which is granted to an organization described in subsection (b)(1)(A) exclusively for conservation purposes.

(C) CONSERVATION PURPOSES DEFINED.—For purposes of subparagraph (B), the term "conservation purposes" means—

(i) the preservation of land areas for public outdoor recreation or education, or scenic enjoyment;

(ii) the preservation of historically important land areas or structures; or

(iii) the protection of natural environmental systems."

• 1977, Tax Reduction and Simplification Act of 1977 (P.L. 95-30)

P.L. 95-30, § 309(a):

Amended clause (iii) of Code Sec. 170(f)(3)(B). **Effective** for contributions or transfers made after 6-13-77, and before 6-14-81. Prior to amendment, clause (iii) read as follows:

"(iii) a lease on, option to purchase, or easement with respect to real property of not less than 30 years' duration granted to an organization described in subsection (b)(1)(A) exclusively for conservation purposes, or".

• 1976, Tax Reform Act of 1976 (P.L 94-455)

P.L. 94-455, § 1307(c):

Added Code Sec. 170(f)(6). Effective for tax years beginning after 12-31-76.

P.L. 94-455, § 1901(a)(28):

Repealed Code Sec. 170(f)(6). **Effective** for tax years beginning after 12-31-76. Prior to repeal, former Code Sec. 170(f)(6) read as follows:

(6) PARTIAL REDUCTION OF UNLIMITED DEDUCTION.—

(A) IN GENERAL.—If the limitations in subsections (b)(1)(A) and (B) do not apply because of the application of subsection (b)(1)(C), the amount otherwise allowable as a deduction under subsection (a) shall be reduced by the amount by which the taxpayer's taxable income computed without regard to this subparagraph is less than the transitional income percentage (determined under subparagraph (C)) of the taxpayer's adjusted gross income. However, in no case shall a taxpayer's deduction under this section be reduced below the amount allowable as a deduction under this section without the applicability of subsection (b)(1)(C).

(B) TRANSITIONAL DEDUCTION PERCENTAGE.—For purposes of applying subsection (b)(1)(C), the term "transitional deduction percentage" means—

(i) in the case of a taxable year beginning before 1970, 90 percent, and

(ii) in the case of a taxable year beginning in—

1970	80 percent
1971	74 percent
1972	68 percent
1973	62 percent
1974	56 percent.

(C) TRANSITIONAL INCOME PERCENTAGE.—For purposes of applying subparagraph (A), the term "transitional income percentage" means, in the case of a taxable year beginning in—

1970	20 percent
1971	26 percent
1972	32 percent
1973	38 percent
1974	44 percent.

P.L. 94-455, §1906(b)(13)(A):

Amended 1954 Code by substituting "Secretary" for "Secretary or his delegate" each place it appeared. **Effective** 2-1-77.

P.L. 94-455, §2124(e) (as amended by P.L. 95-30, §309(b)(2)):

Struck out "or" at the end of Code Sec. 170(f)(3)(B)(i), substituted a comma for the period at the end of clause (ii), and added clauses (iii) and (iv) and subparagraph (C). **Effective** for contributions or transfers made after 6-13-76, and before 6-14-77. However, P.L. 95-30, §309(b)(2), changed this latter date to 6-14-81.

• 1969, Tax Reform Act of 1969 (P.L. 91-172)

P.L. 91-172, §201(a)(1):

Amended Code Sec. 170(f). Code Sec. 170(f)(1) is **effective** for contributions paid after 12-31-69. Paragraphs (2), (3) and (4) of Code Sec. 170(f) apply to transfers in trust and contributions made after 7-31-69.

* * *

[Sec. 170(h)]

(h) QUALIFIED CONSERVATION CONTRIBUTION.—

(1) IN GENERAL.—For purposes of subsection (f)(3)(B)(iii), the term "qualified conservation contribution" means a contribution—

(A) of a qualified real property interest,

(B) to a qualified organization,

(C) exclusively for conservation purposes.

(2) QUALIFIED REAL PROPERTY INTEREST.—For purposes of this subsection, the term "qualified real property interest" means any of the following interests in real property:

(A) the entire interest of the donor other than a qualified mineral interest,

(B) a remainder interest, and

(C) a restriction (granted in perpetuity) on the use which may be made of the real property.

(3) QUALIFIED ORGANIZATION.—For purposes of paragraph (1), the term "qualified organization" means an organization which—

(A) is described in clause (v) or (vi) of subsection (b)(1)(A), or

(B) is described in section 501(c)(3) and—

(i) meets the requirements of section 509(a)(2), or

(ii) meets the requirements of section 509(a)(3) and is controlled by an organization described in subparagraph (A) or in clause (i) of this subparagraph.

(4) CONSERVATION PURPOSE DEFINED.—

(A) IN GENERAL.—For purposes of this subsection, the term "conservation purpose" means—

(i) the preservation of land areas for outdoor recreation by, or the education of, the general public,

(ii) the protection of a relatively natural habitat of fish, wildlife, or plants, or similar ecosystem,

(iii) the preservation of open space (including farmland and forest land) where such preservation is—

(I) for the scenic enjoyment of the general public, or

(II) pursuant to a clearly delineated Federal, State, or local governmental conservation policy,

and will yield a significant public benefit, or

(iv) the preservation of an historically important land area or a certified historic structure.

(B) SPECIAL RULES WITH RESPECT TO BUILDINGS IN REGISTERED HISTORIC DISTRICTS.—In the case of any contribution of a qualified real property interest which is a restriction with respect to the exterior of a building described in subparagraph (C)(ii), such contribution shall not be considered to be exclusively for conservation purposes unless—

(i) such interest—

(I) includes a restriction which preserves the entire exterior of the building (including the front, sides, rear, and height of the building), and

(II) prohibits any change in the exterior of the building which is inconsistent with the historical character of such exterior,

(ii) the donor and donee enter into a written agreement certifying, under penalty of perjury, that the donee—

(I) is a qualified organization (as defined in paragraph (3)) with a purpose of environmental protection, land conservation, open space preservation, or historic preservation, and

(II) has the resources to manage and enforce the restriction and a commitment to do so, and

(iii) in the case of any contribution made in a taxable year beginning after the date of the enactment of this subparagraph, the taxpayer includes with the taxpayer's return for the taxable year of the contribution—

(I) a qualified appraisal (within the meaning of subsection (f)(11)(E)) of the qualified property interest,

(II) photographs of the entire exterior of the building, and

(III) a description of all restrictions on the development of the building.

(C) CERTIFIED HISTORIC STRUCTURE.—For purposes of subparagraph (A)(iv), the term "certified historic structure" means—

(i) any building, structure, or land area which is listed in the National Register, or

(ii) any building which is located in a registered historic district (as defined in section 47(c)(3)(B)) and is certified by the Secretary of the Interior to the Secretary as being of historic significance to the district.

A building, structure, or land area satisfies the preceding sentence if it satisfies such sentence either at the time of the transfer or on the due date (including extensions) for filing the transferor's return under this chapter for the taxable year in which the transfer is made.

(5) EXCLUSIVELY FOR CONSERVATION PURPOSES.—For purposes of this subsection—

(A) CONSERVATION PURPOSE MUST BE PROTECTED.—A contribution shall not be treated as exclusively for conservation purposes unless the conservation purpose is protected in perpetuity.

(B) NO SURFACE MINING PERMITTED.—

(i) IN GENERAL.—Except as provided in clause (ii), in the case of a contribution of any interest where there is a retention of a qualified mineral interest, subparagraph (A) shall not be treated as met if at any time there may be extraction or removal of minerals by any surface mining method.

(ii) SPECIAL RULE.—With respect to any contribution of property in which the ownership of the surface estate and mineral interests has been and remains separated, subparagraph (A) shall be treated as met if the probability of surface mining occurring on such property is so remote as to be negligible.

(6) QUALIFIED MINERAL INTEREST.—For purposes of this subsection, the term "qualified mineral interest" means—

(A) subsurface oil, gas or other minerals, and

(B) the right to access to such minerals.

(7) LIMITATION ON DEDUCTION FOR QUALIFIED CONSERVATION CONTRIBUTIONS MADE BY PASS-THROUGH ENTITIES.—

(A) IN GENERAL.—A contribution by a partnership (whether directly or as a distributive share of a contribution of another partnership) shall not be treated as a qualified conservation contribution for purposes of this section if the amount of such contribution exceeds 2.5 times the sum of each partner's relevant basis in such partnership.

(B) RELEVANT BASIS.—For purposes of this paragraph—

(i) IN GENERAL.—The term "relevant basis" means, with respect to any partner, the portion of such partner's modified basis in the partnership which is allocable (under rules similar to the rules of section 755) to the portion of the real property with respect to which the contribution described in subparagraph (A) is made.

(ii) MODIFIED BASIS.—The term "modified basis" means, with respect to any partner, such partner's adjusted basis in the partnership as determined—

(I) immediately before the contribution described in subparagraph (A),

(II) without regard to section 752, and

(III) by the partnership after taking into account the adjustments described in subclauses (I) and (II) and such other adjustments as the Secretary may provide.

(C) EXCEPTION FOR CONTRIBUTIONS OUTSIDE 3-YEAR HOLDING PERIOD.—Subparagraph (A) shall not apply to any contribution which is made at least 3 years after the latest of—

(i) the last date on which the partnership that made such contribution acquired any portion of the real property with respect to which such contribution is made,

(ii) the last date on which any partner in the partnership that made such contribution acquired any interest in such partnership, and

(iii) if the interest in the partnership that made such contribution is held through 1 or more partnerships—

(I) the last date on which any such partnership acquired any interest in any other such partnership, and

(II) the last date on which any partner in any such partnership acquired any interest in such partnership.

(D) EXCEPTION FOR FAMILY PARTNERSHIPS.—

(i) IN GENERAL.—Subparagraph (A) shall not apply with respect to any contribution made by any partnership if substantially all of the partnership interests in such partnership are held, directly or indirectly, by an individual and members of the family of such individual.

(ii) MEMBERS OF THE FAMILY.—For purposes of this subparagraph, the term "members of the family" means, with respect to any individual—

(I) the spouse of such individual, and

(II) any individual who bears a relationship to such individual which is described in subparagraphs (A) through (G) of section 152(d)(2).

(E) EXCEPTION FOR CONTRIBUTIONS TO PRESERVE CERTIFIED HISTORIC STRUCTURES.—Subparagraph (A) shall not apply to any qualified conservation contribution the conservation purpose of which is the preservation of any building which is a certified historic structure (as defined in paragraph (4)(C)).

(F) APPLICATION TO OTHER PASS-THROUGH ENTITIES.—Except as may be otherwise provided by the Secretary, the rules of this paragraph shall apply to S corporations and other pass-through entities in the same manner as such rules apply to partnerships.

(G) REGULATIONS.—The Secretary shall prescribe such regulations or other guidance as may be necessary or appropriate to carry out the purposes of this paragraph, including regulations or other guidance—

(i) to require reporting, including reporting related to tiered partnerships and the modified basis of partners, and

(ii) to prevent the avoidance of the purposes of this paragraph.

Amendments

• 2022, SECURE 2.0 Act of 2022 (P.L. 117-328)

P.L. 117-328, §605(a)(1):

Amended Code Sec. 170(h) by adding at the end a new paragraph (7). **Effective** for contributions made after 12-29-2022. For a special rule, see Act Sec. 605(c)(2), below.

P.L. 117-328, §605(c)(2), provides:

(2) NO INFERENCE.—No inference is intended as to the appropriate treatment of contributions made in taxable years ending on or before the date specified in paragraph (1), or as to any contribution for which a deduction is not disallowed by reason of section 170(h)(7) of the Internal Revenue Code of 1986, as added by this section.

P.L. 117-328, §605(d), provides:

(d) SAFE HARBORS AND OPPORTUNITY FOR DONOR TO CORRECT CERTAIN DEED ERRORS.—

(1) IN GENERAL.—The Secretary of the Treasury (or such Secretary's delegate) shall, within 120 days after the date of the enactment of this Act, publish safe harbor deed language for extinguishment clauses and boundary line adjustments.

(2) OPPORTUNITY TO CORRECT.—

(A) IN GENERAL.—During the 90-day period beginning on the date of publication of the safe harbor deed language under paragraph (1), a donor may amend an easement deed to substitute the safe harbor language for the corresponding language in the original deed if—

(i) the amended deed is signed by the donor and donee and recorded within such 90-day period, and

(ii) such amendment is treated as effective as of the date of the recording of the original easement deed.

(B) EXCEPTIONS.—Subparagraph (A) shall not apply to an easement deed relating to any contribution—

(i) which—

(I) is part of a reportable transaction (as defined in section 6707A(c)(1) of the Internal Revenue Code of 1986), or

(II) is described in Internal Revenue Service Notice 2017–10,

(ii) which by reason of section 170(h)(7) of such Code, as added by this section, is not treated as a qualified conservation contribution,

(iii) if a deduction for such contribution under section 170 of such Code has been disallowed by the Secretary of the Treasury (or such Secretary's delegate), and the donor is contesting such disallowance in a case which is docketed in a Federal court on a date before the date the amended deed is recorded by the donor, or

(iv) if a claimed deduction for such contribution under section 170 of such Code resulted in an underpayment to which a penalty under section 6662 or 6663 of such Code applies and—

(I) such penalty has been finally determined administratively, or

(II) if such penalty is challenged in court, the judicial proceeding with respect to such penalty has been concluded by a decision or judgment which has become final.

• 2006, Pension Protection Act of 2006 (P.L. 109-280)

P.L. 109-280, §1213(a)(1):

Amended Code Sec. 170(h)(4) by redesignating subparagraph (B) as subparagraph (C) and by inserting after subparagraph (A) a new subparagraph (B). **Effective** for contributions made after 7-25-2006.

P.L. 109-280, §1213(b)(1)-(3):

Amended Code Sec. 170(h)(4)(C), as redesignated by Act Sec. 1213(a), by striking "any building, structure, or land area which", by inserting "any building, structure, or land area which" before "is listed" in clause (i), and by inserting "any building which" before "is located" in clause (ii). **Effective** for contributions made after 8-17-2006.

• 1997, Taxpayer Relief Act of 1997 (P.L. 105-34)

P.L. 105-34, §508(d):

Amended Code Sec. 170(h)(5)(B)(ii). **Effective** for easements granted after 12-31-97. Prior to amendment, Code Sec. 170(h)(5)(B)(ii) read as follows:

(ii) SPECIAL RULE.—With respect to any contribution of property in which the ownership of the surface estate and mineral interests were separated before June 13, 1976, and remain so separated, subparagraph (A) shall be treated as met if the probability of surface mining occurring on such property is so remote as to be negligible.

• 1990, Omnibus Budget Reconciliation Act of 1990 (P.L. 101-508)

P.L. 101-508, §11813(b)(10):

Amended Code Sec. 170(h)(4)(B) by striking "section 48(g)(3)(B)" and inserting "section 47(c)(3)(B)". **Effective**, generally, for property placed in service after 12-31-90. However, for exceptions see Act Sec. 11813(c)(2) below.

P.L. 101-508, §11813(c)(2), provides:

(2) EXCEPTIONS.—The amendments made by this section shall not apply to—

(A) any transition property (as defined in section 49(e) of the Internal Revenue Code of 1986 (as in effect on the day before the date of the enactment of this Act),

(B) any property with respect to which qualified progress expenditures were previously taken into account under section 46(d) of such Code (as so in effect), and

(C) any property described in section 46(b)(2)(C) of such Code (as so in effect).

• 1984, Deficit Reduction Act of 1984 (P.L. 98-369)

P.L. 98-369, §1035(a):

Amended Code Sec. 170(h)(5)(B). **Effective** for contributions made after 7-18-84. Prior to amendment, it read as follows:

(B) NO SURFACE MINING PERMITTED.—In the case of a contribution of any interest where there is a retention of a qualified mineral interest, subparagraph (A) shall not be treated as met if at any time there may be extraction or removal of minerals by any surface mining method.

• 1983, Technical Corrections Act of 1982 (P.L. 97-448)

P.L. 97-448, §102(f)(7):

Amended Code Sec. 170(h)(4)(B)(ii) by striking out "section 191(d)(2)" and inserting in lieu thereof "section 48(g)(3)(B)". **Effective** as if it had been included in the provision of P.L. 97-34 to which it relates.

• 1980 (P.L. 96-541)

P.L. 96-541, §6(b):

Amended Code Sec. 170 by redesignating Code Sec. 170(h) as 170(i) and Code Sec. 170(i) as 170(j), and added a new Code Sec. 170(h). **Effective** for transfers made after 12-17-80, in tax years ending after that date.

* * *

[Sec. 170(q)]

(q) OTHER CROSS REFERENCES.—

(1) For treatment of certain organizations providing child care, see section 501(k).

(2) For charitable contributions of estates and trusts, see section 642(c).

(3) For nondeductibility of contributions by common trust funds, see section 584.

(4) For charitable contributions of partners, see section 702.

(5) For charitable contributions of nonresident aliens, see section 873.

(6) For treatment of gifts for benefit of or use in connection with the Naval Academy as gifts to or for the use of the United States, see section 8473 of title 10, United States Code.

(7) For treatment of gifts accepted by the Secretary of State, the Director of the International Communication Agency, or the Director of the United States International Development Cooperation Agency, as gifts to or for the use of the United States, see section 25 of the State Department Basic Authorities Act of 1956.

(8) For treatment of gifts of money accepted by the Attorney General for credit to the "Commissary Funds, Federal Prisons" as gifts to or for the use of the United States, see section 4043 of title 18, United States Code.

(9) For charitable contributions to or for the use of Indian tribal governments (or their subdivisions), see section 7871.

Amendments

• 2020, Taxpayer Certainty and Disaster Tax Relief Act of 2020 (P.L. 116-260)

P.L. 116-260, §212(a), Div. EE:

Amended Code Sec. 170 by redesignating subsection (p) as subsection (q). **Effective** for tax years beginning after 12-31-2020.

• 2018, John S. McCain National Defense Authorization Act for Fiscal Year 2019 (P.L. 115-232)

P.L. 115-232, §809(h)(1), Div. A:

Amended Code Sec. 170(p)(6) by striking "section 6973 of title 10, United States Code" and inserting "section 8473 of title 10, United States Code". **Effective** 8-13-2018.

• 2006, Pension Protection Act of 2006 (P.L. 109-280)

P.L. 109-280, §1218(a):

Amended Code Sec. 170 by redesignating subsection (o) as subsection (p). **Effective** for contributions, bequests, and gifts made after 8-17-2006.

• 2004, American Jobs Creation Act of 2004 (P.L. 108-357)

P.L. 108-357, §335(a):

Amended Code Sec. 170, as amended by this Act, by redesignating subsection (n) as subsection (o). **Effective** for contributions made after 12-31-2004.

P.L. 108-357, §882(b):

Amended Code Sec. 170 by redesignating subsection (m) as subsection (n). **Effective** for contributions made after 6-3-2004.

• 1990, Omnibus Budget Reconciliation Act of 1990 (P.L. 101-508)

P.L. 101-508, §11801(c)(5):

Amended Code Sec. 170 by redesignating subsection (n) as subsection (m). **Effective** 11-5-90.

P.L. 101-508, §11821(b), provides:

(b) SAVINGS PROVISION.—If—

(1) any provision amended or repealed by this part applied to—

(A) any transaction occurring before the date of the enactment of this Act,

(B) any property acquired before such date of enactment, or

(C) any item of income, loss, deduction, or credit taken into account before such date of enactment, and

(2) the treatment of such transaction, property, or item under such provision would (without regard to the amendments made by this part) affect liability for tax for periods ending after such date of enactment,

nothing in the amendments made by this part shall be construed to affect the treatment of such transaction, property, or item for purposes of determining liability for tax for periods ending after such date of enactment.

• 1988, Technical and Miscellaneous Revenue Act of 1988 (P.L. 100-647)

P.L. 100-647, §6001(a):

Amended Code Sec. 170 by redesignating subsection (m) as subsection (n) and adding after subsection (l) new subsection (m). **Effective**, generally, for tax years beginning after 12-31-83. See Act Sec. 6001(b)(2), below, for a special rule.

P.L. 100-647, §6001(b)(2), provides:

(2) WAIVER OF STATUTE OF LIMITATIONS.—If on the date of the enactment of this Act (or at any time within 1 year after such date of enactment) refund or credit of any overpayment of tax resulting from the application of section 170(m) of the 1986 Code (as added by subsection (a)) is barred by any law or rule of law, refund or credit of such overpayment shall, nevertheless, be made or allowed if claim therefore is filed before the date 1 year after the date of the enactment of this Act.

• 1986, Tax Reform Act of 1986 (P.L. 99-514)

P.L. 99-514, §142(d):

Amended Code Sec. 170 by redesignating subsections (k) and (l) as subsections (l) and (m), respectively. **Effective** for tax years beginning after 12-31-86.

• 1984, Deficit Reduction Act of 1984 (P.L. 98-369)

P.L. 98-369, §1031(a):

Redesignated Code Sec. 170(k) as 170(l). **Effective** for tax years beginning after 1984.

P.L. 98-369, §1032(b)(1):

Amended Code Sec. 170(k), redesignated as (l) by Act Sec. 1031, by redesignating paragraphs (1) through (8) as paragraphs (2) through (9), respectively, and by inserting before paragraph (2) (as so redesignated) new paragraph (1). **Effective** for tax years beginning after 7-18-84.

• 1983 (P.L. 97-473)

P.L. 97-473, §202(b)(4):

Added Code Sec. 170(k)(8). For the **effective** date, see the amendment note for P.L. 97-473, Act Sec. 204 following Code Sec. 7871.

• 1982 (P.L. 97-258)

P.L. 97-258, §3(f)(1):

Amended Code Sec. 170(k)(7) by striking out "section 2 of the Act of May 15, 1952, as amended by the Act of July 9, 1952 (31 U.S.C. 725s-4)" and substituting "section 4043 of title 18, United States Code". **Effective** 9-13-82.

• 1981, Economic Recovery Tax Act of 1981 (P.L. 97-34)

P.L. 97-34, §121(a):

Redesignated Code Sec. 170(j) as 170(k). **Effective** for contributions made after 12-31-81, in tax years beginning after such date.

P.L. 96-541, §6(b):

Redesignated Code Sec. 170(i) as 170(j). **Effective** for transfers made after 12-17-80, in tax years ending after that date.

• 1980, Foreign Service Act of 1980 (P.L. 96-465)

P.L. 96-465, §2206(e)(2):

Amended Code Sec. 170(i)(6). **Effective** 2-15-81. Prior to amendment, paragraph (6) read as follows: "(6) For treatment of gifts accepted by the Secretary of State under the Foreign Service Act of 1946 as gifts to or for the use of the United States, see section 1021(e) of that Act (22 U.S.C. 809(e))."

• 1976, Tax Reform Act of 1976 (P.L. 94-455)

P.L. 94-455, §1901(a)(28):

Amended and redesignated former Code Sec. 170(j) as Code Sec. 170(i). **Effective** for tax years beginning after 12-31-76. Prior to amendment, redesignated Code Sec. 170(i) read as follows:

(j) OTHER CROSS REFERENCES.—

(1) For charitable contributions of estates and trusts, see section 642(c).

(2) For nondeductibility of contributions by common trust funds, see section 584.

(3) For charitable contributions of partners, see section 702.

(4) For charitable contributions of nonresident aliens, see section 873.

(5) For treatment of gifts for benefit of or use in connection with the Naval Academy as gifts to or for the use of the United States, see section 3 of the Act of March 31, 1944 (58 Stat. 135; 34 U.S.C. 1115b).

(6) For treatment of gifts for benefit of the library of the Post Office Department as gifts to or for the use of the United States, see section 2 of the Act of August 8, 1946 (60 Stat. 924; 5 U.S.C. 393).

(7) For treatment of gifts accepted by the Secretary of State under the Foreign Service Act of 1946 as gifts to or for the use of the United States, see section 1021(e) of that Act (60 Stat. 1032; 22 U.S.C. 809(e)).

(8) For treatment of gifts of money accepted by the Attorney General for credit to the "Commissary Funds Federal Prisons" as gifts to or for the use of the United States, see section 2 of the Act of May 15, 1952 (66 Stat. 73, as amended by the Act of July 9, 1952, 66 Stat. 479, 31 U.S.C. 725s-4).

• 1969, Tax Reform Act of 1969 (P.L. 91-172)

P.L. 91-172, §201(a)(1)(A):

Redesignated Code Sec. 170(i) as Code Sec. 170(j). **Effective** 1-1-70.

• 1964, Revenue Act of 1964 (P.L. 88-272)

P.L. 88-272, §209(e):

Redesignated Code Sec. 170(g) as Sec. 170(i). **Effective** 1-1-64.

• 1962, Revenue Act of 1962 (P.L. 87-834)

P.L. 87-834, §13(d):

Redesignated Code Sec. 170(f) as Sec. 170(g). **Effective** for tax years beginning after 12-31-62.

• 1960 (P.L. 86-779)

P.L. 86-779, §7(a)(2):

Redesignated subsection (e) of Code Sec 170 as subsection (f). **Effective** 1-1-60.

* * *

PART VII—ADDITIONAL ITEMIZED DEDUCTIONS FOR INDIVIDUALS

* * *

[Sec. 213]

SEC. 213. MEDICAL, DENTAL, ETC., EXPENSES.

[Sec. 213(a)]

(a) ALLOWANCE OF DEDUCTION.—There shall be allowed as a deduction the expenses paid during the taxable year, not compensated for by insurance or otherwise, for medical care of the taxpayer, his spouse, or a dependent (as defined in section 152, determined without regard to subsections (b)(1), (b)(2), and (d)(1)(B) thereof), to the extent that such expenses exceed 7.5 percent of adjusted gross income.

Amendments

• 2020, Taxpayer Certainty and Disaster Tax Relief Act of 2020 (P.L. 116-260)

P.L. 116-260, §101(a)(1), Div. EE:

Amended Code Sec. 213(a) by striking "10 percent" and inserting "7.5 percent". **Effective** for tax years beginning after 12-31-2020.

• 2010, Patient Protection and Affordable Care Act (P.L. 111-148)

P.L. 111-148, §9013(a):

Amended Code Sec. 213(a) by striking "7.5 percent" and inserting "10 percent". **Effective** for tax years beginning after 12-31-2012.

• 2004, Working Families Tax Relief Act of 2004 (P.L. 108-311)

P.L. 108-311, §207(17):

Amended Code Sec. 213(a) by inserting ", determined without regard to subsections (b)(1), (b)(2), and (d)(1)(B) thereof" after "section 152". **Effective** for tax years beginning after 12-31-2004.

• 1986, Tax Reform Act of 1986 (P.L. 99-514)

P.L. 99-514, §133:

Amended Code Sec. 213(a) by striking out "5 percent" and inserting in lieu thereof "7.5 percent". **Effective** for tax years beginning after 12-31-86.

• 1982, Tax Equity and Fiscal Responsibility Act of 1982 (P.L. 97-248)

P.L. 97-248, §202(a):

Amended Code Sec. 213(a). **Effective** for to tax years beginning after 12-31-82. Prior to amendment, Code Sec. 213(a) read as follows:

"(a) Allowance of Deduction.—There shall be allowed as a deduction the following amounts, not compensated for by insurance or otherwise—

(1) the amount by which the amount of the expenses paid during the taxable year (reduced by any amount deductible under paragraph (2)) for medical care of the taxpayer, his spouse, and dependents (as defined in section 152) exceeds 3 percent of the adjusted gross income, and

(2) an amount (not in excess of $150) equal to one-half of the expenses paid during the taxable year for insurance which constitutes medical care for the taxpayer, his spouse, and dependents."

• 1965, Social Security Amendments of 1965 (P.L. 89-97)

P.L. 89-97, §106(a):

Amended Code Sec. 213(a). **Effective** for tax years beginning after 12-31-66. Prior to amendment, Sec. 213(a) read as follows:

"(a) Allowance of Deduction.—There shall be allowed as a deduction the following amounts of the expenses paid during the taxable year, not compensated for by insurance or otherwise, for medical care of the taxpayer, his spouse, or a dependent (as defined in section 152):

"(1) If neither the taxpayer nor his spouse has attained the age of 65 before the close of the taxable year—

"(A) the amount of such expenses for the care of any dependent who—

"(i) is the mother or father of the taxpayer or of his spouse, and

"(ii) has attained the age of 65 before the close of the taxable year, and

"(B) the amount by which such expenses for the care of the taxpayer, his spouse, and such dependents (other than any dependent described in subparagraph (A)) exceed 3 percent of the adjusted gross income.

"(2) If either the taxpayer or his spouse has attained the age of 65 before the close of the taxable year—

"(A) the amount of such expenses for the care of the taxpayer and his spouse,

"(B) the amount of such expenses for the care of any dependent described in paragraph (1)(A), and

"(C) the amount by which such expenses for the care of such dependents (other than any dependent described in paragraph (1)(A)) exceed 3 percent of the adjusted gross income."

• 1960 (P.L. 86-470)

P.L. 86-470, §3:

Amended Code Sec. 213(a). **Effective** for taxable years beginning after 12-31-59. Prior to amendment, Code Sec. 213(a) read as follows:

"(a) Allowance of Deduction.—There shall be allowed as a deduction the expenses paid during the taxable year, not compensated for by insurance or otherwise, for medical care of the taxpayer, his spouse, or a dependent (as defined in section 152)—

"(1) if neither the taxpayer nor his spouse has attained the age of 65 before the close of the taxable year, to the extent that such expenses exceed 3 percent of the adjusted gross income; or

"(2) if either the taxpayer or his spouse has attained the age of 65 before the close of the taxable year—

"(A) the amount of such expenses for the care of the taxpayer and his spouse, and

"(B) the amount by which such expenses for the care of such dependents exceed 3 percent of the adjusted gross income.".

* * *

[Sec. 213(c)—Repealed]

Amendments

• 1965, Social Security Amendments of 1965 (P.L. 89-97)

P.L. 89-97, §106(d):

Repealed Sec. 213(c). Prior to repeal, it read as follows:

"(c) Maximum Limitations.—Except as provided in subsection (g), the deduction under this section shall not exceed $5,000, multiplied by the number of exemptions allowed for the taxable year as a deduction under section 151 (other than exemptions allowed by reason of subsection (c) or (d), relating to additional exemptions for age or blindness); except that the maximum deduction under this section shall be—

"(1) $10,000, if the taxpayer is single and not the head of a household (as defined in section 1(b)(2)) and not a surviving spouse (as defined in section 2(b)) or is married but files a separate return; or

"(2) $20,000, if the taxpayer files a joint return with his spouse under section 6013, or is the head of a household (as defined in section 1(b)(2)) or a surviving spouse (as defined in section 2(b))."

• 1962 (P.L. 87-863)

P.L. 87-863, §1(a):

Amended Code Sec. 213(c) by substituting "$5,000" for "$2,500," "$10,000" for "$5,000," and "$20,000" for "$10,000." **Effective** 1-1-62.

• 1958, Technical Amendments Act of 1958 (P.L. 85-866)

P.L. 85-866, §17(c):

Struck out the word "The" at the beginning of Sec. 213(c) and substituted the phrase "Except as provided in subsection (g), the". **Effective** 1-1-58.

[Sec. 213(c)]

(c) SPECIAL RULE FOR DECEDENTS.—

(1) TREATMENT OF EXPENSES PAID AFTER DEATH.—For purposes of subsection (a), expenses for the medical care of the taxpayer which are paid out of his estate during the 1-year period beginning with the day after the date of his death shall be treated as paid by the taxpayer at the time incurred.

(2) LIMITATION.—Paragraph (1) shall not apply if the amount paid is allowable under section 2053 as a deduction in computing the taxable estate of the decedent, but this paragraph shall not apply if (within the time and in the manner and form prescribed by the Secretary) there is filed—

(A) a statement that such amount has not been allowed as a deduction under section 2053, and

(B) a waiver of the right to have such amount allowed at any time as a deduction under section 2053.

Amendments

• 1982, Tax Equity and Fiscal Responsibility Act of 1982 (P.L. 97-248)

P.L. 97-248, §202(b)(3)(B):

Redesignated former Code Sec. 213(d) as Code Sec. 213(c). **Effective** for tax years beginning after 1983.

• 1958, Technical Amendments Act of 1958 (P.L. 85-866)

P.L. 85-866, §16:

Struck out the phrase "claimed or" where it preceded the word "allowed" in Sec. 213(d)(2)(A). **Effective** 1-1-54.

* * *

Subchapter C—Corporate Distributions and Adjustments

* * *

PART I—DISTRIBUTIONS BY CORPORATIONS

* * *

Subpart A—Effects on Recipients

* * *

[Sec. 303]

SEC. 303. DISTRIBUTIONS IN REDEMPTION OF STOCK TO PAY DEATH TAXES.

[Sec. 303(a)]

(a) IN GENERAL.—A distribution of property to a shareholder by a corporation in redemption of part or all of the stock of such corporation which (for Federal estate tax purposes) is included in determining the gross estate of a decedent, to the extent that the amount of such distribution does not exceed the sum of—

(1) the estate, inheritance, legacy, and succession taxes (including any interest collected as a part of such taxes) imposed because of such decedent's death, and

(2) the amount of funeral and administration expenses allowable as deductions to the estate under section 2053 (or under section 2106 in the case of the estate of a decedent nonresident, not a citizen of the United States),

shall be treated as a distribution in full payment in exchange for the stock so redeemed.

[Sec. 303(b)]

(b) LIMITATIONS ON APPLICATION OF SUBSECTION (a).—

(1) PERIOD FOR DISTRIBUTION.—Subsection (a) shall apply only to amounts distributed after the death of the decedent and—

(A) within the period of limitations provided in section 6501(a) for the assessment of the Federal estate tax (determined without the application of any provision other than section 6501(a)), or within 90 days after the expiration of such period,

(B) if a petition for redetermination of a deficiency in such estate tax has been filed with the Tax Court within the time prescribed in section 6213, at any time before the expiration of 60 days after the decision of the Tax Court becomes final, or

(C) if an election has been made under section 6166 and if the time prescribed by this subparagraph expires at a later date than the time prescribed by subparagraph (B) of this paragraph, within the time determined under section 6166 for the payment of the installments.

(2) RELATIONSHIP OF STOCK TO DECEDENT'S ESTATE.—

(A) IN GENERAL.—Subsection (a) shall apply to a distribution by a corporation only if the value (for Federal estate tax purposes) of all of the stock of such corporation which is included in determining the value of the decedent's gross estate exceeds 35 percent of the excess of—

(i) the value of the gross estate of such decedent, over

(ii) the sum of the amounts allowable as a deduction under section 2053 or 2054.

(B) SPECIAL RULE FOR STOCK IN 2 OR MORE CORPORATIONS.—For purposes of subparagraph (A), stock of 2 or more corporations, with respect to each of which there is included in determining the value of the decedent's gross estate 20 percent or more in value of the outstanding stock, shall be treated as the stock of a single corporation. For purposes of the 20-percent requirement of the preceding sentence, stock which, at the decedent's death, represents the surviving spouse's interest in property held by the decedent and the surviving spouse as community property or as joint tenants, tenants by the entirety, or tenants in common shall be treated as having been included in determining the value of the decedent's gross estate.

(3) RELATIONSHIP OF SHAREHOLDER TO ESTATE TAX.—Subsection (a) shall apply to a distribution by a corporation only to the extent that the interest of the shareholder is reduced directly (or through a binding obligation to contribute) by any payment of an amount described in paragraph (1) or (2) of subsection (a).

(4) ADDITIONAL REQUIREMENTS FOR DISTRIBUTIONS MADE MORE THAN 4 YEARS AFTER DECEDENT'S DEATH.—In the case of amounts distributed more than 4 years after the date of the decedent's death, subsection (a) shall apply to a distribution by a corporation only to the extent of the lesser of—

(A) the aggregate of the amounts referred to in paragraph (1) or (2) of subsection (a) which remained unpaid immediately before the distribution, or

(B) the aggregate of the amounts referred to in paragraph (1) or (2) of subsection (a) which are paid during the 1-year period beginning on the date of such distribution.

Amendments

• 1981, Economic Recovery Tax Act of 1981 (P.L. 97-34)

P.L. 97-34, §422(b)(1):

Amended Code Sec. 303(b)(2)(A) by striking out "50 percent" and inserting "35 percent". **Effective** for estates of decedents dying after 12-31-81.

P.L. 97-34, §422(b)(2):

Amended Code Sec. 303(b)(2)(B). **Effective** for estates of decedents dying after 12-31-81. Prior to amendment, Code Sec. 303(b)(2)(B) read as follows:

(B) SPECIAL RULE FOR STOCK OF TWO OR MORE CORPORATIONS.—For purposes of the 50 percent requirement of subparagraph (A), stock of two or more corporations, with respect to each of which there is included in determining the value of the decedent's gross estate more than 75 percent in value of the outstanding stock, shall be treated as the stock of a single corporation. For the purpose of the 75 percent requirement of the preceding sentence, stock which, at the decedent's death, represents the surviving spouse's interest in property held by the decedent and the surviving spouse as community property shall be treated as having been included in determining the value of the decedent's gross estate.

P.L. 97-34, §422(e)(1):

Amended Code Sec. 303(b)(1)(C) by striking out "or 6166A" each place it appears. **Effective** for estates of decedents dying after 12-31-81.

• 1976, Tax Reform Act of 1976 (P.L. 94-455)

P.L. 94-455, §2004(e):

Amended Code Sec. 303(b) by striking "or" at the end of paragraph (1)(A), substituting ", or" for the period at the end of paragraph (1)(B), adding paragraph (1)(C), amending paragraph (2)(A), substituting "the 50 percent requirement" for "the 35 percent and 50 percent requirements" in paragraph (2)(B), and adding paragraphs (3) and (4). **Effective** for the estates of decedents dying after 12-31-76. Prior to amendment, Code Sec. 303(b)(2)(A) read as follows:

(A) IN GENERAL.—Subsection (a) shall apply to a distribution by a corporation only if the value (for Federal estate tax purposes) of all of the stock of such corporation which is included in determining the value of the decedent's gross estate is either—

(i) more than 35 percent of the value of the gross estate of such decedent, or

(ii) more than 50 percent of the taxable estate of such decedent.

[Sec. 303(c)]

(c) STOCK WITH SUBSTITUTED BASIS.—If—

(1) a shareholder owns stock of a corporation (referred to in this subsection as "new stock") the basis of which is determined by reference to the basis of stock of a corporation (referred to in this subsection as "old stock"),

(2) the old stock was included (for Federal estate tax purposes) in determining the gross estate of a decedent, and

(3) subsection (a) would apply to a distribution of property to such shareholder in redemption of the old stock,

then, subject to the limitations specified in subsection (b), subsection (a) shall apply in respect of a distribution in redemption of the new stock.

Amendments

• 1976, Tax Reform Act of 1976 (P.L. 94-455)

P.L. 94-455, §2004(e)(4):

Substituted "limitations specified in subsection (b)" for "limitation specified in subsection (b)(1)" in Code Sec. 303(c). **Effective** for the estates of decedents dying after 12-31-76.

[Sec. 303(d)]

(d) SPECIAL RULES FOR GENERATION-SKIPPING TRANSFERS.—Where stock in a corporation is the subject of a generation-skipping transfer (within the meaning of section 2611(a)) occurring at the same time as and as a result of the death of an individual—

(1) the stock shall be deemed to be included in the gross estate of such individual;

(2) taxes of the kind referred to in subsection (a)(1) which are imposed because of the generation-skipping transfer shall be treated as imposed because of such individual's death (and for this purpose the tax imposed by section 2601 shall be treated as an estate tax);

(3) the period of distribution shall be measured from the date of the generation-skipping transfer; and

(4) the relationship of stock to the decedent's estate shall be measured with reference solely to the amount of the generation-skipping transfer.

Amendments

• 1990, Omnibus Budget Reconciliation Act of 1990 (P.L. 101-508)

P.L. 101-508, §11703(c)(3), provides:

(3) Subparagraph (C) of section 1433(b)(2) of the Tax Reform Act of 1986 shall not exempt any generation-skipping transfer from the amendments made by subtitle D of title XVI of such Act to the extent such transfer is attributable to property transferred by gift or by reason of the death of another person to the decedent (or trust) referred to in such subparagraph after August 3, 1990.

• 1988, Technical and Miscellaneous Revenue Act of 1988 (P.L. 100-647)

P.L. 100-647, §1014(h)(5), provides:

(5) Subparagraph (C) of section 1433(b)(2) of the Reform Act shall not exempt any direct skip from the amendments made by subtitle D of title XIV of the Reform Act if—

(A) such direct skip results from the application of section 2044 of the 1986 Code, and

(B) such direct skip is attributable to property transferred to the trust after October 21, 1988.

• 1986, Tax Reform Act of 1986 (P.L. 99-514)

P.L. 99-514, §1432(b):

Amended Code Sec. 303(d). For the **effective** dates, as well as special rules, see P.L. 99-514, §1433, as amended by P.L. 100-647, §1014(h)(1)-(4), below. Prior to amendment, Code Sec. 303(d) read as follows:

(d) SPECIAL RULES FOR GENERATION-SKIPPING TRANSFERS.—Under regulations prescribed by the Secretary, where stock in a corporation is subject to tax under section 2601 as a result of a generation-skipping transfer (within the meaning of section 2611(a)), which occurs at or after the death of the deemed transferor (within the meaning of section 2612)—

(1) the stock shall be deemed to be included in the gross estate of the deemed transferor;

(2) taxes of the kind referred to in subsection (a)(1) which are imposed because of the generation-skipping transfer shall be treated as imposed because of the deemed transferor's death (and for this purpose the tax imposed by section 2601 shall be treated as an estate tax);

(3) the period of distribution shall be measured from the date of the generation-skipping transfer; and

(4) the relationship of stock of the decedent's estate shall be measured with reference solely to the amount of the generation-skipping transfer.

P.L. 99-514, §1433, as amended by P.L. 100-647, §1014(h)(1)-(4), provides:

SEC. 1433. EFFECTIVE DATES.

(a) GENERAL RULE.—Except as provided in subsection (b), the amendments made by this subtitle shall apply to any generation-skipping transfer (within the meaning of section 2611 of the Internal Revenue Code of 1986) made after the date of the enactment of this Act.

(b) SPECIAL RULES.—

(1) TREATMENT OF CERTAIN INTER VIVOS TRANSFERS MADE AFTER SEPTEMBER 25, 1985.—For purposes of subsection (a) (and chapter 13 of the Internal Revenue Code of 1986 as amended by this part), any inter vivos transfer after September 25, 1985, and on or before the date of the enactment of this Act shall be treated as if it were made on the 1st day after the date of enactment of this Act.

(2) EXCEPTIONS.—The amendments made by this subtitle shall not apply to—

(A) any generation-skipping transfer under a trust which was irrevocable on September 25, 1985, but only to the extent that such transfer is not made out of corpus added to the trust after September 25, 1985 (or out of income attributable to corpus so added),

(B) any generation-skipping transfer under a will or revocable trust executed before the date of the enactment of this Act if the decedent dies before January 1, 1987, and

(C) any generation-skipping transfer—

(i) under a trust to the extent such trust consists of property included in the gross estate of a decedent (other than property transferred by the decedent during his life after the date of the enactment of this Act), or reinvestments thereof, or

(ii) which is a direct skip which occurs by reason of the death of any decedent;

but only if such decedent was, on the date of the enactment of this Act, under a mental disability to change the disposition of his property and did not regain his competence to dispose of such property before the date of his death.

(3) TREATMENT OF CERTAIN TRANSFERS TO GRANDCHILDREN.—

(A) IN GENERAL.—For purposes of chapter 13 of the Internal Revenue Code of 1986, the term "direct skip" shall not include any transfer before January 1, 1990, from a transferor to a grandchild of the transferor to the extent the aggregate transfers from such transferor to such grandchild do not exceed $2,000,000.

(B) TREATMENT OF TRANSFERS IN TRUST.—For purposes of subparagraph (A), a transfer in trust for the benefit of a grandchild shall be treated as a transfer to such grandchild if (and only if)—

(i) during the life of the grandchild, no portion of the corpus or income of the trust may be distributed to (or for the benefit of) any person other than such grandchild,

(ii) the assets of the trust will be includible in the gross estate of the grandchild if the grandchild dies before the trust is terminated, and

(iii) all of the income of the trust for periods after the grandchild has attained age 21 will be distributed to (or for the benefit of) such grandchild not less frequently than annually.

(C) COORDINATION WITH SECTION 2653(a) OF THE 1986 CODE.—In the case of any transfer which would be a generation-skipping transfer but for subparagraph (A), the rules of section 2653(a) of the Internal Revenue Code of 1986 shall apply as if such transfer were a generation-skipping transfer.

(D) COORDINATION WITH TAXABLE TERMINATIONS AND TAXABLE DISTRIBUTIONS.—For purposes of chapter 13 of the Internal Revenue Code of 1986, the terms "taxable termination" and "taxable distribution" shall not include any transfer which would be a direct skip but for subparagraph (A).

(4) DEFINITIONS.—Terms used in this section shall have the same respective meanings as when used in chapter 13 of the Internal Revenue Code of 1986; except that section 2612(c)(2) of such Code shall not apply in determining whether an individual is a grandchild of the transferor.

(c) REPEAL OF EXISTING TAX ON GENERATION-SKIPPING TRANSFERS.—

(1) IN GENERAL.—In the case of any tax imposed by chapter 13 of the Internal Revenue Code of 1954 (as in effect on the day before the date of the enactment of this Act), such tax (including interest, additions to tax, and additional amounts) shall not be assessed and if assessed, the assessment shall be abated, and if collected, shall be credited or refunded (with interest) as an overpayment.

(2) WAIVER OF STATUTE OF LIMITATIONS.—If on the date of the enactment of this Act (or at any time within 1 year after such date of enactment) refund or credit of any overpayment of tax resulting from the application of paragraph (1) is barred by any law or rule of law, refund or credit of such overpayment shall, nevertheless, be made or allowed if

claim therefore is filed before the date 1 year after the date of the enactment of this Act.

(d) ELECTION FOR CERTAIN TRANSFERS BENEFITING GRANDCHILD.—

(1) IN GENERAL.—For purposes of chapter 13 of the Internal Revenue Code of 1986 (as amended by this Act) and subsection (b) of this section, any transfer in trust for the benefit of a grandchild of a transferor shall be treated as a direct skip to such grandchild if—

(A) the transfer occurs before the date of enactment of this Act,

(B) the transfer would be a direct skip to a grandchild except for the fact that the trust instrument provides that, if the grandchild dies before vesting of the interest transferred, the interest is transferred to the grandchild's heir (rather than the grandchild's estate), and

(C) an election under this subsection applies to such transfer.

(2) ELECTION.—An election under paragraph (1) shall be made at such time and in such manner as the Secretary of the Treasury or his delegate may prescribe.

Any transfer treated as a direct skip by reason of the preceding sentence shall be subject to Federal estate tax on the grandchild's death in the same manner as if the contingent gift over had been to the grandchild's estate. Unless the grandchild otherwise directs by will, the estate of such grandchild shall be entitled to recover from the person receiving the property on the death of the grandchild any increase in Federal estate tax on the estate of the grandchild by reason of the preceding sentence.

• 1978, Revenue Act of 1978 (P.L. 95-600)

P.L. 95-600, §702(n)(1), (5):

Amended P.L. 95-455, §2006(c) by striking out "April 30, 1976" each place it appears and inserting in place thereof "June 11, 1976".

• 1976, Tax Reform Act of 1976 (P.L. 94-455)

P.L. 94-455, §2006(b)(4), (c):

Added Code Sec. 303(d). **Effective** for any generation-skipping transfer (within the meaning of Code Sec. 2611(a)) made after 6-11-76. Code Sec. 303(d) shall not apply to any generation-skipping transfer: (1) under a trust that was irrevocable on 6-11-76, but only to the extent that the transfer is not made out of corpus added to the trust after 6-11-76, or (2) in the case of a decedent dying before 1-1-82, pursuant to a will (or revocable trust) which was in existence on 6-11-76, and was not amended at any time after that date in any respect that will result in the creation of, or increasing the amount of, any generation-skipping transfer. If a decedent, on 6-11-76, was under a mental disability to change the disposition of his property, the period set forth in (2) shall not expire before the date which is 2 years after the date on which he first regains his competence to dispose of such property. In the case of a trust equivalent within the meaning of Code Sec. 2611(d), the provisions of Code Sec. 2611(d) shall apply. [**Effective** date changed by P.L. 95-600, §702(n)(1), (5).—CCH].

* * *

Subchapter F—Exempt Organizations

* * *

PART VIII—HIGHER EDUCATION SAVINGS ENTITIES

* * *

[Sec. 529]

SEC. 529. QUALIFIED TUITION PROGRAMS.

[Sec. 529(a)]

(a) GENERAL RULE.—A qualified tuition program shall be exempt from taxation under this subtitle. Notwithstanding the preceding sentence, such program shall be subject to the taxes imposed by section 511 (relating to imposition of tax on unrelated business income of charitable organizations).

Amendments

• 2006, Pension Protection Act of 2006 (P.L. 109-280)

P.L. 109-280, §1304(a), provides:

(a) PERMANENT EXTENSION OF MODIFICATIONS.—Section 901 of the Economic Growth and Tax Relief Reconciliation Act of 2001 [P.L. 107-16] (relating to sunset provisions) shall not apply to section 402 of such Act (relating to modifications to qualified tuition programs).

• 2001, Economic Growth and Tax Relief Reconciliation Act of 2001 (P.L. 107-16)

P.L. 107-16, §402(a)(4)(A):

Amended Code Sec. 529 by striking "qualified State tuition" each place it appears and inserting "qualified tuition". **Effective** for tax years beginning after 12-31-2001.

P.L. 107-16, §402(a)(4)(D):

Amended the heading for Code Sec. 529 by striking "**STATE**" following "**QUALIFIED**". **Effective** for tax years beginning after 12-31-2001.

P.L. 107-16, §901(a)-(b), as amended by P.L. 111-312, §101(a)(1), provides [but see P.L. 109-280, §1304(a), above]:

SEC. 901. SUNSET OF PROVISIONS OF ACT.

(a) IN GENERAL.—All provisions of, and amendments made by, this Act shall not apply—

(1) to taxable, plan, or limitation years beginning after December 31, 2012, or

(2) in the case of title V, to estates of decedents dying, gifts made, or generation skipping transfers, after December 31, 2012.

(b) APPLICATION OF CERTAIN LAWS.—The Internal Revenue Code of 1986 and the Employee Retirement Income Security Act of 1974 shall be applied and administered to years, estates, gifts, and transfers described in subsection (a) as if the provisions and amendments described in subsection (a) had never been enacted.

[Sec. 529(b)]

(b) QUALIFIED TUITION PROGRAM.—For purposes of this section—

(1) IN GENERAL.—The term "qualified tuition program" means a program established and maintained by a State or agency or instrumentality thereof or by 1 or more eligible educational institutions—

(A) under which a person—

(i) may purchase tuition credits or certificates on behalf of a designated beneficiary which entitle the beneficiary to the waiver or payment of qualified higher education expenses of the beneficiary, or

(ii) in the case of a program established and maintained by a State or agency or instrumentality thereof, may make contributions to an account which is established for the purpose of meeting the qualified higher education expenses of the designated beneficiary of the account, and

(B) which meets the other requirements of this subsection.

Except to the extent provided in regulations, a program established and maintained by 1 or more eligible educational institutions shall not be treated as a qualified tuition program unless such program provides that amounts are held in a qualified trust and such program has received a ruling or determination that such program meets the applicable requirements for a qualified tuition program. For purposes of the preceding sentence, the term "qualified trust" means a trust which is created or organized in the United States for the exclusive benefit of designated beneficiaries and with respect to which the requirements of paragraphs (2) and (5) of section 408(a) are met.

(2) CASH CONTRIBUTIONS.—A program shall not be treated as a qualified tuition program unless it provides that purchases or contributions may only be made in cash.

(3) SEPARATE ACCOUNTING.—A program shall not be treated as a qualified tuition program unless it provides separate accounting for each designated beneficiary.

(4) LIMITED INVESTMENT DIRECTION.—A program shall not be treated as a qualified tuition program unless it provides that any contributor to, or designated beneficiary under, such program may, directly or indirectly, direct the investment of any contributions to the program (or any earnings thereon) no more than 2 times in any calendar year.

(5) NO PLEDGING OF INTEREST AS SECURITY.—A program shall not be treated as a qualified tuition program if it allows any interest in the program or any portion thereof to be used as security for a loan.

(6) PROHIBITION ON EXCESS CONTRIBUTIONS.—A program shall not be treated as a qualified tuition program unless it provides adequate safeguards to prevent contributions on behalf of a designated beneficiary in excess of those necessary to provide for the qualified higher education expenses of the beneficiary.

Amendments

• 2014, Stephen Beck, Jr., Achieving a Better Life Experience Act of 2014 (P.L. 113-295)

P.L. 113-295, §105(a)(1), Division B:

Amended Code Sec. 529(b)(4) by striking "may not directly or indirectly" and all that follows and inserting "may, directly or indirectly, direct the investment of any contributions to the program (or any earnings thereon) no more than 2 times in any calendar year.". **Effective** for tax years beginning after 12-31-2014. Prior to being stricken, "may not directly or indirectly" and all that follows read as follows: "may not directly or indirectly direct the investment of any contributions to the program (or any earnings theron)".

P.L. 113-295, §105(a)(2), Division B:

Amended the heading of Code Sec. 529(b)(4) by striking "No" and inserting "LIMITED". **Effective** for tax years beginning after 12-31-2014.

• 2006, Pension Protection Act of 2006 (P.L. 109-280)

P.L. 109-280, §1304(a), provides:

(a) PERMANENT EXTENSION OF MODIFICATIONS.—Section 901 of the Economic Growth and Tax Relief Reconciliation Act of 2001 [P.L. 107-16] (relating to sunset provisions) shall not apply to section 402 of such Act (relating to modifications to qualified tuition programs).

• 2001, Economic Growth and Tax Relief Reconciliation Act of 2001 (P.L. 107-16)

P.L. 107-16, §402(a)(1)(A)-(B):

Amended Code Sec. 529(b)(1) by inserting "or by 1 or more eligible educational institutions" after "maintained by a State or agency or instrumentality thereof" in the matter preceding subparagraph (A), and by adding at the end a new flush sentence. **Effective** for tax years beginning after 12-31-2001.

P.L. 107-16, §402(a)(2):

Amended Code Sec. 529(b)(1)(A)(ii) by inserting "in the case of a program established and maintained by a State or agency or instrumentality thereof," before "may make". **Effective** for tax years beginning after 12-31-2001.

P.L. 107-16, §402(a)(3)(A):

Amended Code Sec. 529 by striking paragraph (3) of subsection (b) and by redesignating paragraphs (4), (5), (6), and (7) of such subsection as paragraphs (3), (4), (5), and (6), respectively. **Effective** for tax years beginning after 12-31-2001. Prior to being stricken, Code Sec. 529(b)(3) read as follows:

(3) REFUNDS.—A program shall not be treated as a qualified State tuition program unless it imposes a more than de minimis penalty on any refund of earnings from the account which are not—

(A) used for qualified higher education expenses of the designated beneficiary,

(B) made on account of the death or disability of the designated beneficiary, or

(C) made on account of a scholarship (or allowance or payment described in section 135(d)(1)(B) or (C)) received by the designated beneficiary to the extent the amount of the refund does not exceed the amount of the scholarship, allowance, or payment.

P.L. 107-16, §402(a)(4)(A):

Amended Code Sec. 529 by striking "qualified State tuition" each place it appears and inserting "qualified tuition". **Effective** for tax years beginning after 12-31-2001.

P.L. 107-16, §402(a)(4)(C):

Amended the heading for Code Sec. 529(b) by striking "QUALIFIED STATE TUITION" and inserting "QUALIFIED TUITION". **Effective** for tax years beginning after 12-31-2001.

P.L. 107-16, §901(a)-(b), as amended by P.L. 111-312, §101(a)(1), provides [but see P.L. 109-280, §1304(a), above]:

SEC. 901. SUNSET OF PROVISIONS OF ACT.

(a) IN GENERAL.—All provisions of, and amendments made by, this Act shall not apply—

(1) to taxable, plan, or limitation years beginning after December 31, 2012, or

(2) in the case of title V, to estates of decedents dying, gifts made, or generation skipping transfers, after December 31, 2012.

(b) APPLICATION OF CERTAIN LAWS.—The Internal Revenue Code of 1986 and the Employee Retirement Income Security Act of 1974 shall be applied and administered to years, estates, gifts, and transfers described in subsection (a) as if the provisions and amendments described in subsection (a) had never been enacted.

• 1997, Taxpayer Relief Act of 1997 (P.L. 105-34)

P.L. 105-34, §211(b)(4):

Amended Code Sec. 529(b)(5) by inserting "directly or indirectly" after "may not". **Effective** 1-1-98.

[Sec. 529(c)]

(c) TAX TREATMENT OF DESIGNATED BENEFICIARIES AND CONTRIBUTORS.—

(1) IN GENERAL.—Except as otherwise provided in this subsection, no amount shall be includible in gross income of—

(A) a designated beneficiary under a qualified tuition program, or

(B) a contributor to such program on behalf of a designated beneficiary,

with respect to any distribution or earnings under such program.

(2) GIFT TAX TREATMENT OF CONTRIBUTIONS.—For purposes of chapters 12 and 13—

(A) IN GENERAL.—Any contribution to a qualified tuition program on behalf of any designated beneficiary—

(i) shall be treated as a completed gift to such beneficiary which is not a future interest in property, and

(ii) shall not be treated as a qualified transfer under section 2503(e).

(B) TREATMENT OF EXCESS CONTRIBUTIONS.—If the aggregate amount of contributions described in subparagraph (A) during the calendar year by a donor exceeds the limitation for such year under section 2503(b), such aggregate amount shall, at the election of the donor, be taken into account for purposes of such section ratably over the 5-year period beginning with such calendar year.

(3) DISTRIBUTIONS.—

(A) IN GENERAL.—Any distribution under a qualified tuition program shall be includible in the gross income of the distributee in the manner as provided under section 72 to the extent not excluded from gross income under any other provision of this chapter.

(B) DISTRIBUTIONS FOR QUALIFIED HIGHER EDUCATION EXPENSES.—For purposes of this paragraph—

(i) IN-KIND DISTRIBUTIONS.—No amount shall be includible in gross income under subparagraph (A) by reason of a distribution which consists of providing a benefit to the distributee which, if paid for by the distributee, would constitute payment of a qualified higher education expense.

(ii) CASH DISTRIBUTIONS.—In the case of distributions not described in clause (i), if—

(I) such distributions do not exceed the qualified higher education expenses (reduced by expenses described in clause (i)), no amount shall be includible in gross income, and

(II) in any other case, the amount otherwise includible in gross income shall be reduced by an amount which bears the same ratio to such amount as such expenses bear to such distributions.

(iii) EXCEPTION FOR INSTITUTIONAL PROGRAMS.—In the case of any taxable year beginning before January 1, 2004, clauses (i) and (ii) shall not apply with respect to any distribution during such taxable year under a qualified tuition program established and maintained by 1 or more eligible educational institutions.

(iv) TREATMENT AS DISTRIBUTIONS.—Any benefit furnished to a designated beneficiary under a qualified tuition program shall be treated as a distribution to the beneficiary for purposes of this paragraph.

(v) COORDINATION WITH AMERICAN OPPORTUNITY AND LIFETIME LEARNING CREDITS.—The total amount of qualified higher education expenses with respect to an individual for the taxable year shall be reduced—

(I) as provided in section 25A(g)(2), and

(II) by the amount of such expenses which were taken into account in determining the credit allowed to the taxpayer or any other person under section 25A.

(vi) COORDINATION WITH COVERDELL EDUCATION SAVINGS ACCOUNTS.—If, with respect to an individual for any taxable year—

(I) the aggregate distributions to which clauses (i) and (ii) and section 530(d)(2)(A) apply, exceed

(II) the total amount of qualified higher education expenses otherwise taken into account under clauses (i) and (ii) (after the application of clause (v)) for such year,

the taxpayer shall allocate such expenses among such distributions for purposes of determining the amount of the exclusion under clauses (i) and (ii) and section 530(d)(2)(A).

(C) CHANGE IN BENEFICIARIES OR PROGRAMS.—

(i) ROLLOVERS.—Subparagraph (A) shall not apply to that portion of any distribution which, within 60 days of such distribution, is transferred—

(I) to another qualified tuition program for the benefit of the designated beneficiary,

(II) to the credit of another designated beneficiary under a qualified tuition program who is a member of the family of the designated beneficiary with respect to which the distribution was made, or

(III) before January 1, 2026, to an ABLE account (as defined in section 529A(e)(6)) of the designated beneficiary or a member of the family of the designated beneficiary.

Subclause (III) shall not apply to so much of a distribution which, when added to all other contributions made to the ABLE account for the taxable year, exceeds the limitation under section 529A(b)(2)(B)(i).

(ii) CHANGE IN DESIGNATED BENEFICIARIES.—Any change in the designated beneficiary of an interest in a qualified tuition program shall not be treated as a distribution for purposes of subparagraph (A) if the new beneficiary is a member of the family of the old beneficiary.

(iii) LIMITATION ON CERTAIN ROLLOVERS.—Clause (i)(I) shall not apply to any transfer if such transfer occurs within 12 months from the date of a previous transfer to any qualified tuition program for the benefit of the designated beneficiary.

(D) SPECIAL RULE FOR CONTRIBUTIONS OF REFUNDED AMOUNTS.—In the case of a beneficiary who receives a refund of any qualified higher education expenses from an eligible educational institution, subparagraph (A) shall not apply to that portion of any distribution for the taxable year which is recontributed to a qualified tuition program of which such individual is a beneficiary, but only to the extent such recontribution is made not later than 60 days after the date of such refund and does not exceed the refunded amount.

Caution: Code Sec. 529(c)(3)(E), below, as added by P.L. 117-328, applies with respect to distributions after December 31, 2023.

(E) SPECIAL ROLLOVER TO ROTH IRAS FROM LONG-TERM QUALIFIED TUITION PROGRAMS.—

(i) IN GENERAL.—In the case of a distribution from a qualified tuition program of a designated beneficiary which has been maintained for the 15-year period ending on the date of such distribution, subparagraph (A) shall not apply to so much the portion of such distribution which—

(I) does not exceed the aggregate amount contributed to the program (and earnings attributable thereto) before the 5-year period ending on the date of the distribution, and

(II) is paid in a direct trustee-to-trustee transfer to a Roth IRA maintained for the benefit of such designated beneficiary.

(ii) LIMITATIONS.—

(I) ANNUAL LIMITATION.—Clause (i) shall only apply to so much of any distribution as does not exceed the amount applicable to the designated beneficiary under section 408A(c)(2) for the taxable year (reduced by the amount of aggregate contributions made during the taxable year to all individual retirement plans maintained for the benefit of the designated beneficiary).

(II) AGGREGATE LIMITATION.—This subparagraph shall not apply to any distribution described in clause (i) to the extent that the aggregate amount of such distributions with respect to the designated beneficiary for such taxable year and all prior taxable years exceeds $35,000.

(4) ESTATE TAX TREATMENT.—

(A) IN GENERAL.—No amount shall be includible in the gross estate of any individual for purposes of chapter 11 by reason of an interest in a qualified tuition program.

(B) AMOUNTS INCLUDIBLE IN ESTATE OF DESIGNATED BENEFICIARY IN CERTAIN CASES.—Subparagraph (A) shall not apply to amounts distributed on account of the death of a beneficiary.

(C) AMOUNTS INCLUDIBLE IN ESTATE OF DONOR MAKING EXCESS CONTRIBUTIONS.—In the case of a donor who makes the election described in paragraph (2)(B) and who dies before the close of the 5-year period referred to in such paragraph, notwithstanding subparagraph (A), the gross estate of the donor shall include the portion of such contributions properly allocable to periods after the date of death of the donor.

(5) OTHER GIFT TAX RULES.—For purposes of chapters 12 and 13—

(A) TREATMENT OF DISTRIBUTIONS.—Except as provided in subparagraph (B), in no event shall a distribution from a qualified tuition program be treated as a taxable gift.

(B) TREATMENT OF DESIGNATION OF NEW BENEFICIARY.—The taxes imposed by chapters 12 and 13 shall apply to a transfer by reason of a change in the designated beneficiary under the program (or a rollover to the account of a new beneficiary) unless the new beneficiary is—

(i) assigned to the same generation as (or a higher generation than) the old beneficiary (determined in accordance with section 2651), and

(ii) a member of the family of the old beneficiary.

(6) ADDITIONAL TAX.—The tax imposed by section 530(d)(4) shall apply to any payment or distribution from a qualified tuition program in the same manner as such tax applies to a payment or distribution from a Coverdell education savings account. This paragraph shall not apply to any payment or distribution in any taxable year beginning before January 1, 2004, which is includible in gross income but used for qualified higher education expenses of the designated beneficiary.

(7) TREATMENT OF ELEMENTARY AND SECONDARY TUITION.—Any reference in this subsection to the term "qualified higher education expense" shall include a reference to expenses for tuition in connection with enrollment or attendance at an elementary or secondary public, private, or religious school.

(8) TREATMENT OF CERTAIN EXPENSES ASSOCIATED WITH REGISTERED APPRENTICESHIP PROGRAMS.—Any reference in this subsection to the term "qualified higher education expense" shall include a reference to expenses for fees, books, supplies, and equipment required for the participation of a designated beneficiary in an apprenticeship program registered and certified with the Secretary of Labor under section 1 of the National Apprenticeship Act (29 U.S.C. 50).

(9) TREATMENT OF QUALIFIED EDUCATION LOAN REPAYMENTS.—

(A) IN GENERAL.—Any reference in this subsection to the term "qualified higher education expense" shall include a reference to amounts paid as principal or interest on any qualified education loan (as defined in section 221(d)) of the designated beneficiary or a sibling of the designated beneficiary.

(B) LIMITATION.—The amount of distributions treated as a qualified higher education expense under this paragraph with respect to the loans of any individual shall not exceed $10,000 (reduced by the amount of distributions so treated for all prior taxable years).

(C) SPECIAL RULES FOR SIBLINGS OF THE DESIGNATED BENEFICIARY.—

(i) SEPARATE ACCOUNTING.—For purposes of subparagraph (B) and subsection (d), amounts treated as a qualified higher education expense with respect to the loans of a sibling of the designated beneficiary shall be taken into account with respect to such sibling and not with respect to such designated beneficiary.

(ii) SIBLING DEFINED.—For purposes of this paragraph, the term "sibling" means an individual who bears a relationship to the designated beneficiary which is described in section 152(d)(2)(B).

Amendments

• 2022, SECURE 2.0 Act of 2022 (P.L. 117-328)

P.L. 117-328, §126(a):

Amended Code Sec. 529(c)(3) by adding at the end a new subparagraph (E). **Effective** with respect to distributions after 12-31-2023.

• 2019, Setting Every Community Up for Retirement Enhancement Act of 2019 (P.L. 116-94)

P.L. 116-94, §302(a), Div. O:

Amended Code Sec. 529(c) by adding at the end a new paragraph (8). **Effective** for distributions made after 12-31-2018.

P.L. 116-94, §302(b)(1), Div. O:

Amended Code Sec. 529(c), as amended by Act Sec. 302(a), by adding at the end a new paragraph (9). **Effective** for distributions made after 12-31-2018.

• 2018, Tax Technical Corrections Act of 2018 (P.L. 115-141)

P.L. 115-141, §101(l)(15), Div. U:

Amended the heading of Code Sec. 529(c)(3)(B)(v) by striking "HOPE" and inserting "AMERICAN OPPORTUNITY". **Effective** as if included in the provision of the Protecting Americans from Tax Hikes Act of 2015 to which it relates [**effective** for tax years beginning after 12-18-2015.—CCH].

P.L. 115-141, §401(a)(127), Div. U:

Amended Code Sec. 529(c)(6) by striking "an Coverdell" and inserting "a Coverdell". **Effective** 3-23-2018.

• 2017, Tax Cuts and Jobs Act (P.L. 115-97)

P.L. 115-97, §11025(a):

Amended Code Sec. 529(c)(3)(C)(i) by striking "or" at the end of subclause (I), by striking the period at the end of subclause (II) and inserting ", or", and by adding at the end a new subclause (III) and a new flush sentence. **Effective** for distributions after 12-22-2017.

P.L. 115-97, §11032(a)(1):

Amended Code Sec. 529(c) by adding at the end a new paragraph (7). **Effective** for distributions made after 12-31-2017.

• 2015, Protecting Americans from Tax Hikes Act of 2015 (P.L. 114-113)

P.L. 114-113, §302(b)(1), Div. Q:

Amended Code Sec. 529(c)(3) by striking subparagraph (D). **Effective** for distributions after 12-31-2014. Prior to being stricken, Code Sec. 529(c)(3)(D) read as follows:

(D) OPERATING RULES.—For purposes of applying section 72—

(i) to the extent provided by the Secretary, all qualified tuition programs of which an individual is a designated beneficiary shall be treated as one program,

(ii) except to the extent provided by the Secretary, all distributions during a taxable year shall be treated as one distribution, and

(iii) except to the extent provided by the Secretary, the value of the contract, income on the contract, and investment in the contract shall be computed as of the close of the calendar year in which the taxable year begins.

P.L. 114-113, §302(c)(1), Div. Q:

Amended Code Sec. 529(c)(3), as amended by Act Sec. 302(b)(1), by adding at the end a new subparagraph (D). **Effective** generally with respect to refunds of qualified higher education expenses after 12-31-2014. For a transitional rule, see Act Sec. 302(c)(2)(B), below.

P.L. 114-113, §302(c)(2)(B), Div. Q, provides:

(B) TRANSITION RULE.—In the case of a refund of qualified higher education expenses received after December 31, 2014, and before the date of the enactment of this Act, section 529(c)(3)(D) of the Internal Revenue Code of 1986 (as added by this subsection) shall be applied by substituting "not later than 60 days after the date of the enactment of this subparagraph" for "not later than 60 days after the date of such refund".

• 2006, Pension Protection Act of 2006 (P.L. 109-280)

P.L. 109-280, §1304(a), provides:

(a) PERMANENT EXTENSION OF MODIFICATIONS.—Section 901 of the Economic Growth and Tax Relief Reconciliation Act of 2001 [P.L. 107-16] (relating to sunset provisions) shall not apply to section 402 of such Act (relating to modifications to qualified tuition programs).

•2005, Gulf Opportunity Zone Act of 2005 (P.L. 109-135)

P.L. 109-135, §412(ee)(3):

Amended Code Sec. 529(c)(6) by striking "education individual retirement account" and inserting "Coverdell education savings account". **Effective** 12-21-2005.

• 2004, Working Families Tax Relief Act of 2004 (P.L. 108-311)

P.L. 108-311, §406(a):

Amended Code Sec. 529(c)(5)(B). **Effective** as if included in the provision of the Taxpayer Relief Act of 1997 (P.L. 105-34) to which it relates [**effective** for transfers (including designations of new beneficiaries) made after 8-5-97.—CCH]. Prior to amendment, Code Sec. 529(c)(5)(B) read as follows:

(B) TREATMENT OF DESIGNATION OF NEW BENEFICIARY.—The taxes imposed by chapters 12 and 13 shall apply to a transfer by reason of a change in the designated beneficiary under the program (or a rollover to the account of a new beneficiary) only if the new beneficiary is a generation below the generation of the old beneficiary (determined in accordance with section 2651).

• 2001 (P.L. 107-22)

P.L. 107-22, §1(b)(3)(C):

Amended the heading for Code Sec. 529(c)(3)(B)(vi) by striking "EDUCATION INDIVIDUAL RETIREMENT" and inserting "COVERDELL EDUCATION SAVINGS". **Effective** 7-26-2001.

• 2001, Economic Growth and Tax Relief Reconciliation Act of 2001 (P.L. 107-16)

P.L. 107-16, §402(a)(3)(B):

Amended Code Sec. 529 by adding at the end of subsection (c) a new paragraph (6). **Effective** for tax years beginning after 12-31-2001.

P.L. 107-16, §402(a)(4)(A):

Amended Code Sec. 529 by striking "qualified State tuition" each place it appears and inserting "qualified tuition". **Effective** for tax years beginning after 12-31-2001.

P.L. 107-16, §402(b)(1):

Amended Code Sec. 529(c)(3)(B). **Effective** for tax years beginning after 12-31-2001. Prior to amendment, Code Sec. 529(c)(3)(B) read as follows:

(B) IN-KIND DISTRIBUTIONS.—Any benefit furnished to a designated beneficiary under a qualified State tuition program shall be treated as a distribution to the beneficiary.

P.L. 107-16, §402(c)(1)-(3):

Amended Code Sec. 529(c)(3)(C) by striking "transferred to the credit" in clause (i) and inserting "transferred—" and new subclauses (I) and (II), by adding at the end a new clause (iii), and by inserting "OR PROGRAMS" after "BENEFICIARIES" in the heading. **Effective** for tax years beginning after 12-31-2001.

P.L. 107-16, §402(g)(1)-(2):

Amended Code Sec. 529(c)(3)(D) by inserting "except to the extent provided by the Secretary," before "all distributions" in clause (ii), and by inserting "except to the extent provided by the Secretary," before "the value" in clause (iii). **Effective** for tax years beginning after 12-31-2001.

P.L. 107-16, §901(a)-(b), as amended by P.L. 111-312, §101(a)(1), provides [but see P.L. 109-280, §1304(a), above]:

SEC. 901. SUNSET OF PROVISIONS OF ACT.

(a) IN GENERAL.—All provisions of, and amendments made by, this Act shall not apply—

(1) to taxable, plan, or limitation years beginning after December 31, 2012, or

(2) in the case of title V, to estates of decedents dying, gifts made, or generation skipping transfers, after December 31, 2012.

(b) APPLICATION OF CERTAIN LAWS.—The Internal Revenue Code of 1986 and the Employee Retirement Income Security Act of 1974 shall be applied and administered to years, estates, gifts, and transfers described in subsection (a) as if the provisions and amendments described in subsection (a) had never been enacted.

• 1998, IRS Restructuring and Reform Act of 1998 (P.L. 105-206)

P.L. 105-206, §6004(c)(2):

Amended Code Sec. 529(c)(3)(A) by striking "section 72(b)" and inserting "section 72". **Effective** as if included in the provision of P.L. 105-34 to which it relates [generally **effective** 1-1-98.—CCH].

• 1997, Taxpayer Relief Act of 1997 (P.L. 105-34)

P.L. 105-34, §211(b)(3)(A)(i):

Amended Code Sec. 529(c)(2). **Effective** for transfers (including designations of new beneficiaries) made after 8-5-97. Prior to amendment, Code Sec. 529(c)(2) read as follows:

(2) CONTRIBUTIONS.—In no event shall a contribution to a qualified State tuition program on behalf of a designated beneficiary be treated as a taxable gift for purposes of chapter 12.

P.L. 105-34, §211(b)(3)(A)(ii):

Amended Code Sec. 529(c)(5). **Effective** for transfers (including designations of new beneficiaries) made after 8-5-97. Prior to amendment, Code Sec. 529(c)(5) read as follows:

(5) SPECIAL RULE FOR APPLYING SECTION 2503(e).—For purposes of section 2503(e), the waiver (or payment to an educational institution) of qualified higher education expenses of a designated beneficiary under a qualified State tuition program shall be treated as a qualified transfer.

P.L. 105-34, §211(b)(3)(B):

Amended Code Sec. 529(c)(4). **Effective** for estates of decedents dying after 6-8-97. Prior to amendment, Code Sec. 529(c)(4) read as follows:

(4) ESTATE TAX INCLUSION.—The value of any interest in any qualified State tuition program which is attributable to contributions made by an individual to such program on behalf of any designated beneficiary shall be includible in the gross estate of the contributor for purposes of chapter 11.

P.L. 105-34, §211(d):

Amended Code Sec. 529(c)(3)(A) by striking "section 72" and inserting "section 72(b)". **Effective**, generally, 1-1-98. For a transitional rule, see Act Sec. 211(f)(6), below.

P.L. 105-34, §211(f)(6), provides:

(6) TRANSITION RULE FOR PRE-AUGUST 20, 1996 CONTRACTS.—In the case of any contract issued prior to August 20, 1996, section 529(c)(3)(C) of the Internal Revenue Code of 1986 shall be applied for taxable years ending after August 20, 1996, without regard to the requirement that a distribution be transferred to a member of the family or the requirement that a change in beneficiaries may be made only to a member of the family.

Caution: Code Sec. 529(d), below, prior to amendment by P.L. 117-328, applies with respect to distributions on or before December 31, 2023.

[Sec. 529(d)]

(d) REPORTS.—Each officer or employee having control of the qualified tuition program or their designee shall make such reports regarding such program to the Secretary and to designated beneficiaries with respect to contributions, distributions, and such other matters as the Secretary may require. The reports required by this subsection shall be filed at such time and in such manner and furnished to such individuals at such time and in such manner as may be required by the Secretary.

Caution: Code Sec. 529(d), below, as amended by P.L. 117-328, applies with respect to distributions after December 31, 2023.

[Sec. 529(d)]

(d) REPORTS.—

(1) IN GENERAL.—Each officer or employee having control of the qualified tuition program or their designee shall make such reports regarding such program to the Secretary and to designated beneficiaries with respect to contributions, distributions, and such other matters as the Secretary may require. The reports required by this paragraph shall be filed at such time and in such manner and furnished to such individuals at such time and in such manner as may be required by the Secretary.

(2) ROLLOVER DISTRIBUTIONS.—In the case of any distribution described in subsection (c)(3)(E), the officer or employee having control of the qualified tuition program (or their designee) shall provide a report to the trustee of the Roth IRA to which the distribution is made. Such report shall be filed at such time and in such manner as the Secretary may require and shall include information with respect to the contributions, distributions, and earnings of the qualified tuition program as of the date of the distribution described in subsection (c)(3)(A), together with such other matters as the Secretary may require.

Amendments

• 2022, SECURE 2.0 Act of 2022 (P.L. 117-328)

P.L. 117-328, §126(c)(1)-(3):

Amended Code Sec. 529(d) by striking "Each officer" and inserting

"(1) IN GENERAL.—Each officer",

by striking "by this subsection" and inserting "by this paragraph", and by adding at the end a new paragraph (2). **Effective** with respect to distributions after 12-31-2023.

• 2006, Pension Protection Act of 2006 (P.L. 109-280)

P.L. 109-280, §1304(a), provides:

(a) PERMANENT EXTENSION OF MODIFICATIONS.—Section 901 of the Economic Growth and Tax Relief Reconciliation Act of 2001 [P.L. 107-16] (relating to sunset provisions) shall not apply to section 402 of such Act (relating to modifications to qualified tuition programs).

• 2001, Economic Growth and Tax Relief Reconciliation Act of 2001 (P.L. 107-16)

P.L. 107-16, §402(a)(4)(A):

Amended Code Sec. 529 by striking "qualified State tuition" each place it appears and inserting "qualified tuition". **Effective** for tax years beginning after 12-31-2001.

P.L. 107-16, §901(a)-(b), as amended by P.L. 111-312, §101(a)(1), provides [but see P.L. 109-280, §1304(a), above]:

SEC. 901. SUNSET OF PROVISIONS OF ACT.

(a) IN GENERAL.—All provisions of, and amendments made by, this Act shall not apply—

(1) to taxable, plan, or limitation years beginning after December 31, 2012, or

(2) in the case of title V, to estates of decedents dying, gifts made, or generation skipping transfers, after December 31, 2012.

(b) APPLICATION OF CERTAIN LAWS.—The Internal Revenue Code of 1986 and the Employee Retirement Income Security Act of 1974 shall be applied and administered to years, estates, gifts, and transfers described in subsection (a) as if the provisions and amendments described in subsection (a) had never been enacted.

• 1997, Taxpayer Relief Act of 1997 (P.L. 105-34)

P.L. 105-34, §211(e)(2)(A):

Amended Code Sec. 529(d). **Effective** 1-1-98. Prior to amendment, Code Sec. 529(d) read as follows:

(d) REPORTING REQUIREMENTS.—

(1) IN GENERAL.—If there is a distribution to any individual with respect to an interest in a qualified State tuition program during any calendar year, each officer or employee having control of the qualified State tuition program or their designee shall make such reports as the Secretary may require regarding such distribution to the Secretary and to the designated beneficiary or the individual to whom the distribution was made. Any such report shall include such information as the Secretary may prescribe.

(2) TIMING OF REPORTS.—Any report required by this subsection—

(A) shall be filed at such time and in such matter as the Secretary prescribes, and

(B) shall be furnished to individuals not later than January 31 of the calendar year following the calendar year to which such report relates.

[Sec. 529(e)]

(e) OTHER DEFINITIONS AND SPECIAL RULES.—For purposes of this section—

(1) DESIGNATED BENEFICIARY.—The term "designated beneficiary" means—

(A) the individual designated at the commencement of participation in the qualified tuition program as the beneficiary of amounts paid (or to be paid) to the program,

(B) in the case of a change in beneficiaries described in subsection (c)(3)(C), the individual who is the new beneficiary, and

(C) in the case of an interest in a qualified tuition program purchased by a State or local government (or agency or instrumentality thereof) or an organization described in section 501(c)(3) and exempt from taxation under section 501(a) as part of a scholarship program operated by such government or organization, the individual receiving such interest as a scholarship.

(2) MEMBER OF FAMILY.—The term "member of the family" means, with respect to any designated beneficiary—

(A) the spouse of such beneficiary;

(B) an individual who bears a relationship to such beneficiary which is described in subparagraphs (A) through (G) of section 152(d)(2);

(C) the spouse of any individual described in subparagraph (B); and

(D) any first cousin of such beneficiary.

(3) QUALIFIED HIGHER EDUCATION EXPENSES.—

(A) IN GENERAL.—The term "qualified higher education expenses" means—

(i) tuition, fees, books, supplies, and equipment required for the enrollment or attendance of a designated beneficiary at an eligible educational institution,

(ii) expenses for special needs services in the case of a special needs beneficiary which are incurred in connection with such enrollment or attendance, and

(iii) expenses for the purchase of computer or peripheral equipment (as defined in section 168(i)(2)(B)), computer software (as defined in section 197(e)(3)(B)), or Internet access and related services, if such equipment, software, or services are to be used primarily by the beneficiary during any of the years the beneficiary is enrolled at an eligible educational institution.

Clause (iii) shall not include expenses for computer software designed for sports, games, or hobbies unless the software is predominantly educational in nature. The amount of cash distributions from all qualified tuition programs described in subsection (b)(1)(A)(ii) with respect to a beneficiary during any taxable year shall, in the aggregate, include not more than $10,000 in expenses described in subsection (c)(7) incurred during the taxable year.

(B) ROOM AND BOARD INCLUDED FOR STUDENTS WHO ARE AT LEAST HALF-TIME.—

(i) IN GENERAL.—In the case of an individual who is an eligible student (as defined in section 25A(b)(3)) for any academic period, such term shall also include reasonable costs for such period (as determined under the qualified tuition program) incurred by the designated beneficiary for room and board while attending such institution. For purposes of subsection (b)(6), a designated beneficiary shall be treated as meeting the requirements of this clause.

(ii) LIMITATION.—The amount treated as qualified higher education expenses by reason of clause (i) shall not exceed—

(I) the allowance (applicable to the student) for room and board included in the cost of attendance (as defined in section 472 of the Higher Education Act of 1965 (20 U.S.C. 1087ll), as in effect on the date of the enactment of the Economic Growth and Tax Relief Reconciliation Act of 2001) as determined by the eligible educational institution for such period, or

(II) if greater, the actual invoice amount the student residing in housing owned or operated by the eligible educational institution is charged by such institution for room and board costs for such period.

(4) APPLICATION OF SECTION 514.—An interest in a qualified tuition program shall not be treated as debt for purposes of section 514.

(5) ELIGIBLE EDUCATIONAL INSTITUTION.—The term "eligible educational institution" means an institution—

(A) which is described in section 481 of the Higher Education Act of 1965 (20 U.S.C. 1088), as in effect on the date of the enactment of this paragraph, and

(B) which is eligible to participate in a program under title IV of such Act.

Amendments

• 2018, Tax Technical Corrections Act of 2018 (P.L. 115-141)

P.L. 115-141, §401(a)(128)(A)-(B), Div. U:

Amended Code Sec. 529(e)(3)(A) by striking the semicolon at the end of clause (i) and inserting a comma, and by adding ", and" at the end of clause (ii). **Effective** 3-23-2018.

• 2017, Tax Cuts and Jobs Act (P.L. 115-97)

P.L. 115-97, §11032(a)(2):

Amended Code Sec. 529(e)(3)(A) by adding at the end a new sentence. **Effective** for distributions made after 12-31-2017.

• 2015, Protecting Americans from Tax Hikes Act of 2015 (P.L. 114-113)

P.L. 114-113, §302(a)(1), Div. Q:

Amended Code Sec. 529(e)(3)(A)(iii). **Effective** for tax years beginning after 12-31-2014. Prior to amendment, Code Sec. 529(e)(3)(A)(iii) read as follows:

(iii) expenses paid or incurred in 2009 or 2010 for the purchase of any computer technology or equipment (as defined in section 170(e)(6)(F)(i)) or Internet access and related services, if such technology, equipment, or services are to be used by the beneficiary and the beneficiary's family during any of the years the beneficiary is enrolled at an eligible educational institution.

• 2009, American Recovery and Reinvestment Tax Act of 2009 (P.L. 111-5)

P.L. 111-5, §1005(a):

Amended Code Sec. 529(e)(3)(A) by striking "and" at the end of clause (i), by striking the period at the end of clause (ii), and by adding at the end a new clause (iii) and flush sentence. **Effective** for expenses paid or incurred after 12-31-2008.

• 2006, Pension Protection Act of 2006 (P.L. 109-280)

P.L. 109-280, §1304(a), provides:

(a) PERMANENT EXTENSION OF MODIFICATIONS.—Section 901 of the Economic Growth and Tax Relief Reconciliation Act of 2001 [P.L. 107-16] (relating to sunset provisions) shall not apply to section 402 of such Act (relating to modifications to qualified tuition programs).

• 2004, Working Families Tax Relief Act of 2004 (P.L. 108-311)

P.L. 108-311, §207(21):

Amended Code Sec. 529(e)(2)(B) by striking "paragraphs (1) through (8) of section 152(a)" and inserting "subparagraphs (A) through (G) of section 152(d)(2)". **Effective** for tax years beginning after 12-31-2004.

• 2002, Job Creation and Worker Assistance Act of 2002 (P.L. 107-147)

P.L. 107-147, §417(11):

Amended Code Sec. 529(e)(3)(B)(i) by striking "subsection (b)(7)" and inserting "subsection (b)(6)". **Effective** 3-9-2002.

• 2001, Economic Growth and Tax Relief Reconciliation Act of 2001 (P.L. 107-16)

P.L. 107-16, §402(a)(4)(A):

Amended Code Sec. 529 by striking "qualified State tuition" each place it appears and inserting "qualified tuition". **Effective** for tax years beginning after 12-31-2001.

P.L. 107-16, §402(d):

Amended Code Sec. 529(e)(2) by striking "and" at the end of subparagraph (B), by striking the period at the end of subparagraph (C) and by inserting "; and", and by adding at the end a new subparagraph (D). **Effective** for tax years beginning after 12-31-2001.

P.L. 107-16, §402(e):

Amended Code Sec. 529(e)(3)(B)(ii). **Effective** for tax years beginning after 12-31-2001. Prior to amendment, Code Sec. 529(e)(3)(B)(ii) read as follows:

(ii) LIMITATION.—The amount treated as qualified higher education expenses by reason of the preceding sentence shall not exceed the minimum amount (applicable to the student) included for room and board for such period in the cost of attendance (as defined in section 472 of the Higher Education Act of 1965, 20 U.S.C. 1087ll, as in effect on the date of the enactment of this paragraph) for the eligible educational institution for such period.

P.L. 107-16, §402(f):

Amended Code Sec. 529(e)(3)(A). **Effective** for tax years beginning after 12-31-2001. Prior to amendment, Code Sec. 529(e)(3)(A) read as follows:

(A) IN GENERAL.—The term "qualified higher education expenses" means tuition, fees, books, supplies, and equipment required for the enrollment or attendance of a designated beneficiary at an eligible educational institution.

P.L. 107-16, §901(a)-(b), as amended by P.L. 111-312, §101(a)(1), provides [but see 109-280, §1304(a), above]:

SEC. 901. SUNSET OF PROVISIONS OF ACT.

(a) IN GENERAL.—All provisions of, and amendments made by, this Act shall not apply—

(1) to taxable, plan, or limitation years beginning after December 31, 2012, or

(2) in the case of title V, to estates of decedents dying, gifts made, or generation skipping transfers, after December 31, 2012.

(b) APPLICATION OF CERTAIN LAWS.—The Internal Revenue Code of 1986 and the Employee Retirement Income Security Act of 1974 shall be applied and administered to years, estates, gifts, and transfers described in subsection (a) as if the provisions and amendments described in subsection (a) had never been enacted.

• 2000, Community Renewal Tax Relief Act of 2000 (P.L. 106-554)

P.L. 106-554, §319(5):

Amended the heading for Code Sec. 529(e)(3)(B) by striking "UNDER GUARANTEED PLANS" after "STUDENTS". **Effective** 12-21-2000.

• 1998, IRS Restructuring and Reform Act of 1998 (P.L. 105-206)

P.L. 105-206, §6004(c)(3):

Amended Code Sec. 529(e)(2). **Effective** as if included in the provision of P.L. 105-34 to which it relates [generally **effective** 1-1-98.—CCH]. Prior to amendment, Code Sec. 529(e)(2) read as follows:

(2) MEMBER OF FAMILY.—The term "member of the family" means—

(A) an individual who bears a relationship to another individual which is a relationship described in paragraphs (1) through (8) of section 152(a), and

(B) the spouse of any individual described in subparagraph (A).

• 1997, Taxpayer Relief Act of 1997 (P.L. 105-34)

P.L. 105-34, §211(a):

Amended Code Sec. 529(e)(3). **Effective** as if included in the amendments made by Act Sec. 1806 of P.L. 104-188 [generally **effective** for tax years ending after 8-20-96.—CCH]. Prior to amendment, Code Sec. 529(e)(3) read as follows:

(3) QUALIFIED HIGHER EDUCATION EXPENSES.—The term "qualified higher education expenses" means tuition, fees, books, supplies, and equipment required for the enrollment or attendance of a designated beneficiary at an eligible educational institution (as defined in section 135(c)(3)).

P.L. 105-34, §211(b)(1):

Amended Code Sec. 529(e)(2). **Effective** 1-1-98. Prior to amendment, Code Sec. 529(e)(2) read as follows:

(2) MEMBER OF FAMILY.—The term "member of the family" has the same meaning given such term as section 2032A(e)(2).

P.L. 105-34, §211(b)(2):

Amended Code Sec. 529(e) by adding a new paragraph (5). **Effective** for distributions after 12-31-97, with respect to expenses paid after such date (in tax years ending after such date), for education furnished in academic periods beginning after such date. For a transitional rule, see Act Sec. 211(f)(6), below.

P.L. 105-34, §211(f)(6), provides:

(6) TRANSITION RULE FOR PRE-AUGUST 20, 1996 CONTRACTS.—In the case of any contract issued prior to August 20, 1996, section 529(c)(3)(C) of the Internal Revenue Code of 1986 shall be applied for taxable years ending after August 20, 1996, without regard to the requirement that a distribution be transferred to a member of the family or the requirement that a change in beneficiaries may be made only to a member of the family.

P.L. 105-34, §1601(h)(1)(A):

Amended Code Sec. 529(e)(1)(B) by striking "subsection (c)(2)(C)" and inserting "subsection (c)(3)(C)". **Effective** as if included in the provision of P.L. 104-188 to which it relates [generally **effective** for tax years ending after 8-20-96.—CCH].

P.L. 105-34, §1601(h)(1)(B):

Amended Code Sec. 529(e)(1)(C) by inserting "(or agency or instrumentality thereof)" after "local government". **Effective** as if included in the provision of P.L. 104-188 to which it relates [generally **effective** for tax years ending after 8-20-96.—CCH].

• 1996, Small Business Job Protection Act of 1996 (P.L. 104-188)

P.L. 104-188, §1806(a):

Amended subchapter F of chapter 1 by adding at the end a new part VIII (Code Sec. 529). **Effective** for tax years ending after 8-20-96. For a transitional rule, see Act Sec. 1806(c)(2), below.

P.L. 104-188, §1806(c)(2), as amended by P.L. 105-34, §1601(h)(1)(C), provides:

(2) TRANSITION RULE.—If—

(A) a State or agency or instrumentality thereof maintains, on the date of the enactment of this Act, a program under which persons may purchase tuition credits or certificates on behalf of, or make contributions for education expenses of, a designated beneficiary, and

(B) such program meets the requirements of a qualified State tuition program before the later of—

(i) the date which is 1 year after such date of enactment, or

(ii) the first day of the first calendar quarter after the close of the first regular session of the State legislature that begins after such date of enactment,

then such program (as in effect on August 20, 1996) shall be treated as a qualified State tuition program with respect to contributions (and earnings allocable thereto) pursuant to contracts entered into under such program before the first date on which such program meets such requirements (determined without regard to this paragraph) and the provisions of such program (as so in effect) shall apply in lieu of section 529(b) of the Internal Revenue Code of 1986 with respect to such contributions and earnings.

For purposes of subparagraph (B)(ii), if a State has a 2-year legislative session, each year of such session shall be deemed to be a separate regular session of the State legislature.

[Sec. 529(f)]

(f) REGULATIONS.—Notwithstanding any other provision of this section, the Secretary shall prescribe such regulations as may be necessary or appropriate to carry out the purposes of this section and to prevent abuse of such purposes, including regulations under chapters 11, 12, and 13 of this title.

Amendments

• 2006, Pension Protection Act of 2006 (P.L. 109-280)

P.L. 109-280, §1304(b):

Amended Code Sec. 529 by adding at the end a new subsection (f). **Effective** 8-17-2006.

[Sec. 529A]

SEC. 529A. QUALIFIED ABLE PROGRAMS.

[Sec. 529A(a)]

(a) GENERAL RULE.—A qualified ABLE program shall be exempt from taxation under this subtitle. Notwithstanding the preceding sentence, such program shall be subject to the taxes imposed by section 511 (relating to imposition of tax on unrelated business income of charitable organizations).

[Sec. 529A(b)]

(b) QUALIFIED ABLE PROGRAM.—For purposes of this section—

(1) IN GENERAL.—The term "qualified ABLE program" means a program established and maintained by a State, or agency or instrumentality thereof—

(A) under which a person may make contributions for a taxable year, for the benefit of an individual who is an eligible individual for such taxable year, to an ABLE account which is established for the purpose of meeting the qualified disability expenses of the designated beneficiary of the account,

(B) which limits a designated beneficiary to 1 ABLE account for purposes of this section, and

(C) which meets the other requirements of this section.

(2) CASH CONTRIBUTIONS.—A program shall not be treated as a qualified ABLE program unless it provides that no contribution will be accepted—

(A) unless it is in cash, or

(B) except in the case of contributions under subsection (c)(1)(C), if such contribution to an ABLE account would result in aggregate contributions from all contributors to the ABLE account for the taxable year exceeding the sum of—

(i) the amount in effect under section 2503(b) for the calendar year in which the taxable year begins, plus

(ii) in the case of any contribution by a designated beneficiary described in paragraph (7) before January 1, 2026, the lesser of—

(I) compensation (as defined by section 219(f)(1)) includible in the designated beneficiary's gross income for the taxable year, or

(II) an amount equal to the poverty line for a one-person household, as determined for the calendar year preceding the calendar year in which the taxable year begins.

For purposes of this paragraph, rules similar to the rules of section 408(d)(4) (determined without regard to subparagraph (B) thereof) shall apply. A designated beneficiary (or a person acting on behalf of such beneficiary) shall maintain adequate records for purposes of ensuring, and shall be responsible for ensuring, that the requirements of subparagraph (B)(ii) are met.

(3) SEPARATE ACCOUNTING.—A program shall not be treated as a qualified ABLE program unless it provides separate accounting for each designated beneficiary.

(4) LIMITED INVESTMENT DIRECTION.—A program shall not be treated as a qualified ABLE program unless it provides that any designated beneficiary under such program may, directly or indirectly, direct the investment of any contributions to the program (or any earnings thereon) no more than 2 times in any calendar year.

(5) NO PLEDGING OF INTEREST AS SECURITY.—A program shall not be treated as a qualified ABLE program if it allows any interest in the program or any portion thereof to be used as security for a loan.

(6) PROHIBITION ON EXCESS CONTRIBUTIONS.—A program shall not be treated as a qualified ABLE program unless it provides adequate safeguards to prevent aggregate contributions on behalf of a designated beneficiary in excess of the limit established by the State under section 529(b)(6). For purposes of the preceding sentence, aggregate contributions include contributions under any prior qualified ABLE program of any State or agency or instrumentality thereof.

(7) SPECIAL RULES RELATED TO CONTRIBUTION LIMIT.—For purposes of paragraph (2)(B)(ii)—

(A) DESIGNATED BENEFICIARY.—A designated beneficiary described in this paragraph is an employee (including an employee within the meaning of section 401(c)) with respect to whom—

(i) no contribution is made for the taxable year to a defined contribution plan (within the meaning of section 414(i)) with respect to which the requirements of section 401(a) or 403(a) are met,

(ii) no contribution is made for the taxable year to an annuity contract described in section 403(b), and

(iii) no contribution is made for the taxable year to an eligible deferred compensation plan described in section 457(b).

(B) POVERTY LINE.—The term "poverty line" has the meaning given such term by section 673 of the Community Services Block Grant Act (42 U.S.C. 9902).

Amendments

• 2017, Tax Cuts and Jobs Act (P.L. 115-97)

P.L. 115-97, §11024(a)(1):

Amended Code Sec. 529A(b)(2)(B). **Effective** for tax years beginning after 12-22-2017. Prior to amendment, Code Sec. 529A(b)(2)(B) read as follows:

(B) except in the case of contributions under subsection (c)(1)(C), if such contribution to an ABLE account would result in aggregate contributions from all contributors to the ABLE account for the taxable year exceeding the amount in effect under section 2503(b) for the calendar year in which the taxable year begins.

P.L. 115-97, §11024(a)(2):

Amended Code Sec. 529A(b)(2) by adding at the end a new sentence. **Effective** for tax years beginning after 12-22-2017.

P.L. 115-97, §11024(a)(3):

Amended Code Sec. 529A(b) by adding at the end a new paragraph (7). **Effective** for tax years beginning after 12-22-2017.

• 2015, Protecting Americans from Tax Hikes Act of 2015 (P.L. 114-113)

P.L. 114-113, §303(a), Div. Q:

Amended Code Sec. 529A(b)(1) by striking subparagraph (C), by inserting "and" at the end of subparagraph (B), and by redesignating subparagraph (D) as subparagraph (C). **Effective** for tax years beginning after 12-31-2014. Prior to being stricken, Code Sec. 529A(b)(1)(C) read as follows:

(C) which allows for the establishment of an ABLE account only for a designated beneficiary who is a resident of such State or a resident of a contracting State, and

[Sec. 529A(c)]

(c) TAX TREATMENT.—

(1) DISTRIBUTIONS.—

(A) IN GENERAL.—Any distribution under a qualified ABLE program shall be includible in the gross income of the distributee in the manner as provided under section 72 to the extent not excluded from gross income under any other provision of this chapter.

(B) DISTRIBUTIONS FOR QUALIFIED DISABILITY EXPENSES.—For purposes of this paragraph, if distributions from a qualified ABLE program—

(i) do not exceed the qualified disability expenses of the designated beneficiary, no amount shall be includible in gross income, and

(ii) in any other case, the amount otherwise includible in gross income shall be reduced by an amount which bears the same ratio to such amount as such expenses bear to such distributions.

(C) CHANGE IN DESIGNATED BENEFICIARIES OR PROGRAMS.—

(i) ROLLOVERS FROM ABLE ACCOUNTS.—Subparagraph (A) shall not apply to any amount paid or distributed from an ABLE account to the extent that the amount received is paid, not later than the 60th day after the date of such payment or distribution, into another ABLE account for the benefit of the same designated beneficiary or an eligible individual who is a member of the family of the designated beneficiary.

(ii) CHANGE IN DESIGNATED BENEFICIARIES.—Any change in the designated beneficiary of an interest in a qualified ABLE program during a taxable year shall not be treated as a distribution for purposes of subparagraph (A) if the new beneficiary is an eligible individual for such taxable year and a member of the family of the former beneficiary.

(iii) LIMITATION ON CERTAIN ROLLOVERS.—Clause (i) shall not apply to any transfer if such transfer occurs within 12 months from the date of a previous transfer to any qualified ABLE program for the benefit of the designated beneficiary.

(2) GIFT TAX RULES.—For purposes of chapters 12 and 13—

(A) CONTRIBUTIONS.—Any contribution to a qualified ABLE program on behalf of any designated beneficiary—

(i) shall be treated as a completed gift to such designated beneficiary which is not a future interest in property, and

(ii) shall not be treated as a qualified transfer under section 2503(e).

(B) TREATMENT OF DISTRIBUTIONS.—In no event shall a distribution from an ABLE account to such account's designated beneficiary be treated as a taxable gift.

(C) TREATMENT OF TRANSFER TO NEW DESIGNATED BENEFICIARY.—The taxes imposed by chapters 12 and 13 shall not apply to a transfer by reason of a change in the designated beneficiary under subsection (c)(1)(C).

(3) ADDITIONAL TAX FOR DISTRIBUTIONS NOT USED FOR DISABILITY EXPENSES.—

(A) IN GENERAL.—The tax imposed by this chapter for any taxable year on any taxpayer who receives a distribution from a qualified ABLE program which is includible in gross income shall be increased by 10 percent of the amount which is so includible.

(B) EXCEPTION.—Subparagraph (A) shall not apply if the payment or distribution is made to a beneficiary (or to the estate of the designated beneficiary) on or after the death of the designated beneficiary.

(C) CONTRIBUTIONS RETURNED BEFORE CERTAIN DATE.—Subparagraph (A) shall not apply to the distribution of any contribution made during a taxable year on behalf of the designated beneficiary if—

(i) such distribution is received on or before the day prescribed by law (including extensions of time) for filing such designated beneficiary's return for such taxable year, and

(ii) such distribution is accompanied by the amount of net income attributable to such excess contribution.

Any net income described in clause (ii) shall be included in gross income for the taxable year in which such excess contribution was made.

(4) LOSS OF ABLE ACCOUNT TREATMENT.—If an ABLE account is established for a designated beneficiary, no account subsequently established for such beneficiary shall be treated as an ABLE account. The preceding sentence shall not apply in the case of an account established for purposes of a rollover described in paragraph (1)(C)(i) of this section if the transferor account is closed as of the end of the 60th day referred to in paragraph (1)(C)(i).

Amendments

• 2018, Tax Technical Corrections Act of 2018 (P.L. 115-141)

P.L. 115-141, §101(o), Div. U:

Amended Code Sec. 529A(c)(1) by striking subparagraph (D). **Effective** as if included in the provision of the Protecting Americans from Tax Hikes Act of 2015 to which it relates [**effective** for distributions after 12-31-2014.—CCH]. Prior to being stricken, Code Sec. 529A(c)(1)(D) read as follows:

(D) OPERATING RULES.—For purposes of applying section 72—

(i) except to the extent provided by the Secretary, all distributions during a taxable year shall be treated as one distribution, and

(ii) except to the extent provided by the Secretary, the value of the contract, income on the contract, and investment in the contract shall be computed as of the close of the calendar year in which the taxable year begins.

• 2015, Protecting Americans from Tax Hikes Act of 2015 (P.L. 114-113)

P.L. 114-113, §303(c)(2), Div. Q:

Amended Code Sec. 529A(c)(1)(C)(i) by striking "family member" and inserting "member of the family". **Effective** for tax years beginning after 12-31-2014.

[Sec. 529A(d)]

(d) REPORTS.—

(1) IN GENERAL.—Each officer or employee having control of the qualified ABLE program or their designee shall make such reports regarding such program to the Secretary and to designated beneficiaries with respect to contributions, distributions, the return of excess contributions, and such other matters as the Secretary may require.

(2) CERTAIN AGGREGATED INFORMATION.—For research purposes, the Secretary shall make available to the public reports containing aggregate information, by diagnosis and other relevant characteristics, on contributions and distributions from the qualified ABLE program. In carrying

out the preceding sentence an item may not be made available to the public if such item can be associated with, or otherwise identify, directly or indirectly, a particular individual.

(3) NOTICE OF ESTABLISHMENT OF ABLE ACCOUNT.—A qualified ABLE program shall submit a notice to the Secretary upon the establishment of an ABLE account. Such notice shall contain the name of the designated beneficiary and such other information as the Secretary may require.

(4) ELECTRONIC DISTRIBUTION STATEMENTS.—For purposes of section 103 of the Stephen Beck, Jr., ABLE Act of 2014, States shall submit electronically on a monthly basis to the Commissioner of Social Security, in the manner specified by the Commissioner, statements on relevant distributions and account balances from all ABLE accounts.

(5) REQUIREMENTS.—The reports and notices required by paragraphs (1), (2), and (3) shall be filed at such time and in such manner and furnished to such individuals at such time and in such manner as may be required by the Secretary.

Amendments

• 2018, Tax Technical Corrections Act of 2018 (P.L. 115-141)

P.L. 115-141, §401(a)(129), Div. U:

Amended Code Sec. 529A(d)(4) by striking "Achieving a Better Life Experience Act of 2014" and inserting "Stephen Beck, Jr., ABLE Act of 2014". **Effective** 3-23-2018.

• 2015, Protecting Americans from Tax Hikes Act of 2015 (P.L. 114-113)

P.L. 114-113, §303(b)(1), Div. Q:

Amended the second sentence of Code Sec. 529A(d)(3) by striking "and State of residence" before "of the designated beneficiary". **Effective** for tax years beginning after 12-31-2014.

P.L. 114-113, §303(c)(1), Div. Q:

Amended Code Sec. 529A(d)(4) by striking "section 4" and inserting "section 103". **Effective** for tax years beginning after 12-31-2014.

Caution: Code Sec. 529A(e), below, prior to amendment by P.L. 117-328, applies to tax years beginning on or before December 31, 2025.

[Sec. 529A(e)]

(e) OTHER DEFINITIONS AND SPECIAL RULES.—For purposes of this section—

(1) ELIGIBLE INDIVIDUAL.—An individual is an eligible individual for a taxable year if during such taxable year—

(A) the individual is entitled to benefits based on blindness or disability under title II or XVI of the Social Security Act, and such blindness or disability occurred before the date on which the individual attained age 26, or

(B) a disability certification with respect to such individual is filed with the Secretary for such taxable year.

(2) DISABILITY CERTIFICATION.—

(A) IN GENERAL.—The term "disability certification" means, with respect to an individual, a certification to the satisfaction of the Secretary by the individual or the parent or guardian of the individual that—

(i) certifies that—

(I) the individual has a medically determinable physical or mental impairment, which results in marked and severe functional limitations, and which can be expected to result in death or which has lasted or can be expected to last for a continuous period of not less than 12 months, or is blind (within the meaning of section 1614(a)(2) of the Social Security Act), and

(II) such blindness or disability occurred before the date on which the individual attained age 26, and

(ii) includes a copy of the individual's diagnosis relating to the individual's relevant impairment or impairments, signed by a physician meeting the criteria of section 1861(r)(1) of the Social Security Act.

(B) RESTRICTION ON USE OF CERTIFICATION.—No inference may be drawn from a disability certification for purposes of establishing eligibility for benefits under title II, XVI, or XIX of the Social Security Act.

(3) DESIGNATED BENEFICIARY.—The term "designated beneficiary" in connection with an ABLE account established under a qualified ABLE program means the eligible individual who established an ABLE account and is the owner of such account.

(4) MEMBER OF FAMILY.—The term "member of the family" means, with respect to any designated beneficiary, an individual who bears a relationship to such beneficiary which is described in section 152(d)(2)(B). For purposes of the preceding sentence, a rule similar to the rule of section 152(f)(1)(B) shall apply.

(5) QUALIFIED DISABILITY EXPENSES.—The term "qualified disability expenses" means any expenses related to the eligible individual's blindness or disability which are made for the benefit of an eligible individual who is the designated beneficiary, including the following expenses: education, housing, transportation, employment training and support, assistive technology and

personal support services, health, prevention and wellness, financial management and administrative services, legal fees, expenses for oversight and monitoring, funeral and burial expenses, and other expenses, which are approved by the Secretary under regulations and consistent with the purposes of this section.

(6) ABLE ACCOUNT.—The term "ABLE account" means an account established by an eligible individual, owned by such eligible individual, and maintained under a qualified ABLE program.

»»→ Caution: Code Sec. 529A(e), below, as amended by P.L. 117-328, applies to tax years beginning after December 31, 2025.

[Sec. 529A(e)]

(e) OTHER DEFINITIONS AND SPECIAL RULES.—For purposes of this section—

(1) ELIGIBLE INDIVIDUAL.—An individual is an eligible individual for a taxable year if during such taxable year—

(A) the individual is entitled to benefits based on blindness or disability under title II or XVI of the Social Security Act, and such blindness or disability occurred before the date on which the individual attained age 46, or

(B) a disability certification with respect to such individual is filed with the Secretary for such taxable year.

(2) DISABILITY CERTIFICATION.—

(A) IN GENERAL.—The term "disability certification" means, with respect to an individual, a certification to the satisfaction of the Secretary by the individual or the parent or guardian of the individual that—

(i) certifies that—

(I) the individual has a medically determinable physical or mental impairment, which results in marked and severe functional limitations, and which can be expected to result in death or which has lasted or can be expected to last for a continuous period of not less than 12 months, or is blind (within the meaning of section 1614(a)(2) of the Social Security Act), and

(II) such blindness or disability occurred before the date on which the individual attained age 46, and

(ii) includes a copy of the individual's diagnosis relating to the individual's relevant impairment or impairments, signed by a physician meeting the criteria of section 1861(r)(1) of the Social Security Act.

(B) RESTRICTION ON USE OF CERTIFICATION.—No inference may be drawn from a disability certification for purposes of establishing eligibility for benefits under title II, XVI, or XIX of the Social Security Act.

(3) DESIGNATED BENEFICIARY.—The term "designated beneficiary" in connection with an ABLE account established under a qualified ABLE program means the eligible individual who established an ABLE account and is the owner of such account.

(4) MEMBER OF FAMILY.—The term "member of the family" means, with respect to any designated beneficiary, an individual who bears a relationship to such beneficiary which is described in section 152(d)(2)(B). For purposes of the preceding sentence, a rule similar to the rule of section 152(f)(1)(B) shall apply.

(5) QUALIFIED DISABILITY EXPENSES.—The term "qualified disability expenses" means any expenses related to the eligible individual's blindness or disability which are made for the benefit of an eligible individual who is the designated beneficiary, including the following expenses: education, housing, transportation, employment training and support, assistive technology and personal support services, health, prevention and wellness, financial management and administrative services, legal fees, expenses for oversight and monitoring, funeral and burial expenses, and other expenses, which are approved by the Secretary under regulations and consistent with the purposes of this section.

(6) ABLE ACCOUNT.—The term "ABLE account" means an account established by an eligible individual, owned by such eligible individual, and maintained under a qualified ABLE program.

Amendments

• 2022, SECURE 2.0 Act of 2022 (P.L. 117-328)

P.L. 117-328, §124(a):

Amended Code Sec. 529A(e) by striking "age 26" each place it appears in paragraphs (1)(A) and (2)(A)(i)(II) and inserting "age 46". **Effective** for tax years beginning after 12-31-2025.

• 2018, Tax Technical Corrections Act of 2018 (P.L. 115-141)

P.L. 115-141, §401(a)(130), Div. U:

Amended Code Sec. 529A(e)(4) by striking "subparagraph section" and inserting "section". **Effective** 3-23-2018.

• 2015, Protecting Americans from Tax Hikes Act of 2015 (P.L. 114-113)

P.L. 114-113, §303(b)(2), Div. Q:

Amended Code Sec. 529A(e) by striking paragraph (7). **Effective** for tax years beginning after 12-31-2014. Prior to being stricken, Code Sec. 529A(e)(7) read as follows:

(7) CONTRACTING STATE.—The term "contracting State" means a State without a qualified ABLE program which has entered into a contract with a State with a qualified ABLE program to provide residents of the contracting State access to a qualified ABLE program.

[Sec. 529A(f)]

(f) TRANSFER TO STATE.—Subject to any outstanding payments due for qualified disability expenses, upon the death of the designated beneficiary, all amounts remaining in the qualified ABLE account not in excess of the amount equal to the total medical assistance paid for the designated beneficiary after the establishment of the account, net of any premiums paid from the account or paid by or on behalf of the beneficiary to a Medicaid Buy-In program under any State Medicaid plan established under title XIX of the Social Security Act, shall be distributed to such State upon filing of a claim for payment by such State. For purposes of this paragraph, the State shall be a creditor of an ABLE account and not a beneficiary. Subsection (c)(3) shall not apply to a distribution under the preceding sentence.

[Sec. 529A(g)]

(g) REGULATIONS.—The Secretary shall prescribe such regulations or other guidance as the Secretary determines necessary or appropriate to carry out the purposes of this section, including regulations—

(1) to enforce the 1 ABLE account per eligible individual limit,

(2) providing for the information required to be presented to open an ABLE account,

(3) to generally define qualified disability expenses,

(4) developed in consultation with the Commissioner of Social Security, relating to disability certifications and determinations of disability, including those conditions deemed to meet the requirements of subsection (e)(1)(B),

(5) to prevent fraud and abuse with respect to amounts claimed as qualified disability expenses,

(6) under chapters 11, 12, and 13 of this title, and

(7) to allow for transfers from one ABLE account to another ABLE account.

Amendments

• 2014, Stephen Beck, Jr., Achieving a Better Life Experience Act of 2014 (P.L. 113-295)

P.L. 113-295, §102(a), Division B:

Amended subchapter F of chapter 1 by inserting after section 529 a new Code Sec. 529A. **Effective** generally for tax years beginning after 12-31-2014. For a special rule, see Act Sec. 102(f)(2), Division B, below.

P.L. 113-295, §102(f)(2), Division B, provides:

(2) REGULATIONS.—The Secretary of the Treasury (or the Secretary's designee) shall promulgate the regulations or other guidance required under section 529A(g) of the Internal Revenue Code of 1986, as added by subsection (a), not later than 6 months after the date of the enactment of this Act.

* * *

Subchapter J—Estates, Trusts, Beneficiaries, and Decedents

PART I—ESTATES, TRUSTS, AND BENEFICIARIES

Subpart A—General Rules for Taxation of Estates and Trusts

[Sec. 641]

SEC. 641. IMPOSITION OF TAX.

[Sec. 641(a)]

(a) APPLICATION OF TAX.—The tax imposed by section 1(e) shall apply to the taxable income of estates or of any kind of property held in trust, including—

(1) income accumulated in trust for the benefit of unborn or unascertained persons or persons with contingent interests, and income accumulated or held for future distribution under the terms of the will or trust;

(2) income which is to be distributed currently by the fiduciary to the beneficiaries, and income collected by a guardian of an infant which is to be held or distributed as the court may direct;

(3) income received by estates of deceased persons during the period of administration or settlement of the estate; and

(4) income which, in the discretion of the fiduciary, may be either distributed to the beneficiaries or accumulated.

Amendments

• 1977, Tax Reduction and Simplification Act of 1977 (P.L. 95-30)

P.L. 95-30, §101(d)(8):

Amended Code Sec. 641(a) by striking out "section 1(d)" and inserting in lieu thereof "section 1(e)". **Effective** for tax years beginning after 12-31-76.

• 1969, Tax Reform Act of 1969 (P.L. 91-172)

P.L. 91-172, §803(d)(3):

Amended Code Sec. 641(a) by striking out "The taxes imposed by this chapter on individuals" in the first sentence thereof and inserting "The tax imposed by section 1(d)" in lieu thereof. **Effective** for tax years beginning after 12-31-70.

[Sec. 641(b)]

(b) COMPUTATION AND PAYMENT.—The taxable income of an estate or trust shall be computed in the same manner as in the case of an individual, except as otherwise provided in this part. The tax shall be computed on such taxable income and shall be paid by the fiduciary. For purposes of this subsection, a foreign trust or foreign estate shall be treated as a nonresident alien individual who is not present in the United States at any time.

Amendments

• 1997, Taxpayer Relief Act of 1997 (P.L. 105-34)

P.L. 105-34, §1601(i)(3)(B):

Amended Code Sec. 641(b) by adding at the end a new sentence. **Effective** as if included in the provision of P.L. 104-88 to which it relates [generally **effective** for tax years beginning after 12-31-96.—CCH].

[Sec. 641(c)—Stricken]

Amendments

• 1998, IRS Restructuring and Reform Act of 1998 (P.L. 105-206)

P.L. 105-206, §6007(f)(2):

Amended Code Sec. 641 by striking subsection (c) and by redesignating subsection (d) as subsection (c). **Effective** as if included in the provision of P.L. 105-34 to which it relates [**effective** for sales or exchanges after 8-5-97.—CCH]. Prior to being stricken, Code Sec. 641(c) read as follows:

(c) EXCLUSION OF INCLUDIBLE GAIN FROM TAXABLE INCOME.—

(1) GENERAL RULE.—For purposes of this part, the taxable income of a trust does not include the amount of any includible gain as defined in section 644(b) reduced by any deductions properly allocable thereto.

(2) CROSS REFERENCE.—

For the taxation of any includible gain, see section 644.

• 1976, Tax Reform Act of 1976 (P.L. 94-455)

P.L. 94-455, §701(e)(2):

Added Code Sec. 641(c). **Effective** for transfers in trust made after 5-21-76.

[Sec. 641(c)]

(c) SPECIAL RULES FOR TAXATION OF ELECTING SMALL BUSINESS TRUSTS.—

(1) IN GENERAL.—For purposes of this chapter—

(A) the portion of any electing small business trust which consists of stock in 1 or more S corporations shall be treated as a separate trust, and

(B) the amount of the tax imposed by this chapter on such separate trust shall be determined with the modifications of paragraph (2).

(2) MODIFICATIONS.—For purposes of paragraph (1), the modifications of this paragraph are the following:

(A) Except as provided in section 1(h), the amount of the tax imposed by section 1(e) shall be determined by using the highest rate of tax set forth in section 1(e).

(B) The exemption amount under section 55(d) shall be zero.

(C) The only items of income, loss, deduction, or credit to be taken into account are the following:

(i) The items required to be taken into account under section 1366.

(ii) Any gain or loss from the disposition of stock in an S corporation.

(iii) To the extent provided in regulations, State or local income taxes or administrative expenses to the extent allocable to items described in clauses (i) and (ii).

(iv) Any interest expense paid or accrued on indebtedness incurred to acquire stock in an S corporation.

No deduction or credit shall be allowed for any amount not described in this paragraph, and no item described in this paragraph shall be apportioned to any beneficiary.

(D) No amount shall be allowed under paragraph (1) or (2) of section 1211(b).

(E)(i) Section 642(c) shall not apply.

(ii) For purposes of section 170(b)(1)(G), adjusted gross income shall be computed in the same manner as in the case of an individual, except that the deductions for costs which are paid or incurred in connection with the administration of the trust and which would not have been incurred if the property were not held in such trust shall be treated as allowable in arriving at adjusted gross income.

(3) TREATMENT OF REMAINDER OF TRUST AND DISTRIBUTIONS.—For purposes of determining—

(A) the amount of the tax imposed by this chapter on the portion of any electing small business trust not treated as a separate trust under paragraph (1), and

(B) the distributable net income of the entire trust,

the items referred to in paragraph (2)(C) shall be excluded. Except as provided in the preceding sentence, this subsection shall not affect the taxation of any distribution from the trust.

(4) TREATMENT OF UNUSED DEDUCTIONS WHERE TERMINATION OF SEPARATE TRUST.—If a portion of an electing small business trust ceases to be treated as a separate trust under paragraph (1), any carryover or excess deduction of the separate trust which is referred to in section 642(h) shall be taken into account by the entire trust.

(5) ELECTING SMALL BUSINESS TRUST.—For purposes of this subsection, the term "electing small business trust" has the meaning given such term by section 1361(e)(1).

Amendments

• 2017, Tax Cuts and Jobs Act (P.L. 115-97)

P.L. 115-97, §13542(a):

Amended Code Sec. 641(c)(2) by inserting after subparagraph (D) a new subparagraph (E). **Effective** for tax years beginning after 12-31-2017.

• 2007, Small Business and Work Opportunity Tax Act of 2007 (P.L. 110-28)

P.L. 110-28, §8236(a):

Amended Code Sec. 641(c)(2)(C) by inserting after clause (iii) a new clause (iv). **Effective** for tax years beginning after 12-31-2006.

• 1998, IRS Restructuring and Reform Act of 1998 (P.L. 105-206)

P.L. 105-206, §6007(f)(2):

Amended Code Sec. 641 by striking subsection (c) and by redesignating subsection (d) as subsection (c). **Effective** as if included in the provision of P.L. 105-34 to which it relates [**effective** for sales or exchanges after 8-5-97.—CCH].

• 1996, Small Business Job Protection Act of 1996 (P.L. 104-188)

P.L. 104-188, §1302(d):

Amended Code Sec. 641 by adding at the end a new subsection (d). **Effective** for tax years beginning after 12-31-96.

[Sec. 642]

SEC. 642. SPECIAL RULES FOR CREDITS AND DEDUCTIONS.

[Sec. 642(a)]

(a) FOREIGN TAX CREDIT ALLOWED.—An estate or trust shall be allowed the credit against tax for taxes imposed by foreign countries and possessions of the United States, to the extent allowed by section 901, only in respect of so much of the taxes described in such section as is not properly allocable under such section to the beneficiaries.

Amendments

• 1986, Tax Reform Act of 1986 (P.L. 99-514)

P.L. 99-514, §112(b)(2):

Amended Code Sec. 642(a). **Effective** for tax years beginning after 12-31-86. Prior to amendment, Code Sec. 642(a) read as follows:

(A) CREDITS AGAINST TAX.—

(1) FOREIGN TAXES.—An estate or trust shall be allowed the credit against tax for taxes imposed by foreign countries and possessions of the United States, to the extent allowed by section 901, only in respect of so much of the taxes described in such section as is not properly allocable under such section to the beneficiaries.

(2) POLITICAL CONTRIBUTIONS.—An estate or trust shall not be allowed the credit against tax for political contributions provided by section 24.

• 1984, Deficit Reduction Act of 1984 (P.L. 98-369)

P.L. 98-369, §474(r)(17):

Amended Code Sec. 642(a)(2) by striking out "section 41" and inserting in lieu thereof "section 24". **Effective** for tax years beginning after 12-31-83, and to carrybacks from such years.

• 1976, Tax Reform Act of 1976 (P.L. 94-455)

P.L. 94-455, §1901(b)(1)(H)(i):

Struck out Code Sec. 642(a)(1) and redesignated paragraphs (2) and (3) to be paragraphs (1) and (2), respectively. **Effective** for tax years beginning after 12-31-76. Prior to repeal, Code Sec. 642(a)(1) read as follows:

(1) PARTIALLY TAX-EXEMPT INTEREST.—An estate or trust shall be allowed the credit against tax for partially tax-exempt interest provided by section 35 only in respect of so much of such interest as is not properly allocable to any beneficiary under section 652 or 662. If the estate or trust elects under section 171 to treat as amortizable the premium on bonds with respect to the interest on which the credit is allowable under section 35, such credit (whether allowable to the estate or trust or to the beneficiary) shall be reduced under section 171(a)(3).

• 1971, Revenue Act of 1971 (P.L. 92-178)

P.L. 92-178, §701(b):

Added paragraph (3) to Code Sec. 642(a). **Effective** for tax years ending after 12-31-71, but only with respect to political contributions, payment of which is made after such date.

• 1964, Revenue Act of 1964 (P.L. 88-272)

P.L. 88-272, §201(d)(6)(A):

Amends Code Sec. 642(a) by deleting paragraph (3). **Effective** with respect to dividends received after 12-31-64, in tax years ending after such date. Prior to deletion, Sec. 642(a)(3) read as follows:

"(3) Dividends received by individuals.—An estate or trust shall be allowed the credit against tax for dividends received provided by section 34 only in respect of so much of such dividends as is not properly allocable to any beneficiary under section 652 or 662. For purposes of determining the time of receipt of dividends under section 34 and section 116, the amount of dividends properly allocable to a beneficiary under section 652 or 662 shall be deemed to have been received by the beneficiary ratably on the same dates that the dividends were received by the estate or trust."

[Sec. 642(b)]

(b) DEDUCTION FOR PERSONAL EXEMPTION.—

(1) ESTATES.—An estate shall be allowed a deduction of $600.

(2) TRUSTS.—

(A) IN GENERAL.—Except as otherwise provided in this paragraph, a trust shall be allowed a deduction of $100.

(B) TRUSTS DISTRIBUTING INCOME CURRENTLY.—A trust which, under its governing instrument, is required to distribute all of its income currently shall be allowed a deduction of $300.

(C) DISABILITY TRUSTS.—

(i) IN GENERAL.—A qualified disability trust shall be allowed a deduction equal to the exemption amount under section 151(d), determined—

(I) by treating such trust as an individual described in section 68(b)(1)(C), and

(II) by applying section 67(e) (without the reference to section 642(b)) for purposes of determining the adjusted gross income of the trust.

(ii) QUALIFIED DISABILITY TRUST.—For purposes of clause (i), the term "qualified disability trust" means any trust if—

(I) such trust is a disability trust described in subsection (c)(2)(B)(iv) of section 1917 of the Social Security Act (42 U.S.C. 1396p), and

(II) all of the beneficiaries of the trust as of the close of the taxable year are determined by the Commissioner of Social Security to have been disabled (within the meaning of section 1614(a)(3) of the Social Security Act, 42 U.S.C. 1382c(a)(3)) for some portion of such year.

A trust shall not fail to meet the requirements of subclause (II) merely because the corpus of the trust may revert to a person who is not so disabled after the trust ceases to have any beneficiary who is so disabled.

(iii) YEARS WHEN PERSONAL EXEMPTION AMOUNT IS ZERO.—

(I) IN GENERAL.—In the case of any taxable year in which the exemption amount under section 151(d) is zero, clause (i) shall be applied by substituting "$4,150" for "the exemption amount under section 151(d)".

(II) INFLATION ADJUSTMENT.—In the case of any taxable year beginning in a calendar year after 2018, the $4,150 amount in subparagraph (A) shall be increased in the same manner as provided in section 6334(d)(4)(C).

(3) DEDUCTIONS IN LIEU OF PERSONAL EXEMPTION.—The deductions allowed by this subsection shall be in lieu of the deductions allowed under section 151 (relating to deduction for personal exemption).

Amendments

• 2017, Tax Cuts and Jobs Act (P.L. 115-97)

P.L. 115-97, §11041(b):

Amended Code Sec. 642(b)(2)(C) by adding at the end a new clause (iii). **Effective** for tax years beginning after 12-31-2017.

• 2014, Tax Technical Corrections Act of 2014 (P.L. 113-295)

P.L. 113-295, §202(a), Division A:

Amended Code Sec. 642(b)(2)(C)(i)(I) by striking "section 151(d)(3)(C)(iii)" and inserting "section 68(b)(1)(C)". **Effective** as if included in the provision of the American Taxpayer Relief Act of 2012 (P.L. 112-240) to which it relates [**effective** for tax years beginning after 12-31-2012.—CCH].

• 2002, Victims of Terrorism Tax Relief Act of 2001 (P.L. 107-134)

P.L. 107-134, §116(a):

Amended Code Sec. 642(b). **Effective** for tax years ending on or after 9-11-2001. Prior to amendment, Code Sec 642(b) read as follows:

(b) DEDUCTION FOR PERSONAL EXEMPTION.—An estate shall be allowed a deduction of $600. A trust which, under its governing instrument, is required to distribute all of its income currently shall be allowed a deduction of $300. All other trusts shall be allowed a deduction of $100. The deductions allowed by this subsection shall be in lieu of the deductions allowed under section 151 (relating to deduction for personal exemption).

[Sec. 642(c)]

(c) DEDUCTION FOR AMOUNTS PAID OR PERMANENTLY SET ASIDE FOR A CHARITABLE PURPOSE.—

(1) GENERAL RULE.—In the case of an estate or trust (other than a trust meeting the specifications of subpart B), there shall be allowed as a deduction in computing its taxable income (in lieu of the deduction allowed by section 170(a), relating to deduction for charitable, etc., contributions and gifts) any amount of the gross income, without limitation, which pursuant to the terms of the governing instrument is, during the taxable year, paid for a purpose specified in section 170(c) (determined without regard to section 170(c)(2)(A)). If a charitable contribution is paid after the close of such taxable year and on or before the last day of the year following the close of such taxable year, then the trustee or administrator may elect to treat such contribution as paid during such taxable year. The election shall be made at such time and in such manner as the Secretary prescribes by regulations.

(2) AMOUNTS PERMANENTLY SET ASIDE.—In the case of an estate, and in the case of a trust (other than a trust meeting the specifications of subpart B) required by the terms of its governing instrument to set aside amounts which was—

(A) created on or before October 9, 1969, if—

(i) an irrevocable remainder interest is transferred to or for the use of an organization described in section 170(c), or

(ii) the grantor is at all times after October 9, 1969, under a mental disability to change the terms of the trust; or

(B) established by a will executed on or before October 9, 1969, if—

(i) the testator dies before October 9, 1972, without having republished the will after October 9, 1969, by codicil or otherwise,

(ii) the testator at no time after October 9, 1969, had the right to change the portions of the will which pertain to the trust, or

(iii) the will is not republished by codicil or otherwise before October 9, 1972, and the testator is on such date and at all times thereafter under a mental disability to republish the will by codicil or otherwise,

there shall also be allowed as a deduction in computing its taxable income any amount of the gross income, without limitation, which pursuant to the terms of the governing instrument is, during the taxable year, permanently set aside for a purpose specified in section 170(c), or is to be used exclusively for religious, charitable, scientific, literary, or educational purposes, or for the prevention of cruelty to children or animals, or for the establishment, acquisition, maintenance, or operation of a public cemetery not operated for profit. In the case of a trust, the preceding sentence shall apply only to gross income earned with respect to amounts transferred to the trust before October 9, 1969, or transferred under a will to which subparagraph (B) applies.

➾ Caution: P.L. 98-369, §1001(b)(8), amended Code Sec. 642(c)(3), below, by striking "1 year" and inserting "6 months". This amendment applies to property acquired after June 22, 1984, and before January 1, 1988.

(3) POOLED INCOME FUNDS.—In the case of a pooled income fund (as defined in paragraph (5)), there shall also be allowed as a deduction in computing its taxable income any amount of the gross income attributable to gain from the sale of a capital asset held for more than 6 months [1 year], without limitation, which pursuant to the terms of the governing instrument is, during the taxable year, permanently set aside for a purpose specified in section 170(c).

(4) ADJUSTMENTS.—To the extent that the amount otherwise allowable as a deduction under this subsection consists of gain described in section 1202(a), proper adjustment shall be made for any exclusion allowable to the estate or trust under section 1202. In the case of a trust, the deduction allowed by this subsection shall be subject to section 681 (relating to unrelated business income).

(5) DEFINITION OF POOLED INCOME FUND.—For purposes of paragraph (3), a pooled income fund is a trust—

(A) to which each donor transfers property, contributing an irrevocable remainder interest in such property to or for the use of an organization described in section 170(b)(1)(A) (other than in clauses (vii) or (viii)), and retaining an income interest for the life of one or more beneficiaries (living at the time of such transfer),

(B) in which the property transferred by each donor is commingled with property transferred by other donors who have made or make similar transfers,

(C) which cannot have investments in securities which are exempt from taxes imposed by this subtitle,

(D) which includes only amounts received from transfers which meet the requirements of this paragraph,

(E) which is maintained by the organization to which the remainder interest is contributed and of which no donor or beneficiary of an income interest is a trustee, and

(F) from which each beneficiary of an income interest receives income, for each year for which he is entitled to receive the income interest referred to in subparagraph (A), determined by the rate of return earned by the trust for such year.

For purposes of determining the amount of any charitable contribution allowable by reason of a transfer of property to a pooled fund, the value of the income interest shall be determined on the basis of the highest rate of return earned by the fund for any of the 3 taxable years immediately preceding the taxable year of the fund in which the transfer is made. In the case of funds in existence less than 3 taxable years preceding the taxable year of the fund in which a transfer is made, the rate of return shall be deemed to be 6 percent per annum, except that the Secretary may prescribe a different rate of return.

(6) TAXABLE PRIVATE FOUNDATIONS.—In the case of a private foundation which is not exempt from taxation under section 501(a) for the taxable year, the provisions of this subsection shall not apply and the provisions of section 170 shall apply.

Amendments

• **2018, Tax Technical Corrections Act of 2018 (P.L. 115-141)**

P.L. 115-141, §401(a)(137), Div. U:

Amended Code Sec. 642(c)(1) by striking "other then" and inserting "other than". **Effective** 3-23-2018.

• **1993, Omnibus Budget Reconciliation Act of 1993 (P.L. 103-66)**

P.L. 103-66, §13113(d)(2):

Amended Code Sec. 642(c)(4). **Effective** for stock issued after 8-10-93. Prior to amendment, Code Sec. 642(c)(4) read as follows:

(4) ADJUSTMENTS.—In the case of a trust, the deduction allowed by this subsection shall be subject to section 681 (relating to unrelated business income).

• **1986, Tax Reform Act of 1986 (P.L. 99-514)**

P.L. 99-514, §301(b)(6)(A)-(B):

Amended Code Sec. 642(c)(4) by striking out the 1st sentence. **Effective** for tax years beginning after 12-31-86. Prior to amendment, the 1st sentence of Code Sec. 642(c)(4) read as follows:

To the extent that the amount otherwise allowable as a deduction under this subsection consists of gain from the sale or exchange of capital assets held for more than 6 months, proper adjustment shall be made for any deduction allowable to the estate or trust under section 1202 (relating to deduction for excess of capital gains over capital losses).

• **1984, Deficit Reduction Act of 1984 (P.L. 98-369)**

P.L. 98-369, §1001(b)(8):

Amended Code Sec. 642(c)(3) and (4) by striking out "1 year" each place it appeared and inserting in lieu thereof "6 months". **Effective** for property acquired after 6-22-84, and before 1-1-88.

• **1976, Tax Reform Act of 1976 (P.L. 94-455)**

P.L. 94-455, §1402(b)(1)(J):

§1402(b)(1)(J) substituted "9 months" for "6 months" in Code Sec. 642(c)(3) and (4). **Effective** for tax years beginning in 1977.

P.L. 94-455, §1402(b)(2):

Substituted "1 year" for "9 months" in Code Sec. 642(c)(3) and (4). **Effective** for tax years beginning after 1977.

P.L. 94-455, §1906(b)(13)(A):

Amended 1954 Code by substituting "Secretary" for "Secretary or his delegate" each place it appeared. **Effective** 2-1-77.

• **1969, Tax Reform Act of 1969 (P.L. 91-172)**

P.L. 91-172, §201(b):

Amended Code Sec. 642(c). **Effective** with respect to amounts paid, permanently set aside, or to be used for a charitable purpose in tax years beginning after 12-31-69, except section 642(c)(5) of the Internal Revenue Code of 1954 (as added by subsection (b)) shall apply to transfers in trust made after 7-31-69. Prior to amendment, Code Sec. 642(c), read as follows:

"(c) Deduction for Amounts Paid or Permanently Set Aside for a Charitable Purpose.—In the case of an estate or trust (other than a trust meeting the specifications of subpart B) there shall be allowed as a deduction in computing its taxable income (in lieu of the deductions allowed by section 170(a), relating to deduction for charitable, etc., contributions and gifts) any amount of the gross income, without limitation, which pursuant to the terms of the governing instrument is, during the taxable year, paid or permanently set aside for a purpose specified in section 170(c), or is to be used exclusively for religious, charitable, scientific, literary, or educational purposes, or for the prevention of cruelty to children or animals, or for the establishment, acquisition, maintenance or operation of a public cemetery not operated for profit. For this purpose, to the extent that such amount consists of gain from the sale or exchange of capital assets held for more than 6 months, proper adjustment of the deduction otherwise allowable under this subsection shall be made for any deduction allowable to the estate or trust under section 1202 (relating to deduction for excess of capital gains over capital losses). In the case of a trust, the deduction allowed by this subsection shall be subject to section 681 (relating to unrelated business income and prohibited transactions)."

[Sec. 642(d)]

(d) NET OPERATING LOSS DEDUCTION.—The benefit of the deduction for net operating losses provided by section 172 shall be allowed to estates and trusts under regulations prescribed by the Secretary.

Amendments

• **1976, Tax Reform Act of 1976 (P.L. 94-455)**

P.L. 94-455, §1906(b)(13)(A):

Amended 1954 Code by substituting "Secretary" for "Secretary or his delegate" each place it appeared. **Effective** 2-1-77.

[Sec. 642(e)]

(e) DEDUCTION FOR DEPRECIATION AND DEPLETION.—An estate or trust shall be allowed the deduction for depreciation and depletion only to the extent not allowable to beneficiaries under sections 167(d) and 611(b).

Amendments

• **1990, Omnibus Budget Reconciliation Act of 1990 (P.L. 101-508)**

P.L. 101-508, §11812(b)(9):

Amended Code Sec. 642(e) by striking "167(h)" and inserting "167(d)". **Effective** for property placed in service after 11-5-90. For exceptions, see Act Sec. 11812(c)(2)-(3), below.

P.L. 101-508, §11812(c)(2)-(3), provides:

(2) EXCEPTION.—The amendments made by this section shall not apply to any property to which section 168 of the Internal Revenue Code of 1986 does not apply by reason of subsection (f)(5) thereof.

(3) EXCEPTION FOR PREVIOUSLY GRANDFATHER EXPENDITURES.—The amendments made by this section shall not apply to rehabilitation expenditures described in section 252(f)(5) of the Tax Reform Act of 1986 (as added by section 1002(l)(31) of the Technical and Miscellaneous Revenue Act of 1988).

• **1962, Revenue Act of 1962 (P.L. 87-834)**

P.L. 87-834, §13(c)(2):

Amended Code Sec. 642(e) by substituting "167(h)" for "167(g)" in the last line. **Effective** for tax years beginning after 12-31-61, and ending after 10-16-62.

[Sec. 642(f)]

(f) AMORTIZATION DEDUCTIONS.—The benefit of the deductions for amortization provided by sections 169 and 197 shall be allowed to estates and trusts in the same manner as in the case of an individual. The allowable deduction shall be apportioned between the income beneficiaries and the fiduciary under regulations prescribed by the Secretary.

Amendments

• 1993, Omnibus Budget Reconciliation Act of 1993 (P.L. 103-66)

P.L. 103-66, §13261(f)(2):

Amended Code Sec. 642(f) by striking "section 169" and inserting "sections 169 and 197". **Effective**, generally, with respect to property acquired after 8-10-93. However, for exceptions, see Act Sec. 13261(g)(2)-(3) below.

P.L. 103-66, §13261(g)(2)-(3), provides:

(2) ELECTION TO HAVE AMENDMENTS APPLY TO PROPERTY ACQUIRED AFTER JULY 25, 1991.—

(A) IN GENERAL.—If an election under this paragraph applies to the taxpayer—

(i) the amendments made by this section shall apply to property acquired by the taxpayer after July 25, 1991,

(ii) subsection (c)(1)(A) of section 197 of the Internal Revenue Code of 1986 (as added by this section) (and so much of subsection (f)(9)(A) of such section 197 as precedes clause (i) thereof) shall be applied with respect to the taxpayer by treating July 25, 1991, as the date of the enactment of such section, and

(iii) in applying subsection (f)(9) of such section, with respect to any property acquired by the taxpayer on or before the date of the enactment of this Act, only holding or use on July 25, 1991, shall be taken into account.

(B) ELECTION.—An election under this paragraph shall be made at such time and in such manner as the Secretary of the Treasury or his delegate may prescribe. Such an election by any taxpayer, once made—

(i) may be revoked only with the consent of the Secretary, and

(ii) shall apply to the taxpayer making such election and any other taxpayer under common control with the taxpayer (within the meaning of subparagraphs (A) and (B) of section 41(f)(1) of such Code) at any time after August 2, 1993, and on or before the date on which such election is made.

(3) ELECTIVE BINDING CONTRACT EXCEPTION.—

(A) IN GENERAL.—The amendments made by this section shall not apply to any acquisition of property by the taxpayer if—

(i) such acquisition is pursuant to a written binding contract in effect on the date of the enactment of this Act and at all times thereafter before such acquisition,

(ii) an election under paragraph (2) does not apply to the taxpayer, and

(iii) the taxpayer makes an election under this paragraph with respect to such contract.

(B) ELECTION.—An election under this paragraph shall be made at such time and in such manner as the Secretary of the Treasury or his delegate shall prescribe. Such an election, once made—

(i) may be revoked only with the consent of the Secretary, and

(ii) shall apply to all property acquired pursuant to the contract with respect to which such election was made.

• 1990, Omnibus Budget Reconciliation Act of 1990 (P.L. 101-508)

P.L. 101-508, §11801(c)(6)(B):

Amended Code Sec. 642(f) by striking "sections 169, 184, 187, and 188" and inserting "section 169". **Effective** 11-5-90.

P.L. 101-508, §11821(b), provides:

(b) SAVINGS PROVISION.—If—

(1) any provision amended or repealed by this part applied to—

(A) any transaction occurring before the date of the enactment of this Act,

(B) any property acquired before such date of enactment, or

(C) any item of income, loss, deduction, or credit taken into account before such date of enactment, and

(2) the treatment of such transaction, property, or item under such provision would (without regard to the amendments made by this part) affect liability for tax for periods ending after such date of enactment,

nothing in the amendments made by this part shall be construed to affect the treatment of such transaction, property, or item for purposes of determining liability for tax for periods ending after such date of enactment.

• 1981, Economic Recovery Tax Act of 1981 (P.L. 97-34)

P.L. 97-34, §212(d)(2)(D):

Amended Code Sec. 642(f) by striking out "188, and 191" and inserting in lieu thereof "and 188". **Effective** for expenditures incurred after 12-31-81, in tax years ending after such date.

P.L. 97-34, §212(e)(2), as amended by P.L. 97-448, §102(f)(1), provides:

(2) TRANSITIONAL RULE.—The amendments made by this section shall not apply with respect to any rehabilitation of a building if—

(A) the physical work on such rehabilitation began before January 1, 1982, and

(b) such building does not meet the requirements of paragraph (1) of section 48(g) of the Internal Revenue Code of 1954 (as amended by this Act).

• 1976, Tax Reform Act of 1976 (P.L. 94-455)

P.L. 94-455, §1906(b)(13)(A):

Amended 1954 Code by substituting "Secretary" for "Secretary or his delegate" each place it appeared. **Effective** 2-1-77.

P.L. 94-455, §1951(c)(2)(B):

Struck out "168," after the word "sections". **Effective** for tax years beginning after 12-31-76.

P.L. 94-455, §2124(a)(3)(B):

Substituted "188, and 191" for "and 188". **Effective** for additions to capital account made after 6-14-76 and before 6-15-81.

• 1971, Revenue Act of 1971 (P.L. 92-178)

P.L. 92-178, §303(c)(4):

Amended Code Sec. 642(f) by substituting "187, and 188" for "and 187" in the first sentence. **Effective** for tax years ending after 12-31-71.

• 1969, Tax Reform Act of 1969 (P.L. 91-172)

P.L. 91-172, §704(b)(2):

Amended the heading and first sentence of Code Sec. 642(f). **Effective** for tax years ending after 12-31-68. Prior to amendment, the heading and first sentence read as follows:

(f) Amortization of Emergency or Grain Storage Facilities.—The benefit of the deductions for amortization of emergency and grain storage facilities provided by sections 168 and 169 shall be allowed to estates and trusts in the same manner as in the case of an individual.

[Sec. 642(g)]

(g) DISALLOWANCE OF DOUBLE DEDUCTIONS.—Amounts allowable under section 2053 or 2054 as a deduction in computing the taxable estate of a decedent shall not be allowed as a deduction (or as an offset against the sales price of property in determining gain or loss) in computing the taxable income of the estate or of any other person, unless there is filed, within the time and in the manner and form prescribed by the Secretary, a statement that the amounts have not been allowed as deductions under section 2053 or 2054 and a waiver of the right to have such amounts allowed at any time as deductions under section 2053 or 2054. Rules similar to the rules of the preceding sentence shall apply to amounts which may be taken into account under section 2621(a)(2) or 2622(b). This subsection shall not apply with respect to deductions allowed under part II (relating to income in respect of decedents).

Amendments

• 1996, Small Business Job Protection Act of 1996 (P.L. 104-188)

P.L. 104-188, §1704(t)(8):

Amended Code Sec. 642(g) by striking "under 2621(a)(2)" and inserting "under section 2621(a)(2)". **Effective** 8-20-96.

• 1989, Omnibus Budget Reconciliation Act of 1989 (P.L. 101-239)

P.L. 101-239, §7811(j)(3):

Amended Code Sec. 642(g) by inserting after the first sentence a new sentence. **Effective** as if included in the provision of P.L. 100-647 to which it relates.

• 1976, Tax Reform Act of 1976 (P.L. 94-455)

P.L. 94-455, §1906(b)(13)(A):

Amended 1954 Code by substituting "Secretary" for "Secretary or his delegate" each place it appeared. **Effective** 2-1-77.

P.L. 94-455, §2009(d):

Added "(or as an offset against the sales price of property in determining gain or loss)" to Code Sec. 642(g). **Effective** for tax years ending after 10-4-76.

• 1966 (P.L. 89-621)

P.L. 89-621, §2:

Amended Code Sec. 642(g) by inserting "or of any other person" immediately after "shall not be allowed as a deduction in computing the taxable income of the estate." **Effective** for tax years ending after 10-4-66, but only with respect to amounts paid or incurred, and losses sustained, after that date.

[Sec. 642(h)]

(h) Unused Loss Carryovers and Excess Deductions on Termination Available to Beneficiaries.—If on the termination of an estate or trust, the estate or trust has—

(1) a net operating loss carryover under section 172 or a capital loss carryover under section 1212, or

(2) for the last taxable year of the estate or trust deductions (other than the deductions allowed under subsections (b) or (c)) in excess of gross income for such year,

then such carryover or such excess shall be allowed as a deduction, in accordance with regulations prescribed by the Secretary, to the beneficiaries succeeding to the property of the estate or trust.

Amendments

• 1976, Tax Reform Act of 1976 (P.L. 94-455)

P.L. 94-455, §1906(b)(13)(A):

Amended 1954 Code by substituting "Secretary" for "Secretary or his delegate" each place it appeared. **Effective** 2-1-77.

[Sec. 642(i)]

(i) Certain Distributions by Cemetery Perpetual Care Funds.—In the case of a cemetery perpetual care fund which—

(1) was created pursuant to local law by a taxable cemetery corporation for the care and maintenance of cemetery property, and

(2) is treated for the taxable year as a trust for purposes of this subchapter,

any amount distributed by such fund for the care and maintenance of gravesites which have been purchased from the cemetery corporation before the beginning of the taxable year of the trust and with respect to which there is an obligation to furnish care and maintenance shall be considered to be a distribution solely for purposes of sections 651 and 661, but only to the extent that the aggregate amount so distributed during the taxable year does not exceed $5 multiplied by the aggregate number of such gravesites.

Amendments

• 1978, Revenue Act of 1978 (P.L. 95-600)

P.L. 95-600, §113(a)(2)(B):

Repealed Code Sec. 642(i) and redesignated Code Sec. 642(j) as Code Sec. 642(i). **Effective** for contributions the payment of which is made after 12-31-78, in tax years beginning after such date. Prior to repeal, Code Sec. 642(i) read as follows:

(i) Political Contributions.—An estate or trust shall not be allowed the deduction for contributions to candidates for public office provided by section 218.

• 1976 (P.L. 94-528)

P.L. 94-528, §[(1)](a):

Added Code Sec. 642(j). **Effective** 10-1-77, and shall apply to amounts distributed during tax years ending after 12-31-63.

• 1971, Revenue Act of 1971 (P.L. 92-178)

P.L. 92-178, §702(b);

Added new Code Sec. 642(i) and redesignated former Code Sec. 642(i) as Code Sec. 642(j). **Effective** for tax years ending after 12-31-71, but only with respect to political contributions, payment of which is made after such date.

[Sec. 642(j)—Stricken]

Amendments

• 1986, Tax Reform Act of 1986 (P.L. 99-514)

P.L. 99-514, §612(b)(3):

Amended Code Sec. 642 by striking out subsection (j). **Effective** for tax years beginning after 12-31-86. Prior to amendment, Code Sec. 642(j) read as follows:

(j) Cross References.—

For special rule for determining the time of receipt of dividends by a beneficiary under section 652 or 662, see section 116(c)(3).

• 1978, Revenue Act of 1978 (P.L. 95-600)

P.L. 95-600, § 113(b)(2)(B):

Redesignated Code Sec. 642(k) as Code Sec. 642(j). **Effective** for contributions the payment of which is made after 12-31-78, in tax years beginning after such date.

• 1977, Tax Reduction and Simplification Act of 1977 (P.L. 95-30)

P.L. 95-30, § 101(d)(9):

Amended Code Sec. 642(k). **Effective** for tax years beginning after 12-31-76. Prior to amendment, Code Sec. 642(k) read as follows:

(k) CROSS REFERENCES.—

(1) For disallowance of standard deduction in case of estates and trusts, see section 142(b)(4).

(2) For special rule for determining the time of receipt of dividends by a beneficiary under section 652 or 662, see section 116(c)(3).

• 1976 (P.L. 94-528)

P.L. 94-528, § [(1)](a):

Redesignated former Code Sec. 642(j) as Code Sec. 642(k). **Effective** 10-1-77, and shall apply to amounts distributed during tax years ending after 12-31-63.

• 1971, Revenue Act of 1971 (P.L. 92-178)

P.L. 92-178, § 702(b):

Redesignated former Code Sec. 642(i) as Code Sec. 642(j).

• 1964, Revenue Act of 1964 (P.L. 88-272)

P.L. 88-272, § 201(d)(6)(B):

Amended Code Sec. 642(i) by designating the first sentence as paragraph (1) and by adding paragraph (2). **Effective** with respect to dividends received after 12-31-64, in tax years ending after such date.

[Sec. 643]

SEC. 643. DEFINITIONS APPLICABLE TO SUBPARTS A, B, C, AND D.

[Sec. 643(a)]

(a) DISTRIBUTABLE NET INCOME.—For purposes of this part, the term "distributable net income" means, with respect to any taxable year, the taxable income of the estate or trust computed with the following modifications—

(1) DEDUCTION FOR DISTRIBUTIONS.—No deduction shall be taken under sections 651 and 661 (relating to additional deductions).

(2) DEDUCTION FOR PERSONAL EXEMPTION.—No deduction shall be taken under section 642(b) (relating to deduction for personal exemptions).

(3) CAPITAL GAINS AND LOSSES.—Gains from the sale or exchange of capital assets shall be excluded to the extent that such gains are allocated to corpus and are not (A) paid, credited, or required to be distributed to any beneficiary during the taxable year, or (B) paid, permanently set aside, or to be used for the purposes specified in section 642(c). Losses from the sale or exchange of capital assets shall be excluded, except to the extent such losses are taken into account in determining the amount of gains from the sale or exchange of capital assets which are paid, credited, or required to be distributed to any beneficiary during the taxable year. The exclusion under section 1202 shall not be taken into account.

(4) EXTRAORDINARY DIVIDENDS AND TAXABLE STOCK DIVIDENDS.—For purposes only of subpart B (relating to trusts which distribute current income only), there shall be excluded those items of gross income constituting extraordinary dividends or taxable stock dividends which the fiduciary, acting in good faith, does not pay or credit to any beneficiary by reason of his determination that such dividends are allocable to corpus under the terms of the governing instrument and applicable local law.

(5) TAX-EXEMPT INTEREST.—There shall be included any tax-exempt interest to which section 103 applies, reduced by any amounts which would be deductible in respect of disbursements allocable to such interest but for the provisions of section 265 (relating to disallowance of certain deductions).

(6) INCOME OF FOREIGN TRUST.—In the case of a foreign trust—

(A) There shall be included the amounts of gross income from sources without the United States, reduced by any amounts which would be deductible in respect of disbursements allocable to such income but for the provisions of section 265(a)(1) (relating to disallowance of certain deductions).

(B) Gross income from sources within the United States shall be determined without regard to section 894 (relating to income exempt under treaty).

(C) Paragraph (3) shall not apply to a foreign trust. In the case of such a trust, there shall be included gains from the sale or exchange of capital assets, reduced by losses from such sales or exchanges to the extent such losses do not exceed gains from such sales or exchanges.

(7) ABUSIVE TRANSACTIONS.—The Secretary shall prescribe such regulations as may be necessary or appropriate to carry out the purposes of this part, including regulations to prevent avoidance of such purposes.

If the estate or trust is allowed a deduction under section 642(c), the amount of the modifications specified in paragraphs (5) and (6) shall be reduced to the extent that the amount of income which is paid, permanently set aside, or to be used for the purposes specified in section 642(c) is deemed to consist of items specified in those paragraphs. For this purpose, such amount shall (in the absence of specific provisions in the governing instrument) be deemed to consist of the same proportion of each class of items of income of the estate or trust as the total of each class bears to the total of all classes.

Amendments

• 1996, Small Business Job Protection Act of 1996 (P.L. 104-188)

P.L. 104-188, §1906(b):

Amended Code Sec. 643(a) by inserting after paragraph (6) a new paragraph (7). **Effective** 8-20-96.

• 1993, Omnibus Budget Reconciliation Act of 1993 (P.L. 103-66)

P.L. 103-66, §13113(d)(3):

Amended Code Sec. 643(a)(3) by adding at the end thereof a new sentence. **Effective** for stock issued after 8-10-93.

• 1989, Omnibus Budget Reconciliation Act of 1989 (P.L. 101-239)

P.L. 101-239, §7811(b)(1):

Amended Code Sec. 643(a)(6)(C) by striking "(i)" and by striking ", and (ii)" and all that follows and inserting a period. **Effective** as if included in the provision of P.L. 100-647 to which it relates. Prior to amendment, Code Sec. 643(a)(6)(C) read as follows:

(C) Paragraph (3) shall not apply to a foreign trust. In the case of such a trust, (i) there shall be included gains from the sale or exchange of capital assets, reduced by losses from such sales or exchanges to the extent such losses do not exceed gains from such sales or exchanges, and (ii) the deduction under section 1202 (relating to deduction for excess of capital gains over capital losses) [Code Sec. 1202 was repealed by P.L. 99-514.—CCH.] shall not be taken into account.

P.L. 101-239, §7811(b)(2):

Amended Code Sec. 643(a)(6) by striking subparagraph (D). **Effective** as if included in the provision of P.L. 100-647 to which it relates. Prior to amendment, Code Sec. 643(a)(6)(D) read as follows:

(D) Effective for distributions made in taxable years beginning after December 31, 1975, the undistributed net income of each foreign trust for each taxable year beginning on or before December 31, 1975, remaining undistributed at the close of the last taxable year beginning on or before December 31, 1975, shall be redetermined by taking into account the deduction allowed by section 1202.

P.L. 101-239, §7811(f)(1):

Amended Code Sec. 643(a)(6)(A) by striking "section 265(1)" and inserting "section 265(a)(1)". **Effective** as if included in the provision of P.L. 100-647 to which it relates.

• 1986, Tax Reform Act of 1986 (P.L. 99-514)

P.L. 99-514, §301(b)(7):

Amended Code Sec. 643(a)(3) by striking out the last sentence. **Effective** for tax years beginning after 12-31-86. Prior to amendment, the last sentence read as follows:

The deduction under section 1202 (relating to deduction for excess of capital gains over capital losses) shall not be taken into account.

P.L. 99-514, §612(b)(4):

Repealed Code Sec. 643(a)(7). **Effective** for tax years beginning after 12-31-86. Prior to repeal, Code Sec. 643(a)(7) read as follows:

(7) DIVIDENDS OR INTEREST.—There shall be included the amount of any dividends or interest excluded from gross income pursuant to section 116 (relating to partial exclusion of dividends) or section 128 (relating to certain interest).

• 1983, Technical Corrections Act of 1982 (P.L. 97-448)

P.L. 97-448, §103(a)(3):

Amended Code Sec. 643(a)(7). **Effective** as if included in the provision of P.L. 97-34 to which it relates. Prior to amendment, Code Sec. 643(a)(7) read as follows:

"(7) Dividends or interest.—There shall be included the amount of any dividends or interest excluded from gross income pursuant to section 116 (relating to partial exclusion of dividends or interest received) or section 128 (relating to interest on certain savings certificates)."

• 1981, Economic Recovery Tax Act of 1981 (P.L. 97-34)

P.L. 97-34, §301(b)(4):

Amended Code Sec. 643(a)(7), as in effect for tax years beginning in 1981, by inserting "or section 128 (relating to interest on certain savings certificates)" after "received)". **Effective** for tax years ending after 9-30-81.

P.L. 97-34, §301(b)(6)(B):

Amended Code Sec. 643(a)(7), as in effect for tax years beginning after 12-31-81, by inserting "or interest" after "dividends" each place it appears in the caption or test. **Effective** for tax years beginning after 12-31-81.

• 1980, Crude Oil Windfall Profit Tax Act of 1980 (P.L. 96-223)

P.L. 96-223, §404(b)(4):

Amended Code Sec. 643(a)(7) by inserting "or interest" after "dividends" each place it appeared in the caption and in the text. **Effective** for tax years beginning after 12-31-80 and before 1-1-83. (P.L. 97-34, Act Sec. 302(b)(1), amended Act Sec. 404(c) of the Crude Oil Windfall Profit Tax Act of 1980, P.L. 96-223, by striking out "1983" and inserting "1982".)

• 1976, Tax Reform Act of 1976 (P.L. 94-455)

P.L. 94-455, §1013(c)(1):

Amended Code Sec. 643(a)(6)(C) by striking out "foreign trust created by a United States person" and inserting in lieu thereof "foreign trust". **Effective** for tax years beginning after 12-31-75.

P.L. 94-455, §1013(c)(2):

Added Code Sec. 643(a)(6)(D). **Effective** for tax years beginning after 12-31-75.

• 1962, Revenue Act of 1962 (P.L. 87-834)

P.L. 87-834, §7:

Amended Code Sec. 643(a)(6) by adding subsections (B) and (C). **Effective** with respect to distributions made after 12-31-62. Prior to the amendment, Sec. 643(a)(6) read as follows:

(6) Foreign Income.—In the case of a foreign trust, there shall be included the amounts of gross income from sources without the United States, reduced by any amounts which would be deductible in respect of disbursements allocable to such income but for the provisions of section 265(1) (relating to disallowance of certain deductions).

[Sec. 643(b)]

(b) INCOME.—For purposes of this subpart and subparts B, C, and D, the term "income", when not preceded by the words "taxable", "distributable net", "undistributed net", or "gross", means the amount of income of the estate or trust for the taxable year determined under the terms of the governing instrument and applicable local law. Items of gross income constituting extraordinary dividends or taxable stock dividends which the fiduciary, acting in good faith, determines to be allocable to corpus under the terms of the governing instrument and applicable local law shall not be considered income.

[Sec. 643(c)]

(c) BENEFICIARY.—For purposes of this part, the term "beneficiary" includes heir, legatee, devisee.

[Sec. 643(d)]

(d) COORDINATION WITH BACK-UP WITHHOLDING.—Except to the extent otherwise provided in regulations, this subchapter shall be applied with respect to payments subject to withholding under section 3406—

(1) by allocating between the estate or trust and its beneficiaries any credit allowable under section 31(c) (on the basis of their respective shares of any such payment taken into account under this subchapter),

(2) by treating each beneficiary to whom such credit is allocated as if an amount equal to such credit has been paid to him by the estate or trust, and

(3) by allowing the estate or trust a deduction in an amount equal to the credit so allocated to beneficiaries.

Amendments

• 1984, Deficit Reduction Act of 1984 (P.L. 98-369)

P.L. 98-369, §722(h)(3):

Amended Code Sec. 643 by adding section (d). **Effective** as if included in the amendments made by P.L. 98-67.

• 1983, Interest and Dividend Tax Compliance Act of 1983 (P.L.98-67)

P.L. 98-67, §102(a):

Repealed Code Sec. 643(d) as though it had not been enacted. **Effective** as of the close of 6-30-83. Prior to repeal, Code Sec. 643(d) read as follows:

(d) COORDINATION WITH WITHHOLDING ON INTEREST AND DIVIDENDS.—Except to the extent otherwise provided in regulations, this subchapter shall be applied with respect to payments subject to withholding under subchapter B of chapter 24—

(1) by allocating between the estate or trust and its beneficiaries any credit allowable under section 31(b) (on the basis of their respective shares of interest, dividends, and patronage dividends taken into account under this subchapter),

(2) by treating each beneficiary to whom such credit is allocated as if an amount equal to such credit has been paid to him by the estate or trust, and

(3) by allowing the estate or trust a deduction in an amount equal to the credit so allocated to beneficiaries.

• 1982, Tax Equity and Fiscal Responsibility Act of 1982 (P.L. 97-248)

P.L. 97-248, §302(b)(1):

Amended Code Sec. 643 by inserting at the end thereof new subsection (d). **Effective** for interest, dividends, and patronage dividends paid or credited after 6-30-83, but see amendment notes for P.L. 97-248 following Code Sec. 3451 for special rules.

• 1976, Tax Reform Act of 1976 (P.L. 94-455)

P.L. 94-455, §1013(e)(2):

Repealed Code Sec. 643(d). **Effective** for tax years ending after 12-31-75, but only in the case of foreign trusts created after 5-21-74, and transfers of property to foreign trusts after 5-21-74. Prior to repeal, Code Sec. 643(d) read as follows:

(d) FOREIGN TRUSTS CREATED BY UNITED STATES PERSONS.—For purposes of this part, the term "foreign trust created by a United States person" means that portion of a foreign trust (as defined in section 7701(a)(31)) attributable to money or property transferred directly or indirectly by a United States person (as defined in section 7701(a)(30)), or under the will of a decedent who at the date of his death was a United States citizen or resident.

• 1962, Revenue Act of 1962 (P.L. 87-834)

P.L. 87-834, §7:

Added to Code Sec. 643 a new subsection (d). **Effective** for distributions made after 12-31-62.

[Sec. 643(e)]

(e) TREATMENT OF PROPERTY DISTRIBUTED IN KIND.—

(1) BASIS OF BENEFICIARY.—The basis of any property received by a beneficiary in a distribution from an estate or trust shall be—

(A) the adjusted basis of such property in the hands of the estate or trust immediately before the distribution, adjusted for

(B) any gain or loss recognized to the estate or trust on the distribution.

(2) AMOUNT OF DISTRIBUTION.—In the case of any distribution of property (other than cash), the amount taken into account under sections 661(a)(2) and 662(a)(2) shall be the lesser of—

(A) the basis of such property in the hands of the beneficiary (as determined under paragraph (1)), or

(B) the fair market value of such property.

(3) ELECTION TO RECOGNIZE GAIN.—

(A) IN GENERAL.—In the case of any distribution of property (other than cash) to which an election under this paragraph applies—

(i) paragraph (2) shall not apply,

(ii) gain or loss shall be recognized by the estate or trust in the same manner as if such property had been sold to the distributee at its fair market value, and

(iii) the amount taken into account under sections 661(a)(2) and 662(a)(2) shall be the fair market value of such property.

(B) ELECTION.—Any election under this paragraph shall apply to all distributions made by the estate or trust during a taxable year and shall be made on the return of such estate or trust for such taxable year.

Any such election, once made, may be revoked only with the consent of the Secretary.

(4) EXCEPTION FOR DISTRIBUTIONS DESCRIBED IN SECTION 663(a).—This subsection shall not apply to any distribution described in section 663(a).

Amendments

• **1986, Tax Reform Act of 1986 (P.L. 99-514)**

P.L. 99-514, §1806(a):

Amended Code Sec. 643(e)(3)(B), as redesignated by Act Sec. 1806(c). **Effective** as if included in the provision of P.L. 98-369 to which it relates. Prior to amendment, Code Sec. 64(e)(3)(B) read as follows:

(B) ELECTION—Any election under this paragraph shall be made by the estate or trust on its return for the taxable year for which the distribution was made.

P.L. 99-514, §1806(c)(1) and (2):

Amended Code Sec. 643 by redesignating subsection (d)[e] as subsection (e), and by redesignating subsection (e)[f] as subsection (f). **Effective** as if included in the provision of P.L. 98-369 to which it relates.

• **1984, Deficit Reduction Act of 1984 (P.L. 98-369)**

P.L. 98-369, §81(a):

Amended Code Sec. 643 by adding at the end thereof new subsection (d)[e]. **Effective** for distributions after 6-1-84, in tax years ending after such date. See Act Sec. 81(b)(2), below, for special rules for making elections.

P.L. 98-369, §81(b)(2), provides:

(2) Time for Making Election.—In the case of any distribution before the date of the enactment of this Act—

(A) the time for making an election under section 643(d)(3) of the Internal Revenue Code of 1954 (as added by this section) shall not expire before January 1, 1985, and

(B) the requirement that such election be made on the return of the estate or trust shall not apply.

[Sec. 643(f)]

(f) TREATMENT OF MULTIPLE TRUSTS.—For purposes of this subchapter, under regulations prescribed by the Secretary, 2 or more trusts shall be treated as 1 trust if—

(1) such trusts have substantially the same grantor or grantors and substantially the same primary beneficiary or beneficiaries, and

(2) a principal purpose of such trusts is the avoidance of the tax imposed by this chapter.

For purposes of the preceding sentence, a husband and wife shall be treated as 1 person.

Amendments

• **1988, Technical and Miscellaneous Revenue Act of 1988 (P.L. 100-647)**

P.L. 100-647, §1018(e), provides:

(e) PROVISION RELATED TO SECTION 1806 OF THE REFORM ACT.—If—

(1) on a return for the 1st taxable year of the trusts involved beginning after March 1, 1984, 2 or more trusts were treated as a single trust for purposes of the tax imposed by chapter 1 of the Internal Revenue Code of 1954,

(2) such trusts would have been required to be so treated but for the amendment made by section 1806(b) of the Reform Act, and

(3) such trusts did not accumulate any income during such taxable year and did not make any accumulation distributions during such taxable year,

then, notwithstanding the amendment made by section 1806(b) of the Reform Act, such trusts shall be treated as one trust for purposes of such taxable year.

• **1986, Tax Reform Act of 1986 (P.L. 99-514)**

P.L. 99-514, §1806(c)(1) and (2):

Redesignated subsection (e)[f] as subsection (f). **Effective** for tax years beginning after 3-1-84, except that, in the case of a trust which was irrevocable on 3-1-84, such amendment shall so apply only to that portion of the trust which is attributable to contributions to corpus after 3-1-84.

• **1984, Deficit Reduction Act of 1984 (P.L. 98-369)**

P.L. 98-369, §82(a):

Amended Code Sec. 643 by adding at the end thereof new subsection (e)[f]. **Effective** for tax years beginning after 3-1-84, except that, in the case of a trust which was irrevocable on 3-1-84, such amendment shall so apply only to that portion of the trust which is attributable to contributions to corpus after 3-1-84 [**effective** date changed by P.L. 99-514, §1806(b)].

[Sec. 643(g)]

(g) CERTAIN PAYMENTS OF ESTIMATED TAX TREATED AS PAID BY BENEFICIARY.—

(1) IN GENERAL.—In the case of a trust—

(A) the trustee may elect to treat any portion of a payment of estimated tax made by such trust for any taxable year of the trust as a payment made by a beneficiary of such trust,

(B) any amount so treated shall be treated as paid or credited to the beneficiary on the last day of such taxable year, and

(C) for purposes of subtitle F, the amount so treated—

(i) shall not be treated as a payment of estimated tax made by the trust, but

(ii) shall be treated as a payment of estimated tax made by such beneficiary on January 15 following the taxable year.

(2) TIME FOR MAKING ELECTION.—An election under paragraph (1) shall be made on or before the 65th day after the close of the taxable year of the trust and in such manner as the Secretary may prescribe.

(3) EXTENSION TO LAST YEAR OF ESTATE.—In the case of a taxable year reasonably expected to be the last taxable year of an estate—

(A) any reference in this subsection to a trust shall be treated as including a reference to an estate, and

(B) the fiduciary of the estate shall be treated as the trustee.

Amendments

• **1988, Technical and Miscellaneous Revenue Act of 1988 (P.L. 100-647)**

P.L. 100-647, §1014(d)(3)(A)-(B):

Amended Code Sec. 643(g) by striking out the last sentence of paragraph (1), and by amending paragraph (2). **Effective** as if included in the provision of P.L. 99-514 to which it relates. Prior to amendment, the last sentence of paragraph (1) and paragraph (2) read as follows:

The preceding sentence shall apply only to the extent the payments of estimated tax made by the trust for the taxable year exceed the tax imposed by this chapter shown on its return for the taxable year.

(2) TIME FOR MAKING ELECTION.—An election under paragraph (1) may be made—

(A) only on the trust's return of the tax imposed by this chapter for the taxable year, and

(B) only if such return is filed on or before the 65th day after the close of the taxable year.

P.L. 100-647, §1014(d)(4):

Amended Code Sec. 643(g) by adding at the end thereof a new paragraph (3). **Effective** as if included in the provision of P.L. 99-514 to which it relates.

• 1986, Tax Reform Act of 1986 (P.L. 99-514)

P.L. 99-514, §1404(b):

Amended Code Sec. 643 by adding at the end thereof new subsection (g). **Effective** for tax years beginning after 12-31-86.

[Sec. 643(h)]

(h) DISTRIBUTIONS BY CERTAIN FOREIGN TRUSTS THROUGH NOMINEES.—For purposes of this part, any amount paid to a United States person which is derived directly or indirectly from a foreign trust of which the payor is not the grantor shall be deemed in the year of payment to have been directly paid by the foreign trust to such United States person.

Amendments

• 1996, Small Business Job Protection Act of 1996 (P.L. 104-188)

P.L. 104-188, §1904(c)(1):

Amended Code Sec. 643 by adding at the end a new subsection (h). **Effective** 8-20-96. For special and transitional rules, see Act Sec. 1904(d)(2) and (e), below.

P.L. 104-188, §1904(d)(2) and (e), provides:

(2) EXCEPTION FOR CERTAIN TRUSTS.—The amendments made by this section shall not apply to any trust—

(A) which is treated as owned by the grantor under section 676 or 677 (other than subsection (a)(3) thereof) of the Internal Revenue Code of 1986, and

(B) which is in existence on September 19, 1995.

The preceding sentence shall not apply to the portion of any such trust attributable to any transfer to such trust after September 19, 1995.

(e) TRANSITIONAL RULE.—If—

(1) by reason of the amendments made by this section, any person other than a United States person ceases to be treated as the owner of a portion of a domestic trust, and

(2) before January 1, 1997, such trust becomes a foreign trust, or the assets of such trust are transferred to a foreign trust,

no tax shall be imposed by section 1491 of the Internal Revenue Code of 1986 by reason of such trust becoming a foreign trust or the assets of such trust being transferred to a foreign trust.

[Sec. 643(i)]

(i) LOANS FROM FOREIGN TRUSTS.—For purposes of subparts B, C, and D—

(1) GENERAL RULE.—Except as provided in regulations, if a foreign trust makes a loan of cash or marketable securities (or permits the use of any other trust property) directly or indirectly to or by—

(A) any grantor or beneficiary of such trust who is a United States person, or

(B) any United States person not described in subparagraph (A) who is related to such grantor or beneficiary,

the amount of such loan (or the fair market value of the use of such property) shall be treated as a distribution by such trust to such grantor or beneficiary (as the case may be).

(2) DEFINITIONS AND SPECIAL RULES.—For purposes of this subsection—

(A) CASH.—The term "cash" includes foreign currencies and cash equivalents.

(B) RELATED PERSON.—

(i) IN GENERAL.—A person is related to another person if the relationship between such persons would result in a disallowance of losses under section 267 or 707(b). In applying section 267 for purposes of the preceding sentence, section 267(c)(4) shall be applied as if the family of an individual includes the spouses of the members of the family.

(ii) ALLOCATION.—If any person described in paragraph (1)(B) is related to more than one person, the grantor or beneficiary to whom the treatment under this subsection applies shall be determined under regulations prescribed by the Secretary.

(C) EXCLUSION OF TAX-EXEMPTS.—The term "United States person" does not include any entity exempt from tax under this chapter.

(D) TRUST NOT TREATED AS SIMPLE TRUST.—Any trust which is treated under this subsection as making a distribution shall be treated as not described in section 651.

(E) EXCEPTION FOR COMPENSATED USE OF PROPERTY.—In the case of the use of any trust property other than a loan of cash or marketable securities, paragraph (1) shall not apply to the extent that the trust is paid the fair market value of such use within a reasonable period of time of such use.

(3) SUBSEQUENT TRANSACTIONS.—If any loan (or use of property) is taken into account under paragraph (1), any subsequent transaction between the trust and the original borrower regarding the principal of the loan (by way of complete or partial repayment, satisfaction, cancellation, discharge, or otherwise) or the return of such property shall be disregarded for purposes of this title.

Amendments

• 2010, Hiring Incentives to Restore Employment Act (P.L. 111-147)

P.L. 111-147, §533(a)(1)-(2):

Amended Code Sec. 643(i)(1) by striking "directly or indirectly to" and inserting "(or permits the use of any other trust property) directly or indirectly to or by", and by inserting "(or the fair market value of the use of such property)" after "the amount of such loan". **Effective** for loans made, and uses of property, after 3-18-2010.

P.L. 111-147, §533(b):

Amended Code Sec. 643(i)(2) by adding at the end a new subparagraph (E). **Effective** for loans made, and uses of property, after 3-18-2010.

P.L. 111-147, §533(d)(1)-(3):

Amended Code Sec. 643(i)(3) by inserting "(or use of property)" after "If any loan", by inserting "or the return of such property" before "shall be disregarded", and by striking "REGARDING LOAN PRINCIPAL" following "SUBSEQUENT TRANSACTIONS" in the heading thereof. **Effective** for loans made, and uses of property, after 3-18-2010.

• 1996, Small Business Job Protection Act of 1996 (P.L. 104-188)

P.L. 104-188, §1906(c)(1):

Amended Code Sec. 643 by adding at the end a new subsection (i). **Effective** for loans of cash or marketable securities made after 9-19-95.

[Sec. 644]

SEC. 644. TAXABLE YEAR OF TRUSTS.

[Sec. 644(a)]

(a) IN GENERAL.—For purposes of this subtitle, the taxable year of any trust shall be the calendar year.

[Sec. 644(b)]

(b) EXCEPTION FOR TRUSTS EXEMPT FROM TAX AND CHARITABLE TRUSTS.—Subsection (a) shall not apply to a trust exempt from taxation under section 501(a) or a trust described in section 4947(a)(1).

Amendments

• 1997, Taxpayer Relief Act of 1997 (P.L. 105-34)

P.L. 105-34, §507(b)(1):

Amended subpart A of part I of subchapter J of chapter 1 by striking Code Sec. 644 and by redesignating Code Sec. 645 as Code Sec. 644. **Effective** for sales or exchanges after 8-5-97.

• 1986, Tax Reform Act of 1986 (P.L. 99-514)

P.L. 99-514, §1403(a):

Amended subpart A of part I of subchapter J by adding at the end thereof new Code Sec. 645. **Effective** for tax years beginning after 12-31-86. However, for a transitional rule, see Act Sec. 1403(c)(2), below.

P.L. 99-514, §1403(c)(2), provides:

(2) TRANSITION RULE.—With respect to any trust beneficiary who is required to include in gross income amounts under sections 652(a) or 662(a) of the Internal Revenue Code of 1986 in the 1st taxable year of the beneficiary beginning after December 31, 1986, by reason of any short taxable year of the trust required by the amendments made by this section, such income shall be ratably included in the income of the trust beneficiary over the 4-taxable year period beginning with such taxable year.

[Sec. 644—Stricken]

Amendments

• 1997, Taxpayer Relief Act of 1997 (P.L. 105-34)

P.L. 105-34, §507(b)(1):

Amended subpart A of part I of subchapter J of chapter 1 by striking Code Sec. 644 and by redesignating Code Sec. 645 as Code Sec. 644. **Effective** for sales or exchanges after 8-5-97. Prior to being stricken, Code Sec. 644 read as follows:

SEC. 644. SPECIAL RULE FOR GAIN ON PROPERTY TRANSFERRED TO TRUST AT LESS THAN FAIR MARKET VALUE.

[Sec. 644(a)]

(a) IMPOSITION OF TAX.—

(1) IN GENERAL.—If—

(A) a trust (or another trust to which the property is distributed) sells or exchanges property at a gain not more than 2 years after the date of the initial transfer of the property in trust by the transferor, and

(B) the fair market value of such property at the time of the initial transfer in trust by the transferor exceeds the adjusted basis of such property immediately after such transfer,

there is hereby imposed a tax determined in accordance with paragraph (2) on the includible gain recognized on such sale or exchange.

(2) AMOUNT OF TAX.—The amount of the tax imposed by paragraph (1) on any includible gain recognized on the sale or exchange of any property shall be equal to the sum of—

(A) the excess of—

(i) the tax which would have been imposed under this chapter for the taxable year of the transferor in which the sale or exchange of such property occurs had the amount of the includible gain recognized on such sale or exchange, reduced by any deductions properly allocable to such gain, been included in the gross income of the transferor for such taxable year, over

(ii) the tax actually imposed under this chapter for such taxable year of the transferor, plus

(B) if such sale or exchange occurs in a taxable year of the transferor which begins after the beginning of the taxable year of the trust in which such sale or exchange occurs, an amount equal to the amount determined under subparagraph (A) multiplied by the underpayment rate established under section 6621.

The determination of tax under clause (i) of subparagraph (A) shall be made by not taking into account any carryback, and by not taking into account any loss deduction to the extent that such loss or deduction may be carried by the transferor to any other taxable year.

(3) TAXABLE YEAR FOR WHICH TAX IMPOSED.—The tax imposed by paragraph (1) shall be imposed for the taxable year of the trust which begins with or within the taxable year of the transferor in which the sale or exchange occurs.

(4) TAX TO BE IN ADDITION TO OTHER TAXES.—The tax imposed by this subsection for any taxable year of the trust shall be in addition to any other tax imposed by this chapter for such taxable year.

Amendments

• 1986, Tax Reform Act of 1986 (P.L. 99-514)

P.L. 99-514, §1511(c)(5):

Amended Code Sec. 644(a)(2)(B) by striking out "the annual rate established under section 6621" and inserting in lieu thereof "the underpayment rate established under section 6621". **Effective** for purposes of determining interest for periods after 12-31-86.

• 1978, Revenue Act of 1978 (P.L. 95-600)

P.L. 95-600, §701(p)(1)(A):

Amended Code Sec. 644(a) by striking out "gain realized" wherever it appeared and inserting in lieu thereof "gain recognized". **Effective** for transfers in trust made after 5-21-76.

P.L. 95-600, §701(p)(2):

Amended Code Sec. 644(a)(2) by adding the last sentence. **Effective** for transfers in trust made after 5-21-76.

[Sec. 644(b)]

(b) DEFINITION OF INCLUDIBLE GAIN.—For purposes of this section, the term "includible gain" means the lesser of—

(1) the gain recognized by the trust on the sale or exchange of any property, or

(2) the excess of the fair market value of such property at the time of the initial transfer in trust by the transferor over the adjusted basis of such property immediately after such transfer.

[Sec. 644(c)]

(c) CHARACTER OF INCLUDIBLE GAIN.—For purposes of subsection (a)—

(1) the character of the includible gain shall be determined as if the property had actually been sold or exchanged by the transferor, and any activities of the trust with respect to the sale or exchange of the property shall be deemed to be activities of the transferor, and

(2) the portion of the includible gain subject to the provisions of section 1245 and section 1250 shall be determined in accordance with regulations prescribed by the Secretary.

[Sec. 644(d)]

(d) SPECIAL RULES.—

(1) SHORT SALES.—If the trust sells the property referred to in subsection (a) in a short sale within the 2-year period referred to in such subsection, such 2-year period shall be extended to the date of the closing of such short sale.

(2) SUBSTITUTED BASIS PROPERTY.—For purposes of this section, in the case of any property held by the trust which has a basis determined in whole or in part by reference to the basis of any other property which was transferred to the trust—

(A) the initial transfer of such property in trust by the transferor shall be treated as having occurred on the date of the initial transfer in trust of such other property,

(B) subsections (a)(1)(B) and (b)(2) shall be applied by taking into account the fair market value and the adjusted basis of such other property, and

(C) the amount determined under subsection (b)(2) with respect to such other property shall be allocated (under regulations prescribed by the Secretary) among such other property and all properties held by the trust which have a basis determined in whole or in part by reference to the basis of such other property.

Amendments

• **1978, Revenue Act of 1978 (P.L. 95-600)**

P.L. 95-600, §701(p)(1)(B):

Amended Code Sec. 644(d). **Effective** for transfers in trust made after 5-21-76. Prior to amendment, Code Sec. 644(d) read as follows:

(d) SPECIAL RULE FOR SHORT SALES.—If the trust sells the property referred to in subsection (a) in a short sale within the 2-year period referred to in such subsection, such 2-year period shall be extended to the date of the closing of such short sale.

[Sec. 644(e)]

(e) EXCEPTIONS.—Subsection (a) shall not apply to property—

(1) acquired by the trust from a decedent or which passed to a trust from a decedent (within the meaning of section 1014), or

(2) acquired by a pooled income fund (as defined in section 642(c)(5)), or

(3) acquired by a charitable remainder annuity trust (as defined in section 664(d)(1)) or a charitable remainder unitrust (as defined in sections 664(d)(2) and (3)), or

(4) if the sale or exchange of the property occurred after the death of the transferor.

[Sec. 644(f)]

(f) SPECIAL RULE FOR INSTALLMENT SALES.—If the trust reports income under section 453 on any sale or exchange to which subsection (a) applies, under regulations prescribed by the Secretary—

(1) subsection (a) (other than the 2-year requirement of paragraph (1)(A) thereof) shall be applied as if each installment were a separate sale or exchange of property to which such subsection applies, and

(2) the term "includible gain" shall not include any portion of an installment received by the trust after the death of the transferor.

Amendments

• **1980, Installment Sales Revision Act of 1980 (P.L. 96-471)**

P.L. 96-471, §2(b)(4):

Amended Code Sec. 644(f) by striking out "elects to report income under section 453" and substituting "reports income under section 453". **Effective** for dispositions made after 10-19-80, in tax years ending after that year.

• **1978, Revenue Act of 1978 (P.L. 95-600)**

P.L. 95-600, §701(p)(3):

Amended Code Sec. 644(f)(1) by striking out "subsection (a)" and inserting in lieu thereof "subsection (a) (other than the 2-year requirement of paragraph (1)(A) thereof)". **Effective** for transfers in trust made after 5-21-76.

• **1976, Tax Reform Act of 1976 (P.L. 94-455)**

P.L. 94-455, §701(e):

Added Code Sec. 644. **Effective** for transfers in trust made after 5-21-76.

[Sec. 645]

SEC. 645. CERTAIN REVOCABLE TRUSTS TREATED AS PART OF ESTATE.

[Sec. 645(a)]

(a) GENERAL RULE.—For purposes of this subtitle, if both the executor (if any) of an estate and the trustee of a qualified revocable trust elect the treatment provided in this section, such trust shall be treated and taxed as part of such estate (and not as a separate trust) for all taxable years of the estate ending after the date of the decedent's death and before the applicable date.

[Sec. 645(b)]

(b) DEFINITIONS.—For purposes of subsection (a)—

(1) QUALIFIED REVOCABLE TRUST.—The term "qualified revocable trust" means any trust (or portion thereof) which was treated under section 676 as owned by the decedent of the estate referred to in subsection (a) by reason of a power in the grantor (determined without regard to section 672(e)).

(2) APPLICABLE DATE.—The term "applicable date" means—

(A) if no return of tax imposed by chapter 11 is required to be filed, the date which is 2 years after the date of the decedent's death, and

(B) if such a return is required to be filed, the date which is 6 months after the date of the final determination of the liability for tax imposed by chapter 11.

[Sec. 645(c)]

(c) ELECTION.—The election under subsection (a) shall be made not later than the time prescribed for filing the return of tax imposed by this chapter for the first taxable year of the estate (determined with regard to extensions) and, once made, shall be irrevocable.

Amendments

• 1998, IRS Restructuring and Reform Act of 1998 (P.L. 105-206)

P.L. 105-206, §6013(a)(1):

Redesignated Code Sec. 646 as Code Sec. 645. **Effective** as if included in the provision of P.L. 105-34 to which it relates [**effective** for estates of decedents dying after 8-5-97.—CCH].

• 1997, Taxpayer Relief Act of 1997 (P.L. 105-34)

P.L. 105-34, §1305(a):

Amended subpart A of part I of subchapter J by adding at the end a new Code Sec. 646. **Effective** with respect to estates of decedents dying after 8-5-97.

[Sec. 646]

SEC. 646. TAX TREATMENT OF ELECTING ALASKA NATIVE SETTLEMENT TRUSTS.

[Sec. 646(a)]

(a) IN GENERAL.—If an election under this section is in effect with respect to any Settlement Trust, the provisions of this section shall apply in determining the income tax treatment of the Settlement Trust and its beneficiaries with respect to the Settlement Trust.

[Sec. 646(b)]

(b) TAXATION OF INCOME OF TRUST.—Except as provided in subsection (f)(1)(B)(ii)—

(1) IN GENERAL.—There is hereby imposed on the taxable income of an electing Settlement Trust, other than its net capital gain, a tax at the lowest rate specified in section 1(c).

(2) CAPITAL GAIN.—In the case of an electing Settlement Trust with a net capital gain for the taxable year, a tax is hereby imposed on such gain at the rate of tax which would apply to such gain if the taxpayer were subject to a tax on its other taxable income at only the lowest rate specified in section 1(c).

Any such tax shall be in lieu of the income tax otherwise imposed by this chapter on such income or gain.

[Sec. 646(c)]

(c) ONE-TIME ELECTION.—

(1) IN GENERAL.—A Settlement Trust may elect to have the provisions of this section apply to the trust and its beneficiaries.

(2) TIME AND METHOD OF ELECTION.—An election under paragraph (1) shall be made by the trustee of such trust—

(A) on or before the due date (including extensions) for filing the Settlement Trust's return of tax for the first taxable year of such trust ending after the date of the enactment of this section, and

(B) by attaching to such return of tax a statement specifically providing for such election.

(3) PERIOD ELECTION IN EFFECT.—Except as provided in subsection (f), an election under this subsection—

(A) shall apply to the first taxable year described in paragraph (2)(A) and all subsequent taxable years, and

(B) may not be revoked once it is made.

[Sec. 646(d)]

(d) CONTRIBUTIONS TO TRUST.—

(1) BENEFICIARIES OF ELECTING TRUST NOT TAXED ON CONTRIBUTIONS.—In the case of an electing Settlement Trust, no amount shall be includible in the gross income of a beneficiary of such trust by reason of a contribution to such trust.

(2) EARNINGS AND PROFITS.—The earnings and profits of the sponsoring Native Corporation shall not be reduced on account of any contribution to such Settlement Trust.

[Sec. 646(e)]

(e) TAX TREATMENT OF DISTRIBUTIONS TO BENEFICIARIES.—Amounts distributed by an electing Settlement Trust during any taxable year shall be considered as having the following characteristics in the hands of the recipient beneficiary:

(1) First, as amounts excludable from gross income for the taxable year to the extent of the taxable income of such trust for such taxable year (decreased by any income tax paid by the trust with respect to the income) plus any amount excluded from gross income of the trust under section 103.

(2) Second, as amounts excludable from gross income to the extent of the amount described in paragraph (1) for all taxable years for which an election is in effect under subsection (c) with respect to the trust, and not previously taken into account under paragraph (1).

(3) Third, as amounts distributed by the sponsoring Native Corporation with respect to its stock (within the meaning of section 301(a)) during such taxable year and taxable to the recipient beneficiary as amounts described in section 301(c)(1), to the extent of current or accumulated earnings and profits of the sponsoring Native Corporation as of the close of such taxable year after proper adjustment is made for all distributions made by the sponsoring Native Corporation during such taxable year.

(4) Fourth, as amounts distributed by the trust in excess of the distributable net income of such trust for such taxable year.

Amounts distributed to which paragraph (3) applies shall not be treated as a corporate distribution subject to section 311(b), and for purposes of determining the amount of a distribution for purposes of paragraph (3) and the basis to the recipients, section 643(e) and not section 301(b) or (d) shall apply.

[Sec. 646(f)]

(f) SPECIAL RULES WHERE TRANSFER RESTRICTIONS MODIFIED.—

(1) TRANSFER OF BENEFICIAL INTERESTS.—If, at any time, a beneficial interest in an electing Settlement Trust may be disposed of to a person in a manner which would not be permitted by section 7(h) of the Alaska Native Claims Settlement Act (43 U.S.C. 1606(h)) if such interest were Settlement Common Stock—

(A) no election may be made under subsection (c) with respect to such trust, and

(B) if such an election is in effect as of such time—

(i) such election shall cease to apply as of the first day of the taxable year in which such disposition is first permitted,

(ii) the provisions of this section shall not apply to such trust for such taxable year and all taxable years thereafter, and

(iii) the distributable net income of such trust shall be increased by the current or accumulated earnings and profits of the sponsoring Native Corporation as of the close of such taxable year after proper adjustment is made for all distributions made by the sponsoring Native Corporation during such taxable year.

In no event shall the increase under clause (iii) exceed the fair market value of the trust's assets as of the date the beneficial interest of the trust first becomes so disposable. The earnings and profits of the sponsoring Native Corporation shall be adjusted as of the last day of such taxable year by the amount of earnings and profits so included in the distributable net income of the trust.

(2) STOCK IN CORPORATION.—If—

(A) stock in the sponsoring Native Corporation may be disposed of to a person in a manner which would not be permitted by section 7(h) of the Alaska Native Claims Settlement Act (43 U.S.C. 1606(h)) if such stock were Settlement Common Stock, and

(B) at any time after such disposition of stock is first permitted, such corporation transfers assets to a Settlement Trust,

paragraph (1)(B) shall be applied to such trust on and after the date of the transfer in the same manner as if the trust permitted dispositions of beneficial interests in the trust in a manner not permitted by such section 7(h).

(3) CERTAIN DISTRIBUTIONS.—For purposes of this section, the surrender of an interest in a Native Corporation or an electing Settlement Trust in order to accomplish the whole or partial redemption of the interest of a shareholder or beneficiary in such corporation or trust, or to accomplish the whole or partial liquidation of such corporation or trust, shall be deemed to be a transfer permitted by section 7(h) of the Alaska Native Claims Settlement Act.

[Sec. 646(g)]

(g) TAXABLE INCOME.—For purposes of this title, the taxable income of an electing Settlement Trust shall be determined under section 641(b) without regard to any deduction under section 651 or 661.

[Sec. 646(h)]

(h) DEFINITIONS.—For purposes of this section—

(1) ELECTING SETTLEMENT TRUST.—The term "electing Settlement Trust" means a Settlement Trust which has made the election, effective for a taxable year, described in subsection (c).

(2) NATIVE CORPORATION.—The term "Native Corporation" has the meaning given such term by section 3(m) of the Alaska Native Claims Settlement Act (43 U.S.C. 1602(m)).

(3) SETTLEMENT COMMON STOCK.—The term "Settlement Common Stock" has the meaning given such term by section 3(p) of the Alaska Native Claims Settlement Act (43 U.S.C. 1602(p)).

(4) SETTLEMENT TRUST.—The term "Settlement Trust" means a trust that constitutes a settlement trust under section 3(t) of the Alaska Native Claims Settlement Act (43 U.S.C. 1602(t)).

(5) SPONSORING NATIVE CORPORATION.—The term "sponsoring Native Corporation" means the Native Corporation which transfers assets to an electing Settlement Trust.

[Sec. 646(i)]

(i) SPECIAL LOSS DISALLOWANCE RULE.—Any loss that would otherwise be recognized by a shareholder upon a disposition of a share of stock of a sponsoring Native Corporation shall be reduced (but not below zero) by the per share loss adjustment factor. The per share loss adjustment factor shall be the aggregate of all contributions to all electing Settlement Trusts sponsored by such Native Corporation made on or after the first day each trust is treated as an electing Settlement Trust expressed on a per share basis and determined as of the day of each such contribution.

[Sec. 646(j)]

(j) CROSS REFERENCE.—

For information required with respect to electing Settlement Trusts and sponsoring Native Corporations, see section 6039H.

Amendments

• 2013, American Taxpayer Relief Act of 2012 (P.L. 112-240)

P.L. 112-240, §101(a)(1) and (3), provides:

SEC. 101. PERMANENT EXTENSION AND MODIFICATION OF 2001 TAX RELIEF.

(a) PERMANENT EXTENSION.—

(1) IN GENERAL.—The Economic Growth and Tax Relief Reconciliation Act of 2001 is amended by striking title IX.

* * *

(3) EFFECTIVE DATE.—The amendments made by this subsection shall apply to taxable, plan, or limitation years beginning after December 31, 2012, and estates of decedents dying, gifts made, or generation skipping transfers after December 31, 2012.

• 2001, Economic Growth and Tax Relief Reconciliation Act of 2001 (P.L. 107-16)

P.L. 107-16, §671(a):

Amended subpart A of part I of subchapter J of chapter 1 by adding at the end a new Code Sec. 646. **Effective** for tax years ending after 6-7-2001, and to contributions made to electing Settlement Trusts for such year or any subsequent year.

P.L. 107-16, §901(a)-(b), as amended by P.L. 111-312, §101(a)(1), provides [but see P.L. 112-240, §101(a)(1) and (3), above]:

SEC. 901. SUNSET OF PROVISIONS OF ACT.

(a) IN GENERAL.—All provisions of, and amendments made by, this Act shall not apply—

(1) to taxable, plan, or limitation years beginning after December 31, 2012, or

(2) in the case of title V, to estates of decedents dying, gifts made, or generation skipping transfers, after December 31, 2012.

(b) APPLICATION OF CERTAIN LAWS.—The Internal Revenue Code of 1986 and the Employee Retirement Income Security Act of 1974 shall be applied and administered to years, estates, gifts, and transfers described in subsection (a) as if the provisions and amendments described in subsection (a) had never been enacted.

Subpart B—Trusts Which Distribute Current Income Only

[Sec. 651]

SEC. 651. DEDUCTION FOR TRUSTS DISTRIBUTING CURRENT INCOME ONLY.

[Sec. 651(a)]

(a) DEDUCTION.—In the case of any trust the terms of which—

(1) provide that all of its income is required to be distributed currently, and

(2) do not provide that any amounts are to be paid, permanently set aside, or used for the purposes specified in section 642(c) (relating to deduction for charitable, etc., purposes),

there shall be allowed as a deduction in computing the taxable income of the trust the amount of the income for the taxable year which is required to be distributed currently. This section shall not apply in any taxable year in which the trust distributes amounts other than amounts of income described in paragraph (1).

[Sec. 651(b)]

(b) LIMITATION ON DEDUCTION.—If the amount of income required to be distributed currently exceeds the distributable net income of the trust for the taxable year, the deduction shall be limited to the amount of the distributable net income. For this purpose, the computation of distributable net income shall not include items of income which are not included in the gross income of the trust and the deductions allocable thereto.

[Sec. 652]

SEC. 652. INCLUSION OF AMOUNTS IN GROSS INCOME OF BENEFICIARIES OF TRUSTS DISTRIBUTING CURRENT INCOME ONLY.

[Sec. 652(a)]

(a) INCLUSION.—Subject to subsection (b), the amount of income for the taxable year required to be distributed currently by a trust described in section 651 shall be included in the gross income of the beneficiaries to whom the income is required to be distributed, whether distributed or not. If such amount exceeds the distributable net income, there shall be included in the gross income of each beneficiary an amount which bears the same ratio to distributable net income as the amount of income required to be distributed to such beneficiary bears to the amount of income required to be distributed to all beneficiaries.

[Sec. 652(b)]

(b) CHARACTER OF AMOUNTS.—The amounts specified in subsection (a) shall have the same character in the hands of the beneficiary as in the hands of the trust. For this purpose, the amounts shall be treated as consisting of the same proportion of each class of items entering into the computation of distributable net income of the trust as the total of each class bears to the total distributable net income of the trust, unless the terms of the trust specifically allocate different classes of income to different beneficiaries. In the application of the preceding sentence, the items of deduction entering into the computation of distributable net income shall be allocated among the items of distributable net income in accordance with regulations prescribed by the Secretary.

Amendments

• 1976, Tax Reform Act of 1976 (P.L. 94-455)

P.L. 94-455, §1906(b)(13)(A):

Amended 1954 Code by substituting "Secretary" for "Secretary or his delegate" each place it appeared. **Effective** 2-1-77.

[Sec. 652(c)]

(c) DIFFERENT TAXABLE YEARS.—If the taxable year of a beneficiary is different from that of the trust, the amount which the beneficiary is required to include in gross income in accordance with the provisions of this section shall be based upon the amount of income of the trust for any taxable year or years of the trust ending within or with his taxable year.

Subpart C—Estates and Trusts Which May Accumulate Income or Which Distribute Corpus

[Sec. 661]

SEC. 661. DEDUCTION FOR ESTATES AND TRUSTS ACCUMULATING INCOME OR DISTRIBUTING CORPUS.

[Sec. 661(a)]

(a) DEDUCTION.—In any taxable year there shall be allowed as a deduction in computing the taxable income of an estate or trust (other than a trust to which subpart B applies), the sum of—

(1) any amount of income for such taxable year required to be distributed currently (including any amount required to be distributed which may be paid out of income or corpus to the extent such amount is paid out of income for such taxable year); and

(2) any other amounts properly paid or credited or required to be distributed for such taxable year;

but such deduction shall not exceed the distributable net income of the estate or trust.

Amendments

• 1983, Interest and Dividend Tax Compliance Act of 1983 (P.L. 98-67)

P.L. 98-67, §102(a):

Repealed the amendment made by P.L. 97-248 (see below), as of the close of 6-30-83, as though such amendment had not been made.

• 1982, Tax Equity and Fiscal Responsibility Act of 1982 (P.L. 97-248)

P.L. 97-248, §302(b)(2):

Amended Code Sec. 661(a) by adding at the end thereof the following sentence: "For purposes of paragraph (1), the amount of distributable net income shall be computed without the deduction allowed by section 642(c)." **Effective** for interest, dividends and patronage dividends paid or credited after 6-30-83.

[Sec. 661(b)]

(b) CHARACTER OF AMOUNTS DISTRIBUTED.—The amount determined under subsection (a) shall be treated as consisting of the same proportion of each class of items entering into the computation of distributable net income of the estate or trust as the total of each class bears to the total distributable net income of the estate or trust in the absence of the allocation of different classes of income under the specific terms of the governing instrument. In the application of the preceding sentence, the items of deduction entering into the computation of distributable net income (including the deduction allowed under section 642(c)) shall be allocated among the items of distributable net income in accordance with regulations prescribed by the Secretary.

Amendments

• 1976, Tax Reform Act of 1976 (P.L. 94-455)

P.L. 94-455, §1906(b)(13)(A):

Amended 1954 Code by substituting "Secretary" for "Secretary or his delegate" each place it appeared. **Effective** 2-1-77.

[Sec. 661(c)]

(c) LIMITATION ON DEDUCTION.—No deduction shall be allowed under subsection (a) in respect of any portion of the amount allowed as a deduction under that subsection (without regard to this subsection) which is treated under subsection (b) as consisting of any item of distributable net income which is not included in the gross income of the estate or trust.

[Sec. 662]

SEC. 662. INCLUSION OF AMOUNTS IN GROSS INCOME OF BENEFICIARIES OF ESTATES AND TRUSTS ACCUMULATING INCOME OR DISTRIBUTING CORPUS.

[Sec. 662(a)]

(a) INCLUSION.—Subject to subsection (b), there shall be included in the gross income of a beneficiary to whom an amount specified in section 661(a) is paid, credited, or required to be distributed (by an estate or trust described in section 661), the sum of the following amounts:

(1) AMOUNTS REQUIRED TO BE DISTRIBUTED CURRENTLY.—The amount of income for the taxable year required to be distributed currently to such beneficiary, whether distributed or not. If the amount of income required to be distributed currently to all beneficiaries exceeds the distributable net income (computed without the deduction allowed by section 642(c), relating to deduction for charitable, etc. purposes) of the estate or trust, then, in lieu of the amount provided in the preceding sentence, there shall be included in the gross income of the beneficiary an amount which bears the same ratio to distributable net income (as so computed) as the amount of income required to be distributed currently to such beneficiary bears to the amount required to be distributed currently to all beneficiaries. For purposes of this section, the phrase "the amount of income for the taxable year required to be distributed currently" includes any amount required to be paid out of income or corpus to the extent such amount is paid out of income for such taxable year.

(2) OTHER AMOUNTS DISTRIBUTED.—All other amounts properly paid, credited, or required to be distributed to such beneficiary for the taxable year. If the sum of—

(A) the amount of income for the taxable year required to be distributed currently to all beneficiaries, and

(B) all other amounts properly paid, credited, or required to be distributed to all beneficiaries

exceeds the distributable net income of the estate or trust, then, in lieu of the amount provided in the preceding sentence, there shall be included in the gross income of the beneficiary an amount which bears the same ratio to distributable net income (reduced by the amounts specified in (A)) as the other amounts properly paid, credited or required to be distributed to the beneficiary bear to the other amounts properly paid, credited, or required to be distributed to all beneficiaries.

[Sec. 662(b)]

(b) CHARACTER OF AMOUNTS.—The amounts determined under subsection (a) shall have the same character in the hands of the beneficiary as in the hands of the estate or trust. For this purpose, the amounts shall be treated as consisting of the same proportion of each class of items entering into the computation of distributable net income as the total of each class bears to the total distributable net income of the estate or trust unless the terms of the governing instrument specifically allocate different classes of income to different beneficiaries. In the application of the preceding sentence, the items of deduction entering into the computation of distributable net income (including the deduction allowed under section 642(c)) shall be allocated among the items of distributable net income in accordance with regulations prescribed by the Secretary. In the application of this subsection to the amount determined under paragraph (1) of subsection (a), distributable net income shall be computed without regard to any portion of the deduction under section 642(c) which is not attributable to income of the taxable year.

Amendments

• 1976, Tax Reform Act of 1976 (P.L. 94-455)

P.L. 94-455, § 1906(b)(13)(A):

Amended 1954 Code by substituting "Secretary" for "Secretary or his delegate" each place it appeared. **Effective** 2-1-77.

[Sec. 662(c)]

(c) DIFFERENT TAXABLE YEARS.—If the taxable year of a beneficiary is different from that of the estate or trust, the amount to be included in the gross income of the beneficiary shall be based on the distributable net income of the estate or trust and the amounts properly paid, credited, or required to be distributed to the beneficiary during any taxable year or years of the estate or trust ending within or with his taxable year.

[Sec. 663]

SEC. 663. SPECIAL RULES APPLICABLE TO SECTIONS 661 AND 662 .

[Sec. 663(a)]

(a) EXCLUSIONS.—There shall not be included as amounts falling within section 661(a) or 662(a)—

(1) GIFTS, BEQUESTS, ETC.—Any amount which, under the terms of the governing instrument, is properly paid or credited as a gift or bequest of a specific sum of money or of specific property and which is paid or credited all at once or in not more than 3 installments. For this purpose an amount which can be paid or credited only from the income of the estate or trust shall not be considered as a gift or bequest of a specific sum of money.

(2) CHARITABLE, ETC., DISTRIBUTIONS.—Any amount paid or permanently set aside or otherwise qualifying for the deduction provided in section 642(c) (computed without regard to sections 508(d), 681, and 4948(c)(4)).

(3) DENIAL OF DOUBLE DEDUCTION.—Any amount paid, credited, or distributed in the taxable year, if section 651 or section 661 applied to such amount for a preceding taxable year of an estate or trust because credited or required to be distributed in such preceding taxable year.

Amendments

• 1969, Tax Reform Act of 1969 (P.L. 91-172)

P.L. 91-172, §101(j)(17):

Amended Code Sec. 663(a)(2) by substituting "sections 508(d), 681, and 4948(c)(4)" for "section 681." **Effective** 1-1-70.

[Sec. 663(b)]

(b) DISTRIBUTIONS IN FIRST SIXTY-FIVE DAYS OF TAXABLE YEAR.—

(1) GENERAL RULE.—If within the first 65 days of any taxable year of an estate or a trust, an amount is properly paid or credited, such amount shall be considered paid or credited on the last day of the preceding taxable year.

(2) LIMITATION.—Paragraph (1) shall apply with respect to any taxable year of an estate or a trust only if the executor of such estate or the fiduciary of such trust (as the case may be) elects, in such manner and at such time as the Secretary prescribes by regulations, to have paragraph (1) apply for such taxable year.

Amendments

• 1997, Taxpayer Relief Act of 1997 (P.L. 105-34)

P.L. 105-34, §1306(a):

Amended Code Sec. 663(b) by inserting "an estate or" before "a trust" each place it appears. **Effective** for tax years beginning after 8-5-97.

P.L. 105-34, §1306(b):

Amended Code Sec. 663(b)(2) by striking "the fiduciary of such trust" and inserting "the executor of such estate or the fiduciary of such trust (as the case may be)". **Effective** for tax years beginning after 8-5-97.

• 1976, Tax Reform Act of 1976 (P.L. 94-455)

P.L. 94-455, §1906(b)(13)(A):

Amended 1954 Code by substituting "Secretary" for "Secretary or his delegate" each place it appeared. **Effective** 2-1-77.

• 1969, Tax Reform Act of 1969 (P.L. 91-172)

P.L. 91-172, §331(b):

Amended Code Sec. 663(b)(2). **Effective** for tax years beginning after 12-31-68. Prior to amendment, Code Sec. 663(b)(2) read as follows:

(2) Limitation.—This subsection shall apply only to a trust—

(A) which was in existence prior to January 1, 1954,

(B) which, under the terms of its governing instrument, may not distribute in any taxable year amounts in excess of the income of the preceding taxable year, and

(C) on behalf of which the fiduciary elects to have this subsection apply.

The election authorized by subparagraph (C) shall be made for the first taxable year to which this part is applicable in accordance with such regulations as the Secretary or his delegate shall prescribe and shall be made not later than the time prescribed by law for filing the return for such year (including extensions thereof). If such election is made with respect to a taxable year, this subsection shall apply to all amounts properly paid or credited within the first 65 days of all subsequent taxable years of such trust.

[Sec. 663(c)]

(c) SEPARATE SHARES TREATED AS SEPARATE ESTATES OR TRUSTS.—For the sole purpose of determining the amount of distributable net income in the application of sections 661 and 662, in the case of a single trust having more than one beneficiary, substantially separate and independent shares of different beneficiaries in the trust shall be treated as separate trusts. Rules similar to the rules of the preceding provisions of this subsection shall apply to treat substantially separate and independent shares of different beneficiaries in an estate having more than 1 beneficiary as separate estates. The existence of such substantially separate and independent shares and the manner of treatment as separate trusts or estates, including the application of subpart D, shall be determined in accordance with regulations prescribed by the Secretary.

Amendments

• 1997, Taxpayer Relief Act of 1997 (P.L. 105-34)

P.L. 105-34, §1307(a)(1)-(2):

Amended Code Sec. 663(c) by inserting before the last sentence a new sentence, and by inserting "or estates" after "trusts" in the last sentence. **Effective** for estates of decedents dying after 8-5-97.

P.L. 105-34, §1307(b):

Amended Code Sec. 663(c) by inserting "ESTATES OR" before "TRUSTS" in the subsection heading. **Effective** for estates of decedents dying after 8-5-97.

• 1976, Tax Reform Act of 1976 (P.L. 94-455)

P.L. 94-455, §1906(b)(13)(A):

Amended 1954 Code by substituting "Secretary" for "Secretary or his delegate" each place it appeared. **Effective** 2-1-77.

[Sec. 664]

SEC. 664. CHARITABLE REMAINDER TRUSTS.

[Sec. 664(a)]

(a) GENERAL RULE.—Notwithstanding any other provision of this subchapter, the provisions of this section shall, in accordance with regulations prescribed by the Secretary, apply in the case of a charitable remainder annuity trust and a charitable remainder unitrust.

Amendments

• 1976, Tax Reform Act of 1976 (P.L. 94-455)

P.L. 94-455, §1906(b)(13)(A):

Amended 1954 Code by substituting "Secretary" for "Secretary or his delegate" each place it appeared. **Effective** 2-1-77.

[Sec. 664(b)]

(b) CHARACTER OF DISTRIBUTIONS.—Amounts distributed by a charitable remainder annuity trust or by a charitable remainder unitrust shall be considered as having the following characteristics in the hands of a beneficiary to whom is paid the annuity described in subsection (d)(1)(A) or the payment described in subsection (d)(2)(A):

(1) First, as amounts of income (other than gains, and amounts treated as gains, from the sale or other disposition of capital assets) includible in gross income to the extent of such income of the trust for the year and such undistributed income of the trust for prior years;

(2) Second, as a capital gain to the extent of the capital gain of the trust for the year and the undistributed capital gain of the trust for prior years;

(3) Third, as other income to the extent of such income of the trust for the year and such undistributed income of the trust for prior years; and

(4) Fourth, as a distribution of trust corpus.

For purposes of this section, the trust shall determine the amount of its undistributed capital gain on a cumulative net basis.

[Sec. 664(c)]

(c) TAXATION OF TRUSTS.—

(1) INCOME TAX.—A charitable remainder annuity trust and a charitable remainder unitrust shall, for any taxable year, not be subject to any tax imposed by this subtitle.

(2) EXCISE TAX.—

(A) IN GENERAL.—In the case of a charitable remainder annuity trust or a charitable remainder unitrust which has unrelated business taxable income (within the meaning of section 512, determined as if part III of subchapter F applied to such trust) for a taxable year, there is hereby imposed on such trust or unitrust an excise tax equal to the amount of such unrelated business taxable income.

(B) CERTAIN RULES TO APPLY.—The tax imposed by subparagraph (A) shall be treated as imposed by chapter 42 for purposes of this title other than subchapter E of chapter 42.

(C) TAX COURT PROCEEDINGS.—For purposes of this paragraph, the references in section 6212(c)(1) to section 4940 shall be deemed to include references to this paragraph.

Amendments

• 2006, Tax Relief and Health Care Act of 2006 (P.L. 109-432)

P.L. 109-432, Division A, §424(a):

Amended Code Sec. 664(c). **Effective** for tax years beginning after 12-31-2006. Prior to amendment, Code Sec. 664(c) read as follows:

(c) EXEMPTION FROM INCOME TAXES.—A charitable remainder annuity trust and a charitable remainder unitrust shall, for any taxable year, not be subject to any tax imposed by this subtitle, unless such trust, for such year, has unrelated business taxable income (within the meaning of section 512, determined as if part III of subchapter F applied to such trust).

[Sec. 664(d)]

(d) DEFINITIONS.—

(1) CHARITABLE REMAINDER ANNUITY TRUST.—For purposes of this section, a charitable remainder annuity trust is a trust—

(A) from which a sum certain (which is not less than 5 percent nor more than 50 percent of the initial net fair market value of all property placed in trust) is to be paid, not less often than annually, to one or more persons (at least one of which is not an organization described in section 170(c) and, in the case of individuals, only to an individual who is living at the time of the creation of the trust) for a term of years (not in excess of 20 years) or for the life or lives of such individual or individuals,

(B) from which no amount other than the payments described in subparagraph (A) and other than qualified gratuitous transfers described in subparagraph (C) may be paid to or for the use of any person other than an organization described in section 170(c),

(C) following the termination of the payments described in subparagraph (A), the remainder interest in the trust is to be transferred to, or for the use of, an organization described in section 170(c) or is to be retained by the trust for such a use or, to the extent the remainder interest is in qualified employer securities (as defined in subsection (g)(4)), all or part of such securities are to be transferred to an employee stock ownership plan (as defined in section 4975(e)(7)) in a qualified gratuitous transfer (as defined by subsection (g)), and

(D) the value (determined under section 7520) of such remainder interest is at least 10 percent of the initial net fair market value of all property placed in the trust.

(2) CHARITABLE REMAINDER UNITRUST.—For purposes of this section, a charitable remainder unitrust is a trust—

(A) from which a fixed percentage (which is not less than 5 percent nor more than 50 percent) of the net fair market value of its assets, valued annually, is to be paid, not less often than annually, to one or more persons (at least one of which is not an organization described in section 170(c) and, in the case of individuals, only to an individual who is living at the time of the creation of the trust) for a term of years (not in excess of 20 years) or for the life or lives of such individual or individuals,

(B) from which no amount other than the payments described in subparagraph (A) and other than qualified gratuitous transfers described in subparagraph (C) may be paid to or for the use of any person other than an organization described in section 170(c),

(C) following the termination of the payments described in subparagraph (A), the remainder interest in the trust is to be transferred to, or for the use of, an organization described in section 170(c) or is to be retained by the trust for such a use or, to the extent the remainder interest is in qualified employer securities (as defined in subsection (g)(4)), all or part of such securities are to be transferred to an employee stock ownership plan (as defined in section 4975(e)(7)) in a qualified gratuitous transfer (as defined by subsection (g)), and

(D) with respect to each contribution of property to the trust, the value (determined under section 7520) of such remainder interest in such property is at least 10 percent of the net fair market value of such property as of the date such property is contributed to the trust.

(3) EXCEPTION.—Notwithstanding the provisions of paragraphs (2)(A) and (B), the trust instrument may provide that the trustee shall pay the income beneficiary for any year—

(A) the amount of the trust income, if such amount is less than the amount required to be distributed under paragraph (2)(A), and

(B) any amount of the trust income which is in excess of the amount required to be distributed under paragraph (2)(A), to the extent that (by reason of subparagraph (A)) the aggregate of the amounts paid in prior years was less than the aggregate of such required amounts.

(4) SEVERANCE OF CERTAIN ADDITIONAL CONTRIBUTIONS.—If—

(A) any contribution is made to a trust which before the contribution is a charitable remainder unitrust, and

(B) such contribution would (but for this paragraph) result in such trust ceasing to be a charitable unitrust by reason of paragraph (2)(D),

such contribution shall be treated as a transfer to a separate trust under regulations prescribed by the Secretary.

Amendments

• 2000, Community Renewal Tax Relief Act of 2000 (P.L. 106-554)

P.L. 106-554, §319(7):

Amended Code Sec. 664(d)(1)(C) and (2)(C) by striking the period after "subsection (g))". **Effective** on 12-21-2000.

• 1998, IRS Restructuring and Reform Act of 1998 (P.L. 105-206)

P.L. 105-206, §6010(r):

Amended Code Sec. 664(d)(1)(C) and (2)(C) by adding ", and" at the end. **Effective** as if included in the provision of P.L. 105-34 to which it relates [generally **effective** for transfers in trust after 7-28-97.—CCH].

• 1997, Taxpayer Relief Act of 1997 (P.L. 105-34)

P.L. 105-34, §1089(a)(1):

Amended Code Sec. 664(d)(1)(A) and (2)(A) by inserting "nor more than 50 percent" after "not less than 5 percent". **Effective**, generally, for transfers in trust after 6-18-97. For a special rule, see Act Sec. 1089(b)(6)(B), below.

P.L. 105-34, §1089(b)(1):

Amended Code Sec. 664(d)(1) by striking "and" at the end of subparagraph (B), by striking the period at the end of subparagraph (C), and by adding at the end a new subparagraph (D). **Effective**, generally, for transfers in trust after 7-28-97. For a special rule, see Act Sec. 1089(b)(6)(B), below.

P.L. 105-34, §1089(b)(2):

Amended Code Sec. 664(d)(2) by striking "and" at the end of subparagraph (B), by striking the period at the end of subparagraph (C), and by adding at the end a new subparagraph (D). **Effective**, generally, for transfers in trust after 7-28-97. For a special rule, see Act Sec. 1089(b)(6)(B), below.

P.L. 105-34, §1089(b)(4):

Amended Code Sec. 664(d) by adding at the end a new paragraph (4). **Effective**, generally, for transfers in trust after 7-28-97. For a special rule, see Act Sec. 1089(b)(6)(B), below.

P.L. 105-34, §1089(b)(6)(B), provides:

(B) SPECIAL RULE FOR CERTAIN DECEDENTS.—The amendments made by this subsection shall not apply to transfers in trust under the terms of a will (or other testamentary instrument) executed on or before July 28, 1997, if the decedent—

(i) dies before January 1, 1999, without having republished the will (or amended such instrument) by codicil or otherwise, or

(ii) was on July 28, 1997, under a mental disability to change the disposition of his property and did not regain his competence to dispose of such property before the date of his death.

P.L. 105-34, §1530(a):

Amended Code Sec. 664(d)(1)(C) and (2)(C) by striking the period at the end thereof and inserting "or, to the extent the remainder interest is in qualified employer securities (as defined in subsection (g)(4)), all or part of such securities are to be transferred to an employee stock ownership plan (as defined in section 4975(e)(7)) in a qualified gratuitous transfer (as defined by subsection (g))." **Effective** for transfers made by trusts to, or for the use of, an employee stock ownership plan after 8-5-97.

P.L. 105-34, §1530(c)(5):

Amended Code Sec. 664(d)(1)(B) and (2)(B) by inserting "and other than qualified gratuitous transfers described in subparagraph (C)" after "subparagraph (A)". **Effective** for transfers made by trusts to, or for the use of, an employee stock ownership plan after 8-5-97.

[Sec. 664(e)]

(e) VALUATION OF INTERESTS.—For purposes of determining the amount of any charitable contribution, the remainder interest of a charitable remainder annuity trust or charitable remainder unitrust shall be computed on the basis that an amount equal to 5 percent of the net fair market value of its assets (or a greater amount, if required under the terms of the trust instrument) is to be distributed each year. In the case of the early termination of a trust which is a charitable remainder unitrust by reason of subsection (d)(3), the valuation of interests in such trust for purposes of this section shall be made under rules similar to the rules of the preceding sentence.

Amendments

• 2015, Protecting Americans from Tax Hikes Act of 2015 (P.L. 114-113)

P.L. 114-113, §344(a)(1)-(2), Div. Q:

Amended Code Sec. 664(e) by adding at the end a new sentence, and by striking "FOR PURPOSES OF CHARITABLE CONTRIBUTION" in the heading thereof and inserting "OF INTERESTS". **Effective** for terminations of trusts occurring after 12-18-2015.

• 1969, Tax Reform Act of 1969 (P.L. 91-172)

P.L. 91-172, §201(e)(1):

Added Code Sec. 664. **Effective** with respect to transfers in trust made after 7-31-69.

[Sec. 664(f)]

(f) CERTAIN CONTINGENCIES PERMITTED.—

(1) GENERAL RULE.—If a trust would, but for a qualified contingency, meet the requirements of paragraph (1)(A) or (2)(A) of subsection (d), such trust shall be treated as meeting such requirements.

(2) VALUE DETERMINED WITHOUT REGARD TO QUALIFIED CONTINGENCY.—For purposes of determining the amount of any charitable contribution (or the actuarial value of any interest), a qualified contingency shall not be taken into account.

(3) QUALIFIED CONTINGENCY.—For purposes of this subsection, the term "qualified contingency" means any provision of a trust which provides that, upon the happening of a contingency, the payments described in paragraph (1)(A) or (2)(A) of subsection (d) (as the case may be) will terminate not later than such payments would otherwise terminate under the trust.

Amendments

• 1984, Deficit Reduction Act of 1984 (P.L. 98-369)

P.L. 98-369, §1022(d):

Amended Code Sec. 664 by adding section (f). **Effective** for transfers after 12-31-78. See Act Sec. 1022(e)(3), below, for special rules regarding statute of limitations.

P.L. 98-369, §1022(e)(3), provides:

(3) Statute of Limitations.—

(A) In General.—If on the date of the enactment of this Act (or at any time before the date 1 year after such date of enactment), credit or refund of any overpayment of tax attributable to the amendments made by this section is barred by any law or rule of law, such credit or refund of such overpayment may nevertheless be made if claim therefor is filed before the date 1 year after the date of the enactment of this Act.

(B) No Interest Where Statute Closed on Date of Enactment.—In any case where the making of the credit or refund of the overpayment described in subparagraph (A) is barred on the date of the enactment of this Act, no interest shall be allowed with respect to such overpayment (or any related adjustment) for the period before the date 180 days after the date on which the Secretary of the Treasury (or his delegate) is notified that the reformation has occurred.

[Sec. 664(g)]

(g) QUALIFIED GRATUITOUS TRANSFER OF QUALIFIED EMPLOYER SECURITIES.—

(1) IN GENERAL.—For purposes of this section, the term "qualified gratuitous transfer" means a transfer of qualified employer securities to an employee stock ownership plan (as defined in section 4975(e)(7)) but only to the extent that—

(A) the securities transferred previously passed from a decedent dying before January 1, 1999, to a trust described in paragraph (1) or (2) of subsection (d),

(B) no deduction under section 404 is allowable with respect to such transfer,

(C) such plan contains the provisions required by paragraph (3),

(D) such plan treats such securities as being attributable to employer contributions but without regard to the limitations otherwise applicable to such contributions under section 404, and

(E) the employer whose employees are covered by the plan described in this paragraph files with the Secretary a verified written statement consenting to the application of sections 4978 and 4979A with respect to such employer.

(2) EXCEPTION.—The term "qualified gratuitous transfer" shall not include a transfer of qualified employer securities to an employee stock ownership plan unless—

(A) such plan was in existence on August 1, 1996,

(B) at the time of the transfer, the decedent and members of the decedent's family (within the meaning of section 2032A(e)(2)) own (directly or through the application of section 318(a)) no more than 10 percent of the value of the stock of the corporation referred to in paragraph (4), and

(C) immediately after the transfer, such plan owns (after the application of section 318(a)(4)) at least 60 percent of the value of the outstanding stock of the corporation.

(3) PLAN REQUIREMENTS.—A plan contains the provisions required by this paragraph if such plan provides that—

(A) the qualified employer securities so transferred are allocated to plan participants in a manner consistent with section 401(a)(4),

(B) plan participants are entitled to direct the plan as to the manner in which such securities which are entitled to vote and are allocated to the account of such participant are to be voted,

(C) an independent trustee votes the securities so transferred which are not allocated to plan participants,

(D) each participant who is entitled to a distribution from the plan has the rights described in subparagraphs (A) and (B) of section 409(h)(1),

(E) such securities are held in a suspense account under the plan to be allocated each year, up to the applicable limitation under paragraph (7) (determined on the basis of fair market value of securities when allocated to participants), after first allocating all other annual additions for the limitation year, up to the limitation under section 415(c), and

(F) on termination of the plan, all securities so transferred which are not allocated to plan participants as of such termination are to be transferred to, or for the use of, an organization described in section 170(c).

For purposes of the preceding sentence, the term "independent trustee" means any trustee who is not a member of the family (within the meaning of section 2032A(e)(2)) of the decedent or a 5-percent shareholder. A plan shall not fail to be treated as meeting the requirements of section 401(a) by reason of meeting the requirements of this subsection.

(4) QUALIFIED EMPLOYER SECURITIES.—For purposes of this section, the term "qualified employer securities" means employer securities (as defined in section 409(l)) which are issued by a domestic corporation—

(A) which has no outstanding stock which is readily tradable on an established securities market, and

(B) which has only 1 class of stock.

(5) TREATMENT OF SECURITIES ALLOCATED BY EMPLOYEE STOCK OWNERSHIP PLAN TO PERSONS RELATED TO DECEDENT OR 5-PERCENT SHAREHOLDERS.—

(A) IN GENERAL.—If any portion of the assets of the plan attributable to securities acquired by the plan in a qualified gratuitous transfer are allocated to the account of—

(i) any person who is related to the decedent (within the meaning of section 267(b)) or a member of the decedent's family (within the meaning of section 2032A(e)(2)), or

(ii) any person who, at the time of such allocation or at any time during the 1-year period ending on the date of the acquisition of qualified employer securities by the plan, is a 5-percent shareholder of the employer maintaining the plan, the plan shall be treated as having distributed (at the time of such allocation) to such person or shareholder the amount so allocated.

(B) 5-PERCENT SHAREHOLDER.—For purposes of subparagraph (A), the term "5-percent shareholder" means any person who owns (directly or through the application of section 318(a)) more than 5 percent of the outstanding stock of the corporation which issued such qualified employer securities or of any corporation which is a member of the same controlled group of corporations (within the meaning of section 409(l)(4)) as such corporation. For purposes of the preceding sentence, section 318(a) shall be applied without regard to the exception in paragraph (2)(B)(i) thereof.

(C) CROSS REFERENCE.—

For excise tax on allocations described in subparagraph (A), see section 4979A.

(6) TAX ON FAILURE TO TRANSFER UNALLOCATED SECURITIES TO CHARITY ON TERMINATION OF PLAN.—If the requirements of paragraph (3)(F) are not met with respect to any securities, there is hereby imposed a tax on the employer maintaining the plan in an amount equal to the sum of—

(A) the amount of the increase in the tax which would be imposed by chapter 11 if such securities were not transferred as described in paragraph (1), and

(B) interest on such amount at the underpayment rate under section 6621 (and compounded daily) from the due date for filing the return of the tax imposed by chapter 11.

(7) APPLICABLE LIMITATION.—

(A) IN GENERAL.—For purposes of paragraph (3)(E), the applicable limitation under this paragraph with respect to a participant is an amount equal to the lesser of—

(i) $30,000, or

(ii) 25 percent of the participant's compensation (as defined in section 415(c)(3)).

(B) COST-OF-LIVING ADJUSTMENT.—The Secretary shall adjust annually the $30,000 amount under subparagraph (A)(i) at the same time and in the same manner as under section 415(d), except that the base period shall be the calendar quarter beginning October 1, 1993, and any increase under this subparagraph which is not a multiple of $5,000 shall be rounded to the next lowest multiple of $5,000.

Amendments

• 2018, Tax Technical Corrections Act of 2018 (P.L. 115-141)

P.L. 115-141, §401(b)(27), Div. U:

Amended Code Sec. 664(g)(3)(E) by striking "limitations under sections 415(c) and (e)" and inserting "limitation under section 415(c)". **Effective** 3-23-2018. For a special rule, see Act Sec. 401(e), Div. U, below.

P.L. 115-141, §401(e), Div. U, provides:

(e) GENERAL SAVINGS PROVISION WITH RESPECT TO DEADWOOD PROVISIONS.—If—

(1) any provision amended or repealed by the amendments made by subsection (b) or (d) applied to—

(A) any transaction occurring before the date of the enactment of this Act,

(B) any property acquired before such date of enactment, or

(C) any item of income, loss, deduction, or credit taken into account before such date of enactment, and

(2) the treatment of such transaction, property, or item under such provision would (without regard to the amendments or repeals made by such subsection) affect the liability for tax for periods ending after such date of enactment, nothing in the amendments or repeals made by this section shall be construed to affect the treatment of such transaction, property, or item for purposes of determining liability for tax for periods ending after such date of enactment.

• 2006, Pension Protection Act of 2006 (P.L. 109-280)

P.L. 109-280, §811, provides:

SEC. 811. PENSIONS AND INDIVIDUAL RETIREMENT ARRANGEMENT PROVISIONS OF ECONOMIC GROWTH AND TAX RELIEF RECONCILIATION ACT OF 2001 MADE PERMANENT.

Title IX of the Economic Growth and Tax Relief Reconciliation Act of 2001 [P.L. 107-16] shall not apply to the provisions of, and amendments made by, subtitles A through F of title VI [§§601-666]of such Act (relating to pension and individual retirement arrangement provisions).

P.L. 109-280, §868(a):

Amended Code Sec. 664(g)(3)(E) by inserting "(determined on the basis of fair market value of securities when allocated to participants)" after "paragraph (7)". **Effective** 8-17-2006.

• 2001, Economic Growth and Tax Relief Reconciliation Act of 2001 (P.L. 107-16)

P.L. 107-16, §632(a)(3)(H)(i)-(ii):

Amended Code Sec. 664(g) in paragraph (3)(E) by striking "limitations under section 415(c)" and inserting "applicable limitation under paragraph (7)", and by adding at the end a new paragraph (7). **Effective** for years beginning after 12-31-2001.

P.L. 107-16, §901(a)-(b), as amended by P.L. 111-312, §101(a)(1), provides [but see P.L. 109-280, §811, above]:

SEC. 901. SUNSET OF PROVISIONS OF ACT.

(a) IN GENERAL.—All provisions of, and amendments made by, this Act shall not apply—

(1) to taxable, plan, or limitation years beginning after December 31, 2012, or

(2) in the case of title V, to estates of decedents dying, gifts made, or generation skipping transfers, after December 31, 2012.

(b) APPLICATION OF CERTAIN LAWS.—The Internal Revenue Code of 1986 and the Employee Retirement Income Security Act of 1974 shall be applied and administered to years, estates, gifts, and transfers described in subsection (a) as if the provisions and amendments described in subsection (a) had never been enacted.

• 1997, Taxpayer Relief Act of 1997 (P.L. 105-34)

P.L. 105-34, §1530(b):

Amended Code Sec. 664 by adding at the end a new subsection (g). **Effective** for transfers made by trusts to, or for the use of, an employee stock ownership plan after 8-5-97.

Subpart D—Treatment of Excess Distributions by Trusts

[Sec. 665]

SEC. 665. DEFINITIONS APPLICABLE TO SUBPART D.

[Sec. 665(a)]

(a) UNDISTRIBUTED NET INCOME.—For purposes of this subpart, the term "undistributed net income" for any taxable year means the amount by which the distributable net income of the trust for such taxable year exceeds the sum of—

(1) the amounts for such taxable year specified in paragraphs (1) and (2) of section 661(a), and

(2) the amount of taxes imposed on the trust attributable to such distributable net income.

Amendments

• 1969, Tax Reform Act of 1969 (P.L. 91-172)

P.L. 91-172, §331(a):

Amended Code Sec. 665(a). **Effective** for tax years beginning after 12-31-68. Prior to amendment, Code Sec. 665(a) read as follows:

(a) Undistributed Net Income.—For purposes of this subpart, the term "undistributed net income" for any taxable year means the amount by which distributable net income of the trust for such taxable year exceeds the sum of—

(1) the amounts for such taxable year specified in paragraphs (1) and (2) of section 661(a); and

(2) the amount of taxes imposed on the trust.

[Sec. 665(b)]

(b) ACCUMULATION DISTRIBUTION.—For purposes of this subpart, except as provided in subsection (c), the term "accumulation distribution" means, for any taxable year of the trust, the amount by which—

(1) the amounts specified in paragraph (2) of section 661(a) for such taxable year, exceed

(2) distributable net income for such year reduced (but not below zero) by the amounts specified in paragraph (1) of section 661(a).

For purposes of section 667 (other than subsection (c) thereof, relating to multiple trusts), the amounts specified in paragraph (2) of section 661(a) shall not include amounts properly paid, credited, or required to be distributed to a beneficiary from a trust (other than a foreign trust) as income accumulated before the birth of such beneficiary or before such beneficiary attains the age of 21. If the amounts properly paid, credited, or required to be distributed by the trust for the taxable year do not exceed the income of the trust for such year, there shall be no accumulation distribution for such year.

Amendments

• 1997, Taxpayer Relief Act of 1997 (P.L. 105-34)

P.L. 105-34, §507(a)(2):

Amended Code Sec. 665(b) by inserting "except as provided in subsection (c)," after "subpart,". **Effective** for distributions in tax years beginning after 8-5-97.

• 1976, Tax Reform Act of 1976 (P.L. 94-455)

P.L. 94-455, §701(b):

Added the sentence "For purposes of section 667 (other than subsection (c) thereof, relating to multiple trusts), the amounts specified in paragraph (2) of section 661(a) shall not include amounts properly paid, credited, or required to be distributed to a beneficiary from a trust (other than a foreign trust) as income accumulated before the birth of such beneficiary or before such beneficiary attains the age of 21." **Effective** for distributions made in tax years beginning after 12-31-75.

P.L. 94-455, §701(c):

Added the sentence "If the amounts properly paid, credited, or required to be distributed by the trust for the taxable year do not exceed the income of the trust for such year, there shall be no accumulation distribution for such year." **Effective** for distributions made in tax years beginning after 12-31-75.

• 1969, Tax Reform Act of 1969 (P.L. 91-172)

P.L. 91-172, §331(a), (d)(2)(A):

Amended Code Sec. 665(b). **Effective**, generally, for tax years beginning after 12-31-68. However, see Act Sec. 331(d)(2)(A), below. Before amendment, Code Sec. 665(b) read as follows:

(b) Accumulation Distributions of Trusts Other Than Certain Foreign Trusts.—For purposes of this subpart, in the case of a trust (other than a foreign trust created by a United States person), the term "accumulation distribution" for any taxable year of the trust means the amount (if in excess of $2,000) by which the amounts specified in paragraph (2) of section 661(a) for such taxable year exceed distributable net income reduced by the amounts specified in paragraph (1) of section 661(a). For purposes of this subsection, the amount specified in paragraph (2) of section 661(a) shall be determined without regard to section 666 and shall not include—

(1) amounts paid, credited, or required to be distributed to a beneficiary as income accumulated before the birth of such beneficiary or before such beneficiary attains the age of 21;

(2) amounts properly paid or credited to a beneficiary to meet the emergency needs of such beneficiary;

(3) amounts properly paid or credited to a beneficiary upon such beneficiary's attaining a specified age or ages if—

(A) the total number of such distributions cannot exceed 4 with respect to such beneficiary,

(B) the period between each such distribution to such beneficiary is 4 years or more, and

(C) as of January 1, 1954, such distributions are required by the specific terms of the governing instrument; and

(4) amounts properly paid or credited to a beneficiary as a final distribution of the trust if such final distribution is made more than 9 years after the date of the last transfer to such trust.

P.L. 91-172, §331(d)(2)(A), provides:

(A) Amounts paid, credited, or required to be distributed by a trust (other than a foreign trust created by a United States person) on or before the last day of a taxable year of the trust beginning before January 1, 1974, shall not be deemed to be accumulation distributions to the extent that such amounts were accumulated by a trust in taxable years of such trust beginning before January 1, 1969, and would have been excepted from the definition of an accumulation distribution by reason of paragraphs (1), (2), (3), or (4) of section 665(b) of the Internal Revenue Code of 1954, as in effect on December 31, 1968, if they had been distributed on the last day of the last taxable year of the trust beginning before January 1, 1969.

• 1962, Revenue Act of 1962 (P.L. 87-834)

P.L. 87-834, §7:

Amended Code Sec. 665(b) by striking out "(b) Accumulation Distribution.—For purposes of this subpart," and inserting in lieu thereof the following: "(b) Accumulation Distributions of Trusts Other Than Certain Foreign Trusts.—For purposes of this subpart, in the case of a trust (other than a foreign trust created by a United States person),". **Effective** for distributions made after 12-31-62.

[Sec. 665(c)]

(c) EXCEPTION FOR ACCUMULATION DISTRIBUTIONS FROM CERTAIN DOMESTIC TRUSTS.—For purposes of this subpart—

(1) IN GENERAL.—In the case of a qualified trust, any distribution in any taxable year beginning after the date of the enactment of this subsection shall be computed without regard to any undistributed net income.

(2) QUALIFIED TRUST.—For purposes of this subsection, the term "qualified trust" means any trust other than—

(A) a foreign trust (or, except as provided in regulations, a domestic trust which at any time was a foreign trust), or

(B) a trust created before March 1, 1984, unless it is established that the trust would not be aggregated with other trusts under section 643(f) if such section applied to such trust.

Amendments

• 1997, Taxpayer Relief Act of 1997 (P.L. 105-34)

P.L. 105-34, §507(a)(1):

Amended Code Sec. 665 by inserting after subsection (b) a new subsection (c). **Effective** for distributions in tax years beginning after 8-5-97.

[Sec. 665(c)—Stricken]

Amendments

• 1996, Small Business Job Protection Act of 1996 (P.L. 104-188)

P.L. 104-188, §1904(c)(2):

Amended Code Sec. 665 by striking subsection (c). **Effective** 8-20-96. For special and transitional rules, see Act Sec. 1904(d)(2) and (e), below. Prior to being stricken, Code Sec. 665(c) read as follows:

(c) SPECIAL RULE APPLICABLE TO DISTRIBUTIONS BY CERTAIN FOREIGN TRUSTS.—For purposes of this subpart, any amount paid to a United States person which is from a payor who is not a United States person and which is derived directly or indirectly from a foreign trust created by a United States person shall be deemed in the year of payment to have been directly paid by the foreign trust.

P.L. 104-188, §1904(d)(2) and (e), provides:

(2) EXCEPTION FOR CERTAIN TRUSTS.—The amendments made by this section shall not apply to any trust—

(A) which is treated as owned by the grantor under section 676 or 677 (other than subsection (a)(3) thereof) of the Internal Revenue Code of 1986, and

(B) which is in existence on September 19, 1995.

The preceding sentence shall not apply to the portion of any such trust attributable to any transfer to such trust after September 19, 1995.

(e) TRANSITIONAL RULE.—If—

(1) by reason of the amendments made by this section, any person other than a United States person ceases to be treated as the owner of a portion of a domestic trust, and

(2) before January 1, 1997, such trust becomes a foreign trust, or the assets of such trust are transferred to a foreign trust, no tax shall be imposed by section 1491 of the Internal Revenue Code of 1986 by reason of such trust becoming a foreign trust or the assets of such trust being transferred to a foreign trust.

• 1969, Tax Reform Act of 1969 (P.L. 91-172)

P.L. 91-172, §331(a):

Amended Code Sec. 665(c). **Effective** for tax years beginning after 12-31-68. Prior to amendment, Code Sec. 665(c) read as follows:

(c) Accumulation Distribution of Certain Foreign Trusts.—For purposes of this subpart, in the case of a foreign trust created by a United States person, the term "accumulation distribution" for any taxable year of the trust means the amount by which the amounts specified in paragraph (2) of section 661(a) for such taxable year exceed distributable net income, reduced by the amounts specified in paragraph (1) of section 661(a). For purposes of this subsection, the amount specified in paragraph (2) of section 661(a) shall be determined without regard to section 666. Any amount paid to a United States person which is from a payor who is not a United States person and which is derived directly or indirectly from a foreign trust created by a United States person shall be deemed in the year of payment to have been directly paid by the foreign trust.

• 1962, Revenue Tax of 1962 (P.L. 87-834)

P.L. 87-834, §7:

Redesignated old Code Sec. 665(c) as 665(d); redesignated Sec. 665(d) as Sec. 665(e), and added a new Sec. 665(c). **Effective** with respect to distributions made after 12-31-62.

[Sec. 665(d)]

(d) TAXES IMPOSED ON THE TRUST.—For purposes of this subpart—

(1) IN GENERAL.—The term "taxes imposed on the trust" means the amount of the taxes which are imposed for any taxable year of the trust under this chapter (without regard to this subpart or part IV of subchapter A) and which, under regulations prescribed by the Secretary, are properly allocable to the undistributed portions of distributable net income and gains in excess of losses from sales or exchanges of capital assets. The amount determined in the preceding sentence shall be reduced by any amount of such taxes deemed distributed under section 666(b) and (c) to any beneficiary.

(2) FOREIGN TRUSTS.—In the case of any foreign trust, the term "taxes imposed on the trust" includes the amount, reduced as provided in the last sentence of paragraph (1), of any income, war profits, and excess profits taxes imposed by any foreign country or possession of the United States on such foreign trust which, as determined under paragraph (1), are so properly allocable. Under rules or regulations prescribed by the Secretary, in the case of any foreign trust of which the settlor or another person would be treated as owner of any portion of the trust under subpart E but for section 672(f), the term "taxes imposed on the trust" includes the allocable amount of any income, war profits, and excess profits taxes imposed by any foreign country or possession of the United States on the settlor or such other person in respect of trust income.

Amendments

• 1997, Taxpayer Relief Act of 1997 (P.L. 105-34)

P.L. 105-34, §1604(g)(2):

Amended Code Sec. 665(d)(1) by striking "or 669(d) and (e)" before "to any beneficiary." in the last sentence. **Effective** 8-5-97.

• 1996, Small Business Job Protection Act of 1996 (P.L. 104-188)

P.L. 104-188, §1904(b)(1):

Amended Code Sec. 665(d)(2) by adding at the end a new sentence. **Effective** 8-20-96. For special and transitional rules, see Act Sec. 1904(d)(2) and (e), below.

P.L. 104-188, §1904(d)(2) and (e), provides:

(2) EXCEPTION FOR CERTAIN TRUSTS.—The amendments made by this section shall not apply to any trust—

(A) which is treated as owned by the grantor under section 676 or 677 (other than subsection (a)(3) thereof) of the Internal Revenue Code of 1986, and

(B) which is in existence on September 19, 1995.

The preceding sentence shall not apply to the portion of any such trust attributable to any transfer to such trust after September 19, 1995.

(e) TRANSITIONAL RULE.—If—

(1) by reason of the amendments made by this section, any person other than a United States person ceases to be treated as the owner of a portion of a domestic trust, and

(2) before January 1, 1997, such trust becomes a foreign trust, or the assets of such trust are transferred to a foreign trust,

no tax shall be imposed by section 1491 of the Internal Revenue Code of 1986 by reason of such trust becoming a foreign trust or the assets of such trust being transferred to a foreign trust.

• 1986, Tax Reform Act of 1986 (P.L. 99-514)

P.L. 99-514, §1847(b)(16):

Amended Code Sec. 665(d)(1) by striking out "subpart A of part IV" and inserting in lieu thereof "part IV". **Effective** as if included in the provision of P.L. 98-369 to which it relates.

• 1978, Revenue Act of 1978 (P.L. 95-600)

P.L. 95-600, §701(q)(1)(A):

Amended Code Sec. 665(d). **Effective** for distributions made in tax years beginning after 12-31-75. Prior to amendment, Code Sec. 665(d) read as follows:

(d) TAXES IMPOSED ON THE TRUST.—For purposes of this subpart, the term "taxes imposed on the trust" means the amount of the taxes which are imposed for any taxable year of the trust under this chapter (without regard to this subpart) and which, under regulations prescribed by the Secretary, are properly allocable to the undistributed portions of distributable net income and gains in excess of losses from sales or exchanges of capital assets. The amount determined in the preceding sentence shall be reduced by any amount of such taxes deemed distributed under section 666(b) and (c) or 669(d) and (e) to any beneficiary.

• 1976, Tax Reform Act of 1976 (P.L. 94-455)

P.L. 94-455, §1906(b)(13)(A):

Amended 1954 Code by substituting "Secretary" for "Secretary or his delegate" each place it appeared. **Effective** 2-1-77.

• 1969, Tax Reform Act of 1969 (P.L. 91-172)

P.L. 91-172, §331(a):

Amended Code Sec. 665(d). **Effective** for tax years beginning after 12-31-68. Prior to amendment, Code Sec. 665(d) read as follows:

(d) Taxes Imposed on the Trust.—For purposes of this subpart, the term "taxes imposed on the trust" means the amount of the taxes which are imposed for any taxable year on the trust under this chapter (without regard to this subpart) and which, under regulations prescribed by the Secretary or his delegate, are properly allocable to the undistributed portion of the distributable net income. The amount determined in the preceding sentence shall be reduced by any amount of such taxes allowed, under sections 667 and 668, as a credit to any beneficiary on account of any accumulation distribution determined for any taxable year.

• 1962, Revenue Act of 1962 (P.L. 87-834)

P.L. 87-834, §7:

Redesignated old Code Sec. 665(c) as Sec. 665(d). **Effective** with respect to distributions made after 12-31-62.

[Sec. 665(e)]

(e) PRECEDING TAXABLE YEAR.—For purposes of this subpart—

(1) In the case of a foreign trust created by a United States person, the term "preceding taxable year" does not include any taxable year of the trust to which this part does not apply.

(2) In the case of a preceding taxable year with respect to which a trust qualified, without regard to this subpart, under the provisions of subpart B, for purposes of the application of this subpart to such trust for such taxable year, such trust shall, in accordance with regulations prescribed by the Secretary, be treated as a trust to which subpart C applies.

Amendments

• 1990, Omnibus Budget Reconciliation Act of 1990 (P.L. 101-508)

P.L. 101-508, §11802(f)(2):

Amended Code Sec. 665(e). **Effective** 11-5-90. Prior to amendment, Code Sec. 665(e) read as follows:

(e) PRECEDING TAXABLE YEAR.—For purposes of this subpart—

(1) in the case of a trust (other than a foreign trust created by a United States person), the term "preceding taxable year" does not include any taxable year of the trust—

(A) which precedes by more than 5 years the taxable year of the trust in which an accumulation distribution is made, if it is made in a taxable year beginning before January 1, 1974, or

(B) which begins before January 1, 1969, in the case of an accumulation distribution made during a taxable year beginning after December 31, 1973, and

(2) in the case of a foreign trust created by a United States person, such term does not include any taxable year of the trust to which this part does not apply.

In the case of a preceding taxable year with respect to which a trust qualifies (without regard to this subpart) under the provisions of subpart B, for purposes of the application of this subpart to such trust for such taxable year, such trust shall, in accordance with regulations prescribed by the Secretary, be treated as a trust to which subpart C applies.

P.L. 101-508, §11821(b), provides:

(b) SAVINGS PROVISION.—If—

(1) any provision amended or repealed by this part applied to—

(A) any transaction occurring before the date of the enactment of this Act,

(B) any property acquired before such date of enactment, or

(C) any item of income, loss, deduction, or credit taken into account before such date of enactment, and

(2) the treatment of such transaction, property, or item under such provision would (without regard to the amendments made by this part) affect liability for tax for periods ending after such date of enactment,

nothing in the amendments made by this part shall be construed to affect the treatment of such transaction, property, or item for purposes of determining liability for tax for periods ending after such date of enactment.

• 1976, Tax Reform Act of 1976 (P.L. 94-455)

P.L. 94-455, §701(d)(2):

Struck out Code Sec. 665(e)(1)(C), added "or" at the end of subparagraph (A), and substituted ", and" at the end of subparagraph (B) for ", or". **Effective** for distributions made in tax years beginning after 12-31-75. Prior to repeal, Code Sec. 665(e)(1)(C) read as follows:

(C) which begins before January 1, 1969, in the case of a capital gain distribution made during a taxable year beginning after December 31, 1968, and

P.L. 94-455, §1906(b)(13)(A):

Amended 1954 Code to substitute "Secretary" for "Secretary or his delegate" each place it appeared. **Effective** 2-1-77.

• 1969, Tax Reform Act of 1969 (P.L. 91-172)

P.L. 91-172, §331(a):

Amended Code Sec. 665(e). **Effective** for tax years beginning after 12-31-68. Prior to amendment, Code Sec. 665(e) read as follows:

(e) Preceding Taxable Year.—For purposes of this subpart, the term "preceding taxable year" does not include any taxable year of the trust to which this part does not apply. In the case of a preceding taxable year with respect to which a trust qualifies (without regard to this subpart) under the provisions of subpart B, for purposes of the application of this subpart to such trust for such taxable year, such trust shall, in accordance with regulations prescribed by the Secretary of his delegate, be treated as a trust to which subpart C applies.

• 1962, Revenue Act of 1962 (P.L. 87-834)

P.L. 87-834, §7:

Redesignated old Code Sec. 665(d) as Sec. 665(e). **Effective** with respect to distributions made after 12-31-62.

[Sec. 665(f)—Repealed]

Amendments

• 1976, Tax Reform Act of 1976 (P.L. 94-455)

P.L. 94-455, §701(d)(3):

Repealed Code Sec. 665(f). **Effective** for distributions made in tax years beginning after 12-31-75. Prior to repeal, Code Sec. 665(f) read as follows:

(f) UNDISTRIBUTED CAPITAL GAIN.—For purposes of this subpart, the term "undistributed capital gain" means, for any taxable year of the trust beginning after December 31, 1968, the amount by which—

(1) gains in excess of losses from the sale or exchange of capital assets, to the extent that such gains are allocated to corpus and are not (A) paid, credited, or required to be distributed to any beneficiary during such taxable year, or (B) paid, permanently set aside, or used for the purposes specified in section 642(c), exceed

(2) the amount of taxes imposed on the trust attributable to such gains.

For purposes of paragraph (1), the deduction under section 1202 (relating to deduction for excess of capital gains over capital losses) shall not be taken into account.

• 1969, Tax Reform Act of 1969 (P.L. 91-172)

P.L. 91-172, §331(a):

Added Code Sec. 665(f). **Effective** for tax years ending after 12-31-68.

[Sec. 665(g)—Repealed]

Amendments

• 1976, Tax Reform Act of 1976 (P.L. 94-455)

P.L. 94-455, §701(d)(3):

Repealed Code Sec. 665(g). **Effective** for distributions made in tax years beginning after 12-31-75. Prior to repeal, Code Sec. 665(g) read as follows:

(g) CAPITAL GAIN DISTRIBUTION.—For purposes of this subpart, the term "capital gain distribution" for any taxable year of the trust means, to the extent of undistributed capital gain, that portion of—

(1) the excess of the amounts specified in paragraph (2) of section 661(a) for such taxable year over distributable net income for such year reduced (but not below zero) by the amounts specified in paragraph (1) of section 661(a), over

(2) the undistributed net income of the trust for all preceding taxable years.

• 1971, Revenue Act of 1971 (P.L. 92-178)

P.L. 92-178, §306(a):

Amended the third line of Code Sec. 665(g) by deleting "for such taxable year" which formerly appeared after "undistributed capital gain". **Effective** for tax years beginning after 12-31-68.

• 1969, Tax Reform Act of 1969 (P.L. 91-172)

P.L. 91-172, §331(a):

Added Code Sec. 665(g). **Effective** for tax years beginning after 12-31-68.

[Sec. 666]

SEC. 666. ACCUMULATION DISTRIBUTION ALLOCATED TO PRECEDING YEARS.

[Sec. 666(a)]

(a) AMOUNT ALLOCATED.—In the case of a trust which is subject to subpart C, the amount of the accumulation distribution of such trust for a taxable year shall be deemed to be an amount within the meaning of paragraph (2) of section 661(a) distributed on the last day of each of the preceding taxable years, commencing with the earliest of such years, to the extent that such amount exceeds the total of any undistributed net income for all earlier preceding taxable years. The amount deemed to be distributed in any such preceding taxable year under the preceding sentence shall not exceed the undistributed net income for such preceding taxable year. For purposes of this subsection, undistributed net income for each of such preceding taxable years shall be computed without regard to such accumulation distribution and without regard to any accumulation distribution determined for any succeeding taxable year.

Amendments

• 1969, Tax Reform Act of 1969 (P.L. 91-172)

P.L. 91-172, §331(a)(d)(2)(B):

Amended Code Sec. 666(a). **Effective**, generally, for tax years beginning after 12-31-68. As to first sentence, however, P.L. 91-172, §331(d)(2)(B) provides as follows:

(B) For taxable years of a trust beginning before January 1, 1970, the first sentence of section 666(a) of the Internal Revenue Code of 1954 (as amended by this section) shall not apply, and the amount of the accumulation distribution of the trust for such taxable years shall be deemed to be an amount within the meaning of paragraph (2) of section 661(a) distributed on the last day of each of the preceding taxable years to the extent that such amount exceeds the total of any undistributed net income for any taxable years intervening between the taxable year with respect of which the accumulation distribution is determined and such preceding taxable year.

Prior to amendment, Code Sec. 666(a) read as follows:

(a) Amount Allocated.—In the case of a trust (other than a foreign trust created by a United States person) which for a taxable year beginning after December 31, 1953, is subject to subpart C, the amount of the accumulation distribution of such trust for such taxable year shall be deemed to be an amount within the meaning of paragraph (2) of section 661(a) distributed on the last day of each of the 5 preceding taxable years to the extent that such amount exceeds the total of any undistributed net incomes for any taxable years intervening between the taxable year with respect to which the accumulation distribution is determined and such preceding taxable year. The amount deemed to be distributed in any such preceding taxable year under the preceding sentence shall not exceed the undistributed net income of such preceding taxable year. For purposes of this subsection, undistributed net income for each of such 5 preceding taxable years shall be computed without regard to such accumulation distribution and without regard to any accumulation distribution determined for any succeeding taxable year. In the case of a foreign trust created by a United States person, this subsection shall apply to the preceding taxable years of the trust without regard to any provision of the preceding sentences which would (but for this sentence) limit its application to the 5 preceding taxable years.

• 1962, Revenue Act of 1962 (P.L. 87-834)

P.L. 87-834, §7:

Amended Code Sec. 666(a) by inserting after trust in line 1 the following "(other than a foreign trust created by a United States person)"; and by inserting after the period in line 15 a new sentence. **Effective** with respect to distributions made after 12-31-62.

[Sec. 666(b)]

(b) TOTAL TAXES DEEMED DISTRIBUTED.—If any portion of an accumulation distribution for any taxable year is deemed under subsection (a) to be an amount within the meaning of paragraph (2) of section 661(a) distributed on the last day of any preceding taxable year, and such portion of such distribution is not less than the undistributed net income for such preceding taxable year, the trust shall be deemed to have distributed on the last day of such preceding taxable year an additional amount within the meaning of paragraph (2) of section 661(a). Such additional amount shall be equal to the taxes (other than the tax imposed by section 55) imposed on the trust for such preceding taxable year attributable to the undistributed net income. For purposes of this subsection, the undistributed net income and the taxes imposed on the trust for such preceding taxable year attributable to such undistributed net income shall be computed without regard to such accumulation distribution and without regard to any accumulation distribution determined for any succeeding taxable year.

Amendments

• 1978, Revenue Act of 1978 (P.L. 95-600)

P.L. 95-600, §421(d):

Amended Code Sec. 666(b) by striking out "taxes" in the text and inserting in lieu thereof "taxes (other than the tax imposed by section 55)". **Effective** for tax years beginning after 12-31-78.

• 1969, Tax Reform Act of 1969 (P.L. 91-172)

P.L. 91-172, §331(a):

Amended Code Sec. 666(b). **Effective** for tax years beginning after 12-31-68. Prior to amendment, Code Sec. 666(b) read as follows:

(b) Total Taxes Deemed Distributed.—If any portion of an accumulation distribution for any taxable year is deemed under subsection (a) to be an amount within the meaning of paragraph (2) of section 661(a) distributed on the last day of any preceding taxable year, and such portion of such accumulation distribution is not less than the undistributed net income for such preceding taxable year, the trust shall be deemed to have distributed on the last day of such preceding taxable year an additional amount within the meaning of paragraph (2) of section 661(a). Such additional amount shall be equal to the taxes imposed on the trust for such preceding taxable year. For purposes of this subsection, the undistributed net income and the taxes imposed on the trust for such preceding taxable year shall be computed without regard to such accumulation distribution and without regard to any accumulation distribution determined for any succeeding taxable year.

[Sec. 666(c)]

(c) PRO RATA PORTION OF TAXES DEEMED DISTRIBUTED.—If any portion of an accumulation distribution for any taxable year is deemed under subsection (a) to be an amount within the meaning of paragraph (2) of section 661(a) distributed on the last day of any preceding taxable year and such portion of the accumulation distribution is less than the undistributed net income for such preceding taxable year, the trust shall be deemed to have distributed on the last day of such preceding taxable year an additional amount within the meaning of paragraph (2) of section 661(a). Such additional amount shall be equal to the taxes (other than the tax imposed by section 55) imposed on the trust for such taxable year attributable to the undistributed net income multiplied by the ratio of the portion of the accumulation distribution to the undistributed net income of the trust for such year. For purposes of this subsection, the undistributed net income and the taxes imposed on the trust for such preceding taxable year attributable to such undistributed net income shall be computed without regard to the accumulation distribution and without regard to any accumulation distribution determined for any succeeding taxable year.

Amendments

• 1980, Technical Corrections Act of 1979 (P.L. 96-222)

P.L. 96-222, §104(a)(4)(H)(vi):

Amended Code Sec. 666(c) by adding "(other than the tax imposed by section 55)" after "equal to the taxes". **Effective** for tax years beginning after 12-31-78.

• 1969, Tax Reform Act of 1969 (P.L. 91-172)

P.L. 91-172, §331(a):

Amended Code Sec. 666(c). **Effective** for tax years beginning after 12-31-68. Prior to amendment, Code Sec. 666(c) read as follows:

(c) Pro Rata Portion of Taxes Deemed Distributed.—If any portion of an accumulation distribution for any taxable year is deemed under subsection (a) to be an amount within the meaning of paragraph (2) of section 661(a) distributed on the last day of any preceding taxable year and such portion of the accumulation distribution is less than the undistributed net income for such preceding taxable year, the trust shall be deemed to have distributed on the last day of such preceding taxable year an additional amount within the meaning of paragraph (2) of section 661(a). Such additional amount shall be equal to the taxes imposed on the trust for such taxable year multiplied by the ratio of the portion of the accumulation distribution to the undistributed net income of the trust for such year. For purposes of this subsection, the undistributed net income and the taxes imposed on the trust for such preceding taxable year shall be computed without regard to the accumulation distribution and without regard to any accumulation distribution determined for any succeeding taxable year.

[Sec. 666(d)]

(d) RULE WHEN INFORMATION IS NOT AVAILABLE.—If adequate records are not available to determine the proper application of this subpart to an amount distributed by a trust, such amount shall be deemed to be an accumulation distribution consisting of undistributed net income earned during the earliest preceding taxable year of the trust in which it can be established that the trust was in existence.

Amendments

• 1969, Tax Reform Act of 1969 (P.L. 91-172)

P.L. 91-172, §331(a):

Added Code Sec. 666(d). **Effective** for tax years beginning after 12-31-68.

[Sec. 666(e)]

(e) DENIAL OF REFUND TO TRUSTS AND BENEFICIARIES.—No refund or credit shall be allowed to a trust or a beneficiary of such trust for any preceding taxable year by reason of a distribution deemed to have been made by such trust in such year under this section.

Amendments

• 1976, Tax Reform Act of 1976 (P.L. 94-455)

P.L. 94-455, §701(a)(2):

Added Code Sec. 666(e). **Effective** for distributions made in tax years beginning after 12-31-75.

[Sec. 667]

SEC. 667. TREATMENT OF AMOUNTS DEEMED DISTRIBUTED BY TRUST IN PRECEDING YEARS.

[Sec. 667(a)]

(a) GENERAL RULE.—The total of the amounts which are treated under section 666 as having been distributed by a trust in a preceding taxable year shall be included in the income of a beneficiary of the trust when paid, credited, or required to be distributed to the extent that such total would have been included in the income of such beneficiary under section 662(a)(2) (and, with respect to any tax-exempt interest to which section 103 applies, under section 662(b)) if such total had been paid to such beneficiary on the last day of such preceding taxable year. The tax imposed by this subtitle on a beneficiary for a taxable year in which any such amount is included in his income shall be determined only as provided in this section and shall consist of the sum of—

(1) a partial tax computed on the taxable income reduced by an amount equal to the total of such amounts, at the rate and in the manner as if this section had not been enacted,

(2) a partial tax determined as provided in subsection (b) of this section, and

(3) in the case of a foreign trust, the interest charge determined as provided in section 668.

Amendments

• 1976, Tax Reform Act of 1976 (P.L. 94-455)

P.L. 94-455, §701(a)(1):

Amended Code Sec. 667(a). **Effective** for distributions made in tax years beginning after 12-31-75. Prior to amendment, Code Sec. 667(a) read as follows:

(a) DENIAL OF REFUND TO TRUSTS.—No refund or credit shall be allowed to a trust for any preceding taxable year by reason of a distribution deemed to have been made by such trust in such year under section 666 or 669.

P.L. 94-455, §1014(a):

Struck out "and" at the end of paragraph (1), substituted ", and" for the period at the end of paragraph (2), and added a new paragraph (3). **Effective** for tax years beginning after 12-31-76.

• 1969, Tax Reform Act of 1969 (P.L. 91-172)

P.L. 91-172, §331(a):

Divided Code Sec. 667 into subsections (a) and (b) and amended new Code Sec. 667(a). **Effective** for tax years beginning after 12-31-68. Prior to amendment, Code Sec. 667 read as follows:

Sec. 667. DENIAL OF REFUND TO TRUSTS.

The amount of taxes imposed on the trust under this chapter, which would not have been payable by the trust for any preceding taxable year had the trust in fact made distributions at the times and in the amounts deemed under section 666, shall not be refunded or credited to the trust, but shall be allowed as a credit under section 668(b) against the tax of the beneficiaries who are treated as having received the distributions. For purposes of the preceding sentence, the amount of taxes which may not be refunded or credited to the trust shall be an amount equal to the excess of (1) the taxes imposed on the trust for any preceding taxable year (computed without regard to the accumulation distribution for the taxable year) over (2) the amount of taxes for such preceding taxable year imposed on the undistributed portion of distributable net income of the trust for such preceding taxable year after the application of this subpart on account of the accumulation distribution determined for such taxable year.

[Sec. 667(b)]

(b) TAX ON DISTRIBUTION.—

(1) IN GENERAL.—The partial tax imposed by subsection (a)(2) shall be determined—

(A) by determining the number of preceding taxable years of the trust on the last day of which an amount is deemed under section 666(a) to have been distributed,

(B) by taking from the 5 taxable years immediately preceding the year of the accumulation distribution the 1 taxable year for which the beneficiary's taxable income was the highest and the 1 taxable year for which his taxable income was the lowest,

(C) by adding to the beneficiary's taxable income for each of the 3 taxable years remaining after the application of subparagraph (B) an amount determined by dividing the amount deemed distributed under section 666 and required to be included in income under subsection (a) by the number of preceding taxable years determined under subparagraph (A), and

(D) by determining the average increase in tax for the 3 taxable years referred to in subparagraph (C) resulting from the application of such subparagraph.

The partial tax imposed by subsection (a)(2) shall be the excess (if any) of the average increase in tax determined under subparagraph (D), multiplied by the number of preceding taxable years determined under subparagraph (A), over the amount of taxes (other than the amount of taxes described in section 665(d)(2)) deemed distributed to the beneficiary under sections 666(b) and (c).

(2) TREATMENT OF LOSS YEARS.—For purposes of paragraph (1), the taxable income of the beneficiary for any taxable year shall be deemed to be not less than zero.

(3) CERTAIN PRECEDING TAXABLE YEARS NOT TAKEN INTO ACCOUNT.—For purposes of paragraph (1), if the amount of the undistributed net income deemed distributed in any preceding taxable year of the trust is less than 25 percent of the amount of the accumulation distribution divided by the number of preceding taxable years to which the accumulation distribution is allocated under section 666(a), the number of preceding taxable years of the trust with respect to which an amount is deemed distributed to a beneficiary under section 666(a) shall be determined without regard to such year.

(4) EFFECT OF OTHER ACCUMULATION DISTRIBUTIONS.—In computing the partial tax under paragraph (1) for any beneficiary, the income of such beneficiary for each of his prior taxable years shall include amounts previously deemed distributed to such beneficiary in such year under section 666 as a result of prior accumulation distributions (whether from the same or another trust).

(5) MULTIPLE DISTRIBUTIONS IN THE SAME TAXABLE YEAR.—In the case of accumulation distributions made from more than one trust which are includible in the income of a beneficiary in the same taxable year, the distributions shall be deemed to have been made consecutively in whichever order the beneficiary shall determine.

(6) ADJUSTMENT IN PARTIAL TAX FOR ESTATE AND GENERATION-SKIPPING TRANSFER TAXES ATTRIBUTABLE TO PARTIAL TAX.—

(A) IN GENERAL.—The partial tax shall be reduced by an amount which is equal to the pre-death portion of the partial tax multiplied by a fraction—

(i) the numerator of which is that portion of the tax imposed by chapter 11 or 13, as the case may be, which is attributable (on a proportionate basis) to amounts included in the accumulation distribution, and

(ii) the denominator of which is the amount of the accumulation distribution which is subject to the tax imposed by chapter 11 or 13, as the case may be.

(B) PARTIAL TAX DETERMINED WITHOUT REGARD TO THIS PARAGRAPH.—For purposes of this paragraph, the term "partial tax" means the partial tax imposed by subsection (a)(2) determined under this subsection without regard to this paragraph.

(C) PRE-DEATH PORTION.—For purposes of this paragraph, the pre-death portion of the partial tax shall be an amount which bears the same ratio to the partial tax as the portion of the accumulation distribution which is attributable to the period before the date of the death of the decedent or the date of the generation-skipping transfer bears to the total accumulation distribution.

Amendments

• 1986, Tax Reform Act of 1986 (P.L. 99-514)

P.L. 99-514, §104(b)(10):

Amended Code Sec. 667(b)(2). **Effective** for tax years beginning after 12-31-86. Prior to amendment, Code Sec. 667(b)(2) read as follows:

(2) TREATMENT OF LOSS YEARS.—For purposes of paragraph (1), the taxable income of the beneficiary for any taxable year shall be deemed to be not less than—

(A) in the case of a beneficiary who is an individual, the zero bracket amount for such year, or

(B) in the case of a beneficiary who is a corporation, zero.

• 1978, Revenue Act of 1978 (P.L. 95-600)

P.L. 95-600, §701(q)(1)(C):

Amended Code Sec. 667(b)(1) by inserting "(other than the amount of taxes described in section 665(d)(2))" after "taxes". **Effective** for distributions made in tax years beginning after 12-31-75.

P.L. 95-600, §702(o)(1):

Added 667(b)(6). **Effective** for estates of decedents dying after 12-31-79 and for generation-skipping transfers (within the meaning Code Sec. 2611(a)) made after 6-11-76.

• 1977, Tax Reduction and Simplification Act of 1977 (P.L. 95-30)

P.L. 95-30, §102(b)(8):

Amended paragraph (2) of Code Sec. 667(b). **Effective** for tax years beginning after 12-31-76. Prior to amendment, paragraph (2) of Code Sec. 667(b) read as follows:

(2) TREATMENT OF LOSS YEARS.—For purposes of paragraph (1), the taxable income of the beneficiary for any taxable year shall be deemed not to be less than zero.

• 1976, Tax Reform Act of 1976 (P.L. 94-455)

P.L. 94-455, §701(a)(1):

Amended Code Sec. 667(b). **Effective** for distributions made in tax years beginning after 12-31-75. Prior to amendment, Code Sec. 667(b) read as follows:

(b) AUTHORIZATION OF CREDIT TO BENEFICIARY.—There shall be allowed as a credit (without interest) against the tax imposed by this subtitle on the beneficiary an amount equal to the amount of the taxes deemed distributed to such beneficiary by the trust under sections 666(b) and (c) and 669(d) and (e) during preceding taxable years of the trust on the last day of which the beneficiary was in being, reduced by the amount of the taxes deemed distributed to such beneficiary for such preceding taxable years to the extent that such taxes are taken into account under sections 668(b)(1) and 669(b) in determining the amount of the tax imposed by section 668.

• 1969, Tax Reform Act of 1969 (P.L. 91-172)

P.L. 91-172, §331(a):

Added Code Sec. 667(b). **Effective** for tax years beginning after 12-31-68.

[Sec. 667(c)]

(c) SPECIAL RULE FOR MULTIPLE TRUSTS.—

(1) IN GENERAL.—If, in the same prior taxable year of the beneficiary in which any part of the accumulation distribution from a trust (hereinafter in this paragraph referred to as "third trust") is deemed under section 666(a) to have been distributed to such beneficiary, some part of prior distributions by each of 2 or more other trusts is deemed under section 666(a) to have been distributed to such beneficiary, then subsections (b) and (c) of section 666 shall not apply with respect to such part of the accumulation distribution from such third trust.

(2) ACCUMULATION DISTRIBUTIONS FROM TRUST NOT TAKEN INTO ACCOUNT UNLESS THEY EQUAL OR EXCEED $1,000.—For purposes of paragraph (1), an accumulation distribution from a trust to a beneficiary shall be taken into account only if such distribution, when added to any prior accumulation distributions from such trust which are deemed under section 666(a) to have been distributed to such beneficiary for the same prior taxable year of the beneficiary, equals or exceeds $1,000.

Amendments

• 1976, Tax Reform Act of 1976 (P.L. 94-455)

P.L. 94-455, §701(a)(1):

Added Code Sec. 667(c). **Effective** for distributions made in tax years beginning after 12-31-75.

[Sec. 667(d)]

(d) SPECIAL RULES FOR FOREIGN TRUST.—

(1) FOREIGN TAX DEEMED PAID BY BENEFICIARY.—

(A) IN GENERAL.—In determining the increase in tax under subsection (b)(1)(D) for any computation year, the taxes described in section 665(d)(2) which are deemed distributed under section 666(b) or (c) and added under subsection (b)(1)(C) to the taxable income of the beneficiary for any computation year shall, except as provided in subparagraphs (B) and (C), be treated as a credit against the increase in tax for such computation year under subsection (b)(1)(D).

(B) DEDUCTION IN LIEU OF CREDIT.—If the beneficiary did not choose the benefits of subpart A of part III of subchapter N with respect to the computation year, the beneficiary may in lieu of treating the amounts described in subparagraph (A) (without regard to subparagraph (C)) as a credit may treat such amounts as a deduction in computing the beneficiary's taxable income under subsection (b)(1)(C) for the computation year.

(C) LIMITATION ON CREDIT; RETENTION OF CHARACTER.—

(i) LIMITATION ON CREDIT.—For purposes of determining under subparagraph (A) the amount treated as a credit for any computation year, the limitations under subpart A of part III of subchapter N shall be applied separately with respect to amounts added under subsection (b)(1)(C) to the taxable income of the beneficiary for such computation year. For purposes of computing the increase in tax under subsection (b)(1)(D) for any computation year for which the beneficiary did not choose the benefits of subpart A of part III of subchapter N, the beneficiary shall be treated as having chosen such benefits for such computation year.

(ii) RETENTION OF CHARACTER.—The items of income, deduction, and credit of the Trust shall retain their character (subject to the application of section 904(f)(5)) to the extent necessary to apply this paragraph.

(D) COMPUTATION YEAR.—For purposes of this paragraph, the term "computation year" means any of the three taxable years remaining after application of subsection (b)(1)(B).

Amendments

• 1978, Revenue Act of 1978 (P.L. 95-600)

P.L. 95-600, § 701(q)(1)(B):

Amended Code Sec. 667 by adding subsection (d). **Effective** for distributions made in tax years beginning after 12-31-75.

[Sec. 667(e)]

(e) RETENTION OF CHARACTER OF AMOUNTS DISTRIBUTED FROM ACCUMULATION TRUST TO NONRESIDENT ALIENS AND FOREIGN CORPORATIONS.—In the case of a distribution from a trust to a nonresident alien individual or to a foreign corporation, the first sentence of subsection (a) shall be applied as if the reference to the determination of character under section 662(b) applied to all amounts instead of just to tax-exempt interest.

Amendments

• 1978, Revenue Act of 1978 (P.L. 95-600)

P.L. 95-600, § 701(r)(1):

Amended Code Sec. 667 by adding subsection (e). **Effective** for distributions made in tax years beginning after 12-31-75.

[Sec. 668]

SEC. 668. INTEREST CHARGE ON ACCUMULATION DISTRIBUTIONS FROM FOREIGN TRUSTS.

[Sec. 668(a)]

(a) GENERAL RULE.—For purposes of the tax determined under section 667(a)—

(1) INTEREST DETERMINED USING UNDERPAYMENT RATES.—The interest charge determined under this section with respect to any distribution is the amount of interest which would be determined on the partial tax computed under section 667(b) for the period described in paragraph (2) using the rates and the method under section 6621 applicable to underpayments of tax.

(2) PERIOD.—For purposes of paragraph (1), the period described in this paragraph is the period which begins on the date which is the applicable number of years before the date of the distribution and which ends on the date of the distribution.

(3) APPLICABLE NUMBER OF YEARS.—For purposes of paragraph (2)—

(A) IN GENERAL.—The applicable number of years with respect to a distribution is the number determined by dividing—

(i) the sum of the products described in subparagraph (B) with respect to each undistributed income year, by

(ii) the aggregate undistributed net income.

The quotient determined under the preceding sentence shall be rounded under procedures prescribed by the Secretary.

(B) PRODUCT DESCRIBED.—For purposes of subparagraph (A), the product described in this subparagraph with respect to any undistributed income year is the product of—

(i) the undistributed net income for such year, and

(ii) the sum of the number of taxable years between such year and the taxable year of the distribution (counting in each case the undistributed income year but not counting the taxable year of the distribution).

(4) UNDISTRIBUTED INCOME YEAR.—For purposes of this subsection, the term "undistributed income year" means any prior taxable year of the trust for which there is undistributed net income, other than a taxable year during all of which the beneficiary receiving the distribution was not a citizen or resident of the United States.

(5) DETERMINATION OF UNDISTRIBUTED NET INCOME.—Notwithstanding section 666, for purposes of this subsection, an accumulation distribution from the trust shall be treated as reducing proportionately the undistributed net income for undistributed income years.

(6) PERIODS BEFORE 1996.—Interest for the portion of the period described in paragraph (2) which occurs before January 1, 1996, shall be determined—

(A) by using an interest rate of 6 percent, and

(B) without compounding until January 1, 1996.

Amendments

• 1996, Small Business Job Protection Act of 1996 (P.L. 104-188)

P.L. 104-188, §1906(a):

Amended Code Sec. 668(a). **Effective** for distributions after 8-20-96. Prior to amendment, Code Sec. 668(a) read as follows:

(a) GENERAL RULE.—For purposes of the tax determined under section 667(a), the interest charge is an amount equal to 6 percent of the partial tax computed under section 667(b) multiplied by a fraction—

(1) the numerator of which is the sum of the number of taxable year between each taxable year to which the distribution is allocated under section 666(a) and the taxable year of the distribution (counting in each case the taxable year to which the distribution is allocated but not counting the taxable year of the distribution), and

(2) the denominator of which is the number of taxable years to which the distribution is allocated under section 666(a).

• 1976, Tax Reform Act of 1976 (P.L. 94-455)

P.L. 94-455, §701(a)(3):

Repealed Code Sec. 668(a). **Effective** for distributions made in tax years beginning after 12-31-75. Prior to repeal, Code Sec. 668(a) read as follows:

(a) GENERAL RULE.—The total of the amounts which are treated under sections 666 and 669 as having been distributed by the trust in a preceding taxable year shall be included in the income of a beneficiary of the trust when paid, credited, or required to be distributed to the extent that such total would have been included in the income of such beneficiary under section 662(a)(2) and (b) if such total had been paid to such beneficiary on the last day of such preceding taxable year. The tax imposed by this subtitle on a beneficiary for a taxable year in which any such amount is included in his income shall be determined only as provided in this section and shall consist of the sum of—

(1) a partial tax computed on the taxable income reduced by an amount equal to the total of such amounts, at the rate and in the manner as if this section had not been enacted,

(2) a partial tax determined as provided in subsection (b) of this section, and

(3) in the case of a beneficiary of a trust which is not required to distribute all of its income currently, a partial tax determined as provided in section 669.

For purposes of this subpart, a trust shall not be considered to be a trust which is not required to distribute all of its income currently for any taxable year prior to the first taxable year in which income is accumulated.

P.L. 94-455, §1014(b):

Added a new Code Sec. 668(a). **Effective** for tax years beginning after 12-31-76.

• 1969, Tax Reform Act of 1969 (P.L. 91-172)

P.L. 91-172, §331(a):

Amended Code Sec. 668(a). **Effective** for tax years beginning after 12-31-68. Prior to amendment Code Sec. 668(a) read as follows:

(a) Amounts Treated as Received in Prior Taxable Years.—The total of the amounts which are treated under section 666 as having been distributed by the trust in a preceding taxable year shall be included in the income of a beneficiary or beneficiaries of the trust when paid, credited, or required to be distributed to the extent that such total would have been included in the income of such beneficiary or beneficiaries under section 662(a)(2) and (b) if such total had been paid to such beneficiary or beneficiaries on the last day of such preceding taxable year. The portion of such total included under the preceding sentence in the income of any beneficiary shall be based upon the same ratio as determined under the second sentence of section 662(a)(2) for the taxable year in respect of which the accumulation distribution is determined, except that proper adjustment of such ratio shall be made, in accordance with regulations prescribed by the Secretary or his delegate, for amounts which fall within paragraphs (1) through (4) of section 665(b). The tax of the beneficiaries attributable to the amounts treated as having been received on the last day of such preceding taxable year of the trust shall not be greater than the aggregate of the taxes attributable to those amounts had they been included in the gross income of the beneficiaries on such day in accordance with section 662(a)(2) and (b). Except as provided in section 669, in the case of a foreign trust created by a United States person the preceding sentence shall not apply to any beneficiary who is a United States person.

• 1962, Revenue Act of 1962 (P.L. 87-834)

P.L. 87-834, §7:

Amended Code Sec. 668(a) by inserting after the period in line 18 a new sentence. **Effective** for distributions made after 12-31-62.

[Sec. 668(b)]

(b) LIMITATION.—The total amount of the interest charge shall not, when added to the total partial tax computed under section 667(b), exceed the amount of the accumulation distribution (other than the amount of tax deemed distributed by section 666(b) or (c)) in respect of which such partial tax was determined.

Amendments

• 1976, Tax Reform Act of 1976 (P.L. 94-455)

P.L. 94-455, §701(a)(3):

Repealed Code Sec. 668(a). **Effective** for distributions made in tax years beginning after 12-31-75. Prior to repeal, Code Sec. 668(b) read as follows:

(b) TAX ON DISTRIBUTION.—

(1) ALTERNATIVE METHODS.—Except as provided in paragraph (2), the partial tax imposed by subsection (a)(2) shall be the lesser of—

(A) the aggregate of the taxes attributable to the amounts deemed distributed under section 666 had they been included in the gross income of the beneficiary on the last day of each respective preceding taxable year, or

(B) the tax determined by multiplying, by the number of preceding taxable years of the trust, on the last day of which an amount is deemed under section 666(a) to have been distributed, the average of the increase in tax attributable to recomputing the beneficiary's gross income for each of the beneficiary's 3 taxable years immediately preceding the year of the accumulation distribution by adding to the income of each of such years an amount determined by dividing the amount deemed distributed under section 666 and required to be included in income under subsection (a) by such number of preceding taxable years of the trust, less an amount equal to the amount of taxes deemed distributed to the beneficiary under sections 666(b) and (c).

(2) SPECIAL RULES.—

(A) If a beneficiary was not in existence on the last day of a preceding taxable year of the trust with respect to which a distribution is deemed made under section 666(a), the partial tax under either paragraph (1)(A) or (1)(B) shall be computed as if the beneficiary were in existence on the last day of such year on the basis that the beneficiary had no gross income (other than amounts deemed distributed to him under sections 666 and 669 by the same or other trusts) and no deductions for such year.

(B) The partial tax shall not be computed under the provisions of subparagraph (B) of paragraph (1) if, in the same prior taxable year of the beneficiary in which any part of the accumulation distribution is deemed under section 666(a) to have been distributed to such beneficiary, some part of prior accumulation distributions by each of two or more other trusts is deemed under section 666(a) to have been distributed to such beneficiary.

(C) If the partial tax is computed under paragraph (1)(B), and the amount of the undistributed net income deemed distributed in any preceding taxable year of the trust is less than 25 percent of the amount of the accumulation distribution divided by the number of preceding taxable years to which the accumulation distribution is allocated under section 666(a), the number of preceding taxable years of the trust with respect to which an amount is deemed distributed to a beneficiary under section 666(a) shall be determined without regard to such year.

(3) EFFECT OF OTHER ACCUMULATION DISTRIBUTIONS AND CAPITAL GAIN DISTRIBUTIONS.—In computing the partial tax under paragraph (1) for any beneficiary, the income of such beneficiary for each of his prior taxable years—

(A) shall include amounts previously deemed distributed to such beneficiary in such year under section 666 or 669 as a result of prior accumulation distributions or capital gain distributions (whether from the same or another trust), and

(B) shall not include amounts deemed distributed to such beneficiary in such year under section 669 as a result of a capital gain distribution from the same trust in the current year.

(4) MULTIPLE DISTRIBUTIONS IN THE SAME TAXABLE YEAR.—In the case of accumulation distributions made from more than one trust which are includible in the income of a beneficiary in the same taxable year, the distributions shall be deemed to have been made consecutively in whichever order the beneficiary shall determine.

(5) INFORMATION REQUIREMENTS WITH RESPECT TO BENEFICIARY.—

(A) Except as provided in subparagraph (B), the partial tax shall not be computed under the provisions of paragraph (1)(A) unless the beneficiary supplies such information with respect to his income, for each taxable year with which or in which ends a taxable year of the trust on the last day of which an amount is deemed distributed under section 666(a), as the Secretary or his delegate prescribes by regulations.

(B) If by reason of paragraph (2)(B) the provisions of paragraph (1)(B) do not apply, the determination of the amount of the beneficiary's income for a taxable year for which the beneficiary has not supplied the information required under subparagraph (A) shall be made by the Secretary or his delegate on the basis of information available to him.

P.L. 94-455, §1014(b):

Added a new Code Sec. 668(b). **Effective** for tax years beginning after 12-31-76.

• 1969, Tax Reform Act of 1969 (P.L. 91-172)

P.L. 91-172, §331(a):

Amended Code Sec. 668(b). **Effective** for tax years beginning after 12-31-68. Prior to amendment, Code Sec. 668(b) read as follows:

(b) Credit for Taxes Paid by Trust.—The tax imposed on beneficiaries under this chapter shall be credited with a pro rata portion of the taxes imposed on the trust under this chapter for such preceding taxable year which would not have been payable by the trust for such preceding taxable year had the trust in fact made distributions to such beneficiaries at the times and in the amounts specified in section 666.

[Sec. 668(c)]

(c) INTEREST CHARGE NOT DEDUCTIBLE.—The interest charge determined under this section shall not be allowed as a deduction for purposes of any tax imposed by this title.

Amendments

• 1990, Omnibus Budget Reconciliation Act of 1990 (P.L. 101-508)

P.L. 101-508, §11802(f)(3):

Amended Code Sec. 668(c). **Effective** 11-5-90. Prior to amendment, Code Sec. 668(c) read as follows:

(c) SPECIAL RULES.—

(1) INTEREST CHARGE NOT DEDUCTIBLE.—The interest charge determined under this section shall not be allowed as a deduction for purposes of any tax imposed by this title.

(2) TRANSITIONAL RULE.—For purposes of this section, undistributed net income existing in a trust as of January 1, 1977, shall be treated as allocated under section 666(a) to the first taxable year beginning after December 31, 1976.

P.L. 101-508, §11821(b), provides:

(b) SAVINGS PROVISION.—If—

(1) any provision amended or repealed by this part applied to—

(A) any transaction occurring before the date of the enactment of this Act,

(B) any property acquired before such date of enactment, or

(C) any item of income, loss, deduction, or credit taken into account before such date of enactment, and

(2) the treatment of such transaction, property, or item under such provision would (without regard to the amendments made by this part) affect liability for tax for periods ending after such date of enactment,

nothing in the amendments made by this part shall be construed to affect the treatment of such transaction, property, or item for purposes of determining liability for tax for periods ending after such date of enactment.

• 1976, Tax Reform Act of 1976 (P.L. 94-455)

P.L. 94-455, §1014(b):

Added Code Sec. 668(c). **Effective** for tax years beginning after 12-31-75.

Subpart E—Grantors and Others Treated as Substantial Owners

[Sec. 671]

SEC. 671. TRUST INCOME, DEDUCTIONS, AND CREDITS ATTRIBUTABLE TO GRANTORS AND OTHERS AS SUBSTANTIAL OWNERS.

Where it is specified in this subpart that the grantor or another person shall be treated as the owner of any portion of a trust, there shall then be included in computing the taxable income and credits of the grantor or the other person those items of income, deductions, and credits against tax of the trust which are attributable to that portion of the trust to the extent that such items would be taken into account under this chapter in computing taxable income or credits against the tax of an individual. Any remaining portion of the trust shall be subject to subparts A through D. No items of a trust shall be included in computing the taxable income and credits of the grantor or of any other person solely on the grounds of his dominion and control over the trust under section 61 (relating to definition of gross income) or any other provision of this title, except as specified in this subpart.

[Sec. 672]

SEC. 672. DEFINITIONS AND RULES.

[Sec. 672(a)]

(a) ADVERSE PARTY.—For purposes of this subpart, the term "adverse party" means any person having a substantial beneficial interest in the trust which would be adversely affected by the exercise or nonexercise of the power which he possesses respecting the trust. A person having a general power of appointment over the trust property shall be deemed to have a beneficial interest in the trust.

[Sec. 672(b)]

(b) NONADVERSE PARTY.—For purposes of this subpart, the term "nonadverse party" means any person who is not an adverse party.

[Sec. 672(c)]

(c) RELATED OR SUBORDINATE PARTY.—For purposes of this subpart, the term "related or subordinate party" means any nonadverse party who is—

(1) the grantor's spouse if living with the grantor;

(2) any one of the following: The grantor's father, mother, issue, brother or sister; an employee of the grantor; a corporation or any employee of a corporation in which the stock holdings of the grantor and the trust are significant from the viewpoint of voting control; a subordinate employee of a corporation in which the grantor is an executive.

For purposes of subsection (f) and sections 674 and 675, a related or subordinate party shall be presumed to be subservient to the grantor in respect of the exercise or nonexercise of the powers conferred on him unless such party is shown not to be subservient by a preponderance of the evidence.

Amendments

• 1996, Small Business Job Protection Act of 1996 (P.L. 104-188)

P.L. 104-188, §1904(a)(2):

Amended Code Sec. 672(c) by inserting "subsection (f) and" before "sections 674". **Effective** 8-20-96. For special and transitional rules, see Act Sec. 1904(d)(2) and (e) in the amendment notes following Code Sec. 672(f).

[Sec. 672(d)]

(d) RULE WHERE POWER IS SUBJECT TO CONDITION PRECEDENT.—A person shall be considered to have a power described in this subpart even though the exercise of the power is subject to a precedent giving of notice or takes effect only on the expiration of a certain period after the exercise of the power.

[Sec. 672(e)]

(e) GRANTOR TREATED AS HOLDING ANY POWER OR INTEREST OF GRANTOR'S SPOUSE.—

(1) IN GENERAL.—For purposes of this subpart, a grantor shall be treated as holding any power or interest held by—

(A) any individual who was the spouse of the grantor at the time of the creation of such power or interest, or

(B) any individual who became the spouse of the grantor after the creation of such power or interest, but only with respect to periods after such individual became the spouse of the grantor.

(2) MARITAL STATUS.—For purposes of paragraph (1)(A), an individual legally separated from his spouse under a decree of divorce or of separate maintenance shall not be considered as married.

Amendments

• 1988, Technical and Miscellaneous Revenue Act of 1988 (P.L. 100-647)

P.L. 100-647, §1014(a)(1):

Amended Code Sec. 672(e). **Effective** as if included in the provision of P.L. 99-514 to which it relates. Prior to amendment, Code Sec. 672(e) read as follows:

(e) GRANTOR TREATED AS HOLDING ANY POWER OR INTEREST OF GRANTOR'S SPOUSE.—For purposes of this subpart, if a grantor's spouse is living with the grantor at the time of the creation of any power or interest held by such spouse, the grantor shall be treated as holding such power or interest.

• 1986, Tax Reform Act of 1986 (P.L. 99-514)

P.L. 99-514, §1401(a):

Amended Code Sec. 672 by adding at the end thereof new subsection (e). **Effective** with respect to transfers in trust made after 3-1-86.

[Sec. 672(f)]

(f) SUBPART NOT TO RESULT IN FOREIGN OWNERSHIP.—

(1) IN GENERAL.—Notwithstanding any other provision of this subpart, this subpart shall apply only to the extent such application results in an amount (if any) being currently taken into

account (directly or through 1 or more entities) under this chapter in computing the income of a citizen or resident of the United States or a domestic corporation.

(2) EXCEPTIONS.—

(A) CERTAIN REVOCABLE AND IRREVOCABLE TRUSTS.—Paragraph (1) shall not apply to any portion of a trust if—

(i) the power to revest absolutely in the grantor title to the trust property to which such portion is attributable is exercisable solely by the grantor without the approval or consent of any other person or with the consent of a related or subordinate party who is subservient to the grantor, or

(ii) the only amounts distributable from such portion (whether income or corpus) during the lifetime of the grantor are amounts distributable to the grantor or the spouse of the grantor.

(B) COMPENSATORY TRUSTS.—Except as provided in regulations, paragraph (1) shall not apply to any portion of a trust distributions from which are taxable as compensation for services rendered.

(3) SPECIAL RULES.—Except as otherwise provided in regulations prescribed by the Secretary—

(A) a controlled foreign corporation (as defined in section 957) shall be treated as a domestic corporation for purposes of paragraph (1), and

(B) paragraph (1) shall not apply for purposes of applying section 1297.

(4) RECHARACTERIZATION OF PURPORTED GIFTS.—In the case of any transfer directly or indirectly from a partnership or foreign corporation which the transferee treats as a gift or bequest, the Secretary may recharacterize such transfer in such circumstances as the Secretary determines to be appropriate to prevent the avoidance of the purposes of this subsection.

(5) SPECIAL RULE WHERE GRANTOR IS FOREIGN PERSON.—If—

(A) but for this subsection, a foreign person would be treated as the owner of any portion of a trust, and

(B) such trust has a beneficiary who is a United States person,

such beneficiary shall be treated as the grantor of such portion to the extent such beneficiary has made (directly or indirectly) transfers of property (other than in a sale for full and adequate consideration) to such foreign person. For purposes of the preceding sentence, any gift shall not be taken into account to the extent such gift would be excluded from taxable gifts under section 2503(b).

(6) REGULATIONS.—The Secretary shall prescribe such regulations as may be necessary or appropriate to carry out the purposes of this subsection, including regulations providing that paragraph (1) shall not apply in appropriate cases.

Amendments

• 1998, IRS Restructuring and Reform Act of 1998 (P.L. 105-206)

P.L. 105-206, §6011(c)(1):

Amended Code Sec. 672(f)(3)(B) by striking "section 1296" and inserting "section 1297". **Effective** as if included in the provision of P.L. 105-34 to which it relates [**effective** for tax years of U.S. persons beginning after 12-31-97, and tax years of foreign corporations ending with or within such tax years of U.S. persons.—CCH].

• 1996, Small Business Job Protection Act of 1996 (P.L. 104-188)

P.L. 104-188, §1904(a)(1):

Amended Code Sec. 672(f). **Effective** 8-20-96. For special and transitional rules, see Act Sec. 1904(d)(2) and (e), below. Prior to amendment, Code Sec. 672(f) read as follows:

(f) SPECIAL RULE WHERE GRANTOR IS FOREIGN PERSON.—

(1) IN GENERAL.—If—

(A) but for this subsection, a foreign person would be treated as the owner of any portion of a trust, and

(B) such trust has a beneficiary who is a United States person,

such beneficiary shall be treated as the grantor of such portion to the extent such beneficiary has made transfers of property by gift (directly or indirectly) to such foreign person. For purposes of the preceding sentence, any gift shall not be taken into account to the extent such gift would be excluded from taxable gifts under section 2503(b).

(2) REGULATIONS.—The Secretary shall prescribe such regulations as may be necessary to carry out the purposes of this subsection.

P.L. 104-188, §1904(d)(2) and (e), provides:

(2) EXCEPTIONS FOR CERTAIN TRUSTS.—The amendments made by this section shall not apply to any trust—

(A) which is treated as owned by the grantor under section 676 or 677 (other than subsection (a)(3) thereof) of the Internal Revenue Code of 1986, and

(B) which is in existence on September 19, 1995.

The preceding sentence shall not apply to the portion of any such trust attributable to any transfer to such trust after September 19, 1995.

(e) TRANSITIONAL RULE.—If—

(1) by reason of the amendments made by this section, any person other than a United States person ceases to be treated as the owner of a portion of a domestic trust, and

(2) before January 1, 1997, such trust becomes a foreign trust, or the assets of such trust are transferred to a foreign trust,

no tax shall be imposed by section 1491 of the Internal Revenue Code of 1986 by reason of such trust becoming a foreign trust or the assets of such trust being transferred to a foreign trust.

• 1990, Omnibus Budget Reconciliation Act of 1990 (P.L. 101-508)

P.L. 101-508, §11343(a):

Amended Code Sec. 672 by adding at the end thereof a new subsection (f). **Effective** for any trust created after 11-5-90, and any portion of a trust created on or before such date which is attributable to amounts contributed to the trust after such date.

[Sec. 673]

SEC. 673. REVERSIONARY INTERESTS.

[Sec. 673(a)]

(a) GENERAL RULE.—The grantor shall be treated as the owner of any portion of a trust in which he has a reversionary interest in either the corpus or the income therefrom, if, as of the inception of that portion of the trust, the value of such interest exceeds 5 percent of the value of such portion.

[Sec. 673(b)]

(b) REVERSIONARY INTEREST TAKING EFFECT AT DEATH OF MINOR LINEAL DESCENDANT BENEFICIARY.—In the case of any beneficiary who—

(1) is a lineal descendant of the grantor, and

(2) holds all of the present interests in any portion of a trust,

the grantor shall not be treated under subsection (a) as the owner of such portion solely by reason of a reversionary interest in such portion which takes effect upon the death of such beneficiary before such beneficiary attains age 21.

[Sec. 673(c)]

(c) SPECIAL RULE FOR DETERMINING VALUE OF REVERSIONARY INTEREST.—For purposes of subsection (a), the value of the grantor's reversionary interest shall be determined by assuming the maximum exercise of discretion in favor of the grantor.

[Sec. 673(d)]

(d) POSTPONEMENT OF DATE SPECIFIED FOR REACQUISITION.—Any postponement of the date specified for the reacquisition of possession or enjoyment of the reversionary interest shall be treated as a new transfer in trust commencing with the date on which the postponement is effective and terminating with the date prescribed by the postponement. However, income for any period shall not be included in the income of the grantor by reason of the preceding sentence if such income would not be so includible in the absence of such postponement.

Amendments

• 1988, Technical and Miscellaneous Revenue Act of 1988 (P.L. 100-647)

P.L. 100-647, §1014(b):

Amended Code Sec. 673 by adding at the end thereof new subsections (c) and (d). **Effective** as if included in the provision of P.L. 99-514 to which it relates.

• 1986, Tax Reform Act of 1986 (P.L. 99-514)

P.L. 99-514, §1402(a):

Amended Code Sec. 673. **Effective**, generally, with respect to transfers in trust made after 3-1-86. However, see Act Sec. 1402(c)(2), below.

P.L. 99-514, §1402(c)(2), provides:

(2) TRANSFERS PURSUANT TO PROPERTY SETTLEMENT AGREEMENT.—The amendments made by this section shall not apply to any transfer in trust made after March 1, 1986, pursuant to a binding property settlement agreement entered into on or before March 1, 1986, which required the taxpayer to establish a grantor trust and for the transfer of a specified sum of money or property to the trust by the taxpayer. This paragraph shall apply only to the extent of the amount required to be transferred under the agreement described in the preceding sentence.

Reproduced below is the text of Code Sec. 673 prior to amendment by P.L. 99-514.

SEC. 673. REVERSIONARY INTERESTS.

[Sec. 673(a)]

(a) GENERAL RULE.—The grantor shall be treated as the owner of any portion of a trust in which he has a reversionary interest in either the corpus or the income therefrom if, as of the inception of that portion of the trust, the interest will or may reasonably be expected to take effect in possession or enjoyment within 10 years commencing with the date of the transfer of that portion of the trust.

[Sec. 673(b)—Repealed]

Amendments

• 1969, Tax Reform Act of 1969 (P.L. 91-172)

P.L. 91-172, §201(c):

Repealed Code Sec. 673(b). **Effective** for transfers in trust made after 4-22-69. Prior to repeal, Code Sec. 673(b) read as follows:

(b) EXCEPTION WHERE INCOME IS PAYABLE TO CHARITABLE BENEFICIARIES.—Subsection (a) shall not apply to the extent that the income of a portion of a trust in which the grantor has a reversionary interest is, under the terms of the trust, irrevocably payable for a period of at least 2 years (commencing with the date of the transfer) to a designated beneficiary, which beneficiary is of a type described in section 170 (b)(1)(A)(i), (ii), or (iii).

[Sec. 673(c)]

(c) REVERSIONARY INTEREST TAKING EFFECT AT DEATH OF INCOME BENEFICIARY.—The grantor shall not be treated under subsection (a) as the owner of any portion of a trust where his reversionary interest in such portion is not to take effect in possession or enjoyment until the death of the person or persons to whom the income therefrom is payable.

[Sec. 673(d)]

(d) POSTPONEMENT OF DATE SPECIFIED FOR REACQUISITION.—Any postponement of the date specified for the reacquisition of possession or enjoyment of the reversionary interest shall be treated as a new transfer in trust commencing with the date on which the postponement is effected and terminating with the date prescribed by the postponement. However, income for any period shall not be included in the income of the grantor by reason of the preceding sentence if such income would not be so includible in the absence of such postponement.

[Sec. 674]

SEC. 674. POWER TO CONTROL BENEFICIAL ENJOYMENT.

[Sec. 674(a)]

(a) GENERAL RULE.—The grantor shall be treated as the owner of any portion of a trust in respect of which the beneficial enjoyment of the corpus or the income therefrom is subject to a power of disposition, exercisable by the grantor or a nonadverse party, or both, without the approval or consent of any adverse party.

[Sec. 674(b)]

(b) EXCEPTIONS FOR CERTAIN POWERS.—Subsection (a) shall not apply to the following powers regardless of by whom held:

(1) POWER TO APPLY INCOME TO SUPPORT OF A DEPENDENT.—A power described in section 677(b) to the extent that the grantor would not be subject to tax under that section.

(2) POWER AFFECTING BENEFICIAL ENJOYMENT ONLY AFTER OCCURRENCE OF EVENT.—A power, the exercise of which can only affect the beneficial enjoyment of the income for a period commencing after the occurrence of an event such that a grantor would not be treated as the owner under section 673 if the power were a reversionary interest; but the grantor may be treated as the owner after the occurrence of the event unless the power is relinquished.

(3) POWER EXERCISABLE ONLY BY WILL.—A power exercisable only by will, other than a power in the grantor to appoint by will the income of the trust where the income is accumulated for such disposition by the grantor or may be so accumulated in the discretion of the grantor or a nonadverse party, or both, without the approval or consent of any adverse party.

(4) POWER TO ALLOCATE AMONG CHARITABLE BENEFICIARIES.—A power to determine the beneficial enjoyment of the corpus or the income therefrom if the corpus or income is irrevocably payable for a purpose specified in section 170(c) (relating to definition of charitable contributions) or to an employee stock ownership plan (as defined in section 4975(e)(7)) in a qualified gratuitous transfer (as defined in section 664(g)(1)).

(5) POWER TO DISTRIBUTE CORPUS.—A power to distribute corpus either—

(A) to or for a beneficiary or beneficiaries or to or for a class of beneficiaries (whether or not income beneficiaries) provided that the power is limited by a reasonably definite standard which is set forth in the trust instrument; or

(B) to or for any current income beneficiary, provided that the distribution of corpus must be chargeable against the proportionate share of corpus held in trust for the payment of income to the beneficiary as if the corpus constituted a separate trust.

A power does not fall within the powers described in this paragraph if any person has a power to add to the beneficiary or beneficiaries or to a class of beneficiaries designated to receive the income or corpus, except where such action is to provide for after-born or after-adopted children.

(6) POWER TO WITHHOLD INCOME TEMPORARILY.—A power to distribute or apply income to or for any current income beneficiary or to accumulate the income for him, provided that any accumulated income must ultimately be payable—

(A) to the beneficiary from whom distribution or application is withheld, to his estate, or to his appointees (or persons named as alternate takers in default of appointment) provided that such beneficiary possesses a power of appointment which does not exclude from the class of possible appointees any person other than the beneficiary, his estate, his creditors, or the creditors of his estate, or

(B) on termination of the trust, or in conjunction with a distribution of corpus which is augmented by such accumulated income, to the current income beneficiaries in shares which have been irrevocably specified in the trust instrument.

Accumulated income shall be considered so payable although it is provided that if any beneficiary does not survive a date of distribution which could reasonably have been expected to occur within the beneficiary's lifetime, the share of the deceased beneficiary is to be paid to his appointees or to one or more designated alternate takers (other than the grantor or the grantor's estate) whose shares have been irrevocably specified. A power does not fall within the powers described in this paragraph if any person has a power to add to the beneficiary or beneficiaries or to a class of beneficiaries designated to receive the income or corpus except where such action is to provide for after-born or after-adopted children.

(7) POWER TO WITHHOLD INCOME DURING DISABILITY OF A BENEFICIARY.—A power exercisable only during—

(A) the existence of a legal disability of any current income beneficiary, or

(B) the period during which any income beneficiary shall be under the age of 21 years,

to distribute or apply income to or for such beneficiary or to accumulate and add the income to corpus. A power does not fall within the powers described in this paragraph if any person has a power to add to the beneficiary or beneficiaries or to a class of beneficiaries designated to receive the income or corpus, except where such action is to provide for after-born or after-adopted children.

(8) POWER TO ALLOCATE BETWEEN CORPUS AND INCOME.—A power to allocate receipts and disbursements as between corpus and income, even though expressed in broad language.

Amendments

• 1997, Taxpayer Relief Act of 1997 (P.L. 105-34)

P.L. 105-34, §1530(c)(6):

Amended Code Sec. 674(b)(4) by inserting before the period "or to an employee stock ownership plan (as defined in section 4975(e)(7)) in a qualified gratuitous transfer (as defined in section 664(g)(1))". **Effective** for transfers made by trusts to, or for the use of, an employee stock ownership plan after 8-5-97.

• 1986, Tax Reform Act of 1986 (P.L. 99-514)

P.L. 99-514, §1402(b)(1)(A)-(C):

Amended Code Sec. 674(b)(2) by striking out "the expiration of a period" and inserting in lieu thereof "the occurrence of an event", by striking out "the expiration of the period" and inserting in lieu thereof "the occurrence of the event", and by striking out "EXPIRATION OF 10-YEAR PERIOD" in the heading thereof and inserting in lieu thereof "OCCURRENCE OF EVENT". **Effective**, generally, with respect to transfers in trust made after 3-1-86. However, see Act Sec. 1402(c)(2) following Code Sec. 673.

[Sec. 674(c)]

(c) EXCEPTION FOR CERTAIN POWERS OF INDEPENDENT TRUSTEES.—Subsection (a) shall not apply to a power solely exercisable (without the approval or consent of any other person) by a trustee or trustees, none of whom is the grantor, and no more than half of whom are related or subordinate parties who are subservient to the wishes of the grantor—

(1) to distribute, apportion, or accumulate income to or for a beneficiary or beneficiaries, or to, for, or within a class of beneficiaries; or

(2) to pay out corpus to or for a beneficiary or beneficiaries or to or for a class of beneficiaries (whether or not income beneficiaries).

A power does not fall within the powers described in this subsection if any person has a power to add to the beneficiary or beneficiaries or to a class of beneficiaries designated to receive the income or corpus, except where such action is to provide for after-born or after-adopted children. For periods during which an individual is the spouse of the grantor (within the meaning of section 672(e)(2)), any reference in this subsection to the grantor shall be treated as including a reference to such individual.

Amendments

• 1988, Technical and Miscellaneous Revenue Act of 1988 (P.L. 100-647)

P.L. 100-647, §1014(a)(3):

Amended Code Sec. 674(c) by adding at the end thereof a new sentence. **Effective** as if included in the provision of P.L. 99-514 to which it relates.

[Sec. 674(d)]

(d) POWER TO ALLOCATE INCOME IF LIMITED BY A STANDARD.—Subsection (a) shall not apply to a power solely exercisable (without the approval or consent of any other person) by a trustee or trustees, none of whom is the grantor or spouse living with the grantor, to distribute, apportion, or accumulate income to or for a beneficiary or beneficiaries, or to, for, or within a class of beneficiaries, whether or not the conditions of paragraph (6) or (7) of subsection (b) are satisfied, if such power is limited by a reasonably definite external standard which is set forth in the trust instrument. A power does not fall within the powers described in this subsection if any person has a power to add to the beneficiary or beneficiaries or to a class of beneficiaries designated to receive the income or corpus except where such action is to provide for after-born or after-adopted children.

[Sec. 675]

SEC. 675. ADMINISTRATIVE POWERS.

The grantor shall be treated as the owner of any portion of a trust in respect of which—

(1) POWER TO DEAL FOR LESS THAN ADEQUATE AND FULL CONSIDERATION.—A power exercisable by the grantor or a nonadverse party, or both, without the approval or consent of any adverse party enables the grantor or any person to purchase, exchange, or otherwise deal with or dispose of the corpus or the income therefrom for less than an adequate consideration in money or money's worth.

(2) POWER TO BORROW WITHOUT ADEQUATE INTEREST OR SECURITY.—A power exercisable by the grantor or a nonadverse party, or both, enables the grantor to borrow the corpus or income, directly or indirectly, without adequate interest or without adequate security except where a trustee (other than the grantor) is authorized under a general lending power to make loans to any person without regard to interest or security.

(3) BORROWING OF THE TRUST FUNDS.—The grantor has directly or indirectly borrowed the corpus or income and has not completely repaid the loan, including any interest, before the beginning of the taxable year. The preceding sentence shall not apply to a loan which provides for adequate interest and adequate security, if such loan is made by a trustee other than the grantor and other than a related or subordinate trustee subservient to the grantor. For periods during which an individual is the spouse of the grantor (within the meaning of section 672(e)(2)), any reference in this paragraph to the grantor shall be treated as including a reference to such individual.

(4) GENERAL POWERS OF ADMINISTRATION.—A power of administration is exercisable in a nonfiduciary capacity by any person without the approval or consent of any person in a fiduciary capacity. For purposes of this paragraph, the term "power of administration" means any one or more of the following powers: (A) a power to vote or direct the voting of stock or other securities of a corporation in which the holdings of the grantor and the trust are significant from the viewpoint of voting control; (B) a power to control the investment of the trust funds either by directing investments or reinvestments, or by vetoing proposed investments or reinvestments, to the extent that the trust funds consist of stocks or securities of corporations in which the holdings of the grantor and the trust are significant from the viewpoint of voting

control; or (C) a power to reacquire the trust corpus by substituting other property of an equivalent value.

Amendments

• 1988, Technical and Miscellaneous Revenue Act of 1988 (P.L. 100-647)

P.L. 100-647, §1014(a)(2):

Amended Code Sec. 675(3) by adding at the end thereof a new sentence. **Effective** as if included in the provision of P.L. 99-514 to which it relates.

[Sec. 676]

SEC. 676. POWER TO REVOKE.

[Sec. 676(a)]

(a) GENERAL RULE.—The grantor shall be treated as the owner of any portion of a trust, whether or not he is treated as such owner under any other provision of this part, where at any time the power to revest in the grantor title to such portion is exercisable by the grantor or a nonadverse party, or both.

[Sec. 676(b)]

(b) POWER AFFECTING BENEFICIAL ENJOYMENT ONLY AFTER OCCURRENCE OF EVENT.—Subsection (a) shall not apply to a power the exercise of which can only affect the beneficial enjoyment of the income for a period commencing after the occurrence of an event such that a grantor would not be treated as the owner under section 673 if the power were a reversionary interest. But the grantor may be treated as the owner after the occurrence of such event unless the power is relinquished.

Amendments

• 1986, Tax Reform Act of 1986 (P.L. 99-514)

P.L. 99-514, §1402(b)(2)(A)-(C):

Amended Code Sec. 676(b) by striking out "the expiration of a period" and inserting in lieu thereof "the occurrence of an event", by striking out "the expiration of such period" and inserting in lieu thereof "the occurrence of such event", and by striking out "EXPIRATION OF 10-YEAR PERIOD" in the heading thereof and inserting in lieu thereof "OCCURRENCE OF EVENT". **Effective**, generally, with respect to transfers in trust made after 3-1-86. However, see Act Sec. 1402(c)(2) following Code Sec. 673.

[Sec. 677]

SEC. 677. INCOME FOR BENEFIT OF GRANTOR.

[Sec. 677(a)]

(a) GENERAL RULE.—The grantor shall be treated as the owner of any portion of a trust, whether or not he is treated as such owner under section 674, whose income without the approval or consent of any adverse party is, or, in the discretion of the grantor or a nonadverse party, or both, may be—

(1) distributed to the grantor or the grantor's spouse;

(2) held or accumulated for future distribution to the grantor or the grantor's spouse; or

(3) applied to the payment of premiums on policies of insurance on the life of the grantor or the grantor's spouse (except policies of insurance irrevocably payable for a purpose specified in section 170(c) (relating to definition of charitable contributions)).

This subsection shall not apply to a power the exercise of which can only affect the beneficial enjoyment of the income for a period commencing after the occurrence of an event such that the grantor would not be treated as the owner under section 673 if the power were a reversionary interest; but the grantor may be treated as the owner after the occurrence of the event unless the power is relinquished.

Amendments

• 1986, Tax Reform Act of 1986 (P.L. 99-514)

P.L. 99-514, §1402(b)(3)(A)-(B):

Amended Code Sec. 677(a) by striking out "the expiration of a period" and inserting in lieu thereof "the occurrence of an event", and by striking out "the expiration of the period" and inserting in lieu thereof "the occurrence of the event". **Effective**, generally, with respect to transfers in trust made after 3-1-86. However, see Act Sec. 1402(c)(2) following Code Sec. 673.

• 1969, Tax Reform Act of 1969 (P.L. 91-172)

P.L. 91-172, §332(a)(1):

Amended Code Sec. 677(a)(1), (2) and (3) by striking out "the grantor" each place where it appears and inserting in lieu thereof "the grantor or the grantor's spouse". **Effective** with respect to property transferred in trust after 10-9-69.

[Sec. 677(b)]

(b) OBLIGATIONS OF SUPPORT.—Income of a trust shall not be considered taxable to the grantor under subsection (a) or any other provision of this chapter merely because such income in the discretion of another person, the trustee, or the grantor acting as trustee or co-trustee, may be applied or distributed for the support or maintenance of a beneficiary (other than the grantor's spouse) whom the grantor is legally obligated to support or maintain, except to the extent that such income is so applied or distributed. In cases where the amounts so applied or distributed are paid out of corpus or out of other than income for the taxable year, such amounts shall be considered to be an amount paid or credited within the meaning of paragraph (2) of section 661(a) and shall be taxed to the grantor under section 662.

Amendments

• 1969, Tax Reform Act of 1969 (P.L. 91-172)

P.L. 91-172, §332(a)(2):

Amended Code Sec. 677(b) by striking out "beneficiary" and inserting in lieu thereof "beneficiary (other than the grantor's spouse)". **Effective** with respect to property transferred in trust after 10-9-69.

[Sec. 678]

SEC. 678. PERSON OTHER THAN GRANTOR TREATED AS SUBSTANTIAL OWNER.

[Sec. 678(a)]

(a) GENERAL RULE.—A person other than the grantor shall be treated as the owner of any portion of a trust with respect to which:

(1) such person has a power exercisable solely by himself to vest the corpus or the income therefrom in himself, or

(2) such person has previously partially released or otherwise modified such a power and after the release or modification retains such control as would, within the principles of sections 671 to 677, inclusive, subject a grantor of a trust to treatment as the owner thereof.

[Sec. 678(b)]

(b) EXCEPTION WHERE GRANTOR IS TAXABLE.—Subsection (a) shall not apply with respect to a power over income, as originally granted or thereafter modified, if the grantor of the trust or a transferor (to whom section 679 applies) is otherwise treated as the owner under the provisions of this subpart other than this section.

Amendments

• 1976, Tax Reform Act of 1976 (P.L. 94-455)

P.L. 94-455, §1013(b):

Amended Code Sec. 678(b). **Effective** for tax years ending after 12-31-75, but only in the case of (A) foreign trusts created after 5-21-74, and (B) transfers of property to foreign trusts after 5-21-74. Prior to amendment, Code Sec. 678(b) read as follows:

(b) EXCEPTION WHERE GRANTOR IS TAXABLE.—Subsection (a) shall not apply with respect to a power over income, as originally granted or thereafter modified, if the grantor of the trust is otherwise treated as the owner under sections 671 to 677, inclusive.

[Sec. 678(c)]

(c) OBLIGATIONS OF SUPPORT.—Subsection (a) shall not apply to a power which enables such person, in the capacity of trustee or co-trustee, merely to apply the income of the trust to the support or maintenance of a person whom the holder of the power is obligated to support or maintain except to the extent that such income is so applied. In cases where the amounts so applied or distributed are paid out of corpus or out of other than income of the taxable year, such amounts shall be considered to be an amount paid or credited within the meaning of paragraph (2) of section 661(a) and shall be taxed to the holder of the power under section 662.

[Sec. 678(d)]

(d) EFFECT OF RENUNCIATION OR DISCLAIMER.—Subsection (a) shall not apply with respect to a power which has been renounced or disclaimed within a reasonable time after the holder of the power first became aware of its existence.

[Sec. 678(e)]

(e) CROSS REFERENCE.—

For provision under which beneficiary of trust is treated as owner of the portion of the trust which consists of stock in an S corporation, see section 1361(d).

Amendments

• 2000, Community Renewal Tax Relief Act of 2000 (P.L. 106-554)

P.L. 106-554, §319(8)(A):

Amended Code Sec. 678(e) by striking "an electing small business corporation" and inserting "an S corporation". **Effective** on 12-21-2000.

• 1983, Technical Corrections Act of 1982 (P.L. 97-448)

P.L. 97-448, §102(i)(2):

Added Code Sec. 678(e). **Effective** as if included in the provision of P.L. 97-34 to which it relates.

[Sec. 679]

SEC. 679. FOREIGN TRUSTS HAVING ONE OR MORE UNITED STATES BENEFICIARIES.

[Sec. 679(a)]

(a) TRANSFEROR TREATED AS OWNER.—

(1) IN GENERAL.—A United States person who directly or indirectly transfers property to a foreign trust (other than a trust described in section 6048(a)(3)(B)(ii)) shall be treated as the owner for his taxable year of the portion of such trust attributable to such property if for such year there is a United States beneficiary of any portion of such trust.

(2) EXCEPTIONS.—Paragraph (1) shall not apply—

(A) TRANSFERS BY REASON OF DEATH.—To any transfer by reason of the death of the transferor.

(B) TRANSFERS AT FAIR MARKET VALUE.—To any transfer of property to a trust in exchange for consideration of at least the fair market value of the transferred property. For purposes of the preceding sentence, consideration other than cash shall be taken into account at its fair market value.

(3) CERTAIN OBLIGATIONS NOT TAKEN INTO ACCOUNT UNDER FAIR MARKET VALUE EXCEPTION.—

(A) IN GENERAL.—In determining whether paragraph (2)(B) applies to any transfer by a person described in clause (ii) or (iii) of subparagraph (C), there shall not be taken into account—

(i) except as provided in regulations, any obligation of a person described in subparagraph (C), and

(ii) to the extent provided in regulations, any obligation which is guaranteed by a person described in subparagraph (C).

(B) TREATMENT OF PRINCIPAL PAYMENTS ON OBLIGATION.—Principal payments by the trust on any obligation referred to in subparagraph (A) shall be taken into account on and after the date of the payment in determining the portion of the trust attributable to the property transferred.

(C) PERSONS DESCRIBED.—The persons described in this subparagraph are—

(i) the trust,

(ii) any grantor, owner, or beneficiary of the trust, and

(iii) any person who is related (within the meaning of section 643(i)(2)(B)) to any grantor, owner, or beneficiary of the trust.

(4) SPECIAL RULES APPLICABLE TO FOREIGN GRANTOR WHO LATER BECOMES A UNITED STATES PERSON.—

(A) IN GENERAL.—If a nonresident alien individual has a residency starting date within 5 years after directly or indirectly transferring property to a foreign trust, this section and section 6048 shall be applied as if such individual transferred to such trust on the residency starting date an amount equal to the portion of such trust attributable to the property transferred by such individual to such trust in such transfer.

(B) TREATMENT OF UNDISTRIBUTED INCOME.—For purposes of this section, undistributed net income for periods before such individual's residency starting date shall be taken into account in determining the portion of the trust which is attributable to property transferred by such individual to such trust but shall not otherwise be taken into account.

(C) RESIDENCY STARTING DATE.—For purposes of this paragraph, an individual's residency starting date is the residency starting date determined under section 7701(b)(2)(A).

(5) OUTBOUND TRUST MIGRATIONS.—If—

(A) an individual who is a citizen or resident of the United States transferred property to a trust which was not a foreign trust, and

(B) such trust becomes a foreign trust while such individual is alive,

then this section and section 6048 shall be applied as if such individual transferred to such trust on the date such trust becomes a foreign trust an amount equal to the portion of such trust attributable to the property previously transferred by such individual to such trust. A rule similar to the rule of paragraph (4)(B) shall apply for purposes of this paragraph.

Amendments

• 1997, Taxpayer Relief Act of 1997 (P.L. 105-34)

P.L. 105-34, §1601(i)(2):

Amended Code Sec. 679(a)(3)(C)(ii)-(iii) by inserting ", owner," after "grantor". **Effective** as if included in the provision of P.L. 104-188 to which it relates [**effective** for transfers of property after 2-6-95.—CCH].

• 1996, Small Business Job Protection Act of 1996 (P.L. 104-188)

P.L. 104-188, §1903(a)(1):

Amended Code Sec. 679(a)(2) by striking subparagraph (B) and inserting a new subparagraph (B). **Effective** for transfers of property after 2-6-95. Prior to amendment, Code Sec. 679(a)(2)(B) read as follows:

(B) TRANSFERS WHERE GAIN IS RECOGNIZED TO TRANSFEROR.—To any sale or exchange of the property at its fair market value in a transaction in which all of the gain to the transferor is realized at the time of the transfer and is recognized either at such time or is returned as provided in section 453.

P.L. 104-188, §1903(a)(2):

Amended Code Sec. 679(a) by adding at the end a new paragraph (3). **Effective** for transfers of property after 2-6-95.

P.L. 104-188, §1903(b) (as amended by P.L. 105-206, §6018(g)):

Amended Code Sec. 679(a)(1) by striking "section 404(a)(4) Or [sic] 404A" and inserting "section 6048(a)(3)(B)(ii)". **Effective** for transfers of property after 2-6-95.

P.L. 104-188, §1903(c):

Amended Code Sec. 679(a) by adding at the end new paragraphs (4) and (5). **Effective** for transfers of property after 2-6-95.

• 1980 (P.L. 96-603)

P.L. 96-603, §2(b):

Amended Code Sec. 679(a)(1) by adding "Or [sic] 404A" following the phrase "in section 404(a)(4)". **Effective** with respect to employer contributions or accruals for tax years beginning after 1979. However, see the historical comment for P.L. 96-603 under Code Sec. 404A(h) for details of elections permitting retroactive application of this amendment with respect to foreign subsidiaries and permitting allowance of prior deductions in case of certain funded branch plans.

[Sec. 679(b)]

(b) TRUSTS ACQUIRING UNITED STATES BENEFICIARIES.—If—

(1) subsection (a) applies to a trust for the transferor's taxable year, and

(2) subsection (a) would have applied to the trust for his immediately preceding taxable year but for the fact that for such preceding taxable year there was no United States beneficiary for any portion of the trust,

then, for purposes of this subtitle, the transferor shall be treated as having income for the taxable year (in addition to his other income for such year) equal to the undistributed net income (at the close of such immediately preceding taxable year) attributable to the portion of the trust referred to in subsection (a).

[Sec. 679(c)]

(c) TRUSTS TREATED AS HAVING A UNITED STATES BENEFICIARY.—

(1) IN GENERAL.—For purposes of this section, a trust shall be treated as having a United States beneficiary for the taxable year unless—

(A) under the terms of the trust, no part of the income or corpus of the trust may be paid or accumulated during the taxable year to or for the benefit of a United States person, and

(B) if the trust were terminated at any time during the taxable year, no part of the income or corpus of such trust could be paid to or for the benefit of a United States person.

For purposes of subparagraph (A), an amount shall be treated as accumulated for the benefit of a United States person even if the United States person's interest in the trust is contingent on a future event.

(2) ATTRIBUTION OF OWNERSHIP.—For purposes of paragraph (1), an amount shall be treated as paid or accumulated to or for the benefit of a United States person if such amount is paid to or accumulated for a foreign corporation, foreign partnership, or foreign trust or estate, and—

(A) in the case of a foreign corporation, such corporation is a controlled foreign corporation (as defined in section 957(a)),

(B) in the case of a foreign partnership, a United States person is a partner of such partnership, or

(C) in the case of a foreign trust or estate, such trust or estate has a United States beneficiary (within the meaning of paragraph (1)).

(3) CERTAIN UNITED STATES BENEFICIARIES DISREGARDED.—A beneficiary shall not be treated as a United States person in applying this section with respect to any transfer of property to foreign trust if such beneficiary first became a United States person more than 5 years after the date of such transfer.

(4) SPECIAL RULE IN CASE OF DISCRETION TO IDENTIFY BENEFICIARIES.—For purposes of paragraph (1)(A), if any person has the discretion (by authority given in the trust agreement, by power of appointment, or otherwise) of making a distribution from the trust to, or for the benefit of, any person, such trust shall be treated as having a beneficiary who is a United States person unless—

(A) the terms of the trust specifically identify the class of persons to whom such distributions may be made, and

(B) none of those persons are United States persons during the taxable year.

(5) CERTAIN AGREEMENTS AND UNDERSTANDINGS TREATED AS TERMS OF THE TRUST.—For purposes of paragraph (1)(A), if any United States person who directly or indirectly transfers property to the trust is directly or indirectly involved in any agreement or understanding (whether written, oral, or otherwise) that may result in the income or corpus of the trust being paid or accumulated to or for the benefit of a United States person, such agreement or understanding shall be treated as a term of the trust.

(6) UNCOMPENSATED USE OF TRUST PROPERTY TREATED AS A PAYMENT.—For purposes of this subsection, a loan of cash or marketable securities (or the use of any other trust property) directly or indirectly to or by any United States person (whether or not a beneficiary under the terms of the trust) shall be treated as paid or accumulated for the benefit of a United States person. The preceding sentence shall not apply to the extent that the United States person repays the loan at a market rate of interest (or pays the fair market value of the use of such property) within a reasonable period of time.

Amendments

• 2010, Hiring Incentives to Restore Employment Act (P.L. 111-147)

P.L. 111-147, §531(a):

Amended Code Sec. 679(c)(1) by adding at the end a new sentence. **Effective** 3-18-2010.

P.L. 111-147, §531(b):

Amended Code Sec. 679(c) by adding at the end a new paragraph (4). **Effective** 3-18-2010.

P.L. 111-147, §531(c):

Amended Code Sec. 679(c), as amended by Act Sec. 531(b), by adding at the end a new paragraph (5). **Effective** 3-18-2010.

P.L. 111-147, §533(c):

Amended Code Sec. 679(c), as amended by this Act, by adding at the end a new paragraph (6). **Effective** for loans made, and uses of property, after 3-18-2010.

• 1996, Small Business Job Protection Act of 1996 (P.L. 104-188)

P.L. 104-188, §1903(d):

Amended Code Sec. 679(c) by adding at the end a new paragraph (3). **Effective** for transfers of property after 2-6-95.

P.L. 104-188, §1903(e):

Amended Code Sec. 679(c)(2)(A). **Effective** for transfers of property after 2-6-95. Prior to amendment, Code Sec. 679(c)(2)(A) read as follows:

(A) in the case of a foreign corporation, more than 50 percent of the total combined voting power of all classes of stock entitled to vote of such corporation is owned (within the meaning of section 958(a)) or is considered to be owned (within the meaning of section 958(b)) by United States shareholders (as defined in section 951(b)),

• 1976, Tax Reform Act of 1976 (P.L. 94-455)

P.L. 94-455, §1013(a):

Added Code Sec. 679. **Effective** for tax years ending after 12-31-75, but only in the case of (A) foreign trusts created after 5-21-74, and (B) transfers of property to foreign trusts after 5-21-74.

[Sec. 679(d)]

(d) PRESUMPTION THAT FOREIGN TRUST HAS UNITED STATES BENEFICIARY.—If a United States person directly or indirectly transfers property to a foreign trust (other than a trust described in section 6048(a)(3)(B)(ii)), the Secretary may treat such trust as having a United States beneficiary for purposes of applying this section to such transfer unless such person—

(1) submits such information to the Secretary as the Secretary may require with respect to such transfer, and

(2) demonstrates to the satisfaction of the Secretary that such trust satisfies the requirements of subparagraphs (A) and (B) of subsection (c)(1).

Amendments

• 2010, Hiring Incentives to Restore Employment Act (P.L. 111-147)

P.L. 111-147, §532(a):

Amended Code Sec. 679 by redesignating subsection (d) as subsection (e) and inserting after subsection (c) a new subsection (d). **Effective** for transfers of property after 3-18-2010.

[Sec. 679(e)]

(e) REGULATIONS.—The Secretary shall prescribe such regulations as may be necessary or appropriate to carry out the purposes of this section.

Amendments

• 2010, Hiring Incentives to Restore Employment Act (P.L. 111-147)

P.L. 111-147, §532(a):

Amended Code Sec. 679 by redesignating subsection (d) as subsection (e). **Effective** for transfers of property after 3-18-2010.

• 1996, Small Business Job Protection Act of 1996 (P.L. 104-188)

P.L. 104-188, §1903(f):

Amended Code Sec. 679 by adding at the end a new subsection (d). **Effective** for transfers of property after 2-6-95.

Subpart F—Miscellaneous

[Sec. 681]

SEC. 681. LIMITATION ON CHARITABLE DEDUCTION.

[Sec. 681(a)]

(a) TRADE OR BUSINESS INCOME.—In computing the deduction allowable under section 642(c) to a trust, no amount otherwise allowable under section 642(c) as a deduction shall be allowed as a deduction with respect to income of the taxable year which is allocable to its unrelated business income for such year. For purposes of the preceding sentence, the term "unrelated business income" means an amount equal to the amount which, if such trust were exempt from tax under section 501(a) by reason of section 501(c)(3), would be computed as its unrelated business taxable income under section 512 (relating to income derived from certain business activities and from certain property acquired with borrowed funds).

Amendments

• 1969, Tax Reform Act of 1969 (P.L. 91-172)

P.L. 91-172, §121(d)(2):

Amended Code Sec. 681(a) by changing "certain leases" to "certain property acquired with borrowed funds." **Effective** 1-1-70.

[Sec. 681(b)]

(b) CROSS REFERENCE.—

For disallowance of certain charitable, etc., deductions otherwise allowable under section 642(c), see sections 508(d) and 4948(c)(4).

Amendments

• 1969, Tax Reform Act of 1969 (P.L. 91-172)

P.L. 91-172, §101(j)(18)-(19):

Repealed Code Sec. 681(b) and redesignated former Code Sec. 681(d) as Code Sec. 681(b). **Effective** 1-1-70. Prior to repeal, Code Sec. 681(b) read as follows:

(b) OPERATIONS OF TRUSTS.—

(1) LIMITATION ON CHARITABLE, ETC., DEDUCTION.—The amount otherwise allowable under section 642(c) as a deduction shall not exceed 20 percent of the taxable income of the trust (computed without the benefit of section 642(c) but with the benefit of section 170(b)(1)(A)) if the trust has engaged in a prohibited transaction, as defined in paragraph (2).

(2) PROHIBITED TRANSACTIONS.—For purposes of this subsection, the term "prohibited transaction" means any transaction after July 1, 1950, in which any trust while holding income or corpus which has been permanently set aside or is to be used exclusively for charitable or other purposes described in section 642(c)—

(A) lends any part of such income or corpus, without receipt of adequate security and a reasonable rate of interest, to;

(B) pays any compensation from such income or corpus, in excess of a reasonable allowance for salaries or other compensation for personal services actually rendered, to;

(C) makes any part of its services available on a preferential basis to;

(D) uses such income or corpus to make any substantial purchase of securities or any other property, for more than an adequate consideration in money or money's worth, from;

(E) sells any substantial part of the securities or other property comprising such income or corpus, for less than an adequate consideration in money or money's worth, to; or

(F) engages in any other transaction which results in a substantial diversion of such income or corpus to;

the creator of such trust; any person who has made a substantial contribution to such trust; a member of a family (as defined in section 267(c)(4)) of an individual who is the creator of the trust or who has made a substantial contribution to the trust; or a corporation controlled by any such creator or person through the ownership, directly or indirectly, of 50 percent or more of the total combined voting power of all classes of stock entitled to vote or 50 percent or more of the total value of shares of all classes of stock of the corporation.

(3) TAXABLE YEARS AFFECTED.—The amount otherwise allowable under section 642(c) as a deduction shall be limited as provided in paragraph (1) only for taxable years after the taxable year during which the trust is notified by the Secretary that it has engaged in such transaction, unless such trust entered into such prohibited transaction with the purpose of diverting such corpus or income from the purposes described in section 642(c), and such transaction involved a substantial part of such corpus or income.

(4) FUTURE CHARITABLE, ETC., DEDUCTIONS OF TRUST DENIED DEDUCTION UNDER PARAGRAPH (3).—If the deduction of any trust under section 642(c) has been limited as provided in this subsection, such trust, with respect to any taxable year following the taxable year in which notice is received of limitation of deduction under section 642(c), may, under regulations prescribed by the Secretary or his delegate, file claim for the allowance of the unlimited deduction under section 642(c), and if the Secretary, pursuant to such regulations, is satisfied that such trust will not knowingly again engage in a prohibited transaction, the limitation provided in paragraph (1) shall not apply with respect to taxable years after the year in which such claim is filed.

(5) DISALLOWANCE OF CERTAIN CHARITABLE, ETC., DEDUCTIONS.—No gift or bequest for religious, charitable, scientific, literary, or educational purposes (including the encouragement of art and the prevention of cruelty to children or animals), otherwise allowable as a deduction under section 170, 545 (b) (2), 642 (c), 2055, 2106 (a) (2), or 2522, shall be allowed as a deduction if made in trust and, in the taxable year of the trust in which the gift or bequest is made, the deduction allowed the trust under section 642 (c) is limited by paragraph (1). With respect to any taxable year of a trust in which such deduction has been so limited by reason of entering into a prohibited transaction with the purpose of diverting such corpus or income from the purposes described in section 642(c), and such transaction involved a substantial part of such income or corpus, and which taxable year is the same, or before the, taxable year of the trust in which such prohibited transaction occurred, such deduction shall be disallowed the donor only if such donor or (if such donor is an individual) any member of his family (as defined in section 267(c) (4)) was a party to such prohibited transaction.

(6) DEFINITION.—For purposes of this subsection, the term "gift or bequest" means any gift, contribution, bequest, devise, or legacy, or any transfer without adequate consideration.

[Sec. 681(c)—Repealed]

Amendments

• 1969, Tax Reform Act of 1969 (P.L. 91-172)

P.L. 91-172, §101(j)(18):

Repealed Code Sec. 681(c). **Effective** 1-1-70. Prior to repeal, Code Sec. 681(c) read as follows:

(c) ACCUMULATED INCOME.—If the amounts permanently set aside, or to be used exclusively for the charitable and other purposes described in section 642(c) during the taxable year or any prior taxable year and not actually paid out by the end of the taxable year—

(1) are unreasonable in amount or duration in order to carry out such purposes of the trust;

(2) are used to a substantial degree for purposes other than those prescribed in section 642(c); or

(3) are invested in such a manner as to jeopardize the interests of the religious, charitable, scientific, etc., beneficiaries,

the amount otherwise allowable under section 642(c) as a deduction shall be limited to the amount actually paid out during the taxable year and shall not exceed 20 percent of the taxable income of the trust (computed without the benefit of section 642(c) but with the benefit of section 170(b)(1)(A)). Paragraph (1) shall not apply to income attributable to property of a decedent dying before January 1, 1951, which is transferred under his will to a trust created by such will. Paragraph (1) shall not apply to income attributable to property transferred to a trust before January 1, 1951, by the creator of such trust, if such trust was irrevocable on such date and if such income is required to be accumulated pursuant to the mandatory terms (as in effect on such date and at all times thereafter) of the instrument creating such trust. In the case of a trust created by the will of a decedent dying on or after January 1, 1951, if income is required to be accumulated pursuant to the mandatory terms of the will creating the trust, paragraph (1) shall apply only to income accumulated during a taxable year of the trust beginning more than 21 years after the date of death of the last life in being designated in the trust instrument.

• 1968 (P.L. 90-630)

P.L. 90-630, §6(b):

Amended Code Sec. 681(c) by adding the next to last sentence therein. **Effective** with respect to tax years beginning after 12-31-53, and ending after 8-16-54. For purposes of Section 162(g)(4) of the Internal Revenue Code of 1939, provisions having the same effect as the amendment shall be treated as included in such 1939 section, effective with respect to tax years beginning after 12-31-50.

* * *

[Sec. 683]

SEC. 683. USE OF TRUST AS AN EXCHANGE FUND.

[Sec. 683(a)]

(a) GENERAL RULE.—Except as provided in subsection (b), if property is transferred to a trust in exchange for an interest in other trust property and if the trust would be an investment company (within the meaning of section 351) if it were a corporation, then gain shall be recognized to the transferor.

Amendments

• 1976, Tax Reform Act of 1976 (P.L. 94-455)

P.L. 94-455, §2131(e)(1):

Amended Code Sec. 683(a). **Effective** 4-8-76, in tax years ending on or after such date. Prior to amendment, Code Sec. 683(a) read as follows:

(a) GENERAL RULE.—This part shall apply only to taxable years beginning after December 31, 1953, and ending after the date of the enactment of this title.

[Sec. 683(b)]

(b) EXCEPTION FOR POOLED INCOME FUNDS.—Subsection (a) shall not apply to any transfer to a pooled income fund (within the meaning of section 642(c)(5)).

Amendments

• 1976, Tax Reform Act of 1976 (P.L. 94-455)

P.L. 94-455, §2131(e)(1):

Amended Code Sec. 683(b). **Effective** 4-8-76, in tax years ending on or after such date. Prior to amendment, Code Sec. 683(b) read as follows:

(b) EXCEPTIONS.—In the case of any beneficiary of an estate or trust—

(1) this part shall not apply to any amount paid, credited, or to be distributed by the estate or trust in any taxable year of such estate or trust to which this part does not apply, and

(2) the Internal Revenue Code of 1939 shall apply for purposes of determining the amount includible in the gross income of the beneficiary.

To the extent that any amount paid, credited, or to be distributed by an estate or trust in the first taxable year of such estate or trust to which this part applies would be treated, if the Internal Revenue Code of 1939 were applicable, as paid, credited, or to be distributed on the last day of the preceding taxable year, such amount shall not be taken into account for purposes of this part but shall be taken into account as provided in the Internal Revenue Code of 1939.

[Sec. 684]

SEC. 684. RECOGNITION OF GAIN ON CERTAIN TRANSFERS TO CERTAIN FOREIGN TRUSTS AND ESTATES.

[Sec. 684(a)]

(a) IN GENERAL.—Except as provided in regulations, in the case of any transfer of property by a United States person to a foreign estate or trust, for purposes of this subtitle, such transfer shall be treated as a sale or exchange for an amount equal to the fair market value of the property transferred, and the transferor shall recognize as gain the excess of—

(1) the fair market value of the property so transferred, over

(2) the adjusted basis (for purposes of determining gain) of such property in the hands of the transferor.

Amendments

• 2013, American Taxpayer Relief Act of 2012 (P.L. 112-240)

P.L. 112-240, §101(a)(1)-(3), provides:

SEC. 101. PERMANENT EXTENSION AND MODIFICATION OF 2001 TAX RELIEF.

(a) PERMANENT EXTENSION.—

(1) IN GENERAL.—The Economic Growth and Tax Relief Reconciliation Act of 2001 is amended by striking title IX.

(2) CONFORMING AMENDMENT.—The Tax Relief, Unemployment Insurance Reauthorization, and Job Creation Act of 2010 is amended by striking section 304.

(3) EFFECTIVE DATE.—The amendments made by this subsection shall apply to taxable, plan, or limitation years beginning after December 31, 2012, and estates of decedents dying, gifts made, or generation skipping transfers after December 31, 2012.

• 2010, Tax Relief, Unemployment Insurance Reauthorization, and Job Creation Act of 2010 (P.L. 111-312)

P.L. 111-312, §301(a):

Amended the heading of Code Sec. 684 and Code Sec. 684(a) to read as such provisions would read if subtitle E of title V of the Economic Growth and Tax Relief Reconciliation Act of 2001 (P.L. 107-16) had never been enacted. **Effective** for estates of decedents dying, and transfers made, after 12-31-2009. For a special rule, see Act Sec. 301(c), below. Prior to amendment by P.L. 111-312, the heading of Code Sec. 684 and Code Sec. 684(a) read as follows:

CODE SEC. 684. RECOGNITION OF GAIN ON CERTAIN TRANSFERS TO CERTAIN FOREIGN TRUSTS AND ESTATES AND NONRESIDENT ALIENS.

(a) IN GENERAL.—Except as provided in regulations, in the case of any transfer of property by a United States person to a foreign estate or trust, for purposes of this subtitle, such transfer shall be treated as a sale or exchange for an amount equal to the fair market value of the property transferred, and the transferor shall recognize as gain the excess of—

(1) the fair market value of the property so transferred, over

(2) the adjusted basis (for purposes of determining gain) of such property in the hands of the transferor.

P.L. 111-312, §301(c), provides:

(c) SPECIAL ELECTION WITH RESPECT TO ESTATES OF DECEDENTS DYING IN 2010.—Notwithstanding subsection (a), in the case of an estate of a decedent dying after December 31, 2009, and before January 1, 2011, the executor (within the meaning of section 2203 of the Internal Revenue Code of 1986) may elect to apply such Code as though the amendments made by subsection (a) do not apply with respect to chapter 11 of such Code and with respect to property acquired or passing from such decedent (within the meaning of section 1014(b) of such Code). Such election shall be made at such time and in such manner as the Secretary of the Treasury or the Secretary's delegate shall provide. Such an election once made shall be revocable only with the consent of the Secretary of the Treasury or the Secretary's delegate. For purposes of section 2652(a)(1) of such Code, the determination of whether any property is subject to the tax imposed by such chapter 11 shall be made without regard to any election made under this subsection.

P.L. 111-312, §304, provides [but see P.L. 112-240, §101(a)(2)-(3), above]:

SEC. 304. APPLICATION OF EGTRRA SUNSET TO THIS TITLE.

Section 901 of the Economic Growth and Tax Relief Reconciliation Act of 2001 shall apply to the amendments made by this title.

• 2001, Economic Growth and Tax Relief Reconciliation Act of 2001 (P.L. 107-16)

P.L. 107-16, §542(e)(1)(A):

Amended Code Sec. 684(a) by inserting "or to a nonresident alien" after "or trust". **Effective** for transfers after 12-31-2009.

P.L. 107-16, §542(e)(1)(C):

Amended the section heading for Code Sec. 684 by inserting "**AND NONRESIDENT ALIENS**" after "**ESTATES**". **Effective** for transfers after 12-31-2009.

P.L. 107-16, §901(a)-(b), as amended by P.L. 111-312, §101(a)(1), provides [but see P.L. 112-240, §101(a)(1) and (3), above]:

SEC. 901. SUNSET OF PROVISIONS OF ACT.

(a) IN GENERAL.—All provisions of, and amendments made by, this Act shall not apply—

(1) to taxable, plan, or limitation years beginning after December 31, 2012, or

(2) in the case of title V, to estates of decedents dying, gifts made, or generation skipping transfers, after December 31, 2012.

(b) APPLICATION OF CERTAIN LAWS.—The Internal Revenue Code of 1986 and the Employee Retirement Income Security Act of 1974 shall be applied and administered to years, estates, gifts, and transfers described in subsection (a) as if the provisions and amendments described in subsection (a) had never been enacted.

[Sec. 684(b)]

(b) EXCEPTION.—Subsection (a) shall not apply to a transfer to a trust by a United States person to the extent that any person is treated as the owner of such trust under section 671.

Amendments

• 2013, American Taxpayer Relief Act of 2012 (P.L. 112-240)

P.L. 112-240, §101(a)(1)-(3), provides:

SEC. 101. PERMANENT EXTENSION AND MODIFICATION OF 2001 TAX RELIEF.

(a) PERMANENT EXTENSION.—

(1) IN GENERAL.—The Economic Growth and Tax Relief Reconciliation Act of 2001 is amended by striking title IX.

(2) CONFORMING AMENDMENT.—The Tax Relief, Unemployment Insurance Reauthorization, and Job Creation Act of 2010 is amended by striking section 304.

(3) EFFECTIVE DATE.—The amendments made by this subsection shall apply to taxable, plan, or limitation years beginning after December 31, 2012, and estates of decedents dying, gifts made, or generation skipping transfers after December 31, 2012.

• 2010, Tax Relief, Unemployment Insurance Reauthorization, and Job Creation Act of 2010 (P.L. 111-312)

P.L. 111-312, §301(a):

Amended Code Sec. 684(b) to read as such provision would read if subtitle E of title V of the Economic Growth and Tax Relief Reconciliation Act of 2001 (P.L. 107-16) had never been enacted. **Effective** for estates of decedents dying, and transfers made, after 12-31-2009. For a special rule, see Act Sec. 301(c), below. Prior to amendment by P.L. 111-312, Code Sec. 684(b) read as follows:

(b) EXCEPTIONS.—

(1) TRANSFERS TO CERTAIN TRUSTS.—Subsection (a) shall not apply to a transfer to a trust by a United States person to the extent that any United States person is treated as the owner of such trust under section 671.

(2) LIFETIME TRANSFERS TO NONRESIDENT ALIENS.—Subsection (a) shall not apply to a lifetime transfer to a nonresident alien.

P.L. 111-312, §301(c), provides:

(c) SPECIAL ELECTION WITH RESPECT TO ESTATES OF DECEDENTS DYING IN 2010.—Notwithstanding subsection (a), in the case of an estate of a decedent dying after December 31, 2009, and before January 1, 2011, the executor (within the meaning of section 2203 of the Internal Revenue Code of 1986) may elect to apply such Code as though the amendments made by subsection (a) do not apply with respect to chapter 11 of such Code and with respect to property acquired or passing from such decedent (within the meaning of section 1014(b) of such Code). Such election shall be made at such time and in such manner as the Secretary of the Treasury or the Secretary's delegate shall provide. Such an election once made shall be revocable only with the consent of the Secretary of the Treasury or the Secretary's delegate. For purposes of section 2652(a)(1) of such Code, the determination of whether any property is subject to the tax imposed by such chapter 11 shall be made without regard to any election made under this subsection.

P.L. 111-312, §304, provides [but see P.L. 112-240, §101(a)(2)-(3), above]:

SEC. 304. APPLICATION OF EGTRRA SUNSET TO THIS TITLE.

Section 901 of the Economic Growth and Tax Relief Reconciliation Act of 2001 shall apply to the amendments made by this title.

• 2001, Economic Growth and Tax Relief Reconciliation Act of 2001 (P.L. 107-16)

P.L. 107-16, §542(e)(1)(B):

Amended Code Sec. 684(b). **Effective** for transfers after 12-31-2009. Prior to amendment, Code Sec. 684(b) read as follows:

(b) EXCEPTION.—Subsection (a) shall not apply to a transfer to a trust by a United States person to the extent that any person is treated as the owner of such trust under section 671.

P.L. 107-16, §901(a)-(b), as amended by P.L. 111-312, §101(a)(1), provides [but see P.L. 112-240, §101(a)(1) and (3), above]:

SEC. 901. SUNSET OF PROVISIONS OF ACT.

(a) IN GENERAL.—All provisions of, and amendments made by, this Act shall not apply—

(1) to taxable, plan, or limitation years beginning after December 31, 2012, or

(2) in the case of title V, to estates of decedents dying, gifts made, or generation skipping transfers, after December 31, 2012.

(b) APPLICATION OF CERTAIN LAWS.—The Internal Revenue Code of 1986 and the Employee Retirement Income Security Act of 1974 shall be applied and administered to years, estates, gifts, and transfers described in subsection (a) as if the provisions and amendments described in subsection (a) had never been enacted.

[Sec. 684(c)]

(c) TREATMENT OF TRUSTS WHICH BECOME FOREIGN TRUSTS.—If a trust which is not a foreign trust becomes a foreign trust, such trust shall be treated for purposes of this section as having transferred, immediately before becoming a foreign trust, all of its assets to a foreign trust.

Amendments

• 1997, Taxpayer Relief Act of 1997 (P.L. 105-34)

P.L. 105-34, §1131(b):

Amended subpart F of part I of subchapter J of chapter 1 by adding at the end new section 684. **Effective** 8-5-97.

[Sec. 685]

SEC. 685. TREATMENT OF FUNERAL TRUSTS.

[Sec. 685(a)]

(a) IN GENERAL.—In the case of a qualified funeral trust—

(1) subparts B, C, D, and E shall not apply, and

(2) no deduction shall be allowed by section 642(b).

[Sec. 685(b)]

(b) QUALIFIED FUNERAL TRUST.—For purposes of this subsection, the term "qualified funeral trust" means any trust (other than a foreign trust) if—

(1) the trust arises as a result of a contract with a person engaged in the trade or business of providing funeral or burial services or property necessary to provide such services,

(2) the sole purpose of the trust is to hold, invest, and reinvest funds in the trust and to use such funds solely to make payments for such services or property for the benefit of the beneficiaries of the trust,

(3) the only beneficiaries of such trust are individuals with respect to whom such services or property are to be provided at their death under contracts described in paragraph (1),

(4) the only contributions to the trust are contributions by or for the benefit of such beneficiaries,

(5) the trustee elects the application of this subsection, and

(6) the trust would (but for the election described in paragraph (5)) be treated as owned under subpart E by the purchasers of the contracts described in paragraph (1).

A trust shall not fail to be treated as meeting the requirement of paragraph (6) by reason of the death of an individual but only during the 60-day period beginning on the date of such death.

Amendments

• 1998, IRS Restructuring and Reform Act of 1998 (P.L. 105-206)

P.L. 105-206, §6013(b)(1):

Amended Code Sec. 685(b) by adding at the end a new flush sentence. **Effective** as if included in the provision of P.L. 105-34 to which it relates [**effective** for tax years ending after 8-5-97.—CCH].

[Sec. 685(c)—Repealed]

Amendments

• 2008, Hubbard Act (P.L. 110-317)

P.L. 110-317, §9(a):

Repealed Code Sec. 685(c). **Effective** for tax years beginning after 8-29-2008. Prior to repeal, Code Sec. 685(c) read as follows:

(c) DOLLAR LIMITATION ON CONTRIBUTIONS.—

(1) IN GENERAL.—The term "qualified funeral trust" shall not include any trust which accepts aggregate contributions by or for the benefit of an individual in excess of $7,000.

(2) RELATED TRUSTS.—For purposes of paragraph (1), all trusts having trustees which are related persons shall be treated as 1 trust. For purposes of the preceding sentence, persons are related if—

(A) the relationship between such persons is described in section 267 or 707(b),

(B) such persons are treated as a single employer under subsection (a) or (b) of section 52, or

(C) the Secretary determines that treating such persons as related is necessary to prevent avoidance of the purposes of this section.

(3) INFLATION ADJUSTMENT.—In the case of any contract referred to in subsection (b)(1) which is entered into during any calendar year after 1998, the dollar amount referred to [in] paragraph (1) shall be increased by an amount equal to—

(A) such dollar amount, multiplied by

(B) the cost-of-living adjustment determined under section 1(f)(3) for such calendar year, by substituting "calendar year 1997" for "calendar year 1992" in subparagraph (B) thereof.

If any dollar amount after being increased under the preceding sentence is not a multiple of $100, such dollar amount shall be rounded to the nearest multiple of $100.

[Sec. 685(c)]

(c) APPLICATION OF RATE SCHEDULE.— Section 1(e) shall be applied to each qualified funeral trust by treating each beneficiary's interest in each such trust as a separate trust.

Amendments

• 2008, Hubbard Act (P.L. 110-317)

P.L. 110-317, §9(b):

Redesignated subsection (d) of Code Sec. 685 as subsection (c). **Effective** for tax years beginning after 8-29-2008.

[Sec. 685(d)]

(d) TREATMENT OF AMOUNTS REFUNDED TO PURCHASER ON CANCELLATION.—No gain or loss shall be recognized to a purchaser of a contract described in subsection (b)(1) by reason of any payment from such trust to such purchaser by reason of cancellation of such contract. If any payment referred to in the preceding sentence consists of property other than money, the basis of such property in the hands of such purchaser shall be the same as the trust's basis in such property immediately before the payment.

Amendments

• 2008, Hubbard Act (P.L. 110-317)

P.L. 110-317, §9(b):

Redesignated subsection (e) of Code Sec. 685 as subsection (d). **Effective** for tax years beginning after 8-29-2008.

[Sec. 685(e)]

(e) SIMPLIFIED REPORTING.—The Secretary may prescribe rules for simplified reporting of all trusts having a single trustee and of trusts terminated during the year.

Amendments

• 2008, Hubbard Act (P.L. 110-317)

P.L. 110-317, §9(b):

Redesignated subsection (f) of Code Sec. 685 as subsection (e). **Effective** for tax years beginning after 8-29-2008.

• 1998, IRS Restructuring and Reform Act of 1998 (P.L. 105-206)

P.L. 105-206, §6013(b)(2):

Amended Code Sec. 685(f) by inserting before the period at the end "and of trusts terminated during the year". **Effective** as if included in the provision of P.L. 105-34 to which it relates [**effective** for tax years ending after 8-5-97.—CCH].

• 1997, Taxpayer Relief Act of 1997 (P.L. 105-34)

P.L. 105-34, §1309(a):

Amended subpart F of part I of subchapter J of chapter 1 by adding at the end a new Code Sec. 685. **Effective** for tax years ending after 8-5-97.

PART II—INCOME IN RESPECT OF DECEDENTS

[Sec. 691]

SEC. 691. RECIPIENTS OF INCOME IN RESPECT OF DECEDENTS.

[Sec. 691(a)]

(a) INCLUSION IN GROSS INCOME.—

(1) GENERAL RULE.—The amount of all items of gross income in respect of a decedent which are not properly includible in respect of the taxable period in which falls the date of his death or a prior period (including the amount of all items of gross income in respect of a prior decedent, if the right to receive such amount was acquired by reason of the death of the prior decedent or by bequest, devise, or inheritance from the prior decedent) shall be included in the gross income, for the taxable year when received, of:

(A) the estate of the decedent, if the right to receive the amount is acquired by the decedent's estate from the decedent;

(B) the person who, by reason of the death of the decedent, acquires the right to receive the amount, if the right to receive the amount is not acquired by the decedent's estate from the decedent; or

(C) the person who acquires from the decedent the right to receive the amount by bequest, devise, or inheritance, if the amount is received after a distribution by the decedent's estate of such right.

(2) INCOME IN CASE OF SALE, ETC.—If a right, described in paragraph (1), to receive an amount is transferred by the estate of the decedent or a person who received such right by reason of the death of the decedent or by bequest, devise, or inheritance from the decedent, there shall be included in the gross income of the estate or such person, as the case may be, for the taxable period in which the transfer occurs, the fair market value of such right at the time of such transfer plus the amount by which any consideration for the transfer exceeds such fair market value. For purposes of this paragraph, the term "transfer" includes sale, exchange, or other disposition, or the satisfaction of an installment obligation at other than face value, but does not include transmission at death to the estate of the decedent or a transfer to a person pursuant to the right of such person to receive such amount by reason of the death of the decedent or by bequest, devise, or inheritance from the decedent.

(3) CHARACTER OF INCOME DETERMINED BY REFERENCE TO DECEDENT.—The right, described in paragraph (1), to receive an amount shall be treated, in the hands of the estate of the decedent or any person who acquired such right by reason of the death of the decedent, or by bequest, devise, or inheritance from the decedent, as if it had been acquired by the estate or such person in the transaction in which the right to receive the income was originally derived and the amount includible in gross income under paragraph (1) or (2) shall be considered in the hands of the

estate or such person to have the character which it would have had in the hands of the decedent if the decedent had lived and received such amount.

(4) INSTALLMENT OBLIGATIONS ACQUIRED FROM DECEDENT.—In the case of an installment obligation reportable by the decedent on the installment method under section 453, if such obligation is acquired by the decedent's estate from the decedent or by any person by reason of the death of the decedent or by bequest, devise, or inheritance from the decedent—

(A) an amount equal to the excess of the face amount of such obligation over the basis of the obligation in the hands of the decedent (determined under section 453B) shall, for the purpose of paragraph (1), be considered as an item of gross income in respect of the decedent; and

(B) such obligation shall, for purposes of paragraphs (2) and (3), be considered a right to receive an item of gross income in respect of the decedent, but the amount includible in gross income under paragraph (2) shall be reduced by an amount equal to the basis of the obligation in the hands of the decedent (determined under section 453B).

(5) OTHER RULES RELATING TO INSTALLMENT OBLIGATIONS.—

(A) IN GENERAL.—In the case of an installment obligation reportable by the decedent on the installment method under section 453, for purposes of paragraph (2)—

(i) the second sentence of paragraph (2) shall be applied by inserting "(other than the obligor)" after "or a transfer to a person",

(ii) any cancellation of such an obligation shall be treated as a transfer, and

(iii) any cancellation of such an obligation occurring at the death of the decedent shall be treated as a transfer by the estate of the decedent (or, if held by a person other than the decedent before the death of the decedent, by such person).

(B) FACE AMOUNT TREATED AS FAIR MARKET VALUE IN CERTAIN CASES.—In any case to which the first sentence of paragraph (2) applies by reason of subparagraph (A), if the decedent and the obligor were related persons (within the meaning of section 453(f)(1)), the fair market value of the installment obligation shall be treated as not less than its face amount.

(C) CANCELLATION INCLUDES BECOMING UNENFORCEABLE.—For purposes of subparagraph (A), an installment obligation which becomes unenforceable shall be treated as if it were canceled.

Amendments

• 1987, Revenue Act of 1987 (P.L. 100-203)

P.L. 100-203, §10202(c)(3):

Amended Code Sec. 691(a)(4)-(5) by striking out "or 453A" after "section 453" each place it appears. For the **effective** date, see Act Sec. 10202(e), as amended by P.L. 100-647, §2004(d)(4), below.

P.L. 100-203, §10202(e), as amended by P.L. 100-647, §2004(d)(4), provides:

(e) EFFECTIVE DATES.—

(1) IN GENERAL.—Except as provided in this subsection, the amendments made by this section shall apply to dispositions in taxable years beginning after December 31, 1987.

(2) SPECIAL RULES FOR DEALERS.—

(A) IN GENERAL.—In the case of dealer dispositions (within the meaning of section 453A of the Internal Revenue Code of 1986), the amendments made by subsections (a) and (b) shall apply to installment obligations arising from dispositions after December 31, 1987.

(B) SPECIAL RULES FOR OBLIGATIONS ARISING FROM DEALER DISPOSITIONS AFTER FEBRUARY 28, 1986, AND BEFORE JANUARY 1, 1988.—

(i) IN GENERAL.—In the case of an applicable installment obligation arising from a disposition described in subclause (I) and (II) of section 453C(e)(1)(A)(i) of the Internal Revenue Code of 1986 (as in effect before the amendments made by this section) before January 1, 1988, the amendments made by subsections (a) and (b) shall apply to taxable years beginning after December 31, 1987.

(ii) CHANGE IN METHOD OF ACCOUNTING.—In the case of any taxpayer who is required by clause (i) to change its method of accounting for any taxable year with respect to obligations described in clause (i)—

(I) such change shall be treated as initiated by the taxpayer,

(II) such change shall be treated as made with the consent of the Secretary of the Treasury or his delegate, and

(III) the net amount of adjustments required by section 481 of the Internal Revenue Code of 1986 shall be taken into account over a period not longer than 4 taxable years.

(C) CERTAIN RULES MADE APPLICABLE.—For purposes of this paragraph, rules similar to the rules of paragraphs (4) and (5) of section 812(c) of the Tax Reform Act of 1986 (as added by the Technical and Miscellaneous Revenue Act of 1988) shall apply.

(3) SPECIAL RULE FOR NONDEALERS.—

(A) ELECTION.—A taxpayer may elect, at such time and in such manner as the Secretary of the Treasury or his delegate may prescribe, to have the amendments made by subsections (a) and (c) apply to taxable years ending after December 31, 1986, with respect to dispositions and pledges occurring after August 16, 1986.

(B) PLEDGING RULES.—Except as provided in subparagraph (A)—

(i) IN GENERAL.—Section 453A(d) of the Internal Revenue Code of 1986 shall apply to any installment obligation which is pledged to secure any secured indebtedness (within the meaning of section 453A(d)(4) of such Code) after December 17, 1987, in taxable years ending after such date.

(ii) COORDINATION WITH SECTION 453C.—For purposes of section 453C of such Code (as in effect before its repeal), the face amount of any obligation to which section 453A(d) of such Code applies shall be reduced by the amount treated as payments on such obligation under section 453A(d) of such Code and the amount of any indebtedness secured by it shall not be taken into account.

(4) MINIMUM TAX.—The amendment made by subsection (d) shall apply to dispositions in taxable years beginning after December 31, 1986.

(5) COORDINATION WITH TAX REFORM ACT OF 1986.—The amendments made by this section shall not apply to any installment obligation or to any taxpayer during any period to the extent the amendments made by section 811 of the Tax Reform Act of 1986 do not apply to such obligation or during such period.

• 1980, Installment Sales Revision Act of 1980 (P.L. 96-471)

P.L. 96-471, §2(b)(5)(A):

Amended Code Sec. 691(a)(4) by striking out "received by a decedent on the sale or other disposition of property, the income from which was properly reportable by the decedent on the installment basis under section 453" and substituting "reportable by the decedent on the installment method under section 453 or 453A". **Effective** for dispositions made after 10-19-80, in tax years ending after that date.

P.L. 96-471, §2(b)(5)(B):

Amended Code Sec. 691(a)(4)(A) and (B) by striking out "453(d)" and substituting "453B". **Effective** for dispositions made after 10-19-80, in tax years ending after that date.

P.L. 96-471, §3:

Amended Code Sec. 691(a) by adding paragraph (5). **Effective** in the case of decedents dying after 10-19-80.

[Sec. 691(b)]

(b) ALLOWANCE OF DEDUCTIONS AND CREDIT.—The amount of any deduction specified in section 162, 163, 164, 212, or 611 (relating to deductions for expenses, interest, taxes, and depletion) or credit specified in section 27 (relating to foreign tax credit), in respect of a decedent which is not properly allowable to the decedent in respect of the taxable period in which falls the date of his death, or a prior period, shall be allowed:

(1) EXPENSES, INTEREST, AND TAXES.—In the case of a deduction specified in section 162, 163, 164, or 212 and a credit specified in section 27, in the taxable year when paid—

(A) to the estate of the decedent; except that

(B) if the estate of the decedent is not liable to discharge the obligation to which the deduction or credit relates, to the person who, by reason of the death of the decedent or by bequest, devise, or inheritance acquires, subject to such obligation, from the decedent an interest in property of the decedent.

(2) DEPLETION.—In the case of the deduction specified in section 611, to the person described in subsection (a) (1) (A), (B), or (C) who, in the manner described therein, receives the income to which the deduction relates, in the taxable year when such income is received.

Amendments

• 1984, Deficit Reduction Act of 1984 (P.L. 98-369)

P.L. 98-369, §474(r)(18):

Amended Code Sec. 691(b) by striking out "section 33" each place it appeared and inserting in lieu thereof "section 27". **Effective** for tax years beginning after 12-31-83, and to carrybacks from such years.

[Sec. 691(c)]

(c) DEDUCTION FOR ESTATE TAX.—

(1) ALLOWANCE OF DEDUCTION.—

(A) GENERAL RULE.—A person who includes an amount in gross income under subsection (a) shall be allowed, for the same taxable year, as a deduction an amount which bears the same ratio to the estate tax attributable to the net value for estate tax purposes of all the items described in subsection (a) (1) as the value for estate tax purposes of the items of gross income or portions thereof in respect of which such person included the amount in gross income (or the amount included in gross income, whichever is lower) bears to the value for estate tax purposes of all the items described in subsection (a) (1).

(B) ESTATES AND TRUSTS.—In the case of an estate or trust, the amount allowed as a deduction under subparagraph (A) shall be computed by excluding from the gross income of the estate or trust the portion (if any) of the items described in subsection (a) (1) which is properly paid, credited, or to be distributed to the beneficiaries during the taxable year.

(2) METHOD OF COMPUTING DEDUCTION.—For purposes of paragraph (1)—

(A) The term "estate tax" means the tax imposed on the estate of the decedent or any prior decedent under section 2001 or 2101, reduced by the credits against such tax.

(B) The net value for estate tax purposes of all the items described in subsection (a) (1) shall be the excess of the value for estate tax purposes of all the items described in subsection (a) (1) over the deductions from the gross estate in respect of claims which represent the deductions and credit described in subsection (b). Such net value shall be determined with respect to the provisions of section 421(c)(2), relating to the deduction for estate tax with respect to stock options to which part II of subchapter D applies.

(C) The estate tax attributable to such net value shall be an amount equal to the excess of the estate tax over the estate tax computed without including in the gross estate such net value.

(3) SPECIAL RULE FOR GENERATION-SKIPPING TRANSFERS.—In the case of any tax imposed by chapter 13 on a taxable termination or a direct skip occurring as a result of the death of the transferor, there shall be allowed a deduction (under principles similar to the principles of this subsection) for the portion of such tax attributable to items of gross income of the trust which were not properly includible in the gross income of the trust for periods before the date of such termination.

(4) COORDINATION WITH CAPITAL GAIN PROVISIONS.—For purposes of sections 1(h), 1202, and 1211, the amount taken into account with respect to any item described in subsection (a)(1) shall be reduced (but not below zero) by the amount of the deduction allowable under paragraph (1) of this subsection with respect to such item.

Amendments

• 2017, Tax Cuts and Jobs Act (P.L. 115-97)

P.L. 115-97, §13001(b)(2)(F):

Amended Code Sec. 691(c)(4) by striking "1201," following "sections 1(h),". **Effective** for tax years beginning after 12-31-2017.

• 2004, Working Families Tax Relief Act of 2004 (P.L. 108-311)

P.L. 108-311, §402(a)(4):

Amended Code Sec. 691(c)(4) by striking "of any gain" following "1211, the amount". **Effective** as if included in section 302 of the Jobs and Growth Tax Relief Reconciliation Act of 2003 (P.L. 108-27) [**effective** generally for tax years beginning after 12-31-2002.—CCH].

• 1997, Taxpayer Relief Act of 1997 (P.L. 105-34)

P.L. 105-34, §1073(b)(1):

Amended Code Sec. 691(c)(1) by striking subparagraph (C). **Effective** for estates of decedents dying after 12-31-96. Prior to being stricken, Code Sec. 691(c)(1)(C) read as follows:

(C) EXCESS RETIREMENT ACCUMULATION TAX.—For purposes of this subsection, no deduction shall be allowed for the portion of the estate tax attributable to the increase in such tax under section 4980A(d).

• 1996, Small Business Job Protection Act of 1996 (P.L. 104-188)

P.L. 104-188, §1401(b)(9):

Amended Code Sec. 691(c) by striking paragraph (5). **Effective**, generally, for tax years beginning after 12-31-99. For a special transitional rule, see Act Sec. 1401(c)(2) in the amendment notes following Code Sec. 402(d). Prior to being stricken, Code Sec. 691(c)(5) read as follows:

(5) COORDINATION WITH SECTION 402(d).—For purposes of section 402(d) (other than paragraph (1)(C) thereof), the total taxable amount of any lump sum distribution shall be reduced by the amount of the deduction allowable under paragraph (1) of this subsection which is attributable to the total taxable amount (determined without regard to this paragraph).

• 1993, Omnibus Budget Reconciliation Act of 1993 (P.L. 103-66)

P.L. 103-66, §13113(d)(4):

Amended Code Sec. 691(c)(4) by striking "1201, and 1211" and inserting "1201, 1202, and 1211". **Effective** for stock issued after 8-10-93.

• 1992, Unemployment Compensation Amendments of 1992 (P.L. 102-318)

P.L. 102-318, §521(b)(27), as amended by P.L. 104-188, §1704(t)(73):

Amended Code Sec. 691(c)(5) by striking "402(e)" in the text and heading and inserting "402(d)". **Effective** for distributions after 12-31-92.

• 1990, Omnibus Budget Reconciliation Act of 1990 (P.L. 101-508)

P.L. 101-508, §11101(d)(4):

Amended Code Sec. 691(c)(4) by striking "1(j)" and inserting "1(h)". **Effective** for tax years beginning after 12-31-90.

• 1989, Omnibus Budget Reconciliation Act of 1989 (P.L. 101-239)

P.L. 101-239, §7841(d)(3):

Amended Code Sec. 691(c)(5) by striking "paragraph (1)(D)" and inserting "paragraph (1)(C)". **Effective** 12-19-89.

• 1988, Technical and Miscellaneous Revenue Act of 1988 (P.L. 100-647)

P.L. 100-647, §1011A(g)(10):

Amended Code Sec. 691(c)(1) by adding at the end thereof new subparagraph (C). **Effective** as if included in the provision of P.L. 99-514 to which it relates.

• 1986, Tax Reform Act of 1986 (P.L. 99-514)

P.L. 99-514, §301(b)(8)(A)-(B):

Amended Code Sec. 691(c)(4) by striking out "1201, 1202, and 1211, and for purposes of section 57(a)(9)" and inserting in lieu thereof "1(j), 1201, and 1211", and by striking out "CAPITAL GAIN DEDUCTION, ETC.—" in the paragraph heading and inserting in lieu thereof "CAPITAL GAIN PROVISIONS.—". **Effective** for tax years beginning after 12-31-86.

P.L. 99-514, §1432(a)(3):

Amended Code Sec. 691(c)(3). **Effective**, generally, for any generation-skipping transfer (within the meaning of section 2611 of the Internal Revenue Code of 1986) made after 10-22-86. However, for special rules, see Act Sec. 1433(b)-(d), as amended by P.L. 100-647, §1014(h)(2)-(4), below. Prior to amendment, Code Sec. 691(c)(3) read as follows:

(3) SPECIAL RULE FOR GENERATION-SKIPPING TRANSFERS.—For purposes of this section—

(A) the tax imposed by section 2601 or any State inheritance tax described in section 2602(c)(5)(B) on any generation-skipping transfer shall be treated as a tax imposed by section 2001 on the estate of the deemed transferor (as defined in section 2612(a));

(B) any property transferred in such a transfer shall be treated as if it were included in the gross estate of the deemed transferor at the value of such property taken into account for purposes of the tax imposed by section 2601; and

(C) under regulations prescribed by the secretary, any item of gross income subject to the tax imposed under section 2601 shall be treated as income described in subsection (a) if such item is not properly includible in the gross income of the trust on or before the date of the generation-skipping transfer (within the meaning of section 2611(a)) and if such transfer occurs at or after the death of the deemed transferor (as so defined).

P.L. 99-514, §1433(b)-(d), as amended by P.L. 100-647, §1014(h)(2)-(4), provides:

(b) SPECIAL RULES.—

(1) TREATMENT OF CERTAIN INTER VIVOS TRANSFERS MADE AFTER SEPTEMBER 25, 1985.—For purposes of subsection (a) (and chapter 13 of the Internal Revenue Code of 1986 as amended by this part), any inter vivos transfer after September 25, 1985, and on or before the date of the enactment of this Act shall be treated as if it were made on the 1st day after the date of enactment of this Act.

(2) EXCEPTIONS.—The amendments made by this subtitle shall not apply to—

(A) any generation-skipping transfer under a trust which was irrevocable on September 25, 1985, but only to the extent that such transfer is not made out of corpus added to the trust after September 25, 1985 (or out of income attributable to corpus so added),

(B) any generation-skipping transfer under a will or recovable trust executed before the date of the enactment of this Act if the decedent dies before January 1, 1987, and

(C) any generation-skipping transfer—

(i) under a trust to the extent such trust consists of property included in the gross estate of a decedent (other than property transferred by the decedent during his life after the date of the enactment of this Act), or reinvestments thereof, or

(ii) which is a direct skip which occurs by reason of the death of any decedent;

but only if such decedent was, on the date of the enactment of this Act, under a mental disability to change the disposition of his property and did not regain his competence to dispose of such property before the date of his death.

(3) TREATMENT OF CERTAIN TRANSFERS TO GRANDCHILDREN.—

(A) IN GENERAL.—For purposes of chapter 13 of the Internal Revenue Code of 1986, the term "direct skip" shall not include any transfer before January 1, 1990, from a transferor to a grandchild of the transferor to the extent the aggregate transfers from such transferor to such grandchild do not exceed $2,000,000.

(B) TREATMENT OF TRANSFERS IN TRUST.—For purposes of subparagraph (A), a transfer in trust for the benefit of a grandchild shall be treated as a transfer to such grandchild if (and only if)—

(i) during the life of the grandchild, no portion of the corpus or income of the trust may be distributed to (or for the benefit of) any person other than such grandchild,

(ii) the assets of the trust will be includible in the gross estate of the grandchild if the grandchild dies before the trust is terminated, and

(iii) all of the income of the trust for periods after the grandchild has attained age 21 will be distributed to (or for the benefit of) such grandchild not less frequently than annually.

(C) COORDINATION WITH SECTION 2653(a) OF THE 1986 CODE.—In the case of any transfer which would be a generation-skipping transfer but for subparagraph (A), the rules of section 2653(a) of the Internal Revenue Code of 1986 shall apply as if such transfer were a generation-skipping transfer.

(D) COORDINATION WITH TAXABLE TERMINATIONS AND TAXABLE DISTRIBUTIONS.—For purposes of chapter 13 of the Internal Revenue Code of 1986, the terms "taxable termination" and "taxable distribution" shall not include any transfer which would be a direct skip but for subparagraph (A).

(4) DEFINITIONS.—Terms used in this section shall have the same respective meanings as when used in chapter 13 of the Internal Revenue Code of 1986; except that section 2612(c)(2) of such Code shall not apply in determining whether an individual is a grandchild of the transferor.

(c) REPEAL OF EXISTING TAX ON GENERATION-SKIPPING TRANSFERS.—

(1) IN GENERAL.—In the case of any tax imposed by chapter 13 of the Internal Revenue Code of 1954 (as in effect on the day before the date of the enactment of this Act), such tax (including interest, additions to tax, and additional amounts) shall not be assessed and if assessed, the assessment shall be abated, and if collected, shall be credited or refunded (with interest) as an overpayment.

(2) WAIVER OF STATUTE OF LIMITATIONS.—If on the date of the enactment of this Act (or at any time within 1 year after such date of enactment) refund or credit of any overpayment of tax resulting from the application of paragraph (1) is barred by any law or rule of law, refund or credit of such overpayment shall, nevertheless, be made or allowed if claim therefore is filed before the date 1 year after the date of the enactment of this Act.

(d) ELECTION FOR CERTAIN TRANSFERS BENEFITING GRANDCHILD.—

(1) IN GENERAL.—For purposes of chapter 13 of the Internal Revenue Code of 1986 (as amended by this Act) and subsection (b) of this section, any transfer in trust for the benefit of a grandchild of a transferor shall be treated as a direct skip to such grandchild if—

(A) the transfer occurs before the date of enactment of this Act,

(B) the transfer would be a direct skip to a grandchild except for the fact that the trust instrument provides that, if the grandchild dies before vesting of the interest transferred, the interest is transferred to the grandchild's heir (rather than the grandchild's estate), and

(C) an election under this subsection applies to such transfer.

Any transfer treated as a direct skip by reason of the preceding sentence shall be subject to Federal estate tax on the grandchild's death in the same manner as if the contingent gift over had been to the grandchild's estate. Unless the grandchild otherwise directs by will, the estate of such grandchild shall be entitled to recover from the person receiving the property on the death of the grandchild any increase in Federal estate tax on the estate of the grandchild by reason of the preceding sentence.

(2) ELECTION.—An election under paragraph (1) shall be made at such time and in such manner as the Secretary of the Treasury or his delegate may prescribe.

• 1981, Economic Recovery Tax Act of 1981 (P.L. 97-34)

P.L. 97-34, §403(a)(2)(C):

Amended Code Sec. 691(c)(3)(A) by striking out "section 2602(c)(5)(C)" and inserting "section 2602(c)(5)(B)". **Effective** for estates of decedents dying after 12-31-81.

• 1980, Crude Oil Windfall Profit Tax Act of 1980 (P.L. 96-223)

P.L. 96-223, §401(a), (b):

Repealed Code Sec. 691(c)(2)(A) and (C), as amended by P.L. 94-455, Act Sec. 2005(a)(4). **Effective** with respect to decedents dying after 12-31-76. However, see the amendment note for P.L. 96-223, §401(a), that follows Code Sec. 1014(d), for the text of Act Sec. 401(d) that authorizes the election of the carryover basis rules in the case of a decedent dying after 12-31-76 and before 11-7-78.

• 1980, Technical Corrections Act of 1979 (P.L. 96-222)

P.L. 96-222, §101(a)(8)(A):

Amended Code Sec. 691(c) by adding new paragraph (5). **Effective** with respect to the estates of decedents dying after 4-1-80.

• 1978, Revenue Act of 1978 (P.L. 95-600)

P.L. 95-600, §515(a):

Postponed application of Code Sec. 691(c)(2)(A) and (C), as amended by P.L. 94-455, §2005(a), from estates of decedents dying after 12-31-76, to 12-31-79.

P.L. 95-600, §702(b)(1), (2):

Added Code Sec. 691(c)(4). **Effective** for decedents dying after 11-6-78.

• 1976, Tax Reform Act of 1976 (P.L. 94-455)

P.L. 94-455, §1901(a)(91):

Struck out the last sentence of Code Sec. 691(c)(1)(B). **Effective** for tax years beginning after 12-31-76. Prior to repeal, the last sentence read as follows:

This subparagraph shall apply to the same taxable years, and to the same extent, as is provided in section 683.

P.L. 94-455, §2005(a)(4):

Amended Code Sec. 691(c)(2)(A) and (C). **Effective** for estates of decedents dying after 12-31-79 (effective date amended by P.L. 95-600, 515(a)). Prior to amendment, Code Sec. 691(c)(2)(A) and (C) read as follows:

(A) The term "estate tax" means Federal and State estate taxes (within the meaning of section 1023(f)(3)).

* * *

(C) The estate tax attributable to such net value shall be an amount which bears the same ratio to the estate tax as such net value bears to the value of the gross estate.

P.L. 94-455, §2006(b):

Added Code Sec. 691(c)(3). **Effective** as noted in Act Sec. 2006(c), below.

P.L. 94-455, §2006(c), as amended by P.L. 95-600, §702(n)(1), (n)(5)(B), provides:

(c) EFFECTIVE DATES.—

(1) IN GENERAL.—Except as provided in paragraph (2), the amendments made by this section shall apply to any generation-skipping transfer (within the meaning of section 2611(a) of the Internal Revenue Code of 1954) made after June 11, 1976.

(2) EXCEPTIONS.—The amendments made by this section shall not apply to any generation-skipping transfer—

(A) under a trust which was irrevocable on June 11, 1976, but only to the extent that the transfer is not made out of corpus added to the trust after June 11, 1976, or

(B) in the case of a decedent dying before January 1, 1982, pursuant to a will (or revocable trust) which was in existence on June 11, 1976, and was not amended at any time after that date in any respect which will result in the creation of, or increasing the amount of, any generation-skipping transfer.

For purposes of subparagraph (B), if the decedent on June 11, 1976, was under a mental disability to change the disposition of his property, the period set forth in such subparagraph shall not expire before the date which is 2 years after the date on which he first regains his competence to dispose of such property.

(3) TRUST EQUIVALENTS.—For purposes of paragraph (2), in the case of a trust equivalent within the meaning of subsection (d) of section 2611 of the Internal Revenue Code of 1954, the provisions of such subsection (d) shall apply.

• 1964, Revenue Act of 1964 (P.L. 88-272)

P.L. 88-272, §221(c)(2):

Amended the last sentence of Code Sec. 691(c)(2)(B). **Effective** for tax years ending after 12-31-63. Prior to amendment, the last sentence read as follows:

Such net value shall be determined with regard to the provisions of section 421(d)(6)(B), relating to the deduction for estate tax with respect to restricted stock options.

[Sec. 691(d)]

(d) AMOUNTS RECEIVED BY SURVIVING ANNUITANT UNDER JOINT AND SURVIVOR ANNUITY CONTRACT.—

(1) DEDUCTION FOR ESTATE TAX.—For purposes of computing the deduction under subsection (c) (1) (A), amounts received by a surviving annuitant—

(A) as an annuity under a joint and survivor annuity contract where the decedent annuitant died after the annuity starting date (as defined in section 72(c)(4)), and

(B) during the surviving annuitant's life expectancy period,

shall, to the extent included in gross income under section 72, be considered as amounts included in gross income under subsection (a).

(2) NET VALUE FOR ESTATE TAX PURPOSES.—In determining the net value for estate tax purposes under subsection (c) (2) (B) for purposes of this subsection, the value for estate tax purposes of the items described in paragraph (1) of this subsection shall be computed—

(A) by determining the excess of the value of the annuity at the date of the death of the deceased annuitant over the total amount excludable from the gross income of the surviving annuitant under section 72 during the surviving annuitant's life expectancy period, and

(B) by multiplying the figure so obtained by the ratio which the value of the annuity for estate tax purposes bears to the value of the annuity at the date of the death of the deceased.

(3) DEFINITIONS.—For purposes of this subsection—

(A) The term "life expectancy period" means the period beginning with the first day of the first period for which an amount is received by the surviving annuitant under the contract and ending with the close of the taxable year with or in which falls the termination of the life expectancy of the surviving annuitant. For purposes of this subparagraph, the life expectancy of the surviving annuitant shall be determined, as of the date of the death of the deceased annuitant, with reference to actuarial tables prescribed by the Secretary.

(B) The surviving annuitant's expected return under the contract shall be computed, as of the death of the deceased annuitant, with reference to actuarial tables prescribed by the Secretary.

Amendments

• 2014, Tax Technical Corrections Act of 2014 (P.L. 113-295)

P.L. 113-295, §221(a)(66), Division A:

Amended Code Sec. 691(d)(1)(A) by striking "after December 31, 1953, and" following "the decedent annuitant died". **Effective** generally 12-19-2014. For a special rule, see Act Sec. 221(b)(2), Division A, below.

P.L. 113-295, §221(b)(2), Division A, provides:

(2) SAVINGS PROVISION.—If—

(A) any provision amended or repealed by the amendments made by this section applied to—

(i) any transaction occurring before the date of the enactment of this Act,

(ii) any property acquired before such date of enactment, or

(iii) any item of income, loss, deduction, or credit taken into account before such date of enactment, and

(B) the treatment of such transaction, property, or item under such provision would (without regard to the amendments or repeals made by this section) affect the liability for tax for periods ending after date of enactment, nothing in the amendments or repeals made by this section shall be construed to affect the treatment of such transaction, property, or item for purposes of determining liability for tax for periods ending after such date of enactment.

• 1976, Tax Reform Act of 1976 (P.L. 94-455)

P.L. 94-455, §1906(b)(13)(A):

Amended 1954 Code by substituting "Secretary" for "Secretary or his delegate" each place it appeared. **Effective** 2-1-77.

[Sec. 691(e)]

(e) CROSS REFERENCE.—

For application of this section to income in respect of a deceased partner, see section 753.

Amendments

• 1976, Tax Reform Act of 1976 (P.L. 94-455)

P.L. 94-455, §1951(b)(10)(A):

Repealed Code Sec. 691(e) and redesignated former Code Sec. 691(f) as Code Sec. 691(e). **Effective** for tax years beginning after 12-31-76. Prior to repeal, Code Sec. 691(e) read as follows:

(e) INSTALLMENT OBLIGATIONS TRANSMITTED AT DEATH WHEN PRIOR LAW APPLIED TO TRANSMISSION.—

(1) IN GENERAL.—Effective with respect to the first taxable year to which the election referred to in paragraph (2) applies and to each taxable year thereafter, subsection (a)(4) shall apply in the case of installment obligations in respect of which section 44(d) of the Internal Revenue Code of 1939 (or the corresponding provisions of prior law) did not apply by reason of the filing of the bond referred to in such section or provisions. Subsection (c) of this section shall not apply in respect of any amount included in gross income by reason of this paragraph.

(2) ELECTION.—Installment obligations referred to in paragraph (1) may, at the election of the taxpayer holding such obligations, be treated as obligations in respect of which subsection (a)(4) applies. An election under this subsection

for any taxable year shall be made not later than the time prescribed by law (including extensions thereof) for filing the return for such taxable year. The election shall be made in such manner as the Secretary or his delegate may by regulations prescribe.

(3) RELEASE OF BOND.—The liability under any bond filed under section 44(d) of the Internal Revenue Code of 1939 (or the corresponding provisions or prior law) in respect of which an election under this subsection applies is hereby released with respect to taxable years to which such election applies.

P.L. 94-455, §1951(b)(10)(B), provides:

(B) SAVINGS PROVISION.—Notwithstanding subparagraph (A), any election made under section 691(e) to have subsection (a)(4) of such section apply in the case of an installment obligation shall continue to be effective with respect to taxable years beginning after December 31, 1976. Section 691(c) shall not apply in respect of any amount included in gross income by reason of the preceding sentence. The liability under bond filed under section 44(d) of the Internal Revenue Code of 1939 (or corresponding provisions of prior law) in respect of which such an election applies is hereby released with respect to taxable years to which such election applies.

• 1964 (P.L. 88-570)

P.L. 88-570, §[1]:

Renumbered Code Sec. 691(e) as Code Sec. 691(f) and added Code Sec. 691(e). **Effective**, generally, after 9-2-64. The provision, therefore, will apply with respect to payments received in any year with respect to which the time prescribed by law (including extensions of time) for the filing of the tax return for that year has not yet expired.

[Sec. 692]

SEC. 692. INCOME TAXES OF MEMBERS OF ARMED FORCES, ASTRONAUTS, AND VICTIMS OF CERTAIN TERRORIST ATTACKS ON DEATH.

[Sec. 692(a)]

(a) GENERAL RULE.—In the case of any individual who dies while in active service as a member of the Armed Forces of the United States, if such death occurred while serving in a combat zone (as determined under section 112) or as a result of wounds, disease, or injury incurred while so serving—

(1) any tax imposed by this subtitle shall not apply with respect to the taxable year in which falls the date of his death, or with respect to any prior taxable year ending on or after the first day he so served in a combat zone; and

(2) any tax under this subtitle and under the corresponding provisions of prior revenue laws for taxable years preceding those specified in paragraph (1) which is unpaid at the date of his death (including interest, additions to the tax, and additional amounts) shall not be assessed, and if assessed the assessment shall be abated, and if collected shall be credited or refunded as an overpayment.

Amendments

• 2014, Tax Technical Corrections Act of 2014 (P.L. 113-295)

P.L. 113-295, §221(a)(67), Division A:

Amended Code Sec. 692(a)(1) by striking "after June 24, 1950" following "served in a combat zone". **Effective** generally 12-19-2014. For a special rule, see Act Sec. 221(b)(2), Division A, below.

P.L. 113-295, §221(b)(2), Division A, provides:

(2) SAVINGS PROVISION.—If—

(A) any provision amended or repealed by the amendments made by this section applied to—

(i) any transaction occurring before the date of the enactment of this Act,

(ii) any property acquired before such date of enactment, or

(iii) any item of income, loss, deduction, or credit taken into account before such date of enactment, and

(B) the treatment of such transaction, property, or item under such provision would (without regard to the amendments or repeals made by this section) affect the liability for tax for periods ending after date of enactment, nothing in the amendments or repeals made by this section shall be construed to affect the treatment of such transaction, property, or item for purposes of determining liability for tax for periods ending after such date of enactment.

• 2003, Military Family Tax Relief Act of 2003 (P.L. 108-121)

P.L. 108-121, §110(a)(3)(A):

Amended the heading of Code Sec. 692 by inserting ", ASTRONAUTS," after "FORCES". **Effective** with respect to any astronaut whose death occurs after 12-31-2002.

• 2002, Victims of Terrorism Tax Relief Act of 2001 (P.L. 107-134)

P.L. 107-134, §101(c)(1):

Amended the heading of Code Sec. 692. **Effective** for tax years ending before, on, or after 9-11-2001. For a waiver of limitations, see Act Sec. 101(d)(2), below. Prior to amendment, the heading of Code Sec. 692 read as follows:

SEC. 692. INCOME TAXES OF MEMBERS OF ARMED FORCES ON DEATH.

P.L. 107-134, §101(d)(2), provides:

(2) WAIVER OF LIMITATIONS.—If refund or credit of any overpayment of tax resulting from the amendments made by this section is prevented at any time before the close of the 1-year period beginning on the date of the enactment of this Act by the operation of any law or rule of law (including res judicata), such refund or credit may nevertheless be made or allowed if claim therefor is filed before the close of such period.

• 1976, Tax Reform Act of 1976 (P.L. 94-455)

P.L. 94-455, §1901(a)(92):

Amended the heading to Code Sec. 692. **Effective** for tax years beginning after 12-31-76. Prior to amendment, the section heading read as follows:

SEC. 692. INCOME TAXES ON MEMBERS OF ARMED FORCES ON DEATH.

• 1975 (P.L. 93-597)

P.L. 93-597, §4(a):

Amended Code Sec. 692(a) by substituting at the beginning thereof "(a) General Rule.—In the case of any individual who dies" for "In the case of any individual who dies during an induction period (as defined in section 112(c)(5))". **Effective** with respect to tax years ending on or after 2-28-61. See, also, the historical comment for P.L. 93-597 following the text of Code Sec. 692(b), for a special provision on refunds or credits resulting from this amendment.

[Sec. 692(b)]

(b) INDIVIDUALS IN MISSING STATUS.—For purposes of this section, in the case of an individual who was in a missing status within the meaning of section 6013(f)(3)(A), the date of his death shall be treated as being not earlier than the date on which a determination of his death is made under section 556 of title 37 of the United States Code. Except in the case of the combat zone designated for purposes of the Vietnam conflict, the preceding sentence shall not cause subsection (a)(1) to apply for any taxable year beginning more than 2 years after the date designated under section 112 as the date of termination of combatant activities in a combat zone.

Amendments

• 1986, Tax Reform Act of 1986 (P.L. 99-514)

P.L. 99-514, §1708(a)(2):

Amended the last sentence of Code Sec. 692(b). **Effective** for tax years beginning after 12-31-82. Prior to amendment, the last sentence of Code Sec. 692(b) read as follows:

The preceding sentence shall not cause subsection (a)(1) to apply to any taxable year beginning—

(1) after December 31, 1982, in the case of service in the combat zone designated for purposes of the Vietnam conflict, or

(2) more than 2 years after the date designated under section 112 as the date of termination of combatant activities in that zone, in the case of any combat zone other than that referred to in paragraph (1).

• 1983, Technical Corrections Act of 1982 (P.L. 97-448)

P.L. 97-448, §307(b):

Amended Code Sec. 692(b)(1) by striking out "January 2, 1978" and inserting in lieu thereof "December 31, 1982". **Effective** 1-12-83.

• 1976 (P.L. 94-569)

P.L. 94-569, §2(c):

Amended the second sentence of Code Sec. 692(b). **Effective** with respect to months after the month following the month in which this Act is enacted. Prior to amendment, the second sentence of Code Sec. 692(b) read as follows:

The preceding sentence shall not cause subsection (a)(1) to apply for any taxable year beginning more than 2 years after—

(1) the date of the enactment of this subsection, in the case of service in the combat zone designated for purposes of the Vietnam conflict, or

(2) the date designated under section 112 as the date of termination of combatant activities in that zone, in the case of any combat zone other than that referred to in paragraph (1).

• 1975 (P.L. 93-597)

P.L. 93-597, §4(a):

Added Code Sec. 692(b). **Effective** with respect to tax years ending on or after 2-28-61.

P.L. 93-597, §4(c), provides:

(c) REFUNDS AND CREDITS RESULTING FROM SECTION 692 OF CODE.—If the refund or credit of any overpayment for any taxable year ending on or after February 28, 1961, resulting from the application of section 692 of the Internal Revenue Code of 1954 (as amended by subsection (a) of this section) is prevented at any time before the expiration of one year after the date of the enactment of this Act by the operation of any law or rule of law, but would not have been so prevented if claim for refund or credit therefor were made on the due date for the return for the taxable year of his death (or any later year), refund or credit of such overpayment may, nevertheless, be made or allowed if claim therefor is filed before the expiration of such one-year period.

[Sec. 692(c)]

(c) CERTAIN MILITARY OR CIVILIAN EMPLOYEES OF THE UNITED STATES DYING AS A RESULT OF INJURIES.—

(1) IN GENERAL.—In the case of any individual who dies while a military or civilian employee of the United States, if such death occurs as a result of wounds or injury which was incurred while the individual was a military or civilian employee of the United States and which was incurred in a terroristic or military action, any tax imposed by this subtitle shall not apply—

(A) with respect to the taxable year in which falls the date of his death, and

(B) with respect to any prior taxable year in the period beginning with the last taxable year ending before the taxable year in which the wounds or injury were incurred.

(2) TERRORISTIC OR MILITARY ACTION.—For purposes of paragraph (1), the term "terroristic or military action" means—

(A) any terroristic activity which a preponderance of the evidence indicates was directed against the United States or any of its allies, and

(B) any military action involving the Armed Forces of the United States and resulting from violence or aggression against the United States or any of its allies (or threat thereof).

For purposes of the preceding sentence, the term "military action" does not include training exercises.

(3) TREATMENT OF MULTINATIONAL FORCES.—For purposes of paragraph (2), any multinational force in which the United States is participating shall be treated as an ally of the United States.

Amendments

• 2017, Tax Cuts and Jobs Act (P.L. 115-97)

P.L. 115-97, §11026, provides:

For a special rule, see Act Sec. 11026 in the amendment notes for Code Sec. 112(c).

• 2002, Victims of Terrorism Tax Relief Act of 2001 (P.L. 107-134)

P.L. 107-134, §113(b)(1)-(2):

Amended Code Sec. 692(c) by striking "outside the United States" following "and which was incurred" in paragraph (1); and by striking "SUSTAINED OVERSEAS" before the period in the heading. **Effective** for tax years ending on or after 9-11-2001.

• 1999 (P.L. 106-21)

P.L. 106-21, §1(a)(3), (b) and (d)(1), provide:

SECTION 1. AVAILABILITY OF CERTAIN TAX BENEFITS FOR SERVICES AS PART OF OPERATION ALLIED FORCE.

(a) GENERAL RULE.—For purposes of the following provisions of the Internal Revenue Code of 1986, a qualified hazardous duty area shall be treated in the same manner as if it were a combat zone (as determined under section 112 of such Code):

* * *

(3) Section 692 (relating to income taxes of members of Armed Forces on death).

***

(b) QUALIFIED HAZARDOUS DUTY AREA.—For purposes of this section, the term "qualified hazardous duty area" means any area of the Federal Republic of Yugoslavia (Serbia/Montenegro), Albania, the Adriatic Sea, and the northern Ionian Sea (above the 39th parallel) during the period (which includes the date of the enactment of this Act) that any member of the Armed Forces of the United States is entitled to special pay under section 310 of title 37, United States Code (relating to special pay: duty subject to hostile fire or imminent danger) for services performed in such area.

***

(d) EFFECTIVE DATES.—

(1) IN GENERAL.—Except as provided in paragraph (2), this section shall take effect on March 24, 1999.

• 1996 (P.L. 104-117)

P.L. 104-117, §1(a)(3), (b) and (e)(1), provide:

SECTION 1. TREATMENT OF CERTAIN INDIVIDUALS PERFORMING SERVICES IN CERTAIN HAZARDOUS DUTY AREAS.

(a) GENERAL RULE.—For purposes of the following provisions of the Internal Revenue Code of 1986, a qualified hazardous duty area shall be treated in the same manner as if it were a combat zone (as determined under section 112 of such Code):

***

(3) Section 692 (relating to income taxes of members of Armed Forces on death).

***

(b) QUALIFIED HAZARDOUS DUTY AREA.—For purposes of this section, the term "qualified hazardous duty area" means Bosnia and Herzegovina, Croatia, or Macedonia, if as of the date of the enactment of this section any member of the Armed Forces of the United States is entitled to special pay under section 310 of title 37, United States Code (relating to special pay; duty subject to hostile fire or imminent danger) for services performed in such country. Such term includes any such country only during the period such entitlement is in effect. Solely for purposes of applying section 7508 of the Internal Revenue Code of 1986, in the case of an individual who is performing services as part of Operation Joint Endeavor outside the United States while deployed away from such individual's permanent duty station, the term "qualified hazardous duty area" includes, during the period for which such entitlement is in effect, any area in which such services are performed.

***

(e) EFFECTIVE DATE.—

(1) IN GENERAL.—Except as provided in paragraph (2), the provisions of and amendments made by this section shall take effect on November 21, 1995.

• 1984, Deficit Reduction Act of 1984 (P.L. 98-369)

P.L. 98-369, §722(g)(2):

Amended Code Sec. 692 [(c)](1) by striking out "as a result of wounds or injury incurred" and inserting in lieu thereof "as a result of wounds or injury which was incurred while the individual was a military or civilian employee of the United States and which was incurred". **Effective** as if included in the amendments made by section 1 of P.L. 98-259. See, also, the special rules of Act Sec. 722(g)(4)-(5)(B), below.

P.L. 98-369, §722(g)(3):

Amended Code Sec. 692(c)(2)(A). **Effective** as if included in the amendments made by section 1 of P.L. 98-259. See, also, the special rules of Act Sec. 722(g)(4)-(5)(B), below. Prior to amendment, Code Sec. 692(c)(2)(A) read as follows:

(A) any terroristic activity directed against the United States or any of its allies, and

P.L. 98-369, §722(g)(4) and (5)(B), provide:

(4) TREATMENT OF DIRECTOR GENERAL OF MULTINATIONAL FORCE IN SINAI.—For purposes of section 692(c) of the Internal Revenue Code of 1954, the Director General of the Multinational Force and Observers in the Sinai who died on February 15, 1984, shall be treated as if he were a civilian employee of the United States while he served as such Director General.

[(5)](B) STATUTE OF LIMITATIONS WAIVED.—Notwithstanding section 6511 of the Internal Revenue Code of 1954, the time for filing a claim for credit or refund of any overpayment of tax resulting from the amendments made by this subsection shall not expire before the date 1 year after the date of the enactment of this Act.

• 1984 (P.L. 98-259)

P.L. 98-259, §1(a):

Amended Code Sec. 692 by adding new subsection (c). **Effective** with respect to all tax years (whether beginning before, on, or after 4-10-84) of individuals dying after 11-17-78 [**effective** date changed by P.L. 98-369, §722(g)].

Notwithstanding Code Sec. 6511, the time for filing a claim for credit or refund of any overpayment of tax resulting from the amendment made by subsection (a) shall not expire before the date 1 year after April 10, 1984, of this Act.

[Sec. 692(d)]

(d) INDIVIDUALS DYING AS A RESULT OF CERTAIN ATTACKS.—

(1) IN GENERAL.—In the case of a specified terrorist victim, any tax imposed by this chapter shall not apply—

(A) with respect to the taxable year in which falls the date of death, and

(B) with respect to any prior taxable year in the period beginning with the last taxable year ending before the taxable year in which the wounds, injury, or illness referred to in paragraph (3) were incurred.

(2) $10,000 MINIMUM BENEFIT.—If, but for this paragraph, the amount of tax not imposed by paragraph (1) with respect to a specified terrorist victim is less than $10,000, then such victim shall be treated as having made a payment against the tax imposed by this chapter for such victim's last taxable year in an amount equal to the excess of $10,000 over the amount of tax not so imposed.

(3) TAXATION OF CERTAIN BENEFITS.—Subject to such rules as the Secretary may prescribe, paragraph (1) shall not apply to the amount of any tax imposed by this chapter which would be computed by only taking into account the items of income, gain, or other amounts attributable to—

(A) deferred compensation which would have been payable after death if the individual had died other than as a specified terrorist victim, or

(B) amounts payable in the taxable year which would not have been payable in such taxable year but for an action taken after September 11, 2001.

(4) SPECIFIED TERRORIST VICTIM.—For purposes of this subsection, the term "specified terrorist victim" means any decedent—

(A) who dies as a result of wounds or injury incurred as a result of the terrorist attacks against the United States on April 19, 1995, or September 11, 2001, or

(B) who dies as a result of illness incurred as a result of an attack involving anthrax occurring on or after September 11, 2001, and before January 1, 2002.

Such term shall not include any individual identified by the Attorney General to have been a participant or conspirator in any such attack or a representative of such an individual.

(5) RELIEF WITH RESPECT TO ASTRONAUTS.—The provisions of this subsection shall apply to any astronaut whose death occurs in the line of duty, except that paragraph (3)(B) shall be applied by using the date of the death of the astronaut rather than September 11, 2001.

Amendments

• 2003, Military Family Tax Relief Act of 2003 (P.L. 108-121)

P.L. 108-121, §110(a)(1):

Amended Code Sec. 692(d) by adding at the end a new paragraph (5). **Effective** with respect to any astronaut whose death occurs after 12-31-2002.

• 2002, Victims of Terrorism Tax Relief Act of 2001 (P.L. 107-134)

P.L. 107-134, §101(a):

Amended Code Sec. 692 by adding at the end a new subsection (d). **Effective** for tax years ending before, on, or after 9-11-2001. For a waiver of limitations, see Act Sec. 101(d)(2) in the amendment notes for Code Sec. 692(a).

* * *

Subchapter O—Gain or Loss on Disposition of Property

* * *

PART I—DETERMINATION OF AMOUNT OF AND RECOGNITION OF GAIN OR LOSS

* * *

[Sec. 1001]

SEC. 1001. DETERMINATION OF AMOUNT OF AND RECOGNITION OF GAIN OR LOSS.

[Sec. 1001(a)]

(a) COMPUTATION OF GAIN OR LOSS.—The gain from the sale or other disposition of property shall be the excess of the amount realized therefrom over the adjusted basis provided in section 1011 for determining gain, and the loss shall be the excess of the adjusted basis provided in such section for determining loss over the amount realized.

[Sec. 1001(b)]

(b) AMOUNT REALIZED.—The amount realized from the sale or other disposition of property shall be the sum of any money received plus the fair market value of the property (other than money) received. In determining the amount realized—

(1) there shall not be taken into account any amount received as reimbursement for real property taxes which are treated under section 164(d) as imposed on the purchaser, and

(2) there shall be taken into account amounts representing real property taxes which are treated under section 164(d) as imposed on the taxpayer if such taxes are to be paid by the purchaser.

[Sec. 1001(c)]

(c) RECOGNITION OF GAIN OR LOSS.—Except as otherwise provided in this subtitle, the entire amount of the gain or loss, determined under this section, on the sale or exchange of property shall be recognized.

Amendments

• 1976, Tax Reform Act of 1976 (P.L. 94-455)

P.L. 94-455, §1901(a)(121):

Amended Code Sec. 1001(c). **Effective** for tax years beginning after 12-31-76. Prior to amendment, Code Sec. 1001(c) read as follows:

(c) RECOGNITION OF GAIN OR LOSS.—In the case of a sale or exchange of property, the extent to which the gain or loss determined under this section shall be recognized for purposes of this subtitle shall be determined under section 1002.

[Sec. 1001(d)]

(d) INSTALLMENT SALES.—Nothing in this section shall be construed to prevent (in the case of property sold under contract providing for payment in installments) the taxation of that portion of any installment payment representing gain or profit in the year in which such payment is received.

[Sec. 1001(e)]

(e) CERTAIN TERM INTERESTS.—

(1) IN GENERAL.—In determining gain or loss from the sale or other disposition of a term interest in property, that portion of the adjusted basis of such interest which is determined pursuant to section 1014, 1015, or 1041 (to the extent that such adjusted basis is a portion of the entire adjusted basis of the property) shall be disregarded.

(2) TERM INTEREST IN PROPERTY DEFINED.—For purposes of paragraph (1), the term "term interest in property" means—

(A) a life interest in property,

(B) an interest in property for a term of years, or

(C) an income interest in a trust.

(3) EXCEPTION.—Paragraph (1) shall not apply to a sale or other disposition which is a part of a transaction in which the entire interest in property is transferred to any person or persons.

Amendments

• 1984, Deficit Reduction Act of 1984 (P.L. 98-369)

P.L. 98-369, §421(b)(4):

Amended Code Sec. 1001(e)(1) by striking out "section 1014 or 1015" and inserting in lieu thereof "section 1014, 1015, or 1041". **Effective** for transfers after 7-18-84, in tax years ending after such date.

• 1980, Crude Oil Windfall Profit Tax Act of 1980 (P.L. 96-223)

P.L. 96-223, §401(a):

Repealed Code Sec. 1001(e)(1) as amended by P.L. 95-600, Act Sec. 702(c)(9). **Effective** with respect to decedents dying after 12-31-76. However, see the amendment note for P.L. 96-223, §401(a), that follows Code Sec. 1014(d) for the text of Act Sec. 401(d) that authorizes the election of the carryover basis rules in the case of a decedent dying after 12-31-76 and before 11-7-78. Prior to repeal, Code Sec. 1001(e)(1) read as follows:

(1) IN GENERAL.—In determining gain or loss from the sale or other disposition of a term interest in property, that portion of the adjusted basis of such interest which is determined pursuant to section 1014, 1015, or 1023 (to the extent that such adjusted basis is a portion of the entire adjusted basis of the property) shall be disregarded.

P.L. 96-223, §401(b):

Revived Code Sec. 1001(e)(1) before its amendment by P.L. 96-600, Act Sec. 702(c)(9). **Effective** with respect to decedents dying after 12-31-76. However, see the amendment note for Act Sec. 401(a).

• 1978, Revenue Act of 1978 (P.L. 95-600)

P.L. 95-600, §702(c)(9), (10):

Amended Code Sec. 1001(e)(1) by striking out "section 1014 or 1015" and inserting in place thereof "section 1014, 1015, or 1023". **Effective** as if included in amendments made by P.L. 94-455 [Sec. 2005(f)(1), applicable to estates of decedents dying after 12-31-79, as amended by P.L. 95-600, §515(6)].

• 1969, Tax Reform Act of 1969 (P.L. 91-172)

P.L. 91-172, §516(a):

Amended Code Sec. 1001 by adding section 1001(e). **Effective** for sales or other dispositions after 10-9-69.

[Sec. 1001(f)—Stricken]

Amendments

• 1993, Omnibus Budget Reconciliation Act of 1993 (P.L. 103-66)

P.L. 103-66, §13213(a)(2)(E):

Amended Code Sec. 1001 by striking subsection (f). **Effective** for expenses incurred after 12-31-93. Prior to amendment, subsection (f) read as follows:

(f) CROSS REFERENCE.—For treatment of certain expenses incident to the sale of a residence which were deducted as moving expenses by the taxpayer or his spouse under section 217(a), see section 217(e).

• 1969, Tax Reform Act of 1969 (P.L. 91-172)

P.L. 91-172, §231(c)(2):

Added subsection 1001(f). **Effective** for tax years beginning after 12-31-69.

* * *

PART II—BASIS RULES OF GENERAL APPLICATION

* * *

[Sec. 1011]

SEC. 1011. ADJUSTED BASIS FOR DETERMINING GAIN OR LOSS.

[Sec. 1011(a)]

(a) GENERAL RULE.—The adjusted basis for determining the gain or loss from the sale or other disposition of property, whenever acquired, shall be the basis (determined under section 1012 or other applicable sections of this subchapter and subchapters C (relating to corporate distributions and adjustments), K (relating to partners and partnerships), and P (relating to capital gains and losses)), adjusted as provided in section 1016.

[Sec. 1011(b)]

(b) BARGAIN SALE TO A CHARITABLE ORGANIZATION.—If a deduction is allowable under section 170 (relating to charitable contributions) by reason of a sale, then the adjusted basis for determining the gain from such sale shall be that portion of the adjusted basis which bears the same ratio to the adjusted basis as the amount realized bears to the fair market value of the property.

Amendments

• 1969, Tax Reform Act of 1969 (P.L. 91-172)

P.L. 91-172, §201(f):

Amended Code Sec. 1011. **Effective** with respect to sales made after 12-19-69. Prior to amendment, Code Sec. 1011 read as follows:

"The adjusted basis for determining the gain or loss from the sale or other disposition of property, whenever acquired, shall be the basis (determined under section 1012 or other applicable sections of this subchapter and subchapters C (relating to corporate distributions and adjustments), K (relating to partners and partnerships), and P (relating to capital gains and losses)), adjusted as provided in section 1016."

[Sec. 1012]

SEC. 1012. BASIS OF PROPERTY—COST.

[Sec. 1012(a)]

(a) IN GENERAL.—The basis of property shall be the cost of such property, except as otherwise provided in this subchapter and subchapters C (relating to corporate distributions and adjustments), K (relating to partners and partnerships), and P (relating to capital gains and losses).

[Sec. 1012(b)]

(b) SPECIAL RULE FOR APPORTIONED REAL ESTATE TAXES.—The cost of real property shall not include any amount in respect of real property taxes which are treated under section 164(d) as imposed on the taxpayer.

[Sec. 1012(c)]

(c) DETERMINATIONS BY ACCOUNT.—

(1) IN GENERAL.—In the case of the sale, exchange, or other disposition of a specified security on or after the applicable date, the conventions prescribed by regulations under this section shall be applied on an account by account basis.

(2) APPLICATION TO CERTAIN REGULATED INVESTMENT COMPANIES.—

(A) IN GENERAL.—Except as provided in subparagraph (B), any stock for which an average basis method is permissible under this section which is acquired before January 1, 2012, shall be treated as a separate account from any such stock acquired on or after such date.

(B) ELECTION FOR TREATMENT AS SINGLE ACCOUNT.—If a regulated investment company described in subparagraph (A) elects to have this subparagraph apply with respect to one or more of its stockholders—

(i) subparagraph (A) shall not apply with respect to any stock in such regulated investment company held by such stockholders, and

(ii) all stock in such regulated investment company which is held by such stockholders shall be treated as covered securities described in section 6045(g)(3) without regard to the date of the acquisition of such stock.

A rule similar to the rule of the preceding sentence shall apply with respect to a broker holding such stock as a nominee.

(3) DEFINITIONS.—For purposes of this section, the terms "specified security" and "applicable date" shall have the meaning given such terms in section 6045(g).

Amendments

• 2014, Tax Technical Corrections Act of 2014 (P.L. 113-295)

P.L. 113-295, §210(f)(1)(A)-(C), Division A:

Amended Code Sec. 1012(c)(2) by striking "FUNDS" in the heading and inserting "REGULATED INVESTMENT COMPANIES", by striking "FUND" following "ELECTION" in the heading for subparagraph (B), and by striking "fund" each place it appears in paragraph (2) and inserting "regulated investment company". **Effective** as if included in the provision of the Energy Improvement and Extension Act of 2008 (P.L. 110-343) to which it relates [effective 1-1-2011.—CCH]. Prior to amendment, Code Sec. 1012(c)(2) read as follows:

(2) APPLICATION TO CERTAIN FUNDS.—

(A) IN GENERAL.—Except as provided in subparagraph (B), any stock for which an average basis method is permissible under section 1012 which is acquired before January 1, 2012, shall be treated as a separate account from any such stock acquired on or after such date.

(B) ELECTION FUND FOR TREATMENT AS SINGLE ACCOUNT.—If a fund described in subparagraph (A) elects to have this subparagraph apply with respect to one or more of its stockholders—

(i) subparagraph (A) shall not apply with respect to any stock in such fund held by such stockholders, and

(ii) all stock in such fund which is held by such stockholders shall be treated as covered securities described in section 6045(g)(3) without regard to the date of the acquisition of such stock.

A rule similar to the rule of the preceding sentence shall apply with respect to a broker holding such stock as a nominee.

P.L. 113-295, §220(n), Division A:

Amended Code Sec. 1012(c)(2)(A) by striking "section 1012" and inserting "this section". **Effective** 12-19-2014.

[Sec. 1012(d)]

(d) AVERAGE BASIS FOR STOCK ACQUIRED PURSUANT TO A DIVIDEND REINVESTMENT PLAN.—

(1) IN GENERAL.—In the case of any stock acquired after December 31, 2011, in connection with a dividend reinvestment plan, the basis of such stock while held as part of such plan shall be determined using one of the methods which may be used for determining the basis of stock in a regulated investment company.

(2) TREATMENT AFTER TRANSFER.—In the case of the transfer to another account of stock to which paragraph (1) applies, such stock shall have a cost basis in such other account equal to its basis in the dividend reinvestment plan immediately before such transfer (properly adjusted for any fees or other charges taken into account in connection with such transfer).

(3) SEPARATE ACCOUNTS; ELECTION FOR TREATMENT AS SINGLE ACCOUNT.—

(A) IN GENERAL.—Rules similar to the rules of subsection (c)(2) shall apply for purposes of this subsection.

(B) AVERAGE BASIS METHOD.—Notwithstanding paragraph (1), in the case of an election under rules similar to the rules of subsection (c)(2)(B) with respect to stock held in connection with a dividend reinvestment plan, the average basis method is permissible with respect to all such stock without regard to the date of the acquisition of such stock.

(4) DIVIDEND REINVESTMENT PLAN.—For purposes of this subsection—

(A) IN GENERAL.—The term "dividend reinvestment plan" means any arrangement under which dividends on any stock are reinvested in stock identical to the stock with respect to which the dividends are paid.

(B) INITIAL STOCK ACQUISITION TREATED AS ACQUIRED IN CONNECTION WITH PLAN.—Stock shall be treated as acquired in connection with a dividend reinvestment plan if such stock is acquired pursuant to such plan or if the dividends paid on such stock are subject to such plan.

Amendments

• 2014, Tax Technical Corrections Act of 2014 (P.L. 113-295)

P.L. 113-295, §210(f)(2)(A)-(B), Division A:

Amended Code Sec. 1012(d)(1) by striking "December 31, 2010" and inserting "December 31, 2011", and by striking "an open-end fund" and inserting "a regulated investment company". **Effective** as if included in the provision of the Energy Improvement and Extension Act of 2008 (P.L. 110-343) to which it relates [effective 1-1-2011.—CCH].

P.L. 113-295, §210(f)(3), Division A:

Amended Code Sec. 1012(d)(3). **Effective** as if included in the provision of the Energy Improvement and Extension Act of 2008 (P.L. 110-343) to which it relates [effective 1-1-2011.—CCH]. Prior to amendment, Code Sec. 1012(d)(3) read as follows:

(3) SEPARATE ACCOUNTS; ELECTION FOR TREATMENT AS SINGLE ACCOUNT.—Rules similar to the rules of subsection (c)(2) shall apply for purposes of this subsection.

• 2008, Energy Improvement and Extension Act of 2008 (P.L. 110-343)

P.L. 110-343, Division B, §403(b)(1)-(3):

Amended Code Sec. 1012 by striking "The basis of property" and inserting "(a) IN GENERAL.—The basis of property", by striking "The cost of real property" and inserting "(b) SPECIAL RULE FOR APPORTIONED REAL ESTATE TAXES.—The cost of real property", and by adding at the end new subsections (c)-(d). **Effective** 1-1-2011. Prior to amendment, Code Sec. 1012 read as follows:

SEC. 1012. BASIS OF PROPERTY—COST.

The basis of property shall be the cost of such property, except as otherwise provided in this subchapter and subchapters C (relating to corporate distributions and adjustments), K (relating to partners and partnerships), and P (relating to capital gains and losses). The cost of real property shall not include any amount in respect of real property taxes which are treated under section 164(d) as imposed on the taxpayer.

[Sec. 1013]

SEC. 1013. BASIS OF PROPERTY INCLUDED IN INVENTORY.

If the property should have been included in the last inventory, the basis shall be the last inventory value thereof.

[Sec. 1014]

SEC. 1014. BASIS OF PROPERTY ACQUIRED FROM A DECEDENT.

[Sec. 1014(a)]

(a) IN GENERAL.—Except as otherwise provided in this section, the basis of property in the hands of a person acquiring the property from a decedent or to whom the property passed from a decedent shall, if not sold, exchanged, or otherwise disposed of before the decedent's death by such person, be—

(1) the fair market value of the property at the date of the decedent's death,

(2) in the case of an election under section 2032, its value at the applicable valuation date prescribed by such section,

(3) in the case of an election under section 2032A, its value determined under such section, or

(4) to the extent of the applicability of the exclusion described in section 2031(c), the basis in the hands of the decedent.

Amendments

• 2014, Tax Technical Corrections Act of 2014 (P.L. 113-295)

P.L. 113-295, §221(a)(74)(A), Division A:

Amended Code Sec. 1014(a)(2). **Effective** generally 12-19-2014. For a special rule, see Act Sec. 221(b)(2), Division A, below. Prior to amendment, Code Sec. 1014(a)(2) read as follows:

(2) in the case of an election under either section 2032 or section 811(j) of the Internal Revenue Code of 1939 where the decedent died after October 21, 1942, its value at the applicable valuation date prescribed by those sections,

P.L. 113-295, §221(b)(2), Division A, provides:

(2) SAVINGS PROVISION.—If—

(A) any provision amended or repealed by the amendments made by this section applied to—

(i) any transaction occurring before the date of the enactment of this Act,

(ii) any property acquired before such date of enactment, or

(iii) any item of income, loss, deduction, or credit taken into account before such date of enactment, and

(B) the treatment of such transaction, property, or item under such provision would (without regard to the amendments or repeals made by this section) affect the liability for tax for periods ending after date of enactment, nothing in the amendments or repeals made by this section shall be construed to affect the treatment of such transaction, property, or item for purposes of determining liability for tax for periods ending after such date of enactment.

• 1997, Taxpayer Relief Act of 1997 (P.L. 105-34)

P.L. 105-34, § 508(b):

Amended Code Sec. 1014(a) by striking "or" at the end of paragraphs (1) and (2), by striking the period at the end of paragraph (3) and inserting ", or" and by adding at the end a new paragraph (4). **Effective** for estates of decedents dying after 12-31-97.

• 1980, Technical Corrections Act of 1979 (P.L. 96-222)

P.L. 96-222, § 107(a)(2)(A):

Amended Code Sec. 1014(a)(3) by changing "section 2032.1" to "section 2032A". **Effective** for estates of decedents dying after 12-31-76.

• 1978, Revenue Act of 1978 (P.L. 95-600)

P.L. 95-600, § 702(c)(1)(A), (c)(10):

Amended Code Sec. 1014(a). **Effective** as if included in amendments made by P.L. 94-455 [Sec. 2003(e), applicable to estates of decedents dying after 12-31-76]. Prior to amendment, such section read:

"(a) IN GENERAL.—Except as otherwise provided in this section, the basis of property in the hands of a person acquiring the property from a decedent or to whom the property passed from a decedent shall, if not sold, exchanged, or otherwise disposed of before the decedent's death by such person, be the fair market value of the property at the date of the decedent's death, or, in the case of an election under either section 2032 or section 811(j) of the Internal Revenue Code of 1939 where the decedent died after October 21, 1942, its value at the applicable valuation date prescribed by those sections."

[Sec. 1014(b)]

(b) PROPERTY ACQUIRED FROM THE DECEDENT.—For purposes of subsection (a), the following property shall be considered to have been acquired from or to have passed from the decedent:

(1) Property acquired by bequest, devise, or inheritance, or by the decedent's estate from the decedent;

(2) Property transferred by the decedent during his lifetime in trust to pay the income for life to or on the order or direction of the decedent, with the right reserved to the decedent at all times before his death to revoke the trust;

(3) In the case of decedents dying after December 31, 1951, property transferred by the decedent during his lifetime in trust to pay the income for life to or on the order or direction of the decedent with the right reserved to the decedent at all times before his death to make any change in the enjoyment thereof through the exercise of a power to alter, amend, or terminate the trust;

(4) Property passing without full and adequate consideration under a general power of appointment exercised by the decedent by will;

(5) In the case of decedents dying after August 26, 1937, and before January 1, 2005, property acquired by bequest, devise, or inheritance or by the decedent's estate from the decedent, if the property consists of stock or securities of a foreign corporation, which with respect to its taxable year next preceding the date of the decedent's death was, under the law applicable to such year, a foreign personal holding company. In such case, the basis shall be the fair market value of such property at the date of the decedent's death or the basis in the hands of the decedent, whichever is lower;

(6) In the case of decedents dying after December 31, 1947, property which represents the surviving spouse's one-half share of community property held by the decedent and the surviving spouse under the community property laws of any State, or possession of the United States or any foreign country, if at least one-half of the whole of the community interest in such property was includible in determining the value of the decedent's gross estate under chapter 11 of subtitle B (section 2001 and following, relating to estate tax) or section 811 of the Internal Revenue Code of 1939;

(7) [Stricken.]

(8) [Stricken.]

(9) In the case of decedents dying after December 31, 1953, property acquired from the decedent by reason of death, form of ownership, or other conditions (including property acquired through the exercise or non-exercise of a power of appointment), if by reason thereof the property is required to be included in determining the value of the decedent's gross estate under chapter 11 of subtitle B or under the Internal Revenue Code of 1939. In such case, if the property is acquired before the death of the decedent, the basis shall be the amount determined under subsection (a) reduced by the amount allowed to the taxpayer as deductions in computing taxable income under this subtitle or prior income tax laws for exhaustion, wear and tear, obsolescence, amortization, and depletion on such property before the death of the decedent. Such basis shall be applicable to the property commencing on the death of the decedent. This paragraph shall not apply to—

(A) annuities described in section 72;

(B) property to which paragraph (5) would apply if the property had been acquired by bequest; and

(C) property described in any other paragraph of this subsection.

(10) Property includible in the gross estate of the decedent under section 2044 (relating to certain property for which marital deduction was previously allowed). In any such case, the last 3 sentences of paragraph (9) shall apply as if such property were described in the first sentence of paragraph (9).

Amendments

• 2014, Tax Technical Corrections Act of 2014 (P.L. 113-295)

P.L. 113-295, §221(a)(74)(B), Division A:

Amended Code Sec. 1014(b) by striking paragraphs (7) and (8). **Effective** generally 12-19-2014. For a special rule, see Act Sec. 221(b)(2), Division A, below. Prior to being stricken, Code Sec. 1014(b)(7)-(8) read as follows:

(7) In the case of decedents dying after October 21, 1942, and on or before December 31, 1947, such part of any property, representing the surviving spouse's one-half share of property held by a decedent and the surviving spouse under the community property laws of any State, or possession of the United States or any foreign country, as was included in determining the value of the gross estate of the decedent, if a tax under chapter 3 of the Internal Revenue Code of 1939 was payable on the transfer of the net estate of the decedent. In such case, nothing in this paragraph shall reduce the basis below that which would exist if the Revenue Act of 1948 had not been enacted;

(8) In the case of decedents dying after December 31, 1950, and before January 1, 1954, property which represents the survivor's interest in a joint and survivor's annuity if the value of any part of such interest was required to be included in determining the value of decedent's gross estate under section 811 of the Internal Revenue Code of 1939;

P.L. 113-295, §221(b)(2), Division A, provides:

(2) SAVINGS PROVISION.—If—

(A) any provision amended or repealed by the amendments made by this section applied to—

(i) any transaction occurring before the date of the enactment of this Act,

(ii) any property acquired before such date of enactment, or

(iii) any item of income, loss, deduction, or credit taken into account before such date of enactment, and

(B) the treatment of such transaction, property, or item under such provision would (without regard to the amendments or repeals made by this section) affect the liability for tax for periods ending after date of enactment, nothing in the amendments or repeals made by this section shall be construed to affect the treatment of such transaction, property, or item for purposes of determining liability for tax for periods ending after such date of enactment.

• 2004, American Jobs Creation Act of 2004 (P.L. 108-357)

P.L. 108-357, §413(c)(18):

Amended Code Sec. 1014(b)(5) by inserting "and before January 1, 2005," after "August 26, 1937,". **Effective** for tax years of foreign corporations beginning after 12-31-2004, and for tax years of United States shareholders with or within which such tax years of foreign corporations end.

• 1983, Technical Corrections Act of 1982 (P.L. 97-448)

P.L. 97-448, §104(a)(1)(A):

Added Code Sec. 1014(b)(10). **Effective** as if included in the provision of P.L. 97-34 to which it relates.

• 1976, Tax Reform Act of 1976 (P.L. 94-455)

P.L. 94-455, §1901(c)(8):

Struck out "Territory," following "State," in Code Secs. 1014(b)(6) and 1014(b)(7). **Effective** for tax years beginning after 12-31-76.

[Sec. 1014(c)]

(c) PROPERTY REPRESENTING INCOME IN RESPECT OF A DECEDENT.—This section shall not apply to property which constitutes a right to receive an item of income in respect of a decedent under section 691.

[Sec. 1014(d)]

(d) SPECIAL RULE WITH RESPECT TO DISC STOCK.—If stock owned by a decedent in a DISC or former DISC (as defined in section 992(a)) acquires a new basis under subsection (a), such basis (determined before the application of this subsection) shall be reduced by the amount (if any) which would have been included in gross income under section 995(c) as a dividend if the decedent had lived and sold the stock at its fair market value on the estate tax valuation date. In computing the gain the decedent would have had if he had lived and sold the stock, his basis shall be determined without regard to the last sentence of section 996(e)(2) (relating to reductions of basis of DISC stock). For purposes of this subsection, the estate tax valuation date is the date of the decedent's death or, in the case of an election under section 2032, the applicable valuation date prescribed by that section.

Amendments

• 1980, Crude Oil Windfall Profit Tax Act of 1980 (P.L. 96-223)

P.L. 96-223, §401(a):

Repealed Code Sec. 1014(d) as amended by P.L. 94-455, Act Sec. 2005(a)(1). **Effective** in respect of decedents dying after 12-31-76. However, in the case of a decedent dying after 12-31-76 and before 11-7-78, the executor of an estate may make a special election of the carryover basis rules. The text of Act Sec. 401(d) which authorizes such an election is reproduced below. Prior to repeal, Code Sec. 1014(d) read as follows:

(d) DECEDENTS DYING AFTER DECEMBER 31, 1979.—In the case of a decedent dying after December 31, 1979, this section shall not apply to any property for which a carryover basis is provided by section 1023.

P.L. 96-223, §401(b):

Revived Code Sec. 1014(d) before its amendment by P.L. 94-455 and P.L. 95-600. **Effective** in respect of decedents dying after 12-31-76.

P.L. 96-223, §401(d), provides:

(d) ELECTION OF CARRYOVER BASIS RULES BY CERTAIN ESTATES.—Notwithstanding any other provision of law, in the case of a decedent dying after December 31, 1976, and before November 7, 1978, the executor (within the meaning of section 2203 of the Internal Revenue Code of 1954) of such decedent's estate may irrevocably elect, within 120 days following the date of enactment of this Act and in such manner as the Secretary of the Treasury or his delegate shall prescribe, to have the basis of all property acquired from or passing from the decedent (within the meaning of section 1014(b) of the Internal Revenue Code of 1954) determined for all purposes under such Code as though the provisions of section 2005 of the Tax Reform Act of 1976 (as amended by the provisions of section 702(c) of the Revenue Act of 1978) applied to such property acquired or passing from such decedent.

• 1978, Revenue Act of 1978 (P.L. 95-600)

P.L. 95-600, § 515(1):

Amended Code Sec. 1014(d) by striking out "December 31, 1976" and inserting in place thereof "December 31, 1979" in the caption and text of such section. **Effective** 11-7-78.

• 1976, Tax Reform Act of 1976 (P.L. 94-455)

P.L. 94-455, § 2005(a)(1), (f)(1):

Amended Code Sec. 1014(d). **Effective** in respect of decedents dying after 12-31-79, as amended by P.L. 95-600, § 515(6). Prior to amendment, Code Sec. 1014(d) read as follows:

(d) SPECIAL RULE WITH RESPECT TO DISC STOCK.—If stock owned by a decedent in a DISC or former DISC (as defined in section 992(a)) acquires a new basis under subsection (a), such basis (determined before the application of this subsection) shall be reduced by the amount (if any) which would have been included in gross income under section 995(c) as a dividend if the decedent had lived and sold the stock at its fair market value on the estate tax valuation date. In computing the gain the decedent would have had if he had lived and sold the stock, his basis shall be determined without regard to the last sentence of section 996(e)(2) (relating to reductions of basis of DISC stock). For purposes of this subsection, the estate tax valuation date is the date of the decedent's death or, in the case of an election under section 2032, the applicable valuation date prescribed by that section.

• 1971, Revenue Act of 1971 (P.L. 92-178)

P.L. 92-178, § 502(f):

Added Code Sec. 1014(d). **Effective** date is governed by the effective date for Code Sec. 992.

• 1958 (P.L. 85-320)

P.L. 85-320, § 2:

Repealed 1954 Code Sec. 1014(d). **Effective** with respect to tax years ending after 12-31-56, but only in the case of employees dying after such date. Prior to repeal, Sec. 1014(d) read:

"(d) Employee Stock Options.—This section shall not apply to restricted stock options described in section 421 which the employee has not exercised at death."

[Sec. 1014(e)]

(e) APPRECIATED PROPERTY ACQUIRED BY DECEDENT BY GIFT WITHIN 1 YEAR OF DEATH.—

(1) IN GENERAL.—In the case of a decedent dying after December 31, 1981, if—

(A) appreciated property was acquired by the decedent by gift during the 1-year period ending on the date of the decedent's death, and

(B) such property is acquired from the decedent by (or passes from the decedent to) the donor of such property (or the spouse of such donor),

the basis of such property in the hands of such donor (or spouse) shall be the adjusted basis of such property in the hands of the decedent immediately before the death of the decedent.

(2) DEFINITIONS.—For purposes of paragraph (1)—

(A) APPRECIATED PROPERTY.—The term "appreciated property" means any property if the fair market value of such property on the day it was transferred to the decedent by gift exceeds its adjusted basis.

(B) TREATMENT OF CERTAIN PROPERTY SOLD BY ESTATE.—In the case of any appreciated property described in subparagraph (A) of paragraph (1) sold by the estate of the decedent or by a trust of which the decedent was the grantor, rules similar to the rules of paragraph (1) shall apply to the extent the donor of such property (or the spouse of such donor) is entitled to the proceeds from such sale.

Amendments

• 1981, Economic Recovery Tax Act of 1981 (P.L. 97-34)

P.L. 97-34, § 425(a):

Added Code Sec. 1014(e). **Effective** for property acquired after 8-13-81 by decedents dying after 12-31-81.

[Sec. 1014(f)]

(f) BASIS MUST BE CONSISTENT WITH ESTATE TAX RETURN.—For purposes of this section—

(1) IN GENERAL.—The basis of any property to which subsection (a) applies shall not exceed—

(A) in the case of property the final value of which has been determined for purposes of the tax imposed by chapter 11 on the estate of such decedent, such value, and

(B) in the case of property not described in subparagraph (A) and with respect to which a statement has been furnished under section 6035(a) identifying the value of such property, such value.

(2) EXCEPTION.—Paragraph (1) shall only apply to any property whose inclusion in the decedent's estate increased the liability for the tax imposed by chapter 11 (reduced by credits allowable against such tax) on such estate.

(3) DETERMINATION.—For purposes of paragraph (1), the basis of property has been determined for purposes of the tax imposed by chapter 11 if—

(A) the value of such property is shown on a return under section 6018 and such value is not contested by the Secretary before the expiration of the time for assessing a tax under chapter 11,

(B) in a case not described in subparagraph (A), the value is specified by the Secretary and such value is not timely contested by the executor of the estate, or

(C) the value is determined by a court or pursuant to a settlement agreement with the Secretary.

(4) REGULATIONS.—The Secretary may by regulations provide exceptions to the application of this subsection.

Amendments

• 2015, Surface Transportation and Veterans Health Care Choice Improvement Act of 2015 (P.L. 114-41)

P.L. 114-41, §2004(a):

Amended Code Sec. 1014 by adding at the end a new subsection (f). **Effective** for property with respect to which an estate tax return is filed after 7-31-2015.

[Sec. 1014(f)—Repealed]

Amendments

• 2013, American Taxpayer Relief Act of 2012 (P.L. 112-240)

P.L. 112-240, §101(a)(1)-(3), provides:

SEC. 101. PERMANENT EXTENSION AND MODIFICATION OF 2001 TAX RELIEF.

(a) PERMANENT EXTENSION.—

(1) IN GENERAL.—The Economic Growth and Tax Relief Reconciliation Act of 2001 is amended by striking title IX.

(2) CONFORMING AMENDMENT.—The Tax Relief, Unemployment Insurance Reauthorization, and Job Creation Act of 2010 is amended by striking section 304.

(3) EFFECTIVE DATE.—The amendments made by this subsection shall apply to taxable, plan, or limitation years beginning after December 31, 2012, and estates of decedents dying, gifts made, or generation skipping transfers after December 31, 2012.

• 2010, Tax Relief, Unemployment Insurance Reauthorization, and Job Creation Act of 2010 (P.L. 111-312)

P.L. 111-312, §301(a):

Amended Code Sec. 1014(f) to read as such provision would read if subtitle E of title V of the Economic Growth and Tax Relief Reconciliation Act of 2001 (P.L. 107-16) had never been enacted. [P.L. 107-16, §541, amended Code Sec. 1014 by adding a new subsection (f). Therefore, P.L. 111-312, §301(a), effectively repealed Code Sec. 1014(f).—CCH] **Effective** for estates of decedents dying, and transfers made, after 12-31-2009. For a special rule, see Act Sec. 301(c), below. Prior to amendment by P.L. 111-312, Code Sec. 1014(f) read as follows:

(f) TERMINATION.—This section shall not apply with respect to decedents dying after December 31, 2009.

P.L. 111-312, §301(c), provides:

(c) SPECIAL ELECTION WITH RESPECT TO ESTATES OF DECEDENTS DYING IN 2010.—Notwithstanding subsection (a), in the case of an estate of a decedent dying after December 31, 2009, and before January 1, 2011, the executor (within the meaning of section 2203 of the Internal Revenue Code of 1986) may elect to apply such Code as though the amendments made by subsection (a) do not apply with respect to chapter 11 of such Code and with respect to property acquired or passing from such decedent (within the meaning of section 1014(b) of such Code). Such election shall be made at such time and in such manner as the Secretary of the Treasury or the Secretary's delegate shall provide. Such an election once made shall be revocable only with the consent of the Secretary of the Treasury or the Secretary's delegate. For purposes of section 2652(a)(1) of such Code, the determination of whether any property is subject to the tax imposed by such chapter 11 shall be made without regard to any election made under this subsection.

P.L. 111-312, §304, provides [but see P.L. 112-240, §101(a)(2)-(3), above]:

SEC. 304. APPLICATION OF EGTRRA SUNSET TO THIS TITLE.

Section 901 of the Economic Growth and Tax Relief Reconciliation Act of 2001 shall apply to the amendments made by this title.

• 2001, Economic Growth and Tax Relief Reconciliation Act of 2001 (P.L. 107-16)

P.L. 107-16, §541:

Amended Code Sec. 1014 by adding at the end a new subsection (f). **Effective** 6-7-2001.

P.L. 107-16, §901(a)-(b), as amended by P.L. 111-312, §101(a)(1), provides [but see P.L. 112-240, §101(a)(1) and (3), above]:

SEC. 901. SUNSET OF PROVISIONS OF ACT.

(a) IN GENERAL.—All provisions of, and amendments made by, this Act shall not apply—

(1) to taxable, plan, or limitation years beginning after December 31, 2012, or

(2) in the case of title V, to estates of decedents dying, gifts made, or generation skipping transfers, after December 31, 2012.

(b) APPLICATION OF CERTAIN LAWS.—The Internal Revenue Code of 1986 and the Employee Retirement Income Security Act of 1974 shall be applied and administered to years, estates, gifts, and transfers described in subsection (a) as if the provisions and amendments described in subsection (a) had never been enacted.

[Sec. 1015]

SEC. 1015. BASIS OF PROPERTY ACQUIRED BY GIFTS AND TRANSFERS IN TRUST.

[Sec. 1015(a)]

(a) GIFTS AFTER DECEMBER 31, 1920.—If the property was acquired by gift after December 31, 1920, the basis shall be the same as it would be in the hands of the donor or the last preceding owner by whom it was not acquired by gift, except that if such basis (adjusted for the period before the date of the gift as provided in section 1016) is greater than the fair market value of the property at the time of the gift, then for the purpose of determining loss the basis shall be such fair market value. If the facts necessary to determine the basis in the hands of the donor or the last preceding owner are unknown to the donee, the Secretary shall, if possible, obtain such facts from such donor or last preceding owner, or any other person cognizant thereof. If the Secretary finds it impossible to obtain such facts, the basis in the hands of such donor or last preceding owner shall be the fair market value of such property as found by the Secretary as of the date or approximate date at which, according to the best information that the Secretary is able to obtain, such property was acquired by such donor or last preceding owner.

Amendments

• 1976, Tax Reform Act of 1976 (P.L. 94-455)

P.L. 94-455, §1906(b)(13)(A):

Amended 1954 Code by substituting "Secretary" for "Secretary or his delegate" each place it appeared. **Effective** 2-1-77.

[Sec. 1015(b)]

(b) TRANSFER IN TRUST AFTER DECEMBER 31, 1920.—If the property was acquired after December 31, 1920, by a transfer in trust (other than by a transfer in trust by a gift, bequest, or devise), the basis shall be the same as it would be in the hands of the grantor increased in the amount of gain or decreased in the amount of loss recognized to the grantor on such transfer under the law applicable to the year in which the transfer was made.

[Sec. 1015(c)]

(c) GIFT OR TRANSFER IN TRUST BEFORE JANUARY 1, 1921.—If the property was acquired by gift or transfer in trust on or before December 31, 1920, the basis shall be the fair market value of such property at the time of such acquisition.

[Sec. 1015(d)]

(d) INCREASED BASIS FOR GIFT TAX PAID.—

(1) IN GENERAL.—If—

(A) the property is acquired by gift on or after September 2, 1958, the basis shall be the basis determined under subsection (a), increased (but not above the fair market value of the property at the time of the gift) by the amount of gift tax paid with respect to such gift, or

(B) the property was acquired by gift before September 2, 1958, and has not been sold, exchanged, or otherwise disposed of before such date, the basis of the property shall be increased on such date by the amount of gift tax paid with respect to such gift, but such increase shall not exceed an amount equal to the amount by which the fair market value of the property at the time of the gift exceeded the basis of the property in the hands of the donor at the time of the gift.

(2) AMOUNT OF TAX PAID WITH RESPECT TO GIFT.—For purposes of paragraph (1), the amount of gift tax paid with respect to any gift is an amount which bears the same ratio to the amount of gift tax paid under chapter 12 with respect to all gifts made by the donor for the calendar year (or preceding calendar period) in which such gift is made as the amount of such gift bears to the taxable gifts (as defined in section 2503(a) but computed without the deduction allowed by section 2521) made by the donor during such calendar year or period. For purposes of the preceding sentence, the amount of any gift shall be the amount included with respect to such gift in determining (for the purposes of section 2503(a)) the total amount of gifts made during the calendar year or period, reduced by the amount of any deduction allowed with respect to such gift under section 2522 (relating to charitable deduction) or under section 2523 (relating to marital deduction).

(3) GIFTS TREATED AS MADE ONE-HALF BY EACH SPOUSE.—For purposes of paragraph (1), where the donor and his spouse elected, under section 2513 to have the gift considered as made one-half by each, the amount of gift tax paid with respect to such gift under chapter 12 shall be the sum of the amounts of tax paid with respect to each half of such gift (computed in the manner provided in paragraph (2)).

(4) TREATMENT AS ADJUSTMENT TO BASIS.—For purposes of section 1016(b), an increase in basis under paragraph (1) shall be treated as an adjustment under section 1016(a).

(5) APPLICATION TO GIFTS BEFORE 1955.—With respect to any property acquired by gift before 1955, references in this subsection to any provision of this title shall be deemed to refer to the corresponding provision of the Internal Revenue Code of 1939 or prior revenue laws which was effective for the year in which such gift was made.

(6) SPECIAL RULE FOR GIFTS MADE AFTER DECEMBER 31, 1976.—

(A) IN GENERAL.—In the case of any gift made after December 31, 1976, the increase in basis provided by this subsection with respect to any gift for the gift tax paid under chapter 12 shall be an amount (not in excess of the amount of tax so paid) which bears the same ratio to the amount of tax so paid as—

(i) the net appreciation in value of the gift, bears to

(ii) the amount of the gift.

(B) NET APPRECIATION.—For purposes of paragraph (1), the net appreciation in value of any gift is the amount by which the fair market value of the gift exceeds the donor's adjusted basis immediately before the gift.

Amendments

• 1981, Economic Recovery Tax Act of 1981 (P.L. 97-34)

P.L. 97-34, §442(d)(1):

Amended Code Sec. 1015(d)(2), by striking out "calendar quarter (or calendar year if the gift was made before January 1, 1971)" and inserting "calendar year (or preceding calendar period)", and by striking out "calendar quarter or year" each place it appears and inserting "calendar year or period". **Effective** with respect to estates of decedents dying after 12-31-81.

• 1976, Tax Reform Act of 1976 (P.L. 94-455)

P.L. 94-455, §1901(a)(122):

Substituted "September 2, 1958" for "the date of the enactment of the Technical Amendments Act of 1958" in Code Sec. 1015(d)(1)(A) and (B). **Effective** for tax years beginning after 12-31-76.

P.L. 94-455, §2005(c):

Added Code Sec. 1015(d)(6). **Effective** for gifts made after 12-31-76.

• 1970, Excise, Estate, and Gift Tax Adjustment Act of 1970 (P.L. 91-164)

P.L. 91-614, §102(d)(1):

Amended Code Sec. 1015(d)(2) by substituting "calendar quarter (or calendar year if the gift was made before January 1, 1971)" for "calendar year" in the first sentence and by substituting "calendar quarter or year" for "calendar year" at the end of such sentence. In the second sentence, "calendar quarter or year" was substituted for "calendar year." **Effective** for gifts made after 12-31-70.

• 1958, Technical Amendments Act of 1958 (P.L. 85-866)

P.L. 85-866, §43(a);

Added new subsection (d) to Sec. 1015 to read as prior to amendment by P.L. 91-614 and P.L. 94-455. **Effective** 1-1-54.

[Sec. 1015(e)]

(e) GIFTS BETWEEN SPOUSES.—In the case of any property acquired by gift in a transfer described in section 1041(a), the basis of such property in the hands of the transferee shall be determined under section 1041(b)(2) and not this section.

Amendments

• 1984, Deficit Reduction Act of 1984 (P.L. 98-369)

P.L. 98-369, §421(b)(5):

Amended Code Sec. 1015 by adding at the end thereof a new subsection (e). **Effective** for transfers after 7-18-84, in tax years ending after such date. Special rules appear in Act Sec. 421(d)(2)-(4) following Code Sec. 1041.

[Sec. 1016]

SEC. 1016. ADJUSTMENTS TO BASIS.

* * *

[Sec. 1016(c)]

(c) INCREASE IN BASIS OF PROPERTY ON WHICH ADDITIONAL ESTATE TAX IS IMPOSED.—

(1) TAX IMPOSED WITH RESPECT TO ENTIRE INTEREST.—If an additional estate tax is imposed under section 2032A(c)(1) with respect to any interest in property and the qualified heir makes an election under this subsection with respect to the imposition of such tax, the adjusted basis of such interest shall be increased by an amount equal to the excess of—

(A) the fair market value of such interest on the date of the decedent's death (or the alternate valuation date under section 2032, if the executor of the decedent's estate elected the application of such section), over

(B) the value of such interest determined under section 2032A(a).

(2) PARTIAL DISPOSITIONS.—

(A) IN GENERAL.—In the case of any partial disposition for which an election under this subsection is made, the increase in basis under paragraph (1) shall be an amount—

(i) which bears the same ratio to the increase which would be determined under paragraph (1) (without regard to this paragraph) with respect to the entire interest, as

(ii) the amount of the tax imposed under section 2032A(c)(1) with respect to such disposition bears to the adjusted tax difference attributable to the entire interest (as determined under section 2032A(c)(2)(B)).

(B) PARTIAL DISPOSITION.—For purposes of subparagraph (A), the term "partial disposition" means any disposition or cessation to which subsection (c)(2)(D), (h)(1)(E), or (i)(1)(B) of section 2032A applies.

(3) TIME ADJUSTMENT MADE.—Any increase in basis under this subsection shall be deemed to have occurred immediately before the disposition or cessation resulting in the imposition of the tax under section 2032A(c)(1).

(4) SPECIAL RULE IN THE CASE OF SUBSTITUTED PROPERTY.—If the tax under section 2032A(c)(1) is imposed with respect to qualified replacement property (as defined in section 2032A(h)(3)(B)) or qualified exchange property (as defined in section 2032A(i)(3)), the increase in basis under paragraph (1) shall be made by reference to the property involuntarily converted or exchanged (as the case may be).

(5) ELECTION.—

(A) IN GENERAL.—An election under this subsection shall be made at such time and in such manner as the Secretary shall by regulations prescribe. Such an election, once made, shall be irrevocable.

(B) INTEREST ON RECAPTURED AMOUNT.—If an election is made under this subsection with respect to any additional estate tax imposed under section 2032A(c)(1), for purposes of section 6601 (relating to interest on underpayments), the last date prescribed for payment of such tax shall be deemed to be the last date prescribed for payment of the tax imposed by section 2001 with respect to the estate of the decedent (as determined for purposes of section 6601).

Amendments

• 1981, Economic Recovery Tax Act of 1981 (P.L. 97-34)

P.L. 97-34, §421(g):

Amended Code Sec. 1016(c). **Effective** with respect to decedents dying after 12-31-81. Prior to amendment, Code Sec. 1016(c) read as follows:

(c) INCREASE IN BASIS IN THE CASE OF CERTAIN INVOLUNTARY CONVERSIONS.—

(1) IN GENERAL.—If—

(A) there is a compulsory or involuntary conversion (within the meaning of section 1033) of any property, and

(B) an additional estate tax is imposed on such conversion under section 2032A(c), then the adjusted basis of such property shall be increased by the amount of such tax.

(2) TIME ADJUSTMENT MADE.—Any adjustment under paragraph (1) shall be deemed to have occurred immediately before the compulsory or involuntary conversion.

• 1980, Crude Oil Windfall Profit Tax Act of 1980 (P.L. 96-223)

P.L. 96-223, §401(c)(1):

Amended Code Sec. 1016(c). **Effective** with respect to decedents dying after 12-31-76. See the amendment note for P.L. 96-223, §401(a), that follows Code Sec. 1014(d) for the text of Act Sec. 401(d) that authorizes the election of the carryover basis rules in the case of a decedent dying after 12-31-76 and before 11-7-78. Prior to amendment, Code Sec. 1016(c) read:

(c) INCREASE IN BASIS IN THE CASE OF CERTAIN INVOLUNTARY CONVERSIONS.—

(1) IN GENERAL.—If there is a compulsory or involuntary conversion (within the meaning of section 1033) of any property the basis of which is determined under section 1023 and an additional estate tax is imposed on such conversion under section 2032A(c), then the adjusted basis of such property shall be increased by an amount which bears the same ratio to such tax with respect to the conversion of that property as—

(A) the net appreciation in value of such property, bears to

(B) the excess of—

(i) the value of such property for purposes of chapter 11 as determined with respect to the estate of the decedent without regard to section 2032A; over

(ii) the value of such property for purposes of chapter 11 as determined with respect to the estate of the decedent with regard to section 2032A.

(2) NET APPRECIATION IN VALUE.—For purposes of this subsection, the net appreciation in value of any property shall be determined in accordance with section 1023(f)(2) except that—

(A) the adjusted basis taken into account shall be increased by any adjustment under section 1023,

(B) the fair market value of such property shall be determined without regard to section 2032A, and

(C) any net appreciation in value in excess of the amount determined under paragraph (1)(B) shall be disregarded.

(3) TIME ADJUSTMENT MADE.—Any adjustment under paragraph (1) shall be deemed to have occurred immediately before the compulsory or involuntary conversion.

• 1978 (P.L. 95-472)

P.L. 95-472, §4(b), (d):

Added Code Sec. 1016(c). **Effective** for involuntary conversions after 1976.

* * *

[Sec. 1022—Repealed]

Amendments

• 2013, American Taxpayer Relief Act of 2012 (P.L. 112-240)

P.L. 112-240, §101(a)(1)-(3), provides:

SEC. 101. PERMANENT EXTENSION AND MODIFICATION OF 2001 TAX RELIEF.

(a) PERMANENT EXTENSION.—

(1) IN GENERAL.—The Economic Growth and Tax Relief Reconciliation Act of 2001 is amended by striking title IX.

(2) CONFORMING AMENDMENT.—The Tax Relief, Unemployment Insurance Reauthorization, and Job Creation Act of 2010 is amended by striking section 304.

(3) EFFECTIVE DATE.—The amendments made by this subsection shall apply to taxable, plan, or limitation years beginning after December 31, 2012, and estates of decedents dying, gifts made, or generation skipping transfers after December 31, 2012.

• 2010, Tax Relief, Unemployment Insurance Reauthorization, and Job Creation Act of 2010 (P.L. 111-312)

P.L. 111-312, §301(a):

Amended Code Sec. 1022 to read as such provision would read if subtitle E of title V of the Economic Growth and Tax Relief Reconciliation Act of 2001 (P.L. 107-16) had never been enacted. [P.L. 107-16, §542(a), added a new Code Sec. 1022. Therefore, P.L. 111-312, §301(a), effectively repealed Code Sec. 1022.—CCH] **Effective** for estates of decedents dying, and transfers made, after 12-31-2009. For a special rule, see Act Sec. 301(c), below. Prior to amendment by P.L. 111-312, Code Sec. 1022 read as follows:

SEC. 1022. TREATMENT OF PROPERTY ACQUIRED FROM A DECEDENT DYING AFTER DECEMBER 31, 2009.

[Sec. 1022(a)]

(a) IN GENERAL.—Except as otherwise provided in this section—

(1) property acquired from a decedent dying after December 31, 2009, shall be treated for purposes of this subtitle as transferred by gift, and

(2) the basis of the person acquiring property from such a decedent shall be the lesser of—

(A) the adjusted basis of the decedent, or

(B) the fair market value of the property at the date of the decedent's death.

[Sec. 1022(b)]

(b) BASIS INCREASE FOR CERTAIN PROPERTY.—

(1) IN GENERAL.—In the case of property to which this subsection applies, the basis of such property under subsection (a) shall be increased by its basis increase under this subsection.

(2) BASIS INCREASE.—For purposes of this subsection—

(A) IN GENERAL.—The basis increase under this subsection for any property is the portion of the aggregate basis increase which is allocated to the property pursuant to this section.

(B) AGGREGATE BASIS INCREASE.—In the case of any estate, the aggregate basis increase under this subsection is $1,300,000.

(C) LIMIT INCREASED BY UNUSED BUILT-IN LOSSES AND LOSS CARRYOVERS.—The limitation under subparagraph (B) shall be increased by—

(i) the sum of the amount of any capital loss carryover under section 1212(b), and the amount of any net operating loss carryover under section 172, which would (but for the decedent's death) be carried from the decedent's last taxable year to a later taxable year of the decedent, plus

(ii) the sum of the amount of any losses that would have been allowable under section 165 if the property acquired from the decedent had been sold at fair market value immediately before the decedent's death.

(3) DECEDENT NONRESIDENTS WHO ARE NOT CITIZENS OF THE UNITED STATES.—In the case of a decedent nonresident not a citizen of the United States—

(A) paragraph (2)(B) shall be applied by substituting "$60,000" for "$1,300,000", and

(B) paragraph (2)(C) shall not apply.

[Sec. 1022(c)]

(c) ADDITIONAL BASIS INCREASE FOR PROPERTY ACQUIRED BY SURVIVING SPOUSE.—

(1) IN GENERAL.—In the case of property to which this subsection applies and which is qualified spousal property, the basis of such property under subsection (a) (as increased under subsection (b)) shall be increased by its spousal property basis increase.

(2) SPOUSAL PROPERTY BASIS INCREASE.—For purposes of this subsection—

(A) IN GENERAL.—The spousal property basis increase for property referred to in paragraph (1) is the portion of the aggregate spousal property basis increase which is allocated to the property pursuant to this section.

(B) AGGREGATE SPOUSAL PROPERTY BASIS INCREASE.—In the case of any estate, the aggregate spousal property basis increase is $3,000,000.

(3) QUALIFIED SPOUSAL PROPERTY.—For purposes of this subsection, the term "qualified spousal property" means—

(A) outright transfer property, and

(B) qualified terminable interest property.

(4) OUTRIGHT TRANSFER PROPERTY.—For purposes of this subsection—

(A) IN GENERAL.—The term "outright transfer property" means any interest in property acquired from the decedent by the decedent's surviving spouse.

(B) EXCEPTION.—Subparagraph (A) shall not apply where, on the lapse of time, on the occurrence of an event or contingency, or on the failure of an event or contingency to occur, an interest passing to the surviving spouse will terminate or fail—

(i) (I) if an interest in such property passes or has passed (for less than an adequate and full consideration in money or money's worth) from the decedent to any person other than such surviving spouse (or the estate of such spouse), and

(II) if by reason of such passing such person (or his heirs or assigns) may possess or enjoy any part of such property after such termination or failure of the interest so passing to the surviving spouse, or

(ii) if such interest is to be acquired for the surviving spouse, pursuant to directions of the decedent, by his executor or by the trustee of a trust.

For purposes of this subparagraph, an interest shall not be considered as an interest which will terminate or fail merely because it is the ownership of a bond, note, or similar contractual obligation, the discharge of which would not have the effect of an annuity for life or for a term.

(C) INTEREST OF SPOUSE CONDITIONAL ON SURVIVAL FOR LIMITED PERIOD.—For purposes of this paragraph, an interest passing to the surviving spouse shall not be considered as an interest which will terminate or fail on the death of such spouse if—

(i) such death will cause a termination or failure of such interest only if it occurs within a period not exceeding 6 months after the decedent's death, or only if it occurs as a result of a common disaster resulting in the death of the decedent and the surviving spouse, or only if it occurs in the case of either such event, and

(ii) such termination or failure does not in fact occur.

(5) QUALIFIED TERMINABLE INTEREST PROPERTY.—For purposes of this subsection—

(A) IN GENERAL.—The term "qualified terminable interest property" means property—

(i) which passes from the decedent, and

(ii) in which the surviving spouse has a qualifying income interest for life.

(B) QUALIFYING INCOME INTEREST FOR LIFE.—The surviving spouse has a qualifying income interest for life if—

(i) the surviving spouse is entitled to all the income from the property, payable annually or at more frequent intervals, or has a usufruct interest for life in the property, and

(ii) no person has a power to appoint any part of the property to any person other than the surviving spouse.

Clause (ii) shall not apply to a power exercisable only at or after the death of the surviving spouse. To the extent provided in regulations, an annuity shall be treated in a manner similar to an income interest in property (regardless of whether the property from which the annuity is payable can be separately identified).

(C) PROPERTY INCLUDES INTEREST THEREIN.—The term "property" includes an interest in property.

(D) SPECIFIC PORTION TREATED AS SEPARATE PROPERTY.—A specific portion of property shall be treated as separate property. For purposes of the preceding sentence, the term "specific portion" only includes a portion determined on a fractional or percentage basis.

[Sec. 1022(d)]

(d) DEFINITIONS AND SPECIAL RULES FOR APPLICATION OF SUBSECTIONS (b) AND (c).—

(1) PROPERTY TO WHICH SUBSECTIONS (b) AND (c) APPLY.—

(A) IN GENERAL.—The basis of property acquired from a decedent may be increased under subsection (b) or (c) only if the property was owned by the decedent at the time of death.

(B) RULES RELATING TO OWNERSHIP.—

(i) JOINTLY HELD PROPERTY.—In the case of property which was owned by the decedent and another person as joint tenants with right of survivorship or tenants by the entirety—

(I) if the only such other person is the surviving spouse, the decedent shall be treated as the owner of only 50 percent of the property,

(II) in any case (to which subclause (I) does not apply) in which the decedent furnished consideration for the acquisition of the property, the decedent shall be treated as the owner to the extent of the portion of the property which is proportionate to such consideration, and

(III) in any case (to which subclause (I) does not apply) in which the property has been acquired by gift, bequest, devise, or inheritance by the decedent and any other person as joint tenants with right of survivorship and their interests are not otherwise specified or fixed by law, the decedent shall be treated as the owner to the extent of the value of a fractional part to be determined by dividing the value of the property by the number of joint tenants with right of survivorship.

(ii) REVOCABLE TRUSTS.—The decedent shall be treated as owning property transferred by the decedent during life to a qualified revocable trust (as defined in section 645(b)(1)).

(iii) POWERS OF APPOINTMENT.—The decedent shall not be treated as owning any property by reason of holding a power of appointment with respect to such property.

(iv) COMMUNITY PROPERTY.—Property which represents the surviving spouse's one-half share of community property held by the decedent and the surviving spouse under the community property laws of any State or possession of the United States or any foreign country shall be treated for purposes of this section as owned by, and acquired from, the decedent if at least one-half of the whole of the community interest in such property is treated as owned by, and acquired from, the decedent without regard to this clause.

(C) PROPERTY ACQUIRED BY DECEDENT BY GIFT WITHIN 3 YEARS OF DEATH.—

(i) IN GENERAL.—Subsections (b) and (c) shall not apply to property acquired by the decedent by gift or by inter vivos transfer for less than adequate and full consideration in money or money's worth during the 3-year period ending on the date of the decedent's death.

(ii) EXCEPTION FOR CERTAIN GIFTS FROM SPOUSE.—Clause (i) shall not apply to property acquired by the decedent from the decedent's spouse unless, during such 3-year period, such spouse acquired the property in whole or in part by gift or by inter vivos transfer for less than adequate and full consideration in money or money's worth.

(D) STOCK OF CERTAIN ENTITIES.—Subsections (b) and (c) shall not apply to—

(i) stock or securities of a foreign personal holding company,

(ii) stock of a DISC or former DISC,

(iii) stock of a foreign investment company, or

(iv) stock of a passive foreign investment company unless such company is a qualified electing fund (as defined in section 1295) with respect to the decedent.

(2) FAIR MARKET VALUE LIMITATION.—The adjustments under subsections (b) and (c) shall not increase the basis of any interest in property acquired from the decedent above its fair market value in the hands of the decedent as of the date of the decedent's death.

(3) ALLOCATION RULES.—

(A) IN GENERAL.—The executor shall allocate the adjustments under subsections (b) and (c) on the return required by section 6018.

(B) CHANGES IN ALLOCATION.—Any allocation made pursuant to subparagraph (A) may be changed only as provided by the Secretary.

(4) INFLATION ADJUSTMENT OF BASIS ADJUSTMENT AMOUNTS.—

(A) IN GENERAL.—In the case of decedents dying in a calendar year after 2010, the $1,300,000, $60,000, and $3,000,000 dollar amounts in subsections (b) and (c)(2)(B) shall each be increased by an amount equal to the product of—

(i) such dollar amount, and

(ii) the cost-of-living adjustment determined under section 1(f)(3) for such calendar year, determined by substituting "2009" for "1992" in subparagraph (B) thereof.

(B) ROUNDING.—If any increase determined under subparagraph (A) is not a multiple of—

(i) $100,000 in the case of the $1,300,000 amount,

(ii) $5,000 in the case of the $60,000 amount, and

(iii) $250,000 in the case of the $3,000,000 amount,

such increase shall be rounded to the next lowest multiple thereof.

[Sec. 1022(e)]

(e) PROPERTY ACQUIRED FROM THE DECEDENT.—For purposes of this section, the following property shall be considered to have been acquired from the decedent:

(1) Property acquired by bequest, devise, or inheritance, or by the decedent's estate from the decedent.

(2) Property transferred by the decedent during his lifetime—

(A) to a qualified revocable trust (as defined in section 645(b)(1)), or

(B) to any other trust with respect to which the decedent reserved the right to make any change in the enjoyment thereof through the exercise of a power to alter, amend, or terminate the trust.

(3) Any other property passing from the decedent by reason of death to the extent that such property passed without consideration.

[Sec. 1022(f)]

(f) COORDINATION WITH SECTION 691.—This section shall not apply to property which constitutes a right to receive an item of income in respect of a decedent under section 691.

[Sec. 1022(g)]

(g) CERTAIN LIABILITIES DISREGARDED.—

(1) IN GENERAL.—In determining whether gain is recognized on the acquisition of property—

(A) from a decedent by a decedent's estate or any beneficiary other than a tax-exempt beneficiary, and

(B) from the decedent's estate by any beneficiary other than a tax-exempt beneficiary,

and in determining the adjusted basis of such property, liabilities in excess of basis shall be disregarded.

(2) TAX-EXEMPT BENEFICIARY.—For purposes of paragraph (1), the term "tax-exempt beneficiary" means—

(A) the United States, any State or political subdivision thereof, any possession of the United States, any Indian tribal government (within the meaning of section 7871), or any agency or instrumentality of any of the foregoing,

(B) an organization (other than a cooperative described in section 521) which is exempt from tax imposed by chapter 1,

(C) any foreign person or entity (within the meaning of section 168(h)(2)), and

(D) to the extent provided in regulations, any person to whom property is transferred for the principal purpose of tax avoidance.

[Sec. 1022(h)]

(h) REGULATIONS.—The Secretary shall prescribe such regulations as may be necessary to carry out the purposes of this section.

P.L. 111-312, §301(c), provides:

(c) SPECIAL ELECTION WITH RESPECT TO ESTATES OF DECEDENTS DYING IN 2010.—Notwithstanding subsection (a), in the case of an estate of a decedent dying after December 31, 2009, and before January 1, 2011, the executor (within the meaning of section 2203 of the Internal Revenue Code of 1986) may elect to apply such Code as though the amendments made by subsection (a) do not apply with respect to chapter 11 of such Code and with respect to property acquired or passing from such decedent (within the meaning of section 1014(b) of such Code). Such election shall be made at such time and in such manner as the Secretary of the Treasury or the Secretary's delegate shall provide. Such an election once made shall be revocable only with the consent of the Secretary of the Treasury or the Secretary's delegate. For purposes of section 2652(a)(1) of such Code, the determination of whether any property is subject to the tax imposed by such chapter 11 shall be made without regard to any election made under this subsection.

P.L. 111-312, §304, provides [but see P.L. 112-240, §101(a)(2)-(3), above]:

SEC. 304. APPLICATION OF EGTRRA SUNSET TO THIS TITLE.

Section 901 of the Economic Growth and Tax Relief Reconciliation Act of 2001 shall apply to the amendments made by this title.

Amendments

• 2001, Economic Growth and Tax Relief Reconciliation Act of 2001 (P.L. 107-16)

P.L. 107-16, §542(a):

Amended part II of subchapter O of chapter 1 by inserting after Code Sec. 1021 a new Code Sec. 1022. **Effective** for estates of decedents dying after 12-31-2009.

P.L. 107-16, §901(a)-(b), as amended by P.L. 111-312, §101(a)(1), provides [but see P.L. 112-240, §101(a)(1) and (3), above]:

SEC. 901. SUNSET OF PROVISIONS OF ACT.

(a) IN GENERAL.—All provisions of, and amendments made by, this Act shall not apply—

(1) to taxable, plan, or limitation years beginning after December 31, 2012, or

(2) in the case of title V, to estates of decedents dying, gifts made, or generation skipping transfers, after December 31, 2012.

(b) APPLICATION OF CERTAIN LAWS.—The Internal Revenue Code of 1986 and the Employee Retirement Income Security Act of 1974 shall be applied and administered to years, estates, gifts, and transfers described in subsection (a) as if the provisions and amendments described in subsection (a) had never been enacted.

[Sec. 1022—Repealed]

Amendments

• 1976, Tax Reform Act of 1976 (P.L. 94-455)

P.L. 94-455, §1901(a)(126):

Repealed Code Sec. 1022. **Effective** with respect to stock or securities acquired from a decedent dying after 10-4-76. Prior to repeal, Sec. 1022 read as follows:

SEC. 1022. INCREASE IN BASIS WITH RESPECT TO CERTAIN FOREIGN PERSONAL HOLDING COMPANY STOCK OR SECURITIES.

(a) GENERAL RULE.—The basis (determined under section 1014(b)(5), relating to basis of stock or securities in a foreign personal holding company) of a share of stock or a security, acquired from a decedent dying after December 31, 1963, of a corporation which was a foreign personal holding company for its most recent taxable year ending before the date of the decedent's death shall be increased by its proportionate share of any Federal estate tax attributable to the net appreciation in value of all of such shares and securities determined as provided in this section.

(b) PROPORTIONATE SHARE.—For purposes of subsection (a), the proportionate share of a share of stock or of a security is that amount which bears the same ratio to the aggregate increase determined under subsection (c)(2) as the appreciation in value of such share or security bears to the aggregate appreciation in value of all such shares and securities having appreciation in value.

(c) SPECIAL RULES AND DEFINITIONS.—For purposes of this section—

(1) FEDERAL ESTATE TAX.—The term "Federal estate tax" means only the tax imposed by section 2001 or 2101, reduced by any credit allowable with respect to a tax on prior transfers by section 2013 or 2102.

(2) FEDERAL ESTATE TAX ATTRIBUTABLE TO NET APPRECIATION IN VALUE.—The Federal estate tax attributable to the net appreciation in value of all shares of stock and securities to which subsection (a) applies is that amount which bears the same ratio to the Federal estate tax as the net appreciation in value of all of such shares and securities bears to the value of the gross estate as determined under chapter 11 (including section 2032, relating to alternate valuation).

(3) NET APPRECIATION.—The net appreciation in value of all shares and securities to which subsection (a) applies is the amount by which the fair market value of all such shares and securities exceeds the adjusted basis of such property in the hands of the decedent.

(4) FAIR MARKET VALUE.—For purposes of this section, the term "fair market value" means fair market value determined under chapter 11 (including section 2032, relating to alternate valuation).

(d) LIMITATIONS.—This section shall not apply to any foreign personal holding company referred to in section 342(a)(2).

* * *

PART III—COMMON NONTAXABLE EXCHANGES

* * *

* * *

[Sec. 1040]

SEC. 1040. TRANSFER OF CERTAIN FARM, ETC., REAL PROPERTY.

[Sec. 1040(a)]

(a) GENERAL RULE.—If the executor of the estate of any decedent transfers to a qualified heir (within the meaning of section 2032A(e)(1) any property with respect to which an election was made under section 2032A, then gain on such transfer shall be recognized to the estate only to the extent that, on the date of such transfer, the fair market value of such property exceeds the value of such property for purposes of chapter 11 (determined without regard to section 2032A).

[Sec. 1040(b)]

(b) SIMILAR RULE FOR CERTAIN TRUSTS.—To the extent provided in regulations prescribed by the Secretary, a rule similar to the rule provided in subsection (a) shall apply where the trustee of a trust (any portion of which is included in the gross estate of the decedent) transfers property with respect to which an election was made under section 2032A.

[Sec. 1040(c)]

(c) BASIS OF PROPERTY ACQUIRED IN TRANSFER DESCRIBED IN SUBSECTION (a) OR (b).—The basis of property acquired in a transfer with respect to which gain realized is not recognized by reason of subsection (a) or (b) shall be the basis of such property immediately before the transfer increased by the amount of the gain recognized to the estate or trust on the transfer.

Amendments

• 2013, American Taxpayer Relief Act of 2012 (P.L. 112-240)

P.L. 112-240, §101(a)(1)-(3), provides:

SEC. 101. PERMANENT EXTENSION AND MODIFICATION OF 2001 TAX RELIEF.

(a) PERMANENT EXTENSION.—

(1) IN GENERAL.—The Economic Growth and Tax Relief Reconciliation Act of 2001 is amended by striking title IX.

(2) CONFORMING AMENDMENT.—The Tax Relief, Unemployment Insurance Reauthorization, and Job Creation Act of 2010 is amended by striking section 304.

(3) EFFECTIVE DATE.—The amendments made by this subsection shall apply to taxable, plan, or limitation years beginning after December 31, 2012, and estates of decedents dying, gifts made, or generation skipping transfers after December 31, 2012.

• 2010, Tax Relief, Unemployment Insurance Reauthorization, and Job Creation Act of 2010 (P.L. 111-312)

P.L. 111-312, §301(a):

Amended Code Sec. 1040 to read as such provision would read if subtitle E of title V of the Economic Growth and Tax Relief Reconciliation Act of 2001 (P.L. 107-16) had never been enacted. **Effective** for estates of decedents dying, and transfers made, after 12-31-2009. For a special rule, see Act Sec. 301(c), below. Prior to amendment by P.L. 111-312, Code Sec. 1040 read as follows:

SEC. 1040. USE OF APPRECIATED CARRYOVER BASIS PROPERTY TO SATISFY PECUNIARY BEQUEST.

(a) IN GENERAL.—If the executor of the estate of any decedent satisfies the right of any person to receive a pecuniary bequest with appreciated property, then gain on such exchange shall be recognized to the estate only to the extent that, on the date of such exchange, the fair market value of such property exceeds such value on the date of death.

(b) SIMILAR RULE FOR CERTAIN TRUSTS.—To the extent provided in regulations prescribed by the Secretary, a rule similar to the rule provided in subsection (a) shall apply where—

(1) by reason of the death of the decedent, a person has a right to receive from a trust a specific dollar amount which is the equivalent of a pecuniary bequest, and

(2) the trustee of a trust satisfies such right with property.

(c) BASIS OF PROPERTY ACQUIRED IN EXCHANGE DESCRIBED IN SUBSECTION (a) OR (b).—The basis of property acquired in an exchange with respect to which gain realized is not recognized by reason of subsection (a) or (b) shall be the basis of such property immediately before the exchange increased by the amount of the gain recognized to the estate or trust on the exchange.

P.L. 111-312, §301(c), provides:

(c) SPECIAL ELECTION WITH RESPECT TO ESTATES OF DECEDENTS DYING IN 2010.—Notwithstanding subsection (a), in the case of an estate of a decedent dying after December 31, 2009, and before January 1, 2011, the executor (within the meaning of section 2203 of the Internal Revenue Code of 1986) may elect to apply such Code as though the amendments made by subsection (a) do not apply with respect to chapter 11 of such Code and with respect to property acquired or passing from such decedent (within the meaning of section 1014(b) of such Code). Such election shall be made at such time and in such manner as the Secretary of the Treasury or the Secretary's delegate shall provide. Such an election once made shall be revocable only with the consent of the Secretary of the Treasury or the Secretary's delegate. For purposes of section 2652(a)(1) of such Code, the determination of whether any property is subject to the tax imposed by such chapter 11 shall be made without regard to any election made under this subsection.

P.L. 111-312, §304, provides [but see P.L. 112-240, §101(a)(2)-(3), above]:

SEC. 304. APPLICATION OF EGTRRA SUNSET TO THIS TITLE.

Section 901 of the Economic Growth and Tax Relief Reconciliation Act of 2001 shall apply to the amendments made by this title.

• 2001, Economic Growth and Tax Relief Reconciliation Act of 2001 (P.L. 107-16)

P.L. 107-16, §542(d)(1):

Amended Code Sec. 1040. **Effective** for estates of decedents dying after 12-31-2009. Prior to amendment, Code Sec. 1040 read as follows:

SEC. 1040. TRANSFER OF CERTAIN FARM, ETC., REAL PROPERTY.

[Sec. 1040(a)]

(a) GENERAL RULE.—If the executor of the estate of any decedent transfers to a qualified heir (within the meaning of section 2032A(e)(1) any property with respect to which an election was made under section 2032A, then gain on such transfer shall be recognized to the estate only to the extent that, on the date of such transfer, the fair market value of such property exceeds the value of such property for purposes of chapter 11 (determined without regard to section 2032A).

Amendments

• 1983, Technical Corrections Act of 1982 (P.L. 97-448)

P.L. 97-448, §104(b)(3)(A):

Amended Code Sec. 1040(a) by striking out "such exchange" and inserting in lieu thereof "such transfer". **Effective** as if included in the provision of P.L. 97-34 to which it relates.

• 1981, Economic Recovery Tax Act of 1981 (P.L. 97-34)

P.L. 97-34, §421(j)(2)(B):

Amended Code Sec. 1040(a). **Effective**, generally, for estates of decedents dying after 12-31-76. Prior to amendment, Code Sec. 1040(a) read as follows:

SEC. 1040. USE OF FARM, ETC., REAL PROPERTY TO SATISFY PECUNIARY BEQUEST.

(a) GENERAL RULE.—If the executor of the estate of any decedent satisfies the right of a qualified heir (within the meaning of section 2032A(e)(1)) to receive a pecuniary bequest with property with respect to which an election was made under section 2032A, then gain on such exchange shall be recognized to the estate only to the extent that, on the date of such exchange, the fair market value of such property exceeds the value of such property for purposes of chapter 11 (determined without regard to section 2032A).

P.L. 97-34, §421(k)(5), as amended by P.L. 97-448, §104(b)(4), provides:

(5) CERTAIN AMENDMENTS MADE RETROACTIVE TO 1976.—

(A) IN GENERAL.—The amendments made by subsections (b)(1), (j)(1), and (j)(2) and the provisions of subparagraph (A) of section 2032A(c)(7) of the Internal Revenue Code of 1954 (as added by subsection (c)(2)) shall apply with respect to the estates of decedents dying after December 31, 1976.

(B) TIMELY ELECTION REQUIRED.—Subparagraph (A) shall only apply in the case of an estate if a timely election under section 2032A was made with respect to such estate. If the estate of any decedent would not qualify under section 2032A of the Internal Revenue Code of 1954 but for the amendments described in subparagraph (A) and the time for making an election under section 2032A with respect to such estate would (but for this sentence) expire after July 28, 1980, the time for making such election shall not expire before the close of February 16, 1982.

(C) REINSTATEMENT OF ELECTIONS.—If any election under section 2032A was revoked before the date of the enactment of this Act, such election may be reinstated at any time before February 17, 1982.

(D) STATUTE OF LIMITATIONS.—If on the date of the enactment of this Act (or at any time before February 17, 1982) the making of a credit or refund of any overpayment of tax resulting from the amendments described in subparagraph (A) is barred by any law or rule of law, such credit or refund shall nevertheless be made if claim therefor is made before February 17, 1982.

• 1980, Crude Oil Windfall Profit Tax Act of 1980 (P.L. 96-223)

P.L. 96-223, §401(c)(2)(A):

Amended Code Sec. 1040(a). **Effective** with respect to decedents dying after 12-31-76. However, see the amendment note for P.L. 96-223, Act Sec. 401(a), that follows Code Sec. 1014(d) for the text of Act Sec. 401(d) that authorizes the election of the carryover basis rules in the case of a decedent dying after 12-31-76 and before 11-7-78. Prior to amendment, Code Sec. 1040(a) read:

SEC. 1040. USE OF CERTAIN APPRECIATED CARRYOVER BASIS PROPERTY TO SATISFY PECUNIARY BEQUEST.

(a) GENERAL RULE.—If the executor of the estate of any decedent satisfies the right of any person to receive a pecuniary bequest with appreciated carryover basis property (as defined in section 1023(f)(5)), then gain on such exchange shall be recognized to the estate only to the extent that, on the date of such exchange, the fair market value of such property exceeds the value of such property for purposes of chapter 11 (determined without regard to section 2032A).

• 1980, Technical Corrections Act of 1979 (P.L. 96-222)

P.L. 96-222, §105(a)(5)(B), provides:

(B) PERIOD FOR WHICH SECTION 1040 APPLIES.—Notwithstanding section 515 of the Revenue Act of 1978, section 1040 of the Internal Revenue Code of 1954 (as amended by subparagraph (A)) shall apply with respect to the estates of decedents dying after December 31, 1976.

• 1978, Revenue Act of 1978 (P.L. 95-600)

P.L. 95-600, §702(d)(3), (6):

Amended Code Sec. 1040(a) by adding "(determined without regard to section 2032A)" after "chapter 11". **Effective** for estates of decedents dying after 12-31-76.

• 1976, Tax Reform Act of 1976 (P.L. 94-455)

P.L. 94-455, §2005(b), (f)(1):

Added the heading of Code Sec. 1040 and Code Sec. 1040(a). **Effective** for decedents dying after 12-31-79, as amended by P.L. 95-600, Sec. 515(6).

[Sec. 1040(b)]

(b) SIMILAR RULE FOR CERTAIN TRUSTS.—To the extent provided in regulations prescribed by the Secretary, a rule similar to the rule provided in subsection (a) shall apply where the trustee of a trust (any portion of which is included in the gross estate of the decedent) transfers property with respect to which an election was made under section 2032A.

Amendments

• 1981, Economic Recovery Tax Act of 1981 (P.L. 97-34)

P.L. 97-34, §421(j)(2)(B):

Amended Code Sec. 1040(b). **Effective**, generally, with respect to decedents dying after 12-31-81. For special rules, see the amendment note following Code Sec. 1040(a) at §421(j)(2)(B). Prior to amendment, Code Sec. 1040(b) read as follows:

(b) SIMILAR RULE FOR CERTAIN TRUSTS.—To the extent provided in regulations prescribed by the Secretary, a rule similar to the rule provided in subsection (a) shall apply where—

(1) by reason of the death of the decedent, a qualified heir has a right to receive from a trust a specific dollar amount which is the equivalent of a pecuniary bequest, and

(2) the trustee of the trust satisfies such right with property with respect to which an election was made under section 2032A.

• 1980, Crude Oil Windfall Profit Tax Act of 1980 (P.L. 96-223)

P.L. 96-223, §401(c)(2)(A):

Amended Code Sec. 1040(b). **Effective** with respect to decedents dying after 12-31-76. However, see the amendment note for P.L. 96-223, Act Sec. 401(a), that follows Code Sec. 1014(d) for the text of Act Sec. 401(d) that authorizes the election of the carryover basis rules in the case of a decedent dying after 12-31-76 and before 11-7-78. Prior to amendment Code Sec. 1040(b) read:

(b) SIMILAR RULE FOR CERTAIN TRUSTS.—To the extent provided in regulations prescribed by the Secretary, a rule similar to the rule provided in subsection (a) shall apply where—

(1) by reason of the death of the decedent, a person has a right to receive from a trust a specific dollar amount which is the equivalent of a pecuniary bequest, and

(2) the trustee of the trust satisfies such right with carryover basis property to which section 1023 applies.

• 1976, Tax Reform Act of 1976 (P.L. 94-455)

P.L. 94-455, §2005(b), (f)(1):

Added Code Sec. 1040(b). **Effective** as amended by P.L. 95-600, Sec. 515(6), for decedents dying after 12-31-79.

[Sec. 1040(c)]

(c) BASIS OF PROPERTY ACQUIRED IN TRANSFER DESCRIBED IN SUBSECTION (a) OR (b).—The basis of property acquired in a transfer with respect to which gain realized is not recognized by reason of subsection (a) or (b) shall be the basis of such property immediately before the transfer increased by the amount of the gain recognized to the estate or trust on the transfer.

Amendments

• 1983, Technical Corrections Act of 1982 (P.L. 97-448)

P.L. 97-448, §104(b)(3)(B):

Amended Code Sec. 1040(c) by striking out "an exchange" and inserting in lieu, thereof "a transfer", by striking out "the exchange" each place it appears and inserting in lieu thereof "the transfer", and by striking out "EXCHANGE" in the subsection hearing and inserting in lieu thereof "TRANSFER". **Effective** as if included in the provision of P.L. 97-34 to which it relates.

• 1980, Crude Oil Windfall Profit Tax Act of 1980 (P.L. 96-223)

P.L. 96-223, §401(c)(2)(A):

Amended Code Sec. 1040(c) and repealed Code Sec. 1040(d). **Effective** with respect to decedents dying after 12-31-76. However, see the amendment note for P.L. 96-223, Act Sec. 401(a), that follows Code Sec. 1014(d) for the text of Act Sec. 401(d) that authorizes the election of the carryover basis rules in the case of a decedent dying after 12-31-76 and before 11-7-78. Prior to amendment, Code Sec. 1040(c) and (d) read:

(c) BASIS OF PROPERTY ACQUIRED IN EXCHANGE DESCRIBED IN SUBSECTION (a) OR (b).—The basis of property acquired in an exchange with respect to which gain realized is not recognized by reason of subsection (a) or (b) shall be the basis of such property immediately before the exchange, increased by the amount of the gain recognized to the estate or trust on the exchange.

(d) APPLICATION TO SECTION 2032A PROPERTY.—For purposes of this section, references to carryover basis property shall be treated as including a reference to property the valuation of which is determined under section 2032A.

• 1980, Technical Corrections Act of 1979 (P.L. 96-222)

P.L. 96-222, §105(a)(5):

Added Code Sec. 1040(d). **Effective** for estates of decedents dying after 12-31-76.

• 1976, Tax Reform Act of 1976 (P.L. 94-455)

P.L. 94-455, §2005(b), (f)(1):

Added Code Sec. 1040(c). **Effective** as amended by P.L. 95-600, Sec. 515(6), for decedents dying after 12-31-79.

P.L. 107-16, §901(a)-(b), as amended by P.L. 111-312, §101(a)(1), provides [but see P.L. 112-240, §101(a)(1) and (3), above]:

SEC. 901. SUNSET OF PROVISIONS OF ACT.

(a) IN GENERAL.—All provisions of, and amendments made by, this Act shall not apply—

(1) to taxable, plan, or limitation years beginning after December 31, 2012, or

(2) in the case of title V, to estates of decedents dying, gifts made, or generation skipping transfers, after December 31, 2012.

(b) APPLICATION OF CERTAIN LAWS.—The Internal Revenue Code of 1986 and the Employee Retirement Income Security Act of 1974 shall be applied and administered to years, estates, gifts, and transfers described in subsection (a) as if the provisions and amendments described in subsection (a) had never been enacted.

[Sec. 1041]

SEC. 1041. TRANSFERS OF PROPERTY BETWEEN SPOUSES OR INCIDENT TO DIVORCE.

[Sec. 1041(a)]

(a) GENERAL RULE.—No gain or loss shall be recognized on a transfer of property from an individual to (or in trust for the benefit of)—

(1) a spouse, or

(2) a former spouse, but only if the transfer is incident to the divorce.

[Sec. 1041(b)]

(b) TRANSFER TREATED AS GIFT; TRANSFEREE HAS TRANSFEROR'S BASIS.—In the case of any transfer of property described in subsection (a)—

(1) for purposes of this subtitle, the property shall be treated as acquired by the transferee by gift, and

(2) the basis of the transferee in the property shall be the adjusted basis of the transferor.

[Sec. 1041(c)]

(c) INCIDENT TO DIVORCE.—For purposes of subsection (a)(2), a transfer of property is incident to the divorce if such transfer—

(1) occurs within 1 year after the date on which the marriage ceases, or

(2) is related to the cessation of the marriage.

[Sec. 1041(d)]

(d) SPECIAL RULE WHERE SPOUSE IS NONRESIDENT ALIEN.—Subsection (a) shall not apply if the spouse (or former spouse) of the individual making the transfer is a nonresident alien.

Amendments

• 1988, Technical and Miscellaneous Revenue Act of 1988 (P.L. 100-647)

P.L. 100-647, §1018(l)(3)(A)-(B):

Amended Code Sec. 1041(d) by striking out "Paragraph (1) of subsection (a)" and inserting in lieu thereof "Subsection (a)"; and by striking out "the spouse" and inserting in lieu thereof "the spouse (or former spouse)". **Effective** with respect to transfers after 6-21-88.

[Sec. 1041(e)]

(e) TRANSFERS IN TRUST WHERE LIABILITY EXCEEDS BASIS.—Subsection (a) shall not apply to the transfer of property in trust to the extent that—

(1) the sum of the amount of the liabilities assumed, plus the amount of the liabilities to which the property is subject, exceeds

(2) the total of the adjusted basis of the property transferred.

Proper adjustment shall be made under subsection (b) in the basis of the transferee in such property to take into account gain recognized by reason of the preceding sentence.

Amendments

• 1986, Tax Reform Act of 1986 (P.L. 99-514)

P.L. 99-514, §1842(b):

Amended Code Sec. 1041 by adding at the end thereof new subsection (e). **Effective** as if included in the provision of P.L. 98-369 to which it relates.

• 1984, Deficit Reduction Act of 1984 (P.L. 98-369)

P.L. 98-369, §421(a):

Amended Part III of subchapter O of chapter 1 by adding at the end thereof a new section 1041. **Effective** for transfers after 7-18-84 in tax years ending after such date. Special rules appear in Act Sec. 421(d)(2)-(4), below.

P.L. 98-369, §421(d)(2)-(4), provides:

(2) Election To Have Amendments Apply To Transfers After 1983.—If both spouses or former spouses make an election under this paragraph, the amendments made by this section shall apply to all transfers made by such spouses (or former spouses) after December 31, 1983.

(3) Exception for Transfers Pursuant to Existing Decrees.—Except in the case of an election under paragraph (2), the amendments made by this section shall not apply to transfers under any instrument in effect on or before the date of the enactment of this Act unless both spouses (or former spouses) elect to have such amendments apply to transfers under such instrument.

(4) Election.—Any election under paragraph (2) or (3) shall be made in such manner, at such time, and subject to such conditions, as the Secretary of the Treasury or his delegate may by regulations prescribe.

* * *

Subchapter P—Capital Gains and Losses

* * *

PART III—GENERAL RULES FOR DETERMINING CAPITAL GAINS AND LOSSES

* * *

[Sec. 1221]

SEC. 1221. CAPITAL ASSET DEFINED.

[Sec. 1221(a)]

(a) IN GENERAL.—For purposes of this subtitle, the term "capital asset" means property held by the taxpayer (whether or not connected with his trade or business), but does not include—

(1) stock in trade of the taxpayer or other property of a kind which would properly be included in the inventory of the taxpayer if on hand at the close of the taxable year, or property held by the taxpayer primarily for sale to customers in the ordinary course of his trade or business;

(2) property, used in his trade or business, of a character which is subject to the allowance for depreciation provided in section 167, or real property used in his trade or business;

(3) a patent, invention, model or design (whether or not patented), a secret formula or process, a copyright, a literary, musical, or artistic composition, a letter or memorandum, or similar property, held by—

(A) a taxpayer whose personal efforts created such property,

(B) in the case of a letter, memorandum, or similar property, a taxpayer for whom such property was prepared or produced, or

(C) a taxpayer in whose hands the basis of such property is determined, for purposes of determining gain from a sale or exchange, in whole or part by reference to the basis of such property in the hands of a taxpayer described in subparagraph (A) or (B);

(4) accounts or notes receivable acquired in the ordinary course of trade or business for services rendered or from the sale of property described in paragraph (1);

(5) a publication of the United States Government (including the Congressional Record) which is received from the United States Government or any agency thereof, other than by purchase at the price at which it is offered for sale to the public, and which is held by—

(A) a taxpayer who so received such publication, or

(B) a taxpayer in whose hands the basis of such publication is determined, for purposes of determining gain from a sale or exchange, in whole or in part by reference to the basis of such publication in the hands of a taxpayer described in subparagraph (A);

(6) any commodities derivative financial instrument held by a commodities derivatives dealer, unless—

(A) it is established to the satisfaction of the Secretary that such instrument has no connection to the activities of such dealer as a dealer, and

(B) such instrument is clearly identified in such dealer's records as being described in subparagraph (A) before the close of the day on which it was acquired, originated, or entered into (or such other time as the Secretary may by regulations prescribe);

(7) any hedging transaction which is clearly identified as such before the close of the day on which it was acquired, originated, or entered into (or such other time as the Secretary may by regulations prescribe); or

(8) supplies of a type regularly used or consumed by the taxpayer in the ordinary course of a trade or business of the taxpayer.

Amendments

• 2017, Tax Cuts and Jobs Act (P.L. 115-97)

P.L. 115-97, §13314(a):

Amended Code Sec. 1221(a)(3) by inserting "a patent, invention, model or design (whether or not patented), a secret formula or process," before "a copyright". **Effective** for dispositions after 12-31-2017.

• 2013, American Taxpayer Relief Act of 2012 (P.L. 112-240)

P.L. 112-240, §101(a)(1)-(3), provides:

SEC. 101. PERMANENT EXTENSION AND MODIFICATION OF 2001 TAX RELIEF.

(a) PERMANENT EXTENSION.—

(1) IN GENERAL.—The Economic Growth and Tax Relief Reconciliation Act of 2001 is amended by striking title IX.

(2) CONFORMING AMENDMENT.—The Tax Relief, Unemployment Insurance Reauthorization, and Job Creation Act of 2010 is amended by striking section 304.

(3) EFFECTIVE DATE.—The amendments made by this subsection shall apply to taxable, plan, or limitation years beginning after December 31, 2012, and estates of decedents dying, gifts made, or generation skipping transfers after December 31, 2012.

• 2010, Tax Relief, Unemployment Insurance Reauthorization, and Job Creation Act of 2010 (P.L. 111-312)

P.L. 111-312, §301(a):

Amended Code Sec. 1221(a)(3)(C) to read as such provision would read if subtitle E of title V of the Economic Growth and Tax Relief Reconciliation Act of 2001 (P.L. 107-16) had never been enacted. **Effective** for estates of decedents dying, and transfers made, after 12-31-2009. For a special rule, see Act Sec. 301(c), below.

P.L. 111-312, §301(c), provides:

(c) SPECIAL ELECTION WITH RESPECT TO ESTATES OF DECEDENTS DYING IN 2010.—Notwithstanding subsection (a), in the case of an estate of a decedent dying after December 31, 2009, and before January 1, 2011, the executor (within the meaning of section 2203 of the Internal Revenue Code of 1986) may elect to apply such Code as though the amendments made by subsection (a) do not apply with respect to chapter 11 of such Code and with respect to property acquired or passing from such decedent (within the meaning of section 1014(b) of such Code). Such election shall be made at such time and in such manner as the Secretary of the Treasury or the Secretary's delegate shall provide. Such an election once made shall be revocable only with the consent of the Secretary of the Treasury or the Secretary's delegate. For purposes of section 2652(a)(1) of such Code, the determination of whether any property is subject to the tax imposed by such chapter 11 shall be made without regard to any election made under this subsection.

P.L. 111-312, §304, provides [but see P.L. 112-240, §101(a)(2)-(3), above]:

SEC. 304. APPLICATION OF EGTRRA SUNSET TO THIS TITLE.

Section 901 of the Economic Growth and Tax Relief Reconciliation Act of 2001 shall apply to the amendments made by this title.

• 2001, Economic Growth and Tax Relief Reconciliation Act of 2001 (P.L. 107-16)

P.L. 107-16, §542(e)(2)(A):

Amended Code Sec. 1221(a)(3)(C) by inserting "(other than by reason of section 1022)" after "is determined". **Effective** for estates of decedents dying after 12-31-2009.

P.L. 107-16, §901(a)-(b), as amended by P.L. 111-312, §101(a)(1), provides [but see P.L. 112-240, §101(a)(1) and (3), above]:

SEC. 901. SUNSET OF PROVISIONS OF ACT.

(a) IN GENERAL.—All provisions of, and amendments made by, this Act shall not apply—

(1) to taxable, plan, or limitation years beginning after December 31, 2012, or

(2) in the case of title V, to estates of decedents dying, gifts made, or generation skipping transfers, after December 31, 2012.

(b) APPLICATION OF CERTAIN LAWS.—The Internal Revenue Code of 1986 and the Employee Retirement Income Security Act of 1974 shall be applied and administered to years, estates, gifts, and transfers described in subsection (a) as if the provisions and amendments described in subsection (a) had never been enacted.

• 1999, Tax Relief Extension Act of 1999 (P.L. 106-170)

P.L. 106-170, §532(a)(1)-(3):

Amended Code Sec. 1221 by striking "For purposes" and inserting "(a) IN GENERAL.—For purposes", by striking the period at the end of paragraph (5) and inserting a semicolon, and by adding at the end new paragraphs (6), (7) and (8). **Effective** for any instrument held, acquired, or entered into, any transaction entered into, and supplies held or acquired on or after 12-17-99.

* * *

ESTATE TAX

TABLE OF CONTENTS

SUBTITLE B—ESTATE AND GIFT TAXES

Chapter 11—Estate Tax

SUBCHAPTER A. ESTATES OF CITIZENS OR RESIDENTS

PART I—TAX IMPOSED

PART II—CREDITS AGAINST TAX

PART III—GROSS ESTATE

PART IV—TAXABLE ESTATE

SUBCHAPTER B. ESTATES OF NONRESIDENTS NOT CITIZENS

SUBCHAPTER C. MISCELLANEOUS

SUBTITLE D—MISCELLANEOUS EXCISE TAXES

[Selected Provisions]

Chapter 43—Qualified Pension, Etc., Plans

SUBTITLE B—ESTATE AND GIFT TAXES

CHAPTER 11—ESTATE TAX

Subchapter A—Estates of Citizens or Residents

PART I—TAX IMPOSED

[Sec. 2001]

SEC. 2001. IMPOSITION AND RATE OF TAX.

[Sec. 2001(a)]

(a) IMPOSITION.—A tax is hereby imposed on the transfer of the taxable estate of every decedent who is a citizen or resident of the United States.

[Sec. 2001(b)]

(b) COMPUTATION OF TAX.—The tax imposed by this section shall be the amount equal to the excess (if any) of—

(1) a tentative tax computed under subsection (c) on the sum of—

(A) the amount of the taxable estate, and

(B) the amount of the adjusted taxable gifts, over

(2) the aggregate amount of tax which would have been payable under chapter 12 with respect to gifts made by the decedent after December 31, 1976, if the modifications described in subsection (g) had been applicable at the time of such gifts.

For purposes of paragraph (1)(B), the term "adjusted taxable gifts" means the total amount of the taxable gifts (within the meaning of section 2503) made by the decedent after December 31, 1976, other than gifts which are includible in the gross estate of the decedent.

Amendments

• 2013, American Taxpayer Relief Act of 2012 (P.L. 112-240)

P.L. 112-240, §101(a)(1)-(3), provides:

SEC. 101. PERMANENT EXTENSION AND MODIFICATION OF 2001 TAX RELIEF.

(a) PERMANENT EXTENSION.—

(1) IN GENERAL.—The Economic Growth and Tax Relief Reconciliation Act of 2001 is amended by striking title IX.

(2) CONFORMING AMENDMENT.—The Tax Relief, Unemployment Insurance Reauthorization, and Job Creation Act of 2010 is amended by striking section 304.

(3) EFFECTIVE DATE.—The amendments made by this subsection shall apply to taxable, plan, or limitation years beginning after December 31, 2012, and estates of decedents dying, gifts made, or generation skipping transfers after December 31, 2012.

• 2010, Tax Relief, Unemployment Insurance Reauthorization, and Job Creation Act of 2010 (P.L. 111-312)

P.L. 111-312, §302(d)(1)(A):

Amended Code Sec. 2001(b)(2) by striking "if the provisions of subsection (c) (as in effect at the decedent's death)" and inserting "if the modifications described in subsection (g)". **Effective** for estates of decedents dying, generation-skipping transfers, and gifts made, after 12-31-2009.

P.L. 111-312, §304, provides [but see P.L. 112-240, §101(a)(2)-(3), above]:

SEC. 304. APPLICATION OF EGTRRA SUNSET TO THIS TITLE.

Section 901 of the Economic Growth and Tax Relief Reconciliation Act of 2001 shall apply to the amendments made by this title.

• 2001, Economic Growth and Tax Relief Reconciliation Act of 2001 (P.L. 107-16)

P.L. 107-16, §901(a)-(b), as amended by P.L. 111-312, §101(a)(1), provides [but see P.L. 112-240, §101(a)(1) and (3), above]:

SEC. 901. SUNSET OF PROVISIONS OF ACT.

(a) IN GENERAL.—All provisions of, and amendments made by, this Act shall not apply—

(1) to taxable, plan, or limitation years beginning after December 31, 2012, or

(2) in the case of title V, to estates of decedents dying, gifts made, or generation skipping transfers, after December 31, 2012.

(b) APPLICATION OF CERTAIN LAWS.—The Internal Revenue Code of 1986 and the Employee Retirement Income Security Act of 1974 shall be applied and administered to years, estates, gifts, and transfers described in subsection (a) as if the provisions and amendments described in subsection (a) had never been enacted.

• 1987, Revenue Act of 1987 (P.L. 100-203)

P.L. 100-203, §10401(b)(2)(A)(i)-(ii):

Amended Code Sec. 2001(b) by striking out "in accordance with the rate schedule set forth in subsection (c)" in paragraph (1) and inserting in lieu thereof "under subsection (c)", and by striking out "the rate schedule set forth in subsection (c) (as in effect at the decedent's death)" in paragraph (2) and inserting in lieu thereof "the provisions of subsection (c) (as in effect at the decedent's death)". **Effective** in the case of decedents dying, and gifts made, after 12-31-87.

[Sec. 2001(c)]

(c) RATE SCHEDULE.—

If the amount with respect to which the tentative tax to be computed is:	*The tentative tax is:*
Not over $10,000	18 percent of such amount.
Over $10,000 but not over $20,000	$1,800, plus 20 percent of the excess of such amount over $10,000.
Over $20,000 but not over $40,000	$3,800, plus 22 percent of the excess of such amount over $20,000.
Over $40,000 but not over $60,000	$8,200, plus 24 percent of the excess of such amount over $40,000.
Over $60,000 but not over $80,000	$13,000, plus 26 percent of the excess of such amount over $60,000.
Over $80,000 but not over $100,000	$18,200, plus 28 percent of the excess of such amount over $80,000.
Over $100,000 but not over $150,000	$23,800, plus 30 percent of the excess of such amount over $100,000.
Over $150,000 but not over $250,000	$38,800, plus 32 percent of the excess of such amount over $150,000.
Over $250,000 but not over $500,000	$70,800, plus 34 percent of the excess of such amount over $250,000.
Over $500,000 but not over $750,000	$155,800, plus 37 percent of the excess of such amount over $500,000.
Over $750,000 but not over $1,000,000	$248,300, plus 39 percent of the excess of such amount over $750,000.
Over $1,000,000	$345,800, plus 40 percent of the excess of such amount over $1,000,000.

Amendments

• 2013, American Taxpayer Relief Act of 2012 (P.L. 112-240)

P.L. 112-240, §101(a)(1)-(3), provides:

SEC. 101. PERMANENT EXTENSION AND MODIFICATION OF 2001 TAX RELIEF.

(a) PERMANENT EXTENSION.—

(1) IN GENERAL.—The Economic Growth and Tax Relief Reconciliation Act of 2001 is amended by striking title IX.

(2) CONFORMING AMENDMENT.—The Tax Relief, Unemployment Insurance Reauthorization, and Job Creation Act of 2010 is amended by striking section 304.

(3) EFFECTIVE DATE.—The amendments made by this subsection shall apply to taxable, plan, or limitation years beginning after December 31, 2012, and estates of decedents dying, gifts made, or generation skipping transfers after December 31, 2012.

P.L. 112-240, §101(c)(1):

Amended the table contained in Code Sec. 2001(c), as amended by section 302(a)(2) of the Tax Relief, Unemployment Insurance Reauthorization, and Job Creation Act of 2010 (P.L. 111-312), by striking "Over $500,000" and all that follows and inserting three new table entries. **Effective** for estates of decedents dying, generation-skipping transfers, and gifts made, after 12-31-2012. Prior to being stricken, "Over $500,000" and all that followed read as follows:

Over $500,000	$155,800 plus 35 percent of the excess of such amount over $500,000.

• 2010, Tax Relief, Unemployment Insurance Reauthorization, and Job Creation Act of 2010 (P.L. 111-312)

P.L. 111-312, §302(a)(2)(A)-(C):

Amended Code Sec. 2001(c) by striking "Over $500,000" and all that follows in the table contained in paragraph (1) and inserting a new table row, by striking "(1) IN GENERAL.—" before the table, and by striking paragraph (2). **Effective** for estates of decedents dying, generation-skipping transfers, and gifts made, after 12-31-2009. Prior to amendment, Code Sec. 2001(c)(1) and (2) read as follows:

(1) IN GENERAL.—

If the amount with respect to which the tentative tax to be computed is:	*The tentative tax is:*
Not over $10,000	18 percent of such amount.
Over $10,000 but not over $20,000	$1,800, plus 20 percent of the excess of such amount over $10,000.
Over $20,000 but not over $40,000	$3,800, plus 22 percent of the excess of such amount over $20,000.
Over $40,000 but not over $60,000	$8,200, plus 24 percent of the excess of such amount over $40,000.

If the amount with respect to which the tentative tax to be computed is:	*The tentative tax is:*
Over $60,000 but not over $80,000	$13,000, plus 26 percent of the excess of such amount over $60,000.
Over $80,000 but not over $100,000	$18,200, plus 28 percent of the excess of such amount over $80,000.
Over $100,000 but not over $150,000	$23,800, plus 30 percent of the excess of such amount over $100,000.
Over $150,000 but not over $250,000	$38,800, plus 32 percent of the excess of such amount over $150,000.
Over $250,000 but not over $500,000	$70,800, plus 34 percent of the excess of such amount over $250,000.
Over $500,000	$155,800, plus 35 percent of the excess of such amount over $500,000.
Over $500,000 but not over $750,000	$155,800, plus 37 percent of the excess of such amount over $500,000.
Over $750,000 but not over $1,000,000	$248,300, plus 39 percent of the excess of such amount over $750,000.
Over $1,000,000 but not over $1,250,000	$345,800, plus 41 percent of the excess of such amount over $1,000,000.
Over $1,250,000 but not over $1,500,000	$448,300, plus 43 percent of the excess of such amount over $1,250,000.
Over $1,500,000 but not over $2,000,000	$555,800, plus 45 percent of the excess of such amount over $1,500,000.
Over $2,000,000 but not over $2,500,000	$780,800, plus 49 percent of the excess of such amount over $2,000,000.
Over $2,500,000	$1,025,800, plus 50% of the excess over $2,500,000.

(2) PHASEDOWN OF MAXIMUM RATE OF TAX.—

(A) IN GENERAL.—In the case of estates of decedents dying, and gifts made, in calendar years after 2002 and before 2010, the tentative tax under this subsection shall be determined by using a table prescribed by the Secretary (in lieu of using the table contained in paragraph (1)) which is the same as such table; except that—

(i) the maximum rate of tax for any calendar year shall be determined in the table under subparagraph (B), and

(ii) the brackets and the amounts setting forth the tax shall be adjusted to the extent necessary to reflect the adjustments under subparagraph (A).

(B) MAXIMUM RATE.—

In calendar year:	*The maximum rate is:*
2003	49 percent
2004	48 percent
2005	47 percent
2006	46 percent
2007, 2008, and 2009	45 percent.

P.L. 111-312, §304, provides [but see P.L. 112-240, §101(a)(2)-(3), above]:

SEC. 304. APPLICATION OF EGTRRA SUNSET TO THIS TITLE.

Section 901 of the Economic Growth and Tax Relief Reconciliation Act of 2001 shall apply to the amendments made by this title.

• 2001, Economic Growth and Tax Relief Reconciliation Act of 2001 (P.L. 107-16)

P.L. 107-16, §511(a):

Amended the table contained in Code Sec. 2001(c)(1) by striking the two highest brackets and inserting a new bracket. **Effective** for estates of decedents dying, and gifts made, after 12-31-2001. Prior to amendment, the two highest brackets in the table read as follows:

Over $2,500,000 but not over $3,000,000	$1,025,800, plus 53% of the excess over $2,500,000.
Over $3,000,000	$1,290,800, plus 55% of the excess over $3,000,000

P.L. 107-16, §511(b):

Amended Code Sec. 2001(c) by striking paragraph (2). **Effective** for estates of decedents dying, and gifts made, after 12-31-2001. Prior to being stricken, Code Sec. 2001(c)(2) read as follows:

(1) (2) PHASEOUT OF GRADUATED RATES AND UNIFIED CREDIT.—The tentative tax determined under paragraph (1) shall be increased by an amount equal to 5 percent of so much of the amount (with respect to which the tentative tax is to be computed) as exceeds $10,000,000 but does not exceed the amount at which the average tax rate under this section is 55 percent.

P.L. 107-16, §511(c):

Amended Code Sec. 2001(c), as amended by Act Sec. 511(b), by adding at the end a new paragraph (2). **Effective** for estates of decedents dying, and gifts made, after 12-31-2002.

P.L. 107-16, §901(a)-(b), as amended by P.L. 111-312, §101(a)(1), provides [but see P.L. 112-240, §101(a)(1) and (3), above]:

SEC. 901. SUNSET OF PROVISIONS OF ACT.

(a) IN GENERAL.—All provisions of, and amendments made by, this Act shall not apply—

(1) to taxable, plan, or limitation years beginning after December 31, 2012, or

(2) in the case of title V, to estates of decedents dying, gifts made, or generation skipping transfers, after December 31, 2012.

(b) APPLICATION OF CERTAIN LAWS.—The Internal Revenue Code of 1986 and the Employee Retirement Income Security Act of 1974 shall be applied and administered to years, estates, gifts, and transfers described in subsection (a) as if the provisions and amendments described in subsection (a) had never been enacted.

• 1997, Taxpayer Relief Act of 1997 (P.L. 105-34)

P.L. 105-34, §501(a)(1)(D):

Amended Code Sec. 2001(c)(2) by striking "$21,040,000" and inserting "the amount at which the average tax rate under this section is 55 percent". **Effective** for the estates of decedents dying, and gifts made, after 12-31-97.

• 1993, Omnibus Budget Reconciliation Act of 1993 (P.L. 103-66)

P.L. 103-66, §13208(a):

Amended Code Sec. 2001(c)(1) by striking the last item and inserting two new items. **Effective** in the case of decedents dying and gifts made after 12-31-92. Prior to amendment, the last item in Code Sec. 2001(c)(1) read as follows:

If the amount with respect to which the tentative tax to be computed is:	The tentative tax is:
Over $2,500,000	$1,025,800, plus 50% of the excess of such amount over $2,500,000.

P.L. 103-66, §13208(b)(1):

Amended Code Sec. 2001(c) by striking paragraph (2) and redesignating paragraph (3) as paragraph (2). **Effective** in the case of decedents dying and gifts made after 12-31-92. Prior to being stricken, Code Sec. 2001(c)(2) read as follows:

(2) PHASE-IN OF 50 PERCENT MAXIMUM RATE.—

(A) IN GENERAL.—In the case of decedents dying, and gifts made, before 1993, there shall be substituted for the last item in the schedule contained in paragraph (1) the items determined under this paragraph.

(B) FOR 1982.—In the case of decedents dying, and gifts made, in 1982, the substitution under this paragraph shall be as follows:

If the amount with respect to which the tentative tax to be computed is:	The tentative tax is:
Over $2,500,000 But not over $3,000,000	$1,025,800, plus 53% of the excess over $2,500,000.
Over $3,000,000 But not over $3,500,000	$1,290,800, plus 57% of the excess over $3,000,000.
Over $3,500,000 But not over $4,000,000	$1,575,800, plus 61% of the excess over $3,500,000.
Over $4,000,000	$1,880,800, plus 65% of the excess over $4,000,000.

(C) FOR 1983.—In the case of decedents dying, and gifts made, in 1983, the substitution under this paragraph shall be as follows:

If the amount with respect to which the tentative tax to be computed is:	The tentative tax is:
Over $2,500,000 But not over $3,000,000	$1,025,800, plus 53% of the excess over $2,500,000.
Over $3,000,000 But not over $3,500,000	$1,290,800, plus 57% of the excess over $3,000,000.
Over $3,500,000	$1,575,800, plus 60% of the excess over $3,500,000.

(D) AFTER 1983 AND BEFORE 1993.—In the case of decedents dying, and gifts made, after 1983 and before 1993 the substitution under this paragraph shall be as follows:

If the amount with respect to which the tentative tax to be computed is:	The tentative tax is:
Over $2,500,000 But not over $3,000,000	$1,025,800, plus 53% of the excess over $2,500,000.
Over $3,000,000	$1,290,800, plus 55% of the excess over $3,000,000.

P.L. 103-66, §13208(b)(2):

Amended Code Sec. 2001(c)(2) (as redesignated) by striking "($18,340,000 in the case of decedents dying, and gifts made, after 1992)" before the period. **Effective** in the case of decedents dying and gifts made after 12-31-92.

• 1987, Revenue Act of 1987 (P.L. 100-203)

P.L. 100-203, §10401(a)(1)-(3):

Amended Code Sec. 2001(c)(2) by striking out "1988" in subparagraph (A) and inserting in lieu thereof "1993", by striking out "in 1984, 1985, 1986, or 1987" in the text of subparagraph (D) and inserting in lieu thereof "after 1983 and before 1993", and by amending the heading of subparagraph (D). **Effective** in the case of decedents dying, or gifts made, after 12-31-87. Prior to amendment, the heading for subparagraph (D) read as follows:

(D) FOR 1984, 1985, 1986, OR 1987.—

P.L. 100-203, §10401(b)(1):

Amended Code Sec. 2001(c) by adding at the end thereof new paragraph (3). **Effective** in the case of decedents dying, or gifts made, after 12-31-87.

• 1984, Deficit Reduction Act of 1984 (P.L. 98-369)

P.L. 98-369, §21(a):

Amended Code Sec. 2001(c)(2) by striking out "1985", in subparagraph (A) and inserting in lieu thereof "1988", and by striking out "1984" each place it appears in subparagraph (D) and inserting in lieu thereof "1984, 1985, 1986, or 1987". **Effective** for estates of decedents dying after, and gifts made after, 12-31-83.

[Sec. 2001(d)]

(d) ADJUSTMENT FOR GIFT TAX PAID BY SPOUSE.—For purposes of subsection (b)(2), if—

(1) the decedent was the donor of any gift one-half of which was considered under section 2513 as made by the decedent's spouse, and

(2) the amount of such gift is includible in the gross estate of the decedent,

any tax payable by the spouse under chapter 12 on such gift (as determined under section 2012(d)) shall be treated as a tax payable with respect to a gift made by the decedent.

Amendments

• 1981, Economic Recovery Tax Act of 1981 (P.L. 97-34)

P.L. 97-34, §402(a):

Amended Code Sec. 2001(c) by striking out the item beginning "Over $2,500,000" and all that follows and inserting "Over $2,500,000 . . . $1,025,800, plus 50% of the excess over $2,500,000". **Effective** for estates of decedents dying after, and gifts made after, 12-31-81. (For the text of Code Sec. 2001(c) prior to amendment, see the amendment note at Act Sec. 402(b), below.)

P.L. 97-34, §402(b):

Amended Code Sec. 2001(c) by striking out "(c) Rate Schedule.—" and inserting "(c) Rate Schedule.—(1) In General.—" and by adding a paragraph (2). **Effective** for estates of decedents dying after, and gifts made after, 12-31-81. Prior to amendment, Code Sec. 2001(c) read as follows:

(c) RATE SCHEDULE.—

If the amount with respect to which the tentative tax to be computed is:	The tentative tax is:
Not over $10,000	18 percent of such amount.
Over $10,000 but not over $20,000	$1,800, plus 20 percent of the excess of such amount over $10,000.
Over $20,000 but not over $40,000	$3,800, plus 22 percent of the excess of such amount over $20,000.

Over $40,000 but not over $60,000	$8,200, plus 24 percent of the excess of such amount over $40,000.
Over $60,000 but not over $80,000	$13,000, plus 26 percent of the excess of such amount over $60,000.
Over $80,000 but not over $100,000	$18,200, plus 28 percent of the excess of such amount over $80,000.
Over $100,000 but not over $150,000	$23,800, plus 30 percent of the excess of such amount over $100,000.
Over $150,000 but not over $250,000	$38,800, plus 32 percent of the excess of such amount over $150,000.
Over $250,000 but not over $500,000	$70,800, plus 34 percent of the excess of such amount over $250,000.
Over $500,000 but not over $750,000	$155,800, plus 37 percent of the excess of such amount over $500,000.
Over $750,000 but not over $1,000,000	$248,300, plus 39 percent of the excess of such amount over $750,000.
Over $1,000,000 but not over $1,250,000	$345,800, plus 41 percent of the excess of such amount over $1,000,000.
Over $1,250,000 but not over $1,500,000	$448,300, plus 43 percent of the excess of such amount over $1,250,000.
Over $1,500,000 but not over $2,000,000	$555,800, plus 45 percent of the excess of such amount over $1,500,000.
Over $2,000,000 but not over $2,500,000	$780,800, plus 49 percent of the excess of such amount over $2,000,000.
Over $2,500,000 but not over $3,000,000	$1,025,800, plus 53 percent of the excess of such amount over $2,500,000.
Over $3,000,000 but not over $3,500,000	$1,290,800, plus 57 percent of the excess of such amount over $3,000,000.
Over $3,500,000 but not over $4,000,000	$1,575,800, plus 61 percent of the excess of such amount over $3,500,000.
Over $4,000,000 but not over $4,500,000	$1,880,800, plus 65 percent of the excess of such amount over $4,000,000.
Over $4,500,000 but not over $5,000,000	$2,205,800, plus 69 percent of the excess of such amount over $4,500,000.
Over $5,000,000	$2,550,800, plus 70 percent of the excess of such amount over $5,000,000.

P.L. 97-34, § 402(c):

Amended Code Sec. 2001(b)(2). **Effective** for estates of decedents dying after, and gifts made after, 12-31-81. Prior to amendment, Code Sec. 2001(b)(2) read as follows:

(2) the aggregate amount of tax payable under chapter 12 with respect to gifts made by the decedent after December 31, 1976.

• 1976, Tax Reform Act of 1976 (P.L. 94-455)

P.L. 94-455, § 2001(a)(1), (d)(1):

Amended Code Sec. 2001. **Effective** for estates of decedents dying after 12-31-76. Prior to amendment, Code Sec. 2001 read as follows:

SEC. 2001. RATE OF TAX.

A tax computed in accordance with the following table is hereby imposed on the transfer of the taxable estate, determined as provided in section 2051, of every decedent, citizen or resident of the United States dying after the date of enactment of this title:

If the taxable estate is:	The tax shall be:
Not over $5,000	3% of the taxable estate.
Over $5,000 but not over $10,000	$150, plus 7% of excess over $5,000.
Over $10,000 but not over $20,000	$500, plus 11% of excess over $10,000.
Over $20,000 but not over $30,000	$1,600, plus 14% of excess over $20,000.
Over $30,000 but not over $40,000	$3,000, plus 18% of excess over $30,000
Over $40,000 but not over $50,000	$4,800, plus 22% of excess over $40,000.
Over $50,000 but not over $60,000	$7,000, plus 25% of excess over $50,000.
Over $60,000 but not over $100,000	$9,500, plus 28% of excess over $60,000.
Over $100,000 but not over $250,000	$20,700, plus 30% of excess over $100,000
Over $250,000 but not over $500,000	$65,700, plus 32% of excess over $250,000.
Over $500,000 but not over $750,000	$145,700, plus 35% of excess over $500,000.
Over $750,000 but not over $1,000,000	$233,200, plus 37% of excess over $750,000.
Over $1,000,000 but not over $1,250,000	$325,700, plus 39% of excess over $1,000,000.
Over $1,250,000 but not over $1,500,000	$423,200, plus 42% of excess over $1,250,000.
Over $1,500,000 but not over $2,000,000	$528,200, plus 45% of excess over $1,500,000
Over $2,000,000 but not over $2,500,000	$753,200, plus 49% of excess over $2,000,000.
Over $2,500,000 but not over $3,000,000	$998,200, plus 53% of excess over $2,500,000.

Over $3,000,000 but not over $3,500,000	$1,263,200, plus 56% of excess over $3,000,000.
Over $3,500,000 but not over $4,000,000	$1,543,200, plus 59% of excess over $3,500,000.
Over $4,000,000 but not over $5,000,000	$1,838,200, plus 63% of excess over $4,000,000.
Over $5,000,000 but not over $6,000,000	$2,468,200, plus 67% of excess over $5,000,000.
Over $6,000,000 but not over $7,000,000	$3,138,200, plus 70% of excess over $6,000,000.
Over $7,000,000 but not over $8,000,000	$3,838,200, plus 73% of excess over $7,000,000.
Over $8,000,000 but not over $10,000,000	$4,568,200, plus 76% of excess over $8,000,000.
Over $10,000,000	$6,088,200, plus 77% of excess over $10,000,000.

[Sec. 2001(e)]

(e) COORDINATION OF SECTIONS 2513 AND 2035.—If—

(1) the decedent's spouse was the donor of any gift one-half of which was considered under section 2513 as made by the decedent, and

(2) the amount of such gift is includible in the gross estate of the decedent's spouse by reason of section 2035,

such gift shall not be included in the adjusted taxable gifts of the decedent for purposes of subsection (b)(1)(B), and the aggregate amount determined under subsection (b)(2) shall be reduced by the amount (if any) determined under subsection (d) which was treated as a tax payable by the decedent's spouse with respect to such gift.

Amendments

• 1978, Revenue Act of 1978 (P.L. 95-600)

P.L. 95-600, §702(h)(1):

Added Code Sec. 2001(e). **Effective** for estates of decedents dying after 12-31-76, except that such subsection shall not apply to transfers made before 1-1-77.

[Sec. 2001(f)]

(f) VALUATION OF GIFTS.—

(1) IN GENERAL.—If the time has expired under section 6501 within which a tax may be assessed under chapter 12 (or under corresponding provisions of prior laws) on—

(A) the transfer of property by gift made during a preceding calendar period (as defined in section 2502(b)); or

(B) an increase in taxable gifts required under section 2701(d),

the value thereof shall, for purposes of computing the tax under this chapter, be the value as finally determined for purposes of chapter 12.

(2) FINAL DETERMINATION.—For purposes of paragraph (1), a value shall be treated as finally determined for purposes of chapter 12 if—

(A) the value is shown on a return under such chapter and such value is not contested by the Secretary before the expiration of the time referred to in paragraph (1) with respect to such return;

(B) in a case not described in subparagraph (A), the value is specified by the Secretary and such value is not timely contested by the taxpayer; or

(C) the value is determined by a court or pursuant to a settlement agreement with the Secretary.

For purposes of subparagraph (A), the value of an item shall be treated as shown on a return if the item is disclosed in the return, or in a statement attached to the return, in a manner adequate to apprise the Secretary of the nature of such item.

Amendments

• 1998, Tax and Trade Relief Extension Act of 1998 (P.L. 105-277)

P.L. 105-277, §4003(c):

Amended Code Sec. 2001(f)(2) by adding at the end a new sentence. **Effective** as if included in the provision of P.L. 105-34 to which it relates [**effective** for gifts made after 8-5-97.—CCH].

• 1998, IRS Restructuring and Reform Act of 1998 (P.L. 105-206)

P.L. 105-206, §6007(e)(2)(B):

Amended Code Sec. 2001(f). **Effective** as if included in the provision of P.L. 105-34 to which it relates [**effective** for gifts made after 8-5-97.—CCH]. Prior to amendment, Code Sec. 2001(f) read as follows:

(f) VALUATION OF GIFTS.—If—

(1) the time has expired within which a tax may be assessed under chapter 12 (or under corresponding provisions of prior laws) on the transfer of property by gift made during a preceding calendar period (as defined in section 2502(b)), and

(2) the value of such gift is shown on the return for such preceding calendar period or is disclosed in such return, or in a statement attached to the return, in a manner adequate to apprise the Secretary of the nature of such gift, the value of such gift shall, for purposes of computing the tax under this chapter, be the value of such gift as finally determined for purposes of chapter 12.

• 1997, Taxpayer Relief Act of 1997 (P.L. 107-34)

P.L. 105-34, §506(a):

Amended Code Sec. 2001 by adding at the end a new subsection (f). **Effective** for gifts made after 8-5-97.

[Sec. 2001(g)]

(g) MODIFICATIONS TO TAX PAYABLE.—

(1) MODIFICATIONS TO GIFT TAX PAYABLE TO REFLECT DIFFERENT TAX RATES.—For purposes of applying subsection (b)(2) with respect to 1 or more gifts, the rates of tax under subsection (c) in effect at the decedent's death shall, in lieu of the rates of tax in effect at the time of such gifts, be used both to compute—

(A) the tax imposed by chapter 12 with respect to such gifts, and

(B) the credit allowed against such tax under section 2505, including in computing—

(i) the applicable credit amount under section 2505(a)(1), and

(ii) the sum of the amounts allowed as a credit for all preceding periods under section 2505(a)(2).

(2) MODIFICATIONS TO ESTATE TAX PAYABLE TO REFLECT DIFFERENT BASIC EXCLUSION AMOUNTS.—The Secretary shall prescribe such regulations as may be necessary or appropriate to carry out this section with respect to any difference between—

(A) the basic exclusion amount under section 2010(c)(3) applicable at the time of the decedent's death, and

(B) the basic exclusion amount under such section applicable with respect to any gifts made by the decedent.

Amendments

• 2017, Tax Cuts and Jobs Act (P.L. 115-97)

P.L. 115-97, §11061(b):

Amended Code Sec. 2001(g). **Effective** for estates of decedents dying and gifts made after 12-31-2017. Prior to amendment, Code Sec. 2001(g) read as follows:

(g) MODIFICATIONS TO GIFT TAX PAYABLE TO REFLECT DIFFERENTTAX RATES.—For purposes of applying subsection (b)(2) with respect to 1 or more gifts, the rates of tax under subsection (c) in effect at the decedent's death shall, in lieu of the rates of tax in effect at the time of such gifts, be used both to compute—

(1) the tax imposed by chapter 12 with respect to such gifts, and

(2) the credit allowed against such tax under section 2505, including in computing—

(A) the applicable credit amount under section 2505(a)(1), and

(B) the sum of the amounts allowed as a credit for all preceding periods under section 2505(a)(2).

• 2013, American Taxpayer Relief Act of 2012 (P.L. 112-240)

P.L. 112-240, §101(a)(1)-(3), provides:

SEC. 101. PERMANENT EXTENSION AND MODIFICATION OF 2001 TAX RELIEF.

(a) PERMANENT EXTENSION.—

(1) IN GENERAL.—The Economic Growth and Tax Relief Reconciliation Act of 2001 is amended by striking title IX.

(2) CONFORMING AMENDMENT.—The Tax Relief, Unemployment Insurance Reauthorization, and Job Creation Act of 2010 is amended by striking section 304.

(3) EFFECTIVE DATE.—The amendments made by this subsection shall apply to taxable, plan, or limitation years beginning after December 31, 2012, and estates of decedents dying, gifts made, or generation skipping transfers after December 31, 2012.

• 2010, Tax Relief, Unemployment Insurance Reauthorization, and Job Creation Act of 2010 (P.L. 111-312)

P.L. 111-312, §302(d)(1)(B):

Amended Code Sec. 2001 by adding at the end a new subsection (g). **Effective** for estates of decedents dying, generation-skipping transfers, and gifts made, after 12-31-2009.

P.L. 111-312, §304, provides [but see P.L. 112-240, §101(a)(2)-(3), above]:

SEC. 304. APPLICATION OF EGTRRA SUNSET TO THIS TITLE.

Section 901 of the Economic Growth and Tax Relief Reconciliation Act of 2001 shall apply to the amendments made by this title.

• 2001, Economic Growth and Tax Relief Reconciliation Act of 2001 (P.L. 107-16)

P.L. 107-16, §901(a)-(b), as amended by P.L. 111-312, §101(a)(1), provides [but see P.L. 112-240, §101(a)(1) and (3), above]:

SEC. 901. SUNSET OF PROVISIONS OF ACT.

(a) IN GENERAL.—All provisions of, and amendments made by, this Act shall not apply—

(1) to taxable, plan, or limitation years beginning after December 31, 2012, or

(2) in the case of title V, to estates of decedents dying, gifts made, or generation skipping transfers, after December 31, 2012.

(b) APPLICATION OF CERTAIN LAWS.—The Internal Revenue Code of 1986 and the Employee Retirement Income Security Act of 1974 shall be applied and administered to years, estates, gifts, and transfers described in subsection (a) as if the provisions and amendments described in subsection (a) had never been enacted.

[Sec. 2002]

SEC. 2002. LIABILITY FOR PAYMENT.

The tax imposed by this chapter shall be paid by the executor.

Amendments

• 1989, Omnibus Budget Reconciliation Act of 1989 (P.L. 101-239)

P.L. 101-239, §7304(b)(2)(A):

Amended Code Sec. 2002 by striking "Except as provided in section 2210, the" and inserting "The". **Effective** for estates of decedents dying after 7-12-89.

• 1984, Deficit Reduction Act of 1984 (P.L. 98-369)

P.L. 98-369, §544(b)(1):

Amended Code Sec. 2002. **Effective** for those estates of decedents which are required to file returns on a date (including any extensions) after 7-18-84. Prior to amendment, Code Sec. 2002 read as follows:

SEC. 2002. LIABILITY FOR PAYMENT.

The tax imposed by this chapter shall be paid by the executor.

PART II—CREDITS AGAINST TAX

[Sec. 2010]

SEC. 2010. UNIFIED CREDIT AGAINST ESTATE TAX.

[Sec. 2010(a)]

(a) GENERAL RULE.—A credit of the applicable credit amount shall be allowed to the estate of every decedent against the tax imposed by section 2001.

Amendments

• 1997, Taxpayer Relief Act of 1997 (P.L. 105-34)

P.L. 105-34, § 501(a)(1)(A):

Amended Code Sec. 2010(a) by striking "$192,800" and inserting "the applicable credit amount". **Effective** for estates of decedents dying, and gifts made, after 12-31-97.

• 1981, Economic Recovery Tax Act of 1981 (P.L. 97-34)

P.L. 97-34, § 401(a)(1):

Amended Code Sec. 2010(a) by striking out "$47,000" and inserting "$192,800". **Effective** for estates of decedents dying after 12-31-81.

[Sec. 2010(b)]

(b) ADJUSTMENT TO CREDIT FOR CERTAIN GIFTS MADE BEFORE 1977.—The amount of the credit allowable under subsection (a) shall be reduced by an amount equal to 20 percent of the aggregate amount allowed as a specific exemption under section 2521 (as in effect before its repeal by the Tax Reform Act of 1976) with respect to gifts made by the decedent after September 8, 1976.

Amendments

• 1990, Omnibus Budget Reconciliation Act of 1990 (P.L. 101-508)

P.L. 101-508, § 11801(c)(19)(A):

Amended Code Sec. 2010 by redesignating subsection (c) as subsection (b). **Effective** 11-5-90.

P.L. 101-508, § 11821(b), provides:

(b) SAVINGS PROVISIONS.—If—

(1) any provision amended or repealed by this part applied to—

(A) any transaction occurring before the date of the enactment of this Act,

(B) any property acquired before such date of enactment, or

(C) any item of income, loss, deduction, or credit taken into account before such date of enactment, and

(2) the treatment of such transaction, property, or item under such provision would (without regard to the amendments made by this part) affect liability for tax for periods ending after such date of enactment,

nothing in the amendments made by this part shall be construed to affect the treatment of such transaction, property, or item for purposes of determining liability for tax for periods ending after such date of enactment.

[Sec. 2010(b)—Repealed]

Amendments

• 1990, Omnibus Budget Reconciliation Act of 1990 (P.L. 101-508)

P.L. 101-508, § 11801(a)(39):

Repealed Code Sec. 2010(b). **Effective** 11-5-90. Prior to repeal, Code Sec. 2010(b) read as follows:

(b) PHASE-IN OF CREDIT.—

In the case of decedents dying in:	Subsection (a) shall be applied by substituting for "$192,800" the following amount:
1982	$62,800
1983	79,300
1984	96,300
1985	121,800
1986	155,800

P.L. 101-508, § 11821(b), provides:

(b) SAVINGS PROVISIONS.—If—

(1) any provision amended or repealed by this part applied to—

(A) any transaction occurring before the date of the enactment of this Act,

(B) any property acquired before such date of enactment, or

(C) any item of income, loss, deduction, or credit taken into account before such date of enactment, and

(2) the treatment of such transaction, property, or item under such provision would (without regard to the amendments made by this part) affect liability for tax for periods ending after such date of enactment,

nothing in the amendments made by this part shall be construed to affect the treatment of such transaction, property, or item for purposes of determining liability for tax for periods ending after such date of enactment.

• 1981, Economic Recovery Tax Act of 1981 (P.L. 97-34)

P.L. 97-34, § 401(a)(2)(A):

Amended Code Sec. 2010(b). **Effective** for estates of decedents dying after 12-31-81. Prior to amendment, Code Sec. 2010(b) read as follows:

(b) PHASE-IN of $47,000 CREDIT.—

In the case of decedents dying in:	Subsection (a) shall be applied by substituting for "$47,000" the following amount:
1977	$30,000
1978	34,000
1979	38,000
1980	42,500

[Sec. 2010(c)]

(c) APPLICABLE CREDIT AMOUNT.—

(1) IN GENERAL.—For purposes of this section, the applicable credit amount is the amount of the tentative tax which would be determined under section 2001(c) if the amount with respect to which such tentative tax is to be computed were equal to the applicable exclusion amount.

(2) APPLICABLE EXCLUSION AMOUNT.—For purposes of this subsection, the applicable exclusion amount is the sum of—

(A) the basic exclusion amount, and

(B) in the case of a surviving spouse, the deceased spousal unused exclusion amount.

(3) BASIC EXCLUSION AMOUNT.—

(A) IN GENERAL.—For purposes of this subsection, the basic exclusion amount is $5,000,000.

(B) INFLATION ADJUSTMENT.—In the case of any decedent dying in a calendar year after 2011, the dollar amount in subparagraph (A) shall be increased by an amount equal to—

(i) such dollar amount, multiplied by

(ii) the cost-of-living adjustment determined under section 1(f)(3) for such calendar year by substituting "calendar year 2010" for "calendar year 2016" in subparagraph (A)(ii) thereof.

If any amount as adjusted under the preceding sentence is not a multiple of $10,000, such amount shall be rounded to the nearest multiple of $10,000.

(C) INCREASE IN BASIC EXCLUSION AMOUNT.—In the case of estates of decedents dying or gifts made after December 31, 2017, and before January 1, 2026, subparagraph (A) shall be applied by substituting "$10,000,000" for "$5,000,000".

(4) DECEASED SPOUSAL UNUSED EXCLUSION AMOUNT.—For purposes of this subsection, with respect to a surviving spouse of a deceased spouse dying after December 31, 2010, the term "deceased spousal unused exclusion amount" means the lesser of—

(A) the basic exclusion amount, or

(B) the excess of—

(i) the applicable exclusion amount of the last such deceased spouse of such surviving spouse, over

(ii) the amount with respect to which the tentative tax is determined under section 2001(b)(1) on the estate of such deceased spouse.

(5) SPECIAL RULES.—

(A) ELECTION REQUIRED.—A deceased spousal unused exclusion amount may not be taken into account by a surviving spouse under paragraph (2) unless the executor of the estate of the deceased spouse files an estate tax return on which such amount is computed and makes an election on such return that such amount may be so taken into account. Such election, once made, shall be irrevocable. No election may be made under this subparagraph if such return is filed after the time prescribed by law (including extensions) for filing such return.

(B) EXAMINATION OF PRIOR RETURNS AFTER EXPIRATION OF PERIOD OF LIMITATIONS WITH RESPECT TO DECEASED SPOUSAL UNUSED EXCLUSION AMOUNT.—Notwithstanding any period of limitation in section 6501, after the time has expired under section 6501 within which a tax may be assessed under chapter 11 or 12 with respect to a deceased spousal unused exclusion amount, the Secretary may examine a return of the deceased spouse to make determinations with respect to such amount for purposes of carrying out this subsection.

(6) REGULATIONS.—The Secretary shall prescribe such regulations as may be necessary or appropriate to carry out this subsection.

Amendments

• 2017, Tax Cuts and Jobs Act (P.L. 115-97)

P.L. 115-97, §11002(d)(1)(CC):

Amended Code Sec. 2010(c)(3)(B)(ii) by striking "for 'calendar year 1992' in subparagraph (B)" and inserting "for 'calendar year 2016' in subparagraph (A)(ii)". **Effective** for tax years beginning after 12-31-2017.

P.L. 115-97, §11061(a):

Amended Code Sec. 2010(c)(3) by adding at the end a new subparagraph (C). **Effective** for estates of decedents dying and gifts made after 12-31-2017.

• 2013, American Taxpayer Relief Act of 2012 (P.L. 112-240)

P.L. 112-240, §101(a)(1)-(3), provides:

SEC. 101. PERMANENT EXTENSION AND MODIFICATION OF 2001 TAX RELIEF.

(a) PERMANENT EXTENSION.—

(1) IN GENERAL.—The Economic Growth and Tax Relief Reconciliation Act of 2001 is amended by striking title IX.

(2) CONFORMING AMENDMENT.—The Tax Relief, Unemployment Insurance Reauthorization, and Job Creation Act of 2010 is amended by striking section 304.

(3) EFFECTIVE DATE.—The amendments made by this subsection shall apply to taxable, plan, or limitation years beginning after December 31, 2012, and estates of decedents dying, gifts made, or generation skipping transfers after December 31, 2012.

P.L. 112-240, §101(c)(2):

Amended Code Sec. 2010(c)(4)(B)(i) by striking "basic exclusion amount" and inserting "applicable exclusion amount". **Effective** as if included in the amendments made by section 303 of the Tax Relief, Unemployment Insurance Reauthorization, and Job Creation Act of 2010 (P.L. 111-312) [**effective** for estates of decedents dying and gifts made after 12-31-2010.—CCH].

• 2010, Tax Relief, Unemployment Insurance Reauthorization, and Job Creation Act of 2010 (P.L. 111-312)

P.L. 111-312, §302(a)(1):

Amended Code Sec. 2010(c). **Effective** for estates of decedents dying, generation-skipping transfers, and gifts made, after 12-31-2009. Prior to amendment, Code Sec. 2010(c) read as follows:

(c) APPLICABLE CREDIT AMOUNT.—For purposes of this section, the applicable credit amount is the amount of the tentative tax which would be determined under the rate schedule set forth in section 2001(c) if the amount with respect to which such tentative tax is to be computed were the applicable exclusion amount determined in accordance with the following table:

In the case of estates of decedents dying during:	*The applicable exclusion amount is:*
2002 and 2003	$1,000,000
2004 and 2005	$1,500,000
2006, 2007, and 2008	$2,000,000
2009	$3,500,000.

P.L. 111-312, §303(a):

Amended Code Sec. 2010(c), as amended by Act Sec. 302(a), by striking paragraph (2) and inserting new paragraphs (2)-(6). **Effective** for estates of decedents dying and gifts made after 12-31-2010. Prior to being stricken, Code Sec. 2010(c)(2) read as follows:

(2) APPLICABLE EXCLUSION AMOUNT.—

(A) IN GENERAL.—For purposes of this subsection, the applicable exclusion amount is $5,000,000.

(B) INFLATION ADJUSTMENT.—In the case of any decedent dying in a calendar year after 2011, the dollar amount in subparagraph (A) shall be increased by an amount equal to—

(i) such dollar amount, multiplied by

(ii) the cost-of-living adjustment determined under section 1(f)(3) for such calendar year by substituting "calendar year 2010" for "calendar year 1992" in subparagraph (B) thereof.

If any amount as adjusted under the preceding sentence is not a multiple of $10,000, such amount shall be rounded to the nearest multiple of $10,000.

P.L. 111-312, §304, provides [but see P.L. 112-240, §101(a)(2)-(3), above]:

SEC. 304. APPLICATION OF EGTRRA SUNSET TO THIS TITLE.

Section 901 of the Economic Growth and Tax Relief Reconciliation Act of 2001 shall apply to the amendments made by this title.

• 2001, Economic Growth and Tax Relief Reconciliation Act of 2001 (P.L. 107-16)

P.L. 107-16, §521(a):

Amended Code Sec. 2010(c) by striking the table and inserting a new table. **Effective** for estates of decedents dying, and gifts made, after 12-31-2001. Prior to being stricken, the table read as follows:

In the case of estates of decedents dying, and gifts made, during:	*The applicable exclusion amount is:*
1998	$625,000
1999	$650,000
2000 and 2001	$675,000
2002 and 2003	$700,000
2004	$850,000
2005	$950,000
2006 or thereafter	$1,000,000

P.L. 107-16, §901(a)-(b), as amended by P.L. 111-312, §101(a)(1), provides [but see P.L. 112-240, §101(a)(1) and (3), above]:

SEC. 901. SUNSET OF PROVISIONS OF ACT.

(a) IN GENERAL.—All provisions of, and amendments made by, this Act shall not apply—

(1) to taxable, plan, or limitation years beginning after December 31, 2012, or

(2) in the case of title V, to estates of decedents dying, gifts made, or generation skipping transfers, after December 31, 2012.

(b) APPLICATION OF CERTAIN LAWS.—The Internal Revenue Code of 1986 and the Employee Retirement Income Security Act of 1974 shall be applied and administered to years, estates, gifts, and transfers described in subsection (a) as if the provisions and amendments described in subsection (a) had never been enacted.

• 1997, Taxpayer Relief Act of 1997 (P.L. 105-34)

P.L. 105-34, §501(a)(1)(B):

Amended Code Sec. 2010 by redesignating subsection (c) as subsection (d) and by inserting after subsection (b) a new subsection (c). **Effective** for estates of decedents dying, and gifts made, after 12-31-97.

[Sec. 2010(d)]

(d) LIMITATION BASED ON AMOUNT OF TAX.—The amount of the credit allowed by subsection (a) shall not exceed the amount of the tax imposed by section 2001.

Amendments

• 1997, Taxpayer Relief Act of 1997 (P.L. 105-34)

P.L. 105-34, §501(a)(1)(B):

Amended Code Sec. 2010 by redesignating subsection (c) as subsection (d). **Effective** for estates of decedents dying, and gifts made, after 12-31-97.

• 1990, Omnibus Budget Reconciliation Act of 1990 (P.L. 101-508)

P.L. 101-508, §11801(c)(19)(A):

Amended Code Sec. 2010 by redesignating subsection (d) as subsection (c). **Effective** 11-5-90.

P.L. 101-508, §11821(b), provides:

(b) SAVINGS PROVISION.—If—

(1) any provision amended or repealed by this part applied to—

(A) any transaction occurring before the date of the enactment of this Act,

(B) any property acquired before such date of enactment, or

(C) any item of income, loss, deduction, or credit taken into account before such date of enactment, and

(2) the treatment of such transaction, property, or item under such provision would (without regard to the amendments made by this part) affect liability for tax for periods ending after such date of enactment,

nothing in the amendments made by this part shall be construed to affect the treatment of such transaction, property, or item for purposes of determining liability for tax for periods ending after such date of enactment.

• 1976, Tax Reform Act of 1976 (P.L. 94-455)

P.L. 94-455, §2001(a)(2), (d)(1):

Added Code Sec. 2010. **Effective** for estates of decedents dying after 12-31-76.

[Sec. 2011—Stricken]

Amendments

• 2014, Tax Technical Corrections Act of 2014 (P.L. 113-295)

P.L. 113-295, §221(a)(95)(A)(i), Division A:

Amended part II of subchapter A of chapter 11 by striking Code Sec. 2011. **Effective** generally 12-19-2014. For a special rule, see Act Sec. 221(b)(2), Division A, below.

P.L. 113-295, §221(b)(2), Division A, provides:

(2) SAVINGS PROVISION.—If—

(A) any provision amended or repealed by the amendments made by this section applied to—

(i) any transaction occurring before the date of the enactment of this Act,

(ii) any property acquired before such date of enactment, or

(iii) any item of income, loss, deduction, or credit taken into account before such date of enactment, and

(B) the treatment of such transaction, property, or item under such provision would (without regard to the amendments or repeals made by this section) affect the liability for tax for periods ending after date of enactment, nothing in the amendments or repeals made by this section shall be construed to affect the treatment of such transaction, property, or item for purposes of determining liability for tax for periods ending after such date of enactment.

Prior to being stricken, Code Sec. 2011 read as follows:

SEC. 2011. CREDIT FOR STATE DEATH TAXES.

[Sec. 2011(a)]

(a) IN GENERAL.—The tax imposed by section 2001 shall be credited with the amount of any estate, inheritance, legacy, or succession taxes actually paid to any State or the District of Columbia, in respect of any property included in the gross estate (not including any such taxes paid with respect to the estate of a person other than the decedent).

Amendments

• 1976, Tax Reform Act of 1976 (P.L. 94-455)

P.L. 94-455, §1902(a)(12)(B), (c)(2):

Deleted "or Territory" in Code Sec. 2011(a). **Effective** for gifts made after 12-31-76.

• 1958, Technical Amendments Act of 1958 (P.L. 85-866)

P.L. 85-866, §102(c), (d):

Amended Code Sec. 2011(a) by striking the words "or any possession of the United States," after the words "District of Columbia". **Effective** for estates of decedents dying after 9-2-58.

[Sec. 2011(b)]

(b) AMOUNT OF CREDIT.—

(1) IN GENERAL.—Except as provided in paragraph (2), the credit allowed by this section shall not exceed the appropriate amount stated in the following table:

If the adjusted taxable estate is:	*The maximum tax credit shall be:*
Not over $90,000	8/10ths of 1% of the amount by which the adjusted taxable estate exceeds $40,000.
Over $90,000 but not over $140,000	$400 plus 1.6% of the excess over $90,000.
Over $140,000 but not over $240,000	$1,200 plus 2.4% of the excess over $140,000.
Over $240,000 but not over $440,000	$3,600 plus 3.2% of the excess over $240,000.
Over $440,000 but not over $640,000	$10,000 plus 4% of the excess over $440,000.
Over $640,000 but not over $840,000	$18,000 plus 4.8% of the excess over $640,000.
Over $840,000 but not over $1,040,000	$27,600 plus 5.6% of the excess over $840,000.
Over $1,040,000 but not over $1,540,000	$38,800 plus 6.4% of the excess over $1,040,000.
Over $1,540,000 but not over $2,040,000	$70,800 plus 7.2% of the excess over $1,540,000.
Over $2,040,000 but not over $2,540,000	$106,800 plus 8% of the excess over $2,040,000.
Over $2,540,000 but not over $3,040,000	$146,800 plus 8.8% of the excess over $2,540,000.
Over $3,040,000 but not over $3,540,000	$190,800 plus 9.6% of the excess over $3,040,000.
Over $3,540,000 but not over $4,040,000	$238,800 plus 10.4% of the excess over $3,540,000.
Over $4,040,000 but not over $5,040,000	$290,800 plus 11.2% of the excess over $4,040,000.
Over $5,040,000 but not over $6,040,000	$402,800 plus 12% of the excess over $5,040,000.
Over $6,040,000 but not over $7,040,000	$522,800 plus 12.8% of the excess over $6,040,000.
Over $7,040,000 but not over $8,040,000	$650,800 plus 13.6% of the excess over $7,040,000.
Over $8,040,000 but not over $9,040,000	$786,800 plus 14.4% of the excess over $8,040,000
Over $9,040,000 but not over $10,040,000	$930,800 plus 15.2% of the excess over $9,040,000.
Over $10,040,000	$1,082,800 plus 16% of the excess over $10,040,000.

(2) REDUCTION OF MAXIMUM CREDIT.—

(A) IN GENERAL.—In the case of estates of decedents dying after December 31, 2001, the credit allowed by this section shall not exceed the applicable percentage of the credit otherwise determined under paragraph (1).

(B) APPLICABLE PERCENTAGE.—

In the case of estates of decedents dying during:	*The applicable percentage is:*
2002	75 percent
2003	50 percent
2004	25 percent.

(3) ADJUSTED TAXABLE ESTATE.—For purposes of this section, the term "adjusted taxable estate" means the taxable estate reduced by $60,000.

Amendments

• 2013, American Taxpayer Relief Act of 2012 (P.L. 112-240)

P.L. 112-240, §101(a)(1) and (3), provides:

SEC. 101. PERMANENT EXTENSION AND MODIFICATION OF 2001 TAX RELIEF.

(a) PERMANENT EXTENSION.—

(1) IN GENERAL.—The Economic Growth and Tax Relief Reconciliation Act of 2001 is amended by striking title IX.

* * *

(3) EFFECTIVE DATE.—The amendments made by this subsection shall apply to taxable, plan, or limitation years beginning after December 31, 2012, and estates of decedents dying, gifts made, or generation skipping transfers after December 31, 2012.

• 2001, Economic Growth and Tax Relief Reconciliation Act of 2001 (P.L. 107-16)

P.L. 107-16, §531(a)(1)-(3):

Amended Code Sec. 2011(b) by striking "CREDIT.—The credit allowed" and inserting "CREDIT.—(1) IN GENERAL.—Except as provided in paragraph (2), the credit allowed", by striking "For purposes" and inserting "(3) ADJUSTED TAXABLE ESTATE.—For purposes", and by inserting after paragraph (1) a new paragraph (2). **Effective** for estates of decedents dying after 12-31-2001.

P.L. 107-16, §901(a)-(b), as amended by P.L. 111-312, §101(a)(1), provides [but see P.L. 112-240, §101(a)(1) and (3), above]:

SEC. 901. SUNSET OF PROVISIONS OF ACT.

(a) IN GENERAL.—All provisions of, and amendments made by, this Act shall not apply—

(1) to taxable, plan, or limitation years beginning after December 31, 2012, or

(2) in the case of title V, to estates of decedents dying, gifts made, or generation skipping transfers, after December 31, 2012.

(b) APPLICATION OF CERTAIN LAWS.—The Internal Revenue Code of 1986 and the Employee Retirement Income Security Act of 1974 shall be applied and administered to years, estates, gifts, and transfers described in subsection (a) as if the provisions and amendments described in subsection (a) had never been enacted.

• 1976, Tax Reform Act of 1976 (P.L. 94-455)

P.L. 94-455, §2001(c)(1)(A), (d)(1):

Substituted "adjusted taxable estate" for "taxable estate" each place it appeared in Code Sec. 2011(b); and added at the end of such section a new sentence. **Effective** for estates of decedents dying after 12-31-76.

[Sec. 2011(c)]

(c) PERIOD OF LIMITATIONS ON CREDIT.—The credit allowed by this section shall include only such taxes as were actually paid and credit therefor claimed within 4 years after the filing of the return required by section 6018, except that—

(1) If a petition for redetermination of a deficiency has been filed with the Tax Court within the time prescribed in section 6213(a), then within such 4-year period or before the expiration of 60 days after the decision of the Tax Court becomes final.

(2) If, under section 6161, or 6166 an extension of time has been granted for payment of the tax shown on the return, or of a deficiency, then within such 4-year period or before the date of the expiration of the period of the extension.

(3) If a claim for refund or credit of an overpayment of tax imposed by this chapter has been filed within the time prescribed in section 6511, then within such 4-year period or before the expiration of 60 days from the date of mailing by certified mail or registered mail by the Secretary to the taxpayer of a notice of the disallowance of any part of such claim, or before the expiration of 60 days after a decision by any court of competent jurisdiction becomes final with respect to a timely suit instituted upon such claim, whichever is later.

Refund based on the credit may (despite the provisions of sections 6511 and 6512) be made if claim therefor is filed within the period above provided. Any such refund shall be made without interest.

Amendments

• 1981, Economic Recovery Tax Act of 1981 (P.L. 97-34)

P.L. 97-34, §422(e)(2):

Amended Code Sec. 2011(c)(2) by striking out "6161, 6166 or 6166A" and inserting "6161 or 6166". **Effective** for estates of decedents dying after 12-31-81.

• 1976, Tax Reform Act of 1976 (P.L. 94-455)

P.L. 94-455, §1906(b)(13)(A):

Amended 1954 Code by substituting "Secretary" for "Secretary or his delegate" each place it appeared. **Effective** 2-1-77.

P.L. 94-455, §2004(f)(3):

Amended Code Sec. 2011(c)(2) by striking out "section 6161" and inserting in lieu thereof "6166 or 6166A". **Effective** for estates of decedents dying after 12-31-76.

• 1958, Technical Amendments Act of 1958 (P.L. 85-866)

P.L. 85-866, §65(a):

Amended Code Sec. 2011(c) by adding paragraph (3). **Effective** for estates of decedents dying after 8-16-54.

[Sec. 2011(d)]

(d) LIMITATION IN CASES INVOLVING DEDUCTION UNDER SECTION 2053(d).—In any case where a deduction is allowed under section 2053(d) for an estate, succession, legacy, or inheritance tax imposed by a State or the District of Columbia upon a transfer for public, charitable, or religious uses described in section 2055 or 2106(a)(2), the allowance of the credit under this section shall be subject to the following conditions and limitations:

(1) The taxes described in subsection (a) shall not include any estate, succession, legacy, or inheritance tax for which such deduction is allowed under section 2053(d).

(2) The credit shall not exceed the lesser of—

(A) the amount stated in subsection (b) on a [an] adjusted taxable estate determined by allowing such deduction authorized by section 2053(d), or

(B) that proportion of the amount stated in subsection (b) on a [an] adjusted taxable estate determined without regard to such deduction authorized by section 2053(d) as (i) the amount of the taxes described in subsection (a), as limited by the provisions of paragraph (1) of this subsection, bears to (ii) the amount of the taxes described in subsection (a) before applying the limitation contained in paragraph (1) of this subsection.

(3) If the amount determined under subparagraph (B) of paragraph (2) is less than the amount determined under subparagraph (A) of that paragraph, then for purposes of subsection (d) such lesser amount shall be the maximum credit provided by subsection (b).

Amendments

• 2002, Victims of Terrorism Tax Relief Act of 2001 (P.L. 107-134)

P.L. 107-134, §103(b)(1):

Amended Code Sec. 2011 by striking subsection (d) and redesignating subsection (e) as subsection (d). **Effective** for estates of decedents dying on or after 9-11-2001; and in the case of individuals dying as a result of the 4-19-95 terrorist attack, dying on or after 4-19-95. For a waiver of limitations, see Act Sec. 103(d)(2), below.

P.L. 107-134, §103(d)(2), provides:

(2) WAIVER OF LIMITATIONS.—If refund or credit of any overpayment of tax resulting from the amendments made

by this section is prevented at any time before the close of the 1-year period beginning on the date of the enactment of this Act by the operation of any law or rule of law (including res judicata), such refund or credit may nevertheless be made or allowed if claim therefor is filed before the close of such period.

• 1976, Tax Reform Act of 1976 (P.L. 94-455)

P.L. 94-455, §1902(a)(12)(B), (c):

Deleted "or Territory" in Code Sec. 2011(e). **Effective** for gifts made after 12-31-76.

P.L. 94-455, §2001(c)(1)(A):

Substituted "adjusted taxable estate" for "taxable estate" each place it appeared in Code Sec. 2011(e). **Effective** for estates of decedents dying after 12-31-76.

• 1959 (P.L. 86-175)

P.L. 86-175, §3:

Amended 1954 Code Sec. 2011(e) by striking out "imposed upon a transfer" and by substituting "imposed by a State or Territory or the District of Columbia upon a transfer"; by striking out "for which a deduction" in paragraph (1) and substituting "for which such deduction"; and by striking out "the deduction authorized by" each place it appeared in paragraph (2) and by substituting "such deduction authorized by". **Effective** with respect to the estates of decedents dying on or after 7-1-55.

• 1956 (P.L. 414, 84th Cong.)

P.L. 414, 84th Cong., §3:

Amended Section 2011 by adding after subsection (d) a new subsection (e). **Effective** for the estates of all decedents dying after 12-31-53.

[Sec. 2011(d)—Stricken]

Amendments

• 2002, Victims of Terrorism Tax Relief Act of 2001 (P.L. 107-134)

P.L. 107-134, §103(b)(1):

Amended Code Sec. 2011 by striking subsection (d) and by redesignating subsections (e), (f), and (g) as subsections (d), (e), and (f), respectively. **Effective** for estates of decedents dying on or after 9-11-2001; and in the case of individuals dying as a result of the 4-19-95 terrorist attack, dying on or after 4-19-95. For a waiver of limitations, see Act Sec. 103(d)(2) in the amendment notes for Code Sec. 2011(d). Prior to being stricken, Code Sec. 2011(d) read as follows:

(d) BASIC ESTATE TAX.—The basic estate tax and the estate tax imposed by the Revenue Act of 1926 shall be 125 percent of the amount determined to be the maximum credit provided by subsection (b). The additional estate tax shall be the difference between the tax imposed by section 2001 or 2101 and the basic estate tax.

[Sec. 2011(e)]

(e) LIMITATION BASED ON AMOUNT OF TAX.—The credit provided by this section shall not exceed the amount of the tax imposed by section 2001, reduced by the amount of the unified credit provided by section 2010.

Amendments

• 2002, Victims of Terrorism Tax Relief Act of 2001 (P.L. 107-134)

P.L. 107-134, §103(b)(1):

Amended Code Sec. 2011 by redesignating subsection (f) as subsection (e). **Effective** for estates of decedents dying on or after 9-11-2001; and in the case of individuals dying as a result of the 4-19-95 terrorist attack, dying on or after 4-19-95. For a waiver of limitations, see Act Sec. 103(d)(2) in the amendment notes for Code Sec. 2011(d).

• 1976, Tax Reform Act of 1976 (P.L. 94-455)

P.L. 94-455, §2001(c)(1)(A), (d)(1):

Added new Code Sec. 2011(f). **Effective** for estates of decedents dying after 12-31-76.

[Sec. 2011(f)]

(f) TERMINATION.—This section shall not apply to the estates of decedents dying after December 31, 2004.

Amendments

• 2013, American Taxpayer Relief Act of 2012 (P.L. 112-240)

P.L. 112-240, §101(a)(1) and (3), provides:

SEC. 101. PERMANENT EXTENSION AND MODIFICATION OF 2001 TAX RELIEF.

(a) PERMANENT EXTENSION.—

(1) IN GENERAL.—The Economic Growth and Tax Relief Reconciliation Act of 2001 is amended by striking title IX.

* * *

(3) EFFECTIVE DATE.—The amendments made by this subsection shall apply to taxable, plan, or limitation years beginning after December 31, 2012, and estates of decedents dying, gifts made, or generation skipping transfers after December 31, 2012.

• 2002, Victims of Terrorism Tax Relief Act of 2001 (P.L. 107-134)

P.L. 107-134, §103(b)(1):

Amended Code Sec. 2011 by redesignating subsection (g) as subsection (f). **Effective** for estates of decedents dying on or after 9-11-2001; and in the case of individuals dying as a result of the 4-19-95 terrorist attack, dying on or after 4-19-95. For a waiver of limitations, see Act Sec. 103(d)(2) in the amendment notes for Code Sec. 2011(d).

• 2001, Economic Growth and Tax Relief Reconciliation Act of 2001 (P.L. 107-16)

P.L. 107-16, §532(a):

Amended Code Sec. 2011 by adding at the end a new subsection (g). **Effective** for estates of decedents dying, and generation-skipping transfers, after 12-31-2004.

P.L. 107-16, §901(a)-(b), as amended by P.L. 111-312, §101(a)(1), provides [but see P.L. 112-240, §101(a)(1) and (3), above]:

SEC. 901. SUNSET OF PROVISIONS OF ACT.

(a) IN GENERAL.—All provisions of, and amendments made by, this Act shall not apply—

(1) to taxable, plan, or limitation years beginning after December 31, 2012, or

(2) in the case of title V, to estates of decedents dying, gifts made, or generation skipping transfers, after December 31, 2012.

(b) APPLICATION OF CERTAIN LAWS.—The Internal Revenue Code of 1986 and the Employee Retirement Income Security Act of 1974 shall be applied and administered to years, estates, gifts, and transfers described in subsection (a) as if the provisions and amendments described in subsection (a) had never been enacted.

[Sec. 2012]

SEC. 2012. CREDIT FOR GIFT TAX.

[Sec. 2012(a)]

(a) IN GENERAL.—If a tax on a gift has been paid under chapter 12 (sec. 2501 and following), or under corresponding provisions of prior laws, and thereafter on the death of the donor any amount in respect of such gift is required to be included in the value of the gross estate of the decedent for purposes of this chapter, then there shall be credited against the tax imposed by section 2001 the amount of the tax paid on a gift under chapter 12, or under corresponding provisions of prior laws, with respect to so much of the property which constituted the gift as is included in the gross estate, except that the amount of such credit shall not exceed an amount which bears the same ratio to the tax imposed by section 2001 (after deducting from such tax the unified credit provided by section 2010) as the value (at the time of the gift or at the time of the death, whichever is lower) of so much of the property which constituted the gift as is included in the gross estate bears to the value of the entire gross estate reduced by the aggregate amount of the charitable and marital deductions allowed under sections 2055, 2056, and 2106(a)(2).

Amendments

• 2013, American Taxpayer Relief Act of 2012 (P.L. 112-240)

P.L. 112-240, §101(a)(1) and (3), provides:

SEC. 101. PERMANENT EXTENSION AND MODIFICATION OF 2001 TAX RELIEF.

(a) PERMANENT EXTENSION.—

(1) IN GENERAL.—The Economic Growth and Tax Relief Reconciliation Act of 2001 is amended by striking title IX.

* * *

(3) EFFECTIVE DATE.—The amendments made by this subsection shall apply to taxable, plan, or limitation years beginning after December 31, 2012, and estates of decedents dying, gifts made, or generation skipping transfers after December 31, 2012.

• 2001, Economic Growth and Tax Relief Reconciliation Act of 2001 (P.L. 107-16)

P.L. 107-16, §532(c)(1):

Amended Code Sec. 2012(a) by striking "the credit for State death taxes provided by section 2011 and" following "(after deducting from such tax". **Effective** for estates of decedents dying, and generation-skipping transfers, after 12-31-2004.

P.L. 107-16, §901(a)-(b), as amended by P.L. 111-312, §101(a)(1), provides [but see P.L. 112-240, §101(a)(1) and (3), above]:

SEC. 901. SUNSET OF PROVISIONS OF ACT.

(a) IN GENERAL.—All provisions of, and amendments made by, this Act shall not apply—

(1) to taxable, plan, or limitation years beginning after December 31, 2012, or

(2) in the case of title V, to estates of decedents dying, gifts made, or generation skipping transfers, after December 31, 2012.

(b) APPLICATION OF CERTAIN LAWS.—The Internal Revenue Code of 1986 and the Employee Retirement Income Security Act of 1974 shall be applied and administered to years, estates, gifts, and transfers described in subsection (a) as if the provisions and amendments described in subsection (a) had never been enacted.

• 1976, Tax Reform Act of 1976 (P.L. 94-455)

P.L. 94-455, §2001(c)(1)(B):

Amended Code Sec. 2012(a) by adding "and the unified credit provided by section 2010" after "section 2011". **Effective** for estates of decedents dying after 12-31-76.

[Sec. 2012(b)]

(b) VALUATION REDUCTIONS.—In applying, with respect to any gift, the ratio stated in subsection (a), the value at the time of the gift or at the time of the death, referred to in such ratio, shall be reduced—

(1) by such amount as will properly reflect the amount of such gift which was excluded in determining (for purposes of section 2503(a)), or of corresponding provisions of prior laws, the total amount of gifts made during the calendar quarter (or calendar year if the gift was made before January 1, 1971) in which the gift was made;

(2) if a deduction with respect to such gift is allowed under section 2056(a) (relating to marital deduction), then by the amount of such value, reduced as provided in paragraph (1); and

(3) if a deduction with respect to such gift is allowed under sections 2055 or 2106(a)(2) (relating to charitable deduction), then by the amount of such value, reduced as provided in paragraph (1) of this subsection.

Amendments

• 1981, Economic Recovery Tax Act of 1981 (P.L. 97-34)

P.L. 97-34, §403(a)(2)(A):

Amended Code Sec. 2012(b)(2). **Effective** for estates of decedents dying after 12-31-81. Prior to amendment, Code Sec. 2012(b)(2) read as follows:

(2) if a deduction with respect to such gift is allowed under section 2056(a) (relating to marital deduction), then by an amount which bears the same ratio to such value (reduced as provided in paragraph (1) of this subsection) as the aggregate amount of the marital deductions allowed under section 2056 (a) bears to the aggregate amount of such marital deductions computed without regard to subsection (c) thereof; and

• 1976, Tax Reform Act of 1976 (P.L. 94-455)

P.L. 94-455, §1902(a)(1)(A), (c)(1):

Added the heading "VALUATION REDUCTIONS.—" to Code Sec. 2012(b); and substituted "deduction), then" for "deduction)—then" in paragraphs (2) and (3) of Code Sec. 2012(b). **Effective** for estates of decedents dying after 10-4-76.

• 1970, Excise, Estate, and Gift Tax Adjustment Act of 1970 (P.L. 91-614)

P.L. 91-614, §102(d)(2)(A):

Amended Code Sec. 2012(b)(1) by substituting "the calendar quarter (or calendar year if the gift was made before January 1, 1971)" for "the year." **Effective** for gifts made after 12-31-70.

[Sec. 2012(c)]

(c) WHERE GIFT CONSIDERED MADE ONE-HALF BY SPOUSE.—Where the decedent was the donor of the gift but, under the provisions of section 2513, or corresponding provisions of prior laws, the gift was considered as made one-half by his spouse—

(1) the term "the amount of the tax paid on a gift under chapter 12", as used in subsection (a), includes the amounts paid with respect to each half of such gift, the amount paid with respect to each being computed in the manner provided in subsection (d); and

(2) in applying, with respect to such gift, the ratio stated in subsection (a), the value at the time of the gift or at the time of the death, referred to in such ratio, includes such value with respect to each half of such gift, each such value being reduced as provided in paragraph (1) of subsection (b).

Amendments

• 1976, Tax Reform Act of 1976 (P.L. 94-455)

P.L. 94-455, § 1902(a)(1)(B), (c)(1):

Added the heading "WHERE GIFT CONSIDERED MADE ONE-HALF BY SPOUSE.—" to Code Sec. 2012(c). **Effective** for estates of decedents dying after 10-4-76.

[Sec. 2012(d)]

(d) COMPUTATION OF AMOUNT OF GIFT TAX PAID.—

(1) AMOUNT OF TAX.—For purposes of subsection (a), the amount of tax paid on a gift under chapter 12, or under corresponding provisions of prior laws, with respect to any gift shall be an amount which bears the same ratio to the total tax paid for the calendar quarter (or calendar year if the gift was made before January 1, 1971) in which the gift was made as the amount of such gift bears to the total amount of taxable gifts (computed without deduction of the specific exemption) for such quarter or year.

(2) AMOUNT OF GIFT.—For purposes of paragraph (1), the "amount of such gift" shall be the amount included with respect to such gift in determining (for the purposes of section 2503(a), or of corresponding provisions of prior laws) the total amount of gifts made during such quarter or year, reduced by the amount of any deduction allowed with respect to such gift under section 2522, or under corresponding provisions of prior laws (relating to charitable deduction), or under section 2523 (relating to marital deduction).

Amendments

• 1976, Tax Reform Act of 1976 (P.L. 94-455)

P.L. 94-455, § 1902(a)(1):

Added the heading "COMPUTATION OF AMOUNT OF GIFT TAX PAID.—(1) AMOUNT OF TAX." to Code Sec. 2012(d)(1); and added the heading "AMOUNT OF GIFT.—" to Code Sec. 2012(d)(2). **Effective** for estates of decedents dying after 10-4-76.

• 1970, Excise, Estate, and Gift Tax Adjustment Act of 1970 (P.L. 91-614)

P.L. 91-614, § 102(d)(2)(A), (B):

Amended Code Sec. 2012(d)(1) by substituting "the calendar quarter (or calendar year if the gift was made before January 1, 1971)" for "the year" and by substituting "such quarter or year" for "such year." Also amended Code Sec. 2012(d)(2) by substituting "such quarter or year" for "such year.". **Effective** for gifts made after 12-31-70.

[Sec. 2012(e)]

(e) SECTION INAPPLICABLE TO GIFTS MADE AFTER DECEMBER 31, 1976.—No credit shall be allowed under this section with respect to the amount of any tax paid under chapter 12 on any gift made after December 31, 1976.

Amendments

• 1976, Tax Reform Act of 1976 (P.L. 94-455)

P.L. 94-455, § 2001(a)(3), (d)(1):

Added Code Sec. 2012(e). **Effective** for estates of decedents dying after 12-31-76.

[Sec. 2013]

SEC. 2013. CREDIT FOR TAX ON PRIOR TRANSFERS.

[Sec. 2013(a)]

(a) GENERAL RULE.—The tax imposed by section 2001 shall be credited with all or a part of the amount of the Federal estate tax paid with respect to the transfer of property (including property passing as a result of the exercise or non-exercise of a power of appointment) to the decedent by or from a person (herein designated as a "transferor") who died within 10 years before, or within 2 years after, the decedent's death. If the transferor died within 2 years of the death of the decedent, the credit shall be the amount determined under subsections (b) and (c). If the transferor predeceased the decedent by more than 2 years, the credit shall be the following percentage of the amount so determined—

(1) 80 percent, if within the third or fourth years preceding the decedent's death;

(2) 60 percent, if within the fifth or sixth years preceding the decedent's death;

(3) 40 percent, if within the seventh or eighth years preceding the decedent's death; and

(4) 20 percent, if within the ninth or tenth years preceding the decedent's death.

[Sec. 2013(b)]

(b) COMPUTATION OF CREDIT.—Subject to the limitation prescribed in subsection (c), the credit provided by this section shall be an amount which bears the same ratio to the estate tax paid (adjusted as indicated hereinafter) with respect to the estate of the transferor as the value of the property transferred bears to the taxable estate of the transferor (determined for purposes of the estate tax) decreased by any death taxes paid with respect to such estate. For purposes of the preceding sentence, the estate tax paid shall be the Federal estate tax paid increased by any credits allowed against such estate tax under section 2012, or corresponding provisions of prior laws, on account of gift tax, and for any credits allowed against such estate tax under this section on account of prior transfers where the transferor acquired property from a person who died within 10 years before the death of the decedent.

Amendments

• 1976, Tax Reform Act of 1976 (P.L. 94-455)

P.L. 94-455, §2001(c)(1)(C), (d)(1):

Deleted "and increased by the exemption provided for by 2052 or section 2106(a)(3), or the corresponding provisions of prior laws, in determining the taxable estate of the transferor for purposes of the estate tax" at the end of the first sentence of Code Sec. 2013(b). **Effective** for estates of decedents dying after 12-31-76.

[Sec. 2013(c)]

(c) LIMITATION ON CREDIT.—

(1) IN GENERAL.—The credit provided in this section shall not exceed the amount by which—

(A) the estate tax imposed by section 2001 or section 2101 (after deducting the credits provided for in sections 2010, 2012, and 2014) computed without regard to this section, exceeds

(B) such tax computed by excluding from the decedent's gross estate the value of such property transferred and, if applicable, by making the adjustment hereinafter indicated.

If any deduction is otherwise allowable under section 2055 or section 2106(a)(2) (relating to charitable deduction) then, for the purpose of the computation indicated in subparagraph (B), the amount of such deduction shall be reduced by that part of such deduction which the value of such property transferred bears to the decedent's entire gross estate reduced by the deductions allowed under sections 2053 and 2054, or section 2106(a)(1) (relating to deduction for expenses, losses, etc.). For purposes of this section, the value of such property transferred shall be the value as provided for in subsection (d) of this section.

(2) TWO OR MORE TRANSFERORS.—If the credit provided in this section relates to property received from 2 or more transferors, the limitation provided in paragraph (1) of this subsection shall be computed by aggregating the value of the property so transferred to the decedent. The aggregate limitation so determined shall be apportioned in accordance with the value of the property transferred to the decedent by each transferor.

Amendments

• 2013, American Taxpayer Relief Act of 2012 (P.L. 112-240)

P.L. 112-240, §101(a)(1) and (3), provides:

SEC. 101. PERMANENT EXTENSION AND MODIFICATION OF 2001 TAX RELIEF.

(a) PERMANENT EXTENSION.—

(1) IN GENERAL.—The Economic Growth and Tax Relief Reconciliation Act of 2001 is amended by striking title IX.

* * *

(3) EFFECTIVE DATE.—The amendments made by this subsection shall apply to taxable, plan, or limitation years beginning after December 31, 2012, and estates of decedents dying, gifts made, or generation skipping transfers after December 31, 2012.

• 2001, Economic Growth and Tax Relief Reconciliation Act of 2001 (P.L. 107-16)

P.L. 107-16, §532(c)(2):

Amended Code Sec. 2013(c)(1)(A) by striking "2011," following "in sections 2010,". **Effective** for estates of decedents dying, and generation-skipping transfers, after 12-31-2004.

P.L. 107-16, §901(a)-(b), as amended by P.L. 111-312, §101(a)(1), provides [but see P.L. 112-240, §101(a)(1) and (3), above]:

SEC. 901. SUNSET OF PROVISIONS OF ACT.

(a) IN GENERAL.—All provisions of, and amendments made by, this Act shall not apply—

(1) to taxable, plan, or limitation years beginning after December 31, 2012, or

(2) in the case of title V, to estates of decedents dying, gifts made, or generation skipping transfers, after December 31, 2012.

(b) APPLICATION OF CERTAIN LAWS.—The Internal Revenue Code of 1986 and the Employee Retirement Income Security Act of 1974 shall be applied and administered to years, estates, gifts, and transfers described in subsection (a) as if the provisions and amendments described in subsection (a) had never been enacted.

• 1976, Tax Reform Act of 1976 (P.L. 94-455)

P.L. 94-455, §2001(c)(1)(C), (d)(1):

Amended Code Sec. 2013(c)(1)(A). **Effective** for estates of decedents dying after 12-31-76, Prior to amendment such section read as follows:

(A) the estate tax imposed by section 2001 or section 2101 (after deducting the credits for State death taxes, gift tax, and foreign death taxes provided for in sections 2011, 2012, and 2014) computed without regard to this section, exceeds.

[Sec. 2013(d)]

(d) VALUATION OF PROPERTY TRANSFERRED.—The value of property transferred to the decedent shall be the value used for the purpose of determining the Federal estate tax liability of the estate of the transferor but—

(1) there shall be taken into account the effect of the tax imposed by section 2001 or 2101, or any estate, succession, legacy, or inheritance tax, on the net value to the decedent of such property;

(2) where such property is encumbered in any manner, or where the decedent incurs any obligation imposed by the transferor with respect to such property, such encumbrance or obligation shall be taken into account in the same manner as if the amount of a gift to the decedent of such property was being determined; and

(3) if the decedent was the spouse of the transferor at the time of the transferor's death, the net value of the property transferred to the decedent shall be reduced by the amount allowed under section 2056 (relating to marital deductions) as a deduction from the gross estate of the transferor.

Amendments

• 1976, Tax Reform Act of 1976 (P.L. 94-455)

P.L. 94-455, §1902(a)(2), (c)(1):

Deleted ", or the corresponding provision of prior law," in Code Sec. 2013(d)(3). **Effective** for estates of decedents dying after 10-4-76.

[Sec. 2013(e)]

(e) PROPERTY DEFINED.—For purposes of this section, the term "property" includes any beneficial interest in property, including a general power of appointment (as defined in section 2041).

[Sec. 2013(f)]

(f) TREATMENT OF ADDITIONAL TAX IMPOSED UNDER SECTION 2032A.—If section 2032A applies to any property included in the gross estate of the transferor and an additional tax is imposed with respect to such property under section 2032A(c) before the date which is 2 years after the date of decedent's death, for purposes of this section—

(1) the additional tax imposed by section 2032A(c) shall be treated as a Federal estate tax payable with respect to the estate of the transferor; and

(2) the value of such property and the amount of the taxable estate of the transferor shall be determined as if section 2032A did not apply with respect to such property.

Amendments

• 1976, Tax Reform Act of 1976 (P.L. 94-455)

P.L. 94-455, §2003(c), (e):

Added Code Sec. 2013(f). **Effective** for estates of decedents dying after 12-31-76.

[Sec. 2013(g)—Stricken]

Amendments

• 1997, Taxpayer Relief Act of 1997 (P.L. 105-34)

P.L. 105-34, §1073(b)(2):

Amended Code Sec. 2013 by striking subsection (g). **Effective** for estates of decedents dying after 12-31-96. Prior to being stricken, Code Sec. 2013(g) read as follows:

(g) TREATMENT OF ADDITIONAL TAX UNDER SECTION 4980A.—For purposes of this section, the estate tax paid shall not include any portion of such tax attributable to section 4980A(d).

• 1988, Technical and Miscellaneous Revenue Act of 1988 (P.L. 100-647)

P.L. 100-647, §1011A(g)(7):

Amended Code Sec. 2013 by adding at the end thereof new subsection (g). **Effective** as if included in the provision of P.L. 99-514 to which it relates.

[Sec. 2013(g)—Repealed]

Amendments

• 1986, Tax Reform Act of 1986 (P.L. 99-514)

P.L. 99-514, §1432(c)(2):

Amended Code Sec. 2013 by repealing subsection (g). **Effective**, generally, for any generation-skipping transfer (within the meaning of Code Sec. 2611) made after 10-22-86. However, for special rules see Act Sec. 1433(b)-(d) in the amendments for Code Sec. 2601. Prior to repeal, Code Sec. 2013(g) read as follows:

(g) TREATMENT OF TAX IMPOSED ON CERTAIN GENERATION-SKIPPING TRANSFERS.—If any property was transferred to the decedent in a transfer which is taxable under section 2601 (relating to tax imposed on generation-skipping transfers) and if the deemed transferor (as defined in section 2612) is not alive at the time of such transfer, for purposes of this section—

(1) such property shall be deemed to have passed to the decedent from the deemed transferor;

(2) the tax payable under section 2601 on such transfer shall be treated as a Federal estate tax payable with respect to the estate of the deemed transferor; and

(3) the amount of the taxable estate of the deemed transferor shall be increased by the value of such property as determined for purposes of the tax imposed by section 2601 on the transfer.

• 1976, Tax Reform Act of 1976 (P.L. 94-455)

P.L. 94-455, §2006(b)(2):

Added Code Sec. 2013(g). For **effective** date, see Act Sec. 2006(c), below.

P.L. 94-455, §2006(c), as amended by P.L. 95-600, §702(n)(1), provides:

(c) EFFECTIVE DATES.—

(1) IN GENERAL.—Except as provided in paragraph (2), the amendments made by this section shall apply to any generation-skipping transfer (within the meaning of section 2611(a) of the Internal Revenue Code of 1954) made after June 11, 1976.

(2) EXCEPTIONS.—The amendments made by this section shall not apply to any generation-skipping transfer—

(A) under a trust which was irrevocable on June 11, 1976, but only to the extent that the transfer is not made out of corpus added to the trust after June 11, 1976, or

(B) in the case of a decedent dying before January 1, 1982, pursuant to a will (or revocable trust) which was in existence on June 11, 1976, and was not amended at any time after that date in any respect which will result in the creation of, or increasing the amount of, any generation-skipping transfer.

For purposes of subparagraph (B), if the decedent on June 11, 1976, was under a mental disability to change the disposition of his property, the period set forth in such subparagraph shall not expire before the date which is 2 years after the date on which he first regains his competence to dispose of such property.

(3) TRUST EQUIVALENTS.—For purposes of paragraph (2), in the case of a trust equivalent within the meaning of subsection (d) of section 2611 of the Internal Revenue Code of 1954, the provisions of such subsection (d) shall apply.

[Sec. 2014]

SEC. 2014. CREDIT FOR FOREIGN DEATH TAXES.

[Sec. 2014(a)]

(a) IN GENERAL.—The tax imposed by section 2001 shall be credited with the amount of any estate, inheritance, legacy, or succession taxes actually paid to any foreign country in respect of any property situated within such foreign country and included in the gross estate (not including any such taxes paid with respect to the estate of a person other than the decedent). The determination of the country within which property is situated shall be made in accordance with the rules applicable under subchapter B (sec. 2101 and following) in determining whether property is situated within or without the United States.

Amendments

• 1966, Foreign Investors Tax Act of 1966 (P.L. 89-809)

P.L. 89-809, §106(b)(3):

Amended Code Sec. 2014(a) by deleting the second sentence. **Effective** with respect to estates of decedents dying after 11-13-66. Prior to deletion, the second sentence read as follows:

"If the decedent at the time of his death was not a citizen of the United States, credit shall not be allowed under this section unless the foreign country of which such decedent was a citizen or subject, in imposing such taxes, allows a similar credit in the case of a citizen of the United States resident in such country."

[Sec. 2014(b)]

(b) LIMITATIONS ON CREDIT.—The credit provided in this section with respect to such taxes paid to any foreign country—

(1) shall not, with respect to any such tax, exceed an amount which bears the same ratio to the amount of such tax actually paid to such foreign country as the value of property which is—

(A) situated within such foreign country,

(B) subjected to such tax, and

(C) included in the gross estate

bears to the value of all property subjected to such tax; and

(2) shall not, with respect to all such taxes, exceed an amount which bears the same ratio to the tax imposed by section 2001 (after deducting from such tax the credits provided by sections 2010 and 2012) as the value of property which is—

(A) situated within such foreign country,

(B) subjected to the taxes of such foreign country, and

(C) included in the gross estate

bears to the value of the entire gross estate reduced by the aggregate amount of the deductions allowed under sections 2055 and 2056.

Amendments

• 2013, American Taxpayer Relief Act of 2012 (P.L. 112-240)

P.L. 112-240, §101(a)(1) and (3), provides:

SEC. 101. PERMANENT EXTENSION AND MODIFICATION OF 2001 TAX RELIEF.

(a) PERMANENT EXTENSION.—

(1) IN GENERAL.—The Economic Growth and Tax Relief Reconciliation Act of 2001 is amended by striking title IX.

* * *

(3) EFFECTIVE DATE.—The amendments made by this subsection shall apply to taxable, plan, or limitation years beginning after December 31, 2012, and estates of decedents dying, gifts made, or generation skipping transfers after December 31, 2012.

• 2001, Economic Growth and Tax Relief Reconciliation Act of 2001 (P.L. 107-16)

P.L. 107-16, §532(c)(3):

Amended Code Sec. 2014(b)(2) by striking ", 2011," following "provided by sections 2010". **Effective** for estates of decedents dying, and generation-skipping transfers, after 12-31-2004.

P.L. 107-16, §901(a)-(b), as amended by P.L. 111-312, §101(a)(1), provides [but see P.L. 112-240, §101(a)(1) and (3), above]:

SEC. 901. SUNSET OF PROVISIONS OF ACT.

(a) IN GENERAL.—All provisions of, and amendments made by, this Act shall not apply—

(1) to taxable, plan, or limitation years beginning after December 31, 2012, or

(2) in the case of title V, to estates of decedents dying, gifts made, or generation skipping transfers, after December 31, 2012.

(b) APPLICATION OF CERTAIN LAWS.—The Internal Revenue Code of 1986 and the Employee Retirement Income Security Act of 1974 shall be applied and administered to years, estates, gifts, and transfers described in subsection (a) as if the provisions and amendments described in subsection (a) had never been enacted.

• 1976, Tax Reform Act of 1976 (P.L. 94-455)

P.L. 94-455, §2001(c)(1)(G), (d)(1):

Substituted "sections 2010, 2011, and 2012" for "sections 2011 and 2012" in Code Sec. 2014(b)(2). **Effective** for estates of decedents dying after 12-31-76.

[Sec. 2014(c)]

(c) VALUATION OF PROPERTY.—

(1) The values referred to in the ratio stated in subsection (b)(1) are the values determined for purposes of the tax imposed by such foreign country.

(2) The values referred to in the ratio stated in subsection (b)(2) are the values determined under this chapter; but, in applying such ratio, the value of any property described in subparagraphs (A), (B), and (C) thereof shall be reduced by such amount as will properly reflect, in accordance with regulations prescribed by the Secretary, the deductions allowed in respect of such property under sections 2055 and 2056 (relating to charitable and marital deductions).

Amendments

• 1976, Tax Reform Act of 1976 (P.L. 94-455)

P.L. 94-455, §1906(b)(13)(A):

Amended 1954 Code by substituting "Secretary" for "Secretary or his delegate" each place it appeared. **Effective** 2-1-77.

[Sec. 2014(d)]

(d) PROOF OF CREDIT.—The credit provided in this section shall be allowed only if the taxpayer establishes to the satisfaction of the Secretary—

(1) the amount of taxes actually paid to the foreign country,

(2) the amount and date of each payment thereof,

(3) the description and value of the property in respect of which such taxes are imposed, and

(4) all other information necessary for the verification and computation of the credit.

[Sec. 2014(e)]

(e) PERIOD OF LIMITATION.—The credit provided in this section shall be allowed only for such taxes as were actually paid and credit therefor claimed within 4 years after the filing of the return required by section 6018, except that—

(1) If a petition for redetermination of a deficiency has been filed with the Tax Court within the time prescribed in section 6213(a), then within such 4-year period or before the expiration of 60 days after the decision of the Tax Court becomes final.

(2) If, under section 6161, an extension of time has been granted for payment of the tax shown on the return, or of a deficiency, then within such 4-year period or before the date of the expiration of the period of the extension.

Refund based on such credit may (despite the provisions of sections 6511 and 6512) be made if claim therefor is filed within the period above provided. Any such refund shall be made without interest.

[Sec. 2014(f)]

(f) ADDITIONAL LIMITATION IN CASES INVOLVING A DEDUCTION UNDER SECTION 2053(d).—In any case where a deduction is allowed under section 2053(d) for an estate, succession, legacy, or inheritance tax imposed by and actually paid to any foreign country upon a transfer by the decedent for public, charitable, or religious uses described in section 2055, the property described in subparagraphs (A), (B), and (C) of paragraphs (1) and (2) of subsection (b) of this section shall not include any property in respect of which such deduction is allowed under section 2053(d).

Amendments

• 1959 (P.L. 86-175)

P.L. 86-175, §2:

Amended 1954 Code Sec. 2014 by adding new subsection (f). **Effective** with respect to estates of decedents dying on or after 7-1-55.

[Sec. 2014(g)]

(g) POSSESSION OF UNITED STATES DEEMED A FOREIGN COUNTRY.—For purposes of the credits authorized by this section, each possession of the United States shall be deemed to be a foreign country.

Amendments

• 1959 (P.L. 86-175)

P.L. 86-175, §2:

Amended 1954 Code Sec. 2014 by relettering subsection (f) as subsection (g). **Effective** with respect to the estates of decedents dying on or after 7-1-55.

• 1958, Technical Amendments Act of 1958 (P.L. 85-866)

P.L. 85-866, §102(c), (d):

Added Code Sec. 2014(f). **Effective** for estates of decedents dying after 9-2-58.

[Sec. 2014(h)]

(h) SIMILAR CREDIT REQUIRED FOR CERTAIN ALIEN RESIDENTS.—Whenever the President finds that—

(1) a foreign country, in imposing estate, inheritance, legacy, or succession taxes, does not allow to citizens of the United States resident in such foreign country at the time of death a credit similar to the credit allowed under subsection (a),

(2) such foreign country, when requested by the United States to do so has not acted to provide such a similar credit in the case of citizens of the United States resident in such foreign country at the time of death, and

(3) it is in the public interest to allow the credit under subsection (a) in the case of citizens or subjects of such foreign country only if it allows such a similar credit in the case of citizens of the United States resident in such foreign country at the time of death,

the President shall proclaim that, in the case of citizens or subjects of such foreign country dying while the proclamation remains in effect, the credit under subsection (a) shall be allowed only if such foreign country allows such a similar credit in the case of citizens of the United States resident in such foreign country at the time of death.

Amendments

• 1966, Foreign Investors Tax Act of 1966 (P.L. 89-809)

P.L. 89-809, §106(b)(3):

Added new Code Sec. 2014(h). **Effective** with respect to estates of decedents dying after 11-13-66.

[Sec. 2015]

SEC. 2015. CREDIT FOR DEATH TAXES ON REMAINDERS.

Where an election is made under section 6163(a) to postpone payment of the tax imposed by section 2001 or 2101, such part of any estate, inheritance, legacy, or succession taxes allowable as a credit under section 2014, as is attributable to a reversionary or remainder interest may be allowed as a credit against the tax attributable to such interest, subject to the limitations on the amount of the credit contained in such sections, if such part is paid, and credit therefor claimed, at any time before the expiration of the time for payment of the tax imposed by section 2001 or 2101 as postponed and extended under section 6163.

Amendments

• 2013, American Taxpayer Relief Act of 2012 (P.L. 112-240)

P.L. 112-240, §101(a)(1) and (3), provides:

SEC. 101. PERMANENT EXTENSION AND MODIFICATION OF 2001 TAX RELIEF.

(a) PERMANENT EXTENSION.—

(1) IN GENERAL.—The Economic Growth and Tax Relief Reconciliation Act of 2001 is amended by striking title IX.

* * *

(3) EFFECTIVE DATE.—The amendments made by this subsection shall apply to taxable, plan, or limitation years beginning after December 31, 2012, and estates of decedents dying, gifts made, or generation skipping transfers after December 31, 2012.

• 2001, Economic Growth and Tax Relief Reconciliation Act of 2001 (P.L. 107-16)

P.L. 107-16, §532(c)(4):

Amended Code Sec. 2015 by striking "2011 or" following "a credit under section". **Effective** for estates of decedents dying, and generation-skipping transfers, after 12-31-2004.

P.L. 107-16, §901(a)-(b), as amended by P.L. 111-312, §101(a)(1), provides [but see P.L. 112-240, §101(a)(1) and (3), above]:

SEC. 901. SUNSET OF PROVISIONS OF ACT.

(a) IN GENERAL.—All provisions of, and amendments made by, this Act shall not apply—

(1) to taxable, plan, or limitation years beginning after December 31, 2012, or

(2) in the case of title V, to estates of decedents dying, gifts made, or generation skipping transfers, after December 31, 2012.

(b) APPLICATION OF CERTAIN LAWS.—The Internal Revenue Code of 1986 and the Employee Retirement Income Security Act of 1974 shall be applied and administered to years, estates, gifts, and transfers described in subsection (a) as if the provisions and amendments described in subsection (a) had never been enacted.

• 1958, Technical Amendments Act of 1958 (P.L. 85-866)

P.L. 85-866, §66(a):

Amended Code Sec. 2015 by substituting the phrase "the time for payment of the tax imposed by section 2001 or 2101 as postponed and extended under section 6163" in lieu of the phrase "60 days after the termination of the precedent interest or interests in the property". **Effective** in the case of any reversionary or remainder interest in property only if the precedent interest or interests in the property did not terminate before the beginning of the 60-day period which ends on 9-2-58.

[Sec. 2016]

SEC. 2016. RECOVERY OF TAXES CLAIMED AS CREDIT.

If any tax claimed as a credit under section 2014 is recovered from any foreign country, the executor, or any other person or persons recovering such amount, shall give notice of such recovery to the Secretary at such time and in such manner as may be required by regulations prescribed by him, and the Secretary shall (despite the provisions of section 6501) redetermine the amount of the tax under this chapter and the amount, if any, of the tax due on such redetermination, shall be paid by the executor or such person or persons, as the case may be, on notice and demand. No interest shall be assessed or collected on any amount of tax due on any redetermination by the Secretary resulting from a refund to the executor of tax claimed as a credit under section 2014, for any period before the receipt of such refund, except to the extent interest was paid by the foreign country on such refund.

Amendments

• 2013, American Taxpayer Relief Act of 2012 (P.L. 112-240)

P.L. 112-240, §101(a)(1) and (3), provides:

SEC. 101. PERMANENT EXTENSION AND MODIFICATION OF 2001 TAX RELIEF.

(a) PERMANENT EXTENSION.—

(1) IN GENERAL.—The Economic Growth and Tax Relief Reconciliation Act of 2001 is amended by striking title IX.

* * *

(3) EFFECTIVE DATE.—The amendments made by this subsection shall apply to taxable, plan, or limitation years beginning after December 31, 2012, and estates of decedents dying, gifts made, or generation skipping transfers after December 31, 2012.

• 2002, Job Creation and Worker Assistance Act of 2002 (P.L. 107-147)

P.L. 107-147, §411(h):

Amended Code Sec. 2016 by striking "any State, any possession of the United States, or the District of Columbia," following "any foreign country,". **Effective** as if included in the provision of P.L. 107-16 to which it relates [applicable to estates of decedents dying, and generation-skipping transfers, after 12-31-2004.—CCH].

• 2001, Economic Growth and Tax Relief Reconciliation Act of 2001 (P.L. 107-16)

P.L. 107-16, §532(c)(4):

Amended Code Sec. 2016 by striking "2011 or" following "If any tax claimed as a credit under section". **Effective** for estates of decedents dying, and generation-skipping transfers, after 12-31-2004.

P.L. 107-16, §901(a)-(b), as amended by P.L. 111-312, §101(a)(1), provides [but see P.L. 112-240, §101(a)(1) and (3), above]:

SEC. 901. SUNSET OF PROVISIONS OF ACT.

(a) IN GENERAL.—All provisions of, and amendments made by, this Act shall not apply—

(1) to taxable, plan, or limitation years beginning after December 31, 2012, or

(2) in the case of title V, to estates of decedents dying, gifts made, or generation skipping transfers, after December 31, 2012.

(b) APPLICATION OF CERTAIN LAWS.—The Internal Revenue Code of 1986 and the Employee Retirement Income Security Act of 1974 shall be applied and administered to years, estates, gifts, and transfers described in subsection (a) as if the provisions and amendments described in subsection (a) had never been enacted.

• 1976, Tax Reform Act of 1976 (P.L. 94-455)

P.L. 94-455, §1902(a)(12)(C):

Deleted "Territory or" in Code Sec. 2016. **Effective** for gifts made after 12-31-76.

P.L. 94-455, §1906(b)(13)(A):

Amended 1954 Code by substituting "Secretary" for "Secretary or his delegate" each place it appeared. **Effective** 2-1-77.

PART III—GROSS ESTATE

[Sec. 2031]

SEC. 2031. DEFINITION OF GROSS ESTATE.

[Sec. 2031(a)]

(a) GENERAL.—The value of the gross estate of the decedent shall be determined by including to the extent provided for in this part, the value at the time of his death of all property, real or personal, tangible or intangible, wherever situated.

Amendments

• 1962, Revenue Act of 1962 (P.L. 87-834)

P.L. 87-834, §18(a)(1):

Amended Code Sec. 2031(a) by deleting ", except real property situated outside of the United States". **Effective,** generally, for estates of decedents dying after 10-16-62. For exceptions, see Act Sec. 18(b), below.

P.L. 87-834, §18(b), provides:

(b) EFFECTIVE DATE.—

(1) Except as provided in paragraph (2), the amendments made by subsection (a) shall apply to the estates of decedents dying after the date of the enactment of this Act.

(2) In the case of a decedent dying after the date of the enactment of this Act and before July 1, 1964, the value of real property situated outside of the United States shall not be included in the gross estate (as defined in section 2031(a)) of the decedent—

(A) under section 2033, 2034, 2035(a), 2036(a), 2037(a), or 2038(a) to the extent the real property, or the decedent's interest in it, was acquired by the decedent before February 1, 1962;

(B) under section 2040 to the extent such property or interest was acquired by the decedent before February 1, 1962, or was held by the decedent and the survivor in a joint tenancy or tenancy by the entirety before February 1, 1962; or

(C) under section 2041(a) to the extent that before February 1, 1962, such property or interest was subject to a general power of appointment (as defined in section 2041) possessed by the decedent.

In the case of real property, or an interest therein, situated outside of the United States (including a general power of appointment in respect of such property or interest, and including property held by the decedent and the survivor in a joint tenancy or tenancy by the entirety) which was acquired by the decedent after January 31, 1962, by gift within the meaning of section 2511, or from a prior decedent by devise or inheritance, or by reason of death, form of ownership, or other conditions (including the exercise or nonexercise of a power of appointment), for purposes of this paragraph such property or interest therein shall be deemed to have been acquired by the decedent before February 1, 1962, if before that date the donor or prior decedent had acquired the property or his interest therein or had possessed a power of appointment in respect of the property or interest.

[Sec. 2031(b)]

(b) VALUATION OF UNLISTED STOCK AND SECURITIES.—In the case of stock and securities of a corporation the value of which, by reason of their not being listed on an exchange and by reason of the absence of sales thereof, cannot be determined with reference to bid and asked prices or with reference to sales prices, the value thereof shall be determined by taking into consideration, in addition to all other factors, the value of stock or securities of corporations engaged in the same or a similar line of business which are listed on an exchange.

[Sec. 2031(c)]

(c) ESTATE TAX WITH RESPECT TO LAND SUBJECT TO A QUALIFIED CONSERVATION EASEMENT.—

(1) IN GENERAL.—If the executor makes the election described in paragraph (6), then, except as otherwise provided in this subsection, there shall be excluded from the gross estate the lesser of—

(A) the applicable percentage of the value of land subject to a qualified conservation easement, reduced by the amount of any deduction under section 2055(f) with respect to such land, or

(B) $500,000.

(2) APPLICABLE PERCENTAGE.—For purposes of paragraph (1), the term "applicable percentage" means 40 percent reduced (but not below zero) by 2 percentage points for each percentage point (or fraction thereof) by which the value of the qualified conservation easement is less than 30 percent of the value of the land (determined without regard to the value of such easement and reduced by the value of any retained development right (as defined in paragraph (5))). The values taken into account under the preceding sentence shall be such values as of the date of the contribution referred to in paragraph (8)(B).

(3) [Stricken.]

(4) TREATMENT OF CERTAIN INDEBTEDNESS.—

(A) IN GENERAL.—The exclusion provided in paragraph (1) shall not apply to the extent that the land is debt-financed property.

(B) DEFINITIONS.—For purposes of this paragraph—

(i) DEBT-FINANCED PROPERTY.—The term "debt-financed property" means any property with respect to which there is an acquisition indebtedness (as defined in clause (ii)) on the date of the decedent's death.

(ii) ACQUISITION INDEBTEDNESS.—The term "acquisition indebtedness" means, with respect to debt-financed property, the unpaid amount of—

(I) the indebtedness incurred by the donor in acquiring such property,

(II) the indebtedness incurred before the acquisition of such property if such indebtedness would not have been incurred but for such acquisition,

(III) the indebtedness incurred after the acquisition of such property if such indebtedness would not have been incurred but for such acquisition and the incurrence of such indebtedness was reasonably foreseeable at the time of such acquisition, and

(IV) the extension, renewal, or refinancing of an acquisition indebtedness.

(5) TREATMENT OF RETAINED DEVELOPMENT RIGHT.—

(A) IN GENERAL.—Paragraph (1) shall not apply to the value of any development right retained by the donor in the conveyance of a qualified conservation easement.

(B) TERMINATION OF RETAINED DEVELOPMENT RIGHT.—If every person in being who has an interest (whether or not in possession) in the land executes an agreement to extinguish permanently some or all of any development rights (as defined in subparagraph (D)) retained by the donor on or before the date for filing the return of the tax imposed by section 2001, then any tax imposed by section 2001 shall be reduced accordingly. Such agreement shall be filed with the return of the tax imposed by section 2001. The agreement shall be in such form as the Secretary shall prescribe.

(C) ADDITIONAL TAX.—Any failure to implement the agreement described in subparagraph (B) not later than the earlier of—

(i) the date which is 2 years after the date of the decedent's death, or

(ii) the date of the sale of such land subject to the qualified conservation easement,

shall result in the imposition of an additional tax in the amount of the tax which would have been due on the retained development rights subject to such agreement. Such additional tax shall be due and payable on the last day of the 6th month following such date.

(D) DEVELOPMENT RIGHT DEFINED.—For purposes of this paragraph, the term "development right" means any right to use the land subject to the qualified conservation easement in which such right is retained for any commercial purpose which is not subordinate to and directly supportive of the use of such land as a farm for farming purposes (within the meaning of section 2032A(e)(5)).

(6) ELECTION.—The election under this subsection shall be made on or before the due date (including extensions) for filing the return of tax imposed by section 2001 and shall be made on such return.

(7) CALCULATION OF ESTATE TAX DUE.—An executor making the election described in paragraph (6) shall, for purposes of calculating the amount of tax imposed by section 2001, include the value of any development right (as defined in paragraph (5)) retained by the donor in the conveyance of such qualified conservation easement. The computation of tax on any retained development right prescribed in this paragraph shall be done in such manner and on such forms as the Secretary shall prescribe.

(8) DEFINITIONS.—For purposes of this subsection—

(A) LAND SUBJECT TO A QUALIFIED CONSERVATION EASEMENT.—The term "land subject to a qualified conservation easement" means land—

(i) which is located in the United States or any possession of the United States,

(ii) which was owned by the decedent or a member of the decedent's family at all times during the 3-year period ending on the date of the decedent's death, and

(iii) with respect to which a qualified conservation easement has been made by an individual described in subparagraph (C), as of the date of the election described in paragraph (6).

(B) QUALIFIED CONSERVATION EASEMENT.—The term "qualified conservation easement" means a qualified conservation contribution (as defined in section 170(h)(1)) of a qualified real property interest (as defined in section 170(h)(2)(C)), except that clause (iv) of section 170(h)(4)(A) shall not apply, and the restriction on the use of such interest described in section 170(h)(2)(C) shall include a prohibition on more than a de minimis use for a commercial recreational activity.

(C) INDIVIDUAL DESCRIBED.—An individual is described in this subparagraph if such individual is—

(i) the decedent,

(ii) a member of the decedent's family,

(iii) the executor of the decedent's estate, or

(iv) the trustee of a trust the corpus of which includes the land to be subject to the qualified conservation easement.

(D) MEMBER OF FAMILY.—The term "member of the decedent's family" means any member of the family (as defined in section 2032A(e)(2)) of the decedent.

(9) TREATMENT OF EASEMENTS GRANTED AFTER DEATH.—In any case in which the qualified conservation easement is granted after the date of the decedent's death and on or before the due date (including extensions) for filing the return of tax imposed by section 2001, the deduction under section 2055(f) with respect to such easement shall be allowed to the estate but only if no charitable deduction is allowed under chapter 1 to any person with respect to the grant of such easement.

(10) APPLICATION OF THIS SECTION TO INTERESTS IN PARTNERSHIPS, CORPORATIONS, AND TRUSTS.—This section shall apply to an interest in a partnership, corporation, or trust if at least 30 percent of the entity is owned (directly or indirectly) by the decedent, as determined under the rules described in section 2057(e)(3) (as in effect before its repeal).

Amendments

• 2018, Tax Technical Corrections Act of 2018 (P.L. 115-141)

P.L. 115-141, §401(a)(200), Div. U:

Amended Code Sec. 2031(c)(1) by striking all that follows subparagraph (A) and inserting

"(B) $500,000.".

Effective 3-23-2018. Prior to be stricken, all that follows subparagraph (A) read as follows:

(II) [(B)] $500,000.

P.L. 115-141, §401(a)(201), Div. U:

Amended Code Sec. 2031(c)(2) by striking "paragraph (5))." and inserting "paragraph (5)))."**. Effective** 3-23-2018.

• 2014, Tax Technical Corrections Act of 2014 (P.L. 113-295)

P.L. 113-295, §221(a)(96), Division A:

Amended Code Sec. 2031(c) by striking paragraph (3) and by amending paragraph (1)(B). **Effective** generally 12-19-2014. For a special rule, see Act Sec. 221(b)(2), Division A, below. Prior to being amended and stricken, respectively, Code Sec. 2031(c)(1)(B) and (3) read as follows:

(B) the exclusion limitation.

* * *

(3) EXCLUSION LIMITATION.—For purposes of paragraph (1), the exclusion limitation is the limitation determined in accordance with the following table:

In the case of estates of decedents dying during:	*The exclusion limitation is:*
1998	$100,000
1999	$200,000
2000	$300,000
2001	$400,000
2002 or thereafter	$500,000

P.L. 113-295, §221(a)(97)(B), Division A:

Amended Code Sec. 2031(c)(10) by inserting "(as in effect before its repeal)" immediately before the period at the end thereof. **Effective** generally 12-19-2014. For a special rule, see Act Sec. 221(b)(2), Division A, below.

P.L. 113-295, §221(b)(2), Division A, provides:

(2) SAVINGS PROVISION.—If—

(A) any provision amended or repealed by the amendments made by this section applied to—

(i) any transaction occurring before the date of the enactment of this Act,

(ii) any property acquired before such date of enactment, or

(iii) any item of income, loss, deduction, or credit taken into account before such date of enactment, and

(B) the treatment of such transaction, property, or item under such provision would (without regard to the amendments or repeals made by this section) affect the liability for tax for periods ending after date of enactment, nothing in the amendments or repeals made by this section shall be construed to affect the treatment of such transaction, property, or item for purposes of determining liability for tax for periods ending after such date of enactment.

• 2013, American Taxpayer Relief Act of 2012 (P.L. 112-240)

P.L. 112-240, §101(a)(1) and (3), provides:

SEC. 101. PERMANENT EXTENSION AND MODIFICATION OF 2001 TAX RELIEF.

(a) PERMANENT EXTENSION.—

(1) IN GENERAL.—The Economic Growth and Tax Relief Reconciliation Act of 2001 is amended by striking title IX.

* * *

(3) EFFECTIVE DATE.—The amendments made by this subsection shall apply to taxable, plan, or limitation years beginning after December 31, 2012, and estates of decedents dying, gifts made, or generation skipping transfers after December 31, 2012.

• 2001, Economic Growth and Tax Relief Reconciliation Act of 2001 (P.L. 107-16)

P.L. 107-16, §551(a):

Amended Code Sec. 2031(c)(8)(A)(i). **Effective** for estates of decedents dying after 12-31-2000. Prior to amendment, Code Sec. 2031(c)(8)(A)(i) read as follows:

(i) which is located—

(I) in or within 25 miles of an area which, on the date of the decedent's death, is a metropolitan area (as defined by the Office of Management and Budget),

(II) in or within 25 miles of an area which, on the date of the decedent's death, is a national park or wilderness area designated as part of the National Wilderness Preservation System (unless it is determined by the Secretary that land in or within 25 miles of such a park or wilderness area is not under significant development pressure), or

(III) in or within 10 miles of an area which, on the date of the decedent's death, is an Urban National Forest (as designated by the Forest Service),

P.L. 107-16, §551(b):

Amended Code Sec. 2031(c)(2) by adding at the end a new sentence. **Effective** for estates of decedents dying after 12-31-2000.

P.L. 107-16, §901(a)-(b), as amended by P.L. 111-312, §101(a)(1), provides [but see P.L. 112-240, §101(a)(1) and (3), above]:

SEC. 901. SUNSET OF PROVISIONS OF ACT.

(a) IN GENERAL.—All provisions of, and amendments made by, this Act shall not apply—

(1) to taxable, plan, or limitation years beginning after December 31, 2012, or

(2) in the case of title V, to estates of decedents dying, gifts made, or generation skipping transfers, after December 31, 2012.

(b) APPLICATION OF CERTAIN LAWS.—The Internal Revenue Code of 1986 and the Employee Retirement Income Security Act of 1974 shall be applied and administered to years, estates, gifts, and transfers described in subsection (a) as if the provisions and amendments described in subsection (a) had never been enacted.

• 1998, Tax and Trade Relief Extension Act of 1998 (P.L. 105-277)

P.L. 105-277, §4006(c)(3):

Amended Code Sec. 2031(c)(10) by striking "section 2033A(e)(3)" and inserting "section 2057(e)(3)". **Effective** 10-21-98.

• 1998, IRS Restructuring and Reform Act of 1998 (P.L. 105-206)

P.L. 105-206, §6007(g)(1):

Amended Code Sec. 2031(c) by redesignating paragraph (9) as paragraph (10) and by inserting after paragraph (8) a new paragraph (9). **Effective** as if included in the provision of P.L. 105-34 to which it relates [**effective** for estates of decedents dying after 12-31-97.—CCH].

P.L. 105-206, §6007(g)(2):

Amended the first sentence of Code Sec. 2031(c)(6) by striking all that follows "shall be made" and inserting "on or before the due date (including extensions) for filing the return of tax imposed by section 2001 and shall be made on such return." **Effective** as if included in the provision of P.L. 105-34 to which it relates [**effective** for estates of decedents dying after 12-31-97.—CCH]. Prior to amendment, the first sentence of Code Sec. 2031(c)(6) read as follows:

(6) ELECTION.—The election under this subsection shall be made on the return of the tax imposed by section 2001.

• 1997, Taxpayer Relief Act of 1997 (P.L. 105-34)

P.L. 105-34, §508(a):

Amended Code Sec. 2031 by redesignating subsection (c) as subsection (d) and by inserting after subsection (b) a new subsection (c). **Effective** for estates of decedents dying after 12-31-97.

[Sec. 2031(d)]

(d) CROSS REFERENCE.—

For executor's right to be furnished on request a statement regarding any valuation made by the Secretary within the gross estate, see section 7517.

Amendments

• 1997, Taxpayer Relief Act of 1997 (P.L. 105-34)

P.L. 105-34, §508(a):

Amended Code Sec. 2031 by redesignating subsection (c) as subsection (d). **Effective** for estates of decedents dying after 12-31-97.

• 1976, Tax Reform Act of 1976 (P.L. 94-455)

P.L. 94-455, §2008(a)(2):

Added Code Sec. 2031(c). For the **effective** date, see Act Sec. 2008(d)(1), below.

P.L. 94-455, §2008(d)(1), provides:

(d) EFFECTIVE DATES.—

(1) The amendments made by subsection (a)—

(A) insofar as they relate to the tax imposed under chapter 11 of the Internal Revenue Code of 1954, shall apply to the estates of decedents dying after December 31, 1976, and

(B) insofar as they relate to the tax imposed under chapter 12 of such Code, shall apply to gifts made after December 31, 1976.

[Sec. 2032]

SEC. 2032. ALTERNATE VALUATION.

[Sec. 2032(a)]

(a) GENERAL.—The value of the gross estate may be determined, if the executor so elects, by valuing all the property included in the gross estate as follows:

(1) In the case of property distributed, sold, exchanged, or otherwise disposed of, within 6 months after the decedent's death such property shall be valued as of the date of distribution, sale, exchange, or other disposition.

(2) In the case of property not distributed, sold, exchanged, or otherwise disposed of, within 6 months after the decedent's death such property shall be valued as of the date 6 months after the decedent's death.

(3) Any interest or estate which is affected by mere lapse of time shall be included at its value as of the time of death (instead of the later date) with adjustment for any difference in its value as of the later date not due to mere lapse of time.

Amendments

• 1970, Excise, Estate, and Gift Tax Adjustment Act of 1970 (P.L. 91-614)

P.L. 91-614, §101(a):

Amended paragraphs (1) and (2) of Code Sec. 2032(a) by substituting "6 months" for "1 year" each place it appeared. **Effective** with respect to decedents dying after 12-31-70.

[Sec. 2032(b)]

(b) SPECIAL RULES.—No deduction under this chapter of any item shall be allowed if allowance for such item is in effect given by the alternate valuation provided by this section. Wherever in any other subsection or section of this chapter reference is made to the value of property at the time of the decedent's death, such reference shall be deemed to refer to the value of such property used in determining the value of the gross estate. In case of an election made by the executor under this section, then—

(1) for purposes of the charitable deduction under section 2055 or 2106(a)(2), any bequest, legacy, devise, or transfer enumerated therein, and

(2) for the purpose of the marital deduction under section 2056, any interest in property passing to the surviving spouse,

shall be valued as of the date of the decedent's death with adjustment for any difference in value (not due to mere lapse of time or the occurrence or nonoccurrence of a contingency) of the property as of the date 6 months after the decedent's death (substituting, in the case of property distributed by the executor or trustee, or sold, exchanged, or otherwise disposed of, during such 6-month period, the date thereof).

Amendments

• 1970, Excise, Estate, and Gift Tax Adjustment Act of 1970 (P.L. 91-614)

P.L. 91-614, §101(a):

Amended Code Sec. 2032(b) by substituting "6 months" for "1 year" and "6-month period" for "1-year period" in the last sentence thereof. **Effective** with respect to decedents dying after 12-31-70.

[Sec. 2032(c)]

(c) ELECTION MUST DECREASE GROSS ESTATE AND ESTATE TAX.—No election may be made under this section with respect to an estate unless such election will decrease—

(1) the value of the gross estate, and

(2) the sum of the tax imposed by this chapter and the tax imposed by chapter 13 with respect to property includible in the decedent's gross estate (reduced by credits allowable against such taxes).

Amendments

• 1986, Tax Reform Act of 1986 (P.L. 99-514)

P.L. 99-514, §1432(c)(1):

Amended Code Sec. 2032(c)(2). **Effective**, generally, for any generation-skipping transfer (within the meaning of Code Sec. 2611) made after 10-22-86. However, for special rules see Act Sec. 1433(b)-(d) in the amendment notes following Code Sec. 2601. Prior to amendment, Code Sec. 2032(c)(2) read as follows:

(2) the amount of the tax imposed by this chapter (reduced by credits allowable against such tax).

• 1984, Deficit Reduction Act of 1984 (P.L. 98-369)

P.L. 98-369, §1023(a):

Amended Code Sec. 2032 by redesignating subsection (c) as subsection (d) and by inserting after subsection (b) a new subsection (c). **Effective** with respect to the estates of decedents dying after 7-18-84. For a transitional rule, see Act Sec. 1024(b)(2) in the amendment notes following Code Sec. 2032(d).

[Sec. 2032(d)]

(d) ELECTION.—

(1) IN GENERAL.—The election provided for in this section shall be made by the executor on the return of the tax imposed by this chapter. Such election, once made, shall be irrevocable.

(2) EXCEPTION.—No election may be made under this section if such return is filed more than 1 year after the time prescribed by law (including extensions) for filing such return.

Amendments

• 1984, Deficit Reduction Act of 1984 (P.L. 98-369)

P.L. 98-369, §1023(a):

Amended Code Sec. 2032 by redesignating subsection (c) as subsection (d). **Effective** with respect to the estates of decedents dying after 7-18-84. For a transitional rule, see Act Sec. 1024(b)(2), below.

P.L. 98-369, §1024(a):

Amended Code Sec. 2032(d), as redesignated by Act Sec. 1023. **Effective** with respect to the estates of decedents dying after 7-18-84. For a transitional rule, see Act Sec. 1024(b)(2), below. Prior to amendment, it read as follows:

(c) Time of Election.—The election provided for in this section shall be exercised by the executor on his return if filed within the time prescribed by law or before the expiration of any extension of time granted pursuant to law for the filing of the return.

P.L. 98-369, §1024(b)(2), provides:

(2) Transitional Rule.—In the case of an estate of a decedent dying before the date of the enactment of this Act if—

(A) a credit or refund of the tax imposed by chapter 11 of the Internal Revenue Code of 1954 is not prevented on the date of the enactment of this Act by the operation of any law or rule of law.

(B) the election under section 2032 of the Internal Revenue Code of 1954 would have met the requirements of such section (as amended by this section and section 1023) had the decedent died after the date of enactment of this Act, and

(C) a claim for credit or refund of such tax with respect to such estate is filed not later than the 90th day after the date of the enactment of this Act,

then such election shall be treated as a valid election under such section 2032. The statutory period for the assessment of any deficiency which is attributable to an election under this paragraph shall not expire before the close of the 2-year period beginning on the date of the enactment of this Act.

[Sec. 2032A]

SEC. 2032A. VALUATION OF CERTAIN FARM, ETC., REAL PROPERTY.

[Sec. 2032A(a)]

(a) VALUE BASED ON USE UNDER WHICH PROPERTY QUALIFIES.—

(1) GENERAL RULE.—If—

(A) the decedent was (at the time of his death) a citizen or resident of the United States, and

(B) the executor elects the application of this section and files the agreement referred to in subsection (d)(2),

then, for purposes of this chapter, the value of qualified real property shall be its value for the use under which it qualifies, under subsection (b), as qualified real property.

(2) LIMITATION ON AGGREGATE REDUCTION IN FAIR MARKET VALUE.—The aggregate decrease in the value of qualified real property taken into account for purposes of this chapter which results from the application of paragraph (1) with respect to any decedent shall not exceed $750,000.

(3) INFLATION ADJUSTMENT.—In the case of estates of decedents dying in a calendar year after 1998, the $750,000 amount contained in paragraph (2) shall be increased by an amount equal to—

(A) $750,000, multiplied by

(B) the cost-of-living adjustment determined under section 1(f)(3) for such calendar year by substituting "calendar year 1997" for "calendar year 2016" in subparagraph (A)(ii) thereof.

If any amount as adjusted under the preceding sentence is not a multiple of $10,000, such amount shall be rounded to the next lowest multiple of $10,000.

Amendments

• 2017, Tax Cuts and Jobs Act (P.L. 115-97)

P.L. 115-97, §11002(d)(1)(DD):

Amended Code Sec. 2032A(a)(3)(B) by striking "for 'calendar year 1992' in subparagraph (B)" and inserting "for 'calendar year 2016' in subparagraph (A)(ii)". **Effective** for tax years beginning after 12-31-2017.

• 1997, Taxpayer Relief Act of 1997 (P.L. 105-34)

P.L. 105-34, §501(b):

Amended Code Sec. 2032A(a) by adding a new paragraph (3). **Effective** for the estates of decedents dying, and gifts made, after 12-31-97.

• 1990, Omnibus Budget Reconciliation Act of 1990 (P.L. 101-508)

P.L. 101-508, §11802(f)(5):

Amended Code Sec. 2032A(a)(2). **Effective** 11-5-90. Prior to amendment, Code Sec. 2032A(a)(2) read as follows:

(2) LIMIT ON AGGREGATE REDUCTION IN FAIR MARKET VALUE.—The aggregate decrease in the value of qualified real property taken into account for purposes of this chapter which results from the application of paragraph (1) with respect to any decedent shall not exceed the applicable limit set forth in the following table:

In the case of decedents dying in:	The applicable limit is:
1981	$600,000
1982	700,000
1983	750,000

P.L. 101-508, §11821(b), provides:

(b) SAVINGS PROVISION.—If—

(1) any provision amended or repealed by this part applied to—

(A) any transaction occurring before the date of the enactment of this Act,

(B) any property acquired before such date of enactment, or

(C) any item of income, loss, deduction, or credit taken into account before such date of enactment, and

(2) the treatment of such transaction, property, or item under such provision would (without regard to the amendments made by this part) affect liability for tax for periods ending after such date of enactment,

nothing in the amendments made by this part shall be construed to affect the treatment of such transaction, property, or item for purposes of determining liability for tax for periods ending after such date of enactment.

• 1981, Economic Recovery Tax Act of 1981 (P.L. 97-34)

P.L. 97-34, §421(a):

Amended Code Sec. 2032A(a)(2). **Effective** with respect to the estates of decedents dying after 12-31-80. Prior to amendment, Code Sec. 2032A(a)(2) read as follows:

(2) LIMITATION.—The aggregate decrease in the value of qualified real property taken into account for purposes of this chapter which results from the application of paragraph (1) with respect to any decedent shall not exceed $500,000.

[Sec. 2032A(b)]

(b) QUALIFIED REAL PROPERTY.—

(1) IN GENERAL.—For purposes of this section, the term "qualified real property" means real property located in the United States which was acquired from or passed from the decedent to a qualified heir of the decedent and which, on the date of the decedent's death, was being used for a qualified use by the decedent or a member of the decedent's family, but only if—

(A) 50 percent or more of the adjusted value of the gross estate consists of the adjusted value of real or personal property which—

(i) on the date of the decedent's death, was being used for a qualified use by the decedent or a member of the decedent's family, and

(ii) was acquired from or passed from the decedent to a qualified heir of the decedent.

(B) 25 percent or more of the adjusted value of the gross estate consists of the adjusted value of real property which meets the requirements of subparagraphs (A)(ii) and (C),

(C) during the 8-year period ending on the date of the decedent's death there have been periods aggregating 5 years or more during which—

(i) such real property was owned by the decedent or a member of the decedent's family and used for a qualified use by the decedent or a member of the decedent's family, and

(ii) there was material participation by the decedent or a member of the decedent's family in the operation of the farm or other business, and

(D) such real property is designated in the agreement referred to in subsection (d)(2).

(2) QUALIFIED USE.—For purposes of this section, the term "qualified use" means the devotion of the property to any of the following:

(A) use as a farm for farming purposes, or

(B) use in a trade or business other than the trade or business of farming.

(3) ADJUSTED VALUE.—For purposes of paragraph (1), the term "adjusted value" means—

(A) in the case of the gross estate, the value of the gross estate for purposes of this chapter (determined without regard to this section), reduced by any amounts allowable as a deduction under paragraph (4) of section 2053(a), or

(B) in the case of any real or personal property, the value of such property for purposes of this chapter (determined without regard to this section), reduced by any amounts allowable as a deduction in respect to such property under paragraph (4) of section 2053(a).

(4) DECEDENTS WHO ARE RETIRED OR DISABLED.—

(A) IN GENERAL.—If, on the date of the decedent's death the requirements of paragraph (1)(C)(ii) with respect to the decedent for any property are not met, and the decedent—

(i) was receiving old-age benefits under title II of the Social Security Act for a continuous period ending on such date, or

(ii) was disabled for a continuous period ending on such date,

then paragraph (1)(C)(ii) shall be applied with respect to such property by substituting "the date on which the longer of such continuous periods began" for "the date of the decedent's death" in paragraph (1)(C).

(B) DISABLED DEFINED.—For purposes of subparagraph (A), an individual shall be disabled if such individual has a mental or physical impairment which renders him unable to materially participate in the operation of the farm or other business.

(C) COORDINATION WITH RECAPTURE.—For purposes of subsection (c)(6)(B)(i), if the requirements of paragraph (1)(C)(ii) are met with respect to any decedent by reason of subparagraph (A), the period ending on the date on which the continuous period taken into account under subparagraph (A) began shall be treated as the period immediately before the decedent's death.

(5) SPECIAL RULES FOR SURVIVING SPOUSES.—

(A) IN GENERAL.—If property is qualified real property with respect to a decedent (hereinafter in this paragraph referred to as the "first decedent") and such property was acquired from or passed from the first decedent to the surviving spouse of the first decedent, for purposes of applying this subsection and subsection (c) in the case of the estate of such surviving spouse, active management of the farm or other business by the surviving spouse shall be treated as material participation by such surviving spouse in the operation of such farm or business.

(B) SPECIAL RULE.—For the purposes of subparagraph (A), the determination of whether property is qualified real property with respect to the first decedent shall be made without regard to subparagraph (D) of paragraph (1) and without regard to whether an election under this section was made.

(C) COORDINATION WITH PARAGRAPH (4).—In any case in which to do so will enable the requirements of paragraph (1)(C)(ii) to be met with respect to the surviving spouse, this subsection and subsection (c) shall be applied by taking into account any application of paragraph (4).

Amendments

• 1997, Taxpayer Relief Act of 1997 (P.L. 105-34)

P.L. 105-34, §504(b):

Amended Code Sec. 2032A(b)(5)(A) is amended by striking the last sentence. **Effective** with respect to leases entered into after 12-31-76. Prior to being stricken, the last sentence of Code Sec. 2032A(b)(5)(A) read as follows:

For purposes of subsection (c), such surviving spouse shall not be treated as failing to use such property in a qualified use solely because such spouse rents such property to a member of such spouse's family on a net cash basis.

• 1988, Technical and Miscellaneous Revenue Act of 1988 (P.L. 100-647)

P.L. 100-647, §6151(a):

Amended Code Sec. 2032A(b)(5)(A) by adding at the end thereof a new sentence. **Effective**, generally, with respect to rentals occurring after 12-31-76. See, also, Act Sec. 6151(b)(2), below.

P.L. 100-647, §6151(b)(2), provides:

(2) WAIVER OF STATUTE OF LIMITATIONS.—If on the date of the enactment of this Act (or at any time within 1 year after such date of enactment) refund or credit of any overpayment of tax resulting from the application of the amendment made by subsection (a) is barred by any law or rule of law, refund or credit of such overpayment shall, nevertheless, be made or allowed if claim therefore is filed before the date 1 year after the date of the enactment of this Act.

• 1983, Technical Corrections Act of 1982 (P.L. 97-448)

P.L. 97-448, §104(b)(1):

Amended Code Sec. 2032A(b)(5) by adding at the end thereof new subparagraph (C). **Effective** as if included in the provision of P.L. 97-34 to which it relates.

• 1981, Economic Recovery Tax Act of 1981 (P.L. 97-34)

P.L. 97-34, §421(b)(1):

Amended Code Sec. 2032A(b)(1) by inserting "by the decedent or a member of the decedent's family" after "qualified use" each place it appears. **Effective** with respect to estates of decedents dying after 12-31-76. For special rules, see P.L. 97-34, §421(k)(5), below.

P.L. 97-34, §421(b)(2):

Added Code Sec. 2032A(b)(4) and (5). **Effective** with respect to decedents dying after 12-31-81.

P.L. 97-34, §421(k)(5), as amended by P.L. 97-448, §104(b)(4), provides:

(5) CERTAIN AMENDMENTS MADE RETROACTIVE TO 1976.—

(A) IN GENERAL.—The amendments made by subsections (b)(1), (j)(1), and (j)(2) and the provisions of subparagraph (A) of section 2032A(c)(7) of the Internal Revenue Code of 1954 (as added by subsection (c)(2)) shall apply with respect to the estates of decedents dying after December 31, 1976.

(B) TIMELY ELECTION REQUIRED.—Subparagraph (A) shall only apply in the case of an estate if a timely election under section 2032A was made with respect to such estate. If the estate of any decedent would not qualify under section 2032A of the Internal Revenue Code of 1954 but for the amendments described in subparagraph (A) and the time for making an election under section 2032A with respect to such estate would (but for this sentence) expire after July 28, 1980, the time for making such election shall not expire before the close of February 16, 1982.

(C) REINSTATEMENT OF ELECTIONS.—If any election under section 2032A was revoked before the date of the enactment of this Act, such election may be reinstated at any time before February 17, 1982.

(D) STATUTE OF LIMITATIONS.—If on the date of the enactment of this Act (or at any time before February 17, 1982) the making of a credit or refund of any overpayment of tax resulting from the amendments described in subparagraph (A) is barred by any law or rule of law, such credit or refund shall nevertheless be made if claim therefor is made before February 17, 1982.

• 1978, Revenue Act of 1978 (P.L. 95-600)

P.L. 95-600, §702(d)(1):

Amended Code Sec. 2032A(b)(1) by adding the phrase "which was acquired from or passed to a qualified heir of the decedent and", after "real property located in the United States". **Effective** for estates of decedents dying after 12-31-76.

[Sec. 2032A(c)]

(c) TAX TREATMENT OF DISPOSITIONS AND FAILURES TO USE FOR QUALIFIED USE.—

(1) IMPOSITION OF ADDITIONAL ESTATE TAX.—If, within 10 years after the decedent's death and before the death of the qualified heir—

(A) the qualified heir disposes of any interest in qualified real property (other than by a disposition to a member of his family), or

(B) the qualified heir ceases to use for the qualified use the qualified real property which was acquired (or passed) from the decedent, then there is hereby imposed an additional estate tax.

(2) AMOUNT OF ADDITIONAL TAX.—

(A) IN GENERAL.—The amount of the additional tax imposed by paragraph (1) with respect to any interest shall be the amount equal to the lesser of—

(i) the adjusted tax difference attributable to such interest, or

(ii) the excess of the amount realized with respect to the interest (or, in any case other than a sale or exchange at arm's length, the fair market value of the interest) over the value of the interest determined under subsection (a).

(B) ADJUSTED TAX DIFFERENCE ATTRIBUTABLE TO INTEREST.—For purposes of subparagraph (A), the adjusted tax difference attributable to an interest is the amount which bears the same ratio to the adjusted tax difference with respect to the estate (determined under subparagraph (C)) as—

(i) the excess of the value of such interest for purposes of this chapter (determined without regard to subsection (a)) over the value of such interest determined under subsection (a), bears to

(ii) a similar excess determined for all qualified real property.

(C) ADJUSTED TAX DIFFERENCE WITH RESPECT TO THE ESTATE.—For purposes of subparagraph (B), the term "adjusted tax difference with respect to the estate" means the excess of what would have been the estate tax liability but for subsection (a) over the estate tax liability. For purposes of this subparagraph, the term "estate tax liability" means the tax imposed by section 2001 reduced by the credits allowable against such tax.

(D) PARTIAL DISPOSITIONS.—For purposes of this paragraph, where the qualified heir disposes of a portion of the interest acquired by (or passing to) such heir (or a predecessor qualified heir) or there is a cessation of use of such a portion—

(i) the value determined under subsection (a) taken into account under subparagraph (A)(ii) with respect to such portion shall be its pro rata share of such value of such interest, and

(ii) the adjusted tax difference attributable to the interest taken into account with respect to the transaction involving the second or any succeeding portion shall be reduced by the amount of the tax imposed by this subsection with respect to all prior transactions involving portions of such interest.

(E) SPECIAL RULE FOR DISPOSITION OF TIMBER.—In the case of qualified woodland to which an election under subsection (e)(13)(A) applies, if the qualified heir disposes of (or severs) any standing timber on such qualified woodland—

(i) such disposition (or severance) shall be treated as a disposition of a portion of the interest of the qualified heir in such property, and

(ii) the amount of the additional tax imposed by paragraph (1) with respect to such disposition shall be an amount equal to the lesser of—

(I) the amount realized on such disposition (or, in any case other than a sale or exchange at arm's length, the fair market value of the portion of the interest disposed or severed), or

(II) the amount of additional tax determined under this paragraph (without regard to this subparagraph) if the entire interest of the qualified heir in the qualified woodland had been disposed of, less the sum of the amount of the additional tax imposed with respect to all prior transactions involving such woodland to which this subparagraph applied.

For purposes of the preceding sentence, the disposition of a right to sever shall be treated as the disposition of the standing timber. The amount of additional tax imposed under paragraph (1) in any case in which a qualified heir disposes of his entire interest in the qualified woodland shall be reduced by any amount determined under this subparagraph with respect to such woodland.

(3) ONLY 1 ADDITIONAL TAX IMPOSED WITH RESPECT TO ANY 1 PORTION.—In the case of an interest acquired from (or passing from) any decedent, if subparagraph (A) or (B) of paragraph (1) applies to any portion of an interest, subparagraph (B) or (A), as the case may be, of paragraph (1) shall not apply with respect to the same portion of such interest.

(4) DUE DATE.—The additional tax imposed by this subsection shall become due and payable on the day which is 6 months after the date of the disposition or cessation referred to in paragraph (1).

(5) LIABILITY FOR TAX; FURNISHING OF BOND.—The qualified heir shall be personally liable for the additional tax imposed by this subsection with respect to his interest unless the heir has furnished bond which meets the requirements of subsection (e)(11).

(6) CESSATION OF QUALIFIED USE.—For purposes of paragraph (1)(B), real property shall cease to be used for the qualified use if—

(A) such property ceases to be used for the qualified use set forth in subparagraph (A) or (B) of subsection (b)(2) under which the property qualified under subsection (b), or

(B) during any period of 8 years ending after the date of the decedent's death and before the date of the death of the qualified heir, there had been periods aggregating more than 3 years during which—

(i) in the case of periods during which the property was held by the decedent, there was no material participation by the decedent or any member of his family in the operation of the farm or other business, and

(ii) in the case of periods during which the property was held by any qualified heir, there was no material participation by such qualified heir or any member of his family in the operation of the farm or other business.

(7) SPECIAL RULES.—

(A) NO TAX IF USE BEGINS WITHIN 2 YEARS.—If the date on which the qualified heir begins to use the qualified real property (hereinafter in this subparagraph referred to as the commencement date) is before the date 2 years after the decedent's death—

(i) no tax shall be imposed under paragraph (1) by reason of the failure by the qualified heir to so use such property before the commencement date, and

(ii) the 10-year period under paragraph (1) shall be extended by the period after the decedent's death and before the commencement date.

(B) ACTIVE MANAGEMENT BY ELIGIBLE QUALIFIED HEIR TREATMENT AS MATERIAL PARTICIPATION.—For purposes of paragraph (6)(B)(ii), the active management of a farm or other business by—

(i) an eligible qualified heir, or

(ii) a fiduciary of an eligible qualified heir described in clause (ii) or (iii) of subparagraph (C),

shall be treated as material participation by such eligible qualified heir in the operation of such farm or business. In the case of an eligible qualified heir described in clause (ii), (iii), or (iv) of subparagraph (C), the preceding sentence shall apply only during periods during which such heir meets the requirements of such clause.

(C) ELIGIBLE QUALIFIED HEIR.—For purposes of this paragraph, the term "eligible qualified heir" means a qualified heir who—

(i) is the surviving spouse of the decedent,

(ii) has not attained the age of 21,

(iii) is disabled (within the meaning of subsection (b)(4)(B)), or

(iv) is a student.

(D) STUDENT.—For purposes of subparagraph (C), an individual shall be treated as a student with respect to periods during any calendar year if (and only if) such individual is a student (within the meaning of section 152(f)(2)) for such calendar year.

(E) CERTAIN RENTS TREATED AS QUALIFIED USE.—For purposes of this subsection, a surviving spouse or lineal descendant of the decedent shall not be treated as failing to use qualified real property in a qualified use solely because such spouse or descendant rents such property to a member of the family of such spouse or descendant on a net cash basis. For purposes of the preceding sentence, a legally adopted child of an individual shall be treated as the child of such individual by blood.

(8) QUALIFIED CONSERVATION CONTRIBUTION IS NOT A DISPOSITION.—A qualified conservation contribution (as defined in section 170(h)) by gift or otherwise shall not be deemed a disposition under subsection (c)(1)(A).

Amendments

• 2004, Working Families Tax Relief Act of 2004 (P.L. 108-311)

P.L. 108-311, §207(22):

Amended Code Sec. 2032A(c)(7)(D) by striking "section 151(c)(4)" and inserting "section 152(f)(2)". **Effective** for tax years beginning after 12-31-2004.

• 2001, Economic Growth and Tax Relief Reconciliation Act of 2001 (P.L. 107-16)

P.L. 107-16, §581, provides:

SEC. 581. WAIVER OF STATUTE OF LIMITATION FOR TAXES ON CERTAIN FARM VALUATIONS.

If on the date of the enactment of this Act (or at any time within 1 year after the date of the enactment) a refund or credit of any overpayment of tax resulting from the application of section 2032A(c)(7)(E) of the Internal Revenue Code of 1986 is barred by any law or rule of law, the refund or credit of such overpayment shall, nevertheless, be made or allowed if claim therefor is filed before the date 1 year after the date of the enactment of this Act.

• 1997, Taxpayer Relief Act of 1997 (P.L. 105-34)

P.L. 105-34, §504(a):

Amended Code Sec. 2032A(c)(7) by adding a new subparagraph (E). **Effective** with respect to leases entered into after 12-31-76.

P.L. 105-34, §508(c):

Amended Code Sec. 2032A(c) by adding a new paragraph (8). **Effective** for easements granted after 12-31-97.

• 1986, Tax Reform Act of 1986 (P.L. 99-514)

P.L. 99-514, §104(b)(3):

Amended Code Sec. 2032A(c)(7)(D) by striking out "section 151(e)(4)" and inserting in lieu thereof "section 151(c)(4)". **Effective** for tax years beginning after 12-31-86.

P.L. 99-514, §1421, as amended by P.L. 100-647, §1014(f), provides:

SEC. 1421. INFORMATION NECESSARY FOR VALID SPECIAL USE VALUATION ELECTION.

(a) IN GENERAL.—In the case of any decedent dying before January 1, 1986, if the executor—

(1) made an election under section 2032A of the Internal Revenue Code of 1954 on the return of tax imposed by section 2001 of such Code, and

(2) provided substantially all the information with respect to such election required on such return of tax,

such election shall be a valid election for purposes of section 2032A of such Code.

(b) EXECUTOR MUST PROVIDE INFORMATION.—An election described in subsection (a) shall not be valid if the Secretary of the Treasury or his delegate after the date of the enactment of this Act requests information from the executor with respect to such election and the executor does not provide such information within 90 days of receipt of such request.

(c) EFFECTIVE DATE.—The provisions of this section shall not apply to the estate of any decedent if before the date of the enactment of this Act the statute of limitations has expired with respect to—

(1) the return of tax imposed by section 2001 of the Internal Revenue Code of 1954, and

(2) the period during which a claim for credit or refund may be timely filed.

(d) SPECIAL RULE FOR CERTAIN ESTATE.—Notwithstanding subsection (a)(2), the provisions of this section shall apply to the estate of an individual who died on January 30, 1984, and with respect to which—

(1) a Federal estate tax return was filed on October 30, 1984, electing current use valuation, and

(2) the agreement required under section 2032A was filed on November 9, 1984.

• **1983, Technical Corrections Act of 1982 (P.L. 97-448)**

P.L. 97-448, §104(b)(4)(A):

Amended subparagraph (A) of section 421(k)(5) (relating to effective dates) of P.L. 97-34 by striking out "subsections (b)(1), (c)(2), (j)(1), and (j)(2)" and inserting "subsections (b)(1), (j)(1), and (j)(2) and the provisions of subparagraph (A) of section 2032A(c)(7) of the Internal Revenue Code of 1954 (as added by subsection (c)(2))". [Therefore, the amendment made by P.L. 97-34, §421(c)(2)(B)(ii), is **effective** with respect to estates of decedents dying after 12-31-81.—CCH.]

• **1981, Economic Recovery Tax Act of 1981 (P.L. 97-34)**

P.L. 97-34, §421(c)(1)(A):

Amended Code Sec. 2032A(c)(1) by striking out "15 years" and inserting "10 years". **Effective** with respect to the estates of decedents dying after 12-31-81.

P.L. 97-34, §421(c)(1)(B)(i):

Repealed Code Sec. 2032A(c)(3) and redesignated paragraphs (4) through (7) as (3) through (6), respectively. **Effective** with respect to the estates of decedents dying after 12-31-81. Prior to its repeal, Code Sec. 2032A(c)(3) read as follows:

(3) PHASEOUT OF ADDITIONAL TAX BETWEEN 10TH AND 15TH YEARS.—If the date of the disposition or cessation referred to in paragraph (1) occurs more than 120 months and less than 180 months after the date of the death of the decedent, the amount of the tax imposed by this subsection shall be reduced (but not below zero) by an amount determined by multiplying the amount of such tax (determined without regard to this paragraph) by a fraction—

(A) the numerator of which is the number of full months after such death in excess of 120, and

(B) the denominator of which is 60.

P.L. 97-34, §421(c)(2)(A):

Added Code Sec. 2032A(c)(7). **Effective**, generally, with respect to the estates of decedents dying after 12-31-76. For special rules applicable here relating to certain amendments made retroactive to 1976, see P.L. 97-34, §421(k)(5), as amended by P.L. 97-448, §104(b)(4), in the amendment notes following Code Sec. 2032A(b).

P.L. 97-34, §421(c)(2)(B)(ii):

Amended Code Sec. 2032A(c)(6), after its redesignation by P.L. 97-34, by striking out "3 years or more" and inserting "more than 3 years". **Effective** with respect to estates of decedents dying after 12-31-81.

P.L. 97-34, §421(h)(2):

Added Code Sec. 2032A(c)(2)(E). **Effective** with respect to estates of decedents dying after 12-31-81.

• **1978, Revenue Act of 1978 (P.L. 95-600)**

P.L. 95-600, §702(d)(5)(A):

Amended Code Sec. 2032A(c)(6). **Effective** for estates of decedents dying after 12-31-76. Prior to amendment, Code Sec. 2032A(c)(6) read as follows:

"(6) LIABILITY FOR TAX.—The qualified heir shall be personally liable for the additional tax imposed by this subsection with respect to his interest."

[Sec. 2032A(d)]

(d) ELECTION; AGREEMENT.—

(1) ELECTION.—The election under this section shall be made on the return of the tax imposed by section 2001. Such election shall be made in such manner as the Secretary shall by regulations prescribe. Such an election, once made, shall be irrevocable.

(2) AGREEMENT.—The agreement referred to in this paragraph is a written agreement signed by each person in being who has an interest (whether or not in possession) in any property designated in such agreement consenting to the application of subsection (c) with respect to such property.

(3) MODIFICATION OF ELECTION AND AGREEMENT TO BE PERMITTED.—The Secretary shall prescribe procedures which provide that in any case in which the executor makes an election under paragraph (1) (and submits the agreement referred to in paragraph (2)) within the time prescribed therefor, but—

(A) the notice of election, as filed, does not contain all required information, or

(B) signatures of 1 or more persons required to enter into the agreement described in paragraph (2) are not included on the agreement as filed, or the agreement does not contain all required information,

the executor will have a reasonable period of time (not exceeding 90 days) after notification of such failures to provide such information or signatures.

Amendments

• **1997, Taxpayer Relief Act of 1997 (P.L. 105-34)**

P.L. 105-34, §1313(a):

Amended Code Sec. 2032A(d)(3). **Effective** for estates of decedents dying after 8-5-97. Prior to amendment, Code Sec. 2032A(d)(3) read as follows:

(3) MODIFICATION OF ELECTION AND AGREEMENT TO BE PERMITTED.—The Secretary shall prescribe procedures which provide that in any case in which—

(A) the executor makes an election under paragraph (1) within the time prescribed for filing such election, and

(B) substantially complies with the regulations prescribed by the Secretary with respect to such election, but—

(i) the notice of election, as filed, does not contain all required information, or

(ii) signatures of 1 or more persons required to enter into the agreement described in paragraph (2) are not included on the agreement as filed, or the agreement does not contain all required information,

the executor will have a reasonable period of time (not exceeding 90 days) after notification of such failures to provide such information or agreements.

• **1984, Deficit Reduction Act of 1984 (P.L. 98-369)**

P.L. 98-369, §1025(a):

Amended Code Sec. 2032A(d) by adding paragraph (3). **Effective** for estates of decedents dying after 12-31-76. For a special rule, see Act Sec. 1025(b)(2), below.

P.L. 98-369, §1025(b)(2), provides:

(2) REFUND OR CREDIT OR OVERPAYMENT BARRED BY STATUTE OF LIMITATIONS.—Notwithstanding section 6511(a) of the Internal Revenue Code of 1954 or any other period of limitation or lapse of time, a claim for credit or refund of overpayment of the tax imposed by such Code which arises by reason of this section may be filed by any person at any time within the 1-year period beginning on the date of the enactment of this Act. Sections 6511(b) and 6514 of such Code shall not apply to any claim for credit or refund filed under this subsection within such 1-year period.

• 1981, Economic Recovery Tax Act of 1981 (P.L. 97-34)

P.L. 97-34, §421(j)(3):

Amended Code Sec. 2032A(d)(1). **Effective** for the estates of decedents dying after 12-31-81. Prior to amendment, Code Sec. 2032A(d)(1) read as follows:

(1) ELECTION.—The election under this section shall be made not later than the time prescribed by section 6075(a) for filing the return of tax imposed by section 2001 (including extensions thereof), and shall be made in such manner as the Secretary shall by regulations prescribe.

[Sec. 2032A(e)]

(e) DEFINITIONS; SPECIAL RULES.—For purposes of this section—

(1) QUALIFIED HEIR.—The term "qualified heir" means, with respect to any property, a member of the decedent's family who acquired such property (or to whom such property passed) from the decedent. If a qualified heir disposes of any interest in qualified real property to any member of his family, such member shall thereafter be treated as the qualified heir with respect to such interest.

(2) MEMBER OF FAMILY.—The term "member of the family" means, with respect to any individual, only—

(A) an ancestor of such individual,

(B) the spouse of such individual,

(C) a lineal descendant of such individual, of such individual's spouse, or of a parent of such individual, or

(D) the spouse of any lineal descendant described in subparagraph (C).

For purposes of the preceding sentence, a legally adopted child of an individual shall be treated as the child of such individual by blood.

(3) CERTAIN REAL PROPERTY INCLUDED.—In the case of real property which meets the requirements of subparagraph (C) of subsection (b)(1), residential buildings and related improvements on such real property occupied on a regular basis by the owner or lessee of such real property or by persons employed by such owner or lessee for the purpose of operating or maintaining such real property, and roads, buildings, and other structures and improvements functionally related to the qualified use shall be treated as real property devoted to the qualified use.

(4) FARM.—The term "farm" includes stock, dairy, poultry, fruit, furbearing animal, and truck farms, plantations, ranches, nurseries, ranges, greenhouses or other similar structures used primarily for the raising of agricultural or horticultural commodities, and orchards and woodlands.

(5) FARMING PURPOSES.—The term "farming purposes" means—

(A) cultivating the soil or raising or harvesting any agricultural or horticultural commodity (including the raising, shearing, feeding, caring for, training, and management of animals) on a farm;

(B) handling, drying, packing, grading, or storing on a farm any agricultural or horticultural commodity in its unmanufactured state, but only if the owner, tenant, or operator of the farm regularly produces more than one-half of the commodity so treated; and

(C) (i) the planting, cultivating, caring for, or cutting of trees, or

(ii) the preparation (other than milling) of trees for market.

(6) MATERIAL PARTICIPATION.—Material participation shall be determined in a manner similar to the manner used for purposes of paragraph (1) of section 1402(a) (relating to net earnings from self-employment).

(7) METHOD OF VALUING FARMS.—

(A) IN GENERAL.—Except as provided in subparagraph (B), the value of a farm for farming purposes shall be determined by dividing—

(i) the excess of the average annual gross cash rental for comparable land used for farming purposes and located in the locality of such farm over the average annual State and local real estate taxes for such comparable land, by

(ii) the average annual effective interest rate for all new Federal Land Bank loans.

For purposes of the preceding sentence, each average annual computation shall be made on the basis of the 5 most recent calendar years ending before the date of the decedent's death.

(B) VALUE BASED ON NET SHARE RENTAL IN CERTAIN CASES.—

(i) IN GENERAL.—If there is no comparable land from which the average annual gross cash rental may be determined but there is comparable land from which the average net share rental may be determined, subparagraph (A)(i) shall be applied by substituting "average annual net share rental" for "average annual gross cash rental".

(ii) NET SHARE RENTAL.—For purposes of this paragraph, the term "net share rental" means the excess of—

(I) the value of the produce received by the lessor of the land on which such produce is grown, over

(II) the cash operating expenses of growing such produce which, under the lease, are paid by the lessor.

(C) EXCEPTION.—The formula provided by subparagraph (A) shall not be used—

(i) where it is established that there is no comparable land from which the average annual gross cash rental may be determined and that there is no comparable land from which the average net share rental may be determined, or

(ii) where the executor elects to have the value of the farm for farming purposes determined under paragraph (8).

(8) METHOD OF VALUING CLOSELY HELD BUSINESS INTERESTS, ETC.—In any case to which paragraph (7)(A) does not apply, the following factors shall apply in determining the value of any qualified real property:

(A) The capitalization of income which the property can be expected to yield for farming or closely held business purposes over a reasonable period of time under prudent management using traditional cropping patterns for the area, taking into account soil capacity, terrain configuration, and similar factors,

(B) The capitalization of the fair rental value of the land for farmland or closely held business purposes,

(C) Assessed land values in a State which provides a differential or use value assessment law for farmland or closely held business,

(D) Comparable sales of other farm or closely held business land in the same geographical area far enough removed from a metropolitan or resort area so that nonagricultural use is not a significant factor in the sales price, and

(E) Any other factor which fairly values the farm or closely held business value of the property.

(9) PROPERTY ACQUIRED FROM DECEDENT.—Property shall be considered to have been acquired from or to have passed from the decedent if—

(A) such property is so considered under section 1014(b) (relating to basis of property acquired from a decedent),

(B) such property is acquired by any person from the estate, or

(C) such property is acquired by any person from a trust (to the extent such property is includible in the gross estate of the decedent).

(10) COMMUNITY PROPERTY.—If the decedent and his surviving spouse at any time held qualified real property as community property, the interest of the surviving spouse in such property shall be taken into account under this section to the extent necessary to provide a result under this section with respect to such property which is consistent with the result which would have obtained under this section if such property had not been community property.

(11) BOND IN LIEU OF PERSONAL LIABILITY.—If the qualified heir makes written application to the Secretary for determination of the maximum amount of the additional tax which may be imposed by subsection (c) with respect to the qualified heir's interest, the Secretary (as soon as possible, and in any event within 1 year after the making of such application) shall notify the heir of such maximum amount. The qualified heir, on furnishing a bond in such amount and for such period as may be required, shall be discharged from personal liability for any additional tax imposed by subsection (c) and shall be entitled to a receipt or writing showing such discharge.

(12) ACTIVE MANAGEMENT.—The term "active management" means the making of the management decisions of a business (other than the daily operating decisions).

(13) SPECIAL RULES FOR WOODLANDS.—

(A) IN GENERAL.—In the case of any qualified woodland with respect to which the executor elects to have this subparagraph apply, trees growing on such woodland shall not be treated as a crop.

(B) QUALIFIED WOODLAND.—The term "qualified woodland" means any real property which—

(i) is used in timber operations, and

(ii) is an identifiable area of land such as an acre or other area for which records are normally maintained in conducting timber operations.

(C) TIMBER OPERATIONS.—The term "timber operations" means—

(i) the planting, cultivating, caring for, or cutting of trees, or

(ii) the preparation (other than milling) of trees for market.

(D) ELECTION.—An election under subparagraph (A) shall be made on the return of the tax imposed by section 2001. Such election shall be made in such manner as the Secretary shall by regulations prescribe. Such an election, once made, shall be irrevocable.

(14) TREATMENT OF REPLACEMENT PROPERTY ACQUIRED IN SECTION 1031 OR 1033 TRANSACTIONS.—

(A) IN GENERAL.—In the case of any qualified replacement property, any period during which there was ownership, qualified use, or material participation with respect to the replaced property by the decedent or any member of his family shall be treated as a period during which there was such ownership, use, or material participation (as the case may be) with respect to the qualified replacement property.

(B) LIMITATION.—Subparagraph (A) shall not apply to the extent that the fair market value of the qualified replacement property (as of the date of its acquisition) exceeds the fair market value of the replaced property (as of the date of its disposition).

(C) DEFINITIONS.—For purposes of this paragraph—

(i) QUALIFIED REPLACEMENT PROPERTY.—The term "qualified replacement property" means any real property which is—

(I) acquired in an exchange which qualifies under section 1031, or

(II) the acquisition of which results in the non-recognition of gain under section 1033.

Such term shall only include property which is used for the same qualified use as the replaced property was being used before the exchange.

(ii) REPLACED PROPERTY.—The term "replaced property" means—

(I) the property transferred in the exchange which qualifies under section 1031, or

(II) the property compulsorily or involuntarily converted (within the meaning of section 1033).

Amendments

• 1981, Economic Recovery Tax Act of 1981 (P.L. 97-34)

P.L. 97-34, §421(c)(2)(B)(i):

Added Code Sec. 2032A(e)(12). **Effective** with respect to the estates of decedents dying after 12-31-81. (For the amendment made to section 421(k)(5) of P.L. 97-34 (relating to effective dates), see the amendment note for P.L. 97-448, §104(b)(4)(A), following Code Sec. 2032A(c).)

P.L. 97-34, §421(f)(1):

Amended Code Sec. 2032A(e)(7) by redesignating subparagraph (B) as (C) and by inserting a new subparagraph (B). **Effective** for the estates of decedents dying after 12-31-81.

P.L. 97-34, §421(f)(2):

Amended Code Sec. 2032A(e)(7)(C), after its redesignation by P.L. 97-34, by inserting after "determined" the following: "and that there is no comparable land from which the average net share rental may be determined". **Effective** with respect to the estates of decedents dying after 12-31-81.

P.L. 97-34, §421(h)(1):

Added Code Sec. 2032A(e)(13). **Effective** with respect to the estates of decedents dying after 12-31-81.

P.L. 97-34, §421(i):

Amended Code Sec. 2032A(e)(2). **Effective** with respect to the estates of decedents dying after 12-31-81. Prior to amendment, Code Sec. 2032A(e)(2) read as follows:

(2) MEMBER OF FAMILY.—The term "member of the family" means, with respect to any individual, only such individual's ancestor or lineal descendant, a lineal descendant of a grandparent of such individual, the spouse of such individual, or the spouse of any such descendant. For purposes of the preceding sentence, a legally adopted child of an individual shall be treated as a child of such individual by blood.

P.L. 97-34, §421(j)(2)(A):

Amended Code Sec. 2032A(e)(9)(B) and (C). **Effective**, generally, with respect to the estates of decedents dying after 12-31-76. For special rules applicable here relating to certain amendments made retroactive to 1976, see P.L. 97-34, §412(k)(5), as amended by P.L. 97-448, §104(b)(4), in the amendment notes following Code Sec. 2032A(b). Prior to amendment, Code Sec. 2032A(e)(9)(B) and (C) read as follows:

(B) such property is acquired by any person from the estate in satisfaction of the right of such person to a pecuniary bequest, or

(C) such property is acquired by any person from a trust in satisfaction of a right (which such person has by reason of the death of the decedent) to receive from the trust a specific dollar amount which is the equivalent of a pecuniary bequest.

P.L. 97-34, §421(j)(4):

Added Code Sec. 2032A(e)(14). **Effective** with respect to the estates of decedents dying after 12-3-81.

• 1978, Revenue Act of 1978 (P.L. 95-600)

P.L. 95-600, §702(d)(2), (4), (5)(B):

Added Code Sec. 2032A(e)(9), (10), and (11). **Effective** for estates of decedents dying after 12-31-76.

[Sec. 2032A(f)]

(f) STATUTE OF LIMITATIONS.—If qualified real property is disposed of or ceases to be used for a qualified use, then—

(1) The statutory period for the assessment of any additional tax under subsection (c) attributable to such disposition or cessation shall not expire before the expiration of 3 years from the date the Secretary is notified (in such manner as the Secretary may by regulations prescribe) of such disposition or cessation (or if later in the case of an involuntary conversion or exchange to which subsection (h) or (i) applies, 3 years from the date the Secretary is notified of the replacement of the converted property or of an intention not to replace or of the exchange of property, and

(2) such additional tax may be assessed before the expiration of such 3-year period notwithstanding the provisions of any other law or rule of law which would otherwise prevent such assessment.

Amendments

• 1981, Economic Recovery Tax Act of 1981 (P.L. 97-34)

P.L. 97-34, §421(d)(2)(A):

Amended Code Sec. 2032A(f)(1) by inserting "or exchange" after "conversion", by inserting "or (i)" after "(h)", and by inserting "or of the exchange of property" after "replace". **Effective** with respect to exchanges after 12-31-81.

P.L. 97-34, §421(e)(2):

Amended Code Sec. 2032A(f)(1) by striking out "to which an election under subsection (h)" and inserting "to which subsection (h)". **Effective** with respect to involuntary conversions after 12-31-81.

• 1978 (P.L. 95-472)

P.L. 95-472, §4(c), (d):

Amended Code Sec. 2032A(f)(1) by inserting "(or if later in the case of an involuntary conversion to which an election under subsection (h) applies, 3 years from the date the Secretary is notified of the replacement of the converted property or of an intention not to replace)" immediately before ", and". **Effective** for involuntary conversions after 1976.

• 1976, Tax Reform Act of 1976 (P.L. 94-455)

P.L. 94-455, §2003(a), (e):

Added Code Sec. 2032A(f). **Effective** for estates of decedents dying after 1976.

[Sec. 2032A(g)]

(g) APPLICATION OF THIS SECTION AND SECTION 6324B TO INTERESTS IN PARTNERSHIPS, CORPORATIONS AND TRUSTS.—The Secretary shall prescribe regulations setting forth the application of this section and section 6324B in the case of an interest in a partnership, corporation, or trust which, with respect to the decedent, is an interest in a closely held business (within the meaning of paragraph (1) of section 6166(b)). For purposes of the preceding sentence, an interest in a discretionary trust all the beneficiaries of which are qualified heirs shall be treated as a present interest.

Amendments

• 1981, Economic Recovery Tax Act of 1981 (P.L. 97-34)

P.L. 97-34, §421(j)(1):

Amended Code Sec. 2032A(g) by adding at the end a new sentence. **Effective**, generally, with respect to estates of decedents dying after 12-31-76. For special rules applicable here relating to certain amendments made retroactive to 1976, see P.L. 97-34, §421(k)(5), as amended by P.L. 97-448, §104(b)(4), in the amendment notes, following Code Sec. 2032A(b).

• 1976, Tax Reform Act of 1976 (P.L. 94-455)

P.L. 94-455, §2003(a), (e):

Added Code Sec. 2032A(g). **Effective** for estates of decedents dying after 12-31-76.

[Sec. 2032A(h)]

(h) SPECIAL RULES FOR INVOLUNTARY CONVERSIONS OF QUALIFIED REAL PROPERTY.—

(1) TREATMENT OF CONVERTED PROPERTY.—

(A) IN GENERAL.—If there is an involuntary conversion of an interest in qualified real property—

(i) no tax shall be imposed by subsection (c) on such conversion if the cost of the qualified replacement property equals or exceeds the amount realized on such conversion, or

(ii) if clause (i) does not apply, the amount of the tax imposed by subsection (c) on such conversion shall be the amount determined under subparagraph (B).

(B) AMOUNT OF TAX WHERE THERE IS NOT COMPLETE REINVESTMENT.—The amount determined under this subparagraph with respect to any involuntary conversion is the amount of the tax which (but for this subsection) would have been imposed on such conversion reduced by an amount which—

(i) bears the same ratio to such tax, as

(ii) the cost of the qualified replacement property bears to the amount realized on the conversion.

(2) TREATMENT OF REPLACEMENT PROPERTY.—For purposes of subsection (c)—

(A) any qualified replacement property shall be treated in the same manner as if it were a portion of the interest in qualified real property which was involuntarily converted; except that with respect to such qualified replacement property the 10-year period under paragraph (1) of subsection (c) shall be extended by any period, beyond the 2-year period referred to in section 1033(a)(2)(B)(i), during which the qualified heir was allowed to replace the qualified real property,

(B) any tax imposed by subsection (c) on the involuntary conversion shall be treated as a tax imposed on a partial disposition, and

(C) paragraph (6) of subsection (c) shall be applied—

(i) by not taking into account periods after the involuntary conversion and before the acquisition of the qualified replacement property, and

(ii) by treating material participation with respect to the converted property as material participation with respect to the qualified replacement property.

(3) DEFINITIONS AND SPECIAL RULES.—For purposes of this subsection—

(A) INVOLUNTARY CONVERSION.—The term "involuntary conversion" means a compulsory or involuntary conversion within the meaning of section 1033.

(B) QUALIFIED REPLACEMENT PROPERTY.—The term "qualified replacement property" means—

(i) in the case of an involuntary conversion described in section 1033(a)(1), any real property into which the qualified real property is converted, or

(ii) in the case of an involuntary conversion described in section 1033(a)(2), any real property purchased by the qualified heir during the period specified in section 1033(a)(2)(B) for purposes of replacing the qualified real property.

Such term only includes property which is to be used for the qualified use set forth in subparagraph (A) or (B) of subsection (b)(2) under which the qualified real property qualified under subsection (a).

(4) CERTAIN RULES MADE APPLICABLE.—The rules of the last sentence of section 1033(a)(2)(A) shall apply for purposes of paragraph (3)(B)(ii).

Amendments

• 1981, Economic Recovery Tax Act of 1981 (P.L. 97-34)

P.L. 97-34, §421(c)(1)(B)(ii):

Amended Code Sec. 2032A(h)(2)(A). **Effective** with respect to the estates of decedents dying after 12-31-81. Prior to amendment, Code Sec. 2032A(h)(2)(A) read as follows:

(2) TREATMENT OF REPLACEMENT PROPERTY.—For purposes of subsection (c)—

(A) any qualified replacement property shall be treated in the same manner as if it were a portion of the interest in qualified real property which was involuntarily converted, except that with respect to such qualified replacement property—

(i) the 15-year period under paragraph (1) of subsection (c) shall be extended by any period, beyond the 2-year period referred to in section 1033(a)(2)(B)(i), during which the qualified heir was allowed to replace the qualified real property, and

(ii) the phaseout period under paragraph (3) of subsection (c) shall be appropriately adjusted to take into account the extension referred to in clause (i),

P.L. 97-34, §421(c)(1)(B)(iii):

Amended Code Sec. 2032A(h)(2)(C) by striking out "(7)" and inserting "(6)". **Effective** with respect to decedents dying after 12-31-81.

P.L. 97-34, §421(e)(1)(A):

Amended Code Sec. 2032A(h)(A) by striking out "and the qualified heir makes an election under this subsection". **Effective** with respect to involuntary conversions after 12-31-81.

P.L. 97-34, §421(e)(1)(B):

Repealed Code Sec. 2032A(h)(5). **Effective** with respect to involuntary conversions after 12-31-81. Prior to its repeal, Code Sec. 2032A(h)(5) read as follows:

(5) ELECTION.—Any election under this subsection shall be made at such time and in such manner as the Secretary may by regulations prescribe.

• 1978 (P.L. 95-472)

P.L. 95-472, §4(a):

Added Code Sec. 2032A(h). **Effective** for involuntary conversions after 1976.

[Sec. 2032A(i)]

(i) EXCHANGES OF QUALIFIED REAL PROPERTY.—

(1) TREATMENT OF PROPERTY EXCHANGED.—

(A) EXCHANGES SOLELY FOR QUALIFIED EXCHANGE PROPERTY.—If an interest in qualified real property is exchanged solely for an interest in qualified exchange property in a transaction which qualifies under section 1031, no tax shall be imposed by subsection (c) by reason of such exchange.

(B) EXCHANGES WHERE OTHER PROPERTY RECEIVED.—If an interest in qualified real property is exchanged for an interest in qualified exchange property and other property in a transaction which qualifies under section 1031, the amount of the tax imposed by subsection (c) by reason of such exchange shall be the amount of tax which (but for this subparagraph) would have been imposed on such exchange under subsection (c)(1), reduced by an amount which—

(i) bears the same ratio to such tax, as

(ii) the fair market value of the qualified exchange property bears to the fair market value of the qualified real property exchanged.

For purposes of clause (ii) of the preceding sentence, fair market value shall be determined as of the time of the exchange.

(2) TREATMENT OF QUALIFIED EXCHANGE PROPERTY.—For purposes of subsection (c)—

(A) any interest in qualified exchange property shall be treated in the same manner as if it were a portion of the interest in qualified real property which was exchanged,

(B) any tax imposed by subsection (c) by reason of the exchange shall be treated as a tax imposed on a partial disposition, and

(C) paragraph (6) of subsection (c) shall be applied by treating material participation with respect to the exchanged property as material participation with respect to the qualified exchange property.

(3) QUALIFIED EXCHANGE PROPERTY.—For purposes of this subsection, the term "qualified exchange property" means real property which is to be used for the qualified use set forth in subparagraph (A) or (B) of subsection (b)(2) under which the real property exchanged therefor originally qualified under subsection (a).

Amendments

• 1983, Technical Corrections Act of 1982 (P.L. 97-448)

P.L. 97-448, §104(b)(2)(A):

Amended Code Sec. 2032A(i)(1)(B)(ii) by striking out "the other property" and inserting in lieu thereof "the qualified exchange property". **Effective** as if included in the provision of P.L. 97-34 to which it relates.

P.L. 97-448, §104(b)(2)(B):

Amended Code Sec. 2032A(i)(3) by striking out "subparagraph (A), (B), or (C)" and inserting in lieu thereof "subparagraph (A) or (B)". **Effective** as if included in the provision of P.L. 97-34 to which it relates.

• 1981, Economic Recovery Tax Act of 1981 (P.L. 97-34)

P.L. 97-34, §421(d)(1):

Added Code Sec. 2032A(i). **Effective** with respect to exchanges after 12-31-81.

[Sec. 2033]

SEC. 2033. PROPERTY IN WHICH THE DECEDENT HAD AN INTEREST.

The value of the gross estate shall include the value of all property to the extent of the interest therein of the decedent at the time of his death.

Amendments

• 1962, Revenue Act of 1962 (P.L. 87-834)

P.L. 87-834, §18(a)(2):

Amended Code Sec. 2033 by deleting "(except real property situated outside of the United States)". **Effective,** generally, for estates of decedents dying after 10-16-62. For exceptions, see Act Sec. 18(b) in the amendment notes for Code Sec. 2031(a).

[Sec. 2034]

SEC. 2034. DOWER OR CURTESY INTERESTS.

The value of the gross estate shall include the value of all property to the extent of any interest therein of the surviving spouse, existing at the time of the decedent's death as dower or curtesy, or by virtue of a statute creating an estate in lieu of dower or curtesy.

Amendments

• 1962, Revenue Act of 1962 (P.L. 87-834)

P.L. 87-834, §18(a)(2):

Amended Code Sec. 2034 by deleting "(except real property situated outside of the United States)". **Effective,** generally, for estates of decedents dying after 10-16-62. For exceptions, see Act Sec. 18(b) in the amendment notes for Code Sec. 2031(a).

[Sec. 2035]

SEC. 2035. ADJUSTMENTS FOR CERTAIN GIFTS MADE WITHIN 3 YEARS OF DECEDENT'S DEATH.

[Sec. 2035(a)]

(a) INCLUSION OF CERTAIN PROPERTY IN GROSS ESTATE.—If—

(1) the decedent made a transfer (by trust or otherwise) of an interest in any property, or relinquished a power with respect to any property, during the 3-year period ending on the date of the decedent's death, and

(2) the value of such property (or an interest therein) would have been included in the decedent's gross estate under section 2036, 2037, 2038, or 2042 if such transferred interest or relinquished power had been retained by the decedent on the date of his death, the value of the gross estate shall include the value of any property (or interest therein) which would have been so included.

[Sec. 2035(b)]

(b) INCLUSION OF GIFT TAX ON GIFTS MADE DURING 3 YEARS BEFORE DECEDENT'S DEATH.—The amount of the gross estate (determined without regard to this subsection) shall be increased by the amount of any tax paid under chapter 12 by the decedent or his estate on any gift made by the decedent or his spouse during the 3-year period ending on the date of the decedent's death.

[Sec. 2035(c)]

(c) OTHER RULES RELATING TO TRANSFERS WITHIN 3 YEARS OF DEATH.—

(1) IN GENERAL.—For purposes of—

(A) section 303(b) (relating to distributions in redemption of stock to pay death taxes),

(B) section 2032A (relating to special valuation of certain farms, etc., real property), and

(C) subchapter C of chapter 64 (relating to lien for taxes),

the value of the gross estate shall include the value of all property to the extent of any interest therein of which the decedent has at any time made a transfer, by trust or otherwise, during the 3-year period ending on the date of the decedent's death.

(2) COORDINATION WITH SECTION 6166.—An estate shall be treated as meeting the 35 percent of adjusted gross estate requirement of section 6166(a)(1) only if the estate meets such requirement both with and without the application of subsection (a).

(3) MARITAL AND SMALL TRANSFERS.—Paragraph (1) shall not apply to any transfer (other than a transfer with respect to a life insurance policy) made during a calendar year to any donee if the decedent was not required by section 6019 (other than by reason of section 6019(2)) to file any gift tax return for such year with respect to transfers to such donee.

Amendments

• 2000, Community Renewal Tax Relief Act of 2000 (P.L. 106-554)

P.L. 106-554, §319(14)(A):

Amended Code Sec. 2035(c)(2) by striking "paragraph (1)" and inserting "subsection (a)". **Effective** 12-21-2000.

[Sec. 2035(d)]

(d) EXCEPTION.—Subsection (a) and paragraph (1) of subsection (c) shall not apply to any bona fide sale for an adequate and full consideration in money or money's worth.

Amendments

• 2000, Community Renewal Tax Relief Act of 2000 (P.L. 106-554)

P.L. 106-554, §319(14)(B):

Amended Code Sec. 2035(d) by inserting "and paragraph (1) of subsection (c)" after "Subsection (a)". **Effective** 12-21-2000.

[Sec. 2035(e)]

(e) TREATMENT OF CERTAIN TRANSFERS FROM REVOCABLE TRUSTS.—For purposes of this section and section 2038, any transfer from any portion of a trust during any period that such portion was treated under section 676 as owned by the decedent by reason of a power in the grantor (determined without regard to section 672(e)) shall be treated as a transfer made directly by the decedent.

Amendments

• 1997, Taxpayer Relief Act of 1997 (P.L. 105-34)

P.L. 105-34, §1310(a):

Amended Code Sec. 2035. **Effective** for the estates of decedents dying after 8-5-97. Prior to amendment, Code Sec. 2035 read as follows:

SEC. 2035. ADJUSTMENTS FOR GIFTS MADE WITHIN 3 YEARS OF DECEDENT'S DEATH.

[Sec. 2035(a)]

(a) INCLUSION OF GIFTS MADE BY DECEDENT.—Except as provided in subsection (b), the value of the gross estate shall include the value of all property to the extent of any interest therein of which the decedent has at any time made a transfer, by trust or otherwise, during the 3-year period ending on the date of the decedent's death.

Amendments

• 1976, Tax Reform Act of 1976 (P.L. 94-455)

P.L. 94-455, §2001(a)(5), (d)(1):

Amended Code Sec. 2035(a). **Effective** for estates of decedents dying after 12-31-76, except that it does not apply to transfers made before 1-1-77. Prior to amendment, Code Sec. 2035(a) read as follows:

(a) GENERAL RULE—The value of the gross estate shall include the value of all property to the extent of any interest therein of which the decedent has at any time made a transfer (except in case of a bona fide sale for an adequate and full consideration in money or money's worth), by trust or otherwise, in contemplation of his death.

• 1962, Revenue Act of 1962 (P.L. 87-834)

P.L. 87-834, §18(a)(2):

Amended Code Sec. 2035(a) by deleting "(except real property situated outside of the United States)". **Effective**, generally, for estates of decedents dying after 10-16-62. For exceptions, see Act Sec. 18(b) in the amendment notes for Code Sec. 2031(a).

[Sec. 2035(b)]

(b) EXCEPTIONS.—Subsection (a) shall not apply—

(1) to any bona fide sale for an adequate and full consideration in money or money's worth, and

(2) to any gift to a donee made during a calendar year if the decedent was not required by section 6019 (other than by reason of section 6019(2)) to file any gift tax return for such year with respect to gifts to such donee. Paragraph (2) shall not apply to any transfer with respect to a life insurance policy.

Amendments

• 1983, Technical Corrections Act of 1982 (P.L. 97-448)

P.L. 97-448, §104(a)(9):

Amended Code Sec. 2035(b)(2) by striking out "section 6019(a)(2)" and inserting in lieu thereof "section 6019(2)". **Effective** as if included in the provision of P.L. 97-34 to which it relates.

• 1981, Economic Recovery Tax Act of 1981 (P.L. 97-34)

P.L. 97-34, §403(b)(3)(B):

Amended Code Sec. 2035(b)(2) by inserting after "section 6019" the phrase "(other than by reason of section 6019(a)(2))". **Effective** for estates of decedents dying after 12-31-81.

• 1980, Technical Corrections Act of 1979 (P.L. 96-222)

P.L. 96-222, §107(a)(2)(F)(i)-(ii), provides:

(F)(i) If the executor elects the benefits of this subparagraph with respect to any estate, section 2035(b) of the Internal Revenue Code of 1954 (relating to adjustments for gifts made within 3 years of decedent's death) shall be applied with respect to transfers made by the decedent during 1977 as if paragraph (2) of such section 2035(b) read as follows:

"(2) to any gift to a donee made during 1977 to the extent of the amount of such gift which was excludable in computing taxable gifts by reason of section 2503(b) (relating to $3,000 annual exclusion for purposes of the gift tax) determined without regard to section 2513(a)."

(ii) The election under clause (i) with respect to any estate shall be made on or before the later of—

(I) the due date for filing the estate tax return, or

(II) the day which is 120 days after the date of the enactment of this Act.

• 1978, Revenue Act of 1978 (P.L. 95-600)

P.L. 95-600, §702(f)(1):

Amended Code Sec. 2035(b). **Effective** for estates of decedents dying after 12-31-76. Prior to amendment, Code Sec. 2035(b) read as follows:

"(b) EXCEPTIONS.—Subsection (a) shall not apply to—

"(1) any bona fide sale for an adequate and full consideration in money or money's worth, and

"(2) any gift excludable in computing taxable gifts by reason of section 2503(b) (relating to $3,000 annual exclusion for purposes of the gift tax) determined without regard to section 2513(a)."

• 1976, Tax Reform Act of 1976 (P.L. 94-455)

P.L. 94-455, §2001(a)(5), (d)(1):

Amended Code Sec. 2035(b). **Effective** for estates of decedents dying after 12-31-76, except that it does not apply to transfers made before 1-1-77. Prior to amendment, Code Sec. 2035(b) read as follows:

(b) APPLICATION OF GENERAL RULE.—If the decedent within a period of 3 years ending with the date of his death (except in case of a bona fide sale for an adequate and full consideration in money or money's worth) transferred an interest in property, relinquished a power, or exercised or released a general power of appointment, such transfer, relinquishment, exercise, or release shall, unless shown to the contrary, be deemed to have been made in contemplation of death within the meaning of this section and sections 2038 and 2041 (relating to revocable transfers and powers of appointment); but no such transfer, relinquishment, exercise, or release made before such 3-year period shall be treated as having been made in contemplation of death.

[Sec. 2035(c)]

(c) INCLUSION OF GIFT TAX ON CERTAIN GIFTS MADE DURING 3 YEARS BEFORE DECEDENT'S DEATH.—The amount of the gross estate (determined without regard to this subsection) shall be increased by the amount of any tax paid under chapter 12 by the decedent or his estate on any gift made by the decedent or his spouse after December 31, 1976, and during the 3-year period ending on the date of the decedent's death.

Amendments

• 1976, Tax Reform Act of 1976 (P.L. 94-455)

P.L. 94-455, §2001(a)(5), (d)(1):

Added Code Sec. 2035(c). **Effective** for estates of decedents dying after 12-31-76, except that it does not apply to transfers made before 1-1-77.

[Sec. 2035(d)]

(d) DECEDENTS DYING AFTER 1981.—

(1) IN GENERAL.—Except as otherwise provided in this subsection, subsection (a) shall not apply to the estate of a decedent dying after December 31, 1981.

(2) EXCEPTIONS FOR CERTAIN TRANSFERS.—Paragraph (1) of this subsection and paragraph (2) of subsection (b) shall not apply to a transfer of an interest in property which is included in the value of the gross estate under section 2036, 2037, 2038, or 2042 or would have been included under any of such sections if such interest had been retained by the decedent.

(3) 3-YEAR RULE RETAINED FOR CERTAIN PURPOSES.—Paragraph (1) shall not apply for purposes of—

(A) section 303(b) (relating to distributions in redemption of stock to pay death taxes),

(B) section 2032A (relating to special valuation of certain farm, etc., real property), and

(C) subchapter C of chapter 64 (relating to lien for taxes).

(4) COORDINATION OF 3-YEAR RULE WITH SECTION 6166(a)(1).—An estate shall be treated as meeting the 35-percent of adjusted gross estate requirement of section 6166(a)(1) only if the estate meets such requirement both with and without the application of paragraph (1).

Amendments

• 1983, Technical Corrections Act of 1982 (P.L. 97-448)

P.L. 97-448, §104(d)(1)(A):

Amended Code Sec. 2035(d) by adding at the end thereof new paragraph (4). **Effective** as if included in the provision of P.L. 97-34 to which it relates.

P.L. 97-448, §104(d)(1)(C):

Amended Code Sec. 2035(d)(3) by striking out subparagraph (C), by adding "and" at the end of subparagraph (B), and by redesignating subparagraph (D) as subparagraph (C). **Effective** as if included in the provision of P.L. 97-34 to which it relates. Prior to amendment, subparagraph (C) read as follows:

(C) section 6166 (relating to extension of time for payment of estate tax where estate consists largely of interest in closely held business), and.

P.L. 97-448, §104(d)(2):

Amended Code Sec. 2035(d)(2) by inserting "of this subsection and paragraph (2) of subsection (b)" after "Paragraph (1)", and by striking out "2041,". **Effective** as if included in the provision of P.L. 97-34 to which it relates.

P.L. 97-448, §104(d)(3), provides:

(3) ELECTION TO HAVE AMENDMENTS NOT APPLY.—

(A) In the case of any decedent—

(i) who dies before August 13, 1984, and

(ii) who made a gift (before August 13, 1981, and during the 3-year period ending on the date of the decedent's death) on which tax imposed by chapter 12 of the Internal Revenue Code of 1954 has been paid before April 16, 1982,

such decedent's executor may make an election to have subtitle B of such Code (relating to estate and gift taxes) applied with respect to such decedent without regard to any of the amendments made by title IV of the Economic Recovery Tax Act of 1981.

(B) An election under subparagraph (A) shall be made at such time and in such manner as the Secretary of the Treasury or his delegate shall prescribe.

(C) An election under subparagraph (A), once made, shall be irrevocable.

• 1981, Economic Recovery Tax Act of 1981 (P.L. 97-34)

P.L. 97-34, §424(a):

Added Code Sec. 2035(d). **Effective** for estates of decedents dying after 12-31-81.

[Sec. 2036]

SEC. 2036. TRANSFERS WITH RETAINED LIFE ESTATE.

[Sec. 2036(a)]

(a) GENERAL RULE.—The value of the gross estate shall include the value of all property to the extent of any interest therein of which the decedent has at any time made a transfer (except in case of a bona fide sale for an adequate and full consideration in money or money's worth), by trust or otherwise, under which he has retained for his life or for any period not ascertainable without reference to his death or for any period which does not in fact end before his death—

(1) the possession or enjoyment of, or the right to the income from, the property, or

(2) the right, either alone or in conjunction with any person, to designate the persons who shall possess or enjoy the property or the income therefrom.

Amendments

• 1978, Revenue Act of 1978 (P.L. 95-600)

P.L. 95-600, §702(i)(2):

Amended Code Sec. 2036(a) by deleting from the end thereof the following: "For purposes of paragraph (1), the retention of voting rights in retained stock shall be considered to be a retention of the enjoyment of such stock." **Effective** for transfers made after 6-22-76.

• 1976, Tax Reform Act of 1976 (P.L. 94-455)

P.L. 94-455, §2009(a), (e)(1):

Added the last sentence to Code Sec. 2036(a). **Effective** for transfers made after 6-22-76.

• 1962, Revenue Act of 1962 (P.L. 87-834)

P.L. 87-834, §18(a)(2):

Amended Code Sec. 2036(a) by deleting "(except real property situated outside of the United States)". **Effective**, generally, for estates of decedents dying after 10-16-62. For exceptions, see Act Sec. 18(b) in the amendment notes for Code Sec. 2031(a).

[Sec. 2036(b)]

(b) VOTING RIGHTS.—

(1) IN GENERAL.—For purposes of subsection (a)(1), the retention of the right to vote (directly or indirectly) shares of stock of a controlled corporation shall be considered to be a retention of the enjoyment of transferred property.

(2) CONTROLLED CORPORATION.—For purposes of paragraph (1), a corporation shall be treated as a controlled corporation if, at any time after the transfer of the property and during the 3-year period ending on the date of the decedent's death, the decedent owned (with the application of section 318), or had the right (either alone or in conjunction with any person) to vote stock possessing at least 20 percent of the total combined voting power of all classes of stock.

(3) COORDINATION WITH SECTION 2035.—For purposes of applying section 2035 with respect to paragraph (1), the relinquishment or cessation of voting rights shall be treated as a transfer of property made by the decedent.

Amendments

• 1978, Revenue Act of 1978 (P.L. 95-600)

P.L. 95-600, §702(i)(1):

Added new Code Sec. 2036(b). **Effective** for transfers made after 6-22-76. Prior Code Sec. 2036(b) was redesignated Code Sec. 2036(c).

[Sec. 2036(c)]

(c) LIMITATION ON APPLICATION OF GENERAL RULE.—This section shall not apply to a transfer made before March 4, 1931; nor to a transfer made after March 3, 1931, and before June 7, 1932, unless the property transferred would have been includible in the decedent's gross estate by reason of the amendatory language of the joint resolution of March 3, 1931 (46 Stat. 1516).

Amendments

• 1990, Omnibus Budget Reconciliation Act of 1990 (P.L. 101-508)

P.L. 101-508, §11601(a):

Amended Code Sec. 2036 by striking subsection (c) and by redesignating subsection (d) as subsection (c). **Effective** for property transferred after 12-17-87. Prior to being stricken, subsection (c) read as follows:

(c) INCLUSION RELATED TO VALUATION FREEZES.—

(1) IN GENERAL.—For purposes of subsection (a), if—

(A) any person holds a substantial interest in an enterprise, and

(B) such person in effect transfers after December 17, 1987, property having a disproportionately large share of the potential appreciation in such person's interest in the enterprise while retaining an interest in the income of, or rights in, the enterprise,

then the retention of the retained interest shall be considered to be a retention of the enjoyment of the transferred property.

(2) SPECIAL RULES FOR CONSIDERATION FURNISHED BY FAMILY MEMBERS.—

(A) IN GENERAL.—The exception contained in subsection (a) for a bona fide sale shall not apply to a transfer described in paragraph (1) if such transfer is to a member of the transferor's family.

(B) TREATMENT OF CONSIDERATION.—

(i) IN GENERAL.—In the case of a transfer described in paragraph (1), if—

(I) a member of the transferor's family provides consideration in money or money's worth for such member's interest in the enterprise, and

(II) it is established to the satisfaction of the Secretary that such consideration originally belonged to such member and was never received or acquired (directly or indirectly) by such member from the transferor for less than full and adequate consideration in money or money's worth,

paragraph (1) shall not apply to the applicable fraction of the portion of the enterprise which would (but for this subparagraph) have been included in the gross estate of the transferor by reason of this subsection (determined without regard to any reduction under paragraph (5) for the value of the retained interest).

(ii) APPLICABLE FRACTION.—For purposes of clause (i), the applicable fraction is a fraction—

(I) the numerator of which is the amount of the consideration referred to in clause (i), and

(II) the denominator of which is the value of the portion referred to in clause (i) immediately after the transfer described in paragraph (1).

(iii) SECTION 2043 NOT TO APPLY.—The provisions of this subparagraph shall be lieu of any adjustment under section 2043.

(3) DEFINITIONS.—For purposes of this subsection—

(A) SUBSTANTIAL INTEREST.—A person holds a substantial interest in an enterprise if such person owns (directly or indirectly) 10 percent or more of the voting power or income stream, or both, in such enterprise. For purposes of the preceding sentence, an individual shall be treated as owning any interest in an enterprise which is owned (directly or indirectly) by any member of such individual's family.

(B) FAMILY.—The term "family" means, with respect to any individual, such individual's spouse, any lineal descendant of such individual or of such individual's spouse, any parent or grandparent of such individual, and any spouse of any of the foregoing. For purposes of the preceding sentence, a relationship by legal adoption shall be treated as a relationship by blood.

(C) TREATMENT OF SPOUSE.—Except as provided in regulations, an individual and such individual's spouse shall be treated as 1 person.

(4) TREATMENT OF CERTAIN TRANSFERS.—

(A) IN GENERAL.—For purposes of this subtitle, if, before the death of the original transferor—

(i) the original transferor transfers all (or any portion of) the retained interest referred to in paragraph (1), or

(ii) the original transferee transfers all (or any portion of) the transferred property referred to in paragraph (1) to a person who is not a member of the original transferor's family,

the original transferor shall be treated as having made a transfer by gift of property to the original transferee equal to the paragraph (1) inclusion (or proportionate amount thereof). Proper adjustments shall be made in the amount treated as a gift by reason of the preceding sentence to take into account prior transfers to which this subparagraph applied and take into account any right of recovery (whether or not exercised) under section 2207B.

(B) COORDINATION WITH PARAGRAPH (1).—In any case to which subparagraph (A) applies, nothing in paragraph (1) or section 2035(d)(2) shall require the inclusion of the transferred property (or proportionate amount thereof).

(C) SPECIAL RULE WHERE PROPERTY RETRANSFERRED.—In the case of a transfer described in subparagraph (A)(ii) from the original transferee to the original transferor, the paragraph (1) inclusion (or proportion thereof) shall be reduced by the excess (if any) of—

(i) the fair market value of the property so transferred, over

(ii) the amount of the consideration paid by the original transferor in exchange for such property.

(D) DEFINITIONS.—For purposes of this paragraph—

(i) ORIGINAL TRANSFEROR.—The term "original transferor" means the person making the transfer referred to in paragraph (1).

(ii) ORIGINAL TRANSFEREE.—The term "original transferee" means the person to whom the transfer referred to in paragraph (1) is made. Such term includes any member of the original transferor's family to whom the property is subsequently transferred.

(iii) PARAGRAPH (1) INCLUSION.—The term "paragraph (1) inclusion" means the amount which would have been included in the gross estate of the original transferor under subsection (a) by reason of paragraph (1) (determined without regard to sections 2032 and 2032A) if the original transferor died immediately before the transfer referred to in subparagraph (A). The amount determined under the preceding sentence shall be reduced by the amount (if any) of the taxable gift resulting from the transfer referred to in paragraph (1)(B).

(iv) TRANSFERS TO INCLUDE TERMINATIONS, ETC.—Terminations, lapses, and other changes in any interest in property of the original transferor or original transferee shall be treated as transfers.

(E) CONTINUING INTEREST IN TRANSFERRED PROPERTY MAY NOT BE RETAINED.—A transfer (to which subparagraph (A) would otherwise apply) shall not be taken into account under subparagraph (A) if the original transferor or the original transferee (as the case may be) retains a direct or indirect continuing interest in the property transferred in such transfer.

(5) ADJUSTMENTS.—Appropriate adjustments shall be made in the amount included in the gross estate by reason of this subsection for the value of the retained interest, extraordinary distributions, and changes in the capital structure of the enterprise after the transfer described in paragraph (1).

(6) TREATMENT OF CERTAIN GRANTOR RETAINED INTEREST TRUSTS.—

(A) IN GENERAL.—For purposes of this subsection, any retention of a qualified trust income interest shall be disregarded and the property with respect to which such interest exists shall be treated as held by the transferor while such income interest continues.

(B) QUALIFIED TRUST INCOME INTEREST.—For purposes of subparagraph (A), the term "qualified trust income interest" means any right to receive amounts determined solely by reference to the income from property held in trust if—

(i) such right is for a period not exceeding 10 years,

(ii) the person holding such right transferred the property to the trust, and

(iii) such person is not a trustee of such trust.

(7) EXCEPTIONS.—

(A) IN GENERAL.—Paragraph (1) shall not apply to a transaction solely by reason of 1 or more of the following:

(i) The receipt (or retention) of qualified debt.

(ii) Except as provided in regulations, the existence of an agreement for the sale or lease of goods or other property to be used in the enterprise or the providing of services and—

(I) the agreement is an arm's length agreement for fair market value, and

(II) the agreement does not otherwise involve any change in interests in the enterprise.

(iii) An option or other agreement to buy or sell property at the fair market value of such property as of the time the option is (or the rights under the agreement are) exercised.

(B) LIMITATIONS.—

(i) SERVICES PERFORMED AFTER TRANSFER.—In the case of compensation for services performed after the transfer referred to in paragraph (1)(B), clause (ii) of subparagraph (A) shall not apply if such services were performed under an agreement providing for the performance of services over a period greater than 3 years after the date of the transfer. For purposes of the preceding sentence, the term of any agreement includes any period for which the agreement may be extended at the option of the service provider.

(ii) AMOUNTS MUST NOT BE CONTINGENT ON PROFITS, ETC.—Clause (ii) of subparagraph (A) shall not apply to any amount determined (in whole or in part) by reference to gross receipts, income, profits, or similar items of the enterprise.

(C) QUALIFIED DEBT.—For purposes of this paragraph, except as provided in subparagraph (D), the term "qualified debt" means any indebtedness if—

(i) such indebtedness—

(I) unconditionally requires the payment of a sum certain in money in 1 or more fixed payments on specified dates, and

(II) has a fixed maturity date not more than 15 years from the date of issue (or, in the case of indebtedness secured by real property, not more than 30 years from the date of issue).

(ii) the only other amount payable under such indebtedness is interest determined at—

(I) a fixed rate, or

(II) a rate which bears a fixed relationship to a specified market interest rate,

(iii) the interest payment dates are fixed,

(iv) such indebtedness is not by its terms subordinated to the claims of general creditors,

(v) except in a case where such indebtedness is in default as to interest or principal, such indebtedness does not grant voting rights to the person to whom the debt is owed or place any limitation on the exercise of voting rights by others, and

(vi) such indebtedness—

(I) is not (directly or indirectly) convertible into an interest in the enterprise which would not be qualified debt, and

(II) does not otherwise grant any right to acquire such an interest.

The requirement of clause (i)(I) that the principal be payable on 1 or more specified dates and the requirement of clause (i)(II) shall not apply to indebtedness payable on demand if such indebtedness is issued in return for cash to be used to meet normal business needs of the enterprise.

(D) SPECIAL RULE FOR STARTUP DEBT.—

(i) IN GENERAL.—For purposes of this paragraph, the term "qualified debt" includes any qualified startup debt.

(ii) QUALIFIED STARTUP DEBT.—For purposes of clause (i), the term "qualified startup debt" means any indebtedness if—

(I) such indebtedness unconditionally requires the payment of a sum certain in money,

(II) such indebtedness was received in exchange for cash to be used in any enterprise involving the active conduct of a trade or business,

(III) the person to whom the indebtedness is owed has not at any time (whether before, on, or after the exchange referred to in subclause (II)) transferred any property (including goodwill) which was not cash to the enterprise or transferred customers or other business opportunities to the enterprise,

(IV) the person to whom the indebtedness is owed has not at any time (whether before, on, or after the exchange referred to in subclause (II) held any interest in the enterprise (including an interest as an officer, director, or employee)[)] which was not qualified startup debt,

(V) any person who (but for subparagraph (A)(i)) would have been an original transferee (as defined in paragraph (4)(C)) participates in the active management (as defined in section 2032A(e)(12)) of the enterprise, and

(VI) such indebtedness meets the requirements of clauses (v) and (vi) of subparagraph (C).

(8) REGULATIONS.—The Secretary shall prescribe such regulations as may be necessary or appropriate to carry out the purposes of this subsection, including such regulations as may be necessary or appropriate to prevent avoidance of the purposes of this subsection through distributions or otherwise.

• 1988, Technical and Miscellaneous Revenue Act of 1988 (P.L. 100-647)

P.L. 100-647, §3031(a)(1):

Amended Code Sec. 2036(c)(4). **Effective** in cases where the transfer referred to in section 2036(c)(1)(B) of the 1986 Code is on or after 6-21-88. Prior to amendment, Code Sec. 2036(c)(4) read as follows:

(4) COORDINATION WITH SECTION 2035.—For purposes of applying section 2035, any transfer of the retained interest referred to in paragraph (1) shall be treated as a transfer of an interest in the transferred property referred to in paragraph (1).

P.L. 100-647, §3031(b):

Amended Code Sec. 2036(c) by adding at the end thereof a new paragraph (6). For the **effective** date, see Act Sec. 3031(h), below.

P.L. 100-647, §3031(b)[c]:

Amended Code Sec. 2036(c) by adding at the end thereof new paragraphs (7)-(8). For the **effective** date, see Act Sec. 3031(h), below.

P.L. 100-647, §3031(d):

Amended Code Sec. 2036(c)(3)(C) by striking out "An individual" and inserting in lieu thereof "Except as provided in regulations, an individual". For the **effective** date, see Act Sec. 3031(h), below.

P.L. 100-647, §3031(e):

Amended Code Sec. 2036(c)(1)(B) by striking out "while" and all that follows down through the comma at the end of such subparagraph and inserting in lieu thereof "while retaining an interest in the income of, or rights in, the enterprise,". For the **effective** date, see Act Sec. 3031(h), below. Prior to amendment, Code Sec. 2036(c)(1)(B) read as follows:

(B) such person in effect transfers after December 17, 1987, property having a disproportionately large share of the potential appreciation in such person's interest in the enterprise while retaining a disproportionately large share in the income of, or rights in, the enterprise,

P.L. 100-647, §3031(g)(1):

Amended Code Sec. 2036(c)(2). For the **effective** date, see Act Sec. 3031(h), below. Prior to amendment, Code Sec. 2036(c)(2) read as follows:

(2) SPECIAL RULE FOR SALES TO FAMILY MEMBERS.—The exception contained in subsection (a) for a bona fide sale shall not apply to a transfer described in paragraph (1) if such transfer is to a member of the transferor's family.

P.L. 100-647, §3031(g)(2):

Amended Code Sec. 2036(c)(5). For the **effective** date, see Act Sec. 3031(h), below. Prior to amendment, Code Sec. 2036(c)(5) read as follows:

(5) COORDINATION WITH SECTION 2043.—In lieu of applying section 2043, appropriate adjustments shall be made for the value of the retained interest.

P.L. 100-647, §3031(h), provides:

(h) EFFECTIVE DATE.—

(1) IN GENERAL.—Except as provided in this subsection, any amendment made by this section shall take effect as if included in the provisions of the Revenue Act of 1987 to which such amendment relates.

(2) SUBSECTION (a).—The amendments made by subsection (a) shall apply in cases where the transfer referred to in section 2036(c)(1)(B) of the 1986 Code is on or after June 21, 1988.

(3) SUBSECTION (f).—If an amount is included in the gross estate of a decedent under section 2036 of the 1986 Code other than solely by reason of section 2036(c) of the 1986 Code, the amendments made by subsection (f) shall apply to such amount only with respect to property transferred after the date of the enactment of this Act.

(4) CORRECTION PERIOD.—If section 2036(c)(1) of the 1986 Code would (but for this paragraph) apply to any interest arising from a transaction entered into during the period beginning after December 17, 1987, and ending before January 1, 1990, such section shall not apply to such interest if—

(A) during such period, such actions are taken as are necessary to have such section 2036(c)(1) not apply to such transaction (and any such interest), or

(B) the original transferor and his spouse on January 1, 1990 (or, if earlier, the date of the original transferor's death), does not hold any interest in the enterprise involved.

(5) CLARIFICATION OF EFFECTIVE DATE.—For purposes of section 10402(b) of the Revenue Act of 1987, with respect to property transferred on or before December 17, 1987—

(A) any failure to exercise a right of conversion,

(B) any failure to pay dividends, and

(c) [C] failures to exercise other rights specified in regulations,

shall not be treated as a subsequent transfer.

• 1987, Revenue Act of 1987 (P.L. 100-203)

P.L. 100-203, §10402(a):

Amended Code Sec. 2036 by redesignating subsection (c) as subsection (d) and by inserting after subsection (b) new subsection (c). **Effective** for estates of decedents dying after 12-31-87, but only in the case of property transferred after 12-17-87.

P.L. 100-203, §10402(a):

Amended Code Sec. 2036 by redesignating subsection (c) as subsection (d). **Effective** for estates of decedents dying after 12-31-87, but only in the case of property transferred after 12-17-87.

[Sec. 2037]

SEC. 2037. TRANSFERS TAKING EFFECT AT DEATH.

[Sec. 2037(a)]

(a) GENERAL RULE.—The value of the gross estate shall include the value of all property to the extent of any interest therein of which the decedent has at any time after September 7, 1916, made a transfer (except in case of a bona fide sale for an adequate and full consideration in money or money's worth), by trust or otherwise, if—

(1) possession or enjoyment of the property can, through ownership of such interest, be obtained only by surviving the decedent, and

(2) the decedent has retained a reversionary interest in the property (but in the case of a transfer made before October 8, 1949, only if such reversionary interest arose by the express terms of the instrument of transfer), and the value of such reversionary interest immediately before the death of the decedent exceeds 5 percent of the value of such property.

Amendments

• 1962, Revenue Act of 1962 (P.L. 87-834)

P.L. 87-834, §18(a)(2):

Amended Code Sec. 2037(a) by deleting "(except real property situated outside of the United States)". **Effective**, generally, for estates of decedents dying after 10-16-62. For exceptions, see Act Sec. 18(b) in the amendment notes for Code Sec. 2031(a).

[Sec. 2037(b)]

(b) SPECIAL RULES.—For purposes of this section, the term "reversionary interest" includes a possibility that property transferred by the decedent—

(1) may return to him or his estate, or

(2) may be subject to a power of disposition by him,

but such term does not include a possibility that the income alone from such property may return to him or become subject to a power of disposition by him. The value of a reversionary interest immediately before the death of the decedent shall be determined (without regard to the fact of the decedent's death) by usual methods of valuation, including the use of tables of mortality and actuarial principles, under regulations prescribed by the Secretary. In determining the value of a possibility that property may be subject to a power of disposition by the decedent, such possibility shall be valued as if it were a possibility that such property may return to the decedent or his estate. Notwithstanding the foregoing, an interest so transferred shall not be included in the decedent's gross estate under this section if possession or enjoyment of the property could have been obtained by any beneficiary during the decedent's life through the exercise of a general power of appointment (as defined in section 2041) which in fact was exercisable immediately before the decedent's death.

Amendments

• 1976, Tax Reform Act of 1976 (P.L. 94-455)

P.L. 94-455, §1906(b)(13)(A):

Amended 1954 Code by substituting "Secretary" for "Secretary or his delegate" each place it appeared. **Effective** 2-1-77.

[Sec. 2038]

SEC. 2038. REVOCABLE TRANSFERS.

[Sec. 2038(a)]

(a) IN GENERAL.—The value of the gross estate shall include the value of all property—

(1) TRANSFERS AFTER JUNE 22, 1936.—To the extent of any interest therein of which the decedent has at any time made a transfer (except in case of a bona fide sale for an adequate and full consideration in money or money's worth), by trust or otherwise, where the enjoyment thereof was subject at the date of his death to any change through the exercise of a power (in whatever capacity exercisable) by the decedent alone or by the decedent in conjunction with any other person (without regard to when or from what source the decedent acquired such power), to alter, amend, revoke, or terminate, or where any such power is relinquished during the 3-year period ending on the date of the decedent's death.

(2) TRANSFERS ON OR BEFORE JUNE 22, 1936.—To the extent of any interest therein of which the decedent has at any time made a transfer (except in case of a bona fide sale for an adequate and full consideration in money or money's worth), by trust or otherwise, where the enjoyment thereof was subject at the date of his death to any change through the exercise of a power, either by the decedent alone or in conjunction with any person, to alter, amend, or revoke, or where the decedent relinquished any such power during the 3-year period ending on the date of the decedent's death. Except in the case of transfers made after June 22, 1936, no interest of the decedent of which he has made a transfer shall be included in the gross estate under paragraph (1) unless it is includible under this paragraph.

Amendments

• 1976, Tax Reform Act of 1976 (P.L. 94-455)

P.L. 94-455, §2001(c)(1)(K), (d)(1):

Substituted "during the 3-year period ending on the date of the decedent's death" for "in contemplation of decedent's death" in Code Sec. 2038(a)(1); and substituted "during the 3-year period ending on the date of the decedent's death" for "in contemplation of his death" in Code Sec. 2038(a)(2). **Effective** for estates of decedents dying after 12-31-76, except that the amendments shall not apply to transfers made before 1-1-77.

• 1962, Revenue Act of 1962 (P.L. 87-834)

P.L. 87-834, §18(a)(2):

Amended Code Sec. 2038(a) by deleting "(except real property situated outside of the United States)". **Effective**, generally, for estates of decedents dying after 10-16-62. For exceptions, see Act Sec. 18(b) in the amendment notes for Code Sec. 2031(a).

[Sec. 2038(b)]

(b) DATE OF EXISTENCE OF POWER.—For purposes of this section, the power to alter, amend, revoke, or terminate shall be considered to exist on the date of the decedent's death even though the exercise of the power is subject to a precedent giving of notice or even though the alteration, amendment, revocation, or termination takes effect only on the expiration of a stated period after the exercise of the power, whether or not on or before the date of the decedent's death notice has been given or the power has been exercised. In such cases proper adjustment shall be made representing the interests which would have been excluded from the power if the decedent had lived, and for such purpose, if the notice has not been given or the power has not been exercised on or before the date of his death, such notice shall be considered to have been given, or the power exercised, on the date of his death.

[Sec. 2038(c)—Repealed]

Amendments

• 1976, Tax Reform Act of 1976 (P.L. 94-455)

P.L. 94-455, §1902(a)(3), (c)(1):

Repealed Code Sec. 2038(c). **Effective** for estates of decedents dying after 10-4-76. Prior to repeal, Code Sec. 2038(c) read as follows:

(c) EFFECT OF DISABILITY IN CERTAIN CASES.—For purposes of this section, in the case of a decedent who was (for a continuous period beginning not less than 3 months before December 31, 1947, and ending with his death) under a mental disability to relinquish a power, the term "power" shall not include a power the relinquishment of which on or after January 1, 1940, and on or before December 31, 1947, would, by reason of section 1000(e) of the Internal Revenue Code of 1939, be deemed not to be a transfer of property for purposes of chapter 4 of the Internal Revenue Code of 1939.

• 1959 (P.L. 86-141)

P.L. 86-141, §[1]:

Amended 1954 Code Sec. 2038 by adding Sec. 2038(c). **Effective** only with respect to estates of decedents dying after 8-16-54. No interest shall be allowed or paid on any overpayment resulting from the application of the amendment with respect to any payment made before the date of the enactment of the Act [8-7-59.—CCH].

[Sec. 2039]

SEC. 2039. ANNUITIES.

[Sec. 2039(a)]

(a) GENERAL.—The gross estate shall include the value of an annuity or other payment receivable by any beneficiary by reason of surviving the decedent under any form of contract or agreement entered into after March 3, 1931 (other than as insurance under policies on the life of the decedent), if, under such contract or agreement, an annuity or other payment was payable to the decedent, or the decedent possessed the right to receive such annuity or payment, either alone or in conjunction with another for his life or for any period not ascertainable without reference to his death or for any period which does not in fact end before his death.

[Sec. 2039(b)]

(b) AMOUNT INCLUDIBLE.—Subsection (a) shall apply to only such part of the value of the annuity or other payment receivable under such contract or agreement as is proportionate to that part of the purchase price therefor contributed by the decedent. For purposes of this section, any contribution by the decedent's employer or former employer to the purchase price of such contract or agreement (whether or not to an employee's trust or fund forming part of a pension, annuity, retirement, bonus or profit-sharing plan) shall be considered to be contributed by the decedent if made by reason of his employment.

[Sec. 2039(c)—Repealed]

Amendments

• 1986, Tax Reform Act of 1986 (P.L. 99-514)

P.L. 99-514, § 1852(e)(1)(A):

Repealed Code Sec. 2039(c). **Effective** for estates of decedents dying after 10-22-86. Prior to repeal, Code Sec. 2039(c) read as follows:

(c) EXCEPTION OF CERTAIN ANNUITY INTERESTS CREATED BY COMMUNITY PROPERTY LAWS.—

(1) IN GENERAL.—In the case of an employee on whose behalf contributions or payments were made by his employer or former employer under a trust, plan, or contract to which this subsection applies, if the spouse of such employee predeceases such employee, then notwithstanding any provision of law, there shall be excluded from the gross estate of such spouse the value of any interest of such spouse in such trust, plan, or contract, to the extent such interest—

(A) is attributable to such contributions or payments, and

(B) arises solely by reason of such spouse's interest in community income under the community property laws of a State.

(2) TRUSTS, PLANS, AND CONTRACTS TO WHICH SUBSECTION APPLIES.—This subsection shall apply to—

(A) any trust, plan, or contract which at the time of the decedent's separation from employment (by death or otherwise), or if earlier, at the time of termination of the plan—

(i) formed part of a plan which met the requirements of section 401(a), or

(ii) was purchased pursuant to a plan described in section 403(a), or

(B) a retirement annuity contract purchased for an employee by an employer which is—

(i) an organization referred to in clause (ii) or (vi) of section 170(b)(1)(A), or

(ii) a religious organization (other than a trust) exempt from taxation under section 501(a).

(3) AMOUNT CONTRIBUTED BY EMPLOYEE.—For purposes of this subsection—

(A) contributions or payments made by the decedent's employer or former employer under a trust, plan, or contract described in paragraph (2)(A) shall not be considered to be contributed by the decedent, and

(B) contributions or payments made by the decedent's employer or former employer toward the purchase of an annuity contract described in paragraph (2)(B) shall not be considered to be contributed by the decedent to the extent excludable from gross income under section 403(b).

• 1984, Deficit Reduction Act of 1984 (P.L. 98-369)

P.L. 98-369, § 525(a):

Amended Code Sec. 2039 by striking out subsections (c)-(g) and inserting in lieu thereof subsection (c). **Effective** for the estates of decedents dying after 12-31-84. The amendment does not, however, apply to the estate of any decedent who was a participant in any plan who was in pay status on 12-31-84, and who irrevocably elected before 7-18-84 the form of benefit. Prior to amendment, subsection (c) read as follows:

(c) Exemption of Annuities Under Certain Trusts and Plans.—Subject to the limitation of subsection (g), notwithstanding any other provision of this section or of any provision of law, there shall be excluded from the gross estate the value of an annuity or other payment (other than an amount described in subsection (f)) receivable by any beneficiary (other than the executor) under—

(1) An employees' trust (or under a contract purchased by an employees' trust) forming part of a pension, stock bonus, or profit-sharing plan which, at the time of the decedent's separation from employment (whether by death or otherwise), or at the time of termination of the plan if earlier, met the requirements of section 401(a);

(2) A retirement annuity contract purchased by an employer (and not by an employees' trust) pursuant to a plan which, at the time of decedent's separation from employment (by death or otherwise), or at the time of termination of the plan if earlier, was a plan described in section 403(a);

(3) A retirement annuity contract purchased for an employee by an employer which is an organization referred to in section 170(b)(1)(A)(ii) or (vi), or which is a religious organization (other than a trust), and which is exempt from tax under section 501(a); or

(4) Chapter 73 of title 10 of the United States Code.

If such amounts payable after the death of the decedent under a plan described in paragraph (1) or (2), under a contract described in paragraph (3), or under chapter 73 of title 10 of the United States Code are attributable to any extent to payments or contributions made by the decedent, no exclusion shall be allowed for that part of the value of such amounts in the proportion that the total payments or contributions made by the decedent bears to the total payments or contributions made. For purposes of this subsection, contributions or payments made by the decedent's employer or former employer under a trust or plan described in paragraph (1) or (2) shall not be considered to be contributed by the decedent, and contributions or payments made by the decedent's employer or former employer toward the purchase of an annuity contract described in paragraph (3) shall, to the extent excludable from gross income under section 403(b), not be considered to be contributed by the decedent. The subsection shall apply to all decedents dying after December 31, 1953. For purposes of this subsection, contributions or payments on behalf of the decedent while he was an employee within the meaning of section 401(c)(1) made under a trust or plan described in paragraph (1) or (2) shall, to the extent allowable as a deduction under section 404, be considered to be made by a person other than the decedent and, to the extent not so allowable, shall be considered to be made by the decedent. For purposes of this subsection, amounts payable under chapter 73 of title 10 of the United States Code are attributable to payments or contributions made by the decedent only to the extent of amounts deposited by him pursuant to section 1438 or 1452(d) of such title 10. For purposes of this subsection, any deductible employee contributions (within the meaning of paragraph (5) of section 72(o)) shall be considered as made by a person other than the decedent.

• 1982, Tax Equity and Fiscal Responsibility Act of 1982 (P.L. 97-248)

P.L. 97-248, §245(b):

Amended Code Sec. 2039(c) by striking out "Notwithstanding the provisions of this section", and inserting "Subject to the limitation of subsection (g), notwithstanding any other provision of this section". **Effective** for estates of decedents dying after 12-31-82, except that such amendments shall not apply to the estate of any decedent who was a participant in any plan, who was in pay status on 12-31-82, and who irrevocably elected before 1-1-83, the form of benefit [**effective** date changed by P.L. 98-369].

• 1981, Economic Recovery Tax Act of 1981 (P.L. 97-34)

P.L. 97-34, §311(d)(1):

Amended Code Sec. 2039(c) by adding at the end the following new sentence: "For purposes of this subsection, any deductible employee contributions (within the meaning of paragraph (5) of section 72(o)) shall be made by a person other than the decedent.". **Effective** for estates of decedents dying after 12-31-81 [**effective** date changed by P.L. 97-448, §103(c)(11).—CCH]. The transitional rule provides that, for purposes of the 1954 Code, any amount allowed as a deduction under section 220 of the Code (as in effect before its repeal by P.L. 97-34) shall be treated as if it were allowed by section 219 of the Code.

• 1978, Revenue Act of 1978 (P.L. 95-600)

P.L. 95-600, §142(a):

Amended the first sentence of Code Sec. 2039(c) by substituting "(other than an amount described in subsection (f))" for "(other than a lump sum distribution described in section 402(e)(4), determined without regard to the next to the last sentence of section 402(e)(4)(A))". **Effective** for estates of decedents dying after 12-31-78.

• 1976, Tax Reform Act of 1976 (P.L. 94-455)

P.L. 94-455, §2009(c)(2):

Substituted the fifth sentence of Code Sec. 2039(c). **Effective** for estates of decedents dying after 12-31-76. Prior to amendment, such sentence read as follows:

For purposes of this subsection, contributions or payments on behalf of the decedent while he was an employee within the meaning of section 401(c)(1) made under a trust or plan described in paragraph (1) or (2) shall be considered to be contributions or payments made by the decedent.

P.L. 94-455, §2009(c)(3):

Inserted "(other than a lump sum distribution described in section 402(e)(4), determined without regard to the next to the last sentence of section 402(e)(4)(A))" after "payment" in the first sentence of Code Sec. 2039(c). **Effective** for estates of decedents dying after 12-31-76.

• 1974, Employee Retirement Income Security Act of 1974 (P.L. 93-406)

P.L. 93-406, §2008(b)(4):

Amended Code Sec. 2039(c) by substituting "section 1438 or 1452(d)" for "section 1438". **Effective** for tax years ending on or after 9-21-72.

• 1969, Tax Reform Act of 1969 (P.L. 91-172)

P.L. 91-172, §101(j)(23):

Amended Code Sec. 2039(c)(3) by substituting "section 170(b)(1)(A)(ii) or (vi), or which is a religious organization (other than a trust)," for "section 503(b)(1), (2), or (3),". **Effective** 1-1-70.

• 1966 (P.L. 89-365)

P.L. 89-365, §2:

Amended Code Sec. 2039(c) by striking out "or" at the end of paragraph (2), by substituting "; or" for the period at the end of paragraph (3), by adding a new paragraph (4), by substituting ", under a contract described in paragraph (3), or under chapter 73 of title 10 of the United States Code" for "or under a contract described in paragraph (3)" in the second sentence, and by adding the last sentence. **Effective** with respect to decedents dying after 12-31-65.

• 1962, Self-Employed Individuals Tax Retirement Act of 1962 (P.L. 87-792)

P.L. 87-792, §7:

Amended Code Sec. 2039 by striking out in subsection (c)(2) "met the requirements of section 401(a)(3), (4), (5), and (6)" and inserting in lieu thereof "was a plan described in section 403(a)"; and by adding after the period in line 28 of subsection (c) a new sentence. **Effective** 1-1-63.

• 1958, Technical Amendments Act of 1958 (P.L. 85-866)

P.L. 85-866, §23(e)(1):

Struck out the word "or" at the end of paragraph (1) of Sec. 2039(c), struck out the period at the end of paragraph (2) of Sec. 2039(c) and inserted in lieu thereof ", (4), (5), and (6); or". **Effective** for the estates of decedents dying after 12-31-57.

P.L. 85-866, §23(e)(2):

Added paragraph (3) to Sec. 2039(c). **Effective** for the estates of decedents dying after 12-31-57.

P.L. 85-866, §23(e)(3):

Added after the phrase "under a plan described in paragraph (1) or (2)" in the second sentence of Sec. 2039(c) the phrase "or under a contract described in paragraph (3)". **Effective** for the estates of decedents dying after 12-31-57.

P.L. 85-866, §23(e)(4):

Amended the second to last sentence of Sec. 2039(c). **Effective** for the estates of decedents dying after 12-31-57. Prior to amendment, this sentence read as follows:

For purposes of this subsection, contributions or payments made by the decedent's employer or former employer under a trust or plan described in this subsection shall not be considered to be contributed by the decedent.

P.L. 85-866, §67(a):

Amended Code Sec. 2039(c)(2) by striking out "section 401(a)(3)" and substituting in lieu thereof "section 401(a)(3), (4), (5), and (6)". **Effective** with respect to estates of decedents dying after 12-31-53.

[Sec. 2039(d)—Stricken]

Amendments

• 1984, Deficit Reduction Act of 1984 (P.L. 98-369)

P.L. 98-369, §525(a):

Amended Code Sec. 2039 by striking out subsection (d). **Effective** for the estates of decedents dying after 12-31-84. The amendment does not, however, apply to the estate of any decedent who was a participant in any plan who was in pay status on 12-31-84, and who irrevocably elected before 7-18-84 the form of benefit. Prior to being stricken, Code Sec. 2039(d) read as follows:

(d) EXEMPTION OF CERTAIN ANNUITY INTERESTS CREATED BY COMMUNITY PROPERTY LAWS.—In the case of an employee on whose behalf contributions or payments were made by his employer or former employer under a trust or plan described in subsection (c)(1) or (2), or toward the purchase of a contract described in subsection (c)(3), which under subsection (c) are not considered as contributed by the employee, if the spouse of such employee predeceases him, then, notwithstanding the provisions of this section or of any other provision of law, there shall be excluded from the gross estate of such spouse the value of any interest of such spouse in such trust or plan or such contract, to the extent such interest—

(1) is attributable to such contributions or payments, and

(2) arises solely by reason of such spouse's interest in community income under the community property laws of a State.

• **1972 (P.L. 92-580)**

P.L. 92-580, §2(a):

Added Code Sec. 2039(d). **Effective** with respect to estates of decedents for which the period prescribed for filing of a claim for credit or refund of an overpayment of estate tax ends on or after 10-27-72. No interest shall be allowed or paid on any overpayment of estate tax resulting from the application of the new section for any period prior to 4-25-73.

[Sec. 2039(e)—Stricken]

Amendments

• **1986, Tax Reform Act of 1986 (P.L. 99-514)**

P.L. 99-514, §1848(d):

Amended Code Sec. 2039(e) by striking out "or a bond described in paragraph (3)" in the second sentence. **Effective** as if included in the provision of P.L. 98-369 to which it relates. Prior to amendment, Code Sec. 2039(e) read as follows:

(e) EXCLUSION OF INDIVIDUAL RETIREMENT ACCOUNTS, ETC.—Subject to the limitation of subsection (g), notwithstanding any other provision of this section or of any other provision of law, there shall be excluded from the value of the gross estate the value of an annuity receivable by any beneficiary (other than the executor) under—

(1) an individual retirement account described in section 408(a), or

(2) an individual retirement annuity described in section 408(b).

If any payment to an account described in paragraph (1) or for an annuity described in paragraph (2) or a bond described in paragraph (3) [sic—paragraph (3) is repealed] was not allowable as a deduction under section 219 and was not a rollover contribution described in section 402(a)(5), 403(a)(4), section 403(b)(8) (but only to the extent such contribution is attributable to a distribution from a contract described in section (c)(3)), or 408(d)(3), the preceding sentence shall not apply to that portion of the value of the amount receivable under such account or annuity (as the case may be) which bears the same ratio to the total value of the amount so receivable as the total amount which was paid to or for such account or annuity and which was not allowable as a deduction under section 219 and was not such a rollover contribution bears to the total amount paid to or for such account or annuity. For purposes of this subsection, the term "annuity" means an annuity contract or other arrangement providing for a series of substantially equal periodic payments to be made to a beneficiary (other than the executor) for his life or over a period extending for at least 36 months after the date of the decedent's death.

• **1984, Deficit Reduction Act of 1984 (P.L. 98-369)**

P.L. 98-369, §491(d)(34):

Amended Code Sec. 2039(e) by striking out paragraph (3), by striking out ", or" at the end of paragraph (2) and inserting in lieu thereof a period, by adding "or" at the end of paragraph (1), by striking out "405(d)(3), 408(d)(3), or 409(b)(3)(C)" and inserting in lieu thereof "or 408(d)(3)", and by striking out ", annuity, or bond" each place it appears and inserting in lieu thereof "or annuity". **Effective** for obligations issued after 12-31-83. Prior to amendment Code Sec. 2039(e)(3) read as follows:

(3) a retirement bond described in section 409(a).

P.L. 98-369, §525(a):

Amended Code Sec. 2039 by striking out subsection (e). **Effective** for the estates of decedents dying after 12-31-84. The amendment does not, however, apply to the estate of any decedent who was a participant in any plan who was in pay status on 12-31-84, and who irrevocably elected before 7-18-84 the form of benefit. Prior to being stricken, Code Sec. 2039(e) read as follows:

(e) EXCLUSION OF INDIVIDUAL RETIREMENT ACCOUNTS, ETC.—Subject to the limitation of subsection (g), notwithstanding any other provision of this section or of any other provision of law, there shall be excluded from the value of the gross estate the value of an annuity receivable by any beneficiary (other than the executor) under—

(1) an individual retirement account described in section 408(a), or

(2) an individual retirement annuity described in section 408(b).

If any payment to an account described in paragraph (1) or for an annuity described in paragraph (2) was not allowable as a deduction under section 219 and was not a rollover contribution described in section 402(a)(5), 403(a)(4), section 403(b)(8) (but only to the extent such contribution is attributable to a distribution from a contract described in subsection (c)(3)), or 408(d)(3), the preceding sentence shall not apply to that portion of the value of the amount receivable under such account or annuity (as the case may be) which bears the same ratio to the total value of the amount so receivable as the total amount which was paid to or for such account or annuity and which was not allowable as a deduction under section 219 and was not such a rollover contribution bears to the total amount paid to or for such account or annuity. For purposes of this subsection, the term "annuity" means an annuity contract or other arrangement providing for a series of substantially equal periodic payments to be made to a beneficiary (other than the executor) for his life or over a period extending for at least 36 months after the date of the decedent's death.

• **1982, Tax Equity and Fiscal Responsibility Act of 1982 (P.L. 97-248)**

P.L. 97-248, §245(b):

Amended Code Sec. 2039(e) by striking out "Notwithstanding the provisions of this section", and inserting "Subject to the limitation of subsection (g), notwithstanding any other provision of this section". **Effective** for estates of decedents dying after 12-31-82, except that such amendment shall not apply to the estate of any decedent who was a participant in any plan who was in pay status on 12-31-82, and who irrevocably elected before 1-1-83 the form of benefit [**effective** date changed by P.L. 98-369].

• **1981, Economic Recovery Tax Act of 1981 (P.L. 97-34)**

P.L. 97-34, §311(h)(4):

Amended Code Sec. 2039(e) by striking out "section 219 or 220" each place it appears and inserting "section 219". **Effective** for estates of decedents dying after 12-31-81 [**effective** date changed by P.L. 97-448, §103(c)(11).—CCH]. The transitional rule provides that, for purposes of the 1954 Code, any amount allowed as a deduction under section 220 of the Code (as in effect before its repeal by P.L. 97-34) shall be treated as if it were allowed by Code Sec. 219.

P.L. 97-34, §313(b)(3):

Amended Code Sec. 2039(e) by inserting "405(d)(3)" after "a contract described in subsection (c)(3)),". **Effective** for redemptions after 8-13-81 in tax years ending after 8-31-81.

• **1978, Revenue Act of 1978 (P.L. 95-600)**

P.L. 95-600, §156(c)(4):

Amended the second sentence of Code Sec. 2039(e) by adding after "403(a)(4)" the following: "section 403(b)(8) (but only to the extent such contribution is attributable to a distribution from a contract described in subsection (c)(3)),". **Effective** for distributions or transfers made after 12-31-77, in tax years beginning after such date [**effective** date changed by P.L. 96-222, §101(a)(13)(A).—CCH].

P.L. 95-600, §702(j)(1):

Amended the second sentence of Code Sec. 2039(e) by adding "or 220" after "section 219" in the two places the latter phrase appears. **Effective** for estates of decedents dying after 1976.

• 1976, Tax Reform Act of 1976 (P.L. 94-455)

P.L. 94-455, §2009(c)(1), (e)(3):

Added Code Sec. 2039(e). **Effective** for estates of decedents dying after 12-31-76.

[Sec. 2039(f)—Stricken]

Amendments

• 1984, Deficit Reduction Act of 1984 (P.L. 98-369)

P.L. 98-369, §525(a):

Amended Code Sec. 2039 by striking out subsection (f). **Effective** for estates of decedents dying after 12-31-84. The amendment does not, however, apply to the estate of any decedent who was a participant in any plan who was in pay status on 12-31-84, and who irrevocably elected before 7-18-84 the form of benefit. Prior to being stricken, Code Sec. 2039(f) read as follows:

(f) LUMP SUM DISTRIBUTIONS—

(1) IN GENERAL—An amount is described in this subsection if—

(A) it is a lump sum distribution described in section 402(e)(4) (determined without regard to the third sentence of section 402(e)(4)(A)), or

(B) it is an amount attributable to accumulated deductible employee contributions (as defined in section 72(o)(5)(B)) in any plan taken into account for purposes of determining whether the distribution described in subparagraph (A) qualifies as a lump sum distribution.

(2) EXCEPTION WHERE RECIPIENT ELECTS NOT TO TAKE 10-YEAR AVERAGING—An amount described in paragraph (1) shall be treated as not described in this subsection if the recipient elects irrevocably (at such time and in such manner as the Secretary may by regulations prescribe) to treat the distribution as taxable under section 402(a) (without the application of paragraph (2) thereof) except to the extent that section 402(e)(4)(J) applies to such distribution.

• 1983, Technical Corrections Act of 1982 (P.L. 97-448)

P.L. 97-448, §103(c)(9)(A):

Amended Code Sec. 2039(f)(1). **Effective** with respect to tax years beginning after 12-31-81. Prior to amendment, Code Sec. 2039(f)(1) read as follows:

(1) IN GENERAL.—An amount is described in this subsection if it is a lump sum distribution described in section 402(e)(4) (determined without regard to the next to the last sentence of section 402(e)(4)(A)).

P.L. 97-448, §103(c)(9)(B):

Amended Code Sec. 2039(f)(2) by striking out "A lump sum distribution" and inserting in lieu thereof "An amount". **Effective** as if included in the provision of P.L. 97-34 to which it relates.

• 1980, Technical Corrections Act of 1979 (P.L. 96-222)

P.L. 96-222, §101(a)(8)(B):

Amended Code Sec. 2039(f)(2) by striking out "without the application of paragraph (2) thereof" and inserting "(without the application of paragraph (2) thereof), except to the extent that section 402(e)(4)(J) applies to such distribution". **Effective** for estates of decedents dying after 12-31-78.

• 1978, Revenue Act of 1978 (P.L. 95-600)

P.L. 95-600, §142(b):

Added Code Sec. 2039(f). **Effective** for estates of decedents dying after 12-31-78.

[Sec. 2039(g)—Stricken]

Amendments

• 1984, Deficit Reduction Act of 1984 (P.L. 98-369)

P.L. 98-369, §525(a):

Amended Code Sec. 2039 by striking out subsection (g). **Effective** for estates of decedents dying after 12-31-84. The amendment does not, however, apply to the estate of any decedent who was a participant in any plan who was in pay status on 12-31-84, and who irrevocably elected before 7-18-84 the form of benefit.

Prior to being stricken, Code Sec. 2039(g) read as follows:

(g) $100,000 LIMITATION ON EXCLUSIONS UNDER SUBSECTIONS (c) AND (e).—The aggregate amount excluded from the gross estate of any decedent under subsections (c) and (e) of this section shall not exceed $100,000.

• 1982, Tax Equity and Fiscal Responsibility Act of 1982 (P.L. 97-248)

P.L. 97-248, §245(a):

Amended Code Sec. 2039 by adding subsection (g). **Effective** for estates of decedents dying after 12-31-82.

[Sec. 2040]

SEC. 2040. JOINT INTERESTS.

[Sec. 2040(a)]

(a) GENERAL RULE.—The value of the gross estate shall include the value of all property to the extent of the interest therein held as joint tenants with right of survivorship by the decedent and any other person, or as tenants by the entirety by the decedent and spouse, or deposited, with any person carrying on the banking business, in their joint names and payable to either or the survivor, except such part thereof as may be shown to have originally belonged to such other person and never to have been received or acquired by the latter from the decedent for less than an adequate and full consideration in money or money's worth: *Provided,* That where such property or any part thereof, or part of the consideration with which such property was acquired, is shown to have been at any time acquired by such other person from the decedent for less than an adequate and full consideration in money or money's worth, there shall be excepted only such part of the value of such property as is proportionate to the consideration furnished by such other person: *Provided further,* That where any property has been acquired by gift, bequest, devise, or inheritance, as a tenancy by the entirety by the decedent and spouse, then to the extent of one-half of the value thereof, or, where so acquired by the decedent and any other person as joint tenants with right of survivorship and their interests are not otherwise specified or fixed by law, then to the extent of the value of a fractional part to be determined by dividing the value of the property by the number of joint tenants with right of survivorship.

Amendments

• 1981, Economic Recovery Tax Act of 1981 (P.L. 97-34)

P.L. 97-34, §403(c)(2):

Amended Code Sec. 2040(a) by inserting "with right of survivorship" after "joint tenants" each place it appears. **Effective** for estates of decedents dying after 12-31-81.

• 1976, Tax Reform Act of 1976 (P.L. 94-455)

P.L. 94-455, §2002(c)(3), (d)(3):

Substituted "(a) GENERAL RULE.—The value" for "The value" in Code Sec. 2040. **Effective** for joint interests created after 12-31-76.

• 1962, Revenue Act of 1962 (P.L. 87-834)

P.L. 87-834, §18(a)(2):

Amended Code Sec. 2040 by deleting "(except real property situated outside of the United States)". **Effective**, generally, for estates of decedents dying after 10-16-62. For exceptions, see Act Sec. 18(b) in the amendment notes for Code Sec. 2031(a).

[Sec. 2040(b)]

(b) CERTAIN JOINT INTERESTS OF HUSBAND AND WIFE.—

(1) INTERESTS OF SPOUSE EXCLUDED FROM GROSS ESTATE.—Notwithstanding subsection (a), in the case of any qualified joint interest, the value included in the gross estate with respect to such interest by reason of this section is one-half of the value of such qualified joint interest.

(2) QUALIFIED JOINT INTEREST DEFINED.—For purposes of paragraph (1), the term "qualified joint interest" means any interest in property held by the decedent and the decedent's spouse as—

(A) tenants by the entirety, or

(B) joint tenants with right of survivorship, but only if the decedent and the spouse of the decedent are the only joint tenants.

Amendments

• 1981, Economic Recovery Tax Act of 1981 (P.L. 97-34)

P.L. 97-34, §403(c)(1):

Amended Code Sec. 2040(b)(2). **Effective** for estates of decedents dying after 12-31-81. Prior to amendment, Code Sec. 2040(b)(2) read as follows:

(2) QUALIFIED JOINT INTEREST DEFINED.—For purposes of paragraph (1), the term "qualified joint interest" means any interest in property held by the decedent and the decedent's spouse as joint tenants or as tenants by the entirety, but only if—

(A) such joint interest was created by the decedent, the decedent's spouse, or both,

(B)(i) in the case of personal property, the creation of such joint interest constituted in whole or in part a gift for purposes of chapter 12, or

(ii) in the case of real property, an election under section 2515 applies with respect to the creation of such joint interest, and

(C) in the case of a joint tenancy, only the decedent and the decedent's spouse are joint tenants.

• 1976, Tax Reform Act of 1976 (P.L. 94-455)

P.L. 94-455, §2002(c)(1), (d)(3):

Added Code Sec. 2040(b). **Effective** for joint interests created after 12-31-76.

[Sec. 2040(c)—Repealed]

Amendments

• 1981, Economic Recovery Tax Act of 1981 (P.L. 97-34)

P.L. 97-34, §403(c)(3)(A):

Repealed Code Sec. 2040(c). **Effective** for estates of decedents dying after 12-31-81. Prior to its repeal, Code Sec. 2040(c) read as follows:

(c) VALUE WHERE SPOUSE OF DECEDENT MATERIALLY PARTICIPATED IN FARM OR OTHER BUSINESS.—

(1) IN GENERAL.—Notwithstanding subsection (a), in the case of an eligible joint interest in section 2040(c) property, the value included in the gross estate with respect to such interest by reason of this section shall be—

(A) the value of such interest, reduced by

(B) the sum of—

(i) the section 2040(c) value of such interest, and

(ii) the adjusted consideration furnished by the decedent's spouse.

(2) LIMITATIONS.—

(A) AT LEAST 50 PERCENT OF VALUE TO BE INCLUDED.—Paragraph (1) shall in no event result in the inclusion in the decedent's gross estate of less than 50 percent of the value of the eligible joint interest.

(B) AGGREGATE REDUCTION.—The aggregate decrease in the value of the decedent's gross estate resulting from the application of this subsection shall not exceed $500,000.

(C) AGGREGATE ADJUSTED CONSIDERATION MUST BE LESS THAN VALUE.—Paragraph (1) shall not apply if the sum of—

(i) the adjusted consideration furnished by the decedent, and

(ii) the adjusted consideration furnished by the decedent's spouse, equals or exceeds the value of the interest.

(3) ELIGIBLE JOINT INTEREST DEFINED.—For purposes of paragraph (1) the term "eligible joint interest" means any interest in property held by the decedent and the decedent's spouse as joint tenants or as tenants by the entirety, but only if—

(A) such joint interest was created by the decedent, the decedent's spouse, or both, and

(B) in the case of a joint tenancy, only the decedent and the decedent's spouse are joint tenants.

(4) SECTION 2040(c) PROPERTY DEFINED.—For purposes of paragraph (1), the term "section 2040(c) property" means any interest in any real or tangible personal property which is devoted to use as a farm or used for farming purposes (within the meaning of paragraphs (4) and (5) of section 2032A(e)) or is used in any other trade or business.

(5) SECTION 2040(c) VALUE.—For purposes of paragraph (1), the term "section 2040(c) value" means—

(A) the excess of the value of the eligible joint interest over the adjusted consideration furnished by the decedent, the decedent's spouse, or both, multiplied by

(B) 2 percent for each taxable year in which the spouse materially participated in the operation of the farm or other trade or business but not to exceed 50 percent.

(6) ADJUSTED CONSIDERATION.—For the purpose of this subsection, the term "adjusted consideration" means—

(A) the consideration furnished by the individual concerned (not taking into account any consideration in the form of income or gain from the business of which the section 2040(c) property is a part) determined under rules similar to the rules set forth in subsection (a), and

(B) an amount equal to the amount of interest which the consideration referred to in subparagraph (A) would have earned over the period in which it was invested in the farm or other business if it had been earning interest throughout such period at 6 percent simple interest.

(7) MATERIAL PARTICIPATION.—For purposes of paragraph (1), material participation shall be determined in a manner similar to the manner used for purposes of paragraph (1) of section 1402(a) (relating to net earnings from self-employment).

(8) VALUE.—For purposes of this subsection, except where the context clearly indicates otherwise, the term "value" means value determined without regard to this subsection.

(9) ELECTION TO HAVE SUBSECTION APPLY.—This subsection shall apply with respect to a joint interest only if the estate of the decedent elects to have this subsection apply to such interest. Such an election shall be made not later than the time prescribed by section 6075(a) for filing the return of tax imposed by section 2001 (including extensions thereof), and shall be made in such manner as the Secretary shall by regulations prescribe.

• 1980, Technical Corrections Act of 1979 (P.L. 96-222)

P.L. 96-222, §105(a)(3)(A):

Amended Code Sec. 2040(c)(2) by adding paragraph (c)(2)(C). **Effective** for estates of decedents dying after 12-31-78.

P.L. 96-222, §105(a)(3)(B):

Amended Code Sec. 2040(c)(1) by changing "subsections (a)" to "subsection (a)". **Effective** for estates of decedents dying after 12-31-78.

• 1978, Revenue Act of 1978 (P.L. 95-600)

P.L. 95-600, §511(a):

Added Code Sec. 2040(c). **Effective** for estates of decedents dying after 12-31-78.

[Sec. 2040(d)—Repealed]

Amendments

• 1981, Economic Recovery Tax Act of 1981 (P.L. 97-34)

P.L. 97-34, §403(c)(3)(A):

Repealed Code Sec. 2040(d). **Effective** for estates of decedents dying after 12-31-81. Prior to its repeal, Code Sec. 2040(d) read as follows:

(d) JOINT INTERESTS OF HUSBAND AND WIFE CREATED BEFORE 1977.—Under regulations prescribed by the Secretary—

(1) IN GENERAL.—In the case of any joint interest created before January 1, 1977, which (if created after December 31, 1976) would have constituted a qualified joint interest under subsection (b)(2) (determined without regard to clause (ii) of subsection (b)(2)(B)), the donor may make an election under this subsection to have paragraph (1) of subsection (b) apply with respect to such joint interest.

(2) TIME FOR MAKING ELECTION.—An election under this subsection with respect to any property shall be made for the calendar quarter in 1977, 1978, or 1979 selected by the donor in a gift tax return filed within the time prescribed by law for filing a gift tax return for such quarter. Such an election may be made irrespective of whether or not the amount involved exceeds the exclusion provided by section 2503(b); but no election may be made under this subsection after the death of the donor.

(3) TAX EFFECTS OF ELECTION.—In the case of any property with respect to which an election has been made under this subsection, for purposes of this title—

(A) the donor shall be treated as having made a gift at the close of the calendar quarter selected under paragraph (2), and

(B) the amount of the gift shall be determined under paragraph (4).

(4) AMOUNT OF GIFT.—For purposes of paragraph (3)(B), the amount of any gift is one-half of the amount—

(A) which bears the same ratio to the excess of (i) the value of the property on the date of the deemed making of the gift under paragraph (3)(A), over (ii) the value of such property on the date of the creation of the joint interest, as

(B) the excess of (i) the consideration furnished by the donor at the time of the creation of the joint interest, over (ii) the consideration furnished at such time by the donor's spouse, bears to the total consideration furnished by both spouses at such time.

(5) SPECIAL RULE FOR PARAGRAPH (4)(A).—For purposes of paragraph (4)(A)—

(A) in the case of real property, if the creation was not treated as a gift at the time of the creation, or

(B) in the case of personal property, if the gift was required to be included on a gift tax return but was not so included, and the period of limitations on assessment under section 6501 has expired with respect to the tax (if any) on such gift,

then the value of the property on the date of the creation of the joint interest shall be treated as zero.

(6) SUBSTANTIAL IMPROVEMENTS.—For purposes of this subsection, a substantial improvement of any property shall be treated as the creation of a separate joint interest.

• 1978, Revenue Act of 1978 (P.L. 95-600)

P.L. 95-600, §702(k)(2):

Added Code Sec. 2040(d). **Effective** 11-6-78.

[Sec. 2040(e)—Repealed]

Amendments

• 1981, Economic Recovery Tax Act of 1981 (P.L. 97-34)

P.L. 97-34, §403(c)(3)(A):

Repealed Code Sec. 2040(e). **Effective** for estates of decedents dying after 12-31-81. Prior to its repeal, Code Sec. 2040(e) read as follows:

(e) TREATMENT OF CERTAIN POST-1976 TERMINATIONS.—

(1) IN GENERAL.—If—

(A) before January 1, 1977, a husband and wife had a joint interest in property with right of survivorship,

(B) after December 31, 1976, such joint interest was terminated, and

(C) after December 31, 1976, a joint interest of such husband and wife in such property (or in property the basis of which in whole or in part reflects the basis of such property) was created,

then paragraph (1) of subsection (b) shall apply to the joint interest described in subparagraph (C) only if an election is made under subsection (d).

(2) SPECIAL RULES.—For purposes of applying subsection (d) to property described in paragraph (1) of this subsection—

(A) if the creation described in paragraph (1)(C) occurs after December 31, 1979, the election may be made only with respect to the calendar quarter in which such creation occurs, and

(B) the creation of the joint interest described in paragraphs (4) and (5) of subsection (d) is the creation of the joint interest described in paragraph (1)(A) of this subsection.

• 1978, Revenue Act of 1978 (P.L. 95-600)

P.L. 95-600, §702(k)(2):

Added Code Sec. 2040(e). **Effective** 11-6-78.

[Sec. 2041]

SEC. 2041. POWERS OF APPOINTMENT.

[Sec. 2041(a)]

(a) IN GENERAL.—The value of the gross estate shall include the value of all property—

(1) POWERS OF APPOINTMENT CREATED ON OR BEFORE OCTOBER 21, 1942.—To the extent of any property with respect to which a general power of appointment created on or before October 21, 1942, is exercised by the decedent—

(A) by will, or

(B) by a disposition which is of such nature that if it were a transfer of property owned by the decedent, such property would be includible in the decedent's gross estate under sections 2035 to 2038, inclusive;

but the failure to exercise such a power or the complete release of such a power shall not be deemed an exercise thereof. If a general power of appointment created on or before October 21, 1942, has been partially released so that it is no longer a general power of appointment, the exercise of such power shall not be deemed to be the exercise of a general power of appointment if—

(i) such partial release occurred before November 1, 1951, or

(ii) the donee of such power was under a legal disability to release such power on October 21, 1942, and such partial release occurred not later than 6 months after the termination of such legal disability.

(2) POWERS CREATED AFTER OCTOBER 21, 1942.—To the extent of any property with respect to which the decedent has at the time of his death a general power of appointment created after October 21, 1942, or with respect to which the decedent has at any time exercised or released such a power of appointment by a disposition which is of such nature that if it were a transfer of property owned by the decedent, such property would be includible in the decedent's gross estate under sections 2035 to 2038, inclusive. For purposes of this paragraph (2), the power of appointment shall be considered to exist on the date of the decedent's death even though the exercise of the power is subject to a precedent giving of notice or even though the exercise of the power takes effect only on the expiration of a stated period after its exercise, whether or not on or before the date of the decedent's death notice has been given or the power has been exercised.

(3) CREATION OF ANOTHER POWER IN CERTAIN CASES.—To the extent of any property with respect to which the decedent—

(A) by will, or

(B) by a disposition which is of such nature that if it were a transfer of property owned by the decedent such property would be includible in the decedent's gross estate under section 2035, 2036, or 2037,

exercises a power of appointment created after October 21, 1942, by creating another power of appointment which under the applicable local law can be validly exercised so as to postpone the vesting of any estate or interest in such property, or suspend the absolute ownership or power of alienation of such property, for a period ascertainable without regard to the date of the creation of the first power.

Amendments

• 1976, Tax Reform Act of 1976 (P.L. 94-455)

P.L. 94-455, §2009(b)(4), (e)(2):

Deleted the second sentence of Code Sec. 2041(a)(2). **Effective** for transfers creating an interest in the person disclaiming made after 12-31-76. Prior to deletion, such sentence read as follows: "A disclaimer or renunciation of such a power of appointment shall not be deemed a release of such power."

• 1962, Revenue Act of 1962 (P.L. 87-834)

P.L. 87-834, §18(a)(2):

Amended Code Sec. 2041(a) by deleting "(except real property situated outside of the United States)". **Effective**, generally, for estates of decedents dying after 10-16-62. For exceptions, see Act Sec. 18(b) in the amendment notes for Code Sec. 2031(a).

[Sec. 2041(b)]

(b) DEFINITIONS.—For purposes of subsection (a)—

(1) GENERAL POWER OF APPOINTMENT.—The term "general power of appointment" means a power which is exercisable in favor of the decedent, his estate, his creditors, or the creditors of his estate; except that—

(A) A power to consume, invade, or appropriate property for the benefit of the decedent which is limited by an ascertainable standard relating to the health, education, support, or maintenance of the decedent shall not be deemed a general power of appointment.

(B) A power of appointment created on or before October 21, 1942, which is exercisable by the decedent only in conjunction with another person shall not be deemed a general power of appointment.

(C) In the case of a power of appointment created after October 21, 1942, which is exercisable by the decedent only in conjunction with another person—

(i) If the power is not exercisable by the decedent except in conjunction with the creator of the power—such power shall not be deemed a general power of appointment.

(ii) If the power is not exercisable by the decedent except in conjunction with a person having a substantial interest in the property, subject to the power, which is adverse to exercise of the power in favor of the decedent—such power shall not be deemed a general power of appointment. For the purposes of this clause a person who, after the death of the decedent, may be possessed of a power of appointment (with respect to the property subject to the decedent's power) which he may exercise in his own favor shall be deemed as having an interest in the property and such interest shall be deemed adverse to such exercise of the decedent's power.

(iii) If (after the application of clauses (i) and (ii)) the power is a general power of appointment and is exercisable in favor of such other person—such power shall be deemed a general power of appointment only in respect of a fractional part of the property subject to such power, such part to be determined by dividing the value of such property by the number of such persons (including the decedent) in favor of whom such power is exercisable.

For purposes of clauses (ii) and (iii), a power shall be deemed to be exercisable in favor of a person if it is exercisable in favor of such person, his estate, his creditors, or the creditors of his estate.

(2) LAPSE OF POWER.—The lapse of a power of appointment created after October 21, 1942, during the life of the individual possessing the power shall be considered a release of such power. The preceding sentence shall apply with respect to the lapse of powers during any calendar year only to the extent that the property, which could have been appointed by exercise of such lapsed powers, exceeded in value, at the time of such lapse, the greater of the following amounts:

(A) $5,000, or

(B) 5 percent of the aggregate value, at the time of such lapse, of the assets out of which, or the proceeds of which, the exercise of the lapsed powers could have been satisfied.

(3) DATE OF CREATION OF POWER.—For purposes of this section, a power of appointment created by a will executed on or before October 21, 1942, shall be considered a power created on or before such date if the person executing such will dies before July 1, 1949, without having republished such will, by codicil or otherwise, after October 21, 1942.

[Sec. 2042]

SEC. 2042. PROCEEDS OF LIFE INSURANCE.

The value of the gross estate shall include the value of all property—

(1) RECEIVABLE BY THE EXECUTOR.—To the extent of the amount receivable by the executor as insurance under policies on the life of the decedent.

(2) RECEIVABLE BY OTHER BENEFICIARIES.—To the extent of the amount receivable by all other beneficiaries as insurance under policies on the life of the decedent with respect to which the decedent possessed at his death any of the incidents of ownership, exercisable either alone or in conjunction with any other person. For purposes of the preceding sentence, the term "incident of ownership" includes a reversionary interest (whether arising by the express terms of the policy or other instrument or by operation of law) only if the value of such reversionary interest exceeded 5 percent of the value of the policy immediately before the death of the decedent. As used in this paragraph, the term "reversionary interest" includes a possibility that the policy, or the proceeds of the policy, may return to the decedent or his estate, or may be subject to a power of disposition by him. The value of a reversionary interest at any time shall be determined (without regard to the fact of the decedent's death) by usual methods of valuation, including the use of tables of mortality and actuarial principles, pursuant to regulations prescribed by the Secretary. In determining the value of a possibility that the policy or proceeds thereof may be subject to a power of disposition by the decedent, such possibility shall be valued as if it were a possibility that such policy or proceeds may return to the decedent or his estate.

Amendments

• 1976, Tax Reform Act of 1976 (P.L. 94-455)

P.L. 94-455, §1906(b)(13)(A):

Amended 1954 Code by substituting "Secretary" for "Secretary or his delegate" each place it appeared. **Effective** 2-1-77.

[Sec. 2043]

SEC. 2043. TRANSFERS FOR INSUFFICIENT CONSIDERATION.

[Sec. 2043(a)]

(a) IN GENERAL.—If any one of the transfers, trusts, interests, rights, or powers enumerated and described in sections 2035 to 2038, inclusive, and section 2041 is made, created, exercised, or relinquished for a consideration in money or money's worth, but is not a bona fide sale for an adequate and full consideration in money or money's worth, there shall be included in the gross estate only the excess of the fair market value at the time of death of the property otherwise to be included on account of such transaction, over the value of the consideration received therefor by the decedent.

[Sec. 2043(b)]

(b) MARITAL RIGHTS NOT TREATED AS CONSIDERATION.—

(1) IN GENERAL.—For purposes of this chapter, a relinquishment or promised relinquishment of dower or curtesy, or of a statutory estate created in lieu of dower or curtesy, or of other marital rights in the decedent's property or estate, shall not be considered to any extent a consideration "in money or money's worth".

(2) EXCEPTION.—For purposes of section 2053 (relating to expenses, indebtedness, and taxes), a transfer of property which satisfies the requirements of paragraph (1) of section 2516 (relating to certain property settlements) shall be considered to be made for an adequate and full consideration in money or money's worth.

Amendments

• 1984, Deficit Reduction Act of 1984 (P.L. 98-369)

P.L. 98-369, §425(a)(1):

Amended Code Sec. 2043(b). **Effective** for estates of decedents dying after 7-18-84. Prior to amendment, Code Sec. 2043(b) read as follows:

(b) Marital Rights Not Treated as Consideration.—For purposes of this chapter, a relinquishment or promised relinquishment of dower or curtesy, or of a statutory estate created in lieu of dower or curtesy, or of other marital rights in the decedent's property or estate, shall not be considered to any extent a consideration "in money or money's worth."

[Sec. 2044]

SEC. 2044. CERTAIN PROPERTY FOR WHICH MARITAL DEDUCTION WAS PREVIOUSLY ALLOWED.

[Sec. 2044(a)]

(a) GENERAL RULE.—The value of the gross estate shall include the value of any property to which this section applies in which the decedent had a qualifying income interest for life.

[Sec. 2044(b)]

(b) PROPERTY TO WHICH THIS SECTION APPLIES.—This section applies to any property if—

(1) a deduction was allowed with respect to the transfer of such property to the decedent—

(A) under section 2056 by reason of subsection (b)(7) thereof, or

(B) under section 2523 by reason of subsection (f) thereof, and

(2) section 2519 (relating to dispositions of certain life estates) did not apply with respect to a disposition by the decedent of part or all of such property.

Amendments

• 1981, Economic Recovery Tax Act of 1981 (P.L. 97-34)

P.L. 97-34, §403(d)(3)(A)(i):

Added Code Sec. 2044. **Effective** for estates of decedents dying after 12-31-81.

[Sec. 2044(c)]

(c) PROPERTY TREATED AS HAVING PASSED FROM DECEDENT.—For purposes of this chapter and chapter 13, property includible in the gross estate of the decedent under subsection (a) shall be treated as property passing from the decedent.

Amendments

• 1983, Technical Corrections Act of 1982 (P.L. 97-448)

P.L. 97-448, §104(a)(1)(B):

Amended Code Sec. 2044 by adding at the end thereof new subsection (c). **Effective** as if included in the provision of P.L. 97-34 to which it relates.

[Sec. 2045]

SEC. 2045. PRIOR INTERESTS.

Except as otherwise specifically provided by law, sections 2034 to 2042, inclusive, shall apply to the transfers, trusts, estates, interests, rights, powers, and relinquishment of powers, as severally enumerated and described therein, whenever made, created, arising, existing, exercised, or relinquished.

Amendments

• 1981, Economic Recovery Tax Act of 1981 (P.L. 97-34)

P.L. 97-34, §403(d)(3)(A)(i):

Redesignated Code Sec. 2044 as Code Sec. 2045. **Effective** for estates of decedents dying after 12-31-81.

• 1976, Tax Reform Act of 1976 (P.L. 94-455)

P.L. 94-455, §2001(c)(1)(M):

Substituted "specifically provided by law" for "specifically provided therein" in Code Sec. 2044. **Effective** for estates of decedents dying after 12-31-76.

[Sec. 2046]

SEC. 2046. DISCLAIMERS.

For provisions relating to the effect of a qualified disclaimer for purposes of this chapter, see section 2518.

Amendments

• 1981, Economic Recovery Tax Act of 1981 (P.L. 97-34)

P.L. 97-34, §403(d)(3)(A)(i):

Redesignated Code Sec. 2045 as Code Sec. 2046. **Effective** for estates of decedents dying after 12-31-81.

• 1976, Tax Reform Act of 1976 (P.L. 94-455)

P.L. 94-455, §2009(b)(2):

Added Code Sec. 2045. **Effective** for transfers creating an interest in the person disclaiming made after 12-31-76.

PART IV—TAXABLE ESTATE

[Sec. 2051]

SEC. 2051. DEFINITION OF TAXABLE ESTATE.

For purposes of the tax imposed by section 2001, the value of the taxable estate shall be determined by deducting from the value of the gross estate the deductions provided for in this part.

Amendments

• 1978, Revenue Act of 1978 (P.L. 95-600)

P.L. 95-600, §702(r)(2):

Amended Code Sec. 2051 by deleting "exemption and" after "value of the gross estate the". **Effective** for estates of decedents dying after 1976.

[Sec. 2052—Repealed]

Amendments

• 1976, Tax Reform Act of 1976 (P.L. 94-455)

P.L. 94-455, §2001(a)(4):

Repealed Code Sec. 2052. **Effective** with respect to estates of decedents dying after 12-31-76. Prior to repeal, Code Sec. 2052 read as follows:

SEC. 2052. EXEMPTION.

For purposes of the tax imposed by section 2001, the value of the taxable estate shall be determined by deducting from the value of the gross estate an exemption of $60,000.

[Sec. 2053]

SEC. 2053. EXPENSES, INDEBTEDNESS, AND TAXES.

[Sec. 2053(a)]

(a) GENERAL RULE.—For purposes of the tax imposed by section 2001, the value of the taxable estate shall be determined by deducting from the value of the gross estate such amounts—

(1) for funeral expenses,

(2) for administration expenses,

(3) for claims against the estate, and

(4) for unpaid mortgages on, or any indebtedness in respect of, property where the value of the decedent's interest therein, undiminished by such mortgage or indebtedness, is included in the value of the gross estate,

as are allowable by the laws of the jurisdiction, whether within or without the United States, under which the estate is being administered.

[Sec. 2053(b)]

(b) OTHER ADMINISTRATION EXPENSES.—Subject to the limitations in paragraph (1) of subsection (c), there shall be deducted in determining the taxable estate amounts representing expenses incurred in administering property not subject to claims which is included in the gross estate to the same extent such amounts would be allowable as a deduction under subsection (a) if such property were subject to claims, and such amounts are paid before the expiration of the period of limitation for assessment provided in section 6501.

[Sec. 2053(c)]

(c) LIMITATIONS.—

(1) LIMITATIONS APPLICABLE TO SUBSECTIONS (a) AND (b).—

(A) CONSIDERATION FOR CLAIMS.—The deduction allowed by this section in the case of claims against the estate, unpaid mortgages, or any indebtedness shall, when founded on a promise or agreement, be limited to the extent that they were contracted bona fide and for an adequate and full consideration in money or money's worth; except that in any case in which any such claim is founded on a promise or agreement of the decedent to make a contribution or gift to or for the use of any donee described in section 2055 for the purposes specified therein, the deduction for such claims shall not be so limited, but shall be limited to the extent that it would be allowable as a deduction under section 2055 if such promise or agreement constituted a bequest.

(B) CERTAIN TAXES.—Any income taxes on income received after the death of the decedent, or property taxes not accrued before his death, or any estate, succession, legacy, or inheritance taxes, shall not be deductible under this section.

(C) CERTAIN CLAIMS BY REMAINDERMEN.—No deduction shall be allowed under this section for a claim against the estate by a remainderman relating to any property described in section 2044.

(D) SECTION 6166 INTEREST.—No deduction shall be allowed under this section for any interest payable under section 6601 on any unpaid portion of the tax imposed by section 2001 for the period during which an extension of time for payment of such tax is in effect under section 6166.

(2) LIMITATIONS APPLICABLE ONLY TO SUBSECTION (a).—In the case of the amounts described in subsection (a), there shall be disallowed the amount by which the deductions specified therein exceed the value, at the time of the decedent's death, of property subject to claims, except to the extent that such deductions represent amounts paid before the date prescribed for the filing of the estate tax return. For purposes of this section, the term "property subject to claims" means property includible in the gross estate of the decedent which, or the avails of which, would under the applicable law, bear the burden of the payment of such deductions in the final adjustment and settlement of the estate, except that the value of the property shall be reduced by the amount of the deduction under section 2054 attributable to such property.

Amendments

• 1997, Taxpayer Relief Act of 1997 (P.L. 105-34)

P.L. 105-34, §503(b)(1):

Amended Code Sec. 2053(c)(1) by adding a new subparagraph (D). **Effective**, generally, for estates of decedents dying after 12-31-97. For a special rule, see Act Sec. 503(d)(2), below.

P.L. 105-34, §503(d)(2), provides:

(2) ELECTION.—In the case of the estate of any decedent dying before January 1, 1998, with respect to which there is an election under section 6166 of the Internal Revenue Code of 1986, the executor of the estate may elect to have the amendments made by this section apply with respect to installments due after the effective date of the election; except that the 2-percent portion of such installments shall be equal to the amount which would be the 4-percent portion of such installments without regard to such election. Such an election shall be made before January 1, 1999 in the manner prescribed by the Secretary of the Treasury and, once made, is irrevocable.

P.L. 105-34, §1073(b)(3):

Amended Code Sec. 2053(c)(1)(B) by striking the last sentence. **Effective** for estates of decedents dying after 12-31-96. Prior to being stricken, the last sentence of Code Sec. 2053(c)(1)(B) read as follows:

This subparagraph shall not apply to any increase in the tax imposed by this chapter by reason of section 4980A(d).

• 1988, Technical and Miscellaneous Revenue Act of 1988 (P.L. 100-647)

P.L. 100-647, §1011A(g)(11):

Amended Code Sec. 2053(c)(1)(B) by adding at the end thereof a new sentence. **Effective** as if included in the provision of P.L. 99-514 to which it relates.

• 1984, Deficit Reduction Act of 1984 (P.L. 98-369)

P.L. 98-369, §1027(b):

Amended Code Sec. 2053(c)(1) by adding subparagraph (C). **Effective** as if included in the amendment made by section 403 of P.L. 97-34.

[Sec. 2053(d)]

(d) CERTAIN FOREIGN DEATH TAXES.—

(1) IN GENERAL.—Notwithstanding the provisions of subsection (c)(1)(B), for purposes of the tax imposed by section 2001, the value of the taxable estate may be determined, if the executor so elects before the expiration of the period of limitation for assessment provided in section 6501, by deducting from the value of the gross estate the amount (as determined in accordance with regulations prescribed by the Secretary) of any estate, succession, legacy, or inheritance tax imposed by and actually paid to any foreign country, in respect of any property situated within such foreign country and included in the gross estate of a citizen or resident of the United States, upon a transfer by the decedent for public, charitable, or religious uses described in section 2055. The determination under this paragraph of the country within which property is situated shall be made in accordance with the rules applicable under subchapter B (sec. 2101 and following) in determining whether property is situated within or without the United States. Any election under this paragraph shall be exercised in accordance with regulations prescribed by the Secretary.

(2) CONDITION FOR ALLOWANCE OF DEDUCTION.—No deduction shall be allowed under paragraph (1) for a foreign death tax specified therein unless the decrease in the tax imposed by

section 2001 which results from the deduction provided in paragraph (1) will inure solely for the benefit of the public, charitable, or religious transferees described in section 2055 or section 2106(a)(2). In any case where the tax imposed by section 2001 is equitably apportioned among all the transferees of property included in the gross estate, including those described in sections 2055 and 2106(a)(2) (taking into account any exemptions, credits, or deductions allowed by this chapter), in determining such decrease, there shall be disregarded any decrease in the Federal estate tax which any transferees other than those described in sections 2055 and 2106(a)(2) are required to pay.

(3) EFFECT ON CREDIT FOR FOREIGN DEATH TAXES OF DEDUCTION UNDER THIS SUBSECTION.—

(A) ELECTION.—An election under this subsection shall be deemed a waiver of the right to claim a credit, against the Federal estate tax, under a death tax convention with any foreign country for any tax or portion thereof in respect of which a deduction is taken under this subsection.

(B) CROSS REFERENCE.—

See section 2011(d) for the effect of a deduction taken under this paragraph on the credit for foreign death taxes.

Amendments

• 2013, American Taxpayer Relief Act of 2012 (P.L. 112-240)

P.L. 112-240, §101(a)(1) and (3), provides:

SEC. 101. PERMANENT EXTENSION AND MODIFICATION OF 2001 TAX RELIEF.

(a) PERMANENT EXTENSION.—

(1) IN GENERAL.—The Economic Growth and Tax Relief Reconciliation Act of 2001 is amended by striking title IX.

* * *

(3) EFFECTIVE DATE.—The amendments made by this subsection shall apply to taxable, plan, or limitation years beginning after December 31, 2012, and estates of decedents dying, gifts made, or generation skipping transfers after December 31, 2012.

• 2002, Victims of Terrorism Tax Relief Act of 2001 (P.L. 107-134)

P.L. 107-134, §103(b)(2):

Amended Code Sec. 2053(d)(3)(B) by striking "section 2011(e)" and inserting "section 2011(d)". **Effective** for estates of decedents dying on or after 9-11-2001; and in the case of individuals dying as a result of the 4-19-95 terrorist attack, dying on or after 4-19-95. For a waiver of limitations, see Act Sec. 103(d)(2), below.

P.L. 107-134, §103(d)(2), provides:

(2) WAIVER OF LIMITATIONS.—If refund or credit of any overpayment of tax resulting from the amendments made by this section is prevented at any time before the close of the 1-year period beginning on the date of the enactment of this Act by the operation of any law or rule of law (including res judicata), such refund or credit may nevertheless be made or allowed if claim therefor is filed before the close of such period.

• 2001, Economic Growth and Tax Relief Reconciliation Act of 2001 (P.L. 107-16)

P.L. 107-16, §532(c)(5):

Amended Code Sec. 2053(d). **Effective** for estates of decedents dying, and generation-skipping transfers, after 12-31-2004. Prior to amendment, Code Sec. 2053(d) read as follows:

(d) CERTAIN STATE AND FOREIGN DEATH TAXES.—

(1) GENERAL RULE.—Notwithstanding the provisions of subsection (c)(1)(B) of this section, for purposes of the tax imposed by section 2001 the value of the taxable estate may be determined, if the executor so elects before the expiration of the period of limitation for assessment provided in section 6501, by deducting from the value of the gross estate the amount (as determined in accordance with regulations prescribed by the Secretary) of—

(A) any estate, succession, legacy, or inheritance tax imposed by a State or the District of Columbia upon a transfer by the decedent for public, charitable, or religious uses described in section 2055 or 2106(a)(2), and

(B) any estate, succession, legacy, or inheritance tax imposed by and actually paid to any foreign country, in respect of any property situated within such foreign country and included in the gross estate of a citizen or resident of the United States, upon a transfer by the decedent for public, charitable, or religious uses described in section 2055.

The determination under subparagraph (B) of the country within which property is situated shall be made in accordance with the rules applicable under subchapter B (sec. 2101 and following) in determining whether property is situated within or without the United States. Any election under this paragraph shall be exercised in accordance with regulations prescribed by the Secretary.

(2) CONDITION FOR ALLOWANCE OF DEDUCTION.—No deduction shall be allowed under paragraph (1) for a State death tax or a foreign death tax specified therein unless the decrease in the tax imposed by section 2001 which results from the deduction provided in paragraph (1) will inure solely for the benefit of the public, charitable, or religious transferees described in section 2055 or section 2106(a)(2). In any case where the tax imposed by section 2001 is equitably apportioned among all the transferees of property included in the gross estate, including those described in sections 2055 and 2106(a)(2) (taking into account any exemptions, credits, or deductions allowed by this chapter), in determining such decrease, there shall be disregarded any decrease in the Federal estate tax which any transferees other than those described in sections 2055 and 2106(a)(2) are required to pay.

(3) EFFECT ON CREDITS FOR STATE AND FOREIGN DEATH TAXES OF DEDUCTION UNDER THIS SUBSECTION.—

(A) ELECTION.—An election under this subsection shall be deemed a waiver of the right to claim a credit, against the Federal estate tax, under a death tax convention with any foreign country for any tax or portion thereof in respect of which a deduction is taken under this subsection.

(B) CROSS REFERENCES.—

See section 2011(e) for the effect of a deduction taken under this subsection on the credit for State death taxes, and see section 2014(f) for the effect of a deduction taken under this subsection on the credit for foreign death taxes.

P.L. 107-16, §901(a)-(b), as amended by P.L. 111-312, §101(a)(1), provides [but see P.L. 112-240, §101(a)(1) and (3), above]:

SEC. 901. SUNSET OF PROVISIONS OF ACT.

(a) IN GENERAL.—All provisions of, and amendments made by, this Act shall not apply—

(1) to taxable, plan, or limitation years beginning after December 31, 2012, or

(2) in the case of title V, to estates of decedents dying, gifts made, or generation skipping transfers, after December 31, 2012.

(b) APPLICATION OF CERTAIN LAWS.—The Internal Revenue Code of 1986 and the Employee Retirement Income Security Act of 1974 shall be applied and administered to years, estates, gifts, and transfers described in subsection (a) as if the provisions and amendments described in subsection (a) had never been enacted.

• 1976, Tax Reform Act of 1976 (P.L. 94-455)

P.L. 94-455, §1902(a)(12)(B):

Deleted "or Territory" in Code Sec. 2053(d). **Effective** for gifts made after 12-31-76.

P.L. 94-455, §1906(b)(13)(A):

Amended 1954 Code by substituting "Secretary" for "Secretary or his delegate" each place it appeared. **Effective** 2-1-77.

• 1959 (P.L. 86-175)

P.L. 86-175, §[1]:

Amended 1954 Code Sec. 2053(d). **Effective** with respect to the estates of decedents dying on or after 7-1-55. Prior to amendment, Code Sec. 2053(d) read as follows:

(d) Certain State Death Taxes.—

(1) General rule.—Notwithstanding the provisions of subsection (c)(1)(B) of this section, for purposes of the tax imposed by section 2001 the value of the taxable estate may be determined, if the executor so elects before the expiration of the period of limitation for assessment provided in section 6501, by deducting from the value of the gross estate the amount (as determined in accordance with regulations prescribed by the Secretary or his delegate) of any estate, succession, legacy or inheritance tax imposed by a State or Territory or the District of Columbia, upon a transfer by the decedent for public, charitable, or religious uses described in section 2055 or 2106(a)(2). The election shall be exercised in accordance with regulations prescribed by the Secretary or his delegate.

(2) Condition for allowance of deduction.—No deduction shall be allowed under paragraph (1) for a State death tax specified therein unless the decrease in the tax imposed by section 2001 which results from the deduction provided for in paragraph (1) will inure solely for the benefit of the public, charitable, or religious transferees described in section 2055 or section 2106(a)(2). In any case where the tax imposed by section 2001 is equitably apportioned among all the transferees of property included in the gross estate, including those described in sections 2055 and 2106(a)(2) (taking into account any exemptions, credits, or deductions allowed by this chapter), in determining such decrease, there shall be disregarded any decrease in the Federal estate tax which any transferees other than those described in sections 2055 and 2106(a)(2) are required to pay.

(3) Effect of deduction on credit for state death taxes.—See section 2011(e) for the effect of a deduction taken under this subsection on the credit for State death taxes.

• 1958, Technical Amendments Act of 1958 (P.L. 85-866)

P.L. 85-866, §102(c):

Amended Code Sec. 2053(d)(1) by striking the words "or any possession of the United States," following the words "District of Columbia". **Effective** for estates of decedents dying after 9-2-58.

• 1956 (P.L. 414, 84th Cong.)

P.L. 414, 84th Cong., §2:

Amended Code Sec. 2053 by redesignating subsection (d) as subsection (e) and by adding after subsection (c) a new subsection (d). **Effective** for estates of all decedents dying after 12-31-53.

[Sec. 2053(e)]

(e) MARITAL RIGHTS.—

For provisions treating certain relinquishments of marital rights as consideration in money or money's worth, see section 2043(b)(2).

Amendments

• 1984, Deficit Reduction Act of 1984 (P.L. 98-369)

P.L. 98-369, §425(a)(2):

Amended Code Sec. 2053(e). **Effective** for estates of decedents dying after 7-18-84. Prior to amendment, Code Sec. 2053(e) read as follows:

(e) Marital Rights.—

For provisions that relinquishment of marital rights shall not be deemed a consideration "in money or money's worth," see section 2043(b).

[Sec. 2054]

SEC. 2054. LOSSES.

For purposes of the tax imposed by section 2001, the value of the taxable estate shall be determined by deducting from the value of the gross estate losses incurred during the settlement of estates arising from fires, storms, shipwrecks, or other casualties, or from theft, when such losses are not compensated for by insurance or otherwise.

[Sec. 2055]

SEC. 2055. TRANSFERS FOR PUBLIC, CHARITABLE, AND RELIGIOUS USES.

[Sec. 2055(a)]

(a) IN GENERAL.—For purposes of the tax imposed by section 2001, the value of the taxable estate shall be determined by deducting from the value of the gross estate the amount of all bequests, legacies, devises, or transfers—

(1) to or for the use of the United States, any State, any political subdivision thereof, or the District of Columbia, for exclusively public purposes;

(2) to or for the use of any corporation organized and operated exclusively for religious, charitable, scientific, literary, or educational purposes, including the encouragement of art, or to foster national or international amateur sports competition (but only if no part of its activities involve the provision of athletic facilities or equipment), and the prevention of cruelty to children or animals, no part of the net earnings of which inures to the benefit of any private stockholder or individual, which is not disqualified for tax exemption under section 501(c)(3) by reason of attempting to influence legislation, and which does not participate in, or intervene in (including the publishing or distributing of statements), any political campaign on behalf of (or in opposition to) any candidate for public office;

(3) to a trustee or trustees, or a fraternal society, order, or association operating under the lodge system, but only if such contributions or gifts are to be used by such trustee or trustees, or by such fraternal society, order, or association, exclusively for religious, charitable, scientific, literary, or educational purposes, or for the prevention of cruelty to children or animals, such trust, fraternal society, order, or association would not be disqualified for tax exemption under section 501(c)(3) by reason of attempting to influence legislation, and such trustee or trustees, or such fraternal society, order, or association, does not participate in, or intervene in (including the

publishing or distributing of statements), any political campaign on behalf of (or in opposition to) any candidate for public office;

(4) to or for the use of any veterans' organization incorporated by Act of Congress, or of its departments or local chapters or posts, no part of the net earnings of which inures to the benefit of any private shareholder or individual; or

(5) to an employee stock ownership plan if such transfer qualifies as a qualified gratuitous transfer of qualified employer securities within the meaning of section 664(g).

For purposes of this subsection, the complete termination before the date prescribed for the filing of the estate tax return of a power to consume, invade, or appropriate property for the benefit of an individual before such power has been exercised by reason of the death of such individual or for any other reason shall be considered and deemed to be a qualified disclaimer with the same full force and effect as though he had filed such qualified disclaimer. Rules similar to the rules of section 501(j) shall apply for purposes of paragraph (2).

Amendments

• 1997, Taxpayer Relief Act of 1997 (P.L. 105-34)

P.L. 105-34, §1530(c)(7)(i)-(iii):

Amended Code Sec. 2055(a) by striking "or" at the end of paragraph (3), by striking the period at the end of paragraph (4) and inserting "; or", and by inserting after paragraph (4) a new paragraph (5). **Effective** for transfers made by trusts to, or for the use of, an employee stock ownership plan after 8-5-97.

• 1987, Revenue Act of 1987 (P.L. 100-203)

P.L. 100-203, §10711(a)(3):

Amended Code Sec. 2055(a)(2) and (3) by striking out "on behalf of any candidate" and inserting in lieu thereof "on behalf of (or in opposition to) any candidate". **Effective** with respect to activities after 12-22-87.

• 1982, Tax Equity and Fiscal Responsibility Act of 1982 (P.L. 97-248)

P.L. 97-248, §286(b)(2):

Amended Code Sec. 2055(a) by adding a sentence at the end thereof. **Effective** 10-5-76.

• 1976, Tax Reform Act of 1976 (P.L. 94-455)

P.L. 94-455, §1307(d)(1)(B):

Substituted "which is not disqualified for tax exemption under section 501(c)(3) by reason of attempting to influence legislation," for "no substantial part of the activities of which is carrying on propaganda, or otherwise attempting, to influence legislation (except as otherwise provided in subsection (h))," in Code Sec. 2055(a)(2). **Effective** for tax years beginning after 12-31-76.

P.L. 94-455, §1307(d)(1)(C):

Substituted "such trust, fraternal society, order, or association would not be disqualified for tax exemption under section 501(c)(3) by reason of attempting to influence legislation," for "no substantial part of the activities of such trustee or trustees, or of such fraternal society, order, or association, is carrying on propaganda, or otherwise attempting, to influence legislation," in Code Sec. 2055(a)(3). **Effective** for estates of decedents dying after 12-31-76.

P.L. 94-455, §1313(b)(2):

Added ", or to foster national or international amateur sports competition (but only if no part of its activities involve the provision of athletic facilities or equipment)," after "the encouragement of art" in Code Sec 2055(a)(2). **Effective** 10-5-76.

P.L. 94-455, §1902(a)(12)(A):

Deleted "Territory" in Code Sec. 2055(a)(1). **Effective** for gifts made after 12-31-76.

P.L. 94-455, §2009(b)(4)(B):

Deleted "(including the interest which falls into any such bequest, legacy, devise, or transfer as a result of an irrevocable disclaimer of a bequest, legacy, devise, transfer, or power, if the disclaimer is made before the date prescribed for the filing of the estate tax return)" in the first sentence of Code Sec. 2055(a). **Effective** for transfers creating an interest in the person disclaiming made after 12-31-76.

P.L. 94-455, §2009(b)(4)(C):

Substituted "a qualified" for "an irrevocable" and substituted "such qualified" for "such irrevocable" in the second sentence of Code Sec. 2055(a). **Effective** for transfers creating an interest in the person disclaiming made after 12-31-76.

• 1969, Tax Reform Act of 1969 (P.L. 91-172)

P.L. 91-172, §201(d)(4)(A):

Amended paragraphs (2) and (3) of Code Sec. 2055(a). **Effective** with respect to gifts and transfers in trust made after 12-31-69. Prior to amendment, paragraphs (2) and (3) read as follows:

(2) to or for the use of any corporation organized and operated exclusively for religious, charitable, scientific, literary, or educational purposes, including the encouragement of art and the prevention of cruelty to children or animals, no part of the net earnings of which inures to the benefit of any private stockholder or individual, and no substantial part of the activities of which is carrying on propaganda, or otherwise attempting, to influence legislation;

(3) to a trustee or trustees, or a fraternal society, order, or association operating under the lodge system, but only if such contributions or gifts are to be used by such trustee or trustees, or by such fraternal society, order, or association, exclusively for religious, charitable, scientific, literary, or educational purposes, or for the prevention of cruelty to children or animals, and no substantial part of the activities of such trustee or trustees, or of such fraternal society, order, or association, is carrying on propaganda, or otherwise attempting, to influence legislation; or

[Sec. 2055(b)]

(b) POWERS OF APPOINTMENT.—Property includible in the decedent's gross estate under section 2041 (relating to powers of appointment) received by a donee described in this section shall, for purposes of this section, be considered a bequest of such decedent.

Amendments

• 1976, Tax Reform Act of 1976 (P.L. 94-455)

P.L. 94-455, §1902(a)(4)(A), (c)(1):

Amended Code Sec. 2055(b). **Effective** for estates of decedents dying after 10-4-76. Prior to amendment, Code Sec. 2055(b) read as follows:

(b) POWERS OF APPOINTMENT.—

(1) GENERAL RULE.—Property includible in the decedent's gross estate under section 2041 (relating to powers of appointment) received by a donee described in this section shall, for purposes of this section, be considered a bequest of such decedent.

(2) SPECIAL RULE FOR CERTAIN BEQUESTS SUBJECT TO POWER OF APPOINTMENT.—For purposes of this section, in the case of a bequest in trust, if the surviving spouse of the decedent is entitled for life to all of the net income from the trust and such surviving spouse has a power of appointment over the corpus of such trust exercisable by will in favor of, among others, organizations described in subsection (a)(2), such bequests in trust, reduced by the value of the life estate, shall, to the extent such power is exercised in favor of such organizations, be deemed a transfer to such organizations by the decedent if—

(A) no part of the corpus of such trust is distributed to a beneficiary during the life of the surviving spouse;

(B) such surviving spouse was over 80 years of age at the date of the decedent's death;

(C) such surviving spouse by affidavit executed within 6 months after the death of the decedent specifies the organizations described in subsection (a)(2) in favor of which he intends to exercise the power of appointment and indicates the amount or proportion each such organization is to receive; and

(D) the power of appointment is exercised in favor of such organization and in the amounts or proportions specified in the affidavit required under subparagraph (C).

The affidavit referred to in subparagraph (C) shall be attached to the estate tax return of the decedent and shall constitute a sufficient basis for the allowance of the deduction under this paragraph in the first instance subject to a later disallowance of the deduction if the conditions herein specified are not complied with.

• 1970, Excise, Estate, and Gift Tax Adjustment Act of 1970 (P.L. 91-614)

P.L. 91-614, §101(c):

Amended Code Sec. 2055(b)(2)(C) by substituting "6 months" for "one year." **Effective** with respect to decedents dying after 12-31-70.

• 1956 (P.L. 1011, 84th Cong.)

P.L. 1011, 84th Cong., §[1]:

Amended Sec. 2055(b) by adding "(1) General rule.—" before the word "Property", and by adding paragraph (2). **Effective** in the case of decedents dying after 8-16-54.

[Sec. 2055(c)]

(c) DEATH TAXES PAYABLE OUT OF BEQUESTS.—If the tax imposed by section 2001, or any estate, succession, legacy, or inheritance taxes, are, either by the terms of the will, by the law of the jurisdiction under which the estate is administered, or by the law of the jurisdiction imposing the particular tax, payable in whole or in part out of the bequests, legacies, or devises otherwise deductible under this section, then the amount deductible under this section shall be the amount of such bequests, legacies, or devises reduced by the amount of such taxes.

[Sec. 2055(d)]

(d) LIMITATION ON DEDUCTION.—The amount of the deduction under this section for any transfer shall not exceed the value of the transferred property required to be included in the gross estate.

[Sec. 2055(e)]

(e) DISALLOWANCE OF DEDUCTIONS IN CERTAIN CASES.—

(1) No deduction shall be allowed under this section for a transfer to or for the use of an organization or trust described in section 508(d) or 4948(c)(4) subject to the conditions specified in such sections.

(2) Where an interest in property (other than an interest described in section 170(f)(3)(B)) passes or has passed from the decedent to a person, or for a use, described in subsection (a), and an interest (other than an interest which is extinguished upon the decedent's death) in the same property passes or has passed (for less than an adequate and full consideration in money or money's worth) from the decedent to a person, or for a use, not described in subsection (a), no deduction shall be allowed under this section for the interest which passes or has passed to the person, or for the use, described in subsection (a) unless—

(A) in the case of a remainder interest, such interest is in a trust which is a charitable remainder annuity trust or a charitable remainder unitrust (described in section 664) or a pooled income fund (described in section 642(c)(5)), or

(B) in the case of any other interest, such interest is in the form of a guaranteed annuity or is a fixed percentage distributed yearly of the fair market value of the property (to be determined yearly).

(3) REFORMATIONS TO COMPLY WITH PARAGRAPH (2).—

(A) IN GENERAL.—A deduction shall be allowed under subsection (a) in respect of any qualified reformation.

(B) QUALIFIED REFORMATION.—For purposes of this paragraph, the term "qualified reformation" means a change of a governing instrument by reformation, amendment, construction, or otherwise which changes a reformable interest into a qualified interest but only if—

(i) any difference between—

(I) the actuarial value (determined as of the date of the decedent's death) of the qualified interest, and

(II) the actuarial value (as so determined) of the reformable interest,

does not exceed 5 percent of the actuarial value (as so determined) of the reformable interest,

(ii) in the case of—

(I) a charitable remainder interest, the nonremainder interest (before and after the qualified reformation) terminated at the same time, or

(II) any other interest, the reformable interest and the qualified interest are for the same period, and

(iii) such change is effective as of the date of the decedent's death.

A nonremainder interest (before reformation) for a term of years in excess of 20 years shall be treated as satisfying subclause (I) of clause (ii) if such interest (after reformation) is for a term of 20 years.

(C) REFORMABLE INTEREST.—For purposes of this paragraph—

(i) IN GENERAL.—The term "reformable interest" means any interest for which a deduction would be allowable under subsection (a) at the time of the decedent's death but for paragraph (2).

(ii) BENEFICIARY'S INTEREST MUST BE FIXED.—The term "reformable interest" does not include any interest unless, before the remainder vests in possession, all payments to persons other than an organization described in subsection (a) are expressed either in specified dollar amounts or a fixed percentage of the fair market value of the property. For purposes of determining whether all such payments are expressed as a fixed percentage of the fair market value of the property, section 664(d)(3) shall be taken into account.

(iii) SPECIAL RULE WHERE TIMELY COMMENCEMENT OF REFORMATION.—Clause (ii) shall not apply to any interest if a judicial proceeding is commenced to change such interest into a qualified interest not later than the 90th day after—

(I) if an estate tax return is required to be filed, the last date (including extensions) for filing such return, or

(II) if no estate tax return is required to be filed, the last date (including extensions) for filing the income tax return for the 1st taxable year for which such a return is required to be filed by the trust.

(iv) SPECIAL RULE FOR WILL EXECUTED BEFORE JANUARY 1, 1979, ETC.—In the case of any interest passing under a will executed before January 1, 1979, or under a trust created before such date, clause (ii) shall not apply.

(D) QUALIFIED INTEREST.—For purposes of this paragraph, the term "qualified interest" means an interest for which a deduction is allowable under subsection (a).

(E) LIMITATION.—The deduction referred to in subparagraph (A) shall not exceed the amount of the deduction which would have been allowable for the reformable interest but for paragraph (2).

(F) SPECIAL RULE WHERE INCOME BENEFICIARY DIES.—If (by reason of the death of any individual, or by termination or distribution of a trust in accordance with the terms of the trust instrument) by the due date for filing the estate tax return (including any extension thereof) a reformable interest is in a wholly charitable trust or passes directly to a person or for a use described in subsection (a), a deduction shall be allowed for such reformable interest as if it had met the requirements of paragraph (2) on the date of the decedent's death. For purposes of the preceding sentence, the term "wholly charitable trust" means a charitable trust which, upon the allowance of a deduction, would be described in section 4947(a)(1).

(G) STATUTE OF LIMITATIONS.—The period for assessing any deficiency of any tax attributable to the application of this paragraph shall not expire before the date 1 year after the date on which the Secretary is notified that such reformation (or other proceeding pursuant to subparagraph (J)) has occurred.

(H) REGULATIONS.—The Secretary shall prescribe such regulations as may be necessary to carry out the purposes of this paragraph, including regulations providing such adjustments in the application of the provisions of section 508 (relating to special rules relating to section 501(c)(3) organizations), subchapter J (relating to estates, trusts, beneficiaries, and decedents), and chapter 42 (relating to private foundations) as may be necessary by reason of the qualified reformation.

(I) REFORMATIONS PERMITTED IN CASE OF REMAINDER INTERESTS IN RESIDENCE OR FARM, POOLED INCOME FUNDS, ETC.—The Secretary shall prescribe regulations (consistent with the provisions of this paragraph) permitting reformations in the case of any failure—

(i) to meet the requirements of section 170(f)(3)(B) (relating to remainder interests in personal residence or farm, etc.), or

(ii) to meet the requirements of section 642(c)(5).

(J) VOID OR REFORMED TRUST IN CASES OF INSUFFICIENT REMAINDER INTERESTS.—In the case of a trust that would qualify (or could be reformed to qualify pursuant to subparagraph (B)) but for failure to satisfy the requirement of paragraph (1)(D) or (2)(D) of section 664(d), such trust may be—

(i) declared null and void ab initio, or

(ii) changed by reformation, amendment, or otherwise to meet such requirement by reducing the payout rate or the duration (or both) of any noncharitable beneficiary's interest to the extent necessary to satisfy such requirement,

pursuant to a proceeding that is commenced within the period required in subparagraph (C)(iii). In a case described in clause (i), no deduction shall be allowed under this title for any transfer to the trust and any transactions entered into by the trust prior to being declared void shall be treated as entered into by the transferor.

(4) WORKS OF ART AND THEIR COPYRIGHTS TREATED AS SEPARATE PROPERTIES IN CERTAIN CASES.—

(A) IN GENERAL.—In the case of a qualified contribution of a work of art, the work of art and the copyright on such work of art shall be treated as separate properties for purposes of paragraph (2).

(B) WORK OF ART DEFINED.—For purposes of this paragraph, the term "work of art" means any tangible personal property with respect to which there is a copyright under Federal law.

(C) QUALIFIED CONTRIBUTION DEFINED.—For purposes of this paragraph, the term "qualified contribution" means any transfer of property to a qualified organization if the use of the property by the organization is related to the purpose or function constituting the basis for its exemption under section 501.

(D) QUALIFIED ORGANIZATION DEFINED.—For purposes of this paragraph, the term "qualified organization" means any organization described in section 501(c)(3) other than a private foundation (as defined in section 509). For purposes of the preceding sentence, a private operating foundation (as defined in section 4942(j)(3)) shall not be treated as a private foundation.

(5) CONTRIBUTIONS TO DONOR ADVISED FUNDS.—A deduction otherwise allowed under subsection (a) for any contribution to a donor advised fund (as defined in section 4966(d)(2)) shall only be allowed if—

(A) the sponsoring organization (as defined in section 4966(d)(1)) with respect to such donor advised fund is not—

(i) described in paragraph (3) or (4) of subsection (a), or

(ii) a type III supporting organization (as defined in section 4943(f)(5)(A)) which is not a functionally integrated type III supporting organization (as defined in section 4943(f)(5)(B)), and

(B) the taxpayer obtains a contemporaneous written acknowledgment (determined under rules similar to the rules of section 170(f)(8)(C)) from the sponsoring organization (as so defined) of such donor advised fund that such organization has exclusive legal control over the assets contributed.

Amendments

• 2018, Tax Technical Corrections Act of 2018 (P.L. 115-141)

P.L. 115-141, §401(a)(202), Div. U:

Amended Code Sec. 2055(e)(3)(G) by striking "subparagraph (J)" and inserting "subparagraph (J))". **Effective** 3-23-2018.

• 2006, Pension Protection Act of 2006 (P.L. 109-280)

P.L. 109-280, §1234(b):

Amended Code Sec. 2055(e) by adding at the end a new paragraph (5). **Effective** for contributions made after the date which is 180 days after 8-17-2006.

• 1997, Taxpayer Relief Act of 1997 (P.L. 105-34)

P.L. 105-34, §1089(b)(3):

Amended Code Sec. 2055(e)(3) by adding at the end a new subparagraph (J). **Effective** for transfers in trust after 7-28-97. For a special rule, see Act Sec. 1089(b)(6)(B), below.

P.L. 105-34, §1089(b)(5):

Amended Code Sec. 2055(e)(3)(G) by inserting "(or other proceeding pursuant to subparagraph (J)[)]" after "reformation". **Effective** for transfers in trust after 7-28-97. For a special rule, see Act Sec. 1089(b)(6)(B), below.

P.L. 105-34, §1089(b)(6)(B), provides:

(B) SPECIAL RULES FOR CERTAIN DECEDENTS.—The amendments made by this subsection shall not apply to transfers in trust under the terms of a will (or other testamentary instrument) executed on or before July 28, 1997, if the decedent—

(i) dies before January 1, 1999, without having republished the will (or amended such instrument) by codicil or otherwise, or

(ii) was on July 28, 1997, under a mental disability to change the disposition of his property and did not regain his competence to dispose of such property before the date of his death.

• 1984, Deficit Reduction Act of 1984 (P.L. 98-369)

P.L. 98-369, §1022(a):

Amended Code Sec. 2055(e)(3). **Effective** for reformations after 12-31-78; except that it does not apply to any reformation to which Code Sec. 2055(e)(3) (as in effect on 7-17-84) applies. For purposes of applying Code Sec. 2055(e)(3)(C)(iii) (as amended by Act Sec. 1022), the 90th day described in such clause shall be treated as not occurring before the 90th day after 7-18-84. For statute of limitations provisions, see Act Sec. 1022(e)(3), under the amendment notes for Code Sec. 664(f). Prior to amendment, Code Sec. 2055(e)(3) read as follows:

(3) In the case of a will executed before December 31, 1978, or a trust created before such date, if a deduction is not allowable at the time of the decedent's death because of the failure of an interest in property which passes from the decedent to a person, or for a use described in subsection (a), to meet the requirements of subparagraph (A) or (B) of paragraph (2) of this subsection, and if the governing instrument is amended or conformed on or before December 31, 1981, or, if later, on or before the 30th day after the date on which judicial proceedings begun on or before December 31, 1981 (which are required to amend or conform the governing instrument), become final, so that the interest is in a trust which meets the requirements of such subparagraph (A) or (B) (as the case may be), a deduction shall nevertheless be allowed. The Secretary may, by regulation, provide for the application of the provisions of this paragraph to trusts whose governing instruments are amended or conformed in accordance with this paragraph, and such regulations may provide for any adjustments in the application of the provisions of section 508 (relating to special rules with respect to section 501(c)(3) organizations), subchapter J (relating to estates, trusts, beneficiaries, and decedents), and chapter 42 (relating to private foundations), to such trusts made necessary by the application of this paragraph. If, by the due date for the filing of an estate tax return (including any extension thereof), the interest is in a charitable trust which, upon allowance of a deduction, would be described in section 4947(a)(1), or the interest passes directly to a person or for a use described in subsection (a), a deduction shall be allowed as if the governing instrument was amended or conformed under this paragraph. If the amendment or conformation of the governing instrument is made after the due date for the filing of the estate tax return (including any extension thereof), the deduction shall be allowed upon the filing of a timely claim for credit or refund (as provided for in section 6511) of an overpayment resulting from the application of this paragraph. In the case of a credit or refund as a result of an amendment or conforma-

tion made pursuant to this paragraph, no interest shall be allowed for the period prior to the expiration of the 180th day after the date on which the claim for credit or refund is filed.

• 1981, Economic Recovery Tax Act of 1981 (P.L. 97-34)

P.L. 97-34, §423(a):

Added Code Sec. 2055(e)(4). **Effective** for estates of decedents dying after 12-31-81.

• 1980, Miscellaneous Revenue Act of 1980 (P.L. 96-605)

P.L. 96-605, §301(a)(1) and (2):

Amended the first sentence of Code Sec. 2055(e)(3): (1) by striking out "December 31, 1977" and inserting in lieu thereof "December 31, 1978"; and (2) by striking out "December 31, 1978" each place it appeared and inserting in lieu thereof "December 31, 1981". **Effective** with respect to decedents dying after 12-31-69.

P.L. 95-600, §301(b), provides:

CHARITABLE LEAD TRUSTS AND CHARITABLE REMAINDER TRUSTS IN THE CASE OF INCOME AND GIFT TAXES.—Section 514(b) (and section 514(c) insofar as it relates to section 514(b)) of the Revenue Act of 1978 shall be applied as if the amendment made by subsection (a) [P.L. 96-605, §301(a)(1) and (2), above] had been included in the amendment made by section 514(a) of such Act.

• 1980, Technical Corrections Act of 1979 (P.L. 96-222)

P.L. 96-222, §105(a)(4)(A):

Amended Code Sec. 2055(e)(3) by changing "subparagraph (a) or (B)" to "subparagraph (A) or (B)" and by changing "so that interest" to "so that the interest". For **effective** date, see below.

• 1978, Revenue Act of 1978 (P.L. 95-600)

P.L. 95-600, §514(a):

Amended the first sentence of Code Sec. 2055(e)(3). **Effective** as noted in Act Sec. 514(c), below. Prior to amendment, such sentence read as follows:

"In the case of a will executed before December 31, 1977, or a trust created before such date, if a deduction is not allowable at the time of the decedent's death because of the failure of an interest in property which passes from the decedent to a person, or for a use, described in subsection (a), to meet the requirements of subparagraph (A) of paragraph (2) of this subsection, and if the governing instrument is amended or conformed on or before December 31, 1977, or, if later, on or before the 30th day after the date on which judicial proceedings begun on or before December 31, 1977 (which are required to amend or conform the governing instrument), become final, so that the interest is in a trust which is a charitable remainder annuity trust, a charitable remainder unitrust (described in section 664), or a pooled income fund (described in section 642(c)(5)), a deduction shall nevertheless be allowed."

P.L. 95-600, §514(b), provides:

(b) CHARITABLE LEAD TRUSTS AND CHARITABLE REMAINDER TRUSTS IN THE CASE OF INCOME AND GIFT TAXES.—Under regulations prescribed by the Secretary of the Treasury or his delegate, in the case of trusts created before December 31, 1977, provisions comparable to section 2055(e)(3) of the Internal Revenue Code of 1954 (as amended by subsection (a) [P.L. 95-600, §514(a), above]) shall be deemed to be included in sections 170 and 2522 of the Internal Revenue Code of 1954.

P.L. 95-600, §514(c), as added by P.L. 96-222, §105(a)(4)(B), provides:

(c) EFFECTIVE DATES.—

(1) FOR SUBSECTION (a).—The amendment made by subsection (a) shall apply in the case of decedents dying after December 31, 1969.

(2) FOR SUBSECTION (b).—Subsection (b)—

(A) insofar as it relates to section 170 of the Internal Revenue Code of 1954 shall apply to transfers in trust and contributions made after July 31, 1969, and

(B) insofar as it relates to section 2522 of the Internal Revenue Code of 1954 shall apply to transfers made after December 31, 1969.

• 1976, Tax Reform Act of 1976 (P.L. 94-455)

P.L. 94-455, §1304(a):

Substituted "December 31, 1977," for "September 21, 1974," and substituted "December 31, 1977" for "December 31, 1975" each place it appeared in Code Sec. 2055(e)(3).

P.L. 94-455, §1304(b), provides:

(b) EXTENSION OF PERIOD FOR FILING CLAIM FOR REFUND OF ESTATE TAX PAID.—A claim for refund or credit of an overpayment of the tax imposed by section 2001 of the Internal Revenue Code of 1954 allowable under section 2055(e)(3) of such Code (as amended by subsection (a)) shall not be denied because of the expiration of the time for filing such a claim under section 6511(a) if such claim is filed not later than June 30, 1978.

P.L. 94-455, §1304(c), provides:

The amendments made by this section are **effective** for decedents dying after 12-31-69.

P.L. 94-455, §1906(b)(13)(A):

Amended 1954 Code by substituting "Secretary" for "Secretary or his delegate" each place it appeared. **Effective** 2-1-77.

P.L. 94-455, §2124(e) (as amended by P.L. 95-30, §309(b)(2)):

Substituted "(other than an interest described in section 170(f)(3)(B))" for "(other than a remainder interest in a personal residence or farm or an undivided portion of the decedent's entire interest in property)" in Code Sec. 2055(e)(2). **Effective** for contributions or transfers made after 6-13-76, and before 6-14-77. However, P.L. 95-30, §309(b)(2), changed this latter date to 6-14-81.

• 1974 (P.L. 93-483)

P.L. 93-483, §3:

Amended Code Sec. 2055(e) by adding paragraph (3). **Effective** with respect to decedents dying after 12-31-69.

• 1969, Tax Reform Act of 1969 (P.L. 91-172)

P.L. 91-172, §201(d)(1):

Amended Code Sec. 2055(e). **Effective** in the case of decedents dying after 12-31-69. However, such amendments shall not apply in the case of property passing under the terms of a will executed on or before 10-9-69—

(i) if the decedent dies before October 9, 1972, without having republished the will after October 9, 1969, by codicil or otherwise,

(ii) if the decedent at no time after October 9, 1969, had the right to change the portions of the will which pertain to the passing of the property to, or for the use of, an organization described in section 2055(a), or

(iii) if the will is not republished by codicil or otherwise before October 9, 1972, and the decedent is on such date and at all times thereafter under a mental disability to republish the will by codicil or otherwise.

Such amendment shall not apply in the case of property transferred in trust on or before October 9, 1969—

(i) if the decedent dies before October 9, 1972, without having amended after October 9, 1969, the instrument governing the disposition of the property,

(ii) if the property transferred was an irrevocable interest to, or for the use of, an organization described in section 2055(a), or

(iii) if the instrument governing the disposition of the property was not amended by the decedent before October 9, 1972, and the decedent is on such date and at all times thereafter under a mental disability to change the disposition of the property.

Prior to amendment, Code Sec. 2055(e) read as follows:

(e) Disallowance of Deductions in Certain Cases.—

For disallowance of certain charitable, etc., deductions otherwise allowable under this section, see sections 503 and 681.

• 1958, Technical Amendments Act of 1958 (P.L. 85-866)

P.L. 85-866, §30(d):

Amended Code Sec. 2055(e) by substituting "503" for "504". **Effective** 1-1-54.

[Sec. 2055(f)]

(f) SPECIAL RULE FOR IRREVOCABLE TRANSFERS OF EASEMENTS IN REAL PROPERTY.—A deduction shall be allowed under subsection (a) in respect of any transfer of a qualified real property interest (as defined in section 170(h)(2)(C)) which meets the requirements of section 170(h) (without regard to paragraph (4)(A) thereof).

Amendments

• 1986, Tax Reform Act of 1986 (P.L. 99-514)

P.L. 99-514, §1422(a)(1) and (2):

Amended Code Sec. 2055 by redesignating subsection (f) as subsection (g), and by inserting after subsection (e) new subsection (f). **Effective** for transfers and contributions made after 12-31-86.

[Sec. 2055(g)—Stricken]

Amendments

• 2007, Tax Technical Corrections Act of 2007 (P.L. 110-172)

P.L. 110-172, §3(d)(1):

Amended Code Sec. 2055 by striking subsection (g) and by redesignating subsection (h) as subsection (g). **Effective** as if included in the provision of the Pension Protection Act of 2006 (P.L. 109-280) to which it relates [**effective** for contributions, bequests, and gifts made after 8-17-2006.—CCH]. Prior to being stricken, Code Sec. 2055(g) read as follows:

(g) VALUATION OF SUBSEQUENT GIFTS.—

(1) IN GENERAL.—In the case of any additional contribution, the fair market value of such contribution shall be determined by using the lesser of—

(A) the fair market value of the property at the time of the initial fractional contribution, or

(B) the fair market value of the property at the time of the additional contribution.

(2) DEFINITIONS.—For purposes of this paragraph—

(A) ADDITIONAL CONTRIBUTION.—The term "additional contribution" means a bequest, legacy, devise, or transfer described in subsection (a) of any interest in a property with respect to which the decedent had previously made an initial fractional contribution.

(B) INITIAL FRACTIONAL CONTRIBUTION.—The term "initial fractional contribution" means, with respect to any decedent, any charitable contribution of an undivided portion of the decedent's entire interest in any tangible personal property for which a deduction was allowed under section 170.

• 2006, Pension Protection Act of 2006 (P.L. 109-280)

P.L. 109-280, §1218(b):

Amended Code Sec. 2055 by redesignating subsection (g) as subsection (h) and by inserting after subsection (f) a new subsection (g). **Effective** for contributions, bequests, and gifts made after 8-17-2006.

[Sec. 2055(g)]

(g) CROSS REFERENCES.—

(1) For option as to time for valuation for purpose of deduction under this section, see section 2032.

(2) For treatment of certain organizations providing child care, see section 501(k).

(3) For exemption of gifts and bequests to or for the benefit of Library of Congress, see section 5 of the Act of March 3, 1925, as amended (2 U.S.C. 161).

(4) For treatment of gifts and bequests for the benefit of the Naval Historical Center as gifts or bequests to or for the use of the United States, see section 8622 of title 10, United States Code.

(5) For treatment of gifts and bequests to or for the benefit of National Park Foundation as gifts or bequests to or for the use of the United States, see section 8 of the Act of December 18, 1967 (16 U.S.C. 191).

(6) For treatment of gifts, devises, or bequests accepted by the Secretary of State, the Director of the International Communication Agency, or the Director of the United States International Development Cooperation Agency as gifts, devises, or bequests to or for the use of the United States, see section 25 of the State Department Basic Authorities Act of 1956.

(7) For treatment of gifts or bequests of money accepted by the Attorney General for credit to "Commissary Funds, Federal Prisons" as gifts or bequests to or for the use of the United States, see section 4043 of title 18, United States Code.

(8) For payment of tax on gifts and bequests of United States obligations to the United States, see section 3113(e) of title 31, United States Code.

(9) For treatment of gifts and bequests for benefit of the Naval Academy as gifts or bequests to or for the use of the United States, see section 8473 of title 10, United States Code.

(10) For treatment of gifts and bequests for benefit of the Naval Academy Museum as gifts or bequests to or for the use of the United States, see section 8474 of title 10, United States Code.

(11) For exemption of gifts and bequests received by National Archives Trust Fund Board, see section 2308 of title 44, United States Code.

(12) For treatment of gifts and bequests to or for the use of Indian tribal governments (or their subdivisions), see section 7871.

Amendments

• 2018, John S. McCain National Defense Authorization Act for Fiscal Year 2019 (P.L. 115-232)

P.L. 115-232, §809(h)(2)(A), Div. A:

Amended Code Sec. 2055(g)(4) by striking "section 7222 of title 10, United States Code" and inserting "section 8622 of title 10, United States Code". **Effective** 8-13-2018.

P.L. 115-232, §809(h)(2)(B), Div. A:

Amended Code Sec. 2055(g)(9) by striking "section 6973 of title 10, United States Code" and inserting "section 8473 of title 10, United States Code". **Effective** 8-13-2018.

P.L. 115-232, §809(h)(2)(C), Div. A:

Amended Code Sec. 2055(g)(10) by striking "section 6974 of title 10, United States Code" and inserting "section 8474 of title 10, United States Code". **Effective** 8-13-2018.

• 2007, Tax Technical Corrections Act of 2007 (P.L. 110-172)

P.L. 110-172, §3(d)(1):

Amended Code Sec. 2055 by redesignating subsection (h) as subsection (g). **Effective** as if included in the provision of the Pension Protection Act of 2006 (P.L. 109-280) to which it relates [**effective** for contributions, bequests, and gifts made after 8-17-2006.—CCH].

• 2006, Pension Protection Act of 2006 (P.L. 109-280)

P.L. 109-280, §1218(b):

Amended Code Sec. 2055 by redesignating subsection (g) as subsection (h). **Effective** for contributions, bequests, and gifts made after 8-17-2006.

• 1996, National Defense Authorization Act for Fiscal Year 1997 (P.L. 104-201)

P.L. 104-201, §1073(b)(3):

Amended Code Sec. 2055(h)(4). **Effective** 9-23-96. Prior to amendment, Code Sec. 2055(h)(4) read as follows:

(4) For treatment of gifts and bequests for the benefit of the Office of Naval Records and History as gifts or bequests to or for the use of the United States, see section 7222 of title 10, United States Code.

• 1986, Tax Reform Act of 1986 (P.L. 99-514)

P.L. 99-514, §1422(a)(1)-(2):

Redesignated subsection (f) as subsection (g). **Effective** for transfers and contributions made after 12-31-86.

• 1984, Deficit Reduction Act of 1984 (P.L. 98-369)

P.L. 98-369, §1032(b)(2):

Amended Code Sec. 2055(f) by redesignating paragraphs (2) through (11) as paragraphs (3) through (12), respectively, and by inserting after paragraph (1) a new paragraph (2). **Effective** for tax years beginning after 7-18-84.

• 1983 (P.L. 97-473)

P.L. 97-473, §202(b)(5):

Amended Code Sec. 2055(f) by adding subparagraph (11). For the **effective** date, see the amendment note for Act Sec. 204, following Code Sec. 7871.

• 1982 (P.L. 97-258)

P.L. 97-258, §3(f)(1):

Amended Code Sec. 2055(f)(6) by striking out "section 2 of the Act of May 15, 1952, as amended by the Act of July 9, 1952 (31 U.S.C. 725s-4)" and substituting "section 4043 of title 18, United States Code". **Effective** 9-13-82.

P.L. 97-258, §3(f)(2):

Amended Code Sec. 2055(f)(7) by striking out "section 24 of the Second Liberty Bond Act (31 U.S.C. 757e)" and substituting "section 3113(e) of title 31, United States Code". **Effective** 9-13-82.

• 1980, Foreign Service Act of 1980 (P.L. 96-465)

P.L. 96-465, §2206(e)(4):

Amended Code Sec. 2055(f)(5). **Effective** 2-15-81. Prior to amendment, paragraph (5) read as follows:

"(5) For treatment of gifts, devises, or bequests accepted by the Secretary of State under the Foreign Service Act of 1946 as gifts, devises, or bequests to or for the use of the United States, see section 1021(e) of that Act (22 U.S.C. 809(e)).".

• 1976, Tax Reform Act of 1976 (P.L. 94-455)

P.L. 94-455, §1902(a)(4)(B), (c)(1):

Amended Code Sec. 2055(f). **Effective** for estates of decedents dying after 10-4-76. Prior to amendment, Code Sec. 2055(f) read as follows:

(f) OTHER CROSS REFERENCES.—

(1) For option as to time for valuation for purpose of deduction under this section, see section 2032.

(2) For exemption of bequests to or for benefit of Library of Congress, see section 5 of the Act of March 3, 1925, as amended (56 Stat. 765; 2 U.S.C. 161).

(3) For construction of bequests for benefit of the library of the Post Office Department as bequests to or for the use of the United States, see section 2 of the Act of August 8, 1946 (60 Stat. 924; 5 U.S.C. 393).

(4) For exemption of bequests for benefit of Office of Naval Records and Library, Navy Department, see section 2 of the Act of March 4, 1937 (50 Stat. 25; 5 U.S.C. 419b).

(5) For exemption of bequests to or for benefit of National Park Service, see section 5 of the Act of July 10, 1935 (49 Stat. 478; 16 U.S.C. 19c).

(6) For construction of devises or bequests accepted by the Secretary of State under the Foreign Service Act of 1946 as devises or bequests to or for the use of the United States, see section 1021(e) of that Act (60 Stat. 1032; 22 U.S.C. 809).

(7) For construction of gifts or bequests of money accepted by the Attorney General for credit to "Commissary Funds, Federal Prisons" as gifts or bequests to or for the use of the United States, see section 2 of the Act of May 15, 1952, 66 Stat. 73, as amended by the Act of July 9, 1952, 66 Stat. 479 (31 U.S.C. 725s-4).

(8) For payment of tax on bequests of United States obligations to the United States, see section 24 of the Second Liberty Bond Act, as amended (59 Stat. 48, §4; 31 U.S.C. 757e).

(9) For construction of bequests for benefit of or use in connection with the Naval Academy as bequests to or for the use of the United States, see section 3 of the Act of March 31, 1944 (58 Stat. 135; 34 U.S.C. 1115b).

(10) For exemption of bequests for benefit of Naval Academy Museum, see section 4 of the Act of March 26, 1938 (52 Stat. 119; 34 U.S.C. 1119).

(11) For exemption of bequests received by National Archives Trust Fund Board, see section 7 of the National Archives Trust Fund Board Act (55 Stat. 582; 44 U.S.C. 300gg).

[Sec. 2056]

SEC. 2056. BEQUESTS, ETC., TO SURVIVING SPOUSE.

[Sec. 2056(a)]

(a) ALLOWANCE OF MARITAL DEDUCTION.—For purposes of the tax imposed by section 2001, the value of the taxable estate shall, except as limited by subsection (b), be determined by deducting from the value of the gross estate an amount equal to the value of any interest in property which passes or has passed from the decedent to his surviving spouse, but only to the extent that such interest is included in determining the value of the gross estate.

Amendments

• 1981, Economic Recovery Tax Act of 1981 (P.L. 97-34)

P.L. 97-34, §403(a)(1)(B):

Amended Code Sec. 2056(a) by striking out "subsections (b) and (c)" and inserting "subsection (b)". **Effective** for estates of decedents dying after 12-31-81.

• 1976, Tax Reform Act of 1976 (P.L. 94-455)

P.L. 94-455, §2009(b)(4)(E), (e)(2):

Substituted "subsections (b) and (c)" for "subsections (b), (c), and (d)" in Code Sec. 2056(a). **Effective** for transfers creating an interest in the person disclaiming made after 12-31-76.

[Sec. 2056(b)]

(b) LIMITATION IN THE CASE OF LIFE ESTATE OR OTHER TERMINABLE INTEREST.—

(1) GENERAL RULE.—Where, on the lapse of time, on the occurrence of an event or contingency, or on the failure of an event or contingency to occur, an interest passing to the surviving spouse will terminate or fail, no deduction shall be allowed under this section with respect to such interest—

(A) if an interest in such property passes or has passed (for less than an adequate and full consideration in money or money's worth) from the decedent to any person other than such surviving spouse (or the estate of such spouse); and

(B) if by reason of such passing such person (or his heirs or assigns) may possess or enjoy any part of such property after such termination or failure of the interest so passing to the surviving spouse;

and no deduction shall be allowed with respect to such interest (even if such deduction is not disallowed under subparagraphs (A) and (B))—

(C) if such interest is to be acquired for the surviving spouse, pursuant to directions of the decedent, by his executor or by the trustee of a trust.

For purposes of this paragraph, an interest shall not be considered as an interest which will terminate or fail merely because it is the ownership of a bond, note, or similar contractual obligation, the discharge of which would not have the effect of an annuity for life or for a term.

(2) INTEREST IN UNIDENTIFIED ASSETS.—Where the assets (included in the decedent's gross estate) out of which, or the proceeds of which, an interest passing to the surviving spouse may be satisfied include a particular asset or assets with respect to which no deduction would be allowed if such asset or assets passed from the decedent to such spouse, then the value of such interest passing to such spouse shall, for purposes of subsection (a), be reduced by the aggregate value of such particular assets.

(3) INTEREST OF SPOUSE CONDITIONAL ON SURVIVAL FOR LIMITED PERIOD.—For purposes of this subsection, an interest passing to the surviving spouse shall not be considered as an interest which will terminate or fail on the death of such spouse if—

(A) such death will cause a termination or failure of such interest only if it occurs within a period not exceeding 6 months after the decedent's death, or only if it occurs as a result of a common disaster resulting in the death of the decedent and the surviving spouse, or only if it occurs in the case of either such event; and

(B) such termination or failure does not in fact occur.

(4) VALUATION OF INTEREST PASSING TO SURVIVING SPOUSE.—In determining for purposes of subsection (a) the value of any interest in property passing to the surviving spouse for which a deduction is allowed by this section—

(A) there shall be taken into account the effect which the tax imposed by section 2001, or any estate, succession, legacy, or inheritance tax, has on the net value to the surviving spouse of such interest; and

(B) where such interest or property is encumbered in any manner, or where the surviving spouse incurs any obligation imposed by the decedent with respect to the passing of such interest, such encumbrance or obligation shall be taken into account in the same manner as if the amount of a gift to such spouse of such interest were being determined.

(5) LIFE ESTATE WITH POWER OF APPOINTMENT IN SURVIVING SPOUSE.—In the case of an interest in property passing from the decedent, if his surviving spouse is entitled for life to all the income from the entire interest, or all the income from a specific portion thereof, payable annually or at more frequent intervals, with power in the surviving spouse to appoint the entire interest, or such specific portion (exercisable in favor of such surviving spouse, or of the estate of such surviving spouse, or in favor of either, whether or not in each case the power is exercisable in favor of others), and with no power in any other person to appoint any part of the interest, or such specific portion, to any person other than the surviving spouse—

(A) the interest or such portion thereof so passing shall, for purposes of subsection (a), be considered as passing to the surviving spouse, and

(B) no part of the interest so passing shall, for purposes of paragraph (1)(A), be considered as passing to any person other than the surviving spouse.

This paragraph shall apply only if such power in the surviving spouse to appoint the entire interest, or such specific portion thereof, whether exercisable by will or during life, is exercisable by such spouse alone and in all events.

(6) LIFE INSURANCE OR ANNUITY PAYMENTS WITH POWER OF APPOINTMENT IN SURVIVING SPOUSE.—In the case of an interest in property passing from the decedent consisting of proceeds under a life insurance, endowment, or annuity contract, if under the terms of the contract such proceeds are payable in installments or are held by the insurer subject to an agreement to pay interest thereon (whether the proceeds, on the termination of any interest payments, are payable in a lump sum or in annual or more frequent installments), and such installment or interest payments are payable annually or at more frequent intervals, commencing not later than 13 months after the decedent's death, and all amounts, or a specific portion of all such amounts, payable during the life of the surviving spouse are payable only to such spouse, and such spouse has the power to appoint all amounts, or such specific portion, payable under such contract (exercisable in favor of such surviving spouse, or of the estate of such surviving spouse, or in favor of either, whether or not in each case the power is exercisable in favor of others), with no power in any other person to appoint such amounts to any person other than the surviving spouse—

(A) such amounts shall, for purposes of subsection (a), be considered as passing to the surviving spouse, and

(B) no part of such amounts shall, for purposes of paragraph (1)(A), be considered as passing to any person other than the surviving spouse.

This paragraph shall apply only if, under the terms of the contract, such power in the surviving spouse to appoint such amounts, whether exercisable by will or during life, is exercisable by such spouse alone and in all events.

(7) ELECTION WITH RESPECT TO LIFE ESTATE FOR SURVIVING SPOUSE.—

(A) IN GENERAL.—In the case of qualified terminable interest property—

(i) for purposes of subsection (a), such property shall be treated as passing to the surviving spouse, and

(ii) for purposes of paragraph (1)(A), no part of such property shall be treated as passing to any person other than the surviving spouse.

(B) QUALIFIED TERMINABLE INTEREST PROPERTY DEFINED.—For purposes of this paragraph—

(i) IN GENERAL.—The term "qualified terminable interest property" means property—

(I) which passes from the decedent,

(II) in which the surviving spouse has a qualifying income interest for life, and

(III) to which an election under this paragraph applies.

(ii) QUALIFYING INCOME INTEREST FOR LIFE.—The surviving spouse has a qualifying income interest for life if—

(I) the surviving spouse is entitled to all the income from the property, payable annually or at more frequent intervals, or has a usufruct interest for life in the property, and

(II) no person has a power to appoint any part of the property to any person other than the surviving spouse.

Subclause (II) shall not apply to a power exercisable only at or after the death of the surviving spouse. To the extent provided in regulations, an annuity shall be treated in a manner similar to an income interest in property (regardless of whether the property from which the annuity is payable can be separately identified).

(iii) PROPERTY INCLUDES INTEREST THEREIN.—The term "property" includes an interest in property.

(iv) SPECIFIC PORTION TREATED AS SEPARATE PROPERTY.—A specific portion of property shall be treated as separate property.

(v) ELECTION.—An election under this paragraph with respect to any property shall be made by the executor on the return of tax imposed by section 2001. Such an election, once made, shall be irrevocable.

(C) TREATMENT OF SURVIVOR ANNUITIES.—In the case of an annuity included in the gross estate of the decedent under section 2039 (or, in the case of an interest in an annuity arising under the community property laws of a State, included in the gross estate of the decedent under section 2033) where only the surviving spouse has the right to receive payments before the death of such surviving spouse—

(i) the interest of such surviving spouse shall be treated as a qualifying income interest for life, and

(ii) the executor shall be treated as having made an election under this subsection with respect to such annuity unless the executor otherwise elects on the return of tax imposed by section 2001.

An election under clause (ii), once made, shall be irrevocable.

(8) SPECIAL RULE FOR CHARITABLE REMAINDER TRUSTS.—

(A) IN GENERAL.—If the surviving spouse of the decedent is the only beneficiary of a qualified charitable remainder trust who is not a charitable beneficiary nor an ESOP beneficiary, paragraph (1) shall not apply to any interest in such trust which passes or has passed from the decedent to such surviving spouse.

(B) DEFINITIONS.—For purposes of subparagraph (A)—

(i) CHARITABLE BENEFICIARY.—The term "charitable beneficiary" means any beneficiary which is an organization described in section 170(c).

(ii) ESOP BENEFICIARY.—The term "ESOP beneficiary" means any beneficiary which is an employee stock ownership plan (as defined in section 4975(e)(7)) that holds a remainder interest in qualified employer securities (as defined in section 664(g)(4)) to be transferred to such plan in a qualified gratuitous transfer (as defined in section 664(g)(1)).

(iii) QUALIFIED CHARITABLE REMAINDER TRUST.—The term "qualified charitable remainder trust" means a charitable remainder annuity trust or a charitable remainder unitrust (described in section 664).

(9) DENIAL OF DOUBLE DEDUCTION.—Nothing in this section or any other provision of this chapter shall allow the value of any interest in property to be deducted under this chapter more than once with respect to the same decedent.

(10) SPECIFIC PORTION.—For purposes of paragraphs (5), (6), and (7)(B)(iv), the term "specific portion" only includes a portion determined on a fractional or percentage basis.

Amendments

• 1997, Taxpayer Relief Act of 1997 (P.L. 105-34)

P.L. 105-34, §1311(a):

Amended Code Sec. 2056(b)(7)(C) by inserting "(or, in the case of an interest in an annuity arising under the community property laws of a State, included in the gross estate of the decedent under section 2033)" after "section 2039". **Effective** for estates of decedents dying after 8-5-97.

P.L. 105-34, §1530(c)(8):

Amended Code Sec. 2056(b)(8). **Effective** for transfers made by trusts to, or for the use of, an employee stock ownership plan after 8-5-97. Prior to amendment, Code Sec. 2056(b)(8) read as follows:

(8) SPECIAL RULE FOR CHARITABLE REMAINDER TRUSTS.—

(A) IN GENERAL.—If the surviving spouse of the decedent is the only noncharitable beneficiary of a qualified charitable remainder trust, paragraph (1) shall not apply to any interest in such trust which passes or has passed from the decedent to such surviving spouse.

(B) DEFINITIONS.—For purposes of subparagraph (A)—

(i) NONCHARITABLE BENEFICIARY.—The term "noncharitable beneficiary" means any beneficiary of the qualified charitable remainder trust other than an organization described in section 170(c).

(ii) QUALIFIED CHARITABLE REMAINDER TRUST.—The term "qualified charitable remainder trust" means a charitable remainder annuity trust or charitable remainder unitrust (described in section 664)."

• 1992, Energy Policy Act of 1992 (P.L. 102-486)

P.L. 102-486, §1941(a):

Amended Code Sec. 2056(b) by adding at the end thereof new paragraph (10). For the **effective** date, see Act Sec. 1941(c)(1), below.

P.L. 102-486, §1941(c)(1), provides:

(c) EFFECTIVE DATES.—

(1) SUBSECTION (a).—

(A) IN GENERAL.—Except as provided in subparagraph (B), the amendment made by subsection (a) shall apply to the estates of decedents dying after the date of the enactment of this Act.

(B) EXCEPTION.—The amendment made by subsection (a) shall not apply to any interest in property which passes (or has passed) to the surviving spouse of the decedent pursuant to a will (or revocable trust) in existence on the date of the enactment of this Act if—

(i) the decedent dies on or before the date 3 years after such date of enactment, or

(ii) the decedent was, on such date of enactment, under a mental disability to change the disposition of his property and did not regain his competence to dispose of such property before the date of his death.

The preceding sentence shall not apply if such will (or revocable trust) is amended at any time after such date of enactment in any respect which will increase the amount of the interest which so passes or alters the terms of the transfer by which the interest so passes.

• 1989, Omnibus Budget Reconciliation Act of 1989 (P.L. 101-239)

P.L. 101-239, §7816(q):

Amended Code Sec. 2056(b)(7)(C) by striking "an annuity" and inserting "an annuity included in the gross estate of the decedent under section 2039". **Effective** as if included in the provision of P.L. 100-647 to which it relates.

• 1988, Technical and Miscellaneous Revenue Act of 1988 (P.L. 100-647)

P.L. 100-647, §6152(a):

Amended Code Sec. 2056(b)(7) by adding at the end thereof new subparagraph (C). **Effective**, generally, with respect to decedents dying after 12-31-81. See, also, Act Sec. 6152(c)(2)-(3), below.

P.L. 100-647, §6152(c)(2)-(3), provides:

(2) NOT TO APPLY TO EXTENT INCONSISTENT WITH PRIOR RETURN.—In the case of any estate or gift tax return filed before the date of the enactment of this Act, the amendments made by this section shall not apply to the extent such amendments would be inconsistent with the treatment of the annuity on such return unless the executor or donor (as the case may be) otherwise elects under this paragraph before the day 2 years after the date of the enactment of this Act.

(3) EXTENSION OF TIME FOR ELECTION OUT.—The time for making an election under section 2056(b)(7)(C)(ii) or 2523(f)(6)(B) of the 1986 Code (as added by this subsection) shall not expire before the day 2 years after the date of the enactment of this Act (and, if such election is made within the time permitted under this paragraph, the requirement of such section 2056(b)(7)(C)(ii) that it be made on the return shall not apply).

• 1984, Deficit Reduction Act of 1984 (P.L. 98-369)

P.L. 98-369, §1027(a):

Amended Code Sec. 2056(b)(7)(B)(ii)(1)[(I)] by inserting ", or has a usufruct interest for life in the property" after "intervals". **Effective** as if included in the amendment made by Act Sec. 403 of P.L. 97-34.

• 1983, Technical Corrections Act of 1982 (P.L. 97-448)

P.L. 97-448, §104(a)(2)(A):

Amended Code Sec. 2056(b) by adding at the end thereof new paragraph (9). **Effective** as if included in the provision of P.L. 97-34 to which it relates.

P.L. 97-448, §104(a)(8):

Amended Code Sec. 2056(b)(7)(B)(ii) by adding the sentence at the end thereof. **Effective** as if included in the provision of P.L. 97-34 to which it relates.

• **1981, Economic Recovery Tax Act of 1981 (P.L. 97-34)**

P.L. 97-34, §403(d)(1):

Added Code Sec. 2056(b)(7) and (8). **Effective** for estates of decedents dying after 12-31-81.

[Sec. 2056(c)—Repealed]

Amendments

• **1981, Economic Recovery Tax Act of 1981 (P.L. 97-34)**

P.L. 97-34, §403(a)(1)(A):

Repealed Code Sec. 2056(c). **Effective** for estates of decedents dying after 12-31-81. For a transitional rule, see Act Sec. 403(e)(3), below. Prior to its repeal, Code Sec. 2056(c) read as follows:

(c) LIMITATION ON AGGREGATE OF DEDUCTIONS.—

(1) LIMITATION.—

(A) IN GENERAL.—The aggregate amount of the deductions allowed under this section (computed without regard to this subsection) shall not exceed the greater of—

(i) $250,000, or

(ii) 50 percent of the value of the adjusted gross estate (as defined in paragraph (2)).

(B) ADJUSTMENT FOR CERTAIN GIFTS TO SPOUSE.—If a deduction is allowed to the decedent under section 2523 with respect to any gift made to his spouse after December 31, 1976, the limitation provided by subparagraph (A) (determined without regard to this subparagraph) shall be reduced (but not below zero) by the excess (if any) of—

(i) the aggregate of the deductions allowed to the decedent under section 2523 with respect to gifts made after December 31, 1976, over

(ii) the aggregate of the deductions which would have been allowable under section 2523 with respect to gifts made after December 31, 1976, if the amount deductible under such section with respect to any gift required to be included in a gift tax return were 50 percent of its value.

For purposes of this subparagraph, a gift which is includible in the gross estate of the donor by reason of section 2035 shall not be taken into account.

(C) COMMUNITY PROPERTY ADJUSTMENT.—The $250,000 amount set forth in subparagraph (A)(i) shall be reduced by the excess (if any) of—

(i) the amount of the subtraction determined under clauses (i), (ii), and (iii) of paragraph (2)(B), over

(ii) the excess of the aggregate of the deductions allowed under sections 2053 and 2054 over the amount taken into account with respect to such deductions under clause (iv) of paragraph (2)(B).

(2) COMPUTATION OF ADJUSTED GROSS ESTATE.—

(A) GENERAL RULE.—Except as provided in subparagraph (B) of this paragraph, the adjusted gross estate shall, for purposes of subsection (c)(1), be computed by subtracting from the entire value of the gross estate the aggregate amount of the deductions allowed by sections 2053 and 2054.

(B) SPECIAL RULE IN CASES INVOLVING COMMUNITY PROPERTY.—If the decedent and his surviving spouse at any time, held property as community property under the law of any State, or possession of the United States, or of any foreign country, then the adjusted gross estate shall, for purposes of subsection (c)(1), be determined by subtracting from the entire value of the gross estate the sum of—

(i) the value of property which is at the time of the death of the decedent held as such community property; and

(ii) the value of property transferred by the decedent during his life, if at the time of such transfer the property was held as such community property; and

(iii) the amount receivable as insurance under policies on the life of the decedent, to the extent purchased with premiums or other consideration paid out of property held as such community property; and

(iv) an amount which bears the same ratio to the aggregate of the deductions allowed under sections 2053 and 2054 which the value of the property included in the gross estate, diminished by the amount subtracted under clauses (i), (ii), and (iii) of this subparagraph, bears to the entire value of the gross estate.

For purposes of clauses (i), (ii), and (iii), community property (except property which is considered as community property solely by reason of the provisions of subparagraph (C) of this paragraph) shall be considered as not "held as such community property" as of any moment of time, if, in case of the death of the decedent at such moment, such property (and not merely one-half thereof) would be or would have been includible in determining the value of his gross estate without regard to the provisions of section 402(b) of the Revenue Act of 1942. The amount to be subtracted under clauses (i), (ii), or (iii) shall not exceed the value of the interest in the property described therein which is included in determining the value of the gross estate.

(C) COMMUNITY PROPERTY-CONVERSION INTO SEPARATE PROPERTY.—

(i) AFTER DECEMBER 31, 1941.—If after December 31, 1941, property held as such community property (unless considered by reason of subparagraph (B) of this paragraph as not so held) was by the decedent and the surviving spouse converted, by one transaction or a series of transactions, into separate property of the decedent and his spouse (including any form of coownership by them), the separate property so acquired by the decedent and any property acquired at any time by the decedent in exchange therefor (by one exchange or a series of exchanges) shall, for the purposes of clauses (i), (ii), and (iii) of subparagraph (B), be considered as "held as such community property."

(ii) LIMITATION.—Where the value (at the time of such conversion) of the separate property so acquired by the decedent exceeded the value (at such time) of the separate property so acquired by the decedent's spouse, the rule in clause (i) shall be applied only with respect to the same portion of such separate property of the decedent as the portion which the value (as of such time) of such separate property so acquired by the decedent's spouse is of the value (as of such time) of the separate property so acquired by the decedent.

P.L. 97-34, §403(e)(3), provides:

(3) If—

(A) the decedent dies after December 31, 1981.

(B) by reason of the death of the decedent property passes from the decedent or is acquired from the decedent under a will executed before the date which is 30 days after the date of the enactment of this Act, or a trust created before such date, which contains a formula expressly providing that the spouse is to receive the maximum amount of property qualifying for the marital deduction allowable by Federeal law,

(C) the formula referred to in subparagraph (B) was not amended to refer specifically to an unlimited marital deduction at any time after the date which is 30 days after the date of enactment of this Act, and before the death of the decedent, and

(D) the State does not enact a statute applicable to such estate which construes this type of formula as referring to the marital deduction allowable by Federal law as amended by subsection (a),

then the amendment made by subsection (a) shall not apply to the estate of such decedent.

• **1978, Revenue Act of 1978 (P.L. 95-600)**

P.L. 95-600, §702(g)(1)-(2):

Amended Code Sec. 2056(c)(1)(B) by adding "required to be included in a gift tax return" in clause (ii) and by adding the last sentence in the subparagraph. **Effective** for estates of decedents dying after 1976.

• **1976, Tax Reform Act of 1976 (P.L. 94-455)**

P.L. 94-455, §1902(a)(12)(A):

Deleted "Territory" in Code Sec. 2056(c)(2)(B). **Effective** for gifts made after 12-31-76.

P.L. 94-455, § 2002(a):

Amended Code Sec. 2056(c)(1). For the **effective** date, see Act Sec. 2002(d)(1), below. Prior to amendment, Code Sec. 2056(c)(1) read as follows:

(1) GENERAL RULE.—The aggregate amount of the deductions allowed under this section (computed without regard to this subsection) shall not exceed 50 percent of the value of the adjusted gross estate, as defined in paragraph (2).

P.L. 94-455, § 2002(d)(1), provides:

(d) EFFECTIVE DATES.—

(1)(A) Except as provided in subparagraph (B), the amendment made by subsection (a) shall apply with respect to the estates of decedents dying after December 31, 1976.

(B) If—

(i) the decedent dies after December 31, 1976, and before January 1, 1979,

(ii) by reason of the death of the decedent property passes from the decedent or is acquired from the decedent under a will executed before January 1, 1977, or a trust created before such date, which contains a formula expressly providing that the spouse is to receive the maximum amount of property qualifying for the marital deduction allowable by Federal law,

(iii) the formula referred to in clause (ii) was not amended at any time after December 31, 1976, and before the death of the decedent, and

(iv) the State does not enact a statute applicable to such estate which construes this type of formula as referring to the marital deduction allowable by Federal law as amended by subsection (a),

then the amendment made by subsection (a) shall not apply to the estate of such decedent.

[Sec. 2056(c)]

(c) DEFINITION.—For purposes of this section, an interest in property shall be considered as passing from the decedent to any person if and only if—

(1) such interest is bequeathed or devised to such person by the decedent;

(2) such interest is inherited by such person from the decedent;

(3) such interest is the dower or curtesy interest (or statutory interest in lieu thereof) of such person as surviving spouse of the decedent;

(4) such interest has been transferred to such person by the decedent at any time;

(5) such interest was, at the time of the decedent's death, held by such person and the decedent (or by them and any other person) in joint ownership with right of survivorship;

(6) the decedent had a power (either alone or in conjunction with any person) to appoint such interest and if he appoints or has appointed such interest to such person, or if such person takes such interest in default on the release or nonexercise of such power; or

(7) such interest consists of proceeds of insurance on the life of the decedent receivable by such person.

Except as provided in paragraph (5) or (6) of subsection (b), where at the time of the decedent's death it is not possible to ascertain the particular person or persons to whom an interest in property may pass from the decedent, such interest shall, for purposes of subparagraphs (A) and (B) of subsection (b)(1), be considered as passing from the decedent to a person other than the surviving spouse.

Amendments

• 1981, Economic Recovery Tax Act of 1981 (P.L. 97-34)

P.L. 97-34, § 403(a)(1)(A):

Redesignated Code Sec. 2056(d) as Code Sec. 2056(c). **Effective** for estates of decedents dying after 12-31-81.

• 1976, Tax Reform Act of 1976 (P.L. 94-455)

P.L. 94-455, § 2009(b)(4)(D), (e)(2):

Redesignated Code Sec. 2056(e) as Code Sec. 2056(d). **Effective** for transfers creating an interest in the person disclaiming made after 12-31-76.

[Sec. 2056(d)—Stricken]

Amendments

• 1976, Tax Reform Act of 1976 (P.L. 94-455)

P.L. 94-455, § 2009(b)(4)(D):

Struck Code Sec. 2056(d) and redesignated Code Sec. 2056(e) as Code Sec. 2056(d). **Effective** for transfers creating an interest in the person disclaiming made after 12-31-76. Prior to being stricken, Code Sec. 2056(d) read as follows:

(d) DISCLAIMERS.—

(1) BY SURVIVING SPOUSE.—If under this section an interest would, in the absence of a disclaimer by the surviving spouse, be considered as passing from the decedent to such spouse, and if a disclaimer of such interest is made by such spouse, then such interest shall, for the purposes of this section, be considered as passing to the person or persons entitled to receive such interest as a result of the disclaimer.

(2) BY ANY OTHER PERSON.—If under this section an interest would, in the absence of a disclaimer by any person other than the surviving spouse, be considered as passing from the decedent to such person, and if a disclaimer of such interest is made by such person and as a result of such disclaimer the surviving spouse is entitled to receive such interest, then—

(A) if the disclaimer of such interest is made by such person before the date prescribed for the filing of the estate tax return and if such person does not accept such interest before making the disclaimer, such interest shall, for purposes of this section, be considered as passing from the decedent to the surviving spouse, and

(B) if subparagraph (A) does not apply, such interest shall, for purposes of this section, be considered as passing, not to the surviving spouse, but to the person who made the disclaimer, in the same manner as if the disclaimer had not been made.

• 1966 (P.L. 89-621)

P.L. 89-621, § [1]:

Amended Code Sec. 2056(d)(2). Except as provided, the amendment is **effective** with respect to estates of decedents dying on or after 10-4-66. However, in the case of the estate of a decedent dying before 10-4-66 for which the date prescribed for the filing of the estate tax return (determined without regard to any extension of time for filing) occurs on or after 1-1-65, if, under section 2056 of the Internal Revenue Code of 1954, an interest would, in the absence of a disclaimer by any person other than the surviving spouse, be considered as passing from the decedent to such person, and if a disclaimer of such interest is made by such person and as a result of such disclaimer the surviving spouse is entitled to receive such interest, then such interest shall, for purposes of such section, be considered as passing from the decedent to the surviving spouse, if—

(1) the interest disclaimed was bequeathed or devised to such person,

(2) before the date prescribed for the filing of the estate tax return such person disclaimed all bequests and devises under such will, and

(3) such person did not accept any property under any such bequest or devise before making the disclaimer.
The amount of the deductions allowable under section 2056 of such Code by reason of this subsection, when added to the amount of the deductions allowable under such section without regard to this subsection, shall not exceed the greater of (A) the amount of the deductions which would be allowable under such section without regard to the disclaimer if the surviving spouse elected to take against the will, or (B) an amount equal to one-third of the adjusted gross estate (within the meaning of subsection (c)(2) of such section). Prior to amendment, Sec. 2056(d)(2) read as follows:

"(2) BY ANY OTHER PERSON.—If under this section an interest would, in the absence of a disclaimer by any person other than the surviving spouse, be considered as passing from the decedent to such person, and if a disclaimer of such interest is made by such person and as a result of such disclaimer the surviving spouse is entitled to receive such interest, then such interest shall, for purposes of this section, be considered as passing, not to the surviving spouse, but to the person who made the disclaimer, in the same manner as if the disclaimer had not been made."

[Sec. 2056(d)]

(d) DISALLOWANCE OF MARITAL DEDUCTION WHERE SURVIVING SPOUSE NOT UNITED STATES CITIZEN.—

(1) IN GENERAL.—Except as provided in paragraph (2), if the surviving spouse of the decedent is not a citizen of the United States—

(A) no deduction shall be allowed under subsection (a), and

(B) section 2040(b) shall not apply.

(2) MARITAL DEDUCTION ALLOWED FOR CERTAIN TRANSFERS IN TRUST.—

(A) IN GENERAL.—Paragraph (1) shall not apply to any property passing to the surviving spouse in a qualified domestic trust.

(B) SPECIAL RULE.—If any property passes from the decedent to the surviving spouse of the decedent, for purposes of subparagraph (A), such property shall be treated as passing to such spouse in a qualified domestic trust if—

(i) such property is transferred to such a trust before the date on which the return of the tax imposed by this chapter is made, or

(ii) such property is irrevocably assigned to such a trust under an irrevocable assignment made on or before such date which is enforceable under local law.

(3) ALLOWANCE OF CREDIT TO CERTAIN SPOUSES.—If—

(A) property passes to the surviving spouse of the decedent (hereinafter in this paragraph referred to as the "first decedent"),

(B) without regard to this subsection, a deduction would be allowable under subsection (a) with respect to such property, and

(C) such surviving spouse dies and the estate of such surviving spouse is subject to the tax imposed by this chapter,

the Federal estate tax paid (or treated as paid under section 2056A(b)(7) by the first decedent with respect to such property shall be allowed as a credit under section 2013 to the estate of such surviving spouse and the amount of such credit shall be determined under such section without regard to when the first decedent died and without regard to subsection (d)(3) of such section.

(4) SPECIAL RULE WHERE RESIDENT SPOUSE BECOMES CITIZEN.—Paragraph (1) shall not apply if—

(A) the surviving spouse of the decedent becomes a citizen of the United States before the day on which the return of the tax imposed by this chapter is made, and

(B) such spouse was a resident of the United States at all times after the date of the death of the decedent and before becoming a citizen of the United States.

(5) REFORMATIONS PERMITTED.—

(A) IN GENERAL.—In the case of any property with respect to which a deduction would be allowable under subsection (a) but for this subsection, the determination of whether a trust is a qualified domestic trust shall be made—

(i) as of the date on which the return of the tax imposed by this chapter is made, or

(ii) if a judicial proceeding is commenced on or before the due date (determined with regard to extensions) for filing such return to change such trust into a trust which is a qualified domestic trust, as of the time when the changes pursuant to such proceeding are made.

(B) STATUTE OF LIMITATIONS.—If a judicial proceeding described in subparagraph (A)(ii) is commenced with respect to any trust, the period for assessing any deficiency of tax attributable to any failure of such trust to be a qualified domestic trust shall not expire before the date 1 year after the date on which the Secretary is notified that the trust has been changed pursuant to such judicial proceeding or that such proceeding has been terminated.

Amendments

• 1990, Omnibus Budget Reconciliation Act of 1990 (P.L. 101-508)

P.L. 101-508, §11701(l)(1):

Amended Code Sec. 2056(d) by redesignating paragraph (4)[5]as paragraph (5). **Effective** as if included in the provision of P.L. 101-239 to which it relates.

P.L. 101-508, §11701(l)(2), provides:

(2) The period during which a proceeding may be commenced under section 2056(d)(5)(A)(ii) of the Internal Revenue Code of 1986 (as redesignated by paragraph (1)) shall not expire before the date 6 months after the date of the enactment of this Act.

P.L. 101-508, §11702(g)(5):

Amended Code Sec. 2056(d)(3) by striking "section 2056A(b)(6)" and inserting "section 2056A(b)(7)". **Effective** as if included in the provision of P.L. 100-647 to which it relates.

• 1989, Omnibus Budget Reconciliation Act of 1989 (P.L. 101-239)

P.L. 101-239, §7815(d)(4)(A):

Amended Code Sec. 2056(d)(2)(B). **Effective** as if included in the provision of P.L. 100-647 to which it relates. Prior to amendment, Code Sec. 2056(d)(2)(B) read as follows:

(B) PROPERTY PASSING OUTSIDE OF PROBATE ESTATE.—If any property passes from the decedent to the surviving spouse of the decedent outside of the decedent's probate estate, for purposes of subparagraph (A), such property shall be treated as passing to such spouse in a qualified domestic trust if such property is transferred to such a trust before the day on which the return of the tax imposed by section 2001 is made.

P.L. 101-239, §7815(d)(5):

Amended Code Sec. 2056(d) by adding at the end thereof a new paragraph (4). **Effective** as if included in the provision of P.L. 100-647 to which it relates.

P.L. 101-239, §7815(d)(6)(A)-(B):

Amended Code Sec. 2056(d)(3) by striking "section 2001" and inserting "this chapter", and by inserting "and without regard to subsection (d)(3) of such section" before the period at the end thereof. **Effective** as if included in the provision of P.L. 100-647 to which it relates.

P.L. 101-239, §7815(d)(8):

Amended Code Sec. 2056(d) by adding at the end thereof a new paragraph (4)[5]. **Effective** as if included in the provision of P.L. 100-647 to which it relates.

P.L. 101-239, §7815(d)(4)(B), provides:

(B) In the case of the estate of a decedent dying before the date of the enactment of this Act, the period during which the transfer (or irrevocable assignment) referred to in section 2056(d)(2)(B) of the Internal Revenue Code of 1986 (as amended by subparagraph (A)) may be made shall not expire before the date 1 year after such date of enactment.

P.L. 101-239, §7815(d)(16), provides:

(16) For purposes of applying section 2040(a) of the Internal Revenue Code of 1986 with respect to any joint interest to which section 2040(b) of such Code does not apply solely by reason of section 2056(d)(1)(B) of such Code, any consideration furnished before July 14, 1988, by the decedent for such interest to the extent treated as a gift to the spouse of the decedent for purposes of chapter 12 of such Code (or would have been so treated if the donor were a citizen of the United States) shall be treated as consideration originally belonging to such spouse and never acquired by such spouse from the decedent.

• 1988, Technical and Miscellaneous Revenue Act of 1988 (P.L. 100-647)

P.L. 100-647, §5033(a)(1):

Amended Code Sec. 2056 by adding at the end thereof a new subsection (d). **Effective** for estates of decedents dying after the date of enactment of this Act.

[Sec. 2056A]

SEC. 2056A. QUALIFIED DOMESTIC TRUST.

[Sec. 2056A(a)]

(a) QUALIFIED DOMESTIC TRUST DEFINED.—For purposes of this section and section 2056(d), the term "qualified domestic trust" means, with respect to any decedent, any trust if—

(1) the trust instrument—

(A) except as provided in regulations prescribed by the Secretary, requires that at least 1 trustee of the trust be an individual citizen of the United States or a domestic corporation, and

(B) provides that no distribution (other than a distribution of income) may be made from the trust unless a trustee who is an individual citizen of the United States or domestic corporation has the right to withhold from such distribution the tax imposed by this section on such distribution,

(2) such trust meets such requirements as the Secretary may by regulations prescribe to ensure the collection of any tax imposed by subsection (b), and

(3) an election under this section by the executor of the decedent applies to such trust.

Amendments

• 1997, Taxpayer Relief Act of 1997 (P.L. 105-34)

P.L. 105-34, §1303, provides:

SEC. 1303. TRANSITIONAL RULE UNDER SECTION 2056A.

(a) GENERAL RULE.—In the case of any trust created under an instrument executed before the date of the enactment of the Revenue Reconciliation Act of 1990, such trust shall be treated as meeting the requirements of paragraph (1) of section 2056A(a) of the Internal Revenue Code of 1986 if the trust instrument requires that all trustees of the trust be individual citizens of the United States or domestic corporations.

(b) EFFECTIVE DATE.—The provisions of subsection (a) shall take effect as if included in the provisions of section 11702(g) of the Revenue Reconciliation Act of 1990.

P.L. 105-34, §1314(a):

Amended Code Sec. 2056A(a)(1)(A) by inserting "except as provided in regulations prescribed by the Secretary," before "requires". **Effective** for estates of decedents dying after 8-5-97.

• 1990, Omnibus Budget Reconciliation Act of 1990 (P.L. 101-508)

P.L. 101-508, §11702(g)(2)(A):

Amended Code Sec. 2056A(a)(1). **Effective** as if included in the provision of P.L. 100-647 to which it relates. Prior to amendment, paragraph (1) read as follows:

(1) the trust instrument requires that at least 1 trustee of the trust be an individual citizen of the United States or a domestic corporation and that no distribution from the trust may be made without the approval of such a trustee,

• 1989, Omnibus Budget Reconciliation Act of 1989 (P.L. 101-239)

P.L. 101-239, §7815(d)(7)(A)(i)-(ii):

Amended Code Sec. 2056A(a) by amending paragraph (1), and by striking paragraph (2) and redesignating paragraphs (3) and (4) as paragraphs (2) and (3), respectively. **Effective** as if included in the provision of P.L. 100-647 to which it relates. Prior to amendment, Code Sec. 2056A(a)(1)-(2) read as follows:

(1) the trust instrument requires that all trustees of the trust be individual citizens of the United States or domestic corporations,

(2) the surviving spouse of the decedent is entitled to all the income from the property in such trust, payable annually or at more frequent intervals,

(b) TAX TREATMENT OF TRUST.—

(1) IMPOSITION OF ESTATE TAX.—There is hereby imposed an estate tax on—

(A) any distribution before the date of the death of the surviving spouse from a qualified domestic trust, and

(B) the value of the property remaining in a qualified domestic trust on the date of the death of the surviving spouse.

(2) AMOUNT OF TAX.—

(A) IN GENERAL.—In the case of any taxable event, the amount of the estate tax imposed by paragraph (1) shall be the amount equal to—

(i) the tax which would have been imposed under section 2001 on the estate of the decedent if the taxable estate of the decedent had been increased by the sum of—

(I) the amount involved in such taxable event, plus

(II) the aggregate amount involved in previous taxable events with respect to qualified domestic trusts of such decedent, reduced by

(ii) the tax which would have been imposed under section 2001 on the estate of the decedent if the taxable estate of the decedent had been increased by the amount referred to in clause (i)(II).

(B) TENTATIVE TAX WHERE TAX OF DECEDENT NOT FINALLY DETERMINED.—

(i) IN GENERAL.—If the tax imposed on the estate of the decedent under section 2001 is not finally determined before the taxable event, the amount of the tax imposed by paragraph (1) on such event shall be determined by using the highest rate of tax in effect under section 2001 as of the date of the decedent's death.

(ii) REFUND OF EXCESS WHEN TAX FINALLY DETERMINED.—If—

(I) the amount of the tax determined under clause (i), exceeds

(II) the tax determined under subparagraph (A) on the basis of the final determination of the tax imposed by section 2001 on the estate of the decedent,

such excess shall be allowed as a credit or refund (with interest) if claim therefor is filed not later than 1 year after the date of such final determination.

(C) SPECIAL RULE WHERE DECEDENT HAS MORE THAN 1 QUALIFIED DOMESTIC TRUST.—If there is more than 1 qualified domestic trust with respect to any decedent, the amount of the tax imposed by paragraph (1) with respect to such trusts shall be determined by using the highest rate of tax in effect under section 2001 as of the date of the decedent's death (and the provisions of paragraph (3)(B) shall not apply) unless, pursuant to a designation made by the decedent's executor, there is 1 person—

(i) who is an individual citizen of the United States or a domestic corporation and is responsible for filing all returns of tax imposed under paragraph (1) with respect to such trusts and for paying all tax so imposed, and

(ii) who meets such requirements as the Secretary may by regulations prescribe.

(3) CERTAIN LIFETIME DISTRIBUTIONS EXEMPT FROM TAX.—

(A) INCOME DISTRIBUTIONS.—No tax shall be imposed by paragraph (1)(A) on any distribution of income to the surviving spouse.

(B) HARDSHIP EXEMPTION.—No tax shall be imposed by paragraph (1)(A) on any distribution to the surviving spouse on account of hardship.

(4) TAX WHERE TRUST CEASES TO QUALIFY.—If any qualified domestic trust ceases to meet the requirements of paragraphs (1) and (2) of subsection (a), the tax imposed by paragraph (1) shall apply as if the surviving spouse died on the date of such cessation.

(5) DUE DATE.—

(A) TAX ON DISTRIBUTIONS.—The estate tax imposed by paragraph (1)(A) shall be due and payable on the 15th day of the 4th month following the calendar year in which the taxable event occurs; except that the estate tax imposed by paragraph (1)(A) on distributions during the calendar year in which the surviving spouse dies shall be due and payable not later than the date on which the estate tax imposed by paragraph (1)(B) is due and payable.

(B) TAX AT DEATH OF SPOUSE.—The estate tax imposed by paragraph (1)(B) shall be due and payable on the date 9 months after the date of such death.

(6) LIABILITY FOR TAX.—Each trustee shall be personally liable for the amount of the tax imposed by paragraph (1). Rules similar to the rules of section 2204 shall apply for purposes of the preceding sentence.

(7) TREATMENT OF TAX.—For purposes of section 2056(d), any tax paid under paragraph (1) shall be treated as a tax paid under section 2001 with respect to the estate of the decedent.

(8) LIEN FOR TAX.—For purposes of section 6324, any tax imposed by paragraph (1) shall be treated as an estate tax imposed under this chapter with respect to a decedent dying on the date of the taxable event (and the property involved shall be treated as the gross estate of such decedent).

(9) TAXABLE EVENT.—The term "taxable event" means the event resulting in tax being imposed under paragraph (1).

(10) CERTAIN BENEFITS ALLOWED.—

(A) IN GENERAL.—If any property remaining in the qualified domestic trust on the date of the death of the surviving spouse is includible in the gross estate of such spouse for purposes of this chapter (or would be includible if such spouse were a citizen or resident of the United States), any benefit which is allowable (or would be allowable if such spouse were a citizen or resident of the United States) with respect to such property to the estate of such spouse under section 2014, 2032, 2032A, 2055, 2056, 2058, or 6166 shall be allowed for purposes of the tax imposed by paragraph (1)(B).

(B) SECTION 303.—If the estate of the surviving spouse meets the requirements of section 303 with respect to any property described in subparagraph (A), for purposes of section 303, the tax imposed by paragraph (1)(B) with respect to such property shall be treated as a Federal estate tax payable with respect to the estate of the surviving spouse.

(C) SECTION 6161(a)(2).—The provisions of section 6161(a)(2) shall apply with respect to the tax imposed by paragraph (1)(B), and the reference in such section to the executor shall be treated as a reference to the trustees of the trust.

(11) SPECIAL RULE WHERE DISTRIBUTION TAX PAID OUT OF TRUST.—For purposes of this subsection, if any portion of the tax imposed by paragraph (1)(A) with respect to any distribution is paid out of the trust, an amount equal to the portion so paid shall be treated as a distribution described in paragraph (1)(A).

(12) SPECIAL RULE WHERE SPOUSE BECOMES CITIZEN.—If the surviving spouse of the decedent becomes a citizen of the United States and if—

(A) such spouse was a resident of the United States at all times after the date of the death of the decedent and before such spouse becomes a citizen of the United States,

(B) no tax was imposed by paragraph (1)(A) with respect to any distribution before such spouse becomes such a citizen, or

(C) such spouse elects—

(i) to treat any distribution on which tax was imposed by paragraph (1)(A) as a taxable gift made by such spouse for purposes of—

(I) section 2001, and

(II) determining the amount of the tax imposed by section 2501 on actual taxable gifts made by such spouse during the year in which the spouse becomes a citizen or any subsequent year, and

(ii) to treat any reduction in the tax imposed by paragraph (1)(A) by reason of the credit allowable under section 2010 with respect to the decedent as a credit allowable to such surviving spouse under section 2505 for purposes of determining the amount of the credit allowable under section 2505 with respect to taxable gifts made by the surviving spouse during the year in which the spouse becomes a citizen or any subsequent year,

paragraph (1)(A) shall not apply to any distributions after such spouse becomes such a citizen (and paragraph (1)(B) shall not apply).

(13) COORDINATION WITH SECTION 1015.—For purposes of section 1015, any distribution on which tax is imposed by paragraph (1)(A) shall be treated as a transfer by gift, and any tax paid under paragraph (1)(A) shall be treated as a gift tax.

(14) COORDINATION WITH TERMINABLE INTEREST RULES.—Any interest in a qualified domestic trust shall not be treated as failing to meet the requirements of paragraph (5) or (7) of section 2056(b) merely by reason of any provision of the trust instrument permitting the withholding from any distribution of an amount to pay the tax imposed by paragraph (1) on such distribution.

(15) NO TAX ON CERTAIN DISTRIBUTIONS.—No tax shall be imposed by paragraph (1) on any distribution to the surviving spouse to the extent such distribution is to reimburse such surviving spouse for any tax imposed by subtitle A on any item of income of the trust to which such surviving spouse is not entitled under the terms of the trust.

Amendments

• 2013, American Taxpayer Relief Act of 2012 (P.L. 112-240)

P.L. 112-240, §101(a)(1) and (3), provides:

SEC. 101. PERMANENT EXTENSION AND MODIFICATION OF 2001 TAX RELIEF.

(a) PERMANENT EXTENSION.—

(1) IN GENERAL.—The Economic Growth and Tax Relief Reconciliation Act of 2001 is amended by striking title IX.

* * *

(3) EFFECTIVE DATE.—The amendments made by this subsection shall apply to taxable, plan, or limitation years beginning after December 31, 2012, and estates of decedents dying, gifts made, or generation skipping transfers after December 31, 2012.

• 2001, Economic Growth and Tax Relief Reconciliation Act of 2001 (P.L. 107-16)

P.L. 107-16, §532(c)(6)(A)-(B):

Amended Code Sec. 2056A(b)(10)(A) by striking "2011," following "spouse under section", and by inserting "2058," after "2056,". **Effective** for estates of decedents dying, and generation-skipping transfers, after 12-31-2004.

P.L. 107-16, §901(a)-(b), as amended by P.L. 111-312, §101(a)(1), provides [but see P.L. 112-240, §101(a)(1) and (3), above]:

SEC. 901. SUNSET OF PROVISIONS OF ACT.

(a) IN GENERAL.—All provisions of, and amendments made by, this Act shall not apply—

(1) to taxable, plan, or limitation years beginning after December 31, 2012, or

(2) in the case of title V, to estates of decedents dying, gifts made, or generation skipping transfers, after December 31, 2012.

(b) APPLICATION OF CERTAIN LAWS.—The Internal Revenue Code of 1986 and the Employee Retirement Income Security Act of 1974 shall be applied and administered to years, estates, gifts, and transfers described in subsection (a) as if the provisions and amendments described in subsection (a) had never been enacted.

• 1990, Omnibus Budget Reconciliation Act of 1990 (P.L. 101-508)

P.L. 101-508, §11702(g)(2)(B):

Amended Code Sec. 2056A(b) by adding new paragraphs (14) and (15). **Effective** as if included in the provision of P.L. 100-647 to which it relates.

P.L. 101-508, §11702(g)(4):

Amended Code Sec. 2056A(b)(10)(A) by striking "section 2032" and inserting "section 2011, 2014, 2032". **Effective** as if included in the provision of P.L. 100-647 to which it relates.

P.L. 101-508, §11704(a)(15):

Amended Code Sec. 2056A(b)(2)(B)(ii) by striking "therefore" and inserting "therefor". **Effective** 11-5-90.

• 1989, Omnibus Budget Reconciliation Act of 1989 (P.L. 101-239)

P.L. 101-239, §7815(d)(7)(B):

Amended Code Sec. 2056A(b) by redesignating paragraphs (3) through (8) as paragraphs (4) through (9), respectively, and by inserting after paragraph (2) a new paragraph (3). **Effective** as if included in the provision of P.L. 100-647 to which it relates.

P.L. 101-239, §7815(d)(7)(C):

Amended Code Sec. 2056A(b)(1)(A) by striking "other than a distribution of income required under subsection (a)(2)" after "domestic trust". **Effective** as if included in the provision of P.L. 100-647 to which it relates.

P.L. 101-239, §7815(d)(7)(D):

Amended Code Sec. 2056A(b)(4), as redesignated by subparagraph (B). **Effective** as if included in the provision of P.L. 100-647 to which it relates. Prior to amendment, Code Sec. 2056A(b)(4) read as follows:

(4) TAX IMPOSED WHERE TRUST CEASES TO QUALIFY.—If any person other than an individual citizen of the United States or a domestic corporation becomes a trustee of a qualified domestic trust (or such trust ceases to meet the requirements of subsection (a)(3)), the tax imposed by paragraph (1) shall apply as if the surviving spouse died on the date on which such person became such a trustee or the date of such cessation, as the case may be.

P.L. 101-239, §7815(d)(9):

Amended Code Sec. 2056A(b) by adding at the end thereof new paragraphs (10)-(13). **Effective** as if included in the provision of P.L. 100-647 to which it relates.

P.L. 101-239, §7815(d)(11):

Amended Code Sec. 2056A(b)(2)(B)(ii) by striking "as a credit or refund" and inserting "as a credit or refund (with interest)". **Effective** as if included in the provision of P.L. 100-647 to which it relates.

P.L. 101-239, §7815(d)(12):

Amended Code Sec. 2056A(b)(2) by adding at the end thereof a new subparagraph (C). **Effective** as if included in the provision of P.L. 100-647 to which it relates.

P.L. 101-239, §7815(d)(15):

Amended Code Sec. 2056A(b)(5), as redesignated by section (7)(B). **Effective** as if included in the provision of P.L. 100-647 to which it relates. Prior to amendment, Code Sec. 2056A(b)(5) read as follows:

(5) DUE DATE.—The estate tax imposed by paragraph (1) shall be due and payable on the 15th day of the 4th month following the calendar year in which the taxable event occurs.

[Sec. 2056A(c)]

(c) DEFINITIONS.—For purposes of this section—

(1) PROPERTY INCLUDES INTEREST THEREIN.—The term "property" includes an interest in property.

(2) INCOME.—Except as provided in regulations, the term "income" has the meaning given to such term by section 643(b).

(3) TRUST.—To the extent provided in regulations prescribed by the Secretary, the term "trust" includes other arrangements which have substantially the same effect as a trust.

Amendments

• 1997, Taxpayer Relief Act of 1997 (P.L. 105-34)

P.L. 105-34, §1312(a):

Amended Code Sec. 2056A(c) by adding at the end a new paragraph (3). **Effective** for estates of decedents dying after 8-5-97.

• 1989, Omnibus Budget Reconciliation Act of 1989 (P.L. 101-239)

P.L. 101-239, §7815(d)(10):

Amended Code Sec. 2056A(c)(2) by striking "The term" and inserting "Except as provided in regulations, the term". **Effective** as if included in the provision of P.L. 100-647 to which it relates.

[Sec. 2056A(d)]

(d) ELECTION.—An election under this section with respect to any trust shall be made by the executor on the return of the tax imposed by section 2001. Such an election, once made, shall be irrevocable. No election may be made under this section on any return if such return is filed more than one year after the time prescribed by law (including extensions) for filing such return.

Amendments

• 1990, Omnibus Budget Reconciliation Act of 1990 (P.L. 101-508)

P.L. 101-508, §11702(g)(3)(A):

Amended Code Sec. 2056A(d) by adding at the end thereof a new sentence. Not **effective** for any election made before the date 6 months after 11-5-90.

• 1988, Technical and Miscellaneous Revenue Act of 1988 (P.L. 100-647)

P.L. 100-647, §5033(a)(2):

Amended Part IV of subchapter A of chapter 11 by inserting after section 2056 a new section 2056A. **Effective** for estates of decedents dying after 11-10-88.

[Sec. 2056A(e)]

(e) REGULATIONS.—The Secretary shall prescribe such regulations as may be necessary or appropriate to carry out the purposes of this section, including regulations under which there may be treated as a qualified domestic trust any annuity or other payment which is includible in the decedent's gross estate and is by its terms payable for life or a term of years.

Amendments

• 1989, Omnibus Budget Reconciliation Act of 1989 (P.L. 101-239)

P.L. 101-239, §7815(d)(13):

Amended Code Sec. 2056A by adding at the end thereof a new subsection (e). **Effective** as if included in the provision of P.L. 100-647 to which it relates.

P.L. 101-239, §7815(d)(14), provides:

(14) In the case of the estate of, or gift by, an individual who was not a citizen or resident of the United States but was a resident of a foreign country with which the United States has a tax treaty with respect to estate, inheritance, or gift taxes, the amendments made by section 5033 of the 1988 Act shall not apply to the extent such amendments would be inconsistent with the provisions of such treaty relating to estate, inheritance, or gift tax marital deductions. In the case of the estate of an individual dying before the date 3 years after the date of the enactment of this Act, or a gift by an individual before the date 3 years after the date of the enactment of this Act, the requirement of the preceding sentence that the individual not be a citizen or resident of the United States shall not apply.

[Sec. 2057—Stricken]

Amendments

• 2014, Tax Technical Corrections Act of 2014 (P.L. 113-295)

P.L. 113-295, §221(a)(97)(A), Division A:

Amended part IV of subchapter A of chapter 11 by striking Code Sec. 2057. **Effective** generally 12-19-2014. For a special rule, see Act Sec. 221(b)(2), Division A, below.

P.L. 113-295, §221(b)(2), Division A, provides:

(2) SAVINGS PROVISION.—If—

(A) any provision amended or repealed by the amendments made by this section applied to—

(i) any transaction occurring before the date of the enactment of this Act,

(ii) any property acquired before such date of enactment, or

(iii) any item of income, loss, deduction, or credit taken into account before such date of enactment, and

(B) the treatment of such transaction, property, or item under such provision would (without regard to the amendments or repeals made by this section) affect the liability for tax for periods ending after date of enactment, nothing in the amendments or repeals made by this section shall be construed to affect the treatment of such transaction, property, or item for purposes of determining liability for tax for periods ending after such date of enactment.

Prior to being stricken, Code Sec. 2057 read as follows:

SEC. 2057. FAMILY-OWNED BUSINESS INTERESTS.

[Sec. 2057(a)]

(a) GENERAL RULE.—

(1) ALLOWANCE OF DEDUCTION.—For purposes of the tax imposed by section 2001, in the case of an estate of a decedent to which this section applies, the value of the taxable estate shall be determined by deducting from the value of the gross estate the adjusted value of the qualified family-owned business interests of the decedent which are described in subsection (b)(2).

(2) MAXIMUM DEDUCTION.—The deduction allowed by this section shall not exceed $675,000.

(3) COORDINATION WITH UNIFIED CREDIT.—

(A) IN GENERAL.—Except as provided in subparagraph (B), if this section applies to an estate, the applicable exclusion amount under section 2010 shall be $625,000.

(B) INCREASE IN UNIFIED CREDIT IF DEDUCTION IS LESS THAN $675,000.—If the deduction allowed by this section is less than $675,000, the amount of the applicable exclusion amount under section 2010 shall be increased (but not above the amount which would apply to the estate without regard to this section) by the excess of $675,000 over the amount of the deduction allowed.

Amendments

• 1998, IRS Restructuring and Reform Act of 1998 (P.L. 105-206)

P.L. 105-206, §6007(b)(1)(A):

Amended Code Sec. 2033A by moving it to the end of part IV of subchapter A of chapter 11 and redesignating it as Code Sec. 2057. **Effective** as if included in the provision of P.L. 105-34 to which it relates [**effective** for estates of decedents dying after 12-31-97.—CCH].

P.L. 105-206, §6007(b)(1)(B):

Amended so much of Code Sec. 2057 (as redesignated) as precedes subsection (b). **Effective** as if included in the provision of P.L. 105-34 to which it relates [**effective** for estates of decedents dying after 12-31-97.—CCH]. Prior to amendment, so much of Code Sec. 2057, as redesignated, as precedes subsection (b) read as follows:

SEC. 2033A. FAMILY-OWNED BUSINESS EXCLUSION.

(a) IN GENERAL.—In the case of an estate of a decedent to which this section applies, the value of the gross estate shall not include the lesser of—

(1) the adjusted value of the qualified family-owned business interests of the decedent otherwise includible in the estate, or

(2) the excess of $1,300,000 over the applicable exclusion amount under section 2010(c) with respect to such estate.

[Sec. 2057(b)]

(b) ESTATES TO WHICH SECTION APPLIES.—

(1) IN GENERAL.—This section shall apply to an estate if—

(A) the decedent was (at the date of the decedent's death) a citizen or resident of the United States,

(B) the executor elects the application of this section and files the agreement referred to in subsection (h),

(C) the sum of—

(i) the adjusted value of the qualified family-owned business interests described in paragraph (2), plus

(ii) the amount of the gifts of such interests determined under paragraph (3),

exceeds 50 percent of the adjusted gross estate, and

(D) during the 8-year period ending on the date of the decedent's death there have been periods aggregating 5 years or more during which—

(i) such interests were owned by the decedent or a member of the decedent's family, and

(ii) there was material participation (within the meaning of section 2032A(e)(6)) by the decedent or a member of the decedent's family in the operation of the business to which such interests relate.

(2) INCLUDIBLE QUALIFIED FAMILY-OWNED BUSINESS INTERESTS.—The qualified family-owned business interests described in this paragraph are the interests which—

(A) are included in determining the value of the gross estate, and

(B) are acquired by any qualified heir from, or passed to any qualified heir from, the decedent (within the meaning of section 2032A(e)(9)).

(3) INCLUDIBLE GIFTS OF INTERESTS.—The amount of the gifts of qualified family-owned business interests determined under this paragraph is the sum of—

(A) the amount of such gifts from the decedent to members of the decedent's family taken into account under section 2001(b)(1)(B), plus

(B) the amount of such gifts otherwise excluded under section 2503(b),

to the extent such interests are continuously held by members of such family (other than the decedent's spouse) between the date of the gift and the date of the decedent's death.

Amendments

• 1998, IRS Restructuring and Reform Act of 1998 (P.L. 105-206)

P.L. 105-206, §6007(b)(1)(C):

Amended Code Sec. 2057(b)(2)(A) (as redesignated) by striking "(without regard to this section)" after "the value of the gross estate". **Effective** as if included in the provision of P.L. 105-34 to which it relates [**effective** for estates of decedents dying after 12-31-97.—CCH].

P.L. 105-206, §6007(b)(2):

Amended Code Sec. 2057(b)(3) (as redesignated). **Effective** as if included in the provision of P.L. 105-34 to which it relates [**effective** for estates of decedents dying after 12-31-97.—CCH]. Prior to amendment, Code Sec. 2057(b)(3) read as follows:

(3) INCLUDIBLE GIFTS OF INTERESTS.—The amount of the gifts of qualified family-owned business interests determined under this paragraph is the excess of—

(A) the sum of—

(i) the amount of such gifts from the decedent to members of the decedent's family taken into account under subsection 2001(b)(1)(B), plus

(ii) the amount of such gifts otherwise excluded under section 2503(b),

to the extent such interests are continuously held by members of such family (other than the decedent's spouse) between the date of the gift and the date of the decedent's death, over

(B) the amount of such gifts from the decedent to members of the decedent's family otherwise included in the gross estate.

[Sec. 2057(c)]

(c) ADJUSTED GROSS ESTATE.—For purposes of this section, the term "adjusted gross estate" means the value of the gross estate—

(1) reduced by any amount deductible under paragraph (3) or (4) of section 2053(a), and

(2) increased by the excess of—

(A) the sum of—

(i) the amount of gifts determined under subsection (b)(3), plus

(ii) the amount (if more than de minimis) of other transfers from the decedent to the decedent's spouse (at the time of the transfer) within 10 years of the date of the decedent's death, plus

(iii) the amount of other gifts (not included under clause (i) or (ii)) from the decedent within 3 years of such date, other than gifts to members of the decedent's family otherwise excluded under section 2503(b), over

(B) the sum of the amounts described in clauses (i), (ii), and (iii) of subparagraph (A) which are otherwise includible in the gross estate.

For purposes of the preceding sentence, the Secretary may provide that de minimis gifts to persons other than members of the decedent's family shall not be taken into account.

Amendments

• 1998, IRS Restructuring and Reform Act of 1998 (P.L. 105-206)

P.L. 105-206, §6007(b)(1)(D):

Amended Code Sec. 2057(c) (as redesignated) by striking "(determined without regard to this section)" after "the value of the gross estate". **Effective** as if included in the provision of P.L. 105-34 to which it relates [**effective** for estates of decedents dying after 12-31-97.—CCH].

[Sec. 2057(d)]

(d) ADJUSTED VALUE OF THE QUALIFIED FAMILY-OWNED BUSINESS INTERESTS.—For purposes of this section, the adjusted value of any qualified family-owned business interest is the value of such interest for purposes of this chapter (determined without regard to this section), reduced by the excess of—

(1) any amount deductible under paragraph (3) or (4) of section 2053(a), over

(2) the sum of—

(A) any indebtedness on any qualified residence of the decedent the interest on which is deductible under section 163(h)(3), plus

(B) any indebtedness to the extent the taxpayer establishes that the proceeds of such indebtedness were used for the payment of educational and medical expenses of the decedent, the decedent's spouse, or the decedent's dependents (within the meaning of section 152, determined without regard to subsections (b)(1), (b)(2), and (d)(1)(B) thereof), plus

(C) any indebtedness not described in subparagraph (A) or (B), to the extent such indebtedness does not exceed $10,000.

Amendments

• 2004, Working Families Tax Relief Act of 2004 (P.L. 108-311)

P.L. 108-311, §207(23):

Amended Code Sec. 2057(d)(2)(B) by inserting ", determined without regard to subsections (b)(1), (b)(2), and (d)(1)(B) thereof" after "section 152". **Effective** for tax years beginning after 12-31-2004.

[Sec. 2057(e)]

(e) QUALIFIED FAMILY-OWNED BUSINESS INTEREST.—

(1) IN GENERAL.—For purposes of this section, the term "qualified family-owned business interest" means—

(A) an interest as a proprietor in a trade or business carried on as a proprietorship, or

(B) an interest in an entity carrying on a trade or business, if—

(i) at least—

(I) 50 percent of such entity is owned (directly or indirectly) by the decedent and members of the decedent's family,

(II) 70 percent of such entity is so owned by members of 2 families, or

(III) 90 percent of such entity is so owned by members of 3 families, and

(ii) for purposes of subclause (II) or (III) of clause (i), at least 30 percent of such entity is so owned by the decedent and members of the decedent's family.

For purposes of the preceding sentence, a decedent shall be treated as engaged in a trade or business if any member of the decedent's family is engaged in such trade or business.

(2) LIMITATION.—Such term shall not include—

(A) any interest in a trade or business the principal place of business of which is not located in the United States,

(B) any interest in an entity, if the stock or debt of such entity or a controlled group (as defined in section 267(f)(1)) of which such entity was a member was readily tradable on an established securities market or secondary market (as defined by the Secretary) at any time within 3 years of the date of the decedent's death,

(C) any interest in a trade or business not described in section 542(c)(2), if more than 35 percent of the adjusted ordinary gross income of such trade or business for the taxable year which includes the date of the decedent's death would qualify as personal holding company income (as defined in section 543(a) without regard to paragraph (2)(B) thereof) if such trade or business were a corporation,

(D) that portion of an interest in a trade or business that is attributable to—

(i) cash or marketable securities, or both, in excess of the reasonably expected day-to-day working capital needs of such trade or business, and

(ii) any other assets of the trade or business (other than assets used in the active conduct of a trade or business described in section 542(c)(2)), which produce, or are held for the production of, personal holding company income (as defined in subparagraph (C)) or income described in section 954(c)(1) (determined without regard to subparagraph (A) thereof and by substituting "trade or business" for "controlled foreign corporation").

In the case of a lease of property on a net cash basis by the decedent to a member of the decedent's family, income from such lease shall not be treated as personal holding company income for purposes of subparagraph (C), and such property shall not be treated as an asset described in subparagraph (D)(ii), if such income and property would not be so treated if the lessor had engaged directly in the activities engaged in by the lessee with respect to such property.

(3) RULES REGARDING OWNERSHIP.—

(A) OWNERSHIP OF ENTITIES.—For purposes of paragraph (1)(B)—

(i) CORPORATIONS.—Ownership of a corporation shall be determined by the holding of stock possessing the appropriate percentage of the total combined voting power of all classes of stock entitled to vote and the appropriate percentage of the total value of shares of all classes of stock.

(ii) PARTNERSHIPS.—Ownership of a partnership shall be determined by the owning of the appropriate percentage of the capital interest in such partnership.

(B) OWNERSHIP OF TIERED ENTITIES.—For purposes of this section, if by reason of holding an interest in a trade or business, a decedent, any member of the decedent's family, any qualified heir, or any member of any qualified heir's family is treated as holding an interest in any other trade or business—

(i) such ownership interest in the other trade or business shall be disregarded in determining if the ownership interest in the first trade or business is a qualified family-owned business interest, and

(ii) this section shall be applied separately in determining if such interest in any other trade or business is a qualified family-owned business interest.

(C) INDIVIDUAL OWNERSHIP RULES.—For purposes of this section, an interest owned, directly or indirectly, by or for an entity described in paragraph (1)(B) shall be considered as being owned proportionately by or for the entity's shareholders, partners, or beneficiaries. A person shall be treated as a beneficiary of any trust only if such person has a present interest in such trust.

Amendments

• 1998, IRS Restructuring and Reform Act of 1998 (P.L. 105-206)

P.L. 105-206, §6007(b)(3)(A):

Amended Code Sec. 2057(e)(2)(C) (as redesignated) by striking "(as defined in section 543(a))" and inserting "(as defined in section 543(a) without regard to paragraph (2)(B) thereof) if such trade or business were a corporation". **Effective** as if included in the provision of P.L. 105-34 to which it relates [**effective** for estates of decedents dying after 12-31-97.—CCH].

P.L. 105-206, §6007(b)(3)(B):

Amended Code Sec. 2057(e)(2)(D)(ii) (as redesignated) by striking "income of which is described in section 543(a) or" and inserting "personal holding company income (as defined in subparagraph (C)) or income described". **Effective** as if included in the provision of P.L. 105-34 to which it relates [**effective** for estates of decedents dying after 12-31-97.—CCH].

P.L. 105-206, §6007(b)(3)(C):

Amended Code Sec. 2057(e)(2) (as redesignated) by adding at the end a new flush sentence. **Effective** as if included in the provision of P.L. 105-34 to which it relates [**effective** for estates of decedents dying after 12-31-97.—CCH].

P.L. 105-206, §6007(b)(5)(A):

Amended Code Sec. 2057(e)(1) (as redesignated) by adding at the end a new flush sentence. **Effective** as if included in the provision of P.L. 105-34 to which it relates [**effective** for estates of decedents dying after 12-31-97.—CCH].

[Sec. 2057(f)]

(f) TAX TREATMENT OF FAILURE TO MATERIALLY PARTICIPATE IN BUSINESS OR DISPOSITIONS OF INTERESTS.—

(1) IN GENERAL.—There is imposed an additional estate tax if, within 10 years after the date of the decedent's death and before the date of the qualified heir's death—

(A) the material participation requirements described in section 2032A(c)(6)(B) are not met with respect to the qualified family-owned business interest which was acquired (or passed) from the decedent,

(B) the qualified heir disposes of any portion of a qualified family-owned business interest (other than by a disposition to a member of the qualified heir's family or through a qualified conservation contribution under section 170(h)),

(C) the qualified heir loses United States citizenship (within the meaning of section 877) or with respect to whom an event described in subparagraph (A) or (B) of section 877(e)(1) occurs, and such heir does not comply with the requirements of subsection (g), or

(D) the principal place of business of a trade or business of the qualified family-owned business interest ceases to be located in the United States.

(2) ADDITIONAL ESTATE TAX.—

(A) IN GENERAL.—The amount of the additional estate tax imposed by paragraph (1) shall be equal to—

(i) the applicable percentage of the adjusted tax difference attributable to the qualified family-owned business interest, plus

(ii) interest on the amount determined under clause (i) at the underpayment rate established under section 6621 for the period beginning on the date the estate tax liability was due under this chapter and ending on the date such additional estate tax is due.

(B) APPLICABLE PERCENTAGE.—For purposes of this paragraph, the applicable percentage shall be determined under the following table:

If the event described in paragraph (1) occurs in the following year of material participation:	*The applicable percentage is:*
1 through 6	100
7	80
8	60
9	40
10	20

(C) ADJUSTED TAX DIFFERENCE.—For purposes of subparagraph (A)—

(i) IN GENERAL.—The adjusted tax difference attributable to a qualified family-owned business interest is the amount which bears the same ratio to the adjusted tax difference with respect to the estate (determined under clause (ii)) as the value of such interest bears to the value of all qualified family-owned business interests described in subsection (b)(2).

(ii) ADJUSTED TAX DIFFERENCE WITH RESPECT TO THE ESTATE.—For purposes of clause (i), the term "adjusted tax difference with respect to the estate" means the excess of what would have been the estate tax liability but for the election under this section over the estate tax liability. For purposes of this clause, the term "estate tax liability" means the tax imposed by section 2001 reduced by the credits allowable against such tax.

(3) USE IN TRADE OR BUSINESS BY FAMILY MEMBERS.—A qualified heir shall not be treated as disposing of an interest described in subsection (e)(1)(A) by reason of ceasing to be engaged in a trade or business so long as the property to which such interest relates is used in a trade or business by any member of such individual's family.

Amendments

• 1998, IRS Restructuring and Reform Act of 1998 (P.L. 105-206)

P.L. 105-206, §6007(b)(4)(A)-(B):

Amended Code Sec. 2057(f)(2) (as redesignated) by striking "(as determined under rules similar to the rules of section 2032A(c)(2)(B))" before ", plus", and by adding at the end a new subparagraph (C). **Effective** as if included in the provision of P.L. 105-34 to which it relates [**effective** for estates of decedents dying after 12-31-97.—CCH].

P.L. 105-206, §6007(b)(5)(B):

Amended Code Sec. 2057(f) (as redesignated) by adding at the end a new paragraph (3). **Effective** as if included in the provision of P.L. 105-34 to which it relates [**effective** for estates of decedents dying after 12-31-97.—CCH].

[Sec. 2057(g)]

(g) SECURITY REQUIREMENTS FOR NONCITIZEN QUALIFIED HEIRS.—

(1) IN GENERAL.—Except upon the application of subparagraph (F) of subsection (i)(3), if a qualified heir is not a citizen of the United States, any interest under this section passing to or acquired by such heir (including any interest held by such heir at a time described in subsection (f)(1)(C)) shall be treated as a qualified family-owned business inter-

est only if the interest passes or is acquired (or is held) in a qualified trust.

(2) QUALIFIED TRUST.—The term "qualified trust" means a trust—

(A) which is organized under, and governed by, the laws of the United States or a State, and

(B) except as otherwise provided in regulations, with respect to which the trust instrument requires that at least 1 trustee of the trust be an individual citizen of the United States or a domestic corporation.

Amendments

• 1998, IRS Restructuring and Reform Act of 1998 (P.L. 105-206)

P.L. 105-206, §6007(b)(6):

Amended Code Sec. 2057(g)(1) (as redesignated) by striking "or (M)" after "subparagraph (F)". **Effective** as if included in the provision of P.L. 105-34 to which it relates [**effective** for estates of decedents dying after 12-31-97.—CCH].

[Sec. 2057(h)]

(h) AGREEMENT.—The agreement referred to in this subsection is a written agreement signed by each person in being who has an interest (whether or not in possession) in any property designated in such agreement consenting to the application of subsection (f) with respect to such property.

[Sec. 2057(i)]

(i) OTHER DEFINITIONS AND APPLICABLE RULES.—For purposes of this section—

(1) QUALIFIED HEIR.—The term "qualified heir"—

(A) has the meaning given to such term by section 2032A(e)(1), and

(B) includes any active employee of the trade or business to which the qualified family-owned business interest relates if such employee has been employed by such trade or business for a period of at least 10 years before the date of the decedent's death.

(2) MEMBER OF THE FAMILY.—The term "member of the family" has the meaning given to such term by section 2032A(e)(2).

(3) APPLICABLE RULES.—Rules similar to the following rules shall apply:

(A) Section 2032A(b)(4) (relating to decedents who are retired or disabled).

(B) Section 2032A(b)(5) (relating to special rules for surviving spouses).

(C) Section 2032A(c)(2)(D) (relating to partial dispositions).

(D) Section 2032A(c)(3) (relating to only 1 additional tax imposed with respect to any 1 portion).

(E) Section 2032A(c)(4) (relating to due date).

(F) Section 2032A(c)(5) (relating to liability for tax; furnishing of bond).

(G) Section 2032A(c)(7) (relating to no tax if use begins within 2 years; active management by eligible qualified heir treated as material participation).

(H) Paragraphs (1) and (3) of section 2032A(d) (relating to election; agreement).

(I) Section 2032A(e)(10) (relating to community property).

(J) Section 2032A(e)(14) (relating to treatment of replacement property acquired in section 1031 or 1033 transactions).

(K) Section 2032A(f) (relating to statute of limitations).

(L) Section 2032A(g) (relating to application to interests in partnerships, corporations, and trusts).

(M) Subsections (h) and (i) of section 2032A.

(N) Section 6166(b)(3) (relating to farmhouses and certain other structures taken into account).

(O) Subparagraphs (B), (C), and (D) of section 6166(g)(1) (relating to acceleration of payment).

(P) Section 6324B (relating to special lien for additional estate tax).

Amendments

• 1998, IRS Restructuring and Reform Act of 1998 (P.L. 105-206)

P.L. 105-206, §6007(b)(1)(A):

Amended Code Sec. 2033A by moving it to the end of part IV of subchapter A of chapter 11 and redesignating it as Code Sec. 2057. **Effective** as if included in the provision of P.L. 105-34 to which it relates [**effective** for estates of decedents dying after 12-31-97.—CCH].

P.L. 105-206, §6007(b)(7):

Amended Code Sec. 2057(i)(3) (as redesignated) by redesignating subparagraphs (L), (M), and (N) as subparagraphs (N), (O), and (P), respectively, and by inserting after subparagraph (K) new subparagraphs (L) and (M). **Effective** as if included in the provision of P.L. 105-34 to which it relates [**effective** for estates of decedents dying after 12-31-97.—CCH].

• 1997, Taxpayer Relief Act of 1997 (P.L. 105-34)

P.L. 105-34, §502(a):

Amended part III of subchapter A of chapter 11 by inserting after Code Sec. 2033 a new Code Sec. 2033A. **Effective** for estates of decedents dying after 12-31-97.

[Sec. 2057(j)]

(j) TERMINATION.—This section shall not apply to the estates of decedents dying after December 31, 2003.

Amendments

• 2013, American Taxpayer Relief Act of 2012 (P.L. 112-240)

P.L. 112-240, §101(a)(1) and (3), provides:

SEC. 101. PERMANENT EXTENSION AND MODIFICATION OF 2001 TAX RELIEF.

(a) PERMANENT EXTENSION.—

(1) IN GENERAL.—The Economic Growth and Tax Relief Reconciliation Act of 2001 is amended by striking title IX.

* * *

(3) EFFECTIVE DATE.—The amendments made by this subsection shall apply to taxable, plan, or limitation years beginning after December 31, 2012, and estates of decedents dying, gifts made, or generation skipping transfers after December 31, 2012.

• 2001, Economic Growth and Tax Relief Reconciliation Act of 2001 (P.L. 107-16)

P.L. 107-16, §521(d):

Amended Code Sec. 2057 by adding at the end a new subsection (j). **Effective** for estates of decedents dying, and generation-skipping transfers, after 12-31-2003.

P.L. 107-16, §901(a)-(b), as amended by P.L. 111-312, §101(a)(1), provides [but see P.L. 112-240, §101(a)(1) and (3), above]:

SEC. 901. SUNSET OF PROVISIONS OF ACT.

(a) IN GENERAL.—All provisions of, and amendments made by, this Act shall not apply—

(1) to taxable, plan, or limitation years beginning after December 31, 2012, or

(2) in the case of title V, to estates of decedents dying, gifts made, or generation skipping transfers, after December 31, 2012.

(b) APPLICATION OF CERTAIN LAWS.—The Internal Revenue Code of 1986 and the Employee Retirement Income Security Act of 1974 shall be applied and administered to years, estates, gifts, and transfers described in subsection (a) as if the provisions and amendments described in subsection (a) had never been enacted.

[Sec. 2057—Repealed]

Amendments

• 1989, Omnibus Budget Reconciliation Act of 1989 (P.L. 101-239)

P.L. 101-239, §7304(a)(1):

Repealed Code Sec. 2057. **Effective** for estates of decedents dying after 12-19-89. Prior to repeal, Code Sec. 2057 read as follows:

SEC. 2057. SALES OF EMPLOYER SECURITIES TO EMPLOYEE STOCK OWNERSHIP PLANS OR WORKER-OWNED COOPERATIVES.

(a) GENERAL RULE.—For purposes of the tax imposed by section 2001, the value of the taxable estate shall be determined by deducting from the value of the gross estate an amount equal to 50 percent of the proceeds of any sale of any qualified employer securities to—

(1) an employee stock ownership plan, or

(2) an eligible worker-owned cooperative.

(b) LIMITATIONS.—

(1) MAXIMUM REDUCTION IN TAX LIABILITY.—The amount allowable as a deduction under subsection (a) shall not exceed the amount which would result in an aggregate reduction in the tax imposed by section 2001 (determined without regard to any credit allowable against such tax) equal to $750,000.

(2) DEDUCTION SHALL NOT EXCEED 50 PERCENT OF TAXABLE ESTATE.—The amount of the deduction allowable under subsection (a) shall not exceed 50 percent of the taxable estate (determined without regard to this section).

(c) LIMITATIONS ON PROCEEDS WHICH MAY BE TAKEN INTO ACCOUNT.—

(1) DISPOSITIONS BY PLAN OR COOPERATIVE WITHIN 1 YEAR OF SALE.—

(A) IN GENERAL.—Proceeds from a sale which are taken into account under subsection (a) shall be reduced (but not below zero) by the net sale amount.

(B) NET SALE AMOUNT.—For purposes of subparagraph (A), the term "net sale amount" means the excess (if any) of—

(i) the proceeds of the plan or cooperative from the disposition of employer securities during the 1-year period immediately preceding such sale, over

(ii) the cost of employer securities purchased by such plan or cooperative during such 1-year period.

(C) EXCEPTIONS.—For purposes of subparagraph (B)(i), there shall not be taken into account any proceeds of a plan or cooperative from a disposition described in section 4978A(e).

(D) AGGREGATION RULES.—For purposes of this paragraph, all employee stock ownership plans maintained by an employer shall be treated as 1 plan.

(2) SECURITIES MUST BE ACQUIRED BY PLAN FROM ASSETS WHICH ARE NOT TRANSFERRED ASSETS.—

(A) IN GENERAL.—Proceeds from a sale shall not be taken into account under subsection (a) to the extent that such proceeds (as under paragraph (1)) are attributable to transferred assets. For purposes of the preceding sentence, all assets of a plan or cooperative (other than qualified employer securities) shall be treated as first acquired out of transferred assets.

(B) TRANSFERRED ASSETS.—For purposes of subparagraph (A)—

(i) IN GENERAL.—The term "transferred assets" means assets of an employee stock ownership plan which—

(I) are attributable to assets held by a plan exempt from tax under section 501(a) and meeting the requirements of section 401(a) (other than an employee stock ownership plan of the employer), or

(II) were held by the plan when it was not an employee stock ownership plan.

(ii) EXCEPTION FOR ASSETS HELD ON FEBRUARY 26, 1987.—The term "transferred assets" shall not include any asset held by the employee stock ownership plan on February 26, 1987.

(iii) SECRETARIAL AUTHORITY TO WAIVE TREATMENT AS TRANSFERRED ASSET.—The Secretary may provide that assets or a class of assets shall not be treated as transferred assets if the Secretary finds such treatment is not necessary to carry out the purposes of this paragraph.

(3) OTHER PROCEEDS.—The following proceeds shall not be taken into account under subsection (a):

(A) PROCEEDS FROM SALE AFTER DUE DATE FOR RETURN.—Any proceeds from a sale which occurs after the date on which the return of the tax imposed by section 2001 is required to be filed (determined by taking into account any extension of time for filing).

(B) PROCEEDS FROM SALE OF CERTAIN SECURITIES.—Any proceeds from a sale of employer securities which were received by the decedent—

(i) in a distribution from a plan exempt from tax under section 501(a) and meeting the requirements of section 401(a), or

(ii) as a transfer pursuant to an option or other right to acquire stock to which section 83, 422, 422A, 423, or 424 applies.

Any employer security the basis of which is determined by reference to any employer security described in the preceding sentence shall be treated as an employer security to which this subparagraph applies.

(d) QUALIFIED EMPLOYER SECURITIES.—

(1) IN GENERAL.—The term "qualified employer securities" means employer securities—

(A) which are issued by a domestic corporation which has no stock outstanding which is readily tradable on an established securities market,

(B) which are includible in the gross estate of the decedent,

(C) which would have been includible in the gross estate of the decedent if the decedent had died at any time during the shorter of—

(i) the 5-year period ending on the date of death, or

(ii) the period beginning on October 22, 1986, and ending on the date of death, and

(D) with respect to which the executor elects the application of this section.

Subparagraph (C) shall not apply if the decedent died on or before October 22, 1986.

(2) CERTAIN ASSETS HELD BY SPOUSE.—For purposes of paragraph (1)(C), any employer security which would have been includible in the gross estate of the spouse of a decedent during any period if the spouse had died during such period shall be treated as includible in the gross estate of the decedent during such period.

(3) PERIODS DURING WHICH DECEDENT NOT AT RISK.—For purposes of paragraph (1)(C), employer securities shall not be treated as includible in the gross estate of the decedent during any period described in section 246(c)(4).

(e) WRITTEN STATEMENT REQUIRED.—

(1) IN GENERAL.—No deduction shall be allowed under subsection (a) unless the executor of the estate of the decedent files with the Secretary the statement described in paragraph (2).

(2) STATEMENT.—A statement is described in this paragraph if it is a verified written statement—

(A) which is made by—

(i) the employer whose employees are covered by the employee stock ownership plan, or

(ii) any authorized officer of the eligible worker-owned cooperative, and

(B) which—

(i) acknowledges that the sale of employer securities to the plan or cooperative is a sale to which sections 4978A and 4979A apply, and

(ii) certifies—

(I) the net sale amount for purposes of subsection (c)(1), and

(II) the amount of assets which are not transferred assets for purposes of subsection (c)(2).

(f) OTHER DEFINITIONS AND SPECIAL RULES.—For purposes of this section—

(1) EMPLOYER SECURITIES.—The term "employer securities" has the meaning given such term by section 409(1).

(2) EMPLOYEE STOCK OWNERSHIP PLAN.—The term "employee stock ownership plan" means—

(A) a tax credit employee stock ownership plan (within the meaning of section 409(a)), or

(B) a plan described in section 4975(e)(7).

(3) ELIGIBLE WORKER-OWNED COOPERATIVE.—The term "eligible worker-owned cooperative" has the meaning given such term by section 1042(c).

(4) EMPLOYER.—Except to the extent provided in regulations, the term "employer" includes any person treated as an employer under subsections (b), (c), (m), and (o) of section 414.

(g) TERMINATION.—This section shall not apply to any sale after December 31, 1991.

• 1988, Technical and Miscellaneous Revenue Act of 1988 (P.L. 100-647)

P.L. 100-647, §1011B(g)(3):

Amended Code Sec. 2057(b)(1) by striking out "is" after "plan". **Effective** as if included in the provision of P.L. 99-514 to which it relates.

• 1987, Revenue Act of 1987 (P.L. 100-203)

P.L. 100-203, §10411(a):

Amended Code Sec. 2057 by redesignating subsections (d), (e), and (f) as subsections (e), (f), and (g), respectively, and by inserting after subsection (c) new subsection (d). **Effective** as if included in the amendments made by section 1172 of P.L. 99-514.

P.L. 100-203, §10412(a):

Amended Code Sec. 2057. **Effective**, generally, for sales after 2-26-87. However, see Act Sec. 10412(b)(2)-(4), below, for special provisions. Prior to amendment, Code Sec. 2057 read as follows:

SEC. 2057. SALES OF EMPLOYER SECURITIES TO EMPLOYEE STOCK OWNERSHIP PLANS OR WORKER-OWNED COOPERATIVES.

(a) GENERAL RULE.—For purposes of the tax imposed by section 2001, the value of the taxable estate shall be determined by deducting from the value of the gross estate an amount equal to 50 percent of the qualified proceeds of a qualified sale of employer securities.

(b) QUALIFIED SALE.—For purposes of this section, the term "qualified sale" means any sale of employer securities by the executor of an estate to—

(1) an employee stock ownership plan described in section 4975(e)(7), or

(2) an eligible worker-owned cooperative (within the meaning of section 1042(c)).

(c) QUALIFIED PROCEEDS.—For purposes of this section—

(1) IN GENERAL.—The term "qualified proceeds" means the amount received by the estate from the sale of employer securities at any time before the date on which the return of the tax imposed by section 2001 is required to be filed (including any extensions).

(2) PROCEEDS FROM CERTAIN SECURITIES NOT QUALIFIED.—The term "qualified proceeds" shall not include the proceeds from the sale of any employer securities if such securities were received by the decedent—

(A) in a distribution from a plan exempt from tax under section 501(a) which meets the requirements of section 401(a), or

(B) as a transfer pursuant to an option or other right to acquire stock to which section 83, 422, 422A, 423, or 424 applies.

(d) QUALIFED PROCEEDS FROM QUALIFIED SALES.—

(1) IN GENERAL.—For purposes of this section, the proceeds of a sale of employer securities by an executor to an employee stock ownership plan or an eligible worker-owned cooperative shall not be treated as qualified proceeds from a qualified sale unless—

(A) the decedent directly owned the securities immediately before death, and

(B) after the sale, the employer securities—

(i) are allocated to participants, or

(ii) are held for future allocation in connection with—

(I) an exempt loan under the rules of section 4975, or

(II) a transfer of assets under the rules of section 4980(c)(3).

(2) NO SUBSTITUTION PERMITTED.—For purposes of paragraph (1)(B), except as in the case of a bona fide business transaction (e.g., a substitution of employer securities in connection with a merger of employers), employer securities shall not be treated as allocated or held for future allocation to the extent that such securities are allocated or held for future allocation in substitution of other employer securities that had been allocated or held for future allocation.

(e) WRITTEN STATEMENT REQUIRED.—

(1) IN GENERAL.—No deduction shall be allowed under subsection (a) unless the executor of the estate of the decedent files with the Secretary the statement described in paragraph (2).

(2) STATEMENT.—A statement is described in this paragraph if it is a verified written statement of—

(A) the employer whose employees are covered by the plan described in subsection (b)(1), or

(B) any authorized officer of the cooperative described in subsection (b)(2),

consenting to the application of section 4979A with respect to such employer or cooperative.

(f) EMPLOYER SECURITIES.—For purposes of this section, the term "employer securities" has the meaning given such term by section 409(l).

(g) TERMINATION.—This section shall not apply to any sale after December 31, 1991.

P.L. 100-203, §10412(b)(2)-(4), provides:

(2) PROVISIONS TAKING EFFECT AS IF INCLUDED IN THE TAX REFORM ACT OF 1986.—The following provisions shall take effect as if included in the amendments made by section 1172 of the Tax Reform Act of 1986:

(A) Section 2057(f)(2) of the Internal Revenue Code of 1986, as added, by this section.

(B) The repeal of the requirement that a sale be made by the executor of an estate to qualify for purposes of section 2057 of such Code.

(3) DIRECT OWNERSHIP REQUIREMENT.—If the requirements of section 2057(d)(1)(B) of such Code (as modified by section 2057(d)(2) of such Code), as in effect after the amendments made by this section, are met with respect to any employer securities sold after October 22, 1986, and before February 27, 1987, such securities shall be treated as having been directly owned by the decedent for purposes of section 2057 of such Code, as in effect before such amendments.

(4) REDUCTION FOR SALES ON OR BEFORE FEBRUARY 26, 1987.—In applying the limitations of subsection (b) of section 2057 of such Code to sales after February 26, 1987, there shall be taken into account sales on or before February 26, 1987, to which section 2057 of such Code applied.

• 1986, Tax Reform Act of 1986 (P.L. 99-514)

P.L. 99-514, §1172(a):

Amended Part IV of Subchapter A of chapter 11 by adding new Code Sec. 2057 at the end thereof. **Effective** for sales after 10-22-86 with respect to which an election is made by the executor of an estate who is required to file the return of the tax imposed by the Internal Revenue Code of 1986 on a date (including extensions) after the date of the enactment of this Act.

[Sec. 2057—Repealed]

Amendments

• 1981, Economic Recovery Tax Act of 1981 (P.L. 97-34)

P.L. 97-34, §427(a):

Repealed Code Sec. 2057. **Effective** for estates of decedents dying after 12-31-81. Prior to its repeal, Code Sec. 2057 read as follows:

SEC. 2057. BEQUESTS, ETC., TO CERTAIN MINOR CHILDREN.

(a) ALLOWANCE OF DEDUCTION.—For purposes of the tax imposed by section 2001, if—

(1) the decedent does not have a surviving spouse, and

(2) the decedent is survived by a minor child who, immediately after the death of the decedent, has no known parent,

then the value of the taxable estate shall be determined by deducting from the value of the gross estate an amount equal to the value of any interest in property which passes or has passed from the decedent to such child, but only to the extent that such interest is included in determining the value of the gross estate.

(b) LIMITATION.—The aggregate amount of the deductions allowed under this section (computed without regard to this subsection) with respect to interests in property passing to any minor child shall not exceed an amount equal to $5,000 multiplied by the excess of 21 over the age (in years) which such child has attained on the date of the decedent's death.

(c) LIMITATION IN THE CASE OF LIFE ESTATE OR OTHER TERMINABLE INTEREST.—A deduction shall be allowed under this section with respect to any interest in property passing to a minor child only to the extent that a deduction would have been allowable under section 2056(b) if such interest had passed to a surviving spouse of the decedent. For purposes of this subsection, an interest shall not be treated as terminable solely because the property will pass to another person if the child dies before the youngest child of the decedent attains age 23.

(d) QUALIFIED MINORS' TRUST.—

(1) IN GENERAL.—For purposes of subsection (a), the interest of a minor child in a qualified minors' trust shall be treated as an interest in property which passes or has passed from the decedent to such child.

(2) QUALIFIED MINORS' TRUST.—For purposes of paragraph (1), the term "qualified minors' trust" means a trust—

(A) except as provided in subparagraph (d), all of the beneficiaries of which are minor children of the decedent,

(B) the corpus of which is property which passes or has passed from the decedent to such trust,

(C) except as provided in paragraph (3), all distributions from which to the beneficiaries of the trust before the termination of their interests will be pro rata,

(D) on the death of any beneficiary of which before the termination of the trust, the beneficiary's pro rata share of the corpus and accumulated income remains in the trust for the benefit of the minor children of the decedent who survive the beneficiary or vests in any person, and

(E) on the termination of which, each beneficiary will receive a pro rata share of the corpus and accumulated income.

(3) CERTAIN DISPROPORTIONATE DISTRIBUTIONS PERMITTED.—A trust shall not be treated as failing to meet the requirements of paragraph (2)(C) solely by reason of the fact that the governing instrument of the trust permits the making of disproportionate distributions which are limited by an ascertainable standard relating to the health, education, support, or maintenance of the beneficiaries.

(4) TRUSTEE MAY ACCUMULATE INCOME.—A trust which otherwise qualifies as a qualified minors' trust shall not be disqualified solely by reason of the fact that the trustee has power to accumulate income.

(5) COORDINATION WITH SUBSECTION (c).—In applying subsection (c) to a qualified minors' trust, those provisions of section 2056(b) which are inconsistent with paragraph (3) or (4) of this subsection shall not apply.

(6) DEATH OF BENEFICIARY BEFORE YOUNGEST CHILD REACHES AGE 23.—Nothing in this subsection shall be treated as disqualifying an interest of a minor child in a trust solely because such interest will pass to another person if the child dies before the youngest child of the decedent attains age 23.

(e) DEFINITIONS.—For purposes of this section—

(1) MINOR CHILD.—The term "minor child" means any child of the decedent who has not attained the age of 21 before the date of the decedent's death.

(2) ADOPTED CHILDREN.—A relationship by legal adoption shall be treated as replacing a relationship by blood.

(3) PROPERTY PASSING FROM THE DECEDENT.—The determination of whether an interest in property passes from the decedent to any person shall be made in accordance with section 2056(d).

• 1978, Revenue Act of 1978 (P.L. 95-600)

P.L. 95-600, §702(l)(1):

Redesignated Code Sec. 2057(d) as Code Sec. 2057(e) and added new Code Sec. 2057(d). **Effective** for estates of decedents dying after 1976.

P.L. 95-600, §702(l)(2):

Amended the last sentence of Code Sec. 2057(c) by substituting "23" for "21". **Effective** for estates of decedents dying after 1976.

• 1976, Tax Reform Act of 1976 (P.L. 94-455)

P.L. 94-455, §2007(a), (c):

Added Code Sec. 2057. **Effective** for estates of decedents dying after 12-31-76.

[Sec. 2058]

SEC. 2058. STATE DEATH TAXES.

[Sec. 2058(a)]

(a) ALLOWANCE OF DEDUCTION.—For purposes of the tax imposed by section 2001, the value of the taxable estate shall be determined by deducting from the value of the gross estate the amount of any estate, inheritance, legacy, or succession taxes actually paid to any State or the District of Columbia, in respect of any property included in the gross estate (not including any such taxes paid with respect to the estate of a person other than the decedent).

[Sec. 2058(b)]

(b) PERIOD OF LIMITATIONS.—The deduction allowed by this section shall include only such taxes as were actually paid and deduction therefor claimed before the later of—

(1) 4 years after the filing of the return required by section 6018, or

(2) if—

(A) a petition for redetermination of a deficiency has been filed with the Tax Court within the time prescribed in section 6213(a), the expiration of 60 days after the decision of the Tax Court becomes final,

(B) an extension of time has been granted under section 6161 or 6166 for payment of the tax shown on the return, or of a deficiency, the date of the expiration of the period of the extension, or

(C) a claim for refund or credit of an over-payment of tax imposed by this chapter has been filed within the time prescribed in section 6511, the latest of the expiration of—

(i) 60 days from the date of mailing by certified mail or registered mail by the Secretary to the taxpayer of a notice of the disallowance of any part of such claim,

(ii) 60 days after a decision by any court of competent jurisdiction becomes final with respect to a timely suit instituted upon such claim, or

(iii) 2 years after a notice of the waiver of disallowance is filed under section 6532(a)(3).

Notwithstanding sections 6511 and 6512, refund based on the deduction may be made if the claim for refund is filed within the period provided in the preceding sentence. Any such refund shall be made without interest.

Amendments

• 2013, American Taxpayer Relief Act of 2012 (P.L. 112-240)

P.L. 112-240, §101(a)(1) and (3), provides:

SEC. 101. PERMANENT EXTENSION AND MODIFICATION OF 2001 TAX RELIEF.

(a) PERMANENT EXTENSION.—

(1) IN GENERAL.—The Economic Growth and Tax Relief Reconciliation Act of 2001 is amended by striking title IX.

* * *

(3) EFFECTIVE DATE.—The amendments made by this subsection shall apply to taxable, plan, or limitation years beginning after December 31, 2012, and estates of decedents dying, gifts made, or generation skipping transfers after December 31, 2012.

• 2001, Economic Growth and Tax Relief Reconciliation Act of 2001 (P.L. 107-16)

P.L. 107-16, §532(b):

Amended part IV of subchapter A of chapter 11 by adding at the end a new Code Sec. 2058. **Effective** for estates of decedents dying, and generation-skipping transfers, after 12-31-2004.

P.L. 107-16, §901(a)-(b), as amended by P.L. 111-312, §101(a)(1), provides [but see P.L. 112-240, §101(a)(1) and (3), above]:

SEC. 901. SUNSET OF PROVISIONS OF ACT.

(a) IN GENERAL.—All provisions of, and amendments made by, this Act shall not apply—

(1) to taxable, plan, or limitation years beginning after December 31, 2012, or

(2) in the case of title V, to estates of decedents dying, gifts made, or generation skipping transfers, after December 31, 2012.

(b) APPLICATION OF CERTAIN LAWS.—The Internal Revenue Code of 1986 and the Employee Retirement Income Security Act of 1974 shall be applied and administered to years, estates, gifts, and transfers described in subsection (a) as if the provisions and amendments described in subsection (a) had never been enacted.

Subchapter B—Estates of Nonresidents Not Citizens

[Sec. 2101]

SEC. 2101. TAX IMPOSED.

[Sec. 2101(a)]

(a) IMPOSITION.—Except as provided in section 2107, a tax is hereby imposed on the transfer of the taxable estate (determined as provided in section 2106) of every decedent nonresident not a citizen of the United States.

Amendments

• 1976, Tax Reform Act of 1976 (P.L. 94-455)

P.L. 94-455, §2001(c)(1)(D), (d)(1):

Amended Code Sec. 2101(a). **Effective** for estates of decedents dying after 12-31-76. Prior to amendment, Code Sec. 2101(a) read as follows:

(a) RATE OF TAX.—Except as provided in section 2107, a tax computed in accordance with the following table is hereby imposed on the transfer of the taxable estate, determined as provided in section 2106, of every decedent nonresident not a citizen of the United States:

If the taxable estate is:	The tax shall be:
Not over $100,000	5% of the taxable estate.
Over $100,000 but not over $500,000	$5,000, plus 10% of excess over $100,000.
Over $500,000 but not over $1,000,000	$45,000, plus 15% of excess over $500,000.
Over $1,000,000 but not over $2,000,000	$120,000, plus 20% of excess over $1,000,000
Over $2,000,000	$320,000, plus 25% of excess over $2,000,000.

• 1966, Foreign Investors Tax Act of 1966 (P.L. 89-809)

P.L. 89-809, §108(a):

Amended Code Sec. 2101(a). **Effective** with respect to estates of decedents dying after 11-13-66, the date of enactment. Prior to amendment, Sec. 2101(a) read as follows:

(a) In General.—A tax computed in accordance with the table contained in section 2001 is hereby imposed on the transfer of the taxable estate, determined as provided in section 2106, of every decedent nonresident not a citizen of the United States dying after the date of enactment of this title.

[Sec. 2101(b)]

(b) COMPUTATION OF TAX.—The tax imposed by this section shall be the amount equal to the excess (if any) of—

(1) a tentative tax computed under section 2001(c) on the sum of—

(A) the amount of the taxable estate, and

(B) the amount of the adjusted taxable gifts, over

(2) a tentative tax computed under section 2001(c) on the amount of the adjusted taxable gifts.

For purposes of the preceding sentence, there shall be appropriate adjustments in the application of section 2001(c)(2) to reflect the difference between the amount of the credit provided under section 2102(c) and the amount of the credit provided under section 2010.

Amendments

• 2013, American Taxpayer Relief Act of 2012 (P.L. 112-240)

P.L. 112-240, §101(a)(1) and (3), provides:

SEC. 101. PERMANENT EXTENSION AND MODIFICATION OF 2001 TAX RELIEF.

(a) PERMANENT EXTENSION.—

(1) IN GENERAL.—The Economic Growth and Tax Relief Reconciliation Act of 2001 is amended by striking title IX.

* * *

(3) EFFECTIVE DATE.—The amendments made by this subsection shall apply to taxable, plan, or limitation years beginning after December 31, 2012, and estates of decedents dying, gifts made, or generation skipping transfers after December 31, 2012.

• 2002, Job Creation and Worker Assistance Act of 2002 (P.L. 107-147)

P.L. 107-147, §411(g)(2):

Amended Code Sec. 2101(b) by striking the last sentence. **Effective** as if included in the provision of P.L. 107-16 to which it relates [**effective** for estates of decedents dying, and gifts made, after 12-31-2001.—CCH]. Prior to being stricken, the last sentence of Code Sec. 2101(b) read as follows:

For purposes of the preceding sentence, there shall be appropriate adjustments in the application of section 2001(c)(2) to reflect the difference between the amount of the credit provided under section 2102(c) and the amount of the credit provided under section 2010.

• 2001, Economic Growth and Tax Relief Reconciliation Act of 2001 (P.L. 107-16)

P.L. 107-16, §901(a)-(b), as amended by P.L. 111-312, §101(a)(1), provides [but see P.L. 112-240, §101(a)(1) and (3), above]:

SEC. 901. SUNSET OF PROVISIONS OF ACT.

(a) IN GENERAL.—All provisions of, and amendments made by, this Act shall not apply—

(1) to taxable, plan, or limitation years beginning after December 31, 2012, or

(2) in the case of title V, to estates of decedents dying, gifts made, or generation skipping transfers, after December 31, 2012.

(b) APPLICATION OF CERTAIN LAWS.—The Internal Revenue Code of 1986 and the Employee Retirement Income Security Act of 1974 shall be applied and administered to years, estates, gifts, and transfers described in subsection (a) as if the provisions and amendments described in subsection (a) had never been enacted.

• 1993, Omnibus Budget Reconciliation Act of 1993 (P.L. 103-66)

P.L. 103-66, §13208(b)(3):

Amended Code Sec. 2101(b) by striking "section 2001(c)(3)" and inserting "section 2001(c)(2)". **Effective** in the case of decedents dying and gifts made after 12-31-92.

• 1989, Omnibus Budget Reconciliation Act of 1989 (P.L. 101-239)

P.L. 101-239, §7815(c):

Amended Code Sec. 2101(b) by adding at the end thereof a new sentence. **Effective** as if included in the provision of P.L. 100-647 to which it relates.

• 1988, Technical and Miscellaneous Revenue Act of 1988 (P.L. 100-647)

P.L. 100-647, §5032(a):

Amended Code Sec. 2101(b) by striking out "a tentative tax computed in accordance with the rate schedule set forth in subsection (d)" each place it appears and inserting in lieu thereof "a tentative tax computed under section 2001(c)". **Effective** for estates of decedents dying after the date of enactment of this Act.

• 1976, Tax Reform Act of 1976 (P.L. 94-455)

P.L. 94-455, §2001(c)(1)(D), (d)(1):

Amended Code Sec. 2101(b). **Effective** for estates of decedents dying after 12-31-76. Prior to amendment, Code Sec. 2101(b) read as follows:

(b) PROPERTY HELD BY ALIEN PROPERTY CUSTODIAN.—

For taxes in connection with property or interests transferred to or vested in the Alien Property Custodian, see section 36 of the Trading with the Enemy Act, as added by the Act of August 8, 1946 (60 Stat. 929; 50 U.S.C. App. 36).

[Sec. 2101(c)]

(c) ADJUSTMENTS FOR TAXABLE GIFTS.—

(1) ADJUSTED TAXABLE GIFTS DEFINED.—For purposes of this section, the term "adjusted taxable gifts" means the total amount of the taxable gifts (within the meaning of section 2503 as modified by section 2511) made by the decedent after December 31, 1976, other than gifts which are includible in the gross estate of the decedent.

(2) ADJUSTMENT FOR CERTAIN GIFT TAX.—For purposes of this section, the rules of section 2001(d) shall apply.

Amendments

• 1976, Tax Reform Act of 1976 (P.L. 94-455)

P.L. 94-455, §2001(c)(1)(D), (d)(1):

Added Code Sec. 2101(c). **Effective** for estates of decedents dying after 12-31-76.

[Sec. 2101(d)—Repealed]

Amendments

• 1988, Technical and Miscellaneous Revenue Act of 1988 (P.L. 100-647)

P.L. 100-647, §5032(c):

Repealed Code Sec. 2101(d). **Effective** for estates of decedents dying after 11-10-88. Prior to repeal, Code Sec. 2101(d) read as follows:

(d) RATE SCHEDULE.—

If the amount with respect to which the tentative tax to be computed is:	*The tentative tax is:*
Not over $100,000	6% of such amount.

Over $100,000 but not over $500,000	$6,000, plus 12% of excess over $100,000.
Over $500,000 but not over $1,000,000	$54,000, plus 18% of excess over $500,000.
Over $1,000,000 but not over $2,000,000	$144,000, plus 24% of excess over $1,000,000.
Over $2,000,000	$384,000, plus 30% of excess over $2,000,000.

• 1976, Tax Reform Act of 1976 (P.L. 94-455)

P.L. 94-455, §2001(c)(1)(D), (d)(1):

Added Code Sec. 2101(d). **Effective** for estates of decedents dying after 12-31-76.

[Sec. 2102]

SEC. 2102. CREDITS AGAINST TAX.

[Sec. 2102(a)]

(a) IN GENERAL.—The tax imposed by section 2101 shall be credited with the amounts determined in accordance with sections 2012 and 2013 (relating to gift tax and tax on prior transfers).

Amendments

• 2013, American Taxpayer Relief Act of 2012 (P.L. 112-240)

P.L. 112-240, §101(a)(1) and (3), provides:

SEC. 101. PERMANENT EXTENSION AND MODIFICATION OF 2001 TAX RELIEF.

(a) PERMANENT EXTENSION.—

(1) IN GENERAL.—The Economic Growth and Tax Relief Reconciliation Act of 2001 is amended by striking title IX.

* * *

(3) EFFECTIVE DATE.—The amendments made by this subsection shall apply to taxable, plan, or limitation years beginning after December 31, 2012, and estates of decedents dying, gifts made, or generation skipping transfers after December 31, 2012.

• 2001, Economic Growth and Tax Relief Reconciliation Act of 2001 (P.L. 107-16)

P.L. 107-16, §532(c)(7)(A):

Amended Code Sec. 2102(a). **Effective** for estates of decedents dying, and generation-skipping transfers, after 12-31-2004. Prior to amendment, Code Sec. 2102(a) read as follows:

(a) IN GENERAL.—The tax imposed by section 2101 shall be credited with the amounts determined in accordance with sections 2011 to 2013, inclusive (relating to State death taxes, gift tax, and tax on prior transfers), subject to the special limitation provided in subsection (b).

P.L. 107-16, §901(a)-(b), as amended by P.L. 111-312, §101(a)(1), provides [but see P.L. 112-240, §101(a)(1) and (3), above]:

SEC. 901. SUNSET OF PROVISIONS OF ACT.

(a) IN GENERAL.—All provisions of, and amendments made by, this Act shall not apply—

(1) to taxable, plan, or limitation years beginning after December 31, 2012, or

(2) in the case of title V, to estates of decedents dying, gifts made, or generation skipping transfers, after December 31, 2012.

(b) APPLICATION OF CERTAIN LAWS.—The Internal Revenue Code of 1986 and the Employee Retirement Income Security Act of 1974 shall be applied and administered to years, estates, gifts, and transfers described in subsection (a) as if the provisions and amendments described in subsection (a) had never been enacted.

[Sec. 2102(b)—Stricken]

Amendments

• 2013, American Taxpayer Relief Act of 2012 (P.L. 112-240)

P.L. 112-240, §101(a)(1) and (3), provides:

SEC. 101. PERMANENT EXTENSION AND MODIFICATION OF 2001 TAX RELIEF.

(a) PERMANENT EXTENSION.—

(1) IN GENERAL.—The Economic Growth and Tax Relief Reconciliation Act of 2001 is amended by striking title IX.

* * *

(3) EFFECTIVE DATE.—The amendments made by this subsection shall apply to taxable, plan, or limitation years beginning after December 31, 2012, and estates of decedents dying, gifts made, or generation skipping transfers after December 31, 2012.

• 2001, Economic Growth and Tax Relief Reconciliation Act of 2001 (P.L. 107-16)

P.L. 107-16, §532(c)(7)(B):

Amended Code Sec. 2102 by striking subsection (b) and by redesignating subsection (c) as subsection (b). **Effective** for estates of decedents dying, and generation-skipping transfers, after 12-31-2004. Prior to being stricken, Code Sec. 2102(b) read as follows:

(b) SPECIAL LIMITATION.—The maximum credit allowed under section 2011 against the tax imposed by section 2101 for State death taxes paid shall be an amount which bears the same ratio to the credit computed as provided in section 2011(b) as the value of the property, as determined for purposes of this chapter, upon which State death taxes were paid and which is included in the gross estate under section 2103 bears to the value of the total gross estate under section 2103. For purposes of this subsection, the term "State death taxes" means the taxes described in section 2011(a).

P.L. 107-16, §901(a)-(b), as amended by P.L. 111-312, §101(a)(1), provides [but see P.L. 112-240, §101(a)(1) and (3), above]:

SEC. 901. SUNSET OF PROVISIONS OF ACT.

(a) IN GENERAL.—All provisions of, and amendments made by, this Act shall not apply—

(1) to taxable, plan, or limitation years beginning after December 31, 2012, or

(2) in the case of title V, to estates of decedents dying, gifts made, or generation skipping transfers, after December 31, 2012.

(b) APPLICATION OF CERTAIN LAWS.—The Internal Revenue Code of 1986 and the Employee Retirement Income Security Act of 1974 shall be applied and administered to years, estates, gifts, and transfers described in subsection (a) as if the provisions and amendments described in subsection (a) had never been enacted.

[Sec. 2102(b)]

(b) UNIFIED CREDIT.—

(1) IN GENERAL.—A credit of $13,000 shall be allowed against the tax imposed by section 2101.

(2) RESIDENTS OF POSSESSIONS OF THE UNITED STATES.—In the case of a decedent who is considered to be a "nonresident not a citizen of the United States" under section 2209, the credit under this subsection shall be the greater of—

(A) $13,000, or

(B) that proportion of $46,800 which the value of that part of the decedent's gross estate which at the time of his death is situated in the United States bears to the value of his entire gross estate wherever situated.

(3) SPECIAL RULES.—

(A) COORDINATION WITH TREATIES.—To the extent required under any treaty obligation of the United States, the credit allowed under this subsection shall be equal to the amount which bears the same ratio to the applicable credit amount in effect under section 2010(c) for the calendar year which includes the date of death as the value of the part of the decedent's gross estate which at the time of his death is situated in the United States bears to the value of his entire gross estate wherever situated. For purposes of the preceding sentence, property shall not be treated as situated in the United States if such property is exempt from the tax imposed by this subchapter under any treaty obligation of the United States.

(B) COORDINATION WITH GIFT TAX UNIFIED CREDIT.—If a credit has been allowed under section 2505 with respect to any gift made by the decedent, each dollar amount contained in paragraph (1) or (2) or subparagraph (A) of this paragraph (whichever applies) shall be reduced by the amount so allowed.

(4) LIMITATION BASED ON AMOUNT OF TAX.—The credit allowed under this subsection shall not exceed the amount of the tax imposed by section 2101.

(5) APPLICATION OF OTHER CREDITS.—For purposes of subsection (a), sections 2012 and 2013 shall be applied as if the credit allowed under this subsection were allowed under section 2010.

Amendments

• 2013, American Taxpayer Relief Act of 2012 (P.L. 112-240)

P.L. 112-240, §101(a)(1) and (3), provides:

SEC. 101. PERMANENT EXTENSION AND MODIFICATION OF 2001 TAX RELIEF.

(a) PERMANENT EXTENSION.—

(1) IN GENERAL.—The Economic Growth and Tax Relief Reconciliation Act of 2001 is amended by striking title IX.

* * *

(3) EFFECTIVE DATE.—The amendments made by this subsection shall apply to taxable, plan, or limitation years beginning after December 31, 2012, and estates of decedents dying, gifts made, or generation skipping transfers after December 31, 2012.

• 2001, Economic Growth and Tax Relief Reconciliation Act of 2001 (P.L. 107-16)

P.L. 107-16, §532(c)(7)(B):

Amended Code Sec. 2102 by striking subsection (b) and by redesignating subsection (c) as subsection (b). **Effective** for estates of decedents dying, and generation-skipping transfers, after 12-31-2004. Prior to being stricken, Code Sec. 2102(b) read as follows:

(b) SPECIAL LIMITATION.—The maximum credit allowed under section 2011 against the tax imposed by section 2101 for State death taxes paid shall be an amount which bears the same ratio to the credit computed as provided in section 2011(b) as the value of the property, as determined for purposes of this chapter, upon which State death taxes were paid and which is included in the gross estate under section 2103 bears to the value of the total gross estate under section 2103. For purposes of this subsection, the term "State death taxes" means the taxes described in section 2011(a).

P.L. 107-16, §532(c)(7)(C):

Amended Code Sec. 2102(b)(5), as redesignated by Act Sec. 532(c)(7)(B), by striking "2011 to 2013, inclusive," and inserting "2012 and 2013". **Effective** for estates of decedents dying, and generation-skipping transfers, after 12-31-2004.

P.L. 107-16, §901(a)-(b), as amended by P.L. 111-312, §101(a)(1), provides [but see P.L. 112-240, §101(a)(1) and (3), above]:

SEC. 901. SUNSET OF PROVISIONS OF ACT.

(a) IN GENERAL.—All provisions of, and amendments made by, this Act shall not apply—

(1) to taxable, plan, or limitation years beginning after December 31, 2012, or

(2) in the case of title V, to estates of decedents dying, gifts made, or generation skipping transfers, after December 31, 2012.

(b) APPLICATION OF CERTAIN LAWS.—The Internal Revenue Code of 1986 and the Employee Retirement Income Security Act of 1974 shall be applied and administered to years, estates, gifts, and transfers described in subsection (a) as if the provisions and amendments described in subsection (a) had never been enacted.

• 1997, Taxpayer Relief Act of 1997 (P.L. 105-34)

P.L. 105-34, §501(a)(1)(E):

Amended Code Sec. 2102(c)(3)(A) by striking "$192,800" and inserting "the applicable credit amount in effect under section 2010(c) for the calendar year which includes the date of death". **Effective** for estates of decedents dying, and gifts made, after 12-31-97.

• 1996, Small Business Job Protection Act of 1996 (P.L. 104-188)

P.L. 104-188, §1704(f)(1):

Amended Code Sec. 2102(c)(3)(A) by adding at the end thereof a new sentence. **Effective** 8-20-96.

• 1988, Technical and Miscellaneous Revenue Act of 1988 (P.L. 100-647)

P.L. 100-647, §5032(b)(1)(A)-(B):

Amended Code Sec. 2102(c) by striking out "$3,600" in paragraph (1) and (2)(A) and inserting in lieu thereof "$13,000", and by striking out "$15,075" in paragraph (2)(B) and inserting in lieu thereof "$46,800". **Effective** for estates of decedents dying after 11-10-88.

P.L. 100-647, §5032(b)(2):

Amended Code Sec. 2102(c)(3). **Effective** for estates of decedents dying after 11-10-88. Prior to amendment, Code Sec. 2102(c)(3) read as follows:

(3) PHASE-IN OF PARAGRAPH (2)(B) AMOUNT.—In the case of a decedent dying before 1979, paragraph (2)(B) shall be applied—

(A) in the case of a decedent dying during 1977, by substituting "$8,480" for "$15,075",

(B) in the case of a decedent dying during 1978, by substituting "$10,080" for "$15,075",

(C) in the case of a decedent dying during 1979, by substituting "$11,680" for "$15,075", and

(D) in the case of a decedent dying during 1980, by substituting "$13,388" for "$15,075".

• 1976, Tax Reform Act of 1976 (P.L. 94-455)

P.L. 94-455, §2001(c)(1)(E), (d)(1):

Added Code Sec. 2102(c). **Effective** for estates of decedents dying after 12-31-76.

• 1966, Foreign Investors Tax Act of 1966 (P.L. 89-809)

P.L. 89-809, §108(b):

Amended Code Sec. 2102 by designating Sec. 2102 as Sec. 2102(a), amending it, and adding Sec. 2102(b). **Effective** with respect to estates of decedents dying after 11-13-66. Prior to amendment, Sec. 2102 read as follows:

SEC. 2102. CREDITS AGAINST TAX.

The tax imposed by section 2101 shall be credited with the amounts determined in accordance with sections 2011 to 2013, inclusive (relating to State death taxes, gift tax, and tax on prior transfers).

[Sec. 2103]

SEC. 2103. DEFINITION OF GROSS ESTATE.

For the purpose of the tax imposed by section 2101, the value of the gross estate of every decedent nonresident not a citizen of the United States shall be that part of his gross estate (determined as provided in section 2031) which at the time of his death is situated in the United States.

[Sec. 2104]

SEC. 2104. PROPERTY WITHIN THE UNITED STATES.

[Sec. 2104(a)]

(a) STOCK IN CORPORATION.—For purposes of this subchapter shares of stock owned and held by a nonresident not a citizen of the United States shall be deemed property within the United States only if issued by a domestic corporation.

[Sec. 2104(b)]

(b) REVOCABLE TRANSFERS AND TRANSFERS WITHIN 3 YEARS OF DEATH.—For purposes of this subchapter, any property of which the decedent has made a transfer, by trust or otherwise, within the meaning of sections 2035 to 2038, inclusive, shall be deemed to be situated in the United States, if so situated either at the time of the transfer or at the time of the decedent's death.

Amendments

• 1976, Tax Reform Act of 1976 (P.L. 94-455)

P.L. 94-455, §2001(c)(1)(L), (d)(1):

Substituted "AND TRANSFERS WITHIN 3 YEARS OF DEATH" for "AND TRANSFERS IN CONTEMPLATION OF DEATH" in the heading of Code Sec. 2104(b). **Effective** for estates of decedents dying after 12-31-76, except that the amendment shall not apply to transfers made before 1-1-77.

[Sec. 2104(c)]

(c) DEBT OBLIGATIONS.—For purposes of this subchapter, debt obligations of—

(1) a United States person, or

(2) the United States, a State or any political subdivision thereof, or the District of Columbia,

owned and held by a nonresident not a citizen of the United States shall be deemed property within the United States. Deposits with a domestic branch of a foreign corporation, if such branch is engaged in the commercial banking business, shall, for purposes of this subchapter, be deemed property within the United States. This subsection shall not apply to a debt obligation to which section 2105(b) applies.

Amendments

• 2014, Tax Technical Corrections Act of 2014 (P.L. 113-295)

P.L. 113-295, §221(a)(98), Division A:

Amended Code Sec. 2104(c) by striking "With respect to estates of decedents dying after December 31, 1969, deposits" and inserting "Deposits". **Effective** generally 12-19-2014. For a special rule, see Act Sec. 221(b)(2), Division A, below.

P.L. 113-295, §221(b)(2), Division A, provides:

(2) SAVINGS PROVISION.—If—

(A) any provision amended or repealed by the amendments made by this section applied to—

(i) any transaction occurring before the date of the enactment of this Act,

(ii) any property acquired before such date of enactment, or

(iii) any item of income, loss, deduction, or credit taken into account before such date of enactment, and

(B) the treatment of such transaction, property, or item under such provision would (without regard to the amendments or repeals made by this section) affect the liability for tax for periods ending after date of enactment, nothing in the amendments or repeals made by this section shall be construed to affect the treatment of such transaction, property, or item for purposes of determining liability for tax for periods ending after such date of enactment.

• 2010, (P.L. 111-226)

P.L. 111-226, §217(c)(3):

Amended Code Sec. 2104(c) in the last sentence by striking "or to a debt obligation of a domestic corporation" and all that follows and inserting a period. **Effective** generally for tax years beginning after 12-31-2010. For a grandfather rule, see Act Sec. 217(d)(2), below. Prior to being stricken, "or to a debt obligation of a domestic corporation" and all that followed in the last sentence of Code Sec. 2104(c) read as follows:

or to a debt obligation of a domestic corporation if any interest on such obligation, were such interest received by the decedent at the time of his death, would be treated by reason of section 861(a)(1)(A) as income from sources without the United States.

P.L. 111-226, §217(d)(2), provides:

(2) GRANDFATHER RULE FOR OUTSTANDING DEBT OBLIGATIONS.—

(A) IN GENERAL.—The amendments made by this section shall not apply to payments of interest on obligations issued before the date of the enactment of this Act.

(B) EXCEPTION FOR RELATED PARTY DEBT.—Subparagraph (A) shall not apply to any interest which is payable to a related person (determined under rules similar to the rules of section 954(d)(3)).

(C) SIGNIFICANT MODIFICATIONS TREATED AS NEW ISSUES.—For purposes of subparagraph (A), a significant modification of the terms of any obligation (including any extension of the term of such obligation) shall be treated as a new issue.

• 1996, Small Business Job Protection Act of 1996 (P.L. 104-188)

P.L. 104-188, §1704(t)(38):

Amended Code Sec. 2104(c) by striking "subparagraph (A), (C), or (D) of section 861(a)(1)" and inserting "section 861(a)(1)(A)". **Effective** 8-20-96.

• 1988, Technical and Miscellaneous Revenue Act of 1988 (P.L. 100-647)

P.L. 100-647, §1012(q)(11):

Amended Code Sec. 2104(c) by striking out "section 861(a)(1)(B), section 861(a)(1)(G), or section 861(a)(1)(H)" and inserting in lieu thereof "subparagraph (A), (C), or (D) of section 861(a)(1)". **Effective** as if included in the provision of P.L. 99-514 to which it relates.

• 1975 (P.L. 93-625)

P.L. 93-625, §9(b):

Amended the last sentence of Code Sec. 2104(c) by adding ", or section 861(a)(1)(H)". **Effective** with respect to estates of decedents dying after 1-3-75.

• 1973, Interest Equalization Tax Extension Act of 1973 (P.L. 93-17)

P.L. 93-17, §3(a):

Amended Code Sec. 2104(c) by adding "or section 861(a)(1)(G)" in the last sentence thereof. **Effective** with respect to estates of decedents dying after 12-31-72, except that in the case of the assumption of a debt obligation of a foreign corporation which is treated as issued under section 4912(c)(2) after 12-31-72, and before 1-1-74, the amendment applies with respect to estates of decedents dying after 12-31-73.

• 1969, Tax Reform Act of 1969 (P.L. 91-172)

P.L. 91-172, §435(b):

Amended the second sentence of Sec. 2104(c) by inserting "December 31, 1969" in lieu of "December 31, 1972".

• 1966, Foreign Investors Tax Act of 1966 (P.L. 89-809)

P.L. 89-809, §108(c):

Added Code Sec. 2104(c). **Effective** with respect to estates of decedents dying after 11-13-66.

[Sec. 2105]

SEC. 2105. PROPERTY WITHOUT THE UNITED STATES.

[Sec. 2105(a)]

(a) PROCEEDS OF LIFE INSURANCE.—For purposes of this subchapter, the amount receivable as insurance on the life of a nonresident not a citizen of the the United States shall not be deemed property within the United States.

[Sec. 2105(b)]

(b) BANK DEPOSITS AND CERTAIN OTHER DEBT OBLIGATIONS.—For purposes of this subchapter, the following shall not be deemed property within the United States.—

(1) amounts described in section 871(i)(3), if any interest thereon would not be subject to tax by reason of section 871(i)(1) were such interest received by the decedent at the time of his death,

(2) deposits with a foreign branch of domestic corporation or domestic partnership, if such branch is engaged in the commercial banking business,

(3) debt obligations, if, without regard to whether a statement meeting the requirements of section 871(h)(5) has been received, any interest thereon would be eligible for the exemption from tax under section 871(h)(1) were such interest received by the decedent at the time of his death, and

(4) obligations which would be original issue discount obligations as defined in section 871(g)(1) but for subparagraph (B)(i) thereof, if any interest thereon (were such interest received by the decedent at the time of his death) would not be effectively connected with the conduct of a trade or business within the United States.

Notwithstanding the preceding sentence, if any portion of the interest on an obligation referred to in paragraph (3) would not be eligible for the exemption referred to in paragraph (3) by reason of section 871(h)(4) if the interest were received by the decedent at the time of his death, then an appropriate portion (as determined in a manner prescribed by the Secretary) of the value (as determined for purposes of this chapter) of such debt obligation shall be deemed property within the United States.

Amendments

• 1997, Taxpayer Relief Act of 1997 (P.L. 105-34)

P.L. 105-34, §1304(a):

Amended Code Sec. 2105(b) by striking "and" at the end of paragraph (2), by striking the period at the end of paragraph (3) and inserting ", and", and by inserting after paragraph (3) a new paragraph (4). **Effective** for estates of decedents dying after 8-5-97.

• 1993, Omnibus Budget Reconciliation Act of 1993 (P.L. 103-66)

P.L. 103-66, §13237(b)(1)-(2):

Amended Code Sec. 2105(b) by striking "this subchapter" in the material preceding paragraph (1) and inserting "this subchapter, the following shall not be deemed property within the United States", and by striking paragraph (3) and all that follows down through the period at the end thereof and inserting new paragraph (3) and a flush sentence. **Effective** for estates of decedents dying after 12-31-93. Prior to amendment, paragraph (3) and all that followed read as follows:

(3) debt obligations, if, without regard to whether a statement meeting the requirements of section 871(h)(4) has been received, any interest thereon would be eligible for the exemption from tax under section 871(h)(1) were such interest received by the decedent at the time of his death,

shall not be deemed property within the United States.

• 1988, Technical and Miscellaneous Revenue Act of 1988 (P.L. 100-647)

P.L. 100-647, §1012(g)(4):

Amended Code Sec. 2105(b)(1) by striking out "section 861(c), if any interest thereon would be treated by reason of section 861(a)(1)(A) as income from sources without the United States" and inserting in lieu thereof "section 871(i)(3), if any interest thereon would not be subject to tax by reason of section 871(i)(1)". **Effective** as if included in the provision of P.L. 99-514 to which it relates.

• 1984, Deficit Reduction Act of 1984 (P.L. 98-369)

P.L. 98-369, §127(d):

Amended Code Sec. 2105(b). **Effective** for obligations issued after 7-18-84 with respect to estates of decedents dying after such date. Prior to amendment, Code Sec. 2105(b) read as follows:

(b) Certain Bank Deposits, Etc.—For purposes of this subchapter—

(1) amounts described in section 861(c) if any interest thereon, were such interest received by the decedent at the time of his death, would be treated by reason of section 861(a)(1)(A) as income from sources without the United States, and

(2) deposits with a foreign branch of a domestic corporation or domestic partnership, if such branch is engaged in the commercial banking business,

shall not be deemed property within the United States.

• 1966, Foreign Investors Tax Act of 1966 (P.L. 89-809)

P.L. 89-809, §108(d):

Amended Code Sec. 2105(b). **Effective** with respect to estates of decedents dying after 11-13-66, the date of enactment. Prior to amendment, Code Sec. 2105(b) read as follows:

(b) BANK DEPOSITS.—For purposes of this subchapter, any moneys deposited with any person carrying on the banking business, by or for a nonresident not a citizen of the United States who was not engaged in business in the United States at the time of his death shall not be deemed property within the United States.

[Sec. 2105(c)]

(c) WORKS OF ART ON LOAN FOR EXHIBITION.—For purposes of this subchapter, works of art owned by a nonresident not a citizen of the United States shall not be deemed property within the United States if such works of art are—

(1) imported into the United States solely for exhibition purposes,

(2) loaned for such purposes, to a public gallery or museum, no part of the net earnings of which inures to the benefit of any private stockholder or individual, and

(3) at the time of the death of the owner, on exhibition, or en route to or from exhibition, in such a public gallery or museum.

[Sec. 2105(d)]

(d) STOCK IN A RIC.—

(1) IN GENERAL.—For purposes of this subchapter, stock in a regulated investment company (as defined in section 851) owned by a nonresident not a citizen of the United States shall not be deemed property within the United States in the proportion that, at the end of the quarter of such investment company's taxable year immediately preceding a decedent's date of death (or at such other time as the Secretary may designate in regulations), the assets of the investment company that were qualifying assets with respect to the decedent bore to the total assets of the investment company.

(2) QUALIFYING ASSETS.—For purposes of this subsection, qualifying assets with respect to a decedent are assets that, if owned directly by the decedent, would have been—

(A) amounts, deposits, or debt obligations described in subsection (b) of this section,

(B) debt obligations described in the last sentence of section 2104(c), or

(C) other property not within the United States.

(3) TERMINATION.—This subsection shall not apply to estates of decedents dying after December 31, 2011.

Amendments

• 2010, Tax Relief, Unemployment Insurance Reauthorization, and Job Creation Act of 2010 (P.L. 111-312)

P.L. 111-312, §726(a):

Amended Code Sec. 2105(d)(3) by striking "December 31, 2009" and inserting "December 31, 2011". **Effective** for estates of decedents dying after 12-31-2009.

• 2008, Tax Extenders and Alternative Minimum Tax Relief Act of 2008 (P.L. 110-343)

P.L. 110-343, Division C, §207(a):

Amended Code Sec. 2105(d)(3) by striking "December 31, 2007" and inserting "December 31, 2009". **Effective** for decedents dying after 12-31-2007.

• 2004, American Jobs Creation Act of 2004 (P.L. 108-357)

P.L. 108-357, §411(b):

Amended Code Sec. 2105 by adding at the end a new subsection (d). **Effective** for estates of decedents dying after 12-31-2004.

[Sec. 2106]

SEC. 2106. TAXABLE ESTATE.

[Sec. 2106(a)]

(a) DEFINITION OF TAXABLE ESTATE.—For purposes of the tax imposed by section 2101, the value of the taxable estate of every decedent nonresident not a citizen of the United States shall be determined by deducting from the value of that part of his gross estate which at the time of his death is situated in the United States—

(1) EXPENSES, LOSSES, INDEBTEDNESS, AND TAXES.—That proportion of the deductions specified in sections 2053 and 2054 (other than the deductions described in the following sentence) which the value of such part bears to the value of his entire gross estate, wherever situated. Any deduction allowable under section 2053 in the case of a claim against the estate which was founded on a

promise or agreement but was not contracted for an adequate and full consideration in money or money's worth shall be allowable under this paragraph to the extent that it would be allowable as a deduction under paragraph (2) if such promise or agreement constituted a bequest.

(2) TRANSFERS FOR PUBLIC, CHARITABLE, AND RELIGIOUS USES.—

(A) IN GENERAL.—The amount of all bequests, legacies, devises, or transfers (including the interest which falls into any such bequest, legacy, devise, or transfer as a result of an irrevocable disclaimer of a bequest, legacy, devise, transfer, or power, if the disclaimer is made before the date prescribed for the filing of the estate tax return)—

(i) to or for the use of the United States, any State, any political subdivision thereof, or the District of Columbia, for exclusively public purposes;

(ii) to or for the use of any domestic corporation organized and operated exclusively for religious, charitable, scientific, literary, or educational purposes, including the encouragement of art and the prevention of cruelty to childlren or animals, no part of the net earnings of which inures to the benefit of any private stockholder or individual, which is not disqualified for tax exemption under section 501(c)(3) by reason of attempting to influence legislation, and which does not participate in, or intervene in (including the publishing or distributing of statements), any political campaign on behalf of (or in opposition to) any candidate for public office; or

(iii) to a trustee or trustees, or a fraternal society, order, or association operating under the lodge system, but only if such contributions of gifts are to be used within the United States by such trustee or trustees, or by such faternal society, order, or association, exclusively for religious, charitable, scientific, literary, or educational purposes, or for the prevention of cruelty to children or animals, such trust, fraternal society, order, or association would not be disqualified for tax exemption under section 501(c)(3) by reason of attempting to influence legislation, and such trustee or trustees, or such fraternal society, order, or association, does not participate in, or intervene in (including the publishing or distributing of statements), any political campaign on behalf of (or in opposition to) any candidate for public office.

(B) POWERS OF APPOINTMENT.—Property includible in the decedent's gross estate under section 2041 (relating to powers of appointment) received by a donee described in this paragraph shall, for purposes of this paragraph, be considered a bequest of such decedent.

(C) DEATH TAXES PAYABLE OUT OF BEQUESTS.—If the tax imposed by section 2101, or any estate, succession, legacy, or inheritance taxes, are, either by the terms of the will, by the law of the jurisdiction under which the estate is administered, or by the law of the jurisdiction imposing the particular tax, payable in whole or in part out of the bequest, legacies, or devises otherwise deductible under this paragraph, then the amount deductible under this paragraph shall be the amount of such bequests, legacies, or devises reduced by the amount of such taxes.

(D) LIMITATION ON DEDUCTION.—The amount of the deduction under this paragraph for any transfer shall not exceed the value of the transferred property required to be included in the gross estate.

(E) DISALLOWANCE OF DEDUCTIONS IN CERTAIN CASES.—The provisions of section 2055(e) shall be applied in the determination of the amount allowable as a deduction under this paragraph.

(F) CROSS REFERENCES.—

(i) For option as to time for valuation for purposes of deduction under this section, see section 2032.

(ii) For exemption of certain bequests for the benefit of the United States and for rules of construction for certain bequests, see section 2055(g).

(iii) For treatment of gifts and bequests to or for the use of Indian tribal governments (or their subdivisions), see section 7871.

(3) MARITAL DEDUCTION.—The amount which would be deductible with respect to property situated in the United States at the time of the decedent's death under the principles of section 2056.

(4) STATE DEATH TAXES.—The amount which bears the same ratio to the State death taxes as the value of the property, as determined for purposes of this chapter, upon which State death taxes were paid and which is included in the gross estate under section 2103 bears to the value of the total gross estate under section 2103. For purposes of this paragraph, the term "State death taxes" means the taxes described in section 2058(a).

Amendments

• 2018, Tax Technical Corrections Act of 2018 (P.L. 115-141)

P.L. 115-141, §401(a)(203), Div. U:

Amended Code Sec. 2106(a)(4) by inserting "section" before "2058(a)". **Effective** 3-23-2018.

• 2014, Tax Technical Corrections Act of 2014 (P.L. 113-295)

P.L. 113-295, §221(a)(95)(A)(ii), Division A:

Amended Code Sec. 2106(a)(4) by striking "section 2011(a)" and inserting "[section] 2058(a)". **Effective** generally 12-19-2014. For a special rule, see Act Sec. 221(b)(2), Division A, below.

P.L. 113-295, §221(b)(2), Division A, provides:

(2) SAVINGS PROVISION.—If—

(A) any provision amended or repealed by the amendments made by this section applied to—

(i) any transaction occurring before the date of the enactment of this Act,

(ii) any property acquired before such date of enactment, or

(iii) any item of income, loss, deduction, or credit taken into account before such date of enactment, and

(B) the treatment of such transaction, property, or item under such provision would (without regard to the amendments or repeals made by this section) affect the liability for tax for periods ending after date of enactment, nothing in the amendments or repeals made by this section shall be construed to affect the treatment of such transaction, property, or item for purposes of determining liability for tax for periods ending after such date of enactment.

• 2013, American Taxpayer Relief Act of 2012 (P.L. 112-240)

P.L. 112-240, §101(a)(1) and (3), provides:

SEC. 101. PERMANENT EXTENSION AND MODIFICATION OF 2001 TAX RELIEF.

(a) PERMANENT EXTENSION.—

(1) IN GENERAL.—The Economic Growth and Tax Relief Reconciliation Act of 2001 is amended by striking title IX.

* * *

(3) EFFECTIVE DATE.—The amendments made by this subsection shall apply to taxable, plan, or limitation years beginning after December 31, 2012, and estates of decedents dying, gifts made, or generation skipping transfers after December 31, 2012.

• 2001, Economic Growth and Tax Relief Reconciliation Act of 2001 (P.L. 107-16)

P.L. 107-16, §532(c)(8):

Amended Code Sec. 2106(a) by adding at the end a new paragraph (4). **Effective** for estates of decedents dying, and generation-skipping transfers, after 12-31-2004.

P.L. 107-16, §901(a)-(b), as amended by P.L. 111-312, §101(a)(1), provides [but see P.L. 112-240, §101(a)(1) and (3), above]:

SEC. 901. SUNSET OF PROVISIONS OF ACT.

(a) IN GENERAL.—All provisions of, and amendments made by, this Act shall not apply—

(1) to taxable, plan, or limitation years beginning after December 31, 2012, or

(2) in the case of title V, to estates of decedents dying, gifts made, or generation skipping transfers, after December 31, 2012.

(b) APPLICATION OF CERTAIN LAWS.—The Internal Revenue Code of 1986 and the Employee Retirement Income Security Act of 1974 shall be applied and administered to years, estates, gifts, and transfers described in subsection (a) as if the provisions and amendments described in subsection (a) had never been enacted.

• 1989, Omnibus Budget Reconciliation Act of 1989 (P.L. 101-239)

P.L. 101-239, §7815(d)(3):

Amended Code Sec. 2106(a)(3) by striking "ALLOWED WHERE SPOUSE IS CITIZEN" after "MARITAL DEDUCTION". **Effective** as if included in the provision of P.L. 100-647 to which it relates.

• 1988, Technical and Miscellaneous Revenue Act of 1988 (P.L. 100-647)

P.L. 100-647, §5033(c):

Amended Code Sec. 2106(a) by adding at the end thereof a new paragraph (3). **Effective** for estates of decedents dying after 11-10-88.

• 1987, Revenue Act of 1987 (P.L. 100-203)

P.L. 100-203, §10711(a)(4):

Amended Code Sec. 2106(a)(2)(A)(ii) and (iii) by striking out "on behalf of any candidate" and inserting in lieu thereof "on behalf of (or in opposition to) any candidate". **Effective** with respect to activities after 12-22-87.

• 1986, Tax Reform Act of 1986 (P.L. 99-514)

P.L. 99-514, §1422(c):

Amended Code Sec. 2106(a)(2)(F)(ii) by striking out "section 2055(f)" and inserting in lieu thereof "section 2055(g)". **Effective** for transfers and contributions made after 12-31-86.

• 1983 (P.L. 97-473)

P.L. 97-473, §202(b)(6):

Amended Code Sec. 2106(a)(2)(F). For the **effective** date, see the amendment note for P.L. 97-473, Act Sec. 204, following Code Sec. 7871. Prior to amendment, Code Sec. 2106(a)(2)(F) read as follows:

(F) CROSS REFERENCES.—

(1) For option as to time for valuation for purposes of deduction under this section, see section 2032.

(2) For exemption of certain bequests for the benefit of the United States and for rules of construction for certain bequests, see section 2055(f).

• 1976, Tax Reform Act of 1976 (P.L. 94-455)

P.L. 94-455, §1307(d)(1)(B):

Substituted "which is not disqualified for tax exemption under section 501(c)(3) by reason of attempting to influence legislation," for "no substantial part of the activities of which is carrying on propaganda, or otherwise attempting, to influence legislation," in Code Sec. 2106(a)(2)(A)(ii). **Effective** for estates of decedents dying after 12-31-76.

P.L. 94-455, §1307(d)(1)(C):

Substituted "such trust, fraternal society, order, or association would not be disqualified for tax exemption under section 501(c)(3) by reason of attempting to influence legislation," for "no substantial part of the activities of such trustee or trustees, or of such fraternal society, order, or association, is carrying on propaganda, or otherwise attempting, to influence legislation," in Code Sec. 2106(a)(2)(A)(iii). **Effective** for estates of decedents dying after 12-31-76.

P.L. 94-455, §1902(a)(5)(A):

Amended Code Sec. 2106(a)(2)(F). **Effective** for estates of decedents dying after 10-4-76. Prior to amendment, Code Sec. 2106(a)(2)(F) read as follows:

(F) OTHER CROSS REFERENCES.—

(1) For option as to time for valuation for purpose of deduction under this paragraph [section], see section 2032.

(2) For exemption of bequests to or for benefit of Library of Congress, see section 5 of the Act of March 3, 1925, as amended (56 Stat. 765; 2 U.S.C. 161).

(3) For construction of bequests for benefit of the library of the Post Office Department as bequests to or for the use of the United States, see section 2 of the Act of August 8, 1946 (60 Stat. 924; 5 U.S.C. 393).

(4) For exemption of bequests for benefit of Office of Naval Records and Library, Navy Department, see section 2 of the Act of March 4, 1937 (50 Stat. 25; 5 U.S.C. 419b).

(5) For exemption of bequests to or for benefit of National Park Service, see section 5 of the Act of July 10, 1935 (49 Stat. 478; 16 U.S.C. 19c).

(6) For construction of devises or bequests accepted by the Secretary of State under the Foreign Service Act of 1946 as devises or bequests to or for the use of the United States, see section 1021(e) of that Act (60 Stat. 1032; 22 U.S.C. 809).

(7) For construction of gifts or bequests of money accepted by the Attorney General for credit to "Commissary Funds, Federal Prisons" as gifts or bequests to or for the use of the United States, see section 2 of the Act of May 15, 1952, 66 Stat. 73, as amended by the Act of July 9, 1952, 66 Stat. 479 (31 U.S.C. 725s-4).

(8) For payment of tax on bequests of United States obligations to the United States, see section 24 of the Second Liberty Bond Act, as amended (59 Stat. 48, §4; 31 U.S.C. 757e).

(9) For construction of bequests for benefit of or use in connection with the Naval Academy as bequests to or for the use of the United States, see section 3 of the Act of March 31, 1944 (58 Stat. 135; 34 U.S.C. 1115b).

(10) For exemption of bequests for benefit of Naval Academy Museum, see section 4 of the Act of March 26, 1938 (52 Stat. 119; 34 U.S.C. 1119).

(11) For exemption of bequests received by National Archives Trust Fund Board, see section 7 of the National Archives Trust Fund Board Act (55 Stat. 582; 44 U.S.C. 300gg).

P.L. 94-455, § 1902(a)(12):

Deleted "Territory" in Code Sec. 2106(a)(2)(A)(i). **Effective** for gifts made after 12-31-76.

P.L. 94-455, § 2001(c)(1)(F):

Repealed paragraph (3) of Code Sec. 2106(a). **Effective** for estates of decedents dying after 12-31-76. Prior to repeal, paragraph (3) read as follows:

(3) EXEMPTION.—

(A) GENERAL RULE.—An exemption of $30,000.

(B) RESIDENTS OF POSSESSIONS OF THE UNITED STATES.—In the case of a decedent who is considered to be a "nonresident not a citizen of the United States" under the provisions of section 2209, the exemption shall be the greater of (i) $30,000, or (ii) that proportion of the exemption authorized by section 2052 which the value of that part of the decedent's gross estate which at the time of his death is situated in the United States bears to the value of his entire gross estate wherever situated.

• 1969, Tax Reform Act of 1969 (P.L. 91-172)

P.L. 91-172, § 201(d)(2):

Amended Code Sec. 2106(a)(2)(E). **Effective** in the case of decedents dying after 12-31-69. For exceptions, see Act Sec. 201(g)(4)(B)-(C), below.

P.L. 91-172, § 201(g)(4)(B)-(C), provides:

(B) Such amendments shall not apply in the case of property passing under the terms of a will executed on or before October 9, 1969—

(i) if the decedent dies before October 9, 1972, without having republished the will after October 9, 1969, by codicil or otherwise,

(ii) if the decedent at no time after October 9, 1969, had the right to change the portions of the will which pertain to the passing of the property to, or for the use of, an organization described in section 2055(a), or

(iii) if the will is not republished by codicil or otherwise.

(C) Such amendment shall not apply in the case of property transferred in trust on or before October 9, 1969—

(i) if the decedent dies before October 9, 1972, without having amended after October 9, 1969, the instrument governing the disposition of the property,

(ii) if the property transferred was an irrevocable interest to, or for the use of, an organization described in section 2055(a), or

(iii) if the instrument governing the disposition of the property was not amended by the decedent before October 9, 1972, and the decedent is on such date and at all times thereafter under a mental disability to change the disposition of the property.

Prior to amendment, Code Sec. 2106(a)(2)(E) read as follows:

"(E) Disallowance of Deductions in Certain Cases.—

"For disallowance of certain charitable, etc., deductions otherwise allowable under this paragraph [section]. See sections 503 and 681."

P.L. 91-172, § 201(d)(4)(B):

Amended subparagraphs (A)(ii) and (A)(iii) of Code Sec. 2106(a)(2). **Effective** with respect to gifts and transfers made after 12-31-69. Prior to amendment, subparagraphs (A)(ii) and (A)(iii) of Code Sec. 2106(a)(2) read as follows:

"(ii) to or for the use of any domestic corporation organized and operated exclusively for religious, charitable, scientific, literary, or educational purposes, including the encouragement of art and the prevention of cruelty to children or animals, no part of the net earnings of which inures to the benefit of any private stockholder or individual, and no substantial part of the activities of which is carrying on propaganda, or otherwise attempting, to influence legislation; or

"(iii) to a trustee or trustees, or a fraternal society, order, or association operating under the lodge system, but only if such contributions or gifts are to be used within the United States by such trustee or trustees, or by such fraternal society, order, or association, exclusively for religious, charitable, scientific, literary, or educational purposes, or for the prevention of cruelty to children or animals, and no substantial part of the activities of such trustee or trustees, or of such fraternal society, order, or association, is carrying on propaganda, or otherwise attempting, to influence legislation."

• 1966, Foreign Investors Tax Act of 1966 (P.L. 89-809)

P.L. 89-809, § 108(e):

Amended Code Sec. 2106(a)(3). **Effective** with respect to estates of decedents dying after 11-13-66. Prior to amendment, Sec. 2106(a)(3) read as follows:

(3) EXEMPTION.—

(A) GENERAL RULE.—An exemption of $2,000.

(B) RESIDENTS OF POSSESSIONS OF THE UNITED STATES.—In the case of a decedent who is considered to be a `nonresident not a citizen of the United States' under the provisions of section 2209, the exemption shall be the greater of (i) $2,000, or (ii) that proportion of the exemption authorized by section 2052 which the value of that part of the decedent's gross estate which at the time of his death is situated in the United States bears to the value of his entire gross estate wherever situated.

• 1960 (P.L. 86-779)

P.L. 86-779, § 4(c):

Amended Code Sec. 2106(a)(3). **Effective** for estates of decedents dying after 9-14-60. Prior to amendment, Code Sec. 2106(a)(3) read as follows:

(3) EXEMPTION.—An exemption of $2,000.

• 1958, Technical Amendments Act of 1958 (P.L. 85-866)

P.L. 85-866, § 30(d):

Amended Code Sec. 2106(a)(2)(E) by substituting "503" for "504". **Effective** 1-1-54.

[Sec. 2106(b)]

(b) CONDITION OF ALLOWANCE OF DEDUCTIONS.—No deduction shall be allowed under paragraphs (1) and (2) of subsection (a) in the case of a nonresident not a citizen of the United States unless the executor includes in the return required to be filed under section 6018 the value at the time of his death of that part of the gross estate of such nonresident not situated in the United States.

[Sec. 2106(c)—Repealed]

Amendments

• 1976, Tax Reform Act of 1976 (P.L. 94-455)

P.L. 94-455, § 1902(a)(5)(B), (c)(1):

Repealed Code Sec. 2106(c). **Effective** for estates of decedents dying after 10-4-76. Prior to repeal, Code Sec. 2106(c) read as follows:

(c) UNITED STATES BONDS.—For purposes of section 2103, the value of the gross estate (determined as provided in section 2031) of a decedent who was not engaged in business in the United States at the time of his death—

(1) shall not include obligations issued by the United States before March 1, 1941; and

(2) shall include obligations issued by the United States on or after March 1, 1941.

[Sec. 2107]

SEC. 2107. EXPATRIATION TO AVOID TAX.

[Sec. 2107(a)]

(a) TREATMENT OF EXPATRIATES.—A tax computed in accordance with the table contained in section 2001 is hereby imposed on the transfer of the taxable estate, determined as provided in section 2106, of every decedent nonresident not a citizen of the United States if the date of death occurs during a taxable year with respect to which the decedent is subject to tax under section 877(b).

Amendments

• 2004, American Jobs Creation Act of 2004 (P.L. 108-357)

P.L. 108-357, §804(a)(3):

Amended Code Sec. 2107(a). **Effective** for individuals who expatriate after 6-3-2004. Prior to amendment, Code Sec. 2107(a) read as follows:

(a) TREATMENT OF EXPATRIATES.—

(1) RATE OF TAX.—A tax computed in accordance with the table contained in section 2001 is hereby imposed on the transfer of the taxable estate, determined as provided in section 2106, of every decedent nonresident not a citizen of the United States if, within the 10-year period ending with the date of death, such decedent lost United States citizenship, unless such loss did not have for 1 of its principal purposes the avoidance of taxes under this subtitle or subtitle A.

(2) CERTAIN INDIVIDUALS TREATED AS HAVING TAX AVOIDANCE PURPOSE.—

(A) IN GENERAL.—For purposes of paragraph (1), an individual shall be treated as having a principal purpose to avoid such taxes if such individual is so treated under section 877(a)(2).

(B) EXCEPTION.—Subparagraph (A) shall not apply to a decedent meeting the requirements of section 877(c)(1).

• 1996, Health Insurance Portability and Accountability Act of 1996 (P.L. 104-191)

P.L. 104-191, §511(e)(1)(A):

Amended Code Sec. 2107(a). For the **effective** date, see Act Sec. 511(g), below. Prior to amendment, Code Sec. 2107(a) read as follows:

(a) RATE OF TAX.—A tax computed in accordance with the table contained in section 2001 is hereby imposed on the transfer of the taxable estate, determined as provided in section 2106, of every decedent nonresident not a citizen of the United States dying after November 13, 1966, if after March 8, 1965, and within the 10-year period ending with the date of death such decedent lost United States citizenship, unless such loss did not have for one of its principal purposes the avoidance of taxes under this subtitle or subtitle A.

P.L. 104-191, §511(g), provides:

(g) EFFECTIVE DATE.—

(1) IN GENERAL.—The amendments made by this section shall apply to—

(A) individuals losing United States citizenship (within the meaning of section 877 of the Internal Revenue Code of 1986) on or after February 6, 1995, and

(B) long-term residents of the United States with respect to whom an event described in subparagraph (A) or (B) of section 877(e)(1) of such Code occurs on or after February 6, 1995.

(2) RULING REQUESTS.—In no event shall the 1-year period referred to in section 877(c)(1)(B) of such Code, as amended by this section, expire before the date which is 90 days after the date of the enactment of this Act.

(3) SPECIAL RULE.—

(A) IN GENERAL.—In the case of an individual who performed an act of expatriation specified in paragraph (1), (2), (3), or (4) of section 349(a) of the Immigration and Nationality Act (8 U.S.C. 1481(a)(1)-(4)) before February 6, 1995, but who did not, on or before such date, furnish to the United States Department of State a signed statement of voluntary relinquishment of United States nationality confirming the performance of such act, the amendments made by this section and section 512 shall apply to such individual except that the 10-year period described in section 877(a) of such Code shall not expire before the end of the 10-year period beginning on the date such statement is so furnished.

(B) EXCEPTION.—Subparagraph (A) shall not apply if the individual establishes to the satisfaction of the Secretary of the Treasury that such loss of United States citizenship occurred before February 6, 1994.

• 1976, Tax Reform Act of 1976 (P.L. 94-455)

P.L. 94-455, §1902(a)(6), (c)(1):

Substituted "November 13, 1966" for "the date of enactment of this section" in Code Sec. 2107(a). **Effective** for estates of decedents dying after 10-4-76.

[Sec. 2107(b)]

(b) GROSS ESTATE.—For purposes of the tax imposed by subsection (a), the value of the gross estate of every decedent to whom subsection (a) applies shall be determined as provided in section 2103, except that—

(1) if such decedent owned (within the meaning of section 958(a)) at the time of his death 10 percent or more of the total combined voting power of all classes of stock entitled to vote of a foreign corporation, and

(2) if such decedent owned (within the meaning of section 958(a)), or is considered to have owned (by applying the ownership rules of section 958(b)), at the time of his death, more than 50 percent of—

(A) the total combined voting power of all classes of stock entitled to vote of such corporation, or

(B) the total value of the stock of such corporation,

then that proportion of the fair market value of the stock of such foreign corporation owned (within the meaning of section 958(a)) by such decedent at the time of his death, which the fair market value of any assets owned by such foreign corporation and situated in the United States, at the time of his death, bears to the total fair market value of all assets owned by such foreign corporation at the time of his death, shall be included in the gross estate of such decedent. For purposes of the preceding sentence, a decedent shall be treated as owning stock of a foreign corporation at the time of his death if, at the time of a transfer, by trust or otherwise, within the meaning of sections 2035 to 2038, inclusive, he owned such stock.

Amendments

• 1996, Health Insurance Portability and Accountability Act of 1996 (P.L. 104-191)

P.L. 104-191, §511(e)(1)(C):

Amended Code Sec. 2107(b)(2) by striking "more than 50 percent of" and all that follows and inserting "more than 50 percent of—" and new subparagraphs (A) and (B). For the **effective** date, see Act Sec. 511(g), in the amendment notes following Code Sec. 2107(a). Prior to amendment, Code Sec. 2107(b)(2) read as follows:

(2) if such decedent owned (within the meaning of section 958(a)), or is considered to have owned (by applying the ownership rules of section 958(b)), at the time of his death, more than 50 percent of the total combined voting power of all classes of stock entitled to vote of such foreign corporation,

[Sec. 2107(c)]

(c) CREDITS.—

(1) UNIFIED CREDIT.—

(A) IN GENERAL.—A credit of $13,000 shall be allowed against the tax imposed by subsection (a).

(B) LIMITATION BASED ON AMOUNT OF TAX.—The credit allowed under this paragraph shall not exceed the amount of the tax imposed by subsection (a).

(2) CREDIT FOR FOREIGN DEATH TAXES.—

(A) IN GENERAL.—The tax imposed by subsection (a) shall be credited with the amount of any estate, inheritance, legacy, or succession taxes actually paid to any foreign country in respect of any property which is included in the gross estate solely by reason of subsection (b).

(B) LIMITATION ON CREDIT.—The credit allowed by subparagraph (A) for such taxes paid to a foreign country shall not exceed the lesser of—

(i) the amount which bears the same ratio to the amount of such taxes actually paid to such foreign country as the value of the property subjected to such taxes by such foreign country and included in the gross estate solely by reason of subsection (b) bears to the value of all property subjected to such taxes by such foreign country, or

(ii) such property's proportionate share of the excess of—

(I) the tax imposed by subsection (a), over

(II) the tax which would be imposed by section 2101 but for this section.

(C) PROPORTIONATE SHARE.—In the case of property which is included in the gross estate solely by reason of subsection (b), such property's proportionate share is the percentage which the value of such property bears to the total value of all property included in the gross estate solely by reason of subsection (b).

(3) OTHER CREDITS.—The tax imposed by subsection (a) shall be credited with the amounts determined in accordance with subsections (a) and (b) of section 2102. For purposes of subsection (a) of section 2102, sections 2012 and 2013 shall be applied as if the credit allowed under paragraph (1) were allowed under section 2010.

Amendments

• 2013, American Taxpayer Relief Act of 2012 (P.L. 112-240)

P.L. 112-240, §101(a)(1) and (3), provides:

SEC. 101. PERMANENT EXTENSION AND MODIFICATION OF 2001 TAX RELIEF.

(a) PERMANENT EXTENSION.—

(1) IN GENERAL.—The Economic Growth and Tax Relief Reconciliation Act of 2001 is amended by striking title IX.

* * *

(3) EFFECTIVE DATE.—The amendments made by this subsection shall apply to taxable, plan, or limitation years beginning after December 31, 2012, and estates of decedents dying, gifts made, or generation skipping transfers after December 31, 2012.

• 2001, Economic Growth and Tax Relief Reconciliation Act of 2001 (P.L. 107-16)

P.L. 107-16, §532(c)(7)(C):

Amended Code Sec. 2107(c)(3) by striking "2011 to 2013, inclusive," and inserting "2012 and 2013". **Effective** for estates of decedents dying, and generation-skipping transfers, after 12-31-2004.

P.L. 107-16, §901(a)-(b), as amended by P.L. 111-312, §101(a)(1), provides [but see P.L. 112-240, §101(a)(1) and (3), above]:

SEC. 901. SUNSET OF PROVISIONS OF ACT.

(a) IN GENERAL.—All provisions of, and amendments made by, this Act shall not apply—

(1) to taxable, plan, or limitation years beginning after December 31, 2012, or

(2) in the case of title V, to estates of decedents dying, gifts made, or generation skipping transfers, after December 31, 2012.

(b) APPLICATION OF CERTAIN LAWS.—The Internal Revenue Code of 1986 and the Employee Retirement Income Security Act of 1974 shall be applied and administered to years, estates, gifts, and transfers described in subsection (a) as if the provisions and amendments described in subsection (a) had never been enacted.

• 1997, Taxpayer Relief Act of 1997 (P.L. 105-34)

P.L. 105-34, §1602(g)(6)(A):

Amended Code Sec. 2107(c)(2)(B)(i) by striking "such foreign country in respect of property included in the gross estate as the value of the property" and inserting "such foreign country as the value of the property subjected to such taxes by such foreign country and". **Effective** as if included in the provision of P.L. 104-191 to which such amendment relates [**effective**, generally, for individuals losing U.S. citizenship on or after 2-6-95, and long-term U.S. residents who end U.S. residency or begin foreign residency on or after 2-6-95.—CCH].

P.L. 105-34, §1602(g)(6)(B):

Amended Code Sec. 2107(c)(2)(C). **Effective** as if included in the provision of P.L. 104-191 to which such amendment relates [**effective**, generally, for individuals losing U.S. citizenship on or after 2-6-95, and long-term U.S. residents who end U.S. residency or begin foreign residency on or after 2-6-95.—CCH]. Prior to amendment, Code Sec. 2107(c)(2)(C) read as follows:

(C) PROPORTIONATE SHARE.—For purposes of subparagraph (B), a property's proportionate share is the percentage of the value of the property which is included in the gross estate solely by reason of subsection (b) bears to the total value of the gross estate.

• **1996, Health Insurance Portability and Accountability Act of 1996 (P.L. 104-191)**

P.L. 104-191, §511(e)(1)(B):

Amended Code Sec. 2107(c) by redesignating paragraph (2) as paragraph (3) and by inserting after paragraph (1) a new paragraph (2). For the **effective** date, see Act Sec. 511(g) in the amendment notes following Code Sec. 2107(a).

• **1976, Tax Reform Act of 1976 (P.L. 94-455)**

P.L. 94-455, §2001(c)(1)(E)(ii):

Amended Code Sec. 2107(c). **Effective** for estates of decedents dying after 12-31-76. Prior to amendment, Code Sec. 2107(c) read as follows:

(c) CREDITS.—The tax imposed by subsection (a) shall be credited with the amounts determined in accordance with section 2102.

[Sec. 2107(d)]

(d) BURDEN OF PROOF.—If the Secretary establishes that it is reasonable to believe that an individual's loss of United States citizenship would, but for this section, result in a substantial reduction in the estate, inheritance, legacy, and succession taxes in respect of the transfer of his estate, the burden of proving that such loss of citizenship did not have for one of its principal purposes the avoidance of taxes under this subtitle or subtitle A shall be on the executor of such individual's estate.

Amendments

• **1996, Health Insurance Portability and Accountability Act of 1996 (P.L. 104-191)**

P.L. 104-191, §511(f)(2)(A):

Amended Code Sec. 2107 by striking subsection (d) and by redesignating subsection (e) as subsection (d). For the **effective** date, see Act Sec. 511(g) in the amendment notes following Code Sec. 2107(a). Prior to being stricken, subsection (d) read as follows:

(d) EXCEPTION FOR LOSS OF CITIZENSHIP FOR CERTAIN CAUSES.—Subsection (a) shall not apply to the transfer of the estate of a decedent whose loss of United States citizenship resulted from the application of section 301(b), 350, or 355 of the Immigration and Nationality Act, as amended (8 U. S. C. 1401(b), 1482, or 1487).

[Sec. 2107(e)]

(e) CROSS REFERENCE.—

For comparable treatment of long-term lawful permanent residents who ceased to be taxed as residents, see section 877(e).

Amendments

• **1996, Health Insurance Portability and Accountability Act of 1996 (P.L. 104-191)**

P.L. 104-191, §511(f)(2)(A):

Amended Code Sec. 2107 by striking subsection (d), by redesignating subsection (e) as subsection (d), and by inserting after subsection (d) (as so redesignated) a new subsection (e). For the **effective** date, see Act Sec. 511(g) in the amendment notes following Code Sec. 2107(a).

• **1976, Tax Reform Act of 1976 (P.L. 94-455)**

P.L. 94-455, §1906(b)(13)(A):

Amended 1954 Code by substituting "Secretary" for "Secretary or his delegate" each place it appeared. **Effective** 2-1-77.

• **1966, Foreign Investors Tax Act of 1966 (P.L. 89-809)**

P.L. 89-809, §108(f):

Added Code Sec. 2107. **Effective** with respect to estates of decedents dying after 11-13-66.

[Sec. 2108]

SEC. 2108. APPLICATION OF PRE-1967 ESTATE TAX PROVISIONS.

[Sec. 2108(a)]

(a) IMPOSITION OF MORE BURDENSOME TAX BY FOREIGN COUNTRY.—Whenever the President finds that—

(1) under the laws of any foreign country, considering the tax system of such foreign country, a more burdensome tax is imposed by such foreign country on the transfer of estates of decedents who were citizens of the United States and not residents of such foreign country than the tax imposed by this subchapter on the transfer of estates of decedents who were residents of such foreign country,

(2) such foreign country, when requested by the United States to do so, has not acted to revise or reduce such tax so that it is no more burdensome than the tax imposed by this subchapter on the transfer of estates of decedents who were residents of such foreign country, and

(3) it is in the public interest to apply pre-1967 tax provisions in accordance with this section to the transfer of estates of decedents who were residents of such foreign country,

the President shall proclaim that the tax on the transfer of the estate of every decedent who was a resident of such foreign country at the time of his death shall, in the case of decedents dying after the date of such proclamation, be determined under this subchapter without regard to amendments made to sections 2101 (relating to tax imposed), 2102 (relating to credits against tax), 2106 (relating to taxable estate), and 6018 (relating to estate tax returns) on or after November 13, 1966.

Amendments

• 1976, Tax Reform Act of 1976 (P.L. 94-455)

P.L. 94-455, §1902(a)(6):

Substituted "November 13, 1966" for "the date of enactment of this section" in Code Sec. 2108(a). **Effective** for estates of decedents dying after 10-4-76.

[Sec. 2108(b)]

(b) ALLEVIATION OF MORE BURDENSOME TAX.—Whenever the President finds that the laws of any foreign country with respect to which the President has made a proclamation under subsection (a) have been modified so that the tax on the transfer of estates of decedents who were citizens of the United States and not residents of such foreign country is no longer more burdensome than the tax imposed by this subchapter on the transfer of estates of decedents who were residents of such foreign country, he shall proclaim that the tax on the transfer of the estate of every decedent who was a resident of such foreign country at the time of his death shall, in the case of decedents dying after the date of such proclamation, be determined under this subchapter without regard to subsection (a).

[Sec. 2108(c)]

(c) NOTIFICATION OF CONGRESS REQUIRED.—No proclamation shall be issued by the President pursuant to this section unless, at least 30 days prior to such proclamation, he has notified the Senate and the House of Representatives of his intention to issue such proclamation.

[Sec. 2108(d)]

(d) IMPLEMENTATION BY REGULATIONS.—The Secretary shall prescribe such regulations as may be necessary or appropriate to implement this section.

Amendments

• 1976, Tax Reform Act of 1976 (P.L. 94-455)

P.L. 94-455, §1906(b)(13)(A):

Amended 1954 Code by substituting "Secretary" for "Secretary or his delegate" each place it appeared. **Effective** 2-1-77.

• 1966, Foreign Investors Tax Act of 1966 (P.L. 89-809)

P.L. 89-809, §108(f):

Added Code Sec. 2108. **Effective** with respect to estates of decedents dying after 11-13-66.

Subchapter C—Miscellaneous

[Sec. 2201]

SEC. 2201. COMBAT ZONE-RELATED DEATHS OF MEMBERS OF THE ARMED FORCES, DEATHS OF ASTRONAUTS, AND DEATHS OF VICTIMS OF CERTAIN TERRORIST ATTACKS.

[Sec. 2201(a)]

(a) IN GENERAL.—Unless the executor elects not to have this section apply, in applying sections 2001 and 2101 to the estate of a qualified decedent, the rate schedule set forth in subsection (c) shall be deemed to be the rate schedule set forth in section 2001(c).

Amendments

• 2003, Military Family Tax Relief Act of 2003 (P.L. 108-121)

P.L. 108-121, §110(c)(2)(A):

Amended the heading of Code Sec. 2201 by inserting ", **DEATHS OF ASTRONAUTS**," after "**FORCES**". **Effective** for estates of decedents dying after 12-31-2002.

[Sec. 2201(b)]

(b) QUALIFIED DECEDENT.—For purposes of this section, the term "qualified decedent" means—

(1) any citizen or resident of the United States dying while in active service of the Armed Forces of the United States, if such decedent—

(A) was killed in action while serving in a combat zone, as determined under section 112(c), or

(B) died as a result of wounds, disease, or injury suffered while serving in a combat zone (as determined under section 112(c)), and while in the line of duty, by reason of a hazard to which such decedent was subjected as an incident of such service,

(2) any specified terrorist victim (as defined in section 692(d)(4)), and

(3) any astronaut whose death occurs in the line of duty.

Amendments

• 2003, Military Family Tax Relief Act of 2003 (P.L. 108-121)

P.L. 108-121, §110(c)(1):

Amended Code Sec. 2201(b) by striking "and" at the end of paragraph (1)(B), by striking the period at the end of paragraph (2) and inserting ", and", and by adding at the end a new paragraph (3). **Effective** for estates of decedents dying after 12-31-2002.

[Sec. 2201(c)]

(c) RATE SCHEDULE.—

If the amount with respect to which the tentative tax to be computed is:	*The tentative tax is:*
Not over $150,000	1 percent of the amount by which such amount exceeds $100,000.
Over $150,000 but not over $200,000	$500 plus 2 percent of the excess over $150,000.
Over $200,000 but not over $300,000	$1,500 plus 3 percent of the excess over $200,000.
Over $300,000 but not over $500,000	$4,500 plus 4 percent of the excess over $300,000.
Over $500,000 but not over $700,000	$12,500 plus 5 percent of the excess over $500,000.
Over $700,000 but not over $900,000	$22,500 plus 6 percent of the excess over $700,000.
Over $900,000 but not over $1,100,000	$34,500 plus 7 percent of the excess over $900,000.
Over $1,100,000 but not over $1,600,000	$48,500 plus 8 percent of the excess over $1,100,000.
Over $1,600,000 but not over $2,100,000	$88,500 plus 9 percent of the excess over $1,600,000.
Over $2,100,000 but not over $2,600,000	$133,500 plus 10 percent of the excess over $2,100,000.
Over $2,600,000 but not over $3,100,000	$183,500 plus 11 percent of the excess over $2,600,000.
Over $3,100,000 but not over $3,600,000	$238,500 plus 12 percent of the excess over $3,100,000.
Over $3,600,000 but not over $4,100,000	$298,500 plus 13 percent of the excess over $3,600,000.
Over $4,100,000 but not over $5,100,000	$363,500 plus 14 percent of the excess over $4,100,000.
Over $5,100,000 but not over $6,100,000	$503,500 plus 15 percent of the excess over $5,100,000.
Over $6,100,000 but not over $7,100,000	$653,500 plus 16 percent of the excess over $6,100,000.
Over $7,100,000 but not over $8,100,000	$813,500 plus 17 percent of the excess over $7,100,000.
Over $8,100,000 but not over $9,100,000	$983,500 plus 18 percent of the excess over $8,100,000.
Over $9,100,000 but not over $10,100,000	$1,163,500 plus 19 percent of the excess over $9,100,000.
Over $10,100,000	$1,353,500 plus 20 percent of the excess over $10,100,000.

[Sec. 2201(d)]

(d) DETERMINATION OF UNIFIED CREDIT.—In the case of an estate to which this section applies, subsection (a) shall not apply in determining the credit under section 2010.

Amendments

• 2017, Tax Cuts and Jobs Act (P.L. 115-97)

P.L. 115-97, §11026, provides:

For a special rule, see Act Sec. 11026 in the amendment notes for Code Sec. 112(c).

• 2002, Victims of Terrorism Tax Relief Act of 2001 (P.L. 107-134)

P.L. 107-134, §103(a):

Amended Code Sec. 2201. **Effective** for estates of decedents dying on or after 9-11-2001; and in the case of individuals dying as a result of the 4-19-95 terrorist attack, dying on or after 4-19-95. For a waiver of limitations, see Act Sec. 103(d)(2), below. Prior to amendment, Code Sec. 2201 read as follows:

SEC. 2201. MEMBERS OF THE ARMED FORCES DYING IN COMBAT ZONE OR BY REASON OF COMBAT-ZONE-INCURRED WOUNDS, ETC.

The additional estate tax as defined in section 2011(d) shall not apply to the transfer of the taxable estate of a citizen or resident of the United States dying while in active service as a member of the Armed Forces of the United States, if such decedent—

(1) was killed in action while serving in a combat zone, as determined under section 112(c); or

(2) died as a result of wounds, disease, or injury suffered, while serving in a combat zone (as determined under section 112(c)), and while in line of duty, by reason of a hazard to which he was subjected as an incident of such service.

P.L. 107-134, §103(b)(3):

Retroactively repealed paragraph (9) of section 532(c) of P.L. 107-16, and it never took effect.

P.L. 107-134, §103(d)(2), provides:

(2) WAIVER OF LIMITATIONS.—If refund or credit of any overpayment of tax resulting from the amendments made by this section is prevented at any time before the close of the 1-year period beginning on the date of the enactment of this Act by the operation of any law or rule of law (including res judicata), such refund or credit may nevertheless be made or allowed if claim therefor is filed before the close of such period.

• 2001, Economic Growth and Tax Relief Reconciliation Act of 2001 (P.L. 107-16)

P.L. 107-16, §532(c)(9)(A)-(B) (repealed by P.L. 107-134, §103(b)(3)):

Amended Code Sec. 2201 by striking "as defined in section 2011(d)" following "The additional estate tax", and by adding at the end a new flush sentence. **Effective** for estates of decedents dying, and generation-skipping transfers, after 12-31-2004.

P.L. 107-16, §901(a)-(b), as amended by P.L. 111-312, §101(a)(1), provides:

SEC. 901. SUNSET OF PROVISIONS OF ACT.

(a) IN GENERAL.—All provisions of, and amendments made by, this Act shall not apply—

(1) to taxable, plan, or limitation years beginning after December 31, 2012, or

(2) in the case of title V, to estates of decedents dying, gifts made, or generation skipping transfers, after December 31, 2012.

(b) APPLICATION OF CERTAIN LAWS.—The Internal Revenue Code of 1986 and the Employee Retirement Income Security Act of 1974 shall be applied and administered to years, estates, gifts, and transfers described in subsection (a) as if the provisions and amendments described in subsection (a) had never been enacted.

• 1999 (P.L. 106-21)

P.L. 106-21, §1(a)(4), (b) and (d)(1), provide:

SECTION 1. AVAILABILITY OF CERTAIN TAX BENEFITS FOR SERVICES AS PART OF OPERATION ALLIED FORCE.

(a) GENERAL RULE.—For purposes of the following provisions of the Internal Revenue Code of 1986, a qualified hazardous duty area shall be treated in the same manner as if it were a combat zone (as determined under section 112 of such Code):

* * *

(4) Section 2201 (relating to members of the Armed Forces dying in combat zone or by reason of combat-zone-incurred wounds, etc.).

* * *

(b) QUALIFIED HAZARDOUS DUTY AREA.—For purposes of this section, the term "qualified hazardous duty area" means any area of the Federal Republic of Yugoslavia (Serbia/Montenegro), Albania, the Adriatic Sea, and the northern Ionian Sea (above the 39th parallel) during the period (which includes the date of the enactment of this Act) that any member of the Armed Forces of the United States is entitled to special pay under section 310 of title 37, United States Code (relating to special pay: duty subject to hostile fire or imminent danger) for services performed in such area.

* * *

(d) EFFECTIVE DATES.—

(1) IN GENERAL.—Except as provided in paragraph (2), this section shall take effect on March 24, 1999.

• 1996 (P.L. 104-117)

P.L. 104-117, §1(a)(4), (b) and (e)(1), provide:

SECTION 1. TREATMENT OF CERTAIN INDIVIDUALS PERFORMING SERVICES IN CERTAIN HAZARDOUS DUTY AREAS.

(a) GENERAL RULE.—For purposes of the following provisions of the Internal Revenue Code of 1986, a qualified hazardous duty area shall be treated in the same manner as if it were a combat zone (as determined under section 112 of such Code):

* * *

(4) Section 2201 (relating to members of the Armed Forces dying in combat zone or by reason of combat-zone-incurred wounds, etc.).

* * *

(b) QUALIFIED HAZARDOUS DUTY AREA.—For purposes of this section, the term "qualified hazardous duty area" means Bosnia and Herzegovina, Croatia, or Macedonia, if as of the date of the enactment of this section any member of the Armed Forces of the United States is entitled to special pay under section 310 of title 37, United States Code (relating to special pay; duty subject to hostile fire or imminent danger) for services performed in such country. Such term includes any such country only during the period such entitlement is in effect. Solely for purposes of applying section 7508 of the Internal Revenue Code of 1986, in the case of an individual who is performing services as part of Operation Joint Endeavor outside the United States while deployed away from such individual's permanent duty station, the term "qualified hazardous duty area" includes, during the period for which such entitlement is in effect, any area in which such services are performed.

* * *

(e) EFFECTIVE DATE.—

(1) IN GENERAL.—Except as provided in paragraph (2), the provisions of and amendments made by this section shall take effect on November 21, 1995.

• 1975 (P.L. 93-597)

P.L. 93-597, §6(b):

Amended Code Sec. 2201 by deleting "during an induction period (as defined in sec. 112(c)(5))," that formerly appeared after the word "dying" and by amending the heading of the section. **Effective** 7-1-73. Prior to amendment, the heading read as follows: **"MEMBERS OF THE ARMED FORCES DYING DURING AN INDUCTION PERIOD."**.

[Sec. 2203]

SEC. 2203. DEFINITION OF EXECUTOR.

The term "executor" wherever it is used in this title in connection with the estate tax imposed by this chapter means the executor or administrator of the decedent, or, if there is no executor or administrator appointed, qualified, and acting within the United States, then any person in actual or constructive possession of any property of the decedent.

[Sec. 2204]

SEC. 2204. DISCHARGE OF FIDUCIARY FROM PERSONAL LIABILITY.

[Sec. 2204(a)]

(a) GENERAL RULE.—If the executor makes written application to the Secretary for determination of the amount of the tax and discharge from personal liability therefor, the Secretary (as soon as possible, and in any event within 9 months after the making of such application, or, if the application is made before the return is filed, then within 9 months after the return is filed, but not after the expiration of the period prescribed for the assessment of the tax in section 6501) shall notify the executor of the amount of the tax. The executor, on payment of the amount of which he is notified (other than any amount the time for payment of which is extended under section 6161, 6163, or 6166), and on furnishing any bond which may be required for any amount for which the time for payment is extended, shall be discharged from personal liability for any deficiency in tax thereafter found to be due and shall be entitled to a receipt or writing showing such discharge.

Amendments

• 1981, Economic Recovery Tax Act of 1981 (P.L. 97-34)

P.L. 97-34, §422(e)(3):

Amended Code Sec. 2204(a) by striking out "6166 or 6166A" and inserting "or 6166". **Effective** for estates of decedents dying after 12-31-81.

• 1976, Tax Reform Act of 1976 (P.L. 94-455)

P.L. 94-455, §1906(b)(13)(A):

Amended 1954 Code by substituting "Secretary" for "Secretary or his delegate" each place it appeared. **Effective** 2-1-77.

P.L. 94-455, §2004(f)(6):

Amended Code Sec. 2204(a) by substituting "6166 or 6166A" for "or 6166". **Effective** for estates of decedents dying after 12-31-76.

• 1970, Excise, Estate, and Gift Tax Adjustment Act of 1970 (P.L. 91-614)

P.L. 91-614, §101(d)(1):

Amended Code Sec. 2204. **Effective** with respect to decedents dying after 12-31-70. Prior to amendment, Code Sec. 2204 read as follows:

SEC. 2204. DISCHARGE OF EXECUTOR FROM PERSONAL LIABILITY.

"If the executor makes written application to the Secretary or his delegate for determination of the amount of the tax and discharge from personal liability therefor, the Secretary or his delegate (as soon as possible, and in any event within 1 year after the making of such application, or, if the application is made before the return is filed, then within 1 year after the return is filed, but not after the expiration of the period prescribed for the assessment of the tax in section 6501) shall notify the executor of the amount of the tax. The executor, on payment of the amount of which he is notified, shall be discharged from personal liability for any deficiency in tax thereafter found to be due and shall be entitled to a receipt or writing showing such discharge.

P.L. 91-614, §101(f):

Amended Code Sec. 2204(a) by substituting "9 months" for "1 year." **Effective** with respect to estates of decedents dying after 12-31-73.

[Sec. 2204(b)]

(b) FIDUCIARY OTHER THAN THE EXECUTOR.—If a fiduciary (not including a fiduciary in respect of the estate of a nonresident decedent) other than the executor makes written application to the Secretary for determination of the amount of any estate tax for which the fiduciary may be personally liable, and for discharge from personal liability therefor, the Secretary upon the discharge of the executor from personal liability under subsection (a), or upon the expiration of 6 months after the making of such application by the fiduciary, if later, shall notify the fiduciary (1) of the amount of such tax for which it has been determined the fiduciary is liable, or (2) that it has been determined that the fiduciary is not liable for any such tax. Such application shall be accompanied by a copy of the instrument, if any, under which such fiduciary is acting, a description of the property held by the fiduciary, and such other information for purposes of carrying out the provisions of this section as the Secretary may require by regulations. On payment of the amount of such tax for which it has been determined the fiduciary is liable (other than any amount the time for payment of which has been extended under section 6161, 6163, or 6166), and on furnishing any bond which may be required for any amount for which the time for payment has been extended, or on receipt by him of notification of a determination that he is not liable for any such tax, the fiduciary shall be discharged from personal liability for any deficiency in such tax thereafter found to be due and shall be entitled to a receipt or writing evidencing such discharge.

Amendments

• 1981, Economic Recovery Tax Act of 1981 (P.L. 97-34)

P.L. 97-34, §422(e)(3):

Amended Code Sec. 2204(b) by striking out "6166 or 6166A" and inserting "or 6166". **Effective** for estates of decedents dying after 12-31-81.

• 1976, Tax Reform Act of 1976 (P.L. 94-455)

P.L. 94-455, §1902(a)(9):

Substituted "has been" for "has not been" in the last sentence of Code Sec. 2204(b). **Effective** for estates of decedents dying after 10-4-76.

P.L. 94-455, §1906(b)(13)(A):

Amended the 1954 Code by substituting "Secretary" for "Secretary or his delegate" each place it appeared. **Effective** 2-1-77.

P.L. 94-455, §2004(f)(4):

Substituted "has been extended under" for "has not been extended under" in the last sentence of Code Sec. 2204(b). **Effective** for estates of decedents dying after 12-31-76.

P.L. 94-455, §2004(f)(6):

Substituted "6166 or 6166A" for "or 6166". **Effective** for estates of decedents dying after 12-31-76.

• 1970, Excise, Estate, and Gift Tax Adjustment Act of 1970 (P.L. 91-614)

P.L. 91-614, §101(d)(1):

Amended Code Sec. 2204. **Effective** with respect to decedents dying after 12-31-70. For prior text, see note under Code Sec. 2204(a).

[Sec. 2204(c)]

(c) SPECIAL LIEN UNDER SECTION 6324A.—For purposes of the second sentence of subsection (a) and the last sentence of subsection (b), an agreement which meets the requirements of section 6324A (relating to special lien for estate tax deferred under section 6166) shall be treated as the furnishing of bond with respect to the amount for which the time for payment has been extended under section 6166.

Amendments

• 1981, Economic Recovery Tax Act of 1981 (P.L. 97-34)

P.L. 97-34, §422(e)(1):

Amended Code Sec. 2204(c) by striking out "or 6166A" each place it appears. **Effective** for estates of decedents dying after 12-31-81.

• 1976, Tax Reform Act of 1976 (P.L. 94-455)

P.L. 94-455, §2004(d)(2), (g):

Added Code Sec. 2204(c). **Effective** for estates of decedents dying after 12-31-76.

[Sec. 2204(d)]

(d) GOOD FAITH RELIANCE ON GIFT TAX RETURNS.—If the executor in good faith relies on gift tax returns furnished under section 6103(e)(3) for determining the decedent's adjusted taxable gifts, the executor shall be discharged from personal liability with respect to any deficiency of the tax imposed by this chapter which is attributable to adjusted taxable gifts which—

(1) are made more than 3 years before the date of the decedent's death, and

(2) are not shown on such returns.

Amendments

• 1978, Revenue Act of 1978 (P.L. 95-600)

P.L. 95-600, §702(p)(1):

Added Code Sec. 2204(d). **Effective** for estates of decedents dying after 1976.

[Sec. 2205]

SEC. 2205. REIMBURSEMENT OUT OF ESTATE.

If the tax or any part thereof is paid by, or collected out of, that part of the estate passing to or in the possession of any person other than the executor in his capacity as such, such person shall be entitled to reimbursement out of any part of the estate still undistributed or by a just and equitable contribution by the persons whose interest in the estate of the decedent would have been reduced if the tax had been paid before the distribution of the estate or whose interest is subject to equal or prior liability for the payment of taxes, debts, or other charges against the estate, it being the purpose and intent of this chapter that so far as is practicable and unless otherwise directed by the will of the decedent the tax shall be paid out of the estate before its distribution.

[Sec. 2206]

SEC. 2206. LIABILITY OF LIFE INSURANCE BENEFICIARIES.

Unless the decedent directs otherwise in his will, if any part of the gross estate on which tax has been paid consists of proceeds of policies of insurance on the life of the decedent receivable by a beneficiary other than the executor, the executor shall be entitled to recover from such beneficiary such portion of the total tax paid as the proceeds of such policies bear to the taxable estate. If there is more than one such beneficiary, the executor shall be entitled to recover from such beneficiaries in the same ratio. In the case of such proceeds receivable by the surviving spouse of the decedent for which a deduction is allowed under section 2056 (relating to marital deduction), this section shall not apply to such proceeds except as to the amount thereof in excess of the aggregate amount of the marital deductions allowed under such section.

Amendments

• 1976, Tax Reform Act of 1976 (P.L. 94-455)

P.L. 94-455, §2001(c)(1)(H), (d)(1):

Substituted "the taxable estate" for "the sum of the taxable estate and the amount of the exemption allowed in computing the taxable estate, determined under section 2051" in the first sentence of Code Sec. 2206. **Effective** for estates of decedents dying after 12-31-76.

[Sec. 2207]

SEC. 2207. LIABILITY OF RECIPIENT OF PROPERTY OVER WHICH DECEDENT HAD POWER OF APPOINTMENT.

Unless the decedent directs otherwise in his will, if any part of the gross estate on which the tax has been paid consists of the value of property included in the gross estate under section 2041, the executor shall be entitled to recover from the person receiving such property by reason of the exercise, nonexercise, or release of a power of appointment such portion of the total tax paid as the value of such property bears to the taxable estate. If there is more than one such person, the executor shall be entitled to recover from such persons in the same ratio. In the case of such property received by the surviving spouse of the decedent for which a deduction is allowed under section 2056 (relating to marital deduction), this section shall not apply to such property except as to the value thereof reduced by an amount equal to the excess of the aggregate amount of the marital deductions allowed under section 2056 over the amount of proceeds of insurance upon the life of the decedent receivable by the surviving spouse for which proceeds a marital deduction is allowed under such section.

Amendments

• 1976, Tax Reform Act of 1976 (P.L. 94-455)

P.L. 94-455, §2001(c)(1)(I), (d)(1):

Substituted "the taxable estate" for "the sum of the taxable estate and the amount of the exemption allowed in computing the taxable estate, determined under section 2052, or section 2106(a), as the case may be" in the first sentence of Code Sec. 2207. **Effective** for estates of decedents dying after 12-31-76.

[Sec. 2207A]

SEC. 2207A. RIGHT OF RECOVERY IN THE CASE OF CERTAIN MARITAL DEDUCTION PROPERTY.

[Sec. 2207A(a)]

(a) RECOVERY WITH RESPECT TO ESTATE TAX.—

(1) IN GENERAL.—If any part of the gross estate consists of property the value of which is includible in the gross estate by reason of section 2044 (relating to certain property for which marital deduction was previously allowed), the decedent's estate shall be entitled to recover from the person receiving the property the amount by which—

(A) the total tax under this chapter which has been paid, exceeds

(B) the total tax under this chapter which would have been payable if the value of such property had not been included in the gross estate.

(2) DECEDENT MAY OTHERWISE DIRECT.—Paragraph (1) shall not apply with respect to any property to the extent that the decedent in his will (or a revocable trust) specifically indicates an intent to waive any right of recovery under this subchapter with respect to such property.

Amendments

• 1997, Taxpayer Relief Act of 1997 (P.L. 105-34)

P.L. 105-34, § 1302(a):

Amended Code Sec. 2207A(a)(2). **Effective** with respect to the estates of decedents dying after 8-5-97. Prior to amendment, Code Sec. 2207A(a)(2) read as follows:

(2) DECEDENT MAY OTHERWISE DIRECT BY WILL.—Paragraph (1) shall not apply if the decedent otherwise directs by will.

[Sec. 2207A(b)]

(b) RECOVERY WITH RESPECT TO GIFT TAX.—If for any calendar year tax is paid under chapter 12 with respect to any person by reason of property treated as transferred by such person under section 2519, such person shall be entitled to recover from the person receiving the property the amount by which—

(1) the total tax for such year under chapter 12, exceeds

(2) the total tax which would have been payable under such chapter for such year if the value of such property had not been taken into account for purposes of chapter 12.

[Sec. 2207A(c)]

(c) MORE THAN ONE RECIPIENT OF PROPERTY.—For purposes of this section, if there is more than one person receiving the property, the right of recovery shall be against each such person.

[Sec. 2207A(d)]

(d) TAXES AND INTEREST.—In the case of penalties and interest attributable to additional taxes described in subsections (a) and (b), rules similar to subsections (a), (b), and (c) shall apply.

Amendments

• 1983, Technical Corrections Act of 1982 (P.L. 97-448)

P.L. 97-448, § 104(a)(10):

Amended paragraph (2) of section 403(e) of P.L. 97-34 (relating to effective date) by striking out "and paragraphs (2) and (3)(B) of subsection (d)" and inserting "paragraphs (2) and (3)(B) of subsection (d), and paragraph (4)(A) of subsection (d) (to the extent related to the tax imposed by chapter 12 [gift tax] of the Internal Revenue Code of 1954)". (For the amendment made by P.L. 97-34, Act Sec. 403(d)(4)(A), see below.)

• 1981, Economic Recovery Tax Act of 1981 (P.L. 97-34)

P.L. 97-34, § 403(d)(4)(A):

Added Code Sec. 2207A. **Effective**, generally, for gifts made after 12-31-81. For a special rule applicable to certain wills or trusts executed or created before 9-12-81, see Act Sec. 403(e)(3), below.

P.L. 97-34, § 403(e)(3), provides:

(3) If—

(A) the decedent dies after December 31, 1981,

(B) by reason of the death of the decedent property passes from the decedent or is acquired from the decedent under a will executed before the date which is 30 days after the date of the enactment of this Act, or a trust created before such date, which contains a formula expressly providing that the spouse is to receive the maximum amount of property qualifying for the marital deduction allowable by Federal law,

(C) the formula referred to in subparagraph (B) was not amended to refer specifically to an unlimited marital deduction at any time after the date which is 30 days after the date of enactment of this Act, and before the death of the decedent, and

(D) the State does not enact a statute applicable to such estate which construes this type of formula as referring to the marital deduction allowable by Federal law as amended by subsection (a),

then the amendment made by subsection (a) [relating to the unlimited marital deduction (Code Sec. 2056, as amended by P.L. 97-34)] shall not apply to the estate of such decedent.

[Sec. 2207B]

SEC. 2207B. RIGHT OF RECOVERY WHERE DECEDENT RETAINED INTEREST.

[Sec. 2207B(a)]

(a) ESTATE TAX.—

(1) IN GENERAL.—If any part of the gross estate on which tax has been paid consists of the value of property included in the gross estate by reason of section 2036 (relating to transfers with retained life estate), the decedent's estate shall be entitled to recover from the person receiving

the property the amount which bears the same ratio to the total tax under this chapter which has been paid as—

(A) the value of such property, bears to

(B) the taxable estate.

(2) DECEDENT MAY OTHERWISE DIRECT.—Paragraph (1) shall not apply with respect to any property to the extent that the decedent in his will (or a revocable trust) specifically indicates an intent to waive any right of recovery under this subchapter with respect to such property.

Amendments

• 1997, Taxpayer Relief Act of 1997 (P.L. 105-34)

P.L. 105-34, §1302(b):

Amended Code Sec. 2207B(a)(2). **Effective** with respect to the estates of decedents dying after 8-5-97. Prior to amendment, Code Sec. 2207B(a)(2) read as follows:

(2) DECEDENT MAY OTHERWISE DIRECT BY WILL.—Paragraph (1) shall not apply if the decedent otherwise directs in a provision of his will (or a revocable trust) specifically referring to this section.

[Sec. 2207B(b)]

(b) MORE THAN ONE RECIPIENT.—For purposes of this section, if there is more than 1 person receiving the property, the right of recovery shall be against each such person.

Amendments

• 1990, Omnibus Budget Reconciliation Act of 1990 (P.L. 101-508)

P.L. 101-508, §11601(b)(1)(A):

Amended Code Sec. 2207B by striking subsection (b) and redesignating subsections (c), (d), and (e) as subsections (b), (c), and (d), respectively. **Effective** in the case of property transferred after 12-17-87. Prior to amendment, Code Sec. 2207B(b) read as follows:

(b) GIFT TAX.—If for any calendar year tax is paid under chapter 12 with respect to any person by reason of property treated as transferred by such person under section 2036(c)(4), such person shall be entitled to recover from the original transferee (as defined in section 2036(c)(4)(C)(ii)) the amount which bears the same ratio to the total tax for such year under chapter 12 as—

(1) the value of such property for purposes of chapter 12, bears to

(2) the total amount of the taxable gifts for such year.

[Sec. 2207B(c)]

(c) PENALTIES AND INTEREST.—In the case of penalties and interest attributable to the additional taxes described in subsection (a), rules similar to the rules of subsections (a) and (b) shall apply.

Amendments

• 1990, Omnibus Budget Reconciliation Act of 1990 (P.L. 101-508)

P.L. 101-508, §11601(b)(1)(A):

Redesignated Code Sec. 2207B(d) as subsection (c). **Effective** in the case of property transferred after 12-17-87.

P.L. 101-508, §11601(b)(1)(B):

Amended Code Sec. 2207B(c) (as so redesignated) by striking "subsections (a) and (b)" and inserting "subsection (a)". **Effective** in the case of property transferred after 12-17-87.

P.L. 101-508, §11601(b)(1)(C):

Amended Code Sec. 2207B(c) (as so redesignated) by striking "subsections (a), (b), and (c)" and inserting "subsections (a) and (b)". **Effective** in the case of property transferred after 12-17-87.

[Sec. 2207B(d)]

(d) NO RIGHT OF RECOVERY AGAINST CHARITABLE REMAINDER TRUSTS.—No person shall be entitled to recover any amount by reason of this section from a trust to which section 664 applies (determined without regard to this section).

Amendments

• 1990, Omnibus Budget Reconciliation Act of 1990 (P.L. 101-508)

P.L. 101-508, §11601(b)(1)(A):

Redesignated Code Sec. 2207B(e) as subsection (d). **Effective** in the case of property transferred after 12-17-87.

• 1988, Technical and Miscellaneous Revenue Act of 1988 (P.L. 100-647)

P.L. 100-647, §3031(f)(1):

Amended Subchapter C of chapter 11 by inserting after section 2207A a new section 2207B. **Effective**, generally, as if included in the provision of P.L. 99-514 to which it relates. For a special rule, see Act Sec. 3031(h)(3), below.

P.L. 100-647, §3031(h)(3), provides:

(3) SUBSECTION (f).—If an amount is included in the gross estate of a decedent under section 2036 of the 1986 Code other than solely by reason of section 2036(c) of the 1986 Code, the amendments made by subsection (f) shall apply to such amount only with respect to property transferred after the date of the enactment of this Act.

[Sec. 2208]

SEC. 2208. CERTAIN RESIDENTS OF POSSESSIONS CONSIDERED CITIZENS OF THE UNITED STATES.

A decedent who was a citizen of the United States and a resident of a possession thereof at the time of his death shall, for purposes of the tax imposed by this chapter, be considered a "citizen" of the United States within the meaning of that term wherever used in this title unless he acquired his United States citizenship solely by reason of (1) his being a citizen of such possession of the United States, or (2) his birth or residence within such possession of the United States.

Amendments

• 1958, Technical Amendments Act of 1958 (P.L. 85-866)

P.L. 85-866, §102(a):

Added Code Sec. 2208. **Effective** for estates of decedents dying after 9-2-58.

[Sec. 2209]

SEC. 2209. CERTAIN RESIDENTS OF POSSESSIONS CONSIDERED NONRESIDENTS NOT CITIZENS OF THE UNITED STATES.

A decedent who was a citizen of the United States and a resident of a possession thereof at the time of his death shall, for purposes of the tax imposed by this chapter, be considered a "nonresident not a citizen of the United States" within the meaning of that term wherever used in this title, but only if such person acquired his United States citizenship solely by reason of (1) his being a citizen of such possession of the United States, or (2) his birth or residence within such possession of the United States.

Amendments

• 1960 (P.L. 86-779)

P.L. 86-779, §4(b):

Added Code Sec. 2209. **Effective** for estates of decedents dying after 9-14-60.

[Sec. 2210]

TERMINATION.

[Sec. 2210(a)]

(a) IN GENERAL.—Except as provided in subsection (b), this chapter shall not apply to the estates of decedents dying after December 31, 2009.

[Sec. 2210(b)]

(b) CERTAIN DISTRIBUTIONS FROM QUALIFIED DOMESTIC TRUSTS.—In applying section 2056A with respect to the surviving spouse of a decedent dying before January 1, 2010—

(1) section 2056A(b)(1)(A) shall not apply to distributions made after December 31, 2020, and

(2) section 2056A(b)(1)(B) shall not apply after December 31, 2009.

Amendments

• 2010, Tax Relief, Unemployment Insurance Reauthorization, and Job Creation Act of 2010 (P.L. 111-312)

P.L. 111-312, §301(a):

Amended Code Sec. 2210 to read as such provision would read if subtitle A of title V of the Economic Growth and Tax Relief Reconciliation Act of 2001 (P.L. 107-16) had never been enacted. **Effective** for estates of decedents dying, and transfers made, after 12-31-2009. For a special rule, see Act Sec. 301(c), below.

P.L. 111-312, §301(c), provides:

(c) SPECIAL ELECTION WITH RESPECT TO ESTATES OF DECEDENTS DYING IN 2010.—Notwithstanding subsection (a), in the case of an estate of a decedent dying after December 31, 2009, and before January 1, 2011, the executor (within the meaning of section 2203 of the Internal Revenue Code of 1986) may elect to apply such Code as though the amendments made by subsection (a) do not apply with respect to chapter 11 of such Code and with respect to property acquired or passing from such decedent (within the meaning of section 1014(b) of such Code). Such election shall be made at such time and in such manner as the Secretary of the Treasury or the Secretary's delegate shall provide. Such an election once made shall be revocable only with the consent of the Secretary of the Treasury or the Secretary's delegate. For purposes of section 2652(a)(1) of such Code, the determination of whether any property is subject to the tax imposed by such chapter 11 shall be made without regard to any election made under this subsection.

P.L. 111-312, §304, provides:

SEC. 304. APPLICATION OF EGTRRA SUNSET TO THIS TITLE.

Section 901 of the Economic Growth and Tax Relief Reconciliation Act of 2001 shall apply to the amendments made by this title.

Amendments

• 2001, Economic Growth and Tax Relief Reconciliation Act of 2001 (P.L. 107-16)

P.L. 107-16, §501(a):

Amended subchapter C of chapter 11 of subtitle B by adding at the end a new Code Sec. 2210. **Effective** for the estates of decedents dying, and generation-skipping transfers, after 12-31-2009.

P.L. 107-16, §901(a)-(b), as amended by P.L. 111-312, §101(a)(1), provides:

SEC. 901. SUNSET OF PROVISIONS OF ACT.

(a) IN GENERAL.—All provisions of, and amendments made by, this Act shall not apply—

(1) to taxable, plan, or limitation years beginning after December 31, 2012, or

(2) in the case of title V, to estates of decedents dying, gifts made, or generation skipping transfers, after December 31, 2012.

(b) APPLICATION OF CERTAIN LAWS.—The Internal Revenue Code of 1986 and the Employee Retirement Income Security Act of 1974 shall be applied and administered to years, estates, gifts, and transfers described in subsection (a) as if the provisions and amendments described in subsection (a) had never been enacted.

[Sec. 2210—Repealed]

Amendments

• 1989, Omnibus Budget Reconciliation Act of 1989 (P.L. 101-239)

P.L. 101-239, §7304(b)(1):

Repealed Code Sec. 2210. **Effective** for estates of decedents dying after 7-12-89. Prior to repeal, Code Sec. 2210 read as follows:

SEC. 2210. LIABILITY FOR PAYMENT IN CASE OF TRANSFER OF EMPLOYER SECURITIES TO AN EMPLOYEE STOCK OWNERSHIP PLAN OR A WORKER-OWNED COOPERATIVE.

[Sec. 2210(a)]

(a) IN GENERAL.—If—

(1) employer securities—

(A) are acquired from the decedent by an employee stock ownership plan or by an eligible worker-owned cooperative from any decedent,

(B) pass from the decedent to such a plan or cooperative, or

(C) are transferred by the executor to such a plan or cooperative,

(2) the executor of the estate of the decedent may (without regard to this section) make an election under section 6166 with respect to that portion of the tax imposed by section 2001 which is attributable to employer securities, and

(3) the executor elects the application of this section and files the agreements described in subsection (e) before the due date (including extensions) for filing the return of tax imposed by section 2001,

then the executor is relieved of liability for payment of that portion of the tax imposed by section 2001 which such employee stock ownership plan or cooperative is required to pay under subsection (b).

Amendments

• 1986, Tax Reform Act of 1986 (P.L. 99-514)

P.L. 99-514, §1854(d)(1)(A):

Amended Code Sec. 2210(a) by striking out "and" at the end of paragraph (1), by redesignating paragraph (2) as paragraph (3), and by inserting after paragraph (1) new paragraph (2). **Effective** for the estates of decedents dying after 9-27-85.

[Sec. 2210(b)]

(b) PAYMENT OF TAX BY EMPLOYEE STOCK OWNERSHIP PLAN OR COOPERATIVE.—

(1) IN GENERAL.—An employee stock ownership plan or eligible worker-owned cooperative—

(A) which has acquired employer securities from the decedent, or to which such securities have passed from the decedent or been transferred by the executor, and

(B) with respect to which an agreement described in subsection (e)(1) is in effect,

shall pay that portion of the tax imposed by section 2001 with respect to the taxable estate of the decedent which is described in paragraph (2).

(2) AMOUNT OF TAX TO BE PAID.—The portion of the tax imposed by section 2001 with respect to the taxable estate of the decedent that is referred to in paragraph (1) is equal to the lesser of—

(A) the value of the employer securities described in subsection (a)(1) which is included in the gross estate of the decedent, or

(B) the tax imposed by section 2001 with respect to such taxable estate reduced by the sum of the credits allowable against such tax.

[Sec. 2210(c)]

(c) INSTALLMENT PAYMENTS.—

(1) IN GENERAL.—If—

(A) the executor of the estate of the decedent (without regard to this section) elects to have the provisions of section 6166 (relating to extensions of time for payment of estate tax where estate consists largely of interest in closely held business) apply to payment of that portion of the tax imposed by section 2001 with respect to such estate which is attributable to employer securities, and

(B) the plan administrator or the cooperative provides to the executor the agreement described in subsection (e)(1),

then the plan administrator or any authorized officer of the cooperative may elect, before the due date (including extensions) for filing the return of such tax, to pay all or part of the tax described in subsection (b)(2) in installments under the provisions of section 6166.

(2) INTEREST ON INSTALLMENTS.—In determining the 4-percent portion for purposes of section 6601(j)—

(A) the portion of the tax imposed by section 2001 with respect to an estate for which the executor is liable, and

(B) the portion of such tax for which an employee stock ownership plan or an eligible worker-owned cooperative is liable,

shall be aggregated.

(3) SPECIAL RULES FOR APPLICATION OF SECTION 6166(g).—In the case of any transfer of employer securities to an employee stock ownership plan or eligible worker-owned cooperative to which this section applies—

(A) TRANSFER DOES NOT TRIGGER ACCELERATION.—Such transfer shall not be treated as a disposition or withdrawal to which section 6166(g) applies.

(B) SEPARATE APPLICATION TO ESTATE AND PLAN INTERESTS.—Section 6166(g) shall be applied separately to the interests held after such transfer by the estate and such plan or cooperative.

(C) REQUIRED DISTRIBUTION NOT TAKEN INTO ACCOUNT.—In the case of any distribution of such securities by such plan which is described in section 4978(d)(1)—

(i) such distribution shall not be treated as a disposition or withdrawal for purposes of section 6166(g), and

(ii) such securities shall not be taken into account in applying section 6166(g) to any subsequent disposition or withdrawal.

Amendments

• 1986, Tax Reform Act of 1986 (P.L. 99-514)

P.L. 99-514, §1854(d)(2):

Amended Code Sec. 2210(c) by adding at the end thereof new paragraph (3). **Effective** as if included in the provision of P.L. 98-369 to which it relates.

P.L. 99-514, §1854(d)(4):

Amended Code Sec. 2210(c)(1) by inserting "any authorized officer of" before "the cooperative" in the matter following subparagraph (B). **Effective** as if included in the provision of P.L. 98-369 to which it relates.

[Sec. 2210(d)]

(d) GUARANTEE OF PAYMENTS.—Any employer—

(1) whose employees are covered by an employee stock ownership plan, and

(2) who has entered into an agreement described in subsection (e)(2) which is in effect,

and any eligible worker-owned cooperative shall guarantee (in such manner as the Secretary may prescribe) the payment of any amount such plan or cooperative, repectively, is required to pay under subsection (b).

Amendments

• 1986, Tax Reform Act of 1986 (P.L. 99-514)

P.L. 99-514, §1854(d)(5)(A)-(C):

Amended Code Sec. 2210(d) by inserting "and any eligible worker-owned cooperative" before "shall guarantee" in the matter following paragraph (2), by striking out "such plan" and inserting in lieu thereof "such plan or cooperative, respectively,", and by striking out ", including any interest payable under section 6601 which is attributable to such amount". **Effective** as if included in the provision of P.L. 98-369 to which it relates.

P.L. 99-514, §1899A(37):

Amended Code Sec. 2210(d) by striking out "may prescibe" and inserting in lieu thereof "may prescribe". **Effective** 10-22-86.

[Sec. 2210(e)]

(e) AGREEMENTS.—The agreements described in this subsection are as follows:

(1) A written agreement signed by the plan administrator, or by any authorized officer of the eligible worker-owned cooperative, consenting to the application of subsection (b) to such plan or cooperative.

(2) A written agreement signed by the employer whose employees are covered by the plan described in subsection (b) consenting to the application of subsection (d).

[Sec. 2210(f)]

(f) EXEMPTION FROM TAX ON PROHIBITED TRANSACTIONS.—The assumption under this section by an employee stock ownership plan of any portion of the liability for the tax imposed by section 2001 shall be treated as a loan described in section 4975(d)(3).

[Sec. 2210(g)]

(g) DEFINITIONS.—For purposes of this section—

(1) EMPLOYER SECURITIES.—The term "employer securities" has the meaning given such term by section 409(l).

(2) EMPLOYEE STOCK OWNERSHIP PLAN.—The term "employee stock ownership plan" has the meaning given such term by section 4975(e)(7).

(3) ELIGIBLE WORKER-OWNED COOPERATIVE.—The term "eligible worker-owned cooperative" has the meaning given to such term by section 1041(c)(2).

(4) PLAN ADMINISTRATOR.—The term "plan administrator" has the meaning given such term by section 414(g).

(5) TAX IMPOSED BY SECTION 2001.—The term "tax imposed by section 2001" includes any interest, penalty, addition to tax, or additional amount relating to any tax imposed by section 2001.

Amendments

• 1986, Tax Reform Act of 1986 (P.L. 99-514)

P.L. 99-514, §1854(d)(3):

Amended Code Sec. 2210(g) by adding at the end thereof new paragraph (5). **Effective** as if included in the provision of P.L. 98-369 to which it relates.

P.L. 99-514, §1854(d)(6):

Amended Code Sec. 2210(g)(3) by striking out "section 1041(b)(2)" and inserting in lieu thereof "section 1042(c)(2)". **Effective** as if included in the provision of P.L. 98-369 to which it relates.

• 1984, Deficit Reduction Act of 1984 (P.L. 98-369)

P.L. 98-369, §544(a):

Added Code Sec. 2210. **Effective** for those estates of decedents which are required to file returns on a date (including any extensions) after 7-18-84.

* * *

SUBTITLE D—MISCELLANEOUS EXCISE TAXES

* * *

CHAPTER 43—QUALIFIED PENSION, ETC., PLANS

* * *

[Sec. 4978]

SEC. 4978. TAX ON CERTAIN DISPOSITIONS BY EMPLOYEE STOCK OWNERSHIP PLANS AND CERTAIN COOPERATIVES.

[Sec. 4978(a)]

(a) TAX ON DISPOSITIONS OF SECURITIES TO WHICH SECTION 1042 APPLIES BEFORE CLOSE OF MINIMUM HOLDING PERIOD.—If, during the 3-year period after the date on which the employee stock ownership plan or eligible worker-owned cooperative acquired any qualified securities in a sale to which section 1042 applied or acquired any qualified employer securities in a qualified gratuitous transfer to which section 664(g) applied, such plan or cooperative disposes of any qualified securities and—

(1) the total number of shares held by such plan or cooperative after such disposition is less than the total number of employer securities held immediately after such sale, or

(2) except to the extent provided in regulations, the value of qualified securities held by such plan or cooperative after such disposition is less than 30 percent of the total value of all employer securities as of such disposition (60 percent of the total value of all employer securities as of such disposition in the case of any qualified employer securities acquired in a qualified gratuitous transfer to which section 664(g) applied),

there is hereby imposed a tax on the disposition equal to the amount determined under subsection (b).

Amendments

• 2004, Working Families Tax Relief Act of 2004 (P.L. 108-311)

P.L. 108-311, §408(a)(23):

Amended Code Sec. 4978(a)(2) by striking "60 percent" and inserting "(60 percent". **Effective** 10-4-2004.

• 1997, Taxpayer Relief Act of 1997 (P.L. 105-34)

P.L. 105-34, §1530(c)(11)(A)-(B):

Amended Code Sec. 4978(a) by inserting "or acquired any qualified employer securities in a qualified gratuitous transfer to which section 664(g) applied" after "section 1042 applied", and by inserting before the comma at the end of paragraph (2) "60 percent of the total value of all employer securities as of such disposition in the case of any qualified employer securities acquired in a qualified gratuitous transfer to which section 664(g) applied)". **Effective** for transfers made by trusts to, or for the use of, an employee stock ownership plan after 8-5-97.

• 1986, Tax Reform Act of 1986 (P.L. 99-514)

P.L. 99-514, §1854(e)(1):

Amended Code Sec. 4978(a)(1) by striking out "then" and inserting in lieu thereof "than". **Effective** as if included in the provision of P.L. 98-369 to which it relates.

[Sec. 4978(b)]

(b) AMOUNT OF TAX.—

(1) IN GENERAL.—The amount of the tax imposed by subsection (a) shall be equal to 10 percent of the amount realized on the disposition.

(2) LIMITATION.—The amount realized taken into account under paragraph (1) shall not exceed that portion allocable to qualified securities acquired in the sale to which section 1042

applied or acquired in the qualified gratuitous transfer to which section 664(g) applied determined as if such securities were disposed of—

(A) first from qualified securities to which section 1042 applied or to which section 664(g) applied acquired during the 3-year period ending on the date of the disposition, beginning with the securities first so acquired, and

(B) then from any other employer securities.

If subsection (d) applies to a disposition, the disposition shall be treated as made from employer securities in the opposite order of the preceding sentence.

(3) DISTRIBUTIONS TO EMPLOYEES.—The amount realized on any distribution to an employee for less than fair market value shall be determined as if the qualified security had been sold to the employee at fair market value.

Amendments

• 1997, Taxpayer Relief Act of 1997 (P.L. 105-34)

P.L. 105-34, §1530(c)(12)(A)-(B):

Amended Code Sec. 4978(b)(2) by inserting "or acquired in the qualified gratuitous transfer to which section 664(g) applied" after "section 1042 applied", and by inserting "or to which section 664(g) applied" after "section 1042 applied" in subparagraph (A) thereof. **Effective** for transfers made by trusts to, or for the use of, an employee stock ownership plan after 8-5-97.

• 1996, Small Business Job Protection Act of 1996 (P.L. 104-188)

P.L. 104-188, §1602(b)(4):

Amended Code Sec. 4978(b)(2) by striking subparagraph (A) and all that follows and inserting new subparagraphs (A) and (B) and a flush sentence. For the **effective** date, see Act Sec. 1602(c), below. Prior to amendment, Code Sec. 4978(b)(2)(A)-(D) read as follows:

(A) first, from section 133 securities (as defined in section 4978B(e)(2)) acquired during the 3-year period ending on the date of such disposition, beginning with the securities first so acquired.

(B) second, from section 133 securities (as so defined) acquired before such 3-year period unless such securities (or proceeds from the disposition) have been allocated to accounts of participants or beneficiaries.

(C) third, from qualified securities to which section 1042 applied acquired during the 3-year period ending on the date of the disposition, beginning with the securities first so acquired, and

(D) then from any other employer securities.

If subsection (d) or section 4978B(d) applies to a disposition, the disposition shall be treated as made from employer securities in the opposite order of the preceding sentence.

P.L. 104-188, §1602(c), provides:

(c) EFFECTIVE DATE.—

(1) IN GENERAL.—The amendments made by this section shall apply to loans made after the date of the enactment of this Act.

(2) REFINANCINGS.—The amendments made by this section shall not apply to loans made after the date of the enactment of this Act to refinance securities acquisition loans (determined without regard to section 133(b)(1)(B) of the Internal Revenue Code of 1986, as in effect on the day before the date of the enactment of this Act) made on or before such date or to refinance loans described in this paragraph if—

(A) the refinancing loans meet the requirements of section 133 of such Code (as so in effect),

(B) immediately after the refinancing the principal amount of the loan resulting from the refinancing does not exceed the principal amount of the refinanced loan (immediately before the refinancing), and

(C) the term of such refinancing loan does not extend beyond the last day of the term of the original securities acquisition loan.

For purposes of this paragraph, the term "securities acquisition loan" includes a loan from a corporation to an employee stock ownership plan described in section 133(b)(3) of such Code (as so in effect).

(3) EXCEPTION.—Any loan made pursuant to a binding written contract in effect before June 10, 1996, and at all times thereafter before such loan is made, shall be treated for purposes of paragraphs (1) and (2) as a loan made on or before the date of the enactment of this Act.

• 1989, Omnibus Budget Reconciliation Act of 1989 (P.L. 101-239)

P.L. 101-239, §7304(a)(2)(C)(ii):

Amended Code Sec. 4978(b)(2). **Effective** for the estates of decedents dying after 12-19-89. Prior to amendment, Code Sec. 4978(b)(2) read as follows:

(2) LIMITATION.—The amount realized taken into account under paragraph (1) shall not exceed that portion allocable to qualified securities acquired in the sale to which section 1042 applied (determined as if such securities were disposed of in the order described in section 4978A(e)).

• 1987, Revenue Act of 1987 (P.L. 100-203)

P.L. 100-203, §10413(b)(1):

Amended Code Sec. 4978(b)(2) by striking out the parenthetical and inserting in lieu thereof "(determined as if such securities were disposed of in the order described in section 4978A(e))". **Effective** for taxable events (within the meaning of section 4978A(c) of the Internal Revenue Code of 1986) occurring after 2-26-87. Prior to amendment, the parenthetical read as follows:

(determined as if such securities were disposed of before any other securities)

• 1986, Tax Reform Act of 1986 (P.L. 99-514)

P.L. 99-514, §1854(e)(2):

Amended Code Sec. 4978(b)(1) by striking out "paragraph (1)" and inserting in lieu thereof "subsection (a)". **Effective** as if included in the provision of P.L. 98-369 to which it relates.

[Sec. 4978(c)]

(c) LIABILITY FOR PAYMENT OF TAXES.—The tax imposed by this subsection shall be paid by—

(1) the employer, or

(2) the eligible worker-owned cooperative,

that made the written statement described in section 664(g)(1)(E) or in section 1042(b)(3) (as the case may be).

Amendments

• 1997, Taxpayer Relief Act of 1997 (P.L. 105-34)

P.L. 105-34, §1530(c)(13):

Amended Code Sec. 4978(c) by striking "written statement" and all that follows and inserting "written statement described in section 664(g)(1)(E) or in section 1042(b)(3) (as the case may be)." **Effective** for transfers made by trusts to, or for the use of, an employee stock ownership plan after 8-5-97. Prior to amendment, Code Sec. 4978(c) read as follows:

(c) LIABILITY FOR PAYMENT OF TAXES.—The tax imposed by this subsection shall be paid by—

(1) the employer, or

(2) the eligible worker-owned cooperative,

that made the written statement described in section 1042(b)(3).

• **1986, Tax Reform Act of 1986 (P.L. 99-514)**

P.L. 99-514, §1854(e)(3):

Amended Code Sec. 4978(c) by striking out "section 1042(a)(2)(B)" and inserting in lieu thereof "section 1042(b)(3)". **Effective** as if included in the provision of P.L. 98-369 to which it relates.

[Sec. 4978(d)]

(d) SECTION NOT TO APPLY TO CERTAIN DISPOSITIONS.—

(1) CERTAIN DISTRIBUTIONS TO EMPLOYEES.—This section shall not apply with respect to any distribution of qualified securities (or sale of such securities) which is made by reason of—

(A) the death of the employee,

(B) the retirement of the employee after the employee has attained $59^{1}/_{2}$ years of age,

(C) the disability of the employee (within the meaning of section 72(m)(7)), or

(D) the separation of the employee from service for any period which results in a 1-year break in service (within the meaning of section 411(a)(6)(A)).

(2) CERTAIN REORGANIZATIONS.—In the case of any exchange of qualified securities in any reorganization described in section 368(a)(1) for stock of another corporation, such exchange shall not be treated as a disposition for purposes of this section.

(3) LIQUIDATION OF CORPORATION INTO COOPERATIVE.—In the case of any exchange of qualified securities pursuant to the liquidation of the corporation issuing qualified securities into the eligible worker-owned cooperative in a transaction which meets the requirements of section 332 (determined by substituting "100 percent" for "80 percent" each place it appears in section 332(b)(1)), such exchange shall not be treated as a disposition for purposes of this section.

(4) DISPOSITIONS TO MEET DIVERSIFICATION REQUIREMENTS.—This section shall not apply to any disposition of qualified securities which is required under section 401(a)(28).

Amendments

• **1988, Technical and Miscellaneous Revenue Act of 1988 (P.L. 100-647)**

P.L. 100-647, §1011B(j)(4):

Amended Code Sec. 4978(d) by adding at the end thereof new paragraph (4). **Effective** as if included in the provision of P.L. 99-514 to which it relates.

• **1986, Tax Reform Act of 1986 (P.L. 99-514)**

P.L. 99-514, §1854(e)(4):

Amended Code Sec. 4978(d)(1)(C) by striking out "section 72(m)(5)" and inserting in lieu thereof "section 72(m)(7)". **Effective** as if included in the provision of P.L. 98-369 to which it relates.

P.L. 99-514, §1854(e)(7):

Amended Code Sec. 4978(d) by adding at the end thereof new paragraph (3). **Effective** as if included in the provision of P.L. 98-369 to which it relates.

[Sec. 4978(e)]

(e) DEFINITIONS AND SPECIAL RULES.—For purposes of this section—

(1) EMPLOYEE STOCK OWNERSHIP PLAN.—The term "employee stock ownership plan" has the meaning given to such term by section 4975(e)(7).

(2) QUALIFIED SECURITIES.—The term "qualified securities" has the meaning given to such term by section 1042(c)(1); except that such section shall be applied without regard to subparagraph (B) thereof for purposes of applying this section and section 4979A with respect to securities acquired in a qualified gratuitous transfer (as defined in section 664(g)(1)).

(3) ELIGIBLE WORKER-OWNED COOPERATIVE.—The term "eligible worker-owned cooperative" has the meaning given to such term by section 1042(c)(2).

(4) DISPOSITION.—The term "disposition" includes any distribution.

(5) EMPLOYER SECURITIES.—The term "employer securities" has the meaning given to such term by section 409(l).

Amendments

• **1997, Taxpayer Relief Act of 1997 (P.L. 105-34)**

P.L. 105-34, §1530(c)(14):

Amended Code Sec. 4978(e)(2) by striking the period and inserting "; except that such section shall be applied without regard to subparagraph (B) thereof for purposes of applying this section and section 4979A with respect to securities acquired in a qualified gratuitous transfer (as defined in section 664(g)(1))." **Effective** for transfers made by trusts to, or for the use of, an employee stock ownership plan after 8-5-97.

• **1986, Tax Reform Act of 1986 (P.L. 99-514)**

P.L. 99-514, §1854(e)(5):

Amended Code Sec. 4978(e)(2) by striking out "section 1042(b)(1)" and inserting in lieu thereof "section 1042(c)(1)". **Effective** as if included in the provision of P.L. 98-369 to which it relates.

P.L. 99-514, §1854(e)(6):

Amended Code Sec. 4978(e)(3) by striking out "section 1042(b)(1)" and inserting in lieu thereof "section 1042(c)(2)". **Effective** as if included in the provision of P L. 98-369 to which it relates.

• **1984, Deficit Reduction Act of 1984 (P.L. 98-369)**

P.L. 98-369, §545(a):

Added Code Sec. 4978. **Effective** for tax years beginning after 7-18-84.

* * *

GIFT TAX

TABLE OF CONTENTS

SUBTITLE B—ESTATE AND GIFT TAXES

Chapter 12—Gift Tax

SUBCHAPTER A. DETERMINATION OF TAX LIABILITY

SUBCHAPTER B. TRANSFERS

SUBCHAPTER C. DEDUCTIONS

SUBTITLE B—ESTATE AND GIFT TAXES

* * *

CHAPTER 12—GIFT TAX

Subchapter A—Determination of Tax Liability

[Sec. 2501]

SEC. 2501. IMPOSITION OF TAX.

[Sec. 2501(a)]

(a) TAXABLE TRANSFERS.—

(1) GENERAL RULE.—A tax, computed as provided in section 2502, is hereby imposed for each calendar year on the transfer of property by gift during such calendar year by any individual, resident or nonresident.

(2) TRANSFERS OF INTANGIBLE PROPERTY.—Except as provided in paragraph (3), paragraph (1) shall not apply to the transfer of intangible property by a nonresident not a citizen of the United States.

(3) EXCEPTION.—

(A) CERTAIN INDIVIDUALS.—Paragraph (2) shall not apply in the case of a donor to whom section 877(b) applies for the taxable year which includes the date of the transfer.

(B) CREDIT FOR FOREIGN GIFT TAXES.—The tax imposed by this section solely by reason of this paragraph shall be credited with the amount of any gift tax actually paid to any foreign country in respect of any gift which is taxable under this section solely by reason of this paragraph.

(4) TRANSFERS TO POLITICAL ORGANIZATIONS.—Paragraph (1) shall not apply to the transfer of money or other property to a political organization (within the meaning of section 527(e)(1)) for the use of such organization.

(5) TRANSFERS OF CERTAIN STOCK.—

(A) IN GENERAL.—In the case of a transfer of stock in a foreign corporation described in subparagraph (B) by a donor to whom section 877(b) applies for the taxable year which includes the date of the transfer—

(i) section 2511(a) shall be applied without regard to whether such stock is situated within the United States, and

(ii) the value of such stock for purposes of this chapter shall be its U.S.-asset value determined under subparagraph (C).

(B) FOREIGN CORPORATION DESCRIBED.—A foreign corporation is described in this subparagraph with respect to a donor if—

(i) the donor owned (within the meaning of section 958(a)) at the time of such transfer 10 percent or more of the total combined voting power of all classes of stock entitled to vote of the foreign corporation, and

(ii) such donor owned (within the meaning of section 958(a)), or is considered to have owned (by applying the ownership rules of section 958(b)), at the time of such transfer, more than 50 percent of—

(I) the total combined voting power of all classes of stock entitled to vote of such corporation, or

(II) the total value of the stock of such corporation.

(C) U.S.-ASSET VALUE.—For purposes of subparagraph (A), the U.S.-asset value of stock shall be the amount which bears the same ratio to the fair market value of such stock at the time of transfer as—

(i) the fair market value (at such time) of the assets owned by such foreign corporation and situated in the United States, bears to

(ii) the total fair market value (at such time) of all assets owned by such foreign corporation.

(6) TRANSFERS TO CERTAIN EXEMPT ORGANIZATIONS.—Paragraph (1) shall not apply to the transfer of money or other property to an organization described in paragraph (4), (5), or (6) of section 501(c) and exempt from tax under section 501(a), for the use of such organization.

Amendments

• 2015, Protecting Americans from Tax Hikes Act of 2015 (P.L. 114-113)

P.L. 114-113, §408(a), Div. Q:

Amended Code Sec. 2501(a) by adding at the end a new paragraph (6). **Effective** for gifts made after 12-18-2015. For a special rule, see Act Sec. 408(c), below.

P.L. 114-113, §408(c), Div. Q, provides:

(c) NO INFERENCE.—Nothing in the amendment made by subsection (a) shall be construed to create any inference with respect to whether any transfer of property (whether made before, on, or after the date of the enactment of this Act) to an organization described in paragraph (4), (5), or (6) of section 501(c) of the Internal Revenue Code of 1986 is a transfer of property by gift for purposes of chapter 12 of such Code.

• 2004, American Jobs Creation Act of 2004 (P.L. 108-357)

P.L. 108-357, §804(d)(1):

Amended Code Sec. 2501(a) by striking paragraph (4), by redesignating paragraph (5) as paragraph (4), and by striking paragraph (3) and inserting a new paragraph (3). **Effective** for individuals who expatriate after 6-3-2004. Prior to being stricken, Code Sec. 2501(a)(3)-(4) read as follows:

(3) EXCEPTION.—

(A) CERTAIN INDIVIDUALS.—Paragraph (2) shall not apply in the case of a donor who, within the 10-year period ending with the date of transfer, lost United States citizenship, unless such loss did not have for 1 of its principal purposes the avoidance of taxes under this subtitle or subtitle A.

(B) CERTAIN INDIVIDUALS TREATED AS HAVING TAX AVOIDANCE PURPOSE.—For purposes of subparagraph (A), an individual shall be treated as having a principal purpose to avoid such taxes if such individual is so treated under section 877(a)(2).

(C) EXCEPTION FOR CERTAIN INDIVIDUALS.—Subparagraph (B) shall not apply to a donor meeting the requirements of section 877(c)(1).

(D) CREDIT FOR FOREIGN GIFT TAXES.—The tax imposed by this section solely by reason of this paragraph shall be credited with the amount of any gift tax actually paid to any foreign country in respect of any gift which is taxable under this section solely by reason of this paragraph.

(E) CROSS REFERENCE.—For comparable treatment of long-term lawful permanent residents who ceased to be taxed as residents, see section 877(e).

(4) BURDEN OF PROOF.—If the Secretary establishes that it is reasonable to believe that an individual's loss of United States citizenship would, but for paragraph (3), result in a substantial reduction for the calendar year in the taxes on the transfer of property by gift, the burden of proving that such loss of citizenship did not have for one of its principal purposes the avoidance of taxes under this subtitle or subtitle A shall be on such individual.

P.L. 108-357, §804(d)(2):

Amended Code Sec. 2501(a) by adding at the end a new paragraph (5). **Effective** for individuals who expatriate after 6-3-2004.

• 1997, Taxpayer Relief Act of 1997 (P.L. 105-34)

P.L. 105-34, §1602(g)(5):

Amended Code Sec. 2501(a)(3)(C) by striking "decedent" and inserting "donor". **Effective** as if included in the provision of P.L. 104-191 to which it relates [**effective**, generally, for individuals losing U.S. citizenship on or after 2-6-95, and long-term U.S. residents who end U.S. residency or begin foreign residency on or after 2-6-95.—CCH].

• 1996, Health Insurance Portability and Accountability Act of 1996 (P.L. 104-191)

P.L. 104-191, §511(e)(2)(A):

Amended Code Sec. 2501(a)(3). For the **effective** date, see Act Sec. 511(g), below. Prior to amendment, Code Sec. 2501(a)(3) read as follows:

(3) EXCEPTIONS.—Paragraph (2) shall not apply in the case of a donor who at any time after March 8, 1965, and within the 10-year period ending with the date of transfer lost United States citizenship unless—

(A) such donor's loss of United States citizenship resulted from the application of section 301(b), 350, or 355 of the Immigration and Nationality Act, as amended (8 U. S. C. 1401(b), 1482, or 1487), or

(B) such loss did not have for one of its principal purposes the avoidance of taxes under this subtitle or subtitle A.

P.L. 104-191, §511(f)(2)(B):

Amended Code Sec. 2501(a)(3) (as amended by Act Sec. 511(e)) by adding at the end a new subparagraph (E). For the **effective** date, see Act Sec. 511(g), below.

P.L. 104-191, §511(g), provides:

(g) EFFECTIVE DATE.—

(1) IN GENERAL.—The amendments made by this section shall apply to—

(A) individuals losing United States citizenship (within the meaning of section 877 of the Internal Revenue Code of 1986) on or after February 6, 1995, and

(B) long-term residents of the United States with respect to whom an event described in subparagraph (A) or (B) of section 877(e)(1) of such Code occurs on or after February 6, 1995.

(2) RULING REQUESTS.—In no event shall the 1-year period referred to in section 877(c)(1)(B) of such Code, as amended by this section, expire before the date which is 90 days after the date of the enactment of this Act.

(3) SPECIAL RULE.—

(A) IN GENERAL.—In the case of an individual who performed an act of expatriation specified in paragraph (1), (2), (3), or (4) of section 349(a) of the Immigration and Nationality Act (8 U.S.C. 1481(a)(1)-(4)) before February 6, 1995, but who did not, on or before such date, furnish to the United States Department of State a signed statement of voluntary relinquishment of United States nationality confirming the performance of such act, the amendments made by this section and section 512 shall apply to such individual except that the 10-year period described in section 877(a) of such Code shall not expire before the end of the 10-year period beginning on the date such statement is so furnished.

(B) EXCEPTION.—Subparagraph (A) shall not apply if the individual establishes to the satisfaction of the Secretary of the Treasury that such loss of United States citizenship occurred before February 6, 1994.

• 1981, Economic Recovery Tax Act of 1981 (P.L. 97-34)

P.L. 97-34, §442(a)(1):

Amended Code Sec. 2501(a)(1) and (4) by striking out "calendar quarter" and inserting "calendar year". **Effective** with respect to gifts made after 12-31-81.

• 1976, Tax Reform Act of 1976 (P.L. 94-455)

P.L. 94-455, §1902(a)(10):

Amended Code Sec. 2501(a)(1). **Effective** for estates of decedents dying after 10-4-76. Prior to amendment, Code Sec. 2501(a)(1) read as follows:

(1) GENERAL RULE.—For the first calendar quarter of the calendar year 1971 and each calendar quarter thereafter a tax, computed as provided in section 2502, is hereby imposed on the transfer of property by gift during such calendar quarter by any individual, resident or nonresident.

P.L. 94-455, §1906(b)(13)(A):

Amended 1954 Code by substituting "Secretary" for "Secretary or his delegate" each place it appeared. **Effective** 2-1-77.

• 1975 (P.L. 93-625)

P.L. 93-625, §14(a):

Amended Code Sec. 2501(a) by adding paragraph (5). **Effective** with respect to transfers made after 5-7-74.

• 1970, Excise, Estate, and Gift Tax Adjustment Act of 1970 (P.L. 91-614)

P.L. 91-614, §102(a)(1), (2):

Amended paragraph (1) of Code Sec. 2501(a) by substituting "the first calendar quarter of the calendar year 1971 and each calendar quarter thereafter" for "the calendar year 1955 and each calendar year thereafter" and by substituting "during such calendar quarter" for "during such calendar year." Also amended paragraph (4) by substituting "calendar quarter" for "calendar year.". **Effective** for gifts made after 12-31-70.

• 1966, Foreign Investors Tax Act of 1966 (P.L. 89-809)

P.L. 89-809, §109(a):

Amended Code Sec. 2501(a). **Effective** for the calendar year 1967 and all calendar years thereafter. Prior to amendment, Code Sec. 2501(a) read as follows:

(a) GENERAL RULE.—For the calendar year 1955 and each calendar year thereafter a tax, computed as provided in section 2502, is hereby imposed on the transfer of property by gift during such calendar year by any individual, resident or nonresident, except transfers of intangible property by a nonresident not a citizen of the United States who was not engaged in business in the United States during such calendar year."

• 1960 (P.L. 86-779)

P.L. 86-779, §4(d)(2):

Amended Code Sec. 2501(a) by striking out "nonresident who is not a citizen of the United States and" and by substituting "nonresident not a citizen of the United States". **Effective** for gifts made after 9-14-60.

[Sec. 2501(b)]

(b) CERTAIN RESIDENTS OF POSSESSIONS CONSIDERED CITIZENS OF THE UNITED STATES.—A donor who is a citizen of the United States and a resident of a possession thereof shall, for purposes of the tax imposed by this chapter, be considered a "citizen" of the United States within the meaning of that term wherever used in this title unless he acquired his United States citizenship solely by reason of (1) his being a citizen of such possession of the United States, or (2) his birth or residence within such possession of the United States.

Amendments

• 1958, Technical Amendments Act of 1958 (P.L. 85-866)

P.L. 85-866, §102(b), (d):

Redesignated former Code Sec. 2501(b) as 2501(c) (now (d)) and added new subsection (b). **Effective** for gifts made after 9-2-58.

[Sec. 2501(c)]

(c) CERTAIN RESIDENTS OF POSSESSIONS CONSIDERED NONRESIDENTS NOT CITIZENS OF THE UNITED STATES.—A donor who is a citizen of the United States and a resident of a possession thereof shall, for purposes of the tax imposed by this chapter, be considered a "nonresident not a citizen of the United States" within the meaning of that term wherever used in this title, but only if such donor acquired his United States citizenship solely by reason of (1) his being a citizen of such possession of the United States, or (2) his birth or residence within such possession of the United States.

Amendments

• 1960 (P.L. 86-779)

P.L. 86-779, §4(d)(1):

Redesignated former Code Sec. 2501(c) as 2501(d) and added a new subsection (c). **Effective** for gifts made after 9-14-60.

[Sec. 2501(d)]

(d) CROSS REFERENCES.—

(1) For increase in basis of property acquired by gift for gift tax paid, see section 1015(d).

(2) For exclusion of transfers of property outside the United States by a nonresident who is not a citizen of the United States, see section 2511(a).

Amendments

• 1990, Omnibus Budget Reconciliation Act of 1990 (P.L. 101-508)

P.L. 101-508, §11601(b)(2):

Amended Code Sec. 2051(d) by striking paragraph (3). **Effective** in the case of property transferred after 12-17-87. Prior to being stricken, paragraph (3) read as follows:

(3) For treatment of certain transfers related to estate tax valuation freezes as gifts to which this chapter applies, see section 2036(c)(4).

• 1988, Technical and Miscellaneous Revenue Act of 1988 (P.L. 100-647)

P.L. 100-647, §3031(a)(2):

Amended Code Sec. 2501(d) by adding at the end thereof a new paragraph (3). **Effective** in cases where the Code Sec. 2036(c)(1)(B) transfer is on or after 6-21-88.

• 1960 (P.L. 86-779)

P.L. 86-779, §4(d)(1):

Redesignated former Code Sec. 2501(c) as 2501(d). **Effective** for gifts made after 9-14-60.

• 1958, Technical Amendments Act of 1958 (P.L. 85-866)

P.L. 85-866, §43(b):

Amended former Code Sec. 2501(b). **Effective** 1-1-54. Prior to amendment, Code Sec. 2501(b) read as follows:

"(b) CROSS REFERENCE.—

"For exclusion of transfers of property outside the United States by a nonresident who is not a citizen of the United States, see section 2511(a)."

P.L. 85-866, §102(b):

Redesignated subsection (b) as subsection (c). **Effective** 9-3-58.

[Sec. 2502]

SEC. 2502. RATE OF TAX.

[Sec. 2502(a)]

(a) COMPUTATION OF TAX.—The tax imposed by section 2501 for each calendar year shall be an amount equal to the excess of—

(1) a tentative tax, computed under section 2001(c), on the aggregate sum of the taxable gifts for such calendar year and for each of the preceding calendar periods, over

(2) a tentative tax, computed under such section, on the aggregate sum of the taxable gifts for each of the preceding calendar periods.

Amendments

• 2010, Tax Relief, Unemployment Insurance Reauthorization, and Job Creation Act of 2010 (P.L. 111-312)

P.L. 111-312, §302(b)(2):

Amended Code Sec. 2502(a) to read as such subsection would read if section 511(d) of the Economic Growth and Tax Relief Reconciliation Act of 2001 (P.L. 107-16) had never been enacted. **Effective** on and after 1-1-2011. Prior to amendment by P.L. 111-312, Code Sec. 2502(a) read as follows:

(a) COMPUTATION OF TAX.—

(1) IN GENERAL.—The tax imposed by section 2501 for each calendar year shall be an amount equal to the excess of—

(A) a tentative tax, computed under paragraph (2), on the aggregate sum of the taxable gifts for such calendar year and for each of the preceding calendar periods, over

(B) a tentative tax, computed under paragraph (2), on the aggregate sum of the taxable gifts for each of the preceding calendar periods.

(2) RATE SCHEDULE.—

If the amount with respect to which the tentative tax to be computed is:	*The tentative tax is:*
Not over $10,000	18% of such amount.
Over $10,000 but not over $20,000	$1,800, plus 20% of the excess over $10,000.
Over $20,000 but not over $40,000	$3,800, plus 22% of the excess over $20,000.
Over $40,000 but not over $60,000	$8,200, plus 24% of the excess over $40,000.
Over $60,000 but not over $80,000	$13,000, plus 26% of the excess over $60,000.
Over $80,000 but not over $100,000	$18,200, plus 28% of the excess over $80,000.
Over $100,000 but not over $150,000	$23,800, plus 30% of the excess over $100,000.
Over $150,000 but not over $250,000	$38,800, plus 32% of the excess over $150,000.
Over $250,000 but not over $500,000	$70,800, plus 34% of the excess over $250,000.
Over $500,000	$155,800, plus 35% of the excess over $500,000.

P.L. 111-312, §304, provides:

SEC. 304. APPLICATION OF EGTRRA SUNSET TO THIS TITLE.

Section 901 of the Economic Growth and Tax Relief Reconciliation Act of 2001 shall apply to the amendments made by this title.

• 2001, Economic Growth and Tax Relief Reconciliation Act of 2001 (P.L. 107-16)

P.L. 107-16, § 511(d):

Amended Code Sec. 2502(a). **Effective** for gifts made after 12-31-2009. Prior to amendment, Code Sec. 2502(a) read as follows:

(a) COMPUTATION OF TAX.—The tax imposed by section 2501 for each calendar year shall be an amount equal to the excess of—

(1) a tentative tax, computed under section 2001(c), on the aggregate sum of the taxable gifts for such calendar year and for each of the preceding calendar periods, over

(2) a tentative tax, computed under such section, on the aggregate sum of the taxable gifts for each of the preceding calendar periods.

P.L. 107-16, § 901(a)-(b), as amended by P.L. 111-312, § 101(a)(1), provides:

SEC. 901. SUNSET OF PROVISIONS OF ACT.

(a) IN GENERAL.—All provisions of, and amendments made by, this Act shall not apply—

(1) to taxable, plan, or limitation years beginning after December 31, 2012, or

(2) in the case of title V, to estates of decedents dying, gifts made, or generation skipping transfers, after December 31, 2012.

(b) APPLICATION OF CERTAIN LAWS.—The Internal Revenue Code of 1986 and the Employee Retirement Income Security Act of 1974 shall be applied and administered to years, estates, gifts, and transfers described in subsection (a) as if the provisions and amendments described in subsection (a) had never been enacted.

• 1987, Revenue Act of 1987 (P.L. 100-203)

P.L. 100-203, § 10401(b)(2)(B)(i)-(ii):

Amended Code Sec. 2502(a) by striking out "in accordance with the rate schedule set forth in section 2001(c)" in paragraph (1) and inserting in lieu thereof "under section 2001(c)", and by striking out "in accordance with such rate schedule" in paragraph (2) and inserting in lieu thereof "under such section". **Effective** in the case of decedents dying, and gifts made, after 12-31-87.

• 1981, Economic Recovery Tax Act of 1981 (P.L. 97-34)

P.L. 97-34, § 442(a)(2):

Amended Code Sec. 2502(a). **Effective** with respect to gifts made after 12-31-81. Prior to amendment, Code Sec. 2502(a) read as follows:

(a) COMPUTATION OF TAX.—The tax imposed by section 2501 for each calendar quarter shall be an amount equal to the excess of—

(1) a tentative tax, computed in accordance with the rate schedule set forth in Section 2001(c), on the aggregate sum of the taxable gifts for such calendar quarter and for each of the preceding calendar years and calendar quarters, over

(2) a tentative tax, computed in accordance with such rate schedule, on the aggregate sum of the taxable gifts for each of the preceding calendar years and calendar quarters.

• 1976, Tax Reform Act of 1976 (P.L. 94-455)

P.L. 94-455, § 2001(b)(1), (d)(2):

Amended Code Sec. 2502(a). **Effective** for gifts made after 12-31-76. Prior to amendment, Code Sec. 2502(a) read as follows:

(a) COMPUTATION OF TAX.—The tax imposed by section 2501 for each calendar quarter shall be an amount equal to the excess of—

(1) a tax, computed in accordance with the rate schedule set forth in this subsection, on the aggregate sum of the taxable gifts for such calendar quarter and for each of the preceding calendar years and calendar quarters, over

(2) a tax, computed in accordance with such rate schedule, on the aggregate sum of the taxable gifts for each of the preceding calendar years and calendar quarters.

RATE SCHEDULE

If the taxable gifts are:	The tax shall be:
Not over $5,000	2¼% of the taxable gifts.
Over $5,000 but not over $10,000	$112.50, plus 5¼% of excess over $5,000.
Over $10,000 but not over $20,000	$375, plus 8¼% of excess over $10,000.
Over $20,000 but not over $30,000	$1,200, plus 10½% of excess over $20,000.
Over $30,000 but not over $40,000	$2,250, plus 13½% of excess over $30,000.
Over $40,000 but not over $50,000	$3,600, plus 16½% of excess over $40,000.
Over $50,000 but not over $60,000	$5,250, plus 18¾% of excess over $50,000.
Over $60,000 but not over $100,000	$7,125, plus 21% of excess over $60,000.
Over $100,000 but not over $250,000	$15,525, plus 22½% of excess over $100,000.
Over $250,000 but not over $500,000	$49,275, plus 24% of excess over $250,000.
Over $500,000 but not over $750,000	$109,275, plus 26¼% of excess over $500,000.
Over $750,000 but not over $1,000,000	$174,900, plus 27¾% of excess over $750,000.
Over $1,000,000 but not over $1,250,000	$244,275, plus 29¼% of excess over $1,000,000.
Over $1,250,000 but not over $1,500,000	$317,400, plus 31½% of excess over $1,250,000.
Over $1,500,000 but not over $2,000,000	$396,150 plus 33¾% of excess over $1,500,000.
Over $2,000,000 but not over $2,500,000	$564,900, plus 36¾% of excess over $2,000,000.
Over $2,500,000 but not over $3,000,000	$748,650, plus 39¾% of excess over $2,500,000
Over $3,000,000 but not over $3,500,000	$947,400, plus 42% of excess over $3,000,000.
Over $3,500,000 but not over $4,000,000	$1,157,400, plus 44¼% of excess over $3,500,000.
Over $4,000,000 but not over $5,000,000	$1,378,650, plus 47¼% of excess over $4,000,000.
Over $5,000,000 but not over $6,000,000	$1,851,150, plus 50¼% of excess over $5,000,000.

Over \$6,000,000 but not over \$7,000,000	\$2,353,650, plus 52½% of excess over \$6,000,000.
Over \$7,000,000 but not over \$8,000,000	\$2,878,650, plus 54¾% of excess over \$7,000,000.
Over \$8,000,000 but not over \$10,000,000	\$3,426,150, plus 57% of excess over \$8,000,000.
Over \$10,000,000	\$4,566,150, plus 57¾% of excess over \$10,000,000.

• 1970, Excise, Estate, and Gift Tax Adjustment Act of 1970 (P.L. 91-614)

P.L. 91-614, §102(a)(2)(A):

Amended the matter preceding the tax rate schedule in Code Sec. 2502. **Effective** for gifts made after 12-31-70. Prior to amendment, this matter read as follows:

"(a) Computation of Tax.—The tax imposed by section 2501 for each calendar year shall be an amount equal to the excess of—

"(1) a tax, computed in accordance with the rate schedule set forth in this subsection, on the aggregate sum of the taxable gifts for such calendar year and for each of the preceding calendar years, over

"(2) a tax, computed in accordance with such rate schedule, on the aggregate sum of the taxable gifts for each of the preceding calendar years."

[Sec. 2502(b)]

(b) PRECEDING CALENDAR PERIOD.—Whenever used in this title in connection with the gift tax imposed by this chapter, the term "preceding calendar period" means—

(1) calendar years 1932 and 1970 and all calendar years intervening between calendar year 1932 and calendar year 1970,

(2) the first calendar quarter of calendar year 1971 and all calendar quarters intervening between such calendar quarter and the first calendar quarter of calendar year 1982, and

(3) all calendar years after 1981 and before the calendar year for which the tax is being computed.

For purposes of paragraph (1), the term "calendar year 1932" includes only that portion of such year after June 6, 1932.

Amendments

• 1981, Economic Recovery Tax Act of 1981 (P.L. 97-34)

P.L. 97-34, §442(a)(2):

Amended Code Sec. 2502(b). **Effective** with respect to gifts made after 12-31-81. Prior to amendment Code Sec. 2502(b) read as follows:

(b) CALENDAR QUARTER.—Wherever used in this title in connection with the gift tax imposed by this chapter, the term "calendar quarter" includes only the first calendar quarter of the calendar year 1971 and succeeding calendar quarters.

• 1970, Excise, Estate, and Gift Tax Adjustment Act of 1970 (P.L. 91-614)

P.L. 91-614, §102(a)(2)(B):

Amended Code Sec. 2502(b). **Effective** for gifts made after 12-31-70. Prior to amendment, Code Sec. 2502(b) read as follows:

"(b) Calendar Year.—The term `calendar year' includes only the calendar year 1932 and succeeding calendar years, and, in the case of the calendar year 1932, includes only the portion of such year after June 6, 1932."

[Sec. 2502(c)]

(c) TAX TO BE PAID BY DONOR.—The tax imposed by section 2501 shall be paid by the donor.

Amendments

• 1981, Economic Recovery Tax Act of 1981 (P.L. 97-34)

P.L. 97-34, §442(a)(2):

Amended Code Sec. 2502(c). **Effective** with respect to gifts made after 12-31-81. Prior to amendment, Code Sec. 2502(c) read as follows:

(c) PRECEDING CALENDAR YEARS AND QUARTERS.—Wherever used in this title in connection with the gift tax imposed by this chapter—

(1) The term "preceding calendar years" means calendar years 1932 and 1970 and all calendar years intervening between calendar year 1932 and calendar year 1970. The term "calendar year 1932" includes only the portion of such year after June 6, 1932.

(2) The term "preceding calendar quarters" means the first calendar quarter of calendar year 1971 and all calendar quarters intervening between such calendar quarter and the calendar quarter for which the tax is being computed.

• 1970, Excise, Estate, and Gift Tax Adjustment Act of 1970 (P.L. 91-614)

P.L. 91-614, §102(a)(2)(B):

Amended Code Sec. 2502(c). **Effective** for gifts made after 12-31-70. Prior to amendment, Code Sec. 2502(c) read as follows:

"(c) Preceding Calendar Years.—The term `preceding calendar years' means the calendar year 1932 and all calendar years intervening between the calendar year 1932 and the calendar year for which the tax is being computed."

[Sec. 2502(d)—Repealed]

Amendments

• 1981, Economic Recovery Tax Act of 1981 (P.L. 97-34)

P.L. 97-34, §442(a)(2):

Amended Code Sec. 2502. **Effective** with respect to gifts made after 12-31-81. Code Sec. 2502, as amended, does not include Code Sec. 2502(d). Prior to repeal, Code Sec. 2502(d) read as follows:

(d) TAX TO BE PAID BY DONOR.—The tax imposed by section 2501 shall be paid by the donor.

[Sec. 2503]

SEC. 2503. TAXABLE GIFTS.

[Sec. 2503(a)]

(a) GENERAL DEFINITION.—The term "taxable gifts" means the total amount of gifts made during the calendar year, less the deductions provided in subchapter C (section 2522 and following).

Amendments

• 1981, Economic Recovery Tax Act of 1981 (P.L. 97-34)

P.L. 97-34, §442(a)(3)(A):

Amended Code Sec. 2503(a). **Effective** with respect to gifts made after 12-31-81. Prior to amendment, Code Sec. 2503(a) read as follows:

(a) GENERAL DEFINITION.—The term "taxable gifts" means, in the case of gifts made after December 31, 1970, the total amount of gifts made during the calendar quarter, less the deductions provided in subchapter C (sec. 2521 and following). In the case of gifts made before January 1, 1971, such term means the total amount of gifts made during the calendar year, less the deductions provided in subchapter C.

• 1970, Excise, Estate, and Gift Tax Adjustment Act of 1970 (P.L. 91-614)

P.L. 91-614, §102(a)(3)(A):

Amended Code Sec. 2503(a). **Effective** for gifts made after 12-31-70. Prior to amendment, the section read as follows:

"(a) General Definition.—The term 'taxable gifts' means the total amount of gifts made during the calendar year, less the deductions provided in subchapter C (sec. 2521 and following)."

[Sec. 2503(b)]

(b) EXCLUSIONS FROM GIFTS.—

(1) IN GENERAL.—In the case of gifts (other than gifts of future interests in property) made to any person by the donor during the calendar year, the first $10,000 of such gifts to such person shall not, for purposes of subsection (a), be included in the total amount of gifts made during such year. Where there has been a transfer to any person of a present interest in property, the possibility that such interest may be diminished by the exercise of a power shall be disregarded in applying this subsection, if no part of such interest will at any time pass to any other person.

(2) INFLATION ADJUSTMENT.—In the case of gifts made in a calendar year after 1998, the $10,000 amount contained in paragraph (1) shall be increased by an amount equal to—

(A) $10,000, multiplied by

(B) the cost-of-living adjustment determined under section 1(f)(3) for such calendar year by substituting "calendar year 1997" for "calendar year 2016" in subparagraph (A)(ii) thereof.

If any amount as adjusted under the preceding sentence is not a multiple of $1,000, such amount shall be rounded to the next lowest multiple of $1,000.

Amendments

• 2017, Tax Cuts and Jobs Act (P.L. 115-97)

P.L. 115-97, §11002(d)(1)(EE):

Amended Code Sec. 2503(b)(2)(B) by striking "for 'calendar year 1992' in subparagraph (B)" and inserting "for 'calendar year 2016' in subparagraph (A)(ii)". **Effective** for tax years beginning after 12-31-2017.

• 1997, Taxpayer Relief Act of 1997 (P.L. 105-34)

P.L. 105-34, §501(c)(1)-(3):

Amended Code Sec. 2503(b) by striking the subsection heading and inserting "(b) EXCLUSIONS FROM GIFTS.—(1) IN GENERAL.—", by moving the text 2 ems to the right, and by adding a new paragraph (2). **Effective** for estates of decedents dying, and gifts made, after 12-31-97. Prior to amendment, the heading for Code Sec. 2503(b) read as follows:

(b) EXCLUSIONS FROM GIFTS.—

• 1981, Economic Recovery Tax Act of 1981 (P.L. 97-34)

P.L. 97-34, §441(a):

Amended Code Sec. 2503(b) by striking out "$3,000" and inserting "$10,000". **Effective**, generally, for transfers made after 12-31-81. There is also a special rule applicable to certain instruments creating powers of appointment before 9-12-81.

P.L. 97-34, §441(c), provides:

(c) EFFECTIVE DATES.—

(1) IN GENERAL.—Except as provided in paragraph (2), the amendments made by this section shall apply to transfers after December 31, 1981.

(2) TRANSITIONAL RULE.—If—

(A) an instrument executed before the date which is 30 days after the date of the enactment of this Act provides for a power of appointment which may be exercised during any period after December 31, 1981,

(B) such power of appointment is expressly defined in terms of, or by reference to, the amount of the gift tax exclusion under section 2503(b) of the Internal Revenue Code of 1954 (or the corresponding provision of prior law),

(C) the instrument described in subparagraph (A) has not been amended on or after the date which is 30 days after the date of the enactment of this Act, and

(D) the State has not enacted a statute applicable to such gift under which such power of appointment is to be construed as being defined in terms of, or by reference to, the amount of the exclusion under such section 2503(b) after its amendment by subsection (a),

then the amendment made by subsection (a) shall not apply to such gift.

P.L. 97-34, §442(a)(3)(B):

Amended the first sentence of Code Sec. 2503(b). **Effective** with respect to gifts made after 12-31-81. Prior to amendment, the sentence read as follows:

In computing taxable gifts for the calendar quarter, in the case of gifts (other than gifts of future interests in property) made to any person by the donor during the calendar year 1971 and subsequent calendar years, $3,000 of such gifts to such person less the aggregate of the amounts of such gifts to such person during all preceding calendar quarters of the calendar year shall not, for purposes of subsection (a), be included in the total amount of gifts made during such quarter.

• 1970, Excise, Estate, and Gift Tax Adjustment Act of 1970 (P.L. 91-614)

P.L. 91-614, §102(a)(3)(B):

Amended the first sentence of Code Sec. 2503(b). **Effective** for gifts made after 12-31-70. Prior to amendment, the first sentence read as follows:

"In the case of gifts (other than gifts of future interests in property) made to any person by the donor during the calendar year 1955 and subsequent calendar years, the first $3,000 of such gifts to such person shall not, for purposes of subsection (a), be included in the total amount of gifts made during such year."

[Sec. 2503(c)]

(c) TRANSFER FOR THE BENEFIT OF MINOR.—No part of a gift to an individual who has not attained the age of 21 years on the date of such transfer shall be considered a gift of a future interest in property for purposes of subsection (b) if the property and the income therefrom—

(1) may be expended by, or for the benefit of, the donee before his attaining the age of 21 years, and

(2) will to the extent not so expended—

(A) pass to the donee on his attaining the age of 21 years, and

(B) in the event the donee dies before attaining the age of 21 years, be payable to the estate of the donee or as he may appoint under a general power of appointment as defined in section 2514(c).

[Sec. 2503(d)—Repealed]

Amendments

• 1981, Economic Recovery Tax Act of 1981 (P.L. 97-34)

P.L. 97-34, §311(h)(5):

Repealed Code Sec. 2503(d). **Effective** for transfers after 12-31-81 [**effective** date changed by P.L. 97-448, §103(c)(11).—CCH]. The transitional rule provides that, for purposes of the 1954 Code, any amount allowed as a deduction under section 220 of the Code (as in effect before its repeal by P.L. 97-34) shall be treated as if it were allowed by Code Sec. 219. Prior to repeal, Code Sec. 2503(d) read as follows:

(d) INDIVIDUAL RETIREMENT ACCOUNTS, ETC., FOR SPOUSE.—For purposes of subsection (b), any payment made by an individual for the benefit of his spouse—

(1) to an individual retirement account described in section 408(a),

(2) for an individual retirement annuity described in section 408(b), or

(3) for a retirement bond described in section 409,

shall not be considered a gift of a future interest in property to the extent that such payment is allowable as a deduction under section 220.

• 1978, Revenue Act of 1978 (P.L. 95-600)

P.L. 95-600, §702(j)(2):

Added Code Sec. 2503(d). **Effective** for transfers made after 12-31-76.

[Sec. 2503(e)]

(e) EXCLUSION FOR CERTAIN TRANSFERS FOR EDUCATIONAL EXPENSES OR MEDICAL EXPENSES.—

(1) IN GENERAL.—Any qualified transfer shall not be treated as a transfer of property by gift for purposes of this chapter.

(2) QUALIFIED TRANSFER.—For purposes of this subsection, the term "qualified transfer" means any amount paid on behalf of an individual—

(A) as tuition to an educational organization described in section 170(b)(1)(A)(ii) for the education or training of such individual, or

(B) to any person who provides medical care (as defined in section 213(d)) with respect to such individual as payment for such medical care.

Amendments

• 1988, Technical and Miscellaneous Revenue Act of 1988 (P.L. 100-647)

P.L. 100-647, §1018(u)(52):

Amended Code Sec. 2503(e)(2)(B) by striking out "section 213(e)" and inserting in lieu thereof "section 213(d)". **Effective** as if included in the provision of P.L. 99-514 to which it relates.

• 1981, Economic Recovery Tax Act of 1981 (P.L. 97-34)

P.L. 97-34, §441(b):

Added Code Sec. 2503(e). **Effective** for transfers made after 12-31-81.

[Sec. 2503(f)]

(f) WAIVER OF CERTAIN PENSION RIGHTS.—If any individual waives, before the death of a particpant, any survivor benefit, or right to such benefit, under section 401(a)(11) or 417, such waiver shall not be treated as a transfer of property by gift for purposes of this chapter.

Amendments

• 1986, Tax Reform Act of 1986 (P.L. 99-514)

P.L. 99-514, §1898(h)(1)(B):

Amended Code Sec. 2503 by adding at the end thereof new subsection (f). **Effective** as if included in the provision of P.L. 98-397 to which it relates.

[Sec. 2503(g)]

(g) TREATMENT OF CERTAIN LOANS OF ARTWORKS.—

(1) IN GENERAL.—For purposes of this subtitle, any loan of a qualified work of art shall not be treated as a transfer (and the value of such qualified work of art shall be determined as if such loan had not been made) if—

(A) such loan is to an organization described in section 501(c)(3) and exempt from tax under section 501(c) (other than a private foundation), and

(B) the use of such work by such organization is related to the purpose or function constituting the basis for its exemption under section 501.

(2) DEFINITIONS.—For purposes of this section—

(A) QUALIFIED WORK OF ART.—The term "qualified work of art" means any archaelogical, historic, or creative tangible personal property.

(B) PRIVATE FOUNDATION.—The term "private foundation" has the meaning given such term by section 509, except that such term shall not include any private operating foundation (as defined in section 4942(j)(3)).

Amendments

• 1989, Omnibus Budget Reconciliation Act of 1989 (P.L. 101-239)

P.L. 101-239, §7811(m)(1):

Amended Code Sec. 2503 by redesignating subsection (f), as added by §1018 of P.L. 100-647, as subsection (g). **Effective** as if included in the provision of P.L. 100-647 to which it relates.

• 1988, Technical and Miscellaneous Revenue Act of 1988 (P.L. 100-647)

P.L. 100-647, §1018(s)(2)(A):

Amended Code Sec. 2503 by adding at the end thereof a new subsection (f)[(g)]. **Effective** for loans after 7-31-69.

[Sec. 2504]

SEC. 2504. TAXABLE GIFTS FOR PRECEDING CALENDAR PERIODS.

[Sec. 2504(a)]

(a) IN GENERAL.—In computing taxable gifts for preceding calendar periods for purposes of computing the tax for any calendar year—

(1) there shall be treated as gifts such transfers as were considered to be gifts under the gift tax laws applicable to the calendar period in which the transfers were made,

(2) there shall be allowed such deductions as were provided for under such laws, and

(3) the specific exemption in the amount (if any) allowable under section 2521 (as in effect before its repeal by the Tax Reform Act of 1976) shall be applied in all computations in respect of preceding calendar periods ending before January 1, 1977, for purposes of computing the tax for any calendar year.

Amendments

• 1981, Economic Recovery Tax Act of 1981 (P.L. 97-34)

P.L. 97-34, §442(a)(4)(A):

Amended Code Sec. 2504(a). **Effective** with respect to gifts made after 12-31-81. Prior to amendment, Code Sec. 2504(a) read as follows:

(a) IN GENERAL.—In computing taxable gifts for preceding calendar years or calendar quarters for the purpose of computing the tax for any calendar quarter, there shall be treated as gifts such transfers as were considered to be gifts under the gift tax laws applicable to the years or calendar quarters in which the transfers were made and there shall be allowed such deductions as were provided for under such laws; except that the specific exemption in the amount, if any, allowable under section 2521 (as in effect before its repeal by the Tax Reform Act of 1976) shall be applied in all computations in respect of calendar years or calendar quarters ending before January 1, 1977, for purposes of computing the tax for any calendar quarter.

P.L. 97-34, §442(a)(4)(D):

Amended the section heading for Code Sec. 2504 by striking out "PRECEDING YEARS AND QUARTERS" and inserting "PRECEDING CALENDAR PERIODS". **Effective** with respect to gifts made after 12-31-81.

• 1976, Tax Reform Act of 1976 (P.L. 94-455)

P.L. 94-455, §2001(c)(2)(A), (d)(2):

Substituted "section 2521 (as in effect before its repeal by the Tax Reform Act of 1976) shall be applied in all computations in respect of calendar years or calendar quarters ending before January 1, 1977, for purposes of computing the tax for any calendar quarter" for "section 2521 shall be applied in all computations in respect of previous calendar years or calendar quarters for the purpose of computing the tax for any calendar year or calendar quarter" in Code Sec. 2504(a). **Effective** for gifts made after 12-31-76.

[Sec. 2504(b)]

(b) EXCLUSIONS FROM GIFTS FOR PRECEDING CALENDAR PERIODS.—In the case of gifts made to any person by the donor during preceding calendar periods, the amount excluded, if any, by the provisions of gift tax laws applicable to the periods in which the gifts were made shall not, for purposes of subsection (a), be included in the total amount of the gifts made during such preceding calendar periods.

Amendments

• 1981, Economic Recovery Tax Act of 1981 (P.L. 97-34)

P.L. 97-34, §442(a)(4)(B):

Amended Code Sec. 2504(b) by striking out "preceding calendar years and calendar quarters" and inserting "preceding calendar periods", by striking out "the years and calendar quarters" and inserting "the periods", by striking out "such years and calendar quarters" and inserting "such preceding calendar periods", and by striking out "PRECEDING YEARS AND QUARTERS" in the subsection heading and inserting "PRECEDING CALENDAR PERIODS". **Effective** with respect to gifts made after 12-31-81.

[Sec. 2504(c)]

(c) VALUATION OF GIFTS.—If the time has expired under section 6501 within which a tax may be assessed under this chapter 12 (or under corresponding provisions of prior laws) on—

(1) the transfer of property by gift made during a preceding calendar period (as defined in section 2502(b)); or

(2) an increase in taxable gifts required under section 2701(d),

the value thereof shall, for purposes of computing the tax under this chapter, be the value as finally determined (within the meaning of section 2001(f)(2)) for purposes of this chapter.

Amendments

• 1998, IRS Restructuring and Reform Act of 1998 (P.L. 105-206)

P.L. 105-206, §6007(e)(2)(B)[(C)]:

Amended Code Sec. 2504(c). **Effective** as if included in the provision of P.L. 105-34 to which it relates [**effective** for gifts made after 8-5-97.—CCH]. Prior to amendment, Code Sec. 2504(c) read as follows:

(c) VALUATION OF CERTAIN GIFTS FOR PRECEDING CALENDAR PERIODS.—If the time has expired within which a tax may be assessed under this chapter or under corresponding provisions of prior laws on the transfer of property by gift made during a preceding calendar period, as defined in section 2502(b), the value of such gift made in such preceding calendar period shall, for purposes of computing the tax under this chapter for any calendar year, be the value of such gift which was used in computing the tax for the last preceding calendar period for which a tax under this chapter or under corresponding provisions of prior laws was assessed or paid.

• 1997, Taxpayer Relief Act of 1997 (P.L. 105-34)

P.L. 105-34, §506(d):

Amended Code Sec. 2504(c) by striking ", and if a tax under this chapter or under corresponding provisions of prior laws has been assessed or paid for such preceding calendar period" after "section 2502(b)". **Effective** for gifts made after 8-5-97 [**effective** date changed by P.L. 105-206, §6007(e)(1)].

• 1981, Economic Recovery Tax Act of 1981 (P.L. 97-34)

P.L. 97-34, §442(a)(4)(C):

Amended Code Sec. 2504(c) by striking out "preceding calendar year or calendar quarter" each place it appears and inserting "preceding calendar period", by striking out "under this chapter for any calendar quarter" and inserting "under this chapter for any calendar year", by striking out "section 2502(c)" and inserting "section 2502(b)", and by striking out "PRECEDING CALENDAR YEARS AND QUARTERS" in the subsection heading and inserting "PRECEDING CALENDAR PERIODS". **Effective** with respect to gifts made after 12-31-81.

[Sec. 2504(d)]

(d) NET GIFTS.—The term "net gifts" as used in corresponding provisions of prior laws shall be read as "taxable gifts" for purposes of this chapter.

Amendments

• 1970, Excise, Estate, and Gift Tax Adjustment Act of 1970 (P.L. 91-614)

P.L. 91-614, §102(a)(4)(A):

Amended Code Sec. 2504. **Effective** 1-1-71. Prior to amendment, the section read as follows:

Sec. 2504. Taxable Gifts for Preceding Years.

(a) In General.—In computing taxable gifts for the calendar year 1954 and preceding calendar years for the purpose of computing the tax for the calendar year 1955 or any calendar year thereafter, there shall be treated as gifts such transfers as were considered to be gifts under the gift tax laws applicable to the years in which the transfers were made and there shall be allowed such deductions as were provided for under such laws, except that specific exemption in the amount, if any, allowable under section 2521 shall be applied in all computations in respect of the calendar year 1954 and previous calendar years for the purpose of computing the tax for the calendar year 1955 or any calendar year thereafter.

(b) Exclusions From Gifts for Preceding Years.—In the case of gifts made to any person by the donor during the calendar year 1954 and preceding calendar years, the amount excluded, if any, by the provisions of gift tax laws applicable to the years in which the gifts were made shall not, for purposes of subsection (a), be included in the total amount of the gifts made during such year.

(c) Valuation of Certain Gifts for Preceding Calendar Years.—If the time has expired within which a tax may be assessed under this chapter or under corresponding provisions of prior laws, on the transfer of property by gift made during a preceding calendar year, as defined in section 2502(c), and if a tax under this chapter or under corresponding provisions of prior laws has been assessed or paid for such preceding calendar year, the value of such gift made in such preceding calendar year shall, for purposes of computing the tax under this chapter for the calendar year 1955 and subsequent calendar years, be the value of such gift which was used in computing the tax for the last preceding calendar year, for which a tax under this chapter or under corresponding provisions of prior laws was assessed or paid.

(d) Net Gifts.—For years before the calendar year 1955, the term "net gifts" as used in corresponding provisions of prior laws shall be read as "taxable gifts" for purposes of this chapter.

[Sec. 2505]

SEC. 2505. UNIFIED CREDIT AGAINST GIFT TAX.

[Sec. 2505(a)]

(a) GENERAL RULE.—In the case of a citizen or resident of the United States, there shall be allowed as a credit against the tax imposed by section 2501 for each calendar year an amount equal to—

(1) the applicable credit amount in effect under section 2010(c) which would apply if the donor died as of the end of the calendar year, reduced by

(2) the sum of the amounts allowable as a credit to the individual under this section for all preceding calendar periods.

For purposes of applying paragraph (2) for any calendar year, the rates of tax in effect under section 2502(a)(2) for such calendar year shall, in lieu of the rates of tax in effect for preceding calendar periods, be used in determining the amounts allowable as a credit under this section for all preceding calendar periods.

Amendments

• 2010, Tax Relief, Unemployment Insurance Reauthorization, and Job Creation Act of 2010 (P.L. 111-312)

P.L. 111-312, §301(b):

Amended Code Sec. 2505(a)(1) to read as such paragraph would read if section 521(b)(2) of the Economic Growth and Tax Relief Reconciliation Act of 2001 (P.L. 107-16) had never been enacted. **Effective** on and after 1-1-2011. Prior to amendment by P.L. 111-312, Code Sec. 2505(a)(1) read as follows:

(1) the amount of the tentative tax which would be determined under the rate schedule set forth in section 2502(a)(2) if the amount with respect to which such tentative tax is to be computed were $1,000,000, reduced by

P.L. 111-312, §302(b)(1)(A):

Amended Code Sec. 2505(a)(1), after the application of Act Sec. 301(b), by striking "(determined as if the applicable exclusion amount were $1,000,000)" after "such calendar year". **Effective** for gifts made after 12-31-2010.

P.L. 111-312, §302(d)(2):

Amended Code Sec. 2505(a) by adding at the end a new flush sentence. **Effective** for estates of decedents dying, generation-skipping transfers, and gifts made, after 12-31-2009.

P.L. 111-312, §303(b)(1):

Amended Code Sec. 2505(a)(1), as amended by Act Sec. 302(b)(1). **Effective** for estates of decedents dying and gifts made after 12-31-2010. Prior to amendment, Code Sec. 2505(a)(1) read as follows:

(1) the applicable credit amount in effect under section 2010(c) for such calendar year, reduced by

P.L. 111-312, §304, provides:

SEC. 304. APPLICATION OF EGTRRA SUNSET TO THIS TITLE.

Section 901 of the Economic Growth and Tax Relief Reconciliation Act of 2001 shall apply to the amendments made by this title.

• 2001, Economic Growth and Tax Relief Reconciliation Act of 2001 (P.L. 107-16)

P.L. 107-16, §521(b)(1):

Amended Code Sec. 2505(a)(1) by inserting "(determined as if the applicable exclusion amount were $1,000,000)" after "calendar year". **Effective** for estates of decedents dying, and gifts made, after 12-31-2001.

P.L. 107-16, §521(b)(2):

Amended Code Sec. 2505(a)(1), as amended by Act Sec. 521(b)(1). **Effective** for gifts made after 12-31-2009. Prior to amendment, Code Sec. 2505(a)(1) read as follows:

(1) the applicable credit amount in effect under section 2010(c) for such calendar year (determined as if the applicable exclusion amount were $1,000,000), reduced by

P.L. 107-16, §901(a)-(b), as amended by P.L. 111-312, §101(a)(1), provides:

SEC. 901. SUNSET OF PROVISIONS OF ACT.

(a) IN GENERAL.—All provisions of, and amendments made by, this Act shall not apply—

(1) to taxable, plan, or limitation years beginning after December 31, 2012, or

(2) in the case of title V, to estates of decedents dying, gifts made, or generation skipping transfers, after December 31, 2012.

(b) APPLICATION OF CERTAIN LAWS.—The Internal Revenue Code of 1986 and the Employee Retirement Income Security Act of 1974 shall be applied and administered to years, estates, gifts, and transfers described in subsection (a) as if the provisions and amendments described in subsection (a) had never been enacted.

• 1997, Taxpayer Relief Act of 1997 (P.L. 105-34)

P.L. 105-34, §501(a)(2):

Amended Code Sec. 2505(a)(1) by striking "$192,800" and inserting "the applicable credit amount in effect under section 2010(c) for such calendar year". **Effective** for estates of decedents dying, and gifts made, after 12-31-97.

• 1981, Economic Recovery Tax Act of 1981 (P.L. 97-34)

P.L. 97-34, §401(b)(1):

Amended Code Sec. 2505(a) by striking out "$47,000" and inserting "$192,800". **Effective** for gifts made after 12-31-81.

P.L. 97-34, §442(a)(5)(A):

Amended Code Sec. 2505(a) by striking out "each calendar quarter" and inserting "each calendar year" and by striking out "preceding calendar quarters" and inserting "preceding calendar periods". **Effective** for gifts made after 12-31-81.

[Sec. 2505(b)—Repealed]

Amendments

• 1990, Omnibus Budget Reconciliation Act of 1990 (P.L. 101-508)

P.L. 101-508, §11801(a)(40):

Repealed Code Sec. 2505(b). **Effective** 11-5-90. Prior to repeal, Code Sec. 2505(b) read as follows:

(b) PHASE-IN OF CREDIT.—

In the case of gifts made in:	Subsection (a)(1) shall be applied by substituting for "$192,800" the following amount:
1982	$ 62,800
1983	79,300
1984	96,300
1985	121,800
1986	155,800

P.L. 101-508, §11821(b), provides:

(b) SAVINGS PROVISION.—If—

(1) any provision amended or repealed by this part applied to—

(A) any transaction occurring before the date of the enactment of this Act,

(B) any property acquired before such date of enactment, or

(C) any item of income, loss, deduction, or credit taken into account before such date of enactment, and

(2) the treatment of such transaction, property, or item under such provision would (without regard to the amendments made by this part) affect liability for tax for periods ending after such date of enactment,

nothing in the amendments made by this part shall be construed to affect the treatment of such transaction, property, or item for purposes of determining liability for tax for periods ending after such date of enactment.

• 1981, Economic Recovery Tax Act of 1981 (P.L. 97-34)

P.L. 97-34, §401(b)(2):

Amended Code Sec. 2505(b). **Effective** for gifts made after 12-31-81. Prior to amendment, Code Sec. 2505(b) read as follows:

(b) PHASE-IN OF $47,000 CREDIT.—

In the case of gifts made in:	Subsection (a)(1) shall be applied by substituting for "$192,800" the following amount:
After December 31, 1976, and before July 1, 1977	$ 6,000
After June 30, 1977, and before January 1, 1978	30,000
After December 31, 1977, and before January 1, 1979	34,000
After December 31, 1978, and before January 1, 1980	38,000
After December 31, 1979, and before January 1, 1981	42,500

[Sec. 2505(b)]

(b) ADJUSTMENT TO CREDIT FOR CERTAIN GIFTS MADE BEFORE 1977.—The amount allowable under subsection (a) shall be reduced by an amount equal to 20 percent of the aggregate amount allowed as a specific exemption under section 2521 (as in effect before its repeal by the Tax Reform Act of 1976) with respect to gifts made by the individual after September 8, 1976.

Amendments

• 1990, Omnibus Budget Reconciliation Act of 1990 (P.L. 101-508)

P.L. 101-508, §11801(c)(19)(B):

Amended Code Sec. 2505 by redesignating subsection (c) as subsection (b). **Effective** 11-5-90.

P.L. 101-508, §11821(b), provides:

(b) SAVINGS PROVISION.—If—

(1) any provision amended or repealed by this part applied to—

(A) any transaction occurring before the date of the enactment of this Act,

(B) any property acquired before such date of enactment, or

(C) any item of income, loss, deduction, or credit taken into account before such date of enactment, and

(2) the treatment of such transaction, property, or item under such provision would (without regard to the amendments made by this part) affect liability for tax for periods ending after such date of enactment,

nothing in the amendments made by this part shall be construed to affect the treatment of such transaction, property, or item for purposes of determining liability for tax for periods ending after such date of enactment.

[Sec. 2505(c)]

(c) LIMITATION BASED ON AMOUNT OF TAX.—The amount of the credit allowed under subsection (a) for any calendar year shall not exceed the amount of the tax imposed by section 2501 for such calendar year.

Amendments

• 1990, Omnibus Budget Reconciliation Act of 1990 (P.L. 101-508)

P.L. 101-508, §11801(c)(19)(B):

Amended Code Sec. 2505 by redesignating subsection (d) as subsection (c). **Effective** 11-5-90.

P.L. 101-508, §11821(b), provides:

(b) SAVINGS PROVISION.—If—

(1) any provision amended or repealed by this part applied to—

(A) any transaction occurring before the date of the enactment of this Act,

(B) any property acquired before such date of enactment, or

(C) any item of income, loss, deduction, or credit taken into account before such date of enactment, and

(2) the treatment of such transaction, property, or item under such provision would (without regard to the amendments made by this part) affect liability for tax for periods ending after such date of enactment,

nothing in the amendments made by this part shall be construed to affect the treatment of such transaction, property, or item for purposes of determining liability for tax for periods ending after such date of enactment.

• 1981, Economic Recovery Tax Act of 1981 (P.L. 97-34)

P.L. 97-34, §442(a)(5)(B):

Amended Code Sec. 2505(d) by striking out "calendar quarter" each place it appears and inserting "calendar year". **Effective** with respect to gifts made after 12-31-81.

• 1976, Tax Reform Act of 1976 (P.L. 94-455)

P.L. 94-455, §2001(b)(2), (d)(2):

Added Code Sec. 2505. **Effective** for gifts made after 12-31-76.

Subchapter B—Transfers

[Sec. 2511]

SEC. 2511. TRANSFERS IN GENERAL.

[Sec. 2511(a)]

(a) SCOPE.—Subject to the limitations contained in this chapter, the tax imposed by section 2501 shall apply whether the transfer is in trust or otherwise, whether the gift is direct or indirect, and whether the property is real or personal, tangible or intangible; but in the case of a nonresident not a citizen of the United States, shall apply to a transfer only if the property is situated within the United States.

[Sec. 2511(b)]

(b) INTANGIBLE PROPERTY.—For purposes of this chapter, in the case of a nonresident not a citizen of the United States who is excepted from the application of section 2501(a)(2)—

(1) shares of stock issued by a domestic corporation, and

(2) debt obligations of—

(A) a United States person, or

(B) the United States, a State or any political subdivision thereof, or the District of Columbia,

which are owned and held by such nonresident shall be deemed to be property situated within the United States.

Amendments

• 1966, Foreign Investors Tax Act of 1966 (P.L. 89-809)

P.L. 89-809, §109(b):

Amended Code Sec. 2511(b). **Effective** for the calendar year 1967 and all calendar years thereafter. Prior to amendment, Sec. 2511(b) read as follows:

"(b) Stock in Corporation.—Shares of stock owned and held by a nonresident not a citizen of the United States shall be deemed property within the United States only if issued by a domestic corporation."

[Sec. 2511(c)—Stricken]

Amendments

• 2013, American Taxpayer Relief Act of 2012 (P.L. 112-240)

P.L. 112-240, §101(a)(1) and (3), provides:

SEC. 101. PERMANENT EXTENSION AND MODIFICATION OF 2001 TAX RELIEF.

(a) PERMANENT EXTENSION.—

(1) IN GENERAL.—The Economic Growth and Tax Relief Reconciliation Act of 2001 is amended by striking title IX.

(2) CONFORMING AMENDMENT.—The Tax Relief, Unemployment Insurance Reauthorization, and Job Creation Act of 2010 is amended by striking section 304.

(3) EFFECTIVE DATE.—The amendments made by this subsection shall apply to taxable, plan, or limitation years beginning after December 31, 2012, and estates of decedents dying, gifts made, or generation skipping transfers after December 31, 2012.

• 2010, Tax Relief, Unemployment Insurance Reauthorization, and Job Creation Act of 2010 (P.L. 111-312)

P.L. 111-312, §302(e):

Amended Code Sec. 2511 by striking subsection (c). **Effective** for estates of decedents dying, generation-skipping transfers, and gifts made, after 12-31-2009. Prior to being stricken, Code Sec. 2511(c) read as follows:

(c) TREATMENT OF CERTAIN TRANSFERS IN TRUST.—Notwithstanding any other provision of this section and except as provided in regulations, a transfer in trust shall be treated as a transfer of property by gift, unless the trust is treated as wholly owned by the donor or the donor's spouse under subpart E of part I of subchapter J of chapter 1.

P.L. 111-312, §304, provides [but see P.L. 112-240, §101(a)(2)-(3), above]:

SEC. 304. APPLICATION OF EGTRRA SUNSET TO THIS TITLE.

Section 901 of the Economic Growth and Tax Relief Reconciliation Act of 2001 shall apply to the amendments made by this title.

• 2002, Job Creation and Worker Assistance Act of 2002 (P.L. 107-147)

P.L. 107-147, §411(g)(1):

Amended Code Sec. 2511(c) by striking "taxable gift under section 2503," and inserting "transfer of property by gift,". **Effective** as if included in the provision of P.L. 107-16 to which it relates [**effective** for gifts made after 12-31-2009.—CCH].

• 2001, Economic Growth and Tax Relief Reconciliation Act of 2001 (P.L. 107-16)

P.L. 107-16, §511(e):

Amended Code Sec. 2511 by adding at the end a new subsection (c). **Effective** for gifts made after 12-31-2009.

P.L. 107-16, §901(a)-(b), as amended by P.L. 111-312, §101(a)(1), provides [but see P.L. 112-240, §101(a)(1) and (3), above]:

SEC. 901. SUNSET OF PROVISIONS OF ACT.

(a) IN GENERAL.—All provisions of, and amendments made by, this Act shall not apply—

(1) to taxable, plan, or limitation years beginning after December 31, 2012, or

(2) in the case of title V, to estates of decedents dying, gifts made, or generation skipping transfers, after December 31, 2012.

(b) APPLICATION OF CERTAIN LAWS.—The Internal Revenue Code of 1986 and the Employee Retirement Income Security Act of 1974 shall be applied and administered to years, estates, gifts, and transfers described in subsection (a) as if the provisions and amendments described in subsection (a) had never been enacted.

[Sec. 2512]

SEC. 2512. VALUATION OF GIFTS.

[Sec. 2512(a)]

(a) If the gift is made in property, the value thereof at the date of the gift shall be considered the amount of the gift.

[Sec. 2512(b)]

(b) Where property is transferred for less than an adequate and full consideration in money or money's worth, then the amount by which the value of the property exceeded the value of the consideration shall be deemed a gift, and shall be included in computing the amount of gifts made during the calendar year.

Amendments

• 1981, Economic Recovery Tax Act of 1981 (P.L. 97-34)

P.L. 97-34, §442(b)(1):

Amended Code Sec. 2512(b) by striking out "calendar quarter" and inserting "calendar year". **Effective** with respect to gifts made after 12-31-81.

• 1970, Excise, Estate, and Gift Tax Adjustment Act of 1970 (P.L. 91-614)

P.L. 91-614, §102(b)(1):

Amended Code Sec. 2512(b) by substituting "calendar quarter" for "calendar year". **Effective** for gifts made after 12-31-70.

[Sec. 2512(c)]

(c) CROSS REFERENCE.—

For individual's right to be furnished on request a statement regarding any valuation made by the Secretary of a gift by that individual, see section 7517.

Amendments

• 1976, Tax Reform Act of 1976 (P.L. 94-455)

P.L. 94-455, §2008(a)(2)(B), (d)(1)(B):

Added Code Sec. 2512(c). **Effective** for gifts made after 12-31-76.

[Sec. 2513]

SEC. 2513. GIFT BY HUSBAND OR WIFE TO THIRD PARTY.

[Sec. 2513(a)]

(a) CONSIDERED AS MADE ONE-HALF BY EACH.—

(1) IN GENERAL.—A gift made by one spouse to any person other than his spouse shall, for the purposes of this chapter, be considered as made one-half by him and one-half by his spouse, but only if at the time of the gift each spouse is a citizen or resident of the United States. This paragraph shall not apply with respect to a gift by a spouse of an interest in property if he creates in his spouse a general power of appointment, as defined in section 2514(c), over such interest. For purposes of this section, an individual shall be considered as the spouse of another individual only if he is married to such individual at the time of the gift and does not remarry during the remainder of the calendar year.

(2) CONSENT OF BOTH SPOUSES.—Paragraph (1) shall apply only if both spouses have signified (under the regulations provided for in subsection (b)) their consent to the application of

paragraph (1) in the case of all such gifts made during the calendar year by either while married to the other.

Amendments

• 1981, Economic Recovery Tax Act of 1981 (P.L. 97-34)

P.L. 97-34, §442(b)(2)(A):

Amended Code Sec. 2513(a) by striking out "calendar quarter" each place it appears and inserting "calendar year". **Effective** with respect to gifts made after 12-31-81.

• 1970, Excise, Estate, and Gift Tax Adjustment Act of 1970 (P.L. 91-614)

P.L. 91-614, §102(b)(2)(A):

Amended Code Sec. 2513(a) by substituting "calendar quarter" for "calendar year" in the last line of both paragraphs (1) and (2). **Effective** for gifts made after 12-31-70.

[Sec. 2513(b)]

(b) MANNER AND TIME OF SIGNIFYING CONSENT.—

(1) MANNER.—A consent under this section shall be signified in such manner as is provided under regulations prescribed by the Secretary.

(2) TIME.—Such consent may be so signified at any time after the close of the calendar year in which the gift was made, subject to the following limitations—

(A) The consent may not be signified after the 15th day of April following the close of such year, unless before such 15th day no return has been filed for such year by either spouse, in which case the consent may not be signified after a return for such year is filed by either spouse.

(B) The consent may not be signified after a notice of deficiency with respect to the tax for such year has been sent to either spouse in accordance with section 6212(a).

Amendments

• 1981, Economic Recovery Tax Act of 1981 (P.L. 97-34)

P.L. 97-34, §442(b)(2)(B):

Amended Code Sec. 2513(b)(2) by striking out "calendar quarter" and inserting "calendar year". **Effective** with respect to gifts made after 12-31-81.

P.L. 97-34, §442(b)(2)(C):

Amended Code Sec. 2513(b)(2)(A). **Effective** with respect to gifts made after 12-31-81. Prior to amendment, Code Sec. 2513(b)(2)(A) read as follows:

(A) the consent may not be signified after the 15th day of the second month following the close of such calendar quarter, unless before such 15th day no return has been filed for such calendar quarter by either spouse, in which case the consent may not be signified after a return for such calendar quarter is filed by either spouse;

P.L. 97-34, §442(b)(2)(D):

Amended Code Sec. 2513(b)(2)(B) by striking out "the consent" and inserting "The consent", and by striking out "such calendar quarter" and inserting "such year". **Effective** with respect to gifts made after 12-31-81.

• 1976, Tax Reform Act of 1976 (P.L. 94-455)

P.L. 94-455, §1906(b)(13)(A):

Amended 1954 Code by substituting "Secretary" for "Secretary or his delegate" each place it appeared. **Effective** 2-1-77.

• 1970, Excise, Estate, and Gift Tax Adjustment Act of 1970 (P.L. 91-614)

P.L. 91-614, §102(b)(2)(A)-(C):

Amended Code Sec. 2513(b)(2). **Effective** for gifts made after 12-31-70. Prior to amendment, Code Sec. 2513(b)(2) read as follows:

"(2) Time.—Such consent may be so signified at any time after the close of the calendar year in which the gift was made, subject to the following limitations—

"(A) the consent may not be signified after the 15th day of April following the close of such year, unless before such 15th day no return has been filed for such year by either spouse, in which case the consent may not be signified after a return for such year is filed by either spouse;

"(B) the consent may not be signified after a notice of deficiency with respect to the tax for such year has been sent to either spouse in accordance with section 6212(a)."

[Sec. 2513(c)]

(c) REVOCATION OF CONSENT.—Revocation of a consent previously signified shall be made in such manner as is provided under regulations prescribed by the Secretary, but the right to revoke a consent previously signified with respect to a calendar year—

(1) shall not exist after the 15th day of April following the close of such year if the consent was signified on or before such 15th day; and

(2) shall not exist if the consent was not signified until after such 15th day.

Amendments

• 1981, Economic Recovery Tax Act of 1981 (P.L. 97-34)

P.L. 97-34, §442(b)(2)(E):

Amended Code Sec. 2513(c) by striking out "calendar quarter" and inserting "calendar year", and by striking out "15th day of the second month following the close of such quarter" and inserting "15th day of April following the close of such year". **Effective** with respect to estates of decedents dying after 12-31-81.

• 1976, Tax Reform Act of 1976 (P.L. 94-455)

P.L. 94-455, §1906(b)(13)(A):

Amended 1954 Code by substituting "Secretary" for "Secretary or his delegate" each place it appeared. **Effective** 2-1-77.

• 1970, Excise, Estate, and Gift Tax Adjustment Act of 1970 (P.L. 91-614)

P.L. 91-614, §102(b)(2)(A), (D):

Amended Code Sec. 2513(c). **Effective** for gifts made after 12-31-70. Prior to amendment, the section read as follows:

"(c) Revocation of Consent.—Revocation of a consent previously signified shall be made in such manner as is provided under regulations prescribed by the Secretary or his delegate, but the right to revoke a consent previously signified with respect to a calendar year—

"(1) shall not exist after the 15th day of April following the close of such year if the consent was signified on or before such 15th day; and

"(2) shall not exist if the consent was not signified until after such 15th day."

[Sec. 2513(d)]

(d) JOINT AND SEVERAL LIABILITY FOR TAX.—If the consent required by subsection (a)(2) is signified with respect to a gift made in any calendar year, the liability with respect to the entire tax imposed by this chapter of each spouse for such year shall be joint and several.

Amendments

• 1981, Economic Recovery Tax Act of 1981 (P.L. 97-34)

P.L. 97-34, §442(b)(2)(F):

Amended Code Sec. 2513(d) by striking out "any calendar quarter" and inserting "any calendar year", and by striking out "such calendar quarter" and inserting "such year". **Effective** with respect to estates of decedents dying after 12-31-81.

• 1970, Excise, Estate, and Gift Tax Adjustment Act of 1970 (P.L. 91-614)

P.L. 91-614, §102(b)(2)(E):

Amended Code Sec. 2513(d) by substituting "calendar quarter" for "calendar year" and by substituting "for such calendar quarter" for "for such year." **Effective** for gifts made after 12-31-70.

[Sec. 2514]

SEC. 2514. POWERS OF APPOINTMENT.

[Sec. 2514(a)]

(a) POWERS CREATED ON OR BEFORE OCTOBER 21, 1942.—An exercise of a general power of appointment created on or before October 21, 1942, shall be deemed a transfer of property by the individual possessing such power; but the failure to exercise such a power or the complete release of such a power shall not be deemed an exercise thereof. If a general power of appointment created on or before October 21, 1942, has been partially released so that it is no longer a general power of appointment, the subsequent exercise of such power shall not be deemed to be the exercise of a general power of appointment if—

(1) such partial release occurred before November 1, 1951, or

(2) the donee of such power was under a legal disability to release such power on October 21, 1942, and such partial release occurred not later than six months after the termination of such legal disability.

[Sec. 2514(b)]

(b) POWERS CREATED AFTER OCTOBER 21, 1942.—The exercise or release of a general power of appointment created after October 21, 1942, shall be deemed a transfer of property by the individual possessing such power.

Amendments

• 1976, Tax Reform Act of 1976 (P.L. 94-455)

P.L. 94-455, §2009(b)(4)(F), (e)(2):

Deleted the second sentence of Code Sec. 2514(b). **Effective** for transfers creating an interest in the person disclaiming made after 12-31-76. Prior to deletion, such sentence read as follows:

"A disclaimer or renunciation of such a power of appointment shall not be deemed a release of such power."

[Sec. 2514(c)]

(c) DEFINITION OF GENERAL POWER OF APPOINTMENT.—For purposes of this section, the term "general power of appointment" means a power which is exercisable in favor of the individual possessing the power (hereafter in this subsection referred to as the "possessor"), his estate, his creditors, or the creditors of his estate; except that—

(1) A power to consume, invade, or appropriate property for the benefit of the possessor which is limited by an ascertainable standard relating to the health, education, support, or maintenance of the possessor shall not be deemed a general power of appointment.

(2) A power of appointment created on or before October 21, 1942, which is exercisable by the possessor only in conjunction with another person shall not be deemed a general power of appointment.

(3) In the case of a power of appointment created after October 21, 1942, which is exercisable by the possessor only in conjunction with another person—

(A) if the power is not exercisable by the possessor except in conjunction with the creator of the power—such power shall not be deemed a general power of appointment;

(B) if the power is not exercisable by the possessor except in conjunction with a person having a substantial interest in the property subject to the power, which is adverse to exercise of the power in favor of the possessor—such power shall not be deemed a general power of appointment. For the purposes of this subparagraph a person who, after the death of the possessor, may be possessed of a power of appointment (with respect to the property subject to the possessor's power) which he may exercise in his own favor shall be deemed as having an interest in the property and such interest shall be deemed adverse to such exercise of the possessor's power;

(C) if (after the application of subparagraphs (A) and (B)) the power is a general power of appointment and is exercisable in favor of such other person—such power shall be deemed a general power of appointment only in respect of a fractional part of the property subject to such power, such part to be determined by dividing the value of such property by the number of such persons (including the possessor) in favor of whom such power is exercisable.

For purposes of subparagraphs (B) and (C), a power shall be deemed to be exercisable in favor of a person if it is exercisable in favor of such person, his estate, his creditors, or the creditors of his estate.

[Sec. 2514(d)]

(d) CREATION OF ANOTHER POWER IN CERTAIN CASES.—If a power of appointment created after October 21, 1942, is exercised by creating another power of appointment which, under the applicable local law, can be validly exercised so as to postpone the vesting of any estate or interest in the property which was subject to the first power, or suspend the absolute ownership or power of alienation of such property, for a period ascertainable without regard to the date of the creation of the first power, such exercise of the first power shall, to the extent of the property subject to the second power, be deemed a transfer of property by the individual possessing such power.

[Sec. 2514(e)]

(e) LAPSE OF POWER.—The lapse of a power of appointment created after October 21, 1942, during the life of the individual possessing the power shall be considered a release of such power. The rule of the preceding sentence shall apply with respect to the lapse of powers during any calendar year only to the extent that the property which could have been appointed by exercise of such lapsed powers exceeds in value the greater of the following amounts:

(1) $5,000, or

(2) 5 percent of the aggregate value of the assets out of which, or the proceeds of which, the exercise of the lapsed powers could be satisfied.

[Sec. 2514(f)]

(f) DATE OF CREATION OF POWER.—For purposes of this section a power of appointment created by a will executed on or before October 21, 1942, shall be considered a power created on or before such date if the person executing such will dies before July 1, 1949, without having republished such will, by codicil or otherwise, after October 21, 1942.

[Sec. 2515]

SEC. 2515. TREATMENT OF GENERATION-SKIPPING TRANSFER TAX.

In the case of any taxable gift which is a direct skip (within the meaning of chapter 13), the amount of such gift shall be increased by the amount of any tax imposed on the transferor under chapter 13 with respect to such gift.

Amendments

• 1986, Tax Reform Act of 1986 (P.L. 99-514)

P.L. 99-514, §1432(d)(1):

Amended Subchapter B of chapter 12 by inserting after Code Sec. 2514 new Code Sec. 2515. **Effective**, generally, for any generation-skipping transfer (within the meaning of section 2611 of the Internal Revenue Code of 1986) made after the date of the enactment of this Act. However, for special rules see Act Sec. 1433(b)-(d) in the amendments for Code Sec. 2601.

[Sec. 2515—Repealed]

Amendments

• 1981, Economic Recovery Tax Act of 1981 (P.L. 97-34)

P.L. 97-34, §403(c)(3)(B):

Repealed Code Sec. 2515. **Effective**, generally, for gifts made after 12-31-81. For special rules, see Act Sec. 403(e)(3), below. Prior to its repeal, Code Sec. 2515 read as follows:

SEC. 2515. TENANCIES BY THE ENTIRETY IN REAL PROPERTY.

(a) CREATION.—The creation of a tenancy by the entirety in real property, either by one spouse alone or by both spouses, and additions to the value thereof in the form of improvements, reductions in the indebtedness thereon, or otherwise, shall not be deemed transfers of property for purposes of this chapter, regardless of the proportion of the consideration furnished by each spouse, unless the donor elects to have such creation of a tenancy by the entirety treated as a transfer, as provided in subsection (c).

(b) TERMINATION.—In the case of the termination of a tenancy by the entirety, other than by reason of the death of a spouse, the creation of which, or additions to which, were not deemed to be transfers by reason of subsection (a), a spouse shall be deemed to have made a gift to the extent that the proportion of the total consideration furnished by such spouse multiplied by the proceeds of such termination (whether in form of cash, property, or interests in property) exceeds the value of such proceeds of termination received by such spouse.

(c) EXERCISE OF ELECTION.—

(1) IN GENERAL.—The election provided by subsection (a) shall be exercised by including such creation of a tenancy by the entirety as a transfer by gift, to the extent such transfer constitutes a gift (determined without regard to this section), in the gift tax return of the donor for the calendar quarter in which such tenancy by the entirety was created, filed within the time prescribed by law, irrespective of whether or not the gift exceeds the exclusion provided by section 2503(b).

(2) SUBSEQUENT ADDITIONS IN VALUE.—If the election provided by subsection (a) has been made with respect to the creation of any tenancy by the entirety, such election shall also apply to each addition made to the value of such tenancy by the entirety.

(3) CERTAIN ACTUARIAL COMPUTATIONS NOT REQUIRED.—In the case of any election under subsection (a) with respect to any property, the retained interest of each spouse shall be treated as one-half of the value of their joint interest.

(d) CERTAIN JOINT TENANCIES INCLUDED.—For purposes of this section, the term "tenancy by the entirety" includes a joint tenancy between husband and wife with right of survivorship.

P.L. 97-34, § 403(e)(3), provides:

(3) If—

(A) the decedent dies after December 31, 1981,

(B) by reason of the death of the decedent property passes from the decedent or is acquired from the decedent under a will executed before the date which is 30 days after the date of the enactment of this Act, or a trust created before such date, which contains a formula expressly providing that the spouse is to receive the maximum amount of property qualifying for the marital deduction allowable by Federal law,

(C) the formula referred to in subparagraph (B) was not amended to refer specifically to an unlimited marital deduction at any time after the date which is 30 days after the date of enactment of this Act, and before the death of the decedent, and

(D) the State does not enact a statute applicable to such estate which construes this type of formula as referring to the marital deduction allowable by Federal law as amended by subsection (a),

then the amendment made by subsection (a) [relating to the unlimited marital deduction (Code Sec. 2056, as amended by P.L. 97-34)] shall not apply to the estate of such decedent.

• 1976, Tax Reform Act of 1976 (P.L. 94-455)

P.L. 94-455, § 2002(c)(2):

Amended Code Sec. 2515(c). **Effective** for joint interests created after 12-31-76. Prior to amendment, Code Sec. 2515(c) read as follows:

(c) EXERCISE OF ELECTION.—The election provided by subsection (a) shall be exercised by including such creation of a tenancy by the entirety or additions made to the value thereof as a transfer by gift, to the extent such transfer constitutes a gift, determined without regard to this section, in the gift tax return of the donor for the calendar quarter in which such tenancy by the entirety was created or additions made to the value thereof, filed within the time prescribed by law, irrespective of whether or not the gift exceeds the exclusion provided by section 2503(b).

• 1970, Excise, Estate, and Gift Tax Adjustment Act of 1970 (P.L. 91-614)

P.L. 91-614, § 102(b)(3):

Amended Code Sec. 2515(c) by substituting "calendar quarter" for "calendar year." **Effective** for gifts made after 12-31-70.

[Sec. 2515A—Repealed]

Amendments

• 1981, Economic Recovery Tax Act of 1981 (P.L. 97-34)

P.L. 97-34, § 403(c)(3)(B):

Repealed Code Sec. 2515A. **Effective**, generally, for gifts made after 12-31-81. For special rules, see Act Sec. 403(e)(3), below. Prior to its repeal, Code Sec. 2515A read as follows:

SEC. 2515A. TENANCIES BY THE ENTIRETY IN PERSONAL PROPERTY.

(a) CERTAIN ACTUARIAL COMPUTATIONS NOT REQUIRED.—In the case of—

(1) the creation (either by one spouse alone or by both spouses) of a joint interest of a husband and wife in personal property with right of survivorship, or

(2) additions to the value thereof in the form of improvements, reductions in the indebtedness thereof, or otherwise,

the retained interest of each spouse shall be treated as one-half of the value of their joint interest.

(b) EXCEPTION.—Subsection (a) shall not apply with respect to any joint interest in property if the fair market value of the interest or of the property (determined as if each spouse had a right to sever) cannot reasonably be ascertained except by reference to the life expectancy of one or both spouses.

P.L. 97-34, § 403(e)(3), provides:

(3) If—

(A) the decedent dies after December 31, 1981,

(B) by reason of the death of the decedent property passes from the decedent or is acquired from the decedent under a will executed before the date which is 30 days after the date of the enactment of this Act, or a trust created before such date, which contains a formula expressly providing that the spouse is to receive the maximum amount of property qualifying for the marital deduction allowable by Federal law,

(C) the formula referred to in subparagraph (B) was not amended to refer specifically to an unlimited marital deduction at any time after the date which is 30 days after the date of enactment of this Act, and before the death of the decedent, and

(D) the State does not enact a statute applicable to such estate which construes this type of formula as referring to the marital deduction allowable by Federal law as amended by subsection (a),

then the amendment made by subsection (a) shall not apply to the estate of such decedent.

• 1978, Revenue Act of 1978 (P.L. 95-600)

P.L. 95-600, § 702(k)(1)(A):

Added Code Sec. 2515A. **Effective** for joint interests created after 12-31-76.

[Sec. 2516]

SEC. 2516. CERTAIN PROPERTY SETTLEMENTS.

Where husband and wife enter into a written agreement relative to their marital and property rights and divorce occurs within the 3-year period beginning on the date 1 year before such agreement is entered into (whether or not such agreement is approved by the divorce decree), any transfers of property or interests in property made pursuant to such agreement—

(1) to either spouse in settlement of his or her marital or property rights, or

(2) to provide a reasonable allowance for the support of issue of the marriage during minority,

shall be deemed to be transfers made for a full and adequate consideration in money or money's worth.

Amendments

• 1984, Deficit Reduction Act of 1984 (P.L. 98-369)

P.L. 98-369, §425(b):

Amended Code Sec. 2516 by striking out so much of such section as preceded paragraph (1) thereof and inserting in lieu thereof new material. **Effective** for transfers after 7-18-84. Prior to amendment the material preceding paragraph (1) of Code Sec. 2516 read as follows:

Where husband and wife enter into a written agreement relative to their marital and property rights and divorce occurs within 2 years thereafter (whether or not such agreement is approved by the divorce decree), any transfers of property or interests in property made pursuant to such agreement—

[Sec. 2517—Repealed]

Amendments

• 1986, Tax Reform Act of 1986 (P.L. 99-514)

P.L. 99-514, §1852(e)(2)(A):

Repealed Code Sec. 2517. **Effective** for transfers after 10-22-86. Prior to repeal, Code Sec. 2517 read as follows:

SEC. 2517. CERTAIN ANNUITIES UNDER QUALIFIED PLANS.

[Sec. 2517(a)]

(a) GENERAL RULE.—The exercise or nonexercise by an employee of an election or option whereby an annuity or other payment will become payable to any beneficiary at or after the employee's death shall not be considered a transfer for purposes of this chapter if the option or election and annuity or other payment is provided for under—

(1) an employees' trust (or under a contract purchased by an employees' trust) forming part of a pension, stock bonus, or profit-sharing plan which, at the time of such exercise or nonexercise, or at the time of termination of the plan if earlier, met the requirements of section 401(a);

(2) a retirement annuity contract purchased by an employer (and not by an employees' trust) pursuant to a plan which, at the time of such exercise or nonexercise, or at the time of termination of the plan if earlier, was a plan described in section 403(a);

(3) a retirement annuity contract purchased for an employee by an employer which is an organization referred to in section 170 (b)(1)(A)(ii) or (vi), or which is a religious organization (other than a trust), and which is exempt from tax under section 501(a);

(4) chapter 73 of title 10 of the United States Code; or

(5) an individual retirement account described in section 408(a) or an individual retirement annuity described in section 408(b).

Amendments

• 1984, Deficit Reduction Act of 1984 (P.L. 98-369)

P.L. 98-369, §491(d)(35):

Amended Code Sec. 2517(a)(5) by striking out ", an individual retirement annuity described in section 408(b), or a retirement bond described in section 409(a)" and inserting in lieu thereof "or an individual retirement annuity described in section 408(b)". **Effective** for obligations issued after 12-31-83.

• 1976, Tax Reform Act of 1976 (P.L. 94-455)

P.L. 94-455, §2009(c)(4)(A), (e)(3)(B):

Amended Code Sec. 2517(a) by striking out "or" at the end of paragraph (3); by striking out the period at the end of paragraph (4) and inserting in lieu thereof "; or"; and by adding after paragraph (4) a new paragraph (5). **Effective** for transfers made after 12-31-76.

• 1969, Tax Reform Act of 1969 (P.L. 91-172)

P.L. 91-172, §101(j)(24):

Amended Code Sec. 2517(a)(3) by substituting "section 170(b)(1)(A)(ii) or (vi), or which is a religious organization (other than a trust)," for "section 503(b)(1), (2), or (3),". **Effective** 1-1-70.

• 1966 (P.L. 89-365)

P.L. 89-365, §2:

Amended Code Sec. 2517(a) by striking out "or" at the end of paragraph (2), by substituting "; or" for the period at the end of paragraph (3), and by adding new paragraph (4). **Effective** for calendar years after 1965.

• 1962, Self-Employed Individuals Tax Retirement Act of 1962 (P.L. 87-792)

P.L. 87-792, §7:

Amended Code Sec. 2517(a) by striking out in paragraph (2) "met the requirements of section 401(a)(3), (4), (5), and (6)" and inserting in lieu thereof "was a plan described in section 403(a)". **Effective** 1-1-63.

[Sec. 2517(b)]

(b) TRANSFERS ATTRIBUTABLE TO EMPLOYEE CONTRIBUTIONS.—If the annuity or other payment referred to in subsection (a) (other than paragraphs (4) and (5)) is attributable to any extent to payments or contributions made by the employee, then subsection (a) shall not apply to that part of the value of such annuity or other payment which bears the same proportion to the total value of the annuity or other payment as the total payments or contributions made by the employee bear to the total payments or contributions made. For purposes of the preceding sentence, payments or contributions made by the employee's employer or former employer toward the purchase of an annuity contract described in subsection (a)(3) shall, to the extent not excludable from gross income under section 403(b), be considered to have been made by the employee. For purposes of this subsection, contributions or payments on behalf of an individual while he was an employee within the meaning of section 401(c)(1) made under a trust or plan described in paragraph (1) or (2) of subsection (a) shall, to the extent allowable as a deduction under section 404, be considered to be made by a person other than such individual and, to the extent not so allowable, shall be considered to be made by such individual. For purposes of this subsection, any deductible employee contributions (within the meaning of paragraph (5) of section 72(o)) shall be considered as made by a person other than the employee.

Amendments

• 1983, Technical Corrections Act of 1982 (P.L. 97-448)

P.L. 97-448, §103(c)(11):

Amended subsection (i) of section 311 of P.L. 97-34 so that the amendment made by subsection (d)(2) is **effective** for transfers made after 12-31-81.

• 1981, Economic Recovery Tax Act of 1981 (P.L. 97-34)

P.L. 97-34, §311(d)(2):

Amended Code Sec. 2517(b) by adding at the end the following new sentence: "For purposes of this subsection, any deductible employee contributions (within the meaning of paragraph (5) of section 72(o)) shall be considered as made by a person other than the employee.". **Effective** for transfers after 12-31-81. The transitional rule provides that, for purposes of the 1954 Code, any amount allowed as a deduction under section 220 of the Code (as in effect before its repeal by P. L. 97-34) shall be treated as if it were allowed by section 219 of the Code.

• 1976, Tax Reform Act of 1976 (P.L. 94-455)

P.L. 94-455, §2009(c)(4)(A):

Substituted "other than paragraphs (4) and (5)" for "other than paragraph (4)" in Code Sec. 2517(b). **Effective** for transfers made after 12-31-76.

P.L. 94-455, §2009(c)(4)(B):

Amended the last sentence of Code Sec. 2517(b). **Effective** for transfers made after 12-31-76. Prior to amendment, such sentence read as follows:

"For purposes of this subsection, payments or contributions on behalf of an individual while he was an employee within the meaning of section 401(c)(1) made under a trust or plan described in subsection (a)(1) or (2) shall be considered to be payments or contributions made by the employee."

• 1966 (P.L. 89-365)

P.L. 89-365, §2:

Amended Code Sec. 2517(b) by inserting "(other than paragraph (4))" immediately after "referred to in subsection (a)" in the first sentence. **Effective** for calendar years after 1965.

• 1962, Self-Employed Individuals Tax Retirement Act of 1962 (P.L. 87-792)

P.L. 87-792, §7:

Amended Code Sec. 2517(b) by adding after the period in line 11 a new sentence. **Effective** 1-1-63.

[Sec. 2517(c)]

(c) EXEMPTION OF CERTAIN ANNUITY INTERESTS CREATED BY COMMUNITY PROPERTY LAWS.—Notwithstanding any other provision of law, in the case of an employee on whose behalf contributions or payments are made—

(1) by his employer or former employer under a trust or plan described in paragraph (1) or (2) of subsection (a), or toward the purchase of a contract described in paragraph (3) of subsection (a), which under subsection (b) are not considered as contributed by the employee, or

(2) by the employee to a retirement plan described in paragraph (5) of subsection (a),

a transfer of benefits attributable to such contributions or payments shall, for purposes of this chapter, not be considered as a transfer by the spouse of the employee to the extent that the value of any interest of such spouse in such contributions or payments or in such trust or plan or such contract—

(A) is attributable to such contribution or payments, and

(B) arises solely by reason of such spouse's interest in community income under the community property laws of the State.

Amendments

• 1976, Tax Reform Act of 1976 (P.L. 94-455)

P.L. 94-455, §2009(c)(5), (e)(3)(B):

Redesignated Code Sec. 2517(c) (as amended by paragraph (4)(A)(iii)) as Code Sec. 2517(d) and added after Code Sec. 2517(b) a new subsection (c). **Effective** for transfers made after 12-31-76.

[Sec. 2517(d)]

(d) EMPLOYEE DEFINED.—For purposes of this section, the term "employee" includes a former employee. In the case of a retirement plan described in paragraph (5) of subsection (a), such term means the individual for whose benefit the plan was established.

Amendments

• 1976, Tax Reform Act of 1976 (P.L. 94-455)

P.L. 94-455, §2009(c)(4)(A):

Added a new sentence at the end of Code Sec. 2517(c). **Effective** for transfers made after 12-31-76.

P.L. 94-455, §2009(c)(5):

Redesignated Code Sec. 2517(c) (as amended by paragraph (4)(A)(iii)) as Code Sec. 2517(d). **Effective** for transfers made after 12-31-76.

• 1958, Technical Amendments Act of 1958 (P.L. 85-866)

P.L. 85-866, §68(a):

Added Sec. 2517 to the Code.

P.L. 85-866, §68(c), provides:

"The amendments made by this section shall apply with respect to the calendar year 1955 and all calendar years thereafter. For calendar years before 1955, the determination as to whether the exercise or nonexercise by an employee of an election or option described in section 2517 of the Internal Revenue Code of 1954 (as added by subsection (a)) is a transfer for purposes of chapter 4 of the Internal Revenue Code of 1939 shall be made as if this section had not been enacted and without inferences drawn from the fact that this section is not made applicable with respect to calendar years before 1955."

P.L. 85-866, §23(f), (g):

Amended Code Sec. 2517, as added by §68(a) of P.L. 85-866, by striking out "or" at the end of subsection (a)(1), and by striking out the period at the end of subsection (a)(2) and inserting in lieu thereof "; or", and by inserting after subsection (a)(2) paragraph (3). **Effective** for calendar years after 1957.

[Sec. 2518]

SEC. 2518. DISCLAIMERS.

[Sec. 2518(a)]

(a) GENERAL RULE.—For purposes of this subtitle, if a person makes a qualified disclaimer with respect to any interest in property, this subtitle shall apply with respect to such interest as if the interest had never been transferred to such person.

[Sec. 2518(b)]

(b) QUALIFIED DISCLAIMER DEFINED.—For purposes of subsection (a), the term "qualified disclaimer" means an irrevocable and unqualified refusal by a person to accept an interest in property but only if—

(1) such refusal is in writing,

(2) such writing is received by the transferor of the interest, his legal representative, or the holder of the legal title to the property to which the interest relates not later than the date which is 9 months after the later of—

(A) the date on which the transfer creating the interest in such person is made, or

(B) the day on which such person attains age 21,

(3) such person has not accepted the interest or any of its benefits, and

(4) as a result of such refusal, the interest passes without any direction on the part of the person making the disclaimer and passes either—

(A) to the spouse of the decedent, or

(B) to a person other than the person making the disclaimer.

Amendments

• 2010, Tax Relief, Unemployment Insurance Reauthorization, and Job Creation Act of 2010 (P.L. 111-312)

P.L. 111-312, §301(d)(1), provides:

(1) ESTATE TAX.—In the case of the estate of a decedent dying after December 31, 2009, and before the date of the enactment of this Act, the due date for—

(A) filing any return under section 6018 of the Internal Revenue Code of 1986 (including any election required to be made on such a return) as such section is in effect after the date of the enactment of this Act without regard to any election under subsection (c),

(B) making any payment of tax under chapter 11 of such Code, and

(C) making any disclaimer described in section 2518(b) of such Code of an interest in property passing by reason of the death of such decedent,

shall not be earlier than the date which is 9 months after the date of the enactment of this Act.

• 1978, Revenue Act of 1978 (P.L. 95-600)

P.L. 95-600, §702(m)(1):

Amended paragraph (4) of Code Sec. 2518(b). **Effective** for transfers creating an interest in the person disclaiming made after 1976. Prior to amendment, paragraph (4) read as follows:

"(4) as a result of such refusal, the interest passes to a person other than the person making the disclaimer (without any direction on the part of the person making the disclaimer)."

[Sec. 2518(c)]

(c) OTHER RULES.—For purposes of subsection (a)—

(1) DISCLAIMER OF UNDIVIDED PORTION OF INTEREST.—A disclaimer with respect to an undivided portion of an interest which meets the requirements of the preceding sentence shall be treated as a qualified disclaimer of such portion of the interest.

(2) POWERS.—A power with respect to property shall be treated as an interest in such property.

(3) CERTAIN TRANSFERS TREATED AS DISCLAIMERS.—A written transfer of the transferor's entire interest in the property—

(A) which meets requirements similar to the requirements of paragraphs (2) and (3) of subsection (b), and

(B) which is to a person or persons who would have received the property had the transferor made a qualified disclaimer (within the meaning of subsection (b)), shall be treated as a qualified disclaimer.

Amendments

• 1983, Technical Corrections Act of 1982 (P.L. 97-448)

P.L. 97-448, §104(e):

Amended Code Sec. 2518(c)(3) by striking out "For purposes of subsection (a), a" and inserting in lieu thereof "A". **Effective** as if included in the provision of P.L. 97-34 to which it relates.

• 1981, Economic Recovery Tax Act of 1981 (P.L. 97-34)

P.L. 97-34, §426(a):

Added Code Sec. 2518(c)(3). **Effective** for transfers creating an interest in the person disclaiming made after 12-31-81.

• 1976, Tax Reform Act of 1976 (P.L. 94-455)

P.L. 94-455, §2009(b)(1), (e)(2):

Added Code Sec. 2518. **Effective** for transfers creating an interest in the person disclaiming made after 12-31-76.

[Sec. 2519]

SEC. 2519. DISPOSITIONS OF CERTAIN LIFE ESTATES.

[Sec. 2519(a)]

(a) GENERAL RULE.—For purposes of this chapter and chapter 11, any disposition of all or part of a qualifying income interest for life in any property to which this section applies shall be treated as a transfer of all interests in such property other than the qualifying income interest.

[Sec. 2519(b)]

(b) PROPERTY TO WHICH THIS SUBSECTION APPLIES.—This section applies to any property if a deduction was allowed with respect to the transfer of such property to the donor—

(1) under section 2056 by reason of subsection (b)(7) thereof, or

(2) under section 2523 by reason of subsection (f) thereof.

[Sec. 2519(c)]

(c) CROSS REFERENCE.—

For right of recovery for gift tax in the case of property treated as transferred under this section, see section 2207A(b).

Amendments

• 1983, Technical Corrections Act of 1982 (P.L. 97-448)

P.L. 97-448, §104(a)(3)(A):

Amended Code Sec. 2519(a). **Effective** as if included in the provision of P.L. 97-34 to which it relates. Prior to amendment, Code Sec. 2519(a) read as follows:

"(a) GENERAL RULE.—Any disposition of all or part of a qualifying income interest for life in any property to which this section applies shall be treated as a transfer of such property."

P.L. 97-448, §104(a)(7):

Amended Code Sec. 2519 by adding at the end thereof new subsection (c). **Effective** as if included in the provision of P.L. 97-34 to which it relates.

• 1981, Economic Recovery Tax Act of 1981 (P.L. 97-34)

P.L. 97-34, §403(d)(3)(B)(i):

Added Code Sec. 2519. **Effective**, generally, for gifts made after 12-31-81. See Act Sec. 403(e)(3), below, for a special rule applicable to certain wills and trusts, executed or created, before 9-12-81.

P.L. 97-34, §403(e)(3), provides:

(3) If—

(A) the decedent dies after December 31, 1981,

(B) by reason of the death of the decedent property passes from the decedent or is acquired from the decedent under a will executed before the date which is 30 days after the date of the enactment of this Act, or a trust created before such date, which contains a formula expressly providing that the spouse is to receive the maximum amount of property qualifying for the marital deduction allowable by Federal law,

(C) the formula referred to in subparagraph (B) was not amended to refer specifically to an unlimited marital deduction at any time after the date which is 30 days after the date of enactment of this Act, and before the death of the decedent, and

(D) the State does not enact a statute applicable to such estate which construes this type of formula as referring to the marital deduction allowable by Federal law as amended by subsection (a),

then the amendment made by subsection (a) [relating to the unlimited marital deduction (Code Sec. 2056, as amended by P.L. 97-34)] shall not apply to the estate of such decedent.

Subchapter C—Deductions

[Sec. 2521—Repealed]

Amendments

• 1976, Tax Reform Act of 1976 (P.L. 94-455)

P.L. 94-455, §2001(b)(3):

Repealed Code Sec. 2521. **Effective** for gifts made after 12-31-76. Prior to repeal, Code Sec. 2521 read as follows:

"SEC. 2521. SPECIFIC EXEMPTION.

"In computing taxable gifts for a calendar quarter, there shall be allowed as a deduction in the case of a citizen or resident an exemption of $30,000, less the aggregate of the amounts claimed and allowed as specific exemption in the computation of gift taxes for the calendar year 1932 and all calendar years and calendar quarters intervening between that calendar year and the calendar quarter for which the tax is being computed under the laws applicable to such years or calendar quarters."

[Sec. 2522]

SEC. 2522. CHARITABLE AND SIMILAR GIFTS.

[Sec. 2522(a)]

(a) CITIZENS OR RESIDENTS.—In computing taxable gifts for the calendar year, there shall be allowed as a deduction in the case of a citizen or resident the amount of all gifts made during such year to or for the use of—

(1) the United States, any State, or any political subdivision thereof, or the District of Columbia, for exclusively public purposes;

(2) a corporation, or trust, or community chest, fund, or foundation, organized and operated exclusively for religious, charitable, scientific, literary, or educational purposes, or to foster national or international amateur sports competition (but only if no part of its activities involve the provision of athletic facilities or equipment), including the encouragement of art and the prevention of curelty to children or animals, no part of the net earnings of which inures to the benefit of any private shareholder or individual, which is not disqualified for tax exemption under section 501(c)(3) by reason of attempting to influence legislation, and which does not participate in, or intervene in (including the publishing or distributing of statements), any political campaign on behalf of (or in opposition to) any candidate for public office;

(3) a fraternal society, order, or association, operating under the lodge system, but only if such gifts are to be used exclusively for religious, charitable, scientific, literary, or educational

purposes, including the encouragement of art and the prevention of cruelty to children or animals;

(4) posts or organizations of war veterans, or auxiliary units or societies of any such posts or organizations, if such posts, organizations, units, or societies are organized in the United States or any of its possessions, and if no part of their net earnings inures to the benefit of any private shareholder or individual.

Rules similar to the rules of section 501(j) shall apply for purposes of paragraph (2).

Amendments

• 1987, Revenue Act of 1987 (P.L. 100-203)

P.L. 100-203, §10711(a)(5):

Amended Code Sec. 2522(a)(2) by striking out "on behalf of any candidate" and inserting in lieu thereof "on behalf of (or in opposition to) any candidate". **Effective** with respect to activities after 12-22-87.

• 1982, Tax Equity and Fiscal Responsibility Act of 1982 (P.L. 97-248)

P.L. 97-248, §286(b)(3):

Amended Code Sec. 2522(a) by adding a new sentence at the end thereof. **Effective** 10-5-76.

• 1981, Economic Recovery Tax Act of 1981 (P.L. 97-34)

P.L. 97-34, §442(c):

Amended Code Sec. 2522(a) by striking out "quarter" and inserting "year". **Effective** with respect to estates of decedents dying after 12-31-81.

• 1976, Tax Reform Act of 1976 (P.L. 94-455)

P.L. 94-455, §1307(d)(1)(B)(iv):

Substituted "which is not disqualified for tax exemption under section 501(c)(3) by reason of attempting to influence legislation" for "no substantial part of the activities of which is carrying on propaganda, or otherwise attempting, to influence legislation" in Code Sec. 2522(a)(2). **Effective** for gifts in calendar years beginning after 12-31-76.

P.L. 94-455, §1313(b)(3):

Added after "educational purposes" in Code Sec. 2522(a)(2) the following:", or to foster national or international amateur sports competition (but only if no part of its activities involved the provision of athletic facilities or equipment),". **Effective** 10-5-76.

P.L. 94-455, §1902(a)(12)(D):

Deleted "Territory" in Code Sec. 2522(a)(1). **Effective** for gifts made after 12-31-76.

• 1970, Excise, Estate, and Gift Tax Adjustment Act of 1970 (P.L. 91-614)

P.L. 91-614, §102(c)(2):

Amended Code Sec. 2522(a) by substituting "quarter" for "year" in the line preceding paragraph (1). **Effective** for gifts made after 12-31-70.

• 1969, Tax Reform Act of 1969 (P.L. 91-172)

P.L. 91-172, §201(d)(4)(C):

Amended Code Sec. 2522(a)(2). **Effective** with respect to gifts and transfers made after 12-31-69. Prior to amendment, Code Sec. 2522(a)(2) read as follows:

"(2) a corporation, or trust, or community chest, fund, or foundation, organized and operated exclusively for religious, charitable, scientific, literary, or educational purposes, including the encouragement of art and the prevention of cruelty to children or animals, no part of the net earnings of which inures to the benefit of any private shareholder or individual, and no substantial part of the activities of which is carrying on propaganda, or otherwise attempting, to influence legislation;".

[Sec. 2522(b)]

(b) NONRESIDENTS.—In the case of a nonresident not a citizen of the United States, there shall be allowed as a deduction the amount of all gifts made during such year to or for the use of—

(1) the United States, any State, or any political subdivision thereof, or the District of Columbia, for exclusively public purposes;

(2) a domestic corporation organized and operated exclusively for religious, charitable, scientific, literary, or educational purposes, including the encouragement of art and the prevention of cruelty to children or animals, no part of the net earnings of which inures to the benefit of any private shareholder or individual, which is not disqualified for tax exemption under section 501(c)(3) by reason of attempting to influence legislation, and which does not participate in, or intervene in (including the publishing or distributing of statements), any political campaign on behalf of (or in opposition to) any candidate for public office;

(3) a trust, or community chest, fund, or foundation, organized and operated exclusively for religious, charitable, scientific, literary, or educational purposes, including the encouragement of art and the prevention of cruelty to children or animals, no substantial part of the activities of which is carrying on propaganda, or otherwise attempting, to influence legislation, and which does not participate in, or intervene in (including the publishing or distributing of statements), any political campaign on behalf of (or in opposition to) any candidate for public office; but only if such gifts are to be used within the United States exclusively for such purposes;

(4) a fraternal society, order, or association, operating under the lodge system, but only if such gifts are to be used within the United States exclusively for religious, charitable, scientific, literary, or educational purposes, including the encouragement of art and the prevention of cruelty to children or animals;

(5) posts or organizations of war veterans, or auxiliary units or societies of any such posts or organizations, if such posts, organizations, units, or societies are organized in the United States or any of its possessions, and if no part of their net earnings inures to the benefit of any private shareholder or individual.

Amendments

• 1987, Revenue Act of 1987 (P.L. 100-203)

P.L. 100-203, §10711(a)(6):

Amended Code Sec. 2522(b)(2) and (3) by striking out "on behalf of any candidate" and inserting in lieu thereof "on behalf of (or in opposition to) any candidate". **Effective** with respect to activities after 12-22-87.

• 1981, Economic Recovery Tax Act of 1981 (P.L. 97-34)

P.L. 97-34, §442(c):

Amended Code Sec. 2522(b) by striking out "quarter" and inserting "year". **Effective** with respect to estates of decedents dying after 12-31-81.

• 1976, Tax Reform Act of 1976 (P.L. 94-455)

P.L. 94-455, §1307(d)(1)(B)(v):

Substituted "which is not disqualified for tax exemption under section 501(c)(3) by reason of attempting to influence legislation" for "no substantial part of the activities of which is carrying on propaganda, or otherwise attempting, to influence legislation" in Code Sec. 2522(b)(2). **Effective** for gifts in calendar years beginning after 12-31-76.

P.L. 94-455, §1902(a)(12)(D):

Deleted "territory" in Code Sec. 2522(b)(1). **Effective** for gifts made after 12-31-76.

• 1970, Excise, Estate, and Gift Tax Adjustment Act of 1970 (P.L. 91-614)

P.L. 91-614, §102(c)(2):

Amended Code Sec. 2522(b) by substituting "quarter" for "year" in the line preceding paragraph (1). **Effective** for gifts made after 12-31-70.

• 1969, Tax Reform Act of 1969 (P.L. 91-172)

P.L. 91-172, §201(d)(4)(D):

Amended Code Sec. 2522(b)(2) and (3). **Effective** with respect to gifts and transfers made after 12-31-69. Prior to Amendment, Code Sec. 2522(b)(2) and (3) read as follows:

"(2) a domestic corporation organized and operated exclusively for religious, charitable, scientific, literary, or educational purposes, including the encouragement of art and the prevention of cruelty to children or animals, no part of the net earnings of which inures to the benefit of any private shareholder or individual, and no substantial part of the activities of which is carrying on propaganda, or otherwise attempting, to influence legislation;

(3) a trust, or community chest, fund, or foundation, organized and operated exclusively for religious, charitable, scientific, literary, or educational purposes, including the encouragement of art and the prevention of cruelty to children or animals, no substantial part of the activities of which is carrying on propaganda, or otherwise attempting, to influence legislation; but only if such gifts are to be used within the United States exclusively for such purposes;".

[Sec. 2522(c)]

(c) DISALLOWANCE OF DEDUCTIONS IN CERTAIN CASES.—

(1) No deduction shall be allowed under this section for a gift to or for the use of an organization or trust described in section 508(d) or 4948(c)(4) subject to the conditions specified in such sections.

(2) Where a donor transfers an interest in property (other than an interest described in section 170(f)(3)(B)) to a person, or for a use, described in subsection (a) or (b) and an interest in the same property is retained by the donor, or is transferred or has been transferred (for less than an adequate and full consideration in money or money's worth) from the donor to a person, or for a use, not described in subsection (a) or (b), no deduction shall be allowed under this section for the interest which is, or has been transferred to the person, or for the use, described in subsection (a) or (b), unless—

(A) in the case of a remainder interest, such interest is in a trust which is a charitable remainder annuity trust or a charitable remainder unitrust (described in section 664) or a pooled income fund (described in section 642(c)(5)), or

(B) in the case of any other interest, such interest is in the form of a guaranteed annuity or is a fixed percentage distributed yearly of the fair market value of the property (to be determined yearly).

(3) Rules similar to the rules of section 2055(e)(4) shall apply for purposes of paragraph (2).

(4) REFORMATIONS TO COMPLY WITH PARAGRAPH (2).—

(A) IN GENERAL.—A deduction shall be allowed under subsection (a) in respect of any qualified reformation (within the meaning of section 2055(e)(3)(B)).

(B) RULES SIMILAR TO SECTION 2055(e)(3) TO APPLY.—For purposes of this paragraph, rules similar to the rules of section 2055(e)(3) shall apply.

(5) CONTRIBUTIONS TO DONOR ADVISED FUNDS.—A deduction otherwise allowed under subsection (a) for any contribution to a donor advised fund (as defined in section 4966(d)(2)) shall only be allowed if—

(A) the sponsoring organization (as defined in section 4966(d)(1)) with respect to such donor advised fund is not—

(i) described in paragraph (3) or (4) of subsection (a), or

(ii) a type III supporting organization (as defined in section 4943(f)(5)(A)) which is not a functionally integrated type III supporting organization (as defined in section 4943(f)(5)(B)), and

(B) the taxpayer obtains a contemporaneous written acknowledgment (determined under rules similar to the rules of section 170(f)(8)(C)) from the sponsoring organization (as so defined) of such donor advised fund that such organization has exclusive legal control over the assets contributed.

Amendments

• 2018, Tax Technical Corrections Act of 2018 (P.L. 115-141)

P.L. 115-141, §401(a)(204), Div. U:

Amended Code Sec. 2522(c)(1) by striking "to of for" and inserting "to or for". **Effective** 3-23-2018.

• 2006, Pension Protection Act of 2006 (P.L. 109-280)

P.L. 109-280, §1234(c):

Amended Code Sec. 2522(c) by adding at the end a new paragraph (5). **Effective** for contributions made after the date which is 180 days after 8-17-2006.

• 1984, Deficit Reduction Act of 1984 (P.L. 98-369)

P.L. 98-369, §1022(c):

Amended Code Sec. 2522(c) by adding at the end thereof a new paragraph (4). **Effective** for reformations after 12-31-78, except that such amendments shall not apply to any reformation to which Code Sec. 2055(e)(3) (as in effect on the day before 7-18-84) applies. For purposes of applying Code Sec. 2055(e)(3)(C)(iii) (as amended by this section), the 90th day described in such clause shall be treated as not occurring before the 90th day after 7-18-84.

• 1981, Economic Recovery Tax Act of 1981 (P.L. 97-34)

P.L. 97-34, §423(b):

Added Code Sec. 2522(c)(3). **Effective** for transfers after 12-31-81.

• 1976, Tax Reform Act of 1976 (P.L. 94-455)

P.L. 94-455, §2124(e)(3)-(4) (as amended by P.L. 95-30, §309(b)(2)):

Substituted "(other than an interest described in section 170(f)(3)(B))" for "(other than a remainder interest in a personal residence or farm or an undivided portion of the donor's entire interest in property)" in Code Sec. 2522(c)(2). **Effective** for contributions or transfers made after 6-13-76, and before 6-14-77. However, P.L. 95-30, §309(b)(2), changed this latter date to 6-14-81.

• 1969, Tax Reform Act of 1969 (P.L. 91-172)

P.L. 91-172, §201(d)(3):

Amended Code Sec. 2522(c). **Effective** for gifts made after 12-31-69, except the amendments made to section 2522(c)(2) shall apply to gifts made after 7-31-69. Prior to amendment, Code Sec. 2522(c) read as follows:

"(c) Disallowance of Deductions in Certain Cases.—

"For disallowance of certain charitable, etc., deductions otherwise allowable under this section, see sections 503 and 681."

• 1958, Technical Amendments Act of 1958 (P.L. 85-866)

P.L. 85-866, §30(d):

Amended Code Sec. 2522(c) by substituting "503" for "504". **Effective** 1-1-54.

[Sec. 2522(d)]

(d) SPECIAL RULE FOR IRREVOCABLE TRANSFERS OF EASEMENTS IN REAL PROPERTY.—A deduction shall be allowed under subsection (a) in respect of any transfer of a qualified real property interest (as defined in section 170(h)(2)(C)) which meets the requirements of section 170(h) (without regard to paragraph (4)(A) thereof).

Amendments

• 1986, Tax Reform Act of 1986 (P.L. 99-514)

P.L. 99-514, §1422(b):

Amended Code Sec. 2522 by redesignating subsection (d) as subsection (e) and by inserting after subsection (c) new subsection (d). **Effective** for transfers and contributions made after 12-31-86.

[Sec. 2522(e)]

(e) SPECIAL RULES FOR FRACTIONAL GIFTS.—

(1) DENIAL OF DEDUCTION IN CERTAIN CASES.—

(A) IN GENERAL.—No deduction shall be allowed for a contribution of an undivided portion of a taxpayer's entire interest in tangible personal property unless all interests in the property are held immediately before such contribution by—

(i) the taxpayer, or

(ii) the taxpayer and the donee.

(B) EXCEPTIONS.—The Secretary may, by regulation, provide for exceptions to subparagraph (A) in cases where all persons who hold an interest in the property make proportional contributions of an undivided portion of the entire interest held by such persons.

(2) RECAPTURE OF DEDUCTION IN CERTAIN CASES; ADDITION TO TAX.—

(A) IN GENERAL.—The Secretary shall provide for the recapture of an amount equal to any deduction allowed under this section (plus interest) with respect to any contribution of an undivided portion of a taxpayer's entire interest in tangible personal property—

(i) in any case in which the donor does not contribute all of the remaining interests in such property to the donee (or, if such donee is no longer in existence, to any person described in section 170(c)) on or before the earlier of—

(I) the date that is 10 years after the date of the initial fractional contribution, or

(II) the date of the death of the donor, and

(ii) in any case in which the donee has not, during the period beginning on the date of the initial fractional contribution and ending on the date described in clause (i)—

(I) had substantial physical possession of the property, and

(II) used the property in a use which is related to a purpose or function constituting the basis for the organizations' exemption under section 501.

(B) ADDITION TO TAX.—The tax imposed under this chapter for any taxable year for which there is a recapture under subparagraph (A) shall be increased by 10 percent of the amount so recaptured.

(C) INITIAL FRACTIONAL CONTRIBUTION.—For purposes of this paragraph, the term "initial fractional contribution" means, with respect to any donor, the first gift of an undivided portion of the donor's entire interest in any tangible personal property for which a deduction is allowed under subsection (a) or (b).

Amendments

• 2007, Tax Technical Corrections Act of 2007 (P.L. 110-172)

P.L. 110-172, §3(d)(2)(A)-(C):

Amended Code Sec. 2522(e) by striking paragraphs (2) and (4), by redesignating paragraph (3) as paragraph (2), and by adding at the end of paragraph (2), as so redesignated, a new subparagraph (C). **Effective** as if included in the provision of the Pension Protection Act of 2006 (P.L. 109-280) to which it relates [**effective** for contributions, bequests, and gifts made after 8-17-2006.—CCH]. Prior to being stricken, Code Sec. 2522(e)(2) and (4) read as follows:

(2) VALUATION OF SUBSEQUENT GIFTS.—In the case of any additional contribution, the fair market value of such contribution shall be determined by using the lesser of—

(A) the fair market value of the property at the time of the initial fractional contribution, or

(B) the fair market value of the property at the time of the additional contribution.

* * *

(4) DEFINITIONS.—For purposes of this subsection—

(A) ADDITIONAL CONTRIBUTION.—The term "additional contribution" means any gift for which a deduction is allowed under subsection (a) or (b) of any interest in a property with respect to which the donor has previously made an initial fractional contribution.

(B) INITIAL FRACTIONAL CONTRIBUTION.—The term "initial fractional contribution" means, with respect to any donor, the first gift of an undivided portion of the donor's entire interest in any tangible personal property for which a deduction is allowed under subsection (a) or (b).

P.L. 110-172, §11(a)(16)(A):

Amended Code Sec. 2522(e)(1)(A) by striking "all interest in the property is" and inserting "all interests in the property are". **Effective** 12-29-2007.

P.L. 110-172, §11(a)(16)(B)(i)-(ii):

Amended Code Sec. 2522(e)(2)(A)(i) (as redesignated by Act Sec. 3(d)(2)) by striking "interest" and inserting "interests", and by striking "before" and inserting "on or before". **Effective** 12-29-2007.

• 2006, Pension Protection Act of 2006 (P.L. 109-280)

P.L. 109-280, §1218(c):

Amended Code Sec. 2522 by redesignating subsection (e) as subsection (f) and by inserting after subsection (d) a new subsection (e). **Effective** for contributions, bequests, and gifts made after 8-17-2006.

[Sec. 2522(f)]

(f) CROSS REFERENCES.—

(1) For treatment of certain organizations providing child care, see section 501(k).

(2) For exemption of certain gifts to or for the benefit of the United States and for rules of construction with respect to certain bequests, see section 2055(f).

(3) For treatment of gifts to or for the use of Indian tribal governments (or their subdivisions), see section 7871.

Amendments

• 2006, Pension Protection Act of 2006 (P.L. 109-280)

P.L. 109-280, §1218(c):

Amended Code Sec. 2522 by redesignating subsection (e) as subsection (f). **Effective** for contributions, bequests, and gifts made after 8-17-2006.

• 1986, Tax Reform Act of 1986 (P.L. 99-514)

P.L. 99-514, §1422(b):

Redesignated subsection (d) as subsection (e). **Effective** for transfers and contributions made after 12-31-86.

• 1984, Deficit Reduction Act of 1984 (P.L. 98-369)

P.L. 98-369 §1032(b)(3):

Amended Code Sec. 2522(d) by redesignating paragraphs (1) and (2) as paragraphs (2) and (3), respectively, and by inserting before paragraph (2) (as so redesignated) a new paragraph (1). **Effective** for tax years beginning after 7-18-84.

• 1983 (P.L. 97-473)

P.L. 97-473, §202(b)(7):

Amended Code Sec. 2522(d). For the **effective** date, see the amendment note for P.L. 97-473, Act Sec. 204, following Code Sec. 7871. Prior to amendment, Code Sec. 2522(d) read as follows:

"(d) CROSS REFERENCES.—

For exemption of certain gifts to or for the benefit of the United States and for rules of construction with respect to certain gifts, see section 2055(f)."

• 1976, Tax Reform Act of 1976 (P.L. 94-455)

P.L. 94-455, §1902(a)(11), (c)(1):

Amended Code Sec. 2522(d). **Effective** for estates of decedents dying after 12-31-70. Prior to amendment, Code Sec. 2522(d) read as follows:

(d) OTHER CROSS REFERENCES.—

(1) For exemption of gifts to or for benefit of Library of Congress, see section 5 of the Act of March 3, 1925, as amended (56 Stat. 765; 2 U.S.C. 161).

(2) For construction of gifts for benefit of library of Post Office Department as gifts to or for the use of the United States, see section 2 of the Act of August 8, 1946 (60 Stat. 924; 5 U.S.C. 393).

(3) For exemption of gifts for benefit of Office of Naval Records and Library, Navy Department, see section 2 of the Act of March 4, 1937 (50 Stat. 25; 5 U.S.C. 419b).

(4) For exemption of gifts to or for benefit of National Park Service, see section 5 of the Act of July 10, 1935 (49 Stat. 478; 16 U.S.C. 19c).

(5) For construction of gifts accepted by the Secretary of State under the Foreign Service Act of 1946 as gifts to or for

the use of the United States, see section 1021 (e) of that Act (60 Stat. 1032; 22 U.S.C. 809).

(6) For construction of gifts or bequests of money accepted by the Attorney General for credit to "Commissary Funds, Federal Prisons" as gifts or bequests to or for the use of the United States, see section 2 of the Act of May 15, 1952, 66 Stat. 73, as amended by the Act of July 9, 1952, 66 Stat. 479 (31 U.S.C. 725s-4).

(7) For payment of tax on gifts of United States obligations to the United States, see section 24 of the Second Liberty Bond Act, as amended (59 Stat. 48, §4; 31 U.S.C. 757e).

(8) For construction of gifts for benefit of or use in connection with Naval Academy as gifts to or for the use of the United States, see section 3 of the Act of March 31, 1944 (58 Stat. 135; 34 U.S.C. 1115b).

(9) For exemption of gifts for benefit of Naval Academy Museum, see section 4 of the Act of March 26, 1938 (52 Stat. 119; 34 U.S.C. 1119).

(10) For exemption of gifts received by National Archives Trust Fund Board, see section 7 of the National Archives Trust Fund Board Act (55 Stat. 582; 44 U.S.C. 300gg).

[Sec. 2523]

SEC. 2523. GIFT TO SPOUSE.

[Sec. 2523(a)]

(a) ALLOWANCE OF DEDUCTION.—Where a donor transfers during the calendar year by gift an interest in property to a donee who at the time of the gift is the donor's spouse, there shall be allowed as a deduction in computing taxable gifts for the calendar year an amount with respect to such interest equal to its value.

Amendments

• 1989, Omnibus Budget Reconciliation Act of 1989 (P.L. 101-239)

P.L. 101-239, §7815(d)(2):

Amended Code Sec. 2523(a) by striking "who is a citizen or resident" after "Where a donor". **Effective** as if included in the provision of P.L. 100-647 to which it relates.

• 1981, Economic Recovery Tax Act of 1981 (P.L. 97-34)

P.L. 97-34, §403(b)(1):

Amended Code Sec. 2523(a). **Effective**, generally, for gifts made after 12-31-81. For special rules, see Act Sec. 403(e)(3), below. Prior to amendment, Code Sec. 2523(a) read as follows:

(a) ALLOWANCE OF DEDUCTION.—

(1) IN GENERAL.—Where a donor who is a citizen or resident transfers during the calendar quarter by gift an interest in property to a donee who at the time of the gift is the donor's spouse, there shall be allowed as a deduction in computing taxable gifts for the calendar quarter an amount with respect to such interest equal to its value.

(2) LIMITATION.—The aggregate of the deductions allowed under paragraph (1) for any calendar quarter shall not exceed the sum of—

(A) $100,000 reduced (but not below zero) by the aggregate of the deductions allowed under this section for preceding calendar quarters beginning after December 31, 1976; plus

(B) 50 percent of the lessor of—

(i) the amount of the deductions allowable under paragraph (1) for such calendar quarter (determined without regard to this paragraph); or

(ii) the amount (if any) by which the aggregate of the amounts determined under clause (i) for the calendar quarter and for each preceding calendar quarter beginning after December 31, 1976, exceeds $200,000.

P.L. 97-34, §403(e)(3), provides:

(3) If—

(A) the decedent dies after December 31, 1981,

(B) by reason of the death of the decedent property passes from the decedent or is acquired from the decedent under a will executed before the date which is 30 days after the date of the enactment of this Act, or a trust created before such date, which contains a formula expressly providing that the spouse is to receive the maximum amount of property qualifying for the marital deduction allowable by Federal law,

(C) the formula referred to in subparagraph (B) was not amended to refer specifically to an unlimited marital deduction at any time after the date which is 30 days after the date of enactment of this Act, and before the death of the decedent, and

(D) the State does not enact a staute applicable to such estate which construes this type of formula as referring to the marital deduction allowable by Federal law as amended by subsection (a),

then the amendment made by subsection (a) relating to the unlimited marital deduction (Code Sec. 2056, as amended by P.L. 97-34)] shall not apply to the estate of such decedent.

• 1976, Tax Reform Act of 1976 (P.L. 94-455)

P.L. 94-455, §2002(b), (d)(2):

Amended Code Sec. 2523(a). **Effective** for gifts made after 12-31-76. Prior to amendment, Code Sec. 2523(a) read as follows:

(a) IN GENERAL.—Where a donor who is a citizen or resident transfers during the calendar quarter by gift an interest in property to a donee who at the time of the gift is the donor's spouse, there shall be allowed as a deduction in computing taxable gifts for the calendar quarter an amount with respect to such interest equal to one-half of its value.

• 1970, Excise, Estate, and Gift Tax Adjustment Act of 1970 (P.L. 91-614)

P.L. 91-614, §102(c)(3):

Amended Code Sec. 2523(a) by substituting "calendar quarter" for "calendar year" in the two places such term appears. **Effective** for gifts made after 12-31-70.

[Sec. 2523(b)]

(b) LIFE ESTATE OR OTHER TERMINABLE INTEREST.—Where, on the lapse of time, on the occurrence of an event or contingency, or on the failure of an event or contingency to occur, such interest transferred to the spouse will terminate or fail, no deduction shall be allowed with respect to such interest—

(1) if the donor retains in himself, or transfers or has transferred (for less than an adequate and full consideration in money or money's worth) to any person other than such donee spouse (or the estate of such spouse), an interest in such property, and if by reason of such retention or transfer the donor (or his heirs or assigns) or such person (or his heirs or assigns) may possess or

enjoy any part of such property after such termination or failure of the interest transferred to the donee spouse; or

(2) if the donor immediately after the transfer to the donee spouse has a power to appoint an interest in such property which he can exercise (either alone or in conjunction with any person) in such manner that the appointee may possess or enjoy any part of such property after such termination or failure of the interest transferred to the donee spouse. For purposes of this paragraph, the donor shall be considered as having immediately after the transfer to the donee spouse such power to appoint even though such power cannot be exercised until after the lapse of time, upon the occurrence of an event or contingency, or on the failure of an event or contingency to occur.

An exercise or release at any time by the donor, either alone or in conjunction with any person, of a power to appoint an interest in property, even though not otherwise a transfer, shall, for purposes of paragraph (1), be considered as a transfer by him. Except as provided in subsection (e), where at the time of the transfer it is impossible to ascertain the particular person or persons who may receive from the donor an interest in property so transferred by him, such interest shall, for purposes of paragraph (1), be considered as transferred to a person other than the donee spouse.

[Sec. 2523(c)]

(c) INTEREST IN UNIDENTIFIED ASSETS.—Where the assets out of which, or the proceeds of which, the interest transferred to the donee spouse may be satisfied include a particular asset or assets with respect to which no deduction would be allowed if such asset or assets were transferred from the donor to such spouse, then the value of the interest transferred to such spouse shall, for purposes of subsection (a), be reduced by the aggregate value of such particular assets.

[Sec. 2523(d)]

(d) JOINT INTERESTS.—If the interest is transferred to the donee spouse as sole joint tenant with the donor or as tenant by the entirety, the interest of the donor in the property which exists solely by reason of the possibility that the donor may survive the donee spouse, or that there may occur a severance of the tenancy, shall not be considered for purposes of subsection (b) as an interest retained by the donor in himself.

[Sec. 2523(e)]

(e) LIFE ESTATE WITH POWER OF APPOINTMENT IN DONEE SPOUSE.—Where the donor transfers an interest in property, if by such transfer his spouse is entitled for life to all of the income from the entire interest, or all the income from a specific portion thereof, payable annually or at more frequent intervals, with power in the donee spouse to appoint the entire interest, or such specific portion (exercisable in favor of such donee spouse, or of the estate of such donee spouse, or in favor of either, whether or not in each case the power is exercisable in favor of others), and with no power in any other person to appoint any part of such interest, or such portion, to any person other than the donee spouse—

(1) the interest, or such portion, so transferred shall, for purposes of subsection (a) be considered as transferred to the donee spouse, and

(2) no part of the interest, or such portion, so transferred shall, for purposes of subsection (b)(1), be considered as retained in the donor or transferred to any person other than the donee spouse.

This subsection shall apply only if, by such transfer, such power in the donee spouse to appoint the interest, or such portion, whether exercisable by will or during life, is exercisable by such spouse alone and in all events. For purposes of this subsection, the term "specific portion" only includes a portion determined on a fractional or percentage basis.

Amendments

• 1992, Energy Policy Act of 1992 (P.L. 102-486)

P.L. 102-486, §1941(b)(1):

Amended Code Sec. 2523(e) by adding at the end thereof a new sentence. **Effective** for gifts made after 10-24-92.

[Sec. 2523(f)—Repealed]

Amendments

• 1981, Economic Recovery Tax Act of 1981 (P.L. 97-34)

P.L. 97-34, §403(b)(2):

Repealed Code Sec. 2523(f). **Effective**, generally, for gifts made after 12-31-81. Prior to its repeal, Code Sec. 2523(f) read as follows:

(f) COMMUNITY PROPERTY.—

(1) A deduction otherwise allowable under this section shall be allowed only to the extent that the transfer can be shown to represent a gift of property which is not, at the time of the gift, held as community property under the law of any State, possession of the United States, or of any foreign country.

(2) For purposes of paragraph (1), community property (except property which is considered as community property solely by reason of paragraph (3)) shall not be consid-

ered as "held as community property" if the entire value of such property (and not merely one-half thereof) is treated as the amount of the gift.

(3) If during the calendar year 1942 or in succeeding calendar years, property held as such community property (unless considered by reason of paragraph (2) as not so held) was by the donor and the donee spouse converted, by one transaction or a series of transactions, into separate property of the donor and such spouse (including any form of coownership by them), the separate property so acquired by the donor and any property acquired at any time by the donor in exchange therefor (by one exchange or a series of exchanges) shall, for purposes of paragraph (1), be considered as "held as community property."

(4) Where the value (at the time of such conversion) of the separate property so acquired by the donor exceeded the value (at such time) of the separate property so acquired by such spouse, paragraph (3) shall apply only with respect to the same portion of such separate property of the donor as the portion which the value (as of such time) of such separate property so acquired by such spouse is of the value (as of such time) of the separate property so acquired by the donor.

For the special rule applicable to certain wills or trusts, executed or created, before September 12, 1981, see the historical comment following Code Sec. 2523(a), at P.L. 97-34, § 403(b)(1), above.

• 1976, Tax Reform Act of 1976 (P.L. 94-455)

P.L. 94-455, § 1902(a)(12)(E), (c)(2):

Deleted "Territory, or" in Code Sec. 2523(f)(1). **Effective** for gifts made after 12-31-76.

[Sec. 2523(f)]

(f) ELECTION WITH RESPECT TO LIFE ESTATE FOR DONEE SPOUSE.—

(1) IN GENERAL.—In the case of qualified terminable interest property—

(A) for purposes of subsection (a), such property shall be treated as transferred to the donee spouse, and

(B) for purposes of subsection (b)(1), no part of such property shall be considered as retained in the donor or transferred to any person other than the donee spouse.

(2) QUALIFIED TERMINABLE INTEREST PROPERTY.—For purposes of this subsection, the term "qualified terminable interest property" means any property—

(A) which is transferred by the donor spouse,

(B) in which the donee spouse has a qualifying income interest for life, and

(C) to which an election under this subsection applies.

(3) CERTAIN RULES MADE APPLICABLE.—For purposes of this subsection, rules similar to the rules of clauses (ii), (iii), and (iv) of section 2056(b)(7)(B) shall apply and the rules of section 2056(b)(10) shall apply.

(4) ELECTION.—

(A) TIME AND MANNER.—An election under this subsection with respect to any property shall be made on or before the date prescribed by section 6075(b) for filing a gift tax return with respect to the transfer (determined without regard to section 6019(2)) and shall be made in such manner as the Secretary shall by regulations prescribe.

(B) ELECTION IRREVOCABLE.—An election under this subsection, once made, shall be irrevocable.

(5) TREATMENT OF INTEREST RETAINED BY DONOR SPOUSE.—

(A) IN GENERAL.—In the case of any qualified terminable interest property—

(i) such property shall not be includible in the gross estate of the donor spouse, and

(ii) any subsequent transfer by the donor spouse of an interest in such property shall not be treated as a transfer for purposes of this chapter.

(B) SUBPARAGRAPH (A) NOT TO APPLY AFTER TRANSFER BY DONEE SPOUSE.—Subparagraph (A) shall not apply with respect to any property after the donee spouse is treated as having transferred such property under section 2519, or such property is includible in the donee spouse's gross estate under section 2044.

(6) TREATMENT OF JOINT AND SURVIVOR ANNUITIES.—In the case of a joint and survivor annuity where only the donor spouse and donee spouse have the right to receive payments before the death of the last spouse to die—

(A) the donee spouse's interest shall be treated as a qualifying income interest for life,

(B) the donor spouse shall be treated as having made an election under this subsection with respect to such annuity unless the donor spouse otherwise elects on or before the date specified in paragraph (4)(A),

(C) paragraph (5) and section 2519 shall not apply to the donor spouse's interest in the annuity, and

(D) if the donee spouse dies before the donor spouse, no amount shall be includible in the gross estate of the donee spouse under section 2044 with respect to such annuity. An election under subparagraph (B), once made, shall be irrevocable.

Amendments

• 1992, Energy Policy Act of 1992 (P.L. 102-486)

P.L. 102-486, §1941(b)(2):

Amended Code Sec. 2523(f)(3) by inserting "and the rules of section 2056(b)(10) shall apply" before the period at the end thereof. **Effective** for gifts made after the date of the enactment of this Act.

• 1988, Technical and Miscellaneous Revenue Act of 1988 (P.L. 100-647)

P.L. 100-647, §6152(b):

Amended Code Sec. 2523(f) by adding at the end thereof new paragraph (6). **Effective**, generally, for transfers made after 12-31-81. However, Act Sec. 6152(c)(2) and (3) provide special rules.

P.L. 100-647, §6152(c)(2)-(3), provide:

(2) NOT TO APPLY TO EXTENT INCONSISTENT WITH PRIOR RETURN.—In the case of any estate or gift tax return filed before the date of the enactment of this Act, the amendments made by this section shall not apply to the extent such amendments would be inconsistent with the treatment of the annuity on such return unless the executor or donor (as the case may be) otherwise elects under this paragraph before the day 2 years after the date of the enactment of this Act.

(3) EXTENSION OF TIME FOR ELECTION OUT.—The time for making an election under section 2056(b)(7)(C)(ii) or 2523(f)(6)(B) of the 1986 Code (as added by this subsection) shall not expire before the day 2 years after the date of the enactment of this Act (and, if such election is made within the time permitted under this paragraph, the requirement of such section 2056(b)(7)(C)(ii) that it be made on the return shall not apply).

• 1986, Tax Reform Act of 1986 (P.L. 99-514)

P.L. 99-514, §1879(n)(1):

Amended Code Sec. 2523(f)(4)(A). **Effective** for transfers made after 12-31-85. For a special rule, see Act Sec. 1879(n)(3), below. Prior to amendment, Code Sec. 2523(f)(4)(A) read as follows:

(A) TIME AND MANNER.—An election under this subsection with respect to any property shall be made on or before the first April 15th after the calendar year in which the interest was transferred and shall be made in such manner as the Secretary shall by regulations prescribe.

P.L. 99-514, §1879(n)(3), provides:

(3) SPECIAL RULE FOR CERTAIN TRANSFERS IN OCTOBER 1984.—An election under section 2523(f) of the Internal Revenue Code of 1954 with respect to an interest in property which—

(A) was transferred during October 1984, and

(B) was transferred pursuant to a trust instrument stating that the grantor's intention was that the property of the trust would constitute qualified terminable interest property as to which a Federal gift tax marital deduction would be allowed upon the grantor's election,

shall be made on the return of tax imposed by section 2501 of such Code for the calendar year 1984 which is filed on or before the due date of such return or, if a timely return is not filed, on the first such return filed after the due date of such return and before December 31, 1986.

• 1983, Technical Corrections Act of 1982 (P.L. 97-448)

P.L. 97-448, §104(a)(4):

Amended Code Sec. 2523(f)(4). **Effective** as if included in the provision of P.L. 97-34 to which it relates. Prior to amendment, Code Sec. 2523(f)(4) read as follows:

"(4) ELECTION.—An election under this subsection with respect to any property shall be made on the return of the tax imposed by section 2501 for the calendar year in which the interest was transferred. Such an election, once made, shall be irrevocable."

P.L. 97-448, §104(a)(5):

Amended Code Sec. 2523(f) by adding at the end thereof new paragraph (5). **Effective** as if included in the provision of P.L. 97-34 to which it relates.

P.L. 97-448, §104(a)(6):

Amended Code Sec. 2523(f)(3) by striking out "the rules of" and inserting in lieu thereof "rules similar to the rules of". **Effective** as if included in the provision of P.L. 97-34 to which it relates.

• 1981, Economic Recovery Tax Act of 1981 (P.L. 97-34)

P.L. 97-34, §403(d)(2):

Added Code Sec. 2523(f). **Effective**, generally, for gifts made after 12-31-81. See Act Sec. 403(e)(3), below, for a special rule applicable to certain wills and trusts, executed or created, before 9-12-81.

P.L. 97-34, §403(e)(3), provides:

(3) If—

(A) the decedent dies after December 31, 1981,

(B) by reason of the death of the decedent property passes from the decedent or is acquired from the decedent under a will executed before the date which is 30 days after the date of the enactment of this Act, or a trust created before such date, which contains a formula expressly providing that the spouse is to receive the maximum amount of property qualifying for the marital deduction allowable by Federal law,

(C) the formula referred to in subparagraph (B) was not amended to refer specifically to an unlimited marital deduction at any time after the date which is 30 days after the date of enactment of this Act, and before the death of the decedent, and

(D) the State does not enact a statute applicable to such estate which construes this type of formula as referring to the marital deduction allowable by Federal law as amended by subsection (a),

then the amendment made by subsection (a) [relating to the unlimited marital deduction (Code Sec. 2056, as amended by P.L. 97-34)] shall not apply to the estate of such decedent.

[Sec. 2523(g)]

(g) SPECIAL RULE FOR CHARITABLE REMAINDER TRUSTS.—

(1) IN GENERAL.—If, after the transfer, the donee spouse is the only beneficiary who is not a charitable beneficiary (other than the donor) of a qualified charitable remainder trust, subsection (b) shall not apply to the interest in such trust which is transferred to the donee spouse.

(2) DEFINITIONS.—For purposes of paragraph (1), the terms "charitable beneficiary" and "qualified charitable remainder trust" have the meanings given to such terms by section 2056(b)(8)(B).

Amendments

• 2018, Tax Technical Corrections Act of 2018 (P.L. 115-141)

P.L. 115-141, §401(a)(205), Div. U:

Amended Code Sec. 2523(g)(1) by striking "noncharitable beneficiary" and inserting "beneficiary who is not a charitable beneficiary". **Effective** 3-23-2018.

P.L. 115-141, §401(a)(206), Div. U:

Amended Code Sec. 2523(g)(2) by striking "noncharitable" and inserting "charitable". **Effective** 3-23-2018.

• 1997, Taxpayer Relief Act of 1997 (P.L. 105-34)

P.L. 105-34, §1604(g)(4):

Amended Code Sec. 2523(g)(1) by striking "qualified remainder trust" and inserting "qualified charitable remainder trust". **Effective** 8-5-97.

• 1981, Economic Recovery Tax Act of 1981 (P.L. 97-34)

P.L. 97-34, §403(d)(2):

Added Code Sec. 2523(g). **Effective**, generally, for gifts made after 12-31-81. For the special rule applicable to certain wills and trusts, executed or created, before 9-12-81, see the amendment note following Code Sec. 2523(f).

[Sec. 2523(h)]

(h) DENIAL OF DOUBLE DEDUCTION.—Nothing in this section or any other provision of this chapter shall allow the value of any interest in property to be deducted under this chapter more than once with respect to the same donor.

Amendments

• 1983, Technical Corrections Act of 1982 (P.L. 97-448)

P.L. 97-448, §104(a)(2)(B):

Added Code Sec. 2523(h). **Effective** as if included in the provision of P.L. 97-34 to which it relates.

[Sec. 2523(i)]

(i) DISALLOWANCE OF MARITAL DEDUCTION WHERE SPOUSE NOT CITIZEN.—If the spouse of the donor is not a citizen of the United States—

(1) no deduction shall be allowed under this section,

(2) section 2503(b) shall be applied with respect to gifts which are made by the donor to such spouse and with respect to which a deduction would be allowable under this section but for paragraph (1) by substituting "$100,000" for "$10,000", and

(3) the principles of sections 2515 and 2515A (as such sections were in effect before their repeal by the Economic Recovery Tax Act of 1981) shall apply, except that the provisions of such section 2515 providing for an election shall not apply.

This subsection shall not apply to any transfer resulting from the acquisition of rights under a joint and survivor annuity described in subsection (f)(6).

Amendments

• 1990, Omnibus Budget Reconciliation Act of 1990 (P.L. 101-508)

P.L. 101-508, §11702(g)(1):

Amended Code Sec. 2523(i) by adding at the end thereof a new sentence. **Effective** as if included in the provision of P.L. 100-647 to which it relates.

• 1989, Omnibus Budget Reconciliation Act of 1989 (P.L. 101-239)

P.L. 101-239, §7815(d)(1)(A):

Amended Code Sec. 2523(i)(2) by striking "made by the donor to such spouse" and inserting "which are made by the donor to such spouse and with respect to which a deduction would be allowable under this section but for paragraph (1)". **Effective** with respect to gifts made after 6-29-89.

• 1988, Technical and Miscellaneous Revenue Act of 1988 (P.L. 100-647)

P.L. 100-647, §5033(b):

Amended Code Sec. 2523 by adding at the end thereof a new subsection (i). **Effective** for gifts on or after 7-14-88.

[Sec. 2524]

SEC. 2524. EXTENT OF DEDUCTIONS.

The deductions provided in sections 2522 and 2523 shall be allowed only to the extent that the gifts therein specified are included in the amount of gifts against which such deductions are applied.

GENERATION-SKIPPING TRANSFER TAX

TABLE OF CONTENTS

SUBTITLE B—ESTATE AND GIFT TAXES

Chapter 13—Tax on Generation-Skipping Transfers

SUBTITLE B—ESTATE AND GIFT TAXES

* * *

CHAPTER 13—TAX ON GENERATION-SKIPPING TRANSFERS

Subchapter A—Tax Imposed

[Sec. 2601]

SEC. 2601. TAX IMPOSED.

A tax is hereby imposed on every generation-skipping transfer (within the meaning of subchapter B).

Amendments

• 1990, Omnibus Budget Reconciliation Act of 1990 (P.L. 101-508)

P.L. 101-508, §11703(c)(3), provides:

(3) Subparagraph (C) of section 1433(b)(2) of the Tax Reform Act of 1986 shall not exempt any generation-skipping transfer from the amendments made by subtitle D of title XVI of such Act to the extent such transfer is attributable to property transferred by gift or by reason of the death of another person to the decedent (or trust) referred to in such subparagraph after August 3, 1990.

• 1988, Technical and Miscellaneous Revenue Act of 1988 (P.L. 100-647)

P.L. 100-647, §1014(h)(3)(B) and (h)(5), provide:

(3)(B) Clause (iii) of section 1443[1433](b)(3)(B) of the Reform Act (as amended by subparagraph (A)) shall apply only to transfers after June 10, 1987.

* * *

(5) Subparagraph (C) of section 1433(b)(2) of the Reform Act shall not exempt any direct skip from the amendments made by subtitle D of title XIV of the Reform Act if—

(A) such direct skip results from the application of section 2044 of the 1986 Code, and

(B) such direct skip is attributable to property transferred to the trust after October 21, 1988.

• 1986, Tax Reform Act of 1986 (P.L. 99-514)

P.L. 99-514, §1431(a):

Amended chapter 13 (Code Secs. 2601-2602). **Effective**, generally, for any generation-skipping transfer (within the meaning of section 2611 of the Internal Revenue Code of 1986) made after 10-22-86. However, for special rules, see Act Sec. 1433(b)-(d), below. Prior to amendment by P.L. 99-514, Code Sec. 2601 read as follows:

SEC. 2601. TAX IMPOSED.

A tax is hereby imposed on every generation-skipping transfer in the amount determined under section 2602.

P.L. 99-514, §1433(b)-(d), as amended by P.L. 100-647, §1014(h)(2)-(4), provides:

(b) SPECIAL RULES.—

(1) TREATMENT OF CERTAIN INTER VIVOS TRANSFERS MADE AFTER SEPTEMBER 25, 1985.—For purposes of subsection (a) (and chapter 13 of the Internal Revenue Code of 1986 as amended by this part), any inter vivos transfer after September 25, 1985, and on or before the date of the enactment of this Act shall be treated as if it were made on the 1st day after the date of enactment of this Act.

(2) EXCEPTIONS.—The amendments made by this subtitle shall not apply to—

(A) any generation-skipping transfer under a trust which was irrevocable on September 25, 1985, but only to the extent that such transfer is not made out of corpus added to the trust after September 25, 1985 (or out of income attributable to corpus so added),

(B) any generation-skipping transfer under a will or revocable trust executed before the date of the enactment of this Act if the decedent dies before January 1, 1987, and

(C) any generation-skipping transfer—

(i) under a trust to the extent such trust consists of property included in the gross estate of a decedent (other than property transferred by the decedent during his life after the date of the enactment of this Act), or reinvestments thereof, or

(ii) which is a direct skip which occurs by reason of the death of any decedent;

but only if such decedent was, on the date of the enactment of this Act, under a mental disability to change the disposition of his property and did not regain his competence to dispose of such property before the date of his death.

(3) TREATMENT OF CERTAIN TRANSFERS TO GRANDCHILDREN.—

(A) IN GENERAL.—For purposes of chapter 13 of the Internal Revenue Code of 1986, the term "direct skip" shall not include any transfer before January 1, 1990, from a transferor to a grandchild of the transferor to the extent the aggregate transfers from such transferor to such grandchild do not exceed $2,000,000.

(B) TREATMENT OF TRANSFERS IN TRUST.—For purposes of subparagraph (A), a transfer in trust for the benefit of a grandchild shall be treated as a transfer to such grandchild if (and only if)—

(i) during the life of the grandchild, no portion of the corpus or income of the trust may be distributed to (or for the benefit of) any person other than such grandchild.

(ii) the assets of the trust will be includible in the gross estate of the grandchild if the grandchild dies before the trust is terminated, and

(iii) all of the income of the trust for periods after the grandchild has attained age 21 will be distributed to (or for the benefit of) such grandchild not less frequently than annually.

(C) COORDINATION WITH SECTION 2653(a) OF THE 1986 CODE.—In the case of any transfer which would be a generation-skipping transfer but for subparagraph (A), the rules of section 2653(a) of the Internal Revenue Code of 1986 shall apply as if such transfer were a generation-skipping transfer.

(D) COORDINATION WITH TAXABLE TERMINATIONS AND TAXABLE DISTRIBUTIONS.—For purposes of chapter 13 of the Internal Revenue Code of 1986, the terms "taxable termination" and "taxable distribution" shall not include any transfer which would be a direct skip but for subparagraph (A).

(4) DEFINITIONS.—Terms used in this section shall have the same respective meanings as when used in chapter 13 of the Internal Revenue Code of 1986; except that section 2612(c)(2) of such Code shall not apply in determining whether an individual is a grandchild of the transferor.

(c) REPEAL OF EXISTING TAX ON GENERATION-SKIPPING TRANSFERS.—

(1) IN GENERAL.—In the case of any tax imposed by chapter 13 of the Internal Revenue Code of 1954 (as in effect on the day before the date of the enactment of this Act), such tax (including interest, additions to tax, and additional amounts) shall not be assessed and if assessed, the assessment shall be abated, and if collected, shall be credited or refunded (with interest) as an overpayment.

(2) WAIVER OF STATUTE OF LIMITATIONS.—If on the date of the enactment of this Act (or at any time within 1 year after such date of enactment) refund or credit of any overpayment of tax resulting from the application of paragraph (1) is barred by any law or rule of law, refund or credit of such overpayment shall, nevertheless, be made or allowed if claim therefore is filed before the date 1 year after the date of the enactment of this Act.

(d) ELECTION FOR CERTAIN TRANSFERS BENEFITING GRANDCHILDREN.—

(1) IN GENERAL.—For purposes of chapter 13 of the Internal Revenue Code of 1986 (as amended by this Act) and subsection (b) of this section, any transfer in trust for the benefit of a grandchild of a transferor shall be treated as a direct skip to such grandchild if—

(A) the transfer occurs before the date of enactment of this Act,

(B) the transfer would be a direct skip to a grandchild except for the fact that the trust instrument provides that, if the grandchild dies before vesting of the interest transferred, the interest is transferred to the grandchild's heir (rather than the grandchild's estate), and

(C) an election under this subsection applies to such transfer.

Any transfer treated as a direct skip by reason of the preceding sentence shall be subject to Federal estate tax on the grandchild's death in the same manner as if the contingent gift over had been to the grandchild's estate. Unless the grandchild otherwise directs by will, the estate of such grandchild shall be entitled to recover from the person receiving the property on the death of the grandchild any increase in Federal estate tax on the estate of the grandchild by reason of the preceding sentence.

(2) ELECTION.—An election under paragraph (1) shall be made at such time and in such manner as the Secretary of the Treasury or his delegate may prescribe.

• 1976, Tax Reform Act of 1976 (P.L. 94-455)

P.L. 94-455, §2006(a), (c):

Added Code Sec. 2601. **Effective** as noted in Act Sec. 2006(c), below.

P.L. 94-455, §2006(c) (as amended by P.L. 95-600, §702(n)(1) and P.L. 97-34, §428), provides:

(c) EFFECTIVE DATES.—

(1) IN GENERAL.—Except as provided in paragraph (2), the amendments made by this section shall apply to any generation-skipping transfer (within the meaning of section 2611(a) of the Internal Revenue Code of 1954) made after June 11, 1976.

(2) EXCEPTIONS.—The amendments made by this section shall not apply to any generation-skipping transfer—

(A) under a trust which was irrevocable on June 11, 1976, but only to the extent that the transfer is not made out of corpus added to the trust after June 11, 1976, or

(B) in the case of a decedent dying before January 1, 1983, pursuant to a will (or revocable trust) which was in existence on June 11, 1976, and was not amended at any time after that date in any respect which will result in the creation of, or increasing the amount of, any generation-skipping transfer.

For purposes of subparagraph (B), if the decedent on June 11, 1976, was under a mental disability to change the disposition of his property, the period set forth in such subparagraph shall not expire before the date which is 2 years after the date on which he first regains his competence to dispose of such property.

(3) TRUST EQUIVALENTS.—For purposes of paragraph (2), in the case of a trust equivalent within the meaning of subsection (d) of section 2611 of the Internal Revenue Code of 1954, the provisions of such subsection (d) shall apply.

[Sec. 2602]

SEC. 2602. AMOUNT OF TAX.

The amount of the tax imposed by section 2601 is—

(1) the taxable amount (determined under subchapter C), multiplied by

(2) the applicable rate (determined under subchapter E).

Amendments

• 1986, Tax Reform Act of 1986 (P.L. 99-514)

P.L. 99-514, §1431(a):

Amended Chapter 13 by amending Code Sec. 2602. **Effective**, generally, for any generation-skipping transfer (within the meaning of section 2511 of the Internal Revenue Code of 1986) made after the date of enactment. However, for special rules, see Act Sec. 1433(b)-(d) following Code Sec. 2601. Prior to amendment, Code Sec. 2602 read as follows:

SEC. 2602. AMOUNT OF TAX.

[Sec. 2602(a)]

(a) GENERAL RULE.—The amount of the tax imposed by section 2601 with respect to any transfer shall be the excess of—

(1) a tentative tax computed in accordance with the rate schedule set forth in section 2001(c) (as in effect on the date of transfer) on the sum of—

(A) the fair market value of the property transferred determined as of the date of transfer (or in the case of an election under subsection (d), as of the applicable valuation date prescribed by section 2032),

(B) the aggregate fair market value (determined for purposes of this chapter) of all prior transfers of the deemed transferor to which this chapter applied,

(C) the amount of the adjusted taxable gifts (within the meaning of section 2001(b), as modified by section 2001(e)) made by the deemed transferor before this transfer, and

(D) if the deemed transferor has died at the same time as, or before, this transfer, the taxable estate of the deemed transferor, over

(2) a tentative tax (similarly computed) on the sum of the amounts determined under subparagraphs (B), (C), and (D) of paragraph (1).

Amendments

• 1978, Revenue Act of 1978 (P.L. 95-600)

P.L. 95-600, §702(h)(2):

Amended Code Sec. 2602(a)(C) by adding after section 2001(b) ", as modified by section 2001(e)". **Effective** for estates of decedents dying after 1976, except that such amendment shall not apply to transfers made before 1977.

[Sec. 2602(b)]

(b) MULTIPLE SIMULTANEOUS TRANSFERS.—If two or more transfers which are taxable under section 2601 and which have the same deemed transferor occur by reason of the same event, the tax imposed by section 2601 on each such transfer shall be the amount which bears the same ratio to—

(1) the amount of the tax which would be imposed by section 2601 if the aggregate of such transfers were a single transfer, as

(2) the fair market value of the property transferred in such transfer bears to the aggregate fair market value of all property transferred in such transfers.

[Sec. 2602(c)]

(c) DEDUCTIONS, CREDITS, ETC.—

(1) GENERAL RULE.—Except as otherwise provided in this subsection, no deduction, exclusion, exemption, or credit shall be allowed against the tax imposed by section 2601.

(2) CHARITABLE DEDUCTIONS ALLOWED.—The deduction under section 2055, 2106(a)(2), or 2522, whichever is appropriate, shall be allowed in determining the tax imposed by section 2601.

(3) UNUSED PORTION OF UNIFIED CREDIT.—If the generation-skipping transfer occurs at the same time as, or after, the death of the deemed transferor, then the portion of the credit under section 2010(a) (relating to unified credit) which exceeds the sum of—

(A) the tax imposed by section 2001, and

(B) the taxes theretofore imposed by section 2601 with respect to this deemed transferor,

shall be allowed as a credit against the tax imposed by section 2601. The amount of the credit allowed by the preceding sentence shall not exceed the amount of the tax imposed by section 2601.

(4) CREDIT FOR TAX ON PRIOR TRANSFERS.—The credit under section 2013 (relating to credit for tax on prior transfers) shall be allowed against the tax imposed by section 2601. For purposes of the preceding sentence, section 2013 shall be applied as if so much of the property subject to tax under section 2601 as is not taken into account for purposes of determining the credit allowable by section 2013 with respect to the estate of the deemed transferor passed from the transferor (as defined in section 2013) to the deemed transferor.

(5) COORDINATION WITH ESTATE TAX.—

(A) CERTAIN EXPENSES ATTRIBUTABLE TO GENERATION-SKIPPING TRANSFER.—If the generation-skipping transfer occurs at the same time as, or after, the death of the deemed transferor, for purposes of this section, the amount taken into account with respect to such transfer shall be reduced—

(i) in the case of a taxable termination, by any item referred to in section 2053 or 2054 to the extent that a deduction would have been allowable under such section for such item if the amount of the trust had been includible in the deemed transferor's gross estate and if the deemed transferor had died immediately before such transfer, or

(ii) in the case of a taxable distribution, by any expense incurred in connection with the determination, collection, or refund of the tax imposed by section 2601 on such transfer.

(B) CREDIT FOR STATE INHERITANCE TAX.—If the generation-skipping transfer occurs at the same time as, or after, the death of the deemed transferor, there shall be allowed as a credit against the tax imposed by section 2601 an amount equal to that portion of the estate, inheritance, legacy, or succession tax actually paid to any State or the District of Columbia in respect of any property included in the generation-skipping transfer, but only to the extent of the lesser of—

(i) that portion of such taxes which is levied on such transfer, or

(ii) the excess of the limitation applicable under section 2011(b) if the adjusted taxable estate of the decedent had been increased by the amount of the transfer and all prior generation-skipping transfers to which this subparagraph applied which had the same deemed transferor, over the sum of the amount allowable as a credit under section 2011 with respect to the estate of the decedent plus the aggregate amounts allowable under this subparagraph with respect to such prior generation-skipping transfers.

Amendments

• 1981, Economic Recovery Tax Act of 1981 (P.L. 97-34)

P.L. 97-34, §403(a)(2)(B):

Amended Code Sec. 2602(c)(5) by striking out subparagraph (A) and by redesignating subparagraphs (B) and (C) as (A) and (B), respectively. **Effective** for estates of decedents dying after 12-31-81. Prior to deletion, Code Sec. 2602(c)(5)(A) read as follows:

(A) ADJUSTMENTS TO MARITAL DEDUCTION.—If the generation-skipping transfer occurs at the same time as, or within 9 months after, the death of the deemed transferor, for purposes of section 2056 (relating to bequests, etc., to surviving spouse), the value of the gross estate of the deemed transferor shall be deemed to be increased by the amount of such transfer.

[Sec. 2602(d)]

(d) ALTERNATE VALUATION.—

(1) IN GENERAL.—In the case of—

(A) 1 or more generation-skipping transfers from the same trust which have the same deemed transferor and which are taxable terminations occurring at the same time as the death of such deemed transferor (or at the same time as the death of a beneficiary of the trust assigned to a higher generation than such deemed transferor); or

(B) 1 or more generation-skipping transfers from the same trust with different deemed transferors—

(i) which are taxable terminations occurring on the same day; and

(ii) which would, but for section 2613(b)(2), have occurred at the same time as the death of the individuals who are the deemed transferors with respect to the transfers;

the trustee may elect to value all of the property transferred in such transfers in accordance with section 2032.

(2) SPECIAL RULES.—If the trustee makes an election under paragraph (1) with respect to any generation-skipping transfer, section 2032 shall be applied by taking into account (in lieu of the date of the decedent's death) the following date:

(A) in the case of any generation-skipping transfer described in paragraph (1)(A), the date of the death of the deemed transferor (or beneficiary) described in such paragraph, or

(B) in the case of any generation-skipping transfer described in paragraph (1)(B), the date on which such transfer occurred.

Amendments

• 1978, Revenue Act of 1978 (P.L. 95-600)

P.L. 95-600, §702(n)(4):

Amended Code Sec. 2602(d) by adding "(or at the same time as the death of a beneficiary of the trust assigned to a higher generation than such deemed transferor)" in subparagraph (1)(A) and by adding "(or beneficiary)" in subparagraph (2)(A). **Effective** as if included in chapter 13 (Code Secs. 2601-2603), as added by Sec. 2006 of the Tax Reform Act of 1976.

[Sec. 2602(e)]

(e) TRANSFERS WITHIN 3 YEARS OF DEATH OF DEEMED TRANSFEROR.—Under regulations prescribed by the Secretary, the principles of section 2035 shall apply with respect to transfers made during the 3-year period ending on the date of the deemed transferor's death. In the case of any transfer to which this subsection applies, the amount of the tax imposed by this chapter shall be determined as if the transfer occurred after the death of the deemed transferor and appropriate adjustments shall be made with respect to the amount of any prior transfer which is taken into account under subparagraph (B) or (C) of subsection (a)(1).

Amendments

• 1976, Tax Reform Act of 1976 (P.L. 94-455)

P.L. 94-455, §2006(a):

Added Code Sec. 2602. For **effective** date, see Act Sec. 2006(c) under Code Sec. 2601.

[Sec. 2603]

SEC. 2603. LIABILITY FOR TAX.

[Sec. 2603(a)]

(a) PERSONAL LIABILITY.—

(1) TAXABLE DISTRIBUTIONS.—In the case of a taxable distribution, the tax imposed by section 2601 shall be paid by the transferee.

(2) TAXABLE TERMINATION.—In the case of a taxable termination or a direct skip from a trust, the tax shall be paid by the trustee.

(3) DIRECT SKIP.—In the case of a direct skip (other than a direct skip from a trust), the tax shall be paid by the transferor.

[Sec. 2603(b)]

(b) SOURCE OF TAX.—Unless otherwise directed pursuant to the governing instrument by specific reference to the tax imposed by this chapter, the tax imposed by this chapter on a generation-skipping transfer shall be charged to the property constituting such transfer.

[Sec. 2603(c)]

(c) CROSS REFERENCE.—

For provisions making estate and gift tax provisions with respect to transferee liability, liens, and related matters applicable to the tax imposed by section 2601, see section 2661.

Amendments

• 1986, Tax Reform Act of 1986 (P.L. 99-514)

P.L. 99-514, §1431(a):

Amended Chapter 13 by amending Code Sec. 2603. **Effective**, generally, for any generation-skipping transfer (within the meaning of section 2611 of the Internal Revenue Code of 1986) made after 10-22-86. However, for special rules, see Act Sec. 1433(b)-(d) following Code Sec. 2601. Prior to amendment, Code Sec. 2603 read as follows:

SEC. 2603. LIABILITY FOR TAX.

(a) PERSONAL LIABILITY.—

(1) IN GENERAL.—If the tax imposed by section 2601 is not paid, when due then—

(A) except to the extent provided in paragraph (2), the trustee shall be personally liable for any portion of such tax which is attributable to a taxable termination, and

(B) the distributee of the property shall be personally liable for such tax to the extent provided in paragraph (3).

(2) LIMITATION OF PERSONAL LIABILITY OF TRUSTEE WHO RELIES ON CERTAIN INFORMATION FURNISHED BY THE SECRETARY.—

(A) INFORMATION WITH RESPECT TO RATES.—The trustee shall not be personally liable for any increase in the tax imposed by section 2601 which is attributable to the application to the transfer of rates of tax which exceed the rates of tax furnished by the Secretary to the trustee as being the rates at which the transfer may reasonably be expected to be taxed.

(B) AMOUNT OF REMAINING EXCLUSION.—The trustee shall not be personally liable for any increase in the tax imposed by section 2601 which is attributable to the fact that—

(i) the amount furnished by the Secretary to the trustee as being the amount of the exclusion for a transfer to a grandchild of the grantor of the trust which may reasonably be expected to remain with respect to the deemed transferor, is less than

(ii) the amount of such exclusion remaining with respect to such deemed transferor.

(3) LIMITATION OF PERSONAL LIABILITY OF DISTRIBUTEE.—The distributee of the property shall be personally liable for the tax imposed by section 2601 only to the extent of an amount equal to the fair market value (determined as of the time of the distribution) of the property received by the distributee in the distribution.

(b) LIEN.—The tax imposed by section 2601 on any transfer shall be a lien on the property transferred until the tax is paid in full or becomes unenforceable by reason of lapse of time.

• 1976, Tax Reform Act of 1976 (P.L. 94-455)

P.L. 94-455, §2006(a):

Added Code Sec. 2603. For **effective** date, see Act Sec. 2006(c) under Code Sec. 2601.

[Sec. 2604—Stricken]

Amendments

• 2014, Tax Technical Corrections Act of 2014 (P.L. 113-295)

P.L. 113-295, §221(a)(95)(B)(i), Division A:

Amended subchapter A of chapter 13 by striking Code Sec. 2604. **Effective** generally 12-19-2014. For a special rule, see Act Sec. 221(b)(2), Division A, below.

P.L. 113-295, §221(b)(2), Division A, provides:

(2) SAVINGS PROVISION.—If—

(A) any provision amended or repealed by the amendments made by this section applied to—

(i) any transaction occurring before the date of the enactment of this Act,

(ii) any property acquired before such date of enactment, or

(iii) any item of income, loss, deduction, or credit taken into account before such date of enactment, and

(B) the treatment of such transaction, property, or item under such provision would (without regard to the amendments or repeals made by this section) affect the liability for tax for periods ending after date of enactment, nothing in the amendments or repeals made by this section shall be construed to affect the treatment of such transaction, property, or item for purposes of determining liability for tax for periods ending after such date of enactment.

Prior to being stricken, Code Sec. 2604 read as follows:

SEC. 2604. CREDIT FOR CERTAIN STATE TAXES.

[Sec. 2604(a)]

(a) GENERAL RULE.—If a generation-skipping transfer (other than a direct skip) occurs at the same time as and as a result of the death of an individual, a credit against the tax imposed by section 2601 shall be allowed in an amount equal to the generation-skipping transfer tax actually paid to any State in respect to any property included in the generation-skipping transfer.

[Sec. 2604(b)]

(b) LIMITATION.—The aggregate amount allowed as a credit under this section with respect to any transfer shall not exceed 5 percent of the amount of the tax imposed by section 2601 on such transfer.

Amendments

• 1986, Tax Reform Act of 1986 (P.L. 99-514)

P.L. 99-514, §1431(a):

Amended Chapter 13 by adding Code Sec. 2604. **Effective**, generally, for any generation-skipping transfer (within the meaning of section 2611 of the Internal Revenue Code of 1986) made after 10-22-86. However, for special rules, see Act Sec. 1433(b)-(d) following Code Sec. 2601.

[Sec. 2604(c)]

(c) TERMINATION.—This section shall not apply to the generation-skipping transfers after December 31, 2004.

Amendments

• 2013, American Taxpayer Relief Act of 2012 (P.L. 112-240)

P.L. 112-240, §101(a)(1) and (3), provides:

SEC. 101. PERMANENT EXTENSION AND MODIFICATION OF 2001 TAX RELIEF.

(a) PERMANENT EXTENSION.—

(1) IN GENERAL.—The Economic Growth and Tax Relief Reconciliation Act of 2001 is amended by striking title IX.

* * *

(3) EFFECTIVE DATE.—The amendments made by this subsection shall apply to taxable, plan, or limitation years beginning after December 31, 2012, and estates of decedents dying, gifts made, or generation skipping transfers after December 31, 2012.

• 2001, Economic Growth and Tax Relief Reconciliation Act of 2001 (P.L. 107-16)

P.L. 107-16, §532(c)(10):

Amended Code Sec. 2604 by adding at the end a new subsection (c). **Effective** for estates of decedents dying, and generation-skipping transfers, after 12-31-2004.

P.L. 107-16, §901(a)-(b), as amended by P.L. 111-312, §101(a)(1), provides [but see P.L. 112-240, §101(a)(1) and (3), above]:

SEC. 901. SUNSET OF PROVISIONS OF ACT.

(a) IN GENERAL.—All provisions of, and amendments made by, this Act shall not apply—

(1) to taxable, plan, or limitation years beginning after December 31, 2012, or

(2) in the case of title V, to estates of decedents dying, gifts made, or generation skipping transfers, after December 31, 2012.

(b) APPLICATION OF CERTAIN LAWS.—The Internal Revenue Code of 1986 and the Employee Retirement Income Security Act of 1974 shall be applied and administered to years, estates, gifts, and transfers described in subsection (a) as if the provisions and amendments described in subsection (a) had never been enacted.

Subchapter B—Generation-Skipping Transfers

[Sec. 2611]

SEC. 2611. GENERATION-SKIPPING TRANSFER DEFINED.

[Sec. 2611(a)]

(a) IN GENERAL.—For purposes of this chapter, the term "generation-skipping transfer" means—

(1) a taxable distribution,

(2) a taxable termination, and

(3) a direct skip.

Amendments

• 1988, Technical and Miscellaneous Revenue Act of 1988 (P.L. 100-647)

P.L. 100-647, §1014(g)(1):

Amended Code Sec. 2611(a) by striking out "generation-skipping transfers" and inserting in lieu thereof "generation-skipping transfer". **Effective** as if included in the provision of P.L. 99-514 to which it relates.

P.L. 100-647, §1018(u)(43):

Amended Code Sec. 2611(a) by striking out "mean" and inserting in lieu thereof "means". **Effective** as if included in the provision of P.L. 99-514 to which it relates.

[Sec. 2611(b)]

(b) CERTAIN TRANSFERS EXCLUDED.—The term "generation-skipping transfer" does not include—

(1) any transfer which, if made inter vivos by an individual, would not be treated as a taxable gift by reason of section 2503(e) (relating to exclusion of certain transfers for educational or medical expenses), and

(2) any transfer to the extent—

(A) the property transferred was subject to a prior tax imposed under this chapter,

(B) the transferee in the prior transfer was assigned to the same generation as (or a lower generation than) the generation assignment of the transferee in this transfer, and

(C) such transfers do not have the effect of avoiding tax under this chapter with respect to any transfer.

Amendments

• 1988, Technical and Miscellaneous Revenue Act of 1988 (P.L. 100-647)

P.L. 100-647, §1014(g)(2):

Amended Code Sec. 2611(b) by striking out paragraph (1) and by redesignating paragraphs (2) and (3) as paragraphs (1) and (2) respectively. **Effective** as if included in the provision of P.L. 99-514 to which it relates. Prior to amendment Code Sec. 2611(b)(1) read as follows:

(1) any transfer (other than a direct skip) from a trust, to the extent such transfer is subject to a tax imposed by chapter 11 or 12 with respect to a person in the 1st generation below that of the grantor, and

• 1986, Tax Reform Act of 1986 (P.L. 99-514)

P.L. 99-514, §1431(a):

Amended Chapter 13 by amending Code Sec. 2611. **Effective**, generally, for any generation-skipping transfer (within the meaning of section 2611 of the Internal Revenue Code of 1986) made after 10-22-86. However, for special rules, see Act Sec. 1433(b)-(d) following Code Sec. 2601. Prior to amendment, the table of contents for former subchapter B and Code Sec. 2611 read as follows:

Subchapter B—Definitions and Special Rules

Sec. 2611. Generation-skipping transfer.

Sec. 2612. Deemed transferor.

Sec. 2613. Other definitions.

Sec. 2614. Special rules.

SEC. 2611. GENERATION-SKIPPING TRANSFER.

(a) GENERATION-SKIPPING TRANSFER DEFINED.—For purposes of this chapter, the terms "generation-skipping transfer" and "transfer" mean any taxable distribution or taxable termination with respect to a generation-skipping trust or trust equivalent.

(b) GENERATION-SKIPPING TRUST.—For purposes of this chapter, the term "generation-skipping trust" means any trust having younger generation beneficiaries (within the meaning of section 2613(c)(1)) who are assigned to more than one generation.

(c) ASCERTAINMENT OF GENERATION.—For purposes of this chapter, the generation to which any person (other than the grantor) belongs shall be determined in accordance with the following rules:

(1) an individual who is a lineal descendant of a grandparent of the grantor shall be assigned to that generation which results from comparing the number of generations between the grandparent and such individual with the number of generations between the grandparent and the grantor,

(2) an individual who has been at any time married to a person described in paragraph (1) shall be assigned to the generation of the person so described and an individual who has been at any time married to the grantor shall be assigned to the grantor's generation,

(3) a relationship by the half blood shall be treated as a relationship by the whole blood,

(4) a relationship by legal adoption shall be treated as a relationship by blood,

(5) an individual who is not assigned to a generation by reason of the foregoing paragraphs shall be assigned to a generation on the basis of the date of such individual's birth, with—

(A) an individual born not more than 12½ years after the date of the birth of the grantor assigned to the grantor's generation,

(B) an individual born more than 12½ years but not more than 37½ years after the date of the birth of the grantor assigned to the first generation younger than the grantor, and

(C) similar rules for a new generation every 25 years,

(6) an individual who, but for this paragraph, would be assigned to more than one generation shall be assigned to the youngest such generation, and

(7) if any beneficiary of the trust is an estate or a trust, partnership, corporation, or other entity (other than an organization described in section 511(a)(2) and other than a charitable trust described in section 511(b)(2)), each individual having an indirect interest or power in the trust through such entity shall be treated as a beneficiary of the trust and shall be assigned to a generation under the foregoing provisions of this subsection.

(d) GENERATION-SKIPPING TRUST EQUIVALENT.—

(1) IN GENERAL.—For purposes of this chapter, the term "generation-skipping trust equivalent" means any arrangement which, although not a trust, has substantially the same effect as a generation-skipping trust.

(2) EXAMPLES OF ARRANGEMENTS TO WHICH SUBSECTION RELATES.—Arrangements to be taken into account for purposes of determining whether or not paragraph (1) applies include (but are not limited to) arrangements involving life estates and remainders, estates for years, insurance and annuities, and split interests.

(3) REFERENCES TO TRUST INCLUDE REFERENCES TO TRUST EQUIVALENTS.—Any reference in this chapter in respect of a generation-skipping trust shall include the appropriate reference in respect of a generation-skipping trust equivalent.

• 1976, Tax Reform Act of 1976 (P.L. 94-455)

P.L. 94-455, §2006(a):

Added Code Sec. 2611. For **effective** date, see Act Sec. 2006(c) under Code Sec. 2601.

[Sec. 2612]

SEC. 2612. TAXABLE TERMINATION; TAXABLE DISTRIBUTION; DIRECT SKIP.

[Sec. 2612(a)]

(a) TAXABLE TERMINATION.—

(1) GENERAL RULE.—For purposes of this chapter, the term "taxable termination" means the termination (by death, lapse of time, release of power, or otherwise) of an interest in property held in a trust unless—

(A) immediately after such termination, a non-skip person has an interest in such property, or

(B) at no time after such termination may a distribution (including distributions on termination) be made from such trust to a skip person.

(2) CERTAIN PARTIAL TERMINATIONS TREATED AS TAXABLE.—If, upon the termination of an interest in property held in trust by reason of the death of a lineal descendant of the transferor, a specified portion of the trust's assets are distributed to 1 or more skip persons (or 1 or more trusts for the exclusive benefit of such persons), such termination shall constitute a taxable termination with respect to such portion of the trust property.

Amendments

• 1988, Technical and Miscellaneous Revenue Act of 1988 (P.L. 100-647)

P.L. 100-647, §1014(g)(15):

Amended Code Sec. 2612(a)(2). **Effective** as if included in the provision of P.L. 99-514 to which it relates. Prior to amendment, Code Sec. 2612(a)(2) read as follows:

(2) CERTAIN PARTIAL TERMINATIONS TREATED AS TAXABLE.—If, upon the termination of an interest in property held in a trust, a specified portion of the trust assets are distributed to skip persons who are lineal descendants of the holder of such interest (or to 1 or more trusts for the exclusive benefit of such persons), such termination shall constitute a taxable termination with respect to such portion of the trust property.

[Sec. 2612(b)]

(b) TAXABLE DISTRIBUTION.—For purposes of this chapter, the term "taxable distribution" means any distribution from a trust to a skip person (other than a taxable termination or a direct skip).

[Sec. 2612(c)]

(c) DIRECT SKIP.—For purposes of this chapter—

(1) IN GENERAL.—The term "direct skip" means a transfer subject to a tax imposed by chapter 11 or 12 of an interest in property to a skip person.

(2) LOOK-THRU RULES NOT TO APPLY.—Solely for purposes of determining whether any transfer to a trust is a direct skip, the rules of section 2651(f)(2) shall not apply.

Amendments

• 1997, Taxpayer Relief Act of 1997 (P.L. 105-34)

P.L. 105-34, §511(b)(1):

Amended Code Sec. 2612(c) by striking paragraph (2) and by redesignating paragraph (3) as paragraph (2). **Effective** for terminations, distributions, and transfers occurring after 12-31-97. Prior to being stricken, Code Sec. 2612(c)(2) read as follows:

(2) SPECIAL RULE FOR TRANSFERS TO GRANDCHILDREN.—For purposes of determining whether any transfer is a direct skip, if—

(A) an individual is a grandchild of the transferor (or the transferor's spouse or former spouse), and

(B) as of the time of the transfer, the parent of such individual who is a lineal descendant of the transferor (or the transferor's spouse or former spouse) is dead,

such individual shall be treated as if such individual were a child of the transferor and all of that grandchild's children shall be treated as if they were grandchildren of the transferor. In the case of lineal descendants below a grandchild, the preceding sentence may be reapplied. If any transfer of property to a trust would be a direct skip but for this paragraph, any generation assignment under this paragraph shall apply also for purposes of applying this chapter to transfers from the portion of the trust attributable to such property.

P.L. 105-34, §511(b)(2):

Amended Code Sec. 2612(c)(2), as redesignated by Act Sec. 511(b)(1), by striking "section 2651(e)(2)" and inserting "section 2651(f)(2)". **Effective** for terminations, distributions, and transfers occurring after 12-31-97.

• 1988, Technical and Miscellaneous Revenue Act of 1988 (P.L. 100-647)

P.L. 100-647, §1014(g)(5)(B):

Amended Code Sec. 2612(c) by adding at the end thereof new paragraph (3). **Effective** as if included in the provision of P.L. 99-514 to which it relates.

P.L. 100-647, §1014(g)(7):

Amended Code Sec. 2612(c)(2) adding at the end thereof a new sentence. **Effective** as if included in the provision of P.L. 99-514 to which it relates.

• 1986, Tax Reform Act of 1986 (P.L. 99-514)

P.L. 99-514, §1431(a):

Amended Chapter 13 by amending Code Sec. 2612. **Effective**, generally, for any generation-skipping transfer (within the meaning of section 2611 of the Internal Revenue Code of 1986) made after 10-22-86. However, for special rules, see Act Sec. 1433(b)-(d) following Code Sec. 2601. Prior to amendment, Code Sec. 2612 read as follows:

SEC. 2612. DEEMED TRANSFEROR.

(a) GENERAL RULE.—For purposes of this chapter, the deemed transferor with respect to a transfer is—

(1) except as provided in paragraph (2), the parent of the transferee of the property who is more closely related to the grantor of the trust than the other parent of such transferee (or if neither parent is related to such grantor, the parent having a closer affinity to the grantor), or

(2) if the parent described in paragraph (1) is not a younger generation beneficiary of the trust but 1 or more ancestors of the transferee is a younger generation beneficiary related by blood or adoption to the grantor of the trust, the youngest of such ancestors.

(b) DETERMINATION OF RELATIONSHIP.—For purposes of subsection (a), a parent related to the grantor of the trust by blood or adoption is more closely related than a parent related to such grantor by marriage.

• 1976, Tax Reform Act of 1976 (P.L. 94-455)

P.L. 94-455, §2006(a):

Added Code Sec. 2612. For **effective** date, see Act Sec. 2006(c) under Code Sec. 2601.

[Sec. 2613]

SEC. 2613. SKIP PERSON AND NON-SKIP PERSON DEFINED.

[Sec. 2613(a)]

(a) SKIP PERSON.—For purposes of this chapter, the term "skip person" means—

(1) a natural person assigned to a generation which is 2 or more generations below the generation assignment of the transferor, or

(2) a trust—

(A) if all interests in such trust are held by skip persons, or

(B) if—

(i) there is no person holding an interest in such trust, and

(ii) at no time after such transfer may a distribution (including distributions on termination) be made from such trust to a non-skip person.

[Sec. 2613(b)]

(b) NON-SKIP PERSON.—For purposes of this chapter, the term "non-skip person" means any person who is not a skip person.

Amendments

• 1988, Technical and Miscellaneous Revenue Act of 1988 (P.L. 100-647)

P.L. 100-647, §1014(g)(5)(A):

Amended Code Sec. 2613(a)(1) by striking out "a person assigned" and inserting in lieu thereof "a natural person assigned". **Effective** as if included in the provision of P.L. 99-514 to which it relates.

• 1986, Tax Reform Act of 1986 (P.L. 99-514)

P.L. 99-514, §1431(a):

Amended Chapter 13 by amending Code Sec. 2613. **Effective**, generally, for any generation-skipping transfer (within the meaning of section 2611 of the Internal Revenue Code of 1986) made after 10-22-86. However, for special rules, see Act Sec. 1433(b)-(d) following Code Sec. 2601. Prior to amendment, Code Sec. 2613 read as follows:

SEC. 2613. OTHER DEFINITIONS.

[Sec. 2613(a)]

(a) TAXABLE DISTRIBUTION.—For purposes of this chapter—

(1) IN GENERAL.—The term "taxable distribution" means any distribution which is not out of the income of the trust (within the meaning of section 643(b)) from a generation-skipping trust to any younger generation beneficiary who is assigned to a generation younger than the generation assignment of any other person who is a younger generation beneficiary. For purposes of the preceding sentence, an individual who at no time has had anything other than a future interest or future power (or both) in the trust shall not be considered as a younger generation beneficiary.

(2) SOURCE OF DISTRIBUTION.—If, during the taxable year of the trust, there are distributions out of the income of the trust (within the meaning of section 643(b)) and out of other amounts, for purposes of paragraph (1) the distributions of such income shall be deemed to have been made to the beneficiaries (to the extent of the aggregate distributions made to each such beneficiary during such year) in descending order of generations, beginning with the beneficiaries assigned to the oldest generation.

(3) PAYMENT OF TAX.—If any portion of the tax imposed by this chapter with respect to any transfer is paid out of the income or corpus of the trust, an amount equal to the portion so paid shall be deemed to be a generation-skipping transfer.

(4) CERTAIN DISTRIBUTIONS EXCLUDED FROM TAX.—The term "taxable distribution" does not include—

(A) any transfer to the extent such transfer is to a grandchild of the grantor of the trust and does not exceed the limitation provided by subsection (b)(6), and

(B) any transfer to the extent such transfer is subject to a tax imposed by chapter 11 or 12.

[Sec. 2613(b)]

(b) TAXABLE TERMINATION.—For purposes of this chapter—

(1) IN GENERAL.—The term "taxable termination" means the termination (by death, lapse of time, exercise or nonexercise, or otherwise) of the interest or power in a generation-skipping trust of any younger generation beneficiary who is assigned to any generation older than the generation assignment of any other person who is a younger generation beneficiary of that trust. Such term does not include a termination of the interest or power of any person who at no time has had anything other than a future interest or future power (or both) in the trust.

(2) TIME CERTAIN TERMINATIONS DEEMED TO OCCUR.—

(A) WHERE 2 OR MORE BENEFICIARIES ARE ASSIGNED TO SAME GENERATION.—In any case where 2 or more younger generation beneficiaries of a trust are assigned to the same generation, except to the extent provided in regulations prescribed by the Secretary, the transfer constituting the termination with respect to each such beneficiary shall be treated as occurring at the time when the last such termination occurs.

(B) SAME BENEFICIARY HAS MORE THAN 1 PRESENT INTEREST OR PRESENT POWER.—In any case where a younger generation beneficiary of a trust has both a present interest and a present power, or more than 1 present interest or present power, in the trust, except to the extent provided in regulations prescribed by the Secretary, the termination with respect to each such present interest or present power shall be treated as occurring at the time when the last such termination occurs.

(C) UNUSUAL ORDER OF TERMINATION.—

(i) IN GENERAL.—If—

(I) but for this subparagraph, there would have been a termination (determined after the application of subparagraphs (A) and (B)) of an interest or power of a younger generation beneficiary (hereinafter in this subparagraph referred to as the "younger beneficiary"), and

(II) at the time such termination would have occurred, a beneficiary (hereinafter in this subparagraph referred to as the "older beneficiary") of the trust assigned to a higher generation than the generation of the younger beneficiary has a present interest or power in the trust,

then, except to the extent provided in regulations prescribed by the Secretary, the transfer constituting the termination with respect to the younger beneficiary shall be treated as occurring at the time when the termination of the last present interest or power of the older beneficiary occurs.

(ii) SPECIAL RULES.—If clause (i) applies with respect to any younger beneficiary—

(I) this chapter shall be applied first to the termination of the interest or power of the older beneficiary as if such termination occurred before the termination of the power or interest of the younger beneficiary; and

(II) the value of the property taken into account for purposes of determining the tax (if any) imposed by this chapter with respect to the termination of the interest or power of the younger beneficiary shall be reduced by the tax (if any) imposed by this chapter with respect to the termination of the interest or power of the older beneficiary.

(D) SPECIAL RULE.—Subparagraphs (A) and (C) shall also apply where a person assigned to the same generation as, or a higher generation than, the person whose power or interest terminates has a present power or interest immediately after the termination and such power or interest arises as a result of such termination.

(3) DEEMED TRANSFEREES OF CERTAIN TERMINATIONS.—Where, at the time of any termination, it is not clear who will be the transferee of any portion of the property transferred, except to the extent provided in regulations prescribed by the Secretary, such portion shall be deemed transferred pro rata to all beneficiaries of the trust in accordance with the

amount which each of them would receive under a maximum exercise of discretion on their behalf. For purposes of the preceding sentence, where it is not clear whether discretion will be exercised per stirpes or per capita, it shall be presumed that the discretion will be exercised per stirpes.

(4) TERMINATION OF POWER.—In the case of the termination of any power, the property transferred shall be deemed to be the property subject to the power immediately before the termination (determined without the application of paragraph (2)).

(5) CERTAIN TERMINATIONS EXCLUDED FROM TAX.—The term "taxable termination" does not include—

(A) any transfer to the extent such transfer is to a grandchild of the grantor of the trust and does not exceed the limitation provided by paragraph (6), and

(B) any transfer to the extent such transfer is subject to a tax imposed by chapter 11 or 12.

(6) $250,000 LIMIT ON EXCLUSION OF TRANSFERS TO GRANDCHILDREN.—In the case of any deemed transferor, the maximum amount excluded from the terms "taxable distribution" and "taxable termination" by reason of provisions exempting from such terms transfers to the grandchildren of the grantor of the trust shall be $250,000. The preceding sentence shall be applied to transfers from one or more trusts in the order in which such transfers are made or deemed made.

(7) COORDINATION WITH SUBSECTION (a).—

(A) TERMINATIONS TAKE PRECEDENCE OVER DISTRIBUTIONS.—If—

(i) the death of an individual or any other occurrence is a taxable termination with respect to any property, and

(ii) such occurrence also requires the distribution of part or all of such property in a distribution which would (but for this subparagraph) be a taxable distribution,

then a taxable distribution shall be deemed not to have occurred with respect to the portion described in clause (i).

(B) CERTAIN PRIOR TRANSFERS.—To the extent that—

(i) the deemed transferor in any prior transfer of the property of the trust being transferred in this transfer was assigned to the same generation as (or a lower generation than) the generation assignment of the deemed transferor in this transfer,

(ii) the transferee in such prior transfer was assigned to the same generation as (or a higher generation than) the generation assignment of the transferee in this transfer, and

(iii) such transfers do not have the effect of avoiding tax under this chapter with respect to any transfer,

the terms "taxable termination" and "taxable distribution" do not include this later transfer.

Amendments

• 1978, Revenue Act of 1978 (P.L. 95-600)

P.L. 95-600, § 702(n)(3):

Amended Code Sec. 2613(b)(2)(B) by substituting "a present interest and a present power" for "an interest and a power" and by substituting "present interest of present power" for "interest or power" in the text and heading. **Effective** as if included in chapter 13 (Code Secs. 2601-2603) as added by Act Sec. 2006 of the Tax Reform Act of 1976.

[Sec. 2613(c)]

(c) YOUNGER GENERATION BENEFICIARY; BENEFICIARY.—For purposes of this chapter—

(1) YOUNGER GENERATION BENEFICIARY.—The term "younger generation beneficiary" means any beneficiary who is assigned to a generation younger than the grantor's generation.

(2) TIME FOR ASCERTAINING YOUNGER GENERATION BENEFICIARIES.—A person is a younger generation beneficiary of a trust with respect to any transfer only if such person was a younger generation beneficiary of the trust immediately before the transfer (or, in the case of a series of related transfers, only if such person was a younger generation beneficiary of the trust immediately before the first of such transfers).

(3) BENEFICIARY.—The term "beneficiary" means any person who has a present or future interest or power in the trust.

[Sec. 2613(d)]

(d) INTEREST OR POWER.—For purposes of this chapter—

(1) INTEREST.—A person has an interest in a trust if such person—

(A) has a right to receive income or corpus from the trust, or

(B) is a permissible recipient of such income or corpus.

(2) POWER.—The term "power" means any power to establish or alter benefical enjoyment of the corpus or income of the trust.

[Sec. 2613(e)]

(e) CERTAIN POWERS NOT TAKEN INTO ACCOUNT.—

(1) LIMITED POWER TO APPOINT AMONG LINEAL DESCENDANTS OF THE GRANTOR.—For purposes of this chapter, an individual shall be treated as not having any power in a trust if such individual does not have any present or future power in the trust other than a power to dispose of the corpus of the trust or the income therefrom to a beneficiary or a class of beneficiaries who are lineal descendants of the grantor assigned to a generation younger than the generation assignment of such individual.

(2) POWERS OF INDEPENDENT TRUSTEES.—

(A) IN GENERAL.—For purposes of this chapter, an individual shall be treated as not having any power in a trust if such individual—

(i) is a trustee who has no interest in the trust (other than as a potential appointee under a power of appointment held by another),

(ii) is not a related or subordinate trustee, and

(iii) does not have any present or future power in the trust other than a power to dispose of the corpus of the trust or the income therefrom to a beneficiary or a class of beneficiaries designated in the trust instrument.

(B) RELATED OR SUBORDINATE TRUSTEE DEFINED.—For purposes of subparagraph (A), the term "related or subordinate trustee" means any trustee who is assigned to a younger generation than the grantor's generation and who is—

(i) the spouse of the grantor or of any beneficiary,

(ii) the father, mother, lineal descendant, brother, or sister of the grantor or of any beneficiary,

(iii) an employee of the grantor or of any beneficiary,

(iv) an employee of a corporation in which the stockholdings of the grantor, the trust, and the beneficiaries of the trust are significant from the viewpoint of voting control,

(v) an employee of a corporation in which the grantor or any beneficiary of the trust is an executive,

(vi) a partner of a partnership in which the interest of the grantor, the trust, and the beneficiaries of the trust are significant from the viewpoint of operating control or distributive share of partnership income, or

(vii) an employee of a partnership in which the grantor or any beneficiary of the trust is a partner.

Amendments

• 1980, Technical Corrections Act of 1979 (P.L. 96-222)

P.L. 96-222, § 107(a)(2)(B)(i):

Amended Code Sec. 2613(e)(2)(A)(i) by inserting after "the trust" the phrase "(other than as a potential appointee under a power of appointment held by another)". **Effective** for any generation-skipping transfer made after 6-11-76.

P.L. 96-222, § 107(a)(2)(B)(ii):

Amended Code Sec. 2613(e)(2)(B) by inserting after clause (ii) a new clause, by striking out clause (vi), by redesignating clauses (iii), (iv) and (v) as clauses (iv), (v) and (vi), and by inserting "or" at the end of redesignated clause (vi). **Effective** for any generation-skipping transfer made after 6-11-76. Prior to deletion, clause (vi) read as follows:

(vi) an employee of a corporation in which the grantor or any beneficiary of the trust is an executive, or

• **1978, Revenue Act of 1978 (P.L. 95-600)**

P.L. 95-600, §702(n)(2):

Amended Code Sec. 2613(e). **Effective** as if included in chapter 13 (Code Secs. 2601-2603) as added by Act Sec. 2006 of P.L. 94-455. Prior to amendment, Code Sec. 2613(e) read as follows:

"(e) LIMITED POWER TO APPOINT AMONG LINEAL DESCENDANTS OF GRANTOR NOT TAKEN INTO ACCOUNT IN CERTAIN CASES.—For purposes of this chapter, if any individual does not have any present or future power in the trust other than a power to dispose of the corpus of the trust or the income therefrom to a beneficiary or a class of beneficiaries who are lineal descendents of the grantor assigned to a generation younger than the generation assignment of such individual, then such individual shall be treated as not having any power in the trust."

[Sec. 2613(f)]

(f) EFFECT OF ADOPTION.—For purposes of this chapter, a relationship by legal adoption shall be treated as a relationship by blood.

Amendments

• **1976, Tax Reform Act of 1976 (P.L. 94-455)**

P.L. 94-455, §2006(a):

Added Code Sec. 2613. For **effective** date, see Act Sec. 2006(c) under Code Sec. 2601.

[Sec. 2614—Repealed]

Amendments

• **1986, Tax Reform Act of 1986 (P.L. 99-514)**

P.L. 99-514, §1431(a):

Amended Chapter 13 and removed Code Sec. 2614. **Effective**, generally, for any generation-skipping transfer (within the meaning of section 2611 of the Internal Revenue Code of 1986) made after 10-22-86. However, for special rules, see Act Sec. 1433(b)-(d) following Code Sec. 2601. Prior to amendment, Code Sec. 2614 read as follows:

SEC. 2614. SPECIAL RULES.

[Sec. 2614(a)]

(a) BASIS ADJUSTMENT.—If property is transferred to any person pursuant to a generation-skipping transfer which occurs before the death of the deemed transferor, the basis of such property in the hands of the transferee shall be increased (but not above the fair market value of such property) by an amount equal to that portion of the tax imposed by section 2601 with respect to the transfer which is attributable to the excess of the fair market value of such property over its adjusted basis immediately before the transfer. If property is transferred in a generation-skipping transfer subject to tax under this chapter which occurs at the same time as, or after, the death of the deemed transferor, the basis of such property shall be adjusted in a manner similar to the manner provided under section 1014(a).

Amendments

• **1980, Crude Oil Windfall Profit Tax Act of 1980 (P.L. 96-223)**

P.L. 96-223, §401(c)(3):

Amended the last sentence of Code Sec. 2614(a). **Effective** with respect to decedents dying after 12-31-76. However, see the amendment note for P.L. 96-223, Act Sec. 401(a), that follows Code Sec. 1014(d) for the text of Code Sec. 401(d) that authorizes the election of the carryover basis rules in the case of a decedent dying after 12-31-76 and before 11-7-78. Prior to amendment Code Sec. 2614(a) read:

(a) BASIS ADJUSTMENT.—If property is transferred to any person pursuant to a generation-skipping transfer which occurs before the death of the deemed transferor, the basis of such property in the hands of the transferee shall be increased (but not above the fair market value of such property) by an amount equal to that portion of the tax imposed by section 2601 with respect to the transfer which is attributable to the excess of the fair market value of such property over its adjusted basis immediately before the transfer. If property is transferred in a generation-skipping transfer subject to tax under this chapter which occurs at the same time as, or after, the death of the deemed transferor, the basis of the property shall be adjusted—

(1) in the case of such a transfer occurring after June 11, 1976 and before January 1, 1980, in a manner similar to the manner provided under section 1014(a), and

(2) in the case of such a transfer occurring after December 31, 1979, in a manner similar to the manner provided by section 1023 without regard to subsection (d) thereof (relating to basis of property passing from a decedent dying after December 31, 1979).

• **1978, Revenue Act of 1978 (P.L. 95-600)**

P.L. 95-600, §700(c)(1)(B):

Amended Code Sec. 2614(a). **Effective** as if part of P.L. 94-455. Prior to amendment, Code Sec. 2614(a) read as follows:

"(a) BASIS ADJUSTMENT.—If property is transferred to any person pursuant to a generation-skipping transfer which occurs before the death of the deemed transferor, the basis of such property in the hands of the transferee shall be increased (but not above the fair market value of such property) by an amount equal to that portion of the tax imposed by section 2601 with respect to the transfer which is attributable to the excess of the fair market value of such property over its adjusted basis immediately before the transfer. If property is transferred in a generation-skipping transfer subject to tax under this chapter which occurs at the same time as, or after, the death of the deemed transferor, the basis of such property shall be adjusted in a manner similar to the manner provided by section 1023 without regard to subsection (d) thereof (relating to basis of property passing from a decedent dying after December 31, 1976)."

[Sec. 2614(b)]

(b) NONRESIDENTS NOT CITIZENS OF THE UNITED STATES.—If the deemed transferor of any transfer is, at the time of the transfer, a nonresident not a citizen of the United States and—

(1) if the deemed transferor is alive at the time of the transfer, there shall be taken into account only property which would be taken into account for purposes of chapter 12, or

(2) if the deemed transferor has died at the same time as, or before, the transfer, there shall be taken into account only property which would be taken into account for purposes of chapter 11.

[Sec. 2614(c)]

(c) DISCLAIMERS.—

For provisions relating to the effect of a qualified disclaimer for purposes of this chapter, see section 2518.

Amendments

• **1976, Tax Reform Act of 1976 (P.L. 94-455)**

P.L. 94-455, §2006(a):

Added Code Sec. 2614. For **effective** date, see Act Sec. 2006(c) under Code Sec. 2601.

Subchapter C—Taxable Amount

Sec. 2621. Taxable amount in case of taxable distribution.

Sec. 2622. Taxable amount in case of taxable termination.

[Sec. 2621]

SEC. 2621. TAXABLE AMOUNT IN CASE OF TAXABLE DISTRIBUTION.

[Sec. 2621(a)]

(a) IN GENERAL.—For purposes of this chapter, the taxable amount in the case of any taxable distribution shall be—

(1) the value of the property received by the transferee, reduced by

(2) any expense incurred by the transferee in connection with the determination, collection, or refund of the tax imposed by this chapter with respect to such distribution.

[Sec. 2621(b)]

(b) PAYMENT OF GST TAX TREATED AS TAXABLE DISTRIBUTION.—For purposes of this chapter, if any of the tax imposed by this chapter with respect to any taxable distribution is paid out of the trust, an amount equal to the portion so paid shall be treated as a taxable distribution.

Amendments

• 1986, Tax Reform Act of 1986 (P.L. 99-514)

P.L. 99-514, §1431(a):

Amended Chapter 13 by amending Code Sec. 2621. **Effective**, generally, for any generation-skipping transfer (within the meaning of section 2611 of the Internal Revenue Code of 1986) made after 10-22-86. However, for special rules, see Act Sec. 1433(b)-(d) following Code Sec. 2601. Prior to amendment, the table of contents for former subchapter C and Code Sec. 2621 read as follows:

Subchapter C—Administration

Sec. 2621. Administration.
Sec. 2622. Regulations.

[Sec. 2621]

SEC. 2621. ADMINISTRATION.

[Sec. 2621(a)]

(a) GENERAL RULE.—Insofar as applicable and not inconsistent with the provisions of this chapter—

(1) if the deemed transferor is not alive at the time of the transfer, all provisions of subtitle F (including penalties) applicable to chapter 11 or section 2001 are hereby made applicable in respect of this chapter or section 2601, as the case may be, and

(2) if the deemed transferor is alive at the time of the transfer, all provisions of subtitle F (including penalties) applicable to chapter 12 or section 2501 are hereby made applicable in respect of this chapter or section 2601, as the case may be.

[Sec. 2621(b)]

(b) SECTION 6166 NOT APPLICABLE.—For purposes of this chapter, section 6166 (relating to extension of time for payment of estate tax where estate consists largely of interest in closely held business) shall not apply.

Amendments

• 1981, Economic Recovery Tax Act of 1981 (P.L. 97-34)

P.L. 97-34, §422(e)(4)(A):

Amended Code Sec. 2621(b) by striking out "sections 6166 and 6166A (relating to extensions" and inserting "section 6166 (relating to extension". **Effective** for estates of decedents dying after 12-31-81.

P.L. 97-34, §422(e)(4)(B):

Amended Code Sec. 2621(b) by striking out in the heading "SECTIONS 6166 AND 6166A" and inserting "SECTION 6166". **Effective** for estates of decedents dying after 12-31-81.

[Sec. 2621(c)]

(c) RETURN REQUIREMENTS.—

(1) IN GENERAL.—The Secretary shall prescribe by regulations the person who is required to make the return with respect to the tax imposed by this chapter and the time by which any such return must be filed. To the extent practicable, such regulations shall provide that—

(A) the person who is required to make such return shall be—

(i) in the case of a taxable distribution, the distributee, or

(ii) in the case of a taxable termination, the trustee; and

(B) the return shall be filed—

(i) in the case of a generation-skipping transfer occurring before the death of the deemed transferor, on or before the 90th day after the close of the taxable year of the trust in which such transfer occurred, or

(ii) in the case of a generation-skipping transfer occurring at the same time as, or after, the death of the deemed transferor, on or before the 90th day after the last day prescribed by law (including extensions) for filing the return of tax under chapter 11 with respect to the estate of the deemed transferor (or if later, the day which is 9 months after the day on which such generation-skipping transfer occurred).

(2) INFORMATION RETURNS.—The Secretary may by regulations require the trustee to furnish the Secretary with such information as he determines to be necessary for purposes of this chapter.

Amendments

• 1976, Tax Reform Act of 1976 (P.L. 94-455)

P.L. 94-455, §2006(a):

Added Code Sec. 2621. For **effective** date, see Act Sec. 2006(c) under Code Sec. 2601.

[Sec. 2622]

SEC. 2622. TAXABLE AMOUNT IN CASE OF TAXABLE TERMINATION.

[Sec. 2622(a)]

(a) IN GENERAL.—For purposes of this chapter, the taxable amount in the case of a taxable termination shall be—

(1) the value of all property with respect to which the taxable termination has occurred, reduced by

(2) any deduction allowed under subsection (b).

[Sec. 2622(b)]

(b) DEDUCTION FOR CERTAIN EXPENSES.—For purposes of subsection (a), there shall be allowed a deduction similar to the deduction allowed by section 2053 (relating to expenses, indebtedness, and taxes) for amounts attributable to the property with respect to which the taxable termination has occurred.

Amendments

• 1986, Tax Reform Act of 1986 (P.L. 99-514)

P.L. 99-514, §1431(a):

Amended Chapter 13 by amending Code Sec. 2622. **Effective**, generally, for any generation-skipping transfer (within the meaning of section 2611 of the Internal Revenue Code of 1986) made after 10-22-86. However, for special rules, see Act Sec. 1433(b)-(d) following Code Sec. 2601. Prior to amendment, Code Sec. 2622 read as follows:

SEC. 2622. REGULATIONS.

The Secretary shall prescribe such regulations as may be necessary or appropriate to carry out the purposes of this chapter, including regulations providing the extent to which substantially separate and independent shares of different beneficiaries in the trust shall be treated as separate trusts.

• 1976, Tax Reform Act of 1976 (P.L. 94-455)

P.L. 94-455, §2006(a):

Added Code Sec. 2622. For **effective** date, see Act Sec. 2006(c) under Code Sec. 2601.

[Sec. 2623]

SEC. 2623. TAXABLE AMOUNT IN CASE OF DIRECT SKIP.

For purposes of this chapter, the taxable amount in the case of a direct skip shall be the value of the property received by the transferee.

Amendments

• 1986, Tax Reform Act of 1986 (P.L. 99-514)

P.L. 99-514, §1431(a):

Added Code Sec. 2623. **Effective**, generally, for any generation-skipping transfer (within the meaning of section 2611 of the Internal Revenue Code of 1986) made after 10-22-86. However, for special rules, see Act Sec. 1433(b)-(d) following Code Sec. 2601.

[Sec. 2624]

SEC. 2624. VALUATION.

[Sec. 2624(a)]

(a) GENERAL RULE.—Except as otherwise provided in this chapter, property shall be valued as of the time of the generation-skipping transfer.

[Sec. 2624(b)]

(b) ALTERNATE VALUATION AND SPECIAL USE VALUATION ELECTIONS APPLY TO CERTAIN DIRECT SKIPS.—In the case of any direct skip of property which is included in the transferor's gross estate, the value of such property for purposes of this chapter shall be the same as its value for purposes of chapter 11 (determined with regard to sections 2032 and 2032A).

[Sec. 2624(c)]

(c) ALTERNATE VALUATION ELECTION PERMITTED IN THE CASE OF TAXABLE TERMINATIONS OCCURRING AT DEATH.—If 1 or more taxable terminations with respect to the same trust occur at the same time as and as a result of the death of an individual, an election may be made to value all of the property included in such terminations in accordance with section 2032.

[Sec. 2624(d)]

(d) REDUCTION FOR CONSIDERATION PROVIDED BY TRANSFEREE.—For purposes of this chapter, the value of the property transferred shall be reduced by the amount of any consideration provided by the transferee.

Amendments

• 1986, Tax Reform Act of 1986 (P.L. 99-514)

P.L. 99-514, §1431(a):

Added Code Sec. 2624. **Effective**, generally, for any generation-skipping transfer (within the meaning of section 2611 of the Internal Revenue Code of 1986) made after 10-22-86. However, for special rules, see Act Sec. 1433(b)-(d) following Code Sec. 2601.

Subchapter D—GST Exemption

[Sec. 2631]

SEC. 2631. GST EXEMPTION.

[Sec. 2631(a)]

(a) GENERAL RULE.—For purposes of determining the inclusion ratio, every individual shall be allowed a GST exemption amount which may be allocated by such individual (or his executor) to any property with respect to which such individual is the transferor.

Amendments

• 2013, American Taxpayer Relief Act of 2012 (P.L. 112-240)

P.L. 112-240, §101(a)(1) and (3), provides:

SEC. 101. PERMANENT EXTENSION AND MODIFICATION OF 2001 TAX RELIEF.

(a) PERMANENT EXTENSION.—

(1) IN GENERAL.—The Economic Growth and Tax Relief Reconciliation Act of 2001 is amended by striking title IX.

* * *

(3) EFFECTIVE DATE.—The amendments made by this subsection shall apply to taxable, plan, or limitation years beginning after December 31, 2012, and estates of decedents dying, gifts made, or generation skipping transfers after December 31, 2012.

• 2001, Economic Growth and Tax Relief Reconciliation Act of 2001 (P.L. 107-16)

P.L. 107-16, §521(c)(1):

Amended Code Sec. 2631(a) by striking "of $1,000,000" and inserting "amount". **Effective** for estates of decedents dying, and generation-skipping transfers, after 12-31-2003.

P.L. 107-16, §901(a)-(b), as amended by P.L. 111-312, §101(a)(1), provides [but see P.L. 112-240, §101(a)(1) and (3), above]:

SEC. 901. SUNSET OF PROVISIONS OF ACT.

(a) IN GENERAL.—All provisions of, and amendments made by, this Act shall not apply—

(1) to taxable, plan, or limitation years beginning after December 31, 2012, or

(2) in the case of title V, to estates of decedents dying, gifts made, or generation skipping transfers, after December 31, 2012.

(b) APPLICATION OF CERTAIN LAWS.—The Internal Revenue Code of 1986 and the Employee Retirement Income Security Act of 1974 shall be applied and administered to years, estates, gifts, and transfers described in subsection (a) as if the provisions and amendments described in subsection (a) had never been enacted.

[Sec. 2631(b)]

(b) ALLOCATIONS IRREVOCABLE.—Any allocation under subsection (a), once made, shall be irrevocable.

Amendments

• 1986, Tax Reform Act of 1986 (P.L. 99-514)

P.L. 99-514, §1431(a):

Added Code Sec. 2631. **Effective**, generally, for any generation-skipping transfer (within the meaning of section 2611 of the Internal Revenue Code of 1986) made after 10-22-86. However, for special rules, see Act Sec. 1433(b)-(d) following Code Sec. 2601.

[Sec. 2631(c)]

(c) GST EXEMPTION AMOUNT.—For purposes of subsection (a), the GST exemption amount for any calendar year shall be equal to the basic exclusion amount under section 2010(c) for such calendar year.

Amendments

• 2013, American Taxpayer Relief Act of 2012 (P.L. 112-240)

P.L. 112-240, §101(a)(1)-(3), provides:

SEC. 101. PERMANENT EXTENSION AND MODIFICATION OF 2001 TAX RELIEF.

(a) PERMANENT EXTENSION.—

(1) IN GENERAL.—The Economic Growth and Tax Relief Reconciliation Act of 2001 is amended by striking title IX.

(2) CONFORMING AMENDMENT.—The Tax Relief, Unemployment Insurance Reauthorization, and Job Creation Act of 2010 is amended by striking section 304.

(3) EFFECTIVE DATE.—The amendments made by this subsection shall apply to taxable, plan, or limitation years beginning after December 31, 2012, and estates of decedents dying, gifts made, or generation skipping transfers after December 31, 2012.

• 2010, Tax Relief, Unemployment Insurance Reauthorization, and Job Creation Act of 2010 (P.L. 111-312)

P.L. 111-312, §303(b)(2):

Amended Code Sec. 2631(c) by striking "the applicable exclusion amount" and inserting "the basic exclusion amount". **Effective** for generation-skipping transfers after 12-31-2010.

P.L. 111-312, §304, provides [but see P.L. 112-240, §101(a)(2)-(3), above]:

SEC. 304. APPLICATION OF EGTRRA SUNSET TO THIS TITLE.

Section 901 of the Economic Growth and Tax Relief Reconciliation Act of 2001 shall apply to the amendments made by this title.

• 2001, Economic Growth and Tax Relief Reconciliation Act of 2001 (P.L. 107-16)

P.L. 107-16, §521(c)(2):

Amended Code Sec. 2631(c). **Effective** for estates of decedents dying, and generation-skipping transfers, after 12-31-2003. Prior to amendment, Code Sec. 2631(c) read as follows:

(c) INFLATION ADJUSTMENT.—

(1) IN GENERAL.—In the case of any calendar year after 1998, the $1,000,000 amount contained in subsection (a) shall be increased by an amount equal to—

(A) $1,000,000, multiplied by

(B) the cost-of-living adjustment determined under section 1(f)(3) for such calendar year by substituting "calendar year 1997" for "calendar year 1992" in subparagraph (B) thereof.

If any amount as adjusted under the preceding sentence is not a multiple of $10,000, such amount shall be rounded to the next lowest multiple of $10,000.

(2) ALLOCATION OF INCREASE.—Any increase under paragraph (1) for any calendar year shall apply only to generation-skipping transfers made during or after such calendar year; except that no such increase for calendar years after the calendar year in which the transferor dies shall apply to transfers by such transferor.

P.L. 107-16, §901(a)-(b), as amended by P.L. 111-312, §101(a)(1), provides [but see P.L. 112-240, §101(a)(1) and (3), above]:

SEC. 901. SUNSET OF PROVISIONS OF ACT.

(a) IN GENERAL.—All provisions of, and amendments made by, this Act shall not apply—

(1) to taxable, plan, or limitation years beginning after December 31, 2012, or

(2) in the case of title V, to estates of decedents dying, gifts made, or generation skipping transfers, after December 31, 2012.

(b) APPLICATION OF CERTAIN LAWS.—The Internal Revenue Code of 1986 and the Employee Retirement Income Security Act of 1974 shall be applied and administered to years, estates, gifts, and transfers described in subsection (a) as if the provisions and amendments described in subsection (a) had never been enacted.

• 1998, IRS Restructuring and Reform Act of 1998 (P.L. 105-206)

P.L. 105-206, §6007(a)(1):

Amended Code Sec. 2631(c). **Effective** as if included in the provision of P.L. 105-34 to which it relates [**effective** on 8-5-97.—CCH]. Prior to amendment, Code Sec. 2631(c) read as follows:

(c) INFLATION ADJUSTMENT.—In the case of an individual who dies in any calendar year after 1998, the $1,000,000 amount contained in subsection (a) shall be increased by an amount equal to—

(1) $1,000,000, multiplied by

(2) the cost-of-living adjustment determined under section 1(f)(3) for such calendar year by substituting "calendar year 1997" for "calendar year 1992" in subparagraph (B) thereof.

If any amount as adjusted under the preceding sentence is not a multiple of $10,000, such amount shall be rounded to the next lowest multiple of $10,000.

• 1997, Taxpayer Relief Act of 1997 (P.L. 105-34)

P.L. 105-34, §501(d):

Amended Code Sec. 2631 by adding a new subsection (c). **Effective** 8-5-97 [**effective** date changed by P.L. 105-206, §6007(a)(2)].

[Sec. 2632]

SEC. 2632. SPECIAL RULES FOR ALLOCATION OF GST EXEMPTION.

[Sec. 2632(a)]

(a) TIME AND MANNER OF ALLOCATION.—

(1) TIME.—Any allocation by an individual of his GST exemption under section 2631(a) may be made at any time on or before the date prescribed for filing the estate tax return for such individual's estate (determined with regard to extensions), regardless of whether such a return is required to be filed.

(2) MANNER.—The Secretary shall prescribe by forms or regulations the manner in which any allocation referred to in paragraph (1) is to be made.

[Sec. 2632(b)]

(b) DEEMED ALLOCATION TO CERTAIN LIFETIME DIRECT SKIPS.—

(1) IN GENERAL.—If any individual makes a direct skip during his lifetime, any unused portion of such individual's GST exemption shall be allocated to the property transferred to the extent necessary to make the inclusion ratio for such property zero. If the amount of the direct skip exceeds such unused portion, the entire unused portion shall be allocated to the property transferred.

(2) UNUSED PORTION.—For purposes of paragraph (1), the unused portion of an individual's GST exemption is that portion of such exemption which has not previously been allocated by such individual (or treated as allocated under paragraph (1) or subsection (c)(1)).

(3) SUBSECTION NOT TO APPLY IN CERTAIN CASES.—An individual may elect to have this subsection not apply to a transfer.

Amendments

• 2013, American Taxpayer Relief Act of 2012 (P.L. 112-240)

P.L. 112-240, §101(a)(1) and (3), provides:

SEC. 101. PERMANENT EXTENSION AND MODIFICATION OF 2001 TAX RELIEF.

(a) PERMANENT EXTENSION.—

(1) IN GENERAL.—The Economic Growth and Tax Relief Reconciliation Act of 2001 is amended by striking title IX.

***

(3) EFFECTIVE DATE.—The amendments made by this subsection shall apply to taxable, plan, or limitation years beginning after December 31, 2012, and estates of decedents dying, gifts made, or generation skipping transfers after December 31, 2012.

• 2001, Economic Growth and Tax Relief Reconciliation Act of 2001 (P.L. 107-16)

P.L. 107-16, §561(b):

Amended Code Sec. 2632(b)(2) by striking "with respect to a prior direct skip" and inserting "or subsection (c)(1)". **Effective** for transfers subject to chapter 11 or 12 made after 12-31-2000, and to estate tax inclusion periods ending after 12-31-2000.

P.L. 107-16, §901(a)-(b), as amended by P.L. 111-312, §101(a)(1), provides [but see P.L. 112-240, §101(a)(1) and (3), above]:

SEC. 901. SUNSET OF PROVISIONS OF ACT.

(a) IN GENERAL.—All provisions of, and amendments made by, this Act shall not apply—

(1) to taxable, plan, or limitation years beginning after December 31, 2012, or

(2) in the case of title V, to estates of decedents dying, gifts made, or generation skipping transfers, after December 31, 2012.

(b) APPLICATION OF CERTAIN LAWS.—The Internal Revenue Code of 1986 and the Employee Retirement Income Security Act of 1974 shall be applied and administered to years, estates, gifts, and transfers described in subsection (a) as if the provisions and amendments described in subsection (a) had never been enacted.

• 1988, Technical and Miscellaneous Revenue Act of 1988 (P.L. 100-647)

P.L. 100-647, §1014(g)(16):

Amended Code Sec. 2632(b)(2) by striking out "paragraph (1)) with respect to a prior direct skip" and inserting in lieu thereof "paragraph (1) with respect to a prior direct skip)". **Effective** as if included in the provision of P.L. 99-514 to which it relates.

[Sec. 2632(c)]

(c) DEEMED ALLOCATION TO CERTAIN LIFETIME TRANSFERS TO GST TRUSTS.—

(1) IN GENERAL.—If any individual makes an indirect skip during such individual's lifetime, any unused portion of such individual's GST exemption shall be allocated to the property transferred to the extent necessary to make the inclusion ratio for such property zero. If the amount of the indirect skip exceeds such unused portion, the entire unused portion shall be allocated to the property transferred.

(2) UNUSED PORTION.—For purposes of paragraph (1), the unused portion of an individual's GST exemption is that portion of such exemption which has not previously been—

(A) allocated by such individual,

(B) treated as allocated under subsection (b) with respect to a direct skip occurring during or before the calendar year in which the indirect skip is made, or

(C) treated as allocated under paragraph (1) with respect to a prior indirect skip.

(3) DEFINITIONS.—

(A) INDIRECT SKIP.—For purposes of this subsection, the term "indirect skip" means any transfer of property (other than a direct skip) subject to the tax imposed by chapter 12 made to a GST trust.

(B) GST TRUST.—The term "GST trust" means a trust that could have a generation-skipping transfer with respect to the transferor unless—

(i) the trust instrument provides that more than 25 percent of the trust corpus must be distributed to or may be withdrawn by one or more individuals who are non-skip persons—

(I) before the date that the individual attains age 46,

(II) on or before one or more dates specified in the trust instrument that will occur before the date that such individual attains age 46, or

(III) upon the occurrence of an event that, in accordance with regulations prescribed by the Secretary, may reasonably be expected to occur before the date that such individual attains age 46,

(ii) the trust instrument provides that more than 25 percent of the trust corpus must be distributed to or may be withdrawn by one or more individuals who are non-skip persons and who are living on the date of death of another person identified in the instrument (by name or by class) who is more than 10 years older than such individuals,

(iii) the trust instrument provides that, if one or more individuals who are non-skip persons die on or before a date or event described in clause (i) or (ii), more than 25 percent of the trust corpus either must be distributed to the estate or estates of one or more of such individuals or is subject to a general power of appointment exercisable by one or more of such individuals,

(iv) the trust is a trust any portion of which would be included in the gross estate of a non-skip person (other than the transferor) if such person died immediately after the transfer,

(v) the trust is a charitable lead annuity trust (within the meaning of section 2642(e)(3)(A)) or a charitable remainder annuity trust or a charitable remainder unitrust (within the meaning of section 664(d)), or

(vi) the trust is a trust with respect to which a deduction was allowed under section 2522 for the amount of an interest in the form of the right to receive annual payments of a fixed percentage of the net fair market value of the trust property (determined yearly) and which is required to pay principal to a non-skip person if such person is alive when the yearly payments for which the deduction was allowed terminate.

For purposes of this subparagraph, the value of transferred property shall not be considered to be includible in the gross estate of a non-skip person or subject to a right of withdrawal by reason of such person holding a right to withdraw so much of such property as does not exceed the amount referred to in section 2503(b) with respect to any transferor, and it shall be assumed that powers of appointment held by non-skip persons will not be exercised.

(4) AUTOMATIC ALLOCATIONS TO CERTAIN GST TRUSTS.—For purposes of this subsection, an indirect skip to which section 2642(f) applies shall be deemed to have been made only at the close of the estate tax inclusion period. The fair market value of such transfer shall be the fair market value of the trust property at the close of the estate tax inclusion period.

(5) APPLICABILITY AND EFFECT.—

(A) IN GENERAL.—An individual—

(i) may elect to have this subsection not apply to—

(I) an indirect skip, or

(II) any or all transfers made by such individual to a particular trust, and

(ii) may elect to treat any trust as a GST trust for purposes of this subsection with respect to any or all transfers made by such individual to such trust.

(B) ELECTIONS.—

(i) ELECTIONS WITH RESPECT TO INDIRECT SKIPS.—An election under subparagraph (A)(i)(I) shall be deemed to be timely if filed on a timely filed gift tax return for the calendar year in which the transfer was made or deemed to have been made pursuant to paragraph (4) or on such later date or dates as may be prescribed by the Secretary.

(ii) OTHER ELECTIONS.—An election under clause (i)(II) or (ii) of subparagraph (A) may be made on a timely filed gift tax return for the calendar year for which the election is to become effective.

Amendments

• 2013, American Taxpayer Relief Act of 2012 (P.L. 112-240)

P.L. 112-240, §101(a)(1) and (3), provides:

SEC. 101. PERMANENT EXTENSION AND MODIFICATION OF 2001 TAX RELIEF.

(a) PERMANENT EXTENSION.—

(1) IN GENERAL.—The Economic Growth and Tax Relief Reconciliation Act of 2001 is amended by striking title IX.

* * *

(3) EFFECTIVE DATE.—The amendments made by this subsection shall apply to taxable, plan, or limitation years beginning after December 31, 2012, and estates of decedents dying, gifts made, or generation skipping transfers after December 31, 2012.

• 2001, Economic Growth and Tax Relief Reconciliation Act of 2001 (P.L. 107-16)

P.L. 107-16, §561(a):

Amended Code Sec. 2632 by redesignating subsection (c) as subsection (e) and by inserting after subsection (b) a new subsection (c). **Effective** for transfers subject to chapter 11 or 12 made after 12-31-2000, and to estate tax inclusion periods ending after 12-31-2000.

P.L. 107-16, §901(a)-(b), as amended by P.L. 111-312, §101(a)(1), provides [but see P.L. 112-240, §101(a)(1) and (3), above]:

SEC. 901. SUNSET OF PROVISIONS OF ACT.

(a) IN GENERAL.—All provisions of, and amendments made by, this Act shall not apply—

(1) to taxable, plan, or limitation years beginning after December 31, 2012, or

(2) in the case of title V, to estates of decedents dying, gifts made, or generation skipping transfers, after December 31, 2012.

(b) APPLICATION OF CERTAIN LAWS.—The Internal Revenue Code of 1986 and the Employee Retirement Income Security Act of 1974 shall be applied and administered to years, estates, gifts, and transfers described in subsection (a) as if the provisions and amendments described in subsection (a) had never been enacted.

[Sec. 2632(d)]

(d) RETROACTIVE ALLOCATIONS.—

(1) IN GENERAL.—If—

(A) a non-skip person has an interest or a future interest in a trust to which any transfer has been made,

(B) such person—

(i) is a lineal descendant of a grandparent of the transferor or of a grandparent of the transferor's spouse or former spouse, and

(ii) is assigned to a generation below the generation assignment of the transferor, and

(C) such person predeceases the transferor,

then the transferor may make an allocation of any of such transferor's unused GST exemption to any previous transfer or transfers to the trust on a chronological basis.

(2) SPECIAL RULES.—If the allocation under paragraph (1) by the transferor is made on a gift tax return filed on or before the date prescribed by section 6075(b) for gifts made within the calendar year within which the non-skip person's death occurred—

(A) the value of such transfer or transfers for purposes of section 2642(a) shall be determined as if such allocation had been made on a timely filed gift tax return for each calendar year within which each transfer was made,

(B) such allocation shall be effective immediately before such death, and

(C) the amount of the transferor's unused GST exemption available to be allocated shall be determined immediately before such death.

(3) FUTURE INTEREST.—For purposes of this subsection, a person has a future interest in a trust if the trust may permit income or corpus to be paid to such person on a date or dates in the future.

Amendments

• 2013, American Taxpayer Relief Act of 2012 (P.L. 112-240)

P.L. 112-240, §101(a)(1) and (3), provides:

SEC. 101. PERMANENT EXTENSION AND MODIFICATION OF 2001 TAX RELIEF.

(a) PERMANENT EXTENSION.—

(1) IN GENERAL.—The Economic Growth and Tax Relief Reconciliation Act of 2001 is amended by striking title IX.

* * *

(3) EFFECTIVE DATE.—The amendments made by this subsection shall apply to taxable, plan, or limitation years beginning after December 31, 2012, and estates of decedents dying, gifts made, or generation skipping transfers after December 31, 2012.

• 2001, Economic Growth and Tax Relief Reconciliation Act of 2001 (P.L. 107-16)

P.L. 107-16, §561(a):

Amended Code Sec. 2632 by redesignating subsection (c) as subsection (e) and by inserting after new subsection (c), as added by Act Sec. 561(a), a new subsection (d). **Effective** for deaths of non-skip persons occurring after 12-31-2000.

P.L. 107-16, §901(a)-(b), as amended by P.L. 111-312, §101(a)(1), provides [but see P.L. 112-240, §101(a)(1) and (3), above]:

SEC. 901. SUNSET OF PROVISIONS OF ACT.

(a) IN GENERAL.—All provisions of, and amendments made by, this Act shall not apply—

(1) to taxable, plan, or limitation years beginning after December 31, 2012, or

(2) in the case of title V, to estates of decedents dying, gifts made, or generation skipping transfers, after December 31, 2012.

(b) APPLICATION OF CERTAIN LAWS.—The Internal Revenue Code of 1986 and the Employee Retirement Income Security Act of 1974 shall be applied and administered to years, estates, gifts, and transfers described in subsection (a) as if the provisions and amendments described in subsection (a) had never been enacted.

[Sec. 2632(e)]

(e) ALLOCATION OF UNUSED GST EXEMPTION.—

(1) IN GENERAL.—Any portion of an individual's GST exemption which has not been allocated within the time prescribed by subsection (a) shall be deemed to be allocated as follows—

(A) first, to property which is the subject of a direct skip occurring at such individual's death, and

(B) second, to trusts with respect to which such individual is the transferor and from which a taxable distribution or a taxable termination might occur at or after such individual's death.

(2) ALLOCATION WITHIN CATEGORIES.—

(A) IN GENERAL.—The allocation under paragraph (1) shall be made among the properties described in subparagraph (A) thereof and the trust described in subparagraph (B) thereof, as the case may be, in proportion to the respective amounts (at the time of allocation) of the nonexempt portions of such properties or trusts.

(B) NONEXEMPT PORTION.—For purposes of subparagraph (A), the term "nonexempt portion" means the value (at the time of allocation) of the property or trust, multiplied by the inclusion ratio with respect to such property or trust.

Amendments

• 2013, American Taxpayer Relief Act of 2012 (P.L. 112-240)

P.L. 112-240, §101(a)(1) and (3), provides:

SEC. 101. PERMANENT EXTENSION AND MODIFICATION OF 2001 TAX RELIEF.

(a) PERMANENT EXTENSION.—

(1) IN GENERAL.—The Economic Growth and Tax Relief Reconciliation Act of 2001 is amended by striking title IX.

* * *

(3) EFFECTIVE DATE.—The amendments made by this subsection shall apply to taxable, plan, or limitation years beginning after December 31, 2012, and estates of decedents dying, gifts made, or generation skipping transfers after December 31, 2012.

• 2001, Economic Growth and Tax Relief Reconciliation Act of 2001 (P.L. 107-16)

P.L. 107-16, §561(a):

Amended Code Sec. 2632 by redesignating subsection (c) as subsection (e). **Effective** 6-7-2001.

P.L. 107-16, §901(a)-(b), as amended by P.L. 111-312, §101(a)(1), provides [but see P.L. 112-240, §101(a)(1) and (3), above]:

SEC. 901. SUNSET OF PROVISIONS OF ACT.

(a) IN GENERAL.—All provisions of, and amendments made by, this Act shall not apply—

(1) to taxable, plan, or limitation years beginning after December 31, 2012, or

(2) in the case of title V, to estates of decedents dying, gifts made, or generation skipping transfers, after December 31, 2012.

(b) APPLICATION OF CERTAIN LAWS.—The Internal Revenue Code of 1986 and the Employee Retirement Income Security Act of 1974 shall be applied and administered to years, estates, gifts, and transfers described in subsection (a) as if the provisions and amendments described in subsection (a) had never been enacted.

• 1986, Tax Reform Act of 1986 (P.L. 99-514)

P.L. 99-514, §1431(a):

Added Code Sec. 2632. **Effective**, generally, for any generation-skipping transfer (within the meaning of section

2611 of the Internal Revenue Code of 1986) made after 10-22-86. However, for special rules, see Act Sec. 1433(b)-(d) following Code Sec. 2601.

Subchapter E—Applicable Rate; Inclusion Ratio

[Sec. 2641]

SEC. 2641. APPLICABLE RATE.

[Sec. 2641(a)]

(a) GENERAL RULE.—For purposes of this chapter, the term "applicable rate" means, with respect to any generation-skipping transfer, the product of—

(1) the maximum Federal estate tax rate, and

(2) the inclusion ratio with respect to the transfer.

Amendments

• 2010, Tax Relief, Unemployment Insurance Reauthorization, and Job Creation Act of 2010 (P.L. 111-312)

P.L. 111-312, §302(c), provides:

(c) MODIFICATION OF GENERATION-SKIPPING TRANSFER TAX.—In the case of any generation-skipping transfer made after December 31, 2009, and before January 1, 2011, the applicable rate determined under section 2641(a) of the Internal Revenue Code of 1986 shall be zero.

[Sec. 2641(b)]

(b) MAXIMUM FEDERAL ESTATE TAX RATE.—For purposes of subsection (a), the term "maximum Federal estate tax rate" means the maximum rate imposed by section 2001 on the estates of decedents dying at the time of the taxable distribution, taxable termination, or direct skip, as the case may be.

Amendments

• 1986, Tax Reform Act of 1986 (P.L. 99-514)

P.L. 99-514, §1431(a):

Added Code Sec. 2641. **Effective**, generally, for any generation-skipping transfer (within the meaning of section 2611 of the Internal Revenue Code of 1986) made after 10-22-86. However, for special rules, see Act Sec. 1433(b)-(d) following Code Sec. 2601.

[Sec. 2642]

SEC. 2642. INCLUSION RATIO.

[Sec. 2642(a)]

(a) INCLUSION RATIO DEFINED.—For purposes of this chapter—

(1) IN GENERAL.—Except as otherwise provided in this section, the inclusion ratio with respect to any property transferred in a generation-skipping transfer shall be the excess (if any) of 1 over—

(A) except as provided in subparagraph (B), the applicable fraction determined for the trust from which such transfer is made, or

(B) in the case of a direct skip, the applicable fraction determined for such skip.

(2) APPLICABLE FRACTION.—For purposes of paragraph (1), the applicable fraction is a fraction—

(A) the numerator of which is the amount of the GST exemption allocated to the trust (or in the case of a direct skip, allocated to the property transferred in such skip), and

(B) the denominator of which is—

(i) the value of the property transferred to the trust (or involved in the direct skip), reduced by

(ii) the sum of—

(I) any Federal estate tax or State death tax actually recovered from the trust attributable to such property, and

(II) any charitable deduction allowed under section 2055 or 2522 with respect to such property.

(3) SEVERING OF TRUSTS.—

(A) IN GENERAL.—If a trust is severed in a qualified severance, the trusts resulting from such severance shall be treated as separate trusts thereafter for purposes of this chapter.

(B) QUALIFIED SEVERANCE.—For purposes of subparagraph (A)—

(i) IN GENERAL.—The term "qualified severance" means the division of a single trust and the creation (by any means available under the governing instrument or under local law) of two or more trusts if—

(I) the single trust was divided on a fractional basis, and

(II) the terms of the new trusts, in the aggregate, provide for the same succession of interests of beneficiaries as are provided in the original trust.

(ii) TRUSTS WITH INCLUSION RATIO GREATER THAN ZERO.—If a trust has an inclusion ratio of greater than zero and less than 1, a severance is a qualified severance only if the single trust is divided into two trusts, one of which receives a fractional share of the total value of all trust assets equal to the applicable fraction of the single trust immediately before the severance. In such case, the trust receiving such fractional share shall have an inclusion ratio of zero and the other trust shall have an inclusion ratio of 1.

(iii) REGULATIONS.—The term "qualified severance" includes any other severance permitted under regulations prescribed by the Secretary.

(C) TIMING AND MANNER OF SEVERANCES.—A severance pursuant to this paragraph may be made at any time. The Secretary shall prescribe by forms or regulations the manner in which the qualified severance shall be reported to the Secretary.

Amendments

• 2013, American Taxpayer Relief Act of 2012 (P.L. 112-240)

P.L. 112-240, §101(a)(1) and (3), provides:

SEC. 101. PERMANENT EXTENSION AND MODIFICATION OF 2001 TAX RELIEF.

(a) PERMANENT EXTENSION.—

(1) IN GENERAL.—The Economic Growth and Tax Relief Reconciliation Act of 2001 is amended by striking title IX.

* * *

(3) EFFECTIVE DATE.—The amendments made by this subsection shall apply to taxable, plan, or limitation years beginning after December 31, 2012, and estates of decedents dying, gifts made, or generation skipping transfers after December 31, 2012.

• 2001, Economic Growth and Tax Relief Reconciliation Act of 2001 (P.L. 107-16)

P.L. 107-16, §562(a):

Amended Code Sec. 2642(a) by adding at the end a new paragraph (3). **Effective** for severances after 12-31-2000.

P.L. 107-16, §901(a)-(b), as amended by P.L. 111-312, §101(a)(1), provides [but see P.L. 112-240, §101(a)(1) and (3), above]:

SEC. 901. SUNSET OF PROVISIONS OF ACT.

(a) IN GENERAL.—All provisions of, and amendments made by, this Act shall not apply—

(1) to taxable, plan, or limitation years beginning after December 31, 2012, or

(2) in the case of title V, to estates of decedents dying, gifts made, or generation skipping transfers, after December 31, 2012.

(b) APPLICATION OF CERTAIN LAWS.—The Internal Revenue Code of 1986 and the Employee Retirement Income Security Act of 1974 shall be applied and administered to years, estates, gifts, and transfers described in subsection (a) as if the provisions and amendments described in subsection (a) had never been enacted.

• 1988, Technical and Miscellaneous Revenue Act of 1988 (P.L. 100-647)

P.L. 100-647, §1014(g)(4)(B):

Amended Code Sec. 2642(a)(2) by striking out the last sentence. **Effective** as if included in the provision of P.L. 99-514 to which it relates. Prior to amendment, the last sentence of Code Sec. 2642(a)(2) read as follows:

Except as provided in paragraphs (3) and (4) of subsection (b), the value determined under subparagraph (B)(i) shall be of the property as of the time of the transfer to the trust (or the direct skip).

[Sec. 2642(b)]

(b) VALUATION RULES, ETC.—Except as provided in subsection (f)—

(1) GIFTS FOR WHICH GIFT TAX RETURN FILED OR DEEMED ALLOCATION MADE.—If the allocation of the GST exemption to any transfers of property is made on a gift tax return filed on or before the date prescribed by section 6075(b) for such transfer or is deemed to be made under section 2632(b)(1) or (c)(1)—

(A) the value of such property for purposes of subsection (a) shall be its value as finally determined for purposes of chapter 12 (within the meaning of section 2001(f)(2)), or, in the case of an allocation deemed to have been made at the close of an estate tax inclusion period, its value at the time of the close of the estate tax inclusion period, and

(B) such allocation shall be effective on and after the date of such transfer, or, in the case of an allocation deemed to have been made at the close of an estate tax inclusion period, on and after the close of such estate tax inclusion period.

(2) TRANSFERS AND ALLOCATIONS AT OR AFTER DEATH.—

(A) TRANSFERS AT DEATH.—If property is transferred as a result of the death of the transferor, the value of such property for purposes of subsection (a) shall be its value as finally determined for purposes of chapter 11; except that, if the requirements prescribed by the Secretary respecting allocation of post-death changes in value are not met, the value of such property shall be determined as of the time of the distribution concerned.

(B) ALLOCATIONS TO PROPERTY TRANSFERRED AT DEATH OF TRANSFEROR.—Any allocation to property transferred as a result of the death of the transferor shall be effective on and after the date of the death of the transferor.

(3) ALLOCATIONS TO INTER VIVOS TRANSFERS NOT MADE ON TIMELY FILED GIFT TAX RETURN.—If any allocation of the GST exemption to any property not transferred as a result of the death of the transferor is not made on a gift tax return filed on or before the date prescribed by section 6075(b) and is not deemed to be made under section 2632(b)(1)—

(A) the value of such property for purposes of subsection (a) shall be determined as of the time such allocation is filed with the Secretary, and

(B) such allocation shall be effective on and after the date on which such allocation is filed with the Secretary.

(4) QTIP TRUSTS.—If the value of property is included in the estate of a spouse by virtue of section 2044, and if such spouse is treated as the transferor of such property under section 2652(a), the value of such property for purposes of subsection (a) shall be its value for purposes of chapter 11 in the estate of such spouse.

Amendments

• 2013, American Taxpayer Relief Act of 2012 (P.L. 112-240)

P.L. 112-240, §101(a)(1) and (3), provides:

SEC. 101. PERMANENT EXTENSION AND MODIFICATION OF 2001 TAX RELIEF.

(a) PERMANENT EXTENSION.—

(1) IN GENERAL.—The Economic Growth and Tax Relief Reconciliation Act of 2001 is amended by striking title IX.

* * *

(3) EFFECTIVE DATE.—The amendments made by this subsection shall apply to taxable, plan, or limitation years beginning after December 31, 2012, and estates of decedents dying, gifts made, or generation skipping transfers after December 31, 2012.

• 2001, Economic Growth and Tax Relief Reconciliation Act of 2001 (P.L. 107-16)

P.L. 107-16, §563(a):

Amended Code Sec. 2642(b)(1). **Effective** for transfers subject to chapter 11 or 12 of the Internal Revenue Code of 1986 made after 12-31-2000. Prior to amendment, Code Sec. 2642(b)(1) read as follows:

(1) GIFTS FOR WHICH GIFT TAX RETURN FILED OR DEEMED ALLOCATION MADE.—If the allocation of the GST exemption to any property is made on a gift tax return filed on or before the date prescribed by section 6075(b) or is deemed to be made under section 2632(b)(1)—

(A) the value of such property for purposes of subsection (a) shall be its value for purposes of chapter 12, and

(B) such allocation shall be effective on and after the date of such transfer.

P.L. 107-16, §563(b):

Amended Code Sec. 2642(b)(2)(A). **Effective** for transfers subject to chapter 11 or 12 of the Internal Revenue Code of 1986 made after 12-31-2000. Prior to amendment, Code Sec. 2642(b)(2)(A) read as follows:

(A) TRANSFERS AT DEATH.—If property is transferred as a result of the death of the transferor, the value of such property for purposes of subsection (a) shall be its value for purposes of chapter 11; except that, if the requirements prescribed by the Secretary respecting allocation of post-death changes in value are not met, the value of such property shall be determined as of the time of the distribution concerned.

P.L. 107-16, §901(a)-(b), as amended by P.L. 111-312, §101(a)(1), provides [but see P.L. 112-240, §101(a)(1) and (3), above]:

SEC. 901. SUNSET OF PROVISIONS OF ACT.

(a) IN GENERAL.—All provisions of, and amendments made by, this Act shall not apply—

(1) to taxable, plan, or limitation years beginning after December 31, 2012, or

(2) in the case of title V, to estates of decedents dying, gifts made, or generation skipping transfers, after December 31, 2012.

(b) APPLICATION OF CERTAIN LAWS.—The Internal Revenue Code of 1986 and the Employee Retirement Income Security Act of 1974 shall be applied and administered to years, estates, gifts, and transfers described in subsection (a) as if the provisions and amendments described in subsection (a) had never been enacted.

• 1989, Omnibus Budget Reconciliation Act of 1989 (P.L. 101-239)

P.L. 101-239, §7811(j)(4):

Amended Code Sec. 2642(b)(1) and (3) by striking "a timely filed gift tax return required by section 6019" and inserting "a gift tax return filed on or before the date prescribed by section 6075(b)". **Effective** as if included in the provision of P.L. 100-647 to which it relates.

• 1988, Technical and Miscellaneous Revenue Act of 1988 (P.L. 100-647)

P.L. 100-647, §1014(g)(4)(C):

Amended Code Sec. 2642(b)(2)(A) by inserting before the period at the end thereof the following: "; except that, if the requirements prescribed by the Secretary respecting allocation of post-death changes in value are not met, the value of such property shall be determined as of the time of the distribution concerned." **Effective** as if included in the provision of P.L. 99-514 to which it relates.

P.L. 100-647, §1014(g)(4)(D):

Amended Code Sec. 2642(b) by inserting "Except as provided in subsection (f)—" immediately after the subsection heading. **Effective** as if included in the provision of P.L. 99-514 to which it relates.

P.L. 100-647, §1014(g)(4)(E)(i)-(ii):

Amended Code Sec. 2642(b)(2)(B) by striking out "at or after the death of the transferor" and inserting in lieu thereof "to property transferred as a result of the death of the transferor"; and by striking out "AT OR AFTER DEATH" in the subparagraph heading and inserting in lieu thereof "TO PROPERTY TRANSFERRED AT DEATH". **E ffective** as if included in the provision of P.L. 99-514 to which it relates.

P.L. 100-647, §1014(g)(4)(F)(i)-(ii):

Amended Code Sec. 2642(b)(3) by striking out "to any property is made during the life of the transferor but is" and inserting in lieu thereof "to any property not transferred as a result of the death of the transferor is"; and by striking out "Inter vivos allocations" in the subparagraph heading and inserting in lieu thereof "Allocations to inter vivos transfers". **Effective** as if included in the provision of P.L. 99-514 to which it relates.

[Sec. 2642(c)]

(c) TREATMENT OF CERTAIN DIRECT SKIPS WHICH ARE NONTAXABLE GIFTS.—

(1) IN GENERAL.—In the case of a direct skip which is a nontaxable gift, the inclusion ratio shall be zero.

(2) EXCEPTION FOR CERTAIN TRANSFERS IN TRUST.—Paragraph (1) shall not apply to any transfer to a trust for the benefit of an individual unless—

(A) during the life of such individual, no portion of the corpus or income of the trust may be distributed to (or for the benefit of) any person other than such individual, and

(B) if the trust does not terminate before the individual dies, the assets of such trust will be includible in the gross estate of such individual.

Rules similar to the rules of section 2652(c)(3) shall apply for purposes of subparagraph (A).

(3) NONTAXABLE GIFT.—For purposes of this subsection, the term "nontaxable gift" means any transfer of property to the extent such transfer is not treated as a taxable gift by reason of—

(A) section 2503(b) (taking into account the application of section 2513), or

(B) section 2503(e).

Amendments

• 1990, Omnibus Budget Reconciliation Act of 1990 (P.L. 101-508)

P.L. 101-508, §11703(c)(1):

Amended Code Sec. 2642(c)(2)(B) by striking "such individual dies before the trust is terminated" and inserting "the trust does not terminate before the individual dies". **Effective** for transfers after 3-31-88.

P.L. 101-508, §11703(c)(2):

Amended Code Sec. 2642(c)(2) by adding at the end thereof a new sentence. **Effective** for transfers after 3-31-88.

• 1988, Technical and Miscellaneous Revenue Act of 1988 (P.L. 100-647)

P.L. 100-647, §1014(g)(17)(A):

Amended Code Sec. 2642(c). **Effective** for transfers after 3-31-88. Prior to amendment, Code Sec. 2642(c) read as follows:

(c) TREATMENT OF CERTAIN NONTAXABLE GIFTS.—

(1) DIRECT SKIPS.—In the case of any direct skip which is a nontaxable gift, the inclusion ratio shall be zero.

(2) TREATMENT OF NONTAXABLE GIFTS MADE TO TRUSTS.—

(A) IN GENERAL.—Except as provided in subparagraph (B), any nontaxable gift which is not a direct skip and which is made to a trust shall not be taken into account under subsection (a)(2)(B).

(B) DETERMINATION OF 1ST TRANSFER TO TRUST.—In the case of any nontaxable gift referred to in subparagraph (A) which is the 1st transfer to the trust, the inclusion ratio for such trust shall be zero.

(3) NONTAXABLE GIFT.—For purposes of this section, the term "nontaxable gift" means any transfer of property to the extent such transfer is not treated as a taxable gift by reason of—

(A) section 2503(b) (taking into account the application of section 2513), or

(B) section 2503(e).

[Sec. 2642(d)]

(d) SPECIAL RULES WHERE MORE THAN 1 TRANSFER MADE TO TRUST.—

(1) IN GENERAL.—If a transfer of property is made to a trust in existence before such transfer, the applicable fraction for such trust shall be recomputed as of the time of such transfer in the manner provided in paragraph (2).

(2) APPLICABLE FRACTION.—In the case of any such transfer, the recomputed applicable fraction is a fraction—

(A) the numerator of which is the sum of—

(i) the amount of the GST exemption allocated to property involved in such transfer, plus

(ii) the nontax portion of such trust immediately before such transfer, and

(B) the denominator of which is the sum of—

(i) the value of the property involved in such transfer reduced by the sum of—

(I) any Federal estate tax or State death tax actually recovered from the trust attributable to such property, and

(II) any charitable deduction allowed under section 2055 or 2522 with respect to such property, and

(ii) the value of all of the property in the trust (immediately before such transfer).

(3) NONTAX PORTION.—For purposes of paragraph (2), the term "nontax portion" means the product of—

(A) the value of all of the property in the trust, and

(B) the applicable fraction in effect for such trust.

(4) SIMILAR RECOMPUTATION IN CASE OF CERTAIN LATE ALLOCATIONS.—If—

(A) any allocation of the GST exemption to property transferred to a trust is not made on a timely filed gift tax return required by section 6019, and

(B) there was a previous allocation with respect to property transferred to such trust, the applicable fraction for such trust shall be recomputed as of the time of such allocation under rules similar to the rules of paragraph (2).

Amendments

• **1990, Omnibus Budget Reconciliation Act of 1990 (P.L. 101-508)**

P.L. 101-508, §11074(a)(17):

Amended Code Sec. 2642(d)(2)(B)(i)(I) by striking "state" and inserting "State". **Effective** 11-5-90.

• **1988, Technical and Miscellaneous Revenue Act of 1988 (P.L. 100-647)**

P.L. 100-647, §1014(g)(17)(B):

Amended Code Sec. 2642(d)(1) by striking out "(other than a nontaxable gift)" after "property". **Effective** for transfers after 3-31-88.

P.L. 100-647, §1014(g)(18):

Amended Code Sec. 2642(d)(2)(B)(i). **Effective** as if included in the provision of P.L. 99-514 to which it relates.

Prior to amendment, Code Sec. 2642(d)(2)(B)(i) read as follows:

(i) the value of the property involved in such transfer, reduced by any charitable deduction allowed under section 2055 or 2522 with respect to such property, and

• **1986, Tax Reform Act of 1986 (P.L. 99-514)**

P.L. 99-514, §1431(a):

Added Code Sec. 2642. **Effective**, generally, for any generation-skipping transfer (within the meaning of section 2611 of the Internal Revenue Code of 1986) made after 10-22-86. However, for special rules, see Act Sec. 1433(b)-(d) following Code Sec. 2601.

[Sec. 2642(e)]

(e) SPECIAL RULES FOR CHARITABLE LEAD ANNUITY TRUSTS.—

(1) IN GENERAL.—For purposes of determining the inclusion ratio for any charitable lead annuity trust, the applicable fraction shall be a fraction—

(A) the numerator of which is the adjusted GST exemption, and

(B) the denominator of which is the value of all of the property in such trust immediately after the termination of the charitable lead annuity.

(2) ADJUSTED GST EXEMPTION.—For purposes of paragraph (1), the adjusted GST exemption is an amount equal to the GST exemption allocated to the trust increased by interest determined—

(A) at the interest rate used in determining the amount of the deduction under section 2055 or 2522 (as the case may be) for the charitable lead annuity, and

(B) for the actual period of the charitable lead annuity.

(3) DEFINITIONS.—For purposes of this subsection—

(A) CHARITABLE LEAD ANNUITY TRUST.—The term "charitable lead annuity trust" means any trust in which there is a charitable lead annuity.

(B) CHARITABLE LEAD ANNUITY.—The term "charitable lead annuity" means any interest in the form of a guaranteed annuity with respect to which a deduction was allowed under section 2055 or 2522 (as the case may be).

(4) COORDINATION WITH SUBSECTION (d).—Under regulations, appropriate adjustments shall be made in the application of subsection (d) to take into account the provisions of this subsection.

Amendments

• **1988, Technical and Miscellaneous Revenue Act of 1988 (P.L. 100-647)**

P.L. 100-647, §1014(g)(3)(A):

Amended Code Sec. 2642 by adding at the end thereof new subsection (e). **Effective** for purposes of determining the inclusion ratio with respect to property transferred after 10-13-87.

[Sec. 2642(f)]

(f) SPECIAL RULES FOR CERTAIN INTER VIVOS TRANSFERS.—Except as provided in regulations—

(1) IN GENERAL.—For purposes of determining the inclusion ratio, if—

(A) an individual makes an inter vivos transfer of property, and

(B) the value of such property would be includible in the gross estate of such individual under chapter 11 if such individual died immediately after making such transfer (other than by reason of section 2035),

any allocation of GST exemption to such property shall not be made before the close of the estate tax inclusion period (and the value of such property shall be determined under paragraph (2)). If such transfer is a direct skip, such skip shall be treated as occurring as of the close of the estate tax inclusion period.

(2) VALUATION.—In the case of any property to which paragraph (1) applies, the value of such property shall be—

(A) if such property is includible in the gross estate of the transferor (other than by reason of section 2035), its value for purposes of chapter 11, or

(B) if subparagraph (A) does not apply, its value as of the close of the estate tax inclusion period (or, if any allocation of GST exemption to such property is not made on a timely filed gift tax return for the calendar year in which such period ends, its value as of the time such allocation is filed with the Secretary).

(3) ESTATE TAX INCLUSION PERIOD.—For purposes of this subsection, the term "estate tax inclusion period" means any period after the transfer described in paragraph (1) during which the value of the property involved in such transfer would be includible in the gross estate of the transferor under chapter 11 if he died. Such period shall in no event extend beyond the earlier of—

(A) the date on which there is a generation-skipping transfer with respect to such property, or

(B) the date of the death of the transferor.

(4) TREATMENT OF SPOUSE.—Except as provided in regulations, any reference in this subsection to an individual or transferor shall be treated as including a reference to the spouse of such individual or transferor.

(5) COORDINATION WITH SUBSECTION (d).—Under regulations, appropriate adjustments shall be made in the application of subsection (d) to take into account the provisions of this subsection.

Amendments

• 1988, Technical and Miscellaneous Revenue Act of 1988 (P.L. 100-647)

P.L. 100-647, §1014(g)(4)(A):

Amended Code Sec. 2642 by adding at the end thereof new subsection (f). **Effective** as if included in the provision of P.L. 99-514 to which it relates.

[Sec. 2642(g)]

(g) RELIEF PROVISIONS.—

(1) RELIEF FROM LATE ELECTIONS.—

(A) IN GENERAL.—The Secretary shall by regulation prescribe such circumstances and procedures under which extensions of time will be granted to make—

(i) an allocation of GST exemption described in paragraph (1) or (2) of subsection (b), and

(ii) an election under subsection (b)(3) or (c)(5) of section 2632.

Such regulations shall include procedures for requesting comparable relief with respect to transfers made before the date of the enactment of this paragraph.

(B) BASIS FOR DETERMINATIONS.—In determining whether to grant relief under this paragraph, the Secretary shall take into account all relevant circumstances, including evidence of intent contained in the trust instrument or instrument of transfer and such other factors as the Secretary deems relevant. For purposes of determining whether to grant relief under this paragraph, the time for making the allocation (or election) shall be treated as if not expressly prescribed by statute.

(2) SUBSTANTIAL COMPLIANCE.—An allocation of GST exemption under section 2632 that demonstrates an intent to have the lowest possible inclusion ratio with respect to a transfer or a trust shall be deemed to be an allocation of so much of the transferor's unused GST exemption as produces the lowest possible inclusion ratio. In determining whether there has been substantial compliance, all relevant circumstances shall be taken into account, including evidence of intent contained in the trust instrument or instrument of transfer and such other factors as the Secretary deems relevant.

Amendments

• 2013, American Taxpayer Relief Act of 2012 (P.L. 112-240)

P.L. 112-240, §101(a)(1) and (3), provides:

SEC. 101. PERMANENT EXTENSION AND MODIFICATION OF 2001 TAX RELIEF.

(a) PERMANENT EXTENSION.—

(1) IN GENERAL.—The Economic Growth and Tax Relief Reconciliation Act of 2001 is amended by striking title IX.

***

(3) EFFECTIVE DATE.—The amendments made by this subsection shall apply to taxable, plan, or limitation years beginning after December 31, 2012, and estates of decedents dying, gifts made, or generation skipping transfers after December 31, 2012.

• 2001, Economic Growth and Tax Relief Reconciliation Act of 2001 (P.L. 107-16)

P.L. 107-16, §564(a):

Amended Code Sec. 2642 by adding at the end a new subsection (g). For the **effective** date, see Act Sec. 564(b)(1)-(2), below.

P.L. 107-16, §564(b)(1)-(2), provides:

(b) EFFECTIVE DATES.—

(1) RELIEF FROM LATE ELECTIONS.—Section 2642(g)(1) of the Internal Revenue Code of 1986 (as added by subsection (a)) shall apply to requests pending on, or filed after, December 31, 2000.

(2) SUBSTANTIAL COMPLIANCE.—Section 2642(g)(2) of such Code (as so added) shall apply to transfers subject to chapter 11 or 12 of the Internal Revenue Code of 1986 made after

December 31, 2000. No implication is intended with respect to the availability of relief from late elections or the application of a rule of substantial compliance on or before such date.

P.L. 107-16, §901(a)-(b), as amended by P.L. 111-312, §101(a)(1), provides [but see P.L. 112-240, §101(a)(1) and (3), above]:

SEC. 901. SUNSET OF PROVISIONS OF ACT.

(a) IN GENERAL.—All provisions of, and amendments made by, this Act shall not apply—

(1) to taxable, plan, or limitation years beginning after December 31, 2012, or

(2) in the case of title V, to estates of decedents dying, gifts made, or generation skipping transfers, after December 31, 2012.

(b) APPLICATION OF CERTAIN LAWS.—The Internal Revenue Code of 1986 and the Employee Retirement Income Security Act of 1974 shall be applied and administered to years, estates, gifts, and transfers described in subsection (a) as if the provisions and amendments described in subsection (a) had never been enacted.

Subchapter F—Other Definitions and Special Rules

[Sec. 2651]

SEC. 2651. GENERATION ASSIGNMENT.

[Sec. 2651(a)]

(a) IN GENERAL.—For purposes of this chapter, the generation to which any person (other than the transferor) belongs shall be determined in accordance with the rules set forth in this section.

[Sec. 2651(b)]

(b) LINEAL DESCENDANTS.—

(1) IN GENERAL.—An individual who is a lineal descendant of a grandparent of the transferor shall be assigned to that generation which results from comparing the number of generations between the grandparent and such individual with the number of generations between the grandparent and the transferor.

(2) ON SPOUSE'S SIDE.—An individual who is a lineal descendant of a grandparent of a spouse (or former spouse) of the transferor (other than such spouse) shall be assigned to that generation which results from comparing the number of generations between such grandparent and such individual with the number of generations between such grandparent and such spouse.

(3) TREATMENT OF LEGAL ADOPTIONS, ETC.—For purposes of this subsection—

(A) LEGAL ADOPTIONS.—A relationship by legal adoption shall be treated as a relationship by blood.

(B) RELATIONSHIPS BY HALF-BLOOD.—A relationship by the half-blood shall be treated as a relationship of the whole-blood.

Amendments

• 1988, Technical and Miscellaneous Revenue Act of 1988 (P.L. 100-647)

P.L. 100-647, §1014(g)(19):

Amended Code Sec. 2651(b)(2) by striking out "a spouse of the transferor" and inserting in lieu thereof "a spouse (or former spouse) of the transferor". **Effective** as if included in the provision of P.L. 99-514 to which it relates.

[Sec. 2651(c)]

(c) MARITAL RELATIONSHIP.—

(1) MARRIAGE TO TRANSFEROR.—An individual who has been married at any time to the transferor shall be assigned to the transferor's generation.

(2) MARRIAGE TO OTHER LINEAL DESCENDANTS.—An individual who has been married at any time to an individual described in subsection (b) shall be assigned to the generation of the individual so described.

[Sec. 2651(d)]

(d) PERSONS WHO ARE NOT LINEAL DESCENDANTS.—An individual who is not assigned to a generation by reason of the foregoing provisions of this section shall be assigned to a generation on the basis of the date of such individual's birth with—

(1) an individual born not more than 12½ years after the date of the birth of the transferor assigned to the transferor's generation,

(2) an individual born more than 12½ years but not more than 37½ years after the date of the birth of the transferor assigned to the first generation younger than the transferor, and

(3) similar rules for a new generation every 25 years.

[Sec. 2651(e)]

(e) SPECIAL RULE FOR PERSONS WITH A DECEASED PARENT.—

(1) IN GENERAL.—For purposes of determining whether any transfer is a generation-skipping transfer, if—

(A) an individual is a descendant of a parent of the transferor (or the transferor's spouse or former spouse), and

(B) such individual's parent who is a lineal descendant of the parent of the transferor (or the transferor's spouse or former spouse) is dead at the time the transfer (from which an interest of such individual is established or derived) is subject to a tax imposed by chapter 11 or 12 upon the transferor (and if there shall be more than 1 such time, then at the earliest such time),

such individual shall be treated as if such individual were a member of the generation which is 1 generation below the lower of the transferor's generation or the generation assignment of the youngest living ancestor of such individual who is also a descendant of the parent of the transferor (or the transferor's spouse or former spouse), and the generation assignment of any descendant of such individual shall be adjusted accordingly.

(2) LIMITED APPLICATION OF SUBSECTION TO COLLATERAL HEIRS.—This subsection shall not apply with respect to a transfer to any individual who is not a lineal descendant of the transferor (or the transferor's spouse or former spouse) if, at the time of the transfer, such transferor has any living lineal descendant.

Amendments

• 1997, Taxpayer Relief Act of 1997 (P.L. 105-34)

P.L. 105-34, § 511(a):

Amended Code Sec. 2651 by redesignating subsection (e) as subsection (f) and by inserting after subsection (d) a new subsection (e). **Effective** for terminations, distributions, and transfers occurring after 12-31-97.

[Sec. 2651(f)]

(f) OTHER SPECIAL RULES.—

(1) INDIVIDUALS ASSIGNED TO MORE THAN 1 GENERATION.—Except as provided in regulations, an individual who, but for this subsection, would be assigned to more than 1 generation shall be assigned to the youngest such generation.

(2) INTEREST THROUGH ENTITIES.—Except as provided in paragraph (3), if an estate, trust, partnership, corporation, or other entity has an interest in property, each individual having a beneficial interest in such entity shall be treated as having an interest in such property and shall be assigned to a generation under the foregoing provisions of this subsection.

(3) TREATMENT OF CERTAIN CHARITABLE ORGANIZATIONS AND GOVERNMENTAL ENTITIES.—Any—

(A) organization described in section 511(a)(2),

(B) charitable trust described in section 511(b)(2), and

(C) governmental entity,

shall be assigned to the transferor's generation.

Amendments

• 1997, Taxpayer Relief Act of 1997 (P.L. 105-34)

P.L. 105-34, § 511(a):

Amended Code Sec. 2651 by redesignating subsection (e) as subsection (f). **Effective** for terminations, distributions, and transfers occurring after 12-31-97.

• 1988, Technical and Miscellaneous Revenue Act of 1988 (P.L. 100-647)

P.L. 100-647, § 1014(g)(11):

Amended Code Sec. 2651(e)(3). **Effective** as if included in the provision of P.L. 99-514 to which it relates. Prior to amendment, Code Sec. 2651(e)(3) read as follows:

(3) TREATMENT OF CERTAIN CHARITABLE ORGANIZATIONS.—Any organization described in section 511(a)(2) and any charitable trust described in section 511(b)(2) shall be assigned to the transferor's generation.

• 1986, Tax Reform Act of 1986 (P.L. 99-514)

P.L. 99-514, § 1431(a):

Added Code Sec. 2651. **Effective**, generally, for any generation-skipping transfer (within the meaning of section 2611 of the Internal Revenue Code of 1986) made after 10-22-86. However, for special rules, see Act Sec. 1433(b)-(d) following Code Sec. 2601.

[Sec. 2652]

SEC. 2652. OTHER DEFINITIONS.

[Sec. 2652(a)]

(a) TRANSFEROR.—For purposes of this chapter—

(1) IN GENERAL.—Except as provided in this subsection or section 2653(a), the term "transferor" means—

(A) in the case of any property subject to the tax imposed by chapter 11, the decedent, and

(B) in the case of any property subject to the tax imposed by chapter 12, the donor.

An individual shall be treated as transferring any property with respect to which such individual is the transferor.

(2) GIFT-SPLITTING BY MARRIED COUPLES.—If, under section 2513, one-half of a gift is treated as made by an individual and one-half of such gift is treated as made by the spouse of such individual, such gift shall be so treated for purposes of this chapter.

(3) SPECIAL ELECTION FOR QUALIFIED TERMINABLE INTEREST PROPERTY.—In the case of—

(A) any trust with respect to which a deduction is allowed to the decedent under section 2056 by reason of subsection (b)(7) thereof, and

(B) any trust with respect to which a deduction to the donor spouse is allowed under section 2523 by reason of subsection (f) thereof,

the estate of the decedent or the donor spouse, as the case may be may elect to treat all of the property in such trust for purposes of this chapter as if the election to be treated as qualified terminable interest property had not been made.

Amendments

• 2010, Tax Relief, Unemployment Insurance Reauthorization, and Job Creation Act of 2010 (P.L. 111-312)

P.L. 111-312, §301(c), provides:

(c) SPECIAL ELECTION WITH RESPECT TO ESTATES OF DECEDENTS DYING IN 2010.—Notwithstanding subsection (a), in the case of an estate of a decedent dying after December 31, 2009, and before January 1, 2011, the executor (within the meaning of section 2203 of the Internal Revenue Code of 1986) may elect to apply such Code as though the amendments made by subsection (a) do not apply with respect to chapter 11 of such Code and with respect to property acquired or passing from such decedent (within the meaning of section 1014(b) of such Code). Such election shall be made at such time and in such manner as the Secretary of the Treasury or the Secretary's delegate shall provide. Such an election once made shall be revocable only with the consent of the Secretary of the Treasury or the Secretary's delegate. For purposes of section 2652(a)(1) of such Code, the determination of whether any property is subject to the tax imposed by such chapter 11 shall be made without regard to any election made under this subsection.

• 1988, Technical and Miscellaneous Revenue Act of 1988 (P.L. 100-647)

P.L. 100-647, §1014(g)(9)(A)-(B):

Amended Code Sec. 2652(a)(1) by striking out "a transfer of a kind" each place it appears and inserting in lieu thereof "any property", and by adding at the end thereof a new sentence. **Effective** as if included in the provision of P.L. 99-514 to which it relates.

P.L. 100-647, §1014(g)(14)(A)-(B):

Amended Code Sec. 2652(a)(3) by striking out "any property" in subparagraphs (A) and (B) and inserting in lieu thereof "any trust", and by striking out "may elect to treat such property" and inserting in lieu thereof "may elect to treat all of the property in such trust". **Effective** as if included in the provision of P.L. 99-514 to which it relates.

[Sec. 2652(b)]

(b) TRUST AND TRUSTEE.—

(1) TRUST.—The term "trust" includes any arrangement (other than an estate) which, although not a trust, has substantially the same effect as a trust.

(2) TRUSTEE.—In the case of an arrangement which is not a trust but which is treated as a trust under this subsection, the term "trustee" shall mean the person in actual or constructive possession of the property subject to such arrangement.

(3) EXAMPLES.—Arrangements to which this subsection applies include arrangements involving life estates and remainders, estates for years, and insurance and annuity contracts.

Amendments

• 1998, IRS Restructuring and Reform Act of 1998 (P.L. 105-206)

P.L. 105-206, §6013(a)(3):

Amended Code Sec. 2652(b)(1) by striking "section 646" and inserting "section 645". **Effective** as if included in the provision of P.L. 105-34 to which it relates [**effective** for estates of decedents dying after 8-5-97.—CCH].

P.L. 105-206, §6013(a)(4)(A):

Amended Code Sec. 2652(b)(1) [as amended by Act Sec. 6013(a)(3)]by striking the second sentence. **Effective** as if included in the provision of P.L. 105-34 to which it relates [**effective** for estates of decedents dying after 8-5-97.—CCH]. Prior to being stricken, the second sentence of Code Sec. 2652(b)(1) read as follows:

Such term shall not include any trust during any period the trust is treated as part of an estate under section 645.

• 1997, Taxpayer Relief Act of 1997 (P.L. 105-34)

P.L. 105-34, §1305(b):

Amended Code Sec. 2652(b)(1) by adding at the end a new sentence. **Effective** for estates of decedents dying after 8-5-97.

[Sec. 2652(c)]

(c) INTEREST.—

(1) IN GENERAL.—A person has an interest in property held in trust if (at the time the determination is made) such person—

(A) has a right (other than a future right) to receive income or corpus from the trust,

(B) is a permissible current recipient of income or corpus from the trust and is not described in section 2055(a), or

(C) is described in section 2055(a) and the trust is—

(i) a charitable remainder annuity trust,

(ii) a charitable remainder unitrust within the meaning of section 664, or

(iii) a pooled income fund within the meaning of section 642(c)(5).

(2) CERTAIN INTERESTS DISREGARDED.—For purposes of paragraph (1), an interest which is used primarily to postpone or avoid any tax imposed by this chapter shall be disregarded.

(3) CERTAIN SUPPORT OBLIGATIONS DISREGARDED.—The fact that income or corpus of the trust may be used to satisfy an obligation of support arising under State law shall be disregarded in determining whether a person has an interest in the trust, if—

(A) such use is discretionary, or

(B) such use is pursuant to the provisions of any State law substantially equivalent to the Uniform Gifts to Minors Act.

Amendments

• 1988, Technical and Miscellaneous Revenue Act of 1988 (P.L. 100-647)

P.L. 100-647, §1014(g)(6):

Amended Code Sec. 2652(c) by adding at the end thereof new paragraph (3). **Effective** as if included in the provision of P.L. 99-514 to which it relates.

P.L. 100-647, §1014(g)(8)(A)-(B):

Amended Code Sec. 2652(c)(2) by striking out "NOMINAL INTERESTS" in the paragraph heading and inserting in lieu thereof "INTERESTS", and by striking out "the tax" and inserting in lieu thereof "any tax". **Effective** as if included in the provision of P.L. 99-514 to which it relates.

• 1986, Tax Reform Act of 1986 (P.L. 99-514)

P.L. 99-514, §1431(a):

Added Code Sec. 2652. **Effective**, generally, for any generation-skipping transfer (within the meaning of section 2611 of the Internal Revenue Code of 1986) made after 10-22-86. However, for special rules, see Act Sec. 1433(b)-(d) following Code Sec. 2601.

[Sec. 2652(d)]

(d) EXECUTOR.—For purposes of this chapter, the term "executor" has the meaning given such term by section 2203.

Amendments

• 1988, Technical and Miscellaneous Revenue Act of 1988 (P.L. 100-647)

P.L. 100-647, §1014(g)(20):

Amended Code Sec. 2652 by adding at the end thereof new subsection (d). **Effective** as if included in the provision of P.L. 99-514 to which it relates.

[Sec. 2653]

SEC. 2653. TAXATION OF MULTIPLE SKIPS.

[Sec. 2653(a)]

(a) GENERAL RULE.—For purposes of this chapter, if—

(1) there is a generation-skipping transfer of any property, and

(2) immediately after such transfer such property is held in trust,

for purposes of applying this chapter (other than section 2651) to subsequent transfers from the portion of such trust attributable to such property, the trust will be treated as if the transferor of such property were assigned to the 1st generation above the highest generation of any person who has an interest in such trust immediately after the transfer.

[Sec. 2653(b)]

(b) TRUST RETAINS INCLUSION RATIO.—

(1) IN GENERAL.—Except as provided in paragraph (2), the provisions of subsection (a) shall not affect the inclusion ratio determined with respect to any trust. Under regulations prescribed by the Secretary, notwithstanding the preceding sentence, proper adjustment shall be made to the inclusion ratio with respect to such trust to take into account any tax under this chapter borne by such trust which is imposed by this chapter on the transfer described in subsection (a).

(2) SPECIAL RULE FOR POUR-OVER TRUST.—

(A) IN GENERAL.—If the generation-skipping transfer referred to in subsection (a) involves the transfer of property from 1 trust to another trust (hereinafter in this paragraph referred to as the "pour-over trust"), the inclusion ratio for the pour-over trust shall be determined by treating the nontax portion of such distribution as if it were a part of a GST exemption allocated to such trust.

(B) NONTAX PORTION.—For purposes of subparagraph (A), the nontax portion of any distribution is the amount of such distribution multiplied by the applicable fraction which applies to such distribution.

Amendments

• 1986, Tax Reform Act of 1986 (P.L. 99-514)

P.L. 99-514, §1431(a):

Added Code Sec. 2653. **Effective**, generally, for any generation-skipping transfer (within the meaning of section 2611 of the Internal Revenue Code of 1986) made after 10-22-86. However, for special rules, see Act Sec. 1433(b)-(d) following Code Sec. 2601.

[Sec. 2654]

SEC. 2654. SPECIAL RULES.

[Sec. 2654(a)]

(a) BASIS ADJUSTMENT.—

(1) IN GENERAL.—Except as provided in paragraph (2), if property is transferred in a generation-skipping transfer, the basis of such property shall be increased (but not above the fair market value of such property) by an amount equal to that portion of the tax imposed by section 2601 with respect to the transfer which is attributable to the excess of the fair market value of such property over its adjusted basis immediately before the transfer. The preceding shall be applied after any basis adjustment under section 1015 with respect to transfer.

(2) CERTAIN TRANSFERS AT DEATH.—If property is transferred in a taxable termination which occurs at the same time as and as a result of the death of an individual, the basis of such property shall be adjusted in a manner similar to the manner provided under section 1014(a); except that, if the inclusion ratio with respect to such property is less than 1, any increase or decrease in basis shall be limited by multiplying such increase or decrease (as the case may be) by the inclusion ratio.

Amendments

• 2014, Tax Technical Corrections Act of 2014 (P.L. 113-295)

P.L. 113-295, §221(a)(95)(B)(iii), Division A:

Amended Code Sec. 2654(a)(1) by striking "(computed without regard to section 2604)" following "section 2601". **Effective** generally 12-19-2014. For a special rule, see Act Sec. 221(b)(2), Division A, below.

P.L. 113-295, §221(b)(2), Division A, provides:

(2) SAVINGS PROVISION.—If—

(A) any provision amended or repealed by the amendments made by this section applied to—

(i) any transaction occurring before the date of the enactment of this Act,

(ii) any property acquired before such date of enactment, or

(iii) any item of income, loss, deduction, or credit taken into account before such date of enactment, and

(B) the treatment of such transaction, property, or item under such provision would (without regard to the amendments or repeals made by this section) affect the liability for tax for periods ending after date of enactment, nothing in the amendments or repeals made by this section shall be construed to affect the treatment of such transaction, property, or item for purposes of determining liability for tax for periods ending after such date of enactment.

• 1989, Omnibus Budget Reconciliation Act of 1989 (P.L. 101-239)

P.L. 101-239, §7811(j)(2):

Amended Code Sec. 2654(a)(1) by adding at the end thereof a new sentence. **Effective** as if included in the provision of P.L. 100-647 to which it relates.

• 1988, Technical and Miscellaneous Revenue Act of 1988 (P.L. 100-647)

P.L. 100-647, §1014(g)(12)(A)-(B):

Amended Code Sec. 2654(a)(2) by striking out "any increase" and inserting in lieu thereof "any increase or decrease", and by striking out "such increase" and inserting in lieu thereof "such increase or decrease (as the case may be)". **Effective** as if included in the provision of P.L. 99-514 to which it relates.

[Sec. 2654(b)]

(b) CERTAIN TRUSTS TREATED AS SEPARATE TRUSTS.—For purposes of this chapter—

(1) the portions of a trust attributable to transfers from different transferors shall be treated as separate trusts, and

(2) substantially separate and independent shares of different beneficiaries in a trust shall be treated as separate trusts.

Except as provided in the preceding sentence, nothing in this chapter shall be construed as authorizing a single trust to be treated as 2 or more trusts. For purposes of this subsection, a trust shall be treated as part of an estate during any period that the trust is so treated under section 645.

Amendments

• 1998, IRS Restructuring and Reform Act of 1998 (P.L. 105-206)

P.L. 105-206, §6013(a)(4)(B):

Amended Code Sec. 2654(b) by adding at the end a new sentence. **Effective** as if included in the provision of P.L. 105-34 to which it relates [**effective** for estates of decedents dying after 8-5-97.—CCH].

• 1988, Technical and Miscellaneous Revenue Act of 1988 (P.L. 100-647)

P.L. 100-647, §1014(g)(13):

Amended Code Sec. 2654(b). **Effective** as if included in the provision of P.L. 99-514 to which it relates. Prior to amendment, Code Sec. 2654(b) read as follows:

(b) SEPARATE SHARES TREATED AS SEPARATE TRUSTS.—Substantially separate and independent shares of different beneficiaries in a trust shall be treated as separate trusts.

[Sec. 2654(c)]

(c) DISCLAIMERS.—

For provisions relating to the effect of a qualified disclaimer for purposes of this chapter, see section 2518.

[Sec. 2654(d)]

(d) LIMITATION ON PERSONAL LIABILITY OF TRUSTEE.—A trustee shall not be personally liable for any increase in the tax imposed by section 2601 which is attributable to the fact that—

(1) section 2642(c) (relating to exemption of certain nontaxable gifts) does not apply to a transfer to the trust which was made during the life of the transferor and for which a gift tax return was not filed, or

(2) the inclusion ratio with respect to the trust is greater than the amount of such ratio as computed on the basis of the return on which was made (or was deemed made) an allocation of the GST exemption to property transferred to such trust.

The preceding sentence shall not apply if the trustee has knowledge of facts sufficient reasonably to conclude that a gift tax return was required to be filed or that the inclusion ratio was erroneous.

Amendments

• 1986, Tax Reform Act of 1986 (P.L. 99-514)

P.L. 99-514, §1431(a):

Added Code Sec. 2654. **Effective** for any generation-skipping transfer (within the meaning of section 2611 of the Internal Revenue Code of 1986) made after 10-22-86. However, for special rules, see Act Sec. 1433(b)-(d) following Code Sec. 2601.

Subchapter G—Administration

[Sec. 2661]

SEC. 2661. ADMINISTRATION.

Insofar as applicable and not inconsistent with the provisions of this chapter—

(1) except as provided in paragraph (2), all provisions of subtitle F (including penalties) applicable to the gift tax, to chapter 12, or to section 2501, are hereby made applicable in respect of the generation-skipping transfer tax, this chapter, or section 2601, as the case may be, and

(2) in the case of a generation-skipping transfer occurring at the same time as and as a result of the death of an individual, all provisions of subtitle F (including penalties) applicable to the estate tax, to chapter 11, or to section 2001 are hereby made applicable in respect of the generation-skipping transfer tax, this chapter, or section 2601 (as the case may be).

Amendments

• 1986, Tax Reform Act of 1986 (P.L. 99-514)

P.L. 99-514, §1431(a):

Added Code Sec. 2661. **Effective**, generally, for any generation-skipping transfer (within the meaning of section 2611 of the Internal Revenue Code of 1986) made after 10-22-86. However, for special rules, see Act Sec. 1433(b)-(d) following Code Sec. 2601.

[Sec. 2662]

SEC. 2662. RETURN REQUIREMENTS.

[Sec. 2662(a)]

(a) IN GENERAL.—The Secretary shall prescribe by regulations the person who is required to make the return with respect to the tax imposed by this chapter and the time by which any such return must be filed. To the extent practicable, such regulations shall provide that—

(1) the person who is required to make such return shall be the person liable under section 2603(a) for payment of such tax, and

(2) the return shall be filed—

(A) in the case of a direct skip (other than from a trust), on or before the date on which an estate or gift tax return is required to be filed with respect to the transfer, and

(B) in all other cases, on or before the 15th day of the 4th month after the close of the taxable year of the person required to make such return in which such transfer occurs.

Amendments

• 2010, Tax Relief, Unemployment Insurance Reauthorization, and Job Creation Act of 2010 (P.L. 111-312)

P.L. 111-312, §301(d)(2), provides:

(2) GENERATION-SKIPPING TAX.—In the case of any generation- skipping transfer made after December 31, 2009, and before the date of the enactment of this Act, the due date for filing any return under section 2662 of the Internal Revenue Code of 1986 (including any election required to be made on such a return) shall not be earlier than the date which is 9 months after the date of the enactment of this Act.

[Sec. 2662(b)]

(b) INFORMATION RETURNS.—The Secretary may by regulations require a return to be filed containing such information as he determines to be necessary for purposes of this chapter.

Amendments

• 1986, Tax Reform Act of 1986 (P.L. 99-514)

P.L. 99-514, §1431(a):

Added Code Sec. 2662. **Effective** for any generation-skipping transfer (within the meaning of section 2611 of the Internal Revenue Code of 1986) made after 10-22-86. However, for special rules, see Act Sec. 1433(b)-(d) following Code Sec. 2601.

[Sec. 2663]

SEC. 2663. REGULATIONS.

The Secretary shall prescribe such regulations as may be necessary or appropriate to carry out the purposes of this chapter, including—

(1) such regulations as may be necessary to coordinate the provisions of this chapter with the recapture tax imposed under section 2032A(c),

(2) regulations (consistent with the principles of chapters 11 and 12) providing for the application of this chapter in the case of transferors who are nonresidents not citizens of the United States, and

(3) regulations providing for such adjustments as may be necessary to the application of this chapter in the case of any arrangement which, although not a trust, is treated as a trust under section 2652(b).

Amendments

• 1988, Technical and Miscellaneous Revenue Act of 1988 (P.L. 100-647)

P.L. 100-647, §1014(g)(10):

Amended Code Sec. 2663 by striking out "and" at the end of paragraph (1), by striking out the period at the end of paragraph (2) and inserting in lieu thereof ", and", and by adding at the end thereof new paragraph (3). **Effective** as if included in the provision of P.L. 99-514 to which it relates.

• 1986, Tax Reform Act of 1986 (P.L. 99-514)

P.L. 99-514, §1431(a):

Added Code Sec. 2663. **Effective**, generally, for any generation-skipping transfer (within the meaning of section 2611 of the Internal Revenue Code of 1986) made after 10-22-86. However, for special rules, see Act Sec. 1433(b)-(d) following Code Sec. 2601.

[Sec. 2664]

SEC. 2664. TERMINATION.

This chapter shall not apply to generation-skipping transfers after December 31, 2009.

Amendments

• 2010, Tax Relief, Unemployment Insurance Reauthorization, and Job Creation Act of 2010 (P.L. 111-312)

P.L. 111-312, §301(a):

Amended Code Sec. 2664 to read as such provision would read if subtitle A of title V of the Economic Growth and Tax Relief Reconciliation Act of 2001 (P.L. 107-16) had never been enacted. **Effective** for estates of decedents dying, and transfers made, after 12-31-2009. For a special rule, see Act Sec. 301(c), below. Prior to amendment by P.L. 111-312, Code Sec. 2664 read as follows:

SEC. 2664. TERMINATION.

This chapter shall not apply to generation-skipping transfers after December 31, 2009.

P.L. 111-312, §301(c), provides:

(c) SPECIAL ELECTION WITH RESPECT TO ESTATES OF DECEDENTS DYING IN 2010.—Notwithstanding subsection (a), in the case of an estate of a decedent dying after December 31, 2009, and before January 1, 2011, the executor (within the meaning of section 2203 of the Internal Revenue Code of 1986) may elect to apply such Code as though the amendments made by subsection (a) do not apply with respect to chapter 11 of such Code and with respect to property acquired or passing from such decedent (within the meaning of section 1014(b) of such Code). Such election shall be made at such time and in such manner as the Secretary of the Treasury or the Secretary's delegate shall provide. Such an election once made shall be revocable only with the consent of the Secretary of the Treasury or the Secretary's delegate. For purposes of section 2652(a)(1) of such Code, the determination of whether any property is subject to the tax imposed by such chapter 11 shall be made without regard to any election made under this subsection.

P.L. 111-312, §304, provides:

SEC. 304. APPLICATION OF EGTRRA SUNSET TO THIS TITLE.

Section 901 of the Economic Growth and Tax Relief Reconciliation Act of 2001 shall apply to the amendments made by this title.

• 2001, Economic Growth and Tax Relief Reconciliation Act of 2001 (P.L. 107-16)

P.L. 107-16, §501(b):

Amended subchapter G of chapter 13 of subtitle B by adding at the end a new Code Sec. 2664. **Effective** for the estates of decedents dying, and generation-skipping transfers, after 12-31-2009.

P.L. 107-16, §901(a)-(b), as amended by P.L. 111-312, §101(a)(1), provides:

SEC. 901. SUNSET OF PROVISIONS OF ACT.

(a) IN GENERAL.—All provisions of, and amendments made by, this Act shall not apply—

(1) to taxable, plan, or limitation years beginning after December 31, 2012, or

(2) in the case of title V, to estates of decedents dying, gifts made, or generation skipping transfers, after December 31, 2012.

(b) APPLICATION OF CERTAIN LAWS.—The Internal Revenue Code of 1986 and the Employee Retirement Income Security Act of 1974 shall be applied and administered to years, estates, gifts, and transfers described in subsection (a) as if the provisions and amendments described in subsection (a) had never been enacted.

SPECIAL VALUATION RULES

TABLE OF CONTENTS

SUBTITLE B—ESTATE AND GIFT TAXES

Chapter 14—Special Valuation Rules

Chapter 15—Gifts and Bequests From Expatriates

SUBTITLE B—ESTATE AND GIFT TAXES

* * *

CHAPTER 14—SPECIAL VALUATION RULES

[Sec. 2701]

SEC. 2701. SPECIAL VALUATION RULES IN CASE OF TRANSFERS OF CERTAIN INTERESTS IN CORPORATIONS OR PARTNERSHIPS.

[Sec. 2701(a)]

(a) VALUATION RULES.—

(1) IN GENERAL.—Solely for purposes of determining whether a transfer of an interest in a corporation or partnership to (or for the benefit of) a member of the transferor's family is a gift (and the value of such transfer), the value of any right—

(A) which is described in subparagraph (A) or (B) of subsection (b)(1), and

(B) which is with respect to any applicable retained interest that is held by the transferor or an applicable family member immediately after the transfer,

shall be determined under paragraph (3). This paragraph shall not apply to the transfer of any interest for which market quotations are readily available (as of the date of transfer) on an established securities market.

(2) EXCEPTIONS FOR MARKETABLE RETAINED INTERESTS, ETC.—Paragraph (1) shall not apply to any right with respect to an applicable retained interest if—

(A) market quotations are readily available (as of the date of the transfer) for such interest on an established securities market,

(B) such interest is of the same class as the transferred interest, or

(C) such interest is proportionally the same as the transferred interest, without regard to nonlapsing differences in voting power (or, for a partnership, nonlapsing differences with respect to management and limitations on liability).

Subparagraph (C) shall not apply to any interest in a partnership if the transferor or an applicable family member has the right to alter the liability of the transferee of the transferred property. Except as provided by the Secretary, any difference described in subparagraph (C) which lapses by reason of any Federal or State law shall be treated as a nonlapsing difference for purposes of such subparagraph.

(3) VALUATION OF RIGHTS TO WHICH PARAGRAPH (1) APPLIES.—

(A) IN GENERAL.—The value of any right described in paragraph (1), other than a distribution right which consists of a right to receive a qualified payment, shall be treated as being zero.

(B) VALUATION OF CERTAIN QUALIFIED PAYMENTS.—If—

(i) any applicable retained interest confers a distribution right which consists of the right to a qualified payment, and

(ii) there are 1 or more liquidation, put, call, or conversion rights with respect to such interest,

the value of all such rights shall be determined as if each liquidation, put, call, or conversion right were exercised in the manner resulting in the lowest value being determined for all such rights.

(C) VALUATION OF QUALIFIED PAYMENTS WHERE NO LIQUIDATION, ETC. RIGHTS.—In the case of an applicable retained interest which is described in subparagraph (B)(i) but not subparagraph (B)(ii), the value of the distribution right shall be determined without regard to this section.

(4) MINIMUM VALUATION OF JUNIOR EQUITY.—

(A) IN GENERAL.—In the case of a transfer described in paragraph (1) of a junior equity interest in a corporation or partnership, such interest shall in no event be valued at an amount less than the value which would be determined if the total value of all of the junior equity interests in the entity were equal to 10 percent of the sum of—

(i) the total value of all of the equity interests in such entity, plus

(ii) the total amount of indebtedness of such entity to the transferor (or an applicable family member).

(B) DEFINITIONS.—For purposes of this paragraph—

(i) JUNIOR EQUITY INTEREST.—The term "junior equity interest" means common stock or, in the case of a partnership, any partnership interest under which the rights as to income and capital (or, to the extent provided in regulations, the rights as to either income or capital) are junior to the rights of all other classes of equity interests.

(ii) EQUITY INTEREST.—The term "equity interest" means stock or any interest as a partner, as the case may be.

Amendments

• 1996, Small Business Job Protection Act of 1996 (P.L. 104-188)

P.L. 104-188, §1702(f)(1)(A):

Amended Code Sec. 2701(a)(3) by adding at the end thereof a new subparagraph (C). **Effective** as if included in the provision of P.L. 101-508 to which it relates.

P.L. 104-188, §1702(f)(1)(B):

Amended Code Sec. 2701(a)(3)(B) by inserting "CERTAIN" before "QUALIFIED" in the section heading. **Effective** as if included in the provision of P.L. 101-508 to which it relates.

P.L. 104-188, §1702(f)(2):

Amended Code Sec. 2701(a)(4)(B)(i) by inserting "(or, to the extent provided in regulations, the rights as to either income or capital)" after "income and capital". **Effective** as if included in the provision of P.L. 101-508 to which it relates.

[Sec. 2701(b)]

(b) APPLICABLE RETAINED INTERESTS.—For purposes of this section—

(1) IN GENERAL.—The term "applicable retained interest" means any interest in an entity with respect to which there is—

(A) a distribution right, but only if, immediately before the transfer described in subsection (a)(1), the transferor and applicable family members hold (after application of subsection (e)(3)) control of the entity, or

(B) a liquidation, put, call, or conversion right.

(2) CONTROL.—For purposes of paragraph (1)—

(A) CORPORATIONS.—In the case of a corporation, the term "control" means the holding of at least 50 percent (by vote or value) of the stock of the corporation.

(B) PARTNERSHIPS.—In the case of a partnership, the term "control" means—

(i) the holding of at least 50 percent of the capital or profits interests in the partnership, or

(ii) in the case of a limited partnership, the holding of any interest as a general partner.

(C) APPLICABLE FAMILY MEMBER.—For purposes of this subsection, the term "applicable family member" includes any lineal descendant of any parent of the transferor or the transferor's spouse.

Amendments

• 1996, Small Business Job Protection Act of 1996 (P.L. 104-188)

P.L. 104-188, §1702(f)(3)(A):

Amended Code Sec. 2701(b)(2) by adding at the end a new subparagraph (C). **Effective** as if included in the provision of P.L. 101-508 to which it relates.

[Sec. 2701(c)]

(c) DISTRIBUTION AND OTHER RIGHTS; QUALIFIED PAYMENTS.—For purposes of this section—

(1) DISTRIBUTION RIGHT.—

(A) IN GENERAL.—The term "distribution right" means—

(i) a right to distributions from a corporation with respect to its stock, and

(ii) a right to distributions from a partnership with respect to a partner's interest in the partnership.

(B) EXCEPTIONS.—The term "distribution right" does not include—

(i) a right to distributions with respect to any interest which is junior to the rights of the transferred interest,

(ii) any liquidation, put, call, or conversion right, or

(iii) any right to receive any guaranteed payment described in section 707(c) of a fixed amount.

(2) LIQUIDATION, ETC. RIGHTS.—

(A) IN GENERAL.—The term "liquidation, put, call, or conversion right" means any liquidation, put, call, or conversion right, or any similar right, the exercise or nonexercise of which affects the value of the transferred interest.

(B) EXCEPTION FOR FIXED RIGHTS.—

(i) IN GENERAL.—The term "liquidation, put, call, or conversion right" does not include any right which must be exercised at a specific time and at a specific amount.

(ii) TREATMENT OF CERTAIN RIGHTS.—If a right is assumed to be exercised in a particular manner under subsection (a)(3)(B), such right shall be treated as so exercised for purposes of clause (i).

(C) EXCEPTION FOR CERTAIN RIGHTS TO CONVERT.—The term "liquidation, put, call, or conversion right" does not include any right which—

(i) is a right to convert into a fixed number (or a fixed percentage) of shares of the same class of stock in a corporation as the transferred stock in such corporation under subsection (a)(1) (or stock which would be of the same class but for nonlapsing differences in voting power),

(ii) is nonlapsing,

(iii) is subject to proportionate adjustments for splits, combinations, reclassifications, and similar changes in the capital stock, and

(iv) is subject to adjustments similar to the adjustments under subsection (d) for accumulated but unpaid distributions.

A rule similar to the rule of the preceding sentence shall apply for partnerships.

(3) QUALIFIED PAYMENT.—

(A) IN GENERAL.—Except as otherwise provided in this paragraph, the term "qualified payment" means any dividend payable on a periodic basis under any cumulative preferred stock (or a comparable payment under any partnership interest) to the extent that such dividend (or comparable payment) is determined at a fixed rate.

(B) TREATMENT OF VARIABLE RATE PAYMENTS.—For purposes of subparagraph (A), a payment shall be treated as fixed as to rate if such payment is determined at a rate which bears a fixed relationship to a specified market interest rate.

(C) ELECTIONS.—

(i) IN GENERAL.—Payments under any interest held by a transferor which (without regard to this subparagraph) are qualified payments shall be treated as qualified payments unless the transferor elects not to treat such payments as qualified payments. Payments described in the preceding sentence which are held by an applicable family member shall be treated as qualified payments only if such member elects to treat such payments as qualified payments.

(ii) ELECTION TO HAVE INTEREST TREATED AS QUALIFIED PAYMENT.—A transferor or applicable family member holding any distribution right which (without regard to this subparagraph) is not a qualified payment may elect to treat such right as a qualified payment, to be paid in the amounts and at the times specified in such election. The preceding sentence shall apply only to the extent that the amounts and times so specified are not inconsistent with the underlying legal instrument giving rise to such right.

(iii) ELECTIONS IRREVOCABLE.—Any election under this subparagraph with respect to an interest shall, once made, be irrevocable.

Amendments

• 1996, Small Business Job Protection Act of 1996 (P.L. 104-188)

P.L. 104-188, §1702(f)(4):

Amended Code Sec. 2701(c)(1)(B)(i). **Effective** as if included in the provision of P.L. 101-508 to which it relates. For a special rule, see Act Sec. 1702(f)(5)(C), below. Prior to amendment, Code Sec. 2701(c)(1)(B)(i) read as follows:

(i) a right to distributions with respect to any junior equity interest (as defined in subsection (a)(4)(B)(i));

P.L. 104-188, §1702(f)(5)(A):

Amended Code Sec. 2701(c)(3)(C)(i). **Effective** as if included in the provision of P.L. 101-508 to which it relates. For a special rule, see Act Sec. 1702(f)(5)(C), below. Prior to amendment, Code Sec. 2701(c)(3)(C)(i) read as follows:

(i) WAIVER OF QUALIFIED PAYMENT TREATMENT.—A transferor or applicable family member may elect with respect to payments under any interest specified in such election to treat such payments as payments which are not qualified payments.

P.L. 104-188, §1702(f)(5)(B):

Amended the first sentence of Code Sec. 2701(c)(3)(C)(ii). **Effective** as if included in the provision of P.L. 101-508 to which it relates. For a special rule, see Act Sec. 1702(f)(5)(C), below. Prior to amendment, the first sentence of Code Sec. 2701(c)(3)(C)(ii) read as follows:

A transferor or any applicable family member may elect to treat any distribution right as a qualified payment, to be paid in the amounts and at the times specified in such election.

P.L. 104-188, §1702(f)(5)(C), provides:

(C) The time for making an election under the second sentence of section 2701(c)(3)(C)(i) of the Internal Revenue Code of 1986 (as amended by subparagraph (A)) shall not expire before the due date (including extensions) for filing the transferor's return of the tax imposed by section 2501 of such Code for the first calendar year ending after August 20, 1996.

[Sec. 2701(d)]

(d) TRANSFER TAX TREATMENT OF CUMULATIVE BUT UNPAID DISTRIBUTIONS.—

(1) IN GENERAL.—If a taxable event occurs with respect to any distribution right to which subsection (a)(3)(B) or (C) applied, the following shall be increased by the amount determined under paragraph (2):

(A) The taxable estate of the transferor in the case of a taxable event described in paragraph (3)(A)(i).

(B) The taxable gifts of the transferor for the calendar year in which the taxable event occurs in the case of a taxable event described in paragraph (3)(A)(ii) or (iii).

(2) AMOUNT OF INCREASE.—

(A) IN GENERAL.—The amount of the increase determined under this paragraph shall be the excess (if any) of—

(i) the value of the qualified payments payable during the period beginning on the date of the transfer under subsection (a)(1) and ending on the date of the taxable event determined as if—

(I) all such payments were paid on the date payment was due, and

(II) all such payments were reinvested by the transferor as of the date of payment at a yield equal to the discount rate used in determining the value of the applicable retained interest described in subsection (a)(1), over

(ii) the value of such payments paid during such period computed under clause (i) on the basis of the time when such payments were actually paid.

(B) LIMITATION ON AMOUNT OF INCREASE.—

(i) IN GENERAL.—The amount of the increase under subparagraph (A) shall not exceed the applicable percentage of the excess (if any) of—

(I) the value (determined as of the date of the taxable event) of all equity interests in the entity which are junior to the applicable retained interest, over

(II) the value of such interests (determined as of the date of the transfer to which subsection (a)(1) applied).

(ii) APPLICABLE PERCENTAGE.—For purposes of clause (i), the applicable percentage is the percentage determined by dividing—

(I) the number of shares in the corporation held (as of the date of the taxable event) by the transferor which are applicable retained interests of the same class, by

(II) the total number of shares in such corporation (as of such date) which are of the same class as the class described in subclause (I).

A similar percentage shall be determined in the case of interests in a partnership.

(iii) DEFINITION.—For purposes of this subparagraph, the term "equity interest" has the meaning given such term by subsection (a)(4)(B).

(C) GRACE PERIOD.—For purposes of subparagraph (A), any payment of any distribution during the 4-year period beginning on its due date shall be treated as having been made on such due date.

(3) TAXABLE EVENTS.—For purposes of this subsection—

(A) IN GENERAL.—The term "taxable event" means any of the following:

(i) The death of the transferor if the applicable retained interest conferring the distribution right is includible in the estate of the transferor.

(ii) The transfer of such applicable retained interest.

(iii) At the election of the taxpayer, the payment of any qualified payment after the period described in paragraph (2)(C), but only with respect to such payment.

(B) EXCEPTION WHERE SPOUSE IS TRANSFEREE.—

(i) DEATHTIME TRANSFERS.—Subparagraph (A)(i) shall not apply to any interest includible in the gross estate of the transferor if a deduction with respect to such interest is allowable under section 2056 or 2106(a)(3).

(ii) LIFETIME TRANSFERS.—A transfer to the spouse of the transferor shall not be treated as a taxable event under subparagraph (A)(ii) if such transfer does not result in a taxable gift by reason of—

(I) any deduction allowed under section 2523, or the exclusion under section 2503(b), or

(II) consideration for the transfer provided by the spouse.

(iii) SPOUSE SUCCEEDS TO TREATMENT OF TRANSFEROR.—If an event is not treated as a taxable event by reason of this subparagraph, the transferee spouse or surviving spouse (as the case may be) shall be treated in the same manner as the transferor in applying this subsection with respect to the interest involved.

(4) SPECIAL RULES FOR APPLICABLE FAMILY MEMBERS.—

(A) FAMILY MEMBER TREATED IN SAME MANNER AS TRANSFEROR.—For purposes of this subsection, an applicable family member shall be treated in the same manner as the transferor with respect to any distribution right retained by such family member to which subsection (a)(3)(B) or (C) applied.

(B) TRANSFER TO APPLICABLE FAMILY MEMBER.—In the case of a taxable event described in paragraph (3)(A)(ii) involving the transfer of an applicable retained interest to an applicable family member (other than the spouse of the transferor), the applicable family member shall be treated in the same manner as the transferor in applying this subsection to distributions accumulating with respect to such interest after such taxable event.

(C) TRANSFER TO TRANSFERORS.—In the case of a taxable event described in paragraph (3)(A)(ii) involving a transfer of an applicable retained interest from an applicable family member to a transferor, this subsection shall continue to apply to the transferor during any period the transferor holds such interest.

(5) TRANSFER TO INCLUDE TERMINATION.—For purposes of this subsection, any termination of an interest shall be treated as a transfer.

Amendments

• 1996, Small Business Job Protection Act of 1996 (P.L. 104-188)

P.L. 104-188, §1702(f)(1)(C):

Amended Code Sec. 2701(d)(1) and (d)(4)[A] by striking "subsection (a)(3)(B)" and inserting "subsection (a)(3)(B) or (C)". **Effective** as if included in the provision of P.L. 101-508 to which it relates.

P.L. 104-188, §1702(f)(6):

Amended Code Sec. 2701(d)(3)(A)(iii) by striking "the period ending on the date of" before "such payment". **Effective** as if included in the provision of P.L. 101-508 to which it relates.

P.L. 104-188, §1702(f)(7):

Amended Code Sec. 2701(d)(3)(B)(ii)(I) by inserting "or the exclusion under section 2503(b)," after "section 2523,". **Effective** as if included in the provision of P.L. 101-508 to which it relates.

P.L. 104-188, §1702(f)(9):

Amended Code Sec. 2701(d)(4) by adding at the end thereof a new subparagraph (C). **Effective** as if included in the provision of P.L. 101-508 to which it relates.

[Sec. 2701(e)]

(e) OTHER DEFINITIONS AND RULES.—For purposes of this section—

(1) MEMBER OF THE FAMILY.—The term "member of the family" means, with respect to any transferor—

(A) the transferor's spouse,

(B) a lineal descendant of the transferor or the transferor's spouse, and

(C) the spouse of any such descendant.

(2) APPLICABLE FAMILY MEMBER.—The term "applicable family member" means, with respect to any transferor—

(A) the transferor's spouse,

(B) an ancestor of the transferor or the transferor's spouse, and

(C) the spouse of any such ancestor.

(3) ATTRIBUTION OF INDIRECT HOLDINGS AND TRANSFERS.—An individual shall be treated as holding any interest to the extent such interest is held indirectly by such individual through a corporation, partnership, trust, or other entity. If any individual is treated as holding any interest by reason of the preceding sentence, any transfer which results in such interest being treated as no longer held by such individual shall be treated as a transfer of such interest.

(4) EFFECT OF ADOPTION.—A relationship by legal adoption shall be treated as a relationship by blood.

(5) CERTAIN CHANGES TREATED AS TRANSFERS.—Except as provided in regulations, a contribution to capital or a redemption, recapitalization, or other change in the capital structure of a corporation or partnership shall be treated as a transfer of an interest in such entity to which this section applies if the taxpayer or an applicable family member—

(A) receives an applicable retained interest in such entity pursuant to such transaction, or

(B) under regulations, otherwise holds, immediately after such transaction, an applicable retained interest in such entity.

This paragraph shall not apply to any transaction (other than a contribution to capital) if the interests in the entity held by the transferor, applicable family members, and members of the transferor's family before and after the transaction are substantially identical.

(6) ADJUSTMENTS.—Under regulations prescribed by the Secretary, if there is any subsequent transfer, or inclusion in the gross estate, of any applicable retained interest which was valued under the rules of subsection (a), appropriate adjustments shall be made for purposes of chapter 11, 12, or 13 to reflect the increase in the amount of any prior taxable gift made by the transferor or decedent by reason of such valuation or to reflect the application of subsection (d).

(7) TREATMENT AS SEPARATE INTERESTS.—The Secretary may by regulation provide that any applicable retained interest shall be treated as 2 or more separate interests for purposes of this section.

Amendments

• 1996, Small Business Job Protection Act of 1996 (P.L. 104-188)

P.L. 104-188, §1702(f)(3)(B)(i)-(ii):

Amended Code Sec. 2701(e)(3) by striking subparagraph (B), and by striking so much of paragraph (3) as precedes "shall be treated as holding" and inserting "(3) ATTRIBUTION OF INDIRECT HOLDINGS AND TRANSFERS.—An individual". **Effective** as if included in the provision of P.L. 101-508 to which it relates. Prior to amendment, Code Sec. 2701(e)(3) read as follows:

(3) ATTRIBUTION RULES.—

(A) INDIRECT HOLDINGS AND TRANSFERS.—An individual shall be treated as holding any interest to the extent such interest is held indirectly by such individual through a corporation, partnership, trust, or other entity. If any individual is treated as holding any interest by reason of the preceding sentence, any transfer which results in such interest being treated as no longer held by such individual shall be treated as a transfer of such interest.

(B) CONTROL.—For purposes of subsections (b)(1), an individual shall be treated as holding any interest held by the individual's brothers, sisters, or lineal descendants.

P.L. 104-188, §1702(f)(8)(A)-(B):

Amended Code Sec. 2701(e)(5) by striking "such contribution to capital or such redemption, recapitalization, or other change" in subparagraph (A) and inserting "such transaction", and by striking "the transfer" in subparagraph (B) and inserting "such transaction". **Effective** as if included in the provision of P.L. 101-508 to which it relates.

P.L. 104-188, §1702(f)(10):

Amended Code Sec. 2701(e)(6) by inserting "or to reflect the application of subsection (d)" before the period at the end thereof. **Effective** as if included in the provision of P.L. 101-508 to which it relates.

• 1990, Omnibus Budget Reconciliation Act of 1990 (P.L. 101-508)

P.L. 101-508, §11602(a):

Amended Subtitle B by adding new Code Sec. 2701. For the **effective** date, see Act Sec. 11602(e)(1), below.

P.L. 101-508, §11602(e)(1), provides:

(e) EFFECTIVE DATES.—

(1) SUBSECTION (a).—

(A) IN GENERAL.—The amendments made by subsection (a)—

(i) to the extent such amendments relate to sections 2701 and 2702 of the Internal Revenue Code of 1986 (as added by such amendments), shall apply to transfers after October 8, 1990,

(ii) to the extent such amendments relate to section 2703 of such Code (as so added), shall apply to—

(I) agreements, options, rights, or restrictions entered into or granted after October 8, 1990, and

(II) agreements, options, rights, or restrictions which are substantially modified after October 8, 1990, and

(iii) to the extent such amendments relate to section 2704 of such Code (as so added), shall apply to restrictions or rights (or limitations on rights) created after October 8, 1990.

(B) EXCEPTION.—For purposes of subparagraph (A)(i), with respect to property transferred before October 9, 1990—

(i) any failure to exercise a right of conversion,

(ii) any failure to pay dividends, and

(iii) any failure to exercise other rights specified in regulations,

shall not be treated as a subsequent transfer.

[Sec. 2702]

SEC. 2702. SPECIAL VALUATION RULES IN CASE OF TRANSFERS OF INTERESTS IN TRUSTS.

[Sec. 2702(a)]

(a) VALUATION RULES.—

(1) IN GENERAL.—Solely for purposes of determining—whether a transfer of an interest in trust to (or for the benefit of) a member of the transferor's family is a gift (and the value of such transfer), the value of any interest in such trust retained by the transferor or any applicable family member (as defined in section 2701(e)(2)) shall be determined as provided in paragraph (2).

(2) VALUATION OF RETAINED INTERESTS.—

(A) IN GENERAL.—The value of any retained interest which is not a qualified interest shall be treated as being zero.

(B) VALUATION OF QUALIFIED INTEREST.—The value of any retained interest which is a qualified interest shall be determined under section 7520.

(3) EXCEPTIONS.—

(A) IN GENERAL.—This subsection shall not apply to any transfer—

(i) if such transfer is an incomplete gift,

(ii) if such transfer involves the transfer of an interest in trust all the property in which consists of a residence to be used as a personal residence by persons holding term interests in such trust, or

(iii) to the extent that regulations provide that such transfer is not inconsistent with the purposes of this section.

(B) INCOMPLETE GIFT.—For purposes of subparagraph (A), the term "incomplete gift" means any transfer which would not be treated as a gift whether or not consideration was received for such transfer.

Amendments

• 1996, Small Business Job Protection Act of 1996 (P.L. 104-188)

P.L. 104-188, §1702(f)(11)(A)(i)-(iv):

Amended Code Sec. 2702(a)(3)(A) by striking "to the extent" and inserting "if" in clause (i), by striking "or" at the end of clause (i), by striking the period at the end of clause (ii) and inserting ", or", and by adding at the end thereof a new clause (iii). **Effective** as if included in the provision of P.L. 101-508 to which it relates.

P.L. 104-188, §1702(f)(11)(B)(i):

Amended Code Sec. 2702(a)(3) by striking "incomplete transfer" each place it appears and inserting "incomplete gift". **Effective** as if included in the provision of P.L. 101-508 to which it relates.

P.L. 104-188, §1702(f)(11)(B)(ii):

Amended Code Sec. 2702(a)(3)(B) by striking "INCOMPLETE TRANSFER" in the heading and inserting "INCOMPLETE GIFT". **Effective** as if included in the provision of P.L. 101-508 to which it relates.

[Sec. 2702(b)]

(b) QUALIFIED INTEREST.—For purposes of this section, the term "qualified interest" means—

(1) any interest which consists of the right to receive fixed amounts payable not less frequently than annually,

(2) any interest which consists of the right to receive amounts which are payable not less frequently than annually and are a fixed percentage of the fair market value of the property in the trust (determined annually), and

(3) any noncontingent remainder interest if all of the other interests in the trust consist of interests described in paragraph (1) or (2).

[Sec. 2702(c)]

(c) CERTAIN PROPERTY TREATED AS HELD IN TRUST.—For purposes of this section—

(1) IN GENERAL.—The transfer of an interest in property with respect to which there is 1 or more term interests shall be treated as a transfer of an interest in a trust.

(2) JOINT PURCHASES.—If 2 or more members of the same family acquire interests in any property described in paragraph (1) in the same transaction (or a series of related transactions), the person (or persons) acquiring the term interests in such property shall be treated as having acquired the entire property and then transferred to the other persons the interests acquired by such other persons in the transaction (or series of transactions). Such transfer shall be treated as made in exchange for the consideration (if any) provided by such other persons for the acquisition of their interests in such property.

(3) TERM INTEREST.—The term "term interest" means—

(A) a life interest in property, or

(B) an interest in property for a term of years.

(4) VALUATION RULE FOR CERTAIN TERM INTERESTS.—If the nonexercise of rights under a term interest in tangible property would not have a substantial effect on the valuation of the remainder interest in such property—

(A) subparagraph (A) of subsection (a)(2) shall not apply to such term interest, and

(B) the value of such term interest for purposes of applying subsection (a)(1) shall be the amount which the holder of the term interest establishes as the amount for which such interest could be sold to an unrelated third party.

[Sec. 2702(d)]

(d) TREATMENT OF TRANSFERS OF INTERESTS IN PORTION OF TRUST.—In the case of a transfer of an income or remainder interest with respect to a specified portion of the property in a trust, only such portion shall be taken into account in applying this section to such transfer.

[Sec. 2702(e)]

(e) MEMBER OF THE FAMILY.—For purposes of this section, the term "member of the family" shall have the meaning given such term by section 2704(c)(2).

Amendments

• 1990, Omnibus Budget Reconciliation Act of 1990 (P.L. 101-508)

P.L. 101-508, §11602(a):

Amended Subtitle B by adding new Code Sec. 2702. For the **effective** date, see Act Sec. 11602(e)(1), below.

P.L. 101-508, §11602(e)(1), provides:

(e) EFFECTIVE DATES.—

(1) SUBSECTION (a).—

(A) IN GENERAL.—The amendments made by subsection (a)—

(i) to the extent such amendments relate to sections 2701 and 2702 of the Internal Revenue Code of 1986 (as added by such amendments), shall apply to transfers after October 8, 1990,

(ii) to the extent such amendments relate to section 2703 of such Code (as so added), shall apply to—

(I) agreements, options, rights, or restrictions entered into or granted after October 8, 1990, and

(II) agreements, options, rights, or restrictions which are substantially modified after October 8, 1990, and

(iii) to the extent such amendments relate to section 2704 of such Code (as so added), shall apply to restrictions or rights (or limitations on rights) created after October 8, 1990.

(B) EXCEPTION.—For purposes of subparagraph (A)(i), with respect to property transferred before October 9, 1990—

(i) any failure to exercise a right of conversion,

(ii) any failure to pay dividends, and

(iii) any failure to exercise other rights specified in regulations,

shall not be treated as a subsequent transfer.

[Sec. 2703]

SEC. 2703. CERTAIN RIGHTS AND RESTRICTIONS DISREGARDED.

[Sec. 2703(a)]

(a) GENERAL RULE.—For purposes of this subtitle, the value of any property shall be determined without regard to—

(1) any option, agreement, or other right to acquire or use the property at a price less than the fair market value of the property (without regard to such option, agreement, or right), or

(2) any restriction on the right to sell or use such property.

[Sec. 2703(b)]

(b) EXCEPTIONS.—Subsection (a) shall not apply to any option, agreement, right, or restriction which meets each of the following requirements:

(1) It is a bona fide business arrangement.

(2) It is not a device to transfer such property to members of the decedent's family for less than full and adequate consideration in money or money's worth.

(3) Its terms are comparable to similar arrangements entered into by persons in an arms' length transaction.

Amendments

• 1990, Omnibus Budget Reconciliation Act of 1990 (P.L. 101-508)

P.L. 101-508, §11602(a):

Amended Subtitle B by adding new Code Sec. 2703. For the **effective** date, see Act Sec. 11602(e)(1), below.

P.L. 101-508, §11602(e)(1), provides:

(e) EFFECTIVE DATES.—

(1) SUBSECTION (a).—

(A) IN GENERAL.—The amendments made by subsection (a)—

(i) to the extent such amendments relate to sections 2701 and 2702 of the Internal Revenue Code of 1986 (as added by such amendments), shall apply to transfers after October 8, 1990,

(ii) to the extent such amendments relate to section 2703 of such Code (as so added), shall apply to—

(I) agreements, options, rights, or restrictions entered into or granted after October 8, 1990, and

(II) agreements, options, rights, or restrictions which are substantially modified after October 8, 1990, and

(iii) to the extent such amendments relate to section 2704 of such Code (as so added), shall apply to restrictions or rights (or limitations on rights) created after October 8, 1990.

(B) EXCEPTION.—For purposes of subparagraph (A)(i), with respect to property transferred before October 9, 1990—

(i) any failure to exercise a right of conversion,

(ii) any failure to pay dividends, and

(iii) any failure to exercise other rights specified in regulations,

shall not be treated as a subsequent transfer.

[Sec. 2704]

SEC. 2704. TREATMENT OF CERTAIN LAPSING RIGHTS AND RESTRICTIONS.

[Sec. 2704(a)]

(a) TREATMENT OF LAPSED VOTING OR LIQUIDATION RIGHTS.—

(1) IN GENERAL.—For purposes of this subtitle, if—

(A) there is a lapse of any voting or liquidation right in a corporation or partnership, and

(B) the individual holding such right immediately before the lapse and members of such individual's family hold, both before and after the lapse, control of the entity,

such lapse shall be treated as a transfer by such individual by gift, or a transfer which is includible in the gross estate of the decedent, whichever is applicable, in the amount determined under paragraph (2).

(2) AMOUNT OF TRANSFER.—For purposes of paragraph (1), the amount determined under this paragraph is the excess (if any) of—

(A) the value of all interests in the entity held by the individual described in paragraph (1) immediately before the lapse (determined as if the voting and liquidation rights were nonlapsing), over

(B) the value of such interests immediately after the lapse.

(3) SIMILAR RIGHTS.—The Secretary may by regulations apply this subsection to rights similar to voting and liquidation rights.

[Sec. 2704(b)]

(b) CERTAIN RESTRICTIONS ON LIQUIDATION DISREGARDED.—

(1) IN GENERAL.—For purposes of this subtitle, if—

(A) there is a transfer of an interest in a corporation or partnership to (or for the benefit of) a member of the transferor's family, and

(B) the transferor and members of the transferor's family hold, immediately before the transfer, control of the entity,

any applicable restriction shall be disregarded in determining the value of the transferred interest.

(2) APPLICABLE RESTRICTION.—For purposes of this subsection, the term "applicable restriction" means any restriction—

(A) which effectively limits the ability of the corporation or partnership to liquidate, and

(B) with respect to which either of the following applies:

(i) The restriction lapses, in whole or in part, after the transfer referred to in paragraph (1).

(ii) The transferor or any member of the transferor's family, either alone or collectively, has the right after such transfer to remove, in whole or in part, the restriction.

(3) EXCEPTIONS.—The term "applicable restriction" shall not include—

(A) any commercially reasonable restriction which arises as part of any financing by the corporation or partnership with a person who is not related to the transferor or transferee, or a member of the family of either, or

(B) any restriction imposed, or required to be imposed, by any Federal or State law.

(4) OTHER RESTRICTIONS.—The Secretary may by regulations provide that other restrictions shall be disregarded in determining the value of the transfer of any interest in a corporation or partnership to a member of the transferor's family if such restriction has the effect of reducing the value of the transferred interest for purposes of this subtitle but does not ultimately reduce the value of such interest to the transferee.

[Sec. 2704(c)]

(c) DEFINITIONS AND SPECIAL RULES.—For purposes of this section—

(1) CONTROL.—The term "control" has the meaning given such term by section 2701(b)(2).

(2) MEMBER OF THE FAMILY.—The term "member of the family" means, with respect to any individual—

(A) such individual's spouse,

(B) any ancestor or lineal descendant of such individual or such individual's spouse,

(C) any brother or sister of the individual, and

(D) any spouse of any individual described in subparagraph (B) or (C).

(3) ATTRIBUTION.—The rule of section 2701(e)(3) shall apply for purposes of determining the interests held by any individual.

Amendments

• 1996, Small Business Job Protection Act of 1996 (P.L. 104-188)

P.L. 104-188, §1702(f)(3)(C):

Amended Code Sec. 2704(c)(3) by striking "section 2701(e)(3)(A)" and inserting "section 2701(e)(3)". **Effective** as if included in the provision of P.L. 101-508 to which it relates.

• 1990, Omnibus Budget Reconciliation Act of 1990 (P.L. 101-508)

P.L. 101-508, §11602(a):

Amended Subtitle B by adding new Code Sec. 2704. For the **effective** date, see Act Sec. 11602(e)(1), below.

P.L. 101-508, §11602(e)(1), provides:

(e) EFFECTIVE DATES.—

(1) SUBSECTION (a).—

(A) IN GENERAL.—The amendments made by subsection (a)—

(i) to the extent such amendments relate to sections 2701 and 2702 of the Internal Revenue Code of 1986 (as added by such amendments), shall apply to transfers after October 8, 1990,

(ii) to the extent such amendments relate to section 2703 of such Code (as so added), shall apply to—

(I) agreements, options, rights, or restrictions entered into or granted after October 8, 1990, and

(II) agreements, options, rights, or restrictions which are substantially modified after October 8, 1990, and

(iii) to the extent such amendments relate to section 2704 of such Code (as so added), shall apply to restrictions or rights (or limitations on rights) created after October 8, 1990.

(B) EXCEPTION.—For purposes of subparagraph (A)(i), with respect to property transferred before October 9, 1990—

(i) any failure to exercise a right of conversion,

(ii) any failure to pay dividends, and

(iii) any failure to exercise other rights specified in regulations,

shall not be treated as a subsequent transfer.

PROCEDURE and ADMINISTRATION

Selected Code Sections: Estate and Gift Taxes and Related Income Tax Provisions

TABLE OF CONTENTS

SUBTITLE F—PROCEDURE AND ADMINISTRATION

Chapter 61—Information and Returns

SUBCHAPTER A. RETURNS AND RECORDS

PART VI—EXTENSION OF TIME FOR FILING RETURNS

PART VII—PLACE FOR FILING RETURNS OR OTHER DOCUMENTS

SUBCHAPTER B. MISCELLANEOUS PROVISIONS

Chapter 62—Time and Place for Paying Tax

SUBCHAPTER A. PLACE AND DUE DATE FOR PAYMENT OF TAX

SUBCHAPTER B. EXTENSIONS OF TIME FOR PAYMENT

Chapter 63—Assessment

SUBCHAPTER A. IN GENERAL

SUBCHAPTER B. DEFICIENCY PROCEDURES IN THE CASE OF INCOME, ESTATE, GIFT, AND CERTAIN EXCISE TAXES

Chapter 64—Collection

SUBCHAPTER A. GENERAL PROVISIONS

SUBCHAPTER B. RECEIPT OF PAYMENT

SUBCHAPTER B. INTEREST ON OVERPAYMENTS

SUBCHAPTER C. DETERMINATION OF INTEREST RATE; COMPOUNDING OF INTEREST

SUBCHAPTER D. NOTICE REQUIREMENTS

Chapter 68—Additions to the Tax, Additional Amounts, and Assessable Penalties

SUBCHAPTER A. ADDITIONS TO THE TAX AND ADDITIONAL AMOUNTS

PART I—GENERAL PROVISIONS

PART II—ACCURACY-RELATED AND FRAUD PENALTIES

PART III—APPLICABLE RULES

SUBCHAPTER B. ASSESSABLE PENALTIES

PART I—GENERAL PROVISIONS

Chapter 70—Jeopardy, Receiverships, Etc.

SUBCHAPTER A. JEOPARDY

PART II—JEOPARDY ASSESSMENTS

SUBCHAPTER B. RECEIVERSHIPS, ETC.

Chapter 71—Transferees and Fiduciaries

Chapter 73—Bonds

Chapter 74—Closing Agreements and Compromises

Chapter 75—Crimes, Other Offenses, and Forfeitures

SUBCHAPTER A. CRIMES

PART I—GENERAL PROVISIONS

SUBCHAPTER B. OTHER OFFENSES

Chapter 76—Judicial Proceedings

SUBCHAPTER A. CIVIL ACTIONS BY THE UNITED STATES

SUBCHAPTER B. PROCEEDINGS BY TAXPAYERS AND THIRD PARTIES

SUBCHAPTER C. THE TAX COURT

PART I—ORGANIZATION AND JURISDICTION

PART II—PROCEDURE

SUBCHAPTER B. EFFECTIVE DATE AND RELATED PROVISIONS

SUBCHAPTER C. PROVISIONS AFFECTING MORE THAN ONE SUBTITLE

SUBTITLE F—PROCEDURE AND ADMINISTRATION [SELECTED CODE SECTIONS]

* * *

CHAPTER 61—INFORMATION AND RETURNS

Subchapter A—Returns and Records

* * *

PART I—RECORDS, STATEMENTS, AND SPECIAL RETURNS

* * *

[Sec. 6001]

SEC. 6001. NOTICE OR REGULATIONS REQUIRING RECORDS, STATEMENTS, AND SPECIAL RETURNS.

Every person liable for any tax imposed by this title, or for the collection thereof, shall keep such records, render such statements, make such returns, and comply with such rules and regulations as the Secretary may from time to time prescribe. Whenever in the judgment of the Secretary it is necessary, he may require any person, by notice served upon such person or by regulations, to make such returns, render such statements, or keep such records, as the Secretary deems sufficient to show whether or not such person is liable for tax under this title. The only records which an employer shall be required to keep under this section in connection with charged tips shall be charge receipts, records necessary to comply with section 6053(c), and copies of statements furnished by employees under section 6053(a).

Amendments

• 1982, Tax Equity and Fiscal Responsibility Act of 1982 (P.L. 97-248)

P.L. 97-248, § 314(d):

Amended Code Sec. 6001 by adding ", records necessary to comply with section 6053(c)," after "charge receipts". **Effective** for tax years beginning after 12-31-82. For a special rule for 1983, see the amendment note for P.L. 97-248, following Code Sec. 6053(c).

• 1978, Revenue Act of 1978 (P.L. 95-600)

P.L. 95-600, § 501(a):

Amended Code Sec. 6001 by adding the last sentence. **Effective** for payments made after 12-31-78.

• 1976, Tax Reform Act of 1976 (P.L. 94-455)

P.L. 94-455, § 1906(b)(13)(A):

Amended 1954 Code by substituting "Secretary" for "Secretary or his delegate" each place it appeared. **Effective** 2-1-77.

PART II—TAX RETURNS OR STATEMENTS

Subpart A—General Requirement

* * *

[Sec. 6011]

SEC. 6011. GENERAL REQUIREMENT OF RETURN, STATEMENT, OR LIST.

[Sec. 6011(a)]

(a) GENERAL RULE.—When required by regulations prescribed by the Secretary any person made liable for any tax imposed by this title, or with respect to the collection thereof, shall make a return or statement according to the forms and regulations prescribed by the Secretary. Every person required to make a return or statement shall include therein the information required by such forms or regulations.

Amendments

• 1988, Technical and Miscellaneous Revenue Act of 1988 (P.L. 100-647)

P.L. 100-647, §1015(q)(1):

Amended Code Sec. 6011(a) by striking out "for the collection thereof" and inserting in lieu thereof "with respect to the collection thereof". **Effective** 11-10-88.

• 1976, Tax Reform Act of 1976 (P.L. 94-455)

P.L. 94-455, §1906(b)(13)(A):

Amended 1954 Code by substituting "Secretary" for "Secretary or his delegate" each place it appeared. **Effective** 2-1-77.

* * *

[Sec. 6011(e)]

(e) REGULATIONS REQUIRING RETURNS ON MAGNETIC MEDIA, ETC.—

(1) IN GENERAL.—The Secretary shall prescribe regulations providing standards for determining which returns must be filed on magnetic media or in other machine-readable form. Except as provided in paragraph (3), the Secretary may not require returns of any tax imposed by subtitle A on individuals, estates, and trusts to be other than on paper forms supplied by the Secretary.

(2) REQUIREMENTS OF REGULATIONS.—In prescribing regulations under paragraph (1), the Secretary—

(A) shall not require any person to file returns on magnetic media unless such person is required to file at least the applicable number of returns during the calendar year, and

(B) shall take into account (among other relevant factors) the ability of the taxpayer to comply at reasonable cost with the requirements of such regulations.

(3) SPECIAL RULE FOR TAX RETURN PREPARERS.—

(A) IN GENERAL.—The Secretary shall require that any individual income tax return prepared by a tax return preparer be filed on magnetic media if—

(i) such return is filed by such tax return preparer, and

(ii) such tax return preparer is a specified tax return preparer for the calendar year during which such return is filed.

(B) SPECIFIED TAX RETURN PREPARER.—For purposes of this paragraph, the term "specified tax return preparer" means, with respect to any calendar year, any tax return preparer unless such preparer reasonably expects to file 10 or fewer individual income tax returns during such calendar year.

(C) INDIVIDUAL INCOME TAX RETURN.—For purposes of this paragraph, the term "individual income tax return" means any return of the tax imposed by subtitle A on individuals, estates, or trusts.

(D) EXCEPTION FOR CERTAIN PREPARERS LOCATED IN AREAS WITHOUT INTERNET ACCESS.—The Secretary may waive the requirement of subparagraph (A) if the Secretary determines, on the basis of an application by the tax return preparer, that the preparer cannot meet such requirement by reason of being located in a geographic area which does not have access to internet service (other than dial-up or satellite service).

(4) SPECIAL RULE FOR RETURNS FILED BY FINANCIAL INSTITUTIONS WITH RESPECT TO WITHHOLDING ON FOREIGN TRANSFERS.—The numerical limitation under paragraph (2)(A) shall not apply to any return filed by a financial institution (as defined in section 1471(d)(5)) with respect to tax for which such institution is made liable under section 1461 or 1474(a).

(5) APPLICABLE NUMBER.—

(A) IN GENERAL.—For purposes of paragraph (2)(A), the applicable number shall be—

(i) except as provided in subparagraph (B), in the case of calendar years before 2021, 250,

(ii) in the case of calendar year 2021, 100, and

(iii) in the case of calendar years after 2021, 10.

(B) SPECIAL RULE FOR PARTNERSHIPS FOR 2018, 2019, 2020, AND 2021.—In the case of a partnership, for any calendar year before 2022, the applicable number shall be—

(i) in the case of calendar year 2018, 200,

(ii) in the case of calendar year 2019, 150,

(iii) in the case of calendar year 2020, 100, and

(iv) in the case of calendar year 2021, 50.

(6) PARTNERSHIPS REQUIRED TO FILE ON MAGNETIC MEDIA.—Notwithstanding paragraph (2)(A), the Secretary shall require partnerships having more than 100 partners to file returns on magnetic media.

(6)[(7)]. APPLICATION OF NUMERICAL LIMITATION TO RETURNS RELATING TO DEFERRED COMPENSATION PLANS.—For purposes of applying the numerical limitation under paragraph (2)(A) to any return required under section 6058, information regarding each plan for which information is provided on such return shall be treated as a separate return.

Amendments

• 2019, Setting Every Community Up for Retirement Enhancement Act of 2019 (P.L. 116-94)

P.L. 116-94, §202(d)(1), Div. O:

Amended Code Sec. 6011(e) by adding at the end a new paragraph (6)[(7)]. **Effective** for returns required be filed with respect to plan years beginning after 12-31-2019.

• 2019, Taxpayer First Act (P.L. 116-25)

P.L. 116-25, §2301(a):

Amended Code Sec. 6011(e)(2)(A) by striking "250" and inserting "the applicable number of". **Effective** 7-1-2019.

P.L. 116-25, §2301(b):

Amended Code Sec. 6011(e) by striking paragraph (5) and inserting new paragraphs (5) and (6). **Effective** 7-1-2019. Prior to being stricken, Code Sec. 6011(e)(5) read as follows:

(5) SPECIAL RULES FOR PARTNERSHIPS.—

(A) PARTNERSHIPS PERMITTED TO BE REQUIRED TO FILE ON MAGNETIC MEDIA.—In the case of a partnership, paragraph (2)(A) shall be applied by substituting for "250" the following amount:

(i) In the case of returns and statements relating to calendar year 2018, "200".

(ii) In the case of returns and statements relating to calendar year 2019, "150".

(iii) In the case of returns and statements relating to calendar year 2020, "100".

(iv) In the case of returns and statements relating to calendar year 2021, "50".

(v) In the case of returns and statements relating to calendar years after 2021, "20".

(B) PARTNERSHIPS REQUIRED TO FILE ON MAGNETIC MEDIA.—Notwithstanding subparagraph (A) and paragraph (2)(A), the Secretary shall require partnerships having more than 100 partners to file returns on magnetic media.

P.L. 116-25, §2301(c):

Amended Code Sec. 6011(e)(3) by adding at the end a new subparagraph (D). **Effective** 7-1-2019.

• 2018, Tax Technical Corrections Act of 2018 (P.L. 115-141)

P.L. 115-141, §301(a)(1), Div. U:

Amended Code Sec. 6011(e) by adding at the end a new paragraph (5). **Effective** as if included in section 1101 of the Bipartisan Budget Act of 2015 [**effective** generally for returns filed for partnership tax years beginning after 12-31-2017.—CCH].

P.L. 115-141, §301(a)(2), Div. U:

Amended Code Sec. 6011(e)(2) by striking the last sentence. **Effective** as if included in section 1101 of the Bipartisan Budget Act of 2015 [**effective** generally for returns filed for partnership tax years beginning after 12-31-2017.—CCH]. Prior to being stricken, the last sentence of Code Sec. 6011(e)(2) read as follows:

Notwithstanding the preceding sentence, the Secretary shall require partnerships having more than 100 partners to file returns on magnetic media.

• 2014, Tax Technical Corrections Act of 2014 (P.L. 113-295)

P.L. 113-295, §220(t), Division A:

Amended Code Sec. 6011(e)(3) by striking "shall require than" and inserting "shall require that". **Effective** 12-19-2014.

• 2010, Hiring Incentives to Restore Employment Act (P.L. 111-147)

P.L. 111-147, §522(a):

Amended Code Sec. 6011(e) by adding at the end a new paragraph (4). **Effective** for returns the due date for which (determined without regard to extensions) is after 3-18-2010.

• 2009, Worker, Homeownership, and Business Assistance Act of 2009 (P.L. 111-92)

P.L. 111-92, §17(a):

Amended Code Sec. 6011(e) by adding at the end a new paragraph (3). **Effective** for returns filed after 12-31-2010.

P.L. 111-92, §17(b):

Amended Code Sec. 6011(e)(1) by striking "The Secretary may not" and inserting "Except as provided in paragraph (3), the Secretary may not". **Effective** for returns filed after 12-31-2010.

• 1997, Taxpayer Relief Act of 1997 (P.L. 105-34)

P.L. 105-34, §1224:

Amended Code Sec. 6011(e)(2) by adding at the end a new sentence. **Effective** for partnership tax years beginning after 12-31-97 [**effective** date changed by P.L. 105-206, §6012(e)].

• 1989, Omnibus Budget Reconciliation Act of 1989 (P.L. 101-239)

P.L. 101-239, §7713(a):

Amended Code Sec. 6011(e). **Effective** for returns the due date for which (determined without regard to extensions) is after 12-31-89. Prior to amendment, Code Sec. 6011(e) read as follows:

(e) REGULATIONS REQUIRING RETURNS ON MAGNETIC TAPE, ETC.—

(1) IN GENERAL.—The Secretary shall prescribe regulations providing standards for determining which returns must be filed on magnetic media or in other machine-readable form. The Secretary may not require returns of any tax imposed by subtitle A on individuals, estates, and trusts to be other than on paper forms supplied by the Secretary. In prescribing such regulations, the Secretary shall take into account (among other relevant factors) the ability of the taxpayer to comply at reasonable cost with such a filing requirement.

(2) CERTAIN RETURNS MUST BE FILED ON MAGNETIC MEDIA.—

(A) IN GENERAL.—In the case of any person who is requred to file returns under sections 6042(a), 6044(a), and 6049(a) with respect to more than 50 payees for any calendar year, all returns under such sections shall be on magnetic media.

(B) HARDSHIP EXCEPTION.—Subparagraph (A) shall not apply to any person for any period if such person establishes to the satisfaction of the Secretary that its application to such person for such period would result in undue hardship.

• 1983, Interest and Dividend Tax Compliance Act of 1983 (P.L. 98-67)

P.L. 98-67, §109(a):

Amended Code Sec. 6011(e). **Effective** with respect to payments made after 12-31-83. Prior to amendment, Sec. 6011(e) read as follows:

(e) REGULATIONS REQUIRING RETURNS ON MAGNETIC TAPE, ETC.—The Secretary shall prescribe regulations providing standards for determining which returns must be filed on magnetic media or in other machine-readable form. The Secretary may not require returns of any tax imposed by subtitle A on individuals, estates, and trusts to be other than on paper forms supplied by the Secretary. In prescribing such regulations, the Secretary shall take into account (among other relevant factors) the ability of the taxpayer to comply at a reasonable cost with such a filing requirement.

P.L. 98-67, §109(b), provides:

(b) STUDY OF WAGE RETURNS ON MAGNETIC TAPE.—

(1) STUDY.—The Secretary of the Treasury, in consultation with the Secretary of Health and Human Services, shall conduct a study of the feasibility of requiring persons to file, on magnetic media, returns under section 6011 of the Internal Revenue Code of 1954 containing information described in section 6051(a) of such code (relating to W-2s).

(2) REPORT TO CONGRESS.—Not later than July 1, 1984, the Secretary of the Treasury shall submit to the Committee on Ways and Means of the House of Representatives and the Committee on Finance of the Senate the results of the study conducted under paragraph (1).

• 1982, Tax Equity and Fiscal Responsibility Act of 1982 (P.L. 97-248)

P.L. 97-248, §314(d):

Added Code Sec. 6011(e).

[Sec. 6011(f)]

(f) PROMOTION OF ELECTRONIC FILING.—

(1) IN GENERAL.—The Secretary is authorized to promote the benefits of and encourage the use of electronic tax administration programs, as they become available, through the use of mass communications and other means.

(2) INCENTIVES.—The Secretary may implement procedures to provide for the payment of appropriate incentives for electronically filed returns.

Amendments

• 1998, IRS Restructuring and Reform Act of 1998 (P.L. 105-206)

P.L. 105-206, §2001(c):

Amended Code Sec. 6011 by redesignating subsection (f) as subsection (g) and by inserting after subsection (e) a new subsection (f). **Effective** 7-22-98.

P.L. 105-206, §2001(a)-(b) and (d), provides:

(a) IN GENERAL.—It is the policy of Congress that—

(1) paperless filing should be the preferred and most convenient means of filing Federal tax and information returns;

(2) it should be the goal of the Internal Revenue Service to have at least 80 percent of all such returns filed electronically by the year 2007; and

(3) the Internal Revenue Service should cooperate with and encourage the private sector by encouraging competition to increase electronic filing of such returns.

(b) STRATEGIC PLAN.—

(1) IN GENERAL.—Not later than 180 days after the date of the enactment of this Act, the Secretary of the Treasury or the Secretary's delegate (hereafter in this section referred to as the "Secretary") shall establish a plan to eliminate barriers, provide incentives, and use competitive market forces to increase electronic filing gradually over the next 10 years while maintaining processing times for paper returns at 40 days. To the extent practicable, such plan shall provide that all returns prepared electronically for taxable years beginning after 2001 shall be filed electronically.

(2) ELECTRONIC COMMERCE ADVISORY GROUP.—To ensure that the Secretary receives input from the private sector in the development and implementation of the plan required by paragraph (1), the Secretary shall convene an electronic commerce advisory group to include representatives from the small business community and from the tax practitioner, preparer, and computerized tax processor communities and other representatives from the electronic filing industry.

***

(d) ANNUAL REPORTS.—Not later than June 30 of each calendar year after 1998, the Chairperson of the Internal Revenue Service Oversight Board, the Secretary of the Treasury, and the Chairperson of the electronic commerce advisory group established under subsection (b)(2) shall report to the Committees on Ways and Means, Appropriations, Government Reform and Oversight, and Small Business of the House of Representatives and the Committees on Finance, Appropriations, Governmental Affairs, and Small Business of the Senate on—

(1) the progress of the Internal Revenue Service in meeting the goal of receiving electronically 80 percent of tax and information returns by 2007;

(2) the status of the plan required by subsection (b);

(3) the legislative changes necessary to assist the Internal Revenue Service in meeting such goal; and

(4) the effects on small businesses and the self-employed of electronically filing tax and information returns.

P.L. 105-206, §2003(c)-(e), provides:

(c) ESTABLISHMENT OF PROCEDURES FOR OTHER INFORMATION.—In the case of taxable periods beginning after December 31, 1999, the Secretary of the Treasury or the Secretary's delegate shall, to the extent practicable, establish procedures to accept, in electronic form, any other information, statements, elections, or schedules, from taxpayers filing returns electronically, so that such taxpayers will not be required to file any paper.

(d) INTERNET AVAILABILITY.—In the case of taxable periods beginning after December 31, 1998, the Secretary of the Treasury or the Secretary's delegate shall establish procedures for all tax forms, instructions, and publications created in the most recent 5-year period to be made available electronically on the Internet in a searchable database at approximately the same time such records are available to the public in paper form. In addition, in the case of taxable periods beginning after December 31, 1998, the Secretary of the Treasury or the Secretary's delegate shall, to the extent practicable, establish procedures for other taxpayer guidance to be made available electronically on the Internet in a searchable database at approximately the same time such guidance is available to the public in paper form.

(e) PROCEDURES FOR AUTHORIZING DISCLOSURE ELECTRONICALLY.—The Secretary shall establish procedures for any taxpayer to authorize, on an electronically filed return, the Secretary to disclose information under section 6103(c) of the Internal Revenue Code of 1986 to the preparer of the return.

[Sec. 6011(g)]

(g) DISCLOSURE OF REPORTABLE TRANSACTION TO TAX-EXEMPT ENTITY.—Any taxable party to a prohibited tax shelter transaction (as defined in section 4965(e)(1)) shall by statement disclose to any tax-exempt entity (as defined in section 4965(c)) which is a party to such transaction that such transaction is such a prohibited tax shelter transaction.

Amendments

• 2006, Tax Increase Prevention and Reconciliation Act of 2005 (P.L. 109-222)

P.L. 109-222, §516(b)(2):

Amended Code Sec. 6011 by redesignating subsection (g) as subsection (h) and by inserting after subsection (f) a new subsection (g). **Effective** for disclosures the due date for which are after 5-17-2006.

[Sec. 6011(h)]

(h) MANDATORY E-FILING OF UNRELATED BUSINESS INCOME TAX RETURN.—Any organization required to file an annual return under this section which relates to any tax imposed by section 511 shall file such return in electronic form.

Amendments

• 2019, Taxpayer First Act (P.L. 116-25)

P.L. 116-25, §3101(b)(2):

Amended Code Sec. 6011 by redesignating subsection (h) as subsection (i) and by inserting after subsection (g) a new subsection (h). **Effective** generally for tax years beginning after 7-1-2019. For a transition rule, see Act Sec. 3101(d)(2), below.

P.L. 116-25, §3101(d)(2), provides:

(2) TRANSITIONAL RELIEF.—

(A) SMALL ORGANIZATIONS.—

(i) IN GENERAL.—In the case of any small organizations, or any other organizations for which the Secretary of the Treasury or the Secretary's delegate (hereafter referred to in this paragraph as the "Secretary") determines the application of the amendments made by this section would cause undue burden without a delay, the Secretary may delay the application of such amendments, but such delay shall not apply to any taxable year beginning on or after the date that is 2 years after the enactment of this Act.

(ii) SMALL ORGANIZATION.—For purposes of clause (i), the term "small organization" means any organization—

(I) the gross receipts of which for the taxable year are less than $200,000; and

(II) the aggregate gross assets of which at the end of the taxable year are less than $500,000.

(B) ORGANIZATIONS FILING FORM 990-T.—In the case of any organization described in section 511(a)(2) of the Internal Revenue Code of 1986 which is subject to the tax imposed by section 511(a)(1) of such Code on its unrelated business taxable income, or any organization required to file a return under section 6033 of such Code and include information under subsection (e) thereof, the Secretary may delay the application of the amendments made by this section, but such delay shall not apply to any taxable year beginning on or after the date that is 2 years after the enactment of this Act.

[Sec. 6011(i)]

(i) INCOME, ESTATE, AND GIFT TAXES.—For requirement that returns of income, estate, and gift taxes be made whether or not there is tax liability, see subparts B and C.

Amendments

• 2019, Taxpayer First Act (P.L. 116-25)

P.L. 116-25, §3101(b)(2):

Amended Code Sec. 6011 by redesignating subsection (h) as subsection (i). **Effective** generally for tax years beginning after 7-1-2019.

• 2006, Tax Increase Prevention and Reconciliation Act of 2005 (P.L. 109-222)

P.L. 109-222, §516(b)(2):

Amended Code Sec. 6011 by redesignating subsection (g) as subsection (h). **Effective** for disclosures the due date for which are after 5-17-2006.

• 1998, IRS Restructuring and Reform Act of 1998 (P.L. 105-206)

P.L. 105-206, §2001(c):

Amended Code Sec. 6011 by redesignating subsection (f) as subsection (g). **Effective** 7-22-98.

• 1986, Tax Reform Act of 1986 (P.L. 99-514)

P.L. 99-514, §1899A(52):

Amended Code Sec. 6011(f) by striking out "sections 6012 to 6019, inclusive" and inserting in lieu thereof "subparts B and C". **Effective** 10-22-86.

• 1982, Tax Equity and Fiscal Responsibility Act of 1982 (P.L. 97-248)

P.L. 97-248, §314(d):

Redesignated subsection (e) as subsection (f).

• 1978, Tax Treatment Extension Act of 1978 (P.L. 95-615)

P.L. 95-615, §207(c):

Redesignated Code Sec. 6011(d) as Code Sec. 6011(e).

• 1976, Tax Reform Act of 1976 (P.L. 94-455)

P.L. 94-455, §1904(b)(10)(A)(ii):

Redesignated Code Sec. 6011(f) as Code Sec. 6011(d).

• 1971, Revenue Act of 1971 (P.L. 92-178)

P.L. 92-178, §504(a):

Redesignated subsection (e) of Code Sec. 6011 as subsection (f).

• 1964, Interest Equalization Tax Act (P.L. 88-563)

P.L. 88-563, §3(a):

Redesignated subsection (d) of Code Sec. 6011 as subsection (e).

• 1958, Excise Tax Technical Changes Act of 1958 (P.L. 85-859)

P.L. 85-859, §161:

Redesignated subsection (c) of Code Sec. 6011 as subsection (d).

Subpart B—Income Tax Returns

* * *

[Sec. 6012]

SEC. 6012. PERSONS REQUIRED TO MAKE RETURNS OF INCOME.

[Sec. 6012(a)]

(a) GENERAL RULE.—Returns with respect to income taxes under subtitle A shall be made by the following:

(1)(A) Every individual having for the taxable year gross income which equals or exceeds the exemption amount, except that a return shall not be required of an individual—

(i) who is not married (determined by applying section 7703), is not a surviving spouse (as defined in section 2(a)), is not a head of a household (as defined in section 2(b)), and for the taxable year has gross income of less than the sum of the exemption amount plus the basic standard deduction applicable to such an individual,

(ii) who is a head of a household (as so defined) and for the taxable year has gross income of less than the sum of the exemption amount plus the basic standard deduction applicable to such an individual,

(iii) who is a surviving spouse (as so defined) and for the taxable year has gross income of less than the sum of the exemption amount plus the basic standard deduction applicable to such an individual, or

(iv) who is entitled to make a joint return and whose gross income, when combined with the gross income of his spouse, is, for the taxable year, less than the sum of twice the exemption amount plus the basic standard deduction applicable to a joint return, but only if such individual and his spouse, at the close of the taxable year, had the same household as their home.

Clause (iv) shall not apply if for the taxable year such spouse makes a separate return or any other taxpayer is entitled to an exemption for such spouse under section 151(c).

(B) The amount specified in clause (i), (ii), or (iii) of subparagraph (A) shall be increased by the amount of 1 additional standard deduction (within the meaning of section 63(c)(3)) in the case of an individual entitled to such deduction by reason of section 63(f)(1)(A) (relating to individuals age 65 or more), and the amount specified in clause (iv) of subparagraph (A) shall be increased by the amount of the additional standard deduction for each additional standard deduction to which the individual or his spouse is entitled by reason of section 63(f)(1).

(C) The exception under subparagraph (A) shall not apply to any individual—

(i) who is described in section 63(c)(5) and who has—

(I) income (other than earned income) in excess of the sum of the amount in effect under section 63(c)(5)(A) plus the additional standard deduction (if any) to which the individual is entitled, or

(II) total gross income in excess of the standard deduction, or

(ii) for whom the standard deduction is zero under section 63(c)(6).

(D) For purposes of this subsection—

(i) The terms "standard deduction", "basic standard deduction" and "additional standard deduction" have the respective meanings given such terms by section 63(c).

(ii) The term "exemption amount" has the meaning given such term by section 151(d). In the case of an individual described in section 151(d)(2), the exemption amount shall be zero.

(2) Every corporation subject to taxation under subtitle A;

(3) Every estate the gross income of which for the taxable year is $600 or more;

(4) Every trust having for the taxable year any taxable income, or having gross income of $600 or over, regardless of the amount of taxable income;

(5) Every estate or trust of which any beneficiary is a nonresident alien;

(6) Every political organization (within the meaning of section 527(e)(1)), and every fund treated under section 527(g) as if it constituted a political organization, which has political organization taxable income (within the meaning of section 527(c)(1)) for the taxable year;

(7) Every homeowners association (within the meaning of section 528(c)(1)) which has homeowners association taxable income (within the meaning of section 528(d)) for the taxable year; and

(8) Every estate of an individual under chapter 7 or 11 of title 11 of the United States Code (relating to bankruptcy) the gross income of which for the taxable year is not less than the sum of the exemption amount plus the basic standard deduction under section 63(c)(2)(C);

except that subject to such conditions, limitations, and exceptions and under such regulations as may be prescribed by the Secretary, nonresident alien individuals subject to the tax imposed by section 871 and foreign corporations subject to the tax imposed by section 881 may be exempted from the requirement of making returns under this section.

Amendments

• 2018, Tax Technical Corrections Act of 2018 (P.L. 115-141)

P.L. 115-141, §401(a)(255), Div. U:

Amended Code Sec. 6012(a)(6) by striking "and" at the end. **Effective** 3-23-2018.

P.L. 115-141, §401(a)(256), Div. U:

Amended Code Sec. 6012(a)(7) by striking the period at the end and inserting "; and". **Effective** 3-23-2018.

P.L. 115-141, §401(a)(257), Div. U:

Amended Code Sec. 6012(a)(8) by striking "section 63(c)(2)(D)." and inserting "section 63(c)(2)(C);". **Effective** 3-23-2018.

• 2010, (P.L. 111-226)

P.L. 111-226, §219(b)(1):

Amended Code Sec. 6012(a) by striking paragraph (8) and by redesignating paragraph (9) as paragraph (8). **Effective** for tax years beginning after 12-31-2010. Prior to being stricken, Code Sec. 6012(a)(8) read as follows:

(8) Every individual who receives payments during the calendar year in which the taxable year begins under section 3507 (relating to advance payment of earned income credit).

• 2002 (P.L. 107-276)

P.L. 107-276, §3(a):

Amended Code Sec. 6012(a)(6) by striking "or which has" and all that follows through "section)". **Effective** as if included in the amendments made by P.L. 106-230 [**effective** for returns for tax years beginning after 6-30-2000.—CCH]. Prior to amendment, Code Sec. 6012(a)(6) read as follows:

(6) Every political organization (within the meaning of section 527(e)(1)), and every fund treated under section 527(g) as if it constituted a political organization, which has political organization taxable income (within the meaning of section 527(c)(1)) for the taxable year or which has gross receipts of $25,000 or more for the taxable year (other than an organization to which section 527 applies solely by reason of subsection (f)(1) of such section); and

• 2000 (P.L. 106-230)

P.L. 106-230, §3(a)(1):

Amended Code Sec. 6012(a)(6) by inserting "or which has gross receipts of $25,000 or more for the taxable year (other than an organization to which section 527 applies solely by reason of subsection (f)(1) of such section)" after "taxable year". **Effective** for returns for tax years beginning after 6-30-2000.

• 1998, IRS Restructuring and Reform Act of 1998 (P.L. 105-206)

P.L. 105-206, §2004, provides:

SEC. 2004. RETURN-FREE TAX SYSTEM.

(a) IN GENERAL.—The Secretary of the Treasury or the Secretary's delegate shall develop procedures for the implementation of a return-free tax system under which appropriate individuals would be permitted to comply with the Internal Revenue Code of 1986 without making the return required under section 6012 of such Code for taxable years beginning after 2007.

(b) REPORT.—Not later than June 30 of each calendar year after 1999, the Secretary shall report to the Committee on Ways and Means of the House of Representatives and the Committee on Finance of the Senate on—

(1) what additional resources the Internal Revenue Service would need to implement such a system;

(2) the changes to the Internal Revenue Code of 1986 that could enhance the use of such a system;

(3) the procedures developed pursuant to subsection (a); and

(4) the number and classes of taxpayers that would be permitted to use the procedures developed pursuant to subsection (a).

• 1988, Technical and Miscellaneous Revenue Act of 1988 (P.L. 100-647)

P.L. 100-647, §1001(b)(2):

Amended Code Sec. 6012(a)(1)(C)(i)(I). **Effective** as if included in the provision of P.L. 99-514 to which it relates. Prior to amendment, Code Sec. 6012(a)(1)(C)(i)(I) read as follows:

(I) income (other than earned income) in excess of the amount in effect under section 63(c)(5)(A) (relating to limitation on standard deduction in the case of certain dependents), or

• 1986, Tax Reform Act of 1986 (P.L. 99-514)

P.L. 99-514, §104(a)(1)(A):

Amended Code Sec. 6012(a)(1). **Effective** for tax years beginning after 12-31-86. Prior to amendment, Code Sec. 6012(a)(1) read as follows:

(1)(A) Every individual having for the taxable year a gross income of the exemption amount or more, except that a return shall not be required of an individual (other than an individual described in subparagraph (C))—

(i) who is not married (determined by applying section 143), is not a surviving spouse (as defined in section 2(a)), and for the taxable year has a gross income of less than the sum of the exemption amount plus the zero bracket amount applicable to such an individual,

(ii) who is a surviving spouse (as so defined) and for the taxable year has a gross income of less than the sum of the exemption amount plus the zero bracket amount applicable to such an individual, or

(iii) who is entitled to make a joint return under section 6013 and whose gross income, when combined with the gross income of his spouse, is, for the taxable year, less than the sum of twice the exemption amount plus the zero bracket amount applicable to a joint return but only if such individual and his spouse, at the close of the taxable year, had the same household as their home.

Clause (iii) shall not apply if for the taxable year such spouse makes a separate return or any other taxpayer is entitled to an exemption for such spouse under section 151(e).

(B) The amount specified in clause (i) or (ii) of subparagraph (A) shall be increased by the exemption amount in the case of an individual entitled to an additional personal exemption under section 151(c)(1), and the amount specified in clause (iii) of subparagraph (A) shall be increased by the exemption amount for each additional personal exemption to which the individual or his spouse is entitled under section 151(c).

(C) The exemption under subparagraph (A) shall not apply to—

(i) a nonresident alien individual;

(ii) a citizen of the United States entitled to the benefits of section 931;

(iii) an individual making a return under section 443(a)(1) for a period of less than 12 months on account of a change in his annual accounting period;

(iv) an individual who has income (other than earned income) of the exemption amount or more and who is described in section 63(e)(1)(D); or

(v) an estate or trust.

(D) For purposes of this paragraph—

(i) The term "zero bracket amount" has the meaning given to such term by section 63(d).

(ii) The term "exemption amount" has the meaning given to such term by section 151(f).

P.L. 99-514, §104(a)(1)(B):

Amended Code Sec. 6012(a)(9) by striking out "$2,700 or more" and inserting in lieu thereof "not less than the sum of the exemption amount plus the basic standard deduction under section 63(c)(2)(D)". **Effective** for tax years beginning after 12-31-86.

• 1983, Surface Transportation Act of 1983 (P.L. 97-424)

P.L. 97-424, §542, provides:

SEC. 542. NO RETURN REQUIRED OF INDIVIDUAL WHOSE ONLY GROSS INCOME IS GRANT OF $1,000 FROM STATE.

(a) IN GENERAL.—Nothing in section 6012(a) of the Internal Revenue Code of 1954 shall be construed to require the filing of a return with respect to income taxes under subtitle A of such code by an individual whose only gross income for the taxable year is a grant of $1,000 received from a State which made such grants generally to residents of such State.

(b) EFFECTIVE DATE.—Subsection (a) shall apply to taxable years beginning after December 31, 1981.

• 1981, Economic Recovery Tax Act of 1981 (P.L. 97-34)

P.L. 97-34, §104(d)(1)(A)-(E):

Amended Code Sec. 6012(a)(1)(A)(i) by striking out "$3,300" and inserting in lieu thereof "the sum of the exemption amount plus the zero bracket amount applicable to such an individual". Amended Code Sec. 6012(a)(1)(A)(ii) by striking out "$4,400" and inserting in lieu thereof "the sum of the exemption amount plus the zero bracket amount applicable to such an individual". Amended Code Sec. 6012(a)(1)(A)(iii) by striking out "$5,400" and inserting in lieu thereof "the sum of twice the exemption amount plus the zero bracket amount applicable to a joint return". Amended Code Sec. 6012(a)(1) by striking out "$1,000" each place it appeared and inserting in lieu thereof "the exemption amount". Amended Code Sec. 6012(a)(1) by adding at the end thereof new subparagraph (D). **Effective** for tax years beginning after 12-31-84.

• 1980, Bankruptcy Tax Act of 1980 (P.L. 96-589)

P.L. 96-589, §3(b)(1):

Amended Code Sec. 6012(a) by adding a new paragraph (9). **Effective** for bankruptcy cases commencing on or after 3-25-81.

• 1978, Revenue Act of 1978 (P.L. 95-600)

P.L. 95-600, §§101(c), 102(b)(1):

Amended Code Sec. 6012(a)(1). **Effective** for tax years beginning after 12-31-78. Prior to amendment, Code Sec. 6012(a)(1) read as follows:

"(a) GENERAL RULE.—Returns with respect to income taxes under subtitle A shall be made by the following:

"(1)(A) Every individual having for the taxable year a gross income of $750 or more, except that a return shall not be required of an individual (other than an individual described in subparagraph (C))—

"(i) who is not married (determined by applying section 143), is not a surviving spouse (as defined in section 2(a)), and for the taxable year has a gross income of less than $2,950,

"(ii) who is a surviving spouse (as so defined) and for the taxable year has a gross income of less than $3,950, or

"(iii) who is entitled to make a joint return under section 6013 and whose gross income, when combined with the gross income of his spouse, is, for the taxable year, less than $4,700, but only if such individual and his spouse, at the close of the taxable year, had the same household as their home.

Clause (iii) shall not apply if for the taxable year such spouse makes a separate return or any other taxpayer is entitled to an exemption for such spouse under section 151(e).

"(B) The amount specified in clause (i) or (ii) of subparagraph (A) shall be increased by $750 in the case of an individual entitled to an additional personal exemption under section 151(c)(1), and the amount specified in clause (iii) of subparagraph (A) shall be increased by $750 for each additional personal exemption to which the individual or his spouse is entitled under section 151(c).

"(C) The exception under subparagraph (A) shall not apply to—

"(i) a nonresident alien individual;

"(ii) a citizen of the United States entitled to the benefits of section 931;

"(iii) an individual making a return under section 443(a)(1) for a period of less than 12 months on account of a change in his annual accounting period;

"(iv) an individual who has income (other than earned income) of $750 or more and who is described in section 63(e)(1)(D); or

"(v) an estate or trust."

P.L. 95-600, §105(d):

Amended Code Sec. 6012(a) by adding new paragraph (8). **Effective** for tax years beginning after 12-31-78.

• 1977, Tax Reduction and Simplification Act of 1977 (P.L. 95-30)

P.L. 95-30, §104:

Amended Code Sec. 6012(a)(1)(A). **Effective** for tax years beginning after 12-31-76, Prior to amendment, Sec. 6012(a)(1)(A) read as follows:

"(1)(A) Every individual having for the taxable year a gross income of $750 or more, except that a return shall not be required of an individual (other than an individual referred to in section 142(b))—

"(i) who is not married (determined by applying section 143), is not a surviving spouse (as defined in section 2(a)), and for the taxable year has a gross income of less than $2,450,

"(ii) who is a surviving spouse (as so defined) and for the taxable year has a gross income of less than $2,850, or

"(iii) who is entitled to make a joint return under section 6013 and whose gross income, when combined with the gross income of his spouse, is, for the taxable year, less than $3,600 but only if such individual and his spouse, at the close of the taxable year, had the same household as their home.

Clause (iii) shall not apply if for the taxable year such spouse makes a separate return or any other taxpayer is entitled to an exemption for such spouse under section 151(e).

"(B) The amount specified in clause (i) or (ii) of subparagraph (A) shall be increased by $750 in the case of an individual entitled to an additional personal exemption under section 151(c)(1), and the amount specified in clause (iii) of subparagraph (A) shall be increased by $750 for each additional personal exemption to which the individual or his spouse is entitled under section 151(c);

"(C) Every individual having for the taxable year a gross income of $750 or more and to whom section 141(e) (relating to limitations in case of certain dependent taxpayers) applies;"

• 1976, Tax Reform Act of 1976 (P.L. 94-455)

P.L. 94-455, §401(b)(3):

Amended Code Sec. 6012(a)(1)(A) and (B). **Effective** for tax years ending after 12-31-75. For text of Code Sec. 6012(a)(1)(A) and (B) as it read before the amendment, see below.

P.L. 94-455, §1906(b)(13)(A):

Amended 1954 Code by substituting "Secretary" for "Secretary or his delegate" each place it appeared. **Effective** 2-1-77.

P.L. 94-455, §2101(c):

Added paragraph (7). **Effective** for tax years beginning after 12-31-73.

• 1975, Revenue Adjustment Act of 1975 (P.L. 94-164)

P.L. 94-164, §2(a)(2):

Amended Code Sec. 6012(a)(1)(A) and (B) to read as follows:

(1)(A) Every individual having for the taxable year a gross income of $750 or more, except that a return shall not be required of an individual (other than an individual referred to in section 142(b))—

(i) who is not married (determined by applying section 143), is not a surviving spouse (as defined in section 2(a)), and for the taxable year has a gross income of less than $2,450,

(ii) who is a surviving spouse (as so defined) and for the taxable year has a gross income of less than $2,850, or

(iii) who is entitled to make a joint return under section 6013 and whose gross income, when combined with the gross income of his spouse, is, for the taxable year, less than $3,600 but only if such individual and his spouse, at the close of the taxable year, had the same household as their home.

Clause (iii) shall not apply if for the taxable year such spouse makes a separate return or any other taxpayer is entitled to an exemption for such spouse under section 151(e).

(B) The amount specified in clause (i) or (ii) of subparagraph (A) shall be increased by $750 in the case of an individual entitled to an additional personal exemption under section 151(c)(1), and the amount specified in clause (iii) of subparagraph (A) shall be increased by $750 for each additional personal exemption to which the individual or his spouse is entitled under section 151(c);

Effective for tax years ending after 1975 and before 1977.

• 1975, Tax Reduction Act of 1975 (P.L. 94-12)

P.L. 94-12, §201(b):

Amended Code Sec. 6012(a)(1)(A) and (B) to read as follows:

(1)(A) Every individual having for the taxable year a gross income of $750 or more, except that a return shall not be required of an individual (other than an individual referred to in section 142(b))—

(i) who is not married (determined by applying section 143), is not a surviving spouse (as defined in section 2(a)), and for the taxable year has a gross income of less than $2,350,

(ii) who is a surviving spouse (as so defined) and for the taxable year has a gross income of less than $2,650, or

(iii) who is entitled to make a joint return under section 6013 and whose gross income, when combined with the gross income of his spouse, is, for the taxable year, less than $3,400 but only if such individual and his spouse, at the close of the taxable year, had the same household as their home.

Clause (iii) shall not apply if for the taxable year such spouse makes a separate return or any other taxpayer is entitled to an exemption for such spouse under section 151(e).

(B) The amount specified in clause (i) or (ii) of subparagraph (A) shall be increased by $750 in the case of an individual entitled to an additional personal exemption under section 151(c)(1), and the amount specified in clause (iii) of subparagraph (A) shall be increased by $750 for each additional personal exemption to which the individual or his spouse is entitled under section 151(c);

Effective for tax years ending in 1975.

Code Sec. 6012(a)(1)(A) and (B), as it existed prior to amendment by P.L. 94-12, was again scheduled to become effective for taxable years ending after 1976. Such text of Code Sec. 6012(a)(1)(A) and (B) is reproduced below:

(1)(A) Every individual having for the taxable year a gross income of $750 or more, except that a return shall not be required of an individual (other than an individual referred to in section 142(b))—

(i) who is not married (determined by applying section 143(a)) and for the taxable year has a gross income of less than $2,050, or

(ii) who is entitled to make a joint return under section 6013 and whose gross income, when combined with the gross income of his spouse, is, for the taxable year, less than $2,800 but only if such individual and his spouse, at the close of the taxable year, had the same household as their home.

Clause (ii) shall not apply if for the taxable year such spouse makes a separate return or any other taxpayer is entitled to an exemption for such spouse under section 151(e).

(B) The $2,050 amount specified in subparagraph (A)(i) shall be increased to $2,800 in the case of an individual entitled to an additional personal exemption under section 151(c)(1), and the $2,800 amount specified in subparagraph (A)(ii) shall be increased by $750 for each additional personal exemption to which the individual or his spouse is entitled under section 151(c);

• 1975 (P.L. 93-625)

P.L. 93-625, §10(b):

Amended Code Sec. 6012(a) by deleting "and" at the end of paragraph (4), adding "and" at the end of paragraph (5), adding paragraph (6), and deleting from the end of Code Sec. 6012(a) the following: "The Secretary or his delegate shall, by regulation, exempt from the requirement of making returns under this section any political committee (as defined in section 301(d) of the Federal Election Campaign Act of 1971) having no gross income for the taxable year." **Effective** for tax years beginning after 12-31-74.

P.L. 93-625, §10(f), provides:

"(f) Exemption From Filing Requirement for Prior Years Where Income of Political Party Was $100 or Less.—In the case of a taxable year beginning after December 31, 1971, and before January 1, 1975, nothing in the Internal Revenue Code of 1954 shall be deemed to require any organization described in section 527(e)(1) of such Code to file a return for the taxable year under such Code if such organization would be exempt from so filing under section 6012(a)(6) of such Code if such section applied to such taxable year."

• 1974, Federal Election Campaign Act Amendments of 1974 (P.L. 93-443)

P.L. 93-443, §407:

Amended Code Sec. 6012(a) by adding the last sentence. **Effective** for tax years beginning after 12-31-71.

• 1971, Revenue Act of 1971 (P.L. 92-178)

P.L. 92-178, §204(a):

Amended Code Sec. 6012(a)(1). **Effective** for tax years beginning after 12-31-71. Prior to amendment, Code Sec. 6012(a)(1) read as follows:

"(1)(A) Every individual having for the taxable year a gross income of $600 or more, except that a return shall not be required of an individual (other than an individual referred to in section 142(b))—

"(i) who is not married (determined by applying section 143(a)) and for the taxable year has a gross income of less than $1,700, or

"(ii) who is entitled to make a joint return under section 6013 and whose gross income, when combined with the gross income of his spouse, is, for the taxable year, less than $2,300 but only if such individual and his spouse, at the close of the taxable year, had the same household as their home.

Clause (ii) shall not apply if for the taxable year such spouse makes a separate return or any other taxpayer is entitled to an exemption for such spouse under section 151(e).

"(B) The $1,700 amount specified in subparagraph (A)(i) shall be increased to $2,300 in the case of an individual entitled to an additional personal exemption under section 151(c)(1), and the $2,300 amount specified in subparagraph (A)(ii) shall be increased by $600 for each additional personal exemption to which the individual or his spouse is entitled under section 151(c);"

• 1969, Tax Reform Act of 1969 (P.L. 91-172)

P.L. 91-172, §941(a):

Amended Code Sec. 6012(a)(1). **Effective** for tax years beginning after 12-31-69. Prior to amendment, Code Sec. 6012(a)(1) read as follows:

"(a)(1) Every individual having for the taxable year a gross income of $600 or more (except that any individual who has attained the age of 65 before the close of his taxable year shall be required to make a return only if he has for the taxable year a gross income of $1,200 or more);"

P.L. 91-172, §941(d):

Amended Code Sec. 6012(a)(1) by substituting "$750", "$1,750", and "$2,500" in lieu of "$600", "$1,700", and "$2,300". **Effective** for tax years beginning after 12-31-72.

[Sec. 6012(b)]

(b) RETURNS MADE BY FIDUCIARIES AND RECEIVERS.—

(1) RETURNS OF DECEDENTS.—If an individual is deceased, the return of such individual required under subsection (a) shall be made by his executor, administrator, or other person charged with the property of such decedent.

(2) PERSONS UNDER A DISABILITY.—If an individual is unable to make a return required under subsection (a), the return of such individual shall be made by a duly authorized agent, his committee, guardian, fiduciary or other person charged with the care of the person or property of such individual. The preceding sentence shall not apply in the case of a receiver appointed by authority of law in possession of only a part of the property of an individual.

(3) RECEIVERS, TRUSTEES AND ASSIGNEES FOR CORPORATIONS.—In a case where a receiver, trustee in a case under title 11 of the United States Code or assignee, by order of a court of competent jurisdiction, by operation of law or otherwise, has possession of or holds title to all or substantially all the property or business of a corporation, whether or not such property or business is being operated, such receiver, trustee, or assignee shall make the return of income for such corporation in the same manner and form as corporations are required to make such returns.

(4) RETURNS OF ESTATES AND TRUSTS.—Returns of an estate, a trust, or an estate of an individual under chapter 7 or 11 of title 11 of the United States Code shall be made by the fiduciary thereof.

(5) JOINT FIDUCIARIES.—Under such regulations as the Secretary may prescribe, a return made by one of two or more joint fiduciaries shall be sufficient compliance with the requirements of this section. A return made pursuant to this paragraph shall contain a statement that the fiduciary has sufficient knowledge of the affairs of the person for whom the return is made to enable him to make the return, and that the return is, to the best of his knowledge and belief, true and correct.

(6) IRA SHARE OF PARTNERSHIP INCOME.—In the case of a trust which is exempt from taxation under section 408(e), for purposes of this section, the trust's distributive share of items of gross income and gain of any partnership to which subchapter C or D of chapter 63 applies shall be treated as equal to the trust's distributive share of the taxable income of such partnership.

Amendments

• 1997, Taxpayer Relief Act of 1997 (P.L. 105-34)

P.L. 105-34, §1225:

Amended Code Sec. 6012(b) by adding at the end a new paragraph (6). **Effective** for partnership tax years beginning after 12-31-97 [**effective** date changed by P.L. 105-206, §6012(e)].

• 1984, Deficit Reduction Act of 1984 (P.L. 98-369)

P.L. 98-369, §412(b)(3):

Amended Code Sec. 6012(b)(2) by striking out "or section 6015(a)" following "subsection (a)". **Effective** with respect to tax years beginning after 12-31-84.

• 1980, Bankruptcy Tax Act of 1980 (P.L. 96-589)

P.L. 96-589, §6(i)(5):

Amended Code Sec. 6012(b)(3) by striking out "trustee in bankruptcy" and inserting in lieu thereof "trustee in a case under title 11 of the United States Code". **Effective** 10-1-79, but inapplicable to any proceeding under the Bankruptcy Act commenced before that date.

P.L. 96-589, §3(b)(2):

Amended Code Sec. 6012(b)(4) by striking out "an estate or a trust" and inserting in lieu thereof "an estate, a trust, or an individual under chapter 7 or 11 of title 11 of the United States Code". **Effective** for bankruptcy cases commencing after 3-25-81.

• 1976, Tax Reform Act of 1976 (P.L. 94-455)

P.L. 94-455, §1906(b)(13)(A):

Amended 1954 Code by substituting "Secretary" for "Secretary or his delegate" each place it appeared. **Effective** 2-1-77.

[Sec. 6012(c)]

(c) CERTAIN INCOME EARNED ABROAD OR FROM SALE OF RESIDENCE.—For purposes of this section, gross income shall be computed without regard to the exclusion provided for in section 121 (relating to gain from sale of principal residence) and without regard to the exclusion provided for in section 911 (relating to citizens or residents of the United States living abroad).

Amendments

• 1997, Taxpayer Relief Act of 1997 (P.L. 105-34)

P.L. 105-34, §312(d)(11):

Amended Code Sec. 6012(c) by striking "(relating to one-time exclusion of gain from sale of principal residence by individual who has attained age 55)" and inserting "(relating to gain from sale of principal residence)". **Effective,** generally, for sales and exchanges after 5-6-97.

• 1981, Economic Recovery Tax Act of 1981 (P.L. 97-34)

P.L. 97-34, §111(b)(3):

Amended Code Sec. 6012(c) by striking out "relating to income earned by employees in certain camps" and inserting in lieu thereof "relating to citizens or residents of the United States living abroad". **Effective** with respect to tax years beginning after 12-31-81.

• 1978, Tax Treatment Extension Act of 1978 (P.L. 95-615)

P.L. 95-615, §202(f)(5):

Amended Code Sec. 6012(c) by striking out "relating to earned income from sources without the United States" and inserting in place thereof "relating to income earned by employees of certain camps". **Effective** for tax years beginning after 12-31-77.

• 1978, Revenue Act of 1978 (P.L. 95-600)

P.L. 95-600, §404(c)(8):

Amended Code Sec. 6012(c) by striking out "relating to sale of residence by individual who has attained age 65" and inserting in place thereof "relating to one-time exclusion of gain from sale of principal residence by individual who has attained age 55". **Effective** for sales or exchanges after 7-26-78, in tax years ending after such date.

• 1964, Revenue Act of 1964 (P.L. 88-272)

P.L. 88-272, §206(b)(1):

Amended subsection (c). **Effective** for dispositions after 12-31-63, in tax years ending after such date. Prior to amendment, subsection (c) read as follows:

"(c) Certain Income Earned Abroad.—For purposes of this section, gross income shall be computed without regard to the exclusion provided for in section 911 (relating to earned income from sources without the United States)."

• 1958, Technical Amendments Act of 1958 (P.L. 85-866)

P.L. 85-866, §72(a):

Redesignated Code Sec. 6012(c) as Code Sec. 6012(d) and added new Code Sec. 6012(c). **Effective** for tax years beginning after 12-31-57.

[Sec. 6012(d)]

(d) TAX-EXEMPT INTEREST REQUIRED TO BE SHOWN ON RETURN.—Every person required to file a return under this section for the taxable year shall include on such return the amount of interest received or accrued during the taxable year which is exempt from the tax imposed by chapter 1.

Amendments

• 1986, Tax Reform Act of 1986 (P.L. 99-514)

P.L. 99-514, §1525(a):

Amended Code Sec. 6012 by redesignating subsection (d) as subsection (e) and by inserting after subsection (c) new subsection (d). **Effective** for tax years beginning after 12-31-86.

* * *

[Sec. 6012(f)]

(f) SPECIAL RULE FOR TAXABLE YEARS 2018 THROUGH 2025.—In the case of a taxable year beginning after December 31, 2017, and before January 1, 2026, subsection (a)(1) shall not apply, and every individual who has gross income for the taxable year shall be required to make returns with respect to income taxes under subtitle A, except that a return shall not be required of—

(1) an individual who is not married (determined by applying section 7703) and who has gross income for the taxable year which does not exceed the standard deduction applicable to such individual for such taxable year under section 63, or

(2) an individual entitled to make a joint return if—

(A) the gross income of such individual, when combined with the gross income of such individual's spouse, for the taxable year does not exceed the standard deduction which would be applicable to the taxpayer for such taxable year under section 63 if such individual and such individual's spouse made a joint return,

(B) such individual and such individual's spouse have the same household as their home at the close of the taxable year,

(C) such individual's spouse does not make a separate return, and

(D) neither such individual nor such individual's spouse is an individual described in section 63(c)(5) who has income (other than earned income) in excess of the amount in effect under section 63(c)(5)(A).

Amendments

• 2017, Tax Cuts and Jobs Act (P.L. 115-97)

P.L. 115-97, §11041(e):

Amended Code Sec. 6012 by adding at the end a new subsection (f). **Effective** for tax years beginning after 12-31-2017.

* * *

Subpart C—Estate and Gift Tax Returns

[Sec. 6018]

SEC. 6018. ESTATE TAX RETURNS.

[Sec. 6018(a)]

(a) RETURNS BY EXECUTOR.—

(1) CITIZENS OR RESIDENTS.—In all cases where the gross estate at the death of a citizen or resident exceeds the basic exclusion amount in effect under section 2010(c) for the calendar year which includes the date of death, the executor shall make a return with respect to the estate tax imposed by subtitle B.

(2) NONRESIDENTS NOT CITIZENS OF THE UNITED STATES.—In the case of the estate of every nonresident not a citizen of the United States if that part of the gross estate which is situated in the United States exceeds $60,000, the executor shall make a return with respect to the estate tax imposed by subtitle B.

(3) ADJUSTMENT FOR CERTAIN GIFTS.—The amount applicable under paragraph (1) and the amount set forth in paragraph (2) shall each be reduced (but not below zero) by the sum of—

(A) the amount of the adjusted taxable gifts (within the meaning of section 2001(b)) made by the decedent after December 31, 1976, plus

(B) the aggregate amount allowed as a specific exemption under section 2521 (as in effect before its repeal by the Tax Reform Act of 1976) with respect to gifts made by the decedent after September 8, 1976.

[Sec. 6018(b)]

(b) RETURNS BY BENEFICIARIES.—If the executor is unable to make a complete return as to any part of the gross estate of the decedent, he shall include in his return a description of such part and the name of every person holding a legal or beneficial interest therein. Upon notice from the Secretary such person shall in like manner make a return as to such part of the gross estate.

Amendments

• 2013, American Taxpayer Relief Act of 2012 (P.L. 112-240)

P.L. 112-240, §101(a)(1)-(3), provides:

SEC. 101. PERMANENT EXTENSION AND MODIFICATION OF 2001 TAX RELIEF.

(a) PERMANENT EXTENSION.—

(1) IN GENERAL.—The Economic Growth and Tax Relief Reconciliation Act of 2001 is amended by striking title IX.

(2) CONFORMING AMENDMENT.—The Tax Relief, Unemployment Insurance Reauthorization, and Job Creation Act of 2010 is amended by striking section 304.

(3) EFFECTIVE DATE.—The amendments made by this subsection shall apply to taxable, plan, or limitation years beginning after December 31, 2012, and estates of decedents dying, gifts made, or generation skipping transfers after December 31, 2012.

• 2010, Tax Relief, Unemployment Insurance Reauthorization, and Job Creation Act of 2010 (P.L. 111-312)

P.L. 111-312, §301(a):

Amended Code Sec. 6018 to read as such provision would read if subtitle E of title V of the Economic Growth and Tax Relief Reconciliation Act of 2001 (P.L. 107-16) had never been enacted. **Effective** for estates of decedents dying, and transfers made, after 12-31-2009. For special rules, see Act Sec. 301(c) and (d)(1), below. Prior to amendment by P.L. 111-312, Code Sec. 6018 read as follows:

SEC. 6018. RETURNS RELATING TO LARGE TRANSFERS AT DEATH.

[Sec. 6018(a)]

(a) IN GENERAL.—If this section applies to property acquired from a decedent, the executor of the estate of such decedent shall make a return containing the information specified in subsection (c) with respect to such property.

[Sec. 6018(b)]

(b) PROPERTY TO WHICH SECTION APPLIES.—

(1) LARGE TRANSFERS.—This section shall apply to all property (other than cash) acquired from a decedent if the fair market value of such property acquired from the decedent exceeds the dollar amount applicable under section 1022(b)(2)(B) (without regard to section 1022(b)(2)(C)).

(2) TRANSFERS OF CERTAIN GIFTS RECEIVED BY DECEDENT WITHIN 3 YEARS OF DEATH.—This section shall apply to any appreciated property acquired from the decedent if—

(A) subsections (b) and (c) of section 1022 do not apply to such property by reason of section 1022(d)(1)(C), and

(B) such property was required to be included on a return required to be filed under section 6019.

(3) NONRESIDENTS NOT CITIZENS OF THE UNITED STATES.—In the case of a decedent who is a nonresident not a citizen of the United States, paragraphs (1) and (2) shall be applied—

(A) by taking into account only—

(i) tangible property situated in the United States, and

(ii) other property acquired from the decedent by a United States person, and

(B) by substituting the dollar amount applicable under section 1022(b)(3) for the dollar amount referred to in paragraph (1).

(4) RETURNS BY TRUSTEES OR BENEFICIARIES.—If the executor is unable to make a complete return as to any property acquired from or passing from the decedent, the executor shall include in the return a description of such property and the name of every person holding a legal or beneficial interest therein. Upon notice from the Secretary, such person shall in like manner make a return as to such property.

[Sec. 6018(c)]

(c) INFORMATION REQUIRED TO BE FURNISHED.—The information specified in this subsection with respect to any property acquired from the decedent is—

(1) the name and TIN of the recipient of such property,

(2) an accurate description of such property,

(3) the adjusted basis of such property in the hands of the decedent and its fair market value at the time of death,

(4) the decedent's holding period for such property,

(5) sufficient information to determine whether any gain on the sale of the property would be treated as ordinary income,

(6) the amount of basis increase allocated to the property under subsection (b) or (c) of section 1022, and

(7) such other information as the Secretary may by regulations prescribe.

[Sec. 6018(d)]

(d) PROPERTY ACQUIRED FROM DECEDENT.—For purposes of this section, section 1022 shall apply for purposes of determining the property acquired from a decedent.

[Sec. 6018(e)]

(e) STATEMENTS TO BE FURNISHED TO CERTAIN PERSONS.—Every person required to make a return under subsection (a) shall furnish to each person whose name is required to be set forth in such return (other than the person required to make such return) a written statement showing—

(1) the name, address, and phone number of the person required to make such return, and

(2) the information specified in subsection (c) with respect to property acquired from, or passing from, the decedent to the person required to receive such statement.

The written statement required under the preceding sentence shall be furnished not later than 30 days after the date that the return required by subsection (a) is filed.

P.L. 111-312, §301(c) and (d)(1), provides:

(c) SPECIAL ELECTION WITH RESPECT TO ESTATES OF DECEDENTS DYING IN 2010.—Notwithstanding subsection (a), in the case of an estate of a decedent dying after December 31, 2009, and before January 1, 2011, the executor (within the meaning of section 2203 of the Internal Revenue Code of 1986) may elect to apply such Code as though the amendments made by subsection (a) do not apply with respect to chapter 11 of such Code and with respect to property acquired or passing from such decedent (within the meaning of section 1014(b) of such Code). Such election shall be made at such time and in such manner as the Secretary of the Treasury or the Secretary's delegate shall provide. Such an election once made shall be revocable only with the consent of the Secretary of the Treasury or the Secretary's delegate. For purposes of section 2652(a)(1) of such Code, the determination of whether any property is subject to the tax imposed by such chapter 11 shall be made without regard to any election made under this subsection.

(d) EXTENSION OF TIME FOR PERFORMING CERTAIN ACTS.—

(1) ESTATE TAX.—In the case of the estate of a decedent dying after December 31, 2009, and before the date of the enactment of this Act, the due date for—

(A) filing any return under section 6018 of the Internal Revenue Code of 1986 (including any election required to be made on such a return) as such section is in effect after the date of the enactment of this Act without regard to any election under subsection (c),

(B) making any payment of tax under chapter 11 of such Code, and

(C) making any disclaimer described in section 2518(b) of such Code of an interest in property passing by reason of the death of such decedent,

shall not be earlier than the date which is 9 months after the date of the enactment of this Act.

P.L. 111-312, §303(b)(3):

Amended Code Sec. 6018(a)(1) by striking "the applicable exclusion amount" and inserting "the basic exclusion amount". **Effective** for estates of decedents dying and gifts made after 12-31-2010.

P.L. 111-312, §304, provides [but see P.L. 112-240, §101(a)(2)-(3), above]:

SEC. 304. APPLICATION OF EGTRRA SUNSET TO THIS TITLE.

Section 901 of the Economic Growth and Tax Relief Reconciliation Act of 2001 shall apply to the amendments made by this title.

• 2001, Economic Growth and Tax Relief Reconciliation Act of 2001 (P.L. 107-16)

P.L. 107-16, §542(b)(1):

Amended so much of subpart C of part II of subchapter A of chapter 61 as precedes Code Sec. 6019 (Code Sec. 6018). **Effective** for estates of decedents dying after 12-31-2009. Prior to amendment, so much of subpart C of part II of subchapter A of chapter 61 as preceded section 6019 (Code Sec. 6018) read as follows:

SEC. 6018. ESTATE TAX RETURNS.

[Sec. 6018(a)]

(a) RETURNS BY EXECUTOR.—

(1) CITIZENS OR RESIDENTS.—In all cases where the gross estate at the death of a citizen or resident exceeds the applicable exclusion amount in effect under section 2010(c) for the calendar year which includes the date of death, the executor shall make a return with respect to the estate tax imposed by subtitle B.

(2) NONRESIDENTS NOT CITIZENS OF THE UNITED STATES.—In the case of the estate of every nonresident not a citizen of the United States if that part of the gross estate which is situated in the United States exceeds $60,000, the executor shall make a return with respect to the estate tax imposed by subtitle B.

(3) ADJUSTMENT FOR CERTAIN GIFTS.—The amount applicable under paragraph (1) and the amount set forth in paragraph (2) shall each be reduced (but not below zero) by the sum of—

(A) the amount of the adjusted taxable gifts (within the meaning of section 2001(b)) made by the decedent after December 31, 1976, plus

(B) the aggregate amount allowed as a specific exemption under section 2521 (as in effect before its repeal by the Tax Reform Act of 1976) with respect to gifts made by the decedent after September 8, 1976.

Amendments

• 1997, Taxpayer Relief Act of 1997 (P.L. 105-34)

P.L. 105-34, §501(a)(1)(C):

Amended Code Sec. 6018(a)(1) by striking "$600,000" and inserting "the applicable exclusion amount in effect under section 2010(c) for the calendar year which includes the date of death". **Effective** for the estates of decedents dying, and gifts made, after 12-31-97.

P.L. 105-34, §1073(b)(4):

Amended Code Sec. 6018(a) by striking paragraph (4). **Effective** for estates of decedents dying after 12-31-96. Prior to being stricken, Code Sec. 6018(a)(4) read as follows:

(4) RETURN REQUIRED IF EXCESS RETIREMENT ACCUMULATION TAX.—The executor shall make a return with respect to the estate tax imposed by subtitle B in any case where such tax is increased by reason of section 4980A(d).

• 1990, Omnibus Budget Reconciliation Act of 1990 (P.L. 101-508)

P.L. 101-508, §11801(a)(43):

Repealed Code Sec. 6018(a)(3). **Effective** 11-5-90. Prior to repeal, Code Sec. 6018(a)(3) read as follows:

(3) PHASE-IN OF FILING REQUIREMENT AMOUNT. —

In the case of decedents dying in:	Paragraph (1) shall be applied by substituting for "$600,000" the following amount:
1982	$225,000
1983	275,000
1984	325,000
1985	400,000
1986	500,000

P.L. 101-508, §11801(c)(19)(C):

Amended Code Sec. 6018(a) by redesignating paragraphs (4) and (5) as paragraphs (3) and (4) respectively. **Effective** 11-5-90.

P.L. 101-508, §11821(b), provides:

(b) SAVINGS PROVISION.—If—

(1) any provision amended or repealed by this part applied to—

(A) any transaction occurring before the date of the enactment of this Act,

(B) any property acquired before such date of enactment, or

(C) any item of income, loss, deduction, or credit taken into account before such date of enactment, and

(2) the treatment of such transaction, property, or item under such provision would (without regard to the amendments made by this part) affect liability for tax for periods ending after such date of enactment,

nothing in the amendments made by this part shall be construed to affect the treatment of such transaction, property, or item for purposes of determining liability for tax for periods ending after such date of enactment.

• 1988, Technical and Miscellaneous Revenue Act of 1988 (P.L. 100-647)

P.L. 100-647, §1011A(g)(12):

Amended Code Sec. 6018(a) by adding at the end thereof new paragraph (5). **Effective** as if included in the provision of P.L. 99-514 to which it relates.

• 1981, Economic Recovery Tax Act of 1981 (P.L. 97-34)

P.L. 97-34, §401(a)(2)(B):

Amended Code Sec. 6018(a)(3). **Effective** for estates of decedents dying after 12-31-81. Prior to amendment, Code Sec. 6018(a)(3) read as follows:

(3) PHASE-IN OF FILING REQUIREMENT AMOUNT. —In the case of a decedent dying before 1981, paragraph (1) shall be applied—

(A) in the case of a decedent dying during 1977, by substituting "$120,000" for "$175,000",

(B) in the case of a decedent dying during 1978, by substituting "$134,000" for "$175,000",

(C) in the case of a decedent dying during 1979, by substituting "$147,000" for "$175,000", and

(D) in the case of a decedent dying during 1980, by substituting "$161,000" for "$175,000".

• 1976, Tax Reform Act of 1976 (P.L. 94-455)

P.L. 94-455, §2001(c)(1)(J):

Amended Code Sec. 6018(a) by substituting "$175,000" for "$60,000" in paragraph (1), substituting "$60,000" for "$30,000" in paragraph (2), and adding paragraphs (3) and (4). **Effective** for estates of decedents dying after 12-31-76.

• 1966, Foreign Investors Tax Act of 1966 (P.L. 89-809)

P.L. 89-809, §108(g):

Amended Code Sec. 6018(a)(2) by substituting "$30,000" for "$2,000". **Effective** with respect to estates of decedents dying after 11-13-66, the date of enactment.

[Sec. 6018(b)]

(b) RETURNS BY BENEFICIARIES.—If the executor is unable to make a complete return as to any part of the gross estate of the decedent, he shall include in his return a description of such part and the name of every person holding a legal or beneficial interest therein. Upon notice from the Secretary such person shall in like manner make a return as to such part of the gross estate.

P.L. 107-16, §901(a)-(b), as amended by P.L. 111-312, §101(a)(1), provides [but see P.L. 112-240, §101(a)(1) and (3), above]:

SEC. 901. SUNSET OF PROVISIONS OF ACT.

(a) IN GENERAL.—All provisions of, and amendments made by, this Act shall not apply—

(1) to taxable, plan, or limitation years beginning after December 31, 2012, or

(2) in the case of title V, to estates of decedents dying, gifts made, or generation skipping transfers, after December 31, 2012.

(b) APPLICATION OF CERTAIN LAWS.—The Internal Revenue Code of 1986 and the Employee Retirement Income Security Act of 1974 shall be applied and administered to years, estates, gifts, and transfers described in subsection (a) as if the provisions and amendments described in subsection (a) had never been enacted.

• 1976, Tax Reform Act of 1976 (P.L. 94-455)

P.L. 94-455, §1906(b)(13)(A):

Amended 1954 Code by substituting "Secretary" for "Secretary or his delegate" each place it appeared. **Effective** 2-1-77.

[Sec. 6018(c)—Stricken]

Amendments

• 1989, Omnibus Budget Reconciliation Act of 1989 (P.L. 101-239)

P.L. 101-239, §7304(b)(2)(B):

Amended Code Sec. 6018 by striking subsection (c). **Effective** for estates of decedents dying after 7-12-89. Prior to amendment, Code Sec. 6018(c) read as follows:

(c) ELECTION UNDER SECTION 2210.—In all cases in which subsection (a) requires the filing of a return, if an executor elects the applications of section 2210—

(1) RETURN BY EXECUTOR.—The return which the executor is required to file under the provisions of subsection (a) shall be made with respect to that portion of estate tax imposed by subtitle B which the executor is required to pay.

(2) RETURN BY PLAN ADMINISTRATOR.—The plan administrator of an employee stock ownership plan or the eligible worker-owned cooperative, as the case may be, shall make a return with respect to that portion of the tax imposed by section 2001 which such plan or cooperative is required to pay under section 2210(b).

• 1984, Deficit Reduction Act of 1984 (P.L. 98-369)

P.L. 98-369, §544(b)(3):

Amended Code Sec. 6018 by adding subsection (c). **Effective** for those estates of decedents which are required to file returns on a date (including any extensions) after 7-18-84.

[Sec. 6019]

SEC. 6019. GIFT TAX RETURNS.

Any individual who in any calendar year makes any transfer by gift other than—

(1) a transfer which under subsection (b) or (e) of section 2503 is not to be included in the total amount of gifts for such year,

(2) a transfer of an interest with respect to which a deduction is allowed under section 2523, or

(3) a transfer with respect to which a deduction is allowed under section 2522 but only if—

(A)(i) such transfer is of the donor's entire interest in the property transferred, and

(ii) no other interest in such property is or has been transferred (for less than adequate and full consideration in money or money's worth) from the donor to a person, or for a use, not described in subsection (a) or (b) of section 2522, or

(B) such transfer is described in section 2522(d),

shall make a return for such year with respect to the gift tax imposed by subtitle B.

Amendments

• 2013, American Taxpayer Relief Act of 2012 (P.L. 112-240)

P.L. 112-240, §101(a)(1)-(3), provides:

SEC. 101. PERMANENT EXTENSION AND MODIFICATION OF 2001 TAX RELIEF.

(a) PERMANENT EXTENSION.—

(1) IN GENERAL.—The Economic Growth and Tax Relief Reconciliation Act of 2001 is amended by striking title IX.

(2) CONFORMING AMENDMENT.—The Tax Relief, Unemployment Insurance Reauthorization, and Job Creation Act of 2010 is amended by striking section 304.

(3) EFFECTIVE DATE.—The amendments made by this subsection shall apply to taxable, plan, or limitation years beginning after December 31, 2012, and estates of decedents dying, gifts made, or generation skipping transfers after December 31, 2012.

• 2010, Tax Relief, Unemployment Insurance Reauthorization, and Job Creation Act of 2010 (P.L. 111-312)

P.L. 111-312, §301(a):

Amended Code Sec. 6019 to read as such provision would read if subtitle E of title V of the Economic Growth and Tax Relief Reconciliation Act of 2001 (P.L. 107-16) had never been enacted. **Effective** for estates of decedents dying, and transfers made, after 12-31-2009. For a special rule, see Act Sec. 301(c), below. Prior to amendment by P.L. 111-312, Code Sec. 6019 read as follows:

SEC. 6019. GIFT TAX RETURNS.

[Sec. 6019(a)]

(a) IN GENERAL.—Any individual who in any calendar year makes any transfer by gift other than—

(1) a transfer which under subsection (b) or (e) of section 2503 is not to be included in the total amount of gifts for such year,

(2) a transfer of an interest with respect to which a deduction is allowed under section 2523, or

(3) a transfer with respect to which a deduction is allowed under section 2522 but only if—

(A)(i) such transfer is of the donor's entire interest in the property transferred, and

(ii) no other interest in such property is or has been transferred (for less than adequate and full consideration in money or money's worth) from the donor to a person, or for a use, not described in subsection (a) or (b) of section 2522, or

(B) such transfer is described in section 2522(d),

shall make a return for such year with respect to the gift tax imposed by subtitle B.

[Sec. 6019(b)]

(b) STATEMENTS TO BE FURNISHED TO CERTAIN PERSONS.—Every person required to make a return under subsection (a) shall furnish to each person whose name is required to be set forth in such return (other than the person required to make such return) a written statement showing—

(1) the name, address, and phone number of the person required to make such return, and

(2) the information specified in such return with respect to property received by the person required to receive such statement.

The written statement required under the preceding sentence shall be furnished not later than 30 days after the date that the return required by subsection (a) is filed.

P.L. 111-312, §301(c), provides:

(c) SPECIAL ELECTION WITH RESPECT TO ESTATES OF DECEDENTS DYING IN 2010.—Notwithstanding subsection (a), in the case of an estate of a decedent dying after December 31, 2009, and before January 1, 2011, the executor (within the meaning of section 2203 of the Internal Revenue Code of 1986) may elect to apply such Code as though the amendments made by subsection (a) do not apply with respect to chapter 11 of such Code and with respect to property acquired or passing from such decedent (within the meaning of section 1014(b) of such Code). Such election shall be made at such time and in such manner as the Secretary of the Treasury or the Secretary's delegate shall provide. Such an election once made shall be revocable only with the consent of the Secretary of the Treasury or the Secretary's delegate. For purposes of section 2652(a)(1) of such Code, the determination of whether any property is subject to the tax imposed by such chapter 11 shall be made without regard to any election made under this subsection.

P.L. 111-312, §304, provides [but see P.L. 112-240, §101(a)(2)-(3), above]:

SEC. 304. APPLICATION OF EGTRRA SUNSET TO THIS TITLE.

Section 901 of the Economic Growth and Tax Relief Reconciliation Act of 2001 shall apply to the amendments made by this title.

• 2001, Economic Growth and Tax Relief Reconciliation Act of 2001 (P.L. 107-16)

P.L. 107-16, §542(b)(2)(A):

Amended Code Sec. 6019 by striking "Any individual" and inserting "(a) IN GENERAL.—Any individual". **Effective** for estates of decedents dying after 12-31-2009.

P.L. 107-16, §542(b)(2)(B):

Amended Code Sec. 6019 by adding at the end a new subsection (b). **Effective** for estates of decedents dying after 12-31-2009.

P.L. 107-16, §901(a)-(b), as amended by P.L. 111-312, §101(a)(1), provides [but see P.L. 112-240, §101(a)(1) and (3), above]:

SEC. 901. SUNSET OF PROVISIONS OF ACT.

(a) IN GENERAL.—All provisions of, and amendments made by, this Act shall not apply—

(1) to taxable, plan, or limitation years beginning after December 31, 2012, or

(2) in the case of title V, to estates of decedents dying, gifts made, or generation skipping transfers, after December 31, 2012.

(b) APPLICATION OF CERTAIN LAWS.—The Internal Revenue Code of 1986 and the Employee Retirement Income Security Act of 1974 shall be applied and administered to years, estates, gifts, and transfers described in subsection (a) as if the provisions and amendments described in subsection (a) had never been enacted.

• **1997, Taxpayer Relief Act of 1997 (P.L. 105-34)**

P.L. 105-34, §1301(a):

Amended Code Sec. 6019 by striking "or" at the end of paragraph (1), by adding "or" at the end of paragraph (2), and by inserting after paragraph (2) a new paragraph (3). **Effective** for gifts made after 8-5-97.

• **1981, Economic Recovery Tax Act of 1981 (P.L. 97-34)**

P.L. 97-34, §403(b)(3)(A):

Amended so much of Code Sec. 6019 as followed the heading and preceded subsection (b). **Effective**, generally, for gifts made after 12-31-81. Prior to amendment, that language read as follows:

"(a) IN GENERAL.—Any individual who in any calendar quarter makes any transfers by gift (other than transfers which under section 2503(b) are not to be included in the total amount of gifts for such quarter and other than qualified charitable transfers) shall make a return for such quarter with respect to the gift tax imposed by subtitle B."

There is also a special rule applicable to certain wills or trusts, executed or created, before September 12, 1981.

[Sec. 6019(b)—Repealed]

Amendments

• **1981, Economic Recovery Tax Act of 1981 (P.L. 97-34)**

P.L. 97-34, §442(d)(2):

Repealed Code Sec. 6019(b). **Effective** with respect to estates of decedents dying after 12-31-81. Prior to repeal, Code Sec. 6019(b) read as follows:

(b) QUALIFIED CHARITABLE TRANSFERS.—

(1) RETURN REQUIREMENT.—A return shall be made of any qualified charitable transfer—

(A) for the first calendar quarter, in the calendar year in which the transfer is made, for which a return is required to be filed under subsection (a), or

(B) if no return is required to be filed under subparagraph (A), for the fourth calendar quarter in the calendar year in which such transfer is made.

A return made pursuant to the provisions of this paragraph shall be deemed to be a return with respect to any transfer reported as a qualified charitable transfer for the calendar quarter in which such transfer was made.

(2) DEFINITION OF QUALIFIED CHARITABLE TRANSFER.—For purposes of this section, the term "qualified charitable transfer" means a transfer by gift with respect to which a deduction is allowable under section 2522 in an amount equal to the amount transferred.

[Sec. 6019(c)—Repealed]

Amendments

• **1981, Economic Recovery Tax Act of 1981 (P.L. 97-34)**

P.L. 97-34, §403(c)(3)(B):

Repealed Code Sec. 6019(c). **Effective**, generally, for gifts made after 12-31-81. For the special rule applicable to wills and trusts, executed or created, before 9-12-81, see the amendment note at P.L. 97-34, §403(c)(3)(A). Prior to repeal, Code Sec. 6019(c) read as follows:

(c) TENANCY BY THE ENTIRETY.—

For provisions relating to requirement of return in the case of election as to the treatment of gift by creation of tenancy by the entirety, see section 2515(c).

P.L. 97-34, §403(e)(3), provides:

(3) If—

(A) the decedent dies after December 31, 1981,

(B) by reason of the death of the decedent property passes from the decedent or is acquired from the decedent under a will executed before the date which is 30 days after the date of the enactment of this Act, or a trust created before such date, which contains a formula expressly providing that the spouse is to receive the maximum amount of property qualifying for the marital deduction allowable by Federal law,

(C) the formula referred to in subparagraph (B) was not amended to refer specifically to an unlimited marital deduction at any time after the date which is 30 days after the date of enactment of this Act, and before the death of the decedent, and

(D) the State does not enact a statute applicable to such estate which construes this type of formula as referring to the marital deduction allowable by Federal law as amended by subsection (a),

then the amendment made by subsection (a) [relating to the unlimited marital deduction (Code Sec. 2056, as amended by P.L. 97-34)] shall not apply to the estate of such decedent.

• **1970, Excise, Estate, and Gift Tax Adjustment Act of 1970 (P.L. 91-614)**

P.L. 91-614, §102(d)(3):

Amended Code Sec. 6019 by redesignating former subsection (b) as subsection (c) and by substituting subsections (a) and (b) for the following:

"(a) In General.—Any individual who in any calendar year makes any transfers by gift (except those which under section 2503(b) are not to be included in the total amount of gifts for such year) shall make a return with respect to the gift tax imposed by subtitle B."

Effective for gifts made after 12-31-70.

Subpart D—Miscellaneous Provisions

[Sec. 6020]

SEC. 6020. RETURNS PREPARED FOR OR EXECUTED BY SECRETARY.

[Sec. 6020(a)]

(a) PREPARATION OF RETURN BY SECRETARY.—If any person shall fail to make a return required by this title or by regulations prescribed thereunder, but shall consent to disclose all information necessary for the preparation thereof, then, and in that case, the Secretary may prepare such return, which, being signed by such person, may be received by the Secretary as the return of such person.

Amendments

• **1976, Tax Reform Act of 1976 (P.L. 94-455)**

P.L. 94-455, §1906(b)(13)(A):

Amended 1954 Code by substituting "Secretary" for "Secretary or his delegate" each place it appeared. **Effective** 2-1-77.

[Sec. 6020(b)]

(b) EXECUTION OF RETURN BY SECRETARY.—

(1) AUTHORITY OF SECRETARY TO EXECUTE RETURN.—If any person fails to make any return required by any internal revenue law or regulation made thereunder at the time prescribed therefor, or makes, willfully or otherwise, a false or fraudulent return, the Secretary shall make such return from his own knowledge and from such information as he can obtain through testimony or otherwise.

(2) STATUS OF RETURNS.—Any return so made and subscribed by the Secretary shall be prima facie good and sufficient for all legal purposes.

Amendments

• 1984, Deficit Reduction Act of 1984 (P.L. 98-369)

P.L. 98-369, §412(b)(4):

Amended Code Sec. 6020(b)(1) by striking out "(other than a declaration of estimated tax required under section 6015)". **Effective** with respect to tax years beginning after 12-31-84.

• 1976, Tax Reform Act of 1976 (P.L. 94-455)

P.L. 94-455, §1906(b)(13)(A):

Amended 1954 Code by substituting "Secretary" for "Secretary or his delegate" each place it appeared. **Effective** 2-1-77.

• 1968, Revenue and Expenditure Control Act of 1968 (P.L. 90-364)

P.L. 90-364, §103(e)(3):

Amended Code Sec. 6020(b) by deleting "or 6016" which formerly appeared after "section 6015". **Effective** with respect to tax years beginning after 12-31-67. However, such amendment is to be taken into account only as of 5-31-68. For the **effective** date provisions of P.L. 90-364, see the amendment note following Code Sec. 6154.

[Sec. 6021]

SEC. 6021. LISTING BY SECRETARY OF TAXABLE OBJECTS OWNED BY NONRESIDENTS OF INTERNAL REVENUE DISTRICTS.

Whenever there are in any internal revenue district any articles subject to tax, which are not owned or possessed by or under the care or control of any person within such district, and of which no list has been transmitted to the Secretary, as required by law or by regulations prescribed pursuant to law, the Secretary shall enter the premises where such articles are situated, shall make such inspection of the articles as may be necessary and make lists of the same, according to the forms prescribed. Such lists, being subscribed by the Secretary, shall be sufficient lists of such articles for all purposes.

Amendments

• 1976, Tax Reform Act of 1976 (P.L. 94-455)

P.L. 94-455, §1906(b)(13)(A):

Amended 1954 Code by substituting "Secretary" for "Secretary or his delegate" each place it appeared. **Effective** 2-1-77.

PART III—INFORMATION RETURNS

Subpart A—Information Concerning Persons Subject to Special Provisions

* * *

[Sec. 6034]

SEC. 6034. RETURNS BY CERTAIN TRUSTS.

[Sec. 6034(a)]

(a) SPLIT-INTEREST TRUSTS.—Every trust described in section 4947(a)(2) shall furnish such information with respect to the taxable year as the Secretary may by forms or regulations require.

[Sec. 6034(b)]

(b) TRUSTS CLAIMING CERTAIN CHARITABLE DEDUCTIONS.—

(1) IN GENERAL.—Every trust not required to file a return under subsection (a) but claiming a deduction under section 642(c) for the taxable year shall furnish such information with respect to such taxable year as the Secretary may by forms or regulations prescribe, including—

(A) the amount of the deduction taken under section 642(c) within such year,

(B) the amount paid out within such year which represents amounts for which deductions under section 642(c) have been taken in prior years,

(C) the amount for which such deductions have been taken in prior years but which has not been paid out at the beginning of such year,

(D) the amount paid out of principal in the current and prior years for the purposes described in section 642(c),

(E) the total income of the trust within such year and the expenses attributable thereto, and

(F) a balance sheet showing the assets, liabilities, and net worth of the trust as of the beginning of such year.

(2) EXCEPTIONS.—Paragraph (1) shall not apply to a trust for any taxable year if—

(A) all the net income for such year, determined under the applicable principles of the law of trusts, is required to be distributed currently to the beneficiaries, or

(B) the trust is described in section 4947(a)(1).

Amendments

• 2006, Pension Protection Act of 2006 (P.L. 109-280)

P.L. 109-280, §1201(b)(1):

Amended Code Sec. 6034. **Effective** for returns for tax years beginning after 12-31-2006. Prior to amendment, Code Sec. 6034 read as follows:

SEC. 6034. RETURNS BY TRUSTS DESCRIBED IN SECTION 4947(a)(2) OR CLAIMING CHARITABLE DEDUCTIONS UNDER SECTION 642(c).

[Sec. 6034(a)]

(a) GENERAL RULE.—Every trust described in section 4947(a)(2) or claiming a charitable, etc., deduction under section 642(c) for the taxable year shall furnish such information with respect to such taxable year as the Secretary may by forms or regulations prescribe, including—

(1) the amount of the charitable, etc., deduction taken under section 642(c) within such year,

(2) the amount paid out within such year which represents amounts for which charitable, etc., deductions under section 642(c) have been taken in prior years,

(3) the amount for which charitable, etc., deductions have been taken in prior years but which has not been paid out at the beginning of such year,

(4) the amount paid out of principal in the current and prior years for charitable, etc., purposes,

(5) the total income of the trust within such year and the expenses attributable thereto, and

(6) a balance sheet showing the assets, liabilities, and net worth of the trust as of the beginning of such year.

Amendments

• 1980 (P.L. 96-603)

P.L. 96-603, §1(d)(1):

Amended Code Sec. 6034(a) by striking out "section 4947(a)" and inserting in lieu thereof "section 4947(a)(2)", and amended the title of Code Sec. 6034 by striking out "SECTION 4947(a)" and inserting in lieu thereof "SECTION 4947(a)(2)". **Effective** for tax years beginning after 1980.

• 1976, Tax Reform Act of 1976 (P.L. 94-455)

P.L. 94-455, §1906(b)(13)(A):

Amended 1954 Code by substituting "Secretary" for "Secretary or his delegate" each place it appeared. **Effective** 2-1-77.

• 1969, Tax Reform Act of 1969 (P.L. 91-172)

P.L. 91-172, §101(j)(32), (33):

Amended the matter preceding paragraph (2) in Code Sec. 6034. **Effective** for tax years beginning after 12-31-69. Prior to amendment, Code Sec. 6034 read as follows:

SEC. 6034. RETURNS BY TRUSTS CLAIMING CHARITABLE DEDUCTIONS UNDER SECTION 642(c).

(a) General Rule.—Every trust claiming a charitable, etc., deduction under section 642(c) for the taxable year shall furnish such information with respect to such taxable year as the Secretary or his delegate may by forms or regulations prescribe, setting forth—

(1) the amount of the charitable, etc., deduction taken under section 642(c) within such year (showing separately the amount of such deduction which was paid out and the amount which was permanently set aside for charitable, etc., purposes during such year),

[Sec. 6034(b)]

(b) EXCEPTIONS.—This section shall not apply in the case of a taxable year if all the net income for such year, determined under the applicable principles of the law of trusts, is required to be distributed currently to the beneficiaries. This section shall not apply in the case of a trust described in section 4947(a)(1).

Amendments

• 1980 (P.L. 96-603)

P.L. 96-603, §1(d)(1):

Amended Code Sec. 6034(b) by striking out "EXCEPTION" in the heading and inserting in lieu thereof "EXCEPTIONS" and by adding a new last sentence. **Effective** for tax years beginning after 1980.

[Sec. 6034(c)]

(c) CROSS REFERENCE.—

For provisions relating to penalties for failure to file a return required by this section, see section 6652(c).

Amendments

• 1986, Tax Reform Act of 1986 (P.L. 99-514)

P.L. 99-514, §1501(d)(1)(C):

Amended Code Sec. 6034(c) by striking out "section 6652(d)" and inserting in lieu thereof "section 6652(c)". **Effective** for returns the due date for which (determined without regard to extensions) is after 12-31-86.

• 1969, Tax Reform Act of 1969 (P.L. 91-172)

P.L. 91-172, §101(j)(34):

Added Code Sec. 6034(c). **Effective** for tax years beginning after 12-31-69.

[Sec. 6034A]

SEC. 6034A. INFORMATION TO BENEFICIARIES OF ESTATES AND TRUSTS.

[Sec. 6034A(a)]

(a) GENERAL RULE.—The fiduciary of any estate or trust required to file a return under section 6012(a) for any taxable year shall, on or before the date on which such return was required to be filed, furnish to each beneficiary (or nominee thereof)—

(1) who receives a distribution from such estate or trust with respect to such taxable year, or

(2) to whom any item with respect to such taxable year is allocated,

a statement containing such information required to be shown on such return as the Secretary may prescribe.

Amendments

• 1986, Tax Reform Act of 1986 (P.L. 99-514)

P.L. 99-514, §1501(c)(15)(A)-(C):

Amended Code Sec. 6034A(a) by striking out "making the return required to be filed" and inserting in lieu thereof "required to file a return", by striking out "was filed" and inserting in lieu thereof "was required to be filed", and by striking out "shown on such return" and inserting in lieu thereof "required to be shown on such return". **Effective** for returns the due date for which (determined without regard to extensions) is after 12-31-86.

P.L. 99-514, §1875(d)(3)[4](A)(i)-(iii):

Amended Code Sec. 6034A by striking out "The fiduciary" and inserting in lieu thereof "(a) General Rule.—The fiduciary", by striking out "each beneficiary" and inserting in lieu thereof "each beneficiary (or nominee thereof)", and by adding at the end of Code Sec. 6034A subsection (b). **Effective** for tax years of estates and trusts beginning after 10-22-86.

[Sec. 6034A(b)]

(b) NOMINEE REPORTING.—Any person who holds an interest in an estate or trust as a nominee for another person—

(1) shall furnish to the estate or trust, in the manner prescribed by the Secretary, the name and address of such other person, and any other information for the taxable year as the Secretary may by form and regulations prescribe, and

(2) shall furnish in the manner prescribed by the Secretary to such other person the information provided by the estate or trust under subsection (a).

Amendments

• 1984, Deficit Reduction Act of 1984 (P.L. 98-369)

P.L. 98-369, §714(q)(1):

Added Code Sec. 6034A. **Effective** for tax years beginning after 12-31-84.

[Sec. 6034A(c)]

(c) BENEFICIARY'S RETURN MUST BE CONSISTENT WITH ESTATE OR TRUST RETURN OR SECRETARY NOTIFIED OF INCONSISTENCY.—

(1) IN GENERAL.—A beneficiary of any estate or trust to which subsection (a) applies shall, on such beneficiary's return, treat any reported item in a manner which is consistent with the treatment of such item on the applicable entity's return.

(2) NOTIFICATION OF INCONSISTENT TREATMENT.—

(A) IN GENERAL.—In the case of any reported item, if—

(i)(I) the applicable entity has filed a return but the beneficiary's treatment on such beneficiary's return is (or may be) inconsistent with the treatment of the item on the applicable entity's return, or

(II) the applicable entity has not filed a return, and

(ii) the beneficiary files with the Secretary a statement identifying the inconsistency,

paragraph (1) shall not apply to such item.

(B) BENEFICIARY RECEIVING INCORRECT INFORMATION.—A beneficiary shall be treated as having complied with clause (ii) of subparagraph (A) with respect to a reported item if the beneficiary—

(i) demonstrates to the satisfaction of the Secretary that the treatment of the reported item on the beneficiary's return is consistent with the treatment of the item on the statement furnished under subsection (a) to the beneficiary by the applicable entity, and

(ii) elects to have this paragraph apply with respect to that item.

(3) EFFECT OF FAILURE TO NOTIFY.—In any case—

(A) described in subparagraph (A)(i)(I) of paragraph (2), and

(B) in which the beneficiary does not comply with subparagraph (A)(ii) of paragraph (2), any adjustment required to make the treatment of the items by such beneficiary consistent with the treatment of the items on the applicable entity's return shall be treated as arising out of mathematical or clerical errors and assessed according to section 6213(b)(1). Paragraph (2) of section 6213(b) shall not apply to any assessment referred to in the preceding sentence.

(4) DEFINITIONS.—For purposes of this subsection—

(A) REPORTED ITEM.—The term "reported item" means any item for which information is required to be furnished under subsection (a).

(B) APPLICABLE ENTITY.—The term "applicable entity" means the estate or trust of which the taxpayer is the beneficiary.

(5) ADDITION TO TAX FOR FAILURE TO COMPLY WITH SECTION.—For addition to tax in the case of a beneficiary's negligence in connection with, or disregard of, the requirements of this section, see part II of subchapter A of chapter 68.

Amendments

• 1997, Taxpayer Relief Act of 1997 (P.L. 105-34)

P.L. 105-34, §1027(a):

Amended Code Sec. 6034A by adding at the end a new subsection (c). **Effective** for returns of beneficiaries and owners filed after 8-5-97.

[Sec. 6035]

SEC. 6035. BASIS INFORMATION TO PERSONS ACQUIRING PROPERTY FROM DECEDENT.

[Sec. 6035(a)]

(a) INFORMATION WITH RESPECT TO PROPERTY ACQUIRED FROM DECEDENTS.—

(1) IN GENERAL.—The executor of any estate required to file a return under section 6018(a) shall furnish to the Secretary and to each person acquiring any interest in property included in the decedent's gross estate for Federal estate tax purposes a statement identifying the value of each interest in such property as reported on such return and such other information with respect to such interest as the Secretary may prescribe.

(2) STATEMENTS BY BENEFICIARIES.—Each person required to file a return under section 6018(b) shall furnish to the Secretary and to each other person who holds a legal or beneficial interest in the property to which such return relates a statement identifying the information described in paragraph (1).

(3) TIME FOR FURNISHING STATEMENT.—

(A) IN GENERAL.—Each statement required to be furnished under paragraph (1) or (2) shall be furnished at such time as the Secretary may prescribe, but in no case at a time later than the earlier of—

(i) the date which is 30 days after the date on which the return under section 6018 was required to be filed (including extensions, if any), or

(ii) the date which is 30 days after the date such return is filed.

(B) ADJUSTMENTS.—In any case in which there is an adjustment to the information required to be included on a statement filed under paragraph (1) or (2) after such statement has been filed, a supplemental statement under such paragraph shall be filed not later than the date which is 30 days after such adjustment is made.

[Sec. 6035(b)]

(b) REGULATIONS.—The Secretary shall prescribe such regulations as necessary to carry out this section, including regulations relating to—

(1) the application of this section to property with regard to which no estate tax return is required to be filed, and

(2) situations in which the surviving joint tenant or other recipient may have better information than the executor regarding the basis or fair market value of the property.

Amendments

• 2015, Surface Transportation and Veterans Health Care Choice Improvement Act of 2015 (P.L. 114-41)

P.L. 114-41, §2004(b)(1):

Amended subpart A of part III of subchapter A of chapter 61 by inserting after Code Sec. 6034A a new Code Sec. 6035. **Effective** for property with respect to which an estate tax return is filed after 7-31-2015.

[Sec. 6036]

SEC. 6036. NOTICE OF QUALIFICATION AS EXECUTOR OR RECEIVER.

Every receiver, trustee in a case under title 11 of the United States Code, assignee for benefit of creditors, or other like fiduciary, and every executor (as defined in section 2203), shall give notice of his qualification as such to the Secretary in such manner and at such time as may be required by regulations of the Secretary. The Secretary may by regulation provide such exemptions from the requirements of this section as the Secretary deems proper.

Amendments

• 1980, Bankruptcy Tax Act of 1980 (P.L. 96-589)

P.L. 96-589, §6(i)(6):

Amended Code Sec. 6036 by striking out "trustee in bankruptcy" and inserting in lieu thereof "trustee in a case under title 11 of the United States Code". **Effective** 10-1-79 but inapplicable to any proceeding under the Bankruptcy Act commenced before that date.

• 1976, Tax Reform Act of 1976 (P.L. 94-455)

P.L. 94-455, §1906(b)(13)(A):

Amended 1954 Code by substituting "Secretary" for "Secretary or his delegate" each place it appeared. **Effective** 2-1-77.

* * *

[Sec. 6039A—Repealed]

Amendments

• 1980, Crude Oil Windfall Profit Tax Act of 1980 (P.L. 96-223)

P.L. 96-223, §401(a):

Repealed Code Sec. 6039A as added by P.L. 94-455, Act Sec. 2005(d)(1). **Effective** with respect to decedents dying after 12-31-76. However, see the amendment note for P.L. 96-223, §401(a), that follows Code Sec. 1014(d) that authorizes the election of the carryover basis rules in the case of a decedent dying after 12-31-76 and before 11-7-78. Prior to repeal, Code Sec. 6039A read as follows:

SEC. 6039A. INFORMATION REGARDING CARRYOVER BASIS PROPERTY ACQUIRED FROM A DECEDENT.

(a) IN GENERAL.—Every executor (as defined in section 2203) shall furnish the Secretary such information with respect to carryover basis property to which section 1023 applies as the Secretary may by regulation prescribe.

(b) STATEMENT TO BE FURNISHED TO PERSONS WHO ACQUIRE PROPERTY FROM A DECEDENT.—Every executor who is required to furnish information under subsection (a) shall furnish in writing to each person acquiring an item of such property from the decedent (or to whom the item passes from the decedent) the adjusted basis of such item.

• 1976, Tax Reform Act of 1976 (P.L. 94-455)

P.L. 94-455, §2005(d)(f)(1):

Added Code Sec. 6039A. **Effective** in respect of decedents dying after 12-31-79 (as amended by P.L. 95-600, Act Sec. 515(6)).

* * *

[Sec. 6039F]

SEC. 6039F. NOTICE OF LARGE GIFTS RECEIVED FROM FOREIGN PERSONS.

[Sec. 6039F(a)]

(a) IN GENERAL.—If the value of the aggregate foreign gifts received by a United States person (other than an organization described in section 501(c) and exempt from tax under section 501(a)) during any taxable year exceeds $10,000, such United States person shall furnish (at such time and in such manner as the Secretary shall prescribe) such information as the Secretary may prescribe regarding each foreign gift received during such year.

[Sec. 6039F(b)]

(b) FOREIGN GIFT.—For purposes of this section, the term "foreign gift" means any amount received from a person other than a United States person which the recipient treats as a gift or bequest. Such term shall not include any qualified transfer (within the meaning of section 2503(e)(2)) or any distribution properly disclosed in a return under section 6048(c).

[Sec. 6039F(c)]

(c) PENALTY FOR FAILURE TO FILE INFORMATION.—

(1) IN GENERAL.—If a United States person fails to furnish the information required by subsection (a) with respect to any foreign gift within the time prescribed therefor (including extensions)—

(A) the tax consequences of the receipt of such gift shall be determined by the Secretary, and

(B) such United States person shall pay (upon notice and demand by the Secretary and in the same manner as tax) an amount equal to 5 percent of the amount of such foreign gift for each month for which the failure continues (not to exceed 25 percent of such amount in the aggregate).

(2) REASONABLE CAUSE EXCEPTION.—Paragraph (1) shall not apply to any failure to report a foreign gift if the United States person shows that the failure is due to reasonable cause and not due to willful neglect.

[Sec. 6039F(d)]

(d) COST-OF-LIVING ADJUSTMENT.—In the case of any taxable year beginning after December 31, 1996, the $10,000 amount under subsection (a) shall be increased by an amount equal to the product of such amount and the cost-of-living adjustment for such taxable year under section 1(f)(3), except that subparagraph (A)(ii) thereof shall be applied by substituting "1995" for "2016".

Amendments

• 2017, Tax Cuts and Jobs Act (P.L. 115-97)

P.L. 115-97, §11002(d)(13):

Amended Code Sec. 6039F(d) by striking "subparagraph (B) thereof shall be applied by substituting '1995' for '1992'" and inserting "subparagraph (A)(ii) thereof shall be applied by substituting '1995' for '2016'". **Effective** for tax years beginning after 12-31-2017.

[Sec. 6039F(e)]

(e) REGULATIONS.—The Secretary shall prescribe such regulations as may be necessary or appropriate to carry out the purposes of this section.

Amendments

• 1996, Small Business Job Protection Act of 1996 (P.L. 104-188)

P.L. 104-188, §1905(a):

Amended subpart A of part III of subchapter A of chapter 61 by inserting after section 6039E a new section 6039F. **Effective** for amounts received after 8-20-96, in tax years ending after such date.

* * *

[Sec. 6039H]

SEC. 6039H. INFORMATION WITH RESPECT TO ALASKA NATIVE SETTLEMENT TRUSTS AND NATIVE CORPORATIONS.

[Sec. 6039H(a)]

(a) REQUIREMENT.—The fiduciary of an electing Settlement Trust (as defined in section 646(h)(1)) shall include with the return of income of the trust a statement containing the information required under subsection (c).

Amendments

• 2017, Tax Cuts and Jobs Act (P.L. 115-97)

P.L. 115-97, §13821(c)(1)(A):

Amended Code Sec. 6039H by striking "**SPONSORING**" before "**NATIVE CORPORATIONS**" in the heading. **Effective** for tax years beginning after 12-31-2016.

[Sec. 6039H(b)]

(b) APPLICATION WITH OTHER REQUIREMENTS.—The filing of any statement under this section shall be in lieu of the reporting requirements under section 6034A to furnish any statement to a beneficiary regarding amounts distributed to such beneficiary (and such other reporting rules as the Secretary deems appropriate).

[Sec. 6039H(c)]

(c) REQUIRED INFORMATION.—The information required under this subsection shall include—

(1) the amount of distributions made during the taxable year to each beneficiary,

(2) the treatment of such distribution under the applicable provision of section 646, including the amount that is excludable from the recipient beneficiary's gross income under section 646, and

(3) the amount (if any) of any distribution during such year that is deemed to have been made by the sponsoring Native Corporation (as defined in section 646(h)(5)).

[Sec. 6039H(d)]

(d) SPONSORING NATIVE CORPORATION.—

(1) IN GENERAL.—The electing Settlement Trust shall, on or before the date on which the statement under subsection (a) is required to be filed, furnish such statement to the sponsoring Native Corporation (as so defined).

(2) DISTRIBUTEES.—The sponsoring Native Corporation shall furnish each recipient of a distribution described in section 646(e)(3) a statement containing the amount deemed to have been distributed to such recipient by such corporation for the taxable year.

Amendments

• 2013, American Taxpayer Relief Act of 2012 (P.L. 112-240)

P.L. 112-240, §101(a)(1) and (3), provides:

SEC. 101. PERMANENT EXTENSION AND MODIFICATION OF 2001 TAX RELIEF.

(a) PERMANENT EXTENSION.—

(1) IN GENERAL.—The Economic Growth and Tax Relief Reconciliation Act of 2001 is amended by striking title IX.

***

(3) EFFECTIVE DATE.—The amendments made by this subsection shall apply to taxable, plan, or limitation years beginning after December 31, 2012, and estates of decedents dying, gifts made, or generation skipping transfers after December 31, 2012.

• 2001, Economic Growth and Tax Relief Reconciliation Act of 2001 (P.L. 107-16)

P.L. 107-16, §671(b):

Amended subpart A of part III of subchapter A of chapter 61 of subtitle F by inserting after Code Sec. 6039G a new Code Sec. 6039H. **Effective** for tax years ending after 6-7-2001, and to contributions made to electing Settlement Trusts for such year or any subsequent year.

P.L. 107-16, §901(a)-(b), as amended by P.L. 111-312, §101(a)(1), provides [but see P.L. 112-240, §101(a)(1) and (3), above]:

SEC. 901. SUNSET OF PROVISIONS OF ACT.

(a) IN GENERAL.—All provisions of, and amendments made by, this Act shall not apply—

(1) to taxable, plan, or limitation years beginning after December 31, 2012, or

(2) in the case of title V, to estates of decedents dying, gifts made, or generation skipping transfers, after December 31, 2012.

(b) APPLICATION OF CERTAIN LAWS.—The Internal Revenue Code of 1986 and the Employee Retirement Income Security Act of 1974 shall be applied and administered to years, estates, gifts, and transfers described in subsection (a) as if the provisions and amendments described in subsection (a) had never been enacted.

[Sec. 6039H(e)]

(e) DEDUCTIBLE CONTRIBUTIONS BY NATIVE CORPORATIONS TO ALASKA NATIVE SETTLEMENT TRUSTS.—

(1) IN GENERAL.—Any Native Corporation (as defined in subsection (m) of section 3 of the Alaska Native Claims Settlement Act (43 U.S.C. 1602(m))) which has made a contribution to a

Settlement Trust (as defined in subsection (t) of such section) to which an election under subsection (e) of section 247 applies shall provide such Settlement Trust with a statement regarding such election not later than January 31 of the calendar year subsequent to the calendar year in which the contribution was made.

(2) CONTENT OF STATEMENT.—The statement described in paragraph (1) shall include—

(A) the total amount of contributions to which the election under subsection (e) of section 247 applies,

(B) for each contribution, whether such contribution was in cash,

(C) for each contribution which consists of property other than cash, the date that such property was acquired by the Native Corporation and the adjusted basis and fair market value of such property on the date such property was contributed to the Settlement Trust,

(D) the date on which each contribution was made to the Settlement Trust, and

(E) such information as the Secretary determines to be necessary or appropriate for the identification of each contribution and the accurate inclusion of income relating to such contributions by the Settlement Trust.

Amendments

• 2017, Tax Cuts and Jobs Act (P.L. 115-97)

P.L. 115-97, §13821(c)(1)(B):

Amended Code Sec. 6039H by adding at the end a new subsection (e). **Effective** for tax years beginning after 12-31-2016.

* * *

Subpart B—Information Concerning Transactions With Other Persons

* * *

[Sec. 6048]

SEC. 6048. INFORMATION WITH RESPECT TO CERTAIN FOREIGN TRUSTS.

[Sec. 6048(a)]

(a) NOTICE OF CERTAIN EVENTS.—

(1) GENERAL RULE.—On or before the 90th day (or such later day as the Secretary may prescribe) after any reportable event, the responsible party shall provide written notice of such event to the Secretary in accordance with paragraph (2).

(2) CONTENTS OF NOTICE.—The notice required by paragraph (1) shall contain such information as the Secretary may prescribe, including—

(A) the amount of money or other property (if any) transferred to the trust in connection with the reportable event, and

(B) the identity of the trust and of each trustee and beneficiary (or class of beneficiaries) of the trust.

(3) REPORTABLE EVENT.—For purposes of this subsection—

(A) IN GENERAL.—The term "reportable event" means—

(i) the creation of any foreign trust by a United States person,

(ii) the transfer of any money or property (directly or indirectly) to a foreign trust by a United States person, including a transfer by reason of death, and

(iii) the death of a citizen or resident of the United States if—

(I) the decedent was treated as the owner of any portion of a foreign trust under the rules of subpart E of part I of subchapter J of chapter 1, or

(II) any portion of a foreign trust was included in the gross estate of the decedent.

(B) EXCEPTIONS.—

(i) FAIR MARKET VALUE SALES.—Subparagraph (A)(ii) shall not apply to any transfer of property to a trust in exchange for consideration of at least the fair market value of the transferred property. For purposes of the preceding sentence, consideration other than cash shall be taken into account at its fair market value and the rules of section 679(a)(3) shall apply.

(ii) DEFERRED COMPENSATION AND CHARITABLE TRUSTS.—Subparagraph (A) shall not apply with respect to a trust which is—

(I) described in section 402(b), 404(a)(4), or 404A, or

(II) determined by the Secretary to be described in section 501(c)(3).

(4) RESPONSIBLE PARTY.—For purposes of this subsection, the term "responsible party" means—

(A) the grantor in the case of the creation of an inter vivos trust,

(B) the transferor in the case of a reportable event described in paragraph (3)(A)(ii) other than a transfer by reason of death, and

(C) the executor of the decedent's estate in any other case.

[Sec. 6048(b)]

(b) UNITED STATES OWNER OF FOREIGN TRUST.—

(1) IN GENERAL.—If, at any time during any taxable year of a United States person, such person is treated as the owner of any portion of a foreign trust under the rules of subpart E of part I of subchapter J of chapter 1, such person shall submit such information as the Secretary may prescribe with respect to such trust for such year and shall be responsible to ensure that—

(A) such trust makes a return for such year which sets forth a full and complete accounting of all trust activities and operations for the year, the name of the United States agent for such trust, and such other information as the Secretary may prescribe, and

(B) such trust furnishes such information as the Secretary may prescribe to each United States person (i) who is treated as the owner of any portion of such trust or (ii) who receives (directly or indirectly) any distribution from the trust.

(2) TRUSTS NOT HAVING UNITED STATES AGENT.—

(A) IN GENERAL.—If the rules of this paragraph apply to any foreign trust, the determination of amounts required to be taken into account with respect to such trust by a United States person under the rules of subpart E of part I of subchapter J of chapter 1 shall be determined by the Secretary.

(B) UNITED STATES AGENT REQUIRED.—The rules of this paragraph shall apply to any foreign trust to which paragraph (1) applies unless such trust agrees (in such manner, subject to such conditions, and at such time as the Secretary shall prescribe) to authorize a United States person to act as such trust's limited agent solely for purposes of applying sections 7602, 7603, and 7604 with respect to—

(i) any request by the Secretary to examine records or produce testimony related to the proper treatment of amounts required to be taken into account under the rules referred to in subparagraph (A), or

(ii) any summons by the Secretary for such records or testimony.

The appearance of persons or production of records by reason of a United States person being such an agent shall not subject such persons or records to legal process for any purpose other than determining the correct treatment under this title of the amounts required to be taken into account under the rules referred to in subparagraph (A). A foreign trust which appoints an [agent] described in this subparagraph shall not be considered to have an office or a permanent establishment in the United States, or to be engaged in a trade or business in the United States, solely because of the activities of such agent pursuant to this subsection.

(C) OTHER RULES TO APPLY.—Rules similar to the rules of paragraphs (2) and (4) of section 6038A(e) shall apply for purposes of this paragraph.

Amendments

• 2010, Hiring Incentives to Restore Employment Act (P.L. 111-147)

P.L. 111-147, §534(a):

Amended Code Sec. 6048(b)(1) by inserting "shall submit such information as the Secretary may prescribe with respect to such trust for such year and" before "shall be responsible to ensure". **Effective** for tax years beginning after 3-18-2010.

• 1997, Taxpayer Relief Act of 1997 (P.L. 105-34)

P.L. 105-34, §1601(i)(1):

Amended Code Sec. 6048(b) by striking "GRANTOR" in the heading and inserting "OWNER". **Effective** as if included in the provision of P.L. 104-188 to which it relates [**effective** for tax years of U.S. persons beginning after 12-31-95.—CCH].

[Sec. 6048(c)]

(c) REPORTING BY UNITED STATES BENEFICIARIES OF FOREIGN TRUSTS.—

(1) IN GENERAL.—If any United States person receives (directly or indirectly) during any taxable year of such person any distribution from a foreign trust, such person shall make a return with respect to such trust for such year which includes—

(A) the name of such trust,

(B) the aggregate amount of the distributions so received from such trust during such taxable year, and

(C) such other information as the Secretary may prescribe.

(2) INCLUSION IN INCOME IF RECORDS NOT PROVIDED.—

(A) IN GENERAL.—If adequate records are not provided to the Secretary to determine the proper treatment of any distribution from a foreign trust, such distribution shall be treated as an accumulation distribution includible in the gross income of the distributee under chapter 1. To the extent provided in regulations, the preceding sentence shall not apply if the foreign trust elects to be subject to rules similar to the rules of subsection (b)(2)(B).

(B) APPLICATION OF ACCUMULATION DISTRIBUTION RULES.—For purposes of applying section 668 in a case to which subparagraph (A) applies, the applicable number of years for purposes of section 668(a) shall be 1/2 of the number of years the trust has been in existence.

[Sec. 6048(d)]

(d) SPECIAL RULES.—

(1) DETERMINATION OF WHETHER UNITED STATES PERSON MAKES TRANSFER OR RECEIVES DISTRIBUTION.—For purposes of this section, in determining whether a United States person makes a transfer to, or receives a distribution from, a foreign trust, the fact that a portion of such trust is treated as owned by another person under the rules of subpart E of part I of subchapter J of chapter 1 shall be disregarded.

(2) DOMESTIC TRUSTS WITH FOREIGN ACTIVITIES.—To the extent provided in regulations, a trust which is a United States person shall be treated as a foreign trust for purposes of this section and section 6677 if such trust has substantial activities, or holds substantial property, outside the United States.

(3) TIME AND MANNER OF FILING INFORMATION.—Any notice or return required under this section shall be made at such time and in such manner as the Secretary shall prescribe.

(4) MODIFICATION OF RETURN REQUIREMENTS.—The Secretary is authorized to suspend or modify any requirement of this section if the Secretary determines that the United States has no significant tax interest in obtaining the required information.

(5) UNITED STATES PERSON'S RETURN MUST BE CONSISTENT WITH TRUST RETURN OR SECRETARY NOTIFIED OF INCONSISTENCY.—Rules similar to the rules of section 6034A(c) shall apply to items reported by a trust under subsection (b)(1)(B) and to United States persons referred to in such subsection.

Amendments

• 1997, Taxpayer Relief Act of 1997 (P.L. 105-34)

P.L. 105-34, §1027(b):

Amended Code Sec. 6048(d) by adding at the end a new paragraph (5). **Effective** for returns of beneficiaries and owners filed after 8-5-97.

• 1996, Small Business Job Protection Act of 1996 (P.L. 104-188)

P.L. 104-188, §1901(a):

Amended Code Sec. 6048. For the **effective** date, see Act Sec. 1901(d), below.

P.L. 104-188, §1901(d), provides:

(d) EFFECTIVE DATES.—

(1) REPORTABLE EVENTS.—To the extent related to subsection (a) of section 6048 of the Internal Revenue Code of 1986, as amended by this section, the amendments made by this section shall apply to reportable events (as defined in such section 6048) occurring after the date of the enactment of this Act.

(2) GRANTOR TRUST REPORTING.—To the extent related to subsection (b) of such section 6048, the amendments made by this section shall apply to taxable years of United States persons beginning after December 31, 1995.

(3) REPORTING BY UNITED STATES BENEFICIARIES.—To the extent related to subsection (c) of such section 6048, the amendments made by this section shall apply to distributions received after the date of the enactment of this Act.

Prior to amendment, Code Sec. 6048 read as follows:

SEC. 6048. RETURNS AS TO CERTAIN FOREIGN TRUSTS.

[Sec. 6048(a)]

(a) GENERAL RULE.—On or before the 90th day (or on or before such later day as the Secretary may by regulations prescribe) after—

(1) the creation of any foreign trust by a United States person, or

(2) the transfer of any money or property to a foreign trust by a United States person,

the grantor in the case of an inter vivos trust, the fiduciary of an estate in the case of a testamentary trust, or the transferor, as the case may be, shall make a return in compliance with the provisions of subsection (b).

Amendments

• 1982, Tax Equity and Fiscal Responsibility Act of 1982 (P.L. 97-248)

P.L. 97-248, §341(b)

Amended Code Sec. 6048(a) by inserting "(or on or before such later day as the Secretary may by regulations prescribe)" after "the 90th day". **Effective** for returns filed after 9-3-82.

• 1976, Tax Reform Act of 1976 (P.L. 94-455)

P.L. 94-455, §1013(e):

Amended the heading to Code Sec. 6048. Prior to amendment, the heading read as follows:

SEC. 6048. RETURNS AS TO CREATION OF OR TRANSFER TO CERTAIN FOREIGN TRUSTS.

[Sec. 6048(b)]

(b) FORM AND CONTENTS OF RETURNS.—The returns required by subsection (a) shall be in such form and shall set forth, in respect of the foreign trust, such information as the Secretary prescribes by regulation as necessary for carrying out the provisions of the income tax laws.

Amendments

• 1976, Tax Reform Act of 1976 (P.L. 94-455)

P.L. 94-455, §1906(b)(13)(A):

Amended 1954 Code by substituting "Secretary" for "Secretary or his delegate" each place it appeared. **Effective** 2-1-77.

[Sec. 6048(c)]

(c) ANNUAL RETURNS FOR FOREIGN TRUSTS HAVING ONE OR MORE UNITED STATES BENEFICIARIES.—Each taxpayer subject to tax under section 679 (relating to foreign trusts having one or more United States beneficiaries) for his taxable year with respect to any trust shall make a return with respect to such trust for such year at such time and in such manner, and setting forth such information, as the Secretary may by regulations prescribe.

Amendments

• 1976, Tax Reform Act of 1976 (P.L. 94-455)

P.L. 94-455, §1013(d):

Redesignated former Code Sec. 6048(c) as Code Sec. 6048(d) and added a new Code Sec. 6048(c). **Effective** for tax years ending after 12-31-75, but only in the case of—(A) foreign trusts created after 5-21-74, and (B) transfers of property to foreign trusts after 5-21-74.

[Sec. 6048(d)]

(d) CROSS REFERENCE.—

For provisions relating to penalties for violation of this section, see sections 6677 and 7203.

Amendments

• 1976, Tax Reform Act of 1976 (P.L. 94-455)

P.L. 94-455, §1013(d):

Redesignated former Code Sec. 6048(c) as Code Sec. 6048(d). **Effective** for tax years ending after 12-31-75, but only in the case of—(A) foreign trusts created after 5-21-74, and (B) transfers of property to foreign trusts after 5-21-74.

P.L. 94-455, §1013(e):

Amended redesignated Code Sec. 6048(d). **Effective** for tax years ending after 12-31-75, but only in the case of—(A) foreign trusts created after 5-21-74, and (B) transfers of property to foreign trusts after 5-21-74. Prior to amendment, redesignated Code. Sec. 6048(d) read as follows:

(d) CROSS REFERENCES.—

(1) For provisions relating to penalties for violations of this section, see sections 6677 and 7203.

(2) For definition of the term "foreign trust created by a United States person", see section 643(d).

• **1962, Revenue Act of 1962 (P.L. 87-834)**

P.L. 87-834, §7:

Added Code Sec. 6048. **Effective** 10-17-62.

* * *

Subpart F—Information Concerning Tax Return Preparers

[Sec. 6060]

SEC. 6060. INFORMATION RETURNS OF TAX RETURN PREPARERS.

[Sec. 6060(a)]

(a) GENERAL RULE.—Any person who employs a tax return preparer to prepare any return or claim for refund other than for such person at any time during a return period shall make a return setting forth the name, taxpayer identification number, and place of work of each tax return preparer employed by him at any time during such period. For purposes of this section, any individual who in acting as a tax return preparer is not the employee of another tax return preparer shall be treated as his own employer. The return required by this section shall be filed, in such manner as the Secretary may by regulations prescribe, on or before the first July 31 following the end of such return period.

Amendments

• **2007, Small Business and Work Opportunity Tax Act of 2007 (P.L. 110-28)**

P.L. 110-28, §8246(a)(2)(A)(i):

Amended Code Sec. 6060 by striking "INCOME TAX RETURN PREPARERS" in the heading and inserting "TAX RETURN PREPARERS". **Effective** for returns prepared after 5-25-2007.

P.L. 110-28, §8246(a)(2)(A)(ii)(I)-(III):

Amended Code Sec. 6060(a) by striking "an income tax return preparer" each place it appears and inserting "a tax return preparer", by striking "each income tax return preparer" and inserting "each tax return preparer", and by striking "another income tax return preparer" and inserting "another tax return preparer". **Effective** for returns prepared after 5-25-2007.

[Sec. 6060(b)]

(b) ALTERNATIVE REPORTING.—In lieu of the return required by subsection (a), the Secretary may approve an alternative reporting method if he determines that the necessary information is available to him from other sources.

[Sec. 6060(c)]

(c) RETURN PERIOD DEFINED.—For purposes of subsection (a), the term "return period" means the 12-month period beginning on July 1 of each year.

Amendments

• **2014, Tax Technical Corrections Act of 2014 (P.L. 113-295)**

P.L. 113-295, §221(a)(109), Division A:

Amended Code Sec. 6060(c) by striking "'year'" and all that follows and inserting "year.". **Effective** generally 12-19-2014. For a special rule, see Act Sec. 221(b)(2), Division A, below. Prior to being stricken, "'year'" and all that follows read as follows:

year, except that the first return period shall be the 6-month period beginning on January 1, 1977, and ending on June 30, 1977.

P.L. 113-295, §221(b)(2), Division A, provides:

(2) SAVINGS PROVISION.—If—

(A) any provision amended or repealed by the amendments made by this section applied to—

(i) any transaction occurring before the date of the enactment of this Act,

(ii) any property acquired before such date of enactment, or

(iii) any item of income, loss, deduction, or credit taken into account before such date of enactment, and

(B) the treatment of such transaction, property, or item under such provision would (without regard to the amendments or repeals made by this section) affect the liability for tax for periods ending after date of enactment, nothing in the amendments or repeals made by this section shall be construed to affect the treatment of such transaction, property, or item for purposes of determining liability for tax for periods ending after such date of enactment.

• **1976, Tax Reform Act of 1976 (P.L. 94-455)**

P.L. 94-455, §1203(e):

Added Code Sec. 6060. **Effective** for documents prepared after 12-31-76.

PART IV—SIGNING AND VERIFYING OF RETURNS AND OTHER DOCUMENTS

* * *

[Sec. 6061]

SEC. 6061. SIGNING OF RETURNS AND OTHER DOCUMENTS.

[Sec. 6061(a)]

(a) GENERAL RULE.—Except as otherwise provided by subsection (b) and sections 6062 and 6063, any return, statement, or other document required to be made under any provision of the internal revenue laws or regulations shall be signed in accordance with forms or regulations prescribed by the Secretary.

Amendments

• 1998, IRS Restructuring and Reform Act of 1998 (P.L. 105-206)

P.L. 105-206, §2003(a)(1):

Amended Code Sec. 6061 by striking "Except as otherwise provided by" and inserting "(a) GENERAL RULE.—Except as otherwise provided by subsection (b) and". **Effective** 7-22-98.

• 1976, Tax Reform Act of 1976 (P.L. 94-455)

P.L. 94-455, §1906(b)(13)(A):

Amended 1954 Code by substituting "Secretary" for "Secretary or his delegate" each place it appeared. **Effective** 2-1-77.

[Sec. 6061(b)]

(b) ELECTRONIC SIGNATURES.—

(1) IN GENERAL.—The Secretary shall develop procedures for the acceptance of signatures in digital or other electronic form. Until such time as such procedures are in place, the Secretary may—

(A) waive the requirement of a signature for; or

(B) provide for alternative methods of signing or subscribing,

a particular type or class of return, declaration, statement, or other document required or permitted to be made or written under internal revenue laws and regulations.

(2) TREATMENT OF ALTERNATIVE METHODS.—Notwithstanding any other provision of law, any return, declaration, statement, or other document filed and verified, signed, or subscribed under any method adopted under paragraph (1)(B) shall be treated for all purposes (both civil and criminal, including penalties for perjury) in the same manner as though signed or subscribed.

(3) PUBLISHED GUIDANCE.—

(A) IN GENERAL.—The Secretary shall publish guidance as appropriate to define and implement any waiver of the signature requirements or any method adopted under paragraph (1).

(B) ELECTRONIC SIGNATURES FOR DISCLOSURE AUTHORIZATIONS TO, AND OTHER AUTHORIZATIONS OF, PRACTITIONERS.—Not later than 6 months after the date of the enactment of this subparagraph, the Secretary shall publish guidance to establish uniform standards and procedures for the acceptance of taxpayers' signatures appearing in electronic form with respect to any request for disclosure of a taxpayer's return or return information under section 6103(c) to a practitioner or any power of attorney granted by a taxpayer to a practitioner.

(C) PRACTITIONER.—For purposes of subparagraph (B), the term "practitioner" means any individual in good standing who is regulated under section 330 of title 31, United States Code.

Amendments

• 2019, Taxpayer First Act (P.L. 116-25)

P.L. 116-25, §2302:

Amended Code Sec. 6061(b)(3). **Effective** 7-1-2019. Prior to amendment, Code Sec. 6061(b)(3) read as follows:

(3) PUBLISHED GUIDANCE.—The Secretary shall publish guidance as appropriate to define and implement any waiver of the signature requirements or any method adopted under paragraph (1).

• 1998, IRS Restructuring and Reform Act of 1998 (P.L. 105-206)

P.L. 105-206, §2003(a)(2):

Amended Code Sec. 6061 by adding at the end a new subsection (b). **Effective** 7-22-98. For a special rule, see Act Sec. 2003(c)-(e), below.

P.L. 105-206, §2003(c)-(e), provides:

(c) ESTABLISHMENT OF PROCEDURES FOR OTHER INFORMATION.—In the case of taxable periods beginning after December 31, 1999, the Secretary of the Treasury or the Secretary's delegate shall, to the extent practicable, establish procedures to accept, in electronic form, any other information, statements, elections, or schedules, from taxpayers filing returns electronically, so that such taxpayers will not be required to file any paper.

(d) INTERNET AVAILABILITY.—In the case of taxable periods beginning after December 31, 1998, the Secretary of the Treasury or the Secretary's delegate shall establish procedures for all tax forms, instructions, and publications created in the most recent 5-year period to be made available electronically on the Internet in a searchable database at approximately the same time such records are available to the public in paper form. In addition, in the case of taxable periods beginning after December 31, 1998, the Secretary of the Treasury or the Secretary's delegate shall, to the extent practicable, establish procedures for other taxpayer guidance to be made available electronically on the Internet in a searchable database at approximately the same time such guidance is available to the public in paper form.

(e) PROCEDURES FOR AUTHORIZING DISCLOSURE ELECTRONICALLY.—The Secretary shall establish procedures for any taxpayer to authorize, on an electronically filed return, the Secretary to disclose information under section 6103(c) of the Internal Revenue Code of 1986 to the preparer of the return.

* * *

[Sec. 6064]

SEC. 6064. SIGNATURE PRESUMED AUTHENTIC.

The fact that an individual's name is signed to a return, statement, or other document shall be prima facie evidence for all purposes that the return, statement, or other document was actually signed by him.

[Sec. 6065]

SEC. 6065. VERIFICATION OF RETURNS.

Except as otherwise provided by the Secretary, any return, declaration, statement, or other document required to be made under any provision of the internal revenue laws or regulations shall contain or be verified by a written declaration that it is made under the penalties of perjury.

Amendments

• 1976, Tax Reform Act of 1976 (P.L. 94-455)

P.L. 94-455, §1906(a)(6):

Amended Code Sec. 6065 by striking out subsection (b) and striking out "(a) PENALTIES OF PERJURY.—" in subsection (a). **Effective** for tax years beginning after 12-31-76. Prior to repeal, Code Sec. 6065(b) read as follows:

(b) OATH.—The Secretary or his delegate may by regulations require that any return, statement, or other document required to be made under any provision of the internal revenue laws or regulations shall be verified by an oath. This subsection shall not apply to returns and declarations with respect to income taxes made by individuals.

P.L. 94-455, §1906(b)(13)(A):

Amended the 1954 Code by substituting "Secretary" for "Secretary or his delegate" each place it appeared. **Effective** 2-1-77.

PART V—TIME FOR FILING RETURNS AND OTHER DOCUMENTS

[Sec. 6071]

SEC. 6071. TIME FOR FILING RETURNS AND OTHER DOCUMENTS.

[Sec. 6071(a)]

(a) GENERAL RULE.—When not otherwise provided for by this title, the Secretary shall by regulations prescribe the time for filing any return, statement, or other document required by this title or by regulations.

Amendments

• 1976, Tax Reform Act of 1976 (P.L. 94-455)

P.L. 94-455, §1906(b)(13)(A):

Amended 1954 Code by substituting "Secretary" for "Secretary or his delegate" each place it appeared. **Effective** 2-1-77.

[Sec. 6071(b)]

(b) ELECTRONICALLY FILED INFORMATION RETURNS.—Returns made under subpart B of part III of this subchapter (other than returns and statements required to be filed with respect to nonemployee compensation) which are filed electronically shall be filed on or before March 31 of the year following the calendar year to which such returns relate.

Amendments

• 2015, Protecting Americans from Tax Hikes Act of 2015 (P.L. 114-113)

P.L. 114-113, §201(c), Div. Q:

Amended Code Sec. 6071(b) by striking "subparts B and C of part III of this subchapter" and inserting "subpart B of part III of this subchapter (other than returns and statements required to be filed with respect to nonemployee compensation)". **Effective** for returns and statements relating to calendar years beginning after 12-18-2015.

• 1998, IRS Restructuring and Reform Act of 1998 (P.L. 105-206)

P.L. 105-206, §2002(a):

Amended Code Sec. 6071 by redesignating subsection (b) as subsection (c) and by inserting after subsection (a) a new subsection (b). **Effective** for returns required to be filed after 12-31-99. For a special rule, see Act Sec. 2002(b)(1)-(2), below.

P.L. 105-206, §2002(b)(1)-(2), provides:

(1) IN GENERAL.—The Secretary of the Treasury shall conduct a study evaluating the effect of extending the deadline for providing statements to persons with respect to whom information is required to be furnished under subparts B and C of part III of subchapter A of chapter 61 of the Internal Revenue Code of 1986 (other than section 6051 of such Code) from January 31 to February 15 of the year in which the return to which the statement relates is required to be filed.

(2) REPORT.—Not later than June 30, 1999, the Secretary of the Treasury shall submit a report on the study under paragraph (1) to the Committee on Ways and Means of the House of Representatives and the Committee on Finance of the Senate.

[Sec. 6071(c)]

(c) RETURNS AND STATEMENTS RELATING TO EMPLOYEE WAGE INFORMATION AND NONEMPLOYEE COMPENSATION.—Forms W–2 and W–3 and any returns or statements required by the Secretary to report nonemployee compensation shall be filed on or before January 31 of the year following the calendar year to which such returns relate.

Amendments

• 2015, Protecting Americans from Tax Hikes Act of 2015 (P.L. 114-113)

P.L. 114-113, §201(a), Div. Q:

Amended Code Sec. 6071 by redesignating subsection (c) as subsection (d), and by inserting after subsection (b) a new subsection (c). **Effective** for returns and statements relating to calendar years beginning after 12-18-2015.

[Sec. 6071(d)]

(d) SPECIAL TAXES.—For payment of special taxes before engaging in certain trades and businesses, see section 4901 and section 5732.

Amendments

• 2015, Protecting Americans from Tax Hikes Act of 2015 (P.L. 114-113)

P.L. 114-113, §201(a), Div. Q:

Amended Code Sec. 6071 by redesignating subsection (c) as subsection (d). **Effective** for returns and statements relating to calendar years beginning after 12-18-2015.

• 2005, Safe, Accountable, Flexible, Efficient Transportation Equity Act: A Legacy for Users (P.L. 109-59)

P.L. 109-59, §11125(b)(21):

Amended Code Sec. 6071(c) by striking "section 5142" and inserting "section 5732". **Effective** 7-1-2008, but not applicable to taxes imposed for periods before such date.

• 1998, IRS Restructuring and Reform Act of 1998 (P.L. 105-206)

P.L. 105-206, §2002(a):

Amended Code Sec. 6071 by redesignating subsection (b) as subsection (c). **Effective** for returns required to be filed after 12-31-99.

• 1958, Excise Tax Technical Changes Act of 1958 (P.L. 85-859)

P.L. 85-859, §204(1):

Added the phrase "and section 5142" at the end of Sec. 6071(b). **Effective** 9-3-58.

[Sec. 6072]

SEC. 6072. TIME FOR FILING INCOME TAX RETURNS.

[Sec. 6072(a)]

(a) GENERAL RULE.—In the case of returns under section 6012, 6013, or 6017 (relating to income tax under subtitle A), returns made on the basis of the calendar year shall be filed on or before the 15th day of April following the close of the calendar year and returns made on the basis of a fiscal year shall be filed on or before the 15th day of the fourth month following the close of the fiscal year, except as otherwise provided in the following subsections of this section.

Amendments

• 2015, Surface Transportation and Veterans Health Care Choice Improvement Act of 2015 (P.L. 114-41)

P.L. 114-41, §2006(a)(1)(B):

Amended Code Sec. 6072(a) by striking "6017, or 6031" and inserting "or 6017". **Effective** generally for returns for tax years beginning after 12-31-2015. For an exception, see Act Sec. 2006(a)(3)(B), below.

P.L. 114-41, §2006(a)(3)(B), provides:

(B) SPECIAL RULE FOR C CORPORATIONS WITH FISCAL YEARS ENDING ON JUNE 30.—In the case of any C corporation with a taxable year ending on June 30, the amendments made by this subsection shall apply to returns for taxable years beginning after December 31, 2025.

* * *

[Sec. 6075]

SEC. 6075. TIME FOR FILING ESTATE AND GIFT TAX RETURNS.

[Sec. 6075(a)]

(a) ESTATE TAX RETURNS.—Returns made under section 6018(a) (relating to estate taxes) shall be filed within 9 months after the date of the decedent's death.

Amendments

• 2013, American Taxpayer Relief Act of 2012 (P.L. 112-240)

P.L. 112-240, §101(a)(1)-(3), provides:

SEC. 101. PERMANENT EXTENSION AND MODIFICATION OF 2001 TAX RELIEF.

(a) PERMANENT EXTENSION.—

(1) IN GENERAL.—The Economic Growth and Tax Relief Reconciliation Act of 2001 is amended by striking title IX.

(2) CONFORMING AMENDMENT.—The Tax Relief, Unemployment Insurance Reauthorization, and Job Creation Act of 2010 is amended by striking section 304.

(3) EFFECTIVE DATE.—The amendments made by this subsection shall apply to taxable, plan, or limitation years beginning after December 31, 2012, and estates of decedents dying, gifts made, or generation skipping transfers after December 31, 2012.

• 2010, Tax Relief, Unemployment Insurance Reauthorization, and Job Creation Act of 2010 (P.L. 111-312)

P.L. 111-312, §301(a):

Amended Code Sec. 6075(a) to read as such provision would read if subtitle E of title V of the Economic Growth and Tax Relief Reconciliation Act of 2001 (P.L. 107-16) had never been enacted. **Effective** for estates of decedents dying, and transfers made, after 12-31-2009. For a special rule, see Act Sec. 301(c), below. Prior to amendment by P.L. 111-312, Code Sec. 6075(a) read as follows:

(a) RETURNS RELATING TO LARGE TRANSFERS AT DEATH.—The return required by section 6018 with respect to a decedent shall be filed with the return of the tax imposed by chapter 1 for the decedent's last taxable year or such later date specified in regulations prescribed by the Secretary.

P.L. 111-312, §301(c), provides:

(c) SPECIAL ELECTION WITH RESPECT TO ESTATES OF DECEDENTS DYING IN 2010.—Notwithstanding subsection (a), in the case of an estate of a decedent dying after December 31, 2009, and before January 1, 2011, the executor (within the meaning of section 2203 of the Internal Revenue Code of 1986) may elect to apply such Code as though the amendments made by subsection (a) do not apply with respect to chapter 11 of such Code and with respect to property acquired or passing from such decedent (within the meaning of section 1014(b) of such Code). Such election shall be made at such time and in such manner as the Secretary of the Treasury or the Secretary's delegate shall provide. Such an election once made shall be revocable only with the consent of the Secretary of the Treasury or the Secretary's delegate. For purposes of section 2652(a)(1) of such Code, the determination of whether any property is subject to the tax imposed by such chapter 11 shall be made without regard to any election made under this subsection.

P.L. 111-312, §304, provides [but see P.L. 112-240, §101(a)(2)-(3), above]:

SEC. 304. APPLICATION OF EGTRRA SUNSET TO THIS TITLE.

Section 901 of the Economic Growth and Tax Relief Reconciliation Act of 2001 shall apply to the amendments made by this title.

• 2001, Economic Growth and Tax Relief Reconciliation Act of 2001 (P.L. 107-16)

P.L. 107-16, §542(b)(3)(A):

Amended Code Sec. 6075(a). **Effective** for estates of decedents dying after 12-31-2009. Prior to amendment, Code Sec. 6075(a) read as follows:

(a) ESTATE TAX RETURNS.—Returns made under section 6018 (a) (relating to estate taxes) shall be filed within 9 months after the date of the decedent's death.

P.L. 107-16, §901(a)-(b), as amended by P.L. 111-312, §101(a)(1), provides [but see P.L. 112-240, §101(a)(1) and (3), above]:

SEC. 901. SUNSET OF PROVISIONS OF ACT.

(a) IN GENERAL.—All provisions of, and amendments made by, this Act shall not apply—

(1) to taxable, plan, or limitation years beginning after December 31, 2012, or

(2) in the case of title V, to estates of decedents dying, gifts made, or generation skipping transfers, after December 31, 2012.

(b) APPLICATION OF CERTAIN LAWS.—The Internal Revenue Code of 1986 and the Employee Retirement Income Security Act of 1974 shall be applied and administered to years, estates, gifts, and transfers described in subsection (a) as if the provisions and amendments described in subsection (a) had never been enacted.

• Excise, Estate, and Gift Tax Adjustment Act of 1970 (P.L. 91-614)

P.L. 91-614, §101(b):

Amended Code Sec. 6075(a) by substituting "9 months" for "15 months." **Effective** with respect to decedents dying after 12-31-70.

[Sec. 6075(b)]

(b) GIFT TAX RETURNS.—

(1) GENERAL RULE.—Returns made under section 6019 (relating to gift taxes) shall be filed on or before the 15th day of April following the close of the calendar year.

(2) EXTENSION WHERE TAXPAYER GRANTED EXTENSION FOR FILING INCOME TAX RETURN.—Any extension of time granted the taxpayer for filing the return of income taxes imposed by subtitle A for any taxable year which is a calendar year shall be deemed to be also an extension of time granted the taxpayer for filing the return under section 6019 for such calendar year.

(3) COORDINATION WITH DUE DATE FOR ESTATE TAX RETURN.—Notwithstanding paragraphs (1) and (2), the time for filing the return made under section 6019 for the calendar year which includes the date of death of the donor shall not be later than the time (including extensions) for filing the return made under section 6018 (relating to estate tax returns) with respect to such donor.

Amendments

• 2013, American Taxpayer Relief Act of 2012 (P.L. 112-240)

P.L. 112-240, §101(a)(1)-(3), provides:

SEC. 101. PERMANENT EXTENSION AND MODIFICATION OF 2001 TAX RELIEF.

(a) PERMANENT EXTENSION.—

(1) IN GENERAL.—The Economic Growth and Tax Relief Reconciliation Act of 2001 is amended by striking title IX.

(2) CONFORMING AMENDMENT.—The Tax Relief, Unemployment Insurance Reauthorization, and Job Creation Act of 2010 is amended by striking section 304.

(3) EFFECTIVE DATE.—The amendments made by this subsection shall apply to taxable, plan, or limitation years beginning after December 31, 2012, and estates of decedents dying, gifts made, or generation skipping transfers after December 31, 2012.

• 2010, Tax Relief, Unemployment Insurance Reauthorization, and Job Creation Act of 2010 (P.L. 111-312)

P.L. 111-312, §301(a):

Amended Code Sec. 6075(b)(3) to read as such provision would read if subtitle E of title V of the Economic Growth and Tax Relief Reconciliation Act of 2001 (P.L. 107-16) had never been enacted. **Effective** for estates of decedents dying, and transfers made, after 12-31-2009. For a special rule, see Act Sec. 301(c), below. Prior to amendment by P.L. 111-312, Code Sec. 6075(b)(3) read as follows:

(3) COORDINATION WITH DUE DATE FOR SECTION 6018 RETURN.—Notwithstanding paragraphs (1) and (2), the time for filing the return made under section 6019 for the calendar year which includes the date of death of the donor shall not be later than the time (including extensions) for filing the return made under section 6018 (relating to returns relating to large transfers at death) with respect to such donor.

P.L. 111-312, §301(c), provides:

(c) SPECIAL ELECTION WITH RESPECT TO ESTATES OF DECEDENTS DYING IN 2010.—Notwithstanding subsection (a), in the case of an estate of a decedent dying after December 31, 2009, and before January 1, 2011, the executor (within the meaning of section 2203 of the Internal Revenue Code of 1986) may elect to apply such Code as though the amendments made by subsection (a) do not apply with respect to chapter 11 of such Code and with respect to property acquired or passing from such decedent (within the meaning of section 1014(b) of such Code). Such election shall be made at such time and in such manner as the Secretary of the Treasury or the Secretary's delegate shall provide. Such an election once made shall be revocable only with the consent of the Secretary of the Treasury or the Secretary's delegate. For purposes of section 2652(a)(1) of such Code, the determination of whether any property is subject to the tax imposed by such chapter 11 shall be made without regard to any election made under this subsection.

P.L. 111-312, §304, provides [but see P.L. 112-240, §101(a)(2)-(3), above]:

SEC. 304. APPLICATION OF EGTRRA SUNSET TO THIS TITLE.

Section 901 of the Economic Growth and Tax Relief Reconciliation Act of 2001 shall apply to the amendments made by this title.

• 2001, Economic Growth and Tax Relief Reconciliation Act of 2001 (P.L. 107-16)

P.L. 107-16, §542(b)(3)(B)(i)-(ii):

Amended Code Sec. 6075(b)(3) by striking "ESTATE TAX RETURN" in the heading and inserting "SECTION 6018 RETURN", and by striking "(relating to estate tax returns)" and inserting "(relating to returns relating to large transfers at death)". **Effective** for estates of decedents dying after 12-31-2009.

P.L. 107-16, §901(a)-(b), as amended by P.L. 111-312, §101(a)(1), provides [but see P.L. 112-240, §101(a)(1) and (3), above]:

SEC. 901. SUNSET OF PROVISIONS OF ACT.

(a) IN GENERAL.—All provisions of, and amendments made by, this Act shall not apply—

(1) to taxable, plan, or limitation years beginning after December 31, 2012, or

(2) in the case of title V, to estates of decedents dying, gifts made, or generation skipping transfers, after December 31, 2012.

(b) APPLICATION OF CERTAIN LAWS.—The Internal Revenue Code of 1986 and the Employee Retirement Income Security Act of 1974 shall be applied and administered to years, estates, gifts, and transfers described in subsection (a) as if the provisions and amendments described in subsection (a) had never been enacted.

• 1981, Economic Recovery Tax Act of 1981 (P.L. 97-34)

P.L. 97-34, §442(d)(3):

Amended Code Sec. 6075(b). **Effective** with respect to estates of decedents dying after 12-31-81. Prior to amendment, Code Sec. 6075(b) read as follows:

(b) GIFT TAX RETURNS.—

(1) GENERAL RULE.—Except as provided in paragraph (2), returns made under section 6019 (relating to gift taxes) shall be filed on or before—

(A) in the case of a return for the first, second, or third calendar quarter of any calendar year, the 15th day of the second month following the close of the calendar quarter, or

(B) in the case of a return for the fourth calendar quarter of any calendar year, the 15th day of the fourth month following the close of the calendar quarter.

(2) SPECIAL RULE WHERE GIFTS IN A CALENDAR QUARTER TOTAL $25,000 OR LESS.—If the total amount of taxable gifts made by a person during a calendar quarter is $25,000 or less, the return under section 6019 for such quarter shall be filed on or before the date prescribed by paragraph (1) for filing the return for—

(A) the first subsequent calendar quarter in the calendar year in which the sum of—

(i) the taxable gifts made during such subsequent quarter, plus

(ii) all other taxable gifts made during the calendar year and for which a return has not yet been required to be filed under this subsection,

exceeds $25,000, or

(B) if a return is not required to be filed under subparagraph (A), the fourth calendar quarter of the calendar year.

(3) EXTENSION WHERE TAXPAYER GRANTED EXTENSION FOR FILING INCOME TAX RETURN.—Any extension of time granted the taxpayer for filing the return of income taxes imposed by subtitle A for any taxable year which is a calendar year shall be deemed to be also an extension of time granted the taxpayer for filing the return under section 6019 for the fourth calendar quarter of such taxable year.

(4) NONRESIDENTS NOT CITIZENS OF THE UNITED STATES.—In the case of a nonresident not a citizen of the United States, paragraph (2) shall be applied by substituting "$12,500" for "$25,000" each place it appears.

• 1979 (P.L. 96-167)

P.L. 96-167, §8:

Amended Code Sec. 6075(b). **Effective** for returns for gifts made in calendar years ending after 12-29-79. Prior to amendment, Code Sec. 6075(b) read as follows:

(b) GIFT TAX RETURNS.—

(1) GENERAL RULE.—Except as provided in paragraph (2), returns made under section 6019 (relating to gift taxes) shall be filed on or before the 15th day of the second month following the close of the calendar quarter.

(2) SPECIAL RULE WHERE GIFTS IN A CALENDAR QUARTER TOTAL $25,000 OR LESS.—If the total amount of taxable gifts made by a person during a calendar quarter is $25,000 or less, the return under section 6019 for such quarter shall be filed on or before the 15th day of the second month after—

(A) the close of the first subsequent calendar quarter in the calendar year in which the sum of—

(i) the taxable gifts made during such subsequent quarter, plus

(ii) all other taxable gifts made during the calendar year and for which a return has not yet been required to be filed under this subsection,

exceeds $25,000, or

(B) if a return is not required to be filed under subparagraph (A), the close of the fourth calendar quarter of the calendar year.

(3) NONRESIDENTS NOT CITIZENS OF THE UNITED STATES.—In the case of a nonresident not a citizen of the United States, paragraph (2) shall be applied by substituting "$12,500" for "$25,000" each place it appears.

• 1976, Tax Reform Act of 1976 (P.L. 94-455)

P.L. 94-455, §2008(b):

Amended Code Sec. 6075(b). **Effective** for gifts made after 12-31-76. Prior to amendment, Code Sec. 6075(b) read as follows:

(b) GIFT TAX RETURNS.—Returns made under section 6019 (relating to gift taxes) shall be filed on or before the 15th day of the second month following the close of the calendar quarter.

• Excise, Estate, and Gift Tax Adjustment Act of 1970 (P.L. 91-614)

P.L. 91-614, §102(d)(4):

Amended Code Sec. 6075(b) by substituting "the second month following the close of the calendar quarter" for "April following the close of the calendar year.". **Effective** for gifts made after 12-31-70.

* * *

PART VI—EXTENSION OF TIME FOR FILING RETURNS

* * *

[Sec. 6081]

SEC. 6081. EXTENSION OF TIME FOR FILING RETURNS.

[Sec. 6081(a)]

(a) GENERAL RULE.—The Secretary may grant a reasonable extension of time for filing any return, declaration, statement, or other document required by this title or by regulations. Except in the case of taxpayers who are abroad, no such extension shall be for more than 6 months.

Amendments

• 1976, Tax Reform Act of 1976 (P.L. 94-455)

P.L. 94-455, §1906(b)(13)(A):

Amended 1954 Code by substituting "Secretary" for "Secretary or his delegate" each place it appeared. **Effective** 2-1-77.

* * *

[Sec. 6081(c)]

(c) CROSS REFERENCES.—

For time for performing certain acts postponed by reason of war, see section 7508, and by reason of Presidentially declared disaster or terroristic or military action, see section 7508A.

Amendments

• 2002, Victims of Terrorism Tax Relief Act of 2001 (P.L. 107-134)

P.L. 107-134, §112(d)(2):

Amended Code Sec. 6081(c). **Effective** for disasters and terroristic or military actions occurring on or after 9-11-2001, with respect to any action of the Secretary of the Treasury, the Secretary of Labor, or the Pension Benefit Guaranty Corporation occurring on or after 1-23-2002. Prior to amendment, Code Sec. 6081(c) read as follows:

(c) POSTPONEMENT BY REASON OF WAR.—

For time for performing certain acts postponed by reason of war, see section 7508.

PART VII—PLACE FOR FILING RETURNS OR OTHER DOCUMENTS

* * *

[Sec. 6091]

SEC. 6091. PLACE FOR FILING RETURNS OR OTHER DOCUMENTS.

[Sec. 6091(a)]

(a) GENERAL RULE.—When not otherwise provided for by this title, the Secretary shall by regulations prescribe the place for the filing of any return, declaration, statement, or other document, or copies thereof, required by this title or by regulations.

Amendments

• 1976, Tax Reform Act of 1976 (P.L. 94-455)

P.L. 94-455, §1906(b)(13)(A):

Amended 1954 Code by substituting "Secretary" for "Secretary or his delegate" each place it appeared. **Effective** 2-1-77.

[Sec. 6091(b)]

(b) TAX RETURNS.—In the case of returns of tax required under authority of part II of this subchapter—

(1) PERSONS OTHER THAN CORPORATIONS.—

(A) GENERAL RULE.—Except as provided in subparagraph (B), a return (other than a corporation return) shall be made to the Secretary—

(i) in the internal revenue district in which is located the legal residence or principal place of business of the person making the return, or

(ii) at a service center serving the internal revenue district referred to in clause (i), as the Secretary may by regulations designate.

(B) EXCEPTION.—Returns of—

(i) persons who have no legal residence or principal place of business in any internal revenue district,

(ii) citizens of the United States whose principal place of abode for the period with respect to which the return is filed is outside the United States,

(iii) persons who claim the benefits of section 911 (relating to citizens or residents of the United States living abroad), section 931 (relating to income from sources within Guam, American Samoa, or the Northern Mariana Islands), or section 933 (relating to income from sources within Puerto Rico),

(iv) nonresident alien persons, and

(v) persons with respect to whom an assessment was made under section 6851(a) or 6852(a) (relating to termination assessments) with respect to the taxable year,

shall be made at such place as the Secretary may by regulations designate.

(2) CORPORATIONS.—

(A) GENERAL RULE.—Except as provided in subparagraph (B), a return of a corporation shall be made to the Secretary—

(i) in the internal revenue district in which is located the principal place of business or principal office or agency of the corporation, or

(ii) at a service center serving the internal revenue district referred to in clause (i), as the Secretary may by regulations designate.

(B) EXCEPTION.—Returns of—

(i) corporations which have no principal place of business or principal office or agency in any internal revenue district,

(ii) foreign corporations, and

(iii) corporations with respect to which an assessment was made under section 6851(a) (relating to termination assessments) with respect to the taxable year,

shall be made at such place as the Secretary may by regulations designate.

(3) ESTATE TAX RETURNS.—

(A) GENERAL RULE.—Except as provided in subparagraph (B), returns of estate tax required under section 6018 shall be made to the Secretary—

(i) in the internal revenue district in which was the domicile of the decedent at the time of his death, or

(ii) at a service center serving the internal revenue district referred to in clause (i), as the Secretary may by regulations designate.

(B) EXCEPTION.—If the domicile of the decedent was not in an internal revenue district, or if he had no domicile, the estate tax return required under section 6018 shall be made at such place as the Secretary may by regulations designate.

(4) HAND-CARRIED RETURNS.—Notwithstanding paragraph (1), (2), or (3), a return to which paragraph (1)(A), (2)(A), or (3)(A) would apply, but for this paragraph, which is made to the

Secretary by hand carrying shall, under regulations prescribed by the Secretary, be made in the internal revenue district referred to in paragraph (1)(A)(i), (2)(A)(i), or (3)(A)(i), as the case may be.

(5) EXCEPTIONAL CASES.—Notwithstanding paragraph (1), (2), (3), or (4) of this subsection, the Secretary may permit a return to be filed in any internal revenue district, and may require the return of any officer or employee of the Treasury Department to be filed in any internal revenue district selected by the Secretary.

(6) ALCOHOL, TOBACCO, AND FIREARMS RETURNS, ETC.—In the case of any return of tax imposed by section 4181 or subtitle E (relating to taxes on alcohol, tobacco, and firearms), subsection (a) shall apply (and this subsection shall not apply).

Amendments

• 2018, Tax Technical Corrections Act of 2018 (P.L. 115-141)

P.L. 115-141, §401(a)(266), Div. U:

Amended Code Sec. 6091(b)(2)(B)(ii) by striking "and" at the end. **Effective** 3-23-2018.

P.L. 115-141, §401(d)(1)(D)(xviii), Div. U:

Amended Code Sec. 6091(b)(2)(B) by striking clause (ii) and by redesignating clauses (iii) and (iv) as clauses (ii) and (iii), respectively. **Effective** 3-23-2018. For a special rule, see Act Sec. 401(e), Div. U, below. Prior to being stricken, Code Sec. 6091(b)(2)(B)(ii) read as follows:

(ii) corporations which claim the benefits of section 936 (relating to possession tax credit),

P.L. 115-141, §401(e), Div. U, provides:

(e) GENERAL SAVINGS PROVISION WITH RESPECT TO DEADWOOD PROVISIONS.—If—

(1) any provision amended or repealed by the amendments made by subsection (b) or (d) applied to—

(A) any transaction occurring before the date of the enactment of this Act,

(B) any property acquired before such date of enactment, or

(C) any item of income, loss, deduction, or credit taken into account before such date of enactment, and

(2) the treatment of such transaction, property, or item under such provision would (without regard to the amendments or repeals made by such subsection) affect the liability for tax for periods ending after such date of enactment, nothing in the amendments or repeals made by this section shall be construed to affect the treatment of such transaction, property, or item for purposes of determining liability for tax for periods ending after such date of enactment.

• 1989, Omnibus Budget Reconciliation Act of 1989 (P.L. 101-239)

P.L. 101-239, §7841(f):

Amended Code Sec. 6091(b)(6) by inserting "section 4181 or" before "subtitle E". **Effective** 12-19-89.

• 1987, Revenue Act of 1987 (P.L. 100-203)

P.L. 100-203, §10713(b)(2)(A):

Amended Code Sec. 6091(b)(1)(B)(v) by striking out "section 6851(a)" and inserting in lieu thereof "section 6851(a) or 6852(a)". **Effective** 12-22-87.

• 1986, Tax Reform Act of 1986 (P.L. 99-514)

P.L. 99-514, §1272(d)(10):

Amended Code Sec. 6091(b)(1)(B)(iii) by striking out "possessions of the United States" and inserting in lieu thereof "Guam, American Samoa, or the Northern Mariana Islands". **Effective**, generally, for tax years beginning after 12-31-86. For a special rule, see Act Sec. 1277(b), below.

P.L. 99-514, §1277(b), provides:

(b) SPECIAL RULE FOR GUAM, AMERICAN SAMOA, AND THE NORTHERN MARIANA ISLANDS.—The amendments made by this subtitle shall apply with respect to Guam, American Samoa, or the Northern Mariana Islands (and to residents thereof and corporations created or organized therein) only if (and so long as) an implementing agreement under section 1271 is in effect between the United States and such possession.

See also Act Sec. 1277(e) following Code Sec. 48 for a special rule regarding treatment of certain U.S. persons.

P.L. 99-514, §1879(r)(1):

Amended Code Sec. 6091(b) by adding at the end thereof new paragraph (6). **Effective** on the first day of the first calendar month which begins more than 90 days after 10-22-86.

• 1981, Economic Recovery Tax Act of 1981 (P.L. 97-34)

P.L. 97-34, §111(b)(3):

Amended Code Sec. 6091(b)(1)(B)(iii) by striking out "relating to income earned by employees in certain camps" and inserting in lieu thereof "relating to citizens or residents of the United States living abroad". **Effective** with respect to tax years beginning after 12-31-81.

P.L. 97-34, §112(b)(6):

Amended Code Sec. 6091(b)(1)(B) by striking out "section 913 (relating to deduction for certain expenses of living abroad)". **Effective** with respect to tax years beginning after 12-31-81.

• 1978, Tax Treatment Extension Act of 1978 (P.L. 95-615)

P.L. 95-615, §202(f)(5):

Amended Code Sec. 6091(b)(1)(B)(iii) by striking out "relating to earned income from sources without the United States" and inserting in lieu thereof "relating to income earned by employees in certain camps". **Effective** for tax years beginning after 12-31-77.

P.L. 95-615, §207(b):

Amended Code Sec. 6091(b)(1)(B)(iii) by inserting "section 913 (relating to deduction for certain expenses of living abroad)," before "section 931". **Effective** for tax years beginning after 12-31-77.

• 1976 (P.L. 94-528)

P.L. 94-528, §2(a):

Amended the **effective** date of §1204 of the Tax Reform Act (see below) to change the date from December 31, 1976 to February 28, 1977. **Effective** 10-4-76.

• 1976, Tax Reform Act of 1976 (P.L. 94-455)

P.L. 94-455, §§1051(h), 1052(c), 1053(d):

Amended Code Sec. 6091(b)(2)(B)(ii). **Effective** for tax years beginning after 12-31-75.

P.L. 94-455, §1204(c):

Struck out "and" at the end of paragraph (1)(B)(iii), struck out paragraph (1)(B)(iv), and inserted the material following paragraph (1)(B)(iii). **Effective** with respect to action taken under Code Sec. 6851, 6861, or 6862 of the Internal Revenue Code of 1954 where the notice and demand takes place after 12-31-76 (however, see P.L. 94-528 above). Prior to repeal, Code Sec. 6091(b)(1)(B)(iv) read as follows:

(iv) nonresident alien persons, shall be made at such place as the Secretary or his delegate may by regulations designate.

P.L. 94-455, §1204(c):

Also struck out "and" at the end of paragraph (2)(B)(ii), struck out paragraph (2)(B)(iii), and inserted the material following paragraph (2)(B)(ii). **Effective** with respect to action taken under Code Sec. 6851, 6861, or 6862 of the Internal Revenue Code of 1954 where the notice and demand takes place after 12-31-76 (however, see P.L. 94-528 above). Prior to repeal, Code Sec. 6091(b)(2)(B)(iii) read as follows:

(iii) foreign corporations, shall be made at such place as the Secretary or his delegate may by regulations designate.

P.L. 94-455, §1906(b)(13)(A):

Amended 1954 Code by substituting "Secretary" for "Secretary or his delegate" each place it appeared. **Effective** 2-1-77.

• 1970, Excise, Estate, and Gift Tax Adjustment Act of 1970 (P.L. 91-614)

P.L. 91-614, §101(i)(2):

Amended paragraphs (3) and (4). **Effective** 1-1-71. Prior to amendment, paragraphs (3) and (4) read as follows:

(3) Estate tax returns.—Returns of estate tax required under section 6018 shall be made to the Secretary or his delegate in the internal revenue district in which was the domicile of the decedent at the time of his death or, if there was no such domicile in an internal revenue district, then at such place as the Secretary or his delegate may by regulations prescribe.

(4) Hand-carried returns.—Notwithstanding paragraph (1) or (2), a return to which paragraph (1)(A) or (2)(A) would apply, but for this paragraph, which is made to the Secretary or his delegate by handcarrying shall, under regulations prescribed by the Secretary or his delegate, be made in the internal revenue district referred to in paragraph (1)(A)(i) or (2)(A)(i), as the case may be.

• 1966 (P.L. 89-713)

P.L. 89-713, §1(a):

Redesignated paragraph (4) as paragraph (5), substituted "(3), or (4)" for "or (3)" in newly designated paragraph (5), added a new paragraph (4), and amended paragraphs (1) and (2). **Effective** 11-2-66. Prior to amendment, paragraphs (1) and (2) read as follows:

(1) Individuals.—Returns (other than corporation returns) shall be made to the Secretary or his delegate in the internal revenue district in which is located the legal residence or principal place of business of the person making the return, or, if he has no legal residence or principal place of business in any internal revenue district, then at such place as the Secretary or his delegate may by regulations prescribe.

(2) Corporations.—Returns of corporations shall be made to the Secretary or his delegate in the internal revenue district in which is located the principal place of business or principal office or agency of the corporation, or, if it has no principal place of business or principal office or agency in any internal revenue district, then at such place as the Secretary or his delegate may be regulations prescribe.

* * *

Subchapter B—Miscellaneous Provisions

[Sec. 6101]

SEC. 6101. PERIOD COVERED BY RETURNS OR OTHER DOCUMENTS.

When not otherwise provided for by this title, the Secretary may by regulations prescribe the period for which, or the date as of which, any return, statement, or other document required by this title or by regulations, shall be made.

Amendments

• 1976, Tax Reform Act of 1976 (P.L. 94-455)

P.L. 94-455, §1906(b)(13)(A):

Amended 1954 Code by substituting "Secretary" for "Secretary or his delegate" each place it appeared. **Effective** 2-1-77.

[Sec. 6102]

SEC. 6102. COMPUTATIONS ON RETURNS OR OTHER DOCUMENTS.

[Sec. 6102(a)]

(a) AMOUNTS SHOWN ON INTERNAL REVENUE FORMS.—The Secretary is authorized to provide with respect to any amount required to be shown on a form prescribed for any internal revenue return, statement, or other document, that if such amount of such item is other than a whole-dollar amount, either—

(1) the fractional part of a dollar shall be disregarded; or

(2) the fractional part of a dollar shall be disregarded unless it amounts to one-half dollar or more, in which case the amount (determined without regard to the fractional part of a dollar) shall be increased by $1.

Amendments

• 1976, Tax Reform Act of 1976 (P.L. 94-455)

P.L. 94-455, §1906(b)(13)(A):

Amended 1954 Code by substituting "Secretary" for "Secretary or his delegate" each place it appeared. **Effective** 2-1-77.

[Sec. 6102(b)]

(b) ELECTION NOT TO USE WHOLE DOLLAR AMOUNTS.—Any person making a return, statement, or other document shall be allowed, under regulations prescribed by the Secretary, to make such return, statement, or other document without regard to subsection (a).

Amendments

• 1976, Tax Reform Act of 1976 (P.L. 94-455)

P.L. 94-455, §1906(b)(13)(A):

Amended 1954 Code by substituting "Secretary" for "Secretary or his delegate" each place it appeared. **Effective** 2-1-77.

[Sec. 6102(c)]

(c) INAPPLICABILITY TO COMPUTATION OF AMOUNT.—The provisions of subsections (a) and (b) shall not be applicable to items which must be taken into account in making the computations necessary to determine the amount required to be shown on a form, but shall be applicable only to such final amount.

[Sec. 6103]

SEC. 6103. CONFIDENTIALITY AND DISCLOSURE OF RETURNS AND RETURN INFORMATION.

[Sec. 6103(a)]

(a) GENERAL RULE.—Returns and return information shall be confidential, and except as authorized by this title—

(1) no officer or employee of the United States,

(2) no officer or employee of any State, any local law enforcement agency receiving information under subsection (i)(1)(C) or (7)(A), any local child support enforcement agency, or any local agency administering a program listed in subsection (l)(7)(D) who has or had access to returns or return information under this section or section 6104(c), and

(3) no other person (or officer or employee thereof) who has or had access to returns or return information under subsection (c), subsection (e)(1)(D)(iii), paragraph (10), (13), (14), or (15) of subsection (k), paragraph (6), (10), (12), (13) (other than subparagraphs (D)(v) and (D)(vi) thereof), (16), (19), (20), or (21) of subsection (l), paragraph (2) or (4)(B) of subsection (m), or subsection (n),

shall disclose any return or return information obtained by him in any manner in connection with his service as such an officer or an employee or otherwise or under the provisions of this section. For purposes of this subsection, the term "officer or employee" includes a former officer or employee.

Amendments

• 2020, COVID-related Tax Relief Act of 2020 (P.L. 116-260)

P.L. 116-260, §283(b)(2)(A), Div. N:

Amended Code Sec. 6103(a)(3) by striking "or (14)" and inserting "(14), or (15)". **Effective** for disclosures made on or after 12-27-2020.

P.L. 116-260, §284(a)(3)(A), Div. N:

Amended Code Sec. 6103(a)(3), as amended by section 3516(a)(1) of the CARES Act (P.L. 116-136), by striking "(13)(A), (13)(B), (13)(C), (13)(D)(i)," and inserting "(13) (other than subparagraphs (D)(v) and (D)(vi) thereof),". **Effective** for disclosures made after the date of the enactment of the FUTURE Act (P.L. 116-91) [**effective** for disclosures made after 12-19-2019.—CCH].

• 2020, Consolidated Appropriations Act, 2021 (P.L. 116-260)

P.L. 116-260, §102(b)(2)(A), Div. FF:

Amended Code Sec. 6103(a)(3) by striking "or (14)" and inserting "(14), or (15)". [Note: An identical amendment was made by P.L. 116-260, Act Sec. 283(b)(2)(A), Div. N. Therefore, this amendment cannot be made.—CCH] **Effective** for disclosures made on or after 12-27-2020.

P.L. 116-260, §103(a)(3)(A), Div. FF:

Amended Code Sec. 6103(a)(3), as amended by section 3516(a)(1) of the CARES Act (P.L. 116-136), by striking "(13)(A), (13)(B), (13)(C), (13)(D)(i)," and inserting "(13) (other than subparagraphs (D)(v) and (D)(vi) thereof),". [Note: An identical amendment was made by P.L. 116-260, Act Sec. 284(a)(3)(A), Div. N. Therefore, this amendment cannot be made.—CCH] **Effective** for disclosures made after the date of the enactment of the FUTURE Act (P.L. 116-91) [**effective** for disclosures made after 12-19-2019.—CCH].

• 2020, Coronavirus Aid, Relief, and Economic Security (CARES) Act (P.L. 116-136)

P.L. 116-136, §3516(a)(1):

Amended Code Sec. 6103(a)(3), as amended by the FUTURE Act (P.L. 116-91), by striking "(13), (16)" and inserting "(13)(A), (13)(B), (13)(C), (13)(D)(i), (16)". **Effective** as if included in the enactment of the FUTURE Act (P.L. 116-91) [**effective** for disclosures after 12-19-2019.—CCH].

• 2019, Fostering Undergraduate Talent by Unlocking Resources for Education (FUTURE) Act (P.L. 116-91)

P.L. 116-91, §3(b):

Amended Code Sec. 6103(a)(3) by inserting ", (13)" after "(12)". **Effective** for disclosures after 12-19-2019.

• 2019, Taxpayer First Act (P.L. 116-25)

P.L. 116-25, §1405(a)(2)(A):

Amended Code Sec. 6103(a)(3) by striking "subsection (k)(10)" and inserting "paragraph (10) or (13) of subsection (k)". **Effective** for disclosures made after 7-1-2019.

P.L. 116-25, §2003(c)(2)(A):

Amended Code Sec. 6103(a)(3), as amended by this Act, by striking "or (13)" and inserting ", (13), or (14)". **Effective** 7-1-2019.

P.L. 116-25, §2202(b):

Amended Code Sec. 6103(a)(3) by inserting "subsection (c)," after "return information under". **Effective** for disclosures made after the date which is 180 days after 7-1-2019.

• 2016, Recovering Missing Children Act (P.L. 114-184)

P.L. 114-184, §2(b)(2)(A):

Amended Code Sec. 6103(a)(2) by striking "subsection (i)(7)(A)" and inserting "subsection (i)(1)(C) or (7)(A)". **Effective** for disclosures made after 6-30-2016.

• 2013, American Taxpayer Relief Act of 2012 (P.L. 112-240)

P.L. 112-240, §209(b)(1):

Amended Code Sec. 6103(a)(3) by inserting "subsection (k)(10)," after "subsection (e)(1)(D)(iii),". **Effective** 1-2-2013.

• 2010, Patient Protection and Affordable Care Act (P.L. 111-148)

P.L. 111-148, §1414(b):

Amended Code Sec. 6103(a)(3) by striking "or (20)" and inserting "(20), or (21)". **Effective** 3-23-2010.

• 2008, SSI Extension for Elderly and Disabled Refugees Act (P.L. 110-328)

P.L. 110-328, §3(b)(1):

Amended Code Sec. 6103(a)(3) by inserting "(10)," after "(6),". **Effective** for refunds payable under Code Sec. 6402 on or after 9-30-2008.

• 2006, Pension Protection Act of 2006 (P.L. 109-280)

P.L. 109-280, §1224(b)(1):

Amended Code Sec. 6103(a)(2) by inserting "or section 6104(c)" after "this section". **Effective** 8-17-2006 but shall not apply to requests made before such date.

• 2003, Medicare Prescription Drug, Improvement, and Modernization Act of 2003 (P.L. 108-173)

P.L. 108-173, §105(e)(2):

Amended Code Sec. 6103(a)(3) by striking "or (16)" and inserting "(16), or (19)". **Effective** 12-8-2003.

P.L. 108-173, §811(c)(2)(A):

Amended Code Sec. 6103(a)(3), as amended by Act Sec. 105(e)(1)[(2)], by striking "or (19)" and inserting "(19), or (20)". **Effective** 12-8-2003.

• 2002, Victims of Terrorism Tax Relief Act of 2001 (P.L. 107-134)

P.L. 107-134, §201(c)(1):

Amended Code Sec. 6103(a)(2) by inserting "any local law enforcement agency receiving information under subsection (i)(7)(A)," after "State,". **Effective** for disclosures made on or after 1-23-2002.

• 1997, Balanced Budget Act of 1997 (P.L. 105-33)

P.L. 105-33, §11024(b)(2):

Amended Code Sec. 6103(a)(3) by striking "(6) or (12)" and inserting "(6), (12), or (16)". For the **effective** date, see Act Sec. 11721, below.

P.L. 105-33, §11721, provides:

Except as otherwise provided in this title, the provisions of this title shall take effect on the later of October 1, 1997, or the day the District of Columbia Financial Responsibility and Management Assistance Authority certifies that the financial plan and budget for the District government for fiscal year 1998 meet the requirements of section 201(c)(1) of the District of Columbia Financial Responsibility and Management Assistance Act of 1995, as amended by this title.

• 1996, Personal Responsibility and Work Opportunity Reconciliation Act of 1996 (P.L. 104-193)

P.L. 104-193, §316(g)(4)(B)(i):

Amended Code Sec. 6103(a)(3) by striking "(l)(12)" and inserting "paragraph (6) or (12) of subsection (l)". **Effective** 8-22-96.

• 1989, Omnibus Budget Reconciliation Act of 1989 (P.L. 101-239)

P.L. 101-239, §6202(a)(1)(B)(i):

Amended Code Sec. 6103(a)(3) by inserting "(l)(12)," after "(e)(1)(D)(iii),". **Effective** 12-19-89.

• 1984, Deficit Reduction Act of 1984 (P.L. 98-369)

P.L. 98-369, §2651(k)(2):

Amended Code Sec. 6103(a)(2) by striking out "or of any local child support enforcement agency" and inserting in lieu thereof ", any local child support enforcement agency, or any local agency administering a program listed in subsection (l)(7)(D)". **Effective** 7-18-84.

• 1982, Debt Collection Act of 1982 (P.L. 97-365)

P.L. 97-365, §8(c)(1):

Amended Code Sec. 6103(a)(3) by striking out "subsection (m)(4)(B)" and inserting in lieu thereof "paragraph (2) or (4)(B) of subsection (m)". **Effective** 10-25-82.

• 1978, Revenue Act of 1978 (P.L. 95-600)

P.L. 95-600, §701(bb)(1)(B):

Amended Code Sec. 6103(a)(3) by inserting ", subsection (m)(4)(B)," after "subsection (e)(1)(D)(iii)". **Effective** 1-1-77.

• 1976, Tax Reform Act of 1976 (P.L. 94-455)

P.L. 94-455, §1202(a):

Amended Code Sec. 6103(a). **Effective** 1-1-77. Prior to amendment, Code Sec. 6103(a) read as follows:

(a) PUBLIC RECORD AND INSPECTION.—

(1) Returns made with respect to taxes imposed by chapters 1, 2, 3, and 6 upon which the tax has been determined by the Secretary or his delegate shall constitute public records; but, except as hereinafter provided in this section, they shall be open to inspection only upon order of the President and under rules and regulations prescribed by the Secretary or his delegate and approved by the President.

(2) All returns made with respect to the taxes imposed by chapters 1, 2, 3, 5, 6, 11, 12, and 32, subchapters B and C of chapter 33, subchapter B of chapter 37, and chapter 41 shall constitute public records and shall be open to public examination and inspection to such extent as shall be authorized in rules and regulations promulgated by the President.

(3) Whenever a return is open to the inspection of any person, a certified copy thereof shall, upon request, be furnished to such person under rules and regulations prescribed by the Secretary or his delegate. The Secretary or his delegate may prescribe a reasonable fee for furnishing such copy.

• 1966 (P.L. 89-713)

P.L. 89-713, §4(a):

Amended the heading to Code Sec. 6103 by substituting "AND DISCLOSURE OF INFORMATION AS TO PERSONS FILING INCOME TAX RETURNS" for "LISTS OF TAXPAYERS". **Effective** 11-2-66.

• 1965, Excise Tax Reduction Act of 1965 (P.L. 89-44)

P.L. 89-44, §601(a):

Amended Sec. 6103(a) by substituting "B and C" for "B, C, and D" in paragraph (2).

• 1964, Interest Equalization Tax Act (P.L. 88-563)

P.L. 88-563, §3(c):

Amended Code Sec. 6103(a)(2) by substituting "subchapter B of chapter 37, and chapter 41" for "and subchapter B of chapter 37".

[Sec. 6103(b)]

(b) DEFINITIONS.—For purposes of this section—

(1) RETURN.—The term "return" means any tax or information return, declaration of estimated tax, or claim for refund required by, or provided for or permitted under, the provisions of this title which is filed with the Secretary by, on behalf of, or with respect to any person, and any amendment or supplement thereto, including supporting schedules, attachments, or lists which are supplemental to, or part of, the return so filed.

(2) RETURN INFORMATION.—The term "return information" means—

(A) a taxpayer's identity, the nature, source, or amount of his income, payments, receipts, deductions, exemptions, credits, assets, liabilities, net worth, tax liability, tax withheld, deficiencies, overassessments, or tax payments, whether the taxpayer's return was, is being, or will be examined or subject to other investigation or processing, or any other data, received by, recorded by, prepared by, furnished to, or collected by the Secretary with respect to a return or with respect to the determination of the existence, or possible existence, of liability (or the amount thereof) of any person under this title for any tax, penalty, interest, fine, forfeiture, or other imposition, or offense,

(B) any part of any written determination or any background file document relating to such written determination (as such terms are defined in section 6110(b)) which is not open to public inspection under section 6110,

(C) any advance pricing agreement entered into by a taxpayer and the Secretary and any background information related to such agreement or any application for an advance pricing agreement, and

(D) any agreement under section 7121, and any similar agreement, and any background information related to such an agreement or request for such an agreement,

but such term does not include data in a form which cannot be associated with, or otherwise identify, directly or indirectly, a particular taxpayer. Nothing in the preceding sentence, or in any other provision of law, shall be construed to require the disclosure of standards used or to be used for the selection of returns for examination, or data used or to be used for determining such standards, if the Secretary determines that such disclosure will seriously impair assessment, collection, or enforcement under the internal revenue laws.

(3) TAXPAYER RETURN INFORMATION.—The term "taxpayer return information" means return information as defined in paragraph (2) which is filed with, or furnished to, the Secretary by or on behalf of the taxpayer to whom such return information relates.

(4) TAX ADMINISTRATION.—The term "tax administration"—

(A) means—

(i) the administration, management, conduct, direction, and supervision of the execution and application of the internal revenue laws or related statutes (or equivalent laws and statutes of a State) and tax conventions to which the United States is a party, and

(ii) the development and formulation of Federal tax policy relating to existing or proposed internal revenue laws, related statutes, and tax conventions, and

(B) includes assessment, collection, enforcement, litigation, publication, and statistical gathering functions under such laws, statutes, or conventions.

(5) STATE.—

(A) IN GENERAL.—The term "State" means—

(i) any of the 50 States, the District of Columbia, the Commonwealth of Puerto Rico, the Virgin Islands, Guam, American Samoa, and the Commonwealth of the Northern Mariana Islands,

(ii) for purposes of subsections (a)(2), (b)(4), (d)(1), (h)(4), and (p), any municipality—

(I) with a population in excess of 250,000 (as determined under the most recent decennial United States census data available),

(II) which imposes a tax on income or wages, and

(III) with which the Secretary (in his sole discretion) has entered into an agreement regarding disclosure, and

(iii) for purposes of subsections (a)(2), (b)(4), (d)(1), (h)(4), and (p), any governmental entity—

(I) which is formed and operated by a qualified group of municipalities, and

(II) with which the Secretary (in his sole discretion) has entered into an agreement regarding disclosure.

(B) REGIONAL INCOME TAX AGENCIES.—For purposes of subparagraph (A)(iii)—

(i) QUALIFIED GROUP OF MUNICIPALITIES.—The term "qualified group of municipalities" means, with respect to any governmental entity, 2 or more municipalities—

(I) each of which imposes a tax on income or wages,

(II) each of which, under the authority of a State statute, administers the laws relating to the imposition of such taxes through such entity, and

(III) which collectively have a population in excess of 250,000 (as determined under the most recent decennial United States census data available).

(ii) REFERENCES TO STATE LAW, ETC.—For purposes of applying subparagraph (A)(iii) to the subsections referred to in such subparagraph, any reference in such subsections to State law, proceedings, or tax returns shall be treated as references to the law, proceedings, or tax returns, as the case may be, of the municipalities which form and operate the governmental entity referred to in such subparagraph.

(iii) DISCLOSURE TO CONTRACTORS AND OTHER AGENTS.—Notwithstanding any other provision of this section, no return or return information shall be disclosed to any contractor or other agent of a governmental entity referred to in subparagraph (A)(iii) unless such entity, to the satisfaction of the Secretary—

(I) has requirements in effect which require each such contractor or other agent which would have access to returns or return information to provide safeguards (within the meaning of subsection (p)(4)) to protect the confidentiality of such returns or return information,

(II) agrees to conduct an on-site review every 3 years (or a mid-point review in the case of contracts or agreements of less than 3 years in duration) of each contractor or other agent to determine compliance with such requirements,

(III) submits the findings of the most recent review conducted under subclause (II) to the Secretary as part of the report required by subsection (p)(4)(E), and

(IV) certifies to the Secretary for the most recent annual period that such contractor or other agent is in compliance with all such requirements.

The certification required by subclause (IV) shall include the name and address of each contractor and other agent, a description of the contract or agreement with such contractor or other agent, and the duration of such contract or agreement. The requirements of this clause shall not apply to disclosures pursuant to subsection (n) for purposes of Federal tax administration and a rule similar to the rule of subsection (p)(8)(B) shall apply for purposes of this clause.

(6) TAXPAYER IDENTITY.—The term "taxpayer identity" means the name of a person with respect to whom a return is filed, his mailing address, his taxpayer identifying number (as described in section 6109), or a combination thereof.

(7) INSPECTION.—The terms "inspected" and "inspection" mean any examination of a return or return information.

(8) DISCLOSURE.—The term "disclosure" means the making known to any person in any manner whatever a return or return information.

(9) FEDERAL AGENCY.—The term "Federal agency" means an agency within the meaning of section 551(1) of title 5, United States Code.

(10) CHIEF EXECUTIVE OFFICER.—The term "chief executive officer" means, with respect to any municipality, any elected official and the chief official (even if not elected) of such municipality.

(11) TERRORIST INCIDENT, THREAT, OR ACTIVITY.—The term "terrorist incident, threat, or activity" means an incident, threat, or activity involving an act of domestic terrorism (as defined in section 2331(5) of title 18, United States Code) or international terrorism (as defined in section 2331(1) of such title).

Amendments

• 2007, Tax Technical Corrections Act of 2007 (P.L. 110-172)

P.L. 110-172, §11(a)(34)(A):

Amended Code Sec. 6103(b)(5)(A) by striking "the Canal Zone," following "the Virgin Islands,". **Effective** 12-29-2007.

• 2006, Tax Relief and Health Care Act of 2006 (P.L. 109-432)

P.L. 109-432, Division A, §421(a):

Amended Code Sec. 6103(b)(5). **Effective** for disclosures made after 12-31-2006. Prior to amendment, Code Sec. 6103(b)(5) read as follows:

(5) STATE.—The term "State" means—

(A) any of the 50 States, the District of Columbia, the Commonwealth of Puerto Rico, the Virgin Islands, the Canal Zone, Guam, American Samoa, and the Commonwealth of the Northern Mariana Islands, and

(B) for purposes of subsections (a)(2), (b)(4), (d)(1), (h)(4), and (p) any municipality—

(i) with a population in excess of 250,000 (as determined under the most recent decennial United States census data available),

(ii) which imposes a tax on income or wages, and

(iii) with which the Secretary (in his sole discretion) has entered into an agreement regarding disclosure.

• 2002, Victims of Terrorism Tax Relief Act of 2001 (P.L. 107-134)

P.L. 107-134, §201(c)(2):

Amended Code Sec. 6103(b) by adding at the end a new paragraph (11). **Effective** for disclosures made on or after 1-23-2002.

• 2000, Community Renewal Tax Relief Act of 2000 (P.L. 106-554)

P.L. 106-554, §304(a):

Amended Code Sec. 6103(b)(2) by striking "and" at the end of subparagraph (B), by inserting "and" at the end of subparagraph (C), and by inserting after subparagraph (C) a new subparagraph (D). **Effective** 12-21-2000.

• 1999, Tax Relief Extension Act of 1999 (P.L. 106-170)

P.L. 106-170, §521(a)(1):

Amended Code Sec. 6103(b)(2) by striking "and" at the end of subparagraph (A), by inserting "and" at the end of subparagraph (B), and by inserting after subparagraph (B) a new subparagraph (C). **Effective** 12-17-99.

P.L. 106-170, §521(b)-(c), provides:

(b) ANNUAL REPORT REGARDING ADVANCE PRICING AGREEMENTS.—

(1) IN GENERAL.—Not later than 90 days after the end of each calendar year, the Secretary of the Treasury shall prepare and publish a report regarding advance pricing agreements.

(2) CONTENTS OF REPORT.—The report shall include the following for the calendar year to which such report relates:

(A) Information about the structure, composition, and operation of the advance pricing agreement program office.

(B) A copy of each model advance pricing agreement.

(C) The number of—

(i) applications filed during such calendar year for advance pricing agreements;

(ii) advance pricing agreements executed cumulatively to date and during such calendar year;

(iii) renewals of advance pricing agreements issued;

(iv) pending requests for advance pricing agreements;

(v) pending renewals of advance pricing agreements;

(vi) for each of the items in clauses (ii) through (v), the number that are unilateral, bilateral, and multilateral, respectively;

(vii) advance pricing agreements revoked or canceled, and the number of withdrawals from the advance pricing agreement program; and

(viii) advance pricing agreements finalized or renewed by industry.

(D) General descriptions of—

(i) the nature of the relationships between the related organizations, trades, or businesses covered by advance pricing agreements;

(ii) the covered transactions and the business functions performed and risks assumed by such organizations, trades, or businesses;

(iii) the related organizations, trades, or businesses whose prices or results are tested to determine compliance with transfer pricing methodologies prescribed in advance pricing agreements;

(iv) methodologies used to evaluate tested parties and transactions and the circumstances leading to the use of those methodologies;

(v) critical assumptions made and sources of comparables used;

(vi) comparable selection criteria and the rationale used in determining such criteria;

(vii) the nature of adjustments to comparables or tested parties;

(viii) the nature of any ranges agreed to, including information regarding when no range was used and why, when interquartile ranges were used, and when there was a statistical narrowing of the comparables;

(ix) adjustment mechanisms provided to rectify results that fall outside of the agreed upon advance pricing agreement range;

(x) the various term lengths for advance pricing agreements, including rollback years, and the number of advance pricing agreements with each such term length;

(xi) the nature of documentation required; and

(xii) approaches for sharing of currency or other risks.

(E) Statistics regarding the amount of time taken to complete new and renewal advance pricing agreements.

(F) A detailed description of the Secretary of the Treasury's efforts to ensure compliance with existing advance pricing agreements.

(3) CONFIDENTIALITY.—The reports required by this subsection shall be treated as authorized by the Internal Revenue Code of 1986 for purposes of section 6103 of such Code, but the reports shall not include information—

(A) which would not be permitted to be disclosed under section 6110(c) of such Code if such report were a written determination as defined in section 6110 of such Code; or

(B) which can be associated with, or otherwise identify, directly or indirectly, a particular taxpayer.

(4) FIRST REPORT.—The report for calendar year 1999 shall include prior calendar years after 1990.

(c) REGULATIONS.—The Secretary of the Treasury or the Secretary's delegate shall prescribe such regulations as may be necessary or appropriate to carry out the purposes of section 6103(b)(2)(C), and the last sentence of section 6110(b)(1), of the Internal Revenue Code of 1986, as added by this section.

• 1988, Technical and Miscellaneous Revenue Act of 1988 (P.L. 100-647)

P.L. 100-647, §1012(bb)(3)(B):

Amended Code Sec. 6103(b)(5)(A) by striking out "the Commonwealth of the Northern Mariana Islands, the Republic of the Marshall Islands, the Federated States of Micronesia, and the Republic of Palau" and inserting in lieu thereof "and the Commonwealth of the Northern Mariana Islands". **Effective** 10-22-86.

P.L. 100-647, §6251:

Amended Code Sec. 6103(b)(5)(B)(i) by striking out "2,000,000" and inserting in lieu thereof ["]$250,000". **Effective** 11-10-88.

• 1986, Tax Reform Act of 1986 (P.L. 99-514)

P.L. 99-514, §1568(a)(1) and (a)(2):

Amended Code Sec. 6103(b) by striking out paragraph (5) and adding new paragraph (5), and by adding at the end thereof new paragraph (10). **Effective** 10-22-86. Prior to amendment, Code Sec. 6103(b)(5) read as follows:

(5) STATE.—The term "State" means any of the 50 States, the District of Columbia, the Commonwealth of Puerto Rico, the Virgin Islands, the Canal Zone, Guam, American Samoa, the Commonwealth of the Northern Mariana Islands, and the Trust Territory of the Pacific Islands.

• 1981, Economic Recovery Tax Act of 1981 (P.L. 97-34)

P.L. 97-34, §701:

Added the last sentence to Code Sec. 6103(b)(2). **Effective** for disclosures after 7-19-81.

• 1976, Tax Reform Act of 1976 (P.L. 94-455)

P.L. 94-455, §1202(a):

Amended Code Sec. 6103(b). **Effective** 1-1-77. Prior to amendment, Code Sec. 6103(b) read as follows:

(b) INSPECTION BY STATES.—

(1) STATE OFFICERS.—The proper officers of any State may, upon the request of the governor thereof, have access to the returns of any corporation, or to an abstract thereof showing the name and income of any corporation, at such times and in such manner as the Secretary or his delegate may prescribe.

(2) STATE BODIES OR COMMISSIONS.—All income returns filed with respect to the taxes imposed by chapters 1, 2, 3, and 6 (or copies thereof, if so prescribed by regulations made under this subsection), shall be open to inspection by any official, body, or commission, lawfully charged with the administration of any State tax law, if the inspection is for the purpose of such administration or for the purpose of obtaining information to be furnished to local taxing authorities as provided in this paragraph. The inspection shall be permitted only upon written request of the governor of such State, designating the representative of such official, body, or commission to make the inspection on behalf of such official, body, or commission. The inspection shall be made in such manner, and at such times and places, as shall be prescribed by regulations made by the Secretary or his delegate. Any information thus secured by any official, body, or commission of any State may be used only for the administration of the tax laws of such State, except that upon written request of the governor of such State any such information may be furnished to any official, body, or commission of any political subdivision of such State, lawfully charged with the administration of the tax laws of such political subdivision, but may be furnished only for the purpose of, and may be used only for, the administration of such tax laws.

[Sec. 6103(c)]

(c) DISCLOSURE OF RETURNS AND RETURN INFORMATION TO DESIGNEE OF TAXPAYER.—The Secretary may, subject to such requirements and conditions as he may prescribe by regulations, disclose the return of any taxpayer, or return information with respect to such taxpayer, to such person or persons as the taxpayer may designate in a request for or consent to such disclosure, or to any other person at the taxpayer's request to the extent necessary to comply with a request for information or assistance made by the taxpayer to such other person. However, return information shall not be disclosed to such person or persons if the Secretary determines that such disclosure would seriously impair Federal tax administration. Persons designated by the taxpayer under this subsection to receive return information shall not use the information for any purpose other than the express purpose for which consent was granted and shall not disclose return information to any other person without the express permission of, or request by, the taxpayer.

Amendments

• 2019, Taxpayer First Act (P.L. 116-25)

P.L. 116-25, §2201, provides:

SEC. 2201. DISCLOSURE OF TAXPAYER INFORMATION FOR THIRD-PARTY INCOME VERIFICATION.

(a) IN GENERAL.—Not later than 1 year after the close of the 2-year period described in subsection (d)(1), the Secretary of the Treasury or the Secretary's delegate (hereafter referred to in this section as the "Secretary") shall implement a program to ensure that any qualified disclosure—

(1) is fully automated and accomplished through the internet; and

(2) is accomplished in as close to real-time as is practicable.

(b) QUALIFIED DISCLOSURE.—For purposes of this section, the term "qualified disclosure" means a disclosure under section 6103(c) of the Internal Revenue Code of 1986 of returns or return information by the Secretary to a person seeking to verify the income or creditworthiness of a taxpayer who is a borrower in the process of a loan application.

(c) APPLICATION OF SECURITY STANDARDS.—The Secretary shall ensure that the program described in subsection (a) complies with applicable security standards and guidelines.

(d) USER FEE.—

(1) IN GENERAL.—During the 2-year period beginning on the first day of the sixth calendar month beginning after the date of the enactment of this Act, the Secretary shall assess and collect a fee for qualified disclosures (in addition to any other fee assessed and collected for such disclosures) at such rates as the Secretary determines are sufficient to cover the costs related to implementing the program described in subsection (a), including the costs of any necessary infrastructure or technology.

(2) DEPOSIT OF COLLECTIONS.—Amounts received from fees assessed and collected under paragraph (1) shall be deposited in, and credited to, an account solely for the purpose of carrying out the activities described in subsection (a). Such amounts shall be available to carry out such activities without need of further appropriation and without fiscal year limitation.

P.L. 116-25, §2202(a):

Amended Code Sec. 6103(c) by adding at the end a new sentence. **Effective** for disclosures made after the date which is 180 days after 7-1-2019.

• 1998, IRS Restructuring and Reform Act of 1998 (P.L. 105-206)

P.L. 105-206, §2003(e), provides:

(e) PROCEDURES FOR AUTHORIZING DISCLOSURE ELECTRONICALLY.—The Secretary shall establish procedures for any taxpayer to authorize, on an electronically filed return, the Secretary to disclose information under section 6103(c) of the Internal Revenue Code of 1986 to the preparer of the return.

• 1996, Taxpayer Bill of Rights 2 (P.L. 104-168)

P.L. 104-168, §1207:

Amended Code Sec. 6103(c) by striking "written request for or consent to such disclosure" and inserting "request for or consent to such disclosure". **Effective** 7-30-96.

• 1976, Tax Reform Act of 1976 (P.L. 94-455)

P.L. 94-455, §1202(a):

Amended Code Sec. 6103(c). **Effective** 1-1-77. Prior to amendment, Code Sec. 6103(c) read as follows:

(c) INSPECTION BY SHAREHOLDERS.—All bona fide shareholders of record owning 1 percent or more of the outstanding stock of any corporation shall, upon making request of the Secretary or his delegate, be allowed to examine the annual income returns of such corporation and of its subsidiaries.

[Sec. 6103(d)]

(d) DISCLOSURE TO STATE TAX OFFICIALS AND STATE AND LOCAL LAW ENFORCEMENT AGENCIES.—

(1) IN GENERAL.—Returns and return information with respect to taxes imposed by chapters 1, 2, 6, 11, 12, 21, 23, 24, 31, 32, 44, 51 and 52 and subchapter D of chapter 36 shall be open to inspection by, or disclosure to, any State agency, body, or commission, or its legal representative, which is charged under the laws of such State with responsibility for the administration of State tax laws for the purpose of, and only to the extent necessary in, the administration of such laws, including any procedures with respect to locating any person who may be entitled to a refund. Such inspection shall be permitted, or such disclosure made, only upon written request by the head of such agency, body, or commission, and only to the representatives of such agency, body, or commission designated in such written request as the individuals who are to inspect or to receive the returns or return information on behalf of such agency, body, or commission. Such representatives shall not include any individual who is the chief executive officer of such State or who is neither an employee or legal representative of such agency, body, or commission nor a person described in subsection (n). However, such return information shall not be disclosed to the extent that the Secretary determines that such disclosure would identify a confidential informant or seriously impair any civil or criminal tax investigation.

(2) DISCLOSURE TO STATE AUDIT AGENCIES.—

(A) IN GENERAL.—Any returns or return information obtained under paragraph (1) by any State agency, body, or commission may be open to inspection by, or disclosure to, officers and employees of the State audit agency for the purpose of, and only to the extent necessary in, making an audit of the State agency, body, or commission referred to in paragraph (1).

(B) STATE AUDIT AGENCY.—For purposes of subparagraph (A), the term "State audit agency" means any State agency, body, or commission which is charged under the laws of the State with the responsibility of auditing State revenues and programs.

(3) EXCEPTION FOR REIMBURSEMENT UNDER SECTION 7624.—Nothing in this section shall be construed to prevent the Secretary from disclosing to any State or local law enforcement agency which may receive a payment under section 7624 the amount of the recovered taxes with respect to which such a payment may be made.

(4) AVAILABILITY AND USE OF DEATH INFORMATION.—

(A) IN GENERAL.—No returns or return information may be disclosed under paragraph (1) to any agency, body, or commission of any State (or any legal representative thereof) during any period during which a contract meeting the requirements of subparagraph (B) is not in effect between such State and the Secretary of Health and Human Services.

(B) CONTRACTUAL REQUIREMENTS.—A contract meets the requirements of this subparagraph if—

(i) such contract requires the State to furnish the Secretary of Health and Human Services information concerning individuals with respect to whom death certificates (or equivalent documents maintained by the State of any subdivision thereof) have been officially filed with it, and

(ii) such contract does not include any restriction on the use of information obtained by such Secretary pursuant to such contract, except that such contract may provide that such information is only to be used by the Secretary (or any other Federal agency) for purposes of ensuring that Federal benefits or other payments are not erroneously paid to deceased individuals.

Any information obtained by the Secretary of Health and Human Services under such a contract shall be exempt from disclosure under section 552 of title 5, United States Code, and from the requirements of section 552a of such title 5.

(C) SPECIAL EXCEPTION.—The provisions of subparagraph (A) shall not apply to any State which on July 1, 1993, was not, pursuant to a contract, furnishing the Secretary of Health and Human Services information concerning individuals with respect to whom death certificates (or equivalent documents maintained by the State or any subdivision thereof) have been officially filed with it.

(5) DISCLOSURE FOR COMBINED EMPLOYMENT TAX REPORTING.—

(A) IN GENERAL.—The Secretary may disclose taxpayer identity information and signatures to any agency, body, or commission of any State for the purpose of carrying out with such agency, body, or commission a combined Federal and State employment tax reporting program approved by the Secretary. Subsections (a)(2) and (p)(4) and sections 7213 and 7213A shall not apply with respect to disclosures or inspections made pursuant to this paragraph.

(B) TERMINATION.—The Secretary may not make any disclosure under this paragraph after December 31, 2007.

(6) LIMITATION ON DISCLOSURE REGARDING REGIONAL INCOME TAX AGENCIES TREATED AS STATES.—For purposes of paragraph (1), inspection by or disclosure to an entity described in subsection (b)(5)(A)(iii) shall be for the purpose of, and only to the extent necessary in, the administration of the laws of the member municipalities in such entity relating to the imposition of a tax on income or wages. Such entity may not redisclose any return or return information received pursuant to paragraph (1) to any such member municipality.

Amendments

• 2006, Tax Relief and Health Care Act of 2006 (P.L. 109-432)

P.L. 109-432, Division A, §122(a)(1):

Amended Code Sec. 6103(d)(5)(B) by striking "2006" and inserting "2007". **Effective** for disclosures after 12-31-2006.

P.L. 109-432, Division A, §421(b):

Amended Code Sec. 6103(d) by adding at the end a new paragraph (6). **Effective** for disclosures made after 12-31-2006.

• 2005, Gulf Opportunity Zone Act of 2005 (P.L. 109-135)

P.L. 109-135, §305(a)(1):

Amended Code Sec. 6103(d)(5)(B) by striking "December 31, 2005" and inserting "December 31, 2006". **Effective** for disclosures after 12-31-2005.

• 2004, Working Families Tax Relief Act of 2004 (P.L. 108-311)

P.L. 108-311, §311(a):

Amended Code Sec. 6103(d)(5). **Effective** 10-4-2004. Prior to amendment, Code Sec. 6103(d)(5) read as follows:

(5) DISCLOSURE FOR CERTAIN COMBINED REPORTING PROJECT.—The Secretary shall disclose taxpayer identities and signatures for purposes of the demonstration project described in section 976 of the Taxpayer Relief Act of 1997. Subsections (a)(2) and (p)(4) and sections 7213 and 7213A shall not apply with respect to disclosures or inspections made pursuant to this paragraph.

• 1998, IRS Restructuring and Reform Act of 1998 (P.L. 105-206)

P.L. 105-206, §6009(d):

Amended Code Sec. 6103(d)(5) by striking "section 967 of the Taxpayer Relief Act of 1997." and inserting "section 976 of the Taxpayer Relief Act of 1997. Subsections (a)(2) and (p)(4) and sections 7213 and 7213A shall not apply with respect to disclosures or inspections made pursuant to this paragraph." **Effective** as if included in the provision of P.L. 105-34 to which it relates [**effective** 8-5-97.—CCH].

• 1997, Taxpayer Relief Act of 1997 (P.L. 105-34)

P.L. 105-34, §976(c):

Amended Code Sec. 6103(d) by adding at the end a new paragraph (5). **Effective** 8-5-97.

• 1993, Omnibus Budget Reconciliation Act of 1993 (P.L. 103-66)

P.L. 103-66, §13444(a):

Amended Code Sec. 6103(d) by adding at the end thereof a new paragraph (4). For the **effective** date, see Act Sec. 13444(b), below.

P.L. 103-66, §13444(b), provides:

(b) EFFECTIVE DATE.—

(1) IN GENERAL.—Except as provided in paragraph (2), the amendment made by subsection (a) shall take effect on the date one year after the date of the enactment of this Act.

(2) SPECIAL RULE.—The amendment made by subsection (a) shall take effect on the date 2 years after the date of the enactment of this Act in the case of any State if it is estab-

lished to the satisfaction of the Secretary of the Treasury that—

(A) under the law of such State as in effect on the date of the enactment of this Act, it is impossible for such State to enter into an agreement meeting the requirements of section 6103(d)(4)(B) of the Internal Revenue Code of 1986 (as added by subsection (a)), and

(B) it is likely that such State will enter into such an agreement during the extension period under this paragraph.

• 1989, Omnibus Budget Reconciliation Act of 1989 (P.L. 101-239)

P.L. 101-239, §7841(d)(1):

Amended Code Sec. 6103(d)(1) by striking "45," after "44,". **Effective** 12-19-89.

• 1988, Anti-Drug Abuse Act of 1988 (P.L. 100-690)

P.L. 100-690, §7602(c):

Amended Code Sec. 6103(d) by adding at the end thereof new paragraph (3). **Effective** for information first provided more than 90 days after the date of the enactment of this Act.

P.L. 100-690, §7602(d)(2):

Amended the heading of Code Sec. 6103(d). **Effective** for information first provided more than 90 days after the date of the enactment of this Act. Prior to amendment, the heading for Code Sec. 6103(d) read as follows:

DISCLOSURE TO STATE TAX OFFICIALS.—

P.L. 100-690, §7602(g), provides:

(g) REGULATIONS.—The Secretary of the Treasury shall, not later than 90 days after the date of enactment of this Act, prescribe such rules and regulations as shall be necessary and proper to carry out the provisions of this section, including regulations relating to the definition of information which substantially contributes to the recovery of Federal taxes and the substantiation of expenses required in order to receive a reimbursement.

• 1984, Deficit Reduction Act of 1984 (P.L. 98-369)

P.L. 98-369, §449(a):

Amended Code Sec. 6103(d)(1) by striking out "44, 51" and inserting in lieu thereof "44, 45, 51". **Effective** 7-18-84.

• 1980 (P.L. 96-598)

P.L. 96-598, §3(a):

Amended Code Sec. 6103(d). **Effective** 12-24-80. Prior to amendment, Code Sec. 6103(d) read:

(d) DISCLOSURE TO STATE TAX OFFICIALS.—Returns and return information with respect to taxes imposed by chapters 1, 2, 6, 11, 12, 21, 23, 24, 31, 44, 51, and 52 and subchapter D of chapter 36, shall be open to inspection by or disclosure to any State agency, body, or commission, or its legal representative, which is charged under the laws of such State with responsibility for the administration of State tax laws for the purpose of, and only to the extent necessary in, the administration of such laws, including any procedures with respect to locating any person who may be entitled to a refund. Such inspection shall be permitted, or such disclosure made, only upon written request by the head of such agency, body, or commission, and only to the representatives of such agency, body, or commission designated in such written request as the individuals who are to inspect or to receive the return or return information on behalf of such agency, body, or commission. Such representatives shall not include any individual who is the chief executive officer of such State or who is neither an employee or legal representative of such agency, body, or commission nor a person described in subsection (n). However, such return information shall not be disclosed to the extent that the Secretary determines that such disclosure would identify a confidential informant or seriously impair any civil or criminal tax investigation.

• 1978, Revenue Act of 1978 (P.L. 95-600)

P.L. 95-600, §701(bb)(2):

Amended Code Sec. 6103(d) by inserting "31," after "24,". **Effective** 1-1-77.

• 1976, Tax Reform Act of 1976 (P.L. 94-455)

P.L. 94-455, §1202(a):

Amended Code Sec. 6103(d). **Effective** 1-1-77. Prior to amendment, Code Sec. 6103(d) read as follows:

(d) INSPECTION BY COMMITTEES OF CONGRESS.—

(1) COMMITTEES ON WAYS AND MEANS AND FINANCE.—

(A) The Secretary and any officer or employee of the Treasury Department, upon request from the Committee on Ways and Means of the House of Representatives, the Committee on Finance of the Senate, or a select committee of the Senate or House specially authorized to investigate returns by a resolution of the Senate or House, or a joint committee so authorized by concurrent resolution, shall furnish such committee sitting in executive session with any data of any character contained in or shown by any return.

(B) Any such committee shall have the right, acting directly as a committee, or by or through such examiners or agents as it may designate or appoint, to inspect any or all of the returns at such times and in such manner as it may determine.

(C) Any relevant or useful information thus obtained may be submitted by the committee obtaining it to the Senate or the House, or to both the Senate and the House, as the case may be.

(2) JOINT COMMITTEE ON INTERNAL REVENUE TAXATION.—The Joint Committee on Internal Revenue Taxation shall have the same right to obtain data and to inspect returns as the Committee on Ways and Means or the Committee on Finance, and to submit any relevant or useful information thus obtained to the Senate, the House of Representatives, the Committee on Ways and Means, or the Committee on Finance. The Committee on Ways and Means or the Committee on Finance may submit such information to the House or to the Senate, or to both the House and the Senate, as the case may be.

[Sec. 6103(e)]

(e) DISCLOSURE TO PERSONS HAVING MATERIAL INTEREST.—

(1) IN GENERAL.—The return of a person shall, upon written request, be open to inspection by or disclosure to—

(A) in the case of the return of an individual—

(i) that individual,

(ii) the spouse of that individual if the individual and such spouse have signified their consent to consider a gift reported on such return as made one-half by him and one-half by the spouse pursuant to the provisions of section 2513, or

(iii) the child of that individual (or such child's legal representative) to the extent necessary to comply with the provisions of section (1)(g);

(B) in the case of an income tax return filed jointly, either of the individuals with respect to whom the return is filed;

(C) in the case of the return of a partnership, any person who was a member of such partnership during any part of the period covered by the return;

(D) in the case of the return of a corporation or a subsidiary thereof—

(i) any person designated by resolution of its board of directors or other similar governing body,

(ii) any officer or employee of such corporation upon written request signed by any principal officer and attested to by the secretary or other officer,

(iii) any bona fide shareholder of record owning 1 percent or more of the outstanding stock of such corporation,

(iv) if the corporation was an S corporation, any person who was a shareholder during any part of the period covered by such return during which an election under section 1362(a) was in effect, or

(v) if the corporation has been dissolved, any person authorized by applicable State law to act for the corporation or any person who the Secretary finds to have a material interest which will be affected by information contained therein;

(E) in the case of the return of an estate—

(i) the administrator, executor, or trustee of such estate, and

(ii) any heir at law, next of kin, or beneficiary under the will, of the decedent, but only if the Secretary finds that such heir at law, next of kin, or beneficiary has a material interest which will be affected by information contained therein; and

(F) in the case of the return of a trust—

(i) the trustee or trustees, jointly or separately, and

(ii) any beneficiary of such trust, but only if the Secretary finds that such beneficiary has a material interest which will be affected by information contained therein.

(2) INCOMPETENCY.—If an individual described in paragraph (1) is legally incompetent, the applicable return shall, upon written request, be open to inspection by or disclosure to the committee, trustee, or guardian of his estate.

(3) DECEASED INDIVIDUALS.—The return of a decedent shall, upon written request, be open to inspection by or disclosure to—

(A) the administrator, executor, or trustee of his estate, and

(B) any heir at law, next of kin, or beneficiary under the will, of such decedent, or a donee of property, but only if the Secretary finds that such heir at law, next of kin, beneficiary, or donee has a material interest which will be affected by information contained therein.

(4) TITLE 11 CASES AND RECEIVERSHIP PROCEEDINGS.—If—

(A) there is a trustee in a title 11 case in which the debtor is the person with respect to whom the return is filed, or

(B) substantially all of the property of the person with respect to whom the return is filed is in the hands of a receiver,

such return or returns for prior years of such person shall, upon written request, be open to inspection by or disclosure to such trustee or receiver, but only if the Secretary finds that such trustee or receiver, in his fiduciary capacity, has a material interest which will be affected by information contained therein.

(5) INDIVIDUAL'S TITLE 11 CASE.—

(A) IN GENERAL.—In any case to which section 1398 applies (determined without regard to section 1398(b)(1)), any return of the debtor for the taxable year in which the case commenced or any preceding taxable year shall, upon written request, be open to inspection by or disclosure to the trustee in such case.

(B) RETURN OF ESTATE AVAILABLE TO DEBTOR.—Any return of an estate in a case to which section 1398 applies shall, upon written request, be open to inspection by or disclosure to the debtor in such case.

(C) SPECIAL RULE FOR INVOLUNTARY CASES.—In an involuntary case, no disclosure shall be made under subparagraph (A) until the order for relief has been entered by the court having jurisdiction of such case unless such court finds that such disclosure is appropriate for purposes of determining whether an order for relief should be entered.

(6) ATTORNEY IN FACT.—Any return to which this subsection applies shall, upon written request, also be open to inspection by or disclosure to the attorney in fact duly authorized in writing by any of the persons described in paragraph (1), (2), (3), (4), (5), (8), or (9) to inspect the return or receive the information on his behalf, subject to the conditions provided in such paragraphs.

(7) RETURN INFORMATION.—Return information with respect to any taxpayer may be open to inspection by or disclosure to any person authorized by this subsection to inspect any return of such taxpayer if the Secretary determines that such disclosure would not seriously impair Federal tax administration.

(8) DISCLOSURE OF COLLECTION ACTIVITIES WITH RESPECT TO JOINT RETURN.—If any deficiency of tax with respect to a joint return is assessed and the individuals filing such return are no longer married or no longer reside in the same household, upon request in writing by either of such individuals, the Secretary shall disclose in writing to the individual making the request whether the Secretary has attempted to collect such deficiency from such other individual, the general nature of such collection activities, and the amount collected. The preceding sentence shall not apply to any deficiency which may not be collected by reason of section 6502.

(9) DISCLOSURE OF CERTAIN INFORMATION WHERE MORE THAN 1 PERSON SUBJECT TO PENALTY UNDER SECTION 6672.—If the Secretary determines that a person is liable for a penalty under section 6672(a) with respect to any failure, upon request in writing of such person, the Secretary shall disclose in writing to such person—

(A) the name of any other person whom the Secretary has determined to be liable for such penalty with respect to such failure, and

(B) whether the Secretary has attempted to collect such penalty from such other person, the general nature of such collection activities, and the amount collected.

(10) LIMITATION ON CERTAIN DISCLOSURES UNDER THIS SUBSECTION.—In the case of an inspection or disclosure under this subsection relating to the return of a partnership, S corporation, trust, or an estate, the information inspected or disclosed shall not include any supporting schedule, attachment, or list which includes the taxpayer identity information of a person other than the entity making the return or the person conducting the inspection or to whom the disclosure is made.

(11) DISCLOSURE OF INFORMATION REGARDING STATUS OF INVESTIGATION OF VIOLATION OF THIS SECTION.—In the case of a person who provides to the Secretary information indicating a violation of section 7213, 7213A, or 7214 with respect to any return or return information of such person, the Secretary may disclose to such person (or such person's designee)—

(A) whether an investigation based on the person's provision of such information has been initiated and whether it is open or closed,

(B) whether any such investigation substantiated such a violation by any individual, and

(C) whether any action has been taken with respect to such individual (including whether a referral has been made for prosecution of such individual).

Amendments

• 2015, Protecting Americans from Tax Hikes Act of 2015 (P.L. 114-113)

P.L. 114-113, §403(a), Div. Q:

Amended Code Sec. 6103(e) by adding at the end a new paragraph (11). **Effective** for disclosures made on or after 12-18-2015.

• 2007, Mortgage Forgiveness Debt Relief Act of 2007 (P.L. 110-142)

P.L. 110-142, §8(c)(1):

Amended Code Sec. 6103(e) by adding at the end a new paragraph (10). **Effective** 12-20-2007.

• 2004, American Jobs Creation Act of 2004 (P.L. 108-357)

P.L. 108-357, §413(c)(27):

Amended Code Sec. 6103(e)(1)(D) by striking clause (iv) and redesignating clauses (v) and (vi) as clauses (iv) and (v), respectively. **Effective** for disclosures of return or return information with respect to tax years beginning after 12-31-2004. Prior to being stricken, Code Sec. 6103(e)(1)(D)(iv) read as follows:

(iv) if the corporation was a foreign personal holding company, as defined by section 552, any person who was a shareholder during any part of a period covered by such return if with respect to that period, or any part thereof, such shareholder was required under section 551 to include in his gross income undistributed foreign personal holding company income of such company,

• 2000, Community Renewal Tax Relief Act of 2000 (P.L. 106-554)

P.L. 106-554, §319(8)(B):

Amended Code Sec. 6103(e)(1)(D)(v). **Effective** 12-21-2000. Prior to amendment, Code Sec. 6103(e)(1)(D)(v) read as follows:

(v) if the corporation was an electing small business corporation under subchapter S of chapter 1, any person who was a shareholder during any part of the period covered by such return during which an election was in effect, or

• 1998, IRS Restructuring and Reform Act of 1998 (P.L. 105-206)

P.L. 105-206, §6007(f)(4):

Amended Code Sec. 6103(e)(1)(A) by striking clause (ii) and by redesignating clauses (iii) and (iv) as clauses (ii) and (iii), respectively. **Effective** as if included in the provision of P.L. 105-34 to which it relates [**effective** for sales or exchanges after 8-5-97.—CCH]. Prior to being stricken, Code Sec. 6103(e)(1)(A)(ii) read as follows:

(ii) if property transferred by that individual to a trust is sold or exchanged in a transaction described in section 644, the trustee or trustees, jointly or separately, of such trust to the extent necessary to ascertain any amount of tax imposed upon the trust by section 644,

P.L. 105-206, §6019(c):

Amended Code Sec. 6103(e)(6) by striking "or (5)" and inserting "(5), (8), or (9)". **Effective** 7-22-98.

• 1997, Taxpayer Relief Act of 1997 (P.L. 105-34)

P.L. 105-34, §1201(b)(2):

Amended Code Sec. 6103(e)(1)(A)(iv) by striking "or 59(j)" after "section (1)(g)". **Effective** for tax years beginning after 12-31-97.

• 1996, Small Business Job Protection Act of 1996 (P.L. 104-188)

P.L. 104-188, §1704(t)(41):

Amended Code Sec. 6103(e)(1)(A)(iv) by striking all that follows "provisions of" and inserting "section (1)(g) or 59(j)". **Effective** 8-20-96. Prior to amendment, Code Sec. 6103(e)(1)(A)(iv) read as follows:

(iv) the child of that individual (or such child's legal representative) to the extent necessary to comply with the provisions of section 1(g) or 59(j);

• 1996, Taxpayer Bill of Rights 2 (P.L. 104-168)

P.L. 104-168, §403(a):

Amended Code Sec. 6103(e) by adding at the end a new paragraph (8). **Effective** for requests made after 7-30-96.

P.L. 104-168, §902(a):

Amended Code Sec. 6103(e), as amended by Act Sec. 403, by adding at the end a new paragraph (9). **Effective** 7-30-96.

• 1990, Omnibus Budget Reconciliation Act of 1990 (P.L. 101-508)

P.L. 101-508, §11101(d)(6):

Amended Code Sec. 6103(e)(1)(A)(iv) by striking "section 1(j)" and inserting "section 1(g)". **Effective** for tax years beginning after 12-31-90.

• 1988, Technical and Miscellaneous Revenue Act of 1988 (P.L. 100-647)

P.L. 100-647, §1014(e)(4):

Amended Code Sec. 6103(e)(1)(A)(iv) by striking out "section 1(j)" and inserting in lieu thereof "section 1(j) or 59(j)". **Effective** as if included in the provision of P.L. 99-514 to which it relates.

• **1986, Tax Reform Act of 1986 (P.L. 99-514)**

P.L. 99-514, §1411(b):

Amended Code Sec. 6103(e)(1)(A) by striking out "or" at the end of clause (ii), by inserting "or" at the end of clause (iii), and by adding at the end thereof new clause (iv). **Effective** for tax years beginning after 12-31-86.

• **1980, Bankruptcy Tax Act of 1980 (P.L. 96-589)**

P.L. 96-589, §3(c)(1), (2):

Amended Code Sec. 6103(e) by striking out paragraph (4), redesignating paragraphs (5) and (6) as (6) and (7) and adding new paragraphs (4) and (5). **Effective** for bankruptcy cases commencing on or after 3-25-81. Prior to amendment, Code Sec. 6103(e)(4) provided:

(4) BANKRUPTCY.—If substantially all of the property of the person with respect to whom the return is filed is in the hands of a trustee in bankruptcy or receiver, such return or returns for prior years of such person shall, upon written request, be open to inspection by or disclosure to such trustee or receiver, but only if the Secretary finds that such receiver or trustee, in his fiduciary capacity, has a material interest which will be affected by information contained therein.

P.L. 96-589, §3(c)(2):

Amended Code Sec. 6103(e)(6), as redesignated, by striking out "or (4)" and inserting "(4), or (5)". **Effective** for bankruptcy cases commencing on or after 3-25-81.

• **1976, Tax Reform Act of 1976 (P.L. 94-455)**

P.L. 94-455, §1202(a):

Amended Code Sec. 6103(e). **Effective** 1-1-77. Prior to amendment, Code Sec. 6103(e) read as follows:

(e) DECLARATIONS OF ESTIMATED TAX.—For purposes of this section, a declaration of estimated tax shall be held and considered a return under this chapter.

[Sec. 6103(f)]

(f) DISCLOSURE TO COMMITTEES OF CONGRESS.—

(1) COMMITTEE ON WAYS AND MEANS, COMMITTEE ON FINANCE, AND JOINT COMMITTEE ON TAXATION.—Upon written request from the chairman of the Committee on Ways and Means of the House of Representatives, the chairman of the Committee on Finance of the Senate, or the chairman of the Joint Committee on Taxation, the Secretary shall furnish such committee with any return or return information specified in such request, except that any return or return information which can be associated with, or otherwise identify, directly or indirectly, a particular taxpayer shall be furnished to such committee only when sitting in closed executive session unless such taxpayer otherwise consents in writing to such disclosure.

(2) CHIEF OF STAFF OF JOINT COMMITTEE ON TAXATION.—Upon written request by the Chief of Staff of the Joint Committee on Taxation, the Secretary shall furnish him with any return or return information specified in such request. Such Chief of Staff may submit such return or return information to any committee described in paragraph (1), except that any return or return information which can be associated with, or otherwise identify, directly or indirectly, a particular taxpayer shall be furnished to such committee only when sitting in closed executive session unless such taxpayer otherwise consents in writing to such disclosure.

(3) OTHER COMMITTEES.—Pursuant to an action by, and upon written request by the chairman of, a committee of the Senate or the House of Representatives (other than a committee specified in paragraph (1)) specially authorized to inspect any return or return information by a resolution of the Senate or the House of Representatives or, in the case of a joint committee (other than the joint committee specified in paragraph (1)), by concurrent resolution, the Secretary shall furnish such committee, or a duly authorized and designated subcommittee thereof, sitting in closed executive session, with any return or return information which such resolution authorizes the committee or subcommittee to inspect. Any resolution described in this paragraph shall specify the purpose for which the return or return information is to be furnished and that such information cannot reasonably be obtained from any other source.

(4) AGENTS OF COMMITTEES AND SUBMISSION OF INFORMATION TO SENATE OR HOUSE OF REPRESENTATIVES.—

(A) COMMITTEES DESCRIBED IN PARAGRAPH (1).—Any committee described in paragraph (1) or the Chief of Staff of the Joint Committee on Taxation shall have the authority, acting directly, or by or through such examiners or agents as the chairman of such committee or such chief of staff may designate or appoint, to inspect returns and return information at such time and in such manner as may be determined by such chairman or chief of staff. Any return or return information obtained by or on behalf of such committee pursuant to the provisions of this subsection may be submitted by the committee to the Senate or the House of Representatives, or to both. The Joint Committee on Taxation may also submit such return or return information to any other committee described in paragraph (1), except that any return or return information which can be associated with, or otherwise identify, directly or indirectly, a particular taxpayer shall be furnished to such committee only when sitting in closed executive session unless such taxpayer otherwise consents in writing to such disclosure.

(B) OTHER COMMITTEES.—Any committee or subcommittee described in paragraph (3) shall have the right, acting directly, or by or through no more than four examiners or agents, designated or appointed in writing in equal numbers by the chairman and ranking minority member of such committee or subcommittee, to inspect returns and return information at such time and in such manner as may be determined by such chairman and ranking minority member. Any return or return information obtained by or on behalf of such committee or subcommittee pursuant to the provisions of this subsection may be submitted by the committee to the Senate or the House of Representatives, or to both, except that any return or return information which can be associated with, or otherwise identify, directly or indirectly, a particular taxpayer, shall be furnished to the Senate or the House of Representatives only when sitting in closed executive session unless such taxpayer otherwise consents in writing to such disclosure.

(5) DISCLOSURE BY WHISTLEBLOWER.—Any person who otherwise has or had access to any return or return information under this section may disclose such return or return information to a committee referred to in paragraph (1) or any individual authorized to receive or inspect information under paragraph (4)(A) if such person believes such return or return information may relate to possible misconduct, maladministration, or taxpayer abuse.

Amendments

• 1998, IRS Restructuring and Reform Act of 1998 (P.L. 105-206)

P.L. 105-206, §3708(a):

Amended Code Sec. 6103(f) by adding at the end a new paragraph (5). **Effective** 7-22-98.

• 1976, Tax Reform Act of 1976 (P.L. 94-455)

P.L. 94-455, §1202(a):

Amended Code Sec. 6103(f). **Effective** 1-1-77. Prior to amendment, Code Sec. 6103(f) read as follows:

(f) DISCLOSURE OF INFORMATION AS TO PERSONS FILING INCOME TAX RETURNS.—The Secretary or his delegate shall, upon inquiry as to whether any person has filed an income tax return in a designated internal revenue district for a particular taxable year, furnish to the inquirer, in such manner as the Secretary or his delegate may determine, information showing that such person has, or has not, filed an income tax return in such district for such taxable year.

• 1966 (P.L. 89-713)

P.L. 89-713, §4(a):

Amended Code Sec. 6103(f). **Effective** 11-2-66. Prior to amendment, Sec. 6103(f) read as follows:

"(f) Inspection of List of Taxpayers.—The Secretary or his delegate shall as soon as practicable in each year cause to be prepared and made available to public inspection in such manner as he may determine, in the office of the principal internal revenue officer for the internal revenue district in which the return was filed, and in such other places as he may determine, lists containing the name and the post-office address of each person making an income tax return in such district."

[Sec. 6103(g)]

(g) DISCLOSURE TO PRESIDENT AND CERTAIN OTHER PERSONS.—

(1) IN GENERAL.—Upon written request by the President, signed by him personally, the Secretary shall furnish to the President, or to such employee or employees of the White House Office as the President may designate by name in such request, a return or return information with respect to any taxpayer named in such request. Any such request shall state—

(A) the name and address of the taxpayer whose return or return information is to be disclosed,

(B) the kind of return or return information which is to be disclosed,

(C) the taxable period or periods covered by such return or return information, and

(D) the specific reason why the inspection or disclosure is requested.

(2) DISCLOSURE OF RETURN INFORMATION AS TO PRESIDENTIAL APPOINTEES AND CERTAIN OTHER FEDERAL GOVERNMENT APPOINTEES.—The Secretary may disclose to a duly authorized representative of the Executive Office of the President or to the head of any Federal agency, upon written request by the President or head of such agency, or to the Federal Bureau of Investigation on behalf of and upon the written request by the President or such head, return information with respect to an individual who is designated as being under consideration for appointment to a position in the executive or judicial branch of the Federal Government. Such return information shall be limited to whether such an individual—

(A) has filed returns with respect to the taxes imposed under chapter 1 for not more than the immediately preceding 3 years;

(B) has failed to pay any tax within 10 days after notice and demand, or has been assessed any penalty under this title for negligence, in the current year or immediately preceding 3 years;

(C) has been or is under investigation for possible criminal offenses under the internal revenue laws and the results of any such investigation; or

(D) has been assessed any civil penalty under this title for fraud.

Within 3 days of the receipt of any request for any return information with respect to any individual under this paragraph, the Secretary shall notify such individual in writing that such information has been requested under the provisions of this paragraph.

(3) RESTRICTION ON DISCLOSURE.—The employees to whom returns and return information are disclosed under this subsection shall not disclose such returns and return information to any other person except the President or the head of such agency without the personal written direction of the President or the head of such agency.

(4) RESTRICTION ON DISCLOSURE TO CERTAIN EMPLOYEES.—Disclosure of returns and return information under this subsection shall not be made to any employee whose annual rate of basic pay is less than the annual rate of basic pay specified for positions subject to section 5316 of title 5, United States Code.

(5) REPORTING REQUIREMENTS.—Within 30 days after the close of each calendar quarter, the President and the head of any agency requesting returns and return information under this subsection shall each file a report with the Joint Committee on Taxation setting forth the taxpayers with respect to whom such requests were made during such quarter under this subsection, the returns or return information involved, and the reasons for such requests. The President shall not be required to report on any request for returns and return information

pertaining to an individual who was an officer or employee of the executive branch of the Federal Government at the time such request was made. Reports filed pursuant to this paragraph shall not be disclosed unless the Joint Committee on Taxation determines that disclosure thereof (including identifying details) would be in the national interest. Such reports shall be maintained by the Joint Committee on Taxation for a period not exceeding 2 years unless, within such period, the Joint Committee on Taxation determines that a disclosure to the Congress is necessary.

Amendments

• 1976, Tax Reform Act of 1976 (P.L. 94-455)

P.L. 94-455, §1202(a):

Amended Code Sec. 6103(g). **Effective** 1-1-77. Prior to amendment, Code Sec. 6103(g) read as follows:

(g) DISCLOSURE OF INFORMATION WITH RESPECT TO DEFERRED COMPENSATION PLANS.—The Secretary or his delegate is authorized to furnish—

(1) returns with respect to any tax imposed by this title or information with respect to such returns to the proper officers and employees of the Department of Labor and the Pension Benefit Guaranty Corporation for purposes of administration of Titles I and IV of the Employee Retirement Income Security Act of 1974, and

(2) registration statements (as described in section 6057) and information with respect to such statements to the proper officers and employees of the Department of Health, Education, and Welfare for purposes of administration of section 1131 of the Social Security Act.

• 1974, Employee Retirement Income Security Act of 1974 (P.L. 93-406)

P.L. 93-406, §1022(h):

Added Code Sec. 6103(g). **Effective** 9-2-74.

[Sec. 6103(h)]

(h) DISCLOSURE TO CERTAIN FEDERAL OFFICERS AND EMPLOYEES FOR PURPOSES OF TAX ADMINISTRATION, ETC.—

(1) DEPARTMENT OF THE TREASURY.—Returns and return information shall, without written request, be open to inspection by or disclosure to officers and employees of the Department of the Treasury whose official duties require such inspection or disclosure for tax administration purposes.

(2) DEPARTMENT OF JUSTICE.—In a matter involving tax administration, a return or return information shall be open to inspection by or disclosure to officers and employees of the Department of Justice (including United States attorneys) personally and directly engaged in, and solely for their use in, any proceeding before a Federal grand jury or preparation for any proceeding (or investigation which may result in such a proceeding) before a Federal grand jury or any Federal or State court, but only if—

(A) the taxpayer is or may be a party to the proceeding, or the proceeding arose out of, or in connection with, determining the taxpayer's civil or criminal liability, or the collection of such civil liability in respect of any tax imposed under this title;

(B) the treatment of an item reflected on such return is or may be related to the resolution of an issue in the proceeding or investigation; or

(C) such return or return information relates or may relate to a transactional relationship between a person who is or may be a party to the proceeding and the taxpayer which affects, or may affect, the resolution of an issue in such proceeding or investigation.

(3) FORM OF REQUEST.—In any case in which the Secretary is authorized to disclose a return or return information to the Department of Justice pursuant to the provisions of this subsection—

(A) if the Secretary has referred the case to the Department of Justice, or if the proceeding is authorized by subchapter B of chapter 76, the Secretary may make such disclosure on his own motion, or

(B) if the Secretary receives a written request from the Attorney General, the Deputy Attorney General, or an Assistant Attorney General, for a return of, or return information relating to, a person named in such request and setting forth the need for the disclosure, the Secretary shall disclose return or return the information so requested.

(4) DISCLOSURE IN JUDICIAL AND ADMINISTRATIVE TAX PROCEEDINGS.—A return or return information may be disclosed in a Federal or State judicial or administrative proceeding pertaining to tax administration, but only—

(A) if the taxpayer is a party to the proceeding, or the proceeding arose out of, or in connection with, determining the taxpayer's civil or criminal liability, or the collection of such civil liability, in respect of any tax imposed under this title;

(B) if the treatment of an item reflected on such return is directly related to the resolution of an issue in the proceeding;

(C) if such return or return information directly relates to a transactional relationship between a person who is a party to the proceeding and the taxpayer which directly affects the resolution of an issue in the proceeding; or

(D) to the extent required by order of a court pursuant to section 3500 of title 18, United States Code, or rule 16 of the Federal Rules of Criminal Procedure, such court being authorized in the issuance of such order to give due consideration to congressional policy favoring the confidentiality of returns and return information as set forth in this title.

However, such return or return information shall not be disclosed as provided in subparagraph (A), (B), or (C) if the Secretary determines that such disclosure would identify a confidential informant or seriously impair a civil or criminal tax investigation.

(5) WITHHOLDING OF TAX FROM SOCIAL SECURITY BENEFITS.—Upon written request of the payor agency, the Secretary may disclose available return information from the master files of the Internal Revenue Service with respect to the address and status of an individual as a nonresident alien or as a citizen or resident of the United States to the Social Security Administration or the Railroad Retirement Board (whichever is appropriate) for purposes of carrying out its responsibilities for withholding tax under section 1441 from social security benefits (as defined in section 86(d)).

(6) INTERNAL REVENUE SERVICE OVERSIGHT BOARD.—

(A) IN GENERAL.—Notwithstanding paragraph (1), and except as provided in subparagraph (B), no return or return information may be disclosed to any member of the Oversight Board described in subparagraph (A) or (D) of section 7802(b)(1) or to any employee or detailee of such Board by reason of their service with the Board. Any request for information not permitted to be disclosed under the preceding sentence, and any contact relating to a specific taxpayer, made by any such individual to an officer or employee of the Internal Revenue Service shall be reported by such officer or employee to the Secretary, the Treasury Inspector General for Tax Administration, and the Joint Committee on Taxation.

(B) EXCEPTION FOR REPORTS TO THE BOARD.—If—

(i) the Commissioner or the Treasury Inspector General for Tax Administration prepares any report or other matter for the Oversight Board in order to assist the Board in carrying out its duties, and

(ii) the Commissioner or such Inspector General determines it is necessary to include any return or return information in such report or other matter to enable the Board to carry out such duties, such return or return information (other than information regarding taxpayer identity) may be disclosed to members, employees, or detailees of the Board solely for the purpose of carrying out such duties.

Amendments

• 1998, Tax and Trade Relief Extension Act of 1998 (P.L. 105-277)

P.L. 105-277, §4002(a):

Amended Code Sec. 6103(h) by redesignating paragraph (5) as paragraph (6). **Effective** as if included in the provision of P.L. 105-206 to which it relates [generally **effective** on 7-22-98.—CCH].

• 1998, IRS Restructuring and Reform Act of 1998 (P.L. 105-206)

P.L. 105-206, §1101(b):

Amended Code Sec. 6103(h) by adding at the end a new paragraph (5)[(6)]. **Effective** 7-22-98. For a special rule, see Act Sec. 1101(d)(2)-(3), below.

P.L. 105-206, §1101(d)(2)-(3), provides:

(2) INITIAL NOMINATIONS TO INTERNAL REVENUE SERVICE OVERSIGHT BOARD.—The President shall submit the initial nominations under section 7802 of the Internal Revenue Code of 1986, as added by this section, to the Senate not later than 6 months after the date of the enactment of this Act.

(3) EFFECT ON ACTIONS PRIOR TO APPOINTMENT OF OVERSIGHT BOARD.—Nothing in this section shall be construed to invalidate the actions and authority of the Internal Revenue Service prior to the appointment of the members of the Internal Revenue Service Oversight Board.

P.L. 105-206, §6023(22):

Amended Code Sec. 6103(h)(4)(A) by inserting "if" before "the taxpayer is a party to". **Effective** 7-22-98.

• 1997, Taxpayer Relief Act of 1997 (P.L. 105-34)

P.L. 105-34, §1283(a):

Amended Code Sec. 6103(h) by striking paragraph (5) and by redesignating paragraph (6) as paragraph (5). **Effective** for judicial proceedings commenced after 8-5-97. Prior to amendment, Code Sec. 6103(h)(5) read as follows:

(5) PROSPECTIVE JURORS.—In connection with any judicial proceeding described in paragraph (4) to which the United States is a party, the Secretary shall respond to a written inquiry from an attorney of the Department of Justice (including a United States attorney) involved in such proceeding or any person (or his legal representative) who is a party to such proceeding as to whether an individual who is a prospective juror in such proceeding has or has not been the subject of any audit or other tax investigation by the Internal Revenue Service. The Secretary shall limit such response to an affirmative or negative reply to such inquiry.

• 1983, Social Security Amendments of 1983 (P.L. 98-21)

P.L. 98-21, §121(c)(3)(A):

Amended Code Sec. 6103(h) by adding paragraph (6). **Effective** for benefits received after 12-31-83 in tax years ending after such date. The amendments made by Act Sec. 121 of P.L. 98-21 shall not apply to any portion of a lump-sum payment of social security benefits (as defined in Code Sec. 86(d)) received after 12-31-83 if the generally applicable payment date for such portion was before 1-1-84.

• 1978, Revenue Act of 1978 (P.L. 95-600)

P.L. 95-600, §503(a), (b)(1):

Amended Code Sec. 6103(h)(2). **Effective** 11-7-78. Prior to amendment, Code Sec. 6103(h)(2) read as follows:

"(2) DEPARTMENT OF JUSTICE.—A return or return information shall be open to inspection by or disclosure to attorneys of the Department of Justice (including United States attorneys) personally and directly engaged in, and solely for their use in, preparation for any proceeding (or investigation which may result in such a proceeding) before a Federal grand jury or any Federal or State court in a matter involving tax administration, but only if—

(A) the taxpayer is or may be a party to such proceeding;

(B) the treatment of an item reflected on such return is or may be related to the resolution of an issue in the proceeding or investigation; or

(C) such return or return information relates or may relate to a transactional relationship between a person who is or may be a party to the proceeding and the taxpayer which affects, or may affect, the resolution of an issue in such proceeding or investigation."

P.L. 95-600, §503(b)(2):

Amended Code Sec. 6103(h)(4)(A) by striking out "(A) if the taxpayer is a party to such proceedings," and inserting a new subparagraph (A). **Effective** 11-7-78.

• 1976, Tax Reform Act of 1976 (P.L. 94-455)

P.L. 94-455, §1202(a):

Added Code Sec. 6103(h). **Effective** 1-1-77.

[Sec. 6103(i)]

(i) DISCLOSURE TO FEDERAL OFFICERS OR EMPLOYEES FOR ADMINISTRATION OF FEDERAL LAWS NOT RELATING TO TAX ADMINISTRATION.—

(1) DISCLOSURE OF RETURNS AND RETURN INFORMATION FOR USE IN CRIMINAL INVESTIGATIONS.—

(A) IN GENERAL.—Except as provided in paragraph (6), any return or return information with respect to any specified taxable period or periods shall, pursuant to and upon the grant of an ex parte order by a Federal district court judge or magistrate under subparagraph (B), be open (but only to the extent necessary as provided in such order) to inspection by, or disclosure to, officers and employees of any Federal agency who are personally and directly engaged in—

(i) preparation for any judicial or administrative proceeding pertaining to the enforcement of a specifically designated Federal criminal statute (not involving tax administration) to which the United States or such agency is or may be a party, or pertaining to the case of a missing or exploited child,

(ii) any investigation which may result in such a proceeding, or

(iii) any Federal grand jury proceeding pertaining to enforcement of such a criminal statute to which the United States or such agency is or may be a party, or to such a case of a missing or exploited child,

solely for the use of such officers and employees in such preparation, investigation, or grand jury proceeding.

(B) APPLICATION FOR ORDER.—The Attorney General, the Deputy Attorney General, the Associate Attorney General, any Assistant Attorney General, any United States attorney, any special prosecutor appointed under section 593 of title 28, United States Code, or any attorney in charge of a criminal division organized crime strike force established pursuant to section 510 of title 28, United States Code, may authorize an application to a Federal district court judge or magistrate for the order referred to in subparagraph (A). Upon such application, such judge or magistrate may grant such order if he determines on the basis of the facts submitted by the applicant that—

(i) there is reasonable cause to believe, based upon information believed to be reliable, that a specific criminal act has been committed,

(ii) there is reasonable cause to believe that the return or return information is or may be relevant to a matter relating to the commission of such act, and

(iii) the return or return information is sought exclusively for use in a Federal criminal investigation or proceeding concerning such act (or any criminal investigation or proceeding, in the case of a matter relating to a missing or exploited child), and the information sought to be disclosed cannot reasonably be obtained, under the circumstances, from another source.

(C) DISCLOSURE TO STATE AND LOCAL LAW ENFORCEMENT AGENCIES IN THE CASE OF MATTERS PERTAINING TO A MISSING OR EXPLOITED CHILD.—

(i) IN GENERAL.—In the case of an investigation pertaining to a missing or exploited child, the head of any Federal agency, or his designee, may disclose any return or return information obtained under subparagraph (A) to officers and employees of any State or local law enforcement agency, but only if—

(I) such State or local law enforcement agency is part of a team with the Federal agency in such investigation, and

(II) such information is disclosed only to such officers and employees who are personally and directly engaged in such investigation.

(ii) LIMITATION ON USE OF INFORMATION.—Information disclosed under this subparagraph shall be solely for the use of such officers and employees in locating the missing child, in a grand jury proceeding, or in any preparation for, or investigation which may result in, a judicial or administrative proceeding.

(iii) MISSING CHILD.—For purposes of this subparagraph, the term "missing child" shall have the meaning given such term by section 403 of the Missing Children's Assistance Act (42 U.S.C. 5772).

(iv) EXPLOITED CHILD.—For purposes of this subparagraph, the term "exploited child" means a minor with respect to whom there is reason to believe that a specified offense against a minor (as defined by section 111(7) of the Sex Offender Registration and Notification Act (42 U.S.C. 16911(7))) has or is occurring.

(2) DISCLOSURE OF RETURN INFORMATION OTHER THAN TAXPAYER RETURN INFORMATION FOR USE IN CRIMINAL INVESTIGATIONS.—

(A) IN GENERAL.—Except as provided in paragraph (6), upon receipt by the Secretary of a request which meets the requirements of subparagraph (B) from the head of any Federal agency or the Inspector General thereof, or, in the case of the Department of Justice, the Attorney General, the Deputy Attorney General, the Associate Attorney General, any Assistant Attorney General, the Director of the Federal Bureau of Investigation, the Administrator of the Drug Enforcement Administration, any United States attorney, any special prosecutor appointed under section 593 of title 28, United States Code, or any attorney in charge of a criminal division organized crime strike force established pursuant to section 510 of title 28, United States Code, the Secretary shall disclose return information (other than taxpayer return information) to officers and employees of such agency who are personally and directly engaged in—

(i) preparation for any judicial or administrative proceeding described in paragraph (1)(A)(i),

(ii) any investigation which may result in such a proceeding, or

(iii) any grand jury proceeding described in paragraph (1)(A)(iii),

solely for the use of such officers and employees in such preparation, investigation, or grand jury proceeding.

(B) REQUIREMENTS.—A request meets the requirements of this subparagraph if the request is in writing and sets forth—

(i) the name and address of the taxpayer with respect to whom the requested return information relates;

(ii) the taxable period or periods to which such return information relates;

(iii) the statutory authority under which the proceeding or investigation described in subparagraph (A) is being conducted; and

(iv) the specific reason or reasons why such disclosure is, or may be, relevant to such proceeding or investigation.

(C) TAXPAYER IDENTITY.—For purposes of this paragraph, a taxpayer's identity shall not be treated as taxpayer return information.

(3) DISCLOSURE OF RETURN INFORMATION TO APPRISE APPROPRIATE OFFICIALS OF CRIMINAL OR TERRORIST ACTIVITIES OR EMERGENCY CIRCUMSTANCES.—

(A) POSSIBLE VIOLATIONS OF FEDERAL CRIMINAL LAW.—

(i) IN GENERAL.—Except as provided in paragraph (6), the Secretary may disclose in writing return information (other than taxpayer return information) which may constitute evidence of a violation of any Federal criminal law (not involving tax administration) to the extent necessary to apprise the head of the appropriate Federal agency charged with the responsibility of enforcing such law. The head of such agency may disclose such return information to officers and employees of such agency to the extent necessary to enforce such law.

(ii) TAXPAYER IDENTITY.—If there is return information (other than taxpayer return information) which may constitute evidence of a violation by any taxpayer of any Federal criminal law (not involving tax administration), such taxpayer's identity may also be disclosed under clause (i).

(B) EMERGENCY CIRCUMSTANCES.—

(i) DANGER OF DEATH OR PHYSICAL INJURY.—Under circumstances involving an imminent danger of death or physical injury to any individual, the Secretary may disclose return information to the extent necessary to apprise appropriate officers or employees of any Federal or State law enforcement agency of such circumstances.

(ii) FLIGHT FROM FEDERAL PROSECUTION.—Under circumstances involving the imminent flight of any individual from Federal prosecution, the Secretary may disclose return information to the extent necessary to apprise appropriate officers or employees of any Federal law enforcement agency of such circumstances.

(C) TERRORIST ACTIVITIES, ETC.—

(i) IN GENERAL.—Except as provided in paragraph (6), the Secretary may disclose in writing return information (other than taxpayer return information) that may be related to a terrorist incident, threat, or activity to the extent necessary to apprise the head of the appropriate Federal law enforcement agency responsible for investigating or responding to such terrorist incident, threat, or activity. The head of the agency may disclose such return information to officers and employees of such agency to the extent necessary to investigate or respond to such terrorist incident, threat, or activity.

(ii) DISCLOSURE TO THE DEPARTMENT OF JUSTICE.—Returns and taxpayer return information may also be disclosed to the Attorney General under clause (i) to the extent necessary for, and solely for use in preparing, an application under paragraph (7)(D).

(iii) TAXPAYER IDENTITY.—For purposes of this subparagraph, a taxpayer's identity shall not be treated as taxpayer return information.

(4) USE OF CERTAIN DISCLOSED RETURNS AND RETURN INFORMATION IN JUDICIAL OR ADMINISTRATIVE PROCEEDINGS.—

(A) RETURNS AND TAXPAYER RETURN INFORMATION.—Except as provided in subparagraph (C), any return or taxpayer return information obtained under paragraph (1) or (7)(C) may be disclosed in any judicial or administrative proceeding pertaining to enforcement of a specifically designated Federal criminal statute or related civil forfeiture (not involving tax administration) to which the United States or a Federal agency is a party—

(i) if the court finds that such return or taxpayer return information is probative of a matter in issue relevant in establishing the commission of a crime or the guilt or liability of a party, or

(ii) to the extent required by order of the court pursuant to section 3500 of title 18, United States Code, or rule 16 of the Federal Rules of Criminal Procedure.

(B) RETURN INFORMATION (OTHER THAN TAXPAYER RETURN INFORMATION).—Except as provided in subparagraph (C), any return information (other than taxpayer return information) obtained under paragraph (1), (2), (3)(A) or (C), or (7) may be disclosed in any judicial or administrative proceeding pertaining to enforcement of a specifically designated Federal criminal statute or related civil forfeiture (not involving tax administration) to which the United States or a Federal agency is a party.

(C) CONFIDENTIAL INFORMANT; IMPAIRMENT OF INVESTIGATIONS.—No return or return information shall be admitted into evidence under subparagraph (A)(i) or (B) if the Secretary determines and notifies the Attorney General or his delegate or the head of the Federal agency that such admission would identify a confidential informant or seriously impair a civil or criminal tax investigation.

(D) CONSIDERATION OF CONFIDENTIALITY POLICY.—In ruling upon the admissibility of returns or return information, and in the issuance of an order under subparagraph (A)(ii), the court shall give due consideration to congressional policy favoring the confidentiality of returns and return information as set forth in this title.

(E) REVERSIBLE ERROR.—The admission into evidence of any return or return information contrary to the provisions of this paragraph shall not, as such, constitute reversible error upon appeal of a judgment in the proceeding.

(5) DISCLOSURE TO LOCATE FUGITIVES FROM JUSTICE.—

(A) IN GENERAL.—Except as provided in paragraph (6), the return of an individual or return information with respect to such individual shall, pursuant to and upon the grant of an ex parte order by a Federal district court judge or magistrate under subparagraph (B), be open (but only to the extent necessary as provided in such order) to inspection by, or disclosure to, officers and employees of any Federal agency exclusively for use in locating such individual.

(B) APPLICATION FOR ORDER.—Any person described in paragraph (1)(B) may authorize an application to a Federal district court judge or magistrate for an order referred to in subparagraph (A). Upon such application, such judge or magistrate may grant such order if he determines on the basis of the facts submitted by the applicant that—

(i) a Federal arrest warrant relating to the commission of a Federal felony offense has been issued for an individual who is a fugitive from justice,

(ii) the return of such individual or return information with respect to such individual is sought exclusively for use in locating such individual, and

(iii) there is reasonable cause to believe that such return or return information may be relevant in determining the location of such individual.

(6) CONFIDENTIAL INFORMANTS; IMPAIRMENT OF INVESTIGATIONS.—The Secretary shall not disclose any return or return information under paragraph (1), (2), (3)(A) or (C), (5), (7), or (8) if the Secretary determines (and, in the case of a request for disclosure pursuant to a court order described in paragraph (1)(B) or (5)(B), certifies to the court) that such disclosure would identify a confidential informant or seriously impair a civil or criminal tax investigation.

(7) DISCLOSURE UPON REQUEST OF INFORMATION RELATING TO TERRORIST ACTIVITIES, ETC.—

(A) DISCLOSURE TO LAW ENFORCEMENT AGENCIES.—

(i) IN GENERAL.—Except as provided in paragraph (6), upon receipt by the Secretary of a written request which meets the requirements of clause (iii), the Secretary may disclose return information (other than taxpayer return information) to officers and employees of any Federal law enforcement agency who are personally and directly engaged in the response to or investigation of any terrorist incident, threat, or activity.

(ii) DISCLOSURE TO STATE AND LOCAL LAW ENFORCEMENT AGENCIES.—The head of any Federal law enforcement agency may disclose return information obtained under clause (i) to officers and employees of any State or local law enforcement agency but only if such agency is part of a team with the Federal law enforcement agency in such response or investigation and such information is disclosed only to officers and employees who are personally and directly engaged in such response or investigation.

(iii) REQUIREMENTS.—A request meets the requirements of this clause if—

(I) the request is made by the head of any Federal law enforcement agency (or his delegate) involved in the response to or investigation of any terrorist incident, threat, or activity, and

(II) the request sets forth the specific reason or reasons why such disclosure may be relevant to a terrorist incident, threat, or activity.

(iv) LIMITATION ON USE OF INFORMATION.—Information disclosed under this subparagraph shall be solely for the use of the officers and employees to whom such information is disclosed in such response or investigation.

(v) TAXPAYER IDENTITY.—For purposes of this subparagraph, a taxpayer's identity shall not be treated as taxpayer return information.

(B) DISCLOSURE TO INTELLIGENCE AGENCIES.—

(i) IN GENERAL.—Except as provided in paragraph (6), upon receipt by the Secretary of a written request which meets the requirements of clause (ii), the Secretary may disclose return information (other than taxpayer return information) to those officers and employees of the Department of Justice, the Department of the Treasury, and other Federal intelligence agencies who are personally and directly engaged in the collection or analysis of intelligence and counterintelligence information or investigation concerning any terrorist incident, threat, or activity. For purposes of the preceding sentence, the information disclosed under the preceding sentence shall be solely for the use of such officers and employees in such investigation, collection, or analysis.

(ii) REQUIREMENTS.—A request meets the requirements of this subparagraph if the request—

(I) is made by an individual described in clause (iii), and

(II) sets forth the specific reason or reasons why such disclosure may be relevant to a terrorist incident, threat, or activity.

(iii) REQUESTING INDIVIDUALS.—An individual described in this subparagraph is an individual—

(I) who is an officer or employee of the Department of Justice or the Department of the Treasury who is appointed by the President with the advice and consent of the Senate or who is the Director of the United States Secret Service, and

(II) who is responsible for the collection and analysis of intelligence and counterintelligence information concerning any terrorist incident, threat, or activity.

(iv) TAXPAYER IDENTITY.—For purposes of this subparagraph, a taxpayer's identity shall not be treated as taxpayer return information.

(C) DISCLOSURE UNDER EX PARTE ORDERS.—

(i) IN GENERAL.—Except as provided in paragraph (6), any return or return information with respect to any specified taxable period or periods shall, pursuant to and upon the grant of an ex parte order by a Federal district court judge or magistrate under clause (ii), be open (but only to the extent necessary as provided in such order) to inspection by, or disclosure to, officers and employees of any Federal law enforcement agency or Federal intelligence agency who are personally and directly engaged in any investigation, response to, or analysis of intelligence and counterintelligence information concerning any terrorist incident, threat, or activity. Return or return information opened to inspection or disclosure pursuant to the preceding sentence shall be solely for the use of such officers and employees in the investigation, response, or analysis, and in any judicial, administrative, or grand jury proceedings, pertaining to such terrorist incident, threat, or activity.

(ii) APPLICATION FOR ORDER.—The Attorney General, the Deputy Attorney General, the Associate Attorney General, any Assistant Attorney General, or any United States attorney may authorize an application to a Federal district court judge or magistrate for the order referred to in clause (i). Upon such application, such judge or magistrate may grant such order if he determines on the basis of the facts submitted by the applicant that—

(I) there is reasonable cause to believe, based upon information believed to be reliable, that the return or return information may be relevant to a matter relating to such terrorist incident, threat, or activity, and

(II) the return or return information is sought exclusively for use in a Federal investigation, analysis, or proceeding concerning any terrorist incident, threat, or activity.

(D) SPECIAL RULE FOR EX PARTE DISCLOSURE BY THE IRS.—

(i) IN GENERAL.—Except as provided in paragraph (6), the Secretary may authorize an application to a Federal district court judge or magistrate for the order referred to in subparagraph (C)(i). Upon such application, such judge or magistrate may grant such order if he determines on the basis of the facts submitted by the applicant that the requirements of subparagraph (C)(ii)(I) are met.

(ii) LIMITATION ON USE OF INFORMATION.—Information disclosed under clause (i)—

(I) may be disclosed only to the extent necessary to apprise the head of the appropriate Federal law enforcement agency responsible for investigating or responding to a terrorist incident, threat, or activity, and

(II) shall be solely for use in a Federal investigation, analysis, or proceeding concerning any terrorist incident, threat, or activity.

The head of such Federal agency may disclose such information to officers and employees of such agency to the extent necessary to investigate or respond to such terrorist incident, threat, or activity.

(8) COMPTROLLER GENERAL.—

(A) RETURNS AVAILABLE FOR INSPECTION.—Except as provided in subparagraph (C), upon written request by the Comptroller General of the United States, returns and return information shall be open to inspection by, or disclosure to, officers and employees of the Government Accountability Office for the purpose of, and to the extent necessary in, making—

(i) an audit of the Internal Revenue Service, the Bureau of Alcohol, Tobacco, Firearms, and Explosives, Department of Justice, or the Tax and Trade Bureau, Department of the Treasury, which may be required by section 713 of title 31, United States Code, or

(ii) any audit authorized by subsection (p)(6),

except that no such officer or employee shall, except to the extent authorized by subsection (f) or (p)(6), disclose to any person, other than another officer or employee of such office whose official duties require such disclosure, any return or return information described in section 4424(a) in a form which can be associated with, or otherwise identify, directly or indirectly, a particular taxpayer, nor shall such officer or employee disclose any other return or return information, except as otherwise expressly provided by law, to any person other than such other officer or employee of such office in a form which can be associated with, or otherwise identify, directly or indirectly, a particular taxpayer.

(B) AUDITS OF OTHER AGENCIES.—

(i) IN GENERAL.—Nothing in this section shall prohibit any return or return information obtained under this title by any Federal agency (other than an agency referred to in subparagraph (A)) or by a Trustee as defined in the District of Columbia Retirement Protection Act of 1997, for use in any program or activity from being open to inspection by, or disclosure to, officers and employees of the Government Accountability Office if such inspection or disclosure is—

(I) for purposes of, and to the extent necessary in, making an audit authorized by law of such program or activity, and

(II) pursuant to a written request by the Comptroller General of the United States to the head of such Federal agency.

(ii) INFORMATION FROM SECRETARY.—If the Comptroller General of the United States determines that the returns or return information available under clause (i) are not sufficient for purposes of making an audit of any program or activity of a Federal agency (other than an agency referred to in subparagraph (A)), upon written request by the Comptroller General to the Secretary, returns and return information (of the type authorized by subsection (l) or (m) to be made available to the Federal agency for use in such program or activity) shall be open to inspection by, or disclosure to, officers and employees of the Government Accountability Office for the purpose of, and to the extent necessary in, making such audit.

(iii) REQUIREMENT OF NOTIFICATION UPON COMPLETION OF AUDIT.—Within 90 days after the completion of an audit with respect to which returns or return information were opened to inspection or disclosed under clause (i) or (ii), the Comptroller General of the United States shall notify in writing the Joint Committee on Taxation of such completion. Such notice shall include—

(I) a description of the use of the returns and return information by the Federal agency involved,

(II) such recommendations with respect to the use of returns and return information by such Federal agency as the Comptroller General deems appropriate, and

(III) a statement on the impact of any such recommendations on confidentiality of returns and return information and the administration of this title.

(iv) CERTAIN RESTRICTIONS MADE APPLICABLE.—The restrictions contained in subparagraph (A) on the disclosure of any returns or return information open to inspection or disclosed under such subparagraph shall also apply to returns and return information open to inspection or disclosed under this subparagraph.

(C) DISAPPROVAL BY JOINT COMMITTEE ON TAXATION.—Returns and return information shall not be open to inspection or disclosed under subparagraph (A) or (B) with respect to an audit—

(i) unless the Comptroller General of the United States notifies in writing the Joint Committee on Taxation of such audit, and

(ii) if the Joint Committee on Taxation disapproves such audit by a vote of at least two-thirds of its members within the 30-day period beginning on the day the Joint Committee on Taxation receives such notice.

Amendments

• 2016, Recovering Missing Children Act (P.L. 114-184)

P.L. 114-184, §2(a)(1)-(3):

Amended Code Sec. 6103(i)(1) by inserting "or pertaining to the case of a missing or exploited child," after "may be a party," in subparagraph (A)(i); by inserting "or to such a case of a missing or exploited child," after "may be a party," in subparagraph (A)(iii); and by inserting "(or any criminal investigation or proceeding, in the case of a matter relating to a missing or exploited child)" after "concerning such act" in subparagraph (B)(iii). **Effective** for disclosures made after 6-30-2016.

P.L. 114-184, §2(b)(1):

Amended Code Sec. 6103(i)(1) by adding at the end a new subparagraph (C). **Effective** for disclosures made after 6-30-2016.

• 2008, Tax Extenders and Alternative Minimum Tax Relief Act of 2008 (P.L. 110-343)

P.L. 110-343, Division C, §402(a):

Amended Code Sec. 6103(i)(3)(C) by striking clause (iv). **Effective** for disclosures after 10-3-2008. Prior to being stricken, Code Sec. 6103(i)(3)(C)(iv) read as follows:

(iv) TERMINATION.—No disclosure may be made under this subparagraph after December 31, 2007.

P.L. 110-343, Division C, §402(b):

Amended Code Sec. 6103(i)(7) by striking paragraph (E). **Effective** for disclosures after 10-3-2008. Prior to being stricken, Code Sec. 6103(i)(7)(E) read as follows:

(E) TERMINATION.—No disclosure may be made under this paragraph after December 31, 2007.

• 2006, Tax Relief and Health Care Act of 2006 (P.L. 109-432)

P.L. 109-432, Division A, §122(b)(1):

Amended Code Sec. 6103(i)(3)(C)(iv) and (i)(7)(E) by striking "2006" and inserting "2007". **Effective** for disclosures after 12-31-2006.

• 2005, Gulf Opportunity Zone Act of 2005 (P.L. 109-135)

P.L. 109-135, §305(b)(1):

Amended Code Sec. 6103(i)(3)(C)(iv) and (i)(7)(E) by striking "December 31, 2005" and inserting "December 31, 2006". **Effective** for disclosures after 12-31-2005.

P.L. 109-135, §412(rr)(3):

Amended Code Sec. 6103(i)(8)(A), (i)(8)(B)(i), and (i)(8)(B)(ii) by striking "General Accounting Office" each place it appears therein and inserting "Government Accountability Office". **Effective** 12-21-2005.

• 2004, Working Families Tax Relief Act of 2004 (P.L. 108-311)

P.L. 108-311, §320(a):

Amended Code Sec. 6103(i)(3)(C)(iv) and (7)(E) by striking "December 31, 2003" and inserting "December 31, 2005". **Effective** for disclosures on or after 10-4-2004.

P.L. 108-311, §320(b):

Amended Code Sec. 6103(i)(7)(A) by adding at the end a new clause (v). **Effective** as if included in section 201 of the Victims of Terrorism Tax Relief Act of 2001 (P.L. 107-134) [**effective** for disclosures made on or after 1-23-2002.—CCH].

• 2002, Homeland Security Act of 2002 (P.L. 107-296)

P.L. 107-296, §1112(j):

Amended Code Sec. 6103(i)(8)(A)(i) by striking "or the Bureau of Alcohol, Tobacco and Firearms" and inserting ", the Bureau of Alcohol, Tobacco, Firearms, and Explosives, Department of Justice, or the Tax and Trade Bureau, Department of the Treasury,". **Effective** 60 days after 11-25-2002.

• 2002, Victims of Terrorism Tax Relief Act of 2001 (P.L. 107-134)

P.L. 107-134, §201(a):

Amended Code Sec. 6103(i)(3) by adding at the end a new subparagraph (C). **Effective** for disclosures made on or after 1-23-2002.

P.L. 107-134, §201(b):

Amended Code Sec. 6103(i) by redesignating paragraph (7) as paragraph (8) and by inserting after paragraph (6) a new paragraph (7). **Effective** for disclosures made on or after 1-23-2002.

P.L. 107-134, §201(c)(3):

Amended the heading of Code Sec. 6103(i)(3) by inserting "OR TERRORIST" after "CRIMINAL". **Effective** for disclosures made on or after 1-23-2002.

P.L. 107-134, §201(c)(4)(A)-(B):

Amended Code Sec. 6103(i)(4) in subparagraph (A) by inserting "or (7)(C)" after "paragraph (1)"; and in subparagraph (B) by striking "or (3)(A)" and inserting "(3)(A) or (C), or (7)". **Effective** for disclosures made on or after 1-23-2002.

P.L. 107-134, §201(c)(5)(A)-(B):

Amended Code Sec. 6103(i)(6) by striking "(3)(A)" and inserting "(3)(A) or (C)"; and by striking "or (7)" and inserting "(7), or (8)". **Effective** for disclosures made on or after 1-23-2002.

• 1997, Balanced Budget Act of 1997 (P.L. 105-33)

P.L. 105-33, §11024(b)(3):

Amended Code Sec. 6103(i)(7)(B)(i) by inserting after "(other than an agency referred to in subparagraph (A))" and before the word "for" the words "or by a Trustee as defined in the District of Columbia Retirement Protection Act of 1997,". For the **effective** date, see Act Sec. 11721, below.

P.L. 105-33, §11721, provides:

Except as otherwise provided in this title, the provisions of this title shall take effect on the later of October 1, 1997, or the day the District of Columbia Financial Responsibility and Management Assistance Authority certifies that the financial plan and budget for the District government for fiscal year 1998 meet the requirements of section 201(c)(1) of the District of Columbia Financial Responsibility and Management Assistance Act of 1995, as amended by this title.

• 1996, Taxpayer Bill of Rights 2 (P.L. 104-168)

P.L. 104-168, §1206(b)(1):

Amended Code Sec. 6103(i) by striking paragraph (8). **Effective** 7-30-96. Prior to being stricken, Code Sec. 6103(i)(8) read as follows:

(8) DISCLOSURE OF RETURNS FILED UNDER SECTION 6050I.—The Secretary may, upon written request, disclose returns filed under section 6050I to officers and employees of any Federal agency whose official duties require such disclosure for the administration of Federal criminal statutes not related to tax administration.

• 1988, Anti-Drug Abuse Act of 1988 (P.L. 100-690)

P.L. 100-690, §7601(b)(1):

Amended Code Sec. 6103(i) by adding at the end thereof new paragraph (8). **Effective** for requests made on or after 11-18-88, but disclosures may be made pursuant to such amendments only during the 2-year period beginning on such date.

• 1984, Deficit Reduction Act of 1984 (P.L. 98-369)

P.L. 98-369, §453(b)(5):

Amended P.L. 96-249, §127(a)(1), by redesignating Code Sec. 6103(i)(7), as added by that Act, as Code Sec. 6103(l)(7). **Effective** on the first day of the first calendar month which begins more than 90 days after 7-18-84.

• 1982 (P.L. 97-258)

P.L. 97-258, §3(f)(4):

Amended Code Sec. 6103(i)(6)[7](A)(i) by striking out "section 117 of the Budget and Accounting Procedures Act of 1950 (31 U.S.C. 67)" and substituting "section 713 of title 31, United States Code". **Effective** 9-13-82.

• 1982, Tax Equity and Fiscal Responsibility Act of 1982 (P.L. 97-248)

P.L. 97-248, §356(a):

Amended Code Sec. 6103(i) by redesignating paragraph (6) as paragraph (7) and by striking out paragraphs (1), (2), (3), (4), and (5) and inserting new paragraphs (1)-(6). **Effective** 9-4-82. Prior to amendment, Code Sec. 6103(i)(1) through (5) read as follows:

(1) NONTAX CRIMINAL INVESTIGATION.—

(A) INFORMATION FROM TAXPAYER.—A return or taxpayer return information shall, pursuant to, and upon the grant of, an ex parte order by a Federal district court judge as provided by this paragraph, be open, but only to the extent necessary as provided in such order, to officers and employees of a Federal agency personally and directly engaged in and solely for their use in, preparation for any administrative or judicial proceeding (or investigation which may result in such a proceeding) pertaining to the enforcement of a specifically designated Federal criminal statute (not involving tax administration) to which the United States or such agency is or may be a party.

(B) APPLICATION FOR ORDER.—The head of any Federal agency described in subparagraph (A) or, in the case of the Department of Justice, the Attorney General, the Deputy Attorney General, or an Assistant Attorney General, may authorize an application to a Federal district court judge for the order referred to in subparagraph (A). Upon such application, such judge may grant such order if he determines on the basis of the facts submitted by the applicant that—

(i) there is reasonable cause to believe, based upon information believed to be reliable, that a specific criminal act has been committed;

(ii) there is reason to believe that such return or return information is probative evidence of a matter in issue related to the commission of such criminal act; and

(iii) the information sought to be disclosed cannot reasonably be obtained from any other source, unless it is determined that, notwithstanding the reasonable availability of the information from another source, the return or return information sought constitutes the most probative evidence of a matter in issue relating to the commission of such criminal act.

However, the Secretary shall not disclose any return or return information under this paragraph if he determines and certifies to the court that such disclosure would identify a confidential informant or seriously impair a civil or criminal tax investigation.

(2) RETURN INFORMATION OTHER THAN TAXPAYER RETURN INFORMATION.—Upon written request from the head of a Federal agency described in paragraph (1)(A), or in the case of the Department of Justice, the Attorney General, the Deputy Attorney General, or an Assistant Attorney General, the Secretary shall disclose return information (other than taxpayer return information) to officers and employees of such agency personally and directly engaged in, and solely for their use in preparation for any administrative or judicial proceeding (or investigation which may result in such a proceeding) described in paragraph (1)(A). Such request shall set forth—

(A) the name and address of the taxpayer with respect to whom such return information relates;

(B) the taxable period or periods to which the return information relates;

(C) the statutory authority under which the proceeding or investigation is being conducted; and

(D) the specific reason or reasons why such disclosure is or may be material to the proceeding or investigation.

However, the Secretary shall not disclose any return or return information under this paragraph if he determines that such disclosure would identify a confidential informant or seriously impair a civil or criminal tax investigation. For purposes of this paragraph, the name and address of the taxpayer shall not be treated as taxpayer return information.

(3) DISCLOSURE OF RETURN INFORMATION CONCERNING POSSIBLE CRIMINAL ACTIVITIES.—The Secretary may disclose in writing return information, other than taxpayer return information, which may constitute evidence of a violation of Federal criminal laws to the extent necessary to apprise the head of the appropriate Federal agency charged with the responsibility for enforcing such laws. For purposes of the preceding sentence, the name and address of the taxpayer shall not be treated as taxpayer return information if there is return information (other than taxpayer return information) which may constitute evidence of a violation of Federal criminal laws.

(4) USE IN JUDICIAL OR ADMINISTRATIVE PROCEEDING.—Any return or return information obtained under paragraph (1), (2), or (3) may be entered into evidence in any administrative or judicial proceeding pertaining to enforcement of a specifically designated Federal criminal statute (not involving tax administration) to which the United States or an agency described in paragraph (1)(A) is a party but, in the case of any return or return information obtained under paragraph (1), only if the court finds that such return or return information is probative of a matter in issue relevant in establishing the commission of a crime or the guilt of a party. However, any return or return information obtained under paragraph (1), (2), or (3) shall not be admitted into evidence in such proceeding if the Secretary determines and notifies the Attorney General or his delegate or the head of such agency that such admission would identify a confidential informant or seriously impair a civil or criminal tax investigation. The admission into evidence of any return or return information contrary to the provisions of this paragraph shall not, as such, constitute reversible error upon appeal of a judgment in such proceeding.

(5) RENEGOTIATION OF CONTRACTS.—A return or return information with respect to the tax imposed by chapter 1 upon a taxpayer subject to the provisions of the Renegotiation Act of 1951 shall, upon request in writing by the Chairman of the Renegotiation Board, be open to officers and employees of such board personally and directly engaged in, and solely for their use in, verifying or analyzing financial information required by such Act to be filed with, or otherwise disclosed to, the board, or to the extent necessary to implement the provisions of section 1481 or 1482. The Chairman of the Renegotiation Board may, upon referral of any matter with respect to such Act to the Department of Justice for further legal action, disclose such return and return information to any employee of such department charged with the responsibility for handling such matters.

P.L. 97-248, §358(a):

Amended Code Sec. 6103(i)(7) (as redesignated by P.L. 97-248, §356(a)) by redesignating subparagraph (B) as subparagraph (C) and by adding a new subparagraph (B). **Effective** 9-4-82.

P.L. 97-248, §358(b)(1):

Amended Code Sec. 6103(i)(7)(A) (as redesignated by P.L. 97-248, §356(a)) by striking out "subparagraph (B)" and inserting "subparagraph (C)". **Effective** 9-4-82.

P.L. 97-248, §358(b)(2):

Amended Code Sec. 6102(i)(7)(C) (as redesignated by P.L. 97-248) by striking out "subparagraph (A)" and inserting "subparagraph (A) or (B)". **Effective** 9-4-82.

• 1980, Food Stamp Act Amendments of 1980 (P.L. 96-249)

P.L. 96-249, §127(a)(i):

Erroneously amended Code Sec. 6103(i) by adding a new subsection (7). The new subsection (7) was intended to be added to Code Sec. 6103(l) and is, therefore, reflected at that location.

• 1978, Revenue Act of 1978 (P.L. 95-600)

P.L. 95-600, §701(bb)(3):

Added a new last sentence to Code Sec. 6103(i)(2). **Effective** 1-1-77.

P.L. 95-600, §701(bb)(4):

Added a new last sentence to Code Sec. 6103(i)(3). **Effective** 1-1-77.

• 1976, Tax Reform Act of 1976 (P.L. 94-455)

P.L. 94-455, §1202(a):

Added Code Sec. 6103(i). **Effective** 1-1-77.

[Sec. 6103(j)]

(j) STATISTICAL USE.—

(1) DEPARTMENT OF COMMERCE.—Upon request in writing by the Secretary of Commerce, the Secretary shall furnish—

(A) such returns, or return information reflected thereon, to officers and employees of the Bureau of the Census, and

(B) such return information reflected on returns of corporations to officers and employees of the Bureau of Economic Analysis,

as the Secretary may prescribe by regulation for the purpose of, but only to the extent necessary in, the structuring of censuses and national economic accounts and conducting related statistical activities authorized by law.

(2) FEDERAL TRADE COMMISSION.—Upon request in writing by the Chairman of the Federal Trade Commission, the Secretary shall furnish such return information reflected on any return of a corporation with respect to the tax imposed by chapter 1 to officers and employees of the Division of Financial Statistics of the Bureau of Economics of such commission as the Secretary may prescribe by regulation for the purpose of, but only to the extent necessary in, administration by such division of legally authorized economic surveys of corporations.

(3) DEPARTMENT OF TREASURY.—Returns and return information shall be open to inspection by or disclosure to officers and employees of the Department of the Treasury whose official duties require such inspection or disclosure for the purpose of, but only to the extent necessary in, preparing economic or financial forecasts, projections, analyses, and statistical studies and conducting related activities. Such inspection or disclosure shall be permitted only upon written request which sets forth the specific reason or reasons why such inspection or disclosure is necessary and which is signed by the head of the bureau or office of the Department of the Treasury requesting the inspection or disclosure.

(4) ANONYMOUS FORM.—No person who receives a return or return information under this subsection shall disclose such return or return information to any person other than the taxpayer to whom it relates except in a form which cannot be associated with, or otherwise identify, directly or indirectly, a particular taxpayer.

(5) DEPARTMENT OF AGRICULTURE.—Upon request in writing by the Secretary of Agriculture, the Secretary shall furnish such returns, or return information reflected thereon, as the Secretary may prescribe by regulation to officers and employees of the Department of Agriculture whose official duties require access to such returns or information for the purpose of, but only to the extent necessary in, structuring, preparing, and conducting the census of agriculture pursuant to the Census of Agriculture Act of 1997 (Public Law 105-113).

(6) CONGRESSIONAL BUDGET OFFICE.—Upon written request by the Director of the Congressional Budget Office, the Secretary shall furnish to officers and employees of the Congressional Budget Office return information for the purpose of, but only to the extent necessary for, long-term models of the social security and medicare programs.

Amendments

• 2000, Community Renewal Tax Relief Act of 2000 (P.L. 106-554)

P.L. 106-554, §310(a)(1):

Amended Code Sec. 6103(j) by adding at the end a new paragraph (6). **Effective** 12-21-2000.

• 1998, Tax and Trade Relief Extension Act of 1998 (P.L. 105-277)

P.L. 105-277, §4006(a)(1):

Amended Code Sec. 6103(j) by adding at the end a new paragraph (5). **Effective** for requests made on or after 10-21-98.

• 1976, Tax Reform Act of 1976 (P.L. 94-455)

P.L. 94-455, §1202(a):

Added Code Sec. 6103(j). **Effective** 1-1-77.

[Sec. 6103(k)]

(k) DISCLOSURE OF CERTAIN RETURNS AND RETURN INFORMATION FOR TAX ADMINISTRATION PURPOSES.—

(1) DISCLOSURE OF ACCEPTED OFFERS-IN-COMPROMISE.—Return information shall be disclosed to members of the general public to the extent necessary to permit inspection of any accepted offer-in-compromise under section 7122 relating to the liability for a tax imposed by this title.

(2) DISCLOSURE OF AMOUNT OF OUTSTANDING LIEN.—If a notice of lien has been filed pursuant to section 6323(f), the amount of the outstanding obligation secured by such lien may be disclosed to any person who furnishes satisfactory written evidence that he has a right in the property subject to such lien or intends to obtain a right in such property.

(3) DISCLOSURE OF RETURN INFORMATION TO CORRECT MISSTATEMENTS OF FACT.—The Secretary may, but only following approval by the Joint Committee on Taxation, disclose such return information or any other information with respect to any specific taxpayer to the extent necessary for tax administration purposes to correct a misstatement of fact published or disclosed with respect to such taxpayer's return or any transaction of the taxpayer with the Internal Revenue Service.

(4) DISCLOSURE TO COMPETENT AUTHORITY UNDER TAX CONVENTION.—A return or return information may be disclosed to a competent authority of a foreign government which has an income tax or gift and estate tax convention or other convention or bilateral agreement relating to the exchange of tax information with the United States but only to the extent provided in, and subject to the terms and conditions of, such convention or bilateral agreement.

(5) STATE AGENCIES REGULATING TAX RETURN PREPARERS.—Taxpayer identity information with respect to any tax return preparer, and information as to whether or not any penalty has been assessed against such tax return preparer under section 6694, 6695, or 7216, may be furnished to any agency, body, or commission lawfully charged under any State or local law with the licensing, registration, or regulation of tax return preparers. Such information may be furnished only upon written request by the head of such agency, body, or commission designating the officers or employees to whom such information is to be furnished. Information may be furnished and used under this paragraph only for purposes of the licensing, registration, or regulation of tax return preparers.

(6) DISCLOSURE BY CERTAIN OFFICERS AND EMPLOYEES FOR INVESTIGATIVE PURPOSES.—An internal revenue officer or employee and an officer or employee of the Office of Treasury Inspector General for Tax Administration may, in connection with his official duties relating to any audit, collection activity, or civil or criminal tax investigation or any other offense under the internal revenue laws, disclose return information to the extent that such disclosure is necessary in obtaining information, which is not otherwise reasonably available, with respect to the correct determination of tax, liability for tax, or the amount to be collected or with respect to the enforcement of any other provision of this title. Such disclosures shall be made only in such situations and under such conditions as the Secretary may prescribe by regulation. This paragraph shall not apply to any disclosure to an individual providing information relating to any purpose described in paragraph (1) or (2) of section 7623(a) which is made under paragraph (13)(A).

(7) DISCLOSURE OF EXCISE TAX REGISTRATION INFORMATION.—To the extent the Secretary determines that disclosure is necessary to permit the effective administration of subtitle D, the Secretary may disclose—

(A) the name, address, and registration number of each person who is registered under any provision of subtitle D (and, in the case of a registered terminal operator, the address of each terminal operated by such operator), and

(B) the registration status of any person.

(8) LEVIES ON CERTAIN GOVERNMENT PAYMENTS.—

(A) DISCLOSURE OF RETURN INFORMATION IN LEVIES ON FINANCIAL MANAGEMENT SERVICE.—In serving a notice of levy, or release of such levy, with respect to any applicable government payment, the Secretary may disclose to officers and employees of the Financial Management Service—

(i) return information, including taxpayer identity information,

(ii) the amount of any unpaid liability under this title (including penalties and interest), and

(iii) the type of tax and tax period to which such unpaid liability relates.

(B) RESTRICTION ON USE OF DISCLOSED INFORMATION.—Return information disclosed under subparagraph (A) may be used by officers and employees of the Financial Management Service only for the purpose of, and to the extent necessary in, transferring levied funds in satisfaction of the levy, maintaining appropriate agency records in regard to such levy or the release thereof, notifying the taxpayer and the agency certifying such payment that the levy has been honored, or in the defense of any litigation ensuing from the honor of such levy.

(C) APPLICABLE GOVERNMENT PAYMENT.—For purposes of this paragraph, the term "applicable government payment" means—

(i) any Federal payment (other than a payment for which eligibility is based on the income or assets (or both) of a payee) certified to the Financial Management Service for disbursement, and

(ii) any other payment which is certified to the Financial Management Service for disbursement and which the Secretary designates by published notice.

(9) DISCLOSURE OF INFORMATION TO ADMINISTER SECTION 6311.—The Secretary may disclose returns or return information to financial institutions and others to the extent the Secretary deems necessary for the administration of section 6311. Disclosures of information for purposes other than to accept payments by checks or money orders shall be made only to the extent authorized by written procedures promulgated by the Secretary.

(10) DISCLOSURE OF CERTAIN RETURNS AND RETURN INFORMATION TO CERTAIN PRISON OFFICIALS.—

(A) IN GENERAL.—Under such procedures as the Secretary may prescribe, the Secretary may disclose to officers and employees of the Federal Bureau of Prisons and of any State agency charged with the responsibility for administration of prisons any returns or return information with respect to individuals incarcerated in Federal or State prison systems whom the Secretary has determined may have filed or facilitated the filing of a false or fraudulent return to the extent that the Secretary determines that such disclosure is necessary to permit effective Federal tax administration.

(B) DISCLOSURE TO CONTRACTOR-RUN PRISONS.—Under such procedures as the Secretary may prescribe, the disclosures authorized by subparagraph (A) may be made to contractors responsible for the operation of a Federal or State prison on behalf of such Bureau or agency.

(C) RESTRICTIONS ON USE OF DISCLOSED INFORMATION.—Any return or return information received under this paragraph shall be used only for the purposes of and to the extent necessary in taking administrative action to prevent the filing of false and fraudulent returns, including administrative actions to address possible violations of administrative rules and regulations of the prison facility and in administrative and judicial proceedings arising from such administrative actions.

(D) RESTRICTIONS ON REDISCLOSURE AND DISCLOSURE TO LEGAL REPRESENTATIVES.—Notwithstanding subsection (h)—

(i) RESTRICTIONS ON REDISCLOSURE.—Except as provided in clause (ii), any officer, employee, or contractor of the Federal Bureau of Prisons or of any State agency charged with the responsibility for administration of prisons shall not disclose any information obtained under this paragraph to any person other than an officer or employee or contractor of such Bureau or agency personally and directly engaged in the administration of prison facilities on behalf of such Bureau or agency.

(ii) DISCLOSURE TO LEGAL REPRESENTATIVES.—The returns and return information disclosed under this paragraph may be disclosed to the duly authorized legal representative of the Federal Bureau of Prisons, State agency, or contractor charged with the responsibility for administration of prisons, or of the incarcerated individual accused of filing the false or fraudulent return who is a party to an action or proceeding described in subparagraph (C), solely in preparation for, or for use in, such action or proceeding.

(11) DISCLOSURE OF RETURN INFORMATION TO DEPARTMENT OF STATE FOR PURPOSES OF PASSPORT REVOCATION UNDER SECTION 7345.—

(A) IN GENERAL.—The Secretary shall, upon receiving a certification described in section 7345, disclose to the Secretary of State return information with respect to a taxpayer who has a seriously delinquent tax debt described in such section. Such return information shall be limited to—

(i) the taxpayer identity information with respect to such taxpayer, and

(ii) the amount of such seriously delinquent tax debt.

(B) RESTRICTION ON DISCLOSURE.—Return information disclosed under subparagraph (A) may be used by officers and employees of the Department of State for the purposes of, and to the extent necessary in, carrying out the requirements of section 32101 of the FAST Act.

(12) QUALIFIED TAX COLLECTION CONTRACTORS.—Persons providing services pursuant to a qualified tax collection contract under section 6306 may, if speaking to a person who has identified himself or herself as having the name of the taxpayer to which a tax receivable (within the meaning of such section) relates, identify themselves as contractors of the Internal Revenue Service and disclose the business name of the contractor, and the nature, subject, and reason for the contact. Disclosures under this paragraph shall be made only in such situations and under such conditions as have been approved by the Secretary.

(13) DISCLOSURE TO WHISTLEBLOWERS.—

(A) IN GENERAL.—The Secretary may disclose, to any individual providing information relating to any purpose described in paragraph (1) or (2) of section 7623(a), return information related to the investigation of any taxpayer with respect to whom the individual has provided such information, but only to the extent that such disclosure is necessary in obtaining information, which is not otherwise reasonably available, with respect to the correct determination of tax liability for tax, or the amount to be collected with respect to the enforcement of any other provision of this title.

(B) UPDATES ON WHISTLEBLOWER INVESTIGATIONS.—The Secretary shall disclose to an individual providing information relating to any purpose described in paragraph (1) or (2) of section 7623(a) the following:

(i) Not later than 60 days after a case for which the individual has provided information has been referred for an audit or examination, a notice with respect to such referral.

(ii) Not later than 60 days after a taxpayer with respect to whom the individual has provided information has made a payment of tax with respect to tax liability to which such information relates, a notice with respect to such payment.

(iii) Subject to such requirements and conditions as are prescribed by the Secretary, upon a written request by such individual—

(I) information on the status and stage of any investigation or action related to such information, and

(II) in the case of a determination of the amount of any award under section 7623(b), the reasons for such determination.

Clause (iii) shall not apply to any information if the Secretary determines that disclosure of such information would seriously impair Federal tax administration. Information described in clauses (i), (ii), and (iii) may be disclosed to a designee of the individual providing such information in accordance with guidance provided by the Secretary.

(14) DISCLOSURE OF RETURN INFORMATION FOR PURPOSES OF CYBERSECURITY AND THE PREVENTION OF IDENTITY THEFT TAX REFUND FRAUD.—

(A) IN GENERAL.—Under such procedures and subject to such conditions as the Secretary may prescribe, the Secretary may disclose specified return information to specified ISAC participants to the extent that the Secretary determines such disclosure is in furtherance of effective Federal tax administration relating to the detection or prevention of identity theft tax refund fraud, validation of taxpayer identity, authentication of taxpayer returns, or detection or prevention of cybersecurity threats.

(B) SPECIFIED ISAC PARTICIPANTS.—For purposes of this paragraph—

(i) IN GENERAL.—The term "specified ISAC participant" means—

(I) any person designated by the Secretary as having primary responsibility for a function performed with respect to the information sharing and analysis center described in section 2003(a) of the Taxpayer First Act, and

(II) any person subject to the requirements of section 7216 and which is a participant in such information sharing and analysis center.

(ii) INFORMATION SHARING AGREEMENT.—Such term shall not include any person unless such person has entered into a written agreement with the Secretary setting forth the terms and conditions for the disclosure of information to such person under this paragraph, including requirements regarding the protection and safeguarding of such information by such person.

(C) SPECIFIED RETURN INFORMATION.—For purposes of this paragraph, the term "specified return information" means—

(i) in the case of a return which is in connection with a case of potential identity theft refund fraud—

(I) in the case of such return filed electronically, the internet protocol address, device identification, email domain name, speed of completion, method of authentication, refund method, and such other return information related to the electronic filing characteristics of such return as the Secretary may identify for purposes of this subclause, and

(II) in the case of such return prepared by a tax return preparer, identifying information with respect to such tax return preparer, including the preparer taxpayer identification number and electronic filer identification number of such preparer,

(ii) in the case of a return which is in connection with a case of a [sic] identity theft refund fraud which has been confirmed by the Secretary (pursuant to such procedures as the Secretary may provide), the information referred to in subclauses (I) and (II) of clause (i), the name and taxpayer identification number of the taxpayer as it appears on the return, and any bank account and routing information provided for making a refund in connection with such return, and

(iii) in the case of any cybersecurity threat to the Internal Revenue Service, information similar to the information described in subclauses (I) and (II) of clause (i) with respect to such threat.

(D) RESTRICTION ON USE OF DISCLOSED INFORMATION.—

(i) DESIGNATED THIRD PARTIES.—Any return information received by a person described in subparagraph (B)(i)(I) shall be used only for the purposes of and to the extent necessary in—

(I) performing the function such person is designated to perform under such subparagraph,

(II) facilitating disclosures authorized under subparagraph (A) to persons described in subparagraph (B)(i)(II), and

(III) facilitating disclosures authorized under subsection (d) to participants in such information sharing and analysis center.

(ii) RETURN PREPARERS.—Any return information received by a person described in subparagraph (B)(i)(II) shall be treated for purposes of section 7216 as information furnished to such person for, or in connection with, the preparation of a return of the tax imposed under chapter 1.

(E) DATA PROTECTION AND SAFEGUARDS.—Return information disclosed under this paragraph shall be subject to such protections and safeguards as the Secretary may require in regulations or other guidance or in the written agreement referred to in subparagraph (B)(ii). Such written agreement shall include a requirement that any unauthorized access to information disclosed under this paragraph, and any breach of any system in which such information is held, be reported to the Treasury Inspector General for Tax Administration.

(15) DISCLOSURES TO SOCIAL SECURITY ADMINISTRATION TO IDENTIFY TAX RECEIVABLES NOT ELIGIBLE FOR COLLECTION PURSUANT TO QUALIFIED TAX COLLECTION CONTRACTS.—In the case of any individual involved with a tax receivable which the Secretary has identified for possible collection pursuant to a qualified tax collection contract (as defined in section 6306(b)), the Secretary may disclose the taxpayer identity and date of birth of such individual to officers, employees, and contractors of the Social Security Administration to determine if such tax receivable is not eligible for collection pursuant to such a qualified tax collection contract by reason of section 6306(d)(3)(E).

Amendments

• 2020, COVID-related Tax Relief Act of 2020 (P.L. 116-260)

P.L. 116-260, §283(b)(1), Div. N:

Amended Code Sec. 6103(k) by adding at the end a new paragraph (15). **Effective** for disclosures made on or after 12-27-2020.

• 2020, Consolidated Appropriations Act, 2021 (P.L. 116-260)

P.L. 116-260, §102(b)(1), Div. FF:

Amended Code Sec. 6103(k) by adding at the end a new paragraph (15). [Note: An identical amendment was made by P.L. 116-260, Act Sec. 283(b)(1), Div. N. Therefore, this amendment cannot be made.—CCH] **Effective** for disclosures made on or after 12-27-2020.

• 2019, Taxpayer First Act (P.L. 116-25)

P.L. 116-25, §1405(a)(1):

Amended Code Sec. 6103(k) by adding at the end a new paragraph (13). **Effective** for disclosures made after 7-1-2019.

P.L. 116-25, §1405(a)(2)(C):

Amended Code Sec. 6103(k)(6) by adding at the end a new sentence. **Effective** for disclosures made after 7-1-2019.

P.L. 116-25, §2003(a)-(b), provides:

(a) IN GENERAL.—The Secretary of the Treasury (or the Secretary's delegate) may participate in an information sharing and analysis center to centralize, standardize, and enhance data compilation and analysis to facilitate sharing actionable data and information with respect to identity theft tax refund fraud.

(b) DEVELOPMENT OF PERFORMANCE METRICS.—The Secretary of the Treasury (or the Secretary's delegate) shall develop metrics for measuring the success of such center in detecting and preventing identity theft tax refund fraud.

P.L. 116-25, §2003(c)(1):

Amended Code Sec. 6103(k), as amended by this Act, by adding at the end a new paragraph (14). **Effective** 7-1-2019.

• 2015, Fixing America's Surface Transportation Act (P.L. 114-94)

P.L. 114-94, §32101(c)(1):

Amended Code Sec. 6103(k) by adding at the end a new paragraph (11). **Effective** 12-4-2015.

P.L. 114-94, §32102(d):

Amended Code Sec. 6103(k), as amended by Act Sec. 32101[(c)(1)], by adding at the end a new paragraph (12). **Effective** for disclosures made after 12-4-2015.

• 2013, American Taxpayer Relief Act of 2012 (P.L. 112-240)

P.L. 112-240, §209(a):

Amended Code Sec. 6103(k)(10). **Effective** 1-2-2013. Prior to amendment, Code Sec. 6103(k)(10) read as follows:

(10) DISCLOSURE OF CERTAIN RETURN INFORMATION TO CERTAIN PRISON OFFICIALS.—

(A) IN GENERAL.—Under such procedures as the Secretary may prescribe, the Secretary may disclose to the head of the Federal Bureau of Prisons and the head of any State agency charged with the responsibility for administration of prisons any return information with respect to individuals incarcerated in Federal or State prison whom the Secretary has determined may have filed or facilitated the filing of a false return to the extent that the Secretary determines that such disclosure is necessary to permit effective Federal tax administration.

(B) RESTRICTION ON REDISCLOSURE.—Notwithstanding subsection (n), the head of the Federal Bureau of Prisons and the head of any State agency charged with the responsibility for administration of prisons may not disclose any information obtained under subparagraph (A) to any person other than an officer or employee of such Bureau or agency.

(C) RESTRICTION ON USE OF DISCLOSED INFORMATION.—Return information received under this paragraph shall be used only for purposes of and to the extent necessary in taking administrative action to prevent the filing of false and fraudulent returns, including administrative actions to address possible violations of administrative rules and regulations of the prison facility.

(D) TERMINATION.—No disclosure may be made under this paragraph after December 31, 2011.

• 2010, Homebuyer Assistance and Improvement Act of 2010 (P.L. 111-198)

P.L. 111-198, §4(a)(1)-(2):

Amended Code Sec. 6103(k)(10)(A) by inserting "and the head of any State agency charged with the responsibility for administration of prisons" after "the head of the Federal Bureau of Prisons", and by striking "Federal prison" and inserting "Federal or State prison". **Effective** for disclosures made after 7-2-2010.

P.L. 111-198, §4(b)(1)-(2):

Amended Code Sec. 6103(k)(10)(B) by inserting "and the head of any State agency charged with the responsibility for administration of prisons" after "the head of the Federal Bureau of Prisons", and by inserting "or agency" after "such Bureau". **Effective** for disclosures made after 7-2-2010.

P.L. 111-198, §4(d):

Amended the heading of Code Sec. 6103(k)(10) by striking "OF PRISONERS TO FEDERAL BUREAU OF PRISONS" and inserting "TO CERTAIN PRISON OFFICIALS". **Effective** for disclosures made after 7-2-2010.

• 2008, Inmate Tax Fraud Prevention Act of 2008 (P.L. 110-428)

P.L. 110-428, §2(a):

Amended Code Sec. 6103(k) by adding at the end a new paragraph (10). **Effective** for disclosures made after 12-31-2008.

P.L. 110-428, §2(e), provides:

(e) ANNUAL REPORTS.—The Secretary of the Treasury shall annually submit to Congress and make publicly available a report on the filing of false and fraudulent returns by individuals incarcerated in Federal and State prisons. Such report shall include statistics on the number of false and fraudulent returns associated with each Federal and State prison.

• 2007, Small Business and Work Opportunity Tax Act of 2007 (P.L. 110-28)

P.L. 110-28, §8246(a)(2)(B)(i)-(ii):

Amended Code Sec. 6103(k)(5) by striking "income tax return preparer" each place it appears and inserting "tax return preparer", and by striking "income tax return preparers" each place it appears and inserting "tax return preparers". **Effective** for returns prepared after 5-25-2007.

• 2000, Community Renewal Tax Relief Act of 2000 (P.L. 106-554)

P.L. 106-554, §313(c)(1)-(2):

Amended Code Sec. 6103(k)(6) by inserting "and an officer or employee of the Office of Treasury Inspector General for Tax Administration" after "internal revenue officer or employee", and by striking "INTERNAL REVENUE" in the heading and inserting "CERTAIN". **E ffective** as if included in the provision of P.L. 105-206 to which it relates [**effective** 7-22-98.—CCH].

• 1998, IRS Restructuring and Reform Act of 1998 (P.L. 105-206)

P.L. 105-206, §6012(b)(2):

Amended Code Sec. 6103(k) by redesignating paragraph (8) (as added by Act Sec. 1205(c)(1) of P.L. 105-34) as paragraph (9). **Effective** as if included in the provision of P.L. 105-34 to which it relates [**effective** 5-5-98.—CCH].

• 1997, Taxpayer Relief Act of 1997 (P.L. 105-34)

P.L. 105-34, §1026(a):

Amended Code Sec. 6103(k) by adding at the end a new paragraph (8). **Effective** for levies issued after 8-5-97.

P.L. 105-34, §1205(c)(1):

Amended Code Sec. 6103(k) by adding at the end a new paragraph (8)[(9)]. **Effective** on the day 9 months after 8-5-97.

• 1990, Omnibus Budget Reconciliation Act of 1990 (P.L. 101-508)

P.L. 101-508, §11212(b)(3):

Amended Code Sec. 6103(k) by adding at the end thereof a new paragraph (7). **Effective** 12-1-90.

• 1988, Technical and Miscellaneous Revenue Act of 1988 (P.L. 100-647)

P.L. 100-647, §1012(bb)(3)(A)(i)-(ii):

Amended Code Sec. 6103(k)(4) by striking out "or other convention" and inserting in lieu thereof "or other convention or bilateral agreement", and by striking out "such convention" and inserting in lieu thereof "such convention or bilateral agreement". **Effective** 10-22-86.

• 1978, Revenue Act of 1978 (P.L. 95-600)

P.L. 95-600, §701(bb)(5):

Amended Code Sec. 6103(k)(4). **Effective** 1-1-77. Prior to amendment, Code Sec. 6103(k)(4) read as follows:

(4) DISCLOSURE TO COMPETENT AUTHORITY UNDER INCOME TAX CONVENTION.—A return or return information may be disclosed to a competent authority of a foreign government which has an income tax convention with the United States but only to the extent provided in, and subject to the terms and conditions of, such convention.

• 1976, Tax Reform Act of 1976 (P.L. 94-455)

P.L. 94-455, §1202(a):

Added Code Sec. 6103(k). **Effective** 1-1-77.

[Sec. 6103(l)]

(l) DISCLOSURE OF RETURNS AND RETURN INFORMATION FOR PURPOSES OTHER THAN TAX ADMINISTRATION.—

(1) DISCLOSURE OF CERTAIN RETURNS AND RETURN INFORMATION TO SOCIAL SECURITY ADMINISTRATION AND RAILROAD RETIREMENT BOARD.—The Secretary may, upon written request, disclose returns and return information with respect to—

(A) taxes imposed by chapters 2, 21, and 24, to the Social Security Administration for purposes of its administration of the Social Security Act;

(B) a plan to which part I of subchapter D of chapter 1 applies, to the Social Security Administration for purposes of carrying out its responsibility under section 1131 of the Social Security Act, limited, however to return information described in section 6057(d); and

(C) taxes imposed by chapter 22, to the Railroad Retirement Board for purposes of its administration of the Railroad Retirement Act.

(2) DISCLOSURE OF RETURNS AND RETURN INFORMATION TO THE DEPARTMENT OF LABOR AND PENSION BENEFIT GUARANTY CORPORATION.—The Secretary may, upon written request, furnish returns and return information to the proper officers and employees of the Department of Labor and the Pension Benefit Guaranty Corporation for purposes of, but only to the extent necessary in, the administration of titles I and IV of the Employee Retirement Income Security Act of 1974.

(3) DISCLOSURE THAT APPLICANT FOR FEDERAL LOAN HAS TAX DELINQUENT ACCOUNT.—

(A) IN GENERAL.—Upon written request, the Secretary may disclose to the head of the Federal agency administering any included Federal loan program whether or not an applicant for a loan under such program has a tax delinquent account.

(B) RESTRICTION ON DISCLOSURE.—Any disclosure under subparagraph (A) shall be made only for the purpose of, and to the extent necessary in, determining the creditworthiness of the applicant for the loan in question.

(C) INCLUDED FEDERAL LOAN PROGRAM DEFINED.—For purposes of this paragraph, the term "included Federal loan program" means any program under which the United States or a Federal agency makes, guarantees, or insures loans.

(4) DISCLOSURE OF RETURNS AND RETURN INFORMATION FOR USE IN PERSONNEL OR CLAIMANT REPRESENTATIVE MATTERS.—The Secretary may disclose returns and return information—

(A) upon written request—

(i) to an employee or former employee of the Department of the Treasury, or to the duly authorized legal representative of such employee or former employee, who is or may be a party to any administrative action or proceeding affecting the personnel rights of such employee or former employee; or

(ii) to any person, or to the duly authorized legal representative of such person, whose rights are or may be affected by an administrative action or proceeding under section 330 of title 31, United States Code,

solely for use in the action or proceeding, or in preparation for the action or proceeding, but only to the extent that the Secretary determines that such returns or return information is or may be relevant and material to the action or proceeding; or

(B) to officers and employees of the Department of the Treasury for use in any action or proceeding described in subparagraph (A), or in preparation for such action or proceeding, to the extent necessary to advance or protect the interests of the United States.

(5) SOCIAL SECURITY ADMINISTRATION.—Upon written request by the Commissioner of Social Security, the Secretary may disclose information returns filed pursuant to part III of subchapter A of chapter 61 of this subtitle for the purpose of—

(A) carrying out, in accordance with an agreement entered into pursuant to section 232 of the Social Security Act, an effective return processing program; or

(B) providing information regarding the mortality status of individuals for epidemiological and similar research in accordance with section 1106(d) of the Social Security Act.

(6) DISCLOSURE OF RETURN INFORMATION TO FEDERAL, STATE, AND LOCAL CHILD SUPPORT ENFORCEMENT AGENCIES.—

(A) RETURN INFORMATION FROM INTERNAL REVENUE SERVICE.—The Secretary may, upon written request, disclose to the appropriate Federal, State, or local child support enforcement agency—

(i) available return information from the master files of the Internal Revenue Service relating to the social security account number (or numbers, if the individual involved has more than one such number), address, filing status, amounts and nature of income, and the number of dependents reported on any return filed by, or with respect to, any individual with respect to whom child support obligations are sought to be established or enforced pursuant to the provisions of part D of title IV of the Social Security Act and with respect to any individual to whom such support obligations are owing, and

(ii) available return information reflected on any return filed by, or with respect to, any individual described in clause (i) relating to the amount of such individual's gross income (as defined in section 61) or consisting of the names and addresses of payors of such income and the names of any dependents reported on such return, but only if such return information is not reasonably available from any other source.

(B) DISCLOSURE TO CERTAIN AGENTS.—The following information disclosed to any child support enforcement agency under subparagraph (A) with respect to any individual with respect to whom child support obligations are sought to be established or enforced may be disclosed by such agency to any agent of such agency which is under contract with such agency to carry out the purposes described in subparagraph (C):

(i) The address and social security account number (or numbers) of such individual.

(ii) The amount of any reduction under section 6402(c) (relating to offset of past-due support against overpayments) in any overpayment otherwise payable to such individual.

(C) RESTRICTION ON DISCLOSURE.—Information may be disclosed under this paragraph only for purposes of, and to the extent necessary in, establishing and collecting child support obligations from, and locating, individuals owing such obligations.

(7) DISCLOSURE OF RETURN INFORMATION TO FEDERAL, STATE, AND LOCAL AGENCIES ADMINISTERING CERTAIN PROGRAMS UNDER THE SOCIAL SECURITY ACT, THE FOOD AND NUTRITION ACT OF 2008, OR TITLE 38, UNITED STATES CODE, OR CERTAIN HOUSING ASSISTANCE PROGRAMS.—

(A) RETURN INFORMATION FROM SOCIAL SECURITY ADMINISTRATION.—The Commissioner of Social Security shall, upon written request, disclose return information from returns with respect to net earnings from self-employment (as defined in section 1402), wages (as defined in section 3121(a) or 3401(a)), and payments of retirement income, which have been disclosed to the Social Security Administration as provided by paragraph (1) or (5) of this subsection, to any Federal, State, or local agency administering a program listed in subparagraph (D).

(B) RETURN INFORMATION FROM INTERNAL REVENUE SERVICE.—The Secretary shall, upon written request, disclose current return information from returns with respect to unearned income from the Internal Revenue Service files to any Federal, State, or local agency administering a program listed in subparagraph (D).

(C) RESTRICTION ON DISCLOSURE.—The Commissioner of Social Security and the Secretary shall disclose return information under subparagraphs (A) and (B) only for purposes of, and to the extent necessary in, determining eligibility for, or the correct amount of, benefits under a program listed in subparagraph (D).

(D) PROGRAMS TO WHICH RULE APPLIES.—The programs to which this paragraph applies are:

(i) a State program funded under part A of title IV of the Social Security Act;

(ii) medical assistance provided under a State plan approved under title XIX of the Social Security Act or subsidies provided under section 1860D-14 of such Act;

(iii) supplemental security income benefits provided under title XVI of the Social Security Act, and federally administered supplementary payments of the type described in section 1616(a) of such Act (including payments pursuant to an agreement entered into under section 212(a) of Public Law 93-66);

(iv) any benefits provided under a State plan approved under title I, X, XIV, or XVI of the Social Security Act (as those titles apply to Puerto Rico, Guam, and the Virgin Islands);

(v) unemployment compensation provided under a State law described in section 3304 of this title;

(vi) assistance provided under the Food and Nutrition Act of 2008;

(vii) State-administered supplementary payments of the type described in section 1616(a) of the Social Security Act (including payments pursuant to an agreement entered into under section 212(a) of Public Law 93-66);

(viii)(I) any needs-based pension provided under chapter 15 of title 38, United States Code, or under any other law administered by the Secretary of Veterans Affairs;

(II) parents' dependency and indemnity compensation provided under section 1315 of title 38, United States Code;

(III) health-care services furnished under sections 1710(a)(2)(G), 1710(a)(3), and 1710(b) of such title; and

(IV) compensation paid under chapter 11 of title 38, United States Code, at the 100 percent rate based solely on unemployability and without regard to the fact that the disability or disabilities are not rated as 100 percent disabling under the rating schedule; and

(ix) any housing assistance program administered by the Department of Housing and Urban Development that involves initial and periodic review of an applicant's or participant's income, except that return information may be disclosed under this clause only on written request by the Secretary of Housing and Urban Development and only for use by officers and employees of the Department of Housing and Urban Development with respect to applicants for and participants in such programs.

Only return information from returns with respect to net earnings from self-employment and wages may be disclosed under this paragraph for use with respect to any program described in clause (viii)(IV).

(8) Disclosure of certain return information by Social Security Administration to Federal, State, and local child support enforcement agencies.—

(A) In general.—Upon written request, the Commissioner of Social Security shall disclose directly to officers and employees of a Federal or State or local child support enforcement agency return information from returns with respect to social security account numbers[,]net earnings from self-employment (as defined in section 1402), wages (as defined in section 3121(a) or 3401(a)), and payments of retirement income which have been disclosed to the Social Security Administration as provided by paragraph (1) or (5) of this subsection.

(B) Restriction on disclosure.—The Commissioner of Social Security shall disclose return information under subparagraph (A) only for purposes of, and to the extent necessary in, establishing and collecting child support obligations from, and locating, individuals owing such obligations. For purposes of the preceding sentence, the term "child support obligations" only includes obligations which are being enforced pursuant to a plan described in section 454 of the Social Security Act which has been approved by the Secretary of Health and Human Services under part D of title IV of such Act.

(C) State or local child support enforcement agency.—For purposes of this paragraph, the term "State or local child support enforcement agency" means any agency of a State or political subdivision thereof operating pursuant to a plan described in subparagraph (B).

(9) Disclosure of alcohol fuel producers to administrators of State alcohol laws.—Notwithstanding any other provision of this section, the Secretary may disclose—

(A) the name and address of any person who is qualified to produce alcohol for fuel use under section 5181, and

(B) the location of any premises to be used by such person in producing alcohol for fuel,

to any State agency, body, or commission, or its legal representative, which is charged under the laws of such State with responsibility for administration of State alcohol laws solely for use in the administration of such laws.

(10) Disclosure of certain information to agencies requesting a reduction under subsection (c), (d), (e), or (f) of section 6402.—

(A) Return information from Internal Revenue Service.—The Secretary may, upon receiving a written request, disclose to officers and employees of any agency seeking a reduction under subsection (c), (d), (e) or (f) of section 6402, to officers and employees of the Department of Labor for purposes of facilitating the exchange of data in connection with a notice submitted under subsection (f)(5)(C) of section 6402, and to officers and employees of the Department of the Treasury in connection with such reduction—

(i) taxpayer identity information with respect to the taxpayer against whom such a reduction was made or not made and with respect to any other person filing a joint return with such taxpayer,

(ii) the fact that a reduction has been made or has not been made under such subsection with respect to such taxpayer,

(iii) the amount of such reduction,

(iv) whether such taxpayer filed a joint return, and

(v) the fact that a payment was made (and the amount of the payment) to the spouse of the taxpayer on the basis of a joint return.

(B) RESTRICTION ON USE OF DISCLOSED INFORMATION.—(i) Any officers and employees of an agency receiving return information under subparagraph (A) shall use such information only for the purposes of, and to the extent necessary in, establishing appropriate agency records, locating any person with respect to whom a reduction under subsection (c), (d), (e), or (f) of section 6402 is sought for purposes of collecting the debt with respect to which the reduction is sought, or in the defense of any litigation or administrative procedure ensuing from a reduction made under subsection (c), (d), (e), or (f) of section 6402.

(ii) Notwithstanding clause (i), return information disclosed to officers and employees of the Department of Labor may be accessed by agents who maintain and provide technological support to the Department of Labor's Interstate Connection Network (ICON) solely for the purpose of providing such maintenance and support.

(11) DISCLOSURE OF RETURN INFORMATION TO CARRY OUT FEDERAL EMPLOYEES' RETIREMENT SYSTEM.—

(A) IN GENERAL.—The Commissioner of Social Security shall, on written request, disclose to the Office of Personnel Management return information from returns with respect to net earnings from self-employment (as defined in section 1402), wages (as defined in section 3121(a) or 3401(a)), and payments of retirement income, which have been disclosed to the Social Security Administration as provided by paragraph (1) or (5).

(B) RESTRICTION ON DISCLOSURE.—The Commissioner of Social Security shall disclose return information under subparagraph (A) only for purposes of, and to the extent necessary in, the administration of chapters 83 and 84 of title 5, United States Code.

(12) DISCLOSURE OF CERTAIN TAXPAYER IDENTITY INFORMATION FOR VERIFICATION OF EMPLOYMENT STATUS OF MEDICARE BENEFICIARY AND SPOUSE OF MEDICARE BENEFICIARY.—

(A) RETURN INFORMATION FROM INTERNAL REVENUE SERVICE.—The Secretary shall, upon written request from the Commissioner of Social Security, disclose to the Commissioner available filing status and taxpayer identity information from the individual master files of the Internal Revenue Service relating to whether any medicare beneficiary identified by the Commissioner was a married individual (as defined in section 7703) for any specified year after 1986, and, if so, the name of the spouse of such individual and such spouse's TIN.

(B) RETURN INFORMATION FROM SOCIAL SECURITY ADMINISTRATION.—The Commissioner of Social Security shall, upon written request from the Administrator of the Centers for Medicare & Medicaid Services, disclose to the Administrator the following information:

(i) The name and TIN of each medicare beneficiary who is identified as having received wages (as defined in section 3401(a)), above an amount (if any) specified by the Secretary of Health and Human Services, from a qualified employer in a previous year.

(ii) For each medicare beneficiary who was identified as married under subparagraph (A) and whose spouse is identified as having received wages, above an amount (if any) specified by the Secretary of Health and Human Services, from a qualified employer in a previous year—

(I) the name and TIN of the medicare beneficiary, and

(II) the name and TIN of the spouse.

(iii) With respect to each such qualified employer, the name, address, and TIN of the employer and the number of individuals with respect to whom written statements were furnished under section 6051 by the employer with respect to such previous year.

(C) DISCLOSURE BY CENTERS FOR MEDICARE & MEDICAID SERVICES.—With respect to the information disclosed under subparagraph (B), the Administrator of the Centers for Medicare & Medicaid Services may disclose—

(i) to the qualified employer referred to in such subparagraph the name and TIN of each individual identified under such subparagraph as having received wages from the employer (hereinafter, in this subparagraph referred to as the "employee") for purposes of determining during what period such employee or the employee's spouse may be (or have been) covered under a group health plan of the employer and what benefits are or were covered under the plan (including the name, address, and identifying number of the plan),

(ii) to any group health plan which provides or provided coverage to such an employee or spouse, the name of such employee and the employee's spouse (if the spouse is a medicare beneficiary) and the name and address of the employer, and, for the purpose of presenting a claim to the plan—

(I) the TIN of such employee if benefits were paid under title XVIII of the Social Security Act with respect to the employee during a period in which the plan was a primary plan (as defined in section 1862(b)(2)(A) of the Social Security Act) and

(II) the TIN of such spouse if benefits were paid under such title with respect to the spouse during such period, and

(iii) to any agent of such Administrator the information referred to in subparagraph (B) for purposes of carrying out clauses (i) and (ii) on behalf of such Administrator.

(D) SPECIAL RULES.—

(i) RESTRICTIONS ON DISCLOSURE.—Information may be disclosed under this paragraph only for purposes of, and to the extent necessary in, determining the extent to which any medicare beneficiary is covered under any group health plan.

(ii) TIMELY RESPONSE TO REQUESTS.—Any request made under subparagraph (A) or (B) shall be complied with as soon as possible but in no event later than 120 days afer the date the request was made.

(E) DEFINITIONS.—For purposes of this paragraph—

(i) MEDICARE BENEFICIARY.—The term "medicare beneficiary" means an individual entitled to benefits under part A, or enrolled under part B, of title XVIII of the Social Security Act, but does not include such an individual enrolled in part A under section 1818.

(ii) GROUP HEALTH PLAN.—The term "group health plan" means any group health plan (as defined in section 5000(b)(1)).

(iii) QUALIFIED EMPLOYER.—The term "qualified employer" means, for a calendar year, an employer which has furnished written statements under section 6051 with respect to at least 20 individuals for wages paid in the year.

(13) DISCLOSURE OF RETURN INFORMATION TO CARRY OUT THE HIGHER EDUCATION ACT OF 1965.—

(A) APPLICATIONS AND RECERTIFICATIONS FOR INCOME-CONTINGENT OR INCOME-BASED REPAYMENT.—The Secretary shall, upon written request from the Secretary of Education, disclose to any authorized person, only for the purpose of (and to the extent necessary in) determining eligibility for, or repayment obligations under, income-contingent or income-based repayment plans under title IV of the Higher Education Act of 1965 with respect to loans under part D of such title, the following return information from returns (for any taxable year specified by the Secretary of Education as relevant to such purpose) of an individual certified by the Secretary of Education as having provided approval under section 494(a)(2) of such Act (as in effect on the date of enactment of this paragraph) for such disclosure:

(i) Taxpayer identity information.

(ii) Filing status.

(iii) Adjusted gross income.

(iv) Total number of exemptions claimed, if applicable.

(v) Number of dependents taken into account in determining the credit allowed under section 24.

(vi) If applicable, the fact that there was no return filed.

(B) DISCHARGE OF LOAN BASED ON TOTAL AND PERMANENT DISABILITY.—The Secretary shall, upon written request from the Secretary of Education, disclose to any authorized person, only for the purpose of (and to the extent necessary in) monitoring and reinstating loans under title IV of the Higher Education Act of 1965 that were discharged based on a total and permanent disability (within the meaning of section 437(a) of such Act), the following return information from returns (for any taxable year specified by the Secretary of Education as relevant to such purpose) of an individual certified by the Secretary of Education as having provided approval under section 494(a)(3) of such Act (as in effect on the date of enactment of this paragraph) for such disclosure:

(i) The return information described in clauses (i), (ii), and (vi) of subparagraph (A).

(ii) The return information described in subparagraph (C)(ii).

(C) FEDERAL STUDENT FINANCIAL AID.—The Secretary shall, upon written request from the Secretary of Education, disclose to any authorized person, only for the purpose of (and to the extent necessary in) determining eligibility for, and amount of, Federal student financial aid under a program authorized under subpart 1 of part A, part C, or part D of title IV of the Higher Education Act of 1965 the following return information from returns (for the taxable year used for purposes of section 480(a) of such Act) of an individual certified by the Secretary of Education as having provided approval under section 494(a)(1) of such Act (as in effect on the date of enactment of this paragraph) for such disclosure:

(i) Return information described in clauses (i) through (vi) of subparagraph (A).

(ii) The amount of any net earnings from self employment (as defined in section 1402(a)), wages (as defined in section 3121(a) or 3401(a)), and taxable income from a farming business (as defined in section 263A(e)(4)).

(iii) Amount of total income tax.

(iv) Amount of any credit allowed under section 25A.

(v) Amount of individual retirement account distributions not included in adjusted gross income.

(vi) Amount of individual retirement account contributions and payments to self-employed SEP, Keogh, and other qualified plans which were deducted from income.

(vii) Amount of tax-exempt interest received.

(viii) Amounts from retirement pensions and annuities not included in adjusted gross income.

(ix) If applicable, the fact that any of the following schedules (or equivalent successor schedules) were filed with the return:

(I) Schedule A.

(II) Schedule B.

(III) Schedule D.

(IV) Schedule E.

(V) Schedule F.

(VI) Schedule H.

(x) If applicable, the amount reported on Schedule C (or an equivalent successor schedule) as net profit or loss.

(D) ADDITIONAL USES OF DISCLOSED INFORMATION.—

(i) IN GENERAL.—In addition to the purposes for which information is disclosed under subparagraphs (A), (B), and (C), return information so disclosed may be used by an authorized person, with respect to income-contingent or income-based repayment plans, awards of Federal student financial aid under a program authorized under subpart 1 of part A, part C, or part D of title IV of the Higher Education Act of 1965, and discharges of loans based on a total and permanent disability (within the meaning of section 437(a) of such Act), for purposes of—

(I) reducing the net cost of improper payments under such plans, relating to such awards, or relating to such discharges,

(II) oversight activities by the Office of Inspector General of the Department of Education as authorized by the Inspector General Act of 1978, and

(III) conducting analyses and forecasts for estimating costs related to such plans, awards, or discharges.

(ii) LIMITATION.—The purposes described in clause (i) shall not include the conduct of criminal investigations or prosecutions.

(iii) REDISCLOSURE TO INSTITUTIONS OF HIGHER EDUCATION, STATE HIGHER EDUCATION AGENCIES, AND DESIGNATED SCHOLARSHIP ORGANIZATIONS.—Authorized persons may redisclose return information received under subparagraph (C), solely for the use in the application, award, and administration of financial aid awarded by the Federal government or awarded by a person described in subclause (I), (II), or (III), to the following persons:

(I) An institution of higher education participating in a program under subpart 1 of part A, part C, or part D of title IV of the Higher Education Act of 1965.

(II) A State higher education agency.

(III) A scholarship organization which is an entity designated (prior to the date of the enactment of this clause) by the Secretary of Education under section 483(a)(3)(E) of such Act.

This clause shall only apply to the extent that the taxpayer with respect to whom the return information relates provides written consent for such redisclosure to the Secretary of Education. Under such terms and conditions as may be prescribed by the Secretary, after consultation with the Department of Education, an institution of higher education described in subclause (I) or a State higher education agency described in subclause (II) may designate a contractor of such institution or state agency to receive return information on behalf of such institution or state agency to administer aspects of the institution's or state agency's activities for the application, award, and administration of such financial aid.

(iv) REDISCLOSURE TO OFFICE OF INSPECTOR GENERAL, INDEPENDENT AUDITORS, AND CONTRACTORS.—Any return information which is redisclosed under clause (iii)—

(I) may be further disclosed by persons described in subclauses (I), (II), or (III) of clause (iii) or persons designated in the last sentence of clause (iii) to the Office of Inspector General of the Department of Education and independent auditors conducting audits of such person's administration of the programs for which the return information was received, and

(II) may be further disclosed by persons described in subclauses (I), (II), or (III) of clause (iii) to contractors of such entities,

but only to the extent necessary in carrying out the purposes described in such clause (iii).

(v) REDISCLOSURE TO FAMILY MEMBERS.—In addition to the purposes for which information is disclosed and used under subparagraphs (A) and (C), or redisclosed under clause (iii), any return information so disclosed or redisclosed may be further disclosed to any individual certified by the Secretary of Education as having provided approval under paragraph (1) or (2) of section 494(a) of the Higher Education Act of 1965, as the case may be, for disclosure related to the income-contingent or income-based repayment plan under subparagraph (A) or the eligibility for, and amount of, Federal student financial aid described in subparagraph (C).

(vi) REDISCLOSURE OF FAFSA INFORMATION.—Return information received under subparagraph (C) may be redisclosed in accordance with subsection (c) of section 494 of the Higher Education Act of 1965 as in effect on the date of enactment of the Consolidated Appropriations Act, 2021 to carry out the purposes specified in such subsection.

(E) AUTHORIZED PERSON.—For purposes of this paragraph, the term 'authorized person' means, with respect to information disclosed under subparagraph (A), (B), or (C), any person who—

(i) is an officer, employee, or contractor, of the Department of Education, and

(ii) is specifically authorized and designated by the Secretary of Education for purposes of such subparagraph (applied separately with respect to each such subparagraph).

(F) JOINT RETURNS.—In the case of a joint return, any disclosure authorized under subparagraph (A), (B), or (C), and any redisclosure authorized under clause (iii), (iv)[,] (v), or (vi) of subparagraph (D), with respect to an individual shall be treated for purposes of this paragraph as applying with respect to the taxpayer.

(14) DISCLOSURE OF RETURN INFORMATION TO UNITED STATES CUSTOMS SERVICE.—The Secretary may, upon written request from the Commissioner of the United States Customs Service, disclose to officers and employees of the Department of the Treasury such return information with respect to taxes imposed by chapters 1 and 6 as the Secretary may prescribe by regulations, solely for the purpose of, and only to the extent necessary in—

(A) ascertaining the correctness of any entry in audits as provided for in section 509 of the Tariff Act of 1930 (19 U.S.C. 1509), or

(B) other actions to recover any loss of revenue, or to collect duties, taxes, and fees, determined to be due and owing pursuant to such audits.

(15) DISCLOSURE OF RETURNS FILED UNDER SECTION 6050I.—The Secretary may, upon written request, disclose to officers and employees of—

(A) any Federal agency,

(B) any agency of a State or local government, or

(C) any agency of the government of a foreign country,

information contained on returns filed under section 6050I. Any such disclosure shall be made on the same basis, and subject to the same conditions, as apply to disclosures of information on reports filed under section 5313 of title 31, United States Code; except that no disclosure under this paragraph shall be made for purposes of the administration of any tax law.

(16) DISCLOSURE OF RETURN INFORMATION FOR PURPOSES OF ADMINISTERING THE DISTRICT OF COLUMBIA RETIREMENT PROTECTION ACT OF 1997.—

(A) IN GENERAL.—Upon written request available return information (including such information disclosed to the Social Security Administration under paragraph (1) or (5) of this subsection), relating to the amount of wage income (as defined in section 3121(a) or 3401(a)), the name, address, and identifying number assigned under section 6109, of payors of wage income, taxpayer identity (as defined in section 6103(b)(6)), and the occupational status reflected on any return filed by, or with respect to, any individual with respect to whom eligibility for, or the correct amount of, benefits under the District of Columbia Retirement Protection Act of 1997, is sought to be determined, shall be disclosed by the Commissioner of Social Security, or to the extent not available from the Social Security Administration, by the Secretary, to any duly authorized officer or employee of the Department of the Treasury, or a Trustee or any designated officer or employee of a Trustee (as defined in the District of Columbia Retirement Protection Act of 1997), or any actuary engaged by a Trustee under the terms of the District of Columbia Retirement Protection Act of 1997, whose official duties require such disclosure, solely for the purpose of, and to the extent necessary in, determining an individual's eligibility for, or the correct amount of, benefits under the District of Columbia Retirement Protection Act of 1997.

(B) DISCLOSURE FOR USE IN JUDICIAL OR ADMINISTRATIVE PROCEEDINGS.—Return information disclosed to any person under this paragraph may be disclosed in a judicial or administrative proceeding relating to the determination of an individual's eligibility for, or the correct amount of, benefits under the District of Columbia Retirement Protection Act of 1997.

(17) DISCLOSURE TO NATIONAL ARCHIVES AND RECORDS ADMINISTRATION.—The Secretary shall, upon written request from the Archivist of the United States, disclose or authorize the disclosure of returns and return information to officers and employees of the National Archives and Records Administration for purposes of, and only to the extent necessary in, the appraisal of records for destruction or retention. No such officer or employee shall, except to the extent authorized by subsection (f), (i)(8), or (p), disclose any return or return information disclosed under the preceding sentence to any person other than to the Secretary, or to another officer or employee of the National Archives and Records Administration whose official duties require such disclosure for purposes of such appraisal.

(18) DISCLOSURE OF RETURN INFORMATION FOR PURPOSES OF CARRYING OUT A PROGRAM FOR ADVANCE PAYMENT OF CREDIT FOR HEALTH INSURANCE COSTS OF ELIGIBLE INDIVIDUALS.—The Secretary may disclose to providers of health insurance for any certified individual (as defined in section 7527(c)) return information with respect to such certified individual only to the extent necessary to carry out the program established by section 7527 (relating to advance payment of credit for health insurance costs of eligible individuals).

(19) DISCLOSURE OF RETURN INFORMATION FOR PURPOSES OF PROVIDING TRANSITIONAL ASSISTANCE UNDER MEDICARE DISCOUNT CARD PROGRAM.—

(A) IN GENERAL.—The Secretary, upon written request from the Secretary of Health and Human Services pursuant to carrying out section 1860D-31 of the Social Security Act, shall disclose to officers, employees, and contractors of the Department of Health and Human Services with respect to a taxpayer for the applicable year—

(i) (I) whether the adjusted gross income, as modified in accordance with specifications of the Secretary of Health and Human Services for purposes of carrying out such section, of such taxpayer and, if applicable, such taxpayer's spouse, for the applicable year, exceeds the amounts specified by the Secretary of Health and Human Services in order to apply the 100 and 135 percent of the poverty lines under such section, (II) whether the return was a joint return, and (III) the applicable year, or

(ii) if applicable, the fact that there is no return filed for such taxpayer for the applicable year.

(B) DEFINITION OF APPLICABLE YEAR.—For the purposes of this subsection, the term "applicable year" means the most recent taxable year for which information is available in the Internal Revenue Service's taxpayer data information systems, or, if there is no return filed for such taxpayer for such year, the prior taxable year.

(C) RESTRICTION ON USE OF DISCLOSED INFORMATION.—Return information disclosed under this paragraph may be used only for the purposes of determining eligibility for and administering transitional assistance under section 1860D-31 of the Social Security Act.

(20) DISCLOSURE OF RETURN INFORMATION TO CARRY OUT MEDICARE PART B PREMIUM SUBSIDY ADJUSTMENT AND PART D BASE BENEFICIARY PREMIUM INCREASE.—

(A) IN GENERAL.—The Secretary shall, upon written request from the Commissioner of Social Security, disclose to officers, employees, and contractors of the Social Security Administration return information of a taxpayer whose premium (according to the records of the Secretary) may be subject to adjustment under section 1839(i) or increase under section 1860D–13(a)(7) of the Social Security Act. Such return information shall be limited to—

(i) taxpayer identity information with respect to such taxpayer,

(ii) the filing status of such taxpayer,

(iii) the adjusted gross income of such taxpayer,

(iv) the amounts excluded from such taxpayer's gross income under sections 135 and 911 to the extent such information is available,

(v) the interest received or accrued during the taxable year which is exempt from the tax imposed by chapter 1 to the extent such information is available,

(vi) the amounts excluded from such taxpayer's gross income by sections 931 and 933 to the extent such information is available,

(vii) such other information relating to the liability of the taxpayer as is prescribed by the Secretary by regulation as might indicate in the case of a taxpayer who is an individual described in subsection (i)(4)(B)(iii) of section 1839 of the Social Security Act that the amount of the premium of the taxpayer under such section may be subject to adjustment under subsection (i) of such section or increase under section 1860D–13(a)(7) of such Act and the amount of such adjustment, and

(viii) the taxable year with respect to which the preceding information relates.

(B) RESTRICTION ON USE OF DISCLOSED INFORMATION.—

(i) IN GENERAL.—Return information disclosed under subparagraph (A) may be used by officers, employees, and contractors of the Social Security Administration only for the purposes of, and to the extent necessary in, establishing the appropriate amount of any premium adjustment under such section 1839(i) or increase under such section

1860D-13(a)(7) or for the purpose of resolving taxpayer appeals with respect to any such premium adjustment or increase.

(ii) DISCLOSURE TO OTHER AGENCIES.—Officers, employees, and contractors of the Social Security Administration may disclose—

(I) the taxpayer identity information and the amount of the premium subsidy adjustment or premium increase with respect to a taxpayer described in subparagraph (A) to officers, employees, and contractors of the Centers for Medicare and Medicaid Services, to the extent that such disclosure is necessary for the collection of the premium subsidy amount or the increased premium amount,

(II) the taxpayer identity information and the amount of the premium subsidy adjustment or the increased premium amount with respect to a taxpayer described in subparagraph (A) to officers and employees of the Office of Personnel Management and the Railroad Retirement Board, to the extent that such disclosure is necessary for the collection of the premium subsidy amount or the increased premium amount,

(III) return information with respect to a taxpayer described in subparagraph (A) to officers and employees of the Department of Health and Human Services to the extent necessary to resolve administrative appeals of such premium subsidy adjustment or increased premium, and

(IV) return information with respect to a taxpayer described in subparagraph (A) to officers and employees of the Department of Justice for use in judicial proceedings to the extent necessary to carry out the purposes described in clause (i).

(21) DISCLOSURE OF RETURN INFORMATION TO CARRY OUT ELIGIBILITY REQUIREMENTS FOR CERTAIN PROGRAMS.—

(A) IN GENERAL.—The Secretary, upon written request from the Secretary of Health and Human Services, shall disclose to officers, employees, and contractors of the Department of Health and Human Services return information of any taxpayer whose income is relevant in determining any premium tax credit under section 36B or any cost-sharing reduction under section 1402 of the Patient Protection and Affordable Care Act or eligibility for participation in a State medicaid program under title XIX of the Social Security Act, a State's children's health insurance program under title XXI of the Social Security Act, or a basic health program under section 1331 of Patient Protection and Affordable Care Act. Such return information shall be limited to—

(i) taxpayer identity information with respect to such taxpayer,

(ii) the filing status of such taxpayer,

(iii) the number of individuals for whom a deduction is allowed under section 151 with respect to the taxpayer (including the taxpayer and the taxpayer's spouse),

(iv) the modified adjusted gross income (as defined in section 36B) of such taxpayer and each of the other individuals included under clause (iii) who are required to file a return of tax imposed by chapter 1 for the taxable year,

(v) such other information as is prescribed by the Secretary by regulation as might indicate whether the taxpayer is eligible for such credit or reduction (and the amount thereof), and

(vi) the taxable year with respect to which the preceding information relates or, if applicable, the fact that such information is not available.

(B) INFORMATION TO EXCHANGE AND STATE AGENCIES.—The Secretary of Health and Human Services may disclose to an Exchange established under the Patient Protection and Affordable Care Act or its contractors, or to a State agency administering a State program described in subparagraph (A) or its contractors, any inconsistency between the information provided by the Exchange or State agency to the Secretary and the information provided to the Secretary under subparagraph (A).

(C) RESTRICTION ON USE OF DISCLOSED INFORMATION.—Return information disclosed under subparagraph (A) or (B) may be used by officers, employees, and contractors of the Department of Health and Human Services, an Exchange, or a State agency only for the purposes of, and to the extent necessary in—

(i) establishing eligibility for participation in the Exchange, and verifying the appropriate amount of, any credit or reduction described in subparagraph (A),

(ii) determining eligibility for participation in the State programs described in subparagraph (A).

(22) DISCLOSURE OF RETURN INFORMATION TO DEPARTMENT OF HEALTH AND HUMAN SERVICES FOR PURPOSES OF ENHANCING MEDICARE PROGRAM INTEGRITY.—

(A) IN GENERAL.—The Secretary shall, upon written request from the Secretary of Health and Human Services, disclose to officers and employees of the Department of Health and Human Services return information with respect to a taxpayer who has applied to enroll, or reenroll, as a provider of services or supplier under the Medicare program under title XVIII of the Social Security Act. Such return information shall be limited to—

(i) the taxpayer identity information with respect to such taxpayer;

(ii) the amount of the delinquent tax debt owed by that taxpayer; and

(iii) the taxable year to which the delinquent tax debt pertains.

(B) RESTRICTION ON DISCLOSURE.—Return information disclosed under subparagraph (A) may be used by officers and employees of the Department of Health and Human Services for the purposes of, and to the extent necessary in, establishing the taxpayer's eligibility for enrollment or reenrollment in the Medicare program, or in any administrative or judicial proceeding relating to, or arising from, a denial of such enrollment or reenrollment, or in determining the level of enhanced oversight to be applied with respect to such taxpayer pursuant to section 1866(j)(3) of the Social Security Act.

(C) DELINQUENT TAX DEBT.—For purposes of this paragraph, the term "delinquent tax debt" means an outstanding debt under this title for which a notice of lien has been filed pursuant to section 6323, but the term does not include a debt that is being paid in a timely manner pursuant to an agreement under section 6159 or 7122, or a debt with respect to which a collection due process hearing under section 6330 is requested, pending, or completed and no payment is required.

Amendments

• 2020, COVID-related Tax Relief Act of 2020 (P.L. 116-260)

P.L. 116-260, §284(a)(1)(A)-(B), Div. N:

Amended Code Sec. 6103(l)(13)(D) by inserting at the end of clause (iii) a new sentence, and by adding at the end new clauses (iv)-(vi). **Effective** for disclosures made after the date of the enactment of the FUTURE Act (P.L. 116-91) [**effective** for disclosures made after 12-19-2019.—CCH].

P.L. 116-260, §284(a)(2), Div. N:

Amended Code Sec. 6103(l)(13)(F) by inserting ", and any redisclosure authorized under clause (iii), (iv)[,] (v), or (vi) of subparagraph (D),'" after "or (C)". **Effective** for disclosures made after the date of the enactment of the FUTURE Act (P.L. 116-91) [**effective** for disclosures made after 12-19-2019.—CCH].

• 2020, Consolidated Appropriations Act, 2021 (P.L. 116-260)

P.L. 116-260, §103(a)(1)(A)-(B), Div. FF:

Amended Code Sec. 6103(l)(13)(D) by inserting at the end of clause (iii) a new sentence, and by adding at the end new clauses (iv)-(vi). [Note: With the exception of the text of new clause (vi), an identical amendment was made by P.L. 116-260, Act Sec. 284(a)(1)(A)-(B), Div. N. Therefore, this amendment cannot be made except for the text of new clause (vi).—CCH] **Effective** for disclosures made after the date of the enactment of the FUTURE Act (P.L. 116-91) [**effective** for disclosures made after 12-19-2019.—CCH]. Prior to amendment, Code Sec. 6103(l)(13)(d)(vi) read as follows:

(vi) REDISCLOSURE OF FAFSA INFORMATION.—Return information received under subparagraph (C) may be redisclosed in accordance with subsection (c) of section 494 of the Higher Education Act of 1965 (as in effect on the date of enactment of the COVID-related Tax Relief Act of 2020) to carry out the purposes specified in such subsection.

P.L. 116-260, §103(a)(2), Div. FF:

Amended Code Sec. 6103(l)(13)(F) by inserting ", and any redisclosure authorized under clause (iii), (iv)[,] (v), or (vi) of subparagraph (D)," after "or (C)". [Note: An identical amendment was made by P.L. 116-260, Act Sec. 284(a)(2), Div. N. Therefore, this amendment cannot be made.—CCH] **Effective** for disclosures made after the date of the enactment of the FUTURE Act (P.L. 116-91) [**effective** for disclosures made after 12-19-2019.—CCH].

• 2020, Coronavirus Aid, Relief, and Economic Security (CARES) Act (P.L. 116-136)

P.L. 116-136, §3516(a)(5):

Amended Code Sec. 6103(l)(13)(C)(ii), as added by the FUTURE Act (P.L. 116-91), by striking "section 236A(e)(4)" and inserting "section 263A(e)(4)". **Effective** as if included in the enactment of the FUTURE Act (P.L. 116-91) [**effective** for disclosures after 12-19-2019.—CCH].

• 2019, Fostering Undergraduate Talent by Unlocking Resources for Education (FUTURE) Act (P.L. 116-91)

P.L. 116-91, §3(a):

Amended Code Sec. 6103(l)(13). **Effective** for disclosures after 12-19-2019. Prior to amendment, Code Sec. 6103(l)(13) read as follows:

(13) DISCLOSURE OF RETURN INFORMATION TO CARRY OUT INCOME CONTINGENT REPAYMENT OF STUDENT LOANS.—

(A) IN GENERAL.—The Secretary may, upon written request from the Secretary of Education, disclose to officers and employees of the Department of Education return information with respect to a taxpayer who has received an applicable student loan and whose loan repayment amounts are based in whole or in part on the taxpayer's income. Such return information shall be limited to—

(i) taxpayer identity information with respect to such taxpayer,

(ii) the filing status of such taxpayer, and

(iii) the adjusted gross income of such taxpayer.

(B) RESTRICTION ON USE OF DISCLOSED INFORMATION.—Return information disclosed under subparagraph (A) may be used by officers and employees of the Department of Education only for the purposes of, and to the extent necessary in, establishing the appropriate income contingent repayment amount for an applicable student loan.

(C) APPLICABLE STUDENT LOAN.—For purposes of this paragraph, the term "applicable student loan" means—

(i) any loan made under the program authorized under part D of title IV of the Higher Education Act of 1965, and

(ii) any loan made under part B or E of title IV of the Higher Education Act of 1965 which is in default and has been assigned to the Department of Education.

(D) TERMINATION.—This paragraph shall not apply to any request made after December 31, 2007.

P.L. 116-91, §3(e)-(g), provides:

(e) REQUIREMENT TO DESIGNATE THE INSPECTOR GENERAL OF THE DEPARTMENT OF EDUCATION AS AN AUTHORIZED PERSON.—The Secretary of Education shall authorize and designate the Inspector General of the Department of Education as an authorized person under subparagraph (E)(ii) of section 6103(l)(13) of the Internal Revenue Code of 1986 for purposes of subparagraphs (A), (B), and (C) of such section.

(f) REPORT TO TREASURY.—The Secretary of Education shall annually submit a written report to the Secretary of the Treasury—

(1) regarding redisclosures of return information under subparagraph (D)(iii) of section 6103(l)(13) of the Internal Revenue Code of 1986, including the number of such redisclosures; and

(2) regarding any unauthorized use, access, or disclosure of return information disclosed under such section.

(g) REPORT TO CONGRESS.—The Secretary of the Treasury (or the Secretary's designee) shall annually submit a written report to Congress regarding disclosures under section 6103(l)(13) of the Internal Revenue Code of 1986, including information provided to the Secretary under subsection (f).

• 2018, Tax Technical Corrections Act of 2018 (P.L. 115-141)

P.L. 115-141, §401(a)(267), Div. U:

Amended Code Sec. 6103(l)(7) by striking "OF 1977" following "NUTRITION ACT OF 2008" in the heading thereof. **Effective** 3-23-2018.

P.L. 115-141, §401(a)(268), Div. U:

Amended Code Sec. 6103(l)(10)(A) by striking "request made under subsection (f)(5)" and inserting "notice submitted under subsection (f)(5)(C)". **Effective** 3-23-2018.

P.L. 115-141, §401(a)(269), Div. U:

Amended Code Sec. 6103(l)(10) by striking so much of subparagraph (B) as precedes "Any" and inserting

"(B) RESTRICTION ON USE OF DISCLOSED INFORMATION.—(i)".

Effective 3-23-2018. Prior to being stricken, so much of subparagraph (B) as precedes "Any" read as follows:

(B)(i) RESTRICTION ON USE OF DISCLOSED INFORMATION.—

P.L. 115-141, §401(a)(270), Div. U:

Amended Code Sec. 6103(l)(16)(A) by striking "subsection 6103(b)(6)" and inserting "section 6103(b)(6)". **Effective** 3-23-2018.

• 2010, Preservation of Access to Care for Medicare Beneficiaries and Pension Relief Act of 2010 (P.L. 111-192)

P.L. 111-192, §103(a)(1):

Amended Code Sec. 6103(l) by adding at the end a new paragraph (22). **Effective** 6-25-2010.

• 2010, Health Care and Education Reconciliation Act of 2010 (P.L. 111-152)

P.L. 111-152, §1004(a)(1)(B):

Amended Code Sec. 6103(l)(21)(A)(iv), as added by section 1414 of the Patient Protection and Affordable Care Act (P.L. 111-148), by striking "modified gross" and inserting "modified adjusted gross". **Effective** 3-30-2010.

• 2010, Patient Protection and Affordable Care Act (P.L. 111-148)

P.L. 111-148, §1414(a)(1):

Amended Code Sec. 6103(l) by adding at the end a new paragraph (21). **Effective** 3-23-2010.

P.L. 111-148, §3308(b)(2)(A)-(C):

Amended Code Sec. 6103(l)(20), in the heading, by inserting "AND PART D BASE BENEFICIARY PREMIUM INCREASE" after "PART B PREMIUM SUBSIDY ADJUSTMENT"; in subparagraph (A), in the matter preceding clause (i), by inserting "or increase under section 1860D–13(a)(7)" after "1839(i)"; and in clause (vii), by inserting "or increase under section 1860D–13(a)(7) of such Act" after "subsection (i) of such section"; and in subparagraph (B), by striking "Return information" and inserting "(i) IN GENERAL.—Return information"; by inserting "or increase under such section 1860D–13(a)(7)" before the period at the end; and, as amended by Act Sec. 3308(b)(2)(C)(i), by inserting "or for the purpose of resolving taxpayer appeals with respect to any such premium adjustment or increase" before the period at the end; and by adding at the end a new clause (ii). **Effective** 3-23-2010.

• 2008, SSI Extension for Elderly and Disabled Refugees Act (P.L. 110-328)

P.L. 110-328, §3(b)(2)(A)-(C):

Amended Code Sec. 6103(l)(10) by striking "(c), (d), or (e)" each place it appears in the heading and text and inserting "(c), (d), (e), or (f)", in subparagraph (A) by inserting ", to officers and employees of the Department of Labor for purposes of facilitating the exchange of data in connection with a request made under subsection (f)(5) of section 6402," after "section 6402", and in subparagraph (B) by inserting "(i)" after "(B)"; and by adding at the end a new clause (ii). **Effective** for refunds payable under Code Sec. 6402 on or after 9-30-2008.

• 2008, Food, Conservation, and Energy Act of 2008 (P.L. 110-246)

P.L. 110-246, §4002(b)(1)(B) and (H):

Amended Code Sec. 6103(l)(7) by striking "Food Stamp Act of 1977" and inserting "Food and Nutrition Act of 2008"; and by striking "FOOD STAMP ACT" [sic] in the heading and inserting "FOOD AND NUTRITION ACT OF 2008". **Effective** 10-1-2008.

• 2008, Heroes Earnings Assistance and Relief Tax Act of 2008 (P.L. 110-245)

P.L. 110-245, §108(a):

Amended Code Sec. 6103(l)(7) by striking the last sentence. **Effective** for requests made after 9-30-2008. Prior to being stricken, the last sentence of Code Sec. 6103(l)(7) read as follows:

Clause (viii) shall not apply after September 30, 2008.

P.L. 110-245, §108(b):

Amended Code Sec. 6103(l)(7)(D)(viii)(III) by striking "sections 1710(a)(1)(I), 1710(a)(2), 1710(b), and 1712(a)(2)(B)" and inserting "sections 1710(a)(1)(G), 1710(a)(3), and 1710(b)". **Effective** 6-17-2008.

• 2006, Tax Relief and Health Care Act of 2006 (P.L. 109-432)

P.L. 109-432, Division A, §122(c)(1):

Amended Code Sec. 6103(l)(13)(D) by striking "2006" and inserting "2007". **Effective** for requests made after 12-31-2006.

• 2005, Gulf Opportunity Zone Act of 2005 (P.L. 109-135)

P.L. 109-135, §305(c)(1):

Amended Code Sec. 6103(l)(13)(D) by striking "December 31, 2005" and inserting "December 31, 2006". **Effective** for requests made after 12-31-2005.

P.L. 109-135, §406(a):

Amended Code Sec. 6103(l)(17) by striking "subsection (f), (i)(7), or (p)" and inserting "subsection (f), (i)(8), or (p)". **Effective** as if included in section 201 of the Victims of Terrorism Tax Relief Act of 2001 (P.L. 107-34) [**effective** for disclosures made on or after 1-23-2002.—CCH].

• 2004, Working Families Tax Relief Act of 2004 (P.L. 108-311)

P.L. 108-311, §317:

Amended Code Sec. 6103(l)(13)(D) by striking "December 31, 2004" and inserting "December 31, 2005". **Effective** 10-4-2004.

• 2003, Medicare Prescription Drug, Improvement, and Modernization Act of 2003 (P.L. 108-173)

P.L. 108-173, §101(e)(6):

Amended Code Sec. 6103(l)(7)(D)(ii) by inserting "or subsidies provided under section 1860D-14 of such Act" after "Social Security Act". **Effective** 12-8-2003.

P.L. 108-173, §105(e)(1):

Amended Code Sec. 6103(l) by adding at the end a new paragraph (19). **Effective** 12-8-2003.

P.L. 108-173, §811(c)(1):

Amended Code Sec. 6103(l), as amended by Act Sec. 105(e), by adding at the end a new paragraph (20). **Effective** 12-8-2003.

P.L. 108-173, §900(e)(3)(A)-(B):

Amended Code Sec. 6103(l)(12) in subparagraph (B) by striking "Health Care Financing Administration" in the matter preceding clause (i) and inserting "Centers for Medicare & Medicaid Services"; and in subparagraph (C) by striking "HEALTH CARE FINANCING ADMINISTRATION" in the heading and inserting "CENTERS FOR MEDICARE & MEDICAID SERVICES"; and by striking "Health Care Financing Administration" in the matter preceding clause (i) and inserting "Centers for Medicare & Medicaid Services". **Effective** 12-8-2003.

• 2003 (P.L. 108-89)

P.L. 108-89, §201(a):

Amended Code Sec. 6103(l)(13)(D) by striking "September 30, 2003" and inserting "December 31, 2004". **Effective** for requests made after 9-30-2003.

• 2002, Veterans Benefits Act of 2002 (P.L. 107-330)

P.L. 107-330, §306:

Amended Code Sec. 6103(l)(7)(D) by striking "September 30, 2003" in the second sentence after clause (ix) and inserting "September 30, 2008". **Effective** 12-6-2002.

• 2002, Trade Act of 2002 (P.L. 107-210)

P.L. 107-210, §202(b)(1):

Amended Code Sec. 6103(l) by adding at the end a new paragraph (18). **Effective** 8-6-2002.

• 2002, Job Creation and Worker Assistance Act of 2002 (P.L. 107-147)

P.L. 107-147, §416(c)(1)(A)-(B):

Amended the heading for Code Sec. 6103(l)(8) by striking "STATE AND LOCAL" and inserting "FEDERAL, STATE, AND LOCAL", and in subparagraph (A), by inserting "Federal or" before "State or local". **Effective** 3-9-2002.

• 1998, Tax and Trade Relief Extension Act of 1998 (P.L. 105-277)

P.L. 105-277, §1006:

Amended Code Sec. 6103(l)(13)(D) by striking "September 30, 1998" and inserting "September 30, 2003". **Effective** 10-21-98.

• 1998, IRS Restructuring and Reform Act of 1998 (P.L. 105-206)

P.L. 105-206, §3702(a):

Amended Code Sec. 6103(l) by adding at the end a new paragraph (17). **Effective** for requests made by the Archivist of the United States after 7-22-98.

P.L. 105-206, §3711(b)(1):

Amended Code Sec. 6103(l)(10) by striking "(c) or (d)" each place it appears and inserting "(c), (d), or (e)". **Effective** for refunds payable under Code Sec. 6402 after 12-31-99.

P.L. 105-206, §3711(b)(2):

Amended the paragraph heading of Code Sec. 6103(l)(10) by striking "SECTION 6402(c) OR 6402(d)" and inserting "SUBSECTION (c), (d), OR (e) OF SECTION 6402". **Effective** for refunds payable under Code Sec. 6402 after 12-31-99.

• 1997, Departments of Labor, Health and Human Services and Education, and Related Agencies Appropriations Act, 1998 (P.L. 105-65)

P.L. 105-65, §542(b):

Amended Code Sec. 6103(l)(7)(D) by striking the last sentence. **Effective** 10-27-97. Prior to being stricken, the last sentence of Code Sec. 6103(l)(7)(D) read as follows:

Clause (ix) shall not apply after September 30, 1998.

• 1997, Taxpayer Relief Act of 1997 (P.L. 105-34)

P.L. 105-34, §1023(a):

Amended Code Sec. 6103(l)(7)(D)(viii) by striking "1998" and inserting "2003". **Effective** 8-5-97.

• 1997, Balanced Budget Act of 1997 (P.L. 105-33)

P.L. 105-33, §4631(c)(2):

Amended Code Sec. 6103(l)(12) by striking subparagraph (F). **Effective** 8-5-97. Prior to amendment, Code Sec. 6103(l)(12)(F) read as follows:

(F) TERMINATION.—Subparagraphs (A) and (B) shall not apply to—

(i) any request made after September 30, 1988, and

(ii) any request made before such date for information relating to—

(I) 1997 or thereafter in the case of subparagraph (A), or

(II) 1998 or thereafter in the case of subparagraph (B).

P.L. 105-33, §5514(a)(1):

Struck the amendment made by Act. Sec. 110(l)(4)(A)-(B) of P.L. 104-193, which amended Code Sec. 6103(l)(10) by striking "(c) or (d)" each place it appeared and inserting "(c), (d), or (e)" and which added at the end of subparagraph (B) a new last sentence. Thus, the provisions of law amended by such section are restored as if such section had not been enacted. **Effective** 7-1-97. Prior to the amendment's being stricken, the last sentence of Code Sec. 6103(l)(10)(B), as added by P.L. 104-193, read as follows:

Any return information disclosed with respect to section 6402(e) shall only be disclosed to officers and employees of the State agency requesting such information.

P.L. 105-33, §11024(b)(1):

Amended Code Sec. 6103(l) by adding at the end a new paragraph (16). For the **effective** date, see Act Sec. 11721, below.

P.L. 105-33, §11721, provides:

Except as otherwise provided in this title, the provisions of this title shall take effect on the later of October 1, 1997, or the day the District of Columbia Financial Responsibility and Management Assistance Authority certifies that the financial plan and budget for the District government for fiscal year 1998 meet the requirements of section 201(c)(1) of the District of Columbia Financial Responsibility and Management Assistance Act of 1995, as amended by this title.

• 1996, Personal Responsibility and Work Opportunity Reconciliation Act of 1996 (P.L. 104-193)

P.L. 104-193, §110(l)(3):

Amended Code Sec. 6103(l)(7)(D)(i) by striking "aid to families with dependent children provided under a State plan approved" and inserting "a State program funded". **Effective** 7-1-97.

P.L. 104-193, §110(l)(4)(A)-(B):

Amended Code Sec. 6103(l)(10) by striking "(c) or (d)" each place it appears and inserting "(c), (d), or (e)"; and by adding at the end of subparagraph (B) a new sentence. **Effective** 7-1-97.

P.L. 104-193, §316(g)(4)(A):

Amended Code Sec. 6103(l)(6) by redesignating subparagraph (B) as subparagraph (C) and by inserting after subparagraph (A) a new subparagraph (B). **Effective** 8-22-96.

P.L. 104-193, §316(g)(4)(B)(ii):

Amended Code Sec. 6103(l)(6)(C), as redesignated by subsection (a) [subparagraph (A)]. **Effective** 8-22-96. Prior to amendment, Code Sec. 6103(l)(6)(C) read as follows:

(C) RESTRICTION ON DISCLOSURE.—The Secretary shall disclose return information under subparagraph (A) only for purposes of, and to the extent necessary in, establishing and collecting child support obligations from, and locating, individuals owing such obligations.

• 1996, Taxpayer Bill of Rights 2 (P.L. 104-168)

P.L. 104-168, §1206(a):

Amended Code Sec. 6103(l) by adding at the end a new paragraph (15). **Effective** 7-30-96.

• 1996, Debt Collection Improvement Act of 1996 (P.L. 104-134)

P.L. 104-134, §31001(g)(2):

Amended Code Sec. 6103(l)(10)(A) by inserting "and to officers and employees of the Department of the Treasury in connection with such reduction" after "6402". **Effective** 4-26-96.

P.L. 104-134, §31001(i)(2):

Amended Code Sec. 6103(l)(3)(C). **Effective** 4-26-96. Prior to amendment, Code Sec. 6103(l)(3)(C) read as follows:

(C) INCLUDED FEDERAL LOAN PROGRAM DEFINED.—For purposes of this paragraph, the term "included Federal loan program" means any program—

(i) under which the United States or a Federal agency makes, guarantees, or insures loans, and

(ii) with respect to which there is in effect a determination by the Director of the Office of Management and Budget (which has been published in the Federal Register) that the application of this paragraph to such program will substantially prevent or reduce future delinquencies under such program.

• 1994, Social Security Independence and Program Improvements Act of 1994 (P.L. 103-296)

P.L. 103-296, §108(h)(6)(A)-(B):

Amended Code Sec. 6103(l)(5) by striking "DEPARTMENT OF HEALTH AND HUMAN SERVICES" in the heading and inserting "SOCIAL SECURITY ADMINISTRATION" and by striking "Secretary of Health and Human Services" and inserting "Commissioner of Social Security". **Effective** 3-31-95.

P.L. 103-296, §311(b)(1)-(4):

Amended Code Sec. 6103(l)(5) by striking "for the purpose of" and inserting "for the purpose of—", by striking "carrying out, in accordance with an agreement" and inserting "(A) carrying out, in accordance with an agreement", by striking "program." and inserting "program; or", and by adding at the end thereof a new subparagraph (B). **Effective** with respect to requests for information made after 8-15-94.

• 1993, North American Free Trade Agreement Implementation Act (P.L. 103-182)

P.L. 103-182, §522(a):

Amended Code Sec. 6103(l) by adding at the end thereof new paragraph (14). **Effective** on the date the Agreement enters into force with respect to the United States.

P.L. 103-182, §522(c)(2), provides:

(2) REGULATIONS.—Not later than 90 days after the date of the enactment of this Act, the Secretary of the Treasury or his delegate shall issue temporary regulations to carry out section 6103(l)(14) of the Internal Revenue Code of 1986, as added by this section.

• 1993, Omnibus Budget Reconciliation Act of 1993 (P.L. 103-66)

P.L. 103-66, §13401(a):

Amended Code Sec. 6103(l)(7)(D) by striking "September 30, 1997" in the second sentence following clause (viii) and inserting "September 30, 1998". **Effective** 8-10-93.

P.L. 103-66, §13402(a):

Amended Code Sec. 6103(l) by adding at the end thereof new paragraph (13). **Effective** 8-10-93.

P.L. 103-66, §13403(a)(1)-(4):

Amended Code Sec. 6103(l)(7)(D) by striking "and" at the end of clause (vii); by striking the period at the end of clause (viii) and inserting "; and"; by inserting after clause (viii) a new clause (ix), and by adding at the end of subparagraph (D) a new sentence. **Effective** 8-10-93.

P.L. 103-66, §13403(b):

Amended Code Sec. 6103(l)(7) by inserting ", OR CERTAIN HOUSING ASSISTANCE PROGRAMS" after "CODE" in the heading. **Effective** 8-10-93.

P.L. 103-66, §13561(a)(2)(A)-(C):

Amended Code Sec. 6103(l)(12) by inserting ", above an amount (if any) specified by the Secretary of Health and Human Services," after "section 3401 (a))" in subparagraph (B)(i); by inserting ", above an amount (if any) specified by the Secretary of Health and Human Services," after "wages" in the matter preceding subclause (I) in subparagraph (B)(ii); and in subparagraph (F) by striking "1995" and inserting "1988" in clause (i), by striking "1994" and inserting "1997" in clause (ii)(I), and by striking "1995" and inserting "1998" in clause (ii)(II). **Effective** 8-10-93.

P.L. 103-66, §13561(e)(2)(B):

Amended Code Sec. 6103(l)(12)(E)(ii). **Effective** 8-10-93. Prior to amendment, Code Sec. 6103(l)(12)(E)(ii) read as follows:

(ii) GROUP HEALTH PLAN.—The term "group health plan" means—

(I) any group health plan (as defined in section 5000(b)(1)), and

(II) any large group health plan (as defined in section 5000(b)(2)).

• 1992, Veteran's Benefits Act of 1992 (P.L. 102-568)

P.L. 102-568, §602(b)(1):

Amended Code Sec. 6103(l)(7)(D) by striking out "September 30, 1992" in the last sentence and inserting in lieu thereof "September 30, 1997". **Effective** 10-29-92.

P.L. 102-568, §602(b)(2)(A)-(B):

Amended Code Sec. 6103(l)(7)(D)(viii) by striking "section 415" in subclause (II) and inserting in lieu thereof "section 1315"; and by striking out "section 610(a)(1)(I), 610(a)(2), 610(b), and 612(a)(2)(B)" in subclause (III) and inserting in lieu thereof "sections 1710(a)(1)(I), 1710(a)(2), 1710(b), and 1712(a)(2)(B)". **Effective** 10-29-92.

• 1991, Emergency Unemployment Compensation Act of 1991 (P.L. 102-164)

P.L. 102-164, §401(a):

Amended section 2653(c) of P.L. 98-369 (regarding the **effective** date), as amended by P.L. 100-485, by striking "and on or before January 10, 1994". **Effective** 10-1-91.

• 1990, Omnibus Budget Reconciliation Act of 1990 (P.L. 101-508)

P.L. 101-508, §4203(a)(2)(A)-(C):

Amended Code Sec. 6103(l)(12)(F) by striking "September 30, 1991" in clause (i) and inserting "September 30, 1995"; by striking "1990" in clause (ii)(I) and inserting "1994"; and by striking "1991" in clause (ii)(II) and inserting "1995". **Effective** 11-5-90, and the amendment made by subsection (a)(2)(B) applies to requests made on or after such date.

P.L. 101-508, §8051(a)(1)(A):

Amended Code Sec. 6103(l)(7)(D) by striking out "and" at the end of clause (vi). **Effective** 11-5-90.

P.L. 101-508, §8051(a)(1)(B):

Amended Code Sec. 6103(l)(7)(D) by striking out the period at the end of clause (vii) and inserting in lieu thereof "; and". **Effective** 11-5-90.

P.L. 101-508, §8051(a)(1)(C):

Amended Code Sec. 6103(l)(7)(D) by adding at the end thereof a new clause (viii) and concluding material at the end of subparagraph (D). **Effective** 11-5-90.

P.L. 101-508, §8051(a)(2):

Amended Code Sec. 6103(l)(7) by striking out "OR THE FOOD STAMP ACT OF 1977" and inserting in lieu thereof ", THE FOOD STAMP ACT OF 1977, OR TITLE 38, UNITED STATES CODE". **E ffective** 11-5-90.

• 1989, Omnibus Budget Reconciliation Act of 1989 (P.L. 101-239)

P.L. 101-239, §6202(a)(1)(A):

Amended Code Sec. 6103(l) by adding at the end thereof a new paragraph (12). **Effective** 12-19-89.

• 1988, Family Support Act of 1988 (P.L. 100-485)

P.L. 100-485, §701(a):

Amended section 2653(c) of P.L. 98-369 (regarding the **effective** date) by striking "before July 1, 1988" and inserting "on or before January 10, 1994". For the **effective** date, see Act Sec. 701(b)(3), below.

P.L. 100-485, §701(b)(1):

Amended Code Sec. 6103(l)(10). **Effective**, generally, 10-13-88. However, for a special rule, see Act Sec. 701(b)(3)(B), below. Prior to amendment, Code Sec. 6103(l)(10) read as follows:

(10) DISCLOSURE OF CERTAIN INFORMATION TO AGENCIES REQUESTING A REDUCTION UNDER SECTION 6402(c) OR 6402(d)—

(A) RETURN INFORMATION FROM INTERNAL REVENUE SERVICE.—The Secretary may, upon receiving a written request, disclose to officers and employees of an agency seeking a reduction under section 6402(c) or 6402(d)—

(i) the fact that a reduction has been made or has not been made under such subsection with respect to any person,

(ii) the amount of such reduction, and

(iii) taxpayer identifying information of the person against whom a reduction was made or not made.

(B) RESTRICTION ON USE OF DISCLOSED INFORMATION.—Any officers and employees of an agency receiving return information under subparagraph (A) shall use such information only for the purposes of, and to the extent necessary in, establishing appropriate agency records or in the defense of any litigation or administrative procedure ensuing from reduction made under section 6402(c) or section 6402(d).

P.L. 100-485, §701(b)(2)(A):

Amended Code Sec. 6103(l) by striking paragraph (11) and redesignating paragraph (12) as paragraph (11). **Effective**, generally, 10-13-88. However, for a special rule, see Act. Sec. 701(b)(3)(B), below. Prior to amendment, Code Sec. 6103(l)(11) read as follows:

(11) DISCLOSURE OF CERTAIN INFORMATION TO AGENCIES REQUESTING A REDUCTION UNDER SECTION 6402(c).—

(A) RETURN INFORMATION FROM INTERNAL REVENUE SERVICE.—The Secretary shall, upon receiving a written request, disclose to officers and employees of a State agency seeking a reduction under section 6402(c)—

(i) the fact that a reduction has been made or has not been made under such subsection with respect to any taxpayer,

(ii) the amount of such reduction,

(iii) whether such taxpayer filed a joint return,

(iv) Taxpayer Identity information with respect to the taxpayer against whom a reduction was made or not made and of any other person filing a joint return with such taxpayer; and

(v) the fact that a payment was made (and the amount of the payment) on the basis of a joint return in accordance with section 464(a)(3) of the Social Security Act.

(B) RESTRICTION ON USE OF DISCLOSED INFORMATION.—Any officers and employees of an agency receiving return information under subparagraph (A) shall use such information only for the purposes of, and to the extent necessary in, establishing appropriate agency records or in the defense of any litigation or administrative procedure ensuing from a reduction made under section 6402(c).

P.L. 100-485, §701(b)(3), provides:

(3) EFFECTIVE DATES.—

(A) IN GENERAL.—The amendments made by this subsection shall take effect on the date of enactment of this Act.

(B) SPECIAL RULE.—Nothing in section 2653(c) of the Deficit Reduction Act of 1984 shall be construed to limit the application of paragraph (10) of section 6103(l) of the Internal Revenue Code of 1986 (as amended by this subsection).

• 1986, Tax Reform Act of 1986 (P.L. 99-514)

P.L. 99-514, §1899A(53):

Amended Code Sec. 6103(l)(7)(D)(v) by striking out "this Code" and inserting in lieu thereof "this title". **Effective** 10-22-86.

• 1986 (P.L. 99-335)

P.L. 99-335, §310(a):

Amended Code Sec. 6103(l) by adding at the end thereof new paragraph (12). **Effective** 6-6-86.

• 1984, Child Support Enforcement Amendments of 1984 (P.L. 98-378)

P.L. 98-378, §19(b)(1):

Amended Code Sec. 6103(l)(6)(A)(i) by inserting "social security account number (or numbers, if the individual involved has more than one such number)," before "address". **Effective** 8-16-84.

P.L. 98-378, §19(b)(2):

Amended Code Sec. 6103(l)(8)(A) by inserting "social security account numbers[,]" before "net earnings". **Effective** 8-16-84.

P.L. 98-378, §21(f)(1):

Added Code Sec. 6103(l)(11). **Effective** with respect to refunds payable under Code Sec. 6402 after 12-31-85.

• 1984, Deficit Reduction Act of 1984 (P.L. 98-369)

P.L. 98-369, §453(a):

Amended Code Sec. 6103(l) by adding at the end thereof a new paragraph (9). **Effective** on the first day of the first calendar month which begins more than 90 days after 7-18-84.

P.L. 98-369, §453(b)(5):

Amended P.L. 96-249, Act Sec. 127(a)(1) by redesignating Code Sec. 6103(i)(7) as added by that Act as Code Sec. 6103(l)(7). **Effective** on the first day of the first calendar month which begins more than 90 days after 7-18-84.

P.L. 98-369, §453(b)(6):

Redesignated paragraph (7) of Code Sec. 6103(l) (added by Public Law 96-265) as paragraph (8). **Effective** on the first day of the first calendar month which begins more than 90 days after 7-18-84.

P.L. 98-369, §2651(k)(1):

Amended Code Sec. 6103(l)(7). **Effective** 7-18-84. Prior to amendment, Code Sec. 6103(l)(7) read as follows:

(7) Disclosure of Certain Return Information by Social Security Administration to Department of Agriculture and to State Food Stamp Agencies.—

(A) In General.—The Commissioner of Social Security may disclose return information from returns with respect to net earnings from self-employment (as defined in section 1402), wages (as defined in section 3121(a) or 3401(a)), and payments of retirement income which have been disclosed to the Social Security Administration as provided by paragraph (1) or (5) of this subsection—

(i) upon request, to officers and employees of the Department of Agriculture, and

(ii) upon written request, to officers and employees of a State food stamp agency.

(B) Restriction on Disclosure.—The Commissioner of Social Security shall disclose return information under subparagraph (A) only for purposes of, and to the extent necessary in, determining an individual's eligibility for benefits, or the amounts of benefits, under the food stamp program established under the Food Stamp Act of 1977.

(C) State Food Stamp Agency.—For purposes of this paragraph, the term, "State food stamp agency" means any agency described in section 3(n)(1) of the Food Stamp Act of 1977 which administers the food stamp program established under such Act.

P.L. 98-369, §2653(b)(3)(A):

Amended Code Sec. 6103(l) by adding at the end thereof new paragraph (10). **Effective** with respect to refunds payable under section 6402 of the Internal Revenue Code of 1954 after 12-31-85 [**effective** date changed by P.L. 102-164].

P.L. 98-369, §2663(j)(5)(E):

Amended Code Sec. 6103(l)(5) by striking out "Health, Education, and Welfare" each place it appeared and inserting in lieu thereof "Health and Human Services". **Effective** 7-18-84 but shall not be construed as changing or affecting any right, liability, status, or interpretation which existed (under the provisions of law involved) before that date.

• 1982, Debt Collection Act of 1982 (P.L. 97-365)

P.L. 97-365, §7(a):

Amended Code Sec. 6103(l)(3). **Effective** in the case of loan applications made after 9-30-82.

• 1982 (P.L. 97-258)

P.L. 97-258, §3(f)(5):

Amended Code Sec. 6103(l)(4)(A)(ii) by striking out "section 3 of the Act of July 7, 1884 (23 Stat. 258; 31 U.S.C. 1026)" and substituting "section 330 of title 31, United States Code". **Effective** 9-13-82.

• 1980, Social Security Disability Amendments of 1980 (P.L. 96-265)

P.L. 96-265, §408(a)(1):

Amended Code Sec. 6103(l) by adding new subsection (7) [(8)]. **Effective** 6-9-80. An earlier subsection (7) was added to Code Sec. 6103(l) by P.L. 96-249, but due to an error in the enrollment of that law, the subsection was erroneously added to Code Sec. 6103(i). It is expected that two technical corrections will be enacted: the first clarifying that the earlier subsection (7) was intended to be Code Sec. 6103(l)(7), not Code Sec. 6103(i)(7); and the second redesignating the Code Sec. 6103(l)(7) added by P.L. 96-265 as Code Sec. 6103(l)(8).

• 1980, Food Stamp Act Amendments of 1980 (P.L. 96-249)

P.L. 96-249, §127(a)(1):

Erroneously added the language in subparagraph (7) to Code Sec. 6103(i). **Effective** 5-26-80. It was intended to be added to Code Sec. 6103(l) and has been reflected here for that reason. A technical correction is expected that will correct the error in P.L. 96-249.

• 1976, Tax Reform Act of 1976 (P.L. 94-455)

P.L. 94-455, §1202(a):

Added Code Sec. 6103(l). **Effective** 1-1-77.

[Sec. 6103(m)]

(m) DISCLOSURE OF TAXPAYER IDENTITY INFORMATION.—

(1) TAX REFUNDS.—The Secretary may disclose taxpayer identity information to the press and other media for purposes of notifying persons entitled to tax refunds when the Secretary, after reasonable effort and lapse of time, has been unable to locate such persons.

(2) FEDERAL CLAIMS.—

(A) IN GENERAL.—Except as provided in subparagraph (B), the Secretary may, upon written request, disclose the mailing address of a taxpayer for use by officers, employees, or agents of a Federal agency for purposes of locating such taxpayer to collect or compromise a Federal claim against the taxpayer in accordance with sections 3711, 3717, and 3718 of title 31.

(B) SPECIAL RULE FOR CONSUMER REPORTING AGENCY.—In the case of an agent of a Federal agency which is a consumer reporting agency (within the meaning of section 603(f) of the Fair Credit Reporting Act (15 U.S.C. 1681a(f))), the mailing address of a taxpayer may be disclosed to such agent under subparagraph (A) only for the purpose of allowing such agent to prepare a commercial credit report on the taxpayer for use by such Federal agency in accordance with sections 3711, 3717, and 3718 of title 31.

(3) NATIONAL INSTITUTE FOR OCCUPATIONAL SAFETY AND HEALTH.— Upon written request, the Secretary may disclose the mailing address of taxpayers to officers and employees of the National Institute for Occupational Safety and Health solely for the purpose of locating individuals who are, or may have been, exposed to occupational hazards in order to determine the status of their health or to inform them of the possible need for medical care and treatment.

(4) INDIVIDUALS WHO OWE AN OVERPAYMENT OF FEDERAL PELL GRANTS OR WHO HAVE DEFAULTED ON STUDENT LOANS ADMINISTERED BY THE DEPARTMENT OF EDUCATION.—

(A) IN GENERAL.—Upon written request by the Secretary of Education, the Secretary may disclose the mailing address of any taxpayer—

(i) who owes an overpayment of a grant awarded to such taxpayer under subpart 1 of part A of title IV of the Higher Education Act of 1965, or

(ii) who has defaulted on a loan—

(I) made under part B, D, or E of title IV of the Higher Education Act of 1965, or

(II) made pursuant to section 3(a)(1) of the Migration and Refugee Assistance Act of 1962 to a student at an institution of higher education,

for use only by officers, employees, or agents of the Department of Education for purposes of locating such taxpayer for purposes of collecting such overpayment or loan.

(B) DISCLOSURE TO EDUCATIONAL INSTITUTIONS, ETC.—Any mailing address disclosed under subparagraph (A)(i) may be disclosed by the Secretary of Education to—

(i) any lender, or any State or nonprofit guarantee agency, which is participating under part (B) or (D) of title IV of the Higher Education Act of 1965, or

(ii) any educational institution with which the Secretary of Education has an agreement under subpart 1 of part A, or part D or E, of title IV of such Act,

for use only by officers, employees or agents of such lender, guarantee agency, or institution whose duties relate to the collection of student loans for purposes of locating individuals who have defaulted on student loans made under such loan programs for purposes of collecting such loans.

(5) INDIVIDUALS WHO HAVE DEFAULTED ON STUDENT LOANS ADMINISTERED BY THE DEPARTMENT OF HEALTH AND HUMAN SERVICES.—

(A) IN GENERAL.—Upon written request by the Secretary of Health and Human Services, the Secretary may disclose the mailing address of any taxpayer who has defaulted on a loan made under part C of title VII of the Public Health Service Act or under subpart II of part B of title VIII of such Act, for use only by officers, employees, or agents of the Department of Health and Human Services for purposes of locating such taxpayer for purposes of collecting such loan.

(B) DISCLOSURE TO SCHOOLS AND ELIGIBLE LENDERS.—Any mailing address disclosed under subparagraph (A) may be disclosed by the Secretary of Health and Human Services to—

(i) any school with which the Secretary of Health and Human Services has an agreement under subpart II of part C of title VII of the Public Health Service Act or subpart II of part B of title VIII of such Act, or

(ii) any eligible lender (within the meaning of section 737(4) of such Act) participating under subpart I of part C of title VII of such Act,

for use only by officers, employees, or agents of such school or eligible lender whose duties relate to the collection of student loans for purposes of locating individuals who have defaulted on student loans made under such subparts for the purposes of collecting such loans.

(6) BLOOD DONOR LOCATOR SERVICE.—

(A) IN GENERAL.—Upon written request pursuant to section 1141 of the Social Security Act, the Secretary shall disclose the mailing address of taxpayers to officers and employees of the Blood Donor Locator Services in the Department of Health and Human Services.

(B) RESTRICTION ON DISCLOSURE.—The Secretary shall disclose return information under subparagraph (A) only for purposes of, and to the extent necessary in, assisting under the Blood Donor Locator Service authorized persons (as defined in section 1141(h)(1) of the Social Security Act) in locating blood donors who, as indicated by donated blood or products derived therefrom or by the history of the subsequent use of such blood or blood products, have or may have the virus for acquired immune deficiency syndrome, in order to inform such donors of the possible need for medical care and treatment.

(C) SAFEGUARDS.—The Secretary shall destroy all related blood donor records (as defined in section 1141(h)(2) of the Social Security Act) in the possession of the Department of the Treasury upon completion of their use in making the disclosure required under subparagraph (A), so as to make such records undisclosable.

(7) SOCIAL SECURITY ACCOUNT STATEMENT FURNISHED BY SOCIAL SECURITY ADMINISTRATION.—Upon written request by the Commissioner of Social Security, the Secretary may disclose the mailing address of any taxpayer who is entitled to receive a social security account statement pursuant to section 1143(c) of the Social Security Act, for use only by officers, employees or agents of the Social Security Administration for purposes of mailing such statement to such taxpayer.

Amendments

• 1993, Omnibus Budget Reconciliation Act of 1993 (P.L. 103-66)

P.L. 103-66, §13402(b)(1):

Amended so much of paragraph (4) of Code section 6103(m) as precedes subparagraph (B). **Effective** 8-10-93. Prior to amendment, Code Sec. 6103(m)(4) that preceded subparagraph (B) read as follows:

(4) INDIVIDUALS WHO HAVE DEFAULTED ON STUDENT LOANS ADMINISTERED BY THE DEPARTMENT OF EDUCATION.—

(A) IN GENERAL.—Upon written request by the Secretary of Education, the Secretary may disclose the mailing address of any taxpayer who has defaulted on a loan—

(i) made under part B or E of title IV of the Higher Education Act of 1965, or

(ii) made pursuant to section 3(a)(1) of the Migration and Refugee Assistance Act of 1962 to a student at an institution of higher education,

for use only by officers, employees, or agents of the Department of Education for purposes of locating such taxpayer for purposes of collecting such loan.

P.L. 103-66, §13402(b)(2)(A)-(B):

Amended Code Sec. 6103(m)(4)(B) by striking "under part B" in clause (i) and inserting "under part B or D"; and by striking "under part E" in clause (ii) and inserting "under subpart 1 of part A, or part D or E,". **Effective** 8-10-93.

• 1990, Omnibus Budget Reconciliation Act of 1990 (P.L. 101-508)

P.L. 101-508, §5111(b)(1):

Amended Code Sec. 6103(m) by adding at the end thereof a new paragraph (7). **Effective** 11-5-90.

• 1988, Technical and Miscellaneous Revenue Act of 1988 (P.L. 100-647)

P.L. 100-647, §8008(c)(1):

Amended Code Sec. 6103(m) by adding at the end thereof a new paragraph (6). **Effective** 11-10-88.

• 1985 (P.L. 99-92)

P.L. 99-92, §8(h)(1) and (2):

Amended Code Sec. 6103(m) by inserting "ADMINISTERED BY THE DEPARTMENT OF EDUCATION" before the period in the paragraph heading of paragraph (4), and by adding at the end thereof new paragraph (5). **Effective** 10-1-85.

• 1983 (P.L. 97-452)

P.L. 97-452, §2(c)(4):

Amended Code Sec. 6103(m)(2) by striking out "section 3 of the Federal Claims Collection Act of 1966 (31 U.S.C. 952)" wherever it appeared and inserting "sections 3711, 3717, and 3718 of title 31". **Effective** 1-12-83.

• 1982, Debt Collection Act of 1982 (P.L. 97-365)

P.L. 97-365, §8(a):

Amended Code Sec. 6103(m)(2). **Effective** 10-25-82. Prior to amendment, Code Sec. 6103(m)(2) read as follows:

(2) FEDERAL CLAIMS.—Upon written request, the Secretary may disclose the mailing address of a taxpayer to officers and employees of an agency personally and directly engaged in, and solely for their use in, preparation for any administrative or judicial proceeding (or investigation which may result in such a proceeding) pertaining to the collection or compromise of a Federal claim against such taxpayer in accordance with the provisions of section 3 of the Federal Claims Collection Act of 1966.

P.L. 97-365, §8(e), provides:

(e) Except as otherwise provided in section 4 or 7 of the foregoing provisions of this section, nothing in this Act (or in the amendments made by this Act) shall apply to claims or indebtedness arising under, or amounts payable under, the Internal Revenue Code of 1954, the Social Security Act, or the tariff laws of the United States.

• 1982 (P.L. 97-258)

P.L. 97-258, §3(f)(6):

Amended Code Sec. 6103(m)(2) by striking out "section 3 of the Federal Claims Collection Act of 1966" and substituting "section 3711 of Title 31, United States Code". **Effective** 9-13-82.

• 1980, Omnibus Reconciliation Act of 1980 (P.L. 96-499)

P.L. 96-499, §302(a):

Amended Code Sec. 6103(m)(4). **Effective** 12-5-80. Prior to amendment, Code Sec 6103(m)(4) provided:

(4) INDIVIDUALS WHO HAVE DEFAULTED ON STUDENT LOANS.—

(A) IN GENERAL.—Upon written request by the Commissioner of Education, the Secretary may disclose the mailing address of any taxpayer who has defaulted on a loan made from the student loan fund established under part E of title IV of the Higher Education Act of 1965 for use only for purposes of locating such taxpayer for purposes of collecting such loan.

(B) DISCLOSURE TO INSTITUTIONS.—Any mailing address disclosed under subparagraph (A) may be disclosed by the Commissioner of Education to any educational institution with which he has an agreement under part E of Title IV of the Higher Education Act of 1965 only for use by officers, employees or agents of such institution whose duties relate to the collection of student loans for purposes of locating individuals who have defaulted on student loans made by such institution pursuant to such agreement for purposes of collecting such loans.

• 1978, Revenue Act of 1978 (P.L. 95-600)

P.L. 95-600, §701(bb)(1)(A):

Added Code Sec. 6103(m)(4). **Effective** 1-1-77.

• 1977 (P.L. 95-210)

P.L. 95-210, §5:

Amended subsection (m). **Effective** 12-13-77. Prior to amendment, subsection (m) read as follows:

(m) DISCLOSURE OF TAXPAYER IDENTITY INFORMATION.—The Secretary is authorized—

(1) to disclose taxpayer identity information to the press and other media for purposes of notifying persons entitled to tax refunds when the Secretary, after reasonable effort and lapse of time, has been unable to locate such persons, and

(2) upon written request, to disclose the mailing address of a taxpayer to officers and employees of an agency personally and directly engaged in, and solely for their use in, preparation for any administrative or judicial proceeding (or investigation which may result in such a proceeding) pertaining to the collection or compromise of a Federal claim against such taxpayer in accordance with the provisions of section 3 of the Federal Claims Collection Act of 1966.

• 1976, Tax Reform Act of 1976 (P.L. 94-455)

P.L. 94-455, §1202(a):

Added Code Sec. 6103(m). **Effective** 1-1-77.

[Sec. 6103(n)]

(n) CERTAIN OTHER PERSONS.—Pursuant to regulations prescribed by the Secretary, returns and return information may be disclosed to any person, including any person described in section 7513(a), to the extent necessary in connection with the processing, storage, transmission, and reproduction of such returns and return information, the programming, maintenance, repair, testing, and procurement of equipment, and the providing of other services, for purposes of tax administration.

Amendments

• 1990, Omnibus Budget Reconciliation Act of 1990 (P.L. 101-508)

P.L. 101-508, §11313(a)(1):

Amended Code Sec. 6103(n) by striking "and the programming" and inserting "the programming". **Effective** 11-5-90.

P.L. 101-508, §11313(a)(2):

Amended Code Sec. 6103(n) by inserting after "of equipment," the following "and the providing of other services,". **Effective** 11-5-90.

• 1976, Tax Reform Act of 1976 (P.L. 94-455)

P.L. 94-455, §1202(a):

Added Code Sec. 6103(n). **Effective** 1-1-77.

* * *

[Sec. 6103(p)]

(p) PROCEDURE AND RECORDKEEPING.—

(1) MANNER, TIME, AND PLACE OF INSPECTIONS.—Requests for the inspection or disclosure of a return or return information and such inspection or disclosure shall be made in such manner and at such time and place as shall be prescribed by the Secretary.

(2) PROCEDURE.—

(A) REPRODUCTION OF RETURNS.—A reproduction or certified reproduction of a return shall, upon written request, be furnished to any person to whom disclosure or inspection of such return is authorized under this section. A reasonable fee may be prescribed for furnishing such reproduction or certified reproduction.

(B) DISCLOSURE OF RETURN INFORMATION.—Return information disclosed to any person under the provisions of this title may be provided in the form of written documents, reproductions of such documents, films or photoimpressions, or electronically produced tapes, disks, or records, or by any other mode or means which the Secretary determines necessary or appropriate. A reasonable fee may be prescribed for furnishing such return information.

(C) USE OF REPRODUCTIONS.—Any reproduction of any return, document, or other matter made in accordance with this paragraph shall have the same legal status as the original, and any such reproduction shall, if properly authenticated, be admissible in evidence in any judicial or administrative proceeding as if it were the original, whether or not the original is in existence.

(3) RECORDS OF INSPECTION AND DISCLOSURE.—

(A) SYSTEM OF RECORDKEEPING.—Except as otherwise provided by this paragraph, the Secretary shall maintain a permanent system of standardized records or accountings of all requests for inspection or disclosure of returns and return information (including the reasons for and dates of such requests) and of returns and return information inspected or disclosed under this section and section 6104(c). Notwithstanding the provisions of section 552a(c) of title 5, United States Code, the Secretary shall not be required to maintain a record or accounting of requests for inspection or disclosure of returns and return information, or of returns and return information inspected or disclosed, under the authority of subsection (c), (e), (f)(5), (h)(1), (3)(A), or (4), (i)(4), or (8)(A)(ii), (k)(1), (2), (6), (8), or (9), (l)(1), (4)(B), (5), (7), (8), (9), (10), (11), (12), (13)(D)(iv), (13)(D)(v), (13)(D)(vi)[,] (14), (15), (16), (17), or (18), (m), or (n). The records or accountings required to be maintained under this paragraph shall be available for examination by the Joint Committee on Taxation or the Chief of Staff of such joint committee. Such record or accounting shall also be available for examination by such person or persons as may be, but only to the extent, authorized to make such examination under section 552a(c)(3) of title 5, United States Code.

(B) REPORT BY THE SECRETARY.—The Secretary shall, within 90 days after the close of each calendar year, furnish to the Joint Committee on Taxation a report with respect to, or summary of, the records or accountings described in subparagraph (A) in such form and containing such information as such joint committee or the Chief of Staff of such joint committee may designate. Such report or summary shall not, however, include a record or accounting of any request by the President under subsection (g) for, or the disclosure in response to such request of, any return or return information with respect to any individual who, at the time of such request, was an officer or employee of the executive branch of the Federal Government. Such report or summary, or any part thereof, may be disclosed by such joint committee to such persons and for such purposes as the joint committee may, by record vote of a majority of the members of the joint committee, determine.

(C) PUBLIC REPORT ON DISCLOSURES.—The Secretary shall, within 90 days after the close of each calendar year, furnish to the Joint Committee on Taxation for disclosure to the public a report with respect to the records or accountings described in subparagraph (A) which—

(i) provides with respect to each Federal agency, each agency, body, or commission described in subsection (d), (i)(3)(B)(i) or (7)(A)(ii) or (l)(6), and the Government Accountability Office the number of—

(I) requests for disclosure of returns and return information,

(II) instances in which returns and return information were disclosed pursuant to such requests or otherwise,

(III) taxpayers whose returns, or return information with respect to whom, were disclosed pursuant to such requests, and

(ii) describes the general purposes for which such requests were made.

(4) SAFEGUARDS.—Any Federal agency described in subsection (h)(2), (h)(5), (i)(1), (2), (3), (5), or (7), (j)(1), (2), or (5), (k)(8), (10), (11), or (15), (l)(1), (2), (3), (5), (10), (11), (13)(A), (13)(B), (13)(C), (13)(D)(i), (14), (17), or (22), (o)(1)(A), or (o)(3), the Government Accountability Office, the Congressional Budget Office, or any agency, body, or commission described in subsection (d), (i)(1)(C), (3)(B)(i), or (7)(A)(ii), or (k)(10), (l)(6), (7), (8), (9), (12), (15), or (16), any appropriate State officer (as defined in section 6104(c)), or any other person described in subsection (k)(10) or (15), subsection (l)(10), (13)(A), (13)(B), (13)(C), (13)(D)(i), (16), (18), (19), or (20), or any entity described in subsection (l)(21), shall, as a condition for receiving returns or return information—

(A) establish and maintain, to the satisfaction of the Secretary, a permanent system of standardized records with respect to any request, the reason for such request, and the date of such request made by or of it and any disclosure of return or return information made by or to it;

(B) establish and maintain, to the satisfaction of the Secretary, a secure area or place in which such returns or return information shall be stored;

(C) restrict, to the satisfaction of the Secretary, access to the returns or return information only to persons whose duties or responsibilities require access and to whom disclosure may be made under the provisions of this title;

(D) provide such other safeguards which the Secretary determines (and which he prescribes in regulations) to be necessary or appropriate to protect the confidentiality of the returns or return information;

(E) furnish a report to the Secretary, at such time and containing such information as the Secretary may prescribe, which describes the procedures established and utilized by such agency, body, or commission, the Government Accountability Office, or the Congressional Budget Office for ensuring the confidentiality of returns and return information required by this paragraph; and

(F) upon completion of use of such returns or return information—

(i) in the case of an agency, body, or commission described in subsection (d), (i)(3)(B)(i), (k)(10), or (l)(6), (7), (8), (9), or (16), any appropriate State officer (as defined in section 6104(c)), or any other person described in subsection (k)(10) or (15) or subsection (l)(10), (13)(A), (13)(B), (13)(C), (13)(D)(i), (16), (18), (19), or (20) return to the Secretary such returns or return information (along with any copies made there-from) or make such returns or return information undisclosable in any manner and furnish a written report to the Secretary describing such manner,

(ii) in the case of an agency described in subsection (h)(2), (h)(5), (i)(1), (2), (3), (5) or (7), (j)(1), (2), or (5), (k)(8), (10), (11), or (15), (l)(1), (2), (3), (5), (10), (11), (12), (13)(A), (13)(B), (13)(C), (13)(D)(i), (14), (15), (17), or (22), (o)(1)(A), or (o)(3) or any entity described in subsection (l)(21), the Government Accountability Office, or the Congressional Budget Office, either—

(I) return to the Secretary such returns or return information (along with any copies made therefrom),

(II) otherwise make such returns or return information undisclosable, or

(III) to the extent not so returned or made undisclosable, ensure that the conditions of subparagraphs (A), (B), (C), (D), and (E) of this paragraph continue to be met with respect to such returns or return information, and

(iii) in the case of the Department of Health and Human Services for purposes of subsection (m)(6), destroy all such return information upon completion of its use in providing the notification for which the information was obtained, so as to make such information undisclosable;

except that the conditions of subparagraphs (A), (B), (C), (D), and (E) shall cease to apply with respect to any return or return information if, and to the extent that, such return or return information is disclosed in the course of any judicial or administrative proceeding and made a part of the public record thereof. If the Secretary determines that any such agency, body, or commission, including an agency, an appropriate State officer (as defined in section 6104(c)), or any other person described in subsection (k)(10) or (15) or subsection (l)(10), (13)(A), (13)(B), (13)(C), (13)(D)(i), (16), (18), (19), or (20) or any entity described in subsection (l)(21), or the Government Accountability Office or the Congressional Budget Office, has failed to, or does not, meet the requirements of this paragraph, he may, after any proceedings for review established under paragraph (7), take such actions as are necessary to ensure such requirements are met, including refusing to disclose returns or return information to such agency, body, or commission, including an agency, an appropriate State officer (as defined in section 6104(c)), or any other person described in subsection (k)(10) or (15) or subsection (l)(10), (13)(A), (13)(B), (13)(C), (13)(D)(i), (16), (18), (19), or (20) or any entity described in subsection (l)(21), or the Government Accountability Office or the Congressional Budget Office, until he determines that such requirements have been or will be met. In the case of any agency which receives any mailing address under paragraph (2), (4), (6), or (7) of subsection (m) and which discloses any such mailing address to any agent or which receives any information under paragraph (6)(A), (10), (12)(B), or (16) of subsection (l) and which discloses any such information to any agent, or any person including an agent described in subsection (l)(10), (13)(A), (13)(B), (13)(C), (13)(D)(i), or (16), this paragraph shall apply to such agency and each such agent or other person (except that, in the case of an agent, or any person including an agent described in subsection (l)(10), (13)(A), (13)(B), (13)(C), (13)(D)(i), or (16), any report to the Secretary or other action with respect to the Secretary shall be made or taken through such agency). For purposes of applying this paragraph in any case to which subsection (m)(6) applies, the term "return information" includes related blood donor records (as defined in section 1141(h)(2) of the Social Security Act).

(5) REPORT ON PROCEDURES AND SAFEGUARDS.—After the close of each calendar year, the Secretary shall furnish to each committee described in subsection (f)(1) a report which describes the procedures and safeguards established and utilized by such agencies, bodies, or commissions, the Government Accountability Office, and the Congressional Budget Office for ensuring the confidentiality of returns and return information as required by this subsection. Such report shall also describe instances of deficiencies in, and failure to establish or utilize, such procedures.

(6) AUDIT OF PROCEDURES AND SAFEGUARDS.—

(A) AUDIT BY COMPTROLLER GENERAL.—The Comptroller General may audit the procedures and safeguards established by such agencies, bodies, or commissions and the Congressional Budget Office pursuant to this subsection to determine whether such safeguards and procedures meet the requirements of this subsection and ensure the confidentiality of returns and return information. The Comptroller General shall notify the Secretary before any such audit is conducted.

(B) RECORDS OF INSPECTION AND REPORTS BY THE COMPTROLLER GENERAL.—The Comptroller General shall—

(i) maintain a permanent system of standardized records and accountings of returns and return information inspected by officers and employees of the Government Accountability Office under subsection (i)(8)(A)(ii) and shall, within 90 days after the close of each calendar year, furnish to the Secretary a report with respect to, or summary of, such records or accountings in such form and containing such information as the Secretary may prescribe, and

(ii) furnish an annual report to each committee described in subsection (f) and to the Secretary setting forth his findings with respect to any audit conducted pursuant to subparagraph A.

The Secretary may disclose to the Joint Committee any report furnished to him under clause (i).

(7) ADMINISTRATIVE REVIEW.—The Secretary shall by regulations prescribe procedures which provide for administrative review of any determination under paragraph (4) that any agency, body, or commission described in subsection (d) has failed to meet the requirements of such paragraph.

(8) STATE LAW REQUIREMENTS.—

(A) SAFEGUARDS.—Notwithstanding any other provision of this section, no return or return information shall be disclosed after December 31, 1978, to any officer or employee of any State which requires a taxpayer to attach to, or include in, any State tax return a copy of any portion of his Federal return, or information reflected on such Federal return, unless such State adopts provisions of law which protect the confidentiality of the copy of the Federal return (or portion thereof) attached to, or the Federal return information reflected on, such State tax return.

(B) DISCLOSURE OF RETURNS OR RETURN INFORMATION IN STATE RETURNS.—Nothing in subparagraph (A) or paragraph (9) shall be construed to prohibit the disclosure by an officer or employee of any State of any copy of any portion of a Federal return or any information on a

Federal return which is required to be attached or included in a State return to another officer or employee of such State (or political subdivision of such State) if such disclosure is specifically authorized by State law.

(9) DISCLOSURE TO CONTRACTORS AND OTHER AGENTS.—Notwithstanding any other provision of this section, no return or return information shall be disclosed to any contractor or other agent of a Federal, State, or local agency unless such agency, to the satisfaction of the Secretary—

(A) has requirements in effect which require each such contractor or other agent which would have access to returns or return information to provide safeguards (within the meaning of paragraph (4)) to protect the confidentiality of such returns or return information,

(B) agrees to conduct an on-site review every 3 years (or a mid-point review in the case of contracts or agreements of less than 3 years in duration) of each contractor or other agent to determine compliance with such requirements,

(C) submits the findings of the most recent review conducted under subparagraph (B) to the Secretary as part of the report required by paragraph (4)(E), and

(D) certifies to the Secretary for the most recent annual period that such contractor or other agent is in compliance with all such requirements.

The certification required by subparagraph (D) shall include the name and address of each contractor or other agent, a description of the contract or agreement with such contractor or other agent, and the duration of such contract or agreement. The requirements of this paragraph shall not apply to disclosures pursuant to subsection (n) for purposes of Federal tax administration.

Amendments

• 2020, COVID-related Tax Relief Act of 2020 (P.L. 116-260)

P.L. 116-260, §283(b)(2)(B)(i)-(ii), Div. N:

Amended Code Sec. 6103(p)(4) by striking "(k)(8), (10)[sic] or (11)" both places it appears and inserting "(k)(8), (10), (11), or (15)", and by striking "any other person described in subsection (k)(10)" each place it appears and inserting "any other person described in subsection (k)(10) or (15)". **Effective** for disclosures made on or after 12-27-2020.

P.L. 116-260, §284(a)(3)(B), Div. N:

Amended Code Sec. 6103(p)(3)(A), as amended by section 3516(a)(2) of the CARES Act (P.L. 116-136), by striking "(13)(A), (13)(B), (13)(C), (13)(D)(i),[sic]" and inserting "(13)(D)(iv), (13)(D)(v), (13)(D)(vi)". **Effective** for disclosures made after the date of the enactment of the FUTURE Act (P.L. 116-91) [**effective** for disclosures made after 12-19-2019.—CCH].

• 2020, Consolidated Appropriations Act, 2021 (P.L. 116-260)

P.L. 116-260, §102(b)(2)(B)(i)-(ii), Div. FF:

Amended Code Sec. 6103(p)(4) by striking "(k)(8), (10)[sic] or (11)" both place it appears and inserting "(k)(8), (10), (11), or (15)", and by striking "any other person described in subsection (k)(10)" each place it appears and inserting "any other person described in subsection (k)(10) or (15)". [Note: An identical amendment was made by P.L. 116-260, Act Sec. 283(b)(2)(B)(i)-(ii), Div. N. Therefore, this amendment cannot be made.—CCH] **Effective** for disclosures made on or after 12-27-2020.

P.L. 116-260, §103(a)(3)(B), Div. FF:

Amended Code Sec. 6103(p)(3)(A), as amended by section 3516(a)(2) of the CARES Act (P.L. 116-136), by striking "(13)(A), (13)(B), (13)(C), (13)(D)(i),[sic]" and inserting "(13)(D)(iv), (13)(D)(v), (13)(D)(vi)". [Note: An identical amendment was made by P.L. 116-260, Act Sec. 284(a)(3)(B), Div. N. Therefore, this amendment cannot be made.—CCH] **Effective** for disclosures made after the date of the enactment of the FUTURE Act (P.L. 116–91) [**effective** for disclosures made after 12-19-2019.—CCH].

• 2020, Coronavirus Aid, Relief, and Economic Security (CARES) Act (P.L. 116-136)

P.L. 116-136, §3516(a)(2):

Amended Code Sec. 6103(p)(3)(A), as amended by the FUTURE Act (P.L. 116-91), by striking "(12)," and inserting "(12), (13)(A), (13)(B), (13)(C), (13)(D)(i)". **Effective** as if included in the enactment of the FUTURE Act (P.L. 116-91) [**effective** for disclosures after 12-19-2019.—CCH].

P.L. 116-136, §3516(a)(3):

Amended Code Sec. 6103(p)(4), as amended by the FUTURE Act (P.L. 116-91), by striking "(13) or (16)" each place it appears and inserting "(13), or (16)". **Effective** as if included in the enactment of the FUTURE Act (P.L. 116-91) [**effective** for disclosures after 12-19-2019.—CCH].

P.L. 116-136, §3516(a)(4):

Amended Code Sec. 6103(p)(4), as amended by the FUTURE Act (P.L. 116-91) and by Act Sec. 3516(a)(3), by striking "(13)" each place it appears and inserting "(13)(A), (13)(B), (13)(C), (13)(D)(i)". **Effective** as if included in the enactment of the FUTURE Act (P.L. 116-91) [**effective** for disclosures after 12-19-2019.—CCH].

• 2019, Fostering Undergraduate Talent by Unlocking Resources for Education (FUTURE) Act (P.L. 116-91)

P.L. 116-91, §3(c)(1):

Amended Code Sec. 6103(p)(3)(A) of such Code by striking "(13)" following "(12),". **Effective** for disclosures after 12-19-2019.

P.L. 116-91, §3(c)(2):

Amended Code Sec. 6103(p)(4) of such Code by inserting ", (13)" after "(l)(10)" each place it appears. **Effective** for disclosures after 12-19-2019.

• 2019, Setting Every Community Up for Retirement Enhancement Act of 2019 (P.L. 116-94)

P.L. 116-94, §404(b), Div. O:

Amended Code Sec. 6103(p)(4) by striking "or (o)(1)(A)" each place it appears and inserting ", (o)(1)(A), or (o)(3)". **Effective** 12-20-2019.

• 2019, Taxpayer First Act (P.L. 116-25)

P.L. 116-25, §2004(a):

Amended Code Sec. 6103(p) by adding at the end a new paragraph (9). **Effective** for disclosures made after 12-31-2022.

P.L. 116-25, §2004(b):

Amended Code Sec. 6103(p)(8)(B) by inserting "or paragraph (9)" after "subparagraph (A)". **Effective** for disclosures made after 12-31-2022.

• 2018, Tax Technical Corrections Act of 2018 (P.L. 115-141)

P.L. 115-141, §401(a)(271), Div. U:

Amended Code Sec. 6103(p)(3)(A) by striking "subsections" and inserting "subsection". **Effective** 3-23-2018.

P.L. 115-141, §401(a)(272), Div. U:

Amended Code Sec. 6103(p)(3)(C)(ii) by striking the comma at the end and inserting a period. **Effective** 3-23-2018.

P.L. 115-141, §401(a)(273), Div. U:

Amended Code Sec. 6103(p)(4) by striking "7(A)(ii)" in the matter preceding subparagraph (A) and inserting "(7)(A)(ii)". **Effective** 3-23-2018.

P.L. 115-141, §401(a)(274)(A)-(B), Div. U:

Amended Code Sec. 6103(p)(4)(F)(ii) by striking "subsections" and inserting "subsection", and by striking "subsection (l)(21),,," and inserting "subsection (l)(21),". **Effective** 3-23-2018.

P.L. 115-141, §401(a)(275), Div. U:

Amended Code Sec. 6103(p)(4) by striking "subsection (l)(21),," both places it appears in the flush matter at the end and inserting "subsection (l)(21),". **Effective** 3-23-2018.

• 2016, Recovering Missing Children Act (P.L. 114-184)

P.L. 114-184, §2(b)(2)(B):

Amended Code Sec. 6103(p)(4) by striking "(i)(3)(B)(i)" in the matter preceding subparagraph (A) and inserting "(i)(1)(C), (3)(B)(i),". **Effective** for disclosures made after 6-30-2016.

• 2015, Fixing America's Surface Transportation Act (P.L. 114-94)

P.L. 114-94, §32101(c)(2):

Amended Code Sec. 6103(p)(4) by striking "or (10)" each place it appears in subparagraph (F)(ii) and in the matter preceding subparagraph (A) and inserting ", (10), or (11)". **Effective** 12-4-2015.

• 2013, American Taxpayer Relief Act of 2012 (P.L. 112-240)

P.L. 112-240, §209(b)(2)(A)-(C):

Amended Code Sec. 6103(p)(4) by inserting "subsection (k)(10)," before "subsection (l)(10)," in the matter preceding subparagraph (A), in subparagraph (F)(i) by inserting "(k)(10)," before "or (l)(6),", and by inserting "subsection (k)(10) or" before "subsection (l)(10),", and by inserting "subsection (k)(10) or" before "subsection (l)(10)," both places it appears in the matter following subparagraph (F)(iii). **Effective** 1-2-2013.

• 2010, Homebuyer Assistance and Improvement Act of 2010 (P.L. 111-198)

P.L. 111-198, §4(c):

Amended Code Sec. 6103(p)(4) by inserting "(k)(10)," before "(l)(6)," in the matter preceding subparagraph (A). **Effective** for disclosures made after 7-2-2010.

• 2010, Preservation of Access to Care for Medicare Beneficiaries and Pension Relief Act of 2010 (P.L. 111-192)

P.L. 111-192, §103(a)(2):

Amended Code Sec. 6103(p)(4), as amended by sections 1414 and 3308 of P.L. 111-148, in the matter preceding subparagraph (A) and in subparagraph (F)(ii), by striking "or (17)" and inserting "(17), or (22)" each place it appears. **Effective** 6-25-2010.

• 2010, Patient Protection and Affordable Care Act (P.L. 111-148)

P.L. 111-148, §1414(c)(1)-(3):

Amended Code Sec. 6103(p)(4) by inserting ", or any entity described in subsection (l)(21)," after "or (20)" in the matter preceding subparagraph (A), by inserting "or any entity described in subsection (l)(21)," after "or (o)(1)(A)" in subparagraph (F)(ii), and by inserting "or any entity described in subsection (l)(21)," after "or (20)" both places it appears in the matter after subparagraph (F). **Effective** 3-23-2010.

• 2009, Children's Health Insurance Program Reauthorization Act of 2009 (P.L. 111-3)

P.L. 111-3, §702(f)(2):

Amended Code Sec. 6103(p)(4) by striking "(o)(1)" both places it appears and inserting "(o)(1)(A)". **Effective** on or after 2-4-2009.

• 2008, Inmate Tax Fraud Prevention Act of 2008 (P.L. 110-428)

P.L. 110-428, §2(b):

Amended Code Sec. 6103(p)(4) by striking "(k)(8)" both places it appears and inserting "(k)(8) or (10)". **Effective** for disclosures made after 12-31-2008.

• 2008, SSI Extension for Elderly and Disabled Refugees Act (P.L. 110-328)

P.L. 110-328, §3(b)(3)(A)-(C):

Amended Code Sec. 6103(p)(4) in the matter preceding subparagraph (A), by striking "(l)(16)," and inserting "(l)(10), (16),"; in subparagraph (F)(i), by striking "(l)(16)," and inserting "(l)(10), (16),"; and in the matter following subparagraph (F)(iii), in each of the first two places it appears, by striking "(l)(16)," and inserting "(l)(10), (16),"; by inserting "(10)," after "paragraph (6)(A),"; and in each of the last two places it appears, by striking "(l)(16)" and inserting "(l)(10) or (16)". **Effective** for refunds payable under Code Sec. 6402 on or after 9-30-2008.

• 2006, Pension Protection Act of 2006 (P.L. 109-280)

P.L. 109-280, §1224(b)(2):

Amended Code Sec. 6103(p)(3)(A) by inserting "and section 6104(c)" after "section" in the first sentence. **Effective** 8-17-2006 but shall not apply to requests made before such date.

P.L. 109-280, §1224(b)(3)(A)-(C):

Amended Code Sec. 6103(p)(4) by inserting ", any appropriate State officer (as defined in section 6104(c))," before "or any other person" in the matter preceding subparagraph (A), by inserting "any appropriate State officer (as defined in section 6104(c))," before "or any other person" in subparagraph (F)(i), and by inserting ", an appropriate State officer (as defined in section 6104(c))," after "including an agency" each place it appears in the matter following subparagraph (F). **Effective** 8-17-2006 but shall not apply to requests made before such date.

• 2005, Gulf Opportunity Zone Act of 2005 (P.L. 109-135)

P.L. 109-135, §412(rr)(4):

Amended Code Sec. 6103(p)(3)(C)(i), (p)(4), (p)(5) and (p)(6)(B) by striking "General Accounting Office" each place it appears and inserting "Government Accountability Office". **Effective** 12-21-2005.

P.L. 109-135, §412(yy)(1):

Amended so much of Code Sec. 6103(p)(4) as precedes subparagraph (A). **Effective** 12-21-2005. Prior to amendment, so much of Code Sec. 6103(p)(4) as preceded subparagraph (A) read as follows:

(4) SAFEGUARDS.—Any Federal agency described in subsection (h)(2), (h)(5), (i)(1), (2), (3), (5), or (7), (j)(1), (2), or (5), (k)(8), (l)(1), (2), (3), (5), (10), (11), (13), (14), or (17), or (o)(1), the Government Accountability Office, the Congressional Budget Office, or any agency, body, or commission described in subsection (d), (i)(3)(B)(i) or (7)(A)(ii), or (l)(6), (7), (8), (9), (12), (15), or (16) or any other person described in subsection (l)(16), (18), (19), or (20) shall, as a condition for receiving returns or return information—

P.L. 109-135, §412(yy)(2):

Amended Code Sec. 6103(p)(4)(F)(i). **Effective** 12-21-2005. Prior to amendment, Code Sec. 6103(p)(4)(F)(i) read as follows:

(i) in the case of an agency, body, or commission described in subsection (d), (i)(3)(B)(i), or (l)(6), (7), (8), (9), or (16), or any other person described in subsection (l)(16), (18), (19), or (20) return to the Secretary such returns or return information (along with any copies made therefrom) or make such returns or return information undisclosable in any manner and furnish a written report to the Secretary describing such manner,

P.L. 109-135, §412(yy)(3):

Amended Code Sec. 6103(p)(4) by striking the first full sentence in the matter following subparagraph (F) and inserting a new sentence. **Effective** 12-21-2005. Prior to amendment, the first full sentence in the matter following Code Sec. 6103(p)(4)(F) read as follows:

If the Secretary determines that any such agency, body, or commission, including an agency or any other person described in subsection (l)(16), (18), (19), or (20), or the Government Accountability Office or the Congressional Budget Office has failed to, or does not, meet the requirements of this paragraph, he may, after any proceedings for review established under paragraph (7), take such actions as are necessary to ensure such requirements are met, including refusing to disclose returns or return information to such agency, body, or commission, including an agency or any other person described in subsection (l)(16), (18), (19), or (20), or the Government Accountability Office or the Congressional Budget Office until he determines that such requirements have been or will be met.

• 2004, Miscellaneous Trade and Technical Corrections Act of 2004 (P.L. 108-429)

P.L. 108-429, §2004(a)(22):

Amended Code Sec. 6103(p)(4), as amended by Act Sec. 202(b)(2)(B) of the Trade Act of 2002 (P.L. 107-210), by striking "or (17)" after "any other person described in subsection (l)(16)" each place it appears and inserting "or (18)". **Effective** 12-3-2004.

• 2004, Working Families Tax Relief Act of 2004 (P.L. 108-311)

P.L. 108-311, §408(a)(24):

Amended Code Sec. 6103(p)(4) by striking "subsection (l)(16) or (17)" each place it appears and inserting "subsection (l)(16) or (18)". **Effective** 10-4-2004. [P.L. 108-173, §105(e)(3), struck "(l)(16) or (17)" and inserted "(l)(16), (17), or (19)". Therefore, this amendment cannot be made. However, see the amendment made by P.L. 108-429, §2004(a)(22), above.—CCH.]

• 2003, Medicare Prescription Drug, Improvement, and Modernization Act of 2003 (P.L. 108-173)

P.L. 108-173, §105(e)(3):

Amended Code Sec. 6103(p)(4) by striking "(l)(16) or (17)" each place it appears and inserting "(l)(16), (17), or (19)". **Effective** 12-8-2003.

P.L. 108-173, §811(c)(2)(B):

Amended Code Sec. 6103(p)(4), as amended by Act Sec. 105(e)(3), by striking "(l)(16), (17), or (19)" each place it appears and inserting "(l)(16), (17), (19), or (20)". **Effective** 12-8-2003.

• 2002, Trade Act of 2002 (P.L. 107-210)

P.L. 107-210, §202(b)(2)(A)-(B):

Amended Code Sec. 6103(p) by striking "or (17)" and inserting "(17), or (18)" in paragraph (3)(A), and by inserting "or (17)" after "any other person described in subsection (l)(16)" each place it appears in paragraph (4). **Effective** 8-6-2002.

• 2002, Victims of Terrorism Tax Relief Act of 2001 (P.L. 107-134)

P.L. 107-134, §201(c)(6)(A)-(B):

Amended Code Sec. 6103(p)(3) in subparagraph (A) by striking "(7)(A)(ii)" and inserting "(8)(A)(ii)"; and in subparagraph (C) by striking "(i)(3)(B)(i)" and inserting "(i)(3)(B)(i) or (7)(A)(ii)". **Effective** for disclosures made on or after 1-23-2002.

P.L. 107-134, §201(c)(7)(A)-(B):

Amended Code Sec. 6103(p)(4) in the matter preceding subparagraph (A) by striking "or (5)," the first place it appears and inserting "(5), or (7),"; and by striking "(i)(3)(B)(i)," and inserting "(i)(3)(B)(i) or (7)(A)(ii),"; and in subparagraph (F)(ii) by striking "or (5)," the first place it appears and inserting "(5) or (7),". **Effective** for disclosures made on or after 1-23-2002.

P.L. 107-134, §201(c)(8):

Amended Code Sec. 6103(p)(6)(B)(i) by striking "(i)(7)(A)(ii)" and inserting "(i)(8)(A)(ii)". **Effective** for disclosures made on or after 1-23-2002.

• 2000, Community Renewal Tax Relief Act of 2000 (P.L. 106-554)

P.L. 106-554, §310(a)(2)(A)(i)-(iv):

Amended Code Sec. 6103(p)(4) by inserting "the Congressional Budget Office," after "General Accounting Office," in the matter preceding subparagraph (A), by striking "commission or the General Accounting Office" and inserting "commission, the General Accounting Office, or the Congressional Budget Office" in subparagraph (E), by striking "or the General Accounting Office," and inserting "the General Accounting Office, or the Congressional Budget Office," in subparagraph (F)(ii), and by inserting "or the Congressional Budget Office" after "General Accounting Office" both places it appears in the matter following subparagraph (F). **Effective** 12-21-2000.

P.L. 106-554, §310(a)(2)(B):

Amended Code Sec. 6103(p)(5) by striking "commissions and the General Accounting Office" and inserting "commissions, the General Accounting Office, and the Congressional Budget Office". **Effective** 12-21-2000.

P.L. 106-554, §310(a)(2)(C):

Amended Code Sec. 6103(p)(6)(A) by inserting "and the Congressional Budget Office" after "commissions". **Effective** 12-21-2000.

P.L. 106-554, §319(17)(A):

Amended Code Sec. 6103(p) by striking the second comma after "(13)", and by striking "(7)" and all that follows through "shall, as a condition" and inserting "(7), (8), (9), (12), (15), or (16) or any other person described in subsection (l)(16) shall, as a condition" in the matter preceding subparagraph (4)(A). **Effective** 12-21-2000. Prior to amendment, the matter preceding subparagraph (A) of Code Sec. 6103(p)(4) read as follows:

(4) SAFEGUARDS.—Any Federal agency described in subsection (h)(2), (h)(5), (i)(1), (2), (3), or (5), (j)(1), (2), or (5), (k)(8), (l)(1), (2), (3), (5), (10), (11), (13), (14), or (17), or (o)(1), the General Accounting Office, or any agency, body, or commission described in subsection (d), (i)(3)(B)(i), or (l)(6), (7), (8), (9), (12), or [sic] (15), or (16), or any other person described in subsection (l)(16) shall, as a condition for receiving returns or return information—

P.L. 106-554, §319(17)(B):

Amended Code Sec. 6103(p)(4)(F)(ii) by striking the second comma after "(14)". **Effective** 12-21-2000.

• 1998, Tax and Trade Relief Extension Act of 1998 (P.L. 105-277)

P.L. 105-277, §4002(h):

Amended Code Sec. 6103(p)(3)(A) by inserting "(f)(5)," after "(c), (e),". **Effective** as if included in the provision of P.L. 105-206 to which it relates [**effective** 7-22-98.—CCH].

P.L. 105-277, §4006(a)(2):

Amended Code Sec. 6103(p)(4) by striking "(j)(1) or (2)" in the material preceding subparagraph (A) and in [clause (ii) of]subparagraph (F) and inserting "(j)(1), (2), or (5)". **Effective** for requests made on or after 10-21-98.

• 1998, IRS Restructuring and Reform Act of 1998 (P.L. 105-206)

P.L. 105-206, §3702(b)(1):

Amended Code Sec. 6103(p)(3)(A) by striking "or (16)" and inserting "(16), or (17)". **Effective** for requests made by the Archivist of the United States after 7-22-98.

P.L. 105-206, §3702(b)(2):

Amended Code Sec. 6103(p)(4) by striking "or (14)" and inserting ", (14), or (17)". **Effective** for requests made by the Archivist of the United States after 7-22-98.

P.L. 105-206, §3702(b)(3):

Amended Code Sec. 6103(p)(4)(F)(ii) by striking "or (15)" and inserting ", (15), or (17)". **Effective** for requests made by the Archivist of the United States after 7-22-98.

P.L. 105-206, §6012(b)(4), provides:

Act Sec. 1205(c)(3) of P.L. 105-34 shall be applied as if the amendment to Code Sec. 6103(p)(3)(A) struck "or (8)" and inserted "(8), or (9)". **Effective** 5-5-98.

P.L. 105-206, §2003(e), provides:

(e) PROCEDURES FOR AUTHORIZING DISCLOSURE ELECTRONICALLY.—The Secretary shall establish procedures for any taxpayer to authorize, on an electronically filed return, the Secretary to disclose information under section 6103(c) of the Internal Revenue Code of 1986 to the preparer of the return.

P.L. 105-206, §2005, provides:

SEC. 2005. ACCESS TO ACCOUNT INFORMATION.

(a) IN GENERAL.—Not later than December 31, 2006, the Secretary of the Treasury or the Secretary's delegate shall develop procedures under which a taxpayer filing returns electronically (and their designees under section 6103(c) of the Internal Revenue Code of 1986) would be able to review the taxpayer's account electronically, but only if all necessary safeguards to ensure the privacy of such account information are in place.

(b) REPORT.—Not later than December 31, 2003, the Secretary of the Treasury shall report on the progress the Secretary is making on the development of procedures under subsection (a) to the Committee on Ways and Means of the House of Representatives and the Committee on Finance of the Senate.

P.L. 105-206, §3508, provides:

SEC. 3508. DISCLOSURE TO TAXPAYERS.

The Secretary of the Treasury or the Secretary's delegate shall ensure that any instructions booklet accompanying an individual Federal income tax return form (including forms 1040, 1040A, 1040EZ, and any similar or successor forms) shall include, in clear language, in conspicuous print, and in a conspicuous place, a concise description of the conditions under which return information may be disclosed to any party outside the Internal Revenue Service, including disclosure to any State or agency, body, or commission (or legal representative) thereof.

• 1997, Taxpayer Relief Act of 1997 (P.L. 105-34)

P.L. 105-34, §1026(b)(1)(A):

Amended Code Sec. 6103(p)(3)(A) by striking "(2), or (6)" and inserting "(2), (6), or (8)". **Effective** for levies issued after 8-5-97.

P.L. 105-34, §1026(b)(1)(B):

Amended Code Sec. 6103(p)(4) by inserting "(k)(8)," after "(j)(1) or (2)," each place it appears. **Effective** for levies issued after 8-5-97.

P.L. 105-34, §1205(c)(3):

Amended Code Sec. 6103(p)(3)(A) by striking "or (6)" [sic] and inserting "(6), or (8)". **Effective** on the day 9 months after 8-5-97.

P.L. 105-34, §1283(b):

Amended Code Sec. 6103(p)(4) by striking "(h)(6)" each place it appears and inserting "(h)(5)". **Effective** for judicial proceedings commenced after 8-5-97.

• 1997, Balanced Budget Act of 1997 (P.L. 105-33)

P.L. 105-33, §5514(a)(1):

Struck the amendment made by Act Sec. 110(l)(5)(A)-(B) of P.L. 104-193, which amended Code Sec. 6103(p)(4) in the matter preceding subparagraph (A) by striking "(5), (10)" and inserting "(5)" and by striking "(9), or (12)" and inserting "(9), (10), or (12)". Thus, the provisions of law amended by such section are restored as if such section had not been enacted. **Effective** 7-1-97.

P.L. 105-33, §11024(b)(4):

Amended Code Sec. 6103(p)(3)(A) by striking "or (15)" and inserting "(15), or (16)". For the **effective** date, see Act Sec. 11721, below.

P.L. 105-33, §11024(b)(5):

Amended Code Sec. 6103(p)(4) in the matter preceding subparagraph (A) by striking "or (12)" and inserting "(12), or (16), or any other person described in subsection (l)(16)". For the **effective** date, see Act Sec. 11721, below.

P.L. 105-33, §11024(b)(6):

Amended Code Sec. 6103(p)(4)(F)(i) by striking "or (9)," and inserting "(9), or (16), or any other person described in subsection (l)(16)". For the **effective** date, see Act Sec. 11721, below.

P.L. 105-33, §11024(b)(7)(A)-(F):

Amended Code Sec. 6103(p)(4)(F) in the matter following clause (iii) by inserting after "any such agency, body or commission" and before the words "for [or] the General Accounting Office" the words ", including an agency or any other person described in subsection (l)(16),"; by striking "to such agency, body, or commission" and inserting "to such agency, body, or commission, including an agency or any other person described in subsection (l)(16),"; by striking "or (12)(B)" and inserting ", (12)(B), or (16)"; by inserting after the words "any agent," and before the words "this paragraph shall" the words "or any person including an agent described in subsection (l)(16),"; by inserting after the words "such agent" and before "(except that" the words "or other person"; and by inserting after the words "an agent," and before the words "any report" the words "or any person including an agent described in subsection (l)(16),". For the **effective** date, see Act Sec. 11721, below.

P.L. 105-33, §11721, provides:

Except as otherwise provided in this title, the provisions of this title shall take effect on the later of October 1, 1997, or the day the District of Columbia Financial Responsibility and Management Assistance Authority certifies that the financial plan and budget for the District government for fiscal year 1998 meet the requirements of section 201(c)(1) of the District of Columbia Financial Responsibility and Management Assistance Act of 1995, as amended by this title.

• 1996, Personal Responsibility and Work Opportunity Reconciliation Act of 1996 (P.L. 104-193)

P.L. 104-193, §110(l)(5)(A)-(B):

Amended Code Sec. 6103(p)(4) in the matter preceding subparagraph (A) by striking "(5), (10)" and inserting "(5)"; and by striking "(9), or (12)" and inserting "(9), (10), or (12)". **Effective** 7-1-97.

P.L. 104-193, §316(g)(4)(B)(iii):

Amended Code Sec. 6103(p)(4) in the material following subparagraph (F) by striking "subsection (l)(12)(B)" and inserting "paragraph (6)(A) or (12)(B) of subsection (l)". **Effective** 8-22-96.

• 1996, Taxpayer Bill of Rights 2 (P.L. 104-168)

P.L. 104-168, §1206(b)(2)(A)-(B):

Amended Code Sec. 6103(p)(3)(A) by striking "(7)(A)(ii), or (8)" and inserting "or (7)(A)(ii)", and by striking "or (14)" and inserting "(14), or (15)". **Effective** 7-30-96.

P.L. 104-168, §1206(b)(3)(A)-(C):

Amended the material preceding Code Sec. 6103(p)(4)(A) by striking "(5), or (8)" and inserting "or (5)", by striking "(i)(3)(B)(i), or (8)" and inserting "(i)(3)(B)(i),", and by striking "or (12)" and inserting "(12), or (15)". **Effective** 7-30-96.

P.L. 104-168, §1206(b)(4)(A)-(B):

Amended Code Sec. 6103(p)(4)(F)(ii) by striking "(5), or (8)" and inserting "or (5)", and by striking "or (14)" and inserting "(14), or (15)". **Effective** 7-30-96.

• 1993, North American Free Trade Agreement Implementation Act (P.L. 103-182)

P.L. 103-182, §522(b):

Amended Code Sec. 6103(p)(3)(A) and (4) by striking "or (13) each place it appears and inserting "(13), or (14)". **Effective** on the date the Agreement enters into force with respect to the United States.

• 1993, Omnibus Budget Reconciliation Act of 1993 (P.L. 103-66)

P.L. 103-66, §13402(b)(3)(A):

Amended Code Sec. 6103(p)(3)(A) by striking "(11), or (12), (m)" and inserting "(11), (12), or (13), (m)". **Effective** 8-10-93.

P.L. 103-66, §13402(b)(3)(B)(i):

Amended Code Sec. 6103(p)(4) in the matter preceding subparagraph (A), by striking out "(10), or (11)," and inserting "(10), (11), or (13),". **Effective** 8-10-93.

P.L. 103-66, §13402(b)(3)(B)(ii):

Amended Code Sec. 6103(p)(4)(F)(ii) by striking out "(11), or (12)," and inserting "(11), (12), or (13),". **Effective** 8-10-93.

• 1990, Omnibus Budget Reconciliation Act of 1990 (P.L. 101-508)

P.L. 101-508, §5111(b)(2):

Amended Code Sec. 6103(p)(4) in the matter following subparagraph (F)(iii) by striking "subsection (m)(2), (4), or (6)" and inserting "paragraph (2), (4), (6), or (7) of subsection (m)". **Effective** 11-5-90.

• 1989, Omnibus Budget Reconciliation Act of 1989 (P.L. 101-239)

P.L. 101-239, §6202(a)(1)(B)(ii):

Amended Code Sec. 6103(p)(3)(A) by striking "or (11)" and inserting "(11), or (12)". **Effective** 12-19-89.

P.L. 101-239, §6202(a)(1)(B)(iii):

Amended Code Sec. 6103(p)(4) by striking "or (9) shall" in the material preceding subparagraph (A) and inserting "(9), or (12) shall". **Effective** 12-19-89.

P.L. 101-239, §6202(a)(1)(B)(iv):

Amended Code Sec. 6103(p)(4)(F)(ii) by striking "or (11)" and inserting "(11), or (12)". **Effective** 12-19-89.

P.L. 101-239, §6202(a)(1)(B)(v):

Amended Code Sec. 6103(p)(4) in the next to last sentence by inserting "or which receives any information under subsection (l)(12)(B) and which discloses any such information to any agent" before ", this paragraph". **Effective** 12-19-89.

• 1988, Anti-Drug Abuse Act of 1988 (P.L. 100-690)

P.L. 100-690, §7601(b)(2)(A):

Amended Code Sec. 6103(p)(3)(A) by striking out "or (7)(A)(ii)" and inserting in lieu thereof", (7)(A)(ii), or (8)". **Effective** for requests made on or after 11-18-88, but disclosures may be made pursuant to such amendments only during the 2-year period beginning on such date.

P.L. 100-690, §7601(b)(2)(B)(i)-(ii):

Amended Code Sec. 6103(p)(4) by striking out in the material preceding subparagraph (A) "or (5)" and inserting in lieu thereof "(5), or (8)", and by striking out "(i)(3)(B)(i)," and inserting in lieu thereof "(i)(3)(B)(i), or (8)". **Effective** for requests made on or after 11-18-88, but disclosures may be made pursuant to such amendments only during the 2-year period beginning on such date.

P.L. 100-690, §7601(b)(2)(C):

Amended Code Sec. 6103(p)(4)(F)(ii) by striking out "or (5)" and inserting in lieu thereof "(5), or (8)". **Effective** for requests made on or after 11-18-88, but disclosures may be made pursuant to such amendments only during the 2-year period beginning on such date.

• 1988, Technical and Miscellaneous Revenue Act of 1988 (P.L. 100-647)

P.L. 100-647, §8008(c)(2)(A)(i)-(iii):

Amended Code Sec. 6103(p)(4) in subparagraph (F) by striking "manner; and" at the end of clause (i) and inserting "manner,"; by adding "and" at the end of clause (ii)(III); and by inserting after clause (ii)(III) a new clause (iii); in the last sentence, by striking "subsection (m)(2) or (4)" and inserting "subsection (m)(2), (4), or (6)"; and by adding at the end a new sentence. **Effective** 11-10-88.

P.L. 100-647, §5021, provides:

SEC. 5021. REPEAL OF RULES PERMITTING LOSS TRANSFERS BY ALASKA NATIVE CORPORATIONS.

(a) GENERAL RULE.—Nothing in section 60(b)(5) of the Tax Reform Act of 1984 (as amended by section 1804(e)(4) of the Tax Reform Act of 1986)—

(1) shall allow any loss (or credit) of any corporation which arises after April 26, 1988, to be used to offset the income (or tax) of another corporation if such use would not be allowable without regard to such section 60(b)(5) as so amended, or

(2) shall allow any loss (or credit) of any corporation which arises on or before such date to be used to offset disqualified income (or tax attributable to such income) of another corporation if such use would not be allowable without regard to such section 60(b)(5) as so amended.

(b) EXCEPTION FOR EXISTING CONTRACTS.—

(1) IN GENERAL.—Subsection (a) shall not apply to any loss (or credit) of any corporation if—

(A) such corporation was in existence on April 26, 1988, and

(B) such loss (or credit) is used to offset income assigned (or attributable to property contributed) pursuant to a binding contract entered into before July 26, 1988.

(2) $40,000,000 LIMITATION.—The aggregate amount of losses (and the deduction equivalent of credits as determined in the same manner as under section 469(j)(5) of the 1986 Code) to which paragraph (1) applies with respect to any corporation shall not exceed $40,000,000. For purposes of this paragraph, a Native Corporation and all other corporations all of the stock of which is owned directly by such corporation shall be treated as 1 corporation.

(3) SPECIAL RULE FOR CORPORATIONS UNDER TITLE 11.—In the case of a corporation which on April 26, 1988, was under the jurisdiction of a Federal district court under title 11 of the United States Code—

(A) paragraph (1)(B) shall be applied by substituting the date 1 year after the date of the enactment of this Act for "July 26, 1988",

(B) paragraph (1) shall not apply to any loss or credit which arises on or after the date 1 year after the date of the enactment of this Act, and

(C) paragraph (2) shall be applied by substituting "$99,000,000" for "$40,000,000".

(c) SPECIAL ADMINISTRATIVE RULES.—

(1) NOTICE TO NATIVE CORPORATIONS OF PROPOSED TAX ADJUSTMENTS.—Notwithstanding section 6103 of the 1986 Code, the Secretary of the Treasury or his delegate shall notify a Native Corporation or its designated representative of any proposed adjustment—

(A) of the tax liability of a taxpayer which has contracted with the Native Corporation (or other corporation all of the stock of which is owned directly by the Native Corporation) for the use of loses of such Native Corporation (or such other corporation), and

(B) which is attributable to an asserted overstatement of losses by, or misassignment of income (or income attributable to property contributed) to, an affiliated group of which the Native Corporation (or such other corporation) is a member.

Such notice shall only include information with respect to the transaction between the taxpayer and the Native Corporation.

(2) RIGHTS OF NATIVE CORPORATION.—

(A) IN GENERAL.—If a Native Corporation receives a notice under paragraph (1), the Native Corporation shall have the right to—

(i) submit to the Secretary of the Treasury or his delegate a written statement regarding the proposed adjustment, and

(ii) meet with the Secretary of the Treasury or his delegate with respect to such proposed adjustment.

The Secretary of the Treasury or his delegate may discuss such proposed adjustment with the Native Corporation or its designated representative.

(B) EXTENSION OF STATUTE OF LIMITATIONS.—Subparagraph (A) shall not apply if the Secretary of the Treasury or his delegate determines that an extension of the statute of limitation is necessary to permit the participation described in subparagraph (A) and the taxpayer and the Secretary or his delegate have not agreed to such extension.

(3) JUDICIAL PROCEEDINGS.—In the case of any proceeding in a Federal court or the United States Tax Court involving a proposed adjustment under paragraph (1), the Native Corporation, subject to the rules of such court, may file an amicus brief concerning such adjustment.

(4) FAILURES.—For purposes of the 1986 Code, any failure by the Secretary of the Treasury or his delegate to comply with the provisions of this subsection shall not affect the validity of the determination of the Internal Revenue Service of any adjustment of tax liability of any taxpayer described in paragraph (1).

(d) DISQUALIFIED INCOME DEFINED.—For purposes of subsection (a), the term "disqualified income" means any income assigned (or attributable to property contributed) after April 26, 1988, by a person who is not a Native Corporation or a corporation all the stock of which is owned directly by a Native Corporation.

(e) BASIS DETERMINATION.—For purposes of determining basis for Federal tax purposes, no provision in any law (whether enacted before, on, or after the date of the enactment of this Act) shall affect the date on which the transfer to the Native Corporation is made. The preceding sentence shall apply to all taxable years whether beginning before, on, or after such date of enactment.

• 1988, Family Support Act of 1988 (P.L. 100-485)

P.L. 100-485, §701(b)(2)(B):

Amended Code Sec. 6103(p)(3)(A) and (4) by striking "(10), (11), or (12)" each place it appears and inserting "(10), or (11)". **Effective**, generally, 10-13-88. However, for a special rule, see Act Sec. 701(b)(3)(B), below.

P.L. 100-485, §701(b)(3)(B), provides:

(B) SPECIAL RULE.—Nothing in section 2653(c) of the Deficit Reduction Act of 1984 shall be construed to limit the application of paragraph (10) of section 6103(l) of the Internal Revenue Code of 1986 (as amended by this subsection).

• 1986, Congressional Reports Elimination act of 1986 (P.L. 99-386)

P.L. 99-386, §206(b):

Amended Code Sec. 6103(p)(5) by striking out "quarter" and inserting in lieu thereof "year". **Effective** 8-22-86.

• 1986 (P.L. 99-335)

P.L. 99-335, §310(b)(1):

Amended Code Sec. 6103(p)(3)(A) by striking out "(10), or (11)" and inserting in lieu thereof "(10), (11), or (12)". **Effective** 6-6-86.

P.L. 99-335, §310(b)(2)(A) and (B):

Amended Code Sec 6103(p)(4) by striking out "(10), or (11)" in the material preceding subparagraph (A) and inserting in lieu thereof "(10), (11), or (12)", and by striking out "(10), or (11)" in subparagraph (F)(ii) and inserting in lieu thereof "(10), (11), or (12)". **Effective** 6-6-86.

• 1984, Child Support Enforcement Amendments of 1984 (P.L. 98-378)

P.L. 98-378, §21(f)(2):

Amended Code Sec. 6103(p)(3)(A) by striking out "or (10)" and inserting in lieu thereof "(10), or (11)". **Effective** with respect to refunds payable under Code Sec. 6402 after 12-31-85.

P.L. 98-378, §21(f)(3):

Amended Code Sec. 6103(p)(4) by striking out "or (10)" and inserting in lieu thereof "(10), or (11)". **Effective** with respect to refunds payable under Code Sec. 6402 after 12-31-85.

P.L. 98-378, §21(f)(4):

Amended Code Sec. 6103(p)(4)(F)(ii) by striking out "or (10)" and inserting in lieu thereof "(10), or (11)". **Effective** with respect to refunds payable under Code Sec. 6402 after 12-31-85.

• 1984, Deficit Reduction Act of 1984 (P.L. 98-369)

P.L. 98-369, §453(b)(1):

Amended Code Sec. 6103(p)(3)(A) by striking out "(5), or (7)" and inserting in lieu thereof "(5), (7), (8), or (9)". **Effective** on the first day of the first calendar month which begins more than 90 days after 7-18-84.

P.L. 98-369, §453(b)(2):

Amended Code Sec. 6103(p)(4) by striking out, in the material preceding subparagraph (A), "or 7" and inserting in lieu thereof "(7), (8), or (9)". **Effective** on the first day of the first calendar month which begins more than 90 days after 7-18-84.

P.L. 98-369, §453(b)(3):

Amended Code Sec. 6103(p)(4)(F)(i) by striking out "(l)(6) or (7)" and inserting in lieu thereof "(l)(6), (7), (8), or (9)". **Effective** on the first day of the first calendar month which begins more than 90 days after 7-18-84.

P.L. 98-369, §2653(b)(3)(B)(i):

Amended Code Sec. 6103(p)(3)(A) as so amended by striking out "or (9)" and inserting in lieu thereof "(9), or (10)". **Effective** with respect to refunds payable under section 6402 of the Internal Revenue Code of 1954 after 12-31-85, and on or before 1-10-94 [**effective** date changed by P.L. 100-485].

P.L. 98-369, §2653(b)(3)(B)(ii):

Amended Code Sec. 6103(p)(4), as so amended, by striking out "(l)(1), (2), (3), or (5)" and inserting in lieu thereof "(l)(1), (2), (3), (5), or (10)". **Effective** with respect to refunds payable under section 6402 of the Internal Revenue Code of 1954 after 12-31-85, and on or before 1-10-94 [**effective** date changed by P.L. 100-485].

P.L. 98-369, §2653(b)(3)(B)(iii):

Amended Code Sec. 6103(p)(4)(F)(ii) by striking out "(l)(1), (2), (3), or (5)" and inserting in lieu thereof "(l)(1), (2), (3), (5), or (10)". **Effective** with respect to refunds payable under section 6402 of the Internal Revenue Code of 1954 after 12-31-85, and on or before 1-10-94 [**effective** date changed by P.L. 100-485].

• 1983, Social Security Amendments of 1983 (P.L. 98-21)

P.L. 98-21, §121(c)(3)(B):

Amended Code Sec. 6103(p)(4) by inserting "(h)(6)," after "(h)(2)," in the material preceding subparagraph (A) and in subparagraph (F)(ii) thereof. **Effective** for benefits received after 12-31-83, in tax years ending after such date. The amendments made by Act Sec. 121 do not apply to any portion of a lump-sum payment of social security benefits (as defined in Code Sec. 86(d)) received after 12-31-83, if the generally applicable payment date for such portion was before 1-1-84.

• 1982, Debt Collection Act of 1982 (P.L. 97-365)

P.L. 97-365, §7(b)(1):

Amended Code Sec. 6103(p)(3)(C)(i) by striking out "(l)(3) or (6)" and inserting in lieu thereof "(l)(6)". **Effective** in the case of loan applications made after 9-30-82.

P.L. 97-365, §7(b)(2):

Amended Code Sec. 6103(p)(4) by striking out "(l)(1), (2)," in the matter preceding subparagraph (A) and inserting in lieu thereof "(l)(1), (2), (3),", by striking out "(l)(3), (6)," and inserting in lieu thereof "(l)(6),", and by striking out "(l)(1), (2), or (5), or (o)(1), the commission described in subsection (l)(3)" in subparagraph (F)(ii) and inserting in lieu thereof "(l)(1), (2), (3), or (5), or (o)(1),". **Effective** in the case of loan applications made after 9-30-82.

P.L. 97-365, §8(b):

Amended Code Sec. 6103(p)(4) by adding the last sentence. **Effective** 10-25-82.

• 1982, Tax Equity and Fiscal Responsibility Act of 1982 (P.L. 97-248)

P.L. 97-248, §356(b)(1):

Amended Code Sec. 6103(p) by striking out "(6)(A)(ii)" in paragraph (3)(A) and inserting "(7)(A)(ii)", by striking out "(d)" in paragraph (3)(C)(i) and inserting "(d), (i)(3)(B)(i),", by striking out "such requests" in paragraph (3)(C)(i)(II) and inserting "such requests or otherwise", by striking out "(i)(1), (2), or (5)" each place it appears in paragraph (4) and inserting "(i)(1), (2), (3), or (5)", by striking out "(d)" each place it appears in paragraph (4) and inserting "(d), (i)(3)(B)(i),", and by striking out "subsection (i)(6)(A)(ii)" in paragraph (6)(B)(i) and inserting "subsection (i)(7)(A)(ii)". **Effective** 9-4-82.

• 1980, Social Security Disability Amendments of 1980 (P.L. 96-265)

P.L. 96-265, §408(a)(2)(A), (B) and (C):

Amended Code Sec. 6103(p)(3)(A) by striking out "(l)(1) or (4)(B) or (5)" and substituting "(l)(1), (4)(B), (5), or (7)"; amended Code Sec. 6103(p)(4) by striking out "(l)(3) or (6)" in the first sentence and substituting "(l)(3), (6), or (7)"; and amended Code Sec. 6103(p)(4)(F)(i) by striking out "(l)(6)" and substituting "(l)(6) or (7)". **Effective** 6-9-80. These amendments duplicate prior amendments made to Code Sec. 6103(p) by P.L. 96-249, which added an earlier Code Sec. 6103(l)(7). However, due to an error in the enrollment of P.L. 96-249, the new subsection (7) was added to Code Sec. 6103(i), instead of 6103(l), even though the changes made to Code Sec. 6103(p) properly referred to Code Sec. 6103(l) as the section amended by P.L. 96-249. Thus, P.L. 96-265 added a second Code Sec. 6103(l)(7) because of this error. It is expected that technical corrections will be made, redesignating the subsection (7) added by P.L. 96-265 as subsection (8), and correcting the references contained in Code Sec. 6103(p).

• 1980, Food Stamp Act Amendments of 1980 (P.L. 96-249)

P.L. 96-249, §127(a)(2)(A):

Amended Code Sec. 6103(p)(3)(A) by striking out "(l)(1) or (4)(B) or (5)" and inserting in lieu thereof "(l)(1), (4)(B), (5), or (7)". **Effective** 5-26-80.

P.L. 96-249, §127(a)(2)(B):

Amended Code Sec. 6103(p)(4) by striking out "(l)(3) or (6)" in so much of such paragraph as precedes subparagraph (A), and inserting in lieu thereof "(l)(3), (6), or (7)". **Effective** 5-26-80.

P.L. 96-249, §127(a)(2)(C):

Amended Code Sec. 6103(p)(4)(F)(i) by striking out "(l)(6)" and inserting in lieu thereof "(l)(6) or (7)". **Effective** 5-26-80.

• 1976, Tax Reform Act of 1976 (P.L. 94-455)

P.L. 94-455, §1202(a):

Added Code Sec. 6103(p). **Effective** 1-1-77.

[Sec. 6103(q)]

(q) REGULATIONS.—The Secretary is authorized to prescribe such other regulations as are necessary to carry out the provisions of this section.

Amendments

• 1976, Tax Reform Act of 1976 (P.L. 94-455)

P.L. 94-455, §1202(a):

Added Code Sec. 6103(q). **Effective** 1-1-77.

* * *

[Sec. 6107]

SEC. 6107. TAX RETURN PREPARER MUST FURNISH COPY OF RETURN TO TAXPAYER AND MUST RETAIN A COPY OR LIST.

[Sec. 6107(a)]

(a) FURNISHING COPY TO TAXPAYER.—Any person who is a tax return preparer with respect to any return or claim for refund shall furnish a completed copy of such return or claim to the taxpayer not later than the time such return or claim is presented for such taxpayer's signature.

Amendments

• 2007, Small Business and Work Opportunity Tax Act of 2007 (P.L. 110-28)

P.L. 110-28, §8246(a)(2)(C)(i)(I):

Amended Code Sec. 6107 by striking "INCOME TAX RETURN PREPARER" in the heading and inserting "TAX RETURN PREPARER". **Effective** for returns prepared after 5-25-2007.

P.L. 110-28, §8246(a)(2)(C)(i)(II):

Amended Code Sec. 6107(a) by striking "an income tax return preparer" each place it appears and inserting "a tax return preparer". **Effective** for returns prepared after 5-25-2007.

[Sec. 6107(b)]

(b) COPY OR LIST TO BE RETAINED BY TAX RETURN PREPARER.—Any person who is a tax return preparer with respect to a return or claim for refund shall, for the period ending 3 years after the close of the return period—

(1) retain a completed copy of such return or claim, or retain, on a list, the name and taxpayer identification number of the taxpayer for whom such return or claim was prepared, and

(2) make such copy or list available for inspection upon request by the Secretary.

Amendments

• 2007, Small Business and Work Opportunity Tax Act of 2007 (P.L. 110-28)

P.L. 110-28, §8246(a)(2)(C)(i)(II)-(III):

Amended Code Sec. 6107(b) by striking "an income tax return preparer" each place it appears and inserting "a tax return preparer", and by striking "INCOME TAX RETURN PREPARER" in the heading and inserting "TAX RETURN PREPARER". **Effective** for returns prepared after 5-25-2007.

[Sec. 6107(c)]

(c) REGULATIONS.—The Secretary shall prescribe regulations under which, in cases where 2 or more persons are tax return preparers with respect to the same return or claim for refund, compliance with the requirements of subsection (a) or (b), as the case may be, of one such person shall be deemed to be compliance with the requirements of such subsection by the other persons.

Amendments

• 2007, Small Business and Work Opportunity Tax Act of 2007 (P.L. 110-28)

P.L. 110-28, §8246(a)(2)(C)(i)(IV):

Amended Code Sec. 6107(c) by striking "income tax return preparers" and inserting "tax return preparers". **Effective** for returns prepared after 5-25-2007.

[Sec. 6107(d)]

(d) DEFINITIONS.—For purposes of this section, the terms "return" and "claim for refund" have the respective meanings given to such terms by section 6696(e), and the term "return period" has the meaning given to such term by section 6060(c).

Amendments

• 1976, Tax Reform Act of 1976 (P.L. 94-455)

P.L. 94-455, §1203(c):

Added Code Sec. 6107. **Effective** for documents prepared after 12-31-76.

* * *

[Sec. 6109]

SEC. 6109. IDENTIFYING NUMBERS.

[Sec. 6109(a)]

(a) SUPPLYING OF IDENTIFYING NUMBERS.—When required by regulations prescribed by the Secretary:

(1) INCLUSION IN RETURNS.—Any person required under the authority of this title to make a return, statement, or other document shall include in such return, statement, or other document such identifying number as may be prescribed for securing proper identification of such person.

(2) FURNISHING NUMBER TO OTHER PERSONS.—Any person with respect to whom a return, statement, or other document is required under the authority of this title to be made by another person or whose identifying number is required to be shown on a return of another person shall furnish to such other person such identifying number as may be prescribed for securing his proper identification.

(3) FURNISHING NUMBER OF ANOTHER PERSON.—Any person required under the authority of this title to make a return, statement, or other document with respect to another person shall request from such other person, and shall include in any such return, statement, or other document, such identifying number as may be prescribed for securing proper identification of such other person.

(4) FURNISHING IDENTIFYING NUMBER OF TAX RETURN PREPARER.—Any return or claim for refund prepared by a tax return preparer shall bear such identifying number for securing proper identification of such preparer, his employer, or both, as may be prescribed. For purposes of this paragraph, the terms "return" and "claim for refund" have the respective meanings given to such terms by section 6696(e).

For purposes of paragraphs (1), (2), and (3), the identifying number of an individual (or his estate) shall be such individual's social security account number.

Amendments

• 2007, Small Business and Work Opportunity Tax Act of 2007 (P.L. 110-28)

P.L. 110-28, §8246(a)(2)(D)(i)-(ii):

Amended Code Sec. 6109(a)(4) by striking "an income tax return preparer" and inserting "a tax return preparer", and by striking "INCOME RETURN PREPARER" in the heading and inserting "TAX RETURN PREPARER". **Effective** for returns prepared after 5-25-2007.

• 1998, IRS Restructuring and Reform Act of 1998 (P.L. 105-206)

P.L. 105-206, §3710(a):

Amended the last sentence of Code Sec. 6109(a) by striking "For purposes of this subsection" and inserting "For purposes of paragraphs (1), (2), and (3)". **Effective** 7-22-98.

• 1988, Family Support Act of 1988 (P.L. 100-485)

P.L. 100-485, §703(c)(3):

Amended Code Sec. 6109(a)(2) by striking "shall furnish" and inserting "or whose identifying number is required to be shown on a return of another person shall furnish". **Effective** for tax years beginning after 12-31-88.

• 1976, Tax Reform Act of 1976 (P.L. 94-455)

P.L. 94-455, §1203(d):

Added paragraph (4). **Effective** for documents prepared after 12-31-76.

P.L. 94-455, §1906(b)(13)(A):

Amended 1954 Code by substituting "Secretary" for "Secretary or his delegate" each place it appeared. **Effective** 2-1-77.

[Sec. 6109(b)]

(b) LIMITATION.—

(1) Except as provided in paragraph (2), a return of any person with respect to his liability for tax, or any statement or other document in support thereof, shall not be considered for purposes of paragraphs (2) and (3) of subsection (a) as a return, statement, or other document with respect to another person.

(2) For purposes of paragraphs (2) and (3) of subsection (a), a return of an estate or trust with respect to its liability for tax, and any statement or other document in support thereof, shall be considered as a return, statement, or other document with respect to each beneficiary of such estate or trust.

[Sec. 6109(c)]

(c) REQUIREMENT OF INFORMATION.—For purposes of this section, the Secretary is authorized to require such information as may be necessary to assign an identifying number to any person.

Amendments

• 1976, Tax Reform Act of 1976 (P.L. 94-455)

P.L. 94-455, §1906(b)(13)(A):

Amended 1954 Code by substituting "Secretary" for "Secretary or his delegate" each place it appeared. **Effective** 2-1-77.

• 1961 (P.L. 87-397)

P.L. 87-397, §[1](a):

Added Code Sec. 6109. For the **effective** date, see P.L. 87-397, §[1](d), below.

P.L. 87-397, §[1](d):

(d) EFFECTIVE DATE.—Paragraph (1) of section 6109(a) of the Internal Revenue Code of 1954, as added by subsection (a) of this section, shall apply only in respect of returns, statements, and other documents relating to periods commencing after December 31, 1961. Paragraphs (2) and (3) of such section 6109(a) shall apply only in respect of returns, statements, or other documents relating to periods commencing after December 31, 1962.

[Sec. 6109(d)]

(d) USE OF SOCIAL SECURITY ACCOUNT NUMBER.—The social security account number issued to an individual for purposes of section 205(c)(2)(A) of the Social Security Act shall, except as shall otherwise be specified under regulations of the Secretary, be used as the identifying number for such individual for purposes of this title.

Amendments

• 1976, Tax Reform Act of 1976 (P.L. 94-455)

P.L. 94-455, §1211(c):

Added Code Sec. 6109(d). **Effective** 10-4-76.

[Sec. 6109(e)—Repealed]

Amendments

• 1996, Small Business Job Protection Act of 1996 (P.L. 104-188)

P.L. 104-188, §1615(a)(2)(A):

Repealed Code Sec. 6109(e). **Effective**, generally, with respect to returns the due date for which (without regard to extensions) is on or after the 30th day after 8-20-96. For a special rule, see Act Sec. 1615(d)(2), below. Prior to repeal, Code Sec. 6109(e) read as follows:

(e) FURNISHING NUMBER FOR DEPENDENTS.—Any taxpayer who claims an exemption under section 151 for any dependent on a return for any taxable year shall include on such return the identifying number (for purposes of this title) of such dependent.

P.L. 104-188, §1615(d)(2), provides:

(2) SPECIAL RULE FOR 1995 AND 1996.—In the case of returns for taxable years beginning in 1995 or 1996, a taxpayer shall not be required by the amendments made by this section to provide a taxpayer identification number for a child who is born after October 31, 1995, in the case of a taxable year beginning in 1995 or November 30, 1996, in the case of a taxable year beginning in 1996.

• 1994, Uruguay Round Agreements Act (P.L. 103-465)

P.L. 103-465, §742(b):

Amended Code Sec. 6109(e). **Effective** for returns for tax years beginning after 12-31-94. For exceptions, see Act Sec. 742(c)(2), below. Prior to amendment, Code Sec. 6109(e) read as follows:

(e) FURNISHING NUMBER FOR CERTAIN DEPENDENTS.—If—

(1) any taxpayer claims an exemption under section 151 for any dependent on a return for any taxable year, and

(2) such dependent has attained the age of 1 year before the close of such taxable year,

such taxpayer shall include on such return the identifying number (for purposes of this title) of such dependent.

P.L. 103-465, §742(c)(2), provides:

(2) EXCEPTION.—The amendments made by this section shall not apply to—

(A) returns for taxable years beginning in 1995 with respect to individuals who are born after October 31, 1995, and

(B) returns for taxable years beginning in 1996 with respect to individuals who are born after November 30, 1996.

• 1990, Omnibus Budget Reconciliation Act of 1990 (P.L. 101-508)

P.L. 101-508, §11112(a):

Amended Code Sec. 6109(e)(2) by striking "2 years" and inserting "1 year". **Effective** for returns for tax years beginning after 12-31-90.

• 1988, Family Support Act of 1988 (P.L. 100-485)

P.L. 100-485, §704(a):

Amended Code Sec. 6109(e)(2) by striking "age of 5" and inserting "age of 2". **Effective** for returns the due date for which (determined without regard to extensions) is after 12-31-89.

• 1986, Tax Reform Act of 1986 (P.L. 99-514)

P.L. 99-514, §1524(a):

Amended Code Sec. 6109 by adding at the end thereof new subsection (e). **Effective** for returns the due date for which (determined without regard to extensions) is after 12-31-87.

[Sec. 6109(f)]

(f) ACCESS TO EMPLOYER IDENTIFICATION NUMBERS BY SECRETARY OF AGRICULTURE FOR PURPOSES OF FOOD AND NUTRITION ACT OF 2008.—

(1) IN GENERAL.—In the administration of section 9 of the Food and Nutrition Act of 2008 (7 U.S.C. 2018) involving the determination of the qualifications of applicants under such Act, the Secretary of Agriculture may, subject to this subsection, require each applicant retail store or wholesale food concern to furnish to the Secretary of Agriculture the employer identification number assigned to the store or concern pursuant to this section. The Secretary of Agriculture shall not have access to any such number for any purpose other than the establishment and maintenance of a list of the names and employer identification numbers of the stores and concerns for use in determining those applicants who have been previously sanctioned or convicted under section 12 or 15 of such Act (7 U.S.C. 2021 or 2024).

(2) SHARING OF INFORMATION AND SAFEGUARDS.—

(A) SHARING OF INFORMATION.—The Secretary of Agriculture may share any information contained in any list referred to in paragraph (1) with any other agency or instrumentality of the United States which otherwise has access to employer identification numbers in accordance with this section or other applicable Federal law, except that the Secretary of Agriculture may share such information only to the extent that such Secretary determines such sharing would assist in verifying and matching such information against information maintained by such other agency or instrumentality. Any such information shared pursuant to this subparagraph may be used by such other agency or instrumentality only for the purpose of effective administration and enforcement of the Food and Nutrition Act of 2008 or for the purpose of investigation of violations of other Federal laws or enforcement of such laws.

(B) SAFEGUARDS.—The Secretary of Agriculture, and the head of any other agency or instrumentality referred to in subparagraph (A), shall restrict, to the satisfaction of the Secretary of the Treasury, access to employer identification numbers obtained pursuant to this subsection only to officers and employees of the United States whose duties or responsibilities require access for the purposes described in subparagraph (A). The Secretary of Agriculture, and the head of any agency or instrumentality with which information is shared pursuant to subparagraph (A), shall provide such other safeguards as the Secretary of the Treasury determines to be necessary or appropriate to protect the confidentiality of the employer identification numbers.

(3) CONFIDENTIALITY AND NONDISCLOSURE RULES.—Employer identification numbers that are obtained or maintained pursuant to this subsection by the Secretary of Agriculture or the head of any agency or instrumentality with which this information is shared pursuant to paragraph (2) shall be confidential, and no officer or employee of the United States who has or had access to the employer identification numbers shall disclose any such employer identification number

obtained thereby in any manner. For purposes of this paragraph, the term "officer or employee" includes a former officer or employee.

(4) SANCTIONS.—Paragraphs (1), (2), and (3) of section 7213(a) shall apply with respect to the unauthorized willful disclosure to any person of employer identification numbers maintained pursuant to this subsection by the Secretary of Agriculture or any agency or instrumentality with which information is shared pursuant to paragraph (2) in the same manner and to the same extent as such paragraphs apply with respect to unauthorized disclosures of return and return information described in such paragraphs. Paragraph (4) of section 7213(a) shall apply with respect to the willful offer of any item of material value in exchange for any such employer identification number in the same manner and to the same extent as such paragraph applies with respect to offers (in exchange for any return or return information) described in such paragraph.

Amendments

• 2018, Tax Technical Corrections Act of 2018 (P.L. 115-141)

P.L. 115-141, §401(a)(276), Div. U:

Amended Code Sec. 6109(f) by striking "OF 1977" following "NUTRITION ACT OF 2008" in the heading thereof. **Effective** 3-23-2018.

• 2008, Food, Conservation, and Energy Act of 2008 (P.L. 110-246)

P.L. 110-246, §4002(b)(1)(B) and (G):

Amended Code Sec. 6109(f) by striking "Food Stamp Act of 1977" each place it appears and inserting "Food and Nutrition Act of 2008"; by striking "FOOD STAMP ACT" [sic] in the heading and inserting "FOOD AND NUTRITION ACT OF 2008". **Effective** 10-1-2008.

• 1994, Social Security Independence and Program Improvements Act of 1994 (P.L. 103-296)

P.L. 103-296, §316(b):

Amended Code Sec. 6109(f) by striking out paragraph (2) and adding a new paragraph (2), by striking out "by the Secretary of Agriculture pursuant to this subsection" and inserting "pursuant to this subsection by the Secretary of Agriculture or the head of any agency or instrumentality with which information is shared pursuant to paragraph (2)", and by striking "social security account numbers" and inserting "employer identification numbers" in paragraph (3); and by striking "by the Secretary of Agriculture pursuant to this subsection" and inserting "pursuant to this subsection by the Secretary of Agriculture or any agency or instrumentality with which information is shared pursuant to paragraph (2)" in paragraph (4). **Effective** 8-15-94. Prior to amendment, Code Sec. 6109(f)(2) read as follows:

(2) SAFEGUARDS.—The Secretary of Agriculture shall restrict, to the satisfaction of the Secretary of the Treasury, access to employer identification numbers obtained pursuant to paragraph (1) only to officers and employees of the United States whose duties or responsibilities require access for the administration or enforcement of the Food Stamp Act of 1977. The Secretary of Agriculture shall provide such other safeguards as the Secretary of the Treasury determines to be necessary or appropriate to protect the confidentiality of the employer identification numbers.

• 1990, Food, Agriculture, Conservation, and Trade Act of 1990 (P.L. 101-624)

P.L. 101-624, §1735(c):

Amended Code Sec. 6109 by adding at the end thereof new subsection (f). **Effective** and implemented the 1st day of the month beginning 120 days after the publication of implementing regulations. Such regulations shall be promulgated not later than 10-1-91.

[Sec. 6109(g)]

(g) ACCESS TO EMPLOYER IDENTIFICATION NUMBERS BY FEDERAL CROP INSURANCE CORPORATION FOR PURPOSES OF THE FEDERAL CROP INSURANCE ACT.—

(1) IN GENERAL.—In the administration of section 506 of the Federal Crop Insurance Act, the Federal Crop Insurance Corporation may require each policyholder and each reinsured company to furnish to the insurer or to the Corporation the employer identification number of such policyholder, subject to the requirements of this paragraph. No officer or employee of the Federal Crop Insurance Corporation, or authorized person shall have access to any such number for any purpose other than the establishment of a system of records necessary to the effective administration of such Act. The Manager of the Corporation may require each policyholder to provide to the Manager or authorized person, at such times and in such manner as prescribed by the Manager, the employer identification number of each entity that holds or acquires a substantial beneficial interest in the policyholder. For purposes of this subclause, the term "substantial beneficial interest" means not less than 5 percent of all beneficial interest in the policyholder. The Secretary of Agriculture shall restrict, to the satisfaction of the Secretary of the Treasury, access to employer identification numbers obtained pursuant to this paragraph only to officers and employees of the United States or authorized persons whose duties or responsibilities require access for the administration of the Federal Crop Insurance Act.

(2) CONFIDENTIALITY AND NONDISCLOSURE RULES.—Employer identification numbers maintained by the Secretary of Agriculture or Federal Crop Insurance Corporation pursuant to this subsection shall be confidential, and except as authorized by this subsection, no officer or employee of the United States or authorized person who has or had access to such employer identification numbers shall disclose any such employer identification number obtained thereby in any manner. For purposes of this paragraph, the term "officer or employee" includes a former officer or employee. For purposes of this subsection, the term "authorized person" means an officer or employee of an insurer whom the Manager of the Corporation designates by rule, subject to appropriate safeguards including a prohibition against the release of such social security account numbers (other than to the Corporations) by such person.

(3) SANCTIONS.—Paragraphs (1), (2), and (3) of section 7213 shall apply with respect to the unauthorized willful disclosure to any person of employer identification numbers maintained by the Secretary of Agriculture or the Federal Crop Insurance Corporation pursuant to this subsection in the same manner and to the same extent as such paragraphs apply with respect to unauthorized disclosures of return and return information described in such paragraphs. Para-

graph (4) of section 7213(a) shall apply with respect to the willful offer of any item of material value in exchange for any such employer identification number in the same manner and to the same extent as such paragraph applies with respect to offers (in exchange for any return or return information) described in such paragraph.

Amendments

• 1996, Small Business Job Protection Act of 1996 (P.L. 104-188)

P.L. 104-188, §1704(t)(42):

Amended Code Sec. 6109 by redesignating subsection (f), as added by section 2201(d) of P.L. 101-624, as subsection (g). **Effective** 8-20-96.

• 1990, Food, Agriculture, Conservation, and Trade Act of 1990 (P.L. 101-624)

P.L. 101-624, §2201(d):

Amended Code Sec. 6109 by adding at the end thereof new subsection (f)[g]. **Effective** 11-28-90.

[Sec. 6109(h)]

(h) IDENTIFYING INFORMATION REQUIRED WITH RESPECT TO CERTAIN SELLER-PROVIDED FINANCING.—

(1) PAYOR.—If any taxpayer claims a deduction under section 163 for qualified residence interest on any seller-provided financing, such taxpayer shall include on the return claiming such deduction the name, address, and TIN of the person to whom such interest is paid or accrued.

(2) RECIPIENT.—If any person receives or accrues interest referred to in paragraph (1), such person shall include on the return for the taxable year in which such interest is so received or accrued the name, address, and TIN of the person liable for such interest.

(3) FURNISHING OF INFORMATION BETWEEN PAYOR AND RECIPIENT.—If any person is required to include the TIN of another person on a return under paragraph (1) or (2), such other person shall furnish his TIN to such person.

(4) SELLER-PROVIDED FINANCING.—For purposes of this subsection, the term "seller-provided financing" means any indebtedness incurred in acquiring any residence if the person to whom such indebtedness is owed is the person from whom such residence was acquired.

Amendments

• 1992, Energy Policy Act of 1992 (P.L. 102-486)

P.L. 102-486, §1933(a):

Amended Code Sec. 6109 by adding at the end thereof new subsection (h). **Effective** for tax years beginning after 12-31-91.

[Sec. 6109(i)]

(i) SPECIAL RULES RELATING TO THE ISSUANCE OF ITINS.—

(1) IN GENERAL.—The Secretary is authorized to issue an individual taxpayer identification number to an individual only if the applicant submits an application, using such form as the Secretary may require and including the required documentation—

(A) in the case of an applicant not described in subparagraph (B)—

(i) in person to an employee of the Internal Revenue Service or a community-based certifying acceptance agent approved by the Secretary, or

(ii) by mail, pursuant to rules prescribed by the Secretary, or

(B) in the case of an applicant who resides outside of the United States, by mail or in person to an employee of the Internal Revenue Service, a community-based certifying acceptance agent approved by the Secretary, or a designee of the Secretary at a United States diplomatic mission or consular post.

(2) REQUIRED DOCUMENTATION.—For purposes of this subsection—

(A) IN GENERAL.—The term "required documentation" includes such documentation as the Secretary may require that proves the individual's identity, foreign status, and residency.

(B) VALIDITY OF DOCUMENTS.—The Secretary may accept only original documents or certified copies meeting the requirements of the Secretary.

(3) TERM OF ITIN.—

(A) IN GENERAL.—An individual taxpayer identification number issued after December 31, 2012, shall remain in effect unless the individual to whom such number is issued does not file a return of tax (or is not included as a dependent on the return of tax of another taxpayer) for 3 consecutive taxable years ending after the issuance of such number. In the case of an individual described in the preceding sentence, such number shall expire on the day after the due date for the return of tax for such third consecutive taxable year.

(B) SPECIAL RULE FOR EXISTING ITINS.—In the case of an individual with respect to whom an individual taxpayer identification number was issued before January 1, 2013, such number shall remain in effect until the earlier of—

(i) the applicable date, or

(ii) if the individual does not file a return of tax (or is not included as a dependent on the return of tax of another taxpayer) for 3 consecutive taxable years at least one of which ends after December 18, 2015, the due date for the return of tax for such third consecutive taxable year.

(C) APPLICABLE DATE.—For purposes of subparagraph (B), the term "applicable date" means—

(i) January 1, 2017, in the case of an individual taxpayer identification number issued before January 1, 2008,

(ii) January 1, 2018, in the case of an individual taxpayer identification number issued in 2008,

(iii) January 1, 2019, in the case of an individual taxpayer identification number issued in 2009 or 2010, and

(iv) January 1, 2020, in the case of an individual taxpayer identification number issued in 2011 or 2012.

(4) DISTINGUISHING ITINS ISSUED SOLELY FOR PURPOSES OF TREATY BENEFITS.—The Secretary shall implement a system that ensures that individual taxpayer identification numbers issued solely for purposes of claiming tax treaty benefits are used only for such purposes, by distinguishing such numbers from other individual taxpayer identification numbers issued.

Amendments

• 2018, Tax Technical Corrections Act of 2018 (P.L. 115-141)

P.L. 115-141, §101(g)(1), Div. U:

Amended Code Sec. 6109(i)(1)(A)(i) by striking "community-based certified acceptance agent" and inserting "community-based certifying acceptance agent". **Effective** as if included in the provision of the Protecting Americans from Tax Hikes Act of 2015 to which it relates [**effective**, except to the extent provided in Code Sec. 6109(i)(3), for applications for individual taxpayer identification numbers made after 12-18-2015.—CCH].

P.L. 115-141, §101(g)(2), Div. U:

Amended Code Sec. 6109(i)(1)(B) by striking "Internal Revenue Service" and inserting "Internal Revenue Service, a community-based certifying acceptance agent approved by the Secretary". **Effective** as if included in the provision of the Protecting Americans from Tax Hikes Act of 2015 to which it relates [**effective**, except to the extent provided in Code Sec. 6109(i)(3), for applications for individual taxpayer identification numbers made after 12-18-2015.—CCH].

P.L. 115-141, §101(g)(3)(A)-(B), Div. U:

Amended Code Sec. 6109(i)(3) in subparagraph (A) by inserting "ending after the issuance of such number" before the period at the end of the first sentence, and by striking "on the last day of such third consecutive taxable year" and inserting "on the day after the due date for the return of tax for such third consecutive taxable year", and by striking subparagraph (B)(ii) and inserting a new clause (ii). **Effective** as if included in the provision of the Protecting Americans from Tax Hikes Act of 2015 to which it relates [**effective**, except to the extent provided in Code Sec. 6109(i)(3), for applications for individual taxpayer identification numbers made after 12-18-2015.—CCH]. Prior to being stricken, Code Sec. 6109(i)(3)(B)(ii) read as follows:

(ii) if the individual does not file a return of tax (or is not included as a dependent on the return of tax of another taxpayer) for 3 consecutive taxable years, the earlier of—

(I) the last day of such third consecutive taxable year, or

(II) the last day of the taxable year that includes the date of the enactment of this subsection.

• 2015, Protecting Americans from Tax Hikes Act of 2015 (P.L. 114-113)

P.L. 114-113, §203(a), Div. Q:

Amended Code Sec. 6109 by adding at the end a new subsection (i). **Effective**, except to the extent provided in Code Sec. 6109(i)(3), for applications for individual taxpayer identification numbers made after 12-18-2015 [**effective** date changed by P.L. 115-141, § 101(g)(5), Div. U.—CCH].

[Sec. 6110]

SEC. 6110. PUBLIC INSPECTION OF WRITTEN DETERMINATIONS.

[Sec. 6110(a)]

(a) GENERAL RULE.—Except as otherwise provided in this section, the text of any written determination and any background file document relating to such written determination shall be open to public inspection at such place as the Secretary may by regulations prescribe.

[Sec. 6110(b)]

(b) DEFINITIONS.—For purposes of this section—

(1) WRITTEN DETERMINATION.—

(A) IN GENERAL.—The term "written determination" means a ruling, determination letter, technical advice memorandum, or Chief Counsel advice.

(B) EXCEPTIONS.—Such term shall not include any matter referred to in subparagraph (C) or (D) of section 6103(b)(2).

(2) BACKGROUND FILE DOCUMENT.—The term "background file document" with respect to a written determination includes the request for that written determination, any written material submitted in support of the request, and any communication (written or otherwise) between the Internal Revenue Service and persons outside the Internal Revenue Service in connection with such written determination (other than any communication between the Department of Justice and the Internal Revenue Service relating to a pending civil or criminal case or investigation) received before issuance of the written determination.

(3) REFERENCE AND GENERAL WRITTEN DETERMINATIONS.—

(A) REFERENCE WRITTEN DETERMINATION.—The term "reference written determination" means any written determination which has been determined by the Secretary to have significant reference value.

(B) GENERAL WRITTEN DETERMINATION.—The term "general written determination" means any written determination other than a reference written determination.

Amendments

• 2000, Community Renewal Tax Relief Act of 2000 (P.L. 106-554)

P.L. 106-554, §304(c)(1):

Amended Code Sec. 6110(b)(1). **Effective** 12-21-2000. Prior to amendment, Code Sec. 6110(b)(1) read as follows:

(1) WRITTEN DETERMINATION.—The term "written determination" means a ruling, determination letter, technical advice memorandum, or Chief Counsel advice. Such term shall not include any advance pricing agreement entered into by a taxpayer and the Secretary and any background information related to such agreement or any application for an advance pricing agreement.

• 1999, Tax Relief Extension Act of 1999 (P.L. 106-170)

P.L. 106-170, §521(a)(2):

Amended Code Sec. 6110(b)(1) by adding at the end a new sentence. **Effective** 12-17-99.

P.L. 106-170, §521(c), provides:

(c) REGULATIONS.—The Secretary of the Treasury or the Secretary's delegate shall prescribe such regulations as may be necessary or appropriate to carry out the purposes of section 6103(b)(2)(C), and the last sentence of section 6110(b)(1), of the Internal Revenue Code of 1986, as added by this section.

• 1998, IRS Restructuring and Reform Act of 1998 (P.L. 105-206)

P.L. 105-206, §3509(a):

Amended Code Sec. 6110(b)(1) by striking "or technical advice memorandum" and inserting "technical advice memorandum, or Chief Counsel advice". **Effective** for any Chief Counsel advice issued more than 90 days after 7-22-98. For transition rules, see Act Sec. 3509(d)(2)-(4), below.

P.L. 105-206, §3509(d)(2)-(4), provides:

(2) TRANSITION RULES.—The amendments made by this section shall apply to any Chief Counsel advice issued after December 31, 1985, and before the 91st day after the date of the enactment of this Act by the offices of the associate chief counsel for domestic, employee benefits and exempt organizations, and international, except that any such Chief Counsel advice shall be treated as made available on a timely basis if such advice is made available for public inspection not later than the following dates:

(A) One year after the date of the enactment of this Act, in the case of all litigation guideline memoranda, service center advice, tax litigation bulletins, criminal tax bulletins, and general litigation bulletins.

(B) Eighteen months after such date of enactment, in the case of field service advice and technical assistance to the field issued on or after January 1, 1994.

(C) Three years after such date of enactment, in the case of field service advice and technical assistance to the field issued on or after January 1, 1992, and before January 1, 1994.

(D) Six years after such date of enactment, in the case of any other Chief Counsel advice issued after December 31, 1985.

(3) DOCUMENTS TREATED AS CHIEF COUNSEL ADVICE.—If the Secretary of the Treasury by regulation provides pursuant to section 6110(i)(2) of the Internal Revenue Code of 1986, as added by this section, that any additional advice or instruction issued by the Office of Chief Counsel shall be treated as Chief Counsel advice, such additional advice or instruction shall be made available for public inspection pursuant to section 6110 of such Code, as amended by this section, only in accordance with the effective date set forth in such regulation.

(4) CHIEF COUNSEL ADVICE TO BE AVAILABLE ELECTRONICALLY.—The Internal Revenue Service shall make any Chief Counsel advice issued more than 90 days after the date of the enactment of this Act and made available for public inspection pursuant to section 6110 of such Code, as amended by this section, also available by computer telecommunications within 1 year after issuance.

[Sec. 6110(c)]

(c) EXEMPTIONS FROM DISCLOSURE.—Before making any written determination or background file document open or available to public inspection under subsection (a), the Secretary shall delete—

(1) the names, addresses, and other identifying details of the person to whom the written determination pertains and of any other person, other than a person with respect to whom a notation is made under subsection (d)(1), identified in the written determination or any background file document;

(2) information specifically authorized under criteria established by an Executive order to be kept secret in the interest of national defense or foreign policy, and which is in fact properly classified pursuant to such Executive order;

(3) information specifically exempted from disclosure by any statute (other than this title) which is applicable to the Internal Revenue Service;

(4) trade secrets and commercial or financial information obtained from a person and privileged or confidential;

(5) information the disclosure of which would constitute a clearly unwarranted invasion of personal privacy;

(6) information contained in or related to examination, operating, or condition reports prepared by, or on behalf of, or for use of an agency responsible for the regulation or supervision of financial institutions; and

(7) geological and geophysical information and data, including maps, concerning wells.

The Secretary shall determine the appropriate extent of such deletions and, except in the case of intentional or willful disregard of this subsection, shall not be required to make such deletions (nor be liable for failure to make deletions) unless the Secretary has agreed to such deletions or has been ordered by a court (in a proceeding under subsection (f)(3)) to make such deletions.

[Sec. 6110(d)]

(d) PROCEDURES WITH REGARD TO THIRD PARTY CONTACTS.—

(1) NOTATIONS.—If, before the issuance of a written determination, the Internal Revenue Service receives any communication (written or otherwise) concerning such written determination, any request for such determination, or any other matter involving such written determination from a person other than an employee of the Internal Revenue Service or the person to whom such written determination pertains (or his authorized representative with regard to such written determination), the Internal Revenue Service shall indicate, on the written determination

open to public inspection, the category of the person making such communication and the date of such communication.

(2) EXCEPTION.—Paragraph (1) shall not apply to any communication made by the Chief of Staff of the Joint Committee on Taxation.

(3) DISCLOSURE OF IDENTITY.—In the case of any written determination to which paragraph (1) applies, any person may file a petition in the United States Tax Court or file a complaint in the United States District Court for the District of Columbia for an order requiring that the identity of any person to whom the written determination pertains be disclosed. The court shall order disclosure of such identity if there is evidence in the record from which one could reasonably conclude that an impropriety occurred or undue influence was exercised with respect to such written determination by or on behalf of such person. The court may also direct the Secretary to disclose any portion of any other deletions made in accordance with subsection (c) where such disclosure is in the public interest. If a proceeding is commenced under this paragraph, the person whose identity is subject to being disclosed and the person about whom a notation is made under paragraph (1) shall be notified of the proceeding in accordance with the procedures described in subsection (f)(4)(B) and shall have the right to intervene in the proceeding (anonymously, if appropriate).

(4) PERIOD IN WHICH TO BRING ACTION.—No proceeding shall be commenced under paragraph (3) unless a petition is filed before the expiration of 36 months after the first day that the written determination is open to public inspection.

[Sec. 6110(e)]

(e) BACKGROUND FILE DOCUMENTS.—Whenever the Secretary makes a written determination open to public inspection under this section, he shall also make available to any person, but only upon the written request of that person, any background file document relating to the written determination.

[Sec. 6110(f)]

(f) RESOLUTION OF DISPUTES RELATING TO DISCLOSURE.—

(1) NOTICE OF INTENTION TO DISCLOSE.—Except as otherwise provided by subsection (i), the Secretary shall upon issuance of any written determination, or upon receipt of a request for a background file document, mail a notice of intention to disclose such determination or document to any person to whom the written determination pertains (or a successor in interest, executor, or other person authorized by law to act for or on behalf of such person).

(2) ADMINISTRATIVE REMEDIES.—The Secretary shall prescribe regulations establishing administrative remedies with respect to—

(A) requests for additional disclosure of any written determination or any background file document, and

(B) requests to restrain disclosure.

(3) ACTION TO RESTRAIN DISCLOSURE.—

(A) CREATION OF REMEDY.—Any person—

(i) to whom a written determination pertains (or a successor in interest, executor, or other person authorized by law to act for or on behalf of such person), or who has a direct interest in maintaining the confidentiality of any such written determination or background file document (or portion thereof),

(ii) who disagrees with any failure to make a deletion with respect to that portion of any written determination or any background file document which is to be open or available to public inspection, and

(iii) who has exhausted his administrative remedies as prescribed pursuant to paragraph (2),

may, within 60 days after the mailing by the Secretary of a notice of intention to disclose any written determination or background file document under paragraph (1), together with the proposed deletions, file a petition in the United States Tax Court (anonymously, if appropriate) for a determination with respect to that portion of such written determination or background file document which is to be open to public inspection.

(B) NOTICE TO CERTAIN PERSONS.—The Secretary shall notify any person to whom a written determination pertains (unless such person is the petitioner) of the filing of a petition under this paragraph with respect to such written determination or related background file document, and any such person may intervene (anonymously, if appropriate) in any proceeding conducted pursuant to this paragraph. The Secretary shall send such notice by registered or certified mail to the last known address of such person within 15 days after such petition is served on the Secretary. No person who has received such a notice may thereafter file any petition under this paragraph with respect to such written determination or background file document with respect to which such notice was received.

(4) ACTION TO OBTAIN ADDITIONAL DISCLOSURE.—

(A) CREATION OF REMEDY.—Any person who has exhausted the administrative remedies prescribed pursuant to paragraph (2) with respect to a request for disclosure may file a petition in the United States Tax Court or a complaint in the United States District Court for the District of Columbia for an order requiring that any written determination or background file document (or portion thereof) be made open or available to public inspection. Except where inconsistent with subparagraph (B), the provisions of subparagraphs (C), (D), (E), (F), and (G) of section 552(a)(4) of title 5, United States Code, shall apply to any proceeding under this paragraph. The Court shall examine the matter de novo and without regard to a decision of a court under paragraph (3) with respect to such written determination or background file document, and may examine the entire text of such written determination or background file document in order to determine whether such written determination or background file document or any part thereof shall be open or available to public inspection under this section. The burden of proof with respect to the issue of disclosure of any information shall be on the Secretary and any other person seeking to restrain disclosure.

(B) INTERVENTION.—If a proceeding is commenced under this paragraph with respect to any written determination or background file document, the Secretary shall, within 15 days after notice of the petition filed under subparagraph (A) is served on him, send notice of the commencement of such proceeding to all persons who are identified by name and address in such written determination or background file document. The Secretary shall send such notice by registered or certified mail to the last known address of such person. Any person to whom such determination or background file document pertains may intervene in the proceeding (anonymously, if appropriate). If such notice is sent, the Secretary shall not be required to defend the action and shall not be liable for public disclosure of the written determination or background file document (or any portion thereof) in accordance with the final decision of the court.

(5) EXPEDITION OF DETERMINATION.—The Tax Court shall make a decision with respect to any petition described in paragraph (3) at the earliest practicable date.

(6) PUBLICITY OF TAX COURT PROCEEDINGS.—Notwithstanding sections 7458 and 7461, the Tax Court may, in order to preserve the anonymity, privacy, or confidentiality of any person under this section, provide by rules adopted under section 7453 that portions of hearings, testimony, evidence, and reports in connection with proceedings under this section may be closed to the public or to inspection by the public.

Amendments

• 1998, IRS Restructuring and Reform Act of 1998 (P.L. 105-206)

P.L. 105-206, §3509(c)(1):

Amended Code Sec. 6110(f)(1) by striking "The Secretary" and inserting "Except as otherwise provided by subsection (i), the Secretary". **Effective** for any Chief Counsel advice issued more than 90 days after 7-22-98. For transition rules, see Act Sec. 3509(d)(2)-(4) under the amendment notes to subsection (b), above.

• 1984 (P.L. 98-620)

P.L. 98-620, §402(28)(B):

Amended Code Sec. 6110(f)(5) by striking out "and the Court of Appeals shall expedite any review of such decision in every way possible". **Not effective** for cases pending on 11-8-84.

[Sec. 6110(g)]

(g) TIME FOR DISCLOSURE.—

(1) IN GENERAL.—Except as otherwise provided in this section, the text of any written determination or any background file document (as modified under subsection (c)) shall be open or available to public inspection—

(A) no earlier than 75 days, and no later than 90 days, after the notice provided in subsection (f)(1) is mailed, or, if later,

(B) within 30 days after the date on which a court decision under subsection (f)(3) becomes final.

(2) POSTPONEMENT BY ORDER OF COURT.—The court may extend the period referred to in paragraph (1)(B) for such time as the court finds necessary to allow the Secretary to comply with its decision.

(3) POSTPONEMENT OF DISCLOSURE FOR UP TO 90 DAYS.—At the written request of the person by whom or on whose behalf the request for the written determination was made, the period referred to in paragraph (1)(A) shall be extended (for not to exceed an additional 90 days) until the day which is 15 days after the date of the Secretary's determination that the transaction set forth in the written determination has been completed.

(4) ADDITIONAL 180 DAYS.—If—

(A) the transaction set forth in the written determination is not completed during the period set forth in paragraph (3), and

(B) the person by whom or on whose behalf the request for the written determination was made establishes to the satisfaction of the Secretary that good cause exists for additional delay in opening the written determination to public inspection,

the period referred to in paragraph (3) shall be further extended (for not to exceed an additional 180 days) until the day which is 15 days after the date of the Secretary's determination that the transaction set forth in the written determination has been completed.

(5) SPECIAL RULES FOR CERTAIN WRITTEN DETERMINATIONS, ETC.—Notwithstanding the provisions of paragraph (1), the Secretary shall not be required to make available to the public—

(A) any technical advice memorandum, any Chief Counsel advice, and any related background file document involving any matter which is the subject of a civil fraud or criminal investigation or jeopardy or termination assessment until after any action relating to such investigation or assessment is completed, or

(B) any general written determination and any related background file document that relates solely to approval of the Secretary of any adoption or change of—

(i) the funding method or plan year of a plan under section 412,

(ii) a taxpayer's annual accounting period under section 442,

(iii) a taxpayer's method of accounting under section 446(e), or

(iv) a partnership's or partner's taxable year under section 706,

but the Secretary shall make any such written determination and related background file document available upon the written request of any person after the date on which (except for this subparagraph) such determination would be open to public inspection.

Amendments

• 2000, Community Renewal Tax Relief Act of 2000 (P.L. 106-554)

P.L. 106-554, §313(e):

Amended Code Sec. 6110(g)(5)(A) by inserting ", any Chief Counsel advice," after "technical advice memorandum". **Effective** as if included in the provision of P.L. 105-206 to which it relates **[effective** for Chief Counsel advice issued after 10-20-98, generally.—CCH].

[Sec. 6110(h)]

(h) DISCLOSURE OF PRIOR WRITTEN DETERMINATIONS AND RELATED BACKGROUND FILE DOCUMENTS.—

(1) IN GENERAL.—Except as otherwise provided in this subsection, a written determination issued pursuant to a request made before November 1, 1976, and any background file document relating to such written determination shall be open or available to public inspection in accordance with this section.

(2) TIME FOR DISCLOSURE.—In the case of any written determination or background file document which is to be made open or available to public inspection under paragraph (1)—

(A) subsection (g) shall not apply, but

(B) such written determination or background file document shall be made open or available to public inspection at the earliest practicable date after funds for that purpose have been appropriated and made available to the Internal Revenue Service.

(3) ORDER OF RELEASE.—Any written determination or background file document described in paragraph (1) shall be open or available to public inspection in the following order starting with the most recent written determination in each category:

(A) reference written determinations issued under this title;

(B) general written determinations issued after July 4, 1967; and

(C) reference written determinations issued under the Internal Revenue Code of 1939 or corresponding provisions of prior law.

General written determinations not described in subparagraph (B) shall be open to public inspection on written request, but not until after the written determinations referred to in subparagraphs (A), (B), and (C) are open to public inspection.

(4) NOTICE THAT PRIOR WRITTEN DETERMINATIONS ARE OPEN TO PUBLIC INSPECTION.—Notwithstanding the provisions of subsections (f)(1) and (f)(3)(A), not less than 90 days before making any portion of a written determination described in this subsection open to public inspection, the Secretary shall issue public notice in the Federal Register that such written determination is to be made open to public inspection. The person who received a written determination may, within 75 days after the date of publication of notice under this paragraph, file a petition in the United States Tax Court (anonymously, if appropriate) for a determination with respect to that portion of such written determination which is to be made open to public inspection. The provisions of subsections (f)(3)(B), (5), and (6) shall apply if such a petition is filed. If no petition is filed, the text of any written determination shall be open to public inspection no earlier than 90 days, and no later than 120 days, after notice is published in the Federal Register.

(5) EXCLUSION.—Subsection (d) shall not apply to any written determination described in paragraph (1).

Amendments

• 1976, Tax Reform Act of 1976 (P.L. 94-455)

P.L. 94-455, §1201(b), provides:

(b) EFFECT UPON PENDING REQUESTS.—Any written determination or background file document which is the subject of a judicial proceeding pursuant to section 552 of title 5, United States Code, commenced before January 1, 1976, shall not be treated as a written determination subject to subsection (h)(1), but shall be available to the complainant along with the background file document, if requested, as soon as practicable after July 1, 1976.

[Sec. 6110(i)]

(i) SPECIAL RULES FOR DISCLOSURE OF CHIEF COUNSEL ADVICE.—

(1) CHIEF COUNSEL ADVICE DEFINED.—

(A) IN GENERAL.—For purposes of this section, the term "Chief Counsel advice" means written advice or instruction, under whatever name or designation, prepared by any national office component of the Office of Chief Counsel which—

(i) is issued to field or service center employees of the Service or regional or district employees of the Office of Chief Counsel; and

(ii) conveys—

(I) any legal interpretation of a revenue provision;

(II) any Internal Revenue Service or Office of Chief Counsel position or policy concerning a revenue provision; or

(III) any legal interpretation of State law, foreign law, or other Federal law relating to the assessment or collection of any liability under a revenue provision.

(B) REVENUE PROVISION DEFINED.—For purposes of subparagraph (A), the term "revenue provision" means any existing or former internal revenue law, regulation, revenue ruling, revenue procedure, other published or unpublished guidance, or tax treaty, either in general or as applied to specific taxpayers or groups of specific taxpayers.

(2) ADDITIONAL DOCUMENTS TREATED AS CHIEF COUNSEL ADVICE.—The Secretary may by regulation provide that this section shall apply to any advice or instruction prepared and issued by the Office of Chief Counsel which is not described in paragraph (1).

(3) DELETIONS FOR CHIEF COUNSEL ADVICE.—In the case of Chief Counsel advice and related background file documents open to public inspection pursuant to this section—

(A) paragraphs (2) through (7) of subsection (c) shall not apply, but

(B) the Secretary may make deletions of material in accordance with subsections (b) and (c) of section 552 of title 5, United States Code, except that in applying subsection (b)(3) of such section, no statutory provision of this title shall be taken into account.

(4) NOTICE OF INTENTION TO DISCLOSE.—

(A) NONTAXPAYER-SPECIFIC CHIEF COUNSEL ADVICE.—In the case of Chief Counsel advice which is written without reference to a specific taxpayer or group of specific taxpayers—

(i) subsection (f)(1) shall not apply; and

(ii) the Secretary shall, within 60 days after the issuance of the Chief Counsel advice, complete any deletions described in subsection (c)(1) or paragraph (3) and make the Chief Counsel advice, as so edited, open for public inspection.

(B) TAXPAYER-SPECIFIC CHIEF COUNSEL ADVICE.—In the case of Chief Counsel advice which is written with respect to a specific taxpayer or group of specific taxpayers, the Secretary shall, within 60 days after the issuance of the Chief Counsel advice, mail the notice required by subsection (f)(1) to each such taxpayer. The notice shall include a copy of the Chief Counsel advice on which is indicated the information that the Secretary proposes to delete pursuant to subsection (c)(1). The Secretary may also delete from the copy of the text of the Chief Counsel advice any of the information described in paragraph (3), and shall delete the names, addresses, and other identifying details of taxpayers other than the person to whom the advice pertains, except that the Secretary shall not delete from the copy of the Chief Counsel advice that is furnished to the taxpayer any information of which that taxpayer was the source.

Amendments

• 2007, Tax Technical Corrections Act of 2007 (P.L. 110-172)

P.L. 110-172, §10(a):

Amended Code Sec. 6110(i)(3) by inserting "and related background file documents" after "Chief Counsel advice" in the matter preceding subparagraph (A). **Effective** as if included in the provision of the Internal Revenue Service Restructuring and Reform Act of 1998 (P.L. 105-206) to which it relates [**effective** generally for any Chief Counsel advice issued more than 90 days after 7-22-98. For transition rules, see P.L. 105-206, §3509(d)(2)-(4), in the amendment notes for Code Sec. 6110(b).—CCH].

• 1998, IRS Restructuring and Reform Act of 1998 (P.L. 105-206)

P.L. 105-206, §3509(b):

Amended Code Sec. 6110 by redesignating subsections (i), (j), (k), and (l) as subsections (j), (k), (l), and (m), respectively, and by inserting after subsection (h) a new subsection (i). **Effective** for any Chief Counsel advice issued more than 90 days after 7-22-98. For transition rules, see Act Sec. 3509(d)(2)-(4) in the amendment notes to Code Sec. 6110(b).

[Sec. 6110(j)]

(j) CIVIL REMEDIES.—

(1) CIVIL ACTION.—Whenever the Secretary—

(A) fails to make deletions required in accordance with subsection (c), or

(B) fails to follow the procedures in subsection (g) or (i)(4)(B), the recipient of the written determination or any person identified in the written determination shall have as an exclusive civil remedy an action against the Secretary in the United States Court of Federal Claims, which shall have jurisdiction to hear any action under this paragraph.

(2) DAMAGES.—In any suit brought under the provisions of paragraph (1)(A) in which the Court determines that an employee of the Internal Revenue Service intentionally or willfully failed to delete in accordance with subsection (c), or in any suit brought under subparagraph (1)(B) in which the Court determines that an employee intentionally or willfully failed to act in accordance with subsection (g) or (i)(4)(B), the United States shall be liable to the person in an amount equal to the sum of—

(A) actual damages sustained by the person but in no case shall a person be entitled to receive less than the sum of $1,000, and

(B) the costs of the action together with reasonable attorney's fees as determined by the Court.

Amendments

• 2018, Tax Technical Corrections Act of 2018 (P.L. 115-141)

P.L. 115-141, §401(a)(325)(A), Div. U:

Amended Code Sec. 6110(j)(1)(B) by striking "United States Claims Court" and inserting "United States Court of Federal Claims". [Note: Code Sec. 6110(j)(1)(B) does not contain the text "United States Claims Court". Therefore, this amendment cannot be made.—CCH] **Effective** 3-23-2018.

• 1998, IRS Restructuring and Reform Act of 1998 (P.L. 105-206)

P.L. 105-206, §3509(b):

Amended Code Sec. 6110 by redesignating subsection (i) as subsection (j). **Effective** for any Chief Counsel advice issued more than 90 days after 7-22-98. For transition rules, see Act Sec. 3509(d)(2)-(4) in the amendment notes to subsection (b).

P.L. 105-206, §3509(c)(2):

Amended Code Sec. 6110(j)(1)(B) and (2), as redesignated, by striking " subsection (g)" each place it appears and inserting "subsection (g) or (i)(4)(B)". **Effective** for any Chief Counsel advice issued more than 90 days after 7-22-98. For transition rules, see Act Sec. 3509(d)(2)-(4) in the amendment notes to Code Sec. 6110(b).

• 1992, Court of Federal Claims Technical and Procedural Improvements Act of 1992 (P.L. 102-572)

P.L. 102-572, §902(b)(1):

Amended Code Sec. 6110(j)(1)(B) by striking "United States Claims Court" and inserting "United States Court of Federal Claims". **Effective** 10-29-92.

• 1982, Federal Courts Improvement Act of 1982 (P.L. 97-164)

P.L. 97-164, §160(a)(9):

Amended Code Sec. 6110(i)(1) by striking out "Court of Claims" and inserting in lieu thereof "United States Claims Court". **Effective** 10-1-82.

P.L. 97-164, §403, provides:

SEC. 403. (a) Any case pending before the Court of Claims on the effective date of this Act in which a report on the merits has been filed by a commissioner, or in which there is pending a request for review, and upon which the court has not acted, shall be transferred to the United States Court of Appeals for the Federal Circuit.

(b) Any matter pending before the United States Court of Customs and Patent Appeals on the effective date of this Act shall be transferred to the United States Court of Appeals for the Federal Circuit.

(c) Any petition for rehearing, reconsideration, alteration, modification, or other change in any decision of the United States Court of Claims or the United States Court of Customs and Patent Appeals rendered prior to the effective date of this Act that has not been determined by either of those courts on that date, or that is filed after that date, shall be determined by the United States Court of Appeals for the Federal Circuit.

(d) Any matter pending before a commissioner of the United States Court of Claims on the effective date of this Act, or any pending dispositive motion that the United States Court of Claims has not determined on that date, shall be determined by the United States Claims Court.

(e) Any case in which a notice of appeal has been filed in a district court of the United States prior to the effective date of this Act shall be decided by the court of appeals to which the appeal was taken.

[Sec. 6110(k)]

(k) SPECIAL PROVISIONS.—

(1) FEES.—The Secretary is authorized to assess actual costs—

(A) for duplication of any written determination or background file document made open or available to the public under this section, and

(B) incurred in searching for and making deletions required under subsection (c)(1) or (i)(3) from any written determination or background file document which is available to public inspection only upon written request.

The Secretary shall furnish any written determination or background file document without charge or at a reduced charge if he determines that waiver or reduction of the fee is in the public interest because furnishing such determination or background file document can be considered as primarily benefiting the general public.

(2) RECORDS DISPOSAL PROCEDURES.—Nothing in this section shall prevent the Secretary from disposing of any general written determination or background file document described in subsection (b) in accordance with established records disposition procedures, but such disposal shall, except as provided in the following sentence, occur not earlier than 3 years after such written determination is first made open to public inspection. In the case of any general written determination described in subsection (h), the Secretary may dispose of such determination and any related background file document in accordance with such procedures but such disposal shall not occur earlier than 3 years after such written determination is first made open to public inspection if funds are appropriated for such purpose before January 20, 1979, or not earlier than January 20, 1979, if funds are not appropriated before such date. The Secretary shall not dispose of any reference written determinations and related background file documents.

(3) PRECEDENTIAL STATUS.—Unless the Secretary otherwise establishes by regulations, a written determination may not be used or cited as precedent. The preceding sentence shall not apply to change the precedential status (if any) of written determinations with regard to taxes imposed by subtitle D of this title.

Amendments

• 1998, IRS Restructuring and Reform Act of 1998 (P.L. 105-206)

P.L. 105-206, §3509(b):

Amended Code Sec. 6110 by redesignating subsection (j) as subsection (k). **Effective** for any Chief Counsel advice issued more than 90 days after 7-22-98. For transition rules, see Act Sec. 3509(d)(2)-(4) in the amendment notes to Code Sec. 6110(b).

P.L. 105-206, §3509(c)(3):

Amended Code Sec. 6110(k)(1)(B), as redesignated, by striking "subsection (c)" and inserting "subsection (c)(1) or (i)(3)". **Effective** for any Chief Counsel advice issued more than 90 days after 7-22-98. For transition rules, see Act Sec. 3509(d)(2)-(4) in the amendment notes to Code Sec. 6110(b).

[Sec. 6110(l)]

(l) SECTION NOT TO APPLY.—This section shall not apply to—

(1) any matter to which section 6104 or 6105 applies, or

(2) any—

(A) written determination issued pursuant to a request made before November 1, 1976, with respect to the exempt status under section 501(a) of an organization described in section 501(c) or (d), the status of an organization as a private foundation under section 509(a), or the status of an organization as an operating foundation under section 4942(j)(3),

(B) written determination described in subsection (g)(5)(B) issued pursuant to a request made before November 1, 1976,

(C) determination letter not otherwise described in subparagraph (A), (B), or (E) issued pursuant to a request made before November 1, 1976,

(D) background file document relating to any general written determination issued before July 5, 1967, or

(E) letter or other document described in section 6104(a)(1)(B)(iv) issued before September 2, 1974.

Amendments

• 2000, Community Renewal Tax Relief Act of 2000 (P.L. 106-554)

P.L. 106-554, §304(c)(2):

Amended Code Sec. 6110(l)(1) by inserting "or 6105" after "6104". **Effective** 12-21-2000.

• 1998, IRS Restructuring and Reform Act of 1998 (P.L. 105-206)

P.L. 105-206, §3509(b):

Amended Code Sec. 6110 by redesignating subsection (k) as subsection (l). **Effective** for any Chief Counsel Advice issued more than 90 days after 7-22-98. For transition rules, see Act Sec. 3509(d)(2)-(4) in the amendment notes to Code Sec. 6110(b).

[Sec. 6110(m)]

(m) EXCLUSIVE REMEDY.—Except as otherwise provided in this title, or with respect to a discovery order made in connection with a judicial proceeding, the Secretary shall not be required by any Court to make any written determination or background file document open or available to public inspection, or to refrain from disclosure of any such documents.

Amendments

• 1998, IRS Restructuring and Reform Act of 1998 (P.L. 105-206)

P.L. 105-206, §3509(b):

Amended Code Sec. 6110 by redesignating subsection (l) as subsection (m). **Effective** for any Chief Counsel advice issued more than 90 days after 7-22-98. For transition rules, see Act Sec. 3509(d)(2)-(4) in the amendment notes to Code Sec. 6110(b).

• 1976, Tax Reform Act of 1976 (P.L. 94-455)

P.L. 94-455, §1201(a):

Added Code Sec 6110. **Effective** 11-1-76.

* * *

[Sec. 6114]

SEC. 6114. TREATY-BASED RETURN POSITIONS.

[Sec. 6114(a)]

(a) IN GENERAL.—Each taxpayer who, with respect to any tax imposed by this title, takes the position that a treaty of the United States overrules (or otherwise modifies) an internal revenue law of the United States shall disclose (in such manner as the Secretary may prescribe) such position—

(1) on the return of tax for such tax (or any statement attached to such return), or

(2) if no return of tax is required to be filed, in such form as the Secretary may prescribe.

[Sec. 6114(b)]

(b) WAIVER AUTHORITY.—The Secretary may waive the requirements of subsection (a) with respect to classes of cases for which the Secretary determines that the waiver will not impede the assessment and collection of tax.

Amendments

• 1990, Omnibus Budget Reconciliation Act of 1990 (P.L. 101-508)

P.L. 101-508, §11702(c):

Amended Code Sec. 6114(b) by striking "by regulations" after "the Secretary may". **Effective** as if included in the provision of P.L. 101-647 to which it relates.

* * *

CHAPTER 62—TIME AND PLACE FOR PAYING TAX

Subchapter A—Place and Due Date for Payment of Tax

[Sec. 6151]

SEC. 6151. TIME AND PLACE FOR PAYING TAX SHOWN ON RETURNS.

[Sec. 6151(a)]

(a) GENERAL RULE.—Except as otherwise provided in this subchapter, when a return of tax is required under this title or regulations, the person required to make such return shall, without assessment or notice and demand from the Secretary, pay such tax to the internal revenue officer with whom the return is filed, and shall pay such tax at the time and place fixed for filing the return (determined without regard to any extension of time for filing the return).

Amendments

• 1976, Tax Reform Act of 1976 (P.L. 94-455)

P.L. 94-455, §1906(b)(13)(A):

Amended 1954 Code by substituting "Secretary" for "Secretary or his delegate" each place it appeared. **Effective** 2-1-77.

• 1976, Bank Holding Company Tax Act of 1976 (P.L. 94-452)

P.L. 94-452, §3(c)(2):

Amended Code Sec. 6151(a) by substituting "subchapter" for "section". **Effective** 10-1-77, with respect to sales after 7-7-70, in tax years ending after 7-7-70, but only in the case of qualified bank holding corporations.

• 1966 (P.L. 89-713)

P.L. 89-713, §1(b):

Amended Code Sec. 6151(a) by substituting "to the internal revenue officer with whom the return is filed" for "to the principal internal revenue officer for the internal revenue district in which the return is required to be filed". **Effective** 11-2-66.

[Sec. 6151(b)]

(b) EXCEPTIONS.—

(1) INCOME TAX NOT COMPUTED BY TAXPAYER.—If the taxpayer elects under section 6014 not to show the tax on the return, the amount determined by the Secretary as payable shall be paid within 30 days after the mailing by the Secretary to the taxpayer of a notice stating such amount and making demand therefor.

(2) USE OF GOVERNMENT DEPOSITARIES.—For authority of the Secretary to require payments to Government depositaries, see section 6302(c).

Amendments

• 1976, Tax Reform Act of 1976 (P.L. 94-455)

P.L. 94-455, §1906(b)(13)(A):

Amended 1954 Code by substituting "Secretary" for "Secretary or his delegate" each place it appeared. **Effective** 2-1-77.

[Sec. 6151(c)]

(c) DATE FIXED FOR PAYMENT OF TAX.—In any case in which a tax is required to be paid on or before a certain date, or within a certain period, any reference in this title to the date fixed for payment of such tax shall be deemed a reference to the last day fixed for such payment (determined without regard to any extension of time for paying the tax).

[Sec. 6152—Repealed]

Amendments

• 1986, Tax Reform Act of 1986 (P.L. 99-514)

P.L. 99-514, §1404(c)(1):

Repealed Code Sec. 6152. **Effective** for tax years beginning after 12-31-86. Reproduced immediately below is text of Code Sec. 6152 prior to repeal.

SEC. 6152. INSTALLMENT PAYMENTS.

[Sec. 6152(a)]

(a) PRIVILEGE TO ELECT TO MAKE FOUR INSTALLMENT PAYMENTS BY DECEDENT'S ESTATE.—A decedent's estate subject to the tax imposed by chapter 1 may elect to pay such tax in four equal installments.

Amendments

• **1982, Tax Equity and Fiscal Responsibility Act of 1982 (P.L. 97-248)**

P.L. 97-248, §234(b)(1):

Amended Code Sec. 6152(a). **Effective** for tax years beginning after 12-31-82. Prior to amendment, Code Sec. 6152(a) read as follows:

(a) PRIVILEGE TO ELECT TO MAKE INSTALLMENT PAYMENTS.—

(1) CORPORATIONS.—A corporation subject to the taxes imposed by Chapter 1 may elect to pay the unpaid amount of such taxes in two equal installments.

(2) ESTATES OF DECEDENTS.—A decedent's estate subject to the tax imposed by chapter 1 may elect to pay such tax in four equal installments.

• **1976, Tax Reform Act of 1976 (P.L. 94-455)**

P.L. 94-455, §1906(a)(9):

Amended Code Sec. 6152(a)(1). **Effective** 2-1-77. Prior to amendment, Code Sec. 6152(a)(1) read as follows:

(1) CORPORATIONS.—A corporation subject to the taxes imposed by chapter 1 may elect to pay the unpaid amount of such taxes in installments as follows:

(A) with respect to taxable years ending before December 31, 1954, four installments, the first two of which shall be 45 percent, respectively, of such taxes and the last two of which shall be 5 percent, respectively, of such taxes;

(B) with respect to taxable years ending on or after December 31, 1954, two equal installments.

• **1954 (P.L. 767, 83rd Cong.)**

P.L. 767, 83rd Cong., §3:

Repealed Sec. 6152(a)(3). **Effective** with respect to tax years beginning after 1954. Prior to repeal, Code Sec. 6152(a)(3) read as follows:

(3) EMPLOYERS SUBJECT TO UNEMPLOYMENT TAX.—An employer subject to the tax imposed by section 3301 may elect to pay such tax in four equal installments.

[Sec. 6152(b)]

(b) DATES PRESCRIBED FOR PAYMENT OF FOUR INSTALLMENTS.—In any case (other than payment of estimated income tax) in which the tax may be paid in four installments, the first installment shall be paid on the date prescribed for the payment of the tax, the second installment shall be paid on or before 3 months, the third installment on or before 6 months, and the fourth installment on or before 9 months, after such date.

Amendments

• **1982, Tax Equity and Fiscal Responsibility Act of 1982 (P.L. 97-248)**

P.L. 97-248, §234(b)(1):

Amended Code Sec. 6152(b). **Effective** for tax years beginning after 12-31-82. Prior to amendment, Code Sec. 6152(b) read as follows:

(b) DATES PRESCRIBED FOR PAYMENT OF INSTALLMENTS.—

(1) FOUR INSTALLMENTS.—In any case (other than payment of estimated income tax) in which the tax may be paid in four installments, the first installment shall be paid on the date prescribed for the payment of the tax, the second installment shall be paid on or before 3 months, the third installment on or before 6 months, and the fourth installment on or before 9 months, after such date.

(2) TWO INSTALLMENTS.—In any case (other than payment of estimated income tax) in which the tax may be paid in two installments, the first installment shall be paid on the date prescribed for the payment of the tax, and the second installment shall be paid on or before 3 months after such date.

[Sec. 6152(c)]

(c) PRORATION OF DEFICIENCY TO INSTALLMENTS.—If an election has been made to pay the tax imposed by chapter 1 in installments and a deficiency has been assessed, the deficiency shall be prorated to such installments. Except as provided in section 6861 (relating to jeopardy assessments), that part of the deficiency so prorated to any installment the date for payment of which has not arrived shall be collected at the same time as and as part of such installment. That part of the deficiency so prorated to any installment the date for payment of which has arrived shall be paid upon notice and demand from the Secretary.

Amendments

• **1976, Tax Reform Act of 1976 (P.L. 94-455)**

P.L. 94-455, §1906(b)(13)(A):

Amended 1954 Code by substituting "Secretary" for "Secretary or his delegate" each place it appeared. **Effective** 2-1-77.

[Sec. 6152(d)]

(d) ACCELERATION OF PAYMENT.—If any installment (other than an installment of estimated income tax) is not paid on or before the date fixed for its payment, the whole of the unpaid tax shall be paid upon notice and demand from the Secretary.

Amendments

• **1976, Tax Reform Act of 1976 (P.L. 94-455)**

P.L. 94-455, §1906(b)(13)(A):

Amended 1954 Code by substituting "Secretary" for "Secretary or his delegate" each place it appeared. **Effective** 2-1-77.

* * *

[Sec. 6155]

SEC. 6155. PAYMENT ON NOTICE AND DEMAND.

[Sec. 6155(a)]

(a) GENERAL RULE.—Upon receipt of notice and demand from the Secretary, there shall be paid at the place and time stated in such notice the amount of any tax (including any interest, additional amounts, additions to tax, and assessable penalties) stated in such notice and demand.

Amendments

• **1976, Tax Reform Act of 1976 (P.L. 94-455)**

P.L. 94-455, §1906(b)(13)(A):

Amended 1954 Code by substituting "Secretary" for "Secretary or his delegate" each place it appeared. **Effective** 2-1-77.

[Sec. 6155(b)]

(b) CROSS REFERENCES.—

(1) For restrictions on assessment and collection of deficiency assessments of taxes subject to the jurisdiction of the Tax Court, see sections 6212 and 6213.

(2) For provisions relating to assessment of claims allowed in a receivership proceeding, see section 6873.

(3) For provisions relating to jeopardy assessments, see subchapter A of chapter 70.

Amendments

• 1980, Bankruptcy Tax Act of 1980 (P.L. 96-589)

P.L. 96-589, §6(i)(7):

Amended Code Sec. 6155(b)(2) by striking out "bankruptcy or". **Effective** 10-1-79 but inapplicable to any proceeding under the Bankruptcy Act commenced before that date. Prior to amendment, Code Sec. 6155(b)(2) provided:

"(2) For provisions relating to assessment of claims allowed in a bankruptcy or receivership proceeding, see section 6873.".

* * *

[Sec. 6159]

SEC. 6159. AGREEMENTS FOR PAYMENT OF TAX LIABILITY IN INSTALLMENTS.

[Sec. 6159(a)]

(a) AUTHORIZATION OF AGREEMENTS.—The Secretary is authorized to enter into written agreements with any taxpayer under which such taxpayer is allowed to make payment on any tax in installment payments if the Secretary determines that such agreement will facilitate full or partial collection of such liability.

Amendments

• 2004, American Jobs Creation Act of 2004 (P.L. 108-357)

P.L. 108-357, §843(a)(1)(A)-(B):

Amended Code Sec. 6159(a) by striking "satisfy liability for payment of" and inserting "make payment on", and by inserting "full or partial" after "facilitate". **Effective** for agreements entered into on or after 10-22-2004.

[Sec. 6159(b)]

(b) EXTENT TO WHICH AGREEMENTS REMAIN IN EFFECT.—

(1) IN GENERAL.—Except as otherwise provided in this subsection, any agreement entered into by the Secretary under subsection (a) shall remain in effect for the term of the agreement.

(2) INADEQUATE INFORMATION OR JEOPARDY.—The Secretary may terminate any agreement entered into by the Secretary under subsection (a) if—

(A) information which the taxpayer provided to the Secretary prior to the date such agreement was entered into was inaccurate or incomplete, or

(B) the Secretary believes that collection of any tax to which an agreement under this section relates is in jeopardy.

(3) SUBSEQUENT CHANGE IN FINANCIAL CONDITIONS.—If the Secretary makes a determination that the financial condition of a taxpayer with whom the Secretary has entered into an agreement under subsection (a) has significantly changed, the Secretary may alter, modify, or terminate such agreement.

(4) FAILURE TO PAY AN INSTALLMENT OR ANY OTHER TAX LIABILITY WHEN DUE OR TO PROVIDE REQUESTED FINANCIAL INFORMATION.—The Secretary may alter, modify, or terminate an agreement entered into by the Secretary under subsection (a) in the case of the failure of the taxpayer—

(A) to pay any installment at the time such installment payment is due under such agreement,

(B) to pay any other tax liability at the time such liability is due, or

(C) to provide a financial condition update as requested by the Secretary.

(5) NOTICE REQUIREMENTS.—The Secretary may not take any action under paragraph (2), (3), or (4) unless—

(A) a notice of such action is provided to the taxpayer not later than the day 30 days before the date of such action, and

(B) such notice includes an explanation why the Secretary intends to take such action.

The preceding sentence shall not apply in any case in which the Secretary believes that collection of any tax to which an agreement under this section relates is in jeopardy.

Amendments

• 1996, Taxpayer Bill of Rights 2 (P.L. 104-168)

P.L. 104-168, §201(a):

Amended Code Sec. 6159(b) by adding at the end a new paragraph (5). **Effective** on the date 6 months after 7-30-96.

P.L. 104-168, §201(b):

Amended Code Sec. 6159(b)(3). **Effective** on the date 6 months after 7-30-96. Prior to amendment, Code Sec. 6159(b)(3) read as follows:

(3) SUBSEQUENT CHANGE IN FINANCIAL CONDITIONS.—

(A) IN GENERAL.—If the Secretary makes a determination that the financial condition of a taxpayer with whom the Secretary has entered into an agreement under subsection (a) has significantly changed, the Secretary may alter, modify, or terminate such agreement.

(B) NOTICE.—Action may be taken by the Secretary under subparagraph (A) only if—

(i) notice of such determination is provided to the taxpayer no later than 30 days prior to the date of such action, and

(ii) such notice includes the reasons why the Secretary believes a significant change in the financial condition of the taxpayer has occurred.

• 1988, Technical and Miscellaneous Revenue Act of 1988 (P.L. 100-647)

P.L. 100-647, §6234(a):

Amended subchapter A of chapter 62 by adding at the end thereof a new Section 6159. **Effective** for agreements entered into after 11-10-88.

[Sec. 6159(c)]

(c) SECRETARY REQUIRED TO ENTER INTO INSTALLMENT AGREEMENTS IN CERTAIN CASES.—In the case of a liability for tax of an individual under subtitle A, the Secretary shall enter into an agreement to accept the full payment of such tax in installments if, as of the date the individual offers to enter into the agreement—

(1) the aggregate amount of such liability (determined without regard to interest, penalties, additions to the tax, and additional amounts) does not exceed $10,000;

(2) the taxpayer (and, if such liability relates to a joint return, the taxpayer's spouse) has not, during any of the preceding 5 taxable years—

(A) failed to file any return of tax imposed by subtitle A;

(B) failed to pay any tax required to be shown on any such return; or

(C) entered into an installment agreement under this section for payment of any tax imposed by subtitle A,

(3) the Secretary determines that the taxpayer is financially unable to pay such liability in full when due (and the taxpayer submits such information as the Secretary may require to make such determination);

(4) the agreement requires full payment of such liability within 3 years; and

(5) the taxpayer agrees to comply with the provisions of this title for the period such agreement is in effect.

Amendments

• 2004, American Jobs Creation Act of 2004 (P.L. 108-357)

P.L. 108-357, §843(a)(2):

Amended the matter preceding paragraph (1) of Code Sec. 6159(c) by inserting "full" before "payment". **Effective** for agreements entered into on or after 10-22-2004.

• 1998, IRS Restructuring and Reform Act of 1998 (P.L. 105-206)

P.L. 105-206, §3467(a):

Amended Code Sec. 6159 by redesignating subsection (c) as subsection (d) and by inserting after subsection (b) a new subsection (c). **Effective** 7-22-98.

P.L. 105-206, §3506 (as amended by P.L. 106-554, §302(a)), provides:

SEC. 3506. STATEMENTS REGARDING INSTALLMENT AGREEMENTS.

The Secretary of the Treasury or the Secretary's delegate shall, beginning not later than July 1, 2000, provide each taxpayer who has an installment agreement in effect under section 6159 of the Internal Revenue Code of 1986 an annual statement setting forth the initial balance at the beginning of the year, the payments made during the year, and the remaining balance as of the end of the year.

[Sec. 6159(d)]

(d) SECRETARY REQUIRED TO REVIEW INSTALLMENT AGREEMENTS FOR PARTIAL COLLECTION EVERY TWO YEARS.—In the case of an agreement entered into by the Secretary under subsection (a) for partial collection of a tax liability, the Secretary shall review the agreement at least once every 2 years.

Amendments

• 2004, American Jobs Creation Act of 2004 (P.L. 108-357)

P.L. 108-357, §843(b):

Amended Code Sec. 6159 by redesignating subsections (d) and (e) as subsections (e) and (f), respectively, and inserting after subsection (c) a new subsection (d). **Effective** for agreements entered into on or after 10-22-2004.

[Sec. 6159(e)]

(e) ADMINISTRATIVE REVIEW.—The Secretary shall establish procedures for an independent administrative review of terminations of installment agreements under this section for taxpayers who request such a review.

Amendments

• 2004, American Jobs Creation Act of 2004 (P.L. 108-357)

P.L. 108-357, §843(b):

Amended Code Sec. 6159 by redesignating subsection (d) as subsection (e). **Effective** for agreements entered into on or after 10-22-2004.

• 1998, IRS Restructuring and Reform Act of 1998 (P.L. 105-206)

P.L. 105-206, §3467(a):

Amended Code Sec. 6159 by redesignating subsection (c) as subsection (d). **Effective** 7-22-98.

• 1996, Taxpayer Bill of Rights 2 (P.L. 104-168)

P.L. 104-168, §202(a):

Amended Code Sec. 6159 by adding at the end a new subsection (c). **Effective** 1-1-97.

[Sec. 6159(f)]

(f) INSTALLMENT AGREEMENT FEES.—

(1) LIMITATION ON FEE AMOUNT.—The amount of any fee imposed on an installment agreement under this section may not exceed the amount of such fee as in effect on the date of the enactment of this subsection.

(2) WAIVER OR REIMBURSEMENT.—In the case of any taxpayer with an adjusted gross income, as determined for the most recent year for which such information is available, which does not exceed 250 percent of the applicable poverty level (as determined by the Secretary)—

(A) if the taxpayer has agreed to make payments under the installment agreement by electronic payment through a debit instrument, no fee shall be imposed on an installment agreement under this section, and

(B) if the taxpayer is unable to make payments under the installment agreement by electronic payment through a debit instrument, the Secretary shall, upon completion of the installment agreement, pay the taxpayer an amount equal to any such fees imposed.

Amendments

• 2018, Bipartisan Budget Act of 2018 (P.L. 115-123)

P.L. 115-123, §41105(a), Div. D:

Amended Code Sec. 6159 by redesignating subsection (f) as subsection (g) and by inserting after subsection (e) a new subsection (f). **Effective** for agreements entered into on or after the date which is 60 days after 2-9-2018.

[Sec. 6159(g)]

(g) CROSS REFERENCE.—

For rights to administrative review and appeal, see section 7122(e).

Amendments

• 2018, Bipartisan Budget Act of 2018 (P.L. 115-123)

P.L. 115-123, §41105(a), Div. D:

Amended Code Sec. 6159 by redesignating subsection (f) as subsection (g). **Effective** for agreements entered into on or after the date which is 60 days after 2-9-2018.

• 2006, Tax Increase Prevention and Reconciliation Act of 2005 (P.L. 109-222)

P.L. 109-222, §509(c):

Amended Code Sec. 6159(f) by striking "section 7122(d)" and inserting "section 7122(e)". **Effective** for offers-in-compromise submitted on and after the date which is 60 days after 5-17-2006.

• 2004, American Jobs Creation Act of 2004 (P.L. 108-357)

P.L. 108-357, §843(b):

Amended Code Sec. 6159 by redesignating subsection (e) as subsection (f). **Effective** for agreements entered into on or after 10-22-2004.

• 1998, Tax and Trade Relief Extension Act of 1998 (P.L. 105-277)

P.L. 105-277, §4002(g):

Amended Code Sec. 6159 by redesignating the subsection (d) relating to cross reference as subsection (e). **Effective** as if included in the provision of P.L. 105-206 to which it relates [**effective** 7-22-98.—CCH].

• 1998, IRS Restructuring and Reform Act of 1998 (P.L. 105-206)

P.L. 105-206, §3462(c)(2):

Amended Code Sec. 6159 by adding at the end a new subsection (d) [(e)]. **Effective** for proposed offers-in-compromise and installment agreements submitted after 7-22-98.

* * *

Subchapter B—Extensions of Time for Payment

* * *

[Sec. 6161]

SEC. 6161. EXTENSION OF TIME FOR PAYING TAX.

[Sec. 6161(a)]

(a) AMOUNT DETERMINED BY TAXPAYER ON RETURN.—

(1) GENERAL RULE.—The Secretary, except as otherwise provided in this title, may extend the time for payment of the amount of the tax shown, or required to be shown, on any return or declaration required under authority of this title (or any installment thereof), for a reasonable period not to exceed 6 months (12 months in the case of estate tax) from the date fixed for payment thereof. Such extension may exceed 6 months in the case of a taxpayer who is abroad.

(2) ESTATE TAX.—The Secretary may, for reasonable cause, extend the time for payment of—

(A) any part of the amount determined by the executor as the tax imposed by chapter 11, or

(B) any part of any installment under section 6166 (including any part of a deficiency prorated to any installment under such section),

for a reasonable period not in excess of 10 years from the date prescribed by section 6151(a) for payment of the tax (or, in the case of an amount referred to in subparagraph (B), if later, not beyond the date which is 12 months after the due date for the last installment).

Amendments

• 1981, Economic Recovery Tax Act of 1981 (P.L. 97-34)

P.L. 97-34, §422(e)(1):

Amended Code Sec. 6161(a) by striking out "or 6166A". **Effective** for estates of decedents dying after 12-31-81.

• 1976, Tax Reform Act of 1976 (P.L. 94-455)

P.L. 94-455, §1906(b)(13)(A):

Amended 1954 Code by substituting "Secretary" for "Secretary or his delegate" each place it appeared. **Effective** 2-1-77.

P.L. 94-455, § 2004(c)(1):

Amended Code Sec. 6161(a)(2). **Effective** for the estates of decedents dying after 12-31-76. Prior to amendment, Code Sec. 6161(a)(2) read as follows:

(2) ESTATE TAX.—If the Secretary or his delegate finds—

(A) that the payment, on the due date, of any part of the amount determined by the executor as the tax imposed by chapter 11,

(B) that the payment, on the date fixed for the payment of any installment under section 6166, of any part of such installment (including any part of a deficiency prorated to an installment the date for payment of which had not arrived), or

(C) that the payment upon notice and demand of any part of a deficiency prorated under the provisions of section 6166 to installments the date for payment of which had arrived,

would result in undue hardship to the estate, he may extend the time for payment for a reasonable period not in excess of 10 years from the date prescribed by section 6151(a) for payment of the tax.

• 1970, Excise, Estate, and Gift Tax Adjustment Act of 1970 (P.L. 91-614)

P.L. 91-614, § 101(h):

Amended Code Sec. 6161(a) by adding "(12 months in the case of estate tax)" in the first sentence of paragraph (1). **Effective** 1-1-71.

• 1958, Technical Amendments Act of 1958 (P.L. 85-866)

P.L. 85-866, § 206(c):

Amended paragraph (2) of Sec. 6161(a). For **effective** date, see Act Sec. 206(f), below. Prior to amendment, paragraph (2) read as follows:

"(2) Estate Tax.—If the Secretary or his delegate finds that the payment on the due date of any part of the amount determined by the executor as the tax imposed by chapter 11 would result in undue hardship to the estate, he may extend the time for payment for a reasonable period not in excess of 10 years from the date fixed for payment of the tax."

P.L. 85-866, § 206(f), provides:

"The amendments made by this section shall apply to estates of decedents with respect to which the date for the filing of the estate tax return (including extensions thereof) prescribed by section 6075(a) of the Internal Revenue Code of 1954 is after the date of the enactment of this Act; except that (1) section 6166(i) of such Code as added by this section shall apply to estates of decedents dying after August 16, 1954, but only if the date for the filing of the estate tax return (including extensions thereof) expired on or before the date of the enactment of this Act, and (2) notwithstanding section 6166(a) of such Code, if an election under such section is required to be made before the sixtieth day after the date of the enactment of this Act such an election shall be considered timely if made on or before such sixtieth day."

[Sec. 6161(b)]

(b) AMOUNT DETERMINED AS DEFICIENCY.—

(1) INCOME, GIFT, AND CERTAIN OTHER TAXES.—Under regulations prescribed by the Secretary, the Secretary may extend the time for the payment of the amount determined as a deficiency of a tax imposed by chapter 1, 12, 41, 42, 43, or 44 for a period not to exceed 18 months from the date fixed for the payment of the deficiency, and in exceptional cases, for a further period not to exceed 12 months. An extension under this paragraph may be granted only where it is shown to the satisfaction of the Secretary that payment of a deficiency upon the date fixed for the payment thereof will result in undue hardship to the taxpayer in the case of a tax imposed by chapter 1, 41, 42, 43, or 44, or to the donor in the case of a tax imposed by chapter 12.

(2) ESTATE TAX.—Under regulations prescribed by the Secretary, the Secretary may, for reasonable cause, extend the time for the payment of any deficiency of a tax imposed by chapter 11 for a reasonable period not to exceed 4 years from the date otherwise fixed for the payment of the deficiency.

(3) NO EXTENSION FOR CERTAIN DEFICIENCIES.—No extension shall be granted under this subsection for any deficiency if the deficiency is due to negligence, to intentional disregard of rules and regulations, or to fraud with intent to evade tax.

Amendments

• 1988, Omnibus Trade and Competitiveness Act of 1988 (P.L. 100-418)

P.L. 100-418, § 1941(b)(2)(B)(viii):

Amended Code Sec. 6161(b)(1) by striking "44, or 45" each place it appears and inserting "or 44". **Effective** for crude oil removed from the premises on or after 8-23-88.

• 1980, Crude Oil Windfall Profit Tax Act of 1980 (P.L. 96-223)

P.L. 96-223, § 101(f)(1)(H):

Amended Code Sec. 6161(b)(1) by striking out "or 44" and inserting "44, or 45". For the **effective** date and transitional rules, see P.L. 96-223, § 101(i), following Code Sec. 4986.

• 1976, Tax Reform Act of 1976 (P.L. 94-455)

P.L. 94-455, § 2004(c)(2):

Amended Code Sec. 6161(b). **Effective** for the estates of decedents dying after 12-31-76. Prior to amendment, Code Sec. 6161(b) read as follows:

(b) AMOUNT DETERMINED AS DEFICIENCY.—Under regulations prescribed by the Secretary or his delegate, the Secretary or his delegate may extend, to the extent provided below, the time for payment of the amount determined as a deficiency:

(1) In the case of a tax imposed by chapter 1, 12, 42 or 43, for a period not to exceed 18 months from the date fixed for payment of the deficiency, and, in exceptional cases, for a further period not to exceed 12 months;

(2) In the case of a tax imposed by chapter 11, for a period not to exceed 4 years from the date otherwise fixed for payment of the deficiency.

An extension under this subsection may be granted only where it is shown to the satisfaction of the Secretary or his delegate that the payment of a deficiency upon the date fixed for the payment thereof will result in undue hardship to the taxpayer in the case of a tax imposed by chapter 1, 42, or chapter 43, to the estate in the case of a tax imposed by chapter 11, or to the donor in the case of a tax imposed by chapter 12. No extension shall be granted if the deficiency is due to negligence, to intentional disregard of rules and regulations, or to fraud with intent to evade tax.

P.L. 94-455, § 1307(d):

Amended former Code Sec. 6161(b) by substituting "12, 41" for "12" in paragraph (1) and by substituting "41, 42," for "42" in the second sentence of paragraph (1). The amendments are incorporated in the amendment made by P.L. 94-455, § 2004(c)(2). **Effective** 10-4-76.

P.L. 94-455, § 1605(b)(3):

Amended Code Sec. 6161(b)(1) (as amended by P.L. 94-455, § 1307(d)) by substituting "42, 43, or 44" for "42 or 43" and by substituting "43, or 44" for "or chapter 43". The amendments are incorporated in the amendment made by P.L. 94-455, § 2004(c)(2). **Effective** for tax years of real estate investment trusts beginning after 10-4-76.

• 1974, Employee Retirement Income Security Act of 1974 (P.L. 93-406)

P.L. 93-406, §1016(a)(7):

Amended Code Sec. 6161(b) by changing "or 42" to "42 or 43" in paragraph (1) and by changing "or 42" to "42, or chapter 43" in the second sentence of subsection (b). For **effective** date, see amendment note for P.L. 93-406 under Code Sec. 410.

• 1969, Tax Reform Act of 1969 (P.L. 91-172)

P.L. 91-172, §101(j)(37):

Amended Code Sec. 6161(b) by substituting "chapter 1, 12, or 42," for "chapter 1 or 12," in paragraph (1) and by substituting "chapter 1 or 42," in the first sentence following paragraph (2). **Effective** 1-1-70.

[Sec. 6161(c)]

(c) CLAIMS IN CASES UNDER TITLE 11 OF THE UNITED STATES CODE OR IN RECEIVERSHIP PROCEEDINGS.—Extensions of time for payment of any portion of a claim for tax under chapter 1 or chapter 12, allowed in cases under title 11 of the United States Code or in receivership proceedings, which is unpaid, may be had in the same manner and subject to the same provisions and limitations as provided in subsection (b) in respect of a deficiency in such tax.

Amendments

• 1980, Bankruptcy Tax Act of 1980 (P.L. 96-589)

P.L. 96-589, §6(i)(8):

Amended Code Sec. 6161(c). **Effective** 10-1-79 but inapplicable to any proceeding under the Bankruptcy Act commenced before that date. Prior to amendment, Code Sec. 6161(c) provided:

"(c) CLAIMS IN BANKRUPTCY OR RECEIVERSHIP PROCEEDINGS.—Extensions of time for payment of any portion of a claim for tax under chapter 1 or chapter 12, allowed in bankruptcy or receivership proceedings, which is unpaid, may be had in the same manner and subject to the same provisions and limitations as provided in subsection (b) in respect of a deficiency in such tax."

[Sec. 6161(d)]

(d) CROSS REFERENCES.—

(1) PERIOD OF LIMITATION.—

For extension of the period of limitation in case of an extension under subsection (a)(2) or subsection (b)(2), see section 6503(d).

(2) SECURITY.—

For authority of the Secretary to require security in case of an extension under subsection (a)(2) or subsection (b), see section 6165.

(3) POSTPONEMENT OF CERTAIN ACTS.—

For time for performing certain acts postponed by reason of war, see section 7508, and by reason of Presidentially declared disaster or terroristic or military action, see section 7508A.

Amendments

• 2002, Victims of Terrorism Tax Relief Act of 2001 (P.L. 107-134)

P.L. 107-134, §112(d)(3):

Amended Code Sec. 6161(d) by adding at the end a new paragraph (3). **Effective** for disasters and terroristic or military actions occurring on or after 9-11-01, with respect to any action of the Secretary of the Treasury, the Secretary of Labor, or the Pension Benefit Guaranty Corporation occurring on or after 1-23-02.

• 1976, Tax Reform Act of 1976 (P.L. 94-455)

P.L. 94-455, §1906(b)(13)(A):

Amended 1954 Code by substituting "Secretary" for "Secretary or his delegate" each place it appeared. **Effective** 2-1-77.

[Sec. 6163]

SEC. 6163. EXTENSION OF TIME FOR PAYMENT OF ESTATE TAX ON VALUE OF REVERSIONARY OR REMAINDER INTEREST IN PROPERTY.

[Sec. 6163(a)]

(a) EXTENSION PERMITTED.—If the value of a reversionary or remainder interest in property is included under chapter 11 in the value of the gross estate, the payment of the part of the tax under chapter 11 attributable to such interest may, at the election of the executor, be postponed until 6 months after the termination of the precedent interest or interests in the property, under such regulations as the Secretary may prescribe.

Amendments

• 1976, Tax Reform Act of 1976 (P.L. 94-455)

P.L. 94-455, §1906(b)(13)(A):

Amended 1954 Code by substituting "Secretary" for "Secretary or his delegate" each place it appeared. **Effective** 2-1-77.

[Sec. 6163(b)]

(b) EXTENSION FOR REASONABLE CAUSE.—At the expiration of the period of postponement provided for in subsection (a), the Secretary may, for reasonable cause, extend the time for payment for a reasonable period or periods not in excess of 3 years from the expiration of the period of postponement provided in subsection (a).

Amendments

• 1976, Tax Reform Act of 1976 (P.L. 94-455)

P.L. 94-455, §2004(c)(3):

Amended Code Sec. 6163(b). **Effective** for the estates of decedents dying after 12-31-76. Prior to amendment, Code Sec. 6163(b) read as follows:

(b) EXTENSION TO PREVENT UNDUE HARDSHIP.—If the Secretary or his delegate finds that the payment of the tax at the expiration of the period of postponement provided for in subsection (a) would result in undue hardship to the estate, he may extend the time for payment for a reasonable period or periods not in excess of 3 years from the expiration of such period of postponement.

• 1964, Revenue Act of 1964 (P.L. 88-272)

P.L. 88-272, §240(a):

Amended subsection (b) to insert "or periods not in excess of 3 years" in lieu of "not in excess of 2 years". **Effective** in the case of any reversionary or remainder interest only if the time for payment of the tax under chapter 11 attributable to such interest, including any extensions thereof, has not expired on 2-26-64.

• 1958, Technical Amendments Act of 1958 (P.L. 85-866)

P.L. 85-866, §66(b)(1):

Redesignated subsection (b) of Sec. 6163 as subsection (c) and added a new subsection (b). **Effective** in the case of any reversionary or remainder interest only if the precedent interest or interests in the property did not terminate before the beginning of the 6-month period which ends on 9-2-58.

[Sec. 6163(c)]

(c) CROSS REFERENCE.—

For authority of the Secretary to require security in the case of an extension under this section, see section 6165.

Amendments

• 1976, Tax Reform Act of 1976 (P.L. 94-455)

P.L. 94-455, §1906(b)(13)(A):

Amended 1954 Code by substituting "Secretary" for "Secretary or his delegate" each place it appeared. **Effective** 2-1-77.

• 1975 (P.L. 93-625)

P.L. 93-625, §7(d)(1):

Amended Code Sec. 6163(c). **Effective** 7-1-75. Prior to amendment, this section read as follows:

"(c) Cross References.—

"(1) Interest.—

"For provisions requiring the payment of interest for the period of such extension, see section 6601(b).

"(2) Security.—

"For authority of the Secretary or his delegate to require security in the case of such extension, see section 6165."

• 1958, Technical Amendments Act of 1958 (P.L. 85-866)

P.L. 85-866, §66(b)(1):

Redesignated old subsection (b) as subsection (c). **Effective** 9-2-58.

* * *

[Sec. 6165]

SEC. 6165. BONDS WHERE TIME TO PAY TAX OR DEFICIENCY HAS BEEN EXTENDED.

In the event the Secretary grants any extension of time within which to pay any tax or any deficiency therein, the Secretary may require the taxpayer to furnish a bond in such amount (not exceeding double the amount with respect to which the extension is granted) conditioned upon the payment of the amount extended in accordance with the terms of such extension.

Amendments

• 1976, Tax Reform Act of 1976 (P.L. 94-455)

P.L. 94-455, §1906(b)(13)(A):

Amended 1954 Code by substituting "Secretary" for "Secretary or his delegate" each place it appeared. **Effective** 2-1-77.

[Sec. 6166]

SEC. 6166. EXTENSION OF TIME FOR PAYMENT OF ESTATE TAX WHERE ESTATE CONSISTS LARGELY OF INTEREST IN CLOSELY HELD BUSINESS.

[Sec. 6166(a)]

(a) 5-YEAR DEFERRAL; 10-YEAR INSTALLMENT PAYMENT.—

(1) IN GENERAL.—If the value of an interest in a closely held business, which is included in determining the gross estate of a decedent who was (at the date of his death) a citizen or resident of the United States exceeds 35 percent of the adjusted gross estate, the executor may elect to pay part or all of the tax imposed by section 2001 in 2 or more (but not exceeding 10) equal installments.

(2) LIMITATION.—The maximum amount of tax which may be paid in installments under this subsection shall be an amount which bears the same ratio to the tax imposed by section 2001 (reduced by the credits against such tax) as—

(A) the closely held business amount, bears to

(B) the amount of the adjusted gross estate.

(3) DATE FOR PAYMENT OF INSTALLMENTS.—If an election is made under paragraph (1), the first installment shall be paid on or before the date selected by the executor which is not more than 5 years after the date prescribed by section 6151(a) for payment of the tax, and each succeeding installment shall be paid on or before the date which is 1 year after the date prescribed by this paragraph for payment of the preceding installment.

Amendments

• 1981, Economic Recovery Tax Act of 1981 (P.L. 97-34)

P.L. 97-34, §422(a)(1):

Amended Code Sec. 6166(a)(1) by striking out "65 percent" and inserting "35 percent". **Effective** for estates of decedents dying after 12-31-81.

P.L. 97-34, §422(e)(5)(A):

Repealed Code Sec. 6166(a)(4). **Effective** for estates of decedents dying after 12-31-81. Prior to its repeal, Code Sec. 6166(a)(4) read as follows:

(4) ELIGIBILITY FOR ELECTION.—No election may be made under this section by the executor of the estate of any decedent if an election under section 6166A applies with respect to the estate of such decedent.

P.L. 97-34, §422(e)(5)(B):

Amended Code Sec. 6166 by striking out "ALTERNATE" in the heading. **Effective** for estates of decedents dying after 12-31-81.

[Sec. 6166(b)]

(b) DEFINITIONS AND SPECIAL RULES.—

(1) INTEREST IN CLOSELY HELD BUSINESS.—For purposes of this section, the term "interest in a closely held business" means—

(A) an interest as a proprietor in a trade or business carried on as a proprietorship;

(B) an interest as a partner in a partnership carrying on a trade or business, if—

(i) 20 percent or more of the total capital interest in such partnership is included in determining the gross estate of the decedent, or

(ii) such partnership had 45 or fewer partners; or

(C) stock in a corporation carrying on a trade or business if—

(i) 20 percent or more in value of the voting stock of such corporation is included in determining the gross estate of the decedent, or

(ii) such corporation had 45 or fewer shareholders.

(2) RULES FOR APPLYING PARAGRAPH (1).—For purposes of paragraph (1)—

(A) TIME FOR TESTING.—Determinations shall be made as of the time immediately before the decedent's death.

(B) CERTAIN INTERESTS HELD BY HUSBAND AND WIFE.—Stock or a partnership interest which—

(i) is community property of a husband and wife (or the income from which is community income) under the applicable community property law of a State, or

(ii) is held by a husband and wife as joint tenants, tenants by the entirety, or tenants in common,

shall be treated as owned by one shareholder or one partner, as the case may be.

(C) INDIRECT OWNERSHIP.—Property owned, directly or indirectly, by or for a corporation, partnership, estate, or trust shall be considered as being owned proportionately by or for its shareholders, partners, or beneficiaries. For purposes of the preceding sentence, a person shall be treated as a beneficiary of any trust only if such person has a present interest in the trust.

(D) CERTAIN INTERESTS HELD BY MEMBERS OF DECEDENT'S FAMILY.—All stock and all partnership interests held by the decedent or by any member of his family (within the meaning of section 267(c)(4)) shall be treated as owned by the decedent.

(3) FARMHOUSES AND CERTAIN OTHER STRUCTURES TAKEN INTO ACCOUNT.—For purposes of the 35-percent requirement of subsection (a)(1), an interest in a closely held business which is the business of farming includes an interest in residential buildings and related improvements on the farm which are occupied on a regular basis by the owner or lessee of the farm or by persons employed by such owner or lessee for purposes of operating or maintaining the farm.

(4) VALUE.—For purposes of this section, value shall be value determined for purposes of chapter 11 (relating to estate tax).

(5) CLOSELY HELD BUSINESS AMOUNT.—For purposes of this section, the term "closely held business amount" means the value of the interest in a closely held business which qualifies under subsection (a)(1).

(6) ADJUSTED GROSS ESTATE.—For purposes of this section, the term "adjusted gross estate" means the value of the gross estate reduced by the sum of the amounts allowable as a deduction under section 2053 or 2054. Such sum shall be determined on the basis of the facts and circumstances in existence on the date (including extensions) for filing the return of tax imposed by section 2001 (or, if earlier, the date on which such return is filed).

(7) PARTNERSHIP INTERESTS AND STOCK WHICH IS NOT READILY TRADABLE.—

(A) IN GENERAL.—If the executor elects the benefits of this paragraph (at such time and in such manner as the Secretary shall by regulations prescribe), then—

(i) for purposes of paragraph (1)(B)(i) or (1)(C)(i) (whichever is appropriate) and for purposes of subsection (c), any capital interest in a partnership and any non-readily-tradable stock which (after the application of paragraph (2)) is treated as owned by the decedent shall be treated as included in determining the value of the decedent's gross estate,

(ii) the executor shall be treated as having selected under subsection (a)(3) the date prescribed by section 6151(a), and

(iii) for purposes of applying section 6601(j), the 2-percent portion (as defined in such section) shall be treated as being zero.

(B) NON-READILY-TRADABLE STOCK DEFINED.—For purposes of this paragraph, the term "non-readily-tradable stock" means stock for which, at the time of the decedent's death, there was no market on a stock exchange or in an over-the-counter market.

(8) STOCK IN HOLDING COMPANY TREATED AS BUSINESS COMPANY STOCK IN CERTAIN CASES.—

(A) IN GENERAL.—If the executor elects the benefits of this paragraph, then—

(i) HOLDING COMPANY STOCK TREATED AS BUSINESS COMPANY STOCK.—For purposes of this section, the portion of the stock of any holding company which represents direct ownership (or indirect ownership through 1 or more other holding companies) by such company in a business company shall be deemed to be stock in such business company.

(ii) 5-YEAR DEFERRAL FOR PRINCIPAL NOT TO APPLY.—The executor shall be treated as having selected under subsection (a)(3) the date prescribed by section 6151(a).

(iii) 2-PERCENT INTEREST RATE NOT TO APPLY.—For purposes of applying section 6601(j), the 2-percent portion (as defined in such section) shall be treated as being zero.

(B) ALL STOCK MUST BE NON-READILY-TRADABLE STOCK.—

(i) IN GENERAL.—No stock shall be taken into account for purposes of applying this paragraph unless it is non-readily-tradable stock (within the meaning of paragraph (7)(B)).

(ii) SPECIAL APPLICATION WHERE ONLY HOLDING COMPANY STOCK IS NON-READILY-TRADABLE STOCK.—If the requirements of clause (i) are not met, but all of the stock of each holding company taken into account is non-readily-tradable, then this paragraph shall apply, but subsection (a)(1) shall be applied by substituting "5" for "10".

(C) APPLICATION OF VOTING STOCK REQUIREMENT OF PARAGRAPH (1)(c)(i).—For purposes of clause (i) of paragraph (1)(C), the deemed stock resulting from the application of subparagraph (A) shall be treated as voting stock to the extent that voting stock in the holding company owns directly (or through the voting stock of 1 of more other holding companies) voting stock in the business company.

(D) DEFINITIONS.—For purposes of this paragraph—

(i) HOLDING COMPANY.—The term "holding company" means any corporation holding stock in another corporation.

(ii) BUSINESS COMPANY.—The term "business company" means any corporation carrying on a trade or business.

(9) DEFERRAL NOT AVAILABLE FOR PASSIVE ASSETS.—

(A) IN GENERAL.—For purposes of subsection (a)(1) and determining the closely held business amount (but not for purposes of subsection (g)), the value of any interest in a closely held business shall not include the value of that portion of such interest which is attributable to passive assets held by the business.

(B) PASSIVE ASSET DEFINED.—For purposes of this paragraph—

(i) IN GENERAL.—The term "passive asset" means any asset other than an asset used in carrying on a trade or business.

(ii) STOCK TREATED AS PASSIVE ASSET.—The term "passive asset" includes any stock in another corporation unless—

(I) such stock is treated as held by the decedent by reason of an election under paragraph (8), and

(II) such stock qualified under subsection (a)(1).

(iii) EXCEPTION FOR ACTIVE CORPORATIONS.—If—

(I) a corporation owns 20 percent or more in value of the voting stock of another corporation, or such other corporation has 45 or fewer shareholders, and

(II) 80 percent or more of the value of the assets of each such corporation is attributable to assets used in carrying on a trade or business,

then such corporations shall be treated as 1 corporation for purposes of clause (ii). For purposes of applying subclause (II) to the corporation holding the stock of the other corporation, such stock shall not be taken into account.

(10) STOCK IN QUALIFYING LENDING AND FINANCE BUSINESS TREATED AS STOCK IN AN ACTIVE TRADE OR BUSINESS COMPANY.—

(A) IN GENERAL.—If the executor elects the benefits of this paragraph, then—

(i) STOCK IN QUALIFYING LENDING AND FINANCE BUSINESS TREATED AS STOCK IN AN ACTIVE TRADE OR BUSINESS COMPANY.—For purposes of this section, any asset used in a qualifying lending and finance business shall be treated as an asset which is used in carrying on a trade or business.

(ii) 5-YEAR DEFERRAL FOR PRINCIPAL NOT TO APPLY.—The executor shall be treated as having selected under subsection (a)(3) the date prescribed by section 6151(a).

(iii) 5 EQUAL INSTALLMENTS ALLOWED.—For purposes of applying subsection (a)(1), "5" shall be substituted for "10".

(B) DEFINITIONS.—For purposes of this paragraph—

(i) QUALIFYING LENDING AND FINANCE BUSINESS.—The term "qualifying lending and finance business" means a lending and finance business, if—

(I) based on all the facts and circumstances immediately before the date of the decedent's death, there was substantial activity with respect to the lending and finance business, or

(II) during at least 3 of the 5 taxable years ending before the date of the decedent's death, such business had at least 1 full-time employee substantially all of whose services were the active management of such business, 10 full-time, nonowner employees substantially all of whose services were directly related to such business, and $5,000,000 in gross receipts from activities described in clause (ii).

(ii) LENDING AND FINANCE BUSINESS.—The term "lending and finance business" means a trade or business of—

(I) making loans,

(II) purchasing or discounting accounts receivable, notes, or installment obligations,

(III) engaging in rental and leasing of real and tangible personal property, including entering into leases and purchasing, servicing, and disposing of leases and leased assets,

(IV) rendering services or making facilities available in the ordinary course of a lending or finance business, and

(V) rendering services or making facilities available in connection with activities described in subclauses (I) through (IV) carried on by the corporation rendering services or making facilities available, or another corporation which is a member of the same affiliated group (as defined in section 1504 without regard to section 1504(b)(3)).

(iii) LIMITATION.—The term "qualifying lending and finance business" shall not include any interest in an entity, if the stock or debt of such entity or a controlled group (as defined in section 267(f)(1)) of which such entity was a member was readily tradable on an established securities market or secondary market (as defined by the Secretary) at any time within 3 years before the date of the decedent's death.

Amendments

• 2013, American Taxpayer Relief Act of 2012 (P.L. 112-240)

P.L. 112-240, §101(a)(1) and (3), provides:

SEC. 101. PERMANENT EXTENSION AND MODIFICATION OF 2001 TAX RELIEF.

(a) PERMANENT EXTENSION.—

(1) IN GENERAL.—The Economic Growth and Tax Relief Reconciliation Act of 2001 is amended by striking title IX.

***

(3) EFFECTIVE DATE.—The amendments made by this subsection shall apply to taxable, plan, or limitation years beginning after December 31, 2012, and estates of decedents dying, gifts made, or generation skipping transfers after December 31, 2012.

• 2001, Economic Growth and Tax Relief Reconciliation Act of 2001 (P.L. 107-16)

P.L. 107-16, §571(a):

Amended Code Sec. 6166(b)(1)(B)(ii), (b)(1)(C)(ii), and (b)(9)(B)(iii)(I) by striking "15" and inserting "45". **Effective** for estates of decedents dying after 12-31-2001.

P.L. 107-16, §572(a):

Amended Code Sec. 6166(b) by adding at the end a new paragraph (10). **Effective** for estates of decedents dying after 12-31-2001.

P.L. 107-16, §573(a):

Amended Code Sec. 6166(b)(8)(B). **Effective** for estates of decedents dying after 12-31-2001. Prior to amendment, Code Sec. 6166(b)(8)(B) read as follows:

(B) ALL STOCK MUST BE NON-READILY-TRADABLE STOCK.—No stock shall be taken into account for purposes of applying this paragraph unless it is non-readily-tradable stock (within the meaning of paragraph (7)(B)).

P.L. 107-16, §901(a)-(b), as amended by P.L. 111-312, §101(a)(1), provides [but see P.L. 112-240, §101(a)(1) and (3), above]:

SEC. 901. SUNSET OF PROVISIONS OF ACT.

(a) IN GENERAL.—All provisions of, and amendments made by, this Act shall not apply—

(1) to taxable, plan, or limitation years beginning after December 31, 2012, or

(2) in the case of title V, to estates of decedents dying, gifts made, or generation skipping transfers, after December 31, 2012.

(b) APPLICATION OF CERTAIN LAWS.—The Internal Revenue Code of 1986 and the Employee Retirement Income Security Act of 1974 shall be applied and administered to years, estates, gifts, and transfers described in subsection (a) as if the provisions and amendments described in subsection (a) had never been enacted.

• 1998, IRS Restructuring and Reform Act of 1998 (P.L. 105-206)

P.L. 105-206, §6007(c)(1):

Amended Code Sec. 6166(b)(7)(A)(iii). **Effective** as if included in the provision of P.L. 105-34 to which it relates [**effective** for estates of decedents dying after 12-31-97.—CCH]. Prior to amendment, Code Sec. 6166(b)(7)(A)(iii) read as follows:

(iii) section 6601(j) (relating to 2-percent rate of interest) shall not apply.

P.L. 105-206, §6007(c)(2):

Amended Code Sec. 6166(b)(8)(A)(iii). **Effective** for estates of decedents dying after 12-31-97. Prior to amendment, Code Sec. 6166(b)(8)(A)(iii) read as follows:

(iii) 2-PERCENT INTEREST RATE NOT TO APPLY.—Section 6601(j) (relating to 2-percent rate of interest) shall not apply.

• **1997, Taxpayer Relief Act of 1997 (P.L. 105-34)**

P.L. 105-34, § 503(c)(1):

Amended Code Sec. 6166(b)(7)(A)(iii) and (8)(A)(iii) by striking "4-percent" each place it appears (including the heading) and inserting "2-percent". **Effective** for estates of decedents dying after 12-31-97.

• **1984, Deficit Reduction Act of 1984 (P.L. 98-369)**

P.L. 98-369, § 1021(a):

Amended Code Sec. 6166(b) by adding new paragraph (8). **Effective** with respect to estates of decedents dying after 7-18-84. However, see Act Sec. 1021(d)[(e)](2) following Code Sec. 6166(g) for special rules.

P.L. 98-369, § 1021(b):

Amended Code Sec. 6166(b) by adding at the end thereof new paragraph (9). **Effective** with respect to estates of decedents dying after 7-18-84. However, see Act Sec. 1021(d)[(e)](2) following Code Sec. 6166(g) for special rules.

• **1983, Technical Corrections Act of 1982 (P.L. 97-448)**

P.L. 97-448, § 104(c)(1):

Amended Code Sec. 6166(b)(3) by striking out "65-percent requirement" and inserting in lieu thereof "35-percent requirement". **Effective** as if included in the provision of P.L. 97-34 to which it relates.

• **1978, Revenue Act of 1978 (P.L. 95-600)**

P.L. 95-600, § 512(a), (b):

Added Code Secs. 6166(b)(2)(D) and (b)(7). **Effective** with respect to estates of decedents dying after 11-6-78.

[Sec. 6166(c)]

(c) SPECIAL RULE FOR INTEREST IN 2 OR MORE CLOSELY HELD BUSINESSES.—For purposes of this section, interests in 2 or more closely held businesses, with respect to each of which there is included in determining the value of the decedent's gross estate 20 percent or more of the total value of each such business, shall be treated as an interest in a single closely held business. For purposes of the 20-percent requirement of the preceding sentence, an interest in a closely held business which represents the surviving spouse's interest in property held by the decedent and the surviving spouse as community property or as joint tenants, tenants by the entirety, or tenants in common shall be treated as having been included in determining the value of the decedent's gross estate.

Amendments

• **1981, Economic Recovery Tax Act of 1981 (P.L. 97-34)**

P.L. 97-34, § 422(a)(2):

Amended Code Sec. 6166(c) by striking out "more than 20 percent" and inserting "20 percent or more". **Effective** for estates of decedents dying after 12-31-81.

[Sec. 6166(d)]

(d) ELECTION.—Any election under subsection (a) shall be made not later than the time prescribed by section 6075(a) for filing the return of tax imposed by section 2001 (including extensions thereof), and shall be made in such manner as the Secretary shall by regulations prescribe. If an election under subsection (a) is made, the provisions of this subtitle shall apply as though the Secretary were extending the time for payment of the tax.

[Sec. 6166(e)]

(e) PRORATION OF DEFICIENCY TO INSTALLMENTS.—If an election is made under subsection (a) to pay any part of the tax imposed by section 2001 in installments and a deficiency has been assessed, the deficiency shall (subject to the limitation provided by subsection (a)(2)) be prorated to the installments payable under subsection (a). The part of the deficiency so prorated to any installment the date for payment of which has not arrived shall be collected at the same time as, and as a part of, such installment. The part of the deficiency so prorated to any installment the date for payment of which has arrived shall be paid upon notice and demand from the Secretary. This subsection shall not apply if the deficiency is due to negligence, to intentional disregard of rules and regulations, or to fraud with intent to evade tax.

[Sec. 6166(f)]

(f) TIME FOR PAYMENT OF INTEREST.—If the time for payment of any amount of tax has been extended under this section—

(1) INTEREST FOR FIRST 5 YEARS.—Interest payable under section 6601 of any unpaid portion of such amount attributable to the first 5 years after the date prescribed by section 6151(a) for payment of the tax shall be paid annually.

(2) INTEREST FOR PERIODS AFTER FIRST 5 YEARS.—Interest payable under section 6601 on any unpaid portion of such amount attributable to any period after the 5-year period referred to in paragraph (1) shall be paid annually at the same time as, and as a part of, each installment payment of the tax.

(3) INTEREST IN THE CASE OF CERTAIN DEFICIENCIES.—In the case of a deficiency to which subsection (e) applies which is assessed after the close of the 5-year period referred to in paragraph (1), interest attributable to such 5—year period, and interest assigned under paragraph (2) to any installment the date for payment of which has arrived on or before the date of the assessment of the deficiency, shall be paid upon notice and demand from the Secretary.

(4) SELECTION OF SHORTER PERIOD.—If the executor has selected a period shorter than 5 years under subsection (a)(3), such shorter period shall be substituted for 5 years in paragraphs (1), (2), and (3) of this subsection.

[Sec. 6166(g)]

(g) ACCELERATION OF PAYMENT.—

(1) DISPOSITION OF INTEREST; WITHDRAWAL OF FUNDS FROM BUSINESS.—

(A) If—

(i)(I) any portion of an interest in a closely held business which qualifies under subsection (a)(1) is distributed, sold, exchanged, or otherwise disposed of, or

(II) money and other property attributable to such an interest is withdrawn from such trade or business, and

(ii) the aggregate of such distributions, sales, exchanges, or other dispositions and withdrawals equals or exceeds 50 percent of the value of such interest,

then the extension of time for payment of tax provided in subsection (a) shall cease to apply, and the unpaid portion of the tax payable in installments shall be paid upon notice and demand from the Secretary.

(B) In the case of a distribution in redemption of stock to which section 303 (or so much of section 304 as relates to section 303) applies—

(i) the redemption of such stock, and the withdrawal of money and other property distributed in such redemption, shall not be treated as a distribution or withdrawal for purposes of subparagraph (A), and

(ii) for purposes of subparagraph (A), the value of the interest in the closely held business shall be considered to be such value reduced by the value of the stock redeemed.

This subparagraph shall apply only if, on or before the date prescribed by subsection (a)(3) for the payment of the first installment which becomes due after the date of the distribution (or, if earlier, on or before the day which is 1 year after the date of the distribution), there is paid an amount of the tax imposed by section 2001 not less than the amount of money and other property distributed.

(C) Subparagraph (A)(i) does not apply to an exchange of stock pursuant to a plan of reorganization described in subparagraph (D), (E), or (F) of section 368(a)(1) nor to an exchange to which section 355 (or so much of section 356 as relates to section 355) applies; but any stock received in such an exchange shall be treated for purposes of subparagraph (A)(i) as an interest qualifying under subsection (a)(1).

(D) Subparagraph (A)(i) does not apply to a transfer of property of the decedent to a person entitled by reason of the decedent's death to receive such property under the decedent's will, the applicable law of descent and distribution, or a trust created by the decedent. A similar rule shall apply in the case of a series of subsequent transfers of the property by reason of death so long as each transfer is to a member of the family (within the meaning of section 267(c)(4)) of the transferor in such transfer.

(E) CHANGES IN INTEREST IN HOLDING COMPANY.—If any stock in a holding company is treated as stock in a business company by reason of subsection (b)(8)(A)—

(i) any disposition of any interest in such stock in such holding company which was included in determining the gross estate of the decedent, or

(ii) any withdrawal of any money or other property from such holding company attributable to any interest included in determining the gross estate of the decedent,

shall be treated for purposes of subparagraph (A) as a disposition of (or a withdrawal with respect to) the stock qualifying under subsection (a)(1).

(F) CHANGES IN INTEREST IN BUSINESS COMPANY.—If any stock in a holding company is treated as stock in a business company by reason of subsection (b)(8)(A)—

(i) any disposition of any interest in such stock in the business company by such holding company, or

(ii) any withdrawal of any money or other property from such business company attributable to such stock by such holding company owning such stock,

shall be treated for purposes of subparagraph (A) as a disposition of (or a withdrawal with respect to) the stock qualifying under subsection (a)(1).

(2) UNDISTRIBUTED INCOME OF ESTATE.—

(A) If an election is made under this section and the estate has undistributed net income for any taxable year ending on or after the due date for the first installment, the executor shall, on or before the date prescribed by law for filing the income tax return for such taxable year (including extensions thereof), pay an amount equal to such undistributed net income in liquidation of the unpaid portion of the tax payable in installments.

(B) For purposes of subparagraph (A), the undistributed net income of the estate for any taxable year is the amount by which the distributable net income of the estate for such taxable year (as defined in section 643) exceeds the sum of—

(i) the amounts for such taxable year specified in paragraphs (1) and (2) of section 661(a) (relating to deduction for distributions, etc.);

(ii) the amount of tax imposed for the taxable year on the estate under chapter 1; and

(iii) the amount of the tax imposed by section 2001 (including interest) paid by the executor during the taxable year (other than any amount paid pursuant to this paragraph).

(C) For purposes of this paragraph, if any stock in a corporation is treated as stock in another corporation by reason of subsection (b)(8)(A), any dividends paid by such other corporation to the corporation shall be treated as paid to the estate of the decedent to the extent attributable to the stock qualifying under subsection (a)(1).

(3) FAILURE TO MAKE PAYMENT OF PRINCIPAL OR INTEREST.—

(A) IN GENERAL.—Except as provided in subparagraph (B), if any payment of principal or interest under this section is not paid on or before the date fixed for its payment by this section (including any extension of time), the unpaid portion of the tax payable in installments shall be paid upon notice and demand from the Secretary.

(B) PAYMENT WITHIN 6 MONTHS.—If any payment of principal or interest under this section is not paid on or before the date determined under subparagraph (A) but is paid within 6 months of such date—

(i) the provisions of subparagraph (A) shall not apply with respect to such payment,

(ii) the provisions of section 6601(j) shall not apply with respect to the determination of interest on such payment, and

(iii) there is imposed a penalty in an amount equal to the product of—

(I) 5 percent of the amount of such payment, multiplied by

(II) the number of months (or fractions thereof) after such date and before payment is made.

The penalty imposed under clause (iii) shall be treated in the same manner as a penalty imposed under subchapter B of chapter 68.

Amendments

• 1984, Deficit Reduction Act of 1984 (P.L. 98-369)

P.L. 98-369, §1021(c):

Amended Code Sec. 6166(g)(1) by adding at the end thereof new subparagraphs (E) and (F). **Effective** with respect to estates of decedents dying after 7-18-84. However, see Act Sec. 1021(d)[(e)](2), below, for special rules.

P.L. 98-369, §1021(d):

Amended Code Sec. 6166(g)(2) by adding at the end thereof a new subparagraph (C). **Effective** with respect to estates of decedents dying after 7-18-84. However, see Act Sec. 1021(d)[(e)](2), below, for special rules.

P.L. 98-369, §1021(e)(2), provides:

(2) Special Rule.—

(A) In General.—At the election of the executor, if—

(i) a corporation has 15 or fewer shareholders on June 22, 1984, and at all times thereafter before the date of the decedent's death, and

(ii) stock of such corporation is included in the gross estate of the decedent,

then all other corporations all of the stock of which is owned directly or indirectly by the corporation described in clauses (i) and (ii) shall be treated as one corporation for purposes of section 6166 of the Internal Revenue Code of 1954.

(B) Effect of Election.—Any executor who elects the application of this paragraph shall be treated as having made the election under paragraph (8) of section 6166(b) of such Code.

• 1983, Technical Corrections Act of 1982 (P.L. 97-448)

P.L. 97-448, §104(c)(2):

Amended clauses (i) and (ii) of the first sentence of Code Sec. 6166(g)(1)(B). **Effective** as if included in the provision of P.L. 97-34 to which it relates. Prior to amendment, clauses (i) and (ii) of the first sentence of Code Sec. 6166(g)(1)(B) read as follows:

"(i) subparagraph (A)(i) does not apply with respect to the stock redeemed; and for purposes of such subparagraph the interest in the closely held business shall be considered to be such interest reduced by the value of the stock redeemed, and

(ii) subparagraph (A)(ii) does not apply with respect to withdrawals of money and other property distributed; and for purposes of such subparagraph the value of the trade or business shall be considered to be such value reduced by the amount of money and other property distributed."

• 1981, Economic Recovery Tax Act of 1981 (P.L. 97-34)

P.L. 97-34, §422(c)(1):

Amended Code Sec. 6166(g)(1)(A). **Effective** for estates of decedents dying after 12-31-81. Prior to amendment, Code Sec. 6166(g)(1)(A) read as follows:

(A) If—

(i) one-third or more in value of an interest in a closely held business which qualifies under subsection (a)(1) is distributed, sold, exchanged, or otherwise disposed of, or

(ii) aggregate withdrawals of money and other property from the trade or business, an interest in which qualifies under subsection (a)(1), made with respect to such interest, equal or exceed one-third of the value of such trade or business,

then the extension of time for payment of tax provided in subsection (a) shall cease to apply, and any unpaid portion of the tax payable in installments shall be paid upon notice and demand from the Secretary.

P.L. 97-34, §422(c)(2):

Amended Code Sec. 6166(g)(3). **Effective** for estates of decedents dying after 12-31-81. Prior to amendment, Code Sec. 6166(g)(3) read as follows:

(3) FAILURE TO PAY INSTALLMENT.—If any installment under this section is not paid on or before the date fixed for its payment by this section (including any extension of time for the payment of such installment), the unpaid portion of the tax payable in installments shall be paid upon notice and demand from the Secretary.

P.L. 97-34, §422(c)(3):

Amended Code Sec. 6166(g)(1)(D) by adding the last sentence. **Effective** for transfers after 12-31-81.

[Sec. 6166(h)]

(h) ELECTION IN CASE OF CERTAIN DEFICIENCIES.—

(1) IN GENERAL.—If—

(A) a deficiency in the tax imposed by section 2001 is assessed,

(B) the estate qualifies under subsection (a)(1), and

(C) the executor has not made an election under subsection (a), the executor may elect to pay the deficiency in installments. This subsection shall not apply if the deficiency is due to negligence, to intentional disregard of rules and regulations, or to fraud with intent to evade tax.

(2) TIME OF ELECTION.—An election under this subsection shall be made not later than 60 days after issuance of notice and demand by the Secretary for the payment of the deficiency, and shall be made in such manner as the Secretary shall by regulations prescribe.

(3) EFFECT OF ELECTION ON PAYMENT.—If an election is made under this subsection, the deficiency shall (subject to the limitation provided by subsection (a)(2)) be prorated to the installments which would have been due if an election had been timely made under subsection (a) at the time the estate tax return was filed. The part of the deficiency so prorated to any installment the date for payment of which would have arrived shall be paid at the time of the making of the election under this subsection. The portion of the deficiency so prorated to installments the date for payment of which would not have so arrived shall be paid at the time such installments would have been due if such an election had been made.

[Sec. 6166(i)]

(i) SPECIAL RULE FOR CERTAIN DIRECT SKIPS.—To the extent that an interest in a closely held business is the subject of a direct skip (within the meaning of section 2612(c)) occurring at the same time as and as a result of the decedent's death, then for purposes of this section any tax imposed by section 2601 on the transfer of such interest shall be treated as if it were additional tax imposed by section 2001.

Amendments

• 1986, Tax Reform Act of 1986 (P.L. 99-514)

P.L. 99-514, §1432(e):

Amended Code Sec. 6166 by redesignating subsection (i) and (j) as subsections (j) and (k), respectively, and by inserting after subsection (h), new subsection (i). **Effective**, generally, for any generation-skipping transfer (within the meaning of section 2611 of the Internal Revenue Code of 1986) made after the date of the enactment of this Act. For special rules, see Act Sec. 1433(b)-(d) following Code Sec. 2601.

[Sec. 6166(j)]

(j) REGULATIONS.—The Secretary shall prescribe such regulations as may be necessary to the application of this section.

Amendments

• 1986, Tax Reform Act of 1986 (P.L. 99-514)

P.L. 99-514, §1432(e):

Amended Code Sec. 6166 by redesignating subsection (i) and (j) as subsections (j) and (k), respectively, and by inserting after subsection (h), new subsection (i). **Effective**, generally, for any generation-skipping transfer (within the meaning of section 2611 of the Internal Revenue Code of 1986) made after 10-22-86. For special rules, see Act Sec. 1433(b)-(d) following Code Sec. 2601.

[Sec. 6166(k)]

(k) CROSS REFERENCES.—

(1) SECURITY.—For authority of the Secretary to require security in the case of an extension under this section, see section 6165.

(2) LIEN.—For special lien (in lieu of bond) in the case of an extension under this section, see section 6324A.

(3) PERIOD OF LIMITATION.—For extension of the period of limitation in the case of an extension under this section, see section 6503(d).

(4) INTEREST.—For provisions relating to interest on tax payable in installments under this section, see subsection (j) of section 6601.

(5) TRANSFERS WITHIN 3 YEARS OF DEATH.—For special rule for qualifying an estate under this section where property has been transferred within 3 years of decedent's death, see section 2035(c)(2).

Amendments

• 2000, Community Renewal Tax Relief Act of 2000 (P.L. 106-554)

P.L. 106-554, §319(18):

Amended Code Sec. 6166(k)(5) by striking "2035(d)(4)" and inserting "2035(c)(2)". **Effective** on 12-21-00.

• 1996, Small Business Job Protection Act of 1996 (P.L. 104-188)

P.L. 104-188, §1704(t)(15):

Amended Code Sec. 6166(k) by striking paragraph (6). **Effective** 8-20-96. Prior to being stricken, Code Sec. 6166(k)(6) read as follows:

(6) PAYMENT OF ESTATE TAX BY EMPLOYEE STOCK OWNERSHIP PLAN OR ELIGIBLE WORKER-OWNED COOPERATIVE.—For provision allowing plan administrator or eligible worker-owned cooperative to elect to pay a certain portion of the estate tax in installments under the provisions of this section, see section 2210(c).

• 1986, Tax Reform Act of 1986 (P.L. 99-514)

P.L. 99-514, §1432(e):

Amended Code Sec. 6166 by redesignating subsection (i) and (j) as subsections (j) and (k), respectively, and by inserting after subsection (h), new subsection (i). **Effective**, generally, for any generation-skipping transfer (within the meaning of section 2611 of the Internal Revenue Code of 1986) made after 10-22-86. For special rules, see Act Sec. 1433(b)-(d) following Code Sec. 2601.

• 1984, Deficit Reduction Act of 1984 (P.L. 98-369)

P.L. 98-369 §544(b)(4):

Amended Code Sec. 6166(j) by adding new paragraph (6). **Effective** for those estates of decedents required to file returns on a date (including any extensions) after 7-18-84.

• **1983, Technical Corrections Act of 1982 (P.L. 97-448)**

P.L. 97-448, § 104(d)(1)(B):

Amended Code Sec. 6166(j) by adding at the end thereof new paragraph (5). **Effective** as if included in the provision of P.L. 97-34 to which it relates.

• **1976, Tax Reform Act of 1976 (P.L. 94-455)**

P.L. 94-455, § 2004(a):

Redesignated former Code Sec. 6166 as Code Sec. 6166A and added a new Code Sec. 6166, including Code Sec. 6166(j). **Effective** for estates of decedents dying after 12-31-76.

[Sec. 6166A—Repealed]

Amendments

• **1981, Economic Recovery Tax Act of 1981 (P.L. 97-34)**

P.L. 97-34, § 422(d):

Repealed Code Sec. 6166A. **Effective** for estates of decedents dying after 12-31-81. Prior to its repeal, Code Sec. 6166A read as follows:

SEC. 6166A. EXTENSION OF TIME FOR PAYMENT OF ESTATE TAX WHERE ESTATE CONSISTS LARGELY OF INTEREST IN CLOSELY HELD BUSINESS.

[Sec. 6166A(a)]

(a) EXTENSION PERMITTED.—If the value of an interest in a closely held business which is included in determining the gross estate of a decedent who was (at the date of his death) a citizen or resident of the United States exceeds either—

(1) 35 percent of the value of the gross estate of such decedent, or

(2) 50 percent of the taxable estate of such decedent,

the executor may elect to pay part or all of the tax imposed by section 2001 in two or more (but not exceeding 10) equal installments. Any such election shall be made not later than the time prescribed by section 6075(a) for filing the return of such tax (including extensions thereof), and shall be made in such manner as the Secretary shall by regulations prescribe. If an election under this section is made, the provisions of this subtitle shall apply as though the Secretary were extending the time for payment of the tax. For purposes of this section, value shall be value determined for Federal estate tax purposes.

Amendments

• **1976, Tax Reform Act of 1976 (P.L. 94-455)**

P.L. 94-455, § 1906(b)(13)(A):

Amended 1954 Code by substituting "Secretary" for "Secretary or his delegate" each place it appeared. **Effective** 2-1-77.

[Sec. 6166A(b)]

(b) LIMITATION.—The maximum amount of tax which may be paid in installments as provided in this section shall be an amount which bears the same ratio to the tax imposed by section 2001 (reduced by the credits against such tax) as the value of the interest in a closely held business which qualifies under subsection (a) bears to the value of the gross estate.

[Sec. 6166A(c)]

(c) CLOSELY HELD BUSINESS.—For purposes of this section, the term "interest in a closely held business" means—

(1) an interest as a proprietor in a trade or business carried on as a proprietorship.

(2) an interest as a partner in a partnership carrying on a trade or business, if—

(A) 20 percent or more of the total capital interest in such partnership is included in determining the gross estate of the decedent, or

(B) such partnership had 10 or less partners,

(3) stock in a corporation carrying on a trade or business, if—

(A) 20 percent or more in value of the voting stock of such corporation is included in determining the gross estate of the decedent, or

(B) such corporation had 10 or less shareholders.

For purposes of this subsection, determinations shall be made as of the time immediately before the decedent's death.

[Sec. 6166A(d)]

(d) SPECIAL RULE FOR INTERESTS IN TWO OR MORE CLOSELY HELD BUSINESSES.—For purposes of subsections (a), (b), and (h)(1), interests in two or more closely held businesses, with respect to each of which there is included in determining the value of the decedent's gross estate more than 50 percent of the total value of each such business, shall be treated as an interest in a single closely held business. For purposes of the 50 percent requirement of the preceding sentence, an interest in a closely held business which represents the surviving spouse's interest in property held by the decedent and the surviving spouse as community property shall be treated as having been included in determining the value of the decedent's gross estate.

[Sec. 6166A(e)]

(e) DATE FOR PAYMENT OF INSTALLMENTS.—If an election is made under subsection (a), the first installment shall be paid on or before the date prescribed by section 6151(a) for payment of the tax, and each succeeding installment shall be paid on or before the date which is one year after the date prescribed by this subsection for payment of the preceeding installment.

[Sec. 6166A(f)]

(f) PRORATION OF DEFICIENCY TO INSTALLMENTS.—If an election is made under subsection (a) to pay any part of the tax imposed by section 2001 in installments and a deficiency has been assessed, the deficiency shall (subject to the limitation provided by subsection (b)) be prorated to such installments. The part of the deficiency so prorated to any installment the date for payment of which has not arrived shall be collected at the same time as, and as a part of, such installment. The part of the deficiency so prorated to any installment the date for payment of which has arrived shall be paid upon notice and demand from the Secretary. This subsection shall not apply if the deficiency is due to negligence, to intentional disregard of rules and regulations, or to fraud with intent to evade tax.

Amendments

• **1976, Tax Reform Act of 1976 (P.L. 94-455)**

P.L. 94-455, § 1906(b)(13)(A):

Amended 1954 Code by substituting "Secretary" for "Secretary or his delegate" each place it appeared. **Effective** 2-1-77.

[Sec. 6166A(g)]

(g) TIME FOR PAYMENT OF INTEREST.—If the time for payment of any amount of tax has been extended under this section, interest payable under section 6601 on any unpaid portion of such amount shall be paid annually at the same time as, and as a part of, each installment payment of the tax. Interest, on that part of a deficiency prorated under this section to any installment the date for payment of which has not arrived, for the period before the date fixed for the last installment preceding the assessment of the deficiency, shall be paid upon notice and demand from the Secretary.

Amendments

• **1976, Tax Reform Act of 1976 (P.L. 94-455)**

P.L. 94-455, § 1906(b)(13)(A):

Amended 1954 Code by substituting "Secretary" for "Secretary or his delegate" each place it appeared. **Effective** 2-1-77.

• **1975 (P.L. 93-625)**

P.L. 93-625, § 7(d)(2):

Amended Code Sec. 6166(g) by deleting the following from the end thereof: "In applying section 6601(b) (relating to the application of the 4-percent rate of interest in the case of certain extensions of time to pay estate tax) in the case of a deficiency, the entire amount which is prorated to installments under this section shall be treated as an amount of tax the payment of which is extended under this section." **Effective** 7-1-75.

[Sec. 6166A(h)]

(h) ACCELERATION OF PAYMENT.—

(1) WITHDRAWAL OF FUNDS FROM BUSINESS; DISPOSITION OF INTEREST.—

(A) If—

(i) aggregate withdrawals of money and other property from the trade or business, an interest in which qualifies under subsection (a), made with respect to such interest, equal or exceed 50 percent of the value of such trade or business, or

(ii) 50 percent or more in value of an interest in a closely held business which qualifies under subsection (a) is distributed, sold, exchanged, or otherwise disposed of,

then the extension of time for payment of tax provided in this section shall cease to apply, and any unpaid portion of the tax payable in installments shall be paid upon notice and demand from the Secretary.

(B) In the case of a distribution in redemption of stock to which section 303 (or so much of section 304 as relates to section 303) applies—

(i) subparagraph (A)(i) does not apply with respect to withdrawals of money and other property distributed; and for purposes of such subparagraph the value of the trade or business shall be considered to be such value reduced by the amount of money and other property distributed, and

(ii) subparagraph (A)(ii) does not apply with respect to the stock redeemed; and for purposes of such subparagraph the interest in the closely held business shall be considered to be such interest reduced by the value of the stock redeemed.

This subparagraph shall apply only if, on or before the date prescribed by subsection (e) for payment on the first installment which becomes due after the date of the distribution, there is paid an amount of the tax imposed by section 2001 not less than the amount of money and other property distributed.

(C) Subparagraph (A)(ii) does not apply to an exchange of stock pursuant to a plan of reorganization described in subparagraph (D), (E), or (F) of section 368(a)(1) nor to an exchange to which section 355 (or so much of section 356 as relates to section 355) applies; but any stock received in such an exchange shall be treated for purposes of such subparagraph as an interest qualifying under subsection (a).

(D) Subparagraph (A)(ii) does not apply to a transfer of property of the decedent by the executor to a person entitled to receive such property under the decedent's will or under the applicable law of descent and distribution.

(2) UNDISTRIBUTED INCOME OF ESTATE.—

(A) If an election is made under this section and the estate has undistributed net income for any taxable year after its fourth taxable year, the executor shall, on or before the date prescribed by law for filing the income tax return for such taxable year (including extensions thereof), pay an amount equal to such undistributed net income in liquidation of the unpaid portion of the tax payable in installments.

(B) For purposes of subparagraph (A), the undistributed net income of the estate for any taxable year is the amount by which the distributable net income of the estate for such taxable year (as defined in section 643) exceeds the sum of—

(i) the amounts for such taxable year specified in paragraphs (1) and (2) of section 661(a) (relating to deduction for distributions, etc.);

(ii) the amount of tax imposed for the taxable year on the estate under chapter 1; and,

(iii) the amount of the Federal estate tax (including interest) paid by the executor during the taxable year (other than any amount paid pursuant to this paragraph).

(3) FAILURE TO PAY INSTALLMENT.—If any installment under this section is not paid on or before the date fixed for its payment by this section (including any extension of time for the payment of such installment), the unpaid portion of the tax payable in installments shall be paid upon notice and demand from the Secretary.

Amendments

• 1976, Tax Reform Act of 1976 (P.L. 94-455)

P.L. 94-455, §1906(b)(13)(A):

Amended 1954 Code by substituting "Secretary" for "Secretary or his delegate" each place it appeared. **Effective** 2-1-77.

[Sec. 6166A(i)]

(i) TRANSITIONAL RULES.—

(1) IN GENERAL.—If—

(A) a deficiency in the tax imposed by section 2001 is assessed after the date of the enactment of this section, and

(B) the estate qualifies under paragraph (1) or (2) of subsection (a),

the executor may elect to pay the deficiency in installments. This subsection shall not apply if the deficiency is due to negligence, to intentional disregard of rules and regulations, or to fraud with intent to evade tax.

(2) TIME OF ELECTION.—An election under this subsection shall be made not later than 60 days after issuance of notice and demand by the Secretary for the payment of the deficiency, and shall be made in such manner as the Secretary shall by regulations prescribe.

(3) EFFECT OF ELECTION ON PAYMENT.—If an election is made under this subsection, the deficiency shall (subject to the limitation provided by subsection (b)) be prorated to the installments which would have been due if an election had been timely made under this section at the time the estate tax return was filed. The part of the deficiency so prorated to any installment the date for payment of which would have arrived shall be paid at the time of the making of the election under this subsection. The portion of the deficiency so prorated to installments the date for payment of which would not have so arrived shall be paid at the time such installments would have been due if such an election had been made.

(4) APPLICATION OF SUBSECTION (h)(2).—In the case of an election under this subsection, subsection (h)(2) shall not apply with respect to undistributed net income for any taxable year ending before January 1, 1960.

Amendments

• 1976, Tax Reform Act of 1976 (P.L. 94-455)

P.L. 94-455, §1906(b)(13)(A):

Amended 1954 Code by substituting "Secretary" for "Secretary or his delegate" each place it appeared. **Effective** 2-1-77.

[Sec. 6166A(j)]

(j) REGULATIONS.—The Secretary shall prescribe such regulations as may be necessary to the application of this section.

Amendments

P.L. 94-455, §1906(b)(13)(A):

Amended 1954 Code by substituting "Secretary" for "Secretary or his delegate" each place it appeared. **Effective** 2-1-77.

[Sec. 6166A(k)]

(k) CROSS REFERENCES.—

(1) SECURITY.—

For authority of the Secretary to require security in the case of an extension under this section, see section 6165.

(2) PERIOD OF LIMITATION.—

For extension of the period of limitation in the case of an extension under this section, see section 6503(d).

Amendments

• 1976, Tax Reform Act of 1976 (P.L. 94-455)

P.L. 94-455, §1906(b)(13)(A):

Amended 1954 Code by substituting "Secretary" for "Secretary or his delegate" each place it appeared. **Effective** 2-1-77.

• 1975 (P.L. 93-625)

P.L. 93-625, §7(d)(3):

Amended Code Sec. 6166(k) by deleting former paragraph (1) and renumbering former paragraphs (2) and (3) to be paragraphs (1) and (2), respectively. **Effective** 7-1-75. Prior to amendment, paragraph (1) read as follows:

"(1) Interest.—

"For provisions requiring the payment of interest at the rate of 4 percent per annum for the period of an extension, see section 6601(b)."

• 1958, Technical Amendments Act of 1958 (P.L. 85-866)

P.L. 85-866, §206(a):

Added Sec. 6166. For **effective** date, see Act Sec. 206(f), below.

P.L. 85-866, §206(f), provides:

"The amendments made by this section shall apply to estates of decedents with respect to which the date for the filing of the estate tax return (including extensions thereof) prescribed by section 6075(a) of the Internal Revenue Code of 1954 is after the date of the enactment of this Act; except that (1) section 6166(i) of such Code as added by this section shall apply to estates of decedents dying after August 16, 1954, but only if the date for the filing of the estate tax return (including extensions thereof) expired on or before the date of the enactment of this Act, and (2) notwithstanding section 6166(a) of such Code, if an election under such section is required to be made before the sixtieth day after the date of the enactment of this Act such an election shall be considered timely if made on or before such sixtieth day."

* * *

CHAPTER 63—ASSESSMENT

* * *

Subchapter A—In General

* * *

[Sec. 6201]

SEC. 6201. ASSESSMENT AUTHORITY.

[Sec. 6201(a)]

(a) AUTHORITY OF SECRETARY.—The Secretary is authorized and required to make the inquiries, determinations, and assessments of all taxes (including interest, additional amounts, additions to the tax, and assessable penalties) imposed by this title, or accruing under any former internal revenue law, which have not been duly paid by stamp at the time and in the manner provided by law. Such authority shall extend to and include the following:

(1) TAXES SHOWN ON RETURN.—The Secretary shall assess all taxes determined by the taxpayer or by the Secretary as to which returns or lists (or payments under section 6225(c)(2)(B)(i)) are made under this title.

(2) UNPAID TAXES PAYABLE BY STAMP.—

(A) OMITTED STAMPS.—Whenever any article upon which a tax is required to be paid by means of a stamp is sold or removed for sale or use by the manufacturer thereof or whenever any transaction or act upon which a tax is required to be paid by means of a stamp occurs without the use of the proper stamp, it shall be the duty of the Secretary, upon such information as he can obtain, to estimate the amount of tax which has been omitted to be paid and to make assessment therefor upon the person or persons the Secretary determines to be liable for such tax.

(B) CHECK OR MONEY ORDER NOT DULY PAID.—In any case in which a check or money order received under authority of section 6311 as payment for stamps is not duly paid, the unpaid amount may be immediately assessed as if it were a tax imposed by this title, due at the time of such receipt, from the person who tendered such check or money order.

(3) ERRONEOUS INCOME TAX PREPAYMENT CREDITS.—If on any return or claim for refund of income taxes under subtitle A there is an overstatement of the credit for income tax withheld at the source, or of the amount paid as estimated income tax, the amount so overstated which is allowed against the tax shown on the return or which is allowed as a credit or refund may be assessed by the Secretary in the same manner as in the case of a mathematical or clerical error appearing upon the return, except that the provisions of section 6213(b)(2) (relating to abatement of mathematical or clerical error assessments) shall not apply with regard to any assessment under this paragraph.

(4) CERTAIN ORDERS OF CRIMINAL RESTITUTION.—

(A) IN GENERAL.—The Secretary shall assess and collect the amount of restitution under an order pursuant to section 3556 of title 18, United States Code, for failure to pay any tax imposed under this title in the same manner as if such amount were such tax.

(B) TIME OF ASSESSMENT.—An assessment of an amount of restitution under an order described in subparagraph (A) shall not be made before all appeals of such order are concluded and the right to make all such appeals has expired.

(C) RESTRICTION ON CHALLENGE OF ASSESSMENT.—The amount of such restitution may not be challenged by the person against whom assessed on the basis of the existence or amount of the underlying tax liability in any proceeding authorized under this title (including in any suit or proceeding in court permitted under section 7422).

Amendments

• 2018, Tax Technical Corrections Act of 2018 (P.L. 115-141)

P.L. 115-141, §203(b), Div. U:

Amended Code Sec. 6201(a)(1) by inserting "(or payments under section 6225(c)(2)(B)(i))" after "returns or lists". **Effective** as if included in section 1101 of the Bipartisan Budget Act of 2015 [**effective** generally for returns filed for partnership tax years beginning after 12-31-2017.—CCH].

• 2010, Firearms Excise Tax Improvement Act of 2010 (P.L. 111-237)

P.L. 111-237, §3(a):

Amended Code Sec. 6201(a) by adding at the end a new paragraph (4). **Effective** for restitution ordered after 8-16-2010.

• 1988, Technical and Miscellaneous Revenue Act of 1988 (P.L. 100-647)

P.L. 100-647, §1015(r)(1):

Amended Code Sec. 6201(a) by striking out paragraph (4). **Effective** for notices of deficiencies mailed after 11-10-88. Prior to amendment, Code Sec. 6201(a)(4) read as follows:

(4) ERRONEOUS CREDIT UNDER SECTION 32 OR 34.—If on any return or claim for refund of income taxes under subtitle A there is an overstatement of the credit allowable by section 34 (relating to certain uses of gasoline and special fuels) or section 32 (relating to earned income), the amount so overstated which is allowed against the tax shown on the return or which is allowed as a credit or refund may be assessed by the Secretary in the same manner as in the case of a mathematical or clerical error appearing upon the return, except that the provisions of section 6213(b)(2) (relating to abatement of mathematical or clerical error assessments) shall not apply with regard to any assessment under this paragraph.

• 1984, Deficit Reduction Act of 1984 (P.L. 98-369)

P.L. 98-369, §474(r)(32):

Amended Code Sec. 6201(a)(4) by striking out "section 39" and inserting in lieu thereof "section 34", by striking out "section 43" and inserting in lieu thereof "section 32", and by striking out "Section 39 or 43" in the paragraph heading and inserting in lieu thereof "Section 32 or 34". **Effective** for tax years beginning after 12-31-83, and to carrybacks from such years.

• 1983, Surface Transportation Act of 1983 (P.L. 97-424)

P.L. 97-424, §515(b)(6)(E):

Amended Code Sec. 6201(a)(4) by striking out ", special fuels, and lubricating oil" and inserting "and special fuels". **Effective** with respect to articles sold after 1-6-83.

• 1976, Tax Reform Act of 1976 (P.L. 94-455)

P.L. 94-455, §1206(c)(2)(A):

Substituted "mathematical or clerical error" for "mathematical error" in Code Sec. 6201(a)(3) and 6201(a)(4). **Effective** with respect to returns filed after 12-31-76.

P.L. 94-455, §1206(c)(2)(B):

Added ", except that the provisions of section 6213(b)(2) (relating to abatement of mathematical or clerical error assessments) shall not apply with regard to any assessment under this paragraph" immediately before the period at the end of Code Sec. 6201(a)(3) and 6201(a)(4). **Effective** with respect to returns filed after 12-31-76.

P.L. 94-455, §1906(b)(13)(A):

Amended 1954 Code by substituting "Secretary" for "Secretary or his delegate" each place it appeared. **Effective** 2-1-77.

• 1975, Tax Reduction Act of 1975 (P.L. 94-12)

P.L. 94-12, §204(b)(2):

Amended Code Sec. 6201(a)(4) by inserting "or 43" after "section 39" in the caption of the section and by deleting "oil)," and inserting in lieu thereof "oil) or section 43 (relating to earned income),". **Effective** only for tax years beginning after 1974 (as amended by P.L. 95-600, §103(a), and P.L. 94-164, §2(f)).

• 1970 (P.L. 91-258)

P.L. 91-258, §207(d)(1), (2):

Amended Code Sec. 6201(a)(4) by substituting "UNDER SECTION 39" for "FOR USE OF GASOLINE" in the heading and by adding ", special fuels," in the parenthetical matter in the body. **Effective** 7-1-70.

• 1965, Excise Tax Reduction Act of 1965 (P.L. 89-44)

P.L. 89-44, §809(d)(4):

Amended Sec. 6201(a) by adding paragraph (4). **Effective** 7-1-65.

* * *

[Sec. 6201(d)]

(d) REQUIRED REASONABLE VERIFICATION OF INFORMATION RETURNS.—In any court proceeding, if a taxpayer asserts a reasonable dispute with respect to any item of income reported on an information return filed with the Secretary under subpart B or C of part III of subchapter A of chapter 61 by a third party and the taxpayer has fully cooperated with the Secretary (including providing, within a reasonable period of time, access to and inspection of all witnesses, information, and documents within the control of the taxpayer as reasonably requested by the Secretary), the Secretary shall have the burden of producing reasonable and probative information concerning such deficiency in addition to such information return.

Amendments

• 1996, Taxpayer Bill of Rights 2 (P.L. 104-168)

P.L. 104-168, §602(a):

Amended Code Sec. 6201 by redesignating subsection (d) as subsection (e) and by inserting after subsection (c) a new subsection (d). **Effective** 7-30-96.

[Sec. 6201(e)]

(e) DEFICIENCY PROCEEDINGS.—

For special rules applicable to deficiencies of income, estate, gift, and certain excise taxes, see subchapter B.

Amendments

• 1996, Taxpayer Bill of Rights 2 (P.L. 104-168)

P.L. 104-168, §602(a):

Amended Code Sec. 6201 by redesignating subsection (d) as subsection (e). **Effective** 7-30-96.

• 1976, Tax Reform Act of 1976 (P.L. 94-455)

P.L. 94-455, §1307(d)(2)(D):

Substituted "and certain excise taxes" for "chapter 42, and chapter 43 taxes" in Code Sec. 6201(d). **Effective** 10-4-76.

• 1974, Employee Retirement Income Security Act of 1974 (P.L. 93-406)

P.L. 93-406, §1016(a)(8):

Amended Code Sec. 6201(d) by changing "and chapter 42" to "chapter 42, and chapter 43". For **effective** date, see amendment note for Code Sec. 410.

• **1969, Tax Reform Act of 1969 (P.L. 91-172)**

P.L. 91-172, §101(j)(38):

Amended Code Sec. 6201(d) by substituting "gift, and chapter 42 taxes," for "and gift taxes,". **Effective** 1-1-70.

[Sec. 6202]

SEC. 6202. ESTABLISHMENT BY REGULATIONS OF MODE OR TIME OF ASSESSMENT.

If the mode or time for the assessment of any internal revenue tax (including interest, additional amounts, additions to the tax, and assessable penalties) is not otherwise provided for, the Secretary may establish the same by regulations.

Amendments

• **1976, Tax Reform Act of 1976 (P.L. 94-455)**

P.L. 94-455, §1906(b)(13)(A):

Amended 1954 Code by substituting "Secretary" for "Secretary or his delegate" each place it appeared. **Effective** 2-1-77.

[Sec. 6203]

SEC. 6203. METHOD OF ASSESSMENT.

The assessment shall be made by recording the liability of the taxpayer in the office of the Secretary in accordance with rules or regulations prescribed by the Secretary. Upon request of the taxpayer, the Secretary shall furnish the taxpayer a copy of the record of the assessment.

Amendments

• **1976, Tax Reform Act of 1976 (P.L. 94-455)**

P.L. 94-455, §1906(b)(13)(A):

Amended 1954 Code by substituting "Secretary" for "Secretary or his delegate" each place it appeared. **Effective** 2-1-77.

[Sec. 6204]

SEC. 6204. SUPPLEMENTAL ASSESSMENTS.

[Sec. 6204(a)]

(a) GENERAL RULE.—The Secretary may, at any time within the period prescribed for assessment, make a supplemental assessment whenever it is ascertained that any assessment is imperfect or incomplete in any material respect.

Amendments

• **1976, Tax Reform Act of 1976 (P.L. 94-455)**

P.L. 94-455, §1906(b)(13)(A):

Amended 1954 Code by substituting "Secretary" for "Secretary or his delegate" each place it appeared. **Effective** 2-1-77.

[Sec. 6204(b)]

(b) RESTRICTIONS ON ASSESSMENT.—

For restrictions on assessment of deficiencies in income, estate, gift, and certain excise taxes, see section 6213.

Amendments

• **1974, Employee Retirement Income Security Act of 1974 (P.L. 93-406)**

P.L. 93-406, §1016(a)(27):

Amended Code Sec. 6204(b) by changing "and gift taxes," to "gift, and certain excise taxes". For **effective** date, see amendment note for Code Sec. 410.

* * *

Subchapter B—Deficiency Procedures in the Case of Income, Estate, Gift, and Certain Excise Taxes

* * *

[Sec. 6211]

SEC. 6211. DEFINITION OF A DEFICIENCY.

[Sec. 6211(a)]

(a) IN GENERAL.—For purposes of this title in the case of income, estate, and gift taxes imposed by subtitles A and B and excise taxes imposed by chapters 41, 42, 43, and 44 the term "deficiency" means the amount by which the tax imposed by subtitle A or B, or chapter 41, 42, 43, or 44 exceeds the excess of—

(1) the sum of

(A) the amount shown as the tax by the taxpayer upon his return, if a return was made by the taxpayer and an amount was shown as the tax by the taxpayer thereon, plus

(B) the amounts previously assessed (or collected without assessment) as a deficiency, over—

(2) the amount of rebates, as defined in subsection (b)(2), made.

Amendments

• 1988, Omnibus Trade and Competitiveness Act of 1988 (P.L. 100-418)

P.L. 100-418, §1941(b)(2)(B)(i):

Amended Code Sec. 6211(a) by striking "44, or 45" each place it appears and inserting "or 44". **Effective** for crude oil removed from the premises on or after 8-23-88.

P.L. 100-418, §1941(b)(2)(C):

Amended Code Sec. 6211(a) by striking "44, and 45" and inserting "and 44". **Effective** for crude oil removed from the premises on or after 8-23-88.

• 1980, Crude Oil Windfall Profit Tax Act of 1980 (P.L. 96-223)

P.L. 96-223, §101(f)(1)(A), (f)(2):

Amended Code Sec. 6211(a) by striking out "or 44" and inserting "44, or 45" and by striking out "and 44" and inserting "44, and 45". For the **effective** date and the transitional rules see P.L. 96-223, §101(i), following Code Sec. 4986.

• 1976, Tax Reform Act of 1976 (P.L. 94-455)

P.L. 94-455, §1307(d)(2)(E):

Substituted "chapters 41, 42," for "chapters 42" in Code Sec. 6211(a). **Effective** 10-4-76.

P.L. 94-455, §1307(d)(2)(F)(i):

Substituted "chapter 41, 42," for "chapter 42" in Code Sec. 6211(a).

P.L. 94-455, §1605(b)(4)(A):

Substituted "43, and 44" for "and 43" in Code Sec. 6211(a).

P.L. 94-455, §1608(d), provides:

(d) OTHER AMENDMENTS.—

(1) Except as provided in paragraphs (2) and (3), the amendments made by sections 1603, 1604, and 1605 shall apply to taxable years of real estate investment trusts beginning after the date of the enactment of this Act.

(2) If, as a result of a determination (as defined in section 859(c) of the Internal Revenue Code of 1954), occurring after the date of enactment of this Act, with respect to the real estate investment trust, such trust does not meet the requirement of section 856(a)(4) of the Internal Revenue Code of 1954 (as in effect before the amendment of such section by this Act) for any taxable year beginning on or before the date of the enactment of this Act, such trust may elect, within 60 days after such determination in the manner provided in regulations prescribed by the Secretary of the Treasury or his delegate, to have the provisions of section 1603 (other than paragraphs (1), (2), (3), and (4) of section 1603(c)) apply with respect to such taxable year. Where the provisions of section 1603 apply to a real estate investment trust with respect to any taxable year beginning on or before the date of the enactment of this Act—

(A) credit or refund of any overpayment of tax which results from the application of section 1603 to such taxable year shall be made as if on the date of the determination (as defined in section 859(c) of the Internal Revenue Code of 1954) 2 years remained before the expiration of the period of limitation prescribed by section 6511 of such Code on the filing of claim for refund for the taxable year to which the overpayment relates,

(B) the running of the statute of limitations provided in section 6501 of such Code on the making of assessments, and the bringing of distraint or a proceeding in court for collection, in respect of any deficiency (as defined in section 6211 of such Code) established by such a determination, and all interest, additions to tax, additional amounts, or assessable penalties in respect thereof, shall be suspended for a period of 2 years after the date of such determination, and

(C) the collection of any deficiency (as defined in section 6211 of such Code) established by such determination and all interest, additions to tax, additional amounts, and assessable penalties in respect thereof shall, except in cases of jeopardy, be stayed until the expiration of 60 days after the date of such determination.

No distraint or proceeding in court shall be begun for the collection of an amount the collection of which is stayed under subparagraph (C) during the period for which the collection of such amount is stayed.

(3) Section 856 (g)(3) of the Internal Revenue Code of 1954, as added by section 1604 of this Act, shall not apply with respect to a termination of an election, filed by a taxpayer under section 856(c)(1) of such Code on or before the date of the enactment of this Act, unless the provisions of part II of subchapter M of chapter 1 of subtitle A of such Code apply to such taxpayer for a taxable year ending after the date of the enactment of this Act for which such election is in effect.

P.L. 94-455, §1605(b)(4)(B):

Substituted "43, or 44" for "or 43" in Code Sec. 6211(a). For **effective** date information, see amendatory note for P.L. 94-455, §1605(b)(4)(A).

• 1974, Employee Retirement Income Security Act of 1974 (P.L. 93-406)

P.L. 93-406, §1016(a)(9):

Amended Code Sec. 6211(a) by changing so much of subsection (a) as precedes paragraph (1) to read as prior to amendment by P.L. 94-455. For **effective** date, see amendment note for Code Sec. 410. Prior to amendment it read as follows:

"(a) In General.—For purposes of this title in the case of income, estate, gift, and excise taxes, imposed by subtitles A and B, and chapter 42, the term 'deficiency' means the amount by which the tax imposed by subtitle A or B or chapter 42 exceeds the excess of—"

• 1969, Tax Reform Act of 1969 (P.L. 91-172)

P.L. 91-172, §101(f)(1):

Amended Code Sec. 6211(a). **Effective** 1-1-70. Prior to amendment, the matter preceding paragraph (1) in Code Sec. 6211(a) read as follows:

"(a) In General.—For purposes of this title in the case of income, estate, and gift taxes, imposed by subtitles A and B, the term 'deficiency' means the amount by which the tax imposed by subtitles A or B exceeds the excess of—"

[Sec. 6211(b)]

(b) RULES FOR APPLICATION OF SUBSECTION (a).—For purposes of this section—

(1) The tax imposed by subtitle A and the tax shown on the return shall both be determined without regard to payment on account of estimated tax, without regard to the credit under

section 31, without regard to the credit under section 33, and without regard to any credits resulting from the collection of amounts assessed under section 6851 or 6852 (relating to termination assessments).

(2) The term "rebate" means so much of an abatement, credit, refund, or other repayment, as was made on the ground that the tax imposed by subtitle A or B or chapter 41, 42, 43, or 44 was less than the excess of the amount specified in subsection (a)(1) over the rebates previously made.

(3) The computation by the Secretary, pursuant to section 6014, of the tax imposed by chapter 1 shall be considered as having been made by the taxpayer and the tax so computed considered as shown by the taxpayer upon his return.

Caution: Code Sec. 6211(b)(4), below, prior to amendment by P.L. 117-328, applies to tax years on or before after December 31, 2026.

(4) For purposes of subsection (a)—

(A) any excess of the sum of the credits allowable under sections 21 by reason of subsection (g) thereof, 24 by reason of subsections (d) and (i)(1) thereof, 25A by reason of subsection (i) thereof, 32, 34, 35, 36, 36B, 6428, 6428A, 6428B, and 7527A over the tax imposed by subtitle A (determined without regard to such credits), and

(B) any excess of the sum of such credits as shown by the taxpayer on his return over the amount shown as the tax by the taxpayer on such return (determined without regard to such credits),

shall be taken into account as negative amounts of tax.

Caution: Code Sec. 6211(b)(4), below, as amended by P.L. 117-328, applies to tax years beginning after December 31, 2026.

(4) For purposes of subsection (a)—

(A) any excess of the sum of the credits allowable under sections 21 by reason of subsection (g) thereof, 24 by reason of subsections (d) and (i)(1) thereof, 25A by reason of subsection (i) thereof, 32, 34, 35, 36, 36B, 6428, 6428A, 6428B, 7527A, and 6433 over the tax imposed by subtitle A (determined without regard to such credits), and

(B) any excess of the sum of such credits as shown by the taxpayer on his return over the amount shown as the tax by the taxpayer on such return (determined without regard to such credits),

shall be taken into account as negative amounts of tax.

Amendments

• 2022, SECURE 2.0 Act of 2022 (P.L. 117-328)

P.L. 117-328, §103(c)(1):

Amended Code Sec. 6211(b)(4) by striking "and 7527A" and inserting "7527A, and 6433". **Effective** for tax years beginning after 12-31-2026.

• 2021, American Rescue Plan Act of 2021 (P.L. 117-2)

P.L. 117-2, §9601(c)(1):

Amended Code Sec. 6211(b)(4)(A) by striking "6428, and 6428A" and inserting "6428, 6428A, and 6428B". **Effective** 3-11-2021.

P.L. 117-2, §9611(b)(4)(B)(i)-(ii):

Amended Code Sec. 6211(b)(4)(A), as amended by the preceding provisions of this subtitle, by striking "24(d)" and inserting "24 by reason of subsections (d) and (i)(1) thereof", and by striking "and 6428B" and inserting "6428B, and 7527A". **Effective** for tax years beginning after 12-31-2020.

P.L. 117-2, §9631(c)(1):

Amended Code Sec. 6211(b)(4)(A), as amended by the preceding provisions of this Act, by inserting "21 by reason of subsection (g) thereof," before "24". **Effective** for tax years beginning after 12-31-2020.

• 2020, COVID-related Tax Relief Act of 2020 (P.L. 116-260)

P.L. 116-260, §272(b)(1), Div. N:

Amended Code Sec. 6211(b)(4)(A) by striking "and 6428" and inserting "6428, and 6428A". **Effective** 12-27-2020.

• 2020, Coronavirus Aid, Relief, and Economic Security (CARES) Act (P.L. 116-136)

P.L. 116-136, §2201(b)(1):

Amended Code Sec. 6211(b)(4)(A) by striking "and 36B, 168(k)(4)" and inserting "36B, and 6428". **Effective** 3-27-2020.

• 2018, Tax Technical Corrections Act of 2018 (P.L. 115-141)

P.L. 115-141, §101(l)(17), Div. U:

Amended Code Sec. 6211(b)(4)(A), as amended by this Act, by striking "subsection (i)(5)" and inserting "subsection (i)". **Effective** as if included in the provision of the Protecting Americans from Tax Hikes Act of 2015 to which it relates [**effective** for tax years beginning after 12-18-2015.—CCH].

P.L. 115-141, §106(a), Div. U:

Amended Code Sec. 6211(b)(4)(A) by striking "subsection (i)(6)" and inserting "subsection (i)(5)". **Effective** as if included in section 104 of the American Taxpayer Relief Act of 2012 [**effective** for tax years beginning after 12-31-2011.—CCH].

• 2017, Tax Cuts and Jobs Act (P.L. 115-97)

P.L. 115-97, §13404(c)(3):

Amended Code Sec. 6211(b)(4)(A) by striking ", and 6431" following ", 168(k)(4)" and inserting "and" before "36B". **Effective** for bonds issued after 12-31-2017.

• 2014, Tax Technical Corrections Act of 2014 (P.L. 113-295)

P.L. 113-295, §221(a)(5)(B), Division A:

Amended Code Sec. 6211(b)(4)(A) by striking ", 36A" following "36". **Effective** generally 12-19-2014. For a special rule, see Act Sec. 221(b)(2), Division A, below.

P.L. 113-295, §221(a)(8)(B), Division A:

Amended Code Sec. 6211(b)(4) by striking ", 53(e)" following "36B". **Effective** generally 12-19-2014. For a special rule, see Act Sec. 221(b)(2), Division A, below.

P.L. 113-295, §221(a)(112)(B), Division A:

Amended Code Sec. 6211(b)(4)(A) by striking "6428," following "168(k)(4),". **Effective** generally 12-19-2014. For a special rule, see Act Sec. 221(b)(2), Division A, below.

P.L. 113-295, §221(b)(2), Division A, provides:

(2) SAVINGS PROVISION.—If—

(A) any provision amended or repealed by the amendments made by this section applied to—

(i) any transaction occurring before the date of the enactment of this Act,

(ii) any property acquired before such date of enactment, or

(iii) any item of income, loss, deduction, or credit taken into account before such date of enactment, and

(B) the treatment of such transaction, property, or item under such provision would (without regard to the amendments or repeals made by this section) affect the liability for tax for periods ending after date of enactment, nothing in the amendments or repeals made by this section shall be construed to affect the treatment of such transaction, property, or item for purposes of determining liability for tax for periods ending after such date of enactment.

• 2013, American Taxpayer Relief Act of 2012 (P.L. 112-240)

P.L. 112-240, §101(a)(1) and (3), provides:

SEC. 101. PERMANENT EXTENSION AND MODIFICATION OF 2001 TAX RELIEF.

(a) PERMANENT EXTENSION.—

(1) IN GENERAL.—The Economic Growth and Tax Relief Reconciliation Act of 2001 is amended by striking title IX.

* * *

(3) EFFECTIVE DATE.—The amendments made by this subsection shall apply to taxable, plan, or limitation years beginning after December 31, 2012, and estates of decedents dying, gifts made, or generation skipping transfers after December 31, 2012.

• 2010, Tax Relief, Unemployment Insurance Reauthorization, and Job Creation Act of 2010 (P.L. 111-312)

P.L. 111-312, §101(b)(1):

Amended Code Sec. 6211(b)(4)(A) to read as such provision would read if section 10909 of the Patient Protection and Affordable Care Act (P.L. 111-148) had never been enacted. **Effective** for tax years beginning after 12-31-2011.

• 2010, Patient Protection and Affordable Care Act (P.L. 111-148)

P.L. 111-148, §10105(d):

Amended Act Sec. 1401(d) by adding at the end a new Act Sec. 1401(d)(3), which amends Code Sec. 6211(b)(4)(A) by inserting "36B," after "36A,". **Effective** 3-23-2010.

P.L. 111-148, §10909(b)(2)(N):

Amended Code Sec. 6211(b)(4)(A) by inserting "36C," before "53(e)". **Effective** for tax years beginning after 12-31-2009.

P.L. 111-148, §10909(c), as amended by P.L. 111-312, §101(b)(1), provides:

(c) SUNSET PROVISION.—Each provision of law amended by this section is amended to read as such provision would read if this section had never been enacted. The amendments made by the preceding sentence shall apply to taxable years beginning after December 31, 2011.

• 2009, American Recovery and Reinvestment Tax Act of 2009 (P.L. 111-5)

P.L. 111-5, §1001(e)(1):

Amended Code Sec. 6211(b)(4)(A) by inserting "36A," after "36,". **Effective** for tax years beginning after 12-31-2008.

P.L. 111-5, §1004(b)(7):

Amended Code Sec. 6211(b)(4)(A) by inserting "25A by reason of subsection (i)(6) thereof," after "24(d),". **Effective** for tax years beginning after 12-31-2008.

P.L. 111-5, §1201(a)(3)(B):

Amended Code Sec. 6211(b)(4)(A) by inserting "168(k)(4)," after "53(e),". **Effective** for tax years ending after 3-31-2008.

P.L. 111-5, §1201(b)(2):

Amended Code Sec. 6211(b)(4)(A) by inserting "168(k)(4)," after "53(e),". **Effective** for tax years ending after 3-31-2008. [This amendment cannot be made because the same amendment was made by P.L. 111-5, §1201(a)(3)(B).—CCH].

P.L. 111-5, §1531(c)(4):

Amended Code Sec. 6211(b)(4)(A) by striking "and 6428" and inserting "6428, and 6431". **Effective** for obligations issued after 2-17-2009.

• 2008, Housing Assistance Tax Act of 2008 (P.L. 110-289)

P.L. 110-289, §3011(b)(2):

Amended Code Sec. 6211(b)(4)(A) by striking "34," and all that follows through "6428" and inserting "34, 35, 36, 53(e), and 6428". **Effective** for residences purchased on or after 4-9-2008, in tax years ending on or after such date. Prior to being stricken, "34," and all that follows through "6428" read as follows:

"34, and 35, 53(e), and 6428"

• 2008, Economic Stimulus Act of 2008 (P.L. 110-185)

P.L. 110-185, §101(b)(1):

Amended Code Sec. 6211(b)(4)(A) by striking "and 53(e)" and inserting "53(e), and 6428". **Effective** 2-13-2008.

• 2007, Tax Technical Corrections Act of 2007 (P.L. 110-172)

P.L. 110-172, §11(a)(35):

Amended Code Sec. 6211(b)(4)(A) by striking "and 34" [sic]and inserting "34, and 35". **Effective** 12-29-2007.

• 2006, Tax Relief and Health Care Act of 2006 (P.L. 109-432)

P.L. 109-432, Division A, §402(b)(1):

Amended Code Sec. 6211(b)(4)(A) by striking "and 34" and inserting "34, and 53(e)". **Effective** for tax years beginning after 12-20-2006.

• 2000, Community Renewal Tax Relief Act of 2000 (P.L. 106-554)

P.L. 106-554, §314(a):

Amended Code Sec. 6211(b)(4) by striking "sections 32 and 34" and inserting "sections 24(d), 32, and 34". **Effective** as if included in the provision of the Taxpayer Relief Act of 1997 (P.L. 105-34) to which it relates [**effective** for tax years beginning after 12-31-97.—CCH].

• 1988, Technical and Miscellaneous Revenue Act of 1988 (P.L. 100-647)

P.L. 100-647, §1015(r)(2):

Amended Code Sec. 6211(b)(4). **Effective** for notices of deficiencies mailed after 11-10-88. Prior to amendment, Code Sec. 6211(b)(4) read as follows:

(4) The tax imposed by subtitle A and the tax shown on the return shall both be determined without regard to the credit under section 34, unless, without regard to such credit, the tax imposed by subtitle A exceeds the excess of the amount specified in subsection (a)(1) over the amount specified in subsection (a)(2).

• 1988, Omnibus Trade and Competitiveness Act of 1988 (P.L. 100-418)

P.L. 100-418, §1941(b)(2)(B)(ii):

Amended Code Sec. 6211(b)(2) by striking "44, or 45" each place it appears and inserting "or 44". **Effective** for crude oil removed from the premises on or after 8-23-88.

P.L. 100-418, §1941(b)(2)(D):

Amended Code Sec. 6211(b) by striking paragraphs (5) and (6). **Effective** for crude oil removed from the premises on or after 8-23-88. Prior to amendment, Code Sec. 6211(b)(5) and (6) read as follows:

(5) The amount withheld under section 4995(a) from amounts payable to any producer for crude oil removed during any taxable period (as defined in section 4996(b)(7)) which is not otherwise shown on a return by such producer shall be treated as tax shown by the producer on a return for the taxable period.

(6) Any liability to pay amounts required to be withheld under section 4995(a) shall not be treated as a tax imposed by chapter 45.

• 1987, Revenue Act of 1987 (P.L. 100-203)

P.L. 100-203, §0713(b)(2)(B):

Amended Code Sec. 6211(b)(1) by striking out "section 6851" and inserting in lieu thereof "section 6851 or 6852". **Effective** 12-22-87.

• 1984, Deficit Reduction Act of 1984 (P.L. 98-369)

P.L. 98-369, §474(r)(33)(A):

Amended Code Sec. 6211(b)(1) by striking out "without regard to so much of the credit under section 32 as exceeds 2 percent of the interest on obligations described in section 1451" and inserting in lieu thereof "without regard to the credit under section 33". **Effective** for tax years beginning after 12-31-83, and to carrybacks from such years.

P.L. 98-369, §474(r)(33)(B):

Amended Code Sec. 6211(b)(4) by striking out "section 39" and inserting in lieu thereof "section 34". **Effective** for tax years beginning after 12-31-83, and to carrybacks from such years.

• 1980, Crude Oil Windfall Profit Tax Act of 1980 (P.L. 96-223)

P.L. 96-223, §101(f)(1)(B); (f)(3):

Amended Code Sec. 6211(b) by striking out in paragraph (2) "or 44" and inserting "44, or 45" and by adding paragraphs (5) and (6). For the **effective** date and transitional rules, see P.L. 96-223, §101(i), following Code Sec. 4986.

• 1976, Tax Reform Act of 1976 (P.L. 94-455)

P.L. 94-455, §1204(a)(4):

Struck out "and" following "31," in Code Sec. 6211(b)(1) and added ",and without regard to any credits resulting from the collection of amounts assessed under section 6851 (relating to termination assessments)" before the period at the end of Code Sec. 6211(b)(1). **Effective** with respect to action taken under Code Secs. 6851, 6861, or 6862 where the notice and demand takes place after 2-28-77. [**effective** date changed by P.L. 94-528, §2(a).

P.L. 94-455, §1307(d)(2)(F)(i):

Substituted "chapter 41, 42," for "chapter 42" in Code Sec. 6211(b)(2). **Effective** 10-4-76.

P.L. 94-455, §1605(b)(4)(C):

Substituted "43, or 44" for "or 43" in Code Sec. 6211(b)(2). For **effective** date, see amendatory note for P.L. 94-455, §1605(b)(4)(A), following Code Sec. 6211(a).

P.L. 94-455, §1906(b)(13)(A):

Amended 1954 Code by substituting "Secretary" for "Secretary or his delegate" each place it appeared. **Effective** 2-1-77.

• 1974, Employee Retirement Income Security Act of 1974 (P.L. 93-406)

P.L. 93-406, §1016(a)(9):

Amended Code Sec. 6211(b)(2) by changing "chapter 42" to "chapter 42 or 43". For **effective** date, see amendment note for Code Sec. 410.

• 1969, Tax Reform Act of 1969 (P.L. 91-172)

P.L. 91-172, §101(j)(39):

Amended Code Sec. 6211(b) by substituting "subtitle A or B or chapter 42" for "subtitles A or B" in paragraph (2). **Effective** 1-1-70.

• 1966, Tax Adjustment Act of 1966 (P.L. 89-368)

P.L. 89-368, §102(b)(4):

Amended Code Sec. 6211(b)(1) by substituting "subtitle A" for "chapter 1". **Effective** 1-1-67.

• 1965, Excise Tax Reduction Act of 1965 (P.L. 89-44)

P.L. 89-44, §809(d)(5):

Amended Code Sec. 6211(b) by adding paragraph (4). **Effective** 7-1-65.

[Sec. 6211(c)]

(c) COORDINATION WITH SUBCHAPTER C.—In determining the amount of any deficiency for purposes of this subchapter, adjustments to partnership-related items shall be made only as provided in subchapter C.

Amendments

• 2018, Tax Technical Corrections Act of 2018 (P.L. 115-141)

P.L. 115-141, §201(c)(1), Div. U:

Amended Code Sec. 6211(c). **Effective** as if included in section 1101 of the Bipartisan Budget Act of 2015 [**effective** generally for returns filed for partnership tax years beginning after 12-31-2017.—CCH]. Prior to amendment, Code Sec. 6211(c) read as follows:

(c) COORDINATION WITH SUBCHAPTERS C AND D.—In determining the amount of any deficiency for purposes of this subchapter, adjustments to partnership items shall be made only as provided in subchapters C and D.

• 1998, IRS Restructuring and Reform Act of 1998 (P.L. 105-206)

P.L. 105-206, §6012(f)(1)-(2):

Amended Code Sec. 6211(c) by striking "SUBCHAPTER C" in the heading and inserting "SUBCHAPTERS C AND D", and by striking "subchapter C" in the text and inserting "subchapters C and D". **Effective** as if included in the provision of P.L. 105-34 to which it relates [**effective** for partnership tax years ending after 8-5-97.—CCH].

• 1997, Taxpayer Relief Act of 1997 (P.L. 105-34)

P.L. 105-34, §1231(b):

Amended Code Sec. 6211 by adding at the end a new subsection (c). **Effective** for partnership tax years ending after 8-5-97.

[Sec. 6212]

SEC. 6212. NOTICE OF DEFICIENCY.

[Sec. 6212(a)]

(a) IN GENERAL.—If the Secretary determines that there is a deficiency in respect of any tax imposed by subtitle A or B or chapter 41, 42, 43, or 44, he is authorized to send notice of such deficiency to the taxpayer by certified mail or registered mail. Such notice shall include a notice to the taxpayer of the taxpayer's right to contact a local office of the taxpayer advocate and the location and phone number of the appropriate office.

Amendments

• 1998, IRS Restructuring and Reform Act of 1998 (P.L. 105-206)

P.L. 105-206, §1102(b):

Amended Code Sec. 6212(a) by adding at the end a new sentence. **Effective** 7-22-98. For a special rule, see Act Sec. 1102(f)(3)-(4), below.

P.L. 105-206, §1102(f)(3)-(4), provides:

(3) NATIONAL TAXPAYER ADVOCATE.—Notwithstanding section 7803(c)(1)(B)(iv) of such Code, as added by this section, in appointing the first National Taxpayer Advocate after the date of the enactment of this Act, the Secretary of the Treasury—

(A) shall not appoint any individual who was an officer or employee of the Internal Revenue Service at any time during the 2-year period ending on the date of appointment, and

(B) need not consult with the Internal Revenue Service Oversight Board if the Oversight Board has not been appointed.

(4) CURRENT OFFICERS.—

(A) In the case of an individual serving as Commissioner of Internal Revenue on the date of the enactment of this Act who was appointed to such position before such date, the 5-year term required by section 7803(a)(1) of such Code, as added by this section, shall begin as of the date of such appointment.

(B) Clauses (ii), (iii), and (iv) of section 7803(c)(1)(B) of such Code, as added by this section, shall not apply to the individual serving as Taxpayer Advocate on the date of the enactment of this Act.

P.L. 105-206, §3463(a), provides:

SEC. 3463. NOTICE OF DEFICIENCY TO SPECIFY DEADLINES FOR FILING TAX COURT PETITION.

(a) IN GENERAL.—The Secretary of the Treasury or the Secretary's delegate shall include on each notice of deficiency under section 6212 of the Internal Revenue Code of 1986 the date determined by such Secretary (or delegate) as the last day on which the taxpayer may file a petition with the Tax Court.

P.L. 105-206, §3504, provides:

SEC. 3504. EXPLANATIONS OF APPEALS AND COLLECTION PROCESS.

The Secretary of the Treasury or the Secretary's delegate shall, as soon as practicable, but not later than 180 days after the date of the enactment of this Act, include with any first letter of proposed deficiency which allows the taxpayer an opportunity for administrative review in the Internal Revenue Service Office of Appeals an explanation of the entire process from examination through collection with respect to such proposed deficiency, including the assistance available to the taxpayer from the National Taxpayer Advocate at various points in the process.

• 1988, Omnibus Trade and Competitiveness Act of 1988 (P.L. 100-418)

P.L. 100-418, §1941(b)(2)(B)(iii):

Amended Code Sec. 6212(a) by striking "44, or 45" each place it appears and inserting "or 44". **Effective** for crude oil removed from the premises on or after 8-23-88.

• 1980, Crude Oil Windfall Profit Tax Act of 1980 (P.L. 96-223)

P.L. 96-223, §101(f)(1)(C):

Amended Code Sec. 6212(a) by striking out "or 44" and inserting "44, or 45". For the **effective** date and transitional rules, see P.L. 96-223, §101(i), following Code Sec. 4986.

• 1976, Tax Reform Act of 1976 (P.L. 94-455)

P.L. 94-455, §1307(d)(2)(F)(ii):

Substituted "chapter 41, 42," for "chapter 42" in Code Sec. 6212(a). **Effective** 10-4-76.

P.L. 94-455, §1605(b)(5)(A):

Substituted "43, or 44" for "or 43" in Code Sec. 6212(a). For **effective** date, see amendatory note for P.L. 94-455, §1605(b)(4)(A), following Code Sec. 6211(a).

P.L. 94-455, §1906(b)(13)(A):

Amended 1954 Code by substituting "Secretary" for "Secretary or his delegate" each place it appeared. **Effective** 2-1-77.

• 1974, Employee Retirement Income Security Act of 1974 (P.L. 93-406)

P.L. 93-406, §1016(a)(10):

Amended Code Sec. 6212(a) by changing "chapter 42" to "chapter 42 or 43". For **effective** date, see amendment note for Code Sec. 410.

• 1969, Tax Reform Act of 1969 (P.L. 91-172)

P.L. 91-172, §101(j)(40):

Amended Sec. 6212(a) by substituting "subtitle A or B or chapter 42," for "subtitles A or B,". **Effective** 1-1-70.

• 1958, Technical Amendments Act of 1958 (P.L. 85-866)

P.L. 85-866, §89(b):

Amended Sec. 6212(a) by striking out "registered mail" and substituting "certified mail or registered mail". **Effective** only for mailing after 9-2-58.

[Sec. 6212(b)]

(b) ADDRESS FOR NOTICE OF DEFICIENCY.—

(1) INCOME AND GIFT TAXES AND CERTAIN EXCISE TAXES.—In the absence of notice to the Secretary under section 6903 of the existence of a fiduciary relationship, notice of a deficiency in respect of a tax imposed by subtitle A, chapter 12, chapter 42, chapter 43, or chapter 44 if mailed to the taxpayer at his last known address, shall be sufficient for purposes of subtitle A, chapter 12, chapter 42, chapter 43, chapter 44, and this chapter even if such taxpayer is deceased, or is under a legal disability, or, in the case of a corporation, has terminated its existence.

(2) JOINT INCOME TAX RETURN.—In the case of a joint income tax return filed by husband and wife, such notice of deficiency may be a single joint notice, except that if the Secretary has been notified by either spouse that separate residences have been established, then, in lieu of the single joint notice, a duplicate original of the joint notice shall be sent by certified mail or registered mail to each spouse at his last known address.

(3) ESTATE TAX.—In the absence of notice to the Secretary under section 6903 of the existence of a fiduciary relationship, notice of a deficiency in respect of a tax imposed by chapter 11, if addressed in the name of the decedent or other person subject to liability and mailed to his last known address, shall be sufficient for purposes of chapter 11 and of this chapter.

Amendments

• 1988, Omnibus Trade and Competitiveness Act of 1988 (P.L. 100-418)

P.L. 100-418, §1941(b)(2)(E)(i)-(ii):

Amended Code Sec. 6212(b)(1) by striking "chapter 44, or 45" and inserting "or chapter 44", and by striking "chapter 44, chapter 45, and this chapter" and inserting "chapter 44, and this chapter". **Effective** for crude oil removed from the premises on or after 8-23-88.

• 1980, Crude Oil Windfall Profit Tax Act of 1980 (P.L. 96-223)

P.L. 96-223, §101(f)(4):

Amended Code Sec. 6212(b) by striking out in paragraph (1) "or chapter 44" and "chapter 44, and this chapter" and inserting "chapter 44, or chapter 45" and "chapter 44, chapter 45, and this chapter", respectively, and by striking out "TAXES IMPOSED BY CHAPTER 42" in the paragraph heading and inserting "CERTAIN EXCISE TAXES". For the **effective** date and transitional rules, see P.L. 96-223, § 101(i), following Code Sec. 4986.

• 1976, Tax Reform Act of 1976 (P.L. 94-455)

P.L. 94-455, § 1605(b)(5)(B):

Substituted "chapter 43, or chapter 44" for "or chapter 43" in Code Sec. 6212(b)(1). For **effective** date, see amendatory note for P.L. 94-455, § 1605(b)(4)(A), following Code Sec. 6211(a).

P.L. 94-455, § 1605(b)(5)(C):

Substituted "chapter 43, chapter 44, and this chapter" for "chapter 43, and this chapter" in Code Sec. 6212(b)(1). For **effective** date, see amendatory note for P.L. 94-455, § 1605(b)(4)(A), following Code Sec. 6211(a).

P.L. 94-455, § 1906(b)(13)(A):

Amended 1954 Code by substituting "Secretary" for "Secretary or his delegate" each place it appeared. **Effective** 2-1-77.

• 1974, Employee Retirement Income Security Act of 1974 (P.L. 93-406)

P.L. 93-406, § 1016(a)(10):

Amended Code Sec. 6212(b)(1) by changing "or chapter 42" to "chapter 42, or chapter 43" and by changing "chapter 42, and this chapter" to "chapter 42, chapter 43, and this chapter". For **effective** date, see amendment note for Code Sec. 410.

• 1969, Tax Reform Act of 1969 (P.L. 91-172)

P.L. 91-172, § 101(j)(41):

Amended paragraph (1) of Code Sec. 6212(b) by adding "and taxes imposed by chapter 42" in the heading thereof, by substituting "chapter 12, or chapter 42," for "or chapter 12,", and by adding "chapter 42," after "chapter 12," the last place it appears. **Effective** 1-1-70.

• 1958, Technical Amendments Act of 1958 (P.L. 85-866)

P.L. 85-866, § 76:

Amended Sec. 6212(b) by striking out "chapter 1 or 12" where that phrase followed "a tax imposed by" and substituting "subtitle A or chapter 12", and by striking out "such chapter and" where that phrase followed "for purposes of" and substituting "subtitle A, chapter 12. and". **Effective** 1-1-54.

P.L. 85-866, § 89(b):

Amended Sec. 6212(b)(2) by striking out "registered mail" and substituting "certified mail or registered mail". **Effective** only if the mailing occurs after 9-2-58.

[Sec. 6212(c)]

(c) FURTHER DEFICIENCY LETTERS RESTRICTED.—

(1) GENERAL RULE.—If the Secretary has mailed to the taxpayer a notice of deficiency as provided in subsection (a), and the taxpayer files a petition with the Tax Court within the time prescribed in section 6213(a), the Secretary shall have no right to determine any additional deficiency of income tax for the same taxable year, of gift tax for the same calendar year, of estate tax in respect of the taxable estate of the same decedent, of chapter 41 tax for the same taxable year, of chapter 43 tax for the same taxable year, of chapter 44 tax for the same taxable year, of section 4940 tax for the same taxable year, or of chapter 42 tax (other than under section 4940) with respect to any act (or failure to act) to which such petition relates, except in the case of fraud, and except as provided in section 6214(a) (relating to assertion of greater deficiencies before the Tax Court), in section 6213(b)(1) (relating to mathematical or clerical errors), in section 6851 or 6852 (relating to termination assessments), or in section 6861(c) (relating to the making of jeopardy assessments).

(2) CROSS REFERENCES.—

For assessment as a deficiency notwithstanding the prohibition of further deficiency letters, in the case of—

(A) Deficiency attributable to change of treatment with respect to itemized deductions, see section 63(e)(3).

(B) Deficiency attributable to gain on involuntary conversion, see section 1033(a)(2)(C) and (D).

(C) Deficiency attributable to activities not engaged in for profit, see section 183(e)(4).

For provisions allowing determination of tax in title 11 cases, see section 505(a) of title 11 of the United States Code.

Amendments

• 1997, Taxpayer Relief Act of 1997 (P.L. 105-34)

P.L. 105-34, § 312(d)(12):

Amended Code Sec. 6212(c)(2) by striking subparagraph (C) and by redesignating the succeeding subparagraphs accordingly. **Effective** for sales and exchanges after 5-6-97. Prior to being stricken, Code Sec. 6212(c)(2)(C) read as follows:

(C) Deficiency attributable to gain on sale or exchange of principal residence, see section 1034(j).

• 1988, Omnibus Trade and Competitiveness Act of 1988 (P.L. 100-418)

P.L. 100-418, § 1941(b)(2)(F)(i)-(ii):

Amended Code Sec. 6212(c)(1) by striking out "of chapter 42 tax" and inserting "or of chapter 42 tax", and by striking ", or of chapter 45 tax for the same taxable period" before ", except in the case of fraud". **Effective** for crude oil removed from the premises on or after 8-23-88.

• 1987, Revenue Act of 1987 (P.L. 100-203)

P.L. 100-203, § 10713(b)(2)(C):

Amended Code Sec. 6212(c)(1) by striking out "section 6851" and inserting in lieu thereof "section 6851 or 6852". **Effective** 12-22-87.

• 1986, Tax Reform Act of 1986 (P.L. 99-514)

P.L. 99-514, § 104(b)(17):

Amended Code Sec. 6212(c)(2)(A). **Effective** for tax years beginning after 12-31-86. Prior to amendment, Code Sec. 6212(c)(2)(A) read as follows:

(A) Deficiency attributable to change of treatment with respect to itemized deductions and zero bracket amount, see section 63(g)(5).

• 1984, Economic Recovery Tax Act of 1981 (P.L. 97-34)

P.L. 97-34, §442(d)(4):

Amended Code Sec. 6212(c) by striking out "calendar quarter" and inserting "calendar year". **Effective** with respect to estates of decedents dying after 12-31-81.

• 1980, Bankruptcy Tax Act of 1980 (P.L. 96-589)

P.L. 96-589, §6(d)(2):

Amended Code Sec. 6212(c)(2) by adding a new last sentence. **Effective** 10-1-79, but inapplicable to any proceeding under the Bankruptcy Act commenced before that date.

• 1980, Crude Oil Windfall Profit Tax Act of 1980 (P.L. 96-223)

P.L. 96-223, §101(f)(5):

Amended Code Sec. 6212(c) by striking out "or of chapter 42 tax" and inserting "of chapter 42 tax" and by inserting ", or of chapter 45 tax for the same taxable period" after "to which such petition relates". For the **effective** date and transitional rules, see P.L. 96-223, §101(i), following Code Sec. 4986.

• 1978, Revenue Act of 1978 (P.L. 95-600)

P.L. 95-600, §405(c)(5):

Amended Code Sec. 6212(c)(2)(C) by striking out "personal residence" and inserting in lieu thereof "principal residence". **Effective** for sales and exchanges of residences after 7-26-78, in tax years ending after such date.

• 1977, Tax Reduction and Simplification Act of 1977 (P.L. 95-30)

P.L. 95-30, §101(d)(15):

Amended Code Sec. 6212(c)(2)(A). **Effective** for tax years beginning after 12-31-76. Prior to amendment, Code Sec. 6212(c)(2)(A) read as follows:

"(A) Deficiency attributable to change of election with respect to the standard deduction where taxpayer and his spouse made separate returns, see section 144(b)."

• 1976, Tax Reform Act of 1976 (P.L. 94-455)

P.L. 94-455, §214(b):

Added Code Sec. 6212(c)(2)(E). **Effective** for tax years beginning after 12-31-69; except that Code Sec. 6212(c)(2)(E) shall not apply to any tax year ending before 10-4-76, with respect to which the period for assessing a deficiency has expired before such date.

P.L. 94-455, §1204(c)(5):

Added "in section 6851 (relating to termination assessments)," after "errors)," in Code Sec. 6212(c)(1). P.L. 94-455, §1204(d) provides that the amendment shall be **effective** for action taken under Code Secs. 6851, 6861, or 6862 where the notice or demand takes place after 12-31-76; but P.L. 94-528, §2(a), **effective** 10-4-76, substitutes "February 28, 1977" for "December 31, 1976" in P.L. 94-455, §1204(d).

P.L. 94-455, §1206(c)(3):

Substituted "(relating to mathematical or clerical errors)" for "(relating to mathematical errors)" in Code Sec. 6212(c)(1). **Effective** with respect to returns filed after 12-31-76.

P.L. 94-455, §1605(b)(5)(D):

Added "of chapter 43 tax for the same taxable year, of chapter 44 tax for the same taxable year," in place of "of chapter 43 tax for the same taxable years," (as amended by P.L. 95-600, Sec. 701(t)(3)(B)) in Code Sec. 6212(c)(1). For **effective** date, see amendatory note for P.L. 94-455, §1605(b)(4)(A), following Code Sec. 6211(a).

P.L. 94-455, §1901(b)(31)(C):

Substituted "1033(a)(2)(C) and (D)" for "1033(a)(3)(C) and (D)" in Code Sec. 6212(c)(2)(B). **Effective** for tax years beginning after 12-31-76.

P.L. 94-455, §1901(b)(37)(C):

Struck out Code Sec. 6212(c)(2)(D) (but did not renumber (E)). **Effective** for tax years beginning after 12-31-76. Prior to striking, Code Sec. 6212(c)(2)(D) read as follows:

"(D) Deficiency attributable to war loss recoveries where prior benefit rule is elected, see section 1335."

P.L. 94-455, §1906(b)(13)(A):

Amended 1954 Code by substituting "Secretary" for "Secretary or his delegate" each place it appeared. **Effective** 2-1-77.

• 1974, Employee Retirement Income Security Act of 1974 (P.L. 93-406)

P.L. 93-406, §1016(a)(10):

Amended Code Sec. 6212(c)(1) by changing "of the same decedent," to "of the same decedent, of chapter 43 for the same taxable years,". For **effective** date, see amendment note for Code Sec. 410.

• 1970, Excise, Estate, and Gift Tax Adjustment Act of 1970 (P.L. 91-614)

P.L. 91-614, §102(d)(5):

Amended Code Sec. 6212(c)(1) by substituting "calendar quarter" for "calendar year" in the sixth line. **Effective** for gifts made after 12-31-70.

• 1969, Tax Reform Act of 1969 (P.L. 91-172)

P.L. 91-172, §101(f)(2):

Amended Code Sec. 6212(c)(1). **Effective** 1-1-70. Prior to amendment, paragraph (1) of Code Sec. 6212(c) read as follows:

"(1) General rule.—If the Secretary or his delegate has mailed to the taxpayer a notice of deficiency as provided in subsection (a), and the taxpayer files a petition with the Tax Court within the time prescribed in section 6213(a), the Secretary or his delegate shall have no right to determine any additional deficiency of income tax for the same taxable year, of gift tax for the same calendar year, or of estate tax in respect of the taxable estate of the same decedent, except in the case of fraud, and except as provided in section 6214(a) (relating to assertion of greater deficiencies before the Tax Court), in section 6213(b)(1) (relating to mathematical errors), or in section 6861(c) (relating to the making of jeopardy assessments)."

• 1964, Revenue Act of 1964 (P.L. 88-272)

P.L. 88-272, §112(d)(1):

Amended subparagraph (A) by striking out "to take" and inserting in lieu thereof "with respect to the". **Effective** 1-1-64.

[Sec. 6212(d)]

(d) AUTHORITY TO RESCIND NOTICE OF DEFICIENCY WITH TAXPAYER'S CONSENT.—The Secretary may, with the consent of the taxpayer, rescind any notice of deficiency mailed to the taxpayer. Any notice so rescinded shall not be treated as a notice of deficiency for purposes of subsection (c)(1) (relating to further deficiency letters restricted), section 6213(a) (relating to restrictions applicable to deficiencies; petition to Tax Court), and section 6512(a) (relating to limitations in case of petition to Tax Court), and the taxpayer shall have no right to file a petition with the Tax Court based on such notice. Nothing in this subsection shall affect any suspension of the running of any period of limitations during any period during which the rescinded notice was outstanding.

Amendments

• 1988, Technical and Miscellaneous Revenue Act of 1988 (P.L. 100-647)

P.L. 100-647, §1015(m):

Amended Code Sec. 6212(d) by adding at the end thereof a new sentence. **Effective** as if included in the provision of P.L. 99-514 to which it relates.

• 1986, Tax Reform Act of 1986 (P.L. 99-514)

P.L. 99-514, §1562(a):

Amended Code Sec. 6212 by adding at the end thereof new paragraph (d). **Effective** for notices of deficiency issued on or after 1-1-86.

[Sec. 6213]

SEC. 6213. RESTRICTIONS APPLICABLE TO DEFICIENCIES; PETITION TO TAX COURT.

[Sec. 6213(a)]

(a) TIME FOR FILING PETITION AND RESTRICTION ON ASSESSMENT.—Within 90 days, or 150 days if the notice is addressed to a person outside the United States, after the notice of deficiency authorized in section 6212 is mailed (not counting Saturday, Sunday, or a legal holiday in the District of Columbia as the last day), the taxpayer may file a petition with the Tax Court for a redetermination of the deficiency. Except as otherwise provided in section 6851, 6852, or 6861 no assessment of a deficiency in respect of any tax imposed by subtitle A or B, chapter 41, 42, 43, or 44 and no levy or proceeding in court for its collection shall be made, begun, or prosecuted until such notice has been mailed to the taxpayer, nor until the expiration of such 90-day or 150-day period, as the case may be, nor, if a petition has been filed with the Tax Court, until the decision of the Tax Court has become final. Notwithstanding the provisions of section 7421(a), the making of such assessment or the beginning of such proceeding or levy during the time such prohibition is in force may be enjoined by a proceeding in the proper court, including the Tax Court, and a refund may be ordered by such court of any amount collected within the period during which the Secretary is prohibited from collecting by levy or through a proceeding in court under the provisions of this subsection. The Tax Court shall have no jurisdiction to enjoin any action or proceeding or order any refund under this subsection unless a timely petition for a redetermination of the deficiency has been filed and then only in respect of the deficiency that is the subject of such petition. Any petition filed with the Tax Court on or before the last date specified for filing such petition by the Secretary in the notice of deficiency shall be treated as timely filed.

Amendments

• 1998, IRS Restructuring and Reform Act of 1998 (P.L. 105-206)

P.L. 105-206, §3463(b):

Amended Code Sec. 6213(a) by adding at the end a new sentence. **Effective** for notices mailed after 12-31-98.

P.L. 105-206, §3464(a)(1)-(2):

Amended Code Sec. 6213(a) by striking ", including the Tax Court." and inserting ", including the Tax Court, and a refund may be ordered by such court of any amount collected within the period during which the Secretary is prohibited from collecting by levy or through a proceeding in court under the provisions of this subsection.", and by striking "to enjoin any action or proceeding" and inserting "to enjoin any action or proceeding or order any refund". **Effective** 7-22-98.

• 1988, Technical and Miscellaneous Revenue Act of 1988 (P.L. 100-647)

P.L. 100-647, §6243(a):

Amended Code Sec. 6213(a) by striking out the period at the end of the last sentence and inserting in lieu thereof ", including the Tax Court. The Tax Court shall have no jurisdiction to enjoin any action or proceeding under this subsection unless a timely petition for a redetermination of the deficiency has been filed and then only in respect of the deficiency that is the subject of such petition." **Effective** for orders entered after 11-10-88.

• 1988, Omnibus Trade and Competitiveness Act of 1988 (P.L. 100-418)

P.L. 100-418, §1941(b)(2)(B)(iv):

Amended Code Sec. 6213(a) by striking "44, or 45" each place it appears and inserting "or 44". **Effective** for crude oil removed from the premises on or after 8-23-88.

• 1987, Revenue Act of 1987 (P.L. 100-203)

P.L. 100-203, §10713(b)(2)(D):

Amended Code Sec. 6213(a) by striking out "section 6851 or section 6861" and inserting in lieu thereof "section 6851, 6852, or 6861". **Effective** 12-22-87.

• 1980, Crude Oil Windfall Profit Tax Act of 1980 (P.L. 96-223)

P.L. 96-223, §101(f)(1)(D):

Amended Code Sec. 6213(a) by striking cut "or 44" and inserting "44, or 45". For the **effective** date and transitional rules, see P.L. 96-223, §101(i), following Code Sec. 4986.

• 1976, Tax Reform Act of 1976 (P.L. 94-455)

P.L. 94-455, §1204(c)(6):

Added "section 6851 or" before "section 6861" in Code Sec. 6213(a). **Effective** for action taken under Code Sec. 6851, 6861, or 6862 where the notice and demand takes place after 2-28-77. [P.L. 94-528, §2(a) amended the **effective** date.]

P.L. 94-455, §1307(d)(2)(F)(iii):

Substituted "chapter 41, 42," for "chapter 42" in Code Sec. 6213(a). **Effective** 10-4-76.

P.L. 94-455, §1605(b)(6):

Substituted "43, or 44" for "or 43" in Code Sec. 6213(a). For **effective** date, see amendment note for P.L. 94-455, §1605(b)(4)(A), following Code Sec. 6211(a).

P.L. 94-455, §1906(a)(15):

Substituted "United States" for "States of the Union and the District of Columbia" in Code Sec. 6213(a). **Effective** 2-1-77.

• 1974, Employee Retirement Income Security Act of 1974 (P.L. 93-406)

P.L. 93-406, §1016(a)(11):

Amended Code Sec. 6213(a) by changing "chapter 42" to "chapter 42 or 43". For **effective** date, see amendment note for Code Sec. 410.

• 1969, Tax Reform Act of 1969 (P.L. 91-172)

P.L. 91-172, §101(j)(42):

Amended Code Sec. 6213(a) by adding "or chapter 42" after "subtitle A or B". **Effective** 1-1-70.

[Sec. 6213(b)]

(b) EXCEPTIONS TO RESTRICTIONS ON ASSESSMENT.—

(1) ASSESSMENTS ARISING OUT OF MATHEMATICAL OR CLERICAL ERRORS.—If the taxpayer is notified that, on account of a mathematical or clerical error appearing on the return, an amount of tax in excess of that shown on the return is due, and that an assessment of the tax has been or will be made on the basis of what would have been the correct amount of tax but for the mathematical or clerical error, such notice shall not be considered as a notice of deficiency for the purposes of subsection (a) (prohibiting assessment and collection until notice of the deficiency has been mailed), or of section 6212(c)(1) (restricting further deficiency letters), or of section 6512(a) (prohibiting credits or refunds after petition to the Tax Court), and the taxpayer shall have no right to file a petition with the Tax Court based on such notice, nor shall such assessment or collection be prohibited by the provisions of subsection (a) of this section. Each notice under this paragraph shall set forth the error alleged and an explanation thereof.

(2) ABATEMENT OF ASSESSMENT OF MATHEMATICAL OR CLERICAL ERRORS.—

(A) REQUEST FOR ABATEMENT.—Notwithstanding section 6404(b), a taxpayer may file with the Secretary within 60 days after notice is sent under paragraph (1) a request for an abatement of any assessment specified in such notice, and upon receipt of such request, the Secretary shall abate the assessment. Any reassessment of the tax with respect to which an abatement is made under this subparagraph shall be subject to the deficiency procedures prescribed by this subchapter.

(B) STAY OF COLLECTION.—In the case of any assessment referred to in paragraph (1), notwithstanding paragraph (1), no levy or proceeding in court for the collection of such assessment shall be made, begun, or prosecuted during the period in which such assessment may be abated under this paragraph.

(3) ASSESSMENTS ARISING OUT OF TENTATIVE CARRYBACK OR REFUND ADJUSTMENTS.—If the Secretary determines that the amount applied, credited, or refunded under section 6411 is in excess of the overassessment attributable to the carryback or the amount described in section 1341(b)(1) with respect to which such amount was applied, credited, or refunded, he may assess without regard to the provisions of paragraph (2) the amount of the excess as a deficiency as if it were due to a mathematical or clerical error appearing on the return.

(4) ASSESSMENT OF AMOUNT PAID.—Any amount paid as a tax or in respect of a tax may be assessed upon the receipt of such payment notwithstanding the provisions of subsection (a). In any case where such amount is paid after the mailing of a notice of deficiency under section 6212, such payment shall not deprive the Tax Court of jurisdiction over such deficiency determined under section 6211 without regard to such assessment.

(5) CERTAIN ORDERS OF CRIMINAL RESTITUTION.—If the taxpayer is notified that an assessment has been or will be made pursuant to section 6201(a)(4)—

(A) such notice shall not be considered as a notice of deficiency for the purposes of subsection (a) (prohibiting assessment and collection until notice of the deficiency has been mailed), section 6212(c)(1) (restricting further deficiency letters), or section 6512(a) (prohibiting credits or refunds after petition to the Tax Court), and

(B) subsection (a) shall not apply with respect to the amount of such assessment.

Amendments

• 2019, Taxpayer Certainty and Disaster Tax Relief Act of 2019 (P.L. 116-94)

P.I. 116-94, §204(c), Div. Q, provides:

For a special rule, see Act Sec. 204(c), Div. Q, in the amendment notes for Code Sec. 1400S.

• 2018, Bipartisan Budget Act of 2018 (P.L. 115-123)

P.L. 115-123, §20104(c), Div. B, provides:

For a special rule, see Act Sec. 20104(c), Div. B, in the amendment notes for Code Sec. 1400S(d).

• 2017, Disaster Tax Relief and Airport and Airway Extension Act of 2017 (P.L. 115-63)

P.L. 115-63, §504(c), provides:

For a special rule, see Act Sec. 504(c) in the amendment notes for Code Sec. 1400S(d).

• 2010, Firearms Excise Tax Improvement Act of 2010 (P.L. 111-237)

P.L. 111-237, §3(b)(1):

Amended Code Sec. 6213(b) by adding at the end a new paragraph (5). **Effective** for restitution ordered after 8-16-2010.

• 2005, Katrina Emergency Tax Relief Act of 2005 (P.L. 109-73)

P.L. 109-73, §406 [repealed by P.L. 109-135, §201(b)(4)(B)], provides:

SEC. 406. SPECIAL RULE FOR DETERMINING EARNED INCOME.

(a) IN GENERAL.—In the case of a qualified individual, if the earned income of the taxpayer for the taxable year which includes August 25, 2005, is less than the earned income of the taxpayer for the preceding taxable year, the credits allowed under sections 24(d) and 32 of the Internal Revenue Code of 1986 may, at the election of the taxpayer, be determined by substituting—

(1) such earned income for the preceding taxable year, for

(2) such earned income for the taxable year which includes August 25, 2005.

(b) QUALIFIED INDIVIDUAL.—For purposes of this section, the term "qualified individual" means any individual whose principal place of abode on August 25, 2005, was located—

(1) in the core disaster area, or

(2) in the Hurricane Katrina disaster area (but outside the core disaster area) and such individual was displaced from

such principal place of abode by reason of Hurricane Katrina.

(c) EARNED INCOME.—For purposes of this section, the term "earned income" has the meaning given such term under section 32(c) of such Code.

(d) SPECIAL RULES.—

(1) APPLICATION TO JOINT RETURNS.—For purpose of subsection (a), in the case of a joint return for a taxable year which includes August 25, 2005—

(A) such subsection shall apply if either spouse is a qualified individual, and

(B) the earned income of the taxpayer for the preceding taxable year shall be the sum of the earned income of each spouse for such preceding taxable year.

(2) UNIFORM APPLICATION OF ELECTION.—Any election made under subsection (a) shall apply with respect to both section 24(d) and section 32 of such Code.

(3) ERRORS TREATED AS MATHEMATICAL ERROR.—For purposes of section 6213 of such Code, an incorrect use on a return of earned income pursuant to subsection (a) shall be treated as a mathematical or clerical error.

(4) NO EFFECT ON DETERMINATION OF GROSS INCOME, ETC.—Except as otherwise provided in this section, the Internal Revenue Code of 1986 shall be applied without regard to any substitution under subsection (a).

• **1978, Revenue Act of 1978 (P.L. 95-600)**

P.L. 95-600, § 504(b)(2)(A), (B), (c):

Amended Code Sec. 6213(b)(3). **Effective** for tentative refund claims filed on and after 11-6-78. Prior to amendment, paragraph (3) read:

"(3) ASSESSMENTS ARISING OUT OF TENTATIVE CARRYBACK ADJUSTMENTS.—If the Secretary determines that the amount applied, credited, or refunded under section 6411 is in excess of the overassessment attributable to the carryback with respect to which such amount was applied, credited, or refunded, he may assess without regard to the provisions of paragraph (2) the amount of the excess as a deficiency as if it were due to a mathematical or clerical error appearing on the return."

• **1976, Tax Reform Act of 1976 (P.L. 94-455)**

P.L. 94-455, § 1206(a):

Amended Code Sec. 6213(b) by redesignating paragraph (2) as paragraph (3), redesignating paragraph (3) as paragraph (4), and by substituting paragraphs (1) and (2) above for paragraph (1). **Effective** with respect to returns filed after 12-31-76. Prior to amendment, Code Sec. 6213(b)(1) read as follows:

"(1) MATHEMATICAL ERRORS.—If the taxpayer is notified that, on account of a mathematical error appearing upon the return, an amount of tax in excess of that shown upon the return is due, and that an assessment of the tax has been or will be made on the basis of what would have been the correct amount of tax but for the mathematical error, such notice shall not be considered as a notice of deficiency for the purposes of subsection (a) (prohibiting assessment and collection until notice of the deficiency has been mailed), or of section 6212(c)(1) (restricting further deficiency letters), or section 6512(a) (prohibiting credits or refunds after petition to the Tax Court), and the taxpayer shall have no right to file a petition with the Tax Court based on such notice, nor shall such assessment or collection be prohibited by the provisions of subsection (a) of this section."

P.L. 94-455, § 1206(c)(1):

Substituted "he may assess without regard to the provisions of paragraph (2)" for "he may assess" in Code Sec. 6213(b)(3) (as redesignated), and substituted "mathematical or clerical error" for "mathematical error" in Code Sec. 6213(b)(3). **Effective** with respect to returns filed after 12-31-76.

P.L. 94-455, § 1906(b)(13)(A):

Amended 1954 Code by substituting "Secretary" for "Secretary or his delegate" each place it appeared. **Effective** 2-1-77.

[Sec. 6213(c)]

(c) FAILURE TO FILE PETITION.—If the taxpayer does not file a petition with the Tax Court within the time prescribed in subsection (a), the deficiency, notice of which has been mailed to the taxpayer, shall be assessed, and shall be paid upon notice and demand from the Secretary.

Amendments

• **1976, Tax Reform Act of 1976 (P.L. 94-455)**

P.L. 94-455, § 1906(b)(13)(A):

Amended 1954 Code by substituting "Secretary" for "Secretary or his delegate" each place it appeared. **Effective** 2-1-77.

[Sec. 6213(d)]

(d) WAIVER OF RESTRICTIONS.—The taxpayer shall at any time (whether or not a notice of deficiency has been issued) have the right, by a signed notice in writing filed with the Secretary, to waive the restrictions provided in subsection (a) on the assessment and collection of the whole or any part of the deficiency.

Amendments

• **1976, Tax Reform Act of 1976 (P.L. 94-455)**

P.L. 94-455, § 1906(b)(13)(A):

Amended 1954 Code by substituting "Secretary" for "Secretary or his delegate" each place it appeared. **Effective** 2-1-77.

[Sec. 6213(e)]

(e) SUSPENSION OF FILING PERIOD FOR CERTAIN EXCISE TAXES.—The running of the time prescribed by subsection (a) for filing a petition in the Tax Court with respect to the taxes imposed by section 4941 (relating to taxes on self-dealing), 4942 (relating to taxes on failure to distribute income), 4943 (relating to taxes on excess business holdings), 4944 (relating to investments which jeopardize charitable purpose), 4945 (relating to taxes on taxable expenditures), 4951 (relating to taxes on self-dealing) or 4952 (relating to taxes on taxable expenditures), 4955 (relating to taxes on political expenditures), 4958 (relating to private excess benefit), 4971 (relating to excise taxes on failure to meet minimum funding standard), [or] 4975 (relating to excise taxes on prohibited transactions) shall be suspended for any period during which the Secretary has extended the time allowed for making correction under section 4963(e).

Amendments

• 1996, Taxpayer Bill of Rights 2 (P.L. 104-168)

P.L. 104-168, §1311(c)(3):

Amended Code Sec. 6213(e) by inserting "4958 (relating to private excess benefit)," before "4971". For the **effective** date, see Act Sec. 1311(d)(1)-(2), below.

P.L. 104-168, §1311(d)(1)-(2), provides:

(d) EFFECTIVE DATES.—

(1) IN GENERAL.—The amendments made by this section (other than subsection (b)) shall apply to excess benefit transactions occurring on or after September 14, 1995.

(2) BINDING CONTRACTS.—The amendments referred to in paragraph (1) shall not apply to any benefit arising from a transaction pursuant to any written contract which was binding on September 13, 1995, and at all times thereafter before such transaction occurred.

• 1987, Revenue Act of 1987 (P.L. 100-203)

P.L. 100-203, §10712(c)(1):

Amended Code Sec. 6213(e) by striking out "4971" and inserting in lieu thereof "4955 (relating to taxes on political expenditures), 4971". **Effective** for tax years beginning after 12-22-87.

• 1984, Deficit Reduction Act of 1984 (P.L. 98-369)

P.L. 98-369, §305(b)(4):

Amended Code Sec. 6213(e) by striking out "section 4962(e)" and inserting in lieu thereof "section 4963(e)". **Effective** for taxable events occurring after 12-31-84.

• 1980 (P.L. 96-596)

P.L. 96-596, §2(a)(3):

Amended Code Sec. 6213(e) by striking out "section 4941(e)(4), 4942(j)(2), 4943(d)(3), 4944(e)(3), 4945(i)(2), 4951(e)(4), 4952(e)(2), 4971(c)(3), or 4975(f)(6)." and inserting in lieu thereof "section 4962(e).". **Effective** 12-24-80.

• 1978, Black Lung Benefits Revenue Act of 1977 (P.L. 95-227)

P.L. 95-227, §4(d)(1):

Amended Code Sec. 6213(e) by adding "4951 (relating to taxes on selfdealing), or 4952 (relating to taxes on taxable expenditures)," before "4975 (relating to excise taxes on prohibited transactions", by adding "4951(e)(4), 4952(e)(2)" after "4945(i)(2)", and by substituting "4975(f)(6)" for "4975(f)(4)". For **effective** date, see the historical comment for P.L. 95-227 under Code Sec. 4951.

• 1976, Tax Reform Act of 1976 (P.L. 94-455)

P.L. 94-455, §1906(b)(13)(A):

Amended 1954 Code by substituting "Secretary" for "Secretary or his delegate" each place it appeared. **Effective** 2-1-77.

• 1974, Employee Retirement Income Security Act of 1974 (P.L. 93-406)

P.L. 93-406, §1016(a)(11):

Amended Code Sec. 6213(e) by changing "or 4945 (relating to taxes on taxable expenditures)" to "4945 (relating to taxes on taxable expenditures), 4971 (relating to excise taxes on failure to meet minimum funding standard), 4975 (relating to excise taxes on prohibited transactions)". For **effective** date, see amendment note for Code Sec. 410.

• 1969, Tax Reform Act of 1969 (P.L. 91-172)

P.L. 91-172, §101(f)(3):

Added Code Sec. 6213(e). **Effective** 1-1-70.

[Sec. 6213(f)]

(f) COORDINATION WITH TITLE 11.—

(1) SUSPENSION OF RUNNING OF PERIOD FOR FILING PETITION IN TITLE 11 CASES.—In any case under title 11 of the United States Code, the running of the time prescribed by subsection (a) for filing a petition in the Tax Court with respect to any deficiency shall be suspended for the period during which the debtor is prohibited by reason of such case from filing a petition in the Tax Court with respect to such deficiency, and for 60 days thereafter.

(2) CERTAIN ACTION NOT TAKEN INTO ACCOUNT.—For purposes of the second and third sentences of subsection (a), the filing of a proof of claim or request for payment (or the taking of any other action) in a case under title 11 of the United States Code shall not be treated as action prohibited by such second sentence.

Amendments

• 1980, Bankruptcy Tax Act of 1980 (P.L. 96-589)

P.L. 96-589, §6(b)(1):

Redesignated former Code Sec. 6213(f) as Code Sec. 6213(g) and added a new Code Sec. 6213(f). **Effective** 10-1-79, but inapplicable to any proceeding under the Bankruptcy Act commenced before that date.

[Sec. 6213(g)]

(g) DEFINITIONS.—For purposes of this section—

(1) RETURN.—The term "return" includes any return, statement, schedule, or list, and any amendment or supplement thereto, filed with respect to any tax imposed by subtitle A or B, or chapter 41, 42, 43, or 44.

(2) MATHEMATICAL OR CLERICAL ERROR.—The term "mathematical or clerical error" means—

(A) an error in addition, subtraction, multiplication or division shown on any return,

(B) an incorrect use of any table provided by the Internal Revenue Service with respect to any return if such incorrect use is apparent from the existence of other information on the return,

(C) an entry on a return of an item which is inconsistent with another entry of the same or another item on such return,

(D) an omission of information which is required to be supplied on the return to substantiate an entry on the return,

(E) an entry on a return of a deduction or credit in an amount which exceeds a statutory limit imposed by subtitle A or B, or chapter 41, 42, 43, or 44, if such limit is expressed—

(i) as a specified monetary amount, or

(ii) as a percentage, ratio, or fraction,

and if the items entering into the application of such limit appear on such return,

(F) an omission of a correct taxpayer identification number required under section 32 (relating to the earned income credit) to be included on a return,

(G) an entry on a return claiming the credit under section 32 with respect to net earnings from self-employment described in section 32(c)(2)(A) to the extent the tax imposed by section 1401 (relating to self-employment tax) on such net earnings has not been paid,

(H) an omission of a correct TIN required under section 21 (relating to expenses for household and dependent care services necessary for gainful employment) or section 151 (relating to allowance of deductions for personal exemptions),

(I) an omission of a correct TIN required under section 24(e) (relating to child tax credit) to be included on a return,

(J) an omission of a correct TIN required under section 25A(g)(1) (relating to higher education tuition and related expenses) to be included on a return,

(K) an omission of information required by section 32(k)(2) (relating to taxpayers making improper prior claims of earned income credit) or an entry on the return claiming the credit under section 32 for a taxable year for which the credit is disallowed under subsection (k)(1) thereof,

(L) the inclusion on a return of a TIN required to be included on the return under section 21, 24, 32, 6428, or 6428A if—

(i) such TIN is of an individual whose age affects the amount of the credit under such section, and

(ii) the computation of the credit on the return reflects the treatment of such individual as being of an age different from the individual's age based on such TIN,

(M) the entry on the return claiming the credit under section 32 with respect to a child if, according to the Federal Case Registry of Child Support Orders established under section 453(h) of the Social Security Act, the taxpayer is a non-custodial parent of such child,

(N) an omission of any increase required under section 36(f) with respect to the recapture of a credit allowed under section 36,

(O) the inclusion on a return of an individual taxpayer identification number issued under section 6109(i) which has expired, been revoked by the Secretary, or is otherwise invalid,

(P) an omission of information required by section 24(g)(2) or an entry on the return claiming the credit under section 24 for a taxable year for which the credit is disallowed under subsection (g)(1) thereof,

(Q) an omission of information required by section 25A(b)(4)(B) or an entry on the return claiming the American Opportunity Tax Credit for a taxable year for which such credit is disallowed under section 25A(b)(4)(A),

(R) an omission of information or documentation required under section 25C(b)(6)(B) (relating to home energy audits) to be included on a return,

»»→ *Caution: Code Sec. 6213(g)(2)(S), below, as added by P.L. 117-169, applies to property placed in service after December 31, 2024.*

(S) an omission of a correct product identification number required under section 25C(h) (relating to credit for nonbusiness energy property) to be included on a return,

(T) an omission of a correct vehicle identification number required under section 30D(f)(9) (relating to credit for new clean vehicles) to be included on a return,

(U) an omission of a correct vehicle identification number required under section 25E(d) (relating to credit for previously-owned clean vehicles) to be included on a return, and

(V) an omission of a correct vehicle identification number required under section 45W(e) (relating to commercial clean vehicle credit) to be included on a return.

A taxpayer shall be treated as having omitted a correct TIN for purposes of the preceding sentence if information provided by the taxpayer on the return with respect to the individual whose TIN was provided differs from the information the Secretary obtains from the person issuing the TIN.

Amendments

• 2022, Inflation Reduction Act of 2022 (P.L. 117-169)

P.L. 117-169, §13301(f)(4)(A)-(C):

Amended Code Sec. 6213(g)(2) by striking "and" at the end of subparagraph (P), by striking the period at the end of subparagraph (Q) and inserting ", and", and by inserting after subparagraph (Q) a new subparagraph (R). **Effective** for property placed in service after 12-31-2022.

P.L. 117-169, §13301(g)(2)(A)-(C):

Amended Code Sec. 6213(g)(2), as amended by the preceding provisions of this Act, by striking "and" at the end of subparagraph (Q), by striking the period at the end of subparagraph (R) and inserting ", and", and by inserting after subparagraph (R) a new subparagraph (S). **Effective** for property placed in service after 12-31-2024.

P.L. 117-169, §13401(i)(4)(A)-(C):

Amended Code Sec. 6213(g)(2), as amended by the preceding provisions of this Act, by striking "and" at the end of subparagraph (R), by striking the period at the end of subparagraph (S) and inserting ", and", and by inserting after subparagraph (S) a new subparagraph (T). **Effective** for vehicles placed in service after 12-31-2022.

P.L. 117-169, §13402(c)(1)-(3):

Amended Code Sec. 6213(g)(2), as amended by the preceding provisions of this Act, by striking "and" at the end of subparagraph (S), by striking the period at the end of subparagraph (T) and inserting ", and", and by inserting after subparagraph (T) a new subparagraph (U). **Effective** for vehicles acquired after 12-31-2022.

P.L. 117-169, §13403(b)(2)(A)-(C):

Amended Code Sec. 6213(g)(2), as amended by the preceding provisions of this Act, by striking "and" at the end of subparagraph (T), by striking the period at the end of subparagraph (U) and inserting ", and", and by inserting after subparagraph (U) a new subparagraph (V). **Effective** for vehicles acquired after 12-31-2022.

• 2020, COVID-related Tax Relief Act of 2020 (P.L. 116-260)

P.L. 116-260, §272(b)(2), Div. N:

Amended Code Sec. 6213(g)(2)(L) by striking "or 6428" and inserting "6428, or 6428A". **Effective** 12-27-2020.

• 2020, Coronavirus Aid, Relief, and Economic Security (CARES) Act (P.L. 116-136)

P.L. 116-136, §2201(b)(2):

Amended Code Sec. 6213(g)(2)(L) by striking "or 32" and inserting "32, or 6428". **Effective** 3-27-2020.

• 2018, Tax Technical Corrections Act of 2018 (P.L. 115-141)

P.L. 115-141, §101(l)(18), Div. U:

Amended Code Sec. 6213(g)(2)(Q). **Effective** as if included in the provision of the Protecting Americans from Tax Hikes Act of 2015 to which it relates [**effective** for tax years beginning after 12-18-2015.—CCH]. Prior to amendment, Code Sec. 6213(g)(2)(Q) read as follows:

(Q) an omission of information required by section 25A(i)(8)(B) [25A(i)(7)(B)] or an entry on the return claiming the credit determined under section 25A(i) for a taxable year for which the credit is disallowed under paragraph (8)(A) [(7)(A)] thereof.

P.L. 115-141, §401(a)(277), Div. U:

Amended Code Sec. 6213(g)(2)(O) by adding a comma at the end. **Effective** 3-23-2018.

P.L. 115-141, §401(a)(278)(A)-(B), Div. U:

Amended Code Sec. 6213(g)(2)(P) by striking "section 24(h)(2)" and inserting "section 24(g)(2)", and by striking "subsection (h)(1)" and inserting "subsection (g)(1)". **Effective** 3-23-2018.

• 2015, Protecting Americans from Tax Hikes Act of 2015 (P.L. 114-113)

P.L. 114-113, §203(e), Div. Q:

Amended Code Sec. 6213(g)(2) by striking "and" at the end subparagraph (M), by striking the period at the end of subparagraph (N) and inserting ", and", and by inserting after subparagraph (N) a new subparagraph (O). **Effective**, except to the extent provided in Code Sec. 6109(i)(3), for applications for individual taxpayer identification numbers made after 12-18-2015 [**effective** date changed by P.L. 115-141, §101(g)(5), Div. U.—CCH].

P.L. 114-113, §208(b)(1), Div. Q:

Amended Code Sec. 6213(g)(2)(K) by inserting before the comma at the end "or an entry on the return claiming the credit under section 32 for a taxable year for which the credit is disallowed under subsection (k)(1) thereof". **Effective** for tax years beginning after 12-31-2015.

P.L. 114-113, §208(b)(2), Div. Q:

Amended Code Sec. 6213(g)(2), as amended by this Act, by striking "and" at the end of subparagraph (N), by striking the period at the end of subparagraph (O), and by inserting after subparagraph (O) new subparagraphs (P)-(Q). **Effective** for tax years beginning after 12-31-2015.

• 2014, Tax Technical Corrections Act of 2014 (P.L. 113-295)

P.L. 113-295, §214(a)(1)-(2), Division A:

Amended Code Sec. 6213(g)(2) by striking "32, or 6428" in subparagraph (L) and inserting "or 32", and by striking "and" at the end of subparagraph (O), by striking the period at the end of subparagraph (P) and inserting ", and", and by inserting after subparagraph (P) a new subparagraph (Q). **Effective** as if included in the provision of the Economic Stimulus Act of 2008 (P.L. 110-185) to which it relates [**effective** 2-13-2008.—CCH].

P.L. 113-295, §221(a)(4), Division A:

Amended Code Sec. 6213(g)(2), as amended by Act Sec. 214(a)(2), by striking subparagraph (P). **Effective** generally 12-19-2014. For a special rule, see Act Sec. 221(b)(2), Division A, below. Prior to being stricken, Code Sec. 6213(g)(2)(P) read as follows:

(P) an entry on a return claiming the credit under section 36 if—

(i) the Secretary obtains information from the person issuing the TIN of the taxpayer that indicates that the taxpayer does not meet the age requirement of section 36(b)(4),

(ii) information provided to the Secretary by the taxpayer on an income tax return for at least one of the 2 preceding taxable years is inconsistent with eligibility for such credit, or

(iii) the taxpayer fails to attach to the return the form described in section 36(d)(4), and

P.L. 113-295, §221(a)(5)(C), Division A:

Amended Code Sec. 6213(g)(2) by striking subparagraph (N). **Effective** generally 12-19-2014. For a special rule, see Act Sec. 221(b)(2), Division A, below. Prior to being stricken, Code Sec. 6213(g)(2)(N) read as follows:

(N) an omission of the reduction required under section 36A(c) with respect to the credit allowed under section 36A or an omission of the correct social security account number required under section 36A(d)(1)(B),

P.L. 113-295, §221(a)(112)(C), Division A:

Amended Code Sec. 6213(g)(2), as amended by Act Sec. 214(a)(2) and Act Sec. 221(a)(4) and (5)(C), by striking subparagraph (Q), by redesignating subparagraph (O) as subparagraph (N), by inserting "and" at the end of subparagraph (M), and by striking the comma at the end of subparagraph (N) (as so redesignated) and inserting a period. **Effective** generally 12-19-2014. For a special rule, see Act Sec. 221(b)(2), Division A, below. Prior to being stricken, Code Sec. 6213(g)(2)(Q) read as follows:

(Q) an omission of a correct valid identification number required under section 6428(h) (relating to 2008 recovery rebates for individuals) to be included on a return.

P.L. 113-295, §221(b)(2), Division A, provides:

(2) SAVINGS PROVISION.—If—

(A) any provision amended or repealed by the amendments made by this section applied to—

(i) any transaction occurring before the date of the enactment of this Act,

(ii) any property acquired before such date of enactment, or

(iii) any item of income, loss, deduction, or credit taken into account before such date of enactment, and

(B) the treatment of such transaction, property, or item under such provision would (without regard to the amendments or repeals made by this section) affect the liability for tax for periods ending after date of enactment, nothing in the amendments or repeals made by this section shall be construed to affect the treatment of such transaction, property, or item for purposes of determining liability for tax for periods ending after such date of enactment.

• 2013, American Taxpayer Relief Act of 2012 (P.L. 112-240)

P.L. 112-240, §101(a)(1) and (3), provides:

SEC. 101. PERMANENT EXTENSION AND MODIFICATION OF 2001 TAX RELIEF.

(a) PERMANENT EXTENSION.—

(1) IN GENERAL.—The Economic Growth and Tax Relief Reconciliation Act of 2001 is amended by striking title IX.

* * *

(3) EFFECTIVE DATE.—The amendments made by this subsection shall apply to taxable, plan, or limitation years beginning after December 31, 2012, and estates of decedents dying, gifts made, or generation skipping transfers after December 31, 2012.

• 2009, Worker, Homeownership, and Business Assistance Act of 2009 (P.L. 111-92)

P.L. 111-92, §11(h)(1)-(3):

Amended Code Sec. 6213(g)(2) by striking "and" at the end of subparagraph (M), by striking the period at the end of subparagraph (N) and inserting ", and", and by inserting after subparagraph (N) a new subparagraph (O). **Effective** for tax years ending on or after 4-9-2008.

P.L. 111-92, §12(d):

Amended Code Sec. 6213(g)(2), as amended by this Act, by striking "and" at the end of subparagraph (N), by striking the period at the end of subparagraph (O) and inserting ", and", and by inserting after subparagraph (O) a new subparagraph (P). **Effective** for returns for tax years ending on or after 4-9-2008.

• 2009, American Recovery and Reinvestment Tax Act of 2009 (P.L. 111-5)

P.L. 111-5, §1001(d):

Amended Code Sec. 6213(g)(2) by striking "and" at the end of subparagraph (L)(ii), by striking the period at the end of subparagraph (M) and inserting ", and", and by adding at the end a new subparagraph (N). **Effective** for tax years beginning after 12-31-2008.

• 2008, Economic Stimulus Act of 2008 (P.L. 110-185)

P.L. 110-185, §101(b)(2):

Amended Code Sec. 6213(g)(2)(L) by striking "or 32" and inserting "32, or 6428". **Effective** 2-13-2008.

• 2001, Economic Growth and Tax Relief Reconciliation Act of 2001 (P.L. 107-16)

P.L. 107-16, §303(g):

Amended Code Sec. 6213(g)(2) by striking "and" at the end of subparagraph (K), by striking the period at the end of subparagraph (L) and inserting ", and", and by inserting after subparagraph (L) a new subparagraph (M). **Effective** 1-1-2004.

P.L. 107-16, §901(a)-(b), as amended by P.L. 111-312, §101(a)(1), provides [but see P.L. 112-240, §101(a)(1) and (3), above]:

SEC. 901. SUNSET OF PROVISIONS OF ACT.

(a) IN GENERAL.—All provisions of, and amendments made by, this Act shall not apply—

(1) to taxable, plan, or limitation years beginning after December 31, 2012, or

(2) in the case of title V, to estates of decedents dying, gifts made, or generation skipping transfers, after December 31, 2012.

(b) APPLICATION OF CERTAIN LAWS.—The Internal Revenue Code of 1986 and the Employee Retirement Income Security Act of 1974 shall be applied and administered to years, estates, gifts, and transfers described in subsection (a) as if the provisions and amendments described in subsection (a) had never been enacted.

• 1998, Tax and Trade Relief Extension Act of 1998 (P.L. 105-277)

P.L. 105-277, §3003(a):

Amended Code Sec. 6213(g)(2) by adding at the end a new flush sentence. **Effective** for tax years ending after 10-21-98.

P.L. 105-277, §3003(b):

Amended Code Sec. 6213(g)(2) by striking "and" at the end of subparagraph (J), by striking the period at the end of subparagraph (K) and inserting ", and", and by inserting after subparagraph (K) a new subparagraph (L). **Effective** for tax years ending after 10-21-98.

• 1997, Taxpayer Relief Act of 1997 (P.L. 105-34)

P.L. 105-34, §101(d)(2):

Amended Code Sec. 6213(g)(2) by striking "and" at the end of subparagraph (G), by striking the period at the end of subparagraph (H) and inserting ", and", and by inserting after subparagraph (H) a new subparagraph (I). **Effective** for tax years beginning after 12-31-97.

P.L. 105-34, §201(b):

Amended Code Sec. 6213(g)(2), as amended by Act Sec. 101(d)(2), by striking "and" at the end of subparagraph (H), by striking the period at the end of subparagraph (I) and inserting ", and", and by inserting after subparagraph (I) a new subparagraph (J). **Effective** for expenses paid after 12-31-97 (in tax years ending after such date), for education furnished in academic periods beginning after such date.

P.L. 105-34, §1085(a)(3) (as amended by P.L. 105-206, §6010 (p)(3)):

Amended Code Sec. 6213(g)(2) by striking "and" at the end of subparagraph (I), by striking the period at the end of subparagraph (J) and inserting ", and", and by inserting after subparagraph (J) a new subparagraph (K). **Effective** for tax years beginning after 12-31-96.

• 1996, Personal Responsibility and Work Opportunity Reconciliation Act of 1996 (P.L. 104-193)

P.L. 104-193, §451(c):

Amended Code Sec. 6213(g)(2) by striking "and" at the end of subparagraph (D), by striking the period at the end of subparagraph (E) and inserting a comma, and by inserting after subparagraph (E) new subparagraphs (F) and (G). **Effective** with respect to returns the due date for which (without regard to extensions) is more than 30 days after 8-22-96.

• 1996, Small Business Job Protection Act of 1996 (P.L. 104-188)

P.L. 104-188, §1615(c):

Amended Code Sec. 6213(g)(2), as amended by P.L. 104-193, by striking "and" at the end of subparagraph (F), by striking the period at the end of subparagraph (G) and inserting ", and", and by inserting at the end a new subparagraph (H). **Effective**, generally, with respect to returns the due date for which (without regard to extensions) is on or after the 30th day after 8-20-96. For a special rule, see Act Sec. 1615(d)(2), below.

P.L. 104-188, §1615(d)(2), provides:

(2) SPECIAL RULE FOR 1995 AND 1996.—In the case of returns for taxable years beginning in 1995 or 1996, a taxpayer shall not be required by the amendments made by this section to provide a taxpayer identification number for a child who is born after October 31, 1995, in the case of a taxable year beginning in 1995 or November 30, 1996, in the case of a taxable year beginning in 1996.

• 1988, Omnibus Trade and Competitiveness Act of 1988 (P.L. 100-418)

P.L. 100-418, §1941(b)(2)(B)(v):

Amended Code Sec. 6213(g) by striking "44, or 45" each place it appears and inserting "or 44". **Effective** for crude oil removed from the premises on or after 8-23-88.

• 1980, Bankruptcy Tax Act of 1980 (P.L. 96-589)

P.L. 96-589, §6(b)(1):

Redesignated Code Sec. 6213(f) as 6213(g). **Effective** 10-1-79, but inapplicable to any proceeding under the Bankruptcy Act commenced before 10-1-79.

• 1980, Crude Oil Windfall Profit Tax Act of 1980 (P.L. 96-223)

P.L. 96-223, §101(f)(1)(E):

Amended Code Sec. 6213(f)(2)(E) by striking out "or 44" and inserting "44, or 45". For the **effective** date and transitional rules, see P.L. 96-223, §101(i), following Code Sec. 4986.

• 1978, Black Lung Benefits Revenue Act of 1977 (P.L. 95-227)

P.L. 95-227, §4(d)(2):

Amended Code Sec. 6213(f) by substituting "chapter 41, 42, 43, or 44" for "chapter 42 or 43" in paragraphs (1) and (2)(E). For **effective** date, see the historical comment from P.L. 95-227 under Code Sec. 4951.

• 1976, Tax Reform Act of 1976 (P.L. 94-455)

P.L. 94-455, §1206(b):

Redesignated former Code Sec. 6213(f) as Code Sec. 6213(g) and added a new Code Sec. 6213(f). **Effective** with respect to returns filed after 12-31-76.

[Sec. 6213(h)]

(h) CROSS REFERENCES.—

(1) For assessment as if a mathematical error on the return, in the case of erroneous claims for income tax prepayment credits, see section 6201(a)(3).

(2) For assessments without regard to restrictions imposed by this section in the case of—

(A) Recovery of foreign income taxes, see section 905(c).

(B) Recovery of foreign estate tax, see section 2016.

(3) For provisions relating to application of this subchapter in the case of certain partnership items, etc., see section 6230(a).

Amendments

• 1988, Technical and Miscellaneous Revenue Act of 1988 (P.L. 100-647)

P.L. 100-647, §1015(r)(3):

Amended Code Sec. 6213(h) by striking out paragraph (3) and by redesignating paragraph (4) as paragraph (3). **Effective** for notices of deficiencies mailed after 11-10-88. Prior to amendment, Code Sec. 6213(h)(3) read as follows:

(3) For assessment as if a mathematical error on the return, in the case of erroneous claims for credits under section 32 or 34, see section 6201(a)(4).

• 1986, Tax Reform Act of 1986 (P.L. 99-514)

P.L. 99-514, §1875(d)(2)(B)(i):

Amended Code Sec. 6213(h)(4). **Effective** as if it were included in P.L. 97-248. Prior to amendment, paragraph (4) read as follows:

(4) For provision that this subchapter shall not apply in the case of computational adjustments attributable to partnership items, see section 6230(a).

• 1984, Deficit Reduction Act of 1984 (P.L. 98-369)

P.L. 98-369, §474(r)(34):

Amended Code Sec. 6213(h)(3) by striking out "section 39" and inserting in lieu thereof "section 32 or 34". **Effective** for tax years beginning after 12-31-83, and to carrybacks from such years.

• 1982, Tax Equity and Fiscal Responsibility Act of 1982 (P.L. 97-248)

P.L. 97-248, §402(c)(2):

Amended Code Sec. 6213(h) by adding paragraph (4). **Effective** for partnership tax years beginning after 9-3-82.

• 1980, Bankruptcy Tax Act of 1980 (P.L. 96-589)

P.L. 96-589, §6(b)(1):

Redesignated Code Sec. 6213(g) as 6213(h). **Effective** 10-1-79, but inapplicable to any proceeding under the Bankruptcy Act commenced before 10-1-79.

• 1976, Tax Reform Act of 1976 (P.L. 94-455)

P.L. 94-455, §1206(b):

Redesignated former Code Sec. 6213(f) to be Code Sec. 6213(g). **Effective** with respect to returns filed after 12-31-76.

• 1969, Tax Reform Act of 1969 (P.L. 91-172)

P.L. 91-172, §101(f)(3):

Redesignated Code Sec. 6213(e) as 6213(f). **Effective** 1-1-70.

• 1965, Excise Tax Reduction Act of 1965 (P.L. 89-44)

P.L. 89-44, §809(d)(4):

Added paragraph (3). **Effective** 7-1-65.

[Sec. 6214]

SEC. 6214. DETERMINATIONS BY TAX COURT.

[Sec. 6214(a)]

(a) JURISDICTION AS TO INCREASE OF DEFICIENCY, ADDITIONAL AMOUNTS, OR ADDITIONS TO THE TAX.—Except as provided by section 7463, the Tax Court shall have jurisdiction to redetermine the correct amount of the deficiency even if the amount so redetermined is greater than the amount of the deficiency, notice of which has been mailed to the taxpayer, and to determine whether any additional amount, or any addition to the tax should be assessed, if claim therefor is asserted by the Secretary at or before the hearing or a rehearing.

Amendments

• 1986, Tax Reform Act of 1986 (P.L. 99-514)

P.L. 99-514, §1554(a):

Amended Code Sec. 6214(a) by striking out "addition to the tax" and inserting in lieu thereof "any addition to the tax". **Effective** for any action or proceeding in the Tax Court with respect to which a decision has not become final (as determined under section 7481 of the Internal Revenue Code of 1954) before 10-22-86.

• 1976, Tax Reform Act of 1976 (P.L. 94-455)

P.L. 94-455, §1906(b)(13)(A):

Amended 1954 Code by substituting "Secretary" for "Secretary or his delegate" each place it appeared. **Effective** 2-1-77.

• 1969, Tax Reform Act of 1969 (P.L. 91-172)

P.L. 91-172, §960(a):

Amended Code Sec. 6214(a) by adding the introductory phrase "Except as provided by section 7463,". **Effective** 12-30-70.

[Sec. 6214(b)]

(b) JURISDICTION OVER OTHER YEARS AND QUARTERS.—The Tax Court in redetermining a deficiency of income tax for any taxable year or of gift tax for any calendar year or calendar quarter shall consider such facts with relation to the taxes for other years or calendar quarters as may be necessary correctly to redetermine the amount of such deficiency, but in so doing shall have no jurisdiction to determine whether or not the tax for any other year or calendar quarter has been overpaid or underpaid. Notwithstanding the preceding sentence, the Tax Court may apply the doctrine of equitable recoupment to the same extent that it is available in civil tax cases before the district courts of the United States and the United States Court of Federal Claims.

Amendments

• 2006, Pension Protection Act of 2006 (P.L. 109-280)

P.L. 109-280, §858(a):

Amended Code Sec. 6214(b) by adding at the end a new sentence. **Effective** for any action or proceeding in the United States Tax Court with respect to which a decision has not become final (as determined under Code Sec. 7481) as of 8-17-2006.

• 1970, Excise, Estate, and Gift Tax Adjustment Act of 1970 (P.L. 91-614)

P.L. 91-614, §102(d)(6):

Amended Code Sec. 6214(b). **Effective** 1-1-71 for gifts made after 12-31-70. Prior to amendment, the section read as follows:

(b) JURISDICTION OVER OTHER YEARS.—The Tax Court in redetermining a deficiency of income tax for any taxable year or of gift tax for any calendar year shall consider such facts with relation to the taxes for other years as may be necessary correctly to redetermine the amount of such deficiency, but in so doing shall have no jurisdiction to determine whether or not the tax for any other year has been overpaid or underpaid.

[Sec. 6214(c)]

(c) TAXES IMPOSED BY SECTION 507 OR CHAPTER 41, 42, 43, OR 44.—The Tax Court, in redetermining a deficiency of any tax imposed by section 507 or chapter 41, 42, 43, or 44 for any period, act, or failure to act, shall consider such facts with relation to the taxes under chapter 41, 42, 43, or 44 for other periods, acts, or failures to act as may be necessary correctly to redetermine the amount of such deficiency, but in so doing shall have no jurisdiction to determine whether or not the taxes under chapter 41, 42, 43, or 44 for any other period, act, or failure to act have been overpaid or underpaid. The Tax Court, in redetermining a deficiency of any second tier tax (as defined in section 4963(b)), shall make a determination with respect to whether the taxable event has been corrected.

Amendments

• 1988, Omnibus Trade and Competitiveness Act of 1988 (P.L. 100-418)

P.L. 100-418, §1941(b)(2)(B)(vi):

Amended Code Sec. 6214(c) by striking "44, or 45" each place it appears and inserting "or 44". **Effective** for crude oil removed from the premises on or after 8-23-88.

• 1986, Tax Reform Act of 1986 (P.L. 99-514)

P.L. 99-514, §1833:

Amended Code Sec. 6214(c) by striking out "section 4962(b)" and inserting in lieu thereof "section 4963(b)". **Effective** as if included in the provision of P.L. 98-369 to which it relates.

• 1980 (P.L. 96-596)

P.L. 96-596, §2(b):

Amended Code Sec. 6214(c) by adding the last sentence. **Effective** with respect to second tier taxes assessed after 12-24-80 (except in cases where there is a court decision with regard to which res judicata applies on that date).

• 1980, Crude Oil Windfall Profit Tax Act of 1980 (P.L. 96-223)

P.L. 96-223, §101(f)(1)(F):

Amended Code Sec. 6214(c) by striking out each place it appears "or 44" and inserting ", 44, or 45". For the **effective** date and transitional rules, see P.L. 96-223, §101(i), following Code Sec. 4986.

• 1976, Tax Reform Act of 1976 (P.L. 94-455)

P.L. 94-455, §1307(d)(2)(F)(iv):

Substituted "chapter 41, 42," for "chapter 42" each place it appeared in Code Sec. 6214(c). **Effective** 10-4-76.

P.L. 94-455, §1605(b)(7)(A), (B):

Substituted "43, or 44" for "or 43" each place it appeared in Code Sec. 6214(c). For **effective** date, see amendment note for P.L. 94-455, §1605(b)(4)(A), following Code Sec. 6211(a).

• 1974, Employee Retirement Income Security Act of 1974 (P.L. 93-406)

P.L. 93-406, §1016(a)(12):

Amended Code Sec. 6214(c) by changing "chapter 42" to "chapter 42 or 43" each place it appears. For **effective** date, see amendment note for Code Sec. 410.

• 1969, Tax Reform Act of 1969 (P.L. 91-172)

P.L. 91-172, §101(j)(43):

Added Code Sec. 6214(c). **Effective** 1-1-70.

[Sec. 6214(d)]

(d) FINAL DECISIONS OF TAX COURT.—For purposes of this chapter, chapter 41, 42, 43, or 44 and subtitles A or B the date on which a decision of the Tax Court becomes final shall be determined according to the provisions of section 7481.

Amendments

• 1988, Omnibus Trade and Competitiveness Act of 1988 (P.L. 100-418)

P.L. 100-418, §1941(b)(2)(B)(vii):

Amended Code Sec. 6214(d) by striking "44, or 45" each place it appears and inserting "or 44". **Effective** for crude oil removed from the premises on or after 8-23-88.

• 1980, Crude Oil Windfall Profit Tax Act of 1980 (P.L. 96-223)

P.L. 96-223, §101(f)(1)(G):

Amended Code Sec. 6214(d) by striking out "or 44" and inserting "44, or 45". For the **effective** date and transitional rules, see P.L. 96-223, §101(i), following Code Sec. 4986.

• 1976, Tax Reform Act of 1976 (P.L. 94-455)

P.L. 94-455, §1307(d)(2)(F)(iv):

Substituted "chapter 41, 42," for "chapter 42" in Code Sec. 6214(d). **Effective** 10-4-76.

P.L. 94-455, §1605(b)(7)(C):

Substituted "43, or 44" for "or 43" in Code Sec. 6214(d). For **effective** date, see amendatory note for P.L. 94-455, §1605(b)(4)(A), following Code Sec. 6211(a).

• 1974, Employee Retirement Income Security Act of 1974 (P.L. 93-406)

P.L. 93-406, §1016(a)(12):

Amended Code Sec. 6214(d) by changing "chapter 42" to "chapter 42 or 43". For **effective** date, see amendment note for Code Sec. 410.

• 1969, Tax Reform Act of 1969 (P.L. 91-172)

P.L. 91-172, §101(j)(43), (44):

Redesignated former Code Sec. 6214(c) as Code Sec. 6214(d) and added ", chapter 42," after "chapter". **Effective** 1-1-70.

[Sec. 6214(e)]

(e) CROSS REFERENCE.—

For provision giving Tax Court jurisdiction to order a refund of an overpayment and to award sanctions, see section 6512(b)(2).

Amendments

• 1996, Small Business Job Protection Act of 1996 (P.L. 104-188)

P.L. 104-188, §1704(t)(16):

Amended Code Sec. 6214(e). **Effective** 8-20-96. Prior to amendment, Code Sec. 6214(e) read as follows:

(e) CROSS REFERENCES.—

(1) For provision giving Tax Court jurisdiction to determine whether any portion of deficiency is a substantial underpayment attributable to tax motivated transactions, see section 6621(c)(4).

(2) For provision giving Tax Court jurisdiction to order a refund of an overpayment and to award sanctions, see section 6512(b)(2).

• 1988, Technical and Miscellaneous Revenue Act of 1988 (P.L. 100-647)

P.L. 100-647, §6244(b)(1):

Amended Code Sec. 6214(e) by striking out "REFERENCE.—" and inserting in lieu thereof "REFERENCES.—" in the heading, by designating the undesignated paragraph as paragraph (1), and by adding at the end thereof new paragraph (2). **Effective** for overpayments determined by the Tax Court that have not yet been refunded by the 90th day after 11-10-88.

• 1986, Tax Reform Act of 1986 (P.L. 99-514)

P.L. 99-514, §1511(c)(8):

Amended Code Sec. 6214(e) by striking out "section 6621(d)(4)" and inserting in lieu thereof "section 6621(c)(4)". **Effective** for purposes of determining interest for periods after 12-31-86.

• 1984, Deficit Reduction Act of 1984 (P.L. 98-369)

P.L. 98-369, §144(b):

Amended Code Sec. 6214 by adding new subsection (e). **Effective** with respect to interest accruing after 12-31-84.

[Sec. 6215]

SEC. 6215. ASSESSMENT OF DEFICIENCY FOUND BY TAX COURT.

[Sec. 6215(a)]

(a) GENERAL RULE.—If the taxpayer files a petition with the Tax Court, the entire amount redetermined as the deficiency by the decision of the Tax Court which has become final shall be assessed and shall be paid upon notice and demand from the Secretary. No part of the amount determined as a deficiency by the Secretary but disallowed as such by the decision of the Tax Court which has become final shall be assessed or be collected by levy or by proceeding in court with or without assessment.

Amendments

• 1976, Tax Reform Act of 1976 (P.L. 94-455)

P.L. 94-455, §1906(b)(13)(A):

Amended 1954 Code by substituting "Secretary" for "Secretary or his delegate" each place it appeared. **Effective** 2-1-77.

[Sec. 6215(b)]

(b) CROSS REFERENCES.—

(1) For assessment or collection of the amount of the deficiency determined by the Tax Court pending appellate court review, see section 7485.

(2) For dismissal of petition by Tax Court as affirmation of deficiency as determined by the Secretary, see section 7459(d).

(3) For decision of Tax Court that tax is barred by limitation as its decision that there is no deficiency, see section 7459(e).

(4) For assessment of damages awarded by Tax Court for instituting proceedings merely for delay, see section 6673.

(5) For rules applicable to Tax Court proceedings, see generally subchapter C of chapter 76.

(6) For extension of time for paying amount determined as deficiency, see section 6161(b).

Amendments

• 2018, Tax Technical Corrections Act of 2018 (P.L. 115-141)

P.L. 115-141, §401(b)(46), Div. U:

Amended Code Sec. 6215(b) by striking paragraph (5) and by redesignating paragraphs (6) and (7) as paragraphs (5) and (6), respectively. **Effective** 3-23-2018. For a special rule, see Act Sec. 401(e), Div. U, below. Prior to being stricken, Code Sec. 6215(b)(5) read as follows:

(5) For treatment of certain deficiencies as having been paid, in connection with sale of surplus war-built vessels, see section 9(b)(8) of the Merchant Ship Sales Act of 1946 (50 U. S. C. App. 1742).

P.L. 115-141, §401(e), Div. U, provides:

(e) GENERAL SAVINGS PROVISION WITH RESPECT TO DEADWOOD PROVISIONS.—If—

(1) any provision amended or repealed by the amendments made by subsection (b) or (d) applied to—

(A) any transaction occurring before the date of the enactment of this Act,

(B) any property acquired before such date of enactment, or

(C) any item of income, loss, deduction, or credit taken into account before such date of enactment, and

(2) the treatment of such transaction, property, or item under such provision would (without regard to the amendments or repeals made by such subsection) affect the liability for tax for periods ending after such date of enactment,

nothing in the amendments or repeals made by this section shall be construed to affect the treatment of such transaction, property, or item for purposes of determining liability for tax for periods ending after such date of enactment.

• 1986, Tax Reform Act of 1986 (P.L. 99-514)

P.L. 99-514, §1404(c)(2):

Amended Code Sec. 6215(b) by striking out paragraph (7) and redesignating paragraph (8) as paragraph (7). **Effective** for tax years beginning after 12-31-86. Prior to amendment, Code Sec. 6215(b)(7) read as follows:

(7) For proration of deficiency to installments, see section 6152(c).

• 1976, Tax Reform Act of 1976 (P.L. 94-455)

P.L. 94-455, §1906(a)(16):

Struck out "60 Stat. 48;" before "50 U.S.C. App. 1742" in Code Sec. 6215(b)(5). **Effective** 2-1-77.

* * *

CHAPTER 64—COLLECTION

Subchapter A—General Provisions

* * *

[Sec. 6301]

SEC. 6301. COLLECTION AUTHORITY.

The Secretary shall collect the taxes imposed by the internal revenue laws.

Amendments

• 1976, Tax Reform Act of 1976 (P.L. 94-455)

P.L. 94-455, §1906(b)(13)(A):

Amended 1954 Code by substituting "Secretary" for "Secretary or his delegate" each place it appeared. **Effective** 2-1-77.

[Sec. 6302]

SEC. 6302. MODE OR TIME OF COLLECTION.

[Sec. 6302(a)]

(a) ESTABLISHMENT BY REGULATIONS.—If the mode or time for collecting any tax is not provided for by this title, the Secretary may establish the same by regulations.

Amendments

• 1983, Railroad Retirement Solvency Act of 1983 (P.L. 98-76)

P.L. 98-76, §226, provides:

SEC. 226. DEPOSITARY SCHEDULES.

Effective on and after January 1, 1984, the times for making payments prescribed under section 6302 of the Internal Revenue Code of 1954 with respect to the taxes imposed by chapter 22 of such Code shall be the same as the times prescribed under such section which apply to the taxes imposed by chapters 21 and 24 of such Code.

• 1976, Tax Reform Act of 1976 (P.L. 94-455)

P.L. 94-455, §1906(b)(13)(A):

Amended 1954 Code by substituting "Secretary" for "Secretary or his delegate" each place it appeared. **Effective** 2-1-77.

[Sec. 6302(b)]

(b) DISCRETIONARY METHOD.—Whether or not the method of collecting any tax imposed by chapter 21, 31, 32, or 33, or by section 4481, is specifically provided for by this title, any such tax may, under regulations prescribed by the Secretary, be collected by means of returns, stamps, coupons, tickets, books, or such other reasonable devices or methods as may be necessary or helpful in securing a complete and proper collection of the tax.

Amendments

• 1990, Omnibus Budget Reconciliation Act of 1990 (P.L. 101-508)

P.L. 101-508, §11801(c)(22)(A) (as amended by P.L. 104-188, §1704(t)(52)):

Amended Code Sec. 6302(b) by striking "chapters 21" and all that follows down through "chapter 37," and inserting "chapter 21, 31, 32, or 33, or by section 4481". **Effective** 11-5-90. Prior to amendment, Code Sec. 6302(b) read as follows:

(b) DISCRETIONARY METHOD.—Whether or not the method of collecting any tax imposed by chapters 21, 31, 32, 33, section 4481 of chapter 36, [or]section 4501(a) of chapter 37, is specifically provided for by this title, any such tax may, under regulations prescribed by the Secretary, be collected by means of returns, stamps, coupons, tickets, books, or such other reasonable devices or methods as may be necessary or helpful in securing a complete and proper collection of the tax.

P.L. 101-508, §11821(b), provides:

(b) SAVINGS PROVISION.—If—

(1) any provision amended or repealed by this part applied to—

(A) any transaction occurring before the date of the enactment of this Act,

(B) any property acquired before such date of enactment, or

(C) any item of income, loss, deduction, or credit taken into account before such date of enactment, and

(2) the treatment of such transaction, property, or item under such provision would (without regard to the amendments made by this part) affect liability for tax periods ending after such date of enactment,

nothing in the amendments made by this part shall be construed to affect the treatment of such transaction, property, or item for purposes of determining liability for tax for periods ending after such date of enactment.

• 1976, Tax Reform Act of 1976 (P.L. 94-455)

P.L. 94-455, §1906(a)(17):

Substituted "section 4501(a) of chapter 37" for "sections 4501(a) or 4511 of chapter 37, or section 4701 or 4721 of chapter 39" in Code Sec. 6302(b). **Effective** 2-1-77.

P.L. 94-455, §1906(b)(13)(A):

Amended 1954 Code by substituting "Secretary" for "Secretary or his delegate" each place it appeared. **Effective** 2-1-77.

• 1956 (P.L. 627, 84th Cong.)

P.L. 627, 84th Cong., §206(b):

Amended subsection (b) by inserting "section 4481 of Chapter 36," after "33,". **Effective** 7-1-56.

[Sec. 6302(c)]

(c) USE OF GOVERNMENT DEPOSITARIES.—The Secretary may authorize Federal Reserve banks, and incorporated banks, trust companies, domestic building and loan associations, or credit unions which are depositaries or financial agents of the United States, to receive any tax imposed under the internal revenue laws, in such manner, at such times, and under such conditions as he may prescribe; and he shall prescribe the manner, times, and conditions under which the receipt of such tax by such banks, trust companies, domestic building and loan associations, and credit unions is to be treated as payment of such tax to the Secretary.

Amendments

• 1977 (P.L. 95-147)

P.L. 95-147, §3(a):

Amended Code Sec. 6302(c) by substituting "trust companies, domestic building and loan associations, or credit unions" for "or trust companies" and by substituting "trust companies, domestic building and loan associations, and credit unions" for "and trust companies". **Effective** for amounts deposited after 10-28-77.

• 1976, Tax Reform Act of 1976 (P.L. 94-455)

P.L. 94-455, §1906(b)(13)(A):

Amended 1954 Code by substituting "Secretary" for "Secretary or his delegate" each place it appeared. **Effective** 2-1-77.

[Sec. 6302(d)]

(d) TIME FOR PAYMENT OF MANUFACTURERS' EXCISE TAX ON RECREATIONAL EQUIPMENT.—The taxes imposed by subchapter D of chapter 32 of this title (relating to taxes on recreational equipment) shall be due and payable on the date for filing the return for such taxes.

Amendments

• 2010, Firearms Excise Tax Improvement Act of 2010 (P.L. 111-237)

P.L. 111-237, §2(a):

Amended Code Sec. 6302(d). **Effective** for articles sold by the manufacturer, producer, or importer after 8-16-2010. Prior to amendment, Code Sec. 6302(d) read as follows:

(d) TIME FOR PAYMENT OF MANUFACTURERS' EXCISE TAX ON SPORTING GOODS.—The taxes imposed by subsections (a) and (b) of section 4161 (relating to taxes on sporting goods) shall be due and payable on the date for filing the return for such taxes.

• 1988, Technical and Miscellaneous Revenue Act of 1988 (P.L. 100-647)

P.L. 100-647, §6107(a):

Amended Code Sec. 6302(d). **Effective** with respect to articles sold by the manufacturer, producer, or importer after 12-31-88. Prior to amendment, Code Sec. 6302(d) read as follows:

(d) TIME FOR PAYMENT OF MANUFACTURERS EXCISE TAX ON SPORT FISHING EQUIPMENT.—The tax imposed by section 4161(a) (relating to manufacturers excise tax on sport fishing equipment) shall be due and payable on the date for filing the return for such tax.

• 1984, Deficit Reduction Act of 1984 (P.L. 98-369)

P.L. 98-369, §1015(c):

Amended Code Sec. 6302 by redesignating subsection (d) as subsection (e) and by inserting after subsection (c) new subsection (d). **Effective** with respect to articles sold by the manufacturer, producer, or importer after 9-30-84.

[Sec. 6302(e)]

(e) TIME FOR DEPOSIT OF TAXES ON COMMUNICATIONS SERVICES AND AIRLINE TICKETS.—

(1) IN GENERAL.—Except as provided in paragraph (2), if, under regulations prescribed by the Secretary, a person is required to make deposits of any tax imposed by section 4251 or subsection (a) or (b) of section 4261 with respect to amounts considered collected by such person during any semi-monthly period, such deposit shall be made not later than the 3rd day (not including Saturdays, Sundays, or legal holidays) after the close of the 1st week of the 2nd semimonthly period following the period to which such amounts relate.

(2) SPECIAL RULE FOR TAX DUE IN SEPTEMBER.—

(A) AMOUNTS CONSIDERED COLLECTED.—In the case of a person required to make deposits of the tax imposed by section 4251, 4261, or 4271 with respect to amounts considered collected by such person during any semimonthly period, the amount of such tax included in bills rendered or tickets sold during the period beginning on September 1 and ending on September 11 shall be deposited not later than September 29.

(B) SPECIAL RULE WHERE SEPTEMBER 29 IS ON SATURDAY OR SUNDAY.—If September 29 falls on a Saturday or Sunday, the due date under subparagraph (A) shall be—

(i) in the case of Saturday, the preceding day, and

(ii) in the case of Sunday, the following day.

(C) TAXPAYERS NOT REQUIRED TO USE ELECTRONIC FUNDS TRANSFER.—In the case of deposits not required to be made by electronic funds transfer, subparagraphs (A) and (B) shall be applied by substituting "September 10" for "September 11" and "September 28" for "September 29".

Amendments

• 2018, Tax Technical Corrections Act of 2018 (P.L. 115-141)

P.L. 115-141, §401(a)(279), Div. U:

Amended Code Sec. 6302(e)(2)(A) by striking "sections" and inserting "section". **Effective** 3-23-2018.

• 2014, Tax Technical Corrections Act of 2014 (P.L. 113-295)

P.L. 113-295, §221(a)(110)(A), Division A:

Amended Code Sec. 6302(e)(2)[(A)] by striking "imposed by" and all that follows through "with respect to" and inserting "imposed by sections 4251, 4261, or 4271 with respect to". **Effective** generally 12-19-2014. For a special rule, see Act Sec. 221(b)(2), Division A, below. Prior to amendment, Code Sec. 6302(e)(2)(A) read as follows:

(A) AMOUNTS CONSIDERED COLLECTED.—In the case of a person required to make deposits of the tax imposed by—

(i) section 4251, or

(ii) effective on January 1, 1997, section 4261 or 4271,

with respect to amounts considered collected by such person during any semimonthly period, the amount of such tax included in bills rendered or tickets sold during the period beginning on September 1 and ending on September 11 shall be deposited not later than September 29.

P.L. 113-295, §221(b)(2), Division A, provides:

(2) SAVINGS PROVISION.—If—

(A) any provision amended or repealed by the amendments made by this section applied to—

(i) any transaction occurring before the date of the enactment of this Act,

(ii) any property acquired before such date of enactment, or

(iii) any item of income, loss, deduction, or credit taken into account before such date of enactment, and

(B) the treatment of such transaction, property, or item under such provision would (without regard to the amendments or repeals made by this section) affect the liability for tax for periods ending after date of enactment, nothing in the amendments or repeals made by this section shall be construed to affect the treatment of such transaction, property, or item for purposes of determining liability for tax for periods ending after such date of enactment.

• 2001, Tax-Related Provisions in the Air Transportation Safety and System Stabilization Act (P.L. 107-42)

P.L. 107-42, §301 (as amended by P.L. 107-134, §114), provides:

SEC. 301. EXTENSION OF DUE DATE FOR EXCISE TAX DEPOSITS; TREATMENT OF LOSS COMPENSATION.

(a) EXTENSION OF DUE DATE FOR EXCISE TAX DEPOSITS.—

(1) IN GENERAL.—In the case of an eligible air carrier, any airline-related deposit required under section 6302 of the Internal Revenue Code of 1986 to be made after September 10, 2001, and before November 15, 2001, shall be treated for purposes of such Code as timely made if such deposit is made on or before November 15, 2001. If the Secretary of the Treasury so prescribes, the preceding sentence shall be applied by substituting for "November 15, 2001" each place it appears—

(A) "January 15, 2002"; or

(B) such earlier date after November 15, 2001, as such Secretary may prescribe.

(2) ELIGIBLE AIR CARRIER.—For purposes of this subsection, the term "eligible air carrier" means any domestic corporation engaged in the trade or business of transporting (for hire) persons by air if such transportation is available to the general public.

(3) AIRLINE-RELATED DEPOSIT.—For purposes of this subsection, the term "airline-related deposit" means any deposit of taxes imposed by subchapter C of chapter 33 of such Code (relating to transportation by air).

(b) TREATMENT OF LOSS COMPENSATION.—Nothing in any provision of law shall be construed to exclude from gross income under the Internal Revenue Code of 1986 any compensation received under section 101(a)(2) of this Act.

• 1994, Uruguay Round Agreements Act (P.L. 103-465)

P.L. 103-465, §712(d):

Amended Code Sec. 6302(e). **Effective** 1-1-95. Prior to amendment, Code Sec. 6302(e) read as follows:

(e) TIME FOR DEPOSIT OF TAXES ON COMMUNICATION SERVICES AND AIRLINE TICKETS.—If, under regulations prescribed by the Secretary, a person is required to make deposits of any tax imposed by section 4251 or subsection (a) or (b) of section 4261 with respect to amounts considered collected by such person during any semimonthly period, such deposit shall be made not later than the 3rd day (not including Saturdays, Sundays, or legal holidays) after the close of the 1st week of the 2nd semimonthly period following the period to which such amounts relate.

• 1990, Omnibus Budget Reconciliation Act of 1990 (P.L. 101-508)

P.L. 101-508, §11217(b)(1)(A)-(B):

Amended Code Sec. 6302(e) by inserting "COMMUNICATIONS SERVICES AND" before "AIRLINE", and by inserting "section 4251 or" before "subsection (a) or (b)". **Effective** for payments of taxes considered collected during semimonthly periods beginning after 12-31-90.

• 1989, Omnibus Budget Reconciliation Act of 1989 (P.L. 101-239)

P.L. 101-239, §7502(a):

Amended Code Sec. 6302 by redesignating subsection (e) as subsection (f) and by inserting after subsection (d) a new subsection (e). **Effective** for payments of taxes considered collected for semimonthly periods beginning after 6-30-90.

[Sec. 6302(f)]

(f) TIME FOR DEPOSIT OF CERTAIN EXCISE TAXES.—

(1) GENERAL RULE.—Except as otherwise provided in this subsection and subsection (e), if any person is required under regulations to make deposits of taxes under subtitle D with respect to semi-monthly periods, such person shall make deposits of such taxes for the period beginning on September 16 and ending on September 26 not later than September 29.

(2) TAXES ON OZONE DEPLETING CHEMICALS.—If any person is required under regulations to make deposits of taxes under subchapter D of chapter 38 with respect to semimonthly periods, in lieu of paragraph (1), such person shall make deposits of such taxes for—

(A) the second semimonthly period in August, and

(B) the period beginning on September 1 and ending on September 11,

not later than September 29.

(3) TAXPAYERS NOT REQUIRED TO USE ELECTRONIC FUNDS TRANSFER.—In the case of deposits not required to be made by electronic funds transfer, paragraphs (1) and (2) shall be applied by substituting "September 25" for "September 26", "September 10" for "September 11", and "September 28" for "September 29".

(4) SPECIAL RULE WHERE DUE DATE ON SATURDAY OR SUNDAY.—If, but for this paragraph, the due date under paragraph (1), (2), or (3) would fall on a Saturday or Sunday, such due date shall be deemed to be—

(A) in the case of Saturday, the preceding day, and

(B) in the case of Sunday, the following day.

Amendments

• 2014, Tax Technical Corrections Act of 2014 (P.L. 113-295)

P.L. 113-295, §221(a)(110)(B), Division A:

Amended Code Sec. 6302(f)(1) by striking the last sentence. **Effective** generally 12-19-2014. For a special rule, see Act Sec. 221(b)(2), Division A, below. Prior to being stricken, the last sentence of Code Sec. 6302(f)(1) read as follows:

In the case of taxes imposed by sections 4261 and 4271, this paragraph shall not apply to periods before January 1, 1997.

P.L. 113-295, §221(b)(2), Division A, provides:

(2) SAVINGS PROVISION.—If—

(A) any provision amended or repealed by the amendments made by this section applied to—

(i) any transaction occurring before the date of the enactment of this Act,

(ii) any property acquired before such date of enactment, or

(iii) any item of income, loss, deduction, or credit taken into account before such date of enactment, and

(B) the treatment of such transaction, property, or item under such provision would (without regard to the amendments or repeals made by this section) affect the liability for tax for periods ending after date of enactment, nothing in the amendments or repeals made by this section shall be construed to affect the treatment of such transaction, property, or item for purposes of determining liability for tax for periods ending after such date of enactment.

• 1994, Uruguay Round Agreements Act (P.L. 103-465)

P.L. 103-465, §712(a):

Amended Code Sec. 6302(f). **Effective** 1-1-95. Prior to amendment, Code Sec. 6302(f) read as follows:

(f) TIME FOR DEPOSIT OF TAXES ON GASOLINE AND DIESEL FUEL.—

(1) GENERAL RULE.—Notwithstanding section 518 of the Highway Revenue Act of 1982, any person whose liability for tax under section 4081 is payable with respect to semimonthly periods shall, not later than September 27, make deposits of such tax for the period beginning on September 16 and ending on September 22.

(2) SPECIAL RULE WHERE DUE DATE FALLS ON SATURDAY, SUNDAY, OR HOLIDAY.—If, but for this paragraph, the due date under paragraph (1) would fall on a Saturday, Sunday, or holiday in the District of Columbia, such due date shall be deemed to be the immediately preceding day which is not a Saturday, Sunday, or such a holiday.

• 1993, Omnibus Budget Reconciliation Act of 1993 (P.L. 103-66)

P.L. 103-66, §13242(d)(15):

Amended Code Sec. 6302(f) by inserting "AND DIESEL FUEL" after "GASOLINE" in the heading. **Effective** 1-1-94.

• 1989, Omnibus Budget Reconciliation Act of 1989 (P.L. 101-239)

P.L. 101-239, §7502(a):

Amended Code Sec. 6302 by redesignating subsection (e) as subsection (f). **Effective** for payments of taxes considered collected for semimonthly periods beginning after 6-30-90.

P.L. 101-239, §7507(a):

Amended Code Sec. 6302 by redesignating subsection (f) as subsection (g) and by inserting after subsection (e) a new subsection (f). **Effective** for payments of taxes for tax periods beginning after 12-31-89.

[Sec. 6302(g)]

(g) DEPOSITS OF SOCIAL SECURITY TAXES AND WITHHELD INCOME TAXES.—If, under regulations prescribed by the Secretary, a person is required to make deposits of taxes imposed by chapters 21, 22, and 24 on the basis of eighth-month periods, such person shall make deposits of such taxes on the 1st banking day after any day on which such person has $100,000 or more of such taxes for deposit.

Amendments

• 1996, Small Business Job Protection Act of 1996 (P.L. 104-188)

P.L. 104-188, §1702(c)(3):

Amended Code Sec. 6302(g) by inserting ", 22," after "chapters 21". **Effective** as if included in the provision of P.L. 101-508 to which it relates.

P.L. 104-188, §1809, provides:

Notwithstanding any other provision of law, the increase in the applicable required percentages for fiscal year 1997 in clauses (i)(IV) and (ii)(IV) of section 6302(h)(2)(C) of the Internal Revenue Code of 1986 shall not take effect before July 1, 1997.

• 1990, Omnibus Budget Reconciliation Act of 1990 (P.L. 101-508)

P.L. 101-508, §11334(a):

Amended Code Sec. 6302(g). **Effective** for amounts required to be deposited after 12-31-90. Prior to amendment, Code Sec. 6302(g) read as follows:

(g) DEPOSITS OF SOCIAL SECURITY TAXES AND WITHHELD INCOME TAXES.—

(1) IN GENERAL.—If, under regulations prescribed by the Secretary, a person is required to make deposits of taxes imposed by chapters 21 and 24 on the basis of eighth-month periods, such person shall, for the years specified in paragraph (2), make deposits of such taxes on the applicable banking day after any day on which such person has $100,000 or more of such taxes for deposit.

(2) SPECIFIED YEARS.—For purposes of paragraph (1)—

In the case of:	*The applicable banking day is:*
1990	1st
1991	2d
1992	3rd
1993	1st
1994	1st.

• 1989, Omnibus Budget Reconciliation Act of 1989 (P.L. 101-239)

P.L. 101-239, §7507(a):

Amended Code Sec. 6302 by redesignating subsection (f) as subsection (g). **Effective** for payments of taxes for tax periods beginning after 12-31-89.

P.L. 101-239, §7632(a):

Amended Code Sec. 6302 by redesignating subsection (g) as subsection (h) and by inserting after subsection (f) a new subsection (g). **Effective** for amounts required to be deposited after 7-31-90.

[Sec. 6302(h)]

(h) USE OF ELECTRONIC FUND TRANSFER SYSTEM FOR COLLECTION OF CERTAIN TAXES.—

(1) ESTABLISHMENT OF SYSTEM.—

(A) IN GENERAL.—The Secretary shall prescribe such regulations as may be necessary for the development and implementation of an electronic fund transfer system which is required to be used for the collection of depository taxes. Such system shall be designed in such manner as may be necessary to ensure that such taxes are credited to the general account of the Treasury on the date on which such taxes would otherwise have been required to be deposited under the Federal tax deposit system.

(B) EXEMPTIONS.—The regulations prescribed under subparagraph (A) may contain such exemptions as the Secretary may deem appropriate.

(2) DEFINITIONS.—For purposes of this subsection—

(A) DEPOSITORY TAX.—The term "depository tax" means any tax if the Secretary is authorized to require deposits of such tax.

(B) ELECTRONIC FUND TRANSFER.—The term "electronic fund transfer" means any transfer of funds, other than a transaction originated by check, draft, or similar paper instrument, which is initiated through an electronic terminal, telephonic instrument, or computer or magnetic tape so as to order, instruct, or authorize a financial institution or other financial intermediary to debit or credit an account.

(3) COORDINATION WITH OTHER ELECTRONIC FUND TRANSFER REQUIREMENTS.—Under regulations, any tax required to be paid by electronic fund transfer under section 5061(e) or 5703(b) shall be paid in such a manner as to ensure that the requirements of the second sentence of paragraph (1)(A) of this subsection are satisfied.

Amendments

• 2014, Tax Technical Corrections Act of 2014 (P.L. 113-295)

P.L. 113-295, §221(a)(110)(C)(i)-(ii), Division A:

Amended Code Sec. 6302(h) by striking paragraph (2) and redesignating paragraphs (3) and (4) as paragraphs (2) and (3), respectively, and by amending paragraph (3) (as so redesignated). **Effective** generally 12-19-2014. For a special rule, see Act Sec. 221(b)(2), Division A, below. Prior to being stricken and amended, respectively, Code Sec. 6302(h)(2) and (3) (as redesignated) read as follows:

(2) PHASE-IN REQUIREMENTS.—

(A) IN GENERAL.—Except as provided in subparagraph (B), the regulations referred to in paragraph (1)—

(i) shall contain appropriate procedures to assure that an orderly conversion from the Federal tax deposit system to the electronic fund transfer system is accomplished, and

(ii) may provide for a phase-in of such electronic fund transfer system by classes of taxpayers based on the aggregate undeposited taxes of such taxpayers at the close of specified periods and any other factors the Secretary may deem appropriate.

(B) PHASE-IN REQUIREMENTS.—The phase-in of the electronic fund transfer system shall be designed in such manner as may be necessary to ensure that—

(i) during each fiscal year beginning after September 30, 1993, at least the applicable required percentage of the total depository taxes imposed by chapters 21, 22, and 24 shall be collected by means of electronic fund transfer, and

(ii) during each fiscal year beginning after September 30, 1993, at least the applicable required percentage of the total other depository taxes shall be collected by means of electronic fund transfer.

(C) APPLICABLE REQUIRED PERCENTAGE.—

(i) In the case of the depository taxes imposed by chapters 21, 22, and 24, the applicable required percentage is—

(I) 3 percent for fiscal year 1994,

(II) 16.9 percent for fiscal year 1995,

(III) 20.1 percent for fiscal year 1996,

(IV) 58.3 percent for fiscal years 1997 and 1998, and

(V) 94 percent for fiscal year 1999 and all fiscal years thereafter.

(ii) In the case of other depository taxes, the applicable required percentage is—

(I) 3 percent for fiscal year 1994,

(II) 20 percent for fiscal year 1995,

(III) 30 percent for fiscal year 1996,

(IV) 60 percent for fiscal years 1997 and 1998, and

(V) 94 percent for fiscal year 1999 and all fiscal years thereafter.

(3) COORDINATION WITH OTHER ELECTRONIC FUND TRANSFER REQUIREMENTS.—

(A) COORDINATION WITH CERTAIN EXCISE TAXES.—In determining whether the requirements of subparagraph (B) of paragraph (2) are met, taxes required to be paid by electronic fund transfer under sections 5061(e) and 5703(b) shall be disregarded.

(B) ADDITIONAL REQUIREMENT.—Under regulations, any tax required to be paid by electronic fund transfer under section 5061(e) or 5703(b) shall be paid in such a manner as to ensure that the requirements of the second sentence of paragraph (1)(A) of this subsection are satisfied.

P.L. 113-295, §221(b)(2), Division A, provides:

(2) SAVINGS PROVISION.—If—

(A) any provision amended or repealed by the amendments made by this section applied to—

(i) any transaction occurring before the date of the enactment of this Act,

(ii) any property acquired before such date of enactment, or

(iii) any item of income, loss, deduction, or credit taken into account before such date of enactment, and

(B) the treatment of such transaction, property, or item under such provision would (without regard to the amendments or repeals made by this section) affect the liability for tax for periods ending after date of enactment, nothing in the amendments or repeals made by this section shall be construed to affect the treatment of such transaction, property, or item for purposes of determining liability for tax for periods ending after such date of enactment.

• 1997, Taxpayer Relief Act of 1997 (P.L. 105-34)

P.L. 105-34, §931, provides:

ACT SEC. 931. WAIVER OF PENALTY THROUGH JUNE 30, 1998, ON SMALL BUSINESSES FAILING TO MAKE ELECTRONIC FUND TRANSFERS OF TAXES.

No penalty shall be imposed under the Internal Revenue Code of 1986 solely by reason of a failure by a person to use the electronic fund transfer system established under section 6302(h) of such Code if—

(1) such person is a member of a class of taxpayers first required to use such system on or after July 1, 1997, and

(2) such failure occurs before July 1, 1998.

• 1993, North American Free Trade Agreement Implementation Act (P.L. 103-182)

P.L. 103-182, §523(a):

Amended Code Sec. 6302 by redesignating subsection (h) as subsection (i) and by inserting after subsection (g) new subsection (h). **Effective** on the date the Agreement enters into force with respect to the United States.

P.L. 103-182, §523(b)(2), provides:

(2) REGULATIONS.—Not later than 210 days after the date of the enactment of this Act, the Secretary of the Treasury or his delegate shall prescribe temporary regulations under section 6302(h) of the Internal Revenue Code of 1986 (as added by this section).

[Sec. 6302(i)—Stricken]

Amendments

• 2010, (P.L. 111-226)

P.L. 111-226, §219(b)(2):

Amended Code Sec. 6302 by striking subsection (i). **Effective** for tax years beginning after 12-31-2010. Prior to being stricken, Code Sec. 6302(i) read as follows:

(i) CROSS REFERENCES.—

For treatment of earned income advance amounts as payment of withholding and FICA taxes, see section 3507(d).

• 1993, North American Free Trade Agreement Implementation Act (P.L. 103-182)

P.L. 103-182, §523(a):

Amended Code Sec. 6302 by redesignating subsection (h) as subsection (i). **Effective** on the date the Agreement enters into force with respect to the United States.

• 1989, Omnibus Budget Reconciliation Act of 1989 (P.L. 101-239)

P.L. 101-239, §7632(a):

Amended Code Sec. 6302 by redesignating subsection (g) as subsection (h). **Effective** for amounts required to be deposited after 7-31-90.

• 1988, Omnibus Trade and Competitiveness Act of 1988 (P.L. 100-418)

P.L. 100-418, §1941(b)(2)(G)(i)-(ii):

Amended Code Sec. 6302(e) by striking "(1) For" and inserting "For", and by striking out paragraph (2). **Effective** for crude oil removed from the premises on or after 8-23-88. Prior to amendment, Code Sec. 6320(e)(2) read as follows:

(2) For depositary requirements applicable to the windfall profit tax imposed by section 4986, see section 4995(b).

• 1984, Deficit Reduction Act of 1984 (P.L. 98-369)

P.L. 98-369, §1015(c):

Amended Code Sec. 6302 by redesignating subsection (d) as subsection (e). **Effective** with respect to articles sold by the manufacturer, producer, or importer after 9-30-84.

• 1980, Technical Corrections Act of 1979 (P.L. 96-222)

P.L. 96-222, §101(a)(2)(D):

Amended Act Sec. 105(g)(2) of P.L. 95-600 to change the **effective** date of the addition of Code Sec. 6302(d) from 6-30-78, to 6-30-79.

• 1980, Crude Oil Windfall Profit Tax Act of 1980 (P.L. 96-223)

P.L. 96-223, §101(c)(2):

Amended Code Sec. 6302(d). **Effective** for periods after 2-29-80. Prior to amendment, Code Sec. 6302(d) read:

(d) CROSS REFERENCE.—

For treatment of payment of earned income advance amounts as payment of withholding and FICA taxes, see section 3507(d).

• 1978, Revenue Act of 1978 (P.L. 95-600)

P.L. 95-600, §105(e), (g)(2):

Added Code Sec. 6302(d). **Effective** for remuneration paid after 6-30-78.

[Sec. 6303]

SEC. 6303. NOTICE AND DEMAND FOR TAX.

[Sec. 6303(a)]

(a) GENERAL RULE.—Where it is not otherwise provided by this title, the Secretary shall, as soon as practicable, and within 60 days, after the making of an assessment of a tax pursuant to section 6203, give notice to each person liable for the unpaid tax, stating the amount and demanding payment thereof. Such notice shall be left at the dwelling or usual place of business of such person, or shall be sent by mail to such person's last known address.

Amendments

• 1976, Tax Reform Act of 1976 (P.L. 94-455)

P.L. 94-455, §1906(b)(13)(A):

Amended 1954 Code by substituting "Secretary" for "Secretary or his delegate" each place it appeared. **Effective** 2-1-77.

[Sec. 6303(b)]

(b) ASSESSMENT PRIOR TO LAST DATE FOR PAYMENT.—Except where the Secretary believes collection would be jeopardized by delay, if any tax is assessed prior to the last date prescribed for payment of such tax, payment of such tax shall not be demanded under subsection (a) until after such date.

Amendments

• 1976, Tax Reform Act of 1976 (P.L. 94-455)

P.L. 94-455, §1906(b)(13)(A):

Amended 1954 Code by substituting "Secretary" for "Secretary or his delegate" each place it appeared. **Effective** 2-1-77.

* * *

Subchapter B—Receipt of Payment

* * *

[Sec. 6311]

SEC. 6311. PAYMENT OF TAX BY COMMERCIALLY ACCEPTABLE MEANS.

[Sec. 6311(a)]

(a) AUTHORITY TO RECEIVE.—It shall be lawful for the Secretary to receive for internal revenue taxes (or in payment for internal revenue stamps) any commercially acceptable means that the Secretary deems appropriate to the extent and under the conditions provided in regulations prescribed by the Secretary.

[Sec. 6311(b)]

(b) ULTIMATE LIABILITY.—If a check, money order, or other method of payment, including payment by credit card, debit card, or charge card so received is not duly paid, or is paid and subsequently charged back to the Secretary, the person by whom such check, or money order, or other method of payment has been tendered shall remain liable for the payment of the tax or for the stamps, and for all legal penalties and additions, to the same extent as if such check, money order, or other method of payment had not been tendered.

[Sec. 6311(c)]

(c) LIABILITY OF BANKS AND OTHERS.—If any certified, treasurer's, or cashier's check (or other guaranteed draft), or any money order, or any other means of payment that has been guaranteed by a financial institution (such as a credit card, debit card, or charge card transaction which has been guaranteed expressly by a financial institution) so received is not duly paid, the United States shall, in addition to its right to exact payment from the party originally indebted therefor, have a lien for—

(1) the amount of such check (or draft) upon all assets of the financial institution on which drawn,

(2) the amount of such money order upon all the assets of the issuer thereof, or

(3) the guaranteed amount of any other transaction upon all the assets of the institution making such guarantee,

and such amount shall be paid out of such assets in preference to any other claims whatsoever against such financial institution, issuer, or guaranteeing institution, except the necessary costs and expenses of administration and the reimbursement of the United States for the amount expended in the redemption of the circulating notes of such financial institution.

[Sec. 6311(d)]

(d) PAYMENT BY OTHER MEANS.—

(1) AUTHORITY TO PRESCRIBE REGULATIONS.—The Secretary shall prescribe such regulations as the Secretary deems necessary to receive payment by commercially acceptable means, including regulations that—

(A) specify which methods of payment by commercially acceptable means will be acceptable,

(B) specify when payment by such means will be considered received,

(C) identify types of nontax matters related to payment by such means that are to be resolved by persons ultimately liable for payment and financial intermediaries, without the involvement of the Secretary, and

(D) ensure that tax matters will be resolved by the Secretary, without the involvement of financial intermediaries.

(2) AUTHORITY TO ENTER INTO CONTRACTS.—Notwithstanding section 3718(f) of title 31, United States Code, the Secretary is authorized to enter into contracts to obtain services related to receiving payment by other means where cost beneficial to the Government. The Secretary may not pay any fee or provide any other consideration under any such contract for the use of credit, debit, or charge cards for the payment of taxes imposed by subtitle A. The preceding sentence shall not apply to the extent that the Secretary ensures that any such fee or other consideration is fully recouped by the Secretary in the form of fees paid to the Secretary by persons paying taxes imposed under subtitle A with credit, debit, or charge cards pursuant to such contract. Notwithstanding the preceding sentence, the Secretary shall seek to minimize the amount of any fee or other consideration that the Secretary pays under any such contract.

(3) SPECIAL PROVISIONS FOR USE OF CREDIT CARDS.—If use of credit cards is accepted as a method of payment of taxes pursuant to subsection (a)—

(A) a payment of internal revenue taxes (or a payment for internal revenue stamps) by a person by use of a credit card shall not be subject to section 161 of the Truth in Lending Act (15 U.S.C. 1666), or to any similar provisions of State law, if the error alleged by the person is an error relating to the underlying tax liability, rather than an error relating to the credit card account such as a computational error or numerical transposition in the credit card transaction or an issue as to whether the person authorized payment by use of the credit card,

(B) a payment of internal revenue taxes (or a payment for internal revenue stamps) shall not be subject to section 170 of the Truth in Lending Act (15 U.S.C. 1666i), or to any similar provisions of State law,

(C) a payment of internal revenue taxes (or a payment for internal revenue stamps) by a person by use of a debit card shall not be subject to section 908 of the Electronic Fund Transfer Act (15 U.S.C. 1693f), or to any similar provisions of State law, if the error alleged by the person is an error relating to the underlying tax liability, rather than an error relating to the debit card account such as a computational error or numerical transposition in the debit card transaction or an issue as to whether the person authorized payment by use of the debit card,

(D) the term "creditor" under section 103(g) of the Truth in Lending Act (15 U.S.C. 1602(g)) shall not include the Secretary with respect to credit card transactions in payment of internal revenue taxes (or payment for internal revenue stamps), and

(E) notwithstanding any other provision of law to the contrary, in the case of payment made by credit card or debit card transaction of an amount owed to a person as the result of the correction of an error under section 161 of the Truth in Lending Act (15 U.S.C. 1666) or section 908 of the Electronic Fund Transfer Act (15 U.S.C. 1693f), the Secretary is authorized to provide such amount to such person as a credit to that person's credit card or debit card account through the applicable credit card or debit card system.

Amendments

• 2019, Taxpayer First Act (P.L. 116-25)

P.L. 116-25, §2303:

Amended Code Sec. 6311(d)(2) by adding at the end two new sentences. **Effective** 7-1-2019.

• 2018, Tax Technical Corrections Act of 2018 (P.L. 115-141)

P.L. 115-141, §401(a)(280)(A)-(B), Div. U:

Amended Code Sec. 6311(d)(3)(D) by striking "section 103(f)" and inserting "section 103(g)", and by striking "1602(f)" and inserting "1602(g)". **Effective** 3-23-2018.

• 1998, Tax and Trade Relief Extension Act of 1998 (P.L. 105-277)

P.L. 105-277, §4003(k):

Amended Code Sec. 6311(d)(2) by striking "under such contracts" in the last sentence and inserting "under any such contract for the use of credit, debit, or charge cards for the payment of taxes imposed by subtitle A". **Effective** as if included in the provision of P.L. 105-34 to which it relates [**effective** 5-5-98.—CCH].

[Sec. 6311(e)]

(e) CONFIDENTIALITY OF INFORMATION.—

(1) IN GENERAL.—Except as otherwise authorized by this subsection, no person may use or disclose any information relating to credit or debit card transactions obtained pursuant to section 6103(k)(9) other than for purposes directly related to the processing of such transactions, or the billing or collection of amounts charged or debited pursuant thereto.

(2) EXCEPTIONS.—

(A) Debit or credit card issuers or others acting on behalf of such issuers may also use and disclose such information for purposes directly related to servicing an issuer's accounts.

(B) Debit or credit card issuers or others directly involved in the processing of credit or debit card transactions or the billing or collection of amounts charged or debited thereto may also use and disclose such information for purposes directly related to—

(i) statistical risk and profitability assessment;

(ii) transferring receivables, accounts, or interest therein;

(iii) auditing the account information;

(iv) complying with Federal, State, or local law; and

(v) properly authorized civil, criminal, or regulatory investigation by Federal, State, or local authorities.

(3) PROCEDURES.—Use and disclosure of information under this paragraph shall be made only to the extent authorized by written procedures promulgated by the Secretary.

(4) CROSS REFERENCE.—

For provision providing for civil damages for violation of paragraph (1), see section 7431.

Amendments

• 1998, IRS Restructuring and Reform Act of 1998 (P.L. 105-206)

P.L. 105-206, §6012(b)(1):

Amended Code Sec. 6311(e)(1) by striking "section 6103(k)(8)" and inserting "section 6103(k)(9)". **Effective** as if included in the provision of P.L. 105-34 to which it relates [**effective** 5-5-98.—CCH].

P.L. 105-206, §3703, provides:

SEC. 3703. PAYMENT OF TAXES.

The Secretary of the Treasury or the Secretary's delegate shall establish such rules, regulations, and procedures as are necessary to allow payment of taxes by check or money order made payable to the United States Treasury.

• 1997, Taxpayer Relief Act of 1997 (P.L. 105-34)

P.L. 105-34, §1205(a):

Amended Code Sec. 6311. **Effective** on the day 9 months after 8-5-97. Prior to amendment, Code Sec. 6311 read as follows:

SEC. 6311. PAYMENT BY CHECK OR MONEY ORDER.

[Sec. 6311(a)]

(a) AUTHORITY TO RECEIVE.—It shall be lawful for the Secretary to receive for internal revenue taxes, or in payment for internal revenue stamps, checks or money orders, to the extent and under the conditions provided in regulations prescribed by the Secretary.

Amendments

• 1976, Tax Reform Act of 1976 (P.L. 94-455)

P.L. 94-455, §1906(b)(13)(A):

Amended 1954 Code by substituting "Secretary" for "Secretary or his delegate" each place it appeared. **Effective** 2-1-77.

[Sec. 6311(b)]

(b) CHECK OR MONEY ORDER UNPAID.—

(1) ULTIMATE LIABILITY.—If a check or money order so received is not duly paid, the person by whom such check or money order has been tendered shall remain liable for the payment of the tax or for the stamps, and for all legal penalties and additions, to the same extent as if such check or money order had not been tendered.

(2) LIABILITY OF BANKS AND OTHERS.—If any certified, treasurer's, or cashier's check (or other guaranteed draft) or any money order so received is not duly paid, the United States shall, in addition to its right to exact payment from the party originally indebted therefor, have a lien for the amount of such check (or draft) upon all the assets of the financial institution on which drawn or for the amount of such money order upon all the assets of the issuer thereof; and such amount shall be paid out of such assets in preference to any other claims whatsoever against such financial institution or issuer except the necessary costs and expenses of administration and the reimbursement of the United States for the amount expended in the redemption of the circulating notes of such financial institution.

Amendments

• 1984, Deficit Reduction Act of 1984 (P.L. 98-369)

P.L. 98-369, §448(a):

Amended Code Sec. 6311(b)(2) by striking out "or cashier's check" and inserting in lieu thereof "or cashier's check (or other guaranteed draft)", by striking out "the amount of such check" and inserting in lieu thereof "the amount of such check (or draft)", by striking out "the bank or trust company" and inserting in lieu thereof "the financial institution", and by striking out "such bank" each place it appeared and inserting in lieu thereof "such financial institution". **Effective** 7-18-84.

[Sec. 6312—Repealed]

Amendments

• 1971 (P.L. 92-5)

P.L. 92-5, §4(a)(2):

Repealed Code Sec. 6312. **Effective** with respect to obligations issued after 3-3-71. Prior to repeal, Code Sec. 6312 read as follows:

SEC. 6312. PAYMENT BY UNITED STATES NOTES AND CERTIFICATES OF INDEBTEDNESS.

(a) GENERAL RULE.—It shall be lawful for the Secretary or his delegate to receive, at par with an adjustment for accrued interest, Treasury bills, notes and certificates of indebtedness issued by the United States in payment of any internal revenue taxes, or in payment for internal revenue stamps, to the extent and under the conditions provided in regulations prescribed by the Secretary or his delegate.

(b) CROSS REFERENCES.—

(1) For authority to receive silver certificates, see section 5 of the act of June 19, 1934 (48 Stat. 1178; 31 U.S.C. 405a).

(2) For full legal tender status of all coins and currencies of the United States, see section 43(b)(1) of the Agricultural Adjustment Act, as amended (48 Stat. 52, 113; 31 U.S.C. 462).

(3) For authority to receive obligations under the Second Liberty Bond Act, see section 20(b) of that act, as amended (56 Stat. 189; 31 U.S.C. 754b).

[Sec. 6313]

SEC. 6313. FRACTIONAL PARTS OF A CENT.

In the payment of any tax imposed by this title, a fractional part of a cent shall be disregarded unless it amounts to one-half cent or more, in which case it shall be increased to 1 cent.

Amendments

• 1976, Tax Reform Act of 1976 (P.L. 94-455)

P.L. 94-455, §1906(a)(19):

Struck out "not payable by stamp" following "any tax imposed by this title" in Code Sec. 6313. **Effective** 2-1-77.

[Sec. 6314]

SEC. 6314. RECEIPT FOR TAXES.

[Sec. 6314(a)]

(a) GENERAL RULE.—The Secretary shall, upon request, give receipts for all sums collected by him, excepting only when the same are in payment for stamps sold and delivered; but no receipt shall be issued in lieu of a stamp representing a tax.

Amendments

• 1976, Tax Reform Act of 1976 (P.L. 94-455)

P.L. 94-455, §1906(b)(13)(A):

Amended 1954 Code by substituting "Secretary" for "Secretary or his delegate" each place it appeared. **Effective** 2-1-77.

[Sec. 6314(b)]

(b) DUPLICATE RECEIPTS FOR PAYMENT OF ESTATE TAXES.—The Secretary shall, upon request, give to the person paying the tax under chapter 11 (relating to the estate tax) duplicate receipts, either of which shall be sufficient evidence of such payment, and shall entitle the executor to be credited and allowed the amount thereof by any court having jurisdiction to audit or settle his accounts.

Amendments

• 1976, Tax Reform Act of 1976 (P.L. 94-455)

P.L. 94-455, §1906(b)(13)(A):

Amended 1954 Code by substituting "Secretary" for "Secretary or his delegate" each place it appeared. **Effective** 2-1-77.

[Sec. 6314(c)]

(c) CROSS REFERENCES.—

(1) For receipt required to be furnished by employer to employee with respect to employment taxes, see section 6051.

(2) For receipt of discharge of fiduciary from personal liability, see section 2204.

Amendments

• 1970, Excise, Estate, and Gift Tax Adjustment Act of 1970 (P.L. 91-614)

P.L. 91-614, §101(d)(2):

Amended Code Sec. 6314(c)(2) by substituting "fiduciary" for "executor." **Effective** 1-1-71.

[Sec. 6315]

SEC. 6315. PAYMENTS OF ESTIMATED INCOME TAX.

Payment of the estimated income tax, or any installment thereof, shall be considered payment on account of the income taxes imposed by subtitle A for the taxable year.

* * *

Subchapter C—Lien for Taxes

PART I—DUE PROCESS FOR LIENS

* * *

[Sec. 6320]

SEC. 6320. NOTICE AND OPPORTUNITY FOR HEARING UPON FILING OF NOTICE OF LIEN.

[Sec. 6320(a)]

(a) REQUIREMENT OF NOTICE.—

(1) IN GENERAL.—The Secretary shall notify in writing the person described in section 6321 of the filing of a notice of lien under section 6323.

(2) TIME AND METHOD FOR NOTICE.—The notice required under paragraph (1) shall be—

(A) given in person;

(B) left at the dwelling or usual place of business of such person; or

(C) sent by certified or registered mail to such person's last known address,

not more than 5 business days after the day of the filing of the notice of lien.

(3) INFORMATION INCLUDED WITH NOTICE.—The notice required under paragraph (1) shall include in simple and nontechnical terms—

(A) the amount of unpaid tax;

(B) the right of the person to request a hearing during the 30-day period beginning on the day after the 5-day period described in paragraph (2);

(C) the administrative appeals available to the taxpayer with respect to such lien and the procedures relating to such appeals;

(D) the provisions of this title and procedures relating to the release of liens on property; and

(E) the provisions of section 7345 relating to the certification of seriously delinquent tax debts and the denial, revocation, or limitation of passports of individuals with such debts pursuant to section 32101 of the FAST Act.

Amendments

• 2015, Fixing America's Surface Transportation Act (P.L. 114-94)

P.L. 114-94, §32101(b)(1):

Amended Code Sec. 6320(a)(3) by striking "and" at the end of subparagraph (C), by striking the period at the end of subparagraph (D) and inserting "; and", and by adding at the end a new subparagraph (E). **Effective** 12-4-2015.

[Sec. 6320(b)]

(b) RIGHT TO FAIR HEARING.—

(1) IN GENERAL.—If the person requests a hearing in writing under subsection (a)(3)(B) and states the grounds for the requested hearing, such hearing shall be held by the Internal Revenue Service Independent Office of Appeals.

(2) ONE HEARING PER PERIOD.—A person shall be entitled to only one hearing under this section with respect to the taxable period to which the unpaid tax specified in subsection (a)(3)(A) relates.

(3) IMPARTIAL OFFICER.—The hearing under this subsection shall be conducted by an officer or employee who has had no prior involvement with respect to the unpaid tax specified in subsection (a)(3)(A) before the first hearing under this section or section 6330. A taxpayer may waive the requirement of this paragraph.

(4) COORDINATION WITH SECTION 6330.—To the extent practicable, a hearing under this section shall be held in conjunction with a hearing under section 6330.

Amendments

• 2019, Taxpayer First Act (P.L. 116-25)

P.L. 116-25, §1001(b)(1)(B):

Amended Code Sec. 6320(b)(1) by striking "Internal Revenue Service Office of Appeals" and inserting "Internal Revenue Service Independent Office of Appeals". **Effective** 7-1-2019.

• 2006, Tax Relief and Health Care Act of 2006 (P.L. 109-432)

P.L. 109-432, Division A, §407(c)(1):

Amended Code Sec. 6320(b)(1) by striking "under subsection (a)(3)(B)" and inserting "in writing under subsection (a)(3)(B) and states the grounds for the requested hearing". **Effective** for submissions made and issues raised after the date on which the Secretary first prescribes a list under Code Sec. 6702(c), as amended by Act Sec. 407(a).

[Sec. 6320(c)]

(c) CONDUCT OF HEARING; REVIEW; SUSPENSIONS.—For purposes of this section, subsections (c), (d) (other than paragraph (3)(B) thereof), (e), and (g) of section 6330 shall apply.

Amendments

• **2015, Protecting Americans from Tax Hikes Act of 2015 (P.L. 114-113)**

P.L. 114-113, §424(c), Div. Q:

Amended Code Sec. 6320(c) by striking "(2)(B)" and inserting "(3)(B)". **Effective** 12-18-2015.

• **2006, Tax Relief and Health Care Act of 2006 (P.L. 109-432)**

P.L. 109-432, Division A, §407(c)(2):

Amended Code Sec. 6320(c) by striking "and (e)" and inserting "(e), and (g)". **Effective** for submissions made and issues raised after the date on which the Secretary first prescribes a list under Code Sec. 6702(c), as amended by Act Sec. 407(a).

• **1998, IRS Restructuring and Reform Act of 1998 (P.L. 105-206)**

P.L. 105-206, §3401(a):

Amended subchapter C of chapter 64 by inserting a new Code Sec. 6320. **Effective** for collection actions initiated after the date which is 180 days after 7-22-98.

PART II—LIENS

* * *

[Sec. 6321]

SEC. 6321. LIEN FOR TAXES.

If any person liable to pay any tax neglects or refuses to pay the same after demand, the amount (including any interest, additional amount, addition to tax, or assessable penalty, together with any costs that may accrue in addition thereto) shall be a lien in favor of the United States upon all property and rights to property, whether real or personal, belonging to such person.

Amendments

• **1998, IRS Restructuring and Reform Act of 1998 (P.L. 105-206)**

P.L. 105-206, §3421, provides:

ACT SEC. 3421. APPROVAL PROCESS FOR LIENS, LEVIES, AND SEIZURES.

(a) IN GENERAL.—The Commissioner of Internal Revenue shall develop and implement procedures under which—

(1) a determination by an employee to file a notice of lien or levy with respect to, or to levy or seize, any property or right to property would, where appropriate, be required to be reviewed by a supervisor of the employee before the action was taken; and

(2) appropriate disciplinary action would be taken against the employee or supervisor where the procedures under paragraph (1) were not followed.

(b) REVIEW PROCESS.—The review process under subsection (a)(1) may include a certification that the employee has—

(1) reviewed the taxpayer's information;

(2) verified that a balance is due; and

(3) affirmed that the action proposed to be taken is appropriate given the taxpayer's circumstances, considering the amount due and the value of the property or right to property.

(c) EFFECTIVE DATES.—

(1) IN GENERAL.—Except as provided in paragraph (2), this section shall take effect on the date of the enactment of this Act.

(2) AUTOMATED COLLECTION SYSTEM ACTIONS.—In the case of any action under an automated collection system, this section shall apply to actions initiated after December 31, 2000.

[Sec. 6322]

SEC. 6322. PERIOD OF LIEN.

Unless another date is specifically fixed by law, the lien imposed by section 6321 shall arise at the time the assessment is made and shall continue until the liability for the amount so assessed (or a judgment against the taxpayer arising out of such liability) is satisfied or becomes unenforceable by reason of lapse of time.

Amendments

• **1966, Federal Tax Lien Act of 1966 (P.L. 89-719)**

P.L. 89-719, §113(a):

Amended Code Sec. 6322 by inserting "(or a judgment against the taxpayer arising out of such liability)" immediately after "liability for the amount so assessed". **Effective**, generally, after 11-2-66. However, see the amendment note for Code Sec. 6323 for exceptions to this **effective** date.

[Sec. 6323]

SEC. 6323. VALIDITY AND PRIORITY AGAINST CERTAIN PERSONS.

[Sec. 6323(a)]

(a) PURCHASERS, HOLDERS OF SECURITY INTERESTS, MECHANIC'S LIENORS, AND JUDGMENT LIEN CREDITORS.—The lien imposed by section 6321 shall not be valid as against any purchaser, holder of a security interest, mechanic's lienor, or judgment lien creditor until notice thereof which meets the requirements of subsection (f) has been filed by the Secretary.

Amendments

• **1990, Omnibus Budget Reconciliation Act of 1990 (P.L. 101-508)**

P.L. 101-508, §11704(a)(26):

Amended Code Sec. 6323(a) by striking "Purchases" in the heading and inserting "Purchasers". **Effective** on the date of enactment of this Act.

• **1976, Tax Reform Act of 1976 (P.L. 94-455)**

P.L. 94-455, §1906(b)(13)(A):

Amended 1954 Code by substituting "Secretary" for "Secretary or his delegate" each place it appeared. **Effective** 2-1-77.

[Sec. 6323(b)]

(b) PROTECTION FOR CERTAIN INTERESTS EVEN THOUGH NOTICE FILED.—Even though notice of a lien imposed by section 6321 has been filed, such lien shall not be valid—

(1) SECURITIES.—With respect to a security (as defined in subsection (h)(4))—

(A) as against a purchaser of such security who at the time of purchase did not have actual notice or knowledge of the existence of such lien; and

(B) as against a holder of a security interest in such security who, at the time such interest came into existence, did not have actual notice or knowledge of the existence of such lien.

(2) MOTOR VEHICLES.—With respect to a motor vehicle (as defined in subsection (h)(3)), as against a purchaser of such motor vehicle, if—

(A) at the time of the purchase such purchaser did not have actual notice or knowledge of the existence of such lien, and

(B) before the purchaser obtains such notice or knowledge, he has acquired possession of such motor vehicle and has not thereafter relinquished possession of such motor vehicle to the seller or his agent.

(3) PERSONAL PROPERTY PURCHASED AT RETAIL.—With respect to tangible personal property purchased at retail, as against a purchaser in the ordinary course of the seller's trade or business, unless at the time of such purchase such purchaser intends such purchase to (or knows such purchase will) hinder, evade, or defeat the collection of any tax under this title.

(4) PERSONAL PROPERTY PURCHASED IN CASUAL SALE.—With respect to household goods, personal effects, or other tangible personal property described in section 6334(a) purchased (not for resale) in a casual sale for less than $1,000, as against the purchaser, but only if such purchaser does not have actual notice or knowledge (A) of the existence of such lien, or (B) that this sale is one of a series of sales.

(5) PERSONAL PROPERTY SUBJECT TO POSSESSORY LIEN.—With respect to tangible personal property subject to a lien under local law securing the reasonable price of the repair or improvement of such property, as against a holder of such a lien, if such holder is, and has been, continuously in possession of such property from the time such lien arose.

(6) REAL PROPERTY TAX AND SPECIAL ASSESSMENT LIENS.—With respect to real property, as against a holder of a lien upon such property, if such lien is entitled under local law to priority over security interests in such property which are prior in time, and such lien secures payment of—

(A) a tax of general application levied by any taxing authority based upon the value of such property;

(B) a special assessment imposed directly upon such property by any taxing authority, if such assessment is imposed for the purpose of defraying the cost of any public improvement; or

(C) charges for utilities or public services furnished to such property by the United States, a State or political subdivision thereof, or an instrumentality of any one or more of the foregoing.

(7) RESIDENTIAL PROPERTY SUBJECT TO A MECHANIC'S LIEN FOR CERTAIN REPAIRS AND IMPROVEMENTS.—With respect to real property subject to a lien for repair or improvement of a personal residence (containing not more than four dwelling units) occupied by the owner of such residence, as against a mechanic's lienor, but only if the contract price on the contract with the owner is not more than $5,000.

(8) ATTORNEYS' LIENS.—With respect to a judgment or other amount in settlement of a claim or of a cause of action, as against an attorney who, under local law, holds a lien upon or a contract enforcible against such judgment or amount, to the extent of his reasonable compensation for obtaining such judgment or procuring such settlement, except that this paragraph shall not apply to any judgment or amount in settlement of a claim or of a cause of action against the United States to the extent that the United States offsets such judgment or amount against any liability of the taxpayer to the United States.

(9) CERTAIN INSURANCE CONTRACTS.—With respect to a life insurance, endowment, or annuity contract, as against the organization which is the insurer under such contract, at any time—

(A) before such organization had actual notice or knowledge of the existence of such lien;

(B) after such organization had such notice or knowledge, with respect to advances required to be made automatically to maintain such contract in force under an agreement entered into before such organization had such notice or knowledge; or

(C) after satisfaction of a levy pursuant to section 6332(b), unless and until the Secretary delivers to such organization a notice, executed after the date of such satisfaction, of the existence of such lien.

(10) DEPOSIT-SECURED LOANS.—With respect to a savings deposit, share, or other account, with an institution described in section 581 or 591, to the extent of any loan made by such institution without actual notice or knowledge of the existence of such lien, as against such institution, if such loan is secured by such account.

Amendments

• 1998, IRS Restructuring and Reform Act of 1998 (P.L. 105-206)

P.L. 105-206, §3435(a)(1)(A)-(B):

Amended Code Sec. 6323(b) by striking "$250" and inserting "$1,000" in paragraph (4), and by striking "$1,000" and inserting "$5,000" in paragraph (7). **Effective** 7-22-98.

P.L. 105-206, §3435(b)(1)-(3):

Amended Code Sec. 6323(b)(10) by striking "PASSBOOK LOANS" in the heading and inserting "DEPOSIT-SECURED LOANS", by striking ", evidenced by a passbook,", and by striking all that follows "secured by such account" and inserting a period. **Effective** 7-22-98. Prior to amendment, Code Sec. 6323(b)(10) read as follows:

(10) PASSBOOK LOANS.—With respect to a savings deposit, share, or other account, evidenced by a passbook, with an institution described in section 581 or 591, to the extent of any loan made by such institution without actual notice or knowledge of the existence of such lien, as against such institution, if such loan is secured by such account and if such institution has been continuously in possession of such passbook from the time the loan is made.

• 1976, Tax Reform Act of 1976 (P.L. 94-455)

P.L. 94-455, §1906(b)(13)(A):

Amended 1954 Code by substituting "Secretary" for "Secretary or his delegate" each place it appeared. **Effective** 2-1-77.

[Sec. 6323(c)]

(c) PROTECTION FOR CERTAIN COMMERCIAL TRANSACTIONS FINANCING AGREEMENTS, ETC.—

(1) IN GENERAL.—To the extent provided in this subsection, even though notice of a lien imposed by section 6321 has been filed, such lien shall not be valid with respect to a security interest which came into existence after tax lien filing but which—

(A) is in qualified property covered by the terms of a written agreement entered into before tax lien filing and constituting—

(i) a commercial transactions financing agreement,

(ii) a real property construction or improvement financing agreement, or

(iii) an obligatory disbursement agreement, and

(B) is protected under local law against a judgment lien arising, as of the time of tax lien filing, out of an unsecured obligation.

(2) COMMERCIAL TRANSACTIONS FINANCING AGREEMENT.—For purposes of this subsection—

(A) DEFINITION.—The term "commercial transactions financing agreement" means an agreement (entered into by a person in the course of his trade or business)—

(i) to make loans to the taxpayer to be secured by commercial financing security acquired by the taxpayer in the ordinary course of his trade or business, or

(ii) to purchase commercial financing security (other than inventory) acquired by the taxpayer in the ordinary course of his trade or business;

but such an agreement shall be treated as coming within the term only to the extent that such loan or purchase is made before the 46th day after the date of tax lien filing or (if earlier) before the lender or purchaser had actual notice or knowledge of such tax lien filing.

(B) LIMITATION ON QUALIFIED PROPERTY.—The term "qualified property", when used with respect to a commercial transactions financing agreement, includes only commercial financing security acquired by the taxpayer before the 46th day after the date of tax lien filing.

(C) COMMERCIAL FINANCING SECURITY DEFINED.—The term "commercial financing security" means (i) paper of a kind ordinarily arising in commercial transactions, (ii) accounts receivable, (iii) mortgages on real property, and (iv) inventory.

(D) PURCHASER TREATED AS ACQUIRING SECURITY INTEREST.—A person who satisfies subparagraph (A) by reason of clause (ii) thereof shall be treated as having acquired a security interest in commercial financing security.

(3) REAL PROPERTY CONSTRUCTION OR IMPROVEMENT FINANCING AGREEMENT.—For purposes of this subsection—

(A) DEFINITION.—The term "real property construction or improvement financing agreement" means an agreement to make cash disbursements to finance—

(i) the construction or improvement of real property,

(ii) a contract to construct or improve real property, or

(iii) the raising or harvesting of a farm crop or the raising of livestock or other animals.

For purposes of clause (iii), the furnishing of goods and services shall be treated as the disbursement of cash.

(B) LIMITATION ON QUALIFIED PROPERTY.—The term "qualified property", when used with respect to a real property construction or improvement financing agreement, includes only—

(i) in the case of subparagraph (A)(i), the real property with respect to which the construction or improvement has been or is to be made,

(ii) in the case of subparagraph (A)(ii), the proceeds of the contract described therein, and

(iii) in the case of subparagraph (A)(iii), property subject to the lien imposed by section 6321 at the time of tax lien filing and the crop or the livestock or other animals referred to in subparagraph (A)(iii).

(4) OBLIGATORY DISBURSEMENT AGREEMENT.—For purposes of this subsection—

(A) DEFINITION.—The term "obligatory disbursement agreement" means an agreement (entered into by a person in the course of his trade or business) to make disbursements, but such an agreement shall be treated as coming within the term only to the extent of disbursements which are required to be made by reason of the intervention of the rights of a person other than the taxpayer.

(B) LIMITATION ON QUALIFIED PROPERTY.—The term "qualified property", when used with respect to an obligatory disbursement agreement, means property subject to the lien imposed by section 6321 at the time of tax lien filing and (to the extent that the acquisition is directly traceable to the disbursements referred to in subparagraph (A)) property acquired by the taxpayer after tax lien filing.

(C) SPECIAL RULES FOR SURETY AGREEMENTS.—Where the obligatory disbursement agreement is an agreement ensuring the performance of a contract between the taxpayer and another person—

(i) the term "qualified property" shall be treated as also including the proceeds of the contract the performance of which was ensured, and

(ii) if the contract the performance of which was ensured was a contract to construct or improve real property, to produce goods, or to furnish services, the term "qualified property" shall be treated as also including any tangible personal property used by the taxpayer in the performance of such ensured contract.

[Sec. 6323(d)]

(d) 45-DAY PERIOD FOR MAKING DISBURSEMENTS.—Even though notice of a lien imposed by section 6321 has been filed, such lien shall not be valid with respect to a security interest which came into existence after tax lien filing by reason of disbursements made before the 46th day after the date of tax lien filing, or (if earlier) before the person making such disbursements had actual notice or knowledge of tax lien filing, but only if such security interest—

(1) is in property (A) subject, at the time of tax lien filing, to the lien imposed by section 6321, and (B) covered by the terms of a written agreement entered into before tax lien filing, and

(2) is protected under local law against a judgment lien arising, as of the time of tax lien filing, out of an unsecured obligation.

[Sec. 6323(e)]

(e) PRIORITY OF INTEREST AND EXPENSES.—If the lien imposed by section 6321 is not valid as against a lien or security interest, the priority of such lien or security interest shall extend to—

(1) any interest or carrying charges upon the obligation secured,

(2) the reasonable charges and expenses of an indenture trustee or agent holding the security interest for the benefit of the holder of the security interest,

(3) the reasonable expenses, including reasonable compensation for attorneys, actually incurred in collecting or enforcing the obligation secured,

(4) the reasonable costs of insuring, preserving, or repairing the property to which the lien or security interest relates,

(5) the reasonable costs of insuring payment of the obligation secured, and

(6) amounts paid to satisfy any lien on the property to which the lien or security interest relates, but only if the lien so satisfied is entitled to priority over the lien imposed by section 6321,

to the extent that, under local law, any such item has the same priority as the lien or security interest to which it relates.

[Sec. 6323(f)]

(f) PLACE FOR FILING NOTICE; FORM.—

(1) PLACE FOR FILING.—The notice referred to in subsection (a) shall be filed—

(A) UNDER STATE LAWS.—

(i) REAL PROPERTY.—In the case of real property, in one office within the State (or the county, or other governmental subdivision), as designated by the laws of such State, in which the property subject to the lien is situated; and

(ii) PERSONAL PROPERTY.—In the case of personal property, whether tangible or intangible, in one office within the State (or the county, or other governmental subdivision), as designated by the laws of such State, in which the property subject to the lien is situated, except that State law merely conforming to or reenacting Federal law establishing a national filing system does not constitute a second office for filing as designated by the laws of such State;

(B) WITH CLERK OF DISTRICT COURT.—In the office of the clerk of the United States district court for the judicial district in which the property subject to the lien is situated, whenever the State has not by law designated one office which meets the requirements of subparagraph (A); or

(C) WITH RECORDER OF DEEDS OF THE DISTRICT OF COLUMBIA.—In the office of the Recorder of Deeds of the District of Columbia, if the property subject to the lien is situated in the District of Columbia.

(2) SITUS OF PROPERTY SUBJECT TO LIEN.—For purposes of paragraphs (1) and (4), property shall be deemed to be situated—

(A) REAL PROPERTY.—In the case of real property, at its physical location; or

(B) PERSONAL PROPERTY.—In the case of personal property, whether tangible or intangible, at the residence of the taxpayer at the time the notice of lien is filed.

For purposes of paragraph (2)(B), the residence of a corporation or partnership shall be deemed to be the place at which the principal executive office of the business is located, and the residence of a taxpayer whose residence is without the United States shall be deemed to be in the District of Columbia.

(3) FORM.—The form and content of the notice referred to in subsection (a) shall be prescribed by the Secretary. Such notice shall be valid notwithstanding any other provision of law regarding the form or content of a notice of lien.

(4) INDEXING REQUIRED WITH RESPECT TO CERTAIN REAL PROPERTY.—In the case of real property, if—

(A) under the laws of the State in which the real property is located, a deed is not valid as against a purchaser of the property who (at the time of purchase) does not have actual notice or knowledge of the existence of such deed unless the fact of filing of such deed has been entered and recorded in a public index at the place of filing in such a manner that a reasonable inspection of the index will reveal the existence of the deed, and

(B) there is maintained (at the applicable office under paragraph (1)) an adequate system for the public indexing of Federal tax liens,

then the notice of lien referred to in subsection (a) shall not be treated as meeting the filing requirements under paragraph (1) unless the fact of filing is entered and recorded in the index referred to in subparagraph (B) in such a manner that a reasonable inspection of the index will reveal the existence of the lien.

(5) NATIONAL FILING SYSTEMS.—The filing of a notice of lien shall be governed solely by this title and shall not be subject to any other Federal law establishing a place or places for the filing of liens or encumbrances under a national filing system.

Amendments

• 1988, Technical and Miscellaneous Revenue Act of 1988 (P.L. 100-647)

P.L. 100-647, §1015(s)(1)(A)-(B):

Amended Code Sec. 6323(f) by inserting ", except that State law merely conforming to or reenacting Federal law establishing a national filing system does not constitute a second office for filing as designated by the laws of such State" after "situated" in paragraph (1)(A)(ii) and by adding at the end thereof new paragraph (5). **Effective** 11-10-88.

• 1978, Revenue Act of 1978 (P.L. 95-600)

P.L. 95-600, §702(q)(1), (q)(3):

Amended Code Sec. 6323(f)(4). **Effective** as indicated in Act Sec. 702(q)(3), below. Prior to amendment, paragraph (4) read:

"(4) INDEX.—The notice of lien referred to in subsection (a) shall not be treated as meeting the filing requirements under paragraph (1) unless the fact of filing is entered and recorded in a public index at the district office of the Internal Revenue Service for the district in which the property subject to the lien is situated."

P.L. 95-600, §702(q)(3), provides:

"(3) EFFECTIVE DATE.—

(A) The amendments made by this subsection shall apply with respect to liens, other security interests, and other interests in real property acquired after November 6, 1978.

(B) If, after November 6, 1978, there is a change in the application (or nonapplication) of section 6323(f)(4) of the Internal Revenue Code of 1954 (as amended by paragraph (1)) with respect to any filing jurisdiction, such change shall apply only with respect to liens, other security interests, and other interests in real property acquired after the date of such change."

• 1976, Tax Reform Act of 1976 (P.L. 94-455)

P.L. 94-455, §1906(b)(13)(A):

Amended 1954 Code by substituting "Secretary" for "Secretary or his delegate" each place it appeared. **Effective** 2-1-77.

P.L. 94-455, §2008(c)(1)(A):

Added Code Sec. 6323(f)(4). **Effective,** in the case of liens filed before 10-4-76, on 7-1-77. **Effective,** in the case of liens filed on or after 10-4-76, on 2-1-77.

P.L. 94-455, §2008(c)(1)(B):

Substituted "paragraphs (1) and (4)" for "paragraph (1)" in Code Sec. 6323(f)(2). **Effective,** in the case of liens filed before 10-4-76, on 7-1-77. **Effective,** in the case of liens filed on or after 10-4-76, on 2-1-77.

[Sec. 6323(g)]

(g) REFILING OF NOTICE.—For purposes of this section—

(1) GENERAL RULE.—Unless notice of lien is refiled in the manner prescribed in paragraph (2) during the required refiling period, such notice of lien shall be treated as filed on the date on which it is filed (in accordance with subsection (f)) after the expiration of such refiling period.

(2) PLACE FOR FILING.—A notice of lien refiled during the required refiling period shall be effective only—

(A) if—

(i) such notice of lien is refiled in the office in which the prior notice of lien was filed, and

(ii) in the case of real property, the fact of refiling is entered and recorded in an index to the extent required by subsection (f)(4); and

(B) in any case in which, 90 days or more prior to the date of a refiling of notice of lien under subparagraph (A), the Secretary received written information (in the manner prescribed in regulations issued by the Secretary) concerning a change in the taxpayer's residence, if a notice of such lien is also filed in accordance with subsection (f) in the State in which such residence is located.

(3) REQUIRED REFILING PERIOD.—In the case of any notice of lien, the term "required refiling period" means—

(A) the one-year period ending 30 days after the expiration of 10 years after the date of the assessment of the tax, and

(B) the one-year period ending with the expiration of 10 years after the close of the preceding required refiling period for such notice of lien.

(4) TRANSITIONAL RULE.—Notwithstanding paragraph (3), if the assessment of the tax was made before January 1, 1962, the first required refiling period shall be the calendar year 1967.

Amendments

• 1990, Omnibus Budget Reconciliation Act of 1990 (P.L. 101-508)

P.L. 101-508, §11317(b):

Amended Code Sec. 6323(g)(3) by striking "6 years" each place it appears and inserting "10 years". For the **effective** date, see Act Sec. 11317(c), below.

P.L. 101-508, §11317(c), provides:

(c) EFFECTIVE DATE.—The amendments made by this section shall apply to—

(1) taxes assessed after the date of the enactment of this Act, and

(2) taxes assessed on or before such date if the period specified in section 6502 of the Internal Revenue Code of 1986 (determined without regard to the amendments made by subsection (a)) for collection of such taxes has not expired as of such date.

• 1978, Revenue Act of 1978 (P.L. 95-600)

P.L. 95-600, §702(q)(2), (3):

Amended Code Sec. 6323(g)(2)(A). **Effective**, generally, for liens, other security interests, and other interests in real property acquired after 11-6-78 [see Act Sec. 702(q)(3) in the amendment notes following Code Sec. 6323(f)]. Prior to amendment, subparagraph (A) read:

"(A) if such notice of lien is refiled in the office in which the prior notice of lien was filed and the fact of refiling is entered and recorded in an index in accordance with subsection (f)(4); and"

• 1976, Tax Reform Act of 1976 (P.L. 94-455)

P.L. 94-455, §1906(b)(13)(A):

Amended 1954 Code by substituting "Secretary" for "Secretary or his delegate" each place it appeared. **Effective** 2-1-77.

P.L. 94-455, §2008(c)(2):

Amended Code Sec. 6323(g)(2)(A). **Effective**, in the case of liens filed before 10-4-76, on 7-1-77. **Effective**, in the case of liens filed on or after 10-4-76, on 2-1-77. Prior to amendment, Code Sec. 6323(g)(2)(A) read as follows:

(A) if such notice of lien is refiled in the office in which the prior notice of lien was filed; and

[Sec. 6323(h)]

(h) DEFINITIONS.—For purposes of this section and section 6324—

(1) SECURITY INTEREST.—The term "security interest" means any interest in property acquired by contract for the purpose of securing payment or performance of an obligation or indemnifying against loss or liability. A security interest exists at any time (A) if, at such time the property is in existence and the interest has become protected under local law against a subsequent judgment lien arising out of an unsecured obligation, and (B) to the extent that, at such time, the holder has parted with money or money's worth.

(2) MECHANIC'S LIENOR.—The term "mechanic's lienor" means any person who under local law has a lien on real property (or on the proceeds of a contract relating to real property) for services, labor, or materials furnished in connection with the construction or improvement of such property. For purposes of the preceding sentence, a person has a lien on the earliest date such lien becomes valid under local law against subsequent purchasers without actual notice, but not before he begins to furnish the services, labor, or materials.

(3) MOTOR VEHICLE.—The term "motor vehicle" means a self-propelled vehicle which is registered for highway use under the laws of any State or foreign country.

(4) SECURITY.—The term "security" means any bond, debenture, note, or certificate or other evidence of indebtedness, issued by a corporation or a government or political subdivision thereof, with interest coupons or in registered form, share of stock, voting trust certificate, or any certificate of interest or participation in, certificate of deposit or receipt for, temporary or interim certificate for, or warrant or right to subscribe to or purchase, any of the foregoing; negotiable instrument; or money.

(5) TAX LIEN FILING.—The term "tax lien filing" means the filing of notice (referred to in subsection (a)) of the lien imposed by section 6321.

(6) PURCHASER.—The term "purchaser" means a person who, for adequate and full consideration in money or money's worth, acquires an interest (other than a lien or security interest) in property which is valid under local law against subsequent purchasers without actual notice. In applying the preceding sentence for purposes of subsection (a) of this section, and for purposes of section 6324—

(A) a lease of property,

(B) a written executory contract to purchase or lease property,

(C) an option to purchase or lease property or any interest therein, or

(D) an option to renew or extend a lease of property,

which is not a lien or security interest shall be treated as an interest in property.

[Sec. 6323(i)]

(i) SPECIAL RULES.—

(1) ACTUAL NOTICE OR KNOWLEDGE.—For purposes of this subchapter, an organization shall be deemed for purposes of a particular transaction to have actual notice or knowledge of any fact from the time such fact is brought to the attention of the individual conducting such transaction, and in any event from the time such fact would have been brought to such individual's attention if the organization had exercised due diligence. An organization exercises due diligence if it maintains reasonable routines for communicating significant information to the person conducting the transaction and there is reasonable compliance with the routines. Due diligence does not require an individual acting for the organization to communicate information unless such communication is part of his regular duties or unless he has reason to know of the transaction and that the transaction would be materially affected by the information.

(2) SUBROGATION.—Where, under local law, one person is subrogated to the rights of another with respect to a lien or interest, such person shall be subrogated to such rights for purposes of any lien imposed by section 6321 or 6324.

(3) FORFEITURES.—For purposes of this subchapter, a forfeiture under local law of property seized by a law enforcement agency of a State, county, or other local governmental subdivision shall relate back to the time of seizure, except that this paragraph shall not apply to the extent that under local law the holder of an intervening claim or interest would have priority over the interest of the State, county, or other local governmental subdivision in the property.

(4) COST-OF-LIVING ADJUSTMENT.—In the case of notices of liens imposed by section 6321 which are filed in any calendar year after 1998, each of the dollar amounts under paragraph (4) or (7) of subsection (b) shall be increased by an amount equal to—

(A) such dollar amount, multiplied by

(B) the cost-of-living adjustment determined under section 1(f)(3) for the calendar year, determined by substituting "calendar year 1996" for "calendar year 2016" in subparagraph (A)(ii) thereof.

If any amount as adjusted under the preceding sentence is not a multiple of $10, such amount shall be rounded to the nearest multiple of $10.

Amendments

• 2017, Tax Cuts and Jobs Act (P.L. 115-97)

P.L. 115-97, §11002(d)(1)(HH):

Amended Code Sec. 6323(i)(4)(B) by striking "for 'calendar year 1992' in subparagraph (B)" and inserting "for 'calendar year 2016' in subparagraph (A)(ii)". **Effective** for tax years beginning after 12-31-2017.

• 1998, IRS Restructuring and Reform Act of 1998 (P.L. 105-206)

P.L. 105-206, §3435(a)(2):

Amended Code Sec. 6323(i) by adding at the end a new paragraph (4). **Effective** 7-22-98.

• 1986, Tax Reform Act of 1986 (P.L. 99-514)

P.L. 99-514, §1569(a):

Amended Code Sec. 6323(i) by adding at the end thereof new paragraph (3). **Effective** 10-22-86.

• 1976, Tax Reform Act of 1976 (P.L. 94-455)

P.L. 94-455, §1202(h)(2):

Struck out Code Sec. 6323(i)(3). **Effective** 1-1-77. Prior to striking, Code Sec. 6323(i)(3) read as follows:

(3) DISCLOSURE OF AMOUNT OF OUTSTANDING LIEN.—If a notice of lien has been filed pursuant to subsection (f), the Secretary or his delegate is authorized to provide by regulations the extent to which, and the conditions under which, information as to the amount of outstanding obligation secured by the lien may be disclosed.

• 1966, Federal Tax Lien Act of 1966 (P.L. 89-719)

P.L. 89-719, §101(a):

Amended Code Sec. 6323. Prior to amendment, Sec. 6323 read as follows:

SEC. 6323. VALIDITY AGAINST MORTGAGEES, PLEDGEES, PURCHASERS, AND JUDGMENT CREDITORS.

(a) Invalidity of Lien Without Notice.—Except as otherwise provided in subsections (c) and (d), the lien imposed by section 6321 shall not be valid as against any mortgagee, pledgee, purchaser, or judgment creditor until notice thereof has been filed by the Secretary of his delegate—

(1) Under state or territorial laws.—In the office designated by the law of the State or Territory in which the property subject to the lien is situated, whenever the State or Territory has by law designated an office within the State or Territory for the filing of such notice; or

(2) With clerk of district court.—In the office of the clerk of the United States district court for the judicial district in which the property subject to the lien is situated, whenever the State or Territory has not by law designated an office within the State or Territory for the filing of such notice; or

(3) With Recorder of Deeds of the District of Columbia.—In the office of the Recorder of Deeds of the District of Columbia, if the property subject to the lien is situated in the District of Columbia.

(b) Form of Notice.—If the notice filed pursuant to subsection (a)(1) is in such form as would be valid if filed with the clerk of the United States district court pursuant to subsection (a)(2), such notice shall be valid notwithstanding any law of the State or Territory regarding the form or content of a notice of lien.

(c) Exception in Case of Securities.—

(1) Exception.—Even though notice of a lien provided in section 6321 has been filed in the manner prescribed in subsection (a) of this section, the lien shall not be valid with respect to a security, as defined in paragraph (2) of this subsection, as against any mortgagee, pledgee, or purchaser of such security, for an adequate and full consideration in money or money's worth, if at the time of such mortgage, pledge, or purchase such mortgagee, pledgee, or purchaser is without notice or knowledge of the existence of such lien.

(2) Definition of security.—As used in this subsection, the term 'security' means any bond, debenture, note, or certificate or other evidence of indebtedness, issued by any corporation (incuding one issued by a government or political subdivision thereof), with interest coupons or in registered form, share of stock, voting trust certificate, or any certifi-

cate of interest or participation in, certificate of deposit or receipt for, temporary or interim certificate for, or warrant or right to subscribe to or purchase, any of the foregoing; negotiable instrument; or money.

(d) Exception in Case of Motor Vehicles.—

(1) Exception.—Even though notice of a lien provided in section 6321 has been filed in the manner prescribed in subsection (a) of this section, the lien shall not be valid with respect to a motor vehicle, as defined in paragraph (2) of this subsection, as against any purchaser of such motor vehicle for an adequate and full consideration in money or money's worth if—

(A) at the time of the purchase the purchaser is without notice or knowledge of the existence of such lien, and

(B) before the purchaser obtains such notice or knowledge, he has acquired possession of such motor vehicle and has not thereafter relinquished possession of such motor vehicle to the seller or his agent.

(2) Definition of motor vehicle.—As used in this subsection, the term "motor vehicle" means a self-propelled vehicle which is registered for highway use under the laws of any State or foreign country.

(e) Disclosure of Amount of Outstanding Lien.—If a notice of lien has been filed under subsection (a), the Secretary or his delegate is authorized to provide by rules or regulations the extent to which, and the conditions under which, information as to the amount of the outstanding obligation secured by the lien may be disclosed.

Effective generally after 11-2-66, regardless of when a lien or title of the U. S. arose or when a lien or interest of any other person was acquired. However, the Act provides certain exceptions to the effective date as follows:

(1) The amendments made by the Act are not to apply in any case where the Government has, in effect, completed enforcement of its interest arising under a lien. Thus, the amendments are not to apply where the enforcement proceeding has reached the stage of a civil action or suit which has become final by judgment, sale, or agreement, before the date of enactment.

(2) The amendments are not to apply to any case where they would impair a priority of any person holding a lien or interest prior to the date of enactment; increase the liability of any person; or, shorten the time for bringing suit with respect to any transaction occurring before the date of enactment.

(3) The amendments imposing a liability on third persons who pay wages of employees of another or supply funds for the specific purpose of paying wages of the employees of another are to apply only with respect to wages paid on or after January 1, 1967.

(4) The amendments requiring performance bonds on public works contracts to provide for the payment of withholding are to apply only to contracts entered into pursuant to invitations for bids made by the Government after June 30, 1967.

(5) Where a person has commenced a civil action to clear title to property under the present law (sec. 7424 which, in effect, is repealed by this Act), the action is to be determined in accordance with that section without regard to this Act.

• 1966 (P.L. 89-493)

P.L. 89-493, §17(a):

Amended Code Sec. 6323(a)(3) by substituting "Recorder of Deeds of the District of Columbia" for "Clerk of the United States District Court of the District of Columbia". **Effective** on the first day of the first month which is at least 90 days after 7-5-66.

• 1964, Revenue Act of 1964 (P.L. 88-272)

P.L. 88-272, §236(c)(1):

Amended the first sentence to subsection (a) by inserting "subsections (c) and (d)" in lieu of "subsection (c)". **Effective** with respect to purchases made after 2-26-64.

P.L. 88-272, §236(a):

Added new subsection (d), and redesignated former subsection (d) as subsection (e). **Effective** with respect to purchases made after 2-26-64.

[Sec. 6323(j)]

(j) WITHDRAWAL OF NOTICE IN CERTAIN CIRCUMSTANCES.—

(1) IN GENERAL.—The Secretary may withdraw a notice of a lien filed under this section and this chapter shall be applied as if the withdrawn notice had not been filed, if the Secretary determines that—

(A) the filing of such notice was premature or otherwise not in accordance with administrative procedures of the Secretary,

(B) the taxpayer has entered into an agreement under section 6159 to satisfy the tax liability for which the lien was imposed by means of installment payments, unless such agreement provides otherwise,

(C) the withdrawal of such notice will facilitate the collection of the tax liability, or

(D) with the consent of the taxpayer or the National Taxpayer Advocate, the withdrawal of such notice would be in the best interests of the taxpayer (as determined by the National Taxpayer Advocate) and the United States.

Any such withdrawal shall be made by filing notice at the same office as the withdrawn notice. A copy of such notice of withdrawal shall be provided to the taxpayer.

(2) NOTICE TO CREDIT AGENCIES, ETC.—Upon written request by the taxpayer with respect to whom a notice of a lien was withdrawn under paragraph (1), the Secretary shall promptly make reasonable efforts to notify credit reporting agencies, and any financial institution or creditor whose name and address is specified in such request, of the withdrawal of such notice. Any such request shall be in such form as the Secretary may prescribe.

Amendments

• 1998, IRS Restructuring and Reform Act of 1998 (P.L. 105-206)

P.L. 105-206, §1102(d)(1)(A):

Amended Code Sec. 6323(j)(1)(D) by striking "Taxpayer Advocate" each place it appears and inserting "National Taxpayer Advocate". **Effective** 7-22-98. For special rules, see Act Sec. 1102(f)(3)-(4) in the amendment notes following Code Sec. 7803.

• 1996, Taxpayer Bill of Rights 2 (P.L. 104-168)

P.L. 104-168, §501(a):

Amended Code Sec. 6323 by adding at the end a new subsection (j). **Effective** 7-30-96.

[Sec. 6324]

SEC. 6324. SPECIAL LIENS FOR ESTATE AND GIFT TAXES.

[Sec. 6324(a)]

(a) LIENS FOR ESTATE TAX.—Except as otherwise provided in subsection (c)—

(1) UPON GROSS ESTATE.—Unless the estate tax imposed by chapter 11 is sooner paid in full, or becomes unenforceable by reason of lapse of time, it shall be a lien upon the gross estate of the decedent for 10 years from the date of death, except that such part of the gross estate as is used

for the payment of charges against the estate and expenses of its administration, allowed by any court having jurisdiction thereof, shall be divested of such lien.

(2) LIABILITY OF TRANSFEREES AND OTHERS.—If the estate tax imposed by chapter 11 is not paid when due, then the spouse, transferee, trustee (except the trustee of an employees' trust which meets the requirements of section 401(a)), surviving tenant, person in possession of the property by reason of the exercise, nonexercise, or release of a power of appointment, or beneficiary, who receives, or has on the date of the decedent's death, property included in the gross estate under sections 2034 to 2042, inclusive, to the extent of the value, at the time of the decedent's death, of such property, shall be personally liable for such tax. Any part of such property transferred by (or transferred by a transferee of) such spouse, transferee, trustee, surviving tenant, person in possession, or beneficiary, to a purchaser or holder of a security interest shall be divested of the lien provided in paragraph (1) and a like lien shall then attach to all the property of such spouse, transferee, trustee, surviving tenant, person in possession, or beneficiary, or transferee of any such person, except any part transferred to a purchaser or a holder of a security interest.

(3) CONTINUANCE AFTER DISCHARGE OF FIDUCIARY.—The provisions of section 2204 (relating to discharge of fiduciary from personal liability) shall not operate as a release of any part of the gross estate from the lien for any deficiency that may thereafter be determined to be due, unless such part of the gross estate (or any interest therein) has been transferred to a purchaser or a holder of a security interest, in which case such part (or such interest) shall not be subject to a lien or to any claim or demand for any such deficiency, but the lien shall attach to the consideration received from such purchaser or holder of a security interest, by the heirs, legatees, devisees, or distributees.

Amendments

• 1970, Excise, Estate, and Gift Tax Adjustment Act of 1970 (P.L. 91-614)

P.L. 91-614, §101(d)(2):

Amended Code Sec. 6324(a)(3) by substituting "fiduciary" for "executor" in the heading and in the text. **Effective** for gifts made after 12-31-70.

[Sec. 6324(b)]

(b) LIEN FOR GIFT TAX.—Except as otherwise provided in subsection (c), unless the gift tax imposed by chapter 12 is sooner paid in full or becomes unenforceable by reason of lapse of time, such tax shall be a lien upon all gifts made during the period for which the return was filed, for 10 years from the date the gifts are made. If the tax is not paid when due, the donee of any gift shall be personally liable for such tax to the extent of the value of such gift. Any part of the property comprised in the gift transferred by the donee (or by a transferee of the donee) to a purchaser or holder of a security interest shall be divested of the lien imposed by this subsection and such lien, to the extent of the value of such gift, shall attach to all the property (including after-acquired property) of the donee (or the transferee) except any part transferred to a purchaser or holder of a security interest.

Amendments

• 1970, Excise, Estate, and Gift Tax Adjustment Act of 1970 (P.L. 91-614)

P.L. 91-614, §102(d)(7):

Amended Code Sec. 6324(b) by substituting "period for which the return was filed" for "calendar year" in the first sentence. **Effective** for gifts made after 12-31-70.

[Sec. 6324(c)]

(c) EXCEPTIONS.—

(1) The lien imposed by subsection (a) or (b) shall not be valid as against a mechanic's lienor and, subject to the conditions provided by section 6323(b) (relating to protection for certain interests even though notice filed), shall not be valid with respect to any lien or interest described in section 6323(b).

(2) If a lien imposed by subsection (a) or (b) is not valid as against a lien or security interest, the priority of such lien or security interest shall extend to any item described in section 6323(e) (relating to priority of interest and expenses) to the extent that, under local law, such item has the same priority as the lien or security interest to which it relates.

[Sec. 6324(d)—Repealed]

Amendments

• 1966, Federal Tax Lien Act of 1966 (P.L. 89-719)

P.L. 89-719, §102:

Amended Code Sec. 6324. **Effective**, generally, after 11-2-66, regardless of when a lien or title of the U. S. arose or when a lien or interest of any other person was acquired. However, see the amendment note for Code Sec. 6323 for exceptions to this **effective** date. Prior to amendment, Sec. 6324 read as follows:

Sec. 6324. Special Liens for Estate and Gift Taxes.

(a) Liens for Estate Tax.—Except as otherwise provided in subsection (c) (relating to transfers of securities) and subsection (d) (relating to purchases of motor vehicles)—

(1) Upon gross estate.—Unless the estate tax imposed by chapter 11 is sooner paid in full, it shall be a lien for 10 years upon the gross estate of the decedent, except that such part of the gross estate as is used for the payment of charges against the estate and expenses of its administration, allowed by any court having jurisdiction thereof, shall be divested of such lien.

(2) Liability of transferees and others.—If the estate tax imposed by chapter 11 is not paid when due, then the spouse, transferee, trustee (except the trustee of an employee's [*sic*]trust which meets the requirements of section 401(a)), surviving tenant, person in possession of the property by reason of the exercise, nonexercise, or release of a power of appointment, or beneficiary, who receives, or has on the date of the decedent's death, property included in the gross estate under sections 2034 to 2042, inclusive, to the extent of the value, at the time of the decedent's death, of such property, shall be personally liable for such tax. Any part of such property transferred by (or transferred by a transferee of) such spouse, transferee, trustee, surviving tenant, person in possession of property by reason of the exercise, nonexercise, or release of a power of appointment, or beneficiary, to a bona fide purchaser, mortgagee, or pledgee, for an adequate and full consideration in money or money's worth shall be divested of the lien provided in paragraph (1) and a like lien shall then attach to all the property of such spouse, transferee, trustee, surviving tenant, person in possession, beneficiary, or transferee of any such person, except any part transferred to a bona fide purchaser, mortgagee, or pledgee for an adequate and full consideration in money or money's worth.

(3) Continuance after discharge of executor.—The provisions of section 2204 (relating to discharge of executor from personal liability) shall not operate as a release of any part of the gross estate from the lien for any deficiency that may thereafter be determined to be due, unless such part of the gross estate (or any interest therein) has been transferred to a bona fide purchaser, mortgagee, or pledgee for an adequate and full consideration in money, or money's worth, in which case such part (or such interest) shall not be subject to a lien or to any claim or demand for any such deficiency, but the lien shall attach to the consideration received from such purchaser, mortgagee, or pledgee by the heirs, legatees, devisees, or distributees.

(b) Lien for Gift Tax.—Except as otherwise provided in subsection (c) (relating to transfers of securities) and subsection (d) (relating to purchases of motor vehicles), the gift tax imposed by chapter 12 shall be a lien upon all gifts made during the calendar year, for 10 years from the time the gifts are made. If the tax is not paid when due, the donee of any gift shall be personally liable for such tax to the extent of the value of such gift. Any part of the property comprised in the gift transferred by the donee (or by a transferee of the donee) to a bona fide purchaser, mortgagee, or pledgee for an adequate and full consideration in money or money's worth shall be divested of the lien herein imposed and the lien, to the extent of the value of such gift, shall attach to all the property (including after-acquired property) of the donee (or the transferee) except any part transferred to a bona fide purchaser, mortgagee, or pledgee for an adequate and full consideration in money or money's worth.

(c) Exception in Case of Securities.—The lien imposed by subsection (a) or (b) shall not be valid with respect to a security, as defined in section 6323(c)(2), as against any mortgagee, pledgee, or purchaser of any such security, for an adequate and full consideration in money or money's worth, if at the time of such mortgage, pledge, or purchase such mortgagee, pledgee, or purchaser is without notice or knowledge of the existence of such lien.

(d) Exception in Case of Motor Vehicles.—The lien imposed by subsection (a) or (b) shall not be valid with respect to a motor vehicle, as defined in section 6323(d)(2), as against any purchaser of such motor vehicle for an adequate and full consideration in money or money's worth if—

(1) at the time of the purchase the purchaser is without notice or knowledge of the existence of such lien, and

(2) before the purchaser obtains such notice or knowledge, he has acquired possession of such motor vehicle and has not thereafter relinquished possession of such motor vehicle to the seller or his agent."

• 1964, Revenue Act of 1964 (P.L. 88-272)

P.L. 88-272, §236(c)(2):

Amended subsections (a) and (b) by adding in the first sentence of each "and subsection (d) (relating to purchases of motor vehicles)". **Effective** with respect to purchases made after 2-26-64.

P.L. 88-272, §236(b):

Added subsection (d). **Effective** for purchases made after 2-26-64.

[Sec. 6324A]

SEC. 6324A. SPECIAL LIEN FOR ESTATE TAX DEFERRED UNDER SECTION 6166 .

[Sec. 6324A(a)]

(a) GENERAL RULE.—In the case of any estate with respect to which an election has been made under section 6166, if the executor makes an election under this section (at such time and in such manner as the Secretary shall by regulations prescribe) and files the agreement referred to in subsection (c), the deferred amount (plus any interest, additional amount, addition to tax, assessable penalty, and costs attributable to the deferred amount) shall be a lien in favor of the United States on the section 6166 lien property.

Amendments

• 1981, Economic Recovery Tax Act of 1981 (P.L. 97-34)

P.L. 97-34, §422(e)(6)(A):

Amended Code Sec. 6324A(a) by striking out "6166 or 6166A" and inserting "6166". **Effective** for estates of decedents dying after 12-31-81.

P.L. 97-34, §422(e)(6)(C):

Amended Code Sec. 6324A by striking out in the section heading **"OR 6166A"**. **Effective** for estates of decedents dying after 12-31-81.

[Sec. 6324A(b)]

(b) SECTION 6166 LIEN PROPERTY.—

(1) IN GENERAL.—For purposes of this section, the term "section 6166 lien property" means interests in real and other property to the extent such interests—

(A) can be expected to survive the deferral period, and

(B) are designated in the agreement referred to in subsection (c).

(2) MAXIMUM VALUE OF REQUIRED PROPERTY.—The maximum value of the property which the Secretary may require as section 6166 lien property with respect to any estate shall be a value which is not greater than the sum of—

(A) the deferred amount, and

(B) the required interest amount.

For purposes of the preceding sentence, the value of any property shall be determined as of the date prescribed by section 6151(a) for payment of the tax imposed by chapter 11 and shall be determined by taking into account any encumbrance such as a lien under section 6324B.

(3) PARTIAL SUBSTITUTION OF BOND FOR LIEN.—If the value required as section 6166 lien property pursuant to paragraph (2) exceeds the value of the interests in property covered by the agreement referred to in subsection (c), the Secretary may accept bond in an amount equal to such excess conditioned on the payment of the amount extended in accordance with the terms of such extension.

Amendments

• 1978, Revenue Act of 1978 (P.L. 95-600)

P.L. 95-600, §702(e)(1)(B), (e)(2):

Amended Code Sec. 6324A(b)(2)(B) by striking out "aggregate interest amount" and inserting in place thereof "required interest amount". **Effective** for estates of decedents dying after 12-31-76.

[Sec. 6324A(c)]

(c) AGREEMENT.—The agreement referred to in this subsection is a written agreement signed by each person in being who has an interest (whether or not in possession) in any property designated in such agreement—

(1) consenting to the creation of the lien under this section with respect to such property, and

(2) designating a responsible person who shall be the agent for the beneficiaries of the estate and for the persons who have consented to the creation of the lien in dealings with the Secretary on matters arising under section 6166 or this section.

Amendments

• 1981, Economic Recovery Tax Act of 1981 (P.L. 97-34)

P.L. 97-34, §422(e)(6)(A):

Amended Code Sec. 6324A(c)(2) by striking out "or 6166A" after "section 6166". **Effective** for estates of decedents dying after 12-31-81.

[Sec. 6324A(d)]

(d) SPECIAL RULES.—

(1) REQUIREMENT THAT LIEN BE FILED.—The lien imposed by this section shall not be valid as against any purchaser, holder of a security interest, mechanic's lien, or judgment lien creditor until notice thereof which meets the requirements of section 6323(f) has been filed by the Secretary. Such notice shall not be required to be refiled.

(2) PERIOD OF LIEN.—The lien imposed by this section shall arise at the time the executor is discharged from liability under section 2204 (or, if earlier, at the time notice is filed pursuant to paragraph (1)) and shall continue until the liability for the deferred amount is satisfied or becomes unenforceable by reason of lapse of time.

(3) PRIORITIES.—Even though notice of a lien imposed by this section has been filed as provided in paragraph (1), such lien shall not be valid—

(A) REAL PROPERTY TAX AND SPECIAL ASSESSMENT LIENS.—To the extent provided in section 6323(b)(6).

(B) REAL PROPERTY SUBJECT TO A MECHANIC'S LIEN FOR REPAIRS AND IMPROVEMENTS.—In the case of any real property subject to a lien for repair or improvement, as against a mechanic's lienor.

(C) REAL PROPERTY CONSTRUCTION OR IMPROVEMENT FINANCING AGREEMENT.—As against any security interest set forth in paragraph (3) of section 6323(c) (whether such security interest came into existence before or after tax lien filing).

Subparagraphs (B) and (C) shall not apply to any security interest which came into existence after the date on which the Secretary filed notice (in a manner similar to notice filed under section 6323(f)) that payment of the deferred amount has been accelerated under section 6166(g).

(4) LIEN TO BE IN LIEU OF SECTION 6324 LIEN.—If there is a lien under this section on any property with respect to any estate, there shall not be any lien under section 6324 on such property with respect to the same estate.

(5) ADDITIONAL LIEN PROPERTY REQUIRED IN CERTAIN CASES.—If at any time the value of the property covered by the agreement is less than the unpaid portion of the deferred amount and the required interest amount, the Secretary may require the addition of property to the agreement (but he may not require under this paragraph that the value of the property covered by the agreement exceed such unpaid portion). If property having the required value is not added to the property covered by the agreement (or if other security equal to the required value is not furnished) within 90 days after notice and demand therefor by the Secretary, the failure to comply with the preceding sentence shall be treated as an act accelerating payment of the installments under section 6166(g).

(6) LIEN TO BE IN LIEU OF BOND.—The Secretary may not require under section 6165 the furnishing of any bond for the payment of any tax to which an agreement which meets the requirements of subsection (c) applies.

Amendments

• 1981, Economic Recovery Tax Act of 1981 (P.L. 97-34)

P.L. 97-34, §422(e)(6)(B):

Amended Code Sec. 6324A(d)(3) and (5) by striking out "section 6166(g) or 6166A(h)" and inserting "section 6166(g)". **Effective** for estates of decedents dying after 12-31-81.

• 1978, Revenue Act of 1978 (P.L. 95-600)

P.L. 95-600, §702(e)(1)(C), (e)(2):

Amended Code Sec. 6324A(d)(5). **Effective** for estates of decedents dying after 12-31-76, by striking out "aggregate interest amount" and inserting in place thereof "required interest amount".

[Sec. 6324A(e)]

(e) DEFINITIONS.—For purposes of this section—

(1) DEFERRED AMOUNT.—The term "deferred amount" means the aggregate amount deferred under section 6166 (determined as of the date prescribed by section 6151(a) for payment of the tax imposed by chapter 11).

(2) REQUIRED INTEREST AMOUNT.—The term "required interest amount" means the aggregate amount of interest which will be payable over the first 4 years of the deferral period with respect to the deferred amount (determined as of the date prescribed by section 6151(a) for the payment of the tax imposed by chapter 11).

(3) DEFERRAL PERIOD.—The term "deferral period" means the period for which the payment of tax is deferred pursuant to the election under section 6166.

(4) APPLICATION OF DEFINITIONS IN CASE OF DEFICIENCIES.—In the case of a deficiency, a separate deferred amount, required interest amount, and deferral period shall be determined as of the due date of the first installment after the deficiency is prorated to installments under section 6166.

Amendments

• 1981, Economic Recovery Tax Act of 1981 (P.L. 97-34)

P.L. 97-34, §422(e)(6)(A):

Amended Code Sec. 6324A(e) by striking out "section 6166 or 6166A" and inserting "section 6166" each place it appears. **Effective** for estates of decedents dying after 12-31-81.

• 1978, Revenue Act of 1978 (P.L. 95-600)

P.L. 95-600, §702(e)(1)(A), 702(e)(2):

Amended Code Sec. 6324A(e)(2). **Effective** for estates of decedents dying after 12-31-76. Prior to amendment, paragraph (2) read:

"(2) AGGREGATE INTEREST AMOUNT.—The term 'aggregate interest amount' means the aggregate amount of interest which will be payable over the deferral period with respect to the deferred amount (determined as of the date prescribed by section 6151(a) for payment of the tax imposed by chapter 11)."

P.L. 95-600, §702(e)(1)(D), 702(e)(2):

Amended Code Sec. 6324A(e)(4) by striking out "aggregate interest amount" and inserting in place thereof "required interest amount". **Effective** for estates of decedents dying after 12-31-76.

• 1976, Tax Reform Act of 1976 (P.L. 94-455)

P.L. 94-455, §2004(d)(1):

Added new Code Sec. 6324A. **Effective** for estates of decedents dying after 12-31-76.

[Sec. 6324B]

SEC. 6324B. SPECIAL LIEN FOR ADDITIONAL ESTATE TAX ATTRIBUTABLE TO FARM, ETC., VALUATION.

[Sec. 6324B(a)]

(a) GENERAL RULE.—In the case of any interest in qualified real property (within the meaning of section 2032A(b)), an amount equal to the adjusted tax difference attributable to such interest (within the meaning of section 2032A(c)(2)(B)) shall be a lien in favor of the United States on the property in which such interest exists.

[Sec. 6324B(b)]

(b) PERIOD OF LIEN.—The lien imposed by this section shall arise at the time an election is filed under section 2032A and shall continue with respect to any interest in the qualified real property—

(1) until the liability for tax under subsection (c) of section 2032A with respect to such interest has been satisfied or has become unenforceable by reason of lapse of time, or

(2) until it is established to the satisfaction of the Secretary that no further tax liability may arise under section 2032A(c) with respect to such interest.

Amendments

• 1978, Revenue Act of 1978 (P.L. 95-600)

P.L. 95-600, §702(r)(4), (5):

Amended Code Sec. 6324B(b). **Effective** for estates of decedents dying after 12-31-76, by striking out "qualified farm real property" and inserting in place thereof "qualified real property".

[Sec. 6324B(c)]

(c) CERTAIN RULES AND DEFINITIONS MADE APPLICABLE.—

(1) IN GENERAL.—The rule set forth in paragraphs (1), (3), and (4) of section 6324A(d) shall apply with respect to the lien imposed by this section as if it were a lien imposed by section 6324A.

(2) QUALIFIED REAL PROPERTY.—For purposes of this section, the term "qualified real property" includes qualified replacement property (within the meaning of section 2032A(h)(3)(B)) and qualified exchange property (within the meaning of section 2032A(i)(3)).

Amendments

• 1981, Economic Recovery Tax Act of 1981 (P.L. 97-34)

P.L. 97-34, §421(d)(2)(B):

Amended Code Sec. 6324B(c)(2) by adding before the period "and qualified exchange property (within the meaning of section 2032A(i)(3))". **Effective** with respect to exchanges after 12-31-81.

• 1980, Technical Corrections Act of 1979 (P.L. 96-222)

P.L. 96-222, §108(d):

Amended Code Sec. 6342B(c). Prior to amendment, Code Sec. 6342B(c) read as follows:

(c) CERTAIN RULES MADE APPLICABLE.—The rules set forth in paragraphs (1), (3), and (4) of section 6324A(d) shall apply with respect to the lien imposed by this section as if it were a lien imposed by section 6324A.

[Sec. 6324B(d)]

(d) SUBSTITUTION OF SECURITY FOR LIEN.—To the extent provided in regulations prescribed by the Secretary the furnishing of security may be substituted for the lien imposed by this section.

Amendments

• 1976, Tax Reform Act of 1976 (P.L. 94-455)

P.L. 94-455, §2003(b):

Added new Code Sec. 6324B. **Effective** for estates of decedents dying after 12-31-76.

[Sec. 6325]

SEC. 6325. RELEASE OF LIEN OR DISCHARGE OF PROPERTY.

[Sec. 6325(a)]

(a) RELEASE OF LIEN.—Subject to such regulations as the Secretary may prescribe, the Secretary shall issue a certificate of release of any lien imposed with respect to any internal revenue tax not later than 30 days after the day on which—

(1) LIABILITY SATISFIED OR UNENFORCEABLE.—The Secretary finds that the liability for the amount assessed, together with all interest in respect thereof, has been fully satisfied or has become legally unenforceable; or

(2) BOND ACCEPTED.—There is furnished to the Secretary and accepted by him a bond that is conditioned upon the payment of the amount assessed, together with all interest in respect thereof, within the time prescribed by law (including any extension of such time), and that is in accordance with such requirements relating to terms, conditions, and form of the bond and sureties thereon, as may be specified by such regulations.

Amendments

• 1982, Tax Equity and Fiscal Responsibility Act of 1982 (P.L. 97-248)

P.L. 97-248, §348(a):

Amended so much of subsection (a) as precedes paragraph (1). **Effective** with respect to liens which are filed after 12-31-82 which are satisfied after 12-31-82, or with respect to which the taxpayer after 12-31-82, requests the Secretary of the Treasury or his delegate to issue a certificate of release on the grounds that the liability was satisfied or legally unenforceable. Prior to amendment, so much of subsection (a) as precedes paragraph (1) read as follows:

"(a) RELEASE OF LIEN.—Subject to such regulations as the Secretary may prescribe, the Secretary may issue a certificate of release of any lien imposed with respect to any internal revenue tax if—"

• 1976, Tax Reform Act of 1976 (P.L. 94-455)

P.L. 94-455, §1906(b)(13)(A):

Amended 1954 Code by substituting "Secretary" for "Secretary or his delegate" each place it appeared. **Effective** 2-1-77.

[Sec. 6325(b)]

(b) DISCHARGE OF PROPERTY.—

(1) PROPERTY DOUBLE THE AMOUNT OF THE LIABILITY.—Subject to such regulations as the Secretary may prescribe, the Secretary may issue a certificate of discharge of any part of the property subject to any lien imposed under this chapter if the Secretary finds that the fair market value of that part of such property remaining subject to the lien is at least double the amount of the unsatisfied liability secured by such lien and the amount of all other liens upon such property which have priority over such lien.

(2) PART PAYMENT; INTEREST OF UNITED STATES VALUELESS.—Subject to such regulations as the Secretary may prescribe, the Secretary may issue a certificate of discharge of any part of the property subject to the lien if—

(A) there is paid over to the Secretary in partial satisfaction of the liability secured by the lien an amount determined by the Secretary, which shall not be less than the value, as determined by the Secretary, of the interest of the United States in the part to be so discharged, or

(B) the Secretary determines at any time that the interest of the United States in the part to be so discharged has no value.

In determining the value of the interest of the United States in the part to be so discharged, the Secretary shall give consideration to the value of such part and to such liens thereon as have priority over the lien of the United States.

(3) SUBSTITUTION OF PROCEEDS OF SALE.—Subject to such regulations as the Secretary may prescribe, the Secretary may issue a certificate of discharge of any part of the property subject to the lien if such part of the property is sold and, pursuant to an agreement with the Secretary, the proceeds of such sale are to be held, as a fund subject to the liens and claims of the United States, in the same manner and with the same priority as such liens and claims had with respect to the discharged property.

(4) RIGHT OF SUBSTITUTION OF VALUE.—

(A) IN GENERAL.—At the request of the owner of any property subject to any lien imposed by this chapter, the Secretary shall issue a certificate of discharge of such property if such owner—

(i) deposits with the Secretary an amount of money equal to the value of the interest of the United States (as determined by the Secretary) in the property; or

(ii) furnishes a bond acceptable to the Secretary in a like amount.

(B) REFUND OF DEPOSIT WITH INTEREST AND RELEASE OF BOND.—The Secretary shall refund the amount so deposited (and shall pay interest at the overpayment rate under section 6621), and shall release such bond, to the extent that the Secretary determines that—

(i) the unsatisfied liability giving rise to the lien can be satisfied from a source other than such property; or

(ii) the value of the interest of the United States in the property is less than the Secretary's prior determination of such value.

(C) USE OF DEPOSIT, ETC., IF ACTION TO CONTEST LIEN NOT FILED.—If no action is filed under section 7426(a)(4) within the period prescribed therefor, the Secretary shall, within 60 days after the expiration of such period—

(i) apply the amount deposited, or collect on such bond, to the extent necessary to satisfy the unsatisfied liability secured by the lien; and

(ii) refund (with interest as described in subparagraph (B)) any portion of the amount deposited which is not used to satisfy such liability.

(D) EXCEPTION.—Subparagraph (A) shall not apply if the owner of the property is the person whose unsatisfied liability gave rise to the lien.

Amendments

• 1998, IRS Restructuring and Reform Act of 1998 (P.L. 105-206)

P.L. 105-206, §3106(a):

Amended Code Sec. 6325(b) by adding at the end a new paragraph (4). **Effective** 7-22-98.

• 1976, Tax Reform Act of 1976 (P.L. 94-455)

P.L. 94-455, §1906(b)(13)(A):

Amended 1954 Code by substituting "Secretary" for "Secretary or his delegate" each place it appeared. **Effective** 2-1-77.

[Sec. 6325(c)]

(c) ESTATE OR GIFT TAX.—Subject to such regulations as the Secretary may prescribe, the Secretary may issue a certificate of discharge of any or all of the property subject to any lien imposed by section 6324 if the Secretary finds that the liability secured by such lien has been fully satisfied or provided for.

Amendments

• 1976, Tax Reform Act of 1976 (P.L. 94-455)

P.L. 94-455, §1906(b)(13)(A):

Amended 1954 Code by substituting "Secretary" for "Secretary or his delegate" each place it appeared. **Effective** 2-1-77.

[Sec. 6325(d)]

(d) SUBORDINATION OF LIEN.—Subject to such regulations as the Secretary may prescribe, the Secretary may issue a certificate of subordination of any lien imposed by this chapter upon any part of the property subject to such lien if—

(1) there is paid over to the Secretary an amount equal to the amount of the lien or interest to which the certificate subordinates the lien of the United States,

(2) the Secretary believes that the amount realizable by the United States from the property to which the certificate relates, or from any other property subject to the lien, will ultimately be increased by reason of the issuance of such certificate and that the ultimate collection of the tax liability will be facilitated by such subordination, or

(3) in the case of any lien imposed by section 6324B, if the Secretary determines that the United States will be adequately secured after such subordination.

Amendments

• 1978, Revenue Act of 1978 (P.L. 95-600)

P.L. 95-600, §513(a), (b):

Added Code Sec. 6325(d)(3). **Effective** for estates of decedents dying after 12-31-76.

• 1976, Tax Reform Act of 1976 (P.L. 94-455)

P.L. 94-455, §1906(b)(13)(A):

Amended 1954 Code by substituting "Secretary" for "Secretary or his delegate" each place it appeared. **Effective** 2-1-77.

[Sec. 6325(e)]

(e) NONATTACHMENT OF LIEN.—If the Secretary determines that, because of confusion of names or otherwise, any person (other than the person against whom the tax was assessed) is or may be injured by the appearance that a notice of lien filed under section 6323 refers to such person, the Secretary may issue a certificate that the lien does not attach to the property of such person.

Amendments

• 1976, Tax Reform Act of 1976 (P.L. 94-455)

P.L. 94-455, §1906(b)(13)(A):

Amended 1954 Code by substituting "Secretary" for "Secretary or his delegate" each place it appeared. **Effective** 2-1-77.

[Sec. 6325(f)]

(f) EFFECT OF CERTIFICATE.—

(1) CONCLUSIVENESS.—Except as provided in paragraphs (2) and (3), if a certificate is issued pursuant to this section by the Secretary and is filed in the same office as the notice of lien to which it relates (if such notice of lien has been filed) such certificate shall have the following effect:

(A) in the case of a certificate of release, such certificate shall be conclusive that the lien referred to in such certificate is extinguished;

(B) in the case of a certificate of discharge, such certificate shall be conclusive that the property covered by such certificate is discharged from the lien;

(C) in the case of a certificate of subordination, such certificate shall be conclusive that the lien or interest to which the lien of the United States is subordinated is superior to the lien of the United States; and

(D) in the case of a certificate of nonattachment, such certificate shall be conclusive that the lien of the United States does not attach to the property of the person referred to in such certificate.

(2) REVOCATION OF CERTIFICATE OF RELEASE OR NONATTACHMENT.—If the Secretary determines that a certificate of release or nonattachment of a lien imposed by section 6321 was issued erroneously or improvidently, or if a certificate of release of such lien was issued pursuant to a collateral agreement entered into in connection with a compromise under section 7122 which has been breached, and if the period of limitation on collection after assessment has not expired, the Secretary may revoke such certificate and reinstate the lien—

(A) by mailing notice of such revocation to the person against whom the tax was assessed at his last known address, and

(B) by filing notice of such revocation in the same office in which the notice of lien to which it relates was filed (if such notice of lien had been filed).

Such reinstated lien (i) shall be effective on the date notice of revocation is mailed to the taxpayer in accordance with the provisions of subparagraph (A), but not earlier than the date on which any required filing of notice of revocation is filed in accordance with the provisions of subparagraph (B), and (ii) shall have the same force and effect (as of such date), until the expiration of the period of limitation on collection after assessment, as a lien imposed by section 6321 (relating to lien for taxes).

(3) CERTIFICATES VOID UNDER CERTAIN CONDITIONS.—Notwithstanding any other provision of this subtitle, any lien imposed by this chapter shall attach to any property with respect to which a certificate of discharge has been issued if the person liable for the tax reacquires such property after such certificate has been issued.

Amendments

• 1976, Tax Reform Act of 1976 (P.L. 94-455)

P.L. 94-455, §1906(b)(13)(A):

Amended 1954 Code by substituting "Secretary" for "Secretary or his delegate" each place it appeared. **Effective** 2-1-77.

[Sec. 6325(g)]

(g) FILING OF CERTIFICATES AND NOTICES.—If a certificate or notice issued pursuant to this section may not be filed in the office designated by State law in which the notice of lien imposed by section 6321 is filed, such certificate or notice shall be effective if filed in the office of the clerk of the United States district court for the judicial district in which such office is situated.

[Sec. 6325(h)]

(h) CROSS REFERENCE.—

For provisions relating to bonds, see chapter 73 (sec. 7101 and following).

Amendments

• 1966, Federal Tax Lien Act of 1966 (P.L. 89-719)

P.L. 89-719, §103(a):

Amended Code Sec. 6325 to read as prior to amendment by P.L. 94-455. **Effective**, generally, after 11-2-66, regardless of when a lien or title of the U.S. arose or when a lien or interest of any other person was acquired. However, see the amendment note for Code Sec. 6323 for exceptions to this **effective** date. Prior to amendment, Code Sec. 6325 read as follows:

"Sec. 6325. Release of Lien or Partial Discharge of Property.

"(a) Release of Lien.—Subject to such rules or regulations as the Secretary or his delegate may prescribe, the Secretary or his delegate may issue a certificate of release of any lien imposed with respect to any internal revenue tax if—

"(1) Liability satisfied or unenforceable.—The Secretary or his delegate finds that the liability for the amount assessed, together with all interest in respect thereof, has been fully satisfied or has become legally unenforceable; or

"(2) Bond accepted.—There is furnished to the Secretary or his delegate and accepted by him a bond that is conditioned upon the payment of the amount assessed, together with all interest in respect thereof, within the time prescribed by law (including any extension of such time), and that is in accordance with such requirements relating to terms, conditions, and form of the bond and sureties thereon, as may be specified by such rules or regulations.

"(b) Partial Discharge of Property.—

"(1) Property double the amount of the liability.—Subject to such rules or regulations as the Secretary or his delegate may prescribe, the Secretary or his delegate may issue a certificate of discharge of any part of the property subject to any lien imposed under this chapter if the Secretary or his delegate finds that the fair market value of that part of such property remaining subject to the lien is at least double the amount of the unsatisfied liability secured by such lien and the amount of all other liens upon such property which have priority to such lien.

"(2) Part payment or interest of United States valueless.—Subject to such rules or regulations as the Secretary or his delegate may prescribe, the Secretary or his delegate may issue a certificate of discharge of any part of the property subject to the lien if—

"(A) there is paid over to the Secretary or his delegate in part satisfaction of the liability secured by the lien an amount determined by the Secretary or his delegate, which shall not be less than the value, as determined by the Secretary or his delegate, of the interest of the United States in the part to be so discharged, or

"(B) the Secretary or his delegate determines at any time that the interest of the United States in the part to be so discharged has no value.

In determining the value of the interest of the United States in the part to be so discharged, the Secretary or his delegate shall give consideration to the fair market value of such part and to such liens thereon as have priority to the lien of the United States.

"(c) Estate or Gift Tax.—Subject to such rules or regulations as the Secretary or his delegate may prescribe, the Secretary or his delegate may issue a certificate of discharge of any or all of the property subject to any lien imposed by section 6324 if the Secretary or his delegate finds that the liability secured by such lien has been fully satisfied or provided for.

"(d) Effect of Certificate of Release or Discharge.—A certificate of release or of discharge issued under this section shall be held conclusive that the lien upon the property covered by the certificate is extinguished.

"(e) Cross References.—

"(1) For single bond complying with the requirements of both subsection (a)(2) and section 6165, see section 7102.

"(2) For other provisions relating to bonds, see generally chapter 73.

"(3) For provisions relating to suits to enforce lien, see section 7403.

"(4) For provisions relating to suits to clear title to realty, see section 7424."

• 1958, Technical Amendments Act of 1958 (P.L. 85-866)

P.L. 85-866, §77(1):

Amended Code Sec. 6325(a)(1). **Effective** 1-1-54. Prior to amendment, Code Sec. 6325 (a)(1) read as follows:

"(1) Liability Satisfied or Unenforceable.—The Secretary or his delegate finds that the liability for the amount assessed, together with all interest in respect thereof, has been fully satisfied, has become legally unenforceable, or, in the case of the estate tax imposed by chapter 11 or the gift tax imposed by chapter 12, has been fully satisifed or provided for; or"

P.L. 85-866, §77(2), (3):

Amended Code Sec. 6325 by redesignating subsections (c) and (d) as (d) and (e), respectively, added a new subsection (c), and struck out the word "Partial" where it appeared in the heading and text preceding "Discharge". **Effective** 1-1-54.

[Sec. 6326]

SEC. 6326. ADMINISTRATIVE APPEAL OF LIENS.

[Sec. 6326(a)]

(a) IN GENERAL.—In such form and at such time as the Secretary shall prescribe by regulations, any person shall be allowed to appeal to the Secretary after the filing of a notice of a lien under this subchapter on the property or the rights to property of such person for a release of such lien alleging an error in the filing of the notice of such lien.

[Sec. 6326(b)]

(b) CERTIFICATE OF RELEASE.—If the Secretary determines that the filing of the notice of any lien was erroneous, the Secretary shall expeditiously (and, to the extent practicable, within 14 days after such determination) issue a certificate of release of such lien and shall include in such certificate a statement that such filing was erroneous.

Amendments

• 1988, Technical and Miscellaneous Revenue Act of 1988 (P.L. 100-647)

P.L. 100-647, §6238(a):

Redesignated Code Sec. 6326 as Code Sec. 6327 and inserted new Code Sec. 6326. **Effective** on the date which is 60 days after the date regulations are issued under Act Sec. 6238(b).

P.L. 100-647, §6238(b), provides:

(b) REGULATIONS.—The Secretary of the Treasury or the Secretary's delegate shall prescribe the regulations necessary to implement the administrative appeal provided for in the amendment made by subsection (a) within 180 days after the date of the enactment of this Act.

* * *

Subchapter D—Seizure of Property for Collection of Taxes

* * *

* * *

[Sec. 6331]

SEC. 6331. LEVY AND DISTRAINT.

[Sec. 6331(a)]

(a) AUTHORITY OF SECRETARY.—If any person liable to pay any tax neglects or refuses to pay the same within 10 days after notice and demand, it shall be lawful for the Secretary to collect such tax (and such further sum as shall be sufficient to cover the expenses of the levy) by levy upon all property and rights to property (except such property as is exempt under section 6334) belonging to such person or on which there is a lien provided in this chapter for the payment of such tax. Levy may be made upon the accrued salary or wages of any officer, employee, or elected official, of the United States, the District of Columbia, or any agency or instrumentality of the United States or the District of Columbia, by serving a notice of levy on the employer (as defined in section 3401(d)) of such officer, employee, or elected official. If the Secretary makes a finding that the collection of such tax is in jeopardy, notice and demand for immediate payment of such tax may be made by the Secretary and, upon failure or refusal to pay such tax, collection thereof by levy shall be lawful without regard to the 10-day period provided in this section.

Amendments

• 1998, IRS Restructuring and Reform Act of 1998 (P.L. 105-206)

P.L. 105-206, §3421, provides:

SEC. 3421. APPROVAL PROCESS FOR LIENS, LEVIES, AND SEIZURES.

(a) IN GENERAL.—The Commissioner of Internal Revenue shall develop and implement procedures under which—

(1) a determination by an employee to file a notice of lien or levy with respect to, or to levy or seize, any property or right to property would, where appropriate, be required to be reviewed by a supervisor of the employee before the action was taken; and

(2) appropriate disciplinary action would be taken against the employee or supervisor where the procedures under paragraph (1) were not followed.

(b) REVIEW PROCESS.—The review process under subsection (a)(1) may include a certification that the employee has—

(1) reviewed the taxpayer's information;

(2) verified that a balance is due; and

(3) affirmed that the action proposed to be taken is appropriate given the taxpayer's circumstances, considering the amount due and the value of the property or right to property.

(c) EFFECTIVE DATES.—

(1) IN GENERAL.—Except as provided in paragraph (2), this section shall take effect on the date of the enactment of this Act.

(2) AUTOMATED COLLECTION SYSTEM ACTIONS.—In the case of any action under an automated collection system, this section shall apply to actions initiated after December 31, 2000.

• 1976, Tax Reform Act of 1976 (P.L. 94-455)

P.L. 94-455, §1906(b)(13)(A):

Amended 1954 Code by substituting "Secretary" for "Secretary or his delegate" each place it appeared. **Effective** 2-1-77.

[Sec. 6331(b)]

(b) SEIZURE AND SALE OF PROPERTY.—The term "levy" as used in this title includes the power of distraint and seizure by any means. Except as otherwise provided in subsection (e), a levy shall extend only to property possessed and obligations existing at the time thereof. In any case in which the Secretary may levy upon property or rights to property, he may seize and sell such property or rights to property (whether real or personal, tangible or intangible).

Amendments

• 1984, Deficit Reduction Act of 1984 (P.L. 98-369)

P.L. 98-369, §714(o):

Amended Code Sec. 6331(b) by striking out "subsection (d)(3)" and inserting in lieu thereof "subsection (e)". **Effective** as if included in the provision of P.L. 97-248 to which it relates.

• 1976, Tax Reform Act of 1976 (P.L. 94-455)

P.L. 94-455, §1209(d)(2):

Substituted "Except as otherwise provided in subsection (d)(3), a levy" for "A levy" in the second sentence of Code Sec. 6331(b). **Effective** for levies made after 12-31-76; but P.L. 94-528, §2(c), **effective** 10-4-76, substituted "February 28, 1977" for "December 31, 1976" in P.L. 94-455, §1209(e).

P.L. 94-455, §1906(b)(13)(A):

Amended 1954 Code by substituting "Secretary" for "Secretary or his delegate" each place it appeared. **Effective** 2-1-77.

• 1966, Federal Tax Lien Act of 1966 (P.L. 89-719)

P.L. 89-719, §104(a):

Amended Code Sec. 6331(b) by adding the second sentence. **Effective**, generally, after 11-2-66, the date of enactment. However, see the amendment note for Code Sec. 6323 for exceptions to this **effective** date.

[Sec. 6331(c)]

(c) SUCCESSIVE SEIZURES.—Whenever any property or right to property upon which levy has been made by virtue of subsection (a) is not sufficient to satisfy the claim of the United States for which levy is made, the Secretary may, thereafter, and as often as may be necessary, proceed to levy in like manner upon any other property liable to levy of the person against whom such claim exists, until the amount due from him, together with all expenses, is fully paid.

Amendments

• 1976, Tax Reform Act of 1976 (P.L. 94-455)

P.L. 94-455, §1906(b)(13)(A):

Amended 1954 Code by substituting "Secretary" for "Secretary or his delegate" each place it appeared. **Effective** 2-1-77.

[Sec. 6331(d)]

(d) REQUIREMENT OF NOTICE BEFORE LEVY.—

(1) IN GENERAL.—Levy may be made under subsection (a) upon the salary or wages or other property of any person with respect to any unpaid tax only after the Secretary has notified such person in writing of his intention to make such levy.

(2) 30-DAY REQUIREMENT.—The notice required under paragraph (1) shall be—

(A) given in person,

(B) left at the dwelling or usual place of business of such person, or

(C) sent by certified or registered mail to such person's last known address,

no less than 30 days before the day of the levy.

(3) JEOPARDY.—Paragraph (1) shall not apply to a levy if the Secretary has made a finding under the last sentence of subsection (a) that the collection of tax is in jeopardy.

(4) INFORMATION INCLUDED WITH NOTICE.—The notice required under paragraph (1) shall include a brief statement which sets forth in simple and nontechnical terms—

(A) the provisions of this title relating to levy and sale of property,

(B) the procedures applicable to the levy and sale of property under this title,

(C) the administrative appeals available to the taxpayer with respect to such levy and sale and the procedures relating to such appeals,

(D) the alternatives available to taxpayers which could prevent levy on the property (including installment agreements under section 6159),

(E) the provisions of this title relating to redemption of property and release of liens on property,

(F) the procedures applicable to the redemption of property and the release of a lien on property under this title, and

(G) the provisions of section 7345 relating to the certification of seriously delinquent tax debts and the denial, revocation, or limitation of passports of individuals with such debts pursuant to section 32101 of the FAST Act.

Amendments

• 2015, Fixing America's Surface Transportation Act (P.L. 114-94)

P.L. 114-94, §32101(b)(2):

Amended Code Sec. 6331(d)(4) by striking "and" at the end of subparagraph (E), by striking the period at the end of subparagraph (F) and inserting ", and", and by adding at the end a new subparagraph (G). **Effective** 12-4-2015.

• 1988, Technical and Miscellaneous Revenue Act of 1988 (P.L. 100-647)

P.L. 100-647, §6236(a)(1)-(3):

Amended Code Sec. 6331(d) by striking out "10 days" in paragraph (2) and inserting in lieu thereof "30 days"; by striking out "10-DAY REQUIREMENT" in the heading of paragraph (2) and inserting in lieu thereof "30-DAY REQUIREMENT", and by adding at the end thereof new paragraph (4). **Effective** for levies issued on or after 7-1-89.

• 1982, Tax Equity and Fiscal Responsibility Act of 1982 (P.L. 97-248)

P.L. 97-248, §349(a):

Amended Code Sec. 6331(d). **Effective** for levies made after 12-31-82. Prior to amendment, Code Sec. 6331(d) read as follows:

"(d) SALARY AND WAGES.—

(1) IN GENERAL.—Levy may be made under subsection (a) upon the salary or wages of an individual with respect to any unpaid tax only after the Secretary has notified such individual in writing of his intention to make such levy. Such notice shall be given in person, left at the dwelling or usual place of business of such individual, or shall be sent by mail to such individual's last known address, no less than 10 days before the day of levy.

(2) JEOPARDY.—Paragraph (1) shall not apply to a levy if the Secretary has made a finding under the last sentence of subsection (a) that the collection of tax is in jeopardy.

(3) CONTINUING LEVY ON SALARY AND WAGES.—

(A) EFFECT OF LEVY.—The effect of a levy on salary or wages payable to or received by a taxpayer shall be continuous from the date such levy is first made until the liability out of which such levy arose is satisfied or becomes unenforceable by reason of lapse of time.

(B) RELEASE AND NOTICE OF RELEASE.—With respect to a levy described in subparagraph (A), the Secretary shall promptly release the levy when the liability out of which such levy arose is satisfied or becomes unenforceable by reason of lapse of time, and shall promptly notify the person upon whom such levy was made that such levy has been released."

• 1976, Tax Reform Act of 1976 (P.L. 94-455)

P.L. 94-455, §1209(d)(1):

Added Code Sec. 6331(d)(3). **Effective** for levies made after 2-28-77. [**effective** date amended by P.L. 94-528, §2(c)].

P.L. 94-455, §1209(d)(4):

Struck out the last sentence of Code Sec. 6331(d)(1). For **effective** date, see amendment note for P.L. 94-455, §1209(d)(1). Prior to striking, the last sentence of Code Sec. 6331(d)(1) read as follows:

No additional notice shall be required in the case of successive levies with respect to such tax.

P.L. 94-455, §1906(b)(13)(A):

Amended 1954 Code by substituting "Secretary" for "Secretary or his delegate" each place it appeared. **Effective** 2-1-77.

• 1971, Revenue Act of 1971 (P.L. 92-178)

P.L. 92-178, §211(a):

Added Code Sec. 6331(d) and redesignated former Code Sec. 6331(d) as Code Sec. 6331(e). **Effective** for levies made after 3-31-72.

[Sec. 6331(e)]

(e) CONTINUING LEVY ON SALARY AND WAGES.—The effect of a levy on salary or wages payable to or received by a taxpayer shall be continuous from the date such levy is first made until such levy is released under section 6343.

Amendments

• 1988, Technical and Miscellaneous Revenue Act of 1988 (P.L. 100-647)

P.L. 100-647, §6236(b)(1):

Amended Code Sec. 6331(e). **Effective** for levies issued on or after 7-1-89. Prior to amendment, Code Sec. 6331(e) read as follows:

(e) CONTINUING LEVY ON SALARY AND WAGES.—

(1) EFFECT OF LEVY.—The effect of a levy on salary or wages payable to or received by a taxpayer shall be continuous from the date such levy is first made until the liability out of which such levy arose is satisfied or becomes unenforceable by reason of lapse of time.

(2) RELEASE AND NOTICE OF RELEASE.—With respect to a levy described in paragraph (1), the Secretary shall promptly release the levy when the liability out of which such levy arose is satisfied or becomes unenforceable by reason of lapse of time, and shall promptly notify the person upon whom such levy was made that such levy has been released.

• 1982, Tax Equity and Fiscal Responsibility Act of 1982 (P.L. 97-248)

P.L. 97-248, §349(a):

Added Code Sec. 6331(e). **Effective** for levies made after 12-31-82.

[Sec. 6331(f)]

(f) UNECONOMICAL LEVY.—No levy may be made on any property if the amount of the expenses which the Secretary estimates (at the time of levy) would be incurred by the Secretary with respect to the levy and sale of such property exceeds the fair market value of such property at the time of levy.

Amendments

• 1988, Technical and Miscellaneous Revenue Act of 1988 (P.L. 100-647)

P.L. 100-647, §6236(d):

Amended Code Sec. 6331 by redesignating subsection (f) as subsection (h), and adding new subsection (f). **Effective** for levies issued on or after 7-1-89.

[Sec. 6331(g)]

(g) LEVY ON APPEARANCE DATE OF SUMMONS.—

(1) IN GENERAL.—No levy may be made on the property of any person on any day on which such person (or officer or employee of such person) is required to appear in response to a summons issued by the Secretary for the purpose of collecting any underpayment of tax.

(2) NO APPLICATION IN CASE OF JEOPARDY.—This subsection shall not apply if the Secretary finds that the collection of tax is in jeopardy.

Amendments

• 1988, Technical and Miscellaneous Revenue Act of 1988 (P.L. 100-647)

P.L. 100-647, §6236(d):

Amended Code Sec. 6331 by adding new subsection (g). **Effective** for levies issued on or after 7-1-89.

[Sec. 6331(h)]

(h) CONTINUING LEVY ON CERTAIN PAYMENTS.—

(1) IN GENERAL.—If the Secretary approves a levy under this subsection, the effect of such levy on specified payments to or received by a taxpayer shall be continuous from the date such levy is first made until such levy is released. Notwithstanding section 6334, such continuous levy shall attach to up to 15 percent of any specified payment due to the taxpayer.

(2) SPECIFIED PAYMENT.—For the purposes of paragraph (1), the term "specified payment" means—

(A) any Federal payment other than a payment for which eligibility is based on the income or assets (or both) of a payee,

(B) any payment described in paragraph (4), (7), (9), or (11) of section 6334(a), and

(C) any annuity or pension payment under the Railroad Retirement Act or benefit under the Railroad Unemployment Insurance Act.

(3) INCREASE IN LEVY FOR CERTAIN PAYMENTS.—Paragraph (1) shall be applied by substituting "100 percent" for "15 percent" in the case of any specified payment due to a vendor of property, goods, or services sold or leased to the Federal Government and by substituting "100 percent" for "15 percent" in the case of any specified payment due to a Medicare provider or supplier under title XVIII of the Social Security Act.

Amendments

• 2015, Medicare Access and CHIP Reauthorization Act of 2015 (P.L. 114-10)

P.L. 114-10, §413(a):

Amended Code Sec. 6331(h)(3) by striking "30 percent" and inserting "100 percent". **Effective** for payments made after 180 days after 4-16-2015.

• 2014, Stephen Beck, Jr., Achieving a Better Life Experience Act of 2014 (P.L. 113-295)

P.L. 113-295, §209(a), Division B:

Amended Code Sec. 6331(h)(3) by striking the period at the end and inserting "and by substituting '30 percent' for '15 percent' in the case of any specified payment due to a Medicare provider or supplier under title XVIII of the Social

Security Act.". **Effective** for payments made after 180 days after 12-19-2014.

• 2011, VOW to Hire Heroes Act of 2011 (P.L. 112-56)

P.L. 112-56, §301(a):

Amended Code Sec. 6331(h)(3) by striking "goods or services" and inserting "property, goods, or services". **Effective** for levies issued after 11-21-2011.

• 2004, American Jobs Creation Act of 2004 (P.L. 108-357)

P.L. 108-357, §887(a):

Amended Code Sec. 6331(h) by adding at the end a new paragraph (3). **Effective** 10-22-2004.

• 1998, IRS Restructuring and Reform Act of 1998 (P.L. 105-206)

P.L. 105-206, §6010(f):

Amended Code Sec. 6331(h)(1) by striking "The effect of a levy" and inserting "If the Secretary approves a levy under this subsection, the effect of such levy". **Effective** as if included in the provision of P.L. 105-34 to which it relates [**effective** for levies issued after 8-5-97.—CCH].

P.L. 105-206, §3421, provides:

SEC. 3421. APPROVAL PROCESS FOR LIENS, LEVIES, AND SEIZURES.

(a) IN GENERAL.—The Commissioner of Internal Revenue shall develop and implement procedures under which—

(1) a determination by an employee to file a notice of lien or levy with respect to, or to levy or seize, any property or right to property would, where appropriate, be required to be reviewed by a supervisor of the employee before the action was taken; and

(2) appropriate disciplinary action would be taken against the employee or supervisor where the procedures under paragraph (1) were not followed.

(b) REVIEW PROCESS.—The review process under subsection (a)(1) may include a certification that the employee has—

(1) reviewed the taxpayer's information;

(2) verified that a balance is due; and

(3) affirmed that the action proposed to be taken is appropriate given the taxpayer's circumstances, considering the amount due and the value of the property or right to property.

(c) EFFECTIVE DATES.—

(1) IN GENERAL.—Except as provided in paragraph (2), this section shall take effect on the date of the enactment of this Act.

(2) AUTOMATED COLLECTION SYSTEM ACTIONS.—In the case of any action under an automated collection system, this section shall apply to actions initiated after December 31, 2000.

• 1997, Taxpayer Relief Act of 1997 (P.L. 105-34)

P.L. 105-34, §1024(a)(1)-(2):

Amended Code Sec. 6331 by redesignating subsection (h) as subsection (i), and by inserting after subsection (g) a new subsection (h). **Effective** for levies issued after 8-5-97.

[Sec. 6331(i)]

(i) NO LEVY DURING PENDENCY OF PROCEEDINGS FOR REFUND OF DIVISIBLE TAX.—

(1) IN GENERAL.—No levy may be made under subsection (a) on the property or rights to property of any person with respect to any unpaid divisible tax during the pendency of any proceeding brought by such person in a proper Federal trial court for the recovery of any portion of such divisible tax which was paid by such person if—

(A) the decision in such proceeding would be res judicata with respect to such unpaid tax; or

(B) such person would be collaterally estopped from contesting such unpaid tax by reason of such proceeding.

(2) DIVISIBLE TAX.—For purposes of paragraph (1), the term "divisible tax" means—

(A) any tax imposed by subtitle C; and

(B) the penalty imposed by section 6672 with respect to any such tax.

(3) EXCEPTIONS.—

(A) CERTAIN UNPAID TAXES.—This subsection shall not apply with respect to any unpaid tax if—

(i) the taxpayer files a written notice with the Secretary which waives the restriction imposed by this subsection on levy with respect to such tax; or

(ii) the Secretary finds that the collection of such tax is in jeopardy.

(B) CERTAIN LEVIES.—This subsection shall not apply to—

(i) any levy to carry out an offset under section 6402; and

(ii) any levy which was first made before the date that the applicable proceeding under this subsection commenced.

(4) LIMITATION ON COLLECTION ACTIVITY; AUTHORITY TO ENJOIN COLLECTION.—

(A) LIMITATION ON COLLECTION.—No proceeding in court for the collection of any unpaid tax to which paragraph (1) applies shall be begun by the Secretary during the pendency of a proceeding under such paragraph. This subparagraph shall not apply to—

(i) any counterclaim in a proceeding under such paragraph; or

(ii) any proceeding relating to a proceeding under such paragraph.

(B) AUTHORITY TO ENJOIN.—Notwithstanding section 7421(a), a levy or collection proceeding prohibited by this subsection may be enjoined (during the period such prohibition is in force) by the court in which the proceeding under paragraph (1) is brought.

(5) SUSPENSION OF STATUTE OF LIMITATIONS ON COLLECTION.—The period of limitations under section 6502 shall be suspended for the period during which the Secretary is prohibited under this subsection from making a levy.

(6) PENDENCY OF PROCEEDING.—For purposes of this subsection, a proceeding is pending beginning on the date such proceeding commences and ending on the date that a final order or judgment from which an appeal may be taken is entered in such proceeding.

Amendments

• 1998, IRS Restructuring and Reform Act of 1998 (P.L. 105-206)

P.L. 105-206, §3433(a):

Amended Code Sec. 6331 by redesignating subsection (i) as subsection (j) and by inserting after subsection (h) a new subsection (i). **Effective** for unpaid tax attributable to tax periods beginning after 12-31-98.

• 1997, Taxpayer Relief Act of 1997 (P.L. 105-34)

P.L. 105-34, §1024(a)(1):

Amended Code Sec. 6331 by redesignating subsection (h) as subsection (i). **Effective** for levies issued after 8-5-97.

• 1988, Technical and Miscellaneous Revenue Act of 1988 (P.L. 100-647)

P.L. 100-647, §6236(d):

Amended Code Sec. 6331 by redesignating subsection (f) as subsection (h). **Effective** for levies issued on or after 7-1-89.

P.L. 100-647, §6236(b)(2):

Amended Code Sec. 6331(f), prior to amendment by Act Sec. 6236(d), by adding at the end thereof new paragraph (3). **Effective** for levies issued on or after 7-1-89.

• 1982, Tax Equity and Fiscal Responsibility Act of 1982 (P.L. 97-248)

P.L. 97-248, §349(a):

Redesignated Code Sec. 6331(e) as Code Sec. 6331(f).

• 1971, Revenue Act of 1971 (P.L. 92-178)

P.L. 92-178, §211(a):

Redesignated Code Sec. 6331(d) as Code Sec. 6331(e).

[Sec. 6331(j)]

(j) NO LEVY BEFORE INVESTIGATION OF STATUS OF PROPERTY.—

(1) IN GENERAL.—For purposes of applying the provisions of this subchapter, no levy may be made on any property or right to property which is to be sold under section 6335 until a thorough investigation of the status of such property has been completed.

(2) ELEMENTS IN INVESTIGATION.—For purposes of paragraph (1), an investigation of the status of any property shall include—

(A) a verification of the taxpayer's liability;

(B) the completion of an analysis under subsection (f);

(C) the determination that the equity in such property is sufficient to yield net proceeds from the sale of such property to apply to such liability; and

(D) a thorough consideration of alternative collection methods.

Amendments

• 1998, IRS Restructuring and Reform Act of 1998 (P.L. 105-206)

P.L. 105-206, §3444(a):

Amended Code Sec. 6331, as amended by Act Sec. 3433, by redesignating subsection (j) as subsection (k) and by inserting after subsection (i) a new subsection (j). **Effective** 7-22-98.

[Sec. 6331(k)]

(k) NO LEVY WHILE CERTAIN OFFERS PENDING OR INSTALLMENT AGREEMENT PENDING OR IN EFFECT.—

(1) OFFER-IN-COMPROMISE PENDING.—No levy may be made under subsection (a) on the property or rights to property of any person with respect to any unpaid tax—

(A) during the period that an offer-in-compromise by such person under section 7122 of such unpaid tax is pending with the Secretary; and

(B) if such offer is rejected by the Secretary, during the 30 days thereafter (and, if an appeal of such rejection is filed within such 30 days, during the period that such appeal is pending).

For purposes of subparagraph (A), an offer is pending beginning on the date the Secretary accepts such offer for processing.

(2) INSTALLMENT AGREEMENTS.—No levy may be made under subsection (a) on the property or rights to property of any person with respect to any unpaid tax—

(A) during the period that an offer by such person for an installment agreement under section 6159 for payment of such unpaid tax is pending with the Secretary;

(B) if such offer is rejected by the Secretary, during the 30 days thereafter (and, if an appeal of such rejection is filed within such 30 days, during the period that such appeal is pending);

(C) during the period that such an installment agreement for payment of such unpaid tax is in effect; and

(D) if such agreement is terminated by the Secretary, during the 30 days thereafter (and, if an appeal of such termination is filed within such 30 days, during the period that such appeal is pending).

(3) CERTAIN RULES TO APPLY.—Rules similar to the rules of—

(A) paragraphs (3) and (4) of subsection (i), and

(B) except in the case of paragraph (2)(C), paragraph (5) of subsection (i),

shall apply for purposes of this subsection.

Amendments

• 2002, Job Creation and Worker Assistance Act of 2002 (P.L. 107-147)

P.L. 107-147, §416(e)(1):

Amended Code Sec. 6331(k)(3). **Effective** 3-9-2002. Prior to amendment, Code Sec. 6331(k)(3) read as follows:

(3) CERTAIN RULES TO APPLY.—Rules similar to the rules of paragraphs (3) and (4) of subsection (i) shall apply for purposes of this subsection.

• 2000, Community Renewal Tax Relief Act of 2000 (P.L. 106-554)

P.L. 106-554, §313(b)(3):

Amended Code Sec. 6331(k)(3) by striking "(3), (4), and (5)" and inserting "(3) and (4)". **Effective** 12-21-2000.

• 1998, IRS Restructuring and Reform Act of 1998 (P.L. 105-206)

P.L. 105-206, §3462(b):

Amended Code Sec. 6331, as amended by Act Secs. 3433 and 3444, by redesignating subsection (k) as subsection (l) and by inserting after subsection (j) a new subsection (k). **Effective** for offers-in-compromise pending on or made after 12-31-99.

[Sec. 6331(l)]

(l) CROSS REFERENCES.—

(1) For provisions relating to jeopardy, see subchapter A of chapter 70.

(2) For proceedings applicable to sale of seized property, see section 6335.

(3) For release and notice of release of levy, see section 6343.

Amendments

• 1998, IRS Restructuring and Reform Act of 1998 (P.L. 105-206)

P.L. 105-206, §3433(a):

Amended Code Sec. 6331 by redesignating subsection (i) as subsection (j). **Effective** for unpaid tax attributable to tax periods beginning after 12-31-98.

P.L. 105-206, §3444(a):

Amended Code Sec. 6331, as amended by Act Sec. 3433, by redesignating subsection (j) as subsection (k). **Effective** 7-22-98.

P.L. 105-206, §3462(b):

Amended Code Sec. 6331, as amended by Act Secs. 3433 and 3444, by redesignating subsection (k) as subsection (l). **Effective** for offers-in-compromise pending on or made after 12-31-99.

[Sec. 6332]

SEC. 6332. SURRENDER OF PROPERTY SUBJECT TO LEVY.

[Sec. 6332(a)]

(a) REQUIREMENT.—Except as otherwise provided in this section, any person in possession of (or obligated with respect to) property or rights to property subject to levy upon which a levy has been made shall, upon demand of the Secretary, surrender such property or rights (or discharge such obligation) to the Secretary, except such part of the property or rights as is, at the time of such demand, subject to an attachment or execution under any judicial process.

Amendments

• 1990, Omnibus Budget Reconciliation Act of 1990 (P.L. 101-508)

P.L. 101-508, §11704(a)(27):

Amended Code Sec. 6332(a) by striking "subsections (b) and (c)" and inserting "this section". **Effective** 11-5-90.

• 1988, Technical and Miscellaneous Revenue Act of 1988 (P.L. 100-647)

P.L. 100-647, §6236(e)(2)(A):

Amended Code Sec. 6332(a) by striking out "subsection (b)" and inserting in lieu thereof "subsections (b) and (c)". **Effective** for levies issued on or after 7-1-89.

• 1976, Tax Reform Act of 1976 (P.L. 94-455)

P.L. 94-455, §1906(b)(13)(A):

Amended 1954 Code by substituting "Secretary" for "Secretary or his delegate" each place it appeared. **Effective** 2-1-77.

• 1966, Federal Tax Lien Act of 1966 (P.L. 89-719)

P.L. 89-719, §104(b):

Amended Code Sec. 6332(a) by substituting "Except as otherwise provided in subsection (b), any person" for "Any person". **Effective**, generally, after 11-2-66. However, see the amendment note for Code Sec. 6323 for exceptions to this **effective** date.

[Sec. 6332(b)]

(b) SPECIAL RULE FOR LIFE INSURANCE AND ENDOWMENT CONTRACTS.—

(1) IN GENERAL.—A levy on an organization with respect to a life insurance or endowment contract issued by such organization shall, without necessity for the surrender of the contract document, constitute a demand by the Secretary for payment of the amount described in paragraph (2) and the exercise of the right of the person against whom the tax is assessed to the advance of such amount. Such organization shall pay over such amount 90 days after service of notice of levy. Such notice shall include a certification by the Secretary that a copy of such notice has been mailed to the person against whom the tax is assessed at his last known address.

(2) SATISFACTION OF LEVY.—Such levy shall be deemed to be satisfied if such organization pays over to the Secretary the amount which the person against whom the tax is assessed could have had advanced to him by such organization on the date prescribed in paragraph (1) for the satisfaction of such levy, increased by the amount of any advance (including contractual interest thereon) made to such person on or after the date such organization had actual notice or knowledge (within the meaning of section 6323(i)(1)) of the existence of the lien with respect to which such levy is made, other than an advance (including contractual interest thereon) made

automatically to maintain such contract in force under an agreement entered into before such organization had such notice or knowledge.

(3) ENFORCEMENT PROCEEDINGS.—The satisfaction of a levy under paragraph (2) shall be without prejudice to any civil action for the enforcement of any lien imposed by this title with respect to such contract.

Amendments

• 1976, Tax Reform Act of 1976 (P.L. 94-455)

P.L. 94-455, §1906(b)(13)(A):

Amended 1954 Code by substituting "Secretary" for "Secretary or his delegate" each place it appeared. **Effective** 2-1-77.

• 1966, Federal Tax Lien Act of 1966 (P.L. 89-719)

P.L. 89-719, §104(b):

Amended Code Sec. 6332(b). **Effective,** generally, after 11-2-66. However, see the amendment note for Code Sec. 6323 for exceptions to this **effective** date. Prior to amendment, Code Sec. 6332(b) read as follows:

"(b) Penalty for Violation.—Any person who fails or refuses to surrender as required by subsection (a) any property or rights to property, subject to levy, upon demand by the Secretary or his delegate, shall be liable in his own person and estate to the United States in a sum equal to the value of the property or rights not so surrendered, but not exceeding the amount of the taxes for the collection of which such levy has been made, together with costs and interest on such sum at the rate of 6 percent per annum from the date of such levy."

[Sec. 6332(c)]

(c) SPECIAL RULE FOR BANKS.—Any bank (as defined in section 408(n)) shall surrender (subject to an attachment or execution under judicial process) any deposits (including interest thereon) in such bank only after 21 days after service of levy.

Amendments

• 1988, Technical and Miscellaneous Revenue Act of 1988 (P.L. 100-647)

P.L. 100-647, §6236(e)(1):

Amended Code Sec. 6332, as amended by title I of this Act, by redesignating subsections (c), (d), and (e) as subsections (d), (e), and (f), respectively, and by inserting after subsection (b) new subsection (c). **Effective** for levies issued on or after 7-1-89.

[Sec. 6332(d)]

(d) ENFORCEMENT OF LEVY.—

(1) EXTENT OF PERSONAL LIABILITY.—Any person who fails or refuses to surrender any property or rights to property, subject to levy, upon demand by the Secretary, shall be liable in his own person and estate to the United States in a sum equal to the value of the property or rights not so surrendered, but not exceeding the amount of taxes for the collection of which such levy has been made, together with costs and interest on such sum at the underpayment rate established under section 6621 from the date of such levy (or, in the case of a levy described in section 6331(d)(3), from the date such person would otherwise have been obligated to pay over such amounts to the taxpayer). Any amount (other than costs) recovered under this paragraph shall be credited against the tax liability for the collection of which levy was made.

(2) PENALTY FOR VIOLATION.—In addition to the personal liability imposed by paragraph (1), if any person required to surrender property or rights to property fails or refuses to surrender such property or rights to property without reasonable cause, such person shall be liable for a penalty equal to 50 percent of the amount recoverable under paragraph (1). No part of such penalty shall be credited against the tax liability for the collection of which such levy was made.

Amendments

• 1988, Technical and Miscellaneous Revenue Act of 1988 (P.L. 100-647)

P.L. 100-647, §6236(e)(1):

Amended Code Sec. 6332, as amended by title I of this Act, by redesignating subsection (c) as subsection (d). **Effective** for levies issued on or after 7-1-89.

• 1986, Tax Reform Act of 1986 (P.L. 99-514)

P.L. 99-514, §1511(c)(9):

Amended Code Sec. 6332(c)(1) by striking out "an annual rate established under section 6621" and inserting in lieu thereof "the underpayment rate established under section 6621". **Effective** for purposes of determining interest for periods after 12-31-86.

• 1976, Tax Reform Act of 1976 (P.L. 94-455)

P.L. 94-455, §1209(d)(3):

Added "(or, in the case of a levy described in section 6331(d)(3), from the date such person would otherwise have been obligated to pay over such amounts to the taxpayer)" immediately before the period at the end of the first sentence of Code Sec. 6332(c)(1). **Effective** for levies made after 2-28-77. [**effective** date changed by P.L. 94-528, § 2(c)].

P.L. 94-455, §1906(b)(13)(A):

Amended 1954 Code by substituting "Secretary" for "Secretary or his delegate" each place it appeared. **Effective** 2-1-77.

• 1975 (P.L. 93-625)

P.L. 93-625, §7(a)(2):

Amended Code Sec. 6332(c)(1) by substituting "an annual rate established under section 6621" for "the rate of 6 percent per annum". For **effective** date, see the historical comment for P.L. 93-625 following the text of Code Sec. 6621.

[Sec. 6332(e)]

(e) EFFECT OF HONORING LEVY.—Any person in possession of (or obligated with respect to) property or rights to property subject to levy upon which a levy has been made who, upon demand by the Secretary, surrenders such property or rights to property (or discharges such obligation) to the Secretary (or who pays a liability under subsection (d)(1)) shall be discharged from any obligation or liability to the delinquent taxpayer and any other person with respect to such property or rights to property arising from such surrender or payment.

Amendments

• 1988, Technical and Miscellaneous Revenue Act of 1988 (P.L. 100-647)

P.L. 100-647, §1015(t)(1)(A)-(B):

Amended Code Sec. 6332(d), prior to its redesignation by Act Sec. 6236(e)(1), by inserting "and any other person" after "delinquent taxpayer", and by striking out the last sentence thereof. **Effective** for levies issued after 11-10-88. Prior to being struck out, the last sentence of Code Sec. 6332(d) read as follows:

In the case of a levy which is satisfied pursuant to subsection (b), such organization shall also be discharged from any obligation or liability to any beneficiary arising from such surrender or payment.

P.L. 100-647, §6236(e)(1):

Amended Code Sec. 6332, as amended by title I of this Act, by redesignating subsection (d) as subsection (e). **Effective** for levies issued on or after 7-1-89.

P.L. 100-647, §6236(e)(2)(B):

Amended Code Sec. 6332(e), as redesignated, by striking out "subsection (c)(1)" and inserting in lieu thereof "subsection (d)(1)". **Effective** for levies issued on or after 7-1-89.

• 1976, Tax Reform Act of 1976 (P.L. 94-455)

P.L. 94-455, §1906(b)(13)(A):

Amended 1954 Code by substituting "Secretary" for "Secretary or his delegate" each place it appeared. **Effective** 2-1-77.

• 1966, Federal Tax Lien Act of 1966 (P.L. 89-719)

P.L. 89-719, §104(b):

Added Code Secs. 6332(c) and (d), and redesignated former Code Sec. 6332(c) as Code Sec. 6332(e). **Effective**, generally, after 11-2-66. However, see amendment note for Code Sec. 6323 for exceptions to this **effective** date.

[Sec. 6332(f)]

(f) PERSON DEFINED.—The term "person," as used in subsection (a), includes an officer or employee of a corporation or a member or employee of a partnership, who as such officer, employee, or member is under a duty to surrender the property or rights to property, or to discharge the obligation.

Amendments

• 1988, Technical and Miscellaneous Revenue Act of 1988 (P.L. 100-647)

P.L. 100-647, §6326(e)(1):

Amended Code Sec. 6332, as amended by title I of this Act, by redesignating subsection (e) as subsection (f). **Effective** for levies issued on or after 7-1-89.

• 1966, Federal Tax Lien Act of 1966 (P.L. 89-719)

P.L. 89-719, §104(b):

Redesignated former Code Sec. 6332(c) as Code Sec. 6332(e). **Effective**, generally, after 11-2-66. However, see the amendment note for Code Sec. 6323 for exceptions to this **effective** date.

* * *

[Sec. 6343]

SEC. 6343. AUTHORITY TO RELEASE LEVY AND RETURN PROPERTY.

[Sec. 6343(a)]

(a) RELEASE OF LEVY AND NOTICE OF RELEASE.—

(1) IN GENERAL.—Under regulations prescribed by the Secretary, the Secretary shall release the levy upon all, or part of, the property or rights to property levied upon and shall promptly notify the person upon whom such levy was made (if any) that such levy has been released if—

(A) the liability for which such levy was made is satisfied or becomes unenforceable by reason of lapse of time,

(B) release of such levy will facilitate the collection of such liability,

(C) the taxpayer has entered into an agreement under section 6159 to satisfy such liability by means of installment payments, unless such agreement provides otherwise,

(D) the Secretary has determined that such levy is creating an economic hardship due to the financial condition of the taxpayer, or

(E) the fair market value of the property exceeds such liability and release of the levy on a part of such property could be made without hindering the collection of such liability.

For purposes of subparagraph (C), the Secretary is not required to release such levy if such release would jeopardize the secured creditor status of the Secretary.

(2) EXPEDITED DETERMINATION ON CERTAIN BUSINESS PROPERTY.—In the case of any tangible personal property essential in carrying on the trade or business of the taxpayer, the Secretary shall provide for an expedited determination under paragraph (1) if levy on such tangible personal property would prevent the taxpayer from carrying on such trade or business.

(3) SUBSEQUENT LEVY.—The release of levy on any property under paragraph (1) shall not prevent any subsequent levy on such property.

Amendments

• 1988, Technical and Miscellaneous Revenue Act of 1988 (P.L. 100-647)

P.L. 100-647, §6236(f):

Amended Code Sec. 6343(a). **Effective** for levies issued on or after 7-1-89. Prior to amendment, Code Sec. 6343(a) read as follows:

(a) RELEASE OF LEVY.—It shall be lawful for the Secretary, under regulations prescribed by the Secretary, to release the levy upon all or part of the property or rights to property levied upon where the Secretary determines that such action will facilitate the collection of the liability, but such release shall not operate to prevent any subsequent levy.

• 1976, Tax Reform Act of 1976 (P.L. 94-455)

P.L. 94-455, §1906(b)(13)(A):

Amended 1954 Code by substituting "Secretary" for "Secretary or his delegate" each place it appeared. **Effective** 2-1-77.

[Sec. 6343(b)]

(b) RETURN OF PROPERTY.—If the Secretary determines that property has been wrongfully levied upon, it shall be lawful for the Secretary to return—

(1) the specific property levied upon,

(2) an amount of money equal to the amount of money levied upon, or

(3) an amount of money equal to the amount of money received by the United States from a sale of such property.

Property may be returned at any time. An amount equal to the amount of money levied upon or received from such sale may be returned at any time before the expiration of 2 years from the date of such levy. For purposes of paragraph (3), if property is declared purchased by the United States at a sale pursuant to section 6335(e) (relating to manner and conditions of sale), the United States shall be treated as having received an amount of money equal to the minimum price determined pursuant to such section or (if larger) the amount received by the United States from the resale of such property.

Amendments

• 2017, Tax Cuts and Jobs Act (P.L. 115-97)

P.L. 115-97, §11071(a):

Amended Code Sec. 6343(b) by striking "9 months" and inserting "2 years". For the **effective** date, see Act Sec. 11071(c), below.

P.L. 115-97, §11071(c), provides:

(c) EFFECTIVE DATE.—The amendments made by this section shall apply to—

(1) levies made after the date of the enactment of this Act, and

(2) levies made on or before such date if the 9-month period has not expired under section 6343(b) of the Internal Revenue Code of 1986 (without regard to this section) as of such date.

• 1976, Tax Reform Act of 1976 (P.L. 94-455)

P.L. 94-455, §1906(b)(13)(A):

Amended 1954 Code by substituting "Secretary" for "Secretary or his delegate" each place it appeared. **Effective** 2-1-77.

• 1966, Federal Tax Lien Act of 1966 (P.L. 89-719)

P.L. 89-719, §104(i):

Amended Code Sec. 6343 by adding "AND RETURN PROPERTY" in the title, by adding "(a) Release of Levy.—" immediately before "It shall be lawful", and by adding new subsection (b). **Effective**, generally, after 11-2-66. However, see the amendment note for Code Sec. 6323 for exceptions to this **effective** date.

[Sec. 6343(c)]

(c) INTEREST.—Interest shall be allowed and paid at the overpayment rate established under section 6621—

(1) in a case described in subsection (b)(2), from the date the Secretary receives the money to a date (to be determined by the Secretary) preceding the date of return by not more than 30 days, or

(2) in a case described in subsection (b)(3), from the date of the sale of the property to a date (to be determined by the Secretary) preceding the date of return by not more than 30 days.

Amendments

• 1986, Tax Reform Act of 1986 (P.L. 99-514)

P.L. 99-514, §1511(c)(10):

Amended Code Sec. 6343(c) by striking out "an annual rate established under section 6621" and inserting in lieu thereof "the overpayment rate established under section 6621". **Effective** for purposes of determining interest for periods after 12-31-86.

• 1979 (P.L. 96-167)

P.L. 96-167, §4:

Added new Code Sec. 6343(c). **Effective** for levies made after 12-29-79.

[Sec. 6343(d)]

(d) RETURN OF PROPERTY IN CERTAIN CASES.—If—

(1) any property has been levied upon, and

(2) the Secretary determines that—

(A) the levy on such property was premature or otherwise not in accordance with administrative procedures of the Secretary,

(B) the taxpayer has entered into an agreement under section 6159 to satisfy the tax liability for which the levy was imposed by means of installment payments, unless such agreement provides otherwise,

(C) the return of such property will facilitate the collection of the tax liability, or

(D) with the consent of the taxpayer or the National Taxpayer Advocate, the return of such property would be in the best interests of the taxpayer (as determined by the National Taxpayer Advocate) and the United States,

the provisions of subsection (b) shall apply in the same manner as if such property had been wrongly levied upon, except that no interest shall be allowed under subsection (c).

Amendments

• 1998, IRS Restructuring and Reform Act of 1998 (P.L. 105-206)

P.L. 105-206, §1102(d)(1)(B):

Amended Code Sec. 6343(d)(2)(D) by striking "Taxpayer Advocate" each place it appears and inserting "National Taxpayer Advocate". **Effective** 7-22-98. For a special rule, see Act Sec. 1102 (f)(3)-(4), below.

P.L. 105-206, §1102(f)(3)-(4), provides:

(3) NATIONAL TAXPAYER ADVOCATE.—Notwithstanding section 7803(c)(1)(B)(iv) of such Code, as added by this section, in appointing the first National Taxpayer Advocate after the date of the enactment of this Act, the Secretary of the Treasury—

(A) shall not appoint any individual who was an officer or employee of the Internal Revenue Service at any time during the 2-year period ending on the date of appointment, and

(B) need not consult with the Internal Revenue Service Oversight Board if the Oversight Board has not been appointed.

(4) CURRENT OFFICERS.—

(A) In the case of an individual serving as Commissioner of Internal Revenue on the date of the enactment of this Act who was appointed to such position before such date, the 5-year term required by section 7803(a)(1) of such Code, as added by this section, shall begin as of the date of such appointment.

(B) Clauses (ii), (iii), and (iv) of section 7803(c)(1)(B) of such Code, as added by this section, shall not apply to the individual serving as Taxpayer Advocate on the date of the enactment of this Act.

• 1996, Taxpayer Bill of Rights 2 (P.L. 104-168)

P.L. 104-168, §501(b):

Amended Code Sec. 6343 by adding at the end a new subsection (d). **Effective** 7-30-96.

[Sec. 6343(e)]

(e) RELEASE OF LEVY UPON AGREEMENT THAT AMOUNT IS NOT COLLECTIBLE.—In the case of a levy on the salary or wages payable to or received by the taxpayer, upon agreement with the taxpayer that the tax is not collectible, the Secretary shall release such levy as soon as practicable.

Amendments

• 1998, IRS Restructuring and Reform Act of 1998 (P.L. 105-206)

P.L. 105-206, §3432(a):

Amended Code Sec. 6343 by adding at the end a new subsection (e). **Effective** for levies imposed after 12-31-99.

[Sec. 6343(f)]

(f) INDIVIDUALS HELD HARMLESS ON WRONGFUL LEVY, ETC. ON RETIREMENT PLAN.—

(1) IN GENERAL.—If the Secretary determines that an individual's account or benefit under an eligible retirement plan (as defined in section 402(c)(8)(B)) has been levied upon in a case to which subsection (b) or (d)(2)(A) applies and property or an amount of money is returned to the individual—

(A) the individual may contribute such property or an amount equal to the sum of—

(i) the amount of money so returned by the Secretary, and

(ii) interest paid under subsection (c) on such amount of money,

into such eligible retirement plan if such contribution is permitted by the plan, or into an individual retirement plan (other than an endowment contract) to which a rollover contribution of a distribution from such eligible retirement plan is permitted, but only if such contribution is made not later than the due date (not including extensions) for filing the return of tax for the taxable year in which such property or amount of money is returned, and

(B) the Secretary shall, at the time such property or amount of money is returned, notify such individual that a contribution described in subparagraph (A) may be made.

(2) TREATMENT AS ROLLOVER.—The distribution on account of the levy and any contribution under paragraph (1) with respect to the return of such distribution shall be treated for purposes of this title as if such distribution and contribution were described in section 402(c), 402A(c)(3), 403(a)(4), 403(b)(8), 408(d)(3), 408A(d)(3), or 457(e)(16), whichever is applicable; except that—

(A) the contribution shall be treated as having been made for the taxable year in which the distribution on account of the levy occurred, and the interest paid under subsection (c) shall be treated as earnings within the plan after the contribution and shall not be included in gross income, and

(B) such contribution shall not be taken into account under section 408(d)(3)(B).

(3) REFUND, ETC., OF INCOME TAX ON LEVY.—

(A) IN GENERAL.—If any amount is includible in gross income for a taxable year by reason of a distribution on account of a levy referred to in paragraph (1) and any portion of such amount is treated as a rollover contribution under paragraph (2), any tax imposed by chapter 1 on such portion shall not be assessed, and if assessed shall be abated, and if collected shall be credited or refunded as an overpayment made on the due date for filing the return of tax for such taxable year.

(B) EXCEPTION.—Subparagraph (A) shall not apply to a rollover contribution under this subsection which is made from an eligible retirement plan which is not a Roth IRA or a designated Roth account (within the meaning of section 402A) to a Roth IRA or a designated Roth account under an eligible retirement plan.

(4) INTEREST.—Notwithstanding subsection (d), interest shall be allowed under subsection (c) in a case in which the Secretary makes a determination described in subsection (d)(2)(A) with respect to a levy upon an individual retirement plan.

(5) TREATMENT OF INHERITED ACCOUNTS.—For purposes of paragraph (1)(A), section 408(d)(3)(C) shall be disregarded in determining whether an individual retirement plan is a plan to which a rollover contribution of a distribution from the plan levied upon is permitted.

Amendments

• 2018, Bipartisan Budget Act of 2018 (P.L. 115-123)

P.L. 115-123, §41104(a), Div. D:

Amended Code Sec. 6343 by adding at the end a new subsection (f). **Effective** for amounts paid under Code Sec. 6343(b), (c), and (d)(2)(A) in tax years beginning after 12-31-2017.

* * *

CHAPTER 65—ABATEMENTS, CREDITS, AND REFUNDS

* * *

Subchapter A—Procedure in General

* * *

[Sec. 6401]

SEC. 6401. AMOUNTS TREATED AS OVERPAYMENTS.

[Sec. 6401(a)]

(a) ASSESSMENT AND COLLECTION AFTER LIMITATION PERIOD.—The term "overpayment" includes that part of the amount of the payment of any internal revenue tax which is assessed or collected after the expiration of the period of limitation properly applicable thereto.

* * *

[Sec. 6401(c)]

(c) RULE WHERE NO TAX LIABILITY.—An amount paid as tax shall not be considered not to constitute an overpayment solely by reason of the fact that there was no tax liability in respect of which such amount was paid.

* * *

[Sec. 6402]

SEC. 6402. AUTHORITY TO MAKE CREDITS OR REFUNDS.

[Sec. 6402(a)]

(a) GENERAL RULE.—In the case of any overpayment, the Secretary, within the applicable period of limitations, may credit the amount of such overpayment, including any interest allowed thereon, against any liability in respect of an internal revenue tax on the part of the person who made the overpayment and shall, subject to subsections (c), (d), (e), and (f), refund any balance to such person.

Amendments

• 2018, Tax Technical Corrections Act of 2018 (P.L. 115-141)

P.L. 115-141, §401(a)(285), Div. U:

Amended Code Sec. 6402(a) by striking "(f) refund" and inserting "(f), refund". **Effective** 3-23-2018.

• 2008, SSI Extension for Elderly and Disabled Refugees Act (P.L. 110-328)

P.L. 110-328, §3(d)(1):

Amended Code Sec. 6402(a) by striking "(c), (d), and (e)," and inserting "(c), (d), (e), and (f)". **Effective** for refunds payable under Code Sec. 6402 on or after 9-30-2008.

• 1998, IRS Restructuring and Reform Act of 1998 (P.L. 105-206)

P.L. 105-206, §3711(c)(1):

Amended Code Sec. 6402(a) by striking "(c) and [or] (d)" and inserting "(c), (d), and (e)". **Effective** for refunds payable under Code Sec. 6402 after 12-31-99.

• 1997, Balanced Budget Act of 1997 (P.L. 105-33)

P.L. 105-33, §5514(a)(1):

Struck the changes made by Act Sec. 110(l)(7)(A) of P.L. 104-193, which amended Code Sec. 6402(a) by striking "(c) or (d)" each place it appeared and inserting "(c), (d), or (e)". Thus, the provisions of law amended by such section are restored as if it had not been enacted. **Effective** 7-1-97.

• 1996, Personal Responsibility and Work Opportunity Reconciliation Act of 1996 (P.L. 104-193)

P.L. 104-193, §110(l)(7)(A):

Amended Code Sec. 6402(a) by striking "(c) and (d)" and inserting "(c), (d), and (e)". **Effective** 7-1-97.

• 1984, Deficit Reduction Act of 1984 (P.L. 98-369)

P.L. 98-369, §2653(b)(2):

Amended Code Sec. 6402(a) by striking out "subsection (c)" and inserting in lieu thereof "subsections (c) and (d)". **Effective** with respect to refunds payable under section 6402 of the Internal Revenue Code of 1954 after 12-31-85 [**effective** date changed by P.L. 100-485 and P.L. 102-164].

• 1981, Omnibus Budget Reconciliation Act of 1981 (P.L. 97-35)

P.L. 97-35, §2331(c)(1):

Amended Code Sec. 6402(a) by striking out "shall refund" and inserting in lieu thereof "shall, subject to subsection (c), refund". For the **effective** date, see the historical comment for P.L. 97-35 following Code Sec. 6402(c).

• 1976, Tax Reform Act of 1976 (P.L. 94-455)

P.L. 94-455, §1906(b)(13)(A):

Amended 1954 Code by substituting "Secretary" for "Secretary or his delegate" each place it appeared. **Effective** 2-1-77.

* * *

[Sec. 6402(c)]

(c) OFFSET OF PAST-DUE SUPPORT AGAINST OVERPAYMENTS.—The amount of any overpayment to be refunded to the person making the overpayment shall be reduced by the amount of any past-due support (as defined in section 464(c) of the Social Security Act) owed by that person of which the Secretary has been notified by a State in accordance with section 464 of such Act. The Secretary shall remit the amount by which the overpayment is so reduced to the State collecting such support and notify the person making the overpayment that so much of the overpayment as was necessary to satisfy his obligation for past-due support has been paid to the State. The Secretary shall apply a reduction under this subsection first to an amount certified by the State as past due support under section 464 of the Social Security Act before any other reductions allowed by law. This subsection shall be applied to an overpayment prior to its being credited to a person's future liability for an internal revenue tax.

Amendments

• 2018, Tax Technical Corrections Act of 2018 (P.L. 115-141)

P.L. 115-141, §401(a)(286), Div. U:

Amended Code Sec. 6402(c) by striking "of of" and inserting "of". **Effective** 3-23-2018.

• 2006, Deficit Reduction Act of 2005 (P.L. 109-171)

P.L. 109-171, §7301(d)(1)-(2):

Amended Code Sec. 6402(c) by striking in the first sentence "the Social Security Act." and inserting "of such Act."; and by striking the third sentence and inserting the following: "The Secretary shall apply a reduction under this subsection first to an amount certified by the State as past due support under section 464 of the Social Security Act before any other reductions allowed by law.". **Effective**, generally, 10-1-2009. For a special rule, see Act Sec. 7301(e), below. Prior to being stricken the third sentence of Code Sec. 6402(c) read as follows:

A reduction under this subsection shall be applied first to satisfy any past-due support which has been assigned to the State under section 402(a)(26) or 471(a)(17) of the Social Security Act, and shall be applied to satisfy any other past-due support after any other reductions allowed by law (but before a credit against future liability for an internal revenue tax) have been made.

P.L. 109-171, §7301(e), provides:

(e) EFFECTIVE DATE.—

(1) IN GENERAL.—Except as otherwise provided in this section, the amendments made by the preceding provisions of this section shall take effect on October 1, 2009, and shall apply to payments under parts A and D of title IV of the Social Security Act for calendar quarters beginning on or after such date, and without regard to whether regulations to implement the amendments (in the case of State programs operated under such part D) are promulgated by such date.

(2) STATE OPTION TO ACCELERATE EFFECTIVE DATE.—Notwithstanding paragraph (1), a State may elect to have the amendments made by the preceding provisions of this section apply to the State and to amounts collected by the State (and the payments under parts A and D), on and after such date as the State may select that is not earlier than October 1, 2008, and not later than September 30, 2009.

• 1984, Child Support Enforcement Amendments of 1984 (P.L. 98-378)

P.L. 98-378, §21(e)(1):

Amended Code Sec. 6402(c) by striking out "to which such support has been assigned" and inserting in lieu thereof "collecting such support"; and by inserting before the last sentence thereof "A reduction under this subsection shall be applied first to satisfy any past-due support which has been assigned to the State under section 402(a)(26) or 471(a)(17) of the Social Security Act, and shall be applied to satisfy any other past-due support after any other reductions allowed by law (but before a credit against future liability for an internal revenue tax) have been made." **Effective** with respect to refunds payable under Code Sec. 6402 after 12-31-85.

• 1981, Omnibus Budget Reconciliation Act of 1981 (P.L. 97-35)

P.L. 97-35, §2331(c)(2):

Added Code Sec. 6402(c). **Effective** as noted in Act Sec. 2336, below.

P.L. 97-35, §2336, provides:

SEC. 2336. (a) Except as otherwise specifically provided in the preceding sections of this chapter or in subsection (b), the provisions of this chapter and the amendments and repeals made by this chapter shall become effective on October 1, 1981.

(b) If a State agency administering a plan approved under part D of title IV of the Social Security Act demonstrates, to the satisfaction of the Secretary of Health and Human Services, that it cannot, by reason of State law, comply with the requirements of an amendment made by this chapter to which the effective date specified in subsection (a) applies, the Secretary may prescribe that, in the case of such State, the amendment will become effective beginning with the first month beginning after the close of the first session of such State's legislature ending on or after October 1, 1981. For purposes of the preceding sentence, the term "session of a State's legislature" includes any regular, special, budget, or other session of a State legislature.

[Sec. 6402(d)]

(d) COLLECTION OF DEBTS OWED TO FEDERAL AGENCIES.—

(1) IN GENERAL.—Upon receiving notice from any Federal agency that a named person owes a past-due legally enforceable debt (other than past-due support subject to the provisions of subsection (c)) to such agency, the Secretary shall—

(A) reduce the amount of any overpayment payable to such person by the amount of such debt;

(B) pay the amount by which such overpayment is reduced under subparagraph (A) to such agency; and

(C) notify the person making such overpayment that such overpayment has been reduced by an amount necessary to satisfy such debt.

(2) PRIORITIES FOR OFFSET.—Any overpayment by a person shall be reduced pursuant to this subsection after such overpayment is reduced pursuant to subsection (c) with respect to past-due support collected pursuant to an assignment under section 408(a)(3) of the Social Security Act (42 U.S.C. 608(a)(3)) and before such overpayment is reduced pursuant to subsections (e) and (f) and before such overpayment is credited to the future liability for tax of such person pursuant to subsection (b). If the Secretary receives notice from a Federal agency or agencies of more than one debt subject to paragraph (1) that is owed by a person to such agency or agencies, any overpayment by such person shall be applied against such debts in the order in which such debts accrued.

(3) TREATMENT OF OASDI OVERPAYMENTS.—

(A) REQUIREMENTS.—Paragraph (1) shall apply with respect to an OASDI overpayment only if the requirements of paragraphs (1) and (2) of section 3720A(f) of title 31, United States Code, are met with respect to such overpayment.

(B) NOTICE; PROTECTION OF OTHER PERSONS FILING JOINT RETURN.—

(i) NOTICE.—In the case of a debt consisting of an OASDI overpayment, if the Secretary determines upon receipt of the notice referred to in paragraph (1) that the refund from which the reduction described in paragraph (1)(A) would be made is based upon a joint return, the Secretary shall—

(I) notify each taxpayer filing such joint return that the reduction is being made from a refund based upon such return, and

(II) include in such notification a description of the procedures to be followed, in the case of a joint return, to protect the share of the refund which may be payable to another person.

(ii) ADJUSTMENTS BASED ON PROTECTIONS GIVEN TO OTHER TAXPAYERS ON JOINT RETURN.—If the other person filing a joint return with the person owing the OASDI overpayment takes appropriate action to secure his or her proper share of the refund subject to reduction under this subsection, the Secretary shall pay such share to such other person. The Secretary shall deduct the amount of such payment from amounts which are derived from subsequent reductions in refunds under this subsection and are payable to a trust fund referred to in subparagraph (C).

(C) DEPOSIT OF AMOUNT OF REDUCTION INTO APPROPRIATE TRUST FUND.—In lieu of payment, pursuant to paragraph (1)(B), of the amount of any reduction under this subsection to the Commissioner of Social Security, the Secretary shall deposit such amount in the Federal Old-Age and Survivors Insurance Trust Fund or the Federal Disability Insurance Trust Fund, whichever is certified to the Secretary as appropriate by the Commissioner of Social Security.

(D) OASDI OVERPAYMENT.—For purposes of this paragraph, the term "OASDI overpayment" means any overpayment of benefits made to an individual under title II of the Social Security Act.

Amendments

• 2018, Tax Technical Corrections Act of 2018 (P.L. 115-141)

P.L. 115-141, §401(a)(287), Div. U:

Amended Code Sec. 6402(d)(2) by striking "section 402(a)(26) of the Social Security Act" and inserting "section 408(a)(3) of the Social Security Act (42 U.S.C. 608(a)(3))". **Effective** 3-23-2018.

• 2008, SSI Extension for Elderly and Disabled Refugees Act (P.L. 110-328)

P.L. 110-328, §3(d)(2):

Amended Code Sec. 6402(d)(2) by striking "and before such overpayment is reduced pursuant to subsection (e)" and inserting "and before such overpayment is reduced pursuant to subsections (e) and (f)". **Effective** for refunds payable under Code Sec. 6402 on or after 9-30-2008.

• 1998, IRS Restructuring and Reform Act of 1998 (P.L. 105-206)

P.L. 105-206, §3711(c)(2):

Amended Code Sec. 6402(d)(2) by striking "and before such overpayment" and inserting "and before such overpayment is reduced pursuant to subsection (e) and before such overpayment". **Effective** for refunds payable under Code Sec. 6402 after 12-31-99.

• 1994, Social Security Independence and Program Improvements Act of 1994 (P.L. 103-296)

P.L. 103-296, §108(h)(7):

Amended Code Sec. 6402(d)(3)(C) by striking "Secretary of Health and Human Services" each place it appears and inserting "Commissioner of Social Security". **Effective** 3-31-95.

• 1990, Omnibus Budget Reconciliation Act of 1990 (P.L. 101-508)

P.L. 101-508, §5129(c)(1)(A):

Amended Code Sec. 6402(d)(1) by striking "any OASDI overpayment and" after "other than". **Effective** 1-1-91, and shall not apply to refunds to which the amendments made by section 2653 of the Deficit Reduction Act of 1984 (98 Stat. 1153) do not apply.

P.L. 101-508, §5129(c)(1)(B):

Amended Code Sec. 6402(d) by striking paragraph (3) and inserting new paragraph (3). **Effective** 1-1-91, and shall not apply to refunds to which the amendments made by section 2653 of P.L. 98-369 (98 Stat. 1153) do not apply. Prior to amendment, paragraph (3) read as follows:

(3) DEFINITIONS.—For purposes of this subsection the term "OASDI overpayment" means any overpayment of benefits made to an individual under title II of the Social Security Act.

• 1984, Deficit Reduction Act of 1984 (P.L. 98-369)

P.L. 98-369, §2653(b)(1):

Amended Code Sec. 6402 by adding subsection (d). **Effective** with respect to refunds payable under section 6402 of the Internal Revenue Code of 1954 after 12-31-85 **[effective date changed by P.L. 100-485 and P.L. 102-164]**.

[Sec. 6402(e)]

(e) COLLECTION OF PAST-DUE, LEGALLY ENFORCEABLE STATE INCOME TAX OBLIGATIONS.—

(1) IN GENERAL.—Upon receiving notice from any State that a named person owes a past-due, legally enforceable State income tax obligation to such State, the Secretary shall, under such conditions as may be prescribed by the Secretary—

(A) reduce the amount of any overpayment payable to such person by the amount of such State income tax obligation;

(B) pay the amount by which such overpayment is reduced under subparagraph (A) to such State and notify such State of such person's name, taxpayer identification number, address, and the amount collected; and

(C) notify the person making such overpayment that the overpayment has been reduced by an amount necessary to satisfy a pastdue, legally enforceable State income tax obligation.

If an offset is made pursuant to a joint return, the notice under subparagraph (B) shall include the names, taxpayer identification numbers, and addresses of each person filing such return.

(2) OFFSET PERMITTED ONLY AGAINST RESIDENTS OF STATE SEEKING OFFSET.—Paragraph (1) shall apply to an overpayment by any person for a taxable year only if the address shown on the Federal return for such taxable year of the overpayment is an address within the State seeking the offset.

(3) PRIORITIES FOR OFFSET.—Any overpayment by a person shall be reduced pursuant to this subsection—

(A) after such overpayment is reduced pursuant to—

(i) subsection (a) with respect to any liability for any internal revenue tax on the part of the person who made the overpayment;

(ii) subsection (c) with respect to past-due support; and

(iii) subsection (d) with respect to any past-due, legally enforceable debt owed to a Federal agency; and

(B) before such overpayment is credited to the future liability for any Federal internal revenue tax of such person pursuant to subsection (b).

If the Secretary receives notice from one or more agencies of the State of more than one debt subject to paragraph (1) or subsection (f) that is owed by such person to such an agency, any overpayment by such person shall be applied against such debts in the order in which such debts accrued.

(4) NOTICE; CONSIDERATION OF EVIDENCE.— No State may take action under this subsection until such State—

(A) notifies by certified mail with return receipt the person owing the past-due State income tax liability that the State proposes to take action pursuant to this section;

(B) gives such person at least 60 days to present evidence that all or part of such liability is not past-due or not legally enforceable;

(C) considers any evidence presented by such person and determines that an amount of such debt is past-due and legally enforceable; and

(D) satisfies such other conditions as the Secretary may prescribe to ensure that the determination made under subparagraph (C) is valid and that the State has made reasonable efforts to obtain payment of such State income tax obligation.

(5) PAST-DUE, LEGALLY ENFORCEABLE STATE INCOME TAX OBLIGATION.—For purposes of this subsection, the term "past-due, legally enforceable State income tax obligation" means a debt—

(A)(i) which resulted from—

(I) a judgment rendered by a court of competent jurisdiction which has determined an amount of State income tax to be due; or

(II) a determination after an administrative hearing which has determined an amount of State income tax to be due; and

(ii) which is no longer subject to judicial review; or

(B) which resulted from a State income tax which has been assessed but not collected, the time for redetermination of which has expired, and which has not been delinquent for more than 10 years.

For purposes of this paragraph, the term "State income tax" includes any local income tax administered by the chief tax administration agency of the State.

(6) REGULATIONS.—The Secretary shall issue regulations prescribing the time and manner in which States must submit notices of past-due, legally enforceable State income tax obligations and the necessary information that must be contained in or accompany such notices. The regulations shall specify the types of State income taxes and the minimum amount of debt to which the reduction procedure established by paragraph (1) may be applied. The regulations may require States to pay a fee to reimburse the Secretary for the cost of applying such procedure. Any fee paid to the Secretary pursuant to the preceding sentence shall be used to reimburse appropriations which bore all or part of the cost of applying such procedure.

(7) ERRONEOUS PAYMENT TO STATE.—Any State receiving notice from the Secretary that an erroneous payment has been made to such State under paragraph (1) shall pay promptly to the Secretary, in accordance with such regulations as the Secretary may prescribe, an amount equal to the amount of such erroneous payment (without regard to whether any other amounts payable to such State under such paragraph have been paid to such State).

Amendments

• 2008, SSI Extension for Elderly and Disabled Refugees Act (P.L. 110-328)

P.L. 110-328, §3(d)(3):

Amended the last sentence of Code Sec. 6402(e)(3) by inserting "or subsection (f)" after "paragraph (1)". **Effective** for refunds payable under Code Sec. 6402 on or after 9-30-2008.

• 1998, IRS Restructuring and Reform Act of 1998 (P.L. 105-206)

P.L. 105-206, §3711(a):

Amended Code Sec. 6402, as amended by Act Sec. 3505(a), by redesignating subsections (e) through (j) as subsections (f) through (k), respectively, and by inserting after subsection (d) a new subsection (e). **Effective** for refunds payable under Code Sec. 6402 after 12-31-99.

• 1997, Balanced Budget Act of 1997 (P.L. 105-33)

P.L. 105-33, §5514(a)(1):

Struck the change made by Act Sec. 110(l)(7)(C) of P.L. 104-193, which added a new Code Sec. 6402(e). Thus, subsection (e) of Code Sec. 6402 never took effect, and Code Sec. 6402 is restored as if Act Sec. 110(l)(7)(C) was never enacted. **Effective** 7-1-97. Prior to being stricken, Code Sec. 6402(e) read as follows:

(e) COLLECTION OF OVERPAYMENTS UNDER TITLE IV-A OF THE SOCIAL SECURITY ACT.—The amount of any overpayment to be refunded to the person making the overpayment shall be reduced (after reductions pursuant to subsections (c) and (d), but before a credit against future liability for an internal revenue tax) in accordance with section 405(e) of the Social Security Act (concerning recovery of overpayments to individuals under State plans approved under part A of title IV of such Act).

• 1996, Personal Responsibility and Work Opportunity Reconciliation Act of 1996 (P.L. 104-193)

P.L. 104-193, §110(l)(7)(B)-(C):

Amended Code Sec. 6402 by redesignating subsections (e) through (i) as subsections (f) through (j) respectively; and by inserting after subsection (d) a new subsection (e). **Effective** 7-1-97.

[Sec. 6402(f)]

(f) COLLECTION OF UNEMPLOYMENT COMPENSATION DEBTS.—

(1) IN GENERAL.—Upon receiving notice from any State that a named person owes a covered unemployment compensation debt to such State, the Secretary shall, under such conditions as may be prescribed by the Secretary—

(A) reduce the amount of any overpayment payable to such person by the amount of such covered unemployment compensation debt;

(B) pay the amount by which such overpayment is reduced under subparagraph (A) to such State and notify such State of such person's name, taxpayer identification number, address, and the amount collected; and

(C) notify the person making such overpayment that the overpayment has been reduced by an amount necessary to satisfy a covered unemployment compensation debt.

If an offset is made pursuant to a joint return, the notice under subparagraph (C) shall include information related to the rights of a spouse of a person subject to such an offset.

(2) PRIORITIES FOR OFFSET.—Any overpayment by a person shall be reduced pursuant to this subsection—

(A) after such overpayment is reduced pursuant to—

(i) subsection (a) with respect to any liability for any internal revenue tax on the part of the person who made the overpayment;

(ii) subsection (c) with respect to past-due support; and

(iii) subsection (d) with respect to any past-due, legally enforceable debt owed to a Federal agency; and

(B) before such overpayment is credited to the future liability for any Federal internal revenue tax of such person pursuant to subsection (b).

If the Secretary receives notice from a State or States of more than one debt subject to paragraph (1) or subsection (e) that is owed by a person to such State or States, any overpayment by such person shall be applied against such debts in the order in which such debts accrued.

(3) NOTICE; CONSIDERATION OF EVIDENCE.—No State may take action under this subsection until such State—

(A) notifies the person owing the covered unemployment compensation debt that the State proposes to take action pursuant to this section;

(B) provides such person at least 60 days to present evidence that all or part of such liability is not legally enforceable or is not a covered unemployment compensation debt;

(C) considers any evidence presented by such person and determines that an amount of such debt is legally enforceable and is a covered unemployment compensation debt; and

(D) satisfies such other conditions as the Secretary may prescribe to ensure that the determination made under subparagraph (C) is valid and that the State has made reasonable efforts to obtain payment of such covered unemployment compensation debt.

(4) COVERED UNEMPLOYMENT COMPENSATION DEBT.—For purposes of this subsection, the term "covered unemployment compensation debt" means—

(A) a past-due debt for erroneous payment of unemployment compensation due to fraud or the person's failure to report earnings which has become final under the law of a

State certified by the Secretary of Labor pursuant to section 3304 and which remains uncollected;

(B) contributions due to the unemployment fund of a State for which the State has determined the person to be liable and which remain uncollected; and

(C) any penalties and interest assessed on such debt.

(5) REGULATIONS.—

(A) IN GENERAL.—The Secretary may issue regulations prescribing the time and manner in which States must submit notices of covered unemployment compensation debt and the necessary information that must be contained in or accompany such notices. The regulations may specify the minimum amount of debt to which the reduction procedure established by paragraph (1) may be applied.

(B) FEE PAYABLE TO SECRETARY.—The regulations may require States to pay a fee to the Secretary, which may be deducted from amounts collected, to reimburse the Secretary for the cost of applying such procedure. Any fee paid to the Secretary pursuant to the preceding sentence shall be used to reimburse appropriations which bore all or part of the cost of applying such procedure.

(C) SUBMISSION OF NOTICES THROUGH SECRETARY OF LABOR.—The regulations may include a requirement that States submit notices of covered unemployment compensation debt to the Secretary via the Secretary of Labor in accordance with procedures established by the Secretary of Labor. Such procedures may require States to pay a fee to the Secretary of Labor to reimburse the Secretary of Labor for the costs of applying this subsection. Any such fee shall be established in consultation with the Secretary of the Treasury. Any fee paid to the Secretary of Labor may be deducted from amounts collected and shall be used to reimburse the appropriation account which bore all or part of the cost of applying this subsection.

(6) ERRONEOUS PAYMENT TO STATE.—Any State receiving notice from the Secretary that an erroneous payment has been made to such State under paragraph (1) shall pay promptly to the Secretary, in accordance with such regulations as the Secretary may prescribe, an amount equal to the amount of such erroneous payment (without regard to whether any other amounts payable to such State under such paragraph have been paid to such State).

Amendments

• 2010, Tax Relief, Unemployment Insurance Reauthorization, and Job Creation Act of 2010 (P.L. 111-312)

P.L. 111-312, §503(a):

Amended Code Sec. 6402(f)(3)(C), as amended by section 801 of the Claims Resolution Act of 2010 (P.L. 111-291), by striking "is not a covered unemployment compensation debt" and inserting "is a covered unemployment compensation debt". **Effective** as if included in section 801 of the Claims Resolution Act of 2010 (P.L. 111-291) [**effective** for refunds payable under Code Sec. 6402 on or after 12-8-2010.—CCH].

• 2010, Claims Resolution Act of 2010 (P.L. 111-291)

P.L. 111-291, §801(a)(1)-(4):

Amended Code Sec. 6402(f) by striking "RESULTING FROM FRAUD" following "COMPENSATION DEBTS" in the heading; by striking paragraphs (3) and (8) and redesignating paragraphs (4) through (7) as paragraphs (3) through (6), respectively; in paragraph (3), as so redesignated, by striking "by certified mail with return receipt" following "notifies" in subparagraph (A); by striking "due to fraud" and inserting "is not a covered unemployment compensation debt" in subparagraph (B); by striking " due to fraud" and inserting "is not [sic] a covered unemployment compensation debt" in subparagraph (C); and in paragraph (4), as so redesignated, in subparagraph (A), by inserting "or the person's failure to report earnings" after "due to fraud"; and by striking "for not more than 10 years" following "which remains uncollected"; and in subparagraph (B), by striking "due to fraud" following "the person to be liable"; and by striking "for not more than 10 years" following "which remain uncollected". **Effective** for refunds payable under Code Sec. 6402 on or after 12-8-2010. Prior to being stricken, Code Sec. 6402(f)(3) and (8) read as follows:

(3) OFFSET PERMITTED ONLY AGAINST RESIDENTS OF STATE SEEKING OFFSET.—Paragraph (1) shall apply to an overpayment by any person for a taxable year only if the address shown on the Federal return for such taxable year of the overpayment is an address within the State seeking the offset.

* * *

(8) TERMINATION.—This section shall not apply to refunds payable after the date which is 10 years after the date of the enactment of this subsection.

• 2008, SSI Extension for Elderly and Disabled Refugees Act (P.L. 110-328)

P.L. 110-328, §3(a):

Amended Code Sec. 6402 by redesignating subsections (f) through (k) as subsections (g) through (l), respectively, and by inserting after subsection (e) a new subsection (f). **Effective** for refunds payable under Code Sec. 6402 on or after 9-30-2008.

[Sec. 6402(g)]

(g) REVIEW OF REDUCTIONS.—No court of the United States shall have jurisdiction to hear any action, whether legal or equitable, brought to restrain or review a reduction authorized by subsection (c), (d), (e), or (f). No such reduction shall be subject to review by the Secretary in an administrative proceeding. No action brought against the United States to recover the amount of any such reduction shall be considered to be a suit for refund of tax. This subsection does not preclude any legal, equitable, or administrative action against the Federal agency or State to which the amount of such reduction was paid or any such action against the Commissioner of Social Security which is otherwise available with respect to recoveries of overpayments of benefits under section 204 of the Social Security Act.

Amendments

• 2008, SSI Extension for Elderly and Disabled Refugees Act (P.L. 110-328)

P.L. 110-328, §3(a):

Amended Code Sec. 6402 by redesignating subsection (f) as subsection (g). **Effective** for refunds payable under Code Sec. 6402 on or after 9-30-2008.

P.L. 110-328, §3(d)(4):

Amended Code Sec. 6402(g), as redesignated by Act Sec. 3(a), by striking "(c), (d), or (e)" and inserting "(c), (d), (e), or (f)". **Effective** for refunds payable under Code Sec. 6402 on or after 9-30-2008.

• 1998, IRS Restructuring and Reform Act of 1998 (P.L. 105-206)

P.L. 105-206, §3711(a):

Amended Code Sec. 6402 by redesignating subsection (e) as subsection (f). **Effective** for refunds payable under Code Sec. 6402 after 12-31-99.

P.L. 105-206, §3711(c)(3)(A)-(B):

Amended Code Sec. 6402(f), as redesignated by Act Sec. 3711(a), by striking "(c) or (d)" and inserting "(c), (d), or (e)", and by striking "Federal agency" and inserting "Federal agency or State". **Effective** for refunds payable under Code Sec. 6402 after 12-31-99.

• 1997, Balanced Budget Act of 1997 (P.L. 105-33)

P.L. 105-33, §5514(a)(1):

Struck the change made by Act Sec. 110(l)(7)(B) of P.L. 104-193, which redesignated Code Sec. 6402(e) as Code Sec. 6402(f). The provision of law added by P.L. 104-193 is restored as if Act Sec. 110(l)(7)(B) had not been enacted. Thus, subsection (f) of Code Sec. 6402 is now designated as subsection (e) of Code Sec. 6402. **Effective** 7-1-97.

• 1996, Personal Responsibility and Work Opportunity Reconciliation Act of 1996 (P.L. 104-193)

P.L. 104-193, §110(l)(7)(B):

Amended Code Sec. 6402 by redesignating subsection (e) as subsection (f). **Effective** 7-1-97.

• 1994, Social Security Independence and Program Improvements Act of 1994 (P.L. 103-296)

P.L. 103-296, §108(h)(7):

Amended Code Sec. 6402(e) by striking "Secretary of Health and Human Services" each place it appears and inserting "Commissioner of Social Security". **Effective** 3-31-95.

• 1990, Omnibus Budget Reconciliation Act of 1990 (P.L. 101-508)

P.L. 101-508, §5129(c)(2):

Amended Code Sec. 6402(e) by inserting before the period in the last sentence the following: "or any such action against the Secretary of Health and Human Services which is otherwise available with respect to recoveries of overpayments of benefits under section 204 of the Social Security Act". **Effective** 1-1-91, and shall not apply to refunds to which the Deficit Reduction Act of 1984 (98 Stat. 1153) does not apply.

• 1984, Deficit Reduction Act of 1984 (P.L. 98-369)

P.L. 98-369, §2653(b)(1):

Amended Code Sec. 6402 by adding subsection (e). **Effective** with respect to refunds payable under section 6402 of the Internal Revenue Code of 1954 after 12-31-85 [**effective** date changed by P.L. 100-485 and P.L. 102-164].

[Sec. 6402(h)]

(h) FEDERAL AGENCY.—For purposes of this section, the term "Federal agency" means a department, agency, or instrumentality of the United States, and includes a Government corporation (as such term is defined in section 103 of title 5, United States Code).

Amendments

• 2008, SSI Extension for Elderly and Disabled Refugees Act (P.L. 110-328)

P.L. 110-328, §3(a):

Amended Code Sec. 6402 by redesignating subsection (g) as subsection (h). **Effective** for refunds payable under Code Sec. 6402 on or after 9-30-2008.

• 1998, IRS Restructuring and Reform Act of 1998 (P.L. 105-206)

P.L. 105-206, §3711(a):

Amended Code Sec. 6402 by redesignating subsection (f) as subsection (g). **Effective** for refunds payable under Code Sec. 6402 after 12-31-99.

• 1997, Balanced Budget Act of 1997 (P.L. 105-33)

P.L. 105-33, §5514(a)(1):

Struck the change made by Act Sec. 110(l)(7)(B) of P.L. 104-193, which redesignated Code Sec. 6402(f) as Code Sec. 6402(g). The provision of law added by P.L. 104-193 is restored as if Act Sec. 110(l)(7)(B) had not been enacted. Thus, subsection (g) of Code Sec. 6402 is now designated as subsection (f) of Code Sec. 6402. **Effective** 7-1-97.

• 1996, Personal Responsibility and Work Opportunity Reconciliation Act of 1996 (P.L. 104-193)

P.L. 104-193, §110(l)(7)(B):

Amended Code Sec. 6402 by redesignating subsection (f) as subsection (g). **Effective** 7-1-97.

• 1996, Debt Collection Improvement Act of 1996 (P.L. 104-134)

P.L. 104-134, §31001(u)(2):

Amended Code Sec. 6402(f). **Effective** 4-26-96. Prior to amendment Code Sec. 6402(f) read as follows:

(f) FEDERAL AGENCY.—For purposes of this section, the term "Federal agency" means a department, agency, or instrumentality of the United States (other than an agency subject to section 9 of the Act of May 18, 1933 (48 Stat. 63, chapter 32; 16 U.S.C. 831h)), and includes a Government corporation (as such term is defined in section 103 of title 5, United States Code).

• 1984, Deficit Reduction Act of 1984 (P.L. 98-369)

P.L. 98-369, §2653(b)(1):

Amended Code Sec. 6402 by adding subsection (f). **Effective** with respect to refunds payable under section 6402 of the Internal Revenue Code of 1954 after 12-31-85 [**effective** date changed by P.L. 100-485 and P.L. 102-164].

[Sec. 6402(i)]

(i) TREATMENT OF PAYMENTS TO STATES.—The Secretary may provide that, for purposes of determining interest, the payment of any amount withheld under subsection (c), (e), or (f) to a State shall be treated as a payment to the person or persons making the overpayment.

Amendments

• 2008, SSI Extension for Elderly and Disabled Refugees Act (P.L. 110-328)

P.L. 110-328, §3(a):

Amended Code Sec. 6402 by redesignating subsection (h) as subsection (i). **Effective** for refunds payable under Code Sec. 6402 on or after 9-30-2008.

P.L. 110-328, §3(d)(5):

Amended Code Sec. 6402(i), as redesignated by Act Sec. 3(a), by striking "subsection (c) or (e)" and inserting "subsection (c), (e), or (f)". **Effective** for refunds payable under Code Sec. 6402 on or after 9-30-2008.

• 1998, IRS Restructuring and Reform Act of 1998 (P.L. 105-206)

P.L. 105-206, §3711(a):

Amended Code Sec. 6402 by redesignating subsection (g) as subsection (h). **Effective** for refunds payable under Code Sec. 6402 after 12-31-99.

P.L. 105-206, §3711(c)(4):

Amended Code Sec. 6402(h), as redesignated by Act Sec. 3711(a), by striking "subsection (c)" and inserting "subsection (c) or (e)". **Effective** for refunds payable under Code Sec. 6402 after 12-31-99.

• 1997, Balanced Budget Act of 1997 (P.L. 105-33)

P.L. 105-33, §5514(a)(1):

Struck the change made by Act Sec. 110(l)(7)(B) of P.L. 104-193, which redesignated Code Sec. 6402(g) as Code Sec. 6402(h). The provision of law added by P.L. 104-193 is restored as if Act Sec. 110(l)(7)(B) had not been enacted. Thus, subsection (h) of Code Sec. 6402 is now designated as subsection (g) of Code Sec. 6402. **Effective** 7-1-97.

• 1996, Personal Responsibility and Work Opportunity Reconciliation Act of 1996 (P.L. 104-193)

P.L. 104-193, §110(l)(7)(B):

Amended Code Sec. 6402 by redesignating subsection (g) as subsection (h). **Effective** 7-1-97.

• 1984, Child Support Enforcement Amendments of 1984 (P.L. 98-378)

P.L. 98-378, §21(e)(2):

Amended Code Sec. 6402 by adding at the end thereof new subsection (g). **Effective** with respect to refunds payable under Code Sec. 6402 after 12-31-85.

[Sec. 6402(j)]

(j) CROSS REFERENCE.—

For procedures relating to agency notification of the Secretary, see section 3721 of title 31, United States Code.

Amendments

• 2008, SSI Extension for Elderly and Disabled Refugees Act (P.L. 110-328)

P.L. 110-328, §3(a):

Amended Code Sec. 6402 by redesignating subsection (i) as subsection (j). **Effective** for refunds payable under Code Sec. 6402 on or after 9-30-2008.

• 1998, IRS Restructuring and Reform Act of 1998 (P.L. 105-206)

P.L. 105-206, §3711(a):

Amended Code Sec. 6402 by redesignating subsection (h) as subsection (i). **Effective** for refunds payable under Code Sec. 6402 after 12-31-99.

• 1997, Balanced Budget Act of 1997 (P.L. 105-33)

P.L. 105-33, §5514(a)(1):

Struck the change made by Act Sec. 110(l)(7)(B) of P.L. 104-193, which redesignated Code Sec. 6402(h) as Code Sec. 6402(i). The provision of law added by P.L. 104-193 is restored as if Act Sec. 110(l)(7)(B) had not been enacted. Thus, subsection (i) of Code Sec. 6402 is now designated as subsection (h) of Code Sec. 6402. **Effective** 7-1-97.

• 1996, Personal Responsibility and Work Opportunity Reconciliation Act of 1996 (P.L. 104-193)

P.L. 104-193, §110(l)(7)(B):

Amended Code Sec. 6402 by redesignating subsection (h) as subsection (i). **Effective** 7-1-97.

• 1984, Child Support Enforcement Amendments of 1984 (P.L. 98-378)

P.L. 98-378, §21(e)(2):

Redesignated Code Sec. 6402(g) as (h). **Effective** with respect to refunds payable under Code Sec. 6402 after 12-31-85.

• 1984, Deficit Reduction Act of 1984 (P.L. 98-369)

P.L. 98-369, §2653(b)(1):

Amended Code Sec. 6402 by adding subsection (g). **Effective** with respect to refunds payable under section 6402 of the Internal Revenue Code of 1954 after 12-31-85 [**effective** date changed by P.L. 100-485 and P.L. 102-164].

[Sec. 6402(k)]

(k) REFUNDS TO CERTAIN FIDUCIARIES OF INSOLVENT MEMBERS OF AFFILIATED GROUPS.—Notwithstanding any other provision of law, in the case of an insolvent corporation which is a member of an affiliated group of corporations filing a consolidated return for any taxable year and which is subject to a statutory or court-appointed fiduciary, the Secretary may by regulation provide that any refund for such taxable year may be paid on behalf of such insolvent corporation to such fiduciary to the extent that the Secretary determines that the refund is attributable to losses or credits of such insolvent corporation.

Amendments

• 2008, SSI Extension for Elderly and Disabled Refugees Act (P.L. 110-328)

P.L. 110-328, §3(a):

Amended Code Sec. 6402 by redesignating subsection (j) as subsection (k). **Effective** for refunds payable under Code Sec. 6402 on or after 9-30-2008.

• 1998, IRS Restructuring and Reform Act of 1998 (P.L. 105-206)

P.L. 105-206, §3711(a):

Amended Code Sec. 6402 by redesignating subsection (i) as subsection (j). **Effective** for refunds payable under Code Sec. 6402 after 12-31-99.

• 1997, Balanced Budget Act of 1997 (P.L. 105-33)

P.L. 105-33, §5514(a)(1):

Struck the change made by Act Sec. 110(l)(7)(B) of P.L. 104-193, which redesignated Code Sec. 6402(i) as Code Sec. 6402(j). The provision of law added by P.L. 104-193 is restored as if Act Sec. 110(l)(7)(B) had not been enacted. Thus, subsection (j) of Code Sec. 6402 is now designated as subsection (i) of Code Sec. 6402. **Effective** 7-1-97.

• 1996, Personal Responsibility and Work Opportunity Reconciliation Act of 1996 (P.L. 104-193)

P.L. 104-193, §110(l)(7)(B):

Amended Code Sec. 6402 by redesignating subsection (i) as subsection (j). **Effective** 7-1-97.

• 1988, Technical and Miscellaneous Revenue Act of 1988 (P.L. 100-647)

P.L. 100-647, §6276:

Amended Code Sec. 6402 by adding at the end thereof new subsection (i). **Effective** 11-10-88.

[Sec. 6402(l)]

(l) EXPLANATION OF REASON FOR REFUND DISALLOWANCE.—In the case of a disallowance of a claim for refund, the Secretary shall provide the taxpayer with an explanation for such disallowance.

Amendments

• 2008, SSI Extension for Elderly and Disabled Refugees Act (P.L. 110-328)

P.L. 110-328, §3(a):

Amended Code Sec. 6402 by redesignating subsection (k) as subsection (l). **Effective** for refunds payable under Code Sec. 6402 on or after 9-30-2008.

• 1998, IRS Restructuring and Reform Act of 1998 (P.L. 105-206)

P.L. 105-206, §3505(a):

Amended Code Sec. 6402 by adding at the end a new subsection (j). **Effective** for disallowances after the 180th day after 7-22-98.

P.L. 105-206, §3711(a):

Amended Code Sec. 6402(j), as added by Act Sec. 3505(a), by redesignating subsection (j) as subsection (k). **Effective** for refunds payable under Code Sec. 6402 after 12-31-99.

[Sec. 6402(m)]

(m) EARLIEST DATE FOR CERTAIN REFUNDS.—No credit or refund of an overpayment for a taxable year shall be made to a taxpayer before the 15th day of the second month following the close of such taxable year if a credit is allowed to such taxpayer under section 24 (by reason of subsection (d) thereof) or 32 for such taxable year.

Amendments

• 2015, Protecting Americans from Tax Hikes Act of 2015 (P.L. 114-113)

P.L. 114-113, §201(b), Div. Q:

Amended Code Sec. 6402 by adding at the end a new subsection (m). **Effective** for credits or refunds made after 12-31-2016.

[Sec. 6402(n)]

(n) MISDIRECTED DIRECT DEPOSIT REFUND.—Not later than the date which is 6 months after the date of the enactment of the Taxpayer First Act, the Secretary shall prescribe regulations to establish procedures to allow for—

(1) taxpayers to report instances in which a refund made by the Secretary by electronic funds transfer was not transferred to the account of the taxpayer;

(2) coordination with financial institutions for the purpose of—

(A) identifying the accounts to which transfers described in paragraph (1) were made; and

(B) recovery of the amounts so transferred; and

(3) the refund to be delivered to the correct account of the taxpayer.

Amendments

• 2019, Taxpayer First Act (P.L. 116-25)

P.L. 116-25, §1407:

Amended Code Sec. 6402 by adding at the end a new subsection (n). **Effective** 7-1-2019.

[Sec. 6403]

SEC. 6403. OVERPAYMENT OF INSTALLMENT.

In the case of a tax payable in installments, if the taxpayer has paid as an installment of the tax more than the amount determined to be the correct amount of such installment, the overpayment shall be credited against the unpaid installments, if any. If the amount already paid, whether or not on the basis of installments, exceeds the amount determined to be the correct amount of the tax, the overpayment shall be credited or refunded as provided in section 6402.

[Sec. 6404]

SEC. 6404. ABATEMENTS.

[Sec. 6404(a)]

(a) GENERAL RULE.—The Secretary is authorized to abate the unpaid portion of the assessment of any tax or any liability in respect thereof, which—

(1) is excessive in amount, or

(2) is assessed after the expiration of the period of limitations properly applicable thereto, or

(3) is erroneously or illegally assessed.

Amendments

• 1976, Tax Reform Act of 1976 (P.L. 94-455)

P.L. 94-455, §1906(b)(13)(A):

Amended 1954 Code by substituting "Secretary" for "Secretary or his delegate" each place it appeared. **Effective** 2-1-77.

[Sec. 6404(b)]

(b) NO CLAIM FOR ABATEMENT OF INCOME, ESTATE, AND GIFT TAXES.—No claim for abatement shall be filed by a taxpayer in respect of an assessment of any tax imposed under subtitle A or B.

[Sec. 6404(c)]

(c) SMALL TAX BALANCES.—The Secretary is authorized to abate the unpaid portion of the assessment of any tax, or any liability in respect thereof, if the Secretary determines under uniform rules prescribed by the Secretary that the administration and collection costs involved would not warrant collection of the amount due.

Amendments

• 1976, Tax Reform Act of 1976 (P.L. 94-455)

P.L. 94-455, §1906(b)(13)(A):

Amended 1954 Code by substituting "Secretary" for "Secretary or his delegate" each place it appeared. **Effective** 2-1-77.

[Sec. 6404(d)]

(d) ASSESSMENTS ATTRIBUTABLE TO CERTAIN MATHEMATICAL ERRORS BY INTERNAL REVENUE SERVICE.—In the case of an assessment of any tax imposed by chapter 1 attributable in whole or in part to a mathematical error described in section 6213(g)(2)(A), if the return was prepared by an officer or employee of the Internal Revenue Service acting in his official capacity to provide assistance to taxpayers in the preparation of income tax returns, the Secretary is authorized to abate the assessment of all or any part of any interest on such deficiency for any period ending on or before the 30th day following the date of notice and demand by the Secretary for payment of the deficiency.

Amendments

• 1980, Bankruptcy Tax Act of 1980 (P.L. 96-589)

P.L. 96-589, §6(b)(2):

Amended Code Sec. 6404(d) by striking out "section 6213(f)(2)(A)" and inserting in lieu thereof "section 6213(g)(2)(A)". **Effective** 10-1-79, but inapplicable to any proceeding under the Bankruptcy Act commenced before that date.

• 1976, Tax Reform Act of 1976 (P.L. 94-455)

P.L. 94-455, §1212(a):

Added Code Sec. 6404(d). **Effective** with respect to returns filed for tax years ending after 10-4-76.

[Sec. 6404(e)]

(e) ABATEMENT OF INTEREST ATTRIBUTABLE TO UNREASONABLE ERRORS AND DELAYS BY INTERNAL REVENUE SERVICE.—

(1) IN GENERAL.—In the case of any assessment of interest on—

(A) any deficiency attributable in whole or in part to any unreasonable error or delay by an officer or employee of the Internal Revenue Service (acting in his official capacity) in performing a ministerial or managerial act, or

(B) any payment of any tax described in section 6212(a) to the extent that any unreasonable error or delay in such payment is attributable to such officer or employee being erroneous or dilatory in performing a ministerial or managerial act,

the Secretary may abate the assessment of all or any part of such interest for any period. For purposes of the preceding sentence, an error or delay shall be taken into account only if no significant aspect of such error or delay can be attributed to the taxpayer involved, and after the Internal Revenue Service has contacted the taxpayer in writing with respect to such deficiency or payment.

(2) INTEREST ABATED WITH RESPECT TO ERRONEOUS REFUND CHECK.—The Secretary shall abate the assessment of all interest on any erroneous refund under section 6602 until the date demand for repayment is made, unless—

(A) the taxpayer (or a related party) has in any way caused such erroneous refund, or

(B) such erroneous refund exceeds $50,000.

Amendments

• 1996, Taxpayer Bill of Rights 2 (P.L. 104-168)

P.L. 104-168, §301(a)(1)-(2):

Amended Code Sec. 6404(e)(1) by inserting "unreasonable" before "error" each place it appears in subparagraphs (A) and (B), and by striking "in performing a ministerial act" each place it appears and inserting "in performing a ministerial or managerial act". **Effective** for interest accruing with respect to deficiencies or payments for tax years beginning after 7-30-96.

P.L. 104-168, §301(b)(1)-(2):

Amended Code Sec. 6404(e) by striking "ASSESSMENTS" and inserting "ABATEMENT", and by inserting "UNREASONABLE" before "ERRORS" in the heading. **Effective** for interest accruing with respect to deficiencies or payments for tax years beginning after 7-30-96.

• 1988, Technical and Miscellaneous Revenue Act of 1988 (P.L. 100-647)

P.L. 100-647, §1015(n)(1)-(2):

Amended Code Sec. 6404(e)(1)(B) by inserting "error or" before "delay", and by inserting "erroneous or" before "dilatory". **Effective** as if included in the provision of P.L. 99-514 to which it relates.

• 1986, Tax Reform Act of 1986 (P.L. 99-514)

P.L. 99-514, §1563(a):

Amended Code Sec. 6404 by adding at the end thereof new subsection (e). **Effective** for interest accruing with respect to deficiencies or payments for tax years beginning after 12-31-78. However, see Act Sec. 1563(b)(2), below.

P.L. 99-514, §1563(b)(2), provides:

(2) STATUTE OF LIMITATIONS.—If refund or credit of any amount resulting from the application of the amendment made by subsection (a) is prevented at any time before the close of the date which is 1 year after the date of the enactment of this Act by the operation of any law or rule of law (including res judicata), refund or credit of such amount (to the extent attributable to the application of the amendment made by subsection (a)) may, nevertheless, be made or allowed if claim therefore is filed before the close of such 1-year period.

[Sec. 6404(f)]

(f) ABATEMENT OF ANY PENALTY OR ADDITION TO TAX ATTRIBUTABLE TO ERRONEOUS WRITTEN ADVICE BY THE INTERNAL REVENUE SERVICE.—

(1) IN GENERAL.—The Secretary shall abate any portion of any penalty or addition to tax attributable to erroneous advice furnished to the taxpayer in writing by an officer or employee of the Internal Revenue Service, acting in such officer's or employee's official capacity.

(2) LIMITATIONS.—Paragraph (1) shall apply only if—

(A) the written advice was reasonably relied upon by the taxpayer and was in response to a specific written request of the taxpayer, and

(B) the portion of the penalty or addition to tax did not result from a failure by the taxpayer to provide adequate or accurate information.

Amendments

• 2014, Tax Technical Corrections Act of 2014 (P.L. 113-295)

P.L. 113-295, §221(a)(111), Division A:

Amended Code Sec. 6404(f) by striking paragraph (3). **Effective** 12-19-2014. For a special rule, see Act Sec. 221(b)(2), Division A, below. Prior to being stricken, Code Sec. 6404(f)(3) read as follows:

(3) INITIAL REGULATIONS.—Within 180 days after the date of the enactment of this subsection, the Secretary shall prescribe such initial regulations as may be necessary to carry out this subsection.

P.L. 113-295, §221(b)(2), Division A, provides:

(2) SAVINGS PROVISION.—If—

(A) any provision amended or repealed by the amendments made by this section applied to—

(i) any transaction occurring before the date of the enactment of this Act,

(ii) any property acquired before such date of enactment, or

(iii) any item of income, loss, deduction, or credit taken into account before such date of enactment, and

(B) the treatment of such transaction, property, or item under such provision would (without regard to the amendments or repeals made by this section) affect the liability for tax for periods ending after date of enactment, nothing in the amendments or repeals made by this section shall be construed to affect the treatment of such transaction, property, or item for purposes of determining liability for tax for periods ending after such date of enactment.

• 1988, Technical and Miscellaneous Revenue Act of 1988 (P.L. 100-647)

P.L. 100-647, §6229(a):

Amended Code Sec. 6404 by adding at the end thereof new subsection (f). **Effective** with respect to advice requested on or after 1-1-89.

[Sec. 6404(g)]

(g) SUSPENSION OF INTEREST AND CERTAIN PENALTIES WHERE SECRETARY FAILS TO CONTACT TAXPAYER.—

(1) SUSPENSION.—

(A) IN GENERAL.—In the case of an individual who files a return of tax imposed by subtitle A for a taxable year on or before the due date for the return (including extensions), if the Secretary does not provide a notice to the taxpayer specifically stating the taxpayer's liability and the basis for the liability before the close of the 36-month period beginning on the later of—

(i) the date on which the return is filed; or

(ii) the due date of the return without regard to extensions,

the Secretary shall suspend the imposition of any interest, penalty, addition to tax, or additional amount with respect to any failure relating to the return which is computed by reference to the period of time the failure continues to exist and which is properly allocable to the suspension period.

(B) SEPARATE APPLICATION.—This paragraph shall be applied separately with respect to each item or adjustment.

If, after the return for a taxable year is filed, the taxpayer provides to the Secretary 1 or more signed written documents showing that the taxpayer owes an additional amount of tax for the taxable year, clause (i) shall be applied by substituting the date the last of the documents was provided for the date on which the return is filed.

(2) EXCEPTIONS.—Paragraph (1) shall not apply to—

(A) any penalty imposed by section 6651;

(B) any interest, penalty, addition to tax, or additional amount in a case involving fraud;

(C) any interest, penalty, addition to tax, or additional amount with respect to any tax liability shown on the return;

(D) any interest, penalty, addition to tax, or additional amount with respect to any gross misstatement;

(E) any interest, penalty, addition to tax, or additional amount with respect to any reportable transaction with respect to which the requirement of section 6664(d)(3)(A) is not met and any listed transaction (as defined in 6707A(c)); or

(F) any criminal penalty.

(3) SUSPENSION PERIOD.—For purposes of this subsection, the term "suspension period" means the period—

(A) beginning on the day after the close of the 36-month period under paragraph (1); and

(B) ending on the date which is 21 days after the date on which notice described in paragraph (1)(A) is provided by the Secretary.

Amendments

• 2018, Tax Technical Corrections Act of 2018 (P.L. 115-141)

P.L. 115-141, §401(a)(288), Div. U:

Amended Code Sec. 6404(g)(2)(E) by striking "section 6664(d)(2)(A)" and inserting "section 6664(d)(3)(A)". **Effective** 3-23-2018.

• 2007, Small Business and Work Opportunity Tax Act of 2007 (P.L. 110-28)

P.L. 110-28, §8242(a):

Amended Code Sec. 6404(g)(1)(A) and (3)(A) by striking "18-month period" and inserting "36-month period". **Effective** for notices provided by the Secretary of the Treasury, or his delegate, after the date which is 6 months after 5-25-2007.

• 2005, Gulf Opportunity Zone Act of 2005 (P.L. 109-135)

P.L. 109-135, §303(b)(1):

Amended Code Sec. 6404(g)(1) by adding at the end a new sentence. **Effective** for documents provided on or after 12-21-2005.

• 2004, American Jobs Creation Act of 2004 (P.L. 108-357)

P.L. 108-357, §903(a):

Amended Code Sec. 6404(g) by striking "1-year period (18-month period in the case of taxable years beginning before January 1, 2004)" both places it appears and inserting "18-month period". **Effective** for tax years beginning after 12-31-2003.

P.L. 108-357, §903(b):

Amended Code Sec. 6404(g)(2) by striking "or" at the end of subparagraph (C), by redesignating subparagraph (D) as subparagraph (E), and by inserting after subparagraph (C) a new subparagraph (D). **Effective** for tax years beginning after 12-31-2003.

P.L. 108-357, §903(c):

Amended Code Sec. 6404(g)(2), as amended by Act Sec. 903(b), by striking "or" at the end of subparagraph (D), by redesignating subparagraph (E) as subparagraph (F), and by inserting after subparagraph (D) a new subparagraph (E). **Effective**, generally, with respect to interest accruing after 10-3-2004. For a special rule, see Act Sec. 903(d)(2)(B), below.

P.L. 108-357, §903(d)(2)(B), as added by P.L. 109-135, §303(a)(1), and amended by P.L. 109-432, §426(b)(1), provides:

(B) SPECIAL RULE FOR CERTAIN LISTED AND REPORTABLE TRANSACTIONS.—

(i) IN GENERAL.—Except as provided in clauses (ii), (iii), and (iv), the amendments made by subsection (c) shall also apply with respect to interest accruing on or before October 3, 2004.

(ii) PARTICIPANTS IN SETTLEMENT INITIATIVES.—Clause (i) shall not apply to any transaction if, as of January 23, 2006—

(I) the taxpayer is participating in a settlement initiative described in Internal Revenue Service Announcement 2005-80 with respect to such transaction, or

(II) the taxpayer has entered into a settlement agreement pursuant to such an initiative.

Subclause (I) shall not apply to any taxpayer if, after January 23, 2006, the taxpayer withdraws from, or terminates, participation in the initiative or the Secretary of the Treasury or the Secretary's delegate determines that a settlement agreement will not be reached pursuant to the initiative within a reasonable period of time.

(iii) TAXPAYERS ACTING IN GOOD FAITH.—The Secretary of the Treasury or the Secretary's delegate may except from the application of clause (i) any transaction in which the taxpayer has acted reasonably and in good faith.

(iv) CLOSED TRANSACTIONS.—Clause (i) shall not apply to a transaction if, as of December 14, 2005—

(I) the assessment of all Federal income taxes for the taxable year in which the tax liability to which the interest relates arose is prevented by the operation of any law or rule of law, or

(II) a closing agreement under section 7121 has been entered into with respect to the tax liability arising in connection with the transaction.

• 1998, IRS Restructuring and Reform Act of 1998 (P.L. 105-206)

P.L. 105-206, §3305(a):

Amended Code Sec. 6404 by redesignating subsection (g) as subsection (h) and by inserting after subsection (f) a new subsection (g). **Effective** for tax years ending after 7-22-98.

[Sec. 6404(h)]

(h) JUDICIAL REVIEW OF REQUEST FOR ABATEMENT OF INTEREST.—

(1) IN GENERAL.—The Tax Court shall have jurisdiction over any action brought by a taxpayer who meets the requirements referred to in section 7430(c)(4)(A)(ii) to determine whether the Secretary's failure to abate interest under this section was an abuse of discretion, and may order an abatement, if such action is brought—

(A) at any time after the earlier of—

(i) the date of the mailing of the Secretary's final determination not to abate such interest, or

(ii) the date which is 180 days after the date of the filing with the Secretary (in such form as the Secretary may prescribe) of a claim for abatement under this section, and

(B) not later than the date which is 180 days after the date described in subparagraph (A)(i).

(2) SPECIAL RULES.—

(A) DATE OF MAILING.—Rules similar to the rules of section 6213 shall apply for purposes of determining the date of the mailing referred to in paragraph (1).

(B) RELIEF.—Rules similar to the rules of section 6512(b) shall apply for purposes of this subsection.

(C) REVIEW.—An order of the Tax Court under this subsection shall be reviewable in the same manner as a decision of the Tax Court, but only with respect to the matters determined in such order.

Amendments

• 2015, Protecting Americans from Tax Hikes Act of 2015 (P.L. 114-113)

P.L. 114-113, §421(a)(1)-(2), Div. Q:

Amended Code Sec. 6404(h) by striking "REVIEW OF DENIAL" in the heading and inserting "JUDICIAL REVIEW", and by striking "if such action is brought" and all that follows in paragraph (1) and inserting "if such action is brought—"and new subparagraphs (A)-(B). **Effective** for claims for abatement of interest filed with the Secretary of the Treasury after 12-18-2015. Prior to being stricken, "if such action is brought" and all that follows in Code Sec. 6404(h)(1) read as follows:

if such action is brought within 180 days after the date of the mailing of the Secretary's final determination not to abate such interest.

• 2002, Victims of Terrorism Tax Relief Act of 2001 (P.L. 107-134)

P.L. 107-134, §112(d)(1)(B):

Amended Code Sec. 6404 by redesignating subsection (i) as subsection (h). **Effective** for disasters and terroristic or military actions occurring on or after 9-11-2001, with respect to any action of the Secretary of the Treasury, the Secretary of Labor, or the Pension Benefit Guaranty Corporation occurring on or after 1-23-2002.

• 1998, IRS Restructuring and Reform Act of 1998 (P.L. 105-206)

P.L. 105-206, §3305(a):

Amended Code Sec. 6404 by redesignating subsection (g) as subsection (h). **Effective** for tax years ending after 7-22-98.

P.L. 105-206, §3309(a):

Amended Code Sec. 6404, as amended by Act Sec. 3305(a), by redesignating subsection (h) as subsection (i). **Effective** for disasters declared after 12-31-97, with respect to tax years beginning after 12-31-97. For a special rule, see Act Sec. 3309(c)(1)-(2), below.

P.L. 105-206, §3309(c)(1)-(2), provides:

(c) EMERGENCY DESIGNATION.—

(1) For the purposes of section 252(e) of the Balanced Budget and Emergency Deficit Control Act, Congress designates the provisions of this section as an emergency requirement.

(2) The amendments made by subsections (a) and (b) of this section shall only take effect upon the transmittal by the President to the Congress of a message designating the provisions of subsections (a) and (b) as an emergency requirement pursuant to section 252(e) of the Balanced Budget and Emergency Deficit Control Act.

• 1996, Taxpayer Bill of Rights 2 (P.L. 104-168)

P.L. 104-168, §302(a):

Amended Code Sec. 6404 by adding at the end a new subsection (g). **Effective** for requests for abatement after 7-30-96.

P.L. 104-168, §701(c)(3):

Amended Code Sec. 6404(g) (as amended by Act Sec. 302(a)) by striking "section 7430(c)(4)(A)(iii)" and inserting "section 7430(c)(4)(A)(ii)". **Effective** in the case of proceedings commenced after 7-30-96.

[Sec. 6404(h)—Stricken]

Amendments

• 2002, Victims of Terrorism Tax Relief Act of 2001 (P.L. 107-134)

P.L. 107-134, §112(d)(1)(A):

Amended Code Sec. 6404 by striking subsection (h). **Effective** for disasters and terroristic or military actions occurring on or after 9-11-2001, with respect to any action of the Secretary of the Treasury, the Secretary of Labor, or the Pension Benefit Guaranty Corporation occurring on or after 1-23-2002. Prior to being stricken, Code Sec. 6404(h) read as follows:

(h) ABATEMENT OF INTEREST ON UNDERPAYMENTS BY TAXPAYERS IN PRESIDENTIALLY DECLARED DISASTER AREAS.—

(1) IN GENERAL.—If the Secretary extends for any period the time for filing income tax returns under section 6081 and the time for paying income tax with respect to such returns under section 6161 for any taxpayer located in a Presidentially declared disaster area, the Secretary shall abate for such period the assessment of any interest prescribed under section 6601 on such income tax.

(2) PRESIDENTIALLY DECLARED DISASTER AREA.—For purposes of paragraph (1), the term "Presidentially declared disaster area" means, with respect to any taxpayer, any area which the President has determined warrants assistance by the Federal Government under the Robert T. Stafford Disaster Relief and Emergency Assistance Act.

• 1998, Tax and Trade Relief Extension Act of 1998 (P.L. 105-277)

P.L. 105-277, §4003(e)(2):

Amended Code Sec. 6404(h)(2) by inserting "Robert T. Stafford" before "Disaster". **Effective** as if included in the provision of P.L. 105-34 to which it relates [**effective** for disasters declared after 12-31-96.—CCH].

• 1998, IRS Restructuring and Reform Act of 1998 (P.L. 105-206)

P.L. 105-206, §3305(a):

Amended Code Sec. 6404 by redesignating subsection (g) as subsection (h). **Effective** for tax years ending after 7-22-98.

P.L. 105-206, §3309(a):

Amended Code Sec. 6404, as amended by Act Sec. 3305(a), by redesignating subsection (h) as subsection (i) and by inserting after subsection (g) a new subsection (h). **Effective** for disasters declared after 12-31-97, with respect to tax years beginning after 12-31-97. For a special rule, see Act Sec. 3309(c)(1)-(2), below.

P.L. 105-206, §3309(c)(1)-(2), provides:

(c) EMERGENCY DESIGNATION.—

(1) For the purposes of section 252(e) of the Balanced Budget and Emergency Deficit Control Act, Congress designates the provisions of this section as an emergency requirement.

(2) The amendments made by subsections (a) and (b) of this section shall only take effect upon the transmittal by the President to the Congress of a message designating the provisions of subsections (a) and (b) as an emergency requirement pursuant to section 252(e) of the Balanced Budget and Emergency Deficit Control Act.

[Sec. 6404(i)]

(i) CROSS REFERENCE.—

For authority to suspend running of interest, etc. by reason of Presidentially declared disaster or terroristic or military action, see section 7508A.

Amendments

• 2002, Victims of Terrorism Tax Relief Act of 2001 (P.L. 107-134)

P.L. 107-134, §112(d)(1)(C):

Amended Code Sec. 6404 by adding at the end a new subsection (i). **Effective** for disasters and terroristic or military actions occurring on or after 9-11-2001, with respect to any action of the Secretary of the Treasury, the Secretary of Labor, or the Pension Benefit Guaranty Corporation occurring on or after 1-23-2002.

[Sec. 6405]

SEC. 6405. REPORTS OF REFUNDS AND CREDITS.

[Sec. 6405(a)]

(a) BY TREASURY TO JOINT COMMITTEE.—No refund or credit of any income, war profits, excess profits, estate, or gift tax, or any tax imposed with respect to public charities, private foundations, operators' trust funds, pension plans, or real estate investment trusts under chapter 41, 42, 43, or 44, in excess of $2,000,000 ($5,000,000 in the case of a C corporation) shall be made until after the expiration of 30 days from the date upon which a report giving the name of the person to whom the refund or credit is to be made, the amount of such refund or credit, and a summary of the facts and the decision of the Secretary, is submitted to the Joint Committee on Taxation.

Amendments

• 2014, Tax Increase Prevention Act of 2014 (P.L. 113-295)

P.L. 113-295, §301(a), Division A:

Amended Code Sec. 6405(a) by inserting "($5,000,000 in the case of a C corporation)" after "$2,000,000". **Effective** 12-19-2014, except that such amendment shall not apply with respect to any refund or credit with respect to a report that has been made before such date under Code Sec. 6405.

• 2000, Community Renewal Tax Relief Act of 2000 (P.L. 106-554)

P.L. 106-554, §305(a):

Amended Code Sec. 6405(a) by striking "$1,000,000" and inserting "$2,000,000". **Effective** 12-21-2000, except that such amendment shall not apply with respect to any refund or credit with respect to a report that has been made before such date under Code Sec. 6405.

• 1990, Omnibus Budget Reconciliation Act of 1990 (P.L. 101-508)

P.L. 101-508, §11834(a):

Amended Code Sec. 6405(a) by striking "$200,000" and inserting "$1,000,000." **Effective** 11-5-90, except that such amendment shall not apply with respect to any refund or credit with respect to a report [that] has been made before such date of enactment under section 6405 of the Internal Revenue Code of 1986.

• 1978, Black Lung Benefits Revenue Act of 1977 (P.L. 95-227)

P.L. 95-227, §4(d)(3):

Amended Code Sec. 6405(a) by substituting "public charities, private foundations, operators' trust funds, pension plans, or real estate investment trusts under chapter 41, 42, 43, or 44" for "private foundations and pension plans under chapters 42 and 43". For **effective** date, see the historical comment for P.L. 95-227 under Code Sec. 4951.

• 1976, Tax Reform Act of 1976 (P.L. 94-455)

P.L. 94-455, §1210(a):

Amended Code Sec. 6405(a). **Effective** as indicated in Act Sec. 1210(d)(1), below. Prior to amendment Code Sec. 6405(a) read as follows:

(a) BY TREASURY TO JOINT COMMITTEE.—No refund or credit of any income, war profits, excess profits, estate, or gift tax in excess of $100,000 shall be made until after the expiration of 30 days from the date upon which a report giving the name of the person to whom the refund or credit is to be made, the amount of such refund or credit, and a summary of the facts and the decision of the Secretary or his delegate, is submitted to the Joint Committee on Internal Revenue Taxation.

P.L. 94-455, §1210(d)(1), provides:

(1) The amendments made by subsections (a) and (b) shall take effect on the date of the enactment of this Act [October 4, 1976], except that such amendments shall not apply with respect to any refund or credit with respect to which a report has been made before the date of the enactment of this Act under subsection (a) or (c) of section 6405 of the Internal Revenue Code of 1954.

* * *

[Sec. 6406]

SEC. 6406. PROHIBITION OF ADMINISTRATIVE REVIEW OF DECISIONS.

In the absence of fraud or mistake in mathematical calculation, the findings of fact in and the decision of the Secretary upon the merits of any claim presented under or authorized by the internal revenue laws and the allowance or nonallowance by the Secretary of interest on any credit or refund under the internal revenue laws shall not, except as provided in subchapters C and D of chapter 76 (relating to the Tax Court), be subject to review by any other administrative or accounting officer, employee, or agent of the United States.

Amendments

• 1976, Tax Reform Act of 1976 (P.L. 94-455)

P.L. 94-455, §1906(b)(13)(A):

Amended 1954 Code by substituting "Secretary" for "Secretary or his delegate" each place it appeared. **Effective** 2-1-77.

[Sec. 6407]

SEC. 6407. DATE OF ALLOWANCE OF REFUND OR CREDIT.

The date on which the Secretary first authorizes the scheduling of an overassessment in respect of any internal revenue tax shall be considered as the date of allowance of refund or credit in respect of such tax.

Amendments

• 1976, Tax Reform Act of 1976 (P.L. 94-455)

P.L. 94-455, §1906(b)(13)(A):

Amended 1954 Code by substituting "Secretary" for "Secretary or his delegate" each place it appeared. **Effective** 2-1-77.

[Sec. 6408]

SEC. 6408. STATE ESCHEAT LAWS NOT TO APPLY.

No overpayment of any tax imposed by this title shall be refunded (and no interest with respect to any such overpayment shall be paid) if the amount of such refund (or interest) would escheat to a State or would otherwise become the property of a State under any law relating to the disposition of unclaimed or abandoned property. No refund (or payment of interest) shall be made to the estate of any decedent unless it is affirmatively shown that such amount will not escheat to a State or otherwise become the property of a State under such a law.

Amendments

• 1987, Revenue Act of 1987 (P.L. 100-203)

P.L. 100-203, §10621(a):

Amended subchapter A of chapter 65 by adding at the end thereof new Code Sec. 6408. **Effective** 12-22-87.

* * *

CHAPTER 66—LIMITATIONS

Subchapter A—Limitations on Assessment and Collection

* * *

[Sec. 6501]

SEC. 6501. LIMITATIONS ON ASSESSMENT AND COLLECTION.

[Sec. 6501(a)]

(a) GENERAL RULE.—Except as otherwise provided in this section, the amount of any tax imposed by this title shall be assessed within 3 years after the return was filed (whether or not such return was filed on or after the date prescribed) or, if the tax is payable by stamp, at any time after such tax became due and before the expiration of 3 years after the date on which any part of such tax was paid, and no proceeding in court without assessment for the collection of such tax shall be begun after the expiration of such period. For purposes of this chapter, the term "return" means the return required to be filed by the taxpayer (and does not include a return of any person from whom the taxpayer has received an item of income, gain, loss, deduction, or credit).

Amendments

• 1997, Taxpayer Relief Act of 1997 (P.L. 105-34)

P.L. 105-34, §1284(a):

Amended Code Sec. 6501(a) by adding at the end a new sentence. **Effective** for tax years beginning after 8-5-97.

• 1958, Excise Tax Technical Changes Act of 1958 (P.L. 85-859)

P.L. 85-859, §165(a):

Amended Code Sec. 6501(a) by striking out "within 3 years after such tax became due," and substituting "at any time after such tax became due and before the expiration of 3 years after the date on which any part of such tax was paid,".

[Sec. 6501(b)]

(b) TIME RETURN DEEMED FILED.—

(1) EARLY RETURN.—For purposes of this section, a return of tax imposed by this title, except tax imposed by chapter 3, 4, 21, or 24, filed before the last day prescribed by law or by regulations promulgated pursuant to law for the filing thereof, shall be considered as filed on such last day.

(2) RETURN OF CERTAIN EMPLOYMENT AND WITHHOLDING TAXES.—For purposes of this section, if a return of tax imposed by chapter 3, 4, 21 or 24 for any period ending with or within a calendar year is filed before April 15 of the succeeding calendar year, such return shall be considered filed on April 15 of such calendar year.

(3) RETURN EXECUTED BY SECRETARY.—Notwithstanding the provisions of paragraph (2) of section 6020(b), the execution of a return by the Secretary pursuant to the authority conferred by such section shall not start the running of the period of limitations on assessment and collection.

(4) RETURN OF EXCISE TAXES.—For purposes of this section, the filing of a return for a specified period on which an entry has been made with respect to a tax imposed under a provision of subtitle D (including a return on which an entry has been made showing no liability for such tax for such period) shall constitute the filing of a return of all amounts of such tax which, if properly paid, would be required to be reported on such return for such period.

Amendments

• 2010, Hiring Incentives to Restore Employment Act (P.L. 111-147)

P.L. 111-147, §501(c)(2):

Amended Code Sec. 6501(b)(1) by inserting "4," after "chapter 3,". **Effective** generally for payments made after 12-31-2012. For a special rule, see Act Sec. 501(d)(2), below.

P.L. 111-147, §501(c)(3)(A)-(B):

Amended Code Sec. 6501(b)(2) by inserting "4," after "chapter 3," in the text thereof, and by striking "TAXES AND TAX IMPOSED BY CHAPTER 3" in the heading thereof and inserting "AND WITHHOLDING TAXES". **Effective** generally for payments made after 12-31-2012. For a special rule, see Act Sec. 501(d)(2), below.

P.L. 111-147, §501(d)(2), provides:

(2) GRANDFATHERED TREATMENT OF OUTSTANDING OBLIGATIONS.—The amendments made by this section shall not require any amount to be deducted or withheld from any payment under any obligation outstanding on the date which is 2 years after the date of the enactment of this Act or from the gross proceeds from any disposition of such an obligation.

• 1976, Tax Reform Act of 1976 (P.L. 94-455)

P.L. 94-455, §1906(b)(13)(A):

Amended 1954 Code by substituting "Secretary" for "Secretary or his delegate" each place it appeared. **Effective** 2-1-77.

• 1966, Foreign Investors Tax Act of 1966 (P.L. 89-809)

P.L. 89-809, §105(f)(3):

Amended Code Sec. 6501(b)(1) and (2) by substituting "chapter 3, 21, or 24" for "chapter 21 or 24" and amended Code Sec. 6501(b)(2) by inserting "and Tax Imposed by Chapter 3" after "Taxes" in the heading. **Effective** 11-13-66.

• 1965, Excise Tax Reduction Act of 1965 (P.L. 89-44)

P.L. 89-44, §810(a):

Amended Sec. 6501(b) by adding paragraph (4). **Effective** 7-1-65.

[Sec. 6501(c)]

(c) EXCEPTIONS.—

(1) FALSE RETURN.—In the case of a false or fraudulent return with the intent to evade tax, the tax may be assessed, or a proceeding in court for collection of such tax may be begun without assessment, at any time.

(2) WILLFUL ATTEMPT TO EVADE TAX.—In case of a willful attempt in any manner to defeat or evade tax imposed by this title (other than tax imposed by subtitle A or B), the tax may be assessed, or a proceeding in court for the collection of such tax may be begun without assessment, at any time.

(3) NO RETURN.—In the case of failure to file a return, the tax may be assessed, or a proceeding in court for the collection of such tax may be begun without assessment, at any time.

(4) EXTENSION BY AGREEMENT.—

(A) IN GENERAL.—Where before the expiration of the time prescribed for the assessment of any tax imposed by this title, except the estate tax provided in chapter 11, both the Secretary and the taxpayer have consented in writing to its assessment after such time, the tax may be assessed at any time prior to the expiration of the period agreed upon. The period so agreed upon may be extended by subsequent agreements in writing made before the expiration of the period previously agreed upon.

(B) NOTICE TO TAXPAYER OF RIGHT TO REFUSE OR LIMIT EXTENSION.—The Secretary shall notify the taxpayer of the taxpayer's right to refuse to extend the period of limitations, or to limit such extension to particular issues or to a particular period of time, on each occasion when the taxpayer is requested to provide such consent.

(5) TAX RESULTING FROM CHANGES IN CERTAIN INCOME TAX OR ESTATE TAX CREDITS.—For special rules applicable in cases where the adjustment of certain taxes allowed as a credit against income taxes or estate taxes results in additional tax, see section 905(c) (relating to the foreign tax credit for income tax purposes) and section 2016 (relating to taxes of foreign countries, States, etc., claimed as credit against estate taxes).

(6) TERMINATION OF PRIVATE FOUNDATION STATUS.—In the case of a tax on termination of private foundation status under section 507, such tax may be assessed, or a proceeding in court for the collection of such tax may be begun without assessment, at any time.

(7) SPECIAL RULE FOR CERTAIN AMENDED RETURNS.—Where, within the 60-day period ending on the day on which the time prescribed in this section for the assessment of any tax imposed by subtitle A for any taxable year would otherwise expire, the Secretary receives a written document signed by the taxpayer showing that the taxpayer owes an additional amount of such tax for such taxable year, the period for the assessment of such additional amount shall not expire before the day 60 days after the day on which the Secretary receives such document.

(8) FAILURE TO NOTIFY SECRETARY OF CERTAIN FOREIGN TRANSFERS.—

(A) IN GENERAL.—In the case of any information which is required to be reported to the Secretary pursuant to an election under section 1295(b) or under section 1298(f), 6038, 6038A,

6038B, 6038D, 6046, 6046A, or 6048, the time for assessment of any tax imposed by this title with respect to any tax return, event, or period to which such information relates shall not expire before the date which is 3 years after the date on which the Secretary is furnished the information required to be reported under such section.

(B) APPLICATION TO FAILURES DUE TO REASONABLE CAUSE.—If the failure to furnish the information referred to in subparagraph (A) is due to reasonable cause and not willful neglect, subparagraph (A) shall apply only to the item or items related to such failure.

(9) GIFT TAX ON CERTAIN GIFTS NOT SHOWN ON RETURN.—If any gift of property the value of which (or any increase in taxable gifts required under section 2701(d) which) is required to be shown on a return of tax imposed by chapter 12 (without regard to section 2503(b)), and is not shown on such return, any tax imposed by chapter 12 on such gift may be assessed, or a proceeding in court for the collection of such tax may be begun without assessment, at any time. The preceding sentence shall not apply to any item which is disclosed in such return, or in a statement attached to the return, in a manner adequate to apprise the Secretary of the nature of such item.

(10) LISTED TRANSACTIONS.—If a taxpayer fails to include on any return or statement for any taxable year any information with respect to a listed transaction (as defined in section 6707A(c)(2)) which is required under section 6011 to be included with such return or statement, the time for assessment of any tax imposed by this title with respect to such transaction shall not expire before the date which is 1 year after the earlier of—

(A) the date on which the Secretary is furnished the information so required, or

(B) the date that a material advisor meets the requirements of section 6112 with respect to a request by the Secretary under section 6112(b) relating to such transaction with respect to such taxpayer.

(11) CERTAIN ORDERS OF CRIMINAL RESTITUTION.—In the case of any amount described in section 6201(a)(4), such amount may be assessed, or a proceeding in court for the collection of such amount may be begun without assessment, at any time.

(12) CERTAIN TAXES ATTRIBUTABLE TO PARTNERSHIP ADJUSTMENTS.—In the case of any partnership adjustment determined under subchapter C of chapter 63, the period for assessment of any tax imposed under chapter 2 or 2A which is attributable to such adjustment shall not expire before the date that is 1 year after—

(A) in the case of an adjustment pursuant to the decision of a court in a proceeding brought under section 6234, such decision becomes final, or

(B) in any other case, 90 days after the date on which the notice of the final partnership adjustment is mailed under section 6231.

Amendments

• 2018, Tax Technical Corrections Act of 2018 (P.L. 115-141)

P.L. 115-141, §201(b)(2), Div. U:

Amended Code Sec. 6501(c) by adding at the end a new paragraph (12). **Effective** as if included in section 1101 of the Bipartisan Budget Act of 2015 [**effective** generally for returns filed for partnership tax years beginning after 12-31-2017.—CCH].

P.L. 115-141, §205(b), Div. U:

Amended Code Sec. 6501(c)(4)(A) by striking "in this section" before "for the assessment". **Effective** as if included in section 1101 of the Bipartisan Budget Act of 2015 [**effective** generally for returns filed for partnership tax years beginning after 12-31-2017.—CCH].

• 2010, Firearms Excise Tax Improvement Act of 2010 (P.L. 111-237)

P.L. 111-237, §3(b)(2):

Amended Code Sec. 6501(c) by adding at the end a new paragraph (11). **Effective** for restitution ordered after 8-16-2010.

• 2010, (P.L. 111-226)

P.L. 111-226, §218(a)(1)-(2):

Amended Code Sec. 6501(c)(8) by striking "In the case of any information" and inserting

"(A) IN GENERAL.—In the case of any information"; and

by adding at the end a new subparagraph (B). **Effective** as if included in section 513 of the Hiring Incentives to Restore Employment Act (P.L. 111-147) [**effective** for returns filed after the date of the enactment of P.L. 111-147 [3-18-2010]; and returns filed on or before such date if the period specified in Code Sec. 6501 (determined without regard to the amendment made by section 513) for assessment of such taxes has not expired as of such date.—CCH].

• 2010, Hiring Incentives to Restore Employment Act (P.L. 111-147)

P.L. 111-147, §513(b)(1)-(3):

Amended Code Sec. 6501(c)(8) by inserting "pursuant to an election under section 1295(b) or" before "under section 6038", by inserting "1298(f)," before "6038", and by inserting "6038D," after "6038B,". For the **effective** date, see Act Sec. 513(d), below.

P.L. 111-147, §513(c):

Amended Code Sec. 6501(c)(8) by striking "event" and inserting "tax return, event,". For the **effective** date, see Act Sec. 513(d), below.

P.L. 111-147, §513(d), provides:

(d) EFFECTIVE DATE.—The amendments made by this section shall apply to—

(1) returns filed after the date of the enactment of this Act; and

(2) returns filed on or before such date if the period specified in section 6501 of the Internal Revenue Code of 1986 (determined without regard to such amendments) for assessment of such taxes has not expired as of such date.

• 2005, Gulf Opportunity Zone Act of 2005 (P.L. 109-135)

P.L. 109-135, §403(y):

Amended Code Sec. 6501(c)(10)(B) by striking "(as defined in section 6111)" after "material advisor". **Effective** as if included in the provision of the American Jobs Creation Act of 2004 (P.L. 108-357) to which it relates [**effective** for tax years with respect to which the period for assessing a deficiency did not expire before 10-22-2004.—CCH.]

• 2004, American Jobs Creation Act of 2004 (P.L. 108-357)

P.L. 108-357, §814(a):

Amended Code Sec. 6501(c) by adding at the end a new paragraph (10). **Effective** for tax years with respect to which the period for assessing a deficiency did not expire before 10-22-2004.

• 1998, IRS Restructuring and Reform Act of 1998 (P.L. 105-206)

P.L. 105-206, §3461(b)(1)-(2):

Amended Code Sec. 6501(c)(4) by striking "Where" and inserting "(A) IN GENERAL.—Where", and by adding at the end a new subparagraph (B). **Effective** for requests to extend the period of limitations made after 12-31-99. For a special rule, see Act Sec. 3461(c)(2), below.

P.L. 105-206, §3461(c)(2), provides:

(2) PRIOR REQUEST.—If, in any request to extend the period of limitations made on or before December 31, 1999, a taxpayer agreed to extend such period beyond the 10-year period referred to in section 6502(a) of the Internal Revenue Code of 1986, such extension shall expire on the latest of—

(A) the last day of such 10-year period;

(B) December 31, 2002; or

(C) in the case of an extension in connection with an installment agreement, the 90th day after the end of the period of such extension.

P.L. 105-206, §6007(e)(2)(A):

Amended Code Sec. 6501(c)(9) by striking the last sentence. **Effective** as if included in the provision of P.L. 105-34 to which it relates [**effective** for gifts made in calendar years ending after 8-5-97.—CCH]. Prior to being stricken, the last sentence of Code Sec. 6501(c)(9) read as follows:

The value of any item which is so disclosed may not be redetermined by the Secretary after the expiration of the period under subsection (a).

• 1997, Taxpayer Relief Act of 1997 (P.L. 105-34)

P.L. 105-34, §506(b):

Amended Code Sec. 6501(c)(9). **Effective** for gifts made in calendar years ending after 8-5-97. Prior to amendment, Code Sec. 6501(c)(9) read as follows:

(9) GIFT TAX ON CERTAIN GIFTS NOT SHOWN ON RETURN.—If any gift of property the value of which is determined under section 2701 or 2702 (or any increase in taxable gifts required under section 2701(d)) is required to be shown on a return of tax imposed by chapter 12 (without regard to section 2503(b)), and is not shown on such return, any tax imposed by chapter 12 on such gift may be assessed, or a proceeding in court for the collection of such tax may be begun without assessment, at any time. The preceding sentence shall not apply to any item not shown as a gift on such return if such item is disclosed in such return, or in a statement attached to the return, in a manner adequate to apprise the Secretary of the nature of such item.

P.L. 105-34, §1145(a):

Amended Code Sec. 6501(c)(8). **Effective** for information the due date for the reporting of which is after 8-5-97. Prior to amendment, Code Sec. 6501(c)(8) read as follows:

(8) FAILURE TO NOTIFY SECRETARY UNDER SECTION 6038B.—In the case of any tax imposed on any exchange or distribution by reason of subsection (a), (d), or (e) of section 367, the time for assessment of such tax shall not expire before the date which is 3 years after the date on which the Secretary is notified of such exchange or distribution under section 6038B(a).

• 1990, Omnibus Budget Reconciliation Act of 1990 (P.L. 101-508)

P.L. 101-508, §11602(b):

Amended Code Sec. 6501(c) by adding at the end thereof a new paragraph (9). **Effective** for gifts after 10-8-90.

• 1986, Tax Reform Act of 1986 (P.L. 99-514)

P.L. 99-514, §1810(g)(3)(A), (B):

Amended Code Sec. 6501(c)(8) by striking out "subsection (a) or (d)" and inserting in lieu thereof "subsection (a), (d), or (e)", and by striking out "exchange" each place it appears and inserting in lieu thereof "exchange or distribution". **Effective** as if included in the provision of P.L. 98-369 to which it relates.

• 1984, Deficit Reduction Act of 1984 (P.L. 98-369)

P.L. 98-369, §131(d)(2):

Amended Code Sec. 6501(c) by adding new paragraph (8). **Effective** for transfers or exchanges after 12-31-84, in tax years ending after such date. Special rules appear in Act Sec. 131(g)(2) and (3) following Code Sec. 367.

P.L. 98-369, §211(b)(24)(A):

Amended Code Sec. 6501(c) by striking out paragraph (6) and by redesignating paragraph (7) as paragraph (6). **Effective** for tax years beginning after 12-31-83. Prior to amendment, paragraph (6) read as follows:

(6) Tax Resulting from Certain Distributions or from Termination as Life Insurance Company.—In the case of any tax imposed under section 802(a) by reason of section 802(b)(3) on account of a termination of the taxpayer as an insurance company or as a life insurance company to which section 815(d)(2)(A) applies, or on account of a distribution by the taxpayer to which section 815(d)(2)(B) applies, such tax may be assessed within 3 years after the return was filed (whether or not such return was filed on or after the date prescribed) for the taxable year for which the taxpayer ceases to be an insurance company, the second taxable year for which the taxpayer is not a life insurance company, or the taxable year in which the distribution is actually made, as the case may be.

P.L. 98-369, §447(a):

Amended Code Sec. 6501(c) by adding new paragraph (7). **Effective** with respect to documents received by the Secretary of the Treasury (or his delegate) after 7-18-84.

• 1976, Tax Reform Act of 1976 (P.L. 94-455)

P.L. 94-455, §1906(b)(13)(A):

Amended 1954 Code by substituting "Secretary" for "Secretary or his delegate" each place it appeared. **Effective** 2-1-77.

• 1969, Tax Reform Act of 1969 (P.L. 91-172)

P.L. 91-172, §101(g)(2):

Added paragraph (7) to Code Sec. 6501(c). **Effective** 1-1-70.

• 1962 (P.L. 87-858)

P.L. 87-858, §3(b)(4):

Amended Code Sec. 6501(c)(6) by substituting "802(a)" for "802(a)(1)". **Effective** 1-1-62.

• 1959, Life Insurance Company Income Tax Act of 1959 (P.L. 86-69)

P.L. 86-69, §3(g):

Amended Code Sec. 6501(c) by adding a new paragraph (6). **Effective** for tax years beginning after 12-31-57.

[Sec. 6501(d)]

(d) REQUEST FOR PROMPT ASSESSMENT.—Except as otherwise provided in subsection (c), (e), or (f), in the case of any tax (other than the tax imposed by chapter 11 of subtitle B, relating to estate taxes) for which return is required in the case of a decedent, or by his estate during the period of administration, or by a corporation, the tax shall be assessed, and any proceeding in court without assessment for the collection of such tax shall be begun, within 18 months after written request therefor (filed after the return is made and filed in such manner and such form as may be prescribed by regulations of the Secretary) by the executor, administrator, or other fiduciary representing the estate of such decedent, or by the corporation, but not after the expiration of 3 years after the return was filed. This subsection shall not apply in the case of a corporation unless—

(1)(A) such written request notifies the Secretary that the corporation contemplates dissolution at or before the expiration of such 18-month period, (B) the dissolution is in good faith begun before the expiration of such 18-month period, and (C) the dissolution is completed;

(2)(A) such written request notifies the Secretary that a dissolution has in good faith been begun, and (B) the dissolution is completed; or

(3) a dissolution has been completed at the time such written request is made.

Amendments

• 1976, Tax Reform Act of 1976 (P.L. 94-455)

P.L. 94-455, §1906(b)(13)(A):

Amended 1954 Code by substituting "Secretary" for "Secretary or his delegate" each place it appeared. **Effective** 2-1-77.

• 1958, Technical Amendments Act of 1958 (P.L. 85-866)

P.L. 85-866, §80(a):

Amended the first sentence of Sec. 6501(d) by striking out "subsection (c)" and substituting "subsection (c), (e), or (f)". **Effective** 1-1-54.

P.L. 85-866, §80(b):

Amended paragraphs (1), (2) and (3) of Sec. 6501(d). **Effective** 1-1-54. Prior to amendment, those paragraphs read as follows:

"(1) Such written request notifies the Secretary or his delegate that the corporation contemplates dissolution at or before the expiration of such 18-month period; and

"(2) The dissolution is in good faith begun before the expiration of such 18-month period; and

"(3) The dissolution is completed."

[Sec. 6501(e)]

(e) SUBSTANTIAL OMISSION OF ITEMS.—Except as otherwise provided in subsection (c)—

(1) INCOME TAXES.—In the case of any tax imposed by subtitle A—

(A) GENERAL RULE.—If the taxpayer omits from gross income an amount properly includible therein and—

(i) such amount is in excess of 25 percent of the amount of gross income stated in the return, or

(ii) such amount—

(I) is attributable to one or more assets with respect to which information is required to be reported under section 6038D (or would be so required if such section were applied without regard to the dollar threshold specified in subsection (a) thereof and without regard to any exceptions provided pursuant to subsection (h)(1) thereof), and

(II) is in excess of $5,000,

the tax may be assessed, or a proceeding in court for collection of such tax may be begun without assessment, at any time within 6 years after the return was filed.

(B) DETERMINATION OF GROSS INCOME.—For purposes of subparagraph (A)—

(i) In the case of a trade or business, the term "gross income" means the total of the amounts received or accrued from the sale of goods or services (if such amounts are required to be shown on the return) prior to diminution by the cost of such sales or services;

(ii) An understatement of gross income by reason of an overstatement of unrecovered cost or other basis is an omission from gross income; and

(iii) In determining the amount omitted from gross income (other than in the case of an overstatement of unrecovered cost or other basis), there shall not be taken into account any amount which is omitted from gross income stated in the return if such amount is disclosed in the return, or in a statement attached to the return, in a manner adequate to apprise the Secretary of the nature and amount of such item.

(C) CONSTRUCTIVE DIVIDENDS.—If the taxpayer omits from gross income an amount properly includible therein under section 951(a), the tax may be assessed, or a proceeding in court for the collection of such tax may be done without assessing, at any time within 6 years after the return was filed.

(2) ESTATE AND GIFT TAXES.—In the case of a return of estate tax under chapter 11 or a return of gift tax under chapter 12, if the taxpayer omits from the gross estate or from the total amount of the gifts made during the period for which the return was filed items includible in such gross estate or such total gifts, as the case may be, as exceed in amount 25 percent of the gross estate stated in the return or the total amount of gifts stated in the return, the tax may be assessed, or a proceeding in court for the collection of such tax may be begun without assessment, at any time within 6 years after the return was filed. In determining the items omitted from the gross estate or the total gifts, there shall not be taken into account any item which is omitted from the gross estate or from the total gifts stated in the return if such item is disclosed in the return, or in a statement attached to the return, in a manner adequate to apprise the Secretary of the nature and amount of such item.

(3) EXCISE TAXES.—In the case of a return of a tax imposed under a provision of subtitle D, if the return omits an amount of such tax properly includible thereon which exceeds 25 percent of the amount of such tax reported thereon, the tax may be assessed, or a proceeding in court for the collection of such tax may be begun without assessment, at any time within 6 years after the return is filed. In determining the amount of tax omitted on a return, there shall not be taken into

account any amount of tax imposed by chapter 41, 42, 43, or 44 which is omitted from the return if the transaction giving rise to such tax is disclosed in the return, or in a statement attached to the return, in a manner adequate to apprise the Secretary of the existence and nature of such item.

Amendments

• 2015, Surface Transportation and Veterans Health Care Choice Improvement Act of 2015 (P.L. 114-41)

P.L. 114-41, § 2005(a)(1)-(2)

Amended Code Sec. 6501(e)(1)(B) by striking "and" at the end of clause (i), by redesignating clause (ii) as clause (iii), and by inserting after clause (i) a new clause (ii), and by inserting "(other than in the case of an overstatement of unrecovered cost or other basis)" in clause (iii) (as so redesignated) after "In determining the amount omitted from gross income". For the **effective** date, see Act Sec. 2005(b)(1)-(2), below.

P.L. 114-41, § 2005(b)(1)-(2), provides:

(b) EFFECTIVE DATE.—The amendments made by this section shall apply to—

(1) returns filed after the date of the enactment of this Act, and

(2) returns filed on or before such date if the period specified in section 6501 of the Internal Revenue Code of 1986 (determined without regard to such amendments) for assessment of the taxes with respect to which such return relates has not expired as of such date.

• 2010, Hiring Incentives to Restore Employment Act (P.L. 111-147)

P.L. 111-147, § 513(a)(1):

Amended Code Sec. 6501(e)(1) by redesignating subparagraphs (A) and (B) as subparagraphs (B) and (C), respectively, and by inserting before subparagraph (B) (as so redesignated) a new subparagraph (A). For the **effective** date, see Act Sec. 513(d), below.

P.L. 111-147, § 513(a)(2)(A):

Amended Code Sec. 6501(e)(1)(B), as redesignated by Act Sec. 513(a)(1), by striking all that precedes clause (i) and inserting "(B) DETERMINATION OF GROSS INCOME.—For purposes of subparagraph (A)—". For the **effective** date, see Act Sec. 513(d), below. Prior to being stricken, all that precedes clause (i) of Code Sec. 6501(e)(1)(B) read as follows:

(B) GENERAL RULE.—If the taxpayer omits from gross income an amount properly includible therein which is in excess of 25 percent of the amount of gross income stated in the return, the tax may be assessed, or a proceeding in court for the collection of such tax may be begun without assessment, at any time within 6 years after the return was filed. For purposes of this subparagraph—

P.L. 111-147, § 513(d), provides:

(d) EFFECTIVE DATE.—The amendments made by this section shall apply to—

(1) returns filed after the date of the enactment of this Act; and

(2) returns filed on or before such date if the period specified in section 6501 of the Internal Revenue Code of 1986 (determined without regard to such amendments) for assessment of such taxes has not expired as of such date.

• 2004, American Jobs Creation Act of 2004 (P.L. 108-357)

P.L. 108-357, § 413(c)(28):

Amended Code Sec. 6501(e)(1)(B). **Effective** for tax years of foreign corporations beginning after 12-31-2004, and for tax years of United States shareholders with or within which such tax years of foreign corporations end. Prior to amendment, Code Sec. 6501(e)(1)(B) read as follows:

(B) CONSTRUCTIVE DIVIDENDS.—If the taxpayer omits from gross income an amount properly includible therein under section 551(b) (relating to the inclusion in the gross income of United States shareholders of their distributive shares of the undistributed foreign personal holding company income), the tax may be assessed, or a proceeding in court for the collection of such tax may be begun without assessment, at any time within 6 years after the return was filed.

• 1978, Revenue Act of 1978 (P.L. 95-600)

P.L. 95-600, § 701(t)(3)(A):

Amended Code Sec. 6501(e)(3) by changing ", or 43" to "43, or 44". **Effective** 10-4-76.

• 1978, Black Lung Benefits Revenue Act of 1977 (P.L. 95-227)

P.L. 95-227, § 4(d)(4):

Amended Code Sec. 6501(e)(3) by substituting "43, or 44" for "or 43" in the second sentence thereof. For **effective** date, see the historical comment for P.L. 95-227 under Code Sec. 4951.

• 1976, Tax Reform Act of 1976 (P.L. 94-455)

P.L. 94-455, § 1307(d)(2)(F)(vi):

Substituted "chapter 41, 42," for "chapter 42" in Code Sec. 6501(e)(3). **Effective** 10-4-76.

P.L. 94-455, § 1906(b)(13)(A):

Amended the 1954 Code by substituting "Secretary" for "Secretary or his delegate" each place it appeared. **Effective** 2-1-77.

• 1974, Employee Retirement Income Security Act of 1974 (P.L. 93-406)

P.L. 93-406, § 1016(a)(14):

Amended Code Sec. 6501(e)(3) by changing "chapter 42" to "chapter 42 or 43". For **effective** date, see amendment note for Code Sec. 410.

• 1970, Excise, Estate, and Gift Tax Adjustment Act of 1970 (P.L. 91-614)

P.L. 91-614, § 102(d)(8):

Amended Code Sec. 6501(e) by substituting "period for which the return was filed" for "year" in the first sentence of paragraph (2). **Effective** for gifts made after 12-31-70.

• 1969, Tax Reform Act of 1969 (P.L. 91-172)

P.L. 91-172, § 101(g)(3):

Added the last sentence in Code Sec. 6501(e)(3). **Effective** 1-1-70.

• 1965, Excise Tax Reduction Act of 1965 (P.L. 89-44)

P.L. 89-44, § 810(b):

Amended Code Sec. 6501(e) by adding paragraph (3). **Effective** 7-1-65.

* * *

[Sec. 6501(l)]

(l) SPECIAL RULE FOR CHAPTER 42 AND SIMILAR TAXES.—

(1) IN GENERAL.—For purposes of any tax imposed by section 4912, by chapter 42 (other than section 4940) or by section 4975, the return referred to in this section shall be the return filed by the private foundation, plan, trust, or other organization (as the case may be) for the year in which the act (or failure to act) giving rise to liability for such tax occurred. For purposes of section 4940, such return is the return filed by the private foundation for the taxable year for which the tax is imposed.

(2) CERTAIN CONTRIBUTIONS TO SECTION 501(c)(3) ORGANIZATIONS.—In the case of a deficiency of tax of a private foundation making a contribution in the manner provided in section 4942(g)(3)

(relating to certain contributions to section 501(c)(3) organizations) attributable to the failure of a section 501(c)(3) organization to make the distribution prescribed by section 4942(g)(3), such deficiency may be assessed at any time before the expiration of one year after the expiration of the period within which a deficiency may be assessed for the taxable year with respect to which the contribution was made.

(3) CERTAIN SET-ASIDES DESCRIBED IN SECTION 4942(g)(2).—In the case of a deficiency attributable to the failure of an amount set aside by a private foundation for a specific project to be treated as a qualifying distribution under the provisions of section 4942(g)(2)(B)(ii), such deficiency may be assessed at any time before the expiration of 2 years after the expiration of the period within which a deficiency may be assessed for the taxable year to which the amount set aside relates.

(4) INDIVIDUAL RETIREMENT PLANS.—

(A) IN GENERAL.—For purposes of any tax imposed by section 4973 or 4974 in connection with an individual retirement plan, the return referred to in this section shall include the income tax return filed by the person on whom the tax under such section is imposed for the year in which the act (or failure to act) giving rise to the liability for such tax occurred.

(B) RULE IN CASE OF INDIVIDUALS NOT REQUIRED TO FILE RETURN.—In the case of a person who is not required to file an income tax return for such year—

(i) the return referred to in this section shall be the income tax return that such person would have been required to file but for the fact that such person was not required to file such return, and

(ii) the 3-year period referred to in subsection (a) with respect to the return shall be deemed to begin on the date by which the return would have been required to be filed (excluding any extension thereof).

(C) PERIOD FOR ASSESSMENT IN CASE OF INCOME TAX RETURN.—In any case in which the return with respect to a tax imposed by section 4973 is the individual's income tax return for purposes of this section, subsection (a) shall be applied by substituting a 6-year period in lieu of the 3-year period otherwise referred to in such subsection.

(D) EXCEPTION FOR CERTAIN ACQUISITIONS OF PROPERTY.—In the case of any tax imposed by section 4973 that is attributable to acquiring property for less than fair market value, subparagraph (A) shall not apply.

Amendments

• 2022, SECURE 2.0 Act of 2022 (P.L. 117-328)

P.L. 117-328, §313(a):

Amended Code Sec. 6501(l) by adding at the end a new paragraph (4). **Effective** 12-29-2022.

• 1987, Revenue Act of 1987 (P.L. 100-203)

P.L. 100-203, §10712(c)(2):

Amended Code Sec. 6501(l)(1) by striking out "plan, or trust" and inserting in lieu thereof "plan, trust, or other organization." **Effective** for tax years beginning after 12-22-87.

P.L. 100-203, §10714(c):

Amended Code Sec. 6501(l)(1) by striking out "by chapter 42 (other than section 4940)" and inserting in lieu thereof "by section 4912, by chapter 42 (other than section 4940),". **Effective** for tax years beginning after 12-22-87.

• 1984, Deficit Reduction Act of 1984 (P.L. 98-369)

P.L. 98-369, §163(b)(1):

Amended Code Sec. 6501 by striking subsection (l) and redesignating subsection (n) as (l). **Effective** for expenditures with respect to which the second tax year described in Code Sec. 118(b)(2)(B) ends after 12-31-84. Prior to being stricken, subsection (l) read as follows:

(l) Joint Income Return After Separate Return.—For period of limitations for assessment and collection in the case of a joint income return filed after separate returns have been filed, see section 6013(b)(3) and (4).

P.L. 98-369, §314(a)(3):

Amended Code Sec. 6501(n)(3) [prior to its redesignation as (l)] by striking out "section 4942(g)(2)(B)(i)(II)" and inserting in lieu thereof "section 4942(g)(2)(B)(ii)".

• 1978, Black Lung Benefits Revenue Act of 1977 (P.L. 95-227)

P.L. 95-227, §4(d)(5):

Amended Code Sec. 6501(n) by adding "AND SIMILAR" in the heading and by substituting the first sentence for the following: "For purposes of any tax imposed by chapter 42 (other than section 4940), the return referred to in this section shall be the return filed by the private foundation for the year in which the act (or failure to act) giving rise to liability for such tax occurred." For **effective** date, see the historical comment for P.L. 95-227 under Code Sec. 4951.

• 1976, Tax Reform Act of 1976 (P.L. 94-455)

P.L. 94-455, §1302(b):

Added Code Sec. 6501(n)(3). **Effective** for tax years beginning after 12-31-74.

• 1969, Tax Reform Act of 1969 (P.L. 91-172)

P.L. 91-172, §101(g)(1):

Added Code Sec. 6501(n). **Effective** 1-1-70.

• 1964 (P.L. 88-571)

P.L. 88-571, §3(b):

Redesignated former Code Sec. 6501(k) as Sec. 6501(l).

• 1962, Revenue Act of 1962 (P.L. 87-834)

P.L. 87-834, §2:

Redesignated Code Sec. 6501(j) as 6501(k). **Effective** for tax years ending after 12-31-61.

• 1960 (P.L. 86-780)

P.L. 86-780, §3(c):

Redesignated Sec. 6501(i) as 6501(j). **Effective** for tax years beginning after 12-31-57.

• 1958, Technical Amendments Act of 1958 (P.L. 85-866)

P.L. 85-866, §81(b):

Redesignated Sec. 6501(h) as 6501(i). **Effective** 1-1-54.

[Sec. 6501(m)]

(m) DEFICIENCIES ATTRIBUTABLE TO ELECTION OF CERTAIN CREDITS.—The period for assessing a deficiency attributable to any election under section 30B(h)(9), 30C(e)(4), 30D(f)(6), 35(g)(11), 40(f), 43,

45B, 45C(d)(4), 45H(g), or 51(j) (or any revocation thereof) shall not expire before the date 1 year after the date on which the Secretary is notified of such election (or revocation).

Amendments

• 2022, Inflation Reduction Act of 2022 (P.L. 117-169)

P.L. 117-169, §13401(i)(5):

Amended Code Sec. 6501(m) by striking "30D(e)(4)" and inserting "30D(f)(6)". **Effective** for vehicles placed in service after 12-31-2022.

• 2018, Tax Technical Corrections Act of 2018 (P.L. 115-141)

P.L. 115-141, §401(a)(295), Div. U:

Amended Code Sec. 6501(m) by striking "any election" and all that follows through "(or any" and inserting "any election under section 30B(h)(9), 30C(e)(4), 30D(e)(4), 35(g)(11), 40(f), 43, 45B, 45C(d)(4), 45H(g), or 51(j) (or any". **Effective** 3-23-2018. Prior to being stricken, "any election" and all that follows through "(or any" read as follows:

any election under [section] 30B(h)(9), 30C(e)(5) [30C(e)(4)], 30D(e)(4), 35(g)(11), 40(f), 43, 45B, 45C(d)(4), 45H(g), 45S(h), or 51(j) (or any

• 2017, Tax Cuts and Jobs Act (P.L. 115-97)

P.L. 115-97, §13403(d)(2):

Amended Code Sec. 6501(m) by inserting "45S(h)," after "45H(g),". **Effective** for wages paid in tax years beginning after 12-31-2017.

• 2015, Trade Adjustment Assistance Reauthorization Act of 2015 (P.L. 114-27)

P.L. 114-27, §407(e):

Amended Code Sec. 6501(m) by inserting ", 35(g)(11)" after "30D(e)(4)". **Effective** generally for coverage months in tax years beginning after 12-31-2013. For a transition rule, see Act Sec. 407(f)(3), below.

P.L. 114-27, §407(f)(3), provides:

(3) TRANSITION RULE.—Notwithstanding section 35(g)(11)(B)(i) of the Internal Revenue Code of 1986 (as added by this title), an election to apply section 35 of such Code to an eligible coverage month (as defined in section 35(b) of such Code) (and not to claim the credit under section 36B of such Code with respect to such month) in a taxable year beginning after December 31, 2013, and before the date of the enactment of this Act—

(A) may be made at any time on or after such date of enactment and before the expiration of the 3-year period of limitation prescribed in section 6511(a) with respect to such taxable year; and

(B) may be made on an amended return.

• 2014, Tax Technical Corrections Act of 2014 (P.L. 113-295)

P.L. 113-295, §221(a)(2)(E), Division A:

Amended Code Sec. 6501(m) by striking "section 30(e)(6)," before "30B(h)(9),". **Effective** generally 12-19-2014. For a special rule, see Act Sec. 221(b)(2), Division A, below.

P.L. 113-295, §221(b)(2), Division A, provides:

(2) SAVINGS PROVISION.—If—

(A) any provision amended or repealed by the amendments made by this section applied to—

(i) any transaction occurring before the date of the enactment of this Act,

(ii) any property acquired before such date of enactment, or

(iii) any item of income, loss, deduction, or credit taken into account before such date of enactment, and

(B) the treatment of such transaction, property, or item under such provision would (without regard to the amendments or repeals made by this section) affect the liability for tax for periods ending after date of enactment, nothing in the amendments or repeals made by this section shall be construed to affect the treatment of such transaction, property, or item for purposes of determining liability for tax for periods ending after such date of enactment.

• 2009, American Recovery and Reinvestment Tax Act of 2009 (P.L. 111-5)

P.L. 111-5, §1141(b)(4):

Amended Code Sec. 6501(m) by striking "section [sic] 30D(e)(9)" and inserting "section [sic] 30D(e)(4)". **Effective** for vehicles acquired after 12-31-2009.

P.L. 111-5, §1142(b)(7):

Amended Code Sec. 6501(m) by striking "section 30(d)(4)" and inserting "section 30(e)(6)". **Effective** for vehicles acquired after 2-17-2009. For a transitional rule, see Act Sec. 1142(d) in the amendment notes for Code Sec. 30.

• 2008, Energy Improvement and Extension Act of 2008 (P.L. 110-343)

P.L. 110-343, Division B, §205(d)(3):

Amended Code Sec. 6501(m) by inserting "30D(e)(9)," after "30C(e)(5),". **Effective** for tax years beginning after 12-31-2008.

• 2007, Tax Technical Corrections Act of 2007 (P.L. 110-172)

P.L. 110-172, §7(a)(2)(B):

Amended Code Sec. 6501(m) by inserting "45H(g)," after "45C(d)(4),". **Effective** as if included in the provision of the American Jobs Creation Act of 2004 (P.L. 108-357) to which it relates [**effective** for expenses paid or incurred after 12-31-2002, in tax years ending after such date.—CCH].

• 2005, Energy Tax Incentives Act of 2005 (P.L. 109-58)

P.L. 109-58, §1341(b)(4):

Amended Code Sec. 6501(m) by inserting "30B(h)(9)," after "30(d)(4),". **Effective** for property placed in service after 12-31-2005, in tax years ending after such date.

P.L. 109-58, §1342(b)(4):

Amended Code Sec. 6501(m) by inserting "30C(e)(5)," after "30B(h)(9),". **Effective** for property placed in service after 12-31-2005, in tax years ending after such date.

• 1998, IRS Restructuring and Reform Act of 1998 (P.L. 105-206)

P.L. 105-206, §6023(27):

Amended Code Sec. 6501(m) by striking "election under" and all that follows through "(or any" and inserting "election under section 30(d)(4), 40(f), 43, 45B, 45C(d)(4), or 51(j) (or any". **Effective** 7-22-98. Prior to amendment, Code Sec. 6501(m) read as follows:

(m) DEFICIENCIES ATTRIBUTABLE TO ELECTION OF CERTAIN CREDITS.—The period for assessing a deficiency attributable to any election under section 30(d)(4), 40(f), 43, 45B, or 51(j) (or any revocation thereof) shall not expire before the date 1 year after the date on which the Secretary is notified of such election (or revocation).

• 1996, Small Business Job Protection Act of 1996 (P.L. 104-188)

P.L. 104-188, §1702(e)(3)(A):

Amended Code Sec. 6501 by striking subsection (m) and by redesignating subsections (n) and (o) as subsections (m) and (n), respectively. **Effective** as if included in the provision of P.L. 101-508 to which it relates.

P.L. 104-188, §1702(e)(3)(B):

Amended Code Sec. 6501(m), as redesignated by Act Sec. 1702(e)(3)(A), by striking "section 40(f) or 51(j)" and inserting "section 40(f), 43, or 51(j)". **Effective** as if included in the provision of P.L. 101-508 to which it relates.

P.L. 104-188, §1703(n)(8):

Amended Code Sec. 6501(m), as redesignated by Act Sec. 1702(e)(3)(A), by striking "or 51(j)" and inserting "45B, or 51(j)". **Effective** as if included in the provision of P.L. 103-66 to which it relates.

P.L. 104-188, §1704(j)(4)(B):

Amended Code Sec. 6501(m), as redesignated by Act Sec. 1703(e)(3)(A), by striking "section 40(f)" and inserting "section 30(d)(4), 40(f)". **Effective** 8-20-96.

• 1989, Omnibus Budget Reconciliation Act of 1989 (P.L. 101-239)

P.L. 101-239, §7814(e)(2)(E):

Amended Code Sec. 6501(n) by striking ", 41(h)," after "40(f)". **Effective** as if included in the provision of P.L. 100-647 to which it relates.

• 1988, Technical and Miscellaneous Revenue Act of 1988 (P.L. 100-647)

P.L. 100-647, §4008(c)(2):

Amended Code Sec. 6501(n) by striking out "or 51(j)" and inserting in lieu thereof ", 41(h), or 51(j)". **Effective** for tax years beginning after 12-31-88.

• 1986, Tax Reform Act of 1986 (P.L. 99-514)

P.L. 99-514, §1847(b)(13):

Amended Code Sec. 6501 by redesignating subsection (n) as subsection (o) and by inserting after subsection (m) new subsection (n). **Effective** as if included in the provision of P.L. 98-369 to which it relates.

* * *

[Sec. 6502]

SEC. 6502. COLLECTION AFTER ASSESSMENT.

[Sec. 6502(a)]

(a) LENGTH OF PERIOD.—Where the assessment of any tax imposed by this title has been made within the period of limitation properly applicable thereto, such tax may be collected by levy or by a proceeding in court, but only if the levy is made or the proceeding begun—

(1) within 10 years after the assessment of the tax, or

(2) if—

(A) there is an installment agreement between the taxpayer and the Secretary, prior to the date which is 90 days after the expiration of any period for collection agreed upon in writing by the Secretary and the taxpayer at the time the installment agreement was entered into; or

(B) there is a release of levy under section 6343 after such 10-year period, prior to the expiration of any period for collection agreed upon in writing by the Secretary and the taxpayer before such release.

If a timely proceeding in court for the collection of a tax is commenced, the period during which such tax may be collected by levy shall be extended and shall not expire until the liability for the tax (or a judgment against the taxpayer arising from such liability) is satisfied or becomes unenforceable.

Amendments

• 1998, IRS Restructuring and Reform Act of 1998 (P.L. 105-206)

P.L. 105-206, §3461(a)(1)-(2):

Amended Code Sec. 6502(a) by striking paragraph (2) and inserting a new paragraph (2), and by striking the first sentence in the matter following paragraph (2). **Effective** for requests to extend the period of limitations made after 12-31-99. For a special rule, see Act Sec. 3461(c)(2), below. Prior to amendment, Code Sec. 6502(a)(2) and the first sentence in the matter following paragraph (2) read as follows:

(2) prior to the expiration of any period for collection agreed upon in writing by the Secretary and the taxpayer before the expiration of such 10-year period (or, if there is a release of levy under section 6343 after such 10-year period, then before such release).

The period so agreed upon may be extended by subsequent agreements in writing made before the expiration of the period previously agreed upon.

P.L. 105-206, §3461(c)(2), provides:

(2) PRIOR REQUEST.—If, in any request to extend the period of limitations made on or before December 31, 1999, a taxpayer agreed to extend such period beyond the 10-year period referred to in section 6502(a) of the Internal Revenue Code of 1986, such extension shall expire on the latest of—

(A) the last day of such 10-year period;

(B) December 31, 2002; or

(C) in the case of an extension in connection with an installment agreement, the 90th day after the end of the period of such extension.

• 1990, Omnibus Budget Reconciliation Act of 1990 (P.L. 101-508)

P.L. 101-508, §11317(a)(1):

Amended Code Sec. 6502(a) by striking "6 years" in paragraph (1) and inserting "10 years" and by striking "6-year period" each place it appears in paragraph (2) and inserting "10-year period". For the **effective** date, see Act Sec. 11317(c), below.

P.L. 101-508, §11317(c), provides:

(c) EFFECTIVE DATE.—The amendments made by this section shall apply to—

(1) taxes assessed after the date of the enactment of this Act, and

(2) taxes assessed on or before such date if the period specified in section 6502 of the Internal Revenue Code of 1986 (determined without regard to the amendments made by subsection (a)) for collection of such taxes has not expired as of such date.

• 1989, Omnibus Budget Reconciliation Act of 1989 (P.L. 101-239)

P.L. 101-239, §7811(k)(2):

Amended Code Sec. 6502(a) by striking "enforceable" and inserting "unenforceable" in the last sentence. **Effective** as if included in the provision of P.L. 100-647 to which it relates.

• 1988, Technical and Miscellaneous Revenue Act of 1988 (P.L. 100-647)

P.L. 100-647, §1015(u)(1):

Amended the last sentence of Code Sec. 6502(a). **Effective** for levies issued after 11-10-88. Prior to amendment, the last sentence read as follows:

The period provided by this subsection during which a tax may be collected by levy shall not be extended or curtailed by reason of a judgment against the taxpayer.

• 1976, Tax Reform Act of 1976 (P.L. 94-455)

P.L. 94-455, §1906(b)(13)(A):

Amended 1954 Code by substituting "Secretary" for "Secretary or his delegate" each place it appeared. **Effective** 2-1-77.

• 1966, Federal Tax Lien Act of 1966 (P.L. 89-719)

P.L. 89-719, §113(b):

Amended Code Sec. 6502(a) by adding the last sentence. **Effective**, generally, after 11-2-66. However, see the amendment note for Code Sec. 6323 for exceptions to this **effective** date.

[Sec. 6502(b)]

(b) DATE WHEN LEVY IS CONSIDERED MADE.—The date on which a levy on property or rights to property is made shall be the date on which the notice of seizure provided in section 6335(a) is given.

[Sec. 6503]

SEC. 6503. SUSPENSION OF RUNNING OF PERIOD OF LIMITATION.

[Sec. 6503(a)]

(a) ISSUANCE OF STATUTORY NOTICE OF DEFICIENCY.—

(1) GENERAL RULE.—The running of the period of limitations provided in section 6501 or 6502 on the making of assessments or the collection by levy or a proceeding in court, in respect of any deficiency as defined in section 6211 (relating to income, estate, gift and certain excise taxes), shall (after the mailing of a notice under section 6212(a)) be suspended for the period during which the Secretary is prohibited from making the assessment or from collecting by levy or a proceeding in court (and in any event, if a proceeding in respect of the deficiency is placed on the docket of the Tax Court, until the decision of the Tax Court becomes final), and for 60 days thereafter.

(2) CORPORATION JOINING IN CONSOLIDATED INCOME TAX RETURN.—If a notice under section 6212(a) in respect of a deficiency in tax imposed by subtitle A for any taxable year is mailed to a corporation, the suspension of the running of the period of limitations provided in paragraph (1) of this subsection shall apply in the case of corporations with which such corporation made a consolidated income tax return for such taxable year.

Amendments

• 2018, Tax Technical Corrections Act of 2018 (P.L. 115-141)

P.L. 115-141, §401(a)(296), Div. U:

Amended Code Sec. 6503(a)(1) by striking "section 6230(a))." and inserting "section 6230(a))". **Effective** 3-23-2018. [Note: This amendment cannot be made to the version of Code Sec. 6503(a)(1) in effect 3-23-2018.—CCH.]

• 2015, Bipartisan Budget Act of 2015 (P.L. 114-74)

P.L. 114-74, §1101(f)(4):

Amended Code Sec. 6503(a)(1) by striking "(or section 6229" and all that follows through "of section 6230(a))" following "or 6502". **Effective** generally for returns filed for partnership tax years beginning after 12-31-2017. For a special rule, see Act Sec. 1101(g)(4), below. Prior to being stricken, "(or section 6229" and all that follows through "of section 6230(a))" read as follows:

(or section 6229, but only with respect to a deficiency described in paragraph (2)(A) or (3) of section 6230(a))

P.L. 114-74, §1101(g)(4), provides:

(4) ELECTION.—A partnership may elect (at such time and in such form and manner as the Secretary of the Treasury may prescribe) for the amendments made by this section (other than the election under section 6221(b) of such Code (as added by this Act)) to apply to any return of the partnership filed for partnership taxable years beginning after the date of the enactment of this Act and before January 1, 2018.

• 1997, Taxpayer Relief Act of 1997 (P.L. 105-34)

P.L. 105-34, §1237(c)(2):

Amended Code Sec. 6503(a)(1) by striking "section 6230(a)(2)(A)" and inserting "paragraph (2)(A) or (3) of section 6230(a)". **Effective** as if included in the amendments made by section 402 of P.L. 97-248 [generally effective for partnership tax years beginning after 9-3-82.—CCH].

• 1986, Tax Reform Act of 1986 (P.L. 99-514)

P.L. 99-514, §1875(d)(2)(B)(ii):

Amended Code Sec. 6503(a)(1) by striking out "section 6501 or 6502" and inserting in lieu thereof "section 6501 or 6502 (or section 6229, but only with respect to a deficiency described in section 6230(a)(2)(A))." **Effective** as if included in P.L. 97-248.

• 1976, Tax Reform Act of 1976 (P.L. 94-455)

P.L. 94-455, §1906(b)(13)(A):

Amended 1954 Code by substituting "Secretary" for "Secretary or his delegate" each place it appeared. **Effective** 2-1-77.

• 1974, Employee Retirement Income Security Act of 1974 (P.L. 93-406)

P.L. 93-406, §1016(a)(15):

Amended Code Sec. 6503(a)(1) by changing "chapter 42 taxes" to "certain excise taxes". For **effective** date, see amendment note for Code Sec. 410.

• 1969, Tax Reform Act of 1969 (P.L. 91-172)

P.L. 91-172, §101(j)(46):

Amended Code Sec. 6503(a)(1) by substituting "gift and chapter 42 taxes" for "and gift taxes". **Effective** 1-1-70.

[Sec. 6503(b)]

(b) ASSETS OF TAXPAYER IN CONTROL OR CUSTODY OF COURT.—The period of limitations on collection after assessment prescribed in section 6502 shall be suspended for the period the assets of the taxpayer are in the control or custody of the court in any proceeding before any court of the United States or of any State or of the District of Columbia, and for 6 months thereafter.

Amendments

• 1966, Federal Tax Lien Act of 1966 (P.L. 89-719)

P.L. 89-719, §106(a):

Amended Code Sec. 6503(b) by striking out "(other than the estate of a decedent or of an incompetent)" and "or Territory". **Effective**, generally, after 11-2-66. However, see the amendment note for Code Sec. 6323 for exceptions to this **effective** date.

[Sec. 6503(c)]

(c) TAXPAYER OUTSIDE UNITED STATES.—The running of the period of limitations on collection after assessment prescribed in section 6502 shall be suspended for the period during which the taxpayer is outside the United States if such period of absence is for a continuous period of at least 6 months. If the preceding sentence applies and at the time of the taxpayer's return to the United States the period of limitations on collection after assessment prescribed in section 6502 would expire before the expiration of 6 months from the date of his return, such period shall not expire before the expiration of such 6 months.

Amendments

• 1966, Federal Tax Lien Act of 1966 (P.L. 89-719)

P.L. 89-719, §106(b):

Amended Code Sec. 6503(c). **Effective**, generally, after 11-2-66. However, see the amendment note for Code Sec. 6323 for exceptions to this **effective** date. Prior to amendment, Code Sec. 6503(c) read as follows:

"(c) Location of Property Outside the United States or Removal of Property From the United States.—In case collection is hindered or delayed because property of the taxpayer is situated or held outside the United States or is removed from the United States, the period of limitations on collection after assessment prescribed in section 6502 shall be suspended for the period collection is so hindered or delayed. The total suspension of time under this subsection shall not in the aggregate exceed 6 years."

[Sec. 6503(d)]

(d) EXTENSIONS OF TIME FOR PAYMENT OF ESTATE TAX.—The running of the period of limitations for collection of any tax imposed by chapter 11 shall be suspended for the period of any extension of time for payment granted under the provisions of section 6161(a)(2) or (b)(2) or under provisions of section 6163, or 6166.

Amendments

• 1981, Economic Recovery Tax Act of 1981 (P.L. 97-34)

P.L. 97-34, §422(e)(7):

Amended Code Sec. 6503(d) by striking out "6163, 6166, or 6166A" and inserting "6163, or 6166". **Effective** for estates of decedents dying after 12-31-81.

• 1976, Tax Reform Act of 1976 (P.L. 94-455)

P.L. 94-455, §2004(c)(4):

Substituted "section 6163, 6166, or 6166A" for "section 6166" in Code Sec. 6503(d). **Effective** for estates of decedents dying after 12-31-76.

• 1958, Technical Amendments Act of 1958 (P.L. 85-866)

P.L. 85-866, §206(d):

Amended Sec. 6503(d) by striking out "assessment or" where it preceded the word "collection", and by adding, before the period at the end thereof, the following: "or under the provisions of section 6166". For the **effective** date, see Act Sec. 206(f), below.

P.L. 85-866, §206(f), provides:

"The amendments made by this section shall apply to estates of decedents with respect to which the date for the filing of the estate tax return (including extensions thereof) prescribed by section 6075(a) of the Internal Revenue Code of 1954 is after the date of the enactment of this Act; except that (1) section 6166(i) of such Code as added by this section shall apply to estates of decedents dying after August 16, 1954, but only if the date for the filing of the estate tax return (including extensions thereof) expired on or before the date of the enactment of this Act, and (2) notwithstanding section 6166(a) of such Code, if an election under such section is required to be made before the sixtieth day after the date of the enactment of this Act such an election shall be considered timely if made on or before such sixtieth day."

* * *

[Sec. 6503(f)]

(f) WRONGFUL SEIZURE OF OR LIEN ON PROPERTY OF THIRD PARTY.—

(1) WRONGFUL SEIZURE.—The running of the period under section 6502 shall be suspended for a period equal to the period from the date property (including money) of a third party is wrongfully seized or received by the Secretary to the date the Secretary returns property pursuant to section 6343(b) or the date on which a judgment secured pursuant to section 7426 with respect to such property becomes final, and for 30 days thereafter. The running of such period shall be suspended under this paragraph only with respect to the amount of such assessment equal to the amount of money or the value of specific property returned.

(2) WRONGFUL LIEN.—In the case of any assessment for which a lien was made on any property, the running of the period under section 6502 shall be suspended for a period equal to the period beginning on the date any person becomes entitled to a certificate under section 6325(b)(4) with respect to such property and ending on the date which is 30 days after the earlier of—

(A) the earliest date on which the Secretary no longer holds any amount as a deposit or bond provided under section 6325(b)(4) by reason of such deposit or bond being used to satisfy the unpaid tax or being refunded or released; or

(B) the date that the judgment secured under section 7426(b)(5) becomes final.

The running of such period shall be suspended under this paragraph only with respect to the amount of such assessment equal to the value of the interest of the United States in the property plus interest, penalties, additions to the tax, and additional amounts attributable thereto.

Amendments

• 1998, IRS Restructuring and Reform Act of 1998 (P.L. 105-206)

P.L. 105-206, §3106(b)(3):

Amended Code Sec. 6503(f). **Effective** 7-22-98. Prior to amendment, Code Sec. 6503(f) read as follows:

(f) WRONGFUL SEIZURE OF PROPERTY OF THIRD PARTY.—The running of the period of limitations on collection after assessment prescribed in section 6502 shall be suspended for a period equal to the period from the date property (including money) of a third party is wrongfully seized or received by the Secretary to the date the Secretary returns property pursuant to section 6343(b) or the date on which a judgment secured pursuant to section 7426 with respect to such property becomes final, and for 30 days thereafter. The running of the period of limitations on collection after assessment shall be suspended under this subsection only with respect to the amount of such assessment equal to the amount of money or the value of specific property returned.

• 1976, Tax Reform Act of 1976 (P.L. 94-455)

P.L. 94-455, §1902(b)(2)(A):

Redesignated subsection (g) as Code Sec. 6503(f). **Effective** in the case of estates of decedents dying after 10-4-76.

P.L. 94-455, §1906(b)(13)(A):

Amended the 1954 Code by substituting "Secretary" for "Secretary or his delegate" each place it appeared. **Effective** 2-1-77.

• 1966, Federal Tax Lien Act of 1966 (P.L. 89-719)

P.L. 89-719, §106(c):

Redesignated former Code Sec. 6503(g) as Sec. 6503(h) and added new Code Sec. 6503(g). **Effective**, generally, after 11-2-66. However, see the amendment note for Code Sec. 6323 for exceptions to this **effective** date.

* * *

Subchapter B—Limitations on Credit or Refund

* * *

[Sec. 6511]

SEC. 6511. LIMITATIONS ON CREDIT OR REFUND.

[Sec. 6511(a)]

(a) PERIOD OF LIMITATION ON FILING CLAIM.—Claim for credit or refund of an overpayment of any tax imposed by this title in respect of which tax the taxpayer is required to file a return shall be filed by the taxpayer within 3 years from the time the return was filed or 2 years from the time the tax was paid, whichever of such periods expires the later, or if no return was filed by the taxpayer, within 2 years from the time the tax was paid. Claim for credit or refund of an overpayment of any tax imposed by this title which is required to be paid by means of a stamp shall be filed by the taxpayer within 3 years from the time the tax was paid.

Amendments

• 2016, Combat-Injured Veterans Tax Fairness Act of 2016 (P.L. 114-292)

P.L. 114-292, §3, provides:

SEC. 3. RESTORATION OF AMOUNTS IMPROPERLY WITHHELD FOR TAX PURPOSES FROM SEVERANCE PAYMENTS TO VETERANS WITH COMBAT-RELATED INJURIES.

(a) IN GENERAL.—Not later than 1 year after the date of the enactment of this Act, the Secretary of Defense shall—

(1) identify—

(A) the severance payments—

(i) that the Secretary paid after January 17, 1991;

(ii) that the Secretary computed under section 1212 of title 10, United States Code;

(iii) that were not considered gross income pursuant to section 104(a)(4) of the Internal Revenue Code of 1986; and

(iv) from which the Secretary withheld amounts for tax purposes; and

(B) the individuals to whom such severance payments were made; and

(2) with respect to each person identified under paragraph (1)(B), provide—

(A) notice of—

(i) the amount of severance payments in paragraph (1)(A) which were improperly withheld for tax purposes; and

(ii) such other information determined to be necessary by the Secretary of the Treasury to carry out the purposes of this section; and

(B) instructions for filing amended tax returns to recover the amounts improperly withheld for tax purposes.

(b) EXTENSION OF LIMITATION ON TIME FOR CREDIT OR REFUND.—

(1) PERIOD FOR FILING CLAIM.—If a claim for credit or refund under section 6511(a) of the Internal Revenue Code of 1986 relates to a specified overpayment, the 3-year period of limitation prescribed by such subsection shall not expire before the date which is 1 year after the date the information return described in subsection (a)(2) is provided. The allowable amount of credit or refund of a specified overpayment shall be determined without regard to the amount of tax paid within the period provided in section 6511(b)(2).

(2) SPECIFIED OVERPAYMENT.—For purposes of paragraph (1), the term "specified overpayment" means an overpayment attributable to a severance payment described in subsection (a)(1).

• 1958, Technical Amendments Act of 1958 (P.L. 85-866)

P.L. 85-866, §82(a):

Amended the first sentence of Code Sec. 6511(a). **Effective** 8-17-54. Prior to amendment, that sentence read as follows:

"Claim for credit or refund of an overpayment of any tax imposed by this title in respect of which tax the taxpayer is required to file a return shall be filed by the taxpayer within 3 years from the time the return was required to be filed (determined without regard to any extension of time) or 2 years from the time the tax was paid, whichever of such periods expires the later, or if no return was filed by the taxpayer, within 2 years from the time the tax was paid."

[Sec. 6511(b)]

(b) LIMITATION ON ALLOWANCE OF CREDITS AND REFUNDS.—

(1) FILING OF CLAIM WITHIN PRESCRIBED PERIOD.—No credit or refund shall be allowed or made after the expiration of the period of limitation prescribed in subsection (a) for the filing of a claim for credit or refund, unless a claim for credit or refund is filed by the taxpayer within such period.

(2) LIMIT ON AMOUNT OF CREDIT OR REFUND.—

(A) LIMIT WHERE CLAIM FILED WITHIN 3-YEAR PERIOD.—If the claim was filed by the taxpayer during the 3-year period prescribed in subsection (a), the amount of the credit or refund shall not exceed the portion of the tax paid within the period, immediately preceding the filing of the claim, equal to 3 years plus the period of any extension of time for filing the return. If the tax was required to be paid by means of a stamp, the amount of the credit or refund shall not exceed the portion of the tax paid within the 3 years immediately preceding the filing of the claim.

(B) LIMIT WHERE CLAIM NOT FILED WITHIN 3-YEAR PERIOD.—If the claim was not filed within such 3-year period, the amount of the credit or refund shall not exceed the portion of the tax paid during the 2 years immediately preceding the filing of the claim.

(C) LIMIT IF NO CLAIM FILED.—If no claim was filed, the credit or refund shall not exceed the amount which would be allowable under subparagraph (A) or (B), as the case may be, if claim was filed on the date the credit or refund is allowed.

Amendments

• 1958, Technical Amendments Act of 1958 (P.L. 85-866)

P.L. 85-866, §82(b):

Amended the heading and first sentence of Code Sec. 6511(b)(2)(A). **Effective** 1-1-54. Prior to amendment, they read as follows:

"(A) Limit to amount paid within 3 years.—If the claim was filed by the taxpayer during the 3-year period prescribed in subsection (a), the amount of the credit or refund shall not exceed the portion of the tax paid within the 3 years immediately preceding the filing of the claim."

P.L. 85-866, §82(c):

Amended the heading for Code Sec. 6511(b)(2)(B). **Effective** 1-1-54. Prior to amendment, it read as follows:

"(B) Limit to amount paid within 2 years.—".

[Sec. 6511(c)]

(c) SPECIAL RULES APPLICABLE IN CASE OF EXTENSION OF TIME BY AGREEMENT.—If an agreement under the provisions of section 6501(c)(4) extending the period for assessment of a tax imposed by this title is made within the period prescribed in subsection (a) for the filing of a claim for credit or refund—

(1) TIME FOR FILING CLAIM.—The period for filing claim for credit or refund or for making credit or refund if no claim is filed, provided in subsections (a) and (b)(1), shall not expire prior to 6 months after the expiration of the period within which an assessment may be made pursuant to the agreement or any extension thereof under section 6501(c)(4).

(2) LIMIT ON AMOUNT.—If a claim is filed, or a credit or refund is allowed when no claim was filed, after the execution of the agreement and within 6 months after the expiration of the period within which an assessment may be made pursuant to the agreement or any extension thereof, the amount of the credit or refund shall not exceed the portion of the tax paid after the execution of the agreement and before the filing of the claim or the making of the credit or refund, as the case may be, plus the portion of the tax paid within the period which would be applicable under subsection (b)(2) if a claim had been filed on the date the agreement was executed.

(3) CLAIMS NOT SUBJECT TO SPECIAL RULE.—This subsection shall not apply in the case of a claim filed, or credit or refund allowed if no claim is filed, either—

(A) prior to the execution of the agreement or

(B) more than 6 months after the expiration of the period within which an assessment may be made pursuant to the agreement or any extension thereof.

[Sec. 6511(d)]

(d) SPECIAL RULES APPLICABLE TO INCOME TAXES.—

(1) SEVEN-YEAR PERIOD OF LIMITATION WITH RESPECT TO BAD DEBTS AND WORTHLESS SECURITIES.—If the claim for credit or refund relates to an overpayment of tax imposed by subtitle A on account of—

(A) The deductibility by the taxpayer, under section 166 or section 832(c), of a debt as a debt which became worthless, or, under section 165(g), of a loss from worthlessness of a security, or

(B) The effect that the deductibility of a debt or loss described in subparagraph (A) has on the application to the taxpayer of a carryover,

in lieu of the 3-year period of limitation prescribed in subsection (a), the period shall be 7 years from the date prescribed by law for filing the return for the year with respect to which the claim is made. If the claim for credit or refund relates to an overpayment on account of the effect that the deductibility of such a debt or loss has on the application to the taxpayer of a carryback, the period shall be either 7 years from the date prescribed by law for filing the return for the year of the net operating loss which results in such carryback or the period prescribed in paragraph (2) of this subsection, whichever expires the later. In the case of a claim described in this paragraph the amount of the credit or refund may exceed the portion of the tax paid within the period prescribed in subsection (b)(2) or (c), whichever is applicable, to the extent of the amount of the overpayment attributable to the deductibility of items described in this paragraph.

(2) SPECIAL PERIOD OF LIMITATION WITH RESPECT TO NET OPERATING LOSS OR CAPITAL LOSS CARRYBACKS.—

(A) PERIOD OF LIMITATION.—If the claim for credit or refund relates to an overpayment attributable to a net operating loss carryback or a capital loss carryback, in lieu of the 3-year period of limitation prescribed in subsection (a), the period shall be that period which ends 3 years after the time prescribed by law for filing the return (including extensions thereof) for the taxable year of the net operating loss or net capital loss which results in such carryback, or the period prescribed in subsection (c) in respect of such taxable year, whichever expires later.

In the case of such a claim, the amount of the credit or refund may exceed the portion of the tax paid within the period provided in subsection (b)(2) or (c), whichever is applicable, to the extent of the amount of the overpayment attributable to such carryback.

(B) APPLICABLE RULES.—

(i) IN GENERAL.—If the allowance of a credit or refund of an overpayment of tax attributable to a net operating loss carryback or a capital loss carryback is otherwise prevented by the operation of any law or rule of law other than section 7122 (relating to compromises), such credit or refund may be allowed or made, if claim therefor is filed within the period provided in subparagraph (A) of this paragraph.

(ii) TENTATIVE CARRYBACK ADJUSTMENTS.—If the allowance of an application, credit, or refund of a decrease in tax determined under section 6411(b) is otherwise prevented by the operation of any law or rule of law other than section 7122, such application, credit, or refund may be allowed or made if application for a tentative carryback adjustment is made within the period provided in section 6411(a).

(iii) DETERMINATIONS BY COURTS TO BE CONCLUSIVE.—In the case of any such claim for credit or refund or any such application for a tentative carryback adjustment, the determination by any court, including the Tax Court, in any proceeding in which the decision of the court has become final, shall be conclusive except with respect to—

(I) the net operating loss deduction and the effect of such deduction, and

(II) the determination of a short-term capital loss and the effect of such short-term capital loss, to the extent that such deduction or short-term capital loss is affected by a carryback which was not an issue in such proceeding.

(3) SPECIAL RULES RELATING TO FOREIGN TAX CREDIT.—

(A) SPECIAL PERIOD OF LIMITATION WITH RESPECT TO FOREIGN TAXES PAID OR ACCRUED.—If the claim for credit or refund relates to an overpayment attributable to any taxes paid or accrued to any foreign country or to any possession of the United States for which credit is allowed against the tax imposed by subtitle A in accordance with the provisions of section 901 or the provisions of any treaty to which the United States is a party, in lieu of the 3-year period of limitation prescribed in subsection (a), the period shall be 10 years from the date prescribed by law for filing the return for the year in which such taxes were actually paid or accrued.

(B) EXCEPTION IN THE CASE OF FOREIGN TAXES PAID OR ACCRUED.—In the case of a claim described in subparagraph (A), the amount of the credit or refund may exceed the portion of the tax paid within the period provided in subsection (b) or (c), whichever is applicable, to the extent of the amount of the overpayment attributable to the allowance of a credit for the taxes described in subparagraph (A).

(4) SPECIAL PERIOD OF LIMITATION WITH RESPECT TO CERTAIN CREDIT CARRYBACKS.—

(A) PERIOD OF LIMITATION.—If the claim for credit or refund relates to an overpayment attributable to a credit carryback, in lieu of the 3-year period of limitation prescribed in subsection (a), the period shall be that period which ends 3 years after the time prescribed by law for filing the return (including extensions thereof) for the taxable year of the unused credit which results in such carryback (or, with respect to any portion of a credit carryback from a taxable year attributable to a net operating loss carryback, capital loss carryback, or other credit carryback from a subsequent taxable year, the period shall be that period which ends 3 years after the time prescribed by law for filing the return, including extensions thereof, for such subsequent taxable year) or the period prescribed in subsection (c) in respect of such taxable year, whichever expires later. In the case of such a claim, the amount of the credit or refund may exceed the portion of the tax paid within the period provided in subsection (b)(2) or (c), whichever is applicable, to the extent of the amount of the overpayment attributable to such carryback.

(B) APPLICABLE RULES.—If the allowance of a credit or refund of an overpayment of tax attributable to a credit carryback is otherwise prevented by the operation of any law or rule of law other than section 7122, relating to compromises, such credit or refund may be allowed or made, if claim therefor is filed within the period provided in subparagraph (A) of this paragraph. In the case of any such claim for credit or refund, the determination by any court, including the Tax Court, in any proceeding in which the decision of the court has become final, shall not be conclusive with respect to any credit, and the effect of such credit, to the extent that such credit is affected by a credit carryback which was not in issue in such proceeding.

(C) CREDIT CARRYBACK DEFINED.—For purposes of this paragraph, the term "credit carryback" means any business carryback under section 39.

(5) SPECIAL PERIOD OF LIMITATION WITH RESPECT TO SELF-EMPLOYMENT TAX IN CERTAIN CASES.—If the claim for credit or refund relates to an overpayment of the tax imposed by chapter 2 (relating to the tax on self-employment income) attributable to an agreement, or modification of an agreement, made pursuant to section 218 of the Social Security Act (relating to coverage of State and local employees), and if the allowance of a credit or refund of such overpayment is otherwise

prevented by the operation of any law or rule of law other than section 7122 (relating to compromises), such credit or refund may be allowed or made if claim therefor is filed on or before the last day of the second year after the calendar year in which such agreement (or modification) is agreed to by the State and the Commissioner of Social Security.

(6) SPECIAL PERIOD OF LIMITATION WITH RESPECT TO AMOUNTS INCLUDED IN INCOME SUBSEQUENTLY RECAPTURED UNDER QUALIFIED PLAN TERMINATION.—If the claim for credit or refund relates to an overpayment of tax imposed by subtitle A on account of the recapture, under section 4045 of the Employee Retirement Income Security Act of 1974, of amounts included in income for a prior taxable year, the 3-year period of limitation prescribed in subsection (a) shall be extended, for purposes of permitting a credit or refund of the amount of the recapture, until the date which occurs one year after the date on which such recaptured amount is paid by the taxpayer.

(7) SPECIAL PERIOD OF LIMITATION WITH RESPECT TO SELF-EMPLOYMENT TAX IN CERTAIN CASES.—If—

(A) the claim for credit or refund relates to an overpayment of the tax imposed by chapter 2 (relating to the tax on self-employment income) attributable to Tax Court determination in a proceeding under section 7436, and

(B) the allowance of a credit or refund of such overpayment is otherwise prevented by the operation of any law or rule of law other than section 7122 (relating to compromises),

such credit or refund may be allowed or made if claim therefor is filed on or before the last day of the second year after the calendar year in which such determination becomes final.

(8) SPECIAL RULES WHEN UNIFORMED SERVICES RETIRED PAY IS REDUCED AS A RESULT OF AWARD OF DISABILITY COMPENSATION.—

(A) PERIOD OF LIMITATION ON FILING CLAIM.—If the claim for credit or refund relates to an overpayment of tax imposed by subtitle A on account of—

(i) the reduction of uniformed services retired pay computed under section 1406 or 1407 of title 10, United States Code, or

(ii) the waiver of such pay under section 5305 of title 38 of such Code.

as a result of an award of compensation under title 38 of such Code pursuant to a determination by the Secretary of Veterans Affairs, the 3-year period of limitation prescribed in subsection (a) shall be extended, for purposes of permitting a credit or refund based upon the amount of such reduction or waiver, until the end of the 1-year period beginning on the date of such determination.

(B) LIMITATION TO 5 TAXABLE YEARS.—Subparagraph (A) shall not apply with respect to any taxable year which began more than 5 years before the date of such determination.

Amendments

• 2008, Heroes Earnings Assistance and Relief Tax Act of 2008 (P.L. 110-245)

P.L. 110-245, §106(a):

Amended Code Sec. 6511(d) by adding at the end a new paragraph (8). **Effective** for claims for credit or refund filed after 6-17-2008. For a transitional rule, see Act Sec. 106(c)(1)-(2), below.

P.L. 110-245, §106(c)(1)-(2), provides:

(c) TRANSITION RULES.—In the case of a determination described in paragraph (8) of section 6511(d) of the Internal Revenue Code of 1986 (as added by this section) which is made by the Secretary of Veterans Affairs after December 31, 2000, and before the date of the enactment of this Act [6-17-2008.—CCH], such paragraph—

(1) shall not apply with respect to any taxable year which began before January 1, 2001, and

(2) shall be applied by substituting for "the date of such determination" in subparagraph (A) thereof.

• 1997, Taxpayer Relief Act of 1997 (P.L. 105-34)

P.L. 105-34, §1056(a):

Amended Code Sec. 6511(d)(3)(A) by striking "for the year with respect to which the claim is made" and inserting "for the year in which such taxes were actually paid or accrued". **Effective** for taxes paid or accrued in tax years beginning after 8-5-97.

P.L. 105-34, §1454(b)(1):

Amended Code Sec. 6511(d) by adding at the end a new paragraph (7). **Effective** 8-5-97.

• 1994, Social Security Independence and Program Improvements Act of 1994 (P.L. 103-296)

P.L. 103-296, §108(h)(8):

Amended Code Sec. 6511(d)(5) by striking "Secretary of Health and Human Services" and inserting "Commissioner of Social Security". **Effective** 3-31-95.

• 1990, Omnibus Budget Reconciliation Act of 1990 (P.L. 101-508)

P.L. 101-508, §11801(c)(17)(B):

Amended Code Sec. 6511(d)(2)(A) by striking "; except that" and all that follows down through the period at the end of the first sentence and inserting a period. **Effective** 11-5-90. Prior to amendment, Code Sec. 6511(d)(2)(A) read as follows:

(2) SPECIAL PERIOD OF LIMITATION WITH RESPECT TO NET OPERATING LOSS OR CAPITAL LOSS CARRYBACKS.—

(A) PERIOD OF LIMITATION.—If the claim for credit or refund relates to an overpayment attributable to a net operating loss carryback or a capital loss carryback, in lieu of the 3-year period of limitation prescribed in subsection (a), the period shall be that period which ends 3 years after the time prescribed by law for filing the return (including extensions thereof) for the taxable year of the net operating loss or net capital loss which results in such carryback, or the period prescribed in subsection (c) in respect of such taxable year, whichever expires later; except that with respect to an overpayment attributable to the creation of, or an increase in a net operating loss carryback as a result of the elimination of excessive profits by a renegotiation (as defined in section 1481(a)(1)(A)), the period shall not expire before the expiration of the 12th month following the month in which the agreement or order for the elimination of such excessive profits becomes final.

In the case of such a claim, the amount of the credit or refund may exceed the portion of the tax paid within the period provided in subsection (b)(2) or (c), whichever is applicable, to the extent of the amount of the overpayment attributable to such carryback.

P.L. 101-508, §11821(b)(1)-(2), provides:

(b) SAVINGS PROVISION.—If—

(1) any provision amended or repealed by this part applied to—

(A) any transaction occurring before the date of the enactment of this Act,

(B) any property acquired before such date of enactment, or

(C) any item of income, loss, deduction, or credit taken into account before such date of enactment, and

(2) the treatment of such transaction, property, or item under such provision would (without regard to the amendments made by this part) affect liability for tax for periods ending after such date of enactment,

nothing in the amendments made by this part shall be construed to affect the treatment of such transaction, property, or item for purposes of determining liability for tax for periods ending after such date of enactment.

• 1986, Tax Reform Act of 1986 (P.L. 99-514)

P.L. 99-514, §141(b)(3):

Amended Code Sec. 6511(d)(2)(B). **Effective** for tax years beginning after 12-31-86. Prior to amendment, Code Sec. 6511(d)(2)(B) read as follows:

(B) APPLICABLE RULES.—

(i) If the allowance of a credit or refund of an overpayment of tax attributable to a net operating loss carryback or a capital loss carryback is otherwise prevented by the operation of any law or rule of law other than section 7122, relating to compromises, such credit or refund may be allowed or made, if claim therefor is filed within the period provided in subparagraph (A) of this paragraph. If the allowance of an application, credit, or refund of a decrease in tax determined under section 6411(b) is otherwise prevented by the operation of any law or rule of law other than section 7122, such application, credit, or refund may be allowed or made if application for a tentative carryback adjustment is made within the period provided in section 6411(a). In the case of any such claim for credit or refund or any such application for a tentative carryback adjustment, the determination by any court, including the Tax Court, in any proceeding in which the decision of the court has become final, shall be conclusive except with respect to the net operating loss deduction, and the effect of such deduction, or with respect to the determination of a short-term capital loss, and the effect of such short-term capital loss, to the extent that such deduction or short-term capital loss is affected by a carryback which was not an issue in such proceeding.

(ii) A claim for credit or refund for a computation year (as defined in section 1302(c)(1)) shall be determined to relate to an overpayment attributable to a net operating loss carryback or a capital loss carryback, as the case may be, when such carryback relates to any base period year (as defined in section 1302(c)(3)).

P.L. 99-514, §231(d)(3)(I):

Amended Code Sec. 6511(d)(4)(C) by striking out "and any research credit carryback under section 30(g)(2)". **Effective** for tax years beginning after 12-31-85.

• 1984, Deficit Reduction Act of 1984 (P.L. 98-369)

P.L. 98-369, §211(b)(25):

Amended Code Sec. 6511(d) by striking out paragraph (6) and by redesignating paragraph (7) as paragraph (6). **Effective** for tax years beginning after 12-31-83. Prior to amendment, paragraph (6) read as follows:

(6) Special Period of Limitation with Respect to Reduction of Policyholders Surplus Account of Life Insurance Companies.—

(A) Period of Limitations.—If the claim for credit or refund relates to an overpayment arising by operation of section 815(d)(5) (relating to reduction of policyholders surplus account of life insurance companies for certain unused deductions), in lieu of the 3-year period of limitation prescribed in subsection (a), the period shall be that period which ends with the expiration of the 15th day of the 39th month following the end of the last taxable year to which the loss described in section 815(d)(5)(A) is carried under section 812(b)(2), or the period prescribed in subsection (c), in respect of such taxable year, whichever expires later. In the case of such a claim, the amount of the credit or refund may exceed the portion of the tax paid within the period provided in subsection (b)(2) or (c), whichever is applicable, to the extent of the amount of overpayment arising by operation of section 815(d)(5).

(B) Applicable Rules.—If the allowance of a credit or refund of an overpayment arising by operation of section 815(d)(5) is otherwise prevented by operation of any law or rule of law, other than section 7122 (relating to compromises), such credit or refund may be allowed or made, if claim therefor is filed within the period provided in subparagraph (A) of this paragraph. In the case of any such claim for credit or refund, the determination by any court, including the Tax Court, in any proceeding in which the decision of the court has become final, shall be conclusive except with respect to the effect of the operation of section 815(d)(5), to the extent such effect of the operation of section 815(d)(5) was not in issue in such proceeding.

P.L. 98-369, §474(r)(40):

Amended Code Sec. 6511(d)(4)(C). **Effective** for tax years beginning after 12-31-83, and to carrybacks from such years. Prior to amendment, it read as follows:

(C) Credit Carryback Defined.—For purposes of this paragraph, the term "credit carryback" means any investment credit carryback, work incentive program credit carryback, new employee credit carryback, research credit carryback, and employee stock ownership credit carryback.

P.L. 98-369, §2663(j)(5)(F):

Amended Code Sec. 6511(d)(5) by striking out "Health, Education, and Welfare" each place it appears and inserting in lieu thereof "Health and Human Services". **Effective** 7-18-84. However, it does not change or affect any right, liability, status, or interpretation which existed (under the provisions of law involved) before that date.

• 1981, Economic Recovery Tax Act of 1981 (P.L. 97-34)

P.L. 97-34, §221(b)(2)(A):

Amended Code Sec. 6511(d)(4)(C) by striking out "and new employee credit carryback" and inserting in lieu thereof "new employee credit carryback, and research credit carryback". **Effective** for amounts paid or incurred after 6-30-81 [**effective** date changed by P.L. 99-514, §231(a)].

P.L. 97-34, §221(d)(2), as amended by P.L. 99-514, §231(a), provides the following transitional rule:

(2) TRANSITIONAL RULE.—

(A) IN GENERAL.—If, with respect to the first taxable year to which the amendments made by this section apply and which ends in 1981 or 1982, the taxpayer may only take into account qualified research expenses paid or incurred during a portion of such taxable year, the amount of the qualified research expenses taken into account for the base period of such taxable year shall be the amount which bears the same ratio to the total qualified research expenses for such base period as the number of months in such portion of such taxable year bears to the total number of months in such taxable year.

(B) DEFINITIONS.—For purposes of the preceding sentence, the terms "qualified research expenses" and "base period" have the meanings given to such terms by section 44F of the Internal Revenue Code of 1954 (as added by this section).

P.L. 97-34, §331(d)(2)(A):

Amended Code Sec. 6511(d)(4)(C) by striking out "and research credit carryback" and inserting in lieu thereof "research credit carryback, and employee stock ownership credit carryback". **Effective** for tax years beginning after 12-31-81.

• 1978 (P.L. 95-628)

P.L. 95-628, §8(a):

Amended Code Sec. 6511(d)(2)(A) by striking out "with the expiration of the 15th day of the 40th month (or the 39th month, in the case of a corporation) following the end of" and inserting in lieu thereof "3 years after the time prescribed by law for filing the return (including extensions thereof) for". **Effective** for carrybacks arising in tax years beginning after 11-10-78.

P.L. 95-628, §8(b):

Amended Code Sec. 6511(d) by changing paragraph (d)(4), by deleting paragraphs (d)(7) and (d)(9) and by redesignating paragraph (d)(8) as paragraph (d)(7). **Effective** for carrybacks arising in tax years beginning after 11-10-78. Prior to amendment and deletion, paragraphs (d)(4), (d)(7) and (d)(9) read as follows:

"(4) SPECIAL PERIOD OF LIMITATION WITH RESPECT TO INVESTMENT CREDIT CARRYBACKS.—

(A) PERIOD OF LIMITATION.—If the claim for credit or refund relates to an overpayment attributable to an investment credit carryback, in lieu of the 3-year period of limitation prescribed in subsection (a), the period shall be that period which ends with the expiration of the 15th day of the 40th month (or 39th month, in the case of a corporation) following the end of the taxable year of the unused investment credit which results in such carryback (or, with respect to any portion of an investment credit carryback from a taxable year attributable to a net operating loss carryback or a capital loss carryback from a subsequent taxable year, the period shall be that period which ends with the expiration of the 15th day of the 40th month, or 39th month, in the case of a corporation, following the end of such subsequent taxable year) or the period prescribed in subsection (c) in respect of such taxable year, whichever expires later. In the case of such a claim, the amount of the credit or refund may exceed the portion of the tax paid within the period provided in subsection (b)(2) or (c), whichever is applicable, to the extent of the amount of the overpayment attributable to such carryback.

(B) APPLICABLE RULES.—If the allowance of a credit or refund of an overpayment of tax attributable to an investment credit carryback is otherwise prevented by the operation of any law or rule of law other than section 7122, relating to compromises, such credit or refund may be allowed or made, if claim therefor is filed within the period provided in subparagraph (A) of this paragraph. In the case of any such claim for credit or refund, the determination by any court, including the Tax Court, in any proceeding in which the decision of the court has become final, shall not be conclusive with respect to the investment credit, and the effect of such credit, to the extent that such credit is affected by a carryback which was not in issue in such proceeding."

"(7) SPECIAL PERIOD OF LIMITATION WITH RESPECT TO WORK INCENTIVE PROGRAM CREDIT CARRYBACKS.—

(A) PERIOD OF LIMITATION.—If the claim for credit or refund relates to an overpayment attributable to a work incentive program credit carryback, in lieu of the 3-year period of limitation prescribed in subsection (a), the period shall be that period which ends with the expiration of the 15th day of the 40th month (or 39th month, in the case of a corporation) following the end of the taxable year of the unused work incentive program credit which results in such carryback (or, with respect to any portion of a work incentive program credit carryback from a taxable year attributable to a net operating loss carryback, an investment credit carryback, or a capital loss carryback from a subsequent taxable year, the period shall be that period which ends with the expiration of the 15th day of the 40th month, or 39th month, in the case of a corporation, following the year of such taxable year) or the period prescribed in subsection (c) in respect of such taxable year, whichever expires later. In the case of such a claim, the amount of the credit or refund may exceed the portion of the tax paid within the period provided in subsection (b)(2) or (c), whichever is applicable, to the extent of the amount of the overpayment attributable to such carryback.

(B) APPLICABLE RULES.—If the allowance of a credit or refund of an overpayment of tax attributable to a work incentive program credit carryback is otherwise prevented by the operation of any law or rule of law other than section 7122, relating to compromises, such credit or refund may be allowed or made, if claim therefor is filed within the period provided in subparagraph (A) of this paragraph. In the case of any such claim for credit or refund, the determination by any court, including the Tax Court, in any proceeding in which the decision of the court has become final, shall not be conclusive with respect to the work incentive program credit, and the effect of such credit, to the extent that such credit is affected by a carryback which was not in issue in such proceeding."

"(9) SPECIAL PERIOD OF LIMITATION WITH RESPECT TO NEW EMPLOYEE CREDIT CARRYBACKS.—

(A) PERIOD OF LIMITATIONS.—Of the claim for credit or refund related to an overpayment attributable to a new employee credit carryback, in lieu of the 3-year period of limitation prescribed in subsection (a), the period shall be that period which ends with the expiration of the 15th day of the 40th month (or 39th month, in the case of a corporation) following the end of the taxable year of the unused new employee credit which results in such carryback (or, with respect to any portion of a new employee credit carryback from a taxable year attributable to a net operating loss carryback, an investment credit carryback, a work incentive program credit carryback, or a capital loss carryback from a subsequent taxable year, the period shall be that period which ends with the expiration of the 15th day of the 40th month, or 39th month, in the case of a corporation following the end of such taxable year) or the period prescribed in subsection (c) in respect of such taxable year, whichever expires later. In the case of such a claim, the amount of the credit or refund may exceed the portion of the tax paid within the period provided in subsection (b)(2) or (c), whichever is applicable, to the extent of the amount of the overpayment attributable to such carryback.

(B) APPLICABLE RULES.—If the allowance of a credit or refund of an overpayment of tax attributable to a new employee credit carryback is otherwise prevented by the operation or any law or rule of law other than section 7122, relating to compromises, such credit or refund may be allowed or made, if claim therefor is filed within the period provided in subparagraph (A) of this paragraph. In the case of any such claim for credit or refund, the determination by any court, including the Tax Court, in any proceeding in which the decision of the court has become final shall not be conclusive with respect to the new employee credit, and the effect of such credit, to the extent that such credit is affected by a carryback which was not in issue in such proceeding."

• 1978, Revenue Act of 1978 (P.L. 95-600)

P.L. 95-600, §703(p)(3):

Amended Code Sec. 6511(d)(2)(A). **Effective** with respect to losses sustained in tax years ending after 11-7-78. Prior to amendment, Code Sec. 6511(d)(2)(A) read:

"(A) PERIOD OF LIMITATION.—If the claim for credit or refund relates to an overpayment attributable to a net operating loss carryback or a capital loss carryback, in lieu of the 3-year period of limitation prescribed in subsection (a), the period shall be that period which ends with the expiration of the 15th day of the 40th month (or the 39th month, in the case of a corporation) following the end of the taxable year of the net operating loss or net capital loss which results in such carryback, or the period prescribed in subsection (c) in respect of such taxable year, whichever expires later; except that—

"(i) with respect to an overpayment attributable to a net operating loss carryback to any year on account of a certification issued to the taxpayer under section 317 of the Trade Expansion Act of 1962, the period shall not expire before the expiration of the sixth month following the month in which such certification is issued to the taxpayer, and

"(ii) with respect to an overpayment attributable to the creation of, or an increase in, a net operating loss carryback as a result of the elimination of excessive profits by a renegotiation (as defined in section 1481(a)(1)(A)), the period shall not expire before the expiration of the twelfth month following the month in which the agreement or order for the elimination of such excessive profits becomes final."

• 1977, Tax Reduction and Simplification Act of 1977 (P.L. 95-30)

P.L. 95-30, §202(d)(4)(B):

Amended Code Sec. 6511(d) by adding paragraph (9). **Effective** for tax years beginning after 12-31-76, and for credit carrybacks from such years.

• 1976, Tax Reform Act of 1976 (P.L. 94-455)

P.L. 94-455, §1906(a)(33)(A):

Deleted "September 1, 1959, or" and, "whichever is the later" in Code Sec. 6511(d)(2)(A)(ii). **Effective** 2-1-77.

P.L. 94-455, §1906(a)(33)(B):

Deleted "the later of the following dates: (A)" and ", or (B) December 31, 1965" in Code Sec. 6511(d)(5). **Effective** 2-1-77.

P.L. 94-455, §2107(g)(2)(B):

Inserted ", an investment credit carryback," after "net operating loss carryback" in Code Sec. 6511(d)(7). **Effective** 10-4-76.

• 1974, Employee Retirement Income Security Act of 1974 (P.L. 93-406)

P.L. 93-406, §4081(b):

Amended Code Sec. 6511(d) by adding new paragraph (8). **Effective** 9-2-74.

• **1971, Revenue Act of 1971 (P.L. 92-178)**

P.L. 92-178, §601(d)(2):

Amended Code Sec. 6511(d) by adding paragraph (7). **Effective** for tax years ending after 12-31-71.

• **1969, Tax Reform Act of 1969 (P.L. 91-172)**

P.L. 91-172, §311(d)(3):

Amended Sec. 6511(d)(2)(B)(ii) by substituting references to Code Sec. 1302(c) for references to Code Sec. 1302(e). **Effective** 1-1-70.

P.L. 91-172, §512(e)(2):

Amended Code Sec. 6511(d)(2)(A). **Effective** with respect to net capital losses sustained in tax years beginning after 12-31-69. Prior to amendment, Code Sec. 6511(d)(2)(A) read as follows:

(2) SPECIAL PERIOD OF LIMITATION WITH RESPECT TO NET OPERATING LOSS CARRYBACKS.—

(A) PERIOD OF LIMITATION.—If the claim for credit or refund relates to an overpayment attributable to a net operating loss carryback, in lieu of the 3-year period of limitation prescribed in subsection (a), the period shall be that period which ends with the expiration of the 15th day of the 40th month (or the 39th month, in the case of a corporation) following the end of the taxable year of the net operating loss which results in such carryback, or the period prescribed in subsection (c) in respect of such taxable year, whichever expires later; except that—.

P.L. 91-172, §512(e)(2):

Amended Code Sec. 6511(d)(2)(B)(i) by adding "or a capital loss carryback" after "loss carryback"; and by amending last sentence. **Effective** with respect to net capital losses sustained in tax years beginning after 12-31-69. Prior to amendment, last sentence of Code Sec. 6511(d)(2)(B)(i) read as follows:

"In the case of any such claim for credit or refund or any such application for a tentative carryback adjustment, the determination by any court, including the Tax Court, in any proceeding in which the decision of the court has become final, shall be conclusive except with respect to the net operating loss deduction, and the effect of such deduction, to the extent that such deduction is affected by a carryback which was not in issue in such proceeding."

P.L. 91-172, §512(e)(2):

Amended Code Sec. 6511(d)(2)(B)(ii) by adding "or a capital loss carryback, as the case may be," after "loss carryback". **Effective** with respect to net capital losses sustained in tax years beginning after 12-31-69.

P.L. 91-172, §512(e)(2):

Amended Code Sec. 6511(d)(4)(A) by adding "or a capital loss carryback" after "loss carryback". **Effective** with respect to net capital losses sustained in tax years beginning after 12-31-69.

• **1967 (P.L. 90-225)**

P.L. 90-225, §2(d):

Amended Code Sec. 6511(d)(4)(A) by inserting after "which results in such carryback" in the first sentence the following: "(or, with respect to any portion of a investment credit carryback from a taxable year attributable to a net operating loss carryback from a subsequent taxable year, the period shall be that period which ends with the expiration of the 15th day of the 40th month, or 39th month, in the case of a corporation, following the end of such subsequent taxable year)". **Effective** with respect to investment credit carrybacks attributable to net operating loss carrybacks from tax years ending after 7-31-67.

• **1964 (P.L. 88-571)**

P.L. 88-571, §3(c):

Amended Code Sec. 6511(d) by adding paragraph (6). **Effective** with respect to amounts added to policyholders surplus accounts for tax years beginning after 12-31-58.

• **1964, Revenue Act of 1964 (P.L. 88-272)**

P.L. 88-272, §232(d):

Amended Code Sec. 6511(d)(2)(B) by designating the first paragraph as (i) and by adding new paragraph (ii). **Effective** with respect to tax years beginning after 12-31-63.

P.L. 88-272, §239:

Added to Code Sec. 6511(d) a new paragraph (5).

• **1962, Revenue Act of 1962 (P.L. 87-834)**

P.L. 87-834, §2:

Added to Code Sec. 6511(d) a new paragraph (4). **Effective** for tax years ending after 12-31-61.

• **1962, Trade Expansion Act of 1962 (P.L. 87-794)**

P.L. 87-794, §317(d):

Amended Code Sec. 6511(d)(2)(A). **Effective** with respect to net operating losses for tax years ending after 12-31-55. Prior to amendment, Sec. 6511(d)(2)(A) read as follows:

"(A) Period of limitation.—If the claim for credit or refund relates to an overpayment attributable to a net operating loss carryback, in lieu of the 3-year period of limitation prescribed in subsection (a), the period shall be that period which ends with the expiration of the 15th day of the 40th month (or 39th month, in the case of a corporation) following the end of the taxable year of the net operating loss which results in such carryback, or the period prescribed in subsection (c) in respect of such taxable year, whichever expires later; except that, with respect to an overpayment attributable to the creation of or an increase in a net operating loss carryback as a result of the elimination of excessive profits by a renegotiation (as defined in section 1481(a)(1)(A)), the period shall not expire before September 1, 1959, or the expiration of the twelfth month following the month in which the agreement of order for the elimination of such excessive profits becomes final, whichever is the later. In the case of such a claim, the amount of the credit or refund may exceed the portion of the tax paid within the period provided in subsection (b)(2) or (c), whichever is applicable, to the extent of the amount of the overpayment attributable to such carryback."

• **1959 (P.L. 86-280)**

P.L. 86-280, §1(a):

Added the matter following the semicolon in the first sentence of Code Sec. 6511(d)(2)(A).

P.L. 86-280, §1(c), provides:

"The amendment made by subsection (a) shall apply with respect to claims for credit or refund resulting from the elimination of excessive profits by renegotiation to which section 6511(d)(2) of the Internal Revenue Code of 1954 applies."

• **1958, Technical Amendments Act of 1958 (P.L. 85-866)**

P.L. 85-866, §82(d):

Amended Sec. 6511(d)(2)(A) by striking out the phrase "15th day of the 39th month" and substituting the following: "15th day of the 40th month (or 39th month, in the case of a corporation)". **Effective** 1-1-54.

* * *

[Sec. 6511(i)]

(i) CROSS REFERENCES.—

(1) For time return deemed filed and tax considered paid, see section 6513.

(2) For limitations with respect to certain credits against estate tax, see sections 2014(b) and 2015.

(3) For limitations in case of floor stocks refunds, see section 6412.

(4) For a period of limitations for credit or refund in the case of joint income returns after separate returns have been filed, see section 6013(b)(3).

(5) For limitations in case of payments under section 6420 (relating to gasoline used on farms), see section 6420(b).

(6) For limitations in case of payments under section 6421 (relating to gasoline used for certain nonhighway purposes or by local transit systems), see section 6421(d).

(7) For a period of limitations for refund of an overpayment of penalties imposed under section 6694 or 6695, see section 6696(d)(2).

Amendments

• 2013, American Taxpayer Relief Act of 2012 (P.L. 112-240)

P.L. 112-240, §101(a)(1) and (3), provides:

SEC. 101. PERMANENT EXTENSION AND MODIFICATION OF 2001 TAX RELIEF.

(a) PERMANENT EXTENSION.—

(1) IN GENERAL.—The Economic Growth and Tax Relief Reconciliation Act of 2001 is amended by striking title IX.

***

(3) EFFECTIVE DATE.—The amendments made by this subsection shall apply to taxable, plan, or limitation years beginning after December 31, 2012, and estates of decedents dying, gifts made, or generation skipping transfers after December 31, 2012.

• 2001, Economic Growth and Tax Relief Reconciliation Act of 2001 (P.L. 107-16)

P.L. 107-16, §532(c)(11):

Amended Code Sec. 6511(i)(2) by striking "2011(c), 2014(b)," and inserting "2014(b)". **Effective** for estates of decedents dying, and generation-skipping transfers, after 12-31-2004.

P.L. 107-16, §901(a)-(b), as amended by P.L. 111-312, §101(a)(1), provides [but see P.L. 112-240, §101(a)(1) and (3), above]:

SEC. 901. SUNSET OF PROVISIONS OF ACT.

(a) IN GENERAL.—All provisions of, and amendments made by, this Act shall not apply—

(1) to taxable, plan, or limitation years beginning after December 31, 2012, or

(2) in the case of title V, to estates of decedents dying, gifts made, or generation skipping transfers, after December 31, 2012.

(b) APPLICATION OF CERTAIN LAWS.—The Internal Revenue Code of 1986 and the Employee Retirement Income Security Act of 1974 shall be applied and administered to years, estates, gifts, and transfers described in subsection (a) as if the provisions and amendments described in subsection (a) had never been enacted.

• 1998, IRS Restructuring and Reform Act of 1998 (P.L. 105-206)

P.L. 105-206, §3202(a):

Amended Code Sec. 6511 by redesignating subsection (h) as subsection (i). **Effective** for periods of disability before, on, or after 7-22-98 but does not apply to any claim for credit or refund which (without regard to such amendment) is barred by the operation of any law or rule of law (including res judicata) as of 7-22-98.

• 1988, Technical and Miscellaneous Revenue Act of 1988 (P.L. 100-647)

P.L. 100-647, §1017(c)(11):

Amended Code Sec. 6511(i)[(h)](6) by striking out "section 6421(c)" and inserting in lieu thereof "section 6421(d)". **Effective** as if included in the provision of P.L. 99-514 to which it relates.

• 1988, Omnibus Trade and Competitiveness Act of 1988 (P.L. 100-418)

P.L. 100-418, §1941(b)(2)(I):

Amended Code Sec. 6511 by striking subsection (h) and redesignating subsection (i) as subsection (h). **Effective** for crude oil removed from the premises on or after 8-23-88. Prior to amendment, Code Sec. 6511(h) read as follows:

(h) SPECIAL RULES FOR WINDFALL PROFIT TAXES.—

(1) OIL SUBJECT TO WITHHOLDING.—In the case of any oil to which section 4995(a) applies and with respect to which no return is required, the return referred to in subsection (a) shall be the return (of the person liable for the tax imposed by section 4986) of the taxes imposed by subtitle A for the taxable year in which the removal year (as defined in section 6501(m)(1)(B)) ends.

(2) SPECIAL RULE FOR DOE RECLASSIFICATION.—In the case of any tax imposed by chapter 45, if a Department of Energy change (as defined in section 6501(m)(2)(B)) becomes final, the period for filing a claim for credit or refund for any overpayment attributable to such change shall not expire before the date which is 1 year after the date on which such change becomes final.

(3) CROSS REFERENCE.—

For period of limitation for windfall profit tax items of partnerships, see section 6227(a) and subsections (c) and (d) of section 6230 as made applicable by section 6232.

• 1986, Tax Reform Act of 1986 (P.L. 99-514)

P.L. 99-514, §1847(b)(15)(A) and (B):

Amended Code Sec. 6511(h) by striking out "section 6501(q)(1)(B)" in paragraph (1) and inserting in lieu thereof "section 6501(m)(1)(B)", and by striking out "section 6501(q)(2)(B)" in paragraph (2) and inserting in lieu thereof "section 6501(m)(2)(B)". **Effective** as if included in the provision of P.L. 98-369 to which it relates.

• 1984, Deficit Reduction Act of 1984 (P.L. 98-369)

P.L. 98-369, §714(p)(2)(G):

Amended Code Sec. 6511(h)(3). **Effective** as if included in P.L. 97-248. Prior to amendment, 6511(h)(3) read as follows:

(3) Partnership Items of Federally Registered Partnerships.—Under regulations prescribed by the Secretary, rules similar to the rules of subsection (g) shall apply to the tax imposed by section 4986.

P.L. 98-369, §735(c)(14):

Amended Code Sec. 6511 by striking out subsection (i) and by redesignating subsection (j) as subsection (i). **Effective** as if included in the provision of P.L. 97-424 to which it relates. Prior to amendment, subsection (i) read as follows:

(i) Special Rule for Certain Tread Rubber Tax Credits or Refunds.—The period for allowing a credit or making a refund of any overpayment of tax arising by reason of subparagraph (G)(iii) of section 6416(b)(2) with respect to any adjustment of sales price of a tire pursuant to a warranty or guarantee shall not expire if claim therefore is filed before the date which is one year after the day on which such adjustment is made.

• 1980 (P.L. 96-598)

P.L. 96-598, §1(c):

Redesignated Code Sec. 6511(i) as (j) and inserted a new (i). **Effective** 2-1-81.

• 1980, Crude Oil Windfall Profit Tax Act of 1980 (P.L. 96-223)

P.L. 96-223, §101(g)(2):

Added Code Sec. 6511(h). For the **effective** date and transitional rules, see P.L. 96-223, §101(i), following Code Sec. 4986.

P.L. 96-223, §101(g)(2):

Redesignated Code Sec. 6511(h) as (i). **Effective** for periods beginning after 2-29-80.

• 1978, Revenue Act of 1978 (P.L. 95-600)

P.L. 95-600, §212(b)(1):

Redesignated former Code Sec. 6511(g) as Code Sec. 6511(h).

• 1976, Tax Reform Act of 1976 (P.L. 94-455)

P.L. 94-455, §1203(h)(3):

Added a new paragraph (7) to Code Sec. 6511(g). **Effective** for documents prepared after 12-31-76.

• 1969, Tax Reform Act of 1969 (P.L. 91-172)

P.L. 91-172, §101(h):

Redesignated former Code Sec. 6511(f) as Code Sec. 6511(g). **Effective** 1-1-70.

• 1956 (P.L. 627, 84th Cong.)

P.L. 627, 84th Cong., §208(e)(6):

Amended subsection (f) by adding subparagraph (6). **Effective** 7-1-56.

• 1956 (P.L. 466, 84th Cong.)

P.L. 466, 84th Cong., §4(e):

Added subparagraph (5) to Code Sec. 6511(f).

[Sec. 6512]

SEC. 6512. LIMITATIONS IN CASE OF PETITION TO TAX COURT.

[Sec. 6512(a)]

(a) EFFECT OF PETITION TO TAX COURT.—If the Secretary has mailed to the taxpayer a notice of deficiency under section 6212(a) (relating to deficiencies of income, estate, gift, and certain excise taxes) and if the taxpayer files a petition with the Tax Court within the time prescribed in section 6213(a) (or 7481(c) with respect to a determination of statutory interest or section 7481(d) solely with respect to a determination of estate tax by the Tax Court), no credit or refund of income tax for the same taxable year, of gift tax for the same calendar year or calendar quarter, of estate tax in respect of the taxable estate of the same decedent, or of tax imposed by chapter 41, 42, 43, or 44 with respect to any act (or failure to act) to which such petition relates, in respect of which the Secretary has determined the deficiency shall be allowed or made and no suit by the taxpayer for the recovery of any part of the tax shall be instituted in any court except—

(1) As to overpayments determined by a decision of the Tax Court which has become final, and

(2) As to any amount collected in excess of an amount computed in accordance with the decision of the Tax Court which has become final, and

(3) As to any amount collected after the period of limitation upon the making of levy or beginning a proceeding in court for collection has expired; but in any such claim for credit or refund or in any such suit for refund the decision of the Tax Court which has become final, as to whether such period has expired before the notice of deficiency was mailed, shall be conclusive, and

(4) As to overpayments attributable to partnership items, in accordance with subchapter C of chapter 63, and

(5) As to any amount collected within the period during which the Secretary is prohibited from making the assessment or from collecting by levy or through a proceeding in court under the provisions of section 6213(a), and

(6) As to overpayments the Secretary is authorized to refund or credit pending appeal as provided in subsection (b).

Amendments

• 2000, Community Renewal Tax Relief Act of 2000 (P.L. 106-554)

P.L. 106-554, §319(19):

Amended Code Sec. 6512(a) by striking "; and" at the end of paragraphs (1), (2), and (5) and inserting ", and". **Effective** 12-21-2000.

• 1998, IRS Restructuring and Reform Act of 1998 (P.L. 105-206)

P.L. 105-206, §3464(b):

Amended Code Sec. 6512(a) by striking the period at the end of paragraph (4) and inserting ", and", and by inserting after paragraph (4) new paragraphs (5) and (6). **Effective** 7-22-98.

• 1988, Technical and Miscellaneous Revenue Act of 1988 (P.L. 100-647)

P.L. 100-647, §6246(b)(1):

Amended Code Sec. 6512(a) by inserting after "section 6213(a)" the following: "(or 7481(c) with respect to a determination of statutory interest)". **Effective** for assessments of deficiencies redetermined by the Tax Court made after 11-10-88.

P.L. 100-647, §6247(b)(1):

Amended Code Sec. 6512(a), as amended, by striking out "interest)" and inserting in lieu thereof "interest or section 7481(d) solely with respect to a determination of estate tax by the Tax Court)". **Effective** with respect to Tax Court cases for which the decision is not final on 11-10-88.

• 1988, Omnibus Trade and Competitiveness Act of 1988 (P.L. 100-418)

P.L. 100-418, §1941(b)(2)(J)(i)-(ii):

Amended Code Sec. 6512(a) by striking "of tax imposed by chapter 41" and inserting "or of tax imposed by chapter 41", and by striking, "or of tax imposed by chapter 45 for the same taxable period" after "petition relates". **Effective** for crude oil removed from the premises on or after 8-23-88.

• 1982, Tax Equity and Fiscal Responsibility Act of 1982 (P.L. 97-248)

P.L. 97-248, §402(c)(8):

Amended Code Sec. 6512(a) by striking out the period at the end of paragraph (3) and inserting ", and", and by inserting a new paragraph (4). **Effective** for partnership tax years beginning after 9-3-82, and also to partnership tax years ending after that date if the partnership, each partner, and each indirect partner requests such application and if the Secretary or his delegate consents to such application.

• 1980, Crude Oil Windfall Profit Tax Act of 1980 (P.L. 96-223)

P.L. 96-223, §101(f)(6)(A):

Amended Code Sec. 6512(a) by striking out "chapter 41, 42, 43, or 44 taxes" and inserting "certain excise taxes", by striking out "or of tax imposed by chapter 41" and inserting "of tax imposed by chapter 41", and by inserting ", or of tax imposed by chapter 45 for the same taxable period" after "to which such petition relates". For the **effective** date and transitional rules, see P.L. 96-223, §101(i), following Code Sec. 4986.

• 1976, Tax Reform Act of 1976 (P.L. 94-455)

P.L. 94-455, §1307(d)(2)(F)(vii):

Substituted "chapter 41, 42," for "chapter 42" each place it appeared in Code Sec. 6512(a). **Effective** on and after 10-4-76.

P.L. 94-455, §1605(b)(9):

Substituted "43, or 44" for "or 43" each place it appeared in Code Sec. 6512(a). **Effective** for tax years of real estate investment trusts beginning after 10-4-76.

P.L. 94-455, §1906(b)(13)(A):

Amended 1954 Code by substituting "Secretary" for "Secretary or his delegate" each place it appeared. **Effective** 2-1-77.

• 1970, Excise, Estate, and Gift Tax Adjustment Act of 1970 (P.L. 91-614)

P.L. 91-614, §102(d)(9):

Amended Code Sec. 6512(a) by adding "or calendar quarter" in the sixth line thereof. **Effective** for gifts made after 12-31-70.

• 1969, Tax Reform Act of 1969 (P.L. 91-172)

P.L. 91-172, §101(j)(47):

Amended the first sentence of Code Sec. 6512(a) by substituting "gift, and chapter 42 taxes" for "and gift taxes" and by substituting "of estate tax in respect of the taxable estate of the same decedent, or of tax imposed by chapter 42 with respect to any act (or failure to act) to which such petition relates," for "or of estate tax in respect of the taxable estate of the same decedent,". **Effective** 1-1-70.

[Sec. 6512(b)]

(b) OVERPAYMENT DETERMINED BY TAX COURT.—

(1) JURISDICTION TO DETERMINE.—Except as provided by paragraph (3) and by section 7463, if the Tax Court finds that there is no deficiency and further finds that the taxpayer has made an overpayment of income tax for the same taxable year, of gift tax for the same calendar year or calendar quarter, of estate tax in respect of the taxable estate of the same decedent, or of tax imposed by chapter 41, 42, 43, or 44 with respect to any act (or failure to act) to which such petition relates for the same taxable period, in respect of which the Secretary determined the deficiency, or finds that there is a deficiency but that the taxpayer has made an overpayment of such tax, the Tax Court shall have jurisdiction to determine the amount of such overpayment, and such amount shall, when the decision of the Tax Court has become final, be credited or refunded to the taxpayer. If a notice of appeal in respect of the decision of the Tax Court is filed under section 7483, the Secretary is authorized to refund or credit the overpayment determined by the Tax Court to the extent the overpayment is not contested on appeal.

(2) JURISDICTION TO ENFORCE.—If, after 120 days after a decision of the Tax Court has become final, the Secretary has failed to refund the overpayment determined by the Tax Court, together with the interest thereon as provided in subchapter B of chapter 67, then the Tax Court, upon motion by the taxpayer, shall have jurisdiction to order the refund of such overpayment and interest. An order of the Tax Court disposing of a motion under this paragraph shall be reviewable in the same manner as a decision of the Tax Court, but only with respect to the matters determined in such order.

(3) LIMIT ON AMOUNT OF CREDIT OR REFUND.—No such credit or refund shall be allowed or made of any portion of the tax unless the Tax Court determines as part of its decision that such portion was paid—

(A) after the mailing of the notice of deficiency,

(B) within the period which would be applicable under section 6511(b)(2), (c), or (d), if on the date of the mailing of the notice of deficiency a claim had been filed (whether or not filed) stating the grounds upon which the Tax Court finds that there is an overpayment, or

(C) within the period which would be applicable under section 6511(b)(2), (c), or (d), in respect of any claim for refund filed within the applicable period specified in section 6511 and before the date of the mailing of the notice of deficiency—

(i) which had not been disallowed before that date,

(ii) which had been disallowed before that date and in respect of which a timely suit for refund could have been commenced as of that date, or

(iii) in respect of which a suit for refund had been commenced before that date and within the period specified in section 6532.

In a case described in subparagraph (B) where the date of the mailing of the notice of deficiency is during the third year after the due date (with extensions) for filing the return of tax and no return was filed before such date, the applicable period under subsections (a) and (b)(2) of section 6511 shall be 3 years.

(4) DENIAL OF JURISDICTION REGARDING CERTAIN CREDITS AND REDUCTIONS.—The Tax Court shall have no jurisdiction under this subsection to restrain or review any credit or reduction made by the Secretary under section 6402.

Amendments

• 2015, Bipartisan Budget Act of 2015 (P.L. 114-74)

P.L. 114-74, §1101(f)(7):

Amended Code Sec. 6512(b)(3) by striking the second sentence. **Effective** generally for returns filed for partnership tax years beginning after 12-31-2017. For a special rule, see Act Sec. 1101(g)(4), below. Prior to being stricken, the second sentence of Code Sec. 6512(b)(3) read as follows:

In the case of a credit or refund relating to an affected item (within the meaning of section 6231(a)(5)), the preceding sentence shall be applied by substituting the periods under sections 6229 and 6230(d) for the periods under section 6511(b)(2), (c), and (d).

P.L. 114-74, §1101(g)(4), provides:

(4) ELECTION.—A partnership may elect (at such time and in such form and manner as the Secretary of the Treasury may prescribe) for the amendments made by this section (other than the election under section 6221(b) of such Code (as added by this Act)) to apply to any return of the partnership filed for partnership taxable years beginning after the date of the enactment of this Act and before January 1, 2018.

• 1998, IRS Restructuring and Reform Act of 1998 (P.L. 105-206)

P.L. 105-206, §3464(c):

Amended Code Sec. 6512(b)(1) by adding at the end a new sentence. **Effective** 7-22-98.

• 1997, Taxpayer Relief Act of 1997 (P.L. 105-34)

P.L. 105-34, §1239(c)(2):

Amended Code Sec. 6512(b)(3) by adding at the end a new sentence. **Effective** for partnership tax years ending after 8-5-97.

P.L. 105-34, § 1282(a):

Amended Code Sec. 6512(b)(3) by adding at the end a new flush sentence. **Effective** for claims for credit or refund for tax years ending after 8-5-97.

P.L. 105-34, § 1451(a):

Amended Code Sec. 6512(b)(2) by adding at the end a new sentence. **Effective** 8-5-97.

P.L. 105-34, § 1451(b):

Amended Code Sec. 6512(b) by adding at the end a new paragraph (4). **Effective** 8-5-97.

• 1988, Technical and Miscellaneous Revenue Act of 1988 (P.L. 100-647)

P.L. 100-647, § 6244(a):

Amended Code Sec. 6512(b) by striking out "paragraph (2)" and inserting in lieu thereof "paragraph (3)" in paragraph (1), by redesignating paragraph (2) as paragraph (3) and by inserting new paragraph (2). **Effective** for overpayments determined by the Tax Court which have not yet been refunded by the 90th day after 11-10-88.

• 1988, Omnibus Trade and Competitiveness Act of 1988 (P.L. 100-418)

P.L. 100-418, § 1941(b)(2)(K)(i)-(ii):

Amended Code Sec. 6512(b)(1) by striking "of tax imposed by chapter 41" and inserting "or of tax imposed by chapter 41", and by striking ", or of tax imposed by chapter 45 for the same taxable period" after "petition relates". **Effective** for crude oil removed from the premises on or after 8-23-88.

• 1982, Tax Equity and Fiscal Responsibility Act of 1982 (P.L. 97-248)

P.L. 97-248, § 402(c)(9):

Amended Code Sec. 6512(b)(2) by striking out "(c), (d), or (g)" each place it appeared and inserting "(c), or (d)". For the **effective** date, see the amendment note for P.L. 97-248, following Code Sec. 6512(a).

• 1980, Crude Oil Windfall Profit Tax Act of 1980 (P.L. 96-223)

P.L. 96-223, § 101(f)(6)(B):

Amended Code Sec. 6512(b) by striking out "or of tax imposed by chapter 41" and inserting "of tax imposed by chapter 41" and by inserting ",or of chapter 45 for the same taxable period" after "to which such petition relates". For the **effective** date and transitional rules, see P.L. 96-223, § 101(i), following Code Sec. 4986.

• 1978, Revenue Act of 1978 (P.L. 95-600)

P.L. 95-600, § 212(b)(2):

Amended Code Sec. 6512(b)(2) by changing "(c), or (d)" each place it appeared to "(c), (d), or (g)". **Effective** for partnership items arising in partnership tax years beginning after 12-31-78.

• 1976, Tax Reform Act of 1976 (P.L. 94-455)

P.L. 94-455, § 1307(d)(2)(F)(vii):

Substituted "chapter 41, 42," for "chapter 42" each place it appeared in Code Sec. 6512(b)(1). **Effective** on and after 10-4-76.

P.L. 94-455, § 1605(b)(9):

Substituted "43, or 44" for "or 43" each place it appeared in Code Sec. 6512(b). **Effective** for tax years of real estate investment trusts beginning after 10-4-76.

P.L. 94-455, § 1906(b)(13)(A):

Amended 1954 Code by substituting "Secretary" for "Secretary or his delegate" each place it appeared. **Effective** 2-1-77.

• 1974, Employee Retirement Income Security Act of 1974 (P.L. 93-406)

P.L. 93-406, § 1016(a)(16):

Amended Code Sec. 6512 by changing "chapter 42" to "chapter 42 or 43" each place it appears. For **effective** date, see amendment note for Code Sec. 410.

• 1970, Excise, Estate, and Gift Tax Adjustment Act of 1970 (P.L. 91-614)

P.L. 91-614, § 102(d)(9):

Amended Code Sec. 6512(b) by adding "or calendar quarter" in paragraph (1). **Effective** for gifts made after 12-31-70.

• 1969, Tax Reform Act of 1969 (P.L. 91-172)

P.L. 91-172, § 101(j)(48):

Amended paragraph (1) of Code Sec. 6512(b) by substituting "of estate tax in respect of the taxable estate of the same decedent, or of tax imposed by chapter 42 with respect to any act (or failure to act) to which such petition relates," for "or of estate tax in respect of the taxable estate of the same decedent,". **Effective** 1-1-70.

P.L. 91-172, § 960(b):

Amended Code Sec. 6512(b)(1) by adding the initial phrase "Except as provided by paragraph (2) and section 7463,". **Effective** 12-30-70.

• 1962 (P.L. 87-870)

P.L. 87-870, § 4:

Amended Code Sec. 6512(b)(2) by deleting "or" at the end of subparagraph (A), by deleting the period at the end of subparagraph (B) and inserting in lieu thereof ", or", and by adding after subparagraph (B) a new subparagraph (C). **Effective** 10-24-62.

[Sec. 6512(c)]

(c) CROSS REFERENCES.—

* * *

(2) For provision giving the Tax Court jurisdiction to award reasonable litigation costs in proceedings to enforce an overpayment determined by such court, see section 7430.

Amendments

• 1988, Technical and Miscellaneous Revenue Act of 1988 (P.L. 100-647)

P.L. 100-647, § 6244(b)(2):

Amended Code Sec. 6512(c) by striking out "REFERENCE.—"and inserting in lieu thereof "REFERENCES.—" in the heading, by designating the undesignated paragraph as paragraph (1), and by adding at the end thereof new paragraph (2). **Effective** for overpayments determined by the Tax Court which have not yet been refunded by the 90th day after 11-10-88.

• 1980, Bankruptcy Tax Act of 1980 (P.L. 96-589)

P.L. 96-589, § 6(d)(3):

Added Code Sec. 6512(c). **Effective** 10-1-79, but inapplicable to proceedings under the Bankruptcy Act commenced before that date.

[Sec. 6513]

SEC. 6513. TIME RETURN DEEMED FILED AND TAX CONSIDERED PAID.

[Sec. 6513(a)]

(a) EARLY RETURN OR ADVANCE PAYMENT OF TAX.—For purposes of section 6511, any return filed before the last day prescribed for the filing thereof shall be considered as filed on such last day. For purposes of section 6511(b)(2) and (c) and section 6512, payment of any portion of the tax made before the last day prescribed for the payment of the tax shall be considered made on such last day. For purposes of this subsection, the last day prescribed for filing the return or paying the tax shall be determined without regard to any extension of time granted the taxpayer and without regard to any election to pay the tax in installments.

[Sec. 6513(b)]

(b) PREPAID INCOME TAX.—For purposes of section 6511 or 6512—

(1) Any tax actually deducted and withheld at the source during any calendar year under chapter 24 shall, in respect of the recipient of the income, be deemed to have been paid by him on the 15th day of the fourth month following the close of his taxable year with respect to which such tax is allowable as a credit under section 31.

(2) Any amount paid as estimated income tax for any taxable year shall be deemed to have been paid on the last day prescribed for filing the return under section 6012 for such taxable year (determined without regard to any extension of time for filing such return).

(3) Any tax withheld at the source under chapter 3 or 4 shall, in respect of the recipient of the income, be deemed to have been paid by such recipient on the last day prescribed for filing the return under section 6012 for the taxable year (determined without regard to any extension of time for filing) with respect to which such tax is allowable as a credit under section 1462 or 1474(b). For this purpose, any exemption granted under section 6012 from the requirement of filing a return shall be disregarded.

Amendments

• 2010, Hiring Incentives to Restore Employment Act (P.L. 111-147)

P.L. 111-147, § 501(c)(4)(A)-(B):

Amended Code Sec. 6513(b)(3) by inserting "or 4" after "chapter 3", and by inserting "or 1474(b)" after "section 1462". **Effective** generally for payments made after 12-31-2012. For a special rule, see Act Sec. 501(d)(2), below.

P.L. 111-147, § 501(d)(2), provides:

(2) GRANDFATHERED TREATMENT OF OUTSTANDING OBLIGATIONS.—The amendments made by this section shall not require any amount to be deducted or withheld from any payment under any obligation outstanding on the date which is 2 years after the date of the enactment of this Act or from the gross proceeds from any disposition of such an obligation.

• 1966, Foreign Investors Tax Act of 1966 (P.L. 89-809)

P.L. 89-809, § 105(f)(1):

Amended Code Sec. 6513(b). **Effective** 11-13-66. Prior to amendment, Code Sec. 6513(b) read as follows:

(b) PREPAID INCOME TAX.—For purposes of section 6511 or 6512, any tax actually deducted and withheld at the source during any calendar year under chapter 24 shall, in respect of the recipient of the income, be deemed to have been paid by him on the 15th day of the fourth month following the close of his taxable year with respect to which such tax is allowable as a credit under section 31. For purposes of section 6511 or 6512, any amount paid as estimated income tax for any taxable year shall be deemed to have been paid on the last day prescribed for filing the return under section 6012 for such taxable year (determined without regard to any extension of time for filing such return).

* * *

[Sec. 6514]

SEC. 6514. CREDITS OR REFUNDS AFTER PERIOD OF LIMITATION.

[Sec. 6514(a)]

(a) CREDITS OR REFUNDS AFTER PERIOD OF LIMITATION.—A refund of any portion of an internal revenue tax shall be considered erroneous and a credit of any such portion shall be considered void—

(1) EXPIRATION OF PERIOD FOR FILING CLAIM.—If made after the expiration of the period of limitation for filing claim therefor, unless within such period claim was filed; or

(2) DISALLOWANCE OF CLAIM AND EXPIRATION OF PERIOD FOR FILING SUIT.—In the case of a claim filed within the proper time and disallowed by the Secretary, if the credit or refund was made after the expiration of the period of limitation for filing suit, unless within such period suit was begun by the taxpayer.

(3) RECOVERY OF ERRONEOUS REFUNDS.—

For procedure by the United States to recover erroneous refunds, see sections 6532(b) and 7405.

Amendments

• 1976, Tax Reform Act of 1976 (P.L. 94-455)

P.L. 94-455, § 1906(b)(13)(A):

Amended 1954 Code by substituting "Secretary" for "Secretary of his delegate" each place it appeared. **Effective** 2-1-77.

[Sec. 6514(b)]

(b) CREDIT AFTER PERIOD OF LIMITATION.—Any credit against a liability in respect of any taxable year shall be void if any payment in respect of such liability would be considered an overpayment under section 6401(a).

* * *

Subchapter D—Periods of Limitation in Judicial Proceedings

[Sec. 6531]

SEC. 6531. PERIODS OF LIMITATION ON CRIMINAL PROSECUTIONS.

No person shall be prosecuted, tried, or punished for any of the various offenses arising under the internal revenue laws unless the indictment is found or the information instituted within 3 years next after the commission of the offense, except that the period of limitation shall be 6 years—

(1) for offenses involving the defrauding or attempting to defraud the United States or any agency thereof, whether by conspiracy or not, and in any manner;

(2) for the offense of willfully attempting in any manner to evade or defeat any tax or the payment thereof;

(3) for the offense of willfully aiding or assisting in, or procuring, counseling, or advising, the preparation or presentation under, or in connection with any matter arising under, the internal revenue laws, of a false or fraudulent return, affidavit, claim, or document (whether or not such falsity or fraud is with the knowledge or consent of the person authorized or required to present such return, affidavit, claim, or document);

(4) for the offense of willfully failing to pay any tax, or make any return (other than a return required under authority of part III of subchapter A of chapter 61) at the time or times required by law or regulations;

(5) for offenses described in sections 7206(1) and 7207 (relating to false statements and fraudulent documents);

(6) for the offense described in section 7212(a) (relating to intimidation of officers and employees of the United States);

(7) for offenses described in section 7214(a) committed by officers and employees of the United States; and

(8) for offenses arising under section 371 of Title 18 of the United States Code, where the object of the conspiracy is to attempt in any manner to evade or defeat any tax or the payment thereof.

The time during which the person committing any of the various offenses arising under the internal revenue laws is outside the United States or is a fugitive from justice within the meaning of section 3290 of Title 18 of the United States Code, shall not be taken as any part of the time limited by law for the commencement of such proceedings. (The preceding sentence shall also be deemed an amendment to section 3748(a) of the Internal Revenue Code of 1939, and shall apply in lieu of the sentence in section 3748(a) which relates to the time during which a person committing an offense is absent from the district wherein the same is committed, except that such amendment shall apply only if the period of limitations under section 3748 would, without the application of such amendment, expire more than 3 years after the date of enactment of this title, and except that such period shall not, with the application of this amendment, expire prior to the date which is 3 years after the date of enactment of this title.) Where a complaint is instituted before a commissioner of the United States within the period above limited, the time shall be extended until the date which is 9 months after the date of the making of the complaint before the commissioner of the United States. For the purpose of determining the periods of limitation on criminal prosecutions, the rules of section 6513 shall be applicable.

[Sec. 6532]

SEC. 6532. PERIODS OF LIMITATION ON SUITS.

[Sec. 6532(a)]

(a) SUITS BY TAXPAYERS FOR REFUND.—

(1) GENERAL RULE.—No suit or proceeding under section 7422(a) for the recovery of any internal revenue tax, penalty, or other sum, shall be begun before the expiration of 6 months from the date of filing the claim required under such section unless the Secretary renders a decision thereon within that time, nor after the expiration of 2 years from the date of mailing by certified mail or registered mail by the Secretary to the taxpayer of a notice of the disallowance of the part of the claim to which the suit or proceeding relates.

(2) EXTENSION OF TIME.—The 2-year period prescribed in paragraph (1) shall be extended for such period as may be agreed upon in writing between the taxpayer and the Secretary.

(3) WAIVER OF NOTICE OF DISALLOWANCE.—If any person files a written waiver of the requirement that he be mailed a notice of disallowance, the 2-year period prescribed in paragraph (1) shall begin on the date such waiver is filed.

(4) RECONSIDERATION AFTER MAILING OF NOTICE.—Any consideration, reconsideration, or action by the Secretary with respect to such claim following the mailing of a notice by certified mail or registered mail of disallowance shall not operate to extend the period within which suit may be begun.

(5) CROSS REFERENCE.—

For substitution of 120-day period for the 6-month period contained in paragraph (1) in a title 11 case, see section 505(a)(2) of title 11 of the United States Code.

Amendments

• 1980, Bankruptcy Tax Act of 1980 (P.L. 96-589)

P.L. 96-589, §6(d)(4):

Amended Code Sec. 6532(a) by adding a new paragraph (5). **Effective** 10-1-79, but inapplicable to any proceeding under the Bankruptcy Act commenced before that date.

• 1976, Tax Reform Act of 1976 (P.L. 94-455)

P.L. 94-455, §1906(b)(13)(A):

Amended 1954 Code by substituting "Secretary" for "Secretary or his delegate" each place it appeared. **Effective** 2-1-77.

• 1958, Technical Amendments Act of 1958 (P.L. 85-866)

P.L. 85-866, §89(b):

Amended Sec. 6532(a)(4) by striking out "registered mail" and substituting "certified mail or registered mail". **Effective** 9-3-58.

[Sec. 6532(b)]

(b) SUITS BY UNITED STATES FOR RECOVERY OF ERRONEOUS REFUNDS.—Recovery of an erroneous refund by suit under section 7405 shall be allowed only if such suit is begun within 2 years after the making of such refund, except that such suit may be brought at any time within 5 years from the making of the refund if it appears that any part of the refund was induced by fraud or misrepresentation of a material fact.

Amendments

• 1976, Tax Reform Act of 1976 (P.L. 94-455)

P.L. 94-455, §1906(b)(13)(A):

Amended 1954 Code by substituting "Secretary" for "Secretary or his delegate" each place it appeared. **Effective** 2-1-77.

[Sec. 6532(c)]

(c) SUITS BY PERSONS OTHER THAN TAXPAYERS.—

(1) GENERAL RULE.—Except as provided by paragraph (2), no suit or proceeding under section 7426 shall be begun after the expiration of 2 years from the date of the levy or agreement giving rise to such action.

(2) PERIOD WHEN CLAIM IS FILED.—If a request is made for the return of property described in section 6343(b), the 2-year period prescribed in paragraph (1) shall be extended for a period of 12 months from the date of filing of such request or for a period of 6 months from the date of mailing by registered or certified mail by the Secretary to the person making such request of a notice of disallowance of the part of the request to which the action relates, whichever is shorter.

Amendments

• 2017, Tax Cuts and Jobs Act (P.L. 115-97)

P.L. 115-97, §11071(b)(1)-(2):

Amended Code Sec. 6532(c) by striking "9 months" in paragraph (1) and inserting "2 years", and by striking "9-month" in paragraph (2) and inserting "2-year". For the **effective** date, see Act Sec. 11071(c), below.

P.L. 115-97, §11071(c), provides:

(c) EFFECTIVE DATE.—The amendments made by this section shall apply to—

(1) levies made after the date of the enactment of this Act, and

(2) levies made on or before such date if the 9-month period has not expired under section 6343(b) of the Internal Revenue Code of 1986 (without regard to this section) as of such date.

• 1966, Federal Tax Lien Act of 1966 (P.L. 89-719)

P.L. 89-719, §110(b):

Added new Code Sec. 6532(c). **Effective**, generally, after 11-2-66, but see the amendment note for Code Sec. 6323 for exceptions.

[Sec. 6533]

SEC. 6533. CROSS REFERENCES.

* * *

(2) For extensions of time by reason of armed service in a combat zone, see section 7508.

* * *

CHAPTER 67—INTEREST

Subchapter A—Interest on Underpayments

[Sec. 6601]

SEC. 6601. INTEREST ON UNDERPAYMENT, NONPAYMENT, OR EXTENSIONS OF TIME FOR PAYMENT, OF TAX.

[Sec. 6601(a)]

(a) GENERAL RULE.—If any amount of tax imposed by this title (whether required to be shown on a return, or to be paid by stamp or by some other method) is not paid on or before the last date prescribed for payment, interest on such amount at the underpayment rate established under section 6621 shall be paid for the period from such last date to the date paid.

Amendments

• 1986, Tax Reform Act of 1986 (P.L. 99-514)

P.L. 99-514, §1511(c)(11):

Amended Code Sec. 6601(a) by striking out "an annual rate established under section 6621" and inserting in lieu thereof "the underpayment rate established under section 6621". **Effective** for purposes of determining interest for periods after 12-31-86.

• 1975 (P.L. 93-625)

P.L. 93-625, §7(a)(2):

Amended Code Sec. 6601(a) by substituting "an annual rate established under section 6621" for "the rate of 6 percent per annum". For **effective** date, see the historical comment for P.L. 93-625 following the text of Code Sec. 6621.

[Sec. 6601(b)—Repealed]

Amendments

• 1975 (P.L. 93-625)

P.L. 93-625, §7(b)(1):

Repealed Code Sec. 6601(b) and redesignated the remaining subsections of Code Sec. 6601. **Effective** on 7-1-75, and applicable to amounts outstanding on such date or arising thereafter. Prior to repeal, Code Sec. 6601(b) read as follows:

(b) EXTENSIONS OF TIME FOR PAYMENT OF ESTATE TAX.—If the time for payment of an amount of tax imposed by chapter 11 is extended as provided in section 6161(a)(2) or 6166, or if the time for payment of an amount of such tax is postponed or extended as provided by section 6163, interest shall be paid at the rate of 4 percent, in lieu of 6 percent as provided in subsection (a). Effective 7-1-75.

• 1958, Technical Amendments Act of 1958 (P.L. 85-866)

P.L. 85-866, §66(c):

Amended Sec. 6601(b) by striking out the phrase "if postponement of the payment of an amount of such tax is permitted by section 6163(a)," and substituting the phrase "if the time for payment of an amount of such tax is postponed or extended as provided by section 6163,". For the **effective** date, see Act Sec. 206(f), below.

P.L. 85-866, §206(e):

Amended Sec. 6601(b) by striking out "section 6161(a)(2)" and substituting "section 6161(a)(2) or 6166,". For the **effective** date, see Act Sec. 206(f), below.

P.L. 85-866, §206(f), provides:

"The amendments made by this section shall apply to estates of decedents with respect to which the date for the filing of the estate tax return (including extensions thereof) prescribed by section 6075(a) of the Internal Revenue Code of 1954 is after the date of the enactment of this Act; except that (1) section 6166(i) of such Code as added by this section shall apply to estates of decedents dying after August 16, 1954, but only if the date for the filing of the estate tax return (including extensions thereof) expired on or before the date of the enactment of this Act, and (2) notwithstanding section 6166(a) of such Code, if an election under such section is required to be made before the sixtieth day after the date of the enactment of this Act such an election shall be considered timely if made on or before such sixtieth day." **Effective** 1-1-54.

[Sec. 6601(b)]

(b) LAST DATE PRESCRIBED FOR PAYMENT.—For purposes of this section, the last date prescribed for payment of the tax shall be determined under chapter 62 with the application of the following rules:

(1) EXTENSIONS OF TIME DISREGARDED.—The last date prescribed for payment shall be determined without regard to any extension of time for payment or any installment agreement entered into under section 6159.

(2) JEOPARDY.—The last date prescribed for payment shall be determined without regard to any notice and demand for payment issued, by reason of jeopardy (as provided in chapter 70), prior to the last date otherwise prescribed for such payment.

(3) ACCUMULATED EARNINGS TAX.—In the case of the tax imposed by section 531 for any taxable year, the last date prescribed for payment shall be deemed to be the due date (without regard to extensions) for the return of tax imposed by subtitle A for such taxable year.

(4) LAST DATE FOR PAYMENT NOT OTHERWISE PRESCRIBED.—In the case of taxes payable by stamp and in all other cases in which the last date for payment is not otherwise prescribed, the last date for payment shall be deemed to be the date the liability for tax arises (and in no event shall be later than the date notice and demand for the tax is made by the Secretary).

Amendments

• 2018, Tax Technical Corrections Act of 2018 (P.L. 115-141)

P.L. 115-141, §401(b)(47), Div. U:

Amended Code Sec. 6601(b) by striking paragraph (2) and by redesignating paragraphs (3) through (5) as paragraphs (2) through (4), respectively. **Effective** 3-23-2018. For a special rule, see Act Sec. 401(e), Div. U, below. Prior to being stricken, Code Sec. 6601(b)(2) read as follows:

(2) INSTALLMENT PAYMENTS.—In the case of an election under section 6156(a) to pay the tax in installments—

(A) The date prescribed for payment of each installment of the tax shown on the return shall be determined under section 6156(b), and

(B) The last date prescribed for payment of the first installment shall be deemed the last date prescribed for payment of any portion of the tax not shown on the return.

P.L. 115-141, §401(e), Div. U, provides:

(e) GENERAL SAVINGS PROVISION WITH RESPECT TO DEADWOOD PROVISIONS.—If—

(1) any provision amended or repealed by the amendments made by subsection (b) or (d) applied to—

(A) any transaction occurring before the date of the enactment of this Act,

(B) any property acquired before such date of enactment, or

(C) any item of income, loss, deduction, or credit taken into account before such date of enactment, and

(2) the treatment of such transaction, property, or item under such provision would (without regard to the amendments or repeals made by such subsection) affect the liability for tax for periods ending after such date of enactment,

nothing in the amendments or repeals made by this section shall be construed to affect the treatment of such transaction, property, or item for purposes of determining liability for tax for periods ending after such date of enactment.

• 1990, Omnibus Budget Reconciliation Act of 1990 (P.L. 101-508)

P.L. 101-508, §11801(c)(20)(B)(i)-(iii):

Amended Code Sec. 6601(b)(2) by striking "or 6158(a)" in the material preceding subparagraph (A), by striking "or 6158(a), as the case may be" in subparagraph (A), and by striking the last sentence. **Effective** 11-5-90. Prior to amendment, Code Sec. 6601(b)(2) read as follows:

(2) INSTALLMENT PAYMENTS.—In the case of an election under section 6156(a) or 6158(a) to pay the tax in installments—

(A) The date prescribed for payment of each installment of the tax shown on the return shall be determined under section 6156(b) or 6158(a), as the case may be, and

(B) The last date prescribed for payment of the first installment shall be deemed the last date prescribed for payment of any portion of the tax not shown on the return.

For purposes of subparagraph (A), section 6158(a) shall be treated as providing that the date prescribed for payment of each installment shall not be later than the date prescribed for payment of the 1985 installment.

P.L. 101-508, §11821(b)(1)-(2), provides:

(b) SAVINGS PROVISION.—If—

(1) any provision amended or repealed by this part applied to—

(A) any transaction occurring before the date of the enactment of this Act,

(B) any property acquired before such date of enactment, or

(C) any item of income, loss, deduction, or credit taken into account before such date of enactment, and

(2) the treatment of such transaction, property, or item under such provision would (without regard to the amendments made by this part) affect liability for tax for periods ending after such date of enactment,

nothing in the amendments made by this part shall be construed to affect the treatment of such transaction, property, or item for purposes of determining liability for tax for periods ending after such date of enactment.

• 1988, Technical and Miscellaneous Revenue Act of 1988 (P.L. 100-647)

P.L. 100-647, §6234(b)(1):

Amended Code Sec. 6601(b)(1) by inserting "or any installment agreement entered into under section 6159" after "time for payment". **Effective** for agreements entered into after 11-10-88.

• 1986, Tax Reform Act of 1986 (P.L. 99-514)

P.L. 99-514, §1404(c)(3)(A)-(B):

Amended Code Sec. 6601(b)(2) by striking out "6152(a), 6156(a), 6158(a)" and inserting in lieu thereof "6156(a) or 6158(a)", and by striking out "6152(b), 6156(b), or 6158(a)" in subparagraph (A) and inserting in lieu thereof "6156(b) or 6158(a)". **Effective** for tax years beginning after 12-31-86.

P.L. 99-514, §1512(a):

Amended Code Sec. 6601(b) by redesignating paragraph (4) as paragraph (5) and by inserting after paragraph (3) new paragraph (4). **Effective** for returns the due date for which (determined without regard to extensions) is after 12-31-85.

• 1976, Tax Reform Act of 1976 (P.L. 94-455)

P.L. 94-455, §1906(b)(13)(A):

Amended 1954 Code by substituting "Secretary" for "Secretary or his delegate" each place it appeared. **Effective** 2-1-77.

• 1976, Bank Holding Company Tax Act of 1976 (P.L. 94-452)

P.L. 94-452, §3(c)(3):

Amended Code Sec. 6601(b) by striking out "or 6156(a)" and inserting in lieu thereof ", 6156(a), or 6158(a)", and by striking out "or 6156(b)" and inserting in lieu thereof ", 6156(b), or 6158(a)"; and by adding the new sentence at the end thereof. **Effective** 10-1-77, with respect to sales after 7-7-70, in tax years ending after 7-7-70, but only in the case of qualified bank holding corporations.

• 1975 (P.L. 93-625)

P.L. 93-625, §7(b)(1):

Redesignated Code Sec. 6601(c) as Code Sec. 6601(b). **Effective** 7-1-75.

• 1961, Federal-Aid Highway Act of 1961 (P.L. 87-61)

P.L. 87-61, §203(c)(2):

Amended Sec. 6601(c)(2) by adding "or 6156(a)" and "or 6156(b), as the case may be." **Effective** 7-1-61.

[Sec. 6601(c)]

(c) SUSPENSION OF INTEREST IN CERTAIN INCOME, ESTATE, GIFT, AND CERTAIN EXCISE TAX CASES.—In the case of a deficiency as defined in section 6211 (relating to income, estate, gift, and certain excise taxes), if a waiver of restrictions under section 6213(d) on the assessment of such deficiency has been filed, and if notice and demand by the Secretary for payment of such deficiency is not made within 30 days after the filing of such waiver, interest shall not be imposed on such deficiency for the period beginning immediately after such 30th day and ending with the date of notice and demand and interest shall not be imposed during such period on any interest with respect to such deficiency for any prior period.

Amendments

• 2015, Bipartisan Budget Act of 2015 (P.L. 114-74)

P.L. 114-74, §1101(f)(9):

Amended Code Sec. 6601(c) by striking the last sentence. **Effective** generally for returns filed for partnership tax years beginning after 12-31-2017. For a special rule, see Act Sec. 1101(g)(4), below. Prior to being stricken, the last sentence of Code Sec. 6601(c) read as follows:

In the case of a settlement under section 6224(c) which results in the conversion of partnership items to nonpartnership items pursuant to section 6231(b)(1)(C), the preceding sentence shall apply to a computational adjustment resulting from such settlement in the same manner as if such adjustment were a deficiency and such settlement were a waiver referred to in the preceding sentence.

P.L. 114-74, §1101(g)(4), provides:

(4) ELECTION.—A partnership may elect (at such time and in such form and manner as the Secretary of the Treasury may prescribe) for the amendments made by this section (other than the election under section 6221(b) of such Code (as added by this Act)) to apply to any return of the partnership filed for partnership taxable years beginning after the date of the enactment of this Act and before January 1, 2018.

• 1997, Taxpayer Relief Act of 1997 (P.L. 105-34)

P.L. 105-34, §1242(a):

Amended Code Sec. 6601(c) by adding at the end a new sentence. **Effective** for adjustments with respect to partnership tax years beginning after 8-5-97.

• 1986, Tax Reform Act of 1986 (P.L. 99-514)

P.L. 99-514, §1564(a):

Amended Code Sec. 6601(c) by inserting before the period at the end thereof "and interest shall not be imposed during such period on any interest with respect to such deficiency for any prior period." **Effective** for interest accruing after 12-31-82. However, see Act Sec. 1564(c)(2).

P.L. 99-514, §1564(b)(2), provides:

(2) STATUTE OF LIMITATIONS.—If refund or credit of any amount resulting from the application of the amendment

made by subsection (a) is prevented at any time before the close of the date which is 1 year after the date of the enactment of this Act by the operation of any law or rule of law (including res judicata), refund or credit of such amount (to the extent attributable to the application of the amendment made by subsection (a)) may, nevertheless, be made or allowed if claim therefore is filed before the close of such 1-year period.

• 1980, Crude Oil Windfall Profit Tax Act of 1980 (P.L. 96-223)

P.L. 96-223, §101(f)(7):

Amended Code Sec. 6601(c) by striking out in the subsection heading "CHAPTER 41, 42, 43, OR 44 TAX" and inserting "CERTAIN EXCISE TAX". For the **effective** date and the transitional rules, see P.L. 96-223, §101(i), following Code Sec. 4986.

• 1976, Tax Reform Act of 1976 (P.L. 94-455)

P.L. 94-455, §1307(d)(2)(H):

Substituted "Chapter 41, 42," for "Chapter 42" in the heading of Code Sec. 6601(c). **Effective** on and after 10-4-76.

P.L. 94-455, §1605(b)(10):

Substituted ", 43, or 44" for "or 43" in the heading of Code Sec. 6601(c). **Effective** for tax years of real estate investment trusts beginning after 10-4-76.

P.L. 94-455, §1906(b)(13)(A):

Amended 1954 Code by substituting "Secretary" for "Secretary or his delegate" each place it appeared. **Effective** 2-1-77.

• 1975 (P.L. 93-625)

P.L. 93-625, §7(b)(1):

Redesignated Code Sec. 6601(d) as Code Sec. 6601(c). **Effective** 7-1-75.

• 1974, Employee Retirement Income Security Act of 1974 (P.L. 93-406)

P.L. 93-406, §1016(a)(17):

Amended Code Sec. 6601(d) by adding "or 43" to the heading and by changing "chapter 42" to "certain excise". For **effective** date, see amendment note for Code Sec. 410.

• 1969, Tax Reform Act of 1969 (P.L. 91-172)

P.L. 91-172, §101(j)(49):

Amended Code Sec. 6601(d) by substituting in the heading thereof "Gift, and Chapter 42 Tax Cases" for "and Gift Tax Cases" and by substituting in the body thereof "gift, and chapter 42 taxes" for "and gift taxes". **Effective** 1-1-70.

[Sec. 6601(d)]

(d) INCOME TAX REDUCED BY CARRYBACK OR ADJUSTMENT FOR CERTAIN UNUSED DEDUCTIONS.—

(1) NET OPERATING LOSS OR CAPITAL LOSS CARRYBACK.—If the amount of any tax imposed by subtitle A is reduced by reason of a carryback of a net operating loss or net capital loss, such reduction in tax shall not affect the computation of interest under this section for the period ending with the filing date for the taxable year in which the net operating loss or net capital loss arises.

(2) FOREIGN TAX CREDIT CARRYBACKS.—If any credit allowed for any taxable year is increased by reason of a carryback of tax paid or accrued to foreign countries or possessions of the United States, such increase shall not affect the computation of interest under this section for the period ending with the filing date for the taxable year in which such taxes were in fact paid or accrued, or, with respect to any portion of such credit carryback from a taxable year attributable to a net operating loss carryback or a capital loss carryback from a subsequent taxable year, such increase shall not affect the computation of interest under this section for the period ending with the filing date for such subsequent taxable year.

(3) CERTAIN CREDIT CARRYBACKS.—

(A) IN GENERAL.—If any credit allowed for any taxable year is increased by reason of a credit carryback, such increase shall not affect the computation of interest under this section for the period ending with the filing date for the taxable year in which the credit carryback arises, or, with respect to any portion of a credit carryback from a taxable year attributable to a net operating loss carryback, capital loss carryback, or other credit carryback from a subsequent taxable year, such increase shall not affect the computation of interest under this section for the period ending with the filing date for such subsequent taxable year.

(B) CREDIT CARRYBACK DEFINED.—For purposes of this paragraph, the term "credit carryback" has the meaning given such term by section 6511(d)(4)(C).

(4) FILING DATE.—For purposes of this subsection, the term "filing date" has the meaning given to such term by section 6611(f)(4)(A).

Amendments

• 2005, Gulf Opportunity Zone Act of 2005 (P.L. 109-135)

P.L. 109-135, §409(a)(2):

Amended Code Sec. 6601(d)(4) by striking "6611(f)(3)(A)" and inserting "6611(f)(4)(A)". **Effective** as if included in the provision of the Taxpayer Relief Act of 1997 (P.L. 105-34) to which it relates [**effective** for foreign tax credit carrybacks arising in tax years beginning after 8-5-97.—CCH.]

• 1997, Taxpayer Relief Act of 1997 (P.L. 105-34)

P.L. 105-34, §1055(a):

Amended Code Sec. 6601(d) by redesignating paragraphs (2) and (3) as paragraphs (3) and (4), respectively, and by inserting after paragraph (1) a new paragraph (2). **Effective** for foreign tax credit carrybacks arising in tax years beginning after 8-5-97.

• 1984, Deficit Reduction Act of 1984 (P.L. 98-369)

P.L. 98-369, §211(b)(26):

Amended Code Sec. 6601(d) by striking out paragraph (3) and by redesignating paragraph (4) as paragraph (3). **Effective** for tax years beginning after 12-31-83. Prior to amendment paragraph (3) read as follows:

(3) Adjustment for Certain Unused Deductions of Life Insurance Companies.—If the amount of any tax imposed by subtitle A is reduced by operation of section 815(d)(5) (relating to reduction of policyholders surplus account of life insurance companies for certain unused deductions), such reduction in tax shall not affect the computation of interest under this section for the period ending with the last day of the last taxable year to which the loss described in section 815(d)(5)(A) is carried under section 812(b)(2).

P.L. 98-369, § 714(n)(1):

Corrected an error in P.L. 97-248, Act Sec. 346(c)(2)(B). That section amended Code Sec. 6601(d)(2)(A) by striking out "the last day of the" (instead of "the last day of") and inserted in lieu thereof "the filing date for". **Effective** as if included in P.L. 97-248.

• 1982, Tax Equity and Fiscal Responsibility Act of 1982 (P.L. 97-248)

P.L. 97-248, § 346(c)(2)(A):

Amended Code Sec. 6601(d)(1) by striking out "the last day of the taxable year" and inserting "the filing date for the taxable year". **Effective** for interest accruing after 10-3-82.

P.L. 97-248, § 346(c)(2)(B):

Amended Code Sec. 6601(d)(2)(A) by striking out "the last day of" each place it appeared and inserting "the filing date for". **Effective** for interest accruing after 10-3-82.

P.L. 97-248, § 346(c)(2)(C):

Added Code Sec. 6601(d)(4). **Effective** for interest accruing after 10-3-82.

• 1978 (P.L. 95-628)

P.L. 95-628, § 8(c)(2)(A), (d):

Amended Code Sec. 6601(d)(2). **Effective** for carrybacks arising in tax years beginning after 11-10-78. Prior to amendment, paragraph (2) read:

"(2) INVESTMENT CREDIT CARRYBACK.—If the credit allowed by section 38 for any taxable year is increased by reason of an investment credit carryback, such increase shall not affect the computation of interest under this section for the period ending with the last day of the taxable year in which the investment credit carryback arises, or, with respect to any portion of an investment credit carryback from a taxable year attributable to a net operating loss carryback or a capital loss carryback from a subsequent taxable year, such increase shall not affect the computation of interest under this section for the period ending with the last day of such subsequent taxable year."

P.L. 95-628, § 8(c)(2)(B), (d):

Repealed Code Secs. 6601(d)(4) and (5). **Effective** for carrybacks arising in tax years beginning after 11-10-78. Prior to repeal, such paragraphs read:

"(4) WORK INCENTIVE PROGRAM CREDIT CARRYBACK.—If the credit allowed by section 40 for any taxable year is increased by reason of a work incentive program credit carryback, such increase shall not affect the computation of interest under this section for the period ending with the last day of the taxable year in which the work incentive program credit carryback arises, or, with respect to any portion of a work incentive program carryback from a taxable year attributable to a net operating loss carryback, an investment credit carryback, or a capital loss carryback from a subsequent taxable year, such increase shall not affect the computation of interest under this section for the period ending with the last day of such subsequent taxable year.

"(5) NEW EMPLOYEE CREDIT CARRYBACK.—If the credit allowed by section 44B for any taxable year is increased by reason of a new employee credit carryback, such increase shall not affect the computation of interest under this section for the period ending with the last day of the taxable year in which the new employee credit carryback arises, or, with respect to any portion of a new employee credit carryback from a taxable year attributable to a net operating loss carryback, an investment credit carryback, a work incentive program credit carryback, or a capital loss carryback from a subsequent taxable year, such increase shall not affect the computation of interest under this section for the period ending with the last day of such subsequent taxable year."

• 1977, Tax Reduction and Simplification Act of 1977 (P.L. 95-30)

P.L. 95-30, § 202(d)(4)(C):

Amended Code Sec. 6601(d) by adding paragraph (5). **Effective** for tax years beginning after 12-31-76, and for credit carrybacks from such years.

• 1976, Tax Reform Act of 1976 (P.L. 94-455)

P.L. 94-455, § 2107(g)(2)(C):

Amended Code Sec. 6601(d)(4) by inserting ", an investment credit carryback," after "net operating loss carryback." **Effective** 10-4-76.

• 1975 (P.L. 93-625)

P.L. 93-625, § 7(b)(1):

Redesignated Code Sec. 6601(e) as Code Sec. 6601(d). **Effective** 7-1-75.

• 1971, Revenue Act of 1971 (P.L. 92-178)

P.L. 92-178, § 601(d)(3):

Amended Code Sec. 6601(e) by adding paragraph (4). **Effective** for tax years ending after 12-31-71.

• 1969, Tax Reform Act of 1969 (P.L. 91-172)

P.L. 91-172, § 512(e)(3):

Amended Code Sec. 6601(e)(1) by adding "or Capital Loss" after "Net Operating Loss" in heading; and by adding "or net capital loss" wherever it appears after "operating loss". Amended Code Sec. 6601(e)(2) by adding "or a capital loss carryback" after "loss carryback". **Effective** with respect to net capital losses sustained in tax years beginning after 12-31-69.

• 1967 (P.L. 90-225)

P.L. 90-225, § 2(e):

Amended Code Sec. 6601(e)(2) by inserting at the end thereof the following: ", or, with respect to any portion of an investment credit carryback from a taxable year attributable to a net operating loss carryback from a subsequent taxable year, such increase shall not affect the computation of interest under this section for the period ending with the last day of such subsequent taxable year". **Effective** with respect to investment credit carrybacks attributable to net operating loss carrybacks from tax years ending after 7-31-67.

• 1964 (P.L. 88-571)

P.L. 88-571, § 3(d):

Amended Code Sec. 6601(e) by changing the heading and by adding paragraph (3). **Effective** with respect to amounts added to policyholders surplus accounts for tax years beginning after 12-31-58.

• 1962, Revenue Act of 1962 (P.L. 87-834)

P.L. 87-834, § 2:

Amended Code Sec. 6601(e). **Effective** for tax years ending after 12-31-61. Prior to amendment, Sec. 6601(e) read as follows:

"(e) Income Tax Reduced by Carryback.—If the amount of any tax imposed by subtitle A is reduced by reason of a carryback of a net operating loss, such reduction in tax shall not affect the computation of interest under this section for the period ending with the last day of the taxable year in which the net operating loss arises."

[Sec. 6601(e)]

(e) APPLICABLE RULES.—Except as otherwise provided in this title—

(1) INTEREST TREATED AS TAX.—Interest prescribed under this section on any tax shall be paid upon notice and demand, and shall be assessed, collected, and paid in the same manner as taxes. Any reference in this title (except subchapter B of chapter 63, relating to deficiency procedures) to any tax imposed by this title shall be deemed also to refer to interest imposed by this section on such tax.

(2) INTEREST ON PENALTIES, ADDITIONAL AMOUNTS, OR ADDITIONS TO THE TAX.—

(A) IN GENERAL.—Interest shall be imposed under subsection (a) in respect of any assessable penalty, additional amount, or addition to the tax (other than an addition to tax imposed under section 6651(a)(1) or 6653 or under part II of subchapter A of chapter 68) only if such assessable penalty, additional amount, or addition to the tax is not paid within

21 calendar days from the date of notice and demand therefor (10 business days if the amount for which such notice and demand is made equals or exceeds $100,000), and in such case interest shall be imposed only for the period from the date of the notice and demand to the date of payment.

(B) INTEREST ON CERTAIN ADDITIONS TO TAX.âInterest shall be imposed under this section with respect to any addition to tax imposed by section 6651(a)(1) or 6653 or under part II of subchapter A of chapter 68 for the period whichâ

(i) begins on the date on which the return of the tax with respect to which such addition to tax is imposed is required to be filed (including any extensions), and

(ii) ends on the date of payment of such addition to tax.

(3) PAYMENTS MADE WITHIN SPECIFIED PERIOD AFTER NOTICE AND DEMAND.âIf notice and demand is made for payment of any amount and if such amount is paid within 21 calendar days (10 business days if the amount for which such notice and demand is made equals or exceeds $100,000) after the date of such notice and demand, interest under this section on the amount so paid shall not be imposed for the period after the date of such notice and demand.

Amendments

â¢ 1996, Taxpayer Bill of Rights 2 (P.L. 104-168)

P.L. 104-168, Â§303(a):

Amended Code Sec. 6601(e)(3). **Effective** for any notice and demand given after 12-31-96. Prior to amendment, Code Sec. 6601(e)(3) read as follows:

(3) PAYMENTS MADE WITHIN 10 DAYS AFTER NOTICE AND DEMAND.âIf notice and demand is made for payment of any amount, and if such amount is paid within 10 days after the date of such notice and demand, interest under this section on the amount so paid shall not be imposed for the period after the date of such notice and demand.

P.L. 104-168, Â§303(b)(1):

Amended Code Sec. 6601(e)(2)(A) by striking "10 days from the date of notice and demand therefor" and inserting "21 calendar days from the date of notice and demand therefor (10 business days if the amount for which such notice and demand is made equals or exceeds $100,000)". **Effective** for any notice and demand given after 12-31-96.

â¢ 1989, Omnibus Budget Reconciliation Act of 1989 (P.L. 101-239)

P.L. 101-239, Â§7721(c)(8):

Amended Code Sec. 6601(e)(2) by striking "section 6651(a)(1), 6653, 6659, 6660, or 6661" each place it appears and inserting "section 6651(a)(1) or 6653 or under part II of subchapter A of chapter 68". **Effective** for returns the due date for which (determined without regard to extensions) is after 12-31-89.

â¢ 1988, Technical and Miscellaneous Revenue Act of 1988 (P.L. 100-647)

P.L. 100-647, Â§1015(b)(2)(C):

Amended Code Sec. 6601(e)(2) by striking out "6659" before "6660" each place it appears and inserting in lieu thereof "6653, 6659". **Effective** for returns the due date for which (determined without regard to extensions) is after 12-31-88.

â¢ 1984, Deficit Reduction Act of 1984 (P.L. 98-369)

P.L. 98-369, Â§158(a):

Amended Code Sec. 6601(e)(2). **Effective** for interest accrued after 7-18-84, except with respect to additions to tax for which notice and demand is made before such date. Prior to amendment, Code Sec. 6601(e)(2) read as follows:

(2) Interest on Penalties, Additional Amounts, or Additions to the Tax.âInterest shall be imposed under subsection (a) in respect of any assessable penalty, additional amount, or addition to the tax only if such assessable penalty, additional amount, or addition to the tax is not paid within 10 days from the date of notice and demand therefor, and in such case interest shall be imposed only for the period from the date of the notice and demand to the date of payment.

â¢ 1982, Tax Equity and Fiscal Responsibility Act of 1982 (P.L. 97-248)

P.L. 97-248, Â§344(b)(1):

Amended Code Sec. 6601(e) by striking out paragraph (2) and redesignating paragraphs (3) and (4) as paragraphs (2) and (3), respectively. **Effective** for interest accruing after 12-31-82. Prior to being stricken, such paragraph read:

"(2) No interest on interest.âNo interest under this section shall be imposed on the interest provided by this section."

â¢ 1975 (P.L. 93-625)

P.L. 93-625, Â§7(b)(1):

Redesignated Code Sec. 6601(f) as 6601(e). **Effective** 7-1-75.

[Sec. 6601(f)]

(f) SATISFACTION BY CREDITS.âIf any portion of a tax is satisfied by credit of an overpayment, then no interest shall be imposed under this section on the portion of the tax so satisfied for any period during which, if the credit had not been made, interest would have been allowable with respect to such overpayment. The preceding sentence shall not apply to the extent that section 6621(d) applies.

Amendments

â¢ 1998, IRS Restructuring and Reform Act of 1998 (P.L. 105-206)

P.L. 105-206, Â§3301(b):

Amended Code Sec. 6601(f) by adding at the end a new sentence. **Effective**, generally, for interest for periods beginning after 7-22-98. For a special rule, see Act Sec. 3301(c)(2), below.

P.L. 105-206, Â§3301(c)(2), as amended by P.L. 105-277, Â§4002(d), provides:

(2) SPECIAL RULE.âSubject to any applicable statute of limitation not having expired with regard to either a tax underpayment or a tax overpayment, the amendments made by this section shall apply to interest for periods beginning before the date of the enactment of this Act if the taxpayerâ

(A) reasonably identifies and establishes periods of such tax overpayments and under-payments for which the zero rate applies; and

(B) not later than December 31, 1999, requests the Secretary of the Treasury to apply section 6621(d) of the Internal Revenue Code of 1986, as added by subsection (a), to such periods.

â¢ 1975 (P.L. 93-625)

P.L. 93-625, Â§7(b)(1):

Redesignated Code Sec. 6601(g) as Code Sec. 6601(f). **Effective** 7-1-75.

â¢ 1958, Technical Amendments Act of 1958 (P.L. 85-866)

P.L. 85-866, Â§83(a)(1):

Redesignated subsections (g) and (h) of Sec. 6601 as subsections (i) and (j) and added a new subsection (g). **Effective** for overpayments credited after 12-31-57.

[Sec. 6601(g)]

(g) LIMITATION ON ASSESSMENT AND COLLECTION.—Interest prescribed under this section on any tax may be assessed and collected at any time during the period within which the tax to which such interest relates may be collected.

Amendments

• 1975 (P.L. 93-625)

P.L. 93-625, §7(b)(1):

Redesignated Code Sec. 6601(h) as Code Sec. 6601(g). **Effective** 7-1-75.

• 1958, Technical Amendments Act of 1958 (P.L. 85-866)

P.L. 85-866, §84(a):

Added subsection (h). **Effective** 1-1-54.

* * *

[Sec. 6601(j)]

(j) 2-PERCENT RATE ON CERTAIN PORTION OF ESTATE TAX EXTENDED UNDER SECTION 6166.—

(1) IN GENERAL.—If the time for payment of an amount of tax imposed by chapter 11 is extended as provided in section 6166, then in lieu of the annual rate provided by subsection (a)—

(A) interest on the 2-percent portion of such amount shall be paid at the rate of 2 percent, and

(B) interest on so much of such amount as exceeds the 2-percent portion shall be paid at a rate equal to 45 percent of the annual rate provided by subsection (a).

For purposes of this subsection, the amount of any deficiency which is prorated to installments payable under section 6166 shall be treated as an amount of tax payable in installments under such section.

(2) 2-PERCENT PORTION.—For purposes of this subsection, the term "2-percent portion" means the lesser of—

(A)(i) the amount of the tentative tax which would be determined under the rate schedule set forth in section 2001(c) if the amount with respect to which such tentative tax is to be computed were the sum of $1,000,000 and the applicable exclusion amount in effect under section 2010(c), reduced by

(ii) the applicable credit amount in effect under section 2010(c), or

(B) the amount of the tax imposed by chapter 11 which is extended as provided in section 6166.

(3) INFLATION ADJUSTMENT.—In the case of estates of decedents dying in a calendar year after 1998, the $1,000,000 amount contained in paragraph (2)(A) shall be increased by an amount equal to—

(A) $1,000,000, multiplied by

(B) the cost-of-living adjustment determined under section 1(f)(3) for such calendar year by substituting "calendar year 1997" for "calendar year 2016" in subparagraph (A)(ii) thereof.

If any amount as adjusted under the preceding sentence is not a multiple of $10,000, such amount shall be rounded to the next lowest multiple of $10,000.

(4) TREATMENT OF PAYMENTS.—If the amount of tax imposed by chapter 11 which is extended as provided in section 6166 exceeds the 2-percent portion, any payment of a portion of such amount shall, for purposes of computing interest for periods after such payment, be treated as reducing the 2-percent portion by an amount which bears the same ratio to the amount of such payment as the amount of the 2-percent portion (determined without regard to this paragraph) bears to the amount of the tax which is extended as provided in section 6166.

Amendments

• 2017, Tax Cuts and Jobs Act (P.L. 115-97)

P.L. 115-97, §11002(d)(1)(JJ):

Amended Code Sec. 6601(j)(3)(B) by striking "for 'calendar year 1992' in subparagraph (B)" and inserting "for 'calendar year 2016' in subparagraph (A)(ii)". **Effective** for tax years beginning after 12-31-2017.

• 1997, Taxpayer Relief Act of 1997 (P.L. 105-34)

P.L. 105-34, §501(e):

Amended Code Sec. 6601(j) by redesignating paragraph (3) as paragraph (4) and by inserting after paragraph (2) a new paragraph (3). **Effective** for the estates of decedents dying, and gifts made, after 12-31-97.

P.L. 105-34, §503(a):

Amended Code Sec. 6601(j)(1)-(2). **Effective**, generally, for estates of decedents dying after 12-31-97. For a special rule, see Act Sec. 503(d)(2), below. Prior to amendment, Code Sec. 6601(j)(1)-(2) read as follows:

(1) IN GENERAL.—If the time for payment of an amount of tax imposed by chapter 11 is extended as provided in section 6166, interest on the 4-percent portion of such amount shall (in lieu of the annual rate provided by subsection (a)) be paid at the rate of 4 percent. For purposes of this subsection, the amount of any deficiency which is prorated to installments payable under section 6166 shall be treated as an amount of tax payable in installments under such section.

(2) 4-PERCENT PORTION.—For purposes of this subsection, the term "4-percent portion" means the lesser of—

(A) $345,800 reduced by the amount of the credit allowable under section 2010(a); or

(B) the amount of the tax imposed by chapter 11 which is extended as provided in section 6166.

P.L. 105-34, §503(c)(2):

Amended Code Sec. 6601(j)(4), as redesignated by Act Sec. 501(e), by striking "4-percent" each place it appears and inserting "2-percent". **Effective**, generally, for estates of decedents dying after 12-31-97. For a special rule, see Act Sec. 503(d)(2), below.

P.L. 105-34, §503(c)(3):

Amended Code Sec. 6601(j) by striking "4-PERCENT" in the subsection heading and inserting "2-PERCENT". **Effective**, generally, for estates of decedents dying after 12-31-97. For a special rule, see Act Sec. 503(d)(2), below.

P.L. 105-34, § 503(d)(2), provides:

(2) ELECTION.—In the case of the estate of any decedent dying before January 1, 1998, with respect to which there is an election under section 6166 of the Internal Revenue Code of 1986, the executor of the estate may elect to have the amendments made by this section apply with respect to installments due after the effective date of the election; except that the 2-percent portion of such installments shall be equal to the amount which would be the 4-percent portion of such installments without regard to such election. Such an election shall be made before January 1, 1999 in the manner prescribed by the Secretary of the Treasury and, once made, is irrevocable.

• 1976, Tax Reform Act of 1976 (P.L. 94-455)

P.L. 94-455, § 2004(b):

Redesignated Code Sec. 6601(j) as Code Sec. 6601(k); and inserted after subsection (i) a new subsection (j). **Effective** for estates of decedents dying after 12-31-76.

• 1975 (P.L. 93-625)

P.L. 93-625, § 7(b)(1):

Amended Code Sec. 6601 by striking out subsection (j) and redesignating subsection (l) as subsection (j). **Effective** 7-1-75, and applicable to amounts outstanding on such date or arising thereafter. Prior to being stricken, Code Sec. 6601(j) read as follows:

(j) EXTENSION OF TIME FOR PAYMENT OF TAX ATTRIBUTABLE TO RECOVERIES OF FOREIGN EXPROPRIATION LOSSES.—If the time for payment of an amount of the tax attributable to a recovery of a foreign expropriation loss (within the meaning of section 6167(f)) is extended as provided in subsection (a) or (b) of section 6167, interest shall be paid at the rate of 4 percent, in lieu of 6 percent as provided in subsection (a).

• 1966 (P.L. 89-384)

P.L. 89-384, § 1(f):

Added Code Sec. 6601(j), and redesignated former Code Sec. 6601(j) as Code Sec. 6601(k). **Effective** with respect to amounts received after 12-31-64, in respect of foreign expropriation losses sustained in tax years beginning after 12-31-58.

* * *

[Sec. 6602]

SEC. 6602. INTEREST ON ERRONEOUS REFUND RECOVERABLE BY SUIT.

Any portion of an internal revenue tax (or any interest, assessable penalty, additional amount, or addition to tax) which has been erroneously refunded, and which is recoverable by suit pursuant to section 7405, shall bear interest at the underpayment rate established under section 6621 from the date of the payment of the refund.

Amendments

• 1986, Tax Reform Act of 1986 (P.L. 99-514)

P.L. 99-514, § 1511(c)(12):

Amended Code Sec. 6602 by striking out "an annual rate established under section 6621" and inserting in lieu thereof "the underpayment rate established under section 6621". **Effective** for purposes of determining interest for periods after 12-31-86.

• 1975 (P.L. 93-625)

P.L. 93-625, § 7(a)(2):

Amended Code Sec. 6602 by substituting "an annual rate established under section 6621" for "the rate of 6 percent per annum". For **effective** date, see the historical comment for P.L. 93-625, following the text of Code Sec. 6621.

[Sec. 6603]

SEC. 6603. DEPOSITS MADE TO SUSPEND RUNNING OF INTEREST ON POTENTIAL UNDERPAYMENTS, ETC.

[Sec. 6603(a)]

(a) AUTHORITY TO MAKE DEPOSITS OTHER THAN AS PAYMENT OF TAX.—A taxpayer may make a cash deposit with the Secretary which may be used by the Secretary to pay any tax imposed under subtitle A or B or chapter 41, 42, 43, or 44 which has not been assessed at the time of the deposit. Such a deposit shall be made in such manner as the Secretary shall prescribe.

[Sec. 6603(b)]

(b) NO INTEREST IMPOSED.—To the extent that such deposit is used by the Secretary to pay tax, for purposes of section 6601 (relating to interest on underpayments), the tax shall be treated as paid when the deposit is made.

[Sec. 6603(c)]

(c) RETURN OF DEPOSIT.—Except in a case where the Secretary determines that collection of tax is in jeopardy, the Secretary shall return to the taxpayer any amount of the deposit (to the extent not used for a payment of tax) which the taxpayer requests in writing.

[Sec. 6603(d)]

(d) PAYMENT OF INTEREST.—

(1) IN GENERAL.—For purposes of section 6611 (relating to interest on overpayments), except as provided in paragraph (4), a deposit which is returned to a taxpayer shall be treated as a payment of tax for any period to the extent (and only to the extent) attributable to a disputable tax for such period. Under regulations prescribed by the Secretary, rules similar to the rules of section 6611(b)(2) shall apply.

(2) DISPUTABLE TAX.—

(A) IN GENERAL.—For purposes of this section, the term "disputable tax" means the amount of tax specified at the time of the deposit as the taxpayer's reasonable estimate of the maximum amount of any tax attributable to disputable items.

(B) SAFE HARBOR BASED ON 30-DAY LETTER.—In the case of a taxpayer who has been issued a 30-day letter, the maximum amount of tax under subparagraph (A) shall not be less than the amount of the proposed deficiency specified in such letter.

(3) OTHER DEFINITIONS.—For purposes of paragraph (2)—

(A) DISPUTABLE ITEM.—The term "disputable item" means any item of income, gain, loss, deduction, or credit if the taxpayer—

(i) has a reasonable basis for its treatment of such item, and

(ii) reasonably believes that the Secretary also has a reasonable basis for disallowing the taxpayer's treatment of such item.

(B) 30-DAY LETTER.—The term "30-day letter" means the first letter of proposed deficiency which allows the taxpayer an opportunity for administrative review in the Internal Revenue Service Independent Office of Appeals.

(4) RATE OF INTEREST.—The rate of interest under this subsection shall be the Federal short-term rate determined under section 6621(b), compounded daily.

Amendments

• 2019, Taxpayer First Act (P.L. 116-25)

P.L. 116-25, §1001(b)(1)(D):

Amended Code Sec. 6603(d)(3)(B) by striking "Internal Revenue Service Office of Appeals" and inserting "Internal Revenue Service Independent Office of Appeals". **Effective** 7-1-2019.

[Sec. 6603(e)]

(e) USE OF DEPOSITS.—

(1) PAYMENT OF TAX.—Except as otherwise provided by the taxpayer, deposits shall be treated as used for the payment of tax in the order deposited.

(2) RETURNS OF DEPOSITS.—Deposits shall be treated as returned to the taxpayer on a last-in, first-out basis.

Amendments

• 2004, American Jobs Creation Act of 2004 (P.L. 108-357)

P.L. 108-357, §842(a):

Amended subchapter A of chapter 67 by adding at the end a new Code Sec. 6603. **Effective** generally for deposits made after 10-22-2004. For a special rule, see Act Sec. 842(c)(2), below.

P.L. 108-357, §842(c)(2), provides:

(2) COORDINATION WITH DEPOSITS MADE UNDER REVENUE PROCEDURE 84-58.—In the case of an amount held by the Secretary of the Treasury or his delegate on the date of the enactment of this Act [10-22-2004.—CCH] as a deposit in the nature of a cash bond deposit pursuant to Revenue Procedure 84-58, the date that the taxpayer identifies such amount as a deposit made pursuant to section 6603 of the Internal Revenue Code (as added by this Act) shall be treated as the date such amount is deposited for purposes of such section 6603.

Subchapter B—Interest on Overpayments

* * *

[Sec. 6611]

SEC. 6611. INTEREST ON OVERPAYMENTS.

[Sec. 6611(a)]

(a) RATE.—Interest shall be allowed and paid upon any overpayment in respect of any internal revenue tax at the overpayment rate established under section 6621.

Amendments

• 1986, Tax Reform Act of 1986 (P.L. 99-514)

P.L. 99-514, §1511(c)(13):

Amended Code Sec. 6611(a) by striking out "an annual rate established under section 6621" and inserting in lieu thereof "the overpayment rate established under section 6621". **Effective** for purposes of determining interest for periods after 12-31-86.

• 1975 (P.L. 93-625)

P.L. 93-625, §7(a)(2):

Amended Code Sec. 6611(a) by substituting "an annual rate established under section 6621" for "the rate of 6 percent per annum". For **effective** date, see the historical comment for P.L. 93-625 following the text of Code Sec. 6621.

[Sec. 6611(b)]

(b) PERIOD.—Such interest shall be allowed and paid as follows:

(1) CREDITS.—In the case of a credit, from the date of the overpayment to the due date of the amount against which the credit is taken.

(2) REFUNDS.—In the case of a refund, from the date of the overpayment to a date (to be determined by the Secretary) preceding the date of the refund check by not more than 30 days, whether or not such refund check is accepted by the taxpayer after tender of such check to the taxpayer. The acceptance of such check shall be without prejudice to any right of the taxpayer to claim any additional overpayment and interest thereon.

(3) LATE RETURNS.—Notwithstanding paragraph (1) or (2) in the case of a return of tax which is filed after the last date prescribed for filing such return (determined with regard to extentions), no interest shall be allowed or paid for any day before the date on which the return is filed.

Amendments

• 1982, Tax Equity and Fiscal Responsibility Act of 1982 (P.L. 97-248)

P.L. 97-248, §346(a):

Added Code Sec. 6611(b)(3). **Effective** for returns filed after 10-3-82.

• 1976, Tax Reform Act of 1976 (P.L. 94-455)

P.L. 94-455, §1906(b)(13)(A):

Amended 1954 Code by substituting "Secretary" for "Secretary or his delegate" each place it appeared. **Effective** 2-1-77.

• 1958, Technical Amendments Act of 1958 (P.L. 85-866)

P.L. 85-866, §83(b):

Amended Sec. 6611(b)(1). **Effective** for overpayments credited after 12-31-57. Prior to amendment, Sec. 6611(b)(1) read as follows:

"(1) Credits.—In the case of a credit, from the date of the overpayment to the due date of the amount against which the credit is taken, but if the amount against which the credit is taken is an additional assessment, then to the date of the assessment of that amount."

* * *

[Sec. 6611(e)]

(e) DISALLOWANCE OF INTEREST ON CERTAIN OVERPAYMENTS.—

(1) REFUNDS WITHIN 45 DAYS AFTER RETURN IS FILED.—If any overpayment of tax imposed by this title is refunded within 45 days after the last day prescribed for filing the return of such tax (determined without regard to any extention of time for filing the return) or, in the case of a return filed after such last date, is refunded within 45 days after the date the return is filed, no interest shall be allowed under subsection (a) on such overpayment.

(2) REFUNDS AFTER CLAIM FOR CREDIT OR REFUND.—If—

(A) the taxpayer files a claim for a credit or refund for any overpayment of tax imposed by this title, and

(B) such overpayment is refunded within 45 days after such claim is filed,

no interest shall be allowed on such overpayment from the date the claim is filed until the day the refund is made.

(3) IRS INITIATED ADJUSTMENTS.—If an adjustment initiated by the Secretary, results in a refund or credit of an overpayment, interest on such overpayment shall be computed by subtracting 45 days from the number of days interest would otherwise be allowed with respect to such overpayment.

(4) CERTAIN WITHHOLDING TAXES.—In the case of any overpayment resulting from tax deducted and withheld under chapter 3 or 4, paragraphs (1), (2), and (3) shall be applied by substituting "180 days" for "45 days" each place it appears.

Amendments

• 2010, Hiring Incentives to Restore Employment Act (P.L. 111-147)

P.L. 111-147, §501(b):

Amended Code Sec. 6611(e) by adding at the end a new paragraph (4). For the **effective** date, see Act Sec. 501(d)(3), below.

P.L. 111-147, §501(d)(3), provides:

(3) INTEREST ON OVERPAYMENTS.—The amendment made by subsection (b) shall apply—

(A) in the case of such amendment's application to paragraph (1) of section 6611(e) of the Internal Revenue Code of 1986, to returns the due date for which (determined without regard to extensions) is after the date of the enactment of this Act,

(B) in the case of such amendment's application to paragraph (2) of such section, to claims for credit or refund of any overpayment filed after the date of the enactment of this Act (regardless of the taxable period to which such refund relates), and

(C) in the case of such amendment's application to paragraph (3) of such section, to refunds paid after the date of the enactment of this Act (regardless of the taxable period to which such refund relates).

• 1993, Omnibus Budget Reconciliation Act of 1993 (P.L. 103-66)

P.L. 103-66, §13271(a):

Amended Code Sec. 6611(e). For the **effective** date, see Act Sec. 13271(b). Prior to amendment, Code Sec. 6611(e) read as follows:

(e) INCOME TAX REFUND WITHIN 45 DAYS AFTER RETURN IS FILED.—If any overpayment of tax imposed by subtitle A is refunded within 45 days after the last date prescribed for filing the return of such tax (determined without regard to any extension of time for filing the return) or, in case the return is filed after such last date, is refunded within 45 days after the date the return is filed, no interest shall be allowed under subsection (a) on such overpayment.

P.L. 103-66, §13271(b), provides:

(b) EFFECTIVE DATES.—

(1) Paragraph (1) of section 6611(e) of the Internal Revenue Code of 1986 (as amended by subsection (a)) shall apply in the case of returns the due date for which (determined without regard to extensions) is on or after January 1, 1994.

(2) Paragraph (2) of section 6611(e) of such Code (as so amended) shall apply in the case of claims for credit or refund of any overpayment filed on or after January 1, 1995, regardless of the taxable period to which such refund relates.

(3) Paragraph (3) of section 6611(e) of such Code (as so amended) shall apply in the case of any refund paid on or after January 1, 1995, regardless of the taxable period to which such refund relates.

• 1975, Tax Reduction Act of 1975 (P.L. 94-12)

P.L. 94-12, §101(b), provides:

"(b) No Interest on Individual Income Tax Refunds for 1974 Refunded Within 60 Days After Return Is Filed.—In applying section 6611(e) of the Internal Revenue Code of 1954 (relating to income tax refund within 45 days after return is filed) in the case of any overpayment of tax imposed by subtitle A of such Code by an individual (other than an estate or trust and other than a nonresident alien individual) for a taxable year beginning in 1974, '60 days' shall be substituted for '45 days' each place it appears in such section 6611(e)."

• 1966 (P.L. 89-721)

P.L. 89-721, §[1(a)]:

Amended Code Sec. 6611(e). **Effective** with respect to refunds made more than 45 days after 11-2-66. Prior to amendment, Code Sec. 6611(e) read as follows:

"(e) Income Tax Refund Within 45 Days of Due Date of Tax.—If any overpayment of tax imposed by subtitle A is refunded within 45 days after the last date prescribed for filing the return of such tax (determined without regard to any extension of time for filing the return), no interest shall be allowed under subsection (a) on such overpayment."

* * *

[Sec. 6611(g)]

(g) NO INTEREST UNTIL RETURN IN PROCESSIBLE FORM.—

(1) For purposes of subsections (b)(3) and (e), a return shall not be treated as filed until it is filed in processible form.

(2) For purposes of paragraph (1), a return is in a processible form if—

(A) such return is filed on a permitted form, and

(B) such return contains—

(i) the taxpayer's name, address, and identifying number and the required signature, and

(ii) sufficient required information (whether on the return or on required attachments) to permit the mathematical verification of tax liability shown on the return.

Amendments

• 2000, Community Renewal Tax Relief Act of 2000 (P.L. 106-554)

P.L. 106-554, §319(20):

Amended Code Sec. 6611(g)(1) by striking the comma after "(b)(3)". **Effective** 12-21-2000.

• 1998, IRS Restructuring and Reform Act of 1998 (P.L. 105-206)

P.L. 105-206, §6010(l):

Amended Code Sec. 6611(g)(1) by striking "(e), and (h)" and inserting "and (e)". **Effective** as if included in the provision of P.L. 105-34 to which it relates [**effective** for foreign tax credit carrybacks arising in tax years beginning after 8-5-97.—CCH].

• 1997, Taxpayer Relief Act of 1997 (P.L. 105-34)

P.L. 105-34, §1055(b)(2)(D):

Amended Code Sec. 6611 by striking subsection (g) and by redesignating subsections (h) and (i) as subsections (g) and (h), respectively. **Effective** for foreign tax credit carrybacks arising in tax years beginning after 8-5-97. Prior to being stricken, Code Sec. 6611(g) read as follows:

(g) REFUND OF INCOME TAX CAUSED BY CARRYBACK OF FOREIGN TAXES.—For purposes of subsection (a), if any overpayment of tax results from a carryback of tax paid or accrued to foreign countries or possessions of the United States, such overpayment shall be deemed not to have been paid or accrued prior to the filing date (as defined in subsection (f)(3)) for the taxable year under this subtitle in which such taxes were in fact paid or accrued.

• 1982, Tax Equity and Fiscal Responsibility Act of 1982 (P.L. 97-248)

P.L. 97-248, §346(c)(1)(D):

Amended Code Sec. 6611(g) by striking out "the close of the taxable year" and inserting "the filing date (as defined in subsection (f)(3)) for the taxable year". **Effective** for interest accruing after 10-3-82.

• 1958, Technical Amendments Act of 1958 (P.L. 85-866)

P.L. 85-866, §42(b):

Added new subsection (g) to Sec. 6611. **Effective** for tax years beginning after 12-31-57.

* * *

Subchapter C—Determination of Interest Rate; Compounding of Interest

[Sec. 6621]

SEC. 6621. DETERMINATION OF RATE OF INTEREST.

[Sec. 6621(a)]

(a) GENERAL RULE.—

(1) OVERPAYMENT RATE.—The overpayment rate established under this section shall be the sum of—

(A) the Federal short-term rate determined under subsection (b), plus

(B) 3 percentage points (2 percentage points in the case of a corporation).

To the extent that an overpayment of tax by a corporation for any taxable period (as defined in subsection (c)(3), applied by substituting "overpayment" for "underpayment") exceeds $10,000, subparagraph (B) shall be applied by substituting "0.5 percentage point" for "2 percentage points".

(2) UNDERPAYMENT RATE.—The underpayment rate established under this section shall be the sum of—

(A) the Federal short-term rate determined under subsection (b), plus

(B) 3 percentage points.

Amendments

• 1998, IRS Restructuring and Reform Act of 1998 (P.L. 105-206)

P.L. 105-206, §3302(a):

Amended Code Sec. 6621(a)(1)(B). **Effective** for interest for the second and succeeding calendar quarters beginning after 7-22-98. Prior to amendment, Code Sec. 6621(a)(1)(B) read as follows:

(B) 2 percentage points.

• 1997, Taxpayer Relief Act of 1997 (P.L. 105-34)

P.L. 105-34, §1604(b)(1):

Amended Code Sec. 6621(a)(1) by striking "subsection (c)(3))" in the last sentence and inserting "subsection (c)(3), applied by substituting 'overpayment' for 'underpayment')". **Effective** as if included in the provision of P.L. 103-465 to which it relates [**effective** for determining interest for periods after 12-31-94.—CCH].

• 1994, Uruguay Round Agreements Act (P.L. 103-465)

P.L. 103-465, §713(a):

Amended Code Sec. 6621(a)(1) by adding at the end a new flush sentence. **Effective** for purposes of determining interest for periods after 12-31-94.

• 1988, Technical and Miscellaneous Revenue Act of 1988 (P.L. 100-647)

P.L. 100-647, §1015(d)(1)-(2):

Amended Code Sec. 6621 by striking out "short-term Federal rate" each place it appears in subsections (a) and (b)(1) and inserting in lieu thereof "Federal short-term rate". **Effective** as if included in the provision of P.L. 99-514 to which it relates.

• 1986, Tax Reform Act of 1986 (P.L. 99-514)

P.L. 99-514, §1511(a):

Amended Code Sec. 6621 by striking out subsection (a) and inserting in lieu thereof new subsection (a). **Effective** for purposes of determining interest to periods after 12-31-86. Prior to amendment, Code Sec. 6621(a) read as follows:

(a) IN GENERAL.—The annual rate established under this section shall be such adjusted rate as is established by the Secretary under subsection (b).

• 1979 (P.L. 96-167)

P.L. 96-167, §4:

Amended Code Sec. 6621(a). **Effective** 12-29-79. Prior to amendment, Sec. 6621(a) read as follows:

"(a) IN GENERAL.—The rate of interest under sections 6601(a), 6602, 6611(a), 6332(c)(1), and 7426(g) of this title, and under section 2411(a) of title 28 is 9 percent per annum, or such adjusted rate as is established by the Secretary under subsection (b)."

• 1976, Tax Reform Act of 1976 (P.L. 94-455)

P.L. 94-455, §1906(b)(13)(A):

Amended 1954 Code by substituting "Secretary" for "Secretary or his delegate" each place it appeared. **Effective** 2-1-77.

• 1975 (P.L. 93-625)

P.L. 93-625, §7(a)(1):

Added Code Sec. 6621(a). **Effective** for amounts outstanding on 7-1-75 or arising thereafter.

[Sec. 6621(b)]

(b) FEDERAL SHORT-TERM RATE.—For purposes of this section—

(1) GENERAL RULE.—The Secretary shall determine the Federal short-term rate for the first month in each calendar quarter.

(2) PERIOD DURING WHICH RATE APPLIES.—

(A) IN GENERAL.—Except as provided in subparagraph (B), the Federal short-term rate determined under paragraph (1) for any month shall apply during the first calendar quarter beginning after such month.

(B) SPECIAL RULE FOR INDIVIDUAL ESTIMATED TAX.—In determining the addition to tax under section 6654 for failure to pay estimated tax for any taxable year, the Federal short-term rate which applies during the 3rd month following such taxable year shall also apply during the first 15 days of the 4th month following such taxable year.

(3) FEDERAL SHORT-TERM RATE.—The Federal short-term rate for any month shall be the Federal short-term rate determined during such month by the Secretary in accordance with section 1274(d). Any such rate shall be rounded to the nearest full percent (or, if a multiple of 1/2 of 1 percent, such rate shall be increased to the next highest full percent).

Amendments

• 1988, Technical and Miscellaneous Revenue Act of 1988 (P.L. 100-647)

P.L. 100-647, §1015(d)(1)-(2):

Amended Code Sec. 6621 by striking out "short-term Federal rate" each place it appears in subsections (a) and (b)(1) and inserting in lieu thereof "Federal short-term rate", and by striking out "Short-Term Federal Rate" in the heading of subsection (b) and inserting in lieu thereof "Federal Short-Term Rate". **Effective** as if included in the provision of P.L. 99-514 to which it relates.

• 1986, Tax Reform Act of 1986 (P.L. 99-514)

P.L. 99-514, §1511(a):

Amended Code Sec. 6621 by striking out subsection (b) and inserting in lieu thereof new subsections (a) and (b). **Effective** for purposes of determining interest to periods after 12-31-86. Prior to amendment, Code Sec. 6621(b) read as follows:

(b) ADJUSTMENT OF INTEREST RATE.—

(1) ESTABLISHMENT OF ADJUSTED RATE.—If the adjusted prime rate charged by banks (rounded to the nearest full percent)—

(A) during the 6-month period ending on September 30 of any calendar year, or

(B) during the 6-month period ending on March 31 of any calendar year,

differs from the interest rate in effect under this section on either such date, respectively, then the Secretary shall establish, within 15 days after the close of the applicable 6-month period, an adjusted rate of interest equal to such adjusted prime rate.

(2) EFFECTIVE DATE OF ADJUSTMENT.—Any adjusted rate of interest established under paragraph (1) shall become effective—

(A) on January 1, of the succeeding year in the case of an adjustment attributable to paragraph (1)(A), and

(B) on July 1 of the same year in the case of an adjustment attributable to paragraph (1)(B).

• 1982, Tax Equity and Fiscal Responsibility Act of 1982 (P.L. 97-248)

P.L. 97-248, §345(a):

Amended Code Sec. 6621(b). **Effective** for adjustments taking effect on or after 1-1-83. [**effective** date changed by P.L. 98-369, §714(m).] Prior to amendment, Code Sec. 6621(b) read as follows:

"(b) ADJUSTMENT OF INTEREST RATE.—The Secretary shall establish an adjusted rate of interest for the purpose of subsection (a) not later than October 15 of any year if the adjusted prime rate charged by banks during September of that year, rounded to the nearest full percent, is at least a full percentage point more or less than the interest rate which is then in effect. Any such adjusted rate of interest shall be equal to the adjusted prime rate charged by banks, rounded to the nearest full percent, and shall become effective on January 1 [February 1, effective until 1982] of the immediately succeeding year."

• 1981, Economic Recovery Tax Act of 1981 (P.L. 97-34)

P.L. 97-34, §711(a):

Amended Code Sec. 6621(b) by striking out the last sentence thereof. **Effective** for adjustments made after 8-13-81.

Prior to amendment, the last sentence of Code Sec. 6621(b) read as follows:

An adjustment provided for under this subsection may not be made prior to the expiration of 23 months following the date of any preceding adjustment under this subsection which changes the rate of interest.

P.L. 97-34, §711(c):

Amended Code Sec. 6621(b) by striking out "February 1" and inserting "January 1". **Effective** for adjustments made for periods after 1982.

• 1976, Tax Reform Act of 1976 (P.L. 94-455)

P.L. 94-455, §1906(b)(13)(A):

Amended 1954 Code by substituting "Secretary" for "Secretary or his delegate" each place it appeared. **Effective** 2-1-77.

• 1975 (P.L. 93-625)

P.L. 93-625, §7(a)(1):

Added Code Sec. 6621(b). **Effective** for amounts outstanding on 7-1-75 or arising thereafter.

[Sec. 6621(c)]

(c) INCREASE IN UNDERPAYMENT RATE FOR LARGE CORPORATE UNDERPAYMENTS.—

(1) IN GENERAL.—For purposes of determining the amount of interest payable under section 6601 on any large corporate underpayment for periods after the applicable date, paragraph (2) of subsection (a) shall be applied by substituting "5 percentage points" for "3 percentage points".

(2) APPLICABLE DATE.—For purposes of this subsection—

(A) IN GENERAL.—The applicable date is the 30th day after the earlier of—

(i) the date on which the 1st letter of proposed deficiency which allows the taxpayer an opportunity for administrative review in the Internal Revenue Service Independent Office of Appeals is sent, or

(ii) the date on which the deficiency notice under section 6212 is sent.

The preceding sentence shall be applied without regard to any such letter or notice which is withdrawn by the Secretary.

(B) SPECIAL RULES.—

(i) NONDEFICIENCY PROCEDURES.—In the case of any underpayment of any tax imposed by this title to which the deficiency procedures do not apply, subparagraph (A) shall be applied by taking into account any letter or notice provided by the Secretary which notifies the taxpayer of the assessment or proposed assessment of the tax.

(ii) EXCEPTION WHERE AMOUNTS PAID IN FULL.—For purposes of subparagraph (A), a letter or notice shall be disregarded if, during the 30-day period beginning on the day on which it was sent, the taxpayer makes a payment equal to the amount shown as due in such letter or notice, as the case may be.

(iii) EXCEPTION FOR LETTERS OR NOTICES INVOLVING SMALL AMOUNTS.—For purposes of this paragraph, any letter or notice shall be disregarded if the amount of the deficiency or proposed deficiency (or the assessment or proposed assessment) set forth in such letter or notice is not greater than $100,000 (determined by not taking into account any interest, penalties, or additions to tax).

(3) LARGE CORPORATE UNDERPAYMENT.—For purposes of this subsection—

(A) IN GENERAL.—The term "large corporate underpayment" means any underpayment of a tax by a C corporation for any taxable period if the amount of such underpayment for such period exceeds $100,000.

(B) TAXABLE PERIOD.—For purposes of subparagraph (A), the term "taxable period" means—

(i) in the case of any tax imposed by subtitle A, the taxable year, or

(ii) in the case of any other tax, the period to which the underpayment relates.

Amendments

• 2019, Taxpayer First Act (P.L. 116-25)

P.L. 116-25, §1001(b)(1)(E):

Amended Code Sec. 6621(c)(2)(A)(i) by striking "Internal Revenue Service Office of Appeals" and inserting "Internal Revenue Service Independent Office of Appeals". **Effective** 7-1-2019.

• 1997, Taxpayer Relief Act of 1997 (P.L. 105-34)

P.L. 105-34, §1463(a):

Amended Code Sec. 6621(c)(2)(B) by adding at the end a new clause (iii). **Effective** for purposes of determining interest for periods after 12-31-97.

• 1996, Small Business Job Protection Act of 1996 (P.L. 104-188)

P.L. 104-188, §1702(c)(6):

Amended Code Sec. 6621(c)(2)(A) by adding at the end a new flush sentence. **Effective** as if included in the provision of P.L. 101-508 to which it relates.

P.L. 104-188, §1702(c)(7):

Amended Code Sec. 6621(c)(2)(B)(i) by striking "this subtitle" and inserting "this title". **Effective** as if included in the provision of P.L. 101-508 to which it relates.

• 1990, Omnibus Budget Reconciliation Act of 1990 (P.L. 101-508)

P.L. 101-508, §11341(a):

Amended Code Sec. 6621 by adding at the end thereof a new subsection (c). **Effective** for purposes of determining interest for periods after 12-31-90.

[Sec. 6621(c)—Repealed]

Amendments

• 1989, Omnibus Budget Reconciliation Act of 1989 (P.L. 101-239)

P.L. 101-239, §7721(b):

Repealed Code Sec. 6621(c). **Effective** for returns the due date for which (determined without regard to extensions) is after 12-31-89. Prior to repeal, Code Sec. 6621(c) read as follows:

(c) INTEREST ON SUBSTANTIAL UNDERPAYMENTS ATTRIBUTABLE TO TAX MOTIVATED TRANSACTIONS.—

(1) IN GENERAL.—In the case of interest payable under section 6601 with respect to any substantial underpayment attributable to tax motivated transactions, the rate of interest established under this section shall be 120 percent of the underpayment rate established under this subsection.

(2) SUBSTANTIAL UNDERPAYMENT ATTRIBUTABLE TO TAX MOTIVATED TRANSACTIONS.—For purposes of this subsection, the term "substantial underpayment attributable to tax motivated transactions" means any underpayment of taxes imposed by subtitle A for any taxable year which is attributable to 1 or more tax motivated transactions if the amount of the underpayment for such year so attributable exceeds $1,000.

(3) TAX MOTIVATED TRANSACTIONS.—

(A) IN GENERAL.—For purposes of this subsection, the term "tax motivated transaction" means—

(i) any valuation overstatement (within the meaning of section 6659(c)),

(ii) any loss disallowed by reason of section 465(a) and any credit disallowed under section 46(c)(8),

(iii) any straddle (as defined in section 1092(c) without regard to subsections (d) and (e) of section 1092),

(iv) any use of an accounting method specified in regulations prescribed by the Secretary as a use which may result in a substantial distortion of income for any period, and

(v) any sham or fraudulent transaction.

(B) REGULATORY AUTHORITY.—The Secretary may by regulations specify other types of transactions which will be treated as tax motivated for purposes of this subsection and may by regulations provide that specified transactions being treated as tax motivated will no longer be so treated. In prescribing regulations under the preceding sentence, the Secretary shall take into account—

(i) the ratio of tax benefits to cash invested,

(ii) the methods of promoting the use of this type of transaction, and

(iii) other relevant considerations.

(C) EFFECTIVE DATE FOR REGULATIONS.—Any regulations prescribed under subparagraph (A)(iv) or (B) shall apply only to interest accruing after a date (specified in such regulations) which is after the date on which such regulations are prescribed.

(4) JURISDICTION OF TAX COURT.—In the case of any proceeding in the Tax Court for a redetermination of a deficiency, the Tax Court shall also have jurisdiction to determine the portion (if any) of such deficiency which is a substantial underpayment attributable to tax motivated transactions.

• 1986, Tax Reform Act of 1986 (P.L. 99-514)

P.L. 99-514, §1511(a):

Amended Code Sec. 6621 by striking out subsection (c). **Effective** for purposes of determining interest for periods after 12-31-86. Prior to amendment, Code Sec. 6621(c) read as follows:

(c) DEFINITION OF PRIME RATE.—For purposes of subsection (b), the term "adjusted prime rate charged by banks" means the average predominant prime rate quoted by commercial banks to large businesses, as determined by the Board of Governors of the Federal Reserve System.

P.L. 99-514, §1511(c)(1)(A)-(C):

Amended Code Sec. 6621 by redesignating subsection (d) as subsection (c), by striking out "the adjusted rate established under subsection (b)" in subsection (c)(1) (as so redesignated) and inserting in lieu thereof "the underpayment rate established under this section", and by striking out "annual" in subsection (c)(1) (as so redesignated). **Effective** for purposes of determining interest for periods after 12-31-86.

P.L. 99-514, §1535(a):

Amended Code Sec. 6621(c)(3)(A) (as so redesignated) by striking out "and" at the end of clause (iii), by striking out the period at the end of clause (iv) and inserting in lieu thereof ", and", and by adding at the end thereof new clause (v). **Effective** for interest accruing after 12-31-84, except that it shall not apply in the case of any underpayment with respect to which there was a final court decision before 10-22-86.

P.L. 99-514, §1511(b), provides:

(b) COORDINATION BY REGULATION.—The Secretary of the Treasury or his delegate may issue regulations to coordinate section 6621 of the Internal Revenue Code of 1954 (as amended by this section) with section 6601(f) of such Code. Such regulations shall not apply to any period after the date 3 years after the date of the enactment of this Act.

• 1984, Deficit Reduction Act of 1984 (P.L. 98-369)

P.L. 98-369, §144(a):

Amended Code Sec. 6621 by adding subsection (d). **Effective** with respect to interest accruing after 12-31-84.

• 1981, Economic Recovery Tax Act of 1981 (P.L. 97-34)

P.L. 97-34, §711(b):

Amended Code Sec. 6621(c) by striking out "90 percent of" after "'adjusted prime rate charged by banks' means". **Effective** for adjustments made after 8-13-81.

• 1976, Tax Reform Act of 1976 (P.L. 94-455)

P.L. 94-455, §1906(b)(13)(A):

Amended 1954 Code by substituting "Secretary" for "Secretary or his delegate" each place it appeared. **Effective** 2-1-77.

• 1975 (P.L. 93-625)

P.L. 93-625, §7(a)(1):

Added Code Sec. 6621(c). **Effective** 7-1-75, for amounts outstanding on such date or arising thereafter.

[Sec. 6621(d)]

(d) ELIMINATION OF INTEREST ON OVERLAPPING PERIODS OF TAX OVERPAYMENTS AND UNDERPAYMENTS.—To the extent that, for any period, interest is payable under subchapter A and allowable under subchapter B on equivalent underpayments and overpayments by the same taxpayer of tax imposed by this title, the net rate of interest under this section on such amounts shall be zero for such period.

Amendments

• 1998, IRS Restructuring and Reform Act of 1998 (P.L. 105-206)

P.L. 105-206, §3301(a):

Amended Code Sec. 6621 by adding at the end a new subsection (d). **Effective,** generally, for interest for periods beginning after 7-22-98. For a special rule, see Act Sec. 3301(c)(2), below.

P.L. 105-206, §3301(c)(2), as amended by P.L. 105-277, §4002(d), provides:

(2) SPECIAL RULE.—Subject to any applicable statute of limitation not having expired with regard to either a tax underpayment or a tax overpayment, the amendments made by this section shall apply to interest for periods beginning before the date of the enactment of this Act if the taxpayer—

(A) reasonably identifies and establishes periods of such tax overpayments and under-payments for which the zero rate applies; and

(B) not later than December 31, 1999, requests the Secretary of the Treasury to apply section 6621(d) of the Internal Revenue Code of 1986, as added by subsection (a), to such periods.

[Sec. 6622]

SEC. 6622. INTEREST COMPOUNDED DAILY.

[Sec. 6622(a)]

(a) GENERAL RULE.—In computing the amount of any interest required to be paid under this title or sections 1961(c)(1) or 2411 of title 28, United States Code, by the Secretary or by the taxpayer, or any other amount determined by reference to such amount of interest, such interest and such amount shall be compounded daily.

[Sec. 6622(b)]

(b) EXCEPTION FOR PENALTY FOR FAILURE TO FILE ESTIMATED TAX.—Subsection (a) shall not apply for purposes of computing the amount of any addition to tax under section 6654 or 6655.

Amendments

• 1982, Tax Equity and Fiscal Responsibility Act of 1982 (P.L. 97-248)

P.L. 97-248, §344(a):

Added Code Sec. 6622. **Effective** for interest accruing after 12-31-82.

Subchapter D—Notice Requirements

***

[Sec. 6631]

SEC. 6631. NOTICE REQUIREMENTS.

The Secretary shall include with each notice to an individual taxpayer which includes an amount of interest required to be paid by such taxpayer under this title information with respect to the section of this title under which the interest is imposed and a computation of the interest.

Amendments

• 1998, IRS Restructuring and Reform Act of 1998 (P.L. 105-206)

P.L. 105-206, §3308(a):

Amended chapter 67 by adding at the end a new subchapter D (Code Sec. 6631). **Effective** for notices issued after 12-31-2001. In the case of any notice issued after 6-3-2001, and before 7-1-2003, to which Code Sec. 6631 applies, the requirements of Code Sec. 6631 shall be treated as met if such notice contains a telephone number at which the taxpayer can request a copy of the taxpayer's payment history relating to interest amounts included in such notice [**effective** date changed by P.L. 106-554, §302(c)].

CHAPTER 68—ADDITIONS TO THE TAX, ADDITIONAL AMOUNTS, AND ASSESSABLE PENALTIES

***

Subchapter A—Additions to the Tax and Additional Amounts

PART I—GENERAL PROVISIONS

***

[Sec. 6651]

SEC. 6651. FAILURE TO FILE TAX RETURN OR TO PAY TAX.

[Sec. 6651(a)]

(a) ADDITION TO THE TAX.—In case of failure—

(1) to file any return required under authority of subchapter A of chapter 61 (other than part III thereof), subchapter A of chapter 51 (relating to distilled spirits, wines, and beer), or of

subchapter A of chapter 52 (relating to tobacco, cigars, cigarettes, and cigarette papers and tubes) or of subchapter A of chapter 53 (relating to machine guns and certain other firearms), on the date prescribed therefor (determined with regard to any extension of time for filing), unless it is shown that such failure is due to reasonable cause and not due to willful neglect, there shall be added to the amount required to be shown as tax on such return 5 percent of the amount of such tax if the failure is for not more than 1 month, with an additional 5 percent for each additional month or fraction thereof during which such failure continues, not exceeding 25 percent in the aggregate;

(2) to pay the amount shown as tax on any return specified in paragraph (1) on or before the date prescribed for payment of such tax (determined with regard to any extension of time for payment), unless it is shown that such failure is due to reasonable cause and not due to willful neglect, there shall be added to the amount shown as tax on such return 0.5 percent of the amount of such tax if the failure is for not more than 1 month, with an additional 0.5 percent for each additional month or fraction thereof during which such failure continues, not exceeding 25 percent in the aggregate; or

(3) to pay any amount in respect of any tax required to be shown on a return specified in paragraph (1) which is not so shown (including an assessment made pursuant to section 6213(b)) within 21 calendar days from the date of notice and demand therefor (10 business days if the amount for which such notice and demand is made equals or exceeds $100,000), unless it is shown that such failure is due to reasonable cause and not due to willful neglect, there shall be added to the amount of tax stated in such notice and demand 0.5 percent of the amount of such tax if the failure is for not more than 1 month, with an additional 0.5 percent for each additional month or fraction thereof during which such failure continues, not exceeding 25 percent in the aggregate.

In the case of a failure to file a return of tax imposed by chapter 1 within 60 days of the date prescribed for filing of such return (determined with regard to any extensions of time for filing), unless it is shown that such failure is due to reasonable cause and not due to willful neglect, the addition to tax under paragraph (1) shall not be less than the lesser of $435 or 100 percent of the amount required to be shown as tax on such return.

Amendments

• 2019, Setting Every Community Up for Retirement Enhancement Act of 2019 (P.L. 116-94)

P.L. 116-94, §402(a), Div. O:

Amended the second sentence of Code Sec. 6651(a) by striking "$330" and inserting "$435". **Effective** for returns the due date for which (including extensions) is after 12-31-2019.

• 2019, Taxpayer First Act (P.L. 116-25)

P.L. 116-25, §3201(a):

Amended the second sentence of Code Sec. 6651(a) by striking "$205" and inserting "$330". **Effective** for returns required to be filed after 12-31-2019.

• 2016, Trade Facilitation and Trade Enforcement Act of 2015 (P.L. 114-125)

P.L. 114-125, §921(a):

Amended Code Sec. 6651(a) by striking "$135" in the last sentence and inserting "$205". **Effective** for returns required to be filed in calendar years after 2015.

• 2008, Heroes Earnings Assistance and Relief Tax Act of 2008 (P.L. 110-245)

P.L. 110-245, §303(a):

Amended Code Sec. 6651(a) by striking "$100" in the last sentence and inserting "$135". **Effective** for returns required to be filed after 12-31-2008.

• 1998, IRS Restructuring and Reform Act of 1998 (P.L. 105-206)

P.L. 105-206, §3707, provides:

SEC. 3707. ILLEGAL TAX PROTESTER DESIGNATION.

(a) PROHIBITION.—The officers and employees of the Internal Revenue Service—

(1) shall not designate taxpayers as illegal tax protesters (or any similar designation); and

(2) in the case of any such designation made on or before the date of the enactment of this Act—

(A) shall remove such designation from the individual master file; and

(B) shall disregard any such designation not located in the individual master file.

(b) DESIGNATION OF NONFILERS ALLOWED.—An officer or employee of the Internal Revenue Service may designate any appropriate taxpayer as a nonfiler, but shall remove such designation once the taxpayer has filed income tax returns for 2 consecutive taxable years and paid all taxes shown on such returns.

(c) EFFECTIVE DATE.—The provisions of this section shall take effect on July 22, 1998, except that the removal of any designation under subsection (a)(2)(A) shall not be required to begin before January 1, 1999.

• 1996, Taxpayer Bill of Rights 2 (P.L. 104-168)

P.L. 104-168, §303(b)(2):

Amended Code Sec. 6651(a)(3) by striking "10 days of the date of the notice and demand therefor" and inserting "21 calendar days from the date of notice and demand therefor (10 business days if the amount for which such notice and demand is made equals or exceeds $100,000)". **Effective** in the case of any notice and demand given after 12-31-96.

• 1982, Tax Equity and Fiscal Responsibility Act of 1982 (P.L. 97-248)

P.L. 97-248, §318(a):

Amended Code Sec. 6651(a) by adding at the end a new sentence. **Effective** for returns the due date for the filing of which (including extensions) is after 12-31-82.

[Sec. 6651(b)]

(b) PENALTY IMPOSED ON NET AMOUNT DUE.—For purposes of—

(1) subsection (a)(1), the amount of tax required to be shown on the return shall be reduced by the amount of any part of the tax which is paid on or before the date prescribed for payment of the tax and by the amount of any credit against the tax which may be claimed on the return,

(2) subsection (a)(2), the amount of tax shown on the return shall, for purposes of computing the addition for any month, be reduced by the amount of any part of the tax which is paid on

or before the beginning of such month and by the amount of any credit against the tax which may be claimed on the return, and

(3) subsection (a)(3), the amount of tax stated in the notice and demand shall, for the purpose of computing the addition for any month, be reduced by the amount of any part of the tax which is paid before the beginning of such month.

[Sec. 6651(c)]

(c) LIMITATIONS AND SPECIAL RULE.—

(1) ADDITIONS UNDER MORE THAN ONE PARAGRAPH.—With respect to any return, the amount of the addition under paragraph (1) of subsection (a) shall be reduced by the amount of the addition under paragraph (2) of subsection (a) for any month (or fraction thereof) to which an addition to tax applies under both paragraphs (1) and (2). In any case described in the last sentence of subsection (a), the amount of the addition under paragraph (1) of subsection (a) shall not be reduced under the preceding sentence below the amount provided in such last sentence.

(2) AMOUNT OF TAX SHOWN MORE THAN AMOUNT REQUIRED TO BE SHOWN.—If the amount required to be shown as tax on a return is less than the amount shown as tax on such return, subsections (a)(2) and (b)(2) shall be applied by substituting such lower amount.

Amendments

• 1986, Tax Reform Act of 1986 (P.L. 99-514)

P.L. 99-514, § 1502(b):

Amended Code Sec. 6651(c)(1). **Effective** for amounts assessed after 12-31-86, with respect to failures to pay which begin before, on, or after such date. Prior to amendment, Code Sec. 6651(c)(1) read as follows:

(1) ADDITIONS UNDER MORE THAN ONE PARAGRAPH.—

(A) With respect to any return, the amount of the addition under paragraph (1) of subsection (a) shall be reduced by the amount of the addition under paragraph (2) of subsection (a) for any month to which an addition to tax applies under both paragraphs (1) and (2). In any case described in the last sentence of subsection (a), the amount of the addition under paragraph (1) of subsection (a) shall not be reduced under the preceding sentence below the amount provided in such last sentence.

(B) With respect to any return, the maximum amount of the addition permitted under paragraph (3) of subsection (a) shall be reduced by the amount of the addition under paragraph (1) of subsection (a) (determined without regard to the last sentence of such subsection) which is attributable to the tax for which the notice and demand is made and which is not paid within 10 days of notice and demand.

• 1982, Tax Equity and Fiscal Responsibility Act of 1982 (P.L. 97-248)

P.L. 97-248, § 318(b)(1):

Amended Code Sec. 6651(c)(1)(A) by adding at the end a new sentence. **Effective** for returns the due date for the filing of which (including extensions) is after 12-31-82.

P.L. 97-248, § 318(b)(2):

Amended Code Sec. 6651(c)(1)(B) by inserting "(determined without regard to the last sentence of such subsection)" after "paragraph (1) of subsection (a)". **Effective** for returns the due date for the filing of which (including extensions) is after 12-31-82.

• 1968, Revenue and Expenditure Control Act of 1968 (P.L. 90-364)

P.L. 90-364, § 103(e)(4):

Amended Code Sec. 6651(c) by deleting "or section 6016" which formerly appeared after "section 6015". **Effective** with respect to tax years beginning after 12-31-67.

[Sec. 6651(d)]

(d) INCREASE IN PENALTY FOR FAILURE TO PAY TAX IN CERTAIN CASES.—

(1) IN GENERAL.—In the case of each month (or fraction thereof) beginning after the day described in paragraph (2) of this subsection, paragraphs (2) and (3) of subsection (a) shall be applied by substituting "1 percent" for "0.5 percent" each place it appears.

(2) DESCRIPTION.—For purposes of paragraph (1), the day described in this paragraph is the earlier of—

(A) the day 10 days after the date of which notice is given under section 6331(d), or

(B) the day on which notice and demand for immediate payment is given under the last sentence of section 6331(a).

Amendments

• 1986, Tax Reform Act of 1986 (P.L. 99-514)

P.L. 99-514, § 1502(a):

Amended Code Sec. 6651 by redesignating subsection (d) as subsection (e) and by inserting after subsection (c) new subsection (d). For the **effective** date, see Act Sec. 1502(c)(1), below.

P.L. 99-514, § 1502(c)(1), provides:

(c) EFFECTIVE DATES.—

(1) SUBSECTION (a).—The amendments made by subsection (a) shall apply—

(A) to failures to pay which began after December 31, 1986, and

(B) to failures to pay which begin on or before December 31, 1986, if after December 31, 1986—

(i) notice (or renotice) under section 6331(d) of the Internal Revenue Code of 1954 is given with respect to such failure, or

(ii) notice and demand for immediate payment of the underpayment is made under the last sentence of section 6331(a) of such Code.

In the case of a failure to pay described in subparagraph (B), paragraph (2) of section 6651(d) of such Code (as added by subsection (a)) shall be applied by taking into account the first notice (or renotice) after December 31, 1986.

• 1984, Deficit Reduction Act of 1984 (P.L. 98-369)

P.L. 98-369, § 412(b)(8):

Amended Code Sec. 6651(d). **Effective** with respect to tax years beginning after 12-31-84. Prior to amendment, it read as follows:

(d) EXCEPTION FOR DECLARATION OF ESTIMATED TAX.—This section shall not apply to any failure to file a declaration of estimated tax required by section 6015 or to pay any estimated tax required to be paid by section 6153 or 6154.

* * *

[Sec. 6651(f)]

(f) INCREASE IN PENALTY FOR FRAUDULENT FAILURE TO FILE.—If any failure to file any return is fraudulent, paragraph (1) of subsection (a) shall be applied—

(1) by substituting "15 percent" for "5 percent" each place it appears, and

(2) by substituting "75 percent" for "25 percent".

Amendments

• 1989, Omnibus Budget Reconciliation Act of 1989 (P.L. 101-239)

P.L. 101-239, §7741(a):

Amended Code Sec. 6651 by adding at the end thereof a new subsection (f). **Effective** in the case of failures to file returns the due date for which (determined without regard to extensions) is after 12-31-89.

[Sec. 6651(g)]

(g) TREATMENT OF RETURNS PREPARED BY SECRETARY UNDER SECTION 6020(b).—In the case of any return made by the Secretary under section 6020(b)—

(1) such return shall be disregarded for purposes of determining the amount of the addition under paragraph (1) of subsection (a), but

(2) such return shall be treated as the return filed by the taxpayer for purposes of determining the amount of the addition under paragraphs (2) and (3) of subsection (a).

Amendments

• 1996, Taxpayer Bill of Rights 2 (P.L. 104-168)

P.L. 104-168, §1301(a):

Amended Code Sec. 6651 by adding at the end a new subsection (g). **Effective** in the case of any return the due date for which (determined without regard to extensions) is after 7-30-96.

* * *

[Sec. 6651(i)]

(i) APPLICATION TO IMPUTED UNDERPAYMENT.—For purposes of this section, any failure to comply with section 6226(b)(4)(A)(ii) shall be treated as a failure to pay the amount described in subclause (II) thereof and such amount shall be treated for purposes of this section as an amount shown as tax on a return specified in subsection (a)(1).

Amendments

• 2018, Tax Technical Corrections Act of 2018 (P.L. 115-141)

P.L. 115-141, §206(n)(1), Div. U:

Amended Code Sec. 6651 by redesignating subsection (i) as subsection (j) and by inserting after subsection (h) a new subsection (i). **Effective** as if included in section 1101 of the Bipartisan Budget Act of 2015 [**effective** generally for returns filed for partnership tax years beginning after 12-31-2017.—CCH].

[Sec. 6651(j)]

(j) ADJUSTMENT FOR INFLATION.—

(1) IN GENERAL.—In the case of any return required to be filed in a calendar year beginning after 2020, the $435 dollar amount under subsection (a) shall be increased by an amount equal to such dollar amount multiplied by the cost-of-living adjustment determined under section 1(f)(3) for the calendar year determined by substituting "calendar year 2019" for "calendar year 2016" in subparagraph (A)(ii) thereof.

(2) ROUNDING.—If any amount adjusted under paragraph (1) is not a multiple of $5, such amount shall be rounded to the next lowest multiple of $5.

Amendments

• 2019, Setting Every Community Up for Retirement Enhancement Act of 2019 (P.L. 116-94)

P.L. 116-94, §402(b), Div. O:

Amended Code Sec. 6651(j)(1) by striking "$330" and inserting "$435". **Effective** for returns the due date for which (including extensions) is after 12-31-2019.

• 2019, Taxpayer First Act (P.L. 116-25)

P.L. 116-25, §3201(b)(1)-(3):

Amended Code Sec. 6651(j)(1) by striking "2014" and inserting "2020", by striking "$205" and inserting "$330", and by striking "2013" and inserting "2019". **Effective** for returns required to be filed after 12-31-2019.

• 2018, Tax Technical Corrections Act of 2018 (P.L. 115-141)

P.L. 115-141, §206(n)(1), Div. U:

Amended Code Sec. 6651 by redesignating subsection (i) as subsection (j). **Effective** as if included in section 1101 of the Bipartisan Budget Act of 2015 [**effective** generally for returns filed for partnership tax years beginning after 12-31-2017.—CCH].

P.L. 115-141, §401(a)(299)(A), Div. U:

Amended Code Sec. 6651(i) by inserting "an amount equal to" after "increased by" and by inserting "for the calendar year" after "section 1(f)(3)". **Effective** 3-23-2018.

• 2017, Tax Cuts and Jobs Act (P.L. 115-97)

P.L. 115-97, §11002(d)(1)(KK):

Amended Code Sec. 6651(i)(1) by striking "for 'calendar year 1992' in subparagraph (B)" and inserting "for 'calendar year 2016' in subparagraph (A)(ii)". **Effective** for tax years beginning after 12-31-2017.

• 2016, Trade Facilitation and Trade Enforcement Act of 2015 (P.L. 114-125)

P.L. 114-125, §921(b):

Amended Code Sec. 6651(i)[(1)] by striking "$135" and inserting "$205". **Effective** for returns required to be filed in calendar years after 2015.

• 2014, Stephen Beck, Jr., Achieving a Better Life Experience Act of 2014 (P.L. 113-295)

P.L. 113-295, §208(a), Division B:

Amended Code Sec. 6651 by adding at the end a new subsection (i). **Effective** for returns required to be filed, and statements required to be furnished, after 12-31-2014 [**effective** date changed by P.L. 115-141, §105(a)(1)-(2), Div. U.—CCH]

[Sec. 6652]

SEC. 6652. FAILURE TO FILE CERTAIN INFORMATION RETURNS, REGISTRATION STATEMENTS, ETC.

* * *

[Sec. 6652(c)]

(c) RETURNS BY EXEMPT ORGANIZATIONS AND BY CERTAIN TRUSTS.—

(1) ANNUAL RETURNS UNDER SECTION 6033(a)(1) OR 6012(a)(6).—

(A) PENALTY ON ORGANIZATION.—In the case of—

(i) a failure to file a return required under section 6033(a)(1) (relating to returns by exempt organizations) or section 6012(a)(6) (relating to returns by political organizations) on the date and in the manner prescribed therefor (determined with regard to any extension of time for filing), or

(ii) a failure to include any of the information required to be shown on a return filed under section 6033(a)(1) or section 6012(a)(6) or to show the correct information,

there shall be paid by the exempt organization $20 for each day during which such failure continues. The maximum penalty under this subparagraph on failures with respect to any 1 return shall not exceed the lesser of $10,000 or 5 percent of the gross receipts of the organization for the year. In the case of an organization having gross receipts exceeding $1,000,000 for any year, with respect to the return required under section 6033(a)(1) or section 6012(a)(6) for such year, in applying the first sentence of this subparagraph, the amount of the penalty for each day during which a failure continues shall be $100 in lieu of the amount otherwise specified, and, in lieu of applying the second sentence of this subparagraph, the maximum penalty under this subparagraph shall not exceed $50,000.

(B) MANAGERS.—

(i) IN GENERAL.—The Secretary may make a written demand on any organization subject to penalty under subparagraph (A) specifying therein a reasonable future date by which the return shall be filed (or the information furnished) for purposes of this subparagraph.

(ii) FAILURE TO COMPLY WITH DEMAND.—If any person fails to comply with any demand under clause (i) on or before the date specified in such demand, there shall be paid by the person failing to so comply $10 for each day after the expiration of the time specified in such demand during which such failure continues. The maximum penalty imposed under this subparagraph on all persons for failures with respect to any 1 return shall not exceed $5,000.

(C) PUBLIC INSPECTION OF ANNUAL RETURNS AND REPORTS.—In the case of a failure to comply with the requirements of section 6104(d) with respect to any annual return on the date and in the manner prescribed therefor (determined with regard to any extension of time for filing) or report required under section 527(j), there shall be paid by the person failing to meet such requirements $20 for each day during which such failure continues. The maximum penalty imposed under this subparagraph on all persons for failures with respect to any 1 return or report shall not exceed $10,000.

(D) PUBLIC INSPECTION OF APPLICATIONS FOR EXEMPTION AND NOTICE OF STATUS.—In the case of a failure to comply with the requirements of section 6104(d) with respect to any exempt status application materials (as defined in such section) or notice materials (as defined in such section) on the date and in the manner prescribed therefor, there shall be paid by the person failing to meet such requirements $20 for each day during which such failure continues.

(E) NO PENALTY FOR CERTAIN ANNUAL NOTICES.—This paragraph shall not apply with respect to any notice required under section 6033(i).

(2) RETURNS UNDER SECTION 6034 OR 6043.—

(A) PENALTY ON ORGANIZATION OR TRUST.—In the case of a failure to file a return required under section 6034 (relating to returns by certain trusts) or section 6043(b) (relating to terminations, etc., of exempt organizations), on the date and in the manner prescribed therefor (determined with regard to any extension of time for filing), there shall be paid by the exempt organization or trust failing so to file $10 for each day during which such failure continues, but the total amount imposed under this subparagraph on any organization or trust for failure to file any 1 return shall not exceed $5,000.

(B) MANAGERS.—The Secretary may make written demand on an organization or trust failing to file under subparagraph (A) specifying therein a reasonable future date by which such filing shall be made for purposes of this subparagraph. If such filing is not made on or before such date, there shall be paid by the person failing so to file $10 for each day after the expiration of the time specified in the written demand during which such failure continues, but the total amount imposed under this subparagraph on all persons for failure to file any 1 return shall not exceed $5,000.

(C) SPLIT-INTEREST TRUSTS.—In the case of a trust which is required to file a return under section 6034(a), subparagraphs (A) and (B) of this paragraph shall not apply and paragraph

(1) shall apply in the same manner as if such return were required under section 6033, except that—

(i) the 5 percent limitation in the second sentence of paragraph (1)(A) shall not apply,

(ii) in the case of any trust with gross income in excess of $250,000, in applying the first sentence of paragraph (1)(A), the amount of the penalty for each day during which a failure continues shall be $100 in lieu of the amount otherwise specified, and in lieu of applying the second sentence of paragraph (1)(A), the maximum penalty under paragraph (1)(A) shall not exceed $50,000, and

(iii) the third sentence of paragraph (1)(A) shall be disregarded.

In addition to any penalty imposed on the trust pursuant to this subparagraph, if the person required to file such return knowingly fails to file the return, such penalty shall also be imposed on such person who shall be personally liable for such penalty.

(3) DISCLOSURE UNDER SECTION 6033(a)(2).—

(A) PENALTY ON ENTITIES.—In the case of a failure to file a disclosure required under section 6033(a)(2), there shall be paid by the tax-exempt entity (the entity manager in the case of a tax-exempt entity described in paragraph (4), (5), (6), or (7) of section 4965(c)) $100 for each day during which such failure continues. The maximum penalty under this subparagraph on failures with respect to any 1 disclosure shall not exceed $50,000.

(B) WRITTEN DEMAND.—

(i) IN GENERAL.—The Secretary may make a written demand on any entity or manager subject to penalty under subparagraph (A) specifying therein a reasonable future date by which the disclosure shall be filed for purposes of this subparagraph.

(ii) FAILURE TO COMPLY WITH DEMAND.—If any entity or manager fails to comply with any demand under clause (i) on or before the date specified in such demand, there shall be paid by such entity or manager failing to so comply $100 for each day after the expiration of the time specified in such demand during which such failure continues. The maximum penalty imposed under this subparagraph on all entities and managers for failures with respect to any 1 disclosure shall not exceed $10,000.

(C) DEFINITIONS.—Any term used in this section which is also used in section 4965 shall have the meaning given such term under section 4965.

(4) NOTICES UNDER SECTION 506.—

(A) PENALTY ON ORGANIZATION.—In the case of a failure to submit a notice required under section 506(a) (relating to organizations required to notify Secretary of intent to operate as 501(c)(4)) on the date and in the manner prescribed therefor, there shall be paid by the organization failing to so submit $20 for each day during which such failure continues, but the total amount imposed under this subparagraph on any organization for failure to submit any one notice shall not exceed $5,000.

(B) MANAGERS.—The Secretary may make written demand on an organization subject to penalty under subparagraph (A) specifying in such demand a reasonable future date by which the notice shall be submitted for purposes of this subparagraph. If such notice is not submitted on or before such date, there shall be paid by the person failing to so submit $20 for each day after the expiration of the time specified in the written demand during which such failure continues, but the total amount imposed under this subparagraph on all persons for failure to submit any one notice shall not exceed $5,000.

(5) REASONABLE CAUSE EXCEPTION.—No penalty shall be imposed under this subsection with respect to any failure if it is shown that such failure is due to reasonable cause.

(6) OTHER SPECIAL RULES.—

(A) TREATMENT AS TAX.—Any penalty imposed under this subsection shall be paid on notice and demand of the Secretary and in the same manner as tax.

(B) JOINT AND SEVERAL LIABILITY.—If more than 1 person is liable under this subsection for any penalty with respect to any failure, all such persons shall be jointly and severally liable with respect to such failure.

(C) PERSON.—For purposes of this subsection, the term "person" means any officer, director, trustee, employee, or other individual who is under a duty to perform the act in respect of which the violation occurs.

(7) ADJUSTMENT FOR INFLATION.—

(A) IN GENERAL.—In the case of any failure relating to a return required to be filed in a calendar year beginning after 2014, each of the dollar amounts under paragraphs (1), (2), and (3) shall be increased by an amount equal to such dollar amount multiplied by the cost-of-living adjustment determined under section 1(f)(3) for the calendar year determined by substituting "calendar year 2013" for "calendar year 2016" in subparagraph (A)(ii) thereof.

(B) ROUNDING.—If any amount adjusted under subparagraph (A)—

(i) is not less than $5,000 and is not a multiple of $500, such amount shall be rounded to the next lowest multiple of $500, and

(ii) is not described in clause (i) and is not a multiple of $5, such amount shall be rounded to the next lowest multiple of $5.

Amendments

• 2018, Tax Technical Corrections Act of 2018 (P.L. 115-141)

P.L. 115-141, §401(a)(299)(B), Div. U:

Amended Code Sec. 6652(c)(7)(A) by inserting "an amount equal to" after "increased by" and by inserting "for the calendar year" after "section 1(f)(3)". **Effective** 3-23-2018.

• 2017, Tax Cuts and Jobs Act (P.L. 115-97)

P.L. 115-97, §11002(d)(1)(LL):

Amended Code Sec. 6652(c)(7)(A) by striking "for 'calendar year 1992' in subparagraph (B)" and inserting "for 'calendar year 2016' in subparagraph (A)(ii)". **Effective** for tax years beginning after 12-31-2017.

• 2015, Protecting Americans from Tax Hikes Act of 2015 (P.L. 114-113)

P.L. 114-113, §405(c), Div. Q:

Amended Code Sec. 6652(c) by redesignating paragraphs (4)-(6) as paragraphs (5)-(7), respectively, and by inserting after paragraph (3) a new paragraph (4). For the **effective** date, see Act Sec. 405(f), below.

P.L. 114-113, §405(f), Div. Q, provides:

(f) EFFECTIVE DATE.—

(1) IN GENERAL.—The amendments made by this section shall apply to organizations which are described in section 501(c)(4) of the Internal Revenue Code of 1986 and organized after the date of the enactment of this Act.

(2) CERTAIN EXISTING ORGANIZATIONS.—In the case of any other organization described in section 501(c)(4) of such Code, the amendments made by this section shall apply to such organization only if, on or before the date of the enactment of this Act—

(A) such organization has not applied for a written determination of recognition as an organization described in section 501(c)(4) of such Code, and

(B) such organization has not filed at least one annual return or notice required under subsection (a)(1) or (i) (as the case may be) of section 6033 of such Code.

In the case of any organization to which the amendments made by this section apply by reason of the preceding sentence, such organization shall submit the notice required by section 506(a) of such Code, as added by this Act, not later than 180 days after the date of the enactment of this Act.

• 2014, Stephen Beck, Jr., Achieving a Better Life Experience Act of 2014 (P.L. 113-295)

P.L. 113-295, §208(b)(1), Division B:

Amended Code Sec. 6652(c) by adding at the end a new paragraph (6). **Effective** for returns required to be filed, and statements required to be furnished, after 12-31-2014 [**effective** date changed by P.L. 115-141, §105(a)(1)-(2), Div. U.—CCH].

P.L. 113-295, §208(b)(2)(A), Division B:

Amended the last sentence of Code Sec. 6652(c)(1)(A) by striking "the first sentence of this subparagraph shall be applied by substituting '$100' for '$20' and" and inserting "in applying the first sentence of this subparagraph, the amount of the penalty for each day during which a failure continues shall be $100 in lieu of the amount otherwise specified, and". **Effective** for returns required to be filed, and statements required to be furnished, after 12-31-2014 [**effective** date changed by P.L. 115-141, §105(a)(1)-(2), Div. U.—CCH].

P.L. 113-295, §208(b)(2)(B), Division B:

Amended Code Sec. 6652(c)(2)(C)(ii) by striking "the first sentence of paragraph (1)(A)" and all that follows and inserting "in applying the first sentence of paragraph (1)(A), the amount of the penalty for each day during which a failure continues shall be $100 in lieu of the amount otherwise specified, and in lieu of applying the second sentence of paragraph (1)(A), the maximum penalty under paragraph (1)(A) shall not exceed $50,000, and". **Effective** for returns required to be filed, and statements required to be furnished, after 12-31-2014 [**effective** date changed by P.L. 115-141, §105(a)(1)-(2), Div. U.—CCH]. Prior to being stricken, "the first sentence of paragraph (1)(A)" and all that follows read as follows:

the first sentence of paragraph (1)(A) shall be applied by substituting "$100" for "$20", and the second sentence thereof shall be applied by substituting "$50,000" for "$10,000", and

• 2006, Pension Protection Act of 2006 (P.L. 109-280)

P.L. 109-280, §1201(b)(2):

Amended Code Sec. 6652(c)(2) by adding at the end a new subparagraph (C). **Effective** for returns for tax years beginning after 12-31-2006.

P.L. 109-280, §1223(d):

Amended Code Sec. 6652(c)(1) by adding at the end a new subparagraph (E). **Effective** for notices and returns with respect to annual periods beginning after 2006.

• 2006, Tax Increase Prevention and Reconciliation Act of 2005 (P.L. 109-222)

P.L. 109-222, §516(c)(1):

Amended Code Sec. 6652(c) by redesignating paragraphs (3) and (4) as paragraphs (4) and (5), respectively, and by inserting after paragraph (2) a new paragraph (3). **Effective** for disclosures the due date for which are after 5-17-2006.

P.L. 109-222, §516(c)(2):

Amended Code Sec. 6652(c)(1) by striking "6033" each place it appears in the text and heading thereof and inserting "6033(a)(1)". **Effective** for disclosures the due date for which are after 5-17-2006.

• 2000 (P.L. 106-230)

P.L. 106-230, §1(c)(1)-(2):

Amended Code Sec. 6652(c)(1)(D) by inserting "or notice materials (as defined in such section)" after "section)" and by inserting "AND NOTICE OF STATUS" after "EXEMPTION" in the heading. **Effective** 7-1-2000. For an exception, see Act Sec. 1(d)(2), below.

P.L. 106-230, §1(d)(2), provides:

(2) ORGANIZATIONS ALREADY IN EXISTENCE.—In the case of an organization established before the date of the enactment of this section, the time to file the notice under section 527(i)(2) of the Internal Revenue Code of 1986, as added by this section, shall be 30 days after the date of the enactment of this section.

P.L. 106-230, §2(c)(1)-(3):

Amended Code Sec. 6652(c)(1)(C) by inserting "or report required under section 527(j)" after "filing)"; by inserting "or report" after "1 return"; and by inserting "AND REPORTS" after "RETURNS" in the heading. **Effective** 7-1-2000.

P.L. 106-230, §3(c)(1):

Amended Code Sec. 6652(c)(1)(A)(i) by inserting "or section 6012(a)(6) (relating to returns by political organizations)" after "organizations)". **Effective** for returns for tax years beginning after 6-30-2000.

P.L. 106-230, §3(c)(2):

Amended Code Sec. 6652(c)(1)(A)(ii) by inserting "or section 6012(a)(6)" after "section 6033". **Effective** for returns for tax years beginning after 6-30-2000.

P.L. 106-230, §3(c)(3):

Amended Code Sec. 6652(c)(1)(A) by inserting "or section 6012(a)(6)" after "section 6033" in the third sentence. **Effective** for returns for tax years beginning after 6-30-2000.

P.L. 106-230, §3(c)(4):

Amended Code Sec. 6652(c)(1) by inserting "OR 6012(a)(6)" after "SECTION 6033" in the heading. **Effective** for returns for tax years beginning after 6-30-2000.

• 1998, Tax and Trade Relief Extension Act of 1998 (P.L. 105-277)

P.L. 105-277, §1004(b)(2)(B):

Amended Code Sec. 6652(c)(1)(C) by striking "subsection (d) or (e)(1) of section 6104 (relating to public inspection of annual returns)" and inserting "section 6104(d) with respect to any annual return". **Effective**, generally, for requests made after the later of 12-31-98, or the 60th day after the Secretary of the Treasury first issues the regulations referred to in Code Sec. 6104(d)(4), as amended by Act Sec. 1004. For an exception, see Act Sec. 1004(b)(3)(B), below.

P.L. 105-277, §1004(b)(2)(C):

Amended Code Sec. 6652(c)(1)(D) by striking "section 6104(e)(2) (relating to public inspection of applications for exemption)" and inserting "section 6104(d) with respect to any exempt status application materials (as defined in such section)". **Effective**, generally, for requests made after the later of 12-31-98, or the 60th day after the Secretary of the Treasury first issues the regulations referred to in Code Sec. 6104(d)(4), as amended by Act Sec. 1004. For an exception, see Act Sec. 1004(b)(3)(B), below.

P.L. 105-277, §1004(b)(3)(B), provides:

(B) PUBLICATION OF ANNUAL RETURNS.—Section 6104(d) of such Code, as in effect before the amendments made by this subsection, shall not apply to any return the due date for which is after the date such amendments take effect under subparagraph (A).

• 1996, Small Business Job Protection Act of 1996 (P.L. 104-188)

P.L. 104-188, §1704(s)(1):

Amended Code Sec. 6652(c)(1)(C) by striking "$10" and inserting "$20", and by striking "$5,000" and inserting "$10,000". **Effective** 8-20-96.

P.L. 104-188, §1704(s)(2):

Amended Code Sec. 6652(c)(1)(D) by striking "$10" and inserting "$20". **Effective** 8-20-96.

• 1996, Taxpayer Bill of Rights 2 (P.L. 104-168)

P.L. 104-168, §1314(a):

Amended Code Sec. 6652(c)(1)(A) by striking "$10" and inserting "$20" and by striking "$5,000" and inserting "$10,000". **Effective** for returns for tax years ending on or after 7-30-96.

P.L. 104-168, §1314(b):

Amended Code Sec. 6652(c)(1)(A) by adding at the end a new sentence. **Effective** for returns for tax years ending on or after 7-30-96.

• 1987, Revenue Act of 1987 (P.L. 100-203)

P.L. 100-203, §10704(a):

Amended Code Sec. 6652(c). For the **effective** date, see Act Sec. 10704(d) below. Prior to amendment, Code Sec. 6652(c) read as follows:

(c) RETURNS BY EXEMPT ORGANIZATIONS AND BY CERTAIN TRUSTS.—

(1) PENALTY ON ORGANIZATION OR TRUST.—In the case of a failure to file a return required under section 6033 (relating to returns by exempt organizations), section 6034 (relating to returns by certain trusts), or section 6043(b) (relating to exempt organizations), on the date and in the manner prescribed therefor (determined with regard to any extension of time for filing), unless it is shown that such failure is due to reasonable cause there shall be paid (on notice and demand by the Secretary and in the same manner as tax) by the exempt organization or trust failing so to file, $10 for each day during which such failure continues, but the total amount imposed hereunder on any organization for failure to file any return shall not exceed $5,000.

(2) MANAGERS.—The Secretary may make written demand upon an organization failing to file under paragraph (1) specifying therein a reasonable future date by which such filing shall be made, and if such filing is not made on or before such date, and unless it is shown that failure so to file is due to reasonable cause, there shall be paid (on notice and demand by the Secretary and in the same manner as tax) by the person failing so to file, $10 for each day after the expiration of the time specified in the written demand during which such failure continues, but the total amount imposed hereunder on all persons for such failure to file shall not exceed $5,000. If more than one person is liable under this paragraph for a failure to file, all such persons shall be jointly and severally liable with respect to such failure. The term "person" as used herein means any officer, director, trustee, employee, member, or other individual who is under duty to perform the act in respect of which the violation occurs.

(3) ANNUAL RETURNS.—In the case of a failure to comply with the requirements of section 6104(d) (relating to public inspection of private foundations' annual returns) on the date and in the manner prescribed therefor (determined with regard to any extension of time for filing), unless it is shown that such failure is due to reasonable cause, there shall be paid (on notice and demand by the Secretary and in the same manner as tax) by the person failing to meet such requirement, $10 for each day during which such failure continues, but the total amount imposed hereunder on all such persons for such failure with respect to any one annual return shall not exceed $5,000. If more than one person is liable under this paragraph for a failure to file or comply with the requirements of section 6104(d), all such persons shall be jointly and severally liable with respect to such failure. The term "person" as used herein means any officer, director, trustee, employee, member, or other individual who is under a duty to perform the act in respect of which the violation occurs.

P.L. 100-203, §10704(d), provides:

(d) EFFECTIVE DATE.—The amendments made by this section shall apply—

(1) to returns for years beginning after December 31, 1986, and

(2) on and after the date of the enactment of this Act in the case of applications submitted to the Internal Revenue Service—

(A) after July 15, 1987, or

(B) on or before July 15, 1987, if the organization has a copy of the application on July 15, 1987.

• 1986, Tax Reform Act of 1986 (P.L. 99-514)

P.L. 99-514, §1501(d)(1)(A)(i) and (ii):

Amended Code Sec. 6652 by striking out subsection (a) and by redesignating subsections (b) through (k) as subsections (a) through (j), respectively. **Effective** for returns for which the due date (determined without regard to extensions) is after 12-31-86.

• 1980 (P.L. 96-603)

P.L. 96-603, §1(d)(2):

Amended the heading of Code Sec. 6652(d)(3) by striking out "REPORTS" and inserting in lieu thereof "RETURNS" and by amending the first sentence of such paragraph (3). **Effective** for tax years beginning after 1980. Prior to amendment, the first sentence of Code Sec. 6652(d)(3) provided:

"In the case of a failure to file a report required under section 6056 (relating to annual reports by private foundations) or to comply with the requirements of section 6104(d) (relating to public inspection of private foundations' annual reports), on the date and in the manner prescribed therefor (determined with regard to any extension of time for filing), unless it is shown that such failure is due to reasonable cause, there shall be paid (on notice and demand by the Secretary and in the same manner as tax) by the person failing so to file or meet the publicity requirement, $10 for each day during which such failure continues, but the total amount imposed hereunder on all such persons for such failure to file or comply with the requirements of section 6104(d) with regard to any one annual report shall not exceed $5,000."

• 1976, Tax Reform Act of 1976 (P.L. 94-455)

P.L. 94-455, §1906(b)(13)(A):

Amended 1954 Code by substituting "Secretary" for "Secretary or his delegate" each place it appeared. **Effective** 2-1-77.

• 1969, Tax Reform Act of 1969 (P.L. 91-172)

P.L. 91-172, §101(d)(4):

Added Code Sec. 6652(d). **Effective** for tax years beginning after 12-31-69.

[Sec. 6652(d)]

(d) ANNUAL REGISTRATION AND OTHER NOTIFICATION BY PENSION PLAN.—

(1) REGISTRATION.—In the case of any failure to file a registration statement required under section 6057(a) (relating to annual registration of certain plans) which includes all participants required to be included in such statement, on the date prescribed therefor (determined without

regard to any extension of time for filing), unless it is shown that such failure is due to reasonable cause, there shall be paid (on notice and demand by the Secretary and in the same manner as tax) by the person failing so to file, an amount equal to $10 for each participant with respect to whom there is a failure to file, multiplied by the number of days during which such failure continues, but the total amount imposed under this paragraph on any person for any failure to file with respect to any plan year shall not exceed $50,000.

(2) NOTIFICATION OF CHANGE OF STATUS.—In the case of failure to file a notification required under section 6057(b) (relating to notification of change of status) on the date prescribed therefor (determined without regard to any extension of time for filing), unless it is shown that such failure is due to reasonable cause, there shall be paid (on notice and demand by the Secretary and in the same manner as tax) by the person failing so to file, $10 for each day during which such failure continues, but the total amounts imposed under this paragraph on any person for failure to file any notification shall not exceed $10,000.

Amendments

• 2019, Setting Every Community Up for Retirement Enhancement Act of 2019 (P.L. 116-94)

P.L. 116-94, §403(b)(1)-(3), Div. O:

Amended Code Sec. 6652(d) by striking "$1" both places it appears in paragraphs (1) and (2) and inserting "$10"; by striking "$5,000" in paragraph (1) and inserting "$50,000"; and by striking "$1,000" in paragraph (2) and inserting "$10,000". **Effective** for returns, statements, and notifications required to be filed, and notices required to be provided, after 12-31-2019.

• 1986, Tax Reform Act of 1986 (P.L. 99-514)

P.L. 99-514, §1501(d)(1)(A)(i) and (ii):

Amended Code Sec. 6652 by striking out subsection (a) and by redesignating subsections (b) through (k) as subsections (a) through (j), respectively. **Effective** for returns for which the due date (determined without regard to extensions) is after 12-31-86.

• 1976, Tax Reform Act of 1976 (P.L. 94-455)

P.L. 94-455, §1906(b)(13)(A):

Amended 1954 Code by substituting "Secretary" for "Secretary or his delegate" each place it appeared. **Effective** 2-1-77.

• 1974, Employee Retirement Income Security Act of 1974 (P.L. 93-406)

P.L. 93-406, §1031(b)(1):

Amended Code Sec. 6652 by adding subsection (e). **Effective** 9-2-74.

* * *

[Sec. 6653]

SEC. 6653. FAILURE TO PAY STAMP TAX.

Any person (as defined in section 6671(b)) who—

(1) willfully fails to pay any tax imposed by this title which is payable by stamp, coupons, tickets, books, or other devices or methods prescribed by this title or by regulations under the authority of this title, or

(2) willfully attempts in any manner to evade or defeat any such tax or the payment thereof, shall, in addition to other penalties provided by law, be liable for a penalty of 50 percent of the total amount of the underpayment of the tax.

Amendments

• 1989, Omnibus Budget Reconciliation Act of 1989 (P.L. 101-239)

P.L. 101-239, §7721(c)(1):

Amended Code Sec. 6653. **Effective** for returns the due date for which (determined without regard to extensions) is after 12-31-89. Prior to amendment, Code Sec. 6653 read as follows:

SEC. 6653. ADDITIONS TO TAX FOR NEGLIGENCE AND FRAUD.

[Sec. 6653(a)]

(a) NEGLIGENCE.—

(1) IN GENERAL.—If any part of any underpayment (as defined in subsection (c)) of tax required to be shown on a return is due to negligence (or disregard of rules or regulations), there shall be added to the tax an amount equal to 5 percent of the underpayment.

(2) UNDERPAYMENT TAKEN INTO ACCOUNT REDUCED BY PORTION ATTRIBUTABLE TO FRAUD.—There shall not be taken into account under this subsection any portion of an underpayment attributable to fraud with respect to which a penalty is imposed under subsection (b).

(3) NEGLIGENCE.—For purposes of this subsection, the term "negligence" includes any failure to make a reasonable attempt to comply with the provisions of this title, and the term "disregard" includes any careless, reckless, or intentional disregard.

Amendments

• 1988, Technical and Miscellaneous Revenue Act of 1988 (P.L. 100-647)

P.L. 100-647, §1015(b)(2)(A):

Amended Code Sec. 6653(a)(1). **Effective** for returns the due date for which (determined without regard to extensions) is after 12-31-88. Prior to amendment, Code Sec. 6653(a)(1) read as follows:

(1) IN GENERAL.—If any part of any underpayment (as defined in subsection (c)) is due to negligence or disregard of rules or regulations, there shall be added to the tax an amount equal to the sum of—

(A) 5 percent of the underpayment, and

(B) an amount equal to 50 percent of the interest payable under section 6601 with respect to the portion of such underpayment which is attributable to negligence for the period beginning on the last date prescribed by law for payment of such underpayment (determined without regard to any extension) and ending on the date of the assessment of the tax (or, if earlier, the date of the payment of the tax).

• 1986, Tax Reform Act of 1986 (P.L. 99-514)

P.L. 99-514, §1503(a):

Amended Code Sec. 6653 by striking out subsection (a) and inserting a new subsection (a). **Effective** for returns, the due date for which (determined without regard to extensions) is after 12-31-86. Prior to amendment, Code Sec. 6653(a) read as follows:

(a) NEGLIGENCE OR INTENTIONAL DISREGARD OF RULES AND REGULATIONS WITH RESPECT TO INCOME, GIFT, OR WINDFALL PROFIT TAXES.—

(1) IN GENERAL.—If any part of any underpayment (as defined in subsection (c)(1)) of any tax imposed by subtitle A, by chapter 12 of subtitle B or by chapter 45 (relating to windfall profit tax) is due to negligence or intentional disregard of rules or regulations (but without intent to defraud), there shall be added to the tax an amount equal to 5 percent of the underpayment.

(2) ADDITIONAL AMOUNT FOR PORTION ATTRIBUTABLE TO NEGLIGENCE, ETC.—There shall be added to the tax (in addition to

the amount determined under paragraph (1)) an amount equal to 50 percent of the interest payable under section 6601—

(A) with respect to the portion of the underpayment described in paragraph (1) which is attributable to the negligence or intentional disregard referred to in paragraph (1), and

(B) for the period beginning on the last date prescribed by law for payment of such underpayment (determined without regard to any extension) and ending on the date of the assessment of the tax (or, if earlier, the date of the payment of the tax).

P.L. 99-514, §1503(d)(1):

Amended the heading for Code Sec. 6653. **Effective** for returns, the due date for which (determined without regard to extensions) is after 12-31-86. Prior to amendment, the heading for Code Sec. 6653 read as follows:

SEC. 6653. FAILURE TO PAY TAX.

• 1983, Technical Corrections Act of 1982 (P.L. 97-448)

P.L. 97-448, §107(a)(3):

Amended Code Sec. 6653(a)(2)(B) by inserting "(or, if earlier, the date of the payment of the tax)" after "assessment of the tax". **Effective** as if included in the provision of P.L. 97-34 to which it relates.

• 1981, Economic Recovery Tax Act of 1981 (P.L. 97-34)

P.L. 97-34, §722(b)(1):

Amended Code Sec 6653(a). **Effective** for taxes the last date prescribed for payment of which is after 12-31-81. Prior to amendment, Code Sec. 6653(a) read as follows:

(a) NEGLIGENCE OR INTENTIONAL DISREGARD OF RULES AND REGULATIONS WITH RESPECT TO INCOME, GIFT, OR WINDFALL PROFIT TAXES.—If any part of any underpayment (as defined in subsection (c)(1)) of any tax imposed by subtitle A, by chapter 12 of subtitle B (relating to income taxes and gift taxes), or by chapter 45 (relating to windfall profit tax) is due to negligence or intentional disregard of rules and regulations (but without intent to defraud), there shall be added to the tax an amount equal to 5 percent of the underpayment.

• 1980, Crude Oil Windfall Profit Tax Act of 1980 (P.L. 96-223)

P.L. 96-223, §101(f)(8):

Amended Code Sec. 6653(a) by striking out "or by chapter 12" and inserting ", by chapter 12", by striking out "is due" and inserting ", or by chapter 45 (relating to windfall profit tax) is due", and by striking out "OR GIFT" in the subsection heading and inserting ", GIFT, OR WINDFALL PROFIT". For the **effective** date and transitional rules, see P.L. 96-223, Act Sec. 101(i), following Code Sec. 4986.

[Sec. 6653(b)]

(b) FRAUD.—

(1) IN GENERAL.—If any part of any underpayment (as defined in subsection (c)) of tax required to be shown on a return is due to fraud, there shall be added to the tax an amount equal to 75 percent of the portion of the underpayment which is attributable to fraud.

(2) DETERMINATION OF PORTION ATTRIBUTABLE TO FRAUD.—If the Secretary establishes that any portion of an underpayment is attributable to fraud, the entire underpayment shall be treated as attributable to fraud, except with respect to any portion of the underpayment which the taxpayer establishes is not attributable to fraud.

(3) SPECIAL RULE FOR JOINT RETURNS.—In the case of a joint return, this subsection shall not apply with respect to a spouse unless some part of the underpayment is due to the fraud of such spouse.

Amendments

• 1988, Technical and Miscellaneous Revenue Act of 1988 (P.L. 100-647)

P.L. 100-647, §1015(b)(2)(B):

Amended Code Sec. 6653(b)(1). **Effective** for returns the due date for which (determined without regard to extensions) is after 12-31-88. Prior to amendment, Code Sec. 6653(b)(1) read as follows:

(1) IN GENERAL.—If any part of any underpayment (as defined in subsection (c)) of tax required to be shown on a return is due to fraud, there shall be added to the tax an amount equal to the sum of—

(A) 75 percent of the portion of the underpayment which is attributable to fraud, and

(B) an amount equal to 50 percent of the interest payable under section 6601 with respect to such portion for the period beginning on the last day prescribed by law for payment of such underpayment (determined without regard to any extension) and ending on the date of the assessment of the tax or, if earlier, the date of the payment of the tax.

• 1986, Tax Reform Act of 1986 (P.L. 99-514)

P.L. 99-514, §1503(a):

Amended by Code Sec. 6653 by striking out subsection (b) and inserting new subsection (b). **Effective** for returns the due date for which (determined without regard to extensions) is after 12-31-86. Prior to amendment, Code Sec. 6653(b) read as follows:

(b) FRAUD.—

(1) IN GENERAL.—If any part of any underpayment (as defined in subsection (c)) of tax required to be shown on a return is due to fraud, there shall be added to the tax an amount equal to 50 percent of the underpayment.

(2) ADDITIONAL AMOUNT FOR PORTION ATTRIBUTABLE TO FRAUD.—There shall be added to the tax (in addition to the amount determined under paragraph (1)) an amount equal to 50 percent of the interest payable under section 6601—

(A) with respect to the portion of the underpayment described in paragraph (1) which is attributable to fraud, and

(B) for the period beginning on the last day prescribed by law for payment of such underpayment (determining without regard to any extension) and ending on the date of the assessment of the tax (or, if earlier, the date of the payment of the tax).

(3) NO NEGLIGENCE ADDITION WHEN THERE IS ADDITION FOR FRAUD.—The addition to tax under this subsection shall be in lieu of any amount determined under subsection (a).

(4) SPECIAL RULE FOR JOINT RETURNS.—In the case of a joint return under section 6013, this subsection shall not apply with respect to the tax of the spouse unless some part of the underpayment is due to the fraud of such spouse.

• 1982, Tax Equity and Fiscal Responsibility Act of 1982 (P.L. 97-248)

P.L. 97-248, §325(a):

Amended Code Sec. 6653(b). **Effective** with respect to taxes the last day prescribed by law for payment of which (determined without regard to any extension) is after 9-3-82. Prior to amendment, Code Sec. 6653(b) read as follows:

(b) FRAUD.—If any part of any underpayment (as defined in subsection (c)) of tax required to be shown on a return is due to fraud, there shall be added to the tax an amount equal to 50 percent of the underpayment. In the case of income taxes and gift taxes, this amount shall be in lieu of any amount determined under subsection (a). In the case of a joint return under section 6013, this subsection shall not apply with respect to the tax of a spouse unless some part of the underpayment is due to the fraud of such spouse.

• 1971 (P.L. 91-679)

P.L. 91-679, §2:

Amended subsection 6653(b) by adding new sentence at the end thereof. **Effective** for all tax years in which the Internal Revenue Code of 1954 applies. Corresponding provisions shall be deemed to be included in the Internal Revenue Code of 1939 and shall apply to all tax years to which such Code applies.

[Sec. 6653(c)]

(c) DEFINITION OF UNDERPAYMENT.—For purposes of this section, the term "underpayment" means—

(1) INCOME, ESTATE, GIFT, AND CERTAIN EXCISE TAXES.—In the case of a tax to which section 6211 (relating to income, estate, gift, and certain excise taxes) is applicable, a deficiency as defined in that section (except that, for this purpose, the tax shown on a return referred to in section 6211(a)(1)(A) shall be taken into account only if such return was filed on or before the last day prescribed for the filing of such return, determined with regard to any extension of time for such filing), and

(2) OTHER TAXES.—In the case of any other tax, the amount by which such tax imposed by this title exceeds the excess of—

(A) The sum of—

(i) The amount shown as the tax by the taxpayer upon his return (determined without regard to any credit for an overpayment for any prior period, and without regard to any adjustment under authority of sections 6205(a) and 6413(a)), if a return was made by the taxpayer within the time prescribed for filing such return (determined with regard to any extension of time for such filing) and an amount was shown as the tax by the taxpayer thereon, plus

(ii) Any amount, not shown on the return, paid in respect of such tax, over—

(B) The amount of rebates made.

For purposes of subparagraph (B), the term "rebate" means so much of an abatement, credit, refund, or other repayment, as was made on the ground that the tax imposed was less than the excess of the amount specified in subparagraph (A) over the rebates previously made.

Amendments

• 1974, Employee Retirement Income Security Act of 1974 (P.L. 93-406)

P.L. 93-406, §1016(a)(18):

Amended Code Sec. 6653(c)(1) by changing "chapter 42" to "certain excise". For **effective** date, see amendment note for Code Sec. 410.

• 1969, Tax Reform Act of 1969 (P.L. 91-172)

P.L. 91-172, §101(j)(50):

Amended Code Sec. 6653(c)(1) by substituting in the heading thereof "GIFT, AND CHAPTER 42 TAXES" for "AND GIFT TAXES" and by substituting in the body thereof "gift, and chapter 42 taxes" for "and gift taxes". **Effective** 1-1-70.

• 1958, Technical Amendments Act of 1958 (P.L. 85-866)

P.L. 85-866, §86:

Amended paragraph (1) of Sec. 6653(c) by inserting "on or" after the phrase "such return was filed". **Effective** 1-1-54.

[Sec. 6653(d)]

(d) NO DELINQUENCY PENALTY IF FRAUD ASSESSED.—If any penalty is assessed under subsection (b) (relating to fraud) for an underpayment of tax which is required to be shown on a return, no penalty under section 6651 (relating to failure to file such return or pay tax) shall be assessed with respect to the portion of the underpayment which is attributable to fraud.

Amendments

• 1986, Tax Reform Act of 1986 (P.L. 99-514)

P.L. 99-514, §1503(c)(2):

Amended Code Sec. 6653(d) by striking out "same underpayment" and inserting in lieu thereof "portion of the underpayment which is attributable to fraud". **Effective** for returns the due date for which (determined without regard to extensions) is after 12-31-86.

• 1969, Tax Reform Act of 1969 (P.L. 91-172)

P.L. 91-172, §943(c)(6):

Amended Sec. 6653(d) by inserting "or pay tax" immediately following "such return". **Effective** with respect to returns the date prescribed by law (without regard to any extension of time) for filing of which is after 12-31-69, and with respect to notices and demands for payment of tax made after 12-31-69.

[Sec. 6653(e)]

(e) FAILURE TO PAY STAMP TAX.—Any person (as defined in section 6671 (b)) who willfully fails to pay any tax imposed by this title which is payable by stamp, coupons, tickets, books, or other devices or methods prescribed by this title or by regulations under authority of this title, or willfully attempts in any manner to evade or defeat any such tax or the payment thereof, shall, in addition to other penalties provided by law, be liable to a penalty of 50 percent of the total amount of the underpayment of the tax.

[Sec. 6653(f)]

(f) SPECIAL RULE IN CASES OF FAILURE TO REPORT UNRECOGNIZED GAIN ON POSITION IN PERSONAL PROPERTY.—If—

(1) a taxpayer fails to make the report required under section 1092(a)(3)(B) in the manner prescribed by such section and such failure is not due to reasonable cause, and

(2) such taxpayer has an underpayment of any tax attributable (in whole or in part) to the denial of a deduction of a loss with respect to any position (within the meaning of section 1092(d)(2)),

then such underpayment shall, for purposes of subsection (a), be treated as an underpayment due to negligence.

Amendments

• 1986, Tax Reform Act of 1986 (P.L. 99-514)

P.L. 99-514, §1503(c)(3):

Amended Code Sec. 6653(f) by striking out "or intentional disregard of rules and regulations (but without intent to defraud)" following "negligence". **Effective** for returns the due date for which (determined without regard to extensions) is after 12-31-86.

• 1983, Technical Corrections Act of 1982 (P.L. 97-448)

P.L. 97-448, §105(a)(1)(D)(i):

Amended Code Sec. 6653 by redesignating subsection (g) as subsection (f). **Effective** as if included in the provision of P.L. 97-34 to which it relates.

P.L. 97-448, §105(a)(1)(D)(ii):

Amended the subsection heading of Code Sec. 6653(f) by striking out "Unrealized" and inserting in lieu thereof "Unrecognized". **Effective** as if included in the provision of P.L. 97-34 to which it relates.

• 1981, Economic Recovery Tax Act of 1981 (P.L. 97-34)

P.L. 97-34, §501(b):

Added Code Sec. 6653(g)[f]. **Effective** for property acquired or positions established after 6-23-81, in tax years ending after that date.

[Sec. 6653(g)]

(g) SPECIAL RULE FOR AMOUNTS SHOWN ON INFORMATION RETURNS.—If—

(1) any amount is shown on—

(A) an information return (as defined is section 6724(d)(1)), or

(B) a return filed under section 6031, section 6037, section 6012(a) by an estate or trust, section 6050B, or section 6050E, and

(2) the payee (or other person with respect to whom the return is made) fails to properly show such amount on his return,

any portion of an underpayment attributable to such failure shall be treated, for purposes of subsection (a), as due to negligence in the absence of clear and convincing evidence to the contrary. If any penalty is imposed under subsection (a) by reason of the preceding sentence, only the portion of the underpayment which is attributable to the failure described in the preceding sentence shall be taken into account in determining the amount of the penalty under subsection (a).

Amendments

• 1988, Technical and Miscellaneous Revenue Act of 1988 (P.L. 100-647)

P.L. 100-647, §1015(b)(3):

Amended Code Sec. 6653(g) by adding at the end thereof a new sentence. **Effective** as if included in the provision of P.L. 99-514 to which it relates.

• 1986, Tax Reform Act of 1986 (P.L. 99-514)

P.L. 99-514, §1503(b):

Amended Code Sec. 6653(g). **Effective** for returns the due date for which (determined without regard to extensions) is after 12-31-86. Prior to amendment, Code Sec. 6653(g) read as follows:

(g) SPECIAL RULE IN THE CASE OF INTEREST OR DIVIDEND PAYMENTS.—

(1) IN GENERAL.—If—

(A) any payment is shown on a return made by the payor under section 6042(a), 6044(a), or 6049(a) and

(B) the payee fails to include any portion of such payment in gross income, any portion of an underpayment attributable to such failure shall be treated, for purposes of subsection (a), as due to negligence in the absence of clear and convincing evidence to the contrary.

(2) PENALTY TO APPLY ONLY TO PORTION OF UNDERPAYMENT DUE TO FAILURE TO INCLUDE INTEREST OR DIVIDEND PAYMENT.—If any penalty is imposed under subsection (a) by reason of paragraph (1), the amount of the penalty imposed by paragraph (1) of subsection (a), shall be 5 percent of the portion of the underpayment which is attributable to the failure described in paragraph (1).

• 1983, Interest and Dividend Tax Compliance Act of 1983 (P.L. 98-67)

P.L. 98-67, §106:

Added Code Sec. 6653(g). **Effective** with respect to payments made after 12-31-83.

[Sec. 6653(h)—Repealed]

Amendments

• 1985 (P.L. 99-44)

P.L. 99-44, §1(b):

Repealed P.L. 98-369, §179(b)(3), which amended Code Sec. 6653 by adding at the end thereof subsection (h). **Effective** as if included in the amendments made by P.L. 98-369, §179(b)(3), and the Internal Revenue Code of 1954 shall be applied and administered as if such paragraph (and the amendment made by such paragraph) had not been enacted. Prior to repeal, Code Sec. 6653(h) read as follows:

(h) SPECIAL RULE IN THE CASE OF UNDERPAYMENT ATTRIBUTABLE TO FAILURE TO MEET CERTAIN SUBSTANTIATION REQUIREMENTS.—

(1) IN GENERAL.—Any portion of an underpayment attributable to a failure to comply with the requirements of section 274(d) shall be treated, for purposes of subsection (a), as due to negligence in the absence of clear and convincing evidence to the contrary.

(2) PENALTY TO APPLY ONLY TO PORTION OF UNDERPAYMENT DUE TO FAILURE TO MEET SUBSTANTIATION REQUIREMENTS.—If any penalty is imposed under subsection (a) by reason of paragraph (1), the amount of the penalty imposed by paragraph (1) of subsection (a) shall be 5 percent of the portion of the underpayment which is attributable to the failure described in paragraph (1).

P.L. 99-44, §1(c), provides:

(c) REPEAL OF REGULATIONS.—Regulations issued before the date of the enactment of this Act to carry out the amendments made by paragraphs (1)(C), (2), and (3) of section 179(b) of the Tax Reform Act of 1984 shall have no force and effect.

P.L. 99-44, §5, provides:

Not later than October 1, 1985, the Secretary of the Treasury or his delegate shall prescribe regulations to carry out the provisions of this Act which shall fully reflect such provisions.

• 1984, Deficit Reduction Act of 1984 (P.L. 98-369)

P.L. 98-369, §179(b)(3):

Amended Code Sec. 6653 by adding new subsection (h). **Effective** for tax years beginning after 12-31-84.

* * *

[Sec. 6657]

SEC. 6657. BAD CHECKS.

If any instrument in payment, by any commercially acceptable means, of any amount receivable under this title is not duly paid, in addition to any other penalties provided by law, there shall be paid as a penalty by the person who tendered such instrument, upon notice and demand by the Secretary, in the same manner as tax, an amount equal to 2 percent of the amount of such instrument, except that if the amount of such instrument is less than $1,250, the penalty under this section shall be $25 or the amount of such instrument, whichever is the lesser. This section shall not apply if the person tendered such instrument in good faith and with reasonable cause to believe that it would be duly paid.

Amendments

• 2010, Homebuyer Assistance and Improvement Act of 2010 (P.L. 111-198)

P.L. 111-198, §3(a)(1)-(2):

Amended Code Sec. 6657 by striking "If any check or money order in payment of any amount" and inserting "If any instrument in payment, by any commercially acceptable means, of any amount", and by striking "such check" each place it appears and inserting "such instrument". **Effective** for instruments tendered after 7-2-2010.

• 2007, Small Business and Work Opportunity Tax Act of 2007 (P.L. 110-28)

P.L. 110-28, §8245(a)(1)-(2):

Amended Code Sec. 6657 by striking "$750" and inserting" $1,250", and by striking "$15" and inserting "$25". **Effective** for checks or money orders received after 5-25-2007.

• 1988, Technical and Miscellaneous Revenue Act of 1988 (P.L. 100-647)

P.L. 100-647, §5071(a)(1)-(3):

Amended Code Sec. 6657 by striking out "1 percent" and inserting in lieu thereof "2 percent", by striking out "$500" and inserting in lieu thereof "$750", and by striking out "$5" and inserting in lieu thereof "$15". **Effective** for checks or money orders received after 11-10-88.

• 1976, Tax Reform Act of 1976 (P.L. 94-455)

P.L. 94-455, §1906(b)(13)(A):

Amended 1954 Code by substituting "Secretary" for "Secretary or his delegate" each place it appeared. **Effective** 2-1-77.

* * *

[Sec. 6659—Repealed]

Amendments

• 1989, Omnibus Budget Reconciliation Act of 1989 (P.L. 101-239)

P.L. 101-239, §7721(c)(2):

Repealed Code Sec. 6659. **Effective** for returns the due date for which (determined without regard to extensions) is after 12-31-89. Prior to repeal, Code Sec. 6659 read as follows:

SEC. 6659. ADDITION TO TAX IN THE CASE OF VALUATION OVERSTATEMENTS FOR PURPOSES OF THE INCOME TAX.

[Sec. 6659(a)]

(a) ADDITION TO THE TAX.—If—

(1) an individual, or

(2) a closely held corporation or a personal service corporation,

has an underpayment of the tax imposed by chapter 1 for the taxable year which is attributable to a valuation overstatement, then there shall be added to the tax an amount equal to the applicable percentage of the underpayment so attributable.

[Sec. 6659(b)]

(b) APPLICABLE PERCENTAGE DEFINED.—For purposes of subsection (a), the applicable percentage shall be determined under the following table:

If the valuation claimed is the following percent of the correct valuation—	The applicable percentage is:
150 percent or more but not more than 200 percent	10
More than 200 percent but not more than 250 percent	20
More than 250 percent	30

[Sec. 6659(c)]

(c) VALUATION OVERSTATEMENT DEFINED.—For purposes of this section, there is a valuation overstatement if the value of any property, or the adjusted basis of any property, claimed on any return is 150 percent or more of the amount determined to be the correct amount of such valuation or adjusted basis (as the case may be).

Amendments

• 1984, Deficit Reduction Act of 1984 (P.L. 98-369)

P.L. 98-369, §155(c)(1)(A):

Amended Code Sec. 6659(c). Prior to amendment, Code Sec. 6659(c) read as follows:

(c) Valuation Overstatement Defined.—

(1) In General.—For purposes of this section, there is a valuation overstatement if the value of any property, or the adjusted basis of any property, claimed on any return is 150 percent or more of the amount determined to be the correct amount of such valuation or adjusted basis (as the case may be).

(2) Property Must Have Been Acquired Within Last 5 Years.—This section shall not apply to any property which, as of the close of the taxable year for which there is a valuation overstatement, has been held by the taxpayer for more than 5 years.

[Sec. 6659(d)]

(d) UNDERPAYMENT MUST BE AT LEAST $1,000.—This section shall not apply if the underpayment for the taxable year attributable to valuation overstatements is less than $1,000.

[Sec. 6659(e)]

(e) AUTHORITY TO WAIVE.—The Secretary may waive all or any part of the addition to the tax provided by this section on a showing by the taxpayer that there was a reasonable basis for the valuation or adjusted basis claimed on the return and that such claim was made in good faith.

[Sec. 6659(f)]

(f) SPECIAL RULES FOR OVERSTATEMENT OF CHARITABLE DEDUCTION.—

(1) AMOUNT OF APPLICABLE PERCENTAGE.—In the case of any underpayment attributable to a valuation overstatement with respect to charitable deduction property, the applicable percentage for purposes of subsection (a) shall be 30 percent.

(2) LIMITATION ON AUTHORITY TO WAIVE.—In the case of any underpayment attributable to a valuation overstatement with respect to charitable deduction property, the Secretary may not waive any portion of the addition to tax provided by this section unless the Secretary determines that—

(A) the claimed value of the property was based on a qualified appraisal made by a qualified appraiser, and

(B) in addition to obtaining such appraisal, the taxpayer made a good faith investigation of the value of the contributed property.

(3) DEFINITIONS.—For purposes of this subsection—

(A) CHARITABLE DEDUCTION PROPERTY.—The term "charitable deduction property" means any property contributed by the taxpayer in a contribution for which a deduction was claimed under section 170. For purposes of paragraph (2), such term shall not include any securities for which (as of the date of the contribution) market quotations are readily available on an established securities market.

(B) QUALIFIED APPRAISER.—The term "qualified appraiser" means any appraiser meeting the requirements of the regulations prescribed under section 170(a)(1).

(C) QUALIFIED APPRAISAL.—The term "qualified appraisal" means any appraisal meeting the requirements of the regulations prescribed under section 170(a)(1).

Amendments

• 1984, Deficit Reduction Act of 1984 (P.L. 98-369)

P.L. 98-369, §155(c)(1)(B):

Amended Code Sec. 6659 by redesignating subsection (f) as subsection (g) and adding new subsection (f). **Effective** for returns filed after 12-31-84.

[Sec. 6659(g)]

(g) OTHER DEFINITIONS.—For purposes of this section—

(1) UNDERPAYMENT.—The term "underpayment" has the meaning given to such term by section 6653(c)(1).

(2) CLOSELY HELD CORPORATION.—The term "closely held corporation" means any corporation described in section 465(a)(1)(B).

(3) PERSONAL SERVICE CORPORATION.—The term "personal service corporation" means any corporation which is a service organization (within the meaning of section 414(m)(3)).

Amendments

• 1984, Deficit Reduction Act of 1984 (P.L. 98-369)

P.L. 98-369, §155(c)(1)(B):

Amended Code Sec. 6659 by redesignating subsection (f) as subsection (g). **Effective** for returns filed after 12-31-84.

P.L. 98-369, §721(x)(4):

Amended Code Sec. 6659(f), prior to redesignation by Act Sec. 155(c)(1)(B), by striking out "section 465(a)(1)(C)" and inserting in lieu thereof "section 465(a)(1)(B)". **Effective** as if included in P.L. 97-354.

• 1983, Technical Corrections Act of 1982 (P.L. 97-448)

P.L. 97-448, §107(a)(1):

Amended Code Sec. 6659(d) by striking out "the valuation overstatement" and inserting in lieu thereof "valuation overstatements". **Effective** as if included in the provision of P.L. 97-34 to which it relates.

P.L. 97-448, §107(a)(2):

Amended Code Sec. 6659(c)(1) by striking out "exceeds 150 percent of" and inserting in lieu thereof "is 150 percent or more of". **Effective** as if included in the provision of P.L. 97-34 to which it relates.

• 1981, Economic Recovery Tax Act of 1981 (P.L. 97-34)

P.L. 97-34, §722(a)(1):

Added Code Sec. 6659. **Effective** for returns filed after 12-31-81.

[Sec. 6659A—Repealed]

Amendments

• 1989, Omnibus Budget Reconciliation Act of 1989 (P.L. 101-239)

P.L. 101-239, §7721(c)(2):

Repealed Code Sec. 6659A. **Effective** for returns the due date for which (determined without regard to extensions) is after 12-31-89. Prior to repeal, Code Sec. 6659A read as follows:

SEC. 6659A. ADDITION TO TAX IN CASE OF OVERSTATEMENTS OF PENSION LIABILITIES.

(a) ADDITION TO TAX.—In the case of an underpayment of the tax imposed by chapter 1 on any taxpayer for the taxable year which is attributable to an overstatement of pension liabilities, there shall be added to such tax an amount equal to the applicable percentage of the underpayment so attributable.

(b) APPLICABLE PERCENTAGE DEFINED.—For purposes of subsection (a), the applicable percentage shall be determined under the following table:

If the valuation claimed is the following percent of the correct valuation—	*The applicable percentage is:*
150 percent or more but not more than 200 percent	10
More than 200 percent but not more than 250 percent	20
More than 250 percent	30

(c) OVERSTATEMENT OF PENSION LIABILITIES.—For purposes of this section, there is an overstatement of pension liabilities if the actuarial determination of the liabilities taken into account for purposes of computing the deduction under paragraph (1) or (2) of section 404(a) exceeds the amount determined to be the correct amount of such liability.

(d) UNDERPAYMENT MUST BE AT LEAST $1,000.—This section shall not apply if the underpayment for the taxable year attributable to valuation overstatements is less than $1,000.

(e) AUTHORITY TO WAIVE.—The Secretary may waive all or any part of the addition to the tax provided by this section on a showing by the taxpayer that there was a reasonable basis for the valuation claimed on the return and that such claim was made in good faith.

• 1986, Tax Reform Act of 1986 (P.L. 99-514)

P.L. 99-514, §1138(a):

Amended subchapter A of chapter 68 by inserting after section 6659 new section 6659A. **Effective** for overstatements made after 10-22-86.

[Sec. 6660—Repealed]

Amendments

• 1989, Omnibus Budget Reconciliation Act of 1989 (P.L. 101-239)

P.L. 101-239, §7721(c)(2):

Repealed Code Sec. 6660. **Effective** for returns the due date for which (determined without regard to extensions) is after 12-31-89. Prior to repeal, Code Sec. 6660 read as follows:

SEC. 6660. ADDITION TO TAX IN THE CASE OF VALUATION UNDERSTATEMENT FOR PURPOSES OF ESTATE OR GIFT TAXES.

(a) ADDITION TO THE TAX.—In the case of any underpayment of a tax imposed by subtitle B (relating to estate and gift taxes) which is attributable to a valuation understatement, there shall be added to the tax an amount equal to the applicable percentage of the underpayment so attributed.

(b) APPLICABLE PERCENTAGE.—For purposes of subsection (a), the applicable percentage shall be determined under the following table:

If the valuation claimed is the following percent of the correct valuation—	*The applicable percentage is:*
50 percent or more but not more than 66⅔ percent	10
40 percent of more but less than 50 percent	20
Less than 40 percent	30

(c) VALUATION UNDERSTATEMENT DEFINED.—For purposes of this section, there is a valuation understatement if the value of any property claimed on any return is 66⅔ percent or less of the amount determined to be the correct amount of such valuation.

(d) UNDERPAYMENT MUST BE AT LEAST $1,000.—This section shall not apply if the underpayment is less than $1,000 for any taxable period (or, in the case of the tax imposed by chapter 11, with respect to the estate of the decedent).

(e) AUTHORITY TO WAIVE.—The Secretary may waive all or any part of the addition to the tax provided by this section on a showing by the taxpayer that there was a reasonable basis for the valuation claimed on the return and that such claim was made in good faith.

(f) UNDERPAYMENT DEFINED.—For purposes of this section, the term "underpayment" has the meaning given to such term by section 6653(c)(1).

• 1986, Tax Reform Act of 1986 (P.L. 99-514)

P.L. 99-514, §1811(d):

Amended Code Sec. 6660 by adding at the end thereof new subsection (f). **Effective** as if included in the provision of P.L. 98-369 to which it relates.

P.L. 99-514, §1899A(57):

Amended Code Sec. 6660 by striking out "THE ESTATE" and inserting in lieu thereof "ESTATE" in the heading. **Effective** 10-22-86.

• 1984, Deficit Reduction Act of 1984 (P.L. 98-369)

P.L. 98-369, §155(c)(2)(A):

Added Code Sec. 6660. **Effective** for returns filed after 12-31-84.

[Sec. 6661—Repealed]

Amendments

• 1989, Omnibus Budget Reconciliation Act of 1989 (P.L. 101-239)

P.L. 101-239, §7721:

Repealed Code Sec. 6661. **Effective** for returns the due date for which (determined without regard to extensions) is after 12-31-89. Prior to repeal, Code Sec. 6661 read as follows:

SEC. 6661. SUBSTANTIAL UNDERSTATEMENT OF LIABILITY.

[Sec. 6661(a)]

(a) ADDITION TO TAX.—If there is a substantial understatement of income tax for any taxable year, there shall be added to the tax an amount equal to 25 percent of the amount of any underpayment attributable to such understatement.

Amendments

• 1986, Tax Reform Act of 1986 (P.L. 99-514)

P.L. 99-514, §1504(a) (repealed by P.L. 99-509, §8002(c)):

Amended Code Sec. 6661(a) by striking out "10 percent" and inserting in lieu thereof "20 percent" [see amendment note below.—CCH.] **Effective** for returns the due date for which (determined without regard to extensions) is after 12-31-86.

• 1986, Omnibus Budget Reconciliation Act of 1986 (P.L. 99-509)

P.L. 99-509, §8002(a):

Amended Code Sec. 6661(a). **Effective** for penalties assessed after 10-21-86. Prior to the repeal of P.L. 99-514, §1504(a), Code Sec. 6661(a) read as follows:

(a) ADDITION TO TAX.—If there is a substantial understatement of income tax for any taxable year, there shall be added to the tax an amount equal to 20 percent of the amount of any underpayment attributable to such understatement.

[Sec. 6661(b)]

(b) DEFINITION AND SPECIAL RULE.—

(1) SUBSTANTIAL UNDERSTATEMENT.—

(A) IN GENERAL.—For purposes of this section, there is a substantial understatement of income tax for any taxable year if the amount of the understatement for the taxable year exceeds the greater of—

(i) 10 percent of the tax required to be shown on the return for the taxable year, or

(ii) $5,000.

(B) SPECIAL RULE FOR CORPORATIONS.—In the case of a corporation other than an S corporation or a personal holding company (as defined in section 542), paragraph (1) shall be applied by substituting "$10,000" for "$5,000".

(2) UNDERSTATEMENT.—

(A) IN GENERAL.—For purposes of paragraph (1), the term "Understatement" means the excess of—

(i) the amount of the tax required to be shown on the return for the taxable year, over

(ii) the amount of the tax imposed which is shown on the return, reduced by any rebate (within the meaning of section 6211(b)(2)).

(B) REDUCTION FOR UNDERSTATEMENT DUE TO POSITION OF TAXPAYER OR DISCLOSED ITEM.—The amount of the understatement under subparagraph (A) shall be reduced by that portion of the understatement which is attributable to—

(i) the tax treatment of any item by the taxpayer if there is or was substantial authority for such treatment, or

(ii) any item with respect to which the relevant facts affecting the item's tax treatment are adequately disclosed in the return or in a statement attached to the return.

(C) SPECIAL RULES IN CASES INVOLVING TAX SHELTERS.—

(i) IN GENERAL.—In the case of any item attributable to a tax shelter—

(I) subparagraph (B)(ii) shall not apply, and

(II) subparagraph (B)(i) shall not apply unless (in addition to meeting the requirements of such subparagraph) the taxpayer reasonably believed that the tax treatment of such item by the taxpayer was more likely than not the proper treatment.

(ii) TAX SHELTER.—For purposes of clause (i), the term "tax shelter" means—

(I) a partnership or other entity,

(II) any investment plan or arrangement, or

(III) any other plan or arrangement,

if the principal purpose of such partnership, entity, plan, or arrangement is the avoidance or evasion of Federal income tax.

(3) COORDINATION WITH PENALTY IMPOSED BY SECTION 6659.—For purposes of determining the amount of the addition to tax assessed under subsection (a), there shall not be taken into account that portion of the substantial understatement on which a penalty is imposed under section 6659 (relating to addition to tax in the case of valuation overstatements).

[Sec. 6661(c)]

(c) AUTHORITY TO WAIVE.—The Secretary may waive all or any part of the addition to tax provided by this section on a showing by the taxpayer that there was reasonable cause for the understatement (or part thereof) and that the taxpayer acted in good faith.

Amendments

• 1984, Deficit Reduction Act of 1984 (P.L. 98-369)

P.L. 98-369, §714(h)(3):

Amended Code Sec. 6661(b)(2)(A)(ii) by inserting ", reduced by any rebate (within the meaning of section 6211(b)(2))" after "return". **Effective** as if included in the provision of P.L. 97-248 to which it relates.

• 1982, Subchapter S Revision Act of 1982 (P.L. 97-354)

P.L. 97-354, §5(a)(42):

Amended Code Sec. 6661(b)(1)(B) by striking out "an electing small business corporation (as defined in section 1371(b))" and inserting in lieu thereof "an S corporation". **Effective** for tax years beginning after 12-31-82.

• 1982, Tax Equity and Fiscal Responsibility Act of 1982 (P.L. 97-248)

P.L. 97-248, §323(a):

Added Code Sec. 6661. **Effective** for returns the due date (determined without regard to extension) for filing of which is after 12-31-82.

PART II—ACCURACY-RELATED AND FRAUD PENALTIES

[Sec. 6662]

SEC. 6662. IMPOSITION OF ACCURACY-RELATED PENALTY ON UNDERPAYMENTS.

[Sec. 6662(a)]

(a) IMPOSITION OF PENALTY.—If this section applies to any portion of an underpayment of tax required to be shown on a return, there shall be added to the tax an amount equal to 20 percent of the portion of the underpayment to which this section applies.

Amendments

• 2004, American Jobs Creation Act of 2004 (P.L. 108-357)

P.L. 108-357, §812(e)(1):

Amended the heading for Code Sec. 6662. **Effective** for tax years ending after 10-22-2004. Prior to amendment, the heading for Code Sec. 6662 read as follows:

SEC. 6662. IMPOSITION OF ACCURACY-RELATED PENALTY.

[Sec. 6662(b)]

(b) PORTION OF UNDERPAYMENT TO WHICH SECTION APPLIES.—This section shall apply to the portion of any underpayment which is attributable to 1 or more of the following:

(1) Negligence or disregard of rules or regulations.

(2) Any substantial understatement of income tax.

(3) Any substantial valuation misstatement under chapter 1.

(4) Any substantial overstatement of pension liabilities.

(5) Any substantial estate or gift tax valuation understatement.

(6) Any disallowance of claimed tax benefits by reason of a transaction lacking economic substance (within the meaning of section 7701(o)) or failing to meet the requirements of any similar rule of law.

(7) Any undisclosed foreign financial asset understatement.

(8) Any inconsistent estate basis.

(9) Any overstatement of the deduction provided in section 170(p).

(10) Any disallowance of a deduction by reason of section 170(h)(7).

This section shall not apply to any portion of an underpayment on which a penalty is imposed under section 6663. Except as provided in paragraph (1) or (2)(B) of section 6662A(e), this section shall not apply to the portion of any underpayment which is attributable to a reportable transaction understatement on which a penalty is imposed under section 6662A.

Amendments

• 2022, SECURE 2.0 Act of 2022 (P.L. 117-328)

P.L. 117-328, §605(a)(2)(A):

Amended Code Sec. 6662(b) by inserting after paragraph (9) a new paragraph (10). **Effective** for contributions made after 12-29-2022. For a special rule, see Act Sec. 605(c)(2), below.

P.L. 117-328, §605(c)(2), provides:

(2) NO INFERENCE.—No inference is intended as to the appropriate treatment of contributions made in taxable years ending on or before the date specified in paragraph (1), or as to any contribution for which a deduction is not disallowed by reason of section 170(h)(7) of the Internal Revenue Code of 1986, as added by this section.

• 2020, Taxpayer Certainty and Disaster Tax Relief Act of 2020 (P.L. 116-260)

P.L. 116-260, §212(b)(1), Div. EE:

Amended Code Sec. 6662(b) by inserting after paragraph (8) a new paragraph (9). **Effective** for tax years beginning after 12-31-2020.

• 2015, Surface Transportation and Veterans Health Care Choice Improvement Act of 2015 (P.L. 114-41)

P.L. 114-41, §2004(c)(1):

Amended Code Sec. 6662(b) by inserting after paragraph (7) a new paragraph (8). **Effective** for property with respect to which an estate tax return is filed after 7-31-2015.

• 2010, Health Care and Education Reconciliation Act of 2010 (P.L. 111-152)

P.L. 111-152, §1409(b)(1):

Amended Code Sec. 6662(b) by inserting after paragraph (5) a new paragraph (6). **Effective** for underpayments attributable to transactions entered into after 3-30-2010.

• 2010, Hiring Incentives to Restore Employment Act (P.L. 111-147)

P.L. 111-147, §512(a)(1) (as amended by P.L. 113-295, §208(a), Division A):

Amended Code Sec. 6662, as amended by this Act, in subsection (b) by inserting after paragraph (5) a new paragraph (7). **Effective** for tax years beginning after 3-18-2010.

• 2005, Gulf Opportunity Zone Act of 2005 (P.L. 109-135)

P.L. 109-135, §403(x)(1):

Amended Code Sec. 6662(b) by adding at the end a new sentence. **Effective** as if included in the provision of the American Jobs Creation Act of 2004 (P.L. 108-357) to which it relates [**effective** for tax years ending after 10-22-2004.—CCH].

• 1990, Omnibus Budget Reconciliation Act of 1990 (P.L. 101-508)

P.L. 101-508, §11312(b)(1):

Amended Code Sec. 6662(b)(3). **Effective** for tax years ending after 11-5-90. Prior to amendment, Code Sec. 6662(b)(3) read as follows:

(3) Any substantial valuation overstatement under chapter 1.

[Sec. 6662(c)]

(c) NEGLIGENCE.—For purposes of this section, the term "negligence" includes any failure to make a reasonable attempt to comply with the provisions of this title, and the term "disregard" includes any careless, reckless, or intentional disregard.

[Sec. 6662(d)]

(d) SUBSTANTIAL UNDERSTATEMENT OF INCOME TAX.—

(1) SUBSTANTIAL UNDERSTATEMENT.—

(A) IN GENERAL.—For purposes of this section, there is a substantial understatement of income tax for any taxable year if the amount of the understatement for the taxable year exceeds the greater of—

(i) 10 percent of the tax required to be shown on the return for the taxable year, or

(ii) $5,000.

(B) SPECIAL RULE FOR CORPORATIONS.—In the case of a corporation other than an S corporation or a personal holding company (as defined in section 542), there is a substantial understatement of income tax for any taxable year if the amount of the understatement for the taxable year exceeds the lesser of—

(i) 10 percent of the tax required to be shown on the return for the taxable year (or, if greater, $10,000), or

(ii) $10,000,000.

(C) SPECIAL RULE FOR TAXPAYERS CLAIMING SECTION 199A DEDUCTION.—In the case of any taxpayer who claims any deduction allowed under section 199A for the taxable year, subparagraph (A) shall be applied by substituting "5 percent" for "10 percent".

(2) UNDERSTATEMENT.—

(A) IN GENERAL.—For purposes of paragraph (1), the term "understatement" means the excess of—

(i) the amount of the tax required to be shown on the return for the taxable year, over

(ii) the amount of the tax imposed which is shown on the return, reduced by any rebate (within the meaning of section 6211(b)(2)).

The excess under the preceding sentence shall be determined without regard to items to which section 6662A applies.

(B) REDUCTION FOR UNDERSTATEMENT DUE TO POSITION OF TAXPAYER OR DISCLOSED ITEM.—The amount of the understatement under subparagraph (A) shall be reduced by that portion of the understatement which is attributable to—

(i) the tax treatment of any item by the taxpayer if there is or was substantial authority for such treatment, or

(ii) any item if—

(I) the relevant facts affecting the item's tax treatment are adequately disclosed in the return or in a statement attached to the return, and

(II) there is a reasonable basis for the tax treatment of such item by the taxpayer.

For purposes of clause (ii)(II), in no event shall a corporation be treated as having a reasonable basis for its tax treatment of an item attributable to a multiple-party financing transaction if such treatment does not clearly reflect the income of the corporation.

(C) REDUCTION NOT TO APPLY TO TAX SHELTERS.—

(i) IN GENERAL.—Subparagraph (B) shall not apply to any item attributable to a tax shelter.

(ii) TAX SHELTER.—For purposes of clause (i), the term "tax shelter" means—

(I) a partnership or other entity,

(II) any investment plan or arrangement, or

(III) any other plan or arrangement,

if a significant purpose of such partnership, entity, plan, or arrangement is the avoidance or evasion of Federal income tax.

(3) SECRETARIAL LIST.—The Secretary may prescribe a list of positions which the Secretary believes do not meet 1 or more of the standards specified in paragraph (2)(B)(i), section 6664(d)(3), and section 6694(a)(1). Such list (and any revisions thereof) shall be published in the Federal Register or the Internal Revenue Bulletin.

Amendments

• 2018, Consolidated Appropriations Act, 2018 (P.L. 115-141)

P.L. 115-141, §101(a)(2)(A), Div. T:

Amended Code Sec. 6662(d)(1)(C) by striking "the deduction" and inserting "any deduction". **Effective** as if included in section 11011 of Public Law 115–97 [**effective** for tax years beginning after 12-31-2017.—CCH].

• 2018, Tax Technical Corrections Act of 2018 (P.L. 115-141)

P.L. 115-141, §401(a)(303), Div. U:

Amended Code Sec. 6662(d)(3) by striking "section 6664(d)(2)" and inserting "section 6664(d)(3)". **Effective** 3-23-2018.

• 2017, Tax Cuts and Jobs Act (P.L. 115-97)

P.L. 115-97, §11011(c):

Amended Code Sec. 6662(d)(1) by inserting at the end a new subparagraph (C). **Effective** for tax years beginning after 12-31-2017.

• 2005, Gulf Opportunity Zone Act of 2005 (P.L. 109-135)

P.L. 109-135, §412(aaa):

Amended Code Sec. 6662(d)(3) by striking "the" before "1 or more". **Effective** 12-21-2005.

• 2004, American Jobs Creation Act of 2004 (P.L. 108-357)

P.L. 108-357, §812(b):

Amended Code Sec. 6662(d)(2)(A) by adding at the end a flush sentence. **Effective** for tax years ending after 10-22-2004.

P.L. 108-357, §812(d):

Amended Code Sec. 6662(d)(2)(C). **Effective** for tax years ending after 10-22-2004. Prior to amendment, Code Sec. 6662(d)(2)(C) read as follows:

(C) SPECIAL RULES IN CASES INVOLVING TAX SHELTERS.—

(i) IN GENERAL.—In the case of any item of a taxpayer other than a corporation which is attributable to a tax shelter—

(I) subparagraph (B)(ii) shall not apply, and

(II) subparagraph (B)(i) shall not apply unless (in addition to meeting the requirements of such subparagraph) the taxpayer reasonably believed that the tax treatment of such item by the taxpayer was more likely than not the proper treatment.

(ii) SUBPARAGRAPH (B) NOT TO APPLY TO CORPORATIONS.—Subparagraph (B) shall not apply to any item of a corporation which is attributable to a tax shelter.

(iii) TAX SHELTER.—For purposes of this subparagraph, the term "tax shelter" means—

(I) a partnership or other entity,

(II) any investment plan or arrangement, or

(III) any other plan or arrangement,

if a significant purpose of such partnership, entity, plan, or arrangement is the avoidance or evasion of Federal income tax.

P.L. 108-357, §819(a):

Amended Code Sec. 6662(d)(1)(B). **Effective** for tax years beginning after 10-22-2004. Prior to amendment, Code Sec. 6662(d)(1)(B) read as follows:

(B) SPECIAL RULE FOR CORPORATIONS.—In the case of a corporation other than an S corporation or a personal holding company (as defined in section 542), paragraph (1) shall be applied by substituting "$10,000" for "$5,000".

P.L. 108-357, §819(b)(1):

Amended Code Sec. 6662(d) by adding at the end a new paragraph (3). **Effective** for tax years beginning after 10-22-2004.

P.L. 108-357, §819(b)(2):

Amended Code Sec. 6662(d)(2) by striking subparagraph (D). **Effective** for tax years beginning after 10-22-2004. Prior to being stricken, Code Sec. 6662(d)(2)(D) read as follows:

(D) SECRETARIAL LIST.—The Secretary shall prescribe (and revise not less frequently than annually) a list of positions—

(i) for which the Secretary believes there is not substantial authority, and

(ii) which affect a significant number of taxpayers.

Such list (and any revision thereof) shall be published in the Federal Register.

• 1997, Taxpayer Relief Act of 1997 (P.L. 105-34)

P.L. 105-34, §1028(c)(1):

Amended Code Sec. 6662(d)(2)(B) by adding at the end a new flush sentence. **Effective** for items with respect to transactions entered into after 8-5-97.

P.L. 105-34, §1028(c)(2):

Amended Code Sec. 6662(d)(2)(C)(iii) by striking "the principal purpose" and inserting "a significant purpose". **Effective** for items with respect to transactions entered into after 8-5-97.

• 1994, Uruguay Round Agreements Act (P.L. 103-465)

P.L. 103-465, §744(a):

Amended Code Sec. 6662(d)(2)(C) by redesignating clause (ii) as clause (iii) and by inserting after clause (i) a new clause (ii). **Effective** for items related to transactions occurring after 12-8-94.

P.L. 103-465, §744(b)(1):

Amended Code Sec. 6662(d)(2)(C)(i) by striking "In the case of any item" and inserting "In the case of any item of a taxpayer other than a corporation which is". **Effective** for items related to transactions occurring after 12-8-94.

P.L. 103-465, §744(b)(2):

Amended Code Sec. 6662(d)(2)(C)(iii), as redesignated by Act Sec. 744(a), by striking "clause (i)" and inserting "this subparagraph". **Effective** for items related to transactions occurring after 12-8-94.

• 1993, Omnibus Budget Reconciliation Act of 1993 (P.L. 103-66)

P.L. 103-66, §13251(a):

Amended Code Sec. 6662(d)(2)(B)(ii). **Effective** for returns the due dates for which (determined without regard to extensions) are after 12-31-93. Prior to amendment, Code Sec. 6662(d)(2)(B)(ii) read as follows:

(ii) any item with respect to which the relevant facts affecting the item's tax treatment are adequately disclosed in the return or in a statement attached to the return.

[Sec. 6662(e)]

(e) SUBSTANTIAL VALUATION MISSTATEMENT UNDER CHAPTER 1.—

(1) IN GENERAL.—For purposes of this section, there is a substantial valuation misstatement under chapter 1 if—

(A) the value of any property (or the adjusted basis of any property) claimed on any return of tax imposed by chapter 1 is 150 percent or more of the amount determined to be the correct amount of such valuation or adjusted basis (as the case may be), or

(B)(i) the price for any property or services (or for the use of property) claimed on any such return in connection with any transaction between persons described in section 482 is 200 percent or more (or 50 percent or less) of the amount determined under section 482 to be the correct amount of such price, or

(ii) the net section 482 transfer price adjustment for the taxable year exceeds the lesser of $5,000,000 or 10 percent of the taxpayer's gross receipts.

(2) LIMITATION.—No penalty shall be imposed by reason of subsection (b)(3) unless the portion of the underpayment for the taxable year attributable to substantial valuation misstatements under chapter 1 exceeds $5,000 ($10,000 in the case of a corporation other than an S corporation or a personal holding company (as defined in section 542)).

(3) NET SECTION 482 TRANSFER PRICE ADJUSTMENT.—For purposes of this subsection—

(A) IN GENERAL.—The term "net section 482 transfer price adjustment" means, with respect to any taxable year, the net increase in taxable income for the taxable year (determined without regard to any amount carried to such taxable year from another taxable year) resulting from adjustments under section 482 in the price for any property or services (or for the use of property).

(B) CERTAIN ADJUSTMENTS EXCLUDED IN DETERMINING THRESHOLD.—For purposes of determining whether the threshold requirements of paragraph (1)(B)(ii) are met, the following shall be excluded:

(i) Any portion of the net increase in taxable income referred to in subparagraph (A) which is attributable to any redetermination of a price if—

(I) it is established that the taxpayer determined such price in accordance with a specific pricing method set forth in the regulations prescribed under section 482 and that the taxpayer's use of such method was reasonable,

(II) the taxpayer has documentation (which was in existence as of the time of filing the return) which sets forth the determination of such price in accordance with such a method and which establishes that the use of such method was reasonable, and

(III) the taxpayer provides such documentation to the Secretary within 30 days of a request for such documentation.

(ii) Any portion of the net increase in taxable income referred to in subparagraph (A) which is attributable to a redetermination of price where such price was not determined in accordance with such a specific pricing method if—

(I) the taxpayer establishes that none of such pricing methods was likely to result in a price that would clearly reflect income, the taxpayer used another pricing method to determine such price, and such other pricing method was likely to result in a price that would clearly reflect income,

(II) the taxpayer has documentation (which was in existence as of the time of filing the return) which sets forth the determination of such price in accordance with such other method and which establishes that the requirements of subclause (I) were satisfied, and

(III) the taxpayer provides such documentation to the Secretary within 30 days of a request for such documentation.

(iii) Any portion of such net increase which is attributable to any transaction solely between foreign corporations unless, in the case of any such corporations, the treatment of such transaction affects the determination of income from sources within the United States or taxable income effectively connected with the conduct of a trade or business within the United States.

(C) SPECIAL RULE.—If the regular tax (as defined in section 55(c)) imposed by chapter 1 on the taxpayer is determined by reference to an amount other than taxable income, such amount shall be treated as the taxable income of such taxpayer for purposes of this paragraph.

(D) COORDINATION WITH REASONABLE CAUSE EXCEPTION.—For purposes of section 6664(c) the taxpayer shall not be treated as having reasonable cause for any portion of an underpayment attributable to a net section 482 transfer price adjustment unless such taxpayer meets the requirements of clause (i), (ii), or (iii) of subparagraph (B) with respect to such portion.

Amendments

• 2006, Pension Protection Act of 2006 (P.L. 109-280)

P.L. 109-280, §1219(a)(1)(A):

Amended Code Sec. 6662(e)(1)(A) by striking "200 percent" and inserting "150 percent". **Effective** generally for returns filed after 8-17-2006. For a special rule, see Act Sec. 1219(e)(3), below.

P.L. 109-280, §1219(e)(3), provides:

(3) SPECIAL RULE FOR CERTAIN EASEMENTS.—In the case of a contribution of a qualified real property interest which is a restriction with respect to the exterior of a building described in section 170(h)(4)(C)(ii) of the Internal Revenue Code of 1986, and an appraisal with respect to the contribution, the amendments made by subsections (a) and (b) shall apply to returns filed after July 25, 2006.

• 1993, Omnibus Budget Reconciliation Act of 1993 (P.L. 103-66)

P.L. 103-66, §13236(a):

Amended Code Sec. 6662(e)(1)(B)(ii). **Effective** for tax years beginning after 12-31-93. Prior to amendment, Code Sec. 6662(e)(1)(B)(ii) read as follows:

(ii) the net section 482 transfer price adjustment for the taxable year exceeds $10,000,000.

P.L. 103-66, §13236(b):

Amended Code Sec. 6662(e)(3)(B). **Effective** for tax years beginning after 12-31-93. Prior to amendment, Code Sec. 6662(e)(3)(B) read as follows:

(B) CERTAIN ADJUSTMENTS EXCLUDED IN DETERMINING THRESHOLD.—For purposes of determining whether the $10,000,000 threshold requirement of paragraph (1)(B)(ii) is met, there shall be excluded—

(i) any portion of the net increase in taxable income referred to in subparagraph (A) which is attributable to any redetermination of a price if it is shown that there was a reasonable cause for the taxpayer's determination of such price and that the taxpayer acted in good faith with respect to such price, and

(ii) any portion of such net increase which is attributable to any transaction solely between foreign corporations unless, in the case of any of such corporations, the treatment of such transaction affects the determination of income from sources within the United States or taxable income effectively connected with the conduct of a trade or business within the United States.

P.L. 103-66, §13236(c):

Amended Code Sec. 6662(e)(3) by adding at the end thereof a new subparagraph (D). **Effective** for tax years beginning after 12-31-93.

• 1990, Omnibus Budget Reconciliation Act of 1990 (P.L. 101-508)

P.L. 101-508, §11312(a):

Amended Code Sec. 6662(e). **Effective** for tax years ending after 11-5-90. Prior to amendment, Code Sec. 6662(e) read as follows:

(e) SUBSTANTIAL VALUATION OVERSTATEMENT UNDER CHAPTER 1.—

(1) IN GENERAL.—For purposes of this section, there is a substantial valuation overstatement under chapter 1 if the value of any property (or the adjusted basis of any property) claimed on any return of tax imposed by chapter 1 is 200 percent or more of the amount determined to be the correct amount of such valuation or adjusted basis (as the case may be).

(2) LIMITATION.—No penalty shall be imposed by reason of subsection (b)(3) unless the portion of the underpayment for the taxable year attributable to substantial valuation overstatements under chapter 1 exceeds $5,000 ($10,000 in the case of a corporation other than an S corporation or a personal holding company (as defined in section 542)).

[Sec. 6662(f)]

(f) SUBSTANTIAL OVERSTATEMENT OF PENSION LIABILITIES.—

(1) IN GENERAL.—For purposes of this section, there is a substantial overstatement of pension liabilities if the actuarial determination of the liabilities taken into account for purposes of computing the deduction under paragraph (1) or (2) of section 404(a) is 200 percent or more of the amount determined to be the correct amount of such liabilities.

(2) LIMITATION.—No penalty shall be imposed by reason of subsection (b)(4) unless the portion of the underpayment for the taxable year attributable to substantial overstatements of pension liabilities exceeds $1,000.

[Sec. 6662(g)]

(g) SUBSTANTIAL ESTATE OR GIFT TAX VALUATION UNDERSTATEMENT.—

(1) IN GENERAL.—For purposes of this section, there is a substantial estate or gift tax valuation understatement if the value of any property claimed on any return of tax imposed by subtitle B is 65 percent or less of the amount determined to be the correct amount of such valuation.

(2) LIMITATION.—No penalty shall be imposed by reason of subsection (b)(5) unless the portion of the underpayment attributable to substantial estate or gift tax valuation understatements for the taxable period (or, in the case of the tax imposed by chapter 11, with respect to the estate of the decedent) exceeds $5,000.

Amendments

• 2006, Pension Protection Act of 2006 (P.L. 109-280)

P.L. 109-280, §1219(a)(1)(B):

Amended Code Sec. 6662(g)(1) by striking "50 percent" and inserting "65 percent". **Effective** for returns filed after 8-17-2006. For a special rule, see Act Sec. 1219(e)(3), below.

P.L. 109-280, §1219(e)(3), provides:

(3) SPECIAL RULE FOR CERTAIN EASEMENTS.—In the case of a contribution of a qualified real property interest which is a restriction with respect to the exterior of a building described in section 170(h)(4)(C)(ii) of the Internal Revenue Code of 1986, and an appraisal with respect to the contribution, the amendments made by subsections (a) and (b) shall apply to returns filed after July 25, 2006.

[Sec. 6662(h)]

(h) INCREASE IN PENALTY IN CASE OF GROSS VALUATION MISSTATEMENTS.—

(1) IN GENERAL.—To the extent that a portion of the underpayment to which this section applies is attributable to one or more gross valuation misstatements, subsection (a) shall be applied with respect to such portion by substituting "40 percent" for "20 percent".

(2) GROSS VALUATION MISSTATEMENTS.—The term "gross valuation misstatements" means—

(A) any substantial valuation misstatement under chapter 1 as determined under subsection (e) by substituting—

(i) in paragraph (1)(A), "200 percent" for "150 percent",

(ii) in paragraph (1)(B)(i)—

(I) "400 percent" for "200 percent", and

(II) "25 percent" for "50 percent", and

(iii) in paragraph (1)(B)(ii)—

(I) "$20,000,000" for "$5,000,000", and

(II) "20 percent" for "10 percent".

(B) any substantial overstatement of pension liabilities as determined under subsection (f) by substituting "400 percent" for "200 percent",

(C) any substantial estate or gift tax valuation understatement as determined under subsection (g) by substituting "40 percent" for "65 percent", and

(D) any disallowance of a deduction described in subsection (b)(10).

Amendments

• 2022, SECURE 2.0 Act of 2022 (P.L. 117-328)

P.L. 117-328, §605(a)(2)(B):

Amended Code Sec. 6662(h)(2) by striking "and" at the end of subparagraph (B), by striking the period at the end of subparagraph (C) and inserting ", and", and by adding at the end a new subparagraph (D). **Effective** for contributions made after 12-29-2022. For a special rule, see Act Sec. 605(c)(2), below.

P.L. 117-328, §605(c)(2), provides:

(2) NO INFERENCE.—No inference is intended as to the appropriate treatment of contributions made in taxable years ending on or before the date specified in paragraph (1), or as to any contribution for which a deduction is not disallowed by reason of section 170(h)(7) of the Internal Revenue Code of 1986, as added by this section.

• 2006, Pension Protection Act of 2006 (P.L. 109-280)

P.L. 109-280, §1219(a)(2)(A):

Amended Code Sec. 6662(h)(2)(A)(i)-(ii). **Effective** generally for returns filed after 8-17-2006. For a special rule, see Act Sec. 1219(e)(3), below. Prior to amendment, Code Sec. 6662(h)(2)(A)(i)-(ii) read as follows:

(i) "400 percent" for "200 percent" each place it appears,

(ii) "25 percent" for "50 percent", and

P.L. 109-280, §1219(a)(2)(B):

Amended Code Sec. 6662(h)(2)(C) by striking "'25 percent' for '50 percent'" and inserting "'40 percent' for '65 percent'". **Effective** generally for returns filed after 8-17-2006. For a special rule, see Act Sec. 1219(e)(3), below.

P.L. 109-280, §1219(e)(3), provides:

(3) SPECIAL RULE FOR CERTAIN EASEMENTS.—In the case of a contribution of a qualified real property interest which is a restriction with respect to the exterior of a building described in section 170(h)(4)(C)(ii) of the Internal Revenue Code of 1986, and an appraisal with respect to the contribution, the amendments made by subsections (a) and (b) shall apply to returns filed after July 25, 2006.

• 1993, Omnibus Budget Reconciliation Act of 1993 (P.L. 103-66)

P.L. 103-66, §13236(d):

Amended Code Sec. 6662(h)(2)(A)(iii). **Effective** for tax years beginning after 12-31-93. Prior to amendment, Code Sec. 6662(h)(2)(A)(iii) read as follows:

(iii) "$20,000,000" for "$10,000,000".

• 1990, Omnibus Budget Reconciliation Act of 1990 (P.L. 101-508)

P.L. 101-508, §11312(b)(2):

Amended Code Sec. 6662(h)(2)(A). **Effective** for tax years ending after 11-5-90. Prior to amendment, Code Sec. 6662(h)(2)(A) read as follows:

(A) any substantial valuation overstatement under chapter 1 as determined under subsection (e) by substituting "400 percent" for "200 percent",

• 1989, Omnibus Budget Reconciliation Act of 1989 (P.L. 101-239)

P.L. 101-239, §7721(a):

Amended subchapter A of chapter 68 by striking section 6662 and inserting new Parts II and III. **Effective** for returns the due date for which (determined without regard to extensions) is after 12-31-89. Prior to amendment, Code Sec. 6662 read as follows:

SEC. 6662. APPLICABLE RULES.

(a) ADDITIONS TREATED AS TAX.—Except as otherwise provided in this title—

(1) The additions to the tax, additional amounts, and penalties provided by this chapter shall be paid upon notice and demand and shall be assessed, collected, and paid in the same manner as taxes;

(2) Any reference in this title to "tax" imposed by this title shall be deemed also to refer to the additions to the tax, additional amounts, and penalties provided by this chapter.

(b) PROCEDURE FOR ASSESSING CERTAIN ADDITIONS TO TAX.—For purposes of subchapter B of chapter 63 (relating to deficiency procedures for income, estate, gift, and certain excise taxes), subsection (a) shall not apply to any addition to tax under section 6651, 6654, or 6655; except that it shall apply—

(1) in the case of an addition described in section 6651, to that portion of such addition which is attributable to a deficiency in tax described in section 6211; or

(2) to an addition described in section 6654 or 6655, if no return is filed for the taxable year.

• 1982, Tax Equity and Fiscal Responsibility Act of 1982 (P.L. 97-248)

P.L. 97-248, §323(a):

Redesignated Code Sec. 6660 as Code Sec. 6662. For **effective** date, see the amendment note for P.L. 97-248 following Code Sec. 6661.

• 1981, Economic Recovery Tax Act of 1981 (P.L. 97-34)

P.L. 97-34, §722(a)(1):

Redesignated Code Sec. 6659 as Code Sec. 6660. **Effective** for returns filed after 12-31-81.

• 1974, Employee Retirement Income Security Act of 1974 (P.L. 93-406)

P.L. 93-406, §1016(a)(19):

Amended Code Sec. 6659(b) by changing "chapter 42" to "certain excise". For **effective** date, see amendment note for Code Sec. 410.

• 1969, Tax Reform Act of 1969 (P.L. 91-172)

P.L. 91-172, §101(j)(51):

Amended Code Sec. 6659(b) by substituting "gift, and chapter 42 taxes" for "and gift taxes". **Effective** 1-1-70.

• 1960 (P.L. 86-470)

P.L. 86-470, §§1, 2:

Amended Code Sec. 6659(b). For **effective** date, see §2, below. Prior to amendment, Code Sec. 6659(b) read as follows:

"(b) Additions to Tax for Failure to File Return or Pay Tax.—Any addition under section 6651 or section 6653 to a tax imposed by another subtitle of this title shall be considered a part of such tax for the purpose of applying the provisions of this title relating to the assessment and collection of such tax (including the provisions of subchapter B of chapter 63, relating to deficiency procedures for income, estate, and gift taxes)."

P.L. 86-470, §2, provides:

"The amendment made by the first section of this Act shall apply with respect to assessments made after the date of the enactment of this Act. Any addition to tax under section 6651, 6654, or 6655 of the Internal Revenue Code of 1954, assessed and collected on or before the date of the enactment of this Act, shall not be considered an overpayment solely on the ground that such assessment was invalid, if such assessment would not have been invalid had the amendment made by the first section of this Act applied with respect to such assessment."

[Sec. 6662(i)]

(i) INCREASE IN PENALTY IN CASE OF NONDISCLOSED NONECONOMIC SUBSTANCE TRANSACTIONS.—

(1) IN GENERAL.—In the case of any portion of an underpayment which is attributable to one or more nondisclosed noneconomic substance transactions, subsection (a) shall be applied with respect to such portion by substituting "40 percent" for "20 percent".

(2) NONDISCLOSED NONECONOMIC SUBSTANCE TRANSACTIONS.—For purposes of this subsection, the term "nondisclosed noneconomic substance transaction" means any portion of a transaction described in subsection (b)(6) with respect to which the relevant facts affecting the tax treatment are not adequately disclosed in the return nor in a statement attached to the return.

(3) SPECIAL RULE FOR AMENDED RETURNS.—In no event shall any amendment or supplement to a return of tax be taken into account for purposes of this subsection if the amendment or supplement is filed after the earlier of the date the taxpayer is first contacted by the Secretary regarding the examination of the return or such other date as is specified by the Secretary.

Amendments

• 2018, Tax Technical Corrections Act of 2018 (P.L. 115-141)

P.L. 115-141, §401(a)(304), Div. U:

Amended Code Sec. 6662 by moving subsection (i) before subsection (j). **Effective** 3-23-2018.

• 2010, Health Care and Education Reconciliation Act of 2010 (P.L. 111-152)

P.L. 111-152, §1409(b)(2):

Amended Code Sec. 6662 by adding at the end a new subsection (i). **Effective** for underpayments attributable to transactions entered into after 3-30-2010.

[Sec. 6662(j)]

(j) UNDISCLOSED FOREIGN FINANCIAL ASSET UNDERSTATEMENT.—

(1) IN GENERAL.—For purposes of this section, the term "undisclosed foreign financial asset understatement" means, for any taxable year, the portion of the understatement for such taxable year which is attributable to any transaction involving an undisclosed foreign financial asset.

(2) UNDISCLOSED FOREIGN FINANCIAL ASSET.—For purposes of this subsection, the term "undisclosed foreign financial asset" means, with respect to any taxable year, any asset with respect to which information was required to be provided under section 6038, 6038B, 6038D, 6046A, or 6048 for such taxable year but was not provided by the taxpayer as required under the provisions of those sections.

(3) INCREASE IN PENALTY FOR UNDISCLOSED FOREIGN FINANCIAL ASSET UNDERSTATEMENTS.—In the case of any portion of an underpayment which is attributable to any undisclosed foreign financial asset understatement, subsection (a) shall be applied with respect to such portion by substituting "40 percent" for "20 percent".

Amendments

• 2010, Hiring Incentives to Restore Employment Act (P.L. 111-147)

P.L. 111-147, §512(a)(2):

Amended Code Sec. 6662, as amended by this Act, by adding at the end a new subsection (j). **Effective** for tax years beginning after 3-18-2010.

[Sec. 6662(k)]

(k) INCONSISTENT ESTATE BASIS REPORTING.—For purposes of this section, the term "inconsistent estate basis" means any portion of an underpayment attributable to the failure to comply with section 1014(f).

Amendments

• 2018, Tax Technical Corrections Act of 2018 (P.L. 115-141)

P.L. 115-141, §104(a), Div. U:

Amended Code Sec. 6662(k). **Effective** as if included in the provision of the Surface Transportation and Veterans Health Care Choice Improvement Act of 2015 to which it relates [**effective** for property with respect to which an estate tax return is filed after 7-31-2015.—CCH]. Prior to amendment, Code Sec. 6662(k) read as follows:

(k) INCONSISTENT ESTATE BASIS REPORTING.—For purposes of this section, there is an "inconsistent estate basis" if the basis of property claimed on a return exceeds the basis as determined under section 1014(f).

• 2015, Surface Transportation and Veterans Health Care Choice Improvement Act of 2015 (P.L. 114-41)

P.L. 114-41, §2004(c)(2):

Amended Code Sec. 6662 by adding at the end a new subsection (k). **Effective** for property with respect to which an estate tax return is filed after 7-31-2015.

[Sec. 6662(l)]

(l) INCREASE IN PENALTY IN CASE OF OVERSTATEMENT OF QUALIFIED CHARITABLE CONTRIBUTIONS.—In the case of any portion of an underpayment which is attributable to one or more overstatements of the deduction provided in section 170(p), subsection (a) shall be applied with respect to such portion by substituting "50 percent" for "20 percent".

Amendments

• 2020, Taxpayer Certainty and Disaster Tax Relief Act of 2020 (P.L. 116-260)

P.L. 116-260, §212(b)(2), Div. EE:

Amended Code Sec. 6662 by adding at the end a new subsection (l). **Effective** for tax years beginning after 12-31-2020.

* * *

[Sec. 6663]

SEC. 6663. IMPOSITION OF FRAUD PENALTY.

[Sec. 6663(a)]

(a) IMPOSITION OF PENALTY.—If any part of any underpayment of tax required to be shown on a return is due to fraud, there shall be added to the tax an amount equal to 75 percent of the portion of the underpayment which is attributable to fraud.

[Sec. 6663(b)]

(b) DETERMINATION OF PORTION ATTRIBUTABLE TO FRAUD.—If the Secretary establishes that any portion of an underpayment is attributable to fraud, the entire underpayment shall be treated as attributable to fraud, except with respect to any portion of the underpayment which the taxpayer establishes (by a preponderance of the evidence) is not attributable to fraud.

[Sec. 6663(c)]

(c) SPECIAL RULE FOR JOINT RETURNS.—In the case of a joint return, this section shall not apply with respect to a spouse unless some part of the underpayment is due to the fraud of such spouse.

Amendments

• 1989, Omnibus Budget Reconciliation Act of 1989 (P.L. 101-239)

P.L. 101-239, §7721(a):

Amended subchapter A of chapter 68 by adding a new section 6663. **Effective** for returns the due date for which (determined without regard to extensions) is after 12-31-89.

[Sec. 6664]

SEC 6664. DEFINITIONS AND SPECIAL RULES.

[Sec. 6664(a)]

(a) UNDERPAYMENT.—For purposes of this part, the term "underpayment" means the amount by which any tax imposed by this title exceeds the excess of—

(1) the sum of—

(A) the amount shown as the tax by the taxpayer on his return, plus

(B) amounts not so shown previously assessed (or collected without assessment), over

(2) the amount of rebates made.

For purposes of paragraph (2), the term "rebate" means so much of an abatement, credit, refund, or other repayment, as was made on the ground that tax imposed was less than the excess of the amount specified in paragraph (1) over the rebates previously made. A rule similar to the rule of section 6211(b)(4) shall apply for purposes of this subsection.

Amendments

• 2015, Protecting Americans from Tax Hikes Act of 2015 (P.L. 114-113)

P.L. 114-113, §209(a), Div. Q:

Amended Code Sec. 6664(a) by adding at the end a new sentence. For the **effective** date, see Act Sec. 209(d)(1), below.

P.L. 114-113, §209(d)(1), Div. Q, provides:

(1) UNDERPAYMENT PENALTIES.—The amendment made by subsection (a) shall apply to—

(A) returns filed after the date of the enactment of this Act, and

(B) returns filed on or before such date if the period specified in section 6501 of the Internal Revenue Code of 1986 for assessment of the taxes with respect to which such return relates has not expired as of such date.

[Sec. 6664(b)]

(b) PENALTIES APPLICABLE ONLY WHERE RETURN FILED.—The penalties provided in this part shall apply only in cases where a return of tax is filed (other than a return prepared by the Secretary under the authority of section 6020(b)).

[Sec. 6664(c)]

(c) REASONABLE CAUSE EXCEPTION FOR UNDERPAYMENTS.—

(1) IN GENERAL.—No penalty shall be imposed under section 6662 or 6663 with respect to any portion of an underpayment if it is shown that there was a reasonable cause for such portion and that the taxpayer acted in good faith with respect to such portion.

(2) EXCEPTION.—Paragraph (1) shall not apply to any portion of an underpayment which is attributable to one or more transactions described in section 6662(b)(6) or to any disallowance of a deduction described in section 6662(b)(10).

(3) SPECIAL RULE FOR CERTAIN VALUATION OVERSTATEMENTS.—In the case of any underpayment attributable to a substantial or gross valuation over statement under chapter 1 with respect to charitable deduction property, paragraph (1) shall not apply. The preceding sentence shall not apply to a substantial valuation overstatement under chapter 1 if—

(A) the claimed value of the property was based on a qualified appraisal made by a qualified appraiser, and

(B) in addition to obtaining such appraisal, the taxpayer made a good faith investigation of the value of the contributed property.

(4) DEFINITIONS.—For purposes of this subsection—

(A) CHARITABLE DEDUCTION PROPERTY.—The term "charitable deduction property" means any property contributed by the taxpayer in a contribution for which a deduction was claimed under section 170. For purposes of paragraph (3), such term shall not include any securities for which (as of the date of the contribution) market quotations are readily available on an established securities market.

(B) QUALIFIED APPRAISAL.—The term "qualified appraisal" has the meaning given such term by section 170(f)(11)(E)(i).

(C) QUALIFIED APPRAISER.—The term "qualified appraiser" has the meaning given such term by section 170(f)(11)(E)(ii).

Amendments

• 2022, SECURE 2.0 Act of 2022 (P.L. 117-328)

P.L. 117-328, §605(a)(2)(C):

Amended Code Sec. 6664(c)(2) by inserting "or to any disallowance of a deduction described in section 6662(b)(10)" before the period at the end. **Effective** for contributions made after 12-29-2022. For a special rule, see Act Sec. 605(c)(2), below.

P.L. 117-328, §605(c)(2), provides:

(2) NO INFERENCE.—No inference is intended as to the appropriate treatment of contributions made in taxable years ending on or before the date specified in paragraph (1), or as to any contribution for which a deduction is not disallowed by reason of section 170(h)(7) of the Internal Revenue Code of 1986, as added by this section.

• 2010, Health Care and Education Reconciliation Act of 2010 (P.L. 111-152)

P.L. 111-152, §1409(c)(1)(A)-(C):

Amended Code Sec. 6664(c) by redesignating paragraphs (2) and (3) as paragraphs (3) and (4), respectively; by striking "paragraph (2)" in paragraph (4)(A), as so redesignated, and inserting "paragraph (3)"; and by inserting after paragraph (1) a new paragraph (2). **Effective** for underpayments attributable to transactions entered into after 3-30-2010.

• 2006, Pension Protection Act of 2006 (P.L. 109-280)

P.L. 109-280, §1219(a)(3):

Amended Code Sec. 6664(c)(2) by striking "paragraph (1) shall not apply unless" and inserting "paragraph (1) shall not apply. The preceding sentence shall not apply to a substantial valuation overstatement under chapter 1 if". **Effective** generally for returns filed after 8-17-2006. For a special rule, see Act Sec. 1219(e)(3), below.

P.L. 109-280, §1219(c)(2):

Amended Code Sec. 6664(c)(3)(B)-(C). **Effective** generally for appraisals prepared with respect to returns or submissions filed after 8-17-2006. Prior to amendment, Code Sec. 6664(c)(3)(B)-(C) read as follows:

(B) QUALIFIED APPRAISER.—The term "qualified appraiser" means any appraiser meeting the requirements of the regulations prescribed under section 170(a)(1).

(C) QUALIFIED APPRAISAL.—The term "qualified appraisal" means any appraisal meeting the requirements of the regulations prescribed under section 170(a)(1).

P.L. 109-280, §1219(e)(3), provides:

(3) SPECIAL RULE FOR CERTAIN EASEMENTS.—In the case of a contribution of a qualified real property interest which is a restriction with respect to the exterior of a building described in section 170(h)(4)(C)(ii) of the Internal Revenue Code of 1986, and an appraisal with respect to the contribution, the amendments made by subsections (a) and (b) shall apply to returns filed after July 25, 2006.

• 2004, American Jobs Creation Act of 2004 (P.L. 108-357)

P.L. 108-357, §812(c)(2)(A):

Amended Code Sec. 6664(c)(1) by striking "this part" and inserting "section 6662 or 6663". **Effective** for tax years ending after 10-22-2004.

P.L. 108-357, §812(c)(2)(B):

Amended the heading of Code Sec. 6664(c) by inserting "FOR UNDERPAYMENTS" after "EXCEPTION". **Effective** for tax years ending after 10-22-2004.

• 1989, Omnibus Budget Reconciliation Act of 1989 (P.L. 101-239)

P.L. 101-239, §7721(a):

Amended subchapter A of chapter 68 by adding a new section 6664. **Effective** for returns the due date for which (determined without regard to extensions) is after 12-31-89.

***

PART III—APPLICABLE RULES

* * *

[Sec. 6665]

SEC. 6665. APPLICABLE RULES.

[Sec. 6665(a)]

(a) ADDITIONS TREATED AS TAX.—Except as otherwise provided in this title—

(1) the additions to the tax, additional amounts, and penalties provided by this chapter shall be paid upon notice and demand and shall be assessed, collected, and paid in the same manner as taxes; and

(2) any reference in this title to "tax" imposed by this title shall be deemed also to refer to the additions to the tax, additional amounts, and penalties provided by this chapter.

[Sec. 6665(b)]

(b) PROCEDURE FOR ASSESSING CERTAIN ADDITIONS TO TAX.—For purposes of subchapter B of chapter 63 (relating to deficiency procedures for income, estate, gift, and certain excise taxes), subsection (a) shall not apply to any addition to tax under section 6651, 6654, 6655; except that it shall apply—

(1) in the case of an addition described in section 6651, to that portion of such addition which is attributable to a deficiency in tax described in section 6211; or

(2) to an addition described in section 6654 or 6655, if no return is filed for the taxable year.

Amendments

• 1989, Omnibus Budget Reconciliation Act of 1989 (P.L. 101-239)

P.L. 101-239, §7721(a):

Amended subchapter A of chapter 68 by adding a new part III. **Effective** for returns the due date for which (determined without regard to extensions) is after 12-31-89.

Subchapter B—Assessable Penalties

* * *

PART I—GENERAL PROVISIONS

* * *

* * *

[Sec. 6673]

SEC. 6673. SANCTIONS AND COSTS AWARDED BY COURTS.

[Sec. 6673(a)]

(a) TAX COURT PROCEEDINGS.—

(1) PROCEDURES INSTITUTED PRIMARILY FOR DELAY, ETC.—Whenever it appears to the Tax Court that—

(A) proceedings before it have been instituted or maintained by the taxpayer primarily for delay,

(B) the taxpayer's position in such proceeding is frivolous or groundless, or

(C) the taxpayer unreasonably failed to pursue available administrative remedies,

the Tax Court, in its decision, may require the taxpayer to pay to the United States a penalty not in excess of $25,000.

(2) COUNSEL'S LIABILITY FOR EXCESSIVE COSTS.—Whenever it appears to the Tax Court that any attorney or other person admitted to practice before the Tax Court has multiplied the proceedings in any case unreasonably and vexatiously, the Tax Court may require—

(A) that such attorney or other person pay personally the excess costs, expenses, and attorneys' fees reasonably incurred because of such conduct, or

(B) if such attorney is appearing on behalf of the Commissioner of Internal Revenue, that the United States pay such excess costs, expenses, and attorneys' fees in the same manner as such an award by a district court.

[Sec. 6673(b)]

(b) PROCEEDINGS IN OTHER COURTS.—

(1) CLAIMS UNDER SECTION 7433.—Whenever it appears to the court that the taxpayer's position in the proceedings before the court instituted or maintained by such taxpayer under section 7433 is frivolous or groundless, the court may require the taxpayer to pay to the United States a penalty not in excess of $10,000.

(2) COLLECTION OF SANCTIONS AND COSTS.—In any civil proceeding before any court (other than the Tax Court) which is brought by or against the United States in connection with the determination, collection, or refund of any tax, interest, or penalty under this title, any monetary sanctions, penalties, or costs awarded by the court to the United States may be assessed by the Secretary and, upon notice and demand, may be collected in the same manner as a tax.

(3) SANCTIONS AND COSTS AWARDED BY A COURT OF APPEALS.—In connection with any appeal from a proceeding in the Tax Court or a civil proceeding described in paragraph (2), an order of a United States Court of Appeals or the Supreme Court awarding monetary sanctions, penalties or court costs to the United States may be registered in a district court upon filing a certified copy of such order and shall be enforceable as other district court judgments. Any such sanctions, penalties, or costs may be assessed by the Secretary and, upon notice and demand, may be collected in the same manner as a tax.

Amendments

• 1989, Omnibus Budget Reconciliation Act of 1989 (P.L. 101-239)

P.L. 101-239, §7731(a):

Amended Code Sec. 6673. **Effective** for positions taken after 12-31-89, in proceedings which are pending on, or commenced after such date. Prior to amendment, Code Sec. 6673 read as follows:

SEC. 6673. DAMAGES ASSESSABLE FOR INSTITUTING PROCEEDINGS BEFORE THE TAX COURT PRIMARILY FOR DELAY, ETC.

(a) IN GENERAL.—Whenever it appears to the Tax Court that proceedings before it have been instituted or maintained by the taxpayer primarily for delay, that the taxpayer's position in such proceeding is frivolous or groundless, or that the taxpayer unreasonably failed to pursue available administrative remedies, damages in an amount not in excess of $5,000 shall be awarded to the United States by the Tax Court in its decision. Damages so awarded shall be assessed at the same time as the deficiency and shall be paid upon notice and demand from the Secretary and shall be collected as a part of the tax.

(b) CLAIMS UNDER SECTION 7433.—Whenever it appears to the court that the taxpayer's position in proceedings before the court instituted or maintained by such taxpayer under section 7433 is frivolous or groundless, damages in an amount not in excess of $10,000 shall be awarded to the United States by the court in the court's decision. Damages so awarded shall be assessed at the same time as the decision and shall be paid upon notice and demand from the Secretary.

• 1988, Technical and Miscellaneous Revenue Act of 1988 (P.L. 100-647)

P.L. 100-647, §6241(b)(1):

Amended Code Sec. 6673 by inserting "(a) IN GENERAL.—" before "Whenever" and by adding at the end thereof new subsection (b). **Effective** for actions by officers or employees of the Internal Revenue Service after 11-10-88.

P.L. 100-647, §6241(b)(2):

Amended Code Sec. 6673 by striking out "TAX" before "Court" in the heading. **Effective** for actions by officers or employees of the Internal Revenue Service after 11-10-88.

• 1986, Tax Reform Act of 1986 (P.L. 99-514)

P.L. 99-514, §1552(a):

Amended Code Sec. 6673 by striking out "or that the taxpayer's position in such proceedings is frivolous or groundless" and inserting in lieu thereof ", that the taxpayer's position in such proceeding is frivolous or groundless, or that the taxpayer unreasonably failed to pursue available administrative remedies". **Effective** for proceedings commenced after 10-22-86.

• 1982, Tax Equity and Fiscal Responsibility Act of 1982 (P.L. 97-248)

P.L. 97-248, §292(b):

Amended the first sentence of Code Sec. 6673. **Effective** for any action or proceeding in the Tax Court commenced after 12-31-82 or pending in the United States Tax Court on the day which is 120 days after 7-18-84. Prior to amendment, the first sentence read as follows:

"Whenever it appears to the Tax Court that proceedings before it have been instituted by the taxpayer merely for delay, damages in an amount not in excess of $500 shall be awarded to the United States by the Tax Court in its decision."

P.L. 97-248, §292(d)(2)(A):

Amended the section heading of Code Sec. 6673 by striking out "Merely for Delay." and inserting "Primarily for Delay, Etc.". **Effective** for any action or proceeding in the Tax Court commenced after 12-31-82 or pending in the United States Tax Court on the day which is 120 days after 7-18-84.

• 1976, Tax Reform Act of 1976 (P.L. 94-455)

P.L. 94-455, §1906(b)(13)(A):

Amended 1954 Code by substituting "Secretary" for "Secretary or his delegate" each place it appeared. **Effective** 2-1-77.

* * *

[Sec. 6677]

SEC. 6677. FAILURE TO FILE INFORMATION WITH RESPECT TO CERTAIN FOREIGN TRUSTS.

[Sec. 6677(a)]

(a) CIVIL PENALTY.—In addition to any criminal penalty provided by law, if any notice or return required to be filed by section 6048—

(1) is not filed on or before the time provided in such section, or

(2) does not include all the information required pursuant to such section or includes incorrect information,

the person required to file such notice or return shall pay a penalty equal to the greater of $10,000 or 35 percent of the gross reportable amount. If any failure described in the preceding sentence continues for more than 90 days after the day on which the Secretary mails notice of such failure to the person required to pay such penalty, such person shall pay a penalty (in addition to the amount determined under the preceding sentence) of $10,000 for each 30-day period (or fraction thereof) during which such failure continues after the expiration of such 90-day period. At such time as the gross reportable amount with respect to any failure can be determined by the Secretary, any subsequent penalty imposed under this subsection with respect to such failure shall be reduced as necessary to assure that the aggregate amount of such penalties do not exceed the gross reportable amount (and to the extent that such aggregate amount already exceeds the gross reportable amount the Secretary shall refund such excess to the taxpayer).

Amendments

• 2010, Hiring Incentives to Restore Employment Act (P.L. 111-147)

P.L. 111-147, §535(a)(1)-(2):

Amended Code Sec. 6677(a) by inserting "the greater of $10,000 or" before "35 percent", and by striking the last sentence and inserting a new sentence. **Effective** for notices and returns required to be filed after 12-31-2009. Prior to being stricken, the last sentence of Code Sec. 6677(a) read as follows:

In no event shall the penalty under this subsection with respect to any failure exceed the gross reportable amount.

[Sec. 6677(b)]

(b) SPECIAL RULES FOR RETURNS UNDER SECTION 6048(b).—In the case of a return required under section 6048(b)—

(1) the United States person referred to in such section shall be liable for the penalty imposed by subsection (a), and

(2) subsection (a) shall be applied by substituting "5 percent" for "35 percent".

[Sec. 6677(c)]

(c) GROSS REPORTABLE AMOUNT.—For purposes of subsection (a), the term "gross reportable amount" means—

(1) the gross value of the property involved in the event (determined as of the date of the event) in the case of a failure relating to section 6048(a),

(2) the gross value of the portion of the trust's assets at the close of the year treated as owned by the United States person in the case of a failure relating to section 6048(b)(1), and

(3) the gross amount of the distributions in the case of a failure relating to section 6048(c).

[Sec. 6677(d)]

(d) REASONABLE CAUSE EXCEPTION.—No penalty shall be imposed by this section on any failure which is shown to be due to reasonable cause and not due to willful neglect. The fact that a foreign jurisdiction would impose a civil or criminal penalty on the taxpayer (or any other person) for disclosing the required information is not reasonable cause.

[Sec. 6677(e)]

(e) DEFICIENCY PROCEDURES NOT TO APPLY.—Subchapter B of chapter 63 (relating to deficiency procedures for income, estate, gift, and certain excise taxes) shall not apply in respect of the assessment or collection of any penalty imposed by subsection (a).

Amendments

• 1996, Small Business Job Protection Act of 1996 (P.L. 104-188)

P.L. 104-188, §1901(b):

Amended Code Sec. 6677. For the **effective** date, see Act Sec. 1901(d).

P.L. 104-188, §1901(d), provides:

(d) EFFECTIVE DATES.—

(1) REPORTABLE EVENTS.—To the extent related to subsection (a) of section 6048 of the Internal Revenue Code of 1986, as amended by this section, the amendments made by this section shall apply to reportable events (as defined in such section 6048) occurring after the date of the enactment of this Act.

(2) GRANTOR TRUST REPORTING.—To the extent related to subsection (b) of such section 6048, the amendments made by this section shall apply to taxable years of United States persons beginning after December 31, 1995.

(3) REPORTING BY UNITED STATES BENEFICIARIES.—To the extent related to subsection (c) of such section 6048, the amendments made by this section shall apply to distributions received after the date of the enactment of this Act.

Prior to amendment, Code Sec. 6677 read as follows:

SEC. 6677. FAILURE TO FILE INFORMATION RETURNS WITH RESPECT TO CERTAIN FOREIGN TRUSTS.

[Sec. 6677(a)]

(a) CIVIL PENALTY.—In addition to any criminal penalty provided by law, any person required to file a return under section 6048 who fails to file such return at the time provided in such section, or who files a return which does not show the information required pursuant to such section, shall pay a penalty equal to 5 percent of the amount transferred to a trust (or, in the case of a failure with respect to section 6048(c), equal to 5 percent of the value of the corpus of the trust at the close of the taxable year), but not more than $1,000, unless it is shown that such failure is due to reasonable cause.

Amendments

• 1976, Tax Reform Act of 1976 (P.L. 94-455)

P.L. 94-455, §1013(d)(2):

Substituted "to a trust (or, in the case of a failure with respect to section 6048(c), equal to 5 percent of the value of the corpus of the trust at the close of the taxable year)" for "to a trust" in Code Sec. 6677(a). **Effective** for tax years ending after 12-31-75, but only in the case of—

(A) foreign trusts created after 5-21-74, and

(B) transfers of property to foreign trusts after 5-21-74.

• 1962, Revenue Act of 1962 (P.L. 87-834)

P.L. 87-834, §7:

Added Code Sec. 6677(a). **Effective** 10-17-62.

[Sec. 6677(b)]

(b) DEFICIENCY PROCEDURES NOT TO APPLY.—Subchapter B of chapter 63 (relating to deficiency procedures for income, estate, gift, and certain excise taxes) shall not apply in respect of the assessment or collection of any penalty imposed by subsection (a).

Amendments

• 1974, Employee Retirement Income Security Act of 1974 (P.L. 93-406)

P.L. 93-406, §1016(a)(21):

Amended Code Sec. 6677(b) by changing "chapter 42" to "certain excise". For **effective** date, see amendment note for Code Sec. 410.

• 1969, Tax Reform Act of 1969 (P.L. 91-172)

P.L. 91-172, §101(j)(53):

Amended Code Sec. 6677(b) by substituting "gift, and chapter 42 taxes" for "and gift taxes". **Effective** 1-1-70.

• 1962, Revenue Act of 1962 (P.L. 87-834)

P.L. 87-834, §7:

Added Code Sec. 6677(b). **Effective** 10-17-62.

* * *

[Sec. 6694]

SEC. 6694. UNDERSTATEMENT OF TAXPAYER'S LIABILITY BY TAX RETURN PREPARER.

[Sec. 6694(a)]

(a) UNDERSTATEMENT DUE TO UNREASONABLE POSITIONS.—

(1) IN GENERAL.—If a tax return preparer—

(A) prepares any return or claim of refund with respect to which any part of an understatement of liability is due to a position described in paragraph (2), and

(B) knew (or reasonably should have known) of the position,

such tax return preparer shall pay a penalty with respect to each such return or claim in an amount equal to the greater of $1,000 or 50 percent of the income derived (or to be derived) by the tax return preparer with respect to the return or claim.

(2) UNREASONABLE POSITION.—

(A) IN GENERAL.—Except as otherwise provided in this paragraph, a position is described in this paragraph unless there is or was substantial authority for the position.

(B) DISCLOSED POSITIONS.—If the position was disclosed as provided in section 6662(d)(2)(B)(ii)(I) and is not a position to which subparagraph (C) applies, the position is described in this paragraph unless there is a reasonable basis for the position.

(C) TAX SHELTERS AND REPORTABLE TRANSACTIONS.—If the position is with respect to a tax shelter (as defined in section 6662(d)(2)(C)(ii)) or a reportable transaction to which section 6662A applies, the position is described in this paragraph unless it is reasonable to believe that the position would more likely than not be sustained on its merits.

(3) REASONABLE CAUSE EXCEPTION.—No penalty shall be imposed under this subsection if it is shown that there is reasonable cause for the understatement and the tax return preparer acted in good faith.

Amendments

• 2008, Tax Extenders and Alternative Minimum Tax Relief Act of 2008 (P.L. 110-343)

P.L. 110-343, Division C, §506(a):

Amended Code Sec. 6694(a). For the **effective** date, see Act Sec. 506(b), below. Prior to amendment, Code Sec. 6694(a) read as follows:

(a) UNDERSTATEMENT DUE TO UNREASONABLE POSITIONS.—

(1) IN GENERAL.—Any tax return preparer who prepares any return or claim for refund with respect to which any part of an understatement of liability is due to a position described in paragraph (2) shall pay a penalty with respect to each such return or claim in an amount equal to the greater of—

(A) $1,000, or

(B) 50 percent of the income derived (or to be derived) by the tax return preparer with respect to the return or claim.

(2) UNREASONABLE POSITION.—A position is described in this paragraph if—

(A) the tax return preparer knew (or reasonably should have known) of the position,

(B) there was not a reasonable belief that the position would more likely than not be sustained on its merits, and

(C)(i) the position was not disclosed as provided in section 6662(d)(2)(B)(ii), or

(ii) there was no reasonable basis for the position.

(3) REASONABLE CAUSE EXCEPTION.—No penalty shall be imposed under this subsection if it is shown that there is reasonable cause for the understatement and the tax return preparer acted in good faith.

P.L. 110-343, Division C, §506(b), provides:

(b) EFFECTIVE DATE.—The amendment made by this section shall apply—

(1) in the case of a position other than a position described in subparagraph (C) of section 6694(a)(2) of the Internal Revenue Code of 1986 (as amended by this section), to returns prepared after May 25, 2007, and

(2) in the case of a position described in such subparagraph (C), to returns prepared for taxable years ending after the date of the enactment of this Act [10-3-2008.—CCH].

• 2007, Small Business and Work Opportunity Tax Act of 2007 (P.L. 110-28)

P.L. 110-28, §8246(a)(2)(F)(i)(I):

Amended Code Sec. 6694 by striking "INCOME TAX RETURN PREPARER" in the heading and inserting "TAX

RETURN PREPARER". **Effective** for returns prepared after 5-25-2007.

P.L. 110-28, §8246(a)(2)(F)(i)(II):

Amended Code Sec. 6694 by striking "an income tax return preparer" each place it appears and inserting "a tax return preparer". **Effective** for returns prepared after 5-25-2007.

P.L. 110-28, §8246(b):

Amended Code Sec. 6694(a). **Effective** for returns prepared after 5-25-2007. Prior to amendment, Code Sec. 6694(a) read as follows:

(a) UNDERSTATEMENTS DUE TO UNREALISTIC POSITIONS.—If—

(1) any part of any understatement of liability with respect to any return or claim for refund is due to a position for which there was not a realistic possibility of being sustained on its merits,

(2) any person who is a tax return preparer with respect to such return or claim knew (or reasonably should have known) of such position, and

(3) such position was not disclosed as provided in section 6662(d)(2)(B)(ii) or was frivolous,

such person shall pay a penalty of $250 with respect to such return or claim unless it is shown that there is reasonable cause for the understatement and such person acted in good faith.

• 1989, Omnibus Budget Reconciliation Act of 1989 (P.L. 101-239)

P.L. 101-239, §7732(a):

Amended Code Sec. 6694(a). **Effective** with respect to documents prepared after 12-31-89. Prior to amendment, Code Sec. 6694(a) read as follows:

(a) NEGLIGENT OR INTENTIONAL DISREGARD OF RULES AND REGULATIONS.—If any part of any understatement of liability with respect to any return or claim for refund is due to the negligent or intentional disregard of rules and regulations by any person who is an income tax return preparer with respect to such return or claim, such person shall pay a penalty of $100 with respect to such return or claim.

[Sec. 6694(b)]

(b) UNDERSTATEMENT DUE TO WILLFUL OR RECKLESS CONDUCT.—

(1) IN GENERAL.—Any tax return preparer who prepares any return or claim for refund with respect to which any part of an understatement of liability is due to a conduct described in paragraph (2) shall pay a penalty with respect to each such return or claim in an amount equal to the greater of—

(A) $5,000, or

(B) 75 percent of the income derived (or to be derived) by the tax return preparer with respect to the return or claim.

(2) WILLFUL OR RECKLESS CONDUCT.—Conduct described in this paragraph is conduct by the tax return preparer which is—

(A) a willful attempt in any manner to understate the liability for tax on the return or claim, or

(B) a reckless or intentional disregard of rules or regulations.

(3) REDUCTION IN PENALTY.—The amount of any penalty payable by any person by reason of this subsection for any return or claim for refund shall be reduced by the amount of the penalty paid by such person by reason of subsection (a).

Amendments

• 2015, Protecting Americans from Tax Hikes Act of 2015 (P.L. 114-113)

P.L. 114-113, §210(a), Div. Q:

Amended Code Sec. 6694(b)(1)(B) by striking "50 percent" and inserting "75 percent". **Effective** for returns prepared for tax years ending after 12-18-2015.

• 2007, Small Business and Work Opportunity Tax Act of 2007 (P.L. 110-28)

P.L. 110-28, §8246(a)(2)(F)(i)(II):

Amended Code Sec. 6694 by striking "an income tax return preparer" each place it appears and inserting "a tax return preparer". **Effective** for returns prepared after 5-25-2007.

P.L. 110-28, §8246(b):

Amended Code Sec. 6694(b). **Effective** for returns prepared after 5-25-2007. Prior to amendment, Code Sec. 6694(b) read as follows:

(b) WILLFUL OR RECKLESS CONDUCT.—If any part of any understatement of liability with respect to any return or claim for refund is due—

(1) to a willful attempt in any manner to understate the liability for tax by a person who is a tax return preparer with respect to such return or claim, or

(2) to any reckless or intentional disregard of rules or regulations by any such person,

such person shall pay a penalty of $1,000 with respect to such return or claim. With respect to any return or claim, the amount of the penalty payable by any person by reason of this subsection shall be reduced by the amount of the penalty paid by such person by reason of subsection (a).

• 1989, Omnibus Budget Reconciliation Act of 1989 (P.L. 101-239)

P.L. 101-239, §7732(a):

Amended Code Sec. 6694(b). **Effective** with respect to documents prepared after 12-31-89. Prior to amendment, Code Sec. 6694(b) read as follows:

(b) WILLFUL UNDERSTATEMENT OF LIABILITY.—If any part of any understatement of liability with respect to any return or claim for refund is due to a willful attempt in any manner to understate the liability for a tax by a person who is an income tax return preparer with respect to such return or claim, such person shall pay a penalty of $500 with respect to such return or claim. With respect to any return or claim, the amount of the penalty payable by any person by reason of this subsection shall be reduced by the amount of the penalty paid by such person by reason of subsection (a).

[Sec. 6694(c)]

(c) EXTENSION OF PERIOD OF COLLECTION WHERE PREPARER PAYS 15 PERCENT OF PENALTY.—

(1) IN GENERAL.—If, within 30 days after the day on which notice and demand of any penalty under subsection (a) or (b) is made against any person who is a tax return preparer, such person pays an amount which is not less than 15 percent of the amount of such penalty and files a claim for refund of the amount so paid, no levy or proceeding in court for the collection of the remainder of such penalty shall be made, begun, or prosecuted until the final resolution of a proceeding begun as provided in paragraph (2). Notwithstanding the provisions of section 7421(a), the beginning of such proceeding or levy during the time such prohibition is in force may be enjoined by a proceeding in the proper court. Nothing in this paragraph shall be

construed to prohibit any counterclaim for the remainder of such penalty in a proceeding begun as provided in paragraph (2).

(2) PREPARER MUST BRING SUIT IN DISTRICT COURT TO DETERMINE HIS LIABILITY FOR PENALTY.—If, within 30 days after the day on which his claim for refund of any partial payment of any penalty under subsection (a) or (b) is denied (or, if earlier, within 30 days after the expiration of 6 months after the day on which he filed the claim for refund), the tax return preparer fails to begin a proceeding in the appropriate United States district court for the determination of his liability for such penalty, paragraph (1) shall cease to apply with respect to such penalty, effective on the day following the close of the applicable 30-day period referred to in this paragraph.

(3) SUSPENSION OF RUNNING OF PERIOD OF LIMITATIONS ON COLLECTION.—The running of the period of limitations provided in section 6502 on the collection by levy or by a proceeding in court in respect of any penalty described in paragraph (1) shall be suspended for the period during which the Secretary is prohibited from collecting by levy or a proceeding in court.

Amendments

• 2007, Small Business and Work Opportunity Tax Act of 2007 (P.L. 110-28)

P.L. 110-28, §8246(a)(2)(F)(i)(II):

Amended Code Sec. 6694 by striking "an income tax return preparer" each place it appears and inserting "a tax return preparer". **Effective** for returns prepared after 5-25-2007.

P.L. 110-28, §8246(a)(2)(F)(i)(III):

Amended Code Sec. 6694(c)(2) by striking "the income tax return preparer" and inserting "the tax return preparer". **Effective** for returns prepared after 5-25-2007.

• 1989, Omnibus Budget Reconciliation Act of 1989 (P.L. 101-239)

P.L. 101-239, §7737(a):

Amended Code Sec. 6694(c)(1) by adding at the end thereof a new sentence. **Effective** 12-19-89

[Sec. 6694(d)]

(d) ABATEMENT OF PENALTY WHERE TAXPAYER LIABILITY NOT UNDERSTATED.—If at any time there is a final administrative determination or a final judicial decision that there was no understatement of liability in the case of any return or claim for refund with respect to which a penalty under subsection (a) or (b) has been assessed, such assessment shall be abated, and if any portion of such penalty has been paid the amount so paid shall be refunded to the person who made such payment as an overpayment of tax without regard to any period of limitations which, but for this subsection, would apply to the making of such refund.

[Sec. 6694(e)]

(e) UNDERSTATEMENT OF LIABILITY DEFINED.—For purposes of this section, the term "understatement of liability" means any understatement of the net amount payable with respect to any tax imposed by this title or any overstatement of the net amount creditable or refundable with respect to any such tax. Except as otherwise provided in subsection (d), the determination of whether or not there is an understatement of liability shall be made without regard to any administrative or judicial action involving the taxpayer.

Amendments

• 2007, Small Business and Work Opportunity Tax Act of 2007 (P.L. 110-28)

P.L. 110-28, §8246(a)(2)(F)(i)(IV):

Amended Code Sec. 6694(e) by striking "subtitle A" and inserting "this title". **Effective** for returns prepared after 5-25-2007.

[Sec. 6694(f)]

(f) CROSS REFERENCE.—

For definition of tax return preparer, see section 7701(a)(36).

Amendments

• 2007, Small Business and Work Opportunity Tax Act of 2007 (P.L. 110-28)

P.L. 110-28, §8246(a)(2)(F)(i)(V):

Amended Code Sec. 6694(f) by striking "income tax return preparer" and inserting "tax return preparer". **Effective** for returns prepared after 5-25-2007.

• 1976, Tax Reform Act of 1976 (P.L. 94-455)

P.L. 94-455, §1203(b)(1):

Added Code Sec. 6694. **Effective** for documents prepared after 12-31-76.

[Sec. 6695]

SEC. 6695. OTHER ASSESSABLE PENALTIES WITH RESPECT TO THE PREPARATION OF TAX RETURNS FOR OTHER PERSONS.

[Sec. 6695(a)]

(a) FAILURE TO FURNISH COPY TO TAXPAYER.—Any person who is a tax return preparer with respect to any return or claim for refund who fails to comply with section 6107(a) with respect to such return or claim shall pay a penalty of $50 for such failure, unless it is shown that such failure is due to reasonable cause and not due to willful neglect. The maximum penalty imposed under this subsection on any person with respect to documents filed during any calendar year shall not exceed $25,000.

Amendments

• 2007, Small Business and Work Opportunity Tax Act of 2007 (P.L. 110-28)

P.L. 110-28, §8246(a)(2)(G)(i)(I):

Amended Code Sec. 6695 by striking "INCOME" before "TAX RETURNS" in the heading. **Effective** for returns prepared after 5-25-2007.

P.L. 110-28, §8246(a)(2)(G)(i)(II):

Amended Code Sec. 6695 by striking "an income tax preparer" each place it appears and inserting "a tax return preparer". **Effective** for returns prepared after 5-25-2007.

• 1989, Omnibus Budget Reconciliation Act of 1989 (P.L. 101-239)

P.L. 101-239, §7733(a)(1)-(2):

Amended Code Sec. 6695(a) by striking "$25" and inserting "$50", and by adding at the end thereof a new sentence. **Effective** for documents prepared after 12-31-89.

[Sec. 6695(b)]

(b) FAILURE TO SIGN RETURN.—Any person who is a tax return preparer with respect to any return or claim for refund, who is required by regulations prescribed by the Secretary to sign such return or claim, and who fails to comply with such regulations with respect to such return or claim shall pay a penalty of $50 for such failure, unless it is shown that such failure is due to reasonable cause and not due to willful neglect. The maximum penalty imposed under this subsection on any person with respect to documents filed during any calendar year shall not exceed $25,000.

Amendments

• 2007, Small Business and Work Opportunity Tax Act of 2007 (P.L. 110-28)

P.L. 110-28, §8246(a)(2)(G)(i)(II):

Amended Code Sec. 6695 by striking "an income tax preparer" each place it appears and inserting "a tax return preparer". **Effective** for returns prepared after 5-25-2007.

• 1989, Omnibus Budget Reconciliation Act of 1989 (P.L. 101-239)

P.L. 101-239, §7733(b)(1)-(2):

Amended Code Sec. 6695(b) by striking "$25" and inserting "$50", and by adding at the end thereof a new sentence. **Effective** for documents prepared after 12-31-89.

• 1985 (P.L. 99-44)

P.L. 99-44, §1(b):

Repealed P.L. 98-369, §179(b)(2). **Effective** as if included in the amendment made by P.L. 98-369, §179(b)(2), and the Internal Revenue Code of 1954 shall be applied and administered as if such paragraph (and the amendment made by such paragraph) had not been enacted. Prior to repeal, Code Sec. 6695(b) to read as follows:

(b) FAILURE TO INFORM TAXPAYER OF CERTAIN RECORDKEEPING REQUIREMENTS OR TO SIGN RETURN.—Any person who is an income tax return preparer with respect to any return or claim for refund and who is required by regulations to sign such return or claim—

(1) shall advise the taxpayer of the substantiation requirements of section 274(d) and obtain written confirmation from the taxpayer that such requirements were met with respect to any deduction or credit claimed on such return or claim for refund, and

(2) shall sign such return or claim for refund.

Any person who fails to comply with the requirements of the preceding sentence with respect to any return or claim shall pay a penalty of $25 for such failure, unless it is shown that such failure is due to reasonable cause and not to willful neglect.

P.L. 99-44, §1(c), provides:

(c) REPEAL OF REGULATIONS.—Regulations issued before the date of the enactment of this Act to carry out the amendments made by paragraphs (1)(C), (2), and (3) of section 179(b) of the Tax Reform Act of 1984 shall have no force and effect.

P.L. 99-44, §5, provides:

Not later than October 1, 1985, the Secretary of the Treasury or his delegate shall prescribe regulations to carry out the provisions of this Act which shall fully reflect such provisions.

• 1984, Deficit Reduction Act of 1984 (P.L. 98-369)

P.L. 98-369, §179(b)(2):

Amended Code Sec. 6695(b). **Effective** for tax years beginning after 12-31-84. Prior to amendment, Code Sec. 6695(b) read as follows:

(b) Failure To Sign Return.—Any person who is an income tax return preparer with respect to any return or claim for refund, who is required by regulations prescribed by the Secretary to sign such return or claim, and who fails to comply with such regulations with respect to such return or claim shall pay a penalty of $25 for such failure, unless it is shown that such failure is due to reasonable cause and not due to willful neglect.

[Sec. 6695(c)]

(c) FAILURE TO FURNISH IDENTIFYING NUMBER.—Any person who is a tax return preparer with respect to any return or claim for refund and who fails to comply with section 6109(a)(4) with respect to such return or claim shall pay a penalty of $50 for such failure, unless it is shown that such failure is due to reasonable cause and not due to willful neglect. The maximum penalty imposed under this subsection on any person with respect to documents filed during any calendar year shall not exceed $25,000.

Amendments

• 2007, Small Business and Work Opportunity Tax Act of 2007 (P.L. 110-28)

P.L. 110-28, §8246(a)(2)(G)(i)(II):

Amended Code Sec. 6695 by striking "an income tax preparer" each place it appears and inserting "a tax return preparer". **Effective** for returns prepared after 5-25-2007.

• 1989, Omnibus Budget Reconciliation Act of 1989 (P.L. 101-239)

P.L. 101-239, §7733(c)(1)-(2):

Amended Code Sec. 6695(c) by striking "$25" and inserting "$50", and by adding at the end thereof a new sentence. **Effective** for documents prepared after 12-31-89.

[Sec. 6695(d)]

(d) FAILURE TO RETAIN COPY OR LIST.—Any person who is a tax return preparer with respect to any return or claim for refund who fails to comply with section 6107(b) with respect to such return or claim shall pay a penalty of $50 for each such failure, unless it is shown that such failure is due to reasonable cause and not due to willful neglect. The maximum penalty imposed under this subsection on any person with respect to any return period shall not exceed $25,000.

Amendments

• 2007, Small Business and Work Opportunity Tax Act of 2007 (P.L. 110-28)

P.L. 110-28, §8246(a)(2)(G)(i)(II):

Amended Code Sec. 6695 by striking "an income tax preparer" each place it appears and inserting "a tax return preparer". **Effective** for returns prepared after 5-25-2007.

[Sec. 6695(e)]

(e) FAILURE TO FILE CORRECT INFORMATION RETURNS.—Any person required to make a return under section 6060 who fails to comply with the requirements of such section shall pay a penalty of $50 for—

(1) each failure to file a return as required under such section, and

(2) each failure to set forth an item in the return as required under [such]section,

unless it is shown that such failure is due to reasonable cause and not due to willful neglect. The maximum penalty imposed under this subsection on any person with respect to any return period shall not exceed $25,000.

Amendments

• 1989, Omnibus Budget Reconciliation Act of 1989 (P.L. 101-239)

P.L. 101-239, §7733(d):

Amended Code Sec. 6695(e). **Effective** for documents prepared after 12-31-89. Prior to amendment, Code Sec. 6695(e) read as follows:

(e) FAILURE TO FILE CORRECT INFORMATION RETURN.—Any person required to make a return under section 6060 who fails to comply with the requirements of such section shall pay a penalty of—

(1) $100 for each failure to file a return as required under such section, and

(2) $5 for each failure to set forth an item in the return as required under such section,

unless it is shown that such failure is due to reasonable cause and not due to willful neglect. The maximum penalty imposed under this subsection on any person with respect to any return period shall not exceed $20,000.

[Sec. 6695(f)]

(f) NEGOTIATION OF CHECK.—Any person who is a tax return preparer who endorses or otherwise negotiates (directly or through an agent) any check made in respect of the taxes imposed by this title which is issued to a taxpayer (other than the tax return preparer) shall pay a penalty of $500 with respect to each such check. The preceding sentence shall not apply with respect to the deposit by a bank (within the meaning of section 581) of the full amount of the check in the taxpayer's account in such bank for the benefit of the taxpayer.

Amendments

• 2007, Small Business and Work Opportunity Tax Act of 2007 (P.L. 110-28)

P.L. 110-28, §8246(a)(2)(G)(i)(II):

Amended Code Sec. 6695 by striking "an income tax preparer" each place it appears and inserting "a tax return preparer". **Effective** for returns prepared after 5-25-2007.

P.L. 110-28, §8246(a)(2)(G)(ii)(I)-(II):

Amended Code Sec. 6695(f) by striking "subtitle A" and inserting "this title", and by striking "the income tax return preparer" and inserting "the tax return preparer". **Effective** for returns prepared after 5-25-2007.

• 1978, Revenue Act of 1978 (P.L. 95-600)

P.L. 95-600, §701(cc)(1):

Amended Code Sec. 6695(f). **Effective** for documents prepared after 12-31-76.

• 1976, Tax Reform Act of 1976 (P.L. 94-455)

P.L. 94-455, §1203(f):

Added Code Sec. 6695. **Effective** for documents prepared after 12-31-76.

* * *

[Sec. 6695(h)]

(h) ADJUSTMENT FOR INFLATION.—

(1) IN GENERAL.—In the case of any failure relating to a return or claim for refund filed in a calendar year beginning after 2014, each of the dollar amounts under subsections (a), (b), (c), (d), (e), (f), and (g) shall be increased by an amount equal to such dollar amount multiplied by the cost-of-living adjustment determined under section 1(f)(3) for the calendar year determined by substituting "calendar year 2013" for "calendar year 2016" in subparagraph (A)(ii) thereof.

(2) ROUNDING.—If any amount adjusted under paragraph (1)—

(A) is not less than $5,000 and is not a multiple of $500, such amount shall be rounded to the next lowest multiple of $500, and

(B) is not described in subparagraph (A) and is not a multiple of $5, such amount shall be rounded to the next lowest multiple of $5.

Amendments

• 2018, Tax Technical Corrections Act of 2018 (P.L. 115-141)

P.L. 115-141, §401(a)(299)(C), Div. U:

Amended Code Sec. 6695(h)(1) by inserting "an amount equal to" after "increased by" and by inserting "for the calendar year" after "section 1(f)(3)". **Effective** 3-23-2018.

P.L. 115-141, §401(a)(309), Div. U:

Amended Code Sec. 6695(h)(2) by striking "subparagraph (A)" and inserting "paragraph (1)". **Effective** 3-23-2018.

P.L. 115-141, §401(a)(310), Div. U:

Amended Code Sec. 6695(h)(2)(B) by striking "clause (i)" and inserting "subparagraph (A)". **Effective** 3-23-2018.

• 2017, Tax Cuts and Jobs Act (P.L. 115-97)

P.L. 115-97, § 11002(d)(1)(MM):

Amended Code Sec. 6695(h)(1) by striking "for 'calendar year 1992' in subparagraph (B)" and inserting "for 'calendar year 2016' in subparagraph (A)(ii)". **Effective** for tax years beginning after 12-31-2017.

• 2014, Stephen Beck, Jr., Achieving a Better Life Experience Act of 2014 (P.L. 113-295)

P.L. 113-295, § 208(c), Division B:

Amended Code Sec. 6695 by adding at the end a new subsection (h). **Effective** for returns or claims for refund filed after 12-31-2014 [**effective** date changed by P.L. 115-141, § 105(a)(1)-(3), Div. U.—CCH].

[Sec. 6695A]

SEC. 6695A. SUBSTANTIAL AND GROSS VALUATION MISSTATEMENTS ATTRIBUTABLE TO INCORRECT APPRAISALS.

[Sec. 6695A(a)]

(a) IMPOSITION OF PENALTY.—If—

(1) a person prepares an appraisal of the value of property and such person knows, or reasonably should have known, that the appraisal would be used in connection with a return or a claim for refund, and

(2) the claimed value of the property on a return or claim for refund which is based on such appraisal results in a substantial valuation misstatement under chapter 1 (within the meaning of section 6662(e)), a substantial estate or gift tax valuation understatement (within the meaning of section 6662(g),or a gross valuation misstatement (within the meaning of section 6662(h)), with respect to such property,

then such person shall pay a penalty in the amount determined under subsection (b).

Amendments

• 2007, Tax Technical Corrections Act of 2007 (P.L. 110-172)

P.L. 110-172, § 3(e)(1):

Amended Code Sec. 6695A(a)(2) by inserting "a substantial estate or gift tax valuation understatement (within the meaning of section 6662(g))," before "or a gross valuation misstatement". **Effective** as if included in the provision of the Pension Protection Act of 2006 (P.L. 109-280) to which it relates [**effective** generally for appraisals prepared with respect to returns or submission filed after 8-17-2006. For a special rule, see P.L. 109-432, § 1219(e)(3), in the amendment notes for Code Sec. 6695A(c).—CCH].

P.L. 110-172, § 11(a)(40):

Amended Code Sec. 6695A(a) by striking "then such person" [and all that follows] in paragraph (2) and inserting: "then such person" [and all that follows].

Effective 12-29-2007.

[Sec. 6695A(b)]

(b) AMOUNT OF PENALTY.—The amount of the penalty imposed under subsection (a) on any person with respect to an appraisal shall be equal to the lesser of—

(1) the greater of—

(A) 10 percent of the amount of the underpayment (as defined in section 6664(a)) attributable to the misstatement described in subsection (a)(2), or

(B) $1,000, or

(2) 125 percent of the gross income received by the person described in subsection (a)(1) from the preparation of the appraisal.

[Sec. 6695A(c)]

(c) EXCEPTION.—No penalty shall be imposed under subsection (a) if the person establishes to the satisfaction of the Secretary that the value established in the appraisal was more likely than not the proper value.

Amendments

• 2006, Pension Protection Act of 2006 (P.L. 109-280)

P.L. 109-280, § 1219(b)(1):

Amended part I of subchapter B of chapter 68 by inserting after Code Sec. 6695 a new Code Sec. 6695A. **Effective** generally for appraisals prepared with respect to returns or submissions filed after 8-17-2006. For a special rule, see Act Sec. 1219(e)(3), below.

P.L. 109-280, § 1219(e)(3), provides:

(3) SPECIAL RULE FOR CERTAIN EASEMENTS.—In the case of a contribution of a qualified real property interest which is a restriction with respect to the exterior of a building described in section 170(h)(4)(C)(ii) of the Internal Revenue Code of 1986, and an appraisal with respect to the contribution, the amendments made by subsections (a) and (b) shall apply to returns filed after July 25, 2006.

[Sec. 6696]

SEC. 6696. RULES APPLICABLE WITH RESPECT TO SECTIONS 6694, 6695, AND 6695A.

[Sec. 6696(a)]

(a) PENALTIES TO BE ADDITIONAL TO ANY OTHER PENALTIES.—The penalties provided by sections 6694, 6695, and 6695A shall be in addition to any other penalties provided by law.

Amendments

• 2018, Tax Technical Corrections Act of 2018 (P.L. 115-141)

P.L. 115-141, §401(a)(311), Div. U:

Amended Code Sec. 6696(a) by striking "section 6694," and inserting "sections 6694,". **Effective** 3-23-2018.

• 2006, Pension Protection Act of 2006 (P.L. 109-280)

P.L. 109-280, §1219(b)(2)(A):

Amended Code Sec. 6696 by striking "6694 and 6695" each place it appears in the text and heading thereof and inserting "6694, 6695, and 6695A". **Effective** generally for appraisals prepared with respect to returns or submissions filed after 8-17-2006. For a special rule, see Act Sec. 1219(e)(3), below.

P.L. 109-280, §1219(e)(3), provides:

(3) SPECIAL RULE FOR CERTAIN EASEMENTS.—In the case of a contribution of a qualified real property interest which is a restriction with respect to the exterior of a building described in section 170(h)(4)(C)(ii) of the Internal Revenue Code of 1986, and an appraisal with respect to the contribution, the amendments made by subsections (a) and (b) shall apply to returns filed after July 25, 2006.

[Sec. 6696(b)]

(b) DEFICIENCY PROCEDURES NOT TO APPLY.—Subchapter B of chapter 63 (relating to deficiency procedures for income, estate, gift, and certain excise taxes) shall not apply with respect to the assessment or collection of the penalties provided by sections 6694, 6695, and 6695A.

Amendments

• 2006, Pension Protection Act of 2006 (P.L. 109-280)

P.L. 109-280, §1219(b)(2)(A):

Amended Code Sec. 6696 by striking "6694 and 6695" each place it appears in the text and inserting "6694, 6695, and 6695A". **Effective** generally for appraisals prepared with respect to returns or submissions filed after 8-17-2006. For a special rule, see Act Sec. 1219(e)(3) in the amendment notes for Code Sec. 6696(a).

[Sec. 6696(c)]

(c) PROCEDURE FOR CLAIMING REFUND.—Any claim for credit or refund of any penalty paid under section 6694, 6695, or 6695A shall be filed in accordance with regulations prescribed by the Secretary.

Amendments

• 2006, Pension Protection Act of 2006 (P.L. 109-280)

P.L. 109-280, §1219(b)(2)(B):

Amended Code Sec. 6696 by striking "6694 or 6695" each place it appears in the text and inserting "6694, 6695, or 6695A". **Effective** generally for appraisals prepared with respect to returns or submissions filed after 8-17-2006. For a special rule, see Act Sec. 1219(e)(3) in the amendment notes for Code Sec. 6696(a).

[Sec. 6696(d)]

(d) PERIODS OF LIMITATION.—

(1) ASSESSMENT.—The amount of any penalty under section 6694(a), 6695, or 6695A shall be assessed within 3 years after the return or claim for refund with respect to which the penalty is assessed was filed, and no proceeding in court without assessment for the collection of such tax shall be begun after the expiration of such period. In the case of any penalty under section 6694(b), the penalty may be assessed, or a proceeding in court for the collection of the penalty may be begun without assessment, at any time.

(2) CLAIM FOR REFUND.—Except as provided in section 6694(d), any claim for refund of an overpayment of any penalty assessed under section 6694, 6695, or 6695A shall be filed within 3 years from the time the penalty was paid.

Amendments

• 2018, Tax Technical Corrections Act of 2018 (P.L. 115-141)

P.L. 115-141, §401(a)(312), Div. U:

Amended Code Sec. 6696(d)(1) by striking "section 6695," and inserting "6695,". **Effective** 3-23-2018.

• 2007, Tax Technical Corrections Act of 2007 (P.L. 110-172)

P.L. 110-172, §3(e)(2):

Amended Code Sec. 6696(d)(1) by striking "or under section 6695" and inserting ", section 6695, or 6695A". **Effective** as if included in the provision of the Pension Protection Act of 2006 (P.L. 109-280) to which it relates [**effective** generally for appraisals prepared with respect to returns or submission filed after 8-17-2006. For a special rule, see P.L. 109-280, §1219(e)(3), in the amendment notes for Code Sec. 6696(a).—CCH].

• 2006, Pension Protection Act of 2006 (P.L. 109-280)

P.L. 109-280, §1219(b)(2)(B):

Amended Code Sec. 6696 by striking "6694 or 6695" each place it appears in the text and inserting "6694, 6695, or 6695A". **Effective** generally for appraisals prepared with respect to returns or submissions filed after 8-17-2006. For a special rule, see Act Sec. 1219(e)(3) in the amendment notes for Code Sec. 6696(a).

[Sec. 6696(e)]

(e) DEFINITIONS.—For purposes of sections 6694, 6695, and 6695A—

(1) RETURN.—The term "return" means any return of any tax imposed by this title, any administrative adjustment request under section 6227, and any partnership adjustment tracking report under section 6226(b)(4)(A).

(2) CLAIM FOR REFUND.—The term "claim for refund" means a claim for refund of, or credit against, any tax imposed by this title.

Amendments

• 2018, Tax Technical Corrections Act of 2018 (P.L. 115-141)

P.L. 115-141, §206(n)(3), Div. U:

Amended Code Sec. 6696(e)(1) by inserting ", any administrative adjustment request under section 6227, and any partnership adjustment tracking report under section 6226(b)(4)(A)" before the period at the end. **Effective** as if included in section 1101 of the Bipartisan Budget Act of 2015 [**effective** generally for returns filed for partnership tax years beginning after 12-31-2017.—CCH].

• 2007, Small Business and Work Opportunity Tax Act of 2007 (P.L. 110-28)

P.L. 110-28, §8246(a)(2)(H):

Amended Code Sec. 6696(e) by striking "subtitle A" each place it appears and inserting "this title". **Effective** for returns prepared after 5-25-2007.

• 2006, Pension Protection Act of 2006 (P.L. 109-280)

P.L. 109-280, §1219(b)(2)(A):

Amended Code Sec. 6696 by striking "6694 and 6695" each place it appears in the text and heading thereof and inserting "6694, 6695, and 6695A". **Effective** generally for appraisals prepared with respect to returns or submissions filed after 8-17-2006. For a special rule, see Act Sec. 1219(e)(3) in the amendment notes for Code Sec. 6696(a).

• 1976, Tax Reform Act of 1976 (P.L. 94-455)

P.L. 94-455, §1203(f):

Added Code Sec. 6696. **Effective** for documents prepared after 12-31-76.

* * *

[Sec. 6698A—Repealed]

Amendments

• 1980, Crude Oil Windfall Profit Tax Act of 1980 (P.L. 96-223)

P.L. 96-223, §401(a):

Repealed Code Sec. 6698A(a)-(c), as added by P.L. 94-455, Act Sec. 2005(d)(2), and as redesignated by P.L. 95-600, Act Sec. 702(r)(1)(A), and P.L. 96-222. **Effective** with respect to decedents dying after 1976. However, see the amendment note for P.L. 96-223, Act Sec. 401(a), that follows Code Sec. 1014(d) for the text of Act Sec. 401(d) that authorizes the election of the carryover basis rules in the case of a decedent dying after 12-31-76 and before 11-7-78. Prior to repeal, Code Sec. 6698A read as follows:

SEC. 6698A. FAILURE TO FILE INFORMATION WITH RESPECT TO CARRYOVER BASIS PROPERTY.

[Sec. 6698A(a)]

(a) INFORMATION REQUIRED TO BE FURNISHED TO THE SECRETARY.—Any executor who fails to furnish information required under subsection (a) of section 6039A on the date prescribed therefor (determined with regard to any extension of time for filing), unless it is shown that such failure is due to reasonable cause and not to willful neglect, shall pay a penalty of $100 for each such failure, but the total amount imposed for all such failures shall not exceed $5,000.

Amendments

• 1978, Revenue Act of 1978 (P.L. 95-600)

P.L. 95-600, §702(r)(1)(A):

Redesignated Code Sec. 6694(a) as Code Sec. 6698[A](a). **Effective** for estates of decedents dying after 12-31-76.

• 1976, Tax Reform Act of 1976 (P.L. 94-455)

P.L. 94-455, §2005(d)(2), (f)(1):

Added Code Sec. 6694[A](a). **Effective** in respect of decedents dying after 12-31-79 (as amended by P.L. 95-600, Act Sec. 515(6)).

[Sec. 6698A(b)]

(b) INFORMATION REQUIRED TO BE FURNISHED TO BENEFICIARIES.—Any executor who fails to furnish in writing to each person described in subsection (b) of section 6039A the information required under such subsection, unless it is shown that such failure is due to reasonable cause and not to willful neglect, shall pay a penalty of $50 for each such failure, but the total amount imposed for all such failures shall not exceed $2,500.

Amendments

• 1978, Revenue Act of 1978 (P.L. 95-600)

P.L. 95-600, §702(r)(1)(A):

Redesignated Code Sec. 6694(b) as Code Sec. 6698[A](b). **Effective** for estates of decedents dying after 12-31-76.

• 1976, Tax Reform Act of 1976 (P.L. 94-455)

P.L. 94-455, §2005(d)(2), (f)(1):

Added Code Sec. 6694[A](b). **Effective** in respect of decedents dying after 12-31-79 (as amended by P.L. 95-600, Act Sec. 515(6)).

[Sec. 6698A(c)]

(c) DEFICIENCY PROCEDURES NOT TO APPLY.—Subchapter B of chapter 63 (relating to deficiency procedures for income, estate, gift, and certain excise taxes) shall not apply in respect of the assessment or collection of any penalty imposed by subsection (a).

Amendments

• 1980, Technical Corrections Act of 1979 (P.L. 96-222)

P.L. 96-222, §107(a)(2)(D):

Redesignated Code Sec. 6698 as 6698A. **Effective** for estates of decedents dying after 12-31-76.

• 1978, Revenue Act of 1978 (P.L. 95-600)

P.L. 95-600, §702(r)(1)(B):

Added Code Sec. 6698(c). **Effective** for estates of decedents dying after 12-31-76.

* * *

[Sec. 6712]

SEC. 6712. FAILURE TO DISCLOSE TREATY-BASED RETURN POSITIONS.

[Sec. 6712(a)]

(a) GENERAL RULE.—If a taxpayer fails to meet the requirements of section 6114, there is hereby imposed a penalty equal to $1000 ($10,000 in the case of a C corporation) on each such failure.

[Sec. 6712(b)]

(b) AUTHORITY TO WAIVE.—The Secretary may waive all or any part of the penalty provided by this section on a showing by the taxpayer that there was reasonable cause for the failure and that the taxpayer acted in good faith.

[Sec. 6712(c)]

(c) PENALTY IN ADDITION TO OTHER PENALTIES.—The penalty imposed by this section shall be in addition to any other penalty imposed by law.

Amendments

• 1988, Technical and Miscellaneous Revenue Act of 1988 (P.L. 100-647)

P.L. 100-647, §1012(aa)(5)(B):

Amended part I of subchapter B of chapter 68 by adding section 6712. **Effective** as if included in the provision of P.L. 99-514 to which it relates.

* * *

[Sec. 6716—Repealed]

Amendments

• 2013, American Taxpayer Relief Act of 2012 (P.L. 112-240)

P.L. 112-240, §101(a)(1)-(3), provides:

SEC. 101. PERMANENT EXTENSION AND MODIFICATION OF 2001 TAX RELIEF.

(a) PERMANENT EXTENSION.—

(1) IN GENERAL.—The Economic Growth and Tax Relief Reconciliation Act of 2001 is amended by striking title IX.

(2) CONFORMING AMENDMENT.—The Tax Relief, Unemployment Insurance Reauthorization, and Job Creation Act of 2010 is amended by striking section 304.

(3) EFFECTIVE DATE.—The amendments made by this subsection shall apply to taxable, plan, or limitation years beginning after December 31, 2012, and estates of decedents dying, gifts made, or generation skipping transfers after December 31, 2012.

• 2010, Tax Relief, Unemployment Insurance Reauthorization, and Job Creation Act of 2010 (P.L. 111-312)

P.L. 111-312, §301(a):

Amended Code Sec. 6716 to read as such provision would read if subtitle E of title V of the Economic Growth and Tax Relief Reconciliation Act of 2001 (P.L. 107-16) had never been enacted. [P.L. 107-16, §542(b)(4), added new Code Sec. 6716. Therefore, P.L. 111-312, §301(a), effectively repealed Code Sec. 6716.—CCH] **Effective** for estates of decedents dying, and transfers made, after 12-31-2009. For a special rule, see Act Sec. 301(c), below. Prior to amendment by P.L. 111-312, Code Sec. 6716 read as follows:

SEC. 6716. FAILURE TO FILE INFORMATION WITH RESPECT TO CERTAIN TRANSFERS AT DEATH AND GIFTS.

[Sec. 6716(a)]

(a) INFORMATION REQUIRED TO BE FURNISHED TO THE SECRETARY.—Any person required to furnish any information under section 6018 who fails to furnish such information on the date prescribed therefor (determined with regard to any extension of time for filing) shall pay a penalty of $10,000 ($500 in the case of information required to be furnished under section 6018(b)(2)) for each such failure.

[Sec. 6716(b)]

(b) INFORMATION REQUIRED TO BE FURNISHED TO BENEFICIARIES.—Any person required to furnish in writing to each person described in section 6018(e) or 6019(b) the information required under such section who fails to furnish such information shall pay a penalty of $50 for each such failure.

[Sec. 6716(c)]

(c) REASONABLE CAUSE EXCEPTION.—No penalty shall be imposed under subsection (a) or (b) with respect to any failure if it is shown that such failure is due to reasonable cause.

[Sec. 6716(d)]

(d) INTENTIONAL DISREGARD.—If any failure under subsection (a) or (b) is due to intentional disregard of the requirements under sections 6018 and 6019(b), the penalty under such subsection shall be 5 percent of the fair market value (as of the date of death or, in the case of section 6019(b), the date of the gift) of the property with respect to which the information is required.

[Sec. 6716(e)]

(e) DEFICIENCY PROCEDURES NOT TO APPLY.—Subchapter B of chapter 63 (relating to deficiency procedures for income, estate, gift, and certain excise taxes) shall not apply in respect of the assessment or collection of any penalty imposed by this section.

P.L. 111-312, §301(c), provides:

(c) SPECIAL ELECTION WITH RESPECT TO ESTATES OF DECEDENTS DYING IN 2010.—Notwithstanding subsection (a), in the case of an estate of a decedent dying after December 31, 2009, and before January 1, 2011, the executor (within the meaning of section 2203 of the Internal Revenue Code of 1986) may elect to apply such Code as though the amendments made by subsection (a) do not apply with respect to chapter 11 of such Code and with respect to property acquired or passing from such decedent (within the meaning of section 1014(b) of such Code). Such election shall be made at such time and in such manner as the Secretary of the Treasury or the Secretary's delegate shall provide. Such an election once made shall be revocable only with the consent of the Secretary of the Treasury or the Secretary's delegate. For purposes of section 2652(a)(1) of such Code, the determination of whether any property is subject to the tax imposed by such chapter 11 shall be made without regard to any election made under this subsection.

P.L. 111-312, §304, provides [but see P.L. 112-240, §101(a)(2)-(3), above]:

SEC. 304. APPLICATION OF EGTRRA SUNSET TO THIS TITLE.

Section 901 of the Economic Growth and Tax Relief Reconciliation Act of 2001 shall apply to the amendments made by this title.

• 2001, Economic Growth and Tax Relief Reconciliation Act of 2001 (P.L. 107-16)

P.L. 107-16, §542(b)(4):

Amended part I of subchapter B of chapter 68 by adding at the end a new Code Sec. 6716. **Effective** for estates of decedents dying after 12-31-2009.

P.L. 107-16, §901(a)-(b), as amended by P.L. 111-312, §101(a)(1), provides [but see P.L. 112-240, §101(a)(1) and (3), above]:

SEC. 901. SUNSET OF PROVISIONS OF ACT.

(a) IN GENERAL.—All provisions of, and amendments made by, this Act shall not apply—

(1) to taxable, plan, or limitation years beginning after December 31, 2012, or

(2) in the case of title V, to estates of decedents dying, gifts made, or generation skipping transfers, after December 31, 2012.

(b) APPLICATION OF CERTAIN LAWS.—The Internal Revenue Code of 1986 and the Employee Retirement Income Security Act of 1974 shall be applied and administered to years, estates, gifts, and transfers described in subsection (a) as if the provisions and amendments described in subsection (a) had never been enacted.

* * *

[Sec. 6720]

SEC. 6720. FRAUDULENT ACKNOWLEDGMENTS WITH RESPECT TO DONATIONS OF MOTOR VEHICLES, BOATS, AND AIRPLANES.

Any donee organization required under section 170(f)(12)(A) to furnish a contemporaneous written acknowledgment to a donor which knowingly furnishes a false or fraudulent acknowledgment, or which knowingly fails to furnish such acknowledgment in the manner, at the time, and showing the information required under section 170(f)(12), or regulations prescribed thereunder, shall for each such act, or for each such failure, be subject to a penalty equal to—

(1) in the case of an acknowledgment with respect to a qualified vehicle to which section 170(f)(12)(A)(ii) applies, the greater of—

(A) the product of the highest rate of tax specified in section 1 and the sales price stated on the acknowledgment, or

(B) the gross proceeds from the sale of such vehicle, and

(2) in the case of an acknowledgment with respect to any other qualified vehicle to which section 170(f)(12) applies, the greater of—

(A) the product of the highest rate of tax specified in section 1 and the claimed value of the vehicle, or

(B) $5,000.

Amendments

• 2004, American Jobs Creation Act of 2004 (P.L. 108-357)

P.L. 108-357, §884(b)(1):

Amended part I of subchapter B of chapter 68, as amended by this Act, by inserting after Code Sec. 6719 a new Code Sec. 6720. **Effective** for contributions made after 12-31-2004.

***

CHAPTER 70—JEOPARDY, RECEIVERSHIPS, ETC.

Subchapter A—Jeopardy

***

***

PART II—JEOPARDY ASSESSMENTS

***

[Sec. 6861]

SEC. 6861. JEOPARDY ASSESSMENTS OF INCOME, ESTATE, GIFT, AND CERTAIN EXCISE TAXES.

[Sec. 6861(a)]

(a) AUTHORITY FOR MAKING.—If the Secretary believes that the assessment or collection of a deficiency, as defined in section 6211, will be jeopardized by delay, he shall, notwithstanding the provisions of section 6213(a), immediately assess such deficiency (together with all interest, additional amounts, and additions to the tax provided for by law), and notice and demand shall be made by the Secretary for the payment thereof.

Amendments

• 1976, Tax Reform Act of 1976 (P.L. 94-455)

P.L. 94-455, §1906(b)(13)(A):

Amended 1954 Code by substituting "Secretary" for "Secretary or his delegate" each place it appeared. **Effective** 2-1-77.

• 1974, Employee Retirement Income Security Act of 1974 (P.L. 93-406)

P.L. 93-406, §1016(a)(24):

Amended the heading of Code Sec. 6861 by changing "and gift taxes" to "gift, and certain excise taxes". For **effective** date, see amendment note for Code Sec. 410.

[Sec. 6861(b)]

(b) DEFICIENCY LETTERS.—If the jeopardy assessment is made before any notice in respect of the tax to which the jeopardy assessment relates has been mailed under section 6212(a), then the Secretary shall mail a notice under such subsection within 60 days after the making of the assessment.

Amendments

• 1976, Tax Reform Act of 1976 (P.L. 94-455)

P.L. 94-455, §1906(b)(13)(A):

Amended 1954 Code by substituting "Secretary" for "Secretary or his delegate" each place it appeared. **Effective** 2-1-77.

[Sec. 6861(c)]

(c) AMOUNT ASSESSABLE BEFORE DECISION OF TAX COURT.—The jeopardy assessment may be made in respect of a deficiency greater or less than that notice of which has been mailed to the taxpayer, despite the provisions of section 6212(c) prohibiting the determination of additional deficiencies, and whether or not the taxpayer has theretofore filed a petition with the Tax Court. The Secretary may, at any time before the decision of the Tax Court is rendered, abate such assessment, or any unpaid portion thereof, to the extent that he believes the assessment to be excessive in amount. The Secretary shall notify the Tax Court of the amount of such assessment, or abatement, if the petition is filed with the Tax Court before the making of the assessment or is subsequently filed, and the Tax Court shall have jurisdiction to redetermine the entire amount of the deficiency and of all amounts assessed at the same time in connection therewith.

Amendments

• 1976, Tax Reform Act of 1976 (P.L. 94-455)

P.L. 94-455, §1906(b)(13)(A):

Amended 1954 Code by substituting "Secretary" for "Secretary or his delegate" each place it appeared. **Effective** 2-1-77.

[Sec. 6861(d)]

(d) Amount Assessable After Decision of Tax Court.—If the jeopardy assessment is made after the decision of the Tax Court is rendered, such assessment may be made only in respect of the deficiency determined by the Tax Court in its decision.

[Sec. 6861(e)]

(e) Expiration of Right to Assess.—A jeopardy assessment may not be made after the decision of the Tax Court has become final or after the taxpayer has filed a petition for review of the decision of the Tax Court.

[Sec. 6861(f)]

(f) Collection of Unpaid Amounts.—When the petition has been filed with the Tax Court and when the amount which should have been assessed has been determined by a decision of the Tax Court which has become final, then any unpaid portion, the collection of which has been stayed by bond as provided in section 6863(b) shall be collected as part of the tax upon notice and demand from the Secretary, and any remaining portion of the assessment shall be abated. If the amount already collected exceeds the amount determined as the amount which should have been assessed, such excess shall be credited or refunded to the taxpayer as provided in section 6402, without the filing of claim therefor. If the amount determined as the amount which should have been assessed is greater than the amount actually assessed, then the difference shall be assessed and shall be collected as part of the tax upon notice and demand from the Secretary.

Amendments

• 1976, Tax Reform Act of 1976 (P.L. 94-455)

P.L. 94-455, §1906(b)(13)(A):

Amended 1954 Code by substituting "Secretary" for "Secretary or his delegate" each place it appeared. **Effective** 2-1-77.

* * *

[Sec. 6863]

SEC. 6863. STAY OF COLLECTION OF JEOPARDY ASSESSMENTS.

[Sec. 6863(a)]

(a) Bond to Stay Collection.—When an assessment has been made under section 6851, 6852, 6861, or 6862, the collection of the whole or any amount of such assessment may be stayed by filing with the Secretary, within such time as may be fixed by regulations prescribed by the Secretary, a bond in an amount equal to the amount as to which the stay is desired, conditioned upon the payment of the amount (together with interest thereon) the collection of which is stayed, at the time at which, but for the making of such assessment, such amount would be due. Upon the filing of the bond the collection of so much of the amount assessed as is covered by the bond shall be stayed. The taxpayer shall have the right to waive such stay at any time in respect of the whole or any part of the amount covered by the bond, and if as a result of such waiver any part of the amount covered by the bond is paid, then the bond shall, at the request of the taxpayer, be proportionately reduced. If any portion of such assessment is abated, the bond shall, at the request of the taxpayer, be proportionately reduced.

Amendments

• 2018, Tax Technical Corrections Act of 2018 (P.L. 115-141)

P.L. 115-141, §401(a)(321), Div. U:

Amended Code Sec. 6863(a) by striking "6852,," and inserting "6852,". **Effective** 3-23-2018.

• 1987, Revenue Act of 1987 (P.L. 100-203)

P.L. 100-203, §10713(b)(2)(E)(i)-(iii):

Amended Code Sec. 6863 by striking out "6851" in subsection (a) and inserting in lieu thereof "6851, 6852,", by striking out "6851 or 6861" in subsection (b)(3)(A) and inserting in lieu thereof "6851, 6852, or 6861", and by striking out "6851(a), or 6861(a)" and inserting in lieu thereof "6851(a), 6852(a), or [nor]6861(a)". **Effective** 12-22-87.

• 1976, Tax Reform Act of 1976 (P.L. 94-455)

P.L. 94-455, §1204(c)(7):

Amended Code Sec. 6863(a) by substituting "6851, 6861," for "6861"; by substituting "an assessment" for "a jeopardy assessment" in the first sentence; and by substituting "such assessment" for "the jeopardy assessment" each time it appeared in Code Sec. 6863(a). **Effective** date as provided in Act Sec. 1204(d), below.

P.L. 94-455, §1204(d), as amended by P.L. 94-528, §2(a), provides:

(d) Effective Date.—The amendments made by this section apply with respect to action taken under section 6851, 6861, or 6862 of the Internal Revenue Code of 1954 where the notice and demand takes place after February 28, 1977.

• 1976, Tax Reform Act of 1976 (P.L. 94-455)

P.L. 94-455, §1906(b)(13)(A):

Amended 1954 Code by substituting "Secretary" for "Secretary or his delegate" each place it appeared. **Effective** 2-1-77.

[Sec. 6863(b)]

(b) FURTHER CONDITIONS IN CASE OF INCOME, ESTATE, OR GIFT TAXES.—In the case of taxes subject to the jurisdiction of the Tax Court—

(1) PRIOR TO PETITION TO TAX COURT.—If the bond is given before the taxpayer has filed his petition under section 6213(a), the bond shall contain a further condition that if a petition is not filed within the period provided in such section, then the amount, the collection of which is stayed by the bond, will be paid on notice and demand at any time after the expiration of such period, together with interest thereon from the date of the jeopardy notice and demand to the date of notice and demand under this paragraph.

(2) EFFECT OF TAX COURT DECISION.—The bond shall be conditioned upon the payment of so much of such assessment (collection of which is stayed by the bond) as is not abated by a decision of the Tax Court which has become final. If the Tax Court determines that the amount assessed is greater than the amount which should have been assessed, then when the decision of the Tax Court is rendered the bond shall, at the request of the taxpayer, be proportionately reduced.

(3) STAY OF SALE OF SEIZED PROPERTY PENDING TAX COURT DECISION.—

(A) GENERAL RULE.—Where, notwithstanding the provisions of section 6213(a), an assessment has been made under section 6851, 6852, or 6861, the property seized for collection of the tax shall not be sold—

(i) before the expiration of the periods described in subsection (c)(1)(A) and (B),

(ii) before the issuance of the notice of deficiency described in section 6851(b) or 6861(b), and the expiration of the period provided in section 6213(a) for filing a petition with the Tax Court, and

(iii) if a petition is filed with the Tax Court (whether before or after making of such assessment), before the expiration of the period during which the assessment of the deficiency would be prohibited if neither sections 6851(a), 6852(a), nor 6861(a) were applicable.

Clauses (ii) and (iii) shall not apply in the case of a termination assessment under section 6851 if the taxpayer does not file a return for the taxable year by the due date (determined with regard to any extensions).

(B) EXCEPTIONS.—Such property may be sold if—

(i) the taxpayer consents to the sale,

(ii) the Secretary determines that the expenses of conservation and maintenance will greatly reduce the net proceeds, or

(iii) the property is of the type described in section 6336.

(C) REVIEW BY TAX COURT.—If, but for the application of subparagraph (B), a sale would be prohibited by subparagraph (A)(iii), then the Tax Court shall have jurisdiction to review the Secretary's determination under subparagraph (B) that the property may be sold. Such review may be commenced upon motion by either the Secretary or the taxpayer. An order of the Tax Court disposing of a motion under this paragraph shall be reviewable in the same manner as a decision of the Tax Court.

Amendments

• 1989, Omnibus Budget Reconciliation Act of 1989 (P.L. 101-239)

P.L. 101-239, §7822(d)(2):

Amended Act Sec. 10713(b)(2)(E) of P.L. 100-203, which amended Code Sec. 6863 by striking "6851(a) nor 6861(a)" in subsection (b)(3)(A)(iii) and inserting "6851(a), 6852(a), nor 6861(a)". **Effective** as if included in the provision of P.L. 100-203 to which it relates.

• 1988, Technical and Miscellaneous Revenue Act of 1988 (P.L. 100-647)

P.L. 100-647, §6245(a):

Amended Code Sec. 6863(b)(3) by adding at the end thereof new subparagraph (C). **Effective** on the 90th day after 11-10-88.

• 1987, Revenue Act of 1987 (P.L. 100-203)

P.L. 100-203, §10713(b)(2)(E)(i)-(iii):

Amended Code Sec. 6863 by striking out "6851" in subsection (a) and inserting in lieu thereof "6851, 6852,", by striking out "6851 or 6861" in subsection (b)(3)(A) and inserting in lieu thereof "6851, 6852, or 6861", and by striking out "6851(a), or 6861(a)" and inserting in lieu thereof "6851(a), 6852(a), or [nor]6861(a)". **Effective** 12-22-87.

• 1976, Tax Reform Act of 1976 (P.L. 94-455)

P.L. 94-455, §1204(c)(8):

Amended Code Sec. 6863(b)(3)(A). For the **effective** date, see Act Sec. 1204(d), below. Prior to amendment, Code Sec. 6863(b)(3)(A) read as follows:

(A) GENERAL RULE.—Where, notwithstanding the provisions of section 6213(a), a jeopardy assessment has been made under section 6861 the property seized for the collection of the tax shall not be sold—

(i) if section 6861(b) is applicable, prior to the issuance of the notice of deficiency and the expiration of the time provided in section 6213(a) for filing petition with the Tax Court, and

(ii) if petition is filed with the Tax Court (whether before or after the making of such jeopardy assessment under section 6861), prior to the expiration of the period during which the assessment of the deficiency would be prohibited if section 6861(a) were not applicable.

P.L. 94-455, §1204(d), as amended by P.L. 94-528, §2(a), provides:

(d) Effective Date.—The amendments made by this section apply with respect to action taken under section 6851, 6861, or 6862 of the Internal Revenue Code of 1954 where the notice and demand takes place after February 28, 1977.

P.L. 94-455, §1906(b)(13)(A):

Amended 1954 Code by substituting "Secretary" for "Secretary or his delegate" each place it appeared. **Effective** 2-1-77.

P.L. 94-455, §1906(a)(38):

Amended Code Sec. 6863(b)(3) by striking out subparagraph (C). **Effective** 2-1-77. Prior to amendment, subparagraph (C) read as follows:

(C) APPLICABILITY.—Subparagraphs (A) and (B) shall be applicable only with respect to a jeopardy assessment made on or after January 1, 1955, and shall apply with respect to taxes imposed by this title and with respect to taxes imposed by the Internal Revenue Code of 1939.

[Sec. 6863(c)]

(c) STAY OF SALE OF SEIZED PROPERTY PENDING DISTRICT COURT DETERMINATION UNDER SECTION 7429.—

(1) GENERAL RULE.—Where a jeopardy assessment has been made under section 6862(a), the property seized for the collection of the tax shall not be sold—

(A) if a civil action is commenced in accordance with section 7429(b), on or before the day on which the district court judgment in such action becomes final, or

(B) if subparagraph (A) does not apply, before the day after the expiration of the period provided in section 7429(a) for requesting an administrative review, and if such review is requested, before the day after the expiration of the period provided in section 7429(b), for commencing an action in the district court.

(2) EXCEPTIONS.—With respect to any property described in paragraph (1), the exceptions provided by subsection (b)(3)(B) shall apply.

Amendments

• 1976, Tax Reform Act of 1976 (P.L. 94-455)

P.L. 94-455, §1204(a)(9):

Added Code Sec. 6863(c). For the **effective** date, see Act Sec. 1204(d), below.

P.L. 94-455, §1204(d), as amended by P.L. 94-528, §2(a), provides:

(d) Effective Date.—The amendments made by this section apply with respect to action taken under section 6851, 6861, or 6862 of the Internal Revenue Code of 1954 where the notice and demand takes place after February 28, 1977.

* * *

Subchapter B—Receiverships, Etc.

[Sec. 6871]

SEC. 6871. CLAIMS FOR INCOME, ESTATE, GIFT, AND CERTAIN EXCISE TAXES IN RECEIVERSHIP PROCEEDINGS, ETC.

[Sec. 6871(a)]

(a) IMMEDIATE ASSESSMENT IN RECEIVERSHIP PROCEEDINGS.—On the appointment of a receiver for the taxpayer in any receivership proceeding before any court of the United States or of any State or of the District of Columbia, any deficiency (together with all interest, additional amounts, and additions to the tax provided by law) determined by the Secretary in respect of a tax imposed by subtitle A or B or by chapter 41, 42, 43, or 44 on such taxpayer may, despite the restrictions imposed by section 6213(a) on assessments, be immediately assessed if such deficiency has not theretofore been assessed in accordance with law.

Amendments

• 1989, Omnibus Budget Reconciliation Act of 1989 (P.L. 101-239)

P.L. 101-239, §7841(d)(2):

Amended Code Sec. 6871 by striking "44, or 45" each place it appears and inserting "or 44". **Effective** 12-19-89.

• 1980, Bankruptcy Tax Act of 1980 (P.L. 96-589)

P.L. 96-589, §6(g)(1):

Amended Code Sec. 6871(a). **Effective** 10-1-79, but inapplicable to any proceeding under the Bankruptcy Act commenced before that date. See amendment note for P.L. 96-589 under Code Sec. 6871(c) for the text of Code Sec. 6871(a) prior to amendment.

• 1976, Tax Reform Act of 1976 (P.L. 94-455)

P.L. 94-455, §1906(c)(1):

Amended Code Sec. 6871(a) by striking out "or Territory" after "any State." **Effective** 2-1-77.

P.L. 94-455, §1906(b)(13)(A):

Amended 1954 Code by substituting "Secretary" for "Secretary or his delegate" each place it appeared. **Effective** 2-1-77.

• 1958, Technical Amendments Act of 1958 (P.L. 85-866)

P.L. 85-866, §88(a):

Amended Code Sec. 6871(a) by substituting the phrase "the filing or (where approval is required by the Bankruptcy Act) the approval of a petition of, or the approval of a petition against, any taxpayer" for the phrase "the approval of a petition of, or against, any taxpayer". **Effective** 1-1-54.

[Sec. 6871(b)]

(b) IMMEDIATE ASSESSMENT WITH RESPECT TO CERTAIN TITLE 11 CASES.—Any deficiency (together with all interest, additional amounts, and additions to the tax provided by law) determined by the Secretary in respect of a tax imposed by subtitle A or B or by chapter 41, 42, 43, or 44 on—

(1) the debtor's estate in a case under title 11 of the United States Code, or

(2) the debtor, but only if liability for such tax has become res judicata pursuant to a determination in a case under title 11 of the United States Code,

may, despite the restrictions imposed by section 6213(a) on assessments, be immediately assessed if such deficiency has not theretofore been assessed in accordance with law.

Amendments

• 1989, Omnibus Budget Reconciliation Act of 1989 (P.L. 101-239)

P.L. 101-239, §7841(d)(2):

Amended Code Sec. 6871 by striking "44, or 45" each place it appears and inserting "or 44". **Effective** 12-19-89.

• 1980, Bankruptcy Tax Act of 1980 (P.L. 96-589)

P.L. 96-589, §6(g)(1):

Amended Code Sec. 6871(b). **Effective** 10-1-79, but inapplicable to any proceeding under the Bankruptcy Act commenced before that date. See amendment note for P.L. 96-589 under Code Sec. 6871(c) for the text of Code Sec. 6871(b) prior to amendment.

• 1958, Technical Amendments Act of 1958 (P.L. 85-866)

P.L. 85-866, §88(b):

Amended Code Sec. 6871(b) by substituting the phrase "the filing or (where approval is required by the Bankruptcy Act) the approval of a petition of, or the approval of a petition against, any taxpayer" for the phrase "approval of the petition". **Effective** 1-1-54.

[Sec. 6871(c)]

(c) CLAIM FILED DESPITE PENDENCY OF TAX COURT PROCEEDINGS.—In the case of a tax imposed by subtitle A or B or by chapter 41, 42, 43, or 44—

(1) claims for the deficiency and for interest, additional amounts, and additions to the tax may be presented, for adjudication in accordance with law, to the court before which the receivership proceeding (or the case under title 11 of the United States Code) is pending, despite the pendency of proceedings for the redetermination of the deficiency pursuant to a petition to the Tax Court; but

(2) in the case of a receivership proceeding, no petition for any such redetermination shall be filed with the Tax Court after the appointment of the receiver.

Amendments

• 1989, Omnibus Budget Reconciliation Act of 1989 (P.L. 101-239)

P.L. 101-239, §7841(d)(2):

Amended Code Sec. 6871 by striking "44, or 45" each place it appears and inserting "or 44". **Effective** 12-19-89.

• 1980, Bankruptcy Tax Act of 1980 (P.L. 96-589)

P.L. 96-589, §6(g)(1):

Amended Code Sec. 6871. **Effective** 10-1-79, but inapplicable to any proceeding under the Bankruptcy Act commenced before that date. Prior to amendment, Code Sec. 6871 provided:

"SEC. 6871. CLAIMS FOR INCOME, ESTATE, AND GIFT TAXES IN BANKRUPTCY AND RECEIVERSHIP PROCEEDINGS.

(a) IMMEDIATE ASSESSMENT.—Upon the adjudication of bankruptcy of any taxpayer in any liquidating proceeding, the filing or (where approval is required by the Bankruptcy Act) the approval of a petition of, or the approval of a petition against, any taxpayer in any other bankruptcy proceeding, or the appointment of a receiver for any taxpayer in any receivership proceeding before any court of the United States or of any State or of the District of Columbia, any deficiency (together with all interest, additional amounts, or additions to the tax provided by law) determined by the Secretary in respect of a tax imposed by subtitle A or B upon such taxpayer shall, despite the restrictions imposed by section 6213(a) upon assessments, be immediately assessed if such deficiency has not theretofore been assessed in accordance with law.

(b) CLAIM FILED DESPITE PENDENCY OF TAX COURT PROCEEDINGS.—In the case of a tax imposed by subtitle A or B claims for the deficiency and such interest, additional amounts, and additions to the tax may be presented, for adjudication in accordance with law, to the court before which the bankruptcy or receivership proceeding is pending, despite the pendency of proceedings for the redetermination of the deficiency in pursuance of a petition to the Tax Court; but no petition for any such redetermination shall be filed with the Tax Court after the adjudication of bankruptcy, the filing or (where approval is required by the Bankruptcy Act) the approval of a petition of, or the approval of a petition against, any taxpayer in any other bankruptcy proceeding, or the appointment of the receiver."

[Sec. 6872]

SEC. 6872. SUSPENSION OF PERIOD ON ASSESSMENT.

If the regulations issued pursuant to section 6036 require the giving of notice by any fiduciary in any case under title 11 of the United States Code, or by a receiver in any other court proceeding, to the Secretary of his qualification as such, the running of the period of limitations on the making of assessments shall be suspended for the period from the date of the institution of the proceeding to a date 30 days after the date upon which the notice from the receiver or other fiduciary is received by the Secretary; but the suspension under this sentence shall in no case be for a period in excess of 2 years.

Amendments

• 1980, Bankruptcy Tax Act of 1980 (P.L. 96-589)

P.L. 96-589, §6(i)(12):

Amended Code Sec. 6872 by striking out "any proceeding under the Bankruptcy Act" and inserting in lieu thereof "any case under title 11 of the United States Code". **Effective** 10-1-79 but inapplicable to any proceeding under the Bankruptcy Act commenced before that date.

• 1976, Tax Reform Act of 1976 (P.L. 94-455)

P.L. 94-455, §1906(b)(13)(A):

Amended 1954 Code by substituting "Secretary" for "Secretary or his delegate" each place it appeared. **Effective** 2-1-77.

[Sec. 6873]

SEC. 6873. UNPAID CLAIMS.

[Sec. 6873(a)]

(a) GENERAL RULE.—Any portion of a claim for taxes allowed in a receivership proceeding which is unpaid shall be paid by the taxpayer upon notice and demand from the Secretary after the termination of such proceeding.

Amendments

• 1980, Bankruptcy Tax Act of 1980 (P.L. 96-589)

P.L. 96-589, §6(e)(2):

Amended Code Sec. 6873(a) by striking out "or any proceeding under the Bankruptcy Act" following "receivership proceeding". **Effective** 10-1-79, but inapplicable to any proceeding under the Bankruptcy Act commenced before that date.

• 1976, Tax Reform Act of 1976 (P.L. 94-455)

P.L. 94-455, §1906(b)(13)(A):

Amended 1954 Code by substituting "Secretary" for "Secretary or his delegate" each place it appeared. **Effective** 2-1-77.

* * *

CHAPTER 71—TRANSFEREES AND FIDUCIARIES

[Sec. 6901]

SEC. 6901. TRANSFERRED ASSETS.

[Sec. 6901(a)]

(a) METHOD OF COLLECTION.—The amounts of the following liabilities shall, except as hereinafter in this section provided, be assessed, paid, and collected in the same manner and subject to the same provisions and limitations as in the case of the taxes with respect to which the liabilities were incurred:

(1) INCOME, ESTATE, AND GIFT TAXES.—

(A) TRANSFEREES.—The liability, at law or in equity, of a transferee of property—

(i) of a taxpayer in the case of a tax imposed by subtitle A (relating to income taxes),

(ii) of a decedent in the case of a tax imposed by chapter 11 (relating to estate taxes), or

(iii) of a donor in the case of a tax imposed by chapter 12 (relating to gift taxes),

in respect of the tax imposed by subtitle A or B.

(B) FIDUCIARIES.—The liability of a fiduciary under section 3713(b) of title 31, United States Code, in respect of the payment of any tax described in subparagraph (A) from the estate of the taxpayer, the decedent, or the donor, as the case may be.

(2) OTHER TAXES.—The liability, at law or in equity of a transferee of property of any person liable in respect of any tax imposed by this title (other than a tax imposed by subtitle A or B), but only if such liability arises on the liquidation of a partnership or corporation, or on a reorganization within the meaning of section 368(a).

Amendments

• 2018, Tax Technical Corrections Act of 2018 (P.L. 115-141)

P.L. 115-141, §401(a)(322), Div. U:

Amended Code Sec. 6901(a)(1)(B) by striking "Code in" and inserting "Code, in". **Effective** 3-23-2018.

• 1982 (P.L. 97-258)

P.L. 97-258, §3(f)(10):

Amended Code Sec. 6901(a)(1)(B) by striking out "section 3467 of the Revised Statutes (31 U.S.C. 192)" and substituting "section 3713(b) of title 31, United States Code". **Effective** 9-13-82.

[Sec. 6901(b)]

(b) LIABILITY.—Any liability referred to in subsection (a) may be either as to the amount of tax shown on a return or as to any deficiency or underpayment of any tax.

[Sec. 6901(c)]

(c) PERIOD OF LIMITATIONS.—The period of limitations for assessment of any such liability of a transferee or a fiduciary shall be as follows:

(1) INITIAL TRANSFEREE.—In the case of the liability of an initial transferee, within 1 year after the expiration of the period of limitation for assessment against the transferor;

(2) TRANSFEREE OF TRANSFEREE.—In the case of the liability of a transferee of a transferee, within 1 year after the expiration of the period of limitation for assessment against the preceding transferee, but not more than 3 years after the expiration of the period of limitation for assessment against the initial transferor;

except that if, before the expiration of the period of limitation for the assessment of the liability of the transferee, a court proceeding for the collection of the tax or liability in respect thereof has been begun against the initial transferor or the last preceding transferee, respectively, then the period of limitation for assessment of the liability of the transferee shall expire 1 year after the return of execution in the court proceeding.

(3) FIDUCIARY.—In the case of the liability of a fiduciary, not later than 1 year after the liability arises or not later than the expiration of the period for collection of the tax in respect of which such liability arises, whichever is the later.

[Sec. 6901(d)]

(d) EXTENSION BY AGREEMENT.—

(1) EXTENSION OF TIME FOR ASSESSMENT.—If before the expiration of the time prescribed in subsection (c) for the assessment of the liability, the Secretary and the transferee or fiduciary have both consented in writing to its assessment after such time, the liability may be assessed at any time prior to the expiration of the period agreed upon. The period so agreed upon may be extended by subsequent agreements in writing made before the expiration of the period previously agreed upon. For the purpose of determining the period of limitation on credit or refund to the transferee or fiduciary of overpayments of tax made by such transferee or fiduciary or overpayments of tax made by the transferor of which the transferee or fiduciary is legally entitled to credit or refund, such agreement and any extension thereof shall be deemed an agreement and extension thereof referred to in section 6511(c).

(2) EXTENSION OF TIME FOR CREDIT OR REFUND.—If the agreement is executed after the expiration of the period of limitation for assessment against the taxpayer with reference to whom the liability of such transferee or fiduciary arises, then in applying the limitations under section 6511(c) on the amount of the credit or refund, the periods specified in section 6511(b)(2) shall be increased by the period from the date of such expiration to the date of the agreement.

[Sec. 6901(e)]

(e) PERIOD FOR ASSESSMENT AGAINST TRANSFEROR.—For purposes of this section, if any person is deceased, or is a corporation which has terminated its existence, the period of limitation for assessment against such person shall be the period that would be in effect had death or termination of existence not occurred.

[Sec. 6901(f)]

(f) SUSPENSION OF RUNNING OF PERIOD OF LIMITATIONS.—The running of the period of limitations upon the assessment of the liability of a transferee or fiduciary shall, after the mailing to the transferee or fiduciary of the notice provided for in section 6212 (relating to income, estate, and gift taxes), be suspended for the period during which the Secretary is prohibited from making the assessment in respect of the liability of the transferee or fiduciary (and in any event, if a proceeding in respect of the liability is placed on the docket of the Tax Court, until the decision of the Tax Court becomes final), and for 60 days thereafter.

[Sec. 6901(g)]

(g) ADDRESS FOR NOTICE OF LIABILITY.—In the absence of notice to the Secretary under section 6903 of the existence of a fiduciary relationship, any notice of liability enforceable under this section required to be mailed to such person, shall, if mailed to the person subject to the liability at his last known address, be sufficient for purposes of this title, even if such person is deceased, or is under a legal disability, or, in the case of a corporation, has terminated its existence.

[Sec. 6901(h)]

(h) DEFINITION OF TRANSFEREE.—As used in this section, the term "transferee" includes donee, heir, legatee, devisee, and distributee, and with respect to estate taxes, also includes any person who, under section 6324(a)(2), is personally liable for any part of such tax.

[Sec. 6901(i)]

(i) EXTENSION OF TIME.—

For extensions of time by reason of armed service in a combat zone, see section 7508.

Amendments

• 1976, Tax Reform Act of 1976 (P.L. 94-455)

P.L. 94-455, §1906(b)(13)(A):

Amended Code Sec. 6901 by substituting "Secretary" for "Secretary or his delegate" each place it appeared. **Effective** 2-1-77.

[Sec. 6902]

SEC. 6902. PROVISIONS OF SPECIAL APPLICATION TO TRANSFEREES.

[Sec. 6902(a)]

(a) BURDEN OF PROOF.—In proceedings before the Tax Court the burden of proof shall be upon the Secretary to show that a petitioner is liable as a transferee of property of a taxpayer, but not to show that the taxpayer was liable for the tax.

Amendments

• 1976, Tax Reform Act of 1976 (P.L. 94-455)

P.L. 94-455, §1906(b)(13)(A):

Amended 1954 Code by substituting "Secretary" for "Secretary or his delegate" each place it appeared. **Effective** 2-1-77.

[Sec. 6902(b)]

(b) EVIDENCE.—Upon application to the Tax Court, a transferee of property of a taxpayer shall be entitled, under rules prescribed by the Tax Court, to a preliminary examination of books, papers, documents, correspondence, and other evidence of the taxpayer or a preceding transferee of the taxpayer's property, if the transferee making the application is a petitioner before the Tax Court for the redetermination of his liability in respect of the tax (including interest, additional amounts, and additions to the tax provided by law) imposed upon the taxpayer. Upon such application, the Tax Court may require by subpoena, ordered by the Tax Court or any division thereof and signed by a judge, the production of all such books, papers, documents, correspondence, and other evidence within the United States the production of which, in the opinion of the Tax Court or divisions thereof, is necessary to enable the transferee to ascertain the liability of the taxpayer or preceding transferee and will not result in undue hardship to the taxpayer or preceding transferee. Such examination shall be had at such time and place as may be designated in the subpoena.

[Sec. 6903]

SEC. 6903. NOTICE OF FIDUCIARY RELATIONSHIP.

[Sec. 6903(a)]

(a) RIGHTS AND OBLIGATIONS OF FIDUCIARY.—Upon notice to the Secretary that any person is acting for another person in a fiduciary capacity, such fiduciary shall assume the powers, rights, duties, and privileges of such other person in respect of a tax imposed by this title (except as otherwise specifically provided and except that the tax shall be collected from the estate of such other person), until notice is given that the fiduciary capacity has terminated.

Amendments

• 1976, Tax Reform Act of 1976 (P.L. 94-455)

P.L. 94-455, §1906(b)(13)(A):

Amended 1954 Code by substituting "Secretary" for "Secretary or his delegate" each place it appeared. **Effective** 2-1-77.

[Sec. 6903(b)]

(b) MANNER OF NOTICE.—Notice under this section shall be given in accordance with regulations prescribed by the Secretary.

Amendments

• 1976, Tax Reform Act of 1976 (P.L. 94-455)

P.L. 94-455, §1906(b)(13)(A):

Amended 1954 Code by substituting "Secretary" for "Secretary or his delegate" each place it appeared. **Effective** 2-1-77.

[Sec. 6904]

SEC. 6904. PROHIBITION OF INJUNCTIONS.

For prohibition of suits to restrain enforcement of liability of transferee, or fiduciary, see section 7421(b).

[Sec. 6905]

SEC. 6905. DISCHARGE OF EXECUTOR FROM PERSONAL LIABILITY FOR DECEDENT'S INCOME AND GIFT TAXES.

[Sec. 6905(a)]

(a) DISCHARGE OF LIABILITY.—In the case of liability of a decedent for taxes imposed by subtitle A or by chapter 12, if the executor makes written application (filed after the return with respect to such taxes is made and filed in such manner and such form as may be prescribed by regulations of the Secretary) for release from personal liability for such taxes, the Secretary may notify the executor of the amount of such taxes. The executor, upon payment of the amount of which he is notified, or 9 months after receipt of the application if no notification is made by the Secretary before such date, shall be discharged from personal liability for any deficiency in such tax thereafter found to be due and shall be entitled to a receipt or writing showing such discharge.

Amendments

• 1976, Tax Reform Act of 1976 (P.L. 94-455)

P.L. 94-455, §1906(b)(13)(A):

Amended 1954 Code by substituting "Secretary" for "Secretary or his delegate" each place it appeared. **Effective** 2-1-77.

• 1970, Excise, Estate, and Gift Tax Adjustment Act of 1970 (P.L. 91-614)

P.L. 91-614, §101(f):

Amended Code Sec. 6905(a) by substituting "9 months" for "1 year". **Effective** with respect to estates of decedents dying after 12-31-73.

[Sec. 6905(b)]

(b) DEFINITION OF EXECUTOR.—For purposes of this section, the term "executor" means the executor or administrator of the decedent appointed, qualified, and acting within the United States.

[Sec. 6905(c)]

(c) CROSS REFERENCE.—

For discharge of executor from personal liability for taxes imposed under chapter 11, see section 2204.

Amendments

• 1970, Excise, Estate, and Gift Tax Adjustment Act of 1970 (P.L. 91-614)

P.L. 91-614, §101(e)(1):

Added Code Sec. 6905. **Effective** with respect to decedents dying, or to gifts made, after 12-31-70.

* * *

CHAPTER 73—BONDS

* * *

[Sec. 7101]

SEC. 7101. FORM OF BONDS.

Whenever, pursuant to the provisions of this title (other than section 7485), or rules or regulations prescribed under authority of this title, a person is required to furnish a bond or security—

(1) GENERAL RULE.—Such bond or security shall be in such form and with such surety or sureties as may be prescribed by regulations issued by the Secretary.

(2) UNITED STATES BONDS AND NOTES IN LIEU OF SURETY BONDS.—The person required to furnish such bond or security may, in lieu thereof, deposit bonds or notes of the United States as provided in section 9303 of title 31, United States Code.

Amendments

• 1982 (P.L. 97-258)

P.L. 97-258, §3(f)(11):

Amended Code Sec. 7101(2) by striking out "6 U.S.C. 15" and substituting "section 9303 of title 31, United States Code". **Effective** 9-13-82.

• 1976, Tax Reform Act of 1976 (P.L. 94-455)

P.L. 94-455, §1906(b)(13)(A):

Amended 1954 Code by substituting "Secretary" for "Secretary or his delegate" each place it appeared. **Effective** 2-1-77.

• 1972 (P.L. 92-310)

P.L. 92-310, §230(b):

Amended the first sentence of Code Sec. 7101 by substituting "section 7485" for "sections 7485 and 6803(a)(1)". **Effective** 6-6-72.

[Sec. 7102]

SEC. 7102. SINGLE BOND IN LIEU OF MULTIPLE BONDS.

In any case in which two or more bonds are required or authorized, the Secretary may provide for the acceptance of a single bond complying with the requirements for which the several bonds are required or authorized.

Amendments

• 1976, Tax Reform Act of 1976 (P.L. 94-455)

P.L. 94-455, §1906(b)(13)(A):

Amended 1954 Code by substituting "Secretary" for "Secretary or his delegate" each place it appeared. **Effective** 2-1-77.

* * *

CHAPTER 74—CLOSING AGREEMENTS AND COMPROMISES

* * *

[Sec. 7121]

SEC. 7121. CLOSING AGREEMENTS.

[Sec. 7121(a)]

(a) AUTHORIZATION.—The Secretary is authorized to enter into an agreement in writing with any person relating to the liability of such person (or of the person or estate for whom he acts) in respect of any internal revenue tax for any taxable period.

Amendments

• 1976, Tax Reform Act of 1976 (P.L. 94-455)

P.L. 94-455, §1906(b)(13)(A):

Amended 1954 Code by substituting "Secretary" for "Secretary or his delegate" each place it appeared. **Effective** 2-1-77.

[Sec. 7121(b)]

(b) FINALITY.—If such agreement is approved by the Secretary (within such time as may be stated in such agreement, or later agreed to) such agreement shall be final and conclusive, and, except upon a showing of fraud or malfeasance, or misrepresentation of a material fact—

(1) the case shall not be reopened as to the matters agreed upon or the agreement modified by any officer, employee, or agent of the United States, and

(2) in any suit, action, or proceeding, such agreement, or any determination, assessment, collection, payment, abatement, refund, or credit made in accordance therewith, shall not be annulled, modified, set aside, or disregarded.

Amendments

• 1976, Tax Reform Act of 1976 (P.L. 94-455)

P.L. 94-455, §1906(b)(13)(A):

Amended 1954 Code by substituting "Secretary" for "Secretary or his delegate" each place it appeared. **Effective** 2-1-77.

[Sec. 7122]

SEC. 7122. COMPROMISES.

[Sec. 7122(a)]

(a) AUTHORIZATION.—The Secretary may compromise any civil or criminal case arising under the internal revenue laws prior to reference to the Department of Justice for prosecution or defense; and the Attorney General or his delegate may compromise any such case after reference to the Department of Justice for prosecution or defense.

Amendments

• 1976, Tax Reform Act of 1976 (P.L. 94-455)

P.L. 94-455, §1906(b)(13)(A):

Amended 1954 Code by substituting "Secretary" for "Secretary or his delegate" each place it appeared. **Effective** 2-1-77.

[Sec. 7122(b)]

(b) RECORD.—Whenever a compromise is made by the Secretary in any case, there shall be placed on file in the office of the Secretary the opinion of the General Counsel for the Department of the Treasury or his delegate, with his reasons therefor, with a statement of—

(1) The amount of tax assessed,

(2) The amount of interest, additional amount, addition to the tax, or assessable penalty, imposed by law on the person against whom the tax is assessed, and

(3) The amount actually paid in accordance with the terms of the compromise.

Notwithstanding the foregoing provisions of this subsection, no such opinion shall be required with respect to the compromise of any civil case in which the unpaid amount of tax assessed (including any interest, additional amount, addition to the tax, or assessable penalty) is less than $50,000. However, such compromise shall be subject to continuing quality review by the Secretary.

Amendments

• 1996, Taxpayer Bill of Rights 2 (P.L. 104-168)

P.L. 104-168, §503(a):

Amended Code Sec. 7122(b) by striking "$500." and inserting "$50,000. However, such compromise shall be subject to continuing quality review by the Secretary.". **Effective** 7-30-96.

• 1976, Tax Reform Act of 1976 (P.L. 94-455)

P.L. 94-455, §1906(b)(13)(A):

Amended 1954 Code by substituting "Secretary" for "Secretary or his delegate" each place it appeared. **Effective** 2-1-77.

[Sec. 7122(c)]

(c) RULES FOR SUBMISSION OF OFFERS-IN-COMPROMISE.—

(1) PARTIAL PAYMENT REQUIRED WITH SUBMISSION.—

(A) LUMP-SUM OFFERS.—

(i) IN GENERAL.—The submission of any lump-sum offer-in-compromise shall be accompanied by the payment of 20 percent of the amount of such offer.

(ii) LUMP-SUM OFFER-IN-COMPROMISE.—For purposes of this section, the term "lump-sum offer-in-compromise" means any offer of payments made in 5 or fewer installments.

(B) PERIODIC PAYMENT OFFERS.—

(i) IN GENERAL.—The submission of any periodic payment offer-in-compromise shall be accompanied by the payment of the amount of the first proposed installment.

(ii) FAILURE TO MAKE INSTALLMENT DURING PENDENCY OF OFFER.—Any failure to make an installment (other than the first installment) due under such offer-in-compromise during the period such offer is being evaluated by the Secretary may be treated by the Secretary as a withdrawal of such offer-in-compromise.

(2) RULES OF APPLICATION.—

(A) USE OF PAYMENT.—The application of any payment made under this subsection to the assessed tax or other amounts imposed under this title with respect to such tax may be specified by the taxpayer.

(B) APPLICATION OF USER FEE.—In the case of any assessed tax or other amounts imposed under this title with respect to such tax which is the subject of an offer-in-compromise to which this subsection applies, such tax or other amounts shall be reduced by any user fee imposed under this title with respect to such offer-in-compromise.

(C) WAIVER AUTHORITY.—The Secretary may issue regulations waiving any payment required under paragraph (1) in a manner consistent with the practices established in accordance with the requirements under subsection (d)(3).

(3) EXCEPTION FOR LOW-INCOME TAXPAYERS.—Paragraph (1), and any user fee otherwise required in connection with the submission of an offer-in-compromise, shall not apply to any offer-in-compromise with respect to a taxpayer who is an individual with adjusted gross income, as determined for the most recent taxable year for which such information is available, which does not exceed 250 percent of the applicable poverty level (as determined by the Secretary).

Amendments

• 2019, Taxpayer First Act (P.L. 116-25)

P.L. 116-25, §1102(a):

Amended Code Sec. 7122(c) by adding at the end a new paragraph (3). **Effective** for offers-in-compromise submitted after 7-1-2019.

• 2006, Tax Increase Prevention and Reconciliation Act of 2005 (P.L. 109-222)

P.L. 109-222, §509(a):

Amended Code Sec. 7122 by redesignating subsections (c) and (d) as subsections (d) and (e), respectively, and by inserting after subsection (b) a new subsection (c). **Effective** for offers-in-compromise submitted on and after the date which is 60 days after 5-17-2006.

[Sec. 7122(d)]

(d) STANDARDS FOR EVALUATION OF OFFERS.—

(1) IN GENERAL.—The Secretary shall prescribe guidelines for officers and employees of the Internal Revenue Service to determine whether an offer-in-compromise is adequate and should be accepted to resolve a dispute.

(2) ALLOWANCES FOR BASIC LIVING EXPENSES.—

(A) IN GENERAL.—In prescribing guidelines under paragraph (1), the Secretary shall develop and publish schedules of national and local allowances designed to provide that taxpayers entering into a compromise have an adequate means to provide for basic living expenses.

(B) USE OF SCHEDULES.—The guidelines shall provide that officers and employees of the Internal Revenue Service shall determine, on the basis of the facts and circumstances of each taxpayer, whether the use of the schedules published under subparagraph (A) is appropriate and shall not use the schedules to the extent such use would result in the taxpayer not having adequate means to provide for basic living expenses.

(3) SPECIAL RULES RELATING TO TREATMENT OF OFFERS.—The guidelines under paragraph (1) shall provide that—

(A) an officer or employee of the Internal Revenue Service shall not reject an offer-in-compromise from a low-income taxpayer solely on the basis of the amount of the offer,

(B) in the case of an offer-in-compromise which relates only to issues of liability of the taxpayer—

(i) such offer shall not be rejected solely because the Secretary is unable to locate the taxpayer's return or return information for verification of such liability; and

(ii) the taxpayer shall not be required to provide a financial statement, and

(C) any offer-in-compromise which does not meet the requirements of subparagraph (A)(i) or (B)(i), as the case may be, of subsection (c)(1) may be returned to the taxpayer as unprocessable.

Amendments

• 2006, Tax Increase Prevention and Reconciliation Act of 2005 (P.L. 109-222)

P.L. 109-222, § 509(a):

Amended Code Sec. 7122 by redesignating subsection (c) as subsection (d). **Effective** for offers-in-compromise submitted on and after the date which is 60 days after 5-17-2006.

P.L. 109-222, § 509(b)(1):

Amended Code Sec. 7122(d)(3), as redesignated by Act Sec. 509(a), by striking "; and" at the end of subparagraph (A) and inserting a comma, by striking the period at the end of subparagraph (B) and inserting ", and", and by adding at the end a new subparagraph (C). **Effective** for offers-in-compromise submitted on and after the date which is 60 days after 5-17-2006.

• 1998, IRS Restructuring and Reform Act of 1998 (P.L. 105-206)

P.L. 105-206, § 3462(a):

Amended Code Sec. 7122 by adding at the end a new subsection (c). **Effective** for proposed offers-in-compromise and installment agreements submitted after 7-22-98.

[Sec. 7122(e)]

(e) ADMINISTRATIVE REVIEW.—The Secretary shall establish procedures—

(1) for an independent administrative review of any rejection of a proposed offer-in-compromise or installment agreement made by a taxpayer under this section or section 6159 before such rejection is communicated to the taxpayer; and

(2) which allow a taxpayer to appeal any rejection of such offer or agreement to the Internal Revenue Service Independent Office of Appeals.

Amendments

• 2019, Taxpayer First Act (P.L. 116-25)

P.L. 116-25, § 1001(b)(1)(F):

Amended Code Sec. 7122(e)(2) by striking "Internal Revenue Service Office of Appeals" and inserting "Internal Revenue Service Independent Office of Appeals". **Effective** 7-1-2019.

• 2006, Tax Increase Prevention and Reconciliation Act of 2005 (P.L. 109-222)

P.L. 109-222, § 509(a):

Amended Code Sec. 7122 by redesignating subsection (d) as subsection (e). **Effective** for offers-in-compromise submitted on and after the date which is 60 days after 5-17-2006.

• 1998, IRS Restructuring and Reform Act of 1998 (P.L. 105-206)

P.L. 105-206, § 3462(c)(1):

Amended Code Sec. 7122, as amended by Act Sec. 3462(a), by adding at the end a new subsection (d). **Effective** for proposed offers-in-compromise and installment agreements submitted after 7-22-98.

P.L. 105-206, § 3462(d)(1)-(3), provides:

(d) PREPARATION OF STATEMENT RELATING TO OFFERS-IN-COMPROMISE.—The Secretary of the Treasury shall prepare a statement which sets forth in simple, non-technical terms the rights of a taxpayer and the obligations of the Internal Revenue Service relating to offers-in-compromise. Such statement shall—

(1) advise taxpayers who have entered into a compromise of the advantages of promptly notifying the Internal Revenue Service of any change of address or marital status;

(2) provide notice to taxpayers that in the case of a compromise terminated due to the actions of one spouse or former spouse, the Internal Revenue Service will, upon application, reinstate such compromise with the spouse or former spouse who remains in compliance with such compromise; and

(3) provide notice to the taxpayer that the taxpayer may appeal the rejection of an offer-in-compromise to the Internal Revenue Service Office of Appeals.

[Sec. 7122(f)]

(f) DEEMED ACCEPTANCE OF OFFER NOT REJECTED WITHIN CERTAIN PERIOD.—Any offer-in-compromise submitted under this section shall be deemed to be accepted by the Secretary if such offer is not rejected by the Secretary before the date which is 24 months after the date of the submission of such offer. For purposes of the preceding sentence, any period during which any tax liability which is the subject of such offer-in-compromise is in dispute in any judicial proceeding shall not be taken into account in determining the expiration of the 24-month period.

Amendments

• 2006, Tax Increase Prevention and Reconciliation Act of 2005 (P.L. 109-222)

P.L. 109-222, § 509(b)(2):

Amended Code Sec. 7122, as amended by Act Sec. 509(a), by adding at the end a new subsection (f). **Effective** for offers-in-compromise submitted on and after the date which is 60 days after 5-17-2006.

[Sec. 7122(g)]

(g) FRIVOLOUS SUBMISSIONS, ETC.—Notwithstanding any other provision of this section, if the Secretary determines that any portion of an application for an offer-in-compromise or installment agreement submitted under this section or section 6159 meets the requirement of clause (i) or (ii) of section 6702(b)(2)(A), then the Secretary may treat such portion as if it were never submitted and such portion shall not be subject to any further administrative or judicial review.

Amendments

• **2014, Tax Technical Corrections Act of 2014 (P.L. 113-295)**

P.L. 113-295, §220(y), Division A:

Amended Code Sec. 7122 by redesignating the second subsection (f) (relating to frivolous submissions, etc.) as subsection (g). **Effective** 12-19-2014.

• **2006, Tax Relief and Health Care Act of 2006 (P.L. 109-432)**

P.L. 109-432, Division A, §407(d):

Amended Code Sec. 7122 by adding at the end a new subsection (f)[(g)]. **Effective** for submissions made and issues raised after the date on which the Secretary first prescribes a list under Code Sec. 6702(c), as amended by Act Sec. 407(a).

* * *

CHAPTER 75—CRIMES, OTHER OFFENSES, AND FORFEITURES

* * *

Subchapter A—Crimes

* * *

PART I—GENERAL PROVISIONS

* * *

Caution: See 18 U.S.C. §3571, in the amendment notes, under which a larger fine may be imposed with respect to Code Sec. 7201.

[Sec. 7201]

SEC. 7201. ATTEMPT TO EVADE OR DEFEAT TAX.

Any person who willfully attempts in any manner to evade or defeat any tax imposed by this title or the payment thereof shall, in addition to other penalties provided by law, be guilty of a felony and, upon conviction thereof, shall be fined not more than $100,000 ($500,000 in the case of a corporation), or imprisoned not more than 5 years, or both, together with the costs of prosecution.

Amendments

• **1987 (P.L. 100-185)**

P.L. 100-185, §6:

Amended 18 U.S.C. §3571, which provides as follows:

§3571. Sentence of fine.

(a) IN GENERAL.—A defendant who has been found guilty of an offense may be sentenced to pay a fine.

(b) FINES FOR INDIVIDUALS.—Except as provided in subsection (e) of this section, an individual who has been found guilty of an offense may be fined not more than the greatest of—

(1) the amount specified in the law setting forth the offense;

(2) the applicable amount under subsection (d) of this section;

(3) for a felony, not more than $250,000;

(4) for a misdemeanor resulting in death, not more than $250,000;

(5) for a Class A misdemeanor that does not result in death, not more than $100,000;

(6) for a Class B or C misdemeanor that does not result in death, not more than $5,000; or

(7) for an infraction, not more than $5,000.

(c) FINES FOR ORGANIZATIONS.—Except as provided in subsection (e) of this section, an organization that has been found guilty of an offense may be fined not more than the greatest of—

(1) the amount specified in the law setting forth the offense;

(2) the applicable amount under subsection (d) of this section;

(3) for a felony, not more than $500,000;

(4) for a misdemeanor resulting in death, not more than $500,000;

(5) for a Class A misdemeanor that does not result in death, not more than $200,000;

(6) for a Class B or C misdemeanor that does not result in death, not more than $10,000; and

(7) for an infraction, not more than $10,000.

(d) ALTERNATIVE FINE BASED ON GAIN OR LOSS.—If any person derives pecuniary gain from the offense, or if the offense results in pecuniary loss to a person other than the defendant, the defendant may be fined not more than the greater of twice the gross gain or twice the gross loss, unless imposition of a fine under this subsection would unduly complicate or prolong the sentencing process.

(e) SPECIAL RULE FOR LOWER FINE SPECIFIED IN SUBSTANTIVE PROVISION.—If a law setting forth an offense specifies no fine or a fine that is lower than the fine otherwise applicable under this section and such law, by specific reference, exempts the offense from the applicability of the fine otherwise applicable under this section, the defendant may not be fined more than the amount specified in the law setting forth the offense.

• 1982, Tax Equity and Fiscal Responsibility Act of 1982 (P.L. 97-248)

P.L. 97-248, §329(a):

Amended Code Sec. 7201 by striking out "$10,000" and inserting "$100,000 ($500,000 in the case of a corporation)". **Effective** for offenses committed after 9-3-82.

»» Caution: See 18 U.S.C. §3571, in the amendment notes following Code Sec. 7201, under which a larger fine may be imposed with respect to Code Sec. 7202.

[Sec. 7202]

SEC. 7202. WILLFUL FAILURE TO COLLECT OR PAY OVER TAX.

Any person required under this title to collect, account for, and pay over any tax imposed by this title who willfully fails to collect or truthfully account for and pay over such tax shall, in addition to other penalties provided by law, be guilty of a felony and, upon conviction thereof, shall be fined not more than $10,000, or imprisoned not more than 5 years, or both, together with the costs of prosecution.

[Sec. 7203]

SEC. 7203. WILLFUL FAILURE TO FILE RETURN, SUPPLY INFORMATION, OR PAY TAX.

Any person required under this title to pay any estimated tax or tax, or required by this title or by regulations made under authority thereof to make a return, keep any records, or supply any information, who willfully fails to pay such estimated tax or tax, make such return, keep such records, or supply such information, at the time or times required by law or regulations, shall, in addition to other penalties provided by law, be guilty of a misdemeanor and, upon conviction thereof, shall be fined not more than $25,000 ($100,000 in the case of a corporation), or imprisoned not more than 1 year, or both, together with the costs of prosecution. In the case of any person with respect to whom there is a failure to pay any estimated tax, this section shall not apply to such person with respect to such failure if there is no addition to tax under section 6654 or 6655 with respect to such failure. In the case of a willful violation of any provision of section 6050I, the first sentence of this section shall be applied by substituting "felony" for "misdemeanor" and "5 years" for "1 year".

Amendments

• 1990, Crime Control Act of 1990 (P.L. 101-647)

P.L. 101-647, §3303(a):

Amended Code Sec. 7203 by striking "by substituting" and inserting "by substituting `felony' for `misdemeanor' and". **Effective** for actions, and failures to act, occurring after 11-29-90.

• 1988, Anti-Drug Abuse Act of 1988 (P.L. 100-690)

P.L. 100-690, §7601(a)(2)(B):

Amended Code Sec. 7203 by adding at the end thereof a new sentence. **Effective** for actions after 11-18-88.

• 1984, Deficit Reduction Act of 1984 (P.L. 98-369)

P.L. 98-369, §412(b)(9):

Amended Code Sec. 7203 by striking out "(other than a return required under the [sic] authority of section 6015)", following "to make a return". **Effective** with respect to tax years beginning after 12-31-84.

• 1982, Tax Equity and Fiscal Responsibility Act of 1982 (P.L. 97-248)

P.L. 97-248, §327:

Amended Code Sec. 7203 by adding at the end a new sentence. **Effective** 9-3-82.

P.L. 97-248, §329(b):

Amended Code Sec. 7203 by striking out "$10,000" and inserting "$25,000 ($100,000 in the case of a corporation)". **Effective** for offenses committed after 9-3-82.

• 1968, Revenue and Expenditure Control Act of 1968 (P.L. 90-364)

P.L. 90-364, §103(e)(5):

Amended Code Sec. 7203 by deleting "or section 6016" which formerly appeared after "section 6015" in the third line. **Effective** with respect to tax years beginning after 12-31-67.

* * *

»» Caution: See 18 U.S.C. §3571, in the amendment notes following Code Sec. 7201, under which a larger fine may be imposed with respect to Code Sec. 7206.

[Sec. 7206]

SEC. 7206. FRAUD AND FALSE STATEMENTS.

Any person who—

(1) DECLARATION UNDER PENALTIES OF PERJURY.—Willfully makes and subscribes any return, statement, or other document, which contains or is verified by a written declaration that it is made under the penalties of perjury, and which he does not believe to be true and correct as to every material matter; or

(2) AID OR ASSISTANCE.—Willfully aids or assists in, or procures, counsels, or advises the preparation or presentation under, or in connection with any matter arising under the internal revenue laws, of a return, affidavit, claim, or other document, which is fraudulent or is false as to any material matter, whether or not such falsity or fraud is with the knowledge or consent of the person authorized or required to present such return, affidavit, claim, or document; or

(3) FRAUDULENT BONDS, PERMITS, AND ENTRIES.—Simulates or falsely or fraudulently executes or signs any bond, permit, entry, or other document required by the provisions of the internal

revenue laws, or by any regulation made in pursuance thereof, or procures the same to be falsely or fraudulently executed or advises, aids in, or connives at such execution thereof; or

(4) REMOVAL OR CONCEALMENT WITH INTENT TO DEFRAUD.—Removes, deposits, or conceals, or is concerned in removing, depositing, or concealing, any goods or commodities for or in respect whereof any tax is or shall be imposed, or any property upon which levy is authorized by section 6331, with intent to evade or defeat the assessment or collection of any tax imposed by this title; or

(5) COMPROMISES AND CLOSING AGREEMENTS.—In connection with any compromise under section 7122, or offer of such compromise, or in connection with any closing agreement under section 7121, or offer to enter into any such agreement, willfully—

(A) CONCEALMENT OF PROPERTY.—Conceals from any officer or employee of the United States any property belonging to the estate of a taxpayer or other person liable in respect of the tax, or

(B) WITHHOLDING, FALSIFYING, AND DESTROYING RECORDS.—Receives, withholds, destroys, mutilates, or falsifies any book, document, or record, or makes any false statement, relating to the estate or financial condition of the taxpayer or other person liable in respect of the tax;

shall be guilty of a felony and, upon conviction thereof, shall be fined not more than $100,000 ($500,000 in the case of a corporation) or imprisoned not more than 3 years, or both, together with the costs of prosecution.

Amendments

• 1982, Tax Equity and Fiscal Responsibility Act of 1982 (P.L. 97-248)

P.L. 97-248, §329(c):

Amended Code Sec. 7206 by striking out "$5,000" and inserting "$100,000 ($500,000 in the case of a corporation)". **Effective** for offenses committed after 9-3-82.

[Sec. 7207]

SEC. 7207. FRAUDULENT RETURNS, STATEMENTS, OR OTHER DOCUMENTS.

Any person who willfully delivers or discloses to the Secretary any list, return, account, statement, or other document, known by him to be fraudulent or to be false as to any material matter, shall be fined not more than $10,000 ($50,000 in the case of a corporation), or imprisoned not more than 1 year, or both. Any person required pursuant to section 6047(b), section 6104(d), or subsection (i) or (j) of section 527 to furnish any information to the Secretary or any other person who willfully furnishes to the Secretary or such other person any information known by him to be fraudulent or to be false as to any material matter shall be fined not more than $10,000 ($50,000 in the case of a corporation), or imprisoned not more than 1 year, or both.

Amendments

• 2002 (P.L. 107-276)

P.L. 107-276, §6(d):

Amended Code Sec. 7207 by striking "pursuant to subsection (b) of section 6047 or pursuant to subsection (d) of section 6104" and inserting "pursuant to section 6047(b), section 6104(d), or subsection (i) or (j) of section 527". **Effective** for reports and notices required to be filed on or after 11-2-2002.

• 1998, Tax and Trade Relief Extension Act of 1998 (P.L. 105-277)

P.L. 105-277, §1004(b)(2)(E):

Amended Code Sec. 7207 by striking "or (e)" following "subsection (d)". **Effective**, generally, for requests made after the later of 12-31-98, or the 60th day after the Secretary of the Treasury first issues the regulations referred to in Code Sec. 6104(d)(4), as amended by Act Sec. 1004. For an exception, see Act Sec. 1004(b)(3)(B), below.

P.L. 105-277, §1004(b)(3)(B), provides:

(B) PUBLICATION OF ANNUAL RETURNS.—Section 6104(d) of such Code, as in effect before the amendments made by this subsection, shall not apply to any return the due date for which is after the date such amendments take effect under subparagraph (A).

• 1987, Revenue Act of 1987 (P.L. 100-203)

P.L. 100-203, §10704(c):

Amended Code Sec. 7207 by striking out "subsection (d) of section 6104" and inserting in lieu thereof "subsection (d) or (e) of section 6104". For the **effective** date, see Act Sec. 10704(d), below.

P.L. 100-203, §10704(d), provides:

(d) EFFECTIVE DATE.—The amendments made by this section shall apply—

(1) to returns for years beginning after December 31, 1986, and

(2) on and after the date of the enactment of this Act in the case of applications submitted to the Internal Revenue Service—

(A) after July 15, 1987, or

(B) on or before July 15, 1987, if the organization has a copy of the application on July 15, 1987.

• 1984, Deficit Reduction Act of 1984 (P.L. 98-369)

P.L. 98-369, §491(d)(51):

Amended Code Sec. 7207 by striking out "or (c)" following "subsection (b)". **Effective** for obligations issued after 12-31-83.

• 1982, Tax Equity and Fiscal Responsibility Act of 1982 (P.L. 97-248)

P.L. 97-248, §329(d):

Amended Code Sec. 7207 by striking out "$1,000" each place it appeared and inserting "$10,000 ($50,000 in the case of a corporation)". **Effective** for offenses committed after 9-3-82.

• 1980 (P.L. 96-603)

P.L. 96-603, §1(d)(5):

Amended Code Sec. 7207 by striking out "sections 6047(b) or (c), 6056, or 6104(d)" and inserting in lieu thereof "subsection (b) or (c) of section 6047 or pursuant to subsection (d) of section 6104". **Effective** for tax years beginning after 1980.

• 1976, Tax Reform Act of 1976 (P.L. 94-455)

P.L. 94-455, §1906(b)(13)(A):

Amended 1954 Code by substituting "Secretary" for "Secretary or his delegate" each place it appeared. **Effective** 2-1-77.

• **1969, Tax Reform Act of 1969 (P.L. 91-172)**

P.L. 91-172, §101(e)(5):

Amended Code Sec. 7207 by inserting "sections 6047(b) or (c), 6056, or 6104(d)" in lieu of "section 6047(b) or (c)". **Effective** 1-1-70.

• **1962, Self-Employed Individuals Tax Retirement Act of 1962 (P.L. 87-792)**

P.L. 87-792, §7:

Amended Code Sec. 7207 by inserting after the period in line 4 a new sentence. **Effective** 1-1-63.

* * *

[Sec. 7213A]

SEC. 7213A. UNAUTHORIZED INSPECTION OF RETURNS OR RETURN INFORMATION.

[Sec. 7213A(a)]

(a) PROHIBITIONS.—

(1) FEDERAL EMPLOYEES AND OTHER PERSONS.—It shall be unlawful for—

(A) any officer or employee of the United States, or

(B) any person described in subsection (l)(18) or (n) of section 6103 cr an officer or employee of any such person,

willfully to inspect, except as authorized in this title, any return or return information.

(2) STATE AND OTHER EMPLOYEES.—It shall be unlawful for any person (not described in paragraph (1)) willfully to inspect, except as authorized in this title, any return or return information acquired by such person or another person under a provision of section 6103 referred to in section 7213(a)(2) or under section 6104(c).

Amendments

• **2006, Pension Protection Act of 2006 (P.L. 109-280)**

P.L. 109-280, §1224(b)(6):

Amended Code Sec. 7213A(a)(2) by inserting "or under section 6104(c)" after "7213(a)(2)". **Effective** 8-17-2006 but shall not apply to requests made before such date.

• **2002, Trade Act of 2002 (P.L. 107-210)**

P.L. 107-210, §202(b)(3):

Amended Code Sec. 7213A(a)(1)(B) by striking "section 6103(n)" and inserting "subsection (l)(18) or (n) of section 6103". **Effective** 8-6-2002.

[Sec. 7213A(b)]

(b) PENALTY.—

(1) IN GENERAL.—Any violation of subsection (a) shall be punishable upon conviction by a fine in any amount not exceeding $1,000, or imprisonment of not more than 1 year, or both, together with the costs of prosecution.

(2) FEDERAL OFFICERS OR EMPLOYEES.—An officer or employee of the United States who is convicted of any violation of subsection (a) shall, in addition to any other punishment, be dismissed from office or discharged from employment.

[Sec. 7213A(c)]

(c) DEFINITIONS.—For purposes of this section, the terms "inspect", "return", and "return information" have the respective meanings given such terms by section 6103(b).

Amendments

• **1997, Taxpayer Browsing Protection Act (P.L. 105-35)**

P.L. 105-35, §2(a):

Amended part I of subchapter A of chapter 75 by adding Code Sec. 7213A. **Effective** for violations occurring on and after 8-5-97.

* * *

Subchapter B—Other Offenses

* * *

[Sec. 7269]

SEC. 7269. FAILURE TO PRODUCE RECORDS.

Whoever fails to comply with any duty imposed upon him by section 6018, 6036 (in the case of an executor), or 6075(a), or, having in his possession or control any record, file, or paper, containing or supposed to contain any information concerning the estate of the decedent, or, having in his possession or control any property comprised in the gross estate of the decedent, fails to exhibit the same upon request to the Secretary who desires to examine the same in the performance of his duties under chapter 11 (relating to estate taxes), shall be liable to a penalty of not exceeding $500, to be recovered, with costs of suit, in a civil action in the name of the United States.

Amendments

• **1976, Tax Reform Act of 1976 (P.L. 94-455)**

P.L. 94-455, §1906(b)(13)(A):

Amended 1954 Code by substituting "Secretary" for "Secretary or his delegate" each place it appeared. **Effective** 2-1-77.

* * *

CHAPTER 76—JUDICIAL PROCEEDINGS

Subchapter A—Civil Actions by the United States

* * *

[Sec. 7401]

SEC. 7401. AUTHORIZATION.

No civil action for the collection or recovery of taxes, or of any fine, penalty, or forfeiture, shall be commenced unless the Secretary authorizes or sanctions the proceedings and the Attorney General or his delegate directs that the action be commenced.

Amendments

• 1976, Tax Reform Act of 1976 (P.L. 94-455)

P.L. 94-455, §1906(b)(13)(A):

Amended 1954 Code by substituting "Secretary" for "Secretary or his delegate" each place it appeared. **Effective** 2-1-77.

[Sec. 7402]

SEC. 7402. JURISDICTION OF DISTRICT COURTS.

[Sec. 7402(a)]

(a) TO ISSUE ORDERS, PROCESSES, AND JUDGMENTS.—The district courts of the United States at the instance of the United States shall have such jurisdiction to make and issue in civil actions, writs and orders of injunction, and of *ne exeat republica*, orders appointing receivers, and such other orders and processes, and to render such judgments and decrees as may be necessary or appropriate for the enforcement of the internal revenue laws. The remedies hereby provided are in addition to and not exclusive of any and all other remedies of the United States in such courts or otherwise to enforce such laws.

[Sec. 7402(b)]

(b) TO ENFORCE SUMMONS.—If any person is summoned under the internal revenue laws to appear, to testify, or to produce books, papers, or other data, the district court of the United States for the district in which such person resides or may be found shall have jurisdiction by appropriate process to compel such attendance, testimony, or production of books, papers, or other data.

[Sec. 7402(c)]

(c) FOR DAMAGES TO UNITED STATES OFFICERS OR EMPLOYEES.—Any officer or employee of the United States acting under authority of this title, or any person acting under or by authority of any such officer or employee, receiving any injury to his person or property in the discharge of his duty shall be entitled to maintain an action for damages therefor, in the district court of the United States, in the district wherein the party doing the injury may reside or shall be found.

[Sec. 7402(d)—Repealed]

Amendments

• 1972 (P.L. 92-310)

P.L. 92-310, §230(d):

Repealed Code Sec. 7402(d). **Effective** 6-6-72. Prior to repeal, Code Sec. 7402(d) read as follows:

(d) ACTION ON BONDS.—The United States district courts, concurrently with the courts of the several States, shall have jurisdiction of any action brought on the official bond of any internal revenue officer or employee required to give bond under regulations promulgated by authority of section 7803.

[Sec. 7402(e)]

(e) TO QUIET TITLE.—The United States district courts shall have jurisdiction of any action brought by the United States to quiet title to property if the title claimed by the United States to such property was derived from enforcement of a lien under this title.

Amendments

• 1966, Federal Tax Lien Act of 1966 (P.L. 89-719)

P.L. 89-719, §107(a):

Redesignated Code Sec. 7402(e) as Code Sec. 7402(f) and added new Code Sec. 7402(e). **Effective**, generally, after 11-2-66. However, see the amendment note for Code Sec. 6323 for exceptions to this **effective** date.

[Sec. 7402(f)]

(f) GENERAL JURISDICTION.—

For general jurisdiction of the district courts of the United States in civil actions involving internal revenue, see section 1340 of Title 28 of the United States Code.

[Sec. 7403]

SEC. 7403. ACTION TO ENFORCE LIEN OR TO SUBJECT PROPERTY TO PAYMENT OF TAX.

[Sec. 7403(a)]

(a) FILING.—In any case where there has been a refusal or neglect to pay any tax, or to discharge any liability in respect thereof, whether or not levy has been made, the Attorney General or his delegate, at the request of the Secretary, may direct a civil action to be filed in a district court of the United States to enforce the lien of the United States under this title with respect to such tax or liability or to subject any property, of whatever nature, of the delinquent, or in which he has any right, title, or interest, to the payment of such tax or liability. For the purposes of the preceding sentence, any acceleration of payment under section 6166(g) shall be treated as a neglect to pay tax.

Amendments

• 1981, Economic Recovery Tax Act of 1981 (P.L. 97-34)

P.L. 97-34, §422(e)(8):

Amended Code Sec. 7403(a) by striking out "section 6166(g) or 6166A(h)" and inserting "section 6166(g)". **Effective** for estates of decedents dying after 12-31-81.

• 1976, Tax Reform Act of 1976 (P.L. 94-455)

P.L. 94-455, §1906(b)(13)(A):

Amended 1954 Code by substituting "Secretary" for "Secretary or his delegate" each place it appeared. **Effective** 2-1-77.

P.L. 94-455, §2004(f)(2):

Added the last sentence to Code Sec. 7403(a). **Effective** for the estates of decedents dying after 12-31-76.

[Sec. 7403(b)]

(b) PARTIES.—All persons having liens upon or claiming any interest in the property involved in such action shall be made parties thereto.

[Sec. 7403(c)]

(c) ADJUDICATION AND DECREE.—The court shall, after the parties have been duly notified of the action, proceed to adjudicate all matters involved therein and finally determine the merits of all claims to and liens upon the property, and, in all cases where a claim or interest of the United States therein is established, may decree a sale of such property, by the proper officer of the court, and a distribution of the proceeds of such sale according to the findings of the court in respect to the interests of the parties and of the United States. If the property is sold to satisfy a first lien held by the United States, the United States may bid at the sale such sum, not exceeding the amount of such lien with expenses of sale, as the Secretary directs.

Amendments

• 1976, Tax Reform Act of 1976 (P.L. 94-455)

P.L. 94-455, §1906(b)(13)(A):

Amended 1954 Code by substituting "Secretary" for "Secretary or his delegate" each place it appeared. **Effective** 2-1-77.

• 1966, Federal Tax Lien Act of 1966 (P.L. 89-719)

P.L. 89-719, §107(b):

Amended Code Sec. 7403(c) by adding the last sentence. **Effective**, generally, after 11-2-66. However, see the amendment note for Code Sec. 6323 for exceptions to this **effective** date.

[Sec. 7403(d)]

(d) RECEIVERSHIP.—In any such proceeding, at the instance of the United States, the court may appoint a receiver to enforce the lien, or, upon certification by the Secretary during the pendency of such proceedings that it is in the public interest, may appoint a receiver with all the powers of a receiver in equity.

Amendments

• 1976, Tax Reform Act of 1976 (P.L. 94-455)

P.L. 94-455, §1906(b)(13)(A):

Amended 1954 Code by substituting "Secretary" for "Secretary or his delegate" each place it appeared. **Effective** 2-1-77.

[Sec. 7404]

SEC. 7404. AUTHORITY TO BRING CIVIL ACTION FOR ESTATE TAXES.

If the estate tax imposed by chapter 11 is not paid on or before the due date thereof, the Secretary shall proceed to collect the tax under the provisions of general law; or appropriate proceedings in the name of the United States may be commenced in any court of the United States having jurisdiction to subject the property of the decedent to be sold under the judgment or decree of the court. From the proceeds of such sale the amount of the tax, together with the costs and expenses of every description to be allowed by the court, shall be first paid, and the balance shall be deposited according to the order of the court, to be paid under its direction to the person entitled thereto. This section insofar as it applies to the collection of a deficiency shall be subject to the provisions of sections 6213 and 6601.

Amendments

• 1976, Tax Reform Act of 1976 (P.L. 94-455)

P.L. 94-455, §1906(b)(13)(A):

Amended 1954 Code by substituting "Secretary" for "Secretary or his delegate" each place it appeared. **Effective** 2-1-77.

[Sec. 7405]

SEC. 7405. ACTION FOR RECOVERY OF ERRONEOUS REFUNDS.

[Sec. 7405(a)]

(a) REFUNDS AFTER LIMITATION PERIOD.—Any portion of a tax imposed by this title, refund of which is erroneously made, within the meaning of section 6514, may be recovered by civil action brought in the name of the United States.

[Sec. 7405(b)]

(b) REFUNDS OTHERWISE ERRONEOUS.—Any portion of a tax imposed by this title which has been erroneously refunded (if such refund would not be considered as erroneous under section 6514) may be recovered by civil action brought in the name of the United States.

[Sec. 7405(c)]

(c) INTEREST.—

For provision relating to interest on erroneous refunds, see section 6602.

[Sec. 7405(d)]

(d) PERIODS OF LIMITATION.—

For periods of limitations on actions under this section, see section 6532(b).

* * *

Subchapter B—Proceedings by Taxpayers and Third Parties

[Sec. 7421]

SEC. 7421. PROHIBITION OF SUITS TO RESTRAIN ASSESSMENT OR COLLECTION.

[Sec. 7421(a)]

(a) TAX.—Except as provided in sections 6015(e), 6212(a) and (c), 6213(a), 6232(c), 6330(e)(1), 6331(i), 6672(c), 6694(c), 7426(a) and (b)(1), 7429(b), and 7436, no suit for the purpose of restraining the assessment or collection of any tax shall be maintained in any court by any person, whether or not such person is the person against whom such tax was assessed.

Amendments

• 2015, Bipartisan Budget Act of 2015 (P.L. 114-74)

P.L. 114-74, §1101(f)(10):

Amended Code Sec. 7421(a) by striking "6225(b), 6246(b)" and inserting "6232(c)". **Effective** generally for returns filed for partnership tax years beginning after 12-31-2017. For a special rule, see Act Sec. 1101(g)(4), below.

P.L. 114-74, §1101(g)(4), provides:

(4) ELECTION.—A partnership may elect (at such time and in such form and manner as the Secretary of the Treasury may prescribe) for the amendments made by this section (other than the election under section 6221(b) of such Code (as added by this Act)) to apply to any return of the partnership filed for partnership taxable years beginning after the date of the enactment of this Act and before January 1, 2018.

• 2000, Community Renewal Tax Relief Act of 2000 (P.L. 106-554)

P.L. 106-554, §313(b)(2)(B):

Amended Code Sec. 7421(a) by inserting "6330(e)(1)," after "6246(b),". **Effective** 12-21-2000.

P.L. 106-554, §319(24):

Amended Code Sec. 7421(a) by striking "6672(b)" and inserting "6672(c)". **Effective** 12-21-2000.

• 1998, Tax and Trade Relief Extension Act of 1998 (P.L. 105-277)

P.L. 105-277, §4002(c)(1):

Amended Code Sec. 7421(a) by striking "6015(d)" and inserting "6015(e)". **Effective** as if included in the provision of P.L. 105-206 to which it relates [**effective**, generally, for any tax liability arising after 7-22-98, and any tax liability arising on or before 7-22-98, but remaining unpaid as of such date.—CCH].

P.L. 105-277, §4002(f):

Amended Code Sec. 7421(a) by inserting "6331(i)," after "6246(b),". **Effective** as if included in the provision of P.L. 105-206 to which it relates [**effective**, generally, for any tax liability arising after 7-22-98, and any tax liability arising on or before 7-22-98, but remaining unpaid as of such date.—CCH].

• 1998, IRS Restructuring and Reform Act of 1998 (P.L. 105-206)

P.L. 105-206, §3201(e)(3):

Amended Code Sec. 7421(a) by inserting "6015(d)," after "sections". **Effective** for any liability for tax arising after 7-22-98, and any liability for tax arising on or before such date but remaining unpaid as of such date.

• 1981, Economic Recovery Tax Act of 1981 (P.L. 97-34)

P.L. 105-34, §1222(b)(1):

Amended Code Sec. 7421(a) by inserting "6246(b)," after "6213(a),". **Effective** for partnership tax years beginning after 12-31-97 [**effective** date changed by P.L. 105-206, Act Sec. 6012(e)].

P.L. 105-34, §1239(e)(3):

Amended Code Sec. 7421(a), as amended by Act Sec. 1222, by inserting "6225(b)," after "6213(a),". **Effective** for partnership tax years ending after 8-5-97.

P.L. 105-34, §1454(b)(2):

Amended Code Sec. 7421(a) by striking "and 7429(b)" and inserting "7429(b), and 7436". **Effective** 8-5-97.

• 1978 (P.L. 95-628)

P.L. 95-628, §9(b)(1):

Amended Code Sec. 7421(a) by inserting "6672(b), 6694(c)," after "6213(a),". **Effective** 11-10-78.

• 1976, Tax Reform Act of 1976 (P.L. 94-455)

P.L. 94-455, §1204(c)(11):

Added "and 7429(b)" to Code Sec. 7421(a). For the **effective** date, see Act Sec. 1204(d), below.

P.L. 94-455, §1204(d), as amended by P.L. 94-528, §2(a), provides:

(d) Effective Date.—The amendments made by this section apply with respect to action taken under section 6851, 6861, or 6862 of the Internal Revenue Code of 1954 where the notice and demand takes place after February 28, 1977.

• 1966, Federal Tax Lien Act of 1966 (P.L. 89-719)

P.L. 89-719, §110(c):

Amended Code Sec. 7421(a). **Effective**, generally, after 11-2-66. However, see the amendment note for Code Sec. 6323 for exceptions to this **effective** date. Prior to amendment, Code Sec. 7421(a) read as follows:

"(a) Tax.—Except as provided in sections 6212(a) and (c), and 6213(a), no suit for the purpose of restraining the assessment or collection of any tax shall be maintained in any court."

[Sec. 7421(b)]

(b) LIABILITY OF TRANSFEREE OR FIDUCIARY.—No suit shall be maintained in any court for the purpose of restraining the assessment or collection (pursuant to the provisions of chapter 71) of—

(1) the amount of the liability, at law or in equity, of a transferee of property of a taxpayer in respect of any internal revenue tax, or

(2) the amount of the liability of a fiduciary under section 3713(b) of title 31, United States Code, in respect of any such tax.

Amendments

• 2018, Tax Technical Corrections Act of 2018 (P.L. 115-141)

P.L. 115-141, §401(a)(324), Div. U:

Amended Code Sec. 7421(b)(2) by striking "Code in" and inserting "Code, in". **Effective** 3-23-2018.

• 1982 (P.L. 91-258)

P.L. 97-258, §3(f)(13):

Amended Code Sec. 7421(b)(2) by striking out "section 3467 of the Revised Statutes (31 U.S.C. 192)" and substituting "section 3713(b) of title 31, United States Code". **Effective** 9-13-82.

[Sec. 7422]

SEC. 7422. CIVIL ACTIONS FOR REFUND.

[Sec. 7422(a)]

(a) NO SUIT PRIOR TO FILING CLAIM FOR REFUND.—No suit or proceeding shall be maintained in any court for the recovery of any internal revenue tax alleged to have been erroneously or illegally assessed or collected, or of any penalty claimed to have been collected without authority, or of any sum alleged to have been excessive or in any manner wrongfully collected, until a claim for refund or credit has been duly filed with the Secretary, according to the provisions of law in that regard, and the regulations of the Secretary established in pursuance thereof.

Amendments

• 1976, Tax Reform Act of 1976 (P.L. 94-455)

P.L. 94-455, §1906(b)(13)(A):

Amended 1954 Code by substituting "Secretary" for "Secretary or his delegate" each place it appeared. **Effective** 2-1-77.

[Sec. 7422(b)]

(b) PROTEST OR DURESS.—Such suit or proceeding may be maintained whether or not such tax, penalty or sum has been paid under protest or duress.

[Sec. 7422(c)]

(c) SUITS AGAINST COLLECTION OFFICER A BAR.—A suit against any officer or employee of the United States (or former officer or employee) or his personal representative for the recovery of any internal revenue tax alleged to have been erroneously or illegally assessed or collected, or of any penalty claimed to have been collected without authority, or of any sum alleged to have been excessive or in any manner wrongfully collected shall be treated as if the United States had been a party to such suit in applying the doctrine of res judicata in all suits, in respect of any internal revenue tax, and in all proceedings in the Tax Court and on review of decisions of the Tax Court.

Amendments

• 1976, Tax Reform Act of 1976 (P.L. 94-455)

P.L. 94-455, §1906(a)(44):

Amended Code Sec. 7422(c) by striking out "instituted after June 15, 1942," after "the doctrine of res judicata in all suits" and by striking out "where the petition to the Tax Court was filed after such date" from the end of the subsection. **Effective** 2-1-77.

[Sec. 7422(d)]

(d) CREDIT TREATED AS PAYMENT.—The credit of an overpayment of any tax in satisfaction of any tax liability shall, for the purpose of any suit for refund of such tax liability so satisfied, be deemed to be a payment in respect of such tax liability at the time such credit is allowed.

[Sec. 7422(e)]

(e) STAY OF PROCEEDINGS.—If the Secretary prior to the hearing of a suit brought by a taxpayer in a district court or the United States Court of Federal Claims for the recovery of any income tax, estate tax, gift tax, or tax imposed by chapter 41, 42, 43, or 44 (or any penalty relating to such taxes) mails to the taxpayer a notice that a deficiency has been determined in respect of the tax which is the subject matter of taxpayer's suit, the proceedings in taxpayer's suit shall be stayed during the period of time in which the taxpayer may file a petition with the Tax Court for a redetermination of the asserted deficiency, and for 60 days thereafter. If the taxpayer files a petition with the Tax Court, the district court or the United States Court of Federal Claims, as the case may be, shall lose jurisdiction of taxpayer's suit to whatever extent jurisdiction is acquired by the Tax Court of the subject matter of taxpayer's suit for refund. If the taxpayer does not file a petition with the Tax Court for a redetermination of the asserted deficiency, the United States may counterclaim in the taxpayer's suit, or intervene in the event of a suit as described in subsection (c) (relating to suits against officers or employees of the United States), within the period of the stay of proceedings notwithstanding that the time for such pleading may have otherwise expired. The taxpayer shall have the burden of proof with respect to the issues raised by such counterclaim or intervention of the United States except as to the issue of whether the taxpayer has been guilty of fraud with intent to evade tax. This subsection shall not apply to a suit by a taxpayer which, prior to the date of enactment of this title, is commenced, instituted, or pending in a district court or the United States Court of Federal Claims for the recovery of any income tax, estate tax, or gift tax (or any penalty relating to such taxes).

Amendments

• 2018, Tax Technical Corrections Act of 2018 (P.L. 115-141)

P.L. 115-141, §401(a)(325)(A), Div. U:

Amended Code Sec. 7422(e) by striking "United States Claims Court" and inserting "United States Court of Federal Claims". [Note: Code Sec. 7422(e) does not contain the text "United States Claims Court". Therefore, this amendment cannot be made.—CCH] **Effective** 3-23-2018.

• 1992, Court of Federal Claims Technical and Procedural Improvements Act of 1992 (P.L. 102-572)

P.L. 102-572, §902(b)(1):

Amended Code Sec. 7422(e) by striking "United States Claims Court" and inserting "United States Court of Federal Claims" each place it appears. **Effective** 10-29-92.

• 1988, Omnibus Trade and Competitiveness Act of 1988 (P.L. 100-418)

P.L. 100-418, §1941(b)(2)(B)(x):

Amended Code Sec. 7422(e) by striking "44, or 45" each place it appears and inserting "or 44". **Effective** for crude oil removed from the premises on or after 8-23-88.

• 1982, Federal Courts Improvement Act of 1982 (P.L. 97-164)

P.L. 97-164, §151:

Amended Code Sec. 7422(e) by striking out "Court of Claims" each place it appeared and inserting in lieu thereof "United States Claims Court". **Effective** 10-1-82. For an explanation of the effect of this change on pending cases, see the historical comment for P.L. 97-164, Act Sec. 403, following Code Sec. 6110(i).

• 1980, Crude Oil Windfall Profit Tax Act of 1980 (P.L. 96-223)

P.L. 96-223, §101(f)(1)(J):

Amended Code Sec. 7422(e) by striking out "or 44" and inserting "44, or 45". For the **effective** date and transitional rules, see P.L. 96-223, Act Sec. 101(i), following Code Sec. 4986.

• 1976, Tax Reform Act of 1976 (P.L. 94-455)

P.L. 94-455, §1307(d)(2)(F):

Substituted "chapter 41, 42," for "chapter 42" in Code Sec. 7422(e). **Effective** 10-4-76.

P.L. 94-455, §1605(b)(11):

Substituted "43, or 44" for "or 43" in Code Sec. 7422(e). **Effective** for tax years of real estate investment trusts beginning after 10-4-76.

P.L. 94-455, §1906(b)(13)(A):

Amended 1954 Code by substituting "Secretary" for "Secretary or his delegate" each place it appeared. **Effective** 2-1-77.

• 1974, Employee Retirement Income Security Act of 1974 (P.L. 93-406)

P.L. 93-406, §1016(a)(26):

Amended Code Sec. 7422(e) by changing "chapter 42" to "chapter 42 or 43." For **effective** date, see amendment note for Code Sec. 410.

• 1969, Tax Reform Act of 1969 (P.L. 91-172)

P.L. 91-172, §101(j)(56):

Amended the first sentence of Code Sec. 7422(e) by substituting "gift tax, or tax imposed by chapter 42" for "or gift tax". **Effective** 1-1-70.

[Sec. 7422(f)]

(f) LIMITATION ON RIGHT OF ACTION FOR REFUND.—

(1) GENERAL RULE.—A suit or proceeding referred to in subsection (a) may be maintained only against the United States and not against any officer or employee of the United States (or former officer or employee) or his personal representative. Such suit or proceeding may be maintained against the United States notwithstanding the provisions of section 2502 of title 28 of the United States Code (relating to aliens' privilege to sue) and notwithstanding the provisions of section 1502 of such title 28 (relating to certain treaty cases).

(2) MISJOINDER AND CHANGE OF VENUE.—If a suit or proceeding brought in a United States district court against an officer or employee of the United States (or former officer or employee) or his personal representative is improperly brought solely by virtue of paragraph (1), the court shall order, upon such terms as are just, that the pleadings be amended to substitute the United States as a party for such officer or employee as of the time such action commenced, upon proper service of process on the United States. Such suit or proceeding shall upon request by the United States be transferred to the district or division where it should have been brought if such action initially had been brought against the United States.

Amendments

• 1971, Revenue Act of 1971 (P.L. 92-178)

P.L. 92-178, §309(a):

Added "and notwithstanding the provisions of section 1502 of such title 28 (relating to certain treaty cases)" at the end of Code Sec. 7422(f)(1). **Effective** for suits or proceedings which are instituted after 1-30-67.

• 1966 (P.L. 89-713)

P.L. 89-713, §3(a):

Redesignated Code Sec. 7422(f) as Code Sec. 7422(g) and added new Code Sec. 7422(f). **Effective** for suits brought against officers, employees, or personal representatives referred to therein which are instituted 90 days or more after 11-2-66.

[Sec. 7422(g)]

(g) SPECIAL RULES FOR CERTAIN EXCISE TAXES IMPOSED BY CHAPTER 42 OR 43.—

(1) RIGHT TO BRING ACTIONS.—

(A) IN GENERAL.—With respect to any taxable event, payment of the full amount of the first tier tax shall constitute sufficient payment in order to maintain an action under this section with respect to the second tier tax.

(B) DEFINITIONS.—For purposes of subparagraph (A), the terms "taxable event", "first tier tax", and "second tier tax" have the respective meanings given to such terms by section 4963.

(2) LIMITATION ON SUIT FOR REFUND.—No suit may be maintained under this section for the credit or refund of any tax imposed under section 4941, 4942, 4943, 4944, 4945, 4951, 4952, 4955, 4958, 4971, or 4975 with respect to any act (or failure to act) giving rise to liability for tax under such sections, unless no other suit has been maintained for credit or refund of, and no petition has been filed in the Tax Court with respect to a deficiency in, any other tax imposed by such sections with respect to such act (or failure to act).

(3) FINAL DETERMINATION OF ISSUES.—For purposes of this section, any suit for the credit or refund of any tax imposed under section 4941, 4942, 4943, 4944, 4945, 4951, 4952, 4955, 4958, 4971, or 4975 with respect to any act (or failure to act) giving rise to liability for tax under such sections, shall constitute a suit to determine all questions with respect to any other tax imposed with respect to such act (or failure to act) under such sections, and failure by the parties to such suit to bring any such question before the Court shall constitute a bar to such question.

Amendments

• 1996, Taxpayer Bill of Rights 2 (P.L. 104-168)

P.L. 104-168, §1311(c)(4):

Amended Code Sec. 7422(g)(2) and (3) by inserting "4958," after "4955,". For the **effective** date of the above amendment, see Act Sec. 1311(d)(1)-(2), below.

P.L. 104-168, §1311(d)(1)-(2), provides:

(1) IN GENERAL.—The amendments made by this section (other than subsection (b)) shall apply to excess benefit transactions occurring on or after September 14, 1995.

(2) BINDING CONTRACTS.—The amendments referred to in paragraph (1) shall not apply to any benefit arising from a transaction pursuant to any written contract which was binding on September 13, 1995, and at all times thereafter before such transaction occurred.

• 1987, Revenue Act of 1987 (P.L. 100-203)

P.L. 100-203, §10712:

Amended Code Sec. 7422(g)(2) and (3) by striking out "4952," and inserting in lieu thereof "4952, 4955,". **Effective** for tax years beginning after 12-22-87.

• 1986, Tax Reform Act of 1986 (P.L. 99-514)

P.L. 99-514, §1899A(58):

Amended Code Sec. 7422(g)(1)(B) by striking out "section 4962" and inserting in lieu thereof "section 4963". **Effective** 10-22-86.

• 1980 (P.L. 96-596)

P.L. 96-596, §2(c)(2):

Amended Code Sec. 7422(g)(1). **Effective** with respect to first-tier taxes as if included in the Internal Revenue Code of 1954 when such tax was first imposed. **Effective** for second-tier taxes assessed after 12-24-80 (except in cases where there is a court decision with regard to which res judicata applies on that date). Prior to amendment, Code Sec. 7422(g)(1) read:

(1) RIGHT TO BRING ACTIONS.—With respect to any act (or failure to act) giving rise to liability under section 4941, 4942, 4943, 4944, 4945, 4951, 4952, 4971, or 4975, payment of the full amount of tax imposed under section 4941(a) (relating to initial taxes on self-dealing), section 4942(a) (relating to initial tax on failure to distribute income), section 4943(a) (relating to initial tax on excess business holdings), section 4944(a) (relating to initial taxes on investments which jeopardize charitable purpose), section 4945(a) (relating to initial taxes on taxable expenditures), section 4951(a) (relating to initial taxes on self-dealing), 4952(a) (relating to initial taxes on taxable expenditures), 4971(a) (relating to initial tax on failure to meet minimum funding standard), 4975(a) (relating to initial tax on prohibited transactions), section 4941(b) (relating to additional taxes on self-dealing), section 4942(b) (relating to additional tax on failure to distribute income), section 4943(b) (relating to additional tax on excess business holdings), section 4944(b) (relating to additional taxes on investments which jeopardize charitable purpose), section 4945(b) (relating to additional taxes on taxable expenditures), section 4951(b) (relating to additional taxes on self-dealing), section 4952(b) (relating to additional taxes on taxable expenditures), section 4971(b) (relating to additional tax on failure to meet minimum funding standard), or section 4975(b) (relating to additional tax on prohibited transactions), shall constitute sufficient payment in order to maintain an action under this section with respect to such act (or failure to act).

• 1980, Technical Corrections Act of 1979 (P.L. 96-222)

P.L. 96-222, §108(b)(1)(D), (E), (F):

Amended Code Sec. 7422(g) by changing "4944, 4945" each place it appeared to "4944, 4945, 4951, 4952", by changing "section 4945(a) (relating to initial taxes on taxable expenditures)" to "section 4945(a) (relating to initial taxes on taxable expenditures), section 4951(a) (relating to initial taxes on self-dealing), 4952(a) (relating to initial taxes on taxable expenditures)", and by changing "section 4945(b) (relating to additional taxes on taxable expenditures)" to "section 4945(b) (relating to additional taxes on taxable expenditures), section 4951(b) (relating to additional taxes on self-dealing), section 4952(b) (relating to additional taxes on taxable expenditures)." **Effective** with respect to contributions, acts and expenditures made after 12-31-77.

• 1974, Employee Retirement Income Security Act of 1974 (P.L. 93-406)

P.L. 93-406, §1016(a)(26):

Amended Code Sec. 7422(g). For **effective** date, see amendment note for Code Sec. 410. Prior to amendment, Code Sec. 7422(g) read as follows:

"(g) Special Rules for Certain Excise Taxes Imposed by Chapter 42.—

"(1) Right to bring actions.—With respect to any act (or failure to act) giving rise to liability under section 4941, 4942, 4943, 4944, or 4945, payment of the full amount of tax imposed under section 4941(a) (relating to initial taxes on self-dealing), section 4942(a) (relating to initial tax on failure to distribute income), section 4943(a) (relating to initial tax on excess business holdings), section 4944(a) (relating to initial taxes on investments which jeopardize charitable purpose), section 4945(a) (relating to initial taxes on taxable expenditures), section 4941(b) (relating to additional taxes on self-dealing), section 4942(b) (relating to additional tax on failure to distribute income), section 4943(b) (relating to additional tax on excess business holdings), section 4944(b) (relating to additional taxes on investments which jeopardize charitable purpose), or section 4945(b) (relating to additional taxes on taxable expenditures) shall constitute sufficent payment in order to maintain an action under this section with respect to such act (or failure to act).

"(2) Limitation on suit for refund.—No suit may be maintained under this section for the credit or refund of any tax imposed under section 4941, 4942, 4943, 4944, or 4945 with respect to any act (or failure to act) giving rise to liability for tax under such sections, unless no other suit has been maintained for credit or refund of, and no petition has been filed in the Tax Court with respect to a deficiency in, any other tax imposed by such sections with respect to such act (or failure to act).

"(3) Final determination of issues.—For purposes of this section, any suit for the credit or refund of any tax imposed under section 4941, 4942, 4943, 4944, or 4945 with respect to any act (or failure to act) giving rise to liability for tax under such sections, shall constitute a suit to determine all questions with respect to any other tax imposed with respect to such act (or failure to act) under such sections, and failure by the parties to such suit to bring any such question before the Court shall constitute a bar to such question."

• 1969, Tax Reform Act of 1969 (P.L. 91-172)

P.L. 91-172, §101(i):

Added Code Sec. 7422(g). **Effective** 1-1-70.

[Sec. 7422(h)—Stricken]

Amendments

• 2015, Bipartisan Budget Act of 2015 (P.L. 114-74)

P.L. 114-74, §1101(f)(11):

Amended Code Sec. 7422 by striking subsection (h). **Effective** generally for returns filed for partnership tax years beginning after 12-31-2017. For a special rule, see Act Sec. 1101(g)(4), below. Prior to being stricken, Code Sec. 7422(h) read as follows:

(h) SPECIAL RULE FOR ACTIONS WITH RESPECT TO PARTNERSHIP ITEMS.—No action may be brought for a refund attributable to partnership items (as defined in section 6231(a)(3)) except as provided in section 6228(b) or section 6230(c).

P.L. 114-74, §1101(g)(4), provides:

(4) ELECTION.—A partnership may elect (at such time and in such form and manner as the Secretary of the Treasury may prescribe) for the amendments made by this section (other than the election under section 6221(b) of such Code (as added by this Act)) to apply to any return of the partnership filed for partnership taxable years beginning after the date of the enactment of this Act and before January 1, 2018.

• 1984, Deficit Reduction Act of 1984 (P.L. 98-369)

P.L. 98-369, §714(p)(2)(H):

Amended Code Sec. 7422(h) by striking out "section 6131(a)(3)" and inserting in lieu thereof "section 6231(a)(3)". **Effective** as if included in the provision of P.L. 97-248 to which it relates.

• 1982, Tax Equity and Fiscal Responsibility Act of 1982 (P.L. 97-248)

P.L. 97-248, §402(c)(11):

Added Code Sec. 7422(h). **Effective** for partnership tax years beginning after 9-3-82 and also to partnership tax years ending after that date if the partnership, each partner, and each indirect partner requests such application and the Secretary or his delegate consents to such application.

[Sec. 7422(i)]

(i) SPECIAL RULE FOR ACTIONS WITH RESPECT TO TAX SHELTER PROMOTER AND UNDERSTATEMENT PENALTIES.—No action or proceeding may be brought in the United States Court of Federal Claims for any refund or credit of a penalty imposed by section 6700 (relating to penalty for promoting abusive tax shelters, etc.) or section 6701 (relating to penalties for aiding and abetting understatement of tax liability).

Amendments

• 2018, Tax Technical Corrections Act of 2018 (P.L. 115-141)

P.L. 115-141, §401(a)(325)(A), Div. U:

Amended Code Sec. 7422(i) by striking "United States Claims Court" and inserting "United States Court of Federal Claims". [Note: Code Sec. 7422(i) does not contain the text "United States Claims Court". Therefore, this amendment cannot be made.—CCH] **Effective** 3-23-2018.

• 1992, Court of Federal Claims Technical and Procedural Improvements Act of 1992 (P.L. 102-572)

P.L. 102-572, §902(b)(1):

Amended Code Sec. 7422(i) by striking "United States Claims Court" and inserting "United States Court of Federal Claims". **Effective** 10-29-92.

• 1984, Deficit Reduction Act of 1984 (P.L. 98-369)

P.L. 98-369, §714(g)(1):

Redesignated subsection (i) of Code Sec. 7422 as subsection (j) and inserted new subsection (i). **Effective** for any claim for refund or credit filed after 7-18-84.

[Sec. 7422(j)]

(j) SPECIAL RULE FOR ACTIONS WITH RESPECT TO ESTATES FOR WHICH AN ELECTION UNDER SECTION 6166 IS MADE.—

(1) IN GENERAL.—The district courts of the United States and the United States Court of Federal Claims shall not fail to have jurisdiction over any action brought by the representative of

an estate to which this subsection applies to determine the correct amount of the estate tax liability of such estate (or for any refund with respect thereto) solely because the full amount of such liability has not been paid by reason of an election under section 6166 with respect to such estate.

(2) ESTATES TO WHICH SUBSECTION APPLIES.—This subsection shall apply to any estate if, as of the date the action is filed—

(A) no portion of the installments payable under section 6166 have been accelerated;

(B) all such installments the due date for which is on or before the date the action is filed have been paid;

(C) there is no case pending in the Tax Court with respect to the tax imposed by section 2001 on the estate and, if a notice of deficiency under section 6212 with respect to such tax has been issued, the time for filing a petition with the Tax Court with respect to such notice has expired; and

(D) no proceeding for declaratory judgment under section 7479 is pending.

(3) PROHIBITION ON COLLECTION OF DISALLOWED LIABILITY.—If the court redetermines under paragraph (1) the estate tax liability of an estate, no part of such liability which is disallowed by a decision of such court which has become final may be collected by the Secretary, and amounts paid in excess of the installments determined by the court as currently due and payable shall be refunded.

Amendments

• 1998, IRS Restructuring and Reform Act of 1998 (P.L. 105-206)

P.L. 105-206, §3104(a):

Amended Code Sec. 7422 by redesignating subsection (j) as subsection (k) and by inserting after subsection (i) a new subsection (j). **Effective** for any claim for refund filed after 7-22-98.

[Sec. 7422(k)]

(k) CROSS REFERENCES.—

(1) For provisions relating generally to claims for refund or credit, see chapter 65 (relating to abatements, credit, and refund) and chapter 66 (relating to limitations).

(2) For duty of United States attorneys to defend suits, see section 507 of Title 28 of the United States Code.

(3) For jurisdiction of United States district courts, see section 1346 of Title 28 of the United States Code.

(4) For payment by the Treasury of judgments against internal revenue officers or employees, upon certificate of probable cause, see section 2006 of Title 28 of the United States Code.

Amendments

• 1998, IRS Restructuring and Reform Act of 1998 (P.L. 105-206)

P.L. 105-206, §3104(a):

Amended Code Sec. 7422 by redesignating subsection (j) as subsection (k). **Effective** for any claim for refund filed after 7-22-98.

• 1984, Deficit Reduction Act of 1984 (P.L. 98-369)

P.L. 98-369, §714(g)(1):

Redesignated subsection (i) of Code Sec. 7422 as subsection (j). **Effective** for any claim for refund or credit filed after 7-18-84.

• 1982, Tax Equity and Fiscal Responsibility Act of 1982 (P.L. 97-248)

P.L. 97-248, §402(c)(11):

Redesignated Code Sec. 7422(h) as Code Sec. 7422(i). For **effective** date, see the amendment note for P.L. 97-248, Act Sec. 402(c)(11), following Code Sec. 7422(h) above.

• 1969, Tax Reform Act of 1969 (P.L. 91-172)

P.L. 91-172, §101(i):

Redesignated former Code Sec. 7422(g) as Code Sec. 7422(h). **Effective** 1-1-70.

• 1966 (P.L. 89-713)

P.L. 89-713, §3(a):

Redesignated former Code Sec. 7422(f) as Code Sec. 7422(g). **Effective** as to suits brought against officers, employees, or personal representatives referred to therein which are instituted 90 days or more after 11-2-66.

• 1958, Technical Amendments Act of 1958 (P.L. 85-866)

P.L. 85-866, §78:

Amended paragraph (2) by striking out the word "district" where it appeared in the phrase "United States district attorneys". **Effective** 1-1-54.

* * *

[Sec. 7426]

SEC. 7426. CIVIL ACTIONS BY PERSONS OTHER THAN TAXPAYERS.

[Sec. 7426(a)]

(a) ACTIONS PERMITTED.—

(1) WRONGFUL LEVY.—If a levy has been made on property or property has been sold pursuant to a levy, any person (other than the person against whom is assessed the tax out of which such levy arose) who claims an interest in or lien on such property and that such property was wrongfully levied upon may bring a civil action against the United States in a district court of the United States. Such action may be brought without regard to whether such property has been surrendered to or sold by the Secretary.

(2) SURPLUS PROCEEDS.—If property has been sold pursuant to a levy, any person (other than the person against whom is assessed the tax out of which such levy arose) who claims an interest in or lien on such property junior to that of the United States and to be legally entitled to the surplus proceeds of such sale may bring a civil action against the United States in a district court of the United States.

(3) SUBSTITUTED SALE PROCEEDS.—If property has been sold pursuant to an agreement described in section 6325(b)(3) (relating to substitution of proceeds of sale), any person who claims to be legally entitled to all or any part of the amount held as a fund pursuant to such agreement may bring a civil action against the United States in a district court of the United States.

(4) SUBSTITUTION OF VALUE.—If a certificate of discharge is issued to any person under section 6325(b)(4) with respect to any property, such person may, within 120 days after the day on which such certificate is issued, bring a civil action against the United States in a district court of the United States for a determination of whether the value of the interest of the United States (if any) in such property is less than the value determined by the Secretary. No other action may be brought by such person for such a determination.

Amendments

• 1998, IRS Restructuring and Reform Act of 1998 (P.L. 105-206)

P.L. 105-206, §3106(b)(1):

Amended Code Sec. 7426(a) by adding at the end a new paragraph (4). **Effective** 7-22-98.

• 1976, Tax Reform Act of 1976 (P.L. 94-455)

P.L. 94-455, §1906(b)(13)(A):

Amended 1954 Code by substituting "Secretary" for "Secretary or his delegate" each place it appeared. **Effective** 2-1-77.

[Sec. 7426(b)]

(b) ADJUDICATION.—The district court shall have jurisdiction to grant only such of the following forms of relief as may be appropriate in the circumstances:

(1) INJUNCTION.—If a levy or sale would irreparably injure rights in property which the court determines to be superior to rights of the United States in such property, the court may grant an injunction to prohibit the enforcement of such levy or to prohibit such sale.

(2) RECOVERY OF PROPERTY.—If the court determines that such property has been wrongfully levied upon, the court may—

(A) order the return of specific property if the United States is in possession of such property;

(B) grant a judgment for the amount of money levied upon; or

(C) if such property was sold, grant a judgment for an amount not exceeding the greater of—

(i) the amount received by the United States from the sale of such property, or

(ii) the fair market value of such property immediately before the levy.

For purposes of subparagraph (C), if the property was declared purchased by the United States at a sale pursuant to section 6335(e) (relating to manner and conditions of sale), the United States shall be treated as having received an amount equal to the minimum price determined pursuant to such section or (if larger) the amount received by the United States from the resale of such property.

(3) SURPLUS PROCEEDS.—If the court determines that the interest or lien of any party to an action under this section was transferred to the proceeds of a sale of such property, the court may grant a judgment in an amount equal to all or any part of the amount of the surplus proceeds of such sale.

(4) SUBSTITUTED SALE PROCEEDS.—If the court determines that a party has an interest in or lien on the amount held as a fund pursuant to an agreement described in section 6325(b)(3) (relating to substitution of proceeds of sale), the court may grant a judgment in an amount equal to all or any part of the amount of such fund.

(5) SUBSTITUTION OF VALUE.—If the court determines that the Secretary's determination of the value of the interest of the United States in the property for purposes of section 6325(b)(4) exceeds the actual value of such interest, the court shall grant a judgment ordering a refund of the amount deposited, and a release of the bond, to the extent that the aggregate of the amounts thereof exceeds such value determined by the court.

Amendments

• 1998, IRS Restructuring and Reform Act of 1998 (P.L. 105-206)

P.L. 105-206, §3106(b)(2)(A):

Amended Code Sec. 7426(b) by adding at the end a new paragraph (5). **Effective** 7-22-98.

• 1982, Tax Equity and Fiscal Responsibility Act of 1982 (P.L. 97-248)

P.L. 97-248, §350(a):

Amended Code Sec. 7426(b)(2)(C). **Effective** with respect to levies made after 12-31-82. Prior to amendment, Code Sec. 7426(b)(2)(C) read as follows:

"(C) grant a judgment for an amount not exceeding the amount received by the United States from the sale of such property."

[Sec. 7426(c)]

(c) VALIDITY OF ASSESSMENT.—For purposes of an adjudication under this section, the assessment of tax upon which the interest or lien of the United States is based shall be conclusively presumed to be valid.

[Sec. 7426(d)]

(d) LIMITATION ON RIGHTS OF ACTION.—No action may be maintained against any officer or employee of the United States (or former officer or employee) or his personal representative with respect to any acts for which an action could be maintained under this section.

[Sec. 7426(e)]

(e) SUBSTITUTION OF UNITED STATES AS PARTY.—If an action, which could be brought against the United States under this section, is improperly brought against any officer or employee of the United States (or former officer or employee) or his personal representative, the court shall order, upon such terms as are just, that the pleadings be amended to substitute the United States as a party for such officer or employee as of the time such action was commenced upon proper service of process on the United States.

[Sec. 7426(f)]

(f) PROVISION INAPPLICABLE.—The provisions of section 7422(a) (relating to prohibition of suit prior to filing claim for refund) shall not apply to actions under this section.

[Sec. 7426(g)]

(g) INTEREST.—Interest shall be allowed at the overpayment rate established under section 6621—

(1) in the case of a judgment pursuant to subsection (b)(2)(B), from the date the Secretary receives the money wrongfully levied upon to the date of payment of such judgment;

(2) in the case of a judgment pursuant to subsection (b)(2)(C), from the date of the sale of the property wrongfully levied upon to the date of payment of such judgment; and

(3) in the case of a judgment pursuant to subsection (b)(5) which orders a refund of any amount, from the date the Secretary received such amount to the date of payment of such judgment.

Amendments

• 1998, IRS Restructuring and Reform Act of 1998 (P.L. 105-206)

P.L. 105-206, §3106(b)(2)(B):

Amended Code Sec. 7426(g) by striking "and" at the end of paragraph (1), by striking the period at the end of paragraph (2) and inserting "; and", and by adding at the end a new paragraph (3). **Effective** 7-22-98.

• 1986, Tax Reform Act of 1986 (P.L. 99-514)

P.L. 99-514, §1511(c)(16):

Amended Code Sec. 7426(g) by striking out "an annual rate established under section 6621" and inserting in lieu thereof "the overpayment rate established under section 6621". **Effective** for purposes of determining interest for periods after 12-31-86.

• 1976, Tax Reform Act of 1976 (P.L. 94-455)

P.L. 94-455, §1906(b)(13)(A):

Amended 1954 Code by substituting "Secretary" for "Secretary or his delegate" each place it appeared. **Effective** 2-1-77.

[Sec. 7426(h)]

(h) RECOVERY OF DAMAGES PERMITTED IN CERTAIN CASES.—

(1) IN GENERAL.—Notwithstanding subsection (b), if, in any action brought under this section, there is a finding that any officer or employee of the Internal Revenue Service recklessly or intentionally, or by reason of negligence, disregarded any provision of this title the defendant shall be liable to the plaintiff in an amount equal to the lesser of $1,000,000 ($100,000 in the case of negligence) or the sum of—

(A) actual, direct economic damages sustained by the plaintiff as a proximate result of the reckless or intentional or negligent disregard of any provision of this title by the officer or employee (reduced by any amount of such damages awarded under subsection (b)); and

(B) the costs of the action.

(2) REQUIREMENT THAT ADMINISTRATIVE REMEDIES BE EXHAUSTED; MITIGATION; PERIOD.—The rules of section 7433(d) shall apply for purposes of this subsection.

(3) PAYMENT AUTHORITY.—Claims pursuant to this section shall be payable out of funds appropriated under section 1304 of title 31, United States Code.

Amendments

• 1998, IRS Restructuring and Reform Act of 1998 (P.L. 105-206)

P.L. 105-206, §3102(b):

Amended Code Sec. 7426 by redesignating subsection (h) as subsection (i) and by adding after subsection (g) a new subsection (h). **Effective** for actions of officers or employees of the Internal Revenue Service after 7-22-98.

[Sec. 7426(i)]

(i) CROSS REFERENCE.—

For period of limitation, see section 6532(c).

Amendments

• 1998, IRS Restructuring and Reform Act of 1998 (P.L. 105-206)

P.L. 105-206, §3102(b):

Amended Code Sec. 7426 by redesignating subsection (h) as subsection (i). **Effective** for actions of officers or employees of the Internal Revenue Service after 7-22-98.

• 1976, Tax Reform Act of 1976 (P.L. 94-455)

P.L. 94-455, §1906(b)(13)(A):

Amended 1954 Code by substituting "Secretary" for "Secretary or his delegate" each place it appeared. **Effective** 2-1-77.

• 1975 (P.L. 93-625)

P.L. 93-625, §7(a)(2):

Amended Code Sec. 7426(g) by substituting "an annual rate established under section 6621" for "the rate of 6 percent per annum". For **effective** date, see the historical comment for P.L. 93-625 following the text of Code Sec. 6621.

• 1966, Federal Tax Lien Act of 1966 (P.L. 89-719)

P.L. 89-719, §110(a):

Added Code Sec. 7426. **Effective**, generally, after 11-2-66. However, see the amendment note for Code Sec. 6323 for exceptions to this **effective** date.

* * *

[Sec. 7429]

SEC. 7429. REVIEW OF JEOPARDY LEVY OR ASSESSMENT PROCEDURES.

[Sec. 7429(a)]

(a) ADMINISTRATIVE REVIEW.—

(1) ADMINISTRATIVE REVIEW.—

(A) PRIOR APPROVAL REQUIRED.—No assessment may be made under section 6851(a), 6852(a), 6861(a), or 6862, and no levy may be made under section 6331(a) less than 30 days after notice and demand for payment is made, unless the Chief Counsel for the Internal Revenue Service (or such Counsel's delegate) personally approves (in writing) such assessment or levy.

(B) INFORMATION TO TAXPAYER.—Within 5 days after the day on which such an assessment or levy is made, the Secretary shall provide the taxpayer with a written statement of the information upon which the Secretary relied in making such assessment or levy.

(2) REQUEST FOR REVIEW.—Within 30 days after the day on which the taxpayer is furnished the written statement described in paragraph (1), or within 30 days after the last day of the period within which such statement is required to be furnished, the taxpayer may request the Secretary to review the action taken.

(3) REDETERMINATION BY SECRETARY.—After a request for review is made under paragraph (2), the Secretary shall determine—

(A) whether or not—

(i) the making of the assessment under section 6851, 6861, or 6862, as the case may be, is reasonable under the circumstances, and

(ii) the amount so assessed or demanded as a result of the action taken under section 6851, 6861, or 6862 is appropriate under the circumstances, or

(B) whether or not the levy described in subsection (a)(1) is reasonable under the circumstances.

Amendments

• 1998, IRS Restructuring and Reform Act of 1998 (P.L. 105-206)

P.L. 105-206, §3434(a):

Amended Code Sec. 7429(a)(1). **Effective** for taxes assessed and levies made after 7-22-98. Prior to amendment, Code Sec. 7429(a)(1) read as follows:

(1) INFORMATION TO TAXPAYER.—Within 5 days after the day on which an assessment is made under section 6851(a), 6852(a), 6861(a), or 6862, or levy is made under section 6331(a) less than 30 days after notice and demand for payment is made under section 6331(a), the Secretary shall provide the taxpayer with a written statement of the information upon which the Secretary relies in making such assessment or levy.

• 1988, Technical and Miscellaneous Revenue Act of 1988 (P.L. 100-647)

P.L. 100-647, §6237(a)(1)-(2):

Amended Code Sec. 7429(a)(1) by inserting "or levy is made under section 6331(a) less than 30 days after notice and demand for payment is made under section 6331(a)," after "6862,", and by inserting "or levy" after "such assessment". **Effective** for jeopardy levies issued and assessments made on or after 7-1-89.

P.L. 100-647, §6237(b):

Amended Code Sec. 7429(a)(3). **Effective** for jeopardy levies issued and assessments made on or after 7-1-89. Prior to amendment, Code Sec. 7429(a)(3) read as follows:

(3) REDETERMINATION BY SECRETARY.—After a request for review is made under paragraph (2), the Secretary shall determine whether or not—

(A) the making of the assessment under section 6851, 6852, 6861, or 6862, as the case may be, is reasonable under the circumstances, and

(B) the amount so assessed or demanded as a result of the action taken under section 6851, 6852, 6861, or 6862 is appropriate under the circumstances.

P.L. 100-647, §6237(e)(3):

Amended Code Sec. 7429 by inserting "LEVY OR" after "JEOPARDY". **Effective** for jeopardy levies issued and assessments made on or after 7-1-89.

• 1987, Revenue Act of 1987 (P.L. 100-203)

P.L. 100-203, §10713(b)(2)(F)(i)-(ii):

Amended Code Sec. 7429 by striking out "6851(a)," each place it appears and inserting in lieu thereof "6851(a), 6852(a),", and by striking out "6851," each place it appears and inserting in lieu thereof "6851, 6852,". **Effective** 12-22-87.

[Sec. 7429(b)]

(b) JUDICIAL REVIEW.—

(1) PROCEEDINGS PERMITTED.—Within 90 days after the earlier of—

(A) the day the Secretary notifies the taxpayer of the Secretary's determination described in subsection (a)(3), or

(B) the 16th day after the request described in subsection (a)(2) was made,

the taxpayer may bring a civil action against the United States for a determination under this subsection in the court with jurisdiction determined under paragraph (2).

(2) JURISDICTION FOR DETERMINATION.—

(A) IN GENERAL.—Except as provided in subparagraph (B), the district courts of the United States shall have exclusive jurisdiction over any civil action for a determination under this subsection.

(B) TAX COURT.—If a petition for a redetermination of a deficiency under section 6213(a) has been timely filed with the Tax Court before the making of an assessment or levy that is subject to the review procedures of this section, and 1 or more of the taxes and taxable periods before the Tax Court because of such petition is also included in the written statement that is provided to the taxpayer under subsection (a), then the Tax Court also shall have jurisdiction over any civil action for a determination under this subsection with respect to all the taxes and taxable periods included in such written statement.

(3) DETERMINATION BY COURT.—Within 20 days after a proceeding is commenced under paragraph (1), the court shall determine—

(A) whether or not—

(i) the making of the assessment under section 6851, 6861, or 6862, as the case may be, is reasonable under the circumstances, and

(ii) the amount so assessed or demanded as a result of the action taken under section 6851, 6861, or 6862 is appropriate under the circumstances, or

(B) whether or not the levy described in subsection (a)(1) is reasonable under the circumstances.

If the court determines that proper service was not made on the United States or on the Secretary, as may be appropriate, within 5 days after the date of the commencement of the proceeding, then the running of the 20-day period set forth in the preceding sentence shall not begin before the day on which proper service was made on the United States or on the Secretary, as may be appropriate.

(4) ORDER OF COURT.—If the court determines that the making of such levy is unreasonable, that the making of such assessment is unreasonable, or that the amount assessed or demanded is inappropriate, then the court may order the Secretary to release such levy, to abate such assessment, to redetermine (in whole or in part) the amount assessed or demanded, or to take such other action as the court finds appropriate.

Amendments

• 1988, Technical and Miscellaneous Revenue Act of 1988 (P.L. 100-647)

P.L. 100-647, §6237(c):

Amended Code Sec. 7429(b). **Effective** for jeopardy levies issued or assessments made on or after 7-1-89. Prior to amendment, Code Sec. 7429(b) read as follows:

(b) JUDICIAL REVIEW.—

(1) ACTIONS PERMITTED.—Within 30 days after the earlier of—

(A) the day the Secretary notifies the taxpayer of his determination described in subsection (a)(3), or

(B) the 16th day after the request described in subsection (a)(2) was made,

the taxpayer may bring a civil action against the United States in a district court of the United States for a determination under this subsection.

(2) DETERMINATION BY DISTRICT COURT.—Within 20 days after an action is commenced under paragraph (1), the district court shall determine whether or not—

(A) the making of the assessment under section 6851, 6852, 6861, or 6862, as the case may be, is reasonable under the circumstances, and

(B) the amount so assessed or demanded as a result of the action taken under section 6851, 6852, 6861, or 6862, is appropriate under the circumstances.

If the court determines that proper service was not made on the United States within 5 days after the date of the commencement of the action, the running of the 20-day period set forth in the preceding sentence shall not begin before the day on which proper service was made on the United States.

(3) ORDER OF DISTRICT COURT.—If the court determines that the making of such assessment is unreasonable or that the amount assessed or demanded is inappropriate, the court may order the Secretary to abate such assessment, to redetermine (in whole or in part) the amount assessed or demanded, or to take such other action as the court finds appropriate.

• 1987, Revenue Act of 1987 (P.L. 100-203)

P.L. 100-203, §10713(b)(2)(F)(i)-(ii):

Amended Code Sec. 7429 by striking out "6851(a)," each place it appears and inserting in lieu thereof "6851(a), 6852(a),", and by striking out "6851," each place it appears and inserting in lieu thereof "6851, 6852,". **Effective** 12-22-87.

• 1984, Deficit Reduction Act of 1984 (P.L. 98-369)

P.L. 98-369, §446(a):

Amended Code Sec. 7429(b)(2) by adding at the end thereof a new sentence. **Effective** for actions commenced after 7-18-84.

[Sec. 7429(c)]

(c) EXTENTION OF 20-DAY PERIOD WHERE TAXPAYER SO REQUESTS.—If the taxpayer requests an extension of the 20-day period set forth in subsection (b)(2) and establishes reasonable grounds why such extention should be granted, the court may grant an extension of not more than 40 additional days.

Amendments

• 1988, Technical and Miscellaneous Revenue Act of 1988 (P.L. 100-647)

P.L. 100-647, §6237(e)(1):

Amended Code Sec. 7429(c) by striking out "district" before "court" each place it appears. **Effective** for jeopardy levies issued and assessments made on or after 7-1-89.

[Sec. 7429(d)]

(d) COMPUTATION OF DAYS.—For purposes of this section, Saturday, Sunday, or a legal holiday in the District of Columbia shall not be counted as the last day of any period.

[Sec. 7429(e)]

(e) VENUE.—

(1) DISTRICT COURT.—A civil action in a district court under subsection (b) shall be commenced only in the judicial district described in section 1402(a)(1) or (2) of title 28, United States Code.

(2) TRANSFER OF ACTIONS.—If a civil action is filed under subsection (b) with the Tax Court and such court finds that there is want of jurisdiction because of the jurisdiction provisions of subsection (b)(2), then the Tax Court shall, if such court determines it is in the interest of justice, transfer the civil action to the district court in which the action could have been brought at the time such action was filed. Any civil action so transferred shall proceed as if such action had been filed in the district court to which such action is transferred on the date on which such action was actually filed in the Tax Court from which such action is transferred.

Amendments

• 1988, Technical and Miscellaneous Revenue Act of 1988 (P.L. 100-647)

P.L. 100-647, §6237(d):

Amended Code Sec. 7429(e). **Effective** for jeopardy levies issued and assessments made on or after 7-1-89. Prior to amendment, Code Sec. 7429(e) read as follows:

(e) VENUE.—A civil action under subsection (b) shall be commenced only in the judicial district described in section 1402(a)(1) or (2) of title 28, United States Code.

[Sec. 7429(f)]

(f) FINALITY OF DETERMINATION.—Any determination made by a court under this section shall be final and conclusive and shall not be reviewed by any other court.

Amendments

• 1988, Technical and Miscellaneous Revenue Act of 1988 (P.L. 100-647)

P.L. 100-647, §6237(e)(1):

Amended Code Sec. 7429(f) by striking out "district" before "court" the first place "court" appears in the subsection. **Effective** for jeopardy levies issued and assessments made on or after 7-1-89.

[Sec. 7429(g)]

(g) BURDEN OF PROOF.—

(1) REASONABLENESS OF LEVY, TERMINATION, OR JEOPARDY ASSESSMENT.—In a proceeding under subsection (b) involving the issue of whether the making of a levy described in subsection (a)(1) or the making of an assessment under section 6851, 6852, 6861, or 6862 is reasonable under the circumstances, the burden of proof in respect to such issue shall be upon the Secretary.

(2) REASONABLENESS OF AMOUNT OF ASSESSMENT.—In a proceeding under subsection (b) involving the issue of whether an amount assessed or demanded as a result of action taken under section 6851, 6852, 6861, or 6862 is appropriate under the circumstances, the Secretary shall provide a written statement which contains any information with respect to which his determination of the amount assessed was based, but the burden of proof in respect of such issue shall be upon the taxpayer.

Amendments

• 1988, Technical and Miscellaneous Revenue Act of 1988 (P.L. 100-647)

P.L. 100-647, §6237(e)(2)(A)-(C):

Amended Code Sec. 7429(g) by inserting "the making of a levy described in subsection (a)(1) or" after "whether" in paragraph (1); by striking out "TERMINATION" in the heading of paragraph (1) and inserting in lieu thereof "LEVY, TERMINATION,", and by striking out "an action" and inserting in lieu thereof "a proceeding" in paragraphs (1) and (2). **Effective** for jeopardy levies issued and assessments made on or after 7-1-89.

• 1987, Revenue Act of 1987 (P.L. 100-203)

P.L. 100-203, §10713(b)(2)(F)(i)-(ii):

Amended Code Sec. 7429 by striking out "6851(a)," each place it appears and inserting in lieu thereof "6851(a), 6852(a),", and by striking out "6851," each place it appears and inserting in lieu thereof "6851, 6852,". **Effective** 12-22-87.

• 1976, Tax Reform Act of 1976 (P.L. 94-455)

P.L. 94-455, §1204(a):

Added Code Sec. 7429. For the **effective** date, see Act Sec. 1204(d), below.

P.L. 94-455, §1204(d), as amended by P.L. 94-528, §2(a), provides:

(d) Effective Date.—The amendments made by this section shall apply with respect to action taken under section 6851, 6861, or 6862 of the Internal Revenue Code of 1954 where the notice and demand takes place after February 28, 1977.

[Sec. 7430]

SEC. 7430. AWARDING OF COSTS AND CERTAIN FEES.

[Sec. 7430(a)]

(a) IN GENERAL.—In any administrative or court proceeding which is brought by or against the United States in connection with the determination, collection, or refund of any tax, interest, or penalty under this title, the prevailing party may be awarded a judgment or a settlement for—

(1) reasonable administrative costs incurred in connection with such administrative proceeding within the Internal Revenue Service, and

(2) reasonable litigation costs incurred in connection with such court proceeding.

[Sec. 7430(b)]

(b) LIMITATIONS.—

(1) REQUIREMENT THAT ADMINISTRATIVE REMEDIES BE EXHAUSTED.—A judgment for reasonable litigation costs shall not be awarded under subsection (a) in any court proceeding unless the court determines that the prevailing party has exhausted the administrative remedies available to such party within the Internal Revenue Service. Any failure to agree to an extension of the time for the assessment of any tax shall not be taken into account for purposes of determining whether the prevailing party meets the requirements of the preceding sentence.

(2) ONLY COSTS ALLOCABLE TO THE UNITED STATES.—An award under subsection (a) shall be made only for reasonable litigation and administrative costs which are allocable to the United States and not to any other party.

(3) COSTS DENIED WHERE PARTY PREVAILING PROTRACTS PROCEEDINGS.—No award for reasonable litigation and administrative costs may be made under subsection (a) with respect to any portion of the administrative or court proceeding during which the prevailing party has unreasonably protracted such proceeding.

(4) PERIOD FOR APPLYING TO IRS FOR ADMINISTRATIVE COSTS.—An award may be made under subsection (a) by the Internal Revenue Service for reasonable administrative costs only if the prevailing party files an application with the Internal Revenue Service for such costs before the 91st day after the date on which the final decision of the Internal Revenue Service as to the determination of the tax, interest, or penalty is mailed to such party.

Amendments

• 1998, IRS Restructuring and Reform Act of 1998 (P.L. 105-206)

P.L. 105-206, §6012(h):

Amended Code Sec. 7430(b) by redesignating paragraph (5) as paragraph (4). **Effective** as if included in the provision of P.L. 105-34 to which it relates [**effective** for civil actions or proceedings commenced after 8-5-97.—CCH].

• 1997, Taxpayer Relief Act of 1997 (P.L. 105-34)

P.L. 105-34, §1285(b):

Amended Code Sec. 7430(b) by adding at the end a new paragraph (5)[(4)]. **Effective** for civil actions or proceedings commenced after 8-5-97.

• 1996, Taxpayer Bill of Rights 2 (P.L. 104-168)

P.L. 104-168, §703(a):

Amended Code Sec. 7430(b)(1) by adding at the end a new sentence. **Effective** in the case of proceedings commenced after 7-30-96.

P.L. 104-168, §704(a):

Amended Code Sec. 7430(b) by striking paragraph (3) and by redesignating paragraph (4) as paragraph (3). **Effective** in the case of proceedings commenced after 7-30-96. Prior to amendment, Code Sec. 7430(b)(3) read as follows:

(3) EXCLUSION OF DECLARATORY JUDGMENT PROCEEDINGS.—

(A) IN GENERAL.—No award for reasonable litigation costs may be made under subsection (a) with respect to any declaratory judgment proceeding.

(B) EXCEPTION FOR SECTION 501(c)(3) DETERMINATION REVOCATION PROCEEDINGS.—Subparagraph (A) shall not apply to any proceeding which involves the revocation of a determination that the organization is described in section 501(c)(3).

[Sec. 7430(c)]

(c) DEFINITIONS.—For purposes of this section—

(1) REASONABLE LITIGATION COSTS.—The term "reasonable litigation costs" includes—

(A) reasonable court costs, and

(B) based upon prevailing market rates for the kind or quality of services furnished—

(i) the reasonable expenses of expert witnesses in connection with a court proceeding, except that no expert witness shall be compensated at a rate in excess of the highest rate of compensation for expert witnesses paid by the United States,

(ii) the reasonable cost of any study, analysis, engineering report, test, or project which is found by the court to be necessary for the preparation of the party's case, and

(iii) reasonable fees paid or incurred for the services of attorneys in connection with the court proceeding, except that such fees shall not be in excess of $125 per hour unless the court determines that an increase in the cost of living or a special factor, such as the limited availability of qualified attorneys for such proceeding, the difficulty of the issues presented in the case, or the local availability of tax expertise, justifies a higher rate.

In the case of any calendar year beginning after 1996, the dollar amount referred to in clause (iii) shall be increased by an amount equal to such dollar amount multiplied by the cost-of-living adjustment determined under section 1(f)(3) for such calendar year, by substituting "calendar year 1995" for "calendar year 2016" in subparagraph (A)(ii) thereof. If any dollar amount after being increased under the preceding sentence is not a multiple of $10, such dollar amount shall be rounded to the nearest multiple of $10.

(2) REASONABLE ADMINISTRATIVE COSTS.—The term "reasonable administrative costs" means—

(A) any administrative fees or similar charges imposed by the Internal Revenue Service, and

(B) expenses, costs, and fees described in paragraph (1)(B), except that any determination made by the court under clause (ii) or (iii) thereof shall be made by the Internal Revenue Service in cases where the determination under paragraph (4)(C) of the awarding of reasonable administrative costs is made by the Internal Revenue Service.

Such term shall only include costs incurred on or after whichever of the following is the earliest: (i) the date of the receipt by the taxpayer of the notice of the decision of the Internal Revenue Service Independent Office of Appeals; (ii) the date of the notice of deficiency; or (iii) the date on which the 1st letter of proposed deficiency which allows the taxpayer an opportunity for administrative review in the Internal Revenue Service Independent Office of Appeals is sent.

(3) ATTORNEYS' FEES.—

(A) IN GENERAL.—For purposes of paragraphs (1) and (2), fees for the services of an individual (whether or not an attorney) who is authorized to practice before the Tax Court or before the Internal Revenue Service shall be treated as fees for the services of an attorney.

(B) PRO BONO SERVICES.—The court may award reasonable attorneys' fees under subsection (a) in excess of the attorneys' fees paid or incurred if such fees are less than the reasonable attorneys' fees because an individual is representing the prevailing party for no fee or for a fee which (taking into account all the facts and circumstances) is no more than a nominal fee. This subparagraph shall apply only if such award is paid to such individual or such individual's employer.

(4) PREVAILING PARTY.—

(A) IN GENERAL.—The term "prevailing party" means any party in any proceeding to which subsection (a) applies (other than the United States or any creditor of the taxpayer involved)—

(i) which—

(I) has substantially prevailed with respect to the amount in controversy, or

(II) has substantially prevailed with respect to the most significant issue or set of issues presented, and

(ii) which meets the requirements of the 1st sentence of section 2412(d)(1)(B) of title 28, United States Code (as in effect on October 22, 1986) except to the extent differing procedures are established by rule of court and meets the requirements of section 2412(d)(2)(B) of such title 28 (as so in effect).

(B) EXCEPTION IF UNITED STATES ESTABLISHES THAT ITS POSITION WAS SUBSTANTIALLY JUSTIFIED.—

(i) GENERAL RULE.—A party shall not be treated as the prevailing party in a proceeding to which subsection (a) applies if the United States establishes that the position of the United States in the proceeding was substantially justified.

(ii) PRESUMPTION OF NO JUSTIFICATION IF INTERNAL REVENUE SERVICE DID NOT FOLLOW CERTAIN PUBLISHED GUIDANCE.—For purposes of clause (i), the position of the United States shall be presumed not to be substantially justified if the Internal Revenue Service did not follow its applicable published guidance in the administrative proceeding. Such presumption may be rebutted.

(iii) EFFECT OF LOSING ON SUBSTANTIALLY SIMILAR ISSUES.—In determining for purposes of clause (i) whether the position of the United States was substantially justified, the court shall take into account whether the United States has lost in courts of appeal for other circuits on substantially similar issues.

(iv) APPLICABLE PUBLISHED GUIDANCE.—For purposes of clause (ii), the term "applicable published guidance" means—

(I) regulations, revenue rulings, revenue procedures, information releases, notices, and announcements, and

(II) any of the following which are issued to the taxpayer: private letter rulings, technical advice memoranda, and determination letters.

(C) DETERMINATION AS TO PREVAILING PARTY.—Any determination under this paragraph as to whether a party is a prevailing party shall be made by agreement of the parties or—

(i) in the case where the final determination with respect to the tax, interest, or penalty is made at the administrative level, by the Internal Revenue Service, or

(ii) in the case where such final determination is made by a court, the court.

(D) SPECIAL RULES FOR APPLYING NET WORTH REQUIREMENT.—In applying the requirements of section 2412(d)(2)(B) of title 28, United States Code, for purposes of subparagraph (A)(ii) of this paragraph—

(i) the net worth limitation in clause (i) of such section shall apply to—

(I) an estate but shall be determined as of the date of the decedent's death, and

(II) a trust but shall be determined as of the last day of the taxable year involved in the proceeding, and

(ii) individuals filing a joint return shall be treated as separate individuals for purposes of clause (i) of such section.

(E) SPECIAL RULES WHERE JUDGMENT LESS THAN TAXPAYER'S OFFER.—

(i) IN GENERAL.—A party to a court proceeding meeting the requirements of subparagraph (A)(ii) shall be treated as the prevailing party if the liability of the taxpayer pursuant to the judgment in the proceeding (determined without regard to interest) is equal to or less than the liability of the taxpayer which would have been so determined if the United States had accepted a qualified offer of the party under subsection (g).

(ii) EXCEPTIONS.—This subparagraph shall not apply to—

(I) any judgment issued pursuant to a settlement; or

(II) any proceeding in which the amount of tax liability is not in issue, including any declaratory judgment proceeding, any proceeding to enforce or quash any summons issued pursuant to this title, and any action to restrain disclosure under section 6110(f).

(iii) SPECIAL RULES.—If this subparagraph applies to any court proceeding—

(I) the determination under clause (i) shall be made by reference to the last qualified offer made with respect to the tax liability at issue in the proceeding; and

(II) reasonable administrative and litigation costs shall only include costs incurred on and after the date of such offer.

(iv) COORDINATION.—This subparagraph shall not apply to a party which is a prevailing party under any other provision of this paragraph.

(5) ADMINISTRATIVE PROCEEDINGS.—The term "administrative proceeding" means any procedure or other action before the Internal Revenue Service.

(6) COURT PROCEEDINGS.—The term "court proceeding" means any civil action brought in a court of the United States (including the Tax Court and the United States Court of Federal Claims).

(7) POSITION OF UNITED STATES.—The term "position of the United States" means—

(A) the position taken by the United States in a judicial proceeding to which subsection (a) applies, and

(B) the position taken in an administrative proceeding to which subsection (a) applies as of the earlier of—

(i) the date of the receipt by the taxpayer of the notice of the decision of the Internal Revenue Service Independent Office of Appeals, or

(ii) the date of the notice of deficiency.

Amendments

• 2019, Taxpayer First Act (P.L. 116-25)

P.L. 116-25, §1001(b)(1)(H):

Amended Code Sec. 7430(c)(7)(B)(i) by striking "Internal Revenue Service Office of Appeals" and inserting "Internal Revenue Service Independent Office of Appeals". **Effective** 7-1-2019.

P.L. 116-25, §1001(b)(2):

Amended Code Sec. 7430(c)(2) by striking "Internal Revenue Service Office of Appeals" each place it appears and inserting "Internal Revenue Service Independent Office of Appeals". **Effective** 7-1-2019.

• 2018, Tax Technical Corrections Act of 2018 (P.L. 115-141)

P.L. 115-141, §401(a)(325)(A), Div. U:

Amended Code Sec. 7430(c)(6) by striking "United States Claims Court" and inserting "United States Court of Federal Claims". [Note: Code Sec. 7430(c)(6) does not contain the text "United States Claims Court". Therefore, this amendment cannot be made.—CCH] **Effective** 3-23-2018.

• 2017, Tax Cuts and Jobs Act (P.L. 115-97)

P.L. 115-97, §11002(d)(1)(SS):

Amended Code Sec. 7430(c)(1) by striking "for 'calendar year 1992' in subparagraph (B)" and inserting "for 'calendar year 2016' in subparagraph (A)(ii)". **Effective** for tax years beginning after 12-31-2017.

• 2000, Community Renewal Tax Relief Act of 2000 (P.L. 106-554)

P.L. 106-554, §319(25)(A)-(B):

Amended Code Sec. 7430(c)(3) by striking "ATTORNEYS" and inserting "ATTORNEYS' " in the paragraph heading, and by striking "attorneys fees" each place it appears in subparagraph (B) and inserting "attorneys' fees". **Effective** 12-21-2000.

• 1998, IRS Restructuring and Reform Act of 1998 (P.L. 105-206)

P.L. 105-206, §3101(a)(1):

Amended Code Sec. 7430(c)(1)(B)(iii) by striking "$110" and inserting "$125". **Effective** for costs incurred more than 180 days after 7-22-98.

P.L. 105-206, §3101(a)(2):

Amended Code Sec. 7430(c)(1)(B)(iii) by inserting "the difficulty of the issues presented in the case, or the local availability of tax expertise," before "justifies a higher rate". **Effective** for costs incurred more than 180 days after 7-22-98.

P.L. 105-206, §3101(b):

Amended Code Sec. 7430(c)(2) by striking the last sentence and inserting a new flush sentence. **Effective** for costs incurred more than 180 days after 7-22-98. Prior to being stricken, the last sentence of Code Sec. 7430(c)(2) read as follows:

Such term shall only include costs incurred on or after the earlier of (i) the date of the receipt by the taxpayer of the notice of the decision of the Internal Revenue Service Office of Appeals, or (ii) the date of the notice of deficiency.

P.L. 105-206, §3101(c):

Amended Code Sec. 7430(c)(3). **Effective** for costs incurred and services performed more than 180 days after 7-22-98. Prior to amendment, Code Sec. 7430(c)(3) read as follows:

(3) ATTORNEY'S FEES.—For purposes of paragraphs (1) and (2), fees for the services of an individual (whether or not an

attorney) who is authorized to practice before the Tax Court or before the Internal Revenue Service shall be treated as fees for the services of an attorney.

P.L. 105-206, §3101(d):

Amended Code Sec. 7430(c)(4)(B) by redesignating clause (iii) as clause (iv) and by inserting after clause (ii) a new clause (iii). **Effective** for costs incurred more than 180 days after 7-22-98.

P.L. 105-206, §3101(e)(1):

Amended Code Sec. 7430(c)(4) by adding at the end a new subparagraph (E). **Effective** for costs incurred more than 180 days after 7-22-98.

P.L. 105-206, §6014(e):

Amended Code Sec. 7430(c)(4)(D) by striking "subparagraph (A)(iii)" and inserting "subparagraph (A)(ii)". **Effective** for proceedings commenced after 8-5-97.

• 1997, Taxpayer Relief Act of 1997 (P.L. 105-34)

P.L. 105-34, §1453(a):

Amended Code Sec. 7430(c)(4) by adding at the end a new subparagraph (D). **Effective** as if included in the provision of P.L. 105-34 to which it relates [**effective** for proceedings commenced after 8-5-97.—CCH].

• 1996, Taxpayer Bill of Rights 2 (P.L. 104-168)

P.L. 104-168, §701(a):

Amended Code Sec. 7430(c)(4)(A) by striking clause (i) and by redesignating clauses (ii) and (iii) as clauses (i) and (ii), respectively. **Effective** in the case of proceedings commenced after 7-30-96. Prior to amendment, Code Sec. 7430(c)(4)(A)(i) read as follows:

(i) which establishes that the position of the United States in the proceeding was not substantially justified,

P.L. 104-168, §701(b):

Amended Code Sec. 7430(c)(4) by redesignating subparagraph (B) as subparagraph (C) and by inserting after subparagraph (A) a new subparagraph (B). **Effective** in the case of proceedings commenced after 7-30-96.

P.L. 104-168, §701(c)(1):

Amended Code Sec. 7430(c)(2)(B) by striking "paragraph (4)(B)" and inserting "paragraph (4)(C)". **Effective** in the case of proceedings commenced after 7-30-96.

P.L. 104-168, §701(c)(2):

Amended Code Sec. 7430(c)(4)(C), as redesignated by Act Sec. 701(b), by striking "subparagraph (A)" and inserting "this paragraph". **Effective** in the case of proceedings commenced after 7-30-96.

P.L. 104-168, §702(a)(1)-(3):

Amended Code Sec. 7430(c)(1) by striking "$75" in clause (iii) of subparagraph (B) and inserting "$110", by striking "an increase in the cost of living or" after "determines that" in clause (iii) of subparagraph (B), and by adding after clause (iii) two new sentences. **Effective** in the case of proceedings commenced after 7-30-96.

• 1992, Court of Federal Claims Technical and Procedural Improvements Act of 1992 (P.L. 102-572)

P.L. 102-572, §902(b)(1):

Amended Code Sec. 7430(c) by striking "United States Claims Court" and inserting "United States Court of Federal Claims". **Effective** 10-29-92.

[Sec. 7430(d)]

(d) SPECIAL RULES FOR PAYMENT OF COSTS.—

(1) REASONABLE ADMINISTRATIVE COSTS.—An award for reasonable administrative costs shall be payable out of funds appropriated under section 1304 of title 31, United States Code.

(2) REASONABLE LITIGATION COSTS.—An award for reasonable litigation costs shall be payable in the case of the Tax Court in the same manner as such an award by a district court.

[Sec. 7430(e)]

(e) MULTIPLE ACTIONS.—For purposes of this section, in the case of—

(1) multiple actions which could have been joined or consolidated, or

(2) a case or cases involving a return or returns of the same taxpayer (including joint returns of married individuals) which could have been joined in a single court proceeding in the same court,

such actions or cases shall be treated as 1 court proceeding regardless of whether such joinder or consolidation actually occurs, unless the court in which such action is brought determines, in its discretion, that it would be inappropriate to treat such actions or cases as joined or consolidated.

[Sec. 7430(f)]

(f) RIGHT OF APPEAL.—

(1) COURT PROCEEDINGS.—An order granting or denying (in whole or in part) an award for reasonable litigation or administrative costs under subsection (a) in a court proceeding, may be incorporated as a part of the decision or judgment in the court proceeding and shall be subject to appeal in the same manner as the decision or judgment.

(2) ADMINISTRATIVE PROCEEDINGS.—A decision granting or denying (in whole or in part) an award for reasonable administrative costs under subsection (a) by the Internal Revenue Service shall be subject to the filing of a petition for review with the Tax Court under rules similar to the rules under section 7463 (without regard to the amount in dispute). If the Secretary sends by certified or registered mail a notice of such decision to the petitioner, no proceeding in the Tax Court may be initiated under this paragraph unless such petition is filed before the 91st day after the date of such mailing.

(3) APPEAL OF TAX COURT DECISION.—An order of the Tax Court disposing of a petition under paragraph (2) shall be reviewable in the same manner as a decision of the Tax Court, but only with respect to the matters determined in such order.

Amendments

• 1997, Taxpayer Relief Act of 1997 (P.L. 105-34)

P.L. 105-34, §1285(a):

Amended Code Sec. 7430(f) by adding at the end a new paragraph (3). **Effective** for civil actions or proceedings commenced after 8-5-97.

P.L. 105-34, §1285(c)(1)-(2):

Amended Code Sec. 7430(f)(2) by striking "appeal to" and inserting "the filing of a petition for review with", and by adding at the end a new sentence. **Effective** for civil actions or proceedings commenced after 8-5-97.

• 1988, Technical and Miscellaneous Revenue Act of 1988 (P.L. 100-647)

P.L. 100-647, §6239(a):

Amended Code Sec. 7430. **Effective** for proceedings commencing after 11-10-88. Prior to amendment, Code Sec. 7430 read as follows:

SEC. 7430. AWARDING OF COURT COSTS AND CERTAIN FEES.

[Sec. 7430(a)]

(a) IN GENERAL.—In the case of any civil proceeding which is—

(1) brought by or against the United States in connection with the determination, collection, or refund of any tax, interest, or penalty under this title, and

(2) brought in a court of the United States (including the Tax Court and the United States Claims Court),

the prevailing party may be awarded a judgment (payable in the case of the Tax Court in the same manner as such an award by a district court) for reasonable litigation costs incurred in such proceeding.

Amendments

• 1986, Tax Reform Act of 1986 (P.L. 99-514)

P.L. 99-514, §1551(f):

Amended Code Sec. 7430(a) by inserting "(payable in the case of the Tax Court in the same manner as such an award by a district court)" after "a judgment". **Effective** as if included in the amendments made by P.L. 97-248, Act Sec. 292.

[Sec. 7430(b)]

(b) LIMITATIONS.—

(1) REQUIREMENT THAT ADMINISTRATIVE REMEDIES BE EXHAUSTED.—A judgment for reasonable litigation costs shall not be awarded under subsection (a) unless the court determines that the prevailing party has exhausted the administrative remedies available to such party within the Internal Revenue Service.

(2) ONLY COSTS ALLOCABLE TO THE UNITED STATES.—An award under subsection (a) shall be made only for reasonable litigation costs which are allocable to the United States and not to any other party to the action or proceeding.

(3) EXCLUSION OF DECLARATORY JUDGMENT PROCEEDINGS.—

(A) IN GENERAL.—No award for reasonable litigation costs may be made under subsection (a) with respect to any declaratory judgment proceeding.

(B) EXCEPTION FOR SECTION 501(c)(3) DETERMINATION REVOCATION PROCEEDINGS.—Subparagraph (A) shall not apply to any proceeding which involves the revocation of a determination that the organization is described in section 501(c)(3).

(4) COST DENIED WHERE PARTY PREVAILING PROTRACTS PROCEEDINGS.—No award for reasonable litigation costs may be made under subsection (a) with respect to any portion of the civil proceeding during which the prevailing party has unreasonably protracted such proceeding.

Amendments

• 1986, Tax Reform Act of 1986 (P.L. 99-514)

P.L. 99-514, §1551(a):

Amended Code Sec. 7430(b) by striking out paragraph (1) and redesignating paragraphs (2), (3), and (4) as paragraphs (1), (2), and (3), respectively. **Effective** for amounts paid after 9-30-86, in civil actions or proceedings commenced after 12-31-85. For special rules, see Act Sec. 1551(h)(3) following Code Sec. 7430(c). Prior to amendment, Code Sec. 7430(b)(1) read as follows:

(1) MAXIMUM DOLLAR AMOUNT.—The amount of reasonable litigation costs which may be awarded under subsection (a) with respect to any prevailing party in any civil proceeding shall not exceed $25,000.

P.L. 99-514, §1551(b):

Amended Code Sec. 7430(b) by adding at the end thereof new paragraph (4). **Effective** for amounts paid after 9-30-86, in civil actions or proceedings commenced after 12-31-85. For special rules, see Act Sec. 1551(h)(3) following Code Sec. 7430(c).

[Sec. 7430(c)]

(c) DEFINITIONS.—For purposes of this section—

(1) REASONABLE LITIGATION COSTS.—

(A) IN GENERAL.—The term "reasonable litigation costs" includes—

(i) reasonable court costs, and

(ii) based upon prevailing market rates for the kind or quality of services furnished—

(I) the reasonable expenses of expert witnesses in connection with the civil proceeding, except that no expert witness shall be compensated at a rate in excess of the highest rate of compensation for expert witnesses paid by the United States,

(II) the reasonable cost of any study, analysis, engineering report, test, or project which is found by the court to be necessary for the preparation of the party's case, and

(III) reasonable fees paid or incurred for the services of attorneys in connection with the civil proceeding, except that such fees shall not be in excess of $75 per hour unless the court determines that an increase in the cost of living or a special factor, such as the limited availability of qualified attorneys for such proceeding, justifies a higher rate.

(B) ATTORNEY'S FEES.—In the case of any proceeding in the Tax Court, fees for the services of an individual (whether or not an attorney) who is authorized to practice before the Tax Court shall be treated as fees for the services of an attorney.

(2) PREVAILING PARTY.—

(A) IN GENERAL.—The term "prevailing party" means any party to any proceeding described in subsection (a) (other than the United States or any creditor of the taxpayer involved) which—

(i) establishes that the position of the United States in the civil proceeding was not substantially justified,

(ii)(I) has substantially prevailed with respect to the amount in controversy, or

(II) has substantially prevailed with respect to the most significant issue or set of issues presented, and

(iii) meets the requirements of the 1st sentence of section 2412(d)(1)(B) of title 28, United States Code (as in effect on October 22, 1986) and meets the requirements of section 2412(d)(2)(B) of such title 28 (as so in effect)

(B) DETERMINATION AS TO PREVAILING PARTY.—Any determination under subparagraph (A) as to whether a party is a prevailing party shall be made—

(i) by the court, or

(ii) by agreement of the parties.

(3) CIVIL ACTIONS.—The term "civil proceeding" includes a civil action.

(4) POSITION OF UNITED STATES.—The term "position of the United States" includes—

(A) the position taken by the United States in the civil proceeding, and

(B) any administrative action or inaction by the District Counsel of the Internal Revenue Service (and all subsequent administrative action or inaction) upon which such proceeding is based.

Amendments

• 1988, Technical and Miscellaneous Revenue Act of 1988 (P.L. 100-647)

P.L. 100-647, §1015(i):

Amended Code Sec. 7430(c)(2)(A)(iii). **Effective** as if included in the provision of P.L. 99-514 to which it relates. Prior to amendment, Code Sec. 7430(c)(2)(A)(iii) read as follows:

(iii) meets the requirements of section 504(b)(1)(B) of title 5, United States Code (as in effect on the date of the enactment of the Tax Reform Act of 1986 and applied by taking into account the commencement of the proceeding described in subsection (a) in lieu of the initiation of the adjudication referred to in such section).

• 1986, Tax Reform Act of 1986 (P.L. 99-514)

P.L. 99-514, §1551(c):

Amended Code Sec. 7430(c)(1)(A). **Effective** for amounts paid after 9-30-86, in civil actions or proceedings commenced after 12-31-85. For special rules, see Act Sec. 1551(h)(3), below. Prior to amendment, Code Sec. 7430(c)(1)(A) read as follows:

(A) IN GENERAL.—the term "reasonable litigation costs" includes—

(i) reasonable court costs,

(ii) the reasonable expenses of expert witnesses in connection with the civil proceeding,

(iii) the reasonable cost of any study, analysis, engineering report, test, or project which is found by the court to be necessary for the preparation of the party's case, and

(iv) reasonable fees paid or incurred for the services of attorneys in connection with the civil proceeding.

P.L. 99-514, §1151(d)(1), (2):

Amended Code Sec. 7430(c)(2) by striking out "was unreasonable" in clause (i), and inserting in lieu thereof "was not substantially justified", and by striking out "and" at the end of clause (i), by striking out the period at the end of clause (ii) and inserting in lieu thereof ", and", and by adding at the end thereof new clause (iii). **Effective** for amounts paid after 9-30-86, in civil actions or proceedings commenced after 12-31-85. For special rules, see Act Sec. 1551(h)(3), below.

P.L. 99-514, §1551(e):

Amended Code Sec. 7430(c) by adding at the end thereof new paragraph (4). **Effective** for amounts paid after 9-30-86, in civil actions or proceedings commenced after 12-31-85.

P.L. 99-514, §1551(h)(3), provides:

(3) APPLICABILITY OF AMENDMENTS TO CERTAIN PRIOR CASES.—The amendments made by this section shall apply to any case commenced after December 31, 1985, and finally disposed of before the date of the enactment of this Act, except that in any such case, the 30-day period referred to in section 2412(d)(1)(B) of title 28, United States Code, or Rule 231 of the Tax Court, as the case may be, shall be deemed to commence on the date of the enactment of this Act.

[Sec. 7430(d)]

(d) MULTIPLE ACTIONS.—For purposes of this section, in the case of—

(1) multiple actions which could have been joined or consolidated, or

(2) a case or cases involving a return or returns of the same taxpayer (including joint returns of married individuals) which could have been joined in a single proceeding in the same court,

such actions or cases shall be treated as one civil proceeding regardless of whether such joinder or consolidation actually occurs, unless the court in which such action is brought determines, in its discretion, that would be inappropriate to treat such actions or cases as joined or consolidated for purposes of this section.

[Sec. 7430(e)]

(e) RIGHT OF APPEAL.—An order granting or denying an award for reasonable litigation costs under subsection (a), in whole or in part, shall be incorporated as a part of the decision or judgment in the case and shall be subject to appeal in the same manner as the decision or judgment.

Amendments

• 1986, Tax Reform Act of 1986 (P.L. 99-514)

P.L. 99-514, §1551(g):

Amended Code Sec. 7430 by striking out subsection (f). **Effective** for amounts paid after 9-30-86, in civil actions or proceedings commenced after 12-31-85. See also Act Sec. 1551(h)(3) following Code Sec. 7430(c). Prior to deletion, Code Sec. 7430(f) read as follows:

(f) TERMINATION.—This section shall not apply to any proceeding commenced after December 31, 1985.

• 1984, Deficit Reduction Act of 1984 (P.L. 98-369)

P.L. 98-369, §714(c):

Amended Code Sec. 7430(a)(2) by striking out "including the Tax Court" and inserting in lieu thereof "including the Tax Court and the United States Claims Court". **Effective** as if included in the provision of P.L. 97-248 to which it relates.

• 1982, Tax Equity and Fiscal Responsibility Act of 1982 (P.L. 97-248)

P.L. 97-248, §292(a):

Redesignated Code Sec. 7430 as Code Sec. 7431 and added a new Code Sec. 7430. **Effective** for civil actions or proceedings commenced after 2-28-83, and ceases to apply to any proceeding commenced after 12-31-85.

[Sec. 7430(g)]

(g) QUALIFIED OFFER.—For purposes of subsection (c)(4)—

(1) IN GENERAL.—The term "qualified offer" means a written offer which—

(A) is made by the taxpayer to the United States during the qualified offer period;

(B) specifies the offered amount of the taxpayer's liability (determined without regard to interest);

(C) is designated at the time it is made as a qualified offer for purposes of this section; and

(D) remains open during the period beginning on the date it is made and ending on the earliest of the date the offer is rejected, the date the trial begins, or the 90th day after the date the offer is made.

(2) QUALIFIED OFFER PERIOD.—For purposes of this subsection, the term "qualified offer period" means the period—

(A) beginning on the date on which the 1st letter of proposed deficiency which allows the taxpayer an opportunity for administrative review in the Internal Revenue Service Independent Office of Appeals is sent, and

(B) ending on the date which is 30 days before the date the case is first set for trial.

Amendments

• 2019, Taxpayer First Act (P.L. 116-25)

P.L. 116-25, §1001(b)(1)(H):

Amended Code Sec. 7430(g)(2)(A) by striking "Internal Revenue Service Office of Appeals" and inserting "Internal Revenue Service Independent Office of Appeals". **Effective** 7-1-2019.

• 1998, IRS Restructuring and Reform Act of 1998 (P.L. 105-206)

P.L. 105-206, §3101(e)(2):

Amended Code Sec. 7430 by adding at the end a new subsection (g). **Effective** for costs incurred more than 180 days after 7-22-98.

[Sec. 7431]

SEC. 7431. CIVIL DAMAGES FOR UNAUTHORIZED INSPECTION OR DISCLOSURE OF RETURNS AND RETURN INFORMATION.

[Sec. 7431(a)]

(a) IN GENERAL.—

(1) INSPECTION OR DISCLOSURE BY EMPLOYEE OF UNITED STATES.—If any officer or employee of the United States knowingly, or by reason of negligence, inspects or discloses any return or return information with respect to a taxpayer in violation of any provision of section 6103, such taxpayer may bring a civil action for damages against the United States in a district court of the United States.

(2) INSPECTION OR DISCLOSURE BY A PERSON WHO IS NOT AN EMPLOYEE OF UNITED STATES.—If any person who is not an officer or employee of the United States knowingly, or by reason of negligence, inspects or discloses any return or return information with respect to a taxpayer in violation of any provision of section 6103 or in violation of section 6104(c), such taxpayer may bring a civil action for damages against such person in a district court of the United States.

Amendments

• 2006, Pension Protection Act of 2006 (P.L. 109-280)

P.L. 109-280, §1224(b)(7):

Amended Code Sec. 7431(a)(2) by inserting "or in violation of section 6104(c)" after "6103". **Effective** 8-17-2006 but shall not apply to requests made before such date.

• 1997, Taxpayer Browsing Protection Act (P.L. 105-35)

P.L. 105-35, §3(a)(1)-(2):

Amended Code Sec. 7431(a)(1) and (2) by striking "DISCLOSURE" in the heading and inserting "INSPECTION OR DISCLOSURE" and by striking "discloses" and inserting "inspects or discloses" in the text. **Effective** for inspections and disclosures occurring on and after 8-5-97.

P.L. 105-35, §3(d)(4):

Amended the heading of Code Sec. 7431 by inserting **"INSPECTION OR"** before **"DISCLOSURE"**. **Effective** for inspections and disclosures occurring on and after 8-5-97.

[Sec. 7431(b)]

(b) EXCEPTIONS.—No liability shall arise under this section with respect to any inspection or disclosure—

(1) which results from a good faith, but erroneous, interpretation of section 6103, or

(2) which is requested by the taxpayer.

Amendments

• 1997, Taxpayer Browsing Protection Act (P.L. 105-35)

P.L. 105-35, §3(c):

Amended Code Sec. 7431(b). **Effective** for inspections and disclosures occurring on and after 8-5-97. Prior to amendment, Code Sec. 7431(b) read as follows:

(b) NO LIABILITY FOR GOOD FAITH BUT ERRONEOUS INTERPRETATION.—No liability shall arise under this section with respect to any disclosure which results from a good faith, but erroneous, interpretation of section 6103.

[Sec. 7431(c)]

(c) DAMAGES.—In any action brought under subsection (a), upon a finding of liability on the part of the defendant, the defendant shall be liable to the plaintiff in an amount equal to the sum of—

(1) the greater of—

(A) $1,000 for each act of unauthorized inspection or disclosure of a return or return information with respect to which such defendant is found liable, or

(B) the sum of—

(i) the actual damages sustained by the plaintiff as a result of such unauthorized inspection or disclosure, plus

(ii) in the case of a willful inspection or disclosure or an inspection or disclosure which is the result of gross negligence, punitive damages, plus

(2) the costs of the action, plus

(3) in the case of a plaintiff which is described in section 7430(c)(4)(A)(ii), reasonable attorneys fees, except that if the defendant is the United States, reasonable attorneys fees may be awarded only if the plaintiff is the prevailing party (as determined under section 7430(c)(4)).

Amendments

• 1998, IRS Restructuring and Reform Act of 1998 (P.L. 105-206)

P.L. 105-206, §3101(f):

Amended Code Sec. 7431(c) by striking the period at the end of paragraph (2) and inserting ", plus", and by adding at the end a new paragraph (3). **Effective** for costs incurred more than 180 days after 7-22-98.

• 1997, Taxpayer Browsing Protection Act (P.L. 105-35)

P.L. 105-35, §3(d)(1):

Amended Code Sec. 7431(c)(1)(A) and (B)(i) by inserting "inspection or" before "disclosure". **Effective** for inspections and disclosures occurring on and after 8-5-97.

P.L. 105-35, §3(d)(2):

Amended Code Sec. 7431(c)(1)(B)(ii) by striking "willful disclosure or a disclosure" and inserting "willful inspection or disclosure or an inspection or disclosure". **Effective** for inspections and disclosures occurring on and after 8-5-97.

[Sec. 7431(d)]

(d) PERIOD FOR BRINGING ACTION.—Notwithstanding any other provision of law, an action to enforce any liability created under this section may be brought, without regard to the amount in controversy, at any time within 2 years after the date of discovery by the plaintiff of the unauthorized inspection or disclosure.

Amendments

• 1997, Taxpayer Browsing Protection Act (P.L. 105-35)

P.L. 105-35, §3(d)(1):

Amended Code Sec. 7431(d) by inserting "inspection or" before "disclosure". **Effective** for inspections and disclosures occurring on and after 8-5-97.

[Sec. 7431(e)]

(e) NOTIFICATION OF UNLAWFUL INSPECTION AND DISCLOSURE.—If any person is criminally charged by indictment or information with inspection or disclosure of a taxpayer's return or return information in violation of—

(1) paragraph (1) or (2) of section 7213(a),

(2) section 7213A(a), or

(3) subparagraph (B) of section 1030(a)(2) of title 18, United States Code,

the Secretary shall notify such taxpayer as soon as practicable of such inspection or disclosure. The Secretary shall also notify such taxpayer if the Internal Revenue Service or a Federal or State agency (upon notice to the Secretary by such Federal or State agency) proposes an administrative determination as to disciplinary or adverse action against an employee arising from the employee's unauthorized inspection or disclosure of the taxpayer's return or return information. The notice described in this subsection shall include the date of the unauthorized inspection or disclosure and the rights of the taxpayer under such administrative determination.

Amendments

• 2019, Taxpayer First Act (P.L. 116-25)

P.L. 116-25, §3002(a):

Amended Code Sec. 7431(e) by adding at the end two new sentences. **Effective** for determinations proposed after the date which is 180 days after 7-1-2019.

• 1997, Taxpayer Browsing Protection Act (P.L. 105-35)

P.L. 105-35, §3(b):

Amended Code Sec. 7431 by redesignating subsections (e) and (f) as subsections (f) and (g), respectively, and by inserting after subsection (d) a new subsection (e). **Effective** for inspections and disclosures occurring on and after 8-5-97.

[Sec. 7431(f)]

(f) DEFINITIONS.—For purposes of this section, the terms "inspect", "inspection", "return", and "return information" have the respective meanings given such terms by section 6103(b).

Amendments

• 1997, Taxpayer Browsing Protection Act (P.L. 105-35)

P.L. 105-35, §3(b):

Amended Code Sec. 7431 by redesignating subsection (e) as subsection (f). **Effective** for inspections and disclosures occurring on and after 8-5-97.

P.L. 105-35, §3(d)(3):

Amended Code Sec. 7431(f), as redesignated by Act Sec. 3(b). **Effective** for inspections and disclosures occurring on and after 8-5-97. Prior to amendment, Code Sec. 7431(f) read as follows:

(f) RETURN; RETURN INFORMATION.—For purposes of this section, the terms "return" and "return information" have the respective meanings given such terms in section 6103(b).

[Sec. 7431(g)]

(g) EXTENSION TO INFORMATION OBTAINED UNDER SECTION 3406.—For purposes of this section—

(1) any information obtained under section 3406 (including information with respect to any payee certification failure under subsection (d) thereof) shall be treated as return information, and

(2) any inspection or use of such information other than for purposes of meeting any requirement under section 3406 or (subject to the safeguards set forth in section 6103) for purposes permitted under section 6103 shall be treated as a violation of section 6103.

For purposes of subsection (b), the reference to section 6103 shall be treated as including a reference to section 3406.

Amendments

• 1997, Taxpayer Browsing Protection Act (P.L. 105-35)

P.L. 105-35, §3(b):

Amended Code Sec. 7431 by redesignating subsection (f) as subsection (g). **Effective** for inspections and disclosures occurring on and after 8-5-97.

P.L. 105-35, §3(d)(6):

Amended Code Sec. 7431(g)(2), as redesignated by Act Sec. 3(b), by striking "any use" and inserting "any inspection or use". **Effective** for inspections and disclosures occurring on and after 8-5-97.

• 1983, Interest and Dividend Tax Compliance Act of 1983 (P.L. 98-67)

P.L. 98-67, §104(b):

Added Code Sec. 7431(f).

• 1982, Tax Equity and Fiscal Responsibility Act of 1982 (P.L. 97-248)

P.L. 97-248, §357(a):

Redesignated Code Sec. 7431 as Code Sec. 7432 and added a new Code Sec. 7431. **Effective** with respect to disclosures made after 9-3-82.

[Sec. 7431(h)]

(h) SPECIAL RULE FOR INFORMATION OBTAINED UNDER SECTION 6103(k)(9).—For purposes of this section, any reference to section 6103 shall be treated as including a reference to section 6311(e).

Amendments

• 1998, IRS Restructuring and Reform Act of 1998 (P.L. 105-206)

P.L. 105-206, §6012(b)(3):

Amended Code Sec. 7431 by redesignating subsection (g) as subsection (h) and by striking "(8)" and inserting "(9)" in the heading. **Effective** as if included in the provision of P.L. 105-34 to which it relates [**effective** 5-5-98.—CCH].

• 1997, Taxpayer Relief Act of 1997 (P.L. 105-34)

P.L. 105-34, §1205(c)(2):

Amended Code Sec. 7431 by adding at the end a new subsection (g). **Effective** on the day 9 months after 8-5-97.

* * *

Subchapter C—The Tax Court

PART I—ORGANIZATION AND JURISDICTION

* * *

[Sec. 7441]

SEC. 7441. STATUS.

There is hereby established, under article I of the Constitution of the United States, a court of record to be known as the United States Tax Court. The members of the Tax Court shall be the chief judge and the judges of the Tax Court. The Tax Court is not an agency of, and shall be independent of, the executive branch of the Government.

Amendments

• 2015, Protecting Americans from Tax Hikes Act of 2015 (P.L. 114-113)

P.L. 114-113, §441, Div. Q:

Amended Code Sec. 7441 by adding at the end a new sentence. **Effective** 12-18-2015.

• 1969, Tax Reform Act of 1969 (P.L. 91-172)

P.L. 91-172, §951:

Amended Code Sec. 7441. **Effective** 12-30-69. Prior to amendment, Code Sec. 7441 read as follows:

The Board of Tax Appeals shall be continued as an independent agency in the Executive Branch of the Government, and shall be known as the Tax Court of the United States. The members thereof shall be known as the chief judge and the judges of the Tax Court.

P.L. 91-172, §961, provides:

The United States Tax Court established under the amendment made by section 951 [of P.L. 91-172] is a continuation of the Tax Court of the United States as it existed prior to the date of enactment of this Act [December 30, 1969], the judges of the Tax Court of the United States immediately prior to the date of enactment of this Act shall become the judges of the United States Tax Court upon the enactment of this Act, and no loss of rights or powers, interruption or jurisdiction, or prejudice to matters pending in the Tax Court of the United States before the date of enactment of this Act shall result from the enactment of this Act [P.L. 91-172].

[Sec. 7442]

SEC. 7442. JURISDICTION.

The Tax Court and its divisions shall have such jurisdiction as is conferred on them by this title, by chapters 1, 2, 3, and 4 of the Internal Revenue Code of 1939, by title II and title III of the Revenue Act of 1926 (44 Stat. 10-87), or by laws enacted subsequent to February 26, 1926.

* * *

[Sec. 7443A]

SEC. 7443A. SPECIAL TRIAL JUDGES.

[Sec. 7443A(a)]

(a) APPOINTMENT.—The chief judge may, from time to time, appoint special trial judges who shall proceed under such rules and regulations as may be promulgated by the Tax Court.

[Sec. 7443A(b)]

(b) PROCEEDINGS WHICH MAY BE ASSIGNED TO SPECIAL TRIAL JUDGES.—The chief judge may assign—

(1) any declaratory judgment proceeding,

(2) any proceeding under section 7463,

(3) any proceeding where neither the amount of the deficiency placed in dispute (within the meaning of section 7463) nor the amount of any claimed overpayment exceeds $50,000,

(4) any proceeding under section 6320 or 6330,

(5) any proceeding under section 7436(c),

(6) any proceeding under section 7623(b)(4), and

(7) any other proceeding which the chief judge may designate,

to be heard by the special trial judges of the court.

Amendments

• 2006, Tax Relief and Health Care Act of 2006 (P.L. 109-432)

P.L. 109-432, Division A, §406(a)(2)(A):

Amended Code Sec. 7443A(b) by striking "and" at the end of paragraph (5), by redesignating paragraph (6) as paragraph (7), and by inserting after paragraph (5) a new paragraph (6). **Effective** for information provided on or after 12-20-2006.

• 2006, Pension Protection Act of 2006 (P.L. 109-280)

P.L. 109-280, §857(a):

Amended Code Sec. 7443A(b) by striking "and" at the end of paragraph (4), by redesignating paragraph (5) as paragraph (6), and by inserting after paragraph (4) a new paragraph (5). **Effective** for any proceeding under Code Sec. 7436(c) with respect to which a decision has not become final (as determined under Code Sec. 7481) before 8-17-2006.

• 1998, IRS Restructuring and Reform Act of 1998 (P.L. 105-206)

P.L. 105-206, §3103(b)(1):

Amended Code Sec. 7443A(b)(3) by striking "$10,000" and inserting "$50,000". **Effective** for proceedings commencing after 7-22-98.

P.L. 105-206, §3401(c)(1) (as amended by P.L. 105-277, §4002(e)(1)):

Amended Code Sec. 7443A(b) by striking "and" at the end of paragraph (3), by redesignating paragraph (4) as paragraph (5), and by inserting after paragraph (3) a new paragraph (4). **Effective** for collection actions initiated after the date which is 180 days after 7-22-98.

[Sec. 7443A(c)]

(c) AUTHORITY TO MAKE COURT DECISIONS.—The court may authorize a special trial judge to make the decision of the court with respect to any proceeding described in paragraph (1), (2), (3), (4), (5), or (6) of subsection (b), subject to such conditions and review as the court may provide.

Amendments

• 2006, Tax Relief and Health Care Act of 2006 (P.L. 109-432)

P.L. 109-432, Division A, §406(a)(2)(B):

Amended Code Sec. 7443A(c) by striking "or (5)" and inserting "(5), or (6)". **Effective** for information provided on or after 12-20-2006.

• 2006, Pension Protection Act of 2006 (P.L. 109-280)

P.L. 109-280, §857(b):

Amended Code Sec. 7443A(c) by striking "or 4" and inserting "(4), or (5)". **Effective** for any proceeding under Code Sec. 7436(c) with respect to which a decision has not become final (as determined under Code Sec. 7481) before 8-17-2006.

• 1998, IRS Restructuring and Reform Act of 1998 (P.L. 105-206)

P.L. 105-206, §3401(c)(2) (as amended by P.L. 105-277, §4002(e)(2)):

Amended Code Sec. 7443A(c) by striking "or (3)" and inserting "(3), or (4)". **Effective** for collection actions initiated after the date which is 180 days after 7-22-98.

* * *

[Sec. 7444]

SEC. 7444. ORGANIZATION.

[Sec. 7444(a)]

(a) SEAL.—The Tax Court shall have a seal which shall be judicially noticed.

[Sec. 7444(b)]

(b) DESIGNATION OF CHIEF JUDGE.—The Tax Court shall at least biennially designate a judge to act as chief judge.

[Sec. 7444(c)]

(c) DIVISIONS.—The chief judge may from time to time divide the Tax Court into divisions of one or more judges, assign the judges of the Tax Court thereto, and in case of a division of more than one judge, designate the chief thereof. If a division, as a result of a vacancy or the absence or inability of a judge assigned thereto to serve thereon, is composed of less than the number of judges designated for the division, the chief judge may assign other judges to the division or direct the division to proceed with the transaction of business without awaiting any additional assignment of judges thereto.

[Sec. 7444(d)]

(d) QUORUM.—A majority of the judges of the Tax Court or of any division thereof shall constitute a quorum for the transaction of the business of the Tax Court or of the division, respectively. A vacancy in the Tax Court or in any division thereof shall not impair the powers nor affect the duties of the Tax Court or division nor of the remaining judges of the Tax Court or division, respectively.

[Sec. 7445]

SEC. 7445. OFFICES.

The principal office of the Tax Court shall be in the District of Columbia, but the Tax Court or any of its divisions may sit at any place within the United States.

[Sec. 7446]

SEC. 7446. TIMES AND PLACES OF SESSIONS.

The times and places of the sessions of the Tax Court and of its divisions shall be prescribed by the chief judge with a view to securing reasonable opportunity to taxpayers to appear before the Tax Court or any of its divisions, with as little inconvenience and expense to taxpayers as is practicable.

* * *

PART II—PROCEDURE

[Sec. 7451]

SEC. 7451. PETITIONS.

[Sec. 7451(a)]

(a) FEES.—The Tax Court is authorized to impose a fee in an amount not in excess of $60 to be fixed by the Tax Court for the filing of any petition.

[Sec. 7451(b)]

(b) TOLLING OF TIME IN CERTAIN CASES.—

(1) IN GENERAL.—Notwithstanding any other provision of this title, in any case (including by reason of a lapse in appropriations) in which a filing location is inaccessible or otherwise unavailable to the general public on the date a petition is due, the relevant time period for filing such petition shall be tolled for the number of days within the period of inaccessibility plus an additional 14 days.

(2) FILING LOCATION.—For purposes of this subsection, the term "filing location" means—

(A) the office of the clerk of the Tax Court, or

(B) any on-line portal made available by the Tax Court for electronic filing of petitions.

Amendments

• 2021, Infrastructure Investment and Jobs Act (P.L. 117-58)

P.L. 117-58, §80503(a)(1), Div. H:

Amended Code Sec. 7451 by striking "The Tax Court" and inserting

"(a) FEES.—The Tax Court".

Effective for petitions required to be timely filed (determined without regard to the amendments made by this section) after 11-15-2021.

P.L. 117-58, §80503(a)(2), Div. H:

Amended Code Sec. 7451 by adding at the end a new subsection (b). **Effective** for petitions required to be timely filed (determined without regard to the amendments made by this section) after 11-15-2021.

P.L. 117-58, §80503(b)(1), Div. H:

Amended the heading for Code Sec. 7451 by striking "FEE FOR FILING PETITION" and inserting "PETITIONS". **Effective** for petitions required to be timely filed (determined without regard to the amendments made by this section) after 11-15-2021.

• 2006, Pension Protection Act of 2006 (P.L. 109-280)

P.L. 109-280, §859(a):

Amended Code Sec. 7451 by striking all that follows "petition" and inserting a period. **Effective** 8-17-2006. Prior to being amended, the text of Code Sec. 7451 read as follows:

The Tax Court is authorized to impose a fee in an amount not in excess of $60 to be fixed by the Tax Court for the filing of any petition for the redetermination of a deficiency or for a declaratory judgment under part IV of this subchapter or under section 7428 or for judicial review under section 6226 or section 6228(a).

• 1982, Tax Equity and Fiscal Responsibility Act of 1982 (P.L. 97-248)

P.L. 97-248, §402(c)(12):

Amended Code Sec. 7451 by adding at the end "or for judicial review under section 6226 or section 6228(a)". **Effective** for partnership tax years beginning after 9-3-82, and also to partnership tax years ending after that date if the partnership, each partner, and each indirect partner requests such application and if the Secretary or his delegate consents to such application.

• 1981, Economic Recovery Tax Act of 1981 (P.L. 97-34)

P.L. 97-34, §751(a):

Amended Code Sec. 7451 by striking out "$10" and inserting "$60". **Effective** for petitions filed after 12-31-81.

• 1976, Tax Reform Act of 1976 (P.L. 94-455)

P.L. 94-455, §1306(b)(1):

Amended Code Sec. 7451 by adding "or under section 7428" at the end of the section. For the **effective** date, see Act Sec. 1306(c), below.

P.L. 94-455, §1306(c), provides:

(c) EFFECTIVE DATE.—The amendments made by this section shall apply with respect to pleadings filed with the United States Tax Court, the district court of the United States for the District of Columbia, or the United States

Court of Claims more than 6 months after the date of the enactment of this Act [October 4, 1976] but only with respect to determinations (or requests for determinations) made after January 1, 1976.

• 1974, Employee Retirement Income Security Act of 1974 (P.L. 93-406)

P.L. 93-406, §1041(b)(1):

Amended Code Sec. 7451. **Effective** as to pleadings filed after 9-2-75. Prior to amendment, Code Sec. 7451 read as follows:

SEC. 7451. FEE FOR FILING PETITION.

The Tax Court is authorized to impose a fee in an amount not in excess of $10 to be fixed by the Tax Court for the filing of any petition for the redetermination of a deficiency.

[Sec. 7452]

SEC. 7452. REPRESENTATION OF PARTIES.

The Secretary shall be represented by the Chief Counsel for the Internal Revenue Service or his delegate in the same manner before the Tax Court as he has heretofore been represented in proceedings before such Court. The taxpayer shall continue to be represented in accordance with the rules of practice prescribed by the Court. No qualified person shall be denied admission to practice before the Tax Court because of his failure to be a member of any profession or calling.

Amendments

• 1976, Tax Reform Act of 1976 (P.L. 94-455)

P.L. 94-455, §1906(b)(13)(A):

Amended 1954 Code by substituting "Secretary" for "Secretary or his delegate" each place it appeared. **Effective** 2-1-77.

• 1959 (P.L. 86-368)

P.L. 86-368, §2(a):

Amended Code Sec. 7452 by striking out "Assistant General Counsel of the Treasury Department serving as Chief Counsel of the Internal Revenue Service, or the delegate of such Chief Counsel," and by substituting "Chief Counsel for the Internal Revenue Service or his delegate". **Effective** when the Chief Counsel for the Internal Revenue Service first appointed pursuant to Code Sec. 7801, as amended by P.L. 86-368, Act Sec. 1, qualifies and takes office.

[Sec. 7453]

SEC. 7453. RULES OF PRACTICE, PROCEDURE, AND EVIDENCE.

Except in the case of proceedings conducted under section 7436(c) or 7463, the proceedings of the Tax Court and its divisions shall be conducted in accordance with such rules of practice and procedure (other than rules of evidence) as the Tax Court may prescribe and in accordance with the Federal Rules of Evidence.

Amendments

• 2015, Protecting Americans from Tax Hikes Act of 2015 (P.L. 114-113)

P.L. 114-113, §425(a), Div. Q:

Amended Code Sec. 7453 by striking "the rules of evidence applicable in trials without a jury in the United States District Court of the District of Columbia" and inserting "the Federal Rules of Evidence". **Effective** for proceedings commenced after 12-18-2015 and, to the extent that it is just and practicable, to all proceedings pending on such date.

• 1997, Taxpayer Relief Act of 1997 (P.L. 105-34)

P.L. 105-34, §1454(b)(3):

Amended Code Sec. 7453 by striking "section 7463" and inserting "section 7436(c) or 7463". **Effective** 8-5-97.

• 1969, Tax Reform Act of 1969 (P.L. 91-172)

P.L. 91-172, §960(f):

Amended Code Sec. 7453 by adding the initial phrase "Except in the case of proceedings conducted under section 7463,". **Effective** 12-30-70.

[Sec. 7454]

SEC. 7454. BURDEN OF PROOF IN FRAUD, FOUNDATION MANAGER, AND TRANSFEREE CASES.

[Sec. 7454(a)]

(a) FRAUD.—In any proceeding involving the issue whether the petitioner has been guilty of fraud with intent to evade tax, the burden of proof in respect of such issue shall be upon the Secretary.

Amendments

• 1976, Tax Reform Act of 1976 (P.L. 94-455)

P.L. 94-455, §1906(b)(13)(A):

Amended 1954 Code by substituting "Secretary" for "Secretary or his delegate" each place it appeared. **Effective** 2-1-77.

[Sec. 7454(b)]

(b) FOUNDATION MANAGERS.—In any proceeding involving the issue whether a foundation manager (as defined in section 4946(b)) has "knowingly" participated in an act of self-dealing (within the meaning of section 4941), participated in an investment which jeopardizes the carrying out of exempt purposes (within the meaning of section 4944), or agreed to the making of a taxable expenditure (within the meaning of section 4945), or whether the trustee of a trust described in section 501(c)(21) has "knowingly" participated in an act of self-dealing (within the meaning of section 4951) or agreed to the making of a taxable expenditure (within the meaning of section 4952), or whether an organization manager (as defined in section 4955(f)(2) has "knowingly" agreed to the making of a political expenditure (within the meaning of section 4955), or whether an organization manager (as defined in section 4912(d)(2)) has "knowingly" agreed to the making of disqualifying lobbying expenditures within the meaning of section 4912(b), or whether an organization manager (as defined in section 4958(f)(2)) has "knowingly" participated in an excess benefit transaction (as defined in section 4958(c)) the burden of proof in respect of such issue shall be upon the Secretary.

Amendments

• 2018, Tax Technical Corrections Act of 2018 (P.L. 115-141)

P.L. 115-141, §401(a)(329), Div. U:

Amended Code Sec. 7454(b) by striking "4955),," and inserting "4955),". **Effective** 3-23-2018.

• 1996, Small Business Job Protection Act of 1996 (P.L. 104-188)

P.L. 104-188, §1704(t)(43):

Amended Code Sec. 7454(b) by striking "section 4955(e)(2)" and inserting "section 4955(f)(2)". **Effective** 8-20-96.

• 1996, Taxpayer Bill of Rights 2 (P.L. 104-168)

P.L. 104-168, §1311(c)(5):

Amended Code Sec. 7454(b) by inserting "or whether an organization manager (as defined in section 4958(f)(2)) has `knowingly' participated in an excess benefit transaction (as defined in section 4958(c))," after "section 4912(b),". For the **effective** date, see Act Sec. 1311(d)(1)-(2), below.

P.L. 104-168, §1311(d)(1)-(2), provides:

(d) EFFECTIVE DATES.—

(1) IN GENERAL.—The amendments made by this section (other than subsection (b)) shall apply to excess benefit transactions occurring on or after September 14, 1995.

(2) BINDING CONTRACTS.—The amendments referred to in paragraph (1) shall not apply to any benefit arising from a transaction pursuant to any written contract which was binding on September 13, 1995, and at all times thereafter before such transaction occurred.

• 1987, Revenue Act of 1987 (P.L. 100-203)

P.L. 100-203, §10712(c)(6):

Amended Code Sec. 7454(b) by striking out "the burden of proof" and inserting in lieu thereof "or whether an organization manager (as defined in section 4955(e)(2)) has `knowingly' agreed to the making of a political expenditure (within the meaning of section 4955), the burden of proof". **Effective** for tax years beginning after 12-22-87.

P.L. 100-203, §10714(b):

Amended Code Sec. 7454(b) by striking out "the burden of proof" and inserting in lieu thereof" or whether an organization manager (as defined in section 4912(d)(2)) has `knowingly' agreed to the making of disqualifying lobbying expenditures within the meaning of section 4912(b), the burden of proof". **Effective** for tax years beginning after 12-22-87.

• 1980, Technical Corrections Act of 1979 (P.L. 96-222)

P.L. 96-222, §108(b)(3)(B):

Amended Code Sec. 7454(b) by striking out "502(c)(21)" and inserting "501(c)(21)". **Effective** as if included in the provision of P.L. 95-227 to which it relates.

• 1978, Black Lung Benefits Revenue Act of 1977 (P.L. 95-227)

P.L. 95-227, §4(d)(7):

Amended Code Sec. 7454(b). **Effective** with respect to contributions, acts and expenditures made after 12-31-77, in and for tax years beginning after such date. However, this effective date was contingent upon enactment of P.L. 95-239, which was enacted on 3-1-78. Prior to amendment, Code Sec. 7454(b) read as follows:

"(b) FOUNDATION MANAGERS.—In any proceedings involving the issue whether a foundation manager (as defined in section 4946(b)) has `knowingly, participated in an act of self-dealing (within the meaning of section 4941), participated in an investment which jeopardizes the carrying out of exempt purposes (within the meaning of section 4944), or agreed to the making of a taxable expenditure (within the meaning of section 4945), the burden of proof in respect of such issue shall be upon the Secretary."

• 1976, Tax Reform Act of 1976 (P.L. 94-455)

P.L. 94-455, §1906(b)(13)(A):

Amended 1954 Code by substituting "Secretary" for "Secretary or his delegate" each place it appeared. **Effective** 2-1-77.

[Sec. 7454(c)]

(c) CROSS REFERENCE.—

For provisions relating to burden of proof as to transferee liability, see section 6902(a).

Amendments

• 1976, Tax Reform Act of 1976 (P.L. 94-455)

P.L. 94-455, §1906(b)(13)(A):

Amended 1954 Code by substituting "Secretary" for "Secretary or his delegate" each place it appeared. **Effective** 2-1-77.

• 1969, Tax Reform Act of 1969 (P.L. 91-172)

P.L. 91-172, §101(j)(57):

Amended Code Sec. 7454 by adding ", FOUNDATION MANAGER," in the title, by redesignating subsection (b) to be subsection (c), and by adding a new subsection (b). **Effective** 1-1-70.

* * *

[Sec. 7458]

SEC. 7458. HEARINGS.

Notice and opportunity to be heard upon any proceeding instituted before the Tax Court shall be given to the taxpayer and the Secretary. If an opportunity to be heard upon the proceeding is given before a division of the Tax Court, neither the taxpayer nor the Secretary shall be entitled to notice and opportunity to be heard before the Tax Court upon review, except upon a specific order of the chief judge. Hearings before the Tax Court and its divisions shall be open to the public, and the testimony, and, if the Tax Court so requires, the argument, shall be stenographically reported. The Tax Court is authorized to contract (by renewal of contract or otherwise) for the reporting of such hearings, and in such contract to fix the terms and conditions under which transcripts will be supplied by the contractor to the Tax Court and to other persons and agencies.

Amendments

• 1976, Tax Reform Act of 1976 (P.L. 94-455)

P.L. 94-455, §1906(b)(13)(A):

Amended 1954 Code by substituting "Secretary" for "Secretary or his delegate" each place it appeared. **Effective** 2-1-77.

P.L. 94-455, §1906(b)(13)(L):

Amended Code Sec. 7458 by striking out "nor his delegate" after "Secretary". **Effective** 2-1-77.

[Sec. 7459]

SEC. 7459. REPORTS AND DECISIONS.

[Sec. 7459(a)]

(a) REQUIREMENT.—A report upon any proceeding instituted before the Tax Court and a decision thereon shall be made as quickly as practicable. The decision shall be made by a judge in accordance with the report of the Tax Court, and such decision so made shall, when entered, be the decision of the Tax Court.

[Sec. 7459(b)]

(b) INCLUSION OF FINDINGS OF FACT OR OPINIONS IN REPORT.—It shall be the duty of the Tax Court and of each division to include in its report upon any proceeding its findings of fact or opinion or memorandum opinion. The Tax Court shall report in writing all its findings of fact, opinions, and memorandum opinions. Subject to such conditions as the Tax Court may by rule provide, the requirements of this subsection and of section 7460 are met if findings of fact or opinion are stated orally and recorded in the transcript of the proceedings.

Amendments

• 1982, Miscellaneous Revenue Act of 1982 (P.L. 97-362)

P.L. 97-362, §106(b):

Amended Code Sec. 7459(b) by adding the last sentence. **Effective** 10-25-82.

[Sec. 7459(c)]

(c) DATE OF DECISION.—A decision of the Tax Court (except a decision dismissing a proceeding for lack of jurisdiction) shall be held to be rendered upon the date that an order specifying the amount of the deficiency is entered in the records of the Tax Court or, in the case of a declaratory judgment proceeding under part IV of this subchapter, or under section 7428 or in the case of an action brought under section 6234, the date of the court's order entering the decision. If the Tax Court dismisses a proceeding for reasons other than lack of jurisdiction and is unable from the record to determine the amount of the deficiency determined by the Secretary, or if the Tax Court dismisses a proceeding for lack of jurisdiction, an order to that effect shall be entered in the records of the Tax Court, and the decision of the Tax Court shall be held to be rendered upon the date of such entry.

Amendments

• 2015, Bipartisan Budget Act of 2015 (P.L. 114-74)

P.L. 114-74, §1101(f)(12):

Amended Code Sec. 7459(c) by striking "section 6226" and all that follows through "or 6252" and inserting "section 6234". **Effective** generally for returns filed for partnership tax years beginning after 12-31-2017. For a special rule, see Act Sec. 1101(g)(4), below. Prior to being stricken, "section 6226" and all that follows through "or 6252" read as follows:

section 6226, 6228(a), 6234(c)[,] 6247, or 6252

P.L. 114-74, §1101(g)(4), provides:

(4) ELECTION.—A partnership may elect (at such time and in such form and manner as the Secretary of the Treasury may prescribe) for the amendments made by this section (other than the election under section 6221(b) of such Code (as added by this Act)) to apply to any return of the partnership filed for partnership taxable years beginning after the date of the enactment of this Act and before January 1, 2018.

• 1997, Taxpayer Relief Act of 1997 (P.L. 105-34)

P.L. 105-34, §1222(b)(2):

Amended Code Sec. 7459(c) by striking "or section 6228(a)" and inserting ", 6228(a), 6247, or 6252". **Effective** for partnership tax years beginning after 12-31-97 [**effective** date changed by P.L. 105-206, §6012(e)].

P.L. 105-34, §1239(e)(1):

Amended Code Sec. 7459(c) by striking "or section 6228(a)" [sic] and inserting ", 6228(a), or [sic]6234(c)[,]". **Effective** for partnership tax years ending after 8-5-97.

• 1982, Tax Equity and Fiscal Responsibility Act of 1982 (P.L. 97-248)

P.L. 97-248, §402(c)(14):

Amended Code Sec. 7459(c) by inserting after "or under section 7428" "or in the case of an action brought under section 6226 or section 6228(a)". **Effective** for partnership tax years beginning after 9-3-82 and also to partner tax years ending after that date if the partnership, each partner, and each indirect partner requests such application and if the Secretary or his delegate consents to such application.

• 1976, Tax Reform Act of 1976 (P.L. 94-455)

P.L. 94-455, §1906(b)(13)(A):

Amended 1954 Code by substituting "Secretary" for "Secretary or his delegate" each place it appeared. **Effective** 2-1-77.

P.L. 94-455, §1306(b)(2):

Amended Code Sec. 7459(c) by inserting "or under section 7428" after "under part IV of this subchapter". For the **effective** date, see Act Sec. 1306(c), below.

P.L. 94-455, §1306(c), provides:

(c) EFFECTIVE DATE.—The amendments made by this section shall apply with respect to pleadings filed with the United States Tax Court, the district court of the United States for the District of Columbia, or the United States Court of Claims more than 6 months after the date of the enactment of this Act [October 4, 1976] but only with respect to determinations (or requests for determinations) made after January 1, 1976.

• 1974, Employee Retirement Income Security Act of 1974 (P.L. 93-406)

P.L. 93-406, §1041(b)(2):

Amended Code Sec. 7459(c). **Effective** as to pleadings filed after 9-2-75. Prior to amendment, Code Sec. 7459(c) read as follows:

"(c) Date of Decision.—A decision of the Tax Court (except a decision dismissing a proceeding for lack of jurisdiction) shall be held to be rendered upon the date that an order specifying the amount of the deficiency is entered in the records of the Tax Court. If the Tax Court dismisses a proceeding for reasons other than lack of jurisdiction and is unable from the record to determine the amount of the deficiency determined by the Secretary or his delegate, or if the Tax Court dismisses a proceeding for lack of jurisdiction, an order to that effect shall be entered in the records of the Tax Court, and the decision of the Tax Court shall be held to be rendered upon the date of such entry."

[Sec. 7459(d)]

(d) EFFECT OF DECISION DISMISSING PETITION.—If a petition for a redetermination of a deficiency has been filed by the taxpayer, a decision of the Tax Court dismissing the proceeding shall be considered as its decision that the deficiency is the amount determined by the Secretary. An order specifying such amount shall be entered in the records of the Tax Court unless the Tax Court cannot determine such amount from the record in the proceeding, or unless the dismissal is for lack of jurisdiction.

Amendments

• 1976, Tax Reform Act of 1976 (P.L. 94-455)

P.L. 94-455, §1906(b)(13)(A):

Amended 1954 Code by substituting "Secretary" for "Secretary or his delegate" each place it appeared. **Effective** 2-1-77.

[Sec. 7459(e)]

(e) EFFECT OF DECISION THAT TAX IS BARRED BY LIMITATION.—If the assessment or collection of any tax is barred by any statute of limitations, the decision of the Tax Court to that effect shall be considered as its decision that there is no deficiency in respect of such tax.

[Sec. 7459(f)]

(f) FINDINGS OF FACT AS EVIDENCE.—The findings of the Board of Tax Appeals made in connection with any decision prior to February 26, 1926, shall, notwithstanding the enactment of the Revenue Act of 1926 (44 Stat. 9), continue to be prima facie evidence of the facts therein stated.

[Sec. 7459(g)]

(g) PENALTY.—

For penalty for taxpayer instituting proceedings before Tax Court merely for delay, see section 6673.

* * *

[Sec. 7462]

SEC. 7462. PUBLICATION OF REPORTS.

The Tax Court shall provide for the publication of its reports at the Government Printing Office in such form and manner as may be best adapted for public information and use, and such authorized publication shall be competent evidence of the reports of the Tax Court therein contained in all courts of the United States and of the several States without any further proof or authentication thereof. Such reports shall be subject to sale in the same manner and upon the same terms as other public documents.

[Sec. 7463]

SEC. 7463. DISPUTES INVOLVING $50,000 OR LESS.

[Sec. 7463(a)]

(a) IN GENERAL.—In the case of any petition filed with the Tax Court for a redetermination of a deficiency where neither the amount of the deficiency placed in dispute, nor the amount of any claimed overpayment, exceeds—

(1) $50,000 for any one taxable year, in the case of the taxes imposed by subtitle A,

(2) $50,000, in the case of the tax imposed by chapter 11,

(3) $50,000 for any one calendar year, in the case of the tax imposed by chapter 12, or

(4) $50,000 for any 1 taxable period (or, if there is no taxable period, taxable event) in the case of any tax imposed by subtitle D which is described in section 6212(a) (relating to a notice of deficiency),

at the option of the taxpayer concurred in by the Tax Court or a division thereof before the hearing of the case, proceedings in the case shall be conducted under this section. Notwithstanding the provisions of section 7453, such proceedings shall be conducted in accordance with such rules of evidence, practice, and procedure as the Tax Court may prescribe. A decision, together with a brief summary of the reasons therefor, in any such case shall satisfy the requirements of sections 7459(b) and 7460.

Amendments

• 1998, IRS Restructuring and Reform Act of 1998 (P.L. 105-206)

P.L. 105-206, §3103(a):

Amended Code Sec. 7463 by striking "$10,000" each place it appears (including the section heading) and inserting "$50,000". **Effective** for proceedings commenced after 7-22-98.

• 1984, Deficit Reduction Act of 1984 (P.L. 98-369)

P.L. 98-369, §461(a)(1):

Amended Code Sec. 7463(a) by striking out "$5,000" each place it appeared and inserting in lieu thereof "$10,000". **Effective** 7-18-84.

P.L. 98-369, §461(a)(2)(A):

Amended Code Sec. 7463 by striking out "$5,000" in the heading and inserting in lieu thereof "$10,000". **Effective** 7-18-84.

• 1982, Miscellaneous Revenue Act of 1982 (P.L. 97-362)

P.L. 97-362, §106(a):

Amended Code Sec. 7463(a) by striking out "or" at the end of paragraph (2), by adding "or" at the end of paragraph (3), and by inserting after paragraph (3) the new paragraph (4). **Effective** with respect to petitions filed after 10-25-82.

• **1978, Revenue Act of 1978 (P.L. 95-600)**

P.L. 95-600, §502(a)(1):

Amended Code Sec. 7463(a) by adding paragraphs (1), (2), and (3). **Effective** on the first day of the first calendar month beginning more than 180 days after 11-6-78. Prior to amendment, Code Sec. 7463(a)(1) and (2) read:

"(1) $1,500 for any one taxable year, in the case of the taxes imposed by subtitle A and chapter 12, or

"(2) $1,500, in the case of the tax imposed by chapter 11,".

[Sec. 7463(b)]

(b) FINALITY OF DECISIONS.—A decision entered in any case in which the proceedings are conducted under this section shall not be reviewed in any other court and shall not be treated as a precedent for any other case.

[Sec. 7463(c)]

(c) LIMITATION OF JURISDICTION.—In any case in which the proceedings are conducted under this section, notwithstanding the provisions of sections 6214(a) and 6512(b), no decision shall be entered redetermining the amount of a deficiency, or determining an overpayment, except with respect to amounts placed in dispute within the limits described in subsection (a) and with respect to amounts conceded by the parties.

[Sec. 7463(d)]

(d) DISCONTINUANCE OF PROCEEDINGS.—At any time before a decision entered in a case in which the proceedings are conducted under this section becomes final, the taxpayer or the Secretary may request that further proceedings under this section in such case be discontinued. The Tax Court, or the division thereof hearing such case, may, if it finds that (1) there are reasonable grounds for believing that the amount of the deficiency placed in dispute, or the amount of an overpayment, exceeds the applicable jurisdictional amount described in subsection (a), and (2) the amount of such excess is large enough to justify granting such request, discontinue further proceedings in such case under this section. Upon any such discontinuance, proceedings in such case shall be conducted in the same manner as cases to which the provisions of sections 6214(a) and 6512(b) apply.

Amendments

• **1976, Tax Reform Act of 1976 (P.L. 94-455)**

P.L. 94-455, §1906(b)(13)(A):

Amended 1954 Code by substituting "Secretary" for "Secretary or his delegate" each place it appeared. **Effective** 2-1-77.

[Sec. 7463(e)]

(e) AMOUNT OF DEFICIENCY IN DISPUTE.—For purposes of this section, the amount of any deficiency placed in dispute includes additions to the tax, additional amounts, and penalties imposed by chapter 68, to the extent that the procedures described in subchapter B of chapter 63 apply.

Amendments

• **1969, Tax Reform Act of 1969 (P.L. 91-172)**

P.L. 91-172, §957(a):

Added Code Sec. 7463. **Effective** 12-30-70.

[Sec. 7463(f)]

(f) ADDITIONAL CASES IN WHICH PROCEEDINGS MAY BE CONDUCTED UNDER THIS SECTION.—At the option of the taxpayer concurred in by the Tax Court or a division thereof before the hearing of the case, proceedings may be conducted under this section (in the same manner as a case described in subsection (a)) in the case of—

(1) a petition to the Tax Court under section 6015(e) in which the amount of relief sought does not exceed $50,000,

(2) an appeal under section 6330(d)(1)(A) to the Tax Court of a determination in which the unpaid tax does not exceed $50,000, and

(3) a petition to the Tax Court under section 6404(h) in which the amount of the abatement sought does not exceed $50,000.

Amendments

• **2015, Protecting Americans from Tax Hikes Act of 2015 (P.L. 114-113)**

P.L. 114-113, §422(a)(1)-(3), Div. Q:

Amended Code Sec. 7463(f) by striking "and" at the end of paragraph (1), by striking the period at the end of paragraph (2) and inserting ", and", and by adding at the end a new paragraph (3). **Effective** for cases pending as of the day after the date of the enactment of this Act, and cases commenced after such date of enactment.

• **2000, Community Renewal Tax Relief Act of 2000 (P.L. 106-554)**

P.L. 106-554, §313(b)(1):

Amended Code Sec. 7463 by adding at the end a new subsection (f). **Effective** 12-21-2000.

• **1990, Omnibus Budget Reconciliation Act of 1990 (P.L. 101-508)**

P.L. 101-508, §11801(c)(21)(B):

Amended Code Sec. 7463 by striking subsection (f). **Effective** 11-5-90. Prior to being stricken, Code Sec. 7463(f) read as follows:

(f) QUALIFIED STATE INDIVIDUAL INCOME TAXES.—For purposes of this section, a deficiency placed in dispute or claimed overpayment with regard to a qualified State individual income tax to which subchapter E of chapter 64 applies, for a taxable year, shall be treated as a portion of a deficiency placed in dispute or claimed overpayment of the income tax for that taxable year.

P.L. 101-508, §11821(b), provides:

(b) SAVINGS PROVISION.—If—

(1) any provision amended or repealed by this part applied to—

(A) any transaction occurring before the date of the enactment of this Act,

(B) any property acquired before such date of enactment, or

(C) any item of income, loss, deduction, or credit taken into account before such date of enactment, and

(2) the treatment of such transaction, property, or item under such provision would (without regard to the amendments made by this part) affect liability for tax for periods ending after such date of enactment,

nothing in the amendments made by this part shall be construed to affect the treatment of such transaction, property, or item for purposes of determining liability for tax for periods ending after such date of enactment.

• 1972, State and Local Fiscal Assistance Act of 1972 (P.L. 92-512)

P.L. 92-512, § 203(b):

Amended Code Sec. 7463 by adding subsection (f), by substituting "$1,500" for "$1,000" in the heading of said section, and by making a similar substitution at the beginning of subparagraphs (1) and (2) of subsection (a). **Effective** 1-1-74, for the increase in the jurisdictional amount to $1,500 for the small tax case procedure. The **effective** date of Code Sec. 7463(f) is dependent upon the **effective** date for the federal collection of qualified state individual income taxes. See the amendment note for P.L. 92-512 under Code Sec. 6361.

[Sec. 7463(g)—Repealed]

Amendments

• 1980, Technical Corrections Act of 1979 (P.L. 96-222)

P.L. 96-222, § 105(a)(1)(A):

Repealed Code Sec. 7463(g). **Effective** 4-1-80. Prior to its repeal, Code Sec. 7463(g) read as follows:

"(g) COMMISSIONERS.—The chief judge of the Tax Court may assign proceedings conducted under this section to be heard by the Commissioners of the court, and the court may authorize a commissioner to make the decision of the court with respect to any such proceeding, subject to such conditions and review as the court may by rule provide."

• 1978, Revenue Act of 1978 (P.L. 95-600)

P.L. 95-600, § 502(b):

Added Code Sec. 7463(g). **Effective** 11-6-78.

* * *

[Sec. 7465]

SEC. 7465. PROVISIONS OF SPECIAL APPLICATION TO TRANSFEREES.

(1) For rules of burden of proof in transferee proceedings, see section 6902(a).

(2) For authority of Tax Court to prescribe rules by which a transferee of property of a taxpayer shall be entitled to examine books, records and other evidence, see section 6902(b).

Amendments

• 1980, Bankruptcy Tax Act of 1980 (P.L. 96-589)

P.L. 96-589, § 6(c)(1):

Redesignated former Code Sec. 7464 as Code Sec. 7465. **Effective** 10-1-79, but inapplicable to any proceeding commenced before that date.

• 1969, Tax Reform Act of 1969 (P.L. 91-172)

P.L. 91-172, § 957(a):

Redesignated prior Code Sec. 7463 as Code Sec. 7464. **Effective** 12-30-70.

[Sec. 7466]

SEC. 7466. JUDICIAL CONDUCT AND DISABILITY PROCEDURES.

[Sec. 7466(a)]

(a) IN GENERAL.—The Tax Court shall prescribe rules, consistent with the provisions of chapter 16 of title 28, United States Code, establishing procedures for the filing of complaints with respect to the conduct of any judge or special trial judge of the Tax Court and for the investigation and resolution of such complaints. In investigating and taking action with respect to any such complaint, the Tax Court shall have the powers granted to a judicial council under such chapter.

[Sec. 7466(b)]

(b) JUDICIAL COUNCIL.—The provisions of sections 354(b) through 360 of title 28, United States Code, regarding referral or certification to, and petition for review in the Judicial Conference of the United States, and action thereon, shall apply to the exercise by the Tax Court of the powers of a judicial council under subsection (a). The determination pursuant to section 354(b) or 355 of title 28, United States Code, shall be made based on the grounds for removal of a judge from office under section 7443(f), and certification and transmittal by the Conference of any complaint shall be made to the President for consideration under section 7443(f).

[Sec. 7466(c)]

(c) HEARINGS.—

(1) IN GENERAL.—In conducting hearings pursuant to subsection (a), the Tax Court may exercise the authority provided under section 1821 of title 28, United States Code, to pay the fees and allowances described in that section.

(2) REIMBURSEMENT FOR EXPENSES.—The Tax Court shall have the power provided under section 361 of such title 28 to award reimbursement for the reasonable expenses described in that section. Reimbursements under this paragraph shall be made out of any funds appropriated for purposes of the Tax Court.

Amendments

• 2015, Protecting Americans from Tax Hikes Act of 2015 (P.L. 114-113)

P.L. 114-113, §431(a), Div. Q:

Amended part II of subchapter C of chapter 76 by adding at the end a new Code Sec. 7466. **Effective** for proceedings commenced after the date which is 180 days after 12-18-2015 and, to the extent that it is just and practicable, to all proceedings pending on such date.

PART III—MISCELLANEOUS PROVISIONS

* * *

[Sec. 7470]

SEC. 7470. ADMINISTRATION.

Notwithstanding any other provision of law, the Tax Court may exercise, for purposes of management, administration, and expenditure of funds of the Court, the authorities provided for such purposes by any provision of law (including any limitation with respect to such provision of law) applicable to a court of the United States (as that term is defined in section 451 of title 28, United States Code), except to the extent that such provision of law is inconsistent with a provision of this subchapter.

Amendments

• 2015, Protecting Americans from Tax Hikes Act of 2015 (P.L. 114-113)

P.L. 114-113, §432(a), Div. Q:

Amended part III of subchapter C of chapter 76 by inserting before Code Sec. 7471 new Code Secs. 7470-7470A. **Effective** 12-18-2015.

[Sec. 7470A]

SEC. 7470A. JUDICIAL CONFERENCE.

[Sec. 7470A(a)]

(a) JUDICIAL CONFERENCE.—The chief judge may summon the judges and special trial judges of the Tax Court to an annual judicial conference, at such time and place as the chief judge shall designate, for the purpose of considering the business of the Tax Court and recommending means of improving the administration of justice within the jurisdiction of the Tax Court. The Tax Court shall provide by its rules for representation and active participation at such conferences by persons admitted to practice before the Tax Court and by other persons active in the legal profession.

[Sec. 7470A(b)]

(b) REGISTRATION FEE.—The Tax Court may impose a reasonable registration fee on persons (other than judges and special trial judges of the Tax Court) participating at judicial conferences convened pursuant to subsection (a). Amounts so received by the Tax Court shall be available to the Tax Court to defray the expenses of such conferences.

Amendments

• 2015, Protecting Americans from Tax Hikes Act of 2015 (P.L. 114-113)

P.L. 114-113, §432(a), Div. Q:

Amended part III of subchapter C of chapter 76 by inserting before Code Sec. 7471 new Code Secs. 7470-7470A. **Effective** 12-18-2015.

* * *

PART IV—DECLARATORY JUDGMENTS

* * *

* * *

[Sec. 7477]

SEC. 7477. DECLARATORY JUDGMENTS RELATING TO VALUE OF CERTAIN GIFTS.

[Sec. 7477(a)]

(a) CREATION OF REMEDY.—In a case of an actual controversy involving a determination by the Secretary of the value of any gift shown on the return of tax imposed by chapter 12 or disclosed on such return or in any statement attached to such return, upon the filing of an appropriate pleading, the Tax Court may make a declaration of the value of such gift. Any such declaration shall have the force and effect of a decision of the Tax Court and shall be reviewable as such.

[Sec. 7477(b)]

(b) LIMITATIONS.—

(1) PETITIONER.—A pleading may be filed under this section only by the donor.

(2) EXHAUSTION OF ADMINISTRATIVE REMEDIES.—The court shall not issue a declaratory judgment or decree under this section in any proceeding unless it determines that the petitioner has exhausted all available administrative remedies within the Internal Revenue Service.

(3) TIME FOR BRINGING ACTION.—If the Secretary sends by certified or registered mail notice of his determination as described in subsection (a) to the petitioner, no proceeding may be initiated under this section unless the pleading is filed before the 91st day after the date of such mailing.

Amendments

• 1997, Taxpayer Relief Act of 1997 (P.L. 105-34)

P.L. 105-34, §506(c)(1):

Amended part IV of subchapter C of chapter 76 by inserting after Code Sec. 7476 a new Code Sec. 7477. **Effective** for gifts made after 8-5-97.

[Sec. 7477—Repealed]

Amendments

• 1984, Deficit Reduction Act of 1984 (P.L. 98-369)

P.L. 98-369, §131(e)(1):

Repealed Code Sec. 7477. **Effective** for transfers or exchanges after 12-31-84, in tax years ending after such date. Special rules appear in Act Sec. 131(g)(2)(3) following Code Sec. 367(e). Prior to amendment, Code Sec. 7477 read as follows:

SEC. 7477. DECLARATORY JUDGMENTS RELATING TO TRANSFERS OF PROPERTY FROM THE UNITED STATES.

(a) CREATION OF REMEDY.—

(1) IN GENERAL.—In a case of actual controversy involving—

(A) a determination by the Secretary—

(i) that an exchange described in section 367(a)(1) is in pursuance of a plan having as one of its principal purposes the avoidance of Federal income taxes, or

(ii) of the terms and conditions pursuant to which an exchange described in section 367(a)(1) will be determined not to be in pursuance of a plan having as one of its principal purposes the avoidance of Federal income taxes, or

(B) a failure by the Secretary to make a determination as to whether an exchange described in section 367(a)(1) is in pursuance of a plan having as one of its principal purposes the avoidance of Federal income taxes,

upon the filing of an appropriate pleading, the Tax Court may make the appropriate declaration referred to in paragraph (2). Such declaration shall have the force and effect of a decision of the Tax Court and shall be reviewable as such.

(2) SCOPE OF DECLARATION.—The declaration referred to in paragraph (1) shall be—

(A) in the case of a determination referred to in subparagraph (A) of paragraph (1), whether or not such determination is reasonable, and, if it is not reasonable, a determination of the issue set forth in subparagraph (A)(ii) of paragraph (1), and

(B) in the case of a failure described in subparagraph (B) of paragraph (1), the determination of the issues set forth in subparagraph (A) of paragraph (1).

(b) LIMITATIONS.

(1) PETITIONER.—A pleading may be filed under this section only by a petitioner who is a transferor or transferee of stock, securities, or property transferred in an exchange described in section 367(a)(1).

(2) EXHAUSTION OF ADMINISTRATIVE REMEDIES.—The Tax Court shall not issue a declaratory judgment or decree under this section in any proceeding unless it determines that the petitioner has exhausted administrative remedies available to him within the Internal Revenue Service. A petitioner shall not be deemed to have exhausted his administrative remedies with respect to a failure by the Secretary to make a determination with respect to whether or not an exchange described in section 367(a)(1) is in pursuance of a plan having as one of its principal purposes the avoidance of Federal income taxes before the expiration of 270 days after the request for such determination was made.

(3) EXCHANGE SHALL HAVE BEGUN.—No proceeding may be maintained under this section unless the exchange described in section 367(a)(1) with respect to which a decision of the Tax Court is sought has begun before the filing of the pleading.

(4) TIME FOR BRINGING ACTION.—If the Secretary sends by certified or registered mail to the petitioners referred to in paragraph (1) notice of his determination with respect to whether or not an exchange described in section 367(a)(1) is in pursuance of a plan having as one of its principal purposes the avoidance of Federal income taxes or with respect to the terms and conditions pursuant to which such an exchange will be determined not to be made in pursuance of such a plan, no proceeding may be initiated under this section by any petitioner unless the pleading is filed before the 91st day after the day after such notice is mailed to such petitioner.

• 1978, Revenue Act of 1978 (P.L. 95-600)

P.L. 95-600, §336(b)(2)(B):

Amended Code Sec. 7477 by striking out subsection (c). **Effective** with respect to requests for determinations made after 12-31-78. Prior to deletion, Code Sec. 7477(c) read:

"(c) COMMISSIONERS.—The chief judge of the Tax Court may assign proceedings under this section to be heard by the commissioners of the court, and the court may authorize a commissioner to make the decision of the court with respect to such proceeding, subject to such conditions and review as the court may by rule provide."

• 1976, Tax Reform Act of 1976 (P.L. 94-455)

P.L. 94-455, §1042(d)(1):

Added Code Sec. 7477.

P.L. 94-455, §1042(e)(1), provides:

(1) The amendments made by this section (other than by subsection (d)) shall apply to transfers beginning after October 9, 1975, and to sales, exchanges, and distributions taking place after such date. The amendments made by subsection (d) shall apply with respect to pleadings filed with the Tax Court after the date of the enactment of this Act [October 4, 1976] but only with respect to transfers beginning after October 9, 1975.

* * *

[Sec. 7479]

SEC. 7479. DECLARATORY JUDGMENTS RELATING TO ELIGIBILITY OF ESTATE WITH RESPECT TO INSTALLMENT PAYMENTS UNDER SECTION 6166 .

[Sec. 7479(a)]

(a) CREATION OF REMEDY.—In a case of actual controversy involving a determination by the Secretary of (or a failure by the Secretary to make a determination with respect to)—

(1) whether an election may be made under section 6166 (relating to extension of time for payment of estate tax where estate consists largely of interest in closely held business) with respect to an estate (or with respect to any property included therein), or

(2) whether the extension of time for payment of tax provided in section 6166(a) has ceased to apply with respect to an estate (or with respect to any property included therein),

upon the filing of an appropriate pleading, the Tax Court may make a declaration with respect to whether such election may be made or whether such extension has ceased to apply. Any such declaration shall have the force and effect of a decision of the Tax Court and shall be reviewable as such.

Amendments

• 1998, IRS Restructuring and Reform Act of 1998 (P.L. 105-206)

P.L. 105-206, §6007(d):

Amended Code Sec. 7479(a)(1)-(2) by striking "an estate," and inserting "an estate (or with respect to any property included therein),". **Effective** as if included in the provision of P.L. 105-34 to which it relates [**effective** for estates of decedents dying after 8-5-97.—CCH].

[Sec. 7479(b)]

(b) LIMITATIONS.—

(1) PETITIONER.—A pleading may be filed under this section, with respect to any estate, only—

(A) by the executor of such estate, or

(B) by any person who has assumed an obligation to make payments under section 6166 with respect to such estate (but only if each other such person is joined as a party).

(2) EXHAUSTION OF ADMINISTRATIVE REMEDIES.—The court shall not issue a declaratory judgment or decree under this section in any proceeding unless it determines that the petitioner has exhausted all available administrative remedies within the Internal Revenue Service. A petitioner shall be deemed to have exhausted its administrative remedies with respect to a failure of the Secretary to make a determination at the expiration of 180 days after the date on which the request for such determination was made if the petitioner has taken, in a timely manner, all reasonable steps to secure such determination.

(3) TIME FOR BRINGING ACTION.—If the Secretary sends by certified or registered mail notice of his determination as described in subsection (a) to the petitioner, no proceeding may be initiated under this section unless the pleading is filed before the 91st day after the date of such mailing.

Amendments

• 1997, Taxpayer Relief Act of 1997 (P.L. 105-34)

P.L. 105-34, §505(a):

Amended part IV of subchapter C of chapter 76 by adding Code Sec. 7479. **Effective** for the estates of decedents dying after 8-5-97.

[Sec. 7479(c)]

(c) EXTENSION OF TIME TO FILE REFUND SUIT.—The 2-year period in section 6532(a)(1) for filing suit for refund after disallowance of a claim shall be suspended during the 90-day period after the mailing of the notice referred to in subsection (b)(3) and, if a pleading has been filed with the Tax Court under this section, until the decision of the Tax Court has become final.

Amendments

• 1998, IRS Restructuring and Reform Act of 1998 (P.L. 105-206)

P.L. 105-206, §3104(b):

Amended Code Sec. 7479 by adding at the end a new subsection (c). **Effective** for any claim for refund filed after 7-22-98.

Subchapter D—Court Review of Tax Court Decisions

* * *

[Sec. 7481]

SEC. 7481. DATE WHEN TAX COURT DECISION BECOMES FINAL.

[Sec. 7481(a)]

(a) REVIEWABLE DECISIONS.—Except as provided in subsections (b), (c), and (d), the decision of the Tax Court shall become final—

(1) TIMELY NOTICE OF APPEAL NOT FILED.—Upon the expiration of the time allowed for filing a notice of appeal, if no such notice has been duly filed within such time; or

(2) DECISION AFFIRMED OR APPEAL DISMISSED.—

(A) PETITION FOR CERTIORARI NOT FILED ON TIME.—Upon the expiration of the time allowed for filing a petition for certiorari, if the decision of the Tax Court has been affirmed or the appeal dismissed by the United States Court of Appeals and no petition for certiorari has been duly filed; or

(B) PETITION FOR CERTIORARI DENIED.—Upon the denial of a petition for certiorari, if the decision of the Tax Court has been affirmed or the appeal dismissed by the United States Court of Appeals; or

(C) AFTER MANDATE OF SUPREME COURT.—Upon the expiration of 30 days from the date of issuance of the mandate of the Supreme Court, if such Court directs that the decision of the Tax Court be affirmed or the appeal dismissed.

(3) DECISION MODIFIED OR REVERSED.—

(A) UPON MANDATE OF SUPREME COURT.—If the Supreme Court directs that the decision of the Tax Court be modified or reversed, the decision of the Tax Court rendered in accordance with the mandate of the Supreme Court shall become final upon the expiration of 30 days from the time it was rendered, unless within such 30 days either the Secretary or the taxpayer has instituted proceedings to have such decision corrected to accord with the mandate, in which event the decision of the Tax Court shall become final when so corrected.

(B) UPON MANDATE OF THE COURT OF APPEALS.—If the decision of the Tax Court is modified or reversed by the United States Court of Appeals, and if—

(i) the time allowed for filing a petition for certiorari has expired and no such petition has been duly filed, or

(ii) the petition for certiorari has been denied, or

(iii) the decision of the United States Court of Appeals has been affirmed by the Supreme Court, then the decision of the Tax Court rendered in accordance with the mandate of the United States Court of Appeals shall become final on the expiration of 30 days from the time such decision of the Tax Court was rendered, unless within such 30 days either the Secretary or the taxpayer has instituted proceedings to have such decision corrected so that it will accord with the mandate, in which event the decision of the Tax Court shall become final when so corrected.

(4) REHEARING.—If the Supreme Court orders a rehearing; or if the case is remanded by the United States Court of Appeals to the Tax Court for a rehearing, and if—

(A) the time allowed for filing a petition for certiorari has expired and no such petition has been duly filed, or

(B) the petition for certiorari has been denied, or

(C) the decision of the United States Court of Appeals has been affirmed by the Supreme Court,

then the decision of the Tax Court rendered upon such rehearing shall become final in the same manner as though no prior decision of the Tax Court has been rendered.

(5) DEFINITION OF "MANDATE".—As used in this section, the term "mandate", in case a mandate has been recalled prior to the expiration of 30 days from the date of issuance thereof, means the final mandate.

Amendments

• 1988, Technical and Miscellaneous Revenue Act of 1988 (P.L. 100-647)

P.L. 100-647, §6246(b)(2):

Amended Code Sec. 7481(a) by striking out "subsection (b)" and inserting in lieu thereof "subsections (b) and (c)". **Effective** for assessments of deficiencies redetermined by the Tax Court made after 11-10-88.

P.L. 100-647, §6247(b)(2):

Amended Code Sec. 7481(a), as amended, by striking out "subsections (b) and (c)" and inserting in lieu thereof "subsections (b), (c), and (d)". **Effective** with respect to Tax Court cases for which the decision is not final on 11-10-88.

• 1976, Tax Reform Act of 1976 (P.L. 94-455)

P.L. 94-455, §1906(b)(13)(A):

Amended 1954 Code by substituting "Secretary" for "Secretary or his delegate" each place it appeared. **Effective** 2-1-77.

[Sec. 7481(b)]

(b) NONREVIEWABLE DECISIONS.—The decision of the Tax Court in a proceeding conducted under section 7436(c) or 7463 shall become final upon the expiration of 90 days after the decision is entered.

Amendments

• 1997, Taxpayer Relief Act of 1997 (P.L. 105-34)

P.L. 105-34, §1454(b)(3):

Amended Code Sec. 7481(b) by striking "section 7463" and inserting "section 7436(c) or 7463". **Effective** 8-5-97.

• 1969, Tax Reform Act of 1969 (P.L. 91-172)

P.L. 91-172, §960(h)(1):

Amended Code Sec. 7481 by inserting new subsection (a)(1), by substituting the word "appeal" for the phrase "petition for review" throughout (a)(2) and added new subsection (b). **Effective** 1-29-70. However, in the case of any decision of the Tax Court entered before January 29, 1970, the United States Courts of Appeal shall have jurisdiction to hear an appeal from such decision, if such appeal was filed within the time prescribed by Rule 13(a) of the Federal Rules of Appellate Procedure or by section 7483 of the Internal Revenue Code of 1954, as in effect at the time the decision of the Tax Court was entered. Prior to amendment by P.L. 91-172, paragraph (1) read as follows:

(1) Timely Petition for Review Not Filed.—Upon the expiration of the time allowed for filing a petition for review, if no such petition has been duly filed within such time; or

* * *

[Sec. 7482]

SEC. 7482. COURTS OF REVIEW.

[Sec. 7482(a)]

(a) JURISDICTION.—

(1) IN GENERAL.—The United States Courts of Appeals (other than the United States Court of Appeals for the Federal Circuit) shall have exclusive jurisdiction to review the decisions of the Tax Court, except as provided in section 1254 of Title 28 of the United States Code, in the same manner and to the same extent as decisions of the district courts in civil actions tried without a jury; and the judgment of any such court shall be final, except that it shall be subject to review by the Supreme Court of the United States upon certiorari, in the manner provided in section 1254 of Title 28 of the United States Code.

(2) INTERLOCUTORY ORDERS.—

(A) IN GENERAL.—When any judge of the Tax Court includes in an interlocutory order a statement that a controlling question of law is involved with respect to which there is a substantial ground for difference of opinion and that an immediate appeal from that order may materially advance the ultimate termination of the litigation, the United States Court of Appeals may, in its discretion, permit an appeal to be taken from such order, if application is made to it within 10 days after the entry of such order. Neither the application for nor the granting of an appeal under this paragraph shall stay proceedings in the Tax Court, unless a stay is ordered by a judge of the Tax Court or by the United States Court of Appeals which has jurisdiction of the appeal or a judge of that court.

(B) ORDER TREATED AS TAX COURT DECISION.—For purposes of subsections (b) and (c), an order described in this paragraph shall be treated as a decision of the Tax Court.

(C) VENUE FOR REVIEW OF SUBSEQUENT PROCEEDING.—If a United States Court of Appeals permits an appeal to be taken from an order described in subparagraph (A), except as provided in subsection (b)(2), any subsequent review of the decision of the Tax Court in the proceeding shall be made by such Court of Appeals.

(3) CERTAIN ORDERS ENTERED UNDER SECTION 6213(a).—An order of the Tax Court which is entered under authority of section 6213(a) and which resolves a proceeding to restrain assessment or collection shall be treated as a decision of the Tax Court for purposes of this section and shall be subject to the same review by the United States Court of Appeals as a similar order of a district court.

Amendments

• 1988, Technical and Miscellaneous Revenue Act of 1988 (P.L. 100-647)

P.L. 100-647, §6243(b):

Amended Code Sec. 7482(a) by adding at the end thereof new paragraph (3). **Effective** for orders entered after 11-10-88.

• 1986, Tax Reform Act of 1986 (P.L. 99-514)

P.L. 99-514, §1558(a):

Amended Code Sec. 7482(a) by adding at the end thereof new paragraph (2). **Effective** for any order of the Tax Court entered after 10-22-86.

P.L. 99-514, §1558(b):

Amended Code Sec. 7482(a) (as in effect before the amendment made by Act Sec. 1558(a)) by moving the text below the subsection heading and 2 ems to the right (so that the left margin of such text is aligned with the left margin of the paragraph (2) added by Act Sec. 1558(a)) and by inserting before such text "(1) In General.—". **Effective** for any order of the Tax Court entered after 10-22-86.

• 1982, Federal Courts Improvement Act of 1982 (P.L. 97-164)

P.L. 97-164, §154:

Amended Code Sec. 7482(a) by inserting "(other than the United States Court of Appeals for the Federal Circuit)" after "United States Court of Appeals". For an explanation of the effect of this change on pending cases, see the historical comment for P.L. 97-164, Act Sec. 403, following Code Sec. 6110(i). **Effective** 10-1-82.

[Sec. 7482(b)]

(b) VENUE.—

(1) IN GENERAL.—Except as otherwise provided in paragraphs (2) and (3), such decisions may be reviewed by the United States court of appeals for the circuit in which is located—

(A) in the case of a petitioner seeking redetermination of tax liability other than a corporation, the legal residence of the petitioner,

(B) in the case of a corporation seeking redetermination of tax liability, the principal place of business or principal office or agency of the corporation, or, if it has no principal place of business or principal office or agency in any judicial circuit, then the office to which was made the return of the tax in respect of which the liability arises,

(C) in the case of a person seeking a declaratory decision under section 7476, the principal place of business, or principal office or agency of the employer,

(D) in the case of an organization seeking a declaratory decision under section 7428, the principal office or agency of the organization,

(E) in the case of a petition under section 6234, the principal place of business of the partnership,

(F) in the case of a petition under section 6015(e), the legal residence of the petitioner, or

(G) in the case of a petition under section 6320 or 6330—

(i) the legal residence of the petitioner if the petitioner is an individual, and

(ii) the principal place of business or principal office or agency if the petitioner is an entity other than an individual.

If for any reason no subparagraph of the preceding sentence applies, then such decisions may be reviewed by the Court of Appeals for the District of Columbia. For purposes of this paragraph, the legal residence, principal place of business, or principal office or agency referred to herein shall be determined as of the time the petition seeking redetermination of tax liability was filed with the Tax Court or as of the time the petition seeking a declaratory decision under section 7428 or 7476 or the petition under section 6234 was filed with the Tax Court.

(2) BY AGREEMENT.—Notwithstanding the provisions of paragraph (1), such decisions may be reviewed by any United States Court of Appeals which may be designated by the Secretary and the taxpayer by stipulation in writing.

(3) DECLARATORY JUDGMENT ACTIONS RELATING TO STATUS OF CERTAIN GOVERNMENTAL OBLIGATIONS.—In the case of any decision of the Tax Court in a proceeding under section 7478, such decision may only be reviewed by the Court of Appeals for the District of Columbia.

Amendments

• 2015, Protecting Americans from Tax Hikes Act of 2015 (P.L. 114-113)

P.L. 114-113, §423(a)(1)-(3), Div. Q:

Amended Code Sec. 7482(b)(1) [as amended by P.L. 114-74] by striking "or" at the end of subparagraph (D), by striking the period at the end of subparagraph (E), and by inserting after subparagraph (E) new subparagraphs (F)-(G). **Effective** for petitions filed after 12-18-2015. For a special rule, see Act Sec. 423(b)(2), below.

P.L. 114-113, §423(b)(2), Div. Q, provides:

(2) EFFECT ON EXISTING PROCEEDINGS.—Nothing in this section shall be construed to create any inference with respect to the application of section 7482 of the Internal Revenue Code of 1986 with respect to court proceedings filed on or before the date of the enactment of this Act.

• 2015, Bipartisan Budget Act of 2015 (P.L. 114-74)

P.L. 114-74, §1101(f)(13)(A)-(C):

Amended Code Sec. 7482(b)(1) by striking "section 6226, 6228[(a)], 6247, or 6252" and inserting "section 6234" in subparagraph (E), by striking subparagraph (F), by striking "or" at the end of subparagraph (E) and inserting a period, and by inserting "or" at the end of subparagraph (D), and by striking "section 6226, 6228(a), or 6234(c)" in the last sentence and inserting "section 6234". **Effective** generally for returns filed for partnership tax years beginning after 12-31-2017. For a special rule, see Act Sec. 1101(g)(4), below. Prior to being stricken, Code Sec. 7482(b)(1)(F) read as follows:

(F) in the case of a petition under section 6234(c)—

(i) the legal residence of the petitioner if the petitioner is not a corporation, and

(ii) the place or office applicable under subparagraph (B) if the petitioner is a corporation.

P.L. 114-74, §1101(g)(4), provides:

(4) ELECTION.—A partnership may elect (at such time and in such form and manner as the Secretary of the Treasury may prescribe) for the amendments made by this section (other than the election under section 6221(b) of such Code (as added by this Act)) to apply to any return of the partnership filed for partnership taxable years beginning after the date of the enactment of this Act and before January 1, 2018.

• 1997, Taxpayer Relief Act of 1997 (P.L. 105-34)

P.L. 105-34, §1222(b)(3):

Amended Code Sec. 7482(b)(1)(E) by striking "or 6228(a)" and inserting ", 6228(a), 6247, or 6252". **Effective** for partnership tax years beginning after 12-31-97 [**effective** date changed by P.L. 105-206, §6012(e)].

P.L. 105-34, §1239(d)(1):

Amended Code Sec. 7482(b)(1) by striking "or" at the end of subparagraph (D), by striking the period at the end of subparagraph (E) and inserting ", or", and by inserting after subparagraph (E) a new subparagraph (F). **Effective** for partnership tax years ending after 8-5-97.

P.L. 105-34, §1239(d)(2):

Amended Code Sec. 7482(b)(1) by striking "or 6228(a)" in the last sentence and inserting ", 6228(a), or 6234(c)". **Effective** for partnership tax years ending after 8-5-97.

• 1986, Tax Reform Act of 1986 (P.L. 99-514)

P.L. 99-514, §1810(g)(2):

Amended Code Sec. 7482(b)(1) by striking out "section 7428, 7476 or 7477" and inserting in lieu thereof "section 7428 or 7476". **Effective** as if included in the provision of P.L. 98-369 to which it relates.

P.L. 99-514, §1899A(60):

Amended Code Sec. 7482(b)(1)(E) by striking out "partnership," and inserting in lieu thereof "partnership.". **Effective** 10-22-86.

• 1984, Deficit Reduction Act of 1984 (P.L. 98-369)

P.L. 98-369, §131(e)(2)(A):

Amended Code Sec. 7482(b)(1) by striking out subparagraph (D) and by redesignating subparagraphs (E) and (F) as subparagraphs (D) and (E), respectively. **Effective** for transfers or exchanges after 12-31-84, in tax years ending after such date. Special rules appear in Act Sec. 131(g)(2) and (3) following Code Sec. 367. Prior to amendment, subparagraph (D) read as follows:

(D) in the case of a person seeking a declaratory judgment under section 7477, the legal residence of such person if such person is not a corporation, or the principal place of business or principal office or agency of such person if such person is a corporation,

• 1982, Tax Equity and Fiscal Responsibility Act of 1982 (P.L. 97-248)

P.L. 97-248, §402(c)(15):

Amended Code Sec. 7482(b) by striking out "or" at the end of paragraph (D), by striking out the period at the end of subparagraph (E) and inserting ", or", by adding a new subparagraph (F), and by inserting ", or the petition under section 6226 or 6228(a)," after "or 7477". **Effective** for partnership tax years beginning after 9-3-82 and also to partnership tax years ending after that date if the partnership, each partner, and each indirect partner requests such application and the Secretary or his delegate consents to such application.

• 1978, Revenue Act of 1978 (P.L. 95-600)

P.L. 95-600, §336(c)(1)(A), (B):

Amended Code Sec. 7482(b)(1) by striking out "provided in paragraph (2)" and inserting in lieu thereof "provided in paragraphs (2) and (3)", and added Code Sec. 7482(b)(3). **Effective** for requests for determinations made after 12-31-78.

• 1976, Tax Reform Act of 1976 (P.L. 94-455)

P.L. 94-455, §1042(d)(2)(A):

Amended Code Sec. 7482(b)(1) by striking out "or" at the end of subparagraph (B), by substituting ", or" for the period at the end of subparagraph (C), and by adding a new subparagraph (D). For the **effective** date, see Act Sec. 1042(e)(1), below.

P.L. 94-455, §1042(e)(1), provides:

(1) The amendments made by this section (other than by subsection (d)) shall apply to transfers beginning after October 9, 1975, and to sales, exchanges, and distributions taking place after such date. The amendments made by subsection (d) shall apply with respect to pleadings filed with the Tax Court after the date of the enactment of this Act [October 4, 1976] but only with respect to transfers beginning after October 9, 1975.

P.L. 94-455, §1306(b)(4):

Amended Code Sec. 7482(b) by striking out "or" at the end of subparagraph (C), by substituting ", or" for the period at the end of subparagraph (D), and by adding Sec. 7482(b)(1)(E).

P.L. 94-455, §1306(b)(5):

Amended the last sentence of Code Sec. 7482(b)(1). Prior to amendment, the last sentence of Sec. 7482(b)(1) read as follows:

If for any reason subparagraph (A), (B) and (C) do not apply, then such decisions may be reviewed by the Court of Appeals for the District of Columbia. For purposes of this paragraph, the legal residence, principal place of business, or principal office or agency referred to herein shall be determined as of the time the petition seeking redetermination of tax liability was filed with the Tax Court or as of the time the petition seeking a declaratory decision under section 7476 was filed with the Tax Court.

P.L. 94-455, §1306(c), provides:

(c) EFFECTIVE DATE.—The amendments made by this section shall apply with respect to pleadings filed with the United States Tax Court, the district court of the United States for the District of Columbia, or the United States Court of Claims more than 6 months after the date of the enactment of this Act [October 4, 1976] but only with respect to determinations (or requests for determinations) made after January 1, 1976.

P.L. 94-455, §1906(b)(13)(A):

Amended 1954 Code by substituting "Secretary" for "Secretary or his delegate" each place it appeared. **Effective** 2-1-77.

• 1974, Employee Retirement Income Security Act of 1974 (P.L. 93-406)

P.L. 93-406, §1041(b)(3):

Amended Code Sec. 7482(b)(1). **Effective** to pleadings filed after 9-2-75. Prior to amendment, Code Sec. 7482(b)(1) read as follows:

"(b) Venue.—

"(1) In general.—Except as otherwise provided in paragraph (2), such decisions may be reviewed by the United States court of appeals for the circuit in which is located—

"(A) in the case of a petitioner seeking redetermination of tax liability other than a corporation, the legal residence of the petitioner,

"(B) in the case of a corporation seeking redetermination of tax liability, the principal place of business or principal office or agency of the corporation, or, if it has no principal place of business or principal office or agency in any judicial circuit, then the office to which was made the return of the tax in respect of which the liability arises.

If for any reason neither subparagraph (A) nor (B) applies, then such decisions may be reviewed by the Court of Appeals for the District of Columbia. For purposes of this paragraph, the legal residence, principal place of business, or principal office or agency referred to herein shall be determined as of the time the petition seeking redetermination of tax liability was filed with the Tax Court."

• 1966 (P.L. 89-713)

P.L. 89-713, §3(c):

Amended Code Sec. 7482(b)(1). **Effective** as to all decisions of the Tax Court entered after 11-2-66. Prior to amendment, Sec. 7482(b)(1) read as follows:

"(1) In general.—Except as provided in paragraph (2), such decisions may be reviewed by the United States Court of Appeals for the circuit in which is located the office to which was made the return of the tax in respect of which the liability arises, or, if no return was made, then by the United States Court of Appeals for the District of Columbia."

[Sec. 7482(c)]

(c) POWERS.—

(1) TO AFFIRM, MODIFY, OR REVERSE.—Upon such review, such courts shall have power to affirm or, if the decision of the Tax Court is not in accordance with law, to modify or to reverse the decision of the Tax Court, with or without remanding the case for a rehearing, as justice may require.

(2) TO MAKE RULES.—Rules for review of decisions of the Tax Court shall be those prescribed by the Supreme Court under section 2072 of title 28 of the United States Code.

(3) TO REQUIRE ADDITIONAL SECURITY.—Nothing in section 7483 shall be construed as relieving the petitioner from making or filing such undertakings as the court may require as a condition of or in connection with the review.

(4) TO IMPOSE PENALTIES.—The United States Court of Appeals and the Supreme Court shall have the power to require the taxpayer to pay to the United States a penalty in any case where the decision of the Tax Court is affirmed and it appears that the appeal was instituted or maintained primarily for delay or that the taxpayer's position in the appeal is frivolous or groundless.

Amendments

• 1989, Omnibus Budget Reconciliation Act of 1989 (P.L. 101-239)

P.L. 101-239, §7731(b):

Amended Code Sec. 7482(c)(4). **Effective** for positions taken after 12-31-89, in proceedings which are pending on, or commenced after such date. Prior to amendment, Code Sec. 7482(c)(4) read as follows:

(4) TO IMPOSE DAMAGES.—The United States Court of Appeals and the Supreme Court shall have power to impose damages in any case where the decision of the Tax Court is

affirmed and it appears that the notice of appeal was filed merely for delay.

• 1969, Tax Reform Act of 1969 (P.L. 91-172)

P.L. 91-172, §960(h)(2):

Amended Code Sec. 7482(c)(2) by substituting the phrase "section 2072" for the phrase "section 2074" and by deleting the second sentence, which read as follows: "Until such rules become effective the rules adopted under authority of section 1141(c)(2) of the Internal Revenue Code of 1939 shall remain in effect." (See amendatory note under Code Sec. 7483, below.) Also amended Code Sec. 7482(c)(4) by substituting the phrase "notice of appeal" for the word "petition." **Effective** 1-29-70.

[Sec. 7483]

SEC. 7483. NOTICE OF APPEAL.

Review of a decision of the Tax Court shall be obtained by filing a notice of appeal with the clerk of the Tax Court within 90 days after the decision of the Tax Court is entered. If a timely notice of appeal is filed by one party, any other party may take an appeal by filing a notice of appeal within 120 days after the decision of the Tax Court is entered.

Amendments

• 1969, Tax Reform Act of 1969 (P.L. 91-172)

P.L. 91-172, §959(a):

Amended Code Sec. 7483. **Effective** 1-29-70. However, in the case of any decision of the Tax Court entered before January 29, 1970, the United States Courts of Appeal shall have jurisdiction to hear an appeal from such decision, if such appeal was filed within the time prescribed by Rule 13(a) of the Federal Rules of Appellate Procedure or by section 7483 of the Internal Revenue Code of 1954, as in effect at the time the decision of the Tax Court was entered. Prior to amendment, Sec. 7483 read as follows:

SEC. 7483. PETITION FOR REVIEW.

The decision of the Tax Court may be reviewed by a United States Court of Appeals as provided in section 7482 if a petition for such review is filed by either the Secretary (or his delegate) or the taxpayer within 3 months after the decision is rendered. If, however, a petition for such review is so filed by one party to the proceeding, a petition for review of the decision of the Tax Court may be filed by any other party to the proceeding within 4 months after such decision is rendered.

* * *

Subchapter E—Burden of Proof

* * *

[Sec. 7491]

SEC. 7491. BURDEN OF PROOF.

[Sec. 7491(a)]

(a) BURDEN SHIFTS WHERE TAXPAYER PRODUCES CREDIBLE EVIDENCE.—

(1) GENERAL RULE.—If, in any court proceeding, a taxpayer introduces credible evidence with respect to any factual issue relevant to ascertaining the liability of the taxpayer for any tax imposed by subtitle A or B, the Secretary shall have the burden of proof with respect to such issue.

(2) LIMITATIONS.—Paragraph (1) shall apply with respect to an issue only if—

(A) the taxpayer has complied with the requirements under this title to substantiate any item;

(B) the taxpayer has maintained all records required under this title and has cooperated with reasonable requests by the Secretary for witnesses, information, documents, meetings, and interviews; and

(C) in the case of a partnership, corporation, or trust, the taxpayer is described in section 7430(c)(4)(A)(ii).

Subparagraph (C) shall not apply to any qualified revocable trust (as defined in section 645(b)(1)) with respect to liability for tax for any taxable year ending after the date of the decedent's death and before the applicable date (as defined in section 645(b)(2)).

(3) COORDINATION.—Paragraph (1) shall not apply to any issue if any other provision of this title provides for a specific burden of proof with respect to such issue.

Amendments

• 1998, Tax and Trade Relief Extension Act of 1998 (P.L. 105-277)

P.L. 105-277, §4002(b):

Amended Code Sec. 7491(a)(2) by adding at the end a new flush sentence. **Effective** as if included in the provision of P.L. 105-206 to which it relates [generally effective for court proceedings arising in connection with examinations commencing after 7-22-98.—CCH].

[Sec. 7491(b)]

(b) USE OF STATISTICAL INFORMATION ON UNRELATED TAXPAYERS.—In the case of an individual taxpayer, the Secretary shall have the burden of proof in any court proceeding with respect to any item of income which was reconstructed by the Secretary solely through the use of statistical information on unrelated taxpayers.

[Sec. 7491(c)]

(c) PENALTIES.—Notwithstanding any other provision of this title, the Secretary shall have the burden of production in any court proceeding with respect to the liability of any individual for any penalty, addition to tax, or additional amount imposed by this title.

Amendments

• 1998, IRS Restructuring and Reform Act of 1998 (P.L. 105-206)

P.L. 105-206, §3001(a):

Amended Chapter 76 by adding at the end a new Code Sec. 7491. **Effective**, generally, for court proceedings arising in connection with examinations commencing after 7-22-98. For a special rule, see Act Sec. 3001(c)(2), below.

P.L. 105-206, §3001(c)(2), provides:

(2) TAXABLE PERIODS OR EVENTS AFTER DATE OF ENACTMENT.—In any case in which there is no examination, such amendments shall apply to court proceedings arising in connection with taxable periods or events beginning or occurring after such date of enactment.

CHAPTER 77—MISCELLANEOUS PROVISIONS

* * *

* * *

[Sec. 7502]

SEC. 7502. TIMELY MAILING TREATED AS TIMELY FILING AND PAYING.

[Sec. 7502(a)]

(a) GENERAL RULE.—

(1) DATE OF DELIVERY.—If any return, claim, statement, or other document required to be filed, or any payment required to be made, within a prescribed period or on or before a prescribed date under authority of any provision of the internal revenue laws is, after such period or such date, delivered by United States mail to the agency, officer, or office with which such return, claim, statement, or other document is required to be filed, or to which such payment is required to be made, the date of the United States postmark stamped on the cover in which such return, claim, statement, or other document, or payment, is mailed shall be deemed to be the date of delivery or the date of payment, as the case may be.

(2) MAILING REQUIREMENTS.—This subsection shall apply only if—

(A) the postmark date falls within the prescribed period or on or before the prescribed date—

(i) for the filing (including any extension granted for such filing) of the return, claim, statement, or other document, or

(ii) for making the payment (including any extension granted for making such payment), and

(B) the return, claim, statement, or other document, or payment was, within the time prescribed in subparagraph (A), deposited in the mail in the United States in an envelope or other appropriate wrapper, postage prepaid, properly addressed to the agency, officer, or office with which the return, claim, statement, or other document is required to be filed, or to which such payment is required to be made.

[Sec. 7502(b)]

(b) POSTMARKS.—This section shall apply in the case of postmarks not made by the United States Postal Service only if and to the extent provided by regulations prescribed by the Secretary.

Amendments

• 1976, Tax Reform Act of 1976 (P.L. 94-455)

P.L. 94-455, §1906(b)(13)(A):

Amended 1954 Code by substituting "Secretary" for "Secretary or his delegate" each place it appeared. **Effective** 2-1-77.

P.L. 94-455, §1906(a)(49):

Substituted "United States Postal Service" for "United States Post Office" in Code Sec. 7502(b). **Effective** 2-1-77.

[Sec. 7502(c)]

(c) REGISTERED AND CERTIFIED MAILING; ELECTRONIC FILING.—

(1) REGISTERED MAIL.—For purposes of this section, if any return, claim, statement, or other document, or payment, is sent by United States registered mail—

(A) such registration shall be prima facie evidence that the return, claim, statement, or other document was delivered to the agency, officer, or office to which addressed; and

(B) the date of registration shall be deemed the postmark date.

(2) CERTIFIED MAIL; ELECTRONIC FILING.—The Secretary is authorized to provide by regulations the extent to which the provisions of paragraph (1) with respect to prima facie evidence of delivery and the postmark date shall apply to certified mail and electronic filing.

Amendments

• 1998, IRS Restructuring and Reform Act of 1998 (P.L. 105-206)

P.L. 105-206, §2003(b):

Amended Code Sec. 7502(c). **Effective** 7-22-98. Prior to amendment, Code Sec. 7502(c) read as follows:

(c) REGISTERED AND CERTIFIED MAILING.—

(1) REGISTERED MAIL.—For purposes of this section, if any such return, claim, statement, or other document, or payment, is sent by United States registered mail—

(A) such registration shall be prima facie evidence that the return, claim, statement, or other document was delivered to the agency, officer, or office to which addressed, and

(B) the date of registration shall be deemed the postmark date.

(2) CERTIFIED MAIL.—The Secretary is authorized to provide by regulations the extent to which the provisions of paragraph (1) of this subsection with respect to prima facie evidence of delivery and the postmark date shall apply to certified mail.

• 1976, Tax Reform Act of 1976 (P.L. 94-455)

P.L. 94-455, §1906(b)(13)(A):

Amended 1954 Code by substituting "Secretary" for "Secretary or his delegate" each place it appeared. **Effective** 2-1-77.

[Sec. 7502(d)]

(d) EXCEPTIONS.—This section shall not apply with respect to—

(1) the filing of a document in, or the making of a payment to, any court other than the Tax Court,

(2) currency or other medium of payment unless actually received and accounted for, or

(3) returns, claims, statements, or other documents, or payments, which are required under any provision of the internal revenue laws or the regulations thereunder to be delivered by any method other than by mailing.

* * *

[Sec. 7503]

SEC. 7503. TIME FOR PERFORMANCE OF ACTS WHERE LAST DAY FALLS ON SATURDAY, SUNDAY, OR LEGAL HOLIDAY.

When the last day prescribed under authority of the internal revenue laws for performing any act falls on Saturday, Sunday, or a legal holiday, the performance of such act shall be considered timely if it is performed on the next succeeding day which is not a Saturday, Sunday, or a legal holiday. For purposes of this section, the last day for the performance of any act shall be determined by including any authorized extension of time; the term "legal holiday" means a legal holiday in the District of Columbia; and in the case of any return, statement, or other document required to be filed, or any other act required under authority of the internal revenue laws to be performed, at any office of the Secretary, or at any other office of the United States or any agency thereof, located outside the District of Columbia but within an internal revenue district, the term "legal holiday" also means a Statewide legal holiday in the State where such office is located.

Amendments

• 1976, Tax Reform Act of 1976 (P.L. 94-455)

P.L. 94-455, §1906(b)(13)(A):

Amended 1954 Code by substituting "Secretary" for "Secretary or his delegate" each place it appeared. **Effective** 2-1-77.

[Sec. 7504]

SEC. 7504. FRACTIONAL PARTS OF A DOLLAR.

The Secretary may by regulations provide that in the allowance of any amount as a credit or refund, or in the collection of any amount as a deficiency or underpayment, of any tax imposed by this title, a fractional part of a dollar shall be disregarded, unless it amounts to 50 cents or more, in which case it shall be increased to 1 dollar.

Amendments

• 1976, Tax Reform Act of 1976 (P.L. 94-455)

P.L. 94-455, §1906(b)(13)(A):

Amended 1954 Code by substituting "Secretary" for "Secretary or his delegate" each place it appeared. **Effective** 2-1-77.

* * *

[Sec. 7508]

SEC. 7508. TIME FOR PERFORMING CERTAIN ACTS POSTPONED BY REASON OF SERVICE IN COMBAT ZONE OR CONTINGENCY OPERATION.

[Sec. 7508(a)]

(a) TIME TO BE DISREGARDED.—In the case of an individual serving in the Armed Forces of the United States, or serving in support of such Armed Forces, in an area designated by the President of the United States by Executive order as a "combat zone" for purposes of section 112, or when deployed outside the United States away from the individual's permanent duty station while participating in an operation designated by the Secretary of Defense as a contingency operation (as defined in section 101(a)(13) of title 10, United States Code) or which became such a contingency operation by operation of law, at any time during the period designated by the President by Executive order as the period of combatant activities in such zone for purposes of such section or at any time during the period of such contingency operation, or hospitalized as a result of injury received while serving in such an area or operation during such time, the period of service in such area or operation, plus the period of continuous qualified hospitalization attributable to such injury, and the next 180 days thereafter, shall be disregarded in determining, under the internal revenue laws, in respect of any tax liability (including any interest, penalty, additional amount, or addition to the tax) of such individual—

(1) Whether any of the following acts was performed within the time prescribed therefor:

(A) Filing any return of income, estate, gift, employment, or excise tax;

(B) Payment of any income, estate, gift, employment, or excise tax or any installment thereof or of any other liability to the United States in respect thereof;

(C) Filing a petition with the Tax Court, or filing a notice of appeal from a decision of the Tax Court;

(D) Allowance of a credit or refund of any tax;

(E) Filing a claim for credit or refund of any tax;

(F) Bringing suit upon any such claim for credit or refund;

(G) Assessment of any tax;

(H) Giving or making any notice or demand for the payment of any tax, or with respect to any liability to the United States in respect of any tax;

(I) Collection, by the Secretary, by levy or otherwise, of the amount of any liability in respect of any tax;

(J) Bringing suit by the United States, or any officer on its behalf, in respect of any liability in respect of any tax or in respect of any erroneous refund; and

(K) Any other act required or permitted under the internal revenue laws specified by the Secretary;

(2) The amount of any credit or refund; and

(3) Any certification of a seriously delinquent tax debt under section 7345.

Amendments

• 2021, Infrastructure Investment and Jobs Act (P.L. 117-58)

P.L. 117-58, §80502(a)(1)-(2), Div. H:

Amended Code Sec. 7508(a)(1) by striking subparagraph (C) and inserting a new subparagraph (C), and by inserting "or in respect of any erroneous refund" after "any tax" in subparagraph (J). **Effective** for any period for performing an act which has not expired before 11-15-2021. Prior to being stricken, Code Sec. 7508(a)(1)(C) read as follows:

(C) Filing a petition with the Tax Court for redetermination of a deficiency, or for review of a decision rendered by the Tax Court;

• 2017, Tax Cuts and Jobs Act (P.L. 115-97)

P.L. 115-97, §11026, provides:

For a special rule, see Act Sec. 11026 in the amendment notes for Code Sec. 112(c).

• 2015, Fixing America's Surface Transportation Act (P.L. 114-94)

P.L. 114-94, §32101(d):

Amended Code Sec. 7508(a) by striking the period at the end of paragraph (2) and inserting "; and", and by adding at the end a new paragraph (3). **Effective** 12-4-2015.

• 2005, Katrina Emergency Tax Relief Act of 2005 (P.L. 109-73)

P.L. 109-73, §403(a):

Amended Code Sec. 7508(a)(1)(A)-(B). **Effective** for any period for performing an act which has not expired before 8-25-2005. Prior to amendment, Code Sec. 7508(a)(1)(A)-(B) read as follows:

(A) Filing any return of income, estate, or gift tax (except income tax withheld at source and income tax imposed by subtitle C or any law superseded thereby);

(B) Payment of any income, estate, or gift tax (except income tax withheld at source and income tax imposed by subtitle C or any law superseded thereby) or any installment thereof or of any other liability to the United States in respect thereof;

P.L. 109-73, §403(b) [repealed by P.L. 109-135, §201(b)(4)(B)], provides:

(b) APPLICATION WITH RESPECT TO HURRICANE KATRINA.—In the case of any taxpayer determined by the Secretary of the Treasury to be affected by the Presidentially declared disaster relating to Hurricane Katrina, any relief provided by the Secretary of the Treasury under section 7508A of the Internal Revenue Code of 1986 shall be for a period ending not earlier than February 28, 2006, and shall be treated as applying to the filing of returns relating to, and the payment of, employment and excise taxes.

• 2003, Military Family Tax Relief Act of 2003 (P.L. 108-121)

P.L. 108-121, §104(a)(1)-(4):

Amended Code Sec. 7508(a) by inserting ", or when deployed outside the United States away from the individual's permanent duty station while participating in an operation designated by the Secretary of Defense as a contingency operation (as defined in section 101(a)(13) of title 10, United States Code) or which became such a contingency operation by operation of law" after "section 112", by inserting in the first sentence "or at any time during the period of such contingency operation" after "for purposes of such section", by inserting "or operation" after "such an area", and by inserting "or operation" after "such area". **Effective** for any period for performing an act which has not expired before 11-11-2003.

P.L. 108-121, §104(b)(2):

Amended the heading for Code Sec. 7508 by inserting "OR CONTINGENCY OPERATION" after "COMBAT ZONE". **Effective** for any period for performing an act which has not expired before 11-11-2003.

• 2002, Victims of Terrorism Tax Relief Act of 2001 (P.L. 107-134)

P.L. 107-134, §112(b):

Amended Code Sec. 7508(a)(1)(K) by striking "in regulations prescribed under this section" following "specified". **Effective** for disasters and terroristic or military actions occurring on or after 9-11-2001, with respect to any action of the Secretary of the Treasury, the Secretary of Labor, or the Pension Benefit Guaranty Corporation occurring on or after 10-23-2002.

• 1999 (P.L. 106-21)

P.L. 106-21, §1(a)(8)-(d)(1), provides:

SECTION 1. AVAILABILITY OF CERTAIN TAX BENEFITS FOR SERVICES AS PART OF OPERATION ALLIED FORCE.

(a) GENERAL RULE.—For purposes of the following provisions of the Internal Revenue Code of 1986, a qualified hazardous duty area shall be treated in the same manner as if it were a combat zone (as determined under section 112 of such Code):

* * *

(8) Section 7508 (relating to time for performing certain acts postponed by reason of service in combat zone).

(b) QUALIFIED HAZARDOUS DUTY AREA.—For purposes of this section, the term "qualified hazardous duty area" means any area of the Federal Republic of Yugoslavia (Serbia/Montenegro), Albania, the Adriatic Sea, and the northern Ionian Sea (above the 39th parallel) during the period (which includes the date of the enactment of this Act) that any member of the Armed Forces of the United States is entitled to special pay under section 310 of title 37, United States Code (relating to special pay: duty subject to hostile fire or imminent danger) for services performed in such area.

(c) SPECIAL RULE FOR SECTION 7508.—Solely for purposes of applying section 7508 of the Internal Revenue Code of 1986, in the case of an individual who is performing services as part of Operation Allied Force outside the United States while deployed away from such individual's permanent duty station, the term "qualified hazardous duty area" includes, during the period for which the entitlement referred to in subsection (b) is in effect, any area in which such services are performed.

(d) EFFECTIVE DATES.—

(1) IN GENERAL.—Except as provided in paragraph (2), this section shall take effect on March 24, 1999.

• 1996 (P.L. 104-117)

P.L. 104-117, §1(a)(8), (b) and (e)(1), provide:

SECTION 1. TREATMENT OF CERTAIN INDIVIDUALS PERFORMING SERVICES IN CERTAIN HAZARDOUS DUTY AREAS.

(a) GENERAL RULE.—For purposes of the following provisions of the Internal Revenue Code of 1986, a qualified hazardous duty area shall be treated in the same manner as if it were a combat zone (as determined under section 112 of such Code):

* * *

(8) Section 7508 (relating to time for performing certain acts postponed by reason of service in combat zone).

* * *

(b) QUALIFIED HAZARDOUS DUTY AREA.—For purposes of this section, the term "qualified hazardous duty area" means Bosnia and Herzegovina, Croatia, or Macedonia, if as of the date of the enactment of this section any member of the Armed Forces of the United States is entitled to special pay under section 310 of title 37, United States Code (relating to special pay; duty subject to hostile fire or imminent danger) for services performed in such country. Such term includes any such country only during the period such entitlement is in effect. Solely for purposes of applying section 7508 of the Internal Revenue Code of 1986, in the case of an individual who is performing services as part of Operation Joint Endeavor outside the United States while deployed away from such individual's permanent duty station, the term "qualified hazardous duty area" includes, during the period for which such entitlement is in effect, any area in which such services are performed.

* * *

(e) EFFECTIVE DATE.—

(1) IN GENERAL.—Except as provided in paragraph (2), the provisions of and amendments made by this section shall take effect on November 21, 1995.

• 1991 (P.L. 102-3)

P.L. 102-2, §1(b)(2):

Amended Code Sec. 7508(a)(2) by striking "(including interest)" after "credit or refund". **Effective** 8-2-90.

P.L. 102-2, §1(c)(1)(A):

Amended Code Sec. 7508(a) by striking "outside the United States" the first place it appears after "or hospitalized", and by striking "the period of continuous hospitalization outside the United States" and inserting "the period of continuous qualified hospitalization". **Effective** 8-2-90.

• 1976, Tax Reform Act of 1976 (P.L. 94-455)

P.L. 94-455, §1906(a)(51):

Substituted "SERVICE IN COMBAT ZONE" for "WAR" in the heading of Code Sec. 7508 and substituted "United States" for "States of the Union and the District of Columbia" in Sec. 7508(a). **Effective** 2-1-77.

P.L. 94-455, §1906(b)(13)(A):

Amended 1954 Code by substituting "Secretary" for "Secretary or his delegate" each place it appeared. **Effective** 2-1-77.

[Sec. 7508(b)]

(b) SPECIAL RULE FOR OVERPAYMENTS.—

(1) IN GENERAL.—Subsection (a) shall not apply for purposes of determining the amount of interest on any overpayment of tax.

(2) SPECIAL RULES.—If an individual is entitled to the benefits of subsection (a) with respect to any return and such return is timely filed (determined after the application of such subsection), subsections (b)(3) and (e) of section 6611 shall not apply.

Amendments

• 1991 (P.L. 102-2)

P.L. 102-2, §1(b)(1):

Amended Code Sec. 7508 by redesignating subsections (b), (c), and (d) as subsections (c), (d), and (e), respectively, and by inserting after subsection (a) new subsection (b). **Effective** 8-2-90.

* * *

[Sec. 7508(e)]

(e) EXCEPTIONS.—

(1) TAX IN JEOPARDY; CASES UNDER TITLE 11 OF THE UNITED STATES CODE AND RECEIVERSHIPS; AND TRANSFERRED ASSETS.—Notwithstanding the provisions of subsection (a), any action or proceeding authorized by section 6851 (regardless of the taxable year for which the tax arose), chapter 70, or 71, as well as any other action or proceeding authorized by law in connection therewith, may be taken, begun, or prosecuted. In any other case in which the Secretary determines that collection of the amount of any assessment would be jeopardized by delay, the provisions of subsection (a) shall not operate to stay collection of such amount by levy or otherwise as authorized by law. There shall be excluded from any amount assessed or collected pursuant to this paragraph the amount of interest, penalty, additional amount, and addition to the tax, if any, in respect of the period disregarded under subsection (a). In any case to which this paragraph relates, if the Secretary is required to give any notice to or make any demand upon any person, such requirement shall be deemed to be satisfied if the notice or demand is prepared and signed, in any case in which the address of such person last known to the Secretary is in an area for which United States post offices under instructions of the Postmaster General are not, by reason of the combatant activities, accepting mail for delivery at the time the notice or demand is signed. In such case the notice or demand shall be deemed to have been given or made upon the date it is signed.

(2) ACTION TAKEN BEFORE ASCERTAINMENT OF RIGHT TO BENEFITS.—The assessment or collection of any internal revenue tax or of any liability to the United States in respect of any internal revenue tax, or any action or proceeding by or on behalf of the United States in connection therewith, may be made, taken, begun, or prosecuted in accordance with law, without regard to the provisions of subsection (a), unless prior to such assessment, collection, action, or proceeding it is ascertained that the person concerned is entitled to the benefits of subsection (a).

(3) COLLECTION PERIOD AFTER ASSESSMENT NOT EXTENDED AS A RESULT OF HOSPITALIZATION.—With respect to any period of continuous qualified hospitalization described in subsection (a) and the next 180 days thereafter, subsection (a) shall not apply in the application of section 6502.

Amendments

• 2015, Protecting Americans from Tax Hikes Act of 2015 (P.L. 114-113)

P.L. 114-113, §309(a), Div. Q:

Amended Code Sec. 7508(e) by adding at the end a new paragraph (3). **Effective** for taxes assessed before, on, or after 12-18-2015.

• 1991 (P.L. 102-2)

P.L. 102-2, §1(b)(1):

Redesignated Code Sec. 7508(d) as Code Sec. 7508(e). **Effective** 8-2-90.

• 1980, Bankruptcy Tax Act of 1980 (P.L. 96-589)

P.L. 96-589, §6(i)(14):

Amended the heading of Code Sec. 7508(d)(1) by striking out "BANKRUPTCY AND RECEIVERSHIPS" and inserting in lieu thereof "CASES UNDER TITLE 11 OF THE UNITED STATES CODE AND RECEIVERSHIPS". **Effective** 10-1-79, but inapplicable to any proceeding under the Bankruptcy Act commenced before that date.

• 1976, Tax Reform Act of 1976 (P.L. 94-455)

P.L. 94-455, §1906(b)(13)(A):

Amended 1954 Code by substituting "Secretary" for "Secretary or his delegate" each place it appeared. **Effective** 2-1-77.

• 1975 (P.L. 93-597)

P.L. 93-597, §5(a):

Redesignated former Code Sec. 7508(b) as Code Sec. 7508(d). **Effective** 1-2-75.

* * *

[Sec. 7508A]

SEC. 7508A. AUTHORITY TO POSTPONE CERTAIN DEADLINES BY REASON OF PRESIDENTIALLY DECLARED DISASTER OR TERRORISTIC OR MILITARY ACTIONS.

[Sec. 7508A(a)]

(a) IN GENERAL.—In the case of a taxpayer determined by the Secretary to be affected by a federally declared disaster (as defined by section 165(i)(5)(A)), a significant fire, or a terroristic or military action (as defined in section 692(c)(2)), the Secretary may specify a period of up to 1 year that may be disregarded in determining, under the internal revenue laws, in respect of any tax liability of such taxpayer—

(1) whether any of the acts described in paragraph (1) of section 7508(a) were performed within the time prescribed therefor (determined without regard to extension under any other provision of this subtitle for periods after the date (determined by the Secretary) of such disaster, fire, or action),

(2) the amount of any interest, penalty, additional amount, or addition to the tax for periods after such date, and

(3) the amount of any credit or refund.

Amendments

• 2021, Infrastructure Investment and Jobs Act (P.L. 117-58)

P.L. 117-58, §80504(a)(1), Div. H:

Amended Code Sec. 7508A(a) by inserting ", a significant fire," after "federally declared disaster (as defined in section 165(i)(5)(A))". **Effective** for fires for which assistance is provided after 11-15-2021.

P.L. 117-58, §80504(a)(2), Div. H:

Amended Code Sec. 7508A(a)(1) by inserting", fire," after "disaster" each place it appears. **Effective** for fires for which assistance is provided after 11-15-2021.

P.L. 117-58, §80504(b)(1), Div. H:

Amended the heading for Code Sec. 7508A by striking "PRESIDENTIALLY DECLARED DISASTER" and inserting "FEDERALLY DECLARED DISASTER, SIGNIFICANT FIRE,". **Effective** for fires for which assistance is provided after 11-15-2021.

• 2018, Tax Technical Corrections Act of 2018 (P.L. 115-141)

P.L. 115-141, §401(b)(10)(B), Div. U:

Amended Code Sec. 7508A(a) by striking "section 165(h)(3)(C)(i)" and inserting "section 165(i)(5)(A)". **Effective** 3-23-2018. For a special rule, see Act Sec. 401(e), Div. U, below.

P.L. 115-141, §401(e), Div. U, provides:

(e) GENERAL SAVINGS PROVISION WITH RESPECT TO DEADWOOD PROVISIONS.—If—

(1) any provision amended or repealed by the amendments made by subsection (b) or (d) applied to—

(A) any transaction occurring before the date of the enactment of this Act,

(B) any property acquired before such date of enactment, or

(C) any item of income, loss, deduction, or credit taken into account before such date of enactment, and

(2) the treatment of such transaction, property, or item under such provision would (without regard to the amendments or repeals made by such subsection) affect the liability for tax for periods ending after such date of enactment,

nothing in the amendments or repeals made by this section shall be construed to affect the treatment of such transaction, property, or item for purposes of determining liability for tax for periods ending after such date of enactment.

• 2008, Tax Extenders and Alternative Minimum Tax Relief Act of 2008 (P.L. 110-343)

P.L. 110-343, Division C, §706(a)(2)(D)(vii):

Amended Code Sec. 7508A(a) by striking "Presidentially declared disaster (as defined in section 1033(h)(3))" and inserting "federally declared disaster (as defined by section 165(h)(3)(C)(i))". **Effective** for disasters declared in tax years beginning after 12-31-2007.

• 1997, Taxpayer Relief Act of 1997 (P.L. 105-34)

P.L. 105-34, §911(a):

Amended chapter 77 by inserting after Code Sec. 7508 a new Code Sec. 7508A. **Effective** with respect to any period for performing an act that has not expired before 8-5-97.

[Sec. 7508A(b)]

(b) SPECIAL RULES REGARDING PENSIONS, ETC.—In the case of a pension or other employee benefit plan, or any sponsor, administrator, participant, beneficiary, or other person with respect to such plan, affected by a disaster, fire, or action described in subsection (a), the Secretary may specify a period of up to 1 year which may be disregarded in determining the date by which any action is required or permitted to be completed under this title. No plan shall be treated as failing to be operated in accordance with the terms of the plan solely as the result of disregarding any period by reason of the preceding sentence.

Amendments

• 2021, Infrastructure Investment and Jobs Act (P.L. 117-58)

P.L. 117-58, §80504(a)(2), Div. H:

Amended Code Sec. 7508A(b) by inserting", fire," after "disaster" each place it appears. **Effective** for fires for which assistance is provided after 11-15-2021.

[Sec. 7508A(c)]

(c) SPECIAL RULES FOR OVERPAYMENTS.—The rules of section 7508(b) shall apply for purposes of this section.

Amendments

• 2005, Katrina Emergency Tax Relief Act of 2005 (P.L. 109-73)

P.L. 109-73, §403(b) [repealed by P.L. 109-135, §201(b)(4)(B)], provides:

(b) APPLICATION WITH RESPECT TO HURRICANE KATRINA.—In the case of any taxpayer determined by the Secretary of the Treasury to be affected by the Presidentially declared disaster relating to Hurricane Katrina, any relief provided by the Secretary of the Treasury under section 7508A of the Internal Revenue Code of 1986 shall be for a period ending not earlier than February 28, 2006, and shall be treated as applying to the filing of returns relating to, and the payment of, employment and excise taxes.

• 2002, Victims of Terrorism Tax Relief Act of 2001 (P.L. 107-134)

P.L. 107-134, §112(a):

Amended Code Sec. 7508A. **Effective** for disasters and terroristic or military actions occurring on or after 9-11-2001, with respect to any action of the Secretary of the Treasury, the Secretary of Labor, or the Pension Benefit Guaranty Corporation occurring on or after 1-23-2002. Prior to amendment, Code Sec. 7508A read as follows:

SEC. 7508A. AUTHORITY TO POSTPONE CERTAIN TAX-RELATED DEADLINES BY REASON OF PRESIDENTIALLY DECLARED DISASTER.

(a) IN GENERAL.—In the case of a taxpayer determined by the Secretary to be affected by a Presidentially declared disaster (as defined by section 1033(h)(3), the Secretary may prescribe regulations under which a period of up to 120 days may be disregarded in determining, under the internal revenue laws, in respect of any tax liability (including any penalty, additional amount, or addition to the tax) of such taxpayer—

(1) whether any of the acts described in paragraph (1) of section 7508(a) were performed within the time prescribed therefor, and

(2) the amount of any credit or refund.

(b) INTEREST ON OVERPAYMENTS AND UNDERPAYMENTS.—Subsection (a) shall not apply for the purpose of determining interest on any overpayment or underpayment.

• 2001, Economic Growth and Tax Relief Reconciliation Act of 2001 (P.L. 107-16)

P.L. 107-16, §802(a):

Amended Code Sec. 7508A by striking "90 days" and inserting "120 days". **Effective** 6-7-2001.

P.L. 107-16, §901(a)-(b), as amended by P.L. 111-312, §101(a)(1), provides:

SEC. 901. SUNSET OF PROVISIONS OF ACT.

(a) IN GENERAL.—All provisions of, and amendments made by, this Act shall not apply—

(1) to taxable, plan, or limitation years beginning after December 31, 2012, or

(2) in the case of title V, to estates of decedents dying, gifts made, or generation skipping transfers, after December 31, 2012.

(b) APPLICATION OF CERTAIN LAWS.—The Internal Revenue Code of 1986 and the Employee Retirement Income Security Act of 1974 shall be applied and administered to years, estates, gifts, and transfers described in subsection (a) as if the provisions and amendments described in subsection (a) had never been enacted.

[Sec. 7508A(d)]

(d) MANDATORY 60-DAY EXTENSION.—

(1) IN GENERAL.—In the case of any qualified taxpayer, the period—

(A) beginning on the earliest incident date specified in the declaration to which the disaster area referred to in paragraph (2) relates, and

(B) ending on the date which is 60 days after the later of such earliest incident date described in subparagraph (A) or the date such declaration was issued,

shall be disregarded in determining, under the internal revenue laws, in respect of any tax liability of such qualified taxpayer, whether any of the acts described in subparagraphs (A) through (F) of section 7508(a)(1) were performed within the time prescribed therefor (determined without regard to extension under any other provision of this subtitle for periods after the date determined under subparagraph (B)).

(2) QUALIFIED TAXPAYER.—For purposes of this subsection, the term "qualified taxpayer" means—

(A) any individual whose principal residence (for purposes of section 1033(h)(4)) is located in a disaster area,

(B) any taxpayer if the taxpayer's principal place of business (other than the business of performing services as an employee) is located in a disaster area,

(C) any individual who is a relief worker affiliated with a recognized government or philanthropic organization and who is assisting in a disaster area,

(D) any taxpayer whose records necessary to meet a deadline for an act described in section 7508(a)(1) are maintained in a disaster area,

(E) any individual visiting a disaster area who was killed or injured as a result of the disaster, and

(F) solely with respect to a joint return, any spouse of an individual described in any preceding subparagraph of this paragraph.

(3) DISASTER AREA.—For purposes of this subsection, the term "disaster area" means an area in which a major disaster for which the President provides financial assistance under section 408 of the Robert T. Stafford Disaster Relief and Emergency Assistance Act (42 U.S.C. 5174) occurs.

(4) APPLICATION TO RULES REGARDING PENSIONS.—In the case of any person described in subsection (b), a rule similar to the rule of paragraph (1) shall apply for purposes of subsection (b) with respect to—

(A) making contributions to a qualified retirement plan (within the meaning of section 4974(c)) under section 219(f)(3), 404(a)(6), 404(h)(1)(B), or 404(m)(2),

(B) making distributions under section 408(d)(4),

(C) recharacterizing contributions under section 408A(d)(6), and

(D) making a rollover under section 402(c), 403(a)(4), 403(b)(8), or 408(d)(3).

(5) COORDINATION WITH PERIODS SPECIFIED BY THE SECRETARY.—Any period described in paragraph (1) with respect to any person (including by reason of the application of paragraph (4) shall be in addition to (or concurrent with, as the case may be) any period specified under subsection (a) or (b) with respect to such person.

(6) MULTIPLE DECLARATIONS.—For purposes of paragraph (1), in the case of multiple declarations relating to a disaster area which are issued within a 60-day period, a separate period shall be determined under such paragraph with respect to each such declaration.

Amendments

• 2021, Infrastructure Investment and Jobs Act (P.L. 117-58)

P.L. 117-58, §80501(a)(1)-(3), Div. H:

Amended Code Sec. 7508A(d)(1) by striking "the latest incident date so specified" in subparagraph (B) and inserting "the later of such earliest incident date described in subparagraph (A) or the date such declaration was issued", by striking "in the same manner as a period specified under subsection (a)" and inserting "in determining, under the internal revenue laws, in respect of any tax liability of such qualified taxpayer, whether any of the acts described in subparagraphs (A) through (F) of section 7508(a)(1) were performed within the time prescribed therefor (determined without regard to extension under any other provision of this subtitle for periods after the date determined under subparagraph (B))", by striking paragraph (3) and inserting a new paragraph (3), and by adding at the end a new paragraph (6). **Effective** for federally declared disasters declared after 11-15-2021. Prior to being stricken, Code Sec. 7508A(d)(3) reads as follows:

(3) DISASTER AREA.—For purposes of this subsection, the term "disaster area" has the meaning given such term under subparagraph (B) of section 165(i)(5) with respect to a Federally declared disaster (as defined in subparagraph (A) of such section).

• 2019, Taxpayer Certainty and Disaster Tax Relief Act of 2019 (P.L. 116-94)

P.L. 116-94, § 205(a), Div. Q:

Amended Code Sec. 7508A by adding at the end a new subsection (d). **Effective** for federally declared disasters declared after 12-20-2019.

[Sec. 7508A(e)]

(e) SIGNIFICANT FIRE.—For purposes of this section, the term "significant fire" means any fire with respect to which assistance is provided under section 420 of the Robert T. Stafford Disaster Relief and Emergency Assistance Act.

Amendments

• 2021, Infrastructure Investment and Jobs Act (P.L. 117-58)

P.L. 117-58, § 80504(a)(3), Div. H:

Amended Code Sec. 7508A by adding at the end a new subsection (e). **Effective** for fires for which assistance is provided after 11-15-2021.

* * *

[Sec. 7517]

SEC. 7517. FURNISHING ON REQUEST OF STATEMENT EXPLAINING ESTATE OR GIFT EVALUATION.

[Sec. 7517(a)]

(a) GENERAL RULE.—If the Secretary makes a determination or a proposed determination of the value of an item of property for purposes of the tax imposed under chapter 11, 12, or 13, he shall furnish, on the written request of the executor, donor, or the person required to make the return of the tax imposed by chapter 13 (as the case may be), to such executor, donor, or person a written statement containing the material required by subsection (b). Such statement shall be furnished not later than 45 days after the later of the date of such request or the date of such determination or proposed determination.

[Sec. 7517(b)]

(b) CONTENTS OF STATEMENT.—A statement required to be furnished under subsection (a) with respect to the value of an item of property shall—

(1) explain the basis on which the valuation was determined or proposed,

(2) set forth any computation used in arriving at such value, and

(3) contain a copy of any expert appraisal made by or for the Secretary.

[Sec. 7517(c)]

(c) EFFECT OF STATEMENT.—Except to the extent otherwise provided by law, the value determined or proposed by the Secretary with respect to which a statement is furnished under this section, and the method used in arriving at such value, shall not be binding on the Secretary.

Amendments

• 1976, Tax Reform Act of 1976 (P.L. 94-455)

P.L. 94-455, § 2008(a)(1):

Added Code Sec. 7517.

P.L. 94-455, § 2008(d)(1), provides:

(1) The amendments made by subsection (a)—

(A) insofar as they relate to the tax imposed under chapter 11 of the Internal Revenue Code of 1954, shall apply to the estates of decedents dying after December 31, 1976, and

(B) insofar as they relate to the tax imposed under chapter 12 of such Code, shall apply to gifts made after December 31, 1976.

* * *

[Sec. 7520]

SEC. 7520. VALUATION TABLES.

[Sec. 7520(a)]

(a) GENERAL RULE.—For purposes of this title, the value of any annuity, any interest for life or a term of years, or any remainder or reversionary interest shall be determined—

(1) under tables prescribed by the Secretary, and

(2) by using an interest rate (rounded to the nearest 2/10ths of 1 percent) equal to 120 percent of the Federal midterm rate in effect under section 1274(d)(1) for the month in which the valuation date falls.

If an income, estate, or gift tax charitable contribution is allowable for any part of the property transferred, the taxpayer may elect to use such Federal midterm rate for either of the 2 months preceding the month in which the valuation date falls for purposes of paragraph (2). In the case of transfers of more than 1 interest in the same property with respect to which the taxpayer may use the same rate under paragraph (2), the taxpayer shall use the same rate with respect to each such interest.

[Sec. 7520(b)]

(b) SECTION NOT TO APPLY FOR CERTAIN PURPOSES.—This section shall not apply for purposes of part I of subchapter D of chapter 1 or any other provision specified in regulations.

[Sec. 7520(c)]

(c) TABLES.—

(1) IN GENERAL.—The tables prescribed by the Secretary for purposes of subsection (a) shall contain valuation factors for a series of interest rate categories.

(2) REVISION FOR RECENT MORTALITY CHARGES.—The Secretary shall revise the initial tables prescribed for purposes of subsection (a) to take into account the most recent mortality experience available as of the time of such revision. Such tables shall be revised not less frequently than once each 10 years to take into account the most recent mortality experience available as of the time of the revision.

Amendments

• 2014, Tax Technical Corrections Act of 2014 (P.L. 113-295)

P.L. 113-295, §221(a)(118)(A), Division A:

Amended Code Sec. 7520(c) by striking paragraph (2) and redesignating paragraph (3) as paragraph (2). **Effective** generally 12-19-2014. For a special rule, see Act Sec. 221(b)(2), Division A, below. Prior to being stricken, Code Sec. 7520(c)(2) read as follows:

(2) INITIAL TABLE.—Not later than the day 3 months after the date of the enactment of this section, the Secretary shall prescribe initial tables for purposes of subsection (a). Such tables may be based on the same mortality experience as used for purposes of section 2031 on the date of the enactment of this section.

P.L. 113-295, §221(a)(118)(B)(i)-(ii), Division A:

Amended Code Sec. 7520(c)(2) (as redesignated by Act Sec. 221(a)(118)(A), Division A) by striking "Not later than December 31, 1989, the" and inserting "The", and by striking "thereafter" following "10 years" in the last sentence thereof. **Effective** generally 12-19-2014. For a special rule, see Act Sec. 221(b)(2), Division A, below.

P.L. 113-295, §221(b)(2), Division A, provides:

(2) SAVINGS PROVISION.—If—

(A) any provision amended or repealed by the amendments made by this section applied to—

(i) any transaction occurring before the date of the enactment of this Act,

(ii) any property acquired before such date of enactment, or

(iii) any item of income, loss, deduction, or credit taken into account before such date of enactment, and

(B) the treatment of such transaction, property, or item under such provision would (without regard to the amendments or repeals made by this section) affect the liability for tax for periods ending after date of enactment, nothing in the amendments or repeals made by this section shall be construed to affect the treatment of such transaction, property, or item for purposes of determining liability for tax for periods ending after such date of enactment.

[Sec. 7520(d)]

(d) VALUATION DATE.—For purposes of this section, the term "valuation date" means the date as of which the valuation is made.

[Sec. 7520(e)]

(e) TABLES TO INCLUDE FORMULAS.—For purposes of this section, the term "tables" includes formulas.

Amendments

• 1988, Technical and Miscellaneous Revenue Act of 1988 (P.L. 100-647)

P.L. 100-647, §5031(a):

Amended Chapter 77 by adding at the end thereof a new section 7520. **Effective** in cases where the date the valuation is to be made occurs on or after the 1st day of the 6th calendar month beginning after 11-10-88.

* * *

CHAPTER 78—DISCOVERY OF LIABILITY AND ENFORCEMENT OF TITLE

* * *

Subchapter A—Examination and Inspection

* * *

* * *

[Sec. 7602]

SEC. 7602. EXAMINATION OF BOOKS AND WITNESSES.

[Sec. 7602(a)]

(a) AUTHORITY TO SUMMON, ETC.—For the purpose of ascertaining the correctness of any return, making a return where none has been made, determining the liability of any person for any internal revenue tax or the liability at law or in equity of any transferee or fiduciary of any person in respect of any internal revenue tax, or collecting any such liability, the Secretary is authorized—

(1) To examine any books, papers, records, or other data which may be relevant or material to such inquiry;

(2) To summon the person liable for tax or required to perform the act, or any officer or employee of such person, or any person having possession, custody, or care of books of account containing entries relating to the business of the person liable for tax or required to perform the act, or any other person the Secretary may deem proper, to appear before the Secretary at a time and place named in the summons and to produce such books, papers, records, or other data, and to give such testimony, under oath, as may be relevant or material to such inquiry; and

(3) To take such testimony of the person concerned, under oath, as may be relevant or material to such inquiry.

Amendments

• 1982, Tax Equity and Fiscal Responsibility Act of 1982 (P.L. 97-248)

P.L. 97-248, §333(a):

Amended Code Sec. 7602 by striking out "For the purpose" and inserting "(a) Authority to Summon, Etc.—For the purpose". **Effective** 9-4-82.

• 1976, Tax Reform Act of 1976 (P.L. 94-455)

P.L. 94-455, §1906(b)(13)(A):

Amended 1954 Code by substituting "Secretary" for "Secretary or his delegate" each place it appeared. **Effective** 2-1-77.

* * *

[Sec. 7602(c)]

(c) NOTICE OF CONTACT OF THIRD PARTIES.—

(1) GENERAL NOTICE.—An officer or employee of the Internal Revenue Service may not contact any person other than the taxpayer with respect to the determination or collection of the tax liability of such taxpayer unless such contact occurs during a period (not greater than 1 year) which is specified in a notice which—

(A) informs the taxpayer that contacts with persons other than the taxpayer are intended to be made during such period, and

(B) except as otherwise provided by the Secretary, is provided to the taxpayer not later than 45 days before the beginning of such period.

Nothing in the preceding sentence shall prevent the issuance of notices to the same taxpayer with respect to the same tax liability with periods specified therein that, in the aggregate, exceed 1 year. A notice shall not be issued under this paragraph unless there is an intent at the time such notice is issued to contact persons other than the taxpayer during the period specified in such notice. The preceding sentence shall not prevent the issuance of a notice if the requirement of such sentence is met on the basis of the assumption that the information sought to be obtained by such contact will not be obtained by other means before such contact.

(2) NOTICE OF SPECIFIC CONTACTS.—The Secretary shall periodically provide to a taxpayer a record of persons contacted during such period by the Secretary with respect to the determination or collection of the tax liability of such taxpayer. Such record shall also be provided upon request of the taxpayer.

(3) EXCEPTIONS.—This subsection shall not apply—

(A) to any contact which the taxpayer has authorized;

(B) if the Secretary determines for good cause shown that such notice would jeopardize collection of any tax or such notice may involve reprisal against any person; or

(C) with respect to any pending criminal investigation.

Amendments

• 2019, Taxpayer First Act (P.L. 116-25)

P.L. 116-25, §1206(a):

Amended Code Sec. 7602(c)(1). **Effective** for notices provided, and contacts of persons made, after the date which is 45 days after 7-1-2019. Prior to amendment, Code Sec. 7602(c)(1) read as follows:

(1) GENERAL NOTICE.—An officer or employee of the Internal Revenue Service may not contact any person other than the taxpayer with respect to the determination or collection of the tax liability of such taxpayer without providing reasonable notice in advance to the taxpayer that contacts with persons other than the taxpayer may be made.

• 1998, IRS Restructuring and Reform Act of 1998 (P.L. 105-206)

P.L. 105-206, §3417(a):

Amended Code Sec. 7602, as amended by Act Sec. 3412, by redesignating subsections (c) and (d) as subsections (d) and (e), respectively, and by inserting after subsection (b) a new subsection (c). **Effective** for contacts made after the 180th day after 7-22-98.

* * *

[Sec. 7602(f)]

(f) LIMITATION ON ACCESS OF PERSONS OTHER THAN INTERNAL REVENUE SERVICE OFFICERS AND EMPLOYEES.—The Secretary shall not, under the authority of section 6103(n), provide any books, papers, records, or other data obtained pursuant to this section to any person authorized under section 6103(n), except when such person requires such information for the sole purpose of providing expert evaluation and assistance to the Internal Revenue Service. No person other than an officer or employee of the Internal Revenue Service or the Office of Chief Counsel may, on behalf of the Secretary, question a witness under oath whose testimony was obtained pursuant to this section.

Amendments

• 2019, Taxpayer First Act (P.L. 116-25)

P.L. 116-25, §1208(a):

Amended Code Sec. 7602 by adding at the end a new subsection (f). For the **effective** date, see Act Sec. 1208(b), below.

P.L. 116-25, §1208(b), provides:

(b) EFFECTIVE DATE.—The amendment made by this section—

(1) shall take effect on the date of the enactment of this Act; and

(2) shall not fail to apply to a contract in effect under section 6103(n) of the Internal Revenue Code of 1986 merely because such contract was in effect before the date of the enactment of this Act.

* * *

[Sec. 7603]

SEC. 7603. SERVICE OF SUMMONS.

[Sec. 7603(a)]

(a) IN GENERAL.—A summons issued under section 6420(e)(2), 6421(g)(2), 6427(j)(2), or 7602 shall be served by the Secretary, by an attested copy delivered in hand to the person to whom it is directed, or left at his last and usual place of abode; and the certificate of service signed by the person serving the summons shall be evidence of the facts it states on the hearing of an application for the enforcement of the summons. When the summons requires the production of books, papers, records, or other data, it shall be sufficient if such books, papers, records, or other data are described with reasonable certainty.

Amendments

• 1998, IRS Restructuring and Reform Act of 1998 (P.L. 105-206)

P.L. 105-206, §3416(a):

Amended Code Sec. 7603 by striking "A summons issued" and inserting "(a) IN GENERAL.—A summons issued". **Effective** for summonses served after 7-22-98.

• 1988, Technical and Miscellaneous Revenue Act of 1988 (P.L. 100-647)

P.L. 100-647, §1017(c)(9):

Amended Code Sec. 7603 by striking out "6421(f)(2)" and inserting in lieu thereof "6421(g)(2)". **Effective** as if included in the provision of P.L. 99-514 to which it relates.

• 1986, Tax Reform Act of 1986 (P.L. 99-514)

P.L. 99-514, §1703(e)(2)(G):

Amended Code Sec. 7603 by striking out "6427(i)(2)" and inserting in lieu thereof "6427(j)(2)". **Effective** for gasoline removed (as defined in Code Sec. 4082, as amended) after 12-31-87.

• 1984, Deficit Reduction Act of 1984 (P.L. 98-369)

P.L. 98-369, §911(d)[c](2)(G):

Amended Code Sec. 7603 by striking out "6427(h)(2)" and inserting in lieu thereof "6427(i)(2)". **Effective** 8-1-84.

• 1983, Surface Transportation Act of 1983 (P.L. 97-424)

P.L. 97-424, §515(b)(12):

Amended Code Sec. 7603 by striking out "6424(d)(2)," before "6427(h)(2)". **Effective** 1-6-83.

• 1980, Crude Oil Windfall Profit Tax Act of 1980 (P.L. 96-223)

P.L. 96-223, §232(d)(4)(E):

Amended Code Sec. 7603 by substituting "6427(h)(2)" for "6427(g)(2)". **Effective** 1-1-79.

• 1978, Surface Transportation Assistance Act of 1978 (P.L. 95-599)

P.L. 95-599, §505(c)(5), (d):

Substituted "6427(g)(2)" for "6427(f)(2)" in Code Sec. 7603. **Effective** 1-1-79.

• 1976 (P.L. 94-530)

P.L. 94-530, §1(c)(6):

Substituted "6427(f)(2)" for "6427(e)(2)" in Code Sec. 7603. **Effective** 10-1-76.

• 1976, Tax Reform Act of 1976 (P.L. 94-455)

P.L. 94-455, §1906(b)(13)(A):

Amended 1954 Code by substituting "Secretary" for "Secretary or his delegate" each place it appeared. **Effective** 2-1-77.

• 1970 (P.L. 91-258)

P.L. 91-258, §207(d)(9):

Amended Code Sec. 7603 by adding "6427(e)(2)" in the first line. **Effective** 7-1-70.

• 1965, Excise Tax Reduction Act of 1965 (P.L. 89-44)

P.L. 89-44, §202(c)(4):

Amended Code Sec. 7603 by inserting "6424(d)(2)," after "6421(f)(2),". **Effective** 1-1-66.

• 1956 (P.L. 627, 84th Cong.)

P.L. 627, 84th Cong., §208(d)(4):

Amended Sec. 7603 by inserting after "section 6420(e)(2)" the following: ", 6421(f)(2),". **Effective** 7-1-56.

• 1956 (P.L. 466, 84th Cong.)

P.L. 466, 84th Cong., §4(i):

Amended Code Sec. 7603 by striking out the words "section 7602" in the first sentence and inserting in lieu thereof the words "section 6420(e)(2) or 7602".

[Sec. 7603(b)]

(b) SERVICE BY MAIL TO THIRD-PARTY RECORDKEEPERS.—

(1) IN GENERAL.—A summons referred to in subsection (a) for the production of books, papers, records, or other data by a third-party recordkeeper may also be served by certified or registered mail to the last known address of such recordkeeper.

(2) THIRD-PARTY RECORDKEEPER.—For purposes of paragraph (1), the term "third-party recordkeeper" means—

(A) any mutual savings bank, cooperative bank, domestic building and loan association, or other savings institution chartered and supervised as a savings and loan or similar association under Federal or State law, any bank (as defined in section 581), or any credit union (within the meaning of section 501(c)(14)(A)),

(B) any consumer reporting agency (as defined under section 603(f) of the Fair Credit Reporting Act (15 U.S.C. 1681a(f))),

(C) any person extending credit through the use of credit cards or similar devices,

(D) any broker (as defined in section 3(a)(4) of the Securities Exchange Act of 1934 (15 U.S.C. 78c(a)(4))),

(E) any attorney,

(F) any accountant,

(G) any barter exchange (as defined in section 6045(c)(3)),

(H) any regulated investment company (as defined in section 851) and any agent of such regulated investment company when acting as an agent thereof,

(I) any enrolled agent, and

(J) any owner or developer of a computer software source code (as defined in section 7612(d)(2)).

Subparagraph (J) shall apply only with respect to a summons requiring the production of the source code referred to in subparagraph (J) or the program and data described in section 7612(b)(1)(A)(ii) to which such source code relates.

Amendments

• 2000, Community Renewal Tax Relief Act of 2000 (P.L. 106-554)

P.L. 106-554, §319(26):

Amended Code Sec. 7603(b)(2) by striking the semicolon at the end of subparagraphs (A), (B), (C), (D), (E), (F), and (G) and inserting a comma. **Effective** 12-21-2000.

• 1998, IRS Restructuring and Reform Act of 1998 (P.L. 105-206)

P.L. 105-206, §3413(c):

Amended Code Sec. 7603(b)(2), as amended by Act Sec. 3416(a), by striking "and" at the end of subparagraph (H), by striking a period at the end of subparagraph (I) and inserting ", and", and by adding at the end a new subparagraph (J). **Effective**, generally, for summonses issued and software acquired after 7-22-98. For a special rule, see Act Sec. 3413(e)(2), below.

P.L. 105-206, §3413(e)(2), provides:

(2) SOFTWARE PROTECTION.—In the case of any software acquired on or before such date of enactment, the requirements of section 7612(a)(2) of the Internal Revenue Code of 1986 (as added by such amendments) shall apply after the 90th day after such date. The preceding sentence shall not apply to the requirement under section 7612(c)(2)(G)(ii) of such Code (as so added).

P.L. 105-206, §3416(a):

Amended Code Sec. 7603 by adding at the end a new subsection (b). **Effective** for summonses served after 7-22-98.

[Sec. 7604]

SEC. 7604. ENFORCEMENT OF SUMMONS.

[Sec. 7604(a)]

(a) JURISDICTION OF DISTRICT COURT.—If any person is summoned under the internal revenue laws to appear, to testify, or to produce books, papers, records, or other data, the United States district court for the district in which such person resides or is found shall have jurisdiction by appropriate process to compel such attendance, testimony, or production of books, papers, records, or other data.

[Sec. 7604(b)]

(b) ENFORCEMENT.—Whenever any person summoned under section 6420(e)(2), 6421(g)(2), 6427(j)(2), or 7602 neglects or refuses to obey such summons, or to produce books, papers, records, or other data, or to give testimony, as required, the Secretary may apply to the judge of the district court or to a United States commissioner for the district within which the person so summoned resides or is found for an attachment against him as for a contempt. It shall be the duty of the judge or commissioner to hear the application, and, if satisfactory proof is made, to issue an attachment, directed to some proper officer, for the arrest of such person, and upon his being brought before him to proceed to a hearing of the case; and upon such hearing the judge or the United States commissioner shall have power to make such order as he shall deem proper, not inconsistent with the law for the punishment of contempts, to enforce obedience to the requirements of the summons and to punish such person for his default or disobedience.

Amendments

• 1988, Technical and Miscellaneous Revenue Act of 1988 (P.L. 100-647)

P.L. 100-647, §1017(c)(9):

Amended Code Sec. 7604(b) by striking out "6421(f)(2)" and inserting in lieu thereof "6421(g)(2)". **Effective** as if included in the provision of P.L. 99-514 to which it relates.

• 1986, Tax Reform Act of 1986 (P.L. 99-514)

P.L. 99-514, §1703(e)(2)(G):

Amended Code Sec. 7604(b) and (c)(2) by striking out "6427(i)(2)" and inserting in lieu thereof "6427(j)(2)". **Effective** for gasoline removed (as defined in Code Sec. 4082, as amended) after 12-31-87.

• 1984, Deficit Reduction Act of 1984 (P.L. 98-369)

P.L. 98-369, §911(d)[c](2)(G):

Amended Code Sec. 7604(b) by striking out "6427(h)(2)" each place it appeared and inserting in lieu thereof "6427(i)(2)". **Effective** 8-1-84.

• **1983, Surface Transportation Act of 1983 (P.L. 97-424)**

P.L. 97-424, §515(b)(12):

Amended Code Sec. 7604(b) by striking out "6424(d)(2)," before "6427(h)(2),". **Effective** 1-6-83.

• **1980, Crude Oil Windfall Profit Tax Act of 1980 (P.L. 96-223)**

P.L. 96-223, §232(d)(4)(E):

Amended Code Sec. 7604(b) by substituting "6427(h)(2)" for "6427(g)(2)". **Effective** 1-1-79.

• **1978, Surface Transportation Assistance Act of 1978 (P.L. 95-599)**

P.L. 95-599, §505(c)(5), (d):

Substituted "6427(g)(2)" for "6427(f)(2)" in Code Sec. 7604(b). **Effective** 1-1-79.

• **1976 (P.L. 94-530)**

P.L. 94-530, §1(c)(6):

Substituted "6427(f)(2)" for "6427(e)(2)" in Code Sec. 7604(b). **Effective** 10-1-76.

• **1976, Tax Reform Act of 1976 (P.L. 94-455)**

P.L. 94-455, §1906(b)(13)(A):

Amended 1954 Code by substituting "Secretary" for "Secretary or his delegate" each place it appeared. **Effective** 2-1-77.

• **1970 (P.L. 91-258)**

P.L. 91-258, §207(d)(9):

Amended Code Sec. 7604(b) by adding "6427(e)(2)" in the second line. **Effective** 7-1-70.

• **1965, Excise Tax Reduction Act of 1965 (P.L. 89-44)**

P.L. 89-44, §202(c)(4):

Amended Code Sec. 7604(b) by inserting "6424(d)(2)," after "6421(f)(2),". **Effective** 1-1-66.

• **1956 (P.L. 627, 84th Cong.)**

P.L. 627, 84th Cong., §208(d)(4):

Amended Code Sec. 7604(b) by inserting after "section 6420(e)(2)" the following: ", 6421(f)(2),". **Effective** 7-1-56.

• **1956 (P.L. 466, 84th Cong.)**

P.L. 466, 84th Cong., §4(i):

Amended Code Sec. 7604(b) by striking out the words "section 7602" in the first sentence and inserting in lieu thereof the words "section 6420(e)(2) or 7602".

[Sec. 7604(c)]

(c) CROSS REFERENCES.—

(1) AUTHORITY TO ISSUE ORDERS, PROCESSES, AND JUDGMENTS.—

For authority of district courts generally to enforce the provisions of this title, see section 7402.

(2) PENALTIES.—

For penalties applicable to violation of section 6420(e)(2), 6421(g)(2), 6427(j)(2), or 7602, see section 7210.

Amendments

• **1988, Technical and Miscellaneous Revenue Act of 1988 (P.L. 100-647)**

P.L. 100-647, §1017(c)(9):

Amended Code Sec. 7604(c)(2) by striking out "6421(f)(2)" and inserting in lieu thereof "6421(g)(2)". **Effective** as if included in the provision of P.L. 99-514 to which it relates.

• **1986, Tax Reform Act of 1986 (P.L. 99-514)**

P.L. 99-514, §1703(e)(2)(G):

Amended Code Sec. 7604(c)(2) by striking out "6427(i)(2)" and inserting in lieu thereof "6427(j)(2)". **Effective** for gasoline removed (as defined in Code Sec. 4082, as amended) after 12-31-87.

• **1984, Deficit Reduction Act of 1984 (P.L. 98-369)**

P.L. 98-369, §911(d)[c](2)(G):

Amended Code Sec. 7604(c)(2) by striking out "6427(h)(2)" and inserting in lieu thereof "6427(i)(2)". **Effective** 8-1-84.

• **1983, Surface Transportation Act of 1983 (P.L. 97-424)**

P.L. 97-424, §515(b)(12):

Amended Code Sec. 7604(c) by striking out "6424(d)(2)," before "6427(h)(2)". **Effective** 1-6-83.

• **1980, Crude Oil Windfall Profit Tax Act of 1980 (P.L. 96-223)**

P.L. 96-223, §232(d)(4)(E):

Amended Code Sec. 7604(c) by substituting "6427(h)(2)" for "6427(g)(2)". **Effective** 1-1-79.

• **1978, Surface Transportation Assistance Act of 1978 (P.L. 95-599)**

P.L. 95-599, §505(c)(6), (d):

Substituted "6427(g)(2)" for "6427(e)(2)" in Code Sec. 7604(c)(2). **Effective** 1-1-79.

• **1970 (P.L. 91-258)**

P.L. 91-258, §207(d)(9):

Amended Code Sec. 7604(c)(2) by adding "6427(e)(2)" therein. **Effective** 7-1-70.

• **1965, Excise Tax Reduction Act of 1965 (P.L. 89-44)**

P.L. 89-44, §202(c)(4):

Amended Code Sec. 7604(c)(2) by inserting "6424(d)(2)," after "6421(f)(2),". **Effective** 1-1-66.

• **1956 (P.L. 627, 84th Cong.)**

P.L. 627, 84th Cong., §208(d)(4):

Amended Code Sec. 7604(c)(2) by inserting after "section 6420(e)(2)" the following: ", 6421(f)(2),". **Effective** 7-1-56.

• **1956 (P.L. 466, 84th Cong.)**

P.L. 466, 84th Cong., §4(i):

Amended Code Sec. 7604(c)(2) by striking out the words "section 7602" and inserting in lieu thereof the words "section 6420(e)(2) or 7602".

[Sec. 7605]

SEC. 7605. TIME AND PLACE OF EXAMINATION.

[Sec. 7605(a)]

(a) TIME AND PLACE.—The time and place of examination pursuant to the provisions of section 6420(e)(2), 6421(g)(2), 6427(j)(2), or 7602 shall be such time and place as may be fixed by the Secretary and as are reasonable under the circumstances. In the case of a summons under authority of paragraph (2) of section 7602, or under the corresponding authority of section 6420(e)(2), 6421(g)(2), or 6427(j)(2), the date fixed for appearance before the Secretary shall not be less than 10 days from the date of the summons.

Amendments

• 1988, Technical and Miscellaneous Revenue Act of 1988 (P.L. 100-647)

P.L. 100-647, §1017(c)(9):

Amended Code Sec. 7605(a) by striking out "6421(f)(2)" and inserting in lieu thereof "6421(g)(2)". **Effective** as if included in the provision of P.L. 99-514 to which it relates.

P.L. 100-647, §6228(b), provides:

(b) REGULATIONS WITH RESPECT TO TIME AND PLACE OF EXAMINATION.—The Secretary of the Treasury or the Secretary's delegate shall issue regulations to implement subsection (a) of section 7605 of the 1986 Code (relating to time and place of examination) within 1 year after the date of the enactment of this Act.

• 1986, Tax Reform Act of 1986 (P.L. 99-514)

P.L. 99-514, §1703(e)(2)(G):

Amended Code Sec. 7605(a) by striking out "6427(i)(2)" and inserting in lieu thereof "6427(j)(2)". **Effective** for gasoline removed (as defined in Code Sec. 4082, as amended) after 12-31-87.

• 1984, Deficit Reduction Act of 1984 (P.L. 98-369)

P.L. 98-369, §911(d)[c](2)(G):

Amended Code Sec. 7605(a) by striking out "6427(h)(2)" each place it appeared and inserting in lieu thereof "6427(i)(2)". **Effective** 8-1-84.

• 1983, Surface Transportation Act of 1983 (P.L. 97-424)

P.L. 97-424, §515(b)(12):

Amended Code Sec. 7605(a) by striking out "6424(d)(2)," before "6427(h)(2)" each place it appeared. **Effective** 1-6-83.

• 1980, Crude Oil Windfall Profit Tax Act of 1980 (P.L. 96-223)

P.L. 96-223, §232(d)(4)(E):

Amended Code Sec. 7605(a) by substituting "6427(h)(2)" for "6427(g)(2)". **Effective** 1-1-79.

• 1978, Surface Transportation Assistance Act of 1978 (P.L. 95-599)

P.L. 95-599, §505(c)(5), (d):

Substituted "6427(g)(2)" for "6427(f)(2)" each place it appeared in Code Sec. 7605(a). **Effective** 1-1-79.

• 1976 (P.L. 94-530)

P.L. 94-530, §1(c)(6):

Substituted "6427(f)(2)" for "6427(e)(2)" each place it appeared in Code Sec. 7605(a). **Effective** 10-1-76.

• 1976, Tax Reform Act of 1976 (P.L. 94-455)

P.L. 94-455, §1906(b)(13)(A):

Amended 1954 Code by substituting "Secretary" for "Secretary or his delegate" each place it appeared. **Effective** 2-1-77.

• 1970 (P.L. 91-258)

P.L. 91-258, §207(d)(9):

Amended Code Sec. 7605(a) by adding "6427(e)(2)" in the first sentence and by substituting "6424(d)(2), or 6427(e)(2)" for "or 6424(d)(2)" in the second sentence. **Effective** 7-1-70.

• 1965, Excise Tax Reduction Act of 1965 (P.L. 89-44)

P.L. 89-44, §202(c)(4):

Amended Code Sec. 7605(a) by inserting "6424(d)(2)," after "6421(f)(2)," in the first sentence and by inserting "6420(e)(2), 6421(f)(2), or 6424(d)(2)," in lieu of "6420(e)(2) or 6421(f)(2)," in the second sentence. **Effective** 1-1-66.

• 1956 (P.L. 627, 84th Cong.)

P.L. 627, 84th Cong., §208(d)(4):

Amended Code Sec. 7605(a) by inserting in the first sentence after "section 6420(e)(2)" the following: ", 6421(f)(2),". Amended the second sentence by inserting after "section 6420(e)(2)" the following: "or section 6421(f)(2)". **Effective** 7-1-56.

• 1956 (P.L. 466, 84th Cong.)

P.L. 466, 84th Cong., §4(i):

Amended the first sentence of Code Sec. 7605(a) by striking out the words "section 7602" and inserting in lieu thereof the words "section 6420(e)(2) or 7602". Amended the second sentence of Code Sec. 7605(a) by adding after the words "section 7602" the words ", or under the corresponding authority of section 6420(e)(2),".

[Sec. 7605(b)]

(b) RESTRICTIONS ON EXAMINATION OF TAXPAYER.—No taxpayer shall be subjected to unnecessary examination or investigations, and only one inspection of a taxpayer's books of account shall be made for each taxable year unless the taxpayer requests otherwise or unless the Secretary, after investigation, notifies the taxpayer in writing that an additional inspection is necessary.

Amendments

• 1998, IRS Restructuring and Reform Act of 1998 (P.L. 105-206)

P.L. 105-206, §3503, provides:

SEC. 3503. DISCLOSURE OF CRITERIA FOR EXAMINATION SELECTION.

(a) IN GENERAL.—The Secretary of the Treasury or the Secretary's delegate shall, as soon as practicable, but not later than 180 days after the date of the enactment of this Act, incorporate into the statement required by section 6227 of the Omnibus Taxpayer Bill of Rights (Internal Revenue Service Publication No. 1) a statement which sets forth in simple and nontechnical terms the criteria and procedures for selecting taxpayers for examination. Such statement shall not include any information the disclosure of which would be detrimental to law enforcement, but shall specify the general procedures used by the Internal Revenue Service, including whether taxpayers are selected for examination on the basis of information available in the media or on the basis of information provided to the Internal Revenue Service by informants.

(b) TRANSMISSION TO COMMITTEES OF CONGRESS.—The Secretary shall transmit drafts of the statement required under subsection (a) (or proposed revisions to any such statement) to the Committee on Ways and Means of the House of Representatives and the Committee on Finance of the Senate on the same day.

• 1976, Tax Reform Act of 1976 (P.L. 94-455)

P.L. 94-455, §1906(b)(13)(A):

Amended 1954 Code by substituting "Secretary" for "Secretary or his delegate" each place it appeared. **Effective** 2-1-77.

[Sec. 7605(c)]

(c) CROSS REFERENCE.—

For provisions restricting church tax inquiries and examinations, see section 7611.

Amendments

• 1984, Deficit Reduction Act of 1984 (P.L. 98-369)

P.L. 98-369, §1033(c)(1):

Amended Code Sec. 7605(c). **Effective** with respect to inquiries and examinations beginning after 12-31-84. Prior to amendment, Code Sec. 7605(c) read as follows:

(c) Restriction on Examination of Churches.—No examination of the books of account of a church or convention or association of churches shall be made to determine whether such organization may be engaged in the carrying on of an unrelated trade or business or may be otherwise engaged in activities which may be subject to tax under part III of subchapter F of chapter 1 of this title (sec. 511 and following, relating to taxation of business income of exempt organizations) unless the Secretary (such officer being no lower than a principal internal revenue officer for an internal revenue region) believes that such organization may be so engaged and so notifies the organization in advance of the examination. No examination of the religious activities of such an organization shall be made except to the extent necessary to determine whether such organization is a church or a convention or association of churches, and no examination of the books of account of such an organization shall be made other than to the extent necessary to determine the amount of tax imposed by this title.

• 1976, Tax Reform Act of 1976 (P.L. 94-455)

P.L. 94-455, §1906(b)(13)(A):

Amended 1954 Code by substituting "Secretary" for "Secretary or his delegate" each place it appeared. **Effective** 2-1-77.

• 1969, Tax Reform Act of 1969 (P.L. 91-172)

P.L. 91-172, §121(f):

Added subsection (c) to Code Sec. 7605. **Effective** 1-1-70.

* * *

[Sec. 7609]

SEC. 7609. SPECIAL PROCEDURES FOR THIRD-PARTY SUMMONSES.

[Sec. 7609(a)]

(a) NOTICE.—

(1) IN GENERAL.—If any summons to which this section applies requires the giving of testimony on or relating to, the production of any portion of records made or kept on or relating to, or the production of any computer software source code (as defined in 7612(d)(2)) with respect to, any person (other than the person summoned) who is identified in the summons, then notice of the summons shall be given to any person so identified within 3 days of the day on which such service is made, but no later than the 23rd day before the day fixed in the summons as the day upon which such records are to be examined. Such notice shall be accompanied by a copy of the summons which has been served and shall contain an explanation of the right under subsection (b)(2) to bring a proceeding to quash the summons.

(2) SUFFICIENCY OF NOTICE.—Such notice shall be sufficient if, on or before such third day, such notice is served in the manner provided in section 7603 (relating to service of summons) upon the person entitled to notice, or is mailed by certified or registered mail to the last known address of such person, or, in the absence of a last known address, is left with the person summoned. If such notice is mailed, it shall be sufficient if mailed to the last known address of the person entitled to notice or, in the case of notice to the Secretary under section 6903 of the existence of a fiduciary relationship, to the last known address of the fiduciary of such person, even if such person or fiduciary is then deceased, under a legal disability, or no longer in existence.

(3) NATURE OF SUMMONS.—Any summons to which this subsection applies (and any summons in aid of collection described in subsection (c)(2)(D)) shall identify the taxpayer to whom the summons relates or the other person to whom the records pertain and shall provide such other information as will enable the person summoned to locate the records required under the summons.

Amendments

• 1998, IRS Restructuring and Reform Act of 1998 (P.L. 105-206)

P.L. 105-206, §3415(a):

Amended Code Sec. 7609(a)(1) by striking so much of such paragraph as precedes "notice of the summons" and inserting new material. **Effective** for summonses served after 7-22-98. Prior to amendment, Code Sec. 7609(a)(1) read as follows:

(1) IN GENERAL.—If—

(A) any summons described in subsection (c) is served on any person who is a third-party recordkeeper, and

(B) the summons requires the production of any portion of records made or kept of the business transactions or affairs of any person (other than the person summoned) who is identified in the description of the records contained in the summons,

then notice of the summons shall be given to any person so identified within 3 days of the day on which such service is made, but no later than the 23rd day before the day fixed in the summons as the day upon which such records are to be examined. Such notice shall be accompanied by a copy of the summons which has been served and shall contain an explanation of the right under subsection (b)(2) to bring a proceeding to quash the summons.

P.L. 105-206, §3415(c)(1):

Amended Code Sec. 7609(a) by striking paragraphs (3) and (4), by redesignating paragraph (5) as paragraph (3), and by striking in paragraph (3) (as so redesignated) "subsection (c)(2)(B)" and inserting "subsection (c)(2)(D)". **Effective** for summonses served after 7-22-98. Prior to being stricken, Code Sec. 7609(a)(3)-(4) read as follows:

(3) THIRD-PARTY RECORDKEEPER DEFINED.—For purposes of this subsection, the term "third-party recordkeeper" means—

(A) any mutual savings bank, cooperative bank, domestic building and loan association, or other savings institution chartered and supervised as a savings and loan or similar association under Federal or State law, any bank (as defined in section 581), or any credit union (within the meaning of section 501(c)(14)(A));

(B) any consumer reporting agency (as defined under section 603(d) of the Fair Credit Reporting Act (15 U.S.C. 1681a(f)));

(C) any person extending credit through the use of credit cards or similar devices;

(D) any broker (as defined in section 3(a)(4) of the Securities Exchange Act of 1934 (15 U.S.C. 78c(a)(4)));

(E) any attorney;

(F) any accountant;

(G) any barter exchange (as defined in section 6045(c)(3));

(H) any regulated investment company (as defined in section 851) and any agent of such regulated investment company when acting as an agent thereof; and

(I) any enrolled agent.

(4) EXCEPTIONS.—Paragraph (1) shall not apply to any summons—

(A) served on the person with respect to whose liability the summons is issued, or any officer or employee of such person,

(B) to determine whether or not records of the business transactions or affairs of an identified person have been made or kept, or

(C) described in subsection (f).

• 1996, Taxpayer Bill of Rights 2 (P.L. 104-168)

P.L. 104-168, §1001(a):

Amended Code Sec. 7609(a)(3) by striking "and" at the end of subparagraph (G), by striking the period at the end of subparagraph (H) and inserting "; and", and by adding at the end a new subparagraph (I). **Effective** for summonses issued after 7-30-96.

• 1986, Tax Reform Act of 1986 (P.L. 99-514)

P.L. 99-514, §656(a)(1)-(3):

Amended Code Sec. 7609(a)(3) by striking out "and" at the end of subparagraph (F); by striking out the period at the end of subparagraph (G) and inserting in lieu thereof "; and"; and by adding new subparagraph (H). **Effective** for summonses served after 10-22-86.

• 1982, Tax Equity and Fiscal Responsibility Act of 1982 (P.L. 97-248)

P.L. 97-248, §311(b):

Amended Code Sec. 7609(a)(3) by striking out "and" at the end of subparagraph (E), by striking out the period at the end of subparagraph (F) and inserting "; and", and by adding new subparagraph (G). **Effective** for summonses served after 12-31-82.

P.L. 97-248, §331(d)(1):

Amended Code Sec. 7609(a)(1) by striking out "14th day" and inserting "23rd day" and by striking out the last sentence and inserting a new last sentence. **Effective** for summonses served after 12-31-82. Prior to amendment, the last sentence of Code Sec. 7609(a)(1) read as follows:

Such notice shall be accompanied by a copy of the summons which has been served and shall contain directions for staying compliance with the summons under subsection (b)(2).

[Sec. 7609(b)]

(b) RIGHT TO INTERVENE; RIGHT TO PROCEEDING TO QUASH.—

(1) INTERVENTION.—Notwithstanding any other law or rule of law, any person who is entitled to notice of a summons under subsection (a) shall have the right to intervene in any proceeding with respect to the enforcement of such summons under section 7604.

(2) PROCEEDING TO QUASH.—

(A) IN GENERAL.—Notwithstanding any other law or rule of law, any person who is entitled to notice of a summons under subsection (a) shall have the right to begin a proceeding to quash such summons not later than the 20th day after the day such notice is given in the manner provided in subsection (a)(2). In any such proceeding, the Secretary may seek to compel compliance with the summons.

(B) REQUIREMENT OF NOTICE TO PERSON SUMMONED AND TO SECRETARY.—If any person begins a proceeding under subparagraph (A) with respect to any summons, not later than the close of the 20-day period referred to in subparagraph (A) such person shall mail by registered or certified mail a copy of the petition to the person summoned and to such office as the Secretary may direct in the notice referred to in subsection (a)(1).

(C) INTERVENTION; ETC.—Notwithstanding any other law or rule of law, the person summoned shall have the right to intervene in any proceeding under subparagraph (A). Such person shall be bound by the decision in such proceeding (whether or not the person intervenes in such proceeding).

Amendments

• 1982, Tax Equity and Fiscal Responsibility Act of 1982 (P.L. 97-248)

P.L. 97-248, §331(a):

Amended Code Sec. 7609(b)(2). **Effective** for summonses served after 12-31-82. Prior to amendment, Code Sec. 7609(b)(2) read as follows:

"(2) RIGHT TO STAY COMPLIANCE.—Notwithstanding any other law or rule of law, any person who is entitled to notice of a summons under subsection (a) shall have the right to stay compliance with the summons if, not later than the 14th day after the day such notice is given in the manner provided in subsection (a)(2)—

(A) notice in writing is given to the person summoned not to comply with the summons, and

(B) a copy of such notice not to comply with the summons is mailed by registered or certified mail to such person and to such office as the Secretary may direct in the notice referred to in subsection (a)(1)."

P.L. 97-248, §331(d)(2):

Amended the subsection heading of Code Sec. 7609(b). **Effective** for summonses served after 12-31-82. Prior to amendment, the subsection heading read as follows: "RIGHT TO INTERVENE; RIGHT TO STAY COMPLIANCE.—".

[Sec. 7609(c)]

(c) SUMMONS TO WHICH SECTION APPLIES.—

(1) IN GENERAL.—Except as provided in paragraph (2), this section shall apply to any summons issued under paragraph (2) of section 7602(a) or under section 6420(e)(2), 6421(g)(2), 6427(j)(2), or 7612.

(2) EXCEPTIONS.—This section shall not apply to any summons—

(A) served on the person with respect to whose liability the summons is issued, or any officer or employee of such person;

(B) issued to determine whether or not records of the business transactions or affairs of an identified person have been made or kept;

(C) issued solely to determine the identity of any person having a numbered account (or similar arrangement) with a bank or other institution described in section 7603(b)(2)(A);

(D) issued in aid of the collection of—

(i) an assessment made or judgment rendered against the person with respect to whose liability the summons is issued; or

(ii) the liability at law or in equity of any transferee or fiduciary of any person referred to in clause (i); or

(E)(i) issued by a criminal investigator of the Internal Revenue Service in connection with the investigation of an offense connected with the administration or enforcement of the internal revenue laws; and

(ii) served on any person who is not a third-party recordkeeper (as defined in section 7603(b))

(3) JOHN DOES AND CERTAIN OTHER SUMMONSES.—Subsection (a) shall not apply to any summons described in section (f) or (g).

(4) RECORDS.—For purposes of this section, the term "records" includes books, papers, and other data.

Amendments

• 2005, Gulf Opportunity Zone Act of 2005 (P.L. 109-135)

P.L. 109-135, §408(a)(1):

Amended Code Sec. 7609(c)(2) by inserting" or" at the end of subparagraph (d) by striking ";or" at the end of subparagraph (E) and inserting a period, and by striking subparagraph (F).**Effective** as if included in section 3415 of the Internal Revenue Service Restructuring and Refor Act of 1998 (P.L. 105-206). Prior to being stricken, Code Sec. 7609(c)(2)(F) read as follows:

(F) described in subsection (f) or (g).

P.L. 109-135, §408(a)(2):

Amended Code Sec. 7609(c) by redesignating paragraph (3) as paragraph (4) and by inserting after paragraph (2) a new paragraph (3). **Effective** as if included in section 3415 of the Internal Revenue Service Restructuring and Reform Act of 1998 (P.L. 105-206) [**effective** for summonses served after 7-22-98.—CCH].

• 1998, IRS Restructuring and Reform Act of 1998 (P.L. 105-206)

P.L. 105-206, §3415(c)(2):

Amended Code Sec. 7609(c). **Effective** for summonses served after 7-22-98. Prior to amendment, Code Sec. 7609(c) read as follows:

(c) SUMMONS TO WHICH SECTION APPLIES.—

(1) IN GENERAL.—Except as provided in paragraph (2), a summons is described in this subsection if it is issued under paragraph (2) of section 7602(a) or under section 6420(e)(2), 6421(g)(2), or 6427(j)(2) and requires the production of records.

(2) EXCEPTIONS.—A summons shall not be treated as described in this subsection if—

(A) it is solely to determine the identity of any person having a numbered account (or similar arrangement) with a bank or other institution described in subsection (a)(3)(A), or

(B) it is in aid of the collection of—

(i) the liability of any person against whom an assessment has been made or judgment rendered, or

(ii) the liability at law or in equity of any transferee or fiduciary of any person referred to in clause (i).

(3) RECORDS; CERTAIN RELATED TESTIMONY.—For purposes of this section—

(A) the term "records" includes books, papers, or other data, and

(B) a summons requiring the giving of testimony relating to records shall be treated as a summons requiring the production of such records.

• 1988, Technical and Miscellaneous Revenue Act of 1988 (P.L. 100-647)

P.L. 100-647, §1017(c)(9):

Amended Code Sec. 7609(c)(1) by striking out "6421(f)(2)" and inserting in lieu thereof "6421(g)(2)". **Effective** as if included in the provision of P.L. 99-514 to which it relates.

• 1986, Tax Reform Act of 1986 (P.L. 99-514)

P.L. 99-514, §1703(e)(2)(G):

Amended Code Sec. 7609(c)(1) by striking out "6427(i)(2)" and inserting in lieu thereof "6427(j)(2)". **Effective** for gasoline removed (as defined in Code Sec. 4082, as amended) after 12-31-87.

• 1984, Deficit Reduction Act of 1984 (P.L. 98-369)

P.L. 98-369, §714(i):

Amended Code Sec. 7609(c)(1) by striking out "section 7602" and inserting in lieu thereof "section 7602(a)". **Effective** as if included in P.L. 97-248.

P.L. 98-369, §911(d)[c](2)(G):

Amended Code Sec. 7609(c)(1) by striking out "6427(h)(2)" and inserting in lieu thereof "6427(i)(2)". **Effective** 8-1-84.

• 1983, Surface Transportation Act of 1983 (P.L. 97-424)

P.L. 97-424, §515(b)(12):

Amended Code Sec. 7609(c) by striking out "6424(d)(2)," before "or 6427(h)(2)". **Effective** 1-6-83.

• 1980, Crude Oil Windfall Profit Tax Act of 1980 (P.L. 96-223)

P.L. 96-223, §232(d)(4)(E):

Amended Code Sec. 7609(c)(1) by substituting "6427(h)(2)" for "6427(g)(2)". **Effective** 1-1-79.

• 1978, Revenue Act of 1978 (P.L. 95-600)

P.L. 95-600, §703(1)(4), (r):

Substituted "6427(f)(2)" for "6427(e)(2)" in Code Sec. 7609(c)(1). **Effective** 10-4-76.

• 1978, Surface Transportation Assistance Act of 1978 (P.L. 95-599)

P.L. 95-599, §505(c)(6), (d):

Substituted "6427(g)(2)" for "6427(e)[f](2)" in Code Sec. 7609(c)(1). **Effective** 1-1-79.

[Sec. 7609(d)]

(d) RESTRICTION ON EXAMINATION OF RECORDS.—No examination of any records required to be produced under a summons as to which notice is required under subsection (a) may be made—

(1) before the close of the 23rd day after the day notice with respect to the summons is given in the manner provided in subsection (a)(2), or

(2) where a proceeding under subsection (b)(2)(A) was begun within the 20-day period referred to in such subsection and the requirements of subsection (b)(2)(B) have been met, except

in accordance with an order of the court having jurisdiction of such proceeding or with the consent of the person beginning the proceeding to quash.

Amendments

• 1982, Tax Equity and Fiscal Responsibility Act of 1982 (P.L. 97-248)

P.L. 97-248, §331(b):

Amended Code Sec. 7609(d). **Effective** for summonses served after 12-31-82. Prior to amendment, Code Sec. 7609(d) read as follows:

"(d) RESTRICTION ON EXAMINATION OF RECORDS.—No examination of any records required to be produced under a summons as to which notice is required under subsection (a) may be made—

(1) before the expiration of the 14-day period allowed for the notice not to comply under subsection (b)(2), or

(2) when the requirements of subsection (b)(2) have been met, except in accordance with an order issued by a court of competent jurisdiction authorizing examination of such records or with the consent of the person staying compliance."

[Sec. 7609(e)]

(e) SUSPENSION OF STATUTE OF LIMITATIONS.—

(1) SUBSECTION (b) ACTION.—If any person takes any action as provided in subsection (b) and such person is the person with respect to whose liability the summons is issued (or is the agent, nominee, or other person acting under the direction or control of such person), then the running of any period of limitations under section 6501 (relating to the assessment and collection of tax) or under section 6531 (relating to criminal prosecutions) with respect to such person shall be suspended for the period during which a proceeding, and appeals therein, with respect to the enforcement of such summons is pending.

(2) SUSPENSION AFTER 6 MONTHS OF SERVICE OF SUMMONS.—In the absence of the resolution of the summoned party's response to the summons, the running of any period of limitations under section 6501 or under section 6531 with respect to any person with respect to whose liability the summons is issued (other than a person taking action as provided in subsection (b)) shall be suspended for the period—

(A) beginning on the date which is 6 months after the service of such summons, and

(B) ending with the final resolution of such response.

Amendments

• 1998, IRS Restructuring and Reform Act of 1998 (P.L. 105-206)

P.L. 105-206, §3415(c)(3):

Amended Code Sec. 7609(e)(2) by striking "third-party recordkeeper's" and all that follows through "subsection (f)" and inserting "summoned party's response to the summons". **Effective** for summonses served after 7-22-98. Prior to amendment, Code Sec. 7609(e)(2) read as follows:

(2) SUSPENSION AFTER 6 MONTHS OF SERVICE OF SUMMONS.—In the absence of the resolution of the third-party recordkeeper's response to the summons described in subsection (c), or the summoned party's response to a summons described in subsection (f), the running of any period of limitations under section 6501 or under section 6531 with respect to any person with respect to whose liability the summons is issued (other than a person taking action as provided in subsection (b)) shall be suspended for the period—

(A) beginning on the date which is 6 months after the service of such summons, and

(B) ending with the final resolution of such response.

• 1988, Technical and Miscellaneous Revenue Act of 1988 (P.L. 100-647)

P.L. 100-647, §1014(l)(1)(A)-(B):

Amended Code Sec. 7609(e)(2) by inserting "or the summoned party's response to a summons described in subsection (f)," after "the summons described in subsection (c),", and by striking out "the summons is issued other" and inserting in lieu thereof "the summons is issued". **Effective** on the date of the enactment of this Act.

• 1986, Tax Reform Act of 1986 (P.L. 99-514)

P.L. 99-514, §1561(a):

Amended Code Sec. 7609(e). **Effective** 10-22-86. Prior to amendment, Code Sec. 7609(e) read as follows:

(e) SUSPENSION OF STATUTE OF LIMITATIONS.—If any person takes any action as provided in subsection (b) and such person is the person with respect to whose liability the summons is issued (or is the agent, nominee, or other person acting under the direction or control of such person), then the running of any period of limitations under section 6501 (relating to the assessment and collection of tax) or under section 6531 (relating to criminal prosecutions) with respect to such person shall be suspended for the period during which a proceeding, and appeals therein, with respect to the enforcement of such summons is pending.

[Sec. 7609(f)]

(f) ADDITIONAL REQUIREMENT IN THE CASE OF A JOHN DOE SUMMONS.—Any summons described in subsection (c)(1) which does not identify the person with respect to whose liability the summons is issued may be served only after a court proceeding in which the Secretary establishes that—

(1) the summons relates to the investigation of a particular person or ascertainable group or class of persons,

(2) there is a reasonable basis for believing that such person or group or class of persons may fail or may have failed to comply with any provision of any internal revenue law, and

(3) the information sought to be obtained from the examination of the records or testimony (and the identity of the person or persons with respect to whose liability the summons is issued) is not readily available from other sources.

The Secretary shall not issue any summons described in the preceding sentence unless the information sought to be obtained is narrowly tailored to information that pertains to the failure (or potential failure) of the person or group or class of persons referred to in paragraph (2) to comply with one or more provisions of the internal revenue law which have been identified for purposes of such paragraph.

Amendments

• 2019, Taxpayer First Act (P.L. 116-25)

P.L. 116-25, §1204(a):

Amended Code Sec. 7609(f) by adding at the end a flush sentence. **Effective** for summonses served after the date that is 45 days after 7-1-2019.

• 1998, IRS Restructuring and Reform Act of 1998 (P.L. 105-206)

P.L. 105-206, §3415(c)(4)(A):

Amended Code Sec. 7609(f) by striking "described in subsection (c)" and inserting "described in subsection (c)(1)". **Effective** for summonses served after 7-22-98.

P.L. 105-206, §3415(c)(4)(B):

Amended Code Sec. 7609(f)(3) by inserting "or testimony" after "records". **Effective** for summonses served after 7-22-98.

[Sec. 7609(g)]

(g) SPECIAL EXCEPTION FOR CERTAIN SUMMONSES.—A summons is described in this subsection if, upon petition by the Secretary, the court determines, on the basis of the facts and circumstances alleged, that there is reasonable cause to believe the giving of notice may lead to attempts to conceal, destroy, or alter records relevant to the examination, to prevent the communication of information from other persons through intimidation, bribery, or collusion, or to flee to avoid prosecution, testifying, or production of records.

Amendments

• 1998, IRS Restructuring and Reform Act of 1998 (P.L. 105-206)

P.L. 105-206, §3415(c)(5):

Amended Code Sec. 7609(g) by striking "In the case of any summons described in subsection (c), the provisions of subsections (a)(1) and (b) shall not apply if" and inserting "A summons is described in this subsection if". **Effective** for summonses served after 7-22-98.

[Sec. 7609(h)]

(h) JURISDICTION OF DISTRICT COURT; ETC.—

(1) JURISDICTION.—The United States district court for the district within which the person to be summoned resides or is found shall have jurisdiction to hear and determine any proceedings brought under subsection (b)(2), (f), or (g). An order denying the petition shall be deemed a final order which may be appealed.

(2) SPECIAL RULE FOR PROCEEDINGS UNDER SUBSECTIONS (f) AND (g).—The determinations required to be made under subsections (f) and (g) shall be made ex parte and shall be made solely on the petition and supporting affidavits.

Amendments

• 1984 (P.L. 98-620)

P.L. 98-620, §402(28)(D):

Repealed Code Sec. 7609(h)(3). Not **effective** for cases pending on 11-8-84. Prior to repeal, Code Sec. 7609(h)(3) read as follows:

(3) PRIORITY.—Except as to cases the court considers of greater importance, a proceeding brought for the enforcement of any summons, or a proceeding under this section, and appeals, take precedence on the docket over all other cases and shall be assigned for hearing and decided at the earliest practicable date.

• 1982, Tax Equity and Fiscal Responsibility Act of 1982 (P.L. 97-248)

P.L. 97-248, §331(c):

Amended Code Sec. 7609(h). **Effective** for summonses served after 12-31-82. Prior to amendment, Code Sec. 7609(h) read as follows:

"(h) JURISDICTION OF DISTRICT COURT.—

(1) The United States district court for the district within which the person to be summoned resides or is found shall have jurisdiction to hear and determine proceedings brought under subsections (f) or (g). The determinations required to be made under subsections (f) and (g) shall be made ex parte and shall be made solely upon the petition and supporting affidavits. An order denying the petition shall be deemed a final order which may be appealed.

(2) Except as to cases the court considers of greater importance, a proceeding brought for the enforcement of any summons, or a proceeding under this section, and appeals, take precedence on the docket over all cases and shall be assigned for hearing and decided at the earliest practicable date."

• 1976, Tax Reform Act of 1976 (P.L. 94-455)

P.L. 94-455, §1205(a):

Added Code Sec. 7609. **Effective** with respect to any summons issued after 2-28-77.

* * *

[Sec. 7610]

SEC. 7610. FEES AND COSTS FOR WITNESSES.

[Sec. 7610(a)]

(a) IN GENERAL.—The Secretary shall by regulations establish the rates and conditions under which payment may be made of—

(1) fees and mileage to persons who are summoned to appear before the Secretary, and

(2) reimbursement for such costs that are reasonably necessary which have been directly incurred in searching for, reproducing, or transporting books, papers, records, or other data required to be produced by summons.

[Sec. 7610(b)]

(b) EXCEPTIONS.—No payment may be made under paragraph (2) of subsection (a) if—

(1) the person with respect to whose liability the summons is issued has a proprietary interest in the books, papers, records or other data required to be produced, or

(2) the person summoned is the person with respect to whose liability the summons is issued or an officer, employee, agent, accountant, or attorney of such person who, at the time the summons is served, is acting as such.

[Sec. 7610(c)]

(c) SUMMONS TO WHICH SECTION APPLIES.—This section applies with respect to any summons authorized under section 6420(e)(2), 6421(g)(2), 6427(j)(2), or 7602.

Amendments

• 1988, Technical and Miscellaneous Revenue Act of 1988 (P.L. 100-647)

P.L. 100-647, §1017(c)(9):

Amended Code Sec. 7610(c) by striking out "6421(f)(2)" and inserting in lieu thereof "6421(g)(2)". **Effective** as if included in the provision of P.L. 99-514 to which it relates.

• 1986, Tax Reform Act of 1986 (P.L. 99-514)

P.L. 99-514, §1703(e)(2)(G):

Amended Code Sec. 7610(c) by striking out "6427(i)(2)" and inserting in lieu thereof "6427(j)(2)". **Effective** for gasoline removed (as defined in Code Sec. 4082, as amended) after 12-31-87.

• 1984, Deficit Reduction Act of 1984 (P.L. 98-369)

P.L. 98-369, §911(d)[c](2)(G):

Amended Code Sec. 7610(c) by striking out "6427(h)(2)" and inserting in lieu thereof "6427(i)(2)". **Effective** 8-1-84.

• 1983, Surface Transportation Act of 1983 (P.L. 97-424)

P.L. 97-424, §515(b)(12):

Amended Code Sec. 7610(c) by striking out "6424(d)(2)," before "6427(h)(2)". **Effective** 1-6-83.

• 1980, Crude Oil Windfall Profit Tax Act of 1980 (P.L. 96-223)

P.L. 96-223, §232(d)(4)(E):

Amended Code Sec. 7610(c) by substituting "6427(h)(2)" for "6427(g)(2)". **Effective** 1-1-79.

• 1978, Surface Transportation Assistance Act of 1978 (P.L. 95-599)

P.L. 95-599, §505(c)(6), (d):

Substituted "6427(g)(2)" for "6427(e)(2)" in Code Sec. 7610(c). **Effective** 1-1-79.

• 1976, Tax Reform Act of 1976 (P.L. 94-455)

P.L. 94-455, §1205(a):

Added Code Sec. 7610. **Effective** with respect to any summons issued after 2-28-77.

* * *

Subchapter B—General Powers and Duties

* * *

[Sec. 7621]

SEC. 7621. INTERNAL REVENUE DISTRICTS.

[Sec. 7621(a)]

(a) ESTABLISHMENT AND ALTERATION.—The President shall establish convenient internal revenue districts for the purpose of administering the internal revenue laws. The President may from time to time alter such districts.

[Sec. 7621(b)]

(b) BOUNDARIES.—For the purpose mentioned in subsection (a), the President may subdivide any State or the District of Columbia, or may unite into one district two or more States.

Amendments

• 1976, Tax Reform Act of 1976 (P.L. 94-455)

P.L. 94-455, §1906(a)(53):

Amended Code Sec. 7621(b). **Effective** 2-1-77. Prior to amendment, Code Sec. 7621(b) read as follows:

(b) BOUNDARIES.—For the purpose mentioned in subsection (a), the President may subdivide any State, Territory, or the District of Columbia, or may unite into one District two or more States or a Territory and one or more States.

• 1959, Alaska Omnibus Bill (P.L. 86-70)

P.L. 86-70, §22(e):

Amended 1954 Code Sec. 7621(b). **Effective** 1-3-59. Prior to amendment, Code Sec. 7621(b) read as follows:

(b) BOUNDARIES.—For the purpose mentioned in subsection (a), the President may subdivide any State, Territory, or the District of Columbia, or may unite two or more States or Territories into one district.

* * *

CHAPTER 79—DEFINITIONS

* * *

[Sec. 7701]

SEC. 7701. DEFINITIONS.

[Sec. 7701(a)]

(a) When used in this title, where not otherwise distinctly expressed or manifestly incompatible with the intent thereof—

(1) PERSON.—The term "person" shall be construed to mean and include an individual, a trust, estate, partnership, association, company or corporation.

(2) PARTNERSHIP AND PARTNER.—The term "partnership" includes a syndicate, group, pool, joint venture, or other unincorporated organization, through or by means of which any business, financial operation, or venture is carried on, and which is not, within the meaning of this title, a trust or estate or a corporation; and the term "partner" includes a member in such a syndicate, group, pool, joint venture, or organization.

(3) CORPORATION.—The term "corporation" includes associations, joint-stock companies, and insurance companies.

(4) DOMESTIC.—The term "domestic" when applied to a corporation or partnership means created or organized in the United States or under the law of the United States or of any State unless, in the case of a partnership, the Secretary provides otherwise by regulations.

Amendments

• 1997, Taxpayer Relief Act of 1997 (P.L. 105-34)

P.L. 105-34, §1151(a):

Amended Code Sec. 7701(a)(4) by inserting before the period "unless, in the case of a partnership, the Secretary provides otherwise by regulations". **Effective** 8-5-97. For a special rule, see Act Sec. 1151(b).

P.L. 105-34, §1151(b), provides:

(b) EFFECTIVE DATE.—Any regulations issued with respect to the amendment made by subsection (a) shall apply to partnerships created or organized after the date determined under section 7805(b) of the Internal Revenue Code of 1986 (without regard to paragraph (2) thereof) with respect to such regulations.

• 1976, Tax Reform Act of 1976 (P.L. 94-455)

P.L. 94-455, §1906(c)(3):

Amended Code Sec. 7701(a)(4) by deleting "or Territory" after "State". **Effective** 2-1-77.

(5) FOREIGN.—The term "foreign" when applied to a corporation or partnership means a corporation or partnership which is not domestic.

(6) FIDUCIARY.—The term "fiduciary" means a guardian, trustee, executor, administrator, receiver, conservator, or any person acting in any fiduciary capacity for any person.

(7) STOCK.—The term "stock" includes shares in an association, joint-stock company, or insurance company.

(8) SHAREHOLDER.—The term "shareholder" includes a member in an association, joint-stock company, or insurance company.

(9) UNITED STATES.—The term "United States" when used in a geographical sense includes only the States and the District of Columbia.

Amendments

• 1960, Hawaii Omnibus Act (P.L. 86-624)

P.L. 86-624, §18(i):

Amended 1954 Code Sec. 7701(a)(9) by striking out ", the Territory of Hawaii," immediately after the word "States". **Effective** 8-21-59.

• 1959, Alaska Omnibus Bill (P.L. 86-70)

P.L. 86-70, §22(a):

Amended 1954 Code Sec. 7701(a)(9) by striking out "Territories of Alaska and", and by substituting "Territory of". **Effective** 1-3-59.

(10) STATE.—The term "State" shall be construed to include the District of Columbia, where such construction is necessary to carry out provisions of this title.

Amendments

• 1960, Hawaii Omnibus Act (P.L. 86-624)

P.L. 86-624, §18(j):

Amended 1954 Code Sec. 7701(a)(10) by striking out "the Territory of Hawaii and" immediately after the word "include". **Effective** 8-21-59.

• 1959, Alaska Omnibus Bill (P.L. 86-70)

P.L. 86-70, §22(a):

Amended 1954 Code Sec. 7701(a)(10) by striking out "Territories", and by substituting "Territory of Hawaii". **Effective** 1-3-59.

(11) SECRETARY OF THE TREASURY AND SECRETARY.—

(A) SECRETARY OF THE TREASURY.—The term "Secretary of the Treasury" means the Secretary of the Treasury, personally, and shall not include any delegate of his.

(B) SECRETARY.—The term "Secretary" means the Secretary of the Treasury or his delegate.

Amendments

• 1976, Tax Reform Act of 1976 (P.L. 94-455)

P.L. 94-455, §1906(a)(57)(A):

Amended Code Sec. 7701(a)(11). **Effective** 2-1-77. Prior to amendment, Sec. 7701(a)(11) read as follows:

(11) SECRETARY.—The term "Secretary" means the Secretary of the Treasury.

(12) DELEGATE.—

(A) IN GENERAL.—The term "or his delegate"—

(i) when used with reference to the Secretary of the Treasury, means any officer, employee, or agency of the Treasury Department duly authorized by the Secretary of the Treasury directly, or indirectly by one or more redelegations of authority, to perform the function mentioned or described in the context; and

(ii) when used with reference to any other official of the United States, shall be similarly construed.

(B) PERFORMANCE OF CERTAIN FUNCTIONS IN GUAM OR AMERICAN SAMOA.—The term "delegate", in relation to the performance of functions in Guam or American Samoa with respect to the taxes imposed by chapters 1, 2 and 21, also includes any officer or employee of any other department or agency of the United States, or of any possession thereof, duly authorized by the Secretary (directly, or indirectly by one or more redelegations of authority) to perform such functions.

Amendments

• 1976, Tax Reform Act of 1976 (P.L. 94-455)

P.L. 94-455, §1906(a)(57)(B):

Amended Code Sec. 7701(a)(12)(A). **Effective** 2-1-77. Prior to amendment, Sec. 7701(a)(12)(A) read as follows:

(12) DELEGATE.—

(A) IN GENERAL.—The term "Secretary or his delegate" means the Secretary of the Treasury, or any officer, employee, or agency of the Treasury Department duly authorized by the Secretary (directly, or indirectly by one or more redelegations of authority) to perform the function mentioned or described in the context, and the term "or his delegate" when used in connection with any other official of the United States shall be similarly construed.

• 1972 (P.L. 92-606)

P.L. 92-606, §1(f)(4):

Amended Code Sec. 7701(a)(12)(B) by substituting "chapters 1, 2 and 21" for "chapters 1 and 21". **Effective** with respect to tax years beginning after 12-31-72.

• 1960, Social Security Amendments of 1960 (P.L. 86-778)

P.L. 86-778, §103(t):

Amended paragraph (12). Prior to amendment, it read as follows:

(12) DELEGATE.—The term "Secretary or his delegate" means the Secretary of the Treasury, or any officer, employee, or agency of the Treasury Department duly authorized by the Secretary (directly, or indirectly by one or more redelegations of authority) to perform the function mentioned or described in the context, and the term "or his delegate" when used in connection with any other official of the United States shall be similarly construed.

(13) COMMISSIONER.—The term "Commissioner" means the Commissioner of Internal Revenue.

(14) TAXPAYER.—The term "taxpayer" means any person subject to any internal revenue tax.

(15) MILITARY OR NAVAL FORCES AND ARMED FORCES OF THE UNITED STATES.—The term "military or naval forces of the United States" and the term "Armed Forces of the United States" each includes all regular and reserve components of the uniformed services which are subject to the jurisdiction of the Secretary of Defense, the Secretary of the Army, the Secretary of the Navy, or the Secretary of the Air Force, and each term also includes the Coast Guard. The members of such forces include commissioned officers and personnel below the grade of commissioned officers in such forces.

(16) WITHHOLDING AGENT.—The term "withholding agent" means any person required to deduct and withhold any tax under the provisions of section 1441, 1442, 1443, or 1461.

Amendments

• 1984, Deficit Reduction Act of 1984 (P.L. 98-369)

P.L. 98-369, §474(r)(29)(K):

Amended Code Sec. 7701(a)(16) by striking out "1451,". **Effective** for tax years beginning after 12-31-83, and to carrybacks from such years but does not apply with respect to obligations issued before 1-1-84.

• 1983, Interest and Dividend Tax Compliance Act of 1983 (P.L. 98-67)

P.L. 98-67, §102(a):

Repealed the amendment made to Code Sec. 7701(a)(16) by P.L. 97-248 as though it had not been enacted. **Effective** as of the close of 6-30-83.

• 1982, Tax Equity and Fiscal Responsibility Act of 1982 (P.L. 97-248)

P.L. 97-248, §307(a)(17):

Amended Code Sec. 7701(a)(16) by striking out "or 1461" and inserting "1461 or 3451". **Effective** 7-1-83.

(17) HUSBAND AND WIFE.—As used in section 2516, if the husband and wife therein referred to are divorced, wherever appropriate to the meaning of such section, the term "wife" shall be read "former wife" and the term "husband" shall be read "former husband"; and, if the payments described in such section are made by or on behalf of the wife or former wife to the husband or former husband instead of vice versa, wherever appropriate to the meaning of such section, the term "husband" shall be read "wife" and the term "wife" shall be read "husband."

Amendments

• 2017, Tax Cuts and Jobs Act (P.L. 115-97)

P.L. 115-97, §11051(b)(4)(A)-(B):

Amended Code Sec. 7701(a)(17) by striking "sections 682 and 2516" and inserting "section 2516", and by striking "such sections" each place it appears and inserting "such section". For the **effective** date, see Act Sec. 11051(c)(1)-(2), below.

P.L. 115-97, §11051(c)(1)-(2), provides:

(c) EFFECTIVE DATE.—The amendments made by this section shall apply to—

(1) any divorce or separation instrument (as defined in section 71(b)(2) of the Internal Revenue Code of 1986 as in effect before the date of the enactment of this Act) executed after December 31, 2018, and

(2) any divorce or separation instrument (as so defined) executed on or before such date and modified after such date if the modification expressly provides that the amendments made by this section apply to such modification.

• 2004, Working Families Tax Relief Act of 2004 (P.L. 108-311)

P.L. 108-311, §207(24):

Amended Code Sec. 7701(a)(17) by striking "152(b)(4), 682," and inserting "682". **Effective** for tax years beginning after 12-31-2004.

• 1986, Tax Reform Act of 1986 (P.L. 99-514)

P.L. 99-514, §1842(d):

Amended Code Sec. 7701(a)(17) by striking out "and 682" and inserting in lieu thereof ", 682, and 2516". **Effective** as if included in the provision of P.L. 98-369 to which it relates.

• 1984, Deficit Reduction Act of 1984 (P.L. 98-369)

P.L. 98-369, 422(d)(3):

Amended Code Sec. 7701(a)(17) by striking out "71, 152(b)(4), 215, and 682" and inserting in lieu thereof "152(b)(4) and 682". **Effective** with respect to divorce or separation instruments (as defined in section 71(b)(2) of the Internal Revenue Code of 1954, as amended by this section) executed after 12-31-84. Also **effective** for any divorce or separation instrument (as so defined) executed before 1-1-85, but modified on or after such date if the modification expressly provides that the amendments made by this section shall apply to such modification.

(18) INTERNATIONAL ORGANIZATION.—The term "international organization" means a public international organization entitled to enjoy privileges, exemptions, and immunities as an international organization under the International Organizations Immunities Act (22 U. S. C. 288-288f).

(19) DOMESTIC BUILDING AND LOAN ASSOCIATION.—The term "domestic building and loan association" means a domestic building and loan association, a domestic savings and loan association, and a Federal savings and loan association—

(A) which is subject by law to supervision and examination by State or Federal authority having supervision over such associations;

(B) the business of which consists principally of acquiring the savings of the public and investing in loans; and

(C) at least 60 percent of the amount of the total assets of which (at the close of the taxable year) consists of—

(i) cash,

(ii) obligations of the United States or of a State or political subdivision thereof, and stock or obligations of a corporation which is an instrumentality of the United States or of a State or political subdivision thereof, but not including obligations the interest on which is excludable from gross income under section 103,

(iii) certificates of deposit in, or obligations of, a corporation organized under a State law which specifically authorizes such corporation to insure the deposits or share accounts of member associations,

(iv) loans secured by a deposit or share of a member,

(v) loans (including redeemable ground rents, as defined in section 1055) secured by an interest in real property which is (or, from the proceeds of the loan, will become) residential real property or real property used primarily for church purposes, loans made for the improvement of residential real property or real property used primarily for church purposes, provided that for purposes of this clause, residential real property shall include single or multifamily dwellings, facilities in residential developments dedicated to public use or property used on a nonprofit basis for residents, and mobile homes not used on a transient basis,

(vi) loans secured by an interest in real property located within an urban renewal area to be developed for predominantly residential use under an urban renewal plan approved by the Secretary of Housing and Urban Development under part A or part B of title I of the Housing Act of 1949, as amended, or located within any area covered by a program eligible for assistance under section 103 of the Demonstration Cities and Metropolitan Development Act of 1966, as amended, and loans made for the improvement of any such real property,

(vii) loans secured by an interest in educational, health, or welfare institutions or facilities, including structures designed or used primarily for residential purposes for students, residents, and persons under care, employees, or members of the staff of such institutions or facilities,

(viii) property acquired through the liquidation of defaulted loans described in clause (v), (vi), or (vii),

(ix) loans made for the payment of expenses of college or university education or vocational training, in accordance with such regulations as may be prescribed by the Secretary,

(x) property used by the association in the conduct of the business described in subparagraph (B), and,

(xi) any regular or residual interest in a REMIC, but only in the proportion which the assets of such REMIC consist of property described in any of the preceding clauses of this subparagraph; except that if 95 percent or more of the assets of such REMIC are assets described in clauses (i) through (x), the entire interest in the REMIC shall qualify.

At the election of the taxpayer, the percentage specified in this subparagraph shall be applied on the basis of the average assets outstanding during the taxable year, in lieu of the close of the taxable year, computed under regulations prescribed by the Secretary. For purposes of clause (v), if a multifamily structure securing a loan is used in part for nonresidential purposes, the entire loan is deemed a residential real property loan if the planned residential use exceeds 80 percent of the property's planned use (determined as of the time the loan is made). For purposes of clause (v), loans made to finance the acquisition or development of land shall be deemed to be loans secured by an interest in residential real property if, under regulations prescribed by the Secretary, there is reasonable assurance that the property will become residential real property within a period of 3 years from the date of acquisition of such land; but this sentence shall not apply for any taxable year unless, within such 3-year period, such land becomes residential real property. For purposes of determining whether any interest in a REMIC qualifies under clause (xi), any regular interest in another REMIC held by such REMIC shall be treated as a loan described in a preceding clause under principles similar to the principles of clause (xi); except that, if such REMIC's are part of a tiered structure, they shall be treated as 1 REMIC for purposes of clause (xi).

Amendments

• 2018, Tax Technical Corrections Act of 2018 (P.L. 115-141)

P.L. 115-141, §401(b)(54), Div. U:

Amended Code Sec. 7701(a)(19)(A) by striking "either (i)" and all that follows through "(ii)". **Effective** 3-23-2018. For a special rule, see Act Sec. 401(e), Div. U, below. Prior to amendment, Code Sec. 7701(a)(19)(A) read as follows:

(A) which either (i) is an insured institution within the meaning of section 401(a) of the National Housing Act (12 U. S. C. sec. 1724(a)), or (ii) is subject by law to supervision and examination by State or Federal authority having supervision over such associations;

P.L. 115-141, §401(e), Div. U, provides:

(e) GENERAL SAVINGS PROVISION WITH RESPECT TO DEADWOOD PROVISIONS.—If—

(1) any provision amended or repealed by the amendments made by subsection (b) or (d) applied to—

(A) any transaction occurring before the date of the enactment of this Act,

(B) any property acquired before such date of enactment, or

(C) any item of income, loss, deduction, or credit taken into account before such date of enactment, and

(2) the treatment of such transaction, property, or item under such provision would (without regard to the amendments or repeals made by such subsection) affect the liability for tax for periods ending after such date of enactment,

nothing in the amendments or repeals made by this section shall be construed to affect the treatment of such transaction, property, or item for purposes of determining liability for tax for periods ending after such date of enactment.

• 2004, American Jobs Creation Act of 2004 (P.L. 108-357)

P.L. 108-357, §835(b)(10)(A)-(B):

Amended Code Sec. 7701(a)(19)(C)(xi) by striking "and any regular interest in a FASIT,", and by striking "or FASIT" each place it appears. For the **effective** date, see Act Sec. 835(c), below. Prior to amendment, Code Sec. 7701(a)(19)(C)(xi) read as follows:

(xi) any regular or residual interest in a REMIC, and any regular interest in a FASIT, but only in the proportion which the assets of such REMIC or FASIT consist of property described in any of the preceding clauses of this subparagraph; except that if 95 percent or more of the assets of such REMIC or FASIT are assets described in clauses (i) through (x), the entire interest in the REMIC or FASIT shall qualify.

P.L. 108-357, §835(c), provides:

(c) EFFECTIVE DATE.—

(1) IN GENERAL.—Except as provided in paragraph (2), the amendments made by this section shall take effect on January 1, 2005.

(2) EXCEPTION FOR EXISTING FASITS.—Paragraph (1) shall not apply to any FASIT in existence on the date of the enactment of this Act [10-22-2004.—CCH] to the extent that regular interests issued by the FASIT before such date continue to remain outstanding in accordance with the original terms of issuance.

• 1996, Small Business Job Protection Act of 1996 (P.L. 104-188)

P.L. 104-188, §1621(b)(8):

Amended Code Sec. 7701(a)(19)(C)(xi). **Effective** 9-1-97. Prior to amendment, Code Sec. 7701(a)(19)(C)(xi) read as follows:

(xi) any regular or residual interest in a REMIC, but only in the proportion which the assets of such REMIC consist of property described in any of the preceding clauses of this subparagraph; except that if 95 percent or more of the assets of such REMIC are assets described in clauses (i) through (x), the entire interest in the REMIC shall qualify.

• 1988, Technical and Miscellaneous Revenue Act of 1988 (P.L. 100-647)

P.L. 100-647, §1006(t)(12):

Amended Code Sec. 7701(a)(19)(C)(xi) by striking out "are loans described" and inserting in lieu thereof "are assets described". **Effective** as if included in the provision of P.L. 99-514 to which it relates.

P.L. 100-647, §1006(t)(25)(A):

Amended Code Sec. 7701(a)(19) by adding at the end thereof a new sentence. **Effective** as if included in the provision of P.L. 99-514 to which it relates.

• 1986, Tax Reform Act of 1986 (P.L. 99-514)

P.L. 99-514, §671(b)(3):

Amended Code Sec. 7701(a)(19) by striking out "and" at the end of clause (ix), by striking out the period at the end of clause (x) and inserting in lieu thereof ", and", and by inserting after clause (x) the new clause (xi). **Effective** for tax years beginning after 12-31-86.

• 1976, Tax Reform Act of 1976 (P.L. 94-455)

P.L. 94-455, §1906(b)(13)(A):

Amended 1954 Code by substituting "Secretary" for "Secretary or his delegate" each place it appeared. **Effective** 2-1-77.

• 1969, Tax Reform Act of 1969 (P.L. 91-172)

P.L. 91-172, §432(c):

Amended Code Sec. 7701(a)(19). **Effective** for tax years beginning after 7-11-69. Prior to amendment, Code Sec. 7701(a)(19) read as follows:

(19) DOMESTIC BUILDING AND LOAN ASSOCIATION.—The term "domestic building and loan association" means a domestic building and loan association, a domestic savings and loan association, and a Federal savings and loan association—

(A) which either (i) is an insured institution within the meaning of section 401(a) of the National Housing Act (12 U. S. C., sec. 1724(a)), or (ii) is subject by law to supervision and examination by State or Federal authority having supervision over such associations;

(B) substantially all of the business of which consists of acquiring the savings of the public and investing in loans described in subparagraph (C);

(C) at least 90 percent of the amount of the total assets of which (as of the close of the taxable year) consists of (i) cash, (ii) obligations of the United States or of a State or political subdivision thereof, stock or obligations of a corporation which is an instrumentality of the United States or of a State or political subdivision thereof, and certificates of deposit in, or obligations of, a corporation organized under a State law which specifically authorizes such corporation to insure the deposits or share accounts of member associations, (iii) loans secured by an interest in real property and loans made for the improvement of real property, (iv) loans secured by a deposit or share of a member, (v) property acquired through the liquidation of defaulted loans described in clause (iii), and (vi) property used by the association in the conduct of the business described in subparagraph (B);

(D) of the assets of which taken into account under subparagraph (C) as assets constituting the 90 percent of total assets—

(i) at least 80 percent of the amount of such assets consists of assets described in clauses (i), (ii), (iv), and (vi) of such subparagraph and of loans secured by an interest in real property which is (or, from the proceeds of the loan, will become) residential real property or real property used primarily for church purposes, loans made for the improvement of residential real property or real property used primarily for church purposes, or property acquired through the liquidation of defaulted loans described in this clause; and

(ii) at least 60 percent of the amount of such assets consists of assets described in clauses (i), (ii), (iv), and (vi) of such subparagraph and of loans secured by an interest in real property which is (or, from the proceeds of the loan, will become) residential real property containing 4 or fewer family units or real property used primarily for church purposes, loans made for the improvement of residential real property containing 4 or fewer family units or real property used primarily for church purposes, or property acquired through the liquidation of defaulted loans described in this clause;

(E) not more than 18 percent of the amount of the total assets of which (as of the close of the taxable year) consists of assets other than those described in clause (i) of subparagraph (D), and not more than 36 percent of the amount of the total assets of which (as of the close of the taxable year) consists of assets other than those described in clause (ii) of subparagraph (D); and

(F) except for property described in subparagraph (C), not more than 3 percent of the assets of which consists of stock of any corporation.

The term "domestic building and loan association" also includes any association which, for the taxable year, would satisfy the requirements of the first sentence of this paragraph if "41 percent" were substituted for "36 percent" in subparagraph (E). Except in the case of the taxpayer's first taxable year beginning after the date of the enactment of the Revenue Act of 1962, the second sentence of this paragraph shall not apply to an association for the taxable year unless such association (i) was a domestic building and loan association within the meaning of the first sentence of this paragraph for the first taxable year preceding the taxable year, or (ii) was a domestic building and loan association solely by reason of the second sentence of this paragraph for the first taxable year preceding the taxable year (but not for the second preceding taxable year). At the election of the taxpayer, the percentages specified in this paragraph shall be applied on the basis of the average assets outstanding during the taxable year, in lieu of the close of the taxable year, computed under regulations prescribed by the Secretary or his delegate.

• 1962, Revenue Act of 1962 (P.L. 87-834)

P.L. 87-834, §6:

Amended Code Sec. 7701(a)(19). **Effective** for tax years beginning after 10-16-62. Prior to the amendment Sec. 7701(a)(19) read as follows:

"(19) Domestic building and loan association.—The term `domestic building and loan association' means a domestic building and loan association, a domestic savings and loan association, and a Federal savings and loan association, substantially all the business of which is confined to making loans to members."

(20) EMPLOYEE.—For the purpose of applying the provisions of section 79 with respect to group-term life insurance purchased for employees, for the purpose of applying the provisions of sections 104, 105, and 106 with respect to accident and health insurance or accident and health plans, and for the purpose of applying the provisions of subtitle A with respect to contributions to or under a stock bonus, pension, profit-sharing, or annuity plan, and with respect to distributions under such a plan, or by a trust forming part of such a plan, and for purposes of applying section 125 with respect to cafeteria plans, the term "employee" shall include a full-time life insurance salesman who is considered an employee for the purpose of chapter 21.

Amendments

• 2014, Tax Technical Corrections Act of 2014 (P.L. 113-295)

P.L. 113-295, §221(a)(119), Division A:

Amended Code Sec. 7701(a)(20) by striking "chapter 21" and all that follows and inserting "chapter 21.". **Effective** generally 12-19-2014. For a special rule, see Act Sec. 221(b)(2), Division A, below. Prior to being stricken, "chapter 21" and all that follows read as follows:

chapter 21, or in the case of services performed before January 1, 1951, who would be considered an employee if his services were performed during 1951.

P.L. 113-295, §221(b)(2), Division A, provides:

(2) SAVINGS PROVISION.—If—

(A) any provision amended or repealed by the amendments made by this section applied to—

(i) any transaction occurring before the date of the enactment of this Act,

(ii) any property acquired before such date of enactment, or

(iii) any item of income, loss, deduction, or credit taken into account before such date of enactment, and

(B) the treatment of such transaction, property, or item under such provision would (without regard to the amendments or repeals made by this section) affect the liability for tax for periods ending after date of enactment, nothing in the amendments or repeals made by this section shall be construed to affect the treatment of such transaction, property, or item for purposes of determining liability for tax for periods ending after such date of enactment.

• 1996, Small Business Job Protection Act of 1996 (P.L. 104-188)

P.L. 104-188, §1402(b)(3):

Amended Code Sec. 7701(a)(20) by striking ", for the purpose of applying the provisions of section 101(b) with respect to employees' death benefits" after "accident and health plans". **Effective** with respect to decedents dying after 8-20-96.

• 1988, Technical and Miscellaneous Revenue Act of 1988 (P.L. 100-647)

P.L. 100-647, §1011B(e)(1)-(2):

Amended Code Sec. 7701(a)(20) by striking out "106, and 125" and inserting in lieu thereof "and 106", and by inserting "and for purposes of applying section 125 with respect to cafeteria plans," before "the term". **Effective** as if included in the provision of P.L. 99-514 to which it relates.

• 1986, Tax Reform Act of 1986 (P.L. 99-514)

P.L. 99-514, §1166(a):

Amended Code Sec. 7701(a)(20) by striking out "and 106" and inserting in lieu thereof "106, and 125". **Effective** for tax years beginning after 12-31-85.

• 1964, Revenue Act of 1964 (P.L. 88-272)

P.L. 88-272, §204(a)(3):

Amended the beginning of paragraph (20) to read "For the purpose of applying the provisions of section 79 with respect to group-term life insurance purchased for employees, for the purpose of applying the provisions of section 104" in lieu of "For the purpose of applying the provisions of sections 104". **Effective** 1-1-64.

(21) LEVY.—The term "levy" includes the power of distraint and seizure by any means.

(22) ATTORNEY GENERAL.—The term "Attorney General" means the Attorney General of the United States.

(23) TAXABLE YEAR.—The term "taxable year" means the calendar year, or the fiscal year ending during such calendar year, upon the basis of which the taxable income is computed under subtitle A. "Taxable year" means, in the case of a return made for a fractional part of a year under the provisions of subtitle A or under regulations prescribed by the Secretary, the period for which such return is made.

Amendments

• 1976, Tax Reform Act of 1976 (P.L. 94-455)

P.L. 94-455, §1906(b)(13)(A):

Amended 1954 Code by substituting "Secretary" for "Secretary or his delegate" each place it appeared. **Effective** 2-1-77.

(24) FISCAL YEAR.—The term "fiscal year" means an accounting period of 12 months ending on the last day of any month other than December.

(25) PAID OR INCURRED, PAID OR ACCRUED.—The terms "paid or incurred" and "paid or accrued" shall be construed according to the method of accounting upon the basis of which the taxable income is computed under subtitle A.

(26) TRADE OR BUSINESS.—The term "trade or business" includes the performance of the functions of a public office.

(27) TAX COURT.—The term "Tax Court" means the United States Tax Court.

Amendments

• 1969, Tax Reform Act of 1969 (P.L. 91-172)

P.L. 91-172, §960(j):

Amended Code Sec. 7701(a)(27) by substituting the phrase "United States Tax Court" for the phrase "Tax Court of the United States." **Effective** 12-30-69.

(28) OTHER TERMS.—Any term used in this subtitle with respect to the application of, or in connection with, the provisions of any other subtitle of this title shall have the same meaning as in such provisions.

(29) INTERNAL REVENUE CODE.—The term "Internal Revenue Code of 1986" means this title, and the term "Internal Revenue Code of 1939" means the Internal Revenue Code enacted February 10, 1939, as amended.

Amendments

• 1988, Technical and Miscellaneous Revenue Act of 1988 (P.L. 100-647)

P.L. 100-647, §1(c):

Amended Code Sec. 7701(a)(29) by striking out "of 1954" and inserting in lieu thereof "of 1986". **Effective** as if included in the provision of P.L. 99-514 to which it relates.

(30) UNITED STATES PERSON.—The term "United States person" means—

(A) a citizen or resident of the United States,

(B) a domestic partnership,

(C) a domestic corporation,

(D) any estate (other than a foreign estate, within the meaning of paragraph (31)), and

(E) any trust if—

(i) a court within the United States is able to exercise primary supervision over the administration of the trust, and

(ii) one or more United States persons have the authority to control all substantial decisions of the trust.

Amendments

• 1997, Taxpayer Relief Act of 1997 (P.L. 105-34)

P.L. 105-34, §1601(i)(3)(A):

Amended Code Sec. 7701(a)(30)(E)(ii) by striking "fiduciaries" and inserting "persons". **Effective** as if included in the provision of P.L. 104-188 to which it relates [generally **effective** for tax years beginning after 12-31-96.—CCH].

• 1996, Small Business Job Protection Act of 1996 (P.L. 104-188)

P.L. 104-188, §1907(a)(1):

Amended Code Sec. 7701(a)(30) by striking "and" at the end of subparagraph (C) and by striking subparagraph (D) and by inserting new subparagraphs (D) and (E). **Effective** for tax years beginning after 12-31-96, or at the election of the trusteee of a trust, to tax years ending after the date of the enactment of this Act. Such an election, once made, is irrevocable. For an amendment to this **effective** date, see P.L. 105-34, §1161, below. Prior to amendment, Code Sec. 7701(a)(30)(D) read as follows:

(D) any estate or trust (other than a foreign estate or foreign trust, within the meaning of section 7701(a)(31)).

P.L. 105-34, §1161, provides:

ACT SEC. 1161. TRANSITION RULE FOR CERTAIN TRUSTS.

(a) IN GENERAL.—Paragraph (3) of section 1907(a) of the Small Business Job Protection Act of 1996 is amended by adding at the end the following flush sentence:

To the extent prescribed in regulations by the Secretary of the Treasury or his delegate, a trust which was in existence on August 20, 1996 (other than a trust treated as owned by the grantor under subpart E of part I of subchapter J of chapter 1 of the Internal Revenue Code of 1986), and which was treated as a United States person on the day before the date of the enactment of this Act may elect to continue to be treated as a United States person notwithstanding section 7701(a)(30)(E) of such Code.

(b) EFFECTIVE DATE.—The amendment made by subsection (a) shall take effect as if included in the amendments made by section 1907(a) of the Small Business Job Protection Act of 1996.

• 1962, Revenue Act of 1962 (P.L. 87-834)

P.L. 87-834, §7:

Added paragraph (30) to Code Sec. 7701(a). **Effective** 10-17-62.

(31) FOREIGN ESTATE OR TRUST.—

(A) FOREIGN ESTATE.—The term "foreign estate" means an estate the income of which, from sources without the United States which is not effectively connected with the conduct of a trade or business within the United States, is not includible in gross income under subtitle A.

(B) FOREIGN TRUST.—The term "foreign trust" means any trust other than a trust described in subparagraph (E) of paragraph (30).

Amendments

• 1996, Small Business Job Protection Act of 1996 (P.L. 104-188)

P.L. 104-188, §1907(a)(2):

Amended Code Sec. 7701(a)(31). **Effective** for tax years beginning after 12-31-96, or at the election of the trusteee of a trust, to tax years ending after the date of the enactment of this Act. Such an election, once made, is irrevocable. For an amendment to this **effective** date, see P.L. 105-34, §1161, below. Prior to amendment, Code Sec. 7701(a)(31) read as follows:

(31) FOREIGN ESTATE OR TRUST.—The terms "foreign estate" and "foreign trust" mean an estate or trust, as the case may be, the income of which, from sources without the United States which is not effectively connected with the conduct of a trade or business within the United States, is not includible in gross income under subtitle A.

• 1997, Taxpayer Relief Act of 1997 (P.L. 105-34)

P.L. 105-34, §1161, provides:

ACT SEC. 1161. TRANSITION RULE FOR CERTAIN TRUSTS.

(a) IN GENERAL.—Paragraph (3) of section 1907(a) of the Small Business Job Protection Act of 1996 is amended by adding at the end the following flush sentence:

To the extent prescribed in regulations by the Secretary of the Treasury or his delegate, a trust which was in existence on August 20, 1996 (other than a trust treated as owned by the grantor under subpart E of part I of subchapter J of chapter 1 of the Internal Revenue Code of 1986), and which was treated as a United States person on the day before the date of the enactment of this Act may elect to continue to be treated as a United States person notwithstanding section 7701(a)(30)(E) of such Code.

(b) EFFECTIVE DATE.—The amendment made by subsection (a) shall take effect as if included in the amendments made by section 1907(a) of the Small Business Job Protection Act of 1996.

• 1966, Foreign Investors Tax Act of 1966 (P.L. 89-809)

P.L. 89-809, §103(l)(1):

Amended Code Sec. 7701(a)(31) by substituting ", from sources without the United States which is not effectively connected with the conduct of a trade of business within the United States," for "from sources without the United States". **Effective** 1-1-67.

• 1962, Revenue Act of 1962 (P.L. 87-834)

P.L. 87-834, §7:

Added paragraph (31) to Code Sec. 7701(a). **Effective** 10-17-62.

(32) COOPERATIVE BANK.—The term "cooperative bank" means an institution without capital stock organized and operated for mutual purposes and without profit, which—

(A) is subject by law to supervision and examination by State or Federal authority having supervision over such institutions, and

(B) meets the requirements of subparagraphs (B) and (C) of paragraph (19) of this subsection (relating to definition of domestic building and loan association).

In determining whether an institution meets the requirements referred to in subparagraph (B) of this paragraph, any reference to an association or to a domestic building and loan association contained in paragraph (19) shall be deemed to be a reference to such institution.

Amendments

• 2018, Tax Technical Corrections Act of 2018 (P.L. 115-141)

P.L. 115-141, §401(b)(55), Div. U:

Amended Code Sec. 7701(a)(32)(A). **Effective** 3-23-2018. For a special rule, see Act Sec. 401(e), Div. U, below. Prior to amendment, Code Sec. 7701(a)(32)(A) read as follows:

(A) either—

(i) is an insured institution within the meaning of section 401(a) of the National Housing Act (12 U. S. C., sec. 1724(a)), or

(ii) is subject by law to supervision and examination by State or Federal authority having supervision over such institutions, and

P.L. 115-141, §401(e), Div. U, provides:

(e) GENERAL SAVINGS PROVISION WITH RESPECT TO DEADWOOD PROVISIONS.—If—

(1) any provision amended or repealed by the amendments made by subsection (b) or (d) applied to—

(A) any transaction occurring before the date of the enactment of this Act,

(B) any property acquired before such date of enactment, or

(C) any item of income, loss, deduction, or credit taken into account before such date of enactment, and

(2) the treatment of such transaction, property, or item under such provision would (without regard to the amendments or repeals made by such subsection) affect the liability for tax for periods ending after such date of enactment,

nothing in the amendments or repeals made by this section shall be construed to affect the treatment of such transaction, property, or item for purposes of determining liability for tax for periods ending after such date of enactment.

• 1969, Tax Reform Act of 1969 (P.L. 91-172)

P.L. 91-172, §432(d):

Amended Code Sec. 7701(a)(32)(B) and deleted the third (last) sentence of Code Sec. 7701(a)(32). **Effective** for tax years beginning after 7-11-69. Prior to amendment, Code Sec. 7701(a)(32)(B) read as follows:

(32) Cooperative bank.—The term "cooperative bank" means an institution without capital stock organized and operated for mutual purposes and without profit, which—

(A) either—

(i) is an insured institution within the meaning of section 401(a) of the National Housing Act (12 U. S. C., sec. 1724(a)), or

(ii) is subject by law to supervision and examination by State or Federal authority having supervision over such institutions, and

(B) meets the requirements of subparagraphs (B), (C), (D), (E), and (F) of paragraph (19) of this subsection (relating to definition of domestic building and loan association) determined with the application of the second, third, and fourth sentences of paragraph (19).

In determining whether an institution meets the requirements referred to in subparagraph (B) of this paragraph, any reference to an association or to a domestic building and loan association contained in paragraph (19) shall be deemed to be a reference to such institution. In the case of an institution which, for the taxable year, is a cooperative bank within the meaning of the first sentence of this paragraph by reason of the application of the second and third sentences of paragraph (19) of this subsection, the deduction otherwise allowable under section 166(c) for a reasonable addition to the reserve for bad debts shall, under regulations prescribed by the Secretary or his delegate, be reduced in a manner consistent with the reductions provided by the table contained in section 593(b)(5).

• 1962 (P.L. 87-870)

P.L. 87-870, § 5(a):

Added paragraph (32) to Code Sec. 7701(a). **Effective** 10-17-62.

(33) REGULATED PUBLIC UTILITY.—The term "regulated public utility" means—

(A) A corporation engaged in the furnishing or sale of—

(i) electric energy, gas, water, or sewerage disposal services, or

(ii) transportation (not included in subparagraph (C)) on an intrastate, suburban, municipal, or interurban electric railroad, on an intrastate, municipal, or suburban trackless trolley system, or on a municipal or suburban bus system, or

(iii) transportation (not included in clause (ii)) by motor vehicle—

if the rates for such furnishing or sale, as the case may be, have been established or approved by a State or political subdivision thereof, by an agency or instrumentality of the United States, by a public service or public utility commission or other similar body of the District of Columbia or of any State or political subdivision thereof, or by a foreign country or an agency or instrumentality or political subdivision thereof.

(B) A corporation engaged as a common carrier in the furnishing or sale of transportation of gas by pipe line, if subject to the jurisdiction of the Federal Energy Regulatory Commission.

(C) A corporation engaged as a common carrier (i) in the furnishing or sale of transportation by railroad, if subject to the jurisdiction of the Surface Transportation Board, or (ii) in the furnishing or sale of transportation of oil or other petroleum products (including shale oil) by pipe line, if subject to the jurisdiction of the Federal Energy Regulatory Commission or if the rates for such furnishing or sale are subject to the jurisdiction of a public service or public utility commission or other similar body of the District of Columbia or of any State.

(D) A corporation engaged in the furnishing or sale of telephone or telegraph service, if the rates for such furnishing or sale meet the requirements of subparagraph (A).

(E) A corporation engaged in the furnishing or sale of transportation as a common carrier by air, subject to the jurisdiction of the Secretary of Transportation.

(F) A corporation engaged in the furnishing or sale of transportation by a water carrier subject to jurisdiction under subchapter II of chapter 135 of title 49.

(G) A rail carrier subject to part A of subtitle IV of title 49, if (i) substantially all of its railroad properties have been leased to another such railroad corporation or corporations by an agreement or agreements entered into before January 1, 1954, (ii) each lease is for a term of more than 20 years, and (iii) at least 80 percent or more of its gross income (computed without regard to dividends and capital gains and losses) for the taxable year is derived from such leases and from sources described in subparagraphs (A) through (F), inclusive. For purposes of the preceding sentence, an agreement for lease of railroad properties entered into before January 1, 1954, shall be considered to be a lease including such term as the total number of years of such agreement may, unless sooner terminated, be renewed or continued under the terms of the agreement, and any such renewal or continuance under such agreement shall be considered part of the lease entered into before January 1, 1954.

(H) A common parent corporation which is a common carrier by railroad subject to part A of subtitle IV of title 49 if at least 80 percent of its gross income (computed without regard to capital gains or losses) is derived directly or indirectly from sources described in subparagraphs (A) through (F), inclusive. For purposes of the preceding sentence, dividends and interest, and income from leases described in subparagraph (G), received from a regulated public utility shall be considered as derived from sources described in subparagraphs (A) through (F), inclusive, if the regulated public utility is a member of an affiliated group (as defined in section 1504) which includes the common parent corporation.

The term "regulated public utility" does not (except as provided in subparagraphs (G) and (H)) include a corporation described in subparagraphs (A) through (F), inclusive, unless 80 percent or more of its gross income (computed without regard to dividends and capital gains and losses) for the taxable year is derived from sources described in subparagraphs (A) through (F), inclusive. If the taxpayer establishes to the satisfaction of the Secretary that (i) its revenue from regulated rates described in subparagraph (A) or (D) and its revenue derived from unregulated rates are derived from the operation of a single interconnected and coordinated system or from the operation of more than one such system, and (ii) the unregulated rates have been and are substantially as favorable to users and consumers as are the regulated rates, then such revenue from such unregulated rates shall be considered, for purposes of the preceding sentence, as income derived from sources described in subparagraph (A) or (D).

Amendments

• 1996, Small Business Job Protection Act of 1996 (P.L. 104-188)

P.L. 104-88, §304(e)(1)-(6):

Amended Code Sec. 7701(a)(33) by striking "Federal Power Commission" and inserting in lieu thereof "Federal Energy Regulatory Commission" in subparagraph (B); by striking "Interstate Commerce Commission" and inserting in lieu thereof "Surface Transportation Board" in subparagraph (C)(i); by striking "Interstate Commerce Commission" and inserting in lieu thereof "Federal Energy Regulatory Commission" in subparagraph (C)(ii); by striking "common carrier" and all that follows through "1933" and inserting in lieu thereof "a water carrier subject to jurisdiction under subchapter II of chapter 135 of title 49" in subparagraph (F); by striking "railroad corporation subject to subchapter I of chapter 105" and inserting in lieu thereof "rail carrier subject to part A of subtitle IV" in subparagraph (G); and by striking "subchapter I of chapter 105" and inserting in lieu thereof "part A of subtitle IV" in subparagraph (H). **Effective** 1-1-96. Prior to amendment, Code Sec. 7701(a)(33)(F) read as follows:

(F) A corporation engaged in the furnishing or sale of transportation by common carrier by water, subject to the jurisdiction of the Interstate Commerce Commission under subchapter III of chapter 105 of title 49, or subject to the jurisdiction of the Federal Maritime Board under the Intercoastal Shipping Act, 1933.

• 1984, Civil Aeronautics Board Sunset Act of 1984 (P.L. 98-443)

P.L. 98-443, §9(q):

Amended Code Sec. 7701(a)(33)(E) by striking out "Civil Aeronautics Board" and inserting in lieu thereof "Secretary of Transportation". **Effective** 1-1-85.

• 1984 (P.L. 98-216)

P.L. 98-216, §3(c)(2):

Amended Code Sec. 7701(a)(33)(G) by striking out "part I of the Interstate Commerce Act" and inserting in lieu thereof "subchapter I of chapter 105 of title 49". **Effective** 2-14-84.

• 1983 (P.L. 97-449)

P.L. 97-449, §5(e):

Amended Code Sec. 7701(a)(33) by striking out in subparagraph (F) "part III of the Interstate Commerce Act" and substituting "subchapter III of chapter 105 of title 49"; and by striking out in subparagraph (H) "part I of the Interstate Commerce Act" and substituting "subchapter I of chapter 105 of title 49". **Effective** 1-12-83.

• 1976, Tax Reform Act of 1976 (P.L. 94-455)

P.L. 94-455, §1906(b)(13)(A):

Amended 1954 Code by substituting "Secretary" for "Secretary or his delegate" each place it appeared. **Effective** 2-1-77.

• 1964, Revenue Act of 1964 (P.L. 88-272)

P.L. 88-272, §234(b)(3):

Amended Code Sec. 7701(a) by adding paragraph (33). **Effective** with respect to tax years beginning after 12-31-63.

(34) [Repealed.]

Amendments

• 1984, Deficit Reduction Act of 1984 (P.L. 98-369)

P.L. 98-369, §412(b)(11):

Amended Code Sec. 7701(a) by repealing paragraph (34). **Effective** with respect to tax years beginning after 12-31-84. Prior to amendment, it read as follows:

(34) Estimated Income Tax.—The term "estimated income tax" means—

(A) in the case of an individual, the estimate tax as defined in section 6015(d), or

(B) in the case of a corporation, the estimated tax as defined in section 6154(c).

• 1981, Economic Recovery Tax Act of 1981 (P.L. 97-34)

P.L. 97-34, §725(c)(4):

Amended Code Sec. 7701(a)(34) by striking out "6015(c)" and inserting "6015(d)". **Effective** 1-1-81.

• 1968, Revenue and Expenditure Control Act of 1968 (P.L. 90-364)

P.L. 90-364, §103(e)(6):

Amended Code Sec. 7701(a)(34) by substituting "section 6154(c)" for "section 6016(b)" in subparagraph (B). **Effective** with respect to tax years beginning after 12-31-67. However, the amendment is to be taken into account only as of 5-31-68.

• 1966, Tax Adjustment Act of 1966 (P.L. 89-368)

P.L. 89-368, §102(c)(5):

Added Code Sec. 7701(a)(34). **Effective** 1-1-67.

(35) ENROLLED ACTUARY.—The term "enrolled actuary" means a person who is enrolled by the Joint Board for the Enrollment of Actuaries established under subtitle C of the title III of the Employee Retirement Income Security Act of 1974.

Amendments

• 1974, Employee Retirement Income Security Act of 1974 (P.L. 93-406)

P.L. 93-406, §3043:

Amended Code Sec. 7701(a) by adding paragraph (35). **Effective** 9-2-74.

(36) TAX RETURN PREPARER.—

(A) IN GENERAL.—The term "tax return preparer" means any person who prepares for compensation, or who employs one or more persons to prepare for compensation, any return of tax imposed by this title or any claim for refund of tax imposed by this title. For purposes of the preceding sentence, the preparation of a substantial portion of a return or claim for refund shall be treated as if it were the preparation of such return or claim for refund.

(B) EXCEPTIONS.—A person shall not be a "tax return preparer" merely because such person—

(i) furnishes typing, reproducing, or other mechanical assistance,

(ii) prepares a return or claim for refund of the employer (or of an officer or employee of the employer) by whom he is regularly and continuously employed,

(iii) prepares as a fiduciary a return or claim for refund for any person, or

(iv) prepares a claim for refund for a taxpayer in response to any notice of deficiency issued to such taxpayer or in response to any waiver of restriction after the commencement of an audit of such taxpayer or another taxpayer if a determination in such audit of such other taxpayer directly or indirectly affects the tax liability of such taxpayer.

Amendments

• 2018, Tax Technical Corrections Act of 2018 (P.L. 115-141)

P.L. 115-141, §401(a)(331), Div. U:

Amended Code Sec. 7701(a)(36)(B) by striking "an 'tax" and inserting "a 'tax". **Effective** 3-23-2018.

• 2007, Small Business and Work Opportunity Tax Act of 2007 (P.L. 110-28)

P.L. 110-28, §8246(a)(1)(A)-(B):

Amended Code Sec. 7701(a)(36) by striking "income" each place it appears in the heading and the text, and in subparagraph (A), by striking "subtitle A" each place it appears and inserting "this title". **Effective** for returns prepared after 5-25-2007. Prior to amendment, Code Sec. 7701(a)(36) read as follows:

(36) INCOME TAX RETURN PREPARER.—

(A) IN GENERAL.—The term "income tax return preparer" means any person who prepares for compensation, or who employs one or more persons to prepare for compensation, any return of tax imposed by subtitle A or any claim for refund of tax imposed by subtitle A. For purposes of the preceding sentence, the preparation of a substantial portion of a return or claim for refund shall be treated as if it were the preparation of such return or claim for refund.

(B) EXCEPTIONS.—A person shall not be an "income tax return preparer" merely because such person—

(i) furnishes typing, reproducing, or other mechanical assistance,

(ii) prepares a return or claim for refund of the employer (or of an officer or employee of the employer) by whom he is regularly and continuously employed,

(iii) prepares as a fiduciary a return or claim for refund for any person, or

(iv) prepares a claim for refund for a taxpayer in response to any notice of deficiency issued to such taxpayer or in response to any waiver of restriction after the commencement of an audit of such taxpayer or another taxpayer if a determination in such audit of such other taxpayer directly or indirectly affects the tax liability of such taxpayer.

• 1978, Revenue Act of 1978 (P.L. 95-600)

P.L. 95-600, §701(cc)(2):

Amended Code Sec. 7701(a)(36)(iii). **Effective** with respect to documents prepared after 12-31-76. Prior to amendment, Code Sec. 7701(b)(36)(iii) read:

"(iii) prepares a return or claim for refund for any trust or estate with respect to which he is a fiduciary, or"

• 1976, Tax Reform Act of 1976 (P.L. 94-455)

P.L. 94-455, §1203(a):

Added Code Sec. 7701(a)(36). **Effective** for documents prepared after 12-31-76.

(37) INDIVIDUAL RETIREMENT PLAN.—The term "individual retirement plan" means—

(A) an individual retirement account described in section 408(a), and

(B) an individual retirement annuity described in section 408(b).

Amendments

• 1984, Deficit Reduction Act of 1984 (P.L. 98-369)

P.L. 98-369, §491(d)(53):

Amended Code Sec. 7701(a)(37) by striking out subparagraph (C), by striking out ", and" at the end of subparagraph (B) and inserting in lieu thereof a period, and by adding "and" at the end of subparagraph (A). **Effective** for obligations issued after 12-31-83. Prior to amendment, subparagraph (C) read as follows:

(C) a retirement bond described in section 409.

• 1978, Revenue Act of 1978 (P.L. 95-600)

P.L. 95-600, §157(k)(2):

Added Code Sec. 7701(a)(37). **Effective** for tax years beginning after 12-31-74.

(38) JOINT RETURN.—The term "joint return" means a single return made jointly under section 6013 by a husband and wife.

Amendments

• 1982, Tax Equity and Fiscal Responsibility Act of 1982 (P.L. 97-248)

P.L. 97-248, §201(d)(10):

Added Code Sec. 7701(a)(38). **Effective** for tax years beginning after 12-31-82.

(39) PERSONS RESIDING OUTSIDE UNITED STATES.—If any citizen or resident of the United States does not reside in (and is not found in) any United States judicial district, such citizen or resident shall be treated as residing in the District of Columbia for purposes of any provision of this title relating to—

(A) jurisdiction of courts, or

(B) enforcement of summons.

Amendments

• 1983, Technical Corrections Act of 1982 (P.L. 97-448)

P.L. 97-448, §306(b)(3):

Redesignated Code Sec. 7701(a)(38) (as added by P.L. 97-248) as Code Sec. 7701(a)(39). **Effective** as if included in the provision of P.L 97-248 to which it relates.

• 1982, Tax Equity and Fiscal Responsibility Act of 1982 (P.L. 97-248)

P.L. 97-248, §336(a):

Added Code Sec. 7701(a)(38)[(39)]. **Effective** 9-4-82.

(40) INDIAN TRIBAL GOVERNMENT.—

(A) In general.—The term "Indian tribal government" means the governing body of any tribe, band, community, village, or group of Indians, or (if applicable) Alaska Natives, which is determined by the Secretary, after consultation with the Secretary of the Interior, to exercise governmental functions.

(B) SPECIAL RULE FOR ALASKA NATIVES.—No determination under subparagraph (A) with respect to Alaska Natives shall grant or defer any status or powers other than those enumerated in section 7871. Nothing in the Indian Tribal Governmental Tax Status Act of 1982, or in the amendments made thereby, shall validate or invalidate any claim by Alaska Natives of sovereign authority over lands or people.

Amendments

• 1984 (P.L. 97-473)

P.L. 97-473, §203:

Added Code Sec. 7701(a)(40). For the **effective** date, see the amendment note for P.L. 97-473, §204 following Code Sec. 7871.

(41) TIN.—The term "TIN" means the identifying number assigned to a person under section 6109.

Amendments

• 1983, Interest and Dividend Tax Compliance Act of 1983 (P.L. 98-67)

P.L. 98-67, §104(d)(1):

Added Code Sec. 7701(a)(41). **Effective** with respect to payments made after 12-31-83.

(42) SUBSTITUTED BASIS PROPERTY.—The term "substituted basis property" means property which is—

(A) transferred basis property, or

(B) exchanged basis property.

(43) TRANSFERRED BASIS PROPERTY.—The term "transferred basis property" means property having a basis determined under any provision of subtitle A (or under any corresponding provision of prior income tax law) providing that the basis shall be determined in whole or in part by reference to the basis in the hands of the donor, grantor, or other transferor.

(44) EXCHANGED BASIS PROPERTY.—The term "exchanged basis property" means property having a basis determined under any provision of subtitle A (or under any corresponding provision of prior income tax law) providing that the basis shall be determined in whole or in part by reference to other property held at any time by the person for whom the basis is to be determined.

(45) NONRECOGNITION TRANSACTION.—The term "nonrecognition transaction" means any disposition of property in a transaction in which gain or loss is not recognized in whole or in part for purposes of subtitle A.

Amendments

• 1984, Deficit Reduction Act of 1984 (P.L. 98-369)

P.L. 98-369, §43(a)(1):

Added Code Sec. 7701(a)(42)-(45). **Effective** for tax years ending after 7-18-84.

(46) DETERMINATION OF WHETHER THERE IS A COLLECTIVE BARGAINING AGREEMENT.—In determining whether there is a collective bargaining agreement between employee representatives and 1 or more employers, the term "employee representatives" shall not include any organization more than one-half of the members of which are employees who are owners, officers, or executives of the employer. An agreement shall not be treated as a collective bargaining agreement unless it is a bona fide agreement between bona fide employee representatives and 1 or more employers.

Amendments

• 1986, Tax Reform Act of 1986 (P.L. 99-514)

P.L. 99-514, §1137:

Amended Code Sec. 7701(a)(46) by adding at the end thereof a new sentence. **Effective** 10-22-86.

• 1984, Deficit Reduction Act of 1984 (P.L. 98-369)

P.L. 98-369, §526(c)(1):

Added Code Sec. 7701(a)(46). **Effective** 4-1-84.

(47) [Repealed.]

Amendments

• 2013, American Taxpayer Relief Act of 2012 (P.L. 112-240)

P.L. 112-240, §101(a)(1)-(3), provides:

SEC. 101. PERMANENT EXTENSION AND MODIFICATION OF 2001 TAX RELIEF.

(a) PERMANENT EXTENSION.—

(1) IN GENERAL.—The Economic Growth and Tax Relief Reconciliation Act of 2001 is amended by striking title IX.

(2) CONFORMING AMENDMENT.—The Tax Relief, Unemployment Insurance Reauthorization, and Job Creation Act of 2010 is amended by striking section 304.

(3) EFFECTIVE DATE.—The amendments made by this subsection shall apply to taxable, plan, or limitation years beginning after December 31, 2012, and estates of decedents dying, gifts made, or generation skipping transfers after December 31, 2012.

• 2010, Tax Relief, Unemployment Insurance Reauthorization, and Job Creation Act of 2010 (P.L. 111-312)

P.L. 111-312, §301(a):

Amended Code Sec. 7701(a)(47) to read as such provision would read if subtitle E of title V of the Economic Growth and Tax Relief Reconciliation Act of 2001 (P.L. 107-16) had never been enacted. [P.L. 107-16, §542(e)(3), amended Code Sec. 7701 by adding a new paragraph (47). Therefore, P.L. 111-312, §301(a), effectively repealed Code Sec. 7701(a)(47).—CCH] **Effective** for estates of decedents dying, and transfers made, after 12-31-2009. For a special rule, see Act Sec. 301(c), below. Prior to amendment by P.L. 111-312, Code Sec. 7701(a)(47) read as follows:

(47) EXECUTOR.—The term "executor" means the executor or administrator of the decedent, or, if there is no executor or administrator appointed, qualified, and acting within the United States, then any person in actual or constructive possession of any property of the decedent.

P.L. 111-312, §301(c), provides:

(c) SPECIAL ELECTION WITH RESPECT TO ESTATES OF DECEDENTS DYING IN 2010.—Notwithstanding subsection (a), in the case of an estate of a decedent dying after December 31, 2009, and before January 1, 2011, the executor (within the meaning of section 2203 of the Internal Revenue Code of 1986) may elect to apply such Code as though the amendments made by subsection (a) do not apply with respect to chapter 11 of such Code and with respect to property acquired or passing from such decedent (within the meaning of section 1014(b) of such Code). Such election shall be made at such time and in such manner as the Secretary of the Treasury or the Secretary's delegate shall provide. Such an election once made shall be revocable only with the consent of the Secretary of the Treasury or the Secretary's delegate. For purposes of section 2652(a)(1) of such Code, the determination of whether any property is subject to the tax imposed by such chapter 11 shall be made without regard to any election made under this subsection.

P.L. 111-312, §304, provides [but see P.L. 112-240, §101(a)(2)-(3), above]:

SEC. 304. APPLICATION OF EGTRRA SUNSET TO THIS TITLE.

Section 901 of the Economic Growth and Tax Relief Reconciliation Act of 2001 shall apply to the amendments made by this title.

• 2001, Economic Growth and Tax Relief Reconciliation Act of 2001 (P.L. 107-16)

P.L. 107-16, §542(e)(3):

Amended Code Sec. 7701(a) by adding at the end a new paragraph (47). **Effective** for estates of decedents dying after 12-31-2009.

P.L. 107-16, §901(a)-(b), as amended by P.L. 111-312, §101(a)(1), provides [but see P.L. 112-240, §101(a)(1) and (3), above]:

SEC. 901. SUNSET OF PROVISIONS OF ACT.

(a) IN GENERAL.—All provisions of, and amendments made by, this Act shall not apply—

(1) to taxable, plan, or limitation years beginning after December 31, 2012, or

(2) in the case of title V, to estates of decedents dying, gifts made, or generation skipping transfers, after December 31, 2012.

(b) APPLICATION OF CERTAIN LAWS.—The Internal Revenue Code of 1986 and the Employee Retirement Income Security Act of 1974 shall be applied and administered to years, estates, gifts, and transfers described in subsection (a) as if the provisions and amendments described in subsection (a) had never been enacted.

(48) OFF-HIGHWAY VEHICLES.—

(A) OFF-HIGHWAY TRANSPORTATION VEHICLES.—

(i) IN GENERAL.—A vehicle shall not be treated as a highway vehicle if such vehicle is specially designed for the primary function of transporting a particular type of load other than over the public highway and because of this special design such vehicle's capability to transport a load over the public highway is substantially limited or impaired.

(ii) DETERMINATION OF VEHICLE'S DESIGN.—For purposes of clause (i), a vehicle's design is determined solely on the basis of its physical characteristics.

(iii) DETERMINATION OF SUBSTANTIAL LIMITATION OR IMPAIRMENT.—For purposes of clause (i), in determining whether substantial limitation or impairment exists, account may be taken of factors such as the size of the vehicle, whether such vehicle is subject to the licensing, safety, and other requirements applicable to highway vehicles, and whether such vehicle can transport a load at a sustained speed of at least 25 miles per hour. It is immaterial that a vehicle can transport a greater load off the public highway than such vehicle is permitted to transport over the public highway.

(B) NONTRANSPORTATION TRAILERS AND SEMITRAILERS.—A trailer or semitrailer shall not be treated as a highway vehicle if it is specially designed to function only as an enclosed stationary shelter for the carrying on of an offhighway function at an off-highway site.

Amendments

• 2004, American Jobs Creation Act of 2004 (P.L. 108-357)

P.L. 108-357, §852(a):

Amended Code Sec. 7701(a) by adding at the end a new paragraph (48). **Effective** 10-22-2004. For a special rule, see Act Sec. 852(c)(2), below.

P.L. 108-357, §852(c)(2), provides:

(2) FUEL TAXES.—With respect to taxes imposed under subchapter B of chapter 31 and part III of subchapter A of chapter 32, the amendment made by this section shall apply to taxable periods beginning after the date of the enactment of this Act [10-22-2004.—CCH].

(49) QUALIFIED BLOOD COLLECTOR ORGANIZATION.—The term "qualified blood collector organization" means an organization which is—

(A) described in section 501(c)(3) and exempt from tax under section 501(a),

(B) primarily engaged in the activity of the collection of human blood,

(C) registered with the Secretary for purposes of excise tax exemptions, and

(D) registered by the Food and Drug Administration to collect blood.

Amendments

• 2006, Pension Protection Act of 2006 (P.L. 109-280)

P.L. 109-280, §1207(f):

Amended Code Sec. 7701(a) by inserting at the end a new paragraph (49). **Effective** 1-1-2007.

(50) TERMINATION OF UNITED STATES CITIZENSHIP.—

(A) IN GENERAL.—An individual shall not cease to be treated as a United States citizen before the date on which the individual's citizenship is treated as relinquished under section 877A(g)(4).

(B) DUAL CITIZENS.—Under regulations prescribed by the Secretary, subparagraph (A) shall not apply to an individual who became at birth a citizen of the United States and a citizen of another country.

Amendments

• 2008, Heroes Earnings Assistance and Relief Tax Act of 2008 (P.L. 110-245)

P.L. 110-245, §301(c)(1):

Amended Code Sec. 7701(a) by adding at the end a new paragraph (50). **Effective** for any individual whose expatriation date (as so defined) is on or after 6-17-2008.

[Sec. 7701(b)]

(b) DEFINITION OF RESIDENT ALIEN AND NONRESIDENT ALIEN.—

(1) IN GENERAL.—For purposes of this title (other than subtitle B)—

(A) RESIDENT ALIEN.—An alien individual shall be treated as a resident of the United States with respect to any calendar year if (and only if) such individual meets the requirements of clause (i), (ii), or (iii):

(i) LAWFULLY ADMITTED FOR PERMANENT RESIDENCE.—Such individual is a lawful permanent resident of the United States at any time during such calendar year.

(ii) SUBSTANTIAL PRESENCE TEST.—Such individual meets the substantial presence test of paragraph (3).

(iii) FIRST YEAR ELECTION.—Such individual makes the election provided in paragraph (4).

(B) NONRESIDENT ALIEN.—An individual is a nonresident alien if such individual is neither a citizen of the United States nor a resident of the United States (within the meaning of subparagraph (A)).

(2) SPECIAL RULES FOR FIRST AND LAST YEAR OF RESIDENCY.—

(A) FIRST YEAR OF RESIDENCY.—

(i) IN GENERAL.—If an alien individual is a resident of the United States under paragraph (1)(A) with respect to any calendar year, but was not a resident of the United States at any time during the preceding calendar year, such alien individual shall be treated as a resident of the United States only for the portion of such calendar year which begins on the residency starting date.

(ii) RESIDENCY STARTING DATE FOR INDIVIDUALS LAWFULLY ADMITTED FOR PERMANENT RESIDENCE.—In the case of an individual who is a lawfully permanent resident of the United States at any time during the calendar year, but does not meet the substantial presence test of paragraph (3), the residency starting date shall be the first day in such calendar year on which he was present in the United States while a lawful permanent resident of the United States.

(iii) RESIDENCY STARTING DATE FOR INDIVIDUALS MEETING SUBSTANTIAL PRESENCE TEST.—In the case of an individual who meets the substantial presence test of paragraph (3) with respect to any calendar year, the residency starting date shall be the first day during such calendar year on which the individual is present in the United States.

(iv) RESIDENCY STARTING DATE FOR INDIVIDUALS MAKING FIRST YEAR ELECTION.—In the case of an individual who makes the election provided by paragraph (4) with respect to any calendar year, the residency starting date shall be the 1st day during such calendar year on which the individual is treated as a resident of the United States under that paragraph.

(B) LAST YEAR OF RESIDENCY.—An alien individual shall not be treated as a resident of the United States during a portion of any calendar year if—

(i) such portion is after the last day in such calendar year on which the individual was present in the United States (or, in the case of an individual described in paragraph (1)(A)(i), the last day on which he was so described),

(ii) during such portion the individual has a closer connection to a foreign country than to the United States, and

(iii) the individual is not a resident of the United States at any time during the next calendar year.

(C) CERTAIN NOMINAL PRESENCE DISREGARDED.—

(i) IN GENERAL.—For purposes of subparagraphs (A)(iii) and (B), an individual shall not be treated as present in the United States during any period for which the individual establishes that he has a closer connection to a foreign country than to the United States.

(ii) NOT MORE THAN 10 DAYS DISREGARDED.—Clause (i) shall not apply to more than 10 days on which the individual is present in the United States.

(3) SUBSTANTIAL PRESENCE TEST.—

(A) IN GENERAL.—Except as otherwise provided in this paragraph, an individual meets the substantial presence test of this paragraph with respect to any calendar year (hereinafter in this subsection referred to as the "current year") if—

(i) such individual was present in the United States on at least 31 days during the calendar year, and

(ii) the sum of the number of days on which such individual was present in the United States during the current year and the 2 preceding calendar years (when multiplied by the applicable multiplier determined under the following table) equals or exceeds 183 days:

In the case of days in:	**The applicable multiplier is:**
Current year	1
1st preceding year	1/3
2nd preceding year	1/6

(B) EXCEPTION WHERE INDIVIDUAL IS PRESENT IN THE UNITED STATES DURING LESS THAN ONE-HALF OF CURRENT YEAR AND CLOSER CONNECTION TO FOREIGN COUNTRY IS ESTABLISHED.—An individual shall not be treated as meeting the substantial presence test of this paragraph with respect to any current year if—

(i) such individual is present in the United States on fewer than 183 days during the current year, and

(ii) it is established that for the current year such individual has a tax home (as defined in section 911(d)(3) without regard to the second sentence thereof) in a foreign country and has a closer connection to such foreign country than to the United States.

(C) SUBPARAGRAPH (B) NOT TO APPLY IN CERTAIN CASES.—Subparagraph (B) shall not apply to any individual with respect to any current year if at any time during such year—

(i) such individual had an application for adjustment of status pending, or

(ii) such individual took other steps to apply for status as a lawful permanent resident of the United States.

(D) EXCEPTION FOR EXEMPT INDIVIDUALS OR FOR CERTAIN MEDICAL CONDITIONS.—An individual shall not be treated as being present in the United States on any day if—

(i) such individual is an exempt individual for such day, or

(ii) such individual was unable to leave the United States on such day because of a medical condition which arose while such individual was present in the United States.

(4) FIRST-YEAR ELECTION.—

(A) An alien individual shall be deemed to meet the requirements of this subparagraph if such individual—

(i) is not a resident of the United States under clause (i) or (ii) of paragraph (1)(A) with respect to a calendar year (hereinafter referred to as the "election year"),

(ii) was not a resident of the United States under paragraph (1)(A) with respect to the calendar year immediately preceding the election year,

(iii) is a resident of the United States under clause (ii) of paragraph (1)(A) with respect to the calendar year immediately following the election year, and

(iv) is both—

(I) present in the United States for a period of at least 31 consecutive days in the election year, and

(II) present in the United States during the period beginning with the first day of such 31-day period and ending with the last day of the election year (hereinafter referred to as the "testing period") for a number of days equal to or exceeding 75 percent of the number of days in the testing period (provided that an individual shall be treated for purposes of this subclause as present in the United States for a number of days during the testing period not exceeding 5 days in the aggregate, notwithstanding his absence from the United States on such days).

(B) An alien individual who meets the requirements of subparagraph (A) shall, if he so elects, be treated as a resident of the United States with respect to the election year.

(C) An alien individual who makes the election provided by subparagraph (B) shall be treated as a resident of the United States for the portion of the election year which begins on the 1st day of the earliest testing period during such year with respect to which the individual meets the requirements of clause (iv) of subparagraph (A).

(D) The rules of subparagraph (D)(i) of paragraph (3) shall apply for purposes of determining an individual's presence in the United States under this paragraph.

(E) An election under subparagraph (B) shall be made on the individual's tax return for the election year, provided that such election may not be made before the individual has met the substantial presence test of paragraph (3) with respect to the calendar year immediately following the election year.

(F) An election once made under subparagraph (B) remains in effect for the election year, unless revoked with the consent of the Secretary.

(5) EXEMPT INDIVIDUAL DEFINED.—For purposes of this subsection—

(A) IN GENERAL.—An individual is an exempt individual for any day if, for such day, such individual is—

(i) a foreign government-related individual,

(ii) a teacher or trainee,

(iii) a student, or

(iv) a professional athlete who is temporarily in the United States to compete in a sports event—

(I) which is organized for the primary purpose of benefiting an organization which is described in section 501(c)(3) and exempt from tax under section 501(a),

(II) all of the net proceeds of which are contributed to such organization, and,

(III) which utilizes volunteers for substantially all of the work performed in carrying out such event.

(B) FOREIGN GOVERNMENT-RELATED INDIVIDUAL.—The term "foreign government-related individual" means any individual temporarily present in the United States by reason of—

(i) diplomatic status, or a visa which the Secretary (after consultation with the Secretary of State) determines represents full-time diplomatic or consular status for purposes of this subsection,

(ii) being a full-time employee of an international organization, or

(iii) being a member of the immediate family of an individual described in clause (i) or (ii).

(C) TEACHER OR TRAINEE.—The term "teacher or trainee" means any individual—

(i) who is termporarily present in the United States under subparagraph (J) or (Q) of section 101(15) of the Immigration and Nationality Act (other than as a student), and

(ii) who substantially complies with the requirements for being so present.

(D) STUDENT.—The term "student" means any individual—

(i) who is temporarily present in the United States—

(I) under subparagraph (F) or (M) of section 101(15) of the Immigration and Nationality Act, or

(II) as a student under subparagraph (J) or (Q) of such section 101(15), and

(ii) who substantially complies with the requirements for being so present.

(E) SPECIAL RULES FOR TEACHERS, TRAINEES, AND STUDENTS.—

(i) LIMITATION ON TEACHERS AND TRAINEES.—An individual shall not be treated as an exempt individual by reason of clause (ii) of subparagraph (A) for the current year if, for any 2 calendar years during the preceding 6 calendar years, such person was an exempt person under clause (ii) or (iii) of subparagraph (A). In the case of an individual all of whose compensation is described in section 872(b)(3), the preceding sentence shall be applied by substituting "4 calendar years" for "2 calendar years".

(ii) LIMITATION ON STUDENTS.—For any calendar year after the 5th calendar year for which an individual was an exempt individual under clause (ii) or (iii) of subparagraph (A), such individual shall not be treated as an exempt individual by reason of clause (iii) of subparagraph (A), unless such individual establishes to the satisfaction of the Secretary that such individual does not intend to permanently reside in the United States and that such individual meets the requirements of subparagraph (D)(ii).

(6) LAWFUL PERMANENT RESIDENT.—For purposes of this subsection, an individual is a lawful permanent resident of the United States at any time if—

(A) such individual has the status of having been lawfully accorded the privilege of residing permanently in the United States as an immigrant in accordance with the immigration laws, and

(B) such status has not been revoked (and has not been administratively or judicially determined to have been abandoned).

An individual shall cease to be treated as a lawful permanent resident of the United States if such individual commences to be treated as a resident of a foreign country under the provisions of a tax treaty between the United States and the foreign country, does not waive the benefits of such treaty applicable to residents of the foreign country, and notifies the Secretary of the commencement of such treatment.

(7) PRESENCE IN THE UNITED STATES.—For purposes of this subsection—

(A) IN GENERAL.—Except as provided in subparagraph (B), (C), or (D) an individual shall be treated as present in the United States on any day if such individual is physically present in the United States at any time during such day.

(B) COMMUTERS FROM CANADA OR MEXICO.—If an individual regularly commutes to employment (or self-employment) in the United States from a place of residence in Canada or Mexico, such individual shall not be treated as present in the United States on any day during which he so commutes.

(C) TRANSIT BETWEEN 2 FOREIGN POINTS.—If an individual, who is in transit between 2 points outside the United States, is physically present in the United States for less than 24 hours, such individual shall not be treated as present in the United States on any day during such transit.

(D) CREW MEMBERS TEMPORARILY PRESENT.—An individual who is temporarily present in the United States on any day as a regular member of the crew of a foreign vessel engaged in transportation between the United States and a foreign country or a possession of the United States shall not be treated as present in the United States on such day unless such individual otherwise engages in any trade or business in the United States on such day.

(8) ANNUAL STATEMENTS.—The Secretary may prescribe regulations under which an individual who (but for subparagraph (B) or (D) of paragraph (3)) would meet the substantial presence test of paragraph (3) is required to submit an annual statement setting forth the basis on which such individual claims the benefits of subparagraph (B) or (D) of paragraph (3), as the case may be.

(9) TAXABLE YEAR.—

(A) IN GENERAL.—For purposes of this title, an alien individual who has not established a taxable year for any prior period shall be treated as having a taxable year which is the calendar year.

(B) FISCAL YEAR TAXPAYER.—If—

(i) an individual is treated under paragraph (1) as a resident of the United States for any calendar year, and

(ii) after the application of subparagraph (A), such individual has a taxable year other than a calendar year,

he shall be treated as a resident of the United States with respect to any portion of a taxable year which is within such calendar year.

(10) COORDINATION WITH SECTION 877.—If—

(A) an alien individual was treated as a resident of the United States during any period which includes at least 3 consecutive calendar years (hereinafter referred to as the "initial residency period"), and

(B) such individual ceases to be treated as a resident of the United States but subsequently becomes a resident of the United States before the close of the 3rd calendar year beginning after the close of the initial residency period,

such individual shall be taxable for the period after the close of the initial residency period and before the day on which he subsequently became a resident of the United States in the manner provided in section 877(b). The preceding sentence shall apply only if the tax imposed pursuant to section 877(b) exceeds the tax which, without regard to this paragraph, is imposed pursuant to section 871.

(11) REGULATIONS.—The Secretary shall prescribe such regulations as may be necessary or appropriate to carry out the purposes of this subsection.

Amendments

• 2017, Tax Cuts and Jobs Act (P.L. 115-97)

P.L. 115-97, §13304(a)(2)(F):

Amended Code Sec. 7701(b)(5)(A)(iv). **Effective** for amounts incurred or paid after 12-31-2017. Prior to amendment, Code Sec. 7701(b)(5)(A)(iv) read as follows:

(iv) a professional athlete who is temporarily in the United States to compete in a charitable sports event described in section 274(l)(1)(B).

• 2008, Heroes Earnings Assistance and Relief Tax Act of 2008 (P.L. 110-245)

P.L. 110-245, §301(c)(2)(B):

Amended Code Sec. 7701(b)(6) by adding at the end a new flush sentence. **Effective** for any individual whose expatriation date (as so defined) is on or after 6-17-2008.

• 1997, Taxpayer Relief Act of 1997 (P.L. 105-34)

P.L. 105-34, §1174(b)(1):

Amended Code Sec. 7701(b)(7) by adding at the end a new subparagraph (D). **Effective** for tax years beginning after 12-31-97.

P.L. 105-34, §1174(b)(2):

Amended Code Sec. 7701(b)(7)(A) by striking "or (C)" and inserting ", (C), or (D)". **Effective** for tax years beginning after 12-31-97.

• 1994, Social Security Independence and Program Improvements Act of 1994 (P.L. 103-296)

P.L. 103-296, §320(a)(3):

Amended Code Sec. 7701(b)(5) by striking "subparagraph (J)" in subparagraphs (C)(i) and (D)(i)(II) and inserting "subparagraph (J) or (Q)". **Effective** with the calendar quarter following 8-15-94.

• 1988, Technical and Miscellaneous Revenue Act of 1988 (P.L. 100-647)

P.L. 100-647, §1001(d)(2)(D):

Amended Code Sec. 7701(b)(5)(D)(i)(I) by striking out "subparagraph (F)" and inserting in lieu thereof "subparagraph (F) or (M)". **Effective** as if included in the provision of P.L. 99-514 to which it relates.

P.L. 100-647, §1018(g)(3):

Amended Code Sec. 7701(b)(5)(A)(iv) by striking out "section 274(k)(2)" and inserting in lieu thereof "section 274(l)(1)(B)". **Effective** as if included in the provision of P.L. 99-514 to which it relates.

• 1986, Tax Reform Act of 1986 (P.L. 99-514)

P.L. 99-514, §1810(l)(1):

Amended Code Sec. 7701(b)(4)(E)(i) by adding at the end thereof a new sentence. **Effective** as if included in the provision of P.L. 98-369 to which it relates.

P.L. 99-514, §1810(l)(2)(A) and (B):

Amended Code Sec. 7701(b)(1)(A) by striking out "the requirements of clause (i) or (ii)" and inserting in lieu thereof "the requirements of clause (i), (ii), or (iii)", and by adding at the end thereof new clause (iii). **Effective** as if included in the provision of P.L. 98-369 to which it relates.

P.L. 99-514, §1810(l)(3):

Amended Code Sec. 7701(b)(2)(A) by adding at the end thereof new clause (iv). **Effective** as if included in the provision of P.L. 98-369 to which it relates.

P.L. 99-514, §1810(l)(4):

Amended Code Sec. 7701(b) by redesignating paragraphs (4), (5), (6), (7), (8), (9), and (10) as paragraphs (5), (6), (7), (8), (9), (10), and (11), respectively, and by inserting after paragraph (3) new paragraph (4). **Effective** as if included in the provision of P.L. 98-369 to which it relates.

P.L. 99-514, §1810(l)(5)(A):

Amended Code Sec. 7701(b)(4)(A) by striking out "or" at the end of clause (ii), by striking out the period at the end of clause (iii) and inserting ", or" and by adding after clause (iii) new clause (iv). **Effective** for periods after 10-22-86.

P.L. 99-514, §1899A(63):

Amended Code Sec. 7701(b)(4)(E)(i) by striking out "preceeding" and inserting in lieu thereof "preceding". **Effective** 10-22-86.

• 1984, Deficit Reduction Act of 1984 (P.L. 98-369)

P.L. 98-369, §138(a):

Amended Code Sec. 7701 by redesignating subsections (b), (c), and (d) as subsections (c), (d), and (e), respectively, and by inserting after subsection (a) new subsection (b). **Effective** for tax years beginning after 12-31-84. A transitional rule appears below.

P.L. 98-369, §138(b)(2)-(3), provides:

(2) TRANSITIONAL RULE FOR APPLYING SUBSTANTIAL PRESENCE TEST.—

(A) If an alien individual was not a resident of the United States as of the close of calendar year 1984, the determination of whether such individual meets the substantial presence test of section 7701(b)(3) of the Internal Revenue Code of 1954 (as added by this section) shall be made by only taking into account presence after 1984.

(B) If an alien individual was a resident of the United States as of the close of calendar year 1984, but was not a resident of the United States as of the close of calendar year 1983, the determination of whether such individual meets such substantial presence test shall be made by only taking into account presence in the United States after 1983.

(3) TRANSITIONAL RULE FOR APPLYING LAWFUL RESIDENCE TEST.—In the case of any individual who—

(A) was a lawful permanent resident of the United States (within the meaning of section 7701(b)(5) of the Internal Revenue Code of 1954, as added by this section) throughout calendar year 1984, or

(B) was present in the United States at any time during 1984 while such individual was a lawful permanent resident of the United States (within the meaning of such section 7701(b)(5)), for purposes of section 7701(b)(2)(A) of such Code (as so added), such individual shall be treated as a resident of the United States during 1984.

[Sec. 7701(c)]

(c) INCLUDES AND INCLUDING.—The terms "includes" and "including" when used in a definition contained in this title shall not be deemed to exclude other things otherwise within the meaning of the term defined.

Amendments

• 1984, Deficit Reduction Act of 1984 (P.L. 98-369)

P.L. 98-369, §138(a):

Amended Code Sec. 7701 by redesignating subsection (b) as subsection (c). **Effective** for tax years beginning after 12-31-84.

[Sec. 7701(d)]

(d) COMMONWEALTH OF PUERTO RICO.—Where not otherwise distinctly expressed or manifestly incompatible with the intent thereof, references in this title to possessions of the United States shall be treated as also referring to the Commonwealth of Puerto Rico.

Amendments

• 1984, Deficit Reduction Act of 1984 (P.L. 98-369)

P.L. 98-369, §138(a):

Amended Code Sec. 7701 by redesignating subsection (c) as subsection (d). **Effective** for tax years beginning after 12-31-84.

[Sec. 7701(e)]

(e) TREATMENT OF CERTAIN CONTRACTS FOR PROVIDING SERVICES, ETC.—For purposes of chapter 1—

(1) IN GENERAL.—A contract which purports to be a service contract shall be treated as a lease of property if such contract is properly treated as a lease of property, taking into account all relevant factors including whether or not—

(A) the service recipient is in physical possession of the property,

(B) the service recipient controls the property,

(C) the service recipient has a significant economic or possessory interest in the property,

(D) the service provider does not bear any risk of substantially diminished receipts or substantially increased expenditures if there is nonperformance under the contract,

(E) the service provider does not use the property concurrently to provide significant services to entities unrelated to the service recipient, and

(F) the total contract price does not substantially exceed the rental value of the property for the contract period.

(2) OTHER ARRANGEMENTS.—An arrangement (including a partnership or other pass-thru entity) which is not described in paragraph (1) shall be treated as a lease if such arrangement is properly treated as a lease, taking into account all relevant factors including factors similar to those set forth in paragraph (1).

(3) SPECIAL RULES FOR CONTRACTS OR ARRANGEMENTS INVOLVING SOLID WASTE DISPOSAL, ENERGY, AND CLEAN WATER FACILITIES.—

(A) IN GENERAL.—Notwithstanding paragraphs (1) and (2), and except as provided in paragraph (4), any contract or arrangement between a service provider and a service recipient—

(i) with respect to—

(I) the operation of a qualified solid waste disposal facility,

(II) the sale to the service recipient of electrical or thermal energy produced at a cogeneration or alternative energy facility,

(III) the operation of a water treatment works facility, or

(IV) the operation of a storage facility, and

(ii) which purports to be a service contract,

shall be treated as a service contract.

(B) QUALIFIED SOLID WASTE DISPOSAL FACILITY.—For purposes of subparagraph (A), the term "qualified solid waste disposal facility" means any facility if such facility provides solid waste disposal services for residents of part or all of 1 or more governmental units and substantially all of the solid waste processed at such facility is collected from the general public.

(C) COGENERATION FACILITY.—For purposes of subparagraph (A), the term "cogeneration facility" means a facility which uses the same energy source for the sequential generation of electrical or mechanical power in combination with steam, heat, or other forms of useful energy.

(D) ALTERNATIVE ENERGY FACILITY.—For purposes of subparagraph (A), the term "alternative energy facility" means a facility for producing electrical or thermal energy if the primary energy source for the facility is not oil, natural gas, coal, or nuclear power.

(E) WATER TREATMENT WORKS FACILITY.—For purposes of subparagraph (A), the term "water treatment works facility" means any treatment works within the meaning of section 212(2) of the Federal Water Pollution Control Act.

(F) STORAGE FACILITY.—For purposes of subparagraph (A), the term "storage facility" means a facility which uses energy storage technology within the meaning of section 48(c)(6).

(4) PARAGRAPH (3) NOT TO APPLY IN CERTAIN CASES.—

(A) IN GENERAL.—Paragraph (3) shall not apply to any qualified solid waste disposal facility, cogeneration facility, alternative energy facility, water treatment works facility, or storage facility used under a contract or arrangement if—

(i) the service recipient (or a related entity) operates such facility,

(ii) the service recipient (or a related entity) bears any significant financial burden if there is nonperformance under the contract or arrangement (other than for reasons beyond the control of the service provider),

(iii) the service recipient (or a related entity) receives any significant financial benefit if the operating costs of such facility are less than the standards of performance or operation under the contract or arrangement, or

(iv) the service recipient (or a related entity) has an option to purchase, or may be required to purchase, all or a part of such facility at a fixed and determinable price (other than for fair market value).

For purposes of this paragraph, the term "related entity" has the same meaning as when used in section 168(h).

(B) SPECIAL RULES FOR APPLICATION OF SUBPARAGRAPH (A) WITH RESPECT TO CERTAIN RIGHTS AND ALLOCATIONS UNDER THE CONTRACT.—For purposes of subparagraph (A), there shall not be taken into account—

(i) any right of a service recipient to inspect any facility, to exercise any sovereign power the service recipient may possess, or to act in the event of a breach of contract by the service provider, or

(ii) any allocation of any financial burden or benefits in the event of any change in any law.

(C) SPECIAL RULES FOR APPLICATION OF SUBPARAGRAPH(A) IN THE CASE OF CERTAIN EVENTS.—

(i) TEMPORARY SHUT-DOWNS, ETC.—For purposes of clause (ii) of subparagraph (A), there shall not be taken into account any temporary shut-down of the facility for repairs, maintenance, or capital improvements, or any financial burden caused by the bankruptcy or similar financial difficulty of the service provider.

(ii) REDUCED COSTS.—For purposes of clause (iii) of subparagraph (A), there shall not be taken into account any significant financial benefit merely because payments by the service recipient under the contract or arrangement are decreased by reason of increased production or efficiency or the recovery of energy or other products.

(5) EXCEPTION FOR CERTAIN LOW-INCOME HOUSING.—This subsection shall not apply to any property described in clause (i), (ii), (iii), or (iv) of section 1250(a)(1)(B) (relating to low-income housing) if—

(A) such property is operated by or for an organization described in paragraph (3) or (4) of section 501(c), and

(B) at least 80 percent of the units in such property are leased to low-income tenants (within the meaning of section 167(k)(3)(B)) (as in effect on the day before the date of the enactment of the Revenue Reconciliation Act of 1990).

(6) REGULATIONS.—The Secretary may prescribe such regulations as may be necessary or appropriate to carry out the provisions of this subsection.

Amendments

• 2022, Inflation Reduction Act of 2022 (P.L. 117-169)

P.L. 117-169, §13102(n)(1)-(2):

Amended Code Sec. 7701(e) in paragraph (3)(A)(i) by striking "or" at the end of subclause (II), by striking "and" at the end of subclause (III) and inserting "or", and by adding at the end a new subclause (IV), and by adding at the end a new subparagraph (F); and in paragraph (4), by striking "or water treatment works facility" and inserting "water treatment works facility, or storage facility". **Effective** for property placed in service after 12-31-2022.

• 2018, Tax Technical Corrections Act of 2018 (P.L. 115-141)

P.L. 115-141, §401(a)(332), Div. U:

Amended Code Sec. 7701(e)(5)(B) by striking "Reconcilation" and inserting "Reconciliation". **Effective** 3-23-2018.

• 1990, Omnibus Budget Reconciliation Act of 1990 (P.L. 101-508)

P.L. 101-508, §11812(b)(13):

Amended Code Sec. 7701(e)(5)(B) by inserting before the period at the end thereof "(as in effect on the day before the date of the enactment of the Revenue Reconciliation Act of 1990)". **Effective** for property placed in service after the date of the enactment of this Act. However, for exceptions see Act Sec. 11812(c)(2)-(3) below.

P.L. 101-508, §11812(c)(2)-(3), provides:

(2) EXCEPTION.—The amendments made by this section shall not apply to any property to which section 168 of the Internal Revenue Code of 1986 does not apply by reason of subsection (f)(5) thereof.

(3) EXCEPTION FOR PREVIOUSLY GRANDFATHER EXPENDITURES.—The amendments made by this section shall not apply to rehabilitation expenditures described in section 252(f)(5) of the Tax Reform Act of 1986 (as added by section 1002(l)(31) of the Technical and Miscellaneous Revenue Act of 1988).

• 1986, Tax Reform Act of 1986 (P.L. 99-514)

P.L. 99-514, §201(d)(14)(A):

Amended Code Sec. 7701(e)(4)(A) by striking out "section 168(j)" and inserting in lieu thereof "section 168(h)". For the **effective** date, see Act Sec. 203 under the amendment notes to Code Sec. 168.

P.L. 99-514, §201(d)(14)(B):

Amended Code Sec. 7701(e)(5) by striking out "low-income housing (within the meaning of section 168(c)(2)(F))" and inserting in lieu thereof "property described in clause (i), (ii), (iii), or (iv) of section 1250(a)(1)(B) (relating to low income housing)". For the **effective** date, see Act Sec. 203 under the amendment notes to Code Sec. 168.

P.L. 99-514, §1802(a)(9)(C):

Amended Code Sec. 7701(e)(4)(A) by adding at the end thereof a new sentence. **Effective** as if included in the provision of P.L. 98-369 to which it relates.

P.L. 99-514, §1899A(64):

Amended Code Sec. 7701(e)(5) by striking out "section 168(C)(2)(F))" and inserting in lieu thereof "section 168(c)(2)(F))". **Effective** 10-22-86.

• 1984, Deficit Reduction Act of 1984 (P.L. 98-369)

P.L. 98-369, §31(e):

Amended Code Sec. 7701, as amended by this Act, by redesignating subsection (e) as subsection (f) and by inserting after subsection (d) new subsection (e). **Effective** for property placed in service by the taxpayer after 5-23-83, in tax years ending after such date, and to property placed in service by the taxpayer on or before 5-23-83, if the lease to the tax-exempt entity is entered into after 5-23-83. Special rules appear in Act Sec. 31(g) following Code Sec. 168.

[Sec. 7701(f)]

(f) USE OF RELATED PERSONS OR PASS-THRU ENTITIES.—The Secretary shall prescribe such regulations as may be necessary or appropriate to prevent the avoidance of those provisions of this title which deal with—

(1) the linking of borrowing to investment, or

(2) diminishing risks,

through the use of related persons, pass-thru entities, or other intermediaries.

Amendments

• 1984, Deficit Reduction Act of 1984 (P.L. 98-369)

P.L. 98-369, §53(c):

Amended Code Sec. 7701 by redesignating subsection (f) as (g) and by inserting after subsection (e) new subsection (f). For the **effective** date, see Act Sec. 53(e)(3), below.

P.L. 98-369, §53(e)(3), as amended by P.L. 99-514, §1804(b), provides:

(3) Related Person Provisions.—

(A) In General.—Except as otherwise provided in subparagraph (B), the amendment made by subsection (c) shall take effect on July 18, 1984.

(B) Special Rule for Purposes of Section 265(2).—The amendment made by subsection (c) insofar as it relates to section 265(2) of the Internal Revenue Code of 1954 shall apply to—

(i) term loans made after July 18, 1984, and

(ii) demand loans outstanding after July 18, 1984 (other than any loan outstanding on July 18, 1984, and repaid before September 18, 1984).

(C) Treatment of Renegotiations, Etc.—For purposes of this paragraph, any loan renegotiated, extended, or revised after July 18, 1984, shall be treated as a loan made after such date.

(D) Definition of Term and Demand Loans.—For purposes of this paragraph, the terms "demand loan" and "term loan" have the respective meanings given such terms by paragraphs (5) and (6) of section 7872(f) of the Internal Revenue Code of 1954, except that the second sentence of such paragraph (5) shall not apply.

[Sec. 7701(g)]

(g) CLARIFICATION OF FAIR MARKET VALUE IN THE CASE OF NONRECOURSE INDEBTEDNESS.—For purposes of subtitle A, in determining the amount of gain or loss (or deemed gain or loss) with respect to any property, the fair market value of such property shall be treated as being not less than the amount of any nonrecourse indebtedness to which such property is subject.

Amendments

• 1984, Deficit Reduction Act of 1984 (P.L. 98-369)

P.L. 98-369, §75(c):

Amended Code Sec. 7701, as amended by this Act, by redesignating subsection (g) as subsection (h) and by inserting after subsection (f) new subsection (g). **Effective** for distributions, sales, and exchanges made after 3-31-84, in tax years ending after such date.

[Sec. 7701(h)]

(h) MOTOR VEHICLE OPERATING LEASES.—

(1) IN GENERAL.—For purposes of this title, in the case of a qualified motor vehicle operating agreement which contains a terminal rental adjustment clause—

(A) such agreement shall be treated as a lease if (but for such terminal rental adjustment clause) such agreement would be treated as a lease under this title, and

(B) the lessee shall not be treated as the owner of the property subject to an agreement during any period such agreement is in effect.

(2) QUALIFIED MOTOR VEHICLE OPERATING AGREEMENT DEFINED.—For purposes of this subsection—

(A) IN GENERAL.—The term "qualified motor vehicle operating agreement" means any agreement with respect to a motor vehicle (including a trailer) which meets the requirements of subparagraphs (B), (C), and (D) of this paragraph.

(B) MINIMUM LIABILITY OF LESSOR.—An agreement meets the requirements of this subparagraph if under such agreement the sum of—

(i) the amount the lessor is personally liable to repay, and

(ii) the net fair market value of the lessor's interest in any property pledged as security for property subject to the agreement,

equals or exceeds all amounts borrowed to finance the acquisition of property subject to the agreement. There shall not be taken into account under clause (ii) any property pledged which is property subject to the agreement or property directly or indirectly financed by indebtedness secured by property subject to the agreement.

(C) CERTIFICATION BY LESSEE; NOTICE OF TAX OWNERSHIP.—An agreement meets the requirements of this subparagraph if such agreement contains a separate written statement separately signed by the lessee—

(i) under which the lessee certifies, under penalty of perjury, that it intends that more than 50 percent of the use of the property subject to such agreement is to be in a trade or business of the lessee, and

(ii) which clearly and legibly states that the lessee has been advised that it will not be treated as the owner of the property subject to the agreement for Federal income tax purposes.

(D) LESSOR MUST HAVE NO KNOWLEDGE THAT CERTIFICATION IS FALSE.—An agreement meets the requirements of this subparagraph if the lessor does not know that the certification described in subparagraph (C)(i) is false.

(3) TERMINAL RENTAL ADJUSTMENT CLAUSE DEFINED.—

(A) IN GENERAL.—For purposes of this subsection, the term "terminal rental adjustment clause" means a provision of an agreement which permits or requires the rental price to be adjusted upward or downward by reference to the amount realized by the lessor under the agreement upon sale or other disposition of such property.

(B) SPECIAL RULE FOR LESSEE DEALERS.—The term "terminal rental adjustment clause" also includes a provision of an agreement which requires a lessee who is a dealer in motor vehicles to purchase the motor vehicle for a predetermined price and then resell such vehicle where such provision achieves substantially the same results as a provision described in subparagraph (A).

Amendments

• 1986, Tax Reform Act of 1986 (P.L. 99-514)

P.L. 99-514, §201(c):

Amended Code Sec. 7701 by redesignating subsection (h) as subsection (i) and by inserting after subsection (g) new subsection (h). For the **effective** date, see Act Sec. 203 under the amendment notes to Code Sec. 168.

[Sec. 7701(i)]

(i) TAXABLE MORTGAGE POOLS.—

(1) TREATED AS SEPARATE CORPORATIONS.—A taxable mortgage pool shall be treated as a separate corporation which may not be treated as an includible corporation with any other corporation for purposes of section 1501.

(2) TAXABLE MORTGAGE POOL DEFINED.—For purposes of this title—

(A) IN GENERAL.—Except as otherwise provided in this paragraph, a taxable mortgage pool is any entity (other than a REMIC) if—

(i) substantially all of the assets of such entity consists of debt obligations (or interests therein) and more than 50 percent of such debt obligations (or interests) consists of real estate mortgages (or interests therein),

(ii) such entity is the obligor under debt obligations with 2 or more maturities, and

(iii) under the terms of the debt obligations referred to in clause (ii) (or underlying arrangement), payments on such debt obligations bear a relationship to payments on the debt obligations (or interests) referred to in clause (i).

(B) PORTION OF ENTITIES TREATED AS POOLS.—Any portion of an entity which meets the definition of subparagraph (A) shall be treated as a taxable mortgage pool.

(C) EXCEPTION FOR DOMESTIC BUILDING AND LOAN.—Nothing in this subsection shall be construed to treat any domestic building and loan association (or portion thereof) as a taxable mortgage pool.

(D) TREATMENT OF CERTAIN EQUITY INTERESTS.—To the extent provided in regulations, equity interest of varying classes which correspond to maturity classes of debt shall be treated as debt for purposes of this subsection.

(3) TREATMENT OF CERTAIN REIT'S.—If—

(A) a real estate investment trust is a taxable mortgage pool, or

(B) a qualified REIT subsidiary (as defined in section 856(i)(2)) of a real estate investment trust is a taxable mortgage pool,

under regulations prescribed by the Secretary, adjustments similar to the adjustments provided in section 860E(d) shall apply to the shareholders of such real estate investment trust.

Amendments

• 2004, American Jobs Creation Act of 2004 (P.L. 108-357)

P.L. 108-357, §835(b)(11):

Amended Code Sec. 7701(i)(2)(A) by striking "or a FASIT" after "REMIC". For the **effective** date, see Act Sec. 835(c), below.

P.L. 108-357, §835(c), provides:

(c) EFFECTIVE DATE.—

(1) IN GENERAL.—Except as provided in paragraph (2), the amendments made by this section shall take effect on January 1, 2005.

(2) EXCEPTION FOR EXISTING FASITS.—Paragraph (1) shall not apply to any FASIT in existence on the date of the enactment of this Act [10-22-2004.—CCH] to the extent that regular interests issued by the FASIT before such date continue to remain outstanding in accordance with the original terms of issuance.

• 1996, Small Business Job Protection Act of 1996 (P.L. 104-188)

P.L. 104-188, §1621(b)(9):

Amended Code Sec. 7701(i)(2)(A) by inserting "or a FASIT" after "a REMIC". **Effective** 9-1-97.

• 1986, Tax Reform Act of 1986 (P.L. 99-514)

P.L. 99-514, §673:

Amended Code Sec. 7701, as amended by Act Sec. 201(c), by redesignating subsection (i) as subsection (j) and by inserting after subsection (h) new subsection (i). For the **effective** date, see Act Sec. 675(c), below.

P.L. 99-514, §675(c), provides:

(c) TREATMENT OF TAXABLE MORTGAGE POOLS.—

(1) IN GENERAL.—The amendment made by section 673 shall take effect on January 1, 1992.

(2) TREATMENT OF EXISTING ENTITIES.—The amendment made by section 673 shall not apply to any entity in existence on December 31, 1991. The preceding sentence shall cease to apply with respect to any entity as of the 1st day after December 31, 1991, on which there is a substantial transfer of cash or other property to such entity.

(3) SPECIAL RULE FOR COORDINATION WITH WASH-SALE RULES.—Notwithstanding paragraphs (1) and (2), for purposes of applying section 860F(d) of the Internal Revenue Code of 1986 (as added by this part), the amendment made by section 673 shall apply to taxable years beginning after December 31, 1986.

[Sec. 7701(j)]

(j) TAX TREATMENT OF FEDERAL THRIFT SAVINGS FUND.—

(1) IN GENERAL.—For purposes of this title—

(A) the Thrift Savings Fund shall be treated as a trust described in section 401(a) which is exempt from taxation under section 501(a);

(B) any contribution to, or distribution from, the Thrift Savings Fund shall be treated in the same manner as contributions to or distributions from such a trust; and

(C) subject to section 401(k)(4)(B) and any dollar limitation on the application of section 402(e)(3), contributions to the Thrift Savings Fund shall not be treated as distributed or made available to an employee or Member nor as a contribution made to the Fund by an employee or Member merely because the employee or Member has, under the provisions of subchapter III of chapter 84 of title 5, United States Code, and section 8351 of such title 5, an election whether the contribution will be made to the Thrift Savings Fund or received by the employee or Member in cash.

(2) NONDISCRIMINATION REQUIREMENTS.—Notwithstanding any other provision of the law, the Thrift Savings Fund is not subject to the nondiscrimination requirements applicable to arrangements described in section 401(k) or to matching contributions (as described in section 401(m)), so long as it meets the requirements of this section.

(3) COORDINATION WITH SOCIAL SECURITY ACT.—Paragraph (1) shall not be construed to provide that any amount of the employee's or Member's basic pay which is contributed to the Thrift Savings Fund shall not be included in the term "wages" for the purposes of section 209 of the Social Security Act or section 3121(a) of this title.

(4) DEFINITIONS.—For purposes of this subsection, the terms "Member", "employee", and "Thrift Savings Fund" shall have the same respective meanings as when used in subchapter III of chapter 84 of title 5, United States Code.

(5) COORDINATION WITH OTHER PROVISIONS OF LAW.—No provision of law not contained in this title shall apply for purposes of determining the treatment under this title of the Thrift Savings Fund or any contribution to, or distribution from, such Fund.

Amendments

• 1992, Unemployment Compensation Amendments of 1992 (P.L. 102-318)

P.L. 102-318, §521(b)(43):

Amended Code Sec. 7701(j)(1)(C) by striking "section 402(a)(8)" and inserting "section 402(e)(3)". **Effective** for distributions after 12-31-92.

• 1990, Omnibus Budget Reconciliation Act of 1990 (P.L. 101-508)

P.L. 101-508, §11704(a)(34):

Amended Code Sec. 7701(j)(1)(C) by striking so much of such subparagraph as precedes "contributions to the Thrift" and inserting the following: "(C) subject to section 401(k)(4)(B) and any dollar limitation on the application of section 402(a)(8),". **Effective** 11-5-90. Prior to amendment, subparagraph C read as follows:

(C) subject to section 401(k)(4)(B), [and] any dollar limitation on the application of section 402(a)(8), contributions to the Thrift Savings Fund shall not be treated as distributed or made available to an employee or Member nor as a contribution made to the Fund by an employee or Member merely because the employee or Member has, under the provisions of subchapter III of chapter 84 of title 5, United States Code, and section 8351 of such title 5, an election whether the contribution will be made to the Thrift Savings Fund or received by the employee or Member in cash.

• 1988, Technical and Miscellaneous Revenue Act of 1988 (P.L. 100-647)

P.L. 100-647, §1011A(m)(1):

Amended Code Sec. 7701(j)(1)(C) by inserting ", section 401(k)(4)(B)," after "paragraph (2) [subject to]". **Effective** as if included in the provision of P.L. 99-514 to which it relates.

• 1987, Continuing Appropriations, Fiscal Year 1988 (P.L. 100-202)

P.L. 100-202, §624(a)(1)-(2):

Amended Code Sec. 7701(j) by deleting "the provisions of paragraph (2) and" following "subject to" in paragraph (1)(C) and by amending paragraph (2). **Effective** 12-22-87. Prior to amendment, Code Sec. 7701(j)(2) read as follows:

(2) NONDISCRIMINATION REQUIREMENTS.—Paragraph (1)(C) shall not apply to the Thrift Savings Fund unless the Fund meets the antidiscrimination requirements (other than any requirement relating to coverage) applicable to arrangements described in section 401(k) and to matching contributions. Rules similar to the rules of sections 401(k)(8) and 401(m)(8) (relating to no disqualification if excess contributions distributed) shall apply for purposes of the preceding sentence.

• 1986, Tax Reform Act of 1986 (P.L. 99-514)

P.L. 99-514, §1147(a):

Amended Code Sec. 7701, as amended by Act Secs. 201(d) and 558(b), by redesignating subsection (j) as subsection (k) and by inserting after subsection (i) new subsection (j). **Effective** 10-22-86.

[Sec. 7701(k)]

(k) TREATMENT OF CERTAIN AMOUNTS PAID TO CHARITY.—In the case of any payment which, except for section 13143(b) of title 5, United States Code, might be made to any officer or employee of the Federal Government but which is made instead on behalf of such officer or employee to an organization described in section 170(c)—

(1) such payment shall not be treated as received by such officer or employee for all purposes of this title and for all purposes of any tax law of a State or political subdivision thereof, and

(2) no deduction shall be allowed under any provision of this title (or of any tax law of a State or political subdivision thereof) to such officer or employee by reason of having such payment made to such organization.

For purposes of this subsection, a Senator, a Representative in, or a Delegate or Resident Commissioner to, the Congress shall be treated as an officer or employee of the Federal Government.

Amendments

• 2022, (P.L. 117-286)

2022 (P.L. 117-286), §4(c)(33):

Amended Code Sec. 7701(k) by striking "section 501(b) of the Ethics in Government Act of 1978," and inserting "section 13143(b) of title 5, United States Code," in the matter before paragraph (1). **Effective** 12-27-2022.

• 1991, Legislative Branch Appropriations Act (P.L. 102-90)

P.L. 102-90, §314(e):

Amended the last sentence of Code Sec. 7701(k). **Effective** 1-1-92. Prior to amendment, the last sentence of Code Sec. 7701(k) read as follows:

For purposes of this subsection, a Representative in, or a Delegate or Resident Commissioner to, the Congress shall be treated as an officer or employee of the Federal Government and a Senator or officer (except the Vice President) or employee of the Senate shall not be treated as an officer or employee of the Federal Government.

• 1989, Ethics Reform Act (P.L. 101-194)

P.L. 101-194, §602:

Amended Code Sec. 7701 by redesignating subsection (k) as subsection (l) and by inserting after subsection (j) a new subsection (k). For the **effective** date, see Act Sec. 603, below.

P.L. 101-194, §603, provides:

SEC. 603. EFFECTIVE DATE.

The amendments made by this title shall take effect on January 1, 1991. Such amendments shall cease to be effective if the provisions of section 703 are subsequently repealed, in which case the laws in effect before such amendments shall be deemed to be reenacted.

[Sec. 7701(l)]

(l) REGULATIONS RELATING TO CONDUIT ARRANGEMENTS.—The Secretary may prescribe regulations recharacterizing any multiple-party financing transaction as a transaction directly among any 2 or more of such parties where the Secretary determines that such recharacterization is appropriate to prevent avoidance of any tax imposed by this title.

Amendments

• 1993, Omnibus Budget Reconciliation Act of 1993 (P.L. 103-66)

P.L. 103-66, §13238:

Amended Code Sec. 7701 by redesignating subsection (l) as subsection (m), and by inserting after subsection (k) new subsection (l). **Effective** 8-10-93.

[Sec. 7701(m)]

(m) DESIGNATION OF CONTRACT MARKETS.—Any designation by the Commodity Futures Trading Commission of a contract market which could not have been made under the law in effect on the day before the date of the enactment of the Commodity Futures Modernization Act of 2000 shall apply for purposes of this title except to the extent provided in regulations prescribed by the Secretary.

Amendments

• 2000, Community Renewal Tax Relief Act of 2000 (P.L. 106-554)

P.L. 106-554, §401(i):

Amended Code Sec. 7701 by redesignating subsection (m) as subsection (n) and by inserting after subsection (l) a new subsection (m). **Effective** 12-21-2000.

[Sec. 7701(n)—Stricken]

Amendments

• 2008, Heroes Earnings Assistance and Relief Tax Act of 2008 (P.L. 110-245)

P.L. 110-245, §301(c)(2)(C):

Amended Code Sec. 7701 by striking subsection (n) and by redesignating subsections (o) and (p) as subsections (n) and (o), respectively. **Effective** for any individual whose expatriation date (as so defined) is on or after 6-17-2008. Prior to being stricken, Code Sec. 7701(n) read as follows:

(n) SPECIAL RULES FOR DETERMINING WHEN AN INDIVIDUAL IS NO LONGER A UNITED STATES CITIZEN OR LONG-TERM RESIDENT.—For purposes of this chapter—

(1) UNITED STATES CITIZENS.—An individual who would (but for this paragraph) cease to be treated as a citizen of the United States shall continue to be treated as a citizen of the United States until such individual—

(A) gives notice of an expatriating act (with the requisite intent to relinquish citizenship) to the Secretary of State, and

(B) provides a statement in accordance with section 6039G (if such a statement is otherwise required).

(2) LONG-TERM RESIDENTS.—A long-term resident (as defined in section 877(e)(2)) who would (but for this paragraph) be described in section 877(e)(1) shall be treated as a lawful permanent resident of the United States and as not described in section 877(e)(1) until such individual—

(A) gives notice of termination of residency (with the requisite intent to terminate residency) to the Secretary of Homeland Security, and

(B) provides a statement in accordance with section 6039G (if such a statement is otherwise required).

• 2005, Gulf Opportunity Zone Act of 2005 (P.L. 109-135)

P.L. 109-135, §403(v)(2):

Amended Code Sec. 7701(n). **Effective** as if included in the provision of the American Jobs Creation Act of 2004 (P.L. 108-357) to which it relates [**effective** for individuals who expatriate after 6-30-2004.—CCH]. Prior to amendment, Code Sec. 7701(n) read as follows:

(n) SPECIAL RULES FOR DETERMINING WHEN AN INDIVIDUAL IS NO LONGER A UNITED STATES CITIZEN OR LONG-TERM RESIDENT.—An individual who would (but for this subsection) cease to be treated as a citizen or resident of the United States shall continue to be treated as a citizen or resident of the United States, as the case may be, until such individual—

(1) gives notice of an expatriating act or termination of residency (with the requisite intent to relinquish citizenship or terminate residency) to the Secretary of State or the Secretary of Homeland Security, and

(2) provides a statement in accordance with section 6039G.

• 2004, American Jobs Creation Act of 2004 (P.L. 108-357)

P.L. 108-357, §804(b):

Amended Code Sec. 7701 by redesignating subsection (n) as subsection (o) and by inserting after subsection (m) a new subsection (n). **Effective** for individuals who expatriate after 6-3-2004.

[Sec. 7701(n)]

(n) CONVENTION OR ASSOCIATION OF CHURCHES.—For purposes of this title, any organization which is otherwise a convention or association of churches shall not fail to so qualify merely because the membership of such organization includes individuals as well as churches or because individuals have voting rights in such organization.

Amendments

• 2008, Heroes Earnings Assistance and Relief Tax Act of 2008 (P.L. 110-245)

P.L. 110-245, §301(c)(2)(C):

Amended Code Sec. 7701 by redesignating subsection (o) as subsection (n). **Effective** for any individual whose expatriation date (as so defined) is on or after 6-17-2008.

• 2006, Pension Protection Act of 2006 (P.L. 109-280)

P.L. 109-280, §1222:

Amended Code Sec. 7701 by redesignating subsection (o) as subsection (p) and by inserting after subsection (n) a new subsection (o). **Effective** 8-17-2006.

[Sec. 7701(o)]

(o) CLARIFICATION OF ECONOMIC SUBSTANCE DOCTRINE.—

(1) APPLICATION OF DOCTRINE .—In the case of any transaction to which the economic substance doctrine is relevant, such transaction shall be treated as having economic substance only if—

(A) the transaction changes in a meaningful way (apart from Federal income tax effects) the taxpayer's economic position, and

(B) the taxpayer has a substantial purpose (apart from Federal income tax effects) for entering into such transaction.

(2) SPECIAL RULE WHERE TAXPAYER RELIES ON PROFIT POTENTIAL.—

(A) IN GENERAL .—The potential for profit of a transaction shall be taken into account in determining whether the requirements of subparagraphs (A) and (B) of paragraph (1) are met with respect to the transaction only if the present value of the reasonably expected pre-tax profit from the transaction is substantial in relation to the present value of the expected net tax benefits that would be allowed if the transaction were respected.

(B) TREATMENT OF FEES AND FOREIGN TAXES .—Fees and other transaction expenses shall be taken into account as expenses in determining pre-tax profit under subparagraph (A). The Secretary shall issue regulations requiring foreign taxes to be treated as expenses in determining pre-tax profit in appropriate cases.

(3) STATE AND LOCAL TAX BENEFITS .—For purposes of paragraph (1), any State or local income tax effect which is related to a Federal income tax effect shall be treated in the same manner as a Federal income tax effect.

(4) FINANCIAL ACCOUNTING BENEFITS .—For purposes of paragraph (1)(B), achieving a financial accounting benefit shall not be taken into account as a purpose for entering into a transaction if the origin of such financial accounting benefit is a reduction of Federal income tax.

(5) DEFINITIONS AND SPECIAL RULES .—For purposes of this subsection—

(A) ECONOMIC SUBSTANCE DOCTRINE .—The term "economic substance doctrine" means the common law doctrine under which tax benefits under subtitle A with respect to a transaction are not allowable if the transaction does not have economic substance or lacks a business purpose.

(B) EXCEPTION FOR PERSONAL TRANSACTIONS OF INDIVIDUALS .—In the case of an individual, paragraph (1) shall apply only to transactions entered into in connection with a trade or business or an activity engaged in for the production of income.

(C) DETERMINATION OF APPLICATION OF DOCTRINE NOT AFFECTED .—The determination of whether the economic substance doctrine is relevant to a transaction shall be made in the same manner as if this subsection had never been enacted.

(D) TRANSACTION .—The term "transaction" includes a series of transactions.

Amendments

• 2010, Health Care and Education Reconciliation Act of 2010 (P.L. 111-152)

P.L. 111-152, §1409(a):

Amended Code Sec. 7701 by redesignating subsection (o) as subsection (p) and by inserting after subsection (n) a new subsection (o). **Effective** for transactions entered into after 3-30-2010.

[Sec. 7701(p)]

(p) CROSS REFERENCES.—

(1) OTHER DEFINITIONS.—

For other definitions, see the following sections of Title 1 of the United States Code:

(1) Singular as including plural, section 1.
(2) Plural as including singular, section 1.
(3) Masculine as including feminine, section 1.
(4) Officer, section 1.
(5) Oath as including affirmation, section 1.
(6) County as including parish, section 2.
(7) Vessel as including all means of water transportation, section 3.
(8) Vehicle as including all means of land transportation, section 4.
(9) Company or association as including successors and assigns, section 5.

(2) EFFECT OF CROSS REFERENCES.—

For effect of cross references in this title, see section 7806(a).

Amendments

• 2010, Health Care and Education Reconciliation Act of 2010 (P.L. 111-152)

P.L. 111-152, §1409(a):

Amended Code Sec. 7701 by redesignating subsection (o) as subsection (p). **Effective** for transactions entered into after 3-30-2010.

• 2008, Heroes Earnings Assistance and Relief Tax Act of 2008 (P.L. 110-245)

P.L. 110-245, §301(c)(2)(C):

Amended Code Sec. 7701 by redesignating subsection (p) as subsection (o). **Effective** for any individual whose expatriation date (as so defined) is on or after 6-17-2008.

• **2006, Pension Protection Act of 2006 (P.L. 109-280)**

P.L. 109-280, §1222:

Amended Code Sec. 7701 by redesignating subsection (o) as subsection (p). **Effective** 8-17-2006.

• **2004, American Jobs Creation Act of 2004 (P.L. 108-357)**

P.L. 108-357, §804(b):

Amended Code Sec. 7701 by redesignating subsection (n) as subsection (o). **Effective** for individuals who expatriate after 6-3-2004.

• **2000, Community Renewal Tax Relief Act of 2000 (P.L. 106-554)**

P.L. 106-554, §401(i):

Amended Code Sec. 7701 by redesignating subsection (m) as subsection (n). **Effective** 12-21-2000.

• **1993, Omnibus Budget Reconciliation Act of 1993 (P.L. 103-66)**

P.L. 103-66, §13238:

Amended Code Sec. 7701 by redesignating subsection (l) as subsection (m). **Effective** 8-10-93.

• **1989, Ethics Reform Act (P.L. 101-194)**

P.L. 101-194, §602:

Amended Code Sec. 7701 by redesignating subsection (k) as subsection (l). For the **effective** date, see Act Sec. 603 in the amendment notes following Code Sec. 7701(k).

• **1986, Tax Reform Act of 1986 (P.L. 99-514)**

P.L. 99-514, §1147(a):

Amended Code Sec. 7701, as amended by Act Secs. 201(d) and 558(b), by redesignating subsection (j) as subsection (k). **Effective** 10-22-86.

[Sec. 7702]

SEC. 7702. LIFE INSURANCE CONTRACT DEFINED.

[Sec. 7702(a)]

(a) GENERAL RULE.—For purposes of this title, the term "life insurance contract" means any contract which is a life insurance contract under the applicable law, but only if such contract—

(1) meets the cash value accumulation test of subsection (b), or

(2)(A) meets the guideline premium requirements of subsection (c), and

(B) falls within the cash value corridor of subsection (d).

[Sec. 7702(b)]

(b) CASH VALUE ACCUMULATION TEST FOR SUBSECTION (a)(1).—

(1) IN GENERAL.—A contract meets the cash value accumulation test of this subsection if, by the terms of the contract, the cash surrender value of such contract may not at any time exceed the net single premium which would have to be paid at such time to fund future benefits under the contract.

(2) RULES FOR APPLYING PARAGRAPH (1).—Determinations under paragraph (1) shall be made—

(A) on the basis of interest at the greater of the applicable accumulation test minimum rate or the rate or rates guaranteed on issuance of the contract,

(B) on the basis of the rules of subparagraph (B)(i) (and, in the case of qualified additional benefits, subparagraph (B)(ii)) of subsection (c)(3), and

(C) by taking into account under subparagraphs (A) and (D) of subsection (e)(1) only current and future death benefits and qualified additional benefits.

(3) APPLICABLE ACCUMULATION TEST MINIMUM RATE.—For purposes of paragraph (2)(A), the term "applicable accumulation test minimum rate" means the lesser of—

(A) an annual effective rate of 4 percent, or

(B) the insurance interest rate (as defined in subsection (f)(11)) in effect at the time the contract is issued.

Amendments

• **2020, Taxpayer Certainty and Disaster Tax Relief Act of 2020 (P.L. 116-260)**

P.L. 116-260, §205(a)(1), Div. EE:

Amended Code Sec. 7702(b)(2)(A) by striking "an annual effective rate of 4 percent" and inserting "the applicable accumulation test minimum rate". **Effective** for contracts issued after 12-31-2020.

P.L. 116-260, §205(a)(2), Div. EE:

Amended Code Sec. 7702(b) by adding at the end a new paragraph (3). **Effective** for contracts issued after 12-31-2020.

• **1986, Tax Reform Act of 1986 (P.L. 99-514)**

P.L. 99-514, §1825(a)(2):

Amended Code Sec. 7702(b)(2)(C) by striking out "subparagraphs (A) and (C)" and inserting in lieu thereof "subparagraphs (A) and (D)". **Effective** as if included in the provision of P.L. 98-369 to which it relates.

[Sec. 7702(c)]

(c) GUIDELINE PREMIUM REQUIREMENTS.—For purposes of this section—

(1) IN GENERAL.—A contract meets the guideline premium requirements of this subsection if the sum of the premiums paid under such contract does not at any time exceed the guideline premium limitation as of such time.

(2) GUIDELINE PREMIUM LIMITATION.—The term "guideline premium limitation" means, as of any date, the greater of—

(A) the guideline single premium, or

(B) the sum of the guideline level premiums to such date.

(3) GUIDELINE SINGLE PREMIUM.—

(A) IN GENERAL.—The term "guideline single premium" means the premium at issue with respect to future benefits under the contract.

(B) BASIS ON WHICH DETERMINATION IS MADE.—The determination under subparagraph (A) shall be based on—

(i) reasonable mortality charges which meet the requirements prescribed in regulations to be promulgated by the Secretary or that do not exceed the mortality charges specified in the prevailing commissioners' standard tables as defined in subsection (f)(10),

(ii) any reasonable charges (other than mortality charges) which (on the basis of the company's experience, if any, with respect to similar contracts) are reasonably expected to be actually paid, and

(iii) interest at the greater of the applicable guideline premium minimum rate or the rate or rates guaranteed on issuance of the contract.

(C) WHEN DETERMINATION MADE.—Except as provided in subsection (f)(7), the determination under subparagraph (A) shall be made as of the time the contract is issued.

(D) SPECIAL RULES FOR SUBPARAGRAPH (B)(ii).—

(i) CHARGES NOT SPECIFIED IN THE CONTRACT.—If any charge is not specified in the contract, the amount taken into account under subparagraph (B)(ii) for such charge shall be zero.

(ii) NEW COMPANIES, ETC.—If any company does not have adequate experience for purposes of the determination under subparagraph (B)(ii), to the extent provided in regulations, such determination shall be made on the basis of the industry-wide experience.

(E) APPLICABLE GUIDELINE PREMIUM MINIMUM RATE.—For purposes of subparagraph (B)(iii), the term "applicable guideline premium minimum rate" means the applicable accumulation test minimum rate (as defined in subsection (b)(3)) plus 2 percentage points.

(4) GUIDELINE LEVEL PREMIUM.—The term "guideline level premium" means the level annual amount, payable over a period not ending before the insured attains age 95, computed on the same basis as the guideline single premium, except that paragraph (3)(B)(iii) shall be applied by substituting "the applicable accumulation test minimum rate" for "the applicable guideline premium minimum rate".

Amendments

• 2020, Taxpayer Certainty and Disaster Tax Relief Act of 2020 (P.L. 116-260)

P.L. 116-260, §205(b)(1), Div. EE:

Amended Code Sec. 7702(c)(3)(B)(iii) by striking "an annual effective rate of 6 percent" and inserting "the applicable guideline premium minimum rate". **Effective** for contracts issued after 12-31-2020.

P.L. 116-260, §205(b)(2), Div. EE:

Amended Code Sec. 7702(c)(3) by adding at the end a new subparagraph (E). **Effective** for contracts issued after 12-31-2020.

P.L. 116-260, §205(c)(1)-(2), Div. EE:

Amended Code Sec. 7702(c)(4) by striking "4 percent" and inserting "the applicable accumulation test minimum rate", and by striking "6 percent" and inserting "the applicable guideline premium minimum rate". **Effective** for contracts issued after 12-31-2020.

• 2017, Tax Cuts and Jobs Act (P.L. 115-97)

P.L. 115-97, §13517(a)(4)(A):

Amended Code Sec. 7702(c)(3)(B) by striking clause (i) and inserting a new clause (i). **Effective** generally for tax years beginning after 12-31-2017. For a transition rule, see Act Sec. 13517(c)(2)-(3), below. Prior to being stricken, Code Sec. 7702(c)(3)(B)(i) read as follows:

(i) reasonable mortality charges which meet the requirements (if any) prescribed in regulations and which (except as provided in regulations) do not exceed the mortality charges specified in the prevailing commissioners' standard tables (as defined in section 807(d)(5)) as of the time the contract is issued,

P.L. 115-97, §13517(c)(2)-(3), provides:

(2) TRANSITION RULE.—For the first taxable year beginning after December 31, 2017, the reserve with respect to any contract (as determined under section 807(d) of the Internal Revenue Code of 1986) at the end of the preceding taxable year shall be determined as if the amendments made by this section had applied to such reserve in such preceding taxable year.

(3) TRANSITION RELIEF.—

(A) IN GENERAL.—If—

(i) the reserve determined under section 807(d) of the Internal Revenue Code of 1986 (determined after application of paragraph (2)) with respect to any contract as of the close of the year preceding the first taxable year beginning after December 31, 2017, differs from

(ii) the reserve which would have been determined with respect to such contract as of the close of such taxable year under such section determined without regard to paragraph (2),

then the difference between the amount of the reserve described in clause (i) and the amount of the reserve described in clause (ii) shall be taken into account under the method provided in subparagraph (B).

(B) METHOD.—The method provided in this subparagraph is as follows:

(i) If the amount determined under subparagraph (A)(i) exceeds the amount determined under subparagraph (A)(ii), 1/8 of such excess shall be taken into account, for each of the 8 succeeding taxable years, as a deduction under section 805(a)(2) or 832(c)(4) of such Code, as applicable.

(ii) If the amount determined under subparagraph (A)(ii) exceeds the amount determined under subparagraph (A)(i), 1/8 of such excess shall be included in gross income, for each of the 8 succeeding taxable years, under section 803(a)(2) or 832(b)(1)(C) of such Code, as applicable.

• 1988, Technical and Miscellaneous Revenue Act of 1988 (P.L. 100-647)

P.L. 100-647, §5011(a):

Amended Code Sec. 7702(c)(3)(B) by striking out clauses (i) and (ii) and inserting in lieu thereof new clauses (i) and (ii). **Effective** for contracts entered into on or after 10-21-88. Prior to amendment, Code Sec. 7702(c)(3)(B)(i)-(ii) read as follows:

(i) the mortality charges specified in the contract (or, if none is specified, the mortality charges used in determining the statutory reserves for such contract),

(ii) any charges (not taken into account under clause (i)) specified in the contract (the amount of any charge not so specified shall be treated as zero), and

P.L. 100-647, § 5011(b):

Amended Code Sec. 7702(c)(3) by adding at the end thereof a new subparagraph (D). **Effective** for contracts entered into on or after 10-21-88.

[Sec. 7702(d)]

(d) CASH VALUE CORRIDOR FOR PURPOSES OF SUBSECTION (a)(2)(B).—For purposes of this section—

(1) IN GENERAL.—A contract falls within the cash value corridor of this subsection if the death benefit under the contract at any time is not less than the applicable percentage of the cash surrender value.

(2) APPLICABLE PERCENTAGE.—

In the case of an insured with an attained age as of the beginning of the contract year of:		The applicable percentage shall decrease by a ratable portion for each full year:	
More than:	But not more than:	From:	To:
0	40	250	250
40	45	250	215
45	50	215	185
50	55	185	150
55	60	150	130
60	65	130	120
65	70	120	115
70	75	115	105
75	90	105	105
90	95	105	100

[Sec. 7702(e)]

(e) COMPUTATIONAL RULES.—

(1) IN GENERAL.—For purposes of this section (other than subsection (d))—

(A) the death benefit (and any qualified additional benefit) shall be deemed not to increase,

(B) the maturity date, including the date on which any benefit described in subparagraph (C) is payable, shall be deemed to be no earlier than the day on which the insured attains age 95, and no later than the day on which the insured attains age 100,

(C) the death benefits shall be deemed to be provided until the maturity date determined by taking into account subparagraph (B), and

(D) the amount of any endowment benefit (or sum of endowment benefits, including any cash surrender value on the maturity date determined by taking into account subparagraph (B)) shall be deemed not to exceed the least amount payable as a death benefit at any time under the contract.

(2) LIMITED INCREASES IN DEATH BENEFIT PERMITTED.—Notwithstanding paragraph (1)(A)—

(A) for purposes of computing the guideline level premium, an increase in the death benefit which is provided in the contract may be taken into account but only to the extent necessary to prevent a decrease in the excess of the death benefit over the cash surrender value of the contract,

(B) for purposes of the cash value accumulation test, the increase described in subparagraph (A) may be taken into account if the contract will meet such test at all times assuming that the net level reserve (determined as if level annual premiums were paid for the contract over a period not ending before the insured attains age 95) is substituted for the net single premium,

(C) for purposes of the cash value accumulation test, the death benefit increases may be taken into account if the contract—

(i) has an initial death benefit of $5,000 or less and a maximum death benefit of $25,000 or less,

(ii) provides for a fixed predetermined annual increase not to exceed 10 percent of the initial death benefit or 8 percent of the death benefit at the end of the preceding year, and

(iii) was purchased to cover payment of burial expenses or in connection with prearranged funeral expenses.

For purposes of subparagraph (C), the initial death benefit of a contract shall be determined by treating all contracts issued to the same contract owner as 1 contract.

Amendments

• **1986, Tax Reform Act of 1986 (P.L. 99-514)**

P.L. 99-514, §1825(a)(1)(A)-(D):

Amended Code Sec. 7702(e)(1) by striking out "shall be no earlier than" in subparagraph (B) and inserting in lieu thereof "shall be deemed to be no earlier than", by striking out "and" at the end of subparagraph (B), by redesignating subparagraph (C) as subparagraph (D) and inserting after subparagraph (B) new subparagraph (C), and by striking out "the maturity date described in subparagraph (B)" in subparagraph (D) (as so redesignated) and inserting in lieu thereof "the maturity date determined by taking into account subparagraph (B)". **Effective** as if included in the provision of P.L. 98-369 to which it relates.

P.L. 99-514, §1825(a)(3):

Amended Code Sec. 7702(e)(1) by inserting "(other than subsection (d))" after "section". **Effective** as if included in the provision of P.L. 98-369 to which it relates.

P.L. 99-514, §1825(a)(4)(A)-(C):

Amended Code Sec. 7702(e)(2) by striking out "and" at the end of subparagraph (A), by striking out the period at the end of subparagraph (B), and inserting in lieu thereof a comma and "and", and by adding at the end thereof new subparagraph (C). **Effective** with respect to contracts entered into after 10-22-86 [**effective** date changed by P.L. 100-647, §1018(j)].

[Sec. 7702(f)]

(f) OTHER DEFINITIONS AND SPECIAL RULES.—For purposes of this section—

(1) PREMIUMS PAID.—

(A) IN GENERAL.—The term "premiums paid" means the premiums paid under the contract less amounts (other than amounts includible in gross income) to which section 72(e) applies and less any excess premiums with respect to which there is a distribution described in subparagraph (B) or (E) of paragraph (7) and any other amounts received with respect to the contract which are specified in regulations.

(B) TREATMENT OF CERTAIN PREMIUMS RETURNED TO POLICYHOLDER.—If, in order to comply with the requirements of subsection (a)(2)(A), any portion of any premium paid during any contract year is returned by the insurance company (with interest) within 60 days after the end of a contract year, the amount so returned (excluding interest) shall be deemed to reduce the sum of the premiums paid under the contract during such year.

(C) INTEREST RETURNED INCLUDIBLE IN GROSS INCOME.—Notwithstanding the provisions of section 72(e), the amount of any interest returned as provided in subparagraph (B) shall be includible in the gross income of the recipient.

(2) CASH VALUES.—

(A) CASH SURRENDER VALUE.—The cash surrender value of any contract shall be its cash value determined without regard to any surrender charge, policy loan, or reasonable termination dividends.

(B) NET SURRENDER VALUE.—The net surrender value of any contract shall be determined with regard to surrender charges but without regard to any policy loan.

(3) DEATH BENEFIT.—The term "death benefit" means the amount payable by reason of the death of the insured (determined without regard to any qualified additional benefits).

(4) FUTURE BENEFITS.—The term "future benefits" means death benefits and endowment benefits.

(5) QUALIFIED ADDITIONAL BENEFITS.—

(A) IN GENERAL.—The term "qualified additional benefits" means any—

(i) guaranteed insurability,

(ii) accidental death or disability benefit,

(iii) family term coverage,

(iv) disability waiver benefit, or

(v) other benefit prescribed under regulations.

(B) TREATMENT OF QUALIFIED ADDITIONAL BENEFITS.—For purposes of this section, qualified additional benefits shall not be treated as future benefits under the contract, but the charges for such benefits shall be treated as future benefits.

(C) TREATMENT OF OTHER ADDITIONAL BENEFITS.—In the case of any additional benefit which is not a qualified additional benefit—

(i) such benefit shall not be treated as a future benefit, and

(ii) any charge for such benefit which is not prefunded shall not be treated as a premium.

(6) PREMIUM PAYMENTS NOT DISQUALIFYING CONTRACT.—The payment of a premium which would result in the sum of the premiums paid exceeding the guideline premium limitation shall be disregarded for purposes of subsection (a)(2) if the amount of such premium does not exceed the amount necessary to prevent the termination of the contract on or before the end of the contract year (but only if the contract will have no cash surrender value at the end of such extension period).

(7) ADJUSTMENTS.—

(A) IN GENERAL.—If there is a change in the benefits under (or in other terms of) the contract which was not reflected in any previous determination or adjustment made under this section, there shall be proper adjustments in future determinations made under this section.

(B) Rule for certain changes during first 15 years.—If—

(i) a change described in subparagraph (A) reduces benefits under the contract,

(ii) the change occurs during the 15-year period beginning on the issue date of the contract, and

(iii) a cash distribution is made to the policyholder as a result of such change, section 72 (other than subsection (e)(5) thereof) shall apply to such cash distribution to the extent it does not exceed the recapture ceiling determined under subparagraph (C) or (D) (whichever applies).

(C) Recapture ceiling where change occurs during first 5 years.—If the change referred to in subparagraph (B)(ii) occurs during the 5-year period beginning on the issue date of the contract, the recapture ceiling is—

(i) in the case of a contract to which subsection (a)(1) applies, the excess of—

(I) the cash surrender value of the contract, immediately before the reduction, over

(II) the net single premium (determined under subsection (b)), immediately after the reduction, or

(ii) in the case of a contract to which subsection (a)(2) applies, the greater of—

(I) the excess of the aggregate premiums paid under the contract, immediately before the reduction, over the guideline premium limitation for the contract (determined under subsection (c)(2), taking into account the adjustment described in subparagraph (A)), or

(II) the excess of the cash surrender value of the contract, immediately before the reduction, over the cash value corridor of subsection (d) (determined immediately after the reduction).

(D) Recapture ceiling where change occurs after 5th year and before 16th year.—If the change referred to in subparagraph (B) occurs after the 5-year period referred to under subparagraph (C), the recapture ceiling is the excess of the cash surrender value of the contract, immediately before the reduction, over the cash value corridor of subsection (d) (determined immediately after the reduction and whether or not subsection (d) applies to the contract).

(E) Treatment of certain distributions made in anticipation of benefit reductions.—Under regulations prescribed by the Secretary, subparagraph (B) shall apply also to any distribution made in anticipation of a reduction in benefits under the contract. For purposes of the preceding sentence, appropriate adjustments shall be made in the provisions of subparagraphs (C) and (D); and any distribution which reduces the cash surrender value of a contract and which is made within 2 years before a reduction in benefits under the contract shall be treated as made in anticipation of such reduction.

(8) Correction of errors.—If the taxpayer establishes to the satisfaction of the Secretary that—

(A) the requirements described in subsection (a) for any contract year were not satisfied due to reasonable error, and

(B) reasonable steps are being taken to remedy the error,

the Secretary may waive the failure to satisfy such requirements.

(9) Special rule for variable life insurance contracts.—In the case of any contract which is a variable contract (as defined in section 817), the determination of whether such contract meets the requirements of subsection (a) shall be made whenever the death benefits under such contract change but not less frequently than once during each 12-month period.

(10) Prevailing commissioners' standard tables.—For purposes of subsection (c)(3)(B)(i), the term "prevailing commissioners' standard tables" means the most recent commissioners' standard tables prescribed by the National Association of Insurance Commissioners which are permitted to be used in computing reserves for that type of contract under the insurance laws of at least 26 States when the contract was issued. If the prevailing commissioners' standard tables as of the beginning of any calendar year (hereinafter in this paragraph referred to as the "year of change") are different from the prevailing commissioners' standard tables as of the beginning of the preceding calendar year, the issuer may use the prevailing commissioners' standard tables as of the beginning of the preceding calendar year with respect to any contract issued after the change and before the close of the 3-year period beginning on the first day of the year of change.

(11) Insurance interest rate.—For purposes of this section—

(A) In general.—The term "insurance interest rate" means, with respect to any contract issued in any calendar year, the lesser of—

(i) the section 7702 valuation interest rate for such calendar year (or, if such calendar year is not an adjustment year, the most recent adjustment year), or

(ii) the section 7702 applicable Federal interest rate for such calendar year (or, if such calendar year is not an adjustment year, the most recent adjustment year).

(B) Section 7702 valuation interest rate.—The term "section 7702 valuation interest rate" means, with respect to any adjustment year, the prescribed U.S. valuation interest rate for life insurance with guaranteed durations of more than 20 years (as defined in the

National Association of Insurance Commissioners' Standard Valuation Law) as effective in the calendar year immediately preceding such adjustment year.

(C) SECTION 7702 APPLICABLE FEDERAL INTEREST RATE.—The term "section 7702 applicable Federal interest rate" means, with respect to any adjustment year, the average (rounded to the nearest whole percentage point) of the applicable Federal mid-term rates (as defined in section 1274(d) but based on annual compounding) effective as of the beginning of each of the calendar months in the most recent 60-month period ending before the second calendar year prior to such adjustment year.

(D) ADJUSTMENT YEAR.—The term "adjustment year" means the calendar year following any calendar year that includes the effective date of a change in the prescribed U.S. valuation interest rate for life insurance with guaranteed durations of more than 20 years (as defined in the National Association of Insurance Commissioners' Standard Valuation Law).

(E) TRANSITION RULE.—Notwithstanding subparagraph (A), the insurance interest rate shall be 2 percent in the case of any contract which is issued during the period that—

(i) begins on January 1, 2021, and

(ii) ends immediately before the beginning of the first adjustment year that beings after December 31, 2021.

Amendments

• 2020, Taxpayer Certainty and Disaster Tax Relief Act of 2020 (P.L. 116-260)

P.L. 116-260, §205(d), Div. EE:

Amended Code Sec. 7702(f) by adding at the end a new paragraph (11). **Effective** for contracts issued after 12-31-2020.

• 2017, Tax Cuts and Jobs Act (P.L. 115-97)

P.L. 115-97, §13517(a)(4)(B):

Amended Code Sec. 7702(f) by adding at the end a new paragraph (10). **Effective** generally for tax years beginning after 12-31-2017. For a transition rule, see Act Sec. 13517(c)(2)-(3), below.

P.L. 115-97, §13517(c)(2)-(3), provides:

(2) TRANSITION RULE.—For the first taxable year beginning after December 31, 2017, the reserve with respect to any contract (as determined under section 807(d) of the Internal Revenue Code of 1986) at the end of the preceding taxable year shall be determined as if the amendments made by this section had applied to such reserve in such preceding taxable year.

(3) TRANSITION RELIEF.—

(A) IN GENERAL.—If—

(i) the reserve determined under section 807(d) of the Internal Revenue Code of 1986 (determined after application of paragraph (2)) with respect to any contract as of the close of the year preceding the first taxable year beginning after December 31, 2017, differs from

(ii) the reserve which would have been determined with respect to such contract as of the close of such taxable year under such section determined without regard to paragraph (2),

then the difference between the amount of the reserve described in clause (i) and the amount of the reserve described in clause (ii) shall be taken into account under the method provided in subparagraph (B).

(B) METHOD.—The method provided in this subparagraph is as follows:

(i) If the amount determined under subparagraph (A)(i) exceeds the amount determined under subparagraph (A)(ii), 1/8 of such excess shall be taken into account, for each of the 8 succeeding taxable years, as a deduction under section 805(a)(2) or 832(c)(4) of such Code, as applicable.

(ii) If the amount determined under subparagraph (A)(ii) exceeds the amount determined under subparagraph (A)(i), 1/8 of such excess shall be included in gross income, for each of the 8 succeeding taxable years, under section 803(a)(2) or 832(b)(1)(C) of such Code, as applicable.

• 1986, Tax Reform Act of 1986 (P.L. 99-514)

P.L. 99-514, §1825(b)(1):

Amended Code Sec. 7702(f)(7). **Effective** as if included in the provision of P.L. 98-369 to which it relates. Prior to amendment, Code Sec. 7702(f)(7) read as follows:

(7) ADJUSTMENTS.—

(A) IN GENERAL.—In the event of a change in the future benefits or any qualified additional benefit (or in any other terms) under the contract which was not reflected in any previous determination made under this section, under regulations prescribed by the Secretary, there shall be proper adjustments in future determinations made under this section.

(B) CERTAIN CHANGES TREATED AS EXCHANGE.—In the case of any change which reduces the future benefits under the contract, such change shall be treated as an exchange of the contract for another contract.

P.L. 99-514, §1825(b)(2):

Amended Code Sec. 7702(f)(1)(A) by striking out "less any other amounts received" and inserting in lieu thereof "less any excess premiums with respect to which there is a distribution described in subparagraph (B) or (E) of paragraph (7) and any other amounts received". **Effective** as if included in the provision of P.L. 98-369 to which it relates.

[Sec. 7702(g)]

(g) TREATMENT OF CONTRACTS WHICH DO NOT MEET SUBSECTION(a) TEST.—

(1) INCOME INCLUSION.—

(A) IN GENERAL.—If at any time any contract which is a life insurance contract under the applicable law does not meet the definition of life insurance contract under subsection (a), the income on the contract for any taxable year of the policyholder shall be treated as ordinary income received or accrued by the policyholder during such year.

(B) INCOME ON THE CONTRACT.—For purposes of this paragraph, the term "income on the contract" means, with respect to any taxable year of the policyholder, the excess of—

(i) the sum of—

(I) the increase in the net surrender value of the contract during the taxable year, and

(II) the cost of life insurance protection provided under the contract during the taxable year, over

(ii) the premiums paid (as defined in subsection (f)(1)) under the contract during the taxable year.

(C) CONTRACTS WHICH CEASE TO MEET DEFINITION.—If, during any taxable year of the policyholder, a contract which is a life insurance contract under the applicable law ceases to meet the definition of life insurance contract under subsection (a), the income on the contract for all prior taxable years shall be treated as received or accrued during the taxable year in which such cessation occurs.

(D) COST OF LIFE INSURANCE PROTECTION.—For purposes of this paragraph, the cost of life insurance protection provided under the contract shall be the lesser of—

(i) the cost of individual insurance on the life of the insured as determined on the basis of uniform premiums (computed on the basis of 5-year age brackets) prescribed by the Secretary by regulations, or

(ii) the mortality charge (if any) stated in the contract.

(2) TREATMENT OF AMOUNT PAID ON DEATH OF INSURED.—If any contract which is a life insurance contract under the applicable law does not meet the definition of life insurance contract under subsection (a), the excess of the amount paid by the reason of the death of the insured over the net surrender value of the contract shall be deemed to be paid under a life insurance contract for purposes of section 101 and subtitle B.

(3) CONTRACT CONTINUES TO BE TREATED AS INSURANCE CONTRACT.—If any contract which is a life insurance contract under the applicable law does not meet the definition of life insurance contract under subsection (a), such contract shall, notwithstanding such failure, be treated as an insurance contract for purposes of this title.

Amendments

• 1986, Tax Reform Act of 1986 (P.L. 99-514)

P.L. 99-514, §1825(c):

Amended Code Sec. 7702(g)(1)(B)(ii). **Effective** as if included in the provision of P.L. 98-369 to which it relates.

Prior to amendment, Code Sec. 7702(g)(1)(B)(ii) read as follows:

(ii) the amount of premiums paid under the contract during the taxable year reduced by policyholder dividends received during such taxable year.

[Sec. 7702(h)]

(h) ENDOWMENT CONTRACTS RECEIVE SAME TREATMENT.—

(1) IN GENERAL.—References in subsections (a) and (g) to a life insurance contract shall be treated as including references to a contract which is an endowment contract under the applicable law.

(2) DEFINITION OF ENDOWMENT CONTRACT.—For purposes of this title (other than paragraph (1)), the term "endowment contract" means a contract which is an endowment contract under the applicable law and which meets the requirements of subsection (a).

[Sec. 7702(i)]

(i) TRANSITIONAL RULE FOR CERTAIN 20-PAY CONTRACTS.—

(1) IN GENERAL.—In the case of a qualified 20-pay contract, this section shall be applied by substituting "3 percent" for "4 percent" in subsection (b)(2).

(2) QUALIFIED 20-PAY CONTRACT.—For purposes of paragraph (1), the term "qualified 20-pay contract" means any contract which—

(A) requires at least 20 nondecreasing annual premium payments, and

(B) is issued pursuant to an existing plan of insurance.

(3) EXISTING PLAN OF INSURANCE.—For purposes of this subsection, the term "existing plan of insurance" means, with respect to any contract, any plan of insurance which was filed by the company issuing such contract in 1 or more States before September 28, 1983, and is on file in the appropriate State for such contract.

[Sec. 7702(j)]

(j) CERTAIN CHURCH SELF FUNDED DEATH BENEFIT PLANS TREATED AS LIFE INSURANCE.—

(1) IN GENERAL.—In determining whether any plan or arrangement described in paragraph (2) is a life insurance contract, the requirement of subsection (a) that the contract be a life insurance contract under applicable law shall not apply.

(2) DESCRIPTION.—For purposes of this subsection, a plan or arrangement is described in this paragraph if—

(A) such plan or arrangement provides for the payment of benefits by reason of the death of the individuals covered under such plan or arrangement, and

(B) such plan or arrangement is provided by a church for the benefit of its employees and their beneficiaries, directly or through an organization described in section 414(e)(3)(A) or an organization described in section 414(e)(3)(B)(ii).

(3) DEFINITIONS.—For purposes of this subsection—

(A) CHURCH.—The term "church" means a church or a convention or association of churches.

(B) EMPLOYEE.—The term "employee" includes an employee described in section 414(e)(3)(B).

Amendments

• 2004 (P.L. 108-476)

P.L. 108-476, §1(a)(1) and (4) and (c), provides:

SECTION 1. CERTAIN ARRANGEMENTS MAINTAINED BY THE YMCA RETIREMENT FUND TREATED AS CHURCH PLANS.

(a) RETIREMENT PLANS.—

(1) IN GENERAL.—For purposes of sections 401(a) and 403(b) of the Internal Revenue Code of 1986, any retirement plan maintained by the YMCA Retirement Fund as of January 1, 2003, shall be treated as a church plan (within the meaning of section 414(e) of such Code) which is maintained by an organization described in section 414(e)(3)(A) of such Code.

* * *

(4) SELF-FUNDED DEATH BENEFIT PLAN.—For purposes of section 7702(j) of such Code, a retirement plan described in paragraph (1) shall be treated as an arrangement described in section 7702(j)(2).

* * *

(c) EFFECTIVE DATE.—This section shall apply to plan years beginning after December 31, 2003.

• 1988, Technical and Miscellaneous Revenue Act of 1988 (P.L. 100-647)

P.L. 100-647, §6078(a):

Amended Code Sec. 7702 by inserting after subsection (i) new subsection (j). **Effective** as if included in the amendments made by section 221(a) of P.L. 98-369.

[Sec. 7702(k)]

(k) REGULATIONS.—The Secretary shall prescribe such regulations as may be necessary or appropriate to carry out the purposes of this section.

Amendments

• 1988, Technical and Miscellaneous Revenue Act of 1988 (P.L. 100-647)

P.L. 100-647, §6078(a):

Amended Code Sec. 7702 by redesignating subsection (j) as subsection (k). **Effective** as if included in the amendments made by section 221(a) of P.L. 98-369.

• 1984, Deficit Reduction Act of 1984 (P.L. 98-369)

P.L. 98-369, §221(a):

Added Code Sec. 7702. **Effective** for contracts issued after 12-31-84, in tax years ending after such date. Special rules appear below.

P.L. 98-369, §221(d)(2)-(5), as amended by P.L. 99-514, §1825(e):

(2) Special rule for certain contracts issued after June 30, 1984.—

(A) General rule.—Except as otherwise provided in this paragraph, the amendments made by this section shall apply also to any contract issued after June 30, 1984, which provides an increasing death benefit and has premium funding more rapid than 10-year level premium payments.

(B) Exception for certain contracts.—Subparagraph (A) shall not apply to any contract if—

(i) such contract (whether or not a flexible premium contract) would meet the requirements of section 101(f) of the Internal Revenue Code of 1954,

(ii) such contract is not a flexible premium life insurance contract (within the meaning of section 101(f) of such Code) and would meet the requirements of section 7702 of such Code determined by—

(I) substituting "3 percent" for "4 percent" in section 7702(b)(2) of such Code, and

(II) treating subparagraph (B) of section 7702(e)(1) of such Code as if it read as follows: "the maturity date shall be the latest maturity date permitted under the contract, but not less than 20 years after the date of issue or (if earlier) age 95", or

(iii) under such contract—

(I) the premiums (including any policy fees) will be adjusted from time-to-time to reflect the level amount necessary (but not less than zero) at the time of such adjustment to provide a level death benefit assuming interest crediting and an annual effective interest rate of not less than 3 percent, or

(II) at the option of the insured, in lieu of an adjustment under subclause (I) there will be a comparable adjustment in the amount of the death benefit.

(C) Certain contracts issued before October 1, 1984.—

(i) In general.—Subparagraph (A) shall be applied by substituting "September 30, 1984" for "June 30, 1984" thereof in the case of a contract—

(I) which would meet the requirements of section 7702 of such Code if "3 percent" were substituted for "4 percent" in section 7702(b)(2) of such Code, and the rate or rates guaranteed on issuance of the contract were determined without regard to any mortality charges and any initial excess interest guarantees, and

(II) the cash surrender value of which does not at any time exceed the net single premium which would have to be paid at such time to fund future benefits under the contract.

(ii) Definitions.—For purposes of clause (i)—

(I) In general.—Except as provided in subclause (II), terms used in clause (i) shall have the same meanings as when used in section 7702 of such Code.

(II) Net single premium.—The term "net single premium" shall be determined by substituting "3 percent" for "4 percent" in section 7702(b)(2) of such Code, by using the 1958 standard ordinary mortality and morbidity tables of the National Association of Insurance Commissioners, and by assuming a level death benefit.

(3) Transitional rule for certain existing plans of insurance.—A plan of insurance on file in 1 or more States before September 28, 1983, shall be treated for purposes of section 7702(i)(3) of such Code as a plan of insurance on file in 1 or more States before September 28, 1983, without regard to whether such plan of insurance is modified after September 28, 1983, to permit the crediting of excess interest or similar amounts annually and not monthly under contracts issued pursuant to such plan of insurance.

(4) Extension of flexible premium contract provisions.—The amendments made by subsection (b) shall take effect on January 1, 1984.

(5) Special rule for master contract.—For purposes of this subsection, in the case of a master contract, the date taken into account with respect to any insured shall be the first date on which such insured is covered under such contract.

* * *

CHAPTER 80—GENERAL RULES

Subchapter A—Application of Internal Revenue Laws

* * *

[Sec. 7801]

SEC. 7801. AUTHORITY OF THE DEPARTMENT OF THE TREASURY.

[Sec. 7801(a)]

(a) POWERS AND DUTIES OF SECRETARY.—

(1) IN GENERAL.—Except as otherwise expressly provided by law, the administration and enforcement of this title shall be performed by or under the supervision of the Secretary of the Treasury.

(2) ADMINISTRATION AND ENFORCEMENT OF CERTAIN PROVISIONS BY ATTORNEY GENERAL.—

(A) IN GENERAL.—The administration and enforcement of the following provisions of this title shall be performed by or under the supervision of the Attorney General; and the term "Secretary" or "Secretary of the Treasury" shall, when applied to those provisions, mean the Attorney General; and the term "internal revenue officer" shall, when applied to those provisions, mean any officer of the Bureau of Alcohol, Tobacco, Firearms, and Explosives so designated by the Attorney General:

(i) Chapter 53.

(ii) Chapters 61 through 80, to the extent such chapters relate to the enforcement and administration of the provisions referred to in clause (i).

(B) USE OF EXISTING RULINGS AND INTERPRETATIONS.—Nothing in the Homeland Security Act of 2002 alters or repeals the rulings and interpretations of the Bureau of Alcohol, Tobacco, and Firearms in effect on the effective date of such Act, which concerns the provisions of this title referred to in subparagraph (A). The Attorney General shall consult with the Secretary to achieve uniformity and consistency in administering provisions under chapter 53 of title 26, United States Code.

Amendments

• 2018, Tax Technical Corrections Act of 2018 (P.L. 115-141)

P.L. 115-141, §401(a)(333)(A)-(B), Div. U:

Amended Code Sec. 7801(a)(2)(B) by striking "this Act" and inserting "the Homeland Security Act of 2002", and by striking "effective date of the Homeland Security Act of 2002" and inserting "effective date of such Act". **Effective** 3-23-2018.

• 2002, Homeland Security Act of 2002 (P.L. 107-296)

P.L. 107-296, §1112(k)(1)-(2):

Amended Code Sec. 7801(a) by striking "SECRETARY.—Except" and inserting "SECRETARY.—(1) IN GENERAL.—Except" and by adding at the end a new paragraph (2). **Effective** 60 days after 11-25-2002.

•1998 (P.L. 106-58)

P.L. 106-58, §650, provides:

SEC. 650. ITEMIZED INCOME TAX RECEIPT.

(a) IN GENERAL.—Not later than April 15, 2000, the Secretary of the Treasury shall establish an interactive program on an Internet website where any taxpayer may generate an itemized receipt showing a proportionate allocation (in money terms) of the taxpayer's total tax payments among the major expenditure categories.

(b) INFORMATION NECESSARY TO GENERATE RECEIPT.—For purposes of generating an itemized receipt under subsection (a), the interactive program—

(1) shall only require the input of the taxpayer's total tax payments; and

(2) shall not require any identifying information relating to the taxpayer.

(c) TOTAL TAX PAYMENTS.—For purposes of this section, total tax payments of an individual for any taxable year are—

(1) the tax imposed by subtitle A of the Internal Revenue Code of 1986 for such taxable year (as shown on his return); and

(2) the tax imposed by section 3101 of such Code on wages received during such taxable year.

(d) CONTENT OF TAX RECEIPT.—

(1) MAJOR EXPENDITURE CATEGORIES.—For purposes of subsection (a), the major expenditure categories are:

(A) National defense.

(B) International affairs.

(C) Medicaid.

(D) Medicare.

(E) Means-tested entitlements.

(F) Domestic discretionary.

(G) Social Security.

(H) Interest payments.

(I) All other.

(2) OTHER ITEMS ON RECEIPT.—

(A) IN GENERAL.—In addition, the tax receipt shall include selected examples of more specific expenditure items, including the items listed in subparagraph (B), either at the budget function, subfunction, or program, project, or activity levels, along with any other information deemed appropriate by the Secretary of the Treasury and the Director of the Office of Management and Budget to enhance taxpayer understanding of the Federal budget.

(B) LISTED ITEMS.—The expenditure items listed in this subparagraph are as follows:

(i) Public schools funding programs.

(ii) Student loans and college aid.

(iii) Low-income housing programs.

(iv) Food stamp and welfare programs.

(v) Law enforcement, including the Federal Bureau of Investigation, law enforcement grants to the States, and other Federal law enforcement personnel.

(vi) Infrastructure, including roads, bridges, and mass transit.

(vii) Farm subsidies.

(viii) Congressional Member and staff salaries.

(ix) Health research programs.

(x) Aid to the disabled.

(xi) Veterans health care and pension programs.

(xii) Space programs.

(xiii) Environmental cleanup programs.

(xiv) United States embassies.

(xv) Military salaries.

(xvi) Foreign aid.

(xvii) Contributions to the North Atlantic Treaty Organization.

(xviii) Amtrak.

(xix) United States Postal Service.

(e) COST.—No charge shall be imposed to cover any cost associated with the production or distribution of the tax receipt.

(f) REGULATIONS.—The Secretary of the Treasury may prescribe such regulations as may be necessary to carry out this section.

• 1959 (P.L. 86-368)

P.L. 86-368, §1:

Amended the heading of Code Sec. 7801 by inserting "THE" after "AUTHORITY OF". **Effective** 9-22-59.

[Sec. 7801(b)—Repealed]

Amendments

• 1982 (P.L. 97-258)

P.L. 97-258, §5(b):

Repealed Code Sec. 7801(b). **Effective** 9-13-82. Prior to being repealed, Code Sec. 77801(b) read as follows:

(b) OFFICE OF GENERAL COUNSEL FOR THE DEPARTMENT.—

(1) GENERAL COUNSEL.—There shall be in the Department of the Treasury the office of General Counsel for the Department of the Treasury. The General Counsel shall be appointed by the President, by and with the advice and consent of the Senate. The General Counsel shall be the chief law officer of the Department and shall perform such duties as may be prescribed by the Secretary of the Treasury.

(2) ASSISTANT GENERAL COUNSELS.—The President is authorized to appoint, by and with the advice and consent of the Senate, an Assistant General Counsel who shall be the Chief Counsel for the Internal Revenue Service. The Chief Counsel shall be the chief law officer for the Internal Revenue Service and shall perform such duties as may be prescribed by the Secretary of the Treasury. The Secretary of the Treasury may appoint, without regard to the provisions of the civil service laws, and fix the duties of not to exceed five other assistant General Counsels.

(3) ATTORNEYS.—The Secretary of the Treasury may appoint and fix the duties of such other attorneys as he may deem necessary.

• 1976, Tax Reform Act of 1976 (P.L. 94-455)

P.L. 94-455, §1906(b)(13)(B):

Substituted "Secretary of the Treasury" for "Secretary" each place it appeared in Code Sec. 7801(b). **Effective** 2-1-77.

• 1964, Government Employees Salary Act of 1964 (P.L. 88-426)

P.L. 88-426, §305(39):

Deleted "and shall receive basic compensation at the annual rate of $19,000" from the first sentence of Sec. 7801(b)(2). **Effective** 7-1-64.

• 1959 (P.L. 86-368)

P.L. 86-368, §1:

Amended Code Sec. 7801(b). **Effective** 9-22-59. Prior to amendment, Sec. 7801(b) read as follows:

"(b) General Counsel for the Department.—There shall be in the Department of the Treasury the office of General Counsel for the Department of the Treasury. The General Counsel shall be appointed by the President, by and with the advice and consent of the Senate. The General Counsel shall be the chief law officer of the Department and shall perform such duties as may be prescribed by the Secretary. The Secretary may appoint and fix the duties of an Assistant General Counsel who shall serve as Chief Counsel of the Internal Revenue Service and may appoint and fix the duties of not to exceed five other Assistant General Counsels. All Assistant General Counsels shall be appointed without regard to the provisions of the civil service laws. The Secretary may also appoint and fix the duties of such other attorneys as he may deem necessary."

[Sec. 7801(c)]

(c) FUNCTIONS OF DEPARTMENT OF JUSTICE UNAFFECTED.—Nothing in this section or section 301(f) of title 31 shall be considered to affect the duties, powers, or functions imposed upon, or vested in, the Department of Justice, or any officer thereof, by law existing on May 10, 1934.

Amendments

• 1982 (P.L. 97-258)

P.L. 97-258, §2(f)(1):

Amended Code Sec. 7801(c) by inserting after "in this section" "or section 301(f) of title 31". **Effective** 9-13-82.

• 1959 (P.L. 86-368)

P.L. 86-368, §1:

Amended Code Sec. 7801(c) by inserting a comma preceding and following the phrase "or vested in". **Effective** 9-22-59.

* * *

[Sec. 7805]

SEC. 7805. RULES AND REGULATIONS.

[Sec. 7805(a)]

(a) AUTHORIZATION.—Except where such authority is expressly given by this title to any person other than an officer or employee of the Treasury Department, the Secretary shall prescribe all needful rules and regulations for the enforcement of this title, including all rules and regulations as may be necessary by reason of any alteration of law in relation to internal revenue.

Amendments

• 1976, Tax Reform Act of 1976 (P.L. 94-455)

P.L. 94-455, §1906(b)(13)(A):

Amended 1954 Code by substituting "Secretary" for "Secretary or his delegate" each place it appeared. **Effective** 2-1-77.

[Sec. 7805(b)]

(b) RETROACTIVITY OF REGULATIONS.—

(1) IN GENERAL.—Except as otherwise provided in this subsection, no temporary, proposed, or final regulation relating to the internal revenue laws shall apply to any taxable period ending before the earliest of the following dates:

(A) The date on which such regulation is filed with the Federal Register.

(B) In the case of any final regulation, the date on which any proposed or temporary regulation to which such final regulation relates was filed with the Federal Register.

(C) The date on which any notice substantially describing the expected contents of any temporary, proposed, or final regulation is issued to the public.

(2) EXCEPTION FOR PROMPTLY ISSUED REGULATIONS.—Paragraph (1) shall not apply to regulations filed or issued within 18 months of the date of the enactment of the statutory provision to which the regulation relates.

(3) PREVENTION OF ABUSE.—The Secretary may provide that any regulation may take effect or apply retroactively to prevent abuse.

(4) CORRECTION OF PROCEDURAL DEFECTS.—The Secretary may provide that any regulation may apply retroactively to correct a procedural defect in the issuance of any prior regulation.

(5) INTERNAL REGULATIONS.—The limitation of paragraph (1) shall not apply to any regulation relating to internal Treasury Department policies, practices, or procedures.

(6) CONGRESSIONAL AUTHORIZATION.—The limitation of paragraph (1) may be superseded by a legislative grant from Congress authorizing the Secretary to prescribe the effective date with respect to any regulation.

(7) ELECTION TO APPLY RETROACTIVELY.—The Secretary may provide for any taxpayer to elect to apply any regulation before the dates specified in paragraph (1).

(8) APPLICATION TO RULINGS.—The Secretary may prescribe the extent, if any, to which any ruling (including any judicial decision or any administrative determination other than by regulation) relating to the internal revenue laws shall be applied without retroactive effect.

Amendments

• 1996, Taxpayer Bill of Rights 2 (P.L. 104-168)

P.L. 104-168, §1101(a):

Amended Code Sec. 7805(b). **Effective** with respect to regulations which relate to statutory provisions enacted on or after 7-30-96. Prior to amendment, Code Sec. 7805(b) read as follows:

(b) RETROACTIVITY OF REGULATIONS OR RULINGS.—The Secretary may prescribe the extent, if any, to which any ruling or regulation, relating to the internal revenue laws, shall be applied without retroactive effect.

• 1976, Tax Reform Act of 1976 (P.L. 94-455)

P.L. 94-455, §1906(b)(13)(A):

Amended 1954 Code by substituting "Secretary" for "Secretary or his delegate" each place it appeared. **Effective** 2-1-77.

[Sec. 7805(c)]

(c) PREPARATION AND DISTRIBUTION OF REGULATIONS, FORMS, STAMPS, AND OTHER MATTERS.—The Secretary shall prepare and distribute all the instructions, regulations, directions, forms, blanks, stamps, and other matters pertaining to the assessment and collection of internal revenue.

Amendments

• 1976, Tax Reform Act of 1976 (P.L. 94-455)

P.L. 94-455, §1906(b)(13)(A):

Amended 1954 Code by substituting "Secretary" for "Secretary or his delegate" each place it appeared. **Effective** 2-1-77.

[Sec. 7805(d)]

(d) MANNER OF MAKING ELECTIONS PRESCRIBED BY SECRETARY.—Except to the extent otherwise provided by this title, any election under this title shall be made at such time and in such manner as the Secretary shall prescribe.

Amendments

• 1998, IRS Restructuring and Reform Act of 1998 (P.L. 105-206)

P.L. 105-206, §3704:

Amended Code Sec. 7805(d) by striking "by regulations or forms" after "Secretary shall". **Effective** 7-22-98.

• 1984, Deficit Reduction Act of 1984 (P.L. 98-369)

P.L. 98-369, §43(b):

Amended Code Sec. 7805 by adding at the end thereof new subsection (d). **Effective** for tax years ending after 7-18-84.

[Sec. 7805(e)]

(e) TEMPORARY REGULATIONS.—

(1) ISSUANCE.—Any temporary regulation issued by the Secretary shall also be issued as a proposed regulation.

(2) 3-YEAR DURATION.—Any temporary regulation shall expire within 3 years after the date of issuance of such regulation.

Amendments

• 1988, Technical and Miscellaneous Revenue Act of 1988 (P.L. 100-647)

P.L. 100-647, §6232(a):

Amended Code Sec. 7805 by adding at the end thereof new subsection (e). **Effective** for any regulation issued after 11-20-88.

* * *

Subchapter B—Effective Date and Related Provisions

[Sec. 7851]

SEC. 7851. APPLICABILITY OF REVENUE LAWS.

[Sec. 7851(a)]

(a) GENERAL RULES.—Except as otherwise provided in any section of this title—

(1) SUBTITLE A.—

(A) Chapters 1, 2, and 6 of this title shall apply only with respect to taxable years beginning after December 31, 1953, and ending after the date of enactment of this title, and with respect to such taxable years, chapters 1 (except sections 143 and 144) and 2, and section 3801, of the Internal Revenue Code of 1939 are hereby repealed.

(B) Chapter 3 of this title shall apply with respect to payments and transfers occurring after December 31, 1954, and as to such payments and transfers sections 143 and 144 and chapter 7 of the Internal Revenue Code of 1939 are hereby repealed.

(C) Any provision of subtitle A of this title the applicability of which is stated in terms of a specific date (occurring after December 31, 1953), or in terms of taxable years ending after a specific date (occurring after December 31, 1953), shall apply to taxable years ending after such specific date. Each such provision shall, in the case of a taxable year subject to the Internal Revenue Code of 1939, be deemed to be included in the Internal Revenue Code of 1939, but shall be applicable only to taxable years ending after such specific date. The provisions of the Internal Revenue Code of 1939 superseded by provisions of subtitle A of this title the applicability of which is stated in terms of a specific date (occurring after December 31, 1953) shall be deemed to be included in subtitle A of this title, but shall be applicable only to the period prior to the taking effect of the corresponding provision of subtitle A.

(D) Effective with respect to taxable years ending after March 31, 1954, and subject to tax under chapter 1 of the Internal Revenue Code of 1939—

(i) Sections 13(b)(3), 26(b)(2)(C), 26(h)(1)(C) (including the comma and the word "and" immediately preceding such section), 26(i)(3), 108(k), 207(a)(1)(C), 207(a)(3)(C), and the last sentence of section 362(b)(3) of such Code are hereby repealed; and

(ii) Sections 13(b)(2), 26(b)(2)(B), 26(h)(1)(B), 26(i)(2), 207(a)(1)(B), 207(a)(3)(B), 421(a)(1)(B), and the second sentence of section 362(b)(3) of such Code are hereby amended by striking out "and before April 1, 1954" (and any accompanying punctuation) wherever appearing therein.

(2) SUBTITLE B.—

(A) Chapter 11 of this title shall apply with respect to estates of decedents dying after the date of enactment of this title, and with respect to such estates chapter 3 of the Internal Revenue Code of 1939 is hereby repealed.

(B) Chapter 12 of this title shall apply with respect to the calendar year 1955 and all calendar years thereafter, and with respect to such years chapter 4 of the Internal Revenue Code of 1939 is hereby repealed.

(3) SUBTITLE C.—Subtitle C of this title shall apply only with respect to remuneration paid after December 31, 1954, except that chapter 22 of such subtitle shall apply only with respect to remuneration paid after December 31, 1954, which is for services performed after such date. Chapter 9 of the Internal Revenue Code of 1939 is hereby repealed with respect to remuneration paid after December 31, 1954, except that subchapter B of such chapter (and subchapter E of such chapter to the extent it relates to subchapter B) shall remain in force and effect with respect to remuneration paid after December 31, 1954, for services performed on or before such date.

(4) SUBTITLE D.—Subtitle D of this title shall take effect on January 1, 1955. Subtitles B and C of the Internal Revenue Code of 1939 (except chapters 7, 9, 15, 26, and 28, subchapter B of chapter 25, and parts VII and VIII of subchapter A of chapter 27 of such code) are hereby repealed effective January 1, 1955. Provisions having the same effect as section 6416(b)(2)(H), and so much of section 4082(c) as refers to special motor fuels, shall be considered to be included in the Internal Revenue Code of 1939 effective as of May 1, 1954. Section 2450(a) of the Internal Revenue Code of 1939 (as amended by the Excise Tax Reduction Act of 1954) applies to the period beginning on April 1, 1954, and ending on December 31, 1954.

(5) SUBTITLE E.—Subtitle E shall take effect on January 1, 1955, except that the provisions in section 5411 permitting the use of a brewery under regulations prescribed by the Secretary for the purpose of producing and bottling soft drinks, section 5554, and chapter 53 shall take effect on the day after the date of enactment of this title. Subchapter B of chapter 25, and part VIII of subchapter A of chapter 27, of the Internal Revenue Code of 1939 are hereby repealed effective on the day after the date of enactment of this title. Chapters 15 and 26, and part VII of subchapter A of chapter 27, of the Internal Revenue Code of 1939 are hereby repealed effective January 1, 1955.

(6) SUBTITLE F.—

(A) GENERAL RULE.—The provisions of subtitle F shall take effect on the day after the date of enactment of this title and shall be applicable with respect to any tax imposed by this title. The provisions of subtitle F shall apply with respect to any tax imposed by the Internal

Revenue Code of 1939 only to the extent provided in subparagraphs (B) and (C) of this paragraph.

(B) ASSESSMENT, COLLECTION, AND REFUNDS.—Notwithstanding the provisions of subparagraph (A), and notwithstanding any contrary provision of subchapter A of chapter 63 (relating to assessment), chapter 64 (relating to collection), or chapter 65 (relating to abatements, credits, and refunds) of this title, the provisions of part II of subchapter A of chapter 28 and chapters 35, 36, and 37 (except section 3777) of subtitle D of the Internal Revenue Code of 1939 shall remain in effect until January 1, 1955, and shall also be applicable to the taxes imposed by this title. On and after January 1, 1955, the provisions of subchapter A of chapter 63, chapter 64, and chapter 65 (except section 6405) of this title shall be applicable to all internal revenue taxes (whether imposed by this title or by the Internal Revenue Code of 1939), notwithstanding any contrary provision of part II of subchapter A of chapter 28, or of chapter 35, 36, or 37, of the Internal Revenue Code of 1939. The provisions of section 6405 (relating to reports of refunds and credits) shall be applicable with respect to refunds or credits allowed after the date of enactment of this title, and section 3777 of the Internal Revenue Code of 1939 is hereby repealed with respect to such refunds and credits.

(C) TAXES IMPOSED UNDER THE 1939 CODE.—After the date of enactment of this title, the following provisions of subtitle F shall apply to the taxes imposed by the Internal Revenue Code of 1939, notwithstanding any contrary provisions of such code:

(i) Chapter 73, relating to bonds.

(ii) Chapter 74, relating to closing agreements and compromises.

(iii) Chapter 75, relating to crimes and other offenses, but only insofar as it relates to offenses committed after the date of enactment of this title, and in the case of such offenses, section 6531, relating to periods of limitation on criminal prosecution, shall be applicable. The penalties (other than penalties which may be assessed) provided by the Internal Revenue Code of 1939 shall not apply to offenses, committed after the date of enactment of this title, to which chapter 75 of this title is applicable.

(iv) Chapter 76, relating to judicial proceedings.

(v) Chapter 77, relating to miscellaneous provisions, except that section 7502 shall apply only if the mailing occurs after the date of enactment of this title, and section 7503 shall apply only if the last date referred to therein occurs after the date of enactment of this title.

(vi) Chapter 78, relating to discovery of liability and enforcement of title.

(vii) Chapter 79, relating to definitions.

(viii) Chapter 80, relating to application of internal revenue laws, effective date, and related provisions.

(D) CHAPTER 28 AND SUBTITLE D OF 1939 CODE.—Except as otherwise provided in subparagraphs (B) and (C), the provisions of chapter 28 and of subtitle D of the Internal Revenue Code of 1939 shall remain in effect with respect to taxes imposed by the Internal Revenue Code of 1939.

(7) OTHER PROVISIONS.—If the effective date of any provision of the Internal Revenue Code of 1954 is not otherwise provided in this section or in any other section of this title, such provision shall take effect on the day after the date of enactment of this title. If the repeal of any provision of the Internal Revenue Code of 1939 is not otherwise provided by this section or by any other section of this title, such provision is hereby repealed effective on the day after the date of enactment of this title.

Amendments

• 2018, Tax Technical Corrections Act of 2018 (P.L. 115-141)

P.L. 115-141, §401(a)(335), Div. U:

Amended Code Sec. 7851(a)(1)(A) by striking ", 4" following "1, 2". **Effective** 3-23-2018.

P.L. 115-141, §401(a)(336), Div. U:

Amended Code Sec. 7851(a)(1)(B) by striking "Chapters 3 and 5" and inserting "Chapter 3". **Effective** 3-23-2018.

• 1976, Tax Reform Act of 1976 (P.L. 94-455)

P.L. 94-455, §1906(b)(13)(A):

Amended 1954 Code by substituting "Secretary" for "Secretary or his delegate" each place it appeared. **Effective** 2-1-77.

[Sec. 7851(b)]

(b) EFFECT OF REPEAL OF INTERNAL REVENUE CODE OF 1939.—

(1) EXISTING RIGHTS AND LIABILITIES.—The repeal of any provision of the Internal Revenue Code of 1939 shall not affect any act done or any right accruing or accrued, or any suit or proceeding had or commenced in any civil cause, before such repeal; but all rights and liabilities under such code shall continue, and may be enforced in the same manner, as if such repeal had not been made.

(2) EXISTING OFFICES.—The repeal of any provision of the Internal Revenue Code of 1939 shall not abolish, terminate, or otherwise change—

(A) any internal revenue district,

(B) any office, position, board, or committee, or

(C) the appointment or employment of any officer or employee,

existing immediately preceding the enactment of this title, the continuance of which is not manifestly inconsistent with any provision of this title, but the same shall continue unless and until changed by lawful authority.

(3) EXISTING DELEGATIONS OF AUTHORITY.—Any delegation of authority made pursuant to the provisions of Reorganization Plan Numbered 26 of 1950 or Reorganization Plan Numbered 1 of 1952, including any redelegation of authority made pursuant to any such delegation of authority, and in effect under the Internal Revenue Code of 1939 immediately preceding the enactment of this title shall, notwithstanding the repeal of such code, remain in effect for purposes of this title, unless distinctly inconsistent or manifestly incompatible with the provisions of this title. The preceding sentence shall not be construed as limiting in any manner the power to amend, modify, or revoke any such delegation or redelegation of authority.

[Sec. 7851(c)]

(c) CRIMES AND FORFEITURES.—All offenses committed, and all penalties or forfeitures incurred, under any provision of law hereby repealed, may be prosecuted and punished in the same manner and with the same effect as if this title had not been enacted.

[Sec. 7851(d)]

(d) PERIODS OF LIMITATION.—All periods of limitation, whether applicable to civil causes and proceedings, or to the prosecution of offenses, or for the recovery of penalties or forfeitures, hereby repealed shall not be affected thereby, but all suits, proceedings, or prosecutions, whether civil or criminal, for causes arising, or acts done or committed, prior to said repeal, may be commenced and prosecuted within the same time as if this title had not been enacted.

[Sec. 7851(e)]

(e) REFERENCE TO OTHER PROVISIONS.—For the purpose of applying the Internal Revenue Code of 1939 or the Internal Revenue Code of 1954 to any period, any reference in either such code to another provision of the Internal Revenue Code of 1939 or the Internal Revenue Code of 1954 which is not then applicable to such period shall be deemed a reference to the corresponding provision of the other code which is then applicable to such period.

[Sec. 7852]

SEC. 7852. OTHER APPLICABLE RULES.

[Sec. 7852(a)]

(a) SEPARABILITY CLAUSE.—If any provision of this title, or the application thereof to any person or circumstances, is held invalid, the remainder of the title, and the application of such provision to other persons or circumstances, shall not be affected thereby.

[Sec. 7852(b)]

(b) REFERENCE IN OTHER LAWS TO INTERNAL REVENUE CODE OF 1939.—Any reference in any other law of the United States or in any Executive order to any provision of the Internal Revenue Code of 1939 shall, where not otherwise distinctly expressed or manifestly incompatible with the intent thereof, be deemed also to refer to the corresponding provision of this title.

[Sec. 7852(c)]

(c) ITEMS NOT TO BE TWICE INCLUDED IN INCOME OR DEDUCTED THEREFROM.—Except as otherwise distinctly expressed or manifestly intended, the same item (whether of income, deduction, credit, or otherwise) shall not be taken into account both in computing a tax under subtitle A of this title and a tax under chapter 1 or 2 of the Internal Revenue Code of 1939.

[Sec. 7852(d)]

(d) TREATY OBLIGATIONS.—

(1) IN GENERAL.—For purposes of determining the relationship between a provision of a treaty and any law of the United States affecting revenue, neither the treaty nor the law shall have preferential status by reason of its being a treaty or law.

(2) SAVINGS CLAUSE FOR 1954 TREATIES.—No provision of this title (as in effect without regard to any amendment thereto enacted after August 16, 1954) shall apply in any case where its application would be contrary to any treaty obligation of the United States in effect on August 16, 1954.

Amendments

• 1988, Technical and Miscellaneous Revenue Act of 1988 (P.L. 100-647)

P.L. 100-647, §1012(aa)(1)(A):

Amended Code Sec. 7852(d). **Effective** as if included in the provision of P.L. 99-514 to which it relates. Prior to amendment Code Sec. 7852(d) read as follows:

(d) TREATY OBLIGATIONS.—No provision of this title shall apply in any case where its application would be contrary to any treaty obligation of the United States in effect on the date of enactment of this title.

[Sec. 7852(e)]

(e) PRIVACY ACT OF 1974.—The provisions of subsections (d)(2), (3), and (4), and (g) of section 552a of title 5, United States Code, shall not be applied, directly or indirectly, to the determination of the existence or possible existence of liability (or the amount thereof) of any person for any tax, penalty, interest, fine, forfeiture, or other imposition or offense to which the provisions of this title apply.

Amendments

• 1976, Tax Reform Act of 1976 (P.L. 94-455)

P.L. 94-455, §1202(g):

Added Code Sec. 7852(e). **Effective** 1-1-77.

Subchapter C—Provisions Affecting More than One Subtitle

* * *

[Sec. 7871]

SEC. 7871. INDIAN TRIBAL GOVERNMENTS TREATED AS STATES FOR CERTAIN PURPOSES.

[Sec. 7871(a)]

(a) GENERAL RULE.—An Indian tribal government shall be treated as a State—

(1) for purposes of determining whether and in what amount any contribution or transfer to or for the use of such government (or a political subdivision thereof) is deductible under—

(A) section 170 (relating to income tax deduction for charitable, etc., contributions and gifts),

(B) sections 2055 and 2106(a)(2) (relating to estate tax deduction for transfers of public, charitable, and religious uses), or

(C) section 2522 (relating to gift tax deduction for charitable and similar gifts);

(2) subject to subsection (b), for purposes of any exemption from, credit or refund of, or payment with respect to, an excise tax imposed by—

(A) chapter 31 (relating to tax on special fuels),

(B) chapter 32 (relating to manufacturers excise taxes),

(C) subchapter B of chapter 33 (relating to communications excise tax), or

(D) subchapter D of chapter 36 (relating to tax on use of certain highway vehicles);

(3) for purposes of section 164 (relating to deduction for taxes);

(4) subject to subsection (c), for purposes of section 103 (relating to State and local bonds);

(5) for purposes of section 511(a)(2)(B) (relating to the taxation of colleges and universities which are agencies or instrumentalities of governments or their political subdivisions);

(6) for purposes of—

(A) section 105(e) (relating to accident and health plans),

(B) section 403(b)(1)(A)(ii) (relating to the taxation of contributions of certain employers for employee annuities), and

(C) section 454(b)(2) (relating to discount obligations); and

(7) for purposes of—

(A) chapter 41 (relating to tax on excess expenditures to influence legislation), and

(B) subchapter A of chapter 42 (relating to private foundations).

Amendments

• 1993, Omnibus Budget Reconciliation Act of 1993 (P.L. 103-66)

P.L. 103-66, §13222(d):

Amended Code Sec. 7871(a)(6) by striking subparagraph (B) and by redesignating subparagraphs (C) and (D) as subparagraphs (B) and (C), respectively. **Effective** for amounts paid or incurred after 12-31-93. Prior to amendment, Code Sec. 7871(a)(6)(B) read as follows:

(B) section 162(e) (relating to appearances, etc., with respect to legislation).

• 1986, Tax Reform Act of 1986 (P.L. 99-514)

P.L. 99-514, §112(b)(4):

Amended Code Sec. 7871(a)(6) by striking out subparagraph (A) and by redesignating subparagraphs (B), (C), (D), (E), and (F) as subparagraphs (A), (B), (C), (D), and (E), respectively. **Effective** for tax years beginning after 12-31-86. Prior to amendment, Code Sec. 7871(a)(6)(A) read as follows:

(A) Section 24(c)(4) (defining State for purposes of credit for contribution to candidates for public offices),

P.L. 99-514, §123(b)(3):

Amended Code Sec. 7871(a)(6), as amended by Act Sec. 112(b)(4), by striking out subparagraph (B) and by redesignating subparagraphs (C), (D), and (E) as subparagraphs (B), (C), and (D), respectively. **Effective** for tax years beginning after 12-31-86. Prior to amendment, Code Sec. 7871(a)(6)(B) (as redesignated), read as follows:

(B) section 117(b)(2)(A) (relating to scholarships and fellowship grants), and

P.L. 99-514, §1301(j)(6):

Amended Code Sec. 7871(a)(4) by striking out "(relating to interest on certain governmental obligations)" and inserting in lieu thereof "(relating to State and local bonds)". **Effective** for bonds issued after 8-15-86. However, for transitional rules, see Act Secs. 1311-1318 under the amendment notes to Code Sec. 103.

P.L. 99-514, §1899A(65):

Amended Code Sec. 7871(a)(6)(F) (prior to amendment by Act Secs. 112(b)(4) and 123(b)(3)) by striking out the period at the end thereof and inserting in lieu thereof "; and". **Effective** 10-22-86.

• 1984, Deficit Reduction Act of 1984 (P.L. 98-369)

P.L. 98-369, §474(r)(41):

Amended Code Sec. 7871(a)(6)(A) by striking out "section 41(c)(4)" and inserting in lieu thereof "section 24(c)(4)". **Effective** for tax years beginning after 12-31-83, and for carrybacks from such years.

P.L. 98-369, §1065(b):

Amended Code Sec. 7871(a)(6) by striking out subparagraphs (B) and (C) and inserting in lieu thereof subparagraphs (B)-(F). **Effective** for tax years beginning after 12-31-84. Prior to amendment, subparagraphs (B) and (C) read as follows:

(B) section 117(b)(2)(A) (relating to scholarships and fellowship grants), and

(C) section 403(b)(1)(A)(ii) (relating to the taxation of contributions certain employers for employee annuities); and

• 1983, Social Security Amendments of 1983 (P.L. 98-21)

P.L. 98-21, §122(c)(6):

Amended Code Sec. 7871(a)(6). **Effective** for tax years beginning after 12-31-83. Prior to amendment, Code Sec. 7871(a)(6) read as follows:

(6) for purposes of—

(A) section 37(e)(9)(A) (relating to certain public retirement systems),

(B) section 41(c)(4) (defining State for purposes of credit for contribution to candidates for public offices),

(C) section 117(b)(2)(A) (relating to scholarships and fellowship grants), and

(D) section 403(b)(1)(A)(ii) (relating to the taxation of contributions of certain employers for employee annuities), and

[Sec. 7871(b)]

(b) ADDITIONAL REQUIREMENTS FOR EXCISE TAX EXEMPTIONS.—Paragraph (2) of subsection (a) shall apply with respect to any transaction only if, in addition to any other requirement of this title applicable to similar transactions involving a State or political subdivision thereof, the transaction involves the exercise of an essential governmental function of the Indian tribal government.

[Sec. 7871(c)]

(c) ADDITIONAL REQUIREMENTS FOR TAX-EXEMPT BONDS.—

(1) IN GENERAL.—Subsection (a) of section 103 shall apply to any obligation (not described in paragraph (3)) issued by an Indian tribal government (or subdivision thereof) only if such obligation is part of an issue substantially all of the proceeds of which are to be used in the exercise of any essential governmental function.

(2) NO EXEMPTION FOR PRIVATE ACTIVITY BONDS.—Except as provided in paragraph (3), subsection (a) of section 103 shall not apply to any private activity bond (as defined in section 141(a)) issued by an Indian tribal government (or subdivision thereof).

(3) EXCEPTION FOR CERTAIN PRIVATE ACTIVITY BONDS.—

(A) IN GENERAL.—In the case of an obligation to which this paragraph applies—

(i) paragraph (2) shall not apply,

(ii) such obligation shall be treated for purposes of this title as a qualified small issue bond, and

(iii) section 146 shall not apply.

(B) OBLIGATIONS TO WHICH PARAGRAPH APPLIES.—This paragraph shall apply to any obligation issued as part of an issue if—

(i) 95 percent or more of the net proceeds of the issue are to be used for the acquisition, construction, reconstruction, or improvement of property which is of a character subject to the allowance for depreciation and which is part of a manufacturing facility (as defined in section 144(a)(12)(C)),

(ii) such issue is issued by an Indian tribal government or a subdivision thereof,

(iii) 95 percent or more of the net proceeds of the issue are to be used to finance property which—

(I) is to be located on land which, throughout the 5-year period ending on the date of issuance of such issue, is part of the qualified Indian lands of the issuer, and

(II) is to be owned and operated by such issuer,

(iv) such obligation would not be a private activity bond without regard to subparagraph (C),

(v) it is reasonably expected (at the time of issuance of the issue) that the employment requirement of subparagraph (D)(i) will be met with respect to the facility to be financed by the net proceeds of the issue, and

(vi) no principal user of such facility will be a person (or group of persons) described in section 144(a)(6)(B).

For purposes of clause (iii), section 150(a)(5) shall apply.

(C) PRIVATE ACTIVITY BOND RULES TO APPLY.—An obligation to which this paragraph applies (other than an obligation described in paragraph (1)) shall be treated for purposes of this title as a private activity bond.

(D) EMPLOYMENT REQUIREMENTS.—

(i) IN GENERAL.—The employment requirements of this subparagraph are met with respect to a facility financed by the net proceeds of an issue if, as of the close of each calendar year in the testing period, the aggregate face amount of all outstanding tax-exempt private activity bonds issued to provide financing for the establishment which includes such facility is not more than 20 times greater than the aggregate wages (as defined by section 3121(a)) paid during the preceding calendar year to individuals (who are enrolled members of the Indian tribe of the issuer or the spouse of any such member) for services rendered at such establishment.

(ii) FAILURE TO MEET REQUIREMENTS.—

(I) IN GENERAL.—If, as of the close of any calendar year in the testing period, the requirements of this subparagraph are not met with respect to an establishment, section 103 shall cease to apply to interest received or accrued (on all private activity bonds issued to provide financing for the establishment) after the close of such calendar year.

(II) EXCEPTION.—Subclause (I) shall not apply if the requirements of this subparagraph would be met if the aggregate face amount of all tax-exempt private activity bonds issued to provide financing for the establishment and outstanding at the close of the 90th day after the close of the calendar year were substituted in clause (i) for such bonds outstanding at the close of such calendar year.

(iii) TESTING PERIOD.—For purposes of this subparagraph, the term "testing period" means, with respect to an issue, each calendar year which begins more than 2 years after the date of issuance of the issue (or, in the case of a refunding obligation, the date of issuance of the original issue).

(E) DEFINITIONS.—For purposes of this paragraph—

(i) QUALIFIED INDIAN LANDS.—The term ["]qualified Indian lands["] means land which is held in trust by the United States for the benefit of an Indian tribe.

(ii) INDIAN TRIBE.—The term "Indian tribe" means any Indian tribe, band, nation, or other organized group or community which is recognized as eligible for the special programs and services provided by the United States to Indians because of their status as Indians.

(iii) NET PROCEEDS.—The term "net proceeds" has the meaning given such term by section 150(a)(3).

Amendments

• 2018, Tax Technical Corrections Act of 2018 (P.L. 115-141)

P.L. 115-141, §401(a)(337), Div. U:

Amended Code Sec. 7871(c)(3)(D)(ii)(II) by striking "calender" and inserting "calendar". **Effective** 3-23-2018.

• 1987, Revenue Act of 1987 (P.L. 100-203)

P.L. 100-203, §10632(b)(1):

Amended Code Sec. 7871(c) by adding at the end thereof new paragraph (3). **Effective** for obligations issued after 10-13-87.

P.L. 100-203, §10632(b)(2):

Amended Code Sec. 7871(c)(2) by striking out "Subsection (a)" and inserting in lieu thereof "Except as provided in paragraph (3), subsection (a)". **Effective** for obligations issued after 10-13-87.

• 1986, Tax Reform Act of 1986 (P.L. 99-514)

P.L. 99-514, §1301(j)(7):

Amended Code Sec. 7871(c)(2). **Effective** for bonds issued after 8-15-86. However, for transitional rules, see Act Secs. 1311-1318 under the amendment notes to Code Sec. 103. Prior to amendment, Code Sec. 7871(c)(2) read as follows:

(2) NO EXEMPTION FOR CERTAIN PRIVATE-ACTIVITY BONDS.—Subsection (a) of section 103 shall not apply to any of the following issued by an Indian tribal government (or subdivision thereof):

(A) An industrial development bond (as defined in section 103(b)(2)).

(B) An obligation described in section 103(l)(1)(A) (relating to scholarship bonds).

(C) A mortgage subsidy bond (as defined in paragraph (1) of section 103A(b) without regard to paragraph (2) thereof).

[Sec. 7871(d)]

(d) TREATMENT OF SUBDIVISIONS OF INDIAN TRIBAL GOVERNMENTS AS POLITICAL SUBDIVISIONS.—For the purposes specified in subsection (a), a subdivision of an Indian tribal government shall be treated as a political subdivision of a State if (and only if) the Secretary determines (after consultation with the Secretary of the Interior) that such subdivision has been delegated the right to exercise one or more of the substantial governmental functions of the Indian tribal government.

Amendments

• 1983 (P.L. 97-473)

P.L. 97-473, §202(a) (as amended by P.L. 98-369, §1065(a)):

Added Code Sec. 7871. **Effective** dates provided in §204, below.

P.L. 97-473, §204, provides:

The amendments made by this title—

(1) insofar as they relate to chapter 1 of the Internal Revenue Code of 1954 (other than section 103 thereof), shall apply to taxable years beginning after December 31, 1982,

(2) insofar as they relate to section 103 of such Code, shall apply to obligations issued after December 31, 1982,

(3) insofar as they relate to chapter 11 of such Code, shall apply to estates of decedents dying after December 31, 1982,

(4) insofar as they relate to chapter 12 of such Code, shall apply to gifts made after December 31, 1982, and

(5) insofar as they relate to taxes imposed by subtitle D of such Code, shall take effect on January 1, 1983.

[Sec. 7871(e)]

(e) ESSENTIAL GOVERNMENTAL FUNCTION.—For purposes of this section, the term "essential governmental function' shall not include any function which is not customarily performed by State and local governments with general taxing powers.

Amendments

• 1987, Revenue Act of 1987 (P.L. 100-203)

P.L. 100-203, §10632(a):

Amended Code Sec. 7871 by adding at the end thereof new subsection (e). **Effective** for obligations issued after 10-13-87.

[Sec. 7871(f)]

(f) TRIBAL ECONOMIC DEVELOPMENT BONDS.—

(1) ALLOCATION OF LIMITATION.—

(A) IN GENERAL.—The Secretary shall allocate the national tribal economic development bond limitation among the Indian tribal governments in such manner as the Secretary, in consultation with the Secretary of the Interior, determines appropriate.

(B) NATIONAL LIMITATION.—There is a national tribal economic development bond limitation of $2,000,000,000.

(2) BONDS TREATED AS EXEMPT FROM TAX.—In the case of a tribal economic development bond—

(A) notwithstanding subsection (c), such bond shall be treated for purposes of this title in the same manner as if such bond were issued by a State,

(B) the Indian tribal government issuing such bond and any instrumentality of such Indian tribal government shall be treated as a State for purposes of section 141, and

(C) section 146 shall not apply.

(3) TRIBAL ECONOMIC DEVELOPMENT BOND.—

(A) IN GENERAL.—For purposes of this section, the term "tribal economic development bond" means any bond issued by an Indian tribal government—

(i) the interest on which would be exempt from tax under section 103 if issued by a State or local government, and

(ii) which is designated by the Indian tribal government as a tribal economic development bond for purposes of this subsection.

(B) EXCEPTIONS.—Such term shall not include any bond issued as part of an issue if any portion of the proceeds of such issue are used to finance—

(i) any portion of a building in which class II or class III gaming (as defined in section 4 of the Indian Gaming Regulatory Act) is conducted or housed or any other property actually used in the conduct of such gaming, or

(ii) any facility located outside the Indian reservation (as defined in section 168(j)(6)).

(C) LIMITATION ON AMOUNT OF BONDS DESIGNATED.—The maximum aggregate face amount of bonds which may be designated by any Indian tribal government under subparagraph (A) shall not exceed the amount of national tribal economic development bond limitation allocated to such government under paragraph (1).

Amendments

• 2009, American Recovery and Reinvestment Tax Act of 2009 (P.L. 111-5)

P.L. 111-5, §1402(a):

Amended Code Sec. 7871 by adding at the end a new subsection (f). **Effective** for obligations issued after 2-17-2009.

P.L. 111-5, §1402(b), provides:

(b) STUDY.—The Secretary of the Treasury, or the Secretary's delegate, shall conduct a study of the effects of the amendment made by subsection (a). Not later than 1 year after the date of the enactment of this Act, the Secretary of the Treasury, or the Secretary's delegate, shall report to Congress on the results of the study conducted under this paragraph, including the Secretary's recommendations regarding such amendment.

[Sec. 7872]

SEC. 7872. TREATMENT OF LOANS WITH BELOW-MARKET INTEREST RATES.

[Sec. 7872(a)]

(a) TREATMENT OF GIFT LOANS AND DEMAND LOANS.—

(1) IN GENERAL.—For purposes of this title, in the case of any below-market loan to which this section applies and which is a gift loan or a demand loan, the forgone interest shall be treated as—

(A) transferred from the lender to the borrower, and

(B) retransferred by the borrower to the lender as interest.

(2) TIME WHEN TRANSFERS MADE.—Except as otherwise provided in regulations prescribed by the Secretary, any forgone interest attributable to periods during any calendar year shall be treated as transferred (and retransferred) under paragraph (1) on the last day of such calendar year.

Amendments

• 1996, Small Business Job Protection Act of 1996 (P.L. 104-188)

P.L. 104-188, §1704(t)(58)(A):

Amended Code Sec. 7872(a) by striking "foregone" each place it appears and inserting "forgone". **Effective** 8-20-96.

[Sec. 7872(b)]

(b) TREATMENT OF OTHER BELOW-MARKET LOANS.—

(1) IN GENERAL.—For purposes of this title, in the case of any below-market loan to which this section applies and to which subsection (a)(1) does not apply, the lender shall be treated as having transferred on the date the loan was made (or, if later, on the first day on which this section applies to such loan), and the borrower shall be treated as having received on such date, cash in an amount equal to the excess of—

(A) the amount loaned, over

(B) the present value of all payments which are required to be made under the terms of the loan.

(2) OBLIGATION TREATED AS HAVING ORIGINAL ISSUE DISCOUNT.—For purposes of this title—

(A) IN GENERAL.—Any below-market loan to which paragraph (1) applies shall be treated as having original issue discount in an amount equal to the excess described in paragraph (1).

(B) AMOUNT IN ADDITION TO OTHER ORIGINAL ISSUE DISCOUNT.—Any original issue discount which a loan is treated as having by reason of subparagraph (A) shall be in addition to any other original issue discount on such loan (determined without regard to subparagraph (A)).

[Sec. 7872(c)]

(c) BELOW-MARKET LOANS TO WHICH SECTION APPLIES.—

(1) IN GENERAL.—Except as otherwise provided in this subsection and subsection (g), this section shall apply to—

(A) GIFTS.—Any below-market loan which is a gift loan.

(B) COMPENSATION-RELATED LOANS.—Any below-market loan directly or indirectly between—

(i) an employer and an employee, or

(ii) an independent contractor and a person for whom such independent contractor provides services.

(C) CORPORATION-SHAREHOLDER LOANS.—Any below-market loan directly or indirectly between a corporation and any shareholder of such corporation.

(D) TAX AVOIDANCE LOANS.—Any below-market loan 1 of the principal purposes of the interest arrangements of which is the avoidance of any Federal tax.

(E) OTHER BELOW-MARKET LOANS.—To the extent provided in regulations, any below-market loan which is not described in subparagraph (A), (B), (C), or (F) if the interest arrangements of such loan have a significant effect on any Federal tax liability of the lender or the borrower.

(F) LOANS TO QUALIFIED CONTINUING CARE FACILITIES.—Any loan to any qualified continuing care facility pursuant to a continuing care contract.

(2) $10,000 DE MINIMIS EXCEPTION FOR GIFT LOANS BETWEEN INDIVIDUALS.—

(A) IN GENERAL.—In the case of any gift loan directly between individuals, this section shall not apply to any day on which the aggregate outstanding amount of loans between such individuals does not exceed $10,000.

(B) DE MINIMIS EXCEPTION NOT TO APPLY TO LOANS ATTRIBUTABLE TO ACQUISITION OF INCOME-PRODUCING ASSETS.—Subparagraph (A) shall not apply to any gift loan directly attributable to the purchase or carrying of income-producing assets.

(C) CROSS REFERENCE.—

For limitation on amount treated as interest where loans do not exceed $100,000, see subsection (d)(1).

(3) $10,000 DE MINIMIS EXCEPTION FOR COMPENSATION-RELATED AND CORPORATE-SHAREHOLDER LOANS.—

(A) IN GENERAL.—In the case of any loan described in subparagraph (B) or (C) of paragraph (1), this section shall not apply to any day on which the aggregate outstanding amount of loans between the borrower and lender does not exceed $10,000.

(B) EXCEPTION NOT TO APPLY WHERE 1 OF PRINCIPAL PURPOSES IS TAX AVOIDANCE.—Subparagraph (A) shall not apply to any loan the interest arrangements of which have as 1 of their principal purposes the avoidance of any Federal tax.

Amendments

• 1985 (P.L. 99-121)

P.L. 99-121, §201(b):

Amended Code Sec. 7872(c)(1) by adding at the end thereof new subparagraph (F). **Effective** with respect to loans made after 10-11-85.

P.L. 99-121, §201(c)(1):

Amended Code Sec. 7872(c)(1) by inserting "and subsection (g)" after "subsection". **Effective** with respect to loans made after 10-11-85.

P.L. 99-121, §201(c)(2):

Amended Code Sec. 7872(c)(1)(E) by striking out "or (C)" and inserting in lieu thereof "(C), or (F)". **Effective** with respect to loans made after 10-11-85.

P.L. 99-121, §204(a)(2), provides:

(2) SECTION 7872 NOT TO APPLY TO CERTAIN LOANS.—Section 7872 of the Internal Revenue Code of 1954 shall not apply to loans made on or before the date of the enactment of this Act to any qualified continuing care facility pursuant to a continuing care contract. For purposes of this paragraph, the terms "qualified continuing care facility" and "continuing care contract" have the meanings given such terms by section 7872(g) of such Code (as added by section 201).

[Sec. 7872(d)]

(d) SPECIAL RULES FOR GIFT LOANS.—

(1) LIMITATION ON INTEREST ACCRUAL FOR PURPOSES OF INCOME TAXES WHERE LOANS DO NOT EXCEED $100,000.—

(A) IN GENERAL.—For purposes of subtitle A, in the case of a gift loan directly between individuals, the amount treated as retransferred by the borrower to the lender as of the close of any year shall not exceed the borrower's net investment income for such year.

(B) LIMITATION NOT TO APPLY WHERE 1 OF PRINCIPAL PURPOSES IS TAX AVOIDANCE.—Subparagraph (A) shall not apply to any loan the interest arrangements of which have as 1 of their principal purposes the avoidance of any Federal tax.

(C) SPECIAL RULE WHERE MORE THAN 1 GIFT LOAN OUTSTANDING.—For purposes of subparagraph (A), in any case in which a borrower has outstanding more than 1 gift loan, the net investment income of such borrower shall be allocated among such loans in proportion to the respective amounts which would be treated as retransferred by the borrower without regard to this paragraph.

(D) LIMITATION NOT TO APPLY WHERE AGGREGATE AMOUNT OF LOANS EXCEED $100,000.—This paragraph shall not apply to any loan made by a lender to a borrower for any day on which the aggregate outstanding amount of loans between the borrower and lender exceeds $100,000.

(E) NET INVESTMENT INCOME.—For purposes of this paragraph—

(i) IN GENERAL.—The term "net investment income" has the meaning given such term by section 163(d)(4).

(ii) DE MINIMIS RULE.—If the net investment income of any borrower for any year does not exceed $1,000, the net investment income of such borrower for such year shall be treated as zero.

(iii) ADDITIONAL AMOUNTS TREATED AS INTEREST.—In determining the net investment income of a person for any year, any amount which would be included in the gross income of such person for such year by reason of section 1272 if such section applied to all deferred payment obligations shall be treated as interest received by such person for such year.

(iv) DEFERRED PAYMENT OBLIGATIONS.—The term "deferred payment obligation" includes any market discount bond, short-term obligation, United States savings bond, annuity, or similar obligation.

(2) SPECIAL RULE FOR GIFT TAX.—In the case of any gift loan which is a term loan, subsection (b)(1) (and not subsection (a)) shall apply for purposes of chapter 12.

Amendments

• 1988, Technical and Miscellaneous Revenue Act of 1988 (P.L. 100-647)

P.L. 100-647, §1005(c)(15):

Amended Code Sec. 7872(d)(1)(E)(i) by striking out "section 163(d)(3)" and inserting in lieu thereof "section 163(d)(4)". **Effective** as if included in the provision of P.L. 99-514 to which it relates. See, also, Act Sec. 1005(c)(13), below.

P.L. 100-647, §1005(c)(13), provides:

(13) For purposes of applying the amendments made by this subsection and the amendments made by section 10102 of the Revenue Act of 1987, the provisions of this subsection shall be treated as having been enacted immediately before the enactment of the Revenue Act of 1987.

[Sec. 7872(e)]

(e) DEFINITIONS OF BELOW-MARKET LOAN AND FORGONE INTEREST.—For purposes of this section—

(1) BELOW-MARKET LOAN.—The term "below-market loan" means any loan if—

(A) in the case of a demand loan, interest is payable on the loan at a rate less than the applicable Federal rate, or

(B) in the case of a term loan, the amount loaned exceeds the present value of all payments due under the loan.

(2) FORGONE INTEREST.—The term "forgone interest" means, with respect to any period during which the loan is outstanding, the excess of—

(A) the amount of interest which would have been payable on the loan for the period if interest accrued on the loan at the applicable Federal rate and were payable annually on the day referred to in subsection (a)(2), over

(B) any interest payable on the loan properly allocable to such period.

Amendments

• 1996, Small Business Job Protection Act of 1996 (P.L. 104-188)

P.L. 104-188, §1704(t)(58)(A)-(B):

Amended Code Sec. 7872(e) by striking "foregone" each place it appears in paragraph (2) and inserting "forgone", and by striking "FOREGONE" in the subsection heading and the heading for paragraph (2) and inserting "FORGONE". **Effective** 8-20-96.

[Sec. 7872(f)]

(f) OTHER DEFINITIONS AND SPECIAL RULES.—For purposes of this section—

(1) PRESENT VALUE.—The present value of any payment shall be determined in the manner provided by regulations prescribed by the Secretary—

(A) as of the date of the loan, and

(B) by using a discount rate equal to the applicable Federal rate.

(2) APPLICABLE FEDERAL RATE.—

(A) TERM LOANS.—In the case of any term loan, the applicable Federal rate shall be the applicable Federal rate in effect under section 1274(d) (as of the day on which the loan was made), compounded semiannually.

(B) DEMAND LOANS.—In the case of a demand loan, the applicable Federal rate shall be the Federal short-term rate in effect under section 1274(d) for the period for which the amount of forgone interest is being determined, compounded semiannually.

(3) GIFT LOAN.—The term "gift loan" means any below-market loan where the forgoing of interest is in the nature of a gift.

(4) AMOUNT LOANED.—The term "amount loaned" means the amount received by the borrower.

(5) DEMAND LOAN.—The term "demand loan" means any loan which is payable in full at any time on the demand of the lender. Such term also includes (for purposes other than determining the applicable Federal rate under paragraph (2)) any loan if the benefits of the interest arrangements of such loan are not transferable and are conditioned on the future performance of substantial services by an individual. To the extent provided in regulations, such term also includes any loan with an indefinite maturity.

(6) TERM LOAN.—The term "term loan" means any loan which is not a demand loan.

(7) HUSBAND AND WIFE TREATED AS 1 PERSON.—A husband and wife shall be treated as 1 person.

(8) LOANS TO WHICH SECTION 483, 643(i), OR 1274 APPLIES.—This section shall not apply to any loan to which section 483, 643(i), or 1274 applies.

(9) NO WITHHOLDING.—No amount shall be withheld under chapter 24 with respect to—

(A) any amount treated as transferred or retransferred under subsection (a), and

(B) any amount treated as received under subsection (b).

(10) SPECIAL RULE FOR TERM LOANS.—If this section applies to any term loan on any day, this section shall continue to apply to such loan notwithstanding paragraphs (2) and (3) of subsection (c). In the case of a gift loan, the preceding sentence shall only apply for purposes of chapter 12.

(11) TIME FOR DETERMINING RATE APPLICABLE TO EMPLOYEE RELOCATION LOANS.—

(A) IN GENERAL.—In the case of any term loan made by an employer to an employee the proceeds of which are used by the employee to purchase a principal residence (within the meaning of section 121), the determination of the applicable Federal rate shall be made as of the date the written contract to purchase such residence was entered into.

(B) PARAGRAPH ONLY TO APPLY TO CASES TO WHICH SECTION 217 APPLIES.—Subparagraph (A) shall only apply to the purchase of a principal residence in connection with the commencement of work by an employee or a change in the principal place of work of an employee to which section 217 applies.

Amendments

• 2000, Community Renewal Tax Relief Act of 2000 (P.L. 106-554)

P.L. 106-554, §319(30):

Amended Code Sec. 7872(f)(3) by striking "foregoing" and inserting "forgoing". **Effective** 12-21-2000.

• 1998, IRS Restructuring and Reform Act of 1998 (P.L. 105-206)

P.L. 105-206, §6023(30):

Amended Code Sec. 7872(f)(2)(B) by striking "foregone" and inserting "forgone". **Effective** 7-22-98.

• 1997, Taxpayer Relief Act of 1997 (P.L. 105-34)

P.L. 105-34, §312(d)(1):

Amended Code Sec. 7872(f)(11)(A) by striking "section 1034" and inserting "section 121". **Effective** for sales and exchanges after 5-6-97.

• 1996, Small Business Job Protection Act of 1996 (P.L. 104-188)

P.L. 104-188, §1602(b)(7):

Amended Code Sec. 7872(f) by striking paragraph (12). For the **effective** date, see Act Sec. 1602(c), below. Prior to being stricken, Code Sec. 7872(f)(12) read as follows:

(12) SPECIAL RULE FOR CERTAIN EMPLOYER SECURITY LOANS.—This section shall not apply to any loan between a corporation (or any member of the controlled group of corporations which includes such corporation) and an employee stock ownership plan described in section 4975(e)(7) to the extent that the interest rate on such loan is equal to the interest rate paid on a related securities acquisition loan (as described in section 133(b)) to such corporation.

P.L. 104-188, §1602(c), provides:

(c) EFFECTIVE DATE.—

(1) IN GENERAL.—The amendments made by this section shall apply to loans made after the date of the enactment of this Act.

(2) REFINANCINGS.—The amendments made by this section shall not apply to loans made after the date of the enactment of this Act to refinance securities acquisition loans (determined without regard to section 133(b)(1)(B) of the Internal Revenue Code of 1986, as in effect on the day before the date of the enactment of this Act) made on or before such date or to refinance loans described in this paragraph if—

(A) the refinancing loans meet the requirements of section 133 of such Code (as so in effect),

(B) immediately after the refinancing the principal amount of the loan resulting from the refinancing does not exceed the principal amount of the refinanced loan (immediately before the refinancing), and

(C) the term of such refinancing loan does not extend beyond the last day of the term of the original securities acquisition loan.

For purposes of this paragraph, the term "securities acquisition loan" includes a loan from a corporation to an employee stock ownership plan described in section 133(b)(3) of such Code (as so in effect).

(3) EXCEPTION.—Any loan made pursuant to a binding written contract in effect before June 10, 1996, and at all times thereafter before such loan is made, shall be treated for purposes of paragraphs (1) and (2) as a loan made on or before the date of the enactment of this Act.

P.L. 104-188, §1906(c)(2):

Amended Code Sec. 7872(f)(8) by inserting ", 643(i)," before "or 1274" each place it appears. **Effective** for loans of cash or marketable securities made after 9-19-95.

• 1988, Technical and Miscellaneous Revenue Act of 1988 (P.L. 100-647)

P.L. 100-647, §1018(u)(48):

Amended Code Sec. 7872(f) by redesignating paragraph (11) added by §1854 of P.L. 99-514 as paragraph (12). **Effective** as if included in the provision of P.L 99-514 to which it relates.

• 1986, Tax Reform Act of 1986 (P.L. 99-514)

P.L. 99-514, §1812(b)(2):

Amended Code Sec. 7872(f)(9). **Effective** as if included in the provision of P.L. 98-369 to which it relates. Prior to amendment, Code Sec. 7872(f)(9) read as follows:

(9) NO WITHHOLDING.—No amount shall be withheld under chapter 24 with respect to any amount treated as transferred or retransferred under subsection (a).

P.L. 99-514, §1812(b)(3):

Amended Code Sec. 7872(f)(5). **Effective** as if included in the provision of P.L. 98-369 to which it relates. Prior to amendment, Code Sec. 7872(f)(5) read as follows:

(5) DEMAND LOAN.—The term "demand loan" means any loan which is payable in full at any time on the demand of the lender. Such term also includes (for purposes other than determining the applicable Federal rate under paragraph (2)) any loan which is not transferable and the benefits of the interest arrangements of which is conditioned on the future performance of substantial services by an individual.

P.L. 99-514, §1812(b)(4):

Amended Code Sec. 7872(f)(2)(B) by inserting ", compounded semiannually" immediately before the period at the end thereof. **Effective** as if included in the provision of P.L. 98-369 to which it relates.

P.L. 99-514, §1854(c)(2)(B):

Amended Code Sec. 7872(f) by adding at the end thereof new paragraph (11). **Effective** as if included in the provision of P.L. 98-369 to which it relates.

• 1985 (P.L. 99-121)

P.L. 99-121, §202:

Amended Code Sec. 7872(f) by adding at the end thereof new paragraph (11). **Effective** for contracts entered into after 6-30-85, in tax years ending after such date. For special rules, see Act Secs. 203 and 204(a)(2), following Code Sec. 7872(h).

[Sec. 7872(g)]

(g) EXCEPTION FOR CERTAIN LOANS TO QUALIFIED CONTINUING CARE FACILITIES.—

(1) IN GENERAL.—This section shall not apply for any calendar year to any below-market loan made by a lender to a qualified continuing care facility pursuant to a continuing care contract if the lender (or the lender's spouse) attains age 65 before the close of such year.

(2) $90,000 LIMIT.—Paragraph (1) shall apply only to the extent that the aggregate outstanding amount of any loan to which such paragraph applies (determined without regard to this paragraph), when added to the aggregate outstanding amount of all other previous loans between the lender (or the lender's spouse) and any qualified continuing care facility to which paragraph (1) applies, does not exceed $90,000.

(3) CONTINUING CARE CONTRACT.—For purposes of this section, the term "continuing care contract" means a written contract between an individual and a qualified continuing care facility under which—

(A) the individual or individual's spouse may use a qualified continuing care facility for their life or lives,

(B) the individual or individual's spouse—

(i) will first—

(I) reside in a separate, independent living unit with additional facilities outside such unit for the providing of meals and other personal care, and

(II) not require long-term nursing care, and

(ii) then will be provided long-term and skilled nursing care as the health of such individual or individual's spouse requires, and

(C) no additional substantial payment is required if such individual or individual's spouse requires increased personal care services or long-term and skilled nursing care.

(4) QUALIFIED CONTINUING CARE FACILITY.—

(A) IN GENERAL.—For purposes of this section, the term "qualified continuing care facility" means 1 or more facilities—

(i) which are designed to provide services under continuing care contracts, and

(ii) substantially all of the residents of which are covered by continuing care contracts.

(B) SUBSTANTIALLY ALL FACILITIES MUST BE OWNED OR OPERATED BY BORROWER.—A facility shall not be treated as a qualified continuing care facility unless substantially all facilities which are used to provide services which are required to be provided under a continuing care contract are owned or operated by the borrower.

(C) NURSING HOMES EXCLUDED.—The term "qualified continuing care facility" shall not include any facility which is of a type which is traditionally considered a nursing home.

(5) ADJUSTMENT OF LIMIT FOR INFLATION.—In the case of any loan made during any calendar year after 1986, the dollar amount in paragraph (2) shall be increased by an amount equal to—

(A) such amount, multiplied by

(B) the cost-of-living adjustment determined under section 1(f)(3) for the calendar year in which the taxable year begins, by substituting "calendar year 1985" for "calendar year 2016" in subparagraph (A)(ii) thereof.

Any increase under the preceding sentence shall be rounded to the nearest multiple of $100 (or, if such increase is a multiple of $50, such increase shall be increased to the nearest multiple of $100).

(6) SUSPENSION OF APPLICATION.—Paragraph (1) shall not apply for any calendar year to which subsection (h) applies.

Amendments

• 2017, Tax Cuts and Jobs Act (P.L. 115-97)

P.L. 115-97, §11002(d)(14):

Amended Code Sec. 7872(g)(5). **Effective** for tax years beginning after 12-31-2017. Prior to amendment, Code Sec. 7872(g)(5) read as follows:

(5) ADJUSTMENT OF LIMIT FOR INFLATION.—

(A) IN GENERAL.—In the case of any loan made during any calendar year after 1986 to which paragraph (1) applies, the dollar amount in paragraph (2) shall be increased by the inflation adjustment for such calendar year. Any increase under the preceding sentence shall be rounded to the nearest multiple of $100 (or, if such increase is a multiple of $50, such increase shall be increased to the nearest multiple of $100).

(B) INFLATION ADJUSTMENT.—For purposes of subparagraph (A), the inflation adjustment for any calendar year is the percentage (if any) by which—

(i) the CPI for the preceding calendar year exceeds

(ii) the CPI for calendar year 1985.

For purposes of the preceding sentence, the CPI for any calendar year is the average of the Consumer Price Index as of the close of the 12-month period ending on September 30 of such calendar year.

• 2006, Tax Increase Prevention and Reconciliation Act of 2005 (P.L. 109-222)

P.L. 109-222, §209(b)(1):

Amended Code Sec. 7872(g) by adding at the end a new paragraph (6). **Effective** for calendar years beginning after 12-31-2005, with respect to loans made before, on, or after such date.

• 1986, Tax Reform Act of 1986 (P.L. 99-514)

P.L. 99-514, §1812(b)(5), as amended by P.L. 101-179, §307(a)(1)-(2), provides:

(5) CERTAIN ISRAEL BONDS NOT SUBJECT TO RULES RELATING TO BELOW-MARKET LOANS.—Section 7872 of the Internal Revenue Code of 1954 (relating to treatment of loans with below-market interest rates) shall not apply to any obligation issued by Israel or Poland if—

(A) the obligation is payable in United States dollars, and

(B) the obligation bears interest at an annual rate of not less than 4 percent.

• 1985 (P.L. 99-121)

P.L. 99-121, §201(a):

Amended Code Sec. 7872 by redesignating subsection (g) as subsection (h) and by inserting after subsection (f) new subsection (g). **Effective** with respect to loans made after 10-11-85. For special rules, see the amendment notes following Code Sec. 7872(h).

[Sec. 7872(h)]

(h) EXCEPTION FOR LOANS TO QUALIFIED CONTINUING CARE FACILITIES.—

(1) IN GENERAL.—This section shall not apply for any calendar year to any below-market loan owed by a facility which on the last day of such year is a qualified continuing care facility, if such loan was made pursuant to a continuing care contract and if the lender (or the lender's spouse) attains age 62 before the close of such year.

(2) CONTINUING CARE CONTRACT.—For purposes of this section, the term "continuing care contract" means a written contract between an individual and a qualified continuing care facility under which—

(A) the individual or individual's spouse may use a qualified continuing care facility for their life or lives,

(B) the individual or individual's spouse will be provided with housing, as appropriate for the health of such individual or individual's spouse—

(i) in an independent living unit (which has additional available facilities outside such unit for the provision of meals and other personal care), and

(ii) in an assisted living facility or a nursing facility, as is available in the continuing care facility, and

(C) the individual or individual's spouse will be provided assisted living or nursing care as the health of such individual or individual's spouse requires, and as is available in the continuing care facility.

The Secretary shall issue guidance which limits such term to contracts which provide only facilities, care, and services described in this paragraph.

(3) QUALIFIED CONTINUING CARE FACILITY.—

(A) IN GENERAL.—For purposes of this section, the term "qualified continuing care facility" means 1 or more facilities—

(i) which are designed to provide services under continuing care contracts,

(ii) which include an independent living unit, plus an assisted living or nursing facility, or both, and

(iii) substantially all of the independent living unit residents of which are covered by continuing care contracts.

(B) NURSING HOMES EXCLUDED.—The term "qualified continuing care facility" shall not include any facility which is of a type which is traditionally considered a nursing home.

Amendments

• 2006, Tax Relief and Health Care Act of 2006 (P.L. 109-432)

P.L. 109-432, Division A, §425(a):

Amended Code Sec. 7872(h) by striking paragraph (4). **Effective** as if included in section 209 of the Tax Increase Prevention and Reconciliation Act of 2005 (P.L. 109-222) [**effective** for calendar years beginning after 12-31-2005, with respect to loans made before, on, or after such date.—CCH]. Prior to being stricken, Code Sec. 7872(h)(4) read as follows:

(4) TERMINATION.—This subsection shall not apply to any calendar year after 2010.

• 2006, Tax Increase Prevention and Reconciliation Act of 2005 (P.L. 109-222)

P.L. 109-222, §209(a):

Amended Code Sec. 7872 by redesignating subsection (h) as subsection (i) and inserting after subsection (g) a new subsection (h). **Effective** for calendar years beginning after 12-31-2005, with respect to loans made before, on, or after such date.

[Sec. 7872(i)]

(i) REGULATIONS.—

(1) IN GENERAL.—The Secretary shall prescribe such regulations as may be necessary or appropriate to carry out the purposes of this section, including—

(A) regulations providing that where, by reason of varying rates of interest, conditional interest payments, waivers of interest, disposition of the lender's or borrower's interest in the loan, or other circumstances, the provisions of this section do not carry out the purposes of this section, adjustments to the provisions of this section will be made to the extent necessary to carry out the purposes of this section,

(B) regulations for the purpose of assuring that the positions of the borrower and lender are consistent as to the application (or nonapplication) of this section, and

(C) regulations exempting from the application of this section any class of transactions the interest arrangements of which have no significant effect on any Federal tax liability of the lender or the borrower.

(2) ESTATE TAX COORDINATION.—Under regulations prescribed by the Secretary, any loan which is made with donative intent and which is a term loan shall be taken into account for purposes of chapter 11 in a manner consistent with the provisions of subsection (b).

Amendments

• 2006, Tax Increase Prevention and Reconciliation Act of 2005 (P.L. 109-222)

P.L. 109-222, §209(a):

Amended Code Sec. 7872 by redesignating subsection (h) as subsection (i). **Effective** for calendar years beginning after 12-31-2005, with respect to loans made before, on, or after such date.

• 1986, Tax Reform Act of 1986 (P.L. 99-514)

P.L. 99-514, §1812(b)(5), as amended by P.L. 101-179, §307(a)(1)-(2), provides:

(5) CERTAIN ISRAEL BONDS NOT SUBJECT TO RULES RELATING TO BELOW-MARKET LOANS.—Section 7872 of the Internal Revenue Code of 1954 (relating to treatment of loans with below-market interest rates) shall not apply to any obligation issued by Israel or Poland if—

(A) the obligation is payable in United States dollars, and

(B) the obligation bears interest at an annual rate of not less than 4 percent.

• 1985 (P.L. 99-121)

P.L. 99-121, §201(a):

Redesignated Code Sec. 7872(g) as Code Sec. 7872(h). **Effective** with respect to loans made after 10-11-85.

P.L. 99-121, §203, provides:

SEC. 203. SECTION 7872 OF THE INTERNAL REVENUE CODE SHALL NOT APPLY TO NON-LOAN PAYMENTS TO CERTAIN RESIDENTIAL HOUSING FACILITIES FOR THE ELDERLY.

(a) GENERAL RULE.—For purposes of section 7872 of the Internal Revenue Code of 1954, payments made to a specified independent living facility for the elderly by a payor who is an individual at least 65 years old shall not be treated as loans provided—

(1) the independent living facility is designed and operated to meet some substantial combination of the health, physical, emotional, recreational, social, religious and similar needs of persons over the age of 65;

(2) in exchange for the payment, the payor obtains the right to occupy (or equivalent contractual right) independent living quarters located in the independent living facility;

(3) the amount of the payment is equal to the fair market value of the right to occupy the independent living quarters;

(4) upon leaving the independent living facility, the payor is entitled to receive a payment equal to at least 50 percent of the fair market value at that time of the right to occupy the independent living quarters, the timing of which payment may be contingent on the time when the independent living facility is able to locate a new occupant for such quarters; and

(5) the excess, if any, of the fair market value of the independent living quarters at the time the payor leaves such quarters (less a reasonable amount to cover costs) over the amount paid to the payor is used by an organization

described in section 501(c)(3) of such Code to provide housing and related services for needy elderly persons.

(b) SPECIFIED INDEPENDENT LIVING FACILITY FOR THE ELDERLY.—

For purposes of this section—

(1) IN GENERAL.—The term "specified independent living facility for the elderly" means—

(A) the Our Lady of Life Apartments owned by a Missouri not-for-profit corporation with the same name,

(B) the Laclede Oaks Manor owned by the Lutheran Health Care Association of St. Louis, Missouri, and

(C) the Luther Center Northeast owned by the Lutheran Altenheim Society of Missouri.

(2) REQUIREMENTS.—A facility shall not be considered to be a specified independent living facility for the elderly—

(A) if it is located at any site other than the site which it occupied (or was in the process of occupying through construction) on the date of the enactment of this Act, or

(B) if its ownership is transferred after such date of enactment to a person other than an organization described in section 501(c)(3) of the Internal Revenue Code of 1954.

P.L. 99-121, § 204(a)(2), provides:

(2) SECTION 7872 NOT TO APPLY TO CERTAIN LOANS.—Section 7872 of the Internal Revenue Code of 1954 shall not apply to loans made on or before the date of the enactment of this Act to any qualified continuing care facility pursuant to a continuing care contract. For purposes of this paragraph, the terms "qualified continuing care facility" and "continuing care contract" have the meanings given such terms by section 7872(g) of such Code (as added by section 201).

P.L. 99-121, § 204(c), provides:

(c) SECTION 203.—The provisions of section 203 shall apply as if included in section 172(a) of the Tax Reform Act of 1984.

• 1984, Deficit Reduction Act of 1984 (P.L. 98-369)

P.L. 98-369, § 172(a):

Added Code Sec. 7872. **Effective** for term loans made after 6-6-84, and to demand loans outstanding after 6-6-84. However, see Act Sec. 172(c)(2)-(6), below, for exceptions and special rules.

P.L. 98-369, § 172(c)(2)-(6), provides:

(2) Exception for demand loans outstanding on June 6, 1984, and repaid within 60 days after date of enactment.—The amendments made by this section shall not apply to any demand loan which—

(A) was outstanding on June 6, 1984, and

(B) was repaid before the date 60 days after the date of the enactment of this Act.

(3) Exception for certain existing loans to continuing care facilities.—Nothing in this subsection shall be construed to apply the amendments made by this section to any loan made before June 6, 1984, to a continuing care facility by a resident of such facility which is contingent on continued residence at such facility.

(4) Applicable federal rate for periods before January 1, 1985.—For periods before January 1, 1985, the applicable Federal rate under paragraph (2) of section 7872(f) of the Internal Revenue Code of 1954, as added by this section, shall be 10 percent, compounded semiannually.

(5) Treatment of renegotiations, etc.—For purposes of this subsection, any loan renegotiated, extended, or revised after June 6, 1984, shall be treated as a loan made after such date.

(6) Definition of term and demand loans.—For purposes of this subsection, the terms "demand loan" and "term loan" have the respective meanings given such terms by paragraphs (5) and (6) of section 7872(f) of the Internal Revenue Code of 1954, as added by this section, but the second sentence of such paragraph (5) shall not apply.

* * *

REGULATIONS

Table of Contents

Regulation Sec.

INCOME TAXES

Definition of Gross Income, Adjusted Gross Income, Taxable Income, Etc.

Items Specifically Excluded From Gross Income

Additional Itemized Deductions for Individuals

Distributions by Corporations

Certain Homeowners Associations

Estates, Trusts, and Beneficiaries

Income in Respect of Decedents

Regulation Sec.

Credits Against Tax

Gross Estate

Taxable Estate

Regulation Sec.

Estates of Nonresidents Not Citizens

Miscellaneous

GIFT TAX

Determination of Tax Liability

TAX ON GENERATION-SKIPPING TRANSFERS

Tax Imposed

Generation-Skipping Transfers

GST Exemption

Applicable Rate; Inclusion Ratio

Regulation Sec.

Regulation Sec.

INCOME TAXES

See p. 15 for regulations not amended to reflect law changes

COMPUTATION OF TAXABLE INCOME

Definition of Gross Income, Adjusted Gross Income, Taxable Income, Etc.

[Reg. § 1.67-4]

§ 1.67-4. Costs paid or incurred by estates or non-grantor trusts.—(a) *Deductions.*—(1) *Section 67(e) deductions.*—(i) *In general.*—An estate or trust (including the S portion of an electing small business trust) not described in § 1.67-2T(g)(1)(i) (a non-grantor trust) must compute its adjusted gross income in the same manner as an individual, except that the following deductions (section 67(e) deductions) are allowed in arriving at adjusted gross income:

(A) Costs that are paid or incurred in connection with the administration of the estate or trust that would not have been incurred if the property were not held in such estate or trust; and

(B) Deductions allowable under section 642(b) (relating to the personal exemption) and sections 651 and 661 (relating to distributions).

(ii) *Not disallowed under section 67(g).*—Section 67(e) deductions are not itemized deductions under section 63(d) and are not miscellaneous itemized deductions under section 67(b). Therefore, section 67(e) deductions are not disallowed under section 67(g).

(2) *Deductions subject to 2-percent floor.*—A cost is not a section 67(e) deduction and thus is subject to both the 2-percent floor in section 67(a) and section 67(g) to the extent that it is included in the definition of miscellaneous itemized deductions under section 67(b), is incurred by an estate or non-grantor trust (including the S portion of an electing small business trust), and commonly or customarily would be incurred by a hypothetical individual holding the same property.

(b) *"Commonly" or "Customarily" Incurred.*—(1) *In general.*—In analyzing a cost to determine whether it commonly or customarily would be incurred by a hypothetical individual owning the same property, it is the type of product or service rendered to the estate or non-grantor trust in exchange for the cost, rather than the description of the cost of that product or service, that is determinative. In addition to the types of costs described as commonly or customarily incurred by individuals in paragraphs (b)(2), (3), (4), and (5) of this section, costs that are incurred commonly or customarily by individuals also include, for example, costs incurred in defense of a claim against the estate, the decedent, or the non-grantor trust that are unrelated to the existence, validity, or administration of the estate or trust.

(2) *Ownership costs.*—Ownership costs are costs that are chargeable to or incurred by an owner of property simply by reason of being the owner of the property. Thus, for purposes of section 67(e), ownership costs are commonly or customarily incurred by a hypothetical individual owner of such property. Such ownership costs include, but are not limited to, partnership costs deemed to be passed through to and reportable by a partner if these costs are defined as miscellaneous itemized deductions pursuant to section 67(b), condominium fees, insurance premiums, maintenance and lawn services, and automobile registration and insurance costs. Other expenses incurred merely by reason of the ownership of property may be fully deductible under other provisions of the Code, such as sections 62(a)(4), 162, or 164(a), which would not be miscellaneous itemized deductions subject to section 67(e).

(3) *Tax preparation fees.*—Costs relating to all estate and generationskipping transfer tax returns, fiduciary income tax returns, and the decedent's final individual income tax returns are not subject to the 2-percent floor. The costs of preparing all other tax returns (for example, gift tax returns) are costs commonly and customarily incurred by individuals and thus are subject to the 2-percent floor.

(4) *Investment advisory fees.*—Fees for investment advice (including any related services that would be provided to any individual investor as part of an investment advisory fee) are incurred commonly or customarily by a hypothetical individual investor and therefore are subject to the 2-percent floor. However, certain incremental costs of investment advice beyond the amount that normally would be charged to an individual investor are not subject to the 2-percent floor. For this purpose, such an incremental cost is a special, additional charge that is added solely because the investment advice is rendered to a trust or estate rather than to an individual or attributable to an unusual investment objective or the need for a specialized balancing of the interests of various parties (beyond the usual balancing of the varying interests of current beneficiaries and remaindermen) such that a reasonable comparison with individual investors would be improper. The portion of the investment advisory fees not subject to the 2-percent floor by reason of the preceding sentence is limited to the amount of those fees, if any, that exceeds the fees normally charged to an individual investor.

(5) *Appraisal fees.*—Appraisal fees incurred by an estate or a non-grantor trust to determine the fair market value of assets as of the decedent's date of death (or the alternate valuation

date), to determine value for purposes of making distributions, or as otherwise required to properly prepare the estate's or trust's tax returns, or a generation-skipping transfer tax return, are not incurred commonly or customarily by an individual and thus are not subject to the 2-percent floor. The cost of appraisals for other purposes (for example, insurance) is commonly or customarily incurred by individuals and is subject to the 2-percent floor.

(6) *Certain Fiduciary Expenses.*—Certain other fiduciary expenses are not commonly or customarily incurred by individuals, and thus are not subject to the 2-percent floor. Such expenses include without limitation the following: probate court fees and costs; fiduciary bond premiums; legal publication costs of notices to creditors or heirs; the cost of certified copies of the decedent's death certificate; and costs related to fiduciary accounts.

(c) *Bundled fees.*—(1) *In general.*—If an estate or a non-grantor trust pays a single fee, commission, or other expense (such as a fiduciary's commission, attorney's fee, or accountant's fee) for both costs that are subject to the 2-percent floor and costs (in more than a de minimis amount) that are not, then, except to the extent provided otherwise by guidance published in the Internal Revenue Bulletin, the single fee, commission, or other expense (bundled fee) must be allocated, for purposes of computing the adjusted gross income of the estate or non-grantor trust in compliance with section 67(e), between the costs that are subject to the 2-percent floor and those that are not.

(2) *Exception.*—If a bundled fee is not computed on an hourly basis, only the portion of that fee that is attributable to investment advice is subject to the 2-percent floor; the remaining portion is not subject to that floor.

(3) *Expenses Not Subject to Allocation.*—Out-of-pocket expenses billed to the estate or non-grantor trust are treated as separate from the bundled fee. In addition, payments made from the bundled fee to third parties that would have been subject to the 2-percent floor if they had been paid directly by the estate or non-grantor trust are subject to the 2-percent floor, as are any fees or expenses separately assessed by the fiduciary or other payee of the bundled fee (in addition to the usual or basic bundled fee) for services rendered to the estate or non-grantor trust that are commonly or customarily incurred by an individual.

(4) *Reasonable Method.*—Any reasonable method may be used to allocate a bundled fee between those costs that are subject to the 2-percent floor and those costs that are not, including without limitation the allocation of a portion of a fiduciary commission that is a bundled fee to investment advice. Facts that may be considered in determining whether an allocation is reasonable include, but are not limited to, the percentage of the value of the corpus subject to investment advice, whether a third party advisor would have charged a comparable fee for similar advisory services, and the amount of the fiduciary's attention to the trust or estate that is devoted to investment advice as compared to dealings with beneficiaries and distribution decisions and other fiduciary functions. The reasonable method standard does not apply to determine the portion of the bundled fee attributable to payments made to third parties for expenses subject to the 2-percent floor or to any other separately assessed expense commonly or customarily incurred by an individual, because those payments and expenses are readily identifiable without any discretion on the part of the fiduciary or return preparer.

(d) *Applicability date.*—This section applies to taxable years beginning after December 31, 2014. Paragraph (a) of this section applies to taxable years beginning after October 19, 2020. Taxpayers may choose to apply paragraph (a) of this section to taxable years beginning after December 31, 2017, and on or before October 19, 2020.[Reg. § 1.67-4.]

☐ [*T.D.* 9664, 5-8-2014 (*amended* 7-16-2014). *Amended by T.D.* 9918, 10-16-2020.]

Items Specifically Excluded From Gross Income

***

[Reg. § 1.102-1]

§ 1.102-1. Gifts and inheritances.—(a) *General rule.*—Property received as a gift, or received under a will or under statutes of descent and distribution, is not includible in gross income, although the income from such property is includible in gross income. An amount of principal paid under a marriage settlement is a gift. However, see section 71 and the regulations thereunder for rules relating to alimony or allowances paid upon divorce or separation. Section 102 does not apply to prizes and awards (see section 74 and § 1.74-1) nor to scholarships and fellowship grants (see section 117 and the regulations thereunder).

(b) *Income from gifts and inheritances.*—The income from any property received as a gift, or under a will or statute of descent and distribution shall not be excluded from gross income under paragraph (a) of this section.

(c) *Gifts and inheritances of income.*—If the gift, bequest, devise, or inheritance is of income from property, it shall not be excluded from gross income under paragraph (a) of this section. Section 102 provides a special rule for the treatment of certain gifts, bequests, devises, or inheritances which by their terms are to be paid, credited, or distributed at intervals. Except as provided in section 663(a)(1) and paragraph (d) of this section, to the extent any such gift, bequest, devise, or inheritance is paid, credited, or to be distributed out of income from property, it shall be considered a gift, bequest, devise, or inheritance of income from property. Section 102 provides the same treatment for amounts of income from property which is paid, credited, or to be distributed under a gift or bequest whether the gift or bequest is in terms of a right to payments at intervals (regardless of income) or is in terms of a right to income. To the extent the amounts in either case are paid, credited, or to be distributed at intervals out of income, they are not to be excluded under section 102 from the taxpayer's gross income.

(d) *Effect of subchapter J.*—Any amount required to be included in the gross income of a beneficiary under sections 652, 662, or 668 shall be treated for purposes of this section as a gift, bequest, devise, or inheritance of income from property. On the other hand, any amount excluded from the gross income of a beneficiary under section 663(a)(1) shall be treated for purposes of this section as property acquired by gift, bequest, devise, or inheritance.

(e) *Income taxed to grantor or assignor.*—Section 102 is not intended to tax a donee upon the same income which is taxed to the grantor of a trust or assignor of income under section 61 or sections 671 through 677, inclusive. [Reg. § 1.102-1.]

☐ [*T.D.* 6220, 12-28-56.]

* * *

[Reg. § 1.112-1]

§ 1.112-1. Combat zone compensation of members of the Armed Forces.—(a) *Combat zone compensation exclusion.*—(1) *Amount excluded.*—In addition to the exemptions and credits otherwise applicable, section 112 excludes from gross income the following compensation of members of the Armed Forces:

(i) *Enlisted personnel.*—Compensation received for active service as a member below the grade of commissioned officer in the Armed Forces of the United States for any month during any part of which the member served in a combat zone or was hospitalized at any place as a result of wounds, disease, or injury incurred while serving in the combat zone.

(ii) *Commissioned officers.*—Compensation not exceeding the monthly dollar limit received for active service as a commissioned officer in the Armed Forces of the United States for any month during any part of which the officer served in a combat zone or was hospitalized at any place as a result of wounds, disease, or injury incurred while serving in the combat zone. The monthly dollar limit is the monthly amount excludable from the officer's income under section 112(b) as amended. Beginning in 1966, the monthly dollar limit for periods of active service after 1965 became $500. As of September 10, 1993, the monthly dollar limit continues to be $500.

(2) *Time limits on exclusion during hospitalization.*—Compensation received for service for any month of hospitalization that begins more than 2 years after the date specified by the President in an Executive Order as the date of the termination of combatant activities in the combat zone cannot be excluded under section 112. Furthermore, compensation received while hospitalized after January 1978 for wounds, disease, or injury incurred in the Vietnam combat zone designated by Executive Order 11216 cannot be excluded under section 112.

(3) *Special terms.*—A commissioned warrant officer is not a *commissioned officer* under section 112(b) and is entitled to the exclusion allowed to enlisted personnel under section 112(a). *Compensation*, for the purpose of section 112, does not include pensions and retirement pay. *Armed Forces of the United States* is defined (and members of the Armed Forces are described) in section 7701(a)(15).

(4) *Military compensation only.*—Only compensation paid by the Armed Forces of the United States to members of the Armed Forces can be excluded under section 112, except for compensation paid by an agency or instrumentality of the United States or by an international organization to a member of the Armed Forces whose military active duty status continues during the member's assignment to the agency or instrumentality or organization on official detail. Compensation paid by other employers (whether private enterprises or governmental entities) to members of the Armed Forces cannot be excluded under section 112 even if the payment is made to supplement the member's military compensation or is labeled by the employer as compensation for active service in the Armed Forces of the United States. Compensation paid to civilian employees of the federal government, including civilian employees of the Armed Forces, cannot be excluded under section 112, except as provided in section 112(d)(2) (which extends the exclusion to compensation of civilian employees of the federal government in missing status due to the Vietnam conflict).

(b) *Service in combat zone.*—(1) *Active service.*—The exclusion under section 112 applies only if active service is performed in a combat zone. A member of the Armed Forces is in active service if the member is actually serving in the Armed Forces of the United States. Periods during which a member of the Armed Forces is absent from duty on account of sickness, wounds, leave, internment by the enemy, or other lawful cause are periods of active service. A member of the Armed Forces in active service in a combat zone who becomes a prisoner of war or missing in action in the combat zone is deemed, for the purpose of section 112, to continue in active service in the combat zone for the period for which the member is treated as a prisoner of war or as missing in action for military pay purposes.

(2) *Combat zone status.*—Except as provided in paragraphs (e) and (f) of this section, service is performed in a combat zone only if it is performed in an area which the President of the United States has designated by Executive Order, for the purpose of section 112, as an area in which Armed Forces of the United States are or

have been engaged in combat, and only if it is performed on or after the date designated by the President by Executive Order as the date of the commencing of combatant activities in that zone and on or before the date designated by the President by Executive Order as the date of the termination of combatant activities in that zone.

(3) *Partial month service.*—If a member of the Armed Forces serves in a combat zone for any part of a month, the member is entitled to the exclusion for that month to the same extent as if the member has served in that zone for the entire month. If a member of the Armed Forces is hospitalized for a part of a month as a result of wounds, disease, or injury incurred while serving in that zone, the member is entitled to the exclusion for the entire month.

(4) *Payment time and place.*—The time and place of payment are irrelevant in considering whether compensation is excludable under section 112; rather, the time and place of the entitlement to compensation determine whether the compensation is excludable under section 112. Thus, compensation can be excluded under section 112 whether or not it is received outside a combat zone, or while the recipient is hospitalized, or in a year different from that in which the service was rendered for which the compensation is paid, provided that the member's entitlement to the compensation fully accrued in a month during which the member served in the combat zone or was hospitalized as a result of wounds, disease, or injury incurred while serving in the combat zone. For this purpose, entitlement to compensation fully accrues upon the completion of all actions required of the member to receive the compensation. Compensation received by a member of the Armed Forces for services rendered while in active service can be excluded under section 112 even though payment is received subsequent to discharge or release from active service. Compensation credited to a deceased member's account for a period subsequent to the established date of the member's death and received by the member's estate can be excluded from the gross income of the estate under section 112 to the same extent that it would have been excluded from the gross income of the member had the member lived and received the compensation.

(5) *Examples of combat zone compensation.*—The rules of this section are illustrated by the following examples:

Example 1. On January 5, outside of a combat zone, an enlisted member received basic pay for active duty services performed from the preceding December 1 through December 31. On December 4 (and no other date), the member performed services within a combat zone. The member may exclude from income the entire payment received on January 5, although the member served in the combat zone only one day during December, received the payment outside of the combat zone, and received the payment in a year other than the year in which the combat zone services were performed.

Example 2. From March through December, an enlisted member became entitled to 25 days of annual leave while serving in a combat zone. The member used all 25 days of leave in the following year. The member may exclude from income the compensation received for those 25 days, even if the member performs no services in the combat zone in the year the compensation is received.

Example 3. From March through December, a commissioned officer became entitled to 25 days of annual leave while serving in a combat zone. During that period the officer also received basic pay of $1,000 per month from which the officer excluded from income $500 per month (exhausting the monthly dollar limit under section 112 for that period). The officer used all 25 days of leave in the following year. The officer may not exclude from income any compensation received in the following year related to those 25 days of leave, since the officer had already excluded from income the maximum amount of combat zone compensation for the period in which the leave was earned.

Example 4. In November, while serving in a combat zone, an enlisted member competing for a cash award submitted an employee suggestion. After November, the member neither served in a combat zone nor was hospitalized for wounds incurred in the combat zone. In June of the following year, the member's suggestion was selected as the winner of the competition and the award was paid. The award can be excluded from income as combat zone compensation although granted and received outside of the combat zone, since the member completed the necessary action to win the award (submission of the suggestion) in a month during which the member served in the combat zone.

Example 5. In July, while serving in a combat zone, an enlisted member voluntarily reenlisted. After July, the member neither served in a combat zone nor was hospitalized for wounds incurred in the combat zone. In February of the following year, the member received a bonus as a result of the July reenlistment. The reenlistment bonus can be excluded from income as combat zone compensation although received outside of the combat zone, since the member completed the necessary action for entitlement to the reenlistment bonus in a month during which the member served in the combat zone.

Example 6. In July, while serving outside a combat zone, an enlisted member voluntarily reenlisted. In February of the following year, the member, while performing services in a combat zone, received a bonus as a result of the July reenlistment. The reenlistment bonus cannot be excluded from income as combat zone compensation although received while serving in the combat zone, since the member completed the necessary action for entitlement to the reenlistment bonus in a month during which the member had neither served in the combat zone nor was hospitalized for wounds incurred while serving in a combat zone.

(c) *Hospitalization.*—(1) *Presumption of combat zone injury.*—If an individual is hospitalized for [a] wound, disease, or injury while serving in a combat zone, the wound, disease, or injury will be presumed to have been incurred while serving in a combat zone, unless the contrary clearly appears. In certain cases, however, a wound, disease, or injury may have been incurred while serving in a combat zone even though the individual was not hospitalized for it while so serving. In exceptional cases, a wound, disease, or injury will not have been incurred while serving in a combat zone even though the individual was hospitalized for it while so serving.

(2) *Length of hospitalization.*—An individual is hospitalized only until the date the individual is discharged from the hospital.

(3) *Examples of combat zone injury.*—The rules of this paragraph (c) are illustrated by the following examples:

Example 1. An individual is hospitalized for a disease in the combat zone where the individual has been serving for three weeks. The incubation period of the disease is two to four weeks. The disease is incurred while serving in the combat zone.

Example 2. The facts are the same as in *Example 1* except that the incubation period of the disease is one year. The disease is not incurred while serving in the combat zone.

Example 3. A member of the Air Force, stationed outside the combat zone, is shot while participating in aerial combat over the combat zone, but is not hospitalized until returning to the home base. The injury is incurred while serving in a combat zone.

Example 4. An individual is hospitalized for a disease three weeks after having departed from a combat zone. The incubation period of the disease is two to four weeks. The disease is incurred while serving in a combat zone.

(d) *Married members.*—The exclusion under section 112 applies without regard to the marital status of the recipient of the compensation. If both spouses meet the requirements of the statute, then each spouse is entitled to the benefit of an exclusion. In the case of a husband and wife domiciled in a State recognized for Federal income tax purposes as a community property State, any exclusion from gross income under section 112 operates before apportionment of the gross income of the spouses under community property law. For example, a husband and wife are domiciled in a community property State and the member spouse is entitled, as a commissioned officer, to the benefit of the exclusion under section 112(b) of $500 for each month. The member receives $7,899 as compensation for active service for 3 months in a combat zone. Of that amount, $1,500 is excluded from gross income under section 112(b) and $6,399 is taken into account in determining the gross income of both spouses.

(e) *Service in area outside combat zone.*—(1) *Combat zone treatment.*—For purposes of section 112, a member of the Armed Forces who performs military service in an area outside the area designated by Executive Order as a combat zone is deemed to serve in that combat zone while the member's service is in direct support of military operations in that zone and qualifies the member for the special pay for duty subject to hostile fire or imminent danger authorized under section 310 of title 37 of the United States Code, as amended (37 U.S.C. 310) (hostile fire/imminent danger pay).

(2) *Examples of combat zone treatment.*—The examples in this paragraph (e)(2) are based on the following circumstances: Certain areas, airspace, and adjacent waters are designated as a combat zone for purposes of section 112 as of May 1. Some members of the Armed Forces are stationed in the combat zone; others are stationed in two foreign countries outside the combat zone, named Nearby Country and Destination Country.

Example 1. B is a member of an Armed Forces ground unit stationed in the combat zone. On May 31, B's unit crosses into Nearby Country. B performs military service in Nearby Country in direct support of the military operations in the combat zone from June 1 through June 8 that qualifies B for hostile fire/imminent danger pay. B does not return to the combat zone during June. B is deemed to serve in the combat zone from June 1 through June 8. Accordingly, B is entitled to the exclusion under section 112 for June. Of course, B is also entitled to the exclusion for any month (May, in this example) in which B actually served in the combat zone.

Example 2. B is a member of an Armed Forces ground unit stationed in the combat zone. On May 31, B's unit crosses into Nearby Country. On June 1, B is wounded while performing military service in Nearby Country in direct support of the military operations in the combat zone that qualifies B for hostile fire/imminent danger pay. On June 2, B is transferred for treatment to a hospital in the United States. B is hospitalized from June through October for those wounds. B is deemed to have incurred the wounds while serving in the combat zone on June 1. Accordingly, B is entitled to the exclusion under section 112 for June through October. Of course, B is also entitled to the exclusion for any month (May, in this example) in which B actually served in the combat zone.

Example 3. B is stationed in Nearby Country for the entire month of June as a member of a ground crew servicing combat aircraft operating in the combat zone. B's service in Nearby Country during June does not qualify B for hostile fire/imminent danger pay. Accordingly, B is not deemed to serve in the combat zone during June and is not entitled to the exclusion under section 112 for that month.

Example 4. B is assigned to an air unit stationed in Nearby Country for the entire month of June. In June, members of air units of the Armed Forces stationed in Nearby Country fly combat and supply missions into and over Destination Country in direct support of military operations in the combat zone. B flies combat missions over

Destination Country from Nearby Country from June 1 through June 8. B's service qualifies B for hostile fire/imminent danger pay. Accordingly, B is deemed to serve in the combat zone during June and is entitled to the exclusion under section 112. The result would be the same if B were to fly supply missions into Destination Country from Nearby Country in direct support of operations in the combat zone qualifying B for hostile fire/imminent danger pay.

Example 5. Assigned to an air unit stationed in Nearby Country, B was killed in June when B's plane crashed on returning to the airbase in Nearby Country. B was performing military service in direct support of the military operations in the combat zone at the time of B's death. B's service also qualified B for hostile fire/imminent danger pay. B is deemed to have died while serving in the combat zone or to have died as a result of wounds, disease, or injury incurred while serving in the combat zone for purposes of section 692(a) and section 692(b) (providing relief from certain income taxes for members of the Armed Forces dying in a combat zone or as a result of wounds, disease, or injury incurred while serving in a combat zone) and section 2201 (providing relief from certain estate taxes for members of the Armed Forces dying in a combat zone or by reason of combat-zone-incurred wounds). The result would be the same if B's mission had been a supply mission instead of a combat mission.

Example 6. In June, B was killed as a result of an off-duty automobile accident while leaving the airbase in Nearby Country shortly after returning from a mission over Destination Country. At the time of B's death, B was not performing military duty qualifying B for hostile fire/imminent danger pay. B is not deemed to have died while serving in the combat zone or to have died as the result of wounds, disease, or injury incurred while serving in the combat zone. Accordingly, B does not qualify for the benefits of section 692(a), section 692(b), or section 2201.

Example 7. B performs military service in Nearby Country from June 1 through June 8 in direct support of the military operations in the combat zone. Nearby Country is designated as an area in which members of the Armed Forces qualify for hostile fire/imminent danger pay due to imminent danger, even though members in Nearby Country are not subject to hostile fire. B is deemed to serve in the combat zone from June 1 through June 8. Accordingly, B is entitled to the exclusion under section 112 for June.

(f) *Nonqualifying presence in combat zone.*—(1) *Inapplicability of exclusion.*—The following members of the Armed Forces are not deemed to serve in a combat zone within the meaning of section 112(a)(1) or section 112(b)(1) or to be hospitalized as a result of wounds, disease, or injury incurred while serving in a combat zone within the meaning of section 112(a)(2) or section 112(b)(2)—

(i) Members present in a combat zone while on leave from a duty station located outside a combat zone;

(ii) Members who pass over or through a combat zone during the course of a trip between two points both of which lie outside a combat zone; or

(iii) Members present in a combat zone solely for their own personal convenience.

(2) *Exceptions for temporary duty or special pay.*—Paragraph (f)(1) of this section does not apply to members of the Armed Forces who—

(i) Are assigned on official temporary duty to a combat zone (including official temporary duty to the airspace of a combat zone); or

(ii) Qualify for hostile fire/imminent danger pay.

(3) *Examples of nonqualifying presence and its exceptions.*—The examples in this paragraph (f)(3) are based on the following circumstances: Certain areas, airspace, and adjacent waters are designated as a combat zone for purposes of section 112 as of May 1. Some members of the Armed Forces are stationed in the combat zone; others are stationed in two foreign countries outside the combat zone, named Nearby Country and Destination Country.

Example 1. B is a member of the Armed Forces assigned to a unit stationed in Nearby Country. On June 1, B voluntarily visits a city within the combat zone while on leave. B is not deemed to serve in a combat zone since B is present in a combat zone while on leave from a duty station located outside a combat zone.

Example 2. B is a member of the Armed Forces assigned to a unit stationed in Nearby Country. During June, B takes authorized leave and elects to spend the leave period by visiting a city in the combat zone. While on leave in the combat zone, B is subject to hostile fire qualifying B for hostile fire/imminent danger pay. Although B is present in the combat zone while on leave from a duty station outside the combat zone, B qualifies for the exclusion under section 112 because B qualifies for hostile fire/imminent danger pay while in the combat zone.

Example 3. B is a member of the Armed Forces assigned to a ground unit stationed in the combat zone. During June, B takes authorized leave and elects to spend the leave period in the combat zone. B is not on leave from a duty station located outside a combat zone, nor is B present in a combat zone solely for B's own personal convenience. Accordingly, B's combat zone tax benefits continue while B is on leave in the combat zone.

Example 4. B is assigned as a navigator to an air unit stationed in Nearby Country. On June 4, during the course of a flight between B's home base in Nearby Country and another base in Destination Country, the aircraft on which B serves as a navigator flies over the combat zone. B is not on official temporary duty to the airspace of the combat zone and does not qualify for hostile fire/imminent danger pay as a result of the flight. Accordingly, B is not deemed to serve in a combat zone since B passes over the combat zone during the course of a trip between two points both of which lie outside the combat zone without either being on official temporary duty to the combat zone or qualifying for hostile fire/imminent danger pay.

Example 5. B is a member of the Armed Forces assigned to a unit stationed in Nearby Country. B enters the combat zone on a 3-day pass. B is not on official temporary duty and does not qualify for hostile fire/imminent danger pay while present in the combat zone. Accordingly, B is not deemed to serve in a combat zone since B is present in the combat zone solely for B's own personal convenience.

Example 6. B, stationed in Nearby Country, is a military courier assigned on official temporary duty to deliver military pouches in the combat zone and in Destination Country. On June 1, B arrives in the combat zone from Nearby Country, and on June 2, B departs for Destination Country. Although B passes through the combat zone during the course of a trip between two points outside the combat zone, B is nevertheless deemed to serve in a combat zone while in the combat zone because B is assigned to the combat zone on official temporary duty.

Example 7. B is a member of an Armed Forces ground unit stationed in Nearby Country. On June 1, B took authorized leave and elected to spend the leave period by visiting a city in the combat zone. On June 2, while on leave in the combat zone, B was wounded by hostile fire qualifying B for hostile fire/imminent danger pay. On June 3, B was transferred for treatment to a hospital in the United States. B is hospitalized from June through October for those wounds. Although B was present in the combat zone while on leave from a duty station outside the combat zone, B is deemed to have incurred the wounds while serving in the combat zone on June 2, because B qualified for hostile fire/imminent danger pay while in the combat zone. Accordingly, B is entitled to the exclusion under section 112 for June through October.

Example 8. The facts are the same as in *Example 7* except that B dies on September 1 as a result of the wounds incurred in the combat zone. B is deemed to have died as a result of wounds, disease, or injury incurred while serving in the combat zone for purposes of section 692(a) and section 692(b) (providing relief from certain income taxes for members of the Armed Forces dying in a combat zone or as a result of wounds, disease, or injury incurred while serving in a combat zone) and section 2201 (providing relief from certain estate taxes for members of the Armed Forces dying in a combat zone or by reason of combat-zone-incurred wounds). [Reg. §1.112-1.]

☐ [*T.D.* 6220, 12-28-56. *Amended by T.D.* 6906, 12-28-66; *T.D.* 7066, 11-10-70 *and T.D.* 8489, 9-9-93.]

* * *

Additional Itemized Deductions for Individuals

* * *

[Reg. §1.213-1]

§1.213-1. Medical, dental, etc., expenses.—(a) *Allowance of deduction.*—(1) Section 213 permits a deduction of payments for certain medical expenses (including expenses for medicine and drugs). Except as provided in paragraph (d) of this section (relating to special rule for decedents) a deduction is allowable only to individuals and only with respect to medical expenses actually paid during the taxable year, regardless of when the incident or event which occasioned the expenses occurred and regardless of the method of accounting employed by the taxpayer in making his income tax return. Thus, if the medical expenses are incurred but not paid during the taxable year, no deduction for such expenses shall be allowed for such year.

* * *

(d) *Special rule for decedents.*—(1) For the purpose of section 213(a), expenses for medical care of the taxpayer which are paid out of his estate during the 1-year period beginning with the day after the date of his death shall be treated as paid by the taxpayer at the time the medical services were rendered. However, no credit or refund of tax shall be allowed for any taxable year for which the statutory period for filing a claim has expired. See section 6511 and the regulations thereunder.

(2) The rule prescribed in subparagraph (1) of this paragraph shall not apply where the amount so paid is allowable under section 2053 as a deduction in computing the taxable estate of the decedent unless there is filed in duplicate (i) a statement that such amount has not been allowed as a deduction under section 2053 in computing the taxable estate of the decedent and (ii) a waiver of the right to have such amount allowed at any time as a deduction under section 2053. The statement and waiver shall be filed with or for association with the return, amended return, or claim for credit or refund for the decedent for any taxable year for which such an amount is claimed as a deduction.

* * *

[Reg. §1.213-1.]

☐ [*T.D.* 6279, 12-13-57. *Amended by T.D.* 6451, 2-3-60; *T.D.* 6604, 7-23-62; *T.D.* 6661, 6-26-63; *T.D.* 6761, 9-28-64; *T.D.* 6946, 2-12-68; *T.D.* 6985, 12-26-68; *T.D.* 7114, 5-17-71; *T.D.* 7317, 6-27-74 *and T.D.* 7643, 8-27-79.]

* * *

CORPORATE DISTRIBUTIONS AND ADJUSTMENTS

Distributions by Corporations

* * *

[Reg. §1.303-1]

§1.303-1. General.—Section 303 provides that in certain cases a distribution in redemption of stock, the value of which is included in determining the value of the gross estate of a decedent, shall be treated as a distribution in full payment in exchange for the stock so redeemed. [Reg. § 1.303-1.]

☐ [*T.D.* 6152, 12-2-55.]

[Reg. § 1.303-2]

§ 1.303-2. Requirements.—(a) Section 303 applies only where the distribution is with respect to stock of a corporation the value of whose stock in the gross estate of the decedent for Federal estate tax purposes is an amount in excess of (1) 35 percent of the value of the gross estate of such decedent, or (2) 50 percent of the taxable estate of such decedent. For the purposes of such 35 percent and 50 percent requirements, stock of two or more corporations shall be treated as the stock of a single corporation if more than 75 percent in value of the outstanding stock of each such corporation is included in determining the value of the decedent's gross estate. For the purpose of the 75 percent requirement, stock which, at the decedent's death, represents the surviving spouse's interest in community property shall be considered as having been included in determining the value of the decedent's gross estate.

(b) For the purpose of section 303(b)(2)(A)(i), the term "gross estate" means the gross estate as computed in accordance with section 2031 (or, in the case of the estate of a decedent nonresident not a citizen of the United States, in accordance with section 2103). For the purpose of section 303(b)(2)(A)(ii), the term "taxable estate" means the taxable estate as computed in accordance with section 2051 (or, in the case of the estate of a decedent non-resident not a citizen of the United States, in accordance with section 2106). In case the value of an estate is determined for Federal estate tax purposes under section 2032 (relating to alternate valuation), then, for purposes of section 303(b)(2), the value of the gross estate, the taxable estate, and the stock shall each be determined on the applicable date prescribed in section 2032.

(c)(1) In determining whether the estate of the decedent is comprised of stock of a corporation of sufficient value to satisfy the percentage requirements of section 303(b)(2)(A) and section 303(b)(2)(B), the total value, in the aggregate, of all classes of stock of the corporation includible in determining the value of the gross estate is taken into account. A distribution under section 303(a) may be in redemption of the stock of the corporation includible in determining the value of the gross estate, without regard to the class of such stock.

(2) The above may be illustrated by the following example:

Example. The gross estate of the decedent has a value of $1,000,000, the taxable estate is $700,000, and the sum of the death taxes and funeral and administration expenses is $275,000. Included in determining the gross estate of the decedent is stock of three corporations which, for Federal estate tax purposes, is valued as follows:

Corporation A:	
Common stock	$100,000
Preferred stock	100,000
Corporation B:	
Common stock	50,000
Preferred stock	350,000
Corporation C:	
Common stock	200,000

The stock of Corporation A and Corporation C included in the estate of the decedent constitutes all of the outstanding stock of both corporations. The stock of Corporation A and the stock of Corporation C, treated as the stock of a single corporation under section 303(b)(2)(B), has a value in excess of $350,000 (35 percent of the gross estate or 50 percent of the taxable estate). Likewise, the stock of Corporation B has a value in excess of $350,000. The distribution by one or more of the above corporations, within the period prescribed in section 303(b)(1), of amounts not exceeding, in the aggregate, $275,000, in redemption of preferred stock or common stock of such corporation or corporations, will be treated as in full payment in exchange for the stock so redeemed.

(d) If stock includible in determining the value of the gross estate of a decedent is exchanged for new stock, the basis of which is determined by reference to the basis of the old stock, the redemption of the new stock will be treated the same under section 303 as the redemption of the old stock would have been. Thus, section 303 shall apply with respect to a distribution in redemption of stock received by the estate of a decedent (1) in connection with a reorganization under section 368, (2) in a distribution or exchange under section 355 (or so much of section 356 as relates to section 355), (3) in an exchange under section 1036 or (4) in a distribution to which section 305(a) applies. Similarly, a distribution in redemption of stock will qualify under section 303, notwithstanding the fact that the stock redeemed is section 306 stock to the extent that the conditions of section 303 are met.

(e) Section 303 applies to distributions made after the death of the decedent and (1) before the expiration of the 3-year period of limitations for the assessment of estate tax provided in section 6501(a) (determined without the application of any provisions of law extending or suspending the running of such period of limitations), or within 90 days after the expiration of such period, or (2) if a petition for redetermination of a deficiency in such estate tax has been filed with the Tax Court within the time prescribed in section 6213, at any time before the expiration of 60 days after the decision of the Tax Court becomes final. The extension of the period of distribution provided in section 303(b)(1)(B) has reference solely to bona fide contests in the Tax Court and will not apply in the case of a petition for redetermination of a deficiency which is initiated solely for the purpose of extending the period within which section 303 would otherwise be applicable.

(f) While section 303 will most frequently have application in the case where stock is redeemed from the executor or administrator of an estate, the section is also applicable to distributions in redemption of stock included in the decedent's gross estate and held at the time of the redemption by any person who acquired the stock by any of the means comprehended by Part III, Subchapter A, Chapter 11 of the Code, including the heir, legatee, or donee of the decedent, a surviving joint tenant, surviving spouse, appointee, or taker in default of appointment, or a trustee of a trust created by the decedent. Thus, section 303 may apply with respect to a distribution in redemption of stock from a donee to whom the decedent has transferred stock in contemplation of death where the value of such stock is included in the decedent's gross estate under section 2035. Similarly, section 303 may apply to the redemption of stock from a beneficiary of the estate to whom an executor has distributed the stock pursuant to the terms of the will of the decedent. However, section 303 is not applicable to the case where stock is redeemed from a stockholder who has acquired the stock by gift or purchase from any person to whom such stock has passed from the decedent. Nor is section 303 applicable to the case where stock is redeemed from a stockholder who has acquired the stock from the executor in satisfaction of a specific monetary bequest.

(g)(1) The total amount of the distributions to which section 303 may apply with respect to redemptions of stock included in the gross estate of a decedent may not exceed the sum of the estate, inheritance, legacy, and succession taxes (including any interest collected as a part of such taxes) imposed because of the decedent's death and the amount of funeral and administration expenses allowable as deductions to the estate. Where there is more than one distribution in redemption of stock described in section 303(b)(2) during the period of time prescribed in section 303(b)(1), the distributions shall be applied against the total amount which qualifies for treatment under section 303 in the order in which the distributions are made. For this purpose, all distributions in redemption of such stock shall be taken into account, including distributions which under another provision of the Code are treated as in part or full payment in exchange for the stock redeemed.

(2) Subparagraph (1) of this paragraph may be illustrated by the following example:

Example. (i) The gross estate of the decedent has a value of $800,000, the taxable estate is $500,000, and the sum of the death taxes and funeral and administrative expenses is $225,000. Included in determining the gross estate of the decedent is the stock of a corporation which for Federal estate tax purposes is valued at $450,000. During the first year of administration, one-third of such stock is distributed to a legatee and shortly thereafter this stock is redeemed by the corporation for $150,000. During the second year of administration, another one-third of such stock includible in the estate is redeemed for $150,000.

(ii) The first distribution of $150,000 is applied against the amount that qualifies for treatment under section 303, regardless of whether the first distribution was treated as in payment in exchange for stock under section 302(a). Thus, only $75,000 of the second distribution may be treated as in full payment in exchange for stock under section 303. The tax treatment of the remaining $75,000 would be determined under other provisions of the Code.

(h) For the purpose of section 303, the Federal estate tax or any other estate, inheritance, legacy, or succession tax shall be ascertained after the allowance of any credit, relief, discount, refund, remission or reduction of tax. [Reg. § 1.303-2.]

□ [*T.D.* 6152, 12-2-55. *Amended by T.D.* 6724, 4-20-64 *and T.D.* 7346, 3-6-75.]

[Reg. § 1.303-3]

§ 1.303-3. Application of other sections.—(a) The sole effect of section 303 is to exempt from tax as a dividend a distribution to which such section is applicable when made in redemption of stock includible in a decedent's gross estate. Such section does not, however, in any other manner affect the principles set forth in sections 302 and 306. Thus, if stock of a corporation is owned equally by A, B, and the C Estate, and the corporation redeems one-half of the stock of each shareholder, the determination of whether the distributions to A and B are essentially equivalent to dividends shall be made without regard to the effect which section 303 may have upon the taxability of the distribution to the C Estate.

(b) See section 304 relative to redemption of stock through the use of related corporations. [Reg. § 1.303-3.]

□ [*T.D.* 6152, 12-2-55.]

* * *

Certain Homeowners Associations

[Reg. § 1.529A-0]

§ 1.529A-0. Table of contents.—This section lists the following captions contained in §§ 1.529A-1 through 1.529A-8.

See p. 15 for regulations not amended to reflect law changes

(5) Distribution.
(6) Earnings.
(7) Earnings ratio.
(8) Eligible individual.
(9) Excess contribution.
(10) Excess aggregate contribution.
(11) Investment in the account.
(12) Member of the family.
(13) Program-to-program transfer.
(14) Qualified ABLE program.
(15) Qualified disability expenses.
(16) Rollover.
(c) Applicability date.
§ 1.529A-2 Qualified ABLE program.
(a) In general.
(b) Established and maintained by a State or agency or instrumentality of a State.
(1) Established.
(2) Maintained.
(i) In general.
(ii) Multiple States, agencies, or instrumentalities.
(3) Community Development Financial Institutions (CDFIs).
(c) Establishment of an ABLE account and signature authority.
(1) Establishment of the ABLE account.
(2) Signature authority.
(3) Only one ABLE account.
(4) Beneficial interest.
(d) Eligible individual.
(1) Documentation.
(2) Frequency of recertification.
(3) Loss of qualification as an eligible individual.
(e) Disability certification.
(1) In general.
(2) Marked and severe functional limitations.
(3) Compassionate allowance list.
(4) Additional guidance.
(5) Restriction on use of certification.
(f) Change of designated beneficiary.
(1) In general.
(2) Change effective upon death.
(g) Contributions.
(1) Permissible property.
(2) Annual contributions limit.
(3) Cumulative limit.
(4) Return of excess contributions, excess compensation contributions, and excess aggregate contributions.
(5) Restriction of contributors.
(h) Qualified disability expenses.
(1) In general.
(2) Example.
(i) Separate accounting.
(j) Program-to-program transfers.
(k) Carryover of attributes.
(1) In general.
(2) Annual contribution limit.
(3) Investment direction limit.
(l) Investment direction.
(m) No pledging of interest as security.
(n) No sale or exchange.
(o) Post-death payments.
(p) Reporting requirements.
(q) Applicability date.
§ 1.529A-3 Tax treatment.
(a) Taxation of distributions.
(1) In general.
(2) Additional period.
(b) Additional exclusions from gross income.
(1) Rollover.
(2) Program-to-program transfers.
(3) Change of designated beneficiary.
(4) Payments to creditors post-death.
(c) Computation of earnings.
(d) Additional tax on amounts includible in gross income.
(1) In general.
(2) Exceptions.
(e) Tax on excess contributions.
(f) Filing requirements.
(g) No inference outside section 529A.
(h) Applicability date.
§ 1.529A-4 Gift, estate, and generation-skipping transfer taxes.
(a) Contributions.
(1) In general.
(2) Generation-skipping transfer (GST) tax.
(3) Designated beneficiary as contributor.
(b) Distributions.
(c) Transfer to another designated beneficiary.
(d) Transfer tax on death of designated beneficiary.
(e) Applicability date.
§ 1.529A-5 Reporting of the establishment of and contributions to an ABLE account.
(a) In general.
(b) Additional definitions.
(1) Filer.
(2) TIN.
(c) Requirement to file return.
(1) Form of return.
(2) Information included on return.
(3) Time and manner of filing return.
(d) Requirement to furnish statement.
(1) In general.
(2) Time and manner of furnishing statement.
(3) Copy of Form 5498-QA.
(e) Request for TIN of designated beneficiary.
(f) Penalties.
(1) Failure to file return.
(2) Failure to furnish TIN.
(g) Applicability date.
§ 1.529A-6 Reporting of distributions from and termination of an ABLE account.
(a) In general.
(b) Requirement to file return.
(1) Form of return.
(2) Information included on return.
(3) Information excluded.
(4) Time and manner of filing return.
(c) Requirement to furnish statement.
(1) In general.

(2) Time and manner of furnishing statement.
(3) Copy of Form 1099-QA.
(d) Request for TIN of contributor(s).
(1) In general.
(2) Exception.
(e) Penalties.
(1) Failure to file return.
(2) Failure to furnish TIN.
(f) Applicability date.

§ 1.529A-7 Electronic furnishing of statements to designated beneficiaries and contributors.
(a) Electronic furnishing of statements.
(1) In general.
(2) Consent.
(3) Required disclosures.
(4) Format.
(5) Notice.
(6) Access period.
(b) Applicability date.

§ 1.529A-8 Applicability dates and transition relief.
(a) Applicability dates.
(b) Transition relief.
(1) In general.
(2) Transition period.
(3) Compliance after transition period.

[Reg. § 1.529A-0.]

☐ [*T.D.* 9923, 11-18-2020.]

[Reg. § 1.529A-1]

§ 1.529A-1. Exempt status of qualified ABLE program and definitions.—(a) *In general.*—A qualified ABLE program described in section 529A is exempt from Federal income tax, except for the tax imposed under section 511 on any unrelated business taxable income of that program. See § 1.511-2(e).

(b) *Definitions.*—For purposes of section 529A, this section and § § 1.529A-2 through 1.529A-8—

(1) *ABLE account* means an account established under a qualified ABLE program and owned by the designated beneficiary of that account.

(2) *Contribution* means any payment directly allocated to an ABLE account for the benefit of a designated beneficiary, including amounts transferred to an ABLE account between December 22, 2017, and January 1, 2026, from a qualified tuition program described in section 529.

(3) *Designated beneficiary* means the individual for whom the account was established at a time when he or she was an eligible individual or who has succeeded the former designated beneficiary in that capacity (successor designated beneficiary). The designated beneficiary is the owner of the ABLE account. If the designated beneficiary is not able to exercise signature authority over his or her ABLE account or chooses to have an ABLE account established but not to exercise signature authority, references to the designated beneficiary with respect to his or her actions include actions by the person with signature authority over the account. See § 1.529A-2(c)(1) and (2).

(4) *Disability certification* means a certification to establish a certain level of an individual's physical or mental impairment that meets the requirements described in § 1.529A-2(e).

(5) *Distribution* means any payment from an ABLE account. However, a program-to-program transfer, a Medicaid reimbursement under § 1.529A-2(o), or a payment of administrative or investment fees charged by a qualified ABLE program is not a distribution.

(6) *Earnings* attributable to an ABLE account are the excess of the total account balance on a particular date over the investment in the account as of that date.

(7) *Earnings ratio* as applied to a particular distribution means the amount of earnings attributable to the ABLE account as of the date of the distribution, divided by the total account balance on that same date.

(8) *Eligible individual* for a taxable year means an individual who either:

(i) Is receiving benefits under title II or XVI of the Social Security Act based on blindness or disability or whose entitlement to such benefits under title XVI has been suspended solely due to excess income or resources, provided that such blindness or disability occurred before the date on which the individual attained age 26 (and, for this purpose, an individual is deemed to attain age 26 on his or her 26th birthday); or

(ii) Is the subject of a disability certification filed with the Secretary of the Treasury or his delegate (Secretary) for that taxable year.

(9) *Excess contribution* means the amount by which the amount contributed during the taxable year of the designated beneficiary to an ABLE account exceeds the limit in effect under section 2503(b) for the calendar year in which the taxable year of the designated beneficiary begins.

(10) *Excess aggregate contribution* means—

(i) The amount contributed during the taxable year of the designated beneficiary that causes the total of amounts contributed since the establishment of the ABLE account (or of an ABLE account for the same designated beneficiary that was rolled into the current ABLE account) to exceed the limit in effect under section 529(b)(6); or

(ii) In the context of the safe harbor in § 1.529A-2(g)(3), the amount contributed that causes the account balance to exceed the limit in effect under section 529(b)(6).

(11) *Investment in the account* means—

(i) The sum of all contributions made to the ABLE account, reduced by the aggregate amount of contributions included in distributions, if any, made from the account; or

(ii) In the case of a rollover contribution into an ABLE account, the amount of the rollover contribution that constituted the amount described in paragraph (b)(11)(i) of this section with respect to the ABLE account from which the rollover contribution was made.

(12) *Member of the family* means a sibling, whether by blood or by adoption, and includes a brother, sister, stepbrother, stepsister, half-brother, and half-sister.

(13) *Program-to-program transfer* means—

(i) The direct transfer of the entire balance of an ABLE account into an ABLE account of the same designated beneficiary after which the transferor ABLE account is closed upon completion of the transfer; or

(ii) The direct transfer of part or all of the balance to an ABLE account of another eligible individual who is a member of the family of the former designated beneficiary.

(14) *Qualified ABLE program* means a program established and maintained by a State, or agency or instrumentality of a State, under which an ABLE account may be established by and for the benefit of the account's designated beneficiary who is an eligible individual, and that meets the requirements described in §1.529A-2.

(15) *Qualified disability expenses* means any expenses incurred at a time when the designated beneficiary is an eligible individual that relate to the blindness or disability of the designated beneficiary of an ABLE account, including expenses that are for the benefit of the designated beneficiary in maintaining or improving his or her health, independence, or quality of life. See §1.529A-2(h). However, any expenses incurred at a time when a designated beneficiary is neither disabled nor blind within the meaning of §1.529A-1(b)(8)(i) or §1.529A-2(e)(1)(i), even if the designated beneficiary is an eligible individual for that entire taxable year, do not relate to blindness or disability and therefore are not qualified disability expenses.

(16) *Rollover* means a contribution to an ABLE account of a designated beneficiary (or of an eligible individual who is a member of the family of the designated beneficiary) of all or a portion of an amount distributed from the designated beneficiary's ABLE account, provided the contribution is made within 60 days of the date of the withdrawal and, in the case of a rollover to the designated beneficiary's ABLE account, no rollover has been made to an ABLE account of the designated beneficiary within the 12 month period immediately preceding the rollover to the ABLE account.

(c) *Applicability date.*—This section applies to calendar years beginning on or after January 1, 2021. See §1.529A-8 for the provision of transition relief. [Reg. §1.529A-1.]

☐ [*T.D.* 9923, 11-18-2020.]

[Reg. §1.529A-2]

§1.529A-2. Qualified ABLE program.—(a) *In general.*—A qualified ABLE program is a program established and maintained by a State, or an agency or instrumentality of a State, that satisfies all of the requirements of this section and under which—

(1) An ABLE account may be established for the purpose of meeting the qualified disability expenses of the designated beneficiary of the account;

(2) A designated beneficiary is limited to only one ABLE account at a time except as otherwise provided in paragraph (c)(3) of this section;

(3) Any person may make contributions to such an ABLE account, subject to the limitations described in paragraph (g) of this section; and

(4) Distributions (other than returns of contributions as described in paragraph (g)(4) of this section) may be made only to or for the benefit of the designated beneficiary of the ABLE account.

(b) *Established and maintained by a State or agency or instrumentality of a State.*—(1) *Established.*—A program is established by a State or its agency or instrumentality if the program is initiated by State statute or regulation or by an act of a State official or agency with the authority to act on behalf of the State.

(2) *Maintained.*—(i) *In general.*—A program is maintained by a State or an agency or instrumentality of a State if—

(A) The State or its agency or instrumentality sets all of the terms and conditions of the program, including but not limited to who may contribute to the program, who may be a designated beneficiary of the program, and what benefits the program may provide; and

(B) The State or its agency or instrumentality is actively involved on an ongoing basis in the administration of the program, including supervising the implementation of decisions relating to the investment of assets contributed under the program. Factors that are relevant in determining whether a State or its agency or instrumentality is actively involved in the administration of the program include, but are not limited to: whether the State or its agency or instrumentality provides services to designated beneficiaries that are not provided to persons who are not designated beneficiaries; whether the State or its agency or instrumentality establishes detailed operating rules for administering the program; whether officials of the State or its agency or instrumentality play a substantial role in the operation of the program, including selecting, supervising, monitoring, auditing, and terminating the relationship with any private contractors that provide services under the program; whether the State or its agency or instrumentality holds the private contractors that provide services under the program to the same standards and requirements that apply when private contractors handle funds that belong to the State or its agency or instrumentality or provide services to the State or its agency or instrumentality; whether the State or its agency or instrumentality provides funding for the program; and whether the State or its agency or instrumentality acts as trustee or holds program assets directly or for the benefit of the designated beneficiaries. For example, if the State or its agency or instrumentality exercises the same authority over the funds invested in the program as it does over the investments in or pool of funds of a State employees' defined benefit pension plan, then the State or its agency or instrumentality will be considered actively involved on an ongoing basis in the administration of the program.

(ii) *Multiple States, agencies, or instrumentalities.*—A program may be maintained by two or more States or the agencies or instrumentalities of two or more States if the program meets the requirements of paragraph (b)(2)(i) of this section for each of the States represented. If a State or an agency or instrumentality of a State participates in such a consortium of States or agencies or instrumentalities of States, the consortium's program is considered to be the program of each State represented.

(3) *Community Development Financial Institutions (CDFIs).*—In addition to having the ability to contract with private contractors as provided in paragraph (b)(2)(i)(B) of this section, a State or its agency or instrumentality or qualified ABLE program may contract with one or more Community Development Financial Institutions (CDFIs) (as defined in 12 U.S.C. 4702(5) and 12 CFR 1805.104) to perform some or all of the services described in paragraphs (b)(2)(i)(A) and (B) of this section.

(c) *Establishment of an ABLE account and signature authority.*—(1) *Establishment of the ABLE account.*—(i) *In general.*—A qualified ABLE program must provide that an ABLE account may be established only for an eligible individual.

(A) The ABLE account may be established by the eligible individual;

(B) The ABLE account may be established by a person selected by the eligible individual; or

(C) If an eligible individual (whether a minor or adult) is unable to establish his or her own ABLE account, an ABLE account may be established on behalf of the eligible individual by the eligible individual's agent under a power of attorney or, if none, by a conservator or legal guardian, spouse, parent, sibling, grandparent of the eligible individual, or a representative payee appointed for the eligible individual by the Social Security Administration (SSA), in that order.

(ii) *Authority.*—A qualified ABLE program may accept a certification, made under penalties of perjury, from the person seeking to establish an ABLE account as to the basis for the person's authority to establish the ABLE account, and that there is no other person with a higher priority, under paragraphs (c)(1)(i)(A), (B), and (C) of this section, to establish the ABLE account.

(2) *Signature authority.*—(i) *Signatory.*—In general, the designated beneficiary will have signature authority over his or her ABLE account. However, if an individual other than the designated beneficiary establishes the account in accordance with paragraph (c)(1)(i)(B) or (C) of this section, such individual will have signature authority.

(A) At any time, the designated beneficiary may remove and replace any person with signature authority over the designated beneficiary's ABLE account. The replacement may be the designated beneficiary or any other person selected by the designated beneficiary.

(B) The designated beneficiary may designate a successor to the person with signature authority. In the absence of any designation of a successor by the designated beneficiary, a person with signature authority over the designated beneficiary's ABLE account may designate a successor, consistent with the ordering rules in paragraph (c)(1)(i)(C) of this section.

(ii) *Co-signatories.*—A qualified ABLE program may permit an ABLE account to have co-signatories, consistent with paragraph (c)(1)(i)(C) of this section. If co-signatories are permitted, all of the other provisions of this paragraph (c)(2) continue to apply, and references to the *signatory* refer to the co-signatories acting separately or jointly, as determined by that qualified ABLE program.

(iii) *Authority over sub-accounts.*—The person with signature authority over the ABLE account may appoint and from time to time may remove, replace, or name a successor for any person with signature authority over a sub-account described in paragraph (c)(3)(iii) of this section.

(3) *Only one ABLE account.*—(i) *In general.*—Except as provided in paragraph (c)(3)(ii) of this section, a designated beneficiary is limited to one ABLE account at a time, regardless of where located. To ensure that this requirement is met, a qualified ABLE program must obtain a verification, signed under penalties of perjury by the person establishing the ABLE account, that the individual establishing the ABLE account neither knows nor has reason to know that the eligible individual already has an existing ABLE account (other than an ABLE account that will terminate with the rollover or program-to-program transfer of its assets into the new ABLE account) before that program can permit the establishment of an ABLE account for that eligible individual. In the case of a rollover, the ABLE account from which amounts were distributed must be closed as of the 60th day after the date of the distribution in order to allow the account receiving the rollover to be treated as an ABLE account.

(ii) *Treatment of additional accounts.*—If an individual is the designated beneficiary of an ABLE account established in accordance with paragraph (c)(1) of this section, no other account subsequently established for that individual under a qualified ABLE program (additional account) will be an ABLE account. The preceding sentence does not apply to an additional account, and that additional account is an ABLE account, if—

(A) The additional account is established for the purpose of receiving a rollover or program-to-program transfer;

(B) All of the contributions to the additional account are returned in accordance with the rules that apply to the return of excess contributions and excess aggregate contributions under paragraph (g)(4) of this section; or

(C) All amounts in the additional account are transferred to the designated beneficiary's preexisting ABLE account and any excess contributions and excess aggregate contributions are returned in accordance with the rules that apply to the return of excess contributions and excess aggregate contributions under paragraph (g)(4) of this section.

(iii) *Sub-accounts.*—A qualified ABLE program may establish an ABLE account (primary account) that may include multiple sub-accounts. The person with signature authority over the ABLE account, at any time and from time to time, may create one or more sub-accounts, may transfer funds in the ABLE account to one or more of the sub-accounts, and may close one or more of the sub-accounts, to facilitate the acquisition of certain goods or services for the designated beneficiary. Each sub-account may have a different person with signature authority over that sub-account, appointed in accordance with the rules of paragraph (c)(2)(iii) of this section, and that person's authority is limited to making distributions from that sub-account. The primary account and the sub-accounts collectively constitute a single ABLE account and therefore must be aggregated for all purposes, including without limitation the limit on the number of permissible changes in investment direction under paragraph (l) of this section, the contribution limits under paragraphs (g)(2) and (3) of this section, the computation of gross income and other tax provisions, and the reporting requirements.

(iv) *Investment options.*—A qualified ABLE program may offer different investment options within each ABLE account without violating the only-one-ABLE-account rule in this paragraph (c)(3). For example, an ABLE account may include a cash fund as well as one or more stock or bond funds.

(4) *Beneficial interest.*—A person other than the designated beneficiary with signature authority over the ABLE account of the designated beneficiary may neither have nor acquire any beneficial interest in the ABLE account during the lifetime of the designated beneficiary and must administer the ABLE account for the benefit of the designated beneficiary of the account.

(d) *Eligible individual.*—(1) *Documentation.*—(i) *In general.*—Whether an individual is an eligible individual is determined for each taxable year of that individual, and that determination applies for the entire year. A qualified ABLE program must specify the documentation that an individual must provide, both at the time an ABLE account is established and thereafter, in order to ensure that the designated beneficiary of the ABLE account is, and continues to be, determined an eligible individual. For purposes of determining whether an individual is an eligible individual, a disability certification as described in paragraph (e)(1) of this section will be deemed to be filed with the Secretary once the qualified ABLE program has received the disability certification or a disability certification has been deemed to have been received under the rules of the qualified ABLE program, which information the qualified ABLE program will file in accordance with the filing requirements under §1.529A-5(c)(2)(iv).

(ii) *Safe harbor.*—A qualified ABLE program may establish that an individual is an eligible individual if the person establishing the ABLE account certifies under penalties of perjury—

(A) The basis for the individual's status as an eligible individual (entitlement to benefits based on blindness or disability under title II or XVI of the Social Security Act, or a disability certification described in paragraph (e)(1) of this section);

(B) That the individual is blind or has a medically determinable physical or mental impairment as described in paragraph (e)(1)(i) of this section;

(C) That such blindness or disability occurred before the date on which the individual attained age 26 (and, for this purpose, an individual is deemed to attain age 26 on his or her 26th birthday);

(D) If the basis of the individual's eligibility is a disability certification, that the individual has received and agrees to retain a written diagnosis as described in paragraph (e)(1)(iii) of this section, accompanied by the name and address of the diagnosing physician and the date of the written diagnosis;

(E) The applicable diagnostic code from those listed on Form 5498-QA (or in the instructions to such form) identifying the type of the individual's impairment;

(F) That the person establishing the account is the individual who will be the designated beneficiary of the account or is the person authorized under paragraph (c)(1)(i) of this section to establish the account; and

(G) If required by the qualified ABLE program, the information provided by the diagnosing physician as to the categorization of the disability that may be used to determine, under the particular State's program, the appropriate frequency of required recertifications.

(2) *Frequency of recertification.*—(i) *In general.*—A determination of eligibility must be made annually unless the qualified ABLE program adopts a different method of ensuring a designated beneficiary's continuing status as an eligible individual. Alternative methods may include, without limitation, the use of certifications by the designated beneficiary under penalties of perjury, and the imposition of different recertification frequencies for different types of impairments.

(ii) *Considerations.*—In developing its rules on recertification, a qualified ABLE program may take into consideration whether an impairment is incurable and, if so, the likelihood that a cure may be found in the future. For example, a qualified ABLE program may provide that the initial certification will be deemed to be valid for a stated number of years, which may vary with the type of impairment. Even if the qualified ABLE program imposes an enforceable obligation on the designated beneficiary or other person with signature authority over the ABLE account to promptly report changes in the designated beneficiary's condition that would result in the designated beneficiary's failing to satisfy the definition of an eligible individual, the designated beneficiary will be considered an eligible individual until the end of the taxable year in which the change in the designated beneficiary's condition occurred. A qualified ABLE program that is compliant with the rules regarding recertification will not be considered to be noncompliant solely because a designated beneficiary fails to comply with this enforceable obligation.

(3) *Loss of qualification as an eligible individual.*—If the designated beneficiary of an ABLE account ceases to be an eligible individual, then for each taxable year in which the designated beneficiary is not an eligible individual, the account will continue to be an ABLE account, the designated beneficiary will continue to be the designated beneficiary of the ABLE account (and will be referred to as such), and the ABLE account will not be deemed to have been distributed. However, beginning on the first day of the designated beneficiary's first taxable year for which the designated beneficiary does not satisfy the definition of an eligible individual, additional contributions to the designated beneficiary's ABLE account must not be accepted by the qualified ABLE program. In addition, no expense incurred at a time when a designated beneficiary is neither disabled nor blind within the meaning of § 1.529A-1(b)(8)(i) or § 1.529A-2(e)(1)(i), whichever had applied, is a qualified disability expense even if the individual is an eligible individual for the rest of the year under paragraph (d)(1)(i) of this section. If the designated beneficiary subsequently again satisfies the definition of an eligible individual, contributions to the designated beneficiary's ABLE account again may be accepted, subject to the contribution limits under section 529A, and expenses that are incurred thereafter may meet the definition of a qualified disability expense in § 1.529A-1(b)(15) and paragraph (h) of this section.

(e) *Disability certification.*—(1) *In general.*—Except as provided in paragraph (e)(3) of this section or in additional guidance described in paragraph (e)(4) of this section, a disability certification with respect to an individual, that will be deemed filed with the Secretary as provided in paragraph (d)(1)(i) of this section, and is deemed satisfactory to the Secretary, is a certification signed under penalties of perjury by the individual, or by another individual establishing the ABLE account for the individual, that—

(i) Certifies that the individual—

(A) Has a medically determinable physical or mental impairment that results in marked and severe functional limitations (as defined in paragraph (e)(2) of this section), and that—

(1) Can be expected to result in death; or

(2) Has lasted or can be expected to last for a continuous period of not less than 12 months; or

(B) Is blind (within the meaning of section 1614(a)(2) of the Social Security Act);

(ii) Certifies that such blindness or disability occurred before the date on which the individual attained age 26 (and, for this purpose, an individual is deemed to attain age 26 on his or her 26th birthday); and

(iii) Includes a certification that the individual has obtained and will continue to retain a copy of the individual's diagnosis relating to the individual's relevant impairment or impairments, signed by a physician meeting the criteria of section 1861(r)(1) of the Social Security Act (42 U.S.C. 1395x(r)) and including the name and address of the diagnosing physician and the date of the diagnosis.

(2) *Marked and severe functional limitations.*—For purposes of paragraph (e)(1) of this section, the phrase *marked and severe functional limitations* means the standard of disability in the Social Security Act for children claiming Supplemental Security Income for the Aged, Blind, and Disabled (SSI) benefits based on disability (see 20 CFR 416.906), but without regard to age or to whether the individual engages in substantial gainful activity. Specifically, this is a level of severity that meets, medically equals, or functionally equals the severity of any listing in appendix 1 of subpart P of 20 CFR part 404. See 20 CFR 416.906, 416.924 and 416.926a. Such phrase also includes any impairment or standard of disability identified in future guidance published in the Internal Revenue Bulletin (see § 601.601(d)(2) of this chapter). Consistent with the regulations promulgated by the SSA, the level of severity is determined by taking into account the effect of the individual's prescribed treatment. See 20 CFR 416.930.

(3) *Compassionate allowance list.*—Conditions listed in the "List of Compassionate Allowances Conditions" maintained by the SSA are deemed to meet the requirements of section 529A(e)(1)(B) regarding the filing of a disability certification, if the condition was present and produced marked and severe functional limitations before the date on which the individual attained age 26. To establish that an individual with such a condition satisfies the definition of an eligible individual, the individual must identify the condition and certify to the qualified ABLE program both the presence of the condition and its resulting marked and severe functional limitations prior to age 26, in a manner specified by the qualified ABLE program.

(4) *Additional guidance.*—Additional guidance on conditions deemed to meet the require-

ments of section 529A(e)(1)(B) may be identified in future guidance published in the Internal Revenue Bulletin. See § 601.601(d)(2) of this chapter.

(5) *Restriction on use of certification.*—No inference may be drawn from a disability certification described in this paragraph (e) for purposes of establishing eligibility for benefits under title II, XVI, or XIX of the Social Security Act.

(f) *Change of designated beneficiary.*—(1) *In general.*—A qualified ABLE program must permit a change in the designated beneficiary of an ABLE account made during the life of the designated beneficiary. At the time when the change becomes effective, the successor designated beneficiary must be an eligible individual. However, a qualified ABLE program may limit the change in designated beneficiary to a member of the family as defined in § 1.529A-1(b)(12) of the current designated beneficiary.

(2) *Change effective upon death.*—A qualified ABLE program may permit a change in the designated beneficiary of an ABLE account, made during the life of the designated beneficiary, to take effect upon the death of the designated beneficiary. The amount to be transferred pursuant to such a beneficiary designation is first subject to the payment of any qualified disability expenses incurred before the designated beneficiary's death but not yet paid and those described in paragraph (o) of this section, and is subject to the provisions of § 1.529A-4.

(g) *Contributions.*—(1) *Permissible property.*—Except in the case of a program-to-program transfer or a change in designated beneficiary to a new designated beneficiary who is an eligible individual and a member of the family of the former designated beneficiary, contributions to an ABLE account may be made only in cash. A qualified ABLE program may allow cash contributions to be made in the form of a check, money order, credit card, electronic transfer, after-tax payroll deduction, or similar method.

(2) *Annual contributions limit.*—(i) *In general.*—Except as provided in paragraph (g)(2)(ii) of this section, a qualified ABLE program must provide that no contribution to an ABLE account will be accepted to the extent such contribution, when added to all other contributions (whether from the designated beneficiary or one or more other persons) to that ABLE account made during the designated beneficiary's taxable year causes the total of such contributions during that year to exceed the amount in effect under section 2503(b) for the calendar year in which the designated beneficiary's taxable year begins. See paragraph (k)(2) of this section for purposes of applying the rules in this paragraph (g)(2) to rollovers, program-to-program transfers, and designated beneficiary changes.

(ii) *Additional contributions by an employed designated beneficiary.*—(A) *In general.*—An employed designated beneficiary defined in paragraph (g)(2)(iii)(A) of this section may contribute amounts up to the limit specified in paragraph (g)(2)(ii)(B) of this section in addition to the amount specified in paragraph (g)(2)(i) of this section. Although a designated beneficiary's contributions subject to this compensation income limit do not have to be made from that compensation income, any contribution of the designated beneficiary's compensation income made directly by the designated beneficiary's employer is a contribution made by the designated beneficiary. Once the designated beneficiary has made contributions equal to the limit described in paragraph (g)(2)(ii)(B) of this section, additional contributions by the designated beneficiary may be made if permissible under paragraph (g)(2)(i) of this section.

(B) *Amount of additional permissible contribution.*—Any additional contribution made by the designated beneficiary pursuant to paragraph (g)(2)(ii)(A) of this section is limited to the lesser of—

(1) The designated beneficiary's compensation as defined by section 219(f)(1) for the taxable year; or

(2) An amount equal to the applicable poverty line, as defined in paragraph (g)(2)(iii)(B) of this section, for a one-person household for the calendar year preceding the calendar year in which the designated beneficiary's taxable year begins.

(iii) *Additional definitions.*—In addition to the definitions in § 1.529A-1(b), the following definitions also apply for the purposes of this section—

(A) *Employed designated beneficiary* means a designated beneficiary who is an employee (including an employee within the meaning of section 401(c)), with respect to whom no contribution is made for the taxable year to—

(1) A defined contribution plan (within the meaning of section 414(i)) with respect to which the requirements of sections 401(a) or 403(a) are met;

(2) An annuity contract described in section 403(b); and

(3) An eligible deferred compensation plan described in section 457(b).

(B) *Applicable poverty line* means the amount provided in the poverty guidelines updated periodically in the **Federal Register** by the U.S. Department of Health and Human Services under the authority of 42 U.S.C. 9902(2) for the State of residence of the employed designated beneficiary. If the designated beneficiary lives in more than one State during the taxable year, the applicable poverty line is the poverty line for the State in which the designated beneficiary resided longer than in any other State during that year.

(C) *Excess compensation contribution* means the amount by which the amount contributed during the taxable year of an employed designated beneficiary to the designated beneficiary's ABLE account exceeds the limit in effect under section 529A(b)(2)(B)(ii) and paragraph (g)(2)(ii)(B) of this section for the calendar year in which the taxable year of the employed designated beneficiary begins.

(iv) *Example.*—The provisions of paragraph (g)(2)(ii) of this section may be illustrated by the following example: In 2020, A, an employed designated beneficiary as defined in paragraph (g)(2)(iii)(A) of this section, lives in Hawaii. A's compensation, as defined by section 219(f)(1), for 2020 is $20,000. The poverty line for a one-person household in Hawaii was $14,380 in 2019. Because A's compensation exceeded the applicable poverty line amount, A's additional permissible contribution in 2019 is limited to $14,380, the amount of the 2019 applicable poverty line.

(v) *Ensuring contribution limit is met.*—(A) *Responsibility.*—The employed designated beneficiary, or the person acting on his or her behalf, is solely responsible for ensuring that the requirements in section 529A(b)(2)(B)(ii) and paragraph (g)(2)(ii) of this section are met and for maintaining adequate records for that purpose.

(B) *Certification.*—A qualified ABLE program may allow a designated beneficiary (or the person acting on his or her behalf) to certify, under penalties of perjury, and in the manner specified by the qualified ABLE program that—

(1) The designated beneficiary is an employed designated beneficiary; and

(2) The designated beneficiary's contributions of compensation are not excess compensation contributions.

(3) *Cumulative limit.*—(i) *In general.*—A qualified ABLE program must provide adequate safeguards to prevent aggregate contributions on behalf of a designated beneficiary in excess of the limit established by that State under section 529(b)(6). For purposes of the preceding sentence, aggregate contributions on behalf of a designated beneficiary include contributions to any prior ABLE account maintained by any State or its agency or instrumentality for the same designated beneficiary, or any former designated beneficiary to the extent his or her ABLE account funds were transferred to the designated beneficiary's ABLE account. The transfer of a designated beneficiary's ABLE account from one qualified ABLE program to another with a lower cumulative limit will not violate this rule, but qualified ABLE programs must prohibit subsequent contributions under this general rule. For purposes of this paragraph (g)(3), contributions do not include rollovers, program-to-program transfers or a designated beneficiary change to a new designated beneficiary who is an eligible individual and member of the family of the former designated beneficiary as defined in § 1.529A-1(b)(12).

(ii) *Safe harbor.*—A qualified ABLE program maintained by a State or its agency or instrumentality satisfies the requirement under section 529A(b)(6) if it refuses to accept any additional contribution to an ABLE account (except as provided to the contrary in paragraph (g)(3)(i) of this section) while the balance in that account equals or exceeds the limit established by that State under section 529(b)(6). Nevertheless, without regard to the categories of transfers that caused the account balance to exceed the State limit, once the account balance falls below that limit, additional contributions, subject to the annual contributions limit under paragraph (g)(2) of this section and the limit established by such State under section 529(b)(6), again may be accepted.

(4) *Return of excess contributions, excess compensation contributions, and excess aggregate contributions.*—If an excess contribution as defined in § 1.529A-1(b)(9), an excess compensation contribution as defined in paragraph (g)(2)(iii)(C) of this section, or an excess aggregate contribution as defined in § 1.529A-1(b)(10) is deposited into or allocated to the ABLE account of a designated beneficiary, a qualified ABLE program must return that excess contribution, excess compensation contribution, or excess aggregate contribution, including all net income attributable to that contribution, as determined under the rules set forth in § 1.408-11 (treating references to an IRA as references to an ABLE account and references to returned contributions under section 408(d)(4) as references to excess contributions or excess aggregate contributions), to the person or persons who made that contribution. Each excess contribution, excess compensation contribution, and excess aggregate contribution must be returned to its contributor(s) on a last-in-first-out basis until the entire excess, along with all net income attributable to such excess, has been returned. In the case of an excess compensation contribution, the employed designated beneficiary, or the person acting on the employed designated beneficiary's behalf, is responsible for identifying any excess compensation contribution and for requesting the return of the excess compensation contribution. Returned contributions must be received by the contributor(s) on or before the due date (including extensions) of the Federal income tax return of the designated beneficiary for the taxable year in which the excess contribution or excess aggregate contribution was made. See § 1.529A-3(a) for Federal income tax considerations for the contributor(s). If an excess contribution or excess aggregate contribution and the net income attributable to the excess contribution or excess aggregate contribution are returned to a contributor other than the designated beneficiary, the qualified ABLE program must notify the designated beneficiary of such return at the time of the return. No notification is required if amounts are rejected by the qualified ABLE program before they are deposited into or allocated to the designated beneficiary's ABLE account.

(5) *Restriction of contributors.*—A qualified ABLE program may allow the designated beneficiary, from time to time, to restrict who may make contributions to the designated beneficiary's ABLE account.

(h) *Qualified disability expenses.*—(1) *In general.*—Qualified disability expenses are expenses incurred that relate to the blindness or disability of the designated beneficiary of the ABLE account and are for the benefit of that designated beneficiary in maintaining or improving his or her health, independence, or quality of life. See § 1.529A-1(b)(15). Such expenses include, but are not limited to, expenses related to the designated beneficiary's education, housing, transportation, employment training and support, assistive technology and related services, personal support services, health, prevention and wellness, financial management and administrative services, legal fees, expenses for oversight and monitoring, and funeral and burial expenses, as well as other expenses that may be identified from time to time in future guidance published in the Internal Revenue Bulletin. See § 601.601(d)(2) of this chapter. Qualified disability expenses include basic living expenses and are not limited to items for which there is a medical necessity or which solely benefit an individual with a disability.

(2) *Example*.—The following example illustrates this paragraph (h): B, an individual, has a medically determined mental impairment that causes marked and severe limitations on B's ability to navigate and communicate. A smart phone would enable B to navigate and communicate more safely and effectively, thereby helping B to maintain B's independence and to improve B's quality of life. Therefore, the expense of buying, using, and maintaining a smart phone that is used by B would be a qualified disability expense.

(i) *Separate accounting*.—A program will not be treated as a qualified ABLE program unless it provides separate accounting for each ABLE account. Separate accounting requires that contributions for the benefit of a designated beneficiary and any earnings attributable thereto must be allocated to that designated beneficiary's ABLE account. Whether or not a program provides each designated beneficiary an annual account statement showing the total account balance, the investment in the account, the accrued earnings, and the distributions from the account, the program must give this information to the designated beneficiary upon request.

(j) *Program-to-program transfers*.—A qualified ABLE program may permit a change of qualified ABLE program or a change of designated beneficiary by means of a program-to-program transfer as defined in § 1.529A-1(b)(13). In that event, subject to any contrary provisions or limitations adopted by the qualified ABLE program, rules similar to the rules of § 1.401(a)(31)-1, Q&A-3 and 4 (which apply for purposes of a direct rollover from a qualified plan to an eligible retirement plan) apply for purposes of determining whether an amount is paid in the form of a program-to-program transfer.

(k) *Carryover of attributes*.—(1) *In general*.—Upon a rollover, program-to-program transfer, or change of designated beneficiary, all of the attributes of the former ABLE account relevant for purposes of calculating the investment in the account are applicable to the recipient ABLE account. The portion of the rollover or transfer amount that constituted investment in the account from which the distribution or transfer was made is added to investment in the recipient ABLE account. In addition, the portion of the rollover or transfer amount that constituted earnings of the account from which the distribution or transfer was made is added to the earnings of the recipient ABLE account.

(2) *Annual contribution limit*.—Upon a rollover or program-to-program transfer, for purposes of applying the annual contribution limit under paragraph (g)(2) of this section to the transferee account, annual contributions to the designated beneficiary's transferor ABLE account during the taxable year in which the rollover or program-to-program transfer occurs are included. However, upon a change of designated beneficiary, or upon a rollover or program-to-program transfer to the ABLE account of a different designated beneficiary who is both a member of the family as defined in § 1.529A-1(b)(12) and an eligible individual, no amounts contributed to the prior designated beneficiary's ABLE account are included when applying the annual contribution limit under paragraph (g)(2) of this section.

(3) *Investment direction limit*.—Upon a rollover or program-to-program transfer, the number of investment directions by the designated beneficiary include the number of investment directions made prior to the rollover or program-to-program transfer during the same taxable year for purposes of paragraph (l) of this section. However, upon a change of designated beneficiary, or upon a rollover or program-to-program transfer to the ABLE account of a different designated beneficiary who is both a member of the family as defined in § 1.529A-1(b)(12) and an eligible individual, the number of investment directions made for the prior designated beneficiary's ABLE account are not included in determining the number of investment directions made for the new designated beneficiary's ABLE account in that same year.

(l) *Investment direction*.—A program will not be treated as a qualified ABLE program unless it provides that the designated beneficiary of an ABLE account established under such program may direct, whether directly or indirectly, the investment of any contributions to the program (or any earnings thereon) no more than two times in any calendar year. Such an investment direction does not include a request to transfer any part of the account balance from an investment option to a cash equivalent option to effectuate a distribution, or the automatic rebalancing of the assets of an ABLE account to maintain the asset allocation level chosen when the account was established or by a subsequent investment direction.

(m) *No pledging of interest as security for a loan*.—A program will not be treated as a qualified ABLE program unless the terms of the program, or a State statute or regulation that governs the program, prohibit any interest in the program or any portion thereof from being used as security for a loan. For this purpose, the program administrator's advance of funds to satisfy a withdrawal request during the period between the sale of an asset in the ABLE account (whose value is sufficient to satisfy the withdrawal request) and the clearing or settlement of that sale, does not constitute a loan, pledge, or grant of security for a loan. Similarly, the use of checking accounts or debit cards to facilitate a qualified ABLE program's ability to make distributions will not be treated as a pledge or grant of security for a loan during the period between the use of the check or debit card and the clearing or settlement of that transaction, provided that the ABLE program does not advance funds to a designated beneficiary in excess of the amount in the designated beneficiary's ABLE account.

(n) *No sale or exchange*.—A qualified ABLE program must ensure that no interest in an ABLE account may be sold or exchanged.

(o) *Post-death payments*.—A qualified ABLE program must provide that a portion or all of the balance remaining in the ABLE account of a deceased designated beneficiary must be distributed to a State that files a claim against the designated beneficiary or the ABLE account itself with respect to benefits provided to the designated beneficiary under that State's Medicaid plan established under title XIX of the Social Security Act. The payment of such claim (if any) will be made only after providing for the payment from the designated beneficiary's ABLE account of the designated beneficiary's funeral and burial expenses (including the unpaid balance of a pre-death contract for those services) and all outstanding payments due for his or her other qualified disability expenses, and will be limited to the amount of the total medical assistance paid for the designated beneficiary after the establishment of the ABLE account over the amount of any premiums paid, whether from the ABLE account or otherwise by or on behalf of the designated beneficiary, to a Medicaid Buy-In program under any such State Medicaid plan. The establishment of the ABLE account is the date on which the ABLE account was established or, if earlier, the date on which was established any ABLE account for the same designated beneficiary from which amounts were rolled over or transferred to the ABLE account, but in no event earlier than the date on which the designated beneficiary became the designated beneficiary of the account from which amounts were transferred. After the expiration of the applicable statute of limitations for filing Medicaid claims against the designated beneficiary's estate, a qualified ABLE program may distribute the balance of the ABLE account to the successor designated beneficiary or, if none, to the deceased designated beneficiary's estate. A State law prohibiting the filing of such a claim against either the ABLE account or the designated beneficiary's estate will not prevent that State's program from being a qualified ABLE program.

(p) *Reporting requirements*.—A qualified ABLE program must comply with all applicable reporting requirements, including without limitation those described in §§1.529A-5 through 1.529A-7.

(q) *Applicability date*.—This section applies to calendar years beginning on or after January 1, 2021. See §1.529A-8 for the provision of transition relief. [Reg. §1.529A-2.]

☐ [*T.D.* 9923, 11-18-2020.]

[Reg. §1.529A-3]

§1.529A-3. Tax treatment.—(a) *Taxation of distributions*.—(1) *In general*.—Each distribution from an ABLE account consists of an earnings portion of the account (computed in accordance with paragraph (c) of this section) and investment in the account. If the total amount distributed from an ABLE account to or for the benefit of the designated beneficiary of that ABLE account during his or her taxable year does not exceed the qualified disability expenses of the designated beneficiary paid during that year, no amount distributed is includible in the gross income of the designated beneficiary for that year. If the total amount distributed from an ABLE account to or for the benefit of the designated beneficiary of that ABLE account during his or her taxable year exceeds the qualified disability expenses of the designated beneficiary paid during that year (regardless of when incurred), the distributions from the ABLE account, except to the extent excluded from gross income under this section or any other provision of chapter 1 of the Internal Revenue Code, must be included in the gross income of the designated beneficiary in the manner provided under this section and section 72. The amount to be included in gross income is based on the earnings portion of each distribution, computed in accordance with paragraph (c) of this section. The earnings portion that is includible in gross income is the sum of the earnings portion of all distributions made in that year, reduced by an amount that bears the same ratio to the total earnings portion as the amount of qualified disability expenses paid during the year bears to such total distributions during the year. If an excess contribution or excess aggregate contribution is returned within the time period required in §1.529A-2(g)(4), any net income distributed is includible in the gross income of the contributor(s) in the taxable year in which the excess contribution or excess aggregate contribution was made.

(2) *Additional period*.—The designated beneficiary may treat as having been paid during the preceding taxable year qualified disability expenses paid on or before the 60th day immediately following the end of the designated beneficiary's preceding taxable year. Qualified disability expenses treated, pursuant to the rule in the preceding sentence, as having been paid during the designated beneficiary's taxable year immediately prior to the year of their actual payment may not be included in the total qualified disability expenses for the year in which they were paid.

(b) *Additional exclusions from gross income*.—(1) *Rollover*.—A rollover as defined in

§ 1.529A-1(b)(16) is not included in gross income under paragraph (a) of this section.

(2) *Program-to-program transfers.*—A program-to-program transfer as defined in § 1.529A-1(b)(13) is not a distribution and is not included in gross income under paragraph (a) of this section.

(3) *Change of designated beneficiary.*—(i) *In general.*—A change of designated beneficiary of an ABLE account is not treated as a distribution for purposes of section 529A, and is not included in gross income under paragraph (a) of this section, if the successor designated beneficiary is—

(A) An eligible individual for the taxable year in which the change is made; and

(B) A member of the family (as defined in § 1.529A-1(b)(12)) of the former designated beneficiary.

(ii) *Other designated beneficiary changes.*—In the case of any change of designated beneficiary not described in paragraph (b)(3)(i) of this section, the former designated beneficiary of that ABLE account will be treated as having received a distribution of the fair market value of the assets in that ABLE account on the date on which the change is made to the new designated beneficiary.

(4) *Payments to creditors post-death.*—Distributions made after the death of the designated beneficiary in payment of outstanding obligations due for qualified disability expenses, as well as the funeral and burial expenses of the designated beneficiary, are not included in gross income of the designated beneficiary or his or her estate. Included among these obligations is the post-death payment of any part of a claim filed against the deceased designated beneficiary or his or her estate or ABLE account by a State with respect to benefits provided to the designated beneficiary under that State's Medicaid plan.

(c) *Computation of earnings.*—The earnings portion of a distribution is equal to the product of the amount of the distribution and the earnings ratio, as defined in § 1.529A-1(b)(7). The balance of the distribution (the amount of the distribution minus the earnings portion of that distribution) is the portion of that distribution that constitutes the return of investment in the account.

(d) *Additional tax on amounts includible in gross income.*—(1) *In general.*—If any amount of a distribution from an ABLE account is includible in the gross income of a person for any taxable year under paragraph (a) of this section (includible amount), the income tax imposed on that person by chapter 1 of the Internal Revenue Code will be increased by an amount equal to 10 percent of the includible amount.

(2) *Exceptions.*—(i) *Distributions on or after the death of the designated beneficiary.*—Paragraph (d)(1) of this section does not apply to any distribution made from the ABLE account on or after the death of the designated beneficiary to the estate of the designated beneficiary, to an heir or legatee of the designated beneficiary, or to a creditor described in paragraph (b)(4) of this section.

(ii) *Returned excess contributions and additional accounts.*—Paragraph (d)(1) of this section does not apply to any return made in accordance with § 1.529A-2(g)(4) of an excess contribution as defined in § 1.529A-1(b)(9), an excess compensation contribution as defined in § 1.529A-2(g)(2)(iii)(C), excess aggregate contribution as defined in § 1.529A-1(b)(10), or an additional account as referenced in § 1.529A-2(c)(3)(ii)(A), (B), or (C).

(e) *Tax on excess contributions.*—Under section 4973(h), a contribution to an ABLE account in excess of the annual contributions limit described in § 1.529A-2(g)(2) is subject to an excise tax in an amount equal to 6 percent of the excess contribution. However, any the excess contribution or excess compensation contribution as defined in § 1.529A-2(g)(2)(iii)(C) returned in accordance with the provisions of § 1.529A-2(g)(4) is not treated as a contribution.

(f) *Filing requirements.*—A qualified ABLE program is not required to file Form 990, "Return of Organization Exempt From Income Tax," Form 1041, "U.S. Income Tax Return for Estates and Trusts," or Form 1120, "U.S. Corporation Income Tax Return." However, a qualified ABLE program is required to file Form 990-T, "Exempt Organization Business Income Tax Return," if such filing would be required under the rules of §§ 1.6012-2(e) and 1.6012-3(a)(5) if the ABLE program were an organization described in those sections.

(g) *No inference outside section 529A.*—The rules provided in this section concerning the Federal tax treatment of contributions apply only for purposes of the application of section 529A. No inference is intended with respect to the application of any other Code provisions or Federal tax doctrines. For example, a contribution made by an employer to the ABLE account of an employee or an employee's family member is subject to the rules governing the Federal taxation of compensation.

(h) *Applicability date.*—This section applies to calendar years beginning on or after January 1, 2021. See § 1.529A-8 for the provision of transition relief. [Reg. § 1.529A-3.]

☐ [*T.D.* 9923, 11-18-2020.]

[Reg. § 1.529A-4]

§ 1.529A-4. Gift, estate, and generation-skipping transfer taxes.—(a) *Contributions.*—(1) *In general.*—Each contribution by a person to an ABLE account other than by the designated beneficiary of that account is treated as a completed gift to the designated beneficiary of the account for gift tax purposes. Under the applicable Federal gift tax rules, a contribution from a corporation, partnership, trust, estate, or other entity is treated as a gift by the shareholders, partners, or other beneficial owners in proportion to their respective ownership interests in the entity. See § 25.2511-1(c) and (h) of this chapter. A gift to an ABLE account is not treated as either a gift of a future interest in property, or a qualified transfer under section 2503(e). To the extent a contributor's gifts to the designated beneficiary, including gifts paid into the designated beneficiary's ABLE account, do not exceed the annual limit in section 2503(b), the contribution is not a taxable gift. This provision, however, does not change any other provision applicable to the transfer. For example, a contribution by the employer of the designated beneficiary's parent continues to constitute earned income to the parent and then a gift by the parent to the designated beneficiary. The timely return of an excess contribution or an excess aggregate contribution in accordance with § 1.529A-2(g)(4) is not a taxable gift.

(2) *Generation-skipping transfer (GST) tax.*—To the extent the contribution into an ABLE account is a nontaxable gift for Federal gift tax purposes, the inclusion ratio for purposes of the GST tax will be zero pursuant to section 2642(c)(1).

(3) *Designated beneficiary as contributor.*—A designated beneficiary may make a contribution to fund his or her own ABLE account. That contribution is not a gift.

(b) *Distributions.*—No distribution from an ABLE account to or for the benefit of the designated beneficiary is treated as a taxable gift to that designated beneficiary.

(c) *Transfer to another designated beneficiary.*—Neither gift tax nor generation-skipping transfer tax applies to the transfer (by rollover, program-to-program transfer, or change of beneficiary) of part or all of an ABLE account to the ABLE account of a different designated beneficiary if the successor designated beneficiary is both an eligible individual and a member of the family (as described in § 1.529A-1(b)(12)) of the designated beneficiary. Any other transfer will constitute a gift by the designated beneficiary to the successor designated beneficiary, and the usual gift and GST tax rules will apply.

(d) *Transfer tax on death of designated beneficiary.*—Upon the death of the designated beneficiary, the designated beneficiary's ABLE account is includible in his or her gross estate for estate tax purposes under section 2031. The payment of outstanding qualified disability expenses and the payment of certain claims made by a State under its Medicaid plan may be deductible for estate tax purposes if the requirements of section 2053 are satisfied.

(e) *Applicability date.*—This section applies to calendar years beginning on or after January 1, 2021. See § 1.529A-8 for the provision of transition relief. [Reg. § 1.529A-4.]

☐ [*T.D.* 9923, 11-18-2020.]

[Reg. § 1.529A-5]

§ 1.529A-5. Reporting of the establishment of and contributions to an ABLE account.—(a) *In general.*—A filer defined in paragraph (b)(1) of this section must, with respect to each ABLE account—

(1) File an annual information return, as described in paragraph (c) of this section, with the Internal Revenue Service; and

(2) Furnish an annual statement, as described in paragraph (d) of this section, to the designated beneficiary of the ABLE account.

(b) *Additional definitions.*—In addition to the definitions in § 1.529A-1(b), the following definitions also apply for purposes of this section—

(1) *Filer* means the State or its agency or instrumentality that establishes and maintains the qualified ABLE program under which an ABLE account is established. The filing may be done by either an officer or employee of the State or its agency or instrumentality having control of the qualified ABLE program, or the officer's or employee's designee.

(2) *TIN* means taxpayer identification number as defined in section 7701(a)(41).

(c) *Requirement to file return.*—(1) *Form of return.*—For purposes of reporting the information described in paragraph (c)(2) of this section, the filer must file Form 5498-QA, "ABLE Account Contribution Information," or any successor form, together with Form 1096, "Annual Summary and Transmittal of U.S. Information Returns."

(2) *Information included on return.*—With respect to each ABLE account, the filer must include on the return—

(i) The name, address, and TIN of the designated beneficiary of the ABLE account;

(ii) The name, address, and TIN of the filer;

(iii) Information regarding the establishment of the ABLE account, as required by the form and its instructions;

(iv) Information regarding the disability certification or other basis for eligibility of the designated beneficiary, as required by the form and its instructions. For further information regarding eligibility and disability certification, see § 1.529A-2(d) and (e), respectively;

(v) The total amount of any contributions made with respect to the ABLE account during the calendar year; such contributions do not include any contribution rejected and returned to the contributor before being deposited into or allocated to the ABLE account or any excess contributions, excess compensation contributions, or excess aggregate contributions returned as described in § 1.529A-2(g)(4);

(vi) The fair market value of the ABLE account as of the last day of the calendar year; and

(vii) Any other information required by the form, its instructions, or published guidance. See §§ 601.601(d) and 601.602 of this chapter.

(3) *Time and manner of filing return.*—(i) *In general.*—Except as provided in paragraph (c)(3)(ii) of this section, the information returns required under this paragraph must be filed on or before May 31 of the year following the calen-

dar year with respect to which the return is being filed, in accordance with the forms and their instructions.

(ii) *Extensions of time.*—See §§1.6081-1 and 1.6081-8 for rules relating to extensions of time to file information returns required in this section.

(iii) *Electronic filing.*—See §301.6011-2 of this chapter for rules relating to electronic filing. See also Instructions for Forms 1099-QA and 5498-QA, Distributions From ABLE Accounts and ABLE Account Contribution Information.

(iv) *Substitute forms.*—The filer may file the returns required under this paragraph (c) on an acceptable substitute form. See Publication 1179, "General Rules and Specifications for Substitute Forms 1096, 1098, 1099, 5498, and Certain Other Information Returns."

(d) *Requirement to furnish statement.*—(1) *In general.*—The filer must furnish a statement to the designated beneficiary of the ABLE account for which it is required to file a Form 5498-QA (or any successor form). The statement must include—

(i) The information required under paragraph (c)(2) of this section;

(ii) A legend that identifies the statement as important tax information that is being furnished to the Internal Revenue Service; and

(iii) The name and address of the office or department of the filer that is the information contact for questions regarding the ABLE account to which the Form 5498-QA relates.

(2) *Time and manner of furnishing statement.*—(i) *In general.*—Except as provided in paragraph (d)(2)(ii) of this section, the filer must furnish the statement described in paragraph (d)(1) of this section to the designated beneficiary on or before March 15 of the year following the calendar year with respect to which the statement is being furnished. If mailed, the statement must be sent to the designated beneficiary's last known address. The statement may be furnished electronically, as provided in §1.529A-7.

(ii) *Extensions of time.*—The Internal Revenue Service may, at its discretion, grant an extension of time to furnish statements required in this section.

(3) *Copy of Form 5498-QA.*—The filer may satisfy the requirement of this paragraph (d) by furnishing either a copy of Form 5498-QA (or successor form) or an acceptable substitute form. See Publication 1179, "General Rules and Specifications for Substitute Forms 1096, 1098, 1099, 5498, and Certain Other Information Returns."

(e) *Request for TIN of designated beneficiary.*—The filer must request the TIN of the designated beneficiary at the time the ABLE account is established if the filer does not already have a record of the designated beneficiary's correct TIN. The filer must clearly notify the designated beneficiary that the law requires the designated beneficiary to furnish a TIN so that it may be included on an information return to be filed by the filer. The designated beneficiary may provide his or her TIN in any manner including orally, in writing, or electronically. If the TIN is furnished in writing, no particular form is required. Form W-9, "Request for Taxpayer Identification Number and Certification," may be used, or the request may be incorporated into the forms related to the establishment of the ABLE account.

(f) *Penalties.*—(1) *Failure to file return.*—The section 6693 penalty may apply to the filer that fails to file information returns at the time and in the manner required by this section, unless it is shown that such failure is due to reasonable cause. See section 6693 and §301.6693-1 of this chapter.

(2) *Failure to furnish TIN.*—The section 6723 penalty may apply to any designated beneficiary who fails to furnish his or her TIN to the filer. See section 6723, and §301.6723-1 of this chapter, for rules relating to the penalty for failure to furnish a TIN.

(g) *Applicability date.*—The rules of this section apply to information returns required to be filed, and payee statements required to be furnished, after December 31, 2020. See §1.529A-8 for the provision of transition relief. [Reg. §1.529A-5.]

□ [*T.D.* 9923, 11-18-2020.]

[Reg. §1.529A-6]

§1.529A-6. Reporting of distributions from and termination of an ABLE account.—(a) *In general.*—The filer as defined in §1.529A-5(b)(1) must, with respect to each ABLE account from which any distribution is made or which is terminated during the calendar year—

(1) File an annual information return, as described paragraph (b) of this section, with the Internal Revenue Service; and

(2) Furnish an annual statement, as described in paragraph (c) of this section, to the designated beneficiary of the ABLE account and to each contributor who received a returned contribution in accordance with §1.529A-2(g)(4) attributable to the calendar year.

(b) *Requirement to file return.*—(1) *Form of return.*—For purposes of reporting the information in paragraph (b)(2) of this section, the filer must file Form 1099-QA, "Distributions From ABLE Accounts," or any successor form, together with Form 1096, "Annual Summary and Transmittal of U.S. Information Returns."

(2) *Information included on return.*—The filer must include on the return—

(i) The name, address, and TIN of the recipient of the payment, whether the designated beneficiary of the ABLE account or any contributor who received a returned contribution in accordance with §1.529A-2(g)(4) attributable to the calendar year;

(ii) The name, address, and TIN of the filer;

(iii) Whether the return is being filed with respect to the designated beneficiary or to a contributor;

(iv) The aggregate amount of distributions or returned contributions (including net income attributable to the returned contributions) from the ABLE account to the recipient during the calendar year;

(v) Information as to basis and earnings with respect to such distributions or returns of contributions;

(vi) Information regarding termination (if any) of the ABLE account if the recipient is the designated beneficiary;

(vii) Information regarding each program-to-program transfer from the ABLE account during the designated beneficiary's taxable year; and

(viii) Any other information required by the form, its instructions, or published guidance. See § § 601.601(d) and 601.602 of this chapter.

(3) *Information excluded.*—A State filing a claim against the estate or ABLE account of a deceased designated beneficiary with respect to benefits provided to the designated beneficiary under that State's Medicaid plan is a creditor, and not a beneficiary, so the payment of the claim is not a distribution from the ABLE account and should not be reported as such on the Form 1099-QA for that year.

(4) *Time and manner of filing return.*—(i) *In general.*—Except as provided in paragraph (b)(4)(ii) of this section, the Forms 1099-QA and 1096 must be filed on or before February 28 (March 31 if filing electronically) of the year following the calendar year with respect to which the return is being filed, in accordance with the forms and their instructions.

(ii) *Extensions of time.*—See § § 1.6081-1 and 1.6081-8 for rules relating to extensions of time to file information returns required in this section.

(iii) *Electronic filing.*—See § 301.6011-2 of this chapter for rules relating to electronic filing. See also Instructions for Forms 1099-QA and 5498-QA, Distributions From ABLE Accounts and ABLE Account Contribution Information.

(iv) *Substitute forms.*—The filer may file the return required under this paragraph (b) on an acceptable substitute form. See Publication 1179, "General Rules and Specifications for Substitute Forms 1096, 1098, 1099, 5498, and Certain Other Information Returns."

(c) *Requirement to furnish statement.*—(1) *In general.*—The filer must furnish a statement to the designated beneficiary and each contributor (if any) of the ABLE account for which it is required to file a Form 1099-QA (or any successor form). The statement must include—

(i) The information required under paragraph (b)(2) of this section.

(ii) A legend that identifies the statement as important tax information that is being furnished to the Internal Revenue Service; and

(iii) The name and address of the office or department of the filer that is the information contact for questions regarding the ABLE account to which the Form 1099-QA relates.

(2) *Time and manner of furnishing statement.*—(i) *In general.*—Except as provided in paragraph (c)(2)(ii) of this section, a filer must furnish the statement described in paragraph (c)(1) of this section to the designated beneficiary or contributor on or before January 31 of the year following the calendar year with respect to which the statement is being furnished. If mailed, the statement must be sent to the recipient's last known address. The statement may be furnished electronically, as provided in § 1.529A-7.

(ii) *Extensions of time.*—The Internal Revenue Service may, at its discretion, grant an extension of time to furnish statements required in this section.

(3) *Copy of Form 1099-QA.*—A filer may satisfy the requirement of this paragraph (c) by furnishing either a copy of Form 1099-QA (or successor form) or an acceptable substitute form. See Publication 1179, "General Rules and Specifications for Substitute Forms 1096, 1098, 1099, 5498, and Certain Other Information Returns."

(d) *Request for TIN of contributor(s).*—(1) *In general.*—Except as provided in paragraph (d)(2) of this section, a filer must request the TIN of each contributor to the ABLE account at the time a contribution is made, if the filer does not already have a record of that person's correct TIN.

(2) *Exception.*—If the filer has a system in place to identify and reject amounts that either would constitute an excess contribution or excess aggregate contribution (as defined in § 1.529A-1(b)(9) or (10), respectively) or were contributed to an additional ABLE account as described in § 1.529A-2(c)(3)(ii)(C) (excess amounts) before those excess amounts are deposited into or allocated to an ABLE account, the filer need not request the TIN of each contributor at the time of contribution. A filer with such a system must request a contributor's TIN only if and when an excess contribution or excess aggregate contribution nevertheless is deposited into or allocated to an account and the filer must return the excess amounts including net income to the contributor. The filer must clearly notify each such contributor to the account that the law requires that person to furnish a TIN so that it may be included on an information return to be filed by the filer. The contributor may provide his or her TIN in any manner including orally, in writing, or electronically. If the TIN is furnished in writing, no particular form is required. Form W-9, "Request for Taxpayer Identification Number and Certification," may be used, or the request may be incorporated into the forms related to the establishment of the ABLE account.

(e) *Penalties.*—(1) *Failure to file return.*—The section 6693 penalty may apply to a filer that fails to file information returns at the time and in the manner required by this section, unless it is shown that such failure is due to reasonable cause. See section 6693 and § 301.6693-1 of this chapter.

(2) *Failure to furnish TIN.*—The section 6723 penalty may apply to any contributor who fails to furnish his or her TIN to the filer in accordance with paragraph (d) of this section. See section 6723, and § 301.6723-1 of this chapter, for rules relating to the penalty for failure to furnish a TIN.

(f) *Applicability date.*—The rules of this section apply to information returns required to be filed, and payee statements required to be furnished, after December 31, 2020. See § 1.529A-8 for the provision of transition relief. [Reg. § 1.529A-6.]

☐ [*T.D.* 9923, 11-18-2020.]

[Reg. § 1.529A-7]

§ 1.529A-7. Electronic furnishing of statements to designated beneficiaries and contributors.—(a) *Electronic furnishing of statements.*—(1) *In general.*—A filer required under § 1.529A-5 or § 1.529A-6 to furnish a written statement to a designated beneficiary of or contributor to an ABLE account may furnish the statement in an electronic format in lieu of a paper format. A filer who meets the requirements of paragraphs (a)(2) through (6) of this section is treated as furnishing the required statement.

(2) *Consent.*—(i) *In general.*—The recipient of the statement must have affirmatively consented to receive the statement in an electronic format. The consent may be made electronically in any manner that reasonably demonstrates that the recipient can access the statement in the electronic format in which it will be furnished to the recipient. Alternatively, the consent may be made in a paper document if it is confirmed electronically.

(ii) *Withdrawal of consent.*—The consent requirement of this paragraph (a)(2) is not satisfied if the recipient withdraws the consent and the withdrawal takes effect before the statement is furnished. The filer may provide that a withdrawal of consent takes effect either on the date it is received by the filer or on another date no more than 60 days later. The filer also may provide that a request for a paper statement will be treated as a withdrawal of consent.

(iii) *Change in hardware or software requirements.*—If a change in the hardware or software required to access the statement creates a material risk that the recipient will not be able to access the statement, the filer must, prior to changing the hardware or software, provide the recipient with a notice. The notice must describe the revised hardware and software required to access the statement and inform the recipient that a new consent to receive the statement in the revised electronic format must be provided to the filer if the recipient does not want to withdraw the consent. After implementing the revised hardware and software, the filer must obtain from the recipient, in the manner described in paragraph (a)(2)(i) of this section, a new consent or confirmation of consent to receive the statement electronically.

(iv) *Examples.*—For purposes of the following examples that illustrate the rules of this paragraph (a)(2), assume that the requirements of § 1.529A-7(a)(3) have been met:

(A) *Example 1.*—Filer F sends Recipient R a letter stating that R may consent to receive statements required under § 1.529A-5 or § 1.529A-6 electronically on a website instead of in a paper format. The letter contains instructions explaining how to consent to receive the statements electronically by accessing the website, downloading the consent document, completing the consent document, and e-mailing the completed consent back to F. The consent document posted on the website uses the same electronic format that F will use for the electronically furnished statements. R reads the instructions and submits the consent in the manner provided in the instructions. R has consented to receive the statements electronically in the manner described in paragraph (a)(2)(i) of this section.

(B) *Example 2.*—Filer F sends Recipient R an e-mail stating that R may consent to receive statements required under § 1.529A-5 or § 1.529A-6 electronically instead of in a paper format. The e-mail contains an attachment instructing R how to consent to receive the statements electronically. The e-mail attachment uses the same electronic format that F will use for the electronically furnished statements. R opens the attachment, reads the instructions, and submits the consent in the manner provided in the instructions. R has consented to receive the statements electronically in the manner described in paragraph (a)(2)(i) of this section.

(C) *Example 3.*—Filer F posts a notice on its website stating that Recipient R may receive statements required under § 1.529A-5 or § 1.529A-6 electronically instead of in a paper format. The website contains instructions on how R may access a secure web page and consent to receive the statements electronically. By accessing the secure web page and giving consent, R has consented to receive the statements electronically in the manner described in paragraph (a)(2)(i) of this section.

(3) *Required disclosures.*—(i) *In general.*—Prior to, or at the time of, a recipient's consent, the filer must provide to the recipient a clear and conspicuous disclosure statement containing each of the disclosures described in paragraphs (a)(3)(ii) through (viii) of this section.

(ii) *Paper statement.*—The recipient must be informed that the statement will be furnished on paper if the recipient does not consent to receive it electronically.

(iii) *Scope and duration of consent.*—The recipient must be informed of the scope and duration of the consent. For example, the recipient must be informed whether the consent applies to statements furnished every year after the consent is given until it is withdrawn in the manner described in paragraph (a)(3)(v)(A) of this section, or only to the statement required to be furnished on or before the due date immediately following the date on which the consent is given.

(iv) *Post-consent request for a paper statement.*—The recipient must be informed of any procedure for obtaining a paper copy of the recipient's statement after giving the consent and whether a request for a paper statement will be treated as a withdrawal of consent.

(v) *Withdrawal of consent.*—The recipient must be informed that—

(A) The recipient may withdraw a consent by writing (electronically or on paper) to the person or department whose name, mailing address, and e-mail address is provided in the disclosure statement;

(B) The filer will confirm, in writing (electronically or on paper), the withdrawal and the date on which it takes effect; and

(C) A withdrawal of consent does not apply to a statement that was furnished electronically in the manner described in this paragraph (a) before the date on which the withdrawal of consent takes effect.

(vi) *Notice of termination.*—The recipient must be informed of the conditions under which a filer will cease furnishing statements electronically to the recipient.

(vii) *Updating information.*—The recipient must be informed of the procedures for updating the information needed by the filer to contact the recipient. The filer must inform the recipient of any change in the filer's contact information.

(viii) *Hardware and software requirements.*—The recipient must be provided with a description of the hardware and software required to access, print, and retain the statement, and the date when the statement will no longer be available on the website.

(4) *Format.*—The electronic version of the statement must contain all required information. See Publication 1179, "General Rules and Specifications for Substitute Forms 1096, 1098, 1099, 5498, and Certain Other Information Returns."

(5) *Notice.*—(i) *In general.*—If the statement is furnished on a website, the filer must notify the recipient that the statement is posted on a website. The notice may be delivered by mail, electronic mail, or in person. The notice must provide instructions on how to access and print the statement. The notice must include the following statement in capital letters, "IMPORTANT TAX RETURN DOCUMENT AVAILABLE." If the notice is provided by electronic mail, the foregoing statement must be in the subject line of the electronic mail.

(ii) *Undeliverable electronic address.*—If an electronic notice described in paragraph (a)(5)(i) of this section is returned as undeliverable, and the correct electronic address cannot be obtained from the filer's records or from the recipient, then the filer must furnish the notice by mail or in person within 30 days after the electronic notice is returned.

(iii) *Corrected statements.*—If the filer has corrected a recipient's statement that was furnished electronically, the filer must furnish the corrected statement to the recipient electronically. If the recipient's statement was furnished through a website posting and the filer has corrected the statement, the filer must notify the recipient that it has posted the corrected statement on the website within 30 days of such posting in the manner described in paragraph (a)(5)(i) of this section. The corrected statement or the notice must be furnished by mail or in person if—

(A) An electronic notice of the website posting of an original statement or the corrected statement was returned as undeliverable; and

(B) The recipient has not provided a new e-mail address.

(6) *Access period.*—Statements furnished on a website must be retained on the website through October 15 of the year following the calendar year to which the statements relate (or the first business day after such October 15 if October 15 falls on a Saturday, Sunday, or legal holiday). The filer must maintain access to corrected statements that are posted on the website through October 15 of the year following the calendar year to which the statements relate (or the first business day after such October 15 if October 15 falls on a Saturday, Sunday, or legal holiday) or the date 90 days after the corrected statements are posted, whichever is later. The rules in this paragraph (a)(6) do not replace the filer's obligation to keep records under section 6001 and § 1.6001-1(a).

(b) *Applicability date.*—This section applies to statements required to be furnished after December 31, 2020. See § 1.529A-8 for the provision of transition relief. [Reg. § 1.529A-7.]

☐ [*T.D.* 9923, 11-18-2020.]

[Reg. § 1.529A-8]

§ 1.529A-8. Applicability dates and transition relief.—(a) *Applicability dates.*—Except as otherwise provided in paragraph (b) of this section, § § 1.529A-1 through 1.529A-4 apply for calendar years beginning on or after January 1, 2021, § § 1.529A-5 and 1.529A-6 apply to information returns required to be filed, and payee statements required to be furnished, after December 31, 2020, and § 1.529A-7 applies to statements required to be furnished after December 31, 2020.

(b) *Transition relief.*—(1) *In general.*—Any program purporting to be a qualified ABLE program will not be disqualified during the transition period set forth in paragraph (b)(2) of this section (transition period) solely because of noncompliance with one or more provisions of § § 1.529A-1 through 1.529A-7, provided that the program is established and operated in accordance with a reasonable, good faith interpretation of section 529A. Similarly, no ABLE account established and maintained under a program that meets the requirements of this paragraph will fail to qualify as an ABLE account during the transition period. However, to be a qualified

ABLE program and an ABLE account under such a program after the transition period, the program and each account established and maintained under the program must be in compliance with §§1.529A-1 through 1.529A-7 by the end of the transition period. In no event, however, will a complete failure to file and furnish reports, information returns and payee statements required under section 529A(d)(1) for any accounts established and maintained under the program (including for calendar years beginning prior to January 1, 2021), be deemed to be due to reasonable cause for purposes of avoiding penalties imposed under section 6693.

(2) *Transition period.*—For purposes of paragraph (b)(1) of this section, the transition period begins with the establishment of the program purporting to be a qualified ABLE program and continues through the later of—

(i) November 21, 2022; or

(ii) The day immediately preceding the first day of the qualified ABLE program's first taxable year beginning after the close of the first regular session of the State legislature that begins after November 19, 2020. If a State has a two-year legislative session, each calendar year of such session will be deemed to be a separate regular session of the State legislature for purposes of this paragraph.

(3) *Compliance after transition period.*—After the transition period, a program and an account established and maintained under that program must be in compliance with §§1.529A-1 through 1.529A-7. [Reg. §1.529A-8.]

☐ [*T.D.* 9923, 11-18-2020.]

ESTATES, TRUSTS, BENEFICIARIES, AND DECEDENTS

Estates, Trusts, and Beneficiaries

[Reg. §1.641(a)-0]

§1.641(a)-0. Scope of subchapter J.—(a) *In general.*—Subchapter J (sections 641 and following), chapter 1 of the Code, deals with the taxation of income of estates and trusts and their beneficiaries, and of income in respect of decedents. Part I of subchapter J contains general rules for taxation of estates and trusts (subpart A), specific rules relating to trusts which distribute current income only (subpart B), estates and trusts which may accumulate income or which distribute corpus (subpart C), treatment of excess distributions by trusts (subpart D), grantors and other persons treated as substantial owners (subpart E), and miscellaneous provisions relating to limitations on charitable deductions, income of an estate or trust in case of divorce, and taxable years to which the provisions of subchapter J are applicable (subpart F). Part I has no application to any organization which is not to be classified for tax purposes as a trust under the classification rules of §§301.7701-2, 301.7701-3 and 301.7701-4 of this chapter (Regulations on Procedure and Administration). Part II of subchapter J relates to the treatment of income in respect of decedents. However, the provisions of subchapter J do not apply to employee trusts subject to subchapters D and F, chapter 1 of the Code, and common trust funds subject to subchapter H, chapter 1 of the Code.

(b) *Scope of Subparts A, B, C, and D.*—Subparts A, B, C, and D (sections 641 and following), part I, subchapter J, chapter 1 of the Code, relate to the taxation of estates and trusts and their beneficiaries. These subparts have no application to any portion of the corpus or income of a trust which is to be regarded, within the meaning of the Code, as that of the grantor or others treated as its substantial owners. See subpart E (sections 671 and following), part I, subchapter J, chapter 1 of the Code, and the regulations thereunder for rules for the treatment of any portion of a trust where the grantor (or another person) is treated as the substantial owner. So-called alimony trusts are treated under subparts A, B, C, and D, except to the extent otherwise provided in section 71 or section 682. These subparts have no application to beneficiaries of nonexempt employees' trusts. See section 402(b) and the regulations thereunder.

(c) *Multiple trusts.*—Multiple trusts that have—

(1) No substantially independent purposes (such as independent dispositive purposes),

(2) The same grantor and substantially the same beneficiary, and

(3) The avoidance or mitigation of *(a)* the progressive rates of tax (including mitigation as a result of deferral of tax) or *(b)* the minimum tax for tax preferences imposed by section 56 as their principal purpose, shall be consolidated and treated as one trust for the purposes of subchapter J. [Reg. §1.641(a)-0.]

☐ [*T.D.* 6217, 12-19-56. *Amended by T.D.* 6989, 1-16-69 *and by T.D.* 7204, 8-24-72.]

[Reg. §1.641(a)-1]

§1.641(a)-1. Imposition of tax; application of tax.—For taxable years beginning after December 31, 1970, section 641 prescribes that the taxes imposed by section 1(d), as amended by the Tax Reform Act of 1969, shall apply to the income of estates or of any kind of property held in trust. For taxable years ending before January 1, 1971, section 641 prescribes that the taxes imposed upon individuals by chapter 1 of the Code apply to the income of estates or of any kind of property held in trust. The rates of tax, the statutory provisions respecting gross income, and, with certain exceptions, the deductions and credits allowed to individuals apply also to estates and trusts. [Reg. §1.641(a)-1.]

☐ [*T.D.* 6217, 12-19-56. *Amended by T.D.* 7117, 5-24-71.]

[Reg. § 1.641(a)-2]

§ 1.641(a)-2. Gross income of estates and trusts.—The gross income of an estate or trust is determined in the same manner as that of an individual. Thus, the gross income of an estate or trust consists of all items of gross income received during the taxable year, including:

(a) Income accumulated in trust for the benefit of unborn or unascertained persons or persons with contingent interests;

(b) Income accumulated or held for future distribution under the terms of the will or trust;

(c) Income which is to be distributed currently by the fiduciary to the beneficiaries, and income collected by a guardian of an infant which is to be held or distributed as the court may direct;

(d) Income received by estates of deceased persons during the period of administration or settlement of the estate; and

(e) Income which, in the discretion of the fiduciary, may be either distributed to the beneficiaries or accumulated.

The several classes of income enumerated in this section do not exclude others which also may come within the general purposes of section 641. [Reg. § 1.641(a)-2.]

☐ [*T.D.* 6217, 12-19-56.]

[Reg. § 1.641(b)-1]

§ 1.641(b)-1. Computation and payment of tax; deductions and credits of estates and trusts.—Generally, the deductions and credits allowed to individuals are also allowed to estates and trusts. However, there are special rules for the computation of certain deductions and for the allocation between the estate or trust and the beneficiaries of certain credits and deductions. See section 642 and the regulations thereunder. In addition, an estate or trust is allowed to deduct, in computing its taxable income, the deductions provided by sections 651 and 661 and regulations thereunder, relating to distributions to beneficiaries. [Reg.§ 1.641(b)-1.]

☐ [*T.D.* 6217, 12-19-56.]

[Reg. § 1.641(b)-2]

§ 1.641(b)-2. Filing of returns and payment of the tax.—(a) The fiduciary is required to make and file the return and pay the tax on the taxable income of an estate or of a trust. Liability for the payment of the tax on the taxable income of an estate attaches to the person of the executor or administrator up to and after his discharge if, prior to distribution and discharge, he had notice of his tax obligations or failed to exercise due diligence in ascertaining whether or not such obligations existed. For the extent of such liability, see section 3467 of the Revised Statutes, as amended by section 518 of the Revenue Act of 1934 (31 U.S.C. 192). Liability for the tax also follows the assets of the estate distributed to heirs, devisees, legatees, and distributees, who may be required to discharge the amount of the tax due and unpaid to the extent of the distributive shares received by them. See section 6901. The same considerations apply to trusts.

(b) The estate of an infant, incompetent, or other person under a disability, or, in general, of an individual or corporation in receivership or a corporation in bankruptcy is not a taxable entity separate from the person for whom the fiduciary is acting, in that respect differing from the estate of a deceased person or of a trust. See section 6012(b)(2) and (3) for provisions relating to the obligation of the fiduciary with respect to returns of such persons. [Reg. § 1.641(b)-2.]

☐ [*T.D.* 6217, 12-19-56. *Amended by T.D.* 6580, 12-4-61.]

[Reg. § 1.641(b)-3]

§ 1.641(b)-3. Termination of estates and trusts.—(a) The income of an estate of a deceased person is that which is received by the estate during the period of administration or settlement. The period of administration or settlement is the period actually required by the administrator or executor to perform the ordinary duties of administration, such as the collection of assets and the payment of debts, taxes, legacies, and bequests, whether the period required is longer or shorter than the period specified under the applicable local law for the settlement of estates. For example, where an executor who is also named as trustee under a will fails to obtain his discharge as executor, the period of administration continues only until the duties of administration are complete and he actually assumes his duties as trustee, whether or not pursuant to a court order. However, the period of administration of an estate cannot be unduly prolonged. If the administration of an estate is unreasonably prolonged, the estate is considered terminated for Federal income tax purposes after the expiration of a reasonable period for the performance by the executor of all the duties of administration. Further, an estate will be considered as terminated when all the assets have been distributed except for a reasonable amount which is set aside in good faith for the payment of unascertained or contingent liabilities and expenses (not including a claim by a beneficiary in the capacity of beneficiary). Notwithstanding the above, if the estate has joined in making a valid election under section 645 to treat a qualified revocable trust, as defined under section 645(b)(1), as part of the estate, the estate shall not terminate under this paragraph prior to the termination of the section 645 election period. See section 645 and the regulations thereunder for rules regarding the termination of the section 645 election period.

(b) Generally, the determination of whether a trust has terminated depends upon whether the property held in trust has been distributed to the persons entitled to succeed to the property upon termination of the trust rather than upon the technicality of whether or not the trustee has rendered his final accounting. A trust does not automatically terminate upon the happening of the event by which the duration of the trust is measured. A reasonable time is permitted after such event for the trustee to perform the duties necessary to complete the administration of the trust. Thus, if under the terms of the governing instrument, the trust is to terminate upon the death of the life beneficiary and the corpus is to be distributed to the remainderman, the trust continues after the death of the life beneficiary for a period reasonably necessary to a proper winding up of the affairs of the trust. However, the winding up of a trust cannot be unduly postponed and if the distribution of the trust corpus is unreasonably delayed, the trust is considered terminated for Federal income tax purposes after the expiration of a reasonable period for the trustee to complete the administration of the trust. Further, a trust will be considered as terminated when all the assets have been distributed except for a reasonable amount which is set aside in good faith for the payment of unascertained or contingent liabilities and expenses (not including a claim by a beneficiary in the capacity of beneficiary).

(c)(1) Except as provided in subparagraph (2) of this paragraph, during the period between the occurrence of an event which causes a trust to terminate and the time when the trust is considered as terminated under this section, whether or not the income and the excess of capital gains over capital losses of the trust are to be considered as amounts required to be distributed currently to the ultimate distributee for the year in which they are received depends upon the principles stated in § 1.651(a)-2. See § 1.663 *et seq.* for application of the separate share rule.

(2)(i) Except in cases to which the last sentence of this subdivision applies, for taxable years of a trust ending before September 1, 1957, subparagraph (1) of this paragraph shall not apply and the rule of subdivision (ii) of this subparagraph shall apply unless the trustee elects to have subparagraph (1) of this paragraph apply. Such election shall be made by the trustee in a statement filed on or before April 15, 1959, with the district director with whom such trust's return for any such taxable year was filed. The election provided by this subdivision shall not be available if the treatment given the income and the excess of capital gains over capital losses for taxable years for which returns have been filed was consistent with the provisions of subparagraph (1) of this paragraph.

(ii) The rule referred to in subdivision (i) of this subparagraph is as follows: During the period between the occurrence of an event which causes a trust to terminate and the time when a trust is considered as terminated under this section, the income and the excess of capital gains over capital losses of the trust are in general considered as amounts required to be distributed for the year in which they are received. For example, a trust instrument provides for the payment of income to A during her life, and upon her death for the payment of the corpus to B. The trust reports on the basis of the calendar year. A dies on November 1, 1955, but no distribution is made to B until January 15, 1956. The income of the trust and the excess of capital gains over capital losses for the entire year 1955, to the extent not paid, credited, or required to be distributed to A or A's estate, are treated under sections 661 and 662 as amounts required to be distributed to B for the year 1955.

(d) If a trust or the administration or settlement of an estate is considered terminated under this section for Federal income tax purposes (as for instance, because administration has been unduly prolonged), the gross income, deductions, and credits of the estate or trust are, subsequent to the termination, considered the gross income, deductions, and credits of the person or persons succeeding to the property of the estate or trust. [Reg. § 1.641(b)-3.]

☐ [*T.D.* 6217, 12-19-56. *Amended by T.D.* 6353, 1-13-59; *T.D.* 6462, 5-5-60 *and T.D.* 9032, 12-23-2002.]

[Reg. § 1.641(c)-0]

§ 1.641(c)-0. Table of contents.—This section lists the major captions contained in § 1.641(c)-1.

§ 1.641(c)-1 Electing small business trust.

[Reg. § 1.641(c)-0.]

☐ [*T.D.* 8994, 5-13-2002.]

[Reg. § 1.641(c)-1]

§ 1.641(c)-1. Electing small business trust.—(a) *In general.*—An electing small business trust (ESBT) within the meaning of section 1361(e) is treated as two separate trusts for purposes of chapter 1 of the Internal Revenue Code. The portion of an ESBT that consists of stock in one or more S corporations is treated as one trust. The portion of an ESBT that consists of all the other assets in the trust is treated as a separate trust. The grantor or another person may be treated as the owner of all or a portion of either or both such trusts under subpart E, part I, subchapter J, chapter 1 of the Internal Revenue Code. The ESBT is treated as a single trust for administrative purposes, such as having one taxpayer identification number and filing one tax return. See § 1.1361-1(m).

(b) *Definitions.*—(1) *Grantor portion.*—(i) *In general.*—Subject to paragraph (b)(1)(ii) of this section, the grantor portion of an ESBT is the portion of the trust that is treated as owned by the grantor or another person under subpart E of the Code.

(ii) *Nonresident alien deemed owner.*—If, pursuant to section 672(f)(2)(A)(ii), the deemed owner of a grantor portion of the ESBT is a nonresident alien, as defined in section 7701(b)(1)(B) (NRA), the items of income, deduction, and credit from that grantor portion must be reallocated from the grantor portion to the S portion, as defined in paragraph (b)(2) of this section, of the ESBT.

(2) *S portion.*—(i) *In general.*—Subject to paragraph (b)(2)(ii) of this section, the S portion of an ESBT is the portion of the trust that consists of S corporation stock and that is not treated as owned by the grantor or another person under subpart E of the Code.

(ii) *Nonresident alien (NRA) deemed owner of grantor portion.*—The S portion of an ESBT also includes the grantor portion of the items of income, deduction, and credit reallocated under paragraph (b)(1)(ii) of this section from the grantor portion of the ESBT to the S portion of the ESBT.

(3) *Non-S portion.*—The non-S portion of an ESBT is the portion of the trust that consists of all assets other than S corporation stock and that is not treated as owned by the grantor or another person under subpart E.

(c) *Taxation of grantor portion.*—The grantor or another person who is treated as the owner of a portion of the ESBT includes in computing taxable income items of income, deductions, and credits against tax attributable to that portion of the ESBT under section 671.

(d) *Taxation of S portion.*—(1) *In general.*—The taxable income of the S portion is determined by taking into account only the items of income, loss, deduction, or credit specified in paragraphs (d)(2), (3), and (4) of this section, to the extent not attributable to the grantor portion.

(2) *Section 1366 amounts.*—(i) *In general.*—The S portion takes into account the items of income, loss, deduction, or credit that are taken into account by an S corporation shareholder pursuant to section 1366 and the regulations thereunder. Rules otherwise applicable to trusts apply in determining the extent to which any loss, deduction, or credit may be taken into account in determining the taxable income of the S portion. See § 1.1361-1(m)(3)(iv) for allocation of those items in the taxable year of the S corporation in which the trust is an ESBT for part of the year and an eligible shareholder under section 1361(a)(2)(A)(i) through (iv) for the rest of the year.

(ii) *Special rule for charitable contributions.*—If a deduction described in paragraph (d)(2)(i) of this section is attributable to an amount of the S corporation's gross income that is paid by the S corporation for a charitable purpose specified in section 170(c) (without regard to section 170(c)(2)(A)), the contribution will be deemed to be paid by the S portion pursuant to the terms of the trust's governing instrument within the meaning of section 642(c)(1). The limitations of section 681, regarding unrelated business income, apply in determining whether the contribution is deductible in computing the taxable income of the S portion.

(iii) *Multiple S corporations.*—If an ESBT owns stock in more than one S corporation, items of income, loss, deduction, or credit from all the S corporations are aggregated for purposes of determining the S portion's taxable income.

(3) *Gains and losses on disposition of S stock.*—(i) *In general.*—The S portion takes into account any gain or loss from the disposition of S corporation stock. No deduction is allowed under section 1211(b)(1) and (2) for capital losses that exceed capital gains.

(ii) *Installment method.*—If income from the sale or disposition of stock in an S corporation is reported by the trust on the installment method, the income recognized under this method is taken into account by the S portion. See paragraph (g)(3) of this section for the treatment of interest on the installment obligation. See § 1.1361-1(m)(5)(ii) regarding treatment of a trust as an ESBT upon the sale of all S corporation stock using the installment method.

(iii) *Distributions in excess of basis.*—Gain recognized under section 1368(b)(2) from distributions in excess of the ESBT's basis in its S corporation stock is taken into account by the S portion.

(4) *State and local income taxes and administrative expenses.*—(i) *In general.*—State and local income taxes and administrative expenses directly related to the S portion and those allocated to that portion in accordance with paragraph (h) are taken into account by the S portion.

(ii) *Special rule for certain interest.*—Interest paid by the trust on money borrowed by the trust to purchase stock in an S corporation is allocated to the S portion but is not a deductible administrative expense for purposes of determining the taxable income of the S portion.

(e) *Tax rates and exemption of S portion.*—(1) *Income tax rate.*—Except for capital gains, the highest marginal trust rate provided in section 1(e) is applied to the taxable income of the S portion. See section 1(h) for the rates that apply to the S portion's net capital gain.

(2) *Alternative minimum tax exemption.*—The exemption amount of the S portion under section 55(d) is zero.

(f) *Adjustments to basis of stock in the S portion under section 1367.*—The basis of S corporation stock in the S portion must be adjusted in accordance with section 1367 and the regulations thereunder. If the ESBT owns stock in more than one S corporation, the adjustments to the basis in the S corporation stock of each S corporation must be determined separately with respect to each S corporation. Accordingly, items of income, loss, deduction, or credit of an S corporation that are taken into account by the ESBT under section 1366 can only result in an adjustment to the basis of the stock of that S corporation and cannot affect the basis in the stock of the other S corporations held by the ESBT.

(g) *Taxation of non-S portion.*—(1) *In general.*—The taxable income of the non-S portion is determined by taking into account all items of income, deduction, and credit to the extent not taken into account by either the grantor portion or the S portion. The items attributable to the non-S portion are taxed under subparts A through D of part I, subchapter J, chapter 1 of the Internal Revenue Code. The non-S portion may consist of more than one share pursuant to section 663(c).

(2) *Dividend income under section 1368(c)(2).*—Any dividend income within the meaning of section 1368(c)(2) is includible in the gross income of the non-S portion.

(3) *Interest on installment obligations.*—If income from the sale or disposition of stock in an S corporation is reported by the trust on the installment method, the interest on the installment obligation is includible in the gross income of the non-S portion. See paragraph (d)(3)(ii) of this section for the treatment of income from such a sale or disposition.

(4) *Charitable deduction.*—For purposes of applying section 642(c)(1) to payments made by the trust for a charitable purpose, the amount of gross income of the trust is limited to the gross income of the non-S portion. See paragraph (d)(2)(ii) of this section for special rules concerning charitable contributions paid by the S corporation that are deemed to be paid by the S portion.

(h) *Allocation of state and local income taxes and administration expenses.*—Whenever state and local income taxes or administration expenses relate to more than one portion of an ESBT, they must be allocated between or among the portions to which they relate. These items may be allocated in any manner that is reasonable in light of all the circumstances, including the terms of the governing instrument, applicable local law, and the practice of the trustee with respect to the trust if it is reasonable and consistent. The taxes and expenses apportioned to each portion of the ESBT are taken into account by that portion.

(i) *Treatment of distributions from the trust.*—Distributions to beneficiaries from the S portion or the non-S portion, including distributions of the S corporation stock, are deductible under section 651 or 661 in determining the taxable income of the non-S portion, and are includible in the gross income of the beneficiaries under section 652 or 662. However, the amount of the deduction or inclusion cannot exceed the amount of the distributable net income of the non-S portion. Items of income, loss, deduction, or credit taken into account by the grantor portion or the S portion are excluded for purposes of determining the distributable net income of the non-S portion of the trust.

(j) *Termination or revocation of ESBT election.*—If the ESBT election of the trust terminates pursuant to § 1.1361-1(m)(5) or the ESBT election is revoked pursuant to § 1.1361-1(m)(6), the rules contained in this section are thereafter not applicable to the trust. If, upon termination or revocation, the S portion has a net operating loss under section 172; a capital loss carryover under section 1212; or deductions in excess of gross income; then any such loss, carryover, or excess deductions shall be allowed as a deduction, in accordance with the regulations under section 642(h), to the trust, or to the beneficiaries succeeding to the property of the trust if the entire trust terminates.

(k) *Applicability date.*—This section generally is applicable for taxable years of ESBTs beginning on and after May 14, 2002. However, paragraphs (a), (b), (c), and (l)(1) (*Example 1*) of this section are applicable for taxable years of ESBTs that end on and after December 29, 2000. ESBTs may apply paragraphs (d)(4) and (h) of this section for taxable years of ESBTs beginning after December 31, 1996. Paragraphs (b)(1) and (2) of this section, and *Example 6* in paragraph (l)(6) of this section, apply to all ESBTs after December 31, 2017.

(l) *Examples.*—The following examples illustrate the rules of this section:

(1) *Examples 1. Comprehensive example.*—(i) Trust has a valid ESBT election in effect. Under section 678, *B* is treated as the owner of a portion of Trust consisting of a 10% undivided fractional interest in Trust. No other person is treated as the owner of any other portion of Trust under subpart E. Trust owns stock in *X*, an S corporation, and in *Y*, a C corporation. During 2000, Trust receives a distribution from *X* of $5,100, of which $5,000 is applied against Trust's adjusted basis in the *X* stock in accordance with section 1368(c)(1) and $100 is a dividend under section 1368(c)(2). Trust makes no distributions to its beneficiaries during the year.

(ii) For 2000, Trust has the following items of income and deduction:

Table 1 to paragraph (l)(1)(ii)

Ordinary income attributable to *X* under section 1366	$5,000
Dividend income from *Y*	$900
Dividend from *X* representing C corporation earnings and profits	$100
Total trust income	$6,000
Charitable contributions attributable to *X* under section 1366	$300
Trustee fees	$200
State and local income taxes	$100

(iii) Trust's items of income and deduction are divided into a grantor portion, an S portion, and a non-S portion for purposes of determining the taxation of those items. Income is allocated to each portion as follows:

(A) *B* must take into account the items of income attributable to the grantor portion, that is, 10% of each item, as follows:

Table 2 to paragraph (l)(1)(iii)(A)

Ordinary income from *X*	$500
Dividend income from *Y*	$90
Dividend income from *X*	$10
Total grantor portion income	$600

(B) The total income of the S portion is $4,500, determined as follows:

Table 3 to paragraph (l)(1)(iii)(B)

Ordinary income from *X*	$5,000
Less: Grantor portion	($500)
Total S portion income	$4,500

(C) The total income of the non-S portion is $900 determined as follows:

Table 4 to paragraph (l)(1)(iii)(C)

Dividend income from *Y* (less grantor portion)	$810
Dividend income from *X* (less grantor portion)	$90
Total non-S portion income	$900

(iv) The administrative expenses and the state and local income taxes relate to all three portions and under state law would be allocated ratably to the $6,000 of trust income. Thus, these items would be allocated 10% (600/6000) to the grantor portion, 75% (4500/6000) to the S portion and 15% (900/6000) to the non-S portion.

(v) *B* must take into account the following deductions attributable to the grantor portion of the trust:

Table 5 to paragraph (l)(1)(v)

Charitable contributions from *X*	$30
Trustee fees	$20
State and local income taxes	$10

(vi) The taxable income of the S portion is $4,005, determined as follows:

Table 6 to paragraph (l)(1)(vi)

Ordinary income from *X*	$4,500
Less: Charitable contributions from *X* (less grantor portion)	($270)
75% of trustee fees	($150)
75% of state and local income taxes	($75)
Taxable income of S portion	$4,005

(vii) The taxable income of the non-S portion is $755, determined as follows:

Table 7 to paragraph (l)(1)(vii)

Dividend income from *Y*	$810
Dividend income from *X*	$90

Total non-S portion income	$900
Less: 15% of trustee fees	($30)
15% state and local income taxes	($15)
Personal exemption	($100)
Taxable income of non-S portion	$755

(2) *Examples 2. Sale of S stock.*—Trust has a valid ESBT election in effect and owns stock in *X*, an S corporation. No person is treated as the owner of any portion of Trust under subpart E. In 2003, Trust sells all of its stock in *X* to a person who is unrelated to Trust and its beneficiaries and realizes a capital gain of $5,000. This gain is taken into account by the S portion and is taxed using the appropriate capital gain rate found in section 1(h).

(3) *Example 3.*—(i) *Sale of S stock for an installment note.* Assume the same facts as in *Example 2* in paragraph (l)(2) of this section, except that Trust sells its stock in *X* for a $400,000 installment note payable with stated interest over ten years. After the sale, Trust does not own any S corporation stock.

(ii) *Loss on installment sale.* Assume Trust's basis in its *X* stock was $500,000. Therefore, Trust sustains a capital loss of $100,000 on the sale. Upon the sale, the S portion terminates and the excess loss, after being netted against the other items taken into account by the S portion, is made available to the entire trust as provided in section 641(c)(4).

(iii) *Gain on installment sale.* Assume Trust's basis in its X stock was $300,000 and that the $100,000 gain will be recognized under the installment method of section 453. Interest income will be recognized annually as part of the installment payments. The portion of the $100,000 gain recognized annually is taken into account by the S portion. However, the annual interest income is includible in the gross income of the non-S portion.

(4) *Example 4. Charitable lead annuity trust.*—Trust is a charitable lead annuity trust which is not treated as owned by the grantor or another person under subpart E. Trust acquires stock in *X*, an S corporation, and elects to be an ESBT. During the taxable year, pursuant to its terms, Trust pays $10,000 to a charitable organization described in section 170(c)(2). The non-S portion of Trust receives an income tax deduction for the charitable contribution under section 642(c) only to the extent the amount is paid out of the gross income of the non-S portion. To the extent the amount is paid from the S portion by distributing S corporation stock, no charitable deduction is available to the S portion.

(5) *Example 5. ESBT distributions.*—(i) As of January 1, 2002, Trust owns stock in *X*, a C corporation. No portion of Trust is treated as owned by the grantor or another person under subpart E. *X* elects to be an S corporation effective January 1, 2003, and Trust elects to be an ESBT effective January 1, 2003. On February 1, 2003, *X* makes an $8,000 distribution to Trust, of which $3,000 is treated as a dividend from accumulated earnings and profits under section 1368(c)(2) and the remainder is applied against Trust's basis in the *X* stock under section 1368(b). The trustee of Trust makes a distribution of $4,000 to Beneficiary during 2003. For 2003, Trust's share of *X*'s section 1366 items is $5,000 of ordinary income. For the year, Trust has no other income and no expenses or state or local taxes.

(ii) For 2003, Trust has $5,000 of taxable income in the S portion. This income is taxed to Trust at the maximum rate provided in section 1(e). Trust also has $3,000 of distributable net income (DNI) in the non-S portion. The non-S portion of Trust receives a distribution deduction under section 661(a) of $3,000, which represents the amount distributed to Beneficiary during the year ($4,000), not to exceed the amount of DNI ($3,000). Beneficiary must include this amount in gross income under section 662(a). As a result, the non-S portion has no taxable income.

(6) *Example 6: NRA as potential current beneficiary.*—Domestic Trust (DT) has a valid ESBT election in effect. DT owns S corporation stock. The S corporation owns U.S. and foreign assets. The foreign assets produce foreign source income. B, an NRA, is the grantor and the only trust beneficiary and potential current beneficiary of DT. B is not a resident of a country with which the United States has an income tax treaty. Under section 677(a), B is treated as the owner of DT because, under the trust documents, income and corpus may be distributed only to B during B's lifetime. Paragraph (b)(2)(ii) of this section requires that the S corporation income of the ESBT that otherwise would have been allocated to B under the grantor trust rules must be reallocated from B's grantor portion to the S portion of DT. In the example in this paragraph (l)(6), the S portion of DT is treated as including the grantor portion of the ESBT, and thus all of DT's income from the S corporation is taxable to DT. [Reg. § 1.641(c)-1.]

☐ [*T.D.* 8994, 5-13-2002. *Amended by T.D.* 9868, 6-13-2019.]

[Reg. § 1.642(a)(1)-1]

§ 1.642(a)(1)-1. Partially tax-exempt interest.—An estate or trust is allowed the credit against tax for partially tax-exempt interest provided by section 35 only to the extent that the credit does not relate to interest properly allocable to a beneficiary under section 652 or 662 and the regulations thereunder. A beneficiary of an estate or trust is allowed the credit against tax for partially tax-exempt interest provided by section 35 only to the extent that the credit relates to interest properly allocable to him under section 652 or 662 and the regulations thereunder. If an estate or trust holds partially tax-exempt bonds and elects under section 171 to treat the premium on the bonds as amortizable, the credit allowable under section 35, with respect to the bond interest (whether allowable to the estate or trust or to the beneficiary), is reduced under section 171(a)(3) by reducing the shares of the interest allocable, respectively, to the estate or trust and its beneficiary by the portion of the amortization deduction attributable to the shares. [Reg. § 1.642(a)(1)-1.]

☐ [*T.D.* 6217, 12-19-56.]

[Reg. § 1.642(a)(2)-1]

§ 1.642(a)(2)-1. Foreign taxes.—An estate or trust is allowed the credit against tax for taxes imposed by foreign countries and possessions of the United States to the extent allowed by section 901 only for so much of those taxes as are not properly allocable under that section to the beneficiaries. See section 901(b)(4). For purposes of section 901(b)(4), the term "beneficiaries" includes charitable beneficiaries. [Reg. § 1.642(a)(2)-1.]

☐ [*T.D.* 6217, 12-19-56.]

[Reg. § 1.642(a)(3)-1]

§ 1.642(a)(3)-1. Dividends received by an estate or trust.—An estate or trust is allowed a credit against the tax for dividends received on or before December 31, 1964 (see section 34), only for so much of the dividends as are not properly allocable to any beneficiary under section 652 or 662. Section 642(a)(3), and this section do not apply to amounts received as dividends after December 31, 1964. For treatment of the credit in the hands of the beneficiary see § 1.652(b)-1. [Reg. § 1.642(a)(3)-1.]

☐ [*T.D.* 6217, 12-19-56. *Amended by T.D.* 6777, 12-15-64.]

[Reg. § 1.642(a)(3)-2]

§ 1.642(a)(3)-2. Time of receipt of dividends by beneficiary.—In general, dividends are deemed received by a beneficiary in the taxable year in which they are includible in his gross income under section 652 or 662. For example, a simple trust, reporting on the basis of a fiscal year ending October 30, receives quarterly dividends on November 3, 1954, and February 3, May 3, and August 3, 1955. These dividends are all allocable to beneficiary A, reporting on a calendar year basis, under section 652 and are deemed received by A in 1955. See section 652(c). Accordingly, A may take all these dividends into account in determining his credit for dividends received under section 34 and his dividends exclusion under section 116. However, solely for purposes of determining whether dividends deemed received by individuals from trusts or estates qualify under the time limitations of section 34(a) or section 116(a), section 642(a)(3) provides that the time of receipt of the dividends by the trust or estate is also considered the time of receipt by the beneficiary. For example, a simple trust reporting on the basis of a fiscal year ending October 30 receives quarterly dividends on December 3, 1953, and March 3, June 3, and September 3, 1954. These dividends are all allocable to beneficiary A, reporting on the calendar year basis, under section 652 and are includible in his income for 1954. However, for purposes of section 34(a) or section 116(a), these dividends are deemed received by A on the same dates that the trust received them. Accordingly, A may take into account in determining the credit under section 34 only those dividends received by the trust on September 3, 1954, since the dividend received credit is not allowed under section 34 for dividends received before August 1, 1954 (or after December 31, 1964). Section 642(a)(3) and this section do not apply to amounts received by an estate or trust as dividends after December 31, 1964. However, the rules in this section relating to time of receipt of dividends by a beneficiary are applicable to dividends received by an estate or trust prior to January 1, 1965, and accordingly, such dividends are deemed to be received by the beneficiary (even though received after December 31, 1964) on the same dates that the estate or trust received them for purposes of determining the credit under section 34 or the exclusion under section 116. [Reg. § 1.642(a)(3)-2.]

☐ [*T.D.* 6217, 12-19-56. *Amended by T.D.* 6777, 12-15-64.]

[Reg. § 1.642(a)(3)-3]

§ 1.642(a)(3)-3. Cross reference.—See § 1.683-2(c) for examples relating to the treatment of dividends received by an estate or trust during a fiscal year beginning in 1953 and ending in 1954. [Reg. § 1.642(a)(3)-3.]

☐ [*T.D.* 6217, 12-19-56.]

[Reg. § 1.642(b)-1]

§ 1.642(b)-1. Deduction for personal exemption.—In lieu of the deduction for personal exemptions provided by section 151:

(a) An estate is allowed a deduction of $600,

(b) A trust which, under its governing instrument, is required to distribute currently all of its income for the taxable year is allowed a deduction of $300, and

(c) All other trusts are allowed a deduction of $100.

A trust which, under its governing instrument, is required to distribute all of its income currently is allowed a deduction of $300, even though it also distributes amounts other than income in the taxable year and even though it may be required to make distributions which would qualify for the charitable contributions deduction under section 642(c) (and therefore does not qualify as a "simple trust" under sections 651-652). A trust for the payment of an annuity is allowed a deduction of $300 in a taxable year in which the amount of the annuity required to be paid equals or exceeds all the income of the trust for the taxable year. For the meaning of the term "income required to be distributed currently", see § 1.651(a)-2. [Reg. § 1.642(b)-1.]

☐ [*T.D.* 6217, 12-19-56.]

[Reg. § 1.642(c)-0]

§ 1.642(c)-0. Effective dates.—The provisions of section 642(c) (other than section 642(c)(5)) and of §§ 1.642(c)-1 through 1.642(c)-4 apply to amounts paid, permanently set aside, or to be used for a charitable purpose in taxable years beginning after December 31, 1969. The provisions of section 642(c)(5) and of §§1.642(c)-5 through 1.642(c)-7 apply to transfers in trust made after July 31, 1969. For provisions relating to amounts paid, permanently set aside, or to be used for a charitable purpose in taxable years beginning before January 1, 1970, see 26 CFR 1.642(c) through 1.642(c)-4 (Rev. as of Jan. 1, 1971). [Reg. §1.642(c)-0.]

□ [*T.D. 7357*, 5-30-75.]

[Reg. §1.642(c)-1]

§1.642(c)-1. Unlimited deduction for amounts paid for a charitable purpose.—(a) *In general.*—(1) Any part of the gross income of an estate or trust which, pursuant to the terms of the governing instrument, is paid (or treated under paragraph (b) of this section as paid) during the taxable year for a purpose specified in section 170(c) shall be allowed as a deduction to such estate or trust in lieu of the limited charitable contributions deduction authorized by section 170(a). In applying this paragraph without reference to paragraph (b) of this section, a deduction shall be allowed for an amount paid during the taxable year in respect of gross income received in a previous taxable year, but only if no deduction was allowed for any previous taxable year to the estate or trust, or in the case of a section 645 election, to a related estate, as defined under §1.645-1(b), for the amount so paid.

(2) In determining whether an amount is paid for a purpose specified in section 170(c)(2) the provisions of section 170(c)(2)(A) shall not be taken into account. Thus, an amount paid to a corporation, trust, or community chest, fund, or foundation otherwise described in section 170(c)(2) shall be considered paid for a purpose specified in section 170(c) even though the corporation, trust, or community chest, fund, or foundation is not created or organized in the United States, any State, the District of Columbia, or any possession of the United States.

(3) See section 642(c)(6) and §1.642(c)-4 for disallowance of a deduction under this section to a trust which is, or is treated under section 4947(a)(1) as though it were, a private foundation (as defined in section 509(a) and the regulations thereunder) and not exempt from taxation under section 501(a).

(b) *Election to treat contributions as paid in preceding taxable year.*—(1) *In general.*—For purposes of determining the deduction allowed under paragraph (a) of this section, the fiduciary (as defined in section 7701(a)(6)) of an estate or trust may elect under section 642(c)(1) to treat as paid during the taxable year (whether or not such year begins before January 1, 1970) any amount of gross income received during such taxable year or any preceding taxable year which is otherwise deductible under such paragraph and which is paid after the close of such taxable year but on or before the last day of the next succeeding taxable year of the estate or trust. The preceding sentence applies only in the case of payments actually made in a taxable year which is a taxable year beginning after December 31, 1969. No election shall be made, however, in respect of any amount which was deducted for any previous taxable year or which is deducted for the taxable year in which such amount is paid.

(2) *Time for making election.*—The election under subparagraph (1) of this paragraph shall be made not later than the time, including extensions thereof, prescribed by law for filing the income tax return for the succeeding taxable year. Such election shall, except as provided in subparagraph (4) of this paragraph, become irrevocable after the last day prescribed for making it. Having made the election for any taxable year, the fiduciary may, within the time prescribed for making it, revoke the election without the consent of the Commissioner.

(3) *Manner of making the election.*—The election shall be made by filing with the income tax return (or an amended return) for the taxable year in which the contribution is treated as paid a statement which—

(i) States the name and address of the fiduciary,

(ii) Identifies the estate or trust for which the fiduciary is acting,

(iii) Indicates that the fiduciary is making an election under section 642(c)(1) in respect of contributions treated as paid during such taxable year,

(iv) Gives the name and address of each organization to which any such contribution is paid, and

(v) States the amount of each contribution and date of actual payment or, if applicable, the total amount of contributions paid to each organization during the succeeding taxable year, to be treated as paid in the preceding taxable year.

(4) *Revocation of certain elections with consent.*—An application to revoke with the consent of the Commissioner any election made on or before June 8, 1970, must be in writing and must be filed not later than September 2, 1975. No consent will be granted to revoke an election for any taxable year for which the assessment of a deficiency is prevented by the operation of any law or rule of law. If consent to revoke the election is granted, the fiduciary must attach a copy of the consent to the return (or amended return) for each taxable year affected by the revocation. The application must be addressed to the Commissioner of Internal Revenue, Washington, D.C. 20224, and must indicate—

(i) The name and address of the fiduciary and the estate or trust for which he was acting,

(ii) The taxable year for which the election was made,

(iii) The office of the district director, or the service center, where the return (or amended return) for the year of election was filed, and

(iv) The reason for revoking the election.

[Reg. §1.642(c)-1.]

□ [*T.D.* 6217, 12-19-56. *Amended by T.D.* 7357, 5-30-75 *and T.D.* 9032, 12-23-2002.]

[Reg. § 1.642(c)-2]

§ 1.642(c)-2. Unlimited deduction for amounts permanently set aside for a charitable purpose.—(a) *Estates.*—Any part of the gross income of an estate which pursuant to the terms of the will—

(1) Is permanently set aside during the taxable year for a purpose specified in section 170(c), or

(2) Is to be used (within or without the United States or any of its possessions) exclusively for religious, charitable, scientific, literary, or educational purposes, or for the prevention of cruelty to children or animals, or for the establishment, acquisition, maintenance, or operation of a public cemetery not operated for profit,

shall be allowed as a deduction to the estate in lieu of the limited charitable contributions deduction authorized by section 170(a).

(b) *Certain trusts.*—(1) *In general.*—Any part of the gross income of a trust to which either subparagraph (3) or (4) of this paragraph applies, that by the terms of the governing instrument—

(i) Is permanently set aside during the taxable year for a purpose specified in section 170(c), or

(ii) Is to be used (within or without the United States or any of its possessions) exclusively for religious, charitable, scientific, literary, or educational purposes, or for the prevention of cruelty to children or animals, or for the establishment, acquisition, maintenance, or operation of a public cemetery not operated for profit,

shall be allowed, subject to the limitation provided in subparagraph (2) of this paragraph, as a deduction to the trust in lieu of the limited charitable contributions deduction authorized by section 170(a). The preceding sentence applies only to a trust which is required by the terms of its governing instrument to set amounts aside. See section 642(c)(6) and § 1.642(c)-4 for disallowance of a deduction under this section to a trust which is, or is treated under section 4947(a)(1) as though it were, a private foundation (as defined in section 509(a) and the regulations thereunder) that is not exempt from taxation under section 501(a).

(2) *Limitation of deduction.*—Subparagraph (1) of this paragraph applies only to the gross income earned by a trust with respect to amounts transferred to the trust under a will executed on or before October 9, 1969, and satisfying the requirements of subparagraph (4) of this paragraph or transferred to the trust on or before October 9, 1969. For such purposes, any income, gains, or losses, which are derived at any time from the amounts so transferred to the trust shall also be taken into account in applying subparagraph (1) of this paragraph. If any such amount so transferred to the trust is invested or reinvested at any time, any asset received by the trust upon such investment or reinvestment shall also be treated as an amount which was so transferred to the trust. In the case of a trust to which this paragraph applies which contains (i) amounts transferred pursuant to transfers described in the first sentence of this subparagraph and (ii) amounts transferred pursuant to transfers not so described, subparagraph (1) of this paragraph shall apply only if the amounts described in subdivision (i) of this subparagraph, together with all income, gains, and losses derived therefrom, are separately accounted for from the amounts described in subdivision (ii) of this subparagraph, together with all income, gains, and losses derived therefrom. Such separate accounting shall be carried out consistently with the principles of paragraph (c)(4) of § 53.4947-1 of this chapter (Foundation Excise Tax Regulations), relating to accounting for segregated amounts of split-interest trusts.

(3) *Trusts created on or before October 9, 1969.*—A trust to which this subparagraph applies is a trust, testamentary or otherwise, which was created on or before October 9, 1969, and which qualifies under either subdivision (i) or (ii) of this subparagraph.

(i) *Transfer of irrevocable remainder interest to charity.*—To qualify under this subdivision the trust must have been created under the terms of an instrument granting an irrevocable remainder interest in such trust to or for the use of an organization described in section 170(c). If the instrument granted a revocable remainder interest but the power to revoke such interest terminated on or before October 9, 1969, without the remainder interest having been revoked, the remainder interest will be treated as irrevocable for purposes of the preceding sentence.

(ii) *Grantor under a mental disability to change terms of trust.*—(A) To qualify under this subdivision (ii) the trust must have been created by a grantor who was at all times after October 9, 1969, under a mental disability to change the terms of the trust. The term "mental disability" for this purpose means mental incompetence to change the terms of the trust, whether or not there has been an adjudication of mental incompetence and whether or not there has been an appointment of a committee, guardian, fiduciary, or other person charged with the care of the person or property of the grantor.

(B) If the grantor has not been adjudged mentally incompetent, the trustee must obtain from a qualified physician a certificate stating that the grantor of the trust has been mentally incompetent at all times after October 9, 1969, and that there is no reasonable probability that the grantor's mental capacity will ever improve to the extent that he will be mentally competent to change the terms of the trust. A copy of this certification must be filed with the first return on which a deduction is claimed by reason of this subdivision (ii) and subparagraph (1) of this paragraph. Thereafter, a statement referring to such medical opinion must be attached to any return for a taxable year for which such a deduction is claimed and during which the grantor's mental incompetence continues. The original certificate must be retained by the trustee of the trust.

(C) If the grantor has been adjudged mentally incompetent, a copy of the judgment or decree, and any modification thereof, must be filed with the first return on which a deduction is claimed by reason of this subdivision (ii) and subparagraph (1) of this paragraph. Thereafter, a statement referring to such judgment or decree must be attached to any return for a taxable year for which such a deduction is claimed and during which the grantor's mental incompetence continues. A copy of such judgment or decree must also be retained by the trustee of the trust.

(D) This subdivision (ii) applies even though a person charged with the care of the person or property of the grantor has the power to change the terms of the trust.

(4) *Testamentary trust established by will executed on or before October 9, 1969.*—A trust to which this subparagraph applies is a trust which was established by will executed on or before October 9, 1969, and which qualifies under either subdivision (i), (ii), or (iii) of this subparagraph. This subparagraph does not apply, however, to that portion of any trust, not established by a will executed on or before October 9, 1969, which was transferred to such trust by a will executed on or before October 9, 1969. Nor does it apply to that portion of any trust, not established by a will executed on or before October 9, 1969, which was subject to a testamentary power of appointment that fails by reason of the testator's nonexercise of the power in a will executed on or before October 9, 1969.

(i) *Testator dying within 3 years without republishing his will.*—To qualify under this subdivision the trust must have been established by the will of a testator who died after October 9, 1969, but before October 9, 1972, without having amended any dispositive provision of the will after October 9, 1969, by codicil or otherwise.

(ii) *Testator having no right to change his will.*—To qualify under this subdivision the trust must have been established by the will of a testator who died after October 9, 1969, and who at no time after that date had the right to change any portion of such will pertaining to such trust. This subdivision could apply, for example, where a contract has been entered into for the execution of wills containing reciprocal provisions as well as provisions for the benefit of an organization described in section 170(c) and under applicable local law the surviving testator is prohibited from revoking his will because he has accepted the benefit of the provisions of the will of the other contracting party.

(iii) *Testator under a mental disability to republish his will.*—To qualify under this subdivision the trust must have been established by the will of a testator who died after October 8, 1972, without having amended any dispositive provision of such will after October 9, 1969, and before October 9, 1972, by codicil or otherwise, and who is under a mental disability at all times after October 8, 1972, to amend such will, by codicil or otherwise. The provisions of subparagraph (3)(ii) of this paragraph with respect to mental incompetence apply for purposes of this subdivision.

(iv) *Amendment of dispositive provisions.*—The provisions of paragraph (e)(4) and (5) of § 20.2055-2 of this chapter (Estate Tax Regulations) are to be applied under subdivisions (i) and (iii) of this subparagraph in determining whether there has been an amendment of a dispositive provision of a will.

(c) *Pooled income funds.*—Any part of the gross income of a pooled income fund to which § 1.642(c)-5 applies for the taxable year that is attributable to net long-term capital gain (as defined in section 1222(7)) which, pursuant to the terms of the governing instrument, is permanently set aside during the taxable year for a purpose specified in section 170(c) shall be allowed as a deduction to the fund in lieu of the limited charitable contributions deduction authorized by section 170(a). No amount of net long-term capital gain shall be considered permanently set aside for charitable purposes if, under the terms of the fund's governing instrument and applicable local law, the trustee has the power, whether or not exercised, to satisfy the income beneficiaries' right to income by the payment of either: an amount equal to a fixed percentage of the fair market value of the fund's assets (whether determined annually or averaged on a multiple year basis); or any amount that takes into account unrealized appreciation in the value of the fund's assets. In addition, no amount of net long-term capital gain shall be considered permanently set aside for charitable purposes to the extent the trustee distributes proceeds from the sale or exchange of the fund's assets as income within the meaning of § 1.642(c)-5(a)(5)(i). No deduction shall be allowed under this paragraph for any portion of the gross income of such fund which is (1) attributable to income other than net long-term capital gain or (2) earned with respect to amounts transferred to such fund before August 1, 1969. However, see paragraph (b) of this section for a deduction (subject to the limitations of such paragraph) for amounts permanently set aside by a pooled income fund which meets the requirements of that paragraph. The principles of paragraph (b)(2) of this section with respect to investment, reinvestment, and separate accounting shall apply under this paragraph in the case of amounts transferred to the fund after July 31, 1969.

(d) *Disallowance of deduction for certain amounts not deemed to be permanently set aside for charitable purposes.*—No amount will be considered to be permanently set aside, or to be used, for a purpose described in paragraph (a) or (b)(1) of this section unless under the terms of the governing instrument and the circumstances of the particular case the possibility that the amount set aside, or to be used, will not be devoted to such purpose or use is so remote as to be negligible. Thus, for example, where there is possibility of the invasion of the corpus of a charitable remainder trust, as defined in § 1.664-1(a)(1)(ii), in order to make payment of the annuity amount or unitrust amount, no deduction will be allowed under paragraph (a) of this section in respect of any amount set aside by an estate for distribution to such a charitable remainder trust.

For treatment of distributions by an estate to a charitable remainder trust, see paragraph (a)(5)(iii) of § 1.664-1.

(e) *Effective dates.*—Generally, the second sentence of paragraph (c) of this section, concerning the loss of any charitable deduction for long-term capital gains if the fund's income may be determined by a fixed percentage of the fair market value of the fund's assets or by any amount that takes into account unrealized appreciation in the value of the fund's assets, applies for taxable years beginning after January 2, 2004. In a state whose statute permits income to be determined by reference to a fixed percentage of, or the unrealized appreciation in, the value of the fund's assets, net long-term capital gain of a pooled income fund may be considered to be permanently set aside for charitable purposes if the fund's governing instrument is amended or reformed to eliminate the possibility of determining income in such a manner and if income has not been determined in this manner. For this purpose, a judicial proceeding to reform the fund's governing instrument must be commenced, or a nonjudicial reformation that is valid under state law must be completed, by the date that is nine months after the later of January 2, 2004 or the effective date of the state statute authorizing determination of income in such a manner. [Reg. § 1.642(c)-2.]

☐ [*T.D.* 6217, 12-19-56. *Amended by T.D.* 7357, 5-30-75 *and T.D.* 9102, 12-30-2003.]

[Reg. § 1.642(c)-3]

§ 1.642(c)-3. Adjustments and other special rules for determining unlimited charitable contributions deduction.—(a) *Income in respect of a decedent.*—For purposes of §§ 1.642(c)-1 and 1.642(c)-2, an amount received by an estate or trust which is includible in its gross income under section 691(a)(1) as income in respect of a decedent shall be included in the gross income of the estate or trust.

(b) *Determination of amounts deductible under section 642(c) and the character of such amounts.*—(1) *Reduction of charitable contributions deduction by amounts not included in gross income.*—If an estate, pooled income fund, or other trust pays, permanently sets aside, or uses any amount of its income for a purpose specified in section 642(c)(1), (2), or (3) and that amount includes any items of estate or trust income not entering into the gross income of the estate or trust, the deduction allowable under § 1.642(c)-1 or § 1.642(c)-2 is limited to the gross income so paid, permanently set aside, or used. In the case of a pooled income fund for which a deduction is allowable under paragraph (c) of § 1.642(c)-2 for amounts permanently set aside, only the gross income of the fund which is attributable to net long-term capital gain (as defined in section 1222(7)) shall be taken into account.

(2) *Determination of the character of an amount deductible under section 642(c).*—In determining whether the amounts of income so paid, permanently set aside, or used for a purpose specified in section 642(c)(1), (2), or (3) include particular items of income of an estate or trust, whether or not included in gross income, a provision in the governing instrument or in local law that specifically provides the source out of which amounts are to be paid, permanently set aside, or used for such a purpose controls for Federal tax purposes to the extent such provision has economic effect independent of income tax consequences. See § 1.652(b)-2(b). In the absence of such specific provisions in the governing instrument or in local law, the amount to which section 642(c) applies is deemed to consist of the same proportion of each class of the items of income of the estate or trust as the total of each class bears to the total of all classes. See § 1.643(a)-5(b) for the method of determining the allocable portion of exempt income and foreign income. This paragraph (b)(2) is illustrated by the following examples:

Example 1. A charitable lead annuity trust has the calendar year as its taxable year, and is to pay an annuity of $10,000 annually to an organization described in section 170(c). A provision in the trust governing instrument provides that the $10,000 annuity should be deemed to come first from ordinary income, second from short-term capital gain, third from fifty percent of the unrelated business taxable income, fourth from long-term capital gain, fifth from the balance of unrelated business taxable income, sixth from tax-exempt income, and seventh from principal. This provision in the governing instrument does not have economic effect independent of income tax consequences, because the amount to be paid to the charity is not dependent upon the type of income from which it is to be paid. Accordingly, the amount to which section 642(c) applies is deemed to consist of the same proportion of each class of the items of income of the trust as the total of each class bears to the total of all classes.

Example 2. A trust instrument provides that 100 percent of the trust's ordinary income must be distributed currently to an organization described in section 170(c) and that all remaining items of income must be distributed currently to B, a noncharitable beneficiary. This income ordering provision has economic effect independent of income tax consequences because the amount to be paid to the charitable organization each year is dependent upon the amount of ordinary income the trust earns within that taxable year. Accordingly, for purposes of section 642(c), the full amount distributed to charity is deemed to consist of ordinary income.

(3) *Other examples.*—For examples showing the determination of the character of an amount deductible under § 1.642(c)-1 or § 1.642(c)-2, see examples (1) and (2) in § 1.662(b)-2 and paragraph (e) of the example in § 1.662(c)-4.

See p. 15 for regulations not amended to reflect law changes

(c) *Capital gains included in charitable contribution.*—Where any amount of the income paid, permanently set aside, or used for a purpose specified in section 642(c)(1), (2), or (3) is attributable to net long-term capital gain (as defined in section 1222(7)), the amount of the deduction otherwise allowable under § 1.642(c)-1 or § 1.642(c)-2 must be adjusted for any deduction provided in section 1202 of 50 percent of the excess, if any, of the net long-term capital gain over the net short-term capital loss. For determination of the extent to which the contribution to which § 1.642(c)-1 or § 1.642(c)-2 applies is deemed to consist of net long-term capital gains, see paragraph (b) of this section. The application of this paragraph may be illustrated by the following examples:

Example (1). Under the terms of the trust instrument, the income of a trust described in § 1.642(c)-2(b)(3)(i) is currently distributable to A during his life and capital gains are allocable to corpus. No provision is made in the trust instrument for the invasion of corpus for the benefit of A. Upon A's death the corpus of the trust is to be distributed to M University, an organization described in section 501(c)(3) which is exempt from taxation under section 501(a). During the taxable year ending December 31, 1970, the trust has long-term capital gains of $100,000 from property transferred to it on or before October 9, 1969, which are permanently set aside for charitable purposes. The trust includes $100,000 in gross income but is allowed a deduction of $50,000 under section 1202 for the long-term capital gains and a charitable contributions deduction of $50,000 under section 642(c)(2) ($100,000 permanently set aside for charitable purposes less $50,000 allowed as a deduction under section 1202 with respect to such $100,000).

Example (2). Under the terms of the will, $200,000 of the income (including $100,000 capital gains) for the taxable year 1972 of an estate is distributed, one-quarter to each of two individual beneficiaries and one-half to N University, an organization described in section 501(c)(3) which is exempt from taxation under section 501(a). During 1972 the estate has ordinary income of $200,000, long-term capital gains of $100,000, and no capital losses. It is assumed that for 1972 the estate has no other items of income or any deductions other than those discussed herein. The entire capital gains of $100,000 are included in the gross income of the estate for 1972, and N University receives $100,000 from the estate in such year. However, the amount allowable to the estate under section 642(c)(1) is subject to appropriate adjustment for the deduction allowable under section 1202. In view of the distributions of $25,000 of capital gains to each of the individual beneficiaries, the deduction allowable to the estate under section 1202 is limited by such section to $25,000 [($100,000 capital gains less $50,000 capital gains includible in income of individual beneficiaries under section 662) × 50%]. Since the whole of this $25,000 deduction under section 1202 is attributable to the distribution of $50,000 of capital gains to N University, the deduction allowable to the estate in 1972 under section 642(c)(1) is $75,000 [$100,000 (distributed to N) less $25,000 (proper adjustment for section 1202 deduction)].

Example (3). Under the terms of the trust instrument, 30 percent of the gross income (exclusive of capital gains) of a trust described in § 1.642(c)-2(b)(3)(i) is currently distributed to B, the sole income beneficiary. Net capital gains (capital gain net income for taxable years beginning after December 31, 1976) and undistributed ordinary income are allocable to corpus. No provision is made in the trust instrument for the invasion of corpus for the benefit of B. Upon B's death the remainder of the trust is to be distributed to M Church. During the taxable year 1972, the trust has ordinary income of $100,000, long-term capital gains of $15,000, short-term capital gains of $1,000, long-term capital losses of $5,000, and short-term capital losses of $2,500. It is assumed that the trust has no other items of income or any deductions other than those discussed herein. All the ordinary income and capital gains and losses are attributable to amounts transferred to the trust before October 9, 1969. The trust includes in gross income for 1972 the total amount of $116,000 [$100,000 (ordinary income) + $16,000 (total capital gains determined without regard to capital losses)]. Pursuant to the terms of the governing instrument the trust distributes to B in 1972 the amount of $30,000 ($100,000 × 30%). The balance of $78,500 [($116,000 less $7,500 capital losses) − $30,000 distribution] is available for the set-aside for charitable purposes. In determining taxable income for 1972 the capital losses of $7,500 ($5,000 + $2,500) are allowable in full under section 1211(b)(1). The net capital gain (capital gain net income for taxable years beginning after December 31, 1976) of $8,500 ($16,000 less $7,500) is the excess of the net long-term capital gain of $10,000 ($15,000 less $5,000) over the net short-term capital loss of $1,500 ($2,500 less $1,000). The deduction under section 1202 is $4,250 ($8,500 × 50%), all of which is attributable to the set-aside for charitable purposes. Accordingly, for 1972 the deduction allowable to the trust under section 642(c)(2) is $74,250 [$78,500 (set-aside for M) less $4,250 (proper adjustment for section 1202 deduction)].

Example (4). During the taxable year a pooled income fund, as defined in § 1.642(c)-5, has in addition to ordinary income long-term capital gains of $150,000, short-term capital gains of $15,000, long-term capital losses of $100,000, and short-term capital losses of $10,000. Under the Declaration of Trust and pursuant to State law net long-term capital gain is allocable to corpus and net short-term capital gain is to be distributed to the income beneficiaries of the fund. All the capital gains and losses are attributable to amounts transferred to the fund after July 31, 1969. In view of the distribution of the net short-term capital gain of $5,000 ($15,000 less $10,000) to the income beneficiaries, the deduction allowed to the fund under section 1202 is limited by such section to $25,000 [($150,000 (long-term capital gains) less $100,000 (long-term capital losses)) × 50%]. Since the whole of this deduction under section 1202 is attributable to the set-aside for charitable purposes, the deduction of $50,000 ($150,000 less $100,000) otherwise allowable under section 642(c)(3) is subject to appropriate adjustment under section 642(c)(4) for the deduction allowable under section 1202. Accordingly, the amount of the set-aside deduction is $25,000 [$50,000 (set-aside for public charity) less $25,000 (proper adjustment for section 1202 deduction)].

Example (5). The facts are the same as in example (4) except that under the Declaration of Trust and pursuant to State law all the net capital gain (capital gain net income for taxable years beginning after December 31, 1976) for the taxable year is allocable to corpus of the fund. The fund would thus include in gross income total capital gains of $165,000 ($150,000 + $15,000). In determining taxable income for the taxable year the capital losses of $110,000 ($100,000 + $10,000) are allowable in full under section 1211(b)(1). The net capital gain (capital gain net income for taxable years beginning after December 31, 1976) of $55,000 ($165,000 less $110,000) is available for the set-aside for charitable purposes under section 642(c)(3) only in the amount of the net long-term capital gain of $50,000 ($150,000 long-term gains less $100,000 long-term losses). The deduction under section 1202 is $25,000 ($50,000 × 50%), all of which is attributable to the set-aside for charitable purposes. Accordingly, the deduction allowable to the fund under section 642(c)(3) is $25,000 [$50,000 (set-aside for public charity) less $25,000 (proper adjustment for section 1202 deduction)]. The $5,000 balance of net capital gain (capital gain net income for taxable years beginning after December 31, 1976) is taken into account in determining taxable income of the pooled income fund for the taxable year.

(d) *Disallowance of deduction for amounts allocable to unrelated business income.*—In the case of a trust, the deduction otherwise allowable under § 1.642(c)-1 or § 1.642(c)-2 is disallowed to the extent of amounts allocable to the trust's unrelated business income. See section 681(a) and the regulations thereunder.

(e) *Disallowance of deduction in certain cases.*—For disallowance of certain deductions otherwise allowable under section 642(c)(1), (2), or (3), see sections 508(d) and 4948(c)(4).

(f) *Information returns.*—For rules applicable to the annual information return that must be filed by trusts claiming a deduction under section 642(c) for the taxable year, see section 6034 and the regulations thereunder.

(g) *Payments resulting in state or local tax benefits.*—(1) *In general.*—If the trust or decedent's estate makes a payment of gross income for a purpose specified in section 170(c), and the trust or decedent's estate receives or expects to receive a state or local tax benefit in consideration for such payment, § 1.170A-1(h)(3) applies in determining the charitable contribution deduction under section 642(c).

(2) *Effective/applicability date.*—Paragraph (g)(1) of this section applies to payments of gross income after August 27, 2018. [Reg. § 1.642(c)-3.]

☐ [*T.D.* 6217, 12-19-56. *Amended by T.D.* 7357, 5-30-75; *T.D.* 7728, 10-31-80, *T.D.* 9582, 4-13-2012 *and T.D.* 9864, 6-11-2019.]

[Reg. § 1.642(c)-4]

§ 1.642(c)-4. Nonexempt private foundations.—In the case of a trust which is, or is treated under section 4947(a)(1) as though it were, a private foundation (as defined in section 509(a) and the regulations thereunder) that is not exempt from taxation under section 501(a) for the taxable year, a deduction for amounts paid or permanently set aside, or used for a purpose specified in section 642(c)(1) or (2) shall not be allowed under § 1.642(c)-1 or § 1.642(c)-2, but such trust shall, subject to the provisions applicable to individuals, be allowed a deduction under section 170 for charitable contributions paid during the taxable year. Section 642(c)(6) and this section do not apply to a trust described in section 4947(a)(1) unless such trust fails to meet the requirements of section 508(e). However, if on October 9, 1969, or at any time thereafter, a trust is recognized as being exempt from taxation under section 501(a) as an organization described in section 501(c)(3), if at such time such trust is a private foundation, and if at any time thereafter such trust is determined not to be exempt from taxation under section 501(a) as an organization described in section 501(c)(3), section 642(c)(6) and this section will apply to such trust. See § 1.509(b)-1(b). [Reg. § 1.642(c)-4.]

☐ [*T.D.* 6217, 12-19-56. *Amended by T.D.* 7357, 5-30-75.]

[Reg. § 1.642(c)-5]

§ 1.642(c)-5. Definition of pooled income fund.—(a) *In general.*—(1) *Application of provisions.*—Section 642(c)(5) prescribed certain rules for the valuation of contributions involving transfers to certain funds described in that section as pooled income funds. This section sets forth the requirements for qualifying as a pooled income fund and provides for the manner of allocating the income of the fund to the beneficiaries. Section 1.642(c)-6 provides for the valuation of a remainder interest in property transferred to a pooled income fund. Section 1.642(c)-7 provides transitional rules under which certain funds may be amended so as to qualify as pooled income funds in respect to transfers of property occurring after July 31, 1969.

(2) *Tax status of fund and its beneficiaries.*—Notwithstanding any other provision of this chapter, a fund which meets the requirements of a pooled income fund, as defined in section 642(c)(5) and paragraph (b) of this section, shall not be treated as an association within the meaning of section 7701(a)(3). Such a fund, which need not be a trust under local law, and its beneficiaries shall be taxable under part I, subchapter J, chapter 1 of the Code, but the provisions of subpart E (relating to grantors and

others treated as substantial owners) of such part shall not apply to such fund.

(3) *Recognition of gain or loss on transfer to fund.*—No gain or loss shall be recognized to the donor on the transfer of property to a pooled income fund. In such case, the fund's basis and holding period with respect to property transferred to the fund by a donor shall be determined as provided in sections 1015(b) and 1223(2). If, however, a donor transfers property to a pooled income fund and, in addition to creating or retaining a life income interest therein, receives property from the fund, or transfers property to the fund which is subject to an indebtedness, this subparagraph shall not apply to the gain realized by reason of (i) the receipt of such property or (ii) the amount of such indebtedness, whether or not assumed by the pooled income fund, which is required to be treated as an amount realized on the transfer.
For applicability of the bargain sale rules, see section 1011(b) and the regulations thereunder.

(4) *Charitable contributions deduction.*—A charitable contributions deduction for the value of the remainder interest, as determined under § 1.642(c)-6, may be allowed under section 170, 2055, 2106, or 2522, where there is a transfer of property to a pooled income fund. For a special rule relating to the reduction of the amount of a charitable contribution of certain ordinary income property or capital gain property, see section 170(e)(1)(A) or (B)(i) and the regulations thereunder.

(5) *Definitions.*—For purposes of this section, § 1.642(c)-6, and § 1.642(c)-7—

(i) The term *income* has the same meaning as it does under section 643(b) and the regulations thereunder, except that income generally may not include any long-term capital gains. However, in conformance with the applicable state statute, income may be defined as or satisfied by a unitrust amount, or pursuant to a trustee's power to adjust between income and principal to fulfill the trustee's duty of impartiality, if the state statute both provides for a reasonable apportionment between the income and remainder beneficiaries of the total return of the trust and meets the requirements of § 1.643(b)-1. In exercising a power to adjust, the trustee must allocate to principal, not to income, the proceeds from the sale or exchange of any assets contributed to the fund by any donor or purchased by the fund at least to the extent of the fair market value of those assets on the date of their contribution to the fund or of the purchase price of those assets purchased by the fund. This definition of income applies for taxable years beginning after January 2, 2004.

(ii) The term "donor" includes a decedent who makes a testamentary transfer of property to a pooled income fund.

(iii) The term "governing instrument" means either the governing plan under which the pooled income fund is established and administered or the instrument of transfer, as the context requires.

(iv) The term "public charity" means an organization described in clauses (i) to (vi) of section 170(b)(1)(A). If an organization is described in clauses (i) to (vi) of section 170(b)(1)(A) and is also described in clause (viii) of such section, it shall be treated as a public charity.

(v) The term "fair market value," when used with respect to property, means its value in excess of the indebtedness or charges against such property.

(vi) The term "determination date" means each day within the taxable year of a pooled income fund on which a valuation is made of the property in the fund. The property in the fund shall be valued on the first day of the taxable year of the fund and on at least 3 other days within the taxable year. The period between any two consecutive determination dates within the taxable year shall not be greater than 3 calendar months. In the case of a taxable year of less than 12 months, the property in the fund shall be valued on the first day of such taxable year and on such other days within such year as occur at successive intervals of no greater than 3 calendar months. Where a valuation date falls on a Saturday, Sunday, or legal holiday (as defined in section 7503 and the regulations thereunder), the valuation may be made on either the next preceding day which is not a Saturday, Sunday, or legal holiday or the next succeeding day which is not a Saturday, Sunday, or legal holiday, so long as the next such preceding day or next such succeeding day is consistently used where the valuation date falls on a Saturday, Sunday, or legal holiday.

(6) *Cross references.*—(i) See section 4947(a)(2) and section 4947(b)(3)(B) for the application to pooled income funds of the provisions relating to private foundations and section 508(e) for rules relating to provisions required in the governing instrument prohibiting certain activities specified in section 4947(a)(2).

(ii) For rules postponing the time for deduction of a charitable contribution of a future interest in tangible personal property, see section 170(a)(3) and the regulations thereunder.

(b) *Requirements for qualification as a pooled income fund.*—A pooled income fund to which this section applies must satisfy all of the following requirements:

(1) *Contribution of remainder interest to charity.*—Each donor must transfer property to the fund and contribute an irrevocable remainder interest in such property to or for the use of a public charity, retaining for himself, or creating for another beneficiary or beneficiaries, a life income interest in the transferred property. A contingent remainder interest shall not be treated as an irrevocable remainder interest for purposes of this subparagraph.

(2) *Creation of life income interest.*—Each donor must retain for himself for life an income interest in the property transferred to such fund, or create an income interest in such property for the life of one or more beneficiaries, each of

whom must be living at the time of the transfer of the property to the fund by the donor. The term "one or more beneficiaries" includes those members of a named class who are alive and can be ascertained at the time of the transfer of the property to the fund. In the event more than one beneficiary of the income interest is designated, such beneficiaries may enjoy their shares of income concurrently, consecutively, or both concurrently and consecutively. The donor may retain the power exercisable only by will to revoke or terminate the income interest of any designated beneficiary other than the public charity. The governing instrument must specify at the time of the transfer the particular beneficiary or beneficiaries to whom the income is payable and the share of income distributable to each person so specified. The public charity to or for the use of which the remainder interest is contributed may also be designated as one of the beneficiaries of an income interest. The donor need not retain or create a life interest in all the income from the property transferred to the fund provided any income not payable under the terms of the governing instrument to an income beneficiary is contributed to, and within the taxable year in which it is received is paid to, the same public charity to or for the use of which the remainder interest is contributed. No charitable contributions deduction shall be allowed to the donor for the value of such income interest of the public charity or for the amount of any such income paid to such organization.

(3) *Commingling of property required.*—The property transferred to the fund by each donor must be commingled with, and invested or reinvested with, other property transferred to the fund by other donors satisfying the requirements of subparagraphs (1) and (2) of this paragraph. The governing instrument of the pooled income fund must contain a provision requiring compliance with the preceding sentence. The public charity to or for the use of which the remainder interest is contributed may maintain more than one pooled income fund, provided that each such fund is maintained by the organization and is not a device to permit a group of donors to create a fund which may be subject to their manipulation. The fund must not include property transferred under arrangements other than those specified in section 642(c)(5) and this paragraph. However, a fund shall not be disqualified as a pooled income fund under this paragraph because any portion of its properties is invested or reinvested jointly with other properties, not a part of the pooled income fund, which are held by, or for the use of, the public charity which maintains the fund, as, for example, with securities in the general endowment fund of the public charity to or for the use of which the remainder interest is contributed. Where such joint investment or reinvestment of properties occurs, records must be maintained which sufficiently identify the portion of the total fund which is owned by the pooled income fund and the income earned by, and attributable to, such portion. Such a joint investment or reinvestment of properties shall not be treated as an association or partnership for purposes of the Code. A bank which serves as trustee of more than one pooled income fund may maintain a common trust fund to which section 584 applies for the collective investment and reinvestment of moneys of such funds.

(4) *Prohibition against exempt securities.*—The property transferred to the fund by any donor must not include any securities the income from which is exempt from tax under subtitle A of the Code, and the fund must not invest in such securities. The governing instrument of the fund must contain specific prohibitions against accepting or investing in such securities.

(5) *Maintenance by charitable organization required.*—The fund must be maintained by the same public charity to or for the use of which the irrevocable remainder interest is contributed. The requirement of maintenance will be satisfied where the public charity exercises control directly or indirectly over the fund. For example, this requirement of control shall ordinarily be met when the public charity has the power to remove the trustee or trustees of the fund and designate a new trustee or trustees. A national organization which carries out its purposes through local organizations, chapters, or auxiliary bodies with which it has an identity of aims and purposes may maintain a pooled income fund (otherwise satisfying the requirements of this paragraph) in which one or more local organizations, chapters, or auxiliary bodies which are public charities have been named as recipients of the remainder interests. For example, a national church body may maintain a pooled income fund where donors have transferred property to such fund and contributed an irrevocable remainder interest therein to or for the use of various local churches or educational institutions of such body. The fact that such local organizations or chapters have been separately incorporated from the national organization is immaterial.

(6) *Prohibition against donor or beneficiary serving as trustee.*—The fund must not have, and the governing instrument must prohibit the fund from having, as a trustee a donor to the fund or a beneficiary (other than the public charity to or for the use of which the remainder interest is contributed) of an income interest in any property transferred to such fund. Thus, if a donor or beneficiary (other than such public charity) directly or indirectly has general responsibilities with respect to the fund which are ordinarily exercised by a trustee, such fund does not meet the requirements of section 642(c)(5) and this paragraph. The fact that a donor of property to the fund, or a beneficiary of the fund, is a trustee, officer, director, or other official of the public charity to or for the use of which the remainder interest is contributed ordinarily will not prevent the fund from meeting the requirements of section 642(c)(5) and this paragraph.

(7) *Income of beneficiary to be based on rate of return of fund.*—Each beneficiary entitled to in-

come of any taxable year of the fund must receive such income in an amount determined by the rate of return earned by the fund for such taxable year with respect to his income interest, computed as provided in paragraph (c) of this section. The governing instrument of the fund shall direct the trustee to distribute income currently or within the first 65 days following the close of the taxable year in which the income is earned. Any such payment made after the close of the taxable year shall be treated as paid on the last day of the taxable year. A statement shall be attached to the return of the pooled income fund indicating the date and amount of such payments after the close of the taxable year. Subject to the provisions of part I, subchapter J, chapter 1 of the Code, the beneficiary shall include in his gross income all amounts properly paid, credited, or required to be distributed to the beneficiary during the taxable year or years of the fund ending within or with his taxable year. The governing instrument shall provide that the income interest of any designated beneficiary shall either terminate with the last regular payment which was made before the death of the beneficiary or be prorated to the date of his death.

(8) *Termination of life income interest.*—Upon the termination of the income interest retained or created by any donor, the trustee shall sever from the fund an amount equal to the value of the remainder interest in the property upon which the income interest is based. The value of the remainder interest for such purpose may be either (i) its value as of the determination date next succeeding the termination of the income interest or (ii) its value as of the date on which the last regular payment was made before the death of the beneficiary if the income interest is terminated on such payment date. The amount so severed from the fund must either be paid to, or retained for the use of, the designated public charity, as provided in the governing instrument. However, see subparagraph (3) of this paragraph for rules relating to commingling of property.

(c) *Allocation of income to beneficiary.*—(1) *In general.*—Every income interest retained or created in property transferred to a pooled income fund shall be assigned a proportionate share of the annual income earned by the fund, such share, or unit of participation, being based on the fair market value of such property on the date of transfer, as provided in this paragraph.

(2) *Units of participation.*—(i) *Unit plan.*—*(a)* On each transfer of property by a donor to a pooled income fund, one or more units of participation in the fund shall be assigned to the beneficiary or beneficiaries of the income interest retained or created in such property, the number of units of participation being equal to the number obtained by dividing the fair market value of the property by the fair market value of a unit in the fund at the time of the transfer.

(b) The fair market value of a unit in the fund at the time of the transfer shall be determined by dividing the fair market value of all property in the fund at such time by the number of units then in the fund. The initial fair market value of a unit in a pooled income fund shall be the fair market value of the property transferred to the fund divided by the number of units assigned to the income interest in that property. The value of each unit of participation will fluctuate with each new transfer of property to the fund in relation to the appreciation or depreciation in the fair market value of the property in the fund, but all units in the fund will always have equal value.

(c) The share of income allocated to each unit of participation shall be determined by dividing the income of the fund for the taxable year by the outstanding number of units in the fund at the end of such year, except that, consistently with paragraph (b)(7) of this section, income shall be allocated to units outstanding during only part of such year by taking into consideration the period of time such units are outstanding. For this purpose the actual income of such part of the taxable year, or a prorated portion of the annual income, may be used, after making such adjustments as are reasonably necessary to reflect fluctuations during the year in the fair market value of the property in the fund.

(ii) *Other plans.*—The governing instrument of the fund may provide any other reasonable method not described in subdivision (i) of this subparagraph for assigning units of participation in the fund and allocating income to such units which reaches a result reasonably consistent with the provisions of such subdivision.

(iii) *Transfers between determination dates.*—For purposes of subdivisions (i) and (ii) of this subparagraph, if a transfer of property to the fund by a donor occurs on other than a determination date, the number of units of participation assigned to the income interest in such property may be determined by using the fair market value of the property in the fund on the determination date immediately preceding the date of transfer (determined without regard to the property so transferred), subject, however, to appropriate adjustments on the next succeeding determination date. Such adjustments may be made by any reasonable method, including the use of a method whereby the fair market value of the property in the fund at the time of the transfer is deemed to be the average of the fair market values of the property in the fund on the determination dates immediately preceding and succeeding the date of transfer. For purposes of determining such average any property transferred to the fund between such preceding and succeeding dates, or on such succeeding date, shall be excluded. The application of this subdivision may be illustrated by the following example:

Example. The determination dates of a pooled income fund are the first day of each calendar month. On April 1, 1971, the fair market value of the property in the fund is $100,000, at which time 1,000 units of participation are outstanding with a value of $100 each. On April 15,

1971, B transfers property with a fair market value of $50,000 to the fund, retaining for himself for life an income interest in such property. No other property is transferred to the fund after April 1, 1971. On May 1, 1971, the fair market value of the property in the fund, including the property transferred by B, is $160,000. The average of the fair market values of the property in the fund (excluding the property transferred by B) on April 1 and May 1, 1971, is $105,000 ($100,000 + [$160,000 − $50,000] ÷ 2). Accordingly, the fair market value of a unit of participation in the fund on April 15, 1971, at the time of B's transfer may be deemed to be $105 ($105,000/1,000 units), and B is assigned 476.19 units of participation in the fund ($50,000/$105).

(3) *Special rule for partial allocation of income to charity.*—Notwithstanding subparagraph (2) of this paragraph, the governing instrument may provide that a unit of participation is entitled to share in the income of a fund in a lesser amount than would otherwise be determined under such subparagraph, provided that the income otherwise allocable to the unit under such subparagraph is paid within the taxable year in which it is received to the public charity to or for the use of which the remainder interest is contributed under the governing instrument.

(4) *Illustrations.*—The application of this paragraph may be illustrated by the following examples:

Example (1). On July 1, 1970, A and B transfer separate properties with a fair market value of $20,000 and $10,000, respectively, to a newly created pooled income fund which is maintained by Y University and uses as its taxable year the fiscal year ending June 30. A and B each retain in themselves for life an income interest in such property, the remainder interest being contributed to Y University. The pooled income fund assigns an initial value of $100 to each unit of participation in the fund, and under the governing instruments A receives 200 units, and B receives 100 units, in the fund. On October 1, 1970, which is a determination date, C transfers property to the fund with a fair market value of $12,000, retaining in himself for life an income interest in such property and contributing the remainder interest to Y University. The fair market value of the property in the fund at the time of C's transfer is $36,000. The fair market value of A's and B's units at the time of such transfer is $120 each ($36,000/300). By reason of his transfer of property C is assigned 100 units of participation in the fund ($12,000/$120).

Example (2). Assume that the pooled income fund in example (1) earns $2,600 for its taxable year ending June 30, 1971, and there are no further contributions of property to the fund in such year. Further assume $300 is earned in the first quarter ending September 30, 1970. Therefore, the fund earns $1 per unit for the first quarter ($300 divided by 300 units outstanding) and $5.75 per unit for the remainder of the taxable year ([$2,600 − $300]divided by 400 units outstanding). If the fund distributes its income for the year based on its actual earnings per quarter, the income must be distributed as follows:

Beneficiary	*Share of Income*
A	$1,350 ([200 × $1] + [200 × $5.75])
B	675 ([100 × $1] + [100 × $5.75])
C	575 (100 × $5.75).

Example (3). (a) On July 1, 1970, A and B transfer separate properties with a fair market value of $10,000 and $20,000, respectively, to a newly created pooled income fund which is maintained by X University and uses as its taxable year the fiscal year ending June 30. A and B each retain in themselves an income interest for life in such property, the remainder interest being contributed to X University. The governing instrument provides that each unit of participation in the fund shall have a value of not more than its initial fair market value; the instrument also provides that the income allocable to appreciation in the fair market value of such unit (to the extent in excess of its initial fair market value) at the end of each quarter of the fiscal year is to be distributed currently to X University. On October 1, 1970, which is a determination date, C contributes to the fund property with a fair market value of $60,000 and retains in himself an income interest for life in such property, the remainder interest being contributed to X University. The initial fair market value of the units assigned to A, B, and C is $100. A, B, and C's units of participation are as follows:

Beneficiary	*Units of Participation*
A	100 ($10,000 divided by $100)
B	200 ($20,000 divided by $100)
C	600 ($60,000 divided by $100)

(b) The fair market value of the property in the fund at the time of C's contribution is $40,000. Assuming the fair market value of the property in the fund is $100,000 on December 31, 1970, and that the income of the fund for the second quarter ending December 31, 1970, is $2,000, the income is shared by the income beneficiaries and X University as follows:

Beneficiary	*Allocation of Income*
A, B, and C	90% ($90,000 divided by $100,000)
X University	10% ($10,000 divided by $100,000)

(c) For the quarter ending December 31, 1970, each unit of participation is allocated $2 (90% × $2,000 divided by 900) of the income earned for that quarter. A, B, C and X University share in the income as follows:

Beneficiary	*Share of Income*
A	$ 200 (100 × $2)
B	400 (200 × $2)
C	1,200 (600 × $2)
X University	200 (10% × $2,000)

[Reg. § 1.642(c)-5.]

☐ [*T.D.* 7105, 4-5-71. *Amended by T.D.* 7125, 6-7-71; *T.D.* 7357, 5-30-75; *T.D.* 7633, 7-17-79 *and T.D.* 9102, 12-30-2003.]

[Reg. §1.642(c)-6]

§1.642(c)-6. Valuation of a remainder interest in property transferred to a pooled income fund.—(a) *In general.*—(1) For purposes of sections 170, 2055, 2106, and 2522, the fair market value of a remainder interest in property transferred to a pooled income fund is its present value determined under paragraph (d) of this section.

(2) The present value of a remainder interest at the time of the transfer of property to the pooled income fund is determined by computing the present value (at the time of the transfer) of the life income interest and subtracting that value from the fair market value of the transferred property on the valuation date. The fact that the income beneficiary may not receive the last income payment, as provided in paragraph (b)(7) of §1.642(c)-5, is not taken into account for purposes of determining the value of the life income interest. For purposes of this section, the valuation date is the date on which property is transferred to the fund by the donor except that, for purposes of section 2055 or 2106, it is the alternate valuation date, if elected, under the provisions and limitations set forth in section 2032 and the regulations thereunder.

(3) Any claim for a deduction on any return for the value of the remainder interest in property transferred to a pooled income fund must be supported by a statement attached to the return showing the computation of the present value of the interest.

(b) *Actuarial computations by the Internal Revenue Service.*—The regulations in this and in related sections provide tables of actuarial factors and examples that illustrate the use of the tables in determining the value of remainder interests in property. Section 1.7520-1(c)(2) refers to government publications that provide additional tables of factors and examples of computations for more complex situations. If the computation requires the use of a factor that is not provided in this section, the Commissioner may supply the factor upon a request for a ruling. A request for a ruling must be accompanied by a recitation of the facts including the pooled income fund's highest yearly rate of return for the 3 taxable years immediately preceding the date of transfer, the date of birth of each measuring life, and copies of the relevant documents. A request for a ruling must comply with the instructions for requesting a ruling published periodically in the Internal Revenue Bulletin (see §§601.201 and 601.601(d)(2)(ii)(*b*) of this chapter) and include payment of the required user fee. If the Commissioner furnishes the factor, a copy of the letter supplying the factor should be attached to the tax return in which the deduction is claimed. If the Commissioner does not furnish the factor, the taxpayer must furnish a factor computed in accordance with the principles set forth in this section.

(c) *Computation of pooled income fund's yearly rate of return.*—(1) For purposes of determining the present value of the life income interest, the yearly rate of return earned by a pooled income fund for a taxable year is the percentage obtained by dividing the amount of income earned by the pooled income fund for the taxable year by an amount equal to—

(i) The average fair market value of the property in such fund for that taxable year; less

(ii) The corrective term adjustment.

(2) The average fair market value of the property in a pooled income fund for a taxable year shall be the sum of the amounts of the fair market value of all property held by the pooled income fund on each determination date, as defined in paragraph (a)(5)(vi) of §1.642(c)-5, of such taxable year divided by the number of determination dates in such taxable year. For such purposes the fair market value of property held by the fund shall be determined without including any income earned by the fund.

(3)(i) The corrective term adjustment shall be the sum of the products obtained by multiplying each income payment made by the pooled income fund within its taxable year by the percentage set forth in column (2) of the following table opposite the period within such year, set forth in column (1), which includes the date on which that payment is made:

Table

(1) *Payment Period*	(2) *Percentage of Payment*
Last week of 4th quarter	Zero
Balance of 4th quarter	25
Last week of 3rd quarter	25
Balance of 3rd quarter	50
Last week of 2nd quarter	50
Balance of 2nd quarter	75
Last week of 1st quarter	75
Balance of 1st quarter	100

(ii) If the taxable year of the fund consists of less than 12 months, the corrective term adjustment shall be the sum of the products obtained by multiplying each income payment made by the pooled income fund within such taxable year by the percentage obtained by subtracting from 1 a fraction the numerator of which is the number of days from the first day of such taxable year to the date of such income payment and the denominator of which is 365.

(4) A pooled income fund's method of calculating its yearly rate of return must be supported by a full statement attached to the income tax return of the pooled income fund for each taxable year.

(5) The application of this paragraph may be illustrated by the following examples:

Example (1). (a) The pooled income fund maintained by W University has established determination dates on the first day of each calendar quarter. The pooled income fund is on a calendar-year basis. The pooled income fund earned $5,000 of income during 1971. The fair market value of its property (determined without including any income earned by the fund), and the income paid out, on the first day of each calendar quarter in 1971 are as follows:

Date	*Fair Market Value of Property*	*Income Payment*
Jan. 1	$100,000	$1,200
April 1	105,000	1,200
July 1	95,000	1,200
Oct. 1	100,000	1,400
	400,000	5,000

(b) The average fair market value of the property in the fund for 1971 is $100,000 ($400,000 divided by 4).

(c) The corrective term adjustment for 1971 is $3,050, determined by applying the percentages obtained in column (2) of the table in subparagraph (3) of this paragraph:

Multiplication			*Product*
100%	×	$1,200	$1,200
75%	×	1,200	900
50%	×	1,200	600
25%	×	1,400	350
Sum of Products			3,050

(d) The pooled income fund's yearly rate of return for 1971 is 5.157 percent, determined as follows:

$$\frac{\$5,000}{\$100,000-\$3,050} = .05157$$

Example (2). (a) The pooled income fund maintained by X University has established determination dates on the first day of each calendar quarter. The pooled income fund is on a calendar-year basis. The pooled income fund earned $5,000 of income during 1971 and paid out $3,000 on December 15, 1971, and $2,000 on January 15, 1972, the last amount being treated under paragraph (b)(7) of §1.642(c)-5 as paid on December 31, 1971. The fair market value of its property (determined without including any income earned by the fund) on the determination dates in 1971 and the income paid out during 1971 are as follows:

Date	*Fair Market Value of Property*	*Income Payment*
Jan. 1	$125,000	. . .
April 1	125,000	. . .
July 1	75,000	. . .
Oct. 1	75,000	
Dec. 15		$3,000
Dec. 31		2,000
	400,000	5,000

(b) The average fair market value of the property in the fund for 1971 is $100,000 ($400,000 divided by 4).

(c) The corrective term adjustment for 1971 is $750, determined by applying the percentages obtained in column (2) of the table in subparagraph (3) of this paragraph:

Multiplication		*Product*
0% ×	$2,000	$. .
25% ×	3,000	750
Sum of Products		750

(d) *Valuation.*—The present value of the remainder interest in property transferred to a pooled income fund on or after May 1, 2009, is determined under paragraph (e) of this section. The present value of the remainder interest in property transferred to a pooled income fund for which the valuation date is before May 1, 2009, is determined under the following sections:

Valuation Dates		*Applicable Regulations*
After	*Before*	
-	01-01-52	1.642(c)-6A(a)
12-31-51	01-01-71	1.642(c)-6A(b)
12-31-70	12-01-83	1.642(c)-6A(c)
11-30-83	05-01-89	1.642(c)-6A(d)
04-30-89	05-01-99	1.642(c)-6A(e)
04-30-99	05-01-09	1.642(c)-6A(f)

(e) *Present value of the remainder interest in the case of transfers to pooled income funds for which the valuation date is on or after May 1, 2009.*—(1) *In general.*—In the case of transfers to pooled income funds for which the valuation date is on or after May 1, 2009, the present value of a remainder interest is determined under this section. See, however, §1.7520-3(b) (relating to exceptions to the use of prescribed tables under certain circumstances). The present value of a remainder interest that is dependent on the termination of the life of one individual is computed by the use of Table S in paragraph (e)(6) of this section. For purposes of the computations under this section, the age of an individual is the age at the individual's nearest birthday.

(2) *Transitional rules for valuation of transfers to pooled income funds.*—(i) For purposes of sections 2055, 2106, or 2624, if on May 1, 2009, the decedent was mentally incompetent so that the disposition of the property could not be changed, and the decedent died on or after May 1, 2009, without having regained competency to dispose of the decedent's property, or the decedent died within 90 days of the date that the decedent first regained competency on or after May 1, 2009, the present value of a remainder interest is determined as if the valuation date with respect to the decedent's gross estate is either before or after May 1, 2009, at the option of the decedent's executor.

(ii) For purposes of sections 170, 2055, 2106, 2522, or 2624, in the case of transfers to a pooled income fund for which the valuation date is on or after May 1, 2009, and before July 1, 2009, the present value of the remainder interest under this section is determined by use of the appropriate yearly rate of return for the month in which the valuation date occurs (see §§1.7520-1(b) and 1.7520-2(a)(2)) and the appropriate actuarial tables under either paragraph (e)(6) of this section or §1.642(c)-6A(f)(6), at the option of the donor or the decedent's executor, as the case may be.

(iii) For purposes of paragraphs (e)(2)(i) and (e)(2)(ii) of this section, where the donor or decedent's executor is given the option to use the appropriate actuarial tables under either paragraph (e)(6) of this section or §1.642(c)-6A(f)(6), the donor or decedent's executor must use the same actuarial table with respect to each individual transaction and with respect to all transfers occurring on the valuation date (for example, gift and income tax charitable deductions with respect to the same transfer must be determined based on the same tables, and all assets includible in the gross estate and/or estate tax deductions claimed must be valued based on the same tables).

(3) *Present value of a remainder interest.*—The present value of a remainder interest in property transferred to a pooled income fund is computed on the basis of—

(i) Life contingencies determined from the values of lx that are set forth in Table 2000CM in §20.2031-7(d)(7) of this chapter (see §20.2031-7A for certain prior periods); and

(ii) Discount at a rate of interest, compounded annually, equal to the highest yearly rate of return of the pooled income fund for the 3 taxable years immediately preceding its taxable year in which the transfer of property to the fund is made. For purposes of this paragraph (e), the yearly rate of return of a pooled income fund is determined as provided in paragraph (c) of this section unless the highest rate of return is deemed to be the rate described in paragraph (e)(4) of this section for funds in existence less than 3 taxable years. For purposes of this paragraph (e)(3)(ii), the first taxable year of a pooled income fund is considered a taxable year even though the taxable year consists of less than 12 months. However, appropriate adjustments must be made to annualize the rate of return earned by the fund for that period. Where it appears from the facts and circumstances that the highest yearly rate of return of the fund for the 3 taxable years immediately preceding the taxable year in which the transfer of property is made has been purposely manipulated to be substantially less than the rate of return that would otherwise be reasonably anticipated with the purpose of obtaining an excessive charitable deduction, that rate of return may not be used.

In that case, the highest yearly rate of return of the fund is determined by treating the fund as a pooled income fund that has been in existence for less than 3 preceding taxable years.

(4) *Pooled income funds in existence less than 3 taxable years.*—If a pooled income fund has been in existence less than 3 taxable years immediately preceding the taxable year in which the transfer is made to the fund and the transfer to the fund is made after April 30, 1989, the highest rate of return is deemed to be the interest rate (rounded to the nearest two-tenths of one percent) that is 1 percent less than the highest annual average of the monthly section 7520 rates for the 3 calendar years immediately preceding the calendar year in which the transfer to the pooled income fund is made. The deemed rate of return for transfers to new pooled income funds is recomputed each calendar year using the monthly section 7520 rates for the 3-year period immediately preceding the calendar year in which each transfer to the fund is made until the fund has been in existence for 3 taxable years and can compute its highest rate of return for the 3 taxable years immediately preceding the taxable year in which the transfer of property to the fund is made in accordance with the rules set forth in the first sentence of paragraph (e)(3)(ii) of this section.

(5) *Computation of value of remainder interest.*—(i) The factor that is used in determining the present value of a remainder interest that is dependent on the termination of the life of one individual is the factor from Table S in paragraph (e)(6) of this section under the appropriate yearly rate of return opposite the number that corresponds to the age of the individual upon whose life the value of the remainder interest is based (See § 1.642(c)-6A for certain prior periods). The tables in paragraph (e)(6) of this section include factors for yearly rates of return from 0.2 to 14 percent. Many actuarial factors not contained in the tables in paragraph (e)(6) of this section are contained in Table S in Internal Revenue Service Publication 1457, "Actuarial Valuations Version 3A" (2009). This publication is available, at no charge, electronically via the IRS Internet site at *www.irs.gov*. For other situations, see paragraph (b) of this section. If the yearly rate of return is a percentage that is between the yearly rates of return for which factors are provided, a linear interpolation must be made. The present value of the remainder interest is determined by multiplying the fair market value of the property on the valuation date by the appropriate remainder factor.

(ii) This paragraph (e)(5) may be illustrated by the following example:

Example. A, who is 54 years and 8 months, transfers $100,000 to a pooled income fund, and retains a life income interest in the property. The highest yearly rate of return earned by the fund for its 3 preceding taxable years is 9.47 percent. In Table S, the remainder factor opposite 55 years under 9.4 percent is .16192 and under 9.6 percent is .15755. The present value of the remainder interest is $16,039.00, computed as follows:

Factor at 9.4 percent for age 55	.16192
Factor at 9.6 percent for age 55	.15755
Difference	.00437

Interpolation adjustment:

$$\frac{9.47\% - 9.4\%}{0.2\%} = \frac{x}{.00437}$$

$$x = .00153$$

Factor at 9.4 percent for age 55	.16192
Less: Interpolation adjustment	.00153
Interpolated factor	.16039
Present value of remainder interest: ($100,000 X .16039)	$16,039.00

(6) *Actuarial tables.*—In the case of transfers for which the valuation date is on or after May 1, 2009, the present value of a remainder interest dependent on the termination of one life in the case of a transfer to a pooled income fund is determined by use of the following Table S:

Table S
Based on Life Table 2000CM
Single Life Remainder Factors
Applicable On or After May 1, 2009

	Interest Rate									
AGE	0.2%	0.4%	0.6%	0.8%	1.0%	1.2%	1.4%	1.6%	1.8%	2.0%
0	.85816	.73751	.63478	.54723	.47252	.40872	.35416	.30747	.26745	.23313
1	.85889	.73863	.63604	.54844	.47355	.40948	.35459	.30752	.26711	.23239
2	.86054	.74145	.63968	.55260	.47802	.41409	.35922	.31209	.27155	.23664
3	.86221	.74433	.64339	.55687	.48263	.41887	.36404	.31685	.27619	.24112
4	.86390	.74725	.64716	.56121	.48733	.42374	.36898	.32175	.28098	.24575
5	.86560	.75018	.65097	.56561	.49209	.42871	.37401	.32675	.28588	.25050
6	.86731	.75314	.65482	.57006	.49692	.43375	.37913	.33186	.29090	.25538
7	.86902	.75611	.65868	.57454	.50180	.43885	.38432	.33704	.29601	.26035
8	.87073	.75909	.66258	.57907	.50674	.44403	.38960	.34233	.30122	.26544
9	.87246	.76209	.66651	.58364	.51173	.44928	.39497	.34771	.30654	.27064
10	.87419	.76511	.67046	.58826	.51679	.45459	.40042	.35319	.31197	.27596
11	.87592	.76814	.67445	.59291	.52190	.45998	.40596	.35876	.31750	.28139
12	.87766	.77119	.67845	.59761	.52706	.46544	.41157	.36443	.32313	.28693
13	.87939	.77424	.68247	.60232	.53225	.47094	.41723	.37015	.32884	.29255
14	.88112	.77728	.68649	.60704	.53746	.47646	.42293	.37592	.33460	.29823
15	.88284	.78031	.69050	.61176	.54267	.48199	.42865	.38172	.34038	.30394
16	.88455	.78333	.69449	.61647	.54788	.48752	.43437	.38752	.34619	.30968
17	.88625	.78633	.69848	.62117	.55309	.49307	.44012	.39336	.35203	.31546
18	.88795	.78933	.70246	.62588	.55830	.49863	.44589	.39923	.35791	.32129
19	.88964	.79232	.70644	.63059	.56354	.50422	.45170	.40514	.36385	.32719
20	.89132	.79532	.71044	.63534	.56882	.50987	.45757	.41114	.36987	.33317
21	.89301	.79832	.71445	.64010	.57413	.51555	.46350	.41719	.37597	.33925
22	.89470	.80133	.71847	.64488	.57947	.52129	.46948	.42332	.38216	.34541
23	.89639	.80434	.72251	.64970	.58486	.52708	.47554	.42954	.38844	.35168
24	.89808	.80737	.72658	.65456	.59031	.53295	.48169	.43586	.39484	.35809
25	.89978	.81042	.73068	.65947	.59583	.53890	.48795	.44230	.40137	.36464
26	.90149	.81349	.73482	.66443	.60141	.54494	.49430	.44886	.40804	.37134
27	.90320	.81657	.73899	.66944	.60707	.55107	.50076	.45554	.41484	.37819
28	.90492	.81968	.74319	.67450	.61278	.55728	.50733	.46233	.42178	.38520
29	.90665	.82279	.74741	.67960	.61856	.56356	.51398	.46924	.42884	.39233
30	.90837	.82591	.75165	.68473	.62438	.56990	.52070	.47623	.43601	.39959
31	.91010	.82904	.75592	.68989	.63024	.57631	.52751	.48333	.44329	.40698
32	.91182	.83218	.76020	.69509	.63616	.58278	.53440	.49052	.45068	.41449
33	.91355	.83532	.76449	.70031	.64212	.58931	.54137	.49780	.45818	.42213
34	.91527	.83847	.76880	.70556	.64811	.59589	.54839	.50516	.46578	.42988
35	.91700	.84162	.77312	.71082	.65414	.60253	.55549	.51261	.47347	.43774
36	.91872	.84477	.77744	.71611	.66021	.60921	.56266	.52014	.48127	.44572
37	.92043	.84792	.78178	.72142	.66631	.61594	.56989	.52774	.48916	.45381
38	.92215	.85107	.78613	.72675	.67244	.62272	.57718	.53544	.49715	.46201
39	.92386	.85422	.79048	.73210	.67860	.62955	.58453	.54320	.50523	.47032
40	.92557	.85736	.79483	.73746	.68479	.63641	.59194	.55104	.51340	.47873
41	.92727	.86050	.79918	.74283	.69100	.64331	.59940	.55894	.52165	.48724
42	.92896	.86364	.80354	.74820	.69723	.65024	.60690	.56691	.52998	.49585
43	.93065	.86677	.80789	.75359	.70348	.65721	.61447	.57495	.53840	.50457
44	.93234	.86990	.81225	.75899	.70976	.66422	.62208	.58305	.54690	.51338
45	.93402	.87302	.81660	.76439	.71605	.67125	.62973	.59122	.55547	.52228
46	.93569	.87613	.82095	.76980	.72236	.67832	.63743	.59945	.56413	.53129
47	.93735	.87924	.82530	.77521	.72867	.68541	.64517	.60773	.57286	.54037
48	.93901	.88233	.82964	.78062	.73501	.69253	.65295	.61606	.58166	.54955
49	.94065	.88541	.83397	.78604	.74135	.69967	.66077	.62446	.59053	.55882

AGE	0.2%	0.4%	0.6%	0.8%	1.0%	1.2%	1.4%	1.6%	1.8%	2.0%
50	.94229	.88849	.83830	.79145	.74771	.70684	.66864	.63292	.59949	.56819
51	.94393	.89156	.84263	.79688	.75409	.71404	.67655	.64143	.60852	.57766
52	.94556	.89462	.84695	.80230	.76048	.72127	.68450	.65001	.61763	.58722
53	.94717	.89767	.85126	.80772	.76687	.72852	.69249	.65863	.62680	.59687
54	.94878	.90070	.85555	.81313	.77326	.73577	.70050	.66730	.63603	.60658
55	.95037	.90371	.85983	.81853	.77964	.74302	.70851	.67598	.64530	.61635
56	.95195	.90670	.86406	.82388	.78599	.75024	.71651	.68465	.65457	.62613
57	.95351	.90965	.86827	.82920	.79230	.75744	.72448	.69332	.66384	.63593
58	.95505	.91257	.87243	.83447	.79857	.76459	.73242	.70195	.67309	.64573
59	.95657	.91546	.87655	.83970	.80479	.77170	.74033	.71057	.68233	.65553
60	.95807	.91832	.88064	.84490	.81098	.77879	.74822	.71918	.69158	.66534
61	.95955	.92115	.88469	.85005	.81713	.78584	.75608	.72776	.70081	.67515
62	.96101	.92395	.88869	.85515	.82323	.79283	.76388	.73630	.71001	.68494
63	.96245	.92670	.89265	.86020	.82926	.79977	.77164	.74479	.71917	.69470
64	.96387	.92942	.89655	.86518	.83524	.80665	.77933	.75323	.72828	.70443
65	.96527	.93210	.90040	.87011	.84116	.81346	.78697	.76162	.73735	.71411
66	.96665	.93476	.90423	.87502	.84706	.82027	.79461	.77002	.74645	.72385
67	.96802	.93739	.90803	.87990	.85292	.82705	.80223	.77841	.75554	.73359
68	.96937	.93999	.91179	.88472	.85874	.83378	.80980	.78676	.76461	.74331
69	.97070	.94255	.91549	.88949	.86449	.84044	.81731	.79504	.77362	.75299
70	.97200	.94506	.91914	.89419	.87016	.84702	.82473	.80326	.78256	.76260
71	.97328	.94754	.92273	.89882	.87577	.85353	.83209	.81140	.79143	.77215
72	.97453	.94997	.92626	.90338	.88129	.85996	.83935	.81945	.80021	.78162
73	.97576	.95234	.92972	.90785	.88671	.86627	.84651	.82739	.80888	.79098
74	.97695	.95466	.93310	.91223	.89202	.87247	.85353	.83518	.81741	.80019
75	.97811	.95692	.93638	.91649	.89720	.87851	.86039	.84281	.82577	.80923
76	.97924	.95910	.93957	.92063	.90224	.88440	.86708	.85026	.83393	.81807
77	.98033	.96122	.94267	.92465	.90715	.89013	.87360	.85753	.84191	.82671
78	.98138	.96327	.94567	.92855	.91190	.89571	.87995	.86461	.84968	.83515
79	.98239	.96526	.94857	.93233	.91652	.90112	.88611	.87149	.85725	.84337
80	.98337	.96717	.95138	.93598	.92098	.90635	.89208	.87817	.86460	.85135
81	.98431	.96901	.95408	.93951	.92529	.91141	.89786	.88463	.87172	.85910
82	.98521	.97077	.95667	.94290	.92944	.91629	.90344	.89088	.87861	.86660
83	.98608	.97247	.95917	.94616	.93343	.92099	.90882	.89691	.88526	.87385
84	.98691	.97409	.96156	.94928	.93727	.92551	.91399	.90271	.89166	.88084
85	.98770	.97565	.96384	.95228	.94094	.92984	.91895	.90828	.89782	.88757
86	.98845	.97713	.96602	.95514	.94446	.93398	.92371	.91362	.90373	.89402
87	.98917	.97854	.96810	.95786	.94781	.93794	.92825	.91873	.90939	.90021
88	.98985	.97988	.97008	.96046	.95100	.94171	.93258	.92361	.91479	.90612
89	.99049	.98115	.97196	.96292	.95404	.94530	.93671	.92826	.91994	.91176
90	.99110	.98235	.97373	.96526	.95691	.94871	.94062	.93267	.92484	.91713
91	.99168	.98348	.97541	.96747	.95964	.95193	.94434	.93686	.92949	.92223
92	.99222	.98455	.97700	.96955	.96222	.95498	.94785	.94083	.93390	.92707
93	.99273	.98556	.97849	.97152	.96464	.95786	.95117	.94457	.93806	.93163
94	.99321	.98651	.97989	.97337	.96692	.96057	.95429	.94810	.94199	.93595
95	.99366	.98739	.98121	.97510	.96907	.96312	.95724	.95143	.94569	.94002
96	.99408	.98822	.98244	.97673	.97108	.96551	.95999	.95454	.94916	.94384
97	.99447	.98900	.98359	.97825	.97297	.96774	.96258	.95747	.95242	.94742
98	.99483	.98973	.98467	.97967	.97473	.96984	.96500	.96021	.95547	.95078
99	.99518	.99040	.98568	.98101	.97638	.97180	.96727	.96278	.95834	.95394
100	.99549	.99103	.98661	.98224	.97791	.97362	.96937	.96516	.96100	.95687
101	.99579	.99162	.98750	.98340	.97935	.97534	.97136	.96742	.96351	.95964
102	.99607	.99217	.98831	.98448	.98068	.97692	.97319	.96950	.96583	.96220
103	.99634	.99271	.98911	.98553	.98199	.97848	.97500	.97155	.96812	.96473
104	.99659	.99320	.98984	.98651	.98320	.97992	.97666	.97344	.97023	.96705

See p. 15 for regulations not amended to reflect law changes

AGE	0.2%	0.4%	0.6%	0.8%	1.0%	1.2%	1.4%	1.6%	1.8%	2.0%
105	.99683	.99369	.99056	.98747	.98439	.98134	.97830	.97530	.97231	.96934
106	.99713	.99429	.99146	.98865	.98586	.98309	.98033	.97760	.97488	.97218
107	.99747	.99496	.99246	.98998	.98751	.98506	.98262	.98020	.97779	.97539
108	.99800	.99602	.99404	.99208	.99012	.98818	.98624	.98431	.98240	.98049
109	.99900	.99801	.99702	.99603	.99505	.99407	.99310	.99213	.99116	.99020

Table S
Based on Life Table 2000CM
Single Life Remainder Factors
Applicable On or After May 1, 2009

Interest Rate

AGE	2.2%	2.4%	2.6%	2.8%	3.0%	3.2%	3.4%	3.6%	3.8%	4.0%
0	.20365	.17830	.15648	.13767	.12144	.10741	.09528	.08476	.07564	.06772
1	.20251	.17677	.15458	.13542	.11885	.10451	.09209	.08131	.07194	.06379
2	.20656	.18060	.15817	.13877	.12197	.10740	.09476	.08376	.07420	.06586
3	.21084	.18466	.16200	.14236	.12533	.11054	.09767	.08647	.07670	.06817
4	.21527	.18888	.16600	.14613	.12887	.11385	.10076	.08935	.07938	.07066
5	.21984	.19324	.17013	.15004	.13255	.11730	.10399	.09237	.08220	.07329
6	.22454	.19773	.17440	.15408	.13636	.12089	.10736	.09553	.08515	.07605
7	.22933	.20233	.17879	.15824	.14030	.12460	.11085	.09880	.08822	.07892
8	.23425	.20705	.18330	.16254	.14436	.12844	.11447	.10221	.09142	.08193
9	.23930	.21191	.18795	.16697	.14857	.13243	.11824	.10576	.09476	.08507
10	.24446	.21689	.19273	.17153	.15292	.13655	.12214	.10945	.09824	.08835
11	.24975	.22200	.19764	.17623	.15740	.14081	.12619	.11328	.10187	.09177
12	.25515	.22724	.20268	.18107	.16202	.14521	.13037	.11724	.10563	.09533
13	.26064	.23256	.20782	.18600	.16674	.14972	.13466	.12132	.10949	.09900
14	.26620	.23796	.21303	.19101	.17154	.15430	.13903	.12547	.11344	.10273
15	.27179	.24340	.21829	.19607	.17639	.15894	.14344	.12968	.11743	.10652
16	.27742	.24887	.22358	.20117	.18128	.16361	.14790	.13391	.12145	.11034
17	.28309	.25439	.22893	.20632	.18622	.16834	.15241	.13821	.12554	.11421
18	.28881	.25997	.23434	.21154	.19123	.17314	.15699	.14258	.12969	.11815
19	.29461	.26563	.23983	.21684	.19633	.17803	.16167	.14703	.13393	.12218
20	.30050	.27139	.24543	.22226	.20156	.18304	.16646	.15161	.13829	.12633
21	.30649	.27726	.25114	.22779	.20689	.18817	.17138	.15631	.14277	.13060
22	.31259	.28323	.25697	.23344	.21235	.19342	.17642	.16114	.14739	.13500
23	.31879	.28934	.26293	.23923	.21795	.19882	.18161	.16612	.15215	.13955
24	.32515	.29559	.26904	.24519	.22372	.20440	.18699	.17128	.15710	.14429
25	.33166	.30201	.27534	.25133	.22969	.21018	.19256	.17665	.16226	.14924
26	.33833	.30861	.28182	.25767	.23586	.21616	.19835	.18224	.16764	.15440
27	.34517	.31538	.28849	.26420	.24224	.22236	.20436	.18804	.17324	.15980
28	.35217	.32233	.29535	.27093	.24882	.22877	.21058	.19407	.17907	.16542
29	.35932	.32944	.30237	.27784	.25558	.23537	.21701	.20031	.18511	.17126
30	.36661	.33670	.30956	.28492	.26253	.24216	.22362	.20674	.19135	.17730
31	.37403	.34411	.31691	.29217	.26965	.24914	.23044	.21338	.19779	.18355
32	.38160	.35167	.32442	.29960	.27697	.25631	.23745	.22022	.20445	.19002
33	.38930	.35939	.33211	.30721	.28447	.26368	.24467	.22727	.21133	.19671
34	.39713	.36724	.33993	.31497	.29213	.27123	.25207	.23451	.21839	.20360
35	.40509	.37523	.34792	.32290	.29998	.27896	.25967	.24195	.22567	.21070
36	.41318	.38337	.35606	.33100	.30800	.28688	.26746	.24961	.23317	.21803
37	.42139	.39165	.36435	.33927	.31621	.29499	.27546	.25746	.24087	.22557
38	.42974	.40008	.37281	.34771	.32460	.30330	.28366	.26554	.24880	.23334
39	.43821	.40864	.38141	.35631	.33316	.31179	.29205	.27381	.25694	.24133
40	.44679	.41734	.39016	.36507	.34189	.32046	.30064	.28229	.26529	.24954
41	.45549	.42616	.39906	.37399	.35080	.32932	.30942	.29097	.27386	.25797
42	.46430	.43511	.40809	.38307	.35987	.33836	.31840	.29986	.28264	.26662

AGE	2.2%	2.4%	2.6%	2.8%	3.0%	3.2%	3.4%	3.6%	3.8%	4.0%
43	.47324	.44421	.41729	.39232	.36913	.34760	.32758	.30897	.29165	.27552
44	.48229	.45343	.42663	.40172	.37857	.35702	.33697	.31829	.30088	.28465
45	.49144	.46277	.43611	.41128	.38817	.36663	.34655	.32782	.31033	.29400
46	.50072	.47225	.44574	.42101	.39796	.37644	.35634	.33757	.32002	.30360
47	.51009	.48185	.45550	.43089	.40791	.38642	.36633	.34753	.32992	.31343
48	.51958	.49158	.46540	.44093	.41803	.39660	.37652	.35770	.34006	.32351
49	.52917	.50143	.47545	.45113	.42833	.40696	.38691	.36810	.35043	.33383
50	.53888	.51141	.48566	.46150	.43883	.41754	.39754	.37874	.36106	.34442
51	.54871	.52153	.49602	.47204	.44951	.42832	.40838	.38961	.37194	.35528
52	.55865	.53179	.50653	.48276	.46038	.43931	.41945	.40073	.38307	.36641
53	.56869	.54217	.51718	.49363	.47143	.45050	.43074	.41208	.39446	.37781
54	.57882	.55265	.52796	.50465	.48265	.46186	.44222	.42364	.40607	.38945
55	.58902	.56322	.53884	.51579	.49400	.47338	.45387	.43540	.41789	.40131
56	.59926	.57383	.54978	.52701	.50544	.48501	.46565	.44729	.42987	.41335
57	.60951	.58449	.56078	.53830	.51698	.49675	.47755	.45932	.44201	.42555
58	.61978	.59517	.57182	.54964	.52858	.50858	.48956	.47147	.45427	.43790
59	.63007	.60589	.58290	.56105	.54027	.52050	.50167	.48375	.46668	.45041
60	.64039	.61665	.59405	.57254	.55205	.53253	.51392	.49617	.47925	.46310
61	.65072	.62743	.60524	.58409	.56390	.54465	.52627	.50872	.49196	.47595
62	.66104	.63822	.61645	.59566	.57581	.55683	.53870	.52136	.50478	.48892
63	.67133	.64900	.62766	.60726	.58774	.56907	.55120	.53409	.51770	.50200
64	.68161	.65977	.63887	.61887	.59970	.58134	.56375	.54688	.53071	.51519
65	.69186	.67053	.65009	.63049	.61170	.59367	.57637	.55976	.54381	.52849
66	.70216	.68136	.66140	.64223	.62383	.60615	.58916	.57283	.55713	.54203
67	.71250	.69224	.67277	.65405	.63605	.61874	.60208	.58605	.57062	.55575
68	.72283	.70312	.68416	.66590	.64833	.63140	.61509	.59938	.58423	.56963
69	.73312	.71398	.69553	.67776	.66062	.64409	.62815	.61277	.59793	.58360
70	.74335	.72479	.70688	.68959	.67291	.65680	.64124	.62621	.61168	.59764
71	.75353	.73556	.71819	.70141	.68519	.66951	.65434	.63968	.62549	.61176
72	.76364	.74626	.72945	.71318	.69744	.68220	.66745	.65317	.63933	.62593
73	.77365	.75686	.74061	.72487	.70962	.69484	.68051	.66662	.65315	.64009
74	.78350	.76733	.75164	.73643	.72167	.70735	.69346	.67997	.66688	.65417
75	.79318	.77761	.76249	.74781	.73355	.71971	.70625	.69318	.68048	.66813
76	.80266	.78769	.77314	.75899	.74524	.73187	.71886	.70621	.69390	.68192
77	.81194	.79756	.78358	.76997	.75672	.74382	.73127	.71904	.70713	.69553
78	.82100	.80722	.79380	.78072	.76798	.75556	.74346	.73166	.72016	.70894
79	.82984	.81664	.80378	.79124	.77900	.76706	.75542	.74405	.73296	.72213
80	.83843	.82582	.81351	.80149	.78976	.77830	.76711	.75618	.74550	.73507
81	.84678	.83474	.82298	.81148	.80025	.78927	.77853	.76803	.75777	.74773
82	.85487	.84339	.83217	.82119	.81045	.79994	.78966	.77959	.76974	.76009
83	.86269	.85177	.84107	.83060	.82035	.81030	.80047	.79083	.78139	.77214
84	.87024	.85986	.84968	.83970	.82993	.82035	.81095	.80174	.79271	.78385
85	.87751	.86765	.85798	.84849	.83919	.83005	.82110	.81230	.80368	.79521
86	.88450	.87515	.86597	.85696	.84811	.83942	.83089	.82251	.81428	.80619
87	.89119	.88234	.87363	.86508	.85668	.84843	.84031	.83234	.82450	.81679
88	.89760	.88922	.88099	.87289	.86492	.85708	.84938	.84180	.83434	.82700
89	.90372	.89580	.88801	.88034	.87280	.86537	.85806	.85087	.84378	.83681
90	.90954	.90207	.89471	.88746	.88032	.87329	.86637	.85954	.85282	.84620
91	.91508	.90803	.90109	.89424	.88750	.88085	.87429	.86783	.86146	.85518
92	.92033	.91369	.90714	.90068	.89432	.88803	.88184	.87572	.86969	.86374
93	.92530	.91904	.91287	.90678	.90078	.89484	.88899	.88321	.87751	.87188
94	.92999	.92411	.91830	.91256	.90690	.90130	.89578	.89032	.88493	.87961
95	.93442	.92889	.92342	.91802	.91269	.90741	.90220	.89706	.89197	.88694
96	.93858	.93338	.92824	.92316	.91813	.91316	.90825	.90340	.89859	.89385
97	.94248	.93759	.93276	.92798	.92325	.91857	.91395	.90937	.90484	.90036

See p. 15 for regulations not amended to reflect law changes

AGE	2.2%	2.4%	2.6%	2.8%	3.0%	3.2%	3.4%	3.6%	3.8%	4.0%
98	.94614	.94155	.93701	.93252	.92807	.92367	.91931	.91500	.91073	.90650
99	.94959	.94528	.94101	.93679	.93260	.92846	.92436	.92030	.91628	.91229
100	.95278	.94874	.94473	.94075	.93682	.93292	.92906	.92523	.92144	.91769
101	.95581	.95201	.94824	.94451	.94081	.93715	.93352	.92992	.92635	.92281
102	.95860	.95503	.95149	.94798	.94450	.94105	.93763	.93424	.93088	.92754
103	.96136	.95802	.95470	.95142	.94816	.94492	.94171	.93853	.93538	.93224
104	.96390	.96077	.95766	.95458	.95152	.94848	.94547	.94248	.93951	.93657
105	.96640	.96347	.96057	.95769	.95483	.95199	.94917	.94637	.94359	.94083
106	.96950	.96684	.96420	.96157	.95896	.95636	.95379	.95123	.94868	.94616
107	.97301	.97064	.96829	.96595	.96362	.96131	.95901	.95672	.95445	.95219
108	.97859	.97670	.97482	.97295	.97109	.96923	.96739	.96555	.96373	.96191
109	.98924	.98828	.98733	.98638	.98544	.98450	.98356	.98263	.98170	.98077

Table S
Based on Life Table 2000CM
Single Life Remainder Factors
Applicable On or After May 1, 2009

Interest Rate

AGE	4.2%	4.4%	4.6%	4.8%	5.0%	5.2%	5.4%	5.6%	5.8%	6.0%
0	.06083	.05483	.04959	.04501	.04101	.03749	.03441	.03170	.02931	.02721
1	.05668	.05049	.04507	.04034	.03618	.03254	.02934	.02652	.02403	.02183
2	.05858	.05222	.04665	.04178	.03750	.03373	.03042	.02750	.02492	.02264
3	.06072	.05420	.04848	.04346	.03904	.03516	.03173	.02871	.02603	.02366
4	.06303	.05634	.05046	.04530	.04075	.03674	.03319	.03006	.02729	.02483
5	.06547	.05861	.05258	.04726	.04258	.03844	.03478	.03153	.02866	.02610
6	.06805	.06102	.05482	.04935	.04453	.04026	.03647	.03312	.03014	.02749
7	.07074	.06353	.05717	.05155	.04658	.04217	.03826	.03479	.03171	.02895
8	.07356	.06617	.05964	.05386	.04875	.04421	.04017	.03658	.03338	.03053
9	.07651	.06895	.06225	.05631	.05105	.04637	.04220	.03849	.03518	.03222
10	.07960	.07185	.06499	.05889	.05347	.04865	.04435	.04052	.03709	.03402
11	.08283	.07490	.06786	.06160	.05603	.05106	.04663	.04267	.03912	.03594
12	.08620	.07808	.07087	.06444	.05871	.05360	.04903	.04494	.04127	.03798
13	.08967	.08137	.07397	.06738	.06149	.05623	.05152	.04729	.04351	.04010
14	.09321	.08472	.07715	.07038	.06433	.05892	.05406	.04971	.04579	.04227
15	.09680	.08812	.08036	.07342	.06721	.06164	.05664	.05214	.04810	.04445
16	.10041	.09154	.08360	.07649	.07011	.06438	.05923	.05459	.05041	.04664
17	.10409	.09502	.08689	.07960	.07305	.06716	.06185	.05707	.05276	.04886
18	.10782	.09855	.09024	.08276	.07604	.06998	.06452	.05959	.05514	.05111
19	.11164	.10217	.09366	.08600	.07910	.07288	.06726	.06218	.05758	.05341
20	.11559	.10592	.09721	.08937	.08228	.07589	.07010	.06487	.06012	.05582
21	.11965	.10977	.10087	.09283	.08557	.07900	.07305	.06765	.06276	.05831
22	.12383	.11376	.10465	.09642	.08897	.08223	.07610	.07055	.06550	.06090
23	.12817	.11789	.10859	.10016	.09252	.08559	.07930	.07358	.06837	.06363
24	.13270	.12221	.11270	.10408	.09625	.08914	.08267	.07678	.07141	.06651
25	.13744	.12674	.11703	.10821	.10019	.09289	.08625	.08018	.07465	.06960
26	.14239	.13149	.12158	.11256	.10435	.09686	.09003	.08380	.07810	.07288
27	.14758	.13647	.12636	.11714	.10873	.10106	.09405	.08764	.08177	.07639
28	.15300	.14169	.13137	.12195	.11335	.10549	.09829	.09171	.08567	.08012
29	.15864	.14712	.13660	.12698	.11819	.11013	.10275	.09598	.08977	.08406
30	.16448	.15275	.14203	.13222	.12323	.11498	.10742	.10047	.09408	.08820
31	.17053	.15861	.14769	.13768	.12849	.12006	.11230	.10517	.09860	.09255
32	.17680	.16468	.15357	.14336	.13398	.12535	.11741	.11009	.10335	.09712
33	.18330	.17099	.15968	.14927	.13970	.13088	.12275	.11525	.10832	.10192
34	.19000	.17750	.16599	.15539	.14562	.13661	.12829	.12061	.11350	.10693
35	.19692	.18423	.17253	.16174	.15178	.14258	.13408	.12621	.11892	.11217

AGE	4.2%	4.4%	4.6%	4.8%	5.0%	5.2%	5.4%	5.6%	5.8%	6.0%
36	.20407	.19119	.17931	.16833	.15818	.14879	.14009	.13204	.12457	.11764
37	.21144	.19838	.18631	.17515	.16481	.15523	.14635	.13811	.13046	.12335
38	.21904	.20582	.19357	.18222	.17170	.16193	.15287	.14444	.13661	.12932
39	.22687	.21348	.20105	.18952	.17882	.16887	.15962	.15102	.14300	.13554
40	.23493	.22137	.20878	.19707	.18619	.17606	.16663	.15784	.14965	.14201
41	.24322	.22950	.21674	.20487	.19381	.18350	.17390	.16493	.15656	.14873
42	.25173	.23786	.22494	.21290	.20168	.19120	.18141	.17227	.16372	.15572
43	.26049	.24648	.23342	.22122	.20982	.19918	.18922	.17990	.17118	.16301
44	.26950	.25535	.24214	.22979	.21824	.20742	.19730	.18781	.17892	.17057
45	.27874	.26447	.25112	.23862	.22692	.21595	.20566	.19600	.18694	.17843
46	.28824	.27385	.26038	.24774	.23589	.22476	.21431	.20450	.19527	.18659
47	.29798	.28349	.26989	.25712	.24513	.23386	.22326	.21328	.20390	.19505
48	.30797	.29338	.27967	.26678	.25466	.24325	.23250	.22238	.21283	.20383
49	.31822	.30355	.28974	.27674	.26449	.25294	.24206	.23179	.22210	.21294
50	.32876	.31401	.30011	.28701	.27465	.26298	.25196	.24156	.23172	.22242
51	.33958	.32477	.31079	.29759	.28513	.27335	.26221	.25168	.24170	.23226
52	.35068	.33582	.32178	.30851	.29595	.28407	.27282	.26216	.25206	.24249
53	.36206	.34717	.33308	.31974	.30710	.29513	.28378	.27301	.26279	.25309
54	.37371	.35880	.34467	.33127	.31857	.30651	.29507	.28420	.27388	.26406
55	.38559	.37067	.35652	.34308	.33032	.31820	.30668	.29572	.28529	.27537
56	.39765	.38275	.36859	.35512	.34232	.33014	.31855	.30751	.29699	.28697
57	.40990	.39502	.38086	.36739	.35455	.34233	.33068	.31957	.30898	.29887
58	.42231	.40747	.39333	.37985	.36700	.35474	.34304	.33188	.32121	.31103
59	.43490	.42011	.40600	.39253	.37968	.36740	.35567	.34446	.33374	.32348
60	.44768	.43296	.41890	.40546	.39261	.38033	.36858	.35733	.34656	.33625
61	.46064	.44600	.43200	.41860	.40578	.39351	.38175	.37048	.35968	.34933
62	.47373	.45920	.44527	.43194	.41915	.40690	.39514	.38387	.37305	.36267
63	.48696	.47253	.45870	.44544	.43271	.42049	.40876	.39749	.38666	.37625
64	.50030	.48601	.47229	.45911	.44645	.43428	.42258	.41133	.40051	.39010
65	.51377	.49963	.48603	.47295	.46037	.44827	.43662	.42540	.41460	.40420
66	.52750	.51352	.50007	.48711	.47464	.46262	.45103	.43987	.42911	.41872
67	.54144	.52765	.51436	.50154	.48919	.47727	.46578	.45468	.44397	.43363
68	.55554	.54196	.52885	.51619	.50398	.49218	.48079	.46978	.45915	.44887
69	.56976	.55640	.54349	.53102	.51896	.50731	.49603	.48513	.47458	.46438
70	.58407	.57095	.55826	.54598	.53410	.52260	.51147	.50069	.49025	.48013
71	.59848	.58561	.57316	.56109	.54940	.53808	.52710	.51646	.50615	.49614
72	.61294	.60035	.58815	.57632	.56484	.55371	.54291	.53243	.52225	.51237
73	.62741	.61512	.60318	.59160	.58035	.56943	.55882	.54851	.53849	.52876
74	.64183	.62983	.61818	.60686	.59586	.58516	.57476	.56464	.55480	.54523
75	.65612	.64444	.63309	.62204	.61129	.60083	.59065	.58074	.57109	.56169
76	.67026	.65891	.64786	.63710	.62661	.61640	.60646	.59676	.58731	.57810
77	.68423	.67321	.66248	.65201	.64181	.63186	.62215	.61269	.60345	.59444
78	.69800	.68733	.67692	.66676	.65684	.64717	.63772	.62849	.61948	.61068
79	.71156	.70124	.69116	.68132	.67170	.66230	.65312	.64414	.63537	.62680
80	.72487	.71490	.70516	.69563	.68632	.67721	.66830	.65959	.65106	.64272
81	.73791	.72830	.71890	.70970	.70069	.69188	.68325	.67481	.66654	.65844
82	.75065	.74140	.73235	.72348	.71479	.70628	.69794	.68977	.68176	.67391
83	.76308	.75419	.74548	.73695	.72858	.72037	.71232	.70443	.69669	.68909
84	.77516	.76664	.75828	.75008	.74203	.73413	.72638	.71877	.71130	.70396
85	.78689	.77873	.77072	.76285	.75512	.74753	.74008	.73275	.72556	.71849
86	.79825	.79044	.78278	.77524	.76783	.76055	.75340	.74636	.73944	.73264
87	.80921	.80176	.79443	.78722	.78014	.77316	.76630	.75956	.75292	.74638
88	.81978	.81268	.80569	.79880	.79203	.78536	.77880	.77234	.76598	.75971
89	.82994	.82317	.81651	.80995	.80349	.79712	.79085	.78467	.77859	.77259
90	.83967	.83324	.82690	.82065	.81450	.80843	.80244	.79655	.79073	.78500

See p. 15 for regulations not amended to reflect law changes

AGE	4.2%	4.4%	4.6%	4.8%	5.0%	5.2%	5.4%	5.6%	5.8%	6.0%
91	.84898	.84288	.83685	.83091	.82505	.81928	.81358	.80795	.80241	.79693
92	.85787	.85208	.84636	.84072	.83515	.82966	.82423	.81888	.81360	.80838
93	.86632	.86083	.85541	.85006	.84477	.83955	.83440	.82931	.82428	.81931
94	.87435	.86915	.86402	.85894	.85393	.84898	.84409	.83925	.83447	.82975
95	.88197	.87705	.87219	.86739	.86265	.85795	.85331	.84872	.84419	.83970
96	.88915	.88451	.87991	.87537	.87088	.86643	.86203	.85768	.85338	.84912
97	.89593	.89154	.88720	.88290	.87865	.87444	.87028	.86616	.86208	.85804
98	.90232	.89818	.89408	.89002	.88600	.88202	.87808	.87418	.87031	.86649
99	.90835	.90444	.90057	.89674	.89294	.88918	.88546	.88177	.87811	.87449
100	.91397	.91028	.90663	.90301	.89942	.89587	.89234	.88885	.88539	.88196
101	.91930	.91583	.91238	.90897	.90558	.90223	.89890	.89560	.89233	.88908
102	.92424	.92096	.91771	.91448	.91128	.90811	.90496	.90184	.89875	.89568
103	.92914	.92605	.92300	.91996	.91695	.91397	.91100	.90806	.90514	.90225
104	.93364	.93074	.92786	.92501	.92217	.91935	.91656	.91379	.91103	.90830
105	.93809	.93537	.93266	.92998	.92731	.92467	.92204	.91943	.91683	.91426
106	.94365	.94115	.93867	.93621	.93376	.93133	.92892	.92651	.92413	.92176
107	.94994	.94771	.94549	.94328	.94108	.93890	.93673	.93457	.93242	.93028
108	.96010	.95830	.95651	.95472	.95295	.95118	.94942	.94767	.94593	.94420
109	.97985	.97893	.97801	.97710	.97619	.97529	.97438	.97348	.97259	.97170

Table S
Based on Life Table 2000CM
Single Life Remainder Factors
Applicable On or After May 1, 2009

Interest Rate

AGE	6.2%	6.4%	6.6%	6.8%	7.0%	7.2%	7.4%	7.6%	7.8%	8.0%
0	.02534	.02370	.02223	.02093	.01978	.01874	.01782	.01699	.01625	.01559
1	.01989	.01817	.01664	.01528	.01406	.01298	.01202	.01115	.01037	.00967
2	.02061	.01882	.01722	.01580	.01454	.01340	.01239	.01148	.01066	.00993
3	.02156	.01969	.01802	.01654	.01521	.01403	.01297	.01201	.01115	.01038
4	.02264	.02069	.01896	.01741	.01602	.01478	.01367	.01267	.01176	.01095
5	.02383	.02180	.01999	.01838	.01693	.01563	.01446	.01341	.01246	.01161
6	.02512	.02301	.02113	.01944	.01793	.01657	.01535	.01424	.01325	.01235
7	.02650	.02430	.02234	.02058	.01900	.01758	.01630	.01514	.01410	.01315
8	.02798	.02570	.02365	.02182	.02017	.01868	.01734	.01613	.01503	.01404
9	.02957	.02720	.02507	.02316	.02143	.01988	.01848	.01721	.01606	.01502
10	.03128	.02881	.02659	.02460	.02280	.02118	.01971	.01838	.01718	.01608
11	.03309	.03053	.02823	.02615	.02428	.02258	.02105	.01966	.01839	.01725
12	.03503	.03237	.02997	.02781	.02585	.02408	.02248	.02103	.01971	.01850
13	.03704	.03428	.03179	.02954	.02750	.02565	.02398	.02246	.02108	.01982
14	.03909	.03623	.03364	.03130	.02918	.02726	.02551	.02392	.02248	.02116
15	.04117	.03820	.03551	.03308	.03087	.02886	.02704	.02538	.02387	.02249
16	.04324	.04016	.03737	.03484	.03254	.03046	.02855	.02682	.02524	.02379
17	.04533	.04214	.03924	.03661	.03422	.03205	.03007	.02826	.02661	.02509
18	.04746	.04415	.04114	.03841	.03592	.03366	.03159	.02970	.02798	.02639
19	.04963	.04620	.04309	.04025	.03766	.03530	.03315	.03117	.02937	.02772
20	.05191	.04835	.04512	.04217	.03948	.03702	.03478	.03272	.03083	.02910
21	.05427	.05058	.04723	.04416	.04137	.03881	.03647	.03432	.03235	.03054
22	.05672	.05291	.04943	.04625	.04334	.04067	.03823	.03599	.03394	.03205
23	.05930	.05535	.05174	.04844	.04542	.04265	.04010	.03777	.03562	.03364
24	.06204	.05795	.05421	.05078	.04764	.04476	.04211	.03967	.03743	.03536
25	.06497	.06074	.05687	.05331	.05005	.04705	.04429	.04174	.03940	.03724
26	.06811	.06373	.05972	.05603	.05264	.04952	.04665	.04400	.04155	.03929
27	.07146	.06694	.06278	.05895	.05543	.05219	.04920	.04644	.04389	.04153
28	.07503	.07036	.06605	.06209	.05844	.05507	.05196	.04908	.04642	.04396
29	.07881	.07398	.06953	.06542	.06163	.05814	.05490	.05191	.04913	.04656

See p. 15 for regulations not amended to reflect law changes

AGE	6.2%	6.4%	6.6%	6.8%	7.0%	7.2%	7.4%	7.6%	7.8%	8.0%
30	.08279	.07780	.07319	.06894	.06502	.06138	.05802	.05491	.05202	.04933
31	.08697	.08182	.07707	.07267	.06860	.06483	.06134	.05810	.05509	.05229
32	.09137	.08606	.08115	.07660	.07239	.06848	.06485	.06148	.05835	.05543
33	.09601	.09053	.08546	.08075	.07639	.07234	.06858	.06508	.06182	.05878
34	.10084	.09520	.08996	.08511	.08059	.07640	.07249	.06886	.06547	.06231
35	.10590	.10009	.09470	.08968	.08501	.08067	.07662	.07285	.06933	.06605
36	.11120	.10522	.09966	.09448	.08966	.08517	.08098	.07706	.07341	.06999
37	.11674	.11059	.10486	.09952	.09454	.08990	.08556	.08150	.07771	.07416
38	.12254	.11621	.11032	.10481	.09968	.09487	.09039	.08618	.08225	.07856
39	.12857	.12208	.11601	.11035	.10505	.10009	.09545	.09110	.08702	.08320
40	.13487	.12820	.12196	.11613	.11067	.10555	.10076	.09626	.09204	.08807
41	.14142	.13458	.12817	.12217	.11655	.11127	.10632	.10167	.09730	.09319
42	.14823	.14122	.13464	.12848	.12269	.11725	.11214	.10734	.10282	.09856
43	.15535	.14816	.14141	.13508	.12913	.12353	.11826	.11330	.10863	.10422
44	.16274	.15538	.14847	.14196	.13585	.13008	.12466	.11954	.11472	.11016
45	.17042	.16290	.15581	.14914	.14286	.13694	.13135	.12608	.12110	.11640
46	.17842	.17073	.16348	.15664	.15020	.14411	.13836	.13293	.12780	.12294
47	.18672	.17886	.17145	.16445	.15784	.15159	.14568	.14010	.13481	.12980
48	.19534	.18732	.17974	.17258	.16581	.15940	.15334	.14759	.14215	.13699
49	.20429	.19612	.18838	.18106	.17413	.16757	.16134	.15544	.14984	.14453
50	.21362	.20529	.19740	.18993	.18284	.17612	.16974	.16368	.15793	.15247
51	.22332	.21484	.20680	.19917	.19194	.18506	.17853	.17232	.16642	.16080
52	.23341	.22479	.21660	.20883	.20144	.19442	.18774	.18138	.17533	.16957
53	.24388	.23513	.22681	.21889	.21136	.20419	.19737	.19087	.18467	.17876
54	.25473	.24585	.23739	.22935	.22168	.21437	.20741	.20076	.19442	.18837
55	.26593	.25693	.24835	.24017	.23238	.22494	.21784	.21105	.20458	.19838
56	.27742	.26831	.25962	.25132	.24340	.23583	.22860	.22169	.21508	.20875
57	.28922	.28001	.27121	.26280	.25476	.24707	.23971	.23267	.22593	.21947
58	.30129	.29199	.28309	.27457	.26642	.25862	.25114	.24398	.23712	.23053
59	.31367	.30428	.29529	.28667	.27842	.27051	.26293	.25565	.24867	.24197
60	.32638	.31691	.30784	.29914	.29079	.28278	.27509	.26771	.26062	.25380
61	.33940	.32987	.32073	.31195	.30352	.29542	.28763	.28015	.27295	.26603
62	.35269	.34311	.33391	.32506	.31656	.30837	.30050	.29293	.28564	.27862
63	.36625	.35663	.34738	.33847	.32990	.32165	.31370	.30604	.29867	.29155
64	.38007	.37043	.36113	.35218	.34356	.33524	.32723	.31950	.31204	.30484
65	.39417	.38451	.37519	.36620	.35753	.34917	.34110	.33330	.32577	.31850
66	.40871	.39905	.38972	.38071	.37201	.36361	.35550	.34765	.34006	.33273
67	.42365	.41400	.40468	.39567	.38696	.37853	.37038	.36250	.35487	.34749
68	.43892	.42931	.42001	.41101	.40230	.39387	.38570	.37780	.37014	.36272
69	.45450	.44493	.43567	.42670	.41800	.40958	.40141	.39350	.38582	.37837
70	.47033	.46083	.45162	.44269	.43403	.42563	.41748	.40957	.40189	.39443
71	.48644	.47702	.46788	.45901	.45040	.44203	.43391	.42602	.41835	.41090
72	.50278	.49347	.48441	.47562	.46707	.45877	.45069	.44284	.43520	.42776
73	.51930	.51010	.50115	.49245	.48399	.47575	.46774	.45994	.45234	.44494
74	.53591	.52684	.51802	.50943	.50106	.49291	.48497	.47724	.46970	.46235
75	.55253	.54361	.53492	.52645	.51820	.51015	.50230	.49465	.48719	.47991
76	.56912	.56036	.55182	.54349	.53536	.52742	.51968	.51213	.50475	.49754
77	.58565	.57706	.56868	.56050	.55251	.54471	.53708	.52964	.52236	.51525
78	.60209	.59369	.58549	.57747	.56963	.56197	.55448	.54715	.53999	.53298
79	.61841	.61021	.60219	.59435	.58668	.57917	.57182	.56463	.55760	.55071
80	.63456	.62657	.61875	.61109	.60359	.59625	.58906	.58202	.57512	.56836
81	.65050	.64273	.63512	.62766	.62034	.61318	.60616	.59927	.59252	.58590
82	.66621	.65867	.65127	.64401	.63690	.62992	.62308	.61636	.60977	.60330
83	.68164	.67433	.66716	.66012	.65321	.64642	.63976	.63322	.62680	.62050
84	.69676	.68969	.68275	.67593	.66923	.66265	.65618	.64983	.64358	.63745

See p. 15 for regulations not amended to reflect law changes

AGE	6.2%	6.4%	6.6%	6.8%	7.0%	7.2%	7.4%	7.6%	7.8%	8.0%
85	.71154	.70472	.69801	.69141	.68493	.67856	.67229	.66613	.66007	.65412
86	.72595	.71937	.71290	.70654	.70028	.69412	.68806	.68210	.67623	.67046
87	.73995	.73362	.72740	.72127	.71523	.70929	.70344	.69768	.69201	.68642
88	.75354	.74746	.74148	.73558	.72978	.72406	.71842	.71287	.70739	.70200
89	.76668	.76085	.75511	.74945	.74387	.73837	.73295	.72761	.72234	.71714
90	.77934	.77377	.76827	.76284	.75749	.75222	.74701	.74188	.73681	.73181
91	.79153	.78620	.78094	.77575	.77063	.76558	.76059	.75566	.75080	.74600
92	.80323	.79814	.79312	.78816	.78326	.77843	.77365	.76894	.76428	.75967
93	.81440	.80956	.80477	.80004	.79536	.79074	.78618	.78166	.77721	.77280
94	.82508	.82047	.81591	.81140	.80694	.80253	.79817	.79387	.78961	.78539
95	.83526	.83088	.82654	.82225	.81800	.81380	.80965	.80554	.80148	.79746
96	.84491	.84074	.83662	.83254	.82850	.82450	.82055	.81663	.81276	.80892
97	.85405	.85009	.84617	.84230	.83846	.83466	.83089	.82717	.82348	.81982
98	.86270	.85895	.85523	.85155	.84791	.84430	.84072	.83718	.83367	.83019
99	.87090	.86735	.86382	.86033	.85687	.85345	.85005	.84668	.84335	.84004
100	.87856	.87519	.87185	.86854	.86526	.86201	.85878	.85559	.85242	.84927
101	.88587	.88268	.87952	.87638	.87327	.87019	.86713	.86409	.86109	.85810
102	.89263	.88961	.88662	.88364	.88069	.87777	.87487	.87199	.86913	.86629
103	.89938	.89653	.89370	.89089	.88810	.88534	.88259	.87987	.87717	.87448
104	.90558	.90289	.90021	.89756	.89492	.89231	.88971	.88713	.88456	.88202
105	.91170	.90916	.90664	.90413	.90164	.89917	.89672	.89428	.89186	.88945
106	.91940	.91706	.91474	.91242	.91013	.90784	.90558	.90332	.90108	.89885
107	.92816	.92605	.92395	.92186	.91978	.91772	.91567	.91362	.91159	.90957
108	.94247	.94075	.93904	.93734	.93565	.93396	.93229	.93062	.92895	.92730
109	.97081	.96992	.96904	.96816	.96729	.96642	.96555	.96468	.96382	.96296

Table S
Based on Life Table 2000CM
Single Life Remainder Factors
Applicable On or After May 1, 2009

Interest Rate

AGE	8.2%	8.4%	8.6%	8.8%	9.0%	9.2%	9.4%	9.6%	9.8%	10.0%
0	.01498	.01444	.01395	.01351	.01310	.01273	.01240	.01209	.01181	.01155
1	.00904	.00847	.00796	.00749	.00707	.00668	.00633	.00601	.00572	.00545
2	.00926	.00866	.00812	.00763	.00718	.00677	.00640	.00606	.00575	.00547
3	.00968	.00905	.00848	.00796	.00748	.00705	.00666	.00630	.00597	.00567
4	.01021	.00955	.00894	.00839	.00789	.00744	.00702	.00664	.00629	.00597
5	.01083	.01013	.00949	.00891	.00839	.00790	.00746	.00706	.00669	.00635
6	.01153	.01080	.01012	.00951	.00895	.00844	.00798	.00755	.00715	.00679
7	.01229	.01151	.01081	.01016	.00957	.00903	.00854	.00808	.00767	.00728
8	.01314	.01232	.01157	.01089	.01026	.00969	.00917	.00869	.00825	.00784
9	.01407	.01321	.01242	.01170	.01104	.01044	.00989	.00938	.00891	.00848
10	.01509	.01418	.01335	.01259	.01190	.01126	.01068	.01014	.00965	.00919
11	.01620	.01525	.01437	.01358	.01285	.01218	.01156	.01099	.01047	.00998
12	.01740	.01640	.01549	.01465	.01388	.01317	.01252	.01192	.01137	.01086
13	.01867	.01762	.01665	.01577	.01496	.01422	.01353	.01290	.01231	.01177
14	.01995	.01885	.01784	.01691	.01606	.01527	.01455	.01389	.01327	.01270
15	.02123	.02007	.01901	.01803	.01714	.01632	.01556	.01485	.01420	.01360
16	.02247	.02126	.02015	.01913	.01818	.01732	.01652	.01578	.01509	.01446
17	.02371	.02244	.02127	.02020	.01921	.01830	.01746	.01668	.01596	.01529
18	.02494	.02361	.02239	.02126	.02022	.01926	.01838	.01756	.01680	.01610
19	.02620	.02480	.02352	.02234	.02125	.02024	.01931	.01844	.01764	.01690
20	.02751	.02605	.02471	.02346	.02232	.02126	.02028	.01937	.01853	.01775
21	.02888	.02735	.02593	.02463	.02343	.02231	.02128	.02032	.01944	.01861
22	.03030	.02870	.02722	.02585	.02458	.02341	.02233	.02132	.02038	.01951
23	.03181	.03013	.02858	.02714	.02581	.02458	.02344	.02237	.02139	.02047
24	.03345	.03169	.03006	.02855	.02715	.02586	.02465	.02353	.02249	.02152
25	.03524	.03340	.03169	.03010	.02863	.02727	.02600	.02482	.02373	.02270
26	.03720	.03527	.03348	.03181	.03027	.02884	.02750	.02626	.02510	.02402
27	.03934	.03732	.03544	.03370	.03208	.03057	.02916	.02786	.02664	.02549
28	.04167	.03955	.03759	.03576	.03406	.03247	.03099	.02962	.02833	.02713
29	.04417	.04196	.03990	.03798	.03619	.03453	.03298	.03153	.03017	.02890
30	.04684	.04452	.04237	.04036	.03848	.03674	.03510	.03358	.03215	.03081
31	.04969	.04727	.04501	.04291	.04094	.03911	.03739	.03579	.03428	.03287
32	.05272	.05019	.04783	.04563	.04357	.04165	.03984	.03816	.03657	.03509
33	.05595	.05331	.05085	.04854	.04639	.04437	.04248	.04070	.03904	.03748
34	.05936	.05661	.05403	.05162	.04936	.04725	.04527	.04341	.04166	.04001
35	.06297	.06010	.05741	.05489	.05253	.05032	.04824	.04629	.04445	.04272
36	.06679	.06380	.06100	.05837	.05590	.05358	.05140	.04935	.04742	.04561
37	.07083	.06771	.06479	.06204	.05947	.05704	.05476	.05261	.05059	.04868
38	.07511	.07186	.06881	.06595	.06326	.06072	.05834	.05609	.05397	.05196
39	.07961	.07623	.07306	.07007	.06726	.06462	.06212	.05977	.05754	.05544
40	.08434	.08083	.07753	.07442	.07149	.06873	.06612	.06366	.06133	.05913
41	.08932	.08568	.08225	.07901	.07596	.07308	.07035	.06778	.06534	.06304
42	.09455	.09077	.08720	.08384	.08066	.07766	.07481	.07213	.06958	.06717
43	.10007	.09615	.09245	.08895	.08564	.08251	.07955	.07674	.07408	.07156
44	.10586	.10180	.09796	.09433	.09089	.08763	.08454	.08162	.07884	.07621
45	.11195	.10774	.10376	.09999	.09642	.09303	.08982	.08677	.08387	.08112
46	.11835	.11400	.10987	.10596	.10225	.09873	.09539	.09222	.08920	.08633
47	.12505	.12055	.11629	.11224	.10839	.10474	.10126	.09796	.09482	.09182
48	.13209	.12745	.12303	.11884	.11485	.11106	.10746	.10402	.10075	.09764
49	.13948	.13469	.13013	.12579	.12167	.11774	.11400	.11043	.10703	.10379

See p. 15 for regulations not amended to reflect law changes

AGE	8.2%	8.4%	8.6%	8.8%	9.0%	9.2%	9.4%	9.6%	9.8%	10.0%
50	.14727	.14233	.13762	.13314	.12887	.12481	.12093	.11723	.11370	.11033
51	.15546	.15037	.14551	.14089	.13648	.13228	.12826	.12443	.12077	.11726
52	.16407	.15884	.15384	.14907	.14452	.14018	.13603	.13206	.12826	.12463
53	.17312	.16774	.16260	.15769	.15300	.14852	.14423	.14012	.13620	.13243
54	.18259	.17707	.17179	.16674	.16191	.15729	.15286	.14862	.14456	.14067
55	.19247	.18680	.18139	.17620	.17123	.16648	.16192	.15755	.15335	.14933
56	.20270	.19690	.19135	.18602	.18092	.17603	.17134	.16684	.16251	.15836
57	.21329	.20736	.20167	.19622	.19099	.18596	.18114	.17650	.17205	.16777
58	.22422	.21816	.21235	.20677	.20140	.19625	.19130	.18653	.18195	.17754
59	.23553	.22935	.22341	.21770	.21221	.20693	.20185	.19696	.19225	.18772
60	.24725	.24095	.23489	.22906	.22345	.21805	.21285	.20783	.20300	.19834
61	.25937	.25296	.24679	.24084	.23511	.22959	.22427	.21914	.21419	.20941
62	.27185	.26534	.25906	.25300	.24716	.24153	.23609	.23084	.22577	.22088
63	.28469	.27808	.27169	.26553	.25959	.25384	.24830	.24294	.23776	.23275
64	.29789	.29119	.28471	.27845	.27240	.26656	.26091	.25544	.25016	.24504
65	.31148	.30468	.29812	.29177	.28563	.27969	.27394	.26837	.26299	.25777
66	.32564	.31877	.31213	.30570	.29948	.29345	.28761	.28195	.27647	.27115
67	.34034	.33341	.32671	.32021	.31391	.30780	.30188	.29614	.29057	.28517
68	.35552	.34855	.34179	.33523	.32887	.32270	.31671	.31089	.30524	.29976
69	.37115	.36414	.35734	.35073	.34432	.33809	.33204	.32616	.32045	.31489
70	.38719	.38016	.37332	.36668	.36023	.35396	.34786	.34193	.33616	.33054
71	.40366	.39662	.38977	.38311	.37663	.37032	.36419	.35821	.35240	.34674
72	.42053	.41350	.40665	.39998	.39349	.38716	.38100	.37500	.36916	.36346
73	.43774	.43073	.42389	.41723	.41074	.40441	.39824	.39222	.38636	.38063
74	.45519	.44821	.44140	.43476	.42829	.42197	.41580	.40979	.40391	.39818
75	.47280	.46587	.45910	.45250	.44605	.43975	.43360	.42759	.42173	.41599
76	.49051	.48364	.47693	.47037	.46396	.45770	.45158	.44560	.43975	.43403
77	.50830	.50150	.49486	.48836	.48201	.47580	.46972	.46377	.45795	.45225
78	.52613	.51942	.51286	.50644	.50015	.49400	.48797	.48208	.47630	.47064
79	.54396	.53736	.53089	.52456	.51835	.51227	.50632	.50048	.49476	.48915
80	.56174	.55525	.54888	.54265	.53653	.53054	.52466	.51890	.51325	.50770
81	.57941	.57305	.56681	.56068	.55467	.54878	.54299	.53731	.53174	.52627
82	.59696	.59073	.58461	.57861	.57272	.56693	.56125	.55566	.55018	.54480
83	.61430	.60822	.60224	.59637	.59061	.58494	.57937	.57389	.56851	.56322
84	.63142	.62549	.61966	.61393	.60830	.60276	.59731	.59196	.58669	.58150
85	.64825	.64249	.63682	.63124	.62575	.62035	.61503	.60980	.60465	.59958
86	.66477	.65918	.65367	.64825	.64291	.63765	.63248	.62738	.62236	.61741
87	.68092	.67550	.67016	.66490	.65972	.65462	.64959	.64463	.63975	.63493
88	.69669	.69145	.68628	.68119	.67618	.67123	.66635	.66154	.65680	.65212
89	.71201	.70696	.70198	.69706	.69221	.68742	.68270	.67805	.67345	.66892
90	.72688	.72201	.71721	.71246	.70779	.70317	.69861	.69411	.68966	.68528
91	.74126	.73658	.73196	.72739	.72289	.71844	.71404	.70970	.70541	.70117
92	.75513	.75063	.74620	.74181	.73748	.73320	.72897	.72479	.72066	.71657
93	.76844	.76414	.75988	.75568	.75152	.74741	.74334	.73932	.73535	.73142
94	.78123	.77711	.77303	.76901	.76502	.76108	.75718	.75332	.74951	.74573
95	.79348	.78954	.78565	.78179	.77798	.77421	.77047	.76677	.76312	.75950
96	.80513	.80137	.79765	.79397	.79032	.78671	.78314	.77960	.77610	.77263
97	.81621	.81262	.80908	.80556	.80208	.79864	.79522	.79184	.78849	.78517
98	.82674	.82333	.81995	.81660	.81328	.80999	.80673	.80351	.80031	.79713
99	.83677	.83352	.83030	.82711	.82395	.82082	.81771	.81463	.81158	.80855
100	.84616	.84307	.84001	.83697	.83396	.83097	.82801	.82507	.82216	.81927
101	.85514	.85221	.84930	.84641	.84355	.84070	.83788	.83509	.83231	.82956
102	.86348	.86069	.85792	.85517	.85245	.84974	.84706	.84439	.84175	.83912
103	.87182	.86918	.86655	.86395	.86136	.85880	.85625	.85372	.85121	.84872
104	.87950	.87699	.87450	.87203	.86957	.86713	.86471	.86231	.85992	.85755

AGE	8.2%	8.4%	8.6%	8.8%	9.0%	9.2%	9.4%	9.6%	9.8%	10.0%
105	.88706	.88468	.88232	.87998	.87765	.87534	.87304	.87076	.86849	.86624
106	.89664	.89444	.89225	.89008	.88792	.88577	.88364	.88152	.87941	.87731
107	.90756	.90557	.90358	.90160	.89964	.89768	.89574	.89380	.89188	.88997
108	.92565	.92401	.92238	.92075	.91914	.91753	.91592	.91433	.91274	.91116
109	.96211	.96125	.96041	.95956	.95872	.95788	.95704	.95620	.95537	.95455

Table S
Based on Life Table 2000CM
Single Life Remainder Factors
Applicable On or After May 1, 2009

	Interest Rate									
AGE	10.2%	10.4%	10.6%	10.8%	11.0%	11.2%	11.4%	11.6%	11.8%	12.0%
0	.01132	.01110	.01089	.01071	.01053	.01037	.01022	.01008	.00995	.00983
1	.00520	.00497	.00476	.00457	.00439	.00423	.00407	.00393	.00379	.00367
2	.00521	.00496	.00474	.00454	.00435	.00417	.00401	.00385	.00371	.00358
3	.00539	.00513	.00490	.00468	.00447	.00429	.00411	.00395	.00380	.00366
4	.00567	.00540	.00515	.00492	.00470	.00450	.00432	.00414	.00398	.00383
5	.00603	.00574	.00547	.00523	.00500	.00478	.00459	.00440	.00423	.00407
6	.00646	.00615	.00587	.00560	.00536	.00513	.00492	.00472	.00453	.00436
7	.00693	.00660	.00630	.00602	.00576	.00551	.00529	.00508	.00488	.00469
8	.00747	.00712	.00680	.00650	.00622	.00596	.00572	.00549	.00528	.00509
9	.00808	.00771	.00737	.00705	.00675	.00648	.00622	.00598	.00576	.00555
10	.00877	.00838	.00801	.00767	.00736	.00707	.00679	.00654	.00630	.00608
11	.00954	.00912	.00873	.00838	.00804	.00773	.00744	.00717	.00692	.00668
12	.01038	.00994	.00953	.00915	.00880	.00847	.00816	.00788	.00761	.00735
13	.01127	.01081	.01038	.00998	.00960	.00925	.00893	.00862	.00833	.00806
14	.01217	.01168	.01122	.01080	.01040	.01003	.00969	.00937	.00906	.00878
15	.01305	.01253	.01205	.01160	.01118	.01079	.01042	.01008	.00976	.00946
16	.01387	.01333	.01282	.01234	.01190	.01149	.01110	.01074	.01040	.01009
17	.01467	.01409	.01356	.01306	.01259	.01216	.01175	.01137	.01101	.01067
18	.01544	.01484	.01427	.01374	.01325	.01279	.01236	.01195	.01157	.01122
19	.01621	.01557	.01497	.01442	.01390	.01341	.01295	.01253	.01213	.01175
20	.01702	.01634	.01571	.01512	.01457	.01406	.01357	.01312	.01270	.01230
21	.01784	.01713	.01646	.01584	.01526	.01471	.01420	.01372	.01327	.01285
22	.01870	.01794	.01724	.01658	.01596	.01539	.01485	.01434	.01386	.01342
23	.01961	.01881	.01807	.01737	.01672	.01611	.01554	.01500	.01449	.01402
24	.02062	.01977	.01899	.01825	.01756	.01691	.01630	.01573	.01520	.01469
25	.02175	.02085	.02002	.01924	.01851	.01782	.01718	.01657	.01600	.01547
26	.02301	.02207	.02119	.02036	.01958	.01886	.01817	.01753	.01692	.01635
27	.02443	.02343	.02250	.02162	.02080	.02003	.01930	.01862	.01798	.01737
28	.02600	.02495	.02396	.02303	.02216	.02134	.02057	.01985	.01916	.01852
29	.02771	.02660	.02555	.02457	.02365	.02278	.02197	.02120	.02047	.01979
30	.02956	.02838	.02728	.02624	.02526	.02434	.02348	.02266	.02189	.02116
31	.03155	.03031	.02914	.02804	.02701	.02604	.02512	.02425	.02344	.02266
32	.03370	.03239	.03115	.02999	.02890	.02787	.02690	.02598	.02511	.02429
33	.03601	.03463	.03333	.03210	.03095	.02985	.02883	.02785	.02693	.02606
34	.03847	.03701	.03564	.03434	.03312	.03197	.03088	.02985	.02887	.02795
35	.04109	.03956	.03811	.03675	.03546	.03424	.03308	.03199	.03096	.02998
36	.04390	.04228	.04076	.03932	.03795	.03667	.03545	.03429	.03320	.03216
37	.04688	.04518	.04358	.04206	.04062	.03926	.03798	.03676	.03560	.03450
38	.05007	.04829	.04660	.04500	.04349	.04205	.04069	.03940	.03818	.03701
39	.05346	.05158	.04981	.04812	.04653	.04502	.04358	.04222	.04092	.03969
40	.05705	.05508	.05321	.05144	.04976	.04817	.04666	.04522	.04385	.04255
41	.06086	.05879	.05683	.05497	.05320	.05152	.04993	.04841	.04697	.04559
42	.06488	.06271	.06066	.05870	.05684	.05508	.05340	.05180	.05028	.04882
43	.06917	.06690	.06474	.06269	.06074	.05888	.05711	.05543	.05382	.05229

AGE	10.2%	10.4%	10.6%	10.8%	11.0%	11.2%	11.4%	11.6%	11.8%	12.0%
44	.07370	.07132	.06906	.06691	.06486	.06291	.06105	.05928	.05759	.05598
45	.07850	.07602	.07365	.07139	.06924	.06719	.06524	.06338	.06160	.05990
46	.08360	.08100	.07852	.07616	.07390	.07176	.06970	.06775	.06587	.06409
47	.08897	.08626	.08367	.08120	.07884	.07659	.07443	.07238	.07041	.06853
48	.09466	.09183	.08912	.08654	.08407	.08172	.07946	.07730	.07524	.07326
49	.10069	.09774	.09492	.09222	.08964	.08717	.08481	.08255	.08038	.07831
50	.10711	.10403	.10109	.09827	.09558	.09300	.09053	.08816	.08589	.08371
51	.11392	.11072	.10765	.10472	.10191	.09921	.09663	.09415	.09178	.08950
52	.12116	.11783	.11464	.11159	.10866	.10585	.10315	.10057	.09808	.09569
53	.12883	.12538	.12206	.11889	.11584	.11291	.11010	.10740	.10481	.10231
54	.13694	.13336	.12992	.12662	.12345	.12041	.11748	.11467	.11196	.10936
55	.14547	.14176	.13820	.13478	.13149	.12832	.12528	.12235	.11953	.11682
56	.15437	.15054	.14685	.14330	.13989	.13661	.13345	.13040	.12747	.12464
57	.16365	.15969	.15588	.15221	.14868	.14527	.14199	.13883	.13578	.13284
58	.17330	.16921	.16528	.16149	.15783	.15431	.15091	.14763	.14447	.14141
59	.18335	.17914	.17508	.17117	.16739	.16375	.16023	.15684	.15356	.15039
60	.19385	.18952	.18534	.18131	.17741	.17365	.17001	.16650	.16311	.15982
61	.20480	.20035	.19605	.19189	.18788	.18400	.18025	.17662	.17311	.16971
62	.21615	.21158	.20717	.20290	.19877	.19477	.19090	.18716	.18354	.18003
63	.22791	.22323	.21870	.21431	.21007	.20596	.20198	.19812	.19439	.19077
64	.24009	.23530	.23066	.22616	.22181	.21758	.21349	.20953	.20568	.20195
65	.25271	.24781	.24306	.23846	.23400	.22967	.22547	.22139	.21744	.21360
66	.26600	.26100	.25615	.25145	.24688	.24245	.23814	.23396	.22990	.22596
67	.27992	.27483	.26989	.26509	.26043	.25590	.25150	.24722	.24306	.23901
68	.29443	.28926	.28423	.27934	.27459	.26997	.26548	.26110	.25685	.25271
69	.30950	.30424	.29914	.29417	.28934	.28463	.28005	.27559	.27125	.26703
70	.32508	.31976	.31459	.30955	.30464	.29986	.29520	.29067	.28625	.28194
71	.34122	.33585	.33062	.32552	.32054	.31570	.31097	.30637	.30187	.29749
72	.35790	.35249	.34721	.34205	.33703	.33213	.32734	.32268	.31812	.31367
73	.37505	.36960	.36428	.35909	.35403	.34908	.34425	.33953	.33492	.33042
74	.39258	.38711	.38177	.37655	.37145	.36647	.36160	.35684	.35219	.34764
75	.41039	.40491	.39956	.39432	.38921	.38420	.37931	.37452	.36983	.36525
76	.42843	.42296	.41760	.41236	.40724	.40222	.39731	.39250	.38779	.38318
77	.44668	.44122	.43588	.43065	.42552	.42050	.41559	.41077	.40605	.40143
78	.46510	.45967	.45435	.44914	.44403	.43902	.43411	.42930	.42458	.41995
79	.48365	.47826	.47298	.46780	.46271	.45773	.45284	.44804	.44333	.43871
80	.50226	.49693	.49169	.48655	.48150	.47655	.47169	.46692	.46224	.45763
81	.52090	.51562	.51044	.50536	.50036	.49546	.49064	.48590	.48125	.47668
82	.53951	.53431	.52920	.52418	.51924	.51439	.50963	.50494	.50033	.49580
83	.55802	.55291	.54788	.54294	.53808	.53329	.52859	.52396	.51941	.51493
84	.57640	.57139	.56645	.56159	.55681	.55210	.54747	.54291	.53843	.53401
85	.59459	.58968	.58484	.58008	.57539	.57077	.56623	.56175	.55733	.55298
86	.61254	.60774	.60302	.59836	.59377	.58925	.58479	.58040	.57607	.57180
87	.63019	.62551	.62090	.61635	.61187	.60745	.60309	.59880	.59456	.59038
88	.64751	.64296	.63847	.63405	.62968	.62537	.62112	.61693	.61279	.60871
89	.66444	.66003	.65567	.65137	.64712	.64293	.63880	.63471	.63068	.62670
90	.68094	.67667	.67244	.66827	.66415	.66009	.65607	.65210	.64818	.64431
91	.69699	.69285	.68877	.68473	.68074	.67680	.67291	.66906	.66526	.66150
92	.71254	.70855	.70460	.70071	.69685	.69304	.68928	.68555	.68187	.67823
93	.72753	.72369	.71989	.71613	.71242	.70874	.70510	.70150	.69794	.69442
94	.74200	.73830	.73464	.73103	.72745	.72390	.72040	.71693	.71350	.71010
95	.75591	.75236	.74885	.74538	.74194	.73853	.73516	.73182	.72851	.72524
96	.76920	.76580	.76243	.75909	.75579	.75252	.74928	.74607	.74289	.73974
97	.78188	.77863	.77540	.77220	.76904	.76590	.76279	.75971	.75665	.75363
98	.79399	.79088	.78779	.78473	.78170	.77869	.77571	.77276	.76983	.76693

AGE	10.2%	10.4%	10.6%	10.8%	11.0%	11.2%	11.4%	11.6%	11.8%	12.0%
99	.80555	.80257	.79962	.79670	.79380	.79092	.78807	.78525	.78244	.77966
100	.81641	.81357	.81075	.80796	.80518	.80243	.79971	.79700	.79432	.79165
101	.82683	.82412	.82144	.81877	.81612	.81350	.81089	.80831	.80574	.80320
102	.83652	.83394	.83137	.82882	.82630	.82379	.82130	.81883	.81637	.81394
103	.84624	.84379	.84135	.83892	.83652	.83413	.83176	.82941	.82707	.82475
104	.85519	.85285	.85053	.84822	.84593	.84365	.84139	.83915	.83692	.83470
105	.86400	.86178	.85957	.85737	.85519	.85302	.85087	.84873	.84660	.84449
106	.87523	.87316	.87110	.86905	.86702	.86500	.86299	.86099	.85900	.85703
107	.88806	.88617	.88429	.88242	.88055	.87870	.87686	.87502	.87320	.87139
108	.90958	.90802	.90646	.90490	.90336	.90182	.90028	.89876	.89724	.89573
109	.95372	.95290	.95208	.95126	.95045	.94964	.94883	.94803	.94723	.94643

Table S
Based on Life Table 2000CM
Single Life Remainder Factors
Applicable On or After May 1, 2009

Interest Rate

AGE	12.2%	12.4%	12.6%	12.8%	13.0%	13.2%	13.4%	13.6%	13.8%	14.0%
0	.00972	.00961	.00951	.00941	.00932	.00924	.00916	.00908	.00901	.00894
1	.00355	.00345	.00334	.00325	.00316	.00307	.00299	.00292	.00285	.00278
2	.00346	.00334	.00323	.00313	.00303	.00294	.00286	.00278	.00270	.00263
3	.00353	.00340	.00329	.00318	.00307	.00298	.00289	.00280	.00272	.00264
4	.00369	.00356	.00343	.00332	.00321	.00310	.00300	.00291	.00283	.00274
5	.00392	.00377	.00364	.00352	.00340	.00329	.00318	.00308	.00299	.00290
6	.00420	.00405	.00391	.00377	.00365	.00353	.00342	.00331	.00321	.00311
7	.00452	.00436	.00421	.00406	.00393	.00380	.00368	.00357	.00346	.00336
8	.00490	.00473	.00457	.00441	.00427	.00413	.00400	.00388	.00376	.00365
9	.00535	.00517	.00499	.00483	.00467	.00453	.00439	.00426	.00413	.00402
10	.00587	.00567	.00548	.00531	.00514	.00499	.00484	.00470	.00456	.00444
11	.00645	.00624	.00605	.00586	.00568	.00551	.00536	.00521	.00506	.00493
12	.00711	.00689	.00668	.00648	.00629	.00611	.00595	.00579	.00563	.00549
13	.00781	.00757	.00735	.00714	.00694	.00675	.00657	.00640	.00624	.00609
14	.00851	.00826	.00802	.00780	.00759	.00739	.00720	.00702	.00684	.00668
15	.00918	.00891	.00866	.00842	.00820	.00799	.00779	.00759	.00741	.00724
16	.00979	.00950	.00924	.00899	.00875	.00853	.00832	.00811	.00792	.00774
17	.01035	.01006	.00978	.00951	.00926	.00902	.00880	.00859	.00838	.00819
18	.01088	.01057	.01027	.00999	.00973	.00948	.00924	.00901	.00880	.00860
19	.01139	.01106	.01075	.01045	.01017	.00990	.00965	.00942	.00919	.00898
20	.01192	.01157	.01124	.01092	.01063	.01035	.01008	.00983	.00959	.00936
21	.01245	.01208	.01173	.01139	.01108	.01078	.01050	.01023	.00998	.00974
22	.01300	.01260	.01222	.01187	.01154	.01122	.01092	.01064	.01037	.01011
23	.01357	.01315	.01275	.01238	.01202	.01168	.01137	.01106	.01078	.01051
24	.01422	.01377	.01334	.01294	.01257	.01221	.01187	.01155	.01124	.01095
25	.01496	.01448	.01403	.01361	.01320	.01282	.01246	.01212	.01180	.01149
26	.01582	.01531	.01483	.01438	.01395	.01354	.01316	.01279	.01244	.01211
27	.01680	.01626	.01575	.01527	.01481	.01437	.01396	.01357	.01320	.01285
28	.01791	.01734	.01679	.01628	.01579	.01533	.01489	.01447	.01408	.01370
29	.01914	.01853	.01795	.01740	.01688	.01639	.01592	.01548	.01505	.01465
30	.02048	.01982	.01921	.01862	.01807	.01754	.01704	.01657	.01612	.01569
31	.02193	.02124	.02058	.01996	.01937	.01881	.01828	.01777	.01729	.01683
32	.02351	.02278	.02208	.02142	.02079	.02019	.01962	.01908	.01857	.01808
33	.02523	.02445	.02371	.02300	.02234	.02170	.02109	.02052	.01997	.01944
34	.02707	.02624	.02545	.02470	.02399	.02331	.02267	.02205	.02146	.02091
35	.02905	.02817	.02733	.02653	.02577	.02505	.02436	.02371	.02308	.02249
36	.03117	.03024	.02935	.02850	.02769	.02693	.02619	.02550	.02483	.02419

See p. 15 for regulations not amended to reflect law changes

AGE	12.2%	12.4%	12.6%	12.8%	13.0%	13.2%	13.4%	13.6%	13.8%	14.0%
37	.03345	.03246	.03151	.03061	.02976	.02894	.02816	.02742	.02671	.02603
38	.03590	.03485	.03385	.03289	.03198	.03112	.03029	.02950	.02874	.02802
39	.03852	.03740	.03634	.03533	.03436	.03344	.03256	.03172	.03092	.03015
40	.04131	.04013	.03900	.03793	.03690	.03593	.03499	.03410	.03324	.03242
41	.04428	.04303	.04184	.04070	.03962	.03858	.03759	.03664	.03573	.03486
42	.04744	.04612	.04486	.04366	.04250	.04140	.04035	.03934	.03838	.03745
43	.05083	.04943	.04810	.04683	.04561	.04444	.04333	.04226	.04123	.04025
44	.05443	.05296	.05155	.05021	.04892	.04768	.04650	.04537	.04428	.04324
45	.05827	.05672	.05523	.05381	.05245	.05114	.04989	.04869	.04754	.04643
46	.06237	.06074	.05917	.05767	.05623	.05485	.05352	.05225	.05103	.04986
47	.06673	.06500	.06335	.06177	.06025	.05879	.05739	.05605	.05475	.05351
48	.07137	.06955	.06781	.06614	.06454	.06300	.06152	.06010	.05874	.05742
49	.07632	.07441	.07258	.07082	.06913	.06750	.06595	.06444	.06300	.06161
50	.08162	.07962	.07769	.07584	.07407	.07236	.07071	.06913	.06760	.06614
51	.08731	.08520	.08318	.08124	.07937	.07757	.07583	.07416	.07256	.07101
52	.09340	.09119	.08907	.08703	.08507	.08317	.08135	.07959	.07790	.07627
53	.09991	.09760	.09538	.09324	.09118	.08919	.08728	.08543	.08365	.08193
54	.10685	.10443	.10211	.09987	.09771	.09562	.09361	.09167	.08980	.08799
55	.11420	.11168	.10925	.10690	.10464	.10246	.10035	.09832	.09635	.09445
56	.12191	.11928	.11675	.11430	.11193	.10965	.10745	.10531	.10325	.10126
57	.13001	.12727	.12462	.12207	.11960	.11721	.11491	.11268	.11052	.10843
58	.13846	.13561	.13286	.13020	.12762	.12513	.12273	.12040	.11814	.11595
59	.14732	.14436	.14150	.13873	.13605	.13346	.13095	.12851	.12616	.12388
60	.15665	.15358	.15060	.14772	.14494	.14224	.13962	.13709	.13463	.13225
61	.16642	.16324	.16016	.15717	.15428	.15147	.14875	.14611	.14355	.14107
62	.17663	.17333	.17014	.16704	.16404	.16113	.15830	.15556	.15290	.15031
63	.18726	.18385	.18055	.17734	.17423	.17121	.16828	.16544	.16267	.15999
64	.19833	.19481	.19140	.18809	.18487	.18175	.17871	.17576	.17289	.17010
65	.20987	.20624	.20273	.19931	.19598	.19275	.18961	.18656	.18358	.18069
66	.22213	.21840	.21478	.21125	.20783	.20449	.20125	.19809	.19501	.19202
67	.23508	.23125	.22753	.22390	.22037	.21694	.21360	.21034	.20716	.20407
68	.24868	.24476	.24094	.23722	.23359	.23006	.22662	.22327	.22000	.21681
69	.26291	.25889	.25498	.25117	.24745	.24383	.24030	.23685	.23349	.23020
70	.27773	.27364	.26964	.26574	.26194	.25823	.25461	.25107	.24762	.24425
71	.29321	.28904	.28496	.28099	.27710	.27331	.26961	.26599	.26246	.25900
72	.30933	.30508	.30094	.29689	.29294	.28907	.28530	.28160	.27799	.27446
73	.32602	.32171	.31751	.31340	.30938	.30545	.30160	.29784	.29416	.29056
74	.34319	.33884	.33458	.33042	.32634	.32236	.31845	.31463	.31089	.30723
75	.36076	.35637	.35207	.34786	.34374	.33970	.33575	.33188	.32808	.32437
76	.37867	.37425	.36991	.36567	.36151	.35744	.35344	.34953	.34569	.34192
77	.39690	.39245	.38810	.38383	.37964	.37554	.37151	.36756	.36369	.35989
78	.41541	.41096	.40659	.40231	.39811	.39398	.38993	.38596	.38206	.37823
79	.43418	.42973	.42536	.42107	.41686	.41272	.40866	.40467	.40075	.39691
80	.45311	.44868	.44432	.44003	.43582	.43169	.42763	.42363	.41971	.41585
81	.47219	.46777	.46343	.45916	.45497	.45084	.44679	.44280	.43888	.43502
82	.49135	.48696	.48265	.47841	.47424	.47014	.46610	.46213	.45822	.45437
83	.51052	.50618	.50191	.49771	.49357	.48950	.48549	.48154	.47766	.47383
84	.52966	.52537	.52115	.51700	.51291	.50887	.50490	.50099	.49714	.49334
85	.54870	.54448	.54032	.53622	.53218	.52820	.52428	.52041	.51660	.51284
86	.56759	.56344	.55935	.55532	.55135	.54742	.54356	.53974	.53598	.53227
87	.58626	.58219	.57818	.57422	.57031	.56646	.56266	.55891	.55521	.55155
88	.60468	.60070	.59677	.59290	.58907	.58529	.58157	.57788	.57425	.57066
89	.62277	.61888	.61505	.61126	.60753	.60383	.60018	.59658	.59302	.58950
90	.64048	.63670	.63296	.62927	.62563	.62202	.61846	.61494	.61146	.60803
91	.65778	.65411	.65048	.64689	.64334	.63983	.63636	.63293	.62954	.62619

AGE	12.2%	12.4%	12.6%	12.8%	13.0%	13.2%	13.4%	13.6%	13.8%	14.0%
92	.67462	.67106	.66754	.66406	.66061	.65720	.65383	.65050	.64720	.64393
93	.69094	.68749	.68408	.68071	.67737	.67406	.67079	.66756	.66435	.66118
94	.70673	.70340	.70011	.69685	.69362	.69042	.68725	.68412	.68102	.67794
95	.72199	.71878	.71560	.71246	.70934	.70625	.70319	.70016	.69716	.69419
96	.73662	.73353	.73047	.72743	.72443	.72145	.71850	.71557	.71268	.70981
97	.75063	.74766	.74471	.74180	.73890	.73604	.73319	.73038	.72758	.72482
98	.76405	.76120	.75837	.75557	.75279	.75003	.74730	.74459	.74190	.73923
99	.77690	.77417	.77146	.76877	.76610	.76345	.76083	.75822	75564	.75308
100	.78901	.78639	.78379	.78121	.77866	.77612	.77360	.77110	.76862	.76616
101	.80067	.79816	.79568	.79321	.79076	.78832	.78591	.78351	.78114	.77877
102	.81152	.80912	.80674	.80438	.80203	.79970	.79738	.79508	.79280	.79054
103	.82245	.82016	.81789	.81563	.81339	.81116	.80895	.80676	.80458	.80241
104	.83250	.83031	.82814	.82599	.82384	.82171	.81960	.81750	.81541	.81334
105	.84239	.84030	.83823	.83617	.83412	.83209	.83006	.82806	.82606	.82407
106	.85507	.85311	.85117	.84924	.84733	.84542	.84352	.84164	.83976	.83790
107	.86958	.86779	.86600	.86422	.86246	.86070	.85895	.85721	.85548	.85376
108	.89422	.89272	.89123	.88974	.88826	.88679	.88533	.88386	.88241	.88096
109	.94563	.94484	.94405	.94326	.94248	.94170	.94092	.94014	.93937	.93860

(f) *Effective/applicability date.*—This section applies on and after May 1, 2009. [Reg. § 1.642(c)-6.]

☐ [*T.D.* 7105, 4-5-71. *Amended by T.D.* 7955, 5-10-84; *T.D. 8540*, 6-9-94; *T.D.* 8819, 4-29-99; *T.D.* 8886, 6-9-2000; *T.D.* 9448, 5-1-2009 *and T.D.* 9540, 8-9-2011.]

[Reg. § 1.642(c)-6A]

§ 1.642(c)-6A. Valuation of charitable remainder interests for which the valuation date is before May 1, 2009.—(a) *Valuation of charitable remainder interests for which the valuation date is before January 1, 1952.*—There was no provision for the qualification of pooled income funds under section 642 until 1969. See § 20.2031-7A(a) of this chapter (Estate Tax Regulations) for the determination of the present value of a charitable remainder interest created before January 1, 1952.

(b) *Valuation of charitable remainder interests for which the valuation date is after December 31, 1951, and before January 1, 1971.*—No charitable deduction is allowable for a transfer to a pooled income fund for which the valuation date is after the effective dates of the Tax Reform Act of 1969 unless the pooled income fund meets the requirements of section 642(c)(5). See § 20.2031-7A(b) of this chapter (Estate Tax Regulations) for the determination of the present value of a charitable remainder interest for which the valuation date is after December 31, 1951, and before January 1, 1971.

(c) *Present value of remainder interest in the case of transfers to pooled income funds for which the valuation date is after December 31, 1970, and before December 1, 1983.*—For the determination of the present value of a remainder interest in property transferred to a pooled income fund for which the valuation date is after December 31, 1970, and before December 1, 1983, see § 20.2031-7A(c) of this chapter (Estate Tax Regulations) and former § 1.642(c)-6(e) (as contained in the 26 CFR Part 1 edition revised as of April 1, 1994).

(d) *Present value of remainder interest dependent on the termination of one life in the case of transfers to pooled income funds made after November 30, 1983, for which the valuation date is before May 1, 1989.*—(1) *In general.*—For transfers to pooled income funds made after November 30, 1983, for which the valuation date is before May 1, 1989, the present value of the remainder interest at the time of the transfer of property to the fund is determined by computing the present value (at the time of the transfer) of the life income interest in the transferred property (as determined under paragraph (d)(2) of this section) and subtracting that value from the fair market value of the transferred property on the valuation date. The present value of a remainder interest that is dependent on the termination of the life of one individual is computed by use of Table G in paragraph (d)(4) of this section. For purposes of the computation under this section, the age of an individual is to be taken as the age of the individual at the individual's nearest birthday.

(2) *Present value of life income interest.*—The present value of the life income interest in property transferred to a pooled income fund shall be computed on the basis of:

(i) Life contingencies determined from the values of lx that are set forth in Table LN of § 20.2031-7A(d)(6) of this chapter (Estate Tax Regulations); and

(ii) Discount at a rate of interest, compounded annually, equal to the highest yearly rate of return of the pooled income fund for the 3 taxable years immediately preceding its taxable year in which the transfer of property to the fund is made. For purposes of this paragraph (d)(2), the yearly rate of return of a pooled income fund is determined as provided in § 1.642(c)-6(c) unless the highest yearly rate of return is deemed to be 9 percent. For purposes of this paragraph (d)(2), the first taxable year of a pooled income fund is considered a taxable year even though the taxable year consists of less than 12 months. However, appropriate adjustments must be made to annualize the rate of return earned by the fund for that period. Where it appears from the facts and circumstances that the highest yearly rate of return for the 3 taxable years immediately preceding the taxable year in which the transfer of property is made has been purposely manipulated to be substantially less than the rate of return that would otherwise be reasonably anticipated with the purpose of obtaining an excessive charitable deduction, that rate of return may not be used. In that case, the highest yearly rate of return of the fund is determined by treating the fund as a pooled income fund that has been in existence for less than 3 preceding taxable years. If a pooled income fund has been in existence less than 3 taxable years immediately preceding the taxable year in which the transfer of property to the fund is made, the highest yearly rate of return is deemed to be 9 percent.

(3) *Computation of value of remainder interest.*—The factor which is used in determining the present value of the remainder interest is the factor under the appropriate yearly rate of return in column (2) of Table G opposite the number in column (1) which corresponds to the age of the individual upon whose life the value of the remainder interest is based. If the yearly rate of return is a percentage which is between yearly rates of return for which factors are provided in Table G, a linear interpolation must be made. The present value of the remainder interest is determined by multiplying, by the factor determined under this paragraph (d)(3), the fair market value on the appropriate valuation date. If the yearly rate of return is below 2.2 percent or above 14 percent, see § 1.642(c)-6(b). This paragraph (d)(3) may be illustrated by the following example:

Example. A, who will be 50 years old on April 15, 1985, transfers $100,000 to a pooled income fund on January 1, 1985, and retains a life income interest in such property. The highest yearly rate of return earned by the fund for its 3 preceding taxable years is 9.9 percent. In Table G the figure in column (2) opposite 50 years under 9.8 percent is .15653 and under 10 percent is .15257. The present value of the remainder interest is $15,455, computed as follows:

Factor at 9.8 percent for person aged 50	.15653
Factor at 10 percent for person aged 50	.15257
Difference	.00396

Interpolation adjustment:

$$\frac{9.9\% - 9.8\%}{2\%} = \frac{x}{.00396.2\%}$$

x = .00198

Factor at 9.8 percent for person aged 50	0.15653
Less:	
Interpolation adjustment	.00198
Interpolated factor	.15455
Present value of remainder interest ($100,000 × .15455)	$15,455

(4) *Actuarial tables.*—The following tables shall be used in the application of the provisions of this section.

Table G—Single Life, Unisex—Table Showing the Present Worth of the Remainder Interest in Property Transferred to a Pooled Income Fund Having the Yearly Rate of Return Shown—Applicable for Transfers After November 30, 1983, and Before May 1, 1989

(1)	(2) Yearly Rate of Return									
Age	2.2%	2.4%	2.6%	2.8%	3.0%	3.2%	3.4%	3.6%	3.8%	4.0%
0 . .	.23930	.21334	.19077	.17112	.15401	.13908	.12603	.11461	.10461	.09583
1 . .	.22891	.20224	.17903	.15880	.14114	.12570	.11220	.10036	.08998	.08086
2 . .	.23297	.20610	.18265	.16218	.14429	.12862	.11489	.10284	.09225	.08293
3 . .	.23744	.21035	.18669	.16600	.14787	.13198	.11802	.10576	.09496	.08544
4 . .	.24212	.21485	.19098	.17006	.15171	.13559	.12141	.10893	.09793	.08821
5 . .	.24701	.21955	.19547	.17434	.15577	.13943	.12503	.11234	.10112	.09121
6 . .	.25207	.22442	.20015	.17880	.16001	.14345	.12884	.11593	.10451	.09439
7 . .	.25726	.22944	.20497	.18342	.16441	.14763	.13280	.11968	.10805	.09773
8 . .	.26259	.23461	.20995	.18820	.16898	.15198	.13694	.12360	.11176	.10125
9 . .	.26809	.23995	.21511	.19315	.17373	.15652	.14126	.12771	.11567	.10495
10 . .	.27373	.24544	.22043	.29828	.17865	.16123	.14576	.13200	.11975	.10883
11 . .	.27953	.25110	.22592	.20358	.18375	.16613	.15045	.13648	.12402	.11290
12 . .	.28546	.25690	.23156	.20904	.18902	.17119	.15531	.14113	.12847	.11715
13 . .	.29149	.26280	.23731	.21462	.19440	.17638	.16029	.14591	.13304	.12152
14 . .	.29757	.26877	.24312	.22026	.19986	.18164	.16535	.15076	.13769	.12597
15 . .	.30368	.27476	.24896	.22593	.20535	.18693	.17044	.15565	.14238	.13045
16 . .	.30978	.28075	.25481	.23161	.21085	.19224	.17554	.16055	.14707	.13494
17 . .	.31589	.28676	.26068	.23732	.21637	.19756	.18066	.16547	.15178	.13945
18 . .	.32204	.29280	.26659	.24306	.22193	.20294	.18584	.17044	.15655	.14401

(1)	(2) Yearly Rate of Return									
Age	2.2%	2.4%	2.6%	2.8%	3.0%	3.2%	3.4%	3.6%	3.8%	4.0%
19 . .	.32825	.29892	.27257	.24889	.22759	.20840	.19110	.17550	.16140	.14866
20 . .	.33457	.30514	.27867	.25484	.23336	.21399	.19650	.18069	.16639	.15344
21 . .	.34099	.31148	.28489	.26092	.23927	.21972	.20203	.18602	.17152	.15836
22 . .	.34751	.31794	.29124	.26712	.24532	.22559	.20771	.19151	.17680	.16344
23 . .	.35416	.32452	.29773	.27348	.25152	.23162	.21356	.19716	.18225	.16869
24 . .	.36096	.33127	.30439	.28002	.25791	.23784	.21960	.20301	.18791	.17414
25 . .	.36793	.33821	.31124	.28676	.26452	.24429	.22588	.20910	.19380	.17984
26 . .	.37509	.34535	.31832	.29374	.27136	.25098	.23240	.21545	.19996	.18581
27 . .	.38244	.35269	.32560	.30093	.27844	.25792	.23918	.22206	.20539	.19205
28 . .	.38998	.36023	.33311	.30836	.28577	.26512	.24623	.22894	.21310	.19858
29 . .	.39767	.36795	.34080	.31599	.29330	.27253	.25350	.23605	.22004	.20534
30 . .	.40553	.37584	.34868	.32382	.30104	.28016	.26100	.24341	.22724	.21236
31 . .	.41352	.38388	.35672	.33182	.30897	.28799	.26871	.25097	.23464	.21961
32 . .	.42165	.39208	.36494	.34001	.31710	.29603	.27664	.25877	.24230	.22710
33 . .	.42993	.40044	.37333	.34839	.32543	.30428	.28478	.26679	.25018	.23484
34 . .	.43834	.40894	.38188	.35694	.33395	.31273	.29314	.27504	.25830	.24280
35 . .	.44689	.41760	.39060	.36567	.34266	.32139	.30172	.28351	.26665	.25102
36 . .	.45556	.42640	.39947	.37458	.35156	.33024	.31050	.29220	.27523	.25948
37 . .	.46435	.43534	.40850	.38365	.36063	.33929	.31949	.30111	.28404	.26816
38 . .	.47325	.44440	.41767	.39288	.36987	.34851	.32867	.31022	.29305	.27707
39 . .	.48226	.45358	.42696	.40225	.37927	.35791	.33804	.31953	.30228	.28620
40 . .	.49136	.46288	.43640	.41177	.38884	.36749	.34759	.32904	.31172	.29555
41 . .	.50056	.47228	.44596	.42143	.39856	.37724	.35733	.33874	.32137	.30512
42 . .	.50988	.48182	.45566	.43125	.40846	.38717	.36727	.34866	.33124	.31493
43 . .	.51927	.49145	.46547	.44120	.41850	.39727	.37739	.35877	.34152	.32495
44 . .	.52874	.50118	.47540	.45128	.42869	.40752	.38768	.36906	.35159	.33518
45 . .	.53828	.51099	.48543	.46146	.43899	.41791	.39811	.37952	.36204	.34560
46 . .	.54788	.52088	.49554	.47176	.44943	.42844	.40871	.39014	.37267	.35621
47 . .	.55754	.53083	.50574	.48216	.45998	.43910	.41944	.40092	.38347	.36701
48 . .	.56726	.54087	.51604	.49267	.47065	.44990	.43034	.41188	.39445	.37801
49 . .	.57703	.55097	.52652	.50327	.48144	.46083	.44137	.42299	.40562	.38929
50 . .	.58685	.56114	.53677	.51398	.49234	.47189	.45256	.43427	.41695	.40056
51 . .	.59670	.57136	.54740	.52476	.50333	.48306	.46386	.44567	.42844	.41209
52 . .	.60658	.58161	.55798	.53560	.51441	.49432	.47528	.45721	.44006	.42378
53 . .	.61647	.59189	.56859	.54651	.52556	.50567	.48679	.46886	.45182	.43562
54 . .	.62635	.60217	.57923	.55744	.53675	.51708	.49838	.48060	.46367	.44756

See p. 15 for regulations not amended to reflect law changes

Table G—Continued (1) Table G—Single Life, Unisex—Table Showing the Present Worth of the Remainder Interest in Property Transferred to a Pooled Income Fund Having the Yearly Rate of Return Shown—Applicable for Transfers After November 30, 1983, and Before May 1, 1989

(1)	(2) Yearly Rate of Return									
Age	2.2%	2.4%	2.6%	2.8%	3.0%	3.2%	3.4%	3.6%	3.8%	4.0%
55 . .	.63622	.61246	.58987	.56840	.54798	.52854	.51004	.49242	.47563	.45962
56 . .	.64606	.62273	.60052	.57937	.55923	.54004	.52175	.50430	.48766	.47177
57 . .	.65589	.63299	.61117	.59037	.57052	.55159	.53352	.51626	.49978	.48402
58 . .	.66569	.64324	.62181	.60136	.58183	.56316	.54533	.52827	.51196	.49636
59 . .	.67546	.65347	.63246	.61237	.59316	.57478	.55719	.54036	.52424	.50879
60 . .	.68521	.66368	.64309	.62338	.60450	.58643	.56910	.55250	.53658	.52131
61 . .	.69492	.67388	.65372	.63440	.61587	.59811	.58107	.56471	.54901	.53393
62 . .	.70461	.68406	.66434	.64542	.62726	.60982	.59307	.57697	.56150	.54662
63 . .	.71425	.69420	.67494	.65643	.63865	.62155	.60510	.58928	.57405	.55940
64 . .	.72384	.70430	.68550	.66742	.65002	.63327	.61714	.60161	.58664	.57222
65 . .	.73336	.71434	.69602	.67837	.66137	.64498	.62918	.61395	.59926	.58508
66 . .	.74281	.72431	.70647	.68926	.67267	.67666	.64120	.62628	.61188	.59796
67 . .	.75216	.73419	.71684	.70009	.68391	.66829	.65319	.63859	.62448	.61083
68 . .	.76143	.74399	.72714	.71085	.69509	.67986	.66512	.65086	.63706	.62370
69 . .	.77060	.75370	.73735	.72153	.70622	.69139	.67702	.66311	.64963	.63656
70 . .	.77969	.76334	.74750	.73215	.71728	.70286	.68888	.67533	.66218	.64942
71 . .	.78870	.77290	.75758	.74272	.72830	.71431	.70073	.68754	.67474	.66231
72 . .	.79764	.78240	.76760	.75323	.73928	.72572	.71255	.69974	.68730	.67520
73 . .	.80646	.79178	.77751	.76364	.75016	.73704	.72429	.71188	.69980	.68805
74 . .	.81511	.80099	.78725	.77387	.76086	.74819	.73586	.72384	.71214	.70075
75 . .	.82353	.80995	.79674	.78386	.77132	.75909	.74718	.73557	.72424	.71320
76 . .	.83169	.81866	.80596	.79357	.78149	.76971	.75822	.74700	.73606	.72538
77 . .	.83960	.82710	.81491	.80301	.79139	.78004	.76897	.75815	.74758	.73726
78 . .	.84727	.83530	.82360	.81218	.80101	.79010	.77944	.76902	.75883	.74886
79 . .	.85473	.84328	.83207	.82112	.81041	.79993	.78968	.77965	.76984	.76023
80 . .	.86201	.85106	.84034	.82986	.81960	.80955	.79971	.79008	.78064	.77140
81 . .	.86905	.85861	.84837	.83835	.82853	.81891	.80948	.80024	.79118	.78230
82 . .	.87585	.86589	.85612	.84655	.83717	.82796	.81894	.81009	.80140	.79288
83 . .	.88239	.87291	.86360	.85447	.84552	.83672	.82810	.81962	.81131	.80314
84 . .	.88873	.87971	.87085	.86216	.85362	.84524	.83700	.82891	.82096	.81314
85 . .	.89487	.88630	.87789	.86963	.86150	.85352	.84567	.83795	.83037	.82291
86 . .	.90070	.89258	.88459	.87674	.86901	.86141	.85394	.84659	.83936	.83224
87 . .	.90609	.89838	.89079	.88332	.87597	.86874	.86162	.85461	.84771	.84092
88 . .	.91106	.90372	.89650	.88939	.88234	.87549	.86870	.86201	.85542	.84893
89 . .	.91570	.90872	.90184	.89507	.88839	.88182	.87534	.86895	.86266	.85645
90 . .	.92014	.91350	.90696	.90051	.89416	.88789	.88171	.87562	.86961	.86369
91 . .	.92435	.91804	.91182	.90569	.89964	.89367	.88779	.88198	.87625	.87059
92 . .	.92822	.92222	.91630	.91045	.90469	.89900	.89338	.88784	.88237	.87697
93 . .	.93170	.92597	.92032	.91474	.90923	.90379	.89842	.89312	.88788	.88271
94 . .	.93477	.92929	.92387	.91853	.91325	.90803	.90288	.89780	.89277	.88781
95 . .	.93743	.93216	.92695	.92181	.91673	.91171	.90675	.90185	.89701	.89223
96 . .	.93967	.93458	.92955	.92458	.91966	.91481	.91001	.90527	.90058	.89594
97 . .	.94167	.93674	.93186	.92704	.92228	91757	.91291	.90831	.90376	.89926
98 . .	.94342	.93863	.93389	.92921	.92457	.91999	.91546	.91098	.90655	.90217
99 . .	.94508	.94041	.93580	.93124	.92673	.92227	.91786	.91349	.90917	.90490
100 . .	.94672	.94218	.93770	.93326	.92887	.92453	.92023	.91598	.91177	.90761
101 . .	.94819	.94377	.93940	.93508	.93080	.92656	.92236	.91821	.91410	.91003
102 . .	.94979	.94550	.94125	.93704	.93288	.92875	.92467	.92063	.91662	.91266
103 . .	.95180	.94766	.94357	.93952	.93550	.93152	.92758	.92367	.91980	.91597
104 . .	.95377	.94979	.94585	.94194	.93806	.93423	.93042	.92665	.92291	.91920
105 . .	.95663	.95288	.94916	.94547	.94181	.93818	.93458	.93101	.92747	.92395
106 . .	.96101	.95762	.95425	.95091	.94760	.94430	.94104	.93779	.93457	.93137
107 . .	.96688	.96398	.96110	.95824	.95539	.95256	.94975	.94696	.94418	.94143
108 . .	.97569	.97354	.97141	.96928	.96717	.96507	.96298	.96090	.95883	.95676
109 . .	.98924	.98828	.98733	.98638	.98544	.98450	.98356	.98263	.98170	.98077

See p. 15 for regulations not amended to reflect law changes

Table G—Continued (2) Table G—Single Life, Unisex—Table Showing the Present Worth of the Remainder Interest in Property Transferred to a Pooled Income Fund Having the Yearly Rate of Return Shown—Applicable for Transfers After November 30, 1983, and Before May 1, 1989

(1)	(2) Yearly Rate of Return									
Age	4.2%	4.4%	4.6%	4.8%	5.0%	5.2%	5.4%	5.6%	5.8%	6.0%
0	.08811	.08132	.07534	.07006	.06539	.06126	.05759	.05433	.05143	.04884
1	.07283	.06576	.05952	.05400	.04912	.04480	.04096	.03754	.03450	.03179
2	.07471	.06746	.06106	.05539	.05037	.04591	.04194	.03841	.03527	.03246
3	.07704	.06962	.06304	.05722	.05205	.04745	.04336	.03972	.03646	.03355
4	.07962	.07202	.06528	.05930	.05398	.04924	.04502	.04125	.03789	.03487
5	.08243	.07464	.06773	.06159	.05612	.05124	.04689	.04300	.03952	.03639
6	.08542	.07745	.07037	.06406	.05844	.05342	.04893	.04492	.04131	.03808
7	.08857	.08042	.07316	.06669	.06091	.05574	.05112	.04697	.04324	.03990
8	.09189	.08355	.07612	.06948	.06354	.05822	.05346	.04918	.04533	.04186
9	.09540	.08687	.07926	.07245	.06635	.06089	.05598	.05156	.04759	.04400
10	.09908	.09037	.08258	.07560	.06934	.06372	.05866	.05411	.05000	.04630
11	.10296	.09406	.08609	.07894	.07251	.06673	.06153	.05684	.05260	.04877
12	.10701	.09793	.08977	.08245	.07586	.06992	.06457	.05973	.05536	.05141
13	.11119	.10191	.09358	.08608	.07932	.07322	.06772	.06274	.05824	.05415
14	.11544	.10597	.09745	.08978	.08285	.07659	.07093	.06581	.06117	.05695
15	.11972	.11007	.10136	.09350	.08640	.07998	.07417	.06890	.06411	.05976
16	.12402	.11416	.10527	.09723	.08995	.08337	.07739	.07197	.06704	.06255
17	.12832	.11827	.10919	.10096	.09351	.08675	.08062	.07504	.06996	.06533
18	.13268	.12243	.11315	.10474	.09711	.09018	.08387	.07813	.07290	.06813
19	.13712	.12667	.11720	.10860	.10078	.09367	.08720	.08130	.07591	.07099
20	.14170	.13105	.12138	.11259	.10459	.09730	.09065	.08458	.07904	.07397
21	.14642	.13557	.12570	.11671	.10853	.10106	.09423	.08800	.08229	.07707
22	.15129	.14024	.13017	.12099	.11261	.10496	.09796	.09155	.08568	.08030
23	.15634	.14508	.13481	.12544	.11687	.10903	.10185	.09526	.08923	.08368
24	.16159	.15013	.13967	.13009	.12133	.11330	.10594	.09918	.09297	.08726
25	.16709	.15543	.14477	.13500	.12604	.11782	.11028	.10334	.09696	.09108
26	.17286	.16101	.15014	.14018	.13103	.12262	.11489	.10778	.10122	.09518
27	.17891	.16686	.15580	.14564	.13630	.12771	.11979	.11249	.10576	.09955
28	.18525	.17301	.16175	.15140	.14187	.13309	.12499	.11751	.11060	.10421
29	.19183	.17940	.16796	.15742	.14700	.13873	.13044	.12278	.11570	.10914
30	.19867	.18606	.17443	.16370	.15380	.14464	.13617	.12833	.12107	.11433
31	.20574	.19295	.13114	.17023	.16013	.15079	.14214	.13412	.12668	.11977
32	.21307	.20010	.18811	.17702	.16674	.15722	.14838	.14018	.13256	.12548
33	.22064	.20751	.19535	.18407	.17362	.16391	.15490	.14652	.13873	.13147
34	.22846	.21516	.20283	.19138	.18075	.17087	.16168	.15312	.14515	.13772
35	.23653	.22307	.21058	.19896	.18816	.17811	.16874	.16001	.15186	.14426
36	.24484	.23124	.21859	.20681	.19584	.18562	.17608	.16717	.15886	.15108
37	.25340	.23966	.22685	.21492	.20379	.19340	.18369	.17462	.16613	.15819
38	.26219	.24831	.23536	.22328	.21199	.20144	.19157	.18233	.17368	.16557
39	.27120	.25720	.24411	.23188	.22044	.20974	.19971	.19031	.18149	.17322
40	.28045	.26633	.25311	.24075	.22916	.21830	.20812	.19856	.18959	.18115
41	.28992	.27569	.26236	.24986	.23814	.22714	.21681	.20710	.19797	.18938
42	.29965	.28532	.27188	.25926	.24741	.23627	.22579	.21594	.20665	.19791
43	.30960	.29518	.28163	.26890	.25693	.24566	.23606	.22505	.21562	.20673
44	.31977	.30527	.29164	.27880	.26671	.25532	.24458	.23445	.22488	.21585
45	.33013	.31557	.30185	.28892	.27673	.26522	.25436	.24410	.23440	.22523
46	.34071	.32609	.31230	.29929	.28700	.27538	.26441	.25402	.24420	.23490
47	.35148	.33681	.32296	.30988	.29750	.28579	.27471	.26421	.25427	.24484
48	.36246	.34777	.33387	.32072	.30826	.29647	.28529	.27469	.26463	.25508
49	.37364	.35893	.34499	.33179	.31927	.30739	.29613	.28543	.27527	.26562
50	.38503	.37030	.35634	.34310	.33053	.31859	.30724	.29646	.28620	.27645
51	.39659	.38187	.36790	.35462	.34201	.33001	.31860	.30774	.29740	.28755
52	.40832	.39362	.37965	.36636	.35371	.34167	.33020	.31928	.30885	.29893
53	.42021	.40554	.39158	.37829	.36562	.35355	.34204	.33105	.32057	.31056
54	.43222	.41760	.40367	.39039	.37771	.36562	.35407	.34304	.33250	.32243

See p. 15 for regulations not amended to reflect law changes

Table G—Continued (3) Table G—Single Life, Unisex—Table Showing the Present Worth of the Remainder Interest in Property Transferred to a Pooled Income Fund Having the Yearly Rate of Return Shown—Applicable for Transfers After November 30, 1983, and Before May 1, 1989

(1)	(2) Yearly Rate of Return									
Age	4.2%	4.4%	4.6%	4.8%	5.0%	5.2%	5.4%	5.6%	5.8%	6.0%
55 . .	.44436	.42980	.41591	.41264	.38997	.37787	.36630	.35523	.34465	.33452
56 . .	.45660	.44212	.42828	.41504	.40239	.39029	.37870	.36761	.35699	.34682
57 . .	.46897	.45456	.44079	.42760	.41498	.40289	.39130	.38020	.36956	.35935
58 . .	.48142	.46712	.45342	.44030	.42771	.41565	.40408	.39297	.38231	.37208
59 . .	.49399	.47980	.46620	.45314	.44062	.42859	.41704	.40595	.39529	.38504
60 . .	.50666	.49260	.47910	.46613	.45367	.44170	.43019	.41912	.40847	.39822
61 . .	.51944	.50552	.49214	.47927	.46690	.45499	.44353	.43250	.42187	.41164
62 . .	.53232	.51856	.50531	.49256	.48028	.46845	.45706	.44607	.43548	.42527
63 . .	.54529	.53169	.51860	.50598	.49381	.48208	.47076	.45984	.44930	.43913
64 . .	.55832	.54491	.53198	.51950	.50746	.49583	.48461	.47377	.46329	.45317
65 . .	.57140	.55819	.54544	.53312	.52121	.50971	.49859	.48784	.47744	.46738
66 . .	.58451	.57152	.55895	.54681	.53506	.52369	.51269	.50204	.49173	.48175
67 . .	.59763	.58486	.57251	.56054	.54896	.53774	.52688	.51635	.50614	.49625
68 . .	.61076	.59823	.58609	.57432	.56292	.55187	.54115	.53075	.52066	.51088
69 . .	.62390	.61162	.59971	.58816	.57695	.56607	.55551	.54526	.53530	.52563
70 . .	.63705	.62503	.61337	.60204	.59104	.58035	.56997	.55987	.55006	.54053
71 . .	.65023	.63849	.62709	.61600	.60522	.59474	.58455	.57463	.56498	.55559
72 . .	.66344	.65199	.64086	.63003	.61949	.60923	.59924	.58952	.58004	.57082
73 . .	.67661	.66547	.65463	.64407	.63378	.62375	.61398	.60446	.59518	.58613
74 . .	.68964	.67882	.66827	.65798	.64796	.63818	.62864	.61933	.61026	.60140
75 . .	.70243	.69193	.68168	.67168	.66192	.65240	.64310	.63402	.62515	.61649
76 . .	.71495	.70477	.69482	.68411	.67563	.66636	.65731	.64836	.63981	.63135
77 . .	.72717	.71731	.70768	.69826	.68905	.68005	.67124	.66263	.65420	.64596
78 . .	.73912	.72959	.72026	.71114	.70221	.69347	.68492	.67655	.66836	.66033
79 . .	.75083	.74163	.73262	.72379	.71515	.70669	.69840	.69028	.68232	.67452
80 . .	.76235	.75348	.74479	.73627	.72792	.71973	.71171	.70384	.69613	.68856
81 . .	.77360	.76506	.75669	.74848	.74043	.73252	.72377	.71717	.70970	.70237
82 . .	.78452	.77632	.76827	.76036	.75260	.74499	.73751	.73016	.72295	.71587
83 . .	.79513	.78725	.77952	.77192	.76446	.75713	.74992	.74284	.73589	.72905
84 . .	.80547	.79792	.79051	.78322	.77606	.76901	.76208	.75527	.74857	.74198
85 . .	.81557	.80836	.80126	.79429	.78742	.78067	.77402	.76748	.76104	.75471
86 . .	.82524	.81835	.81157	.80489	.79832	.79185	.78548	.77921	.77304	.76695
87 . .	.83423	.82764	.82115	.81477	.80847	.80228	.79617	.79015	.78423	.77838
88 . .	.84253	.83623	.83002	.82390	.81787	.81193	.80607	.80029	.79460	.78899
89 . .	.85033	.84430	.83836	.83250	.82672	.82102	.81540	.80985	.80438	.79899
90 . .	.85784	.85208	.84639	.84079	.83525	.82979	.82441	.81909	.81384	.80867
91 . .	.86502	.85951	.85408	.84871	.84342	.83820	.83304	.82795	.82292	.81796
92 . .	.87164	.86638	.86118	.85605	.85098	.84598	.84104	.83616	.83134	.82657
93 . .	.87761	.87257	.86759	.86267	.85781	.85300	.84826	.84357	.83894	.83437
94 . .	.88290	.87806	.87327	.86854	.86386	.85924	.85468	.85017	.84570	.84130
95 . .	.88750	.88282	.87820	.87364	.86913	.86466	.86025	.85589	.85158	.84732
96 . .	.89136	.88683	.88236	.87793	.87355	.86922	.86494	.86071	.85652	.85238
97 . .	.89481	.89041	.88606	.88176	.87750	.87329	.86913	.86501	.86093	.85690
98 . .	.89783	.89354	.88930	.88511	.88096	.87685	.87279	.86877	.86479	.86085
99 . .	.90067	.89649	.89235	.88826	.88420	.88019	.87622	.87230	.86814	.86456
100 . .	.90349	.89941	.89538	.89138	.88743	.88351	.87964	.87580	.87200	.86824
101 . .	.90600	.90202	.89807	.89416	.89029	.88646	.88267	.87891	.87519	.87150
102 . .	.90873	.90484	.90099	.89717	.89339	.88965	.88594	.88227	.87863	.87503
103 . .	.91217	.90841	.90468	.90099	.89733	.89370	.89011	.88654	.88301	.87952
104 . .	.91553	.91188	.90827	.90469	.90114	.89763	.89414	.89068	.88725	.88385
105 . .	.92047	.91701	.91358	.91018	.90680	.90345	.90013	.89683	.89356	.89032
106 . .	.92819	.92504	.92191	.91880	.91571	.91265	.90961	.90658	.90358	.90060
107 . .	.93868	.93596	.93325	.93056	.92788	.92522	.92258	.91995	.91734	.91474
108 . .	.95471	.95267	.95064	.94862	.94661	.94461	.94262	.94063	.93866	.93670
109 . .	.97985	.97893	.97801	.97710	.97619	.97529	.97438	.97348	.97259	.97170

See p. 15 for regulations not amended to reflect law changes

Table G—Continued (4) Table G—Single Life, Unisex—Table Showing the Present Worth of the Remainder Interest in Property Transferred to a Pooled Income Fund Having the Yearly Rate of Return Shown—Applicable for Transfers After November 30, 1983, and Before May 1, 1989

(1)	(2) Yearly Rate of Return									
Age	6.2%	6.4%	6.6%	6.8%	7.0%	7.2%	7.4%	7.6%	7.8%	8.0%
0 . .	.04653	.04447	.04262	.04095	.03946	.03811	.03689	.03579	.03479	.03388
1 . .	.02937	.02720	.02525	.02351	.02194	.02052	.01924	.01809	.01704	.01609
2 . .	.02994	.02769	.02567	.02385	.02221	.02074	.01940	.01819	.01710	.01611
3 . .	.03094	.02860	.02650	.02460	.02290	.02136	.01996	.01870	.01756	.01652
4 . .	.03216	.02973	.02755	.02558	.02380	.02219	.02074	.01942	.01822	.01713
5 . .	.03359	.03106	.02879	.02674	.02488	.02321	.02169	.02031	.01905	.01791
6 . .	.03517	.03255	.03019	.02805	.02612	.02437	.02278	.02134	.02203	.01883
7 . .	.93688	.03416	.03171	.02949	.02747	.02565	.02399	.02248	.02111	.01986
8 . .	.03874	.03592	.03337	.03106	.02896	.02706	.02533	.02376	.02232	.02101
9 . .	.04077	.03784	.03519	.03279	.03061	.02863	.02682	.02518	.02367	.02230
10 . .	.04295	.03992	.03717	.03467	.03240	.03034	.02846	.02674	.02517	.02373
11 . .	.04531	.04217	.03931	.03672	.03436	.03221	.03025	.02846	.02682	.02532
12 . .	.04782	.04457	.04161	.03892	.03647	.03424	.03219	.03032	.02861	.02704
13 . .	.05045	.04708	.04402	.04122	.03868	.03635	.03422	.03228	.03049	.02885
14 . .	.05312	.04964	.04646	.04357	.04093	.03851	.03630	.03427	.03240	.03069
15 . .	.05581	.05220	.04891	.04591	.04317	.04066	.03836	.03624	.03430	.03252
16 . .	.05847	.05474	.05134	.04822	.04538	.04277	.04037	.03817	.03615	.03429
17 . .	.06111	.05726	.05374	.05051	.04756	.04485	.04236	.04007	.03796	.03602
18 . .	.06378	.05979	.05615	.05280	.04974	.04693	.04434	.04196	.03976	.03773
19 . .	.06650	.06238	.05861	.05514	.05196	.04904	.04635	.04387	.04159	.03947
20 . .	.06933	.06507	.06117	.05758	.05429	.05125	.04845	.04588	.04349	.04129
21 . .	.07228	.06788	.06384	.06013	.05671	.05356	.05065	.04797	.04549	.04319
22 . .	.07535	.07081	.06664	.06279	.05925	.05597	.05295	.05016	.04758	.04519
23 . .	.07858	.07389	.06958	.06559	.06192	.05853	.05539	.05248	.04979	.04730
24 . .	.08201	.07717	.07270	.06858	.06477	.06125	.05799	.05497	.05217	.04957
25 . .	.08567	.08067	.07606	.07179	.06785	.06420	.06081	.05767	.05475	.05205
26 . .	.08960	.08444	.07968	.07527	.07118	.06739	.06388	.06062	.05758	.05476
27 . .	.09380	.08849	.08357	.07901	.07478	.07086	.06721	.06382	.06067	.05773
28 . .	.09830	.09283	.08775	.08304	.07867	.07460	.07082	.06730	.06402	.06097
29 . .	.10306	.09742	.09218	.08732	.08280	.07859	.07467	.07102	.06762	.06444
30 . .	.10808	.10228	.09688	.09187	.08720	.08284	.07879	.07500	.07146	.06815
31 . .	.11335	.10738	.10182	.09665	.09182	.08733	.08312	.07920	.07553	.07209
32 . .	.11889	.11275	.10704	.10170	.09672	.09207	.08773	.08366	.07986	.07629
33 . .	.12471	.11840	.11252	.10703	.10189	.09709	.09260	.08829	.08445	.08075
34 . .	.13079	.12432	.11827	.11261	.10732	.10237	.09773	.09338	.08929	.08546
35 . .	.13716	.13052	.12431	.11849	.11305	.10794	.10315	.09865	.09442	.09045
36 . .	.14381	.13701	.13063	.12465	.11905	.11379	.10884	.10420	.09983	.09572
37 . .	.15075	.14378	.13724	.13110	.12534	.11992	.11483	.11003	.10552	.10126
38 . .	.15796	.15083	.14412	.13782	.13190	.12633	.12108	.11614	.11148	.10708
39 . .	.16545	.15815	.15129	.14483	.13875	.13302	.12762	.12253	.11772	.11318
40 . .	.17322	.16576	.15874	.15212	.14589	.14000	.13445	.12921	.12425	.11957
41 . .	.18129	.17367	.16649	.15971	.15332	.14728	.14158	.13619	.13109	.12626
42 . .	.18967	.18190	.17456	.16763	.16108	.15490	.14904	.14350	.13825	.13328
43 . .	.19834	.19041	.18293	.17585	.16915	.16281	.15680	.15111	.14572	.14060
44 . .	.20731	.19924	.19160	.18437	.17753	.17104	.16488	.15905	.15351	.14825
45 . .	.21655	.20834	.20055	.19318	.18619	.17955	.17326	.16727	.16159	.15619
46 . .	.22608	.21773	.20981	.20229	.19516	.18838	.18194	.17582	.16999	.16445
47 . .	.23690	.22741	.21935	.21170	.20443	.19751	.19093	.18467	.17870	.17302
48 . .	.24602	.23741	.22922	.22144	.21403	.20698	.20026	.19386	.18776	.18194
49 . .	.25644	.24770	.23939	.23148	.22394	.21676	.20991	.20338	.19715	.19119
50 . .	.26716	.25831	.24989	.24185	.23419	.22689	.21991	.21325	.20689	.20080
51 . .	.27816	.26921	.26068	.25253	.24475	.23732	.23023	.22344	.21695	.21074
52 . .	.28945	.28040	.27176	.26351	.25562	.24808	.24086	.23396	.22735	.22102
53 . .	.30100	.29187	.28313	.27478	.26679	.25914	.25181	.24479	.23807	.23162
54 . .	.31279	.30357	.29475	.28631	.27822	.27047	.26304	.25591	.24908	.24252

See p. 15 for regulations not amended to reflect law changes

Table G—Continued (5) Table G, Single Life, Unisex—Table Showing the Present Worth of the Remainder Interest in Property Transferred to a Pooled Income Fund Having the Yearly Rate of Return Shown—Applicable for Transfers After November 30, 1983, and Before May 1, 1989

(1)	(2) Yearly Rate of Return									
Age	6.2%	6.4%	6.6%	6.8%	7.0%	7.2%	7.4%	7.6%	7.8%	8.0%
55 . .	.32482	.31553	.30663	.29810	.28992	.28208	.27455	.26733	.26039	.25372
56 . .	.33707	.32771	.31875	.31014	.30188	.29395	.28633	.27901	.27197	.26521
57 . .	.34955	.34015	.33112	.32244	.31411	.30610	.29840	.29099	.28386	.27700
58 . .	.36225	.35280	.34372	.33499	.32659	.31851	.31074	.30325	.29604	.28909
59 . .	.37519	.36571	.35659	.34781	.33936	.33122	.32337	.31581	.30853	.30150
60 . .	.38836	.37886	.36971	.36089	.35239	.34420	.33630	.32867	.32132	.31422
61 . .	.41077	.39226	.38309	.37425	.36572	.35748	.34953	.34185	.33444	.32727
62 . .	.41542	.40591	.39674	.38788	.37932	.37106	.36307	.35535	.34788	.34066
63 . .	.42930	.41981	.41064	.40178	.39321	.38492	.37691	.36915	.36165	.35438
64 . .	.44338	.43392	.42477	.41591	.40734	.39905	.39102	.38324	.37571	.36841
65 . .	.45765	.44823	.43910	.43027	.42171	.41342	.40539	.39760	.39005	.38272
66 . .	.47208	.46271	.45364	.44483	.43630	.42803	.42000	.41221	.40465	.39731
67 . .	.48666	.47736	.46834	.45958	.45108	.44283	.43483	.42705	.41949	.41215
68 . .	.50138	.49215	.48320	.47450	.46605	.45784	.44987	.44211	.43457	.42724
69 . .	.51624	.50711	.49824	.48961	.48122	.47307	.46513	.45741	.44990	.44259
70 . .	.53125	.52223	.51345	.50491	.49660	.48851	.48063	.47296	.46549	.45821
71 . .	.54645	.53755	.52899	.52045	.51223	.50422	.49641	.48880	.48139	.47416
72 . .	.56183	.55307	.54453	.53621	.52809	.52018	.51246	.50493	.49758	.49042
73 . .	.57731	.56870	.56030	.55211	.54412	.53631	.52870	.52126	.51400	.50691
74 . .	.59275	.58431	.57606	.56801	.56015	.55247	.54497	.53764	.53048	.52347
75 . .	.60803	.59976	.59168	.58379	.57607	.56852	.56115	.55393	.54687	.53997
76 . .	.62308	.61500	.60709	.59936	.59179	.58439	.57714	.57005	.56311	.55632
77 . .	.63789	.63000	.62227	.61470	.60730	.60005	.59294	.58599	.57917	.57249
78 . .	.65247	.64477	.63723	.62984	.62261	.61551	.60856	.60174	.59506	.58851
79 . .	.66687	.65938	.65203	.64483	.63777	.63084	.62405	.61739	.61085	.60443
80 . .	.68114	.67386	.66672	.65971	.65284	.64609	.63946	.63296	.62657	.62030
81 . .	.69518	.68812	.68119	.67438	.66770	.66114	.65469	.64836	.64213	.63602
82 . .	.70891	.70207	.69535	.68875	.68227	.67589	.66963	.66347	.65742	.65146
83 . .	.72232	.71572	.70922	.70283	.69655	.69037	.68429	.67831	.67342	.66664
84 . .	.73550	.72913	.72285	.71668	.71061	.70463	.69875	.69296	.68726	.68165
85 . .	.74847	.74234	.73630	.73035	.72449	.71872	.71304	.70745	.70194	.69654
86 . .	.76096	.75506	.74925	.74353	.73789	.73233	.72685	.72146	.71614	.71089
87 . .	.77263	.76696	.76137	.75585	.75042	.74507	.73978	.73458	.72944	.72438
88 . .	.78345	.77799	.77261	.76730	.76207	.75691	.75181	.74679	.74183	.73694
89 . .	.79367	.78842	.78323	.77812	.77308	.76810	.76319	.75834	.75355	.74883
90 . .	.80356	.79851	.79353	.78862	.78376	.77897	.77424	.76957	.76496	.76040
91 . .	.81306	.80821	.80344	.79871	.79405	.78945	.78490	.78040	.77596	.77158
92 . .	.82187	.81722	.81263	.80810	.80361	.79919	.79481	.79048	.78621	.78198
93 . .	.82984	.82538	.82096	.81659	.81228	.80801	.80380	.79963	.79550	.79143
94 . .	.83694	.83263	.82837	.83416	.81999	.81587	.81180	.80777	.80379	.79985
95 . .	.84310	.83893	.83481	.83073	.82670	.82271	.81877	.81487	.81100	.80719
96 . .	.84829	.84424	.84023	.83626	.83234	.82846	.82462	.82083	.81707	.81335
97 . .	.85291	.84897	.84506	.84120	.83738	.83360	.82985	.82615	.82248	.81885
98 . .	.85696	.85310	.84929	.84551	.84177	.83808	.83441	.83079	.82720	.82365
99 . .	.86075	.85698	.85325	.84956	.84590	.84228	.83869	.83514	.83163	.82815
100 . .	.86452	.86084	.85719	.85357	.85000	.84645	.84294	.83947	.83603	.83262
101 . .	.86785	.86424	.86066	.85711	.85360	.85012	.84668	.84327	.83988	.83653
102 . .	.87146	.86792	.86442	.86094	.85750	.85409	.85072	.84737	.84405	.84077
103 . .	.87605	.87261	.86921	.86583	.86248	.85917	.85588	.85262	.84939	.84619
104 . .	.88047	.87713	.87382	.87053	.86727	.86403	.86083	.85765	.85449	.85136
105 . .	.88710	.88390	.88073	.87758	.87446	.87136	.86829	.86524	.86221	.85921
106 . .	.89764	.89471	.89179	.88889	.88601	.88315	.88032	.87750	.87470	.87192
107 . .	.91216	.90960	.90705	.90451	.90199	.89949	.89700	.89452	.89206	.88961
108 . .	.93474	.93280	.93086	.92894	.92702	.92511	.92321	.92132	.91944	.91757
109 . .	.97081	.96992	.96904	.96816	.96729	.96642	.96555	.96468	.96382	.96296

Table G—Continued (6) Table G, Single Life, Unisex—Table Showing the Present Worth of the Remainder Interest in Property Transferred to a Pooled Income Fund Having the Yearly Rate of Return Shown—Applicable for Transfers After November 30, 1983, and Before May 1, 1989

(1)	(2) Yearly Rate of Return									
Age	8.2%	8.4%	8.6%	8.8%	9.0%	9.2%	9.4%	9.6%	9.8%	10.0%
0 . .	.03305	.03230	.03161	.03098	.03040	.02987	.02938	.02893	.02851	.02812
1 . .	.01523	.01444	.01372	.01307	.01247	.01192	.01141	.01094	.01051	.01012
2 . .	.01520	.01438	.01362	.01294	.01230	.01173	.01119	.01070	.01025	.00983
3 . .	.01557	.01470	.01391	.01319	.01253	.01192	.01136	.01084	.01036	.00992
4 . .	.01613	.01522	.01439	.01363	.01294	.01229	.01170	.01116	.01066	.01019
5 . .	.01687	.01591	.01504	.01424	.01351	.01283	.01221	.01164	.01111	.01062
6 . .	.01774	.01674	.01582	.01498	.01421	.01350	.01284	.01224	.01168	.01116
7 . .	.01871	.01766	.01670	.01581	.01500	.01425	.01356	.01292	.01233	.01178
8 . .	.01980	.01870	.01769	.01676	.01591	.01512	.01439	.01372	.01309	.01252
9 . .	.02104	.01989	.01883	.01785	.01695	.01612	.01535	.01464	.01398	.01337
10 . .	.02241	.02120	.02009	.01906	.01812	.01724	.01644	.01569	.01499	.01435
11 . .	.02394	.02267	.02150	.02042	.01943	.01851	.01766	.01688	.01615	.01547
12 . .	.02560	.02427	.02305	.02192	.02088	.01991	.01902	.01819	.01742	.01671
13 . .	.02734	.02595	.02467	.02349	.02240	.02139	.02045	.01958	.01877	.01802
14 . .	.02912	.02766	.02632	.02509	.02394	.02288	.02190	.02098	.02013	.01934
15 . .	.03087	.02935	.02795	.02666	.02546	.02435	.02331	.02235	.02146	.02063
16 . .	.03257	.03099	.02952	.02817	.02691	.02575	.02466	.02366	.02272	.02185
17 . .	.03423	.03257	.03104	.02962	.02831	.02709	.02595	.02490	.02391	.02300
18 . .	.03586	.03414	.03253	.03105	.02967	.02839	.02721	.02610	.02507	.02410
19 . .	.03752	.03572	.03414	.03249	.03105	.02971	.02846	.02730	.02621	.02520
20 . .	.03925	.03737	.03562	.03399	.03248	.03108	.02977	.02855	.02741	.02635
21 . .	.04107	.03910	.03727	.03557	.03398	.03251	.03114	.02986	.02866	.02755
22 . .	.04297	.04091	.03899	.03722	.03556	.03402	.03258	.03123	.02998	.02880
23 . .	.04498	.04283	.04083	.03897	.03723	.03562	.03410	.03269	.03137	.03014
24 . .	.04715	.04491	.04282	.04087	.03905	.03735	.03577	.03428	.03290	.03159
25 . .	.04953	.04718	.04499	.04295	.04105	.03927	.03761	.03605	.03459	.03322
26 . .	.05213	.04968	.04740	.04527	.04327	.04141	.03966	.03803	.03649	.03505
27 . .	.05499	.05243	.05005	.04782	.04573	.04377	.04194	.04023	.03861	.03710
28 . .	.05811	.05545	.05295	.05062	.04844	.04639	.04447	.04267	.04098	.03938
29 . .	.06146	.05868	.05608	.05365	.05136	.04922	.04721	.04532	.04354	.04187
30 . .	.06506	.06217	.05945	.05691	.05452	.05228	.05017	.04819	.04633	.04457
31 . .	.06888	.06586	.06303	.06038	.05789	.05554	.05334	.05126	.04930	.04746
32 . .	.07295	.06981	.06687	.06410	.06149	.05904	.05674	.05456	.05251	.05058
33 . .	.07728	.07401	.07095	.06806	.06535	.06279	.06038	.05810	.05595	.05392
34 . .	.08185	.07846	.07527	.07227	.06944	.06677	.06425	.06187	.05962	.05750
35 . .	.08671	.08319	.07988	.07675	.07380	.07102	.06839	.06590	.06355	.06132
36 . .	.09184	.08819	.08475	.08150	.07843	.07553	.07278	.07019	.06773	.06540
37 . .	.09725	.09347	.08989	.08652	.08332	.08030	.07745	.07474	.07217	.06974
38 . .	.10293	.09901	.09531	.09180	.08848	.08534	.08237	.07955	.07687	.07433
39 . .	.10889	.01483	.10099	.09736	.09391	.09065	.08755	.08462	.08182	.07917
40 . .	.11514	.11094	.10697	.10320	.09963	.09624	.09302	.08996	.08706	.08429
41 . .	.12168	.11735	.11324	.10934	.10564	.10212	.09878	.09560	.09258	.08970
42 . .	.12856	.12409	.11984	.11581	.11197	.10833	.10486	.10156	.09842	.09543
43 . .	.13574	.13113	.12675	.12258	.11862	.11484	.11125	.10783	.10456	.10145
44 . .	.14325	.13850	.13398	.12967	.12558	.12167	.11795	.11441	.11102	.10779
45 . .	.15105	.14616	.14150	.13706	.13283	.12880	.12495	.12128	.11777	.11442
46 . .	.15917	.15414	.14935	.14478	.14041	.13625	.13227	.12847	.12484	.12137
47 . .	.16760	.16244	.15751	.15280	.14831	.14402	.13991	.13599	.13223	.12863
48 . .	.17639	.17109	.16602	.16119	.15656	.15214	.14791	.14385	.13997	.13626
49 . .	.18551	.18007	.17488	.16991	.16516	.16060	.15625	.15207	.14806	.14422
50 . .	.19499	.18942	.18410	.17900	.17412	.16944	.16496	.16065	.15653	.15257
51 . .	.20480	.19911	.19366	.18844	.18343	.17862	.17401	.16959	.16534	.16126
52 . .	.21495	.20914	.20357	.19822	.19309	.18816	.18343	.17888	.17451	.17031
53 . .	.22544	.21951	.21381	.20835	.20309	.19805	.19320	.18853	.18404	.17972
54 . .	.23622	.23018	.22437	.21878	.21341	.20825	.20328	.19850	.19390	.18946

See p. 15 for regulations not amended to reflect law changes

Table G—Continued (7) Table G—Single Life, Unisex—Table Showing the Present Worth of the Remainder Interest in Property Transferred to a Pooled Income Fund Having the Yearly Rate of Return Shown—Applicable for Transfers After November 30, 1983, and Before May 1, 1989

(1)	(2) Yearly Rate of Return									
Age	8.2%	8.4%	8.6%	8.8%	9.0%	9.2%	9.4%	9.6%	9.8%	10.0%
55 . .	.24732	.24116	.23524	.22954	.22406	.21878	.21370	.20881	.20409	.19954
56 . .	.25870	.25244	.24641	.24060	.23501	.22963	.22443	.21943	.21460	.20994
57 . .	.27040	.26404	.25791	.25200	.24630	.24081	.23551	.23040	.22546	.22069
58 . .	.28239	.27594	.26971	.26370	.25791	.25231	.24691	.24170	.23665	.23178
59 . .	.29472	.28817	.28186	.27576	.26987	.26418	.25868	.25336	.24822	.24325
60 . .	.30736	.30074	.29434	.28816	.28218	.27640	.27081	.26540	.26016	.25509
61 . .	.32035	.31365	.30718	.30092	.29486	.28899	.28332	.27782	.27249	.26733
62 . .	.33368	.32692	.32038	.31405	.30791	.30197	.29622	.29064	.28523	.27998
63 . .	.34735	.34054	.33394	.32754	.32134	.31533	.30950	.30385	.29836	.29304
64 . .	.36133	.35448	.34783	.34138	.33612	.32905	.32316	.31743	.31188	.30648
65 . .	.37562	.36873	.36204	.35554	.34924	.34311	.33716	.33138	.32576	.32030
66 . .	.39019	.38327	.37655	.37002	.36367	.35751	.35151	.34568	.34001	.33449
67 . .	.40502	.39809	.39134	.38479	.37841	.37221	.36618	.36030	.35459	.34902
68 . .	.42011	.41317	.40642	.39985	.39345	.38723	.38116	.37526	.36950	.36390
69 . .	.43547	.42854	.42179	.41522	.40882	.40257	.39649	.39056	.38478	.37914
70 . .	.45112	.44421	.43748	.43091	.42451	.41826	.41217	.40623	.40043	.39478
71 . .	.46711	.46023	.45352	.44698	.44059	.43435	.42827	.42233	.41642	.41086
72 . .	.48342	.47659	.46992	.46341	.45705	.45084	.44478	.43885	.43305	.42739
73 . .	.49998	.49321	.48660	.48014	.47382	.46765	.46161	.45571	.44994	.44429
74 . .	.51663	.50994	.50339	.49699	.49073	.48460	.47861	.47274	.46700	.46138
75 . .	.53322	.52661	.52014	.51381	.50762	.50155	.49561	.48979	.48409	.47851
76 . .	.54967	.54315	.53678	.53053	.52440	.51841	.41253	.50677	.50112	.49559
77 . .	.56595	.55954	.55326	.54710	.54106	.53514	.52934	.52364	.51806	.51258
78 . .	.58209	.57579	.56961	.56355	.55761	.55177	.54605	.54043	.53492	.52951
79 . .	.59814	.59196	.58590	.57995	.57410	.56837	.56273	.55720	.55177	.54643
80 . .	.61415	.60810	.60217	.59633	.59060	.58497	.57944	.57401	.56866	.56341
81 . .	.63001	.62410	.61830	.61260	.60699	.60148	.59606	.59073	.58548	.58033
82 . .	.64561	.63985	.63419	.62862	.62314	.61775	.61245	.60723	.60210	.59705
83 . .	.66095	.65535	.64983	.64441	.63907	.63381	.62863	.62354	.61852	.61358
84 . .	.67612	.67068	.66533	.66005	.65486	.64974	.64470	.63973	.63484	.63002
85 . .	.69116	.68589	.68070	.67559	.67055	.66558	.66068	.65586	.65110	.64641
86 . .	.70573	.70063	.69561	.69066	.68578	.68096	.67622	.67154	.66692	.66236
87 . .	.71939	.71466	.70961	.70481	.70009	.69542	.69082	.68628	.68180	.67738
88 . .	.73211	.72735	.72265	.71801	.71343	.70891	.70445	.70005	.69570	.69141
89 . .	.74417	.73956	.73501	.73053	.72609	.72172	.71739	.71312	.70891	.70474
90 . .	.75590	.75146	.74707	.74273	.73845	.73422	.73004	.72591	.72182	.71779
91 . .	.76724	.76296	.75873	.75454	.75041	.74632	.74229	.73829	.73435	.73045
92 . .	.77781	.77368	.76960	.76556	.76158	.75763	.75373	.74988	.74606	.74229
93 . .	.78740	.78342	.77948	.77558	.77173	.76791	.76414	.76042	.75673	.75308
94 . .	.79596	.79210	.78829	.78452	.78079	.77710	.77345	.76983	.76626	.76272
95 . .	.80341	.79967	.79597	.79231	.78869	.78510	.78155	.77304	.77457	.77113
96 . .	.80967	.80603	.80242	.79885	.79532	.79183	.78837	.78494	.78155	.77819
97 . .	.81526	.81170	.80818	.80470	.80125	.79783	.79445	.79110	.78779	.78450
98 . .	.82013	.81665	.81320	.80979	.80641	.80306	.79975	.79647	.79322	.79000
99 . .	.82470	.82129	.81791	.81456	.81125	.80797	.80471	.80149	.79830	.79514
100 . .	.82924	.82590	.82258	.81930	.81605	.81283	.80964	.80648	.80335	.80025
101 . .	.83322	.82993	.82667	.82344	.82024	.81708	.81394	.81082	.80774	.80468
102 . .	.83751	.83428	.83108	.82791	.82477	.82165	.81856	.81550	.81247	.80946
103 . .	.84301	.83986	.83674	.83365	.83058	.82754	.82452	.82153	.81857	.81563
104 . .	.84826	.84518	.84213	.83910	.83610	.83312	.83017	.82723	.82433	.82144
105 . .	.85623	.85327	.85033	.84741	.84452	.84165	.83880	.83597	.83316	.83038
106 . .	.86915	.86641	.86369	.86098	.85829	.85562	.85297	.85034	.84772	.84512
107 . .	.88718	.88476	.88236	.87997	.87759	.87523	.87288	.87054	.86822	.86591
108 . .	.91571	.91385	.91201	.91017	.90834	.90652	.90471	.90291	.90111	.89932
109 . .	.96211	.96125	.96041	.95966	.95872	.95788	.95704	.95620	.95537	.95455

See p. 15 for regulations not amended to reflect law changes

Table G—Continued (8) Table G—Single Life, Unisex—Table Showing the Present Worth of the Remainder Interest in Property Transferred to a Pooled Income Fund Having the Yearly Rate of Return Shown—Applicable for Transfers After November 30, 1983, and Before May 1, 1989

(1)	(2) Yearly Rate of Return									
Age	10.2%	10.4%	10.6%	10.8%	11.0%	11.2%	11.4%	11.6%	11.8%	12.0%
0 . .	.02776	.02743	.02712	.02682	.02655	.02630	.02606	.02583	.02562	.02542
1 . .	.00975	.00941	.00909	.00880	.00852	.00827	.00803	.00780	.00759	.00739
2 . .	.00945	.00909	.00875	.00844	.00816	.00789	.00763	.00740	.00718	.00697
3 . .	.00952	.00914	.00879	.00846	.00815	.00787	.00760	.00736	.00712	.00690
4 . .	.00976	.00936	.00899	.00865	.00832	.00802	.00774	.00748	.00723	.00700
5 . .	.01016	.00974	.00935	.00898	.00864	.00832	.00802	.00774	.00748	.00724
6 . .	.01068	.01023	.00981	.00943	.00907	.00873	.00841	.00812	.00784	.00758
7 . .	.01128	.01080	.01036	.00995	.00957	.00921	.00888	.00856	.00827	.00799
8 . .	.01198	.01148	.01101	.01058	.01017	.00979	.00944	.00910	.00879	.00850
9 . .	.01281	.01228	.01179	.01133	.01090	.01049	.01012	.00976	.00943	.00912
10 . .	.01375	.01319	.01267	.01219	.01173	.01131	.01091	.01053	.01018	.00985
11 . .	.01483	.01425	.01370	.01318	.01270	.01225	.01183	.01143	.01106	.01070
12 . .	.01604	.01542	.01484	.01430	.01379	.01331	.01286	.01244	.01205	.01168
13 . .	.01732	.01666	.01605	.01548	.01494	.01444	.01397	.01352	.01311	.01271
14 . .	.01860	.01792	.01727	.01667	.01610	.01558	.01508	.01461	.01417	.01375
15 . .	.01986	.01913	.01845	.01782	.01723	.01667	.01614	.01565	.01519	.01475
16 . .	.02103	.02027	.01956	.01889	.01827	.01768	.01713	.01661	.01612	.01566
17 . .	.02214	.02134	.02059	.01989	.01923	.01862	.01803	.01749	.01697	.01649
18 . .	.02320	.02236	.02157	.02084	.02014	.01949	.01888	.01831	.01776	.01725
19 . .	.02426	.02337	.02254	.02177	.02104	.02035	.01971	.01910	.01853	.01799
20 . .	.02536	.02442	.02355	.02273	.02197	.02124	.02056	.01992	.01932	.01875
21 . .	.02650	.02552	.02460	.02374	.02293	.02217	.02145	.02078	.02014	.01954
22 . .	.02770	.02667	.02570	.02479	.02394	.02313	.02238	.02166	.02099	.02035
23 . .	.02898	.02789	.02687	.02591	.02501	.02416	.02336	.02261	.02190	.02122
24 . .	.03037	.02923	.02815	.02714	.02619	.02529	.02445	.02365	.02290	.02218
25 . .	.03194	.03073	.02960	.02853	.02752	.02657	.02568	.02484	.02404	.02328
26 . .	.03370	.03243	.03123	.03010	.02904	.02804	.02710	.02620	.02536	.02456
27 . .	.05688	.03434	.03307	.03188	.03076	.02970	.02870	.02776	.02686	.02601
28 . .	.03789	.03647	.03614	.03389	.03271	.03159	.03053	.02953	.02858	.02768
29 . .	.04029	.03880	.03740	.03608	.03483	.03365	.03253	.03147	.03047	.02951
30 . .	.04291	.04135	.03987	.03848	.03716	.03591	.03473	.03361	.03255	.03154
31 . .	.04572	.04407	.04252	.04105	.03966	.03834	.03709	.03591	.03478	.03372
32 . .	.04875	.04702	.04538	.04384	.04237	.04098	.03966	.03841	.03722	.03610
33 . .	.05200	.05019	.04847	.04684	.04530	.04383	.04244	.04112	.03987	.03867
34 . .	.05548	.05358	.05177	.05006	.04843	.04689	.04543	.04403	.04271	.04145
35 . .	.05921	.05722	.05532	.05352	.05181	.05019	.04865	.04718	.04578	.04445
36 . .	.06319	.06110	.05911	.05722	.05543	.05372	.05210	.05055	.04907	.04767
37 . .	.06743	.06524	.06315	.06117	.05929	.05749	.05578	.05416	.05260	.05112
38 . .	.07191	.06962	.06744	.06536	.06338	.06150	.05970	.05799	.05636	.05480
39 . .	.07665	.07425	.07197	.06980	.06773	.06575	.06387	.06207	.06035	.05871
40 . .	.08166	.07916	.07677	.07450	.07233	.07026	.06828	.06639	.06459	.06286
41 . .	.08696	.08434	.08185	.07947	.07721	.07504	.07297	.07099	.06909	.06728
42 . .	.09257	.08985	.08725	.08477	.08239	.08018	.07796	.07589	.07390	.07200
43 . .	09848	.09564	.09293	.09034	.08787	.08550	.08323	.08106	.07898	.07699
44 . .	.10470	.10175	.09893	.09623	.09365	.09118	.08881	.08654	.08437	.08228
45 . .	.11121	.10815	.10522	.10241	.09972	.09714	.09467	.09230	.09003	.08784
46 . .	.11805	.11486	.11182	.10890	.10610	.10341	.10084	.09837	.09599	.09371
47 . .	.12519	.12189	.11873	.11569	.11279	.10999	.10731	.10473	.10226	.09988
48 . .	.13269	.12927	.12600	.12285	.11983	.11693	.11414	.11145	.10888	.10639
49 . .	.14054	.13700	.13361	.13035	.12721	.12721	.12130	.11852	.11583	.11325
50 . .	.14876	.14511	.14160	.13822	.13497	.13185	.12884	.12595	.12316	.12047
51 . .	.15734	.15356	.14994	.14645	.14309	.13985	.13674	.13373	.13084	.12805
52 . .	.16627	.16238	.15864	.15504	.15156	.14822	.14499	.14188	.13888	.13598
53 . .	.17557	.17156	.16770	.16399	.16040	.15695	.15361	.15039	.14729	.14428
54 . .	.18519	.18107	.17710	.17327	.16957	.16601	.16256	.15924	.15602	.15292

See p. 15 for regulations not amended to reflect law changes

Table G—Continued (9) Table G—Single Life, Unisex—Table Showing the Present Worth of the Remainder Interest in Property Transferred to a Pooled Income Fund Having The Yearly Rate Of Return Shown—Applicable for Transfers After November 30, 1983, and Before May 1, 1989

(1)	(2) Yearly Rate of Return									
Age	10.2%	10.4%	10.6%	10.8%	11.0%	11.2%	11.4%	11.6%	11.8%	12.0%
55 . .	.19515	.19092	.18684	.18290	.17909	.17542	.17186	.16843	.16511	.16190
56 . .	.20544	.20110	.19691	.19286	.18894	.18516	.18150	.17796	.17454	.17122
57 . .	.21609	.21164	.20734	.20318	.19916	.19527	.19150	.18786	.18733	.18091
58 . .	.22707	.22252	.21811	.21385	.20972	.20573	.20186	.19811	.19448	.19096
59 . .	.23844	.23378	.22928	.22491	.22068	.21659	.21262	.20877	.20504	.20142
60 . .	.25018	.24543	.24082	.23636	.23203	.22784	.22377	.21982	.21599	.21227
61 . .	.26233	.25749	.25279	.24823	.24381	.23952	.23535	.23131	.22738	.22357
62 . .	.27490	.26996	.26517	.26052	.25601	.25163	.24737	.24324	.23922	.23531
63 . .	.28787	.28286	.27798	.27325	.26865	.26418	.25984	.25561	.25151	.24751
64 . .	.30124	.29615	.29120	.28639	.28171	.27716	.27273	.26842	.26423	.26015
65 . .	.31500	.30983	.30481	.29993	.29517	.29054	.28604	.28165	.27738	.27322
66 . .	.32912	.32390	.31881	.31386	.30904	.30434	.29976	.29530	.29096	.28672
67 . .	.34360	.33832	.33318	.32817	.32328	.31852	.31388	.30935	.30494	.30063
68 . .	.35843	.35311	.34791	.34285	.33791	.33310	.32840	.32381	.31933	.31496
69 . .	.37365	.36828	.36305	.35794	.35296	.34809	.34334	.33870	.33417	.32975
70 . .	.38925	.38386	.37860	.37346	.36844	.36353	.35874	.35405	.34948	.34500
71 . .	.40532	.39991	.39463	.38945	.38442	.37948	.37466	.36994	.36532	.36081
72 . .	.42185	.41644	.41115	.40597	.40091	.39595	.39111	.38636	.38172	.37718
73 . .	.43876	.43336	.42807	.42289	.41782	.41286	.40801	.40325	.39859	.39403
74 . .	.45588	.45050	.44522	.44005	.43499	.43004	.42518	.42042	.41575	.41118
75 . .	.47304	.46769	.46244	.45729	.45225	.44730	.44245	.43770	.43304	.42846
76 . .	.49016	.48485	.47963	.47451	.46949	.46457	.45974	.45500	.45035	.44579
77 . .	.50721	.50193	.49676	.49168	.48670	.48181	.47700	.47229	.46766	.46311
78 . .	.52419	.51898	.51385	.50882	.50388	.49903	.49426	.48958	.48497	.48045
79 . .	.54119	.53604	.54097	.52600	.52111	.51631	.51159	.50694	.50238	.49789
80 . .	.55825	.55318	.54819	.54328	.53846	.53371	.52905	.52446	.51994	.51550
81 . .	.57526	.57027	.56536	.56053	.55578	.55110	.54650	.54197	.53752	.53313
82 . .	.59208	.58718	.58236	.57762	.57295	.56835	.56382	.55937	.55497	.55065
83 . .	.60871	.60392	.59920	.59455	.58997	.58546	.58101	.57663	.57231	.56806
84 . .	.62527	.62959	.62597	.61143	.60695	.60253	.59817	.59388	.58965	.58547
85 . .	.64179	.63723	.63273	.62830	.62393	.61961	.61536	.61116	.60703	.60294
86 . .	.65787	.65344	.64907	.64475	.64050	.63630	.63215	.62806	.62402	.62004
87 . .	.67302	.66871	.66446	.66026	.65612	.65203	.64800	.64401	.64007	.63619
88 . .	.68717	.68298	.67885	.67477	.67074	.66676	.66282	.65894	.65510	.65131
89 . .	.70063	.69656	.69255	.68858	.68466	.68079	.67696	.67318	.66944	.66574
90 . .	.71380	.70986	.70597	.70212	.69831	.69455	.69084	.68716	.68353	.67993
91 . .	.72659	.72278	.71901	.71528	.71160	.70795	.70435	.70078	.69726	.69377
92 . .	.73856	.73488	.73123	.72762	.72405	.72052	.71703	.71357	.71015	.70677
93 . .	.74947	.74590	.74236	.73887	.73541	.73198	.72860	.72524	.72192	.71864
94 . .	.75922	.75575	.75233	.74893	.74557	.74225	.73896	.73570	.73248	.72928
95 . .	.76773	.76436	.76102	.75772	.75445	.75121	.74801	.74483	.74169	.73858
96 . .	.77487	.77158	.76832	.76510	.76190	.75874	.75561	.75250	.74943	.74639
97 . .	.78125	.77803	.77485	.77169	.76856	.76546	.76240	.75936	.75635	.75336
98 . .	.78681	.78365	.78052	.77742	.77435	.77131	.76830	.76531	.76235	.75942
99 . .	.79201	.78891	.78583	.78279	.77977	.77678	.77382	.77088	.76798	.76509
100 . .	.79717	.79412	.79111	.78811	.78515	.78221	.77930	.77642	.77356	.77072
101 . .	.80165	.79865	.79568	.79273	.78981	.78691	.78404	.78119	.77837	.77557
102 . .	.80648	.80353	.80060	.79769	.79481	.79196	.78912	.78632	.78353	.78077
103 . .	.81271	.80982	.80695	.80411	.80129	.79849	.79572	.79297	.79024	.78753
104 . .	.81858	.81574	.81292	.81013	.80736	.80460	.80188	.79917	.79648	.79381
105 . .	.82761	.82487	.82214	.81943	.81675	.81408	.81143	.80881	.80620	.80361
106 . .	.84254	.83998	.83743	.83490	.83238	.82989	.82740	.82494	.82249	.82006
107 . .	.86362	.86133	.85906	.85681	.85456	.85233	.85012	.84791	.84572	.84353
108 . .	.89755	.89577	.89401	.89226	.89051	.88877	.88704	.88532	.88361	.88190
109 . .	.95372	.95290	.95208	.95126	.95045	.94964	.94883	.94803	.94723	.94643

Table G—Continued (10) Table G—Single Life, Unisex—Table Showing the Present Worth of the Remainder Interest in Property Transferred to a Pooled Income Fund Having the Yearly Rate of Return Shown—Applicable for Transfers After November 30, 1983, and Before May 1, 1989

(1)	(2) Yearly Rate of Return									
Age	12.2%	12.4%	12.6%	12.8%	13.0%	13.2%	13.4%	13.6%	13.8%	14.0%
0 . .	.02523	.02505	.02488	.02472	.02456	.02442	.02428	.02414	.02402	.02389
1 . .	.00721	.00703	.00687	.00671	.00657	.00643	.00629	.00617	.00605	.00594
2 . .	.00678	.00659	.00642	.00626	.00610	.00596	.00582	.00569	.00556	.00544
3 . .	.00670	.00650	.00632	.00615	.00599	.00583	.00569	.00555	.00542	.00529
4 . .	.00678	.00658	.00638	.00620	.00603	.00586	.00571	.00556	.00542	.00529
5 . .	.00701	.00679	.00658	.00639	.00620	.00603	.00587	.00571	.00556	.00542
6 . .	.00733	.00710	.00688	.00668	.00648	.00630	.00612	.00595	.00580	.00565
7 . .	.00773	.00748	.00725	.00703	.00682	.00663	.00644	.00626	.00610	.00594
8 . .	.00822	.00796	.00771	.00748	.00726	.00705	.00685	.00666	.00648	.00631
9 . .	.00882	.00854	.00828	.00803	.00780	.00757	.00736	.00716	.00697	.00679
10 . .	.00953	.00924	.00896	.00869	.00844	.00821	.00798	.00777	.00756	.00737
11 . .	.01037	.01006	.00976	.00948	.00922	.00896	.00872	.00850	.00828	.00807
12 . .	.01132	.01099	.01068	.01038	.01010	.00983	.00958	.00934	.00911	.00889
13 . .	.01234	.01199	.01166	.01134	.01104	.01076	.01049	.01024	.00999	.00976
14 . .	.01336	.01299	.01264	.01231	.01199	.01170	.01141	.01114	.01088	.01064
15 . .	.01434	.01395	.01358	.01323	.01289	.01258	.01228	.01200	.01172	.01147
16 . .	.01552	.01481	.01442	.01405	.01371	.01337	.01306	.01275	.01247	.01220
17 . .	.01603	.01559	.01518	.01480	.01443	.01408	.01375	.01343	.01313	.01284
18 . .	.01677	.01631	.01588	.01547	.01508	.01471	.01436	.01403	.01371	.01341
19 . .	.01748	.01700	.01654	.01611	.01570	.01531	.01494	.01459	.01426	.01394
20 . .	.01821	.01770	.01722	.01677	.01633	.01592	.01553	.01516	.01481	.01447
21 . .	.01897	.01843	.01792	.01744	.01698	.01655	.01614	.01574	.01537	.01502
22 . .	.01975	.01918	.01864	.01813	.01765	.01719	.01675	.01634	.01594	.01557
23 . .	.02059	.01998	.01941	.01887	.01836	.01787	.01741	.01697	.01655	.01615
24 . .	.02151	.02087	.02027	.01970	.01915	.01863	.01814	.01768	.01723	.01681
25 . .	.02257	.02189	.02125	.02064	.02006	.01952	.01899	.01850	.01802	.01757
26 . .	.02380	.02308	.02240	.02175	.02114	.02056	.02000	.01947	.01897	.01849
27 . .	.02521	.02445	.02373	.02304	.02239	.02177	.02118	.02061	.02008	.01956
28 . .	.02683	.02602	.02525	.02452	.02382	.02317	.02254	.02194	.02137	.02082
29 . .	.02861	.02775	.02694	.02616	.02543	.02472	.02405	.02342	.02281	.02223
30 . .	.03058	.02967	.02881	.02798	.02720	.02645	.02574	.02506	.02441	.02379
31 . .	.03270	.03174	.03082	.02995	.02911	.02832	.02756	.02684	.02615	.02549
32 . .	.03502	.03400	.03303	.03210	.03122	.03037	.02957	.02880	.02806	.02736
33 . .	.03754	.03646	.03543	.03444	.03350	.03261	.03175	.03093	.03015	.02940
34 . .	.04025	.03910	.03801	.03697	.03597	.03502	.03411	.03324	.03241	.03162
35 . .	.04318	.04197	.04081	.03971	.03865	.03764	.03668	.03576	.03488	.03403
36 . .	.04633	.04505	.04383	.04266	.04154	.04048	.03945	.03847	.03754	.03664
37 . .	.04971	.04836	.04707	.04583	.04465	.04352	.04244	.04140	.04040	.03945
38 . .	.05331	.05188	.05052	.04922	.04797	.04677	.04563	.04453	.04347	.04246
39 . .	.05714	.05564	.05420	.05282	.05150	.05024	.04903	.04787	.04675	.04568
40 . .	.06121	.05963	.05812	.05667	.05528	.05394	.05266	.05143	.05025	.04912
41 . .	.06554	.06388	.06229	.06076	.05929	.05789	.05653	.05524	.05399	.05279
42 . .	.07018	.06843	.06675	.06514	.06360	.06212	.06069	.05932	.05800	.05674
43 . .	.07508	.07324	.07148	.06979	.06817	.06661	.06511	.06366	.06227	.06093
44 . .	.08028	.07835	.07651	.07473	.07303	.07138	.06980	.06828	.06682	.06541
45 . .	.08575	.08373	.08180	.07993	.07814	.07642	.07476	.07316	.07162	.07013
46 . .	.09152	.08941	.08738	.08543	.08355	.08174	.08000	.07832	.07670	.07514
47 . .	.09759	.09539	.09326	.09122	.08926	.08736	.08553	.08377	.08207	.08042
48 . .	.10410	.10171	.09949	.09735	.09530	.09331	.09140	.08955	.08776	.08604
49 . .	.11076	.10836	.10605	.10382	.10167	.09959	.09759	.09565	.09378	.09198
50 . .	.11788	.11538	.11297	.11065	.10840	.10624	.10414	.10212	.10016	.09827
51 . .	.12535	.12276	.12025	.11782	.11548	.11322	.11104	.10892	.10688	.10490
52 . .	.13319	.13049	.12788	.12536	.12292	.12057	.11829	.11608	.11395	.11188
53 . .	.14139	.13858	.13588	.13326	.13072	.12827	.12590	.12360	.12138	.11922
54 . .	.14992	.14701	.14420	.14149	.13885	.13631	.13384	.13145	.12913	.12689

See p. 15 for regulations not amended to reflect law changes

Table G—Continued (11) Table G—Single Life, Unisex—Table Showing the Present Worth of the Remainder Interest in Property Transferred to a Pooled Income Fund Having the Yearly Rate of Return Shown—Applicable for Transfers After November 30, 1983, and Before May 1, 1989

(1)	(2) Yearly Rate of Return									
Age	12.2%	12.4%	12.6%	12.8%	13.0%	13.2%	13.4%	13.6%	13.8%	14.0%
55 . .	.15880	.15579	.15288	.15006	.14733	.14469	.14213	.13964	.13724	.13490
56 . .	.16801	.16491	.16190	.15898	.15615	.15341	.15075	.14817	.14567	.14324
57 . .	.17760	.17439	.17128	.16827	.16534	.16250	.15975	.15708	.15448	.15196
58 . .	.18755	.18424	.18103	.17792	.17489	.17196	.16911	.16634	.16365	.16104
59 . .	.19790	.19450	.19119	.18798	.18486	.18183	.17888	.17602	.17324	.17053
60 . .	.20866	.20516	.20175	.19844	.19523	.19210	.18906	.18611	.18323	.18043
61 . .	.21986	.21626	.21276	.20936	.20695	.20283	.19970	.19665	.19368	.19079
62 . .	.23151	.22782	.22423	.22073	.21733	.21402	.21079	.20766	.20460	.20162
63 . .	.24362	.23984	.23616	.23257	.22908	.22568	.22237	.21914	.21600	.21293
64 . .	.25617	.25231	.24854	.24487	.24129	.23780	.23440	.23109	.22786	.22471
65 . .	.26917	.26522	.26137	.25761	.25395	.25038	.24690	.24350	.24019	.23695
66 . .	.28259	.27857	.27464	.27081	.26707	.26342	.25986	.25638	.25298	.24967
67 . .	.29643	.29233	.28833	.28443	.28061	.27689	.27325	.26970	.26623	.26284
68 . .	.31070	.30653	.30246	.29849	.29461	.29081	.28711	.28348	.27994	.27647
69 . .	.32542	.32120	.31707	.31303	.30908	.30523	.30145	.29776	.29415	.29062
70 . .	.34063	.33635	.33217	.32807	.32407	.32015	.31632	.31257	.30890	.30530
71 . .	.35639	.35207	.34784	.34370	.33965	.33568	.33179	.32799	.32426	.32061
72 . .	.37273	.36837	.36410	.35993	.35583	.35182	.34789	.34404	.34027	.33657
73 . .	.38955	.38517	.38088	.37667	.37255	.36815	.36455	.36066	.35685	.35311
74 . .	.40670	.40230	.39799	.39377	.38962	.38555	.38156	.37765	.37381	.37004
75 . .	.42398	.41958	.41526	.41102	.40686	.40278	.39877	.39484	.39098	.38719
76 . .	.44131	.43691	.43259	.42835	.42419	.42010	.41608	.41213	.40826	.40445
77 . .	.45864	.45425	.44994	.44571	.44155	.43746	.43344	.42949	.42561	.42179
78 . .	.47601	.47164	.46734	.46312	.45897	.45489	.45088	.44693	.44305	.43923
79 . .	.49348	.48914	.48487	.48067	.47654	.47248	.46848	.46454	.46067	.45686
80 . .	.51112	.50682	.50259	.49842	.49432	.49028	.48631	.48240	.47854	.47475
81 . .	.52881	.52455	.52036	.51624	.51218	.50818	.50423	.50035	.49653	.49276
82 . .	.54639	.54219	.53805	.53398	.52996	.52600	.52210	.51826	.51447	.51074
83 . .	.56386	.55973	.55566	.55164	.54768	.54377	.53992	.53613	.53238	.52869
84 . .	.58136	.57730	.57329	.56934	.56545	.56160	.55781	.55407	.55038	.54674
85 . .	.59891	.59494	.59102	.58715	.58333	.57956	.57584	.57216	.56854	.56496
86 . .	.61610	.61222	.60839	.60460	.60086	.59717	.59353	.58993	.58638	.58287
87 . .	.63235	.62856	.62481	.62111	.61746	.61385	.61028	.61676	.60328	.59984
88 . .	.64757	.64386	.64021	.63659	.63302	.62950	.62601	.62256	.61915	.61578
89 . .	.66209	.65848	.65491	.65149	.64790	.64445	.64104	.63767	.63434	.63105
90 . .	.67638	.67387	.66939	.66596	.66256	.65920	.65588	.65259	.64934	.64612
91 . .	.69032	.68691	.68353	.68019	.67689	.67362	.67039	.66719	.66402	.66089
92 . .	.70342	.70011	.69683	.69359	.69038	.68720	.68405	.68094	.67786	.67481
93 . .	.71539	.71217	.70899	.70584	.70271	.69962	.69657	.69354	.69054	.68757
94 . .	.72612	.72299	.71989	.71683	.71379	.71078	.70780	.70485	.70193	.69903
95 . .	.73550	.73245	.73943	.72643	.72347	.72053	.71763	.71475	.71189	.70906
96 . .	.74337	.74039	.73743	.73450	.73160	.73872	.72587	.72305	.72026	.71748
97 . .	.75041	.74748	.74458	.74171	.73886	.73604	.73325	.73048	.72773	.72501
98 . .	.75652	.75364	.75079	.74797	.74517	.74329	.73964	.73692	.73422	.73154
99 . .	.76224	.75941	.75660	.75882	.75106	.74833	.74562	.74294	.74028	.73764
100 . .	.76791	.76521	.76237	.75963	.75692	.75423	.75156	.74892	.74630	.74370
101 . .	.77280	.77005	.75732	.76462	.76194	.75928	.75664	.75403	.75144	.74887
102 . .	.77804	.77532	.77263	.76996	.76732	.76469	.76209	.75950	.75694	.75440
103 . .	.78485	.78218	.77954	.77692	.77432	.77174	.76918	.76664	.76413	.76163
104 . .	.79117	.78854	.78594	.78335	.78078	.77824	.77571	.77320	.77071	.76824
105 . .	.80103	.79848	.79595	.79343	.79093	.78845	.78599	.78354	.78111	.77870
106 . .	.81764	.81524	.81285	.81048	.80813	.80579	.80346	.80115	.79885	.79657
107 . .	.84137	.83921	.83706	.83493	.83281	.83070	.82860	.82652	.82444	.82238
108 . .	.88020	.87851	.87682	.87515	.87348	.87182	.87016	.86852	.86688	.86525
109 . .	.94563	.94484	.94405	.94326	.94248	.94170	.94092	.94014	.93937	.93860

(e) *Present value of the remainder interest in the case of transfers to pooled income funds for which the valuation date is after April 30, 1989, and before May 1, 1999.*—

(1) *In general.*—In the case of transfers to pooled income funds for which the valuation date is after April 30, 1989, and before May 1, 1999, the present value of a remainder interest is determined under this section. See, however, § 1.7520-3(b) (relating to exceptions to the use of prescribed tables under certain circumstances). The present value of a remainder interest that is dependent on the termination of the life of one individual is computed by the use of Table S in paragraph (e)(5) of this section. For purposes of the computations under this section, the age of an individual is the age at the individual's nearest birthday. If the valuation date of a transfer to a pooled income fund is after April 30, 1989, and before June 10, 1994, a transferor can rely on Notice 89-24, 1989-1 C.B. 660, or Notice 89-60, 1989-1 C.B. 700, in valuing the transferred interest. (See § 601.601(d)(2)(ii)(*b*) of this chapter.)

(2) *Present value of a remainder interest.*—The present value of a remainder interest in property transferred to a pooled income fund is computed on the basis of—

(i) Life contingencies determined from the values of *lx* that are set forth in Table 80CNSMT in § 20.2031-7A(e)(4) of this chapter (Estate Tax Regulations); and

(ii) Discount at a rate of interest, compounded annually, equal to the highest yearly rate of return of the pooled income fund for the 3 taxable years immediately preceding its taxable year in which the transfer of property to the fund is made. The provisions of § 1.642(c)-6(c) apply for determining the yearly rate of return. However, where the taxable year is less than 12 months, the provisions of § 1.642(c)-6(e)(3)(ii) apply for the determining the yearly rate of return.

(3) *Pooled income funds in existence less than 3 taxable years.*—The provisions of § 1.642(c)-6(e)(4) apply for determining the highest yearly rate of return when the pooled income fund has been in existence less than three taxable years.

(4) *Computation of value of remainder interest.*—The factor that is used in determining the present value of a remainder interest that is dependent on the termination of the life of one individual is the factor from Table S in paragraph (e)(5) of this section under the appropriate yearly rate of return opposite the number that corresponds to the age of the individual upon whose life the value of the remainder interest is based. Table S in paragraph (e)(5) of this section includes factors for yearly rates of return from 4.2 to 14 percent. Many actuarial factors not contained in Table S in paragraph (e)(5) of this section are contained in Table S in Internal Revenue Service Publication 1457, "Actuarial Values, Alpha Volume," (8-89). Publication 1457 is no longer available for purchase from the Superintendent of Documents, United States Government Printing Office, Washington, DC 20402. However, pertinent factors in this publication may be obtained by a written request to: CC:DOM:CORP:R (IRS Publication 1457), room 5226,Internal Revenue Service, POB 7604, Ben Franklin Station, Washington, DC 20044. For other situations, see § 1.642(c)-6(b). If the yearly rate of return is a percentage that is between the yearly rates of return for which factors are provided, a linear interpolation must be made. The present value of the remainder interest is determined by multiplying the fair market value of the property on the valuation date by the appropriate remainder factor. For an example of a computation of the present value of a remainder interest requiring a linear interpolation adjustment, see § 1.642(c)-6(e)(5).

(5) *Actuarial tables.*—In the case of transfers for which the valuation date is after April 30, 1989, and before May 1, 1999, the present value of a remainder interest dependent on the termination of one life in the case of a transfer to a pooled income fund is determined by use of the following tables:

See p. 15 for regulations not amended to reflect law changes

TABLE S
BASED ON LIFE TABLE 80CNSMT
SINGLE LIFE REMAINDER FACTORS
APPLICABLE AFTER APRIL 30, 1989,
AND BEFORE MAY 1, 1999
INTEREST RATE

AGE	*4.2%*	*4.4%*	*4.6%*	*4.8%*	*5.0%*	*5.2%*	*5.4%*	*5.6%*	*5.8%*	*6.0%*
0	.07389	.06749	.06188	.05695	.05261	.04879	.04541	.04243	.03978	.03744
1	.06494	.05832	.05250	.04738	.04287	.03889	.03537	.03226	.02950	.02705
2	.06678	.05999	.05401	.04874	.04410	.03999	.03636	.03314	.03028	.02773
3	.06897	.06200	.05587	.05045	.04567	.04143	.03768	.03435	.03139	.02875
4	.07139	.06425	.05796	.05239	.04746	.04310	.03922	.03578	.03271	.02998
5	.07401	.06669	.06023	.05451	.04944	.04494	.04094	.03738	.03421	.03137
6	.07677	.06928	.06265	.05677	.05156	.04692	.04279	.03911	.03583	.03289
7	.07968	.07201	.06521	.05918	.05381	.04903	.04477	.04097	.03757	.03453
8	.08274	.07489	.06792	.06172	.05621	.05129	.04689	.04297	.03945	.03630
9	.08597	.07794	.07079	.06443	.05876	.05370	.04917	.04511	.04148	.03821
10	.08936	.08115	.07383	.06730	.06147	.05626	.05159	.04741	.04365	.04027
11	.09293	.08453	.07704	.07035	.06436	.05900	.05419	.04988	.04599	.04250
12	.09666	.08807	.08040	.07354	.06739	.06188	.05693	.05248	.04847	.04486
13	.10049	.09172	.08387	.07684	.07053	.06487	.05977	.05518	.05104	.04731
14	.10437	.09541	.08738	.08017	.07370	.06788	.06263	.05791	.05364	.04978
15	.10827	.09912	.09090	.08352	.07688	.07090	.06551	.06064	.05623	.05225
16	.11220	.10285	.09445	.08689	.08008	.07394	.06839	.06337	.05883	.05472
17	.11615	.10661	.09802	.09028	.08330	.07699	.07129	.06612	.06144	.05719
18	.12017	.11043	.10165	.09373	.08656	.08009	.07422	.06890	.06408	.05969
19	.12428	.11434	.10537	.09726	.08992	.08327	.07724	.07177	.06679	.06226
20	.12850	.11836	.10919	.10089	.09337	.08654	.08035	.07471	.06959	.06492
21	.13282	.12248	.11311	.10462	.09692	.08991	.08355	.07775	.07247	.06765
22	.13728	.12673	.11717	.10848	.10059	.09341	.08686	.08090	.07546	.07049
23	.14188	.13113	.12136	.11248	.10440	.09703	.09032	.08418	.07858	.07345
24	.14667	.13572	.12575	.11667	.10839	.10084	.09395	.08764	.08187	.07659
25	.15167	.14051	.13034	.12106	.11259	.10486	.09778	.09130	.08536	.07991
26	.15690	.14554	.13517	.12569	.11703	.10910	.10184	.09518	.08907	.08346
27	.16237	.15081	.14024	.13056	.12171	.11359	.10614	.09930	.09302	.08724
28	.16808	.15632	.14555	.13567	.12662	.11831	.11068	.10366	.09720	.09125
29	.17404	.16208	.15110	.14104	.13179	.12329	.11547	.10827	.10163	.09551
30	.18025	.16808	.15692	.14665	.13721	.12852	.12051	.11313	.10631	.10002
31	.18672	.17436	.16300	.15255	.14291	.13403	.12584	.11827	.11127	.10480
32	.19344	.18090	.16935	.15870	.14888	.13980	.13142	.12367	.11650	.10985
33	.20044	.18772	.17598	.16514	.15513	.14587	.13730	.12936	.12201	.11519
34	.20770	.19480	.18287	.17185	.16165	.15221	.14345	.13533	.12780	.12080
35	.21522	.20215	.19005	.17884	.16846	.15883	.14989	.14159	.13388	.12670
36	.22299	.20974	.19747	.18609	.17552	.16571	.15660	.14812	.14022	.13287
37	.23101	.21760	.20516	.19360	.18286	.17288	.16358	.15492	.14685	.13933
38	.23928	.22572	.21311	.20139	.19048	.18032	.17085	.16201	.15377	.14607
39	.24780	.23409	.22133	.20945	.19837	.18804	.17840	.16939	.16097	.15310
40	.25658	.24273	.22982	.21778	.20654	.19605	.18624	.17706	.16847	.16043
41	.26560	.25163	.23858	.22639	.21499	.20434	.19436	.18502	.17627	.16806
42	.27486	.26076	.24758	.23525	.22370	.21289	.20276	.19326	.18434	.17597
43	.28435	.27013	.25683	.24436	.23268	.22172	.21143	.20177	.19270	.18416
44	.29407	.27975	.26633	.25373	.24191	.23081	.22038	.21057	.20134	.19265
45	.30402	.28961	.27608	.26337	.25142	.24019	.22962	.21966	.21028	.20144
46	.31420	.29970	.28608	.27326	.26120	.24983	.23913	.22904	.21951	.21053
47	.32460	.31004	.29632	.28341	.27123	.25975	.24892	.23870	.22904	.21991
48	.33521	.32058	.30679	.29379	.28151	.26992	.25897	.24862	.23883	.22957
49	.34599	.33132	.31746	.30438	.29201	.28032	.26926	.25879	.24888	.23949
50	.35695	.34224	.32833	.31518	.30273	.29094	.27978	.26921	.25918	.24966
51	.36809	.35335	.33940	.32619	.31367	.30180	.29055	.27987	.26973	.26010
52	.37944	.36468	.35070	.33744	.32486	.31292	.30158	.29081	.28057	.27083
53	.39098	.37622	.36222	.34892	.33629	.32429	.31288	.30203	.29170	.28186
54	.40269	.38794	.37393	.36062	.34795	.33590	.32442	.31349	.30308	.29316
55	.41457	.39985	.38585	.37252	.35983	.34774	.33621	.32522	.31474	.30473
56	.42662	.41194	.39796	.38464	.37193	.35981	.34824	.33720	.32666	.31658
57	.43884	.42422	.41028	.39697	.38426	.37213	.36053	.34945	.33885	.32872
58	.45123	.43668	.42279	.40951	.39682	.38468	.37307	.36196	.35132	.34114
59	.46377	.44931	.43547	.42224	.40958	.39745	.38584	.37471	.36405	.35383
60	.47643	.46206	.44830	.43513	.42250	.41040	.39880	.38767	.37699	.36674
61	.48916	.47491	.46124	.44814	.43556	.42350	.41192	.40080	.39012	.37985
62	.50196	.48783	.47427	.46124	.44874	.43672	.42518	.41408	.40340	.39314
63	.51480	.50081	.48736	.47444	.46201	.45006	.43856	.42749	.41684	.40658
64	.52770	.51386	.50054	.48773	.47540	.46352	.45208	.44105	.43043	.42019
65	.54069	.52701	.51384	.50115	.48892	.47713	.46577	.45480	.44422	.43401
66	.55378	.54029	.52727	.51472	.50262	.49093	.47965	.46876	.45824	.44808
67	.56697	.55368	.54084	.52845	.51648	.50491	.49373	.48293	.47248	.46238
68	.58026	.56717	.55453	.54231	.53049	.51905	.50800	.49729	.48694	.47691
69	.59358	.58072	.56828	.55624	.54459	.53330	.52238	.51179	.50154	.49160
70	.60689	.59427	.58205	.57021	.55874	.54762	.53683	.52638	.51624	.50641
71	.62014	.60778	.59578	.58415	.57287	.56193	.55131	.54100	.53099	.52126

TABLE S
BASED ON LIFE TABLE 80CNSMT
SINGLE LIFE REMAINDER FACTORS
APPLICABLE AFTER APRIL 30, 1989,
AND BEFORE MAY 1, 1999
INTEREST RATE

AGE	4.2%	4.4%	4.6%	4.8%	5.0%	5.2%	5.4%	5.6%	5.8%	6.0%
72	.63334	.62123	.60948	.59808	.58700	.57624	.56579	.55563	.54577	.53617
73	.64648	.63465	.62315	.61198	.60112	.59056	.58029	.57030	.56059	.55113
74	.65961	.64806	.63682	.62590	.61527	.60492	.59485	.58504	.57550	.56620
75	.67274	.66149	.65054	.63987	.62948	.61936	.60950	.59990	.59053	.58140
76	.68589	.67495	.66429	.65390	.64377	.63390	.62427	.61487	.60570	.59676
77	.69903	.68841	.67806	.66796	.65811	.64849	.63910	.62993	.62097	.61223
78	.71209	.70182	.69179	.68199	.67242	.66307	.65393	.64501	.63628	.62775
79	.72500	.71507	.70537	.69588	.68660	.67754	.66867	.65999	.65151	.64321
80	.73768	.72809	.71872	.70955	.70058	.69180	.68320	.67479	.66655	.65849
81	.75001	.74077	.73173	.72288	.71422	.70573	.69741	.68926	.68128	.67345
82	.76195	.75306	.74435	.73582	.72746	.71926	.71123	.70335	.69562	.68804
83	.77346	.76491	.75654	.74832	.74026	.73236	.72460	.71699	.70952	.70219
84	.78456	.77636	.76831	.76041	.75265	.74503	.73756	.73021	.72300	.71592
85	.79530	.78743	.77971	.77212	.76466	.75733	.75014	.74306	.73611	.72928
86	.80560	.79806	.79065	.78337	.77621	.76917	.76225	.75544	.74875	.74216
87	.81535	.80813	.80103	.79404	.78717	.78041	.77375	.76720	.76076	.75442
88	.82462	.81771	.81090	.80420	.79760	.79111	.78472	.77842	.77223	.76612
89	.83356	.82694	.82043	.81401	.80769	.80147	.79533	.78929	.78334	.77747
90	.84225	.83593	.82971	.82357	.81753	.81157	.80570	.79991	.79420	.78857
91	.85058	.84455	.83861	.83276	.82698	.82129	.81567	.81013	.80466	.79927
92	.85838	.85263	.84696	.84137	.83585	.83040	.82503	.81973	.81449	.80933
93	.86557	.86009	.85467	.84932	.84405	.83884	.83370	.82862	.82360	.81865
94	.87212	.86687	.86169	.85657	.85152	.84653	.84160	.83673	.83192	.82717
95	.87801	.87298	.86801	.86310	.85825	.85345	.84872	.84404	.83941	.83484
96	.88322	.87838	.87360	.86888	.86420	.85959	.85502	.85051	.84605	.84165
97	.88795	.88328	.87867	.87411	.86961	.86515	.86074	.85639	.85208	.84782
98	.89220	.88769	.88323	.87883	.87447	.87016	.86589	.86167	.85750	.85337
99	.89612	.89176	.88745	.88318	.87895	.87478	.87064	.86656	.86251	.85850
100	.89977	.89555	.89136	.88722	.88313	.87908	.87506	.87109	.86716	.86327
101	.90326	.89917	.89511	.89110	.88712	.88318	.87929	.87543	.87161	.86783
102	.90690	.90294	.89901	.89513	.89128	.88746	.88369	.87995	.87624	.87257
103	.91076	.90694	.90315	.89940	.89569	.89200	.88835	.88474	.88116	.87760
104	.91504	.91138	.90775	.90415	.90058	.89704	.89354	.89006	.88661	.88319
105	.92027	.91681	.91337	.90996	.90658	.90322	.89989	.89659	.89331	.89006
106	.92763	.92445	.92130	.91816	.91506	.91197	.90890	.90586	.90284	.89983
107	.93799	.93523	.93249	.92977	.92707	.92438	.92170	.91905	.91641	.91378
108	.95429	.95223	.95018	.94814	.94611	.94409	.94208	.94008	.93809	.93611
109	.97985	.97893	.97801	.97710	.97619	.97529	.97438	.97348	.97259	.97170

See p. 15 for regulations not amended to reflect law changes

TABLE S
BASED ON LIFE TABLE 80CNSMT
SINGLE LIFE REMAINDER FACTORS
APPLICABLE AFTER APRIL 30, 1989,
AND BEFORE MAY 1, 1999
INTEREST RATE

AGE	6.2%	6.4%	6.6%	6.8%	7.0%	7.2%	7.4%	7.6%	7.8%	8.0%
0	.03535	.03349	.03183	.03035	.02902	.02783	.02676	.02579	.02492	.02413
1	.02486	.02292	.02119	.01963	.01824	.01699	.01587	.01486	.01395	.01312
2	.02547	.02345	.02164	.02002	.01857	.01727	.01609	.01504	.01408	.01321
3	.02640	.02429	.02241	.02073	.01921	.01785	.01662	.01552	.01451	.01361
4	.02753	.02535	.02339	.02163	.02005	.01863	.01735	.01619	.01514	.01418
5	.02883	.02656	.02453	.02269	.02105	.01956	.01822	.01700	.01590	.01490
6	.03026	.02790	.02578	.02387	.02215	.02060	.01919	.01792	.01677	.01572
7	.03180	.02935	.02714	.02515	.02336	.02174	.02027	.01894	.01773	.01664
8	.03347	.03092	.02863	.02656	.02469	.02300	.02146	.02007	.01881	.01766
9	.03528	.03263	.03025	.02810	.02615	.02438	.02278	.02133	.02000	.01880
10	.03723	.03449	.03201	.02977	.02774	.02590	.02423	.02271	.02133	.02006
11	.03935	.03650	.03393	.03160	.02949	.02757	.02583	.02424	.02279	.02147
12	.04160	.03865	.03598	.03356	.03136	.02936	.02755	.02589	.02438	.02299
13	.04394	.04088	.03811	.03560	.03331	.03123	.02934	.02761	.02603	.02458
14	.04629	.04312	.04025	.03764	.03527	.03311	.03113	.02933	.02768	.02617
15	.04864	.04536	.04238	.03968	.03721	.03496	.03290	.03103	.02930	.02773
16	.05099	.04759	.04451	.04170	.03913	.03679	.03466	.03270	.03090	.02926
17	.05333	.04982	.04662	.04370	.04104	.03861	.03638	.03434	.03247	.03075
18	.05570	.05207	.04875	.04573	.04296	.04044	.03812	.03599	.03404	.03225
19	.05814	.05438	.05095	.04781	.04494	.04231	.03990	.03769	.03565	.03378
20	.06065	.05677	.05321	.04996	.04698	.04424	.04173	.03943	.03731	.03535
21	.06325	.05922	.05554	.05217	.04907	.04623	.04362	.04122	.03901	.03697
22	.06594	.06178	.05797	.05447	.05126	.04831	.04559	.04309	.04078	.03865
23	.06876	.06446	.06051	.05688	.05355	.05048	.04766	.04505	.04265	.04042
24	.07174	.06729	.06321	.05945	.05599	.05281	.04987	.04715	.04465	.04233
25	.07491	.07031	.06609	.06219	.05861	.05530	.05224	.04941	.04680	.04438
26	.07830	.07355	.06918	.06515	.06142	.05799	.05481	.05187	.04915	.04662
27	.08192	.07702	.07250	.06832	.06446	.06090	.05759	.05454	.05170	.04906
28	.08577	.08071	.07603	.07171	.06772	.06402	.06059	.05740	.05445	.05170
29	.08986	.08464	.07981	.07534	.07120	.06736	.06380	.06049	.05742	.05456
30	.09420	.08882	.08383	.07921	.07492	.07095	.06725	.06381	.06061	.05763
31	.09881	.09327	.08812	.08335	.07891	.07479	.07095	.06738	.06405	.06095
32	.10369	.09797	.09267	.08774	.08315	.07888	.07491	.07120	.06774	.06451
33	.10885	.10297	.09750	.09241	.08767	.08325	.07913	.07529	.07170	.06834
34	.11430	.10824	.10261	.09736	.09246	.08790	.08363	.07964	.07592	.07243
35	.12002	.11380	.10800	.10259	.09754	.09282	.08841	.08428	.08041	.07679
36	.12602	.11963	.11366	.10809	.10288	.09800	.09344	.08917	.08516	.08140
37	.13230	.12574	.11961	.11387	.10850	.10347	.09876	.09433	.09018	.08628
38	.13887	.13214	.12584	.11994	.11441	.10922	.10436	.09978	.09549	.09145
39	.14573	.13883	.13237	.12630	.12061	.11527	.11025	.10553	.10109	.09690
40	.15290	.14583	.13920	.13297	.12712	.12162	.11644	.11157	.10698	.10266
41	.16036	.15312	.14633	.13994	.13393	.12827	.12294	.11792	.11318	.10871
42	.16810	.16071	.15375	.14720	.14103	.13522	.12973	.12456	.11967	.11505
43	.17614	.16858	.16146	.15475	.14842	.14245	.13682	.13149	.12645	.12169
44	.18447	.17675	.16948	.16261	.15613	.15000	.14421	.13873	.13355	.12864
45	.19310	.18524	.17780	.17078	.16414	.15787	.15192	.14630	.14096	.13591
46	.20204	.19402	.18644	.17926	.17247	.16604	.15995	.15418	.14870	.14350
47	.21128	.20311	.19538	.18806	.18112	.17454	.16830	.16238	.15676	.15141
48	.22080	.21249	.20462	.19716	.19007	.18335	.17696	.17090	.16513	.15964
49	.23059	.22214	.21413	.20653	.19930	.19244	.18591	.17970	.17379	.16816
50	.24063	.23206	.22391	.21617	.20881	.20180	.19514	.18879	.18274	.17697
51	.25095	.24225	.23398	.22610	.21861	.21147	.20466	.19818	.19199	.18609
52	.26157	.25275	.24436	.23636	.22874	.22147	.21453	.20791	.20159	.19556
53	.27249	.26357	.25505	.24694	.23919	.23180	.22474	.21799	.21154	.20537
54	.28369	.27466	.26604	.25782	.24995	.24244	.23526	.22839	.22181	.21552
55	.29518	.28605	.27734	.26900	.26103	.25341	.24611	.23912	.23243	.22601
56	.30695	.29774	.28893	.28050	.27242	.26469	.25728	.25019	.24338	.23685
57	.31902	.30973	.30084	.29232	.28415	.27632	.26881	.26161	.25469	.24805
58	.33138	.32203	.31306	.30446	.29621	.28829	.28069	.27339	.26637	.25962
59	.34402	.33461	.32558	.31691	.30859	.30059	.29290	.28550	.27839	.27155
60	.35690	.34745	.33836	.32963	.32124	.31317	.30540	.29792	.29073	.28379
61	.36999	.36050	.35137	.34259	.33414	.32601	.31817	.31062	.30334	.29633
62	.38325	.37374	.36458	.35576	.34726	.33907	.33117	.32356	.31621	.30912
63	.39669	.38717	.37799	.36913	.36060	.35236	.34441	.33674	.32933	.32217
64	.41031	.40078	.39159	.38272	.37415	.36588	.35789	.35016	.34270	.33548
65	.42416	.41464	.40545	.39656	.38798	.37968	.37166	.36390	.35639	.34912
66	.43825	.42876	.41958	.41070	.40211	.39380	.38576	.37797	.37043	.36312
67	.45260	.44315	.43399	.42513	.41655	.40824	.40019	.39238	.38482	.37749
68	.46720	.45779	.44868	.43985	.43129	.42299	.41494	.40713	.39956	.39221
69	.48197	.47263	.46357	.45478	.44625	.43798	.42995	.42215	.41458	.40722
70	.49686	.48760	.47861	.46988	.46140	.45316	.44516	.43738	.42983	.42248
71	.51182	.50265	.49374	.48508	.47666	.46847	.46051	.45276	.44523	.43790

See p. 15 for regulations not amended to reflect law changes

TABLE S
BASED ON LIFE TABLE 80CNSMT
SINGLE LIFE REMAINDER FACTORS
APPLICABLE AFTER APRIL 30, 1989,
AND BEFORE MAY 1, 1999
INTEREST RATE

AGE	6.2%	6.4%	6.6%	6.8%	7.0%	7.2%	7.4%	7.6%	7.8%	8.0%
72	.52685	.51778	.50896	.50038	.49203	.48390	.47599	.46829	.46079	.45349
73	.54194	.53298	.52426	.51578	.50751	.49946	.49161	.48397	.47652	.46926
74	.55714	.54832	.53972	.53134	.52317	.51520	.50744	.49986	.49247	.48527
75	.57250	.56382	.55536	.54710	.53904	.53118	.52351	.51601	.50870	.50156
76	.58803	.57951	.57120	.56308	.55515	.54740	.53984	.53245	.52522	.51817
77	.60369	.59535	.58720	.57923	.57144	.56383	.55639	.54912	54200	.53504
78	.61942	.61126	.60329	.59549	.58787	.58040	.57310	.56596	.55896	.55212
79	.63508	.62713	.61935	.61174	.60428	.59698	.58983	.58283	.57597	.56925
80	.65059	.64285	.63527	.62785	.62058	.61345	.60646	.59961	.59290	.58632
81	.66579	.65827	.65090	.64368	.63659	.62965	.62283	.61615	.60959	.60316
82	.68061	.67332	.66616	.65914	.65226	.64550	.63886	.63235	.62595	.61968
83	.69499	.68793	.68099	.67418	.66749	.66092	.65447	.64813	.64191	.63579
84	.70896	.70213	.69541	.68881	.68233	.67595	.66969	.66353	.65748	.65153
85	.72256	.71596	.70947	.70308	.69681	.69063	.68456	.67859	.67271	.66693
86	.73569	.72931	.72305	.71688	.71081	.70484	.69896	.69318	.68748	.68188
87	.74818	.74204	.73599	.73003	.72417	.71839	.71271	.70711	.70159	.69616
88	.76011	.75419	.74836	.74261	.73695	.73137	.72588	.72046	.71512	.70986
89	.77169	.76599	.76037	.75484	.74938	.74400	.73870	.73347	.72831	.72323
90	.78302	.77755	.77215	.76683	.76158	.75640	.75129	.74625	.74128	.73638
91	.79395	.78870	.78352	.77842	.77337	.76840	.76349	.75864	.75385	.74913
92	.80423	.79920	.79423	.78933	.78449	.77971	.77499	.77033	.76572	.76118
93	.81377	.80894	.80417	.79946	.79481	.79022	.78568	.78120	.77677	.77239
94	.82247	.81784	.81325	.80873	.80425	.79983	.79547	.79115	.78688	.78266
95	.83033	.82586	.82145	.81709	.81278	.80852	.80431	.80014	.79602	.79195
96	.83729	.83298	.82872	.82451	.82034	.81622	.81215	.80812	.80414	.80019
97	.84361	.83944	.83532	.83124	.82721	.82322	.81927	.81537	.81151	.80769
98	.84929	.84525	.84126	.83730	.83339	.82952	.82569	.82190	.81815	.81443
99	.85454	.85062	.84674	.84290	.83910	.83534	.83161	.82792	.82427	.82066
100	.85942	.85561	.85184	.84810	.84440	.84074	.83711	.83352	.82997	.82644
101	.86408	.86037	.85670	.85306	.84946	.84589	.84236	.83886	.83539	.83196
102	.86894	.86534	.86177	.85823	.85473	.85126	.84782	.84442	.84104	.83770
103	.87408	.87060	.86714	.86371	.86032	.85695	.85362	.85031	.84703	.84378
104	.87980	.87644	.87311	.86980	.86653	.86328	.86005	.85686	.85369	.85054
105	.88684	.88363	.88046	.87731	.87418	.87108	.86800	.86494	.86191	.85890
106	.89685	.89389	.89095	.88804	.88514	.88226	.87940	.87656	.87374	.87094
107	.91117	.90858	.90600	.90344	.90089	.89836	.89584	.89334	.89085	.88838
108	.93414	.93217	.93022	.92828	.92634	.92442	.92250	.92060	.91870	.91681
109	.97081	.96992	.96904	.96816	.96729	.96642	.96555	.96468	.96382	.96296

See p. 15 for regulations not amended to reflect law changes

TABLE S
BASED ON LIFE TABLE 80CNSMT
SINGLE LIFE REMAINDER FACTORS
APPLICABLE AFTER APRIL 30, 1989,
AND BEFORE MAY 1, 1999
INTEREST RATE

AGE	8.2%	8.4%	8.6%	8.8%	9.0%	9.2%	9.4%	9.6%	9.8%	.10.0%
0	.02341	.02276	.02217	.02163	.02114	.02069	.02027	.01989	.01954	.01922
1	.01237	.01170	.01108	.01052	.01000	.00953	.00910	.00871	.00834	.00801
2	.01243	.01172	.01107	.01048	.00994	.00944	.00899	.00857	.00819	.00784
3	.01278	.01203	.01135	.01073	.01016	.00964	.00916	.00872	.00832	.00795
4	.01332	.01253	.01182	.01116	.01056	.01001	.00951	.00904	.00862	.00822
5	.01400	.01317	.01241	.01172	.01109	.01051	.00998	.00949	.00904	.00862
6	.01477	.01390	.01310	.01238	.01171	.01110	.01054	.01002	.00954	.00910
7	.01563	.01472	.01389	.01312	.01242	.01178	.01118	.01064	.01013	.00966
8	.01660	.01564	.01477	.01396	.01322	.01254	.01192	.01134	.01081	.01031
9	.01770	.01669	.01577	.01492	.01414	.01342	.01276	.01216	.01159	.01107
10	.01891	.01785	.01688	.01599	.01517	.01442	.01372	.01308	.01249	.01194
11	.02026	.01915	.01814	.01720	.01634	.01555	.01481	.01414	.01351	.01293
12	.02173	.02056	.01950	.01852	.01761	.01678	.01601	.01529	.01463	.01402
13	.02326	.02204	.02092	.01989	.01895	.01807	.01726	.01651	.01582	.01517
14	.02478	.02351	.02234	.02126	.02027	.01935	.01850	.01771	.01698	.01630
15	.02628	.02495	.02372	.02259	.02155	.02058	.01969	.01886	.01810	.01738
16	.02774	.02635	.02507	.02388	.02279	.02178	.02084	.01997	.01917	.01842
17	.02917	.02772	.02637	.02513	.02399	.02293	.02194	.02103	.02018	.01940
18	.03059	.02907	.02767	.02637	.02517	.02406	.02302	.02207	.02118	.02035
19	.03205	.03046	.02899	.02763	.02637	.02521	.02412	.02312	.02218	.02131
20	.03355	.03188	.03035	.02892	.02760	.02638	.02524	.02419	.02320	.02229
21	.03509	.03334	.03173	.03024	.02886	.02758	.02638	.02527	.02424	.02328
22	.03669	.03487	.03318	.03162	.03017	.02882	.02757	.02640	.02532	.02430
23	.03837	.03646	.03470	.03306	.03154	.03013	.02881	.02759	.02644	.02538
24	.04018	.03819	.03634	.03463	.03303	.03155	.03016	.02888	.02767	.02655
25	.04214	.04006	.03812	.03633	.03465	.03309	.03164	.03029	.02902	.02784
26	.04428	.04210	.04008	.03820	.03644	.03481	.03328	.03186	.03052	.02928
27	.04662	.04434	.04223	.04025	.03841	.03670	.03509	.03360	.03219	.03088
28	.04915	.04677	.04456	.04249	.04056	.03876	.03708	.03550	.03403	.03264
29	.05189	.04941	.04709	.04493	.04291	.04102	.03925	.03760	.03604	.03458
30	.05485	.05226	.04984	.04757	.04546	.04348	.04162	.03988	.03825	.03671
31	.05805	.05535	.05282	.05045	.04824	.04616	.04421	.04238	.04067	.03905
32	.06149	.05867	.05603	.05356	.05124	.04906	.04702	.04510	.04329	.04160
33	.06520	.06226	.05950	.05692	.05449	.05221	.05007	.04806	.04616	.04438
34	.06916	.06609	.06322	.06052	.05799	.05560	.05336	.05125	.04926	.04738
35	.07339	.07020	.06720	.06439	.06174	.05925	.05690	.05469	.05260	.05063
36	.07787	.07455	.07143	.06850	.06573	.06313	.06068	.05836	.05617	.05411
37	.08262	.07917	.07593	.07287	.06999	.06727	.06470	.06228	.05999	.05783
38	.08765	.08407	.08069	.07751	.07451	.07167	.06899	.06646	.06407	.06180
39	.09296	.08925	.08574	.08243	.07931	.07635	.07356	.07092	.06841	.06604
40	.09858	.09472	.09109	.08765	.08440	.08132	.07841	.07565	.07303	.07055
41	.10449	.10050	.09673	.09316	.08978	.08658	.08355	.08067	.07794	.07535
42	.11069	.10656	.10265	.09895	.09544	.09212	.08896	.08596	.08312	.08041
43	.11718	.11291	.10887	.10503	.10140	.09794	.09466	.09154	.08858	.08576
44	.12399	.11958	.11540	.11143	.10766	.10407	.10067	.09743	.09434	.09141
45	.13111	.12656	.12224	.11814	.11423	.11052	.10699	.10362	.10042	.09736
46	.13856	.13387	.12941	.12516	.12113	.11728	.11362	.11013	.10680	.10363
47	.14633	.14150	.13690	.13252	.12835	.12438	.12059	.11697	.11352	.11022
48	.15442	.14945	.14471	.14020	.13589	.13179	.12787	.12412	.12055	.11713
49	.16280	.15769	.15281	.14816	.14373	.13949	.13544	.13157	.12787	.12433
50	.17147	.16622	.16121	.15643	.15186	.14749	.14331	.13931	.13548	.13182
51	.18045	.17507	.16993	.16501	.16030	.15580	.15150	.14737	.14342	.13963
52	.18979	.18427	.17899	.17394	.16911	.16448	.16004	.15579	.15172	.14780
53	.19947	.19383	.18842	.18324	.17828	.17352	.16896	.16458	.16038	.15635
54	.20950	.20372	.19819	.19288	.18779	.18291	.17822	.17372	.16940	.16524
55	.21986	.21397	.20831	.20288	.19767	.19266	.18785	.18322	.17878	.17450
56	.23058	.22457	.21879	.21324	.20791	.20278	.19785	.19310	.18854	.18414
57	.24167	.23554	.22965	.22399	.21854	.21329	.20824	.20338	.19870	.19419
58	.25314	.24690	.24090	.23512	.22956	.22420	.21904	.21407	.20927	.20464
59	.26497	.25863	.25252	.24664	.24097	.23550	.23023	.22515	.22024	.21551
60	.27712	.27068	.26448	.25849	.25272	.24716	.24178	.23659	.23158	.22674
61	.28956	.28304	.27674	.27067	.26480	.25913	.25366	.24837	.24325	.23831
62	.30228	.29567	.28929	.28312	.27717	.27141	.26584	.26045	.25524	.25020
63	.31525	.30857	.30211	.29586	.28982	.28397	.27832	.27284	.26754	.26240
64	.32851	.32176	.31522	.30890	.30278	.29685	.29111	.28555	.28016	.27493
65	.34209	.33528	.32868	.32229	.31610	.31010	.30429	.29865	.29317	.28787
66	.35604	.34918	.34253	.33609	.32983	.32377	.31788	.31217	.30663	.30124
67	.37037	.36347	.35678	.35028	.34398	.33786	.33191	.32614	.32053	.31508
68	.38508	.37815	.37142	.36489	.35854	.35237	.34638	.34055	.33488	.32937
69	.40008	.39313	.38638	.37982	.37344	.36724	.36120	.35533	.34961	.34405
70	.41533	.40838	.40162	.39504	.38864	.38241	.37634	.37043	.36468	.35907
71	.43076	.42382	.41705	.41047	.40405	.39780	.39171	.38578	.38000	.37436

TABLE S
BASED ON LIFE TABLE 80CNSMT
SINGLE LIFE REMAINDER FACTORS
APPLICABLE AFTER APRIL 30, 1989,
AND BEFORE MAY 1, 1999
INTEREST RATE

AGE	8.2%	8.4%	8.6%	8.8%	9.0%	9.2%	9.4%	9.6%	9.8%	10.0%
72	.44638	.43945	.43269	.42611	.41969	.41344	.40733	.40138	.39558	.38991
73	.46218	.45527	.44854	.44197	.43556	.42931	.42321	.41725	.41143	.40575
74	.47823	.47137	.46466	.45812	.45173	.44549	.43940	.43345	.42763	.42195
75	.49459	.48777	.48112	.47462	.46826	.46205	.45598	.45004	.44424	.43856
76	.51127	.50452	.49793	.49148	.48517	.47900	.47297	.46706	.46129	.45563
77	.52823	.52157	.51505	.50867	.50243	.49632	.49033	.48447	.47873	.47311
78	.54541	.53885	.53242	.52613	.51996	.51392	.50800	.50220	.49652	.49094
79	.56267	.55621	.54989	.54369	.53762	.53166	.52582	.52009	.51448	.50897
80	.57987	.57354	.56733	.56125	.55527	.54941	.54366	.53802	.53248	.52705
81	.59685	.59065	.58457	.57860	.57274	.56699	.56134	.55579	.55035	.54499
82	.61351	.60746	.60151	.59567	.58993	.58429	.57875	.57331	56796	.56270
83	.62978	.62387	.61806	.61236	.60675	.60123	.59581	.59047	58523	.58007
84	.64567	.63992	.63426	.62869	.62321	.61783	.61253	.60731	.60218	.59713
85	.66125	.65565	.65014	.64472	.63938	.63413	.62896	.62387	.61886	.61392
86	.67636	.67092	.66557	.66030	.65511	.65000	.64496	.64000	.63511	.63030
87	.69081	.68554	.68034	.67522	.67018	.66520	.66031	.65548	.55071	.64602
88	.70468	.69957	.69453	.68956	.68466	.67983	.67507	.67037	.56574	.66117
89	.71821	.71326	.70838	.70357	.69882	.69414	.68952	.68495	.58045	.67601
90	.73153	.72676	.72204	.71739	.71280	.70827	.70379	.69938	.69502	.69071
91	.74447	.73986	.73532	.73083	.72640	.72202	.71770	.71343	.70921	.70504
92	.75669	.75225	.74787	.74354	.73927	.73504	.73087	.72674	.72267	.71864
93	.76807	.76379	.75957	.75540	.75127	.74719	.74317	.73918	.73524	.73135
94	.77849	.77437	.77030	.76627	.76229	.75835	.75446	.75061	.74680	.74303
95	.78792	.78394	.78001	.77611	.77226	.76845	.76468	.76096	.75727	.75362
96	.79630	.79244	.78863	.78485	.78112	.77742	.77377	.77015	.76657	.76303
97	.80391	.80016	.79646	.79280	.78917	.78559	.78203	.77852	.77504	.77160
98	.81076	.80712	.80352	.79996	.79643	.79294	.78948	.78606	.78267	.77931
99	.81709	.81354	.81004	.80657	.80313	.79972	.79635	.79302	.78971	.78644
100	.82296	.81950	.81609	.81270	.80934	.80602	.80273	.79947	.79624	.79304
101	.82855	.82518	.82185	.81854	.81526	.81201	.80880	.80561	.80245	.79932
102	.83438	.83110	.82785	.82462	.82142	.81826	.81512	.81200	.80892	.80586
103	.84056	.83737	.83420	.83106	.82795	.82487	.82181	.81878	.81577	.81279
104	.84743	.84433	.84127	.83822	.83521	.83221	.82924	.82630	.82338	.82048
105	.85591	.85295	.85001	.84709	.84419	.84132	.83846	.83563	.83282	.83003
106	.86816	.86540	.86266	.85993	.85723	.85454	.85187	.84922	.84659	.84397
107	.88592	.88348	.88105	.87863	.87623	.87384	.87147	.86911	.86676	.86443
108	.91493	.91306	.91119	.90934	.90749	.90566	.90383	.90201	.90020	.89840
109	.96211	.96125	.96041	.95956	.95872	.95788	.95704	.95620	.95537	.95455

See p. 15 for regulations not amended to reflect law changes

TABLE S
BASED ON LIFE TABLE 80CNSMT
SINGLE LIFE REMAINDER FACTORS
APPLICABLE AFTER APRIL 30, 1989,
AND BEFORE MAY 1, 1999
INTEREST RATE

AGE	10.2%	10.4%	10.6%	10.8%	11.0%	11.2%	11.4%	11.6%	11.8%	12.0%
0	.01891	.01864	.01838	.01814	.01791	.01770	.01750	.01732	.01715	.01698
1	.00770	.00741	.00715	.00690	.00667	.00646	.00626	.00608	.00590	.00574
2	.00751	.00721	.00693	.00667	.00643	.00620	.00600	.00580	.00562	.00544
3	.00760	.00728	.00699	.00671	.00646	.00622	.00600	.00579	.00560	.00541
4	.00786	.00752	.00721	.00692	.00665	.00639	.00616	.00594	.00573	.00554
5	.00824	.00788	.00755	.00724	.00695	.00668	.00643	.00620	.00598	.00578
6	.00869	.00832	.00796	.00764	.00733	.00705	.00678	.00654	.00630	.00608
7	.00923	.00883	.00846	.00811	.00779	.00749	.00720	.00694	.00669	.00646
8	.00986	.00943	.00904	.00867	.00833	.00801	.00771	.00743	.00716	.00692
9	.01059	.01014	.00972	.00933	.00897	.00863	.00831	.00801	.00773	.00747
10	.01142	.01095	.01051	.01009	.00971	.00935	.00901	.00869	.00840	.00812
11	.01239	.01189	.01142	.01098	.01057	.01019	.00983	.00950	.00918	.00889
12	.01345	.01292	.01243	.01197	.01154	.01113	.01075	.01040	.01007	.00975
13	.01457	.01401	.01349	.01300	.01255	.01212	.01172	.01135	.01100	.01067
14	.01567	.01508	.01453	.01402	.01354	.01309	.01267	.01227	.01190	.01155
15	.01672	.01610	.01552	.01498	.01448	.01400	.01356	.01314	.01275	.01238
16	.01772	.01707	.01646	.01589	.01536	.01486	.01439	.01396	.01354	.01315
17	.01866	.01798	.01734	.01674	.01618	.01566	.01516	.01470	.01427	.01386
18	.01958	.01886	.01818	.01755	.01697	.01641	.01590	.01541	.01495	.01452
19	.02050	.01974	.01903	.01837	.01775	.01717	.01662	.01611	.01563	.01517
20	.02143	.02064	.01989	.01919	.01854	.01793	.01735	.01681	.01630	.01582
21	.02238	.02154	.02075	.02002	.01933	.01868	.01807	.01750	.01696	.01646
22	.02336	.02247	.02164	.02087	.02014	.01946	.01882	.01821	.01764	.01711
23	.02438	.02345	.02257	.02176	.02099	.02027	.01959	.01895	.01835	.01778
24	.02550	.02451	.02359	.02273	.02192	.02115	.02044	.01976	.01913	.01853
25	.02673	.02569	.02472	.02381	.02295	.02214	.02138	.02067	.01999	.01936
26	.02811	.02701	.02598	.02502	.02411	.02326	.02246	.02170	.02098	.02031
27	.02965	.02849	.02741	.02639	.02543	.02452	.02367	.02287	.02211	.02140
28	.03134	.03013	.02898	.02790	.02689	.02593	.02503	.02418	.02338	.02262
29	.03322	.03193	.03072	.02958	.02851	.02750	.02654	.02564	.02479	.02398
30	.03527	.03391	.03264	.03143	.03030	.02923	.02821	.02726	.02635	.02550
31	.03753	.03610	.03475	.03348	.03228	.03115	.03008	.02907	.02811	.02720
32	.04000	.03849	.03707	.03573	.03446	.03326	.03213	.03105	.03004	.02907
33	.04269	.04111	.03961	.03819	.03685	.03558	.03438	.03325	.03217	.03115
34	.04561	.04394	.04236	.04087	.03946	.03812	.03685	.03565	.03451	.03342
35	.04877	.04702	.04535	.04378	.04229	.04087	.03953	.03826	.03706	.03591
36	.05215	.05031	.04856	.04690	.04533	.04384	.04242	.04108	.03980	.03859
37	.05578	.05384	.05200	.05025	.04860	.04703	.04553	.04411	.04276	.04148
38	.05965	.05761	.05568	.05385	.05211	.05045	.04888	.04738	.04595	.04460
39	.06379	.06165	.05962	.05770	.05587	.05412	.05247	.05089	.04939	.04795
40	.06820	.06596	.06383	.06181	.05989	.05806	.05631	.05465	.05307	.05155
41	.07288	.07054	.06832	.06620	.06418	.06226	.06042	.05868	.05701	.05541
42	.07784	.07539	.07306	.07085	.06873	.06671	.06479	.06295	.06119	.05952
43	.08308	.08052	.07808	.07576	.07355	.07143	.06941	.06748	.06564	.06387
44	.08861	.08594	.08340	.08097	.07865	.07644	.07432	.07230	.07036	.06851
45	.09445	.09167	.08901	.08648	.08406	.08174	.07953	.07741	.07538	.07343
46	.10060	.09770	.09494	.09230	.08977	.08735	.08503	.08281	.08068	.07865
47	.10707	.10406	.10119	.09843	.09579	.09327	.09085	.08853	.08630	.08417
48	.11386	.11073	.10774	.10487	.10213	.09949	.09697	.09455	.09222	.08999
49	.12094	.11769	.11458	.11160	.10874	.10600	.10337	.10084	.09842	.09609
50	.12831	.12494	.12172	.11862	.11565	.11280	.11006	.10743	.10490	.10247
51	.13600	.13251	.12917	.12596	.12288	.11991	.11706	.11432	.11169	.10915
52	.14405	.14044	.13698	.13366	.13046	.12738	.12442	.12157	.11883	.11619
53	.15247	.14875	.14517	.14172	.13841	.13522	.13215	.12919	.12635	.12360
54	.16124	.15740	.15370	.15014	.14671	.14341	.14023	.13717	.13421	.13136
55	.17039	.16642	.16261	.15893	.15539	.15198	.14868	.14551	.14244	.13948
56	.17991	.17583	.17190	.16811	.16445	.16092	.15752	.15423	.15106	.14799
57	.18984	.18564	.18160	.17769	.17392	.17029	.16677	.16338	.16010	.15692
58	.20018	.19587	.19172	.18770	.18382	.18007	.17645	.17295	.16956	.16628
59	.21093	.20652	.20225	.19812	.19414	.19028	.18655	.18294	.17945	.17606
60	.22206	.21753	.21316	.20893	.20483	.20087	.19703	.19332	.18972	.18624
61	.23353	.22890	.22442	.22009	.21589	.21182	.20788	.20407	.20037	.19678
62	.24532	.24059	.23601	.23158	.22728	.22311	.21907	.21515	.21135	.20767
63	.25742	.25260	.24793	.24339	.23900	.23473	.23060	.22658	.22268	.21890
64	.26987	.26495	.26019	.25556	.25107	.24671	.24248	.23837	.23438	.23050
65	.28271	.27771	.27286	.26815	.26357	.25912	.25480	.25059	.24651	.24254
66	.29601	.29093	.28600	.28120	.27654	.27200	.26760	.26331	.25913	.25507
67	.30978	.30462	.29961	.29474	.29000	.28539	.28090	.27653	.27227	.26813
68	.32401	.31879	.31371	.30877	.30396	.29927	.29471	.29027	.28593	.28171
69	.33863	.33336	.32822	.32322	.31835	.31359	.30896	.30445	.30005	.29576
70	.35361	.34829	.34310	.33804	.33311	.32830	.32361	.31903	.31457	.31021
71	.36886	.36349	.35826	.35316	.34818	.34332	.33858	.33394	.32942	.32500

TABLE S
BASED ON LIFE TABLE 80CNSMT
SINGLE LIFE REMAINDER FACTORS
APPLICABLE AFTER APRIL 30, 1989,
AND BEFORE MAY 1, 1999
INTEREST RATE

AGE	*10.2%*	*10.4%*	*10.6%*	*10.8%*	*11.0%*	*11.2%*	*11.4%*	*11.6%*	*11.8%*	*12.0%*
72	.38439	.37899	.37373	.36858	.36356	.35866	.35387	.34919	.34461	.34015
73	.40021	.39479	.38950	.38432	.37927	.37433	.36950	.36478	.36016	.35565
74	.41639	.41096	.40565	.40046	.39538	.39042	.38556	.38081	.37616	.37161
75	.43301	.42758	.42226	.41706	.41198	.40699	.40212	.39734	.39267	.38809
76	.45009	.44467	.43937	.43417	.42908	.42410	.41921	.41443	.40974	.40514
77	.46761	.46221	.45693	.45175	.44667	.44170	.43682	.43203	.42734	.42274
78	.48548	.48013	.47488	.46973	.46468	.45972	.45486	.45009	.44541	.44082
79	.50356	.49826	.49306	.48795	.48294	.47802	.47319	.46845	.46379	.45922
80	.52171	.51647	.51133	.50628	.50132	.49644	.49166	.48695	.48233	.47779
81	.53974	.53457	.52950	.52451	.51961	.51479	.51006	.50541	.50083	.49633
82	.55753	.55245	.54745	.54254	.53771	.53296	.52828	.52369	.51917	.51472
83	.57500	.57001	.56510	.56026	.55551	.55083	.54623	.54170	.53724	.53285
84	.59216	.58726	.58245	.57770	.57304	.56844	.56391	.55945	.55506	.55074
85	.60906	.60428	.59956	.59492	.59034	.58583	.58139	.57702	.57270	.56845
86	.62555	.62088	.61627	.61173	.60725	.60284	.59849	.59420	.58997	.58580
87	.64139	.63683	.63233	.62790	.62352	.61921	.61495	.61076	.60661	.60253
88	.65666	.65221	.64783	.64350	.63923	.63502	.63086	.62675	.62270	.61871
89	.67163	.66730	.66304	.65882	.65466	.65055	.64650	.64249	.63854	.63463
90	.68646	.68226	.67812	.67402	.66998	.66599	.66204	.65814	.65430	.65049
91	.70093	.69686	.69285	.68888	.68496	.68108	.67725	.67347	.66973	.66604
92	.71466	.71073	.70684	.70300	.69920	.69545	.69173	.68806	.68444	.68085
93	.72750	.72370	.71994	.71622	.71254	.70890	.70530	.70174	.69822	.69474
94	.73931	.73562	.73198	.72838	.72481	.72129	.71780	.71434	.71093	.70755
95	.75001	.74644	.74291	.73941	.73595	.73253	.72914	.72579	.72247	.71919
96	.75953	.75606	.75262	.74923	.74586	.74253	.73924	.73598	.73275	.72955
97	.76819	.76481	.76147	.75816	.75489	.75165	.74844	.74526	.74211	.73899
98	.77599	.77270	.76944	.76621	.76302	.75986	.75672	.75362	.75054	.74750
99	.78319	.77998	.77680	.77365	.77053	.76744	.76437	.76134	.75833	.75535
100	.78987	.78673	.78362	.78054	.77748	.77446	.77146	.76849	.76555	.76263
101	.79622	.79315	.79010	.78708	.78409	.78113	.77819	.77528	.77239	.76953
102	.80283	.79983	.79685	.79390	.79097	.78807	.78519	.78234	.77951	.77671
103	.80983	.80690	.80399	.80111	.79825	.79541	.79260	.78981	.78705	.78430
104	.81760	.81475	.81192	.80912	.80633	.80357	.80083	.79810	.79541	.79273
105	.82726	.82451	.82178	.81907	.81638	.81371	.81106	.80843	.80582	.80322
106	.84137	.83879	.83623	.83368	.83115	.82863	.82614	.82366	.82119	.81874
107	.86211	.85981	.85751	.85523	.85297	.85071	.84847	.84624	.84403	.84182
108	.89660	.89481	.89304	.89127	.88950	.88775	.88601	.88427	.88254	.88081
109	.95372	.95290	.95208	.95126	.95045	.94964	.94883	.94803	.94723	.94643

See p. 15 for regulations not amended to reflect law changes

TABLE S
BASED ON LIFE TABLE 80CNSMT
SINGLE LIFE REMAINDER FACTORS
APPLICABLE AFTER APRIL 30, 1989,
AND BEFORE MAY 1, 1999
INTEREST RATE

AGE	12.2%	12.4%	12.6%	12.8%	13.0%	13.2%	13.4%	13.6%	13.8%	14.0%
0	.01683	.01669	.01655	.01642	.01630	.01618	.01607	.01596	.01586	.01576
1	.00559	.00544	.00531	.00518	.00506	.00494	.00484	.00473	.00464	.00454
2	.00528	.00513	.00499	.00485	.00473	.00461	.00449	.00439	.00428	.00419
3	.00524	.00508	.00493	.00479	.00465	.00453	.00441	.00429	.00419	.00408
4	.00536	.00519	.00503	.00488	.00473	.00460	.00447	.00435	.00423	.00412
5	.00558	.00540	.00523	.00507	.00492	.00477	.00464	.00451	.00439	.00427
6	.00588	.00569	.00550	.00533	.00517	.00502	.00487	.00473	.00460	.00448
7	.00624	.00604	.00584	.00566	.00549	.00532	.00517	.00502	.00488	.00475
8	.00668	.00646	.00626	.00606	.00588	.00570	.00554	.00538	.00523	.00509
9	.00722	.00699	.00677	.00656	.00636	.00617	.00600	.00583	.00567	.00552
10	.00785	.00761	.00737	.00715	.00694	.00674	.00655	.00637	.00620	.00604
11	.00861	.00835	.00810	.00786	.00764	.00743	.00723	.00704	.00686	.00668
12	.00946	.00918	.00891	.00866	.00843	.00820	.00799	.00779	.00760	.00741
13	.01035	.01006	.00978	.00951	.00927	.00903	.00880	.00859	.00839	.00819
14	.01122	.01091	.01061	.01034	.01007	.00982	.00958	.00936	.00914	.00894
15	.01203	.01171	.01140	.01110	.01082	.01056	.01031	.01007	.00985	.00963
16	.01279	.01244	.01211	.01181	.01151	.01123	.01097	.01072	.01048	.01025
17	.01347	.01311	.01276	.01244	.01213	.01184	.01156	.01130	.01104	.01081
18	.01411	.01373	.01336	.01302	.01270	.01239	.01210	.01182	.01155	.01130
19	.01474	.01434	.01396	.01359	.01325	.01293	.01262	.01233	.01205	.01178
20	.01537	.01494	.01454	.01415	.01379	.01345	.01313	.01282	.01252	.01224
21	.01598	.01553	.01510	.01470	.01432	.01396	.01361	.01329	.01298	.01268
22	.01660	.01613	.01568	.01525	.01485	.01446	.01410	.01375	.01343	.01312
23	.01725	.01674	.01627	.01581	.01539	.01498	.01460	.01423	.01388	.01355
24	.01796	.01742	.01692	.01644	.01599	.01556	.01515	.01476	.01439	.01404
25	.01876	.01819	.01765	.01714	.01666	.01621	.01577	.01536	.01497	.01460
26	.01967	.01907	.01850	.01796	.01745	.01696	.01650	.01606	.01565	.01525
27	.02072	.02008	.01948	.01890	.01836	.01784	.01735	.01688	.01644	.01601
28	.02190	.02122	.02057	.01996	.01938	.01883	.01831	.01781	.01734	.01689
29	.02322	.02249	.02181	.02116	.02054	.01996	.01940	.01887	.01836	.01788
30	.02469	.02392	.02319	.02250	.02184	.02122	.02062	.02006	.01952	.01900
31	.02634	.02552	.02475	.02401	.02331	.02264	.02201	.02140	.02083	.02028
32	.02816	.02729	.02647	.02568	.02494	.02423	.02355	.02291	.02229	.02170
33	.03018	.02926	.02838	.02755	.02675	.02600	.02528	.02459	.02393	.02331
34	.03239	.03142	.03048	.02960	.02875	.02795	.02718	.02645	.02575	.02508
35	.03482	.03378	.03279	.03185	.03095	.03009	.02928	.02850	.02775	.02704
36	.03743	.03633	.03528	.03428	.03333	.03242	.03155	.03072	.02992	.02916
37	.04026	.03909	.03798	.03692	.03591	.03494	.03401	.03313	.03228	.03147
38	.04330	.04207	.04089	.03977	.03869	.03767	.03668	.03574	.03484	.03398
39	.04658	.04528	.04403	.04284	.04170	.04061	.03957	.03857	.03762	.03670
40	.05011	.04873	.04741	.04615	.04495	.04379	.04269	.04163	.04061	.03964
41	.05389	.05244	.05104	.04971	.04844	.04721	.04604	.04492	.04384	.04281
42	.05791	.05638	.05491	.05350	.05216	.05086	.04962	.04844	.04729	.04620
43	.06219	.06057	.05902	.05754	.05612	.05475	.05344	.05218	.05098	.04981
44	.06673	.06503	.06340	.06184	.06034	.05890	.05752	.05619	.05491	.05368
45	.07157	.06978	.06806	.06642	.06484	.06332	.06186	.06046	.05911	.05781
46	.07669	.07481	.07301	.07128	.06962	.06802	.06649	.06501	.06358	.06221
47	.08212	.08015	.07826	.07645	.07470	.07302	.07140	.06984	.06834	.06690
48	.08784	.08578	.08380	.08190	.08006	.07830	.07660	.07496	.07338	.07186
49	.09384	.09169	.08961	.08762	.08570	.08384	.08206	.08034	.07868	.07708
50	.10013	.09787	.09570	.09361	.09160	.08966	.08779	.08598	.08424	.08256
51	.10671	.10436	.10209	.09991	.09780	.09577	.09381	.09192	.09009	.08832
52	.11365	.11120	.10883	.10655	.10435	.10222	.10017	.09819	.09628	.09442
53	.12095	.11840	.11593	.11355	.11126	.10904	.10689	.10482	.10282	.10088
54	.12860	.12595	.12338	.12090	.11851	.11619	.11396	.11179	.10970	.10767
55	.13663	.13386	.13120	.12862	.12613	.12372	.12138	.11912	.11694	.11482
56	.14503	.14217	.13940	.13672	.13413	.13162	.12919	.12683	.12456	.12235
57	.15385	.15089	.14801	.14523	.14254	.13994	.13741	.13496	.13259	.13029
58	.16311	.16004	.15706	.15418	.15139	.14868	.14606	.14352	.14105	.13866
59	.17279	.16961	.16654	.16355	.16066	.15786	.15514	.15250	.14994	.14745
60	.18286	.17958	.17640	.17332	.17033	.16743	.16462	.16188	.15922	.15664
61	.19330	.18992	.18665	.18347	.18038	.17738	.17447	.17164	.16889	.16622
62	.20409	.20061	.19724	.19396	.19078	.18768	.18467	.18175	.17891	.17614
63	.21522	.21165	.20818	.20480	.20152	.19833	.19523	.19221	.18928	.18642
64	.22672	.22306	.21949	.21602	.21265	.20937	.20617	.20306	.20003	.19708
65	.23867	.23491	.23125	.22769	.22423	.22085	.21757	.21437	.21125	.20821
66	.25112	.24727	.24353	.23988	.23632	.23286	.22948	.22619	.22299	.21986
67	.26409	.26016	.25633	.25260	.24896	.24541	.24195	.23857	.23528	.23206
68	.27760	.27359	.26968	.26586	.26214	.25851	.25497	.25151	.24814	.24484
69	.29157	.28748	.28350	.27961	.27581	.27211	.26849	.26495	.26150	.25812
70	.30596	.30181	.29775	.29379	.28992	.28614	.28245	.27884	.27532	.27187
71	.32069	.31648	.31236	.30833	.30440	.30055	.29679	.29312	.28952	.28600

TABLE S
BASED ON LIFE TABLE 80CNSMT
SINGLE LIFE REMAINDER FACTORS
APPLICABLE AFTER APRIL 30, 1989,
AND BEFORE MAY 1, 1999
INTEREST RATE

AGE	12.2%	12.4%	12.6%	12.8%	13.0%	13.2%	13.4%	13.6%	13.8%	14.0%
72	.33578	.33151	.32733	.32325	.31925	.31535	.31152	.30778	.30412	.30054
73	.35123	.34691	.34269	.33855	.33450	.33054	.32666	.32286	.31914	.31550
74	.36715	.36279	.35852	.35434	.35024	.34623	.34230	.33845	.33468	.33098
75	.38360	.37921	.37491	.37069	.36656	.36250	.35853	.35464	.35082	.34708
76	.40064	.39623	.39190	.38765	.38349	.37941	.37540	.37148	.36762	.36384
77	.41823	.41381	.40947	.40521	.40103	.39692	.39290	.38895	38507	.38126
78	.43632	.43189	.42755	.42329	.41910	.41499	.41095	.40698	40309	.39926
79	.45473	.45032	.44599	.44173	.43755	.43344	.42940	.42543	.42153	.41770
80	.47333	.46894	.46463	.46040	.45623	.45213	.44811	.44414	.44025	.43642
81	.49191	.48755	.48328	.47907	.47493	.47085	.46684	.46290	.45902	.45520
82	.51034	.50603	.50179	.49762	.49351	.48947	.48549	.48157	.47772	.47392
83	.52852	.52427	.52008	.51595	.51189	.50788	.50394	.50006	.49623	.49246
84	.54648	.54228	.53815	.53407	.53006	.52610	.52221	.51836	.51458	.51084
85	.56426	.56013	.55606	.55205	.54810	.54420	.54035	.53656	.53282	.52913
86	.58169	.57764	.57364	.56970	.56581	.56197	.55818	.55445	.55076	.54713
87	.59850	.59452	.59060	.58673	.58291	.57913	.57541	.57174	.56811	.56453
88	.61476	.61086	.60702	.60322	.59947	.59577	.59212	.58851	.58494	.58142
89	.63078	.62697	.62321	.61950	.61583	.61220	.60862	.60508	.60159	.59813
90	.64674	.64302	.63935	.63573	.63215	.62861	.62511	.62165	.61823	.61485
91	.66238	.65877	.65520	.65167	.64819	.64474	.64133	.63795	.63462	.63132
92	.67730	.67379	.67032	.66689	.66350	.66014	.65682	.65354	.65029	.64708
93	.69130	.68789	.68452	.68119	.67789	.67463	.67140	.66820	.66504	.66191
94	.70421	.70090	.69762	.69438	.69118	.68800	.68486	.68175	.67867	.67563
95	.71594	.71272	.70954	.70639	.70326	.70017	.69712	.69409	.69109	.68812
96	.72638	.72325	.72014	.71707	.71403	.71101	.70803	.70507	.70215	.69925
97	.73590	.73285	.72982	.72682	.72385	.72090	.71799	.71510	.71224	.70941
98	.74448	.74149	.73853	.73560	.73269	.72981	.72696	.72414	.72134	.71856
99	.75240	.74948	.74658	.74371	.74086	.73805	.73525	.73248	.72974	.72702
100	.75974	.75687	.75403	.75121	.74842	.74566	.74292	.74020	.73751	.73484
101	.76669	.76388	.76109	.75833	.75559	.75287	.75018	.74751	.74486	.74223
102	.77393	.77117	.76844	.76573	.76304	.76037	.75773	.75511	.75251	.74993
103	.78158	.77888	.77620	.77355	.77091	.76830	.76571	.76313	.76058	.75805
104	.79007	.78743	.78482	.78222	.77964	.77709	.77455	.77203	.76953	.76705
105	.80065	.79809	.79556	.79304	.79054	.78805	.78559	.78314	.78071	.77829
106	.81631	.81389	.81149	.80911	.80674	.80438	.80204	.79972	.79741	.79511
107	.83963	.83745	.83529	.83313	.83099	.82886	.82674	.82463	.82254	.82045
108	.87910	.87739	.87569	.87400	.87232	.87064	.86897	.86731	.86566	.86401
109	.94563	.94484	.94405	.94326	.94248	.94170	.94092	.94014	.93937	.93860

(f) *Present value of the remainder interest in the case of transfers to pooled income funds for which the valuation date is after April 30, 1999, and before May 1, 2009.*—

(1) *In general.*—In the case of transfers to pooled income funds for which the valuation date is after April 30, 1999, and before May 1, 2009, the present value of a remainder interest is determined under this section. See, however, § 1.7520-3(b) (relating to exceptions to the use of prescribed tables under certain circumstances). The present value of a remainder interest that is dependent on the termination of the life of one individual is computed by the use of Table S in paragraph (f)(6) of this section. For purposes of the computations under this section, the age of an individual is the age at the individual's nearest birthday.

(2) *Transitional rules for valuation of transfers to pooled income funds.*—(i) For purposes of sections 2055, 2106, or 2624, if on May 1, 1999, the decedent was mentally incompetent so that the disposition of the property could not be changed, and the decedent died after April 30, 1999, without having regained competency to dispose of the decedent's property, or the decedent died within 90 days of the date that the decedent first regained competency after April 30, 1999, the present value of a remainder interest is determined as if the valuation date with respect to the decedent's gross estate is either before May 1, 1999, or after April 30, 1999, at the option of the decedent's executor.

(ii) For purposes of sections 170, 2055, 2106, 2522, or 2624, in the case of transfers to a pooled income fund for which the valuation date is after April 30, 1999, and before July 1, 1999, the present value of the remainder interest under this section is determined by use of the section 7520 interest rate for the month in which the valuation date occurs (see §§1.7520-1(b) and 1.7520-2(a)(2) and the appropriate actuarial tables under either paragraph (e)(5) or (f)(6) of this section, at the option of the donor or the decedent's executor, as the case may be.

(iii) For purposes of paragraphs (f)(2)(i) and (f)(2)(ii) of this section, where the donor or decedent's executor is given the option to use the appropriate actuarial tables under either paragraph (e)(5) or (f)(6) of this section, the donor or decedent's executor must use the same actuarial table with respect to each individual transaction and with respect to all transfers occurring on the valuation date (for example, gift and income tax charitable deductions with respect to the same transfer must be determined based on the same tables, and all assets includible in the gross estate and/or estate tax deductions claimed must be valued based on the same tables).

(3) *Present value of a remainder interest.*—The present value of a remainder interest in property transferred to a pooled income fund is computed on the basis of —

(i) Life contingencies determined from the values of *lx* that are set forth in Table 90CM in §20.2031-7A(f)(4); and

(ii) Discount at a rate of interest, compounded annually, equal to the highest yearly rate of return of the pooled income fund for the 3 taxable years immediately preceding its taxable year in which the transfer of property to the fund is made. The provisions of §1.642(c)-6(c) apply for determining the yearly rate of return. However, where the taxable year is less than 12 months, the provisions of §§1.642(c)-6(e)(3)(ii) apply for the determining the yearly rate of return.

(4) *Pooled income funds in existence less than 3 taxable years.*—The provisions of §§1.642(c)-6(e)(4) apply for determining the highest yearly rate of return when the pooled income fund has been in existence less than three taxable years.

(5) *Computation of value of remainder interest.*—The factor that is used in determining the present value of a remainder interest that is dependent on the termination of the life of one individual is the factor from Table S in paragraph (f)(6) of this section under the appropriate yearly rate of return opposite the number that corresponds to the age of the individual upon whose life the value of the remainder interest is based. Table S in paragraph (f)(6) of this section includes factors for yearly rates of return from 4.2 to 14 percent. Many actuarial factors not contained in Table S in paragraph (f)(6) of this section are contained in Table S in Internal Revenue Service Publication 1457, "Actuarial Values, Book Aleph," (7-99). Publication 1457 is no longer available for purchase from the Superintendent of Documents, United States Government Printing Office. However, pertinent factors in this publication may be obtained by a written request to: CC:PA:LPD:PR (IRS Publication 1457), Room 5205, Internal Revenue Service, P.O.Box 7604, Ben Franklin Station, Washington, DC 20044. For other situations, see §1.642(c)-6(b). If the yearly rate of return is a percentage that is between the yearly rates of return for which factors are provided, a linear interpolation must be made. The present value of the remainder interest is determined by multiplying the fair market value of the property on the valuation date by the appropriate remainder factor. For an example of a computation of the present value of a remainder interest requiring a linear interpolation adjustment, see §§1.642(c)-6(e)(5).

(6) *Actuarial tables.*—In the case of transfers for which the valuation date is after April 30, 1999, and before May 1, 2009, the present value of a remainder interest dependent on the termination of one life in the case of a transfer to a pooled income fund is determined by use of the following tables:

TABLE S
BASED ON LIFE TABLE 90CM
SINGLE LIFE REMAINDER FACTORS
[APPLICABLE AFTER APRIL 30, 1999, AND BEFORE MAY 1, 2009]
INTEREST RATE

AGE	4.2%	4.4%	4.6%	4.8%	5.0%	5.2%	5.4%	5.6%	5.8%	6.0%
0	.06752	.06130	.05586	.05109	.04691	.04322	.03998	.03711	.03458	.03233
1	.06137	.05495	.04932	.04438	.04003	.03620	.03283	.02985	.02721	.02487
2	.06325	.05667	.05088	.04580	.04132	.03737	.03388	.03079	.02806	.02563
3	.06545	.05869	.05275	.04752	.04291	.03883	.03523	.03203	.02920	.02668
4	.06784	.06092	.05482	.04944	.04469	.04048	.03676	.03346	.03052	.02791
5	.07040	.06331	.05705	.05152	.04662	.04229	.03845	.03503	.03199	.02928
6	.07310	.06583	.05941	.05372	.04869	.04422	.04025	.03672	.03357	.03076
7	.07594	.06849	.06191	.05607	.05089	.04628	.04219	.03854	.03528	.03236
8	.07891	.07129	.06453	.05853	.05321	.04846	.04424	.04046	.03709	.03407
9	.08203	.07423	.06731	.06115	.05567	.05079	.04643	.04253	.03904	.03592
10	.08532	.07734	.07024	.06392	.05829	.05326	.04877	.04474	.04114	.03790
11	.08875	.08059	.07331	.06683	.06104	.05587	.05124	.04709	.04336	.04002
12	.09233	.08398	.07653	.06989	.06394	.05862	.05385	.04957	.04572	.04226
13	.09601	.08748	.07985	.07304	.06693	.06146	.05655	.05214	.04816	.04458
14	.09974	.09102	.08322	.07624	.06997	.06435	.05929	.05474	.05064	.04694
15	.10350	.09460	.08661	.07946	.07303	.06725	.06204	.05735	.05312	.04930
16	.10728	.09818	.09001	.08268	.07608	.07014	.06479	.05996	.05559	.05164
17	.11108	.10179	.09344	.08592	.07916	.07306	.06755	.06257	.05807	.05399
18	.11494	.10545	.09691	.08921	.08227	.07601	.07034	.06521	.06057	.05636
19	.11889	.10921	.10047	.09259	.08548	.07904	.07322	.06794	.06315	.05880
20	.12298	.11310	.10417	.09610	.08881	.08220	.07622	.07078	.06584	.06135
21	.12722	.11713	.10801	.09976	.09228	.08550	.07935	.07375	.06866	.06403
22	.13159	.12130	.11199	.10354	.09588	.08893	.08260	.07685	.07160	.06682
23	.13613	.12563	.11612	.10748	.09964	.09250	.08601	.08009	.07468	.06975
24	.14084	.13014	.12043	.11160	.10357	.09625	.08958	.08349	.07793	.07284
25	.14574	.13484	.12493	.11591	.10768	.10018	.09334	.08708	.08135	.07611
26	.15084	.13974	.12963	.12041	.11199	.10431	.09728	.09085	.08496	.07956
27	.15615	.14485	.13454	.12513	.11652	.10865	.10144	.09484	.08878	.08322
28	.16166	.15016	.13965	.13004	.12124	.11319	.10580	.09901	.09279	.08706
29	.16737	.15567	.14497	.13516	.12617	.11792	.11035	.10339	.09699	.09109
30	.17328	.16138	.15048	.14047	.13129	.12286	.11510	.10796	.10138	.09532
31	.17938	.16728	.15618	.14599	.13661	.12799	.12004	.11272	.10597	.09974
32	.18568	.17339	.16210	.15171	.14214	.13333	.12520	.11769	.11076	.10435
33	.19220	.17972	.16824	.15766	.14790	.13889	.13058	.12289	.11578	.10920
34	.19894	.18627	.17460	.16383	.15388	.14468	.13618	.12831	.12102	.11426
35	.20592	.19307	.18121	.17025	.16011	.15073	.14204	.13399	.12652	.11958
36	.21312	.20010	.18805	.17691	.16658	.15701	.14814	.13990	.13225	.12514
37	.22057	.20737	.19514	.18382	.17331	.16356	.15450	.14608	.13825	.13096
38	.22827	.21490	.20251	.19100	.18031	.17038	.16113	.15253	.14452	.13705
39	.23623	.22270	.21013	.19845	.18759	.17747	.16805	.15927	.15108	.14344
40	.24446	.23078	.21805	.20620	.19516	.18487	.17527	.16631	.15795	.15013
41	.25298	.23915	.22626	.21425	.20305	.19259	.18282	.17368	.16514	.15715
42	.26178	.24782	.23478	.22262	.21125	.20062	.19069	.18138	.17267	.16450
43	.27087	.25678	.24360	.23129	.21977	.20898	.19888	.18941	.18053	.17220
44	.28025	.26603	.25273	.24027	.22860	.21766	.20740	.19777	.18873	.18023
45	.28987	.27555	.26212	.24953	.23772	.22664	.21622	.20644	.19724	.18858
46	.29976	.28533	.27179	.25908	.24714	.23591	.22536	.21542	.20606	.19725
47	.30987	.29535	.28171	.26889	.25682	.24546	.23476	.22468	.21518	.20621
48	.32023	.30563	.29190	.27897	.26678	.25530	.24447	.23425	.22460	.21549
49	.33082	.31615	.30234	.28931	.27702	.26543	.25447	.24412	.23434	.22509
50	.34166	.32694	.31306	.29995	.28756	.27586	.26479	.25432	.24441	.23502
51	.35274	.33798	.32404	.31085	.29838	.28658	.27541	.26482	.25479	.24528

AGE	4.2%	4.4%	4.6%	4.8%	5.0%	5.2%	5.4%	5.6%	5.8%	6.0%
52	.36402	.34924	.33525	.32200	.30946	.29757	.28630	.27561	.26547	.25584
53	.37550	.36070	.34668	.33339	.32078	.30882	.29746	.28667	.27643	.26669
54	.38717	.37237	.35833	.34500	.33234	.32031	.30888	.29801	.28766	.27782
55	.39903	.38424	.37019	.35683	.34413	.33205	.32056	.30961	.29918	.28925
56	.41108	.39631	.38227	.36890	.35617	.34405	.33250	.32149	.31099	.30097
57	.42330	.40857	.39455	.38118	.36844	.35629	.34469	.33363	.32306	.31297
58	.43566	.42098	.40699	.39364	.38089	.36873	.35710	.34600	.33538	.32522
59	.44811	.43351	.41956	.40623	.39350	.38133	.36968	.35855	.34789	.33768
60	.46066	.44613	.43224	.41896	.40624	.39408	.38243	.37127	.36058	.35033
61	.47330	.45887	.44505	.43182	.41914	.40699	.39535	.38418	.37347	.36318
62	.48608	.47175	.45802	.44485	.43223	.42011	.40848	.39732	.38660	.37629
63	.49898	.48478	.47115	.45807	.44550	.43343	.42184	.41069	.39997	.38966
64	.51200	.49793	.48442	.47143	.45895	.44694	.43539	.42427	.41357	.40326
65	.52512	.51121	.49782	.48495	.47255	.46062	.44912	.43805	.42738	.41709
66	.53835	.52461	.51137	.49862	.48634	.47449	.46307	.45206	.44143	.43118
67	.55174	.53818	.52511	.51250	.50034	.48860	.47727	.46633	.45576	.44556
68	.56524	.55188	.53899	.52654	.51452	.50291	.49168	.48083	.47034	.46020
69	.57882	.56568	.55299	.54071	.52885	.51737	.50627	.49552	.48513	.47506
70	.59242	.57951	.56703	.55495	.54325	.53193	.52096	.51034	.50004	.49007
71	.60598	.59332	.58106	.56918	.55767	.54651	.53569	.52520	.51503	.50516
72	.61948	.60707	.59504	.58338	.57206	.56108	.55043	.54009	.53004	.52029
73	.63287	.62073	.60895	.59751	.58640	.57561	.56513	.55495	.54505	.53543
74	.64621	.63435	.62282	.61162	.60073	.59015	.57985	.56984	.56009	.55061
75	.65953	.64796	.63671	.62575	.61510	.60473	.59463	.58480	.57523	.56591
76	.67287	.66160	.65063	.63995	.62954	.61940	.60952	.59989	.59050	.58135
77	.68622	.67526	.66459	.65419	.64404	.63415	.62450	.61509	.60590	.59694
78	.69954	.68892	.67856	.66845	.65858	.64895	.63955	.63036	.62140	.61264
79	.71278	.70250	.69246	.68265	.67308	.66372	.65457	.64563	.63690	.62836
80	.72581	.71588	.70618	.69668	.68740	.67833	.66945	.66077	.65227	.64396
81	.73857	.72899	.71962	.71045	.70147	.69268	.68408	.67566	.66741	.65933
82	.75101	.74178	.73274	.72389	.71522	.70672	.69840	.69024	.68225	.67441
83	.76311	.75423	.74553	.73700	.72864	.72044	.71240	.70451	.69678	.68919
84	.77497	.76645	.75809	.74988	.74183	.73393	.72618	.71857	.71110	.70377
85	.78665	.77848	.77047	.76260	.75487	.74728	.73982	.73250	.72530	.71823
86	.79805	.79025	.78258	.77504	.76764	.76036	.75320	.74617	.73925	.73245
87	.80904	.80159	.79427	.78706	.77998	.77301	.76615	.75940	.75277	.74624
88	.81962	.81251	.80552	.79865	.79188	.78521	.77865	.77220	.76584	.75958
89	.82978	.82302	.81636	.80980	.80335	.79699	.79072	.78455	.77847	.77248
90	.83952	.83309	.82676	.82052	.81437	.80831	.80234	.79645	.79064	.78492
91	.84870	.84260	.83658	.83064	.82479	.81902	.81332	.80771	.80217	.79671
92	.85716	.85136	.84563	.83998	.83441	.82891	.82348	.81812	.81283	.80761
93	.86494	.85942	.85396	.84858	.84326	.83801	.83283	.82771	.82266	.81767
94	.87216	.86690	.86170	.85657	.85149	.84648	.84153	.83664	.83181	.82704
95	.87898	.87397	.86902	.86412	.85928	.85450	.84977	.84510	.84049	.83592
96	.88537	.88060	.87587	.87121	.86659	.86203	.85751	.85305	.84864	.84427
97	.89127	.88672	.88221	.87775	.87335	.86898	.86467	.86040	.85618	.85200
98	.89680	.89245	.88815	.88389	.87968	.87551	.87138	.86730	.86326	.85926
99	.90217	.89803	.89393	.88987	.88585	.88187	.87793	.87402	.87016	.86633
100	.90738	.90344	.89953	.89567	.89183	.88804	.88428	.88056	.87687	.87322
101	.91250	.90876	.90504	.90137	.89772	.89412	.89054	.88699	.88348	.88000
102	.91751	.91396	.91045	.90696	.90350	.90007	.89668	.89331	.88997	.88666
103	.92247	.91912	.91579	.91249	.90922	.90598	.90276	.89957	.89640	.89326
104	.92775	.92460	.92148	.91839	.91532	.91227	.90924	.90624	.90326	.90031
105	.93290	.92996	.92704	.92415	.92127	.91841	.91558	.91276	.90997	.90719
106	.93948	.93680	.93415	.93151	.92889	.92628	.92370	.92113	.91857	.91604
107	.94739	.94504	.94271	.94039	.93808	.93579	.93351	.93124	.92899	.92675

AGE	4.2%	4.4%	4.6%	4.8%	5.0%	5.2%	5.4%	5.6%	5.8%	6.0%
108	.95950	.95767	.95585	.95404	.95224	.95045	.94867	.94689	.94512	.94336
109	.97985	.97893	.97801	.97710	.97619	.97529	.97438	.97348	.97259	.97170

TABLE S
BASED ON LIFE TABLE 90CM
SINGLE LIFE REMAINDER FACTORS
[APPLICABLE AFTER APRIL 30, 1999, AND BEFORE MAY 1, 2009]
INTEREST RATE

AGE	6.2%	6.4%	6.6%	6.8%	7.0%	7.2%	7.4%	7.6%	7.8%	8.0%
0	.03034	.02857	.02700	.02559	.02433	.02321	.02220	.02129	.02047	.01973
1	.02279	.02094	.01929	.01782	.01650	.01533	.01427	.01331	.01246	.01168
2	.02347	.02155	.01983	.01829	.01692	.01569	.01458	.01358	.01268	.01187
3	.02444	.02243	.02065	.01905	.01761	.01632	.01516	.01412	.01317	.01232
4	.02558	.02349	.02163	.01996	.01846	.01712	.01590	.01481	.01382	.01292
5	.02686	.02469	.02275	.02101	.01945	.01804	.01677	.01562	.01458	.01364
6	.02825	.02600	.02398	.02217	.02053	.01906	.01773	.01653	.01544	.01445
7	.02976	.02742	.02532	.02343	.02172	.02019	.01880	.01754	.01640	.01536
8	.03137	.02894	.02675	.02479	.02301	.02140	.01995	.01864	.01744	.01635
9	.03311	.03059	.02832	.02627	.02442	.02274	.02122	.01985	.01859	.01745
10	.03499	.03237	.03001	.02788	.02595	.02420	.02262	.02118	.01987	.01867
11	.03700	.03428	.03183	.02961	.02760	.02578	.02413	.02262	.02125	.02000
12	.03913	.03632	.03377	.03146	.02937	.02748	.02575	.02418	.02275	.02144
13	.04135	.03843	.03579	.03339	.03122	.02924	.02744	.02580	.02431	.02294
14	.04359	.04057	.03783	.03534	.03308	.03102	.02915	.02744	.02587	.02444
15	.04584	.04270	.03986	.03728	.03493	.03279	.03083	.02905	.02742	.02593
16	.04806	.04482	.04187	.03919	.03674	.03452	.03248	.03063	.02892	.02736
17	.05029	.04692	.04387	.04108	.03855	.03623	.03411	.03218	.03040	.02877
18	.05253	.04905	.04588	.04299	.04036	.03795	.03574	.03373	.03187	.03017
19	.05484	.05124	.04796	.04496	.04222	.03972	.03742	.03532	.03339	.03161
20	.05726	.05354	.05013	.04702	.04418	.04158	.03919	.03700	.03498	.03313
21	.05980	.05595	.05242	.04920	.04625	.04354	.04105	.03877	.03667	.03473
22	.06246	.05847	.05482	.05147	.04841	.04559	.04301	.04063	.03844	.03642
23	.06524	.06112	.05734	.05387	.05069	.04777	.04508	.04260	.04032	.03821
24	.06819	.06392	.06001	.05642	.05312	.05008	.04728	.04470	.04232	.04012
25	.07131	.06690	.06285	.05913	.05570	.05255	.04964	.04695	.04447	.04218
26	.07460	.07005	.06586	.06200	.05845	.05518	.05215	.04936	.04677	.04438
27	.07810	.07340	.06907	.06508	.06140	.05800	.05485	.05195	.04925	.04676
28	.08179	.07693	.07246	.06833	.06451	.06098	.05772	.05469	.05189	.04929
29	.08566	.08065	.07603	.07176	.06780	.06414	.06075	.05761	.05469	.05198
30	.08973	.08456	.07978	.07536	.07127	.06748	.06396	.06069	.05766	.05483
31	.09398	.08865	.08372	.07915	.07491	.07098	.06733	.06394	.06078	.05785
32	.09843	.09294	.08785	.08313	.07875	.07468	.07089	.06737	.06409	.06103
33	.10310	.09745	.09220	.08732	.08279	.07858	.07466	.07100	.06759	.06441
34	.10799	.10217	.09676	.09173	.08705	.08269	.07862	.07483	.07129	.06798
35	.11314	.10715	.10157	.09638	.09155	.08704	.08283	.07890	.07522	.07179
36	.11852	.11236	.10662	.10127	.09628	.09162	.08726	.08319	.07938	.07581
37	.12416	.11783	.11193	.10641	.10126	.09645	.09194	.08772	.08377	.08006
38	.13009	.12359	.11751	.11183	.10652	.10155	.09689	.09253	.08843	.08459
39	.13629	.12962	.12338	.11753	.11206	.10693	.10212	.09761	.09337	.08938
40	.14281	.13597	.12955	.12355	.11791	.11262	.10766	.10299	.09860	.09447
41	.14966	.14264	.13606	.12989	.12409	.11864	.11352	.10870	.10417	.09989
42	.15685	.14966	.14291	.13657	.13061	.12500	.11972	.11475	.11006	.10564
43	.16437	.15702	.15010	.14360	.13747	.13171	.12627	.12115	.11631	.11174
44	.17224	.16472	.15764	.15098	.14469	.13876	.13317	.12789	.12290	.11819
45	.18042	.17274	.16550	.15867	.15223	.14615	.14040	.13496	.12982	.12496
46	.18893	.18110	.17370	.16671	.16011	.15387	.14796	.14238	.13708	.13207
47	.19775	.18975	.18220	.17505	.16830	.16190	.15584	.15010	.14466	.13950
48	.20688	.19873	.19102	.18373	.17682	.17027	.16406	.15817	.15258	.14727

See p. 15 for regulations not amended to reflect law changes

AGE	6.2%	6.4%	6.6%	6.8%	7.0%	7.2%	7.4%	7.6%	7.8%	8.0%
49	.21633	.20804	.20018	.19274	.18568	.17898	.17262	.16658	.16084	.15539
50	.22612	.21769	.20969	.20210	.19490	.18805	.18155	.17536	.16948	.16388
51	.23625	.22769	.21955	.21182	.20448	.19749	.19084	.18452	.17849	.17275
52	.24669	.23799	.22973	.22186	.21438	.20726	.20047	.19400	.18784	.18196
53	.25742	.24861	.24022	.23222	.22461	.21735	.21043	.20383	.19753	.19151
54	.26845	.25952	.25101	.24290	.23516	.22777	.22072	.21399	.20756	.20140
55	.27978	.27074	.26212	.25389	.24604	.23853	.23136	.22450	.21793	.21166
56	.29140	.28227	.27355	.26522	.25725	.24963	.24233	.23535	.22867	.22227
57	.30333	.29411	.28529	.27686	.26879	.26106	.25365	.24656	.23976	.23324
58	.31551	.30621	.29731	.28878	.28061	.27278	.26528	.25807	.25116	.24453
59	.32790	.31854	.30956	.30095	.29269	.28477	.27716	.26986	.26284	.25610
60	.34050	.33107	.32202	.31334	.30500	.29699	.28929	.28190	.27478	.26794
61	.35331	.34384	.33473	.32598	.31757	.30948	.30170	.29422	.28701	.28007
62	.36639	.35688	.34772	.33892	.33044	.32229	.31443	.30687	.29958	.29255
63	.37974	.37020	.36101	.35216	.34363	.33542	.32750	.31986	.31250	.30539
64	.39334	.38378	.37456	.36568	.35711	.34884	.34087	.33317	.32574	.31857
65	.40718	.39761	.38838	.37947	.37087	.36257	.35455	.34681	.33932	.33208
66	.42128	.41172	.40249	.39357	.38496	.37663	.36858	.36079	.35326	.34597
67	.43569	.42616	.41694	.40803	.39941	.39107	.38299	.37518	.36761	.36028
68	.45038	.44089	.43170	.42281	.41419	.40585	.39777	.38994	.38235	.37499
69	.46531	.45587	.44672	.43786	.42927	.42094	.41286	.40503	.39743	.39006
70	.48040	.47103	.46194	.45312	.44456	.43626	.42820	.42038	.41278	.40540
71	.49558	.48629	.47727	.46851	.46000	.45174	.44371	.43591	.42832	.42095
72	.51082	.50162	.49268	.48399	.47554	.46733	.45934	.45157	.44401	.43666
73	.52607	.51697	.50813	.49952	.49114	.48299	.47506	.46733	.45981	.45249
74	.54139	.53241	.52367	.51515	.50686	.49879	.49092	.48325	.47578	.46849
75	.55683	.54798	.53936	.53095	.52276	.51477	.50698	.49938	.49197	.48474
76	.57243	.56373	.55524	.54696	.53888	.53100	.52330	.51579	.50846	.50130
77	.58819	.57965	.57132	.56318	.55523	.54747	.53988	.53247	.52523	.51815
78	.60408	.59572	.58755	.57957	.57177	.56414	.55668	.54939	.54225	.53527
79	.62001	.61184	.60385	.59604	.58840	.58092	.57360	.56644	.55943	.55256
80	.63582	.62786	.62007	.61244	.60497	.59765	.59048	.58347	.57659	.56985
81	.65142	.64367	.63608	.62864	.62135	.61421	.60721	.60034	.59361	.58701
82	.66673	.65920	.65182	.64458	.63748	.63052	.62368	.61698	.61041	.60395
83	.68175	.67444	.66728	.66024	.65334	.64656	.63991	.63338	.62696	.62066
84	.69657	.68950	.68256	.67574	.66904	.66246	.65599	.64964	.64340	.63727
85	.71128	.70446	.69775	.69116	.68467	.67830	.67204	.66587	.65982	.65386
86	.72576	.71919	.71272	.70636	.70010	.69394	.68789	.68193	.67606	.67029
87	.73981	.73349	.72726	.72114	.71511	.70917	.70333	.69757	.69190	.68632
88	.75342	.74735	.74137	.73548	.72968	.72396	.71833	.71279	.70732	.70194
89	.76658	.76076	.75503	.74938	.74381	.73832	.73290	.72757	.72231	.71712
90	.77928	.77371	.76823	.76281	.75748	.75221	.74702	.74190	.73684	.73186
91	.79131	.78600	.78075	.77557	.77046	.76542	.76044	.75553	.75068	.74589
92	.80246	.79737	.79235	.78740	.78250	.77767	.77290	.76818	.76353	.75893
93	.81274	.80788	.80307	.79832	.79363	.78899	.78441	.77989	.77542	.77100
94	.82232	.81766	.81306	.80850	.80401	.79956	.79517	.79082	.78653	.78228
95	.83141	.82695	.82254	.81818	.81387	.80961	.80539	.80122	.79710	.79302
96	.83996	.83569	.83147	.82729	.82316	.81907	.81503	.81103	.80707	.80315
97	.84787	.84378	.83973	.83573	.83176	.82784	.82396	.82012	.81632	.81255
98	.85530	.85138	.84750	.84366	.83985	.83609	.83236	.82867	.82502	.82140
99	.86255	.85880	.85508	.85140	.84776	.84415	.84057	.83703	.83353	.83005
100	.86960	.86601	.86246	.85894	.85546	.85200	.84858	.84519	.84183	.83849
101	.87655	.87313	.86974	.86638	.86305	.85975	.85648	.85324	.85003	.84684
102	.88338	.88012	.87689	.87369	.87052	.86738	.86426	.86116	.85809	.85505
103	.89015	.88706	.88399	.88095	.87793	.87494	.87197	.86903	.86611	.86321
104	.89737	.89446	.89157	.88871	.88586	.88304	.88024	.87745	.87469	.87195

AGE	6.2%	6.4%	6.6%	6.8%	7.0%	7.2%	7.4%	7.6%	7.8%	8.0%
105	.90443	.90170	.89898	.89628	.89360	.89094	.88830	.88568	.88307	.88049
106	.91351	.91101	.90852	.90605	.90359	.90115	.89873	.89632	.89392	.89154
107	.92452	.92230	.92010	.91791	.91573	.91356	.91141	.90927	.90714	.90502
108	.94161	.93987	.93814	.93641	.93469	.93298	.93128	.92958	.92790	.92622
109	.97081	.96992	.96904	.96816	.96729	.96642	.96555	.96468	.96382	.96296

TABLE S
BASED ON LIFE TABLE 90CM
SINGLE LIFE REMAINDER FACTORS
[APPLICABLE AFTER APRIL 30, 1999, AND BEFORE MAY 1, 2009]
INTEREST RATE

AGE	8.2%	8.4%	8.6%	8.8%	9.0%	9.2%	9.4%	9.6%	9.8%	10.0%
0	.01906	.01845	.01790	.01740	.01694	.01652	.01613	.01578	.01546	.01516
1	.01098	.01034	.00977	.00924	.00876	.00833	.00793	.00756	.00722	.00691
2	.01113	.01046	.00986	.00930	.00880	.00834	.00791	.00753	.00717	.00684
3	.01155	.01084	.01020	.00962	.00909	.00860	.00816	.00775	.00737	.00702
4	.01211	.01137	.01069	.01008	.00952	.00900	.00853	.00810	.00770	.00733
5	.01279	.01201	.01130	.01065	.01006	.00952	.00902	.00856	.00814	.00775
6	.01356	.01274	.01199	.01131	.01068	.01011	.00959	.00910	.00865	.00824
7	.01442	.01356	.01277	.01205	.01140	.01079	.01023	.00972	.00925	.00881
8	.01536	.01446	.01363	.01287	.01218	.01154	.01096	.01041	.00991	.00945
9	.01641	.01546	.01460	.01380	.01307	.01240	.01178	.01120	.01068	.01019
10	.01758	.01659	.01567	.01484	.01407	.01336	.01270	.01210	.01154	.01103
11	.01886	.01781	.01686	.01598	.01517	.01442	.01373	.01310	.01251	.01196
12	.02024	.01915	.01814	.01721	.01636	.01558	.01485	.01419	.01357	.01299
13	.02168	.02054	.01948	.01851	.01762	.01679	.01603	.01533	.01467	.01407
14	.02313	.02193	.02083	.01981	.01887	.01801	.01721	.01646	.01578	.01514
15	.02456	.02330	.02214	.02107	.02009	.01918	.01834	.01756	.01634	.01617
16	.02593	.02462	.02340	.02229	.02126	.02030	.01942	.01860	.01735	.01714
17	.02728	.02590	.02463	.02346	.02238	.02138	.02046	.01960	.01880	.01806
18	.02861	.02717	.02584	.02462	.02348	.02243	.02146	.02056	.01972	.01894
19	.02998	.02847	.02708	.02580	.02461	.02351	.02249	.02154	.02066	.01984
20	.03142	.02984	.02839	.02704	.02580	.02465	.02357	.02258	.02165	.02079
21	.03295	.03130	.02978	.02837	.02706	.02585	.02473	.02368	.02271	.02180
22	.03455	.03283	.03124	.02976	.02839	.02712	.02594	.02484	.02382	.02286
23	.03626	.03446	.03279	.03124	.02981	.02847	.02723	.02608	.02500	.02400
24	.03809	.03620	.03446	.03283	.03133	.02993	.02863	.02741	.02628	.02522
25	.04005	.03808	.03625	.03456	.03298	.03151	.03014	.02887	.02768	.02656
26	.04216	.04010	.03819	.03641	.03476	.03322	.03178	.03044	.02919	.02802
27	.04444	.04229	.04029	.03843	.03670	.03508	.03357	.03217	.03085	.02962
28	.04687	.04463	.04254	.04059	.03877	.03708	.03550	.03402	.03263	.03133
29	.04946	.04712	.04493	.04289	.04099	.03922	.03756	.03600	.03455	.03318
30	.05221	.04976	.04748	.04534	.04335	.04149	.03975	.03812	.03659	.03515
31	.05511	.05255	.05017	.04794	.04585	.04390	.04208	.04037	.03876	.03725
32	.05818	.05551	.05302	.05069	.04851	.04647	.04455	.04276	.04107	.03948
33	.06144	.05866	.05606	.05363	.05135	.04921	.04720	.04532	.04355	.04188
34	.06489	.06200	.05928	.05674	.05436	.05212	.05002	.04805	.04619	.04444
35	.06857	.06555	.06273	.06007	.05758	.05524	.05304	.05097	.04902	.04718
36	.07246	.06932	.06638	.06361	.06101	.05856	.05626	.05409	.05205	.05012
37	.07659	.07332	.07025	.06737	.06466	.06210	.05969	.05742	.05528	.05325
38	.08098	.07758	.07439	.07138	.06855	.06588	.06336	.06099	.05874	.05662
39	.08563	.08210	.07878	.07565	.07270	.06992	.06729	.06480	.06245	.06023
40	.09059	.08692	.08347	.08021	.07714	.07423	.07149	.06889	.06643	.06411
41	.09586	.09206	.08848	.08509	.08189	.07886	.07600	.07329	.07072	.06828
42	.10147	.09753	.09381	.09029	.08696	.08381	.08083	.07800	.07531	.07277
43	.10742	.10334	.09948	.09583	.09237	.08909	.08598	.08304	.08024	.07758
44	.11373	.10950	.10551	.10172	.09813	.09472	.09148	.08841	.08549	.08272

See p. 15 for regulations not amended to reflect law changes

AGE	8.2%	8.4%	8.6%	8.8%	9.0%	9.2%	9.4%	9.6%	9.8%	10.0%
45	.12035	.11599	.11185	.10792	.10420	.10066	.09730	.09410	.09106	.08817
46	.12732	.12281	.11853	.11447	.11061	.10694	.10345	.10013	.09696	.09395
47	.13460	.12995	.12553	.12133	.11733	.11353	.10991	.10646	.10317	.10004
48	.14223	.13743	.13287	.12853	.12439	.12046	.11671	.11313	.10972	.10646
49	.15020	.14526	.14056	.13608	.13181	.12774	.12385	.12015	.11661	.11322
50	.15855	.15347	.14862	.14401	.13960	.13540	.13138	.12754	.12388	.12037
51	.16727	.16205	.15707	.15232	.14777	.14344	.13929	.13532	.13153	.12789
52	.17634	.17098	.16587	.16097	.15630	.15183	.14755	.14345	.13953	.13577
53	.18576	.18027	.17501	.16999	.16518	.16057	.15616	.15194	.14789	.14400
54	.19552	.18990	.18451	.17935	.17441	.16968	.16514	.16078	.15661	.15260
55	.20564	.19989	.19437	.18908	.18402	.17915	.17449	.17001	.16571	.16157
56	.21613	.21025	.20461	.19919	.19400	.18901	.18422	.17962	.17519	.17093
57	.22698	.22098	.21522	.20968	.20436	.19925	.19434	.18961	.18507	.18069
58	.23816	.23204	.22616	.22051	.21507	.20984	.20481	.19996	.19530	.19080
59	.24962	.24339	.23740	.23163	.22608	.22073	.21558	.21062	.20584	.20123
60	.26136	.25502	.24892	.24304	.23738	.23192	.22666	.22158	.21669	.21196
61	.27339	.26695	.26075	.25477	.24900	.24343	.23806	.23288	.22787	.22304
62	.28578	.27925	.27295	.26687	.26100	.25533	.24985	.24456	.23945	.23451
63	.29854	.29192	.28553	.27935	.27339	.26762	.26205	.25666	.25145	.24641
64	.31164	.30494	.29846	.29221	.28615	.28030	.27463	.26915	.26384	.25870
65	.32508	.31831	.31177	.30543	.29930	.29336	.28761	.28203	.27663	.27140
66	.33891	.33208	.32547	.31906	.31285	.30684	.30101	.29536	.28987	.28456
67	.35318	.34630	.33963	.33316	.32689	.32081	.31491	.30918	.30363	.29823
68	.36785	.36093	.35422	.34770	.34138	.33524	.32928	.32349	.31787	.31240
69	.38290	.37595	.36920	.36265	.35628	.35009	.34408	.33824	.33256	.32703
70	.39823	.39127	.38450	.37791	.37151	.36529	.35924	.35335	.34762	.34204
71	.41378	.40681	.40003	.39343	.38701	.38076	.37467	.36875	.36298	.35736
72	.42950	.42253	.41575	.40914	.40271	.39644	.39034	.38438	.37858	.37293
73	.44535	.43840	.43162	.42502	.41858	.41231	.40619	.40022	.39440	.38872
74	.46139	.45446	.44771	.44112	.43469	.42842	.42230	.41632	.41049	.40479
75	.47769	.47080	.46408	.45752	.45111	.44485	.43874	.43277	.42693	.42123
76	.49430	.48747	.48079	.47427	.46790	.46167	.45558	.44963	.44380	.43811
77	.51123	.50447	.49786	.49139	.48506	.47888	.47282	.46690	.46111	.45543
78	.52845	.52177	.51523	.50884	.50257	.49645	.49044	.48457	.47881	.47317
79	.54584	.53926	.53282	.52650	.52032	.51426	.50833	.50251	.49681	.49122
80	.56325	.55678	.55044	.54423	.53813	.53216	.52630	.52056	.51492	.50939
81	.58054	.57419	.56797	.56186	.55587	.54999	.54422	.53856	.53300	.52754
82	.59762	.59140	.58530	.57931	.57343	.56766	.56198	.55641	.55094	.54557
83	.61448	.60840	.60243	.59657	.59081	.58515	.57958	.57411	.56874	.56346
84	.63124	.62531	.61949	.61376	.60813	.60259	.59715	.59179	.58652	.58134
85	.64800	.64224	.63657	.63099	.62550	.62010	.61478	.60955	.60441	.59934
86	.66461	.65902	.65351	.64810	.64276	.63751	.63233	.62724	.62222	.61728
87	.68083	.67541	.67008	.66483	.65965	.65455	.64953	.64458	.63970	.63489
88	.69663	.69140	.68624	.68116	.67615	.67121	.66634	.66154	.65680	.65213
89	.71201	.70696	.70199	.69708	.69224	.68747	.68276	.67811	.67353	.66900
90	.72694	.72209	.71730	.71257	.70791	.70330	.69876	.69427	.68984	.68547
91	.74117	.73650	.73190	.72735	.72286	.71842	.71404	.70972	.70545	.70123
92	.75439	.74991	.74548	.74110	.73678	.73251	.72829	.72412	.72000	.71593
93	.76664	.76233	.75806	.75385	.74969	.74557	.74150	.73748	.73350	.72957
94	.77809	.77394	.76983	.76578	.76177	.75780	.75388	.75000	.74616	.74237
95	.78899	.78500	.78106	.77715	.77329	.76947	.76569	.76195	.75826	.75460
96	.79928	.79544	.79165	.78790	.78418	.78050	.77686	.77326	.76970	.76617
97	.80883	.80514	.80149	.79787	.79430	.79075	.78725	.78377	.78033	.77693
98	.81781	.81427	.81075	.80727	.80382	.80041	.79703	.79368	.79036	.78708
99	.82661	.82320	.81982	.81648	.81316	.80988	.80662	.80340	.80020	.79704
100	.83519	.83192	.82868	.82547	.82228	.81913	.81600	.81290	.80982	.80678

AGE	8.2%	8.4%	8.6%	8.8%	9.0%	9.2%	9.4%	9.6%	9.8%	10.0%
101	.84368	.84055	.83744	.83437	.83131	.82829	.82529	.82231	.81936	.81643
102	.85203	.84904	.84607	.84313	.84021	.83731	.83444	.83159	.82876	.82596
103	.86034	.85748	.85465	.85184	.84906	.84629	.84355	.84082	.83812	.83544
104	.86923	.86653	.86385	.86119	.85855	.85593	.85333	.85074	.84818	.84563
105	.87792	.87537	.87283	.87032	.86782	.86534	.86287	.86042	.85799	.85557
106	.88918	.88683	.88450	.88218	.87987	.87758	.87530	.87304	.87079	.86855
107	.90291	.90082	.89873	.89666	.89460	.89255	.89051	.88849	.88647	.88447
108	.92455	.92288	.92123	.91958	.91794	.91630	.91468	.91306	.91145	.90984
109	.96211	.96125	.96041	.95956	.95872	.95788	.95704	.95620	.95537	.95455

TABLE S
BASED ON LIFE TABLE 90CM
SINGLE LIFE REMAINDER FACTORS
[APPLICABLE AFTER APRIL 30, 1999, AND BEFORE MAY 1, 2009]
INTEREST RATE

AGE	10.2%	10.4%	10.6%	10.8%	11.0%	11.2%	11.4%	11.6%	11.8%	12.0%
0	.01488	.01463	.01439	.01417	.01396	.01377	.01359	.01343	.01327	.01312
1	.00662	.00636	.00612	.00589	.00568	.00548	.00530	.00513	.00497	.00482
2	.00654	.00626	.00600	.00576	.00554	.00533	.00514	.00496	.00479	.00463
3	.00670	.00641	.00613	.00588	.00564	.00542	.00522	.00502	.00484	.00468
4	.00699	.00668	.00639	.00612	.00587	.00563	.00542	.00521	.00502	.00484
5	.00739	.00706	.00675	.00646	.00620	.00595	.00571	.00550	.00529	.00510
6	.00786	.00751	.00718	.00687	.00659	.00633	.00608	.00585	.00563	.00543
7	.00841	.00803	.00769	.00736	.00706	.00678	.00652	.00627	.00604	.00582
8	.00902	.00863	.00826	.00791	.00759	.00730	.00702	.00675	.00651	.00628
9	.00973	.00931	.00892	.00856	.00822	.00790	.00760	.00733	.00706	.00682
10	.01055	.01010	.00969	.00930	.00894	.00861	.00829	.00799	.00772	.00746
11	.01146	.01099	.01055	.01014	.00976	.00940	.00907	.00875	.00846	.00818
12	.01246	.01196	.01150	.01106	.01066	.01028	.00993	.00960	.00928	.00899
13	.01351	.01298	.01249	.01204	.01161	.01121	.01084	.01049	.01016	.00985
14	.01455	.01400	.01348	.01300	.01255	.01213	.01173	.01136	.01102	.01069
15	.01555	.01497	.01443	.01392	.01345	.01300	.01259	.01220	.01183	.01148
16	.01648	.01587	.01530	.01477	.01427	.01380	.01336	.01295	.01257	.01220
17	.01737	.01673	.01612	.01556	.01504	.01455	.01408	.01365	.01324	.01286
18	.01822	.01754	.01691	.01632	.01576	.01525	.01476	.01430	.01387	.01347
19	.01908	.01837	.01770	.01708	.01650	.01595	.01544	.01495	.01450	.01407
20	.01999	.01924	.01854	.01788	.01726	.01669	.01615	.01564	.01516	.01471
21	.02096	.02017	.01943	.01874	.01809	.01748	.01691	.01637	.01585	.01539
22	.02197	.02114	.02036	.01963	.01895	.01830	.01770	.01713	.01660	.01610
23	.02306	.02218	.02136	.02059	.01987	.01919	.01855	.01795	.01739	.01686
24	.02424	.02331	.02245	.02163	.02087	.02016	.01948	.01885	.01825	.01769
25	.02552	.02455	.02364	.02278	.02197	.02122	.02051	.01984	.01920	.01861
26	.02692	.02589	.02493	.02403	.02318	.02238	.02162	.02091	.02025	.01961
27	.02846	.02738	.02636	.02541	.02451	.02367	.02287	.02212	.02141	.02074
28	.03012	.02898	.02791	.02690	.02595	.02506	.02422	.02342	.02267	.02196
29	.03190	.03070	.02957	.02851	.02751	.02656	.02567	.02483	.02404	.02329
30	.03381	.03254	.03135	.03023	.02917	.02817	.02723	.02634	.02551	.02471
31	.03583	.03450	.03324	.03206	.03094	.02989	.02890	.02796	.02707	.02623
32	.03799	.03659	.03527	.03402	.03284	.03173	.03068	.02968	.02874	.02785
33	.04031	.03883	.03744	.03612	.03488	.03371	.03260	.03155	.03055	.02961
34	.04279	.04123	.03976	.03838	.03707	.03583	.03465	.03354	.03249	.03149
35	.04545	.04382	.04227	.04081	.03943	.03812	.03688	.03571	.03459	.03354
36	.04830	.04658	.04495	.04341	.04196	.04058	.03927	.03803	.03685	.03573
37	.05134	.04953	.04782	.04620	.04467	.04321	.04183	.04052	.03928	.03809
38	.05462	.05272	.05092	.04921	.04760	.04606	.04461	.04322	.04191	.04066
39	.05812	.05613	.05424	.05245	.05075	.04913	.04760	.04614	.04475	.04343
40	.06190	.05981	.05782	.05594	.05415	.05245	.05083	.04929	.04783	.04643
41	.06597	.06378	.06170	.05972	.05784	.05605	.05435	.05272	.05118	.04970

See p. 15 for regulations not amended to reflect law changes

AGE	10.2%	10.4%	10.6%	10.8%	11.0%	11.2%	11.4%	11.6%	11.8%	12.0%
42	.07035	.06806	.06587	.06380	.06182	.05994	.05815	.05644	.05481	.05326
43	.07505	.07265	.07036	.06818	.06611	.06414	.06225	.06045	.05874	.05710
44	.08008	.07757	.07518	.07290	.07072	.06865	.06667	.06478	.06298	.06125
45	.08542	.08279	.08029	.07791	.07563	.07346	.07138	.06940	.06750	.06569
46	.09108	.08834	.08573	.08324	.08085	.07858	.07640	.07432	.07233	.07043
47	.09705	.09419	.09147	.08886	.08637	.08399	.08172	.07954	.07745	.07545
48	.10335	.10038	.09754	.09482	.09222	.08973	.08735	.08507	.08288	.08078
49	.10999	.10690	.10394	.10111	.09840	.09581	.09332	.09093	.08864	.08644
50	.11701	.11380	.11073	.10778	.10496	.10225	.09965	.09716	.09477	.09247
51	.12441	.12108	.11789	.11482	.11189	.10907	.10636	.10376	.10126	.09886
52	.13217	.12871	.12540	.12222	.11916	.11623	.11341	.11071	.10810	.10560
53	.14028	.13670	.13327	.12997	.12680	.12375	.12082	.11801	.11529	.11268
54	.14875	.14505	.14150	.13808	.13480	.13163	.12859	.12566	.12284	.12012
55	.15760	.15378	.15011	.14657	.14317	.13989	.13674	.13370	.13077	.12794
56	.16684	.16290	.15911	.15546	.15194	.14855	.14528	.14213	.13909	.13615
57	.17648	.17242	.16851	.16474	.16111	.15760	.15422	.15096	.14781	.14477
58	.18647	.18229	.17827	.17438	.17064	.16702	.16353	.16015	.15689	.15374
59	.19678	.19249	.18835	.18435	.18049	.17676	.17316	.16968	.16631	.16305
60	.20740	.20300	.19875	.19464	.19066	.18682	.18311	.17952	.17604	.17268
61	.21837	.21385	.20949	.20527	.20119	.19724	.19341	.18971	.18613	.18266
62	.22973	.22511	.22064	.21631	.21212	.20807	.20414	.20033	.19664	.19306
63	.24152	.23680	.23222	.22779	.22350	.21934	.21530	.21139	.20760	.20392
64	.25372	.24890	.24422	.23969	.23529	.23103	.22690	.22289	.21899	.21521
65	.26633	.26141	.25664	.25201	.24752	.24316	.23893	.23482	.23083	.22695
66	.27940	.27439	.26953	.26481	.26023	.25577	.25145	.24724	.24316	.23918
67	.29299	.28790	.28296	.27815	.27348	.26894	.26453	.26024	.25606	.25200
68	.30709	.30193	.29691	.29202	.28728	.28265	.27816	.27378	.26952	.26537
69	.32166	.31643	.31134	.30639	.30157	.29687	.29230	.28785	.28351	.27928
70	.33661	.33133	.32618	.32116	.31628	.31152	.30688	.30235	.29794	.29364
71	.35188	.34654	.34134	.33627	.33133	.32651	.32181	.31722	.31275	.30838
72	.36742	.36204	.35679	.35168	.34668	.34181	.33706	.33241	.32788	.32345
73	.38317	.37776	.37248	.36733	.36229	.35738	.35257	.34788	.34330	.33882
74	.39923	.39380	.38849	.38330	.37823	.37328	.36844	.36370	.35908	.35455
75	.41566	.41021	.40489	.39968	.39459	.38961	.38474	.37997	.37531	.37074
76	.43254	.42709	.42176	.41655	.41144	.40645	.40156	.39677	.39208	.38749
77	.44988	.44444	.43912	.43391	.42880	.42380	.41891	.41411	.40940	.40479
78	.46765	.46224	.45694	.45174	.44665	.44166	.43677	.43197	.42726	.42265
79	.48574	.48037	.47510	.46993	.46487	.45990	.45502	.45024	.44554	.44094
80	.50397	.49865	.49343	.48830	.48327	.47834	.47349	.46873	.46406	.45947
81	.52219	.51693	.51176	.50669	.50171	.49682	.49201	.48729	.48265	.47809
82	.54029	.53510	.53000	.52499	.52007	.51523	.51047	.50580	.50120	.49667
83	.55826	.55315	.54813	.54319	.53834	.53356	.52886	.52424	.51969	.51522
84	.57624	.57123	.56629	.56144	.55666	.55195	.54732	.54277	.53828	.53386
85	.59435	.58944	.58460	.57984	.57516	.57054	.56599	.56151	.55710	.55275
86	.61241	.60762	.60289	.59824	.59365	.58913	.58468	.58029	.57596	.57170
87	.63015	.62548	.62087	.61633	.61185	.60744	.60309	.59880	.59456	.59039
88	.64753	.64299	.63851	.63409	.62973	.62543	.62118	.61700	.61287	.60879
89	.66454	.66013	.65579	.65150	.64726	.64308	.63895	.63488	.63086	.62689
90	.68115	.67689	.67268	.66853	.66442	.66037	.65637	.65241	.64851	.64465
91	.69706	.69294	.68887	.68486	.68089	.67696	.67309	.66925	.66547	.66173
92	.71190	.70792	.70399	.70011	.69627	.69247	.68872	.68501	.68134	.67771
93	.72569	.72184	.71804	.71429	.71057	.70689	.70326	.69967	.69611	.69259
94	.73861	.73490	.73123	.72759	.72400	.72044	.71692	.71344	.71000	.70659
95	.75097	.74739	.74384	.74033	.73686	.73342	.73002	.72665	.72331	.72001
96	.76267	.75922	.75579	.75240	.74905	.74572	.74243	.73917	.73595	.73275
97	.77356	.77022	.76691	.76363	.76039	.75718	.75399	.75084	.74772	.74463

AGE	10.2%	10.4%	10.6%	10.8%	11.0%	11.2%	11.4%	11.6%	11.8%	12.0%
98	.78382	.78059	.77740	.77423	.77110	.76799	.76491	.76186	.75884	.75584
99	.79390	.79079	.78771	.78465	.78162	.77862	.77565	.77270	.76978	.76688
100	.80376	.80076	.79779	.79485	.79193	.78904	.78617	.78333	.78051	.77771
101	.81353	.81066	.80780	.80497	.80217	.79938	.79662	.79388	.79117	.78847
102	.82318	.82042	.81768	.81496	.81227	.80960	.80694	.80431	.80170	.79911
103	.83278	.83014	.82752	.82491	.82233	.81977	.81723	.81470	.81220	.80971
104	.84310	.84059	.83810	.83563	.83317	.83073	.82831	.82591	.82352	.82115
105	.85318	.85079	.84843	.84607	.84374	.84142	.83911	.83682	.83455	.83229
106	.86633	.86413	.86193	.85975	.85758	.85543	.85329	.85116	.84904	.84694
107	.88247	.88049	.87852	.87656	.87460	.87266	.87073	.86881	.86690	.86500
108	.90825	.90666	.90507	.90350	.90193	.90037	.89881	.89727	.89572	.89419
109	.95372	.95290	.95208	.95126	.95045	.94964	.94883	.94803	.94723	.94643

TABLE S
BASED ON LIFE TABLE 90CM
SINGLE LIFE REMAINDER FACTORS
[APPLICABLE AFTER APRIL 30, 1999, AND BEFORE MAY 1, 2009]
INTEREST RATE

AGE	12.2%	12.4%	12.6%	12.8%	13.0%	13.2%	13.4%	13.6%	13.8%	14.0%
0	.01298	.01285	.01273	.01261	.01250	.01240	.01230	.01221	.01212	.01203
1	.00468	.00455	.00443	.00431	.00420	.00410	.00400	.00391	.00382	.00374
2	.00448	.00435	.00421	.00409	.00398	.00387	.00376	.00366	.00357	.00348
3	.00452	.00437	.00423	.00410	.00398	.00386	.00375	.00365	.00355	.00345
4	.00468	.00452	.00437	.00423	.00410	.00397	.00386	.00375	.00364	.00354
5	.00493	.00476	.00460	.00445	.00431	.00418	.00405	.00393	.00382	.00371
6	.00524	.00506	.00489	.00473	.00458	.00444	.00430	.00418	.00406	.00394
7	.00562	.00543	.00525	.00508	.00492	.00477	.00462	.00449	.00436	.00423
8	.00606	.00586	.00566	.00548	.00531	.00515	.00499	.00485	.00471	.00458
9	.00659	.00637	.00616	.00597	.00579	.00561	.00545	.00529	.00514	.00500
10	.00721	.00698	.00676	.00655	.00636	.00617	.00600	.00583	.00567	.00552
11	.00792	.00767	.00744	.00722	.00701	.00682	.00663	.00645	.00628	.00612
12	.00871	.00845	.00821	.00797	.00775	.00754	.00735	.00716	.00698	.00681
13	.00955	.00928	.00902	.00877	.00854	.00831	.00810	.00790	.00771	.00753
14	.01038	.01009	.00981	.00955	.00930	.00907	.00885	.00864	.00843	.00824
15	.01116	.01085	.01056	.01028	.01002	.00977	.00954	.00932	.00910	.00890
16	.01186	.01153	.01123	.01094	.01066	.01040	.01015	.00992	.00969	.00948
17	.01250	.01215	.01183	.01152	.01124	.01096	.01070	.01045	.01022	.00999
18	.01308	.01272	.01238	.01206	.01175	.01147	.01119	.01093	.01068	.01044
19	.01367	.01329	.01293	.01259	.01227	.01196	.01167	.01140	.01113	.01088
20	.01428	.01388	.01350	.01314	.01280	.01248	.01217	.01188	.01161	.01134
21	.01494	.01451	.01411	.01373	.01337	.01303	.01271	.01240	.01211	.01183
22	.01562	.01517	.01475	.01435	.01397	.01361	.01326	.01294	.01263	.01233
23	.01635	.01588	.01543	.01501	.01460	.01422	.01386	.01351	.01319	.01287
24	.01716	.01665	.01618	.01573	.01530	.01489	.01451	.01415	.01380	.01347
25	.01804	.01751	.01701	.01653	.01608	.01565	.01524	.01485	.01448	.01413
26	.01902	.01845	.01792	.01741	.01693	.01648	.01604	.01563	.01524	.01487
27	.02011	.01951	.01895	.01841	.01790	.01742	.01696	.01652	.01610	.01571
28	.02129	.02066	.02006	.01949	.01895	.01844	.01795	.01748	.01704	.01662
29	.02258	.02191	.02127	.02067	.02009	.01955	.01903	.01853	.01806	.01762
30	.02396	.02325	.02257	.02193	.02132	.02074	.02019	.01966	.01916	.01869
31	.02543	.02467	.02396	.02328	.02263	.02201	.02143	.02087	.02034	.01983
32	.02701	.02621	.02545	.02472	.02404	.02338	.02276	.02217	.02160	.02106
33	.02871	.02786	.02706	.02629	.02556	.02487	.02420	.02357	.02297	.02240
34	.03054	.02964	.02879	.02797	.02720	.02646	.02576	.02509	.02445	.02383
35	.03253	.03158	.03067	.02981	.02898	.02820	.02745	.02674	.02606	.02541
36	.03467	.03366	.03269	.03178	.03090	.03007	.02928	.02852	.02779	.02710
37	.03697	.03590	.03488	.03391	.03298	.03209	.03125	.03044	.02967	.02893
38	.03947	.03833	.03725	.03622	.03524	.03430	.03340	.03254	.03172	.03094

AGE	12.2%	12.4%	12.6%	12.8%	13.0%	13.2%	13.4%	13.6%	13.8%	14.0%
39	.04217	.04096	.03982	.03873	.03768	.03669	.03573	.03482	.03395	.03312
40	.04510	.04383	.04262	.04146	.04035	.03930	.03828	.03732	.03639	.03550
41	.04830	.04695	.04567	.04445	.04327	.04215	.04108	.04005	.03907	.03812
42	.05177	.05035	.04900	.04770	.04646	.04527	.04413	.04304	.04200	.04100
43	.05553	.05404	.05261	.05123	.04992	.04866	.04746	.04630	.04520	.04413
44	.05960	.05802	.05651	.05506	.05368	.05235	.05107	.04985	.04867	.04754
45	.06395	.06229	.06069	.05917	.05770	.05630	.05495	.05365	.05241	.05121
46	.06860	.06685	.06517	.06356	.06202	.06053	.05911	.05774	.05643	.05516
47	.07353	.07169	.06992	.06823	.06660	.06504	.06353	.06209	.06070	.05936
48	.07877	.07684	.07498	.07320	.07149	.06984	.06826	.06673	.06527	.06385
49	.08433	.08231	.08036	.07849	.07669	.07495	.07329	.07168	.07013	.06864
50	.09026	.08814	.08609	.08413	.08224	.08042	.07867	.07698	.07535	.07378
51	.09655	.09433	.09219	.09013	.08815	.08624	.08440	.08262	.08091	.07926
52	.10318	.10086	.09863	.09647	.09439	.09239	.09046	.08860	.08680	.08506
53	.11017	.10774	.10541	.10315	.10098	.09888	.09686	.09491	.09302	.09120
54	.11750	.11498	.11254	.11019	.10792	.10572	.10361	.10156	.09958	.09767
55	.12522	.12258	.12005	.11759	.11522	.11294	.11072	.10859	.10652	.10451
56	.13332	.13059	.12794	.12539	.12292	.12054	.11823	.11599	.11383	.11174
57	.14183	.13899	.13624	.13359	.13102	.12853	.12613	.12380	.12154	.11936
58	.15070	.14775	.14490	.14215	.13948	.13689	.13439	.13197	.12962	.12734
59	.15990	.15685	.15389	.15103	.14826	.14558	.14298	.14046	.13801	.13564
60	.16942	.16626	.16321	.16024	.15737	.15459	.15189	.14927	.14673	.14426
61	.17929	.17603	.17287	.16981	.16684	.16395	.16115	.15844	.15580	.15324
62	.18960	.18623	.18297	.17980	.17673	.17375	.17085	.16803	.16530	.16264
63	.20035	.19688	.19352	.19025	.18708	.18400	.18100	.17809	.17525	.17250
64	.21154	.20797	.20451	.20114	.19787	.19469	.19159	.18859	.18566	.18281
65	.22318	.21951	.21595	.21249	.20912	.20584	.20265	.19955	.19652	.19358
66	.23532	.23156	.22790	.22434	.22088	.21751	.21422	.21102	.20791	.20487
67	.24804	.24419	.24044	.23679	.23324	.22977	.22640	.22311	.21990	.21678
68	.26133	.25740	.25356	.24983	.24618	.24263	.23917	.23579	.23250	.22929
69	.27516	.27114	.26723	.26341	.25969	.25605	.25251	.24905	.24567	.24237
70	.28945	.28536	.28137	.27747	.27367	.26996	.26633	.26279	.25934	.25596
71	.30412	.29996	.29590	.29193	.28806	.28427	.28057	.27696	.27343	.26998
72	.31913	.31491	.31078	.30675	.30281	.29895	.29519	.29150	.28790	.28438
73	.33444	.33016	.32597	.32188	.31788	.31396	.31013	.30638	.30271	.29913
74	.35012	.34579	.34155	.33741	.33335	.32938	.32549	.32168	.31795	.31430
75	.36628	.36190	.35762	.35343	.34932	.34530	.34136	.33750	.33372	.33001
76	.38299	.37858	.37427	.37004	.36589	.36183	.35784	.35394	.35011	.34636
77	.40028	.39585	.39151	.38725	.38307	.37898	.37496	.37103	.36716	.36337
78	.41812	.41368	.40933	.40506	.40086	.39675	.39271	.38874	.38485	.38103
79	.43641	.43198	.42762	.42334	.41914	.41502	.41096	.40698	.40308	.39924
80	.45496	.45054	.44619	.44192	.43772	.43360	.42954	.42556	.42164	.41779
81	.47360	.46920	.46487	.46061	.45643	.45231	.44827	.44429	.44038	.43653
82	.49223	.48785	.48355	.47932	.47516	.47106	.46703	.46307	.45916	.45532
83	.51081	.50648	.50221	.49802	.49388	.48982	.48581	.48187	.47799	.47416
84	.52951	.52523	.52101	.51686	.51277	.50874	.50477	.50086	.49701	.49321
85	.54847	.54425	.54009	.53600	.53196	.52798	.52406	.52019	.51638	.51262
86	.56749	.56335	.55926	.55523	.55126	.54734	.54348	.53966	.53591	.53220
87	.58627	.58221	.57820	.57425	.57035	.56650	.56270	.55895	.55526	.55161
88	.60477	.60079	.59688	.59301	.58919	.58542	.58170	.57802	.57439	.57081
89	.62297	.61909	.61527	.61149	.60776	.60408	.60044	.59685	.59330	.58979
90	.64084	.63707	.63335	.62968	.62604	.62246	.61891	.61540	.61194	.60851
91	.65803	.65437	.65076	.64719	.64366	.64017	.63672	.63330	.62993	.62659
92	.67412	.67058	.66707	.66360	.66017	.65678	.65342	.65010	.64682	.64357
93	.68911	.68567	.68227	.67890	.67557	.67227	.66901	.66578	.66258	.65942
94	.70321	.69988	.69657	.69330	.69006	.68686	.68369	.68055	.67744	.67437

AGE	12.2%	12.4%	12.6%	12.8%	13.0%	13.2%	13.4%	13.6%	13.8%	14.0%
95	.71674	.71351	.71031	.70713	.70399	.70088	.69781	.69476	.69174	.68875
96	.72959	.72646	.72335	.72028	.71724	.71422	.71123	.70828	.70534	.70244
97	.74156	.73853	.73552	.73254	.72959	.72666	.72376	.72089	.71804	.71522
98	.75287	.74993	.74702	.74413	.74126	.73842	.73561	.73282	.73006	.72732
99	.76401	.76117	.75834	.75555	.75277	.75002	.74730	.74459	.74191	.73926
100	.77494	.77219	.76946	.76676	.76408	.76142	.75878	.75616	.75357	.75099
101	.78580	.78315	.78052	.77791	.77532	.77275	.77021	.76768	.76517	.76268
102	.79654	.79399	.79146	.78894	.78645	.78397	.78152	.77908	.77666	.77426
103	.80724	.80479	.80236	.79994	.79755	.79517	.79280	.79046	.78813	.78582
104	.81879	.81646	.81413	.81183	.80954	.80726	.80501	.80276	.80054	.79832
105	.83005	.82782	.82560	.82340	.82121	.81904	.81688	.81474	.81260	.81049
106	.84485	.84277	.84071	.83866	.83662	.83459	.83257	.83057	.82857	.82659
107	.86311	.86124	.85937	.85751	.85566	.85382	.85199	.85017	.84835	.84655
108	.89266	.89114	.88963	.88812	.88662	.88513	.88364	.88216	.88068	.87922
109	.94563	.94484	.94405	.94326	.94248	.94170	.94092	.94014	.93937	.93860

(7) *Effective/applicability dates.*—Paragraphs (f)(1) through (f)(6) apply after April 30, 1999, and before May 1, 2009. [Reg. § 1.642(c)-6A.]

☐ [*T.D.* 8540, 6-9-94. *Amended by T.D.* 8819, 4-29-99; *T.D.* 8886, 6-9-2000; *T.D.* 9448, 5-1-2009 *and T.D.* 9540, 8-9-2011.]

[Reg. § 1.642(c)-7]

§ 1.642(c)-7. Transitional rules with respect to pooled income funds.—(a) *In general.*—(1) *Amendment of certain funds.*—A fund created before May 7, 1971, and not otherwise qualifying as a pooled income fund may be treated as a pooled income fund to which § 1.642(c)-5 applies if on July 31, 1969, or on each date of transfer of property to the fund occurring after July 31, 1969, it possessed the initial characteristics described in paragraph (b) of this section and is amended, in the time and manner provided in paragraph (c) of this section, to meet all the requirements of section 642(c)(5) and § 1.642(c)-5. If a fund to which this subparagraph applies is amended in the time and manner provided in paragraph (c) of this section it shall be treated as provided in paragraph (d) of this section for the period beginning on August 1, 1969, or, if later, on the date of its creation and ending the day before the date on which it meets the requirements of section 642(c)(5) and § 1.642(c)-5.

(2) *Severance of a portion of a fund.*—Any portion of a fund created before May 7, 1971, which consists of property transferred to such fund after July 31, 1969, may be severed from such fund consistently with the principles of paragraph (c)(2) of this section and established before January 1, 1972, as a separate pooled income fund, provided that on and after the date of severance the severed fund meets all the requirements of section 642(c)(5) and § 1.642(c)-5. A separate fund which is established pursuant to this subparagraph shall be treated as provided in paragraph (d) of this section for the period beginning on the day of the first transfer of property which becomes part of the separate fund and ending the day before the day on which the separate fund meets the requirements of section 642(c)(5) and § 1.642(c)-5.

(b) *Initial characteristics required.*—A fund described in paragraph (a)(1) of this section shall not be treated as a pooled income fund to which section 642(c)(5) applies, even though it is amended as provided in paragraph (c) of this section, unless it possessed the following characteristics on July 31, 1969, or on each date of transfer of property to the fund occurring after July 31, 1969:

(1) It satisfied the requirements of section 642(c)(5)(A) other than that the fund be a trust;

(2) It was constituted in a way to attract and contain commingled properties transferred to the fund by more than one donor satisfying such requirements; and

(3) Each beneficiary of a life income interest which was retained or created in any property transferred to the fund was entitled to receive, but not less often than annually, a proportional share of the annual income earned by the fund, such share being based on the fair market value of the property in which such life interest was retained or created.

(c) *Amendment requirements.*—(1) A fund described in paragraph (a)(1) of this section and possessing the initial characteristics described in paragraph (b) of this section on the date prescribed therein shall be treated as a pooled income fund if it is amended to meet all the requirements of section 642(c)(5) and § 1.642(c)-5 before January 1, 1972, or if later, on or before the 30th day after the date on which any judicial proceedings commenced before January 1, 1972, which are required to amend its governing instrument or any other instrument which does not permit it to meet such requirements, become final. However, see paragraph (d) of this section for limitation on the period in which a claim for credit or refund may be filed.

(2) In addition, if the transferred property described in paragraph (b)(2) of this section is commingled with other property, the transferred property must be separated on or before the date specified in subparagraph (1) of this paragraph from the other property and allocated to the fund in accordance with the transferred property's percentage share of the fair market value

of the total commingled property on the date of separation. The percentage share shall be the ratio which the fair market value of the transferred property on the date of separation bears to the fair market value of the total commingled property on that date and shall be computed in a manner consistent with paragraph (c) of § 1.642(c)-5. The property which is so allocated to the fund shall be treated as property received from transfers which meet the requirements of section 642(c)(5), and such transfers shall be treated as made on the dates on which the properties giving rise to such allocation were transferred to the fund by the respective donors. The property so allocated to the fund must be representative of all the commingled property other than securities the income from which is exempt from tax under subtitle A of the Code; compensating increases in other commingled property allocated to the fund shall be made where such tax-exempt securities are not allocated to the fund. The application of this subparagraph may be illustrated by the following example:

Example. (a) The trustees of X fund are in the process of amending it in order to qualify as a pooled income fund. The property transferred to the X fund was commingled with other property transferred to the organization by which the fund was established. After taking into account the various transfers and the appreciation in the fair market value of all the properties, the fair market value of the property allocated to the fund on the various transfer dates is set forth in the following schedule and determined in the manner indicated:

Transfers

Date of Transfer	*Value of All Property Before Transfer (1)*	*Trust Property (2)*	*Other Property (3)*	*Value of All Property After Transfer (4)*	*Property Allocated to Fund (5)*
1/1/68	......	$100,000	$100,000	$200,000	$100,000[1]
9/30/68	$300,000	100,000	......	400,000	250,000[2]
1/15/69	480,000	60,000	......	540,000	360,000[3]
11/11/69	600,000	200,000	......	800,000	600,000[4]

[1] $100,000 = (the amount in column (2))
[2] 250,000 = ([$100,000/$200,000 × $300,000] + $100,000)
[3] 360,000 = ([$250,000/$400,000 × $480,000] + $ 60,000)
[4] 600,000 = ([$360,000/$540,000 × $600,000] + $200,000)

(b) On September 30, 1970, the trustees decide to separate the property of X fund from the other property. The fair market value of all the commingled property is $1,000,000 on September 30, 1970, and there were no additional transfers to the fund after November 11, 1969. Accordingly, the fair market value of the property required to be allocated to X fund must be $750,000 ($600,000/$800,000 × $1,000,000), and X fund's percentage share of the commingled property is 75 percent ($750,000/$1,000,000). Accordingly, assuming that the commingled property consists of Y stock with a fair market value of $800,000 and Z bonds with a fair market value of $200,000, there must be allocated to X fund at the close of September 30, 1970, Y stock with a value of $600,000 ($800,000 × 75%) and Z bonds with a value of $150,000 ($200,000 × 75%).

(d) *Transactions before amendment of or severance from fund.*—(1) A fund which is amended pursuant to paragraph (c) of this section, or is severed from a fund pursuant to paragraph (a)(2) of this section, shall be treated for all purposes, including the allowance of a deduction for any charitable contribution, as if it were before its amendment or severance a pooled income fund to which section 642(c)(5) and § 1.642(c)-5 apply. Thus, for example, where a donor transferred property in trust to such an amended or severed fund on August 1, 1969, but before its amendment or severance under this section, a charitable contributions deduction for the value of the remainder interest may be allowed under section 170, 2055, 2106, or 2522. The deduction may not be allowed, however, until the fund is amended or severed pursuant to this section and shall be allowed only if a claim for credit or refund is filed within the period of limitation prescribed by section 6511(a).

(2) For purposes of determining under § 1.642(c)-6 the highest yearly rate of return earned by a fund (which is amended pursuant to paragraph (c) of this section) for the 3 preceding taxable years, taxable years of the fund preceding its taxable year in which the fund is so amended and qualifies as a pooled income fund under this section shall be used provided that the fund did not at any time during such preceding years hold any investments in securities the income from which is exempt from tax under subtitle A of the Code. If any such tax-exempt securities were held during such period by such amended fund, or if the fund consists of a portion of a fund which is severed pursuant to paragraph (a)(2) of this section, the highest yearly rate of return under § 1.642(c)-6 shall be determined by treating the fund as a pooled income fund which has been in existence for less than 3 taxable years preceding the taxable year in which the transfer of property to the fund is made.

(3) Property transferred to a fund before its amendment pursuant to paragraph (c) of this section, or before its severance under paragraph

(a)(2) of this section, shall be treated as property received from transfers which meet the requirements of section 642(c)(5). [Reg. § 1.642(c)-7.]

☐ [*T.D.* 7105, 4-5-71. *Amended by T.D.* 7125, 6-7-71, *and by T.D.* 8540, 6-9-94.]

[Reg. § 1.642(d)-1]

§ 1.642(d)-1. Net operating loss deduction.—The net operating loss deduction allowed by section 172 is available to estates and trusts generally, with the following exceptions and limitations:

(a) In computing gross income and deductions for the purposes of section 172, a trust shall exclude that portion of the income and deductions attributable to the grantor or another person under sections 671 through 678 (relating to grantors and others treated as substantial owners).

(b) An estate or trust shall not, for the purposes of section 172, avail itself of the deductions allowed by section 642(c) (relating to charitable contributions deductions) and sections 651 and 661 (relating to deductions for distributions). [Reg. § 1.642(d)-1.]

☐ [*T.D.* 6217, 12-19-56.]

[Reg. § 1.642(e)-1]

§ 1.642(e)-1. Depreciation and depletion.—An estate or trust is allowed the deductions for depreciation and depletion, but only to the extent the deductions are not apportioned to beneficiaries under sections 167(h) and 611(b). For purposes of sections 167(h) and 611(b), the term "beneficiaries" includes charitable beneficiaries. See the regulations under those sections. [Reg. § 1.642(e)-1.]

☐ [*T.D.* 6217, 12-19-56. *Amended by T.D.* 6712, 3-23-64.]

[Reg. § 1.642(f)-1]

§ 1.642(f)-1. Amortization deductions.—An estate or trust is allowed amortization deductions with respect to an emergency facility as defined in section 168(d), with respect to a certified pollution control facility as defined in section 169(d), with respect to qualified railroad rolling stock as defined in section 184(d), with respect to certified coal mine safety equipment as defined in section 187(d), with respect to on-the-job training and child-care facilities as defined in section 188(b), and with respect to certain rehabilitations of certified historic structures as defined in section 191, in the same manner and to the same extent as in the case of an individual. However, the principles governing the apportionment of the deductions for depreciation and depletion between fiduciaries and the beneficiaries of an estate or trust (see sections 167(h) and 611(b) and the regulations thereunder) shall be applicable with respect to such amortization deductions. [Reg. § 1.642(f)-1.]

☐ [*T.D.* 6217, 12-19-56. *Amended by T.D.* 6712, 3-23-64, *by T.D.* 7116, 5-17-71, *by T.D.* 7599, 3-12-79, *and by T.D.* 7700, 6-4-80.]

[Reg. § 1.642(g)-1]

§ 1.642(g)-1. Disallowance of double deduction; in general.—Amounts allowable under section 2053(a)(2) (relating to administration expenses) or under section 2054 (relating to losses during administration) as deductions in computing the taxable estate of a decedent are not allowed as deductions in computing the taxable income of the estate unless there is filed a statement, in duplicate, to the effect that the items have not been allowed as deductions from the gross estate of the decedent under section 2053 or 2054 and that all rights to have such items allowed at any time as deductions under section 2053 or 2054 are waived. The statement should be filed with the return for the year for which the items are claimed as deductions or with the district director of internal revenue for the internal revenue district in which the return was filed, for association with the return. The statement may be filed at any time before the expiration of the statutory period of limitation applicable to the taxable year for which the deduction is sought. Allowance of a deduction in computing an estate's taxable income is not precluded by claiming a deduction in the estate tax return, so long as the estate tax deduction is not finally allowed and the statement is filed. However, after a statement is filed under section 642(g) with respect to a particular item or portion of an item, the item cannot thereafter be allowed as a deduction for estate tax purposes since the waiver operates as a relinquishment of the right to have the deduction allowed at any time under section 2053 or 2054. [Reg. § 1.642(g)-1.]

☐ [*T.D.* 6217, 12-19-56.]

[Reg. § 1.642(g)-2]

§ 1.642(g)-2. Deductions included.—It is not required that the total deductions, or the total amount of any deduction, to which section 642(g) is applicable be treated in the same way. One deduction or portion of a deduction may be allowed for income tax purposes if the appropriate statement is filed, while another deduction or portion is allowed for estate tax purposes. Section 642(g) has no application to deductions for taxes, interest, business expenses, and other items accrued at the date of a decedent's death so that they are allowable as a deduction under section 2053(a)(3) for estate tax purposes as claims against the estate, and are also allowable under section 691(b) as deductions in respect of a decedent for income tax purposes. However, section 642(g) is applicable to deductions for interest, business expenses, and other items not accrued at the date of the decedent's death so that they are allowable as deductions for estate tax purposes only as administration expenses under section 2053(a)(2). Although deductible under section 2053(a)(3) in determining the value of the taxable estate of a decedent, medical, dental, etc., expenses of a decedent which are paid by the estate of the decedent are not deductible in computing the taxable income of the estate. See section 213(d) and the regulations thereunder for rules relating to the deductibility of such expenses in computing the taxable income of the decedent. [Reg. § 1.642(g)-2.]

☐ [*T.D.* 6217, 12-19-56.]

[Reg. § 1.642(h)-1]

§ 1.642(h)-1. Unused loss carryovers on termination of an estate or trust.—(a) If, on the final termination of an estate or trust, a net operating loss carryover under section 172 or a capital loss carryover under section 1212 would be allowable to the estate or trust in a taxable year subsequent to the taxable year of termination but for the termination, the carryover or carryovers are allowed under section 642(h)(1) to the beneficiaries succeeding to the property of the estate or trust. See § 1.641(b)-3 for the determination of when an estate or trust terminates.

(b) The net operating loss carryover and the capital loss carryover are the same in the hands of a beneficiary as in the estate or trust, except that the capital loss carryover in the hands of a beneficiary which is a corporation is a short-term loss irrespective of whether it would have been a long-term or short-term capital loss in the hands of the estate or trust. The net operating loss carryover and the capital loss carryover are taken into account in computing taxable income, adjusted gross income, and the tax imposed by section 56 (relating to the minimum tax for tax preferences). The first taxable year of the beneficiary to which the loss shall be carried over is the taxable year of the beneficiary in which or with which the estate or trust terminates. However, for purposes of determining the number of years to which a net operating loss, or a capital loss under paragraph (a) of § 1.1212-1, may be carried over by a beneficiary, the last taxable year of the estate or trust (whether or not a short taxable year) and the first taxable year of the beneficiary to which a loss is carried over each constitute a taxable year, and, in the case of a beneficiary of an estate or trust that is a corporation, capital losses carried over by the estate or trust to any taxable year of the estate or trust beginning after December 31, 1963, shall be treated as if they were incurred in the last taxable year of the estate or trust (whether or not a short taxable year). For the treatment of the net operating loss carryover when the last taxable year of the estate or trust is the last taxable year to which such loss can be carried over, see § 1.642(h)-2.

(c) The application of this section may be illustrated by the following examples:

Example (1). A trust distributes all of its assets to A, the sole remainderman, and terminates on December 31, 1954, when it has a capital loss carryover of $10,000 attributable to transactions during the taxable year 1952. A, who reports on the calendar year basis, otherwise has ordinary income of $10,000 and capital gains of $4,000 for the taxable year 1954. A would offset his capital gains of $4,000 against the capital loss of the trust and, in addition, deduct under section 1211(b) $1,000 on his return for the taxable year 1954. The balance of the capital loss carryover of $5,000 may be carried over only to the years 1955 and 1956, in accordance with paragraph (a) of § 1.1212-1 and the rules of this section.

Example (2). A trust distributes all of its assets, one-half to A, an individual, and one-half to X, a corporation, who are the sole remaindermen, and terminates on December 31, 1966, when it has a short-term capital loss carryover of $20,000 attributable to short-term transactions during the taxable years 1964, 1965 and 1966, and a long-term capital loss carryover of $12,000 attributable to long-term transactions during such years. A, who reports on the calendar year basis, otherwise has ordinary income of $15,000, short-term capital gains of $4,000 and long-term capital gains of $6,000, for the taxable year 1966. A would offset his short-term capital gains of $4,000 against his share of the short-term capital loss carryover of the trust, $10,000 (one-half of $20,000), and, in addition deduct under section 1211(b) $1,000 (treated as a short-term gain for purposes of computing capital loss carryovers) on his return for the taxable year 1966. A would also offset his long-term capital gains of $6,000 against his share of the long-term capital loss carryover of the trust, $6,000 (one-half of 12,000). The balance of A's share of the short-term capital loss carryover, $5,000, may be carried over as a short-term capital loss carryover to the succeeding taxable year and treated as a short-term capital loss incurred in such succeeding taxable year in accordance with paragraph (b) of § 1.1212-1. X, which also reports on the calendar year basis, otherwise has capital gains of $4,000 for the taxable year 1966. X would offset its capital gains of $4,000 against its share of the capital loss carryovers of the trust, $16,000 (the sum of one-half of each the short-term carryover and the long-term carryover of the trust), on its return for the taxable year 1966. The balance of X's share, $12,000, may be carried over as a short-term capital loss only to the years 1967, 1968, 1969, and 1970, in accordance with paragraph (a) of § 1.1212-1 and the rules of this section. [Reg. § 1.642(h)-1.]

☐ [*T.D.* 6217, 12-19-56. *Amended by T.D.* 6828, 6-16-65 *and by T.D.* 7564, 9-11-78.]

[Reg. § 1.642(h)-2]

§ 1.642(h)-2. Excess deductions on termination of an estate or trust.—(a) *Excess deductions.*—(1) *In general.*—If, on the termination of an estate or trust, the estate or trust has for its last taxable year deductions (other than the deductions allowed under section 642(b) (relating to the personal exemption) or section 642(c) (relating to charitable contributions)) in excess of gross income, the excess deductions as determined under paragraph (b) of this section are allowed under section 642(h)(2) as items of deduction to the beneficiaries succeeding to the property of the estate or trust.

(2) *Treatment by beneficiary.*—A beneficiary may claim all or part of the amount of the deductions provided for in paragraph (a) of this section, as determined after application of paragraph (b) of this section, before, after, or together with the same character of deductions

separately allowable to the beneficiary under the Internal Revenue Code for the beneficiary's taxable year during which the estate or trust terminated as provided in paragraph (c) of this section.

(b) *Character and amount of excess deductions.*—(1) *Character.*—The character and amount of the excess deductions on termination of an estate or trust will be determined as provided in this paragraph (b). Each deduction comprising the excess deductions under section 642(h)(2) retains, in the hands of the beneficiary, its character (specifically, as allowable in arriving at adjusted gross income, as a non-miscellaneous itemized deduction, or as a miscellaneous itemized deduction) while in the estate or trust. An item of deduction succeeded to by a beneficiary remains subject to any additional applicable limitation under the Internal Revenue Code and must be separately stated if it could be so limited, as provided in the instructions to Form 1041, *U.S. Income Tax Return for Estates and Trusts*, and the Schedule K–1 (Form 1041), *Beneficiary's Share of Income, Deductions, Credit, etc.*, or successor forms.

(2) *Amount.*—The amount of the excess deductions in the final year is determined as follows:

(i) Each deduction directly attributable to a class of income is allocated in accordance with the provisions in § 1.652(b)-3(a);

(ii) To the extent of any remaining income after application of paragraph (b)(2)(i) of this section, deductions are allocated in accordance with the provisions in § 1.652(b)-3(b) and (d); and

(iii) Deductions remaining after the application of paragraph (b)(2)(i) and (ii) of this section comprise the excess deductions on termination of the estate or trust. These deductions are allocated to the beneficiaries succeeding to the property of the estate of or trust in accordance with § 1.642(h)-4.

(c) *Year of termination.*—(1) *In general.*—The deductions provided for in paragraph (a) of this section are allowable only in the taxable year of the beneficiary in which or with which the estate or trust terminates, whether the year of termination of the estate or trust is of normal duration or is a short taxable year.

(2) *Example.*—Assume that a trust distributes all its assets to B and terminates on December 31, Year X. As of that date, it has excess deductions of $18,000, all characterized as allowable in arriving at adjusted gross income under section 67(e). B, who reports on the calendar year basis, could claim the $18,000 as a deduction allowable in arriving at B's adjusted gross income for Year X. However, if the deduction (when added to other allowable deductions that B claims for the year) exceeds B's gross income, the excess may not be carried over to any year subsequent to Year X.

(d) *Net operating loss carryovers.*—A deduction based upon a net operating loss carryover will never be allowed to beneficiaries under both paragraphs (1) and (2) of section 642(h). Accordingly, a net operating loss deduction which is allowable to beneficiaries succeeding to the property of the estate or trust under the provisions of paragraph (1) of section 642(h) cannot also be considered a deduction for purposes of paragraph (2) of section 642(h) and paragraph (a) of this section. However, if the last taxable year of the estate or trust is the last year in which a deduction on account of a net operating loss may be taken, the deduction, to the extent not absorbed in that taxable year by the estate or trust, is considered an "excess deduction" under section 642(h)(2) and paragraph (a) of this section.

(e) *Items included in net operating loss or capital loss carryovers.* .—Any item of income or deduction, or any part thereof, which is taken into account in determining the net operating loss or capital loss carryover of the estate or trust for its last taxable year shall not be taken into account again in determining excess deductions on termination of the trust or estate within the meaning of section 642(h)(2) and paragraph (a) of this section (see example in § 1.642(h)-5).

(f) *Applicability date.*—Paragraphs (a) through (c) of this section apply to taxable years beginning after October 19, 2020. The rules applicable to taxable years beginning on or before October 19, 2020 are contained in § 1.642(h)-2 as in effect prior to October 19, 2020 (see 26 CFR part 1 revised as of April 1, 2020). Taxpayers may choose to apply paragraphs (a) through (c) of this section to taxable years beginning after December 31, 2017, and on or before October 19, 2020. [Reg. § 1.642(h)-2.]

☐ [*T.D.* 6217, 12-19-56. *Amended by T.D.* 7564, 9-11-78 *and T.D.* 9918, 10-16-2020.]

[Reg. § 1.642(h)-3]

§ 1.642(h)-3. Meaning of "beneficiaries succeeding to the property of the estate or trust".—(a) The phrase "beneficiaries succeeding to the property of the estate or trust" means those beneficiaries upon termination of the estate or trust who bear the burden of any loss for which a carryover is allowed, or of any excess of deductions over gross income for which a deduction is allowed, under section 642(h).

(b) With reference to an intestate estate, the phrase means the heirs and next of kin to whom the estate is distributed, or if the estate is insolvent, to whom it would have been distributed if it had not been insolvent. If a decedent's spouse is entitled to a specified dollar amount of property before any distribution to other heirs and next of kin, and if the estate is less than that amount, the spouse is the beneficiary succeeding to the property of the estate or trust to the extent of the deficiency in amount.

(c) In the case of a testate estate, the phrase normally means the residuary beneficiaries (including a residuary trust), and not specific legatees or devisees, pecuniary legatees, or other nonresiduary beneficiaries. However, the phrase does not include the recipient of a specific sum

See p. 15 for regulations not amended to reflect law changes

of money even though it is payable out of the residue, except to the extent that it is not payable in full. On the other hand, the phrase includes a beneficiary (including a trust) who is not strictly a residuary beneficiary but whose devise or bequest is determined by the value of the decedent's estate as reduced by the loss or deductions in question. Thus the phrase includes:

(1) A beneficiary of a fraction of a decedent's net estate after payment of debts, expenses, etc.;

(2) A nonresiduary legatee or devisee, to the extent of any deficiency in his legacy or devise resulting from the insufficiency of the estate to satisfy it in full;

(3) A surviving spouse receiving a fractional share of an estate in fee under a statutory right of election, to the extent that the loss or deductions are taken into account in determining the share. However, the phrase does not include a recipient of dower or curtesy, or any income beneficiary of the estate or trust from which the loss or excess deduction is carried over.

(d) The principles discussed in paragraph (c) of this section are equally applicable to trust beneficiaries. A remainderman who receives all or a fractional share of the property of a trust as a result of the final termination of the trust is a beneficiary succeeding to the property of the trust. For example, if property is transferred to pay the income to A for life and then to pay $10,000 to B and distribute the balance of the trust corpus to C, C and not B is considered to be the succeeding beneficiary except to the extent that the trust corpus is insufficient to pay B $10,000. [Reg. § 1.642(h)-3.]

☐ [*T.D.* 6217, 12-19-56.]

[Reg. § 1.642(h)-4]

§ 1.642(h)-4. Allocation.—The carryovers and excess deductions to which section 642(h) applies are allocated among the beneficiaries succeeding to the property of an estate or trust (see § 1.642(h)-3) proportionately according to the share of each in the burden of the loss or deductions. A person who qualified as a beneficiary succeeding to the property of an estate or trust with respect to one amount and does not qualify with respect to another amount is a beneficiary succeeding to the property of the estate or trust as to the amount with respect to which he qualifies. The application of this section may be illustrated by the following example:

Example. A decedent's will leaves $100,000 to A, and the residue of his estate equally to B and C. His estate is sufficient to pay only $90,000 to A, and nothing to B and C. There is an excess of deductions over gross income for the last taxable year of the estate or trust of $5,000, and a capital loss carryover of $15,000, to both of which section 642(h) applies. A is a beneficiary succeeding to the property of the estate to the extent of $10,000, and since the total of the excess of deductions and the loss carryover is $20,000, A is entitled to the benefit of one half of each item, and the remaining half is divided equally between B and C. [Reg. § 1.642(h)-4.]

☐ [*T.D.* 6217, 12-19-56.]

[Reg. § 1.642(h)-5]

§ 1.642(h)-5. Examples.—Paragraphs (a) and (b) of this section (Examples 1 and 2) illustrate the application of section 642(h).

(a) *Example 1: Computations under section 642(h) when an estate has a net operating loss.*—(1) *Facts.*—On January 31, 2020, A dies leaving a will that provides for the distribution of all of A's estate equally to B and an existing trust for C. The period of administration of the estate terminates on December 31, 2020, at which time all the property of the estate is distributed to B and the trust. For tax purposes, B and the trust report income on a calendar year basis. During the period of administration, the estate has the following items of income and deductions:

TABLE 1 TO PARAGRAPH (a)(1)

Income		
Taxable interest	$2,500	
Business income	3,000	
Total income		5,500

TABLE 2 TO PARAGRAPH (a)(1)

Deductions		
Business expenses (including administrative expense allocable to business income)	5,000	
Administrative expenses not allocable to business income that would not have been incurred if property had not been held in a trust or estate (section 67(e) deductions)	9,800	
Total deductions		14,800

(2) *Computation of net operating loss.*—(i) The amount of the net operating loss carryover is computed as follows:

TABLE 3 TO PARAGRAPH (a)(2)(i)

Gross income		$5,500
Total deductions	14,800	
Less adjustment under section 172(d)(4) (allowable non-business expenses ($9,800) limited to non-business income ($2,500))	7,300	
Deductions as adjusted		7,500
Net operating loss		2,000

(ii) Under section 642(h)(1), B and the trust are each allocated $1,000 of the $2,000 unused net operating loss carryover of the terminated estate in 2020, with the allowance of any net operating loss carryover to B and the trust determined under section 172. Neither B nor the trust can carry back any of the net operating loss of A's estate made available to them under section 642(h)(1). *See* § 1.642(h)-1(b).

(3) *Section 642(h)(2) excess deductions.*—The $7,300 of non-business deductions not taken into account in determining the net operating loss of the estate are excess deductions on termination of the estate under section 642(h)(2). Under § 1.642(h)-2(b)(1), such deductions retain their character as section 67(e) deductions. Under § 1.642(h)-4, B and the trust each are allocated $3,650 of excess deductions based on B's and the trust's respective shares of the burden of each cost.

(4) *Consequences for C.*—The net operating loss carryover and excess deductions are not allowable directly to C, the trust beneficiary. To the extent the distributable net income of the trust is reduced by the net operating loss carryover and excess deductions, however, C may receive an indirect benefit from the carryover and excess deductions.

(b) *Example 2: Computations under section 642(h)(2).*—(1) *Facts.*—D dies in 2019 leaving an estate of which the residuary legatees are E (75%) and F (25%). The estate's income and deductions in its final year are as follows:

TABLE 4 TO PARAGRAPH (b)(1)

Income		
Dividends	$3,000	
Taxable Interest	500	
Rent	2,000	
Capital Gain	1,000	
Total Income		6,500

TABLE 5 TO PARAGRAPH (b)(1)

Deductions		
Section 62(a)(4) deductions:		
Rental real estate expenses		2,000
Section 67(e) deductions:		
Probate fees	1,500	
Estate tax preparation fees	8,000	
Legal fees	2,500	
Total Section 67(e) deductions		12,000
Non-miscellaneous itemized deductions:		
Personal property taxes		3,500
Total deductions		17,500

(2) *Determination of character.*—Pursuant to § 1.642(h)-2(b)(2), the character and amount of the excess deductions is determined by allocating the deductions among the estate's items of income as provided under § 1.652(b)-3. Under § 1.652(b)-3(a), the $2,000 of rental real estate expenses is allocated to the $2,000 of rental income. In the exercise of the executor's discretion pursuant to § 1.652(b)-3(b), D's executor allocates $3,500 of personal property taxes and $1,000 of section 67(e) deductions to the remaining income. As a result, the excess deductions on termination of the estate are $11,000, all consisting of section 67(e) deductions.

(3) *Allocations among beneficiaries.*—Pursuant to § 1.642(h)-4, the excess deductions are allocated in accordance with E's (75 percent) and F's (25 percent) interests in the residuary estate. E's share of the excess deductions is $8,250, all consisting of section 67(e) deductions. F's share of the excess deductions is $2,750, also all consisting of section 67(e) deductions.

(4) *Separate statement.*—If the executor instead allocated $4,500 of section 67(e) deductions to the remaining income of the estate, the excess deductions on termination of the estate would be $11,000, consisting of $7,500 of section 67(e) deductions and $3,500 of personal property taxes.

The non-miscellaneous itemized deduction for personal property taxes may be subject to limitation on the returns of both B and C's trust under section 164(b)(6)(B) and would have to be separately stated as provided in § 1.642(h)-2(b)(1).

(c) *Applicability date.*—This section is applicable to taxable years beginning after October 19, 2020. Taxpayers may choose to apply this section to taxable years beginning after December 31, 2017, and on or before October 19, 2020. [Reg. § 1.642(h)-5.]

☐ [*T.D.* 6217, 12-19-56. *Amended by T.D.* 6828, 6-16-65 *and T.D.* 9918, 10-16-2020.]

[Reg. § 1.642(i)-1]

§ 1.642(i)-1. Certain distributions by cemetery perpetual care funds.—(a) *In general.*—Section 642(i) provides that amounts distributed during taxable years ending after December 31, 1963 by a cemetery perpetual care fund trust for the care and maintenance of gravesites shall be treated as distributions solely for purposes of sections 651 and 661. The deduction for such a distribution is allowable only if the fund is taxable as a trust. In addition, the fund must have been created pursuant to local law by a taxable cemetery corporation (as defined in § 1.642(i)-2(a)) expressly for the care and maintenance of cemetery property. A care fund will be treated as having been created by a taxable cemetery corporation ("cemetery") if the distributee cemetery is taxable, even though the care fund was created by the distributee cemetery in a year that it was tax-exempt or by a predecessor of such distributee cemetery which was tax-exempt in the year the fund was established. The deduction is the amount of the distributions during the fund's taxable year to the cemetery corporation for such care and maintenance that would be otherwise allowable under section 651 or 661, but in no event is to exceed the limitations described in paragraphs (b) and (c) of this section. The provisions of this paragraph shall not have the effect of extending the period of limitations under section 6511.

(b) *Limitation on amount of deduction.*—The deduction in any taxable year may not exceed the product of $5 multiplied by the aggregate number of gravesites sold by the cemetery corporation before the beginning of the taxable year of the trust. In general, the aggregate number of gravesites sold shall be the aggregate number of interment rights sold by a cemetery corporation (including gravesites sold by the cemetery before a care fund trust law was enacted). In addition, the number of gravesites sold shall include gravesites used to make welfare burials. Welfare burials and pre-trust fund law gravesites shall be included only to the extent that the cemetery cares for and maintains such gravesites. For purposes of this section, a gravesite is sold as of the date on which the purchaser acquires interment rights enforceable under local law. The aggregate number of gravesites includes only those gravesites with respect to which the fund or taxable cemetery corporation has an obligation for care and maintenance.

(c) *Requirements for deductibility of distributions for care and maintenance.*—(1) *Obligation for care and maintenance.*—A deduction is allowed only for distributions for the care and maintenance of gravesites with respect to which the fund or taxable cemetery corporation has an obligation for care and maintenance. Such obligation may be established by the trust instrument, by local law, or by the cemetery's practice of caring for and maintaining gravesites, such as welfare burial plots or gravesites sold before the enactment of a care fund trust law.

(2) *Distribution actually used for care and maintenance.*—The amount of a deduction otherwise allowable for care fund distributions in any taxable year shall not exceed the portion of such distributions expended by the distributee cemetery corporation for the care and maintenance of gravesites before the end of the fund's taxable year following the taxable year in which it makes the distributions. A 6-month extension of time for filing the trust's return may be obtained upon request under section 6081. The failure of a cemetery to expend the care fund's distributions within a reasonable time before the due date for filing the return will be considered reasonable grounds for granting a 6-month extension of time for section 6081. For purposes of this paragraph, any amount expended by the care fund directly for the care and maintenance of gravesites shall be treated as an additional care fund distribution which is expended on the day of distribution by the cemetery corporation. The fund shall be allowed a deduction for such direct expenditure in the fund's taxable year during which the expenditure is made.

(3) *Example.*—The application of paragraph (c)(2) of this section is illustrated by the following example:

A, a calendar-year perpetual care fund trust meeting the requirements of section 642(i), makes a $10,000 distribution on December 1, 1978 to X, a taxable cemetery corporation operating on a May 31 fiscal year. From this $10,000 distribution, the cemetery makes the following expenditures for the care and maintenance of gravesites: $2,000 on December 20, 1978; $4,000 on June 1, 1979; $2,000 on October 1, 1979; and $1,000 on April 1, 1980. In addition, as authorized by the trust instrument, A itself makes a direct $1,000 payment to a contractor on September 1, 1979 for qualifying care and maintenance work performed. As a result of these transactions, A will be allowed an $8,000 deduction for its 1978 taxable year attributable to the cemetery's expenditures, and a $1,000 deduction for its 1979 taxable year attributable to the fund's direct payment. A will not be allowed a deduction for its 1978 taxable year for the cemetery's expenditure of either the $1,000 expended on April 1, 1980 or the remaining unspent portion of the original $10,000 distribution. The trustee may request a 6-month extension in order to allow the fund until October 15, 1979 to file its return for 1978.

(d) *Certified statement made by cemetery officials to fund trustees.*—A trustee of a cemetery perpetual care fund shall not be held personally liable for civil or criminal penalties resulting from false statements on the trust's tax return to the extent that such false statements resulted from the trustee's reliance on a certified statement made by the cemetery specifying the number of interments sold by the cemetery or the amount of the cemetery's expenditures for care and maintenance. The statement must indicate the basis upon which the cemetery determined what portion of its expenditures were made for the care and maintenance of gravesites. The statement must be certified by an officer or employee of the cemetery who has the responsibility to make or account for expenditures for care and maintenance. A copy of this statement shall be retained by the trustee along with the trust's return and shall be made available for inspection upon request by the Secretary. This paragraph does not relieve the care fund trust of its liability to pay the proper amount of tax due and to maintain adequate records to substantiate each of its deductions, including the deduction provided in section 642(i) and this section. [Reg. § 1.642(i)-1.]

□ [*T.D.* 7651, 10-25-79.]

[Reg. § 1.642(i)-2]

§ 1.642(i)-2. Definitions.—(a) *Taxable cemetery corporation.*—For purposes of section 642(i) and this section, the meaning of the term "taxable cemetery corporation" is limited to a corporation (within the meaning of section 7701(a)(3)) engaged in the business of owning and operating a cemetery that either (1) is not exempt from Federal tax, or (2) is subject to tax under section 511 with respect to its cemetery activities.

(b) *Pursuant to local law.*—A cemetery perpetual care fund is created pursuant to local law if:

(1) The governing law of the relevant jurisdiction (State, district, county, parish, etc.) requires or expressly permits the creation of such a fund, or

(2) The legally enforceable bylaws or contracts of a taxable cemetery corporation require a perpetual care fund.

(c) *Gravesite.*—A gravesite is any type of interment right that has been sold by a cemetery, including, but not limited to, a burial lot, mausoleum, lawn crypt, niche, or scattering ground. For purposes of § 1.642(i)-1, the term "gravesites" includes only those gravesites with respect to which the care fund or cemetery has an obligation for care and maintenance within the meaning of § 1.642(i)-1(c)(1).

(d) *Care and maintenance.*—For purposes of section 642(i) and this section, the term "care and maintenance of gravesites" shall be generally defined in accordance with the definition of such term under the local law pursuant to which the cemetery perpetual care fund is created. If the applicable local law contains no definition, care and maintenance of gravesites may include the upkeep, repair and preservation of those portions of cemetery property in which gravesites (as defined in paragraph (c) of this section) have been sold; including gardening, road maintenance, water line and drain repair and other activities reasonably necessary to the preservation of cemetery property. The costs for care and maintenance include, but are not limited to, expenditures for the maintenance, repair and replacement of machinery, tools, and equipment, compensation of employees performing such work, insurance premiums, reasonable payments for employees' pension and other benefit plans, and the costs of maintaining necessary records of lot ownership, transfers and burials. However, if some of the expenditures of the cemetery corporation, such as officers' salaries, are for both care and maintenance and for other purposes, the expenditures must be properly allocated between care and maintenance of gravesites and the other purposes. Only those expenditures that are properly allocable to those portions of cemetery property in which gravesites have been sold qualify as expenditures for care and maintenance of gravesites. [Reg. § 1.642(i)-2.]

□ [*T.D.* 7651, 10-25-79.]

[Reg. § 1.643(a)-0]

§ 1.643(a)-0. Distributable net income; deduction for distributions; in general.—The term "distributable net income" has no application except in the taxation of estates and trusts and their beneficiaries. It limits the deductions allowable to estates and trusts for amounts paid, credited, or required to be distributed to beneficiaries and is used to determine how much of an amount paid, credited, or required to be distributed to a beneficiary will be includible in his gross income. It is also used to determine the character of distributions to the beneficiaries. Distributable net income means for any taxable year, the taxable income (as defined in section 63) of the estate or trust, computed with the modifications set forth in §§ 1.643(a)-1 through 1.643(a)-7. [Reg. § 1.643(a)-0.]

□ [*T.D.* 6217, 12-19-56.]

[Reg. § 1.643(a)-1]

§ 1.643(a)-1. Deduction for distributions.—The deduction allowable to a trust under section 651 and to an estate or trust under section 661 for amounts paid, credited, or required to be distributed to beneficiaries is not allowed in the computation of distributable net income [Reg. § 1.643(a)-1.]

□ [*T.D.* 6217, 12-19-56.]

[Reg. § 1.643(a)-2]

§ 1.643(a)-2. Deduction for personal exemption.—The deduction for personal exemption under section 642(b) is not allowed in the computation of distributable net income. [Reg. § 1.643(a)-2.]

□ [*T.D.* 6217, 12-19-56.]

[Reg. § 1.643(a)-3]

§ 1.643(a)-3. Capital gains and losses.—(a) *In general.*—Except as provided in § 1.643(a)-6 and paragraph (b) of this section, gains from the sale or exchange of capital assets are ordinarily excluded from distributable net income and are not ordinarily considered as paid, credited, or required to be distributed to any beneficiary.

(b) *Capital gains included in distributable net income.*—Gains from the sale or exchange of capital assets are included in distributable net income to the extent they are, pursuant to the terms of the governing instrument and applicable local law, or pursuant to a reasonable and impartial exercise of discretion by the fiduciary (in accordance with a power granted to the fiduciary by applicable local law or by the governing instrument if not prohibited by applicable local law)—

(1) Allocated to income (but if income under the state statute is defined as, or consists of, a unitrust amount, a discretionary power to allocate gains to income must also be exercised consistently and the amount so allocated may not be greater than the excess of the unitrust amount over the amount of distributable net income determined without regard to this subparagraph § 1.643(a)-3(b));

(2) Allocated to corpus but treated consistently by the fiduciary on the trust's books, records, and tax returns as part of a distribution to a beneficiary; or

(3) Allocated to corpus but actually distributed to the beneficiary or utilized by the fiduciary in determining the amount that is distributed or required to be distributed to a beneficiary.

(c) *Charitable contributions included in distributable net income.*—If capital gains are paid, permanently set aside, or to be used for the purposes specified in section 642(c), so that a charitable deduction is allowed under that section in respect of the gains, they must be included in the computation of distributable net income.

(d) *Capital losses.*—Losses from the sale or exchange of capital assets shall first be netted at the trust level against any gains from the sale or exchange of capital assets, except for a capital gain that is utilized under paragraph (b)(3) of this section in determining the amount that is distributed or required to be distributed to a particular beneficiary. See § 1.642(h)-1 with respect to capital loss carryovers in the year of final termination of an estate or trust.

(e) *Examples.*—The following examples illustrate the rules of this section:

Example 1. Under the terms of Trust's governing instrument, all income is to be paid to A for life. Trustee is given discretionary powers to invade principal for A's benefit and to deem discretionary distributions to be made from capital gains realized during the year. During Trust's first taxable year, Trust has $5,000 of dividend income and $10,000 of capital gain from the sale of securities. Pursuant to the terms of the governing instrument and applicable local law, Trustee allocates the $10,000 capital gain to principal. During the year, Trustee distributes to A $5,000, representing A's right to trust income. In addition, Trustee distributes to A $12,000, pursuant to the discretionary power to distribute principal. Trustee does not exercise the discretionary power to deem the discretionary distributions of principal as being paid from capital gains realized during the year. Therefore, the capital gains realized during the year are not included in distributable net income and the $10,000 of capital gain is taxed to the trust. In future years, Trustee must treat all discretionary distributions as not being made from any realized capital gains.

Example 2. The facts are the same as in *Example 1*, except that Trustee intends to follow a regular practice of treating discretionary distributions of principal as being paid first from any net capital gains realized by Trust during the year. Trustee evidences this treatment by including the $10,000 capital gain in distributable net income on Trust's federal income tax return so that it is taxed to A. This treatment of the capital gains is a reasonable exercise of Trustee's discretion. In future years Trustee must treat all discretionary distributions as being made first from any realized capital gains.

Example 3. The facts are the same as in *Example 1*, except that Trustee intends to follow a regular practice of treating discretionary distributions of principal as being paid from any net capital gains realized by Trust during the year from the sale of certain specified assets or a particular class of investments. This treatment of capital gains is a reasonable exercise of Trustee's discretion.

Example 4. The facts are the same as in *Example 1*, except that pursuant to the terms of the governing instrument (in a provision not prohibited by applicable local law), capital gains realized by Trust are allocated to income. Because the capital gains are allocated to income pursuant to the terms of the governing instrument, the $10,000 capital gain is included in Trust's distributable net income for the taxable year.

Example 5. The facts are the same as in *Example 1*, except that Trustee decides that discretionary distributions will be made only to the extent Trust has realized capital gains during the year and thus the discretionary distribution to A is $10,000, rather than $12,000. Because Trustee will use the amount of any realized capital gain to determine the amount of the discretionary distribution to the beneficiary, the $10,000 capital gain is included in Trust's distributable net income for the taxable year.

Example 6. Trust's assets consist of Blackacre and other property. Under the terms of Trust's governing instrument, Trustee is directed to hold Blackacre for ten years and then sell it and distribute all the sales proceeds to A. Because Trustee uses the amount of the sales proceeds that includes any realized capital gain to determine the amount required to be distributed to A, any capital gain realized from the sale of Blackacre is included in Trust's distributable net income for the taxable year.

Example 7. Under the terms of Trust's governing instrument, all income is to be paid to A during the Trust's term. When A reaches 35, Trust is to terminate and all the principal is to be distributed to A. Because all the assets of the trust, including all capital gains, will be actually distributed to the beneficiary at the termination of Trust, all capital gains realized in the year of termination are included in distributable net income. See § 1.641(b)-3 for the determination of the year of final termination and the taxability of capital gains realized after the terminating event and before final distribution.

Example 8. The facts are the same as *Example 7,* except Trustee is directed to pay B $10,000 before distributing the remainder of Trust assets to A. Because the distribution to B is a gift of a specific sum of money within the meaning of section 663(a)(1), none of Trust's distributable net income that includes all of the capital gains realized during the year of termination is allocated to B's distribution.

Example 9. The facts are the same as *Example 7,* except Trustee is directed to distribute one-half of the principal to A when A reaches 35 and the balance to A when A reaches 45. Trust assets consist entirely of stock in corporation M with a fair market value of $1,000,000 and an adjusted basis of $300,000. When A reaches 35, Trustee sells one-half of the stock and distributes the sales proceeds to A. All the sales proceeds, including all the capital gain attributable to that sale, are actually distributed to A and therefore all the capital gain is included in distributable net income.

Example 10. The facts are the same as *Example 9,* except when A reaches 35, Trustee sells all the stock and distributes one-half of the sales proceeds to A. If authorized by the governing instrument and applicable state statute, Trustee may determine to what extent the capital gain is distributed to A. The $500,000 distribution to A may be treated as including a minimum of $200,000 of capital gain (and all of the principal amount of $300,000) and a maximum of $500,000 of the capital gain (with no principal). Trustee evidences the treatment by including the appropriate amount of capital gain in distributable net income on Trust's federal income tax return. If Trustee is not authorized by the governing instrument and applicable state statutes to determine to what extent the capital gain is distributed to A, one-half of the capital gain attributable to the sale is included in distributable net income.

Example 11. The applicable state statute provides that a trustee may make an election to pay an income beneficiary an amount equal to four percent of the fair market value of the trust assets, as determined at the beginning of each taxable year, in full satisfaction of that beneficiary's right to income. State statute also provides that this unitrust amount shall be considered paid first from ordinary and tax-exempt income, then from net short-term capital gain, then from net long-term capital gain, and finally from return of principal. Trust's governing instrument provides that A is to receive each year income as defined under state statute. Trustee makes the unitrust election under state statute. At the beginning of the taxable year, Trust assets are valued at $500,000. During the year, Trust receives $5,000 of dividend income and realizes $80,000 of net long-term gain from the sale of capital assets. Trustee distributes to A $20,000 (4% of $500,000) in satisfaction of A's right to income. Net long-term capital gain in the amount of $15,000 is allocated to income pursuant to the ordering rule of the state statute and is included in distributable net income for the taxable year.

Example 12. The facts are the same as in *Example 11,* except that neither state statute nor Trust's governing instrument has an ordering rule for the character of the unitrust amount, but leaves such a decision to the discretion of Trustee. Trustee intends to follow a regular practice of treating principal, other than capital gain, as distributed to the beneficiary to the extent that the unitrust amount exceeds Trust's ordinary and tax-exempt income. Trustee evidences this treatment by not including any capital gains in distributable net income on Trust's Federal income tax return so that the entire $80,000 capital gain is taxed to Trust. This treatment of the capital gains is a reasonable exercise of Trustee's discretion. In future years Trustee must consistently follow this treatment of not allocating realized capital gains to income.

Example 13. The facts are the same as in *Example 11,* except that neither state statutes nor Trust's governing instrument has an ordering rule for the character of the unitrust amount, but leaves such a decision to the discretion of Trustee. Trustee intends to follow a regular practice of treating net capital gains as distributed to the beneficiary to the extent the unitrust amount exceeds Trust's ordinary and tax-exempt income. Trustee evidences this treatment by including $15,000 of the capital gain in distributable net income on Trust's Federal income tax return. This treatment of the capital gains is a reasonable exercise of Trustee's discretion. In future years Trustee must consistently treat realized capital gain, if any, as distributed to the beneficiary to the extent that the unitrust amount exceeds ordinary and tax-exempt income.

Example 14. Trustee is a corporate fiduciary that administers numerous trusts. State statutes provide that a trustee may make an election to distribute to an income beneficiary an amount equal to four percent of the annual fair market value of the trust assets in full satisfaction of that beneficiary's right to income. Neither state statutes nor the governing instruments of any of the trusts administered by Trustee has an ordering rule for the character of the unitrust amount, but leaves such a decision to the discretion of Trustee. With respect to some trusts, Trustee intends to follow a regular practice of treating principal, other than capital gain, as distributed to the beneficiary to the extent that the unitrust amount exceeds the trust's ordinary and tax-exempt income. Trustee will evidence this treatment by not including any capital gains in distributable net income on the Federal income tax returns for those trusts. With respect to other trusts, Trustee intends to follow a regular practice of treating any net capital gains as distributed to the beneficiary to the extent the unitrust amount exceeds the trust's ordinary and tax-exempt income.

Trustee will evidence this treatment by including net capital gains in distributable net income on the Federal income tax returns filed for these trusts. Trustee's decision with respect to each trust is a reasonable exercise of Trustee's discretion and, in future years, Trustee must treat the capital gains realized by each trust consistently with the treatment by that trust in prior years.

(f) *Effective date.*—This section applies for taxable years of trusts and estates ending after January 2, 2004. [Reg. § 1.643(a)-3.]

☐ [*T.D.* 6217, 12-19-56. *Amended by T.D.* 6989, 1-16-69; *T.D.* 7357, 5-30-75 *and T.D.* 9102, 12-30-2003.]

[Reg. § 1.643(a)-4]

§ 1.643(a)-4. Extraordinary dividends and taxable stock dividends.—In the case solely of a trust which qualifies under subpart B (section 651 and following) as a "simple trust", there are excluded from distributable net income extraordinary dividends (whether paid in cash or in kind) or taxable stock dividends which are not distributed or credited to a beneficiary because the fiduciary in good faith determines that under the terms of the governing instrument and applicable local law such dividends are allocable to corpus. See section 665(e), paragraph (b) of § 1.665(e)-1 and paragraph (b) of § 1.665(e)-1A for the treatment of such dividends upon subsequent distribution. [Reg. § 1.643(a)-4.]

☐ [*T.D.* 6217, 12-19-56. *Amended by T.D.* 6989, 1-16-69 *and by T.D.* 7204, 8-24-72.]

[Reg. § 1.643(a)-5]

§ 1.643(a)-5. Tax-exempt interest.—(a) There is included in distributable net income any tax-exempt interest excluded from gross income under section 103, reduced by disbursements allocable to such interest which would have been deductible under section 212 but for the provisions of section 265 (relating to disallowance of deductions allocable to tax-exempt income).

(b) If the estate or trust is allowed a charitable contributions deduction under section 642(c), the amounts specified in paragraph (a) of this section and § 1.643(a)-6 are reduced by the portion deemed to be included in income paid, permanently set aside, or to be used for the purposes specified in section 642(c). If the governing instrument or local law specifically provides as to the source out of which amounts are paid, permanently set aside, or to be used for such charitable purposes, the specific provision controls for Federal tax purposes to the extent such provision has economic effect independent of income tax consequences. See § 1.652(b)-2(b). In the absence of such specific provisions in the governing instrument or local law, an amount to which section 642(c) applies is deemed to consist of the same proportion of each class of the items of income of the estate or trust as the total of each class bears to the total of all classes. For illustrations showing the determination of the character of an amount deductible under section 642(c), see *Examples 1* and *2* of § 1.662(b)-2 and § 1.662(c)-4(e). [Reg. § 1.643(a)-5.]

☐ [*T.D.* 6217, 12-19-56. *Amended by T.D.* 9582, 4-13-2012.]

[Reg. § 1.643(a)-6]

§ 1.643(a)-6. Income of foreign trust.—(a) *Distributable net income of a foreign trust.*—In the case of a foreign trust (see section 7701(a)(31)), the determination of distributable net income is subject to the following rules:

(1) There is included in distributable net income the amounts of gross income from sources without the United States, reduced by disbursements allocable to such foreign income which would have been deductible but for the provisions of section 265 (relating to disallowance of deductions allocable to tax-exempt income). See paragraph (b) of § 1.643(a)-5 for rules applicable when an estate or trust is allowed a charitable contributions deduction under section 642(c).

(2) In the case of a distribution made by a trust before January 1, 1963, for purposes of determining the distributable net income of the trust for the taxable year in which the distribution is made, or for any prior taxable year,

(i) Gross income from sources within the United States is determined by taking into account the provisions of section 894 (relating to income exempt under treaty); and

(ii) Distributable net income is determined by taking into account the provisions of section 643(a)(3) (relating to exclusion of certain gains from the sale or exchange of capital assets).

(3) In the case of a distribution made by a trust after December 31, 1962, for purposes of determining the distributable net income of the trust for any taxable year, whether ending before January 1, 1963, or after December 31, 1962,

(i) Gross income (for the entire foreign trust) from sources within the United States is determined without regard to the provisions of section 894 (relating to income exempt under treaty);

(ii) In respect of a foreign trust created by a United States person (whether such trust constitutes the whole or only a portion of the entire foreign trust) (see section 643(d) and § 1.643(d)-1), there shall be included in gross income gains from the sale or exchange of capital assets reduced by losses from such sales or exchanges to the extent such losses do not exceed gains from such sales or exchanges, and the deduction under section 1202 (relating to deduction for capital gains) shall not be taken into account; and

(iii) In respect of a foreign trust created by a person other than a United States person (whether such trust constitutes the whole or only a portion of the entire foreign trust) (see section 643(d) and § 1.643(d)-1), distributable net income is determined by taking into account all of the provisions of section 643 except section 643(a)(6)(C) (relating to gains from the sale or exchange of capital assets by a foreign trust created by a United States person).

(b) The application of this section, showing the computation of distributable net income for one of the taxable years for which such a computation must be made, may be illustrated by the following examples:

Example (1). (1) A trust is created in 1952 under the laws of Country X by the transfer to a trustee in Country X of money and property by a United States person. The entire trust constitutes a foreign trust created by a United States person. The income from the trust corpus is to be accumulated until the beneficiary, a resident citizen of the United States who was born in 1944, reaches the age of 21 years, and upon his reaching that age, the corpus and accumulated income are to be distributed to him. The trust instrument provides that capital gains are to be allocated to corpus and are not to be paid, credited, or required to be distributed to any beneficiary during the taxable year or paid, permanently set aside, or to be used for the purposes specified in section 642(c). Under the terms of a tax convention between the United States and Country X, interest income received by the trust from United States sources is exempt from United States taxation. In 1965 the corpus and accumulated income are distributed to the beneficiary. During the taxable year 1964, the trust has the following items of income, loss, and expense:

Interest on bonds of a United States corporation	$10,000
Net long-term capital gain from United States sources	30,000
Gross income from investments in Country X	40,000
Net short-term capital loss from United States sources	5,000
Expenses allocable to gross income from investments in Country X	5,000

(2) The distributable net income for the taxable year 1964 of the foreign trust created by a United States person, determined under section 643(a), is $70,000, computed as follows:

Interest on bonds of a United States corporation		$10,000
Gross income from investments in Country X		40,000
Net long-term capital gain from United States sources	$30,000	
Less: Net short-term capital loss from United States sources	5,000	
Excess of net long-term capital gain over net short-term capital loss		25,000
Total		$75,000
Less: Expenses allocable to income from investments in Country X		5,000
Distributable net income		$70,000

(3) In determining the distributable net income of $70,000, the taxable income of the trust is computed with the following modifications: No deduction is allowed for the personal exemption of the trust (section 643(a)(2)); the interest received on bonds of a United States corporation is included in the trust gross income despite the fact that such interest is exempt from United States tax under the provisions of the tax treaty between Country X and the United States (section 643(a)(6)(B)); the excess of net long-term capital gain over net short-term capital loss allocable to corpus is included in distributable net income, but such excess is not subject to the deduction under section 1202 (section 643(a)(6)(C)); and the amount representing gross income from investments in Country X is included, but such amount is reduced by the amount of the disbursements allocable to such income (section 643(a)(6)(A)).

Example (2). (1) The facts are the same as in example (1) except that money or property has also been transferred to the trust by a person other than a United States person and, pursuant to the provisions of §1.643(d)-1, during 1964 only 60 percent of the entire trust constitutes a foreign trust created by a United States person.

(2) The distributable net income for the taxable year 1964 of the foreign trust created by a United States person, determined under section 643(a), is $42,000 computed as follows:

Interest on bonds of a United States corporation (60% of $10,000)		$ 6,000
Gross income from investments in County X (60% of $40,000)		24,000
Net long-term capital gain from United States sources (60% of $30,000)	$18,000	
Less: Net short-term capital loss from United States sources (60% of $5,000)	$3,000	
Total		$45,000
Less: Expenses allocable to income from investments in Country X (60% of $5,000)		$3,000
Distributable net income		$42,000

(3) The distributable net income for the taxable year 1964 of the portion of the entire foreign trust which does not constitute a foreign trust created by a United States person, determined under section 643(a), is $18,000, computed as follows:

Interest on bonds of a United States corporation (40% of $10,000)	$4,000
Gross income from investments in Country X (40% of $40,000)	16,000
Total	$20,000
Less: Expenses allocable to income from investments in Country X (40% of $5,000)	2,000

(4) The distributable net income of the entire foreign trust for the taxable year 1964 is $60,000, computed as follows:

Distributable net income of the foreign trust created by a United States person	$42,000
Distributable net income of that portion of the entire foreign trust which does not constitute a foreign trust created by a United States person	18,000
Distributable net income of the entire foreign trust	$60,000

It should be noted that the difference between the $70,000 distributable net income of the foreign trust in example (1) and the $60,000 distributable net income of the entire foreign trust in this example is due to the $10,000 (40% of $25,000) net capital gain (capital gain net income for taxable years beginning after December 31, 1976) which under section 643(a)(3) is excluded from the distributable net income of that portion of the foreign trust in example (2) which does not constitute a foreign trust created by a United States person. [Reg. §1.643(a)-6.]

☐ [*T.D. 6217, 12-19-56. Amended by T.D. 6989, 1-16-69 and by T.D. 7728, 10-31-80.*]

[Reg. §1.643(a)-7]

§1.643(a)-7. Dividends.—Dividends excluded from gross income under section 116 (relating to partial exclusion of dividends received) are included in distributable net income. For this purpose, adjustments similar to those required by §1.643(a)-5 with respect to expenses allocable to tax-exempt income and to income included in amounts paid or set aside for charitable purposes are not made. See the regulations under section 642(c). [Reg. §1.643(a)-7.]

☐ [*T.D. 6217, 12-19-56. Amended by T.D. 7357, 5-30-75.*]

[Reg. §1.643(a)-8]

§1.643(a)-8. Certain distributions by charitable remainder trusts.—(a) *Purpose and scope.*—This section is intended to prevent the avoidance of the purposes of the charitable remainder trust rules regarding the characterizations of distributions from those trusts in the hands of the recipients and should be interpreted in a manner consistent with this purpose. This section applies to all charitable remainder trusts described in section 664 and the beneficiaries of such trusts.

(b) *Deemed sale by trust.*—(1) For purposes of section 664(b), a charitable remainder trust shall be treated as having sold, in the year in which a distribution of an annuity or unitrust amount is made from the trust, a pro rata portion of the trust assets to the extent that the distribution of the annuity or unitrust amount would (but for the application of this paragraph (b)) be characterized in the hands of the recipient as being from the category described in section 664(b)(4) and exceeds the amount of the previously undistributed

(i) Cash contributed to the trust (with respect to which a deduction was allowable under section 170, 2055, 2106, or 2522); plus

(ii) Basis in any contributed property (with respect to which a deduction was allowable under section 170, 2055, 2106; or 2522) that was sold by the trust.

(2) Any transaction that has the purpose or effect of circumventing the rules in this paragraph (b) shall be disregarded.

(3) For purposes of paragraph (b)(1) of this section, trust assets do not include cash or assets purchased with the proceeds of a trust borrowing, forward sale, or similar transaction.

(4) Proper adjustment shall be made to any gain or loss subsequently realized for gain or loss taken into account under paragraph (b)(1) of this section.

(c) *Examples*. The following examples illustrate the rules of paragraph (b) of this section:

Example 1. Deemed sale by trust. Donor contributes stock having a fair market value of $2 million to a charitable remainder unitrust with a unitrust amount of 50 percent of the net fair market value of the trust assets and a two-year term. The stock has a total adjusted basis of $400,000. In Year 1, the trust receives dividend income of $20,000. As of the valuation date, the trust's assets have a net fair market value of $2,020,000 ($2 million in stock, plus $20,000 in cash). To obtain additional cash to pay the unitrust amount to the noncharitable beneficiary, the trustee borrows $990,000 against the value of the stock. The trust then distributes $1,010,000 to the beneficiary before the end of Year 1. Under section 664(b)(1), $20,000 of the distribution is characterized in the hands of the beneficiary as dividend income. The rest of the distribution, $990,000, is attributable to an amount received by the trust that did not represent either cash contributed to the trust or a return of basis in any contributed asset sold by the trust during Year 1. Under paragraph (b)(3) of this section, the stock is a trust asset because it was not purchased with the proceeds of the borrowing. Therefore, in Year 1, under paragraph (b)(1) of this section, the trust is treated as having sold $990,000 of stock and as having realized $792,000 of capital gain (the trust's basis in the shares deemed sold is $198,000). Thus, in the hands of the beneficiary, $792,000 of the distribution is characterized as capital gain under section 664(b)(2) and $198,000 is characterized as a tax-free return of corpus under section 664(b)(4). No part of the $990,000 loan is treated as acquisition indebtedness under section 514(c) because the entire loan has been recharacterized as a deemed sale.

Example 2. Adjustment to trust's basis in assets deemed sold. The facts are the same as in *Example 1.* During Year 2, the trust sells the stock for $2,100,000. The trustee uses a portion of the proceeds of the sale to repay the outstanding loan, plus accrued interest. Under paragraph (b)(4) of this section, the trust's adjusted basis in the stock is $1,192,000 ($400,000 plus the $792,000 of gain recognized in Year 1). Therefore, the trust recognizes capital gain (as described in section 664(b)(2)) in Year 2 of $908,000.

Example 3. Distribution of cash contributions. Upon the death of D, the proceeds of a life insurance policy on D's life are payable to T, a charitable remainder annuity trust. The terms of the trust provide that, for a period of three years commencing upon D's death, the trust shall pay an annuity amount equal to $x annually to A, the child of D. After the expiration of such three-year period, the remainder interest in the trust is to be transferred to charity Z. In Year 1, the trust receives payment of the life insurance proceeds and pays the appropriate pro rata portion of the $x annuity to A from the insurance proceeds. During Year 1, the trust has no income. Because the entire distribution is attributable to a cash contribution (the insurance proceeds) to the trust for which a charitable deduction was allowable under section 2055 with respect to the present value of the remainder interest passing to charity, the trust will not be treated as selling a pro rata portion of the trust assets under paragraph (b)(1) of this section. Thus, the distribution is characterized in A's hands as a tax-free return of corpus under section 664(b)(4).

(d) *Effective date.* This section is applicable to distributions made by a charitable remainder trust after October 18, 1999. [Reg. § 1.643(a)-8.]

☐ [*T.D.* 8926, 1-4-2001.]

[Reg. § 1.643(b)-1]

§ 1.643(b)-1. Definition of income.—For purposes of subparts A through D, part I, subchapter J, chapter 1 of the Internal Revenue Code, "income," when not preceded by the words "taxable," "distributable net," "undistributed net," or "gross," means the amount of income of an estate or trust for the taxable year determined under the terms of the governing instrument and applicable local law. Trust provisions that depart fundamentally from traditional principles of income and principal will generally not be recognized. For example, if a trust instrument directs that all the trust income shall be paid to the income beneficiary but defines ordinary dividends and interest as principal, the trust will not be considered one that under its governing instrument is required to distribute all its income currently for purposes of section 642(b) (relating to the personal exemption) and section 651 (relating to simple trusts). Thus, items such as dividends, interest, and rents are generally allocated to income and proceeds from the sale or exchange of trust assets are generally allocated to principal. However, an allocation of amounts between income and principal pursuant to applicable local law will be respected if local law provides for a reasonable apportionment between the income and remainder beneficiaries of the total return of the trust for the year, including ordinary and tax-exempt income, capital gains, and appreciation. For example, a state statute providing that income is a unitrust amount of no less than 3% and no more than 5% of the fair market value of the trust assets, whether determined annually or averaged on a multiple year basis, is a reasonable apportionment of the total return of the trust. Similarly, a state statute that permits the trustee to make adjustments between income and principal to fulfill the trustee's duty of impartiality between the income and remainder beneficiaries is generally a reasonable apportionment of the total return of the trust. Generally, these adjustments are permitted by state statutes when the trustee invests and manages the trust assets under the state's prudent investor standard, the trust describes the amount that may or must be distributed to a beneficiary by referring to the trust's income, and the trustee after applying the state statutory rules regarding the allocation of receipts and disbursements to income and principal, is unable to administer the trust impartially. Allocations pursuant to methods prescribed by such state statutes for apportioning the total return of a trust between income and principal will be respected regardless of whether the trust provides that the income must be distributed to one or more beneficiaries or may be accumulated in whole or in part, and regardless of which alternate permitted method is actually used, provided the trust complies with all requirements of the state statute for switching methods. A switch between methods of determining trust income authorized by state statute will not constitute a recognition event for purposes of section 1001 and will not result in a taxable gift from the trust's grantor or any of the trust's beneficiaries. A switch to a method not specifically authorized by state statute, but valid under state law (including a switch via judicial decision or a binding non-judicial settlement) may constitute a recognition event to the trust or its beneficiaries for purposes of section 1001 and may result in taxable gifts from the trust's grantor and beneficiaries, based on the relevant facts and circumstances. In addition, an allocation to income of all or a part of the gains from the sale or exchange of trust assets will generally be respected if the allocation is made either pursuant to the terms of the governing instrument and applicable local law, or pursuant to a reasonable and impartial exercise of a discretionary power granted to the fiduciary by applicable local law or by the governing instrument, if not prohibited by applicable local law. This section is effective for taxable years of trusts and estates ending after January 2, 2004. [Reg. § 1.643(b)-1.]

☐ [*T.D.* 6217, 12-19-56. *Amended by T.D.* 9102, 12-30-2003.]

[Reg. § 1.643(b)-2]

§ 1.643(b)-2. Dividends allocated to corpus.—Extraordinary dividends or taxable stock dividends which the fiduciary, acting in good faith, determines to be allocable to corpus under the terms of the governing instrument and applicable local law are not considered "income" for purposes of subpart A, B, C, or D, part I, subchapter J, chapter 1 of the Code. See section 643(a)(4), § 1.643(a)-4, § 1.643(d)-2, section 665(e), paragraph (b) of § 1.665(e)-1 and paragraph (b) of § 1.665(e)-1A for the treatment of such items in the computation of distributable net income. [Reg. § 1.643(b)-2.]

☐ [*T.D.* 6217, 12-19-56. *Amended by T.D.* 6989, 1-16-69 *and by T.D.* 7204, 8-24-72.]

[Reg. § 1.643(c)-1]

§ 1.643(c)-1. Definition of "beneficiary".—An heir, legatee, or devisee (including an estate or trust) is a beneficiary. A trust created under a decedent's will is a beneficiary of the decedent's estate. The following persons are treated as beneficiaries:

(a) Any person with respect to an amount used to discharge or satisfy that person's legal obligation as that term is used in § 1.662(a)-4.

(b) The grantor of a trust with respect to an amount applied or distributed for the support of a dependent under the circumstances specified in section 677(b) out of corpus or out of other than income for the taxable year of the trust.

(c) The trustee or cotrustee of a trust with respect to an amount applied or distributed for the support of a dependent under the circumstances specified in section 678(c) out of corpus or out of other than income for the taxable year of the trust. [Reg. § 1.643(c)-1.]

☐ [*T.D.* 6217, 12-19-56.]

[Reg. § 1.643(d)-1]

§ 1.643(d)-1. Definition of "foreign trust created by a United States person".—(a) *In general.*—For the purpose of Part I, subchapter J, chapter 1 of the Internal Revenue Code, the term "foreign trust created by a United States person" means that portion of a foreign trust (as defined in section 7701(a)(31)) attributable to money or property (including all accumulated earnings, profits, or gains attributable to such money or property) of a United States person (as defined in Sec. 7701(a)(30)) transferred directly or indirectly, or under the will of a decedent who at the date of his death was a United States citizen or resident, to the foreign trust. A foreign trust created by a person who is not a United States person, to which a United States person transfers his money or property, is a foreign trust created by a United States person to the extent that the fair market value of the entire foreign trust is attributable to money or property of the United States person transferred to the foreign trust. The transfer of money or property to the foreign trust may be made either directly or indirectly by a United States person. Transfers of money or property to a foreign trust do not include transfers of money or property pursuant to a sale or exchange which is made for a full and adequate consideration. Transfers to which section 643(d) and this section apply are transfers of money or property which establish or increase the corpus of a foreign trust. The rules set forth in this section with respect to transfers by a United States person to a foreign trust also are applicable with respect to transfers under the will of a decedent who at the date of his death was a United States citizen or resident. For provisions relating to the information returns which are required to be filed with respect to the creation of or transfers to foreign trusts, see section 6048.

(b) *Determination of a foreign trust created by a United States person.*—(1) *Transfers of money or property only by a United States person.*—If all the items of money or property constituting the corpus of a foreign trust are transferred to the trust by a United States person, the entire foreign trust is a foreign trust created by a United States person.

(2) *Transfers of money or property by both a United States person and a person other than a United States person; transfers required to be treated as separate funds.*—Where there are transfers of money or property by both a United States person and a person other than a United States person to a foreign trust, and it is necessary, either by reason of the provisions of the governing instrument of the trust or by reason of some other requirement such as local law, that the trustee treat the entire foreign trust as composed of two separate funds, one consisting of the money or property (including all accumulated earnings, profits, or gains attributable to such money or property) transferred by the United States person and the other consisting of the money or property (including all accumulated earnings, profits, or gains attributable to such money or property) transferred by the person other than the United States person, the foreign trust created by a United States person shall be the fund consisting of the money or property transferred by the United States person. See example (1) in paragraph (c) of this section.

(3) *Transfers of money or property by both a United States person and a person other than a United States person; transfers not required to be treated as separate funds.*—Where the corpus of a foreign trust consists of money or property transferred to the trust (simultaneously or at different times) by a United States person and by a person who is not a United States person, the foreign trust created by a United States person within the meaning of section 643(d) is that portion of the entire foreign trust which, immediately after any transfer of money or property to the trust, the fair market value of money or property (including all accumulated earnings, profits, or gains attributable to such money or property) transferred to the foreign trust by the United States person bears to the fair market value of the corpus (including all accumulated earnings, profits, or gains attributable to the corpus) of the entire foreign trust.

(c) The provisions of paragraph (b) of this section may be illustrated by the following examples. Example (1) illustrates the application of paragraph (b)(2) of this section. Example (2) illustrates the application of paragraph (b)(3) of this section in a case where there is no provision in the governing instrument of the trust or elsewhere which would require the trustee to treat the corpus of the trust as composed of more than one fund.

Example (1). On January 1, 1964, the date of the creation of a foreign trust, a United States person transfers to it stock of a United States corporation with a fair market value of $50,000. On the same day, a person other than a United States person transfers to the trust Country X bonds with a fair market value of $25,000. The governing instrument of the trust provides that the income from the stock of the United States corporation is to be accumulated until A, a United States beneficiary, reaches the age of 21 years, and upon his reaching that age, the stock and income accumulated thereon are to be distributed to him. The governing instrument of the trust further provides that the income from the Country X bonds is to be accumulated until B, a United States beneficiary, reaches the age of 21 years, and upon his reaching that age, the bonds and income accumulated thereon are to be distributed to him. To comply with the provisions of the governing instrument of the trust that the income from the stock of the United States corporation be accumulated and distributed to A and that the income from the Country X bonds be accumulated and distributed to B, it is necessary that the trustee treat the transfers as two separate funds. The fund consisting of the stock of the United States corporation is a foreign trust created by a United States person.

Example (2). On January 1, 1964, the date of the creation of a foreign trust, a United States person transfers to it property having a fair market value of $60,000 and a person other than a United States person transfers to it property having a fair market value of $40,000. Immediately after these transfers, the foreign trust created by a United States person is 60 percent of the entire foreign trust, determined as follows:

$$\frac{\$60{,}000 \text{ (Value of property transferred by U.S. person)}}{\$100{,}000 \text{ (Value of entire property transferred to trust)}} = 60 \text{ percent}$$

The undistributed net income for the calendar years 1964 and 1965 is $20,000 which increases the value of the entire foreign trust to $120,000 ($100,000 plus $20,000). Accordingly, as of December 31, 1965, the portion of the foreign trust created by the United States person is $72,000 (60% of $120,000). On January 1, 1966, the United States person transfers property having a fair market value of $40,000 increasing the value of the entire foreign trust to $160,000 ($120,000 plus $40,000) and increasing the value of the portion of the foreign trust created by the United States person to $112,000 ($72,000 plus $40,000). Immediately after this transfer, the foreign trust created by the United States person is 70 percent of the entire foreign trust, determined as follows:

$$\frac{\$112{,}000 \text{ (Value of property transferred by U.S. person)}}{\$160{,}000 \text{ (Value of entire property transferred to the trust)}} = 70 \text{ percent}$$

[Reg. § 1.643(d)-1.]

☐ [*T.D. 6989, 1-16-69. Amended by T.D. 9849*, 3-11-2019.]

[Reg. § 1.643(d)-2]

§ 1.643(d)-2. Illustration of the provisions of section 643.—(a) The provisions of section 643 may be illustrated by the following example:

Example. (1) Under the terms of the trust instrument, the income of a trust is required to be currently distributed to W during her life. Capital gains are allocable to corpus and all expenses are charges against corpus. During the taxable year the trust has the following items of income and expenses:

Dividends for domestic corporations	$30,000
Extraordinary dividends allocated to corpus by the trustee in good faith	20,000
Taxable interest	10,000
Tax-exempt interest	10,000
Long-term capital gains	10,000
Trustee's commissions and miscellaneous expenses allocable to corpus	5,000

(2) The "income" of the trust determined under section 643(b) which is currently distributable to W is $50,000, consisting of dividends of $30,000, taxable interest of $10,000 and tax-exempt interest of $10,000. The trustee's commissions and miscellaneous expenses allocable to tax-exempt interest amount to $1,000 (10,000/50,000 × $5,000).

(3) The "distributable net income" determined under section 643(a) amounts to $45,000, computed as follows:

Dividends from domestic corporations		$30,000
Taxable interest		10,000
Nontaxable interest	$10,000	
Less: Expenses allocable thereto	1,000	9,000
Total		$49,000
Less: Expenses ($5,000 less $1,000 allocable to tax-exempt interest)		$ 4,000
Distributable net income		$45,000

In determining the distributable net income of $45,000, the taxable income of the trust is computed with the following modifications: No deductions are allowed for distributions to W and for personal exemption of the trust (section 643(a)(1) and (2)); capital gains allocable to corpus are excluded and the deduction allowable under section 1202 is not taken into account (section 643(a)(3)); the extraordinary dividends allocated to corpus by the trustee in good faith are excluded (section 643(a)(4)); and the tax-exempt interest (as adjusted for expenses) and the dividend exclusion of $50 are included (section 643(a)(5) and (7)).

(b) See paragraph (c) of the example in § 1.661(c)-2 for the computation of distributable net income where there is a charitable contributions deduction. [Reg. § 1.643(d)-2.]

☐ [*T.D.* 6217, 12-19-56. *Amended by T.D.* 6989, 1-16-69.]

[Reg. § 1.643(f)-1]

§ 1.643(f)-1. Treatment of multiple trusts.—(a) *General rule.*—For purposes of subchapter J of chapter 1 of subtitle A of Title 26 of the United States Code, two or more trusts will be aggregated and treated as a single trust if such trusts have substantially the same grantor or grantors and substantially the same primary beneficiary or beneficiaries, and if a principal purpose for establishing one or more of such trusts or for contributing additional cash or other property to such trusts is the avoidance of Federal income tax. For purposes of applying this rule, spouses will be treated as one person.

(b) *Applicability date.*—The provisions of this section apply to taxable years ending after August 16, 2018. [Reg. § 1.643(f)-1.]

☐ [T.D. 9847, 2-4-2019.]

[Reg. § 1.643(h)-1]

§ 1.643(h)-1. Distributions by certain foreign trusts through intermediaries.—(a) *In general.*—(1) *Principal purpose of tax avoidance.*—Except as provided in paragraph (b) of this section, for purposes of part I of subchapter j, chapter 1 of the Internal Revenue Code, and section 6048, any property (within the meaning of paragraph (f) of this section) that is transferred to a United States person by another person (an intermediary) who has received property from a foreign trust will be treated as property transferred directly by the foreign trust to the United States person if the intermediary received the property from the foreign trust pursuant to a plan one of the principal purposes of which was the avoidance of United States tax.

(2) *Principal purpose of tax avoidance deemed to exist.*—For purposes of paragraph (a)(1) of this section, a transfer will be deemed to have been made pursuant to a plan one of the principal purposes of which was the avoidance of United States tax if the United States person—

(i) Is related (within the meaning of paragraph (e) of this section) to a grantor of the foreign trust, or has another relationship with a grantor of the foreign trust that establishes a reasonable basis for concluding that the grantor of the foreign trust would make a gratuitous transfer (within the meaning of § 1.671-2(e)(2)) to the United States person;

(ii) Receives from the intermediary, within the period beginning twenty-four months before and ending twenty-four months after the intermediary's receipt of property from the foreign trust, either the property the intermediary received from the foreign trust, proceeds from such property, or property in substitution for such property; and

(iii) Cannot demonstrate to the satisfaction of the Commissioner that—

(A) The intermediary has a relationship with the United States person that establishes a reasonable basis for concluding that the intermediary would make a gratuitous transfer to the United States person;

(B) The intermediary acted independently of the grantor and the trustee of the foreign trust;

(C) The intermediary is not an agent of the United States person under generally applicable United States agency principles; and

(D) The United States person timely complied with the reporting requirements of section 6039F, if applicable, if the intermediary is a foreign person.

(b) *Exceptions.*—(1) *Nongratuitous transfers.*—Paragraph (a) of this section does not apply to the extent that either the transfer from the foreign trust to the intermediary or the transfer from the intermediary to the United States person is a transfer that is not a gratuitous transfer within the meaning of § 1.671-2(e)(2).

(2) *Grantor as intermediary.*—Paragraph (a) of this section does not apply if the intermediary is the grantor of the portion of the trust from which the property that is transferred is derived. For the definition of *grantor*, see § 1.671-2(e).

(c) *Effect of disregarding intermediary.*—(1) *General rule.*—Except as provided in paragraph (c)(2) of this section, the intermediary is treated as an agent of the foreign trust, and the property is treated as transferred to the United States person in the year the property is transferred, or made available, by the intermediary to the United States person. The fair market value of the property transferred is determined as of the date of the transfer by the intermediary to the United States person. For purposes of section 665(d)(2),

See p. 15 for regulations not amended to reflect law changes

the term *taxes imposed on the trust* includes any income, war profits, and excess profits taxes imposed by any foreign country or possession of the United States on the intermediary with respect to the property transferred.

(2) *Exception.*—If the Commissioner determines, or if the taxpayer can demonstrate to the satisfaction of the Commissioner, that the intermediary is an agent of the United States person under generally applicable United States agency principles, the property will be treated as transferred to the United States person in the year the intermediary receives the property from the foreign trust. The fair market value of the property transferred will be determined as of the date of the transfer by the foreign trust to the intermediary. For purposes of section 901(b), any income, war profits, and excess profits taxes imposed by any foreign country or possession of the United States on the intermediary with respect to the property transferred will be treated as having been imposed on the United States person.

(3) *Computation of gross income of intermediary.*—If property is treated as transferred directly by the foreign trust to a United States person pursuant to this section, the fair market value of such property is not taken into account in computing the gross income of the intermediary (if otherwise required to be taken into account by the intermediary but for paragraph (a) of this section).

(d) *Transfers not in excess of $10,000.*—This section does not apply if, during the taxable year of the United States person, the aggregate fair market value of all property transferred to such person from all foreign trusts either directly or through one or more intermediaries does not exceed $10,000.

(e) *Related parties.*—For purposes of this section, a United States person is treated as related to a grantor of a foreign trust if the United States person and the grantor are related for purposes of section 643(i)(2)(B), with the following modifications—

(1) For purposes of applying section 267 (other than section 267(f).) and section 707(b)(1), "at least 10 percent" is used instead of "more than 50 percent" each place it appears; and

(2) The principles of section 267(b)(10), using "at least 10 percent" instead of "more than 50 percent," apply to determine whether two corporations are related.

(f) *Definition of property.*—For purposes of this section, the term *property* includes cash.

(g) *Examples.*—The following examples illustrate the rules of this section. In each example, FT is an irrevocable foreign trust that is not treated as owned by any other person and the fair market value of the property that is transferred exceeds $10,000. The examples are as follows:

Example 1. Principal purpose of tax avoidance. FT was created in 1980 by A, a nonresident alien, for the benefit of his children and their descendants. FT's trustee, T, determines that 1000X of accumulated income should be distributed to A's granddaughter, B, who is a resident alien. Pursuant to a plan with a principal purpose of avoiding the interest charge that would be imposed by section 668, T causes FT to make a gratuitous transfer (within the meaning of § 1.671-2(e)(2)) of 1000X to I, a foreign person. I subsequently makes a gratuitous transfer of 1000X to B. Under paragraph (a)(1) of this section, FT is deemed to have made an accumulation distribution of 1000X directly to B.

Example 2. United States person unable to demonstrate that intermediary acted independently. GM and her daughter, M, are both nonresident aliens. M's daughter, D, is a resident alien. GM creates and funds FT for the benefit of her children. On July 1, 2001, FT makes a gratuitous transfer of XYZ stock to M. M immediately sells the XYZ stock and uses the proceeds to purchase ABC stock. On January 1, 2002, M makes a gratuitous transfer of the ABC stock to D. D is unable to demonstrate that M acted independently of GM and the trustee of FT in making the transfer to D. Under paragraph (a)(2) of this section, FT is deemed to have distributed the ABC stock to D. Under paragraph (c)(1) of this section, M is treated as an agent of FT, and the distribution is deemed to have been made on January 1, 2002.

Example 3. United States person demonstrates that specified conditions are satisfied. Assume the same facts as in *Example* 2, except that M receives 1000X cash from FT instead of XYZ stock. M gives 1000X cash to D on January 1, 2002. Also assume that M receives annual income of 5000X from her own investments and that M has given D 1000X at the beginning of each year for the past ten years. Based on this and additional information provided by D, D demonstrates to the satisfaction of the Commissioner that M has a relationship with D that establishes a reasonable basis for concluding that M would make a gratuitous transfer to D, that M acted independently of GM and the trustee of FT, that M is not an agent of D under generally applicable United States agency principles, and that D timely complied with the reporting requirements of section 6039F. FT will not be deemed under paragraph (a)(2) of this section to have made a distribution to D.

Example 4. Transfer to United States person less than 24 months before transfer to intermediary. Several years ago, A, a nonresident alien, created and funded FT for the benefit of his children and their descendants. A has a close friend, C, who also is a nonresident alien. A's granddaughter, B, is a resident alien. On December 31, 2001, C makes a gratuitous transfer of 1000X to B. On January 15, 2002, FT makes a gratuitous transfer of 1000X to C. B is unable to demonstrate that C has a relationship with B that would establish a reasonable basis for concluding that C would make a gratuitous transfer to B or that C acted independently of A and the trustee of FT in making the transfer to B. Under paragraph (a)(2) of this section, FT is deemed to have distributed 1000X directly to B. Under paragraph (c)(1) of this section, C is treated as an agent of FT, and the distribution is deemed to have been made on December 31, 2001.

Example 5. United States person receives property in substitution for property transferred to intermediary. GM and her son, S, are both nonresident aliens. S's daughter, GD, is a resident alien. GM creates and funds FT for the benefit of her children and their descendants. On July 1, 2001, FT makes a gratuitous transfer of ABC stock with a fair market value of approximately 1000X to S. On January 1, 2002, S makes a gratuitous transfer of DEP stock with a fair market value of approximately 1000X to GD. GD is unable to demonstrate that S acted independently of GM and the trustee of FT in transferring the DEF stock to GD. Under paragraph (a)(2) of this section, FT is deemed to have distributed the DEF stock to GD. Under paragraph (c)(1) of this section, S is treated as an agent of FT, and the distribution is deemed to have been made on January 1, 2002.

Example 6. United States person receives indirect loan from foreign trust. Several years ago, A, a nonresident alien, created and funded FT for the benefit of her children and their descendants. A's daughter, B, is a resident alien. B needs funds temporarily while she is starting up her own business. If FT were to loan money directly to B, section 643(i) would apply. FT deposits 500X with FB, a foreign bank, on June 30, 2001. On July 1, 2001, FB loans 400X to B. Repayment of the loan is guaranteed by FT's 500X deposit. B is unable to demonstrate to the satisfaction of the Commissioner that FB has a relationship with B that establishes a reasonable basis for concluding that FB would make a loan to B or that FB acted independently of A and the trustee of FT in making the loan. Under paragraph (a)(2) of this section, FT is deemed to have loaned 400X directly to B on July 1, 2001. Under paragraph (c)(1) of this section, FB is treated as an agent of FT. For the treatment of loans from foreign trusts, see section 643(i).

Example 7. United States person demonstrates that specified conditions are satisfied. GM, a nonresident alien, created and funded FT for the benefit of her children and their descendants. One of GM's children is M, who is a resident alien. During the year 2001, FT makes a gratuitous transfer of 500X to M. M reports the 500X on Form 3520 as a distribution received from a foreign trust. During the year 2002, M makes a gratuitous transfer of 400X to her son, S, who also is a resident alien. M files a Form 709 treating the gratuitous transfer to S as a gift. Based on this and additional information provided by S, S demonstrates to the satisfaction of the Commissioner that M has a relationship with S that establishes a reasonable basis for concluding that M would make a gratuitous transfer to S, that M acted independently of GM and the trustee of FT, and that M is not an agent of S under generally applicable United States agency principles. FT will not be deemed under paragraph (a)(2) of this section to have made a distribution to S.

Example 8. Intermediary as agent of trust; increase in FMV. A, a nonresident alien, created and funded FT for the benefit of his children and their descendants. On December 1, 2001, FT makes a gratuitous transfer of XYZ stock with a fair market value of 85X to B, a nonresident alien. On November 1, 2002, B sells the XYZ stock to a third party in an arm's length transaction for 100X in cash. On November 1, 2002, B makes a gratuitous transfer of 98X to A's grandson, C, a resident alien. C is unable to demonstrate to the satisfaction of the Commissioner that B acted independently of A and the trustee of FT in making the transfer. Under paragraph (a)(2) of this section, FT is deemed to have made a distribution directly to C. Under paragraph (c)(1) of this section, B is treated as an agent of FT, and FT is deemed to have distributed 98X to C on November 1, 2002.

Example 9. Intermediary as agent of United States person; increase in FMV. Assume the same facts as in *Example 8*, except that the Commissioner determines that B is an agent of C under generally applicable United States agency principles. Under paragraph (c)(2) of this section, FT is deemed to have distributed 85X to C on December 1, 2001. C must take the gain of 15X into account in the year 2002.

Example 10. Intermediary as agent of trust; decrease in FMV. Assume the same facts as in *Example 8*, except that the value of the XYZ stock on November 1, 2002, is only 80X. Instead of selling the XYZ stock to a third party and transferring cash to C, B transfers the XYZ stock to C in a gratuitous transfer. Under paragraph (c)(1) of this section, FT is deemed to have distributed XYZ stock with a value of 80X to C on November 1, 2002.

Example 11. Intermediary as agent of United States person; decrease in FMV. Assume the same facts as in *Example 10*, except that the Commissioner determines that B is an agent of C under generally applicable United States agency principles. Under paragraph (c)(2) of this section, FT is deemed to have distributed XYZ stock with a value of 85X to C on December 1, 2001.

(h) *Effective date.*—The rules of this section are applicable to transfers made to United States persons after August 10, 1999. [Reg. § 1.643(h)-1.]

□ [*T.D.* 8831, 8-5-99. *Amended by T.D.* 8890, 7-3-2000.]

[Reg. § 1.645-1]

§ 1.645-1. Election by certain revocable trusts to be treated as part of estate.—(a) *In general.*—If an election is filed for a qualified revocable trust, as defined in paragraph (b)(1) of this section, in accordance with the rules set forth in paragraph (c) of this section, the qualified revocable trust is treated and taxed for purposes of subtitle A of the Internal Revenue Code as part of its related estate, as defined in paragraph (b)(5) of this section (and not as a separate trust) during the election period, as defined in paragraph (b)(6) of this section. Rules regarding the use of taxpayer identification numbers (TINs) and the filing of a Form 1041, "U.S. Income Tax Return for Estates and Trusts," for a qualified revocable trust are in paragraph (d) of this section. Rules regarding the tax treatment of an electing trust and related estate and the general filing requirements for the combined entity during the election period are in paragraph (e)(2) of this section. Rules regarding the tax treatment of an electing trust and its filing requirements during the election period if no executor, as defined in paragraph (b)(4) of this section, is appointed for a related estate are in paragraph (e)(3) of this section. Rules for determining the duration of the section 645 election period are in paragraph (f) of this section. Rules regarding the tax effects of the termination of the election are in paragraph (h) of this section. Rules regarding the tax consequences of the appointment of an executor after a trustee has made a section 645 election believing that an executor would not be appointed for a related estate are in paragraph (g) of this section.

(b) *Definitions.*—For purposes of this section:

(1) *Qualified revocable trust.*—A *qualified revocable trust* (QRT) is any trust (or portion thereof) that on the date of death of the decedent was treated as owned by the decedent under section 676 by reason of a power held by the decedent (determined without regard to section 672(e)). A trust that was treated as owned by the decedent under section 676 by reason of a power that was exercisable by the decedent only with the approval or consent of a nonadverse party or with the approval or consent of the decedent's spouse is a QRT. A trust that was treated as owned by the decedent under section 676 solely by reason of a power held by a nonadverse party or by reason of a power held by the decedent's spouse is not a QRT.

(2) *Electing trust.*—An *electing trust* is a QRT for which a valid section 645 election has been made. Once a section 645 election has been made for the trust, the trust shall be treated as an electing trust throughout the entire election period.

(3) *Decedent.*—The *decedent* is the individual who was treated as the owner of the QRT under section 676 on the date of that individual's death.

(4) *Executor.*—An *executor* is an executor, personal representative, or administrator that has obtained letters of appointment to administer the decedent's estate through formal or informal appointment procedures. Solely for purposes of this paragraph (b)(4), an executor does not include a person that has actual or constructive possession of property of the decedent unless that person is also appointed or qualified as an executor, administrator, or personal representative of the decedent's estate. If more that one jurisdiction has appointed an executor, the executor appointed in the domiciliary or primary proceeding is the executor of the related estate for purposes of this paragraph (b)(4).

(5) *Related estate.*—A *related estate* is the estate of the decedent who was treated as the owner of the QRT on the date of the decedent's death.

(6) *Election period.*—The *election period* is the period of time during which an electing trust is treated and taxed as part of its related estate. The rules for determining the duration of the election period are in paragraph (f) of this section.

(c) *The election.*—(1) *Filing the election if there is an executor.*—(i) *Time and manner for filing the election.*—If there is an executor of the related estate, the trustees of each QRT joining in the election and the executor of the related estate make an election under section 645 and this section to treat each QRT joining in the election as part of the related estate for purposes of subtitle A of the Internal Revenue Code by filing a form provided by the IRS for making the election (election form) properly completed and signed under penalties of perjury, or in any other manner prescribed after December 24, 2002 by forms provided by the Internal Revenue Service (IRS), or by other published guidance for making the election. For the election to be valid, the election form must be filed not later than the time prescribed under section 6072 for filing the Form 1041 for$ the first taxable year of the related estate (regardless of whether there is sufficient income to require the filing of that return). If an extension is granted for the filing of the Form 1041 for the first taxable year of the related estate, the election form will be timely filed if it is filed by the time prescribed for filing the Form 1041 including the extension granted with respect to the Form 1041.

(ii) *Conditions to election.*—In addition to providing the information required by the election form, as a condition to a valid section 645 election, the trustee of each QRT joining in the election and the executor of the related estate agree, by signing the election form under penalties of perjury, that:

(A) With respect to a trustee—

(1) The trustee agrees to the election;

(2) The trustee is responsible for timely providing the executor of the related estate with all the trust information necessary to permit the executor to file a complete, accurate, and timely Form 1041 for the combined electing trust(s) and related estate for each taxable year during the election period;

(3) The trustee of each QRT joining the election and the executor of the related estate have agreed to allocate the tax burden of the combined electing trust(s) and related estate for each taxable year during the election period in a manner that reasonably reflects the tax obligations of each electing trust and the related estate; and

(4) The trustee is responsible for insuring that the electing trust's share of the tax obligations of the combined electing trust(s) and related estate is timely paid to the Secretary.

(B) With respect to the executor—

(1) The executor agrees to the election;

(2) The executor is responsible for filing a complete, accurate, and timely Form 1041 for the combined electing trust(s) and related estate for each taxable year during the election period;

(3) The executor and the trustee of each QRT joining in the election have agreed to allocate the tax burden of the combined electing trust(s) and related estate for each taxable year during the election period in a manner that reasonably reflects the tax obligations of each electing trust and the related estate;

(4) The executor is responsible for insuring that the related estate's share of the tax obligations of the combined electing trust(s) and related estate is timely paid to the Secretary.

(2) *Filing the election if there is no executor.*—(i) *Time and manner for filing the election.*—If there is no executor for a related estate, an election to treat one or more QRTs of the decedent as an estate for purposes of subtitle A of the Internal Revenue Code is made by the trustees of each QRT joining in the election, by filing a properly completed election form, or in any other manner prescribed after December 24, 2002 by forms provided by the IRS, or by other published guidance for making the election. For the election to be valid, the election form must be filed not later than the time prescribed under section 6072 for filing the Form 1041 for the first taxable year of the trust, taking into account the trustee's election to treat the trust as an estate under section 645 (regardless of whether there is sufficient income to require the filing of that return). If an extension is granted for the filing of the Form 1041 for the first taxable year of the electing trust, the election form will be timely filed if it is filed by the time prescribed for filing the Form 1041 including the extension granted with respect to the filing of the Form 1041.

(ii) *Conditions to election.*—In addition to providing the information required by the election form, as a condition to a valid section 645 election, the trustee of each QRT joining in the election agrees, by signing the election form under penalties of perjury, that—

(A) The trustee agrees to the election;

(B) If there is more than one QRT joining in the election, the trustees of each QRT joining in the election have appointed one trustee to be responsible for filing the Form 1041 for the combined electing trusts for each taxable year during the election period (filing trustee) and the filing trustee has agreed to accept that responsibility;

(C) If there is more than one QRT, the trustees of each QRT joining in the election have agreed to allocate the tax liability of the combined electing trusts for each taxable year during the election period in a manner that reasonably reflects the tax obligations of each electing trust;

(D) The trustee agrees to:

(1) Timely file a Form 1041 for the electing trust(s) for each taxable year during the election period; or

(2) If there is more than one QRT and the trustee is not the filing trustee, timely provide the filing trustee with all of the electing trust's information necessary to permit the filing trustee to file a complete, accurate, and timely Form 1041 for the combined electing trusts for each taxable year during the election period;

(3) Insure that the electing trust's share of the tax burden is timely paid to the Secretary;

(E) There is no executor and, to the knowledge and belief of the trustee, one will not be appointed; and

(F) If an executor is appointed after the filing of the election form and the executor agrees to the section 645 election, the trustee will complete and file a revised election form with the executor.

(3) *Election for more than one QRT.*—If there is more than one QRT, the election may be made for some or all of the QRTs. If there is no executor, one trustee must be appointed by the trustees of the electing trusts to file Forms 1041 for the combined electing trusts filing as an estate during the election period.

(d) *TIN and filing requirements for a QRT.*—(1) *Obtaining a TIN.*—Regardless of whether there is an executor for a related estate and regardless of whether a section 645 election will be made for the QRT, a TIN must be obtained for the QRT following the death of the decedent. See § 301.6109-1(a)(3) of this chapter. The trustee must furnish this TIN to the payors of the QRT. See § 301.6109-1(a)(5) of this chapter for the definition of payor.

(2) *Filing a Form 1041 for a QRT.*—(i) *Option not to file a Form 1041 for a QRT for which a section 645 election will be made.*—If a section 645 election will be made for a QRT, the executor of the related estate, if any, and the trustee of the QRT may treat the QRT as an electing trust from the decedent's date of death until the due date for the section 645 election. Accordingly, the trustee of the QRT is not required to file a Form 1041 for the QRT for the short taxable year beginning with the decedent's date of death and ending December 31 of that year. However, if a QRT is treated as an electing trust under this paragraph from the decedent's date of death until the due date for the section 645 election but a valid section 645 election is not made for the QRT, the QRT will be subject to penalties and interest for failing to timely file a Form 1041 and pay the tax due thereon.

(ii) *Requirement to file a Form 1041 for a QRT if paragraph (d)(2)(i) of this section does not apply.*—(A) *Requirement to file Form 1041.*—If the trustee of the QRT and the executor of the related estate, if any, do not treat the QRT as an electing trust as provided under paragraph (d)(2)(i) of this section, or if the trustee of the electing trust and the executor, if any, are uncertain whether a section 645 election will be made for a QRT, the trustee of the QRT must file a Form 1041 for the short taxable year beginning with the decedent's death and ending December 31 of that year (unless the QRT is not required to file a Form 1041 under section 6012 for this period).

(B) *Requirement to amend Form 1041 if a section 645 election is made.*—(*1*) *If there is an executor.*—If there is an executor and a valid section 645 election is made for a QRT after a Form 1041 has been filed for the QRT as a trust (see paragraph (d)(2)(ii)(A) of this section), the trustee must amend the Form 1041. The QRT's items of income, deduction, and credit must be excluded from the amended Form 1041 filed under this paragraph and must be included on the Form 1041 filed for the first taxable year of the combined electing trust and related estate under paragraph (e)(2)(ii)(A) of this section.

(*2*) *If there is no executor.*—If there is no executor and a valid section 645 election is made for a QRT after a Form 1041 has been filed for the QRT as a trust (see paragraph (d)(2)(ii)(A) of this section) for the short taxable year beginning with the decedent's death and ending December 31 of that year, the trustee must file an amended return for the QRT. The amended return must be filed consistent with paragraph (e)(3) of this section and must be filed by the due date of the Form 1041 for the QRT, taking into account the trustee's election under section 645.

(e) *Tax treatment and general filing requirements of electing trust and related estate during the election period.*—(1) *Effect of election.*—The section 645 election once made is irrevocable.

(2) *If there is an executor.*—(i) *Tax treatment of the combined electing trust and related estate.*—If there is an executor, the electing trust is treated, during the election period, as part of the related estate for all purposes of subtitle A of the Internal Revenue Code. Thus, for example, the electing trust is treated as part of the related estate for purposes of the set-aside deduction under section 642(c)(2), the subchapter S shareholder requirements of section 1361(b)(1), and the special offset for rental real estate activities in section 469(i)(4).

(ii) *Filing requirements.*—(A) *Filing the Form 1041 for the combined electing trust and related estate during the election period.*—If there is an executor, the executor files a single income tax return annually (assuming a return is required under section 6012) under the name and TIN of the related estate for the combined electing trust and the related estate. Information regarding the name and TIN of each electing trust must be provided on the Form 1041 as required by the instructions to that form. The period of limitations provided in section 6501 for assessments with respect to an electing trust and the related estate starts with the filing of the return required under this paragraph. Except as required under the separate share rules of section 663(c), for purposes of filing the Form 1041 under this paragraph and computing the tax, the items of income, deduction, and credit of the electing trust and related estate are combined. One personal exemption in the amount of $600 is permitted under section 642(b), and the tax is computed under section 1(e), taking into account section 1(h), for the combined taxable income.

(B) *Filing a Form 1041 for the electing trust is not required.*—Except for any final Form 1041 required to be filed under paragraph (h)(2)(i)(B) of this section, if there is an executor, the trustee of the electing trust does not file a Form 1041 for the electing trust during the election period. Although the trustee is not required to file a Form 1041 for the electing trust, the trustee of the electing trust must timely provide the executor of the related estate with all the trust information necessary to permit the executor to file a complete, accurate and timely Form 1041 for the combined electing trust and related estate. The trustee must also insure that the electing trust's share of the tax obligations of the combined electing trust and related estate is timely paid to the Secretary. In certain situations, the trustee of a QRT may be required to file a Form 1041 for the QRT's short taxable year beginning with the date of the decedent's death and ending December 31 of that year. See paragraph (d)(2) of this section.

(iii) *Application of the separate share rules.*—(A) *Distributions to beneficiaries (other than to a share (or shares) of the combined electing trust and related estate).*—Under the separate share rules of section 663(c), the electing trust and related estate are treated as separate shares for purposes of computing distributable net income (DNI) and applying the distribution provisions of sections 661 and 662. Further, the electing trust share or the related estate share may each contain two or more shares. Thus, if during the taxable year, a distribution is made by the electing trust or the related estate, the DNI of the share making the distribution must be determined and the distribution provisions of sections 661 and 662 must be applied using the separately determined DNI applicable to the distributing share.

(B) *Adjustments to the DNI of the separate shares for distributions between shares to which sections 661 and 662 would apply.*—A distribution from one share to another share to which sections 661 and 662 would apply if made to a beneficiary other than another share of the combined electing trust and related estate affects the computation of the DNI of the share making the distribution and the share receiving the distribution. The share making the distribution reduces its DNI by the amount of the distribution deduction that it would be entitled to under section 661 (determined without regard to section 661(c)), had the distribution been made to another beneficiary, and, solely for purposes of calculating DNI, the share receiving the distribution increases its gross income by the same amount. The distribution has the same character in the hands of the recipient share as in the hands of the distributing share. The following example illustrates the provisions of this paragraph (e)(2)(iii)(B):

Example. (i) A's will provides that, after the payment of debts, expenses, and taxes, the residue of A's estate is to be distributed to Trust, an electing trust. The sole beneficiary of Trust is C. The estate share has $15,000 of gross income, $5,000 of deductions, and $10,000 of taxable income and DNI for the taxable year based on the assets held in A's estate. During the taxable year, A's estate distributes $15,000 to Trust. The distribution reduces the DNI of the estate share by $10,000.

(ii) For the same taxable year, the trust share has $25,000 of gross income and $5,000 of deductions. None of the modifications provided for under section 643(a) apply. In calculating the DNI for the trust share, the gross income of the trust share is increased by $10,000, the amount of the reduction in the DNI of the estate share as a result of the distribution to Trust. Thus, solely for purposes of calculating DNI, the trust share has gross income of $35,000, and taxable income of $30,000. Therefore, the trust share has $30,000 of DNI for the taxable year.

(iii) During the same taxable year, Trust distributes $35,000 to C. The distribution deduction reported on the Form 1041 filed for A's estate and Trust is $30,000. As a result of the distribution by Trust to C, C must include $30,000 in gross income for the taxable year. The gross income reported on the Form 1041 filed for A's estate and Trust is $40,000.

(iv) *Application of the governing instrument requirement of section 642(c).*—A deduction is allowed in computing the taxable income of the combined electing trust and related estate to the extent permitted under section 642(c) for—

(A) Any amount of the gross income of the related estate that is paid or set aside during the taxable year pursuant to the terms of the governing instrument of the related estate for a purpose specified in section 170(c); and

(B) Any amount of gross income of the electing trust that is paid or set aside during the taxable year pursuant to the terms of the governing instrument of the electing trust for a purpose specified in section 170(c).

(3) *If there is no executor.*—(i) *Tax treatment of the electing trust.*—If there is no executor, the trustee treats the electing trust, during the election period, as an estate for all purposes of subtitle A of the Internal Revenue Code. Thus, for example, an electing trust is treated as an estate for purposes of the set-aside deduction under section 642(c)(2), the subchapter S shareholder requirements of section 1361(b)(1), and the special offset for rental real estate activities under section 469(i)(4). The trustee may also adopt a taxable year other than a calendar year.

(ii) *Filing the Form 1041 for the electing trust.*—If there is no executor, the trustee of the electing trust must, during the election period, file a Form 1041, under the TIN obtained by the trustee under § 301.6109-1(a)(3) of this chapter upon the death of the decedent, treating the trust as an estate. If there is more than one electing trust, the Form 1041 must be filed by the filing trustee (see paragraph (c)(2)(ii)(B) of this section) under the name and TIN of the electing trust of the filing trustee. Information regarding the names and TINs of the other electing trusts must be provided on the Form 1041 as required by the instructions to that form. Any return filed in accordance with this paragraph shall be treated as a return filed for the electing trust (or trusts, if there is more than one electing trust) and not as a return filed for any subsequently discovered related estate. Accordingly, the period of limitations provided in section 6501 for assessments with respect to a subsequently discovered related estate does not start until a return is filed with respect to the related estate. See paragraph (g) of this section.

(4) *Application of the section 6654(l)(2) to the electing trust.*—Each electing trust and related estate (if any) is treated as a separate taxpayer for all purposes of subtitle F of the Internal Revenue Code, including, without limitation, the application of section 6654. The provisions of section 6654(l)(2)(A) relating to the two year exception to an estate's obligation to make estimated tax payments, however, will apply to each electing trust for which a section 645 election has been made.

(f) *Duration of election period.*—(1) *In general.*—The election period begins on the date of the decedent's death and terminates on the earlier of the day on which both the electing trust and related estate, if any, have distributed all of their assets, or the day before the applicable date. The election does not apply to successor trusts (trusts that are distributees under the trust instrument).

(2) *Definition of applicable date.*—(i) *Applicable date if no Form 706 "United States Estate (and Generation Skipping Transfer) Tax Return" is required to be filed.*—If a Form 706 is not required to be filed as a result of the decedent's death, the applicable date is the day which is 2 years after the date of the decedent's death.

(ii) *Applicable date if a Form 706 is required to be filed.*—If a Form 706 is required to be filed as a result of the decedent's death, the applicable date is the later of the day that is 2 years after the date of the decedent's death, or the day that is 6 months after the date of final determination of liability for estate tax. Solely for purposes of determining the applicable date under section 645, the date of final determination of liability is the earliest of the following—

(A) The date that is six months after the issuance by the Internal Revenue Service of an estate tax closing letter, unless a claim for refund with respect to the estate tax is filed within twelve months after the issuance of the letter;

(B) The date of a final disposition of a claim for refund, as defined in paragraph (f)(2)(iii) of this section, that resolves the liability for the estate tax, unless suit is instituted within six months after a final disposition of the claim;

(C) The date of execution of a settlement agreement with the Internal Revenue Service that determines the liability for the estate tax;

(D) The date of issuance of a decision, judgment, decree, or other order by a court of competent jurisdiction resolving the liability for the estate tax unless a notice of appeal or a petition for certiorari is filed within 90 days after the issuance of a decision, judgment, decree, or other order of a court; or

(E) The date of expiration of the period of limitations for assessment of the estate tax provided in section 6501.

(iii) *Definition of final disposition of claim for refund.*—For purposes of paragraph (f)(2)(ii)(B) of this section, a claim for refund shall be deemed finally disposed of by the Secretary when all items have been either allowed or disallowed. If a waiver of notification with respect to disallowance is filed with respect to a claim for refund prior to disallowance of the claim, the claim for refund will be treated as disallowed on the date the waiver is filed.

(iv) *Examples.*—The application of this paragraph (f)(2) is illustrated by the following examples:

Example 1. A died on October 20, 2002. The executor of *A's* estate and the trustee of Trust, an electing trust, made a section 645 election. A Form 706 is not required to be filed as a result of *A's* death. The applicable date is October 20, 2004, the day that is two years after *A's* date of death. The last day of the election period is October 19, 2004. Beginning October 20, 2004, Trust will no longer be treated and taxed as part of *A's* estate.

Example 2. Assume the same facts as *Example 1,* except that a Form 706 is required to be filed as the result of *A's* death. The Internal Revenue Service issues an estate tax closing letter accepting the Form 706 as filed on March 15, 2005. The estate does not file a claim for refund by March 15, 2006, the day that is twelve months after the date of issuance of the estate tax closing letter. The date of final determination of liability is September 15, 2005, and the applicable date is March 15, 2006. The last day of the election period is March 14, 2006. Beginning March 15, 2006, Trust will no longer be treated and taxed as part of *A* s estate.

Example 3. Assume the same facts as *Example 1,* except that a Form 706 is required to be filed as the result of *A's* death. The Form 706 is audited, and a notice of deficiency authorized under section 6212 is mailed to the executor of *A's* estate as a result of the audit. The executor files a petition in Tax Court. The Tax Court issues a decision resolving the liability for estate tax on December 14, 2005, and neither party appeals within 90 days after the issuance of the decision. The date of final determination of liability is December 14, 2005. The applicable date is June 14, 2006, the day that is six months after the date of final determination of liability. The last day of the election period is June 13, 2006. Beginning June 14, 2006, Trust will no longer be treated and taxed as part of *A's* estate.

(g) *Executor appointed after the section 645 election is made.*—(1) *Effect on the election.*—If an executor for the related estate is not appointed until after the trustee has made a valid section 645 election, the executor must agree to the trustee's election, and the IRS must be notified of that agreement by the filing of a revised election form (completed as required by the instructions to that form) within 90 days of the appointment of the executor, for the election period to continue past the date of appointment of the executor. If the executor does not agree to the election or a revised election form is not timely filed as required by this paragraph, the election period terminates the day before the appointment of the executor. If the IRS issues other guidance after December 24, 2002 for notifying the IRS of the executor's agreement to the election, the IRS must be notified in the manner provided in that guidance for the election period to continue.

(2) *Continuation of election period.*—(i) *Correction of returns filed before executor appointed.*—If the election period continues under paragraph (g)(1) of this section, the executor of the related estate and the trustee of each electing trust must file amended Forms 1041 to correct the Forms 1041 filed by the trustee before the executor was appointed. The amended Forms 1041 must be filed under the name and TIN of the electing trust and must reflect the items of income, deduction, and credit of the related estate and the electing trust. The name and TIN of the related estate must be provided on the amended Forms 1041 as required in the instructions to that Form. The amended return for the taxable year ending immediately before the executor was appointed must indicate that this Form 1041 is a final return. If the period of limitations for making assessments has expired with respect to the electing trust for any of the Forms 1041 filed by the trustee, the executor must file Forms 1041 for any items of income, deduction, and credit of the related estate that cannot be properly included on amended forms for the electing trust. The personal exemption under section 642(b) is not permitted to be taken on these Forms 1041 filed by the executor.

(ii) *Returns filed after the appointment of the executor.*—All returns filed by the combined electing trust and related estate after the appointment of the executor are to be filed under the name and TIN of the related estate in accordance with paragraph (e)(2) of this section. Regardless of the change in the name and TIN under which the Forms 1041 for the combined electing trust and related estate are filed, the combined electing trust and related estate will be treated as the same entity before and after the executor is appointed.

(3) *Termination of the election period.*—If the election period terminates under paragraph (g)(1) of this section, the executor must file Forms 1041 under the name and TIN of the estate for all taxable years of the related estate ending after the death of the decedent. The trustee of the electing trust is not required to amend any returns filed for the electing trust during the election period. Following termination of the election period, the trustee of the electing trust must obtain a new TIN. See §301.6109-1(a)(4) of this chapter.

(h) *Treatment of an electing trust and related estate following termination of the election.*—(1) *The share (or shares) comprising the electing trust is deemed to be distributed upon termination of the election period.*—On the close of the last day of the election period, the combined electing trust and related estate, if there is an executor, or the electing trust, if there is no executor, is deemed to distribute the share (or shares, as determined under section 663(c)) comprising the electing trust to a new trust in a distribution to which sections 661 and 662 apply. All items of income, including net capital gains, that are attributable to the share (or shares) comprising the electing trust are included in the calculation of the distributable net income of the electing trust and treated as distributed by the combined electing trust and related estate, if there is an executor, or by the electing trust, if there is no executor, to the new trust. The combined electing trust and related estate, if there is an executor, or the electing trust, if there is no executor, is entitled to a distribution deduction to the extent permitted under section 661 in the taxable year in which the election period terminates as a result of the deemed distribution. The new trust shall include the amount of the deemed distribution in gross income to the extent required under section 662.

(2) *Filing of the Form 1041 upon the termination of the section 645 election.*—(i) *If there is an executor.*—(A) *Filing the Form 1041 for the year of termination.*—If there is an executor, the Form 1041 filed under the name and TIN of the related estate for the taxable year in which the election terminates includes—

(1) The items of income, deduction, and credit of the electing trust attributable to the period beginning with the first day of the taxable year of the combined electing trust and related estate and ending with the last day of the election period;

(2) The items of income, deduction, and credit, if any, of the related estate for the entire taxable year; and

(3) A deduction for the deemed distribution of the share (or shares) comprising the electing trust to the new trust as provided for under paragraph (h)(1) of this section.

(B) *Requirement to file a final Form 1041 under the name and TIN of the electing trust.*—If the electing trust terminates during the election period, the trustee of the electing trust must file a Form 1041 under the name and TIN of the electing trust and indicate that the return is a final return to notify the IRS that the electing trust is no longer in existence. The items of income, deduction, and credit of the trust are not reported on this final Form 1041 but on the appropriate Form 1041 filed for the combined electing trust and related estate.

(ii) *If there is no executor.*—If there is no executor, the taxable year of the electing trust closes on the last day of the election period. A Form 1041 is filed in the manner prescribed under paragraph (e)(3)(ii) of this section reporting the items of income, deduction, and credit of the electing trust for the short period ending with the last day of the election period. The Form 1041 filed under this paragraph includes a distribution deduction for the deemed distribution provided for under paragraph (h)(1) of this section. The Form 1041 must indicate that it is a final return.

(3) *Use of TINs following termination of the election.*—(i) *If there is an executor.*—Upon termination of the section 645 election, a former electing trust may need to obtain a new TIN. See § 301.6109-1(a)(4) of this chapter. If the related estate continues after the termination of the election period, the related estate must continue to use the TIN assigned to the estate during the election period.

(ii) *If there is no executor.*—If there is no executor, the former electing trust must obtain a new TIN if the trust will continue after the termination of the election period. See § 301.6109-1(a)(4) of this chapter.

(4) *Taxable year of estate and trust upon termination of the election.*—(i) *Estate.*—Upon termination of the section 645 election period, the taxable year of the estate is the same taxable year used during the election period.

(ii) *Trust.*—Upon termination of the section 645 election, the taxable year of the new trust is the calendar year. See section 644.

(i) *Reserved.*

(j) *Effective date.*—Paragraphs (a), (b), (c), (d), (f), and (g) of this section apply to trusts and estates of decedents dying on or after December 24, 2002. Paragraphs (e) and (h) of this section apply to taxable years ending on or after December 24, 2002. [Reg. § 1.645-1.]

☐ [*T.D.* 9032, 12-23-2002.]

[Reg. § 1.651(a)-1]

§ 1.651(a)-1. Simple trusts; deduction for distributions; in general.—Section 651 is applicable only to a trust the governing instrument of which:

(a) Requires that the trust distribute all of its income currently for the taxable year, and

(b) Does not provide that any amounts may be paid, permanently set aside, or used in the taxable year for the charitable, etc., purposes specified in section 642(c),

and does not make any distribution other than of current income. A trust to which section 651 applies is referred to in this part as a "simple" trust. Trusts subject to section 661 are referred to as "complex" trusts. A trust may be a simple trust for one year and a complex trust for another year. It should be noted that under section 651 a trust qualifies as a simple trust in a taxable year in which it is required to distribute all its income currently and makes no other distributions, whether or not distributions of current income are in fact made. On the other hand a trust is not a complex trust by reason of distributions of amounts other than income unless such distributions are in fact made during the taxable year, whether or not they are required in that year. [Reg. § 1.651(a)-1.]

☐ [*T.D.* 6217, 12-19-56.]

[Reg. §1.651(a)-2]

§1.651(a)-2. Income required to be distributed currently.—

(a) The determination of whether trust income is required to be distributed currently depends upon the terms of the trust instrument and the applicable local law. For this purpose, if the trust instrument provides that the trustee in determining the distributable income shall first retain a reserve for depreciation or otherwise make due allowance for keeping the trust corpus intact by retaining a reasonable amount of the current income for that purpose, the retention of current income for that purpose will not disqualify the trust from being a "simple" trust. The fiduciary must be under a duty to distribute the income currently even if, as a matter of practical necessity, the income is not distributed until after the close of the trust's taxable year. For example: Under the terms of the trust instrument, all of the income is currently distributable to A. The trust reports on the calendar year basis and as a matter of practical necessity makes distribution to A of each quarter's income on the fifteenth day of the month following the close of the quarter. The distribution made by the trust on January 15, 1955, of the income for the fourth quarter of 1954 does not disqualify the trust for treatment in 1955 under section 651, since the income is required to be distributed currently. However, if the terms of a trust require that none of the income be distributed until after the year of its receipt by the trust, the income of the trust is not required to be distributed currently and the trust is not a simple trust. For definition of the term "income" see section 643(b) and §1.643(b)-1.

(b) It is immaterial, for purposes of determining whether all the income is required to be distributed currently, that the amount of income allocated to a particular beneficiary is not specified in the instrument. For example, if the fiduciary is required to distribute all the income currently, but has discretion to "sprinkle" the income among a class of beneficiaries, or among named beneficiaries in such amount as he may see fit, all the income is required to be distributed currently, even though the amount distributable to a particular beneficiary is unknown until the fiduciary has exercised his discretion.

(c) If in one taxable year of a trust its income for that year is required or permitted to be accumulated, and in another taxable year its income for the year is required to be distributed currently (and no other amounts are distributed), the trust is a simple trust for the latter year. For example, a trust under which income may be accumulated until a beneficiary is 21 years old, and thereafter must be distributed currently, is a simple trust for taxable years beginning after the beneficiary reaches the age of 21 years in which no other amounts are distributed.

(d) If a trust distributes property in kind as part of its requirement to distribute currently all the income as defined under section 643(b) and the applicable regulations, the trust shall be treated as having sold the property for its fair market value on the date of distribution. If no amount in excess of the amount of income as defined under section 643(b) and the applicable regulations is distributed by the trust during the year, the trust will qualify for treatment under section 651 even though property in kind was distributed as part of a distribution of all such income. This paragraph (d) applies for taxable years of trusts ending after January 2, 2004. [Reg. §1.651(a)-2.]

□ [*T.D.* 6217, 12-19-56. *Amended by T.D.* 9102, 12-30-2003.]

[Reg. §1.651(a)-3]

§1.651(a)-3. Distribution of amounts other than income.—(a) A trust does not qualify for treatment under section 651 for any taxable year in which it actually distributes corpus. For example, a trust which is required to distribute all of its income currently would not qualify as a simple trust under section 651 in the year of its termination since in that year actual distributions of corpus would be made.

(b) A trust, otherwise qualifying under section 651, which may make a distribution of corpus in the discretion of the trustee, or which is required under the terms of its governing instrument to make a distribution of corpus upon the happening of a specified event, will be disqualified for treatment under section 651 only for the taxable year in which an actual distribution of corpus is made. For example: Under the terms of a trust, which is required to distribute all of its income currently, half of the corpus is to be distributed to beneficiary A when he becomes 30 years of age. The trust reports on the calendar year basis. On December 28, 1954, A becomes 30 years of age and the trustee distributes half of the corpus of the trust to him on January 3, 1955. The trust will be disqualified for treatment under section 651 only for the taxable year 1955, the year in which an actual distribution of corpus is made.

(c) See section 661 and the regulations thereunder for the treatment of trusts which distribute corpus or claim the charitable contributions deduction provided by section 642(c). [Reg. §1.651(a)-3.]

□ [*T.D.* 6217, 12-19-56.]

[Reg. §1.651(a)-4]

§1.651(a)-4. Charitable purposes.—A trust is not considered to be a trust which may pay, permanently set aside, or use any amount for charitable, etc., purposes for any taxable year for which it is not allowed a charitable, etc., deduction under section 642(c). Therefore, a trust with a remainder to a charitable organization is not disqualified for treatment as a simple trust if either (a) the remainder is subject to a contingency, so that no deduction would be allowed for capital gains or other amounts added to corpus as amounts permanently set aside for a charitable, etc., purpose under section 642(c), or (b) the trust receives no capital gains or other income added to corpus for the taxable year for which such a deduction would be allowed. [Reg. §1.651(a)-4.]

□ [*T.D.* 6217, 12-19-56.]

[Reg. § 1.651(a)-5]

§ 1.651(a)-5. Estates.—Subpart B has no application to an estate. [Reg. § 1.651(a)-5.]

☐ [*T.D.* 6217, 12-19-56.]

[Reg. § 1.651(b)-1]

§ 1.651(b)-1. Deduction for distributions to beneficiaries.—In computing its taxable income, a simple trust is allowed a deduction for the amount of income which is required under the terms of the trust instrument to be distributed currently to beneficiaries. If the amount of income [which] is required to be distributed currently exceeds the distributable net income, the deduction allowable to the trust is limited to the amount of the distributable net income. For this purpose the amount of income required to be distributed currently, or distributable net income, whichever is applicable, does not include items of trust income (adjusted for deductions allocable thereto) which are not included in the gross income of the trust. For determination of the character of the income required to be distributed currently, see § 1.652(b)-2. Accordingly, for the purposes of determining the deduction allowable to the trust under section 651, distributable net income is computed without the modifications specified in paragraphs (5), (6), and (7) of section 643(a), relating to tax-exempt interest, foreign income, and excluded dividends. For example: Assume that the distributable net income of a trust as computed under section 643(a) amounts to $99,000 but includes nontaxable income of $9,000. Then distributable net income for the purpose of determining the deduction allowable under section 651 is $90,000 ($99,000 less $9,000 nontaxable income). [Reg. § 1.651(b)-1.]

☐ [*T.D.* 6217, 12-19-56.]

[Reg. § 1.652(a)-1]

§ 1.652(a)-1. Simple trusts; inclusion of amounts in income of beneficiaries.—Subject to the rules in §§ 1.652(a)-2 and 1.652(b)-1, a beneficiary of a simple trust includes in his gross income for the taxable year the amounts of income required to be distributed to him for such year, whether or not distributed. Thus, the income of a simple trust is includible in the beneficiary's gross income for the taxable year in which the income is required to be distributed currently even though, as a matter of practical necessity, the income is not distributed until after the close of the taxable year of the trust. See § 1.642(a)(3)-2 with respect to time of receipt of dividends. See § 1.652(c)-1 for treatment of amounts required to be distributed where a beneficiary and the trust have different taxable years. The term "income required to be distributed currently" includes income required to be distributed currently which is in fact used to discharge or satisfy any person's legal obligation as that term is used in § 1.662(a)-4. [Reg. § 1.652(a)-1.]

☐ [*T.D.* 6217, 12-19-56.]

[Reg. § 1.652(a)-2]

§ 1.652(a)-2. Distributions in excess of distributable net income.—If the amount of income required to be distributed currently to beneficiaries exceeds the distributable net income of the trust (as defined in section 643(a)), each beneficiary includes in his gross income an amount equivalent to his proportionate share of such distributable net income. Thus, if beneficiary A is to receive two-thirds of the trust income and B is to receive one-third, and the income required to be distributed currently is $99,000, A will receive $66,000 and B, $33,000. However, if the distributable net income, as determined under section 643(a) is only $90,000, A will include two-thirds ($60,000) of that sum in his gross income, and B will include one-third ($30,000) in his gross income. See §§ 1.652(b)-1 and 1.652(b)-2, however, for amounts which are not includible in the gross income of a beneficiary because of their tax-exempt character. [Reg. § 1.652(a)-2.]

☐ [*T.D.* 6217, 12-19-56.]

[Reg. § 1.652(b)-1]

§ 1.652(b)-1. Character of amounts.—In determining the gross income of a beneficiary, the amounts includible under § 1.652(a)-1 have the same character in the hands of the beneficiary as in the hands of the trust. For example, to the extent that the amounts specified in § 1.652(a)-1 consist of income exempt from tax under section 103, such amounts are not included in the beneficiary's gross income. Similarly, dividends distributed to a beneficiary retain their original character in the beneficiary's hands for purposes of determining the availability to the beneficiary of the dividends received credit under section 34 (for dividends received on or before December 31, 1964) and the dividend exclusion under section 116. Also, to the extent that the amounts specified in § 1.652(a)-1 consist of "earned income" in the hands of the trust under the provisions of section 1348 such amount shall be treated under section 1348 as "earned income" in the hands of the beneficiary. Similarly, to the extent such amounts consist of an amount received as a part of a lump sum distribution from a qualified plan and to which the provisions of section 72(n) would apply in the hands of the trust, such amount shall be treated as subject to such section in the hands of the beneficiary except where such amount is deemed under section 666(a) to have been distributed in a preceding taxable year of the trust and the partial tax described in section 668(a)(2) is determined under section 668(b)(1)(B). The tax treatment of amounts determined under § 1.652(a)-1 depends upon the beneficiary's status with respect to them not upon the status of the trust. Thus, if a beneficiary is deemed to have received foreign income of a foreign trust, the includibility of such income in his gross income depends upon his taxable status with respect to that income. [Reg. § 1.652(b)-1.]

☐ [*T.D.* 6217, 12-19-56. *Amended by T.D.* 6777, 12-15-64, *and by T.D.* 7204, 8-24-72.]

[Reg. § 1.652(b)-2]

§ 1.652(b)-2. Allocation of income items.—

(a) The amounts specified in § 1.652(a)-1 which are required to be included in the gross income of a beneficiary are treated as consisting of the same proportion of each class of items entering into distributable net income of the trust (as defined in section 643(a)) as the total of each class bears to such distributable net income, unless the terms of the trust specifically allocate different classes of income to different beneficiaries, or unless local law requires such an allocation. For example: Assume that under the terms of the governing instrument, beneficiary A is to receive currently one-half of the trust income and beneficiaries B and C are each to receive currently one-quarter, and the distributable net income of the trust (after allocation of expenses) consists of dividends of $10,000, taxable interest of $10,000, and tax-exempt interest of $4,000. A will be deemed to have received $5,000 of dividends, $5,000 of taxable interest, and $2,000 of tax-exempt interest; B and C will each be deemed to have received $2,500 of dividends, $2,500 of taxable interest, and $1,000 of tax-exempt interest. However, if the terms of the trust specifically allocate different classes of income to different beneficiaries, entirely or in part, or if local law requires such an allocation, each beneficiary will be deemed to have received those items of income specifically allocated to him.

(b) The terms of the trust are considered specifically to allocate different classes of income to different beneficiaries only to the extent that the allocation is required in the trust instrument, and only to the extent that it has an economic effect independent of the income tax consequences of the allocation. For example:

(1) Allocation pursuant to a provision in a trust instrument granting the trustee discretion to allocate different classes of income to different beneficiaries is not a specific allocation by the terms of the trust.

(2) Allocation pursuant to a provision directing the trustee to pay all of one income to A, or $10,000 out of the income to A, and the balance of the income to B, but directing the trustee first to allocate a specific class of income to A's share (to the extent there is income of that class and to the extent it does not exceed A's share) is not a specific allocation by the terms of the trust.

(3) Allocation pursuant to a provision directing the trustee to pay half the class of income (whatever it may be) to A, and the balance of the income to B, is a specific allocation by the terms of the trust. [Reg. § 1.652(b)-2.]

□ [*T.D.* 6217, 12-19-56.]

[Reg. § 1.652(b)-3]

§ 1.652(b)-3. Allocation of deductions.— Items of deduction of a trust that enter into the computation of distributable net income are to be allocated among the items of income in accordance with the following principles:

(a) All deductible items directly attributable to one class of income (except dividends excluded under section 116) are allocated thereto. For example, repairs to, taxes on, and other expenses directly attributable to the maintenance of rental property or the collection of rental income are allocated to rental income. See § 1.642(e)-1 for treatment of depreciation of rental property. Similarly, all expenditures directly attributable to a business carried on by a trust are allocated to the income from such business. If the deductions directly attributable to a particular class of income exceed that income, the excess is applied against other classes of income in the manner provided in paragraph (d) of this section.

(b) The deductions which are not directly attributable to a specific class of income may be allocated to any item of income (including capital gains) included in computing distributable net income, but a portion must be allocated to nontaxable income (except dividends excluded under section 116) pursuant to section 265 and the regulations thereunder. For example, if the income of a trust is $30,000 (after direct expenses), consisting equally of $10,000 of dividends, tax-exempt interest, and rents, and income commissions amount to $3,000, one-third ($1,000) of such commissions should be allocated to tax-exempt interest, but the balance of $2,000 may be allocated to the rents or dividends in such proportions as the trustee may elect. The fact that the governing instrument or applicable local law treats certain items of deduction as attributable to corpus or to income not included in distributable net income does not affect allocation under this paragraph. For instance, if in the example set forth in this paragraph the trust also had capital gains which are allocable to corpus under the terms of the trust instrument, no part of the deductions would be allocable thereto since the capital gains are excluded from the computation of distributable net income under section 643(a)(3).

(c) Examples of expenses which are considered as not directly attributable to a specific class of income are trustee's commissions, the rental of safe deposit boxes, and State income and personal property taxes.

(d) To the extent that any items of deduction which are directly attributable to a class of income exceed that class of income, they may be allocated to any other class of income (including capital gains) included in distributable net income in the manner provided in paragraph (b) of this section, except that any excess deductions attributable to tax-exempt income (other than dividends excluded under section 116) may not be offset against any other class of income. See section 265 and the regulations thereunder. Thus, if the trust has rents, taxable interest, dividends, and tax-exempt interest, and the deductions directly attributable to the rents exceed the rental income, the excess may be allocated to the taxable interest or dividends in such proportions as the fiduciary may elect. However, if the excess deductions are attributable to the tax-exempt interest, they may not be allocated to either the rents, taxable interest, or dividends. [Reg. § 1.652(b)-3.]

□ [*T.D.* 6217, 12-19-56.]

[Reg. §1.652(c)-1]

§1.652(c)-1. Different taxable years.—If a beneficiary has a different taxable year (as defined in section 441 or 442) from the taxable year of the trust, the amount he is required to include in gross income in accordance with section 652(a) and (b) is based on the income of the trust for any taxable year or years ending with or within his taxable year. This rule applies to taxable years of normal duration as well as to so-called short taxable years. Income of the trust for its taxable year or years is determined in accordance with its method of accounting and without regard to that of the beneficiary. [Reg. §1.652(c)-1.]

☐ [*T.D.* 6217, 12-19-56.]

[Reg. §1.652(c)-2]

§1.652(c)-2. Death of individual beneficiaries.—If income is required to be distributed currently to a beneficiary, by a trust for a taxable year which does not end with or within the last taxable year of a beneficiary (because of the beneficiary's death), the extent to which the income is included in the gross income of the beneficiary for his last taxable year or in the gross income of his estate is determined by the computations under section 652 for the taxable year of the trust in which his last taxable year ends. Thus, the distributable net income of the taxable year of the trust determines the extent to which the income required to be distributed currently to the beneficiary is included in his gross income for his last taxable year or in the gross income of his estate. (Section 652(c) does not apply to such amounts.) The gross income for the last taxable year of a beneficiary on the cash basis includes only income actually distributed to the beneficiary before his death. Income required to be distributed, but in fact distributed to his estate, is included in the gross income of the estate as income in respect of a decedent under section 691. See paragraph (e) of §1.663(c)-3 with respect to separate share treatment for the periods before and after the decedent's death. If the trust does not qualify as a simple trust for the taxable year of the trust in which the last taxable year of the beneficiary ends, see section 662(c) and §1.662(c)-2. [Reg. §1.652(c)-2.]

☐ [*T.D.* 6217, 12-19-56.]

[Reg. §1.652(c)-3]

§1.652(c)-3. Termination of existence of other beneficiaries.—If the existence of a beneficiary which is not an individual terminates, the amount to be included under section 652(a) in its gross income for its last taxable year is computed with reference to §§1.652(c)-1 and 1.652(c)-2 as if the beneficiary were a deceased individual, except that income required to be distributed prior to the termination but actually distributed to the beneficiary's successor in interest is included in the beneficiary's income for its last taxable year. [Reg. §1.652(c)-3.]

☐ [*T.D.* 6217, 12-19-56.]

[Reg. §1.652(c)-4]

§1.652(c)-4. Illustration of the provisions of sections 651 and 652.—The rules applicable to a trust required to distribute all of its income currently and to its beneficiaries may be illustrated by the following example:

Example. (a) Under the terms of a simple trust all of the income is to be distributed equally to beneficiaries A and B and capital gains are to be allocated to corpus. The trust and both beneficiaries file returns on the calendar year basis. No provision is made in the governing instrument with respect to depreciation. During the taxable year 1955, the trust had the following items of income and expense:

Rents	$25,000
Dividends of domestic corporations	50,000
Tax-exempt interest on municipal bonds	25,000
Long-term capital gains	15,000
Taxes and expenses directly attributable to rents	5,000
Trustee's commissions allocable to income account	2,600
Trustee's commissions allocable to principal account	1,300
Depreciation	5,000

(b) The income of the trust for fiduciary accounting purposes is $92,400, computed as follows:

Rents		$25,000
Dividends		50,000
Tax-exempt interest		25,000
Total		100,000
Deductions: Expenses directly attributable to rental income	$5,000	
Trustee's commissions allocable to income account	2,600	7,600
Income computed under section 643(b)		92,400

One-half ($46,200) of the income of $92,400 is currently distributable to each beneficiary.

(c) The distributable net income of the trust computed under section 643(a) is $91,100, determined as follows (cents are disregarded in the computation):

Rents		$25,000
Dividends		50,000
Tax-exempt interest	$25,000	
Less: Expenses allocable thereto (25,000/100,000 × $3,900)	975	24,025
Total		99,025
Deductions:		
Expenses directly attributable to rental income	$5,000	
Trustee's commissions ($3,900 less $975 allocable to tax-exempt interest)	2,925	$7,925
Distributable net income		91,100

In computing the distributable net income of $91,100, the taxable income of the trust was computed with the following modifications: No deductions were allowed for distributions to the beneficiaries and for personal exemption of the trust (section 643(a)(1) and (2)); capital gains were excluded and no deduction under section 1202 (relating to the 50 percent deduction for long-term capital gains) was taken into account (section 643(a)(3)); the tax-exempt interest (as adjusted for expenses) and the dividend exclusion of $50 were included (section 643(a)(5) and (7)). Since all of the income of the trust is required to be currently distributed, no deduction is allowable for depreciation in the absence of specific provisions in the governing instrument providing for the keeping of the trust corpus intact. See section 167(h) and the regulations thereunder.

(d) The deduction allowable to the trust under section 651(a) for distributions to the beneficiaries is $67,025, computed as follows:

Distributable net income computed under section 643(a) (see paragraph (c))		$91,100
Less:		
Tax-exempt interest as adjusted	$24,025	
Dividend exclusion	50	24,075
Distributable net income as determined under section 651(b)		67,025

Since the amount of the income ($92,400) required to be distributed currently by the trust exceeds the distributable net income ($67,025) as computed under section 651(b), the deduction allowable under section 651(a) is limited to the distributable net income of $67,025.

(e) The taxable income of the trust is $7,200 computed as follows:

Rents		$25,000
Dividends ($50,000 less $50 exclusion)		49,950
Long-term capital gains		15,000
Gross income		89,950
Deductions:		
Rental expenses	$5,000	
Trustee's commissions	2,925	
Capital gain deduction	7,500	
Distributions to beneficiaries	67,025	
Personal exemption	300	82,750
Taxable income		7,200

The trust is not allowed a deduction for the portion ($975) of the trustee's commissions allocable to tax-exempt interest in computing its taxable income.

(f) In determining the character of the amounts includible in the gross income of A and B, it is assumed that the trustee elects to allocate to rents the expenses not directly attributable to a specific item of income other than the portion ($975) of such expenses allocated to tax-exempt interest. The allocation of expenses among the items of income is shown below:

	Rents	*Dividends*	*Tax-exempt interest*	*Total*
Income for trust accounting purposes	$25,000	$50,000	$25,000	$100,000
Less:				
Rental expenses	5,000			5,000
Trustee's commissions	2,925		975	3,900
Total deductions	7,925	0	975	8,900

	Rents	Dividends	Tax-exempt interest	Total
Character of amounts in the hands of the beneficiaries	17,075	50,000	24,025	[1]91,100

[1] Distributable net income.

Inasmuch as the income of the trust is to be distributed equally to A and B, each is deemed to have received one-half of each item of income; that is, rents of $8,537.50, dividends of $25,000, and tax-exempt interest of $12,012.50. The dividends of $25,000 allocated to each beneficiary are to be aggregated with his other dividends (if any) for purposes of the dividend exclusion provided by section 116 and the dividend received credit allowed under section 34. Also, each beneficiary is allowed a deduction of $2,500 for depreciation of rental property attributable to the portion (one-half) of the income of the trust distributed to him. [Reg. § 1.652(c)-4.]

□ [*T.D.* 6217, 12-19-56. *Amended by T.D.* 6712, 3-23-64.]

[Reg. § 1.661(a)-1]

§ 1.661(a)-1. Estates and trusts accumulating income or distributing corpus; general.—Subpart C, part I, subchapter J, chapter 1 of the Code, is applicable to all decedents' estates and their beneficiaries, and to trusts and their beneficiaries other than trusts subject to the provisions of subpart B of such part I (relating to trusts which distribute current income only, or "simple" trusts). A trust which is required to distribute amounts other than income during the taxable year may be subject to subpart B, and not subpart C, in the absence of an actual distribution of amounts other than income during the taxable year. See §§ 1.651(a)-1 and 1.651(a)-3. A trust to which subpart C is applicable is referred to as a "complex" trust in this part. Section 661 has no application to amounts excluded under section 663(a). [Reg. § 1.661(a)-1.]

□ [*T.D.* 6217, 12-19-56.]

[Reg. § 1.661(a)-2]

§ 1.661(a)-2. Deduction for distributions to beneficiaries.—(a) In computing the taxable income of an estate or trust there is allowed under section 661(a) as a deduction for distributions to beneficiaries the sum of:

(1) The amount of income for the taxable year which is required to be distributed currently, and

(2) Any other amounts properly paid or credited or required to be distributed for such taxable year.

However, the total amount deductible under section 661(a) cannot exceed the distributable net income as computed under section 643(a) and as modified by section 661(c). See § 1.661(c)-1.

(b) The term "income required to be distributed currently" includes any amount required to be distributed which may be paid out of income or corpus (such as an annuity), to the extent it is paid out of income for the taxable year. See § 1.651(a)-2 which sets forth additional rules which are applicable in determining whether income of an estate or trust is required to be distributed currently.

(c) The term "any other amounts properly paid or credited or required to be distributed" includes all amounts properly paid, credited, or required to be distributed by an estate or trust during the taxable year other than income required to be distributed currently. Thus, the term includes the payment of an annuity to the extent it is not paid out of income for the taxable year, and a distribution of property in kind (see paragraph (f) of this section). However, see section 663(a) and regulations thereunder for distributions which are not included. Where the income of an estate or trust may be accumulated or distributed in the discretion of the fiduciary, or where the fiduciary has a power to distribute corpus to a beneficiary, any such discretionary distribution would qualify under section 661(a)(2). The term also includes an amount applied or distributed for the support of a dependent of a grantor or of a trustee or cotrustee under the circumstances described in section 677(b) or section 678(c) out of corpus or out of other than income for the taxable year.

(d) The terms "income required to be distributed currently" and "any other amounts properly paid or credited or required to be distributed" also include any amount used to discharge or satisfy any person's legal obligation as that term is used in § 1.662(a)-4.

(e) The terms "income required to be distributed currently" and "any other amounts properly paid or credited or required to be distributed" include amounts paid, or required to be paid, during the taxable year pursuant to a court order or decree or under local law, by a decedent's estate as an allowance or award for the support of the decedent's widow or other dependent for a limited period during the administration of the estate. The term "any other amounts properly paid or credited or required to be distributed" does not include the value of any interest in real estate owned by a decedent, title to which under local law passes directly from the decedent to his heirs or devisees.

(f) Gain or loss is realized by the trust or estate (or the other beneficiaries) by reason of a distribution of property in kind if the distribution is in satisfaction of a right to receive a distribution of a specific dollar amount, of specific property other than that distributed, or of income as defined under section 643(b) and the applicable regulations, if income is required to be distributed currently. In addition, gain or loss is realized if the trustee or executor makes the election to recognize gain or loss under section 643(e). This paragraph applies for taxable years of trusts and estates ending after January 2, 2004. [Reg. § 1.661(a)-2.]

□ [*T.D.* 6217, 12-19-56. *Amended by T.D.* 7287, 9-26-73 *and T.D.* 9102, 12-30-2003.]

[Reg. § 1.661(b)-1]

§ 1.661(b)-1. Character of amounts distributed; in general.—In the absence of specific provisions in the governing instrument for the allocation of different classes of income, or unless local law requires such an allocation, the amount deductible for distributions to beneficiaries under section 661(a) is treated as consisting of the same proportion of each class of items entering into the computation of distributable net income as the total of each class bears to the total distributable net income. For example, if a trust has distributable net income of $20,000, consisting of $10,000 each of taxable interest and royalties and distributes $10,000 to beneficiary A, the deduction of $10,000 allowable under section 661(a) is deemed to consist of $5,000 each of taxable interest and royalties, unless the trust instrument specifically provides for the distribution or accumulation of different classes of income or unless local law requires such an allocation. See also § 1.661(c)-1. [Reg. § 1.661(b)-1.]

□ [*T.D.* 6217, 12-19-56.]

[Reg. § 1.661(b)-2]

§ 1.661(b)-2. Character of amounts distributed when charitable contributions are made.—In the application of the rule stated in § 1.661(b)-1, the items of deduction which enter into the computation of distributable net income are allocated among the items of income which enter into the computation of distributable net income in accordance with the rules set forth in § 1.652(b)-3, except that, in the absence of specific provisions in the governing instrument, or unless local law requires a different apportionment, amounts paid, permanently set aside, or to be used for the charitable, etc., purposes specified in section 642(c) are first ratably apportioned among each class of items of income entering into the computation of the distributable net income of the estate or trust, in accordance with the rules set out in paragraph (b) of § 1.643(a)-5. [Reg. § 1.661(b)-2.]

□ [*T.D.* 6217, 12-19-56.]

[Reg. § 1.661(c)-1]

§ 1.661(c)-1. Limitation on deduction.—An estate or trust is not allowed a deduction under section 661(a) for any amount which is treated under section 661(b) as consisting of any item of distributable net income which is not included in the gross income of the estate or trust. For example, if in 1962, a trust, which reports on the calendar year basis, has distributable net income of $20,000, which is deemed to consist of $10,000 of dividends and $10,000 of tax-exempt interest, and distributes $10,000 to beneficiary A, the deduction allowable under section 661(a) (computed without regard to section 661(c)) would amount to $10,000 consisting of $5,000 of dividends and $5,000 of tax-exempt interest. The deduction actually allowable under section 661(a) as limited by section 661(c) is $4,975, since no deduction is allowable for the $5,000 of tax-exempt interest and the $25 deemed distributed out of the $50 of dividends excluded under section 116, items of distributable net income which are not included in the gross income of the estate or trust. [Reg. § 1.661(c)-1.]

□ [*T.D.* 6217, 12-19-56. *Amended by T.D.* 6777, 12-15-64.]

[Reg. § 1.661(c)-2]

§ 1.661(c)-2. Illustration of the provisions of section 661.—The provisions of section 661 may be illustrated by the following example:

Example. (a) Under the terms of a trust, which reports on the calendar year basis, $10,000 a year is required to be paid out of income to a designated charity. The balance of the income may, in the trustee's discretion, be accumulated or distributed to beneficiary A. Expenses are allocable against income and the trust instrument requires a reserve for depreciation. During the taxable year 1955 the trustee contributes $10,000 to charity and in his discretion distributes $15,000 of income to A. The trust has the following items of income and expense for the taxable year 1955:

Dividends	$10,000
Partially tax-exempt interest	10,000
Fully tax-exempt interest	10,000
Rents	20,000
Rental expenses	2,000
Depreciation of rental property	3,000
Trustee's commissions	5,000

(b) The income of the trust for fiduciary accounting purposes is $40,000, computed as follows:

Dividends		$10,000
Partially tax-exempt interest		10,000
Fully tax-exempt interest		10,000
Rents		20,000
Total		50,000
Less: Rental expenses	$2,000	

Depreciation	3,000	
Trustee's commissions	5,000	$10,000
Income as computed under section 643(b)		40,000

(c) The distributable net income of the trust as computed under section 643(a) is $30,000, determined as follows:

Rents			$20,000
Dividends			10,000
Partially tax-exempt interest			10,000
Fully tax-exempt interest		$10,000	
Less: Expenses allocable thereto (10,000/50,000 × $5,000)	$1,000		
Charitable contributions allocable thereto (10,000/50,000 × $10,000)	2,000	3,000	7,000
Total			47,000
Deductions:			
Rental expenses		$2,000	
Depreciation of rental property		3,000	
Trustee's commissions ($5,000 less $1,000 allocated to tax-exempt interest)		4,000	
Charitable contributions ($10,000 less $2,000 allocated to tax-exempt interest)		8,000	$17,000
Distributable net income (section 643(a))			30,000

(d) The character of the amounts distributed under section 661(a), determined in accordance with the rules prescribed in §§1.661(b)-1 and 1.661(b)-2 is shown by the following table (for the purpose of this allocation, it is assumed that the trustee elected to allocate the trustee's commissions to rental income except for the amount required to be allocated to tax-exempt interest):

	Rental income	*Taxable Dividends*	*Excluded Dividends*	*Partially tax-exempt interest*	*Tax-exempt interest*	*Total*
Trust income	$20,000	$9,950	$50	$10,000	$10,000	$50,000
Less:						
Charitable contributions	4,000	2,000	....	2,000	2,000	10,000
Rental expenses	2,000	....	....	....	....	2,000
Depreciation	3,000	....	....	....	....	3,000
Trustee's commissions	4,000	....	....	....	1,000	5,000
Total deductions	13,000	2,000	0	2,000	3,000	20,000
Distributable net income	7,000	7,950	50	8,000	7,000	30,000
Amounts deemed distributed under section 661(a) before applying the limitation of section 661(c)	3,500	3,975	25	4,000	3,500	15,000

In the absence of specific provisions in the trust instrument for the allocation of different classes of income, the charitable contribution is deemed to consist of a pro rata portion of the gross amount of each item of income of the trust (except dividends excluded under section 116) and the trust is deemed to have distributed to A a pro rata portion (one-half) of each item of income included in distributable net income.

(e) The taxable income of the trust is $11,375 computed as follows:

Rental income		$20,000
Dividends ($10,000 less $50 exclusion)		9,950
Partially tax-exempt interest		10,000
Gross income		$39,950
Deductions:		
Rental expenses	$2,000	
Depreciation of rental property	3,000	
Trustee's commissions	4,000	
Charitable contributions	8,000	
Distributions to A	11,475	
Personal exemption	100	28,575

In computing the taxable income of the trust no deduction is allowable for the portions of the charitable contributions deduction ($2,000) and trustee's commissions ($1,000) which are treated under section 661(b) as attributable to the tax-exempt interest excludable from gross income. Also, of the dividends of $4,000 deemed to have been distributed to A under section 661(a), $25 (25/50ths of $50) is deemed to have been distributed from the excluded dividends and is not an allowable deduction to the trust. Accordingly, the deduction allowable under section 661 is deemed to be composed of $3,500 rental income, $3,975 of dividends, and $4,000 partially tax-exempt interest. No deduction is allowable for the portion of tax-exempt interest or for the portion of the excluded dividends deemed to have been distributed to the beneficiary.

(f) The trust is entitled to the credit allowed by section 34 with respect to dividends of $5,975 ($9,950 less $3,975 distributed to A) included in gross income. Also, the trust is allowed the credit provided by section 35 with respect to partially tax-exempt interest of $6,000 ($10,000 less $4,000 deemed distributed to A) included in gross income.

(g) Dividends of $4,000 allocable to A are to be aggregated with his other dividends (if any) for purposes of the dividend exclusion under section 116 and the dividend received credit under section 34. [Reg. § 1.661(c)-2.]

☐ [*T.D.* 6217, 12-19-56.]

[Reg. § 1.662(a)-1]

§ 1.662(a)-1. Inclusion of amounts in gross income of beneficiaries of estates and complex trusts; general.—There is included in the gross income of a beneficiary of an estate or complex trust the sum of:

(1) Amounts of income required to be distributed currently to him, and

(2) All other amounts properly paid, credited, or required to be distributed to him by the estate or trust.

The preceding sentence is subject to the rules contained in § 1.662(a)-2 (relating to currently distributable income), § 1.662(a)-3 (relating to other amounts distributed), and §§ 1.662(b)-1 and 1.662(b)-2 (relating to character of amounts). Section 662 has no application to amounts excluded under section 663(a). [Reg. § 1.662(a)-1.]

☐ [*T.D.* 6217, 12-19-56.]

[Reg. § 1.662(a)-2]

§ 1.662(a)-2. Currently distributable income.—(a) There is first included in the gross income of each beneficiary under section 662(a)(1) the amount of income for the taxable year of the estate or trust required to be distributed currently to him, subject to the provisions of paragraph (b) of this section. Such amount is included in the beneficiary's gross income whether or not it is actually distributed.

(b) If the amount of income required to be distributed currently to all beneficiaries exceeds the distributable net income (as defined in section 643(a) but computed without taking into account the payment, crediting, or setting aside of an amount for which a charitable contributions deduction is allowable under section 642(c)) of the estate or trust, then there is included in the gross income of each beneficiary an amount which bears the same ratio to distributable net income (as so computed) as the amount of income required to be distributed currently to the beneficiary bears to the amount required to be distributed currently to all beneficiaries.

(c) The phrase "the amount of income for the taxable year required to be distributed currently" includes any amount required to be paid out of income or corpus to the extent the amount is satisfied out of income for the taxable year. Thus, an annuity required to be paid in all events (either out of income or corpus) would qualify as income required to be distributed currently to the extent there is income (as defined in section 643(b)) not paid, credited, or required to be distributed to other beneficiaries for the taxable year. If an annuity or a portion of an annuity is deemed under this paragraph to be income required to be distributed currently, it is treated in all respects in the same manner as an amount of income actually required to be distributed currently. The phrase "the amount of income for the taxable year required to be distributed currently" also includes any amount required to be paid during the taxable year in all events (either out of income or corpus) pursuant to a court order or decree or under local law, by a decedent's estate as an allowance or award for the support of the decedent's widow or other dependent for a limited period during the administration of the estate to the extent there is income (as defined in section 643(b)) of the estate for the taxable year not paid, credited, or required to be distributed to other beneficiaries.

(d) If an annuity is paid, credited, or required to be distributed tax free, that is, under a provision whereby the executor or trustee will pay the income tax of the annuitant resulting from the receipt of the annuity, the payment of or for the tax by the executor or trustee will be treated as income paid, credited, or required to be distributed currently to the extent it is made out of income.

(e) The application of the rules stated in this section may be illustrated by the following examples:

Example (1). (1) Assume that under the terms of the trust instrument $5,000 is to be paid to X charity out of income each year; that $20,000 of income is currently distributable to A; and that an annuity of $12,000 is to be paid to B out of income or corpus. All expenses are charges against income and capital gains are allocable to corpus. During the taxable year the trust had income of $30,000 (after the payment of expenses) derived from taxable interest and made the payments to X charity and distributions to A and B as required by the governing instrument.

(2) The amounts treated as distributed currently under section 662(a)(1) total $25,000 ($20,000 to A and $5,000 to B). Since the charitable contribution is out of income, the amount of income available for B's annuity is only $5,000. The distributable net income of the trust computed under section 643(a) without taking into consideration the charitable contributions deduction of $5,000 as provided by section 661(a)(1), is $30,000. Since the amounts treated as distributed currently of $25,000 do not exceed the distributable net income (as modified) of $30,000, A is required to include $20,000 in his

gross income and B is required to include $5,000 in his gross income under section 662(a)(1).

Example (2). Assume the same facts as in paragraph (1) of example (1), except that the trust has, in addition, $10,000 of administration expenses, commissions, etc., chargeable to corpus. The amounts treated as distributed currently under section 662(a)(1) total $25,000 ($20,000 to A and $5,000 to B), since trust income under section 643(b) remains the same as in example (1). Distributable net income of the trust computed under section 643(a) but without taking into account the charitable contributions deduction of $5,000 as provided by section 662(a)(1) is only $20,000. Since the amounts treated as distributed currently of $25,000 exceed the distributable net income (as so computed) of $20,000, A is required to include $16,000 (20,000/25,000 of $20,000) in his gross income and B is required to include $4,000 (5,000/25,000 of $20,000) in his gross income under section 662(a)(1). Because A and B are beneficiaries of amounts of income required to be distributed currently, they do not benefit from the reduction of distributable net income by the charitable contributions deduction. [Reg. §1.662(a)-2.]

☐ [*T.D.* 6217, 12-19-56. *Amended by T.D.* 7287, 9-26-73.]

[Reg. §1.662(a)-3]

§1.662(a)-3. Other amounts distributed.—(a) There is included in the gross income of a beneficiary under section 662(a)(2) any amount properly paid, credited, or required to be distributed to the beneficiary for the taxable year, other than (1) income required to be distributed currently, as determined under §1.662(a)-2, (2) amounts excluded under section 663(a) and the regulations thereunder, and (3) amounts in excess of distributable net income (see paragraph (c) below of this section). An amount which is credited or required to be distributed is included in the gross income of a beneficiary whether or not it is actually distributed.

(b) Some of the payments to be included under paragraph (a) of this section are: (1) A distribution made to a beneficiary in the discretion of the fiduciary; (2) a distribution required by the terms of the governing instrument upon the happening of a specified event; (3) an annuity which is required to be paid in all events but which is payable only out of corpus; (4) a distribution of property in kind (see paragraph (f) of §1.661(a)-2); and (5) an amount applied or distributed for the support of a dependent of a grantor or a trustee or cotrustee under the circumstances specified in section 677(b) or section 678(c) out of corpus or out of other than income for the taxable year; and (6) an amount required to be paid during the taxable year pursuant to a court order or decree or under local law, by a decedent's estate as an allowance or award for the support of the decedent's widow or other dependent for a limited period during the administration of the estate which is payable only out of corpus of the estate under the order or decree or local law.

(c) If the sum of the amounts of income required to be distributed currently (as determined under §1.662(a)-2 and other amounts properly paid, credited, or required to be distributed (as determined under paragraph (a) of this section) exceeds distributable net income (as defined in section 643(a)), then such other amounts properly paid, credited, or required to be distributed are included in gross income of the beneficiary but only to the extent of the excess of such distributable net income over the amounts of income required to be distributed currently. If the other amounts are paid, credited, or required to be distributed to more than one beneficiary, each beneficiary includes in gross income his proportionate share of the amount includible in gross income pursuant to the preceding sentence. The proportionate share is an amount which bears the same ratio to distributable net income (reduced by amounts of income required to be distributed currently) as the other amounts (as determined under paragraphs (a) and (d) of this section) distributed to the beneficiary bear to the other amounts distributed to all beneficiaries. For treatment of excess distributions by trusts, see sections 665 to 668, inclusive, and the regulations thereunder.

(d) The application of the rules stated in this section may be illustrated by the following example:

Example. The terms of a trust require the distribution annually of $10,000 of income to A. If any income remains, it may be accumulated or distributed to B, C, and D in amounts in the trustee's discretion. He may also invade corpus for the benefit of A, B, C, or D. In the taxable year, the trust has $20,000 of income after the deduction of all expenses. Distributable net income is $20,000. The trustee distributes $10,000 of income to A. Of the remaining $10,000 of income, he distributes $3,000 each to B, C, and D, and also distributes an additional $5,000 to A. A includes $10,000 in income under section 662(a)(1). The "other amounts distributed" amount to $14,000, includible in the income of the recipients to the extent of $10,000, distributable net income less the income currently distributable to A. A will include an additional $3,571 (5,000/14,000 × $10,000) in income under this section, and B, C, and D will each include $2,143 (3,000/14,000 × $10,000). [Reg. §1.662(a)-3.]

☐ [*T.D.* 6217, 12-19-56. *Amended by T.D.* 7287, 9-26-73.]

[Reg. §1.662(a)-4]

§1.662(a)-4. Amounts used in discharge of a legal obligation.—Any amount which, pursuant to the terms of a will or trust instrument, is used in full or partial discharge or satisfaction of a legal obligation of any person is included in the gross income of such person under section 662(a)(1) or (2), whichever is applicable, as though directly distributed to him as a beneficiary, except in cases to which section 71 (relating to alimony payments) or section 682 (relating to income of a trust in case of divorce, etc.) applies. The term "legal obligation" includes a legal obligation to support another person if, and only if, the obligation is not affected by the adequacy of the dependent's own resources. For example, a parent has a "legal obligation" within the meaning of the preceding sentence to support his minor child if under local law property or income from property owned by the child cannot be used for his support so long as his parent is able to support him. On the other hand, if under local law a mother may use the resources of a child for the child's support in lieu of supporting him herself, no obligation of support exists within the meaning of this paragraph, whether or not income is actually used for support. Similarly, since under local law a child ordinarily is obligated to support his parent only if the parent's earnings and resources are insufficient for the purpose, no obligation exists whether or not the parent's earnings and resources are sufficient. In any event, the amount of trust income which is included in the gross income of a person obligated to support a dependent is limited by the extent of his legal obligation under local law. In the case of a parent's obligation to support his child, to the extent that the parent's legal obligation of support, including education, is determined under local law by the family's station in life and by the means of the parent, it is to be determined without consideration of the trust income in question. [Reg. § 1.662(a)-4.]

☐ [*T.D.* 6217, 12-19-56.]

[Reg. § 1.662(b)-1]

§ 1.662(b)-1. Character of amounts; when no charitable contributions are made.—In determining the amount includible in the gross income of a beneficiary, the amounts which are determined under section 662(a) and §§ 1.662(a)-1 through 1.662(a)-4 shall have the same character in the hands of the beneficiary as in the hands of the estate or trust. The amounts are treated as consisting of the same proportion of each class of items entering into the computation of distributable net income as the total of each class bears to the total distributable net income of the estate or trust unless the terms of the governing instruments specifically allocate different classes of income to different beneficiaries, or unless local law requires such an allocation. For this purpose, the principles contained in § 1.652(b)-1 shall apply. [Reg. § 1.662(b)-1.]

☐ [*T.D.* 6217, 12-19-56.]

[Reg. § 1.662(b)-2]

§ 1.662(b)-2. Character of amounts; when charitable contributions are made.—When a charitable contribution is made, the principles contained in §§ 1.652(b)-1 and 1.662(b)-1 generally apply. However, before the allocation of other deductions among the items of distributable net income, the charitable contributions deduction allowed under section 642(c) is (in the absence of specific allocation under the terms of the governing instrument or the requirement under local law of a different allocation) allocated among the classes of income entering into the computation of estate or trust income in accordance with the rules set forth in paragraph (b) of § 1.643(a)-5. In the application of the preceding sentence, for the purpose of allocating items of income and deductions to beneficiaries to whom income is required to be distributed currently, the amount of the charitable contributions deduction is disregarded to the extent that it exceeds the income of the trust for the taxable year reduced by amounts for the taxable year required to be distributed currently. The application of this section may be illustrated by the following examples (of which example (1) is illustrative of the preceding sentence):

Example (1). (a) A trust instrument provides that $30,000 of its income must be distributed currently to A, and the balance may either be distributed to B, distributed to a designated charity, or accumulated. Accumulated income may be distributed to B and to the charity. The trust for its taxable year has $40,000 of taxable interest and $10,000 of tax-exempt income, with no expenses. The trustee distributed $30,000 to A, $50,000 to charity X, and $10,000 to B.

(b) Distributable net income for the purpose of determining the character of the distribution to A is $30,000 (the charitable contributions deduction, for this purpose, being taken into account only to the extent of $20,000, the difference between the income of the trust for the taxable year, $50,000, and the amount required to be distributed currently, $30,000).

(c) The charitable contributions deduction taken into account, $20,000, is allocated proportionately to the items of income of the trust, $16,000 to taxable interest and $4,000 to tax-exempt income.

(d) Under section 662(a)(1), the amount of income required to be distributed currently to A is $30,000, which consists of the balance of these items, $24,000 of taxable interest and $6,000 of tax-exempt income.

(e) In determining the amount to be included in the gross income of B under section 662 for the taxable year, however, the entire charitable contributions deduction is taken into account, with the result that there is no distributable net income and therefore no amount to be included in gross income.

(f) See subpart D (sections 665 and following), part I, subchapter J, chapter 1 of the Code for application of the throwback provisions to the distribution made to B.

Example (2). The net income of a trust is payable to A for life, with the remainder to a charitable organization. Under the terms of the trust instrument and local law capital gains are added to corpus. During the taxable year the trust receives dividends of $10,000 and realized a long-term capital gain of $10,000, for which a long-term capital gains deduction of $5,000 is allowed under section 1202. Since under the trust instrument and local law the capital gains are allocated to the charitable organization, and since the capital gain deduction is directly attributable to the capital gain, the charitable contributions deduction and the capital gain deduction are both allocable to the capital gain, and dividends in the amount of $10,000 are allocable to A. [Reg. § 1.662(b)-2.]

☐ [*T.D.* 6217, 12-19-56.]

[Reg. § 1.662(c)-1]

§ 1.662(c)-1. Different taxable years.—If a beneficiary has a different taxable year (as defined in section 441 or 442) from the taxable year of an estate or trust, the amount he is required to include in gross income in accordance with section 662(a) and (b) is based upon the distributable net income of the estate or trust and the amounts properly paid, credited, or required to be distributed to the beneficiary for any taxable year or years of the estate or trust ending with or within his taxable year. This rule applies as to so-called short taxable years as well as taxable years of normal duration. Income of an estate or trust for its taxable year or years is determined in accordance with its method of accounting and without regard to that of the beneficiary. [Reg. § 1.662(c)-1.]

☐ [*T.D.* 6217, 12-19-56.]

[Reg. § 1.662(c)-2]

§ 1.662(c)-2. Death of individual beneficiary.—If an amount specified in section 662(a)(1) or (2) is paid, credited, or required to be distributed by an estate or trust for a taxable year which does not end with or within the last taxable year of a beneficiary (because of the beneficiary's death), the extent to which the amount is included in the gross income of the beneficiary for his last taxable year or in the gross income of his estate is determined by the computations under section 662 for the taxable year of the estate or trust in which his last taxable year ends. Thus, the distributable net income and the amounts paid, credited, or required to be distributed for the taxable year of the estate or trust, determine the extent to which the amounts paid, credited, or required to be distributed to the beneficiary are included in his gross income for his last taxable year or in the gross income of his estate. (Section 662(c) does not apply to such amounts.) The gross income for the last taxable year of a beneficiary on the cash basis includes only income actually distributed to the beneficiary before his death. Income required to be distributed, but in fact distributed to his estate, is included in the gross income of the estate as income in respect of a decedent under section 691. See paragraph (e) of § 1.663(c)-3 with respect to separate share treatment for the periods before and after the death of a trust's beneficiary. [Reg. § 1.662(c)-2.]

☐ [*T.D.* 6217, 12-19-56.]

[Reg. § 1.662(c)-3]

§ 1.662(c)-3. Termination of existence of other beneficiaries.—If the existence of a beneficiary which is not an individual terminates, the amount to be included under section 662(a) in its gross income for the last taxable year is computed with reference to §§ 1.662(c)-1 and 1.662(c)-2 as if the beneficiary were a deceased individual, except that income required to be distributed prior to the termination but actually distributed to the beneficiary's successor in interest is included in the beneficiary's income for its last taxable year. [Reg. § 1.662(c)-3.]

☐ [*T.D.* 6217, 12-19-56.]

[Reg. § 1.662(c)-4]

§ 1.662(c)-4. Illustration of the provisions of sections 661 and 662.—The provisions of sections 661 and 662 may be illustrated in general by the following example:

Example. (a) Under the terms of a testamentary trust one-half of the trust income is to be distributed currently to W, the decedent's wife, for her life. The remaining trust income may, in the trustee's discretion, either be paid to D, the grantor's daughter, paid to designated charities, or accumulated. The trust is to terminate at the death of W and the principal will then be payable to D. No provision is made in the trust instrument with respect to depreciation of rental property. Capital gains are allocable to the principal account under the applicable local law. The trust and both beneficiaries file returns on the calendar year basis. The records of the fiduciary show the following items of income and deduction for the taxable year 1955:

Rents	$50,000
Dividends of domestic corporations	50,000
Tax-exempt interest	20,000
Partially tax-exempt interest	10,000
Capital gains (long term)	20,000
Depreciation of rental property	10,000
Expenses attributable to rental income	15,400
Trustee's commissions allocable to income account	2,800
Trustee's commissions allocable to principal account	1,100

(b) The income for trust accounting purposes is $111,800, and the trustee distributes one-half ($55,900) to W and in his discretion makes a contribution of one-quarter ($27,950) to charity X and distributes the remaining one-quarter ($27,950) to D. The total of the distributions to beneficiaries is $83,850, consisting of (1) income required to be distributed currently to W of $55,900 and (2) other amounts properly paid or credited to D of $27,950. The income for trust accounting purposes of $111,800 is determined as follows:

Rents		$50,000
Dividends		50,000
Tax-exempt interest		20,000
Partially tax-exempt interest		10,000
Total		130,000
Less: Rental expenses	$15,400	
Trustee's commissions allocable to income account	2,800	18,200
Income as computed under section 643(b)		111,800

(c) The distributable net income of the trust as computed under section 643(a) is $82,750, determined as follows:

Rents			$50,000
Dividends			50,000
Partially tax-exempt interest			10,000
Tax-exempt interest		$20,000	
Less: Trustee's commissions allocable thereto (20,000/130,000 of $3,900)	$600		
Charitable contributions allocable thereto (20,000/130,000 of $27,950)	4,300	4,900	15,100
Total			$125,100
Deductions:			
Rental expenses		$15,400	
Trustee's commissions ($3,900 less $600 allocated to tax-exempt interest)		3,300	
Charitable deduction ($27,950 less $4,300 attributable to tax-exempt interest)		23,650	42,350
Distributable net income			$82,750

In computing the distributable net income of $82,750, the taxable income of the trust was computed with the following modifications: No deductions were allowed for distributions to beneficiaries and for personal exemption of the trust (section 643(a)(1) and (2)); capital gains were excluded and no deduction under section 1202 (relating to the 50 percent deduction for long-term capital gains) was taken into account (section 643(a)(3)); and the tax-exempt interest (as adjusted for expenses and charitable contributions) and the dividend exclusion of $50 were included (section 643(a)(5) and (7)).

(d) Inasmuch as the distributable net income of $82,750 as determined under section 643(a) is less than the sum of the amounts distributed to W and D of $83,850, the deduction allowable to the trust under section 661(a) is such distributable net income as modified under section 661(c) to exclude therefrom the items of income not included in the gross income of the trust, as follows:

Distributable net income		$82,750
Less: Tax-exempt interest (as adjusted for expenses and the charitable contributions)	$15,100	
Dividend exclusion allowable under section 116	50	15,150
Deduction allowable under section 661(a)		$67,600

(e) For the purpose of determining the character of the amounts deductible under section 642(c) and section 661(a), the trustee elected to offset the trustee's commissions (other than the portion required to be allocated to tax-exempt interest) against the rental income. The following table shows the determination of the character of the amounts deemed distributed to beneficiaries and contributed to charity:

	Rents	*Taxable dividends*	*Excluded dividends*	*Tax-exempt interest*	*Partially tax-exempt interest*	*Total*
Trust income	$50,000	$49,950	$50	$20,000	$10,000	$130,000
Less:						
Charitable contribution	10,750	10,750	.....	4,300	2,150	27,950
Rental expenses	15,400	.....	.....	.....	.....	15,400

	Rents	*Taxable dividends*	*Excluded dividends*	*Tax-exempt interest*	*Partially tax-exempt interest*	*Total*
Trustee's commissions	3,300	. . . . . .	. . . . . .	600	. . . . . .	3,900
Total deductions	29,450	10,750	0	4,900	2,150	47,250
Amounts distributable to beneficiaries	20,550	39,200	50	15,100	7,850	82,750

The character of the charitable contribution is determined by multiplying the total charitable contribution ($27,950) by a fraction consisting of each item of trust income, respectively, over the total trust income, except that no part of the dividends excluded from gross income are deemed included in the charitable contribution. For example, the charitable contribution is deemed to consist of rents of $10,750 (50,000/130,000 × $27,950).

(f) The taxable income of the trust is $9,900 determined as follows:

Rental income		$50,000
Dividends ($50,000 less $50 exclusion)		49,950
Partially tax-exempt interest		10,000
Capital gains		20,000
Gross income		129,950
Deductions:		
Rental expenses	$15,400	
Trustee's commissions	3,300	
Charitable contributions	23,650	
Capital gain deduction	10,000	
Distributions to beneficiaries	67,600	
Personal exemption	100	120,050
Taxable income		9,900

(g) In computing the amount includible in W's gross income under section 662(a)(1), the $55,900 distribution to her is deemed to be composed of the following proportions of the items of income deemed to have been distributed to the beneficiaries by the trust (see paragraph (e) of this example):

Rents (20,550/82,750 × $55,900)	$13,882
Dividends (39,250/82,750 × $55,900)	26,515
Partially tax-exempt interest (7,850/82,750 × $55,900)	5,303
Tax-exempt interest (15,100/82,750 × $55,900)	10,200
Total	55,900

Accordingly, W will exclude $10,200 of tax-exempt interest from gross income and will receive the credits and exclusion for dividends received and for partially tax-exempt interest provided in sections 34, 116, and 35, respectively, with respect to the dividends and partially tax-exempt interest deemed to have been distributed to her, her share of the dividends being aggregated with other dividends received by her for purposes of the dividend credit and exclusion. In addition, she may deduct a share of the depreciation deduction proportionate to the trust income allocable to her; that is, one-half of the total depreciation deduction, or $5,000.

(h) Inasmuch as the sum of the amount of income required to be distributed currently to W ($55,900) and the other amounts properly paid, credited, or required to be distributed to D ($27,950) exceeds the distributable net income ($82,750) of the trust as determined under section 643(a), D is deemed to have received $26,850 ($82,750 less $55,900) for income tax purposes. The character of the amounts deemed distributed to her is determined as follows:

Rents (20,550/82,750 × $26,850)	$ 6,668
Dividends (39,250/82,750 × $26,850)	12,735
Partially tax-exempt interest (7,850/82,750 × $26,850)	2,547
Tax-exempt interest (15,100/82,750 × $26,850)	4,900
Total	26,850

Accordingly, D will exclude $4,900 of tax-exempt interest from gross income and will receive the credits and exclusion for dividends received and for partially tax-exempt interest provided in sections 34, 116, and 35, respectively, with respect to the dividends and partially tax-exempt interest deemed to have been distributed to her, her share of the dividends being aggregated with other dividends received by her for purposes of the dividend credit and exclusion. In addition, she may deduct a share of the depreciation deduction proportionate to the trust income allocable to her; that is, one-fourth of the total depreciation deduction, or $2,500.

(i) [Reserved]

(j) The remaining $2,500 of the depreciation deduction is allocated to the amount distributed to charity X and is hence nondeductible by the trust, W, or D. (See § 1.642(e)-1.) [Reg. § 1.662(c)-4.]

☐ [*T.D.* 6217, 12-19-56.]

[Reg. § 1.663(a)-1]

§ 1.663(a)-1. Special rules applicable to sections 661 and 662; exclusions; gifts, bequests, etc.—(a) *In general.*—A gift or bequest of a specific sum of money or of specific property, which is required by the specific terms of the will or trust instrument and is properly paid or credited to a beneficiary, is not allowed as a deduction to an estate or trust under section 661 and is not included in the gross income of a beneficiary under section 662, unless under the terms of the will or trust instrument the gift or bequest is to be paid or credited to the recipient in more than three installments. Thus, in order for a gift or bequest to be excludable from the gross income of the recipient, (1) it must qualify as a gift or bequest of a specific sum of money or of specific property (see paragraph (b) of this section), and (2) the terms of the governing instrument must not provide for its payment in more than three installments (see paragraph (c) of this section). The date when the estate came into existence or the date when the trust was created is immaterial.

(b) *Definition of a gift or bequest of a specific sum of money or of specific property.*—(1) In order to qualify as a gift or bequest of a specific sum of money or of specific property under section 663(a), the amount of money or the identity of the specific property must be ascertainable under the terms of a testator's will as of the date of his death, or under the terms of an inter vivos trust instrument as of the date of the inception of the trust. For example, bequests to a decedent's son of the decedent's interest in a partnership and to his daughter of a sum of money equal to the value of the partnership interest are bequests of specific property and of a specific sum of money, respectively. On the other hand, a bequest to the decedent's spouse of money or property, to be selected by the decedent's executor, equal in value to a fraction of the decedent's "adjusted gross estate" is neither a bequest of a specific sum of money or of specific property. The identity of the property and the amount of money specified in the preceding sentence are dependent both on the exercise of the executor's discretion and on the payment of administration expenses and other charges, neither of which are facts existing on the date of the decedent's death. It is immaterial that the value of the bequest is determinable after the decedent's death before the bequest is satisfied (so that gain or loss may be realized by the estate in the transfer of property in satisfaction of it).

(2) The following amounts are not considered as gifts or bequests of a sum of money or of specific property within the meaning of this paragraph:

(i) An amount which can be paid or credited only from the income of an estate or trust, whether from the income for the year of payment or crediting, or from the income accumulated from a prior year;

(ii) An annuity, or periodic gifts of specific property in lieu of or having the effect of an annuity;

(iii) A residuary estate or the corpus of a trust; or

(iv) A gift or bequest paid in a lump sum or in not more than three installments, if the gift or bequest is required to be paid in more than three installments under the terms of the governing instrument.

(3) The provisions of subparagraphs (1) and (2) of this paragraph may be illustrated by the following examples, in which it is assumed that the gift or bequest is not required to be made in more than three installments (see paragraph (c)):

Example 1. Under the terms of a will, a legacy of $5,000 was left to A, 1,000 shares of X company stock was left to W, and the balance of the estate was to be divided equally between W and B. No provision was made in the will for the disposition of income of the estate during the period of administration. The estate had income of $25,000 during the taxable year 1954, which was accumulated and added to corpus for estate accounting purposes. During the taxable year, the executor paid the legacy of $5,000 in a lump sum to A, transferred the X company stock to W, and made no other distributions to beneficiaries. The distributions to A and W qualify for the exclusion under section 663(a)(1).

Example 2. Under the terms of a will, the testator's estate was to be distributed to A. No provision was made in the will for the distribution of the estate's income during the period of administration. The estate had income of $50,000 for the taxable year. The estate distributed to A stock with a basis of $40,000 and with a fair market value of $40,000 on the date of distribution. No other distributions were made during the year. The distribution does not qualify for the exclusion under section 663(a)(1), because it is not a specific gift to A required by the terms of the will. Accordingly, the fair market value of the property ($40,000) represents a distribution within the meaning of sections 661(a) and 662(a) (see § 1.661(a)-2(c)).

Example 3. Under the terms of a trust instrument, trust income is to be accumulated for a period of 10 years. During the eleventh year, the trustee is to distribute $10,000 to B, payable from income or corpus, and $10,000 to C, payable out of accumulated income. The trustee is to distribute the balance of the accumulated income to A. Thereafter, A is to receive all the current income until the trust terminates. Only the distribution to B would qualify for the exclusion under section 663(a)(1).

(4) A gift or bequest of a specific sum of money or of specific property is not disqualified under this paragraph solely because its payment is subject to a condition. For example, provision for a payment by a trust to beneficiary A of

See p. 15 for regulations not amended to reflect law changes

$10,000 when he reaches age 25, and $10,000 when he reaches age 30, with payment over to B of any amount not paid to A because of his death, is a gift to A of a specific sum of money payable in two installments, within the meaning of this paragraph, even though the exact amount payable to A cannot be ascertained with certainty under the terms of the trust instrument.

(c) *Installment payments.*—(1) In determining whether a gift or bequest of a specific sum of money or of specific property, as defined in paragraph (b) of this section, is required to be paid or credited to a particular beneficiary in more than three installments—

(i) Gifts or bequests of articles for personal use (such as personal and household effects, automobiles, and the like) are disregarded.

(ii) Specifically devised real property, the title to which passes directly from the decedent to the devisee under local law, is not taken into account, since it would not constitute an amount paid, credited, or required to be distributed under section 661 (see paragraph (e) of § 1.661(a)-2).

(iii) All gifts and bequests under a decedent's will (which are not disregarded pursuant to subdivisions (i) and (ii) of this subparagraph) for which no time of payment or crediting is specified, and which are to be paid or credited in the ordinary course of administration of the decedent's estate, are considered as required to be paid or credited in a single installment.

(iv) All gifts and bequests (which are not disregarded pursuant to subdivisions (i) and (ii) of this subparagraph) payable at any one specified time under the terms of the governing instrument are taken into account as a single installment.

For purposes of determining the number of installments paid or credited to a particular beneficiary, a decedent's estate and a testamentary trust shall each be treated as a separate entity.

(2) The application of the rules stated in subparagraph (1) of this paragraph may be illustrated by the following examples:

Example (1). (i) Under the terms of a decedent's will, $10,000 in cash, household furniture, a watch, an automobile, 100 shares of X company stock, 1,000 bushels of grain, 500 head of cattle, and a farm (title to which passed directly to A under local law) are bequeathed or devised outright to A. The will also provides for the creation of a trust for the benefit of A, under the terms of which there are required to be distributed to A, $10,000 in cash and 100 shares of Y company stock when he reaches 25 years of age, $25,000 in cash and 200 shares of Y company stock when he reaches 30 years of age, and $50,000 in cash and 300 shares of Y company stock when he reaches 35 years of age.

(ii) The furniture, watch, automobile, and the farm are excluded in determining whether any gift or bequest is required to be paid or credited to A in more than three installments. These items qualify for the exclusion under section 663(a)(1) regardless of the treatment of the other items of property bequeathed to A.

(iii) The $10,000 in cash, the shares of X company stock, the grain, the cattle and the assets required to create the trust, to be paid or credited by the estate to A and the trust are considered as required to be paid or credited in a single installment to each, regardless of the manner of payment or distribution by the executor, since no time of payment or crediting is specified in the will. The $10,000 in cash and shares of Y company stock required to be distributed by the trust to A when he is 25 years old are considered as required to be paid or distributed as one installment under the trust. Likewise, the distributions to be made by the trust to A when he is 30 and 35 years old are each considered as one installment under the trust. Since the total number of installments to be made by the estate does not exceed three, all of the items of money and property distributed by the estate qualify for the exclusion under section 663(a)(1). Similarly, the three distributions by the trust qualify.

Example (2). Assume the same facts as in example (1), except that another distribution of a specified sum of money is required to be made by the trust to A when he becomes 40 years old. This distribution would also qualify as an installment, thus making four installments in all under the trust. None of the gifts to A under the trust would qualify for the exclusion under section 663(a)(1). The situation as to the estate, however, would not be changed.

Example (3). A trust instrument provides that A and B are each to receive $75,000 in installments of $25,000, to be paid in alternate years. The trustee distributes $25,000 to A in 1954, 1956, and 1958, and to B in 1955, 1957, and 1959. The gifts to A and B qualify for exclusion under section 663(a)(1), although a total of six payments is made. The gifts of $75,000 to each beneficiary are to be separately treated. [Reg. § 1.663(a)-1.]

☐ [*T.D.* 6217, 12-19-56. *Amended by T.D.* 8849, 12-27-99.]

[Reg. § 1.663(a)-2]

§ 1.663(a)-2. Charitable, etc., distributions.—Any amount paid, permanently set aside, or to be used for the charitable, etc., purposes specified in section 642(c) and which is allowable as a deduction under that section is not allowed as a deduction to an estate or trust under section 661 or treated as an amount distributed for purposes of determining the amounts includible in gross income of beneficiaries under section 662. Amounts paid, permanently set aside, or to be used for charitable, etc., purposes are deductible by estates or trusts only as provided in section 642(c). For purposes of this section, the deduction provided in section 642(c) is computed without regard to the provisions of section 508(d), section 681, or section 4948(c)(4) (concerning unrelated business income and private foundations). [Reg. § 1.663(a)-2.]

☐ [*T.D.* 6217, 12-19-56. *Amended by T.D.* 7428, 8-13-76.]

[Reg. § 1.663(a)-3]

§ 1.663(a)-3. Denial of double deduction.—No amount deemed to have been distributed to a beneficiary in a preceding year under section 651 or 661 is included in amounts falling within section 661(a) or 662(a). For example, assume that all of the income of a trust is required to be distributed currently to beneficiary A and both the trust and A report on the calendar year basis. For administrative convenience, the trustee distributes in January and February 1956 a portion of the income of the trust required to be distributed in 1955. The portion of the income for 1955 which was distributed by the trust in 1956 may not be claimed as a deduction by the trust for 1956 since it is deductible by the trust and includible in A's gross income for the taxable year 1955. [Reg. § 1.663(a)-3.]

☐ [*T.D.* 6217, 12-19-56.]

[Reg. § 1.663(b)-1]

§ 1.663(b)-1. Distributions in first 65 days of taxable year; scope.—(a) *Taxable years beginning after December 31, 1968.*—(1) *General rule.*—With respect to taxable years beginning after December 31, 1968, the fiduciary of a trust may elect under section 663(b) to treat any amount or portion thereof that is properly paid or credited to a beneficiary within the first 65 days following the close of the taxable year as an amount that was properly paid or credited on the last day of such taxable year.

(2) *Effect of election.*—(i) An election is effective only with respect to the taxable year for which the election is made. In the case of distributions made after May 8, 1972, the amount to which the election applies shall not exceed—

(*a*) The amount of income of the trust (as defined in § 1.643(b)-1) for the taxable year for which the election is made, or

(*b*) The amount of distributable net income of the trust (as defined in §§ 1.643(a)-1 through 1.643(a)-7) for such taxable year, if greater, reduced by any amounts paid, credited, or required to be distributed in such taxable year other than those amounts considered paid or credited in a preceding taxable year by reason of section 663(b) and this section. An election shall be made for each taxable year for which the treatment is desired. The application of this paragraph may be illustrated by the following example:

Example. X Trust, a calendar year trust, has $1,000 of income (as defined in § 1.643(b)-1) and $800 of distributable net income (as defined in §§ 1.643(a)-1 through 1.643(a)-7) in 1972. The trust properly pays $550 to A, a beneficiary, on January 15, 1972, which the trustee elects to treat under section 663(b) as paid on December 31, 1971. The trust also properly pays to A $600 on July 19, 1972, and $450 on January 17, 1973. For 1972, the maximum amount that may be elected under this subdivision to be treated as properly paid or credited on the last day of 1972 is $400 ($1,000 − $600). The $550 paid on January 15, 1972, does not reduce the maximum amount to which the election may apply, because that amount is treated as properly paid on December 31, 1971.

(ii) If an election is made with respect to a taxable year of a trust, this section shall apply only to those amounts which are properly paid or credited within the first 65 days following such year and which are so designated by the fiduciary in his election. Any amount considered under section 663(b) as having been distributed in the preceding taxable year shall be so treated for all purposes. For example, in determining the beneficiary's tax liability, such amount shall be considered as having been received by the beneficiary in his taxable year in which or with which the last day of the preceding taxable year of the trust ends.

(b) *Taxable years beginning before January 1, 1969.*—With respect to taxable years of a trust beginning before January 1, 1969, the fiduciary of the trust may elect under section 663(b) to treat distributions wihtin the first 65 days following such taxable year as amounts which were paid or credited on the last day of such taxable year, if:

(1) The trust was in existence prior to January 1, 1954;

(2) An amount in excess of the income of the immediately preceding taxable year may not (under the terms of the governing instrument) be distributed in any taxable year; and

(3) The fiduciary elects (as provided in § 1.663(b)-2) to have section 663(b) apply. [Reg. § 1.663(b)-1.]

☐ [*T.D.* 6217, 12-19-56. *Amended by T.D.* 7204, 8-24-72.]

[Reg. § 1.663(b)-2]

§ 1.663(b)-2. Election.—(a) *Manner and time of election; irrevocability.*—(1) *When return is required to be filed.*—If a trust return is required to be filed for the taxable year of the trust for which the election is made, the election shall be made in the appropriate place on such return. The election under this subparagraph shall be made not later than the time prescribed by law for filing such return (including extensions thereof). Such election shall become irrevocable after the last day prescribed for making it.

(2) *When no return is required to be filed.*—If no return is required to be filed for the taxable year of the trust for which the election is made, the election shall be made in a statement filed with the internal revenue office with which a return by such trust would be filed if such trust were required to file a return for such taxable year. See section 6091 and the regulations thereunder for place for filing return. The election under this subparagraph shall be made not later than the time prescribed by law for filing a return if such trust were required to file a return for such taxable year. Such election shall become irrevocable after the last day prescribed for making it.

(b) *Elections under prior law.*—Elections made pursuant to section 663(b) prior to its amendment by section 331(b) of the Tax Reform Act of 1969 (83 Stat. 598), which, under prior law, were irrevocable for the taxable year for which the election was made and all subsequent years, are not effective for taxable years beginning after December 31, 1968. In the case of a trust for which an election was made under prior law, the fiduciary shall make the election for each taxable year beginning after December 31, 1968, for which the treatment provided by section 663(b) is desired. [Reg. § 1.663(b)-2.]

☐ [*T.D.* 6217, 12-19-56. *Amended by T.D.* 7204, 8-24-72.]

[Reg. § 1.663(c)-1]

§ 1.663(c)-1. Separate shares treated as separate trusts or as separate estates; in general.—(a) If a single trust (or estate) has more than one beneficiary, and if different beneficiaries have substantially separate and independent shares, their shares are treated as separate trusts (or estates) for the sole purpose of determining the amount of distributable net income allocable to the respective beneficiaries under sections 661 and 662. Application of this rule will be significant in, for example, situations in which income is accumulated for beneficiary A but a distribution is made to beneficiary B of both income and corpus in an amount exceeding the share of income that would be distributable to B had there been separate trusts (or estates). In the absence of a separate share rule B would be taxed on income which is accumulated for A. The division of distributable net income into separate shares will limit the tax liability of B. Section 663(c) does not affect the principles of applicable law in situations in which a single trust instrument creates not one but several separate trusts, as opposed to separate shares in the same trust within the meaning of this section.

(b) The separate share rule does not permit the treatment of separate shares as separate trusts (or estates) for any purpose other than the application of distributable net income. It does not, for instance, permit the treatment of separate shares as separate trusts (or estates) for purposes of:

(1) The filing of returns and payment of tax,

(2) The deduction of personal exemption under section 642(b), and

(3) The allowance to beneficiaries succeeding to the trust (or estate) property of excess deductions and unused net operating loss and capital loss carryovers on termination of the trust (or estate) under section 642(h).

(c) The separate share rule may be applicable even though separate and independent accounts are not maintained and are not required to be maintained for each share on the books of account of the trust (or estate), and even though no physical segregation of assets is made or required.

(d) Separate share treatment is not elective. Thus, if a trust (or estate) is properly treated as having separate and independent shares, such treatment must prevail in all taxable years of the trust (or estate) unless an event occurs as a result of which the terms of the trust (or estate) instrument and the requirements of proper administration require different treatment. [Reg. § 1.663(c)-1.]

☐ [*T.D.* 6217, 12-19-56. *Amended by T.D.* 8849, 12-27-99.]

[Reg. § 1.663(c)-2]

§ 1.663(c)-2. Rules of administration.—(a) *When separate shares come into existence.*—A separate share comes into existence upon the earliest moment that a fiduciary may reasonably determine, based upon the known facts, that a separate economic interest exists.

(b) *Computation of distributable net income for each separate share.*—(1) *General rule.*—The amount of distributable net income for any share under section 663(c) is computed as if each share constituted a separate trust or estate. Accordingly, each separate share shall calculate its distributable net income based upon its portion of gross income that is includible in distributable net income and its portion of any applicable deductions or losses.

(2) *Section 643(b) income.*—This paragraph (b)(2) governs the allocation of the portion of gross income includible in distributable net income that is income within the meaning of section 643(b). Such gross income is allocated among the separate shares in accordance with the amount of income that each share is entitled to under the terms of the governing instrument or applicable local law.

(3) *Income in respect of a decedent.*—This paragraph (b)(3) governs the allocation of the portion of gross income includible in distributable net income that is income in respect of a decedent within the meaning of section 691(a) and is not income within the meaning of section 643(b). Such gross income is allocated among the separate shares that could potentially be funded with these amounts irrespective of whether the share is entitled to receive any income under the terms of the governing instrument or applicable local law. The amount of such gross income allocated to each share is based on the relative value of each share that could potentially be funded with such amounts.

(4) *Gross income not attributable to cash.*—This paragraph (b)(4) governs the allocation of the portion of gross income includible in distributable net income that is not attributable to cash received by the estate or trust (for example, original issue discount, a distributive share of partnership tax items, and the pro rata share of an S corporation's tax items). Such gross income is allocated among the separate shares in the same proportion as section 643(b) income from the same source would be allocated under the terms of the governing instrument or applicable local law.

(5) *Deductions and losses.*—Any deduction or any loss which is applicable solely to one separate share of the trust or estate is not available to any other share of the same trust or estate.

(c) *Computations and valuations.*—For purposes of calculating distributable net income for each separate share, the fiduciary must use a reasonable and equitable method to make the allocations, calculations, and valuations required by paragraph (b) of this section. [Reg. § 1.663(c)-2.]

☐ [*T.D.* 6217, 12-19-56. *Amended by T.D.* 8849, 12-27-99.]

[Reg. § 1.663(c)-3]

§ 1.663(c)-3. Applicability of separate share rule to certain trusts.—(a) The applicability of the separate share rule provided by section 663(c) to trusts other than qualified revocable trusts within the meaning of section 645(b)(1) will generally depend upon whether distributions of the trust are to be made in substantially the same manner as if separate trusts had been created. Thus, if an instrument directs a trustee to divide the testator's residuary estate into separate shares (which under applicable law do not constitute separate trusts) for each of the testator's children and the trustee is given discretion, with respect to each share, to distribute or accumulate income or to distribute principal or accumulated income, or to do both, separate shares will exist under section 663(c). In determining whether separate shares exist, it is immaterial whether the principal and any accumulated income of each share is ultimately distributable to the beneficiary of such share, to his descendants, to his appointees under a general or special power of appointment, or to any other beneficiaries (including a charitable organization) designated to receive his share of the trust and accumulated income upon termination of the beneficiary's interest in the share. Thus, a separate share may exist if the instrument provides that upon the death of the beneficiary of the share, the share will be added to the shares of the other beneficiaries of the trust.

(b) Separate share treatment will not be applied to a trust or portion of a trust subject to a power to:

(1) Distribute, apportion, or accumulate income, or

(2) Distribute corpus

to or for one or more beneficiaries within a group or class of beneficiaries, unless payment of income, accumulated income, or corpus of a share of one beneficiary cannot affect the proportionate share of income, accumulated income, or corpus of any shares of the other beneficiaries, or unless substantially proper adjustment must thereafter be made (under the governing instrument) so that substantially separate and independent shares exist.

(c) A share may be considered as separate even though more than one beneficiary has an interest in it. For example, two beneficiaries may have equal, disproportionate, or indeterminate interests in one share which is separate and independent from another share in which one or more beneficiaries have an interest. Likewise, the same person may be a beneficiary of more than one separate share.

(d) Separate share treatment may be given to a trust or portion of a trust otherwise qualifying under this section if the trust or portion of a trust is subject to a power to pay out to a beneficiary of a share (of such trust or portion) an amount of corpus in excess of his proportionate share of the corpus of the trust if the possibility of exercise of the power is remote. For example, if the trust is subject to a power to invade the entire corpus for the health, education, support, or maintenance of A, separate share treatment is applied if exercise of the power requires consideration of A's other income which is so substantial as to make the possibility of exercise of the power remote. If instead it appears that A and B have separate shares in a trust subject to a power to invade the entire corpus for the comfort, pleasure, desire, or happiness of A, separate share treatment shall not be applied.

(e) For taxable years ending before January 1, 1979, the separate share rule may also be applicable to successive interests in point of time, as for instance in the case of a trust providing for a life estate to A and a second life estate or outright remainder to B. In such a case, in the taxable year of a trust in which a beneficiary dies items of income and deduction properly allocable under trust accounting principles to the period before a beneficiary's death are attributed to one share, and those allocable to the period after the beneficiary's death are attributed to the other share. Separate share treatment is not available to a succeeding interest, however, with respect to distributions which would otherwise be deemed distributed in a taxable year of the earlier interest under the throwback provisions of subpart D (section 665 and following), Part I, subchapter J, chapter 1 of the Code. The application of this paragraph may be illustrated by the following example:

Example. A trust instrument directs that the income of a trust is to be paid to A for her life. After her death income may be distributed to B or accumulated. A dies on June 1, 1956. The trust keeps its books on the basis of the calendar year. The trust instrument permits invasions of corpus for the benefit of A and B, and an invasion of corpus was in fact made for A's benefit in 1956. In determining the distributable net income of the trust for the purpose of determining the amounts includible in A's income, income and deductions properly allocable to the period before A's death are treated as income and deductions of a separate share, and for that purpose no account is taken of income and deductions allocable to the period after A's death.

[Reg. § 1.663(c)-3.]

☐ [*T.D.* 6217, 12-19-56. *Amended by T.D.* 7633, 7-17-79 *and T.D.* 8849, 12-27-99.]

[Reg. § 1.663(c)-4]

§ 1.663(c)-4. Applicability of separate share rule to estates and qualified revocable trusts.—(a) *General rule.*—The applicability of the separate share rule provided by section 663(c) to estates and qualified revocable trusts within the meaning of section 645(b)(1) will generally depend upon whether the governing instrument and applicable local law create separate economic interests in one beneficiary or class of beneficiaries of such estate or trust. Ordinarily, a separate share exists if the economic interests of the beneficiary or class of beneficiaries neither affect nor are affected by the economic interests accruing to another beneficiary or class of beneficiaries. Separate shares include, for example, the income on bequeathed property if the recipient of the specific bequest is entitled to such income and a surviving spouse's elective share that under local law is entitled to income and appreciation or depreciation. Furthermore, a qualified revocable trust for which an election is made under section 645 is always a separate share of the estate and may itself contain two or more separate shares. Conversely, a gift or bequest of a specific sum of money or of property as defined in section 663(a)(1) is not a separate share.

(b) *Special rule for certain types of beneficial interests.*—Notwithstanding the provisions of paragraph (a) of this section, a surviving spouse's elective share that under local law is determined as of the date of the decedent's death and is not entitled to income or any appreciation or depreciation is a separate share. Similarly, notwithstanding the provisions of paragraph (a) of this section, a pecuniary formula bequest that, under the terms of the governing instrument or applicable local law, is not entitled to income or to share in appreciation or depreciation constitutes a separate share if the governing instrument does not provide that it is to be paid or credited in more than three installments.

(c) *Shares with multiple beneficiaries and beneficiaries of multiple shares.*—A share may be considered as separate even though more than one beneficiary has an interest in it. For example, two beneficiaries may have equal, disproportionate, or indeterminate interests in one share which is economically separate and independent from another share in which one or more beneficiaries have an interest. Moreover, the same person may be a beneficiary of more than one separate share. [Reg. § 1.663(c)-4.]

☐ [*T.D.* 8849, 12-27-99.]

[Reg. § 1.663(c)-5]

§ 1.663(c)-5. Examples.—Section 663(c) may be illustrated by the following examples:

Example 1. (i) A single trust was created in 1940 for the benefit of A, B, and C, who were aged 6, 4, and 2, respectively. Under the terms of the instrument, the trust income is required to be divided into three equal shares. Each beneficiary's share of the income is to be accumulated until he becomes 21 years of age. When a beneficiary reaches the age of 21, his share of the income may thereafter be either accumulated or distributed to him in the discretion of the trustee. The trustee also has discretion to invade corpus for the benefit of any beneficiary to the extent of his share of the trust estate, and the trust instrument requires that the beneficiary's right to future income and corpus will be proportionately reduced. When each beneficiary reaches 35 years of age, his share of the trust estate shall be paid over to him. The interest in the trust estate of any beneficiary dying without issue and before he has attained the age of 35 is to be equally divided between the other beneficiaries of the trust. All expenses of the trust are allocable to income under the terms of the trust instrument.

(ii) No distributions of income or corpus were made by the trustee prior to 1955, although A became 21 years of age on June 30, 1954. During the taxable year 1955, the trust has income from royalties of $20,000 and expenses of $5,000. The trustee in his discretion distributes $12,000 to A. Both A and the trust report on the calendar year basis.

(iii) The trust qualifies for the separate share treatment under section 663(c) and the distributable net income must be divided into three parts for the purpose of determining the amount deductible by the trust under section 661 and the amount includible in A's gross income under section 662.

(iv) The distributable net income of each share of the trust is $5,000 ($6,667 less $1,667). Since the amount $12,000 distributed to A during 1955 exceeds the distributable net income of $5,000 allocated to his share, the trust is deemed to have distributed to him $5,000 of 1955 income and $7,000 of amounts other than 1955 income. Accordingly, the trust is allowed a deduction of $5,000 under section 661. The taxable income of the trust for 1955 is $9,900, computed as follows:

Royalties		$20,000
Deductions:		
Expenses	$5,000	
Distribution to A	5,000	
Personal exemption . . .	100	10,100
Taxable income		9,900

(v) In accordance with section 662, A must include in his gross income for 1955 an amount equal to the portion ($5,000) of the distributable net income of the trust allocated to his share. Also, the excess distribution of $7,000 made by the trust is subject to the throwback provisions of subpart D (section 665 and following), part I, subchapter J, chapter 1 of the Code, and the regulations thereunder.

Example 2. (i) *Facts.* Testator, who dies in 2000, is survived by a spouse and two children. Testator's will contains a fractional formula bequest dividing the residuary estate between the surviving spouse and a trust for the benefit of the children. Under the fractional formula, the marital bequest constitutes 60% of the estate and the children's trust constitutes 40% of the estate. During the year, the executor makes a partial proportionate distribution of $1,000,0000, ($600,000 to the surviving spouse and $400,000 to the children's trust) and makes no other distributions. The estate receives dividend income of $20,000, and pays expenses of $8,000 that are deductible on the estate's federal income tax return.

(ii) *Conclusion.* The fractional formula bequests to the surviving spouse and to the children's trust are separate shares. Because Testator's will provides for fractional formula residuary bequests, the income and any appreciation in the value of the estate assets are proportionately allocated between the marital share and the trust's share. Therefore, in determining the distributable net income of each share, the income and expenses must be allocated 60% to the marital share and 40% to the trust's share. The distributable net income is $7,200 (60% of income less 60% of expenses) for the marital share and $4,800 (40% of income less 40% of expenses) for the trust's share. Because the amount distributed in partial satisfaction of each bequest exceeds the distributable net income of each share, the estate's distribution deduction under section 661 is limited to the sum of the distributable net income for both shares. The estate is allowed a distribution deduction of $12,000 ($7,200 for the marital share and $4,800 for the trust's share). As a result, the estate has zero taxable income ($20,000 income less $8,000 expenses and $12,000 distribution deduction). Under section 662, the surviving spouse and the trust must include in gross income $7,200 and $4,800, respectively.

Example 3. The facts are the same as in *Example 2*, except that in 2000 the executor makes the payment to partially fund the children's trust but makes no payment to the surviving spouse. The fiduciary must use a reasonable and equitable method to allocate income and expenses to the trust's share. Therefore, depending on when the distribution is made to the trust, it may no longer be reasonable or equitable to determine the distributable net income for the trust's share by allocating to it 40% of the estate's income and expenses for the year. The computation of the distributable net income for the trust's share should take into consideration that after the partial distribution the relative size of the trust's separate share is reduced and the relative size of the spouse's separate share is increased.

Example 4. (i) *Facts.* Testator, who dies in 2000, is survived by a spouse and one child. Testator's will provides for a pecuniary formula bequest to be paid in not more than three installments to a trust for the benefit of the child of the largest amount that can pass free of Federal estate tax and a bequest of the residuary to the surviving spouse. The will provides that the bequest to the child's trust is not entitled to any of the estate's income and does not participate in appreciation or depreciation in estate assets. During the 2000 taxable year, the estate receives dividend income of $200,000 and pays expenses of $15,000 that are deductible on the estate's federal income tax return. The executor partially funds the child's trust by distributing to it securities that have an adjusted basis to the estate of $350,000 and a fair market value of $380,000 on the date of distribution. As a result of this distribution, the estate realizes long-term capital gain of $30,000.

(ii) *Conclusion.* The estate has two separate shares consisting of a formula pecuniary bequest to the child's trust and a residuary bequest to the surviving spouse. Because, under the terms of the will, no estate income is allocated to the bequest to the child's trust, the distributable net income for that trust's share is zero. Therefore, with respect to the $380,000 distribution to the child's trust, the estate is allowed no deduction under section 661, and no amount is included in the trust's gross income under section 662. Because no distributions were made to the spouse, there is no need to compute the distributable net income allocable to the marital share. The taxable income of the estate for the 2000 taxable year is $214,400 ($200,000 (dividend income) plus $30,000 (capital gain) minus $15,000 (expenses) and minus $600 (personal exemption)).

Example 5. The facts are the same as in *Example 4*, except that during 2000 the estate reports on its federal income tax return a pro rata share of an S corporation's tax items and a distributive share of a partnership's tax items allocated on Form K-1s to the estate by the S corporation and by the partnership, respectively. Because, under the terms of the will, no estate income from the S corporation or the partnership would be allocated to the pecuniary bequest to child's trust, none of the tax items attributable to the S corporation stock or the partnership interest is allocated to the trust's separate share. Therefore, with respect to the $380,000 distribution to the trust, the estate is allowed no deduction under section 661, and no amount is included in the trust's gross income under section 662.

Example 6. The facts are the same as in *Example 4*, except that during 2000 the estate receives a distribution of $900,000 from the decedent's individual retirement account that is included in the estate's gross income as income in respect of a decedent under section 691(a). The entire $900,000 is allocated to corpus under applicable local law. Both the separate share for the child's trust and the separate share for the surviving spouse may potentially be funded with the proceeds from the individual retirement account. Therefore, a portion of the $900,000 gross income must be allocated to the trust's separate share. The amount allocated to the trust's share must be based upon the relative values of the two separate shares using a reasonable and equitable method. The estate is entitled to a deduction under section 661 for the portion of the $900,000 properly allocated to the trust's separate share, and the trust must include this amount in income under section 662.

Example 7. (i) *Facts.* Testator, who dies in 2000, is survived by a spouse and three adult children. Testator's will divides the residue of the estate equally among the three children. The surviving spouse files an election under the applicable state's elective share statute. Under this statute, a surviving spouse is entitled to one-third of the decedent's estate after the payment of debts and expenses. The statute also provides that the surviving spouse is not entitled to any of the estate's income and does not participate in appreciation or depreciation of the estate's assets. However, under the statute, the surviving spouse is entitled to interest on the elective share from the date of the court order directing the payment until the executor actually makes payment. During the estate's 2001 taxable year, the estate distributes to the surviving spouse $5,000,000 in partial satisfaction of the elective share and pays $200,000 of interest on the delayed payment of the elective share. During that year, the estate receives dividend income of $3,000,000 and pays expenses of $60,000 that are deductible on the estate's federal income tax return.

(ii) *Conclusion.* The estate has four separate shares consisting of the surviving spouse's elective share and each of the three children's residuary bequests. Because the surviving spouse is not entitled to any estate income under state law, none of the estate's gross income is allocated to the spouse's separate share for purposes of determining that share's distributable net income. Therefore, with respect to the $5,000,000 distribution, the estate is allowed no deduction under section 661, and no amount is included in the spouse's gross income under section 662. The $200,000 of interest paid to the spouse must be included in the spouse's gross income under section 61. Because no distributions were made to any other beneficiaries during the year, there is no need to compute the distributable net income of the other three separate shares. Thus, the taxable income of the estate for the 2000 taxable year is $2,939,400 ($3,000,000 (dividend income) minus $60,000 (expenses) and $600 (personal exemption)). The estate's $200,000 interest payment is a nondeductible personal interest expense described in section 163(h).

Example 8. The will of Testator, who dies in 2000, directs the executor to distribute the X stock and all dividends therefrom to child A and the residue of the estate to child B. The estate has two separate shares consisting of the income on the X stock bequeathed to A and the residue of the estate bequeathed to B. The bequest of the X stock meets the definition of section 663(a)(1) and therefore is not a separate share. If any distributions, other than shares of the X stock, are made during the year to either A or B, then for purposes of determining the distributable net income for the separate shares, gross income attributable to dividends on the X stock must be allocated to A's separate share and any other income must be allocated to B's separate share.

Example 9. The will of Testator, who dies in 2000, directs the executor to divide the residue of the estate equally between Testator's two children, A and B. The will directs the executor to fund A's share first with the proceeds of Testator's individual retirement account. The date of death value of the estate after the payment of debts, expenses, and estate taxes is $9,000,000. During 2000, the $900,000 balance in Testator's individual retirement account is distributed to the estate. The entire $900,000 is allocated to corpus under applicable local law. This amount is income in respect of a decedent within the meaning of section 691(a). The estate has two separate shares, one for the benefit of A and one for the benefit of B. If any distributions are made to either A or B during the year, then, for purposes of determining the distributable net income for each separate share, the $900,000 of income in respect of a decedent must be allocated to A's share.

Example 10. The facts are the same as in *Example 9,* except that the will directs the executor to fund A's share first with X stock valued at $3,000,000, rather than with the proceeds of the individual retirement account. The estate has two separate shares, one for the benefit of A and one for the benefit of B. If any distributions are made to either A or B during the year, then, for purposes of determining the distributable net income for each separate share, the $900,000 of gross income attributable to the proceeds from the individual retirement account must be allocated between the two shares to the extent that they could potentially be funded with those proceeds. The maximum amount of A's share that could potentially be funded with the income in respect of decedent is $1,500,000 ($4,500,000 value of share less $3,000,000 to be funded with stock) and the maximum amount of B's share that could potentially be funded with income in respect of decedent is $4,500,000. Based upon the relative values of these amounts, the gross income attributable to the proceeds of the individual retirement account is allocated $225,000 (or one-fourth) to A's share and $675,000 (or three-fourths) to B's share.

Example 11. The will of Testator, who dies in 2000, provides that after the payment of specific bequests of money, the residue of the estate is to be divided equally among the Testator's three children, A, B, and C. The will also provides that during the period of administration one-half of the income from the residue is to be paid to a designated charitable organization. After the specific bequests of money are paid, the estate initially has three equal separate shares. One share is for the benefit of the charitable organization and A, another share is for the benefit of the charitable organization and B, and the last share is for the benefit of the charitable organization and C. During the period of administration, payments of income to the charitable organization are deductible by the estate to the extent provided in section 642(c) and are not subject to the distribution provisions of sections 661 and 662.

[Reg. § 1.663(c)-5.]

☐ [*T.D.* 6217, 12-19-56. *Redesignated and amended by T.D.* 8849, 12-27-99 (*corrected* 3-27-2000).]

[Reg. § 1.663(c)-6]

§ 1.663(c)-6. Effective dates.—Sections 1.663(c)-1 through 1.663(c)-5 are applicable for estates and qualified revocable trusts within the meaning of section 645(b)(1) with respect to decedents who die on or after December 28, 1999. However, for estates and qualified revocable trusts with respect to decedents who died after the date that section 1307 of the Tax Reform Act of 1997 became effective but before December 28, 1999, the IRS will accept any reasonable interpretation of the separate share provisions, including those provisions provided in 1999-11 I.R.B. 41 (see § 601.601(d)(2)(ii)(b) of this chapter). For trusts other than qualified revocable trusts,

§ 1.663(c)-2 is applicable for taxable years of such trusts beginning after December 28, 1999. [Reg. § 1.663(c)-6.]

☐ [*T.D.* 8849, 12-27-99 (*corrected* 3-27-2000).]

[Reg. § 1.664-1]

§ 1.664-1. Charitable remainder trusts.—(a) *In general.*—(1) *Introduction.*—(i) *General description of a charitable remainder trust.*—Generally, a charitable remainder trust is a trust which provides for a specified distribution, at least annually, to one or more beneficiaries, at least one of which is not a charity, for life or for a term of years, with an irrevocable remainder interest to be held for the benefit of, or paid over to, charity. The specified distribution to be paid at least annually must be a sum certain which is not less than 5 percent of the initial net fair market value of all property placed in trust (in the case of a charitable remainder annuity trust) or a fixed percentage which is not less than 5 percent of the net fair market value of the trust assets, valued annually (in the case of a charitable remainder unitrust). A trust created after July 31, 1969, which is a charitable remainder trust, is exempt from all of the taxes imposed by subtitle A of the Code for any taxable year of the trust, except for a taxable year beginning before January 1, 2007, in which it has unrelated business taxable income. For taxable years beginning after December 31, 2006, an excise tax, treated as imposed by chapter 42, is imposed on charitable remainder trusts that have unrelated business taxable income. See paragraph (c) of this section.

(ii) *Scope.*—This section provides definitions, general rules governing the creation and administration of a charitable remainder trust, and rules governing the taxation of the trust and its beneficiaries. For the application of certain foundation rules to charitable remainder trusts, see paragraph (b) of this section. If the trust has unrelated business taxable income, see paragraph (c) of this section. For the treatment of distributions to recipients, see paragraph (d) of this section. For the treatment of distributions to charity, see paragraph (e) of this section. For the time limitations for amendment of governing instruments, see paragraph (f) of this section. For transitional rules under which particular requirements are inapplicable to certain trusts, see paragraph (g) of this section. Section 1.664-2 provides rules relating solely to a charitable remainder annuity trust. Section 1.664-3 provides rules relating solely to a charitable remainder unitrust. Section 1.664-4 provides rules governing the calculation of the fair market value of the remainder interest in a charitable remainder unitrust. For rules relating to the filing of returns for a charitable remainder trust, see paragraph (a)(6) of § 1.6012-3 and section 6034 and the regulations thereunder.

(iii) *Definitions.*—As used in this section and §§ 1.664-2, 1.664-3, and 1.664-4:

(*a*) *Charitable remainder trust.*—The term "charitable remainder trust" means a trust with respect to which a deduction is allowable under section 170, 2055, 2106, or 2522 and which meets the description of a charitable remainder annuity trust (as described in § 1.664-2) or a charitable remainder unitrust (as described in § 1.664-3).

(*b*) *Annuity amount.*—The term "annuity amount" means the amount described in paragraph (a)(1) of § 1.664-2 which is payable, at least annually, to the beneficiary of a charitable remainder annuity trust.

(*c*) *Unitrust amount.*—The term "unitrust amount" means the amount described in paragraph (a)(1) of § 1.664-3 which is payable, at least annually, to the beneficiary of a charitable remainder unitrust.

(*d*) *Recipient.*—The term "recipient" means the beneficiary who receives the possession or beneficial enjoyment of the annuity amount or unitrust amount.

(*e*) *Governing instrument.*—The term "governing instrument" has the same meaning as in section 508(e) and the regulations thereunder.

(2) *Requirement that the trust must be either a charitable remainder annuity trust or a charitable remainder unitrust.*—A trust is a charitable remainder trust only if it is either a charitable remainder annuity trust in every respect or a charitable remainder unitrust in every respect. For example, a trust which provides for the payment each year to a noncharitable beneficiary of the greater of a sum certain or a fixed percentage of the annual value of the trust assets is not a charitable remainder trust inasmuch as the trust is neither a charitable remainder annuity trust (for the reason that the payment for the year may be a fixed percentage of the annual value of the trust assets which is not a "sum certain") nor a charitable remainder unitrust (for the reason that the payment for the year may be a sum certain which is not a "fixed percentage" of the annual value of the trust assets).

(3) *Restrictions on investments.*—A trust is not a charitable remainder trust if the provisions of the trust include a provision which restricts the trustee from investing the trust assets in a manner which could result in the annual realization of a reasonable amount of income or gain from the sale or disposition of trust assets. In the case of transactions with, or for the benefit of, a disqualified person, see section 4941(d) and the regulations thereunder for rules relating to the definition of self-dealing.

(4) *Requirement that trust must meet definition of and function exclusively as a charitable remainder trust from its creation.*—In order for a trust to be a charitable remainder trust, it must meet the definition of and function exclusively as a charitable remainder trust from the creation of the trust. Solely for the purposes of section 664 and the regulations thereunder, the trust will be deemed to be created at the earliest time that neither the grantor nor any other person is treated as the owner of the entire trust under subpart E, part 1, subchapter J, chapter 1, subtitle A of the Code (relating to grantors and others treated as sub-

stantial owners), but in no event prior to the time property is first transferred to the trust. For purposes of the preceding sentence, neither the grantor nor his spouse shall be treated as the owner of the trust under such subpart E merely because the grantor or his spouse is named as a recipient. See examples 1 through 3 of subparagraph (6) of this paragraph for illustrations of the foregoing rule.

(5) *Rules applicable to testamentary transfers.*—(i) *Deferral of annuity or unitrust amount.*—Notwithstanding subparagraph (4) of this paragraph and §§1.664-2 and 1.664-3, for purposes of sections 2055 and 2106 a charitable remainder trust shall be deemed created at the date of death of the decedent (even though the trust is not funded until the end of a reasonable period of administration or settlement) if the obligation to pay the annuity or unitrust amount with respect to the property passing in trust at the death of the decedent begins as of the date of death of the decedent, even though the requirement to pay such amount is deferred in accordance with the rules provided in this subparagraph. If permitted by applicable local law or authorized by the provisions of the governing instrument, the requirement to pay such amount may be deferred until the end of the taxable year of the trust in which occurs the complete funding of the trust. Within a reasonable period after such time, the trust must pay (in the case of an underpayment) or must receive from the recipient (in the case of an overpayment) the difference between—

(*a*) Any annuity or unitrust amounts actually paid, plus interest on such amounts computed at the rate of interest specified in paragraph (a)(5)(iv) of this section, compounded annually, and

(*b*) The annuity or unitrust amounts payable, plus interest on such amounts computed at the rate of interest specified in paragraph (a)(5)(iv) of this section, compounded annually.

The amounts payable shall be retroactively determined by using the taxable year, valuation method, and valuation dates which are ultimately adopted by the charitable remainder trust. See subdivision (ii) of this subparagraph for rules relating to retroactive determination of the amount payable under a charitable remainder unitrust. See paragraph (d)(4) of this section for rules relating to the year of inclusion in the case of an underpayment to a recipient and the allowance of a deduction in the case of an overpayment to a recipient.

(ii) For purposes of retroactively determining the amount under subdivision (i)(*b*) of this subparagraph, the governing instrument of a charitable remainder unitrust may provide that the amount described in subdivision (i)(*b*) of this subparagraph with respect to property passing in trust at the death of the decedent for the period which begins on the date of death of the decedent and ends on the earlier of the date of death of the last recipient or the end of the taxable year of the trust in which occurs the complete funding of the trust shall be computed by multiplying—

(*a*) The sum of (*1*) the value, on the earlier of the date of death of the last recipient or the last day in such taxable year, of the property held in trust which is attributable to property passing to the trust at the death of the decedent, (*2*) any distributions in respect of unitrust amounts made by the trust or estate before such date, and (*3*) interest on such distributions computed at the rate of interest specified in paragraph (a)(5)(iv) of this section, compounded annually, from the date of distribution to such date by—

(*b*)(*1*) In the case of transfers made after November 30, 1983, for which the valuation date is before May 1, 1989, a factor equal to 1.000000 less the factor under the appropriate adjusted payout rate in Table D in §1.664-4(e)(6) opposite the number of years in column 1 between the date of death of the decedent and the date of the earlier of the death of the last recipient or the last day of such taxable year.

(*2*) In the case of transfers for which the valuation date is after April 30, 1989, a factor equal to 1.000000 less the factor under the appropriate adjusted payout rate in Table D in §1.664-4(e)(6) opposite the number of years in column 1 between the date of death of the decedent and the date of the earlier of the death of the last recipient or the last day of such taxable year. The appropriate adjusted payout rate is determined by using the appropriate Table F contained in §1.664-4(e)(6) for the section 7520 rate for the month of the valuation date.

(*3*) If the number of years between the date of death and the date of the earlier of the death of the last recipient or the last day of such taxable year is between periods for which factors are provided, a linear interpolation must be made.

(iii) *Treatment of distributions.*—The treatment of a distribution to a charitable remainder trust, or to a recipient in respect of an annuity or unitrust amount, paid, credited, or required to be distributed by an estate, or by a trust which is not a charitable remainder trust, shall be governed by the rules of subchapter J of chapter 1 of subtitle A of the Code other than section 664. In the case of a charitable remainder trust which is partially or fully funded during the period of administration of an estate or settlement of a trust (which is not a charitable remainder trust), the treatment of any amounts paid, credited, or required to be distributed by the charitable remainder trust shall be governed by the rules of section 664.

(iv) *Rate of interest.*—The following rates of interest shall apply for purposes of paragraphs (a)(5)(i) through (ii) of this section:

(*a*) The section 7520 rate for the month in which the valuation date with respect to the transfer is (or one of the prior two months if elected under §1.7520-2(b)) after April 30, 1989;

(*b*) 10 percent for instruments executed or amended (other than in the case of a reformation under section 2055(e)(3)) on or after August 9, 1984, and before May 1, 1989, and not subsequently amended;

(*c*) 6 percent or 10 percent for instruments executed or amended (other than in the case of a reformation under section 2055(e)(3)) after October 24, 1983, and before August 9, 1984; and

(*d*) 6 percent for instruments executed before October 25, 1983, and not subsequently amended (other than in the case of a reformation under section 2055(e)(3)).

(6) *Examples.*—The application of the rules in paragraphs (a)(4) and (a)(5) of this section require the use of actuarial factors contained in §§1.664-4(e) and 1.664-4A and may be illustrated by use of the following examples:

Example (1). On September 19, 1971, H transfers property to a trust over which he retains an inter vivos power of revocation. The trust is to pay W 5 percent of the value of the trust assets, valued annually, for her life, remainder to charity. The trust would satisfy all of the requirements of section 664 if it were irrevocable. For purposes of section 664, the trust is not deemed created in 1971 because H is treated as the owner of the entire trust under subpart E. On May 26, 1975, H predeceases W at which time the trust becomes irrevocable. For purposes of section 664, the trust is deemed created on May 26, 1975, because that is the earliest date on which H is not treated as the owner of the entire trust under subpart E. The trust becomes a charitable remainder trust on May 26, 1975, because it meets the definition of a charitable remainder trust from its creation.

Example (2). The facts are the same as in example (1), except that H retains the inter vivos power to revoke only one-half of the trust. For purposes of section 664, the trust is deemed created on September 19, 1971, because on that date the grantor is not treated as the owner of the entire trust under subpart E. Consequently, a charitable deduction is not allowable either at the creation of the trust or at H's death because the trust does not meet the definition of a charitable remainder trust from the date of its creation. The trust does not meet the definition of a charitable remainder trust from the date of its creation because the trust is subject to a partial power to revoke on such date.

Example (3). The facts are the same as in example (1), except that the residue of H's estate is to be paid to the trust and the trust is required to pay H's debts. The trust is not a charitable remainder trust at H's death because it does not function exclusively as a charitable remainder trust from the date of its creation which, in this case, is the date it becomes irrevocable.

Example (4). (i) In 1971, H transfers property to Trust A over which he retains an inter vivos power of revocation. Trust A, which is not a charitable remainder trust, is to provide income or corpus to W until the death of H. Upon H's death the trust is required by its governing instrument to pay the debts and administration expenses of H's estate, and then to terminate and distribute all of the remaining assets to a separate Trust B which meets the definition of a charitable remainder annuity trust.

(ii) Trust B will be charitable remainder trust from the date of its funding because it will function exclusively as a charitable remainder trust from its creation. For purposes of section 2055, Trust B will be deemed created at H's death if the obligation to pay the annuity amount begins on the date of H's death. For purposes of section 664, Trust B becomes a charitable remainder trust as soon as it is partially or completely funded. Consequently, unless Trust B has unrelated business taxable income, the income of the trust is exempt from all taxes imposed by subtitle A of the Code, and any distributions by the trust, even before it is completely funded, are governed by the rules of section 664. Any distributions made by Trust A, including distributions to a recipient in respect of annuity amounts, are governed by the rules of subchapter J, chapter 1, subtitle A of the Code other than section 664.

Example (5). In 1973, H dies testate leaving the net residue of his estate (after payment by the estate of all debts and administration expenses) to a trust which meets the definition of a charitable remainder unitrust. For purposes of section 2055, the trust is deemed created at H's death if the requirement to pay the unitrust amount begins on H's death and is a charitable remainder trust even though the estate is obligated to pay debts and administration expenses. For purposes of section 664, the trust becomes a charitable remainder trust as soon as it is partially or completely funded. Consequently, unless the trust has unrelated business taxable income, the income of the trust is exempt from all taxes imposed by subtitle A of the Code, and any distributions by the trust, even before it is completely funded, are governed by the rules of section 664. Any distributions made by H's estate, including distributions to a recipient in respect of unitrust amounts, are governed by the rules of subchapter J, chapter 1, subtitle A of the Code other than section 664.

Example (6). (i) On January 1, 1974, H dies testate leaving the residue of his estate to a charitable remainder unitrust. The governing instrument provides that, beginning at H's death, the trustee is to make annual payments to W, on December 31 of each year of 5 percent of the net fair market value of the trust assets, valued as of December 31 of each year, for W's life and to pay the remainder to charity at the death of W. The governing instrument also provides that the actual payment of the unitrust amount need not be made until the end of the taxable year of the trust in which occurs the complete funding of the trust. The governing instrument also provides that the amount payable with respect to the period between the date of death and the end of such taxable year shall be computed under the special method provided in subparagraph (5)(ii) of this paragraph. The governing instrument provides that, within a reasonable period after the end of the taxable year of the trust in which occurs the complete funding of the trust, the trustee shall pay (in the case of an underpayment) or shall receive from the recipient (in the case of an overpayment) the difference between the unitrust amounts paid (plus interest at 6 percentage compounded annually) and the amount computed under the special method. The trust is completely funded on September 20, 1976. No amounts were paid before June 30, 1977. The trust adopts a fiscal year of July 1 to June 30. The net fair market value of the trust assets on June 30, 1977, is $100,000.

(ii) Because no amounts were paid prior to the end of the taxable year in which the trust was completely funded, the amount payable at the end of such taxable year is equal to the net fair market value of the trust assets on the last day of such taxable year (June 30, 1977) multiplied by a factor equal to 1.0 minus the factor in Table D corresponding to the number of years in the period between the date of death and the end of such taxable year. The adjusted payout rate (determined under §1.664-4A(c)) is 5 percent. Because the last day of the taxable year in which the trust is completely funded is June 30, 1977, there are 3-181/365 years in such period. Because there is no factor given in Table D for such period, a linear interpolation must be made:

1.0 minus .814506 (factor at 5 percent for 4 years)	.185494
1.0 minus .857375 (factor at 5 percent for 3 years)	.142625
Difference	.042869

$$\frac{181}{365} = \frac{X}{.042869}$$

$$X = .021258$$

1.0 minus .857375 (factor at 5 percent for 3 years)	.142625
Plus: X	.021258
Interpolated factor	.163883

Thus, the amount payable for the period from January 1, 1974, to June 30, 1977, is $16,388.30 ($100,000 × .163883). Thereafter, the trust assets must be valued on December 31 of each year and 5 percent of such value paid annually to W for her life.

(7) *Valuation of unmarketable assets.*—(i) *In general.*—If unmarketable assets are transferred to or held by a trust, the trust will not be a trust with respect to which a deduction is available under section 170, 2055, 2106, or 2522, or will be treated as failing to function exclusively as a charitable remainder trust unless, whenever the trust is required to value such assets, the valuation is—

(a) Performed exclusively by an independent trustee; or

(b) Determined by a current qualified appraisal from a qualified appraiser, as those terms are defined in—

(1) Section 1.170A-13(c)(3) and 1.170A-13(c)(5), respectively, for appraisals prepared for returns or submissions filed on or before August 17, 2006;

(2) Section 3 of Notice 2006-96, 2006-2 CB 902, for appraisals prepared for returns or submissions filed after August 17, 2006, if the donations are made before January 1, 2019; or

(3) Section 1.170A-17(a) and 1.170A-17(b), respectively, for appraisals prepared for returns or submissions for donations made on or after January 1, 2019.

(ii) *Unmarketable assets.*—Unmarketable assets are assets that are not cash, cash equivalents, or other assets that can be readily sold or exchanged for cash or cash equivalents. For example, unmarketable assets include real property, closely-held stock, and an unregistered security for which there is no available exemption permitting public sale.

(iii) *Independent trustee.*—An independent trustee is a person who is not the grantor of the trust, a noncharitable beneficiary, or a related or subordinate party to the grantor, the grantor's spouse, or a noncharitable beneficiary (within the meaning of section 672(c) and the applicable regulations).

(b) *Application of certain foundation rules to charitable remainder trusts.*—See section 4947(a)(2) and section 4947(b)(3)(B) and the regulations thereunder for the application to charitable remainder trusts of certain provisions relating to private foundations. See section 508(e) for rules relating to required provisions in governing instruments prohibiting certain activities specified in section 4947(a)(2).

(c) *Excise tax on charitable remainder trusts.*—(1) *In general.*—For each taxable year beginning after December 31, 2006, in which a charitable remainder annuity trust or a charitable remainder unitrust has any unrelated business taxable income, an excise tax is imposed on that trust in an amount equal to the amount of such unrelated business taxable income. For this purpose, unrelated business taxable income is as defined in section 512, determined as if part III, subchapter F, chapter 1, subtitle A of the Internal Revenue Code applied to such trust. Such excise tax is treated as imposed by chapter 42 (other than subchapter E) and is reported and payable in accordance with the appropriate forms and instructions. Such excise tax shall be allocated to corpus and, therefore, is not deductible in determining taxable income distributed to a beneficiary. (See paragraph (d)(2) of this section.) The charitable remainder trust income that is unrelated business taxable income constitutes income of the trust for purposes of determining the character of the distribution made to the beneficiary. Income of the charitable remainder trust is allocated among the charitable remainder trust income categories in paragraph (d)(1) of this section without regard to whether any part of that income constitutes unrelated business taxable income under section 512.

(2) *Examples.*—The application of the rules in this paragraph (c) may be illustrated by the following examples:

Example 1. For 2007, a charitable remainder annuity trust with a taxable year beginning on

January 1, 2007, has $60,000 of ordinary income, including $10,000 of gross income from a partnership that constitutes unrelated business taxable income to the trust. The trust has no deductions that are directly connected with that income. For that same year, the trust has administration expenses (deductible in computing taxable income) of $16,000, resulting in net ordinary income of $44,000. The amount of unrelated business taxable income is computed by taking gross income from an unrelated trade or business and deducting expenses directly connected with carrying on the trade or business, both computed with modifications under section 512(b). Section 512(b)(12) provides a specific deduction of $1,000 in computing the amount of unrelated business taxable income. Under the facts presented in this example, there are no other modifications under section 512(b). The trust, therefore, has unrelated business taxable income of $9,000 ($10,000 minus the $1,000 deduction under section 512(b)(12)). Undistributed ordinary income from prior years is $12,000 and undistributed capital gains from prior years are $50,000. Under the terms of the trust agreement, the trust is required to pay an annuity of $100,000 for year 2007 to the noncharitable beneficiary. Because the trust has unrelated business taxable income of $9,000, the excise tax imposed under section 664(c) is equal to the amount of such unrelated business taxable income, $9,000. The character of the $100,000 distribution to the noncharitable beneficiary is as follows: $56,000 of ordinary income ($44,000 from current year plus $12,000 from prior years), and $44,000 of capital gains. The $9,000 excise tax is allocated to corpus, and does not reduce the amount in any of the categories of income under paragraph (d)(1) of this section. At the beginning of year 2008, the amount of undistributed capital gains is $6,000, and there is no undistributed ordinary income.

Example 2. During 2007, a charitable remainder annuity trust with a taxable year beginning on January 1, 2007, sells real estate generating gain of $40,000. Because the trust had obtained a loan to finance part of the purchase price of the asset, some of the income from the sale is treated as debt-financed income under section 514 and thus constitutes unrelated business taxable income under section 512. The unrelated debt-financed income computed under section 514 is $30,000. Assuming the trust receives no other income in 2007, the trust will have unrelated business taxable income under section 512 of $29,000 ($30,000 minus the $1,000 deduction under section 512(b)(12)). Except for section 512(b)(12), no other exceptions or modifications under sections 512-514 apply when calculating unrelated business taxable income based on the facts presented in this example. Because the trust has unrelated business taxable income of $29,000, the excise tax imposed under section 664(c) is equal to the amount of such unrelated business taxable income, $29,000. The $29,000 excise tax is allocated to corpus, and does not reduce the amount in any of the categories of income under paragraph (d)(1) of this section. Regardless of how the trust's income might be treated under sections 511-514, the entire $40,000 is capital gain for purposes of section 664 and is allocated accordingly to and within the second of the categories of income under paragraph (d)(1) of this section.

(3) *Effective/applicability date.*—This paragraph (c) is applicable for taxable years beginning after December 31, 2006. The rules that apply with respect to taxable years beginning before January 1, 2007, are contained in § 1.664-1 (c) as in effect prior to June 24, 2008 (See 26 CFR part 1, § 1.664-1(c)(1) revised as of April 1, 2007).

(d) *Treatment of annual distributions to recipients.*—(1) *Character of distributions.*—(i) *Assignment of income to categories and classes at the trust level.*—*(a)* A trust's income, including income includible in gross income and other income, is assigned to one of three categories in the year in which it is required to be taken into account by the trust. These categories are—

(1) Gross income, other than gains and amounts treated as gains from the sale or other disposition of capital assets (referred to as the ordinary income category);

(2) Gains and amounts treated as gains from the sale or other disposition of capital assets (referred to as the capital gains category); and

(3) Other income (including income excluded under part III, subchapter B, chapter 1, subtitle A of the Internal Revenue Code).

(b) Items within the ordinary income and capital gains categories are assigned to different classes based on the Federal income tax rate applicable to each type of income in that category in the year the items are required to be taken into account by the trust. For example, for a trust with a taxable year ending December 31, 2004, the ordinary income category may include a class of qualified dividend income as defined in section 1(h)(11) and a class of all other ordinary income, and the capital gains category may include separate classes for short-term and long-term capital gains and losses, such as a short-term capital gain class, a 28-percent long-term capital gain class (gains and losses from collectibles and section 1202 gains), an unrecaptured section 1250 long-term capital gain class (long-term gains not treated as ordinary income that would be treated as ordinary income if section 1250(b)(1) included all depreciation), a qualified 5-year long-term capital gain class as defined in section 1(h)(9) prior to amendment by the Jobs and Growth Tax Relief Reconciliation Act of 2003 (JGTRRA), Public Law 108-27 (117 Stat. 752), and an all other long-term capital gain class. After items are assigned to a class, the tax rates may change so that items in two or more classes would be taxed at the same rate if distributed to the recipient during a particular year. If the changes to the tax rates are permanent, the undistributed items in those classes are combined into one class. If, however, the changes to the tax rates are only temporary (for example,

the new rate for one class will sunset in a future year), the classes are kept separate.

(ii) *Order of distributions.*—*(a)* The categories and classes of income (determined under paragraph (d)(1)(i) of this section) are used to determine the character of an annuity or unitrust distribution from the trust in the hands of the recipient irrespective of whether the trust is exempt from taxation under section 664(c) for the year of the distribution. The determination of the character of amounts distributed or deemed distributed at any time during the taxable year of the trust shall be made as of the end of that taxable year. The tax rate or rates to be used in computing the recipient's tax on the distribution shall be the tax rates that are applicable, in the year in which the distribution is required to be made, to the classes of income deemed to make up that distribution, and not the tax rates that are applicable to those classes of income in the year the income is received by the trust. The character of the distribution in the hands of the annuity or unitrust recipient is determined by treating the distribution as being made from each category in the following order:

(1) First, from ordinary income to the extent of the sum of the trust's ordinary income for the taxable year and its undistributed ordinary income for prior years.

(2) Second, from capital gain to the extent of the trust's capital gains determined under paragraph (d)(1)(iv) of this section.

(3) Third, from other income to the extent of the sum of the trust's other income for the taxable year and its undistributed other income for prior years.

(4) Finally, from trust corpus (with corpus defined for this purpose as the net fair market value of the trust assets less the total undistributed income (but not loss) in paragraphs (d)(1)(i)*(a)**(1)* through *(3)* of this section).

(b) If the trust has different classes of income in the ordinary income category, the distribution from that category is treated as being made from each class, in turn, until exhaustion of the class, beginning with the class subject to the highest Federal income tax rate and ending with the class subject to the lowest Federal income tax rate. If the trust has different classes of net gain in the capital gains category, the distribution from that category is treated as being made first from the short-term capital gain class and then from each class of long-term capital gain, in turn, until exhaustion of the class, beginning with the class subject to the highest Federal income tax rate and ending with the class subject to the lowest rate. If two or more classes within the same category are subject to the same current tax rate, but at least one of those classes will be subject to a different tax rate in a future year (for example, if the current rate sunsets), the order of that class in relation to other classes in the category with the same current tax rate is determined based on the future rate or rates applicable to those classes. Within each category, if there is more than one type of income in a class, amounts treated as distributed from that class are to be treated as consisting of the same proportion of each type of income as the total of the current and undistributed income of that type bears to the total of the current and undistributed income of all types of income included in that class. For example, if rental income and interest income are subject to the same current and future Federal income tax rate and, therefore, are in the same class, a distribution from that class will be treated as consisting of a proportional amount of rental income and interest income.

(iii) *Treatment of losses at the trust level.*—*(a) Ordinary income category.*—A net ordinary loss for the current year is first used to reduce undistributed ordinary income for prior years that is assigned to the same class as the loss. Any excess loss is then used to reduce the current and undistributed ordinary income from other classes, in turn, beginning with the class subject to the highest Federal income tax rate and ending with the class subject to the lowest Federal income tax rate. If any of the loss exists after all the current and undistributed ordinary income from all classes has been offset, the excess is carried forward indefinitely to reduce ordinary income for future years and retains its class assignment. For purposes of this section, the amount of current income and prior years' undistributed income shall be computed without regard to the deduction for net operating losses provided by section 172 or 642(d).

(b) Other income category.—A net loss in the other income category for the current year is used to reduce undistributed income in this category for prior years and any excess is carried forward indefinitely to reduce other income for future years.

(iv) *Netting of capital gains and losses at the trust level.*—Capital gains of the trust are determined on a cumulative net basis under the rules of this paragraph (d)(1) without regard to the provisions of section 1212. For each taxable year, current and undistributed gains and losses within each class are netted to determine the net gain or loss for that class, and the classes of capital gains and losses are then netted against each other in the following order. First, a net loss from a class of long-term capital gain and loss (beginning with the class subject to the highest Federal income tax rate and ending with the class subject to the lowest rate) is used to offset net gain from each other class of long-term capital gain and loss, in turn, until exhaustion of the class, beginning with the class subject to the highest Federal income tax rate and ending with the class subject to the lowest rate. Second, either—

(a) A net loss from all the classes of long-term capital gain and loss (beginning with the class subject to the highest Federal income tax rate and ending with the class subject to the lowest rate) is used to offset any net gain from the class of short-term capital gain and loss; or

(b) A net loss from the class of short-term capital gain and loss is used to offset any net gain from each class of long-term capital gain and loss, in turn, until exhaustion of the class, beginning with the class subject to the highest Federal income tax rate and ending with the class subject to the lowest Federal income tax rate.

(v) *Carry forward of net capital gain or loss by the trust.*—If, at the end of a taxable year, a trust has, after the application of paragraph (d)(1)(iv) of this section, any net loss or any net gain that is not treated as distributed under paragraph (d)(1)(ii)(*a*)(2) of this section, the net gain or loss is carried over to succeeding taxable years and retains its character in succeeding taxable years as gain or loss from its particular class.

(vi) *Special transitional rules.*—To be eligible to be included in the class of qualified dividend income, dividends must meet the definition of section 1(h)(11) and must be received by the trust after December 31, 2002. Long-term capital gain or loss properly taken into account by the trust before January 1, 1997, is included in the class of all other long-term capital gains and losses. Long-term capital gain or loss properly taken into account by the trust on or after January 1, 1997, and before May 7, 1997, if not treated as distributed in 1997, is included in the class of all other long-term capital gains and losses. Long-term capital gain or loss (other than 28-percent gain (gains and losses from collectibles and section 1202 gains), unrecaptured section 1250 gain (long-term gains not treated as ordinary income that would be treated as ordinary income if section 1250(b)(1) included all depreciation), and qualified 5-year gain as defined in section?1(h)(9) prior to amendment by JGTRRA), properly taken into account by the trust before January 1, 2003, and distributed during 2003 is treated as if it were properly taken into account by the trust after May 5, 2003. Long-term capital gain or loss (other than 28-percent gain, unrecaptured section 1250 gain, and qualified 5-year gain), properly taken into account by the trust on or after January 1, 2003, and before May 6, 2003, if not treated as distributed during 2003, is included in the class of all other long-term capital gain. Qualified 5-year gain properly taken into account by the trust after December 31, 2000, and before May 6, 2003, if not treated as distributed by the trust in 2003 or a prior year, must be maintained in a separate class within the capital gains category until distributed. Qualified 5-year gain properly taken into account by the trust before January 1, 2003, and deemed distributed during 2003 is subject to the same current tax rate as deemed distributions from the class of all other long-term capital gain realized by the trust after May 5, 2003. Qualified 5-year gain properly taken into account by the trust on or after January 1, 2003, and before May 6, 2003, if treated as distributed by the trust in 2003, is subject to the tax rate in effect prior to the amendment of section 1(h)(9) by JGTRRA.

(vii) *Application of section 643(a)(7).*—For application of the anti-abuse rule of section 643(a)(7) to distributions from charitable remainder trusts, see § 1.643(a)-8.

(viii) *Examples.*—The following examples illustrate the rules in this paragraph (d)(1):

Example 1. (i) X, a charitable remainder annuity trust described in section 664(d)(1), is created on January 1, 2003. The annual annuity amount is $100. X's income for the 2003 tax year is as follows:

Interest income	$ 80
Qualified dividend income	50
Capital gains and losses	0
Tax-exempt income	0

(ii) In 2003, the year this income is received by the trust, qualified dividend income is subject to a different rate of Federal income tax than interest income and is, therefore, a separate class of income in the ordinary income category. The annuity amount is deemed to be distributed from the classes within the ordinary income category, beginning with the class subject to the highest Federal income tax rate and ending with the class subject to the lowest rate. Because during 2003 qualified dividend income is taxed at a lower rate than interest income, the interest income is deemed distributed prior to the qualified dividend income. Therefore, in the hands of the recipient, the 2003 annuity amount has the following characteristics:

Interest income	$ 80
Qualified dividend income	20

(iii) The remaining $30 of qualified dividend income that is not treated as distributed to the recipient in 2003 is carried forward to 2004 as undistributed qualified dividend income.

Example 2. (i) The facts are the same as in *Example 1*, and at the end of 2004, X has the following classes of income:

Interest income class	$ 5
Qualified dividend income class ($10 from 2004 and $30 carried forward from 2003)	40
Net short-term capital gain class	15
Net long-term capital loss in 28-percent class	(325)
Net long-term capital gain in unrecaptured section 1250 gain class	175
Net long-term capital gain in all other long-term capital gain class	350

(ii) In 2004, gain in the unrecaptured section 1250 gain class is subject to a 25-percent Federal income tax rate, and gain in the all other long-term capital gain class is subject to a lower rate. The net long-term capital loss in the 28-percent gain class is used to offset the net capital gains in the other classes of long-term capital gain and loss, beginning with the class subject to the highest Federal income tax rate and ending with the class subject to the lowest rate. The $325 net loss in the 28-percent gain class reduces the $175 net gain in the unrecaptured section 1250 gain class to $0. The remaining $150 loss from

See p. 15 for regulations not amended to reflect law changes

the 28-percent gain class reduces the $350 gain in the all other long-term capital gain class to $200. As in *Example 1,* qualified dividend income is taxed at a lower rate than interest income during 2004. The annuity amount is deemed to be distributed from all the classes in the ordinary income category and then from the classes in the capital gains category, beginning with the class subject to the highest Federal income tax rate and ending with the class subject to the lowest rate. In the hands of the recipient, the 2004 annuity amount has the following characteristics:

Interest income	$ 5
Qualified dividend income	40
Net short-term capital gain	15
Net long-term capital gain in all other long-term capital gain class	40

(iii) The remaining $160 gain in the all other long-term capital gain class that is not treated as distributed to the recipient in 2004 is carried forward to 2005 as gain in that same class.

Example 3. (i) The facts are the same as in *Examples 1* and *2,* and at the end of 2005, X has the following classes of income:

Interest income class	$ 5
Qualified dividend income class	20
Net loss in short-term capital gain class	(50)
Net long-term capital gain in 28-percent gain class	10
Net long-term capital gain in unrecaptured section 1250 gain class	135
Net long-term capital gain in all other long-term capital gain class (carried forward from 2004)	160

(ii) There are no long-term capital losses to net against the long-term capital gains. Thus, the net short-term capital loss is used to offset the net capital gains in the classes of long-term capital gain and loss, in turn, until exhaustion of the class, beginning with the class subject to the highest Federal income tax rate and ending with the class subject to the lowest rate. The $50 net short-term loss reduces the $10 net gain in the 28-percent gain class to $0. The remaining $40 net loss reduces the $135 net gain in the unrecaptured section 1250 gain class to $95. As in *Examples 1* and *2,* during 2005, qualified dividend income is taxed at a lower rate than interest income; gain in the unrecaptured section 1250 gain class is taxed at 25 percent; and gain in the all other long-term capital gain class is taxed at a rate lower than 25 percent. The annuity amount is deemed to be distributed from all the classes in the ordinary income category and then from the classes in the capital gains category, beginning with the class subject to the highest Federal income tax rate and ending with the class subject to the lowest rate. Therefore, in the hands of the recipient, the 2005 annuity amount has the following characteristics:

Interest income	$ 5
Qualified dividend income	20
Unrecaptured section 1250 gain	75

(iii) The remaining $20 gain in the unrecaptured section 1250 gain class and the $160 gain in the all other long-term capital gain class that are not treated as distributed to the recipient in 2005 are carried forward to 2006 as gains in their respective classes.

Example 4. (i) The facts are the same as in *Examples 1, 2* and *3,* and at the end of 2006, X has the following classes of income:

Interest income class	$ 95
Qualified dividend income class	10
Net loss in short-term capital gain class	(20)
Net long-term capital loss in 28-percent gain class	(350)
Net long-term capital gain in unrecaptured section 1250 gain class (carried forward from 2005)	20
Net long-term capital gain in all other long-term capital gain class (carried forward from 2005)	160

(ii) A net long-term capital loss in one class is used to offset the net capital gains in the other classes of long-term capital gain and loss, in turn, until exhaustion of the class, beginning with the class subject to the highest Federal income tax rate and ending with the class subject to the lowest rate. The $350 net loss in the 28-percent gain class reduces the $20 net gain in the unrecaptured section 1250 gain class to $0. The remaining $330 net loss reduces the $160 net gain in the all other long-term capital gain class to $0. As in *Examples 1, 2* and *3,* during 2006, qualified dividend income is taxed at a lower rate than interest income. The annuity amount is deemed to be distributed from all the classes in the ordinary income category and then from the classes in the capital gains category, beginning with the class subject to the highest Federal income tax rate and ending with the class subject to the lowest rate. In the hands of the recipient, the 2006 annuity amount has the following characteristics:

Interest income	$ 95
Qualified dividend income	5

(iii) The remaining $5 of qualified dividend income that is not treated as distributed to the recipient in 2006 is carried forward to 2007 as qualified dividend income. The $20 net loss in the short-term capital gain class and the $170 net loss in the 28-percent gain class are carried forward to 2007 as net losses in their respective classes.

Example 5. (i) X, a charitable remainder annuity trust described in section 664(d)(1), is created on January 1, 2002. The annual annuity amount is $100. Except for qualified 5-year gain of $200 realized before May 6, 2003, but not distributed, X has no other gains or losses carried over from former years. X's income for the 2007 tax year is as follows:

Interest income class	$ 10
Net gain in short-term capital gain class	5
Net long-term capital gain in 28-percent gain class	5
Net long-term capital gain in unrecaptured section 1250 gain class	10
Net long-term capital gain in all other long-term capital gain class	10

(ii) The annuity amount is deemed to be distributed from all the classes in the ordinary income category and then from the classes in the capital gains category, beginning with the class subject to the highest Federal income tax rate and ending with the class subject to the lowest rate. In 2007, gains distributed to a recipient from both the qualified 5-year gain class and the all other long-term capital gains class are taxed at a 15/5 percent tax rate. Since after December 31, 2008, gains distributed from the qualified 5-year gain class will be taxed at a lower rate than gains distributed from the other classes of long-term capital gain and loss, distributions from the qualified 5-year gain class are made after distributions from the other classes of long-term capital gain and loss. In the hands of the recipient, the 2007 annuity amount has the following characteristics:

Interest income	$ 10
Short-term capital gain	5
28-percent gain	5
Unrecaptured section 1250 gain	10
All other long-term capital gain	10
Qualified 5-year gain (taxed as all other long-term capital gain)	60

(iii) The remaining $140 of qualified 5-year gain that is not treated as distributed to the recipient in 2007 is carried forward to 2008 as qualified 5-year gain.

(ix) *Effective dates.*—The rules in this paragraph (d)(1) that require long-term capital gains to be distributed in the following order: first, 28-percent gain (gains and losses from collectibles and section 1202 gains); second, unrecaptured section 1250 gain (long-term gains not treated as ordinary income that would be treated as ordinary income if section 1250(b)(1) included all depreciation); and then, all other long-term capital gains are applicable for taxable years ending on or after December 31, 1998. The rules in this paragraph (d)(1) that provide for the netting of capital gains and losses are applicable for taxable years ending on or after December 31, 1998. The rule in the second sentence of paragraph (d)(1)(vi) of this section is applicable for taxable years ending on or after December 31, 1998. The rule in the third sentence of paragraph (d)(1)(vi) of this section is applicable for distributions made in taxable years ending on or after December 31, 1998. All other provisions of this paragraph (d)(1) are applicable for taxable years ending after November 20, 2003.

(2) *Allocation of deductions.*—Items of deduction of the trust for a taxable year of the trust which are deductible in determining taxable income (other than the deductions permitted by sections 642(b), 642(c), 661, and 1202) which are directly attributable to one or more classes of items within a category of income (determined under paragraph (d)(1)(i)(*a*) of this section) or to corpus shall be allocated to such classes of items or to corpus. All other allowable deductions for such taxable year which are not directly attributable to one or more classes of items within a category of income or to corpus (other than the deductions permitted by sections 642(b), 642(c), 661, and 1202) shall be allocated among the classes of items within the category (excluding classes of items with net losses) on the basis of the gross income of such classes for such taxable year reduced by the deductions allocated thereto under the first sentence of this subparagraph, but in no event shall the amount of expenses allocated to any class of items exceed such income of such class for the taxable year. Items of deduction which are not allocable under the above two sentences (other than the deductions permitted by sections 642(b), 642(c), 661, and 1202) may be allocated in any manner. All taxes imposed by chapter 42 of the Code (including without limitation taxes treated under section 664(c)(2) as imposed by chapter 42) and, for taxable years beginning prior to January 1, 2007, all taxes imposed by subtitle A of the Code for which the trust is liable because it has unrelated business taxable income, shall be allocated to corpus. Any expense which is not deductible in determining taxable income and which is not allocable to any class of items described in paragraph (d)(1)(i)(*a*)(*3*) of this section shall be allocated to corpus. The deductions allowable to a trust under sections 642(b), 642(c), 661, and 1202 are not allowed in determining the amount or character of any class of items within a category of income described in paragraph (d)(1)(i)(*a*) of this section or to corpus.

(3) *Allocation of income among recipients.*—If there are two or more recipients, each will be treated as receiving his pro rata portion of the categories of income and corpus. The application of this rule may be illustrated by the following example:

Example. X transfers $40,000 to a charitable remainder annuity trust which is to pay $3,000 per year to X and $2,000 per year to Y for a term of 5 years. During the first taxable year the trust has $3,000 of ordinary income, $500 of capital gain, and $500 of tax exempt income after allocation of all expenses. X is treated as receiving ordinary income of $1,800 ($3,000/$5,000 × $3,000), capital gain of $300 ($3,000/$5,000 × $500), tax exempt income of $300 ($3,000/$5,000 × $500), and corpus of $600 ($3,000/$5,000 × [$5,000 – $4,000]). Y is treated as receiving ordinary income of $1,200 ($2,000/$5,000 × $3,000), capital gain of $200 ($2,000/$5,000 × $500), tax exempt income of $200 ($2,000/$5,000 × $500), and corpus of $400 ($2,000/$5,000 × [$5,000 – $4,000]).

(4) *Year of inclusion.*—(i) *General rule.*—To the extent required by this paragraph, the annu-

ity or unitrust amount is includible in the recipient's gross income for the taxable year in which the annuity or unitrust amount is required to be distributed even though the annuity or unitrust amount is not distributed until after the close of the taxable year of the trust. If a recipient has a different taxable year (as defined in section 441 or 442) from the taxable year of the trust, the amount he is required to include in gross income to the extent required by this paragraph shall be included in his taxable year in which or with which ends the taxable year of the trust in which such amount is required to be distributed.

(ii) Payments resulting from incorrect valuations. Notwithstanding subdivision (i) of this subparagraph, any payments which are made or required to be distributed by a charitable remainder trust pursuant to paragraph (a)(5) of this section, under paragraph (f)(3) of this section because of an amendment to the governing instrument, or under paragraphs (a)(1) of §§1.664-2 and 1.664-3 because of an incorrect valuation, shall, to the extent required by this paragraph, be included in the gross income of the recipient in his taxable year in which or with which ends the taxable year of the trust in which the amount is paid, credited, or required to be distributed. For rules relating to required adjustments of underpayments and overpayments of the annuity or unitrust amounts in respect to payments made prior to the amendment of a governing instrument, see paragraph (f)(3) of this section. There is allowable to a recipient a deduction from gross income for any amounts repaid to the trust because of an overpayment during the reasonable period of administration or settlement or until the trust is fully funded, because of an amendment, or because of an incorrect valuation, to the extent such amounts were included in his gross income. See section 1341 and the regulations thereunder for rules relating to the computation of tax where a taxpayer restores substantial amounts held under a claim of right.

(iii) *Rules applicable to year of recipient's death.*—If the taxable year of the trust does not end with or within the last taxable year of the recipient because of the recipient's death, the extent to which the annuity or unitrust amount required to be distributed to him is included in the gross income of the recipient for his last taxable year, or in the gross income of his estate, is determined by making the computations required under this paragraph for the taxable year of the trust in which his last taxable year ends. (The last sentence of subdivision (i) of this subparagraph does not apply to such amounts.) The gross income for the last taxable year of a recipient on the cash basis includes (to the extent required by this paragraph) amounts actually distributed to the recipient before his death. Amounts required to be distributed which are distributed to his estate are included (to the extent required by this paragraph) in the gross income of the estate as income in respect of a decedent under section 691.

(5) *Distributions in kind.*—The annuity or unitrust amount may be paid in cash or in other property. In the case of a distribution made in other property, the amount paid, credited, or required to be distributed shall be considered as an amount realized by the trust from the sale or other disposition of property. The basis of the property in the hands of the recipient is its fair market value at the time it was paid, credited, or required to be distributed. The application of these rules may be illustrated by the following example:

Example. On January 1, 1971, X creates a charitable remainder annuity trust, whose taxable year is the calendar year, under which X is to receive $5,000 per year. During 1971, the trust receives $500 ordinary income. On December 31, 1971, the trust distributed cash of $500 and a capital asset of the trust having a fair market value of $4,500 and a basis of $2,200. The trust is deemed to have realized a capital gain of $2,300. X treats the distribution of $5,000 as being ordinary income of $500, capital gain of $2,300 and trust corpus of $2,200. The basis of the distributed property is $4,500 in the hands of X.

(e) *Other distributions.*—(1) *Character of distributions.*—An amount distributed by the trust to an organization described in section 170(c) other than the annuity or unitrust amount shall be considered as a distribution of corpus and of those categories of income specified in paragraph (d)(1)(i)(*a*) of this section in an order inverse to that prescribed in such paragraph. The character of such amounts shall be determined as of the end of the taxable year of the trust in which the distribution is made after the character of the annuity or unitrust amount has been determined.

(2) *Distributions in kind.*—In the case of a distribution of an amount to which subparagraph (1) of this paragraph applies, no gain or loss is realized by the trust by reason of a distribution in kind unless such distribution is in satisfaction of a right to receive a distribution of a specific dollar amount or in specific property other than that distributed.

(f) *Effective date.*—(1) *General rule.*—The provisions of this section are effective with respect to transfers in trust made after July 31, 1969. Any trust created (within the meaning of applicable local law) prior to August 1, 1969, is not a charitable remainder trust even if it otherwise satisfies the definition of a charitable remainder trust. The provisions of paragraph §1.664-1(a)(7)(i)(b) apply as provided in that paragraph.

(2) *Transfers to pre-1970 trusts.*—Property transferred to a trust created (within the meaning of applicable local law) before August 1, 1969, whose governing instrument provides that an organization described in section 170(c) receives an irrevocable remainder interest in such trust, shall, for purposes of subparagraphs (1) and (3) of this paragraph, be deemed transferred to a trust created on the date of such transfer provided that the transfer occurs after July 31, 1969, and prior to October 18, 1971, and the

transferred property and any undistributed income therefrom is severed and placed in a separate trust before December 31, 1972, or if later, on or before the 30th day after the date on which any judicial proceedings begun before December 31, 1972, which are required to sever such property, become final.

(3) *Amendment of post-1969 trusts.*—A trust created (within the meaning of applicable local law) subsequent to July 31, 1969, and prior to December 31, 1972, which is not a charitable remainder trust at the date of its creation, may be treated as a charitable remainder trust from the date it would be deemed created under § 1.664-1(a)(4) and (5)(i) for all purposes provided that all the following requirements are met:

(i) At the time of the creation of the trust, the governing instrument provides that an organization described in section 170(c) receives an irrevocable remainder interest in such trust.

(ii) The governing instrument of the trust is amended so that the trust will meet the definition of a charitable remainder trust and, if applicable, will meet the requirement of paragraph (a)(5)(i) of this section that obligation to make payment of the annuity or unitrust amount with respect to property passing at death begin as of the date of death, before December 31, 1972, or if later, on or before the 30th day after the date on which any judicial proceedings which are begun before December 31, 1972, and which are required to amend its governing instrument, become final. In the case of a trust created (within the meaning of applicable local law) subsequent to July 31, 1969, and prior to December 31, 1972, the provisions of section 508(d)(2)(A) shall not apply if the governing instrument of the trust is amended so as to comply with the requirements of section 508(e) before December 31, 1972, or if later, on or before the 30th day after the date on which any judicial proceedings which are begun before December 31, 1972, and which are required to amend its governing instrument, become final. Notwithstanding the provisions of paragraphs (a)(3) and (a)(4) of §§ 1.664-2 and 1.664-3, the governing instrument may grant to the trustee a power to amend the governing instrument for the sole purpose of complying with the requirements of this section and § 1.664-2 or § 1.664-3 provided that at the creation of the trust, the governing instrument (*a*) provides for the payment of a unitrust amount described in § 1.664-3(a)(1)(i) or an annuity which meets the requirements of paragraph (a)(2) of §§ 1.664-2 or 1.664-3, (*b*) designates the recipients of the trust and the period for which the amount described in (*a*) of this subdivision (ii) is to be paid, and (*c*) provides that an organization described in section 170(c) receives an irrevocable remainder interest in such trust. The mere granting of such a power is not sufficient to meet the requirements of this subparagraph that the governing instrument be amended in the manner and within the time limitations of this subparagraph.

(iii)(*a*) Where the amount of the distributions which would have been made by the trust to a recipient if the amended provisions of such trust had been in effect from the time of creation of such trust exceeds the amount of the distributions made by the trust prior to its amendment, the trust pays an amount equal to such excess to the recipient.

(*b*) Where the amount of distributions made to the recipient prior to the amendment of the trust exceeds the amount of the distributions which would have been made by such trust if the amended provisions of such trust had been in effect from the time of creation of such trust, such excess is repaid to the trust by the recipient.

See paragraph (d)(4) of this section for rules relating to the year of inclusion in the case of an underpayment to a recipient and the allowance of a deduction in the case of an overpayment to a recipient. A deduction for a transfer to a charitable remainder trust shall not be allowed until the requirements of this paragraph are met and then only if the deduction is claimed on a timely-filed return (including extensions) or on a claim for refund filed within the period of limitations prescribed by section 6511(a).

(4) *Valuation of unmarketable assets.*—The rules contained in paragraph (a)(7) of this section are applicable for trusts created on or after December 10, 1998. A trust in existence as of December 10, 1998, whose governing instrument requires that an independent trustee value the trust's unmarketable assets may be amended or reformed to permit a valuation method that satisfies the requirements of paragraph (a)(7) of this section for taxable years beginning on or after December 10, 1998.

(g) *Transitional effective date.*—Notwithstanding any other provision of this section, § 1.664-2, or § 1.664-3, the requirement of paragraph (a)(5)(i) of this section that interest accrue on overpayments and underpayments, the requirement of paragraph (a)(5)(ii) of this section that the unitrust amount accruing under the formula provided therein cease with the death of the last recipient, and the requirement that the governing instrument of the trust contain the provisions specified in paragraph (a)(1)(iv) of § 1.664-2 (relating to computation of the annuity amount in certain circumstances), paragraph (a)(1)(v) of § 1.664-3 (relating to computation of the unitrust amount in certain circumstances), paragraphs (b) of §§ 1.664-2 and 1.664-3 (relating to additional contributions), and paragraph (a)(1)(iii) of § 1.664-3 (relating to incorrect valuations), paragraphs (a)(6)(iv) of §§ 1.664-2 and 1.664-3 (relating to alternative remaindermen) shall not apply to:

(1) A will executed on or before December 31, 1972, if:

(i) The testator dies before December 31, 1975, without having republished the will after December 31, 1972 by codicil or otherwise,

(ii) The testator at no time after December 31, 1972, had the right to change the provisions of the will which pertain to the trust, or

(iii) The will is not republished by codicil or otherwise before December 31, 1975, and the testator is on such date and at all times thereafter under a mental disability to republish the will by codicil or otherwise, or

(2) A trust executed on or before December 31, 1972, if:

(i) The grantor dies before December 31, 1975, without having amended the trust after December 31, 1972,

(ii) The trust is irrevocable on December 31, 1972, or

(iii) The trust is not amended before December 31, 1975, and the grantor is on such date and at all times thereafter under a mental disability to change the terms of the trust. [Reg. § 1.664-1.]

☐ [*T.D.* 7202, 8-22-72. *Amended by T.D.* 7955, 5-10-84; *T.D.* 8540, 6-9-94; *T.D.* 8791, 12-9-98; *T.D.* 8819, 4-29-99; *T.D.* 8886, 6-9-2000; *T.D.* 8926, 1-4-2001; *T.D.* 9190, 3-15-2005; *T.D.* 9403, 6-19-2008; *T.D.* 9448, 5-1-2009, *T.D.* 9540, 8-9-2011 *and T.D.* 9836, 7-27-2018.]

[Reg. § 8.1]

§ 8.1. Charitable remainder trusts.—(a) *Certain wills and trusts in existence on September 21, 1974.*—In the case of a will executed before September 21, 1974, or a trust created (within the meaning of applicable local law) after July 31, 1969, and before September 21, 1974, which is amended pursuant to section 2055(e)(3) and § 24.1 of this chapter (Temporary Estate Tax Regulations), a charitable remainder trust resulting from such amendment will be treated as a charitable remainder trust from the date it would be deemed created under § 1.664-1(a)(4) and (5) of this chapter (Income Tax Regulations), whether or not such date is after September 20, 1974.

(b) *Certain transfers to trusts created before August 1, 1969.*—Property transferred to a trust created (within the meaning of applicable local law) before August 1, 1969, whose governing instrument provides that an organization described in section 170(c) receives an irrevocable remainder interest in such trust shall be deemed transferred to a trust created on the date of such transfer, provided that the transfer occurs after July 31, 1969 and prior to October 18, 1971, and pursuant to an amendment provided in § 24.1 of this chapter (Temporary Estate Tax Regulations), the transferred property and any undistributed income therefrom is severed and placed in a separate trust as of the date of the amendment. [Temporary Reg. § 8.1.]

☐ [*T.D.* 7393, 12-16-75.]

[Reg. § 1.664-2]

§ 1.664-2. Charitable remainder annuity trust.—(a) *Description.*—A charitable remainder annuity trust is a trust which complies with the applicable provisions of § 1.664-1 and meets all of the following requirements:

(1) *Required payment of annuity amount.*—(i) *Payment of sum certain at least annually.*—The governing instrument provides that the trust will pay a sum certain not less often than annually to a person or persons described in paragraph (a)(3) of this section for each taxable year of the period specified in paragraph (a)(5) of this section.

(*a*) *General rule applicable to all trusts.*—A trust will not be deemed to have engaged in an act of self-dealing (within the meaning of section 4941), to have unrelated debt-financed income (within the meaning of section 514), to have received an additional contribution (within the meaning of paragraph (b) of this section), or to have failed to function exclusively as a charitable remainder trust (within the meaning of § 1.664-1(a)(4)) merely because the annuity amount is paid after the close of the taxable year if such payment is made within a reasonable time after the close of such taxable year and the entire annuity amount in the hands of the recipient is characterized only as income from the categories described in section 664(b)(1), (2), or (3), except to the extent it is characterized as corpus described in section 664(b)(4) because—

(*1*) The trust pays the annuity amount by distributing property (other than cash) that it owned at the close of the taxable year to pay the annuity amount, and the trustee elects to treat any income generated by the distribution as occurring on the last day of the taxable year in which the annuity amount is due;

(*2*) The trust pays the annuity amount by distributing cash that was contributed to the trust (with respect to which a deduction was allowable under section 170, 2055, 2106, or 2522); or

(*3*) The trust pays the annuity amount by distributing cash received as a return of basis in any asset that was contributed to the trust (with respect to which a deduction was allowable under section 170, 2055, 2106, or 2522), and that is sold by the trust during the year for which the annuity amount is due.

(*b*) *Special rule for trusts created before December 10, 1998.*—In addition, to the circumstances described in paragraph (a)(1)(i)(*a*) of this section, a trust created before December 10, 1998, will not be deemed to have engaged in an act of self-dealing (within the meaning of section 4941), to have unrelated debt-financed income (within the meaning of section 514), to have received an additional contribution (within the meaning of paragraph (b) of this section), or to have failed to function exclusively as a charitable remainder trust (within the meaning of § 1.664-1(a)(4)) merely because the annuity amount is paid after the close of the taxable year if such payment is made within a reasonable time after the close of such taxable year and the sum certain to be paid each year as the annuity amount is 15 percent or less of the initial net fair market value of the property irrevocably passing in trust as determined for federal tax purposes.

(*c*) *Reasonable time.*—For this paragraph (a)(1)(i), a reasonable time will not ordinarily extend beyond the date by which the trustee is required to file Form 5227, "Split-Interest Trust Information Return," (including extensions) for the taxable year.

(d) Example.—The following example illustrates the rules in paragraph (a)(1)(i)(*a*) of this section:

Example. X is a charitable remainder annuity trust described in section 664(d)(1) that was created after December 10, 1998. The prorated annuity amount payable from X for Year 1 is $100. The trustee does not pay the annuity amount to the recipient by the close of Year 1. At the end of Year 1, X has only $95 in the ordinary income category under section 664(b)(1) and no income in the capital gain or tax-exempt income categories under section 664(b)(2) or (3), respectively. By April 15 of Year 2, in addition to $95 in cash, the trustee distributes to the recipient of the annuity a capital asset with a $5 fair market value and a $2 adjusted basis to pay the $100 annuity amount due for Year 1. The trust owned the asset at the end of Year 1. Under § 1.664-1(d)(5), the distribution is treated as a sale by X, resulting in X recognizing a $3 capital gain. The trustee elects to treat the capital gain as occurring on the last day of Year 1. Under § 1.664-1(d)(1), the character of the annuity amount for Year 1 in the recipient's hands is $95 of ordinary income, $3 of capital gain income, and $2 of trust corpus. For Year 1, X satisfied paragraph (a)(1)(i)(*a*) of this section.

(e) Effective date.—This paragraph (a)(1)(i) is applicable for taxable years ending after April 18, 1997. However, paragraphs (a)(1)(i)(*a*)(2) and (3) of this section apply only to distributions made on or after January 5, 2001.

(ii) *Definition of sum certain.*—A sum certain is a stated dollar amount which is the same either as to each recipient or as to the total amount payable for each year of such period. For example, a provision for an amount which is the same every year to A until his death and concurrently an amount which is the same every year to B until his death, with the amount to each recipient to terminate at his death, would satisfy the above rule. Similarly, provision for an amount to A and B for their joint lives and then to the survivor would satisfy the above rule. In the case of a distribution to an organization described in section 170(c) at the death of a recipient or the expiration of a term of years, the governing instrument may provide for a reduction of the stated amount payable after such a distribution provided that:

(a) The reduced amount payable is the same either as to each recipient or as to the total amount payable for each year of the balance of such period, and

(b) The requirements of subparagraph (2)(ii) of this paragraph are met.

(iii) *Sum certain stated as a fraction or percentage.*—The stated dollar amount may be expressed as a fraction or a percentage of the initial net fair market value of the property irrevocably passing in trust as finally determined for Federal tax purposes. If the stated dollar amount is so expressed and such market value is incorrectly determined by the fiduciary, the requirement of this subparagraph will be satisfied if the governing instrument provides that in such event the trust shall pay to the recipient (in the case of an undervaluation) or be repaid by the recipient (in the case of an overvaluation) an amount equal to the difference between the amount which the trust should have paid the recipient if the correct value were used and the amount which the trust actually paid the recipient. Such payments or repayments must be made within a reasonable period after the final determination of such value. Any payment due to a recipient by reason of such incorrect valuation shall be considered to be a payment required to be distributed at the time of such final determination for purposes of paragraph (d)(4)(ii) of § 1.664-1. See paragraph (d)(4) of § 1.664-1 for rules relating to the year of inclusion of such payments and the allowance of a deduction for such repayments. See paragraph (b) of this section for rules relating to future contributions. For rules relating to required adjustments for underpayments or overpayments of the amount described in this paragraph in respect of payments made during a reasonable period of administration, see paragraph (a)(5) of § 1.664-1. The application of the rule permitting the stated dollar amount to be expressed as a fraction or a percentage of the initial net fair market value of the property irrevocably passing in trust as finally determined for Federal tax purposes may be illustrated by the following example:

Example. The will of X provides for the transfer of one-half of his residuary estate to a charitable remainder annuity trust which is required to pay to W for life an annuity equal to 5 percent of the initial net fair market value of the interest passing in trust as finally determined for Federal tax purposes. The annuity is to be paid on December 31 of each year computed from the date of X's death. The will also provides that if such initial net fair market value is incorrectly determined, the trust shall pay to W, in the case of an undervaluation, or be repaid by W, in the case of an overvaluation, an amount equal to the difference between the amount which the trust should have paid if the correct value were used and the amount which the trust actually paid. X dies on March 1, 1971. The executor files an estate tax return showing the value of the residuary estate as $250,000 before reduction for taxes and expenses of $50,000. The executor paid to W $4,192 ([$250,000 – $50,000]× $1/2$ × 5% × 306/365) on December 31, 1971. On January 1, 1972, the executor transfers one-half of the residue of the estate to the trust. The trust adopts the calendar year as its taxable year. The value of the residuary estate is finally determined for Federal tax purposes to be $240,000 ($290,000 – $50,000). Accordingly, the amount which the executor should have paid to W is $5,030 ([$290,000 – $50,000]× $1/2$ × 5% × 306/365). Consequently, an additional amount of $838 ($5,030 – $4,192) must be paid to W within a reasonable period after the final determination of value for Federal tax purposes.

(iv) *Computation of annuity amount in certain circumstances.—(a) Short taxable years.*—The governing instrument provides that, in the case of a taxable year which is for a period of less than 12 months other than the taxable year in which occurs the end of the period specified in subparagraph (5) of this paragraph, the annuity amount determined under subdivision (i) of this subparagraph shall be the amount otherwise determined under that subdivision multiplied by a fraction the numerator of which is the number of days in the taxable year of the trust and the denominator of which is 365 (366 if February 29 is a day included in the numerator).

(b) Last taxable year of period.—The governing instrument provides that, in the case of the taxable year in which occurs the end of the period specified in subparagraph (5) of this paragraph, the annuity amount which must be distributed under subdivision (i) of this subparagraph shall be the amount otherwise determined under that subdivision multiplied by a fraction the numerator of which is the number of days in the period beginning on the first day of such taxable year and ending on the last day of the period specified in subparagraph (5) of this paragraph and the denominator of which is 365 (366 if February 29 is a day included in the numerator). See subparagraph (5) of this paragraph for a special rule allowing termination of payment of the annuity amount with the regular payment next preceding the termination of the period specified therein.

(2) *Minimum annuity amount.*—(i) *General rule.*—The total amount payable under subparagraph (1) of this paragraph is not less than 5 percent of the initial net fair market value of the property placed in trust as finally determined for Federal tax purposes.

(ii) *Reduction of annuity amount in certain cases.*—A trust will not fail to meet the requirements of this subparagraph by reason of the fact that it provides for a reduction of the stated amount payable upon the death of a recipient or the expiration of a term of years provided that:

(a) A distribution is made to an organization described in section 170(c) at the death of such recipient or the expiration of such term of years, and

(b) The total amounts payable each year under subparagraph (1) of this paragraph after such distribution are not less than a stated dollar amount which bears the same ratio to 5 percent of the initial net fair market value of the trust assets as the net fair market value of the trust assets immediately after such distribution bears to the net fair market value of the trust assets immediately before such distribution.

(iii) *Rule applicable to inter vivos trust which does not provide for payment of minimum annuity amount.*—In the case where the grantor of an inter vivos trust underestimates in good faith the initial net fair market value of the property placed in trust as finally determined for Federal tax purposes and specifies a fixed dollar amount for the annuity which is less than 5 percent of the initial net fair market value of the property placed in trust as finally determined for Federal tax purposes, the trust will be deemed to have met the 5 percent requirement if the grantor or his representative consents, by appropriate agreement with the District Director, to accept an amount equal to 20 times the annuity as the fair market value of the property placed in trust for purposes of determining the appropriate charitable contributions deduction.

(3) *Permissible recipients.*—(i) *General rule.*—The amount described in subparagraph (1) of this paragraph is payable to or for the use of a named person or persons, at least one of which is not an organization described in section 170(c). If the amount described in subparagraph (1) of this paragraph is to be paid to an individual or individuals, all such individuals must be living at the time of the creation of the trust. A named person or persons may include members of a named class provided that, in the case of a class which includes any individual, all such individuals must be alive and ascertainable at the time of the creation of the trust unless the period for which the annuity amount is to be paid to such class consists solely of a term of years. For example, in the case of a testamentary trust, the testator's will may provide that an amount shall be paid to his children living at his death.

(ii) *Power to alter amount paid to recipients.*—A trust is not a charitable remainder annuity trust if any person has the power to alter the amount to be paid to any named person other than an organization described in section 170(c) if such power would cause any person to be treated as the owner of the trust, or any portion thereof, if subpart E, Part 1, subchapter J, chapter 1, subtitle A of the Code were applicable to such trust. See paragraph (a)(4) of this section for a rule permitting the retention by a grantor of a testamentary power to revoke or terminate the interest of any recipient other than an organization described in section 170(c). For example, the governing instrument may not grant the trustee the power to allocate the annuity among members of a class unless such power falls within one of the exceptions to section 674(a).

(4) *Other payments.*—No amount other than the amount described in subparagraph (1) of this paragraph may be paid to or for the use of any person other than an organization described in section 170(c). An amount is not paid to or for the use of any person other than an organization described in section 170(c) if the amount is transferred for full and adequate consideration. The trust may not be subject to a power to invade, alter, amend, or revoke for the beneficial use of a person other than an organization described in section 170(c). Notwithstanding the preceding sentence, the grantor may retain the power exercisable only by will to revoke or terminate the interest of any recipient other than an organization described in section 170(c). The governing instrument may provide that any amount other than the amount described in subparagraph (1) of this paragraph shall be paid (or may be paid

in the discretion of the trustee) to an organization described in section 170(c) provided that, in the case of distributions in kind, the adjusted basis of the property distributed is fairly representative of the adjusted basis of the property available for payment on the date of payment. For example, the governing instrument may provide that a portion of the trust assets may be distributed currently, or upon the death of one or more recipients, to an organization described in section 170(c).

(5) *Period of payment of annuity amount.*—(i) *General rules.*—The period for which an amount described in subparagraph (1) of this paragraph is payable begins with the first year of the charitable remainder trust and continues either for the life or lives of a named individual or individuals or for a term of years not to exceed 20 years. Only an individual or an organization described in section 170(c) may receive an amount for the life of an individual. If an individual receives an amount for life, it must be solely for his life. Payment of the amount described in subparagraph (1) of this paragraph may terminate with the regular payment next preceding the termination of the period described in this subparagraph. The fact that the recipient may not receive such last payment shall not be taken into account for purposes of determining the present value of the remainder interest. In the case of an amount payable for a term of years, the length of the term of years shall be ascertainable with certainty at the time of the creation of the trust, except that the term may be terminated by the death of the recipient or by the grantor's exercise by will of a retained power to revoke or terminate the interest of any recipient other than an organization described in section 170(c). In any event, the period may not extend beyond either the life or lives of a named individual or individuals or a term of years not to exceed 20 years. For example, the governing instrument may not provide for the payment of an annuity amount to A for his life and then to B for a term of years because it is possible for the period to last longer than either the lives of recipients in being at the creation of the trust or a term of years not to exceed 20 years. On the other hand, the governing instrument may provide for the payment of an annuity amount to A for his life and then to B for his life or a term of years (not to exceed 20 years), whichever is shorter (but not longer), if both A and B are in being at the creation of the trust because it is not possible for the period to last longer than the lives of recipients in being at the creation of the trust.

(ii) *Relationship to 5 percent requirement.*—The 5 percent requirement provided in subparagraph (2) of this paragraph must be met until the termination of all of the payments described in subparagraph (1) of this paragraph. For example, the following provisions would satisfy the above rules:

(*a*) An amount equal to at least 5 percent of the initial net fair market value of the property placed in trust to A and B for their joint lives and then to the survivor for his life;

(*b*) An amount equal to at least 5 percent of the initial net fair market value of the property placed in trust to A for life or for a term of years not longer than 20 years, whichever is longer (or shorter);

(*c*) An amount equal to at least 5 percent of the initial net fair market value of the property placed in trust to A for a term of years not longer than 20 years and then to B for life (provided B was living at the date of creation of the trust);

(*d*) An amount to A for his life and concurrently an amount to B for his life (the amount to each recipient to terminate at his death) if the amount given to each individual is not less than 5 percent of the initial net fair market value of the property placed in trust; or

(*e*) An amount to A for his life and concurrently an equal amount to B for his life, and at the death of the first to die, the trust to distribute one-half of the then value of its assets to an organization described in section 170(c), if the total of the amounts given to A and B is not less than 5 percent of the initial net fair market value of the property placed in trust.

(6) *Permissible Remaindermen.*—(i) *General rule.*—At the end of the period specified in subparagraph (5) of this paragraph the entire corpus of the trust is required to be irrevocably transferred, in whole or in part, to or for the use of one or more organizations described in section 170(c) or retained, in whole or in part, for such use.

(ii) *Treatment of Trust.*—If all of the trust corpus is to be retained for such use, the taxable year of the trust shall terminate at the end of the period specified in subparagraph (5) of this paragraph and the trust shall cease to be treated as a charitable remainder trust for all purposes. If all or any portion of the trust corpus is to be transferred to or for the use of such organization or organizations, the trustee shall have a reasonable time after the period specified in subparagraph (5) of this paragraph to complete the settlement of the trust. During such time, the trust shall continue to be treated as a charitable remainder trust for all purposes, such as sections 664, 4947(a)(2), and 4947(b)(3)(B). Upon the expiration of such period, the taxable year of the trust shall terminate and the trust shall cease to be treated as a charitable remainder trust for all purposes. If the trust continues in existence, it will be subject to the provisions of section 4947(a)(1) unless the trust is exempt from taxation under section 501(a). For purposes of determining whether the trust is exempt under section 501(a) as an organization described in section 501(c)(3), the trust shall be deemed to have been created at the time it ceases to be treated as a charitable remainder trust.

(iii) *Concurrent or successive remaindermen.*—Where interests in the corpus of the trust are given to more than one organization described in section 170(c) such interests may be enjoyed by them either concurrently or successively.

(iv) *Alternative remaindermen.*—The governing instrument shall provide that if an organization to or for the use of which the trust corpus is to be transferred or for the use of which the trust corpus is to be retained is not an organization described in section 170(c) at the time any amount is to be irrevocably transferred to or for the use of such organization, such amount shall be transferred to or for the use of one or more alternative organizations which are described in section 170(c) at such time or retained for such use. Such alternative organization or organizations may be selected in any manner provided by the terms of the governing instrument.

(b) *Additional contributions.*—A trust is not a charitable remainder annuity trust unless its governing instrument provides that no additional contributions may be made to the charitable remainder annuity trust after the initial contribution. For purposes of this section, all property passing to a charitable remainder annuity trust by reason of death of the grantor shall be considered one contribution.

(c) *Calculation of the fair market value of the remainder interest of a charitable remainder annuity trust.*—For purposes of sections 170, 2055, 2106, and 2522, the fair market value of the remainder interest of a charitable remainder annuity trust (as described in this section) is the net fair market value (as of the appropriate valuation date) of the property placed in trust less the present value of the annuity. For purposes of this section, valuation date means, in general, the date on which the property is transferred to the trust by the donor regardless of when the trust is created. In the case of transfers to a charitable remainder annuity trust for which the valuation date is after April 30, 1999, if an election is made under section 7520 and § 1.7520-2(b) to compute the present value of the charitable interest by use of the interest rate component for either of the 2 months preceding the month in which the transfer is made, the month so elected is the valuation date for purposes of determining the interest rate and mortality tables. For purposes of section 2055 or 2106, the valuation date is the date of death unless the alternate valuation date is elected in accordance with section 2032 in which event, and within the limitations set forth in section 2032 and the regulations thereunder, the valuation date is the alternate valuation date. If the decedent's estate elects the alternate valuation date under section 2032 and also elects, under section 7520 and § 1.7520-2(b), to use the interest rate component for one of the 2 months preceding the alternate valuation date, the month so elected is the valuation date for purposes of determining the interest rate and mortality tables. The present value of an annuity is computed under § 20.2031-7T(d) for transfers for which the valuation date is on or after May 1, 2009, or under § 20.2031-7A(a) through (f), whichever is applicable, for transfers for which the valuation date is before May 1, 2009. See, however, § 1.7520-3(b) (relating to exceptions to the use of prescribed tables under certain circumstances).

(d) *Deduction for transfers to a charitable remainder annuity trust.*—For rules relating to a deduction for transfers to a charitable remainder annuity trust, see sections 170, 2055, 2106 or 2522 and the regulations thereunder. Any claim for deduction on any return for the value of a remainder interest in a charitable remainder annuity trust must be supported by a full statement attached to the return showing the computation of the present value of such interest. The deduction allowed by section 170 is limited to the fair market value of the remainder interest of a charitable remainder annuity trust regardless of whether an organization described in section 170(c) also receives a portion of the annuity. For a special rule relating to the reduction of the amount of a charitable contribution deduction with respect to a contribution of certain ordinary income property or capital gain property, see sections 170(e)(1)(A) or 170(e)(1)(B)(i) and the regulations thereunder. For rules for postponing the time for deduction of a charitable contribution of a future interest in tangible personal property, see section 170(a)(3) and the regulations thereunder.

(e) *Effective/applicability date.*—Paragraph (c)(1) applies after April 30, 1989. [Reg. § 1.664-2.]

☐ [*T.D.* 7202, 8-22-72. *Amended by T.D.* 7955, 5-10-84; *T.D.* 8540, 6-9-94; *T.D.* 8791, 12-9-98; *T.D.* 8819, 4-29-99 (*corrected* 3-8-2000); *T.D.* 8926, 1-4-2001; *T.D.* 9448, 5-1-2009 *and T.D.* 9540, 8-9-2011.]

[Reg. § 1.664-3]

§ 1.664-3. Charitable remainder unitrust.—(a) *Description.*—A charitable remainder unitrust is a trust which complies with the applicable provisions of § 1.664-1 and meets all of the following requirements:

(1) *Required payment of unitrust amount.*—(i) *Payment of fixed percentage at least annually.*—(*a*) *General rule.*—The governing instrument provides that the trust will pay not less often than annually a fixed percentage of the net fair market value of the trust assets determined annually to a person or persons described in paragraph (a)(3) of this section for each taxable year of the period specified in paragraph (a)(5) of this section. This paragraph (a)(1)(i)(*a*) is applicable for taxable years ending after April 18, 1997.

(*b*) *Income exception.*—Instead of the amount described in (*a*) of this subdivision (i), the governing instrument may provide that the trust shall pay for any year either the amount described in (*1*) or the total of the amounts described in (*1*) and (*2*) of this subdivision (*b*).

(*1*) The amount of trust income for a taxable year to the extent that such amount is not more than the amount required to be distributed under paragraph (a)(1)(i)(*a*) of this section.

(*2*) An amount of trust income for a taxable year that is in excess of the amount required to be distributed under paragraph (a)(1)(i)(*a*) of this section for such year to the extent that (by reason of paragraph (a)(1)(i)(*b*)(*1*) of this section) the aggregate of the amounts paid in prior years was less than the aggregate of such required amounts.

(*3*) For purposes of this paragraph (a)(1)(i)(*b*), trust income generally means income as defined under section 643(b) and the applicable regulations. However, trust income may not be determined by reference to a fixed percentage of the annual fair market value of the trust property, notwithstanding any contrary provision in applicable state law. Proceeds from the sale or exchange of any assets contributed to the trust by the donor must be allocated to principal and not to trust income at least to the extent of the fair market value of those assets on the date of their contribution to the trust. Proceeds from the sale or exchange of any assets purchased by the trust must be allocated to principal and not to trust income at least to the extent of the trust's purchase price of those assets. Except as provided in the two preceding sentences, proceeds from the sale or exchange of any assets contributed to the trust by the donor or purchased by the trust may be allocated to income, pursuant to the terms of the governing instrument, if not prohibited by applicable local law. A discretionary power to make this allocation may be granted to the trustee under the terms of the governing instrument but only to the extent that the state statute permits the trustee to make adjustments between income and principal to treat beneficiaries impartially.

(*4*) The rules in paragraph (a)(1)(i)(*b*)(*1*) and (2) of this section are applicable for taxable years ending after April 18, 1997. The rule in the first sentence of paragraph (a)(1)(i)(*b*)(3) is applicable for taxable years ending after April 18, 1997. The rules in the second, fourth, and fifth sentences of paragraph (a)(1)(i)(*b*)(3) are applicable for taxable years ending after January 2, 2004. The rule in the third sentence of paragraph (a)(1)(i)(*b*)(3) is applicable for sales or exchanges that occur after April 18, 1997. The rule in the sixth sentence of paragraph (a)(1)(i)(*b*)(3) is applicable for trusts created after January 2, 2004.

(*c*) *Combination of methods.*—Instead of the amount described in paragraph (a)(1)(i)(*a*) or (*b*) of this section, the governing instrument may provide that the trust will pay not less often than annually the amount described in paragraph (a)(1)(i)(*b*) of this section for an initial period and then pay the amount described in paragraph (a)(1)(i)(*a*) of this section (calculated using the same fixed percentage) for the remaining years of the trust only if the governing instrument provides that—

(*1*) The change from the method prescribed in paragraph (a)(1)(i)(*b*) of this section to the method prescribed in paragraph (a)(1)(i)(*a*) of this section is triggered on a specific date or by a single event whose occurrence is not discretionary with, or within the control of, the trustees or any other persons;

(*2*) The change from the method prescribed in paragraph (a)(1)(i)(*b*) of this section to the method prescribed in paragraph (a)(1)(i)(*a*) of this section occurs at the beginning of the taxable year that immediately follows the taxable year during which the date or event specified under paragraph (a)(1)(i)(*c*)(*1*) of this section occurs; and

(*3*) Following the trust's conversion to the method described in paragraph (a)(1)(i)(*a*) of this section, the trust will pay at least annually to the permissible recipients the amount described only in paragraph (a)(1)(i)(*a*) of this section and not any amount described in paragraph (a)(1)(i)(*b*) of this section.

(*d*) *Triggering event.*—For purposes of paragraph (a)(1)(i)(*c*)(*1*) of this section, a triggering event based on the sale of unmarketable assets as defined in § 1.664-1(a)(7)(ii), or the marriage, divorce, death, or birth of a child with respect to any individual will not be considered discretionary with, or within the control of, the trustees or any other persons.

(*e*) *Examples.*—The following examples illustrate the rules in paragraph (a)(1)(i)(*c*) of this section. For each example, assume that the governing instrument of charitable remainder unitrust *Y* provides that *Y* will initially pay not less often than annually the amount described in paragraph (a)(1)(i)(*b*) of this section and then pay the amount described in paragraph (a)(1)(i)(*a*) of this section (calculated using the same fixed percentage) for the remaining years of the trust and that the requirements of paragraphs (a)(1)(i)(*c*)(2) and (3) of this section are satisfied. The examples are as follows:

Example 1. *Y* is funded with the donor's former personal residence. The governing instrument of *Y* provides for the change in method for computing the annual unitrust amount as of the first day of the year following the year in which the trust sells the residence. *Y* provides for a combination of methods that satisfies paragraph (a)(1)(i)(*c*) of this section.

Example 2. *Y* is funded with cash and an unregistered security for which there is no available exemption permitting public sale under the Securities and Exchange Commission rules. The governing instrument of *Y* provides that the change in method for computing the annual unitrust amount is triggered on the earlier of the date when the stock is sold or at the time the restrictions on its public sale lapse or are otherwise lifted. *Y* provides for a combination of methods that satisfies paragraph (a)(1)(i)(*c*) of this section.

Example 3. *Y* is funded with cash and with a security that may be publicly traded under the Securities and Exchange Commission rules. The governing instrument of *Y* provides that the change in method for computing the annual unitrust amount is triggered when the stock is sold. *Y* does not provide for a combination of methods that satisfies the requirements of paragraph (a)(1)(i)(*c*) of this section because the sale of the publicly-traded stock is within the discretion of the trustee.

Example 4. *S* establishes *Y* for her granddaughter, *G*, when *G* is 10 years old. The governing instrument of *Y* provides for the change in method for computing the annual unitrust amount as of the first day of the year following the year in which *G* turns 18 years old. *Y* provides for a combination of methods that satisfies paragraph (a)(1)(i)(*c*) of this section.

Example 5. The governing instrument of *Y* provides for the change in method for computing the annual unitrust amount as of the first day of the year following the year in which the donor is married. *Y* provides for a combination of methods that satisfies paragraph (a)(1)(i)(*c*) of this section.

Example 6. The governing instrument of *Y* provides that if the donor divorces, the change in method for computing the annual unitrust amount will occur as of the first day of the year following the year of the divorce. *Y* provides for a combination of methods that satisfies paragraph (a)(1)(i)(*c*) of this section.

Example 7. The governing instrument of *Y* provides for the change in method for computing the annual unitrust amount as of the first day of the year following the year in which the noncharitable beneficiary's first child is born. *Y* provides for a combination of methods that satisfies paragraph (a)(1)(i)(*c*) of this section.

Example 8. The governing instrument of *Y* provides for the change in method for computing the annual unitrust amount as of the first day of the year following the year in which the noncharitable beneficiary's father dies. *Y* provides for a combination of methods that satisfies paragraph (a)(1)(i)(*c*) of this section.

Example 9. The governing instrument of *Y* provides for the change in method for computing the annual unitrust amount as of the first day of the year following the year in which the noncharitable beneficiary's financial advisor determines that the beneficiary should begin receiving payments under the second prescribed payment method. Because the change in methods for paying the unitrust amount is triggered by an event that is within a person's control, *Y* does not provide for a combination of methods that satisfies paragraph (a)(1)(i)(*c*) of this section.

Example 10. The governing instrument of *Y* provides for the change in method for computing the annual unitrust amount as of the first day of the year following the year in which the noncharitable beneficiary submits a request to the trustee that the trust convert to the second prescribed payment method. Because the change in methods for paying the unitrust amount is triggered by an event that is within a person's control, *Y* does not provide for a combination of methods that satisfies paragraph (a)(1)(i)(*c*) of this section.

(*f*) *Effective date.*—(1) *General rule.*—Paragraphs (a)(1)(i)(*c*), (*d*), and (*e*) of this section are applicable for charitable remainder trusts created on or after December 10, 1998.

(2) *General rule regarding reformations of combination of method unitrusts.*—If a trust is created on or after December 10, 1998, and contains a provision allowing a change in calculating the unitrust amount that does not comply with the provisions of paragraph (a)(1)(i)(*c*) of this section, the trust will qualify as a charitable remainder unitrust only if it is amended or reformed to use the initial method for computing the unitrust amount throughout the term of the trust, or is reformed in accordance with paragraph (a)(1)(i)(*f*)(3) of this section. If a trust was created before December 10, 1998, and contains a provision allowing a change in calculating the unitrust amount that does not comply with the provisions of paragraph (a)(1)(i)(*c*) of this section, the trust may be reformed to use the initial method for computing the unitrust amount throughout the term of the trust without causing the trust to fail to function exclusively as a charitable remainder unitrust under § 1.664-1(a)(4), or may be reformed in accordance with paragraph (a)(1)(i)(*f*)(3) of this section. Except as provided in paragraph (a)(1)(i)(*f*)(3) of this section, a qualified charitable remainder unitrust will not continue to qualify as a charitable remainder unitrust if it is amended or reformed to add a provision allowing a change in the method for calculating the unitrust amount.

(3) *Special rule for reformations of trusts that begin by June 8, 1999.*—Notwithstanding paragraph (a)(1)(i)(*f*)(2) of this section, if a trust either provides for payment of the unitrust amount under a combination of methods that is not permitted under paragraph (a)(1)(i)(*c*) of this section, or provides for payment of the unitrust amount under only the method prescribed in paragraph (a)(1)(i)(*b*) of this section, then the trust may be reformed to allow for a combination of methods permitted under paragraph (a)(1)(i)(*c*) of this section without causing the trust to fail to function exclusively as a charitable remainder unitrust under § 1.664-1(a)(4) or to engage in an act of self-dealing under section 4941 if the trustee begins legal proceedings to reform by June 8, 1999. The triggering event under the reformed governing instrument may not occur in a year prior to the year in which the court issues the order reforming the trust, except for situations in which the governing instrument prior to reformation already provided for payment of the unitrust amount under a combination of methods that is not permitted under paragraph (a)(1)(i)(*c*) of this section and the triggering event occurred prior to the reformation.

(*g*) *Payment under general rule for fixed percentage trusts.*—When the unitrust amount is computed under paragraph (a)(1)(i)(*a*) of this section, a trust will not be deemed to have engaged in an act of self-dealing (within the meaning of section 4941), to have unrelated debt-financed income (within the meaning of section 514), to have received an additional contribution (within the meaning of paragraph (b) of this section), or to have failed to function exclusively as a charitable remainder trust (within the meaning of § 1.664-1(a)(4)) merely because the unitrust amount is paid after the close of the taxable year if such payment is made within a reasonable time after the close of such taxable year and the entire unitrust amount in the hands of the recipient is characterized only as income from the categories described in section 664(b)(1), (2), or (3), except to the extent it is characterized as corpus described in section 664(b)(4) because—

(1) The trust pays the unitrust amount by distributing property (other than cash) that it owned at the close of the taxable year, and the trustee elects to treat any income generated by the distribution as occurring on the last day of the taxable year in which the unitrust amount is due;

(2) The trust pays the unitrust amount by distributing cash that was contributed to the trust (with respect to which a deduction was allowable under section 170, 2055, 2106, or 2522); or

(3) The trust pays the unitrust amount by distributing cash received as a return of basis in any asset that was contributed to the trust (with respect to which a deduction was allowable under section 170, 2055, 2106, or 2522), and that is sold by the trust during the year for which the unitrust amount is due.

(h) Special rule for fixed percentage trusts created before December 10, 1998.—When the unitrust amount is computed under paragraph (a)(1)(i)(*a*) of this section, a trust created before December 10, 1998, will not be deemed to have engaged in an act of self-dealing (within the meaning of section 4941), to have unrelated debt-financed income (within the meaning of section 514), to have received an additional contribution (within the meaning of paragraph (b) of this section), or to have failed to function exclusively as a charitable remainder trust (within the meaning of § 1.664-1(a)(4)) merely because the unitrust amount is paid after the close of the taxable year if such payment is made within a reasonable time after the close of such taxable year and the fixed percentage to be paid each year as the unitrust amount is 15 percent or less of the net fair market value of the trust assets as determined under paragraph (a)(1)(iv) of this section.

(i) Example.—The following example illustrates the rules in paragraph (a)(1)(i)(*g*) of this section:

Example. X is a charitable remainder unitrust that calculates the unitrust amount under paragraph (a)(1)(i)(*a*) of this section. X was created after December 10, 1998. The prorated unitrust amount payable from X for Year 1 is $100. The trustee does not pay the unitrust amount to the recipient by the end of the Year 1. At the end of Year 1, X has only $95 in the ordinary income category under section 664(b)(1) and no income in the capital gain or tax-exempt income categories under section 664(b)(2) or (3), respectively. By April 15 of Year 2, in addition to $95 in cash, the trustee distributes to the unitrust recipient a capital asset with a $5 fair market value and a $2 adjusted basis to pay the $100 unitrust amount due for Year 1. The trust owned the asset at the end of Year 1. Under § 1.664-1(d)(5), the distribution is treated as a sale by X, resulting in X recognizing a $3 capital gain. The trustee elects to treat the capital gain as occurring on the last day of Year 1. Under § 1.664-1(d)(1), the character of the unitrust amount for Year 1 in the recipient's hands is $95 of ordinary income, $3 of capital gain income, and $2 of trust corpus. For Year 1, X satisfied paragraph (a)(1)(i)(*g*) of this section.

(j) Payment under income exception.—When the unitrust amount is computed under paragraph (a)(1)(i)(*b*) of this section, a trust will not be deemed to have engaged in an act of self-dealing (within the meaning of section 4941), to have unrelated debt-financed income (within the meaning of section 514), to have received an additional contribution (within the meaning of paragraph (b) of this section), or to have failed to function exclusively as a charitable remainder trust (within the meaning of § 1.664-1(a)(4)) merely because payment of the unitrust amount is made after the close of the taxable year if such payment is made within a reasonable time after the close of such taxable year.

(k) Reasonable time.—For paragraphs (a)(1)(i)(*g*), (*h*), and (*j*) of this section, a reasonable time will not ordinarily extend beyond the date by which the trustee is required to file Form 5227, "Split-Interest Trust Information Return," (including extensions) for the taxable year.

(l) Effective date.—Paragraphs (a)(1)(i)(*g*), (*h*), (*i*), (*j*), and (*k*) of this section are applicable for taxable years ending after April 18, 1997. Paragraphs (a)(1)(i)(*g*)(2) and (3) of this section apply only to distributions made on or after January 5, 2001.

(ii) *Definition of fixed percentage.*—The fixed percentage may be expressed either as a fraction or as a percentage and must be payable each year in the period specified in subparagraph (5) of this paragraph. A percentage is fixed if the percentage is the same either as to each recipient or as to the total percentage payable each year of such period. For example, provision for a fixed percentage which is the same every year to A until his death and concurrently a fixed percentage which is the same every year to B until his death, the fixed percentage to each recipient to terminate at his death, would satisfy the rule. Similarly, provision for a fixed percentage to A and B for their joint lives and then to the survivor would satisfy the rule. In the case of a distribution to an organization described in section 170(c) at the death of a recipient or the expiration of a term of years, the governing instrument may provide for a reduction of the fixed percentage payable after such distribution provided that:

(a) The reduced fixed percentage is the same either as to each recipient or as to the total amount payable for each year of the balance of such period, and

(b) The requirements of subparagraph (2)(ii) of this paragraph are met.

(iii) *Rules applicable to incorrect valuations.*—The governing instrument provides that in the case where the net fair market value of the trust assets is incorrectly determined by the fiduciary, the trust shall pay to the recipient (in the case of an undervaluation) or be repaid by the recipient (in the case of an overvaluation) an amount equal to the difference between the amount which the trust should have paid the recipient if the correct value were used and the amount which the trust actually paid the recipient. Such payments or repayments must be made within a reasonable period after the final determination of such value. Any payment due to a recipient by reason of such incorrect valuation shall be considered to be a payment required to be distributed at the time of such final determination for purposes of paragraph (d)(4)(ii) of § 1.664-1. See paragraph (d)(4) of § 1.664-1 for rules relating to the year of inclusion of such payments and the allowance of a deduction for such repayments. See paragraph (b) of this section for rules relating to additional contributions.

(iv) *Rules applicable to valuation.*—In computing the net fair market value of the trust assets there shall be taken into account all assets and liabilities without regard to whether particular items are taken into account in determining the income of the trust. The net fair market value of the trust assets may be determined on any one date during the taxable year of the trust, or by taking the average of valuations made on more than one date during the taxable year of the trust, so long as the same valuation date or dates and valuation methods are used each year. If the governing instrument does not specify the valuation date or dates, the trustee must select such date or dates and indicate the selection on the first return on Form 5227, "Split-Interest Trust Information Return," that the trust must file. The amount described in subdivision (i)(*a*) of this subparagraph which must be paid each year must be based upon the valuation for such year.

(v) *Computation of unitrust amount in certain circumstances.*—*(a) Short taxable years.*—The governing instrument provides that, in the case of a taxable year which is for a period of less than 12 months other than the taxable year in which occurs the end of the period specified in subparagraph (5) of this paragraph:

(1) The amount determined under subdivision (i)(*a*) of this subparagraph shall be the amount otherwise determined under that subdivision multiplied by a fraction the numerator of which is the number of days in the taxable year of the trust and the denominator of which is 365 (366 if February 29 is a day included in the numerator),

(2) The amount determined under subdivison (i)(*b*) of this subparagraph shall be computed by using the amount determined under subdivision (*a*)(*1*) of this subdivision (v), and

(3) If no valuation date occurs before the end of the taxable year of the trust, the trust assets shall be valued as of the last day of the taxable year of the trust.

(b) Last taxable year of period.—*(1)* The governing instrument provides that, in the case of the taxable year in which occurs the end of the period specified in subparagraph (5) of this paragraph:

(i) The unitrust amount which must be distributed under subdivision (i)(*a*) of this subparagraph shall be the amount otherwise determined under that subdivision multiplied by a fraction the numerator of which is the number of days in the period beginning on the first day of such taxable year and ending on the last day of the period specified in subparagraph (5) of this paragraph and the denominator of which is 365 (366 if February 29 is a day included in the numerator),

(ii) The amount determined under subdivision (i)(*b*) of this subparagraph shall be computed by using the amount determined under subdivision (*b*)(*1*)(*i*) of this subdivision (v), and

(iii) If no valuation date occurs before the end of such period, the trust assets shall be valued as of the last day of such period.

(2) See subparagraph (5) of this paragraph for a special rule allowing termination of payment of the unitrust amount with the regular payment next preceding the termination of the period specified therein.

(2) *Minimum unitrust amount.*—(i) *General rule.*—The fixed percentage described in subparagraph (1)(i) of this paragraph with respect to all beneficiaries taken together is not less than 5 percent.

(ii) *Reduction of unitrust amount in certain cases.*—A trust will not fail to meet the requirements of this subparagraph by reason of the fact that it provides for a reduction of the fixed percentage payable upon the death of a recipient or the expiration of a term of years provided that:

(a) A distribution is made to an organization described in section 170(c) at the death of such recipient or the expiration of such term of years, and

(b) The total of the percentage payable under subparagraph (1) of this paragraph after such distribution is not less than 5 percent.

(3) *Permissible recipients.*—(i) *General rule.*—The amount described in subparagraph (1) of this paragraph is payable to or for the use of a named person or persons, at least one of which is not an organization described in section 170(c). If the amount described in subparagraph (1) of this paragraph is to be paid to an individual or individuals, all such individuals must be living at the time of creation of the trust. A named person or persons may include members of a named class except in the case of a class which includes any individual, all such individuals must be alive and ascertainable at the time of the creation of the trust unless the period for which the unitrust amount is to be paid to such class consists solely of a term of years. For example, in

the case of a testamentary trust, the testator's will may provide that the required amount shall be paid to his children living at this death.

(ii) *Power to alter amount paid to recipients.*—A trust is not a charitable remainder unitrust if any person has the power to alter the amount to be paid to any named person other than an organization described in section 170(c) if such power would cause any person to be treated as the owner of the trust, or any portion thereof, if subpart E, part 1, subchapter J, chapter 1, subtitle A of the Code were applicable to such trust. See paragraph (a)(4) of this section for a rule permitting the retention by a grantor of a testamentary power to revoke or terminate the interest of any recipient other than an organization described in section 170(c). For example, the governing instrument may not grant the trustee the power to allocate the fixed percentage among members of a class unless such power falls within one of the exceptions to section 674(a).

(4) *Other payments.*—No amount other than the amount described in subparagraph (1) of this paragraph may be paid to or for the use of any person other than an organization described in section 170(c). An amount is not paid to or for the use of any person other than an organization described in section 170(c) if the amount is transferred for full and adequate consideration. The trust may not be subject to a power to invade, alter, amend, or revoke for the beneficial use of a person other than an organization described in section 170(c). Notwithstanding the preceding sentence, the grantor may retain the power exercisable only by will to revoke or terminate the interest of any recipient other than an organization described in section 170(c). The governing instrument may provide that any amount other than the amount described in subparagraph (1) of this paragraph shall be paid (or may be paid in the discretion of the trustee) to an organization described in section 170(c) provided that, in the case of distributions in kind, the adjusted basis of the property distributed is fairly representative of the adjusted basis of the property available for payment on the date of payment. For example, the governing instrument may provide that a portion of the trust assets may be distributed currently, or upon the death of one or more recipients, to an organization described in section 170(c).

(5) *Period of payment of unitrust amount.*—(i) *General rules.*—The period for which an amount described in subparagraph (1) of this paragraph is payable begins with the first year of the charitable remainder trust and continues either for the life or lives of a named individual or individuals or for a term of years not to exceed 20 years. Only an individual or an organization described in section 170(c) may receive an amount for the life of an individual. If an individual receives an amount for life, it must be solely for his life. Payment of the amount described in subparagrah (1) of this paragraph may terminate with the regular payment next preceding the termination of the period described in this subparagraph. The fact that the recipient may not receive such last payment shall not be taken into account for purposes of determining the present value of the remainder interest. In the case of an amount payable for a term of years, the length of the term of years shall be ascertainable with certainty at the time of the creation of the trust, except that the term may be terminated by the death of the recipient or by the grantor's exercise by will of a retained power to revoke or terminate the interest of any recipient other than an organization described in section 170(c). In any event, the period may not extend beyond either the life or lives of a named individual or individuals or a term of years not to exceed 20 years. For example, the governing instrument may not provide for the payment of a unitrust amount to A for his life and then to B for a term of years because it is possible for the period to last longer than either the lives of recipients in being at the creation of the trust or a term of years not to exceed 20 years. On the other hand, the governing instrument may provide for the payment of an unitrust amount to A for his life and then to B for his life or a term of years (not to exceed 20 years), whichever is shorter (but not longer), if both A and B are in being at the creation of the trust because it is not possible for the period to last longer than the lives of recipients in being at the creation of the trust.

(ii) *Relationship to 5 percent requirement.*—The 5 percent requirement provided in subparagraph (2) of this paragraph must be met until the termination of all the payments described in subparagraph (1) of this paragraph. For example, the following provisions would satisfy the above rules:

(a) A fixed percentage of at least 5 percent to A and B for their joint lives and then to the survivor for his life;

(b) A fixed percentage of at least 5 percent to A for life or for a term of years not longer than 20 years, whichever is longer (or shorter);

(c) A fixed percentage of at least 5 percent to A for a term of years not longer than 20 years and then to B for life (provided B was living at the creation of the trust);

(d) A fixed percentage to A for his life and concurrently a fixed percentage to B for his life (the percentage to each recipient to terminate at his death) if the percentage given to each individual is not less than 5 percent;

(e) A fixed percentage to A for his life and concurrently an equal percentage to B for his life, and at the death of the first to die, the trust to distribute one-half of the then value of its assets to an organization described in section 170(c) if the total of the percentages is not less than 5 percent for the entire period described in this subparagraph.

(6) *Permissible Remaindermen.*—(i) *General Rule.*—At the end of the period specified in subparagraph (5) of this paragraph, the entire corpus of the trust is required to be irrevocably transferred, in whole or in part, to or for the use

of one or more organizations described in section 170(c) or retained, in whole or in part, for such use.

(ii) *Treatment of Trust.*—If all of the trust corpus is to be retained for such use, the taxable year of the trust shall terminate at the end of the period specified in subparagraph (5) of this paragraph and the trust shall cease to be treated as a charitable remainder trust for all purposes. If all or any portion of the trust corpus is to be transferred to or for the use of such organization or organizations, the trustee shall have a reasonable time after the period specified in subparagraph (5) of this paragraph to complete the settlement of the trust. During such time, the trust shall continue to be treated as a charitable remainder trust for all purposes, such as sections 664, 4947(a)(2), and 4947(b)(3)(B). Upon the expiration of such period, the taxable year of the trust shall terminate and the trust shall cease to be treated as a charitable remainder trust for all purposes. If the trust continues in existence, it will be subject to the provisions of section 4947(a)(1) unless the trust is exempt from taxation under section 501(a). For purposes of determining whether the trust is exempt under section 501(a) as an organization described in section 501(c)(3), the trust shall be deemed to have been created at the time it ceases to be treated as a charitable remainder trust.

(iii) *Concurrent or successive remaindermen.*—Where interests in the corpus of the trust are given to more than one organization described in section 170(c) such interests may be enjoyed by them either concurrently or successively.

(iv) *Alternative remaindermen.*—The governing instrument shall provide that if an organization to or for the use of which the trust corpus is to be transferred or for the use of which the trust corpus is to be retained is not an organization described in section 170(c) at the time any amount is to be irrevocably transferred to or for the use of such organization, such amount shall be transferred to or for the use of or retained for the use of one or more alternative organizations which are described in section 170(c) at such time. Such alternative organization or organizations may be selected in any manner provided by the terms of the governing instrument.

(b) *Additional contributions.*—A trust is not a charitable remainder unitrust unless its governing instrument either prohibits additional contributions to the trust after the initial contribution or provides that for the taxable year of the trust in which the additional contribution is made:

(1) Where no valuation date occurs after the time of the contribution and during the taxable year in which the contribution is made, the additional property shall be valued as of the time of contribution; and

(2) The amount described in paragraph (a)(1)(i)(*a*) of this section shall be computed by multiplying the fixed percentage by the sum of (i) the net fair market value of the trust assets (excluding the value of the additional property and any earned income from and any appreciation on such property after its contribution), and (ii) that proportion of the value of the additional property (that was excluded under subdivision (i) of this paragraph), which the number of days in the period which begins with the date of contribution and ends with the earlier of the last day of such taxable year or the last day of the period described in paragraph (a)(5) of this section bears to the number of days in the period which begins with the first day of such taxable year and ends with the earlier of the last day of such taxable year or the last day of the period described in paragraph (a)(5) of this section.

For purposes of this section, all property passing to a charitable remainder unitrust by reason of death of the grantor shall be considered one contribution. The application of the preceding rules may be illustrated by the following examples:

Example (1). On March 2, 1971, X makes an additional contribution of property to a charitable remainder unitrust. The taxable year of the trust is the calendar year and the regular valuation date is January 1 of each year. For purposes of computing the required payout with respect to the additional contribution for the year of contribution, the additional contribution is valued on March 2, 1971, the time of contribution. The property had a value on that date of $5,000. Income from such property in the amount of $250 was received on December 31, 1971. The required payout with respect to the additional contribution for the year of contribution is $208 (5 percent × $5,000 × 305/365). The income earned after the date of the contribution and after the regular valuation date does not enter into the computation.

Example (2). On July 1, 1971, X makes an additional contribution of $10,000 to a charitable remainder unitrust. The taxable year of the trust is the calendar year and the regular valuation date is December 31 of each year. The fixed percentage is 5 percent. Between July 1, 1971, and December 31, 1971, the additional property appreciates in value to $12,500 and earns $500 of income. Because the regular valuation date for the year of contribution occurs after the date of the additional contribution, the additional contribution including income earned by it is valued on the regular valuation date. Thus, the required payout with respect to the additional contribution is $325.87 (5 percent × [$12,500 + $500] × 183/365).

(c) *Calculation of the fair market value of the remainder interest of a charitable remainder unitrust.*—See § 1.664-4 for rules relating to the calculation of the fair market value of the remainder interest of a charitable remainder unitrust.

(d) *Deduction for transfers to a charitable remainder unitrust.*—For rules relating to a deduction for transfers to a charitable remainder unitrust, see sections 170, 2055, 2106 or 2522 and the regulations thereunder. The deduction allowed by section 170 for transfers to charity is limited to the fair market value of the remainder interest of a charitable remainder unitrust regardless of whether an organization described in section 170(c) also receives a portion of the amount described in § 1.664-3(a)(1). For a special rule relating to the reduction of the amount of a charitable contribution deduction with respect to a contribution of certain ordinary income property or capital gain property, see section 170(e)(1)(A) or (B)(i) and the regulations thereunder. For rules for postponing the time for deduction of a charitable contribution of a future interest in tangible personal property, see section 170(a)(3) and the regulations thereunder. [Reg. § 1.664-3.]

☐ [*T.D.* 7202, 8-22-72. *Amended by T.D.* 8791, 12-9-98; *T.D.* 8926, 1-4-2001 *and T.D.* 9102, 12-30-2003.]

[Reg. § 1.664-4]

§ 1.664-4. Calculation of the fair market value of the remainder interest in a charitable remainder unitrust.—(a) *Rules for determining present value.*—For purposes of sections 170, 2055, 2106, and 2522, the fair market value of a remainder interest in a charitable remainder unitrust (as described in § 1.664-3) is its present value determined under paragraph (d) of this section. The present value determined under this section shall be computed on the basis of—

(1) Life contingencies determined as to each life involved, from the values of *lx* set forth in Table 2000CM contained in § 20.2031-7(d)(7) of this chapter in the case of transfers for which the valuation date is on or after May 1, 2009; or from Table 90CM contained in § 20.2031-7A(f)(4) in the case of transfers for which the valuation date is after April 30, 1999, and before May 1, 2009. See § 20.2031-7A(a) through (e), whichever is applicable, for transfers for which the valuation date is before May 1, 1999;

(2) Interest at the section 7520 rate in the case of transfers for which the valuation date is after April 30, 1989, or 10 percent in the case of transfers to charitable remainder unitrusts made after November 30, 1983, for which the valuation date is before May 1, 1989. See § 20.2031-7A(a) through (c) of this chapter, whichever is applicable, for transfers for which the valuation date is before December 1, 1983; and

(3) The assumption that the amount described in § 1.664-3(a)(1)(*i*)(*a*) is distributed in accordance with the payout sequence described in the governing instrument. If the governing instrument does not prescribe when the distribution is made during the period for which the payment is made, for purposes of this section, the distribution is considered payable on the first day of the period for which the payment is made.

(b) *Actuarial Computations by the Internal Revenue Service.*—The regulations in this and in related sections provide tables of actuarial factors and examples that illustrate the use of the tables in determining the value of remainder interests in property. Section 1.7520-1(c)(2) refers to government publications that provide additional tables of factors and examples of computations for more complex situations. If the computation requires the use of a factor that is not provided in this section, the Commissioner may supply the factor upon a request for a ruling. A request for a ruling must be accompanied by a recitation of the facts including the date of birth of each measuring life, and copies of the relevant documents. A request for a ruling must comply with the instructions for requesting a ruling published periodically in the Internal Revenue Bulletin (See § 601.601(d)(2)(ii)(*b*) of this chapter) and include payment of the required user fee. If the Commissioner furnishes the factor, a copy of the letter supplying the factor should be attached to the tax return in which the deduction is claimed. If the Commissioner does not furnish the factor, the taxpayer must furnish a factor computed in accordance with the principles set forth in this section.

(c) *Statement supporting deduction required.*—Any claim for a deduction on any return for the value of a remainder interest in a charitable remainder unitrust must be supported by a full statement attached to the return showing the computation of the present value of such interest.

(d) *Valuation.*—The fair market value of a remainder interest in a charitable remainder unitrust (as described in § 1.664-3) for transfers for which the valuation date is on or after May 1, 2009, is its present value determined under paragraph (e) of this section. The fair market value of a remainder interest in a charitable remainder unitrust (as described in § 1.664-3) for transfers for which the valuation date is before May 1, 2009, is its present value determined under the following sections:

Valuation Dates		*Applicable Regulations*
After	*Before*	
-	01-01-52	1.664-4A(a)
12-31-51	01-01-71	1.664-4A(b)
12-31-70	12-01-83	1.664-4A(c)
11-30-83	05-01-89	1.664-4A(d)
04-30-89	05-01-99	1.664-4A(e)
04-30-99	05-01-09	1.664-4A(f)

(e) *Valuation of charitable remainder unitrusts having certain payout sequences for transfers for which the valuation date is on or after May 1, 2009.*—(1) *In general.*—Except as otherwise provided in paragraph (e)(2) of this section, in the case of transfers for which the valuation date is on or after May 1, 2009, the present value of a remainder interest is determined under paragraphs (e)(3) through (e)(7) of this section, provided that the amount of the payout as of any payout date during any taxable year of the trust is not larger than the amount that the trust could distribute on such date under § 1.664-3(a)(1)(v) if the taxable year of the trust were to end on such date. See, however, § 1.7520-3(b) (relating to exceptions to the use of the prescribed tables under certain circumstances).

(2) *Transitional rules for valuation of charitable remainder unitrusts.*—

(i) For purposes of sections 2055, 2106, or 2624, if on May 1, 2009, the decedent was mentally incompetent so that the disposition of the property could not be changed, and the decedent died on or after May 1, 2009, without having regained competency to dispose of the decedent's property, or the decedent died within 90 days of the date that the decedent first regained competency on or after May 1, 2009, the present value of a remainder interest under this section is determined as if the valuation date with respect to the decedent's gross estate is either before or after May 1, 2009, at the option of the decedent's executor.

(ii) For purposes of sections 170, 2055, 2106, 2522, or 2624, in the case of transfers to a charitable remainder unitrust for which the valuation date is on or after May 1, 2009, and before July 1, 2009, the present value of a remainder interest based on one or more measuring lives is determined under this section by use of the section 7520 interest rate for the month in which the valuation date occurs (see §§ 1.7520-1(b) and 1.7520-2(a)(2)) and the appropriate actuarial tables under either paragraph (e)(7) of this section or § 1.664-4A(f)(6), at the option of the donor or the decedent's executor, as the case may be.

(iii) For purposes of paragraphs (e)(2)(i) and (e)(2)(ii) of this section, where the donor or decedent's executor is given the option to use the appropriate actuarial tables under either paragraph (e)(7) of this section or § 1.664-4A(f)(6), the donor or decedent's executor must use the same actuarial table with respect to each individual transaction and with respect to all transfers occurring on the valuation date (for example, gift and income tax charitable deductions with respect to the same transfer must be determined based on the same tables, and all assets includible in the gross estate and/or estate tax deductions claimed must be valued based on the same tables).

(3) *Adjusted payout rate.*—For transfers for which the valuation date is after April 30, 1989, the adjusted payout rate is determined by using the appropriate Table F in paragraph (e)(6) of this section, for the section 7520 interest rate applicable to the transfer. If the interest rate is between 4.2 and 14 percent, see paragraph (e)(6) of this section. If the interest rate is below 4.2 percent or greater than 14 percent, see paragraph (b) of this section. The adjusted payout rate is determined by multiplying the fixed percentage described in § 1.664-3(a)(1)(i)(*a*) by the factor describing the payout sequence of the trust and the number of months by which the valuation date for the first full taxable year of the trust precedes the first payout date for such taxable year. If the governing instrument does not prescribe when the distribution or distributions shall be made during the taxable year of the trust, see paragraph (a) of this section. In the case of a trust having a payout sequence for which no figures have been provided by the appropriate table, and in the case of a trust that determines the fair market value of the trust assets by taking the average of valuations on more than one date during the taxable year, see paragraph (b) of this section.

(4) *Period is a term of years.*—If the period described in § 1.664-3(a)(5) is a term of years, the factor that is used in determining the present value of the remainder interest for transfers for which the valuation date is after November 30, 1983, is the factor under the appropriate adjusted payout rate in Table D of paragraph (e)(6) of this section corresponding to the number of years in the term. If the adjusted payout rate is an amount that is between adjusted payout rates for which factors are provided in Table D, a linear interpolation must be made. The present value of the remainder interest is determined by multiplying the net fair market value (as of the appropriate valuation date) of the property placed in trust by the factor determined under this paragraph. For purposes of this section, the valuation date is, in the case of an inter vivos transfer, the date on which the property is transferred to the trust by the donor. However, if an election is made under section 7520 and § 1.7520-2(b) to compute the present value of the charitable interest by use of the interest rate component for either of the 2 months preceding the month in which the date of transfer falls, the month so elected is the valuation date for purposes of determining the interest rate and mortality tables. In the case of a testamentary transfer under section 2055, 2106, or 2624, the valuation date is the date of death, unless the alternate valuation date is elected under section 2032, in which event, and within the limitations set forth in section 2032 and the regulations thereunder, the valuation date is the alternate valuation date. If the decedent's estate elects the alternate valuation date under section 2032 and also elects, under section 7520 and § 1.7520-2(b), to use the interest rate component for one of the 2 months preceding the alternate valuation date, the month so elected is the valuation date for purposes of determining the interest rate and mortality tables. The application of this paragraph (e)(4) may be illustrated by the following example:

Example. D transfers $100,000 to a charitable remainder unitrust on January 1. The trust instrument requires that the trust pay 8 percent of the fair market value of the trust assets as of January 1st for a term of 12 years to D in quarterly payments (March 31, June 30, September 30, and December 31). The section 7520 rate for January (the month that the transfer occurred) is 9.6 percent. Under Table F(9.6) in paragraph(e)(6) of this section, the appropriate adjustment factor is .944628 for quarterly payments payable at the end of each quarter. The adjusted payout rate is 7.557 (8% × .944628). Based on the remainder factors in Table D in paragraph(e)(6) of this section, the present value of the remainder interest is $38,950.30, computed as follows:

Factor at 7.4 percent for 12 years		.397495
Factor at 7.6 percent for 12 years		.387314
Difference		.010181
Interpolation adjustment:		
7.557% – 7.4% / 0.2%	=	x / .010181
x	=	.007992
Factor at 7.4 percent for 12 years		.397495
Less: Interpolation adjustment		.007992
Interpolated factor		.389503
Present value of remainder interest: ($100,000 × .389503)		$38,950.30

(5) *Period is the life of one individual.*—(i) If the period described in § 1.664-3(a)(5) is the life of one individual, the factor that is used in determining the present value of the remainder interest for transfers for which the valuation date is on or after May 1, 2009, is the factor in Table U(1) in paragraph (e)(7) of this section under the appropriate adjusted payout. For purposes of the computations described in this paragraph (e)(5), the age of an individual is the age of that individual at the individual's nearest birthday. If the adjusted payout rate is an amount that is between adjusted payout rates for which factors are provided in the appropriate table, a linear interpolation must be made. The present value of the remainder interest is determined by multiplying the net fair market value (as of the valuation date as determined in paragraph (e)(4) of this section) of the property placed in trust by the factor determined under this paragraph (e)(5). If the adjusted payout rate is between 4.2 and 14 percent, see paragraph (e)(7) of this section. If the adjusted payout rate is below 4.2 percent or greater than 14 percent, see paragraph (b) of this section.

(ii) The application of paragraph (e)(5)(i) of this section may be illustrated by the following example:

Example. A, who is 44 years and 11 months old, transfers $100,000 to a charitable remainder unitrust on January 1st. The trust instrument requires that the trust pay to A semiannually (on June 30 and December 31) 8 percent of the fair market value of the trust assets as of January 1st during A's life. The section 7520 rate for January is 6.6 percent. Under Table F(6.6) in paragraph (e)(6) of this section, the appropriate adjustment factor is .917 for semiannual payments payable at the end of the semiannual period. The adjusted payout rate is 7.627% (8% X .953317). Based on the remainder factors in Table U(1) in this section, the present value of the remainder interest is $11,075.00, computed as follows:

Factor at 7.6 percent at age 45		.11141
Factor at 7.8 percent at age 45		.10653
Difference		.00488
Interpolation adjustment:		
7.627% - 7.6% / 0.2%	=	x / .00488
x	=	.00066
Factor at 7.6 percent at age 45		.11141
Less: Interpolation adjustment		.00066
Interpolated Factor		.11075
Present value of remainder interest: ($100,000 X .11075)		$11,075.00

(6) *Actuarial Table D and F (4.2 through 14.0) for transfers for which the valuation date is after April 30, 1989.*—For transfers for which the valuation date is after April 30, 1989, the present value of a charitable remainder unitrust interest that is dependent upon a term of years is determined by using the section 7520 rate and the tables in this paragraph (e)(6). For transfers for which the valuation date is on or after May 1, 2009, where the present value of a charitable remainder unitrust interest is dependent on the termination of a life interest, see paragraph (e)(5) of this section. See, however, § 1.7520-3(b) (relating to exceptions to the use of prescribed tables under certain circumstances). Many actuarial factors not contained in the following tables are contained in Internal Revenue Service Publication 1458, "Actuarial Valuations Version 3B" (2009). This publication will be available beginning May 1, 2009, at no charge, electronically via the IRS Internet site at *www.irs.gov*.

See p. 15 for regulations not amended to reflect law changes

TABLE D
SHOWING THE PRESENT WORTH OF A REMAINDER INTEREST POSTPONED FOR A TERM CERTAIN IN A CHARITABLE REMAINDER UNITRUST
APPLICABLE AFTER APRIL 30, 1989
ADJUSTED PAYOUT RATE

YEARS	*4.2%*	*4.4%*	*4.6%*	*4.8%*	*5.0%*	*5.2%*	*5.4%*	*5.6%*	*5.8%*	*6.0%*
1	.958000	.956000	.954000	.952000	.950000	.948000	.946000	.944000	.942000	.940000
2	.917764	.913936	.910116	.906304	.902500	.898704	.894916	.891136	.887364	.883600
3	.879218	.873723	.868251	.862801	.857375	.851971	.846591	.841232	835897	.830584
4	.842291	.835279	.828311	.821387	.814506	.807669	.800875	.794123	.787415	.780749
5	.806915	.798527	.790209	.781960	.773781	.765670	.757627	.749652	.741745	.733904
6	.773024	.763392	.753859	.744426	.735092	.725855	.716716	.707672	.698724	.689870
7	.740557	.729802	.719182	.708694	.698337	.688111	.678013	.668042	.658198	.648478
8	.709454	.697691	.686099	.674677	.663420	.652329	.641400	.630632	.620022	.609569
9	.679657	.666993	.654539	.642292	.630249	.618408	.606765	.595317	.584061	.572995
10	.651111	.637645	.624430	.611462	.598737	.586251	.573999	.561979	.550185	.538615
11	.623764	.609589	.595706	.582112	.568800	.555766	.543003	.530508	.518275	.506298
12	.597566	.582767	.568304	.554170	.540360	.526866	.513681	.500800	.488215	.475920
13	.572469	.557125	.542162	.527570	.513342	.499469	.485942	.472755	.459898	.447365
14	.548425	.532611	.517222	.502247	.487675	.473496	.459701	.446281	.433224	.420523
15	.525391	.509177	.493430	.478139	.463291	.448875	.434878	.421289	.408097	.395292
16	.503325	.486773	.470732	.455188	.440127	.425533	.411394	.397697	.384427	.371574
17	.482185	.465355	.449079	.433339	.418120	.403405	.389179	.375426	.362131	.349280
18	.461933	.444879	.428421	.412539	.397214	.382428	.368163	.354402	.341127	.328323
19	.442532	.425304	.408714	.392737	.377354	.362542	.348282	.334555	.321342	.308624
20	.423946	.406591	.389913	.373886	.358486	.343690	.329475	.315820	.302704	.290106

TABLE D
SHOWING THE PRESENT WORTH OF A REMAINDER INTEREST POSTPONED FOR A TERM CERTAIN IN A CHARITABLE REMAINDER UNITRUST
APPLICABLE AFTER APRIL 30, 1989
ADJUSTED PAYOUT RATE

YEARS	*6.2%*	*6.4%*	*6.6%*	*6.8%*	*7.0%*	*7.2%*	*7.4%*	*7.6%*	*7.8%*	*8.0%*
1	.938000	.936000	.934000	.932000	.930000	.928000	.926000	.924000	.922000	.920000
2	.879844	.876096	.872356	.868624	.864900	.861184	.857476	.853776	.850084	.846400
3	.825294	.820026	.814781	.809558	.804357	.799179	.794023	.788889	.783777	.778688
4	.774125	.767544	.761005	.754508	.748052	.741638	.735265	.728933	.722643	.716393
5	.726130	.718421	.710779	.703201	.695688	.688240	.680855	.673535	.666277	.659082
6	.681110	.672442	.663867	.655383	.646990	.638687	.630472	.622346	.614307	.606355
7	.638881	.629406	.620052	.610817	.601701	.592701	.583817	.575048	.566391	.557847
8	.599270	.589124	.579129	.569282	.559582	.550027	.540615	.531344	.522213	.513219
9	.562115	.551420	.540906	.530571	.520411	.510425	.500609	.490962	.481480	.472161
10	.527264	.516129	.505206	.494492	.483982	.473674	.463564	.453649	.443925	.434388
11	.494574	.483097	.471863	.460866	.450104	.439570	.429260	.419171	.409298	.399637
12	.463910	.452179	.440720	.429527	.418596	.407921	.397495	.387314	.377373	.367666
13	.435148	.423239	.411632	.400320	.389295	.378550	.368081	.357879	.347938	.338253
14	.408169	.396152	.384465	.373098	.362044	.351295	.340843	.330680	.320799	.311193
15	.382862	.370798	.359090	.347727	.336701	.326002	.315620	.305548	.295777	.286297
16	.359125	.347067	.335390	.324082	.313132	.302529	.292264	.282326	.272706	.263394
17	.336859	.324855	.313254	.302044	.291213	.280747	.270637	.260870	.251435	.242322
18	.315974	.304064	.292579	.281505	.270828	.260533	.250610	.241044	.231823	.222936
19	.296383	.284604	.273269	.262363	.251870	.241775	.232065	.222724	.213741	.205101
20	.278008	.266389	.255233	.244522	.234239	.224367	.214892	.205797	.197069	.188693

TABLE D
SHOWING THE PRESENT WORTH OF A REMAINDER INTEREST
POSTPONED FOR A TERM CERTAIN IN A CHARITABLE
REMAINDER UNITRUST
APPLICABLE AFTER APRIL 30, 1989
ADJUSTED PAYOUT RATE

YEARS	*8.2%*	*8.4%*	*8.6%*	*8.8%*	*9.0%*	*9.2%*	*9.4%*	*9.6%*	*9.8%*	*10.0%*
1	.918000	.916000	.914000	.912000	.910000	.908000	.906000	.904000	.902000	.900000
2	.842724	.839056	.835396	.831744	.828100	.824464	.820836	.817216	.813604	.810000
3	.773621	.768575	.763552	.758551	.753571	.748613	.743677	.738763	.733871	.729000
4	.710184	.704015	.697886	.691798	.685750	.679741	.673772	.667842	.661951	.656100
5	.651949	.644878	.637868	.630920	.624032	.617205	.610437	.603729	.597080	.590490
6	.598489	.590708	.583012	.575399	.567869	.560422	.553056	.545771	.538566	.531441
7	.549413	.541089	.532873	.524764	.516761	.508863	.501069	.493377	.485787	.478297
8	.504361	.495637	.487046	.478585	.470253	.462048	.453968	.446013	.438180	.430467
9	.463003	.454004	.445160	.436469	.427930	.419539	.411295	.403196	.395238	.387420
10	.425037	.415867	.406876	.398060	.389416	.380942	.372634	.364489	.356505	.348678
11	.390184	.380934	.371885	.363031	.354369	.345895	.337606	.329498	.321567	.313811
12	.358189	.348936	.339902	.331084	.322475	.314073	.305871	.297866	.290054	.282430
13	.328817	.319625	.310671	.301949	.293453	.285178	.277119	.269271	.261628	.254187
14	.301854	.292777	.283953	.275377	.267042	.258942	.251070	.243421	.235989	.228768
15	.277102	.268184	.259533	.251144	.243008	.235119	.227469	.220053	.212862	.205891
16	.254380	.245656	.237213	.229043	.221137	.213488	.206087	.198928	.192001	.185302
17	.233521	.225021	.216813	.208887	.201235	.193847	.186715	.179830	.173185	.166772
18	.214372	.206119	.198167	.190505	.183124	.176013	.169164	.162567	.156213	.150095
19	.196794	.188805	.181125	.173741	.166643	.159820	.153262	.146960	.140904	.135085
20	.180657	.172946	.165548	.158452	.151645	.145117	.138856	.132852	.127096	.121577

TABLE D
SHOWING THE PRESENT WORTH OF A REMAINDER INTEREST
POSTPONED FOR A TERM CERTAIN IN A CHARITABLE
REMAINDER UNITRUST
APPLICABLE AFTER APRIL 30, 1989
ADJUSTED PAYOUT RATE

YEARS	*10.2%*	*10.4%*	*10.6%*	*10.8%*	*11.0%*	*11.2%*	*11.4%*	*11.6%*	*11.8%*	*12.0%*
1	.898000	.896000	.894000	.892000	.890000	.888000	.886000	.884000	.882000	.880000
2	.806404	.802816	.799236	.795664	.792100	.788544	.784996	.781456	.777924	.774400
3	.724151	.719323	.714517	.709732	.704969	.700227	.695506	.690807	.686129	.681472
4	.650287	.644514	.638778	.633081	.627422	.621802	.616219	.610673	.605166	.599695
5	.583958	.577484	.571068	.564708	.558406	.552160	.545970	.539835	.533756	.527732
6	.524394	.517426	.510535	.503720	.496981	.490318	.483729	.477214	.470773	.464404
7	.470906	.463613	.456418	.449318	.442313	.435402	.428584	.421858	.415222	.408676
8	.422874	.415398	.408038	.400792	.393659	.386637	.379726	.372922	.366226	.359635
9	.379741	.372196	.364786	.357506	.350356	.343334	.336437	.329663	.323011	.316478
10	.341007	.333488	.326118	.318896	.311817	.304881	.298083	.291422	.284896	.278501
11	.306224	.298805	.291550	.284455	.277517	.270734	.264102	.257617	.251278	.245081
12	.274989	.267729	.260645	.253734	.246990	.240412	.233994	.227734	.221627	.215671
13	.246941	.239886	.233017	.226331	.219821	.213486	.207319	.201317	.195475	.189791
14	.221753	.214937	.208317	.201887	.195641	.189575	.183684	.177964	.172409	.167016
15	.199134	.192584	.186236	.180083	.174121	.168343	.162744	.157320	.152065	.146974
16	.178822	.172555	.166495	.160634	.154967	.149488	.144191	.139071	.134121	.129337
17	.160582	.154609	.148846	.143286	.137921	.132746	.127754	.122939	.118295	.113817
18	.144203	.138530	.133069	.127811	.122750	.117878	.113190	.108678	.104336	.100159
19	.129494	.124123	.118963	.114007	.109247	.104676	.100286	.096071	.092024	.088140
20	.116286	.111214	.106353	.101694	.097230	.092952	.088853	.084927	.081166	.077563

See p. 15 for regulations not amended to reflect law changes

TABLE D
SHOWING THE PRESENT WORTH OF A REMAINDER INTEREST POSTPONED FOR A TERM CERTAIN IN A CHARITABLE REMAINDER UNITRUST
APPLICABLE AFTER APRIL 30, 1989
ADJUSTED PAYOUT RATE

YEARS	*12.2%*	*12.4%*	*12.6%*	*12.8%*	*13.0%*	*13.2%*	*13.4%*	*13.6%*	*13.8%*	*14.0%*
1	.878000	.876000	.874000	.872000	.870000	.868000	.866000	.864000	.862000	.860000
2	.770884	.767376	.763876	.760384	.756900	.753424	.749956	.746496	.743044	.739600
3	.676836	.672221	.667628	.663055	.658503	.653972	.649462	.644973	.640504	.636056
4	.594262	.588866	.583507	.578184	.572898	.567648	.562434	.557256	.552114	.547008
5	.521762	.515847	.509985	.504176	.498421	.492718	.487068	.481469	.475923	.470427
6	.458107	.451882	.445727	.439642	.433626	.427679	.421801	.415990	.410245	.404567
7	.402218	.395848	.389565	.383368	.377255	.371226	.365279	.359415	.353631	.347928
8	.353147	.346763	.340480	.334297	.328212	.322224	.316332	.310535	.304830	.299218
9	.310063	.303764	.297579	.291507	.285544	.279690	.273944	.268302	.262764	.257327
10	.272236	.266098	.260084	.254194	.248423	.242771	.237235	.231813	.226502	.221302
11	.239023	.233102	.227314	.221657	.216128	.210725	.205446	.200286	.195245	.190319
12	.209862	.204197	.198672	.193285	.188032	.182910	.177916	.173047	.168301	.163675
13	.184259	.178877	.173640	.168544	.163588	.158766	.154075	.149513	.145076	.140760
14	.161779	.156696	.151761	.146971	.142321	.137809	.133429	.129179	.125055	.121054
15	.142042	.137266	.132639	.128158	.123819	.119618	.115550	.111611	.107798	.104106
16	.124713	.120245	.115927	.111754	.107723	.103828	.100066	.096432	.092922	.089531
17	.109498	.105334	.101320	.097450	.093719	.090123	.086657	.083317	.080098	.076997
18	.096139	.092273	.088554	.084976	.081535	.078227	.075045	.071986	.069045	.066217
19	.084410	.080831	.077396	.074099	.070936	.067901	.064989	.062196	.059517	.056947
20	.074112	.070808	.067644	.064614	.061714	.058938	.056280	.053737	.051303	.048974

TABLE F(4.2), WITH INTEREST AT 4.2 PERCENT, SHOWING FACTORS FOR COMPUTATION OF THE ADJUSTED PAYOUT RATE FOR CERTAIN VALUATIONS APPLICABLE AFTER APRIL 30, 1989

1 NUMBER OF MONTHS BY WHICH THE VALUATION DATE FOR THE FIRST FULL TAXABLE YEAR OF THE TRUST PRECEDES THE FIRST PAYOUT		2 FACTORS FOR PAYOUT AT THE END OF EACH PERIOD			
AT LEAST	*BUT LESS THAN*	*ANNUAL PERIOD*	*SEMIANNUAL PERIOD*	*QUARTERLY PERIOD*	*MONTHLY PERIOD*
. .	1	1.000000	.989820	.984755	.981389
1	2	.996577	.986432	.981385	.978030
2	3	.993166	.983056	.978026	
3	4	.989767	.979691	.974679	
4	5	.986380	.976338		
5	6	.983004	.972996		
6	7	.979639	.969666		
7	8	.976286			
8	9	.972945			
9	10	.969615			
10	11	.966296			
11	12	.962989			
12	. .	.959693			

TABLE F(4.4), WITH INTEREST AT 4.4 PERCENT, SHOWING FACTORS FOR COMPUTATION OF THE ADJUSTED PAYOUT RATE FOR CERTAIN VALUATIONS APPLICABLE AFTER APRIL 30, 1989

1 NUMBER OF MONTHS BY WHICH THE VALUATION DATE FOR THE FIRST FULL TAXABLE YEAR OF THE TRUST PRECEDES THE FIRST PAYOUT		2 FACTORS FOR PAYOUT AT THE END OF EACH PERIOD			
AT LEAST	*BUT LESS THAN*	*ANNUAL PERIOD*	*SEMIANNUAL PERIOD*	*QUARTERLY PERIOD*	*MONTHLY PERIOD*
. .	1	1.000000	.989350	.984054	.980533
1	2	.996418	.985806	.980529	.977021
2	3	.992849	.982275	.977017	
3	4	.989293	.978757	.973517	
4	5	.985749	.975251		
5	6	.982219	.971758		
6	7	.978700	.968277		
7	8	.975195			
8	9	.971702			
9	10	.968221			
10	11	.964753			
11	12	.961298			
12	. .	.957854			

TABLE F(4.6), WITH INTEREST AT 4.6 PERCENT, SHOWING FACTORS FOR COMPUTATION OF THE ADJUSTED PAYOUT RATE FOR CERTAIN VALUATIONS APPLICABLE AFTER APRIL 30, 1989

1 NUMBER OF MONTHS BY WHICH THE VALUATION DATE FOR THE FIRST FULL TAXABLE YEAR OF THE TRUST PRECEDES THE FIRST PAYOUT		2 FACTORS FOR PAYOUT AT THE END OF EACH PERIOD			
AT LEAST	*BUT LESS THAN*	*ANNUAL PERIOD*	*SEMIANNUAL PERIOD*	*QUARTERLY PERIOD*	*MONTHLY PERIOD*
. .	1	1.000000	.988882	.983354	.979680
1	2	.996259	.985183	.979676	.976015
2	3	.992532	.981498	.976011	
3	4	.988820	.977826	.972360	
4	5	.985121	.974168		
5	6	.981436	.970524		
6	7	.977764	.966894		
7	8	.974107			
8	9	.970463			
9	10	.966832			
10	11	.963216			
11	12	.959613			
12	. .	.956023			

See p. 15 for regulations not amended to reflect law changes

TABLE F(4.8), WITH INTEREST AT 4.8 PERCENT, SHOWING FACTORS FOR COMPUTATION OF THE ADJUSTED PAYOUT RATE FOR CERTAIN VALUATIONS APPLICABLE AFTER APRIL 30, 1989

1 NUMBER OF MONTHS BY WHICH THE VALUATION DATE FOR THE FIRST FULL TAXABLE YEAR OF THE TRUST PRECEDES THE FIRST PAYOUT		2 FACTORS FOR PAYOUT AT THE END OF EACH PERIOD			
AT LEAST	*BUT LESS THAN*	*ANNUAL PERIOD*	*SEMIANNUAL PERIOD*	*QUARTERLY PERIOD*	*MONTHLY PERIOD*
. .	1	1.000000	.988415	.982657	.978830
1	2	.996101	.984561	.978825	.975013
2	3	.992217	.980722	.975008	
3	4	.988348	.976898	.971206	
4	5	.984494	.973089		
5	6	.980655	.969294		
6	7	.976831	.965515		
7	8	.973022			
8	9	.969228			
9	10	.965448			
10	11	.961684			
11	12	.957934			
12	. .	.954198			

TABLE F(5.0), WITH INTEREST AT 5.0 PERCENT, SHOWING FACTORS FOR COMPUTATION OF THE ADJUSTED PAYOUT RATE FOR CERTAIN VALUATIONS APPLICABLE AFTER APRIL 30, 1989

1 NUMBER OF MONTHS BY WHICH THE VALUATION DATE FOR THE FIRST FULL TAXABLE YEAR OF THE TRUST PRECEDES THE FIRST PAYOUT		2 FACTORS FOR PAYOUT AT THE END OF EACH PERIOD			
AT LEAST	*BUT LESS THAN*	*ANNUAL PERIOD*	*SEMIANNUAL PERIOD*	*QUARTERLY PERIOD*	*MONTHLY PERIOD*
. .	1	1.000000	.987950	.981961	.977982
1	2	.995942	.983941	.977977	.974014
2	3	.991901	.979949	.974009	
3	4	.987877	.975973	.970057	
4	5	.983868	.972013		
5	6	.979876	.968069		
6	7	.975900	.964141		
7	8	.971940			
8	9	.967997			
9	10	.964069			
10	11	.960157			
11	12	.956261			
12	. .	.952381			

TABLE F(5.2), WITH INTEREST AT 5.2 PERCENT, SHOWING FACTORS FOR COMPUTATION OF THE ADJUSTED PAYOUT RATE FOR CERTAIN VALUATIONS APPLICABLE AFTER APRIL 30, 1989

1 NUMBER OF MONTHS BY WHICH THE VALUATION DATE FOR THE FIRST FULL TAXABLE YEAR OF THE TRUST PRECEDES THE FIRST PAYOUT		2 FACTORS FOR PAYOUT AT THE END OF EACH PERIOD			
AT LEAST	*BUT LESS THAN*	*ANNUAL PERIOD*	*SEMIANNUAL PERIOD*	*QUARTERLY PERIOD*	*MONTHLY PERIOD*
. .	1	1.000000	.987486	.981268	.977137
1	2	.995784	.983323	.977132	.973018
2	3	.991587	.979178	.973012	
3	4	.987407	.975050	.968911	
4	5	.983244	.970940		
5	6	.979099	.966847		
6	7	.974972	.962771		
7	8	.970862			
8	9	.966769			
9	10	.962694			
10	11	.958636			
11	12	.954594			
12	. .	.950570			

TABLE F(5.4), WITH INTEREST AT 5.4 PERCENT, SHOWING FACTORS FOR COMPUTATION OF THE ADJUSTED PAYOUT RATE FOR CERTAIN VALUATIONS APPLICABLE AFTER APRIL 30, 1989

1 NUMBER OF MONTHS BY WHICH THE VALUATION DATE FOR THE FIRST FULL TAXABLE YEAR OF THE TRUST PRECEDES THE FIRST PAYOUT		2 FACTORS FOR PAYOUT AT THE END OF EACH PERIOD			
AT LEAST	*BUT LESS THAN*	*ANNUAL PERIOD*	*SEMIANNUAL PERIOD*	*QUARTERLY PERIOD*	*MONTHLY PERIOD*
. .	1	1.000000	.987023	.980577	.976295
1	2	.995627	.982707	.976289	.972026
2	3	.991273	.978409	.972019	
3	4	.986938	.974131	.967769	
4	5	.982622	.969871		
5	6	.978325	.965629		
6	7	.974047	.961407		
7	8	.969787			
8	9	.965546			
9	10	.961323			
10	11	.957119			
11	12	.952934			
12	. .	.948767			

TABLE F(5.6), WITH INTEREST AT 5.6 PERCENT, SHOWING FACTORS FOR COMPUTATION OF THE ADJUSTED PAYOUT RATE FOR CERTAIN VALUATIONS APPLICABLE AFTER APRIL 30, 1989

1 NUMBER OF MONTHS BY WHICH THE VALUATION DATE FOR THE FIRST FULL TAXABLE YEAR OF THE TRUST PRECEDES THE FIRST PAYOUT		2 FACTORS FOR PAYOUT AT THE END OF EACH PERIOD			
AT LEAST	*BUT LESS THAN*	*ANNUAL PERIOD*	*SEMIANNUAL PERIOD*	*QUARTERLY PERIOD*	*MONTHLY PERIOD*
.	1	1.000000	.986562	.979888	.975455
1	2	.995470	.982092	.975449	.971036
2	3	.990960	.977643	.971029	
3	4	.986470	.973214	.966630	
4	5	.982001	.968805		
5	6	.977552	.964416		
6	7	.973124	.960047		
7	8	.968715			
8	9	.964326			
9	10	.959958			
10	11	.955609			
11	12	.951279			
12	.	.946970			

TABLE F(5.8), WITH INTEREST AT 5.8 PERCENT, SHOWING FACTORS FOR COMPUTATION OF THE ADJUSTED PAYOUT RATE FOR CERTAIN VALUATIONS APPLICABLE AFTER APRIL 30, 1989

1 NUMBER OF MONTHS BY WHICH THE VALUATION DATE FOR THE FIRST FULL TAXABLE YEAR OF THE TRUST PRECEDES THE FIRST PAYOUT		2 FACTORS FOR PAYOUT AT THE END OF EACH PERIOD			
AT LEAST	*BUT LESS THAN*	*ANNUAL PERIOD*	*SEMIANNUAL PERIOD*	*QUARTERLY PERIOD*	*MONTHLY PERIOD*
.	1	1.000000	.986102	.979201	.974618
1	2	.995313	.981480	.974611	.970050
2	3	.990647	.976879	.970043	
3	4	.986004	.972300	.965496	
4	5	.981382	.967743		
5	6	.976782	.963206		
6	7	.972203	.958692		
7	8	.967646			
8	9	.963111			
9	10	.958596			
10	11	.954103			
11	12	.949631			
12	.	.945180			

See p. 15 for regulations not amended to reflect law changes

TABLE F(6.0), WITH INTEREST AT 6.0 PERCENT, SHOWING FACTORS FOR COMPUTATION OF THE ADJUSTED PAYOUT RATE FOR CERTAIN VALUATIONS APPLICABLE AFTER APRIL 30, 1989

1 NUMBER OF MONTHS BY WHICH THE VALUATION DATE FOR THE FIRST FULL TAXABLE YEAR OF THE TRUST PRECEDES THE FIRST PAYOUT		2 FACTORS FOR PAYOUT AT THE END OF EACH PERIOD			
AT LEAST	*BUT LESS THAN*	*ANNUAL PERIOD*	*SEMIANNUAL PERIOD*	*QUARTERLY PERIOD*	*MONTHLY PERIOD*
.	1	1.000000	.985643	.978516	.973784
1	2	.995156	.980869	.973776	.969067
2	3	.990336	.976117	.969059	
3	4	.985538	.971389	.964365	
4	5	.980764	.966684		
5	6	.976014	.962001		
6	7	.971286	.957341		
7	8	.966581			
8	9	.961899			
9	10	.957239			
10	11	.952603			
11	12	.947988			
12	.	.943396			

TABLE F(6.2), WITH INTEREST AT 6.2 PERCENT, SHOWING FACTORS FOR COMPUTATION OF THE ADJUSTED PAYOUT RATE FOR CERTAIN VALUATIONS APPLICABLE AFTER APRIL 30, 1989

1 NUMBER OF MONTHS BY WHICH THE VALUATION DATE FOR THE FIRST FULL TAXABLE YEAR OF THE TRUST PRECEDES THE FIRST PAYOUT		2 FACTORS FOR PAYOUT AT THE END OF EACH PERIOD			
AT LEAST	*BUT LESS THAN*	*ANNUAL PERIOD*	*SEMIANNUAL PERIOD*	*QUARTERLY PERIOD*	*MONTHLY PERIOD*
.	1	1.000000	.985185	.977833	.972952
1	2	.995000	.980259	.972944	.968087
2	3	.990024	.975358	.968079	
3	4	.985074	.970481	.963238	
4	5	.980148	.965628		
5	6	.975247	.960799		
6	7	.970371	.955995		
7	8	.965519			
8	9	.960691			
9	10	.955887			
10	11	.951107			
11	12	.946352			
12	.	.941620			

See p. 15 for regulations not amended to reflect law changes

TABLE F(6.4), WITH INTEREST AT 6.4 PERCENT, SHOWING FACTORS FOR COMPUTATION OF THE ADJUSTED PAYOUT RATE FOR CERTAIN VALUATIONS APPLICABLE AFTER APRIL 30, 1989

1 NUMBER OF MONTHS BY WHICH THE VALUATION DATE FOR THE FIRST FULL TAXABLE YEAR OF THE TRUST PRECEDES THE FIRST PAYOUT		2 FACTORS FOR PAYOUT AT THE END OF EACH PERIOD			
AT LEAST	*BUT LESS THAN*	*ANNUAL PERIOD*	*SEMIANNUAL PERIOD*	*QUARTERLY PERIOD*	*MONTHLY PERIOD*
.	1	1.000000	.984729	.977152	.972122
1	2	.994844	.979652	.972114	.967110
2	3	.989714	.974600	.967101	
3	4	.984611	.969575	.962115	
4	5	.979534	.964576		
5	6	.974483	.959602		
6	7	.969458	.954654		
7	8	.964460			
8	9	.959487			
9	10	.954539			
10	11	.949617			
11	12	.944721			
12	.	.939850			

TABLE F(6.6), WITH INTEREST AT 6.6 PERCENT, SHOWING FACTORS FOR COMPUTATION OF THE ADJUSTED PAYOUT RATE FOR CERTAIN VALUATIONS APPLICABLE AFTER APRIL 30, 1989

1 NUMBER OF MONTHS BY WHICH THE VALUATION DATE FOR THE FIRST FULL TAXABLE YEAR OF THE TRUST PRECEDES THE FIRST PAYOUT		2 FACTORS FOR PAYOUT AT THE END OF EACH PERIOD			
AT LEAST	*BUT LESS THAN*	*ANNUAL PERIOD*	*SEMIANNUAL PERIOD*	*QUARTERLY PERIOD*	*MONTHLY PERIOD*
.	1	1.000000	.984274	.976473	.971295
1	2	.994688	.979046	.971286	.966136
2	3	.989404	.973845	.966127	
3	4	.984149	.968672	.960995	
4	5	.978921	.963527		
5	6	.973721	.958408		
6	7	.968549	.953317		
7	8	.963404			
8	9	.958286			
9	10	.953196			
10	11	.948132			
11	12	.943096			
12	.	.938086			

TABLE F(6.8), WITH INTEREST AT 6.8 PERCENT, SHOWING FACTORS FOR COMPUTATION OF THE ADJUSTED PAYOUT RATE FOR CERTAIN VALUATIONS APPLICABLE AFTER APRIL 30, 1989

1		2			
NUMBER OF MONTHS BY WHICH THE VALUATION DATE FOR THE FIRST FULL TAXABLE YEAR OF THE TRUST PRECEDES THE FIRST PAYOUT		FACTORS FOR PAYOUT AT THE END OF EACH PERIOD			
AT LEAST	*BUT LESS THAN*	*ANNUAL PERIOD*	*SEMIANNUAL PERIOD*	*QUARTERLY PERIOD*	*MONTHLY PERIOD*
.	1	1.000000	.983821	.975796	.970471
1	2	.994533	.978442	.970461	.965165
2	3	.989095	.973092	.965156	
3	4	.983688	.967772	.959879	
4	5	.978309	.962481		
5	6	.972961	.957219		
6	7	.967641	.951985		
7	8	.962351			
8	9	.957089			
9	10	.951857			
10	11	.946653			
11	12	.941477			
12	.	.936330			

TABLE F(7.0), WITH INTEREST AT 7.0 PERCENT, SHOWING FACTORS FOR COMPUTATION OF THE ADJUSTED PAYOUT RATE FOR CERTAIN VALUATIONS APPLICABLE AFTER APRIL 30, 1989

1		2			
NUMBER OF MONTHS BY WHICH THE VALUATION DATE FOR THE FIRST FULL TAXABLE YEAR OF THE TRUST PRECEDES THE FIRST PAYOUT		FACTORS FOR PAYOUT AT THE END OF EACH PERIOD			
AT LEAST	*BUT LESS THAN*	*ANNUAL PERIOD*	*SEMIANNUAL PERIOD*	*QUARTERLY PERIOD*	*MONTHLY PERIOD*
. .	1	1.000000	.983368	.975122	.969649
1	2	.994378	.977839	.969639	.964198
2	3	.988787	.972342	.964187	
3	4	.983228	.966875	.958766	
4	5	.977700	.961439		
5	6	.972203	.956033		
6	7	.966736	.950658		
7	8	.961301			
8	9	.955896			
9	10	.950522			
10	11	.945178			
11	12	.939864			
12	. .	.934579			

TABLE F(7.2), WITH INTEREST AT 7.2 PERCENT, SHOWING FACTORS FOR COMPUTATION OF THE ADJUSTED PAYOUT RATE FOR CERTAIN VALUATIONS APPLICABLE AFTER APRIL 30, 1989

1 NUMBER OF MONTHS BY WHICH THE VALUATION DATE FOR THE FIRST FULL TAXABLE YEAR OF THE TRUST PRECEDES THE FIRST PAYOUT		2 FACTORS FOR PAYOUT AT THE END OF EACH PERIOD			
AT LEAST	*BUT LESS THAN*	*ANNUAL PERIOD*	*SEMIANNUAL PERIOD*	*QUARTERLY PERIOD*	*MONTHLY PERIOD*
. .	1	1.000000	.982917	.974449	.968830
1	2	.994223	.977239	.968819	.963233
2	3	.988479	.971593	.963222	
3	4	.982769	.965980	.957658	
4	5	.977091	.960400		
5	6	.971446	.954851		
6	7	.965834	.949335		
7	8	.960255			
8	9	.954707			
9	10	.949192			
10	11	.943708			
11	12	.938256			
12	. .	.932836			

TABLE F(7.4), WITH INTEREST AT 7.4 PERCENT, SHOWING FACTORS FOR COMPUTATION OF THE ADJUSTED PAYOUT RATE FOR CERTAIN VALUATIONS APPLICABLE AFTER APRIL 30, 1989

1 NUMBER OF MONTHS BY WHICH THE VALUATION DATE FOR THE FIRST FULL TAXABLE YEAR OF THE TRUST PRECEDES THE FIRST PAYOUT		2 FACTORS FOR PAYOUT AT THE END OF EACH PERIOD			
AT LEAST	*BUT LESS THAN*	*ANNUAL PERIOD*	*SEMIANNUAL PERIOD*	*QUARTERLY PERIOD*	*MONTHLY PERIOD*
. .	1	1.000000	.982467	.973778	.968013
1	2	.994068	.976640	.968002	.962271
2	3	.988172	.970847	.962260	
3	4	.982311	.965088	.956552	
4	5	.976484	.959364		
5	6	.970692	.953673		
6	7	.964935	.948017		
7	8	.959211			
8	9	.953521			
9	10	.947866			
10	11	.942243			
11	12	.936654			
12	. .	.931099			

TABLE F(7.6), WITH INTEREST AT 7.6 PERCENT, SHOWING FACTORS FOR COMPUTATION OF THE ADJUSTED PAYOUT RATE FOR CERTAIN VALUATIONS APPLICABLE AFTER APRIL 30, 1989

1		2			
NUMBER OF MONTHS BY WHICH THE VALUATION DATE FOR THE FIRST FULL TAXABLE YEAR OF THE TRUST PRECEDES THE FIRST PAYOUT		FACTORS FOR PAYOUT AT THE END OF EACH PERIOD			
AT LEAST	*BUT LESS THAN*	*ANNUAL PERIOD*	*SEMIANNUAL PERIOD*	*QUARTERLY PERIOD*	*MONTHLY PERIOD*
. .	1	1.000000	.982019	.973109	.967199
1	2	.993914	.976042	.967187	.961313
2	3	.987866	.970103	.961301	
3	4	.981854	.964199	.955451	
4	5	.975879	.958331		
5	6	.969940	.952499		
6	7	.964037	.946703		
7	8	.958171			
8	9	.952340			
9	10	.946544			
10	11	.940784			
11	12	.935058			
12	. .	.929368			

TABLE F(7.8), WITH INTEREST AT 7.8 PERCENT, SHOWING FACTORS FOR COMPUTATION OF THE ADJUSTED PAYOUT RATE FOR CERTAIN VALUATIONS APPLICABLE AFTER APRIL 30, 1989

1		2			
NUMBER OF MONTHS BY WHICH THE VALUATION DATE FOR THE FIRST FULL TAXABLE YEAR OF THE TRUST PRECEDES THE FIRST PAYOUT		FACTORS FOR PAYOUT AT THE END OF EACH PERIOD			
AT LEAST	*BUT LESS THAN*	*ANNUAL PERIOD*	*SEMIANNUAL PERIOD*	*QUARTERLY PERIOD*	*MONTHLY PERIOD*
. .	1	1.000000	.981571	.972442	.966387
1	2	.993761	.975447	.966374	.960357
2	3	.987560	.969361	.960345	
3	4	.981398	.963312	.954353	
4	5	.975275	.957302		
5	6	.969190	.951329		
6	7	.963143	.945393		
7	8	.957133			
8	9	.951161			
9	10	.945227			
10	11	.939329			
11	12	.933468			
12	. .	.927644			

TABLE F(8.0), WITH INTEREST AT 8.0 PERCENT, SHOWING FACTORS FOR COMPUTATION OF THE ADJUSTED PAYOUT RATE FOR CERTAIN VALUATIONS APPLICABLE AFTER APRIL 30, 1989

1 NUMBER OF MONTHS BY WHICH THE VALUATION DATE FOR THE FIRST FULL TAXABLE YEAR OF THE TRUST PRECEDES THE FIRST PAYOUT		2 FACTORS FOR PAYOUT AT THE END OF EACH PERIOD			
AT LEAST	*BUT LESS THAN*	*ANNUAL PERIOD*	*SEMIANNUAL PERIOD*	*QUARTERLY PERIOD*	*MONTHLY PERIOD*
. .	1	1.000000	.981125	.971777	.965578
1	2	.993607	.974853	.965564	.959405
2	3	.987255	.968621	.959392	
3	4	.980944	.962429	.953258	
4	5	.974673	.956276		
5	6	.968442	.950162		
6	7	.962250	.944088		
7	8	.956099			
8	9	.949987			
9	10	.943913			
10	11	.937879			
11	12	.931883			
12	. .	.925926			

TABLE F(8.2), WITH INTEREST AT 8.2 PERCENT, SHOWING FACTORS FOR COMPUTATION OF THE ADJUSTED PAYOUT RATE FOR CERTAIN VALUATIONS APPLICABLE AFTER APRIL 30, 1989

1 NUMBER OF MONTHS BY WHICH THE VALUATION DATE FOR THE FIRST FULL TAXABLE YEAR OF THE TRUST PRECEDES THE FIRST PAYOUT		2 FACTORS FOR PAYOUT AT THE END OF EACH PERIOD			
AT LEAST	*BUT LESS THAN*	*ANNUAL PERIOD*	*SEMIANNUAL PERIOD*	*QUARTERLY PERIOD*	*MONTHLY PERIOD*
. .	1	1.000000	.980680	.971114	.964771
1	2	.993454	.974261	.964757	.958455
2	3	.986951	.967883	.958441	
3	4	.980490	.961547	.952167	
4	5	.974072	.955253		
5	6	.967695	.949000		
6	7	.961361	.942788		
7	8	.955068			
8	9	.948816			
9	10	.942605			
10	11	.936434			
11	12	.930304			
12	. .	.924214			

TABLE F(8.4), WITH INTEREST AT 8.4 PERCENT, SHOWING FACTORS FOR COMPUTATION OF THE ADJUSTED PAYOUT RATE FOR CERTAIN VALUATIONS APPLICABLE AFTER APRIL 30, 1989

1 NUMBER OF MONTHS BY WHICH THE VALUATION DATE FOR THE FIRST FULL TAXABLE YEAR OF THE TRUST PRECEDES THE FIRST PAYOUT		2 FACTORS FOR PAYOUT AT THE END OF EACH PERIOD			
AT LEAST	*BUT LESS THAN*	*ANNUAL PERIOD*	*SEMIANNUAL PERIOD*	*QUARTERLY PERIOD*	*MONTHLY PERIOD*
. .	1	1.000000	.980237	.970453	.963966
1	2	.993301	.973670	.963952	.957509
2	3	.986647	.967148	.957494	
3	4	.980037	.960669	.951080	
4	5	.973472	.954233		
5	6	.966951	.947841		
6	7	.960473	.941491		
7	8	.954039			
8	9	.947648			
9	10	.941300			
10	11	.934994			
11	12	.928731			
12	. .	.922509			

TABLE F(8.6), WITH INTEREST AT 8.6 PERCENT, SHOWING FACTORS FOR COMPUTATION OF THE ADJUSTED PAYOUT RATE FOR CERTAIN VALUATIONS APPLICABLE AFTER APRIL 30, 1989

1 NUMBER OF MONTHS BY WHICH THE VALUATION DATE FOR THE FIRST FULL TAXABLE YEAR OF THE TRUST PRECEDES THE FIRST PAYOUT		2 FACTORS FOR PAYOUT AT THE END OF EACH PERIOD			
AT LEAST	*BUT LESS THAN*	*ANNUAL PERIOD*	*SEMIANNUAL PERIOD*	*QUARTERLY PERIOD*	*MONTHLY PERIOD*
. .	1	1.000000	.979794	.969794	.963164
1	2	.993148	.973081	.963149	.956565
2	3	.986344	.966414	.956550	
3	4	.979586	.959793	.949996	
4	5	.972874	.953217		
5	6	.966209	.946686		
6	7	.959589	.940199		
7	8	.953014			
8	9	.946484			
9	10	.940000			
10	11	.933559			
11	12	.927163			
12	. .	.920810			

See p. 15 for regulations not amended to reflect law changes

TABLE F(8.8), WITH INTEREST AT 8.8 PERCENT, SHOWING FACTORS FOR COMPUTATION OF THE ADJUSTED PAYOUT RATE FOR CERTAIN VALUATIONS APPLICABLE AFTER APRIL 30, 1989

1 NUMBER OF MONTHS BY WHICH THE VALUATION DATE FOR THE FIRST FULL TAXABLE YEAR OF THE TRUST PRECEDES THE FIRST PAYOUT		2 FACTORS FOR PAYOUT AT THE END OF EACH PERIOD			
AT LEAST	*BUT LESS THAN*	*ANNUAL PERIOD*	*SEMIANNUAL PERIOD*	*QUARTERLY PERIOD*	*MONTHLY PERIOD*
. .	1	1.000000	.979353	.969136	.962364
1	2	.992996	.972494	.962349	.955624
2	3	.986041	.965683	.955609	
3	4	.979135	.958919	.948916	
4	5	.972278	.952203		
5	6	.965468	.945534		
6	7	.958706	.938912		
7	8	.951992			
8	9	.945324			
9	10	.938703			
10	11	.932129			
11	12	.925600			
12	. .	.919118			

TABLE F(9.0), WITH INTEREST AT 9.0 PERCENT, SHOWING FACTORS FOR COMPUTATION OF THE ADJUSTED PAYOUT RATE FOR CERTAIN VALUATIONS APPLICABLE AFTER APRIL 30, 1989

1 NUMBER OF MONTHS BY WHICH THE VALUATION DATE FOR THE FIRST FULL TAXABLE YEAR OF THE TRUST PRECEDES THE FIRST PAYOUT		2 FACTORS FOR PAYOUT AT THE END OF EACH PERIOD			
AT LEAST	*BUT LESS THAN*	*ANNUAL PERIOD*	*SEMIANNUAL PERIOD*	*QUARTERLY PERIOD*	*MONTHLY PERIOD*
. .	1	1.000000	.978913	.968481	.961567
1	2	.992844	.971908	.961551	.954686
2	3	.985740	.964954	.954670	
3	4	.978686	.958049	.947839	
4	5	.971683	.951193		
5	6	.964730	.944387		
6	7	.957826	.937629		
7	8	.950972			
8	9	.944167			
9	10	.937411			
10	11	.930703			
11	12	.924043			
12	. .	.917431			

TABLE F(9.2), WITH INTEREST AT 9.2 PERCENT, SHOWING FACTORS FOR COMPUTATION OF THE ADJUSTED PAYOUT RATE FOR CERTAIN VALUATIONS APPLICABLE AFTER APRIL 30, 1989

1 NUMBER OF MONTHS BY WHICH THE VALUATION DATE FOR THE FIRST FULL TAXABLE YEAR OF THE TRUST PRECEDES THE FIRST PAYOUT		2 FACTORS FOR PAYOUT AT THE END OF EACH PERIOD			
AT LEAST	*BUT LESS THAN*	*ANNUAL PERIOD*	*SEMIANNUAL PERIOD*	*QUARTERLY PERIOD*	*MONTHLY PERIOD*
. .	1	1.000000	.978474	.967827	.960772
1	2	.992693	.971324	.960755	.953752
2	3	.985439	.964226	.953734	
3	4	.978238	.957180	.946765	
4	5	.971089	.950186		
5	6	.963993	.943242		
6	7	.956949	.936350		
7	8	.949956			
8	9	.943014			
9	10	.936123			
10	11	.929283			
11	12	.922492			
12	. .	.915751			

TABLE F(9.4), WITH INTEREST AT 9.4 PERCENT, SHOWING FACTORS FOR COMPUTATION OF THE ADJUSTED PAYOUT RATE FOR CERTAIN VALUATIONS APPLICABLE AFTER APRIL 30, 1989

1 NUMBER OF MONTHS BY WHICH THE VALUATION DATE FOR THE FIRST FULL TAXABLE YEAR OF THE TRUST PRECEDES THE FIRST PAYOUT		2 FACTORS FOR PAYOUT AT THE END OF EACH PERIOD			
AT LEAST	*BUT LESS THAN*	*ANNUAL PERIOD*	*SEMIANNUAL PERIOD*	*QUARTERLY PERIOD*	*MONTHLY PERIOD*
. .	1	1.000000	.978037	.967176	.959980
1	2	.992541	.970742	.959962	.952820
2	3	.985138	.963501	.952802	
3	4	.977790	.956315	.945695	
4	5	.970497	.949182		
5	6	.963258	.942102		
6	7	.956074	.935075		
7	8	.948942			
8	9	.941865			
9	10	.934839			
10	11	.927867			
11	12	.920946			
12	. .	.914077			

See p. 15 for regulations not amended to reflect law changes

TABLE F(9.6), WITH INTEREST AT 9.6 PERCENT, SHOWING FACTORS FOR COMPUTATION OF THE ADJUSTED PAYOUT RATE FOR CERTAIN VALUATIONS APPLICABLE AFTER APRIL 30, 1989

1		2			
NUMBER OF MONTHS BY WHICH THE VALUATION DATE FOR THE FIRST FULL TAXABLE YEAR OF THE TRUST PRECEDES THE FIRST PAYOUT		FACTORS FOR PAYOUT AT THE END OF EACH PERIOD			
AT LEAST	*BUT LESS THAN*	*ANNUAL PERIOD*	*SEMIANNUAL PERIOD*	*QUARTERLY PERIOD*	*MONTHLY PERIOD*
. .	1	1.000000	.977600	.966526	.959190
1	2	.992390	.970161	.959171	.951890
2	3	.984838	.962778	.951872	
3	4	.977344	.955452	.944628	
4	5	.969906	.948181		
5	6	.962526	.940965		
6	7	.955201	.933805		
7	8	.947932			
8	9	.940718			
9	10	.933560			
10	11	.926455			
11	12	.919405			
12	. .	.912409			

TABLE F(9.8), WITH INTEREST AT 9.8 PERCENT, SHOWING FACTORS FOR COMPUTATION OF THE ADJUSTED PAYOUT RATE FOR CERTAIN VALUATIONS APPLICABLE AFTER APRIL 30, 1989

1		2			
NUMBER OF MONTHS BY WHICH THE VALUATION DATE FOR THE FIRST FULL TAXABLE YEAR OF THE TRUST PRECEDES THE FIRST PAYOUT		FACTORS FOR PAYOUT AT THE END OF EACH PERIOD			
AT LEAST	*BUT LESS THAN*	*ANNUAL PERIOD*	*SEMIANNUAL PERIOD*	*QUARTERLY PERIOD*	*MONTHLY PERIOD*
. .	1	1.000000	.977165	.965878	.958402
1	2	.992239	.969582	.958382	.950964
2	3	.984539	.962057	.950945	
3	4	.976898	.954591	.943565	
4	5	.969317	.947183		
5	6	.961795	.939832		
6	7	.954331	.932539		
7	8	.946924			
8	9	.939576			
9	10	.932284			
10	11	.925049			
11	12	.917870			
12	. .	.910747			

TABLE F(10.0), WITH INTEREST AT 10.0 PERCENT, SHOWING FACTORS FOR COMPUTATION OF THE ADJUSTED PAYOUT RATE FOR CERTAIN VALUATIONS APPLICABLE AFTER APRIL 30, 1989

1 NUMBER OF MONTHS BY WHICH THE VALUATION DATE FOR THE FIRST FULL TAXABLE YEAR OF THE TRUST PRECEDES THE FIRST PAYOUT		2 FACTORS FOR PAYOUT AT THE END OF EACH PERIOD			
AT LEAST	*BUT LESS THAN*	*ANNUAL PERIOD*	*SEMIANNUAL PERIOD*	*QUARTERLY PERIOD*	*MONTHLY PERIOD*
..	1	1.000000	.976731	.965232	.957616
1	2	.992089	.969004	.957596	.950041
2	3	.984240	.961338	.950021	
3	4	.976454	.953733	.942505	
4	5	.968729	.946188		
5	6	.961066	.938703		
6	7	.953463	.931277		
7	8	.945920			
8	9	.938436			
9	10	.931012			
10	11	.923647			
11	12	.916340			
12	..	.909091			

TABLE F(10.2), WITH INTEREST AT 10.2 PERCENT, SHOWING FACTORS FOR COMPUTATION OF THE ADJUSTED PAYOUT RATE FOR CERTAIN VALUATIONS APPLICABLE AFTER APRIL 30, 1989

1 NUMBER OF MONTHS BY WHICH THE VALUATION DATE FOR THE FIRST FULL TAXABLE YEAR OF THE TRUST PRECEDES THE FIRST PAYOUT		2 FACTORS FOR PAYOUT AT THE END OF EACH PERIOD			
AT LEAST	*BUT LESS THAN*	*ANNUAL PERIOD*	*SEMIANNUAL PERIOD*	*QUARTERLY PERIOD*	*MONTHLY PERIOD*
..	1	1.000000	.976298	.964588	.956833
1	2	.991939	.968428	.956812	.949120
2	3	.983943	.960622	.949099	
3	4	.976011	.952878	.941448	
4	5	.968143	.945196		
5	6	.960338	.937577		
6	7	.952597	.930019		
7	8	.944918			
8	9	.937301			
9	10	.929745			
10	11	.922250			
11	12	.914816			
12	..	.907441			

TABLE F(10.4), WITH INTEREST AT 10.4 PERCENT, SHOWING FACTORS FOR COMPUTATION OF THE ADJUSTED PAYOUT RATE FOR CERTAIN VALUATIONS APPLICABLE AFTER APRIL 30, 1989

1 NUMBER OF MONTHS BY WHICH THE VALUATION DATE FOR THE FIRST FULL TAXABLE YEAR OF THE TRUST PRECEDES THE FIRST PAYOUT		2 FACTORS FOR PAYOUT AT THE END OF EACH PERIOD			
AT LEAST	*BUT LESS THAN*	*ANNUAL PERIOD*	*SEMIANNUAL PERIOD*	*QUARTERLY PERIOD*	*MONTHLY PERIOD*
. .	1	1.000000	.975867	.963946	.956052
1	2	.991789	.967854	.956031	.948202
2	3	.983645	.959907	.948181	
3	4	.975568	.952025	.940395	
4	5	.967558	.944208		
5	6	.959613	.936455		
6	7	.951734	.928765		
7	8	.943919			
8	9	.936168			
9	10	.928481			
10	11	.920858			
11	12	.913296			
12	. .	.905797			

TABLE F(10.6), WITH INTEREST AT 10.6 PERCENT, SHOWING FACTORS FOR COMPUTATION OF THE ADJUSTED PAYOUT RATE FOR CERTAIN VALUATIONS APPLICABLE AFTER APRIL 30, 1989

1 NUMBER OF MONTHS BY WHICH THE VALUATION DATE FOR THE FIRST FULL TAXABLE YEAR OF THE TRUST PRECEDES THE FIRST PAYOUT		2 FACTORS FOR PAYOUT AT THE END OF EACH PERIOD			
AT LEAST	*BUT LESS THAN*	*ANNUAL PERIOD*	*SEMIANNUAL PERIOD*	*QUARTERLY PERIOD*	*MONTHLY PERIOD*
. .	1	1.000000	.975436	.963305	.955274
1	2	.991639	.967281	.955252	.947287
2	3	.983349	.959194	.947265	
3	4	.975127	.951174	.939345	
4	5	.966974	.943222		
5	6	.958890	.935336		
6	7	.950873	.927516		
7	8	.942923			
8	9	.935039			
9	10	.927222			
10	11	.919470			
11	12	.911782			
12	. .	.904159			

See p. 15 for regulations not amended to reflect law changes

TABLE F(10.8), WITH INTEREST AT 10.8 PERCENT, SHOWING FACTORS FOR COMPUTATION OF THE ADJUSTED PAYOUT RATE FOR CERTAIN VALUATIONS APPLICABLE AFTER APRIL 30, 1989

1 NUMBER OF MONTHS BY WHICH THE VALUATION DATE FOR THE FIRST FULL TAXABLE YEAR OF THE TRUST PRECEDES THE FIRST PAYOUT		2 FACTORS FOR PAYOUT AT THE END OF EACH PERIOD			
AT LEAST	*BUT LESS THAN*	*ANNUAL PERIOD*	*SEMIANNUAL PERIOD*	*QUARTERLY PERIOD*	*MONTHLY PERIOD*
. .	1	1.000000	.975007	.962667	.954498
1	2	.991490	.966710	.954475	.946375
2	3	.983052	.958483	.946352	
3	4	.974687	.950327	.938299	
4	5	.966392	.942239		
5	6	.958168	.934221		
6	7	.950014	.926271		
7	8	.941930			
8	9	.933914			
9	10	.925966			
10	11	.918086			
11	12	.910273			
12	. .	.902527			

TABLE F(11.0), WITH INTEREST AT 11.0 PERCENT, SHOWING FACTORS FOR COMPUTATION OF THE ADJUSTED PAYOUT RATE FOR CERTAIN VALUATIONS APPLICABLE AFTER APRIL 30, 1989

1 NUMBER OF MONTHS BY WHICH THE VALUATION DATE FOR THE FIRST FULL TAXABLE YEAR OF THE TRUST PRECEDES THE FIRST PAYOUT		2 FACTORS FOR PAYOUT AT THE END OF EACH PERIOD			
AT LEAST	*BUT LESS THAN*	*ANNUAL PERIOD*	*SEMIANNUAL PERIOD*	*QUARTERLY PERIOD*	*MONTHLY PERIOD*
. .	1	1.000000	.974579	.962030	.953724
1	2	.991341	.966140	.953700	.945466
2	3	.982757	.957774	.945442	
3	4	.974247	.949481	.937255	
4	5	.965811	.941260		
5	6	.957449	.933109		
6	7	.949158	.925029		
7	8	.940939			
8	9	.932792			
9	10	.924715			
10	11	.916708			
11	12	.908770			
12	. .	.900901			

See p. 15 for regulations not amended to reflect law changes

TABLE F(11.2), WITH INTEREST AT 11.2 PERCENT, SHOWING FACTORS FOR COMPUTATION OF THE ADJUSTED PAYOUT RATE FOR CERTAIN VALUATIONS APPLICABLE AFTER APRIL 30, 1989

1 NUMBER OF MONTHS BY WHICH THE VALUATION DATE FOR THE FIRST FULL TAXABLE YEAR OF THE TRUST PRECEDES THE FIRST PAYOUT		2 FACTORS FOR PAYOUT AT THE END OF EACH PERIOD			
AT LEAST	*BUT LESS THAN*	*ANNUAL PERIOD*	*SEMIANNUAL PERIOD*	*QUARTERLY PERIOD*	*MONTHLY PERIOD*
. .	1	1.000000	.974152	.961395	.952952
1	2	.991192	.965572	.952927	.944559
2	3	.982462	.957068	.944534	
3	4	.973809	.948638	.936215	
4	5	.965232	.940283		
5	6	.956731	.932001		
6	7	.948304	.923792		
7	8	.939952			
8	9	.931673			
9	10	.923467			
10	11	.915333			
11	12	.907272			
12	. .	.899281			

TABLE F(11.4), WITH INTEREST AT 11.4 PERCENT, SHOWING FACTORS FOR COMPUTATION OF THE ADJUSTED PAYOUT RATE FOR CERTAIN VALUATIONS APPLICABLE AFTER APRIL 30, 1989

1 NUMBER OF MONTHS BY WHICH THE VALUATION DATE FOR THE FIRST FULL TAXABLE YEAR OF THE TRUST PRECEDES THE FIRST PAYOUT		2 FACTORS FOR PAYOUT AT THE END OF EACH PERIOD			
AT LEAST	*BUT LESS THAN*	*ANNUAL PERIOD*	*SEMIANNUAL PERIOD*	*QUARTERLY PERIOD*	*MONTHLY PERIOD*
. .	1	1.000000	.973726	.960762	.952183
1	2	.991044	.965005	.952157	.943655
2	3	.982168	.956363	.943630	
3	4	.973372	.947798	.935178	
4	5	.964654	.939309		
5	6	.956015	.930896		
6	7	.947452	.922559		
7	8	.938967			
8	9	.930557			
9	10	.922223			
10	11	.913964			
11	12	.905778			
12	. .	.897666			

See p. 15 for regulations not amended to reflect law changes

TABLE F(11.6), WITH INTEREST AT 11.6 PERCENT, SHOWING FACTORS FOR COMPUTATION OF THE ADJUSTED PAYOUT RATE FOR CERTAIN VALUATIONS APPLICABLE AFTER APRIL 30, 1989

1		2			
NUMBER OF MONTHS BY WHICH THE VALUATION DATE FOR THE FIRST FULL TAXABLE YEAR OF THE TRUST PRECEDES THE FIRST PAYOUT		FACTORS FOR PAYOUT AT THE END OF EACH PERIOD			
AT LEAST	*BUT LESS THAN*	*ANNUAL PERIOD*	*SEMIANNUAL PERIOD*	*QUARTERLY PERIOD*	*MONTHLY PERIOD*
. .	1	1.000000	.973302	.960130	.951416
1	2	.990896	.964440	.951389	.942754
2	3	.981874	.955660	.942728	
3	4	.972935	.946959	.934145	
4	5	.964077	.938338		
5	6	.955300	.929795		
6	7	.946603	.921330		
7	8	.937985			
8	9	.929445			
9	10	.920984			
10	11	.912599			
11	12	.904290			
12	. .	.896057			

TABLE F(11.8), WITH INTEREST AT 11.8 PERCENT, SHOWING FACTORS FOR COMPUTATION OF THE ADJUSTED PAYOUT RATE FOR CERTAIN VALUATIONS APPLICABLE AFTER APRIL 30, 1989

1		2			
NUMBER OF MONTHS BY WHICH THE VALUATION DATE FOR THE FIRST FULL TAXABLE YEAR OF THE TRUST PRECEDES THE FIRST PAYOUT		FACTORS FOR PAYOUT AT THE END OF EACH PERIOD			
AT LEAST	*BUT LESS THAN*	*ANNUAL PERIOD*	*SEMIANNUAL PERIOD*	*QUARTERLY PERIOD*	*MONTHLY PERIOD*
. .	1	1.000000	.972878	.959501	.950651
1	2	.990748	.963877	.950624	.941855
2	3	.981582	.954959	.941828	
3	4	.972500	.946124	.933114	
4	5	.963502	.937370		
5	6	.954588	.928698		
6	7	.945756	.920105		
7	8	.937006			
8	9	.928337			
9	10	.919748			
10	11	.911238			
11	12	.902807			
12	. .	.894454			

See p. 15 for regulations not amended to reflect law changes

TABLE F(12.0), WITH INTEREST AT 12.0 PERCENT, SHOWING FACTORS FOR COMPUTATION OF THE ADJUSTED PAYOUT RATE FOR CERTAIN VALUATIONS APPLICABLE AFTER APRIL 30, 1989

1 NUMBER OF MONTHS BY WHICH THE VALUATION DATE FOR THE FIRST FULL TAXABLE YEAR OF THE TRUST PRECEDES THE FIRST PAYOUT		2 FACTORS FOR PAYOUT AT THE END OF EACH PERIOD			
AT LEAST	*BUT LESS THAN*	*ANNUAL PERIOD*	*SEMIANNUAL PERIOD*	*QUARTERLY PERIOD*	*MONTHLY PERIOD*
. .	1	1.000000	.972456	.958873	.949888
1	2	.990600	.963315	.949860	.940960
2	3	.981289	.954260	.940932	
3	4	.972065	.945290	.932087	
4	5	.962928	.936405		
5	6	.953877	.927603		
6	7	.944911	.918884		
7	8	.936029			
8	9	.927231			
9	10	.918515			
10	11	.909882			
11	12	.901329			
12	. .	.892857			

TABLE F(12.2), WITH INTEREST AT 12.2 PERCENT, SHOWING FACTORS FOR COMPUTATION OF THE ADJUSTED PAYOUT RATE FOR CERTAIN VALUATIONS APPLICABLE AFTER APRIL 30, 1989

1 NUMBER OF MONTHS BY WHICH THE VALUATION DATE FOR THE FIRST FULL TAXABLE YEAR OF THE TRUST PRECEDES THE FIRST PAYOUT		2 FACTORS FOR PAYOUT AT THE END OF EACH PERIOD			
AT LEAST	*BUT LESS THAN*	*ANNUAL PERIOD*	*SEMIANNUAL PERIOD*	*QUARTERLY PERIOD*	*MONTHLY PERIOD*
. .	1	1.000000	.972034	.958247	.949128
1	2	.990453	.962754	.949099	.940067
2	3	.980997	.953563	.940038	
3	4	.971632	.944460	.931063	
4	5	.962356	.935443		
5	6	.953168	.926512		
6	7	.944069	.917667		
7	8	.935056			
8	9	.926129			
9	10	.917287			
10	11	.908530			
11	12	.899856			
12	. .	.891266			

See p. 15 for regulations not amended to reflect law changes

TABLE F(12.4), WITH INTEREST AT 12.4 PERCENT, SHOWING FACTORS FOR COMPUTATION OF THE ADJUSTED PAYOUT RATE FOR CERTAIN VALUATIONS APPLICABLE AFTER APRIL 30, 1989

1 NUMBER OF MONTHS BY WHICH THE VALUATION DATE FOR THE FIRST FULL TAXABLE YEAR OF THE TRUST PRECEDES THE FIRST PAYOUT		2 FACTORS FOR PAYOUT AT THE END OF EACH PERIOD			
AT LEAST	*BUT LESS THAN*	*ANNUAL PERIOD*	*SEMIANNUAL PERIOD*	*QUARTERLY PERIOD*	*MONTHLY PERIOD*
. .	1	1.000000	.971614	.957623	.948370
1	2	.990306	.962195	.948340	.939176
2	3	.980706	.952868	.939147	
3	4	.971199	.943631	.930043	
4	5	.961785	.934484		
5	6	.952461	.925425		
6	7	.943228	.916454		
7	8	.934085			
8	9	.925030			
9	10	.916063			
10	11	.907183			
11	12	.898389			
12	. .	.889680			

TABLE F(12.6), WITH INTEREST AT 12.6 PERCENT, SHOWING FACTORS FOR COMPUTATION OF THE ADJUSTED PAYOUT RATE FOR CERTAIN VALUATIONS APPLICABLE AFTER APRIL 30, 1989

1 NUMBER OF MONTHS BY WHICH THE VALUATION DATE FOR THE FIRST FULL TAXABLE YEAR OF THE TRUST PRECEDES THE FIRST PAYOUT		2 FACTORS FOR PAYOUT AT THE END OF EACH PERIOD			
AT LEAST	*BUT LESS THAN*	*ANNUAL PERIOD*	*SEMIANNUAL PERIOD*	*QUARTERLY PERIOD*	*MONTHLY PERIOD*
. .	1	1.000000	.971195	.957000	.947614
1	2	.990159	.961638	.947583	.938289
2	3	.980416	.952175	.938258	
3	4	.970768	.942805	.929025	
4	5	.961215	.933527		
5	6	.951756	.924341		
6	7	.942390	.915245		
7	8	.933117			
8	9	.923934			
9	10	.914842			
10	11	.905840			
11	12	.896926			
12	. .	.888099			

See p. 15 for regulations not amended to reflect law changes

TABLE F(12.8), WITH INTEREST AT 12.8 PERCENT, SHOWING FACTORS FOR COMPUTATION OF THE ADJUSTED PAYOUT RATE FOR CERTAIN VALUATIONS APPLICABLE AFTER APRIL 30, 1989

1 NUMBER OF MONTHS BY WHICH THE VALUATION DATE FOR THE FIRST FULL TAXABLE YEAR OF THE TRUST PRECEDES THE FIRST PAYOUT		2 FACTORS FOR PAYOUT AT THE END OF EACH PERIOD			
AT LEAST	*BUT LESS THAN*	*ANNUA PERIOD*	*SEMIANNUAL PERIOD*	*QUARTERLY PERIOD*	*MONTHLY PERIOD*
. .	1	1.000000	.970777	.956379	.946860
1	2	.990013	.961082	.946828	.937403
2	3	.980126	.951484	.937372	
3	4	.970337	.941981	.928011	
4	5	.960647	.932574		
5	6	.951053	.923260		
6	7	.941554	.914040		
7	8	.932151			
8	9	.922842			
9	10	.913625			
10	11	.904501			
11	12	.895468			
12	. .	.886525			

TABLE F(13.0), WITH INTEREST AT 13.0 PERCENT, SHOWING FACTORS FOR COMPUTATION OF THE ADJUSTED PAYOUT RATE FOR CERTAIN VALUATIONS APPLICABLE AFTER APRIL 30, 1989

1 NUMBER OF MONTHS BY WHICH THE VALUATION DATE FOR THE FIRST FULL TAXABLE YEAR OF THE TRUST PRECEDES THE FIRST PAYOUT		2 FACTORS FOR PAYOUT AT THE END OF EACH PERIOD			
AT LEAST	*BUT LESS THAN*	*ANNUAL PERIOD*	*SEMIANNUAL PERIOD*	*QUARTERLY PERIOD*	*MONTHLY PERIOD*
. .	1	1.000000	.970360	.955760	.946108
1	2	.989867	.960528	.946075	.936521
2	3	.979836	.950795	.936489	
3	4	.969908	.941160	.926999	
4	5	.960079	.931623		
5	6	.950351	.922183		
6	7	.940721	.912838		
7	8	.931188			
8	9	.921753			
9	10	.912412			
10	11	.903167			
11	12	.894015			
12	. .	.884956			

TABLE F(13.2), WITH INTEREST AT 13.2 PERCENT, SHOWING FACTORS FOR COMPUTATION OF THE ADJUSTED PAYOUT RATE FOR CERTAIN VALUATIONS APPLICABLE AFTER APRIL 30, 1989

1 NUMBER OF MONTHS BY WHICH THE VALUATION DATE FOR THE FIRST FULL TAXABLE YEAR OF THE TRUST PRECEDES THE FIRST PAYOUT		2 FACTORS FOR PAYOUT AT THE END OF EACH PERIOD			
AT LEAST	*BUT LESS THAN*	*ANNUAL PERIOD*	*SEMIANNUAL PERIOD*	*QUARTERLY PERIOD*	*MONTHLY PERIOD*
. .	1	1.000000	.969945	.955143	.945359
1	2	.989721	.959975	.945325	.935641
2	3	.979548	.950107	.935608	
3	4	.969479	.940341	.925991	
4	5	.959514	.930675		
5	6	.949651	.921109		
6	7	.939889	.911641		
7	8	.930228			
8	9	.920667			
9	10	.911203			
10	11	.901837			
11	12	.892567			
12	. .	.883392			

TABLE F(13.4), WITH INTEREST AT 13.4 PERCENT, SHOWING FACTORS FOR COMPUTATION OF THE ADJUSTED PAYOUT RATE FOR CERTAIN VALUATIONS APPLICABLE AFTER APRIL 30, 1989

1 NUMBER OF MONTHS BY WHICH THE VALUATION DATE FOR THE FIRST FULL TAXABLE YEAR OF THE TRUST PRECEDES THE FIRST PAYOUT		2 FACTORS FOR PAYOUT AT THE END OF EACH PERIOD			
AT LEAST	*BUT LESS THAN*	*ANNUAL PERIOD*	*SEMIANNUAL PERIOD*	*QUARTERLY PERIOD*	*MONTHLY PERIOD*
. .	1	1.000000	.969530	.954527	.944611
1	2	.989575	.959423	.944577	.934764
2	3	.979260	.949422	.934730	
3	4	.969051	.939524	.924986	
4	5	.958949	.929730		
5	6	.948953	.920038		
6	7	.939060	.910447		
7	8	.929271			
8	9	.919584			
9	10	.909998			
10	11	.900511			
11	12	.891124			
12	. .	.881834			

See p. 15 for regulations not amended to reflect law changes

TABLE F(13.6), WITH INTEREST AT 13.6 PERCENT, SHOWING FACTORS FOR COMPUTATION OF THE ADJUSTED PAYOUT RATE FOR CERTAIN VALUATIONS APPLICABLE AFTER APRIL 30, 1989

1 NUMBER OF MONTHS BY WHICH THE VALUATION DATE FOR THE FIRST FULL TAXABLE YEAR OF THE TRUST PRECEDES THE FIRST PAYOUT		2 FACTORS FOR PAYOUT AT THE END OF EACH PERIOD			
AT LEAST	*BUT LESS THAN*	*ANNUAL PERIOD*	*SEMIANNUAL PERIOD*	*QUARTERLY PERIOD*	*MONTHLY PERIOD*
. .	1	1.000000	.969117	.953913	.943866
1	2	.989430	.958873	.943831	.933890
2	3	.978972	.948738	.933854	
3	4	.968624	.938710	.923984	
4	5	.958386	.928788		
5	6	.948256	.918971		
6	7	.938233	.909257		
7	8	.928316			
8	9	.918504			
9	10	.908796			
10	11	.899190			
11	12	.889686			
12	. .	.880282			

TABLE F(13.8), WITH INTEREST AT 13.8 PERCENT, SHOWING FACTORS FOR COMPUTATION OF THE ADJUSTED PAYOUT RATE FOR CERTAIN VALUATIONS APPLICABLE AFTER APRIL 30, 1989

1 NUMBER OF MONTHS BY WHICH THE VALUATION DATE FOR THE FIRST FULL TAXABLE YEAR OF THE TRUST PRECEDES THE FIRST PAYOUT		2 FACTORS FOR PAYOUT AT THE END OF EACH PERIOD			
AT LEAST	*BUT LESS THAN*	*ANNUAL PERIOD*	*SEMIANNUAL PERIOD*	*QUARTERLY PERIOD*	*MONTHLY PERIOD*
. .	1	1.000000	.968704	.953301	.943123
1	2	.989285	.958325	.943087	.933018
2	3	.978685	.948056	.932982	
3	4	.968199	.937898	.922985	
4	5	.957824	.927849		
5	6	.947561	.917907		
6	7	.937408	.908072		
7	8	.927364			
8	9	.917428			
9	10	.907598			
10	11	.897873			
11	12	.888252			
12	. .	.878735			

TABLE F(14.0), WITH INTEREST AT 14.0 PERCENT, SHOWING FACTORS FOR COMPUTATION OF THE ADJUSTED PAYOUT RATE FOR CERTAIN VALUATIONS APPLICABLE AFTER APRIL 30, 1989

1 NUMBER OF MONTHS BY WHICH THE VALUATION DATE FOR THE FIRST FULL TAXABLE YEAR OF THE TRUST PRECEDES THE FIRST PAYOUT		2 FACTORS FOR PAYOUT AT THE END OF EACH PERIOD			
AT LEAST	*BUT LESS THAN*	*ANNUAL PERIOD*	*SEMIANNUAL PERIOD*	*QUARTERLY PERIOD*	*MONTHLY PERIOD*
. .	1	1.000000	.968293	.952691	.942382
1	2	.989140	.957778	.942345	.932148
2	3	.978399	.947377	.932111	
3	4	.967774	.937088	.921989	
4	5	.957264	.926912		
5	6	.946868	.916846		
6	7	.936586	.906889		
7	8	.926415			
8	9	.916354			
9	10	.906403			
10	11	.896560			
11	12	.886824			
12	. .	.877193			

(7) *Actuarial Table U(1) for transfers for which the valuation date is on or after May 1, 2009.*—For transfers for which the valuation date is on or after May 1, 2009, the present value of a charitable remainder unitrust interest that is dependent on the termination of a life interest is determined by using the section 7520 rate, Table U(1) in this paragraph (e)(7) and Table F(4.2) through (14.0) in paragraph (e)(6) of this section. See, however, § 1.7520-3(b) (relating to exceptions to the use of prescribed tables under certain circumstances). Many actuarial factors not contained in the following tables are contained in Internal Revenue Service Publication 1458, "Actuarial Valuations Version 3B" (2009). This publication is available, at no charge, electronically via the IRS Internet site at *www.irs.gov*.

Table U(1) - Unitrust Single Life Remainder Factors Based on Life Table 2000CM Applicable On or After May 1, 2009

Adjusted Payout Rate

AGE	4.2%	4.4%	4.6%	4.8%	5.0%	5.2%	5.4%	5.6%	5.8%	6.0%
0	.05527	.04953	.04455	.04023	.03648	.03321	.03037	.02789	.02573	.02383
1	.05095	.04501	.03986	.03538	.03148	.02809	.02513	.02255	.02029	.01831
2	.05269	.04659	.04128	.03666	.03264	.02913	.02606	.02338	.02103	.01896
3	.05468	.04841	.04295	.03818	.03403	.03040	.02722	.02443	.02199	.01984
4	.05684	.05039	.04477	.03986	.03557	.03181	.02852	.02563	.02309	.02085
5	.05912	.05251	.04672	.04166	.03723	.03335	.02993	.02694	.02429	.02197
6	.06154	.05475	.04880	.04359	.03901	.03500	.03146	.02835	.02561	.02319
7	.06407	.05709	.05097	.04561	.04089	.03673	.03308	.02985	.02700	.02448
8	.06672	.05956	.05328	.04775	.04288	.03859	.03481	.03146	.02850	.02588
9	.06951	.06217	.05571	.05002	.04500	.04057	.03665	.03319	.03012	.02739
10	.07244	.06491	.05827	.05241	.04724	.04266	.03861	.03503	.03134	.02901
11	.07550	.06778	.06096	.05494	.04961	.04489	.04070	.03698	.03368	.03074
12	.07869	.07078	.06378	.05759	.05210	.04723	.04290	.03906	.03563	.03258
13	.08199	.07389	.06670	.06034	.05468	.04966	.04519	.04121	.03767	.03450
14	.08536	.07706	.06969	.06315	.05733	.05215	.04754	.04342	.03975	.03646
15	.08877	.08027	.07271	.06599	.06000	.05467	.04990	.04565	.04184	.03844
16	.09221	.08351	.07576	.06885	.06269	.05719	.05228	.04788	.04394	.04041
17	.09570	.08679	.07885	.07176	.06542	.05975	.05468	.05014	.04606	.04240
18	.09925	.09014	.08199	.07471	.06820	.06236	.05712	.05243	.04821	.04442
19	.10289	.09356	.08522	.07774	.07104	.06503	.05963	.05478	.05041	.04648
20	.10665	.09711	.08856	.08089	.07400	.06781	.06224	.05723	.05272	.04864
21	.11052	.10077	.09201	.08413	.07706	.07068	.06495	.05977	.05510	.05088
22	.11452	.10455	.09558	.08750	.08023	.07367	.06776	.06241	.05759	.05322
23	.11867	.10848	.09929	.09101	.08354	.07680	.07070	.06519	.06019	.05567
24	.12300	.11259	.10319	.09470	.08703	.08009	.07381	.06812	.06297	.05829
25	.12755	.11691	.10730	.09860	.09073	.08359	.07713	.07126	.06593	.06109

See p. 15 for regulations not amended to reflect law changes

AGE	4.2%	4.4%	4.6%	4.8%	5.0%	5.2%	5.4%	5.6%	5.8%	6.0%
26	.13232	.12146	.11163	.10272	.09464	.08731	.08065	.07460	.06910	.06409
27	.13732	.12624	.11619	.10706	.09878	.09125	.08440	.07816	.07248	.06731
28	.14255	.13125	.12098	.11164	.10315	.09542	.08837	.08195	.07609	.07074
29	.14799	.13647	.12598	.11644	.10773	.09980	.09256	.08594	.07990	.07438
30	.15365	.14191	.13120	.12144	.11252	.10438	.09694	.09014	.08391	.07821
31	.15952	.14756	.13664	.12666	.11754	.10919	.10155	.09455	.08813	.08225
32	.16561	.15343	.14230	.13210	.12277	.11422	.10637	.09918	.09257	.08650
33	.17193	.15954	.14819	.13778	.12824	.11948	.11143	.10403	.09724	.09098
34	.17845	.16585	.15429	.14367	.13391	.12495	.11670	.10910	.10211	.09566
35	.18520	.17239	.16062	.14979	.13982	.13065	.12219	.11440	.10721	.10057
36	.19218	.17916	.16718	.15614	.14597	.13659	.12793	.11993	.11254	.10571
37	.19938	.18617	.17398	.16274	.15236	.14276	.13390	.12570	.11812	.11110
38	.20683	.19342	.18103	.16958	.15900	.14920	.14013	.13173	.12395	.11673
39	.21450	.20090	.18832	.17667	.16588	.15588	.14661	.13801	.13003	.12261
40	.22241	.20862	.19585	.18400	.17301	.16281	.15334	.14454	.13636	.12875
41	.23055	.21659	.20362	.19158	.18040	.17000	.16033	.15133	.14295	.13514
42	.23892	.22479	.21164	.19942	.18804	.17744	.16757	.15838	.14980	.14180
43	.24756	.23326	.21994	.20753	.19596	.18517	.17511	.16572	.15695	.14875
44	.25644	.24198	.22849	.21590	.20415	.19318	.18293	.17334	.16438	.15599
45	.26557	.25096	.23731	.22455	.21263	.20147	.19103	.18125	.17210	.16352
46	.27496	.26021	.24641	.23349	.22139	.21006	.19943	.18947	.18013	.17136
47	.28460	.26972	.25578	.24270	.23044	.21893	.20813	.19799	.18846	.17951
48	.29451	.27950	.26542	.25220	.23978	.22811	.21714	.20682	.19712	.18798
49	.30468	.28957	.27536	.26201	.24944	.23761	.22648	.21599	.20611	.19679
50	.31515	.29994	.28562	.27214	.25943	.24746	.23617	.22552	.21547	.20598
51	.32591	.31062	.29620	.28260	.26976	.25765	.24621	.23541	.22520	.21554
52	.33697	.32161	.30710	.29340	.28045	.26821	.25663	.24568	.23531	.22550
53	.34832	.33291	.31833	.30453	.29148	.27912	.26741	.25632	.24582	.23585
54	.35995	.34449	.32985	.31598	.30283	.29037	.27855	.26733	.25669	.24658
55	.37183	.35635	.34166	.32773	.31450	.30194	.29001	.27868	.26791	.25768
56	.38390	.36841	.35370	.33971	.32642	.31378	.30175	.29032	.27943	.26907
57	.39618	.38069	.36596	.35194	.33859	.32588	.31377	.30224	.29125	.28077
58	.40862	.39316	.37842	.36438	.35099	.33822	.32605	.31443	.30334	.29276
59	.42126	.40583	.39110	.37705	.36364	.35083	.33859	.32691	.31574	.30506
60	.43410	.41873	.40403	.38999	.37656	.36372	.35145	.33970	.32846	.31770
61	.44714	.43183	.41718	.40316	.38974	.37689	.36458	.35279	.34149	.33067
62	.46033	.44510	.43052	.41653	.40313	.39028	.37796	.36614	.35480	.34391
63	.47366	.45853	.44402	.43010	.41673	.40390	.39157	.37974	.36836	.35744
64	.48712	.47212	.45770	.44385	.43053	.41773	.40542	.39358	.38219	.37123
65	.50073	.48586	.47156	.45779	.44454	.43179	.41951	.40768	.39629	.38531
66	.51461	.49990	.48573	.47207	.45891	.44623	.43400	.42220	.41083	.39985
67	.52872	.51419	.50018	.48665	.47360	.46100	.44884	.43710	.42576	.41481
68	.54302	.52869	.51484	.50147	.48854	.47605	.46398	.45231	.44103	.43011
69	.55744	.54333	.52968	.51648	.50371	.49134	.47938	.46780	.45659	.44573
70	.57198	.55810	.54467	.53165	.51905	.50683	.49500	.48352	.47241	.46163
71	.58662	.57300	.55980	.54700	.53458	.52253	.51084	.49950	.48849	.47781
72	.60134	.58800	.57505	.56247	.55026	.53840	.52688	.51569	.50481	.49425
73	.61608	.60303	.59035	.57803	.56604	.55439	.54305	.53203	.52131	.51087
74	.63077	.61804	.60565	.59358	.58184	.57041	.55928	.54844	.53789	.52761
75	.64536	.63295	.62085	.60907	.59759	.58639	.57548	.56485	.55447	.54436
76	.65980	.64772	.63594	.62445	.61323	.60229	.59162	.58120	.57102	.56110
77	.67408	.66234	.65089	.63970	.62877	.61809	.60766	.59747	.58751	.57779
78	.68817	.67679	.66567	.65479	.64416	.63376	.62359	.61364	.60392	.59440
79	.70205	.69104	.68026	.66971	.65938	.64927	.63937	.62968	.62019	.61090
80	.71569	.70504	.69461	.68439	.67438	.66457	.65495	.64553	.63629	.62724

AGE	4.2%	4.4%	4.6%	4.8%	5.0%	5.2%	5.4%	5.6%	5.8%	6.0%
81	.72905	.71878	.70871	.69883	.68914	.67963	.67031	.66116	.65219	.64339
82	.74213	.73224	.72252	.71299	.70363	.69444	.68541	.67655	.66785	.65930
83	.75489	.74538	.73603	.72684	.71781	.70894	.70022	.69165	.68323	.67495
84	.76731	.75818	.74919	.74036	.73167	.72312	.71471	.70644	.69830	.69029
85	.77937	.77062	.76200	.75352	.74516	.73694	.72884	.72087	.71302	.70529
86	.79106	.78268	.77443	.76629	.75828	.75038	.74260	.73493	.72738	.71993
87	.80235	.79434	.78645	.77866	.77098	.76341	.75595	.74858	.74132	.73416
88	.81324	.80560	.79806	.79062	.78328	.77603	.76888	.76182	.75486	.74798
89	.82371	.81643	.80924	.80214	.79513	.78821	.78137	.77461	.76794	.76134
90	.83375	.82682	.81998	.81321	.80653	.79992	.79339	.78693	.78055	.77424
91	.84336	.83678	.83027	.82383	.81747	.81117	.80494	.79878	.79268	.78665
92	.85253	.84629	.84011	.83399	.82794	.82194	.81601	.81014	.80433	.79857
93	.86126	.85534	.84948	.84367	.83792	.83222	.82658	.82099	.81545	.80997
94	.86956	.86395	.85840	.85289	.84743	.84202	.83666	.83134	.82608	.82086
95	.87744	.87213	.86687	.86166	.85648	.85135	.84626	.84122	.83621	.83125
96	.88487	.87985	.87488	.86994	.86504	.86017	.85535	.85056	.84581	.84109
97	.89188	.88714	.88244	.87776	.87312	.86852	.86395	.85941	.85490	.85042
98	.89850	.89402	.88958	.88516	.88077	.87641	.87208	.86778	.86351	.85927
99	.90475	.90053	.89632	.89215	.88800	.88388	.87978	.87571	.87167	.86765
100	.91057	.90658	.90261	.89867	.89475	.89085	.88697	.88312	.87929	.87548
101	.91610	.91234	.90860	.90487	.90117	.89749	.89382	.89018	.88655	.88295
102	.92122	.91767	.91413	.91061	.90711	.90363	.90017	.89672	.89328	.88987
103	.92630	.92296	.91963	.91632	.91303	.90975	.90648	.90323	.89999	.89677
104	.93097	.92783	.92470	.92158	.91847	.91537	.91229	.90922	.90616	.90312
105	.93558	.93263	.92969	.92676	.92383	.92092	.91802	.91513	.91225	.90938
106	.94135	.93864	.93594	.93325	.93057	.92789	.92522	.92256	.91991	.91726
107	.94789	.94546	.94304	.94062	.93821	.93580	.93340	.93101	.92861	.92623
108	.95844	.95648	.95453	.95258	.95063	.94868	.94673	.94478	.94284	.94090
109	.97900	.97800	.97700	.97600	.97500	.97400	.97300	.97200	.97100	.97000

Table U(1) - Unitrust Single Life Remainder Factors
Based on Life Table 2000CM
Applicable On or After May 1, 2009

	Adjusted Payout Rate									
AGE	6.2%	6.4%	6.6%	6.8%	7.0%	7.2%	7.4%	7.6%	7.8%	8.0%
0	.02217	.02071	.01942	.01829	.01729	.01640	.01561	.01491	.01429	.01373
1	.01657	.01504	.01369	.01250	.01145	.01053	.00970	.00897	.00831	.00773
2	.01715	.01555	.01415	.01290	.01180	.01082	.00996	.00918	.00850	.00788
3	.01795	.01628	.01481	.01350	.01235	.01132	.01041	.00960	.00887	.00822
4	.01888	.01714	.01560	.01423	.01302	.01194	.01098	.01013	.00936	.00867
5	.01991	.01809	.01648	.01505	.01378	.01265	.01164	.01074	.00993	.00921
6	.02104	.01914	.01746	.01597	.01463	.01345	.01239	.01144	.01059	.00982
7	.02225	.02027	.01851	.01695	.01555	.01430	.01319	.01219	.01130	.01049
8	.02356	.02149	.01965	.01802	.01656	.01525	.01408	.01303	.01209	.01124
9	.02497	.02282	.02090	.01919	.01766	.01629	.01506	.01396	.01296	.01207
10	.02649	.02425	.02224	.02046	.01885	.01742	.01613	.01497	.01392	.01298
11	.02812	.02578	.02369	.02182	.02015	.01865	.01729	.01608	.01498	.01398
12	.02986	.02742	.02525	.02329	.02154	.01997	.01855	.01727	.01612	.01508
13	.03167	.02914	.02687	.02483	.02300	.02135	.01987	.01853	.01732	.01622
14	.03352	.03089	.02852	.02640	.02449	.02276	.02121	.01981	.01854	.01738
15	.03538	.03264	.03018	.02797	.02597	.02417	.02255	.02107	.01974	.01853
16	.03724	.03439	.03183	.02952	.02744	.02556	.02385	.02231	.02092	.01965
17	.03911	.03615	.03348	.03107	.02890	.02694	.02516	.02354	.02208	.02075
18	.04100	.03792	.03515	.03264	.03037	.02832	.02646	.02477	.02323	.02184
19	.04294	.03974	.03685	.03424	.03188	.02973	.02778	.02602	.02441	.02294

See p. 15 for regulations not amended to reflect law changes

AGE	6.2%	6.4%	6.6%	6.8%	7.0%	7.2%	7.4%	7.6%	7.8%	8.0%
20	.04497	.04165	.03864	.03592	.03345	.03121	.02918	.02732	.02564	.02410
21	.04707	.04362	.04049	.03766	.03508	.03275	.03062	.02868	.02691	.02530
22	.04926	.04568	.04243	.03948	.03679	.03435	.03212	.03009	.02824	.02655
23	.05157	.04785	.04447	.04140	.03860	.03605	.03372	.03160	.02965	.02788
24	.05404	.05017	.04666	.04346	.04054	.03788	.03545	.03322	.03119	.02932
25	.05668	.05268	.04902	.04569	.04265	.03987	.03733	.03500	.03287	.03091
26	.05953	.05537	.05157	.04811	.04494	.04204	.03938	.03695	.03472	.03267
27	.06258	.05827	.05433	.05072	.04742	.04440	.04163	.03908	.03674	.03459
28	.06585	.06138	.05729	.05354	.05011	.04695	.04406	.04140	.03895	.03670
29	.06932	.06469	.06044	.05655	.05297	.04969	.04667	.04389	.04132	.03896
30	.07298	.06818	.06378	.05974	.05602	.05260	.04944	.04654	.04386	.04139
31	.07684	.07188	.06732	.06312	.05925	.05569	.05241	.04937	.04657	.04399
32	.08092	.07578	.07106	.06670	.06268	.05898	.05556	.05239	.04947	.04676
33	.08522	.07991	.07501	.07050	.06633	.06247	.05891	.05561	.05256	.04972
34	.08972	.08423	.07917	.07449	.07016	.06615	.06244	.05901	.05582	.05286
35	.09444	.08878	.08354	.07869	.07420	.07004	.06618	.06260	.05928	.05619
36	.09940	.09355	.08814	.08312	.07846	.07415	.07013	.06641	.06294	.05972
37	.10459	.09856	.09297	.08777	.08295	.07847	.07431	.07043	.06682	.06346
38	.11004	.10382	.09805	.09268	.08769	.08304	.07872	.07469	.07093	.06742
39	.11573	.10932	.10337	.09782	.09266	.08784	.08336	.07917	.07526	.07161
40	.12167	.11508	.10893	.10321	.09787	.09289	.08824	.08389	.07982	.07602
41	.12787	.12109	.11476	.10885	.10334	.09818	.09336	.08885	.08463	.08068
42	.13433	.12736	.12085	.11476	.10906	.10373	.09874	.09406	.08968	.08557
43	.14109	.13393	.12723	.12095	.11508	.10957	.10441	.09957	.09502	.09075
44	.14814	.14078	.13389	.12744	.12138	.11569	.11036	.10534	.10063	.09620
45	.15548	.14793	.14086	.13421	.12797	.12211	.11659	.11141	.10653	.10193
46	.16313	.15540	.14814	.14131	.13488	.12884	.12315	.11779	.11274	.10798
47	.17109	.16318	.15573	.14871	.14210	.13588	.13001	.12448	.11925	.11432
48	.17938	.17128	.16364	.15645	.14966	.14325	.13721	.13150	.12610	.12100
49	.18801	.17973	.17191	.16453	.15756	.15098	.14475	.13887	.13330	.12803
50	.19702	.18856	.18057	.17301	.16586	.15910	.15270	.14663	.14089	.13545
51	.20642	.19778	.18961	.18188	.17456	.16762	.16104	.15480	.14889	.14328
52	.21621	.20741	.19907	.19117	.18367	.17656	.16981	.16340	.15732	.15153
53	.22641	.21745	.20894	.20087	.19321	.18593	.17901	.17243	.16617	.16022
54	.23699	.22788	.21922	.21098	.20316	.19571	.18862	.18188	.17546	.16934
55	.24794	.23868	.22987	.22148	.21350	.20589	.19865	.19174	.18516	.17888
56	.25920	.24981	.24085	.23232	.22418	.21642	.20902	.20195	.19521	.18877
57	.27078	.26126	.25217	.24349	.23521	.22730	.21975	.21253	.20563	.19904
58	.28266	.27301	.26379	.25498	.24656	.23851	.23081	.22345	.21640	.20965
59	.29486	.28510	.27576	.26682	.25827	.25009	.24225	.23474	.22755	.22065
60	.30740	.29754	.28810	.27905	.27037	.26206	.25409	.24645	.23911	.23208
61	.32029	.31033	.30079	.29164	.28285	.27442	.26632	.25855	.25109	.24391
62	.33347	.32344	.31381	.30455	.29567	.28712	.27891	.27102	.26343	.25613
63	.34693	.33684	.32713	.31779	.30881	.30017	.29185	.28385	.27614	.26872
64	.36069	.35054	.34076	.33135	.32229	.31356	.30515	.29704	.28922	.28169
65	.37474	.36455	.35472	.34525	.33612	.32731	.31881	.31061	.30270	.29506
66	.38927	.37905	.36919	.35968	.35049	.34161	.33304	.32476	.31676	.30903
67	.40423	.39401	.38413	.37458	.36535	.35643	.34780	.33946	.33138	.32357
68	.41956	.40935	.39947	.38991	.38066	.37170	.36303	.35464	.34650	.33863
69	.43522	.42504	.41518	.40562	.39636	.38739	.37869	.37026	.36208	.35415
70	.45118	.44104	.43121	.42168	.41243	.40346	.39475	.38629	.37809	.37012
71	.46744	.45737	.44759	.43810	.42888	.41992	.41122	.40276	.39455	.38656
72	.48398	.47399	.46429	.45486	.44568	.43676	.42808	.41964	.41143	.40344
73	.50072	.49084	.48123	.47187	.46276	.45389	.44526	.43685	.42866	.42068
74	.51759	.50784	.49833	.48907	.48004	.47124	.46267	.45431	.44616	.43821

See p. 15 for regulations not amended to reflect law changes

AGE	6.2%	6.4%	6.6%	6.8%	7.0%	7.2%	7.4%	7.6%	7.8%	8.0%
75	.53450	.52488	.51550	.50635	.49743	.48872	.48022	.47192	.46383	.45592
76	.55140	.54194	.53270	.52368	.51487	.50626	.49785	.48964	.48161	.47377
77	.56828	.55898	.54990	.54102	.53234	.52385	.51555	.50744	.49950	.49173
78	.58509	.57598	.56707	.55835	.54981	.54146	.53328	.52528	.51744	.50977
79	.60181	.59290	.58417	.57562	.56725	.55904	.55100	.54313	.53541	.52785
80	.61837	.60967	.60114	.59278	.58458	.57653	.56865	.56091	.55333	.54589
81	.63475	.62627	.61795	.60979	.60177	.59391	.58619	.57861	.57117	.56386
82	.65091	.64267	.63457	.62661	.61880	.61112	.60358	.59617	.58888	.58173
83	.66681	.65881	.65094	.64321	.63560	.62812	.62077	.61353	.60642	.59942
84	.68241	.67466	.66703	.65952	.65214	.64487	.63771	.63067	.62373	.61691
85	.69768	.69019	.68280	.67553	.66837	.66132	.65437	.64753	.64078	.63414
86	.71259	.70536	.69822	.69120	.68427	.67744	.67070	.66406	.65752	.65107
87	.72709	.72012	.71325	.70647	.69977	.69317	.68666	.68023	.67389	.66764
88	.74119	.73449	.72787	.72134	.71489	.70852	.70223	.69602	.68989	.68384
89	.75483	.74840	.74204	.73576	.72955	.72342	.71736	.71138	.70546	.69962
90	.76800	.76183	.75573	.74971	.74375	.73785	.73202	.72626	.72056	.71493
91	.78069	.77479	.76895	.76317	.75745	.75180	.74620	.74067	.73519	.72977
92	.79288	.78724	.78165	.77613	.77065	.76524	.75987	.75456	.74930	.74409
93	.80453	.79915	.79382	.78854	.78331	.77812	.77299	.76790	.76286	.75787
94	.81568	.81055	.80547	.80043	.79544	.79048	.78557	.78071	.77588	.77110
95	.82633	.82144	.81660	.81180	.80704	.80231	.79763	.79298	.78837	.78380
96	.83642	.83177	.82717	.82259	.81806	.81356	.80909	.80465	.80025	.79588
97	.84598	.84157	.83719	.83284	.82853	.82424	.81998	.81576	.81156	.80739
98	.85505	.85086	.84670	.84257	.83847	.83439	.83034	.82631	.82232	.81835
99	.86365	.85968	.85573	.85181	.84791	.84404	.84019	.83636	.83255	.82877
100	.87169	.86792	.86418	.86045	.85675	.85307	.84941	.84577	.84215	.83855
101	.87936	.87579	.87224	.86871	.86520	.86171	.85823	.85477	.85133	.84791
102	.88647	.88309	.87972	.87637	.87304	.86972	.86642	.86313	.85986	.85660
103	.89356	.89036	.88718	.88402	.88086	.87772	.87460	.87149	.86839	.86531
104	.90008	.89706	.89405	.89105	.88807	.88509	.88213	.87918	.87624	.87331
105	.90652	.90366	.90082	.89799	.89517	.89236	.88955	.88676	.88398	.88120
106	.91462	.91199	.90937	.90675	.90414	.90154	.89895	.89636	.89378	.89121
107	.92385	.92147	.91910	.91673	.91437	.91201	.90966	.90731	.90497	.90263
108	.93896	.93702	.93509	.93316	.93123	.92930	.92737	.92544	.92352	.92160
109	.96900	.96800	.96700	.96600	.96500	.96400	.96300	.96200	.96100	.96000

Table U(1) - Unitrust Single Life Remainder Factors Based on Life Table 2000CM Applicable On or After May 1, 2009

	Adjusted Payout Rate									
AGE	8.2%	8.4%	8.6%	8.8%	9.0%	9.2%	9.4%	9.6%	9.8%	10.0%
0	.01323	.01279	.01238	.01202	.01169	.01139	.01112	.01088	.01065	.01044
1	.00721	.00674	.00632	.00594	.00559	.00528	.00500	.00474	.00451	.00430
2	.00733	.00683	.00639	.00598	.00562	.00529	.00499	.00472	.00447	.00425
3	.00764	.00711	.00664	.00622	.00583	.00548	.00516	.00487	.00461	.00437
4	.00806	.00750	.00700	.00655	.00614	.00577	.00543	.00513	.00485	.00459
5	.00856	.00797	.00744	.00696	.00653	.00614	.00578	.00545	.00515	.00488
6	.00914	.00852	.00795	.00745	.00699	.00657	.00619	.00584	.00552	.00523
7	.00976	.00911	.00851	.00798	.00749	.00704	.00664	.00627	.00593	.00562
8	.01047	.00978	.00915	.00858	.00806	.00759	.00716	.00677	.00640	.00607
9	.01126	.01053	.00986	.00926	.00871	.00821	.00775	.00734	.00695	.00660
10	.01213	.01136	.01065	.01002	.00944	.00891	.00842	.00798	.00757	.00720
11	.01309	.01227	.01153	.01086	.01024	.00968	.00917	.00870	.00827	.00787
12	.01413	.01327	.01249	.01178	.01113	.01054	.00999	.00950	.00904	.00862
13	.01523	.01432	.01350	.01275	.01206	.01144	.01086	.01034	.00985	.00940
14	.01634	.01539	.01452	.01373	.01301	.01235	.01174	.01118	.01067	.01020

See p. 15 for regulations not amended to reflect law changes

AGE	8.2%	8.4%	8.6%	8.8%	9.0%	9.2%	9.4%	9.6%	9.8%	10.0%
15	.01743	.01643	.01552	.01469	.01393	.01323	.01259	.01200	.01146	.01096
16	.01849	.01744	.01648	.01561	.01480	.01407	.01339	.01277	.01220	.01167
17	.01953	.01843	.01742	.01650	.01565	.01488	.01416	.01351	.01290	.01235
18	.02056	.01940	.01834	.01737	.01648	.01566	.01491	.01422	.01358	.01299
19	.02160	.02038	.01927	.01824	.01730	.01644	.01565	.01492	.01424	.01362
20	.02270	.02141	.02024	.01916	.01817	.01726	.01642	.01565	.01494	.01428
21	.02382	.02247	.02124	.02010	.01906	.01810	.01721	.01640	.01565	.01495
22	.02500	.02358	.02228	.02108	.01998	.01897	.01803	.01717	.01638	.01564
23	.02625	.02476	.02339	.02213	.02097	.01990	.01891	.01800	.01716	.01638
24	.02761	.02604	.02460	.02327	.02205	.02092	.01988	.01891	.01802	.01719
25	.02912	.02747	.02595	.02455	.02326	.02206	.02096	.01994	.01900	.01812
26	.03078	.02904	.02744	.02597	.02461	.02335	.02218	.02110	.02010	.01917
27	.03261	.03079	.02910	.02755	.02611	.02478	.02355	.02241	.02135	.02037
28	.03462	.03270	.03093	.02929	.02778	.02637	.02507	.02387	.02274	.02170
29	.03678	.03477	.03291	.03118	.02959	.02811	.02673	.02546	.02427	.02316
30	.03910	.03699	.03503	.03322	.03154	.02997	.02852	.02717	.02592	.02475
31	.04159	.03937	.03731	.03541	.03364	.03199	.03046	.02903	.02770	.02646
32	.04425	.04192	.03976	.03776	.03589	.03416	.03254	.03104	.02963	.02832
33	.04710	.04466	.04239	.04029	.03832	.03650	.03479	.03320	.03172	.03033
34	.05011	.04756	.04518	.04297	.04090	.03898	.03718	.03551	.03394	.03247
35	.05331	.05064	.04815	.04582	.04366	.04163	.03974	.03798	.03632	.03477
36	.05671	.05391	.05130	.04887	.04659	.04446	.04247	.04061	.03887	.03723
37	.06032	.05739	.05466	.05210	.04972	.04748	.04539	.04343	.04159	.03986
38	.06415	.06109	.05823	.05556	.05305	.05070	.04850	.04644	.04450	.04268
39	.06819	.06500	.06201	.05921	.05658	.05412	.05181	.04964	.04760	.04568
40	.07246	.06913	.06601	.06308	.06033	.05774	.05532	.05304	.05089	.04887
41	.07697	.07349	.07023	.06717	.06429	.06158	.05904	.05664	.05439	.05226
42	.08171	.07809	.07469	.07149	.06848	.06564	.06298	.06046	.05809	.05585
43	.08674	.08297	.07942	.07608	.07293	.06997	.06717	.06453	.06204	.05969
44	.09203	.08810	.08441	.08092	.07764	.07454	.07161	.06885	.06624	.06377
45	.09760	.09352	.08967	.08604	.08261	.07938	.07632	.07342	.07068	.06809
46	.10348	.09925	.09524	.09146	.08789	.08451	.08131	.07828	.07542	.07270
47	.10967	.10527	.10111	.09717	.09345	.08992	.08659	.08342	.08042	.07757
48	.11618	.11161	.10730	.10321	.09933	.09566	.09217	.08887	.08573	.08275
49	.12304	.11831	.11383	.10958	.10555	.10173	.09810	.09465	.09137	.08825
50	.13029	.12540	.12076	.11635	.11216	.10818	.10440	.10081	.09739	.09413
51	.13795	.13289	.12808	.12351	.11917	.11504	.11110	.10736	.10379	.10040
52	.14604	.14081	.13584	.13111	.12661	.12232	.11823	.11434	.11062	.10708
53	.15456	.14917	.14404	.13914	.13448	.13004	.12580	.12175	.11789	.11420
54	.16352	.15796	.15266	.14761	.14279	.13819	.13379	.12959	.12558	.12175
55	.17289	.16717	.16171	.15650	.15152	.14676	.14221	.13786	.13370	.12971
56	.18262	.17674	.17113	.16576	.16062	.15570	.15100	.14650	.14218	.13805
57	.19273	.18669	.18092	.17539	.17010	.16503	.16017	.15552	.15105	.14677
58	.20319	.19700	.19107	.18539	.17994	.17472	.16971	.16490	.16029	.15586
59	.21404	.20770	.20162	.19579	.19019	.18481	.17965	.17470	.16993	.16535
60	.22532	.21884	.21261	.20663	.20088	.19536	.19005	.18494	.18003	.17530
61	.23702	.23040	.22403	.21790	.21201	.20634	.20089	.19564	.19058	.18571
62	.24911	.24235	.23584	.22958	.22355	.21774	.21214	.20674	.20154	.19653
63	.26157	.25468	.24805	.24165	.23548	.22954	.22380	.21827	.21293	.20777
64	.27442	.26742	.26065	.25413	.24783	.24175	.23588	.23021	.22474	.21944
65	.28768	.28056	.27368	.26703	.26061	.25441	.24841	.24261	.23700	.23158
66	.30156	.29433	.28735	.28059	.27405	.26773	.26161	.25569	.24995	.24440
67	.31601	.30870	.30161	.29476	.28812	.28169	.27545	.26942	.26357	.25790
68	.33100	.32360	.31643	.30949	.30275	.29622	.28989	.28375	.27779	.27201
69	.34646	.33900	.33177	.32474	.31793	.31131	.30489	.29865	.29259	.28671

AGE	8.2%	8.4%	8.6%	8.8%	9.0%	9.2%	9.4%	9.6%	9.8%	10.0%
70	.36239	.35488	.34758	.34049	.33361	.32692	.32041	.31409	.30795	.30197
71	.37880	.37125	.36391	.35677	.34983	.34308	.33651	.33011	.32389	.31784
72	.39566	.38809	.38073	.37355	.36657	.35977	.35315	.34670	.34041	.33429
73	.41291	.40534	.39796	.39077	.38376	.37693	.37027	.36377	.35744	.35126
74	.43046	.42290	.41552	.40833	.40131	.39446	.38778	.38125	.37489	.36867
75	.44821	.44068	.43332	.42614	.41913	.41227	.40558	.39904	39266	.38641
76	.46611	.45862	.45130	.44415	.43715	.43031	.42363	.41709	.41069	.40444
77	.48414	.47671	.46944	.46233	.45537	.44856	.44189	.43536	.42898	.42272
78	.50226	.49490	.48770	.48065	.47374	.46697	.46034	.45384	.44747	.44123
79	.52043	.51317	.50604	.49906	.49222	.48551	.47892	.47247	.46614	.45993
80	.53859	.53142	.52440	.51750	.51074	.50410	.49758	.49118	.48491	.47874
81	.55669	.54964	.54273	.53593	.52926	.52271	.51627	.50995	.50373	.49763
82	.57469	.56778	.56099	.55431	.54774	.54129	.53494	.52871	.52257	.51654
83	.59254	.58577	.57911	.57256	.56612	.55978	.55354	.54740	.54136	.53541
84	.61019	.60358	.59706	.59065	.58434	.57812	.57200	.56597	.56003	.55419
85	.62759	.62114	.61479	.60853	.60236	.59628	.59028	.58438	.57856	.57282
86	.64470	.63843	.63224	.62614	.62012	.61419	.60833	.60256	.59687	.59125
87	.66146	.65537	.64936	.64342	.63757	.63179	.62608	.62045	.61489	.60941
88	.67786	.67196	.66613	.66037	.65469	.64907	.64352	.63804	.63263	.62728
89	.69384	.68813	.68249	.67691	.67140	.66595	.66057	.65525	.64999	.64479
90	.70936	.70385	.69840	.69301	.68768	.68241	.67719	.67204	.66693	.66189
91	.72440	.71909	.71384	.70864	.70349	.69840	.69336	.68837	.68344	.67855
92	.73894	.73383	.72878	.72377	.71881	.71390	.70904	.70422	.69945	.69473
93	.75292	.74801	.74316	.73834	.73357	.72885	.72416	.71952	.71492	.71037
94	.76636	.76166	.75700	.75238	.74780	.74326	.73876	.73429	.72986	.72547
95	.77926	.77476	.77030	.76587	.76148	.75712	.75280	.74851	.74426	.74004
96	.79155	.78725	.78298	.77874	.77453	.77036	.76622	.76210	.75802	.75397
97	.80325	.79915	.79507	.79101	.78699	.78300	.77903	.77509	.77117	.76729
98	.81440	.81048	.80659	.80272	.79887	.79505	.79126	.78749	.78375	.78002
99	.82502	.82128	.81757	.81388	.81021	.80656	.80294	.79934	.79576	.79220
100	.83497	.83141	.82788	.82436	.82086	.81738	.81392	.81048	.80706	.80365
101	.84451	.84112	.83776	.83441	.83107	.82776	.82446	.82117	.81791	.81466
102	.85337	.85014	.84693	.84374	.84056	.83740	.83425	.83112	.82800	.82490
103	.86223	.85918	.85613	.85310	.85008	.84708	.84409	.84111	.83814	.83519
104	.87040	.86749	.86460	.86172	.85885	.85599	.85314	.85030	.84748	.84466
105	.87844	.87568	.87294	.87020	.86748	.86476	.86205	.85935	.85666	.85398
106	.88865	.88609	.88354	.88100	.87846	.87594	.87341	.87090	.86839	.86590
107	.90030	.89797	.89565	.89333	.89102	.88871	.88641	.88411	.88181	.87952
108	.91968	.91776	.91585	.91394	.91203	.91012	.90821	.90630	.90440	.90250
109	.95900	.95800	.95700	.95600	.95500	.95400	.95300	.95200	.95100	.95000

Table U(1) - Unitrust Single Life Remainder Factors
Based on Life Table 2000CM
Applicable On or After May 1, 2009

Adjusted Payout Rate

AGE	10.2%	10.4%	10.6%	10.8%	11.0%	11.2%	11.4%	11.6%	11.8%	12.0%
0	.01025	.01008	.00992	.00977	.00963	.00950	.00938	.00927	.00917	.00907
1	.00410	.00392	.00376	.00361	.00347	.00334	.00322	.00310	.00300	.00290
2	.00404	.00385	.00367	.00351	.00336	.00322	.00310	.00298	.00287	.00276
3	.00415	.00394	.00376	.00359	.00343	.00328	.00314	.00301	.00290	.00279
4	.00435	.00414	.00394	.00375	.00358	.00342	.00328	.00314	.00302	.00290
5	.00463	.00439	.00418	.00398	.00380	.00363	.00348	.00333	.00319	.00307
6	.00496	.00471	.00448	.00427	.00408	.00390	.00373	.00357	.00343	.00329
7	.00533	.00507	.00483	.00460	.00439	.00420	.00402	.00385	.00369	.00355
8	.00577	.00549	.00523	.00499	.00476	.00456	.00436	.00418	.00402	.00386

AGE	10.2%	10.4%	10.6%	10.8%	11.0%	11.2%	11.4%	11.6%	11.8%	12.0%
9	.00627	.00598	.00570	.00544	.00520	.00498	.00478	.00458	.00440	.00423
10	.00685	.00653	.00624	.00596	.00571	.00547	.00525	.00505	.00485	.00467
11	.00750	.00716	.00685	.00656	.00629	.00603	.00580	.00558	.00537	.00518
12	.00823	.00787	.00753	.00722	.00693	.00667	.00642	.00618	.00596	.00576
13	.00899	.00861	.00826	.00793	.00762	.00734	.00707	.00682	.00659	.00637
14	.00976	.00935	.00898	.00863	.00831	.00801	.00772	.00746	.00722	.00698
15	.01050	.01007	.00967	.00931	.00896	.00864	.00835	.00807	.00781	.00756
16	.01118	.01073	.01031	.00992	.00956	.00922	.00891	.00861	.00834	.00808
17	.01183	.01135	.01091	.01050	.01011	.00976	.00942	.00911	.00882	.00855
18	.01244	.01194	.01147	.01104	.01063	.01025	.00990	.00957	.00926	.00897
19	.01304	.01251	.01202	.01156	.01113	.01073	.01035	.01001	.00968	.00937
20	.01367	.01311	.01258	.01209	.01164	.01122	.01082	.01045	.01011	.00978
21	.01430	.01371	.01315	.01263	.01215	.01171	.01129	.01090	.01053	.01019
22	.01496	.01432	.01373	.01319	.01268	.01220	.01176	.01134	.01095	.01059
23	.01565	.01498	.01436	.01377	.01323	.01273	.01225	.01181	.01140	.01101
24	.01642	.01571	.01505	.01443	.01386	.01332	.01282	.01235	.01191	.01149
25	.01731	.01655	.01585	.01519	.01458	.01401	.01347	.01297	.01250	.01206
26	.01831	.01751	.01676	.01606	.01541	.01480	.01423	.01370	.01320	.01273
27	.01945	.01860	.01780	.01706	.01637	.01572	.01511	.01454	.01401	.01351
28	.02073	.01982	.01898	.01819	.01745	.01676	.01611	.01551	.01494	.01440
29	.02213	.02117	.02027	.01943	.01865	.01791	.01722	.01658	.01597	.01540
30	.02365	.02263	.02168	.02079	.01995	.01917	.01844	.01775	.01710	.01649
31	.02531	.02422	.02321	.02226	.02138	.02054	.01976	.01902	.01833	.01768
32	.02709	.02595	.02487	.02387	.02292	.02204	.02120	.02042	.01968	.01899
33	.02903	.02782	.02668	.02561	.02461	.02366	.02278	.02194	.02116	.02041
34	.03110	.02981	.02860	.02747	.02640	.02540	.02446	.02357	.02273	.02194
35	.03332	.03195	.03067	.02947	.02834	.02728	.02627	.02533	.02444	.02359
36	.03569	.03425	.03290	.03162	.03042	.02929	.02823	.02722	.02627	.02537
37	.03824	.03671	.03528	.03393	.03266	.03146	.03032	.02925	.02824	.02729
38	.04097	.03936	.03784	.03641	.03506	.03379	.03259	.03145	.03037	.02936
39	.04387	.04217	.04057	.03905	.03763	.03628	.03500	.03380	.03265	.03157
40	.04696	.04517	.04347	.04187	.04036	.03893	.03758	.03630	.03509	.03394
41	.05025	.04836	.04657	.04488	.04328	.04177	.04034	.03898	.03769	.03647
42	.05374	.05174	.04986	.04807	.04638	.04478	.04326	.04183	.04046	.03917
43	.05747	.05537	.05338	.05150	.04971	.04802	.04641	.04489	.04344	.04207
44	.06143	.05922	.05712	.05514	.05325	.05147	.04977	.04816	.04663	.04517
45	.06564	.06331	.06111	.05901	.05703	.05514	.05335	.05164	.05002	.04848
46	.07012	.06768	.06536	.06315	.06106	.05907	.05718	.05538	.05366	.05203
47	.07487	.07231	.06987	.06755	.06535	.06325	.06125	.05935	.05754	.05581
48	.07992	.07723	.07467	.07223	.06991	.06770	.06560	.06359	.06168	.05985
49	.08529	.08247	.07978	.07722	.07479	.07246	.07024	.06813	.06611	.06418
50	.09103	.08808	.08526	.08258	.08002	.07757	.07524	.07301	.07088	.06885
51	.09716	.09407	.09112	.08831	.08562	.08306	.08060	.07826	.07601	.07387
52	.10370	.10047	.09739	.09445	.09163	.08894	.08637	.08390	.08154	.07928
53	.11068	.10731	.10409	.10101	.09806	.09524	.09254	.08996	.08748	.08510
54	.11808	.11457	.11121	.10800	.10492	.10197	.09914	.09642	.09382	.09133
55	.12590	.12225	.11875	.11540	.11218	.10910	.10614	.10330	.10057	.09795
56	.13409	.13029	.12665	.12316	.11981	.11659	.11350	.11053	.10768	.10493
57	.14266	.13872	.13494	.13130	.12781	.12446	.12123	.11813	.11515	.11228
58	.15160	.14751	.14359	.13981	.13618	.13269	.12933	.12609	.12298	.11998
59	.16095	.15672	.15264	.14873	.14495	.14132	.13783	.13446	.13121	.12808
60	.17076	.16638	.16216	.15810	.15419	.15042	.14678	.14328	.13990	.13663
61	.18101	.17649	.17213	.16793	.16388	.15997	.15619	.15255	.14904	.14564
62	.19169	.18703	.18253	.17818	.17399	.16994	.16603	.16225	.15860	.15507
63	.20279	.19799	.19335	.18886	.18453	.18034	.17629	.17238	.16859	.16493

See p. 15 for regulations not amended to reflect law changes

AGE	10.2%	10.4%	10.6%	10.8%	11.0%	11.2%	11.4%	11.6%	11.8%	12.0%
64	.21433	.20939	.20461	.19998	.19551	.19119	.18700	.18295	.17903	.17523
65	.22633	.22125	.21633	.21158	.20697	.20251	.19819	.19400	.18994	.18601
66	.23903	.23382	.22877	.22388	.21914	.21455	.21010	.20578	.20159	.19752
67	.25240	.24707	.24190	.23688	.23202	.22730	.22271	.21827	.21395	.20975
68	.26640	.26095	.25566	.25053	.24554	.24070	.23600	.23143	.22698	.22267
69	.28099	.27544	.27004	.26480	.25970	.25474	.24992	.24523	.24067	.23623
70	.29616	.29051	.28501	.27966	.27446	.26939	.26446	.25966	.25499	.25044
71	.31194	.30620	.30062	.29517	.28987	.28471	.27968	.27478	27000	.26534
72	.32833	.32251	.31684	.31132	.30593	.30068	.29556	.29057	.28569	.28094
73	.34524	.33936	.33363	.32804	.32258	.31725	.31205	.30697	.30201	.29717
74	.36260	.35667	.35089	.34523	.33971	.33432	.32905	.32390	.31887	.31395
75	.38031	.37435	.36852	.36282	.35725	.35180	.34647	.34126	.33617	.33118
76	.39832	.39233	.38647	.38074	.37513	.36964	.36427	.35901	.35386	.34882
77	.41660	.41060	.40473	.39898	.39335	.38783	.38242	.37713	.37194	.36685
78	.43512	.42913	.42326	.41750	.41186	.40632	.40090	.39558	.39036	.38524
79	.45384	.44787	.44201	.43626	.43062	.42509	.41966	.41432	.40909	.40396
80	.47269	.46675	.46092	.45519	.44957	.44404	.43862	.43329	.42806	.42291
81	.49163	.48574	.47994	.47425	.46866	.46316	.45775	.45244	.44722	.44208
82	.51061	.50478	.49904	.49340	.48784	.48238	.47701	.47173	.46653	.46141
83	.52956	.52380	.51813	.51255	.50705	.50165	.49632	.49108	.48592	.48083
84	.54843	.54275	.53716	.53166	.52623	.52089	.51562	.51044	.50532	.50029
85	.56716	.56159	.55609	.55067	.54533	.54006	.53487	.52975	.52470	.51972
86	.58571	.58024	.57485	.56953	.56428	.55910	.55399	.54894	.54397	.53906
87	.60399	.59864	.59337	.58815	.58301	.57793	.57291	.56795	.56306	.55823
88	.62200	.61678	.61162	.60653	.60150	.59653	.59161	.58676	.58196	.57722
89	.63965	.63457	.62954	.62458	.61967	.61481	.61001	.60526	.60057	.59593
90	.65690	.65196	.64707	.64224	.63746	.63273	.62805	.62342	.61884	.61431
91	.67371	.66892	.66418	.65949	.65485	.65025	.64570	.64119	.63673	.63231
92	.69005	.68542	.68083	.67628	.67178	.66732	.66290	.65852	.65419	.64989
93	.70585	.70137	.69694	.69254	.68819	.68387	.67959	.67534	.67114	.66697
94	.72112	.71681	.71253	.70828	.70407	.69990	.69576	.69166	.68759	.68355
95	.73585	.73170	.72758	.72349	.71943	.71541	.71141	.70745	.70352	.69961
96	.74995	.74595	.74199	.73806	.73415	.73027	.72642	.72260	.71881	.71505
97	.76343	.75960	.75579	.75201	.74826	.74453	.74083	.73715	.73350	.72987
98	.77633	.77265	.76900	.76538	.76177	.75819	.75463	.75110	.74759	.74410
99	.78866	.78514	.78165	.77817	.77472	.77129	.76787	.76448	.76111	.75775
100	.80027	.79690	.79356	.79023	.78692	.78363	.78036	.77710	.77386	.77065
101	.81143	.80821	.80502	.80183	.79867	.79552	.79239	.78927	.78617	.78308
102	.82181	.81874	.81568	.81264	.80961	.80659	.80359	.80060	.79763	.79467
103	.83225	.82933	.82641	.82351	.82062	.81774	.81488	.81203	.80919	.80636
104	.84186	.83907	.83629	.83351	.83076	.82801	.82527	.82254	.81982	.81712
105	.85131	.84865	.84600	.84336	.84072	.83810	.83548	.83288	.83028	.82769
106	.86340	.86092	.85844	.85597	.85351	.85105	.84860	.84616	.84372	.84130
107	.87724	.87496	.87268	.87041	.86815	.86589	.86363	.86138	.85914	.85690
108	.90060	.89870	.89681	.89492	.89303	.89114	.88925	.88736	.88548	.88360
109	.94900	.94800	.94700	.94600	.94500	.94400	.94300	.94200	.94100	.94000

Table U(1) - Unitrust Single Life Remainder Factors
Based on Life Table 2000CM
Applicable On or After May 1, 2009

Adjusted Payout Rate

AGE	12.2%	12.4%	12.6%	12.8%	13.0%	13.2%	13.4%	13.6%	13.8%	14.0%
0	.00898	.00889	.00881	.00873	.00866	.00859	.00853	.00846	.00840	.00835
1	.00281	.00273	.00265	.00257	.00250	.00244	.00237	.00232	.00226	.00221
2	.00267	.00258	.00249	.00241	.00234	.00227	.00220	.00214	.00208	.00202

See p. 15 for regulations not amended to reflect law changes

AGE	12.2%	12.4%	12.6%	12.8%	13.0%	13.2%	13.4%	13.6%	13.8%	14.0%
3	.00268	.00259	.00249	.00241	.00233	.00225	.00218	.00212	.00205	.00199
4	.00279	.00268	.00258	.00249	.00241	.00233	.00225	.00218	.00211	.00205
5	.00295	.00284	.00273	.00263	.00254	.00245	.00237	.00229	.00222	.00215
6	.00316	.00304	.00293	.00283	.00273	.00263	.00254	.00246	.00238	.00230
7	.00341	.00328	.00316	.00305	.00294	.00284	.00274	.00265	.00256	.00248
8	.00371	.00357	.00344	.00332	.00320	.00310	.00299	.00289	.00280	.00271
9	.00408	.00393	.00379	.00366	.00353	.00341	.00330	.00320	.00310	.00300
10	.00450	.00434	.00419	.00405	.00392	.00379	.00367	.00356	.00345	.00335
11	.00500	.00483	.00467	.00452	.00438	.00424	.00411	.00399	.00387	.00376
12	.00557	.00538	.00521	.00505	.00490	.00476	.00462	.00449	.00436	.00425
13	.00617	.00597	.00579	.00562	.00546	.00531	.00516	.00502	.00489	.00477
14	.00677	.00656	.00637	.00619	.00602	.00585	.00570	.00555	.00541	.00528
15	.00733	.00712	.00691	.00672	.00654	.00636	.00620	.00605	.00590	.00576
16	.00784	.00761	.00739	.00719	.00700	.00681	.00664	.00648	.00632	.00618
17	.00829	.00805	.00782	.00761	.00741	.00721	.00703	.00686	.00670	.00654
18	.00870	.00845	.00821	.00798	.00777	.00756	.00737	.00719	.00702	.00685
19	.00909	.00882	.00856	.00832	.00810	.00788	.00768	.00749	.00731	.00713
20	.00948	.00919	.00892	.00867	.00843	.00821	.00799	.00779	.00760	.00741
21	.00986	.00956	.00927	.00901	.00875	.00851	.00829	.00807	.00787	.00767
22	.01024	.00992	.00962	.00933	.00906	.00881	.00857	.00834	.00813	.00792
23	.01065	.01030	.00998	.00968	.00939	.00912	.00887	.00862	.00839	.00818
24	.01110	.01074	.01040	.01007	.00977	.00948	.00921	.00895	.00870	.00847
25	.01165	.01126	.01089	.01055	.01022	.00991	.00962	.00934	.00908	.00884
26	.01228	.01187	.01148	.01111	.01076	.01043	.01012	.00982	.00955	.00928
27	.01303	.01259	.01217	.01178	.01140	.01105	.01072	.01040	.01010	.00982
28	.01390	.01342	.01297	.01255	.01215	.01178	.01142	.01108	.01076	.01046
29	.01486	.01435	.01387	.01342	.01299	.01259	.01221	.01185	.01150	.01117
30	.01591	.01537	.01486	.01437	.01392	.01348	.01307	.01269	.01232	.01197
31	.01707	.01649	.01594	.01542	.01493	.01447	.01403	.01361	.01322	.01284
32	.01833	.01771	.01713	.01657	.01605	.01555	.01508	.01464	.01421	.01381
33	.01971	.01905	.01843	.01784	.01728	.01674	.01624	.01576	.01531	.01487
34	.02119	.02049	.01982	.01919	.01859	.01802	.01748	.01697	.01648	.01602
35	.02280	.02204	.02133	.02065	.02001	.01940	.01883	.01828	.01775	.01726
36	.02452	.02372	.02296	.02224	.02155	.02090	.02028	.01969	.01913	.01860
37	.02638	.02553	.02471	.02394	.02321	.02252	.02185	.02123	.02063	.02006
38	.02839	.02748	.02661	.02579	.02501	.02427	.02356	.02289	.02225	.02164
39	.03055	.02957	.02865	.02777	.02694	.02615	.02539	.02467	.02399	.02333
40	.03285	.03181	.03083	.02990	.02901	.02816	.02735	.02658	.02585	.02515
41	.03531	.03421	.03316	.03217	.03122	.03032	.02946	.02863	.02785	.02710
42	.03793	.03676	.03565	.03459	.03358	.03262	.03170	.03082	.02999	.02919
43	.04076	.03952	.03833	.03721	.03613	.03510	.03413	.03319	.03230	.03144
44	.04378	.04246	.04120	.04000	.03886	.03777	.03672	.03573	.03477	.03386
45	.04701	.04561	.04427	.04299	.04178	.04062	.03950	.03844	.03743	.03645
46	.05047	.04898	.04757	.04621	.04492	.04368	.04250	.04137	.04029	.03925
47	.05416	.05258	.05108	.04964	.04827	.04696	.04570	.04449	.04334	.04224
48	.05810	.05644	.05484	.05332	.05186	.05047	.04913	.04785	.04662	.04545
49	.06233	.06057	.05888	.05727	.05572	.05424	.05282	.05146	.05016	.04890
50	.06690	.06503	.06325	.06154	.05990	.05833	.05683	.05538	.05399	.05266
51	.07181	.06984	.06796	.06615	.06442	.06275	.06116	.05962	.05815	.05673
52	.07712	.07504	.07305	.07114	.06931	.06755	.06585	.06423	.06267	.06116
53	.08282	.08063	.07853	.07652	.07458	.07272	.07093	.06921	.06756	.06596
54	.08893	.08663	.08442	.08229	.08025	.07829	.07640	.07458	.07283	.07114
55	.09544	.09302	.09070	.08846	.08631	.08424	.08224	.08032	.07847	.07669
56	.10230	.09976	.09732	.09497	.09270	.09052	.08842	.08639	.08444	.08256
57	.10952	.10686	.10430	.10183	.09945	.09716	.09495	.09281	.09075	.08877

See p. 15 for regulations not amended to reflect law changes

AGE	12.2%	12.4%	12.6%	12.8%	13.0%	13.2%	13.4%	13.6%	13.8%	14.0%
58	.11709	.11431	.11162	.10904	.10654	.10413	.10181	.09956	.09739	.09530
59	.12506	.12215	.11934	.11663	.11402	.11149	.10905	.10669	.10441	.10221
60	.13349	.13045	.12751	.12468	.12194	.11929	.11674	.11426	.11187	.10955
61	.14236	.13919	.13613	.13317	.13031	.12754	.12486	.12227	.11976	.11733
62	.15166	.14836	.14517	.14208	.13909	.13620	.13340	.13069	.12806	.12551
63	.16138	.15795	.15463	.15141	.14830	.14528	.14235	.13952	.13677	.13410
64	.17155	.16799	.16453	.16119	.15794	.15480	.15175	.14879	.14592	.14313
65	.18220	.17850	.17492	.17144	.16806	.16479	.16161	.15853	.15553	.15262
66	.19358	.18975	.18604	.18243	.17893	.17552	.17222	.16901	.16589	.16285
67	.20568	.20173	.19788	.19415	.19052	.18699	.18356	.18022	.17698	.17382
68	.21847	.21439	.21042	.20656	.20280	.19915	.19560	.19213	.18877	.18549
69	.23191	.22771	.22362	.21964	.21577	.21199	.20831	.20473	.20124	.19784
70	.24601	.24169	.23748	.23339	.22939	.22550	.22171	.21801	.21440	.21088
71	.26080	.25638	.25206	.24785	.24375	.23974	.23584	.23202	.22830	.22467
72	.27630	.27178	.26736	.26305	.25884	.25473	.25071	.24679	.24296	.23922
73	.29244	.28782	.28331	.27890	.27460	.27039	.26628	.26226	.25833	.25449
74	.30914	.30444	.29984	.29535	.29096	.28666	.28245	.27834	.27432	.27038
75	.32630	.32153	.31686	.31229	.30782	.30344	.29915	.29496	.29085	.28682
76	.34389	.33905	.33432	.32968	.32514	.32069	.31633	.31205	.30787	.30376
77	.36187	.35698	.35220	.34750	.34290	.33839	.33396	.32963	.32537	.32120
78	.38022	.37530	.37047	.36573	.36108	.35652	.35204	.34765	.34333	.33910
79	.39891	.39396	.38910	.38433	.37965	.37504	.37053	.36609	.36173	.35744
80	.41786	.41290	.40802	.40323	.39852	.39389	.38934	.38486	.38047	.37615
81	.43703	.43207	.42719	.42238	.41766	.41302	.40845	.40395	.39953	.39518
82	.45638	.45143	.44655	.44175	.43703	.43238	.42781	.42330	.41887	.41450
83	.47583	.47090	.46604	.46126	.45655	.45191	.44734	.44284	43840	.43403
84	.49532	.49043	.48561	.48085	.47617	.47155	.46700	.46251	.45808	.45372
85	.51480	.50996	.50518	.50047	.49582	.49124	.48671	.48225	.47785	.47351
86	.53421	.52943	.52470	.52004	.51544	.51090	.50642	.50200	.49763	.49332
87	.55346	.54875	.54409	.53950	.53496	.53047	.52604	.52167	.51734	.51307
88	.57254	.56791	.56333	.55881	.55434	.54992	.54555	.54124	.53697	.53275
89	.59134	.58680	.58231	.57788	.57349	.56914	.56485	.56060	.55640	.55225
90	.60982	.60538	.60099	.59665	.59234	.58809	.58388	.57971	.57558	.57150
91	.62794	.62361	.61932	.61508	.61087	.60671	.60259	.59851	.59447	.59046
92	.64564	.64142	.63725	.63311	.62901	.62495	.62093	.61694	.61299	.60907
93	.66284	.65874	.65468	.65066	.64667	.64272	.63880	.63491	.63106	.62724
94	.67955	.67558	.67164	.66773	.66386	.66002	.65621	.65243	.64868	.64496
95	.69574	.69190	.68809	.68431	.68055	.67683	.67313	.66946	.66582	.66221
96	.71131	.70760	.70391	.70025	.69662	.69302	.68944	.68588	.68235	.67885
97	.72626	.72268	.71913	.71560	.71209	.70861	.70515	.70171	.69829	.69490
98	.74063	.73718	.73376	.73035	.72697	.72361	.72027	.71695	.71365	.71037
99	.75442	.75111	.74781	.74454	.74128	.73804	.73483	.73163	.72844	.72528
100	.76744	.76426	.76109	.75794	.75481	.75169	.74860	.74551	.74245	.73940
101	.78001	.77695	.77392	.77089	.76788	.76489	.76191	.75895	.75600	.75306
102	.79172	.78879	.78587	.78297	.78008	.77720	.77434	.77149	.76865	.76582
103	.80354	.80074	.79795	.79517	.79240	.78965	.78690	.78417	.78145	.77874
104	.81442	.81174	.80906	.80640	.80374	.80110	.79847	.79584	.79323	.79063
105	.82511	.82254	.81998	.81742	.81488	.81234	.80982	.80730	.80479	.80229
106	.83887	.83646	.83405	.83165	.82926	.82687	.82449	.82212	.81975	.81739
107	.85466	.85243	.85020	.84798	.84576	.84355	.84134	.83914	.83694	.83474
108	.88172	.87984	.87797	.87610	.87423	.87236	.87049	.86862	.86676	.86490
109	.93900	.93800	.93700	.93600	.93500	.93400	.93300	.93200	.93100	.93000

(f) *Effective/applicability dates.*—This section applies on and after May 1, 2009. [Reg. § 1.664-4.]

☐ [*T.D.* 7202, 8-22-72. *Amended by T.D.* 7955, 5-10-84; *T.D.* 8540, 6-9-94; *T.D.* 8819, 4-29-99; *T.D.* 8886, 6-9-2000 *T.D.* 9448, 5-1-2009 *and T.D.* 9540, 8-9-2011.]

[Reg. § 1.664-4A]

§ 1.664-4A. Valuation of charitable remainder interests for which the valuation date is before May 1, 2009.—(a) *Valuation of charitable remainder interests for which the valuation date is before January 1, 1952.*—There was no provision for the qualification of a charitable remainder unitrust under section 664 until 1969. See § 20.2031-7A(a) of this chapter (Estate Tax Regulations) for the determination of the present value of a charitable interest for which the valuation date is before January 1, 1952.

(b) *Valuation of charitable remainder interests for which the valuation date is after December 31, 1951, and before January 1, 1971.*—No charitable deduction is allowable for a transfer to a unitrust for which the valuation date is after the effective dates of the Tax Reform Act of 1969 unless the unitrust meets the requirements of section 664. See § 20.2031-7A(b) of this chapter (Estate Tax Regulations) for the determination of the present value of a charitable remainder interest for which the valuation date is after December 31, 1951, and before January 1, 1971.

(c) *Valuation of charitable remainder unitrusts having certain payout sequences for transfers for which the valuation date is after December 31, 1970, and before December 1, 1983.*—For the determination of the present value of a charitable remainder unitrust for which the valuation date is after December 31, 1970, and before December 1, 1983, see § 20.2031-7A(c) of this chapter (Estate Tax Regulations) and former § 1.664-4(d) (as contained in the 26 CFR Part 1 edition revised as of April 1, 1994).

(d) *Valuation of charitable remainder unitrusts having certain payout sequences for transfers for which the valuation date is after November 30, 1983, and before May 1, 1989.*—(1) *In general.*—Except as otherwise provided in paragraph (d)(2) of this section, in the case of transfers made after November 30, 1983, for which the valuation date is before May 1, 1989, the present value of a remainder interest that is dependent on a term of years or the termination of the life of one individual is determined under paragraphs (d)(3) through (d)(6) of this section, provided that the amount of the payout as of any payout date during any taxable year of the trust is not larger than the amount that the trust could distribute on such date under § 1.664-3(a)(1)(v) if the taxable year of the trust were to end on such date. The present value of the remainder interest in the trust is determined by computing the adjusted payout rate (as defined in paragraph (d)(3) of this section) and following the procedure outlined in paragraph (d)(4) or (d)(5) of this section, whichever is applicable. The present value of a remainder interest that is dependent on a term of years is computed under paragraph (d)(4) of this section. The present value of a remainder interest that is dependent on the termination of the life of one individual is computed under paragraph (d)(5) of this section. See paragraph (d)(2) of this section for testamentary transfers for which the valuation date is after November 30, 1983, and before August 9, 1984.

(2) *Rules for determining the present value for testamentary transfers where the decedent dies after November 30, 1983, and before August 9, 1984.*—For purposes of section 2055 or 2106, if—

(i) The decedent dies after November 30, 1983, and before August 9, 1984; or

(ii) On December 1, 1983, the decedent was mentally incompetent so that the disposition of the property could not be changed, and the decedent died after November 30, 1983, without regaining competency to dispose of the decedent's property, or died within 90 days of the date on which the decedent first regained competency, the present value determined under this section of a remainder interest is determined in accordance with paragraph (d)(1) and paragraphs (d)(3) through (d)(6) of this section, or § 1.664-4A(c), at the option of the taxpayer.

(3) *Adjusted payout rate.*—The adjusted payout rate is determined by multiplying the fixed percentage described in paragraph (a)(1)(i)*(a)* of § 1.664-3 by the figure in column (2) of Table F(1) which describes the payout sequence of the trust opposite the number in column (1) of Table F(1) which corresponds to the number of months by which the valuation date for the first full taxable year of the trust precedes the first payout date for such taxable year. If the governing instrument does not prescribe when the distribution shall be made during the taxable year of the trust, see § 1.664-4(a). In the case of a trust having a payout sequence for which no figures have been provided by Table F(1) and in the case of a trust which determines the fair market value of the trust assets by taking the average of valuations on more than one date during the taxable year, see § 1.664-4(b).

(4) *Period is a term of years.*—If the period described in § 1.664-3(a)(5) is a term of years, the factor which is used in determining the present

value of the remainder interest is the factor under the appropriate adjusted payout rate in Table D in § 1.664-4(e)(6) that corresponds to the number of years in the term. If the adjusted payout rate is an amount which is between adjusted payout rates for which factors are provided in Table D, a linear interpolation must be made. The present value of the remainder interest is determined by multiplying the net fair market value (as of the appropriate valuation date) of the property placed in trust by the factor determined under this paragraph (d)(4). For purposes of this section, the term "appropriate valuation date" means the date on which the property is transferred to the trust by the donor except that, for purposes of section 2055 or 2106, it means the date of death unless the alternate valuation date is elected in accordance with section 2032 and the regulations thereunder in which event it means the alternate valuation date. If the adjusted payout rate is greater than 14 percent, see § 1.664-4(b) of this section. The application of this paragraph (d)(4) may be illustrated by the following example:

Example. D transfers $100,000 to a charitable remainder unitrust on January 1, 1985. The trust instrument requires that the trust pay to D semi-annually (on June 30 and December 31) 10 percent of the fair market value of the trust assets as of June 30th for a term of 15 years. The adjusted payout rate is 9.767 percent (10% × 0.976731). The present value of the remainder interest is $21,404.90, computed as follows:

Factor at 9.6 percent for 15 years	0.220053
Factor at 9.8 percent for 15 years	.212862
Difference	.007191

$$\frac{9.767\% - 9.6\%}{0.2\%} = \frac{X}{.007191}$$

$$X = .006004$$

Factor at 9.6 percent for 15 years	0.220053
Less: X	.006004
Interpolated factor	.214049

Present value of remainder interest =
$100,000 × 0.214049 = $21,404.90

(5) *Period is the life of one individual.*—If the period described in paragraph (a)(5) of § 1.664-3 is the life of one individual, the factor that is used in determining the present value of the remainder interest is the factor under the appropriate adjusted payout rate in column (2) of Table E in paragraph (d)(6) of this section opposite the number in column (1) that corresponds to the age of the individual whose life measures the period. For purposes of the computations described in this paragraph (b)(5), the age of an individual is to be taken as the age of that individual at the individual's nearest birthday. If the adjusted payout rate is an amount which is between adjusted payout rates for which factors are provided for in Table E, a linear interpolation must be made. The present value of the remainder interest is determined by multiplying the net fair market value (as of the appropriate valuation date) of the property placed in trust by the factor determined under this paragraph (b)(5). If the adjusted payout rate is greater than 14 percent, see § 1.664-4(b). The application of this paragraph may be illustrated by the following example:

Example. A, who will be 50 years old on April 15, 1985, transfers $100,000 to a charitable remainder unitrust on January 1, 1985. The trust instrument requires that the trust pay to A at the end of each taxable year of the trust 10 percent of the fair market value of the trust assets as of the beginning of each taxable year of the trust. The adjusted payout rate is 9.091 percent (10 percent × .909091). The present value of the remainder interest is $15,259.00 computed as follows:

Factor at 9 percent at age 50	0.15472
Factor at 9.2 percent at age 50	.15003
Difference	.00469

$$9.091\% - 9\% \div 0.2\% = X \div 0.00469$$
$$x = 0.00213$$

Factor at 9 percent at age 50	.15472
Less: X	.00213
Interpolated factor	.15259

Present value of remainder interest =
$100,000 × 0.15259 = $15,259.00

(6) *Actuarial tables for transfers for which the valuation date is after November 30, 1983, and before May 1, 1989.*—Table D in § 1.664-4(e)(6) and the following tables shall be used in the application of the provisions of this section:

See p. 15 for regulations not amended to reflect law changes

Table E—Single Life, Unisex—Table Showing the Present Worth of the Remainder Interest in Property Transferred to a Unitrust Having the Adjusted Payout Rate Shown—Applicable for Transfers After November 30, 1983, and Before May 1, 1989

(1)	(2) Adjusted Payout Rate									
Age	2.2%	2.4%	2.6%	2.8%	3.0%	3.2%	3.4%	3.6%	3.8%	4.0%
0 . . .	.23253	.20635	.18364	.16394	.14683	.13196	.11901	.10774	.09791	.08933
1 . . .	.22196	.19506	.17170	.15139	.13372	.11834	.10493	.09324	.08303	.07410
2 . . .	.22597	.19884	.17523	.15468	.13676	.12113	.10749	.09557	.08514	.07601
3 . . .	.23039	.20304	.17920	.15840	.14024	.12437	.11050	.09835	.08770	.07837
4 . . .	.23053	.20747	.18340	.16237	.14397	.12787	.11376	.10138	.09052	.08098
5 . . .	.23988	.21211	.18783	.16656	.14793	.13159	.11725	.10465	.09357	.08382
6 . . .	.24489	.21693	.19243	.17094	.15207	.13549	.12092	.10810	.09680	.08684
7 . . .	.25004	.22189	.19718	.17546	.15637	.13956	.12476	.11171	.10019	.09002
8 . . .	.25534	.22701	.20209	.18016	.16084	.14380	.12877	.11549	.10376	.09337
9 . . .	.26080	.23230	.20718	.18503	.16549	.14822	.13296	.11946	.10751	.09691
10 . . .	.26640	.23774	.21243	.19008	.17031	.15282	.13734	.12361	.11144	.10063
11 . . .	.27217	.24335	.21786	.19530	.17532	.15761	.14190	.12795	.11556	.10454
12 . . .	.27807	.24911	.22344	.20068	.18049	.16257	.14663	.13247	.11986	.10863
13 . . .	.28407	.25497	.22913	.20618	.18579	.16764	.15149	.13711	.12428	.11283
14 . . .	.29013	.26089	.23489	.21175	.19115	.17279	.15643	.14182	.12878	.11712
15 . . .	.29621	.26684	.24067	.21735	.19655	.17798	.16140	.14657	.13331	.12143
16 . . .	.30229	.27279	.24647	.22296	.20196	.18318	.16638	.15133	.13785	.12576
17 . . .	.30838	.27876	.25228	.22859	.20739	.18840	.17138	.15611	.14241	.13010
18 . . .	.31451	.28477	.25813	.23427	.21287	.19367	.17643	.16094	.14702	.13449
19 . . .	.32070	.29085	.26407	.24003	.21844	.19903	.18157	.16586	.15172	.13897
20 . . .	.32699	.29704	.27012	.24591	.22413	.20452	.18685	.17092	.15655	.14358
21 . . .	.33339	.30335	.27629	.25192	.22996	.21014	.19226	.17612	.16153	.14833
22 . . .	.33991	.30977	.28259	.25807	.23592	.21591	.19783	.18146	.16665	.15324
23 . . .	.34655	.31634	.28904	.26437	.24205	.22185	.20356	.18698	.17195	.15832
24 . . .	.35334	.32306	.29566	.27085	.24836	.22798	.20949	.19270	.17746	.16361
25 . . .	.36031	.32998	.30248	.27754	.25490	.23434	.21565	.19866	.18321	.16914
26 . . .	.36746	.33710	.30952	.28446	.26167	.24094	.22207	.20489	.18922	.17494
27 . . .	.37481	.34443	.31678	.29161	.26869	.24780	.22875	.21138	.19551	.18102
28 . . .	.38236	.35197	.32427	.29901	.27596	.25492	.23570	.21814	.20208	.18739
29 . . .	.39006	.35968	.33194	.30660	.28344	.26226	.24288	.22514	.20889	.19400
30 . . .	.39793	.36757	.33980	.31439	.29113	.26982	.25029	.23239	.21596	.20088
31 . . .	.40594	.37561	.34783	.32237	.29902	.27759	.25792	.23985	.22324	.20798
32 . . .	.41410	.38383	.35605	.33054	.30711	.28557	.26577	.24755	.23078	.21533
33 . . .	.42240	.39220	.36444	.33890	.31541	.29377	.27385	.25548	.23855	.22293
34 . . .	.43084	.40072	.37299	.34744	.32389	.30217	.28214	.26364	.24656	.23077
35 . . .	.43942	.40941	.38172	.35617	.33258	.31079	.29065	.27203	.25481	.23887
36 . . .	.44813	.41824	.39061	.36508	.34146	.31961	.29939	.28065	.26330	.24721
37 . . .	.45696	.42720	.39966	.37416	.35053	.32863	.30833	.28950	.27202	.25579
38 . . .	.46591	.43630	.40885	.38339	.35977	.33784	.31747	.29855	.28096	.26460
39 . . .	.47496	.44552	.41818	.39378	.36917	.34722	.32680	.30780	.29011	.27363
40 . . .	.48412	.45486	.42765	.40232	.37875	.35679	.33633	.31727	.29948	.28290
41 . . .	.49338	.46432	.43725	.41201	.38849	.36654	.34606	.32693	.30908	.29239
42 . . .	.50275	.47391	.44700	.42187	.39840	.37648	.35599	.33683	.31890	.30213
43 . . .	.51221	.48360	.45686	.43186	.40847	.38659	.36610	.34691	.32894	.31209
44 . . .	.52175	.49340	.46685	.44199	.41870	.39687	.37640	.35720	.33918	.32227
45 . . .	.53136	.50327	.47693	.45223	.42905	.40728	.38685	.36765	.34961	.33265
46 . . .	.54104	.51323	.48712	.46259	.43953	.41785	.39746	.37828	.36023	.34323
47 . . .	.55077	.52327	.49739	.47305	.45013	.42856	.40823	.38908	.37103	.35400
48 . . .	.56058	.53339	.50777	.48363	.46087	.43941	.41917	.40006	.38202	.36499
49 . . .	.57043	.54358	.51823	.49432	.47173	.45040	.43025	.41121	.39320	.37617
50 . . .	.58035	.55384	.52879	.50510	.48271	.46153	.44149	.42252	.40457	.38756
51 . . .	.59029	.56415	.53940	.51597	.49379	.47277	.45286	.43398	.41609	.39911
52 . . .	.60027	.57450	.55008	.52692	.50496	.48412	.46435	.44558	.42776	.41084
53 . . .	.61026	.58488	.56080	.53793	.51620	.49556	.47595	.45731	.43958	.42272
54 . . .	.62025	.59528	.57154	.54897	.52750	.50707	.48763	.46913	.45151	.43473
55 . . .	.63022	.60567	.58230	.56004	.53884	.51864	.49939	.48104	.46354	.44685
56 . . .	.64018	.61606	.59306	.57113	.55021	.53026	.51121	.49303	.47567	.45908
57 . . .	.65012	.62644	.60384	.58225	.56163	.54192	.52310	.50510	.48789	.47143
58 . . .	.66004	.63681	.61461	.59337	.57306	.55363	.53503	.51723	.50019	.48387
59 . . .	.66993	.64717	.62538	.60452	.58453	.56538	.54703	.52945	.51258	.49642
60 . . .	.67979	.65751	.63615	.61567	.59602	.57717	.55909	.54173	.52506	.50906
61 . . .	.68963	.66784	.64692	.62683	.60754	.58901	.57120	.55408	.53763	.52181

(1)	(2) Adjusted Payout Rate									
Age	2.2%	2.4%	2.6%	2.8%	3.0%	3.2%	3.4%	3.6%	3.8%	4.0%
62 . . .	.69944	.67815	.65769	.63801	.61908	.60087	.58336	.56650	.55028	.53466
63 . . .	.70922	.68844	.66843	.64918	.63063	.61277	.59556	.57898	.56300	.54760
64 . . .	.71893	.69868	.67915	.66032	.64217	.62467	.60778	.59149	.57577	.56060
65 . . .	.72859	.70886	.68982	.67144	.65369	.63655	.62000	.60402	.58857	.57365
66 . . .	.73817	.71897	.70043	.68250	.66517	.64842	.63221	.61654	.60139	.58672
67 . . .	.74766	.72901	.71096	.69350	.67660	.66023	.64439	.62905	.61420	.59980
68 . . .	.75706	.73896	.72142	.70443	.68796	.67200	.65653	.64154	.62699	.61289
69 . . .	.76637	.74882	.73181	.71530	.69928	.68373	.66865	.65400	.63978	.62598
70 . . .	.77559	.75861	.74212	.72610	.71053	.69541	.68072	.66645	.65257	.63908
71 . . .	.78475	.76833	.75237	.73685	.72176	.70708	.69279	.67890	.66538	.65222
72 . . .	.79383	.77799	.76257	.74756	.73294	.71870	.70484	.69134	.67819	.66538
73 . . .	.80279	.78753	.77266	.75816	.74403	.73025	.71682	.70372	.69095	.67850
74 . . .	.81158	.79689	.78256	.76858	.75494	.74163	.72863	.71595	.70356	.69147
75 . . .	.82013	.80602	.79223	.77876	.76561	.75275	.74019	.72792	.71593	.70421
76 . . .	.82844	.81488	.80163	.78867	.77599	.76360	.75147	.73962	.72802	.71667
77 . . .	.83648	.82347	.81075	.79829	.78609	.77415	.76246	.75102	.73981	.72883
78 . . .	.84428	.83182	.81961	.80764	.79592	.78443	.77318	.76214	.75133	.74073
79 . . .	.85187	.83994	.82824	.81677	.80552	.79448	.78365	.77303	.76261	.75238
80 . . .	.85927	.84787	.83668	.82569	.81491	.80432	.79392	.78371	.77369	.76384
81 . . .	.86645	.85556	.84487	.83437	.82404	.81390	.80393	.79413	.78450	.77504
82 . . .	.87336	.86299	.85278	.84275	.83288	.82317	.81362	.80423	.79499	.78590
83 . . .	.88003	.87014	.86042	.85084	.84142	.83214	.82301	.81402	.80517	.79645
84 . . .	.88648	.87708	.86782	.85870	.84971	.84086	.83214	.82355	.81508	.80674
85 . . .	.89273	.88381	.87501	.86633	.85778	.84935	.84104	.83284	.82476	.81679
86 . . .	.89868	.89021	.88185	.87360	.86547	.85745	.84953	.84172	.83401	.82640
87 . . .	.90417	.89613	.88818	.88034	.87260	.86496	.85741	.84996	.84260	.83533
88 . . .	.90923	.90158	.89402	.88655	.87917	.87189	.86468	.85757	.85054	.84359
89 . . .	.91396	.90668	.89948	.89237	.88533	.87838	.87150	.86471	.85799	.85135
90 . . .	.91849	.91156	.90471	.89794	.89124	.88461	.87806	.87157	.86516	.85881
91 . . .	.92278	.91620	.90968	.90324	.89686	.89055	.88430	.87812	.87200	.86594
92 . . .	.92673	.92046	.91426	.90812	.90204	.89602	.89006	.88416	.87831	.87252
93 . . .	.93027	.92429	.91837	.91251	.90670	.90094	.89524	.88959	.88400	.87846
94 . . .	.93341	.92768	.92201	.91639	.91082	.90530	.89983	.89441	.88904	.88372
95 . . .	.93612	.93062	.92516	.91976	.91440	.90908	.90381	.89859	.89341	.88828
96 . . .	.93841	.93309	.92782	.92259	.91740	.91226	.90716	.90211	.89709	.89212
97 . . .	.94044	.93529	.93018	.92512	.92009	.91510	.91015	.90525	.90038	.89555
98 . . .	.94223	.93723	.93226	.92733	.92244	.91759	.91277	.90800	.90326	.89855
99 . . .	.94392	.93905	.93421	.92942	.92466	.91993	.91524	.91058	.90596	.90137
100 . . .	.94559	.94086	.93615	.93149	.92685	.92225	.91768	.91315	.90865	.90417
101 . . .	.94709	.94248	.93790	.93334	.92882	.92433	.91987	.91544	.91104	.90667
102 . . .	.94873	.94424	.93979	.93536	.93096	.92659	.92225	.91793	.91364	.90938
103 . . .	.95077	.94645	.94216	.93789	.93365	.92943	.92524	.92107	.91692	.91280
104 . . .	.95278	.94862	.94449	.94037	.93628	.93221	.92816	.92413	.92012	.91614
105 . . .	.95570	.95178	.94787	.94399	.94012	.93627	.93244	.92863	.92483	.92105
106 . . .	.96017	.95662	.95309	.94957	.94607	.94257	.93909	.93562	.93217	.92872
107 . . .	.96616	.96313	.96010	.95709	.95408	.95107	.94808	.94509	.94211	.93914
108 . . .	.97515	.97291	.97067	.96843	.96620	.96396	.96173	.95950	.95728	.95505
109 . . .	.98900	.98800	.98700	.98600	.98500	.98400	.98300	.98200	.98100	.98000

See p. 15 for regulations not amended to reflect law changes

Table E—Continued. Single Life, Unisex—Table Showing the Present Worth of the Remainder Interest in Property Transferred to a Unitrust Having the Adjusted Payout Rate Shown—Applicable for Transfers After November 30, 1983, and Before May 1, 1989

(1)	(2) Adjusted Payout Rate									
Age	4.2%	4.4%	4.6%	4.8%	5.0%	5.2%	5.4%	5.6%	5.8%	6.0%
0 . . .	.08183	.07527	.06952	.06448	.06005	.05615	.05272	.04969	.04701	.04464
1 . . .	.06629	.05945	.05344	.04817	.04354	.03945	.03585	.03268	.02986	.02737
2 . . .	.06801	.06098	.05481	.04939	.04460	.04039	.03667	.03337	.03046	.02787
3 . . .	.07017	.06297	.05663	.05104	.04611	.04176	.03791	.03450	.03147	.02879
4 . . .	.07259	.06520	.05868	.05294	.04786	.04336	.03938	.03585	.03272	.02993
5 . . .	.07523	.06765	.06096	.05505	.04982	.04518	.04107	.03741	.03416	.03127
6 . . .	.07805	.07029	.06342	.05734	.05195	.04717	.04292	.03914	.03577	.03276
7 . . .	.08103	.07307	.06603	.05978	.05423	.04929	.04490	.04099	.03750	.03438
8 . . .	.08418	.07603	.06880	.06238	.05666	.05158	.04704	.04300	.03938	.03615
9 . . .	.08752	.07917	.07175	.06516	.05928	.05404	.04936	.04518	.04143	.03808
10 . . .	.09103	.08249	.07488	.06811	.06206	.05666	.05183	.04751	.04364	.04016
11 . . .	.09473	.08600	.07820	.07125	.06503	.05947	.05449	.05003	.04602	.04242
12 . . .	.09861	.08968	.08169	.07456	.06817	.06245	.05731	.05271	.04856	.04484
13 . . .	.10261	.09348	.08530	.07799	.07142	.06554	.06025	.05549	.05121	.04735
14 . . .	.10669	.09735	.08899	.08148	.07474	.06869	.06324	.05834	.05391	.04992
15 . . .	.11080	.10126	.09269	.08500	.07808	.07186	.06625	.06119	.05662	.05250
16 . . .	.11491	.10516	.09640	.08852	.08142	.07502	.06924	.05403	.05931	.05504
17 . . .	.11903	.10908	.10012	.09204	.08475	.07817	.07223	.06685	.06199	.05757
18 . . .	.12321	.11304	.10387	.09560	.08812	.08136	.07524	.06970	.06468	.06012
19 . . .	.12747	.11709	.10771	.09923	.09156	.08462	.07832	.07261	.06743	.06272
20 . . .	.13186	.12126	.11168	.10300	.09513	.08800	.08152	.07564	.07029	.06542
21 . . .	.13639	.12558	.11578	.10690	.09883	.09151	.08485	.07879	.07327	.06824
22 . . .	.14108	.13005	.12004	.11094	.10268	.09516	.08831	.08207	.07638	.07119
23 . . .	.14594	.13469	.12446	.11516	.10669	.09897	.09193	.08551	.07964	.07428
24 . . .	.15101	.13954	.12910	.11958	.11091	.10299	.09576	.08915	.08310	.07756
25 . . .	.15632	.14464	.13398	.12426	.11537	.10725	.09982	.09302	.08679	.08108
26 . . .	.16191	.15001	.13914	.12920	.12011	.11179	.10416	.09717	.09075	.08486
27 . . .	.16778	.15567	.14459	.13444	.12514	.11661	.10878	.10160	.09500	.08892
28 . . .	.17394	.16162	.15032	.13997	.13046	.12173	.11370	.10632	.09953	.09328
29 . . .	.18035	.16782	.15632	.14575	.13604	.12710	.11888	.11130	.10432	.09788
30 . . .	.18702	.17429	.16259	.15181	.14189	.13276	.12433	.11656	.10938	.10276
31 . . .	.19393	.18100	.16909	.15811	.14799	.13865	.13002	.12205	.11469	.10787
32 . . .	.20109	.18797	.17586	.16468	.15436	.14482	.13599	.12783	.12026	.11326
33 . . .	.20851	.19520	.18290	.17152	.16100	.15126	.14223	.13387	.12612	.11892
34 . . .	.21618	.20268	.19018	.17861	.16789	.15796	.14874	.14018	.13223	.12485
35 . . .	.22411	.21043	.19775	.18599	.17508	.16494	.15553	.14678	.13864	.13107
36 . . .	.23228	.21844	.20558	.19363	.18253	.17221	.16260	.15366	.14533	.13757
37 . . .	.24071	.22670	.21367	.20154	.19026	.17975	.16996	.16082	.15231	.14435
38 . . .	.24938	.23521	.22201	.20971	.19825	.18756	.17758	.16826	.15955	.15142
39 . . .	.25827	.24396	.23060	.21814	.20650	.19563	.18547	.17597	.16708	.15875
40 . . .	.26741	.25295	.23945	.22682	.21502	.20397	.19364	.18395	.17488	.16638
41 . . .	.27679	.26220	.24855	.23577	.22381	.21259	.20209	.19223	.18298	.17430
42 . . .	.28642	.27172	.25793	.24501	.23289	.22152	.21084	.20082	.19140	.18254
43 . . .	.29629	.28147	.26756	.25450	.24224	.23071	.21988	.20969	.20010	.19107
44 . . .	.30639	.29147	.27745	.26426	.25186	.24019	.22920	.21885	.20910	.19991
45 . . .	.31669	.30169	.28756	.27426	.26173	.24992	.23878	.22828	.21837	.20902
46 . . .	.32722	.31213	.29791	.28450	.27185	.25991	.24864	.23799	.22793	.21842
47 . . .	.33795	.32280	.30849	.29498	.28222	.27016	.25876	.24798	.23777	.22812
48 . . .	.34890	.33370	.31932	.30573	.29287	.28070	.26918	.25826	.24792	.23812
49 . . .	.36007	.34482	.33039	.31672	.30377	.29150	.27987	.26883	.25837	.24843
50 . . .	.37144	.35617	.34170	.32797	.31494	.30258	.29084	.27970	.26911	.25905
51 . . .	.38301	.36773	.35322	.33944	.32635	.31391	.30208	.29084	.28014	.26996
52 . . .	.39476	.37948	.36495	.35113	.33799	.32548	.31358	.30224	.29144	.28115
53 . . .	.40668	.39141	.37688	.36304	.34986	.33729	.32532	.31390	.30302	.29263
54 . . .	.41874	.40350	.38897	.37512	.36191	.34931	.33728	.32579	.31482	.30434
55 . . .	.43093	.41574	.40123	.38739	.37416	.36152	.34945	.33790	.32686	.31631
56 . . .	.44324	.42811	.41364	.39980	.38657	.37392	.36181	.35022	.33912	.32850
57 . . .	.45568	.44062	.42620	.41240	.39918	.38652	.37438	.36276	.35162	.34093
58 . . .	.48623	.45325	.43890	.42514	.41194	.39929	.38715	.37550	.36432	.35359
59 . . .	.48091	.46603	.45175	.43805	.42489	.41226	.40013	.38847	.37727	.36650
60 . . .	.49370	.47893	.46475	.45112	.43802	.42542	.41331	.40165	.39044	.37965
61 . . .	.50661	.49198	.47790	.46436	.45133	.43878	.42670	.41506	.40386	.39306

See p. 15 for regulations not amended to reflect law changes

(1)	(2) Adjusted Payout Rate									
Age	4.2%	4.4%	4.6%	4.8%	5.0%	5.2%	5.4%	5.6%	5.8%	6.0%
62 . . .	.51963	.50515	.49120	.47776	.46481	.45233	.44029	.42869	.41750	.40671
63 . . .	.53275	.51844	.50463	.49131	.47846	.46606	.45409	.44253	.43138	.42060
64 . . .	.54596	.53182	.51817	.50498	.49225	.47994	.46805	.45656	.44545	.43471
65 . . .	.55922	.54528	.53180	.51877	.50616	.49397	.48217	.47076	.45971	.44902
66 . . .	.57253	.55880	.54551	.53264	.52018	.50811	.49642	.48510	47413	.46350
67 . . .	.58586	.57235	.55926	.54657	.53427	.52235	.51079	.49957	.48869	.47814
68 . . .	.59921	.58594	.57306	.56057	.54845	.53668	.52525	.51416	.50339	.49293
69 . . .	.61258	.59956	.58692	.57463	.56270	.55110	.53983	.52888	.51823	.50788
70 . . .	.62597	.61322	.60082	.58877	.57704	.56563	.55453	.54373	.53322	.52299
71 . . .	.63941	.62695	.61481	.60300	.59149	.58029	.56938	.55875	.54839	.53830
72 . . .	.65289	.64073	.62887	.61731	.60605	.59507	.58436	.57392	.56374	.55380
73 . . .	.66635	.65449	.64293	.63165	.62064	.60990	.59941	.58917	.57918	.56942
74 . . .	.67976	.66814	.65688	.64588	.63514	.62465	.61439	.60437	.59458	.58502
75 . . .	.69275	.68156	.67061	.65990	.64944	.63920	.62919	.61940	.60983	.60046
76 . . .	.70557	.69470	.68407	.67366	.66348	.65351	.64375	.63419	.62484	.61568
77 . . .	.71809	.70756	.69724	.68714	.67724	.66755	.65804	.64873	.63961	.63066
78 . . .	.73033	.72014	.71015	.70036	.69075	.68133	.67209	.66303	.65414	.64542
79 . . .	.74235	.73251	.72284	.71336	.70405	.69492	.68595	.67714	.66850	.66001
80 . . .	.75417	.74468	.73535	.72619	.71718	.70834	.69965	.69111	.68272	.67448
81 . . .	.76573	.75659	.74759	.73875	.73006	.72151	.71311	.70484	.69671	.68872
82 . . .	.77696	.76816	.75951	.75099	.74261	.73436	.72624	.71825	.71039	.70265
83 . . .	.78787	.77942	.77110	.76291	.75484	.74689	.73906	.73135	.72376	.71627
84 . . .	.79852	.79042	.78243	.77457	.76681	.75917	.75163	.74421	.73688	.72967
85 . . .	.80893	.80118	.79353	.78599	.77856	.77122	.76398	.75685	.74980	.74286
86 . . .	.81889	.81148	.80417	.79695	.78983	.78280	.77586	.76901	.76224	.75556
87 . . .	.82816	.82107	.81408	.80716	.80034	.79359	.78693	.78036	.77386	.76744
88 . . .	.83673	.82994	.82324	.81662	.81007	.80360	.79720	.79088	.78463	.77846
89 . . .	.84478	.83828	.83186	.82551	.81923	.81302	.80688	.80081	.79480	.78886
90 . . .	.85253	.84632	.84018	.83410	.82808	.82213	.81624	.81041	.80455	.79894
91 . . .	.85994	.85401	.84813	.84232	.83656	.83086	.82522	.81963	.81410	.80862
92 . . .	.86679	.86111	.85549	.84993	.84441	.83895	.83354	.82818	.82287	.81762
93 . . .	.87296	.86752	.86213	.85679	.85150	.84626	.84106	.83591	.83081	.82575
94 . . .	.87844	.87321	.86803	.86289	.85780	.85275	.84774	.84278	.83787	.83299
95 . . .	.88319	.87815	.87314	.86818	.86327	.85839	.85355	.84876	.84400	.83929
96 . . .	.88719	.88230	.87745	.87264	.86787	.86313	.85844	.85378	.84915	.84458
97 . . .	.89076	.88601	.88129	.87661	.87197	.86737	.86280	.85826	.85377	.84930
98 . . .	.89388	.88925	.88465	.88009	.87556	.87107	.86661	.86218	.85779	.85343
99 . . .	.89682	.89230	.88781	.88336	.87894	.87455	.87019	.86586	.86157	.85730
100 . . .	.89973	.89533	.89095	.88660	.88228	.87800	.87374	.86951	.86532	.86115
101 . . .	.90233	.89802	.89374	.88948	.88526	.88106	.87689	.87275	.86863	.86455
102 . . .	.90515	.90094	.89676	.89260	.88848	.88437	.88030	.87625	.87222	.86822
103 . . .	.90871	.90464	.90059	.89656	.89256	.88858	.88463	.88070	.87679	.87290
104 . . .	.91217	.90823	.90431	.90040	.89652	.89266	.88882	.88500	.88120	.87741
105 . . .	.91729	.91354	.90981	.90610	.90240	.89872	.89506	.89141	.88778	.88417
106 . . .	.92529	.92187	.91846	.91507	.91169	.90832	.90496	.90161	.89828	.89496
107 . . .	.93617	.93322	.93027	.92732	.92439	.92146	.91854	.91562	.91271	.90981
108 . . .	.95283	.95062	.94840	.94619	.94398	.94177	.93956	.93736	.93516	.93296
109 . . .	.97900	.97800	.97700	.97600	.97500	.97400	.97300	.97200	.97100	.97000

See p. 15 for regulations not amended to reflect law changes

Table E—Continued. Single Life, Unisex—Table Showing the Present Worth of the Remainder Interest in Property Transferred to a Unitrust Having the Adjusted Payout Rate Shown—Applicable for Transfers After November 30, 1983, and Before May 1, 1989

(1)	(2) Adjusted Payout Rate									
Age	6.2%	6.4%	6.6%	6.8%	7.0%	7.2%	7.4%	7.6%	7.8%	8.0%
0 . . .	.04253	.04066	.03899	.03751	.03618	.03499	.03392	.03296	.03209	.03130
1 . . .	.02516	.02320	.02145	.01989	.01850	.01725	.01613	.01513	.01422	.01340
2 . . .	.02557	.02353	.02171	.02008	.01862	.01732	.01615	.01509	.01414	.01329
3 . . .	.02640	.02427	.02237	.02067	.01915	.01778	.01656	.01545	.01446	.01356
4 . . .	.02744	.02523	.02325	.02147	.01988	.01846	.01717	.01601	.01497	.01402
5 . . .	.02868	.02638	.02431	.02246	.02080	.01930	.01796	.01674	.01574	.01465
6 . . .	.03008	.02767	.02552	.02359	.02185	.02029	.01888	.01761	.01645	.01541
7 . . .	.03159	.02909	.02685	.02483	.02302	.02138	.01991	.01857	.01736	.01627
8 . . .	.03325	.03065	.02831	.02621	.02432	.02261	.02106	.01966	.01839	.01724
9 . . .	.03507	.03236	.02993	.02774	.02576	.02397	.02236	.02089	.01956	.01835
10 . . .	.03704	.03423	.03170	.02941	.02735	.02548	.02379	.02225	.02086	.01959
11 . . .	.03918	.03626	.03363	.03125	.02910	.02715	.02538	.02377	.02231	.02098
12 . . .	.04148	.03845	.03571	.03323	.03099	.02895	.02710	.02542	.02389	.02240
13 . . .	.04387	.04073	.03788	.03531	.03297	.03085	.02892	.02716	.02556	.02410
14 . . .	.04632	.04305	.04010	.03742	.03499	.03278	.03076	.02893	.02725	.02572
15 . . .	.04876	.04538	.04231	.03953	.03699	.03469	.03259	.03067	.02892	.02732
16 . . .	.05118	.04767	.04449	.04159	.03896	.03656	.03437	.03237	.03054	.02286
17 . . .	.05357	.04994	.04663	.04362	.04088	.03938	.03610	.03401	.03210	.03035
18 . . .	.05598	.05221	.04878	.04565	.04280	.04020	.03782	.03564	.03364	.03181
19 . . .	.05843	.05453	.05097	.04772	.04476	.04204	.03956	.03729	.03520	.03328
20 . . .	.06099	.05694	.05325	.04988	.04679	.04397	.04138	.03901	.03683	.03483
21 . . .	.06365	.05946	.05564	.05213	.04893	.04599	.04329	.04081	.03853	.03644
22 . . .	.06644	.06210	.05813	.05449	.05116	.04810	.04529	.04270	.04032	.03813
23 . . .	.06937	.06488	.06076	.05699	.05352	.05033	.04740	.04470	.04222	.03992
24 . . .	.07249	.06784	.06357	.05965	.05605	.05273	.04968	.04686	.04427	.04187
25 . . .	.07584	.07103	.06660	.06254	.05879	.05534	.05216	.04922	.04651	.04400
26 . . .	.07945	.07447	.06989	.06567	.06178	.05819	.05488	.05182	.04890	.04636
27 . . .	.08334	.07819	.07345	.06907	.06503	.06130	.05785	.05466	.05170	.04896
28 . . .	.08751	.08219	.07729	.07275	.06856	.06468	.06109	.05777	.05468	.05182
29 . . .	.09194	.08645	.08137	.07667	.07233	.06830	.06457	.06110	.05789	.05490
30 . . .	.09663	.09096	.08572	.08086	.07635	.07217	.06829	.06469	.06134	.05822
31 . . .	.10156	.09572	.09030	.08527	.08060	.07627	.07224	.06849	.06500	.06174
32 . . .	.10677	.10074	.09515	.08995	.08512	.08062	.07644	.07254	.06891	.06552
33 . . .	.11224	.10604	.10027	.09490	.08990	.08524	.08090	.07686	.07308	.06955
34 . . .	.11798	.11159	.10564	.10010	.09494	.09012	.08562	.08142	.07749	.07382
35 . . .	.12401	.11744	.11131	.10560	.10026	.09528	.09062	.08626	.08218	.07836
36 . . .	.13033	.12357	.11727	.11137	.10586	.10071	.09589	.09137	.08714	.08317
37 . . .	.13693	.12999	.12350	.11743	.11175	.10643	.10144	.09676	.09237	.08825
38 . . .	.14380	.13668	.13002	.12377	.11791	.11242	.10727	.10243	.09788	.09361
39 . . .	.15096	.14366	.13681	.13038	.12436	.11869	.11337	.10837	.10366	.09923
40 . . .	.15841	.15092	.14390	.13729	.13109	.12526	.11977	.11460	.10973	.10514
41 . . .	.16615	.15848	.15128	.14450	.13812	.13212	.12646	.12113	.11609	.11135
42 . . .	.17421	.16637	.15899	.15204	.14549	.13931	.13349	.12799	.12279	.11789
43 . . .	.18257	.17456	.16700	.15988	.15316	.14681	.14082	.13515	.12980	.12473
44 . . .	.19124	.18306	.17533	.16804	.16115	.15463	.14847	.14264	.13712	.13189
45 . . .	.20018	.19184	.18395	.17649	.16943	.16274	.15642	.15042	.14474	.13935
46 . . .	.20943	.20092	.19287	.18524	.17802	.17117	.16468	.15853	.15268	.14713
47 . . .	.21897	.21030	.20209	.19431	.18692	.17991	.17326	.16694	.16094	.15523
48 . . .	.22883	.22001	.21165	.20371	.19616	.18900	.18219	.17571	.16955	.16368
49 . . .	.23900	.23004	.22152	.21343	.20573	.19841	.19145	.18481	.17850	.17248
50 . . .	.24948	.24039	.23173	.22349	.21565	.20818	.20106	.19428	.18781	.18163
51 . . .	.26027	.25104	.24225	.23387	.22589	.21827	.21101	.20407	.19745	.19113
52 . . .	.27135	.26200	.25308	.24457	.23645	.22869	.22129	.21421	.20745	.20098
53 . . .	.28271	.27325	.26421	.25558	.24733	.23944	.23190	.22468	.21778	.21117
54 . . .	.29433	.28476	.27561	.26686	.25848	.25047	.24280	.23545	.22841	.22167
55 . . .	.30621	.29654	.28728	.27842	.26993	.26180	.25400	.24653	.23936	.23249
56 . . .	.31832	.30856	.29921	.29025	.28165	.27341	.26550	.25790	.25061	.24361
57 . . .	.33068	.32085	.31142	.30236	.29367	.28532	.27729	.26959	.26218	.25505
58 . . .	.34329	.33339	.32388	.31474	.30595	.29751	.28938	.28157	.27405	.26681
59 . . .	.35615	.34620	.33662	.32741	.31855	.31001	.30180	.29388	.28626	.27892
60 . . .	.36927	.35927	.34964	.34037	.33143	.32282	.31452	.30652	.29880	.29136
61 . . .	.38265	.37262	.37295	.35362	.34463	.33595	.32758	.31950	.31169	.30416

See p. 15 for regulations not amended to reflect law changes

(1) Age	(2) Adjusted Payout Rate 6.2%	6.4%	6.6%	6.8%	7.0%	7.2%	7.4%	7.6%	7.8%	8.0%
62 . . .	.39630	.38625	.37655	.36718	.35814	.34941	.34097	.33282	.32494	.31733
63 . . .	.41020	.40014	.39043	.38104	.37196	.36318	.35469	.34648	.33854	.33085
64 . . .	.42432	.41428	.40456	.39516	.38606	.37725	.36872	.36046	.35246	.34472
65 . . .	.43866	.42864	.41893	.40953	.40042	.39159	.38304	.37474	.36670	.35891
66 . . .	.45320	.44321	.43353	.42414	.41503	.40620	.39763	.38931	.38124	.37340
67 . . .	.46790	.45796	.44832	.43896	.42987	.42104	.41247	.40414	.39605	.38819
68 . . .	.48277	.47289	.46330	.45398	.44492	.43611	.42755	.41923	41113	.40326
69 . . .	.49781	.48802	.47849	.46923	.46021	.45144	.44290	.43459	.42650	.41863
70 . . .	.51303	.50333	.49389	.48470	.47574	.46702	.45852	.45025	.44218	.43432
71 . . .	.52847	.51888	.50954	.50044	.49156	.48291	.47447	.46623	.45820	.45037
72 . . .	.54412	.53466	.52544	.51644	.50766	.49909	.49072	.48255	.47458	.46679
73 . . .	.55990	.55059	.54151	.53263	.52396	.51549	.50721	.49912	.49122	.48349
74 . . .	.57566	.56652	.55758	.54885	.54030	.53195	.52377	.51578	.50796	.50031
75 . . .	.59129	.58232	.57354	.56496	.55655	.54832	.54027	.53238	.52466	.51710
76 . . .	.60671	.59792	.58932	.58089	.57263	.56454	.55661	.54884	.54123	.53377
77 . . .	.62189	.61330	.60487	.59661	.58851	.58057	.57278	.56514	.55765	.55030
78 . . .	.63687	.62847	.62024	.61215	.60422	.59644	.58879	.58129	.57393	.56670
79 . . .	.65168	.64349	.63546	.62756	.61981	.61219	.60471	.59736	.59013	.58304
80 . . .	.66637	.65841	.65058	.64289	.63532	.62788	.62057	.61338	.60632	.59936
81 . . .	.68085	.67312	.66551	.65802	.65066	.64341	.63628	.62926	.62236	.61556
82 . . .	.69503	.68753	.68014	.67287	.66571	.65866	.65172	.64488	.63815	.63151
83 . . .	.70890	.70164	.69448	.68743	.68048	.67364	.66689	.66024	.65369	.64723
84 . . .	.72255	.71553	.70861	.70179	.69506	.68843	.68189	.67544	.66907	.66279
85 . . .	.73600	.72924	.72257	.71598	.70948	.70307	.69674	.69050	.68433	.67825
86 . . .	.74897	.7446	.73693	.72969	.72342	.71723	.71112	.70508	.69912	.69323
87 . . .	.76109	.75483	.74864	.74252	.73647	.73050	.72460	.71877	.71300	.70731
88 . . .	.77235	.76631	.76035	.75445	.74862	.74285	.73715	.73151	.72593	.72042
89 . . .	.78298	.77717	.77142	.76573	.76011	.75454	.74903	.74358	.73819	.73286
90 . . .	.79329	.78770	.78217	.77669	.77127	.76591	.76060	.75534	.75014	.74499
91 . . .	.80320	.79783	.79252	.78725	.78204	.77688	.77176	.76670	.76159	.75672
92 . . .	.81241	.80725	.80214	.79708	.79206	.78709	.78217	.77729	.77245	.76766
93 . . .	.82074	.81578	.81086	.80598	.80115	.79635	.79160	.78690	.78223	.77761
94 . . .	.82816	.82337	.81862	.81391	.80924	.80461	.80002	.79547	.79096	.78648
95 . . .	.83461	.82997	.82537	.82081	.81629	.81180	.80735	.80394	.79856	.79421
96 . . .	.84003	.83552	.83105	.82661	.82221	.81784	.81351	.80921	.80494	.80071
97 . . .	.84487	.84048	.83612	.83179	.82750	.82324	.81901	.81481	.81065	.80651
98 . . .	.84910	.84481	.84054	.83631	.83211	.82794	.82380	.81969	.81562	.81157
99 . . .	.85307	.84887	.84469	.84055	.83644	.83235	.82830	.82427	.82028	.81631
100 . . .	.85701	.85290	.84882	.84476	.84073	.83674	.83276	.82882	.82490	.82101
101 . . .	.86049	.85645	.85244	.84846	.84451	.84058	.83668	.83280	.82895	.82512
102 . . .	.86424	.86029	.85637	.85247	.84859	.84474	.84091	.83710	.83332	.82956
103 . . .	.86904	.86520	.86138	.85758	.85381	.85006	.84633	.84262	.83893	.83526
104 . . .	.87365	.86991	.86619	.86249	.85880	.85514	.85150	.84787	.84427	.84068
105 . . .	.88058	.87700	.87343	.86988	.86635	.86284	.85934	.85585	.85239	.84893
106 . . .	.89165	.88835	.88506	.88179	.87852	.87527	.87204	.86881	.86559	.86239
107 . . .	.90692	.90404	.90116	.89829	.89542	.89257	.88972	.88688	.88404	.88121
108 . . .	.93077	.92858	.92639	.92420	.92201	.91983	.91765	.91547	.91330	.91113
109 . . .	.96900	.96800	.96700	.96600	.96500	.96400	.96300	.96200	.96100	.96000

Table E—Continued. Single Life, Unisex—Table Showing the Present Worth of the Remainder Interest in Property Transferred to a Unitrust Having the Adjusted Payout Rate Shown—Applicable for Transfers After November 30, 1983, and Before May 1, 1989

(1)	(2) Adjusted Payout Rate									
Age	8.2%	8.4%	8.6%	8.8%	9.0%	9.2%	9.4%	9.6%	9.8%	10.0%
0 . . .	.03059	.02995	.02936	.02882	.02833	.02788	.02747	.02709	.02673	.02641
1 . . .	.01267	.01200	.01139	.01084	.01033	.00987	.00945	.00906	.00871	.00838
2 . . .	.01251	.01181	.01117	.01059	.01006	.00957	.00913	.00872	.00835	.00800
3 . . .	.01274	.01200	.01133	.01072	.01016	.00965	.00918	.00875	.00836	.00799
4 . . .	.01316	.01239	.01168	.01103	.01044	.00991	.00941	.00896	.00854	.00815
5 . . .	.01375	.01293	.01218	.01150	.01088	.01031	.00979	.00931	.00887	.00846
6 . . .	.01446	.01360	.01281	.01209	.01144	.01084	.01028	.00978	.00931	.00888
7 . . .	.01527	.01436	.01353	.01277	.01208	.01144	.01086	.01032	.00983	.00937
8 . . .	.01619	.01523	.01436	.01356	.01283	.01216	.01154	.01097	.01044	.00996
9 . . .	.01725	.01624	.01532	.01448	.01370	.01299	.01234	.01174	.01118	.01067
10 . . .	.01843	.01737	.01640	.01551	.01470	.01395	.01326	.01262	.01204	.01149
11 . . .	.01976	.01865	.01763	.01669	.01583	.01504	.01432	.01364	.01302	.01245
12 . . .	.02122	.02055	.01898	.01800	.01709	.01626	.01549	.01478	.01413	.01352
13 . . .	.02276	.02153	.02041	.01937	.01842	.01755	.01674	.01599	.01530	.01466
14 . . .	.02432	.02303	.02185	.02077	.01977	.01885	.01800	.01721	.01648	.01581
15 . . .	.02585	.02451	.02327	.02213	.02108	.02011	.01922	.01839	.01762	.01691
16 . . .	.02732	.02591	.02462	.02342	.02232	.02130	.02036	.01949	.01869	.01794
17 . . .	.02874	.02726	.02590	.02465	.02349	.02243	.02144	.02052	.01967	.01888
18 . . .	.03013	.02858	.02715	.02584	.02462	.02350	.02246	.02150	.02061	.01978
19 . . .	.03152	.02990	.02841	.02703	.02575	.02457	.02348	.02247	.02153	.02065
20 . . .	.03298	.03128	.02971	.02826	.02692	.02569	.02454	.02347	.02248	.02156
21 . . .	.03451	.03272	.03108	.02956	.02815	.02685	.02564	.02452	.02347	.02250
22 . . .	.03611	.03424	.03251	.03091	.02944	.02806	.02679	.02561	.02451	.02348
23 . . .	.03781	.03585	.03404	.03236	.03081	.02936	.02802	.02677	.02561	.02453
24 . . .	.03965	.03760	.03570	.03393	.03230	.03078	.02937	.02805	.02683	.02569
25 . . .	.04168	.03953	.03753	.03568	.03396	.03236	.03087	.02949	.02820	.02699
26 . . .	.04393	.04168	.03958	.03764	.03583	.03415	.03258	.03112	.02975	.02848
27 . . .	.04642	.04406	.04186	.03982	.03792	.03615	.03450	.03295	.03151	.03017
28 . . .	.04916	.04669	.04439	.04224	.04025	.03838	.03664	.03502	.03350	.03208
29 . . .	.05212	.04953	.04712	.04487	.04277	.04081	.03898	.03727	.03567	.03416
30 . . .	.05531	.05260	.05008	.04772	.04552	.04346	.04154	.03973	.03804	.03646
31 . . .	.05871	.05588	.05324	.05077	.04846	.04630	.04427	.04237	.04059	.03892
32 . . .	.06236	.05940	.05663	.05405	.05163	.04936	.04723	.04523	.04335	.04159
33 . . .	.06625	.06316	.06027	.05756	.05502	.05264	.05041	.04831	.04633	.04448
34 . . .	.07038	.06716	.06414	.06131	.05865	.05615	.05381	.05160	.04952	.04757
35 . . .	.07478	.07142	.06827	.06531	.06253	.05992	.05746	.05514	.05296	.05090
36 . . .	.07944	.07595	.07266	.06957	.06667	.06393	.06135	.05892	.05663	.05447
37 . . .	.08438	.08074	.07732	.07410	.07106	.06820	.06550	.06295	.06055	.05828
38 . . .	.08958	.08580	.08223	.07888	.07571	.07272	.06990	.06723	.06471	.06233
39 . . .	.09506	.09112	.08742	.08392	.08061	.07749	.07454	.07175	.06912	.06662
40 . . .	.10081	.09673	.09288	.08924	.08580	.08254	.07946	.07655	.07379	.07117
41 . . .	.10687	.10263	.09863	.09484	.09126	.08787	.08466	.08162	.07873	.07599
42 . . .	.11325	.10886	.10471	.10078	.09705	.09352	.09018	.08700	.08399	.08112
43 . . .	.11993	.11539	.11109	.10701	.10314	.09947	.09599	.09268	.08953	.08654
44 . . .	.12694	.12224	.11779	.11356	.10955	.10573	.10211	.09866	.09539	.09227
45 . . .	.13424	.12939	.12478	.12040	.11624	.11229	.10852	.10494	.10152	.09827
46 . . .	.14186	.13686	.13210	.12757	.12326	.11916	.11525	.11153	.10798	.10459
47 . . .	.14980	.14464	.13973	.13505	.13059	.12634	.12229	.11843	.11474	.11122
48 . . .	.15810	.15278	.14772	.14289	.13828	.13388	.12969	.12568	.12186	.11820
49 . . .	.16674	.16127	.15605	.15107	.14631	.14177	.13743	.13329	.12932	.12553
50 . . .	.17574	.17012	.16475	.15962	.15472	.15003	.14555	.14126	.13716	.13322
51 . . .	.18510	.17932	.17381	.16853	.16348	.15865	.15402	.14959	.14534	.14127
52 . . .	.19480	.18888	.18322	.17779	.17260	.16763	.16286	.15828	.15390	.14969
53 . . .	.20484	.19878	.19298	.18741	.18208	.17696	.17205	.16734	.16281	.15847
54 . . .	.21520	.20901	.20306	.19735	.19188	.18662	.18157	.17672	.17206	.16758
55 . . .	.22589	.21955	.21347	.20763	.20202	.19662	.19144	.18645	.18165	.17703
56 . . .	.23688	.23041	.22420	.21822	.21248	.20695	.20163	.19651	.19157	.18682
57 . . .	.24820	.24161	.23527	.22917	.22329	.21763	.21218	.20693	.20186	.19698
58 . . .	.25984	.25313	.24667	.24044	.23444	.22865	.22307	.21769	.21250	.20749
59 . . .	.27184	.26501	.25843	.25209	.24596	.24005	.23435	.22885	.22353	.21839
60 . . .	.28417	.27724	.27055	.26409	.25786	.25183	.24601	.24038	.23494	.22969
61 . . .	.29688	.28985	.28306	.27650	.27015	.26401	.25808	.25234	.24678	.24141

See p. 15 for regulations not amended to reflect law changes

(1) Age	(2) Adjusted Payout Rate 8.2%	8.4%	8.6%	8.8%	9.0%	9.2%	9.4%	9.6%	9.8%	10.0%
62 . . .	.30996	.30284	.29596	.28929	.28285	.27661	.27056	.26471	.25905	.25356
63 . . .	.32341	.31621	.30924	.30249	.29595	.28961	.28347	.27752	.27175	.26615
64 . . .	.33721	.32994	.32289	.31605	.30943	.30300	.29677	.29072	.28486	.27916
65 . . .	.35134	.34401	.33689	.32999	.32329	.31678	.31046	.30433	.29837	.29259
66 . . .	.36580	.35841	.35124	.34427	.33750	.33093	.32454	.31832	.31228	.30641
67 . . .	.38055	.37312	.36590	.35889	.35206	.34542	.33897	.33268	.32657	.32062
68 . . .	.39559	.38814	.38089	.37383	.36696	.36027	.35376	.34742	34124	.33522
69 . . .	.41096	.40349	.39622	.38913	.38222	.37550	.36894	.36255	35632	.35024
70 . . .	.42665	.41918	.41190	.40480	.39787	.39111	.38452	.37809	.37182	.36570
71 . . .	.44273	.43527	.42799	.42089	.41395	.40719	.40058	.39412	.38782	.38166
72 . . .	.45919	.45176	.44450	.43741	.43049	.42372	.41710	.41064	.40432	.39814
73 . . .	.47594	.46856	.46134	.45428	.44738	.44062	.43402	.42756	.42124	.41506
74 . . .	.49283	.48550	.47834	.47132	.46446	.45774	.45116	.44471	.43840	.43223
75 . . .	.50969	.50244	.49534	.48838	.48157	.47489	.46834	.46193	.45565	.44949
76 . . .	.52646	.51929	.51226	.50537	.49862	.49199	.48550	.47913	.47288	.46675
77 . . .	.54309	.53601	.52907	.52226	.51558	.50902	.50258	.49626	.49006	.48397
78 . . .	.55960	.55263	.54579	.53907	.53247	.52598	.51962	.51336	.50721	.50117
79 . . .	.57606	.56921	.56248	.55586	.54935	.54295	.53667	.53049	.52441	.51843
80 . . .	.59253	.58580	.57919	.57269	.56629	.55999	.55380	.54771	.54171	.53581
81 . . .	.60887	.60229	.59581	.58943	.58315	.57697	.57088	.56489	.55899	.55317
82 . . .	.62498	.61855	.61221	.60597	.59982	.59375	.58778	.58190	.57610	.57039
83 . . .	.64086	.63459	.62840	.62230	.61629	.61036	.60451	.59875	.59306	.58746
84 . . .	.65660	.65049	.64447	.63852	.63266	.62687	.62116	.61553	.60997	.60448
85 . . .	.67224	.66631	.66046	.65468	.64898	.64335	.63779	.63230	.62688	.62152
86 . . .	.68742	.68167	.67600	.67040	.66486	.65939	.65398	.64864	.64337	.63816
87 . . .	.70168	.69611	.69061	.68518	.67980	.67449	.66924	.66405	.65892	.65384
88 . . .	.71497	.70958	.70425	.69897	.69376	.68860	.68350	.67845	.67346	.66852
89 . . .	.72758	.72236	.71720	.71208	.70702	.70202	.69706	.69216	.68731	.68250
90 . . .	.73989	.73484	.72985	.72490	.72000	.71515	.71035	.70559	.70088	.69622
91 . . .	.75180	.74693	.74210	.73732	.73259	.72790	.72325	.71865	.71409	.70957
92 . . .	.76292	.75821	.75355	.74894	.74436	.73982	.73533	.73087	.72646	.72208
93 . . .	.77302	.76848	.76397	.75951	.75508	.75069	.74634	.74202	.73774	.73350
94 . . .	.78204	.77764	.77328	.76895	.76466	.76040	.75618	.75199	.74734	.74372
95 . . .	.78991	.78563	.78139	.77719	.77302	.76888	.76477	.76070	.75666	.75265
96 . . .	.79651	.79234	.78821	.78411	.78003	.77599	.77199	.76801	.76406	.76014
97 . . .	.80241	.79834	.79430	.79029	.78630	.78235	.77843	.77454	.77067	.76684
98 . . .	.80755	.80356	.79960	.79567	.79176	.78789	.78404	.78022	.77642	.77266
99 . . .	.81236	.80845	.80456	.80071	.79687	.79307	.78929	.78554	.78181	.77811
100 . . .	.81715	.81331	.80949	.80571	.80195	.79821	.79450	.79081	.78715	.78351
101 . . .	.82132	.81754	.81379	.81006	.80636	.80268	.79902	.79539	.79173	.78819
102 . . .	.82582	.82211	.81842	.81476	.81111	.80749	.80389	.80031	.79676	.79322
103 . . .	.83162	.82799	.82439	.82080	.81724	.81370	.81018	.80668	.80319	.79973
104 . . .	.83711	.83356	.83003	.82652	.82302	.81955	.81609	.81265	.80923	.80582
105 . . .	.84550	.84208	.83867	.83528	.83191	.82855	.82520	.82187	.81856	.81526
106 . . .	.85920	.85602	.85285	.84969	.84655	.84341	.84029	.83718	.83408	.83099
107 . . .	.87839	.87558	.87277	.86997	.86718	.86439	.86162	.85884	.85608	.85332
108 . . .	.90896	.90679	.90463	.90246	.90030	.89815	.89599	.89384	.89169	.88955
109 . . .	.95900	.95800	.95700	.95600	.95500	.95400	.95300	.95200	.95100	.95000

See p. 15 for regulations not amended to reflect law changes

Table E—Continued. Single Life, Unisex—Table Showing the Present Worth of the Remainder Interest in Property Transferred to a Unitrust Having the Adjusted Payout Rate Shown—Applicable for Transfers After November 30, 1983, and Before May 1, 1989

(1)	(2) Adjusted Payout Rate									
Age	10.2%	10.4%	10.6%	10.8%	11.0%	11.2%	11.4%	11.6%	11.8%	12.0%
0 . . .	.02610	.02582	.02556	.02531	.02508	.02487	.02466	.02447	.02429	.02412
1 . . .	.00807	.00779	.00753	.00729	.00707	.00686	.00666	.00648	.00631	.00615
2 . . .	.00769	.00739	.00712	.00686	.00663	.00641	.00620	.00601	.00583	.00566
3 . . .	.00766	.00735	.00706	.00679	.00654	.00631	.00609	.00589	.00570	.00552
4 . . .	.00780	.00747	.00716	.00688	.00662	.00637	.00614	.00593	.00573	.00554
5 . . .	.00808	.00773	.00741	.00711	.00683	.00657	.00633	.00610	.00588	.00568
6 . . .	.00848	.00811	.00776	.00744	.00715	.00687	.00661	.00637	.00614	.00593
7 . . .	.00894	.00855	.00819	.00785	.00753	.00724	.00696	.00670	.00646	.00623
8 . . .	.00951	.00909	.00871	.00835	.00801	.00770	.00740	.00713	.00687	.00633
9 . . .	.01019	.00975	.00934	.00896	.00860	.00827	.00795	.00766	.00739	.00713
10 . . .	.01099	.01052	.01008	.00967	.00930	.00894	.00861	.00830	.00800	.00773
11 . . .	.01191	.01142	.01095	.01052	.01012	.00974	.00939	.00906	.00875	.00846
12 . . .	.01295	.01243	.01194	.01148	.01106	.01066	.01029	.00993	.00961	.00929
13 . . .	.01406	.01351	.01299	.01251	.01206	.01164	.01124	.01087	.01052	.01019
14 . . .	.01518	.01459	.01405	.01354	.01306	.01262	.01220	.01181	.01144	.01109
15 . . .	.01625	.01563	.01506	.01452	.01402	.01355	.01311	.01270	.01231	.01194
16 . . .	.01724	.01659	.01599	.01542	.01489	.01440	.01394	.01350	.01309	.01271
17 . . .	.01815	.01747	.01683	.01624	.01568	.01516	.01467	.01421	.01378	.01337
18 . . .	.01901	.01829	.01761	.01699	.01640	.01585	.01534	.01485	.01440	.01397
19 . . .	.01984	.01908	.01837	.01771	.01709	.01651	.01597	.01546	.01498	.01453
20 . . .	.02070	.01990	.01915	.01846	.01780	.01719	.01662	.01608	.01557	.01510
21 . . .	.02160	.02075	.01996	.01923	.01854	.01789	.01728	.01672	.01618	.01568
22 . . .	.02253	.02164	.02080	.02003	.01930	.01861	.01797	.01737	.01680	.01627
23 . . .	.02352	.02258	.02170	.02088	.02010	.01938	.01870	.01806	.01746	.01689
24 . . .	.02462	.02362	.02269	.02182	.02100	.02023	.01951	.01883	.01819	.01759
25 . . .	.02586	.02481	.02382	.02289	.02203	.02121	.02045	.01973	.01905	.01841
26 . . .	.02729	.02617	.02512	.02414	.02322	.02236	.02155	.02078	.02006	.01938
27 . . .	.02891	.02772	.02662	.02558	.02460	.02368	.02282	.02200	.02124	.02051
28 . . .	.03074	.02949	.02832	.02722	.02618	.02521	.02429	.02342	.02261	.02183
29 . . .	.03276	.03143	.03019	.02902	.02792	.02689	.02591	.02499	.02412	.02330
30 . . .	.03497	.03357	.03225	.03102	.02985	.02875	.02772	.02674	.02581	.02494
31 . . .	.03735	.03587	.03448	.03317	.03193	.03076	.02966	.02863	.02764	.02671
32 . . .	.03993	.03837	.03690	.03551	.03420	.03297	.03180	.03070	.02965	.02866
33 . . .	.04273	.04108	.03952	.03806	.03667	.03536	.03412	.03295	.03184	.03079
34 . . .	.04572	.04399	.04234	.04079	.03933	.03794	.03663	.03539	.03421	.03309
35 . . .	.04896	.04713	.04539	.04376	.04221	.04074	.03935	.03803	.03678	.03559
36 . . .	.05243	.05049	.04867	.04694	.04530	.04375	.04228	.04089	.03956	.03830
37 . . .	.05613	.05410	.05217	.05035	.04862	.04699	.04543	.04395	.04255	.04122
38 . . .	.06007	.05793	.05591	.05399	.05217	.05044	.04879	.04723	.04575	.04433
39 . . .	.06425	.06200	.05987	.05785	.05593	.05411	.05238	.05073	.04916	.04766
40 . . .	.06869	.06633	.06409	.06197	.05995	.05802	.05620	.05445	.05279	.05121
41 . . .	.07339	.07092	.06857	.06634	.06421	.06219	.06026	.05843	.05668	.05500
42 . . .	.07840	.07581	.07335	.07101	.06878	.06665	.06462	.06269	.06084	.05908
43 . . .	.08370	.08099	.07841	.07595	.07361	.07138	.06924	.06721	.06526	.06341
44 . . .	.08930	.08646	.08377	.08119	.07874	.07639	.07415	.07202	.06997	.06801
45 . . .	.09517	.09222	.08940	.08670	.08413	.08168	.07933	.07708	.07493	.07287
46 . . .	.10136	.09828	.09533	.09252	.08983	.08726	.08480	.08244	.08018	.07802
47 . . .	.10786	.10464	.10157	.09864	.09582	.09313	.09056	.08809	.08572	.08345
48 . . .	.11470	.11136	.10816	.10510	.10216	.09935	.09666	.09408	.09160	.08922
49 . . .	.12189	.11842	.11509	.11190	.10884	.10591	.10309	.10039	.09780	.09531
50 . . .	.12946	.12585	.12239	.11907	.11588	.11282	.10989	.10707	.10436	.10176
51 . . .	.13737	.13363	.13003	.12659	.12327	.12009	.11703	.11409	.11127	.10855
52 . . .	.14565	.14177	.13805	.13447	.13103	.12772	.12454	.12147	.11853	.11569
53 . . .	.15429	.15028	.14642	.14271	.13914	.13571	.13340	.12922	.12615	.12319
54 . . .	.16327	.15912	.15513	.15129	.14759	.14403	.14060	.13729	.13410	.13102
55 . . .	.17259	.16831	.16419	.16022	.15639	.15270	.14914	.14571	.14240	.13920
56 . . .	.18225	.17784	.17358	.16948	.16553	.16171	.15802	.15447	.15103	.14771
57 . . .	.19227	.18773	.18335	.17912	.17503	.17109	.16728	.16360	.16004	.15660
58 . . .	.20265	.19798	.19347	.18911	.18490	.18083	.17690	.17309	.16941	.16585
59 . . .	.21343	.20863	.20400	.19951	.19518	.19098	.18692	.18299	.17919	.17551
60 . . .	.22460	.21968	.21492	.21032	.20586	.20154	.19736	.19331	.18938	.18558
61 . . .	.23620	.23117	.22629	.22156	.21698	.21254	.20824	.20407	.20003	.19610

See p. 15 for regulations not amended to reflect law changes

(1) Age	(2) Adjusted Payout Rate 10.2%	10.4%	10.6%	10.8%	11.0%	11.2%	11.4%	11.6%	11.8%	12.0%
62 . . .	.24824	.24309	.23810	.23325	.22856	.22400	.21958	.21530	.21113	.20709
63 . . .	.26073	.25546	.25036	.24540	.24060	.23593	.23139	.22699	.22272	.21856
64 . . .	.27364	.26827	.26306	.25800	.25308	.24830	.24366	.23915	.23476	.23050
65 . . .	.28696	.28150	.27619	.27103	.26601	.26113	.25638	.25176	.24727	.24290
66 . . .	.30070	.29515	.28974	.28449	.27937	.27439	.26955	.26483	.26023	.25576
67 . . .	.31483	.30919	.30371	.29836	.29316	.28808	.28314	.27833	.27364	.26906
68 . . .	.32936	.32365	.31808	.31266	.30737	.30221	.29718	.29228	28750	.28283
69 . . .	.34432	.33854	.33290	.32741	.32204	.31681	.31170	.30672	30185	.29710
70 . . .	.35972	.35389	.34820	.34264	.33721	.33190	.32673	.32167	.31672	.31189
71 . . .	.37565	.36977	.36403	.35842	.35294	.34758	.34234	.33721	.33220	.32731
72 . . .	.39210	.38619	.38042	.37477	.36924	.36384	.35855	.35337	.34831	.34335
73 . . .	.40900	.40308	.39728	.39161	.38605	.38061	.37529	.37007	.36496	.35996
74 . . .	.42618	.42025	.41444	.40876	.40318	.39772	.39237	.38713	.38199	.37695
75 . . .	.44345	.43753	.43173	.42604	.42046	.41499	.40962	.40436	.39920	.39413
76 . . .	.46073	.45483	.44904	.44336	.43779	.43232	.42695	.42168	.41650	.41142
77 . . .	.47799	.47212	.46635	.46069	.45513	.44967	.44431	.43904	.43386	.42878
78 . . .	.49524	.48941	.48368	.47805	.47252	.46708	.46173	.45647	.45130	.44622
79 . . .	.51256	.50678	.50110	.49551	.49001	.48460	.47928	.47405	.45890	.46383
80 . . .	.53001	.52429	.51867	.51313	.50769	.50232	.49705	.49185	.48673	.48169
81 . . .	.54745	.54181	.53626	.53079	.52541	.52010	.51487	.50973	.50465	.49965
82 . . .	.56476	.55921	.55374	.54835	.54303	.53779	.53263	.52754	.52252	.51757
83 . . .	.58193	.57648	.57110	.56579	.56056	.55540	.55031	.54529	.54033	.53544
84 . . .	.59907	.59373	.58845	.58325	.57811	.57304	.56804	.56309	.55822	.55340
85 . . .	.61624	.61102	.60586	.60077	.59574	.59077	.58586	.58102	.57623	.57150
86 . . .	.63300	.62791	.62289	.61791	.61300	.60815	.60335	.59860	.59392	.58928
87 . . .	.64883	.64387	.63896	.63411	.62932	.62458	.61989	.61525	.61066	.60613
88 . . .	.66363	.65880	.65402	.64929	.64461	.63998	.63540	.63086	.62638	.62194
89 . . .	.67775	.67304	.66838	.66377	.65921	.65469	.65022	.64579	.64141	.63707
90 . . .	.69160	.68703	.68250	.67802	.67357	.66918	.66482	.66050	.65623	.65199
91 . . .	.70509	.70066	.69626	.69191	.68760	.68332	.67909	.67489	.67073	.66661
92 . . .	.71775	.71345	.70919	.70496	.70078	.69662	.69251	.68843	.68439	.68038
93 . . .	.72929	.72512	.72099	.71689	.71282	.70879	.70479	.70082	.69689	.69299
94 . . .	.73964	.73559	.73157	.72758	.72362	.71970	.71581	.71195	.70812	.70432
95 . . .	.74867	.74472	.74081	.73692	.73306	.72924	.72544	.72167	.71793	.71422
96 . . .	.75625	.75239	.74856	.74476	.74099	.73724	.73353	.72984	.72618	.72254
97 . . .	.76303	.75925	.75550	.75177	.74807	.74440	.74076	.73714	.73354	.72998
98 . . .	.76892	.76521	.76152	.75786	.75422	.75061	.74703	.74347	.73994	.73643
99 . . .	.77443	.77078	.76715	.76355	.75998	.75642	.75290	.74939	.74591	.74245
100 . . .	.77990	.77631	.77275	.76921	.76569	.76219	.75872	.75527	.75184	.74844
101 . . .	.78463	.78109	.77757	.77407	.77060	.76715	.76372	.76031	.75692	.75356
102 . . .	.78971	.78622	.78275	.77930	.77587	.77246	.76908	.76571	.76236	.75904
103 . . .	.79629	.79287	.78947	.78608	.78272	.77937	.77605	.77274	.76945	.76618
104 . . .	.80244	.79907	.79572	.79239	.78907	.78577	.78249	.77923	.77598	.77275
105 . . .	.81198	.80871	.80546	.80222	.79900	.79579	.79259	.78941	.78625	.78310
106 . . .	.82792	.82485	.82180	.81876	.81572	.81270	.80969	.80670	.80371	.80073
107 . . .	.85057	.84783	.84509	.84237	.83964	.83693	.83422	.83152	.82883	.82614
108 . . .	.88740	.88526	.88312	.88098	.87885	.87672	.87459	.87246	.87034	.86822
109 . . .	.94900	.94800	.94700	.94600	.94500	.94400	.94300	.94200	.94100	.94000

See p. 15 for regulations not amended to reflect law changes

Table E—Continued. Single Life, Unisex—Table Showing the Present Worth of the Remainder Interest in Property Transferred to a Unitrust Having the Adjusted Payout Rate Shown—Applicable for Transfers After November 30, 1983, and Before May 1, 1989

(1)	(2) Adjusted Payout Rate									
Age	12.2%	12.4%	12.6%	12.8%	13.0%	13.2%	13.4%	13.6%	13.8%	14.0%
0 . .	.02396	.02380	.02366	.02352	.02338	.02325	.02313	.02301	.02290	.02279
1 . .	.00600	.00585	.00572	.00559	.00547	.00536	.00525	.00514	.00505	.00495
2 . .	.00550	.00535	.00521	.00508	.00495	.00484	.00472	.00462	.00451	.00442
3 . .	.00536	.00520	.00505	.00491	.00478	.00465	.00453	.00442	.00431	.00421
4 . .	.00536	.00519	.00504	.00489	.00475	.00461	.00449	.00437	.00426	.00415
5 . .	.00549	.00532	.00515	.00499	.00484	.00470	.00457	.00444	.00432	.00421
6 . .	.00572	.00554	.00536	.00519	.00503	.00488	.00474	.00460	.00447	.00435
7 . .	.00602	.00582	.00563	.00545	.00528	.00512	.00496	.00482	.00468	.00455
8 . .	.00640	.00618	.00598	.00579	.00561	.00543	.00527	.00512	.00497	.00483
9 . .	.00688	.00665	.00644	.00623	.00604	.00585	.00568	.00551	.00536	.00521
10 . .	.00747	.00723	.00699	.00678	.00657	.00637	.00619	.00601	.00584	.00568
11 . .	.00818	.00792	.00767	.00744	.00722	.00701	.00681	.00662	.00644	.00627
12 . .	.00900	.00873	.00846	.00822	.00798	.00776	.00755	.00735	.00716	.00697
13 . .	.00988	.00959	.00931	.00905	.00880	.00857	.00834	.00813	.00793	.00773
14 . .	.01077	.01046	.01017	.00989	.00963	.00938	.00914	.00892	.00870	.00850
15 . .	.01160	.01127	.01097	.01067	.01040	.01014	.00989	.00965	.00942	.00921
16 . .	.01234	.01200	.01167	.01137	.01108	.01080	.01054	.01029	.01005	.00983
17 . .	.01299	.01263	.01229	.01197	.01166	.01137	.01109	.01083	.01058	.01035
18 . .	.01357	.01319	.01283	.01249	.01217	.01186	.01157	.01130	.01103	.01078
19 . .	.01410	.01370	.01332	.01297	.01263	.01230	.01200	.01171	.01143	.01117
20 . .	.01465	.01422	.01382	.01345	.01309	.01275	.01243	.01212	.01183	.01155
21 . .	.01520	.01475	.01433	.01393	.01355	.01319	.01285	.01253	.01222	.01193
22 . .	.01576	.01529	.01484	.01442	.01402	.01364	.01328	.01293	.01261	.01230
23 . .	.01636	.01586	.01538	.01493	.01450	.01410	.01372	.01336	.01301	.01268
24 . .	.01703	.01649	.01599	.01551	.01505	.01463	.01422	.01383	.01347	.01312
25 . .	.01781	.01724	.01670	.01619	.01571	.01525	.01482	.01441	.01401	.01364
26 . .	.01874	.01813	.01756	.01701	.01650	.01601	.01555	.01511	.01469	.01430
27 . .	.01983	.01918	.01857	.01799	.01744	.01692	.01643	.01596	.01551	.01509
28 . .	.02111	.02042	.01976	.01915	.01856	.01800	.01748	.01697	.01650	.01604
29 . .	.02253	.02179	.02110	.02044	.01981	.01922	.01865	.01812	.01760	.01712
30 . .	.02411	.02333	.02259	.02188	.02121	.02058	.01998	.01940	.01886	.01833
31 . .	.02583	.02500	.02421	.02345	.02274	.02206	.02142	.02080	.02022	.01966
32 . .	.02772	.02683	.02599	.02519	.02443	.02370	.02301	.02236	.02173	.02113
33 . .	.02979	.02885	.02795	.02709	.02628	.02550	.02477	.02407	.02340	.02276
34 . .	.03203	.03102	.03006	.02915	.02829	.02746	.02667	.02592	.02521	.02452
35 . .	.03447	.03340	.03238	.03141	.03048	.02960	.02876	.02796	.02719	.02646
36 . .	.03710	.03597	.03488	.03385	.03286	.03193	.03103	.03017	.02936	.02858
37 . .	.03995	.03874	.03758	.03649	.03544	.03444	.03348	.03257	.03170	.03087
38 . .	.04299	.04170	.04048	.03931	.03820	.03714	.03612	.03515	.03422	.03333
39 . .	.04623	.04487	.04358	.04234	.04115	.04002	.03894	.03791	.03692	.03597
40 . .	.04970	.04826	.04689	.04558	.04432	.04312	.04197	.04087	.03981	.03880
41 . .	.05341	.05189	.05043	.04904	.04771	.04643	.04521	.04404	.04292	.04185
42 . .	.05739	.05578	.05424	.05277	.05136	.05001	.04871	.04747	.04628	.04514
43 . .	.06163	.05993	.05830	.05674	.05525	.05382	.05245	.05113	.04987	.04865
44 . .	.06614	.06435	.06263	.06099	.05941	.05789	.05644	.05505	.05371	.05242
45 . .	.07090	.06901	.06720	.06547	.06380	.06220	.06067	.05919	.05777	.05641
46 . .	.07595	.07396	.07206	.07023	.06847	.06678	.06516	.06360	.06210	.06065
47 . .	.08128	.07919	.07718	.07525	.07340	.07162	.06991	.06826	.06668	.06515
48 . .	.08693	.08474	.08263	.08061	.07866	.07678	.07498	.07324	.07157	.06996
49 . .	.09291	.09061	.08840	.08627	.08423	.08225	.08035	.07852	.07676	.07506
50 . .	.09925	.09684	.09452	.09229	.09014	.08807	.08607	.08415	.08229	.08050
51 . .	.10593	.10341	.10098	.09864	.09638	.09421	.09211	.09009	.08814	.08625
52 . .	.11296	.11032	.10778	.10534	.10297	.10070	.09850	.09637	.09432	.09234
53 . .	.12034	.11759	.11494	.11238	.10991	.10753	.10523	.10300	.10085	.09877
54 . .	.12805	.12519	.12243	.11976	.11718	.11468	.11227	.10994	.10769	.10551
55 . .	.13611	.13313	.13025	.12747	.12478	.12218	.11966	.11722	.11487	.11258
56 . .	.14451	.14141	.13841	.13551	.13271	.12999	.12737	.12483	.12236	.11998
57 . .	.15327	.15005	.14694	.14393	.14101	.13818	.13545	.13279	.13022	.12773
58 . .	.16240	.15906	.15583	.15270	.14967	14673	.14388	.14112	.13844	.13584
59 . .	.17194	.16848	.16513	.16189	.15874	.15568	.15272	.14985	.14706	.14435
60 . .	.18189	.17831	.17485	.17148	.16822	.16505	.16198	.15899	.15609	.15327
61 . .	.19230	.18860	.18502	.18154	.17816	.17488	.17169	.16859	.16558	.16265

(1) Age	(2) Adjusted Payout Rate 12.2%	12.4%	12.6%	12.8%	13.0%	13.2%	13.4%	13.6%	13.8%	14.0%
62 . .	.20317	.19936	.19566	.19207	.18857	.18518	.18187	.17866	.17554	.17251
63 . .	.21453	.21060	.20679	.20308	.19947	.19596	.19255	.18923	.18600	.18285
64 . .	.22635	.22231	.21839	.21457	.21085	.20723	.20371	.20028	.19694	.19368
65 . .	.23864	.23450	.23046	.22653	.22271	.21898	.21535	.21181	.20836	.20500
66 . .	.25140	.24715	.24301	.23898	.23505	.23121	.22748	.22383	.22028	.21681
67 . .	.26461	.26026	.25602	.25188	.24785	.24392	.24008	.23633	.23267	.22910
68 . .	.27828	.27384	.26950	.26527	.26114	.25711	.25317	.24932	.24556	.24189
69 . .	.29246	.28793	.28350	.27918	.27496	.27083	.26680	.26285	25900	.25523
70 . .	.30718	.30256	.29805	.29364	.28933	.28512	.28100	.27697	.27302	.26916
71 . .	.32251	.31783	.31324	.30876	.30437	.30007	.29587	.29176	.28773	.28378
72 . .	.33850	.33375	.32910	.32455	.32009	.31572	.31145	.30726	.30315	.29913
73 . .	.35506	.35026	.34555	.34094	.33642	.33199	.32765	.32340	.31923	.31514
74 . .	.37201	.36716	.36241	.35776	.35319	.34871	.34431	.34000	.33577	.33162
75 . .	.38916	.38429	.37950	.37481	.37020	.36568	.36124	.35688	.35260	.34840
76 . .	.40644	.40154	.39673	.39200	.38737	.38281	.37833	.37393	.36961	.36537
77 . .	.42378	.41887	.41404	.40930	.40464	.40006	.39555	.39113	.38677	.38249
78 . .	.44123	.43631	.43148	.42673	.42205	.41745	.41293	.40848	.40410	.39980
79 . .	.45885	.45394	.44911	.44436	.43969	.43508	.43055	.42609	.42170	.41737
80 . .	.47673	.47184	.46703	.46229	.45763	.45303	.44850	.44404	.43964	.43531
81 . .	.49473	.48987	.48509	.48037	.47573	.47115	.46663	.46218	.45779	.45347
82 . .	.51269	.50787	.50313	.49845	.49383	.48928	.48479	.48036	.47599	.47168
83 . .	.53062	.52586	.52116	.51653	.51195	.50744	.50298	.49858	.49424	.48995
84 . .	.54864	.54395	.53931	.53473	.53021	.52575	.52134	.51698	.51268	.50843
85 . .	.56683	.56221	.55765	.55314	.54869	.54429	.53994	.53564	.53139	.52720
86 . .	.58470	.58017	.57570	.57127	.56689	.56257	.55829	.55406	.54988	.54574
87 . .	.60164	.59720	.59281	.58847	.58417	.57993	.57572	.57156	.56745	.56338
88 . .	.61754	.61320	.60889	.60464	.60042	.59625	.59212	.58804	.58399	.57999
89 . .	.63277	.62851	.62430	.62013	.61600	.61191	.60786	.60384	.59987	.59594
90 . .	.64780	.64364	.63953	.63545	.63141	.62741	.62344	.61952	.61562	.61177
91 . .	.66252	.65848	.65446	.65049	.64655	.64264	.63877	.63493	.63113	.62736
92 . .	.67640	.67246	.66856	.66468	.66084	.65703	.65326	.64951	.64580	.64212
93 . .	.68912	.68528	.68148	.67770	.67396	.67024	.66656	.66291	.65928	.65568
94 . .	.70055	.69680	.69309	.68941	.68576	.68213	.67854	.67497	.67142	.66791
95 . .	.71054	.70689	.70326	.69966	.69609	.69255	.68903	.68554	.68207	.67863
96 . .	.71893	.71535	.71180	.70827	.70476	.70128	.69783	.69440	.69100	.68762
97 . .	.72643	.72292	.71943	.71596	.71252	.70910	.70570	.70233	.69899	.69566
98 . .	.73294	.72948	.72604	.72263	.71924	.71587	.71252	.70920	.70590	.70263
99 . .	.73902	.73561	.73222	.72886	.72551	.72219	.71889	.71562	.71236	.70913
100 . .	.74506	.74170	.73836	.73504	.73174	.72847	.72522	.72189	.71877	.71558
101 . .	.75021	.74689	.74359	.74030	.73704	.73380	.73058	.72738	.72420	.72104
102 . .	.75573	.75244	.74918	.74593	.74270	.73949	.73630	.73313	.72998	.72685
103 . .	.76293	.75970	.75649	.75329	.75011	.74695	.74381	.74068	.73758	.73449
104 . .	.76954	.76634	.76316	.76000	.75685	.75372	.75060	.74751	.74442	.74136
105 . .	.77996	.77684	.77373	.77064	.76756	.76449	.76144	.75840	.75538	.75237
106 . .	.79777	.79481	.79187	.78894	.78602	.78311	.78021	.77732	.77444	.77157
107 . .	.82346	.82078	.81812	.81546	.81281	.81016	.80752	.80489	.80227	.79965
108 . .	.86610	.86398	.86187	.85976	.85765	.85554	.85344	.85134	.84924	.84715
109 . .	.93900	.93800	.93700	.93600	.93500	.93400	.93300	.93200	.93100	.93000

Table F(1)—10 Percent—Table Showing Factors for Computations of the Adjusted Payout Rate for Certain Valuations and Payout Sequences—Applicable for Transfers After November 30, 1983, and Before May 1, 1989

1 Number of Months by Which the Valuation Date Precedes the First Payout		2 Factors for Payout at the End of Each.			
At least	*But Less than*	*Annual Period*	*Semiannual Period*	*Quarterly Period*	*Monthly Period*
.	1		.976731	.965232	.957616
1	2	.992089	.969004	.957596	.950041
2	3	.984240	.961338	.950021	
3	4	.976454	.953733	.942505	
4	5	.968729	.946188		
5	6	.961066	.938703		
6	7	.953463	.931277		
7	8	.945920			
8	9	.938436			
9	10	.931012			
10	11	.923647			
11	12	.916340			
12	.	.909091			

(e) *Valuation of charitable remainder unitrusts having certain payout sequences for transfers for which the valuation date is after April 30, 1989, and before May 1, 1999.*—(1) *In general.*—Except as otherwise provided in paragraph (e)(2) of this section, in the case of transfers for which the valuation date is after April 30, 1989, and before May 1, 1999, the present value of a remainder interest is determined under paragraphs (e)(3) through (e)(6) of this section, provided that the amount of the payout as of any payout date during any taxable year of the trust is not larger than the amount that the trust could distribute on such date under § 1.664-3(a)(1)(v) if the taxable year of the trust were to end on such date. See, however, § 1.7520-3(b) (relating to exceptions to the use of the prescribed tables under certain circumstances).

(2) *Transitional rules for valuation of charitable remainder unitrusts.*—(i) If the valuation date of a transfer to a charitable remainder unitrust is after April 30, 1989, and before June 10, 1994, a transferor can rely upon Notice 89-24, 1989-1 C.B. 660, or Notice 89-60, 1989-1 C.B. 700, in valuing the transferred interest. (See § 601.601(d)(2)(ii)(*b*) of this chapter.)

(ii) For purposes of sections 2055, 2106, or 2624, if on May 1, 1989, the decedent was mentally incompetent so that the disposition of the property could not be changed, and the decedent died after April 30, 1989, without having regained competency to dispose of the decedent's property, or the decedent died within 90 days of the date that the decedent first regained competency after April 30, 1989, the present value of a remainder interest determined under this section is determined as if the valuation date with respect to the decedent's gross estate is either before May 1, 1989, or after April 30, 1989, at the option of the decedent's executor.

(3) *Adjusted payout rate.*—For transfers for which the valuation date is after April 30, 1989, and before May 1, 1999, the adjusted payout rate is determined by using the appropriate Table F, contained in § 1.664-4(e)(6), for the section 7520 interest rate applicable to the transfer. If the interest rate is between 4.2 and 14 percent, see § 1.664-4(e)(6). If the interest rate is below 4.2 percent or greater than 14 percent, see § 1.664-4(b). See § 1.664-4(e) for rules applicable in determining the adjusted payout rate.

(4) *Period is a term of years.*—If the period described in § 1.664-3(a)(5) is a term of years, the factor that is used in determining the present value of the remainder interest for transfers for which the valuation date is after April 30, 1989, and before May 1, 1999, is the factor under the appropriate adjusted payout rate in Table D in § 1.664-4(e)(6) corresponding to the number of years in the term. If the adjusted payout rate is an amount that is between adjusted payout rates for which factors are provided in Table D, a linear interpolation must be made. The present value of the remainder interest is determined by multiplying the net fair market value (as of the appropriate valuation date) of the property placed in trust by the factor determined under this paragraph. Generally, for purposes of this section, the valuation date is, in the case of an inter vivos transfer, the date on which the property is transferred to the trust by the donor, and, in the case of a testamentary transfer under sections 2055, 2106, or 2624, the valuation date is the date of death. See § 1.664-4(e)(4) for additional rules regarding the valuation date. See § 1.664-4(e)(4) for an example that illustrates the application of this paragraph (e)(4).

(5) *Period is the life of one individual.*—If the period described in § 1.664-3(a)(5) is the life of one individual, the factor that is used in determining the present value of the remainder interest for transfers for which the valuation date is after April 30, 1989, and before May 1, 1999, is the factor in Table U(1) in paragraph (e)(6) of this section under the appropriate adjusted payout. For purposes of the computations described in this paragraph (e)(5), the age of an individual is the age of that individual at the individual's nearest birthday. If the adjusted payout rate is an amount that is between adjusted payout rates for which factors are provided in the appropriate

See p. 15 for regulations not amended to reflect law changes

table, a linear interpolation must be made. The rules provided in § 1.664-4(e)(5) apply for determining the present value of the remainder interest. See § 1.664-4(e)(5) for an example illustrating the application of this paragraph (e)(5)(using current actuarial tables).

(6) *Actuarial tables for transfers for which the valuation date is after April 30, 1989, and before May 1, 1999.*—For transfers for which the valuation date is after April 30, 1989, and before May 1, 1999, the present value of a charitable remainder unitrust interest that is dependent on a term of years or the termination of a life interest is determined by using the section 7520 rate and Table D, Tables F(4.2) through F(14.0) in § 1.664-4(e)(6) and Table U(1) of this paragraph (e)(6), as applicable. See, however, § 1.7520-3(b) (relating to exceptions to the use of prescribed tables under certain circumstances). Many actuarial factors not contained in the following tables are contained in Internal Revenue Service Publication 1458, "Actuarial Values, Beta Volume," (8-89). Publication 1458 is no longer available for purchase from the Superintendent of Documents, United States Government Printing Office, Washington, DC 20402. However, pertinent factors in this publication may be obtained by a written request to: CC:DOM:CORP:R (IRS Publication 1458), room 5226, Internal Revenue Service, POB 7604, Ben Franklin Station, Washington, DC 20044.

See p. 15 for regulations not amended to reflect law changes

TABLE U(1)

BASED ON LIFE TABLE 80CNSMT
UNITRUST SINGLE LIFE REMAINDER FACTORS
APPLICABLE FOR TRANSFERS AFTER APRIL 30, 1989,
AND BEFORE MAY 1, 1999
ADJUSTED PAYOUT RATE

AGE	4.2%	4.4%	4.6%	4.8%	5.0%	5.2%	5.4%	5.6%	5.8%	6.0%
0	.06797	.06181	.05645	.05177	.04768	.04410	.04096	.03820	.03578	.03364
1	.05881	.05243	.04686	.04199	.03773	.03400	.03072	.02784	.02531	.02308
2	.06049	.05394	.04821	.04319	.03880	.03494	.03155	.02856	.02593	.02361
3	.06252	.05579	.04990	.04473	.04020	.03621	.03270	.02961	.02688	.02446
4	.06479	.05788	.05182	.04650	.04183	.03771	.03408	.03087	.02804	.02553
5	.06724	.06016	.05393	.04845	.04363	.03937	.03562	.03230	.02936	.02675
6	.06984	.06257	.05618	.05054	.04557	.04117	.03729	.03385	.03080	.02809
7	.07259	.06513	.05856	.05276	.04764	.04310	.03909	.03552	.03236	.02954
8	.07548	.06784	.06109	.05513	.04985	.04517	.04102	.03733	.03405	.03113
9	.07854	.07071	.06378	.05765	.05221	.04738	.04310	.03928	.03588	.03285
10	.08176	.07374	.06663	.06033	.05473	.04976	.04533	.04138	.03786	.03471
11	.08517	.07695	.06966	.06319	.05743	.05230	.04772	.04364	.04000	.03673
12	.08872	.08031	.07284	.06619	.06026	.05498	.05026	.04604	.04227	.03889
13	.09238	.08378	.07612	.06929	.06320	.05776	.05289	.04853	.04463	.04113
14	.09608	.08728	.07943	.07243	.06616	.06056	.05554	.05104	.04701	.04338
15	.09981	.09081	.08276	.07557	.06914	.06337	.05820	.05356	.04938	.04563
16	.10356	.09435	.08612	.07874	.07213	.06619	.06086	.05607	.05176	.04787
17	.10733	.09792	.08949	.08192	.07513	.06902	.06353	.05858	.05413	.05010
18	.11117	.10155	.09291	.08515	.07817	.07189	.06623	.06113	.05652	.05236
19	.11509	.10526	.09642	.08847	.08130	.07484	.06901	.06375	.05899	.05469
20	.11913	.10908	.10003	.09188	.08452	.07788	.07188	.06645	.06154	.05708
21	.12326	.11300	.10375	.09539	.08784	.08101	.07483	.06923	.06416	.05955
22	.12753	.11705	.10758	.09902	.09127	.08426	.07789	.07212	.06688	.06212
23	.13195	.12125	.11156	.10279	.09484	.08763	.08109	.07514	.06973	.06481
24	.13655	.12563	.11573	.10675	.09860	.09119	.08446	.07833	.07274	.06766
25	.14136	.13022	.12010	.11091	.10255	.09495	.08802	.08171	.07595	.07069
26	.14640	.13504	.12471	.11530	.10674	.09893	.09181	.08531	.07937	.07394
27	.15169	.14011	.12956	.11994	.11117	.10316	.09584	.08915	.08302	.07742
28	.15721	.14542	.13465	.12482	.11583	.10762	.10010	.09322	.08691	.08112
29	.16299	.15097	.13999	.12994	.12075	.11233	.10461	.09753	.09104	.08507
30	.16901	.15678	.14559	.13533	.12592	.11729	.10937	.10210	.09541	.08926
31	.17531	.16287	.15146	.14099	.13137	.12254	.11441	.10694	.10006	.09372
32	.18186	.16921	.15759	.14691	.13709	.12804	.11972	.11205	.10497	.09844
33	.18869	.17584	.16401	.15312	.14309	.13384	.12531	.11744	.11017	.10345
34	.19578	.18273	.17070	.15961	.14937	.13992	.13119	.12312	.11565	.10874
35	.20315	.18990	.17767	.16637	.15593	.14628	.13735	.12908	.12142	.11431
36	.21076	.19732	.18490	.17340	.16276	.15291	.14377	.13531	.12745	.12016
37	.21863	.20501	.19239	.18071	.16987	.15982	.15049	.14182	.13377	.12628
38	.22676	.21296	.20016	.18828	.17725	.16701	.15748	.14862	.14037	.13269
39	.23515	.22118	.20820	.19614	.18492	.17448	.16476	.15571	.14727	.13940
40	.24379	.22967	.21652	.20428	.19288	.18225	.17234	.16310	.15447	.14641
41	.25270	.23842	.22511	.21270	.20112	.19031	.18021	.17078	.16197	.15372
42	.26184	.24742	.23395	.22137	.20962	.19864	.18836	.17875	.16975	.16132
43	.27123	.25666	.24305	.23031	.21840	.20724	.19679	.18700	.17782	.16921
44	.28085	.26616	.25241	.23952	.22745	.21613	.20551	.19554	.18618	.17739
45	.29072	.27591	.26203	.24901	.23678	.22530	.21452	.20438	.19485	.18589
46	.30082	.28591	.27191	.25875	.24639	.23476	.22381	.21352	.20382	.19468
47	.31116	.29616	.28204	.26877	.25626	.24449	.23340	.22295	.21309	.20379
48	.32171	.30663	.29241	.27902	.26640	.25449	.24326	.23265	.22264	.21318
49	.33245	.31730	.30300	.28950	.27676	.26473	.25336	.24262	.23246	.22285
50	.34338	.32816	.31379	.30020	.28735	.27521	.26371	.25283	.24253	.23277
51	.35449	.33923	.32479	.31112	.29818	.28593	.27431	.26331	.25287	.24297
52	.36582	.35053	.33603	.32230	.30927	.29692	.28520	.27408	.26352	.25349
53	.37736	.36205	.34751	.33372	.32063	.30819	.29637	.28514	.27446	.26431
54	.38909	.37376	.35921	.34537	.33221	.31970	.30780	.29647	.28569	.27542
55	.40099	.38568	.37111	.35724	.34404	.33146	.31949	.30807	.29719	.28681
56	.41308	.39779	.38322	.36934	.35610	.34348	.33143	.31994	.30898	.29851
57	.42536	.41011	.39555	.38167	.36841	.35575	.34366	.33210	.32106	.31051
58	.43781	.42262	.40810	.39422	.38096	.36828	.35615	.34454	.33344	.32281
59	.45043	.43530	.42083	.40698	.39373	.38104	.36888	.35724	.34609	.33540
60	.46318	.44813	.43372	.41992	.40668	.39400	.38183	.37017	.35898	.34824

See p. 15 for regulations not amended to reflect law changes

BASED ON LIFE TABLE 80CNSMT
UNITRUST SINGLE LIFE REMAINDER FACTORS
APPLICABLE FOR TRANSFERS AFTER APRIL 30, 1989,
AND BEFORE MAY 1, 1999
ADJUSTED PAYOUT RATE

AGE	4.2%	4.4%	4.6%	4.8%	5.0%	5.2%	5.4%	5.6%	5.8%	6.0%
61	.47602	.46107	.44674	.43299	.41979	.40713	.39497	.38329	.37207	.36129
62	.48893	.47410	.45986	.44617	.43303	.42039	.40825	.39657	.38534	.37454
63	.50190	.48720	.47306	.45946	.44638	.43379	.42168	.41001	.39878	.38796
64	.51494	.50038	.48636	.47286	.45986	.44733	.43526	.42362	.41240	.40158
65	.52808	.51368	.49980	.48641	.47350	.46104	.44903	.43743	.42624	.41544
66	.54134	.52711	.51338	.50013	.48733	.47496	.46302	.45148	.44033	.42956
67	.55471	.54068	.52712	.51401	.50134	.48908	.47723	.46577	.45467	.44394
68	.56820	.55437	.54100	.52805	.51552	.50339	.49165	.48027	.46925	.45858
69	.58172	.56812	.55495	.54219	.52982	.51783	.50620	.49494	.48401	.47341
70	.59526	.58190	.56894	.55637	.54417	.53234	.52086	.50971	.49889	.48838
71	.60874	.59564	.58291	.57055	.55854	.54687	.53554	.52453	.51382	.50342
72	.62218	.60934	.59685	.58471	.57291	.56143	.55026	.53939	.52882	.51854
73	.63557	.62301	.61078	.59887	.58728	.57600	.56501	.55431	.54389	.53373
74	.64896	.63669	.62472	.61307	.60171	.59064	.57985	.56932	.55906	.54906
75	.66237	.65040	.63872	.62733	.61622	.60538	.59480	.58447	.57439	.56455
76	.67581	.66416	.65279	.64168	.63083	.62023	.60988	.59977	.58989	.58023
77	.68925	.67793	.66688	.65606	.64550	.63516	.62506	.61517	.60551	.59605
78	.70263	.69166	.68093	.67044	.66016	.65010	.64026	.63062	.62119	.61195
79	.71585	.70525	.69486	.68468	.67471	.66495	.65538	.64600	.63681	.62780
80	.72885	.71860	.70856	.69872	.68906	.67959	.67031	.66120	.65227	.64350
81	.74150	.73162	.72193	.71242	.70308	.69392	.68492	.67609	.66742	.65890
82	.75376	.74425	.73490	.72572	.71671	.70785	.69915	.69059	.68219	.67393
83	.76559	.75643	.74744	.73859	.72989	.72134	.71293	.70466	.69652	.68852
84	.77700	.76821	.75955	.75104	.74266	.73441	.72629	.71831	.71044	.70270
85	.78805	.77961	.77130	.76311	.75505	.74711	.73929	.73158	.72399	.71652
86	.79866	.79056	.78258	.77472	.76697	.75933	.75180	.74438	.73707	.72985
87	.80870	.80094	.79329	.78574	.77829	.77095	.76370	.75656	.74951	.74255
88	.81825	.81081	.80348	.79623	.78908	.78202	.77506	.76818	.76139	.75469
89	.82746	.82035	.81332	.80638	.79952	.79275	.78606	.77945	.77292	.76647
90	.83643	.82963	.82291	.81627	.80971	.80322	.79681	.79047	.78420	.77801
91	.84503	.83854	.83212	.82578	.81950	.81330	.80716	.80109	.79509	.78915
92	.85308	.84689	.84076	.83470	.82870	.82276	.81689	.81107	.80532	.79963
93	.86052	.85460	.84875	.84295	.83721	.83152	.82590	.82033	.81481	.80935
94	.86729	.86163	.85602	.85046	.84496	.83951	.83412	.82877	.82348	.81823
95	.87338	.86795	.86257	.85723	.85195	.84672	.84153	.83639	.83129	.82624
96	.87877	.87354	.86836	.86323	.85814	.85309	.84809	.84313	.83822	.83334
97	.88365	.87861	.87362	.86867	.86375	.85888	.85405	.84926	.84450	.83979
98	.88805	.88318	.87835	.87356	.86880	.86409	.85941	.85477	.85016	.84559
99	.89210	.88739	.88271	.87807	.87347	.86890	.86436	.85986	.85539	.85095
100	.89588	.89131	.88678	.88227	.87780	.87337	.86896	.86459	.86024	.85593
101	.89949	.89506	.89066	.88629	.88195	.87764	.87336	.86911	.86488	.86069
102	.90325	.89897	.89471	.89047	.88627	.88209	.87794	.87381	.86971	.86564
103	.90724	.90311	.89900	.89491	.89085	.88681	.88279	.87880	.87484	.87089
104	.91167	.90770	.90376	.89983	.89593	.89205	.88819	.88435	.88053	.87673
105	.91708	.91333	.90959	.90587	.90217	.89848	.89481	.89116	.88752	.88391
106	.92470	.92126	.91782	.91440	.91100	.90760	.90422	.90085	.89749	.89414
107	.93545	.93246	.92948	.92650	.92353	.92057	.91762	.91467	.91173	.90880
108	.95239	.95016	.94792	.94569	.94346	.94123	.93900	.93678	.93456	.93234
109	.97900	.97800	.97700	.97600	.97500	.97400	.97300	.97200	.97100	.97000

TABLE U(1)

BASED ON LIFE TABLE 80CNSMT
UNITRUST SINGLE LIFE REMAINDER FACTORS
APPLICABLE FOR TRANSFERS AFTER APRIL 30, 1989,
AND BEFORE MAY 1, 1999
ADJUSTED PAYOUT RATE

AGE	6.2%	6.4%	6.6%	6.8%	7.0%	7.2%	7.4%	7.6%	7.8%	8.0%
0	.03176	.03009	.02861	.02730	.02613	.02509	.02416	.02333	.02258	.02191
1	.02110	.01936	.01781	.01644	.01522	.01413	.01316	.01229	.01150	.01080
2	.02156	.01974	.01812	.01669	.01541	.01427	.01325	.01234	.01152	.01078
3	.02233	.02043	.01875	.01725	.01591	.01471	.01364	.01268	.01182	.01105
4	.02330	.02132	.01956	.01800	.01660	.01535	.01422	.01322	.01231	.01149
5	.02443	.02237	.02054	.01890	.01743	.01612	.01494	.01389	.01293	.01208
6	.02568	.02353	.02162	.01990	.01837	.01700	.01576	.01465	.01365	.01275
7	.02704	.02480	.02280	.02102	.01941	.01798	.01668	.01552	.01446	.01351
8	.02852	.02619	.02411	.02224	.02057	.01906	.01770	.01648	.01537	.01437
9	.03014	.02772	.02554	.02360	.02184	.02027	.01885	.01756	.01640	.01535
10	.03190	.02938	.02711	.02508	.02325	.02160	.02012	.01877	.01755	.01645
11	.03381	.03119	.02883	.02672	.02481	.02308	.02153	.02012	.01884	.01768
12	.03585	.03313	.03068	.02847	.02648	.02468	.02305	.02157	.02023	.01902
13	.03798	.03515	.03260	.03030	.02822	.02635	.02464	.02310	.02170	.02042
14	.04012	.03718	.03453	.03213	.02997	.02801	.02623	.02462	.02315	.02181
15	.04225	.03919	.03644	.03395	.03169	.02965	.02779	.02611	.02457	.02317
16	.04436	.04120	.03833	.03574	.03339	.03126	.02932	.02756	.02595	.02449
17	.04647	.04319	.04021	.03752	.03507	.03285	.03082	.02898	.02730	.02577
18	.04860	.04519	.04210	.03930	.03675	.03443	.03232	.03040	.02864	.02703
19	.05079	.04725	.04404	.04113	.03847	.03606	.03386	.03185	.03001	.02833
20	.05304	.04938	.04604	.04301	.04025	.03773	.03543	.03333	.03141	.02965
21	.05537	.05157	.04811	.04495	.04208	.03945	.03705	.03486	.03285	.03101
22	.05779	.05385	.05025	.04698	.04398	.04125	.03874	.03645	.03435	.03242
23	.06032	.05623	.05250	.04910	.04598	.04313	.04052	.03812	.03592	.03390
24	.06302	.05878	.05491	.05136	.04812	.04515	.04242	.03992	.03762	.03550
25	.06589	.06150	.05748	.05380	.05042	.04733	.04448	.04187	.03946	.03725
26	.06897	.06442	.06025	.05643	.05292	.04969	.04673	.04400	.04148	.03916
27	.07228	.06757	.06325	.05928	.05563	.05227	.04917	.04632	.04369	.04126
28	.07582	.07094	.06646	.06234	.05854	.05504	.05182	.04884	.04609	.04355
29	.07958	.07454	.06990	.06562	.06167	.05804	.05468	.05157	.04870	.04604
30	.08360	.07838	.07357	.06913	.06504	.06125	.05775	.05452	.05152	.04874
31	.08788	.08249	.07751	.07291	.06866	.06472	.06108	.05771	.05457	.05167
32	.09242	.08685	.08170	.07694	.07252	.06844	.06465	.06113	.05786	.05483
33	.09724	.09149	.08617	.08124	.07666	.07242	.06848	.06482	.06141	.05824
34	.10234	.09641	.09091	.08581	.08107	.07667	.07257	.06876	.06521	.06191
35	.10773	.10161	.09594	.09066	.08575	.08119	.07694	.07298	.06928	.06583
36	.11338	.10708	.10122	.09577	.09070	.08597	.08156	.07744	.07360	.07001
37	.11932	.11283	.10680	.10117	.09592	.09102	.08645	.08217	.07818	.07444
38	.12554	.11887	.11265	.10685	.10142	.09636	.09162	.08719	.08304	.07915
39	.13206	.12521	.11880	.11282	.10722	.10198	.09708	.09249	.08818	.08414
40	.13888	.13184	.12526	.11909	.11332	.10791	.10284	.09808	.09361	.08942
41	.14601	.13878	.13201	.12567	.11972	.11414	.10890	.10398	.09935	.09499
42	.15342	.14601	.13906	.13254	.12641	.12066	.11525	.11016	.10537	.10086
43	.16112	.15353	.14640	.13970	.13340	.12747	.12189	.11663	.11168	.10701
44	.16913	.16136	.15406	.14718	.14070	.13460	.12885	.12342	.11830	.11347
45	.17745	.16951	.16202	.15497	.14832	.14204	.13612	.13053	.12525	.12025
46	.18608	.17796	.17030	.16308	.15625	.14981	.14372	.13796	.13251	.12735
47	.19501	.18673	.17890	.17150	.16451	.15790	.15164	.14571	.14010	.13478
48	.20425	.19579	.18780	.18024	.17308	.16630	.15987	.15378	.14800	.14252
49	.21375	.20514	.19698	.18926	.18193	.17499	.16840	.16214	.15620	.15056
50	.22352	.21476	.20644	.19856	.19107	.18396	.17721	.17080	.16470	.15890
51	.23358	.22467	.21620	.20816	.20051	.19325	.18634	.17976	.17350	.16755
52	.24396	.23490	.22628	.21809	.21030	.20288	.19581	.18908	.18267	.17655
53	.25465	.24545	.23670	.22836	.22042	.21285	.20563	.19875	.19218	.18592
54	.26563	.25631	.24742	.23895	.23086	.22315	.21579	.20876	.20204	.19562
55	.27692	.26747	.25846	.24986	.24164	.23379	.22628	.21911	.21225	.20568
56	.28850	.27895	.26982	.26109	.25275	.24476	.23712	.22981	.22281	.21611
57	.30041	.29076	.28152	.27267	.26421	.25610	.24833	.24089	.23376	.22691
58	.31263	.30288	.29355	.28460	.27602	.26780	.25991	.25234	.24508	.23811
59	.32515	.31532	.30590	.29685	.28817	.27984	.27184	.26416	.25677	.24968
60	.33793	.32803	.31853	.30940	.30062	.29219	.28409	.27630	.26880	.26159
61	.35093	.34098	.33141	.32220	.31335	.30483	.29663	.28873	.28113	.27381

BASED ON LIFE TABLE 80CNSMT
UNITRUST SINGLE LIFE REMAINDER FACTORS
APPLICABLE FOR TRANSFERS AFTER APRIL 30, 1989,
AND BEFORE MAY 1, 1999
ADJUSTED PAYOUT RATE

AGE	6.2%	6.4%	6.6%	6.8%	7.0%	7.2%	7.4%	7.6%	7.8%	8.0%
62	.36414	.35414	.34451	.33524	.32631	.31771	.30942	.30144	.29374	.28631
63	.37754	.36750	.35783	.34850	.33951	.33084	.32247	.31440	.30661	.29910
64	.39115	.38108	.37137	.36200	.35296	.34422	.33579	.32765	.31978	.31217
65	.40500	.39493	.38519	.37579	.36670	.35792	.34943	.34122	.33328	.32560
66	.41914	.40906	.39932	.38990	.38079	.37197	.36343	.35517	.34717	.33943
67	.43355	.42350	.41376	.40434	.39521	.38636	.37780	.36950	.36145	.35365
68	.44824	.43822	.42851	.41909	.40996	.40111	.39252	.38419	.37611	.36827
69	.46313	.45316	.44348	.43409	.42498	.41613	.40754	.39919	.39109	.38322
70	.47818	.46827	.45864	.44929	.44020	.43137	.42279	.41445	.40634	.39845
71	.49331	.48348	.47391	.46461	.45557	.44677	.43821	.42988	.42177	.41388
72	.50853	.49879	.48930	.48007	.47108	.46233	.45380	.44550	.43741	.42952
73	.52384	.51421	.50482	.49566	.48674	.47805	.46957	.46130	.45324	.44538
74	.53930	.52979	.52050	.51145	.50261	.49399	.48557	.47736	.46934	.46152
75	.55495	.54557	.53641	.52747	.51873	.51020	.50187	.49372	.48577	.47799
76	.57079	.56157	.55256	.54374	.53513	.52670	.51847	.51041	.50253	.49483
77	.58680	.57775	.56890	.56024	.55176	.54346	.53534	.52739	.51960	.51198
78	.60291	.59405	.58537	.57687	.56855	.56040	.55241	.54458	.53691	.52940
79	.61898	.61032	.60184	.59353	.58537	.57738	.56954	.56185	.55431	.54691
80	.63491	.62647	.61819	.61007	.60210	.59428	.58660	.57907	.57167	.56441
81	.65054	.64234	.63427	.62636	.61858	.61094	.60344	.59606	.58882	.58170
82	.66582	.65784	.65000	.64229	.63472	.62727	.61994	.61274	.60566	.59870
83	.68065	.67291	.66530	.65781	.65044	.64319	.63605	.62903	.62212	.61532
84	.69508	.68758	.68020	.67293	.66577	.65872	.65178	.64495	.63821	.63158
85	.70915	.70190	.69475	.68770	.68076	.67392	.66718	.66054	.65399	.64754
86	.72274	.71573	.70882	.70200	.69528	.68865	.68212	.67567	.66931	.66304
87	.73569	.72892	.72224	.71565	.70915	.70273	.69639	.69014	.68397	.67788
88	.74807	.74154	.73509	.72872	.72243	.71622	.71009	.70403	.69805	.69214
89	.76010	.75381	.74759	.74144	.73537	.72937	.72344	.71758	.71179	.70607
90	.77189	.76584	.75985	.75394	.74809	.74230	.73659	.73093	.72534	.71981
91	.78327	.77746	.77171	.76603	.76040	.75484	.74933	.74388	.73850	.73316
92	.79399	.78841	.78289	.77743	.77202	.76667	.76137	.75613	.75093	.74579
93	.80394	.79858	.79328	.78803	.78283	.77768	.77258	.76753	.76252	.75757
94	.81303	.80788	.80278	.79773	.79272	.78776	.78284	.77797	.77315	.76837
95	.82124	.81628	.81136	.80649	.80166	.79687	.79213	.78742	.78276	.77814
96	.82851	.82372	.81897	.81426	.80959	.80496	.80036	.79581	.79129	.78682
97	.83512	.83048	.82588	.82132	.81679	.81230	.80785	.80343	.79905	.79471
98	.84106	.83656	.83210	.82767	.82328	.81892	.81459	.81030	.80604	.80181
99	.84655	.84218	.83785	.83354	.82927	.82503	.82082	.81664	.81249	.80837
100	.85165	.84740	.84318	.83899	.83483	.83070	.82660	.82252	.81848	.81446
101	.85652	.85238	.84827	.84419	.84013	.83611	.83210	.82813	.82418	.82026
102	.86159	.85757	.85358	.84960	.84566	.84174	.83784	.83397	.83012	.82630
103	.86697	.86307	.85920	.85535	.85152	.84771	.84392	.84016	.83642	.83270
104	.87295	.86919	.86544	.86172	.85802	.85434	.85068	.84704	.84341	.83981
105	.88030	.87672	.87315	.86959	.86605	.86253	.85903	.85554	.85207	.84861
106	.89081	.88749	.88418	.88088	.87760	.87433	.87106	.86782	.86458	.86135
107	.90588	.90296	.90005	.89715	.89425	.89137	.88849	.88561	.88275	.87989
108	.93013	.92791	.92570	.92350	.92129	.91909	.91689	.91469	.91250	.91031
109	.96900	.96800	.96700	.96600	.96500	.96400	.96300	.96200	.96100	.96000

See p. 15 for regulations not amended to reflect law changes

TABLE U(1)

BASED ON LIFE TABLE 80CNSMT
UNITRUST SINGLE LIFE REMAINDER FACTORS
APPLICABLE FOR TRANSFERS AFTER APRIL 30, 1989,
AND BEFORE MAY 1, 1999
ADJUSTED PAYOUT RATE

AGE	*8.2%*	*8.4%*	*8.6%*	*8.8%*	*9.0%*	*9.2%*	*9.4%*	*9.6%*	*9.8%*	*10.0%*
0	.02130	.02075	.02025	.01980	.01939	.01901	.01867	.01835	.01806	.01779
1	.01017	.00960	.00908	.00861	.00819	.00780	.00745	.00712	.00683	.00655
2	.01011	.00951	.00897	.00848	.00803	.00762	.00725	.00690	.00659	.00630
3	.01035	.00971	.00914	.00862	.00815	.00771	.00732	.00696	.00663	.00632
4	.01076	.01009	.00948	.00894	.00843	.00798	.00756	.00718	.00683	.00650
5	.01130	.01059	.00996	.00938	.00885	.00836	.00792	.00752	.00714	.00680
6	.01193	.01119	.01051	.00990	.00934	.00883	.00836	.00793	.00754	.00717
7	.01265	.01187	.01116	.01051	.00992	.00938	.00888	.00842	.00800	.00762
8	.01347	.01264	.01189	.01121	.01058	.01001	.00948	.00900	.00856	.00815
9	.01440	.01353	.01274	.01201	.01135	.01075	.01019	.00968	.00921	.00877
10	.01544	.01453	.01369	.01293	.01223	.01159	.01101	.01046	.00997	.00950
11	.01662	.01566	.01478	.01398	.01324	.01257	.01195	.01137	.01085	.01036
12	.01791	.01690	.01597	.01513	.01435	.01364	.01298	.01238	.01182	.01131
13	.01926	.01820	.01722	.01634	.01552	.01477	.01408	.01344	.01285	.01231
14	.02059	.01948	.01846	.01752	.01667	.01588	.01515	.01448	.01386	.01328
15	.02189	.02072	.01965	.01867	.01777	.01694	.01617	.01547	.01481	.01421
16	.02315	.02192	.02080	.01977	.01882	.01795	.01714	.01640	.01572	.01508
17	.02436	.02308	.02190	.02082	.01982	.01891	.01806	.01728	.01656	.01589
18	.02556	.02422	.02298	.02184	.02080	.01983	.01894	.01812	.01736	.01665
19	.02679	.02537	.02408	.02288	.02178	.02077	.01983	.01897	.01817	.01742
20	.02804	.02656	.02519	.02394	.02278	.02172	.02073	.01982	.01898	.01819
21	.02932	.02776	.02633	.02501	.02380	.02268	.02164	.02068	.01979	.01896
22	.03065	.02902	.02751	.02613	.02485	.02367	.02258	.02157	.02063	.01976
23	.03204	.03033	.02876	.02730	.02595	.02471	.02356	.02249	.02150	.02058
24	.03356	.03176	.03010	.02857	.02716	.02585	.02463	.02351	.02246	.02149
25	.03520	.03332	.03158	.02997	.02848	.02710	.02582	.02463	.02352	.02249
26	.03702	.03504	.03321	.03152	.02995	.02850	.02714	.02589	.02472	.02363
27	.03902	.03695	.03502	.03324	.03159	.03006	.02863	.02730	.02607	.02492
28	.04120	.03902	.03700	.03513	.03339	.03178	.03027	.02887	.02757	.02635
29	.04358	.04129	.03917	.03720	.03537	.03367	.03208	.03061	.02923	.02794
30	.04616	.04376	.04154	.03947	.03754	.03575	.03408	.03251	.03106	.02969
31	.04897	.04646	.04413	.04195	.03993	.03804	.03627	.03463	.03309	.03165
32	.05200	.04938	.04693	.04465	.04252	.04053	.03867	.03693	.03531	.03378
33	.05529	.05254	.04998	.04758	.04534	.04325	.04130	.03946	.03775	.03614
34	.05883	.05595	.05326	.05075	.04840	.04620	.04414	.04221	.04040	.03870
35	.06262	.05961	.05680	.05417	.05170	.04939	.04723	.04520	.04329	.04149
36	.06665	.06351	.06057	.05781	.05523	.05280	.05053	.04839	.04638	.04449
37	.07094	.06766	.06459	.06171	.05900	.05646	.05407	.05182	.04971	.04771
38	.07550	.07208	.06888	.06586	.06303	.06037	.05786	.05550	.05327	.05118
39	.08034	.07678	.07344	.07029	.06733	.06454	.06191	.05943	.05709	.05489
40	.08547	.08177	.07828	.07499	.07190	.06898	.06623	.06363	.06118	.05886
41	.09090	.08704	.08341	.07998	.07675	.07371	.07083	.06811	.06553	.06310
42	.09661	.09260	.08882	.08525	.08188	.07870	.07569	.07284	.07015	.06760
43	.10260	.09844	.09451	.09080	.08729	.08397	.08083	.07785	.07503	.07236
44	.10891	.10459	.10051	.09666	.09300	.08954	.08626	.08316	.08021	.07741
45	.11553	.11106	.10683	.10282	.09902	.09542	.09201	.08876	.08568	.08276
46	.12247	.11784	.11346	.10930	.10536	.10161	.09806	.09468	.09146	.08841
47	.12974	.12496	.12042	.11611	.11202	.10813	.10443	.10091	.09756	.09438
48	.13732	.13238	.12769	.12323	.11899	.11495	.11111	.10745	.10397	.10065
49	.14520	.14011	.13526	.13064	.12625	.12207	.11809	.11429	.11066	.10721
50	.15338	.14812	.14312	.13836	.13381	.12948	.12535	.12141	.11765	.11405
51	.16187	.15646	.15130	.14639	.14169	.13721	.13294	.12885	.12495	.12121
52	.17072	.16516	.15985	.15478	.14993	.14531	.14088	.13665	.13261	.12873
53	.17993	.17422	.16876	.16353	.15854	.15377	.14920	.14482	.14064	.13662
54	.18949	.18362	.17801	.17264	.16750	.16258	.15787	.15335	.14902	.14486
55	.19940	.19339	.18763	.18212	.17683	.17176	.16690	.16224	.15777	.15348
56	.20968	.20353	.19762	.19196	.18654	.18132	.17632	.17152	.16691	.16247
57	.22035	.21406	.20802	.20222	.19665	.19129	.18615	.18121	.17646	.17189
58	.23142	.22499	.21881	.21287	.20717	.20168	.19640	.19132	.18643	.18172
59	.24286	.23630	.23000	.22393	.21809	.21247	.20705	.20184	.19682	.19198
60	.25465	.24797	.24154	.23534	.22938	.22363	.21808	.21274	.20759	.20262
61	.26676	.25996	.25341	.24710	.24101	.23513	.22946	.22399	.21871	.21361

BASED ON LIFE TABLE 80CNSMT
UNITRUST SINGLE LIFE REMAINDER FACTORS
APPLICABLE FOR TRANSFERS AFTER APRIL 30, 1989,
AND BEFORE MAY 1, 1999
ADJUSTED PAYOUT RATE

AGE	8.2%	8.4%	8.6%	8.8%	9.0%	9.2%	9.4%	9.6%	9.8%	10.0%
62	.27916	.27225	.26559	.25916	.25295	.24695	.24117	.23557	.23017	.22495
63	.29184	.28483	.27806	.27152	.26520	.25909	.25319	.24748	.24196	.23661
64	.30483	.29772	.29085	.28421	.27779	.27157	.26555	.25973	.25409	.24863
65	.31817	.31098	.30402	.29729	.29076	.28444	.27832	.27240	.26665	.26108
66	.33192	.32466	.31762	.31079	.30418	.29777	.29155	.28552	.27968	.27400
67	.34609	.33876	.33164	.32474	.31805	.31156	.30525	.29913	.29319	.28742
68	.36066	.35328	.34610	.33914	.33238	.32581	.31943	.31323	.30720	.30134
69	.37558	.36815	.36093	.35391	.34709	.34045	.33400	.32773	.32163	.31569
70	.39078	.38332	.37606	.36900	.36213	.35545	.34894	.34260	.33643	.33042
71	.40620	.39872	.39144	.38435	.37744	.37071	.36415	.35776	.35153	.34547
72	.42184	.41435	.40706	.39994	.39301	.38625	.37965	.37322	.36694	.36082
73	.43771	.43023	.42293	.41581	.40886	.40207	.39545	.38899	.38267	.37651
74	.45387	.44641	.43912	.43201	.42505	.41826	.41163	.40514	.39881	.39261
75	.47039	.46296	.45570	.44861	.44167	.43488	.42824	.42175	.41541	.40920
76	.48729	.47991	.47269	.46563	.45872	.45196	.44534	.43886	.43251	.42630
77	.50452	.49722	.49006	.48305	.47619	.46946	.46287	.45642	.45009	.44389
78	.52203	.51481	.50773	.50079	.49399	.48732	.48078	.47437	.46808	.46191
79	.53966	.53254	.52556	.51870	.51198	.50538	.49891	.49255	.48632	.48019
80	.55728	.55028	.54340	.53665	.53002	.52351	.51712	.51083	.50466	.49860
81	.57471	.56784	.56109	.55445	.54792	.54151	.53521	.52901	.52292	.51692
82	.59186	.58512	.57850	.57199	.56558	.55927	.55307	.54697	.54097	.53506
83	.60863	.60204	.59556	.58918	.58289	.57671	.57062	.56462	.55872	.55290
84	.62505	.61862	.61228	.60604	.59989	.59383	.58786	.58198	.57618	.57047
85	.64118	.63491	.62873	.62263	.61663	.61070	.60486	.59911	.59343	.58783
86	.65685	.65075	.64473	.63879	.63294	.62716	.62145	.61583	.61027	.60479
87	.67187	.66594	.66008	.65430	.64859	.64296	.63739	.63190	.62647	.62112
88	.68631	.68054	.67485	.66923	.66367	.65818	.65276	.64740	.64211	.63688
89	.70042	.69483	.68930	.68384	.67845	.67311	.66784	.66262	.65747	.65237
90	.71434	.70894	.70359	.69830	.69307	.68790	.68278	.67772	.67271	.66775
91	.72789	.72266	.71750	.71239	.70733	.70232	.69736	.69246	.68760	.68280
92	.74070	.73567	.73068	.72574	.72085	.71601	.71121	.70647	.70176	.69711
93	.75266	.74780	.74298	.73821	.73348	.72880	.72417	.71957	.71502	.71051
94	.76363	.75893	.75428	.74967	.74510	.74057	.73608	.73163	.72722	.72285
95	.77356	.76901	.76451	.76005	.75562	.75123	.74688	.74257	.73829	.73405
96	.78237	.77797	.77360	.76927	.76497	.76071	.75648	.75229	.74813	.74401
97	.79039	.78612	.78187	.77766	.77348	.76934	.76523	.76115	.75710	.75308
98	.79762	.79345	.78932	.78522	.78115	.77711	.77310	.76913	.76518	.76126
99	.80429	.80023	.79620	.79220	.78823	.78429	.78038	.77649	.77264	.76881
100	.81047	.80651	.80258	.79867	.79479	.79094	.78712	.78332	.77955	.77580
101	.81636	.81249	.80865	.80483	.80104	.79727	.79352	.78981	.78611	.78244
102	.82250	.81872	.81497	.81124	.80754	.80386	.80020	.79656	.79295	.78936
103	.82900	.82532	.82167	.81804	.81442	.81083	.80726	.80371	.80018	.79667
104	.83622	.83266	.82911	.82558	.82207	.81858	.81510	.81165	.80821	.80479
105	.84517	.84174	.83833	.83494	.83156	.82819	.82485	.82151	.81820	.81489
106	.85814	.85494	.85175	.84857	.84540	.84225	.83911	.83598	.83286	.82975
107	.87704	.87420	.87136	.86853	.86571	.86290	.86009	.85729	.85450	.85171
108	.90812	.90593	.90375	.90156	.89939	.89721	.89504	.89286	.89070	.88853
109	.95900	.95800	.95700	.95600	.95500	.95400	.95300	.95200	.95100	.95000

TABLE U(1)

BASED ON LIFE TABLE 80CNSMT
UNITRUST SINGLE LIFE REMAINDER FACTORS
APPLICABLE FOR TRANSFERS AFTER APRIL 30, 1989,
AND BEFORE MAY 1, 1999
ADJUSTED PAYOUT RATE

AGE	10.2%	10.4%	10.6%	10.8%	11.0%	11.2%	11.4%	11.6%	11.8%	12.0%
0	.01754	.01731	.01710	.01690	.01671	.01654	.01638	.01622	.01608	.01594
1	.00630	.00607	.00585	.00565	.00547	.00530	.00514	.00499	.00485	.00472
2	.00604	.00579	.00557	.00536	.00516	.00498	.00481	.00465	.00451	.00437
3	.00604	.00578	.00554	.00532	.00511	.00492	.00474	.00458	.00442	.00427
4	.00621	.00593	.00568	.00544	.00522	.00502	.00483	.00465	.00448	.00433
5	.00648	.00619	.00592	.00567	.00544	.00522	.00502	.00483	.00465	.00449
6	.00684	.00653	.00624	.00597	.00572	.00549	.00528	.00507	.00489	.00471
7	.00726	.00693	.00663	.00634	.00608	.00583	.00560	.00539	.00518	.00499
8	.00777	.00742	.00709	.00679	.00651	.00624	.00600	.00577	.00555	.00535
9	.00837	.00800	.00765	.00733	.00703	.00675	.00649	.00625	.00602	.00580
10	.00908	.00868	.00832	.00797	.00765	.00736	.00708	.00682	.00657	.00634
11	.00991	.00949	.00910	.00874	.00840	.00808	.00779	.00751	.00725	.00700
12	.01083	.01039	.00997	.00959	.00923	.00890	.00858	.00829	.00801	.00775
13	.01181	.01134	.01090	.01049	.01012	.00976	.00943	.00912	.00883	.00855
14	.01275	.01226	.01180	.01137	.01097	.01060	.01025	.00992	.00961	.00932
15	.01365	.01313	.01264	.01219	.01177	.01138	.01101	.01066	.01034	.01003
16	.01449	.01394	.01343	.01295	.01251	.01209	.01171	.01134	.01100	.01068
17	.01526	.01469	.01415	.01365	.01318	.01274	.01233	.01195	.01159	.01125
18	.01600	.01539	.01482	.01430	.01380	.01334	.01291	.01251	.01213	.01177
19	.01673	.01609	.01550	.01494	.01442	.01393	.01348	.01305	.01265	.01227
20	.01747	.01679	.01616	.01557	.01502	.01451	.01403	.01358	.01316	.01276
21	.01820	.01748	.01682	.01620	.01562	.01508	.01457	.01409	.01365	.01323
22	.01895	.01819	.01749	.01683	.01622	.01565	.01511	.01461	.01414	.01369
23	.01972	.01893	.01818	.01749	.01684	.01624	.01567	.01514	.01464	.01417
24	.02058	.01974	.01895	.01822	.01753	.01689	.01629	.01572	.01519	.01469
25	.02154	.02064	.01981	.01903	.01830	.01762	.01698	.01638	.01582	.01529
26	.02262	.02167	.02079	.01996	.01919	.01847	.01779	.01715	.01655	.01599
27	.02385	.02284	.02191	.02103	.02021	.01944	.01872	.01804	.01740	.01680
28	.02521	.02415	.02316	.02222	.02135	.02053	.01977	.01904	.01836	.01772
29	.02673	.02561	.02455	.02357	.02264	.02177	.02095	.02018	.01946	.01877
30	.02842	.02723	.02611	.02506	.02407	.02315	.02227	.02146	.02068	.01996
31	.03030	.02903	.02784	.02673	.02568	.02470	.02377	.02290	.02207	.02130
32	.03235	.03101	.02976	.02857	.02746	.02641	.02543	.02450	.02362	.02279
33	.03463	.03321	.03188	.03062	.02944	.02833	.02728	.02629	.02535	.02447
34	.03711	.03561	.03419	.03286	.03161	.03043	.02931	.02826	.02726	.02632
35	.03981	.03822	.03672	.03531	.03398	.03273	.03154	.03042	.02936	.02836
36	.04271	.04103	.03945	.03796	.03655	.03522	.03396	.03277	.03164	.03057
37	.04584	.04407	.04239	.04081	.03932	.03791	.03657	.03531	.03411	.03297
38	.04920	.04733	.04556	.04389	.04231	.04082	.03940	.03806	.03679	.03558
39	.05280	.05083	.04897	.04721	.04554	.04396	.04246	.04103	.03968	.03840
40	.05667	.05459	.05263	.05077	.04901	.04733	.04575	.04424	.04280	.04144
41	.06080	.05861	.05655	.05459	.05272	.05096	.04928	.04768	.04617	.04472
42	.06518	.06289	.06071	.05864	.05668	.05482	.05305	.05136	.04975	.04822
43	.06982	.06742	.06513	.06296	.06089	.05893	.05706	.05528	.05358	.05196
44	.07475	.07223	.06983	.06754	.06537	.06330	.06133	.05945	.05766	.05595
45	.07998	.07733	.07481	.07242	.07014	.06796	.06588	.06390	.06202	.06021
46	.08550	.08273	.08010	.07758	.07519	.07290	.07072	.06864	.06665	.06474
47	.09134	.08845	.08569	.08306	.08055	.07815	.07586	.07367	.07157	.06957
48	.09748	.09446	.09158	.08882	.08619	.08368	.08128	.07898	.07678	.07467
49	.10391	.10076	.09775	.09487	.09212	.08949	.08697	.08456	.08225	.08003
50	.11062	.10734	.10420	.10120	.09832	.09557	.09293	.09041	.08798	.08566
51	.11764	.11423	.11096	.10783	.10483	.10195	.09919	.09655	.09401	.09158
52	.12503	.12148	.11807	.11481	.11168	.10868	.10581	.10304	.10039	.09784
53	.13278	.12909	.12556	.12216	.11891	.11578	.11278	.10989	.10712	.10445
54	.14088	.13706	.13339	.12986	.12648	.12322	.12009	.11709	.11419	.11141
55	.14936	.14540	.14159	.13793	.13442	.13103	.12778	.12464	.12163	.11872
56	.15821	.15412	.15018	.14639	.14274	.13923	.13584	.13258	.12944	.12642
57	.16749	.16326	.15918	.15526	.15148	.14784	.14433	.14094	.13768	.13453
58	.17719	.17282	.16862	.16456	.16065	.15688	.15324	.14973	.14634	.14306
59	.18731	.18281	.17847	.17429	.17025	.16634	.16258	.15894	.15543	.15203
60	.19782	.19319	.18872	.18440	.18023	.17621	.17231	.16855	.16491	.16139
61	.20869	.20393	.19934	.19489	.19060	.18644	.18242	.17854	.17477	.17113

BASED ON LIFE TABLE 80CNSMT
UNITRUST SINGLE LIFE REMAINDER FACTORS
APPLICABLE FOR TRANSFERS AFTER APRIL 30, 1989,
AND BEFORE MAY 1, 1999
ADJUSTED PAYOUT RATE

AGE	10.2%	10.4%	10.6%	10.8%	11.0%	11.2%	11.4%	11.6%	11.8%	12.0%
62	.21990	.21502	.21029	.20573	.20131	.19703	.19289	.18887	.18499	.18123
63	.23144	.22644	.22159	.21690	.21236	.20796	.20370	.19956	.19556	.19167
64	.24335	.23823	.23326	.22845	.22379	.21927	.21489	.21063	.20651	.20250
65	.25568	.25045	.24537	.24044	.23566	.23103	.22653	.22216	.21791	.21379
66	.26850	.26316	.25797	.25293	.24804	.24329	.23868	.23420	.22984	.22560
67	.28182	.27637	.27108	.26594	.26095	.25609	.25137	.24678	.24231	.23797
68	.29565	.29011	.28472	.27949	.27439	.26943	.26461	.25991	.25534	.25089
69	.30991	.30429	.29882	.29349	.28830	.28325	.27833	.27354	.26887	.26432
70	.32457	.31887	.31332	.30791	.30264	.29750	.29249	.28760	28284	.27820
71	.33955	.33378	.32816	.32267	.31732	.31210	.30701	.30204	.29719	.29246
72	.35485	.34902	.34333	.33778	.33236	.32707	.32190	.31686	.31193	.30711
73	.37049	.36461	.35887	.35326	.34778	.34242	.33719	.33207	.32707	.32218
74	.38656	.38064	.37485	.36920	.36366	.35825	.35296	.34778	.34272	.33776
75	.40312	.39717	.39136	.38566	.38009	.37464	.36930	.36407	.35895	.35394
76	.42022	.41426	.40842	.40271	.39711	.39163	.38625	.38099	.37583	.37077
77	.43782	.43187	.42603	.42031	.41470	.40920	.40380	.39851	.39332	.38823
78	.45586	.44992	.44410	.43839	.43278	.42728	.42188	.41658	.41138	.40627
79	.47418	.46828	.46248	.45679	.45120	.44572	.44033	.43503	.42983	.42472
80	.49264	.48679	.48103	.47538	.46982	.46436	.45900	.45372	.44853	.44343
81	.51103	.50524	.49954	.49394	.48843	.48301	.47768	.47243	.46727	.46219
82	.52925	.52352	.51789	.51235	.50690	.50153	.49624	.49104	.48591	.48087
83	.54718	.54154	.53598	.53051	.52512	.51981	.51459	.50943	.50436	.49936
84	.56484	.55930	.55383	.54844	.54313	.53789	.53273	.52764	.52262	.51767
85	.58231	.57686	.57149	.56619	.56096	.55581	.55072	.54571	.54076	.53588
86	.59939	.59405	.58878	.58358	.57845	.57339	.56839	.56346	.55858	.55377
87	.61583	.61061	.60545	.60035	.59532	.59035	.58545	.58060	.57581	.57108
88	.63171	.62661	.62156	.61658	.61165	.60678	.60196	.59721	.59251	.58786
89	.64733	.64235	.63742	.63255	.62774	.62298	.61827	.61361	.60900	.60444
90	.66285	.65801	.65321	.64847	.64377	.63913	.63453	.62998	.62548	.62103
91	.67804	.67334	.66868	.66407	.65950	.65498	.65050	.64607	.64169	.63735
92	.69250	.68793	.68341	.67893	.67450	.67011	.66575	.66144	.65718	.65295
93	.70604	.70162	.69723	.69288	.68858	.68431	.68008	.67589	.67174	.66762
94	.71852	.71422	.70997	.70575	.70156	.69742	.69331	.68923	.68519	.68119
95	.72984	.72567	.72154	.71744	.71337	.70934	.70534	.70137	.69744	.69354
96	.73992	.73586	.73183	.72784	.72388	.71995	.71605	.71218	.70835	.70454
97	.74910	.74514	.74122	.73733	.73346	.72963	.72582	.72205	.71830	.71458
98	.75737	.75351	.74967	.74587	.74209	.73835	.73463	.73093	.72727	.72363
99	.76501	.76123	.75748	.75376	.75007	.74640	.74276	.73914	.73555	.73198
100	.77208	.76838	.76471	.76107	.75745	.75385	.75028	.74673	.74321	.73971
101	.77879	.77517	.77157	.76800	.76444	.76092	.75741	.75392	.75046	.74702
102	.78579	.78224	.77871	.77521	.77173	.76827	.76483	.76141	.75801	.75463
103	.79318	.78971	.78626	.78283	.77942	.77604	.77266	.76931	.76598	.76267
104	.80139	.79801	.79464	.79129	.78796	.78465	.78136	.77808	.77482	.77157
105	.81161	.80834	.80508	.80184	.79861	.79540	.79220	.78902	.78585	.78270
106	.82665	.82357	.82049	.81743	.81438	.81134	.80831	.80530	.80229	.79930
107	.84893	.84616	.84340	.84064	.83789	.83515	.83241	.82969	.82696	.82425
108	.88637	.88421	.88205	.87989	.87774	.87559	.87344	.87129	.86915	.86701
109	.94900	.94800	.94700	.94600	.94500	.94400	.94300	.94200	.94100	.94000

See p. 15 for regulations not amended to reflect law changes

TABLE U(1)
BASED ON LIFE TABLE 80CNSMT
UNITRUST SINGLE LIFE REMAINDER FACTORS
APPLICABLE FOR TRANSFERS AFTER APRIL 30, 1989,
AND BEFORE MAY 1, 1999
ADJUSTED PAYOUT RATE

AGE	12.2%	12.4%	12.6%	12.8%	13.0%	13.2%	13.4%	13.6%	13.8%	14.0%
0	.01581	.01569	.01557	.01546	.01536	.01526	.01516	.01507	.01499	.01490
1	.00459	.00448	.00437	.00426	.00417	.00407	.00399	.00390	.00382	.00375
2	.00424	.00412	.00400	.00389	.00379	.00369	.00360	.00352	.00343	.00335
3	.00414	.00401	.00389	.00377	.00366	.00356	.00346	.00337	.00328	.00320
4	.00418	.00404	.00391	.00379	.00368	.00357	.00347	.00337	.00327	.00319
5	.00433	.00418	.00405	.00391	.00379	.00368	.00357	.00346	.00336	.00327
6	.00454	.00439	.00424	.00410	.00397	.00384	.00372	.00361	.00351	.00341
7	.00482	.00465	.00449	.00434	.00420	.00407	.00394	.00382	.00371	.00360
8	.00516	.00498	.00481	.00465	.00450	.00436	.00422	.00410	.00397	.00386
9	.00560	.00541	.00523	.00505	.00489	.00474	.00459	.00446	.00433	.00420
10	.00613	.00592	.00573	.00555	.00537	.00521	.00505	.00491	.00477	.00463
11	.00677	.00655	.00635	.00615	.00597	.00580	.00563	.00547	.00532	.00518
12	.00751	.00728	.00706	.00685	.00666	.00647	.00629	.00613	.00597	.00581
13	.00829	.00805	.00782	.00760	.00739	.00719	.00701	.00683	.00666	.00650
14	.00905	.00879	.00854	.00831	.00809	.00789	.00769	.00750	.00732	.00715
15	.00974	.00947	.00921	.00897	.00874	.00852	.00831	.00811	.00793	.00775
16	.01037	.01009	.00982	.00956	.00932	.00909	.00887	.00866	.00846	.00827
17	.01093	.01063	.01034	.01007	.00982	.00958	.00935	.00913	.00892	.00873
18	.01143	.01112	.01082	.01053	.01027	.01001	.00977	.00954	.00933	.00912
19	.01192	.01159	.01127	.01097	.01069	.01043	.01017	.00993	.00970	.00949
20	.01239	.01204	.01170	.01139	.01109	.01081	.01055	.01029	.01005	.00983
21	.01283	.01246	.01211	.01178	.01147	.01117	.01089	.01063	.01037	.01013
22	.01328	.01288	.01251	.01216	.01183	.01152	.01122	.01094	.01067	.01042
23	.01372	.01331	.01292	.01254	.01219	.01186	.01155	.01125	.01097	.01070
24	.01422	.01378	.01336	.01297	.01260	.01225	.01191	.01160	.01130	.01101
25	.01479	.01432	.01388	.01346	.01306	.01269	.01233	.01200	.01168	.01138
26	.01545	.01495	.01448	.01404	.01362	.01322	.01284	.01248	.01214	.01182
27	.01623	.01570	.01520	.01472	.01427	.01385	.01344	.01306	.01270	.01235
28	.01712	.01655	.01601	.01551	.01503	.01457	.01414	.01373	.01334	.01298
29	.01813	.01752	.01695	.01641	.01589	.01541	.01494	.01451	.01409	.01370
30	.01927	.01862	.01801	.01743	.01688	.01635	.01586	.01539	.01495	.01452
31	.02056	.01987	.01922	.01859	.01801	.01745	.01692	.01642	.01594	.01548
32	.02201	.02127	.02057	.01990	.01927	.01868	.01811	.01757	.01706	.01657
33	.02363	.02284	.02209	.02138	.02071	.02007	.01946	.01888	.01833	.01781
34	.02543	.02458	.02378	.02302	.02230	.02162	.02096	.02034	.01975	.01919
35	.02741	.02651	.02565	.02484	.02407	.02333	.02264	.02197	.02134	.02073
36	.02956	.02859	.02768	.02681	.02599	.02520	.02446	.02374	.02307	.02242
37	.03189	.03087	.02990	.02897	.02809	.02725	.02645	.02569	.02496	.02427
38	.03443	.03334	.03230	.03131	.03037	.02948	.02862	.02781	.02703	.02628
39	.03718	.03602	.03491	.03386	.03285	.03190	.03099	.03011	.02928	.02849
40	.04015	.03891	.03774	.03662	.03555	.03453	.03355	.03262	.03173	.03088
41	.04335	.04204	.04079	.03959	.03846	.03737	.03633	.03534	.03439	.03348
42	.04677	.04538	.04405	.04278	.04157	.04042	.03931	.03825	.03724	.03627
43	.05042	.04894	.04754	.04619	.04491	.04368	.04250	.04138	.04030	.03926
44	.05432	.05276	.05127	.04984	.04848	.04718	.04593	.04473	.04358	.04248
45	.05849	.05684	.05526	.05375	.05231	.05092	.04960	.04832	.04710	.04593
46	.06292	.06118	.05952	.05792	.05639	.05492	.05352	.05217	.05087	.04963
47	.06765	.06581	.06405	.06237	.06075	.05920	.05771	.05628	.05491	.05359
48	.07265	.07071	.06886	.06708	.06537	.06373	.06216	.06064	.05919	.05779
49	.07791	.07587	.07392	.07204	.07024	.06851	.06685	.06525	.06371	.06223
50	.08343	.08129	.07923	.07726	.07536	.07354	.07178	.07009	.06847	.06690
51	.08924	.08699	.08483	.08276	.08076	.07884	.07699	.07520	.07349	.07183
52	.09539	.09303	.09076	.08858	.08648	.08446	.08251	.08064	.07883	.07708
53	.10189	.09942	.09704	.09475	.09255	.09043	.08838	.08640	.08450	.08266
54	.10872	.10614	.10365	.10126	.09894	.09672	.09456	.09249	.09049	.08855
55	.11592	.11322	.11062	.10811	.10569	.10335	.10110	.09892	.09682	.09478
56	.12350	.12068	.11796	.11534	.11281	.11036	.10800	.10571	.10350	.10137
57	.13148	.12855	.12572	.12298	.12033	.11777	.11530	.11291	.11060	.10836
58	.13990	.13685	.13389	.13104	.12828	.12561	.12303	.12053	.11811	.11576
59	.14875	.14557	.14250	.13953	.13665	.13387	.13118	.12856	.12604	.12359
60	.15799	.15469	.15150	.14841	.14542	.14253	.13972	.13700	.13436	.13180
61	.16761	.16419	.16088	.15768	.15457	.15156	.14864	.14580	.14305	.14039

BASED ON LIFE TABLE 80CNSMT
UNITRUST SINGLE LIFE REMAINDER FACTORS
APPLICABLE FOR TRANSFERS AFTER APRIL 30, 1989,
AND BEFORE MAY 1, 1999
ADJUSTED PAYOUT RATE

AGE	12.2%	12.4%	12.6%	12.8%	13.0%	13.2%	13.4%	13.6%	13.8%	14.0%
62	.17758	.17404	.17062	.16729	.16407	.16094	.15791	.15496	.15210	.14932
63	.18791	.18425	.18071	.17726	.17392	.17068	.16753	.16447	.16150	.15861
64	.19862	.19484	.19118	.18762	.18417	.18081	.17754	.17437	.17129	.16829
65	.20979	.20590	.20212	.19845	.19487	.19140	.18802	.18474	.18154	.17843
66	.22149	.21748	.21359	.20980	.20612	.20253	.19904	.19564	.19233	.18911
67	.23374	.22962	.22562	.22172	.21792	.21423	.21062	.20712	.20370	.20037
68	.24656	.24234	.23822	.23422	.23031	.22651	.22280	.21919	.21566	.21222
69	.25988	.25556	.25134	.24724	.24323	.23932	.23551	.23179	.22816	.22461
70	.27367	.26925	.26493	.26073	.25662	.25261	.24870	.24488	.24115	.23750
71	.28784	.28333	.27892	.27462	.27042	.26631	.26230	.25839	.25456	.25082
72	.30241	.29781	.29332	.28893	.28464	.28044	.27634	.27233	.26841	.26457
73	.31740	.31272	.30815	.30368	.29930	.29502	.29084	.28674	.28273	.27880
74	.33291	.32817	.32352	.31897	.31452	.31016	.30589	.30171	.29762	.29361
75	.34903	.34422	.33951	.33490	.33038	.32595	.32161	.31735	.31318	.30909
76	.36581	.36095	.35619	.35152	.34694	.34245	.33805	.33373	.32949	.32533
77	.38324	.37835	.37354	.36883	.36420	.35966	.35520	.35083	.34654	.34232
78	.40126	.39634	.39150	.38676	.38210	.37752	.37302	.36861	.36427	.36001
79	.41970	.41476	.40992	.40515	.40047	.39587	.39135	.38690	.38253	.37823
80	.43842	.43348	.42864	.42387	.41918	.41456	.41002	.40556	.40117	.39685
81	.45719	.45228	.44744	.44267	.43799	.43337	.42883	.42436	.41996	.41562
82	.47590	.47101	.46619	.46145	.45677	.45217	.44764	.44317	.43877	.43443
83	.49443	.48957	.48478	.48007	.47542	.47084	.46632	.46187	.45748	.45315
84	.51279	.50798	.50324	.49856	.49394	.48939	.48490	.48048	.47611	.47180
85	.53106	.52630	.52161	.51698	.51241	.50790	.50345	.49906	.49473	.49045
86	.54902	.54434	.53971	.53514	.53062	.52616	.52176	.51741	.51312	.50888
87	.56640	.56178	.55722	.55271	.54826	.54386	.53951	.53521	.53097	.52677
88	.58326	.57872	.57423	.56979	.56541	.56107	.55678	.55254	.54834	.54420
89	.59994	.59548	.59107	.58671	.58240	.57813	.57391	.56973	.56560	.56152
90	.61662	.61226	.60794	.60367	.59944	.59526	.59112	.58702	.58296	.57894
91	.63305	.62879	.62457	.62040	.61627	.61217	.60812	.60411	.60013	.59619
92	.64876	.64461	.64050	.63643	.63239	.62839	.62443	.62051	.61662	.61277
93	.66355	.65950	.65550	.65153	.64759	.64369	.63983	.63600	.63220	.62843
94	.67722	.67328	.66938	.66551	.66167	.65786	.65409	.65035	.64664	.64296
95	.68967	.68583	.68203	.67825	.67451	.67079	.66711	.66345	.65983	.65623
96	.70076	.69701	.69330	.68961	.68595	.68231	.67871	.67513	.67158	.66806
97	.71089	.70722	.70359	.69998	.69640	.69284	.68931	.68581	.68234	.67888
98	.72001	.71642	.71286	.70933	.70582	.70233	.69887	.69544	.69203	.68864
99	.72844	.72492	.72143	.71796	.71452	.71110	.70770	.70433	.70098	.69765
100	.73623	.73278	.72935	.72594	.72256	.71920	.71586	.71254	.70924	.70597
101	.74361	.74021	.73684	.73349	.73016	.72685	.72356	.72029	.71704	.71382
102	.75128	.74794	.74463	.74133	.73806	.73480	.73157	.72835	.72515	.72198
103	.75938	.75610	.75284	.74961	.74639	.74319	.74000	.73684	.73369	.73056
104	.76835	.76514	.76194	.75877	.75561	.75246	.74934	.74623	.74313	.74005
105	.77956	.77643	.77332	.77023	.76714	.76408	.76102	.75798	.75496	.75195
106	.79632	.79334	.79038	.78743	.78449	.78157	.77865	.77575	.77285	.76997
107	.82154	.81884	.81615	.81346	.81079	.80811	.80545	.80279	.80014	.79750
108	.86487	.86274	.86061	.85848	.85635	.85423	.85210	.84998	.84787	.84575
109	.93900	.93800	.93700	.93600	.93500	.93400	.93300	.93200	.93100	.93000

(f) *Valuation of charitable remainder unitrusts having certain payout sequences for transfers for which the valuation date is after April 30, 1999, and before May 1, 2009.*—(1) *In general.*—Except as otherwise provided in paragraph (f)(2) of this section, in the case of transfers for which the valuation date is after April 30, 1999, and before May 1, 2009, the present value of a remainder interest is determined under paragraphs (f)(3) through (f)(6) of this section, provided that the amount of the payout as of any payout date during any taxable year of the trust is not larger than the amount that the trust could distribute on such date under § 1.664-3(a)(1)(v) if the taxable year of the trust were to end on such date. See, however, § 1.7520-3(b) (relating to exceptions to the use of the prescribed tables under certain circumstances).

(2) *Transitional rules for valuation of charitable remainder unitrusts.*—(i) For purposes of sections 2055, 2106, or 2624, if on May 1, 1999, the decedent was mentally incompetent so that the disposition of the property could not be changed, and the decedent died after April 30, 1999, without having regained competency to dispose of the decedent's property, or the decedent died within 90 days of the date that the decedent first regained competency after April 30, 1999, the present value of a remainder interest under this section is determined as if the valuation date with respect to the decedent's gross estate is either before May 1, 1999, or after April 30, 1999, at the option of the decedent's executor.

(ii) For purposes of sections 170, 2055, 2106, 2522, or 2624, in the case of transfers to a charitable remainder unitrust for which the valuation date is after April 30, 1999, and before July 1, 1999, the present value of a remainder interest based on one or more measuring lives is determined under this section by use of the section 7520 interest rate for the month in which the valuation date occurs (see §§ 1.7520-1(b) and 1.7520-2(a)(2) and the appropriate actuarial tables under either paragraph (e)(6) or (f)(6) of this section, at the option of the donor or the decedent's executor, as the case may be.

(iii) For purposes of paragraphs (f)(2)(i) and (f)(2)(ii) of this section, where the donor or decedent's executor is given the option to use the appropriate actuarial tables under either paragraph (e)(6) or (f)(6) of this section, the donor or decedent's executor must use the same actuarial table with respect to each individual transaction and with respect to all transfers occurring on the valuation date (for example, gift and income tax charitable deductions with respect to the same transfer must be determined based on the same tables, and all assets includible in the gross estate and/or estate tax deductions claimed must be valued based on the same tables).

(3) *Adjusted payout rate.*—For transfers for which the valuation date is after April 30, 1999, and before May 1, 2009, the adjusted payout rate is determined by using the appropriate Table F, contained in § 1.664-4(e)(6), for the section 7520 interest rate applicable to the transfer. If the interest rate is between 4.2 and 14 percent, see § 1.664-4(e)(6). If the interest rate is below 4.2 percent or greater than 14 percent, see § 1.664-4(b). See § 1.664-4(e) for rules applicable in determining the adjusted payout rate.

(4) *Period is a term of years.*—If the period described in § 1.664-3(a)(5) is a term of years, the factor that is used in determining the present value of the remainder interest for transfers for which the valuation date is after April 30, 1999, and before May 1, 2009, is the factor under the appropriate adjusted payout rate in Table D in § 1.664-4(e)(6) corresponding to the number of years in the term. If the adjusted payout rate is an amount that is between adjusted payout rates for which factors are provided in Table D, a linear interpolation must be made. The present value of the remainder interest is determined by multiplying the net fair market value (as of the appropriate valuation date) of the property placed in trust by the factor determined under this paragraph. Generally, for purposes of this section, the valuation date is, in the case of an inter vivos transfer, the date on which the property is transferred to the trust by the donor, and, in the case of a testamentary transfer under sections 2055, 2106, or 2624, the valuation date is the date of death. See § 1.664-4(e)(4) for additional rules regarding the valuation date. See § 1.664-4(e)(4) for an example that illustrates the application of this paragraph (f)(4).

(5) *Period is the life of one individual.*—If the period described in § 1.664-3(a)(5) is the life of one individual, the factor that is used in determining the present value of the remainder interest for transfers for which the valuation date is after April 30, 1999, and before May 1, 2009, is the factor in Table U(1) in paragraph (f)(6) of this section under the appropriate adjusted payout. For purposes of the computations described in this paragraph (f)(5), the age of an individual is the age of that individual at the individual's nearest birthday. If the adjusted payout rate is an amount that is between adjusted payout rates for which factors are provided in the appropriate table, a linear interpolation must be made. The rules provided in § 1.664-4(e)(5) apply for determining the present value of the remainder interest. See § 1.664-4(e)(5) for an example illustrating the application of this paragraph (f)(5) (using current actuarial tables).

(6) *Actuarial Table U(1) for transfers for which the valuation date is after April 30, 1999, and before May 1, 2009.*—For transfers for which the valuation date is after April 30, 1999, and before May 1, 2009, the present value of a charitable remainder unitrust interest that is dependent on the termination of a life interest is determined by using the section 7520 rate, Table U(1) in this paragraph (f)(6), and Tables F(4.2) through F(14.0) in § 1.664-4(e)(6). See, however, § 1.7520-3(b) (relating to exceptions to the use of prescribed tables under certain circumstances). Many actuarial factors not contained in the following tables are contained in Internal Revenue Service Publication 1458, "Actuarial Values, Book Beth," (7-1999). Publication 1458 is no longer available for purchase from the Superintendent of Documents, United States Government Printing Office. However, pertinent factors in this publication may be obtained by a written request to: CC:PA:LPD:PR (IRS Publication 1458), Room 5205, Internal Revenue Service, P.O.Box 7604, Ben Franklin Station, Washington, DC 20044.

TABLE U(1)
BASED ON LIFE TABLE 90CM
UNITRUST SINGLE LIFE REMAINDER FACTORS
[APPLICABLE FOR TRANSFERS AFTER APRIL 30, 1999, AND BEFORE MAY 1, 2009]
ADJUSTED PAYOUT RATE

AGE	*4.2%*	*4.4%*	*4.6%*	*4.8%*	*5.0%*	*5.2%*	*5.4%*	*5.6%*	*5.8%*	*6.0%*
0	.06177	.05580	.05061	.04609	.04215	.03871	.03570	.03307	.03075	.02872
1	.05543	.04925	.04388	.03919	.03509	.03151	.02838	.02563	.02321	.02109
2	.05716	.05081	.04528	.04045	.03622	.03252	.02927	.02642	.02391	.02170
3	.05920	.05268	.04699	.04201	.03765	.03382	.03046	.02750	.02490	.02260
4	.06143	.05475	.04889	.04376	.03926	.03530	.03182	.02876	.02605	.02366
5	.06384	.05697	.05095	.04567	.04103	.03694	.03334	.03016	.02735	.02487
6	.06637	.05933	.05315	.04771	.04292	.03870	.03497	.03168	.02876	.02618
7	.06905	.06183	.05547	.04987	.04494	.04058	.03673	.03332	.03029	.02761
8	.07186	.06445	.05792	.05216	.04708	.04258	.03859	.03506	.03192	.02914
9	.07482	.06722	.06052	.05460	.04936	.04471	.04060	.03694	.03369	.03079
10	.07793	.07015	.06327	.05718	.05179	.04700	.04274	.03896	.03559	.03259
11	.08120	.07323	.06617	.05991	.05435	.04942	.04502	.04111	.03762	.03450
12	.08461	.07645	.06920	.06277	.05706	.05197	.04744	.04339	.03978	.03655
13	.08812	.07976	.07234	.06574	.05985	.05461	.04993	.04576	.04202	.03867
14	.09168	.08313	.07552	.06874	.06269	.05729	.05247	.04815	.04428	.04081
15	.09527	.08652	.07872	.07176	.06554	.05999	.05501	.05055	.04655	.04296
16	.09886	.08991	.08192	.07478	.06839	.06267	.05754	.05294	.04880	.04508
17	.10249	.09334	.08515	.07782	.07126	.06537	.06008	.05533	.05105	.04720
18	.10616	.09680	.08842	.08090	.07415	.06809	.06264	.05774	.05332	.04933
19	.10994	.10037	.09178	.08407	.07714	.07091	.06529	.06023	.05566	.05153
20	.11384	.10406	.09527	.08737	.08025	.07383	.06805	.06283	.05811	.05384
21	.11790	.10790	.09891	.09080	.08349	.07690	.07094	.06555	.06068	.05626
22	.12208	.11188	.10267	.09436	.08686	.08008	.07395	.06839	.06336	.05879
23	.12643	.11601	.10659	.09808	.09038	.08342	.07710	.07138	.06618	.06146
24	.13095	.12031	.11069	.10197	.09408	.08692	.08042	.07452	.06915	.06427
25	.13567	.12481	.11497	.10605	.09795	.09060	.08392	.07784	.07230	.06726
26	.14058	.12950	.11945	.11032	.10202	.09447	.08760	.08134	.07563	.07042
27	.14571	.13442	.12415	.11481	.10631	.09856	.09149	.08505	.07916	.07379
28	.15104	.13953	.12904	.11949	.11078	.10284	.09558	.08895	.08288	.07733
29	.15656	.14484	.13414	.12438	.11546	.10731	.09986	.09304	.08679	.08106
30	.16229	.15034	.13943	.12946	.12034	.11198	.10433	.09732	.09089	.08498
31	.16821	.15605	.14493	.13474	.12541	.11685	.10900	.10179	.09517	.08909
32	.17433	.16196	.15063	.14023	.13069	.12193	.11387	.10647	.09966	.09339
33	.18068	.16810	.15655	.14595	.13620	.12723	.11897	.11137	.10437	.09791
34	.18724	.17446	.16270	.15189	.14193	.13275	.12430	.11650	.10930	.10265
35	.19405	.18107	.16910	.15808	.14791	.13853	.12987	.12187	.11448	.10764
36	.20109	.18791	.17574	.16451	.15414	.14456	.13569	.12749	.11990	.11287
37	.20838	.19500	.18263	.17120	.16062	.15083	.14177	.13337	.12558	.11835
38	.21593	.20236	.18979	.17816	.16739	.15739	.14813	.13953	.13154	.12412
39	.22374	.20998	.19723	.18540	.17443	.16423	.15477	.14597	.13779	.13017
40	.23183	.21789	.20496	.19294	.18177	.17138	.16172	.15272	.14434	.13653
41	.24021	.22611	.21299	.20079	.18943	.17885	.16899	.15980	.15123	.14322
42	.24889	.23463	.22134	.20896	.19741	.18665	.17660	.16721	.15845	.15025
43	.25786	.24344	.23000	.21744	.20572	.19477	.18453	.17496	.16601	.15762
44	.26712	.25257	.23896	.22625	.21435	.20322	.19281	.18305	.17391	.16534
45	.27665	.26196	.24821	.23534	.22328	.21198	.20139	.19145	.18213	.17338
46	.28644	.27163	.25774	.24472	.23251	.22105	.21028	.20018	.19068	.18174
47	.29647	.28155	.26754	.25438	.24201	.23040	.21947	.20919	.19952	.19041
48	.30676	.29173	.27760	.26431	.25181	.24004	.22896	.21852	.20868	.19941
49	.31729	.30217	.28794	.27453	.26190	.24999	.23876	.22817	.21817	.20873
50	.32808	.31289	.29856	.28505	.27229	.26026	.24889	.23814	.22799	.21839
51	.33912	.32387	.30946	.29585	.28299	.27083	.25933	.24845	.23815	.22840

AGE	4.2%	4.4%	4.6%	4.8%	5.0%	5.2%	5.4%	5.6%	5.8%	6.0%
52	.35038	.33507	.32060	.30691	.29395	.28168	.27005	.25904	.24861	.23872
53	.36185	.34651	.33198	.31821	.30517	.29280	.28106	.26993	.25937	.24934
54	.37352	.35815	.34358	.32976	.31664	.30418	.29234	.28110	.27042	.26026
55	.38539	.37002	.35542	.34155	.32836	.31583	.30390	.29256	.28177	.27149
56	.39746	.38209	.36748	.35358	.34034	.32774	.31574	.30431	.29342	.28303
57	.40971	.39437	.37976	.36584	.35257	.33992	.32785	.31634	.30536	.29488
58	.42212	.40682	.39222	.37829	.36500	.35231	.34019	.32862	.31756	.30699
59	.43464	.41939	.40482	.39090	.37759	.36488	.35272	.34109	.32996	.31932
60	.44726	.43207	.41754	.40364	.39034	.37761	.36542	.35375	.34257	.33186
61	.45999	.44488	.43041	.41655	.40326	.39053	.37833	.36662	.35540	.34463
62	.47286	.45785	.44345	.42964	.41639	.40367	.39146	.37974	.36848	.35767
63	.48589	.47098	.45667	.44293	.42972	.41703	.40484	.39311	.38184	.37100
64	.49903	.48426	.47005	.45638	.44324	.43060	.41843	.40671	.39544	.38458
65	.51229	.49766	.48357	.47001	.45694	.44435	.43223	.42054	.40927	.39841
66	.52568	.51121	.49726	.48381	.47084	.45833	.44626	.43461	.42337	.41252
67	.53924	.52495	.51115	.49784	.48498	.47256	.46056	.44898	.43778	.42696
68	.55293	.53883	.52521	.51205	.49932	.48701	.47511	.46360	.45246	.44169
69	.56671	.55283	.53940	.52640	.51382	.50165	.48985	.47844	.46738	.45666
70	.58052	.56687	.55365	.54084	.52843	.51639	.50473	.49342	.48245	.47181
71	.59431	.58091	.56791	.55529	.54306	.53118	.51966	.50847	.49761	.48707
72	.60804	.59490	.58213	.56973	.55768	.54598	.53461	.52357	.51283	.50239
73	.62168	.60881	.59629	.58411	.57227	.56076	.54955	.53866	.52806	.51774
74	.63528	.62268	.61042	.59848	.58686	.57555	.56453	.55380	.54335	.53316
75	.64887	.63657	.62458	.61290	.60151	.59041	.57959	.56904	.55875	.54872
76	.66249	.65049	.63880	.62739	.61625	.60538	.59478	.58443	.57432	.56446
77	.67612	.66446	.65307	.64194	.63108	.62046	.61009	.59995	.59005	.58037
78	.68975	.67843	.66736	.65654	.64596	.63561	.62548	.61558	.60590	.59643
79	.70330	.69233	.68160	.67109	.66081	.65074	.64088	.63123	.62178	.61253
80	.71666	.70605	.69566	.68548	.67550	.66573	.65615	.64676	.63755	.62853
81	.72975	.71950	.70946	.69961	.68995	.68047	.67117	.66205	.65310	.64433
82	.74250	.73263	.72293	.71342	.70407	.69490	.68589	.67705	.66837	.65984
83	.75493	.74542	.73608	.72690	.71788	.70902	.70031	.69175	.68333	.67506
84	.76712	.75798	.74900	.74016	.73147	.72292	.71451	.70624	.69810	.69010
85	.77913	.77037	.76175	.75326	.74491	.73668	.72859	.72061	.71276	.70503
86	.79086	.78248	.77423	.76610	.75808	.75019	.74241	.73474	.72719	.71974
87	.80218	.79418	.78628	.77850	.77083	.76326	.75580	.74844	.74118	.73402
88	.81307	.80544	.79790	.79047	.78313	.77589	.76874	.76169	.75473	.74786
89	.82355	.81628	.80909	.80200	.79500	.78808	.78125	.77450	.76783	.76125
90	.83360	.82668	.81985	.81309	.80642	.79982	.79330	.78685	.78048	.77418
91	.84308	.83650	.83000	.82357	.81721	.81092	.80470	.79855	.79246	.78645
92	.85182	.84556	.83937	.83325	.82718	.82119	.81525	.80937	.80356	.79780
93	.85985	.85390	.84800	.84215	.83637	.83064	.82497	.81936	.81379	.80829
94	.86732	.86164	.85601	.85044	.84491	.83944	.83402	.82865	.82333	.81806
95	.87437	.86895	.86359	.85827	.85300	.84778	.84260	.83746	.83237	.82733
96	.88097	.87582	.87070	.86563	.86060	.85561	.85066	.84575	.84088	.83605
97	.88708	.88216	.87727	.87243	.86762	.86285	.85811	.85341	.84875	.84413
98	.89280	.88810	.88343	.87880	.87420	.86964	.86511	.86061	.85614	.85171
99	.89836	.89388	.88943	.88501	.88062	.87626	.87193	.86763	.86336	.85911
100	.90375	.89948	.89525	.89103	.88685	.88269	.87856	.87445	.87037	.86632
101	.90905	.90500	.90097	.89696	.89298	.88902	.88509	.88118	.87729	.87342
102	.91424	.91040	.90658	.90278	.89900	.89524	.89150	.88778	.88408	.88040
103	.91939	.91575	.91214	.90854	.90496	.90139	.89785	.89432	.89081	.88732
104	.92485	.92144	.91805	.91467	.91131	.90796	.90463	.90131	.89800	.89471
105	.93020	.92701	.92383	.92067	.91751	.91437	.91125	.90813	.90502	.90193
106	.93701	.93411	.93122	.92834	.92546	.92260	.91974	.91689	.91405	.91122
107	.94522	.94268	.94013	.93760	.93507	.93254	.93002	.92750	.92499	.92249

AGE	4.2%	4.4%	4.6%	4.8%	5.0%	5.2%	5.4%	5.6%	5.8%	6.0%
108	.95782	.95583	.95385	.95187	.94989	.94791	.94593	.94396	.94199	.94002
109	.97900	.97800	.97700	.97600	.97500	.97400	.97300	.97200	.97100	.97000

TABLE U(1)
BASED ON LIFE TABLE 90CM
UNITRUST SINGLE LIFE REMAINDER FACTORS
[APPLICABLE FOR TRANSFERS AFTER APRIL 30, 1999, AND BEFORE MAY 1, 2009]
ADJUSTED PAYOUT RATE

AGE	6.2%	6.4%	6.6%	6.8%	7.0%	7.2%	7.4%	7.6%	7.8%	8.0%
0	.02693	.02534	.02395	.02271	.02161	.02063	.01976	.01898	.01828	.01765
1	.01922	.01756	.01610	.01480	.01365	.01263	.01171	.01090	.01017	.00951
2	.01975	.01802	.01650	.01514	.01393	.01286	.01190	.01104	.01028	.00959
3	.02056	.01876	.01717	.01575	.01449	.01336	.01235	.01145	.01064	.00992
4	.02155	.01967	.01800	.01652	.01520	.01401	.01296	.01201	.01116	.01039
5	.02266	.02071	.01896	.01741	.01603	.01479	.01368	.01269	.01179	.01098
6	.02389	.02184	.02003	.01841	.01696	.01566	.01450	.01345	.01251	.01166
7	.02522	.02309	.02120	.01950	.01799	.01663	.01540	.01431	.01332	.01242
8	.02665	.02444	.02246	.02069	.01910	.01768	.01640	.01524	.01420	.01326
9	.02821	.02590	.02384	.02199	.02033	.01884	.01750	.01629	.01520	.01421
10	.02990	.02750	.02535	.02342	.02169	.02013	.01872	.01745	.01631	.01526
11	.03172	.02922	.02698	.02497	.02316	.02153	.02006	.01872	.01752	.01643
12	.03365	.03106	.02872	.02663	.02474	.02303	.02149	.02010	.01884	.01769
13	.03566	.03297	.03054	.02835	.02638	.02460	.02299	.02154	.02021	.01901
14	.03770	.03490	.03237	.03010	.02804	.02619	.02450	.02298	.02159	.02033
15	.03973	.03682	.03419	.03182	.02968	.02775	.02599	.02439	.02294	.02162
16	.04173	.03871	.03598	.03352	.03129	.02926	.02743	.02576	.02424	.02286
17	.04372	.04059	.03775	.03519	.03287	.03076	.02884	.02710	.02551	.02406
18	.04573	.04248	.03953	.03686	.03444	.03224	.03024	.02842	.02676	.02524
19	.04780	.04443	.04137	.03859	.03607	.03378	.03169	.02978	.02804	.02646
20	.04997	.04647	.04329	.04040	.03778	.03539	.03321	.03122	.02940	.02773
21	.05226	.04862	.04532	.04232	.03958	.03709	.03481	.03274	.03083	.02909
22	.05465	.05088	.04745	.04432	.04148	.03888	.03650	.03433	.03234	.03052
23	.05716	.05325	.04969	.04645	.04348	.04077	.03830	.03603	.03394	.03203
24	.05983	.05578	.05208	.04871	.04562	.04280	.04021	.03784	.03566	.03367
25	.06266	.05846	.05463	.05112	.04791	.04497	.04227	.03980	.03752	.03543
26	.06566	.06131	.05734	.05369	.05035	.04729	.04448	.04189	.03951	.03732
27	.06887	.06436	.06024	.05646	.05298	.04979	.04686	.04416	.04168	.03939
28	.07225	.06758	.06331	.05938	.05577	.05245	.04940	.04658	.04398	.04159
29	.07581	.07099	.06656	.06248	.05873	.05528	.05210	.04916	.04645	.04394
30	.07956	.07457	.06998	.06575	.06186	.05827	.05495	.05189	.04906	.04644
31	.08348	.07833	.07358	.06920	.06515	.06142	.05797	.05478	.05182	.04908
32	.08761	.08228	.07736	.07282	.06863	.06475	.06116	.05783	.05475	.05189
33	.09195	.08645	.08136	.07666	.07231	.06828	.06454	.06108	.05786	.05488
34	.09651	.09082	.08557	.08070	.07619	.07200	.06812	.06452	.06117	.05805
35	.10131	.09545	.09002	.08498	.08030	.07596	.07193	.06818	.06459	.06144
36	.10635	.10031	.09470	.08949	.08465	.08015	.07596	.07206	.06842	.06503
37	.11165	.10542	.09963	.09424	.08923	.08457	.08022	.07617	.07238	.06885
38	.11722	.11081	.10484	.09927	.09409	.08926	.08475	.08054	.07661	.07293
39	.12308	.11648	.11032	.10458	.09922	.09422	.08955	.08518	.08109	.07726
40	.12925	.12246	.11612	.11020	.10466	.09949	.09465	.09011	.08587	.08189
41	.13575	.12877	.12225	.11614	.11043	.10508	.10007	.09537	.09097	.08683
42	.14259	.13542	.12871	.12243	.11654	.11101	.10583	.10097	.09640	.09210
43	.14977	.14242	.13552	.12905	.12298	.11729	.11193	.10690	.10217	.09771
44	.15731	.14976	.14269	.13604	.12979	.12391	.11838	.11318	.10828	.10367
45	.16516	.15743	.15017	.14334	.13691	.13086	.12516	.11979	.11472	.10994
46	.17334	.16544	.15800	.15099	.14438	.13816	.13228	.12674	.12150	.11656
47	.18184	.17375	.16613	.15895	.15217	.14576	.13972	.13400	.12860	.12349
48	.19066	.18240	.17461	.16724	.16029	.15371	.14749	.14161	.13604	.13077

See p. 15 for regulations not amended to reflect law changes

AGE	6.2%	6.4%	6.6%	6.8%	7.0%	7.2%	7.4%	7.6%	7.8%	8.0%
49	.19981	.19138	.18342	.17588	.16875	.16201	.15562	.14956	.14383	.13839
50	.20931	.20072	.19259	.18489	.17759	.17067	.16412	.15790	.15199	.14639
51	.21917	.21042	.20212	.19426	.18679	.17971	.17299	.16660	.16054	.15477
52	.22933	.22043	.21198	.20395	.19633	.18909	.18220	.17566	.16943	.16350
53	.23981	.23076	.22216	.21399	.20621	.19881	.19176	.18506	.17867	.17258
54	.25060	.24141	.23267	.22434	.21642	.20886	.20166	.19480	.18826	.18201
55	.26171	.25239	.24351	.23504	.22697	.21927	.21192	.20491	.19821	.19182
56	.27313	.26369	.25468	.24608	.23787	.23003	.22254	.21538	.20854	.20199
57	.28487	.27531	.26618	.25746	.24912	.24114	.23351	.22621	.21923	.21254
58	.29688	.28722	.27798	.26914	.26067	.25257	.24481	.23738	.23025	.22343
59	.30913	.29937	.29002	.28107	.27249	.26427	.25639	.24882	.24157	.23461
60	.32159	.31175	.30231	.29325	.28457	.27623	.26823	.26055	.25317	.24608
61	.33429	.32437	.31485	.30571	.29692	.28848	.28037	.27257	.26507	.25786
62	.34728	.33730	.32770	.31847	.30960	.30106	.29285	.28495	.27734	.27001
63	.36057	.35053	.34087	.33157	.32262	.31400	.30569	.29769	.28998	.28255
64	.37412	.36404	.35433	.34498	.33596	.32726	.31887	.31078	.30298	.29545
65	.38794	.37783	.36809	.35868	.34961	.34085	.33239	.32422	.31633	.30871
66	.40205	.39193	.38216	.37272	.36361	.35479	.34628	.33804	.33008	.32238
67	.41650	.40639	.39661	.38715	.37800	.36915	.36059	.35230	.34428	.33651
68	.43126	.42117	.41139	.40193	.39277	.38390	.37530	.36697	.35890	.35108
69	.44628	.43622	.42648	.41703	.40787	.39898	.39037	.38201	.37391	.36604
70	.46150	.45149	.44178	.43236	.42321	.41433	.40571	.39735	.38922	.38132
71	.47683	.46689	.45723	.44785	.43873	.42987	.42126	.41290	.40476	.39685
72	.49225	.48238	.47279	.46346	.45439	.44556	.43697	.42862	.42048	.41257
73	.50770	.49793	.48841	.47915	.47013	.46135	.45280	.44447	.43635	.42844
74	.52324	.51358	.50416	.49498	.48603	.47731	.46880	.46051	.45242	.44454
75	.53894	.52939	.52008	.51100	.50214	.49349	.48505	.47681	.46877	.46092
76	.55483	.54543	.53624	.52728	.51852	.50996	.50160	.49344	.48546	.47766
77	.57091	.56167	.55263	.54380	.53516	.52671	.51845	.51038	.50247	.49475
78	.58716	.57809	.56922	.56053	.55203	.54372	.53557	.52760	.51980	.51216
79	.60346	.59459	.58590	.57738	.56904	.56086	.55286	.54501	.53732	.52978
80	.61969	.61102	.60252	.59419	.58601	.57800	.57014	.56243	.55487	.54745
81	.63571	.62726	.61897	.61082	.60283	.59499	.58729	.57974	.57232	.56503
82	.65146	.64324	.63515	.62722	.61942	.61176	.60423	.59683	.58957	.58242
83	.66693	.65893	.65108	.64335	.63575	.62828	.62093	.61371	.60660	.59962
84	.68222	.67447	.66684	.65934	.65195	.64468	.63753	.63049	.62356	.61674
85	.69742	.68993	.68255	.67528	.66812	.66106	.65411	.64727	.64053	.63389
86	.71241	.70517	.69805	.69102	.68410	.67727	.67054	.66390	.65736	.65091
87	.72696	.72000	.71313	.70635	.69967	.69307	.68656	.68014	.67381	.66756
88	.74108	.73438	.72777	.72125	.71480	.70845	.70217	.69597	.68985	.68380
89	.75475	.74832	.74198	.73571	.72951	.72339	.71734	.71137	.70547	.69963
90	.76796	.76180	.75572	.74971	.74376	.73788	.73207	.72633	.72065	.71503
91	.78049	.77460	.76878	.76302	.75732	.75168	.74610	.74058	.73512	.72972
92	.79211	.78647	.78089	.77537	.76990	.76449	.75913	.75383	.74858	.74338
93	.80283	.79743	.79208	.78679	.78154	.77634	.77119	.76610	.76105	.75604
94	.81283	.80765	.80253	.79744	.79240	.78741	.78247	.77756	.77270	.76789
95	.82233	.81737	.81245	.80757	.80274	.79795	.79320	.78849	.78382	.77918
96	.83126	.82651	.82180	.81712	.81248	.80788	.80332	.79880	.79431	.78985
97	.83953	.83498	.83046	.82597	.82152	.81710	.81271	.80836	.80404	.79976
98	.84731	.84294	.83860	.83429	.83002	.82577	.82155	.81737	.81321	.80908
99	.85490	.85071	.84656	.84243	.83832	.83425	.83020	.82618	.82219	.81822
100	.86229	.85828	.85431	.85035	.84642	.84252	.83864	.83478	.83095	.82714
101	.86958	.86575	.86195	.85818	.85442	.85069	.84698	.84329	.83962	.83597
102	.87674	.87310	.86947	.86587	.86229	.85873	.85518	.85166	.84815	.84466
103	.88384	.88038	.87694	.87351	.87010	.86671	.86334	.85998	.85663	.85331
104	.89143	.88817	.88492	.88169	.87847	.87526	.87207	.86889	.86573	.86258

AGE	6.2%	6.4%	6.6%	6.8%	7.0%	7.2%	7.4%	7.6%	7.8%	8.0%
105	.89885	.89578	.89272	.88967	.88664	.88361	.88060	.87760	.87461	.87163
106	.90840	.90559	.90278	.89999	.89720	.89442	.89165	.88888	.88613	.88338
107	.91999	.91750	.91501	.91253	.91005	.90758	.90511	.90265	.90019	.89774
108	.93805	.93609	.93412	.93216	.93020	.92824	.92629	.92434	.92239	.92044
109	.96900	.96800	.96700	.96600	.96500	.96400	.96300	.96200	.96100	.96000

TABLE U(1)
BASED ON LIFE TABLE 90CM
UNITRUST SINGLE LIFE REMAINDER FACTORS
[APPLICABLE FOR TRANSFERS AFTER APRIL 30, 1999, AND BEFORE MAY 1, 2009]
ADJUSTED PAYOUT RATE

AGE	8.2%	8.4%	8.6%	8.8%	9.0%	9.2%	9.4%	9.6%	9.8%	10.0%
0	.01709	.01658	.01612	.01570	.01532	.01497	.01466	.01437	.01410	.01386
1	.00892	.00839	.00791	.00747	.00708	.00672	.00639	.00609	.00582	.00557
2	.00896	.00840	.00790	.00744	.00702	.00664	.00629	.00598	.00569	.00542
3	.00926	.00867	.00814	.00765	.00721	.00681	.00644	.00611	.00580	.00552
4	.00970	.00908	.00851	.00800	.00753	.00711	.00672	.00636	.00604	.00574
5	.01026	.00960	.00900	.00846	.00796	.00751	.00710	.00672	.00637	.00606
6	.01089	.01019	.00956	.00899	.00846	.00799	.00755	.00715	.00678	.00644
7	.01161	.01088	.01021	.00960	.00905	.00854	.00808	.00765	.00726	.00690
8	.01241	.01163	.01093	.01029	.00970	.00917	.00867	.00822	.00781	.00743
9	.01331	.01249	.01175	.01107	.01045	.00988	.00936	.00889	.00845	.00804
10	.01432	.01346	.01268	.01196	.01131	.01071	.01016	.00965	.00918	.00875
11	.01543	.01453	.01370	.01295	.01226	.01162	.01104	.01051	.01001	.00956
12	.01664	.01569	.01482	.01403	.01330	.01263	.01202	.01145	.01093	.01045
13	.01791	.01691	.01600	.01516	.01440	.01369	.01304	.01245	.01190	.01139
14	.01918	.01813	.01717	.01629	.01548	.01474	.01406	.01343	.01285	.01231
15	.02041	.01931	.01831	.01738	.01653	.01576	.01504	.01437	.01376	.01320
16	.02160	.02044	.01938	.01841	.01752	.01670	.01595	.01525	.01460	.01401
17	.02274	.02152	.02041	.01940	.01846	.01760	.01680	.01607	.01539	.01476
18	.02386	.02258	.02142	.02035	.01936	.01846	.01762	.01685	.01613	.01547
19	.02500	.02367	.02245	.02132	.02029	.01933	.01845	.01764	.01689	.01619
20	.02621	.02481	.02353	.02235	.02126	.02025	.01933	.01847	.01768	.01694
21	.02749	.02603	.02468	.02344	.02229	.02124	.02026	.01936	.01852	.01774
22	.02884	.02730	.02589	.02458	.02338	.02227	.02124	.02029	.01940	.01859
23	.03028	.02867	.02718	.02581	.02454	.02337	.02229	.02128	.02035	.01949
24	.03183	.03013	.02857	.02713	.02580	.02456	.02342	.02236	.02138	.02047
25	.03350	.03172	.03008	.02857	.02717	.02587	.02467	.02355	.02251	.02155
26	.03530	.03344	.03172	.03013	.02865	.02729	.02602	.02484	.02375	.02273
27	.03727	.03532	.03351	.03183	.03028	.02885	.02751	.02627	.02511	.02404
28	.03937	.03732	.03543	.03367	.03204	.03052	.02911	.02780	.02658	.02545
29	.04162	.03947	.03748	.03564	.03392	.03233	.03084	.02946	.02818	.02698
30	.04401	.04176	.03967	.03773	.03593	.03425	.03269	.03124	.02988	.02861
31	.04654	.04419	.04200	.03996	.03807	.03630	.03466	.03312	.03169	.03035
32	.04923	.04676	.04447	.04233	.04034	.03849	.03676	.03514	.03363	.03221
33	.05210	.04952	.04711	.04487	.04278	.04083	.03901	.03731	.03571	.03422
34	.05515	.05245	.04993	.04758	.04538	.04333	.04142	.03962	.03794	.03637
35	.05841	.05558	.05295	.05048	.04818	.04603	.04401	.04212	.04035	.03869
36	.06187	.05892	.05616	.05358	.05116	.04890	.04678	.04480	.04293	.04118
37	.06555	.06247	.05958	.05688	.05435	.05198	.04975	.04766	.04570	.04385
38	.06949	.06627	.06325	.06043	.05777	.05528	.05295	.05075	.04868	.04674
39	.07368	.07032	.06717	.06421	.06143	.05882	.05637	.05406	.05189	.04984
40	.07816	.07465	.07137	.06827	.06537	.06263	.06006	.05764	.05535	.05320
41	.08295	.07930	.07587	.07264	.06960	.06674	.06405	.06150	.05910	.05683
42	.08807	.08427	.08069	.07733	.07415	.07116	.06833	.06567	.06315	.06077
43	.09352	.08957	.08585	.08233	.07902	.07589	.07294	.07014	.06750	.06500
44	.09932	.09521	.09134	.08768	.08423	.08096	.07787	.07495	.07218	.06956

See p. 15 for regulations not amended to reflect law changes

AGE	8.2%	8.4%	8.6%	8.8%	9.0%	9.2%	9.4%	9.6%	9.8%	10.0%
45	.10543	.10117	.09715	.09334	.08974	.08634	.08311	.08005	.07716	.07441
46	.11189	.10747	.10329	.09933	.09559	.09204	.08867	.08548	.08245	.07958
47	.11866	.11408	.10974	.10564	.10174	.09805	.09454	.09121	.08805	.08504
48	.12577	.12103	.11654	.11228	.10823	.10439	.10074	.09727	.09397	.09083
49	.13323	.12833	.12368	.11926	.11506	.11107	.10728	.10366	.10022	.09695
50	.14107	.13601	.13120	.12663	.12228	.11813	.11419	.11043	.10685	.10344
51	.14928	.14407	.13910	.13437	.12987	.12558	.12149	.11758	.11386	.11031
52	.15785	.15248	.14735	.14247	.13781	.13337	.12913	.12508	.12122	.11752
53	.16678	.16124	.15597	.15093	.14612	.14153	.13714	.13294	.12893	.12509
54	.17606	.17037	.16493	.15974	.15478	.15004	.14550	.14116	.13700	.13302
55	.18570	.17986	.17428	.16893	.16382	.15893	.15424	.14976	.14546	.14134
56	.19573	.18974	.18400	.17851	.17325	.16821	.16338	.15875	.15430	.15004
57	.20613	.20000	.19412	.18848	.18307	.17789	.17291	.16814	.16355	.15914
58	.21688	.21060	.20458	.19880	.19325	.18792	.18280	.17788	.17316	.16861
59	.22793	.22151	.21535	.20943	.20374	.19827	.19301	.18795	.18309	.17840
60	.23927	.23272	.22642	.22036	.21454	.20893	.20354	.19834	.19334	.18851
61	.25092	.24425	.23782	.23163	.22567	.21993	.21440	.20907	.20393	.19898
62	.26295	.25616	.24961	.24329	.23721	.23134	.22568	.22021	.21494	.20985
63	.27538	.26847	.26180	.25537	.24916	.24316	.23738	.23179	.22639	.22117
64	.28817	.28116	.27438	.26783	.26150	.25539	.24949	.24377	.23825	.23291
65	.30134	.29423	.28735	.28069	.27426	.26803	.26201	.25618	.25054	.24508
66	.31493	.30772	.30075	.29399	.28746	.28113	.27500	.26906	.26331	.25774
67	.32899	.32170	.31464	.30780	.30118	.29475	.28852	.28248	.27663	.27095
68	.34349	.33614	.32901	.32209	.31538	.30887	.30256	.29643	.29047	.28469
69	.35841	.35100	.34381	.33683	.33005	.32346	.31707	.31085	.30481	.29894
70	.37366	.36620	.35896	.35193	.34509	.33844	.33197	.32568	.31957	.31362
71	.38916	.38167	.37440	.36732	.36043	.35372	.34720	.34084	.33466	.32864
72	.40486	.39736	.39006	.38295	.37602	.36927	.36270	.35629	.35005	.34396
73	.42074	.41323	.40591	.39878	.39182	.38504	.37843	.37198	.36568	.35955
74	.43685	.42934	.42202	.41488	.40791	.40110	.39446	.38798	.38165	.37547
75	.45326	.44577	.43846	.43132	.42435	.41754	.41088	.40438	.39802	.39181
76	.47004	.46259	.45530	.44818	.44122	.43442	.42776	.42125	.41488	.40865
77	.48718	.47979	.47255	.46547	.45853	.45175	.44511	.43861	.43225	.42601
78	.50467	.49735	.49017	.48314	.47626	.46951	.46290	.45643	.45008	.44386
79	.52239	.51515	.50806	.50110	.49427	.48758	.48102	.47459	.46828	.46209
80	.54018	.53304	.52603	.51916	.51242	.50580	.49930	.49292	.48666	.48052
81	.55788	.55085	.54396	.53718	.53053	.52399	.51757	.51126	.50507	.49898
82	.57540	.56851	.56173	.55506	.54851	.54207	.53574	.52951	.52339	.51737
83	.59274	.58598	.57933	.57279	.56635	.56001	.55378	.54765	.54161	.53567
84	.61002	.60341	.59690	.59049	.58418	.57796	.57184	.56582	.55988	.55403
85	.62734	.62090	.61454	.60828	.60211	.59603	.59004	.58414	.57832	.57258
86	.64455	.63828	.63210	.62600	.61999	.61406	.60821	.60244	.59675	.59113
87	.66139	.65531	.64930	.64337	.63752	.63175	.62605	.62043	.61488	.60939
88	.67783	.67194	.66612	.66037	.65469	.64908	.64354	.63807	.63267	.62733
89	.69387	.68817	.68254	.67698	.67148	.66605	.66068	.65537	.65012	.64493
90	.70947	.70398	.69855	.69318	.68786	.68261	.67742	.67228	.66719	.66217
91	.72437	.71908	.71385	.70867	.70354	.69847	.69345	.68848	.68357	.67870
92	.73823	.73314	.72810	.72310	.71816	.71326	.70841	.70361	.69886	.69415
93	.75109	.74618	.74132	.73650	.73173	.72700	.72232	.71768	.71308	.70852
94	.76312	.75839	.75370	.74905	.74445	.73988	.73536	.73087	.72643	.72202
95	.77459	.77004	.76552	.76104	.75660	.75220	.74783	.74350	.73920	.73494
96	.78543	.78105	.77670	.77238	.76810	.76386	.75964	.75546	.75131	.74720
97	.79550	.79128	.78709	.78293	.77880	.77470	.77063	.76659	.76258	.75860
98	.80498	.80091	.79687	.79286	.78888	.78492	.78099	.77709	.77322	.76937
99	.81428	.81036	.80647	.80261	.79877	.79496	.79117	.78741	.78367	.77995
100	.82336	.81959	.81586	.81214	.80845	.80478	.80113	.79751	.79390	.79032

AGE	8.2%	8.4%	8.6%	8.8%	9.0%	9.2%	9.4%	9.6%	9.8%	10.0%
101	.83234	.82873	.82515	.82158	.81804	.81451	.81101	.80753	.80406	.80062
102	.84119	.83774	.83431	.83089	.82750	.82412	.82076	.81742	.81409	.81078
103	.84999	.84670	.84342	.84016	.83691	.83368	.83046	.82726	.82408	.82091
104	.85944	.85632	.85321	.85011	.84703	.84396	.84090	.83786	.83483	.83182
105	.86866	.86570	.86276	.85982	.85690	.85399	.85109	.84820	.84532	.84245
106	.88065	.87792	.87520	.87248	.86978	.86708	.86440	.86172	.85905	.85638
107	.89530	.89286	.89042	.88799	.88557	.88315	.88073	.87833	.87592	.87352
108	.91849	.91654	.91460	.91266	.91072	.90879	.90685	.90492	90299	.90106
109	.95900	.95800	.95700	.95600	.95500	.95400	.95300	.95200	.95100	.95000

TABLE U(1)
BASED ON LIFE TABLE 90CM
UNITRUST SINGLE LIFE REMAINDER FACTORS
[APPLICABLE FOR TRANSFERS AFTER APRIL 30, 1999, AND BEFORE MAY 1, 2009]
ADJUSTED PAYOUT RATE

AGE	10.2%	10.4%	10.6%	10.8%	11.0%	11.2%	11.4%	11.6%	11.8%	12.0%
0	.01363	.01342	.01323	.01305	.01288	.01272	.01258	.01244	.01231	.01219
1	.00534	.00512	.00493	.00474	.00458	.00442	.00427	.00414	.00401	.00389
2	.00518	.00495	.00474	.00455	.00437	.00421	.00405	.00391	.00377	.00365
3	.00526	.00502	.00480	.00459	.00440	.00422	.00406	.00391	.00376	.00363
4	.00546	.00521	.00497	.00475	.00455	.00436	.00419	.00402	.00387	.00373
5	.00576	.00549	.00524	.00501	.00479	.00459	.00440	.00423	.00406	.00391
6	.00613	.00584	.00557	.00532	.00509	.00488	.00468	.00449	.00432	.00415
7	.00657	.00626	.00598	.00571	.00547	.00524	.00502	.00482	.00464	.00446
8	.00707	.00675	.00644	.00616	.00590	.00565	.00542	.00521	.00501	.00482
9	.00766	.00732	.00699	.00669	.00641	.00615	.00591	.00568	.00547	.00527
10	.00835	.00798	.00764	.00732	.00702	.00675	.00649	.00624	.00602	.00580
11	.00913	.00874	.00838	.00804	.00772	.00743	.00715	.00689	.00665	.00642
12	.01000	.00959	.00920	.00884	.00851	.00819	.00790	.00762	.00737	.00712
13	.01091	.01048	.01007	.00969	.00933	.00900	.00869	.00840	.00813	.00787
14	.01181	.01135	.01092	.01052	.01014	.00979	.00947	.00916	.00887	.00860
15	.01267	.01218	.01173	.01130	.01091	.01054	.01019	.00987	.00956	.00928
16	.01345	.01294	.01246	.01201	.01160	.01121	.01084	.01050	.01018	.00988
17	.01418	.01364	.01313	.01266	.01222	.01181	.01143	.01107	.01073	.01041
18	.01486	.01429	.01375	.01326	.01279	.01236	.01196	.01158	.01122	.01088
19	.01554	.01494	.01438	.01385	.01336	.01291	.01248	.01208	.01170	.01135
20	.01626	.01562	.01503	.01448	.01396	.01348	.01303	.01260	.01220	.01183
21	.01702	.01635	.01573	.01514	.01460	.01409	.01361	.01316	.01274	.01235
22	.01782	.01711	.01645	.01584	.01526	.01472	.01422	.01374	.01330	.01288
23	.01868	.01793	.01724	.01658	.01597	.01540	.01487	.01437	.01390	.01345
24	.01962	.01883	.01809	.01740	.01675	.01615	.01558	.01505	.01455	.01408
25	.02065	.01981	.01903	.01830	.01762	.01698	.01638	.01581	.01523	.01478
26	.02178	.02089	.02006	.01929	.01856	.01789	.01725	.01665	.01609	.01556
27	.02303	.02209	.02122	.02040	.01963	.01891	.01824	.01760	.01700	.01644
28	.02439	.02339	.02247	.02160	.02079	.02002	.01931	.01863	.01800	.01740
29	.02585	.02480	.02382	.02290	.02204	.02123	.02047	.01976	.01908	.01845
30	.02742	.02631	.02527	.02430	.02339	.02253	.02172	.02096	.02025	.01957
31	.02910	.02793	.02683	.02579	.02482	.02391	.02306	.02225	.02149	.02077
32	.03089	.02965	.02849	.02739	.02636	.02540	.02449	.02363	.02282	.02206
33	.03282	.03151	.03028	.02912	.02803	.02701	.02604	.02513	.02427	.02346
34	.03489	.03350	.03220	.03097	.02982	.02873	.02771	.02674	.02583	.02497
35	.03713	.03567	.03429	.03299	.03177	.03061	.02953	.02850	.02753	.02661
36	.03953	.03798	.03653	.03515	.03386	.03263	.03148	.03039	.02936	.02838
37	.04211	.04048	.03894	.03748	.03611	.03481	.03359	.03243	.03134	.03030
38	.04490	.04318	.04155	.04001	.03856	.03719	.03589	.03466	.03350	.03239
39	.04791	.04609	.04437	.04274	.04120	.03975	.03837	.03707	.03583	.03466
40	.05116	.04924	.04742	.04571	.04408	.04254	.04108	.03970	.03839	.03714
41	.05469	.05267	.05075	.04894	.04722	.04559	.04405	.04258	.04119	.03987

AGE	10.2%	10.4%	10.6%	10.8%	11.0%	11.2%	11.4%	11.6%	11.8%	12.0%
42	.05851	.05638	.05436	.05245	.05063	.04891	.04728	.04573	.04425	.04285
43	.06263	.06039	.05827	.05625	.05433	.05252	.05079	.04915	.04759	.04610
44	.06707	.06472	.06248	.06035	.05834	.05642	.05459	.05286	.05121	.04963
45	.07180	.06933	.06698	.06474	.06262	.06059	.05867	.05684	.05509	.05342
46	.07685	.07425	.07178	.06943	.06720	.06507	.06304	.06110	.05926	.05750
47	.08218	.07946	.07687	.07440	.07205	.06981	.06768	.06564	.06369	.06183
48	.08784	.08499	.08228	.07969	.07722	.07487	.07262	.07047	.06842	.06646
49	.09382	.09085	.08801	.08530	.08271	.08024	.07788	.07562	.07346	.07140
50	.10018	.09707	.09410	.09127	.08856	.08597	.08349	.08112	.07885	.07667
51	.10691	.10367	.10057	.09761	.09477	.09206	.08946	.08697	.08459	.08231
52	.11399	.11061	.10738	.10429	.10132	.09849	.09577	.09316	.09066	.08826
53	.12142	.11791	.11454	.11132	.10823	.10526	.10242	.09969	.09707	.09456
54	.12921	.12556	.12206	.11870	.11548	.11239	.10942	.10657	.10383	.10120
55	.13738	.13359	.12995	.12646	.12311	.11989	.11679	.11382	.11096	.10820
56	.14595	.14202	.13824	.13462	.13113	.12778	.12456	.12146	.11847	.11560
57	.15491	.15084	.14693	.14317	.13955	.13607	.13272	.12949	.12638	.12338
58	.16424	.16004	.15599	.15209	.14834	.14473	.14125	.13789	.13465	.13153
59	.17390	.16955	.16537	.16134	.15746	.15371	.15010	.14662	.14325	.14001
60	.18387	.17939	.17507	.17091	.16689	.16302	.15927	.15566	.15217	.14880
61	.19420	.18958	.18513	.18084	.17669	.17268	.16881	.16506	.16145	.15795
62	.20494	.20020	.19561	.19119	.18691	.18277	.17877	.17490	.17115	.16753
63	.21613	.21126	.20654	.20199	.19758	.19331	.18918	.18518	.18131	.17757
64	.22774	.22274	.21791	.21322	.20869	.20429	.20004	.19592	.19192	.18805
65	.23979	.23467	.22971	.22490	.22025	.21573	.21135	.20710	.20299	.19899
66	.25233	.24709	.24202	.23709	.23231	.22767	.22318	.21881	.21457	.21045
67	.26543	.26009	.25489	.24985	.24496	.24021	.23560	.23111	.22676	.22252
68	.27908	.27363	.26833	.26319	.25819	.25332	.24860	.24400	.23954	.23519
69	.29324	.28769	.28230	.27705	.27195	.26699	.26216	.25746	.25288	.24843
70	.30783	.30219	.29671	.29137	.28618	.28112	.27619	.27139	.26672	.26216
71	.32277	.31706	.31150	.30608	.30079	.29564	.29063	.28573	.28096	.27631
72	.33803	.33225	.32661	.32112	.31575	.31052	.30542	.30044	.29559	.29084
73	.35356	.34772	.34201	.33645	.33101	.32571	.32053	.31547	.31053	.30571
74	.36943	.36354	.35778	.35215	.34666	.34129	.33604	.33091	.32590	.32100
75	.38574	.37980	.37400	.36833	.36278	.35735	.35205	.34686	.34178	.33681
76	.40256	.39660	.39076	.38505	.37947	.37400	.36864	.36340	.35827	.35324
77	.41991	.41394	.40808	.40235	.39674	.39124	.38585	.38056	.37539	.37032
78	.43777	.43180	.42594	.42020	.41457	.40906	.40365	.39834	.39314	.38803
79	.45602	.45007	.44422	.43849	.43287	.42735	.42193	.41661	.41139	.40627
80	.47449	.46856	.46275	.45704	.45143	.44592	.44051	.43519	.42997	.42484
81	.49300	.48712	.48134	.47566	.47008	.46460	.45921	.45391	.44870	.44357
82	.51145	.50563	.49990	.49427	.48873	.48328	.47792	.47265	.46746	.46235
83	.52983	.52407	.51841	.51284	.50735	.50195	.49663	.49139	.48624	.48116
84	.54828	.54261	.53702	.53151	.52609	.52075	.51549	.51030	.50519	.50015
85	.56693	.56135	.55586	.55044	.54510	.53983	.53464	.52952	.52447	.51949
86	.58560	.58013	.57474	.56943	.56418	.55901	.55390	.54886	.54389	.53898
87	.60398	.59864	.59337	.58817	.58303	.57795	.57294	.56799	.56310	.55828
88	.62206	.61685	.61170	.60662	.60159	.59663	.59173	.58688	.58209	.57736
89	.63980	.63474	.62972	.62477	.61987	.61503	.61024	.60551	.60083	.59620
90	.65719	.65227	.64741	.64259	.63783	.63312	.62846	.62385	.61928	.61477
91	.67388	.66912	.66440	.65973	.65511	.65053	.64600	.64152	.63708	.63269
92	.68949	.68487	.68030	.67577	.67129	.66685	.66245	.65809	.65378	.64950
93	.70401	.69954	.69511	.69072	.68637	.68205	.67778	.67355	.66935	.66519
94	.71765	.71332	.70902	.70477	.70055	.69636	.69222	.68810	.68403	.67998
95	.73072	.72653	.72237	.71825	.71416	.71010	.70608	.70209	.69813	.69421
96	.74311	.73906	.73504	.73105	.72709	.72316	.71926	.71539	.71155	.70774
97	.75465	.75073	.74684	.74297	.73914	.73533	.73155	.72780	.72407	.72037

AGE	10.2%	10.4%	10.6%	10.8%	11.0%	11.2%	11.4%	11.6%	11.8%	12.0%
98	.76555	.76175	.75798	.75424	.75052	.74683	.74317	.73953	.73591	.73232
99	.77626	.77260	.76895	.76534	.76174	.75817	.75462	.75109	.74759	.74411
100	.78676	.78323	.77971	.77622	.77274	.76929	.76586	.76245	.75906	.75569
101	.79719	.79379	.79040	.78703	.78368	.78035	.77704	.77375	.77048	.76722
102	.80749	.80422	.80096	.79772	.79450	.79130	.78811	.78494	.78178	.77864
103	.81775	.81461	.81149	.80838	.80529	.80221	.79914	.79609	.79306	.79003
104	.82881	.82582	.82284	.81988	.81693	.81399	.81106	.80815	.80525	.80236
105	.83959	.83674	.83391	.83108	.82826	.82546	.82267	.81988	.81711	.81435
106	.85373	.85108	.84844	.84581	.84319	.84058	.83797	.83537	.83278	.83020
107	.87113	.86875	.86636	.86399	.86161	.85925	.85689	.85453	.85218	.84984
108	.89913	.89721	.89529	.89337	.89145	.88953	.88762	.88571	.38380	.88189
109	.94900	.94800	.94700	.94600	.94500	.94400	.94300	.94200	.94100	.94000

TABLE U(1)
BASED ON LIFE TABLE 90CM
UNITRUST SINGLE LIFE REMAINDER FACTORS
[APPLICABLE FOR TRANSFERS AFTER APRIL 30, 1999, AND BEFORE MAY 1, 2009]
ADJUSTED PAYOUT RATE

AGE	12.2%	12.4%	12.6%	12.8%	13.0%	13.2%	13.4%	13.6%	13.8%	14.0%
0	.01208	.01197	.01187	.01177	.01168	.01159	.01151	.01143	.01135	.01128
1	.00378	.00367	.00358	.00348	.00340	.00331	.00323	.00316	.00309	.00302
2	.00353	.00342	.00331	.00322	.00312	.00304	.00295	.00288	.00280	.00273
3	.00350	.00339	.00327	.00317	.00307	.00298	.00289	.00281	.00273	.00265
4	.00359	.00347	.00335	.00324	.00313	.00303	.00294	.00285	.00276	.00268
5	.00377	.00363	.00351	.00339	.00327	.00317	.00306	.00297	.00288	.00279
6	.00400	.00386	.00372	.00359	.00347	.00335	.00325	.00314	.00305	.00295
7	.00430	.00414	.00400	.00386	.00373	.00360	.00349	.00338	.00327	.00317
8	.00465	.00448	.00432	.00417	.00403	.00390	.00378	.00366	.00354	.00344
9	.00508	.00490	.00473	.00457	.00442	.00428	.00414	.00402	.00389	.00378
10	.00560	.00541	.00523	.00506	.00490	.00475	.00460	.00446	.00433	.00421
11	.00620	.00600	.00581	.00563	.00546	.00529	.00514	.00499	.00485	.00472
12	.00689	.00668	.00647	.00628	.00610	.00593	.00576	.00560	.00545	.00531
13	.00763	.00740	.00718	.00698	.00678	.00660	.00642	.00626	.00610	.00595
14	.00834	.00810	.00787	.00766	.00745	.00726	.00707	.00689	.00673	.00657
15	.00901	.00875	.00851	.00828	.00807	.00786	.00767	.00748	.00730	.00714
16	.00959	.00932	.00907	.00883	.00860	.00839	.00818	.00799	.00730	.00762
17	.01011	.00983	.00956	.00930	.00907	.00884	.00862	.00842	.00822	.00804
18	.01057	.01027	.00999	.00972	.00947	.00923	.00900	.00879	.00858	.00839
19	.01101	.01070	.01040	.01012	.00985	.00960	.00936	.00914	.00892	.00871
20	.01148	.01115	.01083	.01054	.01026	.00999	.00974	.00950	.00927	.00905
21	.01197	.01162	.01129	.01098	.01068	.01040	.01014	.00988	.00964	.00941
22	.01249	.01211	.01176	.01143	.01112	.01082	.01054	.01027	.01002	.00978
23	.01304	.01264	.01227	.01192	.01159	.01127	.01098	.01069	.01042	.01017
24	.01364	.01322	.01283	.01246	.01210	.01177	.01145	.01115	.01087	.01060
25	.01431	.01387	.01345	.01306	.01268	.01233	.01199	.01168	.01137	.01109
26	.01506	.01459	.01415	.01373	.01333	.01295	.01260	.01226	.01194	.01163
27	.01591	.01541	.01494	.01449	.01407	.01367	.01329	.01293	.01259	.01226
28	.01684	.01631	.01580	.01533	.01488	.01445	.01405	.01367	.01330	.01296
29	.01785	.01728	.01675	.01624	.01577	.01531	.01488	.01447	.01408	.01372
30	.01893	.01833	.01776	.01723	.01672	.01623	.01578	.01534	.01493	.01453
31	.02010	.01946	.01885	.01828	.01773	.01722	.01673	.01627	.01582	.01540
32	.02134	.02066	.02002	.01940	.01883	.01828	.01776	.01726	.01679	.01634
33	.02270	.02197	.02128	.02063	.02002	.01943	.01887	.01835	.01784	.01736
34	.02415	.02338	.02265	.02195	.02130	.02067	.02008	.01951	.01897	.01846
35	.02574	.02492	.02414	.02340	.02270	.02203	.02140	.02080	.02022	.01967
36	.02746	.02658	.02575	.02496	.02422	.02350	.02283	.02218	.02157	.02098
37	.02932	.02838	.02750	.02666	.02586	.02510	.02438	.02369	.02303	.02241
38	.03135	.03035	.02941	.02851	.02766	.02685	.02608	.02534	.02464	.02397

AGE	12.2%	12.4%	12.6%	12.8%	13.0%	13.2%	13.4%	13.6%	13.8%	14.0%
39	.03355	.03249	.03149	.03053	.02962	.02876	.02793	.02715	.02640	.02568
40	.03596	.03484	.03377	.03275	.03178	.03086	.02998	.02914	.02833	.02757
41	.03861	.03742	.03628	.03520	.03416	.03318	.03224	.03134	.03048	.02966
42	.04152	.04025	.03903	.03788	.03678	.03573	.03473	.03377	.03285	.03198
43	.04468	.04333	.04205	.04082	.03965	.03853	.03746	.03644	.03546	.03453
44	.04813	.04670	.04533	.04403	.04278	.04159	.04045	.03936	.03832	.03732
45	.05183	.05032	.04887	.04748	.04616	.04489	.04368	.04252	.04141	.04034
46	.05582	.05421	.05267	.05121	.04980	.04846	.04717	.04593	.04475	.04362
47	.06006	.05836	.05673	.05518	.05369	.05226	.05089	.04958	.04832	.04711
48	.06459	.06279	.06107	.05943	.05785	.05634	.05488	.05349	.05216	.05087
49	.06942	.06752	.06571	.06397	.06230	.06070	.05916	.05768	.05626	.05490
50	.07459	.07259	.07068	.06884	.06708	.06538	.06376	.06219	.06069	.05924
51	.08012	.07801	.07599	.07406	.07220	.07041	.06869	.06703	.06544	.06391
52	.08596	.08375	.08163	.07959	.07763	.07574	.07392	.07218	.07049	.06887
53	.09214	.08982	.08759	.08544	.08338	.08139	.07948	.07763	.07586	.07415
54	.09867	.09623	.09389	.09164	.08946	.08737	.08536	.08342	.08154	.07974
55	.10556	.10301	.10055	.09819	.09591	.09371	.09159	.08955	.08757	.08567
56	.11283	.11016	.10759	.10511	.10272	.10042	.09819	.09605	.09397	.09197
57	.12050	.11771	.11502	.11243	.10993	.10751	.10518	.10293	.10075	.09864
58	.12852	.12562	.12281	.12011	.11749	.11496	.11252	.11016	.10787	.10567
59	.13687	.13385	.13092	.12810	.12537	.12273	.12017	.11770	.11531	.11299
60	.14554	.14240	.13935	.13641	.13356	.13080	.12813	.12555	.12305	.12063
61	.15457	.15130	.14813	.14507	.14210	.13923	.13644	.13375	.13113	.12860
62	.16402	.16063	.15734	.15415	.15107	.14808	.14518	.14237	.13964	.13699
63	.17393	.17042	.16700	.16370	.16049	.15738	.15437	.15144	.14860	.14584
64	.18429	.18065	.17712	.17369	.17036	.16714	.16400	.16096	.15800	.15513
65	.19511	.19135	.18769	.18415	.18070	.17735	.17410	.17094	.16787	.16488
66	.20645	.20257	.19880	.19513	.19157	.18810	.18473	.18146	.17827	.17517
67	.21841	.21441	.21052	.20673	.20305	.19947	.19599	.19259	.18929	.18608
68	.23096	.22685	.22284	.21895	.21515	.21146	.20786	.20436	.20094	.19762
69	.24409	.23987	.23575	.23175	.22784	.22404	.22033	.21672	.21320	.20976
70	.25772	.25339	.24918	.24507	.24106	.23715	.23333	.22961	.22598	.22244
71	.27178	.26735	.26304	.25882	.25471	.25070	.24679	.24296	.23923	.23559
72	.28622	.28170	.27729	.27298	.26877	.26467	.26065	.25673	.25290	.24915
73	.30100	.29639	.29189	.28749	.28320	.27899	.27489	.27087	.26694	.26310
74	.31621	.31152	.30694	.30246	.29807	.29378	.28959	.28548	.28146	.27753
75	.33195	.32719	.32253	.31797	.31351	.30914	.30486	.30067	.29657	.29255
76	.34832	.34350	.33877	.33415	.32961	.32517	.32082	.31656	.31238	.30828
77	.36535	.36047	.35570	.35101	.34642	.34192	.33750	.33317	.32892	.32475
78	.38302	.37811	.37329	.36856	.36392	.35937	.35490	.35051	.34621	.34198
79	.40124	.39630	.39145	.38669	.38201	.37742	.37291	.36848	.36413	.35985
80	.41980	.41485	.40998	.40520	.40050	.39588	.39134	.38688	.38249	.37818
81	.43854	.43358	.42871	.42392	.41921	.41457	.41001	.40553	.40112	.39678
82	.45733	.45238	.44752	.44273	.43802	.43338	.42881	.42431	.41989	.41553
83	.47616	.47123	.46638	.46161	.45690	.45227	.44770	.44320	.43877	.43441
84	.49519	.49030	.48548	.48073	.47604	.47143	.46688	.46239	.45797	.45361
85	.51458	.50974	.50496	.50025	.49560	.49102	.48650	.48204	.47763	.47329
86	.53413	.52935	.52463	.51998	.51538	.51084	.50636	.50194	.49758	.49327
87	.55351	.54881	.54416	.53957	.53503	.53055	.52613	.52176	.51744	.51317
88	.57268	.56806	.56349	.55898	.55451	.55010	.54574	.54144	.53718	.53296
89	.59162	.58710	.58262	.57819	.57382	.56949	.56520	.56097	.55678	.55263
90	.61030	.60588	.60151	.59718	.59290	.58866	.58447	.58032	.57621	.57214
91	.62834	.62403	.61977	.61554	.61136	.60722	.60312	.59907	.59505	.59107
92	.64527	.64107	.63692	.63280	.62872	.62468	.62068	.61672	.61279	.60890
93	.66107	.65699	.65294	.64893	.64495	.64101	.63711	.63323	.62940	.62559
94	.67597	.67200	.66806	.66415	.66027	.65643	.65262	.64884	.64509	.64138

See p. 15 for regulations not amended to reflect law changes

AGE	12.2%	12.4%	12.6%	12.8%	13.0%	13.2%	13.4%	13.6%	13.8%	14.0%
95	.69031	.68645	.68262	.67881	.67504	.67130	.66759	.66390	.66025	.65662
96	.70396	.70021	.69648	.69279	.68912	.68548	.68186	.67828	.67471	.67118
97	.71670	.71305	.70943	.70584	.70227	.69872	.69520	.69171	.68824	.68480
98	.72875	.72521	.72169	.71819	.71472	.71127	.70784	.70444	.70106	.69770
99	.74065	.73721	.73379	.73040	.72703	.72368	.72035	.71704	.71375	.71048
100	.75234	.74901	.74570	.74241	.73914	.73589	.73265	.72944	.72625	.72307
101	.76399	.76077	.75757	.75438	.75122	.74807	.74494	.74183	.73873	.73565
102	.77552	.77241	.76932	.76625	.76319	.76015	.75712	.75411	75111	.74813
103	.78703	.78404	.78106	.77809	.77514	.77221	.76929	.76638	.76348	.76060
104	.79948	.79662	.79377	.79093	.78810	.78528	.78248	.77969	.77691	.77414
105	.81159	.80885	.80612	.80340	.80069	.79799	.79530	.79262	.78995	.78729
106	.82763	.82506	.82250	.81995	.81741	.81488	.81235	.80983	.80732	.80482
107	.84749	.84516	.84283	.84051	.83819	.83587	.83356	.83126	.82896	.82666
108	.87999	.87808	.87618	.87428	.87238	.87049	.86859	.86670	.86481	.86293
109	.93900	.93800	.93700	.93600	.93500	.93400	.93300	.93200	.93100	.93000

(7) *Effective/applicability dates.*—Paragraphs (f)(1) through (f)(6) apply after April 30, 1999, and before May 1, 2009. [Reg. § 1.664-4A.]

☐ [*T.D.* 8540, 6-9-94. *Amended by T.D.* 8819, 4-29-99; *T.D.* 8886, 6-9-2000; *T.D.* 9448, 5-1-2009 *and T.D.* 9540, 8-9-2011.]

[Reg. § 1.665(a)-0A]

§ 1.665(a)-0A. Excess distributions by trusts; scope of subpart D.—(a) *In general.*—(1) Subpart D (section 665 and following), part I, subchapter J, chapter 1 of the Code, as amended by the Tax Reform Act of 1969, is designed to tax the beneficiary of a trust that accumulates, rather than distributes, all or part of its income currently (i.e., an accumulation trust), in most cases, as if the income had been currently distributed to the beneficiary instead of accumulated by the trust. Accordingly, subpart D provides special rules for the treatment of amounts paid, credited, or required to be distributed by a complex trust (one that is subject to subpart C (section 661 and following) of such part I) in any year in excess of "distributable net income" (as defined in section 643(a)) for that year. Such an excess distribution is an "accumulation distribution" (as defined in section 665(b)). The special rules of subpart D are generally inapplicable to amounts paid, credited, or required to be distributed by a trust in a taxable year in which it qualifies as a simple trust (one that is subject to subpart B (section 651 and following) of such part I). However, see § 1.665(e)-1A(b) for rules relating to the treatment of a simple trust as a complex trust.

(2) An accumulation distribution is deemed to consist of, first, "undistributed net income" (as defined in section 665(a)) of the trust from preceding taxable years, and, after all the undistributed net income for all preceding taxable years has been deemed distributed, "undistributed capital gain" (as defined in section 665(f)) of the trust for all preceding taxable years commencing with the first year such amounts were accumulated. An accumulation distribution of undistributed capital gain is a "capital gain distribution" (as defined in section 665(g)). To the extent an accumulation distribution exceeds the "undistributed net income" and "undistributed capital gain" so determined, it is deemed to consist of corpus.

(3) The accumulation distribution is "thrown back" to the earliest "preceding taxable year" of the trust, which, in the case of distributions made for a taxable year beginning after December 31, 1973, from a trust (other than a foreign trust created by a United States person), is any taxable year beginning after December 31, 1968. Special transitional rules apply for distributions made in taxable years beginning before January 1, 1974. In the case of a foreign trust created by a United States person, a "preceding taxable year" is any year of the trust to which the Code applies.

(4) A distribution of undistributed net income (included in an accumulation distribution) and a capital gain distribution will be included in the income of the beneficiary in the year they are actually paid, credited, or required to be distributed to him. The tax on the distribution will be approximately the amount of tax the beneficiary would have paid with respect to the distribution had the income and capital gain been distributed to the beneficiary in the year earned by the trust. An additional amount equal to the "taxes imposed on the trust" for the preceding year is also deemed distributed. To prevent double taxation, however, the beneficiary receives a credit for such taxes.

(b) *Effective dates.*—All regulations sections under subpart D (sections 665 through 669) which have an "A" suffix (such as §§ 1.665(a)A and 1.666(b)-1A) are applicable to taxable years beginning on or after January 1, 1969, and all references therein to sections 665 through 669 are references to such sections as amended by the Tax Reform Act of 1969. Sections without the "A" suffix (such as §§ 1.665(a) and 1.666(b)-1) are applicable only to taxable years beginning before January 1, 1969, and all references therein to sections 665 through 669 are references to such sections before amendment by the Tax Reform Act of 1969.

(c) *Examples.*—Where examples contained in the regulations under subpart D refer to tax rates for years after 1968, such tax rates are not necessarily the actual rates for such years, but are only used for example purposes.

(d) *Applicability to estates.*—Subpart D does not apply to any estate. [Reg. § 1.665(a)-0A].

☐ [*T.D.* 7204, 8-24-72.]

[Reg. § 1.665(a)-1A]

§ 1.665(a)-1A. Undistributed net income.—(a) *Domestic trusts.*—The term "undistributed net income", in the case of a trust (other than a foreign trust created by a U.S. person) means, for any taxable year beginning after December 31, 1968, the distributable net income of the trust for that year (as determined under section 643(a)), less:

(1) The amount of income required to be distributed currently and any other amounts properly paid or credited or required to be distributed to beneficiaries in the taxable year as specified in section 661(a), and

(2) The amount of taxes imposed on the trust allocable to such distributable net income, as defined in § 1.665(d)-1A.

The application of the rule in this paragraph to a taxable year of a trust in which income is accumulated may be illustrated by the following example:

Example. Under the terms of the trust, $10,000 of income is required to be distributed currently to A and the trustee has discretion to make additional distributions to A. During the taxable year 1971 the trust had distributable net income of $30,100 derived from royalties and the trustee made distributions of $20,000 to A. The taxable income of the trust is $10,000 on which a tax of $2,190 is paid. The undistributed net income of the trust for the taxable year 1971 is $7,910, computed as follows:

Distributable net income		$30,100
Less:		
Income currently distributable to A	$10,000	
Other amounts distributed to A	10,000	
Taxes imposed on the trust attributable to the undistributed net income (see § 1.665(d)-1A)	2,190	
		22,190
Undistributed net income		7,910

(b) *Foreign trusts.*—The undistributed net income of a foreign trust created by a U.S. person for any taxable year is the distributable net income of such trust (see § 1.643(a)-6 and the examples set forth in paragraph (b) thereof), less:

(1) The amount of income required to be distributed currently and any other amounts properly paid or credited or required to be distributed to beneficiaries in the taxable year as specified in section 661(a), and

(2) The amount of taxes imposed on such trust by chapter 1 of the Internal Revenue Code, which are attributable to items of income which are required to be included in such distributable net income.

For purposes of subparagraph (2) of this paragraph, the amount of taxes imposed on the trust for any taxable year by chapter 1 of the Internal Revenue Code is the amount of taxes imposed pursuant to section 871 (relating to tax on nonresident alien individuals) which is properly allocable to the undistributed portion of the distributable net income. See § 1.665(d)-1A. The amount of taxes imposed pursuant to section 871 is the difference between the total tax imposed pursuant to that section on the foreign trust created by a U.S. person for the year and the amount which would have been imposed on such trust had all the distributable net income, as determined under section 643(a), been distributed. The application of the rule in this paragraph may be illustrated by the following examples:

Example (1). A trust was created in 1952 under the laws of Country X by the transfer to a trustee in Country X of property by U.S. person. The entire trust constitutes a foreign trust created by a U.S. person. The governing instrument of the trust provides that $7,000 of income is required to be distributed currently to a U.S. beneficiary and gives the trustee discretion to make additional distributions to the beneficiary. During the taxable year 1973 the trust had income of $10,000 from dividends of a U.S. corporation (on which Federal income taxes of $3,000 were imposed pursuant to section 871 and withheld under section 1441, resulting in the receipt by the trust of cash in the amount of $7,000), $20,000 in capital gains from the sale of stock of a Country Y corporation and $30,000 from dividends of a Country X corporation, none of the gross income of which was derived from sources within the United States. No income taxes were required to be paid to Country X or Country Y in 1973. The trustee did not file a U.S. income tax return for the taxable year 1973. The distributable net income of the trust before distributions to the beneficiary for 1973 is $60,000 ($57,000 of which is cash). During 1973 the trustee made distributions to the U.S. beneficiary equaling one-half of the trust's distributable net income. Thus, the U.S. beneficiary is treated as having had distributed to him $5,000 (composed of $3,500 as a cash distribution and $1,500 as the tax imposed pursuant to section 871 and withheld under section 1441), representing one-half of the income from U.S. sources; $10,000 in cash, representing one-half of the capital gains from the sale of stock of the Country Y corporation; and $15,000 in cash, representing one-half of the income from Country X sources for a total of $30,000. The undistributed net income of the trust at the close of taxable year 1973 is $28,500 computed as follows:

Distributable net income		$60,000
Less:		
(1) Amounts distributed to the beneficiary		
Income currently distributed to the beneficiary	$7,000	
Other amounts distributed to the beneficiary	21,500	
Taxes under sec. 871 deemed distributed to the beneficiary	1,500	
Total amounts distributed to the beneficiary	30,000	
(2) Amount of taxes imposed on the trust under chapter 1 of the Code attributable to the undistributed net income (See § 1.665(d)-1A) ($3,000 less $1,500)	1,500	
Total		31,500
Undistributed net income		28,500

Example (2). The facts are the same as in example (1) except that property has been transferred to the trust by a person other than a U.S. person, and during 1973 the foreign trust created by a U.S. person was 60 percent of the entire foreign trust. The trustee paid no income taxes to Country X or Country Y in 1973.

(1) The undistributed net income of the portion of the entire trust which is a foreign trust created by a U.S. person for 1973 is $17,100, computed as follows:

Distributable net income (60% of each item of gross income of entire trust):		
60% of $10,000 U.S. dividends		$ 6,000
60% of $20,000 Country X capital gains		12,000
60% of $30,000 Country X dividends		18,000
Total		36,000
Less:		
(i) Amounts distributed to the beneficiary—		
Income currently distributed to the beneficiary (60% of $7,000)	$ 4,200	
Other amounts distributed to the beneficiary (60% of $21,500)	12,900	
Taxes under sec. 871 deemed distributed to the beneficiary (60% of $1,500)	900	
Total amounts distributed to the beneficiary	18,000	
(ii) Amount of taxes imposed on the trust under chapter 1 of the Code attributable to the undistributed net income (See § 1.665(d)-1A) (60% of $1,500)	$ 900	
Total		$18,900
Undistributed net income		17,100

(2) The undistributed net income of the portion of the entire trust which is not a foreign trust created by a U.S. person for 1973 is $11,400, computed as follows:

Distributable net income (40% of each item of gross income of entire trust)		
40% of $10,000 U.S. dividends		$ 4,000
40% of $30,000 Country X dividends		12,000
Total		24,000
Less:		
(i) Amounts distributed to the beneficiary—		
Income currently distributed to the beneficiary (40% of $7,000)	$ 2,800	
Other amounts distributed to the beneficiary (40% of $21,500)	8,600	
Taxes under sec. 871 deemed distributed to the beneficiary (40% of $1,500)	600	
Total amounts distributed to the beneficiary	12,000	
(ii) Amount of taxes imposed on the trust under chapter 1 of the Code attributable to the undistributed net income (See § 1.665(d)-1A) (40% of $1,500)	$ 600	
Total		$12,600
Undistributed net income		11,400

(c) *Effect of prior distributions.*—The undistributed net income for any year to which an accumulation distribution for a later year may be thrown back will be reduced by accumulation distributions in intervening years that are required to be thrown back to such year. For example, if a trust has undistributed net income for 1975, and an accumulation distribution is made in 1980, there must be taken into account the effect on undistributed net income for 1975 of any accumulation distribution made in 1976, 1977, 1978, or 1979. However, undistributed net income for any year will not be reduced by any distributions in intervening years that are excluded under section 663(a)(1), relating to gifts, bequests, etc. See paragraph (d) of §1.666(a)-1A for an illustration of the reduction of undistributed net income for any year by a subsequent accumulation distribution.

(d) *Distributions made in taxable years beginning before January 1, 1974.*—For special rules relating to accumulation distributions of undistributed net income made in taxable years of the trust beginning before January 1, 1974, see §1.665(b)-2A. [Reg. §1.665(a)-1A.]

☐ [*T.D. 7204, 8-24-72.*]

[Reg. §1.665(b)-1A]

§1.665(b)-1A. Accumulation distributions.—(a) *In general.*—(1) For any taxable year of a trust the term "accumulation distribution" means an amount by which the amounts properly paid, credited, or required to be distributed within the meaning of section 661(a)(2) (*i.e.*, all amounts properly paid, credited, or required to be distributed to the beneficiary other than income required to be distributed currently within the meaning of section 661(a)(1)) for that year exceed the distributable net income (determined under section 643(a)) of the trust, reduced (but not below zero) by the amount of income required to be distributed currently. To the extent provided in section 663(b) and the regulations thereunder, distributions made within the first 65 days following a taxable year may be treated as having been distributed on the last day of such taxable year.

(2) An accumulation distribution also includes, for a taxable year of the trust, any amount to which section 661(a)(2) and the preceding paragraph are inapplicable and which is paid, credited, or required to be distributed during the taxable year of the trust by reason of the exercise of a power to appoint, distribute, consume, or withdraw corpus of the trust or income of the trust accumulated in a preceding taxable year. No accumulation distribution is deemed to be made solely because the grantor or any other person is treated as owner of a portion of the trust by reason of an unexercised power to appoint, distribute, consume, or withdraw corpus or accumulated income of the trust. Nor will an accumulation distribution be deemed to have been made by reason of the exercise of a power that may affect only taxable income previously attributed to the holders of such power under subpart E (section 671 and following). See example 4 of paragraph (d) of this section for an example of an accumulation distribution occurring as a result of the exercise of a power of withdrawal.

(3) Although amounts properly paid or credited under section 661(a) do not exceed the income of the trust during the taxable year, an accumulation distribution may result if the amounts properly paid or credited under section 661(a)(2) exceed distributable net income reduced (but not below zero) by the amount required to be distributed currently under section 661(a)(1). This may occur, for example, when expenses, interest, taxes, or other items allocable to corpus are taken into account in determining taxable income and hence causing distributable net income to be less than the trust's income.

(b) *Payments that are accumulation distributions.*—The following are some instances in which an accumulation distribution may arise:

(1) *One trust to another.*—A distribution from one trust to another trust is generally an accumulation distribution. See §1.643(c)-1. This general rule will apply regardless of whether the distribution is to an existing trust or to a newly created trust and regardless of whether the trust to which the distribution is made was created by the same person who created the trust from which the distribution is made or a different person. However, a distribution made from one trust to a second trust will be deemed an accumulation distribution by the first trust to an ultimate beneficiary of the second trust if the primary purpose of the distribution to the second trust is to avoid the capital gain distribution provisions (see section 669 and the regulations thereunder). An amount passing from one separate share of a trust to another separate share of the same trust is not an accumulation distribution. See §1.665(g)-2A. For rules relating to the computation of the beneficiary's tax under section 668 by reason of an accumulation distribution from the second trust, see paragraphs (b)(1) and (c)(1)(i) of §1.668(b)-1A and paragraphs (b)(1) and (c)(1)(i) of §1.669(b)-1A.

(2) *Income accumulated during minority.*—A distribution of income accumulated during the minority of the beneficiary is generally an accumulation distribution. For example, if a trust accumulates income until the beneficiary's 21st birthday, and then distributes the income to the beneficiary, such a distribution is an accumulation distribution. However, see §1.665(b)-2A for rules governing income accumulated in taxable years beginning before January 1, 1969.

(3) *Amounts paid for support.*—To the extent that amounts forming all or part of an accumulation distribution are applied or distributed for the support of a dependent under the circumstances specified in section 677(b) or section 678(c) or are used to discharge or satisfy any person's legal obligation as that term is used in §1.662(a)-4, such amounts will be considered as having been distributed directly to the person whose obligation is being satisfied.

(c) *Payments which are not accumulation distributions.*—(1) *Gifts, bequests, etc., described in section 663(a)(1).*—A gift or bequest of a specific sum of money or of specific property described in section 663(a)(1) is not an accumulation distribution.

(2) *Charitable payments.*—Any amount paid, permanently set aside, or used for the purposes specified in section 642(c) is not an accumulation distribution, even though no charitable deduction is allowed under such section with respect to such payment.

(3) *Income required to be distributed currently.*—No accumulation distribution will arise by reason of a payment of income required to be distributed currently even though such income exceeds the distributable net income of the trust because the payment is an amount specified in section 661(a)(1).

(d) *Examples.*—The provisions of this section may be illustrated by the following examples:

Example (1). A trustee properly makes a distribution to a beneficiary of $20,000 during the taxable year 1976, of which $10,000 is income required to be distributed currently to the beneficiary. The distributable net income of the trust is $15,000. There is an accumulation distribution of $5,000 computed as follows.

Total distribution		$20,000
Less: Income required to be distributed currently (section 661(a)(1))		10,000
Other amounts distributed (section 661(a)(2))		10,000
Distributable net income	$15,000	
Less: Income required to be distributed currently	10,000	
Balance of distributable net income		5,000
Accumulation distribution		5,000

Example (2). Under the terms of the trust instrument, an annuity of $15,000 is required to be paid to A out of income each year and the trustee may in his discretion make distributions out of income or corpus to B. During the taxable year the trust had income of $18,000, as defined in section 643(b), and expenses allocable to corpus of $5,000. Distributable net income amounted to $13,000. The trustee distributed $15,000 of income to A and, in the exercise of his discretion, paid $5,000 to B. There is an accumulation distribution of $5,000 computed as follows:

Total distribution		$20,000
Less: Income required to be distributed currently to A (section 661(a)(1))		15,000
Other amounts distributed (section 661(a)(2))		5,000
Distributable net income	$13,000	
Less: Income required to be distributed currently to A	15,000	
Balance of distributable net income		$ 0
Accumulation distribution to B		5,000

Example (3). Under the terms of a trust instrument, the trustee may either accumulate the trust income or make distributions to A and B. The trustee may also invade corpus for the benefit of A and B. During the taxable year, the trust had income as defined in section 643(b) of $22,000 and expenses of $5,000 allocable to corpus. Distributable net income amounts to $17,000. The trustee distributed $10,000 each to A and B during the taxable year. There is an accumulation distribution of $3,000 computed as follows:

Total distribution		$20,000
Less: Income required to be distributed currently		0
Other amounts distributed (section 661(a)(2))		20,000
Distributable net income	$17,000	
Less: Income required to be distributed currently	0	
Balance of distributable net income		17,000
Accumulation distribution		3,000

Example (4). A dies in 1974 and bequeaths one-half the residue of his estate in trust. His widow, W, is given a power, exercisable solely by her, to require the trustee to pay her each year of the trust $5,000 from corpus. W's right to exercise such power was exercisable at any time during the year but was not cumulative, so that, upon her failure to exercise it before the end of any taxable year of the trust, her right as to that year lapsed. The trust's taxable year is the calendar year. During the calendar years 1975 and 1976, W did not exercise her right and it lapsed as to those years. In the calendar years 1977 and 1978, in which years the trust had no distributable net income, she exercised her right and withdrew $4,000 in 1977 and $5,000 in 1978. No accumulation distribution was made by the trust in the calendar years 1975 and 1976. An accumulation distribution of $4,000 was made in 1977 and an accumulation distribution of $5,000 was made in 1978. The accumulation distribution for the years 1977 and 1978 is not reduced by any amount of income of the trust attributable to her under section 678 by reason of her power of withdrawal. [Reg. § 1.665(b)-1A.]

☐ [*T.D.* 7204, 8-24-72.]

[Reg. § 1.665(b)-2A]

§ 1.665(b)-2A. Special rules for accumulation distributions made in taxable years beginning before January 1, 1974.—(a) *General rule.*—Section 331(d)(2)(A) of the Tax Reform Act of 1969 excludes certain accumulated income from the tax imposed by section 668(a)(2) by providing certain exceptions from the definition of an "accumulation distribution". Any amount paid, credited, or required to be distributed by a trust (other than a foreign trust created by a U.S. person) during a taxable year of the trust beginning after December 31, 1968, and before January 1, 1974, shall not be subject to the tax imposed by section 668(a)(2) to the extent of the portion of such amount that (1) would be allocated under section 666(a) to a preceding taxable year of the trust beginning before January 1, 1969, and (2) would not have been deemed an accumulation distribution because of the provisions of paragraphs (1), (2), (3), or (4) of section 665(b) as in effect on December 31, 1968, had the trust distributed such amounts on the last day of its last taxable year beginning before January 1, 1969. However, the $2,000 *de minimis* exception formerly in section 665(b) does not apply in the case of any distribution made in a taxable year of a trust beginning after December 31, 1968. Amounts to which this exclusion applies shall reduce the undistributed net income of the trust for the preceding taxable year or years to which such amounts would be allocated under section 666(a). However, since section 668(a)(2) does not apply to such amounts, no amount of taxes imposed on the trust allocable to such undistributed net income is deemed distributed under section 666(b) and (c).

(b) *Application of general rule.*—The rule expressed in paragraph (a) of this section is applied to the exceptions formerly in section 665(b) as follows:

(1) *Distributions from amounts accumulated while beneficiary is under 21.*—(i) Paragraph (1) of section 665(b) as in effect on December 31, 1968, provided that amounts paid, credited, or required to be distributed to a beneficiary as income accumulated before the birth of such beneficiary or before such beneficiary attains the age of 21 were not to be considered to be accumulation distributions. If an accumulation distribution is made in a taxable year of the trust beginning after December 31, 1968, and before January 1, 1974, and under section 666(a) such accumulation distribution would be allocated to a preceding taxable year beginning before January 1, 1969, no tax shall be imposed under section 668(a)(2) to the extent the income earned by the trust for such preceding taxable year would be deemed under § 1.665(b)-2(b)(1) to have been accumulated before the beneficiary's birth or before his 21st birthday. The provisions of this subparagraph may be illustrated by the following example:

Example. A trust on the calendar year basis was established on January 1, 1965, to accumulate the income during the minority of B, and to pay the accumulated income over to B upon his attaining the age of 21. B's 21st birthday is January 1, 1973. On January 2, 1973, the trustee pays over to B all the accumulated income of the trust. The distribution is an accumulation distribution that may be allocated under section 666(a) to 1968, 1969, 1970, 1971, and 1972 (the five preceding taxable years as defined in § 1.665(e)-1A). To the extent the distribution is allocated to 1968, no tax is imposed under section 668(a)(2).

(ii) As indicated in paragraph (a), a distribution of an amount excepted from the tax otherwise imposed under section 668(a)(2) will reduce undistributed net income for the purpose of determining the effect of a future distribution. Thus, under the facts of the example in subdivision (i) of this paragraph, the undistributed net income for the trust's taxable year 1968 would be reduced by the amount of the distribution allocated to that year under section 666(a).

(2) *Emergency distributions.*—Paragraph (2) of section 665(b) as in effect on December 31, 1968, provided an exclusion from the definition of an accumulation distribution for amounts properly paid or credited to a beneficiary to meet his emergency needs. Therefore, if an accumulation distribution is made from a trust in a taxable year beginning before January 1, 1974, and under section 666(a) such accumulation distribution would be allocated to a preceding taxable year of the trust beginning before January 1, 1969, no tax shall be imposed under section 668(a)(2) if such distribution would have been considered an emergency distribution under § 1.665(b)-2(b)(2) had it been made in a taxable year of the trust beginning before January 1, 1969. For example, assume a trust on a calendar year basis in 1972 makes an accumulation distribution which under § 1.665(b)-2(b)(2) would be considered an emergency distribution and under section 666(a) the distribution would be allocated to the years 1967, 1968, and 1969. To the extent such amount is allocated to 1967 and 1968, no tax would be imposed under section 668(a)(2).

(3) *Certain distributions at specified ages.*—Paragraph (3) of section 665(b) as in effect on December 31, 1968, provided an exclusion (in the case of certain trusts created before January 1, 1954) from the definition of an accumulation distribution for amounts properly paid or credited to a beneficiary upon his attaining a specified age or ages, subject to certain restrictions (see § 1.665(b)-2(b)(3)). Therefore, a distribution from a trust in a taxable year beginning after December 31, 1968, will not be subject to the tax imposed under section 668(a)(2) to the extent such distribution would be allocated to a preceding taxable year of the trust beginning before January 1, 1969, if such distribution would have qualified under the provisions of § 1.665(b)-2(b)(3) had it been made in a taxable year of the trust to which such section was applicable.

(4) *Certain final distributions.*—Paragraph (4) of section 665(b) as in effect on December 31, 1968, provided an exclusion from the definition of an accumulation distribution for amounts properly paid or credited to a beneficiary as a final distribution of the trust if such final distribution was made more than 9 years after the date of the last transfer to such trust. Therefore, amounts properly paid or credited to a beneficiary as a final distribution of a trust in a taxable year of the trust beginning after December 31, 1968, and before January 1, 1974, will not be subject to the tax imposed under section 668(a)(2) to the extent such distribution would be allocated to a preceding taxable year of the trust beginning before January 1, 1969, if such final distribution was made more than 9 years after the date of the last transfer to such trust. The provisions of this subparagraph may be illustrated by the following example:

Example. A trust on a calendar year basis was established on January 1, 1958, and no additional transfers were made to it. On January 1, 1973, the trustee terminates the trust and on the same day he makes a final distribution to the beneficiary, B. The distribution is an accumulation distribution that may be allocated under section 666(a) to 1968, 1969, 1970, 1971, and 1972 (the 5 preceding taxable years as defined in § 1.665(e)-1A). Because more than 9 years elapsed between the date of the last transfer to the trust and the date of final distribution, the distribution is not taxed under section 668(a)(2) to the extent it would be allocated to 1968 under section 666(a). [Reg. § 1.665(b)-2A.]

☐ [*T.D.* 7204, 8-24-72.]

[Reg. § 1.665(c)-1A]

§ 1.665(c)-1A. Special rule applicable to distributions by certain foreign trusts.—(a) *In general.*—Except as provided in paragraph (b) of this section, for purposes of section 665 any amount paid to a U.S. person which is from a payor who is not a U.S. person and which is derived directly or indirectly from a foreign trust created by a U.S. person shall be deemed in the year of payment to the U.S. person to have been directly paid to the U.S. person by the trust. For example, if a nonresident alien receives a distribution from a foreign trust created by a U.S. person and then pays the amount of the distribution over to a U.S. person, the payment of such amount to the U.S. person represents an accumulation distribution to the U.S. person from the trust to the extent that the amount received would have been an accumulation distribution had the trust paid the amount directly to the U.S. person in the year in which the payment was received by the U.S. person. This section also applies in a case where a nonresident alien receives indirectly an accumulation distribution from a foreign trust created by a U.S. person and then pays it over to a U.S. person. An example of such a transaction is one where the foreign trust created by a U.S. person makes the distribution to an intervening foreign trust created by either a U.S. person or a person other than a U.S. person and the intervening trust distributes the amount received to a nonresident alien who in turn pays it over to a U.S. person. Under these circumstances, it is deemed that the payment received by the U.S. person was received directly from a foreign trust created by a U.S. person.

(b) *Limitation.*—In the case of a distribution to a beneficiary who is a U.S. person, paragraph (a) of this section does not apply if the distribution is received by such beneficiary under circumstances indicating lack of intent on the part of the parties to circumvent the purposes for which section 7 of the Revenue Act of 1962 (76 Stat. 985) was enacted. [Reg. § 1.665(c)-1A.]

☐ [*T.D.* 7204, 8-24-72.]

[Reg. § 1.665(d)-1A]

§ 1.665(d)-1A. Taxes imposed on the trust.—(a) *In general.*—(1) For the purpose of subpart D, the term "taxes imposed on the trust" means the amount of Federal income taxes properly imposed for any taxable year on the trust that are attributable to the undistributed portions of distributable net income and gains in excess of losses from the sales or exchanges of capital assets. Except as provided in paragraph (c)(2) of this section, the minimum tax for tax preferences imposed by section 56 is not a tax attributable to the undistributed portions of distributable net income and gains in excess of losses from the sales or exchanges of capital assets. See section 56 and the regulations thereunder.

(2) In the case of a trust that has received an accumulation distribution from another trust, the term "taxes imposed on the trust" also includes the amount of taxes deemed distributed under §§ 1.666(b)-1A, 1.666(c)-1A, 1.669(d)-1A, and 1.669(e)-1A (whichever are applicable) as a result of such accumulation distribution, to the extent that they were taken into account under paragraphs (b)(2) or (c)(1)(vi) of § 1.668(b)-1A and (b)(2) or (c)(1)(vi) of § 1.669(b)-1A in computing the partial tax on such accumulation distribution. For example, assume that trust A, a calendar year trust, makes an accumulation distribution in 1975 to trust B, also on the calendar year basis, in connection with which $500 of taxes are deemed under § 1.666(b)-1A to be distributed to trust B. The partial tax on the accumulation distribution is computed under paragraph (b) of § 1.668(b)-1A (the exact method) to be $600 and all of the $500 is used under paragraph (b)(2) of § 1.668(b)-1A to reduce the partial tax to $100. The taxes imposed on trust B for 1975 will, in addition to the $100 partial tax, also include the $500 used to reduce the partial tax.

(b) *Taxes imposed on the trust attributable to undistributed net income.*—(1) For the purpose of subpart D, the term "taxes imposed on the trust attributable to the undistributed net income" means the amount of Federal income taxes for the taxable year properly allocable to the undistributed portion of the distributable net income for such taxable year. This amount is (i) an amount that bears the same relationship to the total taxes of the trust for the year (other than the minimum tax for tax preferences imposed by section 56), computed after the allowance of credits under section 642(a), as (*a*) the taxable income of the trust, other than the capital gains not included in distributable net income less their share of section 1202 deduction, bears to (*b*) the total taxable income of the trust for such year or, (ii) if the alternative tax computation under section 1201(b) is used and there are no net short-term gains, an amount equal to such total taxes less the amount of the alternative tax imposed on the trust and attributable to the capital gain. Thus, for the purposes of subpart D, in determining the amount of taxes imposed on the trust attributable to the undistributed net income, that portion of the taxes paid by the trust attributable to capital gain allocable to corpus is excluded. The rule stated in this subparagraph may be illustrated by the following example, which assumes that the alternative tax computation is not used:

Example. (1) Under the terms of a trust, which reports on the calendar year basis, the income may be accumulated or distributed to A in the discretion of the trustee and capital gains are allocable to corpus. During the taxable year 1974, the trust had income of $20,000 from royalties, long-term capital gains of $10,000, and expenses of $2,000. The trustee in his discretion made a distribution of $10,000 to A. The taxes imposed on the trust for such year attributable to the undistributed net income are $2,319, determined as shown below.

(2) The distributable net income of the trust computed under section 643(a) is $18,000 (royalties of $20,000 less expenses of $2,000). The total taxes paid by the trust are $3,787, computed as follows:

Royalties		$20,000
Capital gain allocable to corpus		10,000
Gross income		30,000
Deductions:		
Expenses	$2,000	
Distributions to A	10,000	
Capital gain deduction	5,000	
Personal exemption	100	
		17,100
Taxable income		$12,900
Total income taxes		3,787

(3) Taxable income other than capital gains less the section 1202 deduction is $7,900 ($12,900 – ($10,000 – $5,000)). Therefore, the amount of taxes imposed on the trust attributable to the undistributed net income is $2,319, computed as follows:

$3,787 (total taxes) × $7,900 (taxable income other than capital gains not included in d.n.i. less the 1202 deduction) divided by $12,900 (taxable income) $2,319

(2) If in any taxable year an accumulation distribution of undistributed net income is made by the trust which results in a throwback to a prior year, the taxes of the prior year imposed on the trust attributable to any remaining undistributed net income of such prior year are the taxes prescribed in subparagraph (1) of this paragraph reduced by the taxes of the prior year deemed distributed under section 666(b) or (c). The provisions of this subparagraph may be illustrated by the following example:

Example. Assume the same facts as in the example in subparagraph (1) of this paragraph. In 1975 the trust makes an accumulation distribution, of which an amount of undistributed net income is deemed distributed in 1974. Taxes imposed on the trust (in the amount of $1,000) attributable to the undistributed net income are therefore deemed distributed in such year. Consequently, the taxes imposed on the trust subsequent to the 1975 distribution attributable to the remaining undistributed net income are $1,319 ($2,319 less $1,000).

(c) *Taxes imposed on the trust attributable to undistributed capital gain.*—(1) *Regular tax.*—For the purpose of subpart D, the term "taxes imposed on the trust attributable to undistributed capital gain" means the amount of Federal income taxes for the taxable year properly attributable to that portion of the excess of capital gains over capital losses of the trust which is allocable to corpus for such taxable year. Such amount is the total of—

(i) the amount computed under subparagraph (2) of this paragraph (the minimum tax), plus

(ii) the amount which bears the same relationship to the total taxes of the trust for the year, (other than the minimum tax), computed after the allowance of credits under section 642(a), as (*a*) the excess of capital gains over capital losses for such year that are not included in distributable net income, computed after its share of the deduction under section 1202 (relating to the deduction for capital gains) has been taken into account, bears to the greater of (*b*) the total taxable income of the trust for such year, or (*c*) the amount of capital gains computed under (*a*) of this subdivision. However, if the alternative tax computation under section 1201(b) is used and there are no net short-term gains, the amount is the amount of the alternative tax imposed on the trust and attributable to the capital gain. The application of this subparagraph may be illustrated by the following example, which assumes that the alternative tax computation is not used:

Example. Assume the facts as in the example in paragraph (b)(1). The capital gains not included in d.n.i. are $10,000, and the deduction under section 1202 is $5,000. The amount of taxes imposed on the trust attributable to undistributed capital gain is $1,468, computed as follows:

$3,787 (total taxes) × $5,000 (capital gains not included in d.n.i. less sec. 1202 deductions) divided by $12,900 (taxable income) $1,468

(2) *Minimum tax.*—The term "taxes imposed on the trust attributable to the undistributed capital gain" also includes the minimum tax for tax preferences imposed on the trust by section 56 with respect to the undistributed capital gain. The amount of such minimum tax so included bears the same relation to the total amount of minimum tax imposed on the trust by section 56 for the taxable year as one-half the net capital gain (net section 1201 gain for taxable years beginning before January 1, 1977) (as defined in section 1222(11)) from such taxable year bears to the sum of the items of tax preference of the trust for such taxable year which are apportioned to the trust in accordance with § 1.58-3(a)(1).

(3) *Reduction for prior distribution.*—If in any taxable year a capital gain distribution is made by the trust which results in a throwback to a prior year, the taxes of the prior year imposed on the trust attributable to any remaining undistributed capital gain of the prior year are the taxes prescribed in subparagraph (1) of this paragraph reduced by the taxes of the prior year deemed distributed under section 669(d) or (e). The provisions of this subparagraph may be illustrated by the following example:

Example. Assume the same facts as in the example in subparagraph (1) of this paragraph. In 1976, the trust makes a capital gain distribution, of which an amount of undistributed capital gain is deemed distributed in 1974. Taxes imposed on the trust (in the amount of $500) attributable to the undistributed capital gain are therefore deemed distributed in such year. Consequently, the taxes imposed on the trust attributable to the remaining undistributed capital gain are $968 ($1,468 less $500). [Reg. § 1.665(d)-1A.]

☐ [*T.D.* 7204, 8-24-72. *Amended by T.D.* 7728, 10-31-80.]

[Reg. § 1.665(e)-1A]

§ 1.665(e)-1A. Preceding taxable year.—(a) *Definition.*—(1) *Domestic trusts.*—(i) *In general.*—For purposes of subpart D, in the case of a trust other than a foreign trust created by a U.S. person, the term "preceding taxable year" serves to identify and limit the taxable years of a trust to which an accumulation distribution consisting of undistributed net income or undistributed capital gain may be allocated (or "thrown back") under sections 666(a) and 669(a). An accumulation distribution consisting of undistributed net income or undistributed capital gain may not be allocated or "thrown back" to a taxable year of a trust if such year is not a "preceding taxable year."

(ii) *Accumulation distributions.*—In the case of an accumulation distribution consisting of undistributed net income made in a taxable year beginning before January 1, 1974, any taxable year of the trust that precedes by more than five years the taxable year of the trust in which such accumulation distribution was made is not a "preceding taxable year." Thus, for a domestic trust on a calendar year basis, calendar year 1967 is not a "preceding taxable year" with respect to an accumulation distribution made in calendar year 1973, whereas calendar year 1968 is a "preceding taxable year." In the case of an accumulation distribution made during a taxable year beginning after December 31, 1973, any taxable year of the trust that begins before January 1, 1969, is not a "preceding taxable year." Thus, for a domestic trust on a calendar year basis, calendar year 1968 is not a "preceding taxable year" with respect to an accumulation distribution made in calendar year 1975, whereas calendar year 1969 is a "preceding taxable year."

(iii) *Capital gain distributions.*—In the case of an accumulation distribution that is a capital gain distribution, any taxable year of the trust that (*a*) begins before January 1, 1969, or (*b*) is prior to the first year in which income is accumulated, whichever occurs later, is not a "preceding taxable year." Thus, for the purpose of capital gain distributions and section 669, only taxable years beginning after December 31, 1968, can be "preceding taxable years." See § 1.668(a)-1A(c).

(2) *Foreign trusts created by United States persons.*—For purposes of subpart D, in the case of a foreign trust created by a U.S. person, the term "preceding taxable year" does not include any taxable year to which part I of subchapter J does not apply. See section 683 and regulations thereunder. Accordingly, the provisions of subpart D may not, in the case of a foreign trust created by a U.S. person, be applied to any taxable year which begins before 1954 or ends before August 17, 1954. For example, if a foreign trust created by a U.S. person (reporting on the calendar year basis) makes a distribution during the calendar year 1970 of income accumulated during prior years, the earliest year of the trust to which the accumulation distribution may be allocated under such subpart D is 1954, but it may not be allocated to 1953 and prior years, since the Internal Revenue Code of 1939 applies to those years.

(b) *Simple trusts.*—A taxable year of a trust during which the trust was a simple trust (that is, was subject to subpart B) for the entire year shall not be considered a "preceding taxable year" unless during such year the trust received "outside income" or unless the trustee did not distribute all of the income of the trust that was required to be distributed currently for such year. In such event, undistributed net income for such year shall not exceed the greater of the "outside income" or income not distributed during such year. For purposes of this paragraph, the term "outside income" means amounts that are included in distributable net income of the trust for the year but that are not "income" of the trust as that term is defined in § 1.643(b)-1. Some examples of "outside income" are:

(1) Income taxable to the trust under section 691;

(2) Unrealized accounts receivable that were assigned to the trusts; and

(3) Distributions from another trust that include distributable net income or undistributed net income of such other trust.

The term "outside income", however, does not include amounts received as distributions from an estate, other than income specified in (1) and (2), for which the estate was allowed a deduction under section 661(a). The application of this paragraph may be illustrated by the following examples:

Example (1). By his will D creates a trust for his widow W. The terms of the trust require that the income be distributed currently (*i.e.,* it is a simple trust), and authorize the trustee to make discretionary payments of corpus to W. Upon W's death the trust corpus is to be distributed to D's then living issue. The executor of D's will makes a $10,000 distribution of corpus to the trust that carries out estate income consisting of dividends and interest to the trust under section 662(a)(2). The trust reports this income as its only income on its income tax return for its taxable year in which ends the taxable year of the estate in which the $10,000 distribution was made, and pays a tax thereon of $2,106. Thus, the trust has undistributed net income of $7,894 ($10,000 – $2,106). Several years later the trustee makes a discretionary corpus payment of $15,000 to W. This payment is an accumulation distribution under section 665(b). However, since the trust had no "outside income" in the year of the estate distribution, such year is not a preceding taxable year. Thus, W is not treated as receiving undistributed net income of $7,894 and taxes thereon of $2,106 for the purpose of including the same in her gross income under section 668. The result would be the same if the invasion power were not exercised and the accumulation distribution occurred as a result of the distribution of the corpus to D's issue upon the death of W.

Example (2). Trust A, a simple trust on the calendar year basis, received in 1972 extraordinary dividends or taxable stock dividends that the trustee in good faith allocated to corpus, but that are determined in 1974 to have been currently distributable to the beneficiary. See section 643(a)(4) and § 1.643(a)-4. Trust A would qualify for treatment under subpart C for 1974, the year of distribution of the extraordinary dividends or taxable stock dividends, because the distribution is not out of income of the current taxable year and is treated as an other amount properly paid or credited or required to be distributed for such taxable year within the meaning of section 661(a)(2). Also, the distribution in 1974 qualifies as an accumulation distribution for the purposes of subpart D. For purposes only of such subpart D, trust A would be treated as subject to the provisions of such subpart C for 1972, the preceding taxable year in which the extraordinary or taxable stock dividends were received, and, in computing undistributed net income for 1972, the extraordinary or taxable stock dividends would be included in distributable net income under section 643(a). The rule stated in the preceding sentence would also apply if the distribution in 1974 was made out of corpus without regard to a determination that the extraordinary dividends or taxable stock dividends in question were currently distributable to the beneficiary. [Reg. § 1.665(e)-1A.]

☐ [*T.D.* 7204, 8-24-72.]

[Reg. § 1.665(f)-1A]

§ 1.665(f)-1A. [Reserved].

☐ [*T.D.* 7204, 8-24-72. *Removed and reserved by T.D.* 9849, 3-11-2019.]

[Reg. § 1.665(g)-1A]

§ 1.665(g)-1A. [Reserved].

☐ [*T.D.* 7204, 8-24-72. *Removed and reserved by T.D.* 9849, 3-11-2019.]

[Reg. § 1.665(g)-2A]

§ 1.665(g)-2A. Application of separate share rule.—(a) *In general.*—If the separate share rule of section 663(c) is applicable for any taxable year of a trust, subpart D is applied as if each share were a separate trust except as provided in paragraph (c) of this section and in § 1.668(a)-1A(c). Thus, the amounts of an "accumulation distribution", "undistributed net income", "undistributed capital gain", and "capital gain distribution" are computed separately for each share.

(b) *Allocation of taxes—undistributed net income.*—The "taxes imposed on the trust attributable to the undistributed net income" are allocated as follows:

(1) There is first allocated to each separate share that portion of the "taxes imposed on the trust attributable to the undistributed net income" (as defined in § 1.665(d)-1A(b)), computed before the allowance of any credits under section 642(a), that bears the same relation to the total of such taxes that the distributable net income of the separate share bears to the distributable net income of the trust, adjusted for this purpose as follows:

(i) There is excluded from distributable net income of the trust and of each separate share any tax-exempt interest, foreign income of a foreign trust, and excluded dividends, to the extent such amounts are included in distributable net income pursuant to section 643(a)(5), (6), and (7); and

(ii) The distributable net income of the trust is reduced by any deductions allowable under section 661 for amounts paid, credited, or required to be distributed during the taxable year, and the distributable net income of each separate share is reduced by any such deduction allocable to that share.

(2) The taxes so determined for each separate share are then reduced by that portion of the credits against tax allowable to the trust under

section 642(a) in computing the "taxes imposed on the trust" that bears the same relation to the total of such credits that the items of distributable net income allocable to the separate share with respect to which the credit is allowed bear to the total of such items of the trust.

(c) *Allocation of taxes—undistributed capital gain.*—The "taxes imposed on the trust attributable to undistributed capital gain" are allocated as follows:

(1) There is first allocated to each separate share that portion of the "taxes imposed on the trust attributable to undistributed capital gain" (as defined in § 1.665(d)-1A(c)), computed before the allowance of any credits under section 642(a), that bears the same relation to the total of such taxes that the undistributed capital gain (prior to the deduction of taxes under section 665(c)(2)) of the separate share bears to the total such undistributed capital gain of the trust.

(2) The taxes so determined for each separate share are then reduced by that portion of the credits against tax allowable to the trust under section 642(a) in computing the "taxes imposed on the trust" that bears the same relation to the total of such credits that the capital gain allocable to the separate share with respect to which the credit is allowed bear to the total of such capital gain of the trust.

(d) *Termination of a separate share.*—(1) If upon termination of a separate share, an amount is properly paid, credited, or required to be distributed by the trust under section 661(a)(2) to a beneficiary from such share, an accumulation distribution will be deemed to have been made to the extent of such amount. In determining the distributable net income of such share, only those items of income and deduction for the taxable year of the trust in which such share terminates, properly allocable to such share, shall be taken into consideration.

(2) No accumulation distribution will be deemed to have been made upon the termination of a separate share to the extent that the property constituting such share, or a portion thereof, continues to be held as a part of the same trust. The undistributed net income, undistributed capital gain, and the taxes imposed on the trust attributable to such items, if any, for all preceding taxable years (reduced by any amounts deemed distributed under sections 666(a) and 669(a) by reason of any accumulation distribution of undistributed net income or undistributed capital gain in prior years or the current taxable year), which were allocable to the terminating share, shall be treated as being applicable to the trust itself. However, no adjustment will be made to the amounts deemed distributed under sections 666 and 669 by reason of an accumulation distribution of undistributed net income or undistributed capital gain from the surviving share or shares made in years prior to the year in which the terminating share was added to such surviving share or shares.

(3) The provisions of this paragraph may be illustrated by the following example:

Example. A trust was established under the will of X for the benefit of his wife and upon her death the property was to continue in the same trust for his two sons, Y and Z. The separate share rule is applicable to this trust. The trustee had discretion to pay or accumulate the income to the wife, and after her death was to pay each son's share to him after he attained the age of 25. When the wife died, Y was 23 and Z was 28.

(1) Upon the death of X's widow, there is no accumulation distribution. The entire trust is split into two equal shares, and therefore the undistributed net income and the undistributed capital gain of the trust are split into two shares.

(2) The distribution to Z of his share after his mother's death is an accumulation distribution of his separate share of one-half of the undistributed net income and undistributed capital gain. [Reg. § 1.665(g)-2A.]

☐ [*T.D.* 7204, 8-24-72.]

[Reg. § 1.666(a)-1A]

§ 1.666(a)-1A. Amount allocated.—(a) *In general.*—In the case of a trust that is subject to subpart C of part I of subchapter J of chapter 1 of the Code (relating to estates and trusts which may accumulate income or which distribute corpus), section 666(a) prescribes rules for determining the taxable years from which an accumulation distribution will be deemed to have been made and the extent to which the accumulation distribution is considered to consist of undistributed net income. In general, an accumulation distribution made in taxable years beginning after December 31, 1969, is deemed to have been made first from the earliest preceding taxable year of the trust for which there is undistributed net income. An accumulation distribution made in a taxable year beginning before January 1, 1970, is deemed to have been made first from the most recent preceding taxable year of the trust for which there is undistributed net income. See § 1.665(e)-1A for the definition of "preceding taxable year."

(b) *Distributions by domestic trusts.*—(1) *Taxable years beginning after December 31, 1973.*—An accumulation distribution made by a trust (other than a foreign trust created by a U.S. person) in any taxable year beginning after December 31, 1973, is allocated to the preceding taxable years of the trust (defined in § 1.665(e)-1A(a)(1)(ii) as those beginning after December 31, 1968) according to the amount of undistributed net income of the trust for such years. For this purpose, an accumulation distribution is first allocated to the earliest such preceding taxable year in which there is undistributed net income and shall then be allocated in turn, beginning with the next earliest, to any remaining preceding taxable years of the trust. The portion of the accumulation distribution allocated to the earliest preceding taxable year is the amount of the undistributed net income for that preceding taxable year. The portion of the accumulation distribution allocated to any preceding taxable year subsequent to the earliest such preceding taxable year is the excess of the accumulation distribution over the aggregate of the undistributed net income for all earlier preceding taxable years. See paragraph (d) of this section for adjustments to undistributed net income for prior distributions. The provisions of this subparagraph may be illustrated by the following example:

Example. In 1977, a domestic trust reporting on the calendar year basis makes an accumulation distribution of $33,000. Therefore, years before 1969 are ignored. In 1969, the trust had $6,000 of undistributed net income; in 1970, $4,000; in 1971, none; in 1972, $7,000; in 1973, $5,000; in 1974, $8,000; in 1975, $6,000; and $4,000 in 1976. The accumulation distribution is deemed distributed $6,000 in 1969, $4,000 in 1970, none in 1971, $7,000 in 1972, $5,000 in 1973, $8,000 in 1974, and $3,000 in 1975.

(2) *Taxable years beginning after December 31, 1969, and before January 1, 1974.*—If a trust (other than a foreign trust created by a U.S. person) makes an accumulation distribution in a taxable year beginning after December 31, 1969, and before January 1, 1974, the distribution will be deemed distributed in the same manner as accumulation distributions qualifying under subparagraph (1) of this paragraph, except that the first year to which the distribution may be thrown back cannot be earlier than the fifth taxable year of the trust preceding the year in which the accumulation distribution is made. Thus, for example, in the case of an accumulation distribution made in the taxable year of a domestic trust which begins on January 1, 1972, the taxable year of the trust beginning on January 1, 1967, would be the first year in which the distribution was deemed made, assuming that there was undistributed net income for 1967. See also § 1.665(e)-1A(a)(1). The provisions of this subparagraph may be illustrated by the following example:

Example. In 1973, a domestic trust, reporting on the calendar year basis, makes an accumulation distribution of $25,000. In 1968, the fifth year preceding 1973, the trust had $7,000 of undistributed net income; in 1969, none; in 1970, $12,000; in 1971, $4,000; in 1972, $4,000. The accumulation distribution is deemed distributed in the amounts of $7,000 in 1968, none in 1969, $12,000 in 1970, $4,000 in 1971, and $2,000 in 1972.

(3) *Taxable years beginning after December 31, 1968, and before January 1, 1970.*—Accumulation distributions made in taxable years of the trust beginning after December 31, 1968, and before January 1, 1970, are allocated to prior years according to § 1.666(a)-1.

(c) *Distributions by foreign trusts.*—(1) *Foreign trusts created solely by U.S. persons.*—(i) *Taxable years beginning after December 31, 1969.*—If a foreign trust created by a U.S. person makes an accumulation distribution in any taxable year beginning after December 31, 1969, the distribution is allocated to the trust's preceding taxable years (defined in § 1.665(e)-1A(a)(2) as those beginning after December 31, 1953, and ending after August 16, 1954) according to the amount of undistributed net income of the trust for such years. For this purpose, an accumulation distribution is first allocated to the earliest such preceding taxable year in which there is undistributed net income and shall then be allocated in turn, beginning with the next earliest, to any remaining preceding taxable years of the trust. The portion of the accumulation distribution allocated to the earliest preceding taxable year is the amount of the undistributed net income for that preceding taxable year. The portion of the accumulation distribution allocated to any preceding taxable year subsequent to the earliest such preceding taxable year is the excess of the accumulation distribution over the aggregate of the undistributed net income for all earlier preceding taxable years. See paragraph (d) of this section for adjustments to undistributed net income for prior distributions. The provisions of this subdivision may be illustrated by the following example:

Example. In 1971, a foreign trust created by a U.S. person, reporting on the calendar year basis, makes an accumulation distribution of $50,000. In 1961, the trust had $12,000 of undistributed net income; in 1962, none; in 1963, $10,000; in 1964, $8,000; in 1965, $5,000; in 1966, $14,000; in 1967, none; in 1968, $3,000; in 1969, $2,000; and in 1970, $1,000. The accumulation distribution is deemed distributed in the amounts of $12,000 in 1961, none in 1962, $10,000 in 1963, $8,000 in 1964, $5,000 in 1965, $14,000 in 1966, none in 1967, and $1,000 in 1968.

(ii) *Taxable years beginning after December 31, 1968, and before January 1, 1970.*—Accumulation distributions made in taxable years of the trust beginning after December 31, 1968, and before January 1, 1970, are allocated to prior years according to § 1.666(a)-1.

(2) *Foreign trusts created partly by U.S. persons.*—(i) *Taxable years beginning after December 31, 1969.*—If a trust that is in part a foreign trust created by a U.S. person and in part a foreign trust created by a person other than a U.S. person makes an accumulation distribution in any year after December 31, 1969, the distribution is deemed made from the undistributed net income of the foreign trust created by a U.S. person in the proportion that the total undistributed net income for all preceding years of the foreign trust created by the U.S. person bears to the total undistributed net income for all years of the entire foreign trust. In addition, such distribution is deemed made from the undistributed net income of the foreign trust created by a person other than a U.S. person in the proportion that the total undistributed net income for all preceding years of the foreign trust created by a person other than a U.S. person bears to the total undistributed net income for all years of the entire foreign trust. Accordingly, an accumulation distribution of such a trust is composed of two portions with one portion relating to the undistributed net income of the foreign trust created by the U.S. person and the other portion relating to the undistributed net income of the foreign trust created by the person other than a U.S. person. For these purposes, each portion of an

accumulation distribution made in any taxable year is first allocated to each of such preceding taxable years in turn, beginning with the earliest preceding taxable year, as defined in § 1.665(e)-1A(a), of the applicable foreign trusts, to the extent of the undistributed net income for the such [sic] trust for each of those years. Thus, each portion of an accumulation distribution is deemed to have been made from the earliest accumulated income of the applicable trust. If the foreign trust created by a U.S. person makes an accumulation distribution in any year beginning after December 31, 1969, the distribution is included in the beneficiary's income for that year to the extent of the undistributed net income of the trust for the trust's preceding taxable years which began after December 31, 1953, and ended after August 16, 1954. The provisions of this subdivision may be illustrated by the following example:

Example. A trust is created in 1962 under the laws of Country X by the transfer to a trustee in Country X of property by both a United States person and a person other than a United States person. Both the trust and the only beneficiary of the trust (who is a U.S. person) report their taxable income on a calendar year basis. On March 31, 1974, the trust makes an accumulation distribution of $150,000 to the beneficiary. The distributable net income of both the portion of the trust which is a foreign trust created by a U.S. person and the portion of the trust which is a foreign trust created by a person other than a U.S. person for each year is computed in accordance with the provisions of paragraph (b)(3) of § 1.643(d)-1 and the undistributed net income for each portion of the trust for each year is computed as described in paragraph (b) of § 1.665(a)-1A. For taxable years 1962 through 1973, the portion of the trust which is a foreign trust created by a United States person and the portion of the trust which is a foreign trust created by a person other than a U.S. person had the following amounts of undistributed net income:

Year	*Undistributed net income-portion of the trust created by a U.S. person*	*Undistributed net income-portion of the trust created by a person other than a U.S. person*
1962	$7,000	$4,000
1963	12,000	7,000
1964	None	None
1965	11,000	5,000
1966	8,000	3,000
1967	None	None
1968	4,000	2,000
1969	17,000	8,000
1970	16,000	9,000
1971	None	None
1972	25,000	12,000
1973	20,000	10,000
Totals	120,000	60,000

The accumulation distribution in the amount of $150,000 is deemed to have been distributed in the amount of $100,000 (120,000/180,000 × $150,000) from the portion of the trust which is a foreign trust created by a U.S. person and in the amount of $39,000, which is less than $50,000 (60,000/180,000 × $150,000), from the portion of the trust which is a foreign trust created by a person other than a U.S. person computed as follows:

Year	*Throwback to preceding years of foreign trust created by a U.S. person*	*Throwback to preceding years of portion of the entire foreign trust which is not a foreign trust created by a U.S. person*
1962	$7,000	None
1963	12,000	None
1964	None	None
1965	11,000	None
1966	8,000	None
1967	None	None
1968	4,000	None
1969	17,000	$8,000
1970	16,000	9,000
1971	None	None
1972	25,000	12,000
1973	None	10,000
Totals	$100,000	$39,000

Pursuant to this paragraph, the accumulation distribution in the amount of $100,000 from the portion of the trust which is a foreign trust created by a U.S. person is included in the beneficiary's income for 1974, as the amount represents undistributed net income of the trust for the trust's preceding taxable years which began after December 31, 1953, and ended after August 16,

1954. The accumulation distribution in the amount of $50,000 from the portion of the trust which is a foreign trust created by a person other than a U.S. person is included in the beneficiary's income for 1974 to the extent of the undistributed net income of the trust for the preceding years beginning after December 31, 1968. Accordingly, with respect to the portion of the trust which is a foreign trust created by a person other than a U.S. person, only the undistributed net income for the years 1969 through 1973, which totals $39,000, is includible in the beneficiary's income for 1974. Thus, of the $150,000 distribution made in 1974, the beneficiary is required to include a total of $139,000 in his income for 1974. The balance of $11,000 is deemed to represent a distribution of corpus.

(ii) *Taxable years beginning after December 31, 1968 and before January 1, 1970.*—Accumulation distributions made in taxable years of the trust beginning after December 31, 1968, and before January 1, 1970, are allocated to prior years according to § 1.666(a)-1.

(3) *Foreign trusts created by non-U.S. persons.*—To the extent that a foreign trust is a foreign trust created by a person other than a U.S. person, an accumulation distribution is included in the beneficiary's income for the year paid, credited, or required to be distributed to the extent provided under paragraph (b) of this section.

(d) *Reduction of undistributed net income for prior accumulation distributions.*—For the purposes of allocating to any preceding taxable year an accumulation distribution of the taxable year, the undistributed net income of such preceding taxable year is reduced by the amount from such year deemed distributed in any accumulation distribution of undistributed net income made in any taxable year intervening between such preceding taxable year and the taxable year. Accordingly, for example, if a trust has undistributed net income for 1974 and makes accumulation distributions during the taxable years 1978 and 1979, in determining that part of the 1979 accumulation distribution that is thrown back to 1974 the undistributed net income for 1974 is first reduced by the amount of the undistributed net income for 1974 deemed distributed in the 1978 accumulation distribution.

(e) *Rule when no undistributed net income.*—If, before the application of the provisions of subpart D to an accumulation distribution for the taxable year, there is no undistributed net income for a preceding taxable year, then no portion of the accumulation distribution is undistributed net income deemed distributed on the last day of such preceding taxable year. Thus, if an accumulation distribution is made during the taxable year 1975 from a trust whose earliest preceding taxable year is taxable year 1970, and the trust had no undistributed net income for 1970, then no portion of the 1975 accumulation distribution is undistributed net income deemed distributed on the last day of 1970. [Reg. § 1.666(a)-1A.]

□ [*T.D.* 7204, 8-24-72.]

[Reg. § 1.666(b)-1A]

§ 1.666(b)-1A. Total taxes deemed distributed.—(a) If an accumulation distribution is deemed under § 1.666(a)-1A to be distributed on the last day of a preceding taxable year and the amount is not less than the undistributed net income for such preceding taxable year, then an additional amount equal to the "taxes imposed on the trust attributable to the undistributed net income" (as defined in § 1.665(d)-1A(b)) for such preceding taxable year is also deemed distributed under section 661(a)(2). For example, a trust has undistributed net income of $8,000 for the taxable year 1974. The taxes imposed on the trust attributable to the undistributed net income are $3,032. During the taxable year 1977, an accumulation distribution of $8,000 is made to the beneficiary, which is deemed under § 1.666(a)-1A to have been distributed on the last day of 1974. The 1977 accumulation distribution is not less than the 1974 undistributed net income. Accordingly, the taxes of $3,032 imposed on the trust attributable to the undistributed net income for 1974 are also deemed to have been distributed on the last day of 1974. Thus, a total of $11,032 will be deemed to have been distributed on the last day of 1974.

(b) For the purpose of paragraph (a) of this section, the undistributed net income of any preceding taxable year and the taxes imposed on the trust for such preceding taxable year attributable to such undistributed net income are computed after taking into account any accumulation distributions of taxable years intervening between such preceding taxable year and the taxable year. See paragraph (d) of § 1.666(a)-1A. [Reg. § 1.666(b)-1A.]

□ [*T.D.* 7204, 8-24-72.]

[Reg. § 1.666(c)-1A]

§ 1.666(c)-1A. Pro rata portion of taxes deemed distributed.—(a) If an accumulation distribution is deemed under § 1.666(a)-1A to be distributed on the last day of a preceding taxable year and the amount is less than the undistributed net income for such preceding taxable year, then an additional amount is also deemed distributed under section 661(a)(2). The additional amount is equal to the "taxes imposed on the trust attributable to the undistributed net income" (as defined in § 1.665(a)-1A(b)) for such preceding taxable year, multiplied by a fraction, the numerator of which is the amount of the accumulation distribution allocated to such preceding taxable year and the denominator of which is the undistributed net income for such preceding taxable year. See paragraph (b) of example (1) and paragraphs (c) and (f) of example (2) in § 1.666(c)-2A for illustrations of this paragraph.

(b) For the purpose of paragraph (a) of this section, the undistributed net income of any preceding taxable year and the taxes imposed on the trust for such preceding taxable year attributable to such undistributed net income are computed after taking into account any accumulation distributions of any taxable years intervening between such preceding taxable year and the taxable year. See paragraph (d) of § 1.666(a)-1A and paragraph (c) of example (1) and paragraphs (e) and (h) of example (2) in § 1.666(c)-2A. [Reg. § 1.666(c)-1A.]

☐ [*T.D. 7204, 8-24-72.*]

[Reg. § 1.666(c)-2A]

§ 1.666(c)-2A. Illustration of the provisions of section 666(a), (b), and (c).—The application of the provisions of §§ 1.666(a)-1A, 1.666(b)-1A, and 1.666(c)-1A may be illustrated by the following examples:

Example (1). (a) A trust created on January 1, 1974, makes accumulation distributions as follows:

1979	$7,000
1980	26,000

For 1974 through 1978, the undistributed portion of distributable net income, taxes imposed on the trust attributable to the undistributed net income, and undistributed net income are as follows:

Year	*Undistributed portion of distributable net income*	*Taxes imposed on the trust attributable to the undistributed net income*	*Undistributed net income*
1974	$12,100	$3,400	$8,700
1975	16,100	5,200	10,900
1976	6,100	1,360	4,740
1977	None	None	None
1978	10,100	2,640	7,460

The trust has no undistributed capital gain.

(b) Since the entire amount of the accumulation distribution for 1979 ($7,000) is less than the undistributed net income for 1974 ($8,700), an additional amount of $2,736 (7,000/8,700 × $3,400) is deemed distributed under section 666(c).

(c) In allocating the accumulation distribution for 1980, the amount of undistributed net income for 1974 will reflect the accumulation distribution for 1979. The undistributed net income for 1974 will then be $1,700 and the taxes imposed on the trust for 1974 will be $664, determined as follows:

Undistributed net income as of the close of 1974	$8,700
Less:	
Accumulation distribution (1979)	7,000
Balance (undistributed net income as of the close of 1979)	$1,700
Taxes imposed on the trust attributable to the undistributed net income as of the close of 1979 (1,700/8,700 × $3,400)	$664

(d) The accumulation distribution of $26,000 for 1980 is deemed to have been made on the last day of the preceding taxable years of the trust to the extent of $24,800, the total of the undistributed net income for such years, as shown in the tabulation below. In addition, $9,864, the total taxes imposed on the trust attributable to the undistributed net income for such years is also deemed to have been distributed on the last day of such years, as shown below:

Year	*Undistributed net income*	*Taxes imposed on the trust*
1974	$ 1,700	$ 664
1975	10,900	5,200
1976	4,740	1,360
1977	None	None
1978	7,460	2,640
1979	None	None

Example (2). (a) Under the terms of a trust instrument, the trustee has discretion to accumulate or distribute the income to X and to invade corpus for the benefit of X. The entire income of the trust is from royalties. Both X and the trust report on the calendar year basis. All of the income for 1974 was accumulated. The distributable net income of the trust for the taxable year 1974 is $20,100 and the income taxes paid by the trust for 1974 attributable to the undistributed net income are $7,260. All of the income for 1975 and 1976 was distributed and in addition the trustee made accumulation distributions within the meaning of section 665(b) of $5,420 for each year.

(b) The undistributed net income of the trust determined under section 665(a) as of the close of 1974, is $12,840, computed as follows:

Distributable net income	$20,100
Less: Taxes imposed on the trust attributable to the undistributed net income	7,260
Undistributed net income as of the close of 1974	$12,840

(c) The accumulation distribution of $5,420 made during the taxable year 1975 is deemed under section 666(a) to have been made on December 31, 1974. Since this accumulation distribution is less than the 1974 undistributed net income of $12,840, a portion of the taxes imposed on the trust for 1974 is also deemed under section 666(c) to have been distributed on December 31, 1974. The total amount deemed to have been distributed to X on December 31, 1974 is $8,484, computed as follows:

Accumulation distribution	$5,420
Taxes deemed distributed (5,420/12,840 × $7,260)	3,064
Total	$8,484

(d) After the application of the provisions of subpart D to the accumulation distribution of 1975, the undistributed net income of the trust for 1974 is $7,420, computed as follows:

Undistributed net income as of the close of 1974	$12,840
Less: 1975 accumulation distribution deemed distributed on December 31, 1974 (paragraph (c) of this example)	5,420
Undistributed net income for 1974 as of the close of 1975	$7,420

(e) The taxes imposed on the trust attributable to the undistributed net income for the taxable year 1974, as adjusted to give effect to the 1975 accumulation distribution, amount to $4,196, computed as follows:

Taxes imposed on the trust attributable to undistributed net income as of the close of 1974	$7,260
Less: Taxes deemed distributed in 1974	3,064
Taxes attributable to the undistributed net income determined as of the close of 1975	$4,196

(f) The accumulation distribution of $5,420 made during the taxable year 1976 is, under section 666(a), deemed a distribution to X on December 31, 1974, within the meaning of section 661(a)(2). Since the accumulation distribution is less than the 1974 adjusted undistributed net income of $7,420, the trust is deemed under section 666(c) also to have distributed on December 31, 1974, a portion of the taxes imposed on the trust for 1974. The total amount deemed to be distributed on December 31, 1974, with respect to the accumulation distribution made in 1976, is $8,484, computed as follows:

Accumulation distribution	$5,420
Taxes deemed distributed (5,420/7,420 × $4,196)	3,064
Total	$8,484

(g) After the application of the provisions of subpart D to the accumulation distribution of 1976, the undistributed net income of the trust for 1974 is $2,000, computed as follows:

Undistributed net income for 1974 as of the close of 1975	$7,420
Less: 1976 accumulation distribution deemed distributed on December 31, 1974 (paragraph (f) of this example)	5,420
Undistributed net income for 1974 as of the close of 1976	$2,000

(h) The taxes imposed on the trust attributable to the undistributed net income of the trust for the taxable year 1974, determined as of the close of the taxable year 1976, amount to $1,132 ($4,196 less $3,064). [Reg. § 1.666(c)-2A.]

☐ [*T.D.* 7204, 8-24-72.]

[Reg. § 1.666(d)-1A]

§ 1.666(d)-1A. Information required from trusts.—(a) *Adequate records required.*—For all taxable years of a trust, the trustee must retain copies of the trust's income tax return as well as information pertaining to any adjustments in the tax shown as due on the return. The trustee shall also keep the records of the trust required to be retained by section 6001 and the regulations thereunder for each taxable year as to which the period of limitations on assessment of tax under section 6501 has not expired. If the trustee fails to produce such copies and records, and such failure is due to circumstances beyond the reasonable control of the trustee or any predecessor trustee, the trustee may reconstruct the amount of corpus, accumulated income, etc., from competent sources (including, to the extent permissible, Internal Revenue Service records). To the extent that an accurate reconstruction can be made for a taxable year, the requirements of this paragraph shall be deemed satisfied for such year.

(b) *Rule when information is not available.*—(1) *Accumulation distributions.*—If adequate records (as required by paragraph (a) of this section) are not available to determine the proper application of subpart D to an accumulation distribution made in a taxable year by a trust, such accumulation distribution shall be deemed to consist of undistributed net income earned during the earliest preceding taxable year (as defined in § 1.665(e)-1A) of the trust in which it can be established that the trust was in existence. If adequate records are available for some years, but not for others, the accumulation distribution shall be allocated first to the earliest preceding taxable year of the trust for which there are adequate records and then to each subsequent preceding taxable year for which there are adequate records. To the extent that the distribution is not allocated in such manner to years for which adequate records are available, it will be deemed distributed on the last day of the earliest preceding taxable year of the trust in which it is established that the trust was in existence and for which the trust has no records. The provisions of this subparagraph may be illustrated by the following example:

Example. A trust makes a distribution in 1975 of $100,000. The trustee has adequate records for 1973, 1974, and 1975. The records show that the trust is on the calendar year basis, had distributable net income in 1975 of $20,000, and undistributed net income in 1974 of $15,000, and in 1973 of $16,000. The trustee has no other records of the trust except for a copy of the trust instrument showing that the trust was established on January 1, 1965. He establishes that the loss of the records was due to circumstances beyond his control. Since the distribution is made in 1975, the earliest "preceding taxable year," as defined in § 1.665(e)-1A, is 1969. Since $80,000 of the distribution is an accumulation distribution and $31,000 thereof is allocated to 1974 and 1973, $49,000 is deemed to have been distributed on the last day of 1969.

(2) *Taxes.*—(i) If an amount is deemed under this paragraph to be undistributed net income allocated to a preceding taxable year for which adequate records are not available, there shall be deemed to be "taxes imposed on the trust" for such preceding taxable year an amount equal to the taxes that the trust would have paid if the deemed undistributed net income were the amount remaining when the taxes were subtracted from taxable income of the trust for such year. For example, assume that an accumulation distribution in 1975 of $100,000 is deemed to be undistributed net income from 1971, and that the taxable income required to produce $100,000 after taxes in 1971 would be $284,966. Therefore the amount deemed to be "taxes imposed on the trust" for such preceding taxable year is $184,966.

(ii) The credit allowed by section 667(b) shall not be allowed for any amount deemed under this subparagraph to be "taxes imposed on the trust". [Reg. § 1.666(d)-1A.]

☐ [*T.D.* 7204, 8-24-72.]

[Reg. § 1.667(a)-1A]

§ 1.667(a)-1A. [Reserved].

☐ [*T.D.* 7204, 8-24-72. *Removed and reserved by T.D.* 9849, 3-11-2019.]

[Reg. § 1.667(b)-1A]

§ 1.667(b)-1A. Authorization of credit to beneficiary for taxes imposed on the trust.—(a) *Determination of credit.*—(1) *In general.*—Section 667(b) allows under certain circumstances a credit (without interest) against the tax imposed by subtitle A of the Code on the beneficiary for the taxable year in which the accumulation distribution is required to be included in income under section 668(a). In the case of an accumulation distribution consisting only of undistributed net income, the amount of such credit is the total of the taxes deemed distributed to such beneficiary under section 666(b) and (c) as a result of such accumulation distribution for preceding taxable years of the trust on the last day of which such beneficiary was in being, less the amount of such taxes for such preceding taxable years taken into account in reducing the amount of partial tax determined under § 1.668(b)-1A. In the case of an accumulation distribution consisting only of undistributed capital gain, the amount of such credit is the total of the taxes deemed distributed as a result of the accumulation distribution to such beneficiary under section 669(d) and (e) for preceding taxable years of the trust on the last day of which such beneficiary was in being, less the amount of such taxes for such preceding taxable years taken into account in reducing the amount of partial tax determined under § 1.669(b)-1A. In the case of an accumulation distribution consisting of both undistributed net income and undistributed capital gain, a credit will not be available unless the total taxes deemed distributed to the beneficiary for all preceding taxable years as a result of the accumulation distribution exceeds the beneficiary's partial tax determined under §§ 1.668(b)-1A and 1.669(b)-1A without reference to the taxes deemed distributed. A credit is not allowed for any taxes deemed distributed as a result of an accumulation distribution to a beneficiary by reason of sections 666(b) and (c) or sections 669(d) and (e) for a preceding taxable year of the trust before the beneficiary was born or created. However, if as a result of an accumulation distribution the total taxes deemed distributed under section 668(a)(2) and 668(a)(3) in preceding taxable years before the beneficiary was born or created exceed the partial taxes attributable to amounts deemed distributed in such years, such excess may be used to offset any liability for partial taxes attributable to amounts deemed distributed as a result of the same accumulation distribution in preceding taxable years after the beneficiary was born or created.

(2) *Exact method.*—In the case of the tax computed under the exact method provided in §§ 1.668(b)-1A(b) and 1.669(b)-1A(b), the credit allowed by this section is computed as follows:

(i) Compute the total taxes deemed distributed under §§ 1.666(b)-1A and 1.666(c)-1A or §§ 1.669(d)-1A and 1.669(e)-1A, whichever are appropriate for the preceding taxable years of the trust on the last day of which the beneficiary was in being.

(ii) Compute the total of the amounts of tax determined under § 1.668(b)-1A(b)(1) or § 1.669(b)-1A(b)(1), whichever is appropriate, for the prior taxable years of the beneficiary in which he was in being.

If the amount determined under subdivision (i) does not exceed the amount determined under subdivision (ii), no credit is allowable. If the amount determined under subdivision (i) exceeds the amount determined under subdivision (ii), the credit allowable is the lesser of the amount of such excess or the amount of taxes deemed distributed to the beneficiary for all preceding taxable years to the extent that such taxes are not used in § 1.668(b)-1A(b)(2) or

§1.669(b)-1A(b)(2) in determining the beneficiary's partial tax under section 668(a)(2) or 668(a)(3). The application of this subparagraph may be illustrated by the following example:

Example. An accumulation distribution made in 1975 is deemed distributed in 1973 and 1974, years in which the beneficiary was in being. The taxes deemed distributed in such years are $4,000 and $2,000, respectively, totaling $6,000. The amounts of tax computed under §1.668(b)-1A(b)(1) attributable to the amounts thrown back are $3,000 and $2,000, respectively, totaling $5,000. The credit allowable under this subparagraph is therefore $1,000 ($6,000 less $5,000).

(3) *Short-cut method.*—In the case of the tax computed under the short-cut method provided in §1.668(b)-1A(c) or 1.669(b)-1A(c), the credit allowed by this section is computed as follows:

(i) Compute the total taxes deemed distributed in all preceding taxable years of the trust under §§1.666(b)-1A and 1.666(c)-1A or §§1.669(d)-1A and 1.669(e)-1A, whichever are appropriate.

(ii) Compute the beneficiary's partial tax determined under either §1.668(b)-1A(c)(1)(v) or §1.669(b)-1A(c)(1)(v), whichever is appropriate.

If the amount determined under subdivision (i) does not exceed the amount determined under subdivision (ii), no credit is allowable. If the amount determined under subdivision (i) exceeds the amount determined under subdivision (ii),

(iii) Compute the total taxes deemed distributed under §§1.666(b)-1A and 1.666(c)-1A or §§1.669(d)-1A and 1.669(e)-1A, which are appropriate, for the preceding taxable years of the trust on the last day of which the beneficiary was in being.

(iv) Multiply the amount by which subdivision (i) exceeds subdivision (ii) by a fraction, the numerator of which is the amount determined under subdivision (iii) of this subparagraph and the denominator of which is the amount determined under subdivision (i) of this subparagraph.

The result is the allowable credit. The application of this subparagraph may be illustrated by the following example:

Example. An accumulation distribution that consists only of undistributed net income is made in 1975. The taxes deemed distributed in the preceding years under §§1.666(b)-1A and 1.666(c)-1A are $15,000. The amount determined under §1.668(b)-1A(c)(1)(v) is $12,000. The beneficiary was in being on the last day of all but one preceding taxable year in which the accumulation distribution was deemed made, and the taxes deemed distributed in those years was $10,000. Therefore, the excess of the subdivision (i) amount over the subdivision (ii) amount is $3,000, and is multiplied by 10,000/15,000, resulting in an answer of $2,000, which is the credit allowable when computed under the short-cut method.

(b) *Year of credit.*—The credit to which a beneficiary is entitled under this section is allowed for the taxable year in which the accumulation distribution (to which the credit relates) is required to be included in the income of the beneficiary under section 668(a). Any excess over the total tax liability of the beneficiary for such year is treated as an overpayment of tax by the beneficiary. See section 6401(b) and the regulations thereunder. [Reg. §1.667(b)-1A.]

☐ [*T.D.* 7204, 8-24-72.]

[Reg. §1.671-1]

§1.671-1. Grantors and others treated as substantial owners; scope.—(a) Subpart E (section 671 and following), part I, subchapter J, chapter 1 of the Code, contains provisions taxing income of a trust to the grantor or another person under certain circumstances even though he is not treated as a beneficiary under subparts A through D (section 641 and following) of such part I. Section 671 and 672 contain general provisions relating to the entire subpart. Sections 673 through 677 define the circumstances under which income of a trust is taxed to a grantor. These circumstances are in general as follows:

(1) If the grantor has retained a reversionary interest in the trust, within specified time limits (section 673);

(2) If the grantor or a nonadverse party has certain powers over the beneficial interests under the trust (section 674);

(3) If certain administrative powers over the trust exist under which the grantor can or does benefit (section 675);

(4) If the grantor or a nonadverse party has a power to revoke the trust or return the corpus to the grantor (section 676); or

(5) If the grantor or a nonadverse party has the power to distribute income to or for the benefit of the grantor or the grantor's spouse (section 677).

Under section 678, income of a trust is taxed to a person other than the grantor to the extent that he has the sole power to vest corpus or income in himself.

(b) Sections 671 and 677 do not apply if the income of a trust is taxable to a grantor's spouse under section 71 or 682 (relating respectively to alimony and separate maintenance payments, and the income of an estate or trust in the case of divorce, etc.).

(c) Except as provided in such subpart E, income of a trust is not included in computing the taxable income and credits of a grantor or another person solely on the grounds of his dominion and control over the trust. However, the provisions of subpart E do not apply in situations involving an assignment of future income, whether or not the assignment is to a trust. Thus, for example, a person who assigns his right to future income under an employment contract may be taxed on that income even though the assignment is to a trust over which the assignor has retained none of the controls specified in sections 671 through 677. Similarly, a bondholder who assigns his right to interest may be taxed on interest payments even though the assignment is to an uncontrolled trust. Nor are the rules as to family partnerships affected by the provisions of subpart E even though a partnership interest is held in trust. Likewise, these sections have no application in determining the right of a grantor to deductions for payments to a trust under a transfer and leaseback arrangement. In addition, the limitation of the last sentence of section 671 does not prevent any person from being taxed on the income of a trust when it is used to discharge his legal obligation. See § 1.662(a)-4. He is then treated as a beneficiary under subparts A through D or treated as an owner under section 677 because the income is distributed for his benefit, and not because of his dominion or control over the trust.

(d) The provisions of subpart E are not applicable with respect to a pooled income fund as defined in paragraph (5) of section 642(c) and the regulations thereunder, a charitable remainder annuity trust as defined in paragraph (1) of section 664(d) and the regulations thereunder, or a charitable remainder unitrust as defined in paragraph (2) of section 664(d) and the regulations thereunder.

(e) For the effective date of subpart E see section 683 and the regulations thereunder.

(f) For rules relating to the treatment of liabilities resulting on the sale or other disposition of encumbered trust property due to a renunciation of powers by the grantor or other owner, see § 1.1001-2. [Reg. § 1.671-1.]

☐ [*T.D.* 6217, 12-19-56. *Amended by T.D.* 7148, 10-28-71, *and by T.D.* 7741, 12-11-80.]

[Reg. § 1.671-2]

§ 1.671-2. Applicable principles.—(a) Under section 671 a grantor or another person includes in computing his taxable income and credits those items of income, deduction, and credit against tax which are attributable to or included in any portion of a trust of which he is treated as the owner. Sections 673 through 678 set forth the rules for determining when the grantor or another person is treated as the owner of any portion of a trust. The rules for determining the items of income, deduction, and credit against tax that are attributable to or included in a portion of the trust are set forth in § 1.671-3.

(b) Since the principle underlying subpart E (section 671 and following), part I, subchapter J, chapter 1 of the Code, is in general that income of a trust over which the grantor or another person has retained substantial dominion or control should be taxed to the grantor or other person rather than to the trust which receives the income or to the beneficiary to whom the income may be distributed it is ordinarily immaterial whether the income involved constitutes income or corpus for trust accounting purposes. Accordingly, when it is stated in the regulations under subpart E that "income" is attributed to the grantor or another person, the reference, unless specifically limited, is to income determined for tax purposes and not to income for trust accounting purposes. When it is intended to emphasize that income for trust accounting purposes (determined in accordance with the provisions set forth in § 1.643(b)-1), is meant, the phrase "ordinary income" is used.

(c) An item of income, deduction, or credit included in computing the taxable income and credits of a grantor or another person under section 671 is treated as if it had been received or paid directly by the grantor or other person (whether or not an individual). For example, a charitable contribution made by a trust which is attributed to the grantor (an individual) under sections 671 through 677 will be aggregated with his other charitable contributions to determine their deductibility under the limitations of section 170(b)(1). Likewise, dividends received by a trust from sources in a particular foreign country which are attributed to a grantor or another person under subpart E will be aggregated with his other income from sources within that country to determine whether the taxpayer is subject to the limitations of section 904 with respect to credit for the tax paid to that country.

(d) Items of income, deduction, and credit not attributed to or included in any portion of a trust of which the grantor or another person is treated as the owner under subpart E are subject to the provisions of subparts A through D (section 641 and following), of such part I.

(e)(1) For purposes of part I of subchapter J, chapter 1 of the Internal Revenue Code, a grantor includes any person to the extent such person either creates a trust, or directly or indirectly makes a gratuitous transfer (within the meaning of paragraph (e)(2) of this section) of property to a trust. For purposes of this section, the term *property* includes cash. If a person creates or funds a trust on behalf of another person, both persons are treated as grantors of the trust. (See section 6048 for reporting requirements that apply to grantors of foreign trusts.) However, a person who creates a trust but makes no gratuitous transfers to the trust is not treated as an owner of any portion of the trust under sections 671 through 677 or 679. Also, a person who funds a trust with an amount that is directly reimbursed to such person within a reasonable period of time and who makes no other transfers to the trust that constitute gratuitous transfers is not treated as an owner of any portion of the trust under sections 671 through 677 or 679. See also § 1.672(f)-5(a).

(2)(i) A gratuitous transfer is any transfer other than a transfer for fair market value. A transfer of property to a trust may be considered a gratuitous transfer without regard to whether the transfer is treated as a gift for gift tax purposes.

(ii) For purposes of this paragraph (e), a transfer is for fair market value only to the extent of the value of property received from the trust, services rendered by the trust, or the right to use property of the trust. For example, rents, royalties, interest, and compensation paid to a trust are transfers for fair market value only to the extent that the payments reflect an arm's length price for the use of the property of, or for the services rendered by, the trust. For purposes of this determination, an interest in the trust is not property received from the trust. In addition, a person will not be treated as making a transfer for fair market value merely because the transferor recognizes gain on the transaction. See, for example, section 684 regarding the recognition of gain on certain transfers to foreign trusts.

(iii) For purposes of this paragraph (e), a gratuitous transfer does not include a distribution to a trust with respect to an interest held by such trust in either a trust described in paragraph (e)(3) of this section or an entity other than a trust. For example, a distribution to a trust by a corporation with respect to its stock described in section 301 is not a gratuitous transfer.

(3) A grantor includes any person who acquires an interest in a trust from a grantor of the trust if the interest acquired is an interest in certain investment trusts described in §301.7701-4(c) of this chapter, liquidating trusts described in §301.7701-4(d) of this chapter, or environmental remediation trusts described in §301.7701-4(e) of this chapter.

(4) If a gratuitous transfer is made by a partnership or corporation to a trust and is for a business purpose of the partnership or corporation, the partnership or corporation will generally be treated as the grantor of the trust. For example, if a partnership makes a gratuitous transfer to a trust in order to secure a legal obligation of the partnership to a third party unrelated to the partnership, the partnership will be treated as the grantor of the trust. However, if a partnership or a corporation makes a gratuitous transfer to a trust that is not for a business purpose of the partnership or corporation but is for the personal purposes of one or more of the partners or shareholders, the gratuitous transfer will be treated as a constructive distribution to such partners or shareholders under federal tax principles and the partners or the shareholders will be treated as the grantors of the trust. For example, if a partnership makes a gratuitous transfer to a trust that is for the benefit of a child of a partner, the gratuitous transfer will be treated as a distribution to the partner under section 731 and a subsequent gratuitous transfer by the partner to the trust.

(5) If a trust makes a gratuitous transfer of property to another trust, the grantor of the transferor trust generally will be treated as the grantor of the transferee trust. However, if a person with a general power of appointment over the transferor trust exercises that power in favor of another trust, then such person will be treated as the grantor of the transferee trust, even if the grantor of the transferor trust is treated as the owner of the transferor trust under subpart E of part I, subchapter J, chapter 1 of the Internal Revenue Code.

(6) The following examples illustrate the rules of this paragraph (e). Unless otherwise indicated, all trusts are domestic trusts, and all other persons are United States persons. The examples are as follows:

Example 1. A creates and funds a trust, T, for the benefit of her children. B subsequently makes a gratuitous transfer to T. Under paragraph (e)(1) of this section, both A and B are grantors of T.

Example 2. A makes an investment in a fixed investment trust, T, that is classified as a trust under §301.7701-4(c)(1) of this chapter. A is a grantor of T. B subsequently acquires A's entire interest in T. Under paragraph (e)(3) of this section, B is a grantor of T with respect to such interest.

Example 3. A, an attorney, creates a foreign trust, FT, on behalf of A's client, B, and transfers $100 to FT out of A's funds. A is reimbursed by B for the $100 transferred to FT. The trust instrument states that the trustee has discretion to distribute the income or corpus of FT to B and B's children. Both A and B are treated as grantors of FT under paragraph (e)(1) of this section. In addition, B is treated as the owner of the entire trust under section 677. Because A is reimbursed for the $100 transferred to FT on behalf of B, A is not treated as transferring any property to FT. Therefore, A is not an owner of any portion of FT under sections 671 through 677 regardless of whether A retained any power over or interest in FT described in sections 673 through 677. Furthermore, A is not treated as an owner of any portion of FT under section 679. Both A and B are responsible parties for purposes of the requirements in section 6048.

Example 4. A creates and funds a trust, T. A does not retain any power or interest in T that would cause A to be treated as an owner of any portion of the trust under sections 671 through 677. B holds an unrestricted power, exercisable solely by B, to withdraw certain amounts contributed to the trust before the end of the calendar year and to vest those amounts in B. B is treated as an owner of the portion of T that is subject to the withdrawal power under section 678(a)(1). However, B is not a grantor of T under paragraph (e)(1) of this section because B neither created T nor made a gratuitous transfer to T.

Example 5. A transfers cash to a trust, T, through a broker, in exchange for units in T. The units in T are not property for purposes of determining whether A has received fair market value under paragraph (e)(2)(ii) of this section. Therefore, A has made a gratuitous transfer to T, and, under paragraph (e)(1) of this section, A is a grantor of T.

Example 6. A borrows cash from T, a trust. A has not made any gratuitous transfers to T. Arm's length interest payments by A to T will not be treated as gratuitous transfers under paragraph (e)(2)(ii) of this section. Therefore, under paragraph (e)(1) of this section, A is not a grantor of T with respect to the interest payments.

Example 7. A, B's brother, creates a trust, T, for B's benefit and transfers $50,000 to T. The trustee invests the $50,000 in stock of Company X. C, B's uncle, purportedly sells property with a fair market value of $1,000,000 to T in exchange for the stock when it has appreciated to a fair market value of $100,000. Under paragraph (e)(2)(ii) of this section, the $900,000 excess value is a gratuitous transfer by C. Therefore, under paragraph (e)(1) of this section, A is a grantor with respect to the portion of the trust valued at $100,000, and C is a grantor of T with respect to the portion of the trust valued at $900,000. In addition, A or C or both will be treated as the owners of the respective portions of the trust of which each person is a grantor if A or C or both retain powers over or interests in such portions under sections 673 through 677.

Example 8. G creates and funds a trust, T1, for the benefit of G's children and grandchildren. After G's death, under authority granted to the trustees in the trust instrument, the trustees of T1 transfer a portion of the assets of T1 to another trust, T2, and retain a power to revoke T2 and revest the assets of T2 in T1. Under paragraphs (e)(1) and (5) of this section, G is the grantor of T1 and T2. In addition, because the trustees of T1 have retained a power to revest the assets of T2 in T1, T1 is treated as the owner of T2 under section 678(a).

Example 9. G creates and funds a trust, T1, for the benefit of B. G retains a power to revest the assets of T1 in G within the meaning of section 676. Under the trust agreement, B is given a general power of appointment over the assets of T1. B exercises the general power of appointment with respect to one-half of the corpus of T1 in favor of a trust, T2, that is for the benefit of C, B's child. Under paragraph (e)(1) of this section, G is the grantor of T1, and under paragraphs (e)(1) and (5) of this section, B is the grantor of T2.

(7) The rules of this section are applicable to any transfer to a trust, or transfer of an interest in a trust, on or after August 10, 1999. [Reg. § 1.671-2.]

☐ [*T.D.* 6217, 12-19-56. *Amended by T.D.* 8831, 8-5-99 *and T.D.* 8890, 7-3-2000.]

[Reg. § 1.671-3]

§ 1.671-3. Attribution or inclusion of income, deductions, and credits against tax.—(a) When a grantor or another person is treated under subpart E (section 671 and following) as the owner of any portion of a trust, there are included in computing his tax liability those items of income, deduction, and credit against tax attributable to or included in that portion. For example—

(1) If a grantor or another person is treated as the owner of an entire trust (corpus as well as ordinary income), he takes into account in computing his income tax liability all items of income, deduction, and credit (including capital gains and losses) to which he would have been entitled had the trust not been in existence during the period he is treated as owner.

(2) If the portion treated as owned consists of specific trust property and its income, all items directly related to that property are attributable to the portion. Items directly related to trust property not included in the portion treated as owned by the grantor or other person are governed by the provisions of subparts A through D (section 641 and following), part I, subchapter J, chapter 1 of the Code. Items that relate both to the portion treated as owned by the grantor and to the balance of the trust must be apportioned in a manner that is reasonable in the light of all the circumstances of each case, including the terms of the governing instrument, local law, and the practice of the trustee if it is reasonable and consistent.

(3) If the portion of a trust treated as owned by a grantor or another person consists of an undivided fractional interest in the trust, or of an interest represented by a dollar amount, a pro rata share of each item of income, deduction, and credit is normally allocated to the portion. Thus, where the portion owned consists of an interest in or a right to an amount of corpus only, a fraction of each item (including items allocated to corpus, such as capital gains) is attributed to the portion. The numerator of this fraction is the amount which is subject to the control of the grantor or other person and the denominator is normally the fair market value of the trust corpus at the beginning of the taxable year in question. The share not treated as owned by the grantor or other person is governed by the provisions of subparts A through D. See the last three sentences of paragraph (c) of this section for the principles applicable if the portion treated as owned consists of an interest in part of the ordinary income in contrast to an interest in corpus alone.

(b) If a grantor or another person is treated as the owner of a portion of a trust, that portion may or may not include both ordinary income and other income allocable to corpus. For example—

(1) Only ordinary income is included by reason of an interest in or a power over ordinary income alone. Thus, if a grantor is treated under section 673 as an owner by reason of a reversionary interest in ordinary income only, items of income allocable to corpus will not be included in the portion he is treated as owning. Similarly, if a grantor or another person is treated under sections 674-678 as an owner of a portion by reason of a power over ordinary income only, items of income allocable to corpus are not included in that portion. (See paragraph (c) of this section to determine the treatment of deductions and credits when only ordinary income is included in the portion.)

(2) Only income allocable to corpus is included by reason of an interest in or a power over corpus alone, if satisfaction of the interest or an exercise of the power will not result in an interest in or the exercise of a power over ordinary income which would itself cause that income to be included. For example, if a grantor has a reversionary interest in a trust which is not such as to require that he be treated as an owner under section 673, he may nevertheless be treated as an owner under section 677(a)(2) since any income allocable to corpus is accumulated for future distribution to him, but items of income included in determining ordinary income are not included in the portion he is treated as

owning. Similarly, he may have a power over corpus which is such that he is treated as an owner under section 674 or 676(a), but ordinary income will not be included in the portion he owns, if his power can only affect income received after a period of time such that he would not be treated as an owner of the income if the power were a reversionary interest. (See paragraph (c) of this section to determine the treatment of deductions and credits when only income allocated to corpus is included in the portion.)

(3) Both ordinary income and other income allocable to corpus are included by reason of an interest in or a power over both ordinary income and corpus, or an interest in or a power over corpus alone which does not come within the provisions of subparagraph (2) of this paragraph. For example, if a grantor is treated under section 673 as the owner of a portion of a trust by reason of a reversionary interest in corpus, both ordinary income and other income allocable to corpus are included in the portion. Further, a grantor includes both ordinary income and other income allocable to corpus in the portion he is treated as owning if he is treated under section 674 or 676 as an owner because of a power over corpus which can affect income received within a period such that he would be treated as an owner under section 673 if the power were a reversionary interest. Similarly, a grantor or another person includes both ordinary income and other income allocable to corpus in the portion he is treated as owning if he is treated as an owner under section 675 or 678 because of a power over corpus.

(c) If only income allocable to corpus is included in computing a grantor's tax liability, he will take into account in that computation only those items of income, deduction, and credit which would not be included under subparts A through D in the computation of the tax liability of the current income beneficiaries if all distributable net income had actually been distributed to those beneficiaries. On the other hand, if the grantor or another person is treated as an owner solely because of his interest in or power over ordinary income alone, he will take into account in computing his tax liability those items which would be included in computing the tax liability of a current income beneficiary, including expenses allocable to corpus which enter into the computation of distributable net income. If the grantor or other person is treated as an owner because of his power over or right to a dollar amount of ordinary income, he will first take into account a portion of those items of income and expense entering into the computation of ordinary income under the trust instrument or local law sufficient to produce income of the dollar amount required. There will then be attributable to him a pro rata portion of other items entering into the computation of distributable net income under subparts A through D, such as expenses allocable to corpus, and a pro rata portion of credits of the trust. For examples of computations under this paragraph, see paragraph (g) of § 1.677(a)-1. [Reg. § 1.671-3.]

☐ [*T.D.* 6217, 12-19-56. *Amended by T.D.* 6989, 1-16-69.]

[Reg. § 1.671-4]

§ 1.671-4. Method of reporting.—(a) *Portion of trust treated as owned by the grantor or another person.*—Except as otherwise provided in paragraph (b) of this section and § 1.671-5, items of income, deduction, and credit attributable to any portion of a trust that, under the provisions of subpart E (section 671 and following), part I, subchapter J, chapter 1 of the Internal Revenue Code, is treated as owned by the grantor or another person, are not reported by the trust on Form 1041, "U.S. Income Tax Return for Estates and Trusts," but are shown on a separate statement to be attached to that form. Section 1.671-5 provides special reporting rules for widely held fixed investment trusts. Section 301.7701-4(e)(2) of this chapter provides guidance regarding the application of the reporting rules in this paragraph (a) to an environmental remediation trust.

(b) *A trust all of which is treated as owned by one or more grantors or other persons.*—(1) *In general.*—In the case of a trust all of which is treated as owned by one or more grantors or other persons, and which is not described in paragraph (b)(6) or (7) of this section, the trustee may, but is not required to, report by one of the methods described in this paragraph (b) rather than by the method described in paragraph (a) of this section. A trustee may not report, however, pursuant to paragraph (b)(2)(i)(A) of this section unless the grantor or other person treated as the owner of the trust provides to the trustee a complete Form W-9 or acceptable substitute Form W-9 signed under penalties of perjury. See section 3406 and the regulations thereunder for the information to include on, and the manner of executing, the Form W-9, depending upon the type of reportable payments made.

(2) *A trust all of which is treated as owned by one grantor or by one other person.*—(i) *In general.*—In the case of a trust all of which is treated as owned by one grantor or one other person, the trustee reporting under this paragraph (b) must either—

(A) Furnish the name and taxpayer identification number (TIN) of the grantor or other person treated as the owner of the trust, and the address of the trust, to all payors during the taxable year, and comply with the additional requirements described in paragraph (b)(2)(ii) of this section; or

(B) Furnish the name, TIN, and address of the trust to all payors during the taxable year, and comply with the additional requirements described in paragraph (b)(2)(iii) of this section.

(ii) *Additional obligations of the trustee when name and TIN of the grantor or other person treated as the owner of the trust and the address of the trust are furnished to payors.*—(A) Unless the grantor or other person treated as the owner of the trust is the trustee or a co-trustee of the trust, the trustee must furnish the grantor or other person treated as the owner of the trust with a statement that—

(1) Shows all items of income, deduction, and credit of the trust for the taxable year;

(2) Identifies the payor of each item of income;

(3) Provides the grantor or other person treated as the owner of the trust with the information necessary to take the items into account in computing the grantor's or other person's taxable income; and

(4) Informs the grantor or other person treated as the owner of the trust that the items of income, deduction and credit and other information shown on the statement must be included in computing the taxable income and credits of the grantor or other person on the income tax return of the grantor or other person.

(B) The trustee is not required to file any type of return with the Internal Revenue Service.

(iii) *Additional obligations of the trustee when name, TIN, and address of the trust are furnished to payors.*—(A) *Obligation to file Forms 1099.*—The trustee must file with the Internal Revenue Service the appropriate Forms 1099, reporting the income or gross proceeds paid to the trust during the taxable year, and showing the trust as the payor and the grantor or other person treated as the owner of the trust as the payee. The trustee has the same obligations for filing the appropriate Forms 1099 as would a payor making reportable payments, except that the trustee must report each type of income in the aggregate, and each item of gross proceeds separately. See paragraph (b)(5) of this section regarding the amounts required to be included on any Forms 1099 filed by the trustee.

(B) *Obligation to furnish statement.*—*(1)* Unless the grantor or other person treated as the owner of the trust is the trustee or a co-trustee of the trust, the trustee must also furnish to the grantor or other person treated as the owner of the trust a statement that—

(i) Shows all items of income, deduction, and credit of the trust for the taxable year;

(ii) Provides the grantor or other person treated as the owner of the trust with the information necessary to take the items into account in computing the grantor's or other person's taxable income; and

(iii) Informs the grantor or other person treated as the owner of the trust that the items of income, deduction and credit and other information shown on the statement must be included in computing the taxable income and credits of the grantor or other person on the income tax return of the grantor or other person.

(2) By furnishing the statement, the trustee satisfies the obligation to furnish statements to recipients with respect to the Forms 1099 filed by the trustee.

(iv) *Examples.*—The following examples illustrate the provisions of this paragraph (b)(2):

Example 1. G, a United States citizen, creates an irrevocable trust which provides that the ordinary income is to be payable to him for life and that on his death the corpus shall be distributed to B, an unrelated person. Except for the right to receive income, G retains no right or power which would cause him to be treated as an owner under sections 671 through 679. Under the applicable local law, capital gains must be added to corpus. Since G has a right to receive income, he is treated as an owner of a portion of the trust under section 677. The tax consequences of any items of capital gain of the trust are governed by the provisions of subparts A, B, C, and D (section 641 and following), part I, subchapter J, chapter 1 of the Internal Revenue Code. Because not all of the trust is treated as owned by the grantor or another person, the trustee may not report by the methods described in paragraph (b)(2) of this section.

Example 2. (i)(A) On January 2, 1996, G, a United States citizen, creates a trust all of which is treated as owned by G. The trustee of the trust is T. During the 1996 taxable year the trust has the following items of income and gross proceeds:

Interest	$2,500
Dividends	3,205
Proceeds from sale of B stock	2,000

(B) The trust has no items of deduction or credit.

(ii)(A) The payors of the interest paid to the trust are X ($2,000), Y ($300), and Z ($200). The payors of the dividends paid to the trust are A ($3,200), and D ($5). The payor of the gross proceeds paid to the trust is D, a brokerage firm, which held the B stock as the nominee for the trust. The B stock was purchased by T for $1,500 on January 3, 1996, and sold by T on November 29, 1996. T chooses to report pursuant to paragraph (b)(2)(i)(B) of this section, and therefore furnishes the name, TIN, and address of the trust to X, Y, Z, A, and D. X, Y, and Z each furnish T with a Form 1099-INT showing the trust as the payee. A furnishes T with a Form 1099-DIV showing the trust as the payee. D does not furnish T with a Form 1099-DIV because D paid a dividend of less than $10 to T. D furnishes T with a Form 1099-B showing the trust as the payee.

(B) On or before February 28, 1997, T files a Form 1099-INT with the Internal Revenue Service on which T reports interest attributable to G, as the owner of the trust, of $2,500; a Form 1099-DIV on which T reports dividends attributable to G, as the owner of the trust, of $3,205; and a Form 1099-B on which T reports gross proceeds from the sale of B stock attributable to G, as the owner of the trust, of $2,000. On or before April 15, 1997, T furnishes a statement to G which lists the following items of income and information necessary for G to take the items into account in computing G's taxable income:

Interest	$2,500
Dividends	3,205
Gain from sale of B stock	500

Information regarding sale of B stock:

Proceeds	$2,000
Basis	1,500
Date acquired	1/03/96
Date sold	11/29/96

(C) T informs G that any items of income, deduction and credit and other information shown on the statement must be included in computing the taxable income and credits of the grantor or other person on the income tax return of the grantor or other person.

(D) T has complied with T's obligations under this section.

(iii)(A) Same facts as paragraphs (i) and (ii) of this *Example 2,* except that G contributed the B stock to the trust on January 2, 1996. On or before April 15, 1997, T furnishes a statement to G which lists the following items of income and information necessary for G to take the items into account in computing G's taxable income:

Interest	$2,500
Dividends	3,205
Information regarding sale of B stock:	
Proceeds	$2,000
Date sold	11/29/96

(B) T informs G that any items of income, deduction and credit and other information shown on the statement must be included in computing the taxable income and credits of the grantor or other person on the income tax return of the grantor or other person.

(C) T has complied with T's obligations under this section.

Example 3. On January 2, 1996, G, a United States citizen, creates a trust all of which is treated as owned by G. The trustee of the trust is T. The only asset of the trust is an interest in C, a common trust fund under section 584(a). T chooses to report pursuant to paragraph (b)(2)(i)(B) of this section and therefore furnishes the name, TIN, and address of the trust to C. C files a Form 1065 and a Schedule K-1 (Partner's Share of Income, Credits, Deductions, etc.) showing the name, TIN, and address of the trust with the Internal Revenue Service and furnishes a copy to T. Because the trust did not receive any amounts described in paragraph (b)(5) of this section, T does not file any type of return with the Internal Revenue Service. On or before April 15, 1997, T furnishes G with a statement that shows all items of income, deduction, and credit of the trust for the 1996 taxable year. In addition, T informs G that any items of income, deduction and credit and other information shown on the statement must be included in computing the taxable income and credits of the grantor or other person on the income tax return of the grantor or other person. T has complied with T's obligations under this section.

(3) *A trust all of which is treated as owned by two or more grantors or other persons.*—(i) *In general.*—In the case of a trust all of which is treated as owned by two or more grantors or other persons, the trustee must furnish the name, TIN, and address of the trust to all payors for the taxable year, and comply with the additional requirements described in paragraph (b)(3)(ii) of this section.

(ii) *Additional obligations of trustee.*—(A) *Obligation to file Forms 1099.*—The trustee must file with the Internal Revenue Service the appropriate Forms 1099, reporting the items of income paid to the trust by all payors during the taxable year attributable to the portion of the trust treated as owned by each grantor or other person, and showing the trust as the payor and each grantor or other person treated as an owner of the trust as the payee. The trustee has the same obligations for filing the appropriate Forms 1099 as would a payor making reportable payments, except that the trustee must report each type of income in the aggregate, and each item of gross proceeds separately. See paragraph (b)(5) of this section regarding the amounts required to be included on any Forms 1099 filed by the trustee.

(B) *Obligation to furnish statement.*—*(1)* The trustee must also furnish to each grantor or other person treated as an owner of the trust a statement that—

(i) Shows all items of income, deduction, and credit of the trust for the taxable year attributable to the portion of the trust treated as owned by the grantor or other person;

(ii) Provides the grantor or other person treated as an owner of the trust with the information necessary to take the items into account in computing the grantor's or other person's taxable income; and

(iii) Informs the grantor or other person treated as the owner of the trust that the items of income, deduction and credit and other information shown on the statement must be included in computing the taxable income and credits of the grantor or other person on the income tax return of the grantor or other person.

(2) Except for the requirements pursuant to section 3406 and the regulations thereunder, by furnishing the statement, the trustee satisfies the obligation to furnish statements to recipients with respect to the Forms 1099 filed by the trustee.

(4) *Persons treated as payors.*—(i) *In general.*—For purposes of this section, the term payor means any person who is required by any provision of the Internal Revenue Code and the regulations thereunder to make any type of information return (including Form 1099 or Schedule K-1) with respect to the trust for the taxable year, including persons who make payments to the trust or who collect (or otherwise act as middlemen with respect to) payments on behalf of the trust.

(ii) *Application to brokers and customers.*—For purposes of this section, a broker, within the meaning of section 6045, is considered a payor. A customer, within the meaning of section 6045, is considered a payee.

(5) *Amounts required to be included on Forms 1099 filed by the trustee.*—(i) *In general.*—The amounts that must be included on any Forms

1099 required to be filed by the trustee pursuant to this section do not include any amounts that are reportable by the payor on an information return other than Form 1099. For example, in the case of a trust which owns an interest in a partnership, the trust's distributive share of the income and gain of the partnership is not includible on any Forms 1099 filed by the trustee pursuant to this section because the distributive share is reportable by the partnership on Schedule K-1.

(ii) *Example.*—The following example illustrates the provisions of this paragraph (b)(5):

Example. (i)(A) On January 2, 1996, G, a United States citizen, creates a trust all of which is treated as owned by G. The trustee of the trust is T. The assets of the trust during the 1996 taxable year are shares of stock in X, an S corporation, a limited partnership interest in P, shares of stock in M, and shares of stock in N. T chooses to report pursuant to paragraph (b)(2)(i)(B) of this section and therefore furnishes the name, TIN, and address of the trust to X, P, M, and N. M furnishes T with a Form 1099-DIV showing the trust as the payee. N does not furnish T with a Form 1099-DIV because N paid a dividend of less than $10 to T. X and P furnish T with Schedule K-1 (Shareholder's Share of Income, Credits, Deductions, etc.) and Schedule K-1 (Partner's Share of Income, Credits, Deductions, etc.), respectively, showing the trust's name, TIN, and address.

(B) For the 1996 taxable year the trust has the following items of income and deduction:

Dividends paid by M	$12
Dividends paid by N	6
Administrative expense	$20

Items reported by X on Schedule K-1 attributable to trust's shares of stock in X:

Interest	$20
Dividends	35

Items reported by P on Schedule K-1 attributable to trust's limited partnership interest in P:

Ordinary income	$300

(ii)(A) On or before February 28, 1997, T files with the Internal Revenue Service a Form 1099-DIV on which T reports dividends attributable to G as the owner of the trust in the amount of $18. T does not file any other returns.

(B) T has complied with T's obligation under paragraph (b)(2)(iii)(A) of this section to file the appropriate Forms 1099.

(6) *Trusts that cannot report under this paragraph (b).*—The following trusts cannot use the methods of reporting described in this paragraph (b)—

(i) A common trust fund as defined in section 584(a);

(ii) A trust that has its situs or any of its assets located outside the United States;

(iii) A trust that is a qualified subchapter S trust as defined in section 1361(d)(3);

(iv) A trust all of which is treated as owned by one grantor or one other person whose taxable year is a fiscal year;

(v) A trust all of which is treated as owned by one grantor or one other person who is not a United States person; or

(vi) A trust all of which is treated as owned by two or more grantors or other persons, one of whom is not a United States person.

(7) *Grantors or other persons who are treated as owners of the trust and are exempt recipients for information reporting purposes.*—(i) *Trust treated as owned by one grantor or one other person.*—The trustee of a trust all of which is treated as owned by one grantor or one other person may not report pursuant to this paragraph (b) if the grantor or other person is an exempt recipient for information reporting purposes.

(ii) *Trust treated as owned by two or more grantors or other persons.*—The trustee of a trust, all of which is treated as owned by two or more grantors or other persons, may not report pursuant to this paragraph (b) if one or more grantors or other persons treated as owners are exempt recipients for information reporting purposes unless—

(A) At least one grantor or one other person who is treated as an owner of the trust is a person who is not an exempt recipient for information reporting purposes; and

(B) The trustee reports without regard to whether any of the grantors or other persons treated as owners of the trust are exempt recipients for information reporting purposes.

(8) *Husband and wife who make a single return jointly.*—A trust all of which is treated as owned by a husband and wife who make a single return jointly of income taxes for the taxable year under section 6013 is considered to be owned by one grantor for purposes of this paragraph (b).

(c) *Due date for Forms 1099 required to be filed by trustee.*—The due date for any Forms 1099 required to be filed with the Internal Revenue Service by a trustee pursuant to this section is the due date otherwise in effect for filing Forms 1099.

(d) *Due date and other requirements with respect to statement required to be furnished by trustee.*—(1) *In general.*—The due date for the statement required to be furnished by a trustee to the grantor or other person treated as an owner of the trust pursuant to this section is the date specified by section 6034A(a). The trustee must maintain in its records a copy of the statement furnished to the grantor or other person treated as an owner of the trust for a period of three years from the due date for furnishing such statement specified in this paragraph (d).

(2) *Statement for the taxable year ending with the death of the grantor or other person treated as the owner of the trust.*—If a trust ceases to be treated as owned by the grantor, or other person, by reason of the death of that grantor or other person (decedent), the due date for the statement required to be furnished for the taxable year

ending with the death of the decedent shall be the date specified by section 6034A(a) as though the decedent had lived throughout the decedent's last taxable year. See paragraph (h) of this section for special reporting rules for a trust or portion of the trust that ceases to be treated as owned by the grantor or other person by reason of the death of the grantor or other person.

(e) *Backup withholding requirements.*—(1) *Trustee reporting under paragraph (b)(2)(i)(A) of this section.*—In order for the trustee to be able to report pursuant to paragraph (b)(2)(i)(A) of this section and to furnish to all payors the name and TIN of the grantor or other person treated as the owner of the trust, the grantor or other person must provide a complete Form W-9 to the trustee in the manner provided in paragraph (b)(1) of this section, and the trustee must give the name and TIN shown on that Form W-9 to all payors. In addition, if the Form W-9 indicates that the grantor or other person is subject to backup withholding, the trustee must notify all payors of reportable interest and dividend payments of the requirement to backup withhold. If the Form W-9 indicates that the grantor or other person is not subject to backup withholding, the trustee does not have to notify the payors that backup withholding is not required. The trustee should not give the Form W-9, or a copy thereof, to a payor because the Form W-9 contains the address of the grantor or other person and paragraph (b)(2)(i)(A) of this section requires the trustee to furnish the address of the trust to all payors and not the address of the grantor or other person. The trustee acts as the agent of the grantor or other person for purposes of furnishing to the payors the information required by this paragraph (e)(1). Thus, a payor may rely on the name and TIN provided to the payor by the trustee, and, if given, on the trustee's statement that the grantor is subject to backup withholding.

(2) *Other backup withholding requirements.*—Whether a trustee is treated as a payor for purposes of backup withholding is determined pursuant to section 3406 and the regulations thereunder.

(f) *Penalties for failure to file a correct Form 1099 or furnish a correct statement.*—A trustee who fails to file a correct Form 1099 or to furnish a correct statement to a grantor or other person treated as an owner of the trust as required by paragraph (b) of this section is subject to the penalties provided by sections 6721 and 6722 and the regulations thereunder.

(g) *Changing reporting methods.*—(1) *Changing from reporting by filing Form 1041 to a method described in paragraph (b) of this section.*—If the trustee has filed a Form 1041 for any taxable year ending before January 1, 1996 (and has not filed a final Form 1041 pursuant to § 1.6714(b)(3) (as contained in the 26 CFR part 1 edition revised as of April 1, 1995)), or files a Form 1041 for any taxable year thereafter, the trustee must file a final Form 1041 for the taxable year which ends after January 1, 1995, and which immediately precedes the first taxable year for which the trustee reports pursuant to paragraph (b) of this section, on the front of which form the trustee must write: "Pursuant to § 1.671-4(g), this is the final Form 1041 for this grantor trust.".

(2) *Changing from reporting by a method described in paragraph (b) of this section to the filing of a Form 1041.*—The trustee of a trust who reported pursuant to paragraph (b) of this section for a taxable year may report pursuant to paragraph (a) of this section for subsequent taxable years. If the trustee reported pursuant to paragraph (b)(2)(i)(A) of this section, and therefore furnished the name and TIN of the grantor to all payors, the trustee must furnish the name, TIN, and address of the trust to all payors for such subsequent taxable years. If the trustee reported pursuant to paragraph (b)(2)(i)(B) or (b)(3)(i) of this section, and therefore furnished the name and TIN of the trust to all payors, the trustee must indicate on each Form 1096 (Annual Summary and Transmittal of U.S. Information Returns) that it files (or appropriately on magnetic media) for the final taxable year for which the trustee so reports that it is the final return of the trust.

(3) *Changing between methods described in paragraph (b) of this section.*—(i) *Changing from furnishing the TIN of the grantor to furnishing the TIN of the trust.*—The trustee of a trust who reported pursuant to paragraph (b)(2)(i)(A) of this section for a taxable year, and therefore furnished the name and TIN of the grantor to all payors, may report pursuant to paragraph (b)(2)(i)(B) of this section, and furnish the name and TIN of the trust to all payors, for subsequent taxable years.

(ii) *Changing from furnishing the TIN of the trust to furnishing the TIN of the grantor.*—The trustee of a trust who reported pursuant to paragraph (b)(2)(i)(B) of this section for a taxable year, and therefore furnished the name and TIN of the trust to all payors, may report pursuant to paragraph (b)(2)(i)(A) of this section, and furnish the name and TIN of the grantor to all payors, for subsequent taxable years. The trustee, however, must indicate on each Form 1096 (Annual Summary and Transmittal of U.S. Information Returns) that it files (or appropriately on magnetic media) for the final taxable year for which the trustee reports pursuant to paragraph (b)(2)(i)(B) of this section that it is the final return of the trust.

(4) *Example.*—The following example illustrates the provisions of paragraph (g) of this section:

Example. (i) On January 3, 1994, G, a United States citizen, creates a trust all of which is treated as owned by G. The trustee of the trust is T. On or before April 17, 1995, T files with the Internal Revenue Service a Form 1041 with an attached statement for the 1994 taxable year showing the items of income, deduction, and credit of the trust. On or before April 15, 1996, T files with the Internal Revenue Service a Form 1041 with an attached statement for the 1995 taxable year showing the items of income, deduction, and credit of the trust. On the Form 1041, T states that "pursuant to § 1.671-4(g), this is the final Form 1041 for this grantor trust." T may report pursuant to paragraph (b) of this section for the 1996 taxable year.

(ii) T reports pursuant to paragraph (b)(2)(i)(B) of this section, and therefore furnishes the name, TIN, and address of the trust to all payors, for the 1996 and 1997 taxable years. T chooses to report pursuant to paragraph (a) of this section for the 1998 taxable year. On each Form 1096 (Annual Summary and Transmittal of U.S. Information Returns) which T files for the 1997 taxable year (or appropriately on magnetic media), T indicates that it is the trust's final return. On or before April 15, 1999, T files with the Internal Revenue Service a Form 1041 with an attached statement showing the items of income, deduction, and credit of the trust. On the Form 1041, T uses the same TIN which T used on the Forms 1041 and Forms 1099 it filed for previous taxable years. T has complied with T's obligations under paragraph (g)(2) of this section.

(h) *Reporting rules for a trust, or portion of a trust, that ceases to be treated as owned by a grantor or other person by reason of the death of the grantor or other person.*—(1) *Definition of decedent.*—For purposes of this paragraph (h), the *decedent* is the grantor or other person treated as the owner of the trust, or portion of the trust, under subpart E, part I, subchapter J, chapter 1 of the Internal Revenue Code on the date of death of that person.

(2) *In general.*—The provisions of this section apply to a trust, or portion of a trust, treated as owned by a decedent for the taxable year that ends with the decedent's death. Following the death of the decedent, the trust or portion of a trust that ceases to be treated as owned by the decedent, by reason of the death of the decedent, may no longer report under this section. A trust, all of which was treated as owned by the decedent, must obtain a new TIN upon the death of the decedent, if the trust will continue after the death of the decedent. See § 301.6109-1(a)(3)(i) of this chapter for rules regarding obtaining a TIN upon the death of the decedent.

(3) *Special rules.*—(i) *Trusts reporting pursuant to paragraph (a) of this section for the taxable year ending with the decedent's death.*—The due date for the filing of a return pursuant to paragraph (a) of this section for the taxable year ending with the decedent's death shall be the due date provided for under § 1.6072-1(a)(2). The return filed under this paragraph for a trust all of which was treated as owned by the decedent must indicate that it is a final return.

(ii) *Trust reporting pursuant to paragraph (b)(2)(B) of this section for the taxable year of the decedent's death.*—A trust that reports pursuant to paragraph (b)(2)(B) of this section for the taxable year ending with the decedent's death must indicate on each Form 1096 "Annual Summary and Transmittal of the U.S. Information Returns" that it files (or appropriately on magnetic media) for the taxable year ending with the death of the decedent that it is the final return of the trust.

(iii) *Trust reporting under paragraph (b)(3) of this section.*—If a trust has been reporting under paragraph (b)(3) of this section, the trustee may not report under that paragraph if any portion of the trust has a short taxable year by reason of the death of the decedent and the portion treated as owned by the decedent does not terminate on the death of the decedent.

(i) *Effective date and transition rule.*—(1) *Effective date.*—The trustee of a trust any portion of which is treated as owned by one or more grantors or other persons must report pursuant to paragraphs (a), (b), (c), (d)(1), (e), (f), and (g) of this section for taxable years beginning on or after January 1, 1996.

(2) *Transition rule.*—For taxable years beginning prior to January 1, 1996, the Internal Revenue Service will not challenge the manner of reporting of—

(i) A trustee of a trust all of which is treated as owned by one or more grantors or other persons who did not report in accordance with § 1.671-4(a) (as contained in the 26 CFR part 1 edition revised as of April 1, 1995) as in effect for taxable years beginning prior to January 1, 1996, but did report in a manner substantially similar to one of the reporting methods described in paragraph (b) of this section; or

(ii) A trustee of two or more trusts all of which are treated as owned by one or more grantors or other persons who filed a single Form 1041 for all of the trusts, rather than a separate Form 1041 for each trust, provided that the items of income, deduction, and credit of each trust were shown on a statement attached to the single Form 1041.

(3) *Effective date for paragraphs (d)(2) and (h) of this section.*—Paragraphs (d)(2) and (h) of this section apply for taxable years ending on or after December 24, 2002.

(j) *Cross-reference.*—For rules relating to employer identification numbers, and to the obligation of a payor of income or proceeds to the trust to furnish to the payee a statement to recipient, see § 301.6109-1(a)(2) of this chapter. [Reg. § 1.671-4.]

□ [*T.D.* 6217, 12-19-56. *Amended by T.D.* 7796, 11-23-81; *T.D.* 8633, 12-20-95; *T.D.* 8668, 4-30-96 *T.D.* 9032, 12-23-2002 *and T.D.* 9241, 1-23-2006.]

[Reg. § 1.671-5]

§ 1.671-5. Reporting for widely held fixed investment trusts.—(a) *Table of contents.*—This table of contents lists the major paragraph headings for this section.

(iv) Gross income requirement.

(2) Information to be reported by all WHFITs.

(i) Trust identification and calculation period chosen.

(ii) Items of income, expense, and credit.

(iii) Non pro-rata partial principal payments.

(iv) Asset sales and dispositions.

(v) Redemptions and sales of WHFIT interests.

(vi) Information regarding bond premium.

(vii) Information regarding market discount.

(viii) Other information.

(3) Identifying the representative who will provide trust information.

(4) Time and manner of providing information.

(i) Time.

(ii) Manner.

(iii) Inclusion of information with respect to all calculation periods.

(5) Requesting information from a WHFIT.

(i) In general.

(ii) Manner of requesting information.

(iii) Period of time during which a requesting person may request WHFIT information.

(6) Trustee's requirement to retain records.

(d) Form 1099 requirement for trustees and middlemen.

(1) Obligation to file Form 1099 with the IRS.

(i) In general.

(ii) Forms 1099 not required for exempt recipients.

(iii) Reporting and withholding with respect to foreign persons.

(2) Information to be reported.

(i) Determining amounts to be provided on Forms 1099.

(ii) Information to be provided on Forms 1099.

(3) Time and manner of filing Forms 1099.

(i) Time and place.

(ii) Reporting trust sales proceeds, redemption asset proceeds, redemption proceeds, sales asset proceeds, sales proceeds, and non pro-rata partial principal payments.

(e) Requirement to furnish a written tax information statement to the TIH.

(1) In general.

(2) Information required.

(i) WHFIT information.

(ii) Identification of the person furnishing the statement.

(iii) Items of income, expense, and credit.

(iv) Non pro-rata partial principal payments.

(v) Asset sales and dispositions.

(vi) Redemption or sale of a trust interest.

(vii) Information regarding market discount and bond premium.

(viii) Other information.

(ix) Required statement.

(3) Due date and other requirements

(4) Requirement to retain records

(f) Safe harbor for providing information for certain NMWHFITs.

(1) Safe harbor for trustee reporting of NMWHFIT information.

(i) In general.

(ii) Reporting NMWHFIT income and expenses.

(iii) Reporting non pro-rata partial principal payments under the safe harbor.

(iv) Reporting sales and dispositions of NMWHFIT assets under the safe harbor.

(v) Reporting redemptions under the safe harbor.

(vi) Reporting the sale of a trust interest under the safe harbor.

(vii) Reporting OID information under the safe harbor.

(viii) Reporting market discount information under the safe harbor.

(ix) Reporting bond premium information under the safe harbor.

(x) Reporting additional information.

(2) Use of information provided by trustees under the safe harbor for NMWHFITs.

(i) In general.

(ii) Determining NMWHFIT income and expenses under the safe harbor.

(iii) Reporting non pro-rata partial principal payments under the safe harbor.

(iv) Reporting sales and dispositions of NMWHFIT assets under the safe harbor.

(v) Reporting redemptions under the safe harbor.

(vi) Reporting sales of trust interests under the safe harbor.

(vii) Reporting OID information under the safe harbor.

(viii) Reporting market discount information under the safe harbor.

(ix) Reporting bond premium information under the safe harbor.

(3) Example of the use of the safe harbor for NMWHFITs.

(i) Facts.

(ii) Trustee reporting.

(iii) Brokers' use of information provided by Trustee.

(g) Safe Harbor for certain WHMTs.

(1) Safe harbor for trustees of certain WHMTs for reporting information.

(i) In general.

(ii) Requirements.

(iii) Reporting WHMT income, expenses, non pro-rata partial principal payments, and sales and dispositions under the safe harbor

(iv) Reporting OID information under the safe harbor

(v) Reporting market discount information under the safe harbor.

(vi) Reporting bond premium information under the safe harbor.

(2) Use of information provided by a trustee under the safe harbor.

(i) In general.

(ii) Reporting WHMT income, expenses, non pro-rata partial principal payments, and sales and dispositions under the safe harbor.

(iii) Reporting OID information under the safe harbor.

(iv) Requirement to provide market discount information under the safe harbor.

(v) Requirement to provide bond premium information under the safe harbor.

(3) Example of safe harbor in paragraph (g)(1) of this section.

(i) Facts.

(ii) Trustee reporting.

(iii) Broker's use of the information provided by Trustee.

(h) Additional safe harbors.

(1) Temporary safe harbors.

(2) Additional safe harbors provided by other published guidance.

(i) Reserved.

(j) Requirement that middlemen furnish information to beneficial owners that are exempt recipients and non calendar year beneficial owners.

(1) In general.

(2) Time for providing information.

(3) Manner of providing information

(4) Clearing organization.

(k) Coordination with other information reporting rules.

(l) Backup withholding requirements.

(m) Penalties for failure to comply.

(n) Effective date.

(b) *Definitions.*—Solely for purposes of this section:

(1) An *asset* includes any real or personal, tangible or intangible property held by the trust, including an interest in a contract.

(2) An *affected expense* is an expense described in § 1.67-2T(i)(1).

(3) A *beneficial owner* is a trust interest holder (TIH) (as defined in paragraph (b)(20) of this section) that holds a beneficial interest in a widely held fixed investment trust (WHFIT) (as defined in paragraph (b)(22) of this section.)

(4) The *calculation period* is the period the trustee chooses under paragraph (c)(1)(ii) of this section for calculating the trust information required to be provided under paragraph (c) of this section.

(5) The *cash held for distribution* is the amount of cash held by the WHFIT (other than trust sales proceeds and proceeds from sales described in paragraphs (c)(2)(iv)(D)(4), (G), and (H) of this section) less reasonably required reserve funds as of the date that the amount of a distribution is required to be determined under the WHFIT's governing document.

(6) A *clean-up call* is the redemption of all trust interests in termination of the WHFIT when the administrative costs of the WHFIT outweigh the benefits of maintaining the WHFIT.

(7) An *exempt recipient* is—

(i) Any person described in § 1.6049-4(c)(1)(ii);

(ii) A middleman (as defined in paragraph (b)(10) of this section);

(iii) A real estate mortgage investment conduit (as defined in section 860(D)(a)) (REMIC);

(iv) A WHFIT; or

(v) A trust or an estate for which the trustee or middleman of the WHFIT is also required to file a Form 1041, "U.S. Income Tax Return for Estates and Trusts," in its capacity as a fiduciary of that trust or estate.

(8) An *in-kind redemption* is a redemption in which a beneficial owner receives a pro-rata share of each of the assets of the WHFIT that the beneficial owner is deemed to own under section 671. For example, for purposes of this paragraph (b)(8), if beneficial owner A owns a one percent interest in a WHFIT that holds 100 shares of X corporation stock, so that A is considered to own a one percent interest in each of the 100 shares, A's pro-rata share of the X corporation stock for this purpose is one share of X corporation stock.

(9) An *item* refers to an item of income, expense, or credit as well as any trust event (for example, the sale of an asset) or any characteristic or attribute of the trust that affects the income, deductions, and credits reported by a beneficial owner in any taxable year that the beneficial owner holds an interest in the trust. An item may refer to an individual item or a group of items depending on whether the item must be reported separately under paragraphs (c)(1)(i) and (e)(1) of this section.

(10) A *middleman* is any TIH, other than a qualified intermediary as defined in § 1.1031(k)-1(g), who, at any time during the calendar year, holds an interest in a WHFIT on behalf of, or for the account of, another TIH, or who otherwise acts in a capacity as an intermediary for the account of another person. A middleman includes, but is not limited to—

(i) A custodian of a person's account, such as a bank, financial institution, or brokerage firm acting as custodian of an account;

(ii) A nominee;

(iii) A joint owner of an account or instrument other than—

(A) A joint owner who is the spouse of the other owner; and

(B) A joint owner who is the beneficial owner and whose name appears on the Form 1099 filed with respect to the trust interest under paragraph (d) of this section; and

(iv) A broker (as defined in section 6045(c)(1) and § 1.6045-1(a)(1))), holding an interest for a customer in street name.

(11) A *mortgage* is an obligation that is principally secured by an interest in real property within the meaning of § 1.860G-2(a)(5), except that a mortgage does not include an interest in another WHFIT or mortgages held by another WHFIT.

(12) A *non-mortgage widely held fixed investment trust* (NMWHFIT) is a WHFIT other than a widely held mortgage trust (as defined in paragraph (b)(23) of this section).

(13) A *non pro-rata partial principal payment* is any partial payment of principal received on a debt instrument which does not retire the debt instrument and which is not a pro-rata prepayment described in § 1.1275-2(f)(2).

(14) The *redemption asset proceeds* equal the redemption proceeds (as defined in paragraph (b)(15) of this section) less the cash held for distribution with respect to the redeemed trust interest.

(15) The *redemption proceeds* equal the total amount paid to a redeeming TIH as the result of a redemption of a trust interest.

(16) A *requesting person* is—

(i) A middleman;

(ii) A beneficial owner who is a broker;

(iii) A beneficial owner who is an exempt recipient who holds a trust interest directly and not through a middleman;

(iv) A noncalendar-year beneficial owner who holds a trust interest directly and not through a middleman; or

(v) A representative or agent of a person specified in this paragraph (b)(16).

(17) The *sales asset proceeds* equal the sales proceeds (as defined in paragraph (b)(18) of this section) less the cash held for distribution with respect to the sold trust interest at the time of the sale.

(18) The *sales proceeds* equal the total amount paid to a selling TIH in consideration for the sale of a trust interest.

(19) The *start-up date* is the date on which substantially all of the assets have been deposited with the trustee of the WHFIT.

(20) A *trust interest holder* (TIH) is any person who holds a direct or indirect interest, including a beneficial interest, in a WHFIT at any time during the calendar year.

(21) *Trust sales proceeds* equal the amount paid to a WHFIT for the sale or disposition of an asset held by the WHFIT, including principal payments received by the WHFIT that completely retire a debt instrument (other than a final scheduled principal payment) and pro-rata partial principal prepayments described under § 1.1275-2(f)(2). Trust sales proceeds do not include amounts paid for any interest income that would be required to be reported under § 1.6045-1(d)(3). Trust sales proceeds also do not include amounts paid to a NMWHFIT as the result of pro-rata sales of trust assets to effect a redemption described in paragraph (c)(2)(iv)(G) of this section or the value of assets received as a result of a tax-free corporate reorganization as described in paragraph (c)(2)(iv)(H) of this section.

(22) A *widely held fixed investment trust* (WHFIT) is an arrangement classified as a trust under § 301.7701-4(c) of this chapter, provided that—

(i) The trust is a United States person under section 7701(a)(30)(E);

(ii) The beneficial owners of the trust are treated as owners under subpart E, part I, subchapter J, chapter 1 of the Internal Revenue Code; and

(iii) At least one interest in the trust is held by a middleman.

(23) A *widely held mortgage trust* (WHMT) is a WHFIT, the assets of which consist only of one or more of the following—

(i) Mortgages;

(ii) Regular interests in a REMIC;

(iii) Interests in another WHMT;

(iv) Reasonably required reserve funds;

(v) Amounts received on the assets described in paragraphs (b)(23)(i), (ii), (iii), and (iv) of this section pending distribution to TIHs; and

(vi) During a brief initial funding period, cash and short-term contracts for the purchase of the assets described in paragraphs (b)(23)(i), (ii), and (iii).

(c) *Trustee's obligation to report information.*—(1) *In general.*—Upon the request of a requesting person (as defined in paragraph (b)(16) of this section), a trustee of a WHFIT must report the information described in paragraph (c)(2) of this section to the requesting person. The trustee must determine such information in accordance with the following rules—

(i) *Calculation.*—WHFIT information may be calculated in any manner that enables a requesting person to determine with reasonable accuracy the WHFIT items described in paragraph (c)(2) of this section that are attributable (or, if permitted under paragraphs (c)(2)(iv)(B) or (f)(2)(iii) of this section, distributed) to a beneficial owner for the taxable year of that owner. The manner of calculation must generally conform with industry practice for calculating the WHFIT items described in paragraph (c)(2) of this section for the type of asset or assets held by the WHFIT, and must enable a requesting person to separately state any WHFIT item that, if taken into account separately by a beneficial owner, would result in an income tax liability different from that which would result if the owner did not take the item into account separately.

(ii) *Calculation period.*—WHFIT information may be calculated on the basis of a calendar month, calendar quarter, or half or full calendar year, provided that a trustee uses the same calculation period for the life of the WHFIT and the information provided by the trustee meets the requirements of paragraph (c)(1)(i) of this section. Regardless of the calculation period chosen by the trustee, the trustee must provide information requested by a requesting person under paragraph (c)(5) on a calendar year basis. The trustee may provide additional information to requesting persons throughout the calendar year at the trustee's discretion.

(iii) *Accounting method.*—(A) *General rule.*—WHFIT information must be calculated and reported using the cash receipts and disbursements method of accounting unless another method is required by the Internal Revenue Code or regulations with respect to a specific trust item. Accordingly, a trustee must provide information necessary for TIHs to comply with the rules of subtitle A, chapter 1, subchapter P, part V, subpart A of the Internal Revenue Code, which require the inclusion of accrued amounts with respect to OID, and section 860B(b), which requires the inclusion of accrued amounts with respect to a REMIC regular interest.

(B) *Exception for WHFITs marketed predominantly to taxpayers on the accrual method.*—If the trustee or the trust's sponsor knows or reasonably should know that a WHFIT is marketed primarily to accrual method TIHs and the WHFIT holds assets for which the timing of the recognition of income is materially affected by the use of the accrual method of accounting, the trustee must calculate and report trust information using the accrual method of accounting.

(iv) *Gross income requirement.*—The amount of income required to be reported by the trustee is the gross income (as defined in section 61) generated by the WHFIT's assets. Thus, in the case of a WHFIT that receives a payment of income from which an expense (or expenses) has been deducted, the trustee, in calculating the income to be reported under paragraph (c)(2)(ii) of this section, must report the income earned on the trusts assets unreduced by the deducted expense or expenses and separately report the deducted expense or expenses. See paragraph (c)(2)(iv) of this section regarding reporting with respect to sales and dispositions.

(2) *Information to be reported by all WHFITs.*—With respect to all WHFITs—

(i) *Trust identification and calculation period chosen.*—The trustee must report information identifying the WHFIT, including—

(A) The name of the WHFIT;

(B) The employer identification number of the WHFIT;

(C) The name and address of the trustee;

(D) The Committee on Uniform Security Identification Procedure (CUSIP) number, account number, serial number, or other identifying number of the WHFIT;

(E) The classification of the WHFIT as either a WHMT or NMWHFIT; and

(F) The calculation period used by the trustee.

(ii) *Items of income, expense, and credit.*—The trustee must report information detailing—

(A) All items of gross income (including OID, except than OID is not required to be included for a WHMT that has a start-up date (as defined in paragraph (b)(19) of this section) prior to August 13, 1998).

(B) All items of expense (including affected expenses); and

(C) All items of credit.

(iii) *Non pro-rata partial principal payments.*—The trustee must report information detailing non pro-rata partial principal payments (as defined in paragraph (b)(13) of this section) received by the WHFIT.

(iv) *Asset sales and dispositions.*—The trustee must report information regarding sales and dispositions of WHFIT assets as required in this paragraph (c)(2)(iv). For purposes of this paragraph (c)(2)(iv), a payment (other than a final scheduled payment) that completely retires a debt instrument (including a mortgage held by a WHMT) or a pro-rata prepayment on a debt instrument (see § 1.1275-2(f)(2)) held by a WHFIT must be reported as a full or partial sale or disposition of the debt instrument. Pro-rata sales of trust assets to effect redemptions, as defined in paragraph (c)(2)(iv)(G) of this section, or exchanges of trust assets as the result of a corporate reorganization under paragraph (c)(2)(iv)(H) of this section, are not reported as sales or dispositions under this paragraph (c)(2)(iv).

(A) *General rule.*—Except as provided in paragraph (c)(2)(iv)(B) (regarding the exception for certain NMWHFITs) or paragraph (c)(2)(iv)(C) (regarding the exception for certain WHMTs) of this section, the trustee must report with respect to each sale or disposition of a WHFIT asset—

(1) The date of each sale or disposition;

(2) Information that enables a requesting person to determine the amount of trust sales proceeds (as defined in paragraph (b)(21) of this section) attributable to a beneficial owner as a result of each sale or disposition; and

(3) Information that enables a beneficial owner to allocate, with reasonable accuracy, a portion of the owner's basis in its trust interest to each sale or disposition.

(B) *Exception for certain NMWHFITs.*—If a NMWHFIT meets paragraph (c)(2)(iv)(D)(*1*)(regarding the general de minimis test), paragraph (c)(2)(iv)(E) (regarding the qualified NMWHFIT exception), or paragraph (c)(2)(iv)(F) (regarding the NMWHFIT final calendar year exception) of this section, the trustee is not required to report under paragraph (c)(2)(iv)(A) of this section. Instead, the trustee must report sufficient information to enable a requesting person to determine the amount of trust sales proceeds distributed to a beneficial owner during the calendar year with respect to each sale or disposition of a trust asset. The trustee also must provide requesting persons with a statement that the NMWHFIT is permitted to report under this paragraph (c)(2)(iv)(B).

(C) *Exception for certain WHMTs.*—If a WHMT meets either the general or the special de minimis test of paragraph (c)(2)(iv)(D) of this section for the calendar year, the trustee is not required to report under paragraph (c)(2)(iv)(A) of this section. Instead, the trustee must report information to enable a requesting person to determine the amount of trust sales proceeds attributable to a beneficial owner as a result of the sale or disposition. The trustee also must provide requesting persons with a statement that the WHMT is permitted to report under this paragraph (c)(2)(iv)(C).

(D) *De minimis tests.*—*(1) General WHFIT de minimis test.*—The general WHFIT de minimis test is satisfied if trust sales proceeds for the calendar year are not more than five percent of the net asset value of the trust (aggregate fair market value of the trust's assets less the trust's liabilities) as of the later of January 1 and the start-up date (as defined paragraph (b)(19) of this section); or, if the trustee chooses, the later of January 1 and the measuring date. The measuring date is the date of the last deposit of assets into the WHFIT (not including any deposit of assets into the WHFIT pursuant to a distribution reinvestment program), not to exceed 90 days after the date the registration statement of the WHFIT becomes effective under the Securities Act of 1933.

(2) Special WHMT de minimis test.—A WHMT that meets the asset requirement of paragraph (g)(1)(ii)(E) of this section satisfies the special WHMT de minimis test in this paragraph (c)(2)(iv)(D)(*2*) if trust sales proceeds for the calendar year are not more than five percent of the aggregate outstanding principal balance of the WHMT (as defined in paragraph (g)(1)(iii)(D) of this section) as of the later of January 1 of that year or the trust's start-up date. For purposes of applying the special WHMT de minimis test in this paragraph (c)(2)(iv)(D)(*2*), amounts that result from the complete or partial payment of the outstanding principal balance of the mortgages held by the trust are not included in the amount of trust sales proceeds. The IRS and the Treasury Department may provide by revenue ruling, or by other published guidance, that the special de minimis test of this paragraph (c)(2)(iv)(D)(*2*) may be applied to WHFITs holding debt instruments other than those described in paragraph (g)(1)(ii)(E) of this section.

(3) Effect of clean-up call.—If a WHFIT fails to meet either de minimis test described in this paragraph (c)(2)(iv)(D) solely as the result of a clean-up call, as defined in paragraph (b)(6) of this section, the WHFIT will be treated as having met the de minimis test.

(4) Exception for certain fully reported sales.—*(i) Rule.*—If a trustee of a NMWHFIT reports the sales described in paragraph (c)(2)(iv)(D)(*4*)(*ii*) of this section as provided under paragraph (c)(2)(iv)(A) of this section (regardless of whether the general minimis test in paragraph (c)(2)(iv)(D)(*1*) of this section is satisfied for a particular calendar year) consistently throughout the life of the WHFIT, a trustee may exclude the trust sales proceeds received by the WHFIT as a result of those sales from the trust sales proceeds used to determine whether a WHFIT has satisfied the general de minimis test in paragraph (c)(2)(iv)(D)(*1*) of this section.

(ii) Applicable sales and dispositions.—This paragraph (c)(2)(iv)(D)(*4*) applies to sales and dispositions resulting from corporate reorganizations and restructurings for which the trust receives cash, the sale of assets received by the trust in corporate reorganizations and restructurings (including conversions of closed-end investment companies to open-end investment companies), principal prepayments, bond calls, bond maturities, and the sale of securities by the trustee as required by the governing document or applicable law governing fiduciaries in order to maintain the sound investment character of the trust, and any other nonvolitional dispositions of trust assets.

(iii) Certain small sales and dispositions.—If the amount of trust sales proceeds from a sale or disposition described in paragraph (c)(2)(iv)(D)(*4*)(*ii*) of this section is less than .01 percent of the net fair market value of the WHFIT as determined for applying the de minimis test for the calendar year, the trustee is not required to report the sale or disposition under paragraph (c)(2)(iv)(A) of this section provided the trustee includes the trust sales proceeds, received for purposes of determining whether the trust has met the general de minimis test of paragraph (c)(2)(iv)(D)(*1*) of this section.

(E) *Qualified NMWHFIT exception.*—The qualified NMWHFIT exception is satisfied if—

(1) The NMWHFIT has a start-up date (as defined in paragraph (b)(19) of this section) before February 23, 2006;

(2) The registration statement of the NMWHFIT becomes effective under the Securities Act of 1933, as amended (15 U.S.C. 77a, et. seq.) and trust interests are offered for sale to the public before February 23, 2006; or

(3) The registration statement of the NMWHFIT becomes effective under the Securities Act of 1933 and trust interests are offered for sale to the public on or after February 23, 2006, and before July 31, 2006, and the NMWHFIT is fully funded before October 1, 2006. For purposes of determining whether a NMWHFIT is fully funded under this paragraph (c)(2)(iv)(E), deposits to the NMWHFIT after October 1, 2006, that are made pursuant to a distribution reinvestment program that is consistent with the requirements of § 301.7701-4(c) of this chapter are disregarded.

(F) *NMWHFIT final calendar year exception.*—The NMWHFIT final calendar year exception is satisfied if—

(1) The NMWHFIT terminates on or before December 31 of the year for which the trustee is reporting;

(2) Beneficial owners exchange their interests for cash or are treated as having ex-

changed their interests for cash upon termination of the trust; and

(3) The trustee makes reasonable efforts to engage in pro-rata sales of trust assets to effect redemptions.

(G) *Pro-rata sales of trust assets to effect a redemption.—(1) Rule.*—Pro-rata sales of trust assets to effect redemptions are not required to be reported under this paragraph (c)(2)(iv).

(2) Definition.—Pro-rata sales of trust assets to effect redemptions occur when—

(i) One or more trust interests are tendered for redemption;

(ii) The trustee identifies the pro-rata shares of the trust assets that are deemed to be owned by the trust interest or interests tendered for redemption (See paragraph (b)(8) of this section for a description of how pro-rata is to be applied for purposes of this paragraph (c)(2)(iv)(G)) and sells those assets as soon as practicable;

(iii) Proceeds from the sales of the assets identified in paragraph (c)(2)(iv)(G)(2)*(ii)* of this section are used solely to effect redemptions; and

(iv) The redemptions are reported as required under paragraph (c)(2)(v) of this section by the trustee.

(3) Additional rules.—(i) Calendar month aggregation.—The trustee may compare the aggregate pro-rata share of the assets deemed to be owned by the trust interests tendered for redemption during the calendar month with the aggregate sales of assets to effect redemptions for the calendar month to determine the pro-rata sales of trust assets to effect redemptions for the calendar month. If the aggregate pro-rata share of an asset deemed to be owned by the trust interests tendered for redemption for the month is a fractional amount, the trustee may round that number up to the next whole number for the purpose of determining the pro-rata sales to effect redemptions for the calendar month;

(ii) Sales of assets to effect redemptions may be combined with sales of assets for other purposes.—Sales of assets to effect redemptions may be combined with the sales of assets to obtain cash for other purposes but the proceeds from the sales of assets to effect redemptions must be used solely to provide cash for redemptions and the sales of assets to obtain cash for other purposes must be reported as otherwise provided in this paragraph (c)(2)(iv). For example, if a trustee sells assets and the proceeds are used by the trustee to pay trust expenses, these amounts are to be included in the amounts reported under paragraph (c)(2)(iv)(A) or (B), as appropriate.

(4) Example.—(i) January 1, 2008.—Trust has one million trust interests and all interests have equal value and equal rights. The number of shares of stock in corporations A through J and the pro-rata share of each stock that a trust interest is deemed to own as of the January 1, 2008, is as follows:

STOCK	TOTAL SHARES	PER TRUST INTEREST
A	24,845	.024845
B	28,273	.028273
C	35,575	.035575
D	13,866	.013866
E	25,082	.C25082
F	39,154	.039154
G	16,137	.016137
H	14,704	.014704
I	17,436	.017436
J	31,133	.031133

(ii) Transactions of January 2, 2008.—On January 2, 2008, 50,000 trust interests are tendered for redemption. The deemed pro-rata ownership of stocks A through J represented by the 50,000 redeemed trust interests and the stocks sold to provide cash for the redemptions are set out in the following table:

STOCK	DEEMED PRO-RATA OWNERSHIP	SHARES SOLD
A	1,242.25	1,242
B	1,413.65	1,413
C	1,778.75	1,779
D	693.30	694
E	1,254.10	1,254
F	1,957.70	1,957
G	806.85	807
H	735.20	735
I	871.80	872
J	1,556.65	1.557

(iii) Transactions on January 15 through 17 2008.—On January 15, 2008, 10,000 trust interests are tendered for redemption. Trustee lends money to Trust for redemptions. On January 16, B merges into C at a rate of .55 per share. On January 17, Trustee sells stock to obtain cash to be reimbursed the cash loaned to Trust to effect the redemptions. The pro-rata share of the stock deemed to be owned by the 10,000 redeemed trust interests and the stock sold by the trustee to effect the redemptions are set out in the following table:

STOCK	DEEMED PRO-RATA OWNERSHIP	SHARES SOLD
A	248.45	249
B	00	00
C	511.25	512
D	138.66	138

STOCK	DEEMED PRO-RATA OWNERSHIP	SHARES SOLD
E	250.82	251
F	391.54	392
G	161.37	162
H	147.04	148
I	174.36	174
J	311.33	311

(iv) Transactions on January 28 and 29, 2008.—On January 28, 2008, the value of the H stock is $30.00 per share and Trustee, pursuant to Trust's governing document, sells the H stock to preserve the financial integrity of Trust and receives $414, 630. Trustee intends to report this sale under paragraph (c)(2)(iv)(A) of this section and to distribute the proceeds of the sale pro-rata to trust interest holders on Trust's next scheduled distribution date. On January 29, 2008, while trustee still holds the proceeds from the January 28 sale, 10,000 trust interests are tendered for redemption. The pro-rata share of the stock deemed to be owned by the 10,000 redeemed trust interests and the stock sold by the trustee to effect the redemptions are set out in the following table:

STOCK	DEEMED PRO-RATA OWNERSHIP	SHARES SOLD
A	248.45	248
B	0	0
C	511.25	511
D	138.66	139
E	250.82	251
F	391.54	391
G	161.37	161
H	0 Share of cash proceeds: $4,458.39	0
I	174.36	175
J	311.33	312

(v) Monthly amounts.—To determine the pro-rata sales to effect redemptions for January, trustee compares the aggregate pro-rata share of stocks A through J (rounded to the next whole number) deemed to be owned by the trust interests tendered for redemption during the month of January with the sales of stocks A through J to effect redemptions:

STOCK	DEEMED PRO-RATA OWNERSHIP	SHARES SOLD
A	1740	1739
B	0	0
C	3579	3579
D	971	971
E	1756	1756
F	2741	2741
G	1130	1130
H	883	883
I	1221	1221
J	2180	2180

(vi) Pro-rata sales to effect redemptions for the month of January.—For the month of January, the deemed pro-rata ownership of shares of stocks A through J equal or exceed the sales of stock to effect redemptions for the month. Accordingly, all of the sales to effect redemptions during the month of January are considered to be pro-rata and are not required to be reported under this paragraph (c)(2)(iv).

(H) *Corporate Reorganizations.*—The exchange of trust assets for other assets of equivalent value pursuant to a tax free corporate reorganization is not required to be reported as a sale or disposition under this paragraph (c)(2)(iv).

(v) *Redemptions and sales of WHFIT interests.*—(A) *Redemptions.*—*(1) In general.*—Unless paragraph (c)(2)(v)(C) of this section applies, for each date on which the amount of a redemption proceeds for the redemption of a trust interest is determined, the trustee must provide information to enable a requesting person to determine—

(i) The redemption proceeds (as defined in paragraph (b)(15) of this section) per trust interest on that date;

(ii) The redemption asset proceeds (as defined in paragraph (b)(14) of this section) per trust interest on that date; and

(iii) The gross income that is attributable to the redeeming beneficial owner for the portion of the calendar year that the redeeming beneficial owner held its interest (including income earned by the WHFIT after the date of the last income distribution.

(2) In kind redemptions.—The value of the assets received with respect to an in-kind redemption (as defined in paragraph (b)(8) of this section) is not required to be reported under this paragraph (c)(2)(v)(A). Information regarding the income attributable to a redeeming beneficial owner must, however, be reported under paragraph (c)(2)(v)(A)*(1)(iii)* of this section.

(B) *Sale of a trust interest.*—Under paragraph (c)(2)(v)(C) of this section applies, if a secondary market for interests in the WHFIT is established, the trustee must provide, for each day of the calendar year, information to enable requesting persons to determine—

(1) The sale assets proceeds (as defined in paragraph (b)(17) of this section) per trust interest on that date; and

(2) The gross income that is attributable to a selling beneficial owner and to a purchasing beneficial owner for the portion of the calendar year that each held the trust interest.

(C) *Simplified Reporting for Certain NMWHFITs.—(1) In general.*—The trustee of a NMWHFIT described in paragraph (c)(2)(v)(C)(*2*) of this section is not required to report the information described in paragraph (c)(2)(v)(A) of this section (regarding redemptions) or (c)(2)(v)(B) of this section (regarding sales). However, the trustee must report to requesting persons, for each date on which the amount of redemption proceeds to be paid for the redemption of a trust interest is determined, information that will enable requesting persons to determine the redemption proceeds per trust interest on that date. The trustee also must provide requesting persons with a statement that this paragraph applies to the NMWHFIT.

(2) NMWHFITs that qualify for the exception.—This paragraph (c)(2)(v)(C) applies to a NMWHFIT if—

(i) Substantially all the assets of the NMWHFIT produce income that is treated as interest income (but only if these assets trade on a recognized exchange or securities market without a price component attributable to accrued interest) or produce dividend income (as defined in section 6042(b) and the regulations under that section). (Trust sales proceeds and gross proceeds from sales described in paragraphs (c)(2)(iv)(G) and (H) of this section are ignored for the purpose of determining if substantially all of a NMWHFIT's assets produce dividend or the interest income described in this paragraph); and

(ii) The qualified NMWHFIT exception of paragraph (c)(2)(iv)(E) of this section is satisfied, or the trustee is required by the governing document of the NMWHFIT to determine and distribute all cash held for distribution (as defined in paragraph (b)(5) of this section) no less frequently than monthly. A NMWHFIT will be considered to have satisfied this paragraph (c)(2)(v)(C)(*2*)(*i*) notwithstanding that the governing document of the NMWHFIT permits the trustee to forego making a required monthly or more frequent distribution, if the cash held for distribution is less than 0.1 percent of the aggregate net asset value of the trust as of the date specified in the governing document for calculating the amount of the monthly distribution.

(vi) *Information regarding bond premium.*—The trustee generally must report information that enables a beneficial owner to determine, in any manner that is reasonably consistent with section 171, the amount of the beneficial owner's amortizable bond premium, if any, for each calendar year. However, if a NMWHFIT meets the general de minimis test in paragraph (c)(2)(iv)(D)(*1*) of this section, the qualified NMWHFIT exception of paragraph (c)(2)(iv)(E) of this section, or the NMWHFIT final calendar year exception of paragraph (c)(2)(iv)(F) of this section, the trustee of the NMWHFIT is not required to report information regarding bond premium.

(vii) *Information regarding market discount.*—The trustee generally must report information that enables a beneficial owner to determine, in any manner reasonably consistent with section 1276 (including section 1276(a)(3)), the amount of market discount that has accrued during the calendar year. However, if a NMWHFIT meets the general de minimis test in paragraph (c)(2)(iv)(D) of this section, the qualified NMWHFIT exception of paragraph (c)(2)(iv)(E) of this section, or the NMWHFIT final calendar year exception of paragraph (c)(2)(iv)(F) of this section, the trustee of such NMWHFIT is not required to provide information regarding market discount.

(viii) *Other information.*—The trustee must provide any other information necessary for a beneficial owner of a trust interest to report, with reasonable accuracy, the items (as defined in paragraph (b)(9) of this section) attributable to the portion of the trust treated as owned by the beneficial owner under section 671.

(3) *Identifying the representative who will provide trust information.*—The trustee must identify a representative of the WHFIT who will provide the information specified in this paragraph (c). The trustee also may identify an Internet website at which the trustee will provide the information specified in this paragraph (c). This information must be—

(i) Printed in a publication generally read by, and available to, requesting persons;

(ii) Stated in the trust's prospectus; or

(iii) Posted at the trustee's Internet website.

(4) *Time and manner of providing information.*—(i) *Time.*—(A) *In general.*—Except as provided in paragraph (c)(4)(i)(B) of this section, a trustee must provide the information specified in this paragraph (c) to requesting persons on or before the later of—

(1) The 30th day after the close of the calendar year to which the request relates; or

(2) The day that is 14 days after the receipt of the request.

(B) *Trusts holding interests in other WHFITs or in REMICs.*—If the WHFIT holds an interest in one or more other WHFITs or holds one or more REMIC regular interests, or holds both, a trustee must provide the information specified in this paragraph (c) to requesting persons on or before the later of—

(1) The 44th day after the close of the calendar year to which the request relates; or

(2) The day that is 28 days after the receipt of the request.

(ii) *Manner.*—The information specified in this paragraph (c) must be provided—

(A) By written statement sent by first class mail to the address provided by the requesting person;

(B) By causing it to be printed in a publication generally read by and available to requesting persons and by notifying requesting persons in writing of the publication in which it will appear, the date on which it will appear, and, if possible, the page on which it will appear;

(C) By causing it to be posted at an Internet website, provided the trustee identifies the website under paragraph (c)(3) of this section;

(D) By electronic mail provided that the requesting person requests that the trustee furnish the information by electronic mail and the person furnishes an electronic address; or

(E) By any other method agreed to by the trustee and the requesting person.

(iii) *Inclusion of information with respect to all calculation periods.*—If a trustee calculates WHFIT information using a calculation period other than a calendar year, the trustee must provide information for each calculation period that falls within the calendar year requested.

(5) *Requesting information from a WHFIT.*—(i) *In general.*—Requesting persons may request the information specified in this paragraph (c) from a WHFIT.

(ii) *Manner of requesting information.*—In requesting WHFIT information, a requesting person must specify the WHFIT and the calendar year for which information is requested.

(iii) *Period of time during which a requesting person may request WHFIT information.*—For the life of the WHFIT and for five years following the date of the WHFIT's termination, a requesting person may request the information specified in this paragraph (c) for any calendar year of the WHFIT's existence beginning with the 2007 calendar year.

(6) *Trustee's requirement to retain records.*—For the life of the WHFIT and for five years following the date of termination of the WHFIT, the trustee must maintain in its records a copy of the information required to be provided to requesting persons this paragraph (c) for each calendar year beginning with the 2007 calendar year. For a period of five years following the close of the calendar year to which the data pertains, the trustee also must maintain in its records such supplemental data as may be necessary to establish that the information provided to requesting persons is correct and meets the requirements of this paragraph (c).

(d) *Form 1099 requirement for trustees and middlemen.*—(1) *Obligation to file Form 1099 with the IRS.*—(i) *In general.*—Except as provided in paragraphs (d)(1)(ii) and (iii) of this section—

(A) The trustee must file with the IRS the appropriate Forms 1099, reporting the information specified in paragraph (d)(2) of this section with respect to any TIH who holds an interest in the WHFIT directly and not through a middleman; and

(B) Every middleman must file with the IRS the appropriate Forms 1099, reporting the information specified in paragraph (d)(2) of this section with respect to any TIH on whose behalf or account the middleman holds an interest in the WHFIT or acts as an intermediary.

(ii) *Forms 1099 not required for exempt recipients.*—(A) *In general.*—A Form 1099 is not required with respect to a TIH who is an exempt recipient (as defined in paragraph (b)(7) of this section), unless the trustee or middleman backup withholds under section 3406 on payments made to an exempt recipient (because, for example, the exempt recipient has failed to furnish a Form W-9 on request). If the trustee or middleman backup withholds, then the trustee or middleman is required to file a Form 1099 under this paragraph (d) unless the trustee or middleman refunds the amount withheld in accordance with § 31.6413(a)-3 of this chapter.

(B) *Exempt recipients must include WHFIT information in computing taxable income.*—A beneficial owner who is an exempt recipient must obtain WHFIT information and must include the items (as defined in paragraph (b)(9) of this section) of the WHFIT in computing its taxable income on its federal income tax return. Paragraphs (c)(3) and (h) of this section provide rules for exempt recipients to obtain information from a WHFIT.

(iii) *Reporting and withholding with respect to foreign persons.*—The items of the WHFIT attributable to a TIH who is not a United States person must be reported, and amounts must be withheld, as provided under subtitle A, chapter 3 of the Internal Revenue Code (sections 1441 through 1464) and the regulations thereunder and not reported under this paragraph (d).

(2) *Information to be reported.*—(i) *Determining amounts to be provided on Forms 1099.*—The amounts reported to the IRS for a calendar year by a trustee or middleman on the appropriate Form 1099 must be consistent with the information provided by the trustee under paragraph (c) of this section and must reflect with reasonable accuracy the amount of each item required to be reported on a Form 1099 that is attributable (or if permitted under paragraphs (d)(2)(ii)(D) and (E) of this section, distributed) to the TIH. If the trustee, in providing WHFIT information, uses the safe harbors in paragraph (f)(1) or (g)(1) of this section, then the trustee or middleman must calculate the information to be provided to the IRS on the Forms 1099 in accordance with paragraph (f)(2) or (g)(2) of this section, as appropriate.

(ii) *Information to be provided on Forms 1099.*—The trustee or middleman must include on the appropriate Forms 1099:

(A) *Taxpayer information.*—The name, address, and taxpayer identification number of the TIH;

(B) *Information regarding the person filing the Form 1099.*—The name, address, taxpayer identification number, and telephone number of the person required to file the Form 1099;

(C) *Gross income.*—All items of gross income of the WHFIT attributable to the TIH for the calendar year (including OID (unless the exception for certain WHMTs applies (see paragraph (c)(2)(ii)(A) of this section)) and all amounts of income attributable to a selling, purchasing, or redeeming TIH for the portion of the calendar year that the TIH held its interest (unless paragraph (c)(2)(v)(C) of this section (regarding an exception for certain NMWHFITs) applies));

(D) *Non pro-rata partial principal payments.*—All non pro-rata partial principal payments (as defined in paragraph (b)(13) of this section) received by the WHFIT that are attributable (or distributed, in the case of a trustee or middleman reporting under paragraph (f)(2)(iii) of this section) to the TIH;

(E) *Trust sales proceeds.*—All trust sales proceeds (as defined in paragraph (b)(21) of this section) that are attributable to the TIH for the calendar year, if any, or, if paragraph (c)(2)(iv)(B) of this section (regarding certain NMWHFITs) applies, the amount of trust sales proceeds distributed to the TIH for the calendar year;

(F) *Reporting Redemptions.*—All redemption asset proceeds (as defined in paragraph (b)(14) of this section) paid to the TIH for the calendar year, if any, or if paragraph (c)(2)(v)(C) of this section (regarding an exception for certain NMWHFITs) applies, all redemption proceeds (as defined in paragraph (b)(15) of this section) paid to the TIH for the calendar year;

(G) *Reporting sales of a trust interest on a secondary market.*—All sales asset proceeds (as defined in paragraph (b)(17) of this section) paid to the TIH for the sale of a trust interest or interests on a secondary market established for the NMWHFIT for the calendar year, if any, or, if paragraph (c)(2)(v)(C) of this section (regarding an exception for certain NMWHFITs) applies, all sales proceeds (as defined in paragraph (b)(18) of this section) paid to the TIH for the calendar year; and

(H) *Other information.*—Any other information required by the Form 1099.

(3) *Time and manner of filing Forms 1099.*—(i) *Time and place.*—The Forms 1099 required to be filed under this paragraph (d) must be filed on or before February 28 (March 31, if filed electronically) of the year following the year for which the Forms 1099 are being filed. The returns must be filed with the appropriate Internal Revenue Service Center, at the address listed in the instructions for the Forms 1099. For extensions of time for filing returns under this section, see § 1.6081-1, the instructions for the Forms 1099, and applicable revenue procedures (see § 601.601(d)(2) of this chapter). For magnetic media filing requirements, see § 301.6011-2 of this chapter.

(ii) *Reporting trust sales proceeds, redemption asset proceeds, redemption proceeds, sale asset proceeds, sales proceeds and non pro-rata partial principal payments.*—(A) *Form to be used.*—Trust sales proceeds, redemption asset proceeds, redemption proceeds, sale asset proceeds, sales proceeds, and non pro-rata partial principal payments are to be reported on the same type of Form 1099 as that required for reporting gross proceeds under section 6045.

(B) *Appropriate reporting for in-kind redemptions.*—The value of the assets distributed with respect to an in-kind redemption is not required to be reported to the IRS. Unless paragraph (c)(2)(v)(C) of this section applies, the trustee or middleman must report the gross income attributable to the redeemed trust interest for the calendar year up to the date of the redemption under paragraph (d)(2)(ii)(C) of this section.

(e) *Requirement to furnish a written tax information statement to the TIH.*—(1) *In general.*—Every trustee or middleman required to file appropriate Forms 1099 under paragraph (d) of this section with respect to a TIH must furnish to that TIH (the person whose identifying number is required to be shown on the form) a written tax information statement showing the information described in paragraph (e)(2) of this section. The amount of a trust item reported to a TIH under this paragraph (e) must be consistent with the information reported to the IRS with respect to the TIH under paragraph (d) of this section. Information provided in this written statement must be determined in accordance with the rules provided in paragraph (d)(2)(i) of this section (regardless of whether the information was required to be provided on a Form 1099). Further, the trustee or middleman must separately state on the written tax information statement any items that, if taken into account separately by that TIH, would result in an income tax liability that is different from the income tax liability that would result if the items were not taken into account separately.

(2) *Information required.*—For the calendar year, the written tax information statement must meet the following requirements:

(i) *WHFIT information.*—The written tax information statement must include the name of the WHFIT and the identifying number of the WHFIT;

(ii) *Identification of the person furnishing the statement.*—The written tax information statement must include the name, address, and taxpayer identification number of the person required to furnish the statement;

(iii) *Items of income, expense, and credit.*—The written tax information statement must include information regarding the items of income (that is, the information required to be reported to the IRS on Forms 1099), expense (including affected expenses), and credit that are attributable to the TIH for the calendar year;

(iv) *Non pro-rata partial principal payments.*—The written tax information statement must include the information required to be reported to the IRS on Forms 1099 under paragraph (d)(2)(ii)(D) of this section (regarding the non prorata partial principal payments that are attributable (or distributed, in the case of a trustee or middleman reporting under paragraph (f)(2)(iii) of this section) to the TIH for the calendar year).

(v) *Asset sales and dispositions.*—(A) *General rule.*—Unless paragraph (c)(2)(iv)(B) (regarding the exception for certain NMWHFITs) or (c)(2)(iv)(C) (regarding the exception for certain WHMTs) of this section applies, the written tax information statement must include, with respect to each sale or disposition of a WHFIT asset for the calendar year—

(1) The date of sale or disposition;

(2) Information regarding the trust sales proceeds that are attributable to the TIH as a result of the sale or disposition; and

(3) Information that will enable the TIH to allocate with reasonable accuracy a portion of the TIH's basis in the TIH's trust interest to the sale or disposition.

(B) *Special rule for certain NMWHFITs and WHMTs.*—In the case of a NMWHFIT to which paragraph (c)(2)(iv)(B) of this section applies or in the case of a WHMT to which paragraph (c)(2)(iv)(C) of this section applies, the written tax information statement must include, with respect to asset sales and dispositions, only the information required to be reported to the IRS on Form 1099 under paragraph (d)(2)((ii)(E) of this section.

(vi) *Redemption or sale of a trust interest.*—The written tax information statement must include the information required to be reported to the IRS on Forms 1099 under paragraphs (d)(2)(ii)(F) and (G) of this section (regarding the sales and redemptions of trust interests made by the TIH for the calendar year);

(vii) *Information regarding market discount and bond premium.*—The written tax information statement must include the information required to be reported by the trustee under paragraphs (c)(2)(vi) and (vii) of this section (regarding bond premium and market discount);

(viii) *Other information.*—The written tax information statement must include any other information necessary for the TIH to report, with reasonable accuracy for the calendar year, the items (as defined in paragraph (b)(9) of this section) attributable to the portion of the trust treated as owned by the TIH under section 671. The written tax information statement may include information with respect to a trust item on a per trust interest basis if the trustee has reported (or calculated) the information with respect to that item on a per trust interest basis and information with respect to that item is not required to be reported on a Form 1099; and

(ix) *Required statement.*—The written tax information statement must inform the TIH that the items of income, deduction, and credit, and any other information shown on the statement must be taken into account in computing the taxable income and credits of the TIH on the Federal income tax return of the TIH. If the written tax information statement reports that an amount of qualified dividend income is attributable to the TIH, the written tax information statement also must inform the TIH that the TIH must meet the requirements of section 1(h)(11)(B)(iii) to treat the dividends as qualified dividends.

(3) *Due date and other requirements.*—The written tax information statement must be furnished to the TIH on or before March 15 of the year following the calendar year for which the statement is being furnished.

(4) *Requirement to retain records.*—For a period of no less than five years from the due date for furnishing the written tax information statement, a trustee or middleman must maintain in its records a copy of any written tax information statement furnished to a TIH, and such supplemental data as may be required to establish the correctness of the statement.

(f) *Safe harbor for providing information for certain NMWHFITs.*—(1) *Safe harbor for trustee reporting of NMWHFIT information.*—The trustee of a NMWHFIT that meets the requirements of paragraph (f)(1)(i) of this section is deemed to satisfy paragraph (c)(1)(i) of this section, if the trustee calculates and provides WHFIT information in the manner described in this paragraph (f) and provides a statement to a requesting person giving notice that information has been calculated in accordance with this paragraph (f)(1).

(i) *In general.*—(A) *Eligibility to report under this safe harbor.*—Only NMWHFITs that meet the requirements set forth in paragraphs (f)(1)(i)(A)*(1)* and *(2)* of this section may report under this safe harbor. For purposes of determining whether the requirements of paragraph (f)(1)(i)(A)*(1)* of this section are met, trust sales proceeds and gross proceeds from sales described in paragraphs (c)(2)(iv)(G) and (H) of this section are ignored.

(1) Substantially all of the NMWHFIT's income is from dividends or interest; and

(2) All trust interests have identical value and rights.

(B) *Consistency Requirements.*—The trustee must—

(1) Calculate all trust items subject to the safe harbor consistent with the safe harbor; and,

(2) Report under this paragraph (f)(1) for the life of the NMWHFIT; or, if the NMWHFIT has a start-up date before January 1, 2007, the NMWHFIT must begin reporting under this paragraph (f)(1) as of January 1, 2007 and must continue to report under this paragraph for the life of the NMWHFIT.

(ii) *Reporting NMWHFIT income and expenses.*—A trustee must first determine the total amount of NMWHFIT distributions (both actual and deemed) for the calendar year and then express each income or expense item as a fraction of the total amount of NMWHFIT distributions. These fractions (hereinafter referred to as factors) must be accurate to at least four decimal places.

(A) *Step One: Determine the total amount of NMWHFIT distributions for the calendar year.*—The trustee must determine the total amount of NMWHFIT distributions (actual and deemed) for the calendar year. If the calculation of the total amount of NMWHFIT distributions under this paragraph (f)(1)(ii)(A) results in a zero or a negative number, the trustee may not determine income and expense information under this paragraph (f)(1)(ii)(A) (but may report all other applicable items under this paragraph (f)(1)). The total amount of NMWHFIT distributions equals the amount of NMWHFIT funds paid out to all TIHs (including all trust sales proceeds, all principal receipts, and all redemption proceeds) for the calendar year—

(*1*) Increased by—

(*i*) All amounts that would have been distributed during the calendar year, but were instead reinvested pursuant to a reinvestment plan; and

(*ii*) All cash held for distribution to TIHs as of December 31 of the year for which the trustee is reporting; and

(*2*) Decreased by—

(*i*) All cash distributed during the current year that was included in a year-end cash allocation factor (see paragraph (f)(1)(ii)(C)(*1*) of this section) for a prior year;

(*ii*) All redemption asset proceeds paid for the calendar year, or if paragraph (c)(2)(v)(C) of this section applies to the NMWHFIT, all redemption proceeds paid for the calendar year;

(*iii*) All trust sales proceeds distributed during the calendar year; and

(*iv*) All non pro-rata partial principal payments distributed during the calendar year.

(*3*) For the purpose of determining the amount of all redemption asset proceeds or redemption proceeds paid for the calendar year with respect to paragraph (f)(1)(ii)(A)(*2*)(*ii*) of this section, the value of the assets (not including cash) distributed with respect to an in-kind redemption is disregarded. Any cash distributed as part of the redemption must be included in the total amount of NMWHFIT distributions.

(B) *Step Two: Determine factors that express the ratios of NMWHFIT income and expenses to the total amount of NMWHFIT distributions.*—The trustee must determine factors that express the ratios of NMWHFIT income and expenses to the total amount of NMWHFIT distributions as follows:

(*1*) *Income factors.*—For each item of income generated by the NMWHFIT's assets for the calendar year, the trustee must determine the ratio of the gross amount of that item of income to the total amount of NMWHFIT distributions for the calendar year; and

(*2*) *Expense factors.*—For each item of expense paid by a NMWHFIT during the calendar year, the trustee must determine the ratio of the gross amount of that item of expense to the total amount of NMWHFIT distributions for the calendar year.

(C) *Step Three: Determine adjustments for reconciling the total amount of NMWHFIT distributions (determined under Step One) with amounts actually paid to TIHs.*—Paragraph (f)(1)(ii)(B) of this section (Step Two) requires an item of income or expense to be expressed as a ratio of that item to the total amount of NMWHFIT distributions as determined in paragraph (f)(1)(ii)(A) of this section (Step One). A TIH's share of the total amount of NMWHFIT distributions may differ from the amount actually paid to that TIH. A trustee, therefore, must provide information that can be used to compute a TIH's share of the total amount of NMWHFIT distributions based on the amount actually paid to the TIH. A trustee satisfies this requirement by providing a current year-end cash allocation factor, a prior year cash allocation factor, and the date on which the prior year cash was distributed to TIHs (prior year cash distribution date).

(*1*) *The current year-end cash allocation factor.*—The current year-end cash allocation factor is the amount of cash held for distribution to TIHs by the NMWHFIT as of December 31 of the calendar year for which the trustee is reporting, divided by the number of trust interests outstanding as of that date.

(*2*) *The prior year cash allocation factor.*—The prior year cash allocation factor is the amount of the distribution during the calendar year for which the trustee is reporting that was included in determining a year-end cash allocation factor for a prior year, divided by the number of trust interests outstanding on the date of the distribution.

(iii) *Reporting non pro-rata partial principal payments under the safe harbor.*—The trustee must provide a list of dates on which non pro-rata partial principal payments were distributed by the trust, and the amount distributed, per trust interest.

(iv) *Reporting sales and dispositions of NMWHFIT assets under the safe harbor.*—(A) *NMWHFITs that must report under the general rule.*—(*1*) *In general.*—If a NMWHFIT must report under the general rule of paragraph (c)(2)(iv)(A) of this section, the trustee must provide a list of dates (from earliest to latest) on which sales or dispositions of NMWHFIT assets occurred during the calendar year for which the trustee is reporting and, for each date identified, provide—

(*i*) The trust sales proceeds received by the trust, per trust interest, with respect to the sales and dispositions, on that date;

(ii) The trust sales proceeds distributed to TIHs, per trust interest, with respect to the sales and dispositions on that date, and the date that the trust sales proceeds were distributed to the TIHs; and

(iii) The ratio (expressed as a percentage) of the assets sold or disposed of on that date to all assets held by the NMWHFIT.

(2) Determination of the portion of all assets held by the NMWHFIT that the assets sold or disposed of represented—

(i) If a NMWHFIT terminates within twenty-four months of its start-up date, the ratio of the assets sold or disposed of on that date to all assets held by the NMWHFIT is based on the fair market value of the NMWHFIT's assets as of the start-up date; or

(ii) If a NMWHFIT terminates more than twenty-four months after its start-up date, the ratio of the assets sold or disposed of on that date to all assets held by the NMWHFIT is based on the fair market value of the NMWHFIT's assets as of the date of the sale or disposition.

(B) *NMWHFITs excepted from the general rule*.—If paragraph (c)(2)(iv)(B) of this section applies to the NMWHFIT, the trustee must provide a list of dates on which trust sales proceeds were distributed, and the amount of trust sales proceeds, per trust interest, that were distributed on that date. The trustee also must also provide requesting persons with the statement required by paragraph (c)(2)(iv)(B) of this section.

(v) *Reporting redemptions under the safe harbor*.—(A) *In general*.—The trustee must:

(1) Provide a list of dates on which the amount of redemption proceeds paid for the redemption of a trust interest was determined and the amount of the redemption asset proceeds determined per trust interest on that date, or if paragraph (c)(2)(v)(C) of this section applies to the NMWHFIT, the amount of redemption proceeds determined on that date; or

(2) Provide to each requesting person that held (either for its own behalf or for the behalf of a TIH) a trust interest that was redeemed during the calendar year, the date of the redemption and the amount of the redemption asset proceeds per trust interest determined on that date, or if paragraph (c)(2)(v)(C) of this section applies to the NMWHFIT, the amount of the redemption proceeds determined for that date; and

(B) *Paragraph (c)(2)(v)(C) statement*.—If paragraph (c)(2)(v)(C) of this section applies to the NMWHFIT, the trustee must provide a statement to requesting persons to the effect that the trustee is providing information consistent with paragraph (c)(2)(v)(C) of this section.

(vi) *Reporting the sale of a trust interest under the safe harbor*.—If paragraph (c)(2)(v)(C) of this section does not apply to the NMWHFIT, the trustee must provide, for each day of the calendar year, the amount of cash held for distribution, per trust interest, by the NMWHFIT on that date. If the trustee is able to identify the date on which trust interests were sold on the secondary market, the trustee alternatively may provide information for each day on which sales of trust interests occurred rather than for each day during the calendar year. If paragraph (c)(2)(v)(C) of this section applies to the NMWHFIT, the trustee is not required to provide any information under this paragraph (f)(1)(vi), other than a statement that the NMWHFIT meets the requirements to report under paragraph (c)(2)(v)(C) of this section.

(vii) *Reporting OID information under the safe harbor*.—The trustee must provide, for each calculation period, the average aggregate daily accrual of OID per $1,000 of original principal amount.

(viii) *Reporting market discount information under the safe harbor*.—(A) *In general*.—*(1) Trustee required to provide market discount information*.—If the trustee is required to provide information regarding market discount under paragraph (c)(2)(vii) of this section, the trustee must provide—

(i) The information required to be provided under paragraph (f)(1)(iv)(A)(*1*)(*iii*) of this section; and

(ii) If the NMWHFIT holds debt instruments with OID, a list of the aggregate adjusted issue prices of the debt instruments per trust interest calculated as of the start-up date or measuring date (see paragraph (c)(2)(iv)(D)(*4*) of this section) (whichever provides more accurate information) and as of January 1 for each subsequent year of the NMWHFIT.

(2) Trustee not required to provide market discount information.—If the trustee is not required to provide market discount information under paragraph (c)(2)(vii) of this section (because the NMWHFIT meets the general de minimis test of paragraph (c)(2)(iv)(D)(*1*) of this section, the qualified NMWHFIT exception of paragraph (c)(2)(iv)(E) of this section, or the NMWHFIT final year exception of paragraph (c)(2)(iv)(F) of this section), the trustee is not required under this paragraph (f) to provide any information regarding market discount.

(B) *Reporting market discount information under the safe harbor when the yield of the debt obligations held by the WHFIT is expected to be affected by prepayments*.—[Reserved.]

(ix) *Reporting bond premium information under the safe harbor*.—[Reserved.]

(x) *Reporting additional information*.—If a requesting person cannot use the information provided by the trustee under paragraphs (f)(1)(ii) through (ix) of this section to determine with reasonable accuracy the trust items that are attributable to a TIH, the requesting person must request, and the trustee must provide, additional information to enable the requesting person to determine the trust items that are attributable to the TIH. See, for example, paragraph (f)(2)(ii)(A)(*4*) of this section which requires a middleman to request additional information from the trustee when the total amount of WHFIT distributions attributable to a TIH equals zero or less.

(2) *Use of information provided by trustees under the safe harbor for NMWHFITs.*—(i) *In general.*—If a trustee reports NMWHFIT items in accordance with paragraph (f)(1) of this section, the information provided with respect to those items on the Forms 1099 required under paragraph (d) of this section to be filed with the IRS and on the statement required under paragraph (e) of this section to be furnished to the TIH must be determined as provided in this paragraph (f)(2).

(ii) *Determining NMWHFIT income and expense under the safe harbor.*—The trustee or middleman must determine the amount of each item of income and expense attributable to a TIH as follows—

(A) *Step One: Determine the total amount of NMWHFIT distributions attributable to the TIH.*—To determine the total amount of NMWHFIT distributions attributable to a TIH for the calendar year, the total amount paid to, or credited to the account of, the TIH during the calendar year (including amounts paid as trust sales proceeds or partial non-pro rata principal payments, redemption proceeds, and sales proceeds) is—

(1) Increased by—

(i) All amounts that would have been distributed during the calendar year to the TIH, but that were reinvested pursuant to a reinvestment plan (unless another person (for example, the custodian of the reinvestment plan) is responsible for reporting these amounts under paragraph (d) of this section); and

(ii) An amount equal to the current year-end cash allocation factor (provided by the trustee in accordance with paragraph (f)(1)(ii)(C)(*1*) of this section) multiplied by the number of trust interests held by the TIH as of December 31 of the calendar year for which the trustee is reporting; and

(2) Decreased by—

(i) An amount equal to the prior year cash allocation factor (provided by the trustee in accordance with paragraph (f)(1)(ii)(C)(2) of this section) multiplied by the number of trust interests held by the TIH on the date of the distribution;

(ii) An amount equal to all redemption asset proceeds paid to the TIH for the calendar year, or if paragraph (c)(2)(v)(C) of this section applies to the NMWHFIT, an amount equal to all redemption proceeds paid to the TIH for the calendar year;

(iii) An amount equal to all sale asset proceeds paid to the TIH for the calendar year, or if paragraph (c)(2)(v)(C) of this section applies to the NMWHFIT, the amount of sales proceeds paid to the TIH for the calendar year;

(iv) In the case of a TIH that purchased a trust interest in a NMWHFIT to which paragraph (c)(2)(v)(C) of this section does not apply, an amount equal to the cash held for distribution per trust interest on the date that the TIH acquired its interest, multiplied by the trust interests acquired on that date;

(v) The amount of the trust sales proceeds distributed to the TIH, calculated as provided in paragraph (f)(2)(iv)(A)(3) of this section; and

(vi) The amount of non pro-rata partial principal prepayments distributed to the TIH during the calendar year, calculated as provided in paragraph (f)(2)(iii) of this section.

(3) *Treatment of in-kind distributions under this paragraph (f)(2)(i).*—The value of the assets (not including cash) received with respect to an in-kind redemption is not included in the amount used in paragraph (f)(2)(ii)(A)(2)(*ii*) of this section. The cash distributed as part of the redemption, however, must be included in the total amount of NMWHFIT distributions paid to the TIH.

(4) The total amount of distributions attributable to a TIH calculated under this paragraph (f)(2)(i)(A) equals zero or less.—If the total amount of distributions attributable to a TIH, calculated under this paragraph (f)(2)(i)(A), equals zero or less, the trustee or middleman may not report the income and expense attributable to the TIH under this paragraph (f)(2)(i). The trustee or middleman must request additional information from the trustee of the NMWHFIT to enable the trustee or middleman to determine with reasonable accuracy the items of income and expense that are attributable to the TIH. The trustee or middleman must report the other items subject to paragraph (f)(1) of this section in accordance with this paragraph (f)(2).

(B) *Step Two: Apply the factors provided by the trustee to determine the items of income and expense that are attributable to the TIH.*—The amount of each item of income (other than OID) and each item of expense attributable to a TIH is determined as follows—

(1) Application of income factors.—For each income factor, the trustee or middleman must multiply the income factor by the total amount of NMWHFIT distributions attributable to the TIH for the calendar year (as determined in paragraph (f)(2)(i)(A) of this section).

(2) Application of expense factors.—For each expense factor, the trustee or middleman must multiply the expense factor by the total amount of NMWHFIT distributions attributable to the TIH for the calendar year (as determined in paragraph (f)(2)(i)(A) of this section).

(iii) *Reporting non pro-rata partial principal payments under the safe harbor.*—To determine the amount of non pro-rata partial principal payments that are distributed to a TIH for the calendar year, the trustee or middleman must aggregate the amount of non pro-rata partial principal payments distributed to a TIH for each day that non pro-rata principal payments were distributed. To determine the amount of non pro-rata principal payments that are distributed to a TIH on each distribution date, the trustee or middleman must multiply the amount of non-pro rata principal payments per trust interest distributed on that date by the number of trust interests held by the TIH.

(iv) *Reporting sales and dispositions of NMWHFIT assets under the safe harbor.*—(A) *Reporting under the safe harbor if the general rules apply to the NMWHFIT.*—Unless paragraph (c)(2)(iv)(B) of this section applies, the trustee or middleman must comply with paragraphs (f)(2)(iv)(A)(*1*), (*2*), and (*3*) of this section.

(*1*) *Form 1099.*—The trustee or middleman must report the amount of trust sales proceeds attributable to the TIH for the calendar year on Form 1099. To determine the amount of trust sales proceeds attributable to a TIH for the calendar year, the trustee or middleman must aggregate the total amount of trust sales proceeds attributable to the TIH for each date on which the NMWHFIT sold or disposed of an asset or assets. To determine the total amount of trust sales proceeds attributable to a TIH for each date that the NMWHFIT sold or disposed of an asset or assets, the trustee or middleman multiplies the amount of trust sales proceeds received by the NMWHFIT per trust interest on that date by the number of trust interests held by the TIH on that date.

(*2*) *The written tax information statement furnished to the TIH.*—The written tax information statement required to be furnished to the TIH under paragraph (e) of this section must include a list of dates (in order, from earliest to latest) on which sales or dispositions of trust assets occurred during the calendar year and provide, for each date identified—

(*i*) The trust sales proceeds received by the trust, per trust interest, with respect to the sales or dispositions of trust assets on that date; and

(*ii*) The information provided by the trustee under paragraph (f)(1)(iv)(B)(2) of this section regarding the ratio of the assets sold or disposed of on that date to all the assets of the NMWHFIT held on that date, prior to such sale or disposition.

(*3*) *Calculating the total amount of trust sales proceeds distributed to the TIH.*—To determine the total amount of NMWHFIT distributions attributable to a TIH, the trustee or middleman must calculate the amount of trust sales proceeds distributed to the TIH for the calendar year. (See paragraph (f)(2)(ii)(A)(2)(*v*) of this section.) To determine the amount of trust sales proceeds distributed to a TIH for the calendar year, the trustee or middleman must aggregate the total amount of trust sales proceeds distributed to the TIH for each date on which the NMWHFIT distributed trust sales proceeds. To determine the total amount of trust sales proceeds distributed to a TIH for each date that the NMWHFIT distributed trust sales proceeds, the trustee or middleman must multiply the amount of trust sales proceeds distributed by the NMWHFIT per trust interest on that date by the number of trust interests held by the TIH on that date.

(B) *Reporting under the safe harbor if paragraph (c)(2)(iv)(B) of this section applies to the NMWHFIT.*—If paragraph (c)(2)(iv)(B) of this section applies, the trustee or middleman must calculate, in the manner provided in paragraph (f)(2)(iv)(A)(*3*) of this section, the amount of trust sales proceeds distributed to the TIH for the calendar year. The trustee or middleman must report this amount on the Form 1099 filed for the TIH and on the written tax information statement furnished to the TIH.

(v) *Reporting redemptions under the safe harbor.*—(A) Except as provided in paragraph (f)(2)(v)(B) or (C) of this section, if the trustee has provided a list of dates for which the amount of the redemption proceeds to be paid for the redemption of a trust interest was determined and the redemption asset proceeds paid for that date, the trustee or middleman must multiply the redemption asset proceeds determined per trust interest for that date by the number of trust interests redeemed by the TIH on that date.

(B) If paragraph (c)(2)(v)(C) of this section applies, and the trustee has provided a list of dates for which the amount of the redemption proceeds to be paid for the redemption of a trust interest was determined and the redemption proceeds determined per trust interest on each date, the trustee or middleman must multiply the redemption proceeds per trust interest for each date by the number of trust interests redeemed by the TIH on that date.

(C) If the trustee has provided the requesting person with information regarding the redemption asset proceeds paid for each redemption of a trust interest held by the middleman for the calendar year, or if paragraph (c)(2)(v)(C) of this section applies and the trustee has provided the amount of redemption proceeds paid for each redemption of a trust interest held by the middleman during the calendar year, the requesting person may use this information to determine the amount of the redemption asset proceeds or redemption proceeds paid to the TIH for the calendar year.

(vi) *Reporting sales of trust interests under the safe harbor.*—(A) Except as provided in paragraph (f)(2)(vi)(B) of this section, the trustee or middleman must subtract the amount of cash held for distribution per trust interest on the date of the sale from the sales proceeds paid to the TIH to determine the sale asset proceeds that are to be reported to the TIH for each sale of a trust interest.

(B) If paragraph (c)(2)(v)(C) of this section applies, the trustee or middleman must report the sales proceeds paid to the TIH as a result of each sale of a trust interest.

(vii) *Reporting OID information under the safe harbor.*—The trustee or middleman must aggregate the amounts of OID that are allocable to each trust interest held by a TIH for each calculation period. The amount of OID that is allocable to a trust interest, with respect to each calculation period, is determined by multiplying—

(A) The product of the OID factor and the original principal balance of the trust interest, divided by 1,000; by

(B) The number of days during the OID calculation period in that calendar year that the TIH held the trust interest.

(viii) *Reporting market discount information under the safe harbor.*—(A) Except as provided in paragraph (f)(2)(viii)(B) of this section, the trustee or middleman must provide the TIH with the information provided under paragraph (f)(1)(viii) of this section.

(B) If paragraph (c)(2)(iv)(B) of this section applies, the trustee and middleman are not required under this paragraph (f)(2) to provide any information regarding market discount.

(ix) *Reporting bond premium information under the safe harbor.*—[Reserved]

(3) *Example of the use of the safe harbor for NMWHFITs.*—The following example illustrates the use of the factors in this paragraph (f) to calculate and provide NMWHFIT information:

Example: (i) *Facts*—(A) *In general*—(*1*) Trust is a NMWHFIT that holds common stock in ten different corporations and has 100 trust interests outstanding. The start-up date for Trust is December 15, 2006, and Trust's registration statement under the Securities Act of 1933 became effective after July 31, 2006. Trust terminates on March 15, 2008. The agreement governing Trust requires Trust to distribute cash held by Trust reduced by accrued but unpaid expenses on April 15, July 15, and October 15 of the 2007 calendar year. The agreement also provides that the trust interests will be redeemed by the Trust for an amount equal to the value of the trust interest, as of the close of business, on the day the trust interest is tendered for redemption. There is no reinvestment plan. A secondary market for interests in Trust will be created by Trust's sponsor and Trust's sponsor will provide Trustee with a list of dates on which sales occurred on this secondary market.

(*2*) As of December 31, 2006, Trust holds $12x for distribution to TIHs on the next distribution date and has no accrued but unpaid expenses. Trustee includes the $12x in determining the year-end cash allocation factor for December 31, 2006.

(B) *Events occurring during the 2007 calendar year*— (*1*) As of January 1, 2007, Broker1 holds ten trust interests in Trust in street name for each of *J* and *A* and Broker2 holds ten trust interests in Trust in street name for *S*. *J*, *A*, and *S* are individual, cash method taxpayers.

(*2*) As of January 1, 2007, the fair market value of the Trust's assets equals $10,000x.

(*3*) During 2007, Trust receives $588x in dividend income. Trustee determines that $400x of the dividend income received during 2007 meets the definition of a qualified dividend in section 1(h)(11)(B)(i) and the holding period requirement in section 1(h)(11)(B)(iii) with respect to the Trust. During 2007, Trust also receives $12x in interest income from investment of Trust's funds pending distribution to TIHs, and pays $45x in expenses, all of which are affected expenses.

(*4*) On April 15, 2007, Trustee distributes $135x, which includes the $12x included in determining the year-end cash allocation factor for December 31, 2006. As a result of the distribution, Broker1 credits *J*'s account and *A*'s account for $13.50x each. Broker2 credits *S*'s account for $13.50x.

(*5*) On June 1, 2007, Trustee sells shares of stock for $1000×to preserve the soundness of the trust. The stock sold on June 1, 2007, equaled 20¶ of the aggregate fair market value of the assets held by Trust on the start-up date of Trust. Trustee has chosen not to report sales described in paragraph (c)(2)(iv)(*4*)(*ii*) of Trust's assets under paragraph (c)(2)(iv)(D)(*4*) of this section.

(*6*) On July 15, 2007, Trustee distributes $1,135x, which includes the $1,000x of trust sales proceeds received by Trust for the sale of assets on June 1, 2007. As a result of the distribution, Broker1 credits *J*'s account and *A*'s account for $113.50x each. Broker 2 credits *S*'s account for $113.50x.

(*7*) On September 30 2007, *J*, through Trust's sponsor, sells a trust interest to *S* for $115.35x. Trustee determines that the cash held for distribution per trust interest on September 30 is $1.35x. As a result of the sale, Broker1 credits *J*'s account for $115.35x.

(*8*) On October 15, 2007, Trustee distributes $123x. As a result of the distribution, Broker1 credits *J*'s account for $11.07x and *A*'s account for $12.30x. Broker2 credits *S*'s account for $13.53x.

(*9*) On December 10, 2007, *J* tenders a trust interest to Trustee for redemption through Broker1. Trustee determines that the amount of the redemption proceeds to be paid for a trust interest that is tendered for redemption on December 10, 2007 is $116x, of which $115x represents the redemption asset proceeds. Trustee pays this amount to Broker1 on *J*'s behalf. On December 12, 2007, trustee engages in a non pro-rata sale of shares of common stock for $115x to effect *J*'s redemption of a trust interest. The stock sold on December 12, 2007, equals 2% of the aggregate fair market value of all the assets of Trust as of the start-up date.

(*10*) On December 10, 2007, *J*, through Trust's sponsor, also sells a trust interest to *S* for $116x. Trustee determines that the cash held for distribution per trust interest on that date is $1x. As a result of the sale, Broker1 credits J's account for $116x.

(*11*) As of December 31, 2007, Trust holds cash of $173x and has incurred $15x in expenses that Trust has not paid. *J* is the only TIH to redeem a trust interest during the calendar year. The sale of two trust interests in Trust by *J* to *S* are the only sales that occurred on the secondary market established by Trust's sponsor during 2007.

(ii) *Trustee reporting*—(A) *Summary of information provided by Trustee.* Trustee meets the requirements of paragraph (f)(1) of this section if

Trustee provides the following information to requesting persons:

(*1*) Income and expense information:

Factor for ordinary dividend income	0.3481
Factor for qualified dividend income	0.7407
Factor for interest income	0.0222
Factor for affected expenses	0.0833
Current year-end cash allocation factor	1.5960
Prior year cash allocation factor	0.1200
Prior year cash distribution date	April 15

(*2*) Information regarding asset sales and distributions:

Date of sale	*Trust sales proceeds Received*	*Trust sales proceeds Distributed and Date Distributed*	*% of Trust Sold*
June 1	$10.0000x	$10.0000x (July 15)	20%
December 12	$ 1.1616x	$ 0.0000x	2%

(*3*) Information regarding redemptions:

Date	*Redemption asset proceeds*
December 10	$115x

(*4*) Information regarding sales of trust interests

Date	*Cash held for distribution per trust interest*
September 30	$1.35x
December 10	1.00x

(B) *Trustee determines this information as follows:*

(*1*) *Step One: Trustee determines the total amount of NMWHFIT distributions for the calendar year.* The total amount of NMWHFIT distributions (actual and deemed) for the calendar year for purposes of determining the safe harbor factors is $540x. This amount consists of the amounts paid on each scheduled distribution date during the calendar year ($1135x, $135x, and $123x), plus the total amount paid to *J* as a result of *J*'s redemption of a trust interest ($116x) ($1,135x + $135x + $123x + $116x = $1,509x)—

(*i*) Increased by all cash held for distribution to TIHs as of December 31, 2007 ($158x), which is the cash held as of December 31, 2007 ($173x) reduced by the accrued but unpaid expenses as of December 31, 2007 ($15x), and

(*ii*) Decreased by all amounts distributed during the calendar year but included in the year-end cash allocation factor from a prior year ($12x); all redemption asset proceeds paid for the calendar year ($115x); and all trust sales proceeds distributed during the calendar year ($1,000x).

(*2*) *Step Two: Trustee determines factors that express the ratio of NMWHFIT income (other than OID) and expenses to the total amount of NMWHFIT distributions.* Trustee determines the factors for each item of income earned by Trust and each item of expense as follows:

(*i*) *Ordinary dividend income factor.* The ordinary dividend income factor is 0.3481, which represents the ratio of the gross amount of ordinary dividends ($188x) to the total amount of NMWHFIT distributions for the calendar year ($540x).

(*ii*) *Qualified dividend income factor.* The qualified dividend income factor is 0.7407 which represents the ratio of the gross amount of qualified dividend income ($400x) to the total amount of NMWHFIT distributions for the calendar year ($540x).

(*iii*) *Interest income factor.* The interest income factor is 0.0222, which represents the ratio of the gross amount of interest income ($12x) to the total amount of NMWHFIT distributions for the calendar year ($540x).

(*iv*) *Expense factor.* The affected expenses factor is 0.0833, which represents the ratio of the gross amount of affected expenses paid by Trust for the calendar year ($45x) to the total amount of NMWHFIT distributions for the calendar year ($540x).

(*3*) *Step Three: Trustee determines adjustments for reconciling the total amount of NMWHFIT distributions with amounts paid to TIHs.* To enable requesting persons to determine the total amount of NMWHFIT distributions that are attributable to a TIH based on amounts actually paid to the TIH, the trustee must provide both a current year-end cash allocation factor and a prior year cash allocation factor.

(*i*) *Current year-end cash allocation factor.* The adjustment factor for cash held by Trust at year end is 1.5960, which represents the cash held for distribution as of December 31, 2007 ($158x) (the amount of cash held by Trust on December 31, 2007 ($173x) reduced by accrued, but unpaid, expenses ($15x)), divided by the number of trust interests outstanding at year-end (99).

(*ii*) *Prior Year Cash Allocation Factor.* The adjustment factor for distributions of year-end cash from the prior year is 0.1200, which represents the amount of the distribution during the current calendar year that was included in a year-end cash allocation factor for a prior year ($12x), divided by the number of trust interests outstanding at the time of the distribution (100). The prior year cash distribution date is April 15, 2007.

(*4*) *Reporting sales and dispositions of trust assets*—(*i*) *Application of the de minimis test.* The aggregate fair market value of the assets of Trust as of January 1, 2007, was $10,000x. During the 2007 calendar year, Trust received trust sales proceeds of $1115x. The trust sales proceeds received by Trust for the 2007 calendar year equal 11.15% of Trust's fair market value as of January 1, 2007. Accordingly, the de minimis test is not satisfied for the 2007 calendar year. The qualified NMWHFIT exception in paragraph (c)(2)(iv)(E) of this section and the NMWHFIT final calendar year exception in (c)(2)(iv)(F) of this section also do not apply to Trust for the 2007 calendar year.

(ii) *Information to be provided.* To satisfy the requirements of paragraph (f)(1) of this section with respect to sales and dispositions of Trust's assets, Trustee provides a list of dates on which trust assets were sold during the calendar year, and provides, for each date: the trust sales proceeds (per trust interest) received on that date; the trust sales proceeds distributed to TIHs (per trust interest) with respect to sales or dispositions on that date; the date those trust sales proceeds were distributed, and the ratio of the assets sold or disposed of on that day to all the assets held by Trust. Because Trust will terminate within 15 months of its start-up date, Trustee must use the fair market value of the assets as of the start-up date to determine the portion of Trust sold or disposed of on any particular date.

(5) *Reporting redemptions.* Because Trust is not required to make distributions at least as frequently as monthly, and Trust does not satisfy the qualified NMWHFIT exception in paragraph (c)(2)(iv)(E) of this section, the exception in paragraph (c)(2)(v)(C) does not apply to Trust. To satisfy the requirements of paragraph (f)(1) of this section, Trustee provides a list of dates for which the redemption proceeds to be paid for the redemption of a trust interest was determined for the 2007 calendar year and the redemptions asset proceeds paid for each date. During 2007, Trustee only determined the amount of redemption proceeds paid for the redemption of a trust interest once, for December 10, 2007 and the redemption asset proceeds determined for that date was $115x.

(6) *Reporting sales of trust interest.* Because trust is not required to make distributions at least as frequently as monthly, and Trust does not satisfy the qualified NMWHFIT exception in paragraph (c)(2)(iv)(E) of this section, the exception in paragraph (c)(2)(v)(C) of this section does not apply to Trust. Sponsor, in accordance with the trust agreement, provides Trustee with a list of dates on which sales on the secondary market occurred. To satisfy the requirements of paragraph (f)(1) of this section, Trustee provides requesting persons with a list of dates on which sales on the secondary market occurred and the amount of cash held for distribution, per trust interest, on each date. The first sale during the 2007 calendar year occurred on September 30, 2007, and the amount of cash held for distribution, per trust interest, on that date is $1.35x. The second sale occurred on December 10, 2007, and the amount of cash held for distribution, per trust interest, on that date is $1.00x.

(iii) *Brokers' use of information provided by Trustee.* (A) Broker1 and Broker2 use the information furnished by Trustee under the safe harbor to determine that the following items are attributable to *J*, *A*, and *S*—

With respect to *J*	
Ordinary Dividend Income	$ 17.89x
Qualified Dividend Income	38.07x
Interest Income	1.14x
Affected Expenses	4.28x
Trust sales proceeds reported on Form 1099	108.13x
Redemption asset proceeds	
For redemption on December 10	115.00x
Sale asset proceeds	
For sale on September 30	114.00x
For sale on December 10	115.00x
With respect to *A*	
Ordinary Dividend Income	$ 18.82x
Qualified Dividend Income	40.04x
Interest Income	1.20x
Affected Expenses	4.50x
Trust sales proceeds reported on Form 1099	11.62x
With respect to *S*	
Ordinary Dividend Income	$ 19.54x
Qualified Dividend Income	41.58x
Interest Income	1.25x
Affected Expenses	4.68x
Trust sales proceeds reported on Form 1099	113.94x

With respect to *J*, *A*, and *S* (regarding the sales and dispositions executed by Trust during the calendar year)

Date	*Trust sales proceeds received per trust interest*	*% of Trust sold*
June 15	$10.0000x	20%
December 12	1.1616x	2%

(B) The brokers determine the information provided to *J*, *A*, and *S* as follows—

(*1*) *Step One: Brokers determine the total amount of NMWHFIT distributions attributable to J, A, and S.* Broker1 determines that the total amount of NMWHFIT distributions attributable to *J* is $51.39x and the total amount of NMWHFIT distributions attributable to *A* is $54.06x. Broker2 determines that the total amount of NMWHFIT distributions attributable to *S* is $56.13x.

(*i*) To calculate these amounts the brokers begin by determining the total amount paid to *J*, *A*, and *S* for the calendar year—

(*A*) The total amount paid to *J* for the calendar year equals $485.42x and includes the April 15, 2007, distribution of $13.50x, the July 15, 2007, distribution of $113.50x, the sales proceeds for the September 30, 2007, sale of $115.35x, the October 15, 2007, distribution of $11.07x, and the redemption proceeds of $116x and sales proceeds of $116x for the redemption and sale on December 10, 2007.

(*B*) The total amount paid to *A* for the calendar year equals $139.30x and includes the April 15, 2007, distribution of $13.50x, the July 15, 2007, distribution of $113.50x and the October 15, 2007, distribution of $12.30x.

(*C*) The total amount paid to *S* for the calendar year equals $140.53x and includes the April 15, 2007, distribution of $13.50x, the July 15, 2007, distribution of $113.50x and the October 15, 2007, distribution of $13.53x.

(*ii*) The brokers increase the total amount paid to *J*, *A*, and *S* by an amount equal to the current year-end cash allocation factor (1.5960) multiplied by the number of trust interests held by *J* (7), *A* (10), and *S* (12) as of December 31, 2007; that is for *J*, $11.17x; for *A*, $15.96x; and for *S*, $19.15x.

(*iii*) The brokers reduce the amount paid to *J*, *A*, and *S* as follows—

(*A*) An amount equal to the prior year cash allocation factor (0.1200), multiplied by the number of trust interests held by *J* (10), *A* (10), and *S* (10) on the date of the prior year cash distribution; that is for *J*, *A*, and *S*, $1.20x, each;

(*B*) An amount equal to all redemption asset proceeds paid to a TIH for the calendar year; that is, for *J*, $115x;

(*C*) An amount equal to all sales asset proceeds attributable to the TIH for the calendar year; that is for *J*, $229x (for the September 30, 2007, sale: $115.35x — 1.35x (cash held for distribution per trust interest on that date)= $114x; and for the December 10, 2007, sale: $116x-1.00 (cash held for distribution per trust interest on that date)=$115x));

(*D*) In the case of a purchasing TIH, an amount equal to the amount of cash held for distribution per trust interest at the time the TIH purchased its trust interest, multiplied by the number of trust interests purchased; that is for *S*, $2.35x ($1.35x with respect to the September 30, 2007, sale and $1x with respect to the December 10, 2007, sale);

(*E*) All amounts of trust sales proceeds distributed to the TIH for the calendar year; that is for *J*, *A*, and *S*, $100. ($100 each, with respect to the June 15, 2007, sale of assets by Trust, and $0 each, with respect to the December 12, 2007, sale of assets by Trust).

(*2*) *Step two: The brokers apply the factors provided by Trustee to determine the Trust's income and expenses that are attributable to J, A, and S.* The amounts of each item of income (other than OID) and expense that are attributable to *J*, *A*, and *S* are determined by multiplying the factor for that type of income or expense by the total amount of NMWHFIT distributions attributable to *J*, *A*, and *S* as follows:

(*i*) *Application of factor for ordinary dividends.* The amount of ordinary dividend income attributable to *J* is $17.89x, to *A* is $18.82x, and to *S* is $19.54x. The brokers determine these amounts by multiplying the total amount of NMWHFIT distributions attributable to *J*, *A*, and *S* ($51.39x, $54.06x, and $56.13x, respectively) by the factor for ordinary dividends (0.3481).

(*ii*) *Application of factor for qualified dividend income.* The amount of qualified dividend income attributable to *J* is $38.07x, to *A* is $40.04x, and to *S* is $41.58x. The brokers determine these amounts by multiplying the total amount of NMWHFIT distributions attributable to *J*, *A*, and *S* ($51.39x, $54.06x, and $56.13x, respectively) by the factor for qualified dividends (0.7407).

(*iii*) *Application of factor for interest income.* The amount of interest income attributable to *J* is $1.14x, to *A* is $1.20x, and to *S* is $1.25x. The brokers determine these amounts by multiplying the total amount of NMWHFIT distributions attributable to *J*, *A*, and *S* ($51.39x, $54.06x, and $56.13x, respectively) by the factor for interest (0.0222).

(*iv*) *Application of factor for affected expenses.* The amount of affected expenses attributable to *J* is $4.28x, to *A* is $4.50x, and to *S* is $4.68x. The brokers determine these amounts by multiplying the total amount of NMWHFIT distributions attributable to *J*, *A*, and *S* ($51.39x, $54.06x, and $56.13x, respectively) by the factor for affected expenses (0.0833).

(*3*) *Brokers reporting of sales and dispositions of trust assets*—(*1*) *Determining the amount of trust sales proceeds to be reported on Form 1099 for J, A, and S.* The amount of trust sales proceeds to be reported on Form 1099 with respect to *J* is $108.13x, to *A* is $111.62x, and to *S* is $113.94x. To determine these amounts, the brokers aggregate the amount of trust sales proceeds attributable to *J*, *A*, and *S* for each date on which Trust sold or disposed of assets. The brokers determine the amount of trust sales proceeds to be reported with respect to the June 15, 2007, asset sale by multiplying the number of trust interests held by *J* (10), *A* (10) and *S* (10) on that date by the trust sales proceeds received per trust interest on that date ($10x). The brokers determine the amount of trust sales proceeds to be reported with respect to the December 12, 2007, asset sale by multiplying the number of trust interests held by *J* (7), *A* (10) and *S* (12) on that date by the trust sales proceeds received per trust interest on that date ($1.1616x).

(*ii*) *Information provided on the tax information statements furnished to J, A, and S.* The tax information statements furnished to *J*, *A*, and *S* must include the dates of each sale or disposition (June 15, 2007, and December 12, 2007); the amount of trust sales proceeds per trust interest received on those dates ($10.00x and $1.1616x, respectively); and, the percentage of Trust sold or disposed of on that date (20% and 2%, respectively).

(*4*) *Reporting redemptions.* Broker1 reports on Form 1099 and on the written tax information statement furnished to *J* that *J* received $115x in redemption asset proceeds for the calendar year.

(*5*) *Reporting sales of trust interests on the secondary market.* Broker1 reports on *J*'s two sales of trust interests. With respect to the sale on September 30, 2007, the sale asset proceeds equals $114x ($115.35x sale proceeds — $1.35x cash held for distribution on that date) and with respect to the sale on December 10, 2007, the sale asset proceeds equal $115x ($116x sale proceeds - $1x cash held for distribution on that date). Broker1 reports these amounts on Form 1099 and on the tax information statement furnished to *J*.

(g) *Safe Harbor for certain WHMTs.*—(1) *Safe harbor for trustee of certain WHMTs for reporting information.*—(i) *In general.*—The trustee of a WHMT that meets the requirements of paragraph (g)(1)(ii) of this section is deemed to satisfy paragraph (c)(1)(i) of this section, if the trustee calculates and provides WHFIT information in the manner described in this paragraph (g) and provides a statement to the requesting person giving notice that information has been calculated in accordance with this paragraph (g)(1).

(ii) *Requirements.*—A WHMT must meet the following requirements—

(A) The WHMT must make monthly distributions of the income and principal payments received by the WHMT to its TIHs;

(B) All trust interests in the WHMT must represent the right to receive an equal pro-rata share of both the income and the principal payments received by the WHMT on the mortgages it holds (for example, a WHMT that holds or issues trust interests that qualify as stripped interests under section 1286 may not report under this safe harbor);

(C) The WHMT must—

(*1*) Report under this paragraph (g)(1)(ii) for the life of the WHMT; or

(*2*) If the WHMT has a start-up date before January 1, 2007, the WHMT must begin reporting under this paragraph (g)(1)(ii) as of January 1, 2007, and must continue to report under this paragraph for the life of the WHMT;

(D) The WHMT must calculate all items subject to the safe harbor consistent with the safe harbor;

(E) The assets of the WHMT must be limited to—

(*1*) Mortgages with uniform characteristics;

(*2*) Reasonably required reserve funds; and

(*3*) Amounts received on mortgages or reserve funds and held for distribution to TIHs; and

(F) The aggregate outstanding principal balance (as defined in paragraph (g)(1)(iii)(D) of this section) as of the WHMT's start-up date must equal the aggregate of the original face amounts of all issued trust interests.

(iii) *Reporting WHMT income, expenses, non pro-rata partial principal payments, and sales and dispositions under the safe harbor.*—A trustee must comply with each step provided in this paragraph (g)(1)(iii).

(A) *Step One: Determine monthly pool factors.*—The trustee must, for each month of the calendar year and for January of the following calendar year, calculate and provide the ratio (expressed as a decimal carried to at least eight places and called a *pool factor*) of—

(*1*) The amount of the aggregate outstanding principal balance of the WHMT as of the first business day of the month; to

(*2*) The amount of the aggregate outstanding principal balance of the WHMT as of the start-up date.

(B) *Step Two: Determine monthly expense factors.*—For each month of the calendar year and for each item of expense paid by the WHMT during that month, the trustee must calculate and provide the ratio (expressed as a decimal carried to at least eight places and called an *expense factor*) of—

(*1*) The gross amount, for the month, of each item of expense; to

(*2*) The amount that represents the aggregate outstanding principal balance of the WHMT as of the start-up date, divided by 1,000.

(C) *Step Three: Determine monthly income factors.*—For each month of the calendar year and for each item of gross income earned by the WHMT during that month, the trustee must calculate and provide the ratio (expressed as a decimal carried to at least eight places and called an *income factor*) of—

(*1*) The gross amount, for the month, of each item of income, to

(*2*) The amount that represents the aggregate outstanding principal balance of the WHMT as of the start-up date, divided by 1,000.

(D) *Definition of aggregate outstanding principal balance.*—For purposes of this paragraph (g)(1)(iii), the amount of the aggregate outstanding principal balance of a WHMT is the aggregate of—

(1) The outstanding principal balance of all mortgages held by the WHMT;

(2) The amounts received on mortgages as principal payments and held for distribution by the WHMT; and

(3) The amount of the reserve fund (exclusive of undistributed income).

(iv) *Reporting OID information under the safe harbor.*—(A) *Reporting OID prior to the issuance of final regulations under section 1272(a)(6)(C)(iii).*—*(1)* For calendar years prior to the effective date of final regulations under section 1272(a)(6)(C)(iii), the trustee must provide, for each month during the calendar year, the aggregate daily accrual of OID per $1,000 of aggregate outstanding principal balance as of the start-up date (daily portion). For purposes of this paragraph (g)(1)(iv), the daily portion of OID is determined by allocating to each day of the month its ratable portion of the excess (if any) of—

(i) The sum of the present value (determined under section 1272(a)(6)(B)) of all remaining payments under the mortgages held by the WHMT at the close of the month, and the payments during the month of amounts included in the stated redemption price of the mortgages, over

(ii) The aggregate of each mortgage's adjusted issue price as of the beginning of the month.

(2) In calculating the daily portion of OID, the trustee must use the prepayment assumption used in pricing the original issue of trust interests. If the WHMT has a start-up date prior to January 24, 2006, and the trustee, after a good faith effort to ascertain that information, does not know the prepayment assumption used in pricing the original issue of trust interests, the trustee may use any reasonable prepayment assumption to calculate OID provided it continues to use the same prepayment assumption consistently thereafter.

(B) *Reporting OID after the issuance of final regulations under section 1272(a)(6)(C)(iii).*—[Reserved.]

(v) *Reporting market discount information under the safe harbor.*—(A) *Reporting market discount information prior to the issuance of final regulations under sections 1272(a)(6)(C)(iii) and 1276(b)(3).*—For calendar years prior to the effective date of final regulations under sections 1272(a)(6)(C)(iii) and 1276(b)(3), the trustee must provide—

(1) In the case of a WHMT holding mortgages issued with OID, the ratio (expressed as a decimal carried to at least eight places) of—

(i) The OID accrued during the month (calculated in accordance with paragraph (g)(1)(iv) of this section); to

(ii) The total remaining OID as of the beginning of the month (as determined under paragraph (g)(1)(v)(A)(3) of this section); or

(2) In the case of a WHMT holding mortgages issued without OID, the ratio (expressed as a decimal carried to at least eight places) of—

(i) The amount of stated interest paid to the WHMT during the month; to

(ii) The total amount of stated interest remaining to be paid to the WHMT as of the beginning of the month (as determined under paragraph (g)(1)(v)(A)(3) of this section).

(3) Computing the total amount of stated interest remaining to be paid and the total remaining OID at the beginning of the month.—To compute the total amount of stated interest remaining to be paid to the WHMT as of the beginning of the month and the total remaining OID as of the beginning of the month, the trustee must use the prepayment assumption used in pricing the original issue of trust interests. If the WHMT has a start-up date prior to January 24, 2006, and the trustee, after a good faith effort to ascertain that information, does not know the prepayment assumption used in pricing the original issue of trust interests, the trustee may use any reasonable prepayment assumption to calculate these amounts provided it continues to use the same prepayment assumption consistently thereafter.

(B) *Reporting market discount information under the safe harbor following the issuance of final regulations under sections 1272(a)(6)(C)(iii) and 1276(b)(3).*—[Reserved.]

(vi) *Reporting bond premium information under the safe harbor.*—[Reserved]

(2) *Use of information provided by a trustee under the safe harbor.*—(i) *In general.*—If a trustee reports WHMT items in accordance with paragraph (g)(1) of this section, the information provided with respect to those items on the Forms 1099 required to be filed with the IRS under paragraph (d) of this section and on the statement required to be furnished to the TIH under paragraph (e) of this section must be determined as provided in this paragraph (g)(2).

(ii) *Reporting WHMT income, expenses, non pro-rata partial principal payments, and sales and dispositions under the safe harbor.*—The amount of each item of income, the amount of each item of expense, and the combined amount of non pro-rata partial principal payments and trust sales proceeds that are attributable to a TIH for each month of the calendar year must be computed as follows:

(A) *Step One: Determine the aggregate of the non pro-rata partial principal payments and trust sales proceeds that are attributable to the TIH for the calendar year.*—For each month of the calendar year that a trust interest was held on the record date—

(1) Determine the monthly amounts per trust interest.—The trustee or middleman must determine the aggregate amount of non pro-rata partial principal payments and the trust sales proceeds that are attributable to each trust interest for each month by multiplying—

(*i*) The original face amount of the trust interest; by

(*ii*) The difference between the pool factor for the current month and the pool factor for the following month.

(*2*) *Determine the amount for the calendar year*.—The trustee or middleman must multiply the monthly amount per trust interest by the number of trust interests held by the TIH on the record date of each month. The trustee or middleman then must aggregate these monthly amounts, and report the aggregate amount on the Form 1099 filed with the IRS and on the tax information statement furnished to the TIH as trust sales proceeds. No other information is required to be reported to the IRS or the TIH to satisfy the requirements of paragraphs (d) and (e) of this section under this paragraph (g) with respect to sales and dispositions and non pro-rata partial principal payments.

(B) *Step Two: Determine the amount of each item of expense that is attributable to a TIH*.—(*1*) *Determine the monthly amounts per trust interest*.—For each month of the calendar year that a trust interest was held on the record date, the trustee or middleman must determine the amount of each item of expense that is attributable to each trust interest by multiplying—

(*i*) The original face amount of the trust interest, divided by 1000; by

(*ii*) The expense factor for that month and that item of expense.

(*2*) *Determine the amount for the calendar year*.—The trustee or middleman must multiply the monthly amount of each item of expense per trust interest by the number of trust interests held by the TIH on the record date of each month. The trustee or middleman then must aggregate the monthly amounts for each item of expense to determine the total amount of each item of expense that is attributable to the TIH for the calendar year.

(C) *Step Three: Determine the amount of each item of income that is attributable to the TIH for the calendar year*.—(*1*) *Determine the monthly amounts per trust interest*.—For each month of the calendar year that a trust interest was held on the record date, the trustee or middleman must determine the amount of each item of income that is attributable to each trust interest by multiplying—

(*i*) The original face amount of the trust interest, divided by 1,000; by

(*ii*) The income factor for that month and that item of income.

(*2*) *Determine the amount for the calendar year*.—The trustee or middleman must multiply the monthly amount of each item of income per trust interest by the number of trust interests held by the TIH on the record date of each month. The trustee or middleman then must aggregate the monthly amounts for each item of income to determine the total amount of each item of income that is attributable to the TIH for the calendar year.

(D) *Definitions for this paragraph (g)(2)*.—For purposes of this paragraph (g)(2)(ii)—

(*1*) The *record date* is the date used by the WHMT to determine the owner of the trust interest for the purpose of distributing the payment for the month.

(*2*) The *original face amount of the trust interest* is the original principal amount of a trust interest on its issue date.

(iii) *Reporting OID information under the safe harbor*.—With respect to each month, trustee or middleman must determine the amount of OID that is attributable to each trust interest held by a TIH by multiplying—

(A) The product of the OID factor multiplied by the original face amount of the trust interest, divided by 1,000; by

(B) The number of days during the month that the TIH held the trust interest.

(iv) *Requirement to provide market discount information under the safe harbor*.—The trustee or middleman must provide the market discount information in accordance with paragraph (g)(1)(v) of this section to the TIH in, or with, the written statement required to be furnished to the TIH under paragraph (e) of this section.

(v) *Requirement to provide bond premium information under the safe harbor*.—[Reserved]

(3) *Example of safe harbor in paragraph (g)(1) of this section*.—The following example illustrates the use of the factors in this paragraph (g) to calculate and provide WHMT information:

Example. (i) *Facts*—(A) *In general*. *X* is a WHMT. *X*'s start-up date is January 1, 2007. As of that date, *X*'s assets consist of 100 15-year mortgages, each having an unpaid principal balance of $125,000 and a fixed, annual interest rate of 7.25 percent. None of the mortgages were issued with OID. *X*'s TIHs are entitled to monthly, pro-rata distributions of the principal payments received by X. *X*'s TIHs are also entitled to monthly, pro-rata distributions of the interest earned on the mortgages held by *X*, reduced by expenses. Trust interests are issued in increments of $5,000 with a $25,000 minimum. The prepayment assumption used in pricing the original issue of trust interests is six percent. Broker holds a trust interest in X, with an original face amount of $25,000, in street name, for *C* during the entire 2007 calendar year.

(B) *Trust events during the 2007 calendar year*. During the 2007 calendar year, *X* collects all interest and principal payments when due and makes all monthly distributions when due. One mortgage is repurchased from *X* in July 2007 for $122,249, the mortgage's unpaid principal balance plus accrued, but unpaid, interest at the time. During November 2007, another mortgage is prepaid in full. *X* earns $80 interest income each month from the temporary investment of *X*'s funds pending distribution to the TIHs. All of *X*'s expenses are affected expenses. The aggregate outstanding principal balance of *X*'s mortgages, *X*'s interest income, and *X*'s expenses, for each month of the 2007 calendar year, along with the aggregate outstanding principal balance of X as of January 2008, are as follows:

Month	Principal Balance	Income	Expenses
January	$12,500,000	$75,601	$5,288
February	12,461,413	75,368	5,273
March	12,422,593	75,133	5,256
April	12,383,538	74,897	5,240
May	12,344,247	74,660	5,244
June	12,304,719	74,421	5,207
July	12,264,952	74,181	5,191
August	12,102,696	73,200	5,122
September	12,062,849	72,960	5,106
October	12,022,762	72,718	5,089
November	11,982,432	72,474	5,073
December	11,821,234	71,500	5,006
January	11,780,829		

(ii) *Trustee reporting.* (A) Trustee, X's fiduciary, comes within the safe harbor of paragraph (g)(1)(ii) of this section by providing the following information to requesting persons:

Month	Pool Factor	Income Factor	Expense Factor
January	1.00000000	6.04806667	0.42304000
February	0.99691304	6.02941628	0.42184000
March	0.99380744	6.01065328	0.42048000
April	0.99068304	5.99177670	0.41920000
May	0.98753976	5.97278605	0.41952000
June	0.98437752	5.95368085	0.41656000
July	0.98119616	5.93446013	0.41528000
August	0.96821564	5.85603618	0.40976000
September	0.96502792	5.83677704	0.40848000
October	0.96182096	5.81740161	0.40712000
November	0.95859459	5.79790896	0.40584000
December	0.94569875	5.71999659	0.40048000
January	0.94246631		

(B) Trustee determines this information as follows:

(1) *Step One: Trustee determines monthly pool factors.* Trustee calculates and provides X's pool factor for each month of the 2007 calendar year. For example, for the month of January 2007 the pool factor is 1.0, which represents the ratio of—

(*i*) The amount that represents the aggregate outstanding principal balance of X ($12,500,000) as of the first business day of January; divided by

(*ii*) The amount that represents the aggregate outstanding principal balance of X ($12,500,000) as of the start-up day.

(2) *Step Two: Trustee determines monthly expense factors.* Trustee calculates and provides the expense factors for each month of the 2007 calendar year. During 2007, X has only affected expenses, and therefore, will have only one expense factor for each month. For example, the expense factor for the month of January 2007 is 0.42304000, which represents the ratio of—

(*i*) The gross amount of expenses paid during January by X ($5,288); divided by

(*ii*) The amount that represents the aggregate outstanding principal balance of X as of the start-up date ($12,500,000) divided by 1,000 ($12,500).

(3) *Step Three: Trustee determines monthly income factors.* Trustee calculates and provides the income factors for each month of the 2007 calendar year. During 2007, X has only interest income, and therefore, will have only one income factor for each month. For example, the income factor for the month of January 2007 is 6.04806667, which represents the ratio of—

(*i*) The gross amount of interest income earned by X during January ($75,601); divided by (*ii*) The amount that represents that aggregate outstanding principal balance of *X* as of the start-up date ($12,500,000), divided by 1,000 ($12,500).

(4) *Step Four: Trustee calculates and provides monthly market discount fractions.* Trustee calculates and provides a market discount fraction for each month of the 2007 calendar year using a prepayment assumption of 6% and a stated interest rate of 7.25%.

(iii) *Broker's use of the information provided by Trustee.* (A) Broker uses the information provided by Trustee under paragraph (g) of this section to determine that the following trust items are attributable to *C*:

Month	Aggregate trust sales proceeds and non pro-rata partial principal payments	Affected expenses	Gross interest income
January	$ 77.17	$ 10.58	$ 151.20
February	77.64	10.55	150.74
March	78.11	10.51	150.27
April	78.58	10.48	149.79
May	79.06	10.49	149.32
June	79.53	10.41	148.84
July	324.51	10.38	148.36
August	79.69	10.24	146.40
September	80.17	10.21	145.92
October	80.66	10.18	145.43
November	322.40	10.15	144.95
December	80.81	10.01	143.00
Total	$1438.33	$124.19	$1774.22

(B) Broker determines this information as follows:

(1) *Step One: Broker determines the amount of the non pro-rata partial principal payments and trust sales proceeds received by X that are attributable to C for the 2007 calendar year.* Broker determines the amount of the non pro-rata partial principal payments and trust sales proceeds received by *X* that are attributable to *C* for each month of the 2007 calendar year. For example, for the month of January, Broker determines that the amount of principal receipts and the amount of trust sales proceeds that are attributable to *C* is $77.17. Broker determines this by multiplying the original face amount of *C*'s trust interest ($25,000) by 0.00308696, the difference between the pool factor for January 2007 (1.00000000) and the pool factor for the following month of February 2007 (0.99691304). Broker reports the aggregate of the monthly amounts of non pro-rata partial principal payments and trust sales proceeds that are attributable to *C* for the 2007 calendar year as trust sales proceeds on the Form 1099 filed with the IRS.

(2) *Step Two: Broker applies the expense factors provided by Trustee to determine the amount of expenses that are attributable to C for the 2007 calendar year.* Broker determines the amount of *X*'s expenses that are attributable to *C* for each month of the calendar year. For example, for the month of January 2007, Broker determines that the amount of expenses attributable to *C* is $10.58. Broker determines this by multiplying the original face amount of *C*'s trust interest ($25,000), divided by 1,000 ($25) by the expense factor for January 2007 (0.42304000). Broker determines the expenses that are attributable to *C* for the 2007 calendar year by aggregating the monthly amounts.

(3) *Step Three: Broker applies the income factors provided by Trustee to determine the amount of gross interest income attributable to C for the 2007 calendar year.* Broker determines the amount of gross interest income that is attributable to *C* for each month of the calendar year. For example, for the month of January 2007, Broker determines that the amount of gross interest income attributable to *C* is $151.20. Broker determines this by multiplying the original face amount of *C*'s trust interest ($25,000), divided by 1,000 ($25), by the income factor for January 2007 (6.04806667). Broker determines the amount of the gross interest income that is attributable to *C* for the 2007 calendar year by aggregating the monthly amounts.

(4) *Step Four: Broker provides market discount information to C.* Broker provides *C* with the market discount fractions calculated and provided by the trustee of *X* under paragraph (g)(3)(ii)(D) of this section.

(h) *Additional safe harbors.*—(1) *Temporary safe harbor for WHMTs.*—(i) *Application.*—Pending the issuance of additional guidance, the safe harbor in this paragraph applies to trustees and middlemen of WHMTs that are not eligible to report under the WHMT safe harbor in paragraph (g) of this section because they hold interests in another WHFIT, in a REMIC, or hold or issue stripped interests.

(ii) *Safe harbor.*—A trustee is deemed to satisfy the requirements of paragraph (c) of this section, if the trustee calculates and provides trust information in a manner that enables a requesting person to provide trust information to a beneficial owner of a trust interest that enables the owner to reasonably accurately report the tax consequences of its ownership of a trust interest on its federal income tax return. Additionally, to be deemed to satisfy the requirements of paragraph (c) of this section, the trustee must calculate and provide trust information regarding market discount and OID by any reasonable manner consistent with section 1272(a)(6). A middleman or a trustee may satisfy its obligation to furnish information to the IRS under paragraph (d) of this section and to the trust interest holder under paragraph (e) of this section by providing information consistent with the information provided under this paragraph by the trustee.

(2) *Additional safe harbors provided by other published guidance.*—The IRS and the Treasury Department may provide additional safe harbor reporting procedures for complying with this section or a specific paragraph of this section by other published guidance (see § 601.601(d)(2) of this chapter).

(i) [Reserved.]

(j) *Requirement that middlemen furnish information to beneficial owners that are exempt recipients and noncalendar-year beneficial owners.*—(1) *In general.*—A middleman that holds a trust interest on behalf of, or for the account of, either a beneficial owner that is an exempt recipient defined in paragraph (b)(7) of this section or a noncalendar-year beneficial owner, must provide to such beneficial owner, upon request, the information provided by the trustee to the middleman under paragraph (c) of this section.

(2) *Time for providing information.*—The middleman must provide the requested information to any beneficial owner making a request under paragraph (h)(1) of this section on or before the later of the 44th day after the close of the calendar year for which the information was requested, or the day that is 28 days after the receipt of the request. A middleman must provide information with respect to a WHFIT holding an interest in another WHFIT, or a WHFIT holding an interest in a REMIC, on or before the later of the 58th day after the close of the calendar year for which the information was requested, or the 42nd day after the receipt of the request.

(3) *Manner of providing information.*—The requested information must be provided—

(i) By written statement sent by first class mail to the address provided by the person requesting the information;

(ii) By electronic mail provided that the person requesting the information requests that the middleman furnish the information by electronic mail and the person furnishes an electronic address;

(iii) At an Internet website of the middleman or the trustee, provided that the beneficial owner requesting the information is notified that the requested information is available at the Internet website and is furnished the address of the site; or

(iv) Any other manner agreed to by the middleman and the beneficial owner requesting the information.

(4) *Clearing organization.*—A clearing organization described in § 1.163-5(c)(2)(i)(D)(8) is not required to furnish information to exempt recipients or non-calendar-year TIHs under this paragraph (h).

(k) *Coordination with other information reporting rules.*—In general, in cases in which reporting is required for a WHFIT under both this section and subpart B, part III, subchapter A, chapter 61 of the Internal Revenue Code (Sections 6041 through 6050S) (Information Reporting Sections), the reporting rules for WHFITs under this section must be applied. The provisions of the Information Reporting Sections and the regulations thereunder are incorporated into this section as applicable, but only to the extent that such provisions are not inconsistent with the provisions of this section.

(l) *Backup withholding requirements.*—Every trustee and middleman required to file a Form 1099 under this section is a payor within the meaning of § 31.3406(a)-2, and must backup withhold as required under section 3406 and any regulations thereunder.

(m) *Penalties for failure to comply.*—(1) *In general.*—Every trustee or middleman who fails to comply with the reporting obligations imposed by this section is subject to penalties under sections 6721, 6722, and any other applicable penalty provisions.

(2) *Penalties not imposed on trustees and middlemen of certain WHMTs for failure to report OID.*—Penalties will not be imposed as a result of a failure to provide OID information for a WHMT that has a start-up date on or after August 13, 1998 and on or before January 24, 2006, if the trustee of the WHMT does not have the historic information necessary to provide this information and the trustee demonstrates that it has attempted in good faith, but without success, to obtain this information. For purposes of calculating a market discount fraction under paragraph (g)(1)(v) of this section, for a WHMT described in this paragraph, it may be assumed that the WHMT is holding mortgages that were issued without OID. A trustee availing itself of this paragraph must include a statement to that effect when providing information to requesting persons under paragraph (c) of these regulations.

(n) *Effective date.*—These regulations are applicable January 1, 2007. Trustees must calculate and provide trust information with respect to the 2007 calendar year and all subsequent years consistent with these regulations Information returns required to be filed with the IRS and the tax information statements required to be furnished to trust interest holders after December 31, 2007 must be consistent with these regulations. [Reg. § 1.671-5.]

☐ [*T.D.* 9241, 1-23-2006. *Amended by T.D.* 9279, 7-28-2006 *and T.D.* 9308, 12-26-2006.]

[Reg. § 1.672(a)-1]

§ 1.672(a)-1. Definition of adverse party.—(a) Under section 672(a) an adverse party is defined as any person having a substantial beneficial interest in a trust which would be adversely affected by the exercise or nonexercise of a power which he possesses respecting the trust. A trustee is not an adverse party merely because of his interest as trustee. A person having a general power of appointment over the trust property is deemed to have a beneficial interest in the trust. An interest is a substantial interest if its value in relation to the total value of the property subject to the power is not insignificant.

(b) Ordinarily, a beneficiary will be an adverse party, but if his right to share in the income or corpus of a trust is limited to only a part, he may be an adverse party only as to that part. Thus, if A, B, C, and D are equal income beneficiaries of a trust and the grantor can revoke with A's consent, the grantor is treated as the owner of a portion which represents three-fourths of the trust; and items of income, deduction, and credit attributable to that portion are included in determining the tax of the grantor.

(c) The interest of an ordinary income beneficiary of a trust may or may not be adverse with respect to the exercise of a power over corpus. Thus, if the income of a trust is payable to A for life, with a power (which is not a general power of appointment) in A to appoint the corpus to the grantor either during his life or by will, A's interest is adverse to the return of the corpus to the grantor during A's life, but is not adverse to a return of the corpus after A's death. In other words, A's interest is adverse as to ordinary income but is not adverse as to income allocable to corpus. Therefore, assuming no other relevant facts exist, the grantor would not be taxable on the ordinary income of the trust under sections 674, 676, or 677, but would be taxable under section 677 on income allocable to corpus (such as capital gains), since it may in the discretion of a nonadverse party be accumulated for future distribution to the grantor. Similarly, the interest of a contingent income beneficiary is adverse to a return of corpus to the grantor before the termination of his interest but not to a return of corpus after the termination of his interest.

(d) The interest of a remainderman is adverse to the exercise of any power over the corpus of a trust, but not to the exercise of a power over any income interest preceding his remainder. For example, if the grantor creates a trust which provides for income to be distributed to A for 10 years and then for the corpus to go to X if he is then living, a power exercisable by X to revest corpus in the grantor is a power exercisable by an adverse party; however, a power exercisable by X to distribute part or all of the ordinary income to the grantor may be a power exercisable by a nonadverse party (which would cause the ordinary income to be taxed to the grantor). [Reg. § 1.672(a)-1.]

☐ [*T.D.* 6217, 12-19-56.]

[Reg. § 1.672(b)-1]

§ 1.672(b)-1. Nonadverse party.—A "nonadverse party" is any person who is not an adverse party. [Reg. § 1.672(b)-1.]

☐ [*T.D.* 6217, 12-19-56.]

[Reg. § 1.672(c)-1]

§ 1.672(c)-1. Related or subordinate party.—Section 672(c) defines the term "related or subordinate party". The term, as used in sections 674(c) and 675(3), means any nonadverse party who is the grantor's spouse if living with the grantor; the grantor's father, mother, issue, brother or sister; an employee of the grantor; a corporation or any employee of a corporation in which the stock holdings of the grantor and the trust are significant from the viewpoint of voting control; or a subordinate employee of a corporation in which the grantor is an executive. For purposes of sections 674(c) and 675(3), these persons are presumed to be subservient to the grantor in respect of the exercise or nonexercise of the powers conferred on them unless shown not to be subservient by a preponderance of the evidence. [Reg. § 1.672(c)-1.]

☐ [*T.D.* 6217, 12-19-56.]

[Reg. § 1.672(d)-1]

§ 1.672(d)-1. Power subject to condition precedent.—Section 672(d) provides that a person is considered to have a power described in subpart E (section 671 and following), part I, subchapter J, chapter 1 of the Code, even though the exercise of the power is subject to a precedent giving of notice or takes effect only after the expiration of a certain period of time. However, although a person may be considered to have such a power, the grantor will nevertheless not be treated as an owner by reason of the power if its exercise can only affect beneficial enjoyment of income received after the expiration of a period of time such that, if the power were a reversionary interest, he would not be treated as an owner under section 673. See sections 674(b)(2), 676(b), and the last sentence of section 677(a). Thus, for example, if a grantor creates a trust for the benefit of his son and retains a power to revoke which takes effect only after the expiration of 2 years from the date of exercise, he is treated as an owner from the inception of the trust. However, if the grantor retains a power to revoke, exercisable at any time, which can only affect the beneficial enjoyment of the ordinary income of a trust received after the expiration of 10 years commencing with the date of the transfer in trust, or after the death of the income beneficiary, the power does not cause him to be treated as an owner with respect to ordinary income during the first 10 years of the trust or during the income beneficiary's life, as the case may be. See section 676(b). [Reg. § 1.672(d)-1.]

☐ [*T.D.* 6217, 12-19-56.]

See p. 15 for regulations not amended to reflect law changes

[Reg. §1.672(f)-1]

§1.672(f)-1. Foreign persons not treated as owners.—(a) *General rule.*—(1) *Application of the general rule.*—Section 672(f)(1) provides that subpart E of part I, subchapter J, chapter 1 of the Internal Revenue Code (the grantor trust rules) shall apply only to the extent such application results in an amount (if any) being currently taken into account (directly or through one or more entities) in computing the income of a citizen or resident of the United States or a domestic corporation. Accordingly, the grantor trust rules apply to the extent that any portion of the trust, upon application of the grantor trust rules without regard to section 672(f), is treated as owned by a United States citizen or resident or domestic corporation. The grantor trust rules do not apply to any portion of the trust to the extent that, upon application of the grantor trust rules without regard to section 672(f), that portion is treated as owned by a person other than a United States citizen or resident or domestic corporation, unless the person is described in §1.672(f)-2(a) (relating to certain foreign corporations treated as domestic corporations), or one of the exceptions set forth in §1.672(f)-3 is met, (relating to: trusts where the grantor can revest trust assets; trusts where the only amounts distributable are to the grantor or the grantor's spouse; and compensatory trusts). Section 672(f) applies to domestic and foreign trusts. Any portion of the trust that is not treated as owned by a grantor or another person is subject to the rules of subparts A through D (section 641 and following), part I, subchapter J, chapter 1 of the Internal Revenue Code.

(2) *Determination of portion based on application of the grantor trust rules.*—The determination of the portion of a trust treated as owned by the grantor or other person is to be made based on the terms of the trust and the application of the grantor trust rules and section 671 and the regulations thereunder.

(b) *Example.*—The following example illustrates the rules of this section:

Example. (i) A, a nonresident alien, funds an irrevocable domestic trust, DT, for the benefit of his son, B, who is a United States citizen, with stock of Corporation X. A's brother, C, who also is a United States citizen, contributes stock of Corporation Y to the trust for the benefit of B. A has a reversionary interest within the meaning of section 673 in the X stock that would cause A to be treated as the owner of the X stock upon application of the grantor trust rules without regard to section 672(f). C has a reversionary interest within the meaning of section 673 in the Y stock that would cause C to be treated as the owner of the Y stock upon application of the grantor trust rules without regard to section 672(f). The trustee has discretion to accumulate or currently distribute income of DT to B.

(ii) Because A is a nonresident alien, application of the grantor trust rules without regard to section 672(f) would not result in the portion of the trust consisting of the X stock being treated as owned by a United States citizen or resident. None of the exceptions in §1.672(f)-3 applies because A cannot revest the X stock in A, amounts may be distributed during A's lifetime to B, who is neither a grantor nor a spouse of a grantor, and the trust is not a compensatory trust. Therefore, pursuant to paragraph (a)(1) of this section, A is not treated as an owner under subpart E of part I, subchapter J, chapter 1 of the Internal Revenue Code, of the portion of the trust consisting of the X stock. Any distributions from such portion of the trust are subject to the rules of subparts A through D (641 and following), part I, subchapter J, chapter 1 of the Internal Revenue Code.

(iii) Because C is a United States citizen, paragraph (a)(1) of this section does not prevent C from being treated under section 673 as the owner of the portion of the trust consisting of the Y stock.

(c) *Effective date.*—The rules of this section are applicable to taxable years of a trust beginning after August 10, 1999. [Reg. §1.672(f)-1.]

☐ [*T.D.* 8831, 8-5-99.]

[Reg. §1.672(f)-2]

§1.672(f)-2. Certain foreign corporations.—(a) *Application of general rule in this section.*—Subject to the provisions of paragraph (b) of this section, if the owner of any portion of a trust upon application of the grantor trust rules without regard to section 672(f) is a controlled foreign corporation or a passive foreign investment company (as defined in section 1297), the corporation is treated as a domestic corporation for purposes of applying the rules of §1.672(f)-1. For purposes of this section, a controlled foreign corporation has the meaning provided in section 957, determined without applying section 318(a)(3)(A), (B), and (C) so as to consider a United States person as owning stock which is owned by a person who is not a United States person.

(b) *Gratuitous transfers to United States persons.*—(1) *Transfer from trust to which corporation made a gratuitous transfer.*—If a trust for (or portion of a trust) to which a controlled foreign corporation, passive foreign investment company, or foreign personal holding company has made a gratuitous transfer (within the meaning of §1.671-2(e)(2)), makes a gratuitous transfer to a United States person, the controlled foreign corporation, passive foreign investment company, or foreign personal holding company, as the case may be, is treated as a foreign corporation for purposes of §1.672(f)-4(c), relating to gratuitous transfers from trusts (or portions of trusts) to which a partnership or foreign corporation has made a gratuitous transfer.

(2) *Transfer from trust over which corporation has a section 678 power.*—If a trust (or portion of a trust) that a controlled foreign corporation, passive foreign investment company, or foreign personal holding company is treated as owning under section 678 makes a gratuitous transfer to a United States person, the controlled foreign

corporation, passive foreign investment company, or foreign personal holding company, as the case may be, is treated as a foreign corporation that had made a gratuitous transfer to the trust (or portion of a trust) and the rules of § 1.672(f)-4(c) apply.

(c) *Special rules for passive foreign investment companies.*—(1) *Application of section 1297.*—For purposes of determining whether a foreign corporation is a passive foreign investment company as defined in section 1297, the grantor trust rules apply as if section 672(f) had not come into effect.

(2) *References to renumbered Internal Revenue Code section.*—For taxable years of shareholders beginning on or before December 31, 1997, and taxable years of passive foreign investment companies ending with or within such taxable years of the shareholders, all references in this § 1.672(f)-2 to section 1297 are deemed to be references to section 1296.

(d) *Examples.*—The following examples illustrate the rules of this section. In each example, FT is an irrevocable foreign trust, and CFC is a controlled foreign corporation. The examples are as follows:

Example 1. Application of general rule. CFC creates and funds FT. CFC is the grantor of FT within the meaning of § 1.671-2(e). CFC has a reversionary interest in FT within the meaning of section 673 that would cause CFC to be treated as the owner of FT upon application of the grantor trust rules without regard to section 672(f). Under paragraph (a) of this section, CFC is treated as a domestic corporation for purposes of applying the general rule of § 1.672(f)-1. Thus, § 1.672(f)-1 does not prevent CFC from being treated as the owner of FT under section 673.

Example 2. Distribution from trust to which CFC made gratuitous transfer. A, a nonresident alien, owns 40 percent of the stock of CFC. A's brother B, a resident alien, owns the other 60 percent of the stock of CFC. CFC makes a gratuitous transfer to FT. FT makes a gratuitous transfer to A's daughter, C, who is a resident alien. Under paragraph (b)(1) of this section, CFC will be treated as a foreign corporation for purposes of § 1.672(f)-4(c). For further guidance, see § 1.672(f)-4(g) *Example 2* through *Example 4*.

(e) *Applicability dates.*—Except as provided in this paragraph (e), the rules of this section apply to taxable years of shareholders of controlled foreign corporations and passive foreign investment companies beginning after August 10, 1999, and taxable years of controlled foreign corporations and passive foreign investment companies ending with or within such taxable years of the shareholders. The provisions in paragraph (a) of this section relating to the controlled foreign corporations taken into account for purposes of this section apply to taxable years of foreign corporations ending on or after October 1, 2019, and taxable years of United States shareholders in which or with which such taxable years of foreign corporations end. For taxable years of foreign corporations ending before October 1, 2019, and taxable years of United States shareholders in which or with which such taxable years of foreign corporations end, a taxpayer may apply such provisions to the last taxable year of a foreign corporation beginning before January 1, 2018, and each subsequent taxable year of the foreign corporation, and to taxable years of United States shareholders in which or with which such taxable years of the foreign corporation end, provided that the taxpayer and United States persons that are related (within the meaning of section 267 or 707) to the taxpayer consistently apply such provisions with respect to all foreign corporations. For taxable years of foreign corporations ending before October 1, 2019, and taxable years of United States shareholders in which or with which such taxable years of foreign corporations end, where the taxpayer does not apply the provisions of paragraph (a) of this section relating to controlled foreign corporations, see paragraph (a) of this section as in effect and contained in 26 CFR part 1, as revised April 1, 2020. [Reg. § 1.672(f)-2.]

☐ [*T.D.* 8831, 8-5-99. *Amended by T.D.* 8890, 7-3-2000 *and T.D.* 9908, 9-21-2020.]

[Reg. § 1.672(f)-3]

§ 1.672(f)-3. Exceptions to general rule.—(a) *Certain revocable trusts.*—(1) *In general.*—Subject to the provisions of paragraph (a)(2) of this section, the general rule of § 1.672(f)-1 does not apply to any portion of a trust for a taxable year of the trust if the power to revest absolutely in the grantor title to such portion is exercisable solely by the grantor (or, in the event of the grantor's incapacity, by a guardian or other person who has unrestricted authority to exercise such power on the grantor's behalf) without the approval or consent of any other person. If the grantor can exercise such power only with the approval of a related or subordinate party who is subservient to the grantor, such power is treated as exercisable solely by the grantor. For the definition of *grantor*, see § 1.671-2(e). For the definition of *related or subordinate party*, see § 1.672(c)-1. For purposes of this paragraph (a), a related or subordinate party is subservient to the grantor unless the presumption in the last sentence of § 1.672(c)-1 is rebutted by a preponderance of the evidence. A trust (or portion of a trust) that fails to qualify for the exception provided by this paragraph (a) for a particular taxable year of the trust will be subject to the general rule of § 1.672(f)-1 for that taxable year and all subsequent taxable years of the trust.

(2) *183-day rule.*—For purposes of paragraph (a)(1) of this section, the grantor is treated as having a power to revest for a taxable year of the trust only if the grantor has such power for a total of 183 or more days during the taxable year of the trust. If the first or last taxable year of the trust (including the year of the grantor's death) is less than 183 days, the grantor is treated as having a power to revest for purposes of paragraph (a)(1) of this section if the grantor has such power for each day of the first or last taxable year, as the case may be.

(3) *Grandfather rule for certain revocable trusts in existence on September 19, 1995.*—Subject to the rules of paragraph (d) of this section (relating to separate accounting for gratuitous transfers to the trust after September 19, 1995), the general rule of §1.672(f)-1 does not apply to any portion of a trust that was treated as owned by the grantor under section 676 on September 19, 1995, as long as the trust would continue to be so treated thereafter. However, the preceding sentence does not apply to any portion of the trust attributable to gratuitous transfers to the trust after September 19, 1995.

(4) *Examples.*—The following examples illustrate the rules of this paragraph (a):

Example 1. Grantor is owner. FP1, a foreign person, creates and funds a revocable trust, T, for the benefit of FP1's children, who are resident aliens. The trustee is a foreign bank, FB, that is owned and controlled by FP1 and FP2, who is FP1's brother. The power to revoke T and revest absolutely in FP1 title to the trust property is exercisable by FP1, but only with the approval or consent of FB. The trust instrument contains no standard that FB must apply in determining whether to approve or consent to the revocation of T. There are no facts that would suggest that FB is not subservient to FP1. Therefore, the exception in paragraph (a)(1) of this section is applicable.

Example 2. Death of grantor. Assume the same facts as in *Example 1*, except that FP1 dies. After FP1's death, FP2 has the power to withdraw the assets of T, but only with the approval of FB. There are no facts that would suggest that FB is not subservient to FP2. However, the exception in paragraph (a)(1) of this section is no longer applicable, because FP2 is not a grantor of T within the meaning of §1.671-2(e).

Example 3. Trustee is not related or subordinate party. Assume the same facts as in *Example 1*, except that neither FP1 nor any member of FP1's family has any substantial ownership interest or other connection with FB. FP1 can remove and replace FB at any time for any reason. Although FP1 can replace FB with a related or subordinate party if FB refuses to approve or consent to FP1's decision to revest the trust property in himself, FB is not a related or subordinate party. Therefore, the exception in paragraph (a)(1) of this section is not applicable.

Example 4. Unrelated trustee will consent to revocation. FP, a foreign person, creates and funds an irrevocable trust, T. The trustee is a foreign bank, FB, that is not a related or subordinate party within the meaning of §1.672(c)-1. FB has the discretion to distribute trust income or corpus to beneficiaries of T, including FP. Even if FB would in fact distribute all the trust property to FP if requested to do so by FP, the exception in paragraph (a)(1) of this section is not applicable, because FP does not have the power to revoke T.

(b) *Certain trusts that can distribute only to the grantor or the spouse of the grantor.*—(1) *In general.*—The general rule of §1.672(f)-1 does not apply to any trust (or portion of a trust) if at all times during the lifetime of the grantor the only amounts distributable (whether income or corpus) from such trust (or portion thereof) are amounts distributable to the grantor or the spouse of the grantor. For purposes of this paragraph (b), payments of amounts that are not gratuitous transfers (within the meaning of §1.671-2(e)(2)) are not amounts distributable. For the definition of *grantor*, see §1.671-2(e).

(2) *Amounts distributable in discharge of legal obligations.*—(i) *In general.*—A trust (or portion of a trust) does not fail to satisfy paragraph (b)(1) of this section solely because amounts are distributable from the trust (or portion thereof) in discharge of a legal obligation of the grantor or the spouse of the grantor. Subject to the provisions of paragraph (b)(2)(ii) of this section, an obligation is considered a legal obligation for purposes of this paragraph (b)(2)(i) if it is enforceable under the local law of the jurisdiction in which the grantor (or the spouse of the grantor) resides.

(ii) *Related parties.*—(A) *In general.*—Except as provided in paragraph (b)(2)(ii)(B) of this section, an obligation to a person who is a related person for purposes of §1.643(h)-1(e) (other than an individual who is legally separated from the grantor under a decree of divorce or of separate maintenance) is not a legal obligation for purposes of paragraph (b)(2)(i) of this section unless it was contracted bona fide and for adequate and full consideration in money or money's worth (see §20.2043-1 of this chapter).

(B) *Exceptions.*—*(1) Amounts distributable in support of certain individuals.*—Paragraph (b)(2)(ii)(A) of this section does not apply with respect to amounts that are distributable from the trust (or portion thereof) to support an individual who—

(i) Would be treated as a dependent of the grantor or the spouse of the grantor under section 152(a)(1) through (9), without regard to the requirement that over half of the individual's support be received from the grantor or the spouse of the grantor; and

(ii) Is either permanently and totally disabled (within the meaning of section 22(e)(3)), or less than 19 years old.

(2) Certain potential support obligations.—The fact that amounts might become distributable from a trust (or portion of a trust) in discharge of a potential obligation under local law to support an individual other than an individual described in paragraph (b)(2)(ii)(B)(*1*) of this section is disregarded if such potential obligation is not reasonably expected to arise under the facts and circumstances.

(3) Reinsurance trusts.—[Reserved]

(3) *Grandfather rule for certain section 677 trusts in existence on September 19, 1995.*—Subject to the rules of paragraph (d) of this section (relating to separate accounting for gratuitous transfers to the trust after September 19, 1995), the general rule of §1.672(f)-1 does not apply to any portion of a trust that was treated as owned by

the grantor under section 677 (other than section 677(a)(3)) on September 19, 1995, as long as the trust would continue to be so treated thereafter. However, the preceding sentence does not apply to any portion of the trust attributable to gratuitous transfers to the trust after September 19, 1995.

(4) *Examples.*—The following examples illustrate the rules of this paragraph (b):

Example 1. Amounts distributable only to grantor or grantor's spouse. H and his wife, W, are both nonresident aliens. H is 70 years old, and W is 65. H and W have a 30-year-old child, C, a resident alien. There is no reasonable expectation that H or W will ever have an obligation under local law to support C or any other individual. H creates and funds an irrevocable trust, FT, using only his separate property. H is the grantor of FT within the meaning of § 1.671-2(e). Under the terms of FT, the only amounts distributable (whether income or corpus) from FT as long as either H or W is alive are amounts distributable to H or W. Upon the death of both H and W, C may receive distributions from FT. During H's lifetime, the exception in paragraph (b)(1) of this section is applicable.

Example 2. Effect of grantor's death. Assume the same facts as in *Example 1*. H predeceases W. Assume that W would be treated as owning FT under section 678 if the grantor trust rules were applied without regard to section 672(f). The exception in paragraph (b)(1) of this section is no longer applicable, because W is not a grantor of FT within the meaning of § 1.671-2(e).

Example 3. Amounts temporarily distributable to person other than grantor or grantor's spouse. Assume the same facts as in *Example 1*, except that C (age 30) is a law student at the time FT is created and the trust instrument provides that, as long as C is in law school, amounts may be distributed from FT to pay C's expenses. Thereafter, the only amounts distributable from FT as long as either H or W is alive will be amounts distributable to H or W. Even assuming there is an enforceable obligation under local law for H and W to support C while he is in school, distributions from FT in payment of C's expenses cannot qualify as distributions in discharge of a legal obligation under paragraph (b)(2) of this section, because C is neither permanently and totally disabled nor less than 19 years old. The exception in paragraph (b)(1) of this section is not applicable. After C graduates from law school, the exception in paragraph (b)(1) still will not be applicable, because amounts were distributable to C during the lifetime of H.

Example 4. Fixed investment trust. FC, a foreign corporation, invests in a domestic fixed investment trust, DT, that is classified as a trust under § 301.7701-4(c)(1) of this chapter. Under the terms of DT, the only amounts that are distributable from FC's portion of DT are amounts distributable to FC. The exception in paragraph (b)(1) of this section is applicable to FC's portion of DT.

Example 5. Reinsurance trust. A domestic insurance company, DI, reinsures a portion of its business with an unrelated foreign insurance company, FI. To satisfy state regulatory requirements, FI places the premiums in an irrevocable domestic trust, DT. The trust funds are held by a United States bank and may be used only to pay claims arising out of the reinsurance policies, which are legally enforceable under the local law of the jurisdiction in which FT resides. On the termination of DT, any assets remaining will revert to FI. Because the only amounts that are distributable from DT are distributable either to FI or in discharge of FI's legal obligations within the meaning of paragraph (b)(2)(i) of this section, the exception in paragraph (b)(1) of this section is applicable.

Example 6. Trust that provides security for loan. FC, a foreign corporation, borrows money from B, an unrelated bank, to finance the purchase of an airplane. FC creates a foreign trust, FT, to hold the airplane as security for the loan from B. The only amounts that are distributable from FT while the loan is outstanding are amounts distributable to B in the event that FC defaults on its loan from B. When FC repays the loan, the trust assets will revert to FC. The loan is a legal obligation of FC within the meaning of paragraph (b)(2)(i) of this section, because it is enforceable under the local law of the country in which FC is incorporated. Paragraph (b)(2)(ii) of this section is not applicable, because B is not a related person for purposes of § 1.643(h)-1(e). The exception in paragraph (b)(1) of this section is applicable.

(c) *Compensatory trusts.*—(1) *In general.*—The general rule of § 1.672(f)-1 does not apply to any portion of—

(i) A nonexempt employees' trust described in section 402(b), including a trust created on behalf of a self-employed individual;

(ii) A trust, including a trust created on behalf of a self-employed individual, that would be a nonexempt employees' trust described in section 402(b) but for the fact that the trust's assets are not set aside from the claims of creditors of the actual or deemed transferor within the meaning of § 1.83-3(e); and

(iii) Any additional category of trust that the Commissioner may designate in revenue procedures, notices, or other guidance published in the Internal Revenue Bulletin (see § 601.601(d)(2) of this chapter).

(2) *Exceptions.*—The Commissioner may, in revenue rulings, notices, or other guidance published in the Internal Revenue Bulletin (see § 601.601(d)(2) of this chapter), designate categories of compensatory trusts to which the general rule of paragraph (c)(1) of this section does not apply.

(d) *Separate accounting for gratuitous transfers to grandfathered trusts after September 19, 1995.*—If a trust that was treated as owned by the grantor under section 676 or 677 (other than section 677(a)(3)) on September 19, 1995, contains both amounts held in the trust on September 19, 1995, and amounts that were gratuitously transferred to the trust after September 19, 1995, paragraphs (a)(3) and (b)(3) of this section apply only if the amounts that were gratuitously transferred to the trust after September 19, 1995, are treated as a separate portion of the trust that is accounted for under the rules of §1.671-3(a)(2). If the amounts that were gratuitously transferred to the trust after September 19, 1995 are not so accounted for, the general rule of §1.672(f)-1 applies to the entire trust. If such amounts are so accounted for, and without regard to whether there is physical separation of the assets, the general rule of §1.672(f)-1 does not apply to the portion of the trust that is attributable to amounts that were held in the trust on September 19, 1995.

(e) *Effective date.*—The rules of this section are generally applicable to taxable years of a trust beginning after August 10, 1999. The initial separate accounting required by paragraph (d) of this section must be prepared by the due date (including extensions) for the tax return of the trust for the first taxable year of the trust beginning after August 10, 1999. [Reg. §1.672(f)-3.]

☐ [*T.D.* 8831, 8-5-99. *Amended by T.D.* 8890, 7-3-2000.]

[Reg. §1.672(f)-4]

§1.672(f)-4. Recharacterization of purported gifts.—(a) *In general.*—(1) *Purported gifts from partnerships.*—Except as provided in paragraphs (b), (e), and (f) of this section, and without regard to the existence of any trust, if a United States person (United States donee) directly or indirectly receives a purported gift or bequest (as defined in paragraph (d) of this section) from a partnership, the purported gift or bequest must be included in the United States donee's gross income as ordinary income.

(2) *Purported gifts from foreign corporations.*—Except as provided in paragraphs (b), (e), and (f) of this section, and without regard to the existence of any trust, if a United States donee directly or indirectly receives a purported gift or bequest (as defined in paragraph (d) of this section) from any foreign corporation, the purported gift or bequest must be included in the United States donee's gross income as if it were a distribution from the foreign corporation. If the foreign corporation is a passive foreign investment company (within the meaning of section 1297), the rules of section 1291 apply. For purposes of section 1012, the United States donee is not treated as having basis in the stock of the foreign corporation. However, for purposes of section 1223, the United States donee is treated as having a holding period in the stock of the foreign corporation on the date of the deemed distribution equal to the weighted average of the holding periods of the actual interest holders (other than any interest holders who treat the portion of the purported gift attributable to their interest in the foreign corporation in the manner described in paragraph (b)(1) of this section). For purposes of section 902, a United States donee that is a domestic corporation is not treated as owning any voting stock of the foreign corporation.

(b) *Exceptions.*—(1) *Partner or shareholder treats transfer as distribution and gift.*—Paragraph (a) of this section does not apply to the extent the United States donee can demonstrate to the satisfaction of the Commissioner that either—

(i) A United States citizen or resident alien individual who directly or indirectly holds an interest in the partnership or foreign corporation treated and reported the purported gift or bequest for United States tax purposes as a distribution to such individual and a subsequent gift or bequest to the United States donee; or

(ii) A nonresident alien individual who directly or indirectly holds an interest in the partnership or foreign corporation treated and reported the purported gift or bequest for purposes of the tax laws of the nonresident alien individual's country of residence as a distribution to such individual and a subsequent gift or bequest to the United States donee, and the United States donee timely complied with the reporting requirements of section 6039F, if applicable.

(2) *All beneficial owners of domestic partnership are United States citizens or residents or domestic corporations.*—Paragraph (a)(1) of this section does not apply to a purported gift or bequest from a domestic partnership if the United States donee can demonstrate to the satisfaction of the Commissioner that all beneficial owners (within the meaning of §1.1441-1(c)(6)) of the partnership are United States citizens or residents or domestic corporations.

(3) *Contribution to capital of corporate United States donee.*—Paragraph (a) of this section does not apply to the extent a United States donee that is a corporation can establish that the purported gift or bequest was treated for United States tax purposes as a contribution to the capital of the United States donee to which section 118 applies.

(4) *Charitable transfers.*—Paragraph (a) of this section does not apply if either—

(i) The United States donee is described in section 170(c); or

(ii) The transferor has received a ruling or determination letter, which has been neither revoked nor modified, from the Internal Revenue Service recognizing its exempt status under section 501(c)(3), and the transferor made the transfer pursuant to an exempt purpose for which the transferor was created or organized. For purposes of the preceding sentence, a ruling or determination letter recognizing exemption may not be relied upon if there is a material change, inconsistent with exemption, in the character, the purpose, or the method of operation of the organization.

(c) *Certain transfers from trusts to which a partnership or foreign corporation has made a gratuitous transfer.*—(1) *Generally treated as distribution from partnership or foreign corporation.*—Except as provided in paragraphs (c)(2) and (3) of this section, if a United States donee receives a gratuitous transfer (within the meaning of §1.671-2(e)(2)) from a trust (or portion of a trust) to which a partnership or foreign corporation has made a gratuitous transfer, the United States donee must treat the transfer as a purported gift or bequest from the partnership or foreign corporation that is subject to the rules of paragraph (a) of this section (including the exceptions in paragraphs (b) and (f) of this section). This paragraph (c) applies without regard to who is treated as the grantor of the trust (or portion thereof) under §1.671-2(e)(4).

(2) *Alternative rule.*—Except as provided in paragraph (c)(3) of this section, if the United States tax computed under the rules of paragraphs (a) and (c)(1) of this section does not exceed the United States tax that would be due if the United States donee treated the transfer as a distribution from the trust (or portion thereof), paragraph (c)(1) of this section does not apply and the United States donee must treat the transfer as a distribution from the trust (or portion thereof) that is subject to the rules of subparts A through D (section 641 and following), part I, subchapter J, chapter 1 of the Internal Revenue Code. For purposes of paragraph (f) of this section, the transfer is treated as a purported gift or bequest from the partnership or foreign corporation that made the gratuitous transfer to the trust (or portion thereof).

(3) *Exception.*—Neither paragraph (c)(1) of this section nor paragraph (c)(2) of this section applies to the extent the United States donee can demonstrate to the satisfaction of the Commissioner that the transfer represents an amount that is, or has been, taken into account for United States tax purposes by a United States citizen or resident or a domestic corporation. A transfer will be deemed to be made first out of amounts that have not been taken into account for United States tax purposes by a United States citizen or resident or a domestic corporation, unless the United States donee can demonstrate to the satisfaction of the Commissioner that another ordering rule is more appropriate.

(d) *Definition of purported gift or bequest.*—(1) *In general.*—Subject to the provisions of paragraphs (d)(2) and (3) of this section, *a purported gift or bequest* for purposes of this section is any transfer of property by a partnership or foreign corporation other than a transfer for fair market value (within the meaning of §1.671-2(e)(2)(ii)) to a person who is not a partner in the partnership or a shareholder of the foreign corporation (or to a person who is a partner in the partnership or a shareholder of a foreign corporation, if the amount transferred is inconsistent with the partner's interest in the partnership or the shareholder's interest in the corporation, as the case may be). For purposes of this section, the term *property* includes cash.

(2) *Transfers for less than fair market value.*—(i) *Excess treated as purported gift or bequest.*—Except as provided in paragraph (d)(2)(ii) of this section, if a transfer described in paragraph (d)(1) of this section is for less than fair market value, the excess of the fair market value of the property transferred over the value of the property received, services rendered, or the right to use property is treated as a purported gift or bequest.

(ii) *Exception for transfers to unrelated parties.*—No portion of a transfer described in paragraph (d)(1) of this section will be treated as a purported gift or bequest for purposes of this section if the United States donee can demonstrate to the satisfaction of the Commissioner that the United States donee is not related to a partner or shareholder of the transferor within the meaning of §1.643(h)-1(e) or does not have another relationship with a partner or shareholder of the transferor that establishes a reasonable basis for concluding that the transferor would make a gratuitous transfer to the United States donee.

(e) *Prohibition against affirmative use of recharacterization by taxpayers.*—A taxpayer may not use the rules of this section if a principal purpose for using such rules is the avoidance of any tax imposed by the Internal Revenue Code. Thus, with respect to such taxpayer, the Commissioner may depart from the rules of this section and recharacterize (for all purposes of the Internal Revenue Code) the transfer in accordance with its form or its economic substance.

(f) *Transfers not in excess of $10,000.*—This section does not apply if, during the taxable year of the United States donee, the aggregate amount of purported gifts or bequests that is transferred to such United States donee directly or indirectly from all partnerships or foreign corporations that are related (within the meaning of section 643(i)) does not exceed $10,000. The aggregate amount must include gifts or bequests from persons that the United States donee knows or has reason to know are related to the partnership or foreign corporation (within the meaning of section 643(i)).

(g) *Examples.*—The following examples illustrate the rules of this section. In each example, the amount that is transferred exceeds $10,000. The examples are as follows:

Example 1. Distribution from foreign corporation. FC is a foreign corporation that is wholly owned by A, a nonresident alien who is resident in Country C. FC makes a gratuitous transfer of property directly to A's daughter, B, who is a resident alien. Under paragraph (a)(2) of this section, B generally must treat the transfer as a dividend from FC to the extent of FC's earnings and profits and as an amount received in excess of basis thereafter. If FC is a passive foreign investment company, B must treat the amount received as a distribution under section 1291. B will be treated as having the same holding period as A. However, under paragraph (b)(1)(ii) of this section, if B can establish to the satisfaction of the Commissioner that, for purposes of the tax laws of Country C, A treated (and reported, if applicable) the transfer as a distribution to himself and a subsequent gift to B, B may treat the transfer as a gift (provided B timely complied with the reporting requirements of section 6039F, if applicable).

Example 2. Distribution of corpus from trust to which foreign corporation made gratuitous transfer. FC is a foreign corporation that is wholly owned by A, a nonresident alien who is resident in Country C. FC makes a gratuitous transfer to a foreign trust, FT, that has no other assets. FT immediately makes a gratuitous transfer in the same amount to A's daughter, B, who is a resident alien. Under paragraph (c)(1) of this section, B must treat the transfer as a transfer from FC that is subject to the rules of paragraph (a)(2) of this section. Under paragraph (a)(2) of this section, B must treat the transfer as a dividend from FC unless she can establish to the satisfaction of the Commissioner that, for purposes of the tax laws of Country C, A treated (and reported, if applicable) the transfer as a distribution to himself and a subsequent gift to B and that B timely complied with the reporting requirements of section 6039F, if applicable. The alternative rule in paragraph (c)(2) of this section would not apply as long as the United States tax computed under the rules of paragraph (a)(2) of this section is equal to or greater than the United States tax that would be due if the transfer were treated as a distribution from FT.

Example 3. Accumulation distribution from trust to which foreign corporation made gratuitous transfer. FC is a foreign corporation that is wholly owned by A, a nonresident alien. FC is not a passive foreign investment company (as defined in section 1297). FC makes a gratuitous transfer of 100X to a foreign trust, FT, on January 1, 2001. FT has no other assets on January 1, 2001. Several years later, FT makes a gratuitous transfer of 1000X to A's daughter, B, who is a United States resident. Assume that the section 668 interest charge on accumulation distributions will apply if the transfer is treated as a distribution from FT. Under the alternative rule of paragraph (c)(2) of this section, B must treat the transfer as an accumulation distribution from FT, because the resulting United States tax liability is greater than the United States tax that would be due if the transfer were treated as a transfer from FC that is subject to the rules of paragraph (a) of this section.

Example 4. Transfer from trust that is treated as owned by United States citizen. Assume the same facts as in *Example 3*, except that A is a United States citizen. Assume that A treats and reports the transfer to FT as a constructive distribution to himself, followed by a gratuitous transfer to FT, and that A is properly treated as the grantor of FT within the meaning of §1.671-2(e). A is treated as the owner of FT under section 679 and, as required by section 671 and the regulations thereunder, A includes all of FT's items of income, deductions, and credit in computing his taxable income and credits. Neither paragraph (c)(1) nor paragraph (c)(2) of this section is applicable, because the exception in paragraph (c)(3) of this section applies.

Example 5. Transfer for less than fair market value. FC is a foreign corporation that is wholly owned by A, a nonresident alien. On January 15, 2001, FC transfers property directly to A's daughter, B, a resident alien, in exchange for 90X. The Commissioner later determines that the fair market value of the property at the time of the transfer was 100X. Under paragraph (d)(2)(i) of this section, 10X will be treated as a purported gift to B on January 15, 2001.

(h) *Effective date.*—The rules of this section are generally applicable to any transfer after August 10, 1999, by a partnership or foreign corporation, or by a trust to which a partnership or foreign corporation makes a gratuitous transfer after August 10, 1999. [Reg. §1.672(f)-4.]

☐ [*T.D.* 8831, 8-5-99. *Amended by T.D.* 8890, 7-3-2000.]

[Reg. §1.672(f)-5]

§1.672(f)-5. Special rules.—(a) *Transfers by certain beneficiaries to foreign grantor.*—(1) *In general.*—If, but for section 672(f)(5), a foreign person would be treated as the owner of any portion of a trust, any United States beneficiary of the trust is treated as the grantor of a portion of the trust to the extent the United States beneficiary directly or indirectly made transfers of property to such foreign person (without regard to whether the United States beneficiary was a United States beneficiary at the time of any transfer) in excess of transfers to the United States beneficiary from the foreign person. The rule of this paragraph (a) does not apply to the extent the United States beneficiary can demonstrate to the satisfaction of the Commissioner that the transfer by the United States beneficiary to the foreign person was wholly unrelated to any transaction involving the trust. For purposes of this paragraph (a), the term property includes cash, and a transfer of property does not include a transfer that is not a gratuitous transfer (within the meaning of §1.671-2(e)(2)). In addition, a gift is not taken into account to the extent such gift would not be characterized as a taxable gift under section 2503(b). For a definition of United States beneficiary, see section 679.

(2) *Examples.*—The following examples illustrate the rules of this section:

Example 1. A, a nonresident alien, contributes property to FC, a foreign corporation that is wholly owned by A. FC creates a foreign trust, FT, for the benefit of A and A's children. FT is revocable by FC without the approval or consent of any other person. FC funds FT with the property received from A. A and A's family move to the United States. Under paragraph (a)(1) of this section, A is treated as a grantor of FT. (A may also be treated as an owner of FT under section 679(a)(4).)

Example 2. B, a United States citizen, makes a gratuitous transfer of $1 million to B's uncle, C, a nonresident alien. C creates a foreign trust, FT, for the benefit of B and B's children. FT is revocable by C without the approval or consent of any other person. C funds FT with the property received from B. Under paragraph (a)(1) of this section, B is treated as a grantor of FT. (B also would be treated as an owner of FT as a result of section 679.)

(b) *Entity characterization.*—Entities generally are characterized under United States tax principles for purposes of § § 1.672(f)-1 through 1.672(f)-5. See § § 301.7701-1 through 301.7701-4 of this chapter. However, solely for purposes of § 1.672(f)-4, a transferor that is a wholly owned business entity is treated as a corporation, separate from its single owner.

(c) *Effective date.*—The rules in paragraph (a) of this section are applicable to transfers to trusts on or after August 10, 1999. The rules in paragraph (b) of this section are applicable August 10, 1999. [Reg. § 1.672(f)-5.]

☐ [*T.D.* 8831, 8-5-99. *Amended by T.D.* 8890, 7-3-2000.]

[Reg. § 1.673(a)-1]

§ 1.673(a)-1. Reversionary interests; income payable to beneficiaries other than certain charitable organizations; general rule.—(a) Under section 673(a), a grantor, in general, is treated as the owner of any portion of a trust in which he has a reversionary interest in either the corpus or income if, as of the inception of that portion of the trust, the grantor's interest will or may reasonably be expected to take effect in possession or enjoyment within 10 years commencing with the date of transfer of that portion of the trust. However, the following types of reversionary interests are excepted from the general rule of the preceding sentence:

(1) A reversionary interest after the death of the income beneficiary of a trust (see paragraph (b) of this section); and

(2) Except in the case of transfers in trust made after April 22, 1969, a reversionary interest in a charitable trust meeting the requirements of section 673(b) (see § 1.673(b)-1).

Even though the duration of the trust may be such that the grantor is not treated as its owner under section 673, and therefore is not taxed on the ordinary income, he may nevertheless be treated as an owner under section 677(a)(2) if he has a reversionary interest in the corpus. In the latter case, items of income, deduction, and credit allocable to corpus, such as capital gains and losses, will be included in the portion he owns. See § 1.671-3 and the regulations under section 677. See § 1.673(d)-1 with respect to a postponement of the date specified for reacquisition of a reversionary interest.

(b) Section 673(c) provides that a grantor is not treated as the owner of any portion of a trust by reason of section 673 if his reversionary interest in the portion is not to take effect in possession or enjoyment until the death of the person or persons to whom the income of the portion is payable, regardless of the life expectancies of the income beneficiaries. If his reversionary interest is to take effect on or after the death of an income beneficiary or upon the expiration of a specific term of years, whichever is earlier, the grantor is treated as the owner if the specific term of years is less than 10 years (but not if the term is 10 years or longer).

(c) Where the grantor's reversionary interest in a portion of a trust is to take effect in possession or enjoyment by reason of some event other than the expiration of a specific term of years or the death of the income beneficiary, the grantor is treated as the owner of the portion if the event may reasonably be expected to occur within 10 years from the date of transfer of that portion, but he is not treated as the owner under section 673 if the event may not reasonably be expected to occur within 10 years from that date. For example, if the reversionary interest in any portion of a trust is to take effect on or after the death of the grantor (or any person other than the person to whom the income is payable) the grantor is treated under section 673 as the owner of the portion if the life expectancy of the grantor (or other person) is less than 10 years on the date of transfer of the portion, but not if the life expectancy is 10 years or longer. If the reversionary interest in any portion is to take effect on or after the death of the grantor (or any person other than the person to whom the income is payable) or upon the expiration of a specific term of years, whichever is earlier, the grantor is treated as the owner of the portion if on the date of transfer of the portion either the life expectancy of the grantor (or other person) or the specific term is less than 10 years; however, if both the life expectancy and the specific term are 10 years or longer the grantor is not treated as the owner of the portion under section 673. Similarly, if the grantor has a reversionary interest in any portion which will take effect at the death of the income beneficiary or the grantor, whichever is earlier, the grantor is not treated as an owner of the portion unless his life expectancy is less than 10 years.

(d) It is immaterial that a reversionary interest in corpus or income is subject to a contingency if the reversionary interest may, taking the contingency into consideration, reasonably be expected to take effect in possession or enjoyment within 10 years. For example, the grantor is taxable where the trust income is to be paid to the grantor's son for 3 years, and the corpus is then to be returned to the grantor if he survives that period, or to be paid to the grantor's son if he is already deceased.

(e) See section 671 and § § 1.671-2 and 1.671-3 for rules for treatment of items of income, deduction, and credit when a person is treated as the owner of all or only a portion of a trust. [Reg. § 1.673(a)-1.]

☐ [*T.D.* 6217, 12-19-56. *Amended by T.D.* 7357, 5-30-75.]

[Reg. § 1.673(b)-1]

§ 1.673(b)-1. Income payable to charitable beneficiaries (before amendment by Tax Reform Act of 1969).—(a) Pursuant to section 673(b) a grantor is not treated as an owner of any portion of a trust under section 673, even though he has a reversionary interest which will take effect within 10 years, to the extent that, under the terms of the trust, the income of the portion is irrevocably payable for a period of at least 2 years (commencing with the date of the transfer) to a designated beneficiary of the type described in section 170(b)(1)(A).

(b) Income must be irrevocably payable to a designated beneficiary for at least 2 years commencing with the date of the transfer before the benefit of section 673(b) will apply. Thus, section 673(b) will not apply if income of a trust is irrevocably payable to University A for 1 year and then to University B for the next year; or if income of a trust may be allocated among two or more charitable beneficiaries in the discretion of the trustee or any other person. On the other hand, section 673(b) will apply if half the income of a trust is irrevocably payable to University A and the other half is irrevocably payable to University B for two years.

(c) Section 673(b) applies to the period of 2 years or longer during which income is paid to a designated beneficiary of the type described in section 170(b)(1)(A)(i), (ii), or (iii), even though the trust term is to extend beyond that period. However, the other provisions of section 673 apply to the part of the trust term, if any, that extends beyond that period. This paragraph may be illustrated by the following example:

Example. G transfers property in trust with the ordinary income payable to University C (which qualifies under section 170(b)(1)(A)(ii)) for 3 years, and then to his son, B, for 5 years. At the expiration of the term the trust reverts to G. G is not taxed under section 673 on the trust income payable to University C for the first 3 years because of the application of section 673(b). However, he is taxed on income for the next 5 years because he has a reversionary interest which will take effect within 10 years commencing with the date of the transfer. On the other hand, if the income were payable to University C for 3 years and then to B for 7 years so that the trust corpus would not be returned to G within 10 years, G would not be taxable under section 673 on income payable to University C and to B during any part of the term.

(d) This section does not apply to transfers in trust made after April 22, 1969. [Reg. §1.673(b)-1.]

□ [*T.D.* 6217, 12-19-56. *Amended by T.D.* 6605, 8-14-62, *and by T.D.* 7357, 5-30-75.]

[Reg. §1.673(c)-1]

§1.673(c)-1. Reversionary interest after income beneficiary's death.—The subject matter of section 673(c) is covered in paragraph (b) of §1.673(a)-1. [Reg. §1.673(c)-1.]

□ [*T.D.* 6217, 12-19-56.]

[Reg. §1.673(d)-1]

§1.673(d)-1. Postponement of date specified for reacquisition.—Any postponement of the date specified for the reacquisition of possession or enjoyment of any reversionary interest is considered a new transfer in trust commencing with the date on which the postponement is effected and terminating with the date prescribed by the postponement. However, the grantor will not be treated as the owner of any portion of a trust for any taxable year by reason of the foregoing sentence if he would not be so treated in the absence of any postponement. The rules contained in this section may be illustrated by the following example:

Example. G places property in trust for the benefit of his son B. Upon the expiration of 12 years or the earlier death of B the property is to be paid over to G or his estate. After the expiration of 9 years G extends the term of the trust for an additional 2 years. G is considered to have made a new transfer in trust for a term of 5 years (the remaining 3 years of the original transfer plus the 2-year extension). However, he is not treated as the owner of the trust under section 673 for the first 3 years of the new term because he would not be so treated if the term of the trust had not been extended. G is treated as the owner of the trust, however, for the remaining 2 years. [Reg. §1.673(d)-1.]

□ [*T.D.* 6217, 12-19-56.]

[Reg. §1.674(a)-1]

§1.674(a)-1. Power to control beneficial enjoyment; scope of section 674.—(a) Under section 674, the grantor is treated as the owner of a portion of trust if the grantor or a nonadverse party has a power, beyond specified limits, to dispose of the beneficial enjoyment of the income or corpus, whether the power is a fiduciary power, a power of appointment, or any other power. Section 674(a) states in general terms that the grantor is treated as the owner in every case in which he or a nonadverse party can affect the beneficial enjoyment of a portion of a trust, the limitations being set forth as exceptions in subsections (b), (c), and (d) of section 674. These exceptions are discussed in detail in §§1.674(b)-1 through 1.674(d)-1. Certain limitations applicable to sections 674(b), (c), and (d) are set forth in §1.674(d)-2. Section 674(b) describes powers which are excepted regardless of who holds them. Section 674(c) describes additional powers of trustees which are excepted if at least half the trustees are independent, and if the grantor is not a trustee. Section 674(d) describes a further power which is excepted if it is held by trustees other than the grantor or his spouse (if living with the grantor).

(b) In general terms the grantor is treated as the owner of a portion of a trust if he or a nonadverse party or both has a power to dispose of the beneficial enjoyment of the corpus or income unless the power is one of the following:

(1) *Miscellaneous powers over either ordinary income or corpus.*—(i) A power that can only affect the beneficial enjoyment of income (including capital gains) received after a period of time such that the grantor would not be treated as an owner under section 673 if the power were a reversionary interest (section 674(b)(2));

(ii) A testamentary power held by anyone (other than a testamentary power held by the grantor over accumulated income) (section 674(b)(3));

(iii) A power to choose between charitable beneficiaries or to affect the manner of their enjoyment of a beneficial interest (section 674(b)(4));

(iv) A power to allocate receipts and disbursements between income and corpus (section 674(b)(8)).

(2) *Powers of distribution primarily affecting only one beneficiary.*—(i) *A power to distribute corpus.*—to or for a current income beneficiary, if the distribution must be charged against the share of corpus from which the beneficiary may receive income (section 674(b)(5)(B));

(ii) *A power to distribute income.*—to or for a current income beneficiary or to accumulate it either (*a*) if accumulated income must either be payable to the beneficiary from whom it was withheld or as described in paragraph (b)(6) of § 1.674(b)-1 (section 674(b)(6)); (*b*) if the power is to apply income to the support of a dependent of the grantor, and the income is not so applied (section 674(b)(1)); or (*c*) if the beneficiary is under 21 or under a legal disability and accumulated income is added to corpus (section 674(b)(7)).

(3) *Powers of distribution affecting more than one beneficiary.*—A power to distribute corpus or income to or among one or more beneficiaries or to accumulate income, either (i) if the power is held by a trustee or trustees other than the grantor, at least half of whom are independent (section 674(c)), or (ii) if the power is limited by a reasonably definite standard in the trust instrument, and in the case of a power over income, if in addition the power is held by a trustee or trustees other than the grantor and the grantor's spouse living with the grantor (sections 674(b)(5)(A) and (d)). (These powers include both powers to "sprinkle" income or corpus among current beneficiaries, and powers to shift income or corpus between current beneficiaries and remaindermen; however, certain of the powers described under subparagraph (2) of this paragraph can have the latter effect incidentally.)

(c) See section 671 and §§ 1.671-2 and 1.671-3 for rules for the treatment of income, deductions, and credits when a person is treated as the owner of all or only a portion of a trust. [Reg. § 1.674(a)-1.]

☐ [*T.D.* 6217, 12-19-56.]

[Reg. § 1.674(b)-1]

§ 1.674(b)-1. Excepted powers exercisable by any person.—(a) Paragraph (b)(1) through (8) of this section sets forth a number of powers which may be exercisable by any person without causing the grantor to be treated as an owner of a trust under section 674(a). Further, with the exception of powers described in paragraph (b)(1) of this section, it is immaterial whether these powers are held in the capacity of trustee. It makes no difference under section 674(b) that the person holding the power is the grantor, or a related or subordinate party (with the qualifications noted in paragraph (b)(1) and (3) of this section).

(b) The exceptions referred to in paragraph (a) of this section are as follows (see, however, the limitations set forth in § 1.674(d)-2):

(1) *Powers to apply income to support of a dependent.*—Section 674(b)(1) provides, in effect, that regardless of the general rule of section 674(a), the income of a trust will not be considered as taxable to the grantor merely because in the discretion of any person (other than a grantor who is not acting as a trustee or cotrustee) it may be used for the support of a beneficiary whom the grantor is legally obligated to support, except to the extent that it is in fact used for that purpose. See section 677(b) and the regulations thereunder.

(2) *Powers affecting beneficial enjoyment only after a period.*—Section 674(b)(2) provides an exception to section 674(a) if the exercise of a power can only affect the beneficial enjoyment of the income of a trust received after a period of time which is such that a grantor would not be treated as an owner under section 673 if the power were a reversionary interest. See §§ 1.673(a)-1 and 1.673(b)-1. For example, if a trust created on January 1, 1955, provides for the payment of income to the grantor's son, and the grantor reserves the power to substitute other beneficiaries of income or corpus in lieu of his son on or after January 1, 1965, the grantor is not treated under section 674 as the owner of the trust with respect to ordinary income received before January 1, 1965. But the grantor will be treated as an owner on and after that date unless the power is relinquished. If the beginning of the period during which the grantor may substitute beneficiaries is postponed, the rules set forth in § 1.673(d)-1 are applicable in order to determine whether the grantor should be treated as an owner during the period following the postponement.

(3) *Testamentary powers.*—Under paragraph (3) of section 674(b) a power in any person to control beneficial enjoyment exercisable only by will does not cause a grantor to be treated as an owner under section 674(a). However, this exception does not apply to income accumulated for testamentary disposition by the grantor or to income which may be accumulated for such distribution in the discretion of the grantor or a nonadverse party, or both, without the approval or consent of any adverse party. For example, if a trust instrument provides that the income is to be accumulated during the grantor's life and that the grantor may appoint the accumulated income by will, the grantor is treated as the owner of the trust. Moreover, if a trust instrument provides that the income is payable to another person for his life, but the grantor has a testamentary power of appointment over the remainder, and under the trust instrument and local law capital gains are added to corpus, the grantor is treated as the owner of a portion of the trust and capital gains and losses are included in that portion. (See § 1.671-3.)

(4) *Powers to determine beneficial enjoyment of charitable beneficiaries.*—Under paragraph (4) of

See p. 15 for regulations not amended to reflect law changes

section 674(b) a power in any person to determine the beneficial enjoyment of corpus or income which is irrevocably payable (currently or in the future) for purposes specified in section 170(c) (relating to definition of charitable contributions) will not cause the grantor to be treated as an owner under section 674(a). For example, if a grantor creates a trust, the income of which is irrevocably payable solely to educational or other organizations that qualify under section 170(c), he is not treated as an owner under section 674 although he retains the power to allocate the income among such organizations.

(5) *Powers to distribute corpus.*—Paragraph (5) of section 674(b) provides an exception to section 674(a) for powers to distribute corpus, subject to certain limitations, as follows:

(i) If the power is limited by a reasonably definite standard which is set forth in the trust instrument, it may extend to corpus distributions to any beneficiary or beneficiaries or class of beneficiaries (whether income beneficiaries or remaindermen) without causing the grantor to be treated as an owner under section 674. See section 674(b)(5)(A). It is not required that the standard consist of the needs and circumstances of the beneficiary. A clearly measurable standard under which the holder of a power is legally accountable is deemed a reasonably definite standard for this purpose. For instance, a power to distribute corpus for the education, support, maintenance, or health of the beneficiary; for his reasonable support and comfort; or to enable him to maintain his accustomed standard of living; or to meet an emergency, would be limited by a reasonably definite standard. However, a power to distribute corpus for the pleasure, desire, or happiness of a beneficiary is not limited by a reasonably definite standard. The entire context of a provision of a trust instrument granting a power must be considered in determining whether the power is limited by a reasonably definite standard. For example, if a trust instrument provides that the determination of the trustee shall be conclusive with respect to the exercise or nonexercise of a power, the power is not limited by a reasonably definite standard. However, the fact that the governing instrument is phrased in discretionary terms is not in itself an indication that no reasonably definite standard exists.

(ii) If the power is not limited by a reasonably definite standard set forth in the trust instrument, the exception applies only if distributions of corpus may be made solely in favor of current income beneficiaries, and any corpus distribution to the current income beneficiary must be chargeable against the proportionate part of corpus held in trust for payment of income to that beneficiary as if it constituted a separate trust (whether or not physically segregated). See section 674(b)(5)(B).

(iii) This subparagraph may be illustrated by the following examples:

Example (1). A trust instrument provides for payment of the income to the grantor's two brothers for life, and for payment of the corpus to the grantor's nephews in equal shares. The grantor reserves the power to distribute corpus to pay medical expenses that may be incurred by his brothers or nephews. The grantor is not treated as an owner by reason of this power because section 674(b)(5)(A) excepts a power, exercisable by any person, to invade corpus for any beneficiary, including a remainderman, if the power is limited by a reasonably definite standard which is set forth in the trust instrument. However, if the power were also exercisable in favor of a person (for example, a sister) who was not otherwise a beneficiary of the trust, section 674(b)(5)(A) would not be applicable.

Example (2). The facts are the same as in example (1) except that the grantor reserves the power to distribute any part of the corpus to his brothers or to his nephews for their happiness. The grantor is treated as the owner of the trust. Paragraph (5)(A) of section 674(b) is inapplicable because the power is not limited by a reasonably definite standard. Paragraph (5)(B) is inapplicable because the power to distribute corpus permits a distribution of corpus to persons other than current income beneficiaries.

Example (3). A trust instrument provides for payment of the income to the grantor's two adult sons in equal shares for 10 years, after which the corpus is to be distributed to his grandchildren in equal shares. The grantor reserves the power to pay over to each son up to one-half of the corpus during the 10-year period, but any such payment shall proportionately reduce subsequent income and corpus payments made to the son receiving the corpus. Thus, if one-half of the corpus is paid to one son, all the income from the remaining half is thereafter payable to the other son. The grantor is not treated as an owner under section 674(a) by reason of this power because it qualifies under the exception of section 674(b)(5)(B).

(6) *Powers to withhold income temporarily.*—(i) Section 674(b)(6) excepts a power which, in general, enables the holder merely to effect a postponement in the time when the ordinary income is enjoyed by a current income beneficiary. Specifically, there is excepted a power to distribute or apply ordinary income to or for a current income beneficiary or to accumulate the income, if the accumulated income must ultimately be payable either:

(a) To the beneficiary from whom it was withheld, his estate, or his appointees (or persons designated by name, as a class, or otherwise as alternate takers in default of appointment) under a power of appointment held by the beneficiary which does not exclude from the class of possible appointees any person other than the beneficiary, his estate, his creditors, or the creditors of his estate (section 674(b)(6)(A));

(b) To the beneficiary from whom it was withheld, or if he does not survive a date of distribution which could reasonably be expected to occur within his lifetime, to his appointees (or alternate takers in default of appointment) under any power of appointment, general or special, or if he has no power of appointment to one or

more designated alternate takers (other than the grantor or the grantor's estate) whose shares have been irrevocably specified in the trust instrument (section 674(b)(6)(A) and the flush material following); or

(*c*) On termination of the trust, or in conjunction with a distribution of corpus which is augmented by the accumulated income, to the current income beneficiaries in shares which have been irrevocably specified in the trust instrument, or if any beneficiary does not survive a date of distribution which would reasonably be expected to occur within his lifetime, to his appointees (or alternate takers in default of appointment) under any power of appointment, general or special, or if he has no power of appointment to one or more designated alternate takers (other than the grantor or the grantor's estate) whose shares have been irrevocably specified in the trust instrument (section 674(b)(6)(B) and the flush material following). (In the application of (*a*) above of this subdivision, if the accumulated income of a trust is ultimately payable to the estate of the current income beneficiary, or is ultimately payable to his appointees, or takers in default of appointment, under a power of the type described in (*a*) of this subdivision, it need not be payable to the beneficiary from whom it was withheld under any circumstances. Furthermore, if a trust otherwise qualifies for the exception in (*a*) of this subdivision the trust income will not be considered to be taxable to the grantor under section 677 by reason of the existence of the power of appointment referred to in (*a*) of this subdivision.) In general, the exception in section 674(b)(6) is not applicable if the power is in substance one to shift ordinary income from one beneficiary to another. Thus, a power will not qualify for this exception if ordinary income may be distributed to beneficiary A, or may be added to corpus which is ultimately payable to beneficiary B, a remainderman who is not a current income beneficiary. However, section 674(b)(6)(B), and (*c*) of this subdivision, permit a limited power to shift ordinary income among current income beneficiaries, as illustrated in example (1) below of this subparagraph.

(ii) The application of section 674(b)(6) may be illustrated by the following examples:

Example (1). A trust instrument provides that the income shall be paid in equal shares to the grantor's two adult daughters but the grantor reserves the power to withhold from either beneficiary any part of that beneficiary's share of income and to add it to the corpus of the trust until the younger daughter reaches the age of 30 years. When the younger daughter reaches the age of 30, the trust is to terminate and the corpus is to be divided equally between the two daughters or their estates. Although exercise of this power may permit the shifting of accumulated income from one beneficiary to the other (since the corpus with the accumulations is to be divided equally) the power is excepted under section 674(b)(6)(B) and subdivision (i)(*c*) above of this subparagraph.

Example (2). The facts are the same as in example (1), except that the grantor of the trust reserves the power to distribute accumulated income to the beneficiaries in such shares as he chooses. The combined powers are not excepted by section 674(b)(6)(B) since income accumulated pursuant to the first power is neither required to be payable only in conjunction with a corpus distribution nor required to be payable in shares specified in the trust instrument. See, however, section 674(c) and §1.674(c)-1 for the effect of such a power if it is exercisable only by independent trustees.

Example (3). A trust provides for payment of income to the grantor's adult son with the grantor retaining the power to accumulate the income until the grantor's death, when all accumulations are to be paid to the son. If the son predeceases the grantor, all accumulations are, at the death of the grantor, to be paid to his daughter, or if she is not living, to alternate takers (which do not include the grantor's estate) in specified shares. The power is excepted under section 674(b)(6)(A) since the date of distribution (the date of the grantor's death) may, in the usual case, reasonably be expected to occur during the beneficiary's (the son's) lifetime. It is not necessary that the accumulations be payable to the son's estate or his appointees if he should predecease the grantor for this exception to apply.

(7) *Power to withhold income during disability.*—Section 674(b)(7) provides an exception for a power which, in general, will permit ordinary income to be withheld during the legal disability of an income beneficiary or while he is under 21. Specifically, there is excepted a power, exercisable only during the existence of a legal disability of any current income beneficiary or the period during which any income beneficiary is under the age of 21 years, to distribute or apply ordinary income to or for that beneficiary or to accumulate the income and add it to corpus. To qualify under this exception it is not necessary that the income ultimately be payable to the income beneficiary from whom it was withheld, his estate, or his appointees; that is, the accumulated income may be added to corpus and ultimately distributed to others. For example, the grantor is not treated as an owner under section 674 if the income of a trust is payable to his son for life, remainder to his grandchildren, although he reserves the power to accumulate income and add it to corpus while his son is under 21.

(8) *Powers to allocate between corpus and income.*—Paragraph (8) of section 674(b) provides that a power to allocate receipts and disbursements between corpus and income, even though expressed in broad language, will not cause the grantor to be treated as an owner under the general rule of section 674(a). [Reg. §1.674(b)-1.]

☐ [*T.D.* 6217, 12-19-56.]

[Reg. §1.674(c)-1]

§1.674(c)-1. Excepted powers exercisable only by independent trustees.—Section 674(c) provides an exception to the general rule of section 674(a) for certain powers that are exercisable by independent trustees. This exception is in addition to those provided for under section 674(b) which may be held by any person including an independent trustee. The powers to which section 674(c) apply are powers (a) to distribute, apportion, or accumulate income to or for a beneficiary or beneficiaries, or to, for, or within a class of beneficiaries, or (b) to pay out corpus to or for a beneficiary or beneficiaries or to or for a class of beneficiaries (whether or not income beneficiaries). In order for such a power to fall within the exception of section 674(c) it must be exercisable solely (without the approval or consent of any other person) by a trustee or trustees none of whom is the grantor and no more than half of whom are related or subordinate parties who are subservient to the wishes of the grantor. (See section 672(c) for definitions of these terms.) An example of the application of section 674(c) is a trust whose income is payable to the grantor's three adult sons with power in an independent trustee to allocate without restriction the amounts of income to be paid to each son each year. Such a power does not cause the grantor to be treated as the owner of the trust. See, however, the limitations set forth in § 1.674(d)-2. [Reg. § 1.674(c)-1.]

☐ [*T.D.* 6217, 12-19-56.]

[Reg. § 1.674(d)-1]

§ 1.674(d)-1. Excepted powers exercisable by any trustees other than grantor or spouse.—Section 674(d) provides an additional exception to the general rule of section 674(a) for a power to distribute, apportion, or accumulate income to or for a beneficiary or beneficiaries or to, for, or within a class of beneficiaries, whether or not the conditions of section 674(b)(6) or (7) are satisfied, if the power is solely exercisable (without the approval or consent of any other person) by a trustee or trustees none of whom is the grantor or spouse living with the grantor, and if the power is limited by a reasonably definite external standard set forth in the trust instrument (see paragraph (b)(5) of § 1.674(b)-1 with respect to what constitutes a reasonably definite standard). See, however, the limitations set forth in § 1.674(d)-2. [Reg. § 1.674(d)-1.]

☐ [*T.D.* 6217, 12-19-56.]

[Reg. § 1.674(d)-2]

§ 1.674(d)-2. Limitations on exceptions in section 674(b), (c), and (d).—(a) *Power to remove trustee.*—A power in the grantor to remove, substitute, or add trustees (other than a power exercisable only upon limited conditions which do not exist during the taxable year, such as the death or resignation of, or breach of fiduciary duty by, an existing trustee) may prevent a trust from qualifying under section 674(c) or (d). For example, if a grantor has an unrestricted power to remove an independent trustee and substitute any person including himself as trustee, the trust will not qualify under section 674(c) or (d). On the other hand if the grantor's power to remove, substitute, or add trustees is limited so that its exercise could not alter the trust in a manner that would disqualify it under section 674(c) or (d), as the case may be, the power itself does not disqualify the trust. Thus, for example, a power in the grantor to remove or discharge an independent trustee on the condition that he substitute another independent trustee will not prevent a trust from qualifying under section 674(c).

(b) *Power to add beneficiaries.*—The exceptions described in section 674(b)(5), (6), and (7), (c), and (d) are not applicable if any person has a power to add to the beneficiary or beneficiaries or to a class of beneficiaries designated to receive the income or corpus, except where the action is to provide for after-born or after-adopted children. This limitation does not apply to a power held by a beneficiary to substitute other beneficiaries to succeed to his interest in the trust (so that he would be an adverse party as to the exercise or non-exercise of that power). For example, the limitation does not apply to a power in a beneficiary of a nonspendthrift trust to assign his interest. Nor does the limitation apply to a power held by any person which would qualify as an exception under section 674(b)(3) (relating to testamentary powers). [Reg. § 1.674(d)-2.]

☐ [*T.D.* 6217, 12-19-56.]

[Reg. § 1.675-1]

§ 1.675-1. Administrative powers.—(a) *General rule.*—Section 675 provides in effect that the grantor is treated as the owner of any portion of a trust if under the terms of the trust instrument or circumstances attendant on its operation administrative control is exercisable primarily for the benefit of the grantor rather than the beneficiaries of the trust. If a grantor retains a power to amend the administrative provisions of a trust instrument which is broad enough to permit an amendment causing the grantor to be treated as the owner of a portion of the trust under section 675, he will be treated as the owner of the portion from its inception. See section 671 and §§ 1.671-2 and 1.671-3 for rules for treatment of items of income, deduction, and credit when a person is treated as the owner of all or only a portion of a trust.

(b) *Prohibited controls.*—The circumstances which cause administrative controls to be considered exercisable primarily for the benefit of the grantor are specifically described in paragraphs (1) through (4) of section 675 as follows:

(1) The existence of a power, exercisable by the grantor or a non-adverse party, or both, without the approval or consent of any adverse party, which enables the grantor or any other person to purchase, exchange, or otherwise deal with or dispose of the corpus or the income of the trust for less than adequate consideration in money or money's worth. Whether the existence of the power itself will constitute the holder an adverse party will depend on the particular circumstances.

(2) The existence of a power exercisable by the grantor or a non-adverse party, or both, which enables the grantor to borrow the corpus

or income of the trust, directly or indirectly, without adequate interest or adequate security. However, this paragraph does not apply where a trustee (other than the grantor acting alone) is authorized under a general lending power to make loans to any person without regard to interest or security. A general lending power in the grantor, acting alone as trustee, under which he has power to determine interest rates and the adequacy of security is not in itself an indication that the grantor has power to borrow the corpus or income without adequate interest or security.

(3) The circumstance that the grantor has directly or indirectly borrowed the corpus or income of the trust and has not completely repaid the loan, including any interest, before the beginning of the taxable year. The preceding sentence does not apply to a loan which provides for adequate interest and adequate security, if it is made by a trustee other than the grantor or a related or subordinate trustee subservient to the grantor. See section 672(c) for definition of "a related or subordinate party."

(4) The existence of certain powers of administration exercisable in a nonfiduciary capacity by any nonadverse party without the approval or consent of any person in a fiduciary capacity. The term "powers of administration" means one or more of the following powers:

(i) A power to vote or direct the voting of stock or other securities of a corporation in which the holdings of the grantor and the trust are significant from the viewpoint of voting control;

(ii) A power to control the investment of the trust funds either by directing investments or reinvestments, or by vetoing proposed investments or reinvestments, to the extent that the trust funds consist of stocks or securities of corporations in which the holdings of the grantor and the trust are significant from the viewpoint of voting control; or

(iii) A power to reacquire the trust corpus by substituting other property of an equivalent value.

If a power is exercisable by a person as trustee, it is presumed that the power is exercisable in a fiduciary capacity primarily in the interests of the beneficiaries. This presumption may be rebutted only by clear and convincing proof that the power is not exercisable primarily in the interests of the beneficiaries. If a power is not exercisable by a person as trustee, the determination of whether the power is exercisable in a fiduciary or a nonfiduciary capacity depends on all the terms of the trust and the circumstances surrounding its creation and administration.

(c) *Authority of trustee.*—The mere fact that a power exercisable by a trustee is described in broad language does not indicate that the trustee is authorized to purchase, exchange, or otherwise deal with or dispose of the trust property or income for less than an adequate and full consideration in money or money's worth, or is authorized to lend the trust property or income to the grantor without adequate interest. On the other hand, such authority may be indicated by the actual administration of the trust. [Reg. § 1.675-1.]

☐ [*T.D.* 6217, 12-19-56.]

[Reg. § 1.676(a)-1]

§ 1.676(a)-1. Power to revest title to portion of trust property in grantor; general rule.—If a power to revest in the grantor title to any portion of a trust is exercisable by the grantor or a nonadverse party, or both, without the approval or consent of an adverse party, the grantor is treated as the owner of that portion, except as provided in section 676(b) (relating to powers affecting beneficial enjoyment of income only after the expiration of certain periods of time). If the title to a portion of the trust will revest in the grantor upon the exercise of a power by the grantor or a nonadverse party, or both, the grantor is treated as the owner of that portion regardless of whether the power is a power to revoke, to terminate, to alter or amend, or to appoint. See section 671 and §§ 1.671-2 and 1.671-3 for rules for treatment of items of income, deduction, and credit when a person is treated as the owner of all or only a portion of a trust. [Reg. § 1.676(a)-1.]

☐ [*T.D.* 6217, 12-19-56.]

[Reg. § 1.676(b)-1]

§ 1.676(b)-1. Powers exercisable only after a period of time.—Section 676(b) provides an exception to the general rule of section 676(a) when the exercise of a power can only affect the beneficial enjoyment of the income of a trust received after the expiration of a period of time which is such that a grantor would not be treated as an owner under section 673 if the power were a reversionary interest. See §§ 1.673(a)-1 and 1.673(b)-1. Thus, for example, a grantor is excepted from the general rule of section 676 (a) with respect to ordinary income if exercise of a power to revest corpus in him cannot affect the beneficial enjoyment of the income received within 10 years after the date of transfer of that portion of the trust. It is immaterial for this purpose that the power is vested at the time of the transfer. However, the grantor is subject to the general rule of section 676(a) after the expiration of the period unless the power is relinquished. Thus, in the above example, the grantor may be treated as the owner and be taxed on all income in the eleventh and succeeding years if exercise of the power can affect beneficial enjoyment of income received in those years. If the beginning of the period during which the grantor may revest is postponed, the rules set forth in § 1.673(d)-1 are applicable to determine whether the grantor should be treated as an owner during the period following the postponement. [Reg. § 1.676(b)-1.]

☐ [*T.D.* 6217, 12-19-56.]

[Reg. § 1.677(a)-1]

§ 1.677(a)-1. Income for benefit of grantor; general rule.—(a)(1) *Scope.*—Section 677 deals with the treatment of the grantor of a trust as the owner of a portion of the trust because he has retained an interest in the income from that portion. For convenience, "grantor" and "spouse" are generally referred to in the masculine and feminine genders, respectively, but if the grantor is a woman the reference to "grantor" is to her and the reference to "spouse" is to her husband. Section 677 also deals with the treatment of the grantor of a trust as the owner of a portion of the trust because the income from property transferred in trust after October 9, 1969, is, or may be, distributed to his spouse or applied to the payment of premiums on policies of insurance on the life of his spouse. However, section 677 does not apply when the income of a trust is taxable to a grantor's spouse under section 71 (relating to alimony and separate maintenance payments) or section 682 (relating to income of an estate or trust in the case of divorce, etc.). See § 1.671-1(b).

(2) *Cross references.*—See section 671 and §§ 1.671-2 and 1.671-3 for rules for treatment of items of income, deduction, and credit when a person is treated as the owner of all or a portion of a trust.

(b) *Income for benefit of grantor or his spouse; general rule.*—(1) *Property transferred in trust prior to October 10, 1969.*—With respect to property transferred in trust prior to October 10, 1969, the grantor is treated, under section 677, in any taxable year as the owner (whether or not he is treated as an owner under section 674) of a portion of a trust of which the income for the taxable year or for a period not within the exception described in paragraph (e) of this section is, or in the discretion of the grantor or a nonadverse party, or both (without the approval or consent of any adverse party) may be:

(i) Distributed to the grantor;

(ii) Held or accumulated for future distribution to the grantor; or

(iii) Applied to the payment of premiums on policies of insurance on the life of the grantor, except policies of insurance irrevocably payable for a charitable purpose specified in section 170(c).

(2) *Property transferred in trust after October 9, 1969.*—With respect to property transferred in trust after October 9, 1969, the grantor is treated, under section 677, in any taxable year as the owner (whether or not he is treated as an owner under section 674) of a portion of a trust of which the income for the taxable year or for a period not within the exception described in paragraph (e) of this section is, or in the discretion of the grantor, or his spouse, or a nonadverse party, or any combination thereof (without the approval or consent of any adverse party other than the grantor's spouse) may be:

(i) Distributed to the grantor or the grantor's spouse;

(ii) Held or accumulated for future distribution to the grantor or the grantor's spouse; or

(iii) Applied to the payment of premiums on policies of insurance on the life of the grantor or the grantor's spouse, except policies of insurance irrevocably payable for a charitable purpose specified in section 170(c).

With respect to the treatment of a grantor as the owner of a portion of a trust solely because its income is, or may be, distributed or held or accumulated for future distribution to a beneficiary who is his spouse or applied to the payment of premiums for insurance on the spouse's life, section 677(a) applies to the income of a trust solely during the period of the marriage of the grantor to a beneficiary. In the case of divorce or separation, see sections 71 and 682 and the regulations thereunder.

(c) *Constructive distribution; cessation of interest.*—Under section 677 the grantor is treated as the owner of a portion of a trust if he has retained any interest which might, without the approval or consent of an adverse party, enable him to have the income from that portion distributed to him at some time either actually or constructively (subject to the exception described in paragraph (e) of this section). In the case of a transfer in trust after October 9, 1969, the grantor is also treated as the owner of a portion of a trust if he has granted or retained any interest which might, without the approval or consent of an adverse party (other than the grantor's spouse), enable his spouse to have the income from the portion at some time, whether or not within the grantor's life time, distributed to the spouse either actually or constructively. See paragraph (b)(2) of this section for additional rules relating to the income of a trust prior to the grantor's marriage to a beneficiary. Constructive distribution to the grantor or to his spouse includes payment on behalf of the grantor or his spouse to another in obedience to his or her direction and payment of premiums upon policies of insurance on the grantor's, or his spouse's, life (other than policies of insurance irrevocably payable for charitable purposes specified in section 170(c)). If the grantor (in the case of property transferred prior to October 10, 1969) or the grantor and his spouse (in the case of property transferred after October 9, 1969) are divested permanently and completely of every interest described in this paragraph, the grantor is not treated as an owner under section 677 after that divesting. The word "interest" as used in this paragraph does not include the possibility that the grantor or his spouse might receive back from a beneficiary an interest in a trust by inheritance. Further, with respect to transfers in trust prior to October 10, 1969, the word "interest" does not include the possibility that the grantor might receive back from a beneficiary an interest in a trust as a surviving spouse under a statutory right of election or a similar right.

(d) *Discharge of legal obligation of grantor or his spouse.*—Under section 677 a grantor is, in general, treated as the owner of a portion of a trust whose income is, or in the discretion of the grantor or a nonadverse party, or both, may be applied in discharge of a legal obligation of the grantor (or his spouse in the case of property transferred in trust by the grantor after October 9, 1969). However, see § 1.677(b)-1 for special rules for trusts whose income may not be applied for the discharge of any legal obligation of the grantor or the grantor's spouse other than the support or maintenance of a beneficiary (other than the grantor's spouse) whom the grantor or grantor's spouse is legally obligated to support. See § 301.7701-4(e) of this chapter for rules on the classification of and application of section 677 to an environmental remediation trust.

(e) *Exception for certain discretionary rights affecting income.*—The last sentence of section 677(a) provides that a grantor shall not be treated as the owner when a discretionary right can only affect the beneficial enjoyment of the income of a trust received after a period of time during which a grantor would not be treated as an owner under section 673 if the power were a reversionary interest. See §§ 1.673(a)-1 and 1.673(b)-1. For example, if the ordinary income of a trust is payable to B for 10 years and then in the grantor's discretion income or corpus may be paid to B or to the grantor (or his spouse in the case of property transferred in trust by the grantor after October 9, 1969), the grantor is not treated as an owner with respect to the ordinary income under section 677 during the first 10 years. He will be treated as an owner under section 677 after the expiration of the 10-year period unless the power is relinquished. If the beginning of the period during which the grantor may substitute beneficiaries is postponed, the rules set forth in § 1.673(d)-1 are applicable in determining whether the grantor should be treated as an owner during the period following the postponement.

(f) *Accumulation of income.*—If income is accumulated in any taxable year for future distribution to the grantor (or his spouse in the case of property transferred in trust by the grantor after October 9, 1969), section 677(a)(2) treats the grantor as an owner for that taxable year. The exception set forth in the last sentence of section 677(a) does not apply merely because the grantor (or his spouse in the case of property transferred in trust by the grantor after October 9, 1969) must await the expiration of a period of time before he or she can receive or exercise discretion over previously accumulated income of the trust, even though the period is such that the grantor would not be treated as an owner under section 673 if a reversionary interest were involved. Thus, if income (including capital gains) of a trust is to be accumulated for 10 years and then will be, or at the discretion of the grantor, or his spouse in the case of property transferred in trust after October 9, 1969, or a nonadverse party, may be, distributed to the grantor (or his spouse in the case of property transferred in trust after October 9, 1969), the grantor is treated as the owner of the trust from its inception. If income attributable to transfers after October 9, 1969 is accumulated in any taxable year during the grantor's lifetime for future distribution to his spouse, section 677(a)(2) treats the grantor as an owner for that taxable year even though his spouse may not receive or exercise discretion over such income prior to the grantor's death.

(g) *Examples.*—The application of section 677(a) may be illustrated by the following examples:

Example (1). G creates an irrevocable trust which provides that the ordinary income is to be payable to him for life and that on his death the corpus shall be distributed to B, an unrelated person. Except for the right to receive income, G retains no right or power which would cause him to be treated as an owner under sections 671 through 677. Under the applicable local law capital gains must be applied to corpus. During the taxable year 1970 the trust has the following items of gross income and deductions:

Dividends	$5,000
Capital gain	1,000
Expenses allocable to income	200
Expenses allocable to corpus	100

Since G has a right to receive income he is treated as an owner of a portion of the trust under section 677. Accordingly, he should include the $5,000 of dividends, $200 income expense, and $100 corpus expense in the computation of his taxable income for 1970. He should not include the $1,000 capital gain since that is not attributable to the portion of the trust that he owns. See § 1.671-3(b). The tax consequences of the capital gain are governed by the provisions of subparts A, B, C, and D (section 641 and following), part I, subchapter J, chapter 1 of the Code. Had the trust sustained a capital loss in any amount the loss would likewise not be included in the computation of G's taxable income, but would also be governed by the provisions of such subparts.

Example (2). G creates a trust which provides that the ordinary income is payable to his adult son. Ten years and one day from the date of transfer or on the death of his son, whichever is earlier, corpus is to revert to G. In addition, G retains a discretionary right to receive $5,000 of ordinary income each year. (Absent the exercise of this right all the ordinary income is to be distributed to his son.) G retained no other right or power which would cause him to be treated as an owner under subpart E (section 671 and following). Under the terms of the trust instrument and applicable local law capital gains must be applied to corpus. During the taxable year 1970 the trust had the following items of income and deductions:

Dividends	$10,000
Capital gain	2,000
Expenses allocable to income	400
Expenses allocable to corpus	200

Since the capital gain is held or accumulated for future distributions to G, he is treated under section 677(a)(2) as an owner of a portion of the trust to which the gain is attributable. See § 1.671-3(b).

Therefore, he must include the capital gain in the computation of his taxable income. (Had the trust sustained a capital loss in any amount, G would likewise include that loss in the computation of his taxable income.) In addition, because of G's discretionary right (whether exercised or not) he is treated as the owner of a portion of the trust which will permit a distribution of income to him of $5,000. Accordingly, G includes dividends of $5,208.33 and income expenses of $208.33 in computing his taxable income, determined in the following manner:

Total dividends	$10,000.00
Less: Expenses allocable to income	400.00
Distributable income of the trust	9,600.00
Portion of dividends attributable to G (5,000/9,600 × $10,000)	5,208.33
Portion of income expenses attributable to G (5,000/9,600 × $400)	208.33
Amount of income subject to discretionary right	5,000.00

In accordance with §1.671-3(c), G also takes into account $104.17 (5,000/9,600×$200) of corpus expenses in computing his tax liability. The portion of the dividends and expenses of the trust not attributable to G are governed by the provisions of subparts A through D. [Reg. §1.677(a)-1.]

□ [*T.D.* 6217, 12-19-56. *Amended by T.D.* 7148, 10-28-71 *and T.D.* 8668, 4-30-96.]

[Reg. §1.677(b)-1]

§1.677(b)-1. Trusts for support.—(a) Section 677(b) provides that a grantor is not treated as the owner of a trust merely because its income may in the discretion of any person other than the grantor (except when he is acting as trustee or cotrustee) be applied or distributed for the support or maintenance of a beneficiary (other than the grantor's spouse in the case of income from property transferred in trust after October 9, 1969), such as the child of the grantor, whom the grantor or his spouse is legally obligated to support. If income of the current year of the trust is actually so applied or distributed the grantor may be treated as the owner of any portion of the trust under section 677 to that extent, even though it might have been applied or distributed for other purposes. In the case of property transferred to a trust before October 10, 1969, for the benefit of the grantor's spouse, the grantor may be treated as the owner to the extent income of the current year is actually applied for the support or maintenance of his spouse.

(b) If any amount applied or distributed for the support of a beneficiary, including the grantor's spouse in the case of property transferred in trust before October 10, 1969, whom the grantor is legally obligated to support is paid out of corpus or out of income other than income of the current year, the grantor is treated as a beneficiary of the trust, and the amount applied or distributed is considered to be an amount paid within the meaning of section 661(a)(2), taxable to the grantor under section 662. Thus, he is subject to the other relevant portions of subparts A through D (section 641 and following), part I, subchapter J, chapter 1 of the Code. Accordingly, the grantor may be taxed on an accumulation distribution or a capital gain distribution under subpart D (section 665 and following) of such part I. Those provisions are applied on the basis that the grantor is the beneficiary.

(c) For the purpose of determining the items of income, deduction, and credit of a trust to be included under this section in computing the grantor's tax liability, the income of the trust for the taxable year of distribution will be deemed to have been first distributed. For example, in the case of a trust reporting on the calendar year basis, a distribution made on January 1, 1956, will be deemed to have been made out of ordinary income of the trust for the calendar year 1956 to the extent of the income for that year even though the trust had received no income as of January 1, 1956. Thus, if a distribution of $10,000 is made on January 1, 1956, for the support of the grantor's dependent, the grantor will be treated as the owner of the trust for 1956 to that extent. If the trust received dividends of $5,000 and incurred expenses of $1,000 during that year but subsequent to January 1, he will take into account dividends of $5,000 and expenses of $1,000 in computing his tax liability for 1956. In addition, the grantor will be treated as a beneficiary of the trust with respect to the $6,000 ($10,000 less distributable income of $4,000 (dividends of $5,000 less expenses of $1,000)) paid out of corpus or out of other than income of the current year. See paragraph (b) of this section.

(d) The exception provided in section 677(b) relates solely to the satisfaction of the grantor's legal obligation to support or maintain a beneficiary. Consequently, the general rule of section 677(a) is applicable when in the discretion of the grantor or nonadverse parties income of a trust may be applied in discharge of a grantor's obligations other than his obligation of support or maintenance falling within section 677(b). Thus, if the grantor creates a trust the income of which may in the discretion of a nonadverse party be applied in the payment of the grantor's debts, such as the payment of his rent or other household expenses, he is treated as an owner of the trust regardless of whether the income is actually so applied.

(e) The general rule of section 677(a), and not section 677(b), is applicable if discretion to apply or distribute income of a trust rests solely in the grantor, or in the grantor in conjunction with other persons, unless in either case the grantor has such discretion as trustee or cotrustee.

(f) The general rule of section 677(a), and not section 677(b), is applicable to the extent that income is required, without any discretionary determination, to be applied to the support of a beneficiary whom the grantor is legally obligated to support. [Reg. §1.677(b)-1.]

□ [*T.D.* 6217, 12-19-56. *Amended by T.D.* 7148, 10-28-71.]

[Reg. § 1.678(a)-1]

§ 1.678(a)-1. Person other than grantor treated as substantial owner; general rule.—(a) Where a person other than the grantor of a trust has a power exercisable solely by himself to vest the corpus or the income of any portion of a testamentary or inter vivos trust in himself, he is treated under section 678(a) as the owner of that portion, except as provided in section 678(b) (involving taxation of the grantor) and section 678(c) (involving an obligation of support). The holder of such a power also is treated as an owner of the trust even though he has partially released or otherwise modified the power so that he can no longer vest the corpus or income in himself, if he has retained such control of the trust as would, if retained by a grantor, subject the grantor to treatment as the owner under sections 671 to 677, inclusive. See section 671 and § § 1.671-2 and 1.671-3 for rules for treatment of items of income, deduction, and credit where a person is treated as the owner of all or only a portion of a trust.

(b) Section 678(a) treats a person as an owner of a trust if he has a power exercisable solely by himself to apply the income or corpus for the satisfaction of his legal obligations, other than an obligation to support a dependent (see § 1.678(c)-1) subject to the limitation of section 678(b). Section 678 does not apply if the power is not exercisable solely by himself. However, see § 1.662(a)-4 for principles applicable to income of a trust which, pursuant to the terms of the trust instrument, is used to satisfy the obligations of a person other than the grantor. [Reg. § 1.678(a)-1.]

□ [*T.D.* 6217, 12-19-56.]

[Reg. § 1.678(b)-1]

§ 1.678(b)-1. If grantor is treated as the owner.—Section 678(a) does not apply with respect to a power over income, as originally granted or thereafter modified, if the grantor of the trust is treated as the owner under sections 671 to 677, inclusive. [Reg. § 1.678(b)-1.]

□ [*T.D.* 6217, 12-19-56.]

[Reg. § 1.678(c)-1]

§ 1.678(c)-1. Trusts for support.—(a) Section 678(a) does not apply to a power which enables the holder, in the capacity of trustee or cotrustee, to apply the income of the trust to the support or maintenance of a person whom the holder is obligated to support, except to the extent the income is so applied. See paragraph (a), (b), and (c) of § 1.677(b)-1 for applicable principles where any amount is applied for the support or maintenance of a person whom the holder is obligated to support.

(b) The general rule in section 678(a) (and not the exception in section 678(c)) is applicable in any case in which the holder of a power exercisable solely by himself is able, in any capacity other than that of trustee or cotrustee, to apply the income in discharge of his obligation of support or maintenance.

(c) Section 678(c) is concerned with the taxability of income subject to a power described in section 678(a). It has no application to the taxability of income which is either required to be applied pursuant to the terms of the trust instrument or is applied pursuant to a power which is not described in section 678(a), the taxability of such income being governed by other provisions of the Code. See § 1.662(a)-4. [Reg. § 1.678(c)-1.]

□ [*T.D.* 6217, 12-19-56.]

[Reg. § 1.678(d)-1]

§ 1.678(d)-1. Renunciation of power.—Section 678(a) does not apply to a power which has been renounced or disclaimed within a reasonable time after the holder of the power first became aware of its existence. [Reg. § 1.678(d)-1.]

□ [*T.D.* 6217, 12-19-56.]

[Reg. § 1.679-0]

§ 1.679-0. Outline of major topics.—This section lists the major paragraphs contained in § § 1.679-1 through 1.679-7 as follows:

§ 1.679-1 U.S. transferor treated as owner of foreign trust.

(a) In general.

(b) Interaction with sections 673 through 678.

(c) Definitions.

(1) U.S. transferor.

(2) U.S. person.

(3) Foreign trust.

(4) Property.

(5) Related person.

(6) Obligation.

(d) Examples.

§ 1.679-2 Trusts treated as having a U.S. beneficiary.

(a) Existence of U.S. beneficiary.

(1) In general.

(2) Benefit to a U.S. person

(i) In general.

(ii) Certain unexpected beneficiaries.

(iii) Examples.

(3) Changes in beneficiary's status.

(i) In general.

(ii) Examples.

(4) General rules.

(i) Records and documents.

(ii) Additional factors.

(iii) Examples.

(b) Indirect U.S. beneficiaries.

(1) Certain foreign entities.

(2) Other indirect beneficiaries.

(3) Examples.

(c) Treatment of U.S. transferor upon foreign trust's acquisition or loss of U.S. beneficiary.

(1) Trusts acquiring a U.S. beneficiary.

(2) Trusts ceasing to have a U.S. beneficiary.

(3) Examples.

§ 1.679-3 Transfers.

(a) In general.

(b) Transfers by certain trusts.

(1) In general.

(2) Example.

(c) Indirect transfers.
(1) Principal purpose of tax avoidance.
(2) Principal purpose of tax avoidance deemed to exist.
(3) Effect of disregarding intermediary.
(i) In general.
(ii) Special rule.
(iii) Effect on intermediary.
(4) Related parties.
(5) Examples.
(d) Constructive transfers.
(1) In general.
(2) Examples.
(e) Guarantee of trust obligations.
(1) In general.
(2) Amount transferred.
(3) Principal repayments.
(4) Guarantee.
(5) Examples.
(f) Transfers to entities owned by a foreign trust.
(1) General rule.
(2) Examples.

§1.679-4 Exceptions to general rule.
(a) In general.
(b) Transfers for fair market value.
(1) In general.
(2) Special rule.
(i) Transfers for partial consideration.
(ii) Example.
(c) Certain obligations not taken into account.
(d) Qualified obligations.
(1) In general.
(2) Additional loans.
(3) Obligations that cease to be qualified.
(4) Transfers resulting from failed qualified obligations.
(5) Renegotiated loans.
(6) Principal repayments.
(7) Examples.

§1.679-5 Pre-immigration trusts.
(a) In general.
(b) Special rules.
(1) Change in grantor trust status.
(2) Treatment of undistributed income.
(c) Examples.

§1.679-6 Outbound migrations of domestic trusts.
(a) In general.
(b) Amount deemed transferred.
(c) Example.

§1.679-7 Effective dates.
(a) In general.
(b) Special rules.

[Reg. §1.679-0.]

☐ [*T.D.* 8955, 7-19-2001.]

[Reg. §1.679-1]

§1.679-1. U.S. transferor treated as owner of foreign trust.—(a) *In general.*—A U.S. transferor who transfers property to a foreign trust is treated as the owner of the portion of the trust attributable to the property transferred if there is a U.S. beneficiary of any portion of the trust, unless an exception in §1.679-4 applies to the transfer.

(b) *Interaction with sections 673 through 678.*—The rules of this section apply without regard to whether the U.S. transferor retains any power or interest described in sections 673 through 677. If a U.S. transferor would be treated as the owner of a portion of a foreign trust pursuant to the rules of this section and another person would be treated as the owner of the same portion of the trust pursuant to section 678, then the U.S. transferor is treated as the owner and the other person is not treated as the owner.

(c) *Definitions.*—The following definitions apply for purposes of this section and §§1.679-2 through 1.679-7:

(1) *U.S. transferor.*—The term *U.S. transferor* means any U.S. person who makes a transfer (as defined in §1.679-3) of property to a foreign trust.

(2) *U.S. person.*—The term *U.S. person* means a United States person as defined in section 7701(a)(30), a nonresident alien individual who elects under section 6013(g) to be treated as resident of the United States, and an individual who is a dual resident taxpayer within the meaning of §301.7701(b)-7(a) of this chapter.

(3) *Foreign trust.*—Section 7701(a)(31)(B) defines the term *foreign trust.* See also §301.7701-7 of this chapter.

(4) *Property.*—The term *property* means any property including cash.

(5) *Related person.*—A person is a *related person* if, without regard to the transfer at issue, the person is—

(i) A grantor of any portion of the trust (within the meaning of §1.671-2(e)(1));

(ii) An owner of any portion of the trust under sections 671 through 679;

(iii) A beneficiary of the trust; or

(iv) A person who is related (within the meaning of section 643(i)(2)(B)) to any grantor, owner or beneficiary of the trust.

(6) *Obligation.*—The term *obligation* means any bond, note, debenture, certificate, bill receivable, account receivable, note receivable, open account, or other evidence of indebtedness, and, to the extent not previously described, any annuity contract.

(d) *Examples.*—The following examples illustrate the rules of paragraph (a) of this section. In these examples, *A* is a resident alien, *B* is *A*'s son, who is a resident alien, *C* is *A*'s father, who is a resident alien, *D* is *A*'s uncle, who is a nonresident alien, and *FT* is a foreign trust. The examples are as follows:

Example 1. Interaction with section 678. A creates and funds *FT*. *FT* may provide for the education of *B* by paying for books, tuition, room and board. In addition, *C* has the power to vest the trust corpus or income in himself within the meaning of section 678(a)(1). Under paragraph (b) of this section, *A* is treated as the owner of the portion of *FT* attributable to the property transferred to *FT* by *A* and *C* is not treated as the owner thereof.

Example 2. U.S. person treated as owner of a portion of FT. D creates and funds *FT* for the benefit of *B*. *D* retains a power described in section 676 and § 1.672(f)-3(a)(1). *A* transfers property to *FT*. Under sections 676 and 672(f), *D* is treated as the owner of the portion of *FT* attributable to the property transferred by *D*. Under paragraph (a) of this section, *A* is treated as the owner of the portion of *FT* attributable to the property transferred by *A*.

[Reg. § 1.679-1.]

☐ [*T.D.* 8955, 7-19-2001.]

[Reg. § 1.679-2]

§ 1.679-2. Trusts treated as having a U.S. beneficiary.—(a) *Existence of U.S. beneficiary.*—(1) *In general.*—The determination of whether a foreign trust has a U.S. beneficiary is made on an annual basis. A foreign trust is treated as having a U.S. beneficiary unless during the taxable year of the U.S. transferor—

(i) No part of the income or corpus of the trust may be paid or accumulated to or for the benefit of, directly or indirectly, a U.S. person; and

(ii) If the trust is terminated at any time during the taxable year, no part of the income or corpus of the trust could be paid to or for the benefit of, directly or indirectly, a U.S. person.

(2) *Benefit to a U.S. person.*—(i) *In general.*—For purposes of paragraph (a)(1) of this section, income or corpus may be paid or accumulated to or for the benefit of a U.S. person during a taxable year of the U.S. transferor if during that year, directly or indirectly, income may be distributed to, or accumulated for the benefit of, a U.S. person, or corpus may be distributed to, or held for the future benefit of, a U.S. person. This determination is made without regard to whether income or corpus is actually distributed to a U.S. person during that year, and without regard to whether a U.S. person's interest in the trust income or corpus is contingent on a future event.

(ii) *Certain unexpected beneficiaries.*—Notwithstanding paragraph (a)(2)(i) of this section, for purposes of paragraph (a)(1) of this section, a person who is not named as a beneficiary and is not a member of a class of beneficiaries as defined under the trust instrument is not taken into consideration if the U.S. transferor demonstrates to the satisfaction of the Commissioner that the person's contingent interest in the trust is so remote as to be negligible. The preceding sentence does not apply with respect to persons to whom distributions could be made pursuant to a grant of discretion to the trustee or any other person. A class of beneficiaries generally does not include heirs who will benefit from the trust under the laws of intestate succession in the event that the named beneficiaries (or members of the named class) have all deceased (whether or not stated as a named class in the trust instrument).

(iii) *Examples.*—The following examples illustrate the rules of paragraphs (a)(1) and (2) of this section. In these examples, *A* is a resident alien, *B* is *A*'s son, who is a resident alien, *C* is *A*'s daughter, who is a nonresident alien, and *FT* is a foreign trust. The examples are as follows:

Example 1. Distribution of income to U.S. person. A transfers property to *FT*. The trust instrument provides that all trust income is to be distributed currently to *B*. Under paragraph (a)(1) of this section, *FT* is treated as having a U.S. beneficiary.

Example 2. Income accumulation for the benefit of a U.S. person. In 2001, *A* transfers property to *FT*. The trust instrument provides that from 2001 through 2010, the trustee of *FT* may distribute trust income to *C* or may accumulate the trust income. The trust instrument further provides that in 2011, the trust will terminate and the trustee may distribute the trust assets to either or both of *B* and *C*, in the trustee's discretion. If the trust terminates unexpectedly prior to 2011, all trust assets must be distributed to *C*. Because it is possible that income may be accumulated in each year, and that the accumulated income ultimately may be distributed to *B*, a U.S. person, under paragraph (a)(1) of this section *FT* is treated as having a U.S. beneficiary during each of *A*'s tax years from 2001 through 2011. This result applies even though no U.S. person may receive distributions from the trust during the tax years 2001 through 2010.

Example 3. Corpus held for the benefit of a U.S. person. The facts are the same as in *Example 2*, except that from 2001 through 2011, all trust income must be distributed to *C*. In 2011, the trust will terminate and the trustee may distribute the trust corpus to either or both of *B* and *C*, in the trustee's discretion. If the trust terminates unexpectedly prior to 2011, all trust corpus must be distributed to *C*. Because during each of *A*'s tax years from 2001 through 2011 trust corpus is held for possible future distribution to *B*, a U.S. person, under paragraph (a)(1) of this section *FT* is treated as having a U.S. beneficiary during each of those years. This result applies even though no U.S. person may receive distributions from the trust during the tax years 2001 through 2010.

Example 4. Distribution upon U.S. transferor's death. A transfers property to *FT*. The trust instrument provides that all trust income must be distributed currently to *C* and, upon *A*'s death, the trust will terminate and the trustee may distribute the trust corpus to either or both of *B* and *C*. Because *B* may receive a distribution of corpus upon the termination of *FT*, and *FT* could terminate in any year, *FT* is treated as having a U.S. beneficiary in the year of the transfer and in subsequent years.

Example 5. Distribution after U.S. transferor's death. The facts are the same as in *Example 4*, except the trust instrument provides that the trust will not terminate until the year following

See p. 15 for regulations not amended to reflect law changes

A's death. Upon termination, the trustee may distribute the trust assets to either or both of *B* and *C*, in the trustee's discretion. All trust assets are invested in the stock of *X*, a foreign corporation, and *X* makes no distributions to *FT*. Although no U.S. person may receive a distribution until the year after *A*'s death, and *FT* has no realized income during any year of its existence, during each year in which *A* is living corpus may be held for future distribution to *B*, a U.S. person. Thus, under paragraph (a)(1) of this section *FT* is treated as having a U.S. beneficiary during each of *A*'s tax years from 2001 through the year of *A*'s death.

Example 6. Constructive benefit to U.S. person. A transfers property to *FT*. The trust instrument provides that no income or corpus may be paid directly to a U.S. person. However, the trust instrument provides that trust corpus may be used to satisfy *B*'s legal obligations to a third party by making a payment directly to the third party. Under paragraphs (a)(1) and (2) of this section, *FT* is treated as having a U.S. beneficiary.

Example 7. U.S. person with negligible contingent interest. A transfers property to *FT*. The trust instrument provides that all income is to be distributed currently to *C*, and upon *C*'s death, all corpus is to be distributed to whomever of *C*'s three children is then living. All of *C*'s children are nonresident aliens. Under the laws of intestate succession that would apply to *FT*, if all of *C*'s children are deceased at the time of *C*'s death, the corpus would be distributed to *A*'s heirs. *A*'s living relatives at the time of the transfer consist solely of two brothers and two nieces, all of whom are nonresident aliens, and two first cousins, one of whom, *E*, is a U.S. citizen. Although it is possible under certain circumstances that *E* could receive a corpus distribution under the applicable laws of intestate succession, for each year the trust is in existence *A* is able to demonstrate to the satisfaction of the Commissioner under paragraph (a)(2)(ii) of this section that *E*'s contingent interest in *FT* is so remote as to be negligible. Provided that paragraph (a)(4) of this section does not require a different result, *FT* is not treated as having a U.S. beneficiary.

Example 8. U.S. person with non-negligible contingent interest. A transfers property to *FT*. The trust instrument provides that all income is to be distributed currently to *D*, *A*'s uncle, who is a nonresident alien, and upon *A*'s death, the corpus is to be distributed to D if he is then living. Under the laws of intestate succession that would apply to *FT*, *B* and *C* would share equally in the trust corpus if *D* is not living at the time of *A*'s death. *A* is unable to demonstrate to the satisfaction of the Commissioner that *B*'s contingent interest in the trust is so remote as to be negligible. Under paragraph (a)(2)(ii) of this section, *FT* is treated as having a U.S. beneficiary as of the year of the transfer.

Example 9. U.S. person as member of class of beneficiaries. A transfers property to *FT*. The trust instrument provides that all income is to be distributed currently to *D*, *A*'s uncle, who is a nonresident alien, and upon *A*'s death, the corpus is to be distributed to *D* if he is then living. If *D* is not then living, the corpus is to be distributed to *D*'s descendants. *D*'s grandson, *E*, is a resident alien. Under paragraph (a)(2)(ii) of this section, *FT* is treated as having a U.S. beneficiary as of the year of the transfer.

Example 10. Trustee's discretion in choosing beneficiaries. A transfers property to *FT*. The trust instrument provides that the trustee may distribute income and corpus to, or accumulate income for the benefit of, any person who is pursuing the academic study of ancient Greek, in the trustee's discretion. Because it is possible that a U.S. person will receive distributions of income or corpus, or will have income accumulated for his benefit, *FT* is treated as having a U.S. beneficiary. This result applies even if, during a tax year, no distributions or accumulations are actually made to or for the benefit of a U.S. person. *A* may not invoke paragraph (a)(2)(ii) of this section because a U.S. person could benefit pursuant to a grant of discretion in the trust instrument.

Example 11. Appointment of remainder beneficiary. A transfers property to *FT*. The trust instrument provides that the trustee may distribute current income to C, or may accumulate income, and, upon termination of the trust, trust assets are to be distributed to C. However, the trust instrument further provides that *D*, *A*'s uncle, may appoint a different remainder beneficiary. Because it is possible that a U.S. person could be named as the remainder beneficiary, and because corpus could be held in each year for the future benefit of that U.S. person, *FT* is treated as having a U.S. beneficiary for each year.

Example 12. Trust not treated as having a U.S. beneficiary. A transfers property to *FT*. The trust instrument provides that the trustee may distribute income and corpus to, or accumulate income for the benefit of *C*. Upon termination of the trust, all income and corpus must be distributed to *C*. Assume that paragraph (a)(4) of this section is not applicable under the facts and circumstances and that A establishes to the satisfaction of the Commissioner under paragraph (a)(2)(ii) of this section that no U.S. persons are reasonably expected to benefit from the trust. Because no part of the income or corpus of the trust may be paid or accumulated to or for the benefit of, either directly or indirectly, a U.S. person, and if the trust is terminated no part of the income or corpus of the trust could be paid to or for the benefit of, either directly or indirectly, a U.S. person, *FT* is not treated as having a U.S. beneficiary.

Example 13. U.S. beneficiary becomes non-U.S. person. In 2001, *A* transfers property to *FT*. The trust instrument provides that, as long as *B* remains a U.S. resident, no distributions of income or corpus may be made from the trust to *B*. The trust instrument further provides that if *B* becomes a nonresident alien, distributions of income (including previously accumulated income) and corpus may be made to him. If *B* remains a U.S. resident at the time of *FT*'s termination, all accumulated income and corpus is to be distributed to *C*. In 2007, *B* becomes a nonresident alien and remains so thereafter. Because income may be accumulated during the years 2001 through 2007 for the benefit of a person who is a U.S. person during those years, *FT* is treated as having a U.S. beneficiary under paragraph (a)(1) of this section during each of those years. This result applies even though *B* cannot receive distributions from *FT* during the years he is a resident alien and even though *B* might remain a resident alien who is not entitled to any distribution from *FT*. Provided that paragraph (a)(4) of this section does not require a different result and that *A* establishes to the satisfaction of the Commissioner under paragraph (a)(2)(ii) of this section that no other U.S. persons are reasonably expected to benefit from the trust, *FT* is not treated as having a U.S. beneficiary under paragraph (a)(1) of this section during tax years after 2007.

(3) *Changes in beneficiary's status.*—(i) *In general.*—For purposes of paragraph (a)(1) of this section, the possibility that a person that is not a U.S. person could become a U.S. person will not cause that person to be treated as a U.S. person for purposes of paragraph (a)(1) of this section until the tax year of the U.S. transferor in which that individual actually. becomes a U.S. person. However, if a person who is not a U.S. person becomes a U.S. person for the first time more than 5 years after the date of a transfer to the foreign trust by a U.S. transferor, that person is not treated as a U.S. person for purposes of applying paragraph (a)(1) of this section with respect to that transfer.

(ii) *Examples.*—The following examples illustrate the rules of paragraph (a)(3) of this section. In these examples, *A* is a resident alien, *B* is *A*'s son, who is a resident alien, *C* is *A*'s daughter, who is a nonresident alien, and *FT* is a foreign trust. The examples are as follows:

Example 1. Non-U.S. beneficiary becomes U.S. person. In 2001, *A* transfers property to *FT*. The trust instrument provides that all income is to be distributed currently to *C* and that, upon the termination of *FT*, all corpus is to be distributed to *C*. Assume that paragraph (a)(4) of this section is not applicable under the facts and circumstances and that *A* establishes to the satisfaction of the Commissioner under paragraph (a)(2)(ii) of this section that no U.S. persons are reasonably expected to benefit from the trust. Under paragraph (a)(3)(i) of this section, *FT* is not treated as having a U.S. beneficiary during the tax years of *A* in which *C* remains a nonresident alien. If *C* first becomes a resident alien in 2004, *FT* is treated as having a U.S. beneficiary commencing in that year under paragraph (a)(3) of this section. See paragraph (c) of this section regarding the treatment of *A* upon *FT*'s acquisition of a U.S. beneficiary.

Example 2. Non-U.S. beneficiary becomes U.S. person more than 5 years after transfer. The facts are the same as in *Example 1*, except *C* first becomes a resident alien in 2007. *FT* is treated as not having a U.S. beneficiary under paragraph (a)(3)(i) of this section with respect to the property transfer by *A*. However, if *C* had previously been a U.S. person during any prior period, the 5-year exception in paragraph (a)(3)(i) of this section would not apply in 2007 because it would not have been the first time *C* became a U.S. person.

(4) *General rules.*—(i) *Records and documents.*—Even if, based on the terms of the trust instrument, a foreign trust is not treated as having a U.S. beneficiary within the meaning of paragraph (a)(1) of this section. the trust may nevertheless be treated as having a U.S. beneficiary pursuant to paragraph (a)(1) of this section based on the following—

(A) All written and oral agreements and understandings relating to the trust;

(B) Memoranda or letters of wishes;

(C) All records that relate to the actual distribution of income and corpus; and

(D) All other documents that relate to the trust, whether or not of any purported legal effect.

(ii) *Additional factors.*—For purposes of determining whether a foreign trust is treated as having a U.S. beneficiary within the meaning of paragraph (a)(1) of this section, the following additional factors are taken into account—

(A) If the terms of the trust instrument allow the trust to be amended to benefit a U.S. person, all potential benefits that could be provided to a U.S. person pursuant to an amendment must be taken into account;

(B) If the terms of the trust instrument do not allow the trust to be amended to benefit a U.S. person, but the law applicable to a foreign trust may require payments or accumulations of income or corpus to or for the benefit of a U.S. person (by judicial reformation or otherwise), all potential benefits that could be provided to a U.S. person pursuant to the law must be taken into account, unless the U.S. transferor demonstrates to the satisfaction of the Commissioner that the law is not reasonably expected to be applied or invoked under the facts and circumstances; and

(C) If the parties to the trust ignore the terms of the trust instrument, or if it is reasonably expected that they will do so, all benefits that have been, or are reasonably expected to be, provided to a U.S. person must be taken into account.

(iii) *Examples.*—The following examples illustrate the rules of paragraph (a)(4) of this section. In these examples, *A* is a resident alien, *B* is *A*'s son, who is a resident alien, *C* is *A*'s daughter, who is a nonresident alien, and *FT* is a foreign trust. The examples are as follows:

Example 1. Amendment pursuant to local law. A creates and funds *FT* for the benefit of *C*. The terms of *FT* (which, according to the trust instrument, cannot be amended) provide that no part of the income or corpus of *FT* may be paid or accumulated during the taxable year to or for the benefit of any U.S. person, either during the existence of *FT* or at the time of its termination. However, pursuant to the applicable foreign law, *FT* can be amended to provide for additional beneficiaries, and there is an oral understanding between *A* and the trustee that *B* can be added as a beneficiary. Under paragraphs (a)(1) and (a)(4)(ii)(B) of this section, *FT* is treated as having a U.S. beneficiary.

Example 2. Actions in violation of the terms of the trust. A transfers property to *FT*. The trust instrument provides that no U.S. person can receive income or corpus from *FT* during the term of the trust or at the termination of *FT*. Notwithstanding the terms of the trust instrument, a letter of wishes directs the trustee of *FT* to provide for the educational needs of *B*, who is about to begin college. The letter of wishes contains a disclaimer to the effect that its contents are only suggestions and recommendations and that the trustee is at all times bound by the terms of the trust as set forth in the trust instrument. Under paragraphs (a)(1) and (a)(4)(ii)(C) of this section, *FT* is treated as having a U.S. beneficiary.

(b) *Indirect U.S. beneficiaries.*—(1) *Certain foreign entities.*—For purposes of paragraph (a)(1) of this section, an amount is treated as paid or accumulated to or for the benefit of a U.S. person if the amount is paid to or accumulated for the benefit of—

(i) A controlled foreign corporation, as defined in section 957(a);

(ii) A foreign partnership, if a U.S. person is a partner of such partnership; or

(iii) A foreign trust or estate, if such trust or estate has a U.S. beneficiary (within the meaning of paragraph (a)(1) of this section).

(2) *Other indirect beneficiaries.*—For purposes of paragraph (a)(1) of this section, an amount is treated as paid or accumulated to or for the benefit of a U.S. person if the amount is paid to or accumulated for the benefit of a U.S. person through an intermediary, such as an agent or nominee, or by any other means where a U.S. person may obtain an actual or constructive benefit.

(3) *Examples.*—The following examples illustrate the rules of this paragraph (b). Unless otherwise noted, *A* is a resident alien. *B* is *A's* son and is a resident alien. *FT* is a foreign trust. The examples are as follows:

Example 1. Trust benefitting foreign corporation. A transfers property to *FT*. The beneficiary of *FT* is *FC*, a foreign corporation. *FC* has outstanding solely 100 shares of common stock. *B* owns 49 shares of the *FC* stock and *FC2*, also a foreign corporation, owns the remaining 51 shares. *FC2* has outstanding solely 100 shares of common stock. *B* owns 49 shares of *FC2* and nonresident alien individuals own the remaining 51 *FC2* shares. *FC* is a controlled foreign corporation (as defined in section 957(a), after the application of section 958(a)(2)). Under paragraphs (a)(1) and (b)(1)(i) of this section, *FT* is treated as having a U.S. beneficiary.

Example 2. Trust benefitting another trust. A transfers property to *FT*. The terms of *FT* permit current distributions of income to *B*. *A* transfers property to another foreign trust, *FT2*. The terms of *FT2* provide that no U.S. person can benefit either as to income or corpus, but permit current distributions of income to *FT*. Under paragraph (a)(1) of this section, *FT* is treated as having a U.S. beneficiary and, under paragraphs (a)(1) and (b)(1)(iii) of this section, *FT2* is treated as having a U.S. beneficiary.

Example 3. Trust benefitting another trust after transferor's death. A transfers property to *FT*. The terms of *FT* require that all income from *FT* be accumulate during *A's* lifetime. In the year following *A's* death, a share of *FT* is to be distributed to *FT2*, another foreign trust, for the benefit of *B*. Under paragraphs (a)(1) and (b)(1)(iii) of this section, *FT* is treated as having a U.S. beneficiary beginning with the year of *A's* transfer of property to *FT*.

Example 4. Indirect benefit through use of debit card. A transfers property to *FT*. The trust instrument provides that no U.S. person can benefit either as to income or corpus. However, *FT* maintains an account with *FB*, a foreign bank, and *FB* issues a debit card to *B* against the account maintained by *FT* and *B* is allowed to make withdrawals. Under paragraphs (a)(1) and (b)(2) of this section, *FT* is treated as having a U.S. beneficiary.

Example 5. Other indirect benefit. A transfers property to *FT*. *FT* is administered by *FTC*, a foreign trust company. *FTC* forms *IBC*, an international business corporation formed under the laws of a foreign jurisdiction. *IBC* is the beneficiary of *FT*. *IBC* maintains an account with *FB*, a foreign bank. *FB* issues a debit card to *B* against the account maintained by *IBC* and *B* is allowed to make withdrawals. Under paragraphs (a)(1) and (b)(2) of this section, *FT* is treated as having a U.S. beneficiary.

(c) *Treatment of U.S. transferor upon foreign trust's acquisition or loss of U.S. beneficiary.*—(1) *Trusts acquiring a U.S. beneficiary.*—If a foreign trust to which a U.S. transferor has transferred property is not treated as having a U.S. beneficiary (within the meaning of paragraph (a) of this section) for any taxable year of the U.S. transferor, but the trust is treated as having a U.S. beneficiary (within the meaning of paragraph (a) of this section) in any subsequent taxable year, the U.S. transferor is treated as having additional income in the first such taxable year of the U.S. transferor in which the trust is treated as having a U.S. beneficiary. The amount of the additional income is equal to the trust's undistributed net income, as defined in section 665(a), at the end of the U.S. transferor's immediately preceding taxable year and is subject to the rules of section 668, providing for an interest charge on accumulation distributions from foreign trusts.

(2) *Trusts ceasing to have a U.S. beneficiary.*—If, for any taxable year of a U.S. transferor, a foreign trust that has received a transfer of property from the U.S. transferor ceases to be treated as having a U.S. beneficiary, the U.S. transferor ceases to be treated as the owner of the portion

of the trust attributable to the transfer beginning in the first taxable year following the last taxable year of the U.S. transferor during which the trust was treated as having a U.S. beneficiary (unless the U.S. transferor is treated as an owner thereof pursuant to sections 673 through 677). The U.S. transferor is treated as making a transfer of property to the foreign trust on the first day of the first taxable year following the last taxable year of the U.S. transferor during which the trust was treated as having a U.S. beneficiary. The amount of the property deemed to be transferred to the trust is the portion of the trust attributable to the prior transfer to which paragraph (a)(1) of this section applied. For rules regarding the recognition of gain on transfers to foreign trusts, see section 684.

(3) *Examples.*—The rules of this paragraph (c) are illustrated by the following examples. *A* is a resident alien, *B* is *A*'s son, and *FT* is a foreign trust. The examples are as follows:

Example 1. Trust acquiring U.S. beneficiary. (i) In 2001, *A* transfers stock with a fair market value of $100,000 to *FT*. The stock has an adjusted basis of $50,000 at the time of the transfer. The trust instrument provides that income may be paid currently to, or accumulated for the benefit of, *B* and that, upon the termination of the trust, all income and corpus is to be distributed to *B*. At the time of the transfer, *B* is a nonresident alien. *A* is not treated as the owner of any portion of *FT* under sections 673 through 677. *FT* accumulates a total of $30,000 of income during the taxable years 2001 through 2003. In 2004, *B* moves to the United States and becomes a resident alien. Assume paragraph (a)(4) of this section is not applicable under the facts and circumstances.

(ii) Under paragraph (c) (1) of this section, *A* is treated as receiving an accumulation distribution in the amount of $30,000 in 2004 and immediately transferring that amount back to the trust. The accumulation distribution is subject to the rules of section 668, providing for an interest charge on accumulation distributions.

(iii) Under paragraphs (a)(1) and (3) of this section, beginning in 2005, *A* is treated as the owner of the portion of *FT* attributable to the stock transferred by *A* to *FT* in 2001 (which includes the portion attributable to the accumulated income deemed to be retransferred in 2004).

Example 2. Trust ceasing to have U.S. beneficiary. (i) The facts are the same as in *Example 1*. In 2008, *B* becomes a nonresident alien. On the date *B* becomes a nonresident alien, the stock transferred by *A* to *FT* in 2001 has a fair market value of $125,000 and an adjusted basis of $50,000.

(ii) Under paragraph (c)(2) of this section, beginning in 2009, *FT* is not treated as having a U.S. beneficiary, and *A* is not treated as the owner of the portion of the trust attributable to the prior transfer of stock. For rules regarding the recognition of gain on the termination of ownership status, see section 684.

[Reg. §1.679-2.]

□ [*T.D.* 8955, 7-19-2001.]

[Reg. §1.679-3]

§1.679-3. Transfers.—(a) *In general.*—A transfer means a direct, indirect, or constructive transfer.

(b) *Transfers by certain trusts.*—(1) *In general.*—If any portion of a trust is treated as owned by a U.S. person, a transfer of property from that portion of the trust to a foreign trust is treated as a transfer from the owner of that portion to the foreign trust.

(2) *Example.*—The following example illustrates this paragraph (b):

Example. In 2001, *A*, a U.S. citizen, creates and funds *DT*, a domestic trust. *A* has the power to revest absolutely in himself the title to the property in *DT* and is treated as the owner of *DT* pursuant to section 676. In 2004, *DT* transfers property to *FT*, a foreign trust. *A* is treated as having transferred the property to *FT* in 2004 for purposes of this section.

(c) *Indirect transfers.*—(1) *Principal purpose of tax avoidance.*—A transfer to a foreign trust by any person (intermediary) to whom a U.S. person transfers property is treated as an indirect transfer by a U.S. person to the foreign trust if such transfer is made pursuant to a plan one of the principal purposes of which is the avoidance of United States tax.

(2) *Principal purpose of tax avoidance deemed to exist.*—For purposes of paragraph (c)(1) of this section, a transfer is deemed to have been made pursuant to a plan one of the principal purposes of which was the avoidance of United States tax if—

(i) The U.S. person is related (within the meaning of paragraph (c)(4) of this section) to a beneficiary of the foreign trust, or has another relationship with a beneficiary of the foreign trust that establishes a reasonable basis for concluding that the U.S. transferor would make a transfer to the foreign trust; and

(ii) The U.S. person cannot demonstrate to the satisfaction of the Commissioner that—

(A) The intermediary has a relationship with a beneficiary of the foreign trust that establishes a reasonable basis for concluding that the intermediary would make a transfer to the foreign trust;

(B) The intermediary acted independently of the U.S. person;

(C) The intermediary is not an agent of the U.S. person under generally applicable United States agency principles; and

(D) The intermediary timely complied with the reporting requirements of section 6048, if applicable.

(3) *Effect of disregarding intermediary.*—(i) *In general.*—Except as provided in paragraph (c)(3)(ii) of this section, if a transfer is treated as an indirect transfer pursuant to paragraph (c)(1) of this section, then the intermediary is treated as an agent of the U.S. person, and the property is treated as transferred to the foreign trust by the U.S. person in the year the property is trans-

ferred, or made available, by the intermediary to the foreign trust. The fair market value of the property transferred is determined as of the date of the transfer by the intermediary to the foreign trust.

(ii) *Special rule.*—If the Commissioner determines, or if the taxpayer can demonstrate to the satisfaction of the Commissioner, that the intermediary is an agent of the foreign trust under generally applicable United states agency principles, the property will be treated as transferred to the foreign trust in the year the U.S. person transfers the property to the intermediary. The fair market value of the property transferred will be determined as of the date of the transfer by the U.S. person to the intermediary.

(iii) *Effect on intermediary.*—If a transfer of property is treated as an indirect transfer under paragraph (c)(1) of this section, the intermediary is not treated as having transferred the property to the foreign trust.

(4) *Related parties.*—For purposes of this paragraph (c), a U.S. transferor is treated as related to a U.S. beneficiary of a foreign trust if the U.S. transferor and the beneficiary are related for purposes of section 643(i)(2)(B), with the following modifications—

(i) For purposes of applying section 267 (other than section 267(f)) and section 707(b)(1), "at least 10 percent" is used instead of "more than 50 percent" each place it appears; and

(ii) The principles of section 267(b)(10), using "at least 10 percent" instead of "more than 50 percent," apply to determine whether two corporations are related.

(5) *Examples.*—The rules of this paragraph (c) are illustrated by the following examples:

Example 1. Principal purpose of tax avoidance. *A*, a U.S. citizen, creates and funds *FT*, a foreign trust, for the benefit of *A*'s children, who are U.S. citizens. In 2004, *A* decides to transfer an additional 1000X to the foreign trust. Pursuant to a plan with a principal purpose of avoiding the application of section 679, *A* transfers 1000X to *I*, a foreign person. *I* subsequently transfers 1000X to *FT*. Under paragraph (c)(1) of this section, *A* is treated as having made a transfer of 1000X to *FT*.

Example 2. U.S. person unable to demonstrate that intermediary acted independently. *A*, a U.S. citizen, creates and funds *FT*, a foreign trust, for the benefit of *A*'s children, who are U.S. citizens. On July 1, 2004, *A* transfers XYZ stock to *D*, *A*'s uncle, who is a nonresident alien. *D* immediately sells the XYZ stock and uses the proceeds to purchase ABC stock. On January 1, 2007, *D* transfers the ABC stock to *FT*. *A* is unable to demonstrate to the satisfaction of the Commissioner, pursuant to paragraph (c)(2) of this section, that D acted independently of *A* in making the transfer to *FT*. Under paragraph (c)(1) of this section, *A* is treated as having transferred the ABC stock to *FT*. Under paragraph (c)(3) of this section, *D* is treated as an agent of *A*, and the transfer is deemed to have been made on January 1, 2007.

Example 3. Indirect loan to foreign trust. *A*, a U.S. citizen, previously created and funded *FT*, a foreign trust, for the benefit of *A*'s children, who are U.S. citizens. On July 1, 2004, *A* deposits 500X with *FB*, a foreign bank. On January 1, 2005, *FB* loans 450X to *FT*. *A* is unable to demonstrate to the satisfaction of the Commissioner, pursuant to paragraph (c)(2) of this section, that *FB* has a relationship with *FT* that establishes a reasonable basis for concluding that *FB* would make a loan to *FT* or that *FB* acted independently of *A* in making the loan. Under paragraph (c)(1) of this section, *A* is deemed to have transferred 450X directly to *FT* on January 1, 2005. Under paragraph (c)(3) of this section, *FB* is treated as an agent of *A*. For possible exceptions with respect to qualified obligations of the trust, and the treatment of principal repayments with respect to obligations of the trust that are not qualified obligations, see § 1.679-4.

Example 4. Loan to foreign trust prior to deposit of funds in foreign bank. The facts are the same as in *Example 3*, except that *A* makes the 500X deposit with *FB* on January 2, 2005, the day after *FB* makes the loan to *FT*. The result is the same as in *Example 3*.

(d) *Constructive transfers.*—(1) *In general.*—For purposes of paragraph (a) of this section, a constructive transfer includes any assumption or satisfaction of a foreign trust's obligation to a third party.

(2) *Examples.*—The rules of this paragraph (d) are illustrated by the following examples. In each example, *A* is a U.S. citizen and *FT* is a foreign trust. The examples are as follows:

Example 1. Payment of debt of foreign trust. *FT* owes 1000X to *Y*, an unrelated foreign corporation, for the performance of services by *Y* for *FT*. In satisfaction of FT's liability to *Y*, *A* transfers to *Y* property with a fair market value of 1000X. Under paragraph (d) (1) of this section, *A* is treated as having made a constructive transfer of the property to *FT*.

Example 2. Assumption of liability of foreign trust. *FT* owes 1000X to *Y*, an unrelated foreign corporation, for the performance of services by *Y* for *FT*. *A* assumes *FT*'s liability to pay *Y*. Under paragraph (d) (1) of this section, *A* is treated as having made a constructive transfer of property with a fair market value of 1000X to *FT*.

(e) *Guarantee of trust obligations.*—(1) *In general.*—If a foreign trust borrows money or other property from any person who is not a related person (within the meaning of § 1.679-1(c)(5)) with respect to the trust (lender) and a U.S. person (U.S. guarantor) that is a related person with respect to the trust guarantees (within the meaning of paragraph (e)(4) of this section) the foreign trust's obligation, the U.S. guarantor is treated for purposes of this section as a U.S. transferor that has made a transfer to the trust on the date of the guarantee in an amount determined under paragraph (e)(2) of this section. To the extent this paragraph causes the U.S. guarantor to be treated as having made a transfer to the trust, a lender that is a U.S. person shall not be treated as having transferred that amount to the foreign trust.

(2) *Amount transferred.*—The amount deemed transferred by a U.S. guarantor described in paragraph (e)(1) of this section is the guaranteed portion of the adjusted issue price of the obligation (within the meaning of § 1.1275-1(b)) plus any accrued but unpaid qualified stated interest (within the meaning of § 1.1273-1(c)).

(3) *Principal repayments.*—If a U.S. person is treated under this paragraph (e) having made a transfer by reason of the guarantee of an obligation, payments of principal to the lender by the foreign trust with respect to the obligation are taken into account on and after the date of the payment in determining the portion of the trust attributable to the property deemed transferred by the U.S. guarantor.

(4) *Guarantee.*—For purposes of this section, the term guarantee—

(i) Includes any arrangement under which a person, directly or indirectly, assures, on a conditional or unconditional basis, the payment of another's obligation;

(ii) Encompasses any form of credit support, and includes a commitment to make a capital contribution to the debtor or otherwise maintain its financial viability; and

(iii) Includes an arrangement reflected in a comfort letter, regardless of whether the arrangement gives rise to a legally enforceable obligation. If an arrangement is contingent upon the occurrence of an event, in determining whether the arrangement is a guarantee, it is assumed that the event has occurred.

(5) *Examples.*—The rules of this paragraph (e) are illustrated by the following examples. In all of the examples, *A* is a U.S. resident and *FT* is a foreign trust. The examples are as follows:

Example 1. Foreign lender. X, a foreign corporation, loans 1000X of cash to *FT* in exchange for *FT*'s obligation to repay the loan. *A* guarantees the repayment of 600X of *FT*'s obligation. Under paragraph (e)(2) of this section, *A* is treated as having transferred 600X to *FT*.

Example 2. Unrelated U.S. lender. The facts are the same as in *Example 1*, except *X* is a U.S. person that is not a related person within the meaning of § 1.679-1(c)(5). The result is the same as in *Example 1*.

(f) *Transfers to entities owned by a foreign trust.*—(1) *General rule.*—If a U.S. person is a related person (as defined in § 1.679-1(c)(5)) with respect to a foreign trust, any transfer of property by the U.S. person to an entity in which the foreign trust holds an ownership interest is treated as a transfer of such property by the U.S. person to the foreign trust followed by a transfer of the property from the foreign trust to the entity owned by the foreign trust, unless the U.S. person demonstrates to the satisfaction of the Commissioner that the transfer to the entity is properly attributable to the U.S. person's ownership interest in the entity.

(2) *Examples.*—The rules of this paragraph (f) are illustrated by the following examples. In all of the examples, *A* is a U.S. citizen, *FT* is a foreign trust, and *FC* is a foreign corporation. The examples are as follows:

Example 1. Transfer treated as transfer to trust. A creates and funds *FT*, which is treated as having a U.S. beneficiary under § 1.679-2. *FT* owns all of the outstanding stock of *FC*. *A* transfers property directly to *FC*. Because *FT* is the sole shareholder of *FC*, *A* is unable to demonstrate to the satisfaction of the Commissioner that the transfer is properly attributable to *A*'s ownership interest in *FC*. Accordingly, under this paragraph (f), *A* is treated as having transferred the property to *FT*, followed by a transfer of such property by *FT* to *FC*. Under § 1.679-1(a), *A* is treated as the owner of the portion of *FT* attributable to the property treated as transferred directly to *FT*. Under § 1.367(a)-1T(c)(4)(ii), the transfer of property by *FT* to *FC* is treated as a transfer of the property by *A* to *FC*.

Example 2. Transfer treated as transfer to trust. The facts are the same as in *Example 1*, except that *FT* is not treated as having a U.S. beneficiary under § 1.679-2. Under this paragraph (f), *A* is treated as having transferred the property to *FT*, followed by a transfer of such property by *FT* to *FC*. *A* is not treated as the owner of *FT* for purposes of § 1.679-1(a). For rules regarding the recognition of gain on the transfer, see section 684.

Example 3. Transfer not treated as transfer to trust. A creates and funds *FT*. *FC* has outstanding solely 100 shares of common stock. *FT* owns 50 shares of *FC* stock, and *A* owns the remaining 50 shares. On July 1, 2001, *FT* and *A* each transfer 1000X to *FC*. *A* is able to demonstrate to the satisfaction of the Commissioner that *A*'s transfer to *FC* is properly attributable to *A*'s ownership interest in *FC*. Accordingly, under this paragraph (f), *A*'s transfer to *FC* is not treated as a transfer to *FT*.

[Reg. § 1.679-3.]

☐ [*T.D. 8955, 7-19-2001.*]

[Reg. § 1.679-4]

§ 1.679-4. Exceptions to general rule.—(a) *In general.*—Section 1.679-1 does not apply to—

(1) Any transfer of property to a foreign trust by reason of the death of the transferor;

(2) Any transfer of property to a foreign trust described in sections 402(b), 404(a)(4), or 404A;

(3) Any transfer of property to a foreign trust described in section 501(c)(3) (without regard to the requirements of section 508(a)); and

(4) Any transfer of property to a foreign trust to the extent the transfer is for fair market value.

(b) *Transfers for fair market value.*—(1) *In general.*—For purposes of this section, a transfer is for fair market value only to the extent of the value of property received from the trust, services rendered by the trust, or the right to use property of the trust. For example, rents, royalties, interest, and compensation paid to a trust are transfers for fair market value only to the extent that the payments reflect an arm's length price for the use of the property of, or for the services rendered by, the trust. For purposes of this determination, an interest in the trust is not property received from the trust. For purposes of this section, a distribution to a trust with respect to an interest held by such trust in an entity other than a trust or an interest in certain investment trusts described in § 301.7701-4(c) of this chapter, liquidating trusts described in § 301.7701-4(d) of this chapter, or environmental remediation trusts described in § 301.7701-4(e) of this chapter is considered to be a transfer for fair market value.

(2) *Special rule.*—(i) *Transfers for partial consideration.*—For purposes of this section, if a person transfers property to a foreign trust in exchange for property having a fair market value that is less than the fair market value of the property transferred, the exception in paragraph (a)(4) of this section applies only to the extent of the fair market value of the property received.

(ii) *Example.*—This paragraph (b) is illustrated by the following example:

Example. A, a U.S. citizen, transfers property that has a fair market value of 1000X to *FT*, a foreign trust, in exchange for 600X of cash. Under this paragraph (b), § 1.679-1 applies with respect to the transfer of 400X (1000X less 600X) to *FT*.

(c) *Certain obligations not taken into account.*—Solely for purposes of this section, in determining whether a transfer by a U.S. transferor that is a related person (as defined in § 1.679-1(c)(5)) with respect to the foreign trust is for fair market value, any obligation (as defined in § 1.679-1(c)(6)) of the trust or a related person (as defined in § 1.679-1(c)(5)) that is not a qualified obligation within the meaning of paragraph (d)(1) of this section shall not be taken into account.

(d) *Qualified obligations.*—(1) *In general.*—For purposes of this section, an obligation is treated as a qualified obligation only if—

(i) The obligation is reduced to writing by an express written agreement;

(ii) The term of the obligation does not exceed five years (for purposes of determining the term of an obligation, the obligation's maturity date is the last possible date that the obligation can be outstanding under the terms of the obligation);

(iii) All payments on the obligation are denominated in U.S. dollars;

(iv) The yield to maturity is not less than 100 percent of the applicable Federal rate and not greater that 130 percent of the applicable Federal rate (the applicable Federal rate for an obligation is the applicable Federal rate in effect under section 1274(d) for the day on which the obligation is issued, as published in the Internal Revenue Bulletin (see § 601.601(d)(2) of this chapter));

(v) The U.S. transferor extends the period for assessment of any income or transfer tax attributable to the transfer and any consequential income tax changes for each year that the obligation is outstanding, to a date not earlier than three years after the maturity date of the obligation (this extension is not necessary if the maturity date of the obligation does not extend beyond the end of the U.S. transferor's taxable year for the year of the transfer and is paid within such period); when properly executed and filed, such an agreement is deemed to be consented to for purposes of § 301.6501(c)-1(d) of this chapter; and

(vi) The U.S. transferor reports the status of the loan, including principal and interest payments, on Form 3520 for every year that the loan is outstanding.

(2) *Additional loans.*—If, while the original obligation is outstanding, the U.S. transferor or a person related to the trust (within the meaning of § 1.679-1(c)(5)) directly or indirectly obtains another obligation issued by the trust, or if the U.S. transferor directly or indirectly obtains another obligation issued by a person related to the trust, the original obligation is deemed to have the maturity date of any such subsequent obligation in determining whether the term of the original obligation exceeds the specified 5-year term. In addition, a series of obligations issued and repaid by the trust (or a person related to the trust) is treated as a single obligation if the transactions giving rise to the obligations are structured with a principal purpose to avoid the application of this provision.

(3) *Obligations that cease to be qualified.*—If an obligation treated as a qualified obligation subsequently fails to be a qualified obligation (e.g., renegotiation of the terms of the obligation causes the term of the obligation to exceed five years), the U.S. transferor is treated as making a transfer to the trust in an amount equal to the original obligation's adjusted issue price (within the meaning of § 1.1275-1(b)) plus any accrued but unpaid qualified stated interest (within the meaning of § 1.1273-1(c)) as of the date of the subsequent event that causes the obligation to no longer be a qualified obligation. If the maturity date is extended beyond five years by reason of the issuance of a subsequent obligation by the trust (or person related to the trust), the amount of the transfer will not exceed the issue price of the subsequent obligation. The subsequent obligation is separately tested to determine if it is a qualified obligation.

(4) *Transfers resulting from failed qualified obligations.*—In general, a transfer resulting from a failed qualified obligation is deemed to occur on the date of the subsequent event that causes the obligation to no longer be a qualified obligation. However, based on all of the facts and circumstances, the Commissioner may deem a transfer to have occurred on any date on or after the issue date of the original obligation. For example, if at the time the original obligation was issued, the transferor knew or had reason to

know that the obligation would not be repaid, the Commissioner could deem the transfer to have occurred on the issue date of the original obligation.

(5) *Renegotiated loans.*—Any loan that is renegotiated, extended, or revised is treated as a new loan, and any transfer of funds to a foreign trust after such renegotiation, extension, or revision under a pre-existing loan agreement is treated as a transfer subject to this section.

(6) *Principal repayments.*—The payment of principal with respect to any obligation that is not treated as a qualified obligation under this paragraph is taken into account on and after the date of the payment in determining the portion of the trust attributable to the property transferred.

(7) *Examples.*—The rules of this paragraph (d) are illustrated by the following examples. In the examples, *A* and *B* are U.S. residents and *FT* is a foreign trust. The examples are as follows:

Example 1. Demand loan. A transfers 500X to *FT* in exchange for a demand note that permits *A* to require repayment by *FT* at any time. *A* is a related person (as defined in § 1.679-1(c)(5)) with respect to *FT*. Because *FT*'s obligation to *A* could remain outstanding for more than five years, the obligation is not a qualified obligation within the meaning of paragraph (d) of this section and, pursuant to paragraph (c) of this section, it is not taken into account for purposes of determining whether *A*'s transfer is eligible for the fair market value exception of paragraph (a)(4) of this section. Accordingly, § 1.679-1 applies with respect to the full 500X transfer to *FT*.

Example 2. Private annuity. A transfers 4000X to *FT* in exchange for an annuity from the foreign trust that will pay *A* 100X per year for the rest of *A*'s life. *A* is a related person (as defined in § 1.679-1(c)(5)) with respect to *FT*. Because *FT*'s obligation to *A* could remain outstanding for more than five years, the obligation is not a qualified obligation within the meaning of paragraph (d)(1) of this section and, pursuant to paragraph (c) of this section, it is not taken into account for purposes of determining whether *A*'s transfer is eligible for the fair market value exception of paragraph (a)(4) of this section. Accordingly, § 1.679-1 applies with respect to the full 4000X transfer to *FT*.

Example 3. Loan to unrelated foreign trust. B transfers 1000X to *FT* in exchange for an obligation of the trust. The term of the obligation is fifteen years. *B* is not a related person (as defined in § 1.679-1(c)(5)) with respect to *FT*. Because *B* is not a related person, the fair market value of the obligation received by *B* is taken into account for purposes of determining whether *B*'s transfer is eligible for the fair market value exception of paragraph (a)(4) of this section, even though the obligation is not a qualified obligation within the meaning of paragraph (d)(1) of this section.

Example 4. Transfer for an obligation with term in excess of 5 years. A transfers property that has a fair market value of 5000X to *FT* in exchange for an obligation of the trust. The term of the obligation is ten years. *A* is a related person (as defined in § 1.679-1(c)(5)) with respect to *FT*. Because the term of the obligation is greater than five years, the obligation is not a qualified obligation within the meaning of paragraph (d)(1) of this section and, pursuant to paragraph (c) of this section, it is not taken into account for purposes of determining whether *A*'s transfer is eligible for the fair market value exception of paragraph (a)(4) of this section. Accordingly, § 1.679-1 applies with respect to the full 5000X transfer to *FT*.

Example 5. Transfer for a qualified obligation. The facts are the same as in *Example 4*, except that the term of the obligation is 3 years. Assuming the other requirements of paragraph (d)(1) of this section are satisfied, the obligation is a qualified obligation and its adjusted issue price is taken into account for purposes of determining whether *A*'s transfer is eligible for the fair market value exception of paragraph (a)(4) of this section.

Example 6. Effect of subsequent obligation on original obligation. A transfers property that has a fair market value of 1000X to *FT* in exchange for an obligation that satisfies the requirements of paragraph (d)(1) of this section. *A* is a related person (as defined in § 1. 679-1(c)(5)) with respect to *FT*. Two years later, *A* transfers an additional 2000X to *FT* and receives another obligation from *FT* that has a maturity date four years from the date that the second obligation was issued. Under paragraph (d)(2) of this section, the original obligation is deemed to have the maturity date of the second obligation. Under paragraph (a) of this section, *A* is treated as having made a transfer in an amount equal to the original obligation's adjusted issue price (within the meaning of § 1.1275-1(b)) plus any accrued but unpaid qualified stated interest (within the meaning of § 1.1273-1(c)) as of the date of issuance of the second obligation. The second obligation is tested separately to determine whether it is a qualified obligation for purposes of applying paragraph (a) of this section to the second transfer.

[Reg. § 1.679-4.]

☐ [*T.D. 8955*, 7-19-2001.]

[Reg. § 1.679-5]

§ 1.679-5. Pre-immigration trusts.—(a) *In general.*—If a nonresident alien individual becomes a U.S. person and the individual has a residency starting date (as determined under section 7701(b)(2)(A)) within 5 years after directly or indirectly transferring property to a foreign trust (the original transfer), the individual is treated as having transferred to the trust on the residency starting date an amount equal to the portion of the trust attributable to the property transferred by the individual in the original transfer.

(b) *Special rules.*—(1) *Change in grantor trust status.*—For purposes of paragraph (a) of this section, if a nonresident alien individual who is treated as owning any portion of a trust under the provisions of subpart E of part I of subchapter J, chapter 1 of the Internal Revenue Code, subsequently ceases to be so treated, the individual is treated as having made the original transfer to the foreign trust immediately before the trust ceases to be treated as owned by the individual.

(2) *Treatment of undistributed income.*—For purposes of paragraph (a) of this section, the property deemed transferred to the foreign trust on the residency starting date includes undistributed net income, as defined in section 665(a), attributable to the property deemed transferred. Undistributed net income for periods before the individual's residency starting date is taken into account only for purposes of determining the amount of the property deemed transferred.

(c) *Examples.*—The rules of this section are illustrated by the following examples:

Example 1. Nonresident alien becomes resident alien. On January 1, 2002, *A*, a nonresident alien individual, transfers property to a foreign trust, *FT*. On January 1, 2006, *A* becomes a resident of the United States within the meaning of section 7701(b)(1)(A) and has a residency starting date of January 1, 2006, within the meaning of section 7701(b)(2)(A). Under paragraph (a) of this section, *A* is treated as a U.S. transferor and is deemed to transfer the property to *FT* on January 1, 2006. Under paragraph (b)(2) of this section, the property deemed transferred to *FT* on January 1, 2006, includes the undistributed net income of the trust, as defined in section 665(a), attributable to the property originally transferred.

Example 2. Nonresident alien loses power to revest property. On January 1, 2002, *A*, a nonresident alien individual, transfers property to a foreign trust, *FT*. *A* has the power to revest absolutely in himself the title to such property transferred and is treated as the owner of the trust pursuant to sections 676 and 672(f). On January 1, 2008, the terms of *FT* are amended to remove *A*'s power to revest in himself title to the property transferred, and *A* ceases to be treated as the owner of *FT*. On January 1, 2010, *A* becomes a resident of the United States. Under paragraph (b)(1) of this section, for purposes of paragraph (a) of this section *A* is treated as having originally transferred the property to *FT* on January 1, 2008. Because this date is within five years of *A*'s residency starting date, *A* is deemed to have made a transfer to the foreign trust on January 1, 2010, his residency starting date. Under paragraph (b)(2) of this section, the property deemed transferred to the foreign trust on January 1, 2010, includes the undistributed net income of the trust, as defined in section 665(a), attributable to the property deemed transferred.

[Reg. § 1.679-5.]

☐ [*T.D.* 8955, 7-19-2001.]

[Reg. § 1.679-6]

§ 1.679-6. Outbound migrations of domestic trusts.—(a) *In general.*—Subject to the provisions of paragraph (b) of this section, if an individual who is a U.S. person transfers property to a trust that is not a foreign trust, and such trust becomes a foreign trust while the U.S. person is alive, the U.S. individual is treated as a U.S. transferor and is deemed to transfer the property to a foreign trust on the date the domestic trust becomes a foreign trust.

(b) *Amount deemed transferred.*—For purposes of paragraph (a) of this section, the property deemed transferred to the trust when it becomes a foreign trust includes undistributed net income, as defined in section 665(a), attributable to the property previously transferred. Undistributed net income for periods prior to the migration is taken into account only for purposes of determining the portion of the trust that is attributable to the property transferred by the U.S. person.

(c) *Example.*—The following example illustrates the rules of this section. For purposes of the example, *A* is a resident alien, *B* is *A*'s son, who is a resident alien, and *DT* is a domestic trust. The example is as follows:

Example. Outbound migration of domestic trust. On January 1, 2002, *A* transfers property to *DT*, for the benefit of *B*. On January 1, 2003, *DT* acquires a foreign trustee who has the power to determine whether and when distributions will be made to *B*. Under section 7701(a)(30)(E) and § 301.7701-7(d)(ii)(A) of this chapter, *DT* becomes a foreign trust on January 1, 2003. Under paragraph (a) of this section, *A* is treated as transferring property to a foreign trust on January 1, 2003. Under paragraph (b) of this section, the property deemed transferred to the trust when it becomes a foreign trust includes undistributed net income, as defined in section 665(a), attributable to the property deemed transferred.

[Reg. § 1.679-6.]

☐ [*T.D.* 8955, 7-19-2001.]

[Reg. § 1.679-7]

§ 1.679-7. Effective dates.—(a) *In general.*—Except as provided in paragraph (b) of this section, the rules of §§ 1.679-1, 1.679-2, 1.679-3, and 1.679-4 apply with respect to transfers after August 7, 2000.

(b) *Special rules.*—(1) The rules of § 1.679-4(c) and (d) apply to an obligation issued after February 6, 1995, whether or not in accordance with a pre-existing arrangement or understanding. For purposes of the rules of § 1.679-4(c) and (d), if an obligation issued on or before February 6, 1995, is modified after that date, and the modification is a significant modification within the meaning of § 1.1001-3, the obligation is treated as if it were issued on the date of the modification. However, the penalty provided in section 6677 applies only to a failure to report transfers in exchange for obligations issued after August 20, 1996.

(2) The rules of § 1.679-5 apply to persons whose residency starting date is after August 7, 2000.

(3) The rules of § 1.679-6 apply to trusts that become foreign trusts after August 7, 2000. [Reg. § 1.679-7.]

☐ [*T.D.* 8955, 7-19-2001.]

[Reg. § 1.681(a)-1]

§ 1.681(a)-1. Limitation on charitable contributions deductions of trusts; scope of section 681.—Under section 681, the unlimited charitable contributions deduction otherwise allowable to a trust under section 642(c) is, in general, subject to percentage limitations, corresponding to those applicable to contributions by an individual under section 170(b)(1)(A) and (B), under the following circumstances:

(a) To the extent that the deduction is allocable to "unrelated business income";

(b) For taxable years beginning before January 1, 1970, if the trust has engaged in a prohibited transaction;

(c) For taxable years beginning before January 1, 1970, if income is accumulated for a charitable purpose and the accumulation is (1) unreasonable, (2) substantially diverted to a noncharitable purpose, or (3) invested against the interests of the charitable beneficiaries.

Further, if the circumstance set forth in paragraph (a) or (c) of this section is applicable, the deduction is limited to income actually paid out for charitable purposes, and is not allowed for income only set aside or to be used for those purposes. If the circumstance set forth in paragraph (b) of this section is applicable, deductions for contributions to the trust may be disallowed. The provisions of section 681 are discussed in detail in §§ 1.681(a)-2 through 1.681(c)-1. For definition of the term "income," see section 643(b) and § 1.643(b)-1. [Reg. § 1.681(a)-1.]

☐ [*T.D.* 6269, 11-15-57. *Amended by T.D.* 7428, 8-13-76.]

[Reg. § 1.681(a)-2]

§ 1.681(a)-2. Limitation on charitable contributions deduction of trusts with trade or business income.—(a) *In general.*—No charitable contributions deduction is allowable to a trust under section 642(c) for any taxable year for amounts allocable to the trust's unrelated business income for the taxable year. For the purpose of section 681(a) the term "unrelated business income" of a trust means an amount which would be computed as the trust's unrelated business taxable income under section 512 and the regulations thereunder, if the trust were an organization exempt from tax under section 501(a) by reason of section 501(c)(3). For the purpose of the computation under section 512, the term "unrelated trade or business" includes a trade or business carried on by a partnership of which a trust is a member, as well as one carried on by the trust itself. While the charitable contributions deduction under section 642(c) is entirely disallowed by section 681(a) for amounts allocable to "unrelated business income," a partial deduction is nevertheless allowed for such amounts by the operation of section 512(b)(11), as illustrated in paragraphs (b) and (c) of this section. This partial deduction is subject to the percentage limitations applicable to contributions by an individual under section 170(b)(1)(A) and (B), and is not allowed for amounts set aside or to be used for charitable purposes but not actually paid out during the taxable year. Charitable contributions deductions otherwise allowable under section 170, 545(b)(2), or 642(c) for contributions to a trust are not disallowed solely because the trust has unrelated business income.

(b) *Determination of amounts allocable to unrelated business income.*—In determining the amount for which a charitable contributions deduction would otherwise be allowable under section 642(c) which are allocable to unrelated business income, and therefore not allowable as a deduction, the following steps are taken:

(1) There is first determined the amount which would be computed as the trust's unrelated business taxable income under section 512 and the regulations thereunder if the trust were an organization exempt from tax under section 501(a) by reason of section 501(c)(3), but without taking the charitable contributions deduction allowed under section 512(b)(11).

(2) The amount for which a charitable contributions deduction would otherwise be allowable under section 642(c) is then allocated between the amount determined in subparagraph (1) of this paragraph and any other income of the trust. Unless the facts clearly indicate to the contrary, the allocation to the amount determined in subparagraph (1) of this paragraph is made on the basis of the ratio (but not in excess of 100 percent) of the amount determined in subparagraph (1) of this paragraph to the taxable income of the trust, determined without the deduction for personal exemption under section 642(b), the charitable contributions deduction under section 642(c), or the deduction for distributions to beneficiaries under section 661(a).

(3) The amount for which a charitable contributions deduction would otherwise be allowable under section 642(c) which is allocable to unrelated business income as determined in subparagraph (2) of this paragraph, and therefore not allowable as a deduction, is the amount determined in subparagraph (2) of this paragraph reduced by the charitable contributions deduction which would be allowed under section 512(b)(11) if the trust were an organization exempt from tax under section 501(a) by reason of section 501(c)(3).

(c) *Examples.*—(1) The application of this section may be illustrated by the following examples, in which it is assumed that the Y charity is not a charitable organization qualifying under section 170(b)(1)(A) (see subparagraph (2) of this paragraph):

Example (1). The X trust has income of $50,000. There is included in this amount a net profit of $31,000 from the operation of a trade or business. The trustee is required to pay half of the trust income to A, an individual, and the balance of the trust income to the Y charity, an organization described in section 170(c)(2). The trustee pays each beneficiary $25,000. Under these facts, the unrelated business income of the trust (computed before the charitable contributions deduction which would be allowed under section 512(b)(11)) is $30,000 ($31,000 less the deduction of $1,000 allowed by section 512(b)(12)). The deduction otherwise allowable under section 642(c) is $25,000, the amount paid to the Y charity. The portion allocable to the unrelated business income (computed as prescribed in paragraph (b)(2) of this section) is $15,000, that is, an amount which bears the same ratio to $25,000 as $30,000 bears to $50,000. The portion allocable to the unrelated business income, and therefore disallowed as a deduction, is $15,000 reduced by $6,000 (20 percent of $30,000, the charitable contributions deduction which would be allowable under section 512(b)(11)), or $9,000.

Example (2). Assume the same facts as in example (1), except that the trustee has discretion as to the portion of the trust income to be paid to each beneficiary, and the trustee pays $40,000 to A and $10,000 to the Y charity. The deduction otherwise allowable under section 642(c) is $10,000. The portion allocable to the unrelated business income computed as prescribed in paragraph (b)(2) of this section is $6,000, that is, an amount which bears the same ratio to $10,000 as $30,000 bears to $50,000. Since this amount does not exceed the charitable contributions deduction which would be allowable under section 512(b)(11) ($6,000, determined as in example (1)), no portion of it is disallowed as a deduction.

Example (3). Assume the same facts as in example (1), except that the terms of the trust instrument require the trustee to pay to the Y charity the trust income, if any, derived from the trade or business, and to pay to A all the trust income derived from other sources. The trustee pays $31,000 to the Y charity and $19,000 to A. The deduction otherwise allowable under section 642(c) is $31,000. Since the entire income from the trade or business is paid to Y charity, the amount allocable to the unrelated business income computed before the charitable contributions deduction under section 512(b)(11) is $30,000 ($31,000 less the deduction of $1,000 allowed by section 512(b)(12)). The amount allocable to the unrelated business income and therefore disallowed as a deduction is $24,000 ($30,000 less $6,000).

Example (4). (i) Under the terms of the trust, the trustee is required to pay half of the trust income to A, an individual, for his life, and the balance of the trust income to the Y charity, an organization described in section 170(c)(2). Capital gains are allocable to corpus and upon A's death the trust is to terminate and the corpus is to be distributed to the Y charity. The trust has taxable income of $50,000 computed without any deduction for personal exemption, charitable contributions, or distributions. The amount of $50,000 includes $10,000 capital gains, $30,000 ($31,000 less the $1,000 deduction allowed under section 512(b)(12)) unrelated business income (computed before the charitable contributions deduction which would be allowed under section 512(b)(11)) and other income of $9,000. The trustee pays each beneficiary $20,000.

(ii) The deduction otherwise allowable under section 642(c) is $30,000 ($20,000 paid to Y charity and $10,000 capital gains allocated to corpus and permanent set aside for charitable purposes). The portion allocable to the unrelated business income is $15,000, that is, an amount which bears the same ratio to $20,000 (the amount paid to Y charity) as $30,000 bears to $40,000 ($50,000 less $10,000 capital gains allocable to corpus). The portion allocable to the unrelated business income, and therefore disallowed as a deduction, is $15,000 reduced by $6,000 (the charitable contributions deduction which would be allowable under section 512(b)(11)), or $9,000.

(2) If, in the examples in subparagraph (1) of this paragraph, the Y charity were a charitable organization qualifying under section 170(b)(1)(A), then the deduction allowable under section 512(b)(11) would be computed at a rate of 30 percent. [Reg. § 1.681(a)-2.]

☐ [*T.D.* 6269, 11-15-57. *Amended by T.D.* 6605, 8-14-62.]

[Reg. § 1.681(b)-1]

§ 1.681(b)-1. Cross reference.—For disallowance of certain charitable, etc., deductions otherwise allowable under section 642(c), see sections 508(d) and 4948(c)(4). See also 26 CFR §§ 1.681(b)-1 and 1.681(c)-1 (rev. as of Apr. 1, 1974) for provisions applying before January 1, 1970. [Reg. § 1.681(b)-1.]

☐ [*T.D.* 7428, 8-13-76.]

[Reg. § 1.682(a)-1]

§ 1.682(a)-1. Income of trust in case of divorce, etc.—(a) *In general.*—(1) Section 682(a) provides rules in certain cases for determining the taxability of income of trusts as between spouses who are divorced, or who are separated under a decree of separate maintenance or a written separation agreement. In such cases, the spouse actually entitled to receive payments from the trust is considered the beneficiary rather than the spouse in discharge of whose obligations the payments are made, except to the extent that the payments are specified to be for the support of the obligor spouse's minor children in the divorce or separate maintenance decree, the separation agreement or the governing trust instrument. For convenience, the beneficiary spouse will hereafter in this section and in § 1.682(b)-1 be referred to as the "wife" and the obligor spouse from whom she is divorced or legally separated as the "husband". (See section 7701(a)(17).) Thus, under section 682(a) income of a trust—

(i) Which is paid, credited, or required to be distributed to the wife in a taxable year of the wife, and

(ii) Which, except for the provisions of section 682, would be includible in the gross income of her husband,

is includible in her gross income and is not includible in his gross income.

(2) Section 682(a) does not apply in any case to which section 71 applies. Although section 682(a) and section 71 seemingly cover some of

the same situations, there are important differences between them. Thus, section 682(a) applies, for example, to a trust created before the divorce or separation and not in contemplation of it, while section 71 applies only if the creation of the trust or payments by a previously created trust are in discharge of an obligation imposed upon or assumed by the husband (or made specific) under the court order or decree divorcing or legally separating the husband and wife, or a written instrument incident to the divorce status or legal separation status, or a written separation agreement. If section 71 applies, it requires inclusion in the wife's income of the full amount of periodic payments received attributable to property in trust (whether or not out of trust income), while, if section 71 does not apply, section 682(a) requires amounts paid, credited, or required to be distributed to her to be included only to the extent they are includible in the taxable income of a trust beneficiary under subparts A through D (section 641 and following), part I, subchapter J, chapter 1 of the Code.

(3) Section 682(a) is designed to produce uniformity as between cases in which, without section 682(a), the income of a so-called alimony trust would be taxable to the husband because of his continuing obligation to support his wife or former wife, and other cases in which the income of a so-called alimony trust is taxable to the wife or former wife because of the termination of the husband's obligation. Furthermore, section 682(a) taxes trust income to the wife in all cases in which the husband would otherwise be taxed not only because of the discharge of his alimony obligation but also because of his retention of control over the trust income or corpus. Section 682(a) applies whether the wife is the beneficiary under the terms of the trust instrument or is an assignee of a beneficiary.

(4) The application of section 682(a) may be illustrated by the following examples, in which it is assumed that both the husband and wife make their income tax returns on a calendar year basis:

Example (1). Upon the marriage of H and W, H irrevocably transfers property in trust to pay the income to W for her life for support, maintenance, and all other expenses. Some years later, W obtains a legal separation from H under an order of court. W, relying upon the income from the trust payable to her, does not ask for any provision for her support and the decree recites that since W is adequately provided for by the trust, no further provision is being made for her. Under these facts, section 682(a), rather than section 71, is applicable. Under the provisions of section 682(a), the income of the trust which becomes payable to W after the order of separation is includible in her income and is deductible by the trust. No part of the income is includible in H's income or deductible by him.

Example (2). H transfers property in trust for the benefit of W, retaining the power to revoke the trust at any time. H, however, promises that if he revokes the trust he will transfer to W property in the value of $100,000. The transfer in trust and the agreement were not incident to divorce, but some years later W divorces H. The court decree is silent as to alimony and the trust. After the divorce, income of the trust which becomes payable to W is taxable to her, and is not taxable to H or deductible by him. If H later terminates the trust and transfers $100,000 of property to W, the $100,000 is not income to W nor deductible by H.

(b) *Alimony trust income designated for support of minor children.*—Section 682(a) does not require the inclusion in the wife's income of trust income which the terms of the divorce or separate maintenance decree, separation agreement, or trust instrument fix in terms of an amount of money or a portion of the income as a sum which is payable for the support of minor children of the husband. The portion of the income which is payable for the support of the minor children is includible in the husband's income. If in such a case trust income fixed in terms of an amount of money is to be paid but a lesser amount becomes payable, the trust income is considered to be payable for the support of the husband's minor children to the extent of the sum which would be payable for their support out of the originally specified amount of trust income. This rule is similar to that provided in the case of periodic payments under section 71. See §1.71-1. [Reg. §1.682(a)-1.]

☐ [*T.D.* 6269, 12-15-57.]

[Reg. §1.682(b)-1]

§1.682(b)-1. Application of trust rules to alimony payments.—(a) For the purpose of the application subparts A through D (section 641 and following), part I, subchapter J, chapter 1 of the Code, the wife described in section 682 or section 71 who is entitled to receive payments attributable to property in trust is considered a beneficiary of the trust, whether or not the payments are made for the benefit of the husband in discharge of his obligations. A wife treated as a beneficiary of a trust under this section is also treated as the beneficiary of such trust for purposes of the tax imposed by section 56 (relating to the minimum tax for tax preferences). For rules relating to the treatment of items of tax preference with respect to a beneficiary of a trust, see §1.58-3.

(b) A periodic payment includible in the wife's gross income under section 71 attributable to property in trust is included in full in her gross income in her taxable year in which any part is required to be included under section 652 or 662. Assume, for example, in a case in which both the wife and the trust file income tax returns on the calendar year basis, that an annuity of $5,000 is to be paid to the wife by the trustee every December 31 (out of trust income if possible and, if not, out of corpus) pursuant to the terms of a divorce decree. Of the $5,000 distributable on December 31, 1954, $4,000 is payable out of income and $1,000 out of corpus. The actual distribution is made in 1955. Although the periodic payment is received by the wife in 1955, since under section 662 the $4,000 income distributable on December 31, 1954, is to be included in the wife's income for 1954, the $1,000 payment out of corpus is also to be included in her income for 1954. [Reg. § 1.682(b)-1.]

☐ [*T.D.* 6269, 11-15-57. *Amended by T.D.* 7564, 9-11-78.]

[Reg. § 1.682(c)-1]

§ 1.682(c)-1. Definitions.—For definitions of the terms "husband" and "wife" as used in section 682, see section 7701(a)(17) and the regulations thereunder. [Reg. § 1.682(c)-1.]

☐ [*T.D.* 6269, 12-15-57.]

[Reg. § 1.683-1]

§ 1.683-1. Applicability of provisions; general rule.—Part I (section 641 and following), subchapter J, chapter 1 of the Code, applies to estates and trusts and to beneficiaries only with respect to taxable years which begin after December 31, 1953, and end after August 16, 1954, the date of enactment of the Internal Revenue Code of 1954. In the case of an estate or trust, the date on which a trust is created or amended or on which an estate commences, and the taxable years of beneficiaries, grantors, or decedents concerned are immaterial. This provision applies equally to taxable years of normal and of abbreviated length. [Reg. § 1.683-1.]

☐ [*T.D.* 6269, 12-15-57.]

[Reg. § 1.683-2]

§ 1.683-2. Exceptions.—(a) In the case of any beneficiary of an estate or trust, sections 641 through 682 do not apply to any amount paid, credited, or to be distributed by an estate or trust in any taxable year of the estate or trust which begins before January 1, 1954, or which ends before August 17, 1954. Whether an amount so paid, credited, or to be distributed is to be included in the gross income of a beneficiary is determined with reference to the Internal Revenue Code of 1939. Thus, if a trust in its fiscal year ending June 30, 1954, distributed its current income to a beneficiary on June 30, 1954, the extent to which the distribution is includible in the beneficiary's gross income for his taxable year (the calendar year 1954) and the character of such income will be determined under the Internal Revenue Code of 1939. The Internal Revenue Code of 1954, however, determines the beneficiary's tax liability for a taxable year of the beneficiary to which such Code applies, with respect even to gross income of the beneficiary determined under the Internal Revenue Code of 1939 in accordance with this paragraph. Accordingly, the beneficiary is allowed credits and deductions pursuant to the Internal Revenue Code of 1954 for a taxable year governed by the Internal Revenue Code of 1954. See subparagraph (ii) of example (1) in paragraph (c) of this section.

(b) For purposes of determining the time of receipt of dividends under sections 34 (for purposes of the credit for dividends received on or before December 31, 1964) and 116, the dividends paid, credited, or to be distributed to a beneficiary are deemed to have been received by the beneficiary ratably on the same dates that the dividends were received by the estate or trust.

(c) The application of this section may be illustrated by the following examples:

Example (1). (i) A trust, reporting on the fiscal year basis, receives in its taxable year ending November 30, 1954, dividends on December 3, 1953, and April 3, July 5, and October 4, 1954. It distributes the dividends to A, its sole beneficiary (who reports on the calendar year basis) on November 30, 1954. Since the trust has received dividends in a taxable year ending after July 31, 1954, it will receive a dividend credit under section 34 with respect to dividends received which otherwise qualify under that section, in this case dividends received on October 4, 1954 (i.e., received after July 31, 1954). See section 7851(a)(1)(C). This credit, however, is reduced to the extent the dividends are allocable to the beneficiary as a result of income being paid, credited, or required to be distributed to him. The trust will also be permitted the dividend exclusion under section 116, since it received its dividends in a taxable year ending after July 31, 1954.

(ii) A is entitled to the section 34 credit with respect to the portion of the October 4, 1954, dividends which is distributed to him even though the determination of whether the amount distributed to him is includible in his gross income is made under the Internal Revenue Code of 1939. The credit allowable to the trust is reduced proportionately to the extent A is deemed to have received the October 4 dividends. A is not entitled to a credit with respect to the dividends received by the trust on December 3, 1953, and April 3, and July 5, 1954, because, although he receives after July 31, 1954, the distribution resulting from the trust's receipt of dividends, he is deemed to have received the dividends ratably with the trust on dates prior to July 31, 1954. In determining the exclusion under section 116 to which he is entitled, all the dividends received by the trust in 1954 and distributed to him are aggregated with any other dividends received by him in 1954, since he is deemed to have received such dividends in 1954 and therefore within a taxable year ending after July 31, 1954. He is not, however, entitled to the exclusion for the dividends received by the trust in December 1953.

Example (2). (i) A simple trust reports on the basis of a fiscal year ending July 31. It receives dividends on October 3, 1953, and January 4, April 3, and July 5, 1954. It distributes the dividends to A, its sole beneficiary, on September 1, 1954. The trust, receiving dividends in a taxable year ending prior to August 17, 1954, is entitled neither to the dividend received credit under section 34 nor the dividend exclusion under section 116.

(ii) A (reporting on the calendar year basis) is not entitled to the section 34 credit, because, although he receives after July 31, 1954, the distribution resulting from the trust's receipt of dividends, he is deemed to have received the dividends ratably with the trust, that is, on October 3, 1953, and January 4, April 3, and July 5, 1954. He is, however, entitled to the section 116 exclusion with respect to the dividends received by the trust in 1954 (along with other dividends received by him in 1954) and distributed to him, since he is deemed to have received such dividends on January 4, April 3, and July 5, 1954, each a date in his taxable year ending after July 31, 1954. He is entitled to no exclusion for the dividends received by the trust on October 3, 1953, since he is deemed to receive the resulting distribution on the same date, which falls within a taxable year of his which ends before August 1, 1954, although he is required to include the October 1953 dividends in his 1954 income. See section 164 of the Internal Revenue Code of 1939.

Example (3). A simple trust on a fiscal year ending July 31, 1954 receives dividends August 5 and November 4, 1953. It distributes the dividends to A, its sole beneficiary (who is on a calendar year basis), on September 1, 1954. Neither the trust nor A is entitled to a credit under section 34 or an exclusion under section 116. [Reg. § 1.683-2.]

☐ [*T.D.* 6217, 12-19-56. *Amended by T.D.* 6777, 12-15-64.]

[Reg. § 1.683-3]

§ 1.683-3. Application of the 65-day rule of the Internal Revenue Code of 1939.—If an amount is paid, credited, or to be distributed in the first 65 days of the first taxable year of an estate or trust (heretofore subject to the provisions of the Internal Revenue Code of 1939) to which the Internal Revenue Code of 1954 applies and the amount would be treated, if the Internal Revenue Code of 1939 were applicable, as if paid, credited, or to be distributed on the last day of the preceding taxable year, sections 641 through 682 do not apply to the amount. The amount so paid, credited, or to be distributed is taken into account as provided in the Internal Revenue Code of 1939. See 26 CFR (1939) § 39.162-2(c) and (d) (Regulations 118). [Reg. § 1.683-3.]

☐ [*T.D.* 6217, 12-19-56.]

[Reg. § 1.684-1]

§ 1.684-1. Recognition of gain on transfers to certain foreign trusts and estates.—(a) *Immediate recognition of gain.*—(1) *In general.*—Any U.S. person who transfers property to a foreign trust or foreign estate shall be required to recognize gain at the time of the transfer equal to the excess of the fair market value of the property transferred over the adjusted basis (for purposes of determining gain) of such property in the hands of the U.S. transferor unless an exception applies under the provisions of § 1.684-3. The amount of gain recognized is determined on an asset-by-asset basis.

(2) *No recognition of loss.*—Under this section a U.S. person may not recognize loss on the transfer of an asset to a foreign trust or foreign estate. A U.S. person may not offset gain realized on the transfer of an appreciated asset to a foreign trust or foreign estate by a loss realized on the transfer of a depreciated asset to the foreign trust or foreign estate.

(b) *Definitions.*—The following definitions apply for purposes of this section:

(1) *U.S. person.*—The term *U.S. person* means a United States person as defined in section 7701(a)(30), and includes a nonresident alien individual who elects under section 6013(g) to be treated as a resident of the United States.

(2) *U.S. transferor.*—The term *U.S. transferor* means any U.S. person who makes a transfer (as defined in § 1.684-2) of property to a foreign trust or foreign estate.

(3) *Foreign trust.*—Section 7701(a)(31)(B) defines foreign trust. See also § 301.7701-7 of this chapter.

(4) *Foreign estate.*—Section 7701(a)(31)(A) defines foreign estate.

(c) *Reporting requirements.*—A U.S. person who transfers property to a foreign trust or foreign estate must comply with the reporting requirements under section 6048.

(d) *Examples.*—The following examples illustrate the rules of this section. In all examples, *A* is a U.S. person and *FT* is a foreign trust. The examples are as follows:

Example 1. Transfer to foreign trust. A transfers property that has a fair market value of 1000X to *FT. A*'s adjusted basis in the property is 400X. *FT* has no U.S. beneficiary within the meaning of § 1.679-2, and no person is treated as owning any portion of *FT*. Under paragraph (a)(1) of this section, *A* recognizes gain at the time of the transfer equal to 600X.

Example 2. Transfer of multiple properties. A transfers property Q, with a fair market value of 1000X, and property R, with a fair market value of 2000X, to *FT*. At the time of the transfer, *A*'s adjusted basis in property Q is 700X, and *A*'s adjusted basis in property R is 2200X. *FT* has no U.S. beneficiary within the meaning of § 1.679-2, and no person is treated as owning any portion of *FT*. Under paragraph (a)(1) of this section, *A* recognizes the 300X of gain attributable to property Q. Under paragraph (a)(2) of this section, *A* does not recognize the 200X of loss attributable to property R, and may not offset that loss against the gain attributable to property Q.

Example 3. Transfer for less than fair market value. A transfers property that has a fair market value of 1000X to *FT* in exchange for 400X of cash. *A*'s adjusted basis in the property is 200X. *FT* has no U.S. beneficiary within the meaning of § 1.679-2, and no person is treated as owning any portion of *FT*. Under paragraph (a)(1) of this section, *A* recognizes gain at the time of the transfer equal to 800X.

Example 4. Exchange of property for private annuity. A transfers property that has a fair market value of 1000X to *FT* in exchange for *FT*'s obligation to pay *A* 50X per year for the rest of *A*'s life. *A*'s adjusted basis in the property is 100X. *FT* has no U.S. beneficiary within the meaning of § 1.679-2, and no person is treated as owning any portion of *FT*. *A* is required to recognize gain equal to 900X immediately upon transfer of the property to the trust. This result applies even though *A* might otherwise have been allowed to defer recognition of gain under another provision of the Internal Revenue Code.

Example 5. Transfer of property to related foreign trust in exchange for qualified obligation. *A* transfers property that has a fair market value of 1000X to *FT* in exchange for *FT*'s obligation to make payments to *A* during the next four years. *FT* is related to *A* as defined in § 1.679-1(c)(5). The obligation is treated as a qualified obligation within the meaning of § 1.679-4(d), and no person is treated as owning any portion of *FT*. *A*'s adjusted basis in the property is 100X. *A* is required to recognize gain equal to 900X immediately upon transfer of the property to the trust. This result applies even though *A* might otherwise have been allowed to defer recognition of gain under another provision of the Internal Revenue Code. Section 1.684-3(d) provides rules relating to transfers for fair market value to unrelated foreign trusts.

[Reg. § 1.684-1.]

☐ [*T.D.* 8956, 7-19-2001.]

[Reg. § 1.684-2]

§ 1.684-2. Transfers.—(a) *In general.*—A transfer means a direct, indirect, or constructive transfer.

(b) *Indirect transfers.*—(1) *In general.*—Section 1.679-3(c) shall apply to determine if a transfer to a foreign trust or foreign estate, by any person, is treated as an indirect transfer by a U.S. person to the foreign trust or foreign estate.

(2) *Examples.*—The following examples illustrate the rules of this paragraph (b). In all examples, *A* is a U.S. citizen, *FT* is a foreign trust, and *I* is *A*'s uncle, who is a nonresident alien. The examples are as follows:

Example 1. Principal purpose of tax avoidance. *A* creates and funds *FT* for the benefit of *A*'s cousin, who is a nonresident alien. *FT* has no U.S. beneficiary within the meaning of § 1.679-2, and no person is treated as owning any portion of *FT*. In 2004, *A* decides to transfer additional property with a fair market value of 1000X and an adjusted basis of 600X to *FT*. Pursuant to a plan with a principal purpose of avoiding the application of section 684, *A* transfers the property to *I*. *I* subsequently transfers the property to *FT*. Under paragraph (b) of this section and § 1.679-3(c), *A* is treated as having transferred the property to *FT*.

Example 2. U.S. person unable to demonstrate that intermediary acted independently. *A* creates and funds *FT* for the benefit of *A*'s cousin, who is a nonresident alien. *FT* has no U.S. beneficiary within the meaning of § 1.679-2, and no person is treated as owning any portion of *FT*. On July 1, 2004, *A* transfers property with a fair market value of 1000X and an adjusted basis of 300X to *I*, a foreign person. On January 1, 2007, at a time when the fair market value of the property is 1100X, *I* transfers the property to *FT*. *A* is unable to demonstrate to the satisfaction of the Commissioner, under § 1.679-3(c)(2)(ii), that *I* acted independently of *A* in making the transfer to *FT*. Under paragraph (b) of this section and § 1.679-3(c), *A* is treated as having transferred the property to *FT*. Under paragraph (b) of this section and § 1.679-3(c)(3), *I* is treated as an agent of *A*, and the transfer is deemed to have been made on January 1, 2007. Under § 1.684-1(a), *A* recognizes gain equal to 800X on that date.

(c) *Constructive transfers.*—Section 1.679-3(d) shall apply to determine if a transfer to a foreign trust or foreign estate is treated as a constructive transfer by a U.S. person to the foreign trust or foreign estate.

(d) *Transfers by certain trusts.*—(1) *In general.*—If any portion of a trust is treated as owned by a U.S. person, a transfer of property from that portion of the trust to a foreign trust is treated as a transfer from the owner of that portion to the foreign trust.

(2) *Examples.*—The following examples illustrate the rules of this paragraph (d). In all examples, *A* is a U.S. person, *DT* is a domestic trust, and *FT* is a foreign trust. The examples are as follows:

Example 1. Transfer by a domestic trust. On January 1, 2001, *A* transfers property which has a fair market value of 1000X and an adjusted basis of 200X to *DT*. *A* retains the power to revoke *DT*. On January 1, 2003, *DT* transfers property which has a fair market value of 500X and an adjusted basis of 100X to *FT*. At the time of the transfer, *FT* has no U.S. beneficiary as defined in § 1.679-2 and no person is treated as owning any portion of *FT*. *A* is treated as having transferred the property to *FT* and is required to recognize gain of 400X, under § 1.684-1, at the time of the transfer by *DT* to *FT*.

Example 2. Transfer by a foreign trust. On January 1, 2001, *A* transfers property which has a fair market value of 1000X and an adjusted basis of 200X to *FT1*. At the time of the transfer, *FT1* has a U.S. beneficiary as defined in § 1.679-2 and *A* is treated as the owner of *FT1* under section 679. On January 1, 2003, *FT1* transfers property which has a fair market value of 500X and an adjusted basis of 100X to *FT2*. At the time of the transfer, *FT2* has no U.S. beneficiary as defined in § 1.679-2 and no person is treated as owning any portion of *FT2*. *A* is treated as having transferred the property to *FT2* and is required to recognize gain of 400X, under § 1.684-1, at the time of the transfer by *FT1* to *FT2*.

(e) *Deemed transfers when foreign trust no longer treated as owned by a U.S. person.*—(1) *In general.*—If any portion of a foreign trust is treated as owned by a U.S. person under subpart E of part I of subchapter J, chapter 1 of the Internal Revenue Code, and such portion ceases to be treated as owned by that person under such subpart (other than by reason of an actual transfer of property from the trust to which § 1.684-2(d) applies), the U.S. person shall be treated as having transferred, immediately before (but on the same date that) the trust is no longer treated as owned by that U.S. person, the assets of such portion to a foreign trust.

(2) *Examples.*—The following examples illustrate the rules of this paragraph (e). In all examples, *A* is a U.S. citizen and *FT* is a foreign trust. The examples are as follows:

Example 1. Loss of U.S. beneficiary. (i) On January 1, 2001, *A* transfers property, which has a fair market value of 1000X and an adjusted basis of 400X, to *FT*. At the time of the transfer, *FT* has a U.S. beneficiary within the meaning of § 1.679-2, and *A* is treated as owning *FT* under section 679. Under § 1.684-3(a), § 1.684-1 does not cause *A* to recognize gain at the time of the transfer.

(ii) On July 1, 2003, *FT* ceases to have a U.S. beneficiary as defined in § 1.679-2(c) and as of that date neither *A* nor any other person is treated as owning any portion of *FT*. Pursuant to § 1.679-2(c)(2), if *FT* ceases to be treated as having a U.S. beneficiary, *A* will cease to be treated as owner of *FT* beginning on the first day of the first taxable year following the last taxable year in which there was a U.S. beneficiary. Thus, on January 1, 2004, *A* ceases to be treated as owner of *FT*. On that date, the fair market value of the property is 1200X and the adjusted basis is 350X. Under paragraph (e)(1) of this section, *A* is treated as having transferred the property to *FT* on January 1, 2004, and must recognize 850X of gain at that time under § 1.684-1.

Example 2. Death of grantor. (i) The initial facts are the same as in paragraph (i) of *Example 1.*

(ii) On July 1, 2003, *A* dies, and as of that date no other person is treated as the owner of *FT*. On that date, the fair market value of the property is 1200X, and its adjusted basis equals 350X. Under paragraph (e)(1) of this section, *A* is treated as having transferred the property to *FT* immediately before his death, and generally is required to recognize 850X of gain at that time under § 1.684-1. However, an exception may apply under § 1.684-3(c).

Example 3. Release of a power. (i) On January 1, 2001, *A* transfers property that has a fair market value of 500X and an adjusted basis of 200X to *FT*. At the time of the transfer, FT does not have a U.S. beneficiary within the meaning of § 1.679-2. However, *A* retains the power to revoke the trust. *A* is treated as the owner of the trust under section 676 and, therefore, under § 1.684-3(a), *A* is not required to recognize gain under § 1.684-1 at the time of the transfer.

(ii) On January 1, 2007, *A* releases the power to revoke the trust and, as of that date, neither *A* nor any other person is treated as owning any portion of FT. On that date, the fair market value of the property is 900X, and its adjusted basis is 200X. Under paragraph (e)(1) of this section, *A* is treated as having transferred the property to *FT* on January 1, 2007, and must recognize 700X of gain at that time.

(f) *Transfers to entities owned by a foreign trust.*—Section 1.679-3(f) provides rules that apply with respect to transfers of property by a U.S. person to an entity in which a foreign trust holds an ownership interest. [Reg. § 1.684-2.]

☐ [*T.D.* 8956, 7-19-2001.]

[Reg. § 1.684-3]

§ 1.684-3. Exceptions to general rule of gain recognition.—(a) *Transfers to grantor trusts.*—The general rule of gain recognition under § 1.684-1 shall not apply to any transfer of property by a U.S. person to a foreign trust to the extent that any person is treated as the owner of the trust under section 671. Section 1.684-2(e) provides rules regarding a subsequent change in the status of the trust.

(b) *Transfers to charitable trusts.*—The general rule of gain recognition under § 1.684-1 shall not apply to any transfer of property to a foreign trust that is described in section 501(c)(3) (without regard to the requirements of section 508(a)).

(c) *Certain transfers at death.*—(1) *Section 1014 basis.*—The general rule of gain recognition under § 1.684-1 shall not apply to any transfer of property to a foreign trust or foreign estate or, in the case of a transfer of property by a U.S. transferor decedent dying in 2010, to a foreign trust, foreign estate, or a nonresident alien, by reason of death of the U.S. transferor, if the basis of the property in the hands of the transferee is determined under section 1014(a).

(2) *Section 1022 basis election.*—For U.S. transferor decedents dying in 2010, the general rule of gain recognition under § 1.684-1 shall apply to any transfer of property by reason of death of the U.S. transferor if the basis of the property in the hands of the foreign trust, foreign estate, or the nonresident alien individual is determined under section 1022. The gain on the transfer shall be calculated as set out under § 1.684-1(a), except that adjusted basis will reflect any increases allocated to such property under section 1022.

(d) *Transfers for fair market value to unrelated trusts.*—The general rule of gain recognition under § 1.684-1 shall not apply to any transfer of property for fair market value to a foreign trust that is not a related foreign trust as defined in § 1.679-1(c)(5). Section 1.671-2(e)(2)(ii) defines fair market value.

(e) *Transfers to which section 1032 applies.*—The general rule of gain recognition under § 1.684-1 shall not apply to any transfer of stock (including treasury stock) by a domestic corporation to a foreign trust if the domestic corporation is not required to recognize gain on the transfer under section 1032.

(f) *Certain distributions to trusts.*—For purposes of this section, a transfer does not include a distribution to a trust with respect to an interest held by such trust in an entity other than a trust or an interest in certain investment trusts described in § 301.7701-4(c) of this chapter, liquidating trusts described in § 301.7701-4(d) of this chapter, or environmental remediation trusts described in § 301.7701-4(e) of this chapter.

(g) *Examples.*—The following examples illustrate the rules of this section. In all examples, *A* is a U.S. citizen and *FT* is a foreign trust. The examples are as follows:

Example 1. Transfer to owner trust. In 2001, *A* transfers property which has a fair market value of 1000X and an adjusted basis equal to 400X to *FT*. At the time of the transfer, *FT* has a U.S. beneficiary within the meaning of § 1.679-2, and *A* is treated as owning *FT* under section 679. Under paragraph (a) of this section, § 1.684-1 does not cause *A* to recognize gain at the time of the transfer. See § 1.684-2(e) for rules that may require *A* to recognize gain if the trust is no longer owned by *A*.

Example 2. Transfer of property at death: Basis determined under section 1014(a). (i) The initial facts are the same as *Example 1*.

(ii) *A* dies on July 1, 2004. The fair market value at *A*'s death of all property transferred to *FT* by *A* is 1500X. The basis in the property is 400X. *A* retained the power to revoke *FT*, thus, the value of all property owned by *FT* at *A*'s death is includible in *A*'s gross estate for U.S. estate tax purposes. Pursuant to paragraph (c) of this section, *A* is not required to recognize gain under § 1.684-1 because the basis of the property in the hands of the foreign trust is determined under section 1014(a).

Example 3. Transfer of property at death: Basis not determined under section 1014(a). (i) The initial facts are the same as *Example 1*.

(ii) *A* dies on July 1, 2004. The fair market value at *A*'s death of all property transferred to *FT* by *A* is 1500X. The basis in the property is 400X. *A* retains no power over *FT*, and *FT*'s basis in the property transferred is not determined under section 1014(a). Under § 1.684-2(e)(1), *A* is treated as having transferred the property to *FT* immediately before his death, and must recognize 1100X of gain at that time under § 1.684-1.

Example 4. Transfer of property for fair market value to an unrelated foreign trust. *A* sells a house with a fair market value of 1000X to *FT* in exchange for a 30-year note issued by *FT*. *A* is not related to *FT* as defined in § 1.679-1(c)(5). *FT* is not treated as owned by any person. Pursuant to paragraph (d) of this section, *A* is not required to recognize gain under § 1.684-1.

[Reg. § 1.684-3.]

☐ [*T.D.* 8956, 7-19-2001. *Amended by T.D.* 9811, 1-18-2017.]

[Reg. § 1.684-4]

§ 1.684-4. Outbound migrations of domestic trusts.—(a) *In general.*—If a U.S. person transfers property to a domestic trust, and such trust becomes a foreign trust, and neither trust is treated as owned by any person under subpart E of part I of subchapter J, chapter 1 of the Internal Revenue Code, the trust shall be treated for purposes of this section as having transferred all of its assets to a foreign trust and the trust is required to recognize gain on the transfer under § 1.684-1(a). The trust must also comply with the rules of section 6048.

(b) *Date of transfer.*—The transfer described in this section shall be deemed to occur immediately before, but on the same date that, the trust meets the definition of a foreign trust set forth in section 7701(a)(31)(B).

(c) *Inadvertent migrations.*—In the event of an inadvertent migration, as defined in § 301.7701-7(d)(2) of this chapter, a trust may avoid the application of this section by complying with the procedures set forth in § 301.7701-7(d)(2) of this chapter.

(d) *Examples.*—The following examples illustrate the rules of this section. In all examples, *A* is a U.S. citizen, *B* is a U.S. citizen, *C* is a nonresident alien, and *T* is a trust. The examples are as follows:

Example 1. Migration of domestic trust with U.S. beneficiaries. *A* transfers property which has a fair market value of 1000X and an adjusted basis equal to 400X to *T*, a domestic trust, for the benefit of *A*'s children who are also U.S. citizens. *B* is the trustee of *T*. On January 1, 2001, while *A* is still alive, *B* resigns as trustee and *C* becomes successor trustee under the terms of the trust. Pursuant to § 301.7701-7(d) of this chapter, *T* becomes a foreign trust. *T* has U.S. beneficiaries within the meaning of § 1.679-2 and *A* is, therefore, treated as owning *FT* under section 679. Pursuant to § 1.684-3(a), neither *A* nor *T* is required to recognize gain at the time of the migration. Section 1.684-2(e) provides rules that may require *A* to recognize gain upon a subsequent change in the status of the trust.

Example 2. Migration of domestic trust with no U.S. beneficiaries. *A* transfers property which has a fair market value of 1000X and an adjusted basis equal to 400X to *T*, a domestic trust for the benefit of *A*'s mother who is not a citizen or resident of the United States. *T* is not treated as owned by another person. *B* is the trustee of *T*. On January 1, 2001, while *A* is still alive, B resigns as trustee and *C* becomes successor trustee under the terms of the trust. Pursuant to § 301.7701-7(d) of this chapter, *T* becomes a foreign trust, *FT*. *FT* has no U.S. beneficiaries within the meaning of § 1.679-2 and no person is treated as owning any portion of *FT*. *T* is required to recognize gain of 600X on January 1, 2001. Paragraph (c) of this section provides rules with respect to an inadvertent migration of a domestic trust.

[Reg. § 1.684-4.]

☐ [*T.D.* 8956, 7-19-2001.]

[Reg. § 1.684-5]

§ 1.684-5. Effective/applicability dates.—(a) Sections 1.684-1 through 1.684-4 apply to transfers of property to foreign trusts and foreign estates after August 7, 2000, except as provided in paragraph (b) of this section.

(b) In the case a U.S. transferor decedent dying in 2010, § 1.684-3(c) applies to transfers of property to foreign trusts, foreign estates, and nonresident aliens after December 31, 2009, and before January 1, 2011. [Reg. § 1.684-5.]

☐ [*T.D.* 8956, 7-19-2001. *Amended by T.D.* 9811, 1-18-2017.]

Income in Respect of Decedents

[Reg. §1.691(a)-1]

§1.691(a)-1. Income in respect of a decedent.—(a) *Scope of section 691.*—In general, the regulations under section 691 cover: (1) The provisions requiring that amounts which are not includible in gross income for the decedent's last taxable year or for a prior taxable year be included in the gross income of the estate or persons receiving such income to the extent that such amounts constitute "income in respect of a decedent"; (2) the taxable effect of a transfer of the right to such income; (3) the treatment of certain deductions and credit in respect of a decedent which are not allowable to the decedent for the taxable period ending with his death or for a prior taxable year; (4) the allowance to a recipient of income in respect of a decedent of a deduction for estate taxes attributable to the inclusion of the value of the right to such income in the decedent's estate; (5) special provisions with respect to installment obligations acquired from a decedent and with respect to the allowance of a deduction for estate taxes to a surviving annuitant under a joint and survivor annuity contract; and (6) special provisions relating to installment obligations transmitted at death when prior law applied to the transmission.

(b) *General definition.*—In general, the term "income in respect of a decedent" refers to those amounts to which a decedent was entitled as gross income but which were not properly includible in computing his taxable income for the taxable year ending with the date of his death or for a previous taxable year under the method of accounting employed by the decedent. See the regulations under section 451. Thus, the term includes—

(1) All accrued income of a decedent who reported his income by use of the cash receipts and disbursements method:

(2) Income accrued solely by reason of the decedent's death in case of a decedent who reports his income by use of an accrual method of accounting; and

(3) Income to which the decedent had a contingent claim at the time of his death.

See sections 736 and 753 and the regulations thereunder for "income in respect of a decedent" in the case of a deceased partner.

(c) *Prior decedent.*—The term "income in respect of a decedent" also includes the amount of all items of gross income in respect of a prior decedent, if (1) the right to receive such amount was acquired by the decedent by reason of the death of the prior decedent or by bequest, devise, or inheritance from the prior decedent and if (2) the amount of gross income in respect of the prior decedent was not properly includible in computing the decedent's taxable income for the taxable year ending with the date of his death or for a previous taxable year. See example (2) of paragraph (b) of §1.691(a)-2.

(d) *Items excluded from gross income.*—Section 691 applies only to the amount of items of gross income in respect of a decedent, and items which are excluded from gross income under subtitle A of the Code are not within the provisions of section 691.

(e) *Cross reference.*—For items deemed to be income in respect of a decedent for purposes of the deduction for estate taxes provided by section 691(c), see paragraph (c) of §1.691(c)-1. [Reg. §1.691(a)-1.]

☐ [*T.D. 6257, 10-7-57. Amended by T.D. 6808, 3-15-65.*]

[Reg. §1.691(a)-2]

§1.691(a)-2. Inclusion in gross income by recipients.—(a) Under section 691(a)(1), income in respect of a decedent shall be included in the gross income, for the taxable year when received, of—

(1) The estate of the decedent, if the right to receive the amount is acquired by the decedent's estate from the decedent;

(2) The person who, by reason of the death of the decedent, acquires the right to receive the amount, if the right to receive the amount is not acquired by the decedent's estate from the decedent; or

(3) The person who acquires from the decedent the right to receive the amount by bequest, devise, or inheritance, if the amount is received after a distribution by the decedent's estate of such right.

These amounts are included in the income of the estate or of such persons when received by them whether or not they report income by use of the cash receipts and disbursements method.

(b) The application of paragraph (a) of this section may be illustrated by the following examples, in each of which it is assumed that the decedent kept his books by use of the cash receipts and disbursements method:

Example (1). The decedent was entitled at the date of his death to a large salary payment to be made in equal annual installments over five years. His estate, after collecting two installments, distributed the right to the remaining installment payments to the residuary legatee of the estate. The estate must include in its gross income the two installments received by it, and the legatee must include in his gross income each of the three installments received by him.

Example (2). A widow acquired, by bequest from her husband, the right to receive renewal commissions on life insurance sold by him in his lifetime, which commissions were payable over a period of years. The widow died before having received all of such commissions, and her son inherited the right to receive the rest of the commissions. The commissions received by the widow were includible in her gross income. The commissions received by the son were not includible in the widow's gross income but must be included in the gross income of the son.

Example (3). The decedent owned a Series E United States savings bond, with his wife as co-owner or beneficiary, but died before the payment of such bond. The entire amount of interest accruing on the bond and not includible in income by the decedent, nor just the amount accruing after the death of the decedent, would be treated as income to his wife when the bond is paid.

Example (4). A, prior to his death, acquired 10,000 shares of the capital stock of the X Corporation at a cost of $100 per share. During his lifetime, A had entered into an agreement with X Corporation whereby X Corporation agreed to purchase and the decedent agreed that his executor would sell the 10,000 shares of X Corporation stock owned by him at the book value of the stock at the date of A's death. Upon A's death, the shares are sold by A's executor for $500 a share pursuant to the agreement. Since the sale of stock is consummated after A's death, there is no income in respect of a decedent with respect to the appreciation in value of A's stock to the date of his death. If, in this example, A had in fact sold the stock during his lifetime but payment had not been received before his death, any gain on the sale would constitute income in respect of a decedent when the proceeds were received.

Example (5). (1) A owned and operated an apple orchard. During his lifetime, A sold and delivered 1,000 bushels of apples to X, a canning factory, but did not receive payment before his death. A also entered into negotiations to sell 3,000 bushels of apples to Y, a canning factory, but did not complete the sale before his death. After A's death, the executor received payment from X. He also completed the sale to Y and transferred to Y 1,200 bushels of apples on hand at A's death and harvested and transferred an additional 1,800 bushels. The gain from the sale of apples by A to X constitutes income in respect of a decedent when received. On the other hand, the gain from the sale of apples by the executor to Y does not.

(2) Assume that, instead of the transaction entered into with Y, A had disposed of the 1,200 bushels of harvested apples by delivering them to Z, a cooperative association, for processing and sale. Each year the association commingles the fruit received from all of its members into a pool and assigns to each member a percentage interest in the pool based on the fruit delivered by him. After the fruit is processed and the products are sold, the association distributes the net proceeds from the pool to its members in proportion to their interests in the pool. After A's death, the association made distributions to the executor with respect to A's share of the proceeds from the pool in which A had an interest. Under such circumstances, the proceeds from the disposition of the 1,200 bushels of apples constitute income in respect of a decedent. [Reg. § 1.691(a)-2.]

☐ [*T.D.* 6257, 10-7-57.]

[Reg. § 1.691(a)-3]

§ 1.691(a)-3. Character of gross income.—(a) The right to receive an amount of income in respect of a decedent shall be treated in the hands of the estate, or by the person entitled to receive such amount by bequest, devise, or inheritance from the decedent or by reason of his death, as if it had been acquired in the transaction by which the decedent (or a prior decedent) acquired such right, and shall be considered as having the same character it would have had if the decedent (or a prior decedent) had lived and received such amount. The provisions of section 1014(a), relating to the basis of property acquired from a decedent, and section 1022, relating to the basis of property acquired from certain decedents who died in 2010, do not apply to these amounts in the hands of the estate and such persons. See sections 1014(c) and 1022(f).

(b) The application of paragraph (a) of this section may be illustrated by the following:

(1) If the income would have been capital gain to the decedent, if he had lived and had received it, from the sale of property held for more than 1 year (6 months for taxable years beginning before 1977; 9 months for taxable years beginning in 1977), the income, when received, shall be treated in the hands of the estate or of such person as capital gain from the sale of the property, held for more than 1 year (6 months for taxable years beginning before 1977; 9 months for taxable years beginning in 1977), in the same manner as if such person had held the property for the period the decedent held it, and had made the sale.

(2) If the income is interest on United States obligations which were owned by the decedent, such income shall be treated as interest on United States obligations in the hands of the person receiving it, for the purpose of determining the credit provided by section 35, as if such person had owned the obligations with respect to which such interest is paid.

(3) If the amounts received would be subject to special treatment under part I (section 1301 and following), subchapter Q, chapter 1 of the Code, relating to income attributable to several taxable years, as in effect for taxable years beginning before January 1, 1964, if the decedent had lived and included such amounts in his gross income, such sections apply with respect to the recipient of the income.

(4) The provisions of sections 632 and 1347, relating to the tax attributable to the sale of certain oil or gas property and to certain claims against the United States, apply to any amount included in gross income, the right to which was obtained by the decedent by a sale or claim within the provisions of those sections.

(c) *Effective/applicability dates.*—The last two sentences of paragraph (a) of this section apply on and after January 19, 2017. For rules before January 19, 2017, see § 1.691(a)-3 as contained in

26 CFR part 1 revised as of April 1, 2016. [Reg. § 1.691(a)-3.]

☐ [*T.D.* 6257, 10-7-57. *Amended by T.D.* 6885, 6-1-66, *T.D.* 7728, 10-31-80 *and T.D.* 9811, 1-18-2017.]

[Reg. § 1.691(a)-4]

§ 1.691(a)-4. Transfer of right to income in respect of a decedent.—(a) Section 691(a)(2) provides the rules governing the treatment of income in respect of a decedent (or a prior decedent) in the event a right to receive such income is transferred by the estate or person entitled thereto by bequest, devise, or inheritance, or by reason of the death of the decedent. In general, the transferor must include in his gross income for the taxable period in which the transfer occurs the amount of the consideration, if any, received for the right or the fair market value of the right at the time of the transfer, whichever is greater. Thus, upon a sale of such right by the estate or person entitled to receive it, the fair market value of the right or the amount received upon the sale, whichever is greater, is included in the gross income of the vendor. Similarly, if such right is disposed of by gift, the fair market value of the right at the time of the gift must be included in the gross income of the donor. In the case of a satisfaction of an installment obligation at other than face value, which is likewise considered a transfer under section 691(a)(2), see § 1.691(a)-5.

(b) If the estate of a decedent or any person transmits the right to income in respect of a decedent to another who would be required by section 691(a)(1) to include such income when received in his gross income, only the transferee will include such income when received in his gross income. In this situation, a transfer within the meaning of section 691(a)(2) has not occurred. This paragraph may be illustrated by the following:

(1) If a person entitled to income in respect of a decedent dies before receiving such income, only his estate or other person entitled to such income by bequest, devise, or inheritance from the latter decedent, or by reason of the death of the latter decedent, must include such amount in gross income when received.

(2) If a right to income in respect of a decedent is transferred by an estate to a specific or residuary legatee, only the specific or residuary legatee must include such income in gross income when received.

(3) If a trust to which is bequeathed a right of a decedent to certain payments of income terminates and transfers the right to a beneficiary, only the beneficiary must include such income in gross income when received. If the transferee described in subparagraphs (1), (2), and (3) of this paragraph transfers his right to receive the amounts in the manner described in paragraph (a) of this section, the principles contained in paragraph (a) are applied to such transfer. On the other hand, if the transferee transmits his right in the manner described in this paragraph, the principles of this paragraph are again applied to such transfer. [Reg. § 1.691(a)-4.]

☐ [*T.D.* 6257, 10-7-57.]

[Reg. § 1.691(a)-5]

§ 1.691(a)-5. Installment obligations acquired from decedent.—(a) Section 691(a)(4) has reference to an installment obligation which remains uncollected by a decedent (or a prior decedent) and which was originally acquired in a transaction the income from which was properly reportable by the decedent on the installment method under section 453. Under the provisions of section 691(a)(4), an amount equal to the excess of the face value of the obligation over its basis in the hands of the decedent (determined under section 453(d)(2) and the regulations thereunder) shall be considered an amount of income in respect of a decedent and shall be treated as such. The decedent's estate (or the person entitled to receive such income by bequest or inheritance from the decedent or by reason of the decedent's death) shall include in its gross income when received the same proportion of any payment in satisfaction of such obligations as would be returnable as income by the decedent if he had lived and received such payment. No gain on account of the transmission of such obligations by the decedent's death is required to be reported as income in the return of the decedent for the year of his death. See § 1.691(e)-1 for special provisions relating to the filing of an election to have the provisions of section 691(a)(4) apply in the case of installment obligations in respect of which section 44(d) of the Internal Revenue Code of 1939 (or corresponding provisions of prior law) would have applied but for the filing of a bond referred to therein.

(b) If an installment obligation described in paragraph (a) of this section is transferred within the meaning of section 691(a)(2) and paragraph (a) of § 1.691(a)-4, the entire installment obligation transferred shall be considered a right to income in respect of a decedent but the amount includible in the gross income of the transferor shall be reduced by an amount equal to the basis of the obligation in the hands of the decedent (determined under section 453(d)(2) and the regulations thereunder) adjusted, however, to take into account the receipt of any installment payments after the decedent's death and before such transfer. Thus, the amount includible in the gross income of the transferor shall be the fair market value of such obligation at the time of the transfer or the consideration received for the transfer of the installment obligation, whichever is greater, reduced by the basis of the obligation as described in the preceding sentence. For purposes of this paragraph, the term "transfer" in section 691(a)(2) and paragraph (a) of § 1.691(a)-4, includes the satisfaction of an installment obligation at other than face value.

(c) The application of this section may be illustrated by the following example:

Example. An heir of a decedent is entitled to collect an installment obligation with a face value of $100, a fair market value of $80, and a basis in the hands of the decedent of $60. If the heir collects the obligation at face value, the excess of the amount collected over the basis is considered income in respect of a decedent and includible in the gross income of the heir under section 691(a)(1). In this case, the amount includible would be $40 ($100 less $60). If the heir collects the obligation at $90, an amount other than face value, the entire obligation is considered a right to receive income in respect of a decedent but the amount ordinarily required to be included in the heir's gross income under section 691(a)(2) (namely, the consideration received in satisfaction of the installment obligation or its fair market value, whichever is greater) shall be reduced by the amount of the basis of the obligation in the hands of the decedent. In this case, the amount includible would be $30 ($90 less $60). [Reg. § 1.691(a)-5.]

☐ [*T.D.* 6257, 10-7-57. *Amended by T.D.* 6808, 3-15-65.]

[Reg. § 1.691(b)-1]

§ 1.691(b)-1. Allowance of deductions and credit in respect of decedents.—(a) Under section 691(b), the expenses, interest, and taxes described in sections 162, 163, 164, and 212 for which the decedent (or a prior decedent) was liable, which were not properly allowable as a deduction in his last taxable year or any prior taxable year, are allowed when paid—

(1) As a deduction by the estate; or

(2) If the estate was not liable to pay such obligation, as a deduction by the person who by bequest, devise, or inheritance from the decedent or by reason of the death of the decedent acquires, subject to such obligation, an interest in property of the decedent (or the prior decedent). Similar treatment is given to the foreign tax credit provided by section 33. For the purposes of subparagraph (2) of this paragraph, the right to receive an amount of gross income in respect of a decedent is considered property of the decedent; on the other hand, it is not necessary for a person, otherwise within the provisions of subparagraph (2) of this paragraph, to receive the right to any income in respect of a decedent. Thus, an heir who receives a right to income in respect of a decedent (by reason of the death of the decedent) subject to an income tax imposed by a foreign country during the decedent's life, which tax must be satisfied out of such income, is entitled to the credit provided by section 33 when he pays the tax. If a decedent who reported income by use of the cash receipts and disbursements method owned real property on which accrued taxes had become a lien, and if such property passed directly to the heir of the decedent in a jurisdiction in which real property does not become a part of a decedent's estate, the heir, upon paying such taxes, may take the same deduction under section 164 that would be allowed to the decedent if, while alive, he had made such payment.

(b) The deduction for percentage depletion is allowable only to the person (described in section 691(a)(1)) who receives the income in respect of the decedent to which the deduction relates, whether or not such person receives the property from which such income is derived. Thus, an heir who (by reason of the decedent's death) receives income derived from sales of units of mineral by the decedent (who reported income by use of the cash receipts and disbursements method) shall be allowed the deduction for percentage depletion, computed on the gross income from such number of units as if the heir had the same economic interest in the property as the decedent. Such heir need not also receive any interest in the mineral property other than such income. If the decedent did not compute his deduction for depletion on the basis of percentage depletion, any deduction for depletion to which the decedent was entitled at the date of his death would be allowable in computing his taxable income for his last taxable year, and there can be no deduction in respect of the decedent by any other person for such depletion. [Reg. § 1.691(b)-1.]

☐ [*T.D.* 6257, 10-7-57.]

[Reg. § 1.691(c)-1]

§ 1.691(c)-1. Deduction for estate tax attributable to income in respect of a decedent.—(a) *In general.*—A person who is required to include in gross income for any taxable year an amount of income in respect of a decedent may deduct for the same taxable year that portion of the estate tax imposed upon the decedent's estate which is attributable to the inclusion in the decedent's estate of the right to receive such amount. The deduction is determined as follows:

(1) Ascertain the net value in the decedent's estate of the items which are included under section 691 in computing gross income. This is the excess of the value included in the gross estate on account of the items of gross income in respect of the decedent (see § 1.691(a)-1 and paragraph (c) of this section) over the deductions from the gross estate for claims which represent the deductions and credit in respect of the decedent (see § 1.691(b)-1). But see section 691(d) and paragraph (b) of § 1.691(d)-1 for computation of the special value of a survivor's annuity to be used in computing the net value for estate tax purposes in cases involving joint and survivor annuities.

(2) Ascertain the portion of the estate tax attributable to the inclusion in the gross estate of such net value. This is the excess of the estate tax over the estate tax computed without including such net value in the gross estate. In computing the estate tax without including such net value in the gross estate, any estate tax deduction (such as the marital deduction) which may be based upon the gross estate shall be recomputed so as to take into account the exclusion of such net value from the gross estate. See example (2), paragraph (e) of § 1.691(d)-1.

For purposes of this section, the term "estate tax" means the tax imposed under section 2001 or 2101 (or the corresponding provisions of the Internal Revenue Code of 1939), reduced by the credits against such tax. Each person including in gross income an amount of income in respect of a decedent may deduct as his share of the portion of the estate tax (computed under subparagraph (2) of this paragraph) an amount which bears the same ratio to such portion as the value in the gross estate of the right to the income included by such person in gross income (or the amount included in gross income if lower) bears to the value in the gross estate of all the items of gross income in respect of the decedent.

(b) *Prior decedent.*—If a person is required to include in gross income an amount of income in respect of a prior decedent, such person may deduct for the same taxable year that portion of the estate tax imposed upon the prior decedent's estate which is attributable to the inclusion in the prior decedent's estate of the value of the right to receive such amount. This deduction is computed in the same manner as provided in paragraph (a) of this section and is in addition to the deduction for estate tax imposed upon the decedent's estate which is attributable to the inclusion in the decedent's estate of the right to receive such amount.

(c) *Amounts deemed to be income in respect of a decedent.*—For purposes of allowing the deduction under section 691(c), the following items are also considered to be income in respect of a decedent under section 691(a):

(1) The value for estate tax purposes of stock options in respect of which amounts are includible in gross income under section 421(b) (prior to amendment by section 221(a) of the Revenue Act of 1964), in the case of taxable years ending before January 1, 1964, or under section 422(c)(1), 423(c), or 424(c)(1), whichever is applicable, in the case of taxable years ending after December 31, 1963. See section 421(d)(6) (prior to amendment by section 221(a) of the Revenue Act of 1964), in the case of taxable years ending before January 1, 1964, and section 421(c)(2), in the case of taxable years ending after December 31, 1963.

(2) Amounts received by a surviving annuitant during his life expectancy period as an annuity under a joint and survivor annuity contract to the extent included in gross income under section 72. See section 691(d).

(d) *Examples.*—Paragraphs (a) and (b) of this section may be illustrated by the following examples:

Example (1). X, an attorney who kept his books by use of the cash receipts and disbursements method, was entitled at the date of his death to a fee for services rendered in a case not completed at the time of his death, which fee was valued in his estate at $1,000, and to accrued bond interest, which was valued in his estate at $500. In all, $1,500 was included in his gross estate in respect of income described in section 691(a)(1). There were deducted as claims against his estate $150 for business expenses for which his estate was liable and $50 for taxes accrued on certain property which he owned. In all, $200 was deducted for claims which represent amounts described in section 691(b) which are allowable as deductions to his estate or to the beneficiaries of his estate. His gross estate was $185,000 and, considering deductions of $15,000 and an exemption of $60,000, his taxable estate amounted to $110,000. The estate tax on this amount is $23,700 from which is subtracted a $75 credit for State death taxes leaving an estate tax liability of $23,625. In the year following the closing of X's estate, the fee in the amount of $1,200 was collected by X's son, who was the sole beneficiary of the estate. This amount was included under section 691(a)(1)(C) in the son's gross income. The son may deduct, in computing his taxable income for such year, $260 on account of the estate tax attributable to such income, computed as follows:

(1)	(i)	Value of income described in section 691(a)(1) included in computing gross estate	$ 1,500
	(ii)	Deductions in computing gross estate for claims representing deductions described in section 691(b)	200
	(iii)	Net value of items described in section 691(a)(1)	1,300
(2)	(i)	Estate tax	23,625
	(ii)	Less: Estate tax computed without including $1,300 (item (1)(iii)) in gross estate	23,235
	(iii)	Portion of estate tax attributable to net value of items described in section 691(a)(1)	390
(3)	(i)	Value in gross estate of items described in section 691(a)(1) received in taxable year (fee)	1,000
	(ii)	Value in gross estate of all income items described in section 691(a)(1) (item (1)(i))	1,500
	(iii)	Part of estate tax deductible on account of receipt of $1,200 fee (1,000/1,500 of $390)	260

Although $1,200 was later collected as the fee, only the $1,000 actually included in the gross estate is used in the above computations. However, to avoid distortion, section 691(c) provides that if the value included in the gross estate is greater than the amount finally collected, only the amount collected shall be used in the above computations. Thus, if the amount collected as the fee were only $500, the estate tax deductible on the receipt of such amount would be 500/1,500 of $390, or $130. With respect to taxable years ending before January 1, 1964, see paragraph (d)(3) of § 1.421-5 for a similar example involving a restricted stock option. With respect to taxable years ending after December 31, 1963, see paragraph (c)(3) of § 1.421-8 for a similar example involving a stock option subject to the provisions of part II of subchapter D.

Example (2). Assume that in example (1) the fee valued at $1,000 had been earned by prior decedent Y and had been inherited by X who died before collecting it. With regard to the son, the fee would be considered income in respect of a prior decedent. Assume further that the fee was valued at $1,000 in Y's estate, that the net value in Y's estate of items described in section 691(a)(1) was $5,000 and that the estate tax imposed on Y's estate attributable to such net value was $550. In such case, the portion of such estate tax attributable to the fee would be 1,000/5,000 of $550, or $110. When the son collects the $1,200 fee, he will receive for the same taxable year a deduction of $110 with respect to the estate tax imposed on the estate of prior decedent Y as well as the deduction of $260 (as computed in example (1)) with respect to the estate tax imposed on the estate of decedent X. [Reg. § 1.691(c)-1.]

☐ [*T.D. 6257, 10-7-57. Amended by T.D. 6887, 6-23-66.*]

[Reg. § 1.691(c)-2]

§ 1.691(c)-2. Estates and trusts.—(a) In the case of an estate or trust, the deduction prescribed in section 691(c) is determined in the same manner as described in § 1.691(c)-1, with the following exceptions:

(1) If any amount properly paid, credited, or required to be distributed by an estate or trust to a beneficiary consists of income in respect of a decedent received by the estate or trust during the taxable year—

(i) Such income shall be excluded in determining the income in respect of the decedent with respect to which the estate or trust is entitled to a deduction under section 691(c), and

(ii) Such income shall be considered income in respect of a decedent to such beneficiary for purposes of allowing the deduction under section 691(c) to such beneficiary.

(2) For determination of the amount of income in respect of a decedent received by the beneficiary, see sections 652 and 662, and §§ 1.652(b)-2 and 1.662(b)-2. However, for this purpose, distributable net income as defined in section 643(a) and the regulations thereunder shall be computed without taking into account the estate tax deduction provided in section 691(c) and this section. Distributable net income as modified under the preceding sentence shall be applied for other relevant purposes of subchapter J, chapter 1 of the Code, such as the deduction provided by section 651 or 661, or subpart D, part I of subchapter J, relating to excess distributions by trusts.

(3) The rule stated in subparagraph (1) of this paragraph does not apply to income in respect of a decedent which is properly allocable to corpus by the fiduciary during the taxable year but which is distributed to a beneficiary in a subsequent year. The deduction provided by section 691(c) in such a case is allowable only to the estate or trust. If any amount properly paid, credited, or required to be distributed by a trust qualifies as a distribution under section 666, the fact that a portion thereof constitutes income in respect of a decedent shall be disregarded for the purposes of determining the deduction of the trust and of the beneficiaries under section 691(c) since the deduction for estate taxes was taken into consideration in computing the undistributed net income of the trust for the preceding taxable year.

(b) This section shall apply only to amounts properly paid, credited, or required to be distributed in taxable years of an estate or trust beginning after December 31, 1953, and ending after August 16, 1954, except as otherwise provided in paragraph (c) of this section.

(c) In the case of an estate or trust heretofore taxable under the provisions of the Internal Revenue Code of 1939, amounts paid, credited, or to be distributed during its first taxable year subject to the Internal Revenue Code of 1954 which would have been treated as paid, credited, or to be distributed on the last day of the preceding taxable year if the Internal Revenue Code of 1939 were still applicable shall not be subject to the provisions of section 691(c)(1)(B) or this section. See section 683 and the regulations thereunder.

(d) The provisions of this section may be illustrated by the following example, in which it is assumed that the estate and the beneficiary make their returns on the calendar year basis:

Example. (1) The fiduciary of an estate receives taxable interest of $5,500 and income in respect of a decedent of $4,500 during the taxable year. Neither the will of the decedent nor local law requires the allocation to corpus of income in respect of a decedent. The estate tax attributable to the income in respect of a decedent is $1,500. In his discretion, the fiduciary distributes $2,000 (falling within sections 661(a) and 662(a)) to a beneficiary during that year. On these facts the fiduciary and beneficiary are respectively entitled to estate tax deductions of $1,200 and $300, computed as follows:

(2) Distributable net income computed under section 643(a) without regard to the estate tax deduction under section 691(c) is $10,000, computed as follows:

Taxable interest	$5,500
Income in respect of a decedent	4,500
Total	$10,000

(3) Inasmuch as the distributable net income of $10,000 exceeds the amount of $2,000 distributed to the beneficiary, the deduction allowable to the estate under section 661(a), and the amount taxable to the beneficiary under section 662(a), is $2,000.

(4) The character of the amounts distributed to the beneficiary under section 662(b) is shown in the following table:

	Taxable interest	Income in respect of a decedent	Total
Distributable net income	$5,500	$4,500	$10,000
Amount deemed distributed under section 662(b)	1,100	900	2,000

(5) Accordingly, the beneficiary will be entitled to an estate tax deduction of $300 (900/4,500 × $1,500) and the estate will be entitled to an estate tax deduction of $1,200 (3,600/4,500 × $1,500).

(6) The taxable income of the estate is $6,200, computed as follows:

Gross income		$10,000
Less:		
Distributions to the beneficiary	$2,000	
Estate tax deduction under section 691(c)	1,200	
Personal exemption	600	3,800
Taxable income		$6,200

[Reg. § 1.691(c)-2.]

☐ [*T.D.* 6257, 10-7-57.]

[Reg. § 1.691(d)-1]

§ 1.691(d)-1. Amounts received by surviving annuitant under joint and survivor annuity contract.—(a) *In general.*—Under section 691(d), annuity payments received by a surviving annuitant under a joint and survivor annuity contract (to the extent indicated in paragraph (b) of this section) are treated as income in respect of a decedent under section 691(a) for the purpose of allowing the deduction for estate tax provided for in section 691(c)(1)(A). This section applies only if the deceased annuitant died after December 31, 1953, and after the annuity starting date as defined in section 72(c)(4).

(b) *Special value for surviving annuitant's payments.*—Section 691(d) provides a special value for the surviving annuitant's payments to determine the amount of the estate tax deduction provided for in section 691(c)(1)(A). This special value is determined by multiplying—

(1) The excess of the value of the annuity at the date of death of the deceased annuitant over the total amount excludable from the gross income of the surviving annuitant under section 72 during his life expectancy period (see paragraph (d)(1)(i) of this section) by

(2) A fraction consisting of the value of the annuity for estate tax purposes over the value of the annuity at the date of death of the deceased annuitant.

This special value is used for the purpose of determining the net value for estate tax purposes (see section 691(c)(2)(B) and paragraph (a)(1) of § 1.691(c)-1) and for the purpose of determining the portion of estate tax attributable to the survivor's annuity (see paragraph (a) of § 1.691(c)-1).

(c) *Amount of deduction.*—The portion of estate tax attributable to the survivor's annuity (see paragraph (a) of § 1.691(c)-1) is allowable as a deduction to the surviving annuitant over his life expectancy period. If the surviving annuitant continues to receive annuity payments beyond this period, there is no further deduction under section 691(d). If the surviving annuitant dies before expiration of such period, there is no compensating adjustment for the unused deduction.

(d) *Definitions.*—(1) For purposes of section 691(d) and this section—

(i) The term "life expectancy period" means the period beginning with the first day of the first period for which an amount is received by the surviving annuitant under the contract and ending with the close of the taxable year with or in which falls the termination of the life expectancy of the surviving annuitant.

(ii) The life expectancy of the surviving annuitant shall be determined as of the date of the deceased annuitant, with reference to actuarial Table I set forth in § 1.72-9 (but without making any adjustment under paragraph (a)(2) of § 1.72-5).

(iii) The value of the annuity at the date of death of the deceased annuitant shall be the entire value of the survivor's annuity determined by reference to the principles set forth in section 2031 and the regulations thereunder, relating to the valuation of annuities for estate tax purposes.

(iv) The value of the annuity for estate tax purposes shall be that portion of the value determined under subdivision (iii) of this subparagraph which was includible in the deceased annuitant's gross estate.

(2) The determination of the "life expectancy period" of the survivor for purposes of section 691(d) may be illustrated by the following example:

Example. H and W file their income tax returns on the calendar year basis. H dies on July 15, 1955, on which date W is 70 years of age. On August 1, 1955, W receives a monthly payment under a joint and survivor annuity contract. W's life expectancy determined as of the date of H's death is 15 years as determined from Table I in

§ 1.72-9; thus her life expectancy ends on July 14, 1970. Under the provisions of section 691(d), her life expectancy period begins as of July 1, 1955, and ends as of December 31, 1970, thus giving her a life expectancy period of 15 ½ years.

(e) *Examples.*—The application of section 691(d) and this section may be illustrated by the following examples:

Example (1). (1) H and W, husband and wife, purchased a joint and survivor annuity contract for $203,800 providing for monthly payments of $1,000 starting January 28, 1954, and continuing for their joint lives and for the remaining life of the survivor. H contributed $152,850 and W contributed $50,950 to the cost of the annuity. As of the annuity starting date, January 1, 1954, H's age at his nearest birthday was 70 and W's age at her nearest birthday was 67. H dies on January 1, 1957, and beginning on January 28, 1957, W receives her monthly payments of $1,000. The value of the annuity at the date of H's death is $159,000 (see paragraph (d)(1)(iii) of this section), and the value of the annuity for estate tax purposes (see paragraph (d)(1)(iv) of this section) is $119,250 (152,850/203,800 of $159,000). As of the date of H's death, W's age is 70 and her life expectancy period is 15 years (see paragraph (d) of this section for method of computation). Both H and W reported income by use of the cash receipts and disbursements method and filed income tax returns on the calendar year basis.

(2) The following computations illustrate the application of section 72 in determining the excludable portions of the annuity payments to W during her life expectancy period:

Amount of annuity payments per year (12 × $1,000)	$ 12,000
Life expectancy of H and W as of the annuity starting date (see section 72(c)(3)(A) and Table II of § 1.72-9 (male, age 70; female, age 67))	19.7
Expected return as of the annuity starting date, January 1, 1954 ($12,000 × 19.7 as determined under section 72(c)(3)(A) and paragraph (b) of § 1.72-5)	$236,400
Investment in the contract as of the annuity starting date, Jan. 1, 1954 (see section 72(c)(1) and paragraph (a) of § 1.72-6)	$203,800
Exclusion ratio (203,800/236,400 as determined under section 72(b) and § 1.72-4) (percent)	86.2
Exclusion per year under section 72 ($12,000 × 86.2 percent)	$ 10,344
Excludable during W's life expectancy period ($10,344 × 15)	$155,160

(3) For the purpose of computing the deduction for estate tax under section 691(c), the value for estate tax purposes of the amounts includible in W's gross income and considered income in respect of a decedent by virtue of section 691(d)(1) is $2,880. This amount is arrived at in accordance with the formula contained in section 691(d)(2), as follows:

Value of annuity at date of H's death	$159,000
Total amount excludable from W's gross income under section 72 during W's life expectancy period (see subparagraph (2) of this example)	$155,160
Excess	$3,840
Ratio which value of annuity for estate tax purposes bears to value of annuity at date of H's death (119,250/159,000) (percent)	75
Value for estate tax purposes (75 percent of $3,840)	$2,880

This amount ($2,880) is included in the items of income under section 691(a)(1) for the purpose of determining the estate tax attributable to each item under section 691(c)(1)(A). The estate tax determined to be attributable to the item of $2,880 is then allowed as a deduction to W over her 15-year life expectancy period (see example (2) of this paragraph).

Example (2). Assume, in addition to the facts contained in example (1) of this paragraph, that H was an attorney and was entitled at the date of his death to a fee for services rendered in a case not completed at the time of his death, which fee was valued at $1,000, and to accrued bond interest, which was valued at $500. Taking into consideration the annuity payments of example (1), valued at $2,880, a total of $4,380 was included in his gross estate in respect of income described in section 691(a)(1). There was deducted as claims against his estate $280 for business expenses for which his estate was liable and $100 for taxes accrued on certain property which he owned. In all, $380 was deducted for claims which represent amounts described in section 691(b) which are allowable as deductions to his estate or to the beneficiaries of his estate. His gross estate was $404,250 and considering deductions of $15,000, a marital deduction of $119,250 (assuming the annuity to be the only qualifying gift) and an exemption of $60,000, his taxable estate amounted to $210,000. The estate tax on this amount is $53,700 from which is subtracted a $175 credit for State death taxes, leaving an estate tax liability of $53,525. W may deduct, in computing her taxable income during each year of her 15-year life expectancy period, $14.73 on account of the estate tax attributable to the value for estate tax purposes of that portion of the annuity payments considered income in respect of a decedent, computed as follows:

(1)	(i) Value of income described in section 691(a)(1) included in computing gross estate	$ 4,380.00
	(ii) Deductions in computing gross estate for claims representing deductions described in section 691(b)	380.00
	(iii) Net value of items described in section 691(a)(1)	4,000.00

(2)	(i) Estate tax	53,525.00
	(ii) Less: Estate tax computed without including $4,000 (item (1)(iii)) in gross estate and by reducing marital deduction by $2,880 (portion of item (1)(iii) allowed as a marital deduction)	53,189.00
	(iii) Portion of estate tax attributable to net value of income items	336.00
(3)	(i) Value in gross estate of income attributable to annuity payments	2,880.00
	(ii) Value in gross estate of all income items described in section 691(a)(1) (item (1)(i))	4,380.00
	(iii) Part of estate tax attributable to annuity income (2,880/4,380 of $336)	220.93
	(iv) Deduction each year on account of estate tax attributable to annuity income ($220.93 ÷ 15 (life expectancy period))	14.73

[Reg. § 1.691(d)-1.]

☐ [*T.D.* 6257, 10-7-57.]

[Reg. § 1.691(e)-1]

§ 1.691(e)-1. Installment obligations transmitted at death when prior law applied.—(a) *In general.*—(1) *Application of prior law.*—Under section 44(d) of the Internal Revenue Code of 1939 and corresponding provisions of prior law, gains and losses on account of the transmission of installment obligations at the death of a holder of such obligations were required to be reported in the return of the decedent for the year of his death. However, an exception to this rule was provided if there was filed with the Commissioner a bond assuring the return as income of any payment in satisfaction of these obligations in the same proportion as would have been returnable as income by the decedent had he lived and received such payments. Obligations in respect of which such bond was filed are referred to in this section as "obligations assured by bond".

(2) *Application of present law.*—Section 691(a)(4) of the Internal Revenue Code of 1954 (effective for taxable years beginning after December 31, 1953, and ending after August 16, 1954) in effect makes the exception which under prior law applied to obligations assured by bond the general rule for obligations transmitted at death, but contains no requirement for a bond. Section 691(e)(1) provides that if the holder of the installment obligation makes a proper election, the provisions of section 691(a)(4) shall apply in the case of obligations assured by bond. Section 691(e)(1) further provides that the estate tax deduction provided by section 691(c)(1) is not allowable for any amount included in gross income by reason of filing such an election.

(b) *Manner and scope of election.*—(1) *In general.*—The election to have obligations assured by bond treated as obligations to which section 691(a)(4) applies shall be made by the filing of a statement with respect to each bond to be released, containing the following information:

(i) The name and address of the decedent from whom the obligations assured by bond were transmitted, the date of his death, the internal revenue district in which the last income tax return of the decedent was filed.

(ii) A schedule of all obligations assured by the bond on which is listed—

(*a*) The name and address of the obligors, face amount, date of maturity, and manner of payment of each obligation,

(*b*) The name, identifying number (provided under section 6109 and the regulations thereunder), and address of each person holding the obligations, and

(*c*) The name, identifying number, and address, of each person who at the time of the election possesses an interest in each obligation, and a description of such interest.

(iii) The total amount of income in respect of the obligations which would have been reportable as income by the decedent if he had lived and received such payment.

(iv) The amount of income referred to in subdivision (iii) of this subparagraph which has previously been included in gross income.

(v) An unqualified statement, signed by all persons holding the obligations, that they elect to have the provisions of section 691(a)(4) apply to such obligations and that such election shall be binding upon them, all current beneficiaries, and any person to whom the obligations may be transmitted by gift, bequest, or inheritance.

(vi) A declaration that the election is made under the penalties of perjury.

(2) *Filing of statement.*—The statement with respect to each bond to be released shall be filed in duplicate with the district director of internal revenue for the district in which the bond is maintained. The statement shall be filed not later than the time prescribed for filing the return for the first taxable year (including any extension of time for such filing) to which the election applies.

(3) *Effect of election.*—The election referred to in subparagraph (1) of this paragraph shall be irrevocable. Once an election is made with respect to an obligation assured by bond, it shall apply to all payments made in satisfaction of such obligation which were received during the first taxable year to which the election applies and to all such payments received during each taxable year thereafter, whether the recipient is the person who made the election, a current beneficiary, or a person to whom the obligation may be transmitted by gift, bequest, or inheritance. Therefore, all payments received to which the election applies shall be treated as payments made on installment obligations to which section 691(a)(4) applies. However, the estate tax deduc-

tion provided by section 691(c) is not allowable for any such payment. The application of this subparagraph may be illustrated by the following example:

Example. A, the holder of an installment obligation, died in 1952. The installment obligation was transmitted at A's death to B who filed a bond on Form 1132 pursuant to paragraph (c) of §39.44-5 of Regulations 118 (26 CFR Part 39, 1939 ed.) for the necessary amount. On January 1, 1965, B, a calendar year taxpayer, filed an election under section 691(e) to treat the obligation assured by bond as an obligation to which section 691(a)(4) applies, and B's bond was released by 1964 and subsequent taxable years. B died on June 1, 1965, and the obligation was bequeathed to C. On January 1, 1966, C received an installment payment on the obligation which had been assured by the bond. Because B filed an election with respect to the obligation assured by bond, C is required to treat the proper proportion of the January 1, 1966, payment and all subsequent payments made in satisfaction of this obligation as income in respect of a decedent. However, no estate tax deduction is allowable to C under section 691(c)(1) for any estate tax attributable to the inclusion of the value of such obligation in the estate of either A or B.

(c) *Release of bond.*—If an election according to the provisions of paragraph (b) of this section is filed, the liability under any bond filed under section 44(d) of the 1939 Code (or the corresponding provisions of prior law) shall be released with respect to each taxable year to which such election applies. However, the liability under any such bond for an earlier taxable year to which the election does not apply shall not be released until the district director of internal revenue for the district in which the bond is maintained is assured that the proper portion of each installment payment received in such taxable year has been reported and the tax thereon paid. [Reg. §1.691(e)-1.]

☐ [*T.D.* 6808, 3-15-65.]

[Reg. §1.691(f)-1]

§1.691(f)-1. Cross reference.—See section 753 and the regulations thereunder for application of section 691 to income in respect of a deceased partner. [Reg. §1.691(f)-1.]

☐ [*T.D.* 6257, 10-7-57. *Amended by T.D.* 6808, 3-15-65.]

[Reg. §1.692-1]

§1.692-1. Abatement of income taxes of certain members of the Armed Forces of the United States upon death.—(a)(1) This section applies if—

(i) An individual dies while in active service as a member of the Armed Forces of the United States, and

(ii) His death occurs while he is serving in a combat zone (as determined under section 112), or at any place as a result of wounds, disease, or injury incurred while he was serving in a combat zone.

(2) If an individual dies as described in paragraph (a)(1), the following liabilities for tax, under subtitle A of the Internal Revenue Code of 1954 or under chapter 1 of the Internal Revenue Code of 1939, are canceled:

(i) The liability of the deceased individual, for his last taxable year, ending on the date of his death, and for any prior taxable year ending on or after the first day he served in a combat zone in active service as a member of the U.S. Armed Forces after June 24, 1950, and

(ii) The liability of any other person to the extent the liability is attributable to an amount received after the individual's death (including income in respect of a decedent under section 691) which would have been includible in the individual's gross income for his taxable year in which the date of his death falls (determined as if he had survived).

If the tax (including interest, additions to the tax, and additional amounts) is assessed, the assessment will be abated. If the amount of the tax is collected (regardless of the date of collection), the amount so collected will be credited or refunded as an overpayment.

(3) If an individual dies as described in paragraph (a)(1), there will not be assessed any amount of tax of the individual for taxable years preceding the years specified in paragraph (a)(2), under subtitle A of the Internal Revenue Code of 1954, chapter 1 of the Internal Revenue Code of 1939, or corresponding provisions of prior revenue laws, remaining unpaid as of the date of death. If any such unpaid tax (including interest, additions to the tax, and additional amounts) has been assessed, the assessments will be abated. If the amount of any such unpaid tax is collected after the date of death, the amount so collected will be credited or refunded as an overpayment.

(4) As to what constitutes active service as a member of the Armed Forces, service in a combat zone, and wounds, disease, or injury incurred while serving in a combat zone, see section 112. As to who are members of the Armed Forces, see section 7701(a)(15). As to the period of time within which any claim for refund must be filed, see sections 6511(a) and 7508(a)(1)(E).

(b) If such an individual and his spouse have for any such year filed a joint return, the tax abated, credited, or refunded pursuant to the provisions of section 692 for such year shall be an amount equal to that portion of the joint tax liability which is the same percentage of such joint tax liability as a tax computed upon the separate income of such individual is of the sum of the taxes computed upon the separate income of such individual and his spouse, but with respect to taxable years ending before June 24, 1950, and with respect to taxable years ending before the first day such individual served in a combat zone, as determined under section 112, the amount so abated, credited or refunded shall not exceed the amount unpaid at the date of death. For such purpose, the separate tax of each spouse—

(1) For taxable years beginning after December 31, 1953, and ending after August 16, 1954, shall be the tax computed under subtitle A of the Internal Revenue Code of 1954 before the application of sections 31, 32 6401(b), and 6402, but after the application of section 33, as if such spouse were required to make a separate income tax return; and

(2) For taxable years beginning before January 1, 1954, and for taxable years beginning after December 31, 1953, and ending before August 17, 1954, shall be the tax computed under chapter 1 of the Internal Revenue Code of 1939 before the application of sections 32, 35, and 322(a) but after the application of section 31, as if such spouse were required to make a separate income tax return.

(c) If such an individual and his spouse filed a joint declaration of estimated tax for the taxable year ending with the date of his death, the estimated tax paid pursuant to such declaration may be treated as the estimated tax of either such individual or his spouse, may be divided between them, in such manner as his legal representative and such spouse may agree. Should they agree to treat such estimated tax, or any portion thereof, as the estimated tax of such individual, the estimated tax so paid shall be credited or refunded as an overpayment for the taxable year ending with the date of his death.

(d) For the purpose of determining the tax which is unpaid at the date of death, amounts deducted and withheld under chapter 24, subtitle C of the Internal Revenue Code of 1954, or under subchapter D, chapter 9 of the Internal Revenue Code of 1939 (relating to income tax withheld at source on wages), constitute payment of tax imposed under subtitle A of the Internal Revenue Code of 1954 or under chapter 1 of the Internal Revenue Code of 1939, as the case may be.

(e) This section shall have no application whatsoever with respect to the liability of an individual as a transferee of property of a taxpayer where such liability relates to the tax imposed upon the taxpayer by subtitle A of the Internal Revenue Code of 1954 or by chapter 1 of the Internal Revenue Code of 1939. [Reg. § 1.692-1.]

☐ [*T.D.* 6257, 10-7-57. *Amended by T.D.* 7543, 5-4-78.]

* * *

GAIN OR LOSS ON DISPOSITION OF PROPERTY

Determination of Amount of and Recognition of Gain or Loss

[Reg. § 1.1001-1]

§ 1.1001-1. Computation of gain or loss.—(a) *General Rule.*—Except as otherwise provided in subtitle A of the Code, the gain or loss realized from the conversion of property into cash, or from the exchange of property for other property differing materially either in kind or in extent, is treated as income or as loss sustained. The amount realized from a sale or other disposition of property is the sum of any money received plus the fair market value of any property (other than money) received. The fair market value of property is a question of fact, but only in rare and extraordinary cases will property be considered to have no fair market value. The general method of computing such gain or loss is prescribed by section 1001(a) through (d) which contemplates that from the amount realized upon the sale or exchange there shall be withdrawn a sum sufficient to restore the adjusted basis prescribed by section 1011 and the regulations thereunder (i.e., the cost or other basis adjusted for receipts, expenditures, losses, allowances, and other items chargeable against and applicable to such cost or other basis). The amount which remains after the adjusted basis has been restored to the taxpayer constitutes the realized gain. If the amount realized upon the sale or exchange is insufficient to restore to the taxpayer the adjusted basis of the property, a loss is sustained to the extent of the difference between such adjusted basis and the amount realized. The basis may be different depending upon whether gain or loss is being computed. For example, see section 1015(a) and the regulations thereunder. Section 1001(e) and paragraph (f) of this section prescribe the method of computing gain or loss upon the sale or other disposition of a term interest in property the adjusted basis (or a portion) of which is determined pursuant, or by reference, to section 1014 (relating to the basis of property acquired from a decedent), section 1015 (relating to the basis of property acquired by gift or by a transfer in trust), or section 1022 (relating to the basis of property acquired from certain decedents who died in 2010).

(b) *Real estate taxes as amounts received.*—(1) Section 1001(b) and section 1012 state rules applicable in making an adjustment upon a sale of real property with respect to the real property taxes apportioned between seller and purchaser under section 164(d). Thus, if the seller pays (or agrees to pay) real property taxes attributable to the real property tax year in which the sale occurs, he shall not take into account, in determining the amount realized from the sale under section 1001(b), any amount received as reimbursement for taxes which are treated under section 164(d) as imposed upon the purchaser. Similarly, in computing the cost of the property under section1012, the purchaser shall not take into account any amount paid to the seller as reimbursement for real property taxes which are treated under section 164(d) as imposed upon the purchaser. These rules apply whether or not the contract of sale calls for the purchaser to reimburse the seller for such real property taxes paid or to be paid by the seller.

(2) On the other hand, if the purchaser pays (or is to pay) an amount representing real property taxes which are treated under section 164(d) as imposed upon the seller, that amount shall be taken into account both in determining the amount realized from the sale under section 1001(b) and in computing the cost of the property under section 1012. It is immaterial whether or not the contract of sale specifies that the sale price has been reduced by, or is in any way intended to reflect, the taxes allocable to the seller. See also paragraph (b) of § 1.1012-1.

(3) Subparagraph (1) of this paragraph shall not apply to a seller who, in a taxable year prior to the taxable year of sale, pays an amount representing real property taxes which are treated under section 164(d) as imposed on the purchaser, if such seller has elected to capitalize such amount in accordance with section 266 and the regulations thereunder (relating to election to capitalize certain carrying charges and taxes).

(4) The application of this paragraph may be illustrated by the following examples:

Example (1). Assume that the contract price on the sale of a parcel of real estate is $50,000 and that real property taxes thereon in the amount of $1,000 for the real property tax year in which occurred the date of sale were previously paid by the seller. Assume further that $750 of the taxes are treated under section 164(d) as imposed upon the purchaser and that he reimburses the seller in that amount in addition to the contract price. The amount realized by the seller is $50,000. Similarly, $50,000 is the purchaser's cost. If, in this example, the purchaser made no payment other than the contract price of $50,000, the amount realized by the seller would be $49,250, since the sales price would be deemed to include $750 paid to the seller in reimbursement for real property taxes imposed upon the purchaser. Similarly, $49,250 would be the purchaser's cost.

Example (2). Assume that the purchaser in example (1) above, paid all of the real property taxes. Assume further that $250 of the taxes are treated under section 164(d) as imposed upon the seller. The amount realized by the seller is $50,250. Similarly, $50,250 is the purchaser's cost, regardless of the taxable year in which the purchaser makes actual payment of the taxes.

Example (3). Assume that the seller described in the first part of example (1), above, paid the real property taxes of $1,000 in the taxable year prior to the taxable year of sale and elected under section 266 to capitalize the $1,000 of taxes. In such a case, the amount realized is $50,750. Moreover, regardless of whether the seller elected to capitalize the real property taxes, the purchaser in that case could elect under section 266 to capitalize the $750 of taxes treated under section 164(d) as imposed upon him, in which case his adjusted basis would be $50,750 (cost of $50,000 plus capitalized taxes of $570 [$750]).

(c) *Other rules.*—(1) Even though property is not sold or otherwise disposed of, gain is realized if the sum of all the amounts received which are required by section 1016 and other applicable provisions of subtitle A of the Code to be applied against the basis of the property exceeds such basis. Except as otherwise provided in section 301(c)(3)(B) with respect to distributions out of increase in value of property accrued prior to March 1, 1913, such gain is includible in gross income under section 61 as "income from whatever source derived". On the other hand, a loss is not ordinarily sustained prior to the sale or other disposition of the property, for the reason that until such sale or other disposition occurs there remains the possibility that the taxpayer may recover or recoup the adjusted basis of the property. Until some identifiable event fixes the actual sustaining of a loss and the amount thereof, it is not taken into account.

(2) The provisions of subparagraph (1) of this paragraph may be illustrated by the following example:

Example. A, an individual on a calendar year basis, purchased certain shares of stock subsequent to February 28, 1913, for $10,000. On January 1, 1954, A's adjusted basis for the stock had been reduced to $1,000 by reason of receipts and distributions described in sections 1016(a)(1) and 1016(a)(4). He received in 1954 a further distribution of $5,000, being a distribution covered by section 1016(a)(4), other than a distribution out of increase of value of property accrued prior to March 1, 1913. This distribution applied against the adjusted basis as required by section 1016(a)(4) exceeds that basis by $4,000. The $4,000 excess is a gain realized by A in 1954 and is includible in gross income in his return for that calendar year. In computing gain from the stock, as in adjusting basis, no distinction is made between items of receipts or distributions described in section 1016. If A sells the stock in 1955 for $5,000, he realizes in 1955 a gain of $5,000, since the adjusted basis of the stock for the purpose of computing gain or loss from the sale is zero.

(d) *Installment sales.*—In the case of property sold on the installment plan, special rules for the taxation of the gain are prescribed in section 453.

(e) *Transfers in part a sale and in part a gift.*—(1) Where a transfer of property is in part a sale and in part a gift, the transferor has a gain to the extent that the amount realized by him exceeds his adjusted basis in the property. However, no loss is sustained on such a transfer if the amount realized is less than the adjusted basis. For determination of basis of the property in the hands of the transferee, see § 1.1015-4. For the allocation of the adjusted basis of property in the case of a bargain sale to a charitable organization, see § 1.1011-2.

(2) *Examples.*—The provisions of subparagraph (1) may be illustrated by the following examples:

Example (1). A transfers property to his son for $60,000. Such property in the hands of A has an adjusted basis of $30,000 (and a fair market value of $90,000). A's gain is $30,000, the excess of $60,000, the amount realized, over the adjusted basis, $30,000. He has made a gift of

$30,000, the excess of $90,000, the fair market value, over the amount realized, $60,000.

Example (2). A transfers property to his son for $30,000. Such property in the hands of A has an adjusted basis of $60,000 (and a fair market value of $90,000). A has no gain or loss, and has made a gift of $60,000, the excess of $90,000, the fair market value, over the amount realized, $30,000.

Example (3). A transfers property to his son for $30,000. Such property in A's hands has an adjusted basis of $30,000 (and a fair market value of $60,000). A has no gain and has made a gift of $30,000, the excess of $60,000, the fair market value, over the amount realized, $30,000.

Example (4). A transfers property to his son for $30,000. Such property in A's hands has an adjusted basis of $90,000 (and a fair market value of $60,000). A has sustained no loss, and has made a gift of $30,000, the excess of $60,000, the fair market value, over the amount realized, $30,000.

(f) *Sale or other disposition of a term interest in property.*—(1) *General rule.*—Except as otherwise provided in paragraph (f)(3) of this section, for purposes of determining gain or loss from the sale or other disposition after October 9, 1969, of a term interest in property (as defined in paragraph (f)(2) of this section), a taxpayer shall not take into account that portion of the adjusted basis of such interest that is determined pursuant, or by reference, to section 1014 (relating to the basis of property acquired from a decedent), section 1015 (relating to the basis of property acquired by gift or by a transfer in trust), or section 1022 (relating to the basis of property acquired from certain decedents who died in 2010) to the extent that such adjusted basis is a portion of the adjusted uniform basis of the entire property (as defined in § 1.1014-5). Where a term interest in property is transferred to a corporation in connection with a transaction to which section 351 applies and the adjusted basis of the term interest:

(i) Is determined pursuant to sections 1014, 1015, or 1022; and

(ii) Is also a portion of the adjusted uniform basis of the entire property, a subsequent sale or other disposition of such term interest by the corporation will be subject to the provisions of section 1001(e) and this paragraph (f) to the extent that the basis of the term interest so sold or otherwise disposed of is determined by reference to its basis in the hands of the transferor as provided by section 362(a). See paragraph (f)(2) of this section for rules relating to the characterization of stock received by the transferor of a term interest in property in connection with a transaction to which section 351 applies. That portion of the adjusted uniform basis of the entire property that is assignable to such interest at the time of its sale or other disposition shall be determined under the rules provided in § 1.1014-5. Thus, gain or loss realized from a sale or other disposition of a term interest in property shall be determined by comparing the amount of the proceeds of such sale with that part of the adjusted basis of such interest that is not a portion of the adjusted uniform basis of the entire property.

(2) *Term interest defined.*—For purposes of section 1001(e) and this paragraph, a "term interest in property" means—

(i) A life interest in property,

(ii) An interest in property for a term of years, or

(iii) An income interest in a trust.

Generally subdivisions (i), (ii), and (iii) refer to an interest, present or future, in the income from property or the right to use property which will terminate or fail on the lapse of time, on the occurrence of an event or contingency, or on the failure of an event or contingency to occur. Such divisions do not refer to remainder or reversionary interests in the property itself or other interests in the property which will ripen into ownership of the entire property upon termination or failure of a preceding term interest. A "term interest in property" also includes any property received upon a sale or other disposition of a life interest in property, an interest in property for a term of years, or an income interest in a trust by the original holder of such interest, but only to the extent that the adjusted basis of the property received is determined by reference to the adjusted basis of the term interest so transferred.

(3) *Exception.*—Paragraph (1) of section 1001(e) and subparagraph (1) of this paragraph shall not apply to a sale or other disposition of a term interest in property as a part of a single transaction in which the entire interest in the property is transferred to a third person or to two or more other persons, including persons who acquire such entire interest as joint tenants, tenants by the entirety, or tenants in common. See § 1.1014-5 for computation of gain or loss upon such a sale or other disposition where the property has been acquired from a decedent or by gift or transfer in trust.

(4) *Illustrations.*—For examples illustrating the application of this paragraph, see paragraph (d) of § 1.1014-5.

(g) *Debt instruments issued in exchange for property.*—(1) *In general.*—If a debt instrument is issued in exchange for property, the amount realized attributable to the debt instrument is the issue price of the debt instrument as determined under § 1.1273-2 or § 1.1274-2; whichever is applicable. If, however, the issue price of the debt instrument is determined under section 1273(b)(4), the amount realized attributable to the debt instrument is its stated principal amount reduced by any unstated interest (as determined under section 483).

(2) *Certain debt instruments that provide for contingent payments.*—(i) *In general.*—Paragraph (g)(1) of this section does not apply to a debt instrument subject to either § 1.483-4 or § 1.1275-4(c) (certain contingent payment debt instruments issued for nonpublicly traded property).

(ii) *Special rule to determine amount realized.*—If a debt instrument subject to § 1.1275-4(c) is issued in exchange for property, and the income from the exchange is not reported under the installment method of section 453, the amount realized attributable to the debt instrument is the issue price of the debt instrument as determined under § 1.1274-2(g), increased by the fair market value of the contingent payments payable on the debt instrument. If a debt instrument subject to § 1.483-4 is issued in exchange for property, and the income from the exchange is not reported under the installment method of section 453, the amount realized attributable to the debt instrument is its stated principal amount, reduced by any unstated interest (as determined under section 483), and increased by the fair market value of the contingent payments payable on the debt instrument. This paragraph (g)(2)(ii), however, does not apply to a debt instrument if the fair market value of the contingent payments is not reasonably ascertainable. Only in rare and extraordinary cases will the fair market value of the contingent payments be treated as not reasonably ascertainable.

(3) *Coordination with section 453.*—If a debt instrument is issued in exchange for property, and the income from the exchange is not reported under the installment method of section 453, this paragraph (g) applies rather than § 15a.453-1(d)(2) to determine the taxpayer's amount realized attributable to the debt instrument.

(4) *Effective date.*—This paragraph (g) applies to sales or exchanges that occur on or after August 13, 1996.

(h) *Severances of trusts.*—(1) *In general.*—The severance of a trust (including without limitation a severance that meets the requirements of § 26.2642-6 or of § 26.2654-1(b) of this chapter) is not an exchange of property for other property differing materially either in kind or in extent if—

(i) An applicable state statute or the governing instrument authorizes or directs the trustee to sever the trust; and

(ii) Any non-pro rata funding of the separate trusts resulting from the severance (including non-pro rata funding as described in § 26.2642-6(d)(4) or § 26.2654-1(b)(1)(ii)(C) of this chapter), whether mandatory or in the discretion of the trustee, is authorized by an applicable state statute or the governing instrument.

(2) *Effective/applicability date.*—This paragraph (h) applies to severances occurring on or after August 2, 2007. Taxpayers may apply this paragraph (h) to severances occurring on or after August 24, 2004, and before August 2, 2007.

(i) *Effective/applicability date.*—Except as provided in paragraphs (g) and (h) of this section, this section applies on and after January 19, 2017. For rules before January 19, 2017, see § 1.1001-1 as contained in 26 CFR part 1 revised as of April 1, 2016. [Reg. § 1.1001-1.]

☐ [*T.D.* 6265, 11-6-57. *Amended by T.D.* 7142, 9-23-71; *T.D.* 7207, 10-3-72; *T.D.* 7213, 10-17-72; *T.D.* 8517, 1-27-94; *T.D.* 8674, 6-11-96, *T.D.* 9348, 8-1-2007, *T.D.* 9729, 8-11-15 *and T.D.* 9811, 1-18-2017.]

* * *

Basis Rules of General Application

[Reg. § 1.1011-1]

§ 1.1011-1. Adjusted basis.—The adjusted basis for determining the gain or loss from the sale or other disposition of property is the cost or other basis prescribed in section 1012 or other applicable provisions of subtitle A of the Code, adjusted to the extent provided in sections 1016, 1017, and 1018 or as otherwise specifically provided for under applicable provisions of internal revenue laws. [Reg. § 1.1011-1.]

☐ [*T.D.* 6265, 11-6-57.]

[Reg. § 1.1011-2]

§ 1.1011-2. Bargain sale to a charitable organization.—(a) *In general.*—(1) If for the taxable year a charitable contributions deduction is allowable under section 170 by reason of a sale or exchange of property, the taxpayer's adjusted basis of such property for purposes of determining gain from such sale or exchange must be computed as provided in section 1011(b) and paragraph (b) of this section. If after applying the provisions of section 170 for the taxable year, including the percentage limitations of section 170(b), no deduction is allowable under that section by reason of the sale or exchange of the property, section 1011(b) does not apply and the adjusted basis of the property is not required to be apportioned pursuant to paragraph (b) of this section. In such case the entire adjusted basis of the property is to be taken into account in determining gain from the sale or exchange, as provided in § 1.1011-1(e). In ascertaining whether or not a charitable contributions deduction is allowable under section 170 for the taxable year for such purposes, that section is to be applied without regard to this section and the amount by which the contributed portion of the property must be reduced under section 170(e)(1) is the amount determined by taking into account the amount of gain which would have been ordinary income or long-term capital gain if the contributed portion of the property had been sold by the donor at its fair market value at the time of the sale or exchange.

(2) If in the taxable year there is a sale or exchange of property which gives rise to a charitable contribution which is carried over under section 170(b)(1)(D)(ii) or section 170(d) to a subsequent taxable year or is postponed under section 170(a)(3) to a subsequent taxable year, section 1011(b) and paragraph (b) of this section must be applied for purposes of apportioning the adjusted basis of the property for the year of

the sale or exchange, whether or not such contribution is allowable as a deduction under section 170 in such subsequent year.

(3) If property is transferred subject to an indebtedness, the amount of the indebtedness must be treated as an amount realized for purposes of determining whether there is a sale or exchange to which section 1011(b) and this section apply, even though the transferee does not agree to assume or pay the indebtedness.

(4)(i) Section 1011(b) and this section apply where property is sold or exchanged in return for an obligation to pay an annuity and a charitable contributions deduction is allowable under section 170 by reason of such sale or exchange.

(ii) If in such case the annuity received in exchange for the property is nonassignable, or is assignable but only to the charitable organization to which the property is sold or exchanged, and if the transferor is the only annuitant or the transferor and a designated survivor annuitant or annuitants are the only annuitants, any gain on such exchange is to be reported as provided in example (8) in paragraph (c) of this section. In determining the period over which gain may be reported as provided in such example, the life expectancy of the survivor annuitant may not be taken into account. The fact that the transferor may retain the right to revoke the survivor's annuity or relinquish his own right to the annuity will not be considered, for purposes of this subdivision, to make the annuity assignable to someone other than the charitable organization. Gain on an exchange of the type described in this subdivision pursuant to an agreement which is entered into after December 19, 1969, and before May 3, 1971, may be reported as provided in example (8) in paragraph (c) of this section, even though the annuity is assignable.

(iii) In the case of an annuity to which subdivision (ii) of this subparagraph applies, the gain unreported by the transferor with respect to annuity payments not yet due when the following events occur is not required to be included in gross income of any person where—

(a) The transferor dies before the entire amount of gain has been reported and there is no surviving annuitant, or

(b) The transferor relinquishes the annuity to the charitable organization. If the transferor dies before the entire amount of gain on a two-life annuity has been reported, the unreported gain is required to be reported by the surviving annuitant or annuitants with respect to the annuity payments received by them.

(b) *Apportionment of adjusted basis.*—For purposes of determining gain on a sale or exchange to which this paragraph applies, the adjusted basis of the property which is sold or exchanged shall be that portion of the adjusted basis of the entire property which bears the same ratio to the adjusted basis as the amount realized bears to the fair market value of the entire property. The amount of such gain which shall be treated as ordinary income (or long-term capital gain) shall be that amount which bears the same ratio to the ordinary income (or long-term capital gain) which would have been recognized if the entire property had been sold by the donor at its fair market value at the time of the sale or exchange as the amount realized on the sale or exchange bears to the fair market value of the entire property at such time. The terms "ordinary income" and "long-term capital gain", as used in this section, have the same meaning as they have in paragraph (a) of § 1.170A-4. For determining the portion of the adjusted basis, ordinary income, and long-term capital gain allocated to the contributed portion of the property for purposes of applying section 170(e)(1) and paragraph (a) of § 1.170A-4 to the contributed portion of the property, and for determining the donee's basis in such contributed portion, see paragraph (c)(2) and (4) of § 1.170A-4. For determining the holding period of such contributed portion, see section 1223(2) and the regulations thereunder.

(c) *Illustrations.*—The application of this section may be illustrated by the following examples, which are supplemented by other examples in paragraph (d) of § 1.170A-4:

Example (1). In 1970, a calendar-year individual taxpayer, sells to a church for $4,000 stock held for more than 6 months which has an adjusted basis of $4,000 and a fair market value of $10,000. A's contribution base for 1970, as defined in section 170(b)(1)(F), is $100,000, and during that year he makes no other charitable contributions. Thus, A makes a charitable contribution to the church of $6,000 ($10,000 value – $4,000 amount realized). Without regard to this section, A is allowed a deduction under section 170 of $6,000 for his charitable contribution to the church, since there is no reduction under section 170(e)(1) with respect to the long-term capital gain. Accordingly, under paragraph (b) of this section the adjusted basis for determining gain on the bargain sale is $1,600 ($4,000 adjusted basis × $4,000 amount realized/$10,000 value of property). A has recognized long-term capital gain of $2,400 ($4,000 amount realized – $1,600 adjusted basis) on the bargain sale.

Example (2). The facts are the same as in Example (1) except that A also makes a charitable contribution in 1970 of $50,000 cash to the church. By reason of section 170(b)(1)(A), the deduction allowed under section 170 for 1970 is $50,000 for the amount of cash contributed to the church; however, the $6,000 contribution of property is carried over to 1971 under section 170(d). Under paragraphs (a)(2) and (b) of this section the adjusted basis for determining gain for 1970 on the bargain sale in that year is $1,600 ($4,000 × $4,000/$10,000). A has a recognized long-term capital gain for 1970 of $2,400 ($4,000 – $1,600) on the sale.

Example (3). In 1970, C, a calendar-year individual taxpayer, makes a charitable contribution of $50,000 cash to a church. In addition, he sells for $4,000 to a private foundation not described in section 170(b)(1)(E) stock held for more than 6 months which has an adjusted basis of $4,000 and a fair market value of $10,000. Thus, C makes a charitable contribution of $6,000 of such property to the private foundation ($10,000 value

– $4,000 amount realized). C's contribution base for 1970, as defined in section 170(b)(1)(F), is $100,000, and during that year he makes no other charitable contributions. By reason of section 170(b)(1)(A), the deduction allowed under section 170 for 1970 is $50,000 for the amount of cash contributed to the church. Under section 170(e)(1)(B)(ii) and paragraphs (a)(1) and (c)(2)(i) of § 1.170A-4, the $6,000 contribution of stock is reduced to $4,800 ($6,000 – [50% × ($6,000 value of contributed portion of stock – $3,600 adjusted basis)]). However, by reason of section 170(b)(1)(B)(ii), applied without regard to section 1011(b), no deduction is allowed under section 170 for 1970 or any other year for the reduced contribution of $4,800 to the private foundation. Accordingly, paragraph (b) of this section does not apply for purposes of apportioning the adjusted basis of the stock sold to the private foundation, and under section 1.1011-1(e) the recognized gain on the bargain sale is $0 ($4,000 amount realized – $4,000 adjusted basis).

Example (4). In 1970, B, a calendar-year individual taxpayer, sells to a church for $2,000 stock held for not more than 6 months which has an adjusted basis of $4,000 and a fair market value of $10,000. B's contribution base for 1970, as defined in section 170(b)(1)(F), is $20,000 and during such year B makes no other charitable contributions. Thus, he makes a charitable contribution to the church of $8,000 ($10,000 value – $2,000 amount realized). Under paragraph (b) of this section the adjusted basis for determining gain on the bargain sale is $800 ($4,000 adjusted basis × $2,000 amount realized/$10,000 value of stock). Accordingly, B has a recognized short-term capital gain of $1,200 ($2,000 amount realized – $800 adjusted basis) on the bargain sale. After applying section 1011(b) and paragraphs (a)(1) and (c)(2)(i) of § 1.170A-4, B is allowed a charitable contributions deduction for 1970 of $3,200 ($8,000 value of gift – [$8,000 – ($4,000 adjusted basis of property × $8,000 value of gift/$10,000 value of property)]).

Example (5). The facts are the same as in Example (4) except that B sells the property to the church for $4,000. Thus, B makes a charitable contribution to the church of $6,000 ($10,000 value – $4,000 amount realized). Under paragraph (b) of this section the adjusted basis for determining gain on the bargain sale is $1,600 ($4,000 adjusted basis × $4,000 amount realized/$10,000 value of stock). Accordingly, B has a recognized short-term capital gain of $2,400 ($4,000 amount realized – $1,600 adjusted basis) on the bargain sale. After applying section 1011(b) and paragraphs (a)(1) and (c)(2)(i) of § 1.170A-4, B is allowed a charitable contributions deduction for 1970 of $2,400 ($6,000 value of gift – [$6,000 – ($4,000 adjusted basis of property × $6,000 value of gift/$10,000 value of property)]).

Example (6). The facts are the same as in Example (4) except that B sells the property to the church for $6,000. Thus, B makes a charitable contribution to the church of $4,000 ($10,000 value – $6,000 amount realized). Under paragraph (b) of this section the adjusted basis for determining gain on the bargain sale is $2,400 ($4,000 adjusted basis × $6,000 amount realized/$10,000 value of stock). Accordingly, B has a recognized short-term capital gain of $3,600 ($6,000 amount realized – $2,400 adjusted basis) on the bargain sale. After applying section 1011(b) and paragraphs (a)(1) and (c)(2)(i) of § 1.170A-4, B is allowed a charitable contributions deduction for 1970 of $1,600 ($4,000 value of gift – [$4,000 – ($4,000 adjusted basis of property × $4,000 value of gift/$10,000 value of property)]).

Example (7). In 1970, C, a calendar-year individual taxpayer, sells to a church for $4,000 tangible personal property used in his business for more than 6 months which has an adjusted basis of $4,000 and a fair market value of $10,000. Thus, C makes a charitable contribution to the church of $6,000 ($10,000 value – $4,000 adjusted basis). C's contribution base for 1970, as defined in section 170(b)(1)(F), is $100,000 and during such year he makes no other charitable contributions. If C had sold the property at its fair market value at the time of its contribution, it is assumed that under section 1245 $4,000 of the gain of $6,000 ($10,000 value – $4,000 adjusted basis) would have been treated as ordinary income. Thus, there would have been long-term capital gain of $2,000. It is also assumed that the church does not put the property to an unrelated use, as defined in paragraph (b)(3) of § 1.170A-4. Under paragraph (b) of this section the adjusted basis for determining gain on the bargain sale is $1,600 ($4,000 adjusted basis × $4,000 amount realized/$10,000 value of property). Accordingly, C has a recognized gain of $2,400 ($4,000 amount realized – $1,600 adjusted basis) on the bargain sale, consisting of ordinary income of $1,600 ($4,000 ordinary income × $4,000 amount realized/$10,000 value of property) and of long-term capital gain of $800 ($2,000 long-term gain × $4,000 amount realized/$10,000 value of property). After applying section 1011(b) and paragraphs (a) and (c)(2)(i) of § 1.170A-4, C is allowed a charitable contributions deduction for 1970 of $3,600 ($6,000 gift – [$4,000 ordinary income × $6,000 value of gift/$10,000 value of property]).

Example (8). (*a*) On January 1, 1970, A, a male of age 65, transfers capital assets consisting of securities held for more than 6 months to a church in exchange for a promise by the church to pay A a nonassignable annuity of $5,000 per year for life. The annuity is payable monthly with the first payment to be made on February 1, 1970. A's contribution base for 1970, as defined in section 170(b)(1)(F), is $200,000, and during that year he makes no other charitable contributions. On the date of transfer the securities have a fair market value of $100,000 and an adjusted basis to A of $20,000.

(*b*) The present value of the right of a male age 65 to receive a life annuity of $5,000 per annum, payable in equal installments at the end of each monthly period, is $59,755 ($5,000 × [11.469 + 0.482]), determined in accordance with section 101(b) of the Code, paragraph (e)(1)(iii)(b)(2) of

§1.101-2, and section 3 of Rev. Rul. 62-216, C.B. 1962-2, 30. Thus, A makes a charitable contribution to the church of $40,245 ($100,000 – $59,755). See Rev. Rul. 84-162, 1984-2 C.B. 200, for transfers for which the valuation date falls after November 23, 1984. (See §601.601(d)(2)(ii)(*b*) of this chapter). For the applicable valuation tables in connection therewith, see §20.2031-7(d)(6) of this chapter. See, however, §1.7520-3(b) (relating to exceptions to the use of standard actuarial factors in certain circumstances).

(*c*) Under paragraph (*b*) of this section, the adjusted basis for determining gain on the bargain sale is $11,951 ($20,000 × $59,775/$100,000). Accordingly, A has a recognized long-term capital gain of $47,804 ($59,755 – $11,951) on the bargain sale. Such gain is to be reported by A ratably over the period of years measured by the expected return multiple under the contract but only from that portion of the annual payments which is a return of his investment in the contract under section 72 of the Code. For such purposes, the investment in the contract is $59,755, that is, the present value of the annuity.

(*d*) The computation and application of the exclusion ratio, the gain, and the ordinary annuity income are as follows, determined by using the expected return multiple of 15.0 applicable under Table I of §1.72-9:

A's expected return (annual payments of $5,000 × 15)	$75,000.00
Exclusion ratio ($59,755 investment in contract divided by expected return of $75,000)	79.7%
Annual exclusion (annual payments of $5,000 × 79.7%)	3,985.00
Ordinary annuity income ($5,000 – $3,985)	1,015.00
Long-term capital gain per year ($47,804/15) with respect to the annual exclusion	3,186.93

(*e*) The exclusion ratio of 79.7 percent applies throughout the life of the contract. During the first 15 years of the annuity, A is required to report ordinary income of $1,015 and long-term capital gain of $3,186.93 with respect to the annuity payments he receives. After the total long-term capital gain of $47,804 has been reported by A, he is required to report only ordinary income of $1,015.00 per annum with respect to the annuity payments he receives.

(d) *Effective date.*—This section applies only to sales and exchanges made after December 19, 1969.

(e) *Cross reference.*—For rules relating to the treatment of liabilities in a bargain sale transaction, see §1.1001-2. [Reg. §1.1011-2.]

☐ [*T.D.* 7207, 10-3-72. *Amended by T.D.* 7741, 12-11-80, *T.D.* 8176, 2-24-88 *and T.D.* 8540, 6-9-94.]

[Reg. §1.1012-1]

§1.1012-1. Basis of property.—(a) *General rule.*—In general, the basis of property is the cost thereof. The cost is the amount paid for such property in cash or other property. This general rule is subject to exceptions stated in subchapter O (relating to gain or loss on the disposition of property), subchapter C (relating to corporate distributions and adjustments), subchapter K (relating to partners and partnerships), and subchapter P (relating to capital gains and losses), chapter 1 of the Code.

(b) *Real estate taxes as part of cost.*—In computing the cost of real property, the purchaser shall not take into account any amount paid to the seller as reimbursement for real property taxes which are treated under section 164(d) as imposed upon the purchaser. This rule applies whether or not the contract of sale calls for the purchaser to reimburse the seller for such real estate taxes paid or to be paid by the seller. On the other hand, where the purchaser pays (or assumes liability for) real estate taxes which are treated under section 164(d) as imposed upon the seller, such taxes shall be considered part of the cost of the property. It is immaterial whether or not the contract of sale specifies that the sale price has been reduced by, or is in any way intended to reflect, real estate taxes allocable to the seller under section 164(d). For illustrations of the application of the paragraph, see paragraph (b) of §1.1001-1.

(c) *Sale of stock.*—(1) *In general.*—(i) Except as provided in paragraph (e)(2) of this section (dealing with stock for which the average basis method is permitted), if a taxpayer sells or transfers shares of stock in a corporation that the taxpayer purchased or acquired on different dates or at different prices and the taxpayer does not adequately identify the lot from which the stock is sold or transferred, the stock sold or transferred is charged against the earliest lot the taxpayer purchased or acquired to determine the basis and holding period of the stock. If the earliest lot purchased or acquired is held in a stock certificate that represents multiple lots of stock, and the taxpayer does not adequately identify the lot from which the stock is sold or transferred, the stock sold or transferred is charged against the earliest lot included in the certificate. See paragraphs (c)(2), (c)(3), and (c)(4) of this section for rules on what constitutes an adequate identification.

(ii) A taxpayer must determine the basis of identical stock (within the meaning of paragraph (e)(4) of this section) by averaging the cost of each share if the stock is purchased at separate times on the same calendar day in executing a single trade order and the broker executing the trade provides a single confirmation that reports an aggregate total cost or an average cost per share. However, the taxpayer may determine the basis of the stock by the actual cost per share if the taxpayer notifies the broker in writing of this intent. The taxpayer must notify the broker by the earlier of the date of the sale of any of the stock for which the taxpayer received the confirmation or one year after the date of the confirmation. A broker may extend the one-year period but the taxpayer must notify the broker no later than the date of sale of any of the stock.

(2) *Identification of stock.*—An adequate identification is made if it is shown that certificates representing shares of stock from a lot which was purchased or acquired on a certain date or for a certain price were delivered to the taxpayer's transferee. Except as otherwise provided in subparagraph (3) or (4) of this paragraph, such stock certificates delivered to the transferee constitute the stock sold or transferred by the taxpayer. Thus, unless the requirements of subparagraph (3) or (4) of this paragraph are met, the stock sold or transferred is charged to the lot to which the certificates delivered to the transferee belong, whether or not the taxpayer intends, or instructs his broker or other agent, to sell or transfer stock from a lot purchased or acquired on a different date or for a different price.

(3) *Identification on confirmation document.*—(i) Where the stock is left in the custody of a broker or other agent, an adequate identification is made if—

(*a*) At the time of the sale or transfer, the taxpayer specifies to such broker or other agent having custody of the stock the particular stock to be sold or transferred, and

(*b*) Within a reasonable time thereafter, confirmation of such specification is set forth in a written document from such broker or other agent.

Stock identified pursuant to this subdivision is the stock sold or transferred by the taxpayer, even though stock certificates from a different lot are delivered to the taxpayer's transferee.

(ii) Where a single stock certificate represents stock from different lots, where such certificate is held by the taxpayer rather than his broker or other agent, and where the taxpayer sells a part of the stock represented by such certificate through a broker or other agent, an adequate identification is made if—

(*a*) At the time of the delivery of the certificate to the broker or other agent, the taxpayer specifies to such broker or other agent the particular stock to be sold or transferred, and

(*b*) Within a reasonable time thereafter, confirmation of such specification is set forth in a written document from such broker or agent.

Where part of stock represented by a single certificate is sold or transferred directly by the taxpayer to the purchaser or transferee instead of through a broker or other agent, an adequate identification is made if the taxpayer maintains a written record of the particular stock which he intended to sell or transfer.

(4) *Stock held by a trustee, executor, or administrator.*—(i) A trustee or executor or administrator of an estate holding stock (not left in the custody of a broker) makes an adequate identification if the trustee, executor, or administrator—

(*a*) Specifies in writing in the books and records of the trust or estate the particular stock to be sold, transferred, or distributed;

(*b*) In the case of a distribution, furnishes the distributee with a written document identifying the particular stock distributed; and

(*c*) In the case of a sale or transfer through a broker or other agent, specifies to the broker or agent the particular stock to be sold or transferred, and within a reasonable time thereafter the broker or agent confirms the specification in a written document.

(ii) The stock the trust or estate identifies under paragraph (c)(4)(i) of this section is the stock treated as sold, transferred, or distributed, even if the trustee, executor, or administrator delivers stock certificates from a different lot.

(5) *Subsequent sales.*—If stock identified under subparagraph (3) or (4) of this paragraph as belonging to a particular lot is sold, transferred, or distributed, the stock so identified shall be deemed to have been sold, transferred, or distributed, and such sale, transfer, or distribution will be taken into consideration in identifying the taxpayer's remaining stock for purposes of subsequent sales, transfers, or distributions.

(6) *Bonds.*—Paragraphs (1) through (5), (8), and (9) of this section apply to the sale or transfer of bonds.

(7) *Book-entry securities.*—(i) In applying the provisions of subparagraph (3)(i)(*a*) of this paragraph in the case of a sale or transfer of a book-entry security (as defined in subdivision (iii)(*a*) of this subparagraph) which is made after December 31, 1970, pursuant to a written instruction by the taxpayer, a specification by the taxpayer of the unique lot number which he has assigned to the lot which contains the securities being sold or transferred shall constitute specification as required by such subparagraph. The specification of the lot number shall be made either—

(*a*) In such written instruction, or

(*b*) In the case of a taxpayer in whose name the book entry by the Reserve Bank is made, in a list of lot numbers with respect to all book-entry securities on the books of the Reserve Bank sold or transferred on that date by the taxpayer, provided such list is mailed to or received by the Reserve Bank on or before the Reserve Bank's next business day.

This subdivision shall apply only if the taxpayer assigns lot numbers in numerical sequence to successive purchases of securities of the same loan title (series) and maturity date, except that securities of the same loan title (series) and maturity date which are purchased at the same price on the same date may be included within the same lot.

(ii) In applying paragraph (c)(3)(i)(*b*) of this section to a sale or transfer of a bookentry security pursuant to a taxpayer's written instruction, a confirmation is made by furnishing to the taxpayer a written advice of transaction from the Reserve Bank or other person through whom the taxpayer sells or transfers the securities. The confirmation document must describe the securities and specify the date of the transaction and amount of securities sold or transferred.

(iii) For purposes of this paragraph (c)(7):

(*a*) The term *book-entry security* means a transferable Treasury bond, note, certificate of indebtedness, or bill issued under the Second Liberty Bond Act (31 U.S.C. 774(2)), as amended, or other security of the United States (as defined in paragraph (c)(7)(iii)(*b*) of this section) in the form of an entry made as prescribed in 31 CFR Part 306, or other comparable Federal regulations, on the records of a Reserve Bank.

(*b*) The term "other security of the United States" means a bond, note, certificate of indebtedness, bill, debenture, or similar obligation which is subject to the provisions of 31 CFR Part 306 or other comparable Federal regulations and which is issued by (*1*) any department or agency of the Government of the United States, or (*2*) the Federal National Mortgage Association, the Federal Home Loan Banks, the Federal Home Loan Mortgage Corporation, the Federal Land Banks, the Federal Intermediate Credit Banks, the Banks for Cooperatives, or the Tennessee Valley Authority;

(*c*) The term "serially-numbered advice of transaction" means the confirmation (prescribed in 31 CFR 306.116) issued by the Reserve Bank which is identifiable by a unique number and indicates that a particular written instruction to the Reserve Bank with respect to the deposit or withdrawal of a specified book-entry security (or securities) has been executed; and

(*d*) The term "Reserve Bank" means a Federal Reserve Bank and its branches acting as Fiscal Agent of the United States.

(8) *Time for making identification.*—For purposes of this paragraph (c), an adequate identification of stock is made at the time of sale, transfer, delivery, or distribution if the identification is made no later than the earlier of the settlement date or the time for settlement required by Rule 15c6-1 under the Securities Exchange Act of 1934, 17 CFR 240.15c6-1 (or its successor). A standing order or instruction for the specific identification of stock is treated as an adequate identification made at the time of sale, transfer, delivery, or distribution.

(9) *Method of writing.*—(i) A written confirmation, record, document, instruction, notification, or advice includes a writing in electronic format.

(ii) A broker or agent may include the written confirmation required under this paragraph (c) in an account statement or other document the broker or agent periodically provides to the taxpayer if the broker or agent provides the statement or other document within a reasonable time after the sale or transfer.

(10) *Method for determining basis of stock.*—A method of determining the basis of stock, including a method of identifying stock sold under this paragraph (c) and the average basis method described in paragraph (e) of this section, is not a method of accounting. Therefore, a change in a method of determining the basis of stock is not a change in method of accounting to which sections 446 and 481 apply.

(11) *Effective/applicability date.*—Paragraphs (c)(1), (c)(4), (c)(6), (c)(7)(ii), (c)(7)(iii)(*a*), (c)(8), (c)(9), and (c)(10) of this section apply for taxable years beginning after October 18, 2010.

(d) *Obligations issued as part of an investment unit.*—For purposes of determining the basis of the individual elements of an investment unit (as defined in paragraph (b)(2)(ii)(*a*) of § 1.1232-3) consisting of an obligation and an option (which is not an excluded option under paragraph (b)(1)(iii)(*c*) of § 1.1232-3), security, or other property, the cost of such investment unit shall be allocated to such individual elements on the basis of their respective fair market values. In the case of the initial issuance of an investment unit consisting of an obligation and an option, security, or other property, where neither the obligation nor the option, security, or other property has a readily ascertainable fair market value, the portion of the cost of the unit which is allocable to the obligation shall be an amount equal to the issue price of the obligation as determined under paragraph (b)(2)(ii)(*a*) of § 1.1232-3.

(e) *Election to use average basis method.*—(1) *In general.*—Notwithstanding paragraph (c) of this section, and except as provided in paragraph (e)(8) of this section, a taxpayer may use the average basis method described in paragraph (e)(7) of this section to determine the cost or other basis of identical shares of stock if—

(i) The taxpayer leaves shares of stock in a regulated investment company (as defined in paragraph (e)(5) of this section) or shares of stock acquired after December 31, 2010, in connection with a dividend reinvestment plan (as defined in paragraph (e)(6) of this section) with a custodian or agent in an account maintained for the acquisition or redemption, sale, or other disposition of shares of the stock; and

(ii) The taxpayer acquires identical shares of stock at different prices or bases in the account.

(2) *Determination of method.*—(i) If a taxpayer places shares of stock described in paragraph (e)(1)(i) of this section acquired on or after January 1, 2012, in the custody of a broker (as defined by section 6045(c)(1)), including by transfer from an account with another broker, the basis of the shares is determined in accordance with the broker's default method, unless the taxpayer notifies the broker that the taxpayer elects another permitted method. The taxpayer must report gain or loss using the method the taxpayer elects or, if the taxpayer fails to make an election, the broker's default method. *See* paragraphs (e)(9)(i) and (e)(9)(v), *Example 2*, of this section.

(ii) The provisions of this paragraph (e)(2) are illustrated by the following example:

Example. (i) In connection with a dividend reinvestment plan, Taxpayer B acquires 100 shares of G Company in 2012 and 100 shares of

G Company in 2013, in an account B maintains with R Broker. B notifies R in writing that B elects to use the average basis method to compute the basis of the shares of G Company. In 2014, B transfers the shares of G Company to an account with S Broker. B does not notify S of the basis determination method B chooses to use for the shares of G Company, and S's default method is first-in, first-out. In 2015, B purchases 200 shares of G Company in the account with S. In 2016, B instructs S to sell 150 shares of G Company.

(ii) Because B does not notify S of a basis determination method for the shares of G Company, under paragraph (e)(2)(i) of this section, the basis of the 150 shares of G Company S sells for B in 2016 must be determined under S's default method, first-in, first-out.

(3) *Shares of stock.*—For purposes of this paragraph (e), securities issued by unit investment trusts described in paragraph (e)(5) of this section are treated as shares of stock and the term *share* or *shares* includes fractions of a share.

(4) *Identical stock.*—For purposes of this paragraph (e), *identical shares of stock* means stock with the same Committee on Uniform Security Identification Procedures (CUSIP) number or other security identifier number as permitted in published guidance of general applicability, *see* § 601.601(d)(2) of this chapter.

(5) *Regulated investment company.*—(i) For purposes of this paragraph, a "regulated investment company" means any domestic corporation (other than a personal holding company as defined in section 542) which meets the limitations of section 851(b) and § 1.851-2, and which is registered at all times during the taxable year under the Investment Company Act of 1940, as amended (15 U.S.C. 80a-1 to 80b-2), either as a management company, or as a unit investment trust.

(ii) Notwithstanding subdivision (i), this paragraph shall not apply in the case of a unit investment trust unless it is one—

(a) Substantially all of the assets of which consist *(1)* of securities issued by a single management company (as defined in such Act) and securities acquired pursuant to subdivision *(b)* of this subdivision (ii), or *(2)* securities issued by a single other corporation, and

(b) Which has no power to invest in any other securities except securities issued by a single other management company, when permitted by such Act or the rules and regulations of the Securities and Exchange Commission.

(6) *Dividend reinvestment plan.*—(i) *In general.*—For purposes of this paragraph (e), the term *dividend reinvestment plan* means any written plan, arrangement, or program under which at least 10 percent of every dividend (within the meaning of section 316) on any share of stock is reinvested in stock identical to the stock on which the dividend is paid. A plan is a dividend reinvestment plan if the plan documents require that at least 10 percent of any dividend paid is reinvested in identical stock even if the plan includes stock on which no dividends have ever been declared or paid or on which an issuer ceases paying dividends. A plan that holds one or more different stocks may permit a taxpayer to reinvest a different percentage of dividends in the stocks held. A dividend reinvestment plan may reinvest other distributions on stock, such as capital gain distributions, non-taxable returns of capital, and cash in lieu of fractional shares. The term dividend reinvestment plan includes both issuer administered dividend reinvestment plans and non-issuer administered dividend reinvestment plans.

(ii) *Acquisition of stock.*—Stock is acquired in connection with a dividend reinvestment plan if the stock is acquired under that plan, arrangement, or program, or if the dividends and other distributions paid on the stock are subject to that plan, arrangement, or program. Shares of stock acquired in connection with a dividend reinvestment plan include the initial purchase of stock in the dividend reinvestment plan, transfers of identical stock into the dividend reinvestment plan, additional periodic purchases of identical stock in the dividend reinvestment plan, and identical stock acquired through reinvestment of the dividends or other distributions paid on the stock held in the plan.

(iii) *Dividends and other distributions paid after reorganization.*—For purposes of this paragraph (e)(6), dividends and other distributions declared or announced before or pending a corporate action (such as a merger, consolidation, acquisition, split-off, or spin-off) involving the issuer and subsequently paid and reinvested in shares of stock in the successor entity or entities are treated as reinvested in shares of stock identical to the shares of stock of the issuer.

(iv) *Withdrawal from or termination of plan.*—If a taxpayer withdraws stock from a dividend reinvestment plan or the plan administrator terminates the dividend reinvestment plan, the shares of identical stock the taxpayer acquires after the withdrawal or termination are not acquired in connection with a dividend reinvestment plan. The taxpayer may not use the average basis method after the withdrawal or termination but may use any other permissible basis determination method. See paragraph (e)(7)(v) of this section for the basis of the shares after withdrawal or termination.

(7) *Computation of average basis.*—(i) *In general.*—Average basis is determined by averaging the basis of all shares of identical stock in an account regardless of holding period. However, for this purpose, shares of stock in a dividend reinvestment plan are not identical to shares of stock with the same CUSIP number that are not in a dividend reinvestment plan. The basis of each share of identical stock in the account is the aggregate basis of all shares of that stock in the account divided by the aggregate number of shares. Unless a single-account election is in effect, see paragraph (e)(11) of this section, a taxpayer may not average together the basis of identical stock held in separate accounts that the

taxpayer sells, exchanges, or otherwise disposes of on or after January 1, 2012.

(ii) *Order of disposition of shares sold or transferred.*—In the case of the sale or transfer of shares of stock to which the average basis method election applies, shares sold or transferred are deemed to be the shares first acquired. Thus, the first shares sold or transferred are those with a holding period of more than 1 year (long-term shares) to the extent that the account contains long-term shares. If the number of shares sold or transferred exceeds the number of long-term shares in the account, the excess shares sold or transferred are deemed to be shares with a holding period of 1 year or less (short-term shares). Any gain or loss attributable to shares held for more than 1 year constitutes long-term gain or loss, and any gain or loss attributable to shares held for 1 year or less constitutes short-term gain or loss. For example, if a taxpayer sells 50 shares from an account containing 100 long-term shares and 100 short-term shares, the shares sold or transferred are all long-term shares. If, however, the account contains 40 long-term shares and 100 short-term shares, the taxpayer has sold 40 long-term shares and 10 short-term shares.

(iii) *Transition rule from double-category method.*—This paragraph (e)(7)(iii) applies to stock for which a taxpayer uses the double-category method under §1.1012-1(e)(3) (April 1, 2010), that the taxpayer acquired before April 1, 2011, and that the taxpayer sells, exchanges, or otherwise disposes of on or after that date. The taxpayer must calculate the average basis of this stock by averaging together all identical shares of stock in the account on April 1, 2011, regardless of holding period.

(iv) *Wash sales.*—A taxpayer must apply section 1091 and the associated regulations (dealing with wash sales of substantially identical securities) in computing average basis regardless of whether the stock or security sold or otherwise disposed of and the stock acquired are in the same account or in different accounts.

(v) *Basis after change from average basis method.*—Unless a taxpayer revokes an average basis method election under paragraph (e)(9)(iii) of this section, if a taxpayer changes from the average basis method to another basis determination method (including a change resulting from a withdrawal from or termination of a dividend reinvestment plan), the basis of each share of stock immediately after the change is the same as the basis immediately before the change. *See* paragraph (e)(9)(iv) of this section for rules for changing from the average basis method.

(vi) The provisions of this paragraph (e)(7) are illustrated by the following examples:

Example 1. (i) In 2011, Taxpayer C acquires 100 shares of H Company and enrolls them in a dividend reinvestment plan administered by T Custodian. C elects to use the average basis method for the shares of H Company enrolled in the dividend reinvestment plan. T also acquires for C's account 50 shares of H Company and does not enroll these shares in the dividend reinvestment plan.

(ii) Under paragraph (e)(7)(i) of this section, the 50 shares of H Company not in the dividend reinvestment plan are not identical to the 100 shares of H Company enrolled in the dividend reinvestment plan, even if they have the same CUSIP number. Accordingly, under paragraphs (e)(1) and (e)(7)(i) of this section, C may not average the basis of the 50 shares of H Company with the basis of the 100 shares of H Company. Under paragraph (e)(1)(i) of this section, C may not use the average basis method for the 50 shares of H Company because the shares are not acquired in connection with a dividend reinvestment plan.

Example 2. (i) Taxpayer D enters into an agreement with W Custodian establishing an account for the periodic acquisition of shares of L Company, a regulated investment company. W acquires for D's account shares of L Company stock on the following dates and amounts:

Date	*Number of shares*	*Cost*
January 8, 2010	25 shares	$200
February 8, 2010	24 shares	200
March 8, 2010	20 shares	200
April 8, 2010	20 shares	200

(ii) At D's direction, W sells 40 shares from the account on January 15, 2011, for $10 per share or a total of $400. D elects to use the average basis method for the shares of L Company. The average basis for the shares sold on January 15, 2011, is $8.99 (total cost of shares, $800, divided by the total number of shares, 89).

(iii) Under paragraph (e)(7)(ii) of this section, the shares sold are the shares first acquired. Thus, D realizes $25.25 ($1.01 * 25) long-term capital gain for the 25 shares acquired on January 8, 2010, and $15.15 ($1.01 * 15) short-term capital gain for 15 of the shares acquired on February 8, 2010.

Example 3. (i) The facts are the same as in *Example 2,* except that on February 8, 2011, D changes to the first-in, first-out basis determination method. W purchases 25 shares of L Company for D on March 8, 2011, at $12 per share. D sells 40 shares on May 8, 2011, and 34 shares on July 8, 2012.

(ii) Because D uses the first-in, first-out method, the 40 shares sold on May 8, 2011 are 9 shares purchased on February 8, 2010, 20 shares purchased on March 8, 2010, and 11 shares purchased on April 8, 2010. Because, under paragraph (e)(7)(v) of this section, the basis of the shares D owns when D changes from the average basis method remains the same, the basis of the shares sold on May 8, 2011, is $8.99 per share, not the original cost of $8.33 per share for the shares purchased on February 8, 2010, or $10 per share for the shares purchased on March 8, 2010, and April 8, 2010. The basis of the shares sold on July 8, 2012, is $8.99 per share for 9 shares purchased on April 8, 2010, and $12 per share for 25 shares purchased on March 8, 2011.

Example 4. (i) The facts are the same as in *Example 2,* except that D uses the first-in, first-out method for the 40 shares sold on January 15, 2011. W purchases 25 shares of L Company for D on March 8, 2011, at $12 per share. D sells 40 shares on May 8, 2011, and elects the average basis method.

(ii) Because D uses the first-in, first-out method for the sale on January 15, 2011, the 40 shares sold are the 25 shares acquired on January 8, 2010, for $200 (basis $8 per share) and 15 of the 24 shares purchased on February 8, 2010, for $200 (basis $8.33 per share).

(iii) Under paragraph (e)(7)(i) of this section, under the average basis method, the basis of all of the shares of identical stock in D's account is averaged. Thus, the basis of each share D sells on May 8, 2011, after electing the average basis method, is $10.47. This figure is the total cost of the shares in D's account ($74.97 for the 9 shares acquired on February 8, 2010, $200 for the 20 shares acquired on March 8, 2010, $200 for the 20 shares acquired on April 8, 2010, and $300 for the 25 shares acquired on March 8, 2011) divided by 74, the total number of shares ($774.97/74).

(8) *Limitation on use of average basis method for certain gift shares.*—(i) Except as provided in paragraph (e)(8)(ii) of this section, a taxpayer may not use the average basis method for shares of stock a taxpayer acquires by gift after December 31, 1920, if the basis of the shares (adjusted for the period before the date of the gift as provided in section 1016) in the hands of the donor or the last preceding owner by whom the shares were not acquired by gift was greater than the fair market value of the shares at the time of the gift. This paragraph (e)(8)(i) does not apply to shares the taxpayer acquires as a result of a taxable dividend or capital gain distribution on the gift shares.

(ii) Notwithstanding paragraph (e)(8)(i) of this section, a taxpayer may use the average basis method if the taxpayer states in writing that the taxpayer will treat the basis of the gift shares as the fair market value of the shares at the time the taxpayer acquires the shares. The taxpayer must provide this statement when the taxpayer makes the election under paragraph (e)(9) of this section or when transferring the shares to an account for which the taxpayer has made this election, whichever occurs later. The statement must be effective for any gift shares identical to the gift shares to which the average basis method election applies that the taxpayer acquires at any time and must remain in effect as long as the election remains in effect.

(iii) The provisions of this paragraph (e)(8) are illustrated by the following examples:

Example 1. (i) Taxpayer E owns an account for the periodic acquisition of shares of M Company, a regulated investment company. On April 15, 2010, E acquires identical shares of M Company by gift and transfers those shares into the account. These shares had an adjusted basis in the hands of the donor that was greater than the fair market value of the shares on that date. On June 15, 2010, E sells shares from the account and elects to use the average basis method.

(ii) Under paragraph (e)(8)(ii) of this section, E may elect to use the average basis method for shares sold or transferred from the account if E includes a statement with E's election that E will treat the basis of the gift shares in the account as the fair market value of the shares at the time E acquired them. *See* paragraph (e)(9)(ii) of this section.

Example 2. (i) The facts are the same as in *Example 1,* except E acquires the gift shares on April 15, 2012, transfers those shares into the account, and used the average basis method for sales of shares of M Company before acquiring the gift shares. E sells shares of M Company on June 15, 2012.

(ii) Under paragraph (e)(8)(ii) of this section, the basis of the gift shares may be averaged with the basis of the other shares of M Company in E's account if, when E transfers the gift shares to the account, E provides a statement to E's broker that E will treat the basis of the gift shares in the account as the fair market value of the shares at the time E acquired them. *See* paragraph (e)(9)(i) of this section.

(9) *Time and manner for making the average basis method election.*—(i) *In general.*—A taxpayer makes an election to use the average basis method for shares of stock described in paragraph (e)(1)(i) of this section that are covered securities (within the meaning of section 6045(g)(3)) by notifying the custodian or agent in writing by any reasonable means. For purposes of this paragraph (e), a writing may be in electronic format. A taxpayer has not made an election within the meaning of this section if the taxpayer fails to notify a broker of the taxpayer's basis determination method and basis is determined by the broker's default method under paragraph (e)(2) of this section. A taxpayer may make the average basis method election at any time, effective for sales or other dispositions of stock occurring after the taxpayer notifies the custodian or agent. The election must identify each account with that custodian or agent and each stock in that account to which the election applies. The election may specify that it applies to all accounts with a custodian or agent, including accounts the taxpayer later establishes with the custodian or agent. If the election applies to gift shares, the taxpayer must provide the statement required by paragraph (e)(8)(ii) of this section, if applicable, to the custodian or agent with the taxpayer's election.

(ii) *Average basis method election for securities that are noncovered securities.*—A taxpayer makes an election to use the average basis method for shares of stock described in paragraph (e)(1)(i) of this section that are noncovered securities (as described in § 1.6045-1(a)(16) on the taxpayer's income tax return for the first taxable year for which the election applies. A taxpayer may make the election on an amended return filed no later than the time prescribed (including extensions) for filing the original return for the taxable year for which the election applies. The taxpayer must indicate on the return that the taxpayer used the average basis method in reporting gain or loss on the sale or other disposition. A taxpayer must attach to the return the statement described in paragraph (e)(8)(ii) of this section, if applicable. A taxpayer making the election must maintain records necessary to substantiate the average basis reported.

(iii) *Revocation of election.*—A taxpayer may revoke an election under paragraph (e)(9)(i) of this section by the earlier of one year after the taxpayer makes the election or the date of the first sale, transfer, or disposition of that stock following the election. A custodian or agent may extend the one-year period but a taxpayer may not revoke an election after the first sale, transfer, or disposition of the stock. A revocation applies to all stock the taxpayer holds in an account that is identical to the shares of stock for which the taxpayer revokes the election. A revocation is effective when the taxpayer notifies, in writing by any reasonable means, the custodian or agent holding the stock to which the revocation applies. After revocation, the taxpayer's basis in the shares of stock to which the revocation applies is the basis before averaging.

(iv) *Change from average basis method.*—A taxpayer may change basis determination methods from the average basis method to another method prospectively at any time. A change from the average basis method applies to all identical stock the taxpayer sells or otherwise disposes of before January 1, 2012, that was held in any account. A change from the average basis method applies on an account by account basis (within the meaning of paragraph (e)(10) of this section) to all identical stock the taxpayer sells or otherwise disposes of on or after January 1, 2012. The taxpayer must notify, in writing by any reasonable means, the custodian or agent holding the stock to which the change applies. Unless paragraph (e)(9)(iii) of this section applies, the basis of each share of stock to which the change applies remains the same as the basis immediately before the change. *See* paragraph (e)(7)(v) of this section.

(v) *Examples.*—The provisions of this paragraph (e)(9) are illustrated by the following examples:

Example 1. (i) Taxpayer F enters into an agreement with W Custodian establishing an account for the periodic acquisition of shares of N Company, a regulated investment company. W acquires for F's account shares of N Company on the following dates and amounts:

Date	*Number of shares*	*Cost*
January 8, 2012	25 shares	$200
February 8, 2012	24 shares	200
March 8, 2012	20 shares	200

(ii) F notifies W that F elects, under paragraph (e)(9)(i) of this section, to use the average basis method for the shares of N Company. On May 8, 2012, under paragraph (e)(9)(iii) of this section, F notifies W that F revokes the average basis method election. On June 1, 2012, F sells 60 shares of N Company using the first-in, first-out basis determination method.

(iii) Under paragraph (e)(9)(iii) of this section, the basis of the N Company shares upon revocation, and for purposes of determining gain on the sale, is $8.00 per share for each of the 25 shares purchased on January 8, 2012, $8.34 per share for each of the 24 shares purchased on February 8, 2012, and $10 per share for the remaining 11 shares purchased on March 8, 2012.

Example 2. (i) The facts are the same as in *Example 1*, except that F does not notify W that F elects a basis determination method. W's default basis determination method is the average basis method and W maintains an averaged basis for F's shares of N Company on W's books and records.

(ii) F has not elected the average basis method under paragraph (e)(9)(i) of this section. Therefore, F's notification to W on May 8, 2012, is not an effective revocation under paragraph (e)(9)(iii) of this section. F's attempted revocation is, instead, notification of a change from the average basis method under paragraph (e)(9)(iv) of this section. Accordingly, the basis of each share of stock F sells on June 1, 2012, is the basis immediately before the change, $8.70 (total cost of shares, $600, divided by the total number of shares, 69).

(10) *Application of average basis method account by account.*—(i) *In general.*—For sales, exchanges, or other dispositions on or after January 1, 2012, of stock described in paragraph (e)(1)(i) of this section, the average basis method applies on an account by account basis. A taxpayer may use the average basis method for stock in a regulated investment company or stock acquired in connection with a dividend reinvestment plan in one account but use a different basis determination method for identical stock in a different account. If a taxpayer uses the average basis method for a stock described in paragraph (e)(1)(i) of this section, the taxpayer must use the average basis method for all identical stock within that account. The taxpayer may use different basis determination methods for stock within an account that is not identical. Except as provided in paragraph (e)(10)(ii) of this section, a taxpayer must make separate elections to use the average basis method for stock held in separate accounts.

(ii) *Account rule for stock sold before 2012.*—A taxpayer's election to use the average basis method for shares of stock described in paragraph (e)(1)(i) of this section that a taxpayer sells, exchanges, or otherwise disposes of before January 1, 2012, applies to all identical shares of stock the taxpayer holds in any account.

(iii) *Separate account.*—Unless the single-account election described in paragraph (e)(11)(i) of this section applies, stock described in paragraph (e)(1)(i) of this section that is a covered security (within the meaning of section 6045(g)(3)) is treated as held in a separate account from stock that is a noncovered security (as described in § 1.6045-1(a)(16), regardless of when acquired.

(iv) *Examples.*—The provisions of this paragraph (e)(10) are illustrated by the following examples:

Example 1. (i) In 2012, Taxpayer G enters into an agreement with Y Broker establishing three accounts (G-1, G-2, and G-3) for the periodic acquisition of shares of P Company, a regulated investment company. Y makes periodic purchases of P Company for each of G's accounts. G elects to use the average basis method for account G-1. On July 1, 2013, G sells shares of P Company from account G-1.

(ii) G is not required to use the average basis method for the shares of P Company that G holds in accounts G-2 and G-3 because, under paragraph (e)(10)(i) of this section, the average basis method election applies to shares sold after 2011 on an account by account basis.

Example 2. The facts are the same as in *Example 1*, except that G also instructs Y to acquire shares of Q Company, a regulated investment company, for account G-1. Under paragraph (e)(10)(i) of this section, G may use any permissible basis determination method for the shares of Q Company because, under paragraph (e)(4) of this section, the shares of Q Company are not identical to the shares of P Company.

Example 3. (i) The facts are the same as in *Example 1*, except that G establishes the accounts in 2011 and Y sells shares of P Company from account G-1 on July 1, 2011.

(ii) For sales before 2012, under paragraph (e)(10)(ii) of this section, G's election applies to all accounts in which G holds identical stock. G must average together the basis of the shares in all accounts to determine the basis of the shares sold from account G-1.

Example 4. (i) In 2011, Taxpayer H acquires 80 shares of R Company and enrolls them in R Company's dividend reinvestment plan. In 2012, H acquires 50 shares of R Company in the dividend reinvestment plan. H elects to use the average basis method for the shares of R Company in the dividend reinvestment plan. R Company does not make the single-account election under paragraph (e)(11)(i) of this section.

(ii) Under section 6045(g)(3) and § 1.6045-1(a)(16), the 80 shares acquired in 2011 are noncovered securities and the 50 shares acquired in 2012 are covered securities. Therefore, under paragraph (e)(10)(iii) of this section, the 80 shares are treated as held in a separate account from the 50 shares. H must make a separate average basis method election for each account and must average the basis of the shares in each account separately from the shares in the other account.

Example 5. (i) B Broker maintains an account for Taxpayer J for the periodic acquisition of shares of S Company, a regulated investment company. In 2013, B purchases shares of S Company for J's account that are covered securities within the meaning of section 6045(g)(3). On April 15, 2014, J inherits shares of S Company that are noncovered securities and transfers the shares into the account with B.

(ii) Under paragraph (e)(10)(iii) of this section, J must treat the purchased shares and the inherited shares of S Company as held in separate accounts. J may elect to apply the average basis method to all the shares of S Company, but must make a separate election for each account, and must average the basis of the shares in each account separately from the shares in the other account.

Example 6. (i) In 2010, Taxpayer K purchases stock in T Company in an account with C Broker. In 2012, K purchases additional T Company stock and enrolls that stock in a dividend reinvestment plan maintained by C. K elects the average basis method for the T Company stock. In 2013, K transfers the T Company stock purchased in 2010 into the dividend reinvestment plan.

(ii) Under paragraphs (e)(1)(i) and (e)(6)(ii) of this section, the stock purchased in 2010 is not stock acquired after December 31, 2010, in connection with a dividend reinvestment plan before transfer into the dividend reinvestment plan. Therefore, the stock is not eligible for the average basis method at that time.

(iii) Once transferred into the dividend reinvestment plan in 2013, the stock K purchased in 2010 is acquired after December 31, 2010, in connection with a dividend reinvestment plan within the meaning of paragraph (e)(6)(ii) of this section and is eligible for the average basis method. Because stock purchased in 2010 is a noncovered security under § 1.6045-1(a)(16), under paragraph (e)(10)(iii) of this section, the 2010 stock and the 2012 stock must be treated as held in separate accounts. Under paragraph (e)(7)(i) of this section, the basis of the 2010 shares may not be averaged with the basis of the 2012 shares.

Example 7. The facts are the same as in *Example 6*, except that K purchases the initial T Company stock in January 2011. Because this stock is a covered security under section 6045(g)(3) and § 1.6045-1(a)(15)(iv)(A), the 2011 stock and the 2012 stock are not required under paragraph (e)(10)(iii) of this section to be treated as held in separate accounts. Under paragraph (e)(7)(i) of this section, the basis of the 2011 shares must be averaged with the basis of the 2012 shares.

Example 8. (i) The facts are the same as in *Example 7*, except that K purchases the additional T Company stock and enrolls in the dividend reinvestment plan in March 2011. In September 2011, K transfers the T Company stock purchased in January 2011 into the dividend reinvestment plan. K sells some of the T Company stock in 2012.

(ii) Under section 6045(g)(3) and § 1.6045-1(a)(16), the stock K purchases in January 2011 is a covered security at the time of purchase but the stock K purchases and enrolls in the dividend reinvestment plan in March 2011 is a noncovered security. However, under § 1.6045-1(a)(15)(iv)(A), the stock purchased in January 2011 becomes a noncovered security after it is transferred to the dividend reinvestment plan. Because all the shares in the dividend reinvestment plan in September 2011 are noncovered securities, when K sells stock in 2012, the January 2011 stock and the March 2011 stock are not required under paragraph (e)(10)(iii) of this section to be treated as held in separate accounts. Under paragraph (e)(7)(i) of this section, the basis of the January 2011 shares must be averaged with the basis of the March 2011 shares.

(11) *Single-account election.*—(i) *In general.*—Paragraph (e)(10)(iii) of this section does not apply if a regulated investment company or dividend reinvestment plan elects to treat all identical shares of stock described in paragraph (e)(1)(i) of this section as held in a single account (single-account election). The single-account election applies only to stock for which a taxpayer elects to use the average basis method that is held in separate accounts or treated as held in separate accounts maintained for the taxpayer and only to accounts with the same ownership. If a broker (as defined by section 6045(c)(1)) holds the stock as a nominee, the broker, and not the regulated investment company or dividend reinvestment plan, makes the election. The single-account election is irrevocable, but is void if the taxpayer revokes the average basis election under paragraph (e)(9)(iii) of this section.

(ii) *Scope of election.*—A company, plan, or broker may make a single-account election for one or more taxpayers for which it maintains an account, and for one or more stocks it holds for a taxpayer. The company, plan, or broker may make the election only for the shares of stock for which it has accurate basis information. A company, plan, or broker has accurate basis information if the company, plan, or broker neither knows nor has reason to know that the basis information is inaccurate. *See* also section 6724 and the associated regulations regarding standards for relief from information reporting penalties. Stock for which accurate basis information is unavailable may not be included in the single-account election and must be treated as held in a separate account.

(iii) *Effect of single-account election.*—If a company, plan, or broker makes the single-account election, the basis of all identical shares of stock to which the election applies must be averaged together regardless of when the taxpayer acquires the shares, and all the shares are treated as covered securities. The single-account election applies to all identical stock a taxpayer later acquires in the account that is a covered security (within the meaning of section 6045(g)(3)). A company, plan, or broker may make another single-account election if, for example, the broker later acquires accurate basis information for a stock, or a taxpayer acquires identical stock in the account that is a noncovered security (as described in § 1.6045-1(a)(16) for which the company, plan, or broker has accurate basis information.

(iv) *Time and manner for making the single-account election.*—A company, plan, or broker makes the single-account election by clearly noting it on its books and records. The books and records must reflect the date of the election; the taxpayer's name, account number, and taxpayer identification number; the stock subject to the election; and the taxpayer's basis in the stock. The company, plan, or broker must provide copies of the books and records regarding the election to the taxpayer upon request. A company, plan, or broker may make the single-account election at any time.

(v) *Notification to taxpayer.*—A company, plan, or broker making the singleaccount election must use reasonable means to notify the taxpayer of the election. Reasonable means include mailings, circulars, or electronic mail sent separately to the taxpayer or included with the taxpayer's account statement, or other means reasonably calculated to provide actual notice to the taxpayer. The notice must identify the securities subject to the election and advise the taxpayer that the securities will be treated as covered securities regardless of when acquired.

(vi) *Examples.*—The provisions of this paragraph (e)(11) are illustrated by the following examples:

Example 1. (i) E Broker maintains Accounts A and B for Taxpayer M for the acquisition and disposition of shares of T Company, a regulated investment company. In 2011, E purchases 100 shares of T Company for M's Account A. E has accurate basis information for these shares. In 2012, E purchases 150 shares of T Company for M's Account A and 80 shares of T Company for M's Account B. M elects to use the average basis method for all shares of T Company. E makes a single-account election for M's T Company stock.

(ii) The shares of T Company in Accounts A and B are held in separate accounts. Under section 6045(g)(3) and § 1.6045-1(a)(16), of the shares purchased in Account A, the 100 shares purchased in 2011 are noncovered securities and the 150 shares purchased in 2012 are covered securities. Under paragraph (e)(10)(iii) of this section, the 100 shares are treated as held in a separate account from the 150 shares. Under paragraph (e)(11)(i) of this section, the single-account election applies to all 330 shares of T Company in Accounts A and B. Thus, under paragraph (e)(11)(iii) of this section, the basis of the 330 shares of stock is averaged together and all the shares are treated as covered securities.

Example 2. The facts are the same as in *Example 1,* except that M owns Account B jointly with Taxpayer N. E may make a single-account election for the 250 shares of stock in M's Account A. However, under paragraph (e)(11)(i) of this section, E may not make a single-account election for Accounts A and B because the accounts do not have the same ownership.

Example 3. (i) C Broker maintains an account for Taxpayer K for the acquisition and disposition of shares of T Company, a regulated investment company, and shares of V Company that K enrolls in C's dividend reinvestment plan. In 2011, C purchases for K's account 100 shares of T Company in multiple lots and 80 shares of V Company in multiple lots that are enrolled in the dividend reinvestment plan. C has accurate basis information for all 100 shares of T Company and 80 shares of V Company. In 2012, C acquires for K's account 150 shares of T Company and 160 shares of V Company that are enrolled in the dividend reinvestment plan. K elects to use the average basis method for all the shares of T Company and V Company.

(ii) Under paragraphs (e)(11)(i) and (ii) of this section, C may make a singleaccount election for the T Company stock or the V Company stock, or both. After making a single-account election for each stock, under paragraph (e)(11)(iii) of this section, the basis of all T Company stock is averaged together and the basis of all V Company stock is averaged together, regardless of when acquired, and all the shares of T Company and V Company are treated as covered securities.

Example 4. The facts are the same as in *Example 3,* except that K transfers the 100 shares of T Company acquired in 2011 from an account with another broker into K's account with C. C does not have accurate basis information for 30 of the 100 shares of T Company, which K had acquired in two lots. Under paragraph (e)(11)(ii) of this section, C may make the single-account election only for the 70 shares of T Company stock for which C has accurate basis information. C must treat the 30 shares of T Company for which C does not have accurate basis information as held in a separate account. K may use the average basis method for the 30 shares of T Company, but must make a separate average basis method election for these shares and must average the basis of these shares separately from the 70 shares subject to C's single-account election.

Example 5. The facts are the same as in *Example 3,* except that C has made the single-account election and in 2013 K acquires additional shares of T Company that are covered securities in K's account with C. Under paragraph (e)(11)(iii) of this section, these shares of T Company are subject to C's single-account election.

Example 6. The facts are the same as in *Example 3,* except that C has made the single-account election and in 2013 K inherits shares of T Company that are noncovered securities and transfers the shares into the account with C. C has accurate basis information for these shares. Under paragraph (e)(11)(iii) of this section, C may make a second single-account election to include the inherited T Company shares.

Example 7. (i) Between 2002 and 2011, Taxpayer L acquires 1500 shares of W Company, a regulated investment company, in an account with D Broker, for which L uses the average basis method, and sells 500 shares. On January 5, 2012, based on accurate basis information, the averaged basis of L's remaining 1000 shares of W Company is $24 per share. On January 5, 2012, L acquires 100 shares of W Company for $28 per share and makes an average basis election for those shares under paragraph (e)(9)(i) of this section.

(ii) On February 1, 2012, D makes a single-account election that includes all 1100 of L's shares in W Company. Thereafter, the basis of L's shares of W Company is $24.36 per share (($24,000 + $2,800) / 1100). On September 12, 2012, under paragraph (e)(9)(iii) of this section, L revokes the average basis election for the 100 shares acquired on January 5, 2012.

(iii) Under paragraph (e)(11)(i) of this section, D's single-account election is void. Therefore, the basis of the 1000 shares of W Company that L acquires before 2012 is $24 per share and the basis of the 100 shares of W Company that L acquires in 2012 is $28 per share.

(12) *Effective/applicability date.*—Except as otherwise provided in paragraphs (e)(1), (e)(2), (e)(7), (e)(9), and (e)(10) of this section, this paragraph (e) applies for taxable years beginning after October 18, 2010.

(f) *Special rules.*—For special rules for determining the basis for gain or loss in the case of certain vessels acquired through the Maritime Commission (or its successors) or pursuant to an agreement with the Secretary of Commerce, see sections 510, 511, and 607 of the Merchant Marine Act, 1936, as amended (46 U.S.C. 1160, 1161) and 26 CFR Parts 2 and 3. For special rules for determining the unadjusted basis of property recovered in respect of war losses, see section 1336. For special rules with respect to taxable years beginning before January 1, 1964, for determining the basis for gain or loss in the case of a disposition of a share of stock acquired pursuant to the timely exercise of a restricted stock option where the option price was between 85 percent and 95 percent of the fair market value of the stock at the time the option was granted, see paragraph (b) of §1.421-5. See sections 423(c)(1) or 424(c)(1), whichever is applicable, for special rules with respect to taxable years ending after December 31, 1963, for determining the basis for gain or loss in the case of the disposition of a share of stock acquired pursuant to the timely exercise of a stock option described in such sections. See section 422(c)(1) for special rules with respect to taxable years ending after December 31, 1963, for determining the basis for gain or loss in the case of an exercise of a qualified stock option.

(g) *Debt instruments issued in exchange for property.*—(1) *In general.*—For purposes of paragraph (a) of this section, if a debt instrument is issued in exchange for property, the cost of the property that is attributable to the debt instrument is the issue price of the debt instrument as determined under § 1.1273-2 or § 1.1274-2, whichever is applicable. If, however, the issue price of the debt instrument is determined under section 1273(b)(4), the cost of the property attributable to the debt instrument is its stated principal amount reduced by any unstated interest (as determined under section 483).

(2) *Certain tax-exempt obligations.*—This paragraph (g)(2) applies to a tax-exempt obligation (as defined in section 1275(a)(3)) that is issued in exchange for property and that has an issue price determined under § 1.1274-2(j) (concerning tax-exempt contingent payment obligations and certain tax-exempt variable rate debt instruments subject to section 1274). Notwithstanding paragraph (g)(1) of this section, if this paragraph (g)(2) applies to a tax-exempt obligation, for purposes of paragraph (a) of this section, the cost of the property that is attributable to the obligation is the sum of the present values of the noncontingent payments (as determined under § 1.1274-2(c)).

(3) *Effective date.*—This paragraph (g) applies to sales or exchanges that occur on or after August 13, 1996. [Reg. § 1.1012-1.]

□ [*T.D.* 6265, 11-6-57. *Amended by T.D.* 6311, 9-10-58; *T.D.* 6837, 7-12-65; *T.D.* 6887, 6-23-66; *T.D.* 6934, 11-13-67; *T.D.* 6984, 12-23-68; *T.D.* 7015, 6-19-69; *T.D.* 7081, 12-30-70; *T.D.* 7129, 7-6-71; *T.D.* 7154, 12-27-71; *T.D.* 7213, 10-17-72; *T.D.* 7568, 10-11-78; *T.D.* 7728, 10-31-80; *T.D.* 8517, 1-27-94; *T.D.* 8674, 6-11-96 *and T.D.* 9504, 10-12-2010.]

[Reg. § 1.1012-2]

§ 1.1012-2. Transfers in part a sale and in part a gift.—For rules relating to basis of property acquired in a transfer which is in part a gift and in part a sale, see § 1.170A-4(c), § 1.1011-2(b), and § 1.1015-4. [Reg. § 1.1012-2.]

□ [*T.D.* 6265, 11-6-57. *Amended by T.D.* 7207, 10-3-72.]

[Reg. § 1.1013-1]

§ 1.1013-1. Property included in inventory.—The basis of property required to be included in inventory is the last inventory value of such property in the hands of the taxpayer. The requirements with respect to the valuation of an inventory are stated in subpart D (sections 471 and following), part II, or subchapter E, chapter 1 of the Code, and the regulations thereunder. [Reg. § 1.1013-1.]

□ [*T.D.* 6265, 11-6-57.]

[Reg. § 1.1014-1]

§ 1.1014-1. Basis of property acquired from a decedent.—(a) *General rule.*—The purpose of section 1014 is, in general, to provide a basis for property acquired from a decedent that is equal to the value placed upon such property for purposes of the federal estate tax. Accordingly, the general rule is that the basis of property acquired from a decedent is the fair market value of such property at the date of the decedent's death, or, if the decedent's executor so elects, at the alternate valuation date prescribed in section 2032, or in section 811(j) of the Internal Revenue Code (Code) of 1939. However, the basis of property acquired from certain decedents who died in 2010 is determined under section 1022, if the decedent's executor made an election under section 301(c) of the Tax Relief, Unemployment Insurance Reauthorization, and Job Creation Act of 2010, Public Law 111-312 (124 Stat. 3296, 3300 (2010)). See section 1022. Property acquired from a decedent includes, principally, property acquired by bequest, devise, or inheritance, and, in the case of decedents dying after December 31, 1953, property required to be included in determining the value of the decedent's gross estate under any provision of the Code of 1954 or the Code of 1939. The general rule governing basis of property acquired from a decedent, as well as other rules prescribed elsewhere in this section, shall have no application if the property is sold, exchanged, or otherwise disposed of before the decedent's death by the person who acquired the property from the decedent. For general rules on the applicable valuation date where the executor of a decedent's estate elects under section 2032, or under section 811(j) of the Code of 1939, to value the decedent's gross estate at the alternate valuation date prescribed in such sections, see § 1.1014-3(e).

(b) *Scope and application.*—With certain limitations, the general rule described in paragraph (a) of this section is applicable to the classes of property described in paragraphs (a) and (b) of § 1.1014-2, including stock in a DISC or former DISC. In the case of stock in a DISC or former DISC, the provisions of this section and §§ 1.1014-2 through 1.1014-8 are applicable, except as provided in § 1.1014-9. Special basis rules with respect to the basis of certain other property acquired from a decedent are set forth in paragraph (c) of § 1.1014-2. These special rules concern certain stock or securities of a foreign personal holding company and the surviving spouse's one-half share of community property held with a decedent dying after October 21, 1942, and on or before December 31, 1947. In this section and §§ 1.1014-2 to 1.1014-6, inclusive, whenever the words "property acquired from a decedent" are used, they shall also mean "property passed from a decedent", and the phrase "person who acquired it from the decedent" shall include the "person to whom it passed from the decedent."

(c) *Property to which section 1014 does not apply.*—Section 1014 shall have no application to the following classes of property:

(1) Property which constitutes a right to receive an item of income in respect of a decedent under section 691; and

(2) Restricted stock options described in section 421 which the employee has not exercised at death if the employee died before January 1, 1957. In the case of employees dying after December 31, 1956, see paragraph (d)(4) of § 1.421-5. In the case of employees dying in a taxable year ending after December 31, 1963, see paragraph (c)(4) of § 1.421-9 with respect to an option described in part II of subchapter D.

(d) *Effective/applicability date.*—This section applies on and after January 19, 2017. For rules before January 19, 2017, see § 1.1014-1 as contained in 26 CFR part 1 revised as of April 1, 2016. [Reg. § 1.1014-1.]

☐ [*T.D.* 6265, 11-6-57. *Amended by T.D.* 6527, 1-18-61, *T.D.* 6887, 6-23-66, *T.D.* 7283, 8-2-73 *and T.D.* 9811, 1-18-2017.]

[Reg. § 1.1014-2]

§ 1.1014-2. Property acquired from a decedent.—(a) *In general.*—The following property, except where otherwise indicated, is considered to have been acquired from a decedent and the basis thereof is determined in accordance with the general rule in § 1.1014-1:

(1) Without regard to the date of the decedent's death, property acquired by bequest, devise, or inheritance, or by the decedent's estate from the decedent, whether the property was acquired under the decedent's will or under the law governing the descent and distribution of the property of decedents. However, see paragraph (c)(1) of this section if the property was acquired by bequest or inheritance from a decedent dying after August 26, 1937, and if such property consists of stock or securities of a foreign personal holding company.

(2) Without regard to the date of the decedent's death, property transferred by the decedent during his lifetime in trust to pay the income for life to or on the order or direction of the decedent, with the right reserved to the decedent at all times before his death to revoke the trust.

(3) In the case of decedents dying after December 31, 1951, property transferred by the decedent during his lifetime in trust to pay the income for life to or on the order or direction of the decedent with the right reserved to the decedent at all times before his death to make any change in the enjoyment thereof through the exercise of a power to alter, amend, or terminate the trust.

(4) Without regard to the date of the decedent's death, property passing without full and adequate consideration under a general power of appointment exercised by the decedent by will. (See section 2041(b) for definition of general power of appointment.)

(5) In the case of decedents dying after December 31, 1947, property which represents the surviving spouse's one-half share of community property held by the decedent and the surviving spouse under the community property laws of any State, Territory, or possession of the United States or any foreign country, if at least one-half of the whole of the community interest in that property was includible in determining the value of the decedent's gross estate under part III, chapter 11 of the Internal Revenue Code of 1954 (relating to the estate tax) or section 811 of the Internal Revenue Code of 1939. It is not necessary for the application of this subparagraph that an estate tax return be required to be filed for the estate of the decedent or that an estate tax be payable.

(6) In the case of decedents dying after December 31, 1950, and before January 1, 1954, property which represents the survivor's interest in a joint and survivor's annuity if the value of any part of that interest was required to be included in determining the value of the decedent's gross estate under section 811 of the Internal Revenue Code of 1939. It is necessary only that the value of a part of the survivor's interest in the annuity be includible in the gross estate under section 811. It is not necessary for the application of this subparagraph that an estate tax return be required to be filed for the estate of the decedent or that an estate tax be payable.

(b) *Property acquired from a decedent dying after December 31, 1953.*—(1) *In general.*—In addition to the property described in paragraph (a) of this section, and except as otherwise provided in subparagraph (3) of this paragraph, in the case of a decedent dying after December 31, 1953, property shall also be considered to have been acquired from the decedent to the extent that both of the following conditions are met: (i) the property was acquired from the decedent by reason of death, form of ownership, or other conditions (including property acquired through the exercise or non-exercise of a power of appointment), and (ii) the property is includible in the decedent's gross estate under the provisions of the Internal Revenue Code of 1954, or the Internal Revenue Code of 1939, because of such acquisition. The basis of such property in the hands of the person who acquired it from the decedent shall be determined in accordance with the general rule in § 1.1014-1. See, however, § 1.1014-6 for special adjustments if such property is acquired before the death of the decedent. See also subparagraph (3) of this paragraph for a description of property not within the scope of this paragraph.

(2) *Rules for the application of subparagraph (1) of this paragraph.*—Except as provided in subparagraph (3) of this paragraph, this paragraph generally includes all property acquired from a decedent, which is includible in the gross estate of the decedent if the decedent died after December 31, 1953. It is not necessary for the application of this paragraph that an estate tax return be required to be filed for the estate of the decedent or that an estate tax be payable. Property acquired prior to the death of a decedent which is includible in the decedent's gross estate, such as property transferred by a decedent in contemplation of death, and property held by a taxpayer and the decedent as joint tenants or as tenants by the entireties is within the scope of this paragraph. Also, this paragraph includes

property acquired through the exercise or nonexercise of a power of appointment where such property is includible in the decedent's gross estate. It does not include property not includible in the decedent's gross estate such as property not situated in the United States acquired from a nonresident who is not a citizen of the United States.

(3) *Exceptions to application of this paragraph.*—The rules of this paragraph are not applicable to the following property:

(i) Annuities described in section 72;

(ii) Stock or securities of a foreign personal holding company as described in section 1014(b)(5) (see paragraph (c)(1) of this section);

(iii) Property described in any paragraph other than paragraph (9) of section 1014(b). See paragraphs (a) and (c) of this section.

In illustration of subdivision (ii), assume that A acquired by gift stock of a character described in paragraph (c)(1) of this section from a donor and upon the death of the donor the stock was includible in the donor's estate as being a gift in contemplation of death. A's basis in the stock would not be determined by reference to its fair market value at the donor's death under the general rule in section 1014(a). Furthermore, the special basis rules prescribed in paragraph (c)(1) are not applicable to such property acquired by gift in contemplation of death. It will be necessary to refer to the rules in section 1015(a) to determine the basis.

(c) *Special basis rules with respect to certain property acquired from a decedent.*—(1) *Stock or securities of a foreign personal holding company.*—The basis of certain stock or securities of a foreign corporation which was a foreign personal holding company with respect to its taxable year next preceding the date of the decedent's death is governed by a special rule. If such stock was acquired from a decedent dying after August 26, 1937, by bequest or inheritance, or by the decedent's estate from the decedent, the basis of the property in the hands of the person who so acquired it (notwithstanding any other provision of section 1014) shall be the fair market value of such property at the date of the decedent's death or the adjusted basis of the stock in the hands of the decedent, whichever is lower.

(2) *Spouse's interest in community property of decedent dying after October 21, 1942, and on or before December 31, 1947.*—In the case of a decedent dying after October 21, 1942, and on or before December 31, 1947, a special rule is provided for determining the basis of such part of any property, representing the surviving spouse's one-half share of property held by the decedent and the surviving spouse under the community property laws of any State, Territory, or possession of the United States or any foreign country, as was included in determining the value of the decedent's gross estate, if a tax under chapter 3 of the Internal Revenue Code of 1939 was payable upon the decedent's net estate. In such case the basis shall be the fair market value of such part of the property at the date of death (or the optional valuation elected under section 811(j) of the Internal Revenue Code of 1939) or the adjusted basis of the property determined without regard to this subparagraph, whichever is the higher. [Reg. § 1.1014-2.]

☐ [*T.D.* 6265, 11-6-57.]

[Reg. § 1.1014-3]

§ 1.1014-3. Other basis rules.—(a) *Fair market value.*—For purposes of this section and § 1.1014-1, the value of property as of the date of the decedent's death as appraised for the purpose of the Federal estate tax or the alternate value as appraised for such purpose, whichever is applicable, shall be deemed to be its fair market value. If no estate tax return is required to be filed under section 6018 (or under section 821 or 864 of the Internal Revenue Code of 1939), the value of the property appraised as of the date of the decedent's death for the purpose of State inheritance or transmission taxes shall be deemed to be its fair market value and no alternative valuation date shall be applicable.

(b) *Property acquired from a decedent dying before March 1, 1913.*—If the decedent died before March 1, 1913, the fair market value on that date is taken in lieu of the fair market value on the date of death, but only to the same extent and for the same purposes as the fair market value on March 1, 1913, is taken under section 1053.

(c) *Reinvestments by a fiduciary.*—The basis of property acquired after the death of the decedent by a fiduciary as an investment is the cost or other basis of such property to the fiduciary, and not the fair market value of such property at the death of the decedent. For example, the executor of an estate purchases stock of X company at a price of $100 per share with the proceeds of the sale of property acquired from a decedent. At the date of the decedent's death the fair market value of such stock was $98 per share. The basis of such stock to the executor or to a legatee, assuming the stock is distributed, is $100 per share.

(d) *Reinvestments of property transferred during life.*—Where property is transferred by a decedent during life and the property is sold, exchanged, or otherwise disposed of before the decedent's death by the person who acquired the property from the decedent, the general rule stated in paragraph (a) of § 1.1014-1 shall not apply to such property. However, in such a case, the basis of any property acquired by such donee in exchange for the original property, or of any property acquired by the donee through reinvesting the proceeds of the sale of the original property, shall be the fair market value of the property thus acquired at the date of the decedent's death (or applicable alternate valuation date) if the property thus acquired is properly included in the decedent's gross estate for Federal estate tax purposes. These rules also apply to property acquired by the donee in any further exchanges or in further reinvestments. For example, on January 1, 1956, the decedent made a gift of real property to a trust for the benefit of his children, reserving to himself the power to revoke the trust at will. Prior to the decedent's death, the trustee sold the real property and invested the proceeds in stock of the Y company at $50 per share. At the time of the decedent's death, the value of such stock was $75 per share. The corpus of the trust was required to be included in the decedent's gross estate owing to his reservation of the power of revocation. The basis of the Y company stock following the decedent's death is $75 per share. Moreover, if the trustee sold the Y company stock before the decedent's death for $65 a share and reinvested the proceeds in Z company stock which increased in value to $85 per share at the time of the decedent's death, the basis of the Z company stock following the decedent's death would be $85 per share.

(e) *Alternate valuation dates.*—Section 1014(a) provides a special rule applicable in determining the basis of property described in § 1.1014-2 where—

(1) The property is includible in the gross estate of a decedent who died after October 21, 1942, and

(2) The executor elects for estate tax purposes under section 2032, or section 811(j) of the Internal Revenue Code of 1939, to value the decedent's gross estate at the alternate valuation date prescribed in such sections.

In those cases, the value applicable in determining the basis of the property is not the value at the date of the decedent's death but (with certain limitations) the value at the date one year after his death if not distributed, sold, exchanged, or otherwise disposed of in the meantime. If such property was distributed, sold, exchanged, or otherwise disposed of within one year after the date of the decedent's death by the person who acquired it from the decedent, the value applicable in determining the basis is its value as of the date of such distribution, sale, exchange, or other disposition. For illustrations of the operation of this paragraph, see the estate tax regulations under section 2032. [Reg. § 1.1014-3.]

☐ [*T.D.* 6265, 11-6-57.]

[Reg. § 1.1014-4]

§ 1.1014-4. Uniformity of basis; adjustment to basis.—(a) *In general.*—(1) The basis of property acquired from a decedent, as determined under section 1014(a) or section 1022, is uniform in the hands of every person having possession or enjoyment of the property at any time under the will or other instrument or under the laws of descent and distribution. The principle of uniform basis means that the basis of the property (to which proper adjustments must, of course, be made) will be the same, or uniform, whether the property is possessed or enjoyed by the executor or administrator, the heir, the legatee or devisee, or the trustee or beneficiary of a trust created by a will or an inter vivos trust. In determining the amount allowed or allowable to a taxpayer in computing taxable income as deductions for depreciation or depletion under section 1016(a)(2), the uniform basis of the property shall at all times be used and adjusted. The sale, exchange, or other disposition by a life tenant or remainderman of his interest in property will, for purposes of this section, have no effect upon the uniform basis of the property in the hands of those who acquired it from the decedent. Thus, gain or loss on sale of trust assets by the trustee will be determined without regard to the prior sale of any interest in the property. Moreover, any adjustment for depreciation shall be made to the uniform basis of the property without regard to such prior sale, exchange, or other disposition.

(2) Under the law governing wills and the distribution of the property of decedents, all titles to property acquired by bequest, devise, or inheritance relate back to the death of the decedent, even though the interest of the person taking the title was, at the date of death of the decedent, legal, equitable, vested, contingent, general, specific, residual, conditional, executory, or otherwise. Accordingly, there is a common acquisition date for all titles to property acquired from a decedent within the meaning of section 1014 or section 1022, and, for this reason, a common or uniform basis for all such interests. For example, if distribution of personal property left by a decedent is not made until one year after his death, the basis of such property in the hands of the legatee is its fair market value at the time when the decedent died, and not when the legatee actually received the property. If the bequest is of the residue to trustees in trust, and the executors do not distribute the residue to such trustees until five years after the death of the decedent, the basis of each piece of property left by the decedent and thus received, in the hands of the trustees, is its fair market value at the time when the decedent dies. If the bequest is to trustees in trust to pay to A during his lifetime the income of the property bequeathed, and after his death to distribute such property to the survivors of a class, and upon A's death the property is distributed to the taxpayer as the sole survivor, the basis of such property, in the hands of the taxpayer, is its fair market value at the time when the decedent died. The purpose of the Code in prescribing a general uniform basis rule for property acquired from a decedent is, on the one hand, to tax the gain, in respect of such property, to him who realizes it (without regard to the circumstance that at the death of the decedent it may have been quite uncertain whether the taxpayer would take or gain anything); and, on the other hand, not to recognize as gain any element of value resulting solely from the circumstance that the possession or enjoyment of the taxpayer was postponed. Such postponement may be, for example, until the administration of the decedent's estate is completed, until the period of the possession or enjoyment of another has terminated, or until an uncertain event has happened. It is the increase or decrease in the value of property reflected in a sale or other disposition which is recognized as the measure of gain or loss.

(3) The principles stated in subparagraphs (1) and (2) of this paragraph do not apply to property transferred by an executor, administra-

tor or trustee, to an heir, legatee, devisee or beneficiary under circumstances such that the transfer constitutes a sale or exchange. In such a case, gain or loss must be recognized by the transferor to the extent required by the revenue laws, and the transferee acquires a basis equal to the fair market value of the property on the date of the transfer. Thus, for example, if the trustee of a trust created by will transfers to a beneficiary, in satisfaction of a specific bequest of $10,000, securities which had a fair market value of $9,000 on the date of the decedent's death (the applicable valuation date) and $10,000 on the date of the transfer, the trust realizes a taxable gain of $1,000 and the basis of the securities in the hands of the beneficiary would be $10,000. As a further example, if the executor of an estate transfers to a trust property worth $200,000, which had a fair market value of $175,000 on the date of the decedent's death (the applicable valuation date), in satisfaction of the decedent's bequest in trust for the benefit of his wife of cash or securities to be selected by the executor in an amount sufficient to utilize the marital deduction to the maximum extent authorized by law (after taking into consideration any other property qualifying for the marital deduction), capital gain in the amount of $25,000 would be realized by the estate and the basis of the property in the hands of the trustees would be $200,000. If, on the other hand, the decedent bequeathed a fraction of his residuary estate to a trust for the benefit of his wife, which fraction will not change regardless of any fluctuations in value of property in the decedent's estate after his death, no gain or loss would be realized by the estate upon transfer of property to the trust, and the basis of the property in the hands of the trustee would be its fair market value on the date of the decedent's death or on the alternate valuation date.

(b) *Multiple interests.*—Where more than one person has an interest in property acquired from a decedent, the basis of such property shall be determined and adjusted without regard to the multiple interests. The basis for computing gain or loss on the sale of any one of such multiple interests shall be determined under § 1.1014-5. Thus, the deductions for depreciation and for depletion allowed or allowable, under sections 167 and 611, to a legal life tenant as if the life tenant were the absolute owner of the property, constitute an adjustment to the basis of the property not only in the hands of the life tenant, but also in the hands of the remainderman and every other person to whom the same uniform basis is applicable. Similarly, the deductions allowed or allowable under sections 167 and 611, both to the trustee and to the trust beneficiaries, constitute an adjustment to the basis of the property not only in the hands of the trustee, but also in the hands of the trust beneficiaries and every other person to whom the uniform basis is applicable. See, however, section 262. Similarly, adjustments in respect of capital expenditures or losses, tax-free distributions, or other distributions applicable in reduction of basis, or other items for which the basis is adjustable are made without regard to which one of the persons to whom the same uniform basis is applicable makes the capital expenditures or sustains the capital losses, or to whom the tax-free or other distributions are made, or to whom the deductions are allowed or allowable. See § 1.1014-6 for adjustments in respect of property acquired from a decedent prior to his death.

(c) *Records.*—The executor or other legal representative of the decedent, the fiduciary of a trust under a will, the life tenant and every other person to whom a uniform basis under this section is applicable, shall maintain records showing in detail all deductions, distributions, or other items for which adjustment to basis is required to be made by sections 1016 and 1017, and shall furnish to the district director such information with respect to those adjustments as he may require.

(d) *Effective/applicability date.*—This section applies on and after January 19, 2017. For rules before January 19, 2017, see § 1.1014-4 as contained in 26 CFR part 1 revised as of April 1, 2016. [Reg. § 1.1014-4.]

□ [*T.D.* 6265, 11-6-57. *Amended by T.D.* 9811, 1-18-2017.]

[Reg. § 1.1014-5]

§ 1.1014-5. Gain or loss.—(a) *Sale or other disposition of a life interest, remainder interest, or other interest in property acquired from a decedent.*—(1) Except as provided in paragraph (b) or (c) of this section with respect to the sale or other disposition after October 9, 1969, of a term interest in property, gain or loss from a sale or other disposition of a life interest, remainder interest, or other interest in property acquired from a decedent is determined by comparing the amount of the proceeds with the amount of that part of the adjusted uniform basis which is assignable to the interest so transferred. The adjusted uniform basis is the uniform basis of the entire property adjusted to the date of sale or other disposition of any such interest as required by sections 1016 and 1017. The uniform basis is the unadjusted basis of the entire property determined immediately after the decedent's death under the applicable sections of part II of subchapter O of chapter 1 of the Code.

(2) Except as provided in paragraph (b) of this section, the proper measure of gain or loss resulting from a sale or other disposition of an interest in property acquired from a decedent is so much of the increase or decrease in the value of the entire property as is reflected in such sale or other disposition. Hence, in ascertaining the basis of a life interest, remainder interest, or other interest which has been so transferred, the uniform basis rule contemplates that proper adjustments will be made to reflect the change in relative value of the interests on account of the passage of time.

(3) The factors set forth in the tables contained in § 20.2031-7 or, for certain prior periods, § 20.2031-7A of Part 20 of this chapter (Estate Tax Regulations) shall be used in the manner pro-

vided therein in determining the basis of the life interest, the remainder interest, or the term certain interest in the property on the date such interest is sold. The basis of the life interest, the remainder interest, or the term certain interest is computed by multiplying the uniform basis (adjusted to the time of the sale) by the appropriate factor. In the case of the sale of a life interest or a remainder interest, the factor used is the factor (adjusted where appropriate) which appears in the life interest or the remainder interest column of the table opposite the age (on the date of the sale) of the person at whose death the life interest will terminate. In the case of the sale of a term certain interest, the factor used is the factor (adjusted where appropriate) which appears in the term certain column of the table opposite the number of years remaining (on the date of sale) before the term certain interest will terminate.

(b) *Sale or other disposition of certain term interests.*—(1) *In general.*—In determining gain or loss from the sale or other disposition after October 9, 1969, of a term interest in property (as defined in § 1.1001-1(f)(2)) the adjusted basis of which is determined pursuant, or by reference, to section 1014 (relating to the basis of property acquired from a decedent), section 1015 (relating to the basis of property acquired by gift or by a transfer in trust), or section 1022 (relating to the basis of property acquired from certain decedents who died in 2010), that part of the adjusted uniform basis assignable under the rules of paragraph (a) of this section to the interest sold or otherwise disposed of shall be disregarded to the extent and in the manner provided by section 1001(e) and § 1.1001-1(f).

(2) *Effective/applicability date.*—The provisions of paragraph (b)(1) of this section relating to section 1022 are effective on and after January 19, 2017. For rules before January 19, 2017, see § 1.1014-5 as contained in 26 CFR part 1 revised as of April 1, 2016.

(c) *Sale or other disposition of a term interest in a tax-exempt trust.*—(1) *In general.*—In the case of any sale or other disposition by a taxable beneficiary of a term interest (as defined in § 1.1001-1(f)(2)) in a tax-exempt trust (as defined in paragraph (c)(2) of this section) to which section 1001(e)(3) applies, the taxable beneficiary's share of adjusted uniform basis, determined as of (and immediately before) the sale or disposition of that interest, is—

(i) That part of the adjusted uniform basis assignable to the term interest of the taxable beneficiary under the rules of paragraph (a) of this section reduced, but not below zero, by

(ii) An amount determined by applying the same actuarial share applied in paragraph (c)(1)(i) of this section to the sum of—

(A) The trust's undistributed net ordinary income within the meaning of section 664(b)(1) and § 1.664-1(d)(1)(ii)(*a*)(*1*) for the current and prior taxable years of the trust, if any; and

(B) The trust's undistributed net capital gains within the meaning of section 664(b)(2) and § 1.664-1(d)(1)(ii)(*a*)(*1*) for the current and prior taxable years of the trust, if any.

(2) *Tax-exempt trust defined.*—For purposes of this section, the term *tax-exempt trust* means a charitable remainder annuity trust or a charitable remainder unitrust as defined in section 664.

(3) *Taxable beneficiary defined.*—For purposes of this section, the term *taxable beneficiary* means any person other than an organization described in section 170(c) or exempt from taxation under section 501(a).

(4) *Effective/applicability date.*—This paragraph (c) and paragraph (d) *Example 7* and *Example 8* of this section apply to sales and other dispositions of interests in tax-exempt trusts occurring on or after January 16, 2014, except for sales or dispositions occurring pursuant to a binding commitment entered into before January 16, 2014.

(d) *Illustrations.*—The application of this section may be illustrated by the following examples, in which references are made to the actuarial tables contained in Part 20 of this chapter (Estate Tax Regulations):

Example (1). Securities worth $500,000 at the date of decedent's death on January 1, 1971, are bequeathed to his wife, W, for life, with remainder over to his son, S. W is 48 years of age when the life interest is acquired. The estate does not elect the alternate valuation allowed by section 2032. By reference to § 20.2031-7A(c), the life estate factor for age 48, female, is found to be 0.77488 and the remainder factor for such age is found to be 0.22512. Therefore, the present value of the portion of the uniform basis assigned to W's life interest is $387,440 ($500,000 × 0.77488), and the present value of the portion of the uniform basis assigned to S's remainder interest is $112,560 ($500,000 × 0.22512). W sells her life interest to her nephew, A, on February 1, 1971, for $370,000, at which time W is still 48 years of age. Pursuant to section 1001(e), W realizes no loss; her gain is $370,000, the amount realized from the sale. A has a basis of $370,000 which he can recover by amortization deductions over W's life expectancy.

Example (2). The facts are the same as in example (1) except that W retains the life interest for 12 years, until she is 60 years of age, and then sells it to A on February 1, 1983, when the fair market value of the securities has increased to $650,000. By reference to § 20.2031-7A(c), the life estate factor for age 60, female, is found to be 0.63226 and the remainder factor for such age is found to be 0.36774. Therefore, the present value on February 1, 1983, of the portion of the uniform basis assigned to W's life interest is $316,130 ($500,000 × 0.63226) and the present value on that date of the portion of the uniform basis assigned to S's remainder interest is $183,870 ($500,000 × 0.36774). W sells her life interest for $410,969, that being the commuted value of her remaining life interest in the securities as appreciated ($650,000 × 0.63226). Pursuant to section 1001(e), W's gain is $410,969, the amount realized. A has a basis of $410,969 which he can recover by amortization deductions over W's life expectancy.

Example (3). Unimproved land having a fair market value of $18,800 at the date of the decedent's death on January 1, 1970, is devised to A, a male, for life, with remainder over to B, a female. The estate does not elect the alternate valuation allowed by section 2032. On January 1, 1971, A sells his life interest to S for $12,500. S is not related to A or B. At the time of the sale, A is 39 years of age. By reference to § 20.2031-7A(c), the life estate factor for age 39, male, is found to be 0.79854. Therefore, the present value of the portion of the uniform basis assigned to A's life interest is $15,012.55 ($18,800 × 0.79854). This portion is disregarded under section 1001(e). A realized no loss; his gain is $12,500, the amount realized. S has a basis of $12,500 which he can recover by amortization deductions over A's life expectancy.

Example (4). The facts are the same as in example (3) except that on January 1, 1971, A and B jointly sell the entire property to S for $25,000 and divide the proceeds equally between them. A and B are not related, and there is no element of gift or compensation in the transaction. By reference to § 20.2031-7A(c), the remainder factor for age 39, male, is found to be 0.20146. Therefore, the present value of the uniform basis assigned to B's remainder interest is $3,787.45 ($18,800 × 0.20146). On the sale A realizes a loss of $2,512.55 ($15,012.55 less $12,500), the portion of the uniform basis assigned to his life interest not being disregarded by reason of section 1001(e)(3). B's gain on the sale is $8,712.55 ($12,500 less $3,787.45). S has a basis in the entire property of $25,000, no part of which, however, can be recovered by amortization deductions over A's life expectancy.

Example (5). (a) Nondepreciable property having a fair market value of $54,000 at the date of decedent's death on January 1, 1971, is devised to her husband, H, for life and, after his death, to her daughter, D, for life, with remainder over to her grandson, G. The estate does not elect the alternate valuation allowed by section 2032. On January 1, 1973, H sells his life interest to D for $32,000. At the date of the sale, H is 62 years of age, and D is 45 years of age. By reference to § 20.2031-7A(c), the life estate factor for age 62, male, is found to be 0.52321. Therefore, the present value on January 1, 1973, of the portion of the adjusted uniform basis assigned to H's life interest is $28,253 ($54,000 × 0.52321). Pursuant to section 1001(e), H realizes no loss; his gain is $32,000, the amount realized from the sale. D has a basis of $32,000 which she can recover by amortization deductions over H's life expectancy.

(b) On January 1, 1976, D sells both life estates to G for $40,000. During each of the years 1973 through 1975, D is allowed a deduction for the amortization of H's life interest. At the date of the sale H is 65 years of age, and D is 48 years of age. For purposes of determining gain or loss on the sale by D, the portion of the adjusted uniform basis assigned to H's life interest and the portion assigned to D's life interest are not taken into account under section 1001(e). However, pursuant to § 1.1001-1(f)(1), D's cost basis in H's life interest, minus deductions for the amortization of such interest, is taken into account. On the sale, D realizes gain of $40,000 minus an amount which is equal to the $32,000 cost basis (for H's life estate) reduced by amortization deductions. G is entitled to amortize over H's life expectancy that part of the $40,000 cost which is attributable to H's life interest. That part of the $40,000 cost which is attributable to D's life interest is not amortizable by G until H dies.

Example (6). Securities worth $1,000,000 at the date of decedent's death on January 1, 1971, are bequeathed to his wife, W, for life, with remainder over to his son, S. W is 48 years of age when the life interest is acquired. The estate does not elect the alternate valuation allowed by section 2032. By reference to § 20.2031-7A(c), the life estate factor for age 48, female, is found to be 0.77488, and the remainder factor for such age is found to be 0.22512. Therefore, the present value of the portion of the uniform basis assigned to W's life interest is $774,880 ($1,000,000 × 0.77488), and the present value of the portion of the uniform basis assigned to S's remainder interest is $225,120 ($1,000,000 × 0.22512). On February 1, 1971, W transfers her life interest to Corporation X in exchange for all of the stock of X pursuant to a transaction in which no gain or loss is recognized by reason of section 351. On February 1, 1972, W sells all of her stock in X to S for $800,000. Pursuant to section 1001(e) and § 1.1001-1(f)(2), W realizes no loss; her gain is $800,000, the amount realized from the sale. On February 1, 1972, X sells to N for $900,000 the life interest transferred to it by W. Pursuant to section 1001(e) and § 1.1001-1(f)(1), X realizes no loss; its gain is $900,000, the amount realized from the sale. N has a basis of $900,000 which he can recover by amortization deductions over W's life expectancy.

Example 7. (a) Grantor creates a charitable remainder unitrust (CRUT) on Date 1 in which Grantor retains a unitrust interest and irrevocably transfers the remainder interest to Charity. Grantor is an individual taxpayer subject to income tax. CRUT meets the requirements of section 664 and is exempt from income tax.

(b) Grantor's basis in the shares of X stock used to fund CRUT is $10x. On Date 2, CRUT sells the X stock for $100x. The $90x of gain is exempt from income tax under section 664(c)(1). On Date 3, CRUT uses the $100x proceeds from its sale of the X stock to purchase Y stock. On Date 4, CRUT sells the Y stock for $110x. The $10x of gain on the sale of the Y stock is exempt from income tax under section 664(c)(1). On Date 5, CRUT uses the $110x proceeds from its sale of Y stock to buy Z stock. On Date 5, CRUT's basis in its assets is $110x and CRUT's total undistributed net capital gains are $100x.

(c) Later, when the fair market value of CRUT's assets is $150x and CRUT has no undistributed net ordinary income, Grantor and Charity sell all of their interests in CRUT to a third person. Grantor receives $100x for the retained unitrust interest, and Charity receives $50x for its interest. Because the entire interest in CRUT is transferred to the third person, section 1001(e)(3) prevents section 1001(e)(1) from applying to the transaction. Therefore, Grantor's gain on the sale of the retained unitrust interest in CRUT is determined under section 1001(a), which provides that Grantor's gain on the sale of that interest is the excess of the amount realized, $100x, over Grantor's adjusted basis in the interest.

(d) Grantor's adjusted basis in the unitrust interest in CRUT is that portion of CRUT's adjusted uniform basis that is assignable to Grantor's interest under § 1.1014-5, which is Grantor's actuarial share of the adjusted uniform basis. In this case, CRUT's adjusted uniform basis in its sole asset, the Z stock, is $110x. However, paragraph (c) of this section applies to the transaction. Therefore, Grantor's actuarial share of CRUT's adjusted uniform basis (determined by applying the factors set forth in the tables contained in § 20.2031-7 of this chapter) is reduced by an amount determined by applying the same factors to the sum of CRUT's $0 of undistributed net ordinary income and its $100x of undistributed net capital gains.

(e) In determining Charity's share of the adjusted uniform basis, Charity applies the factors set forth in the tables contained in § 20.2031-7 of this chapter to the full $110x of basis.

Example 8. (a) Grantor creates a charitable remainder annuity trust (CRAT) on Date 1 in which Grantor retains an annuity interest and irrevocably transfers the remainder interest to Charity. Grantor is an individual taxpayer subject to income tax. CRAT meets the requirements of section 664 and is exempt from income tax.

(b) Grantor funds CRAT with shares of X stock having a basis of $50x. On Date 2, CRAT sells the X stock for $150x. The $100x of gain is exempt from income tax under section 664(c)(1). On Date 3, CRAT distributes $10x to Grantor, and uses the remaining $140x of net proceeds from its sale of the X stock to purchase Y stock. Grantor treats the $10x distribution as capital gain, so that CRAT's remaining undistributed net capital gains amount described in section 664(b)(2) and § 1.664-1(d) is $90x.

(c) On Date 4, when the fair market value of CRAT's assets, which consist entirely of the Y stock, is still $140x, Grantor and Charity sell all of their interests in CRAT to a third person. Grantor receives $126x for the retained annuity interest, and Charity receives $14x for its remainder interest. Because the entire interest in CRAT is transferred to the third person, section 1001(e)(3) prevents section 1001(e)(1) from applying to the transaction. Therefore, Grantor's gain on the sale of the retained annuity interest in CRAT is determined under section 1001(a), which provides that Grantor's gain on the sale of that interest is the excess of the amount realized, $126x, over Grantor's adjusted basis in that interest.

(d) Grantor's adjusted basis in the annuity interest in CRAT is that portion of CRAT's adjusted uniform basis that is assignable to Grantor's interest under § 1.1014-5, which is Grantor's actuarial share of the adjusted uniform basis. In this case, CRAT's adjusted uniform basis in its sole asset, the Y stock, is $140x. However, paragraph (c) of this section applies to the transaction. Therefore, Grantor's actuarial share of CRAT's adjusted uniform basis (determined by applying the factors set forth in the tables contained in § 20.2031-7 of this chapter) is reduced by an amount determined by applying the same factors to the sum of CRAT's $0 of undistributed net ordinary income and its $90x of undistributed net capital gains.

(e) In determining Charity's share of the adjusted uniform basis, Charity applies the factors set forth in the tables contained in § 20.2031-7 of this chapter to determine its actuarial share of the full $140x of basis. [Reg. § 1.1014-5.]

□ [*T.D.* 6265, 11-6-57. *Amended by T.D.* 7142, 9-23-71, *T.D.* 8540, 6-9-94, *T.D.* 9729, 8-11-15 *and T.D.* 9811, 1-18-2017.]

[Reg. § 1.1014-6]

§ 1.1014-6. Special rule for adjustments to basis where property is acquired from a decedent prior to his death.—(a) *In general.*—(1) The basis of property described in section 1014(b)(9) which is acquired from a decedent prior to his death shall be adjusted for depreciation, obsolescence, amortization, and depletion allowed the taxpayer on such property for the period prior to the decedent's death. Thus, in general, the adjusted basis of such property will be its fair market value at the decedent's death, or the applicable alternate valuation date, less the amount allowed (determined with regard to section 1016(a)(2)(B)) to the taxpayer as deductions for exhaustion, wear and tear, obsolescence, amortization and depletion for the period held by the taxpayer prior to the decedent's death. The deduction allowed for a taxable year in which the decedent dies shall be an amount properly allocable to that part of the year prior to his death. For a discussion of the basis adjustment required by section 1014(b)(9) where property is held in trust, see paragraph (c) of this section.

(2) Where property coming within the purview of subparagraph (1) of this paragraph was held by the decedent and his surviving spouse as tenants by the entirety or as joint tenants with right of survivorship, and joint income tax returns were filed by the decedent and the surviving spouse in which the deductions referred to in subparagraph (1) were taken, there shall be allocated to the surviving spouse's interest in the property that proportion of the deductions allowed for each period for which the joint returns were filed which her income from the property bears to the total income from the property. Each spouse's income from the property shall be determined in accordance with local law.

(3) The application of this paragraph may be illustrated by the following examples:

Example (1). The taxpayer acquired income-producing property by gift on January 1, 1954.

The property had a fair market value of $50,000 on the date of the donor's death, January 1, 1956, and was included in his gross estate at that amount for estate tax purposes as a transfer in contemplation of death. Depreciation in the amount of $750 per year was allowable for each of the taxable years 1954 and 1955. However, the taxpayer claimed depreciation in the amount of $500 for each of these years (resulting in a reduction in his taxes) and his income tax returns were accepted as filed. The adjusted basis of the property as of the date of the decedent's death is $49,000 ($50,000, the fair market value at the decedent's death, less $1,000, the total of the amounts actually allowed as deductions).

Example (2). On July 1, 1952, H purchased for $30,000 income-producing property which he conveyed to himself and W, his wife, as tenants by the entirety. Under local law each spouse was entitled to one-half of the income therefrom. H died on January 1, 1955, at which time the fair market value of the property was $40,000. The entire value of the property was included in H's gross estate. H and W filed joint income tax returns for the years 1952, 1953, and 1954. The total depreciation allowance for the year 1952 was $500 and for each of the other years 1953 and 1954 was $1,000. One-half of the $2,500 depreciation will be allocated to W. The adjusted basis of the property in W's hands [as] of January 1, 1955, was $38,750 ($40,000, value on the date of H's death, less $1,250, depreciation allocated to W for periods before H's death). However, if, under local law, all of the income from the property was allocable to H, no adjustment under this paragraph would be required and W's basis for the property as of the date of H's death would be $40,000.

(b) *Multiple interests in property described in section 1014(b)(9) and acquired from a decedent prior to his death.*—(1) Where more than one person has an interest in property described in section 1014(b)(9) which was acquired from a decedent before his death, the basis of such property and of each of the several interests therein shall, in general, be determined and adjusted in accordance with the principles contained in §§1.1014-4 and 1.1014-5, relating to the uniformity of basis rule. Application of these principles to the determination of basis under section 1014(b)(9) is shown in the remaining subparagraphs of this paragraph in connection with certain commonly encountered situations involving multiple interests in property acquired from a decedent before his death.

(2) Where property is acquired from a decedent before his death, and the entire property is subsequently included in the decedent's gross estate for estate tax purposes, the uniform basis of the property, as well as the basis of each of the several interests in the property, shall be determined by taking into account the basis adjustments required by section 1014(a) owing to such inclusion of the entire property in the decedent's gross estate. For example, suppose that the decedent transfers property in trust, with a life estate to A, and the remainder to B or his estate. The transferred property consists of 100 shares of the common stock of X Corporation, with a basis of $10,000 at the time of the transfer. At the time of the decedent's death the value of the stock is $20,000. The transfer is held to have been made in contemplation of death and the entire value of the trust is included in the decedent's gross estate. Under section 1014(a), the uniform basis of the property in the hands of the trustee, the life tenant, and the remainderman, is $20,000. If immediately prior to the decedent's death, A's share of the uniform basis of $10,000 was $6,000, and B's share was $4,000, then, immediately after the decedent's death, A's share of the uniform basis of $20,000 is $12,000, and B's share is $8,000.

(3)(i) In cases where, due to the operation of the estate tax, only a portion of property acquired from a decedent before his death is included in the decedent's gross estate, as in cases where the decedent retained a reversion to take effect upon the expiration of a life estate in another, the uniform basis of the entire property shall be determined by taking into account any basis adjustments required by section 1014(a) owing to such inclusion of a portion of the property in the decedent's gross estate. In such cases the uniform basis is the adjusted basis of the entire property immediately prior to the decedent's death increased (or decreased) by an amount which bears the same relation to the total appreciation (or diminution) in value of the entire property (over the adjusted basis of the entire property immediately prior to the decedent's death) as the value of the property included in the decedent's gross estate bears to the value of the entire property. For example, assume that the decedent creates a trust to pay the income to A for life, remainder to B or his estate. The trust instrument further provides that if the decedent should survive A, the income shall be paid to the decedent for life. Assume that the decedent predeceases A, so that, due to the operation of the estate tax, only the present value of the remainder interest is included in the decedent's gross estate. The trust consists of 100 shares of the common stock of X Corporation with an adjusted basis immediately prior to the decedent's death of $10,000 (as determined under section 1015). At the time of the decedent's death the value of the stock is $20,000, and the value of the remainder interest in the hands of B is $8,000. The uniform basis of the entire property following the decedent's death is $14,000, computed as follows:

Uniform basis prior to decedent's death	$10,000
plus	
Increase in uniform basis (determined by the following formula)	4,000

$$\frac{\text{Increase in uniform basis (to be determined)}}{\$10{,}000\ \text{(total appreciation)}} = \frac{\$8{,}000\ \text{(value of property included in gross estate)}}{\$20{,}000\ \text{(value of entire property)}}$$

Uniform basis under section 1014(a) $14,000

(ii) In cases of the type described in subdivision (i) of this subparagraph, the basis of any interest which is included in the decedent's gross estate may be ascertained by adding to (or subtracting from) the basis of such interest determined immediately prior to the decedent's death the increase (or decrease) in the uniform basis of the property attributable to the inclusion of the interest in the decedent's gross estate. Where the interest is sold or otherwise disposed of at any time after the decedent's death, proper adjustment must be made in order to reflect the change in value of the interest on account of the passage of time, as provided in § 1.1014-5. For an illustration of the operation of this subdivision, see step 6 of the example in § 1.1014-7.

(iii) In cases of the type described in subdivision (i) of this subparagraph (cases where, due to the operation of the estate tax, only a portion of the property is included in the decedent's gross estate), the basis for computing the depreciation, amortization, or depletion allowance shall be the uniform basis of the property determined under section 1014(a). However, the manner of taking into account such allowance computed with respect to such uniform basis is subject to the following limitations:

(a) In cases where the value of the life interest is not included in the decedent's gross estate, the amount of such allowance to the life tenant under section 167(h) (or section 611(b)) shall not exceed (or be less than) the amount which would have been allowable to the life tenant if no portion of the basis of the property was determined under section 1014(a). Proper adjustment shall be made for the amount allowable to the life tenant, as required by section 1016. Thus, an appropriate adjustment shall be made to the uniform basis of the property in the hands of the trustee, to the basis of the life interest in the hands of the life tenant, and to the basis of the remainder in the hands of the remainderman.

(b) Any remaining allowance (that is, the increase in the amount of depreciation, amortization, or depletion allowable resulting from any increase in the uniform basis of the property under section 1014(a)) shall not be allowed to the life tenant. The remaining allowance shall, instead, be allowed to the trustee to the extent that the trustee both (*1*) is required or permitted, by the governing trust instrument (or under local law), to maintain a reserve for depreciation, amortization, or depletion, and (*2*) actually maintains such a reserve. If, in accordance with the preceding sentence, the trustee does maintain such a reserve, the remaining allowance shall be taken into account, under section 1016, in adjusting the uniform basis of the property in the hands of the trustee and in adjusting the basis of the remainder interest in the hands of the remainderman, but shall not be taken into account, under section 1016, in determining the basis of the life interest in the hands of the life tenant. For an example of the operation of this subdivision, see paragraph (b) of § 1.1014-7.

(4) In cases where the basis of any interest in property is not determined under section 1014(a), as where such interest (i) is not included in the decedent's gross estate, or (ii) is sold, exchanged or otherwise disposed of before the decedent's death, the basis of such interest shall be determined under other applicable provisions of the Code. To illustrate, in the example shown in subparagraph (3)(i) of this paragraph the basis of the life estate in the hands of A shall be determined under section 1015, relating to the basis of property acquired by gift. If, on the other hand, A had sold his life interest prior to the decedent's death, the basis of the life estate in the hands of A's transferee would be determined under section 1012.

(c) *Adjustments for deductions allowed prior to the decedent's death.*—(1) As stated in paragraph (a) of this section, section 1014(b)(9) requires a reduction in the uniform basis of property acquired from a decedent before his death for certain deductions allowed in respect of such property during the decedent's lifetime. In general, the amount of the reduction in basis required by section 1014(b)(9) shall be the aggregate of the deductions allowed in respect of the property, but shall not include deductions allowed in respect of the property to the decedent himself. In cases where, owing to the operation of the estate tax, only a part of the value of the entire property is included in the decedent's gross estate, the amount of the reduction required by section 1014(b)(9) shall be an amount which bears the same relation to the total of all deductions (described in paragraph (a) of this section) allowed in respect of the property as the value of the property included in the decedent's gross estate bears to the value of the entire property.

(2) The application of this paragraph may be illustrated by the following examples:

Example (1). The decedent creates a trust to pay the income to A for life, remainder to B or his estate. The property transferred in trust consists of an apartment building with a basis of $50,000 at the time of the transfer. The decedent dies 2 years after the transfer is made and the gift is held to have been made in contemplation of death. Depreciation on the property was allowed in the amount of $1,000 annually. At the time of the decedent's death the value of the property is $58,000. The uniform basis of the property in the hands of the trustee, the life tenant, and the remainderman, immediately after the decedent's death is $56,000 ($58,000, fair market value of the property immediately after the decedent's death, reduced by $2,000, deductions for depreciation allowed prior to the decedent's death).

Example (2). The decedent creates a trust to pay the income to A for life, remainder to B or his estate. The trust instrument provides that if the decedent should survive A, the income shall be paid to the decedent for life. The decedent predeceases A and the present value of the remainder interest is included in the decedent's gross estate for estate tax purposes. The property transferred consists of an apartment building with a basis of $110,000 at the time of the transfer. Following the creation of the trust and during the balance of the decedent's life, deductions for depreciation were allowed on the property in the amount of $10,000. At the time of decedent's death the value of the entire property is $150,000, and the value of the remainder interest is $100,000. Accordingly, the uniform basis of the property in the hands of the trustee, the life tenant, and the remainderman, as adjusted under section 1014(b)(9), is $126,666, computed as follows:

Uniform basis prior to decedent's death	$100,000
plus	
Increase in uniform basis—before reduction (determined by the following formula)	33,333

$$\frac{\text{Increase in uniform basis (to be determined)}}{\text{\$50,000 (total appreciation of property since time of transfer)}} = \frac{\text{\$100,000 (value of property included in gross estate)}}{\text{\$150,000 (value of entire property)}}$$

	$133,333
less	
Deductions allowed prior to decedent's death—taken into account under section 1014(b)(9) (determined by the following formula)	6,667

$$\frac{\text{Prior deductions taken into account (to be determined)}}{\text{\$10,000 (total deductions allowed prior to decedent's death)}} = \frac{\text{\$100,000 (value of property included in gross estate)}}{\text{\$150,000 (value of entire property)}}$$

Uniform basis under section 1014	$126,666

[Reg. § 1.1014-6.]

☐ [*T.D.* 6265, 11-6-57. *Amended by T.D.* 6712, 3-23-64 *and T.D.* 7142, 9-23-71.]

[Reg. § 1.1014-7]

§ 1.1014-7. Example applying rules of §§ 1.1014-4 through 1.1014-6 to case involving multiple interests.—(a) On January 1, 1950, the decedent creates a trust to pay the income to A for life, remainder to B or his estate. The trust instrument provides that if the decedent should survive A, the income shall be paid to the decedent for life. The decedent, who died on January 1, 1955, predeceases A, so that, due to the operation of the estate tax, only the present value of the remainder interest is included in the decedent's gross estate. The trust consists of an apartment building with a basis of $30,000 at the time of transfer. Under the trust instrument the trustee is required to maintain a reserve for depreciation. During the decedent's lifetime depreciation is allowed in the amount of $800 annually. At the time of the decedent's death the value of the apartment building is $45,000. A, the life tenant, is 43 years of age at the time of the decedent's death. Immediately after the decedent's death, the uniform basis of the entire property under section 1014(a) is $32,027; A's basis for the life interest is $15,553; and B's basis for the remainder interest is $16,474, computed as follows:

Step 1. Uniform basis (adjusted) immediately prior to decedent's death:	
Basis at time of transfer	$30,000
less	
Depreciation allowed under section 1016 before decedent's death ($800 × 5)	4,000
	$26,000
Step 2. Value of property included in decedent's gross estate:	
0.40180 (remainder factor, age 43) × $45,000 (value of entire property)	$18,081
Step 3. Uniform basis of property under section 1014(a), before reduction required by section 1014(b)(9):	
Uniform basis (adjusted) prior to decedent's death	26,000
Increase in uniform basis (determined by the following formula) . .	7,634

See p. 15 for regulations not amended to reflect law changes

Increase in uniform basis (to be determined)	=	$18,081 (value of property included in gross estate)
$19,000 (total appreciation, $45,000—$26,000)		$45,000 (value of entire propery)

$33,634

Step 4. Uniform basis reduced as required by section 1014(b)(9) for deductions allowed prior to death:

Uniform basis before reduction		33,634
less		
Deductions allowed prior to decedent's death—taken into account under section 1014(b)(9) (determined by the following formula)		1,607

Prior deductions taken into account (to be determined)	=	$18,081 (value of property included in gross estate)
$4,000 (total deductions allowed prior to decedent's death)		$45,000 (value of entire property)

$32,027

Step 5. A's basis for the life interest at the time of the decedent's death, determined under section 1015:

0.59820 (life factor, age 43) × $26,000	15,553	

Step 6. B's basis for the remainder interest, determined under section 1014(a):

Basis prior to the decedent's death:		
0.40180 (remainder factor, age 43) × $26,000		10,447
plus		
Increase in uniform basis owing to decedent's death:		
Increase in uniform basis	$7,634	
Reduction required by section 1014(b)(9)	$1,607	$6,027
		$16,474

(b) Assume the same facts as in (a) of this section. Assume further, that following the decedent's death depreciation is allowed in the amount of $1,000 annually. As of January 1, 1964, when A's age is 52, the adjusted uniform basis of the entire property is $23,027; A's basis for the life interest is $9,323; and B's basis for the remainder interest is $13,704, computed as follows:

Step 7. Uniform basis (adjusted) as of January 1, 1964:

Uniform basis determined under section 1014(a), reduced as required by section 1014(b)(9)	$32,027
Depreciation allowed since decedent's death ($1,000 × 9)	9,000
	$23,027

Step 8. Allocable share of adjustment for depreciation allowable in the nine years since the decedent's death:

A's interest	
0.49587 (life factor, age 52) × $7,200 ($800, depreciation attributable to uniform basis before increase under section 1014(a), × 9)	3,570
B's interest	
0.50413 (remainder factor, age 52) × $7,200 ($800, depreciation attributable to uniform basis before increase under section 1014(a), × 9)	3,630
plus	
$200 (annual depreciation attributable to increase in uniform basis under section 1014(a)) × 9	1,800
	$5,430

Step 9. Tentative bases of A's and B's interests as of January 1, 1964 (before adjustment for depreciation).

A's interest	
0.49587 (life factor, age 52) × $26,000 (adjusted uniform basis immediately before decedent's death)	12,893
B's interest	

0.50413 (remainder factor, age 52) × $26,000 (adjusted uniform basis immediately before decedent's death)	13,107
plus	
Increase in uniform basis owing to inclusion of remainder in decedent's gross estate	6,027
	$19,134

Step 10. Bases of A's and B's interests as of January 1, 1964

A	
Tentative basis (Step 9)	$12,893
less	
Allocable depreciation (Step 8)	3,570
	$9,323
B	
Tentative basis (Step 9)	$19,134
less	
Allocable depreciation (Step 8)	5,430
	$13,704

[Reg. § 1.1014-7.]

☐ [*T.D.* 6265, 11-6-57.]

[Reg. § 1.1014-8]

§ 1.1014-8. Bequest, devise, or inheritance of a remainder interest.—(a)(1) Where property is transferred for life, with remainder in fee, and the remainderman dies before the life tenant, no adjustment is made to the uniform basis of the property on the death of the remainderman (see paragraph (a) of § 1.1014-4). However, the basis of the remainderman's heir, legatee, or devisee for the remainder interest is determined by adding to (or subtracting from) the part of the adjusted uniform basis assigned to the remainder interest (determined in accordance with the principles set forth in § § 1.1014-4 through 1.1014-6) the difference between—

(i) The value of the remainder interest included in the remainderman's estate, and

(ii) The basis of the remainder interest immediately prior to the remainderman's death.

(2) The basis of any property distributed to the heir, legatee, or devisee upon termination of a trust (or legal life estate) or at any other time (unless included in the gross income of the legatee or devisee) shall be determined by adding to (or subtracting from) the adjusted uniform basis of the property thus distributed the difference between—

(i) The value of the remainder interest in the property included in the remainderman's estate, and

(ii) The basis of the remainder interest in the property immediately prior to the remainderman's death.

(b) The provisions of paragraph (a) of this section are illustrated by the following examples:

Example (1). Assume that, under the will of a decedent, property consisting of common stock with a value of $1,000 at the time of the decedent's death is transferred in trust, to pay the income to A for life, remainder to B or to B's estate. B predeceases A and bequeaths the remainder interest to C. Assume that B dies on January 1, 1956, and that the value of the stock originally transferred is $1,600 at B's death. A's age at that time is 37. The value of the remainder interest included in B's estate is $547 (0.34185, remainder factor age 37, × $1,600), and hence $547 is C's basis for the remainder interest immediately after B's death. Assume that C sells the remainder interest on January 1, 1961, when A's age is 42. C's basis for the remainder interest at the time of such sale is $596, computed as follows:

Basis of remainder interest computed with respect to uniform basis of entire property (0.39131, remainder factor age 42, × $1,000, uniform basis of entire property)		$391
plus		
Value of remainder interest included in B's estate	$547	
less		
Basis of remainder interest immediately prior to B's death (0.34185, remainder factor of age 37, × $1,000)	342	205
Basis of C's remainder interest at the time of sale		$596

Example (2). Assume the same facts as in example (1), except that C does not sell the remainder interest. Upon A's death terminating the trust, C's basis for the stock distributed to him is computed as follows:

Uniform basis of the property, adjusted to date of termination of the trust		$1,000
plus		
Value of remainder interest in the property at the time of B's death	$547	
less		
B's share of uniform basis of the property at the time of his death	342	205
C's basis for the stock distributed to him upon the termination of the trust		$1,205

Example (3). Assume the same facts as in example (2), except that the property transferred is depreciable. Assume further that $100 of depreciation was allowed prior to B's death and that $50 of depreciation is allowed between the time of B's death and the termination of the trust. Upon A's death terminating the trust, C's basis for the property distributed to him is computed as follows:

Uniform basis of the property, adjusted to date of termination of the trust:		
Uniform basis immediately after decedent's death	$1,000	
Depreciation allowed following decedent's death	150	$850
plus		
Value of remainder interest in the property at the time of B's death .	$547	
less		
B's share of uniform basis of the property at the time of his death (0.34185 × $900, uniform basis at B's death)	$308	$239
C's basis for the property distributed to him upon the termination of the trust		$1,089

(c) The rules stated in paragraph (a) of this section do not apply where the basis of the remainder interest in the hands of the remainderman's transferee is determined by reference to its cost to such transferee. See, also, paragraph (a) of § 1.1014-4. Thus, if, in example *(1)* of paragraph (b) of this section, B sold his remainder interest to C for $547 in cash, C's basis for the stock distributed to him upon the death of A terminating the trust is $547. [Reg. § 1.1014-8.]

☐ [*T.D.* 6265, 11-6-57.]

[Reg. § 1.1014-9]

§ 1.1014-9. Special rule with respect to DISC stock.—(a) *In general.*—If property consisting of stock of a DISC or former DISC (as defined in section 992(a)(1) or (3) as the case may be) is considered to have been acquired from a decedent (within the meaning of paragraph (a) or (b) of § 1.1014-2), the uniform basis of such stock under section 1014, as determined pursuant to §§ 1.1014-1 through 1.1014-8 shall be reduced as provided in this section. Such uniform basis shall be reduced by the amount (hereinafter referred to in this section as the amount of reduction), if any, which the decedent would have included in his gross income under section 995(c) as a dividend if the decedent had lived and sold such stock at its fair market value on the estate tax valuation date. If the alternate valuation date for Federal estate tax purposes is elected under section 2032, in computing the gain which the decedent would have had if he had lived and sold the stock on the alternate valuation date, the decedent's basis shall be determined with reduction for any distributions with respect to the stock which may have been made, after the date of the decedent's death and on or before the alternate valuation date, from the DISC's previously taxed income (as defined in section 996(f)(2)). For this purpose, the last sentence of section 996(e)(2) (relating to reductions of basis of DISC stock) shall not apply. For purposes of this section, if the corporation is not a DISC or former DISC at the date of the decedent's death but is a DISC for a taxable year which begins after such date and on or before the alternate valuation date, the corporation will be considered to be a DISC or former DISC only if the alternate valuation date is elected. The provisions of this paragraph apply with respect to stock of a DISC or former DISC which is included in the gross estate of the decedent, including but not limited to property which—

(1) Is acquired from the decedent before his death, and the entire property is subsequently included in the decedent's gross estate for estate tax purposes, or

(2) Is acquired property described in paragraph (d) of § 1.1014-3.

(b) *Portion of property acquired from decedent before his death included in decedent's gross estate.*—(1) *In general.*—In cases where, due to the operation of the estate tax, only a portion of property which consists of stock of a DISC or former DISC and which is acquired from a decedent before his death is included in the decedent's gross estate, the uniform basis of such stock under section 1014, as determined pursuant to § 1.1014-1 through § 1.1014-8, shall be reduced by an amount which bears the same ratio to the amount of reduction which would have been determined under paragraph (a) of this section if the entire property consisting of such stock were included in the decedent's gross estate as the value of such property included in the decedent's gross estate bears to the value of the entire property.

(2) *Example.*—The provisions of this paragraph may be illustrated by the following example:

Example. The decedent creates a trust during his lifetime to pay the income to A for life, remainder to B or his estate. The trust instrument further provides that if the decedent should survive A, the income shall be paid to the decedent for life. The decedent predeceases A, so that, due to the operation of the estate tax, only the present value of the remainder interest is included in the decedent's gross estate. The trust consists of 100 shares of the stock of X Corporation (which is a DISC at the time the shares are transferred to the trust and at the time of the decedent's death) with an adjusted basis immediately prior to the decedent's death of $10,000 (as determined under section 1015). At the time of the decedent's death the value of the stock is $20,000, and the value of the remainder interest in the hands of B is $8,000. Applying the principles of paragraph (b)(3)(i) of §1.1014-6, the uniform basis of the entire property following the decedent's death, prior to reduction pursuant to this paragraph, is $14,000. The amount of reduction which would have been determined under paragraph (a) of this section if the entire property consisting of such stock of X Corporation were included in the decedent's gross estate is $5,000. The uniform basis of the entire property following the decedent's death, as reduced pursuant to this paragraph, is $12,000, computed as follows:

Uniform basis under section 1014(a), prior to reduction pursuant to this paragraph	$14,000
Less decrease in uniform basis (determined by the following formula)	2,000

$$\frac{\text{Reduction in uniform basis (to be determined)}}{\text{\$5,000 (amount of reduction if paragraph (a) applied)}} = \frac{\text{\$8,000 (value of property included in gross estate)}}{\text{\$20,000 (value of entire property)}}$$

Uniform basis under section 1014(a) reduced pursuant to this paragraph	$12,000

(c) *Estate tax valuation date.*—For purposes of section 1014(d) and this section, the estate tax valuation date is the date of the decedent's death or, in the case of an election under section 2032, the applicable valuation date prescribed by that section.

(d) *Examples.*—The provisions of this section may be illustrated by the following examples:

Example (1). At the date of A's death, his DISC stock has a fair market value of $100. The estate does not elect the alternate valuation allowed by section 2032, and A's basis in such stock is $60 at the date of his death. The person who acquires such stock from the decedent will take as a basis for such stock its fair market value at A's death ($100), reduced by the amount which would have been included in A's gross income under section 995(c) as a dividend if A had sold stock on the date he died. Thus, if the amount that would have been treated as a dividend under section 995(c) were $30, such person will take a basis of $70 for such stock ($100, reduced by $30). If such person were immediately to sell the DISC stock so received for $100, $30 of the proceeds from the sale would be treated as a dividend by such person under section 995(c).

Example (2). Assume the same facts as in example (1) except that the estate elects the alternate valuation allowed by section 2032, the DISC stock has a fair market value of $140 on the alternate valuation date, the amount that would have been treated as a dividend under section 995(c) in the event of a sale on such date is $50 and the DISC has $20 of previously taxed income which accrued after the date of the decedent's death and before the alternate valuation date. The basis of the person who acquires such stock will be $90 determined as follows:

(1) Fair market value of DISC stock at alternate valuation date	$140
(2) Less: Amount which would have been treated as a dividend under section 995(c)	50
(3) Basis of person who acquires DISC stock	$90

If a distribution of $20 attributable to such previously taxed income had been made by the DISC on or before the alternate valuation date (with the DISC stock having a fair market value of $120 after such distribution), the basis of the person who acquires such stock will be $70 determined as follows:

(1) Fair market value of DISC stock at alternate valuation date	$120
(2) Less: Amount which would have been treated as a dividend under section 995(c)	50
(3) Basis of person who acquires DISC stock	$70

[Reg. § 1.1014-9.]

☐ [*T.D.* 7283, 8-2-73.]

[Reg. § 1.1015-1]

§ 1.1015-1. Basis of property acquired by gift after December 31, 1920.—(a) *General rule.*—(1) In the case of property acquired by gift after December 31, 1920 (whether by a transfer in trust or otherwise), the basis of the property for the purpose of determining gain is the same as it would be in the hands of the donor or the last preceding owner by whom it was not acquired by gift. The same rule applies in determining loss unless the basis (adjusted for the period prior to the date of gift in accordance with sections 1016 and 1017) is greater than the fair market value of the property at the time of the gift. In such case, the basis for determining loss is the fair market value at the time of the gift.

(2) The provisions of subparagraph (1) of this paragraph may be illustrated by the following example.

Example. A acquires by gift income-producing property which has an adjusted basis of $100,000 at the date of gift. The fair market value of the property at the date of gift is $90,000. A later sells the property for $95,000. In such case there is neither gain nor loss. The basis for determining loss is $90,000; therefore, there is no loss. Furthermore, there is no gain, since the basis for determining gain is $100,000.

(3) If the facts necessary to determine the basis of property in the hands of the donor or the last preceding owner by whom it was not acquired by gift are unknown to the donee, the district director shall, if possible, obtain such

facts from such donor or last preceding owner, or any other person cognizant thereof. If the district director finds it impossible to obtain such facts, the basis in the hands of such donor or last preceding owner shall be the fair market value of such property as found by the district director as of the date or approximate date at which, according to the best information the district director is able to obtain, such property was acquired by such donor or last preceding owner. See paragraph (e) of this section for rules relating to fair market value.

(b) *Uniform basis; proportionate parts of.*—Property acquired by gift has a single or uniform basis although more than one person may acquire an interest in such property. The uniform basis of the property remains fixed subject to proper adjustment for items under sections 1016 and 1017. However, the value of the proportionate parts of the uniform basis represented, for instance, by the respective interests of the life tenant and remainderman are adjustable to reflect the change in the relative values of such interest on account of the lapse of time. The portion of the basis attributable to an interest at the time of its sale or other disposition shall be determined under the rule provided in § 1.1014-5. In determining gain or loss from the sale or other disposition after October 9, 1969, of a term interest in property (as defined in § 1.1001-1(f)(2)) the adjusted basis of which is determined pursuant, or by reference, to section 1015, that part of the adjusted uniform basis assignable under the rules of § 1.1014-5(a) to the interest sold or otherwise disposed of shall be disregarded to the extent and in the manner provided by section 1001(e) and § 1.1001-1(f).

(c) *Time of acquisition.*—The date that the donee acquires an interest in property by gift is when the donor relinquishes dominion over the property and not necessarily when title to the property is acquired by the donee. Thus, the date that the donee acquires an interest in property by gift where he is a successor in interest, such as in the case of a remainderman of a life estate or a beneficiary of the distribution of the corpus of a trust, is the date such interests are created by the donor and not the date the property is actually acquired.

(d) *Property acquired by gift from a decedent dying after December 31, 1953.*—If an interest in property was acquired by the taxpayer by gift from a donor dying after December 31, 1953, under conditions which require the inclusion of the property in the donor's gross estate for estate tax purposes, and the property had not been sold, exchanged, or otherwise disposed of by the taxpayer before the donor's death, see the rules prescribed in section 1014 and the regulations thereunder.

(e) *Fair market value.*—For the purposes of this section, the value of property as appraised for the purpose of the Federal gift tax, or, if the gift is not subject to such tax, its value as appraised for the purpose of a State gift tax, shall be deemed to be the fair market value of the property at the time of the gift.

(f) *Reinvestments by fiduciary.*—If the property is an investment by the fiduciary under the terms of the gift (as, for example, in the case of a sale by the fiduciary of property transferred under the terms of the gift, and the reinvestment of the proceeds), the cost or other basis to the fiduciary is taken in lieu of the basis specified in paragraph (a) of this section.

(g) *Records.*—To insure a fair and adequate determination of the proper basis under section 1015, persons making or receiving gifts of property should preserve and keep accessible a record of the facts necessary to determine the cost of the property and, if pertinent, its fair market value as of March 1, 1913, or its fair market value as of the date of the gift. [Reg. § 1.1015-1.]

☐ [*T.D.* 6265, 11-6-57. *Amended by T.D.* 6693, 12-2-63 *and T.D.* 7142, 9-23-71.]

[Reg. § 1.1015-2]

§ 1.1015-2. Transfer of property in trust after December 31, 1920.—(a) *General rule.*—(1) In the case of property acquired after December 31, 1920, by transfer in trust (other than by a transfer in trust by a gift, bequest, or devise) the basis of property so acquired is the same as it would be in the hands of the grantor increased in the amount of gain or decreased in the amount of loss recognized to the grantor upon such transfer under the law applicable to the year in which the transfer was made. If the taxpayer acquired the property by a transfer in trust, this basis applies whether the property be in the hands of the trustee, or the beneficiary, and whether acquired prior to the termination of the trust and distribution of the property, or thereafter.

(2) The principles stated in paragraph (b) of § 1.1015-1 concerning the uniform basis are applicable in determining the basis of property where more than one person acquires an interest in property by transfer in trust after December 31, 1920.

(b) *Reinvestment by fiduciary.*—If the property is an investment made by the fiduciary (as, for example, in the case of a sale by the fiduciary of property transferred by the grantor, and the reinvestment of the proceeds), the cost or other basis to the fiduciary is taken in lieu of the basis specified in paragraph (a) of this section. [Reg. § 1.1015-2.]

☐ [*T.D.* 6265, 11-6-57.]

[Reg. § 1.1015-3]

§ 1.1015-3. Gift or transfer in trust before January 1, 1921.—(a) In the case of property acquired by gift or transfer in trust before January 1, 1921, the basis of such property is the fair market value thereof at the time of the gift or at the time of the transfer in trust.

(b) The principles stated in paragraph (b) of § 1.1015-1 concerning the uniform basis are applicable in determining the basis of property where more than one person acquires an interest in property by gift or transfer in trust before

January 1, 1921. In addition, if an interest in such property was acquired from a decedent and the property had not been sold, exchanged, or otherwise disposed of before the death of the donor, the rules prescribed in section 1014 and the regulations thereunder are applicable in determining the basis of such property in the hands of the taxpayer. [Reg. § 1.1015-3.]

☐ [*T.D.* 6265, 11-6-57.]

[Reg. § 1.1015-4]

§ 1.1015-4. Transfers in part a gift and in part a sale.—(a) *General rule.*—Where a transfer of property is in part a sale and in part a gift, the unadjusted basis of the property in the hands of the transferee is the sum of—

(1) Whichever of the following is the greater:

(i) The amount paid by the transferee for the property, or

(ii) The transferor's adjusted basis for the property at the time of the transfer, and

(2) The amount of increase, if any, in basis authorized by section 1015(d) for gift tax paid (see § 1.1015-5).

For determining loss, the unadjusted basis of the property in the hands of the transferee shall not be greater than the fair market value of the property at the time of such transfer. For determination of gain or loss of the transferor, see § 1.1001-1(e) and § 1.1011-2. For special rule where there has been a charitable contribution of less than a taxpayer's entire interest in property, see section 170(e)(2) and § 1.170A-4(c).

(b) *Examples.*—The rule of paragraph (a) of this section is illustrated by the following examples:

Example (1). If A transfers property to his son for $30,000, and such property at the time of the transfer has an adjusted basis of $30,000 in A's hands (and a fair market value of $60,000), the unadjusted basis of the property in the hands of the son is $30,000.

Example (2). If A transfers property to his son for $60,000, and such property at the time of transfer had an adjusted basis of $30,000 in A's hands (and a fair market value of $90,000), the unadjusted basis of such property in the hands of the son is $60,000.

Example (3). If A transfers property to his son for $30,000, and such property at the time of transfer has an adjusted basis in A's hands of $60,000 (and a fair market value of $90,000), the unadjusted basis of such property in the hands of the son is $60,000.

Example (4). If A transfers property to his son for $30,000 and such property at the time of transfer has an adjusted basis of $90,000 in A's hands (and a fair market value of $60,000), the unadjusted basis of the property in the hands of the son is $90,000. However, since the adjusted basis of the property in A's hands at the time of the transfer was greater than the fair market value at that time, for the purpose of determining any loss on a later sale or other disposition of the property by the son its unadjusted basis in his hands is $60,000. [Reg. § 1.1015-4.]

☐ [*T.D.* 6265, 11-6-57. *Amended by T.D.* 6693, 12-2-63 *and T.D.* 7207, 10-3-72.]

[Reg. § 1.1015-5]

§ 1.1015-5. Increased basis for gift tax paid.—(a) *General rule in the case of gifts made on or before December 31, 1976.*—(1)(i) Subject to the conditions and limitations provided in section 1015(d), as added by the Technical Amendments Act of 1958, the basis (as determined under section 1015(a) and paragraph (a) of § 1.1015-1) of property acquired by gift is increased by the amount of gift tax paid with respect to the gift of such property. Under section 1015(d)(1)(A), such increase in basis applies to property acquired by gift on or after September 2, 1958 (the date of enactment of the Technical Amendments Act of 1958). Under section 1015(d)(1)(B), such increase in basis applies to property acquired by gift before September 2, 1958, and not sold, exchanged, or otherwise disposed of before such date. If section 1015(d)(1)(A) applies, the basis of the property is increased as of the date of the gift regardless of the date of payment of the gift tax. For example, if the property was acquired by gift on September 8, 1958, and sold by the donee on October 15, 1958, the basis of the property would be increased (subject to the limitation of section 1015(d)) as of September 8, 1958 (the date of the gift), by the amount of gift tax applicable to such gift even though such tax was not paid until March 1, 1959. If section 1015 (d)(1)(B) applies, any increase in the basis of the property due to gift tax paid (regardless of date of payment) with respect to the gift is made as of September 2, 1958. Any increase in basis under section 1015(d) can be no greater than the amount by which the fair market value of the property at the time of the gift exceeds the basis of such property in the hands of the donor at the time of the gift. See paragraph (b) of this section for rules for determining the amount of gift tax paid in respect of property transferred by gift.

(ii) With respect to property acquired by gift before September 2, 1958, the provisions of section 1015(d) and this section do not apply if, before such date, the donee has sold, exchanged, or otherwise disposed of such property. The phrase "sold, exchanged, or otherwise disposed of" includes the surrender of a stock certificate for corporate assets in complete or partial liquidation of a corporation pursuant to section 331. It also includes the exchange of property for property of a like kind such as the exchange of one apartment house for another. The phrase does not, however, extend to transactions which are mere changes in form. Thus, it does not include a transfer of assets to a corporation in exchange for its stock in a transaction with respect to which no gain or loss would be recognizable for income tax purposes under section 351. Nor does it include an exchange of stock or securities in a corporation for stock or securities in the same corporation or another corporation in a transaction such as a merger, recapitalization, reorganization, or other transaction described in section 368(a) or 355, with respect to which no gain or loss is recognizable for income tax purposes under section 354 or 355. If a binding contract for the sale, exchange, or other disposition of property is entered into, the property is considered as sold, exchanged, or otherwise disposed of on the effective date of the contract, unless the contract is not subsequently carried out substantially in accordance with its terms. The effective date of a contract is normally the date it is entered into (and not the date it is consummated, or the date legal title to the property passes) unless the contract specifies a different effective date. For purposes of this subdivision, in determining whether a transaction comes within the phrase "sold, exchanged, or otherwise disposed of", if a transaction would be treated as a mere change in the form of the property if it occurred in a taxable year subject to the Internal Revenue Code of 1954, it will be so treated if the transaction occurred in a taxable year subject to the Internal Revenue Code of 1939 or prior revenue law.

(2) Application of the provisions of subparagraph (1) of this paragraph may be illustrated by the following examples:

Example (1). In 1938, A purchased a business building at a cost of $120,000. On September 2, 1958, at which time the property had an adjusted basis in A's hands of $60,000, he gave the property to his nephew, B. At the time of the gift to B, the property had a fair market value of $65,000 with respect to which A paid a gift tax in the amount of $7,545. The basis of the property in B's hands at the time of the gift, as determined under section 1015(a) and § 1.1015-1, would be the same as the adjusted basis in A's hands at the time of the gift, or $60,000. Under section 1015(d) and this section, the basis of the building in B's hands as of the date of the gift would be increased by the amount of the gift tax paid with respect to such gift, limited to an amount by which the fair market value of the property at the time of the gift exceeded the basis of the property in the hands of A at the time of gift, or $5,000. Therefore, the basis of the property in B's hands immediately after the gift, both for determining gain or loss on the sale of the property, would be $65,000.

Example (2). C purchased property in 1938 at a cost of $100,000. On October 1, 1952, at which time the property had an adjusted basis of $72,000 in C's hands, he gave the property to his daughter, D. At the date of the gift to D, the property had a fair market value of $85,000 with respect to which C paid a gift tax in the amount of $11,745. On September 2, 1958, D still held the property which then had an adjusted basis in her hands of $65,000. Since the excess of the fair market value of the property at the time of the gift to D over the adjusted basis of the property in C's hands at such time is greater than the amount of gift tax paid, the basis of the property in D's hands would be increased as of September 2, 1958, by the amount of the gift tax paid, or $11,745. The adjusted basis of the property in D's hands, both for determining gain or loss on the sale of the property, would then be $76,745 ($65,000 plus $11,745).

Example (3). On December 31, 1951, E gave to his son, F, 500 shares of common stock of the X Corporation which shares had been purchased earlier by E at a cost of $100 per share, or a total cost of $50,000. The basis in E's hands was still $50,000 on the date of the gift to F. On the date of the gift, the fair market value of the 500 shares was $80,000 with respect to which E paid a gift tax in the amount of $10,695. In 1956, the 500 shares of X Corporation stock were exchanged for 500 shares of common stock of the Y Corporation in a reorganization with respect to which no gain or loss was recognized for income tax purposes under section 354. F still held the 500 shares of Y Corporation stock on September 2, 1958. Under such circumstances, the 500 shares of X Corporation stock would not, for purposes of section 1015(d) and this section, be considered as having been "sold, exchanged, or otherwise disposed of" by F before September 2, 1958. Therefore, the basis of the 500 shares of Y Corporation stock held by F as of such date would, by reason of section 1015(d) and this section, be increased by $10,695, the amount of gift tax paid with respect to the gift to F of the X Corporation stock.

Example (4). On November 15, 1953, G gave H property which had a fair market value of $53,000 and a basis in the hands of G of $20,000. G paid gift tax of $5,250 on the transfer. On November 16, 1956, H gave the property to J who still held it on September 2, 1958. The value of the property on the date of the gift to J was $63,000 and H paid gift tax of $7,125 on the transfer. Since the property was not sold, exchanged, or otherwise disposed of by J before September 2, 1958, and the gift tax paid on the transfer to J did not exceed $43,000 ($63,000, fair market value of property at time of gift to J, less $20,000, basis of property in H's hands at that time), the basis of property in his hands is increased on September 2, 1958, by $7,125, the amount of gift tax paid by H on the transfer. No increase in basis is allowed for the $5,250 gift tax paid by G on the transfer to H, since H had sold, exchanged, or otherwise disposed of the property before September 2, 1958.

(b) *Amount of gift tax paid with respect to gifts made on or before December 31, 1976.*—(1)(i) If only one gift was made during a certain "calendar period" (as defined in § 25.2502-1(c)(1)), the entire amount of the gift tax paid under chapter 12 or the corresponding provisions of prior revenue laws for that calendar period is the amount of the gift tax paid with respect to the gift.

(ii) If more than one gift was made during a certain calendar period, the amount of the gift tax paid under chapter 12 or the corresponding provisions of prior revenue laws with respect to any specified gift made during that calendar period is an amount, A, which bears the same ratio to B (the total gift tax paid for that calendar period) as C (the "amount of the gift," computed as described in this paragraph (b)(1)(ii)) bears to

D (the total taxable gifts for the calendar period computed without deduction for the gift tax specific exemption under section 2521 (as in effect prior to its repeal by the Tax Reform Act of 1976) or the corresponding provisions of prior revenue laws).

(iii) If a gift consists of more than one item of property, the gift tax paid with respect to each item shall be computed by allocating to each item a proportionate part of the gift tax paid with respect to the gift, computed in accordance with the provisions of this paragraph.

(2) For purposes of this paragraph, it is immaterial whether the gift tax is paid by the donor or the donee. Where more than one gift of a present interest in property is made to the same donee during a "calendar period" (as defined in § 25.2502-1(c)(1)), the annual exclusion shall apply to the earliest of such gifts in point of time.

(3) Where the donor and his spouse elect under section 2513 or the corresponding provisions of prior law to have any gifts made by either of them considered as made one-half by each, the amount of gift tax paid with respect to such a gift is the sum of the amounts of tax (computed separately) paid with respect to each half of the gift by the donor and his spouse.

(4) The method described in section 1015(d)(2) and this paragraph for computing the amount of gift tax paid in respect of a gift may be illustrated by the following examples:

Example (1). Prior to 1959 H made no taxable gifts. On July 1, 1959, he made a gift to his wife, W, of land having a value for gift tax purposes of $60,000 and gave to his son, S, certain securities valued at $60,000. During the year 1959, H also contributed $5,000 in cash to a charitable organization described in section 2522. H filed a timely gift tax return for 1959 with respect to which he paid gift tax in the amount of $6,000, computed as follows:

Value of land given to W		$60,000	
Less: Annual exclusion	$ 3,000		
Marital deduction	30,000	33,000	
Included amount of gift			$27,000
Value of securities given to S		$60,000	
Less: Annual exclusion		3,000	
Included amount of gift			57,000
Gift to charitable organization		$5,000	
Less: Annual exclusion	$3,000		
Charitable deduction	2,000	5,000	
Included amount of gift			None
Total included gifts			84,000
Less: Specific exemption allowed			30,000
Taxable gifts for 1959			54,000
Gift tax on $54,000			$ 6,000

In determining the gift tax paid with respect to the land given to W, amount C of the ratio set forth in subparagraph (1)(ii) of this paragraph is $60,000, value of property given to W, less $33,000 (the sum of $3,000, the amount excluded under section 2503(b), and $30,000, the amount deducted under section 2523), or $27,000. Amount D of the ratio is $84,000 (the amount of taxable gifts, $54,000, plus the gift tax specific exemption, $30,000). The gift tax paid with respect to the land given to W is $1,928.57, computed as follows:

$$\frac{\$27{,}000\ (C)}{\$84{,}000\ (D)} \times \$6{,}000\ (B)$$

Example (2). The facts are the same as in example (1) except that H made his gifts to W and S on July 1, 1971, and that prior to 1971, H made no taxable gifts. Furthermore, H made his charitable contribution on August 12, 1971. These were the only gifts made by H during 1971. H filed his gift tax return for the third quarter of 1971 on November 15, 1971, as required by section 6075(b). With respect to the above gifts, H paid a gift tax in the amount of $6,000, on total taxable gifts of $54,000 for the third quarter of 1971. The gift tax paid with respect to the land given to W is $1,928.57. The computations for these figures are identical to those used in example (1).

Example (3). On January 15, 1956, A made a gift to his nephew, N, of land valued at $86,000, and on June 30, 1956, gave N securities valued at $40,000. On July 1, 1956, A gave to his sister, S, $46,000 in cash. A and his wife, B, were married during the entire calendar year 1956. The amount of A's taxable gifts for prior years was zero although in arriving at that amount A had used in full the specific exemption authorized by section 2521. B did not make any gifts before 1956. A and B elected under section 2513 to have all gifts made by either during 1956 treated as made one-half by A and one-half by B. Pursuant to that election, A and B each filed a gift tax return for 1956. A paid gift tax of $11,325 and B paid gift tax of $5,250, computed as follows:

	A	*B*
Value of land given to N	$43,000	$43,000
Less: exclusion	3,000	3,000
Included amount of gift	$40,000	$40,000
Value of securities given to N	$20,000	$20,000
Less: exclusion	none	none

Included amount of gift	20,000	20,000
Cash gift to S	23,000	23,000
Less: exclusion	3,000	3,000
Included amount of gift	20,000	20,000
Total included gifts	80,000	80,000
Less: specific exemption	none	30,000
Taxable gifts for 1956	80,000	50,000
Gift tax for 1956	11,325	5,250

The amount of the gift tax paid by A with respect to the land given to N is computed as follows:

$$\frac{\$40{,}000\ (C)}{\$80{,}000\ (D)} \times \$11{,}325\ (B) = \$5{,}662.50$$

The amount of the gift tax paid by B with respect to the land given to N is computed as follows:

$$\frac{\$40{,}000\ (C)}{\$80{,}000\ (D)} \times \$5{,}250\ (B) = \$2{,}625$$

The amount of the gift tax paid with respect to the land is $5,662.50 plus $2,625, or $8,287.50. Computed in a similar manner, the amount of gift tax paid by A with respect to the securities given to N is $2,831.25, and the amount of gift tax paid by B with respect thereto is $1,312.50, or a total of $4,143.75.

Example (4). The facts are the same as in example (3) except that A gave the land to N on January 15, 1972, the securities to N on February 3, 1972, and the cash to S on March 7, 1972. As in example (3), the amount of A's taxable gifts for taxable years prior to 1972 was zero, although in arriving at that amount A had used in full the specific exemption authorized by section 2521. B did not make any gifts before 1972. Pursuant to the election under section 2513, A and B treated all gifts made by either during 1972 as made one-half by A and one-half by B. A and B each filed a gift tax return for the first quarter of 1972 on May 15, 1972, as required by section 6075(b). A paid gift tax of $11,325 on taxable gifts of $80,000 and B paid gift tax of $5,250 on taxable gifts of $50,000. The amount of the gift tax paid by A and B with respect to the land given to N is $5,662.50 and $2,625, respectively. The computations for these figures are identical to those used in example (3).

(c) *Special rule for increased basis for gift tax paid in the case of gifts made after December 31, 1976.*—(1) *In general.*—With respect to gifts made after December 31, 1976 (other than gifts between spouses described in section 1015(e)), the increase in basis for gift tax paid is determined under section 1015(d)(6). Under section 1015(d)(6)(A), the increase in basis with respect to gift tax paid is limited to the amount (not in excess of the amount of gift tax paid) that bears the same ratio to the amount of gift tax paid as the net appreciation in value of the gift bears to the amount of the gift.

(2) *Amount of gift.*—In general, for purposes of section 1015(d)(6)(A)(ii), the amount of the gift is determined in conformance with the provisions of paragraph (b) of this section. Thus, the amount of the gift is the amount included with respect to the gift in determining (for purposes of section 2503(a)) the total amount of gifts made during the calendar year (or calendar quarter in the case of a gift made on or before December 31, 1981), reduced by the amount of any annual exclusion allowable with respect to the gift under section 2503(b), and any deductions allowed with respect to the gift under section 2522 (relating to the charitable deduction) and section 2523 (relating to the marital deduction). Where more than one gift of a present interest in property is made to the same donee during a calendar year, the annual exclusion shall apply to the earliest of such gifts in point of time.

(3) *Amount of gift tax paid with respect to the gift.*—In general, for purposes of section 1015(d)(6), the amount of gift tax paid with respect to the gift is determined in conformance with the provisions of paragraph (b) of this section. Where more than one gift is made by the donor in a calendar year (or quarter in the case of gifts made on or before December 31, 1981), the amount of gift tax paid with respect to any specific gift made during that period is the amount which bears the same ratio to the total gift tax paid for that period (determined after reduction for any gift tax unified credit available under section 2505) as the amount of the gift (computed as described in paragraph (c)(2) of this section) bears to the total taxable gifts for the period.

(4) *Qualified domestic trusts.*—For purposes of section 1015(d)(6), in the case of a qualified domestic trust (QDOT) described in section 2056A(a), any distribution during the noncitizen surviving spouse's lifetime with respect to which a tax is imposed under section 2056A(b)(1)(A) is treated as a transfer by gift, and any estate tax paid on the distribution under section 2056A(b)(1)(A) is treated as a gift tax. The rules under this paragraph apply in determining the extent to which the basis in the assets distributed is increased by the tax imposed under section 2056A(b)(1)(A).

(5) *Examples.*—Application of the provisions of this paragraph (c) may be illustrated by the following examples:

Example 1. (i) Prior to 1995, *X* exhausts *X*'s gift tax unified credit available under section 2505. In 1995, *X* makes a gift to *X*'s child *Y*, of a parcel of real estate having a fair market value of $100,000. *X*'s adjusted basis in the real estate immediately before making the gift was $70,000. Also in 1995, *X* makes a gift to *X*'s child *Z*, of a painting having a fair market value of $70,000. *X* timely files a gift tax return for 1995 and pays gift tax in the amount of $55,500, computed as follows:

Value of real estate transferred to *Y*	$100,000	
Less: Annual exclusion	10,000	
Included amount of gift (C)		$90,000
Value of painting transferred to *Z*	$70,000	
Less: annual exclusion	10,000	
Included amount of gift		60,000
Total included gifts (D)		$150,000
Total gift tax liability for 1995 gifts (B)		$55,500

(ii) The gift tax paid with respect to the real estate transferred to *Y*, is determined as follows:

$$\frac{\$90{,}000(C)}{\$150{,}000(D)} \times \$55{,}500 = \$33{,}300$$

(iii) (A) The amount by which *Y*'s basis in the real property is increased is determined as follows:

$$\frac{\$30{,}000 \text{ (net appreciation)}}{\$90{,}000 \text{ (amount of gift)}} \times \$33{,}300 = \$11{,}000$$

(B) *Y*'s basis in the real property is $70,000 plus $11,100, or $81,100. If *X* had not exhausted any of *X*'s unified credit, no gift tax would have been paid and, as a result, *Y*'s basis would not be increased.

Example 2. (i) *X* dies in 1995. *X*'s spouse, *Y*, is not a United States citizen. In order to obtain the marital deduction for property passing to *X*'s spouse, *X* established a QDOT in *X*'s will. In 1996, the trustee of the QDOT makes a distribution of principal from the QDOT in the form of shares of stock having a fair market value of $70,000 on the date of distribution. The trustee's basis in the stock (determined under section 1014) is $50,000. An estate tax is imposed on the distribution under section 2056A(b)(1)(A) in the amount $38,500, and is paid. *Y*'s basis in the shares of stock is increased by a portion of the section 2056A estate tax paid determined as follows:

$$\frac{\$20{,}000 \text{ (net appreciation)}}{\$70{,}000 \text{ (distribution)}} \times \$38{,}500 \text{ (section 2056a estate tax)} = \$11{,}000$$

(ii) *Y*'s basis in the stock is $50,000 plus $11,000, or $61,000.

(6) *Effective date.*—The provisions of this paragraph (c) are effective for gifts made after August 22, 1995.

(d) *Treatment as adjustment to basis.*—Any increase in basis under section 1015(d) and this section shall for purposes of section 1016(b) (relating to adjustments to a substituted basis), be treated as an adjustment under section 1016(a) to the basis of the donee's property to which such increase applies. See paragraph (p) of § 1.1016-5. [Reg. § 1.1015-5.]

☐ [*T.D.* 6693, 12-2-63. *Amended by T.D.* 7238, 12-28-72; *T.D.* 7910, 9-6-83 *and T.D.* 8612, 8-21-95.]

[Reg. § 1.1016-1]

§ 1.1016-1. Adjustments to basis; scope of section.—Section 1016 and §§ 1.1016-2 to 1016-10, inclusive, contain the rules relating to the adjustments to be made to the basis of property to determine the adjusted basis as defined in section 1011. However, if the property was acquired from a decedent before his death, see § 1.1014-6 for adjustments on account of certain deductions allowed the taxpayer for the period between the date of acquisition of the property and the date of death of the decedent. If an election has been made under the Retirement-Straight Line Adjustment Act of 1958 (26 U.S.C. 1016 note), see § 1.9001-1 for special rules for determining adjusted basis in the case of a taxpayer who has changed from the retirement to the straight-line method of computing depreciation allowances. [Reg. § 1.1016-1.]

☐ [*T.D.* 6265, 11-6-57. *Amended by T.D.* 6418, 10-9-59.]

* * *

Common Nontaxable Exchanges

* * *

[Reg. § 1.1041-1T]

§ 1.1041-1T. Treatment of transfer of property between spouses or incident to divorce (temporary).—

Q-1. How is the transfer of property between spouses treated under section 1041?

A-1. Generally, no gain or loss is recognized on a transfer of property from an individual to (or in trust for the benefit of) a spouse or, if the transfer is incident to a divorce, a former spouse. The following questions and answers describe more fully the scope, tax consequences and other rules which apply to transfers of property under section 1041.

(a) *Scope of section 1041 in general.*

Q-2. Does section 1041 apply only to transfers of property incident to divorce?

A-2. No. Section 1041 is not limited to transfers of property incident to divorce. Section 1041 applies to any transfer of property between spouses regardless of whether the transfer is a gift or is a sale or exchange between spouses acting at arm's length (including a transfer in exchange for the relinquishment of property or marital rights or an exchange otherwise governed by another nonrecognition provision of the Code). A divorce or legal separation need not be contemplated between the spouses at the time of the transfer nor must a divorce or legal separation ever occur.

Example (1). A and B are married and file a joint return. A is the sole owner of a condominium unit. A sale or gift of the condominium from A to B is a transfer which is subject to the rules of section 1041.

Example (2). A and B are married and file separate returns. A is the owner of an independent sole proprietorship, X Company. In the ordinary course of business, X Company makes a sale of property to B. This sale is a transfer of property between spouses and is subject to the rules of section 1041.

Example (3). Assume the same facts as in example (2), except that X Company is a corporation wholly owned by A. This sale is not a sale between spouses subject to the rules of section 1041. However, in appropriate circumstances, general tax principles, including the step-transaction doctrine, may be applicable in recharacterizing the transaction.

Q-3. Do the rules of section 1041 apply to a transfer between spouses if the transferee spouse is a nonresident alien?

A-3. No. Gain or loss (if any) is recognized (assuming no other nonrecognition provision applies) at the time of a transfer of property if the property is transferred to a spouse who is a nonresident alien.

Q-4. What kinds of transfers are governed by section 1041?

A-4. Only transfers of property (whether real or personal, tangible or intangible) are governed by section 1041. Transfers of services are not subject to the rules of section 1041.

Q-5. Must the property transferred to a former spouse have been owned by the transferor spouse during the marriage?

A-5. No. A transfer of property acquired after the marriage ceases may be governed by section 1041.

(b) *Transfer incident to the divorce.*

Q-6. What is a transfer of property "incident to the divorce"?

A-6. A transfer of property is "incident to the divorce" in either of the following 2 circumstances—

(1) the transfer occurs not more than one year after the date on which the marriage ceases, or

(2) the transfer is related to the cessation of the marriage.

Thus, a transfer of property occurring not more than one year after the date on which the marriage ceases need not be related to the cessation of the marriage to qualify for section 1041 treatment. (See A-7 for transfers occurring more than one year after the cessation of the marriage.)

Q-7. When is a transfer of property "related to the cessation of the marriage"?

A-7. A transfer of property is treated as related to the cessation of the marriage if the transfer is pursuant to a divorce or separation instrument, as defined in section 71(b)(2), and the transfer occurs not more than 6 years after the date on which the marriage ceases. A divorce or separation instrument includes a modification or amendment to such decree or instrument. Any transfer not pursuant to a divorce or separation instrument and any transfer occurring more than 6 years after the cessation of the marriage is presumed to be not related to the cessation of the marriage. This presumption may be rebutted only by showing that the transfer was made to effect the division of property owned by the former spouses at the time of the cessation of the marriage. For example, the presumption may be rebutted by showing that (a) the transfer was not made within the one- and six-year periods described above because of factors which hampered an earlier transfer of the property, such as legal or business impediments to transfer or disputes concerning the value of the property owned at the time of the cessation of the marriage, and (b) the transfer is effected promptly after the impediment to transfer is removed.

Q-8. Do annulments and the cessations of marriages that are void *ab initio* due to violations of state law constitute divorces for purposes of section 1041?

A-8. Yes.

(c) *Transfers on behalf of a spouse.*

Q-9. May transfers of property to third parties on behalf of a spouse (or former spouse) qualify under section 1041?

A-9. Yes. There are three situations in which a transfer of property to a third party on behalf of a spouse (or former spouse) will qualify under section 1041, provided all other requirements of the section are satisfied. The first situation is where the transfer to the third party is required by a divorce or separation instrument. The second situation is where the transfer to the third party is pursuant to the written request of the other spouse (or former spouse). The third situation is where the transferor receives from the other spouse (or former spouse) a written consent or ratification of the transfer to the third party. Such consent or ratification must state that the parties intend the transfer to be treated as a transfer to the nontransferring spouse (or former spouse) subject to the rules of section 1041 and must be received by the transferor prior to the date of filing of the transferor's first return of tax for the taxable year in which the transfer was made. In the three situations described above, the transfer of property will be treated as made directly to the nontransferring spouse (or former spouse) and the nontransferring spouse will be treated as immediately transferring the property to the third party. The deemed transfer from the nontransferring spouse (or former spouse) to the third party is not a transaction that qualifies for nonrecognition of gain under section 1041. This A-9 shall not apply to transfers to which § 1.1041-2 applies.

(d) *Tax consequences of transfers subject to section 1041.*

Q-10. How is the transferor of property under section 1041 treated for income tax purposes?

A-10. The transferor of property under section 1041 recognizes no gain or loss on the transfer even if the transfer was in exchange for the release of marital rights or other consideration. This rule applies regardless of whether the transfer is of property separately owned by the transferor or is a division (equal or unequal) of community property. Thus, the result under section 1041 differs from the result in *United States v. Davis,* 370 U.S. 65 (1962).

Q-11. How is the transferee of property under section 1041 treated for income tax purposes?

A-11. The transferee of property under section 1041 recognizes no gain or loss upon receipt of the transferred property. In all cases, the basis of the transferred property in the hands of the transferee is the adjusted basis of such property in the hands of the transferor immediately before the transfer. Even if the transfer is a bona fide sale, the transferee does not acquire a basis in the transferred property equal to the transferee's cost (the fair market value). This carryover basis rule applies whether the adjusted basis of the transferred property is less than, equal to, or greater than its fair market value at the time of transfer (or the value of any consideration provided by the transferee) and applies for purposes of determining loss as well as gain upon the subsequent disposition of the property by the transferee. Thus, this rule is different from the rule applied in section 1015(a) for determining the basis of property acquired by gift.

Q-12. Do the rules described in A-10 and A-11 apply even if the transferred property is subject to liabilities which exceed the adjusted basis of the property?

A-12. Yes. For example, assume A owns property having a fair market value of $10,000 and an adjusted basis of $1,000. In contemplation of making a transfer of this property incident to a divorce from B, A borrows $5,000 from a bank, using the property as security for the borrowing. A then transfers the property to B and B assumes, or takes the property subject to, the liability to pay the $5,000 debt. Under section 1041, A recognizes no gain or loss upon the transfer of the property, and the adjusted basis of the property in the hands of B is $1,000.

Q-13. Will a transfer under section 1041 result in a recapture of investment tax credits with respect to the property transferred?

A-13. In general, no. Property transferred under section 1041 will not be treated as being disposed of by, or ceasing to be section 38 property with respect to, the transferor. However, the transferee will be subject to investment tax credit recapture if, upon or after transfer, the property is disposed of by, or ceases to be section 38 property with respect to, the transferee. For example, as part of a divorce property settlement, B receives a car from A that has been used in A's business for two years and for which an investment tax credit was taken by A. No part of A's business is transferred to B and B's use of the car is solely personal. B is subject to recapture of the investment tax credit previously taken by A.

(e) *Notice and recordkeeping requirement with respect to transactions under section 1041.*

Q-14. Does the transferor of property in a transaction described in section 1041 have to supply, at the time of the transfer, the transferee with records sufficient to determine the adjusted basis and holding period of the property at the time of the transfer and (if applicable) with notice that the property transferred under section 1041 is potentially subject to recapture of the investment tax credit?

A-14. Yes. A transferor of property under section 1041 must, at the time of the transfer, supply the transferee with records sufficient to determine the adjusted basis and holding period of the property as of the date of the transfer. In addition, in the case of a transfer of property which carries with it a potential liability for investment tax credit recapture, the transferor must, at the time of the transfer, supply the transferee with records sufficient to determine the amount and period of such potential liability. Such records must be preserved and kept accessible by the transferee.

(f) *Property settlements—effective dates, transitional periods and elections.*

Q-15. When does section 1041 become effective?

A-15. Generally, section 1041 applies to all transfers after July 18, 1984. However, it does not apply to transfers after July 18, 1984 pursuant to instruments in effect on or before July 18, 1984. (See A-16 with respect to exceptions to the general rule.)

Q-16. Are there any exceptions to the general rule stated in A-15 above?

A-16. Yes. Two transitional rules provide exceptions to the general rule stated in A-15. First, section 1041 will apply to transfers after July 18, 1984 under instruments that were in effect on or before July 18, 1984 if both spouses (or former spouses) elect to have section 1041 apply to such transfers. Second, section 1041 will apply to all transfers after December 31, 1983 (including transfers under instruments in effect on or before July 18, 1984) if both spouses (or former spouses) elect to have section 1041 apply. (See A-18 relating to the time and manner of making the elections under the first or second transitional rule.)

Q-17. Can an election be made to have section 1041 apply to some, but not all, transfers made after December 31, 1983, or to some, but not all, transfers made after July 18, 1984 under instruments in effect on or before July 18, 1984?

A-17. No. Partial elections are not allowed. An election under either of the two elective transitional rules applies to all transfers governed by that election whether before or after the election is made, and is irrevocable.

(g) *Property settlements—time and manner of making the elections under section 1041.*

Q-18. How do spouses (or former spouses) elect to have section 1041 apply to transfers after December 31, 1983, or to transfers after July 18, 1984 under instruments in effect on or before July 18, 1984?

A-18. In order to make an election under section 1041 for property transfers after December 31, 1983, or property transfers under instruments that were in effect on or before July 18, 1984, both spouses (or former spouses) must elect the application of the rules of section 1041 by attaching to the transferor's first filed income tax return for the taxable year in which the first transfer occurs, a statement signed by both spouses (or former spouses) which includes each spouse's social security number and is in substantially the form set forth at the end of this answer.

In addition, the transferor must attach a copy of such statement to his or her return for each subsequent taxable year in which a transfer is made that is governed by the transitional election. A copy of the signed statement must be kept by both parties.

The election statements shall be in substantially the following form:

In the case of an election regarding transfers after 1983:

Section 1041 Election

The undersigned hereby elect to have the provisions of section 1041 of the Internal Revenue Code apply to all qualifying transfers of property after December 31, 1983. The undersigned understand that section 1041 applies to all property transferred between spouses, or former spouses incident to divorce. The parties further understand that the effects for Federal income tax purposes of having section 1041 apply are that (1) no gain or loss is recognized by the transferor spouse or former spouse as a result of this transfer; and (2) the basis of the transferred property in the hands of the transferee is the adjusted basis of the property in the hands of the transferor immediately before the transfer, whether or not the adjusted basis of the transferred property is less than, equal to, or greater than its fair market value at the time of the transfer. The undersigned understand that if the transferee spouse or former spouse disposes of the property in a transaction in which gain is recognized, the amount of gain which is taxable may be larger than it would have been if this election had not been made.

In the case of an election regarding preexisting decrees:

Section 1041 Election

The undersigned hereby elect to have the provisions of section 1041 of the Internal Revenue Code apply to all qualifying transfers of property after July 18, 1984 under any instrument in effect on or before July 18, 1984. The undersigned understand that section 1041 applies to all property transferred between spouses, or former spouses incident to the divorce. The parties further understand that the effects for Federal income tax purposes of having section 1041 apply are that (1) no gain or loss is recognized by the transferor spouse or former spouse as a result of this transfer; and (2) the basis of the transferred property in the hands of the transferee is the adjusted basis of the property in the hands of the transferor immediately before the transfer, whether or not the adjusted basis of the transferred property is less than, equal to, or greater than its fair market value at the time of the transfer. The undersigned understand that if the transferee spouse or former spouse disposes of the property in a transaction in which gain is recognized, the amount of gain which is taxable may be larger than it would have been if this election had not been made. [Temp. Reg. §1.1041-1T.]

☐ [*T.D.* 7973, 8-30-84. *Amended by T.D.* 9035, 1-10-2003.]

[Reg. §1.1041-2]

§1.1041-2. Redemptions of stock.—(a) *In general.*—(1) *Redemptions of stock not resulting in constructive distributions.*—Notwithstanding Q&A-9 of §1.1041-1T(c), if a corporation redeems stock owned by a spouse or former spouse (transferor spouse), and the transferor spouse's receipt of property in respect of such redeemed stock is not treated, under applicable tax law, as resulting in a constructive distribution to the other spouse or former spouse (nontransferor spouse), then the form of the stock redemption shall be respected for Federal income tax purposes. Therefore, the transferor spouse will be treated as having received a distribution from the corporation in redemption of stock.

(2) *Redemptions of stock resulting in constructive distributions.*—Notwithstanding Q&A-9 of §1.1041-1T(c), if a corporation redeems stock owned by a transferor spouse, and the transferor spouse's receipt of property in respect of such redeemed stock is treated, under applicable tax law, as resulting in a constructive distribution to the nontransferor spouse, then the redeemed stock shall be deemed first to be transferred by the transferor spouse to the nontransferor spouse and then to be transferred by the nontransferor spouse to the redeeming corporation. Any property actually received by the transferor spouse from the redeeming corporation in respect of the redeemed stock shall be deemed first to be transferred by the corporation to the nontransferor spouse in redemption of such spouse's stock and then to be transferred by the nontransferor spouse to the transferor spouse.

(b) *Tax consequences.*—(1) *Transfers described in paragraph (a)(1) of this section.*—Section 1041 will not apply to any of the transfers described in paragraph (a)(1) of this section. See section 302 for rules relating to the tax consequences of certain redemptions; redemptions characterized as distributions under section 302(d) will be subject to section 301 if received from a Subchapter C corporation or section 1368 if received from a Subchapter S corporation.

(2) *Transfers described in paragraph (a)(2) of this section.*—The tax consequences of each deemed transfer described in paragraph (a)(2) of this section are determined under applicable provisions of the Internal Revenue Code as if the spouses had actually made such transfers. Accordingly, section 1041 applies to any deemed transfer of the stock and redemption proceeds between the transferor spouse and the nontransferor spouse, provided the requirements of section 1041 are otherwise satisfied with respect to such deemed transfer. Section 1041, however, will not apply to any deemed transfer of stock by the nontransferor spouse to the redeeming corporation in exchange for the redemption proceeds. See section 302 for rules relating to the tax consequences of certain redemptions; redemptions characterized as distributions under section 302(d) will be subject to section 301 if received from a Subchapter C corporation or section 1368 if received from a Subchapter S corporation.

(c) *Special rules in case of agreements between spouses or former spouses.*—(1) *Transferor spouse taxable.*—Notwithstanding applicable tax law, a transferor spouse's receipt of property in respect of the redeemed stock shall be treated as a distribution to the transferor spouse in redemption of such stock for purposes of paragraph (a)(1) of this section, and shall not be treated as resulting in a constructive distribution to the nontransferor spouse for purposes of paragraph (a)(2) of this section, if a divorce or separation instrument, or a valid written agreement between the transferor spouse and the nontransferor spouse, expressly provides that—

(i) Both spouses or former spouses intend for the redemption to be treated, for Federal income tax purposes, as a redemption distribution to the transferor spouse; and

(ii) Such instrument or agreement supersedes any other instrument or agreement concerning the purchase, sale, redemption, or other disposition of the stock that is the subject of the redemption.

(2) *Nontransferor spouse taxable.*—Notwithstanding applicable tax law, a transferor spouse's receipt of property in respect of the redeemed stock shall be treated as resulting in a constructive distribution to the nontransferor spouse for purposes of paragraph (a)(2) of this section, and shall not be treated as a distribution to the transferor spouse in redemption of such stock for purposes of paragraph (a)(1) of this section, if a divorce or separation instrument, or a valid written agreement between the transferor spouse and the nontransferor spouse, expressly provides that—

(i) Both spouses or former spouses intend for the redemption to be treated, for Federal income tax purposes, as resulting in a constructive distribution to the nontransferor spouse; and

(ii) Such instrument or agreement supersedes any other instrument or agreement concerning the purchase, sale, redemption, or other disposition of the stock that is the subject of the redemption.

(3) *Execution of agreements.*—For purposes of this paragraph (c), a divorce or separation instrument must be effective, or a valid written agreement must be executed by both spouses or former spouses, prior to the date on which the transferor spouse (in the case of paragraph (c)(1) of this section) or the nontransferor spouse (in the case of paragraph (c)(2) of this section) files such spouse's first timely filed Federal income tax return for the year that includes the date of the stock redemption, but no later than the date such return is due (including extensions).

(d) *Examples.*—The provisions of this section may be illustrated by the following examples:

Example 1. Corporation X has 100 shares outstanding. A and B each own 50 shares. A and B divorce. The divorce instrument requires B to purchase A's shares, and A to sell A's shares to B, in exchange for $100x. Corporation X redeems A's shares for $100x. Assume that, under applicable tax law, B has a primary and unconditional obligation to purchase A's stock, and therefore the stock redemption results in a constructive distribution to B. Also assume that the special rule of paragraph (c)(1) of this section does not apply. Accordingly, under paragraphs (a)(2) and (b)(2) of this section, A shall be treated as transferring A's stock of Corporation X to B in a transfer to which section 1041 applies (assuming the requirements of section 1041 are otherwise satisfied), B shall be treated as transferring the Corporation X stock B is deemed to have received from A to Corporation X in exchange for $100x in an exchange to which section 1041 does not apply and sections 302(d) and 301 apply, and B shall be treated as transferring the $100x to A in a transfer to which section 1041 applies.

Example 2. Assume the same facts as *Example 1*, except that the divorce instrument provides as follows: "A and B agree that the redemption will be treated for Federal income tax purposes as a redemption distribution to A." The divorce instrument further provides that it "supersedes all other instruments or agreements concerning the purchase, sale, redemption, or other disposition of the stock that is the subject of the redemption." By virtue of the special rule of paragraph (c)(1) of this section and under paragraphs (a)(1) and (b)(1) of this section, the tax consequences of the redemption shall be determined in accordance with its form as a redemption of A's shares by Corporation X and shall not be treated as resulting in a constructive distribution to B. See section 302.

Example 3. Assume the same facts as *Example 1*, except that the divorce instrument requires A to sell A's shares to Corporation X in exchange for a note. B guarantees Corporation X's payment of the note. Assume that, under applicable tax law, B does not have a primary and unconditional obligation to purchase A's stock, and therefore the stock redemption does not result in a constructive distribution to B. Also assume that the special rule of paragraph (c)(2) of this section does not apply. Accordingly, under paragraphs (a)(1) and (b)(1) of this section, the tax consequences of the redemption shall be determined in accordance with its form as a redemption of A's shares by Corporation X. See section 302.

Example 4. Assume the same facts as *Example 3,* except that the divorce instrument provides as follows: "A and B agree the redemption shall be treated, for Federal income tax purposes, as resulting in a constructive distribution to B." The divorce instrument further provides that it "supersedes any other instrument or agreement concerning the purchase, sale, redemption, or other disposition of the stock that is the subject of the redemption." By virtue of the special rule of paragraph (c)(2) of this section, the redemption is treated as resulting in a constructive distribution to B for purposes of paragraph (a)(2) of this section. Accordingly, under paragraphs (a)(2) and (b)(2) of this section, A shall be treated as transferring A's stock of Corporation X to B in a transfer to which section 1041 applies (assuming the requirements of section 1041 are otherwise satisfied), B shall be treated as transferring the Corporation X stock B is deemed to have received from A to Corporation X in exchange for a note in an exchange to which section 1041 does not apply and sections 302(d) and 301 apply, and B shall be treated as transferring the note to A in a transfer to which section 1041 applies.

(e) *Effective date.*—Except as otherwise provided in this paragraph, this section is applicable to redemptions of stock on or after January 13, 2003, except for redemptions of stock that are pursuant to instruments in effect before January 13, 2003. For redemptions of stock before January 13, 2003 and redemptions of stock that are pursuant to instruments in effect before January 13, 2003, see § 1.1041-1T(c), A-9. However, these regulations will be applicable to redemptions described in the preceding sentence of this paragraph (e) if the spouses or former spouses execute a written agreement on or after August 3, 2001 that satisfies the requirements of one of the special rules in paragraph (c) of this section with respect to such redemption. A divorce or separation instrument or valid written agreement executed on or after August 3, 2001, and before May 13, 2003 that meets the requirements of the special rule in Regulations Project REG-107151-00 published in 2001-2 C.B. 370 (see § 601.601(d)(2) of this chapter) will be treated as also meeting the requirements of the special rule in paragraph (c)(2) of this section. [Reg. § 1.1041-2.]

☐ [*T.D.* 9035, 1-10-2003.]

* * *

General Rules for Determining Capital Gains and Losses

[Reg. § 1.1221-1]

§ 1.1221-1. Meaning of terms.—(a) The term "capital assets" includes all classes of property not specifically excluded by section 1221. In determining whether property is a "capital asset", the period for which held is immaterial.

(b) Property used in the trade or business of a taxpayer of a character which is subject to the allowance for depreciation provided in section 167 and real property used in the trade or business of a taxpayer is excluded from the term "capital assets". Gains and losses from the sale or exchange of such property are not treated as gains and losses from the sale or exchange of capital assets, except to the extent provided in section 1231. See § 1.1231-1. Property held for the production of income, but not used in a trade or business of the taxpayer, is not excluded from the term "capital assets" even though depreciation may have been allowed with respect to such property under section 23(1) of the Internal Revenue Code of 1939 before its amendment by section 121(c) of the Revenue Act of 1942 (56 Stat. 819). However, gain or loss upon the sale or exchange of land held by a taxpayer primarily for sale to customers in the ordinary course of his business, as in the case of a dealer in real estate, is not subject to the provisions of subchapter P (section 1201 and following), chapter 1 of the Code.

(c)(1) A copyright, a literary, musical, or artistic composition, and similar property are excluded from the term "capital assets" if held by a taxpayer whose personal efforts created such property, or if held by a taxpayer in whose hands the basis of such property is determined, for purposes of determining gain from a sale or exchange, in whole or in part by reference to the basis of such property in the hands of a taxpayer whose personal efforts created such property. For purposes of this subparagraph, the phrase "similar property" includes, for example, such property as a theatrical production, a radio program, a newspaper cartoon strip, or any other property eligible for copyright protection (whether under statute or common law), but does not include a patent or an invention, or a design which may be protected only under the patent law and not under the copyright law.

(2) In the case of sales and other dispositions occurring after July 25, 1969, a letter, a memorandum, or similar property is excluded from the term "capital asset" if held by (i) a taxpayer whose personal efforts created such property, (ii) a taxpayer for whom such property was prepared or produced, or (iii) a taxpayer in whose hands the basis of such property is determined, for purposes of determining gain from a sale or exchange, in whole or in part by reference to the basis of such property in the hands of a taxpayer described in subdivision (i) or (ii) of this subparagraph. In the case of a collection of letters, memorandums, or similar property held by a person who is a taxpayer described in subdivision (i), (ii), or (iii) of this subparagraph as to some of such letters, memorandums, or similar property but not as to others, this subparagraph shall apply only to those letters, memorandums, or similar property as to which such person is a taxpayer described in such subdivision. For purposes of this subparagraph, the phrase "similar property" includes, for example, such property as a draft of a speech, a manuscript, a research

paper, an oral recording of any type, a transcript of an oral recording, a transcript of an oral interview or of dictation, a personal or business diary, a log or journal, a corporate archive, including a corporate charter, office correspondence, a financial record, a drawing, a photograph, or a dispatch. A letter, memorandum, or property similar to a letter or memorandum, addressed to a taxpayer shall be considered as prepared or produced for him. This subparagraph does not apply to property, such as a corporate archive, office correspondence, or a financial record, sold or disposed of as part of a going business if such property has no significant value separate and apart from its relation to and use in such business; it also does not apply to any property to which subparagraph (1) of this paragraph applies (i.e., property to which section 1221(3) applied before its amendment by section 514(a) of the Tax Reform Act of 1969 (83 Stat. 643).

(3) For purposes of this paragraph, in general property is created in whole or in part by the personal efforts of a taxpayer if such taxpayer performs literary, theatrical, musical, artistic, or other creative or productive work which affirmatively contributes to the creation of the property, or if such taxpayer directs and guides others in the performance of such work. A taxpayer, such as corporate executive, who merely has administrative control of writers, actors, artists, or personnel and who does not substantially engage in the direction and guidance of such persons in the performance of their work, does not create property by his personal efforts. However, for purposes of subparagraph (2) of this paragraph, a letter or memorandum, or property similar to a letter or memorandum, which is prepared by personnel who are under the administrative control of a taxpayer, such as a corporate executive, shall be deemed to have been prepared or produced for him whether or not such letter, memorandum, or similar property is reviewed by him.

(4) For the application of section 1231 to the sale or exchange of property to which this paragraph applies, see § 1.1231-1. For the application of section 170 to the charitable contribution of property to which this paragraph applies, see section 170(e) and the regulations thereunder.

(d) Section 1221(4) excludes from the definition of "capital asset" accounts or notes receivable acquired in the ordinary course of trade or business for services rendered or from the sale of stock in trade or inventory or property held for sale to customers in the ordinary course of trade or business. Thus, if a taxpayer acquires a note receivable for services rendered, reports the fair market value of the note as income, and later sells the note for less than the amount previously reported, the loss is an ordinary loss. On the other hand, if the taxpayer later sells the note for more than the amount originally reported, the excess is treated as ordinary income.

(e) Obligations of the United States or any of its possessions, or of a State or Territory, or any political subdivision thereof, or of the District of Columbia, issued on or after March 1, 1941, on a discount basis and payable without interest at a fixed maturity date not exceeding one year from the date of issue, are excluded from the term "capital assets." An obligation may be issued on a discount basis even though the price paid exceeds the face amount. Thus, although the Second Liberty Bond Act (31 U.S.C. 754) provides that United States Treasury bills shall be issued on a discount basis, the issuing price paid for a particular bill may, by reason of competitive bidding, actually exceed the face amount of the bill. Since the obligations of the type described in this paragraph are excluded from the term "capital assets", gains or losses from the sale or exchange of such obligations are not subject to the limitations provided in such subchapter P. It is, therefore, not necessary for a taxpayer (other than a life insurance company taxable under part I (section 801 and following), subchapter L, chapter 1 of the Code, as amended by the Life Insurance Company Tax Act of 1955 (70 Stat. 36), and, in the case of taxable years beginning before January 1, 1955, subject to taxation only on interest, dividends, and rents) to segregate the original discount accrued and the gain or loss realized upon the sale or other disposition of any such obligation. See section 454(b) with respect to the original discount accrued. The provisions of this paragraph may be illustrated by the following examples:

Example (1). A (not a life insurance company) buys a $100,000, 90-day Treasury bill upon issuance for $99,998. As of the close of the forty-fifth day of the life of such bill, he sells it to B (not a life insurance company) for $99,999.50. The entire net gain to A of $1.50 may be taken into account as a single item of income, without allocating $1 to interest and $0.50 to gain. If B holds the bill until maturity his net gain of $0.50 may similarly be taken into account as a single item of income, without allocating $1 to interest and $0.50 to loss.

Example (2). The facts in this example are the same as in example (1) except that the selling price to B is $99,998.50. The net gain to A of $0.50 may be taken into account without allocating $1 to interest and $0.50 to loss, and, similarly, if B holds the bill until maturity his entire net gain of $1.50 may be taken into account as a single item of income without allocating $1 to interest and $0.50 to gain. [Reg. § 1.1221-1.]

□ [*T.D. 6243, 7-23-57. Amended by T.D. 7369, 7-15-75.*]

* * *

[Reg. § 1.1221-3]

§ 1.1221-3. Time and manner for electing capital asset treatment for certain self-created musical works.—(a) *Description.*—Section 1221(b)(3) allows an electing taxpayer to treat the sale or exchange of a musical composition or a copyright in a musical work created by the taxpayer's personal efforts (or having a basis determined by reference to the basis of such property in the hands of a taxpayer whose personal efforts created such property) as the sale or exchange of a capital asset. As a consequence, gain or loss from the sale or exchange is treated as capital gain or loss.

(b) *Time and manner for making the election.*—An election described in this section is made separately for each musical composition (or copyright in a musical work) sold or exchanged during the taxable year. An election must be made on or before the due date (including extensions) of the income tax return for the taxable year of the sale or exchange. The election is made on Schedule D, "Capital Gains and Losses," of the appropriate income tax form (for example, Form 1040, "U.S. Individual Income Tax Return;" Form 1065, "U.S. Return of Partnership Income;" Form 1120, "U.S. Corporation Income Tax Return") by treating the sale or exchange as the sale or exchange of a capital asset, in accordance with the form and its instructions.

(c) *Revocability of election.*—The election described in this section is revocable with the consent of the Commissioner. To seek consent to revoke the election, a taxpayer must submit a request for a letter ruling under the applicable administrative procedures. Alternatively, an automatic extension of 6 months from the due date of the taxpayer's income tax return (excluding extensions) is granted to revoke the election, provided the taxpayer timely filed the taxpayer's income tax return and, within this 6-month extension period, the taxpayer files an amended income tax return that treats the sale or exchange as the sale or exchange of property that is not a capital asset.

(d) *Effective/applicability date.*—This section applies to elections under section 1221(b)(3) in taxable years beginning after May 17, 2006. [Reg. § 1.1221-3.]

□ [*T.D.* 9514, 2-4-2011.]

ESTATE AND GIFT TAXES

See p. 15 for regulations not amended to reflect law changes

Estate Tax

ESTATES OF CITIZENS OR RESIDENTS

Tax Imposed

[Reg. § 20.0-1]

§ 20.0-1. Introduction.—(a) *In general.*—(1) The regulations in this part (Part 20, Subchapter B, Chapter I, Title 26, Code of Federal Regulations) are designated "Estate Tax Regulations". These regulations pertain to (i) the Federal estate tax imposed by chapter 11 of subtitle B of the Internal Revenue Code on the transfer of estates of decedents dying after August 16, 1954, and (ii) certain related administrative provisions of subtitle F of the Code. It should be noted that the application of many of the provisions of these regulations may be affected by the provisions of an applicable death tax convention with a foreign country. Unless otherwise indicated, references in the regulations to the "Internal Revenue Code" or the "Code" are references to the Internal Revenue Code of 1954, as amended, and references to a section or other provision of law are references to a section or other provision of the Internal Revenue Code of 1954, as amended. Unless otherwise provided, the Estate Tax Regulations are applicable to the estates of decedents dying after August 16, 1954, and supersede the regulations contained in Part 81 of this chapter (1939) (Regulations 105, Estate Tax), as prescribed and made applicable to the Internal Revenue Code of 1954 by Treasury Decision 6091, signed August 16, 1954 (19 F.R. 5167, August 17, 1954).

(2) Section 2208 makes the provisions of chapter 11 of the Code apply to the transfer of the estates of certain decedents dying after September 2, 1958, who were citizens of the United States and residents of a possession thereof at the time of death. Section 2209 makes the provisions of chapter 11 apply to the transfer of the estates of certain other decedents dying after September 14, 1960, who were citizens of the United States and residents of a possession thereof at the time of death. See §§ 20.2208-1 and 20.2209-1. Except as otherwise provided in §§ 20.2208-1 and 20.2209-1, the provisions of these regulations do not apply to the estates of such decedents.

(b) *Scope of regulations.*—(1) *Estates of citizens or residents.*—Subchapter A of chapter 11 of the Code pertains to the taxation of the estate of a person who was a citizen or a resident of the United States at the time of his death. A "resident" decedent is a decedent who, at the time of his death, had his domicile in the United States. The term "United States," as used in the Estate Tax Regulations, includes only the States and the District of Columbia. The term also includes the Territories of Alaska and Hawaii prior to their admission as States. See section 7701(a)(9). A person acquires a domicile in a place by living there, for even a brief period of time, with no definite present intention of later removing therefrom. Residence without the requisite intention to remain indefinitely will not suffice to constitute domicile, nor will intention to change domicile effect such a change unless accompanied by actual removal. For the meaning of the term "citizen of the United States" as applied in a case where the decedent was a resident of a possession of the United States, see § 20.2208-1. The regulations pursuant to subchapter A are set forth in §§ 20.2001 to 20.2056(d)-1.

(2) *Estates of nonresidents not citizens.*—Subchapter B of Chapter 11 of the Code pertains to the taxation of the estate of a person who was a nonresident not a citizen of the United States at the time of his death. A "nonresident" decedent is a decedent who, at the time of his death, had his domicile outside the United States under the principles set forth in subparagraph (1) of this paragraph. (See, however, section 2202 with respect to missionaries in foreign service.) The regulations pursuant to subchapter B are set forth in §§ 20.2101 to 20.2108.

(3) *Miscellaneous substantive provisions.*—Subchapter C of chapter 11 of the Code contains a number of miscellaneous substantive provisions. The regulations pursuant to subchapter C are set forth in §§ 20.2203-1 through 20.2209-1.

(4) *Procedure and administration provisions.*—Subtitle F of the Internal Revenue Code contains some sections which are applicable to the Federal estate tax. The regulations pursuant to those sections are set forth in §§ 20.6001 to 20.7404. Such regulations do not purport to be all the regulations on procedure and administration which are pertinent to estate tax matters. For the remainder of the regulations on procedure and administration which are pertinent to estate tax matters, see Part 301 (Procedure and Administration Regulations) of this chapter.

(c) *Arrangement and numbering.*—Each section of the regulations in this part (other than this section and § 20.0-2) is designated by a number composed of the part number followed by a decimal point (20.); the section of the Internal Revenue Code which it interprets; a hyphen (-); and a number identifying the section. By use of these designations one can ascertain the sections of the regulations relating to a provision of the Code. For example, the regulations pertaining to section 2012 of the Code are designated § 20.2012-1. [Reg. § 20.0-1.]

☐ [*T.D.* 6296, 6-23-58. *Amended by T.D.* 6526, 1-18-61; *T.D.* 7238, 12-28-72; *T.D.* 7296, 12-11-73;

T.D. 7665, 1-24-80, *T.D.* 8522, 2-28-94 *and T.D.* 9849, 3-11-2019.]

[Reg. § 20.0-2]

§ 20.0-2. General description of tax.—(a) *Nature of tax.*—The Federal estate tax is neither a property tax nor an inheritance tax. It is a tax imposed upon the transfer of the entire taxable estate and not upon any particular legacy, devise, or distributive share. Escheat of a decedent's property to the State for lack of heirs is a transfer which causes the property to be included in the decedent's gross estate.

(b) *Method of determining tax; estate of citizen or resident.*—(1) *In general.*—Subparagraphs (2) to (5) of this paragraph contain a general description of the method to be used in determining the Federal estate tax imposed upon the transfer of the estate of a decedent who was a citizen or resident of the United States at the time of his death.

(2) *Gross estate.*—The first step in determining the tax is to ascertain the total value of the decedent's gross estate. The value of the gross estate includes the value of all property to the extent of the interest therein of the decedent at the time of his death. (For certain exceptions in the case of real property situated outside the United States, see paragraphs (a) and (c) of § 20.2031-1.) In addition, the gross estate may include property in which the decedent did not have an interest at the time of his death. A decedent's gross estate for Federal estate tax purposes may therefore be very different from the decedent's estate for local probate purposes. Examples of items which may be included in a decedent's gross estate and not in his probate estate are the following: certain property transferred by the decedent during his lifetime without adequate consideration; property held jointly by the decedent and others; property over which the decedent had a general power of appointment; proceeds of certain policies of insurance on the decedent's life; annuities; and dower or curtesy of a surviving spouse or a statutory estate in lieu thereof. For a detailed explanation of the method of ascertaining the value of the gross estate, see sections 2031 through 2044, and the regulations thereunder.

(3) *Taxable estate.*—The second step in determining the tax is to ascertain the value of the decedent's taxable estate. The value of the taxable estate is determined by subtracting from the value of the gross estate the authorized exemption and deductions. Under various conditions and limitations, deductions are allowable for expenses, indebtedness, taxes, losses, charitable transfers, and transfers to a surviving spouse. For a detailed explanation of the method of ascertaining the value of the taxable estate, see sections 2051 through 2056, and the regulations thereunder.

(4) *Gross estate tax.*—The third step is the determination of the gross estate tax. This is accomplished by the application of certain rates to the value of the decedent's taxable estate. In this connection, see section 2001 and the regulations thereunder.

(5) *Net estate tax payable.*—The final step is the determination of the net estate tax payable. This is done by subtracting from the gross estate tax the authorized credits against tax. Under certain conditions and limitations, credits are allowable for the following (computed in the order stated below):

(i) State death taxes paid in connection with the decedent's estate (section 2011);

(ii) Gift taxes paid on inter-vivos transfers by the decedent of property included in his gross estate (section 2012);

(iii) Foreign death taxes paid in connection with the decedent's estate (section 2014); and

(iv) Federal estate taxes paid on transfers of property to the decedent (section 2013).

Sections 2015 and 2016 contain certain further rules for the application of the credits for State and foreign death taxes.

Sections 25.2701-5 and 25.2702-6 of this chapter contain rules that provide additional adjustments to mitigate double taxation in cases where the amount of the decedent's gift was previously determined under the special valuation provisions of section 2701 and 2702. For a detailed explanation of the credits against tax, see sections 2011 through 2016 and the regulations thereunder.

(c) *Method of determining tax; estate of nonresident not a citizen.*—In general, the method to be used in determining the Federal estate tax imposed upon the transfer of an estate of a decedent who was a nonresident not a citizen of the United States is similar to that described in paragraph (b) of this section with respect to the estate of a citizen or resident. Briefly stated, the steps are as follows: First, ascertain the sum of the value of that part of the decedent's "entire gross estate" which at the time of his death was situated in the United States (see §§ 20.2103-1 and 20.2014-1) and, in the case of an estate of an expatriate to which section 2107 applies, any amounts includible in his gross estate under section 2107(b) (see paragraph (b) of § 20.2107-1); second, determine the value of the taxable estate by subtracting from the amount determined under the first step the amount of the allowable deductions (see § 20.2106-1); third, compute the gross estate tax on the taxable estate (see § 20.2106-1); and fourth, subtract from the gross estate tax the total amount of any allowable credits in order to arrive at the net estate tax payable (see § 20.2102-1 and paragraph (c) of § 20.2107-1). [Reg. § 20.0-2.]

☐ [*T.D.* 6296, 6-23-58. *Amended by T.D.* 6684, 10-23-63; *T.D.* 7296, 12-11-73 *and T.D.* 8395, 1-28-92.]

[Reg. § 20.2001-1]

§ 20.2001-1. Valuation of adjusted taxable gifts and section 2701(d) taxable events.—(a) *Adjusted taxable gifts made prior to August 6, 1997.*—For purposes of determining the value of adjusted taxable gifts as defined in section 2001(b), if the gift was made prior to August 6, 1997, the value of the gift may be adjusted at any time, even if the time within which a gift tax may be assessed has expired under section 6501. This paragraph (a) also applies to adjustments involving issues other than valuation for gifts made prior to August 6, 1997.

(b) *Adjusted taxable gifts and section 2701(d) taxable events occurring after August 5, 1997.*—For purposes of determining the amount of adjusted taxable gifts as defined in section 2001(b), if, under section 6501, the time has expired within which a gift tax may be assessed under chapter 12 of the Internal Revenue Code (or under corresponding provisions of prior laws) with respect to a gift made after August 5, 1997, or with respect to an increase in taxable gifts required under section 2701(d) and §25.2701-4 of this chapter, then the amount of the taxable gift will be the amount as finally determined for gift tax purposes under chapter 12 of the Internal Revenue Code and the amount of the taxable gift may not thereafter be adjusted. The rule of this paragraph (b) applies to adjustments involving all issues relating to the gift, including valuation issues and legal issues involving the interpretation of the gift tax law.

(c) *Finally determined.*—For purposes of paragraph (b) of this section, the amount of a taxable gift as finally determined for gift tax purposes is—

(1) The amount of the taxable gift as shown on a gift tax return, or on a statement attached to the return, if the Internal Revenue Service does not contest such amount before the time has expired under section 6501 within which gift taxes may be assessed;

(2) The amount as specified by the Internal Revenue Service before the time has expired under section 6501 within which gift taxes may be assessed on the gift, if such specified amount is not timely contested by the taxpayer;

(3) The amount as finally determined by a court of competent jurisdiction; or

(4) The amount as determined pursuant to a settlement agreement entered into between the taxpayer and the Internal Revenue Service.

(d) *Definitions.*—For purposes of paragraph (b) of this section, the amount is finally determined by a court of competent jurisdiction when the court enters a final decision, judgment, decree or other order with respect to the amount of the taxable gift that is not subject to appeal. See, for example, section 7481 regarding the finality of a decision by the U.S. Tax Court. Also, for purposes of paragraph (b) of this section, a settlement agreement means any agreement entered into by the Internal Revenue Service and the taxpayer that is binding on both. The term includes a closing agreement under section 7121, a compromise under section 7122, and an agreement entered into in settlement of litigation involving the amount of the taxable gift.

(e) *Expiration of period of assessment.*—For purposes of determining if the time has expired within which a tax may be assessed under chapter 12 of the Internal Revenue Code, see §301.6501(c)-1(e) and (f) of this chapter.

(f) *Effective dates.*—Paragraph (a) of this section applies to transfers of property by gift made prior to August 6, 1997, if the estate tax return for the donor/decedent's estate is filed after December 3, 1999. Paragraphs (b) through (e) of this section apply to transfers of property by gift made after August 5, 1997, if the gift tax return for the calendar period in which the gift is made is filed after December 3, 1999. [Reg. §20.2001-1.]

☐ [*T.D. 6296, 6-23-58. Amended by T.D. 8845, 12-2-99.*]

[Reg. §20.2001-2]

§20.2001-2. Valuation of adjusted taxable gifts for purposes of determining the deceased spousal unused exclusion amount of last deceased spouse.—(a) *General rule.*—Notwithstanding §20.2001-1(b), §§20.2010-2(d) and 20.2010-3(d) provide additional rules regarding the authority of the Internal Revenue Service to examine any gift or other tax return(s), even if the time within which a tax may be assessed under section 6501 has expired, for the purpose of determining the deceased spousal unused exclusion amount available under section 2010(c) of the Internal Revenue Code.

(b) *Effective/applicability date.*—Paragraph (a) of this section applies to the estates of decedents dying on or after June 12, 2015. See 26 CFR 20.2001-2T(a), as contained in 26 CFR part 20, revised as of April 1, 2015, for the rules applicable to estates of decedents dying on or after January 1, 2011, and before June 12, 2015. [Reg. §20.2001-2.]

☐ [*T.D. 9725, 6-12-2015.*]

[Reg. §20.2002-1]

§20.2002-1. Liability for payment of tax.—The Federal estate tax imposed both with respect to the estates of citizens or residents and with respect to estates of nonresidents not citizens is payable by the executor or administrator of the decedent's estate. This duty applies to the entire tax, regardless of the fact that the gross estate consists in part of property which does not come within the possession of the executor or administrator. If there is no executor or administrator appointed, qualified, and acting in the United States, any person in actual or constructive possession of any property of the decedent is required to pay the entire tax to the extent of the value of the property in his possession. See section 2203, defining the term "executor". The personal liability of the executor or such other person is described in section 3467 of the Revised Statutes (31 U.S.C. 192) as follows:

> Every executor, administrator, or assignee, or other person, who pays, in whole or in part, any debt due by the person or estate for whom or for which he acts before he satisfies and pays the debts due to the United States from such person or estate, shall become answerable in his own person

and estate to the extent of such payments for the debts so due to the United States, or for so much thereof as may remain due and unpaid.

As used in said section, the word "debt" includes a beneficiary's distributive share of an estate. Thus, if the executor pays a debt due by the decedent's estate or distributes any portion of the estate before all the estate tax is paid, he is personally liable, to the extent of the payment or distribution, for so much of the estate tax as remains due and unpaid. In addition, section 6324(a)(2) provides that if the estate tax is not paid when due, then the spouse, transferee, trustee (except the trustee of an employee's trust which meets the requirements of section 401(a)), surviving tenant, person in possession of the property by reason of the exercise, nonexercise, or release of a power of appointment, or beneficiary, who receives, or has on the date of the decedent's death, property included in the gross estate under sections 2034 through 2042, is personally liable for the tax to the extent of the value, at the time of the decedent's death, of such property. See also the following related sections of the Internal Revenue Code: section 2204, discharge of executor from personal liability; section 2205, reimbursement out of estate; sections 2206 and 2207, liability of life insurance beneficiaries and recipients of property over which decedent had power of appointment; sections 6321 through 6325, concerning liens for taxes; and section 6901(a)(1), concerning the liabilities of transferees and fiduciaries. [Reg. § 20.2002-1.]

☐ [*T.D.* 6296, 6-23-58.]

Credits Against Tax

[Reg. § 20.2010-0]

§ 20.2010-0. Table of contents.—This section lists the table of contents for §§ 20.2010-1 through 20.2010-3.

[Reg. § 20.2010-0.]

☐ [*T.D.* 9725, 6-12-2015. *Amended by T.D.* 9884, 11-22-2019.]

[Reg. § 20.2010-1]

§ 20.2010-1. Unified credit against estate tax; in general.—(a) *General rule.*—Section 2010(a) allows the estate of every decedent a credit against the estate tax imposed by section 2001. The allowable credit is the applicable credit amount. See paragraph (e)(1) of this section for an explanation of the term *applicable credit amount.*

(b) *Special rule in case of certain gifts made before 1977.*—The applicable credit amount allowable under paragraph (a) of this section must be reduced by an amount equal to 20 percent of the aggregate amount allowed as a specific exemption under section 2521 (as in effect before its repeal by the Tax Reform Act of 1976) for gifts made by the decedent after September 8, 1976, and before January 1, 1977.

(c) *Special rule in the case of a difference between the basic exclusion amount applicable to gifts and that applicable at the donor's date of death.*—Changes in the basic exclusion amount that occur between the date of a donor's gift and the date of the donor's death may cause the basic exclusion amount allowable on the date of a gift to exceed that allowable on the date of death. If the total of the amounts allowable as a credit in computing the gift tax payable on the decedent's post-1976 gifts, within the meaning of section 2001(b)(2), to the extent such credits are based solely on the basic exclusion amount as defined and adjusted in section 2010(c)(3), exceeds the credit allowable within the meaning of section 2010(a) in computing the estate tax, again only to the extent such credit is based solely on such basic exclusion amount, in each case by applying the tax rates in effect at the decedent's death, then the portion of the credit allowable in computing the estate tax on the decedent's taxable estate that is attributable to the basic exclusion amount is the sum of the amounts attributable to the basic exclusion amount allowable as a credit in computing the gift tax payable on the decedent's post-1976 gifts.

(1) *Computational rules.*—For purposes of this paragraph (c):

(i) In determining the amounts allowable as a credit:

(A) The amount allowable as a credit in computing gift tax payable for any calendar period may not exceed the tentative tax on the gifts made during that period (section 2505(c)); and

(B) The amount allowable as a credit in computing the estate tax may not exceed the net tentative tax on the taxable estate (section 2010(d)).

(ii) In determining the extent to which an amount allowable as a credit in computing gift tax payable is based solely on the basic exclusion amount:

(A) Any deceased spousal unused exclusion (DSUE) amount available to the decedent is deemed to be applied to gifts made by the decedent before the decedent's basic exclusion amount is applied to those gifts (see §§ 20.2010-3(b) and 25.2505-2(b));

(B) In a calendar period in which the applicable exclusion amount allowable with regard to gifts made during that period includes amounts other than the basic exclusion amount, the allowable basic exclusion amount may not exceed that necessary to reduce the tentative gift tax to zero; and

(C) In a calendar period in which the applicable exclusion amount allowable with regard to gifts made during that period includes amounts other than the basic exclusion amount, the portion of the credit based solely on the basic exclusion amount is that which corresponds to the result of dividing the basic exclusion amount allocable to those gifts by the applicable exclusion amount allocable to those gifts.

(iii) In determining the extent to which an amount allowable as a credit in computing the estate tax is based solely on the basic exclusion amount, the credit is computed as if the applicable exclusion amount were limited to the basic exclusion amount.

(2) *Examples.*—All basic exclusion amounts include hypothetical inflation adjustments. Unless otherwise stated, in each example the decedent's date of death is after 2025.

(i) *Example 1.* Individual A (never married) made cumulative post-1976 taxable gifts of $9 million, all of which were sheltered from gift tax by the cumulative total of $11.4 million in basic exclusion amount allowable on the dates of the gifts. The basic exclusion amount on A's date of death is $6.8 million. A was not eligible for any restored exclusion amount pursuant to Notice 2017-15. Because the total of the amounts allowable as a credit in computing the gift tax payable on A's post-1976 gifts (based on the $9 million of basic exclusion amount used to determine those credits) exceeds the credit based on the $6.8 million basic exclusion amount allowable on A's date of death, this paragraph (c) applies, and the credit for purposes of computing A's estate tax is based on a basic exclusion amount of $9 million, the amount used to determine the credits allowable in computing the gift tax payable on A's post-1976 gifts.

(ii) *Example 2.* Assume that the facts are the same as in *Example 1* of paragraph (c)(2)(i) of this section except that A made cumulative post-1976 taxable gifts of $4 million. Because the total of the amounts allowable as a credit in computing the gift tax payable on A's post-1976 gifts is less than the credit based on the $6.8 million basic exclusion amount allowable on A's date of death, this paragraph (c) does not apply. The credit to be applied for purposes of computing A's estate tax is based on the $6.8 million basic exclusion amount as of A's date of death, subject to the limitation of section 2010(d).

(iii) *Example 3.* Individual B's predeceased spouse, C, died before 2026, at a time when the basic exclusion amount was $11.4 million. C had made no taxable gifts and had no taxable estate. C's executor elected, pursuant to § 20.2010-2, to allow B to take into account C's $11.4 million DSUE amount. B made no taxable gifts and did not remarry. The basic exclusion amount on B's date of death is $6.8 million. Because the total of the amounts allowable as a credit in computing the gift tax payable on B's post-1976 gifts attributable to the basic exclusion amount (zero) is less than the credit based on the basic exclusion amount allowable on B's date of death, this paragraph (c) does not apply. The credit to be applied for purposes of computing B's estate tax is based on B's $18.2 million applicable exclusion amount, consisting of the $6.8 million basic exclusion amount on B's date of death plus the $11.4 million DSUE amount, subject to the limitation of section 2010(d).

(iv) *Example 4.* Assume the facts are the same as in *Example 3* of paragraph (c)(2)(iii) of this section except that, after C's death and before 2026, B makes taxable gifts of $14 million in a year when the basic exclusion amount is $12 million. B is considered to apply the DSUE amount to the gifts before applying B's basic exclusion amount. The amount allowable as a credit in computing the gift tax payable on B's post-1976 gifts for that year ($5,545,800) is the tax on $14 million, consisting of $11.4 million in DSUE amount and $2.6 million in basic exclusion amount. This basic exclusion amount is 18.6 percent of the $14 million exclusion amount allocable to those gifts, with the result that $1,031,519 (0.186 x $5,545,800) of the amount allowable as a credit for that year in computing gift tax payable is based solely on the basic exclusion amount. The amount allowable as a credit based solely on the basic exclusion amount for purposes of computing B's estate tax ($2,665,800) is the tax on the $6.8 million basic exclusion amount on B's date of death. Because the portion of the credit allowable in computing the gift tax payable on B's post-1976 gifts based solely on the basic exclusion amount ($1,031,519) is less than the credit based solely on the basic exclusion amount ($2,665,800) allowable on B's date of death, this paragraph (c) does not apply. The credit to be applied for purposes of computing B's estate tax is based on B's $18.2 million applicable exclusion amount, consisting of the $6.8 million basic exclusion amount on B's date of death plus the $11.4 million DSUE amount, subject to the limitation of section 2010(d).

(3) [Reserved]

(d) *Credit limitation.*—The applicable credit amount allowed under paragraph (a) of this section cannot exceed the amount of the estate tax imposed by section 2001.

(e) *Explanation of terms.*—The explanation of terms in this section applies to this section and to §§20.2010-2 and 20.2010-3.

(1) *Applicable credit amount.*—The term *applicable credit amount* refers to the allowable credit against estate tax imposed by section 2001 and gift tax imposed by section 2501. The applicable credit amount equals the amount of the tentative tax that would be determined under section 2001(c) if the amount on which such tentative tax is to be computed were equal to the applicable exclusion amount. The applicable credit amount is determined by applying the unified rate schedule in section 2001(c) to the applicable exclusion amount.

(2) *Applicable exclusion amount.*—The *applicable exclusion amount* equals the sum of the basic exclusion amount and, in the case of a surviving spouse, the deceased spousal unused exclusion (DSUE) amount.

(3) *Basic exclusion amount.*—Except to the extent provided in paragraph (e)(3)(iii) of this section, the *basic exclusion amount* is the sum of the amounts described in paragraphs (e)(3)(i) and (ii) of this section.

(i) For any decedent dying in calendar year 2011 or thereafter, $5,000,000; and

(ii) For any decedent dying after calendar year 2011 and before calendar year 2018, $5,000,000 multiplied by the cost-of-living adjustment determined under section 1(f)(3) for the calendar year of the decedent's death by substituting "calendar year 2010" for "calendar year 1992" in section 1(f)(3)(B) and by rounding to the nearest multiple of $10,000. For any decedent dying after calendar year 2017, $5,000,000 multiplied by the cost-of-living adjustment determined under section 1(f)(3) for the calendar year of the decedent's death by substituting "calendar year 2010" for "calendar year 2016" in section 1(f)(3)(A)(ii) and rounded to the nearest multiple of $10,000.

(iii) For any decedent dying after calendar year 2017, and before calendar year 2026, paragraphs (e)(3)(i) and (ii) of this section will be applied by substituting "$10,000,000" for "$5,000,000."

(4) *Deceased spousal unused exclusion (DSUE) amount.*—The term *DSUE amount* refers, generally, to the unused portion of a decedent's applicable exclusion amount to the extent this amount does not exceed the basic exclusion amount in effect in the year of the decedent's death. For the rules on computing the DSUE amount, see §§20.2010-2(c) and 20.2010-3(b).

(5) *Last deceased spouse.*—The term *last deceased spouse* means the most recently deceased individual who, at that individual's death after December 31, 2010, was married to the surviving spouse. See §§20.2010-3(a) and 25.2505-2(a) for additional rules pertaining to the identity of the last deceased spouse for purposes of determining the applicable exclusion amount of the surviving spouse.

(f) *Applicability dates.*—(1) *In general.*—Except as provided in paragraph (f)(2) of this section, this section applies to the estates of decedents dying after June 11, 2015. For the rules applicable to estates of decedents dying after December 31, 2010, and before June 12, 2015, see §20.2010-1T, as contained in 26 CFR part 20, revised as of April 1, 2015.

(2) *Exceptions.*—Paragraphs (c) and (e)(3) of this section apply to estates of decedents dying on and after November 26, 2019. However, paragraph (e)(3) of this section may be applied by estates of decedents dying after December 31, 2017, and before November 26, 2019. For the explanation of the basic exclusion amount applicable to estates of decedents dying after June 11, 2015, and before January 1, 2018, see §20.2010-1(d)(3), as contained in 26 CFR part 20, revised as of April 1, 2019. [Reg. §20.2010-1.]

□ [*T.D. 9725, 6-12-2015. Amended by T.D. 9884, 11-22-2019.*]

[Reg. §20.2010-2]

§20.2010-2. Portability provisions applicable to estate of a decedent survived by a spouse.—(a) *Election required for portability.*—To allow a decedent's surviving spouse to take into account that decedent's deceased spousal unused exclusion (DSUE) amount, the executor of the decedent's estate must elect portability of the DSUE amount on a timely filed Form 706, "United States Estate (and Generation-Skipping Transfer) Tax Return" (estate tax return). This election is referred to in this section and in § 20.2010-3 as the portability election.

(1) *Timely filing required.*—An estate that elects portability will be considered, for purposes of subtitle B and subtitle F of the Internal Revenue Code (Code), to be required to file a return under section 6018(a). Accordingly, the due date of an estate tax return required to elect portability is nine months after the decedent's date of death or the last day of the period covered by an extension (if an extension of time for filing has been obtained). See §§ 20.6075-1 and 20.6081-1 for additional rules relating to the time for filing estate tax returns. An extension of time to elect portability under this paragraph (a) will not be granted under § 301.9100-3 of this chapter to an estate that is required to file an estate tax return under section 6018(a), as determined without regard to this paragraph (a). Such an extension, however, may be available under the procedures applicable under §§ 301.9100-1 and 301.9100-3 of this chapter to an estate that is not required to file a return under section 6018(a), as determined without regard to this paragraph (a).

(2) *Portability election upon filing of estate tax return.*—Upon the timely filing of a complete and properly prepared estate tax return, an executor of an estate of a decedent survived by a spouse will have elected portability of the decedent's DSUE amount unless the executor chooses not to elect portability and satisfies the requirement in paragraph (a)(3)(i) of this section. See paragraph (a)(7) of this section for the return requirements related to the portability election.

(3) *Portability election not made; requirements for election not to apply.*—The executor of the estate of a decedent survived by a spouse will not make or be considered to make the portability election if either of the following applies:

(i) The executor states affirmatively on a timely filed estate tax return, or in an attachment to that estate tax return, that the estate is not electing portability under section 2010(c)(5). The manner in which the executor may make this affirmative statement on the estate tax return is as set forth in the instructions issued with respect to such form ("Instructions for Form 706").

(ii) The executor does not timely file an estate tax return in accordance with paragraph (a)(1) of this section.

(4) *Election irrevocable.*—An executor of the estate of a decedent survived by a spouse who timely files an estate tax return may make or may supersede a portability election previously made, provided that the estate tax return reporting the election or the superseding election is filed on or before the due date of the return, including extensions actually granted. However, see paragraph (a)(6) of this section when contrary elections are made by more than one person permitted to make the election. The portability election, once made, becomes irrevocable once the due date of the estate tax return, including extensions actually granted, has passed.

(5) *Estates eligible to make the election.*—An executor may elect portability on behalf of the estate of a decedent survived by a spouse if the decedent dies on or after January 1, 2011. However, an executor of the estate of a nonresident decedent who was not a citizen of the United States at the time of death may not elect portability on behalf of that decedent, and the timely filing of such a decedent's estate tax return will not constitute the making of a portability election.

(6) *Persons permitted to make the election.*—(i) *Appointed executor.*—An executor or administrator of the estate of a decedent survived by a spouse that is appointed, qualified, and acting within the United States, within the meaning of section 2203 (an appointed executor), may timely file the estate tax return on behalf of the estate of the decedent and, in so doing, elect portability of the decedent's DSUE amount. An appointed executor also may elect not to have portability apply pursuant to paragraph (a)(3) of this section.

(ii) *Non-appointed executor.*—If there is no appointed executor, any person in actual or constructive possession of any property of the decedent (a non-appointed executor) may timely file the estate tax return on behalf of the estate of the decedent and, in so doing, elect portability of the decedent's DSUE amount, or, by complying with paragraph (a)(3) of this section, may elect not to have portability apply. A portability election made by a non-appointed executor when there is no appointed executor for that decedent's estate can be superseded by a subsequent contrary election made by an appointed executor of that same decedent's estate on an estate tax return filed on or before the due date of the return, including extensions actually granted. An election to allow portability made by a non-appointed executor cannot be superseded by a contrary election to have portability not apply made by another non-appointed executor of that same decedent's estate (unless such other non-appointed executor is the successor of the non-appointed executor who made the election). See § 20.6018-2 for additional rules relating to persons permitted to file the estate tax return.

(7) *Requirements of return.*—(i) *General rule.*—An estate tax return will be considered complete and properly prepared for purposes of this section if it is prepared in accordance with the instructions issued for the estate tax return (Instructions for Form 706) and if the requirements of §§ 20.6018-2, 20.6018-3, and 20.6018-4 are satisfied. However, see paragraph (a)(7)(ii) of this section for reduced requirements applicable to certain property of certain estates.

(ii) *Reporting of value not required for certain property.*—(A) *In general.*—A special rule applies with respect to certain property of estates in which the executor is not required to file an estate tax return under section 6018(a), as determined without regard to paragraph (a)(1) of this section. With respect to such an estate, for bequests, devises, or transfers of property included in the gross estate, the value of which is deductible under section 2056 or 2056A (marital deduction property) or under section 2055(a) (charitable deduction property), an executor is not required to report a value for such property on the estate tax return (except to the extent provided in this paragraph (a)(7)(ii)(A)) and will be required to report only the description, ownership, and/or beneficiary of such property, along with all other information necessary to establish the right of the estate to the deduction in accordance with §§20.2056(a)-1(b)(i) through (iii) and 20.2055-1(c), as applicable. However, this rule does not apply in certain circumstances as provided in this paragraph (a) and as may be further described in guidance issued from time to time by publication in the Internal Revenue Bulletin (see §601.601(d)(2)(ii)(b) of this chapter). In particular, this rule does not apply to marital deduction property or charitable deduction property if—

(1) The value of such property relates to, affects, or is needed to determine, the value passing from the decedent to a recipient other than the recipient of the marital or charitable deduction property;

(2) The value of such property is needed to determine the estate's eligibility for the provisions of sections 2032, 2032A, or another estate or generation-skipping transfer tax provision of the Code for which the value of such property or the value of the gross estate or adjusted gross estate must be known (not including section 1014 of the Code);

(3) Less than the entire value of an interest in property includible in the decedent's gross estate is marital deduction property or charitable deduction property; or

(4) A partial disclaimer or partial qualified terminable interest property (QTIP) election is made with respect to a bequest, devise, or transfer of property includible in the gross estate, part of which is marital deduction property or charitable deduction property.

(B) *Return requirements when reporting of value not required for certain property.*—Paragraph (a)(7)(ii)(A) of this section applies only if the executor exercises due diligence to estimate the fair market value of the gross estate, including the property described in paragraph (a)(7)(ii)(A) of this section. Using the executor's best estimate of the value of properties to which paragraph (a)(7)(ii)(A) of this section applies, the executor must report on the estate tax return, under penalties of perjury, the amount corresponding to the particular range within which falls the executor's best estimate of the total gross estate, in accordance with the Instructions for Form 706.

(C) *Examples.*—The following examples illustrate the application of paragraph (a)(7)(ii) of this section. In each example, assume that Husband (H) dies in 2015, survived by his wife (W), that both H and W are U.S. citizens, that H's gross estate does not exceed the excess of the applicable exclusion amount for the year of his death over the total amount of H's adjusted taxable gifts and any specific exemption under section 2521, and that H's executor (E) timely files Form 706 solely to make the portability election.

Example 1. (i) *Facts.* The assets includible in H's gross estate consist of a parcel of real property and bank accounts held jointly with W with rights of survivorship, a life insurance policy payable to W, and a survivor annuity payable to W for her life. H made no taxable gifts during his lifetime.

(ii) *Application.* E files an estate tax return on which these assets are identified on the proper schedule, but E provides no information on the return with regard to the date of death value of these assets in accordance with paragraph (a)(7)(ii)(A) of this section. To establish the estate's entitlement to the marital deduction in accordance with §20.2056(a)-1(b) (except with regard to establishing the value of the property) and the instructions for the estate tax return, E includes with the estate tax return evidence to verify the title of each jointly held asset, to confirm that W is the sole beneficiary of both the life insurance policy and the survivor annuity, and to verify that the annuity is exclusively for W's life. Finally, E reports on the estate return E's best estimate, determined by exercising due diligence, of the fair market value of the gross estate in accordance with paragraph (a)(7)(ii)(B) of this section. The estate tax return is considered complete and properly prepared and E has elected portability.

Example 2. (i) *Facts.* H's will, duly admitted to probate and not subject to any proceeding to challenge its validity, provides that H's entire estate is to be distributed outright to W. The non-probate assets includible in H's gross estate consist of a life insurance policy payable to H's children from a prior marriage, and H's individual retirement account (IRA) payable to W. H made no taxable gifts during his lifetime.

(ii) *Application.* E files an estate tax return on which all of the assets includible in the gross estate are identified on the proper schedule. In the case of the probate assets and the IRA, no information is provided with regard to date of death value in accordance with paragraph (a)(7)(ii)(A) of this section. However, E attaches a copy of H's will and describes each such asset and its ownership to establish the estate's entitlement to the marital deduction in accordance with the instructions for the estate tax return and §20.2056(a)-1(b) (except with regard to establishing the value of the property). In the case of the life insurance policy payable to H's children, all of the regular return requirements, including reporting and establishing the fair market value of such asset, apply. Finally, E reports on the estate return E's best estimate, determined by exercising due diligence, of the fair market value of the gross estate in accordance with paragraph (a)(7)(ii)(B) of this section. The estate tax return is considered complete and properly prepared and E has elected portability.

Example 3. (i) *Facts.* H's will, duly admitted to probate and not subject to any proceeding to challenge its validity, provides that 50 percent of the property passing under the terms of H's will is to be paid to a marital trust for W and 50 percent is to be paid to a trust for W and their descendants.

(ii) *Application.* The amount passing to the non-marital trust cannot be verified without knowledge of the full value of the property passing under the will. Therefore, the value of the property of the marital trust relates to or affects the value passing to the trust for W and the descendants of H and W. Accordingly, the general return requirements apply to all of the property includible in the gross estate and the provisions of paragraph (a)(7)(ii) of this section do not apply.

(b) *Requirement for DSUE computation on estate tax return.*—Section 2010(c)(5)(A) requires an executor of a decedent's estate to include a computation of the DSUE amount on the estate tax return to elect portability and thereby allow the decedent's surviving spouse to take into account that decedent's DSUE amount. This requirement is satisfied by the timely filing of a complete and properly prepared estate tax return, as long as the executor has not elected out of portability as described in paragraph(a)(3)(i) of this section. See paragraph (a)(7) of this section for the requirements for a return to be considered complete and properly prepared.

(c) *Computation of the DSUE amount.*—(1) *General rule.*—Subject to paragraphs (c)(2) through (4) of this section, the DSUE amount of a decedent with a surviving spouse is the lesser of the following amounts—

(i) The basic exclusion amount in effect in the year of the death of the decedent; or

(ii) The excess of—

(A) The decedent's applicable exclusion amount; over

(B) The sum of the amount of the taxable estate and the amount of the adjusted taxable gifts of the decedent, which together is the amount on which the tentative tax on the decedent's estate is determined under section 2001(b)(1).

(2) *Special rule to consider gift taxes paid by decedent.*—Solely for purposes of computing the decedent's DSUE amount, the amount of the adjusted taxable gifts of the decedent referred to in paragraph (c)(1)(ii)(B) of this section is reduced by the amount, if any, on which gift taxes were paid for the calendar year of the gift(s).

(3) *Impact of applicable credits.*—An estate's eligibility under sections 2012 through 2015 for credits against the tax imposed by section 2001 does not impact the computation of the DSUE amount.

(4) *Special rule in case of property passing to qualified domestic trust.*—(i) *In general.*—When property passes for the benefit of a surviving spouse in a qualified domestic trust (QDOT) as defined in section 2056A(a), the DSUE amount of the decedent is computed on the decedent's estate tax return for the purpose of electing portability in the same manner as this amount is computed under paragraph (c)(1) of this section, but this DSUE amount is subject to subsequent adjustments. The DSUE amount of the decedent must be redetermined upon the occurrence of the final distribution or other event (generally, the termination of all QDOTs created by or funded with assets passing from the decedent or the death of the surviving spouse) on which estate tax is imposed under section 2056A. See § 20.2056A-6 for the rules on determining the estate tax under section 2056A. See § 20.2010-3(c)(3) regarding the timing of the availability of the decedent's DSUE amount to the surviving spouse.

(ii) *Surviving spouse becomes a U.S. citizen.*—If the surviving spouse becomes a U.S. citizen and if the requirements of section 2056A(b)(12) and the corresponding regulations are satisfied, the estate tax imposed under section 2056A(b)(1) ceases to apply. Accordingly, no estate tax will be imposed under section 2056A either on subsequent QDOT distributions or on the property remaining in the QDOT on the surviving spouse's death and the decedent's DSUE amount is no longer subject to adjustment.

(5) *Examples.*—The following examples illustrate the application of this paragraph (c):

Example 1. Computation of DSUE amount. (i) *Facts.* In 2002, having made no prior taxable gift, Husband (H) makes a taxable gift valued at $1,000,000 and reports the gift on a timely filed gift tax return. Because the amount of the gift is equal to the applicable exclusion amount for that year ($1,000,000), $345,800 is allowed as a credit against the tax, reducing the gift tax liability to zero. H dies in 2015, survived by Wife (W). H and W are U.S. citizens and neither has any prior marriage. H's taxable estate is $1,000,000. The executor of H's estate timely files H's estate tax return and elects portability, thereby allowing W to benefit from H's DSUE amount.

(ii) *Application.* The executor of H's estate computes H's DSUE amount to be $3,430,000 (the lesser of the $5,430,000 basic exclusion amount in 2015, or the excess of H's $5,430,000 applicable exclusion amount over the sum of the $1,000,000 taxable estate and the $1,000,000 amount of adjusted taxable gifts).

Example 2. Computation of DSUE amount when gift tax paid. (i) *Facts.* The facts are the same as in *Example 1* of this paragraph (c)(5) except that the value of H's taxable gift in 2002 is $2,000,000. After application of the applicable credit amount, H owes gift tax on $1,000,000, the amount of the gift in excess of the applicable exclusion amount for that year. H pays the gift tax owed on the 2002 transfer.

(ii) *Application*. On H's death, the executor of H's estate computes the DSUE amount to be $3,430,000 (the lesser of the $5,430,000 basic exclusion amount in 2015, or the excess of H's $5,430,000 applicable exclusion amount over the sum of the $1,000,000 taxable estate and $1,000,000 of adjusted taxable gifts sheltered from tax by H's applicable credit amount). H's adjusted taxable gifts of $2,000,000 were reduced for purposes of this computation by $1,000,000, the amount of taxable gifts on which gift taxes were paid.

Example 3. Computation of DSUE amount when QDOT created. (i) *Facts*. Husband (H), a U.S. citizen, makes his first taxable gift in 2002, valued at $1,000,000, and reports the gift on a timely filed gift tax return. No gift tax is due because the applicable exclusion amount for that year ($1,000,000) equals the fair market value of the gift. H dies in 2015 with a gross estate of $2,000,000. H's surviving spouse (W) is a resident, but not a citizen, of the United States and, under H's will, a pecuniary bequest of $1,500,000 passes to a QDOT for the benefit of W. H's executor timely files an estate tax return and makes the QDOT election for the property passing to the QDOT, and H's estate is allowed a marital deduction of $1,500,000 under section 2056(d) for the value of that property. H's taxable estate is $500,000. On H's estate tax return, H's executor computes H's preliminary DSUE amount to be $3,930,000 (the lesser of the $5,430,000 basic exclusion amount in 2015, or the excess of H's $5,430,000 applicable exclusion amount over the sum of the $500,000 taxable estate and the $1,000,000 adjusted taxable gifts). No taxable events within the meaning of section 2056A occur during W's lifetime with respect to the QDOT, and W makes no taxable gifts. At all times since H's death, W has been a U.S. resident. In 2017, W dies and the value of the assets of the QDOT is $1,800,000.

(ii) *Application*. H's DSUE amount is redetermined to be $2,130,000 (the lesser of the $5,430,000 basic exclusion amount in 2015, or the excess of H's $5,430,000 applicable exclusion amount over $3,300,000 (the sum of the $500,000 taxable estate augmented by the $1,800,000 of QDOT assets and the $1,000,000 adjusted taxable gifts)).

Example 4. Computation of DSUE amount when surviving spouse with QDOT becomes a U.S. citizen. (i) *Facts*. The facts are the same as in *Example 3* of this paragraph (c)(5) except that W becomes a U.S. citizen in 2016 and dies in 2018. The U.S. Trustee of the QDOT notifies the IRS that W has become a U.S. citizen by timely filing a final estate tax return (Form 706-QDT). Pursuant to section 2056A(b)(12), the estate tax under section 2056A no longer applies to the QDOT property.

(ii) *Application*. Because H's DSUE amount no longer is subject to adjustment once W becomes a citizen of the United States, H's DSUE amount is $3,930,000, as it was preliminarily determined as of H's death. Upon W's death in 2018, the value of the QDOT property is includible in W's gross estate.

(d) *Authority to examine returns of decedent.*—The IRS may examine returns of a decedent in determining the decedent's DSUE amount, regardless of whether the period of limitations on assessment has expired for that return. See § 20.2010-3(d) for additional rules relating to the IRS's authority to examine returns. See also section 7602 for the IRS's authority, when ascertaining the correctness of any return, to examine any returns that may be relevant or material to such inquiry.

(e) *Effective/applicability date.*—This section applies to the estates of decedents dying on or after June 12, 2015. See 26 CFR 20.2010-2T, as contained in 26 CFR part 20, revised as of April 1, 2015, for the rule applicable to estates of decedents dying on or after January 1, 2011, and before June 12, 2015. [Reg. § 20.2010-2.]

□ [*T.D.* 9725, 6-12-2015.]

[Reg. § 20.2010-3]

§ 20.2010-3. Portability provisions applicable to the surviving spouse's estate.—(a) *Surviving spouse's estate limited to DSUE amount of last deceased spouse.*—(1) *In general.*—The deceased spousal unused exclusion (DSUE) amount of a decedent, computed under § 20.2010-2(c), is included in determining the surviving spouse's applicable exclusion amount under section 2010(c)(2), provided—

(i) Such decedent is the last deceased spouse of such surviving spouse within the meaning of § 20.2010-1(e)(5) on the date of the death of the surviving spouse; and

(ii) The executor of the decedent's estate elected portability (see § 20.2010-2(a) and (b) for applicable requirements).

(2) *No DSUE amount available from last deceased spouse.*—If the last deceased spouse of such surviving spouse had no DSUE amount, or if the executor of such a decedent's estate did not make a portability election, the surviving spouse's estate has no DSUE amount (except as provided in paragraph (b)(1)(ii) of this section) to be included in determining the applicable exclusion amount, even if the surviving spouse previously had a DSUE amount available from another decedent who, prior to the death of the last deceased spouse, was the last deceased spouse of such surviving spouse. See paragraph (b) of this section for a special rule in the case of multiple deceased spouses and a previously applied DSUE amount.

(3) *Identity of last deceased spouse unchanged by subsequent marriage or divorce.*—A decedent is the last deceased spouse (as defined in § 20.2010-1(e)(5)) of a surviving spouse even if, on the date of the death of the surviving spouse, the surviving spouse is married to another (then-living) individual. If a surviving spouse marries again and that marriage ends in divorce or an annulment, the subsequent death of the divorced spouse does not end the status of the prior deceased spouse as the last deceased spouse of the

surviving spouse. The divorced spouse, not being married to the surviving spouse at death, is not the last deceased spouse as that term is defined in § 20.2010-1(e)(5).

(b) *Special rule in case of multiple deceased spouses and previously-applied DSUE amount.*—(1) *In general.*—A special rule applies to compute the DSUE amount included in the applicable exclusion amount of a surviving spouse who previously has applied the DSUE amount of one or more deceased spouses to taxable gifts in accordance with § 25.2505-2(b) and (c). If a surviving spouse has applied the DSUE amount of one or more (successive) last deceased spouses to the surviving spouse's transfers during life, and if any of those last deceased spouses is different from the surviving spouse's last deceased spouse as defined in § 20.2010-1(e)(5) at the time of the surviving spouse's death, then the DSUE amount to be included in determining the applicable exclusion amount of the surviving spouse at the time of the surviving spouse's death is the sum of—

(i) The DSUE amount of the surviving spouse's last deceased spouse as described in paragraph (a)(1) of this section; and

(ii) The DSUE amount of each other deceased spouse of the surviving spouse, to the extent that such amount was applied to one or more taxable gifts of the surviving spouse.

(2) *Example.*—The following example, in which all described individuals are U.S. citizens, illustrates the application of this paragraph (b):

Example. (i) *Facts.* Husband 1 (H1) dies in 2011, survived by Wife (W). Neither has made any taxable gifts during H1's lifetime. H1's executor elects portability of H1's DSUE amount. The DSUE amount of H1 as computed on the estate tax return filed on behalf of H1's estate is $5,000,000. In 2012, W makes taxable gifts to her children valued at $2,000,000. W reports the gifts on a timely filed gift tax return. W is considered to have applied $2,000,000 of H1's DSUE amount to the amount of taxable gifts, in accordance with § 25.2505-2(c), and, therefore, W owes no gift tax. W has an applicable exclusion amount remaining in the amount of $8,120,000 ($3,000,000 of H1's remaining DSUE amount plus W's own $5,120,000 basic exclusion amount). W marries Husband 2 (H2) in 2013. H2 dies in 2014. H2's executor elects portability of H2's DSUE amount, which is properly computed on H2's estate tax return to be $2,000,000. W dies in 2015.

(ii) *Application.* The DSUE amount to be included in determining the applicable exclusion amount available to W's estate is $4,000,000, determined by adding the $2,000,000 DSUE amount of H2 and the $2,000,000 DSUE amount of H1 that was applied by W to W's 2012 taxable gifts. The $4,000,000 DSUE amount added to W's $5,430,000 basic exclusion amount (for 2015), causes W's applicable exclusion amount to be $9,430,000.

(c) *Date DSUE amount taken into consideration by surviving spouse's estate.*—(1) *General rule.*—A portability election made by an executor of a decedent's estate (see § 20.2010-2(a) and (b) for applicable requirements) generally applies as of the date of the decedent's death. Thus, such decedent's DSUE amount is included in the applicable exclusion amount of the decedent's surviving spouse under section 2010(c)(2) and will be applicable to transfers made by the surviving spouse after the decedent's death (subject to the limitations in paragraph (a) of this section). However, such decedent's DSUE amount will not be included in the applicable exclusion amount of the surviving spouse, even if the surviving spouse had made a transfer in reliance on the availability or computation of the decedent's DSUE amount:

(i) If the executor of the decedent's estate supersedes the portability election by filing a subsequent estate tax return in accordance with § 20.2010-2(a)(4);

(ii) To the extent that the DSUE amount subsequently is reduced by a valuation adjustment or the correction of an error in calculation; or

(iii) To the extent that the surviving spouse cannot substantiate the DSUE amount claimed on the surviving spouse's return.

(2) *Exception when surviving spouse not a U.S. citizen on date of deceased spouse's death.*—If a surviving spouse becomes a citizen of the United States after the death of the surviving spouse's last deceased spouse, the DSUE amount of the surviving spouse's last deceased spouse becomes available to the surviving spouse on the date the surviving spouse becomes a citizen of the United States (subject to the limitations in paragraph (a) of this section). However, when the special rule regarding qualified domestic trusts in paragraph (c)(3) of this section applies, the earliest date on which a decedent's DSUE amount may be included in the applicable exclusion amount of such decedent's surviving spouse who becomes a U.S. citizen is as provided in paragraph (c)(3) of this section.

(3) *Special rule when property passes to surviving spouse in a qualified domestic trust.*—(i) *In general.*—When property passes from a decedent for the benefit of the decedent's surviving spouse in one or more qualified domestic trusts (QDOT) as defined in section 2056A(a) and the decedent's executor elects portability, the DSUE amount available to be included in the applicable exclusion amount of the surviving spouse under section 2010(c)(2) is the DSUE amount of the decedent as redetermined in accordance with § 20.2010-2(c)(4) (subject to the limitations in paragraph (a) of this section). The earliest date on which such decedent's DSUE amount may be included in the applicable exclusion amount of the surviving spouse under section 2010(c)(2) is the date of the occurrence of the final QDOT distribution or final other event (generally, the termination of all QDOTs created by or funded with assets passing from the decedent or the death of the surviving spouse) on which tax under section 2056A is imposed. However, the decedent's DSUE amount as redetermined in ac-

cordance with § 20.2010-2(c)(4) may be applied to certain taxable gifts of the surviving spouse. See § 25.2505-2(d)(3)(i).

(ii) *Surviving spouse becomes a U.S. citizen.*—If a surviving spouse for whom property has passed from a decedent in one or more QDOTs becomes a citizen of the United States and the requirements in section 2056A(b)(12) and the corresponding regulations are satisfied, then the date on which such decedent's DSUE amount may be included in the applicable exclusion amount of the surviving spouse under section 2010(c)(2) (subject the limitations in paragraph (a) of this section) is the date on which the surviving spouse becomes a citizen of the United States. See § 20.2010-2(c)(4) for the rules for computing the decedent's DSUE amount in the case of a qualified domestic trust.

(d) *Authority to examine returns of deceased spouses.*—For the purpose of determining the DSUE amount to be included in the applicable exclusion amount of a surviving spouse, the Internal Revenue Service (IRS) may examine returns of each of the surviving spouse's deceased spouses whose DSUE amount is claimed to be included in the surviving spouse's applicable exclusion amount, regardless of whether the period of limitations on assessment has expired for any such return. The IRS's authority to examine returns of a deceased spouse applies with respect to each transfer by the surviving spouse to which a DSUE amount is or has been applied. Upon examination, the IRS may adjust or eliminate the DSUE amount reported on such a return of a deceased spouse; however, the IRS may assess additional tax on that return only if that tax is assessed within the period of limitations on assessment under section 6501 applicable to the tax shown on that return. See also section 7602 for the IRS's authority, when ascertaining the correctness of any return, to examine any returns that may be relevant or material to such inquiry. For purposes of these examinations to determine the DSUE amount, the surviving spouse is considered to have a material interest that is affected by the return information of the deceased spouse within the meaning of section 6103(e)(3).

(e) *Availability of DSUE amount for estates of nonresidents who are not citizens.*—The estate of a nonresident surviving spouse who is not a citizen of the United States at the time of such surviving spouse's death shall not take into account the DSUE amount of any deceased spouse of such surviving spouse within the meaning of § 20.2010-1(e)(5) except to the extent allowed under any applicable treaty obligation of the United States. See section 2102(b)(3).

(f) *Effective/applicability date.*—This section applies to the estates of decedents dying on or after June 12, 2015. See 26 CFR 20.2010-3T, as contained in 26 CFR part 20, revised as of April 1, 2015, for the rules applicable to estates of decedents dying on or after January 1, 2011, and before June 12, 2015. [Reg. § 20.2010-3.]

☐ [*T.D. 9725, 6-12-2015. Amended by T.D. 9884, 11-22-2019.*]

[Reg. § 20.2011-1]

§ 20.2011-1. Credit for State death taxes.—(a) *In general.*—A credit is allowed under section 2011 against the Federal estate tax for estate, inheritance, legacy or succession taxes actually paid to any State, Territory, or the District of Columbia, or in the case of decedents dying before September 3, 1958, any possession of the United States (hereafter referred to as "State death taxes"). The credit, however, is allowed only for State death taxes paid (1) with respect to property included in the decedent's gross estate, and (2) with respect to the decedent's estate. The amount of the credit is subject to the limitation described in paragraph (b) of this section. It is subject to further limitations described in § 20.2011-2 if a deduction is allowed under section 2053(d) for State death taxes paid with respect to a charitable gift. See paragraph (a) of § 20.2014-1 as to the allowance of a credit for death taxes paid to a possession of the United States in a case where the decedent died after September 2, 1958.

(b) *Amount of credit.*—(1) If the decedent's taxable estate does not exceed $40,000, the credit for State death taxes is zero. If the decedent's taxable estate does exceed $40,000, the credit for State death taxes is limited to an amount computed in accordance with the following table:

TABLE FOR COMPUTATION OF MAXIMUM CREDIT FOR STATE DEATH TAXES

(A) *Taxable estate equal to or more than—*	(B) *Taxable estate less than—*	(C) *Credit on amount in column (A)*	(D) *Rates of credit on excess over amount in column (A)*
			Percent
$40,000	$90,000	.....	.8
90,000	140,000	$400	1.6
140,000	240,000	1,200	2.4
240,000	440,000	3,600	3.2
440,000	640,000	10,000	4.0
640,000	840,000	18,000	4.8
840,000	1,040,000	27,600	5.6
1,040,000	1,540,000	38,800	6.4
1,540,000	2,040,000	70,800	7.2
2,040,000	2,540,000	106,800	8.0

(A) Taxable estate equal to or more than—	(B) Taxable estate less than—	(C) Credit on amount in column (A)	(D) Rates of credit on excess over amount in column (A)
2,540,000	3,040,000	146,800	8.8
3,040,000	3,540,000	190,800	9.6
3,540,000	4,040,000	238,800	10.4
4,040,000	5,040,000	290,800	11.2
5,040,000	6,040,000	402,800	12.0
6,040,000	7,040,000	522,800	12.8
7,040,000	8,040,000	650,800	13.6
8,040,000	9,040,000	786,800	14.4
9,040,000	10,040,000	930,800	15.2
10,040,000	....	1,082,800	16.0

(2) Subparagraph (1) of this paragraph may be illustrated by the following example:

Example. (i) The decedent died January 1, 1955, leaving a taxable estate of $150,000. On January 1, 1956, inheritance taxes totaling $2,500 were actually paid to a State with respect to property included in the decedent's gross estate. Reference to the table discloses that the specified amount in column (A) nearest to but less than the value of the decedent's taxable estate is $140,000. The maximum credit in respect of this amount, as indicated in column (C), is $1,200. The amount by which the taxable estate exceeds the same specified amount is $10,000. The maximum credit in respect of this amount, computed at the rate of 2.4 percent indicated in column (D), is $240. Thus, the maximum credit in respect of the decedent's taxable estate of $150,000 is $1,440, even though $2,500 in inheritance taxes was actually paid to the State.

(ii) If, in subdivision (i) of this example, the amount actually paid to the State was $950, the credit for State death taxes would be limited to $950. If, in subdivision (i) of this example, the decedent's taxable estate was $35,000, no credit for State death taxes would be allowed.

(c) *Miscellaneous limitations and conditions to credit.*—(1) *Period of limitations.*—The credit for State death taxes is limited under section 2011(c) to those taxes which were actually paid and for which a credit was claimed within four years after the filing of the estate tax return for the decedent's estate. If, however, a petition has been filed with the Tax Court of the United States for the redetermination of a deficiency within the time prescribed in section 6213(a), the credit is limited to those taxes which were actually paid and for which a credit was claimed within four years after the filing of the return or within 60 days after the decision of the Tax Court becomes final, whichever period is the last to expire. Similarly, if an extension of time has been granted under section 6161 for payment of the tax shown on the return, or of a deficiency, the credit is limited to those taxes which were actually paid and for which a credit was claimed within four years after the filing of the return, or before the date of the expiration of the period of the extension, whichever period is last to expire. If a claim for refund or credit of an overpayment of the Federal estate tax is filed within the time prescribed in section 6511, the credit for State death taxes is limited to such taxes as were actually paid and credit therefor claimed within four years after the filing of the return or before the expiration of 60 days from the date of mailing by certified or registered mail by the district director to the taxpayer of a notice of disallowance of any part of the claim, or before the expiration of 60 days after a decision by any court of competent jurisdiction becomes final with respect to a timely suit instituted upon the claim, whichever period is the last to expire. See section 2015 for the applicable period of limitations for credit for State death taxes on reversionary or remainder interests if an election is made under section 6163(a) to postpone payment of the estate tax attributable to reversionary or remainder interests. If a claim for refund based on the credit for State death taxes is filed within the applicable period described in this subparagraph, a refund may be made despite the general limitation provisions of sections 6511 and 6512. Any refund based on the credit described in this section shall be made without interest.

(2) *Submission of evidence.*—Before the credit for State death taxes is allowed, evidence that such taxes have been paid must be submitted to the district director. The district director may require the submission of a certificate from the proper officer of the taxing State, Territory, or possession of the United States, or the District of Columbia, showing: (i) the total amount of tax imposed (before adding interest and penalties and before allowing discount); (ii) the amount of any discount allowed; (iii) the amount of any penalties and interest imposed or charged; (iv) the total amount actually paid in cash; and (v) the date or dates of payment. If the amount of these taxes has been redetermined, the amount finally determined should be stated. The required evidence should be filed with the return, but if that is not convenient or possible, then it should be submitted as soon thereafter as practicable. The district director may require the submission of such additional proof as is deemed necessary to establish the right to the credit. For example, he may require the submission of a certificate of the proper officer of the taxing jurisdiction showing (vi) whether a claim for refund of any part of the State death tax is pending and (vii) whether a refund of any part thereof has been authorized, and if a refund has been made, its date and amount, and a description of the property or interest in respect of which the refund was made. The district director may also

require an itemized list of the property in respect of which State death taxes were imposed certified by the officer having custody of the records pertaining to those taxes. In addition, he may require the executor to submit a written statement (containing a declaration that it is made under penalties of perjury) stating whether, to his knowledge, any person has instituted litigation or taken an appeal (or contemplates doing so), the final determination of which may affect the amount of those taxes. See section 2016 concerning the redetermination of the estate tax if State death taxes claimed as credit are refunded.

(d) *Definition of "basic estate tax".*—Section 2011(d) provides definitions of the terms "basic estate tax" and "additional estate tax", used in the Internal Revenue Code of 1939, and "estate tax imposed by the Revenue Act of 1926", for the purpose of supplying a means of computing State death taxes under local statutes using those terms, and for use in determining the exemption provided for in section 2201 for estates of certain members of the Armed Forces. See section 2011(e)(3) for a modification of these definitions if a deduction is allowed under section 2053(d) for State death taxes paid with respect to a charitable gift. [Reg. § 20.2011-1.]

☐ [*T.D.* 6296, 6-23-58. *Amended by T.D.* 6526, 1-18-61.]

[Reg. § 20.2011-2]

§ 20.2011-2. Limitation on credit if a deduction for State death taxes is allowed under section 2053(d).—If a deduction is allowed under section 2053(d) for State death taxes paid with respect to a charitable gift, the credit for State death taxes is subject to special limitations. Under these limitations, the credit cannot exceed the least of the following:

(a) The amount of State death taxes paid other than those for which a deduction is allowed under section 2053(d);

(b) The amount indicated in section 2011(b) to be the maximum credit allowable with respect to the decedent's taxable estate; or

(c) An amount, A, which bears the same ratio to B (the amount which would be the maximum credit allowable under section 2011(b) if the deduction under section 2053(d) for State death taxes were not allowed in computing the decedent's taxable estate) as C (the amount of State death taxes paid other than those for which a deduction is allowed under section 2053(d)) bears to D (the total amount of State death taxes paid). For the purpose of this computation, in determining what the decedent's taxable estate would be if the deduction for State death taxes under section 2053(d) were not allowed, adjustment must be made for the decrease in the deduction for charitable gifts under section 2055 or 2106(a)(2) (for estates of nonresidents not citizens) by reason of any increase in Federal estate tax which would be charged against the charitable gifts.

The application of this section may be illustrated by the following example:

Example. The decedent died January 1, 1955, leaving a gross estate of $925,000. Expenses, indebtedness, etc., amounted to $25,000. The decedent bequeathed $400,000 to his son with the direction that the son bear the State death taxes on the bequest. The residuary estate was left to a charitable organization. Except as noted above, all Federal and State death taxes were payable out of the residuary estate. The State imposed death taxes of $60,000 on the son's bequest and death taxes of $75,000 on the bequest to charity. No death taxes were imposed by a foreign country with respect to any property in the gross estate. The decedent's taxable estate (determined without regard to the limitation imposed by section 2011(e)(2)(B)) is computed as follows:

Gross estate				$925,000.00
Expenses, indebtedness, etc.			$25,000.00	
Exemption			60,000.00	
Deduction under section 2053(d)			75,000.00	
Charitable deduction:				
Gross estate		$925,000.00		
Expenses, etc.	$25,000.00			
Bequest to son	400,000.00			
State death tax paid from residue	75,000.00			
Federal estate tax paid from residue	122,916.67	622,916.67	302,083.33	462,083.33
Taxable estate				$462,916.67

If the deduction under section 2053(d) were not allowed, the decedent's taxable estate would be computed as follows:

Gross estate				$925,000.00
Expenses, indebtedness, etc.			$25,000.00	
Exemption			$60,000.00	
Charitable deduction:				
Gross estate		$925,000.00		

Expenses, etc.	$25,000.00			
Bequest to son	400,000.00			
State death tax paid from residue	75,000.00			
Federal estate tax paid from residue .	155,000.00	655,000.00	270,000.00	$355,000.00
Taxable estate				$570,000.00

On a taxable estate of $570,000, the maximum credit allowable under section 2011(b) would be $15,200. Under these facts, the credit for State death taxes is determined as follows:

(1)	Amount of State death taxes paid other than those for which a deduction is allowed under section 2053(d) ($135,000 – $75,000)	$60,000.00
(2)	Amount indicated in section 2011(b) to be the maximum credit allowable with respect to the decedent's taxable estate of $462,916.67	10,916.67
(3)	Amount determined by use of the ratio described in paragraph (c) above $\frac{\$60,000}{\$135,000} \times \$15,200$	6,755.56
(4)	Credit for State death taxes (least of subparagraphs (1) through (3) above) . .	6,755.56

[Reg. § 20.2011-2]

☐ [*T.D. 6296, 6-23-58. Amended by T.D. 6600, 5-28-62.*]

[Reg. § 20.2012-1]

§ 20.2012-1. Credit for gift tax.—(a) *In general.*—With respect to gifts made before 1977, a credit is allowed under section 2012 against the Federal estate tax for gift tax paid under chapter 12 of the Internal Revenue Code, or corresponding provisions of prior law, on a gift by the decedent of property subsequently included in the decedent's gross estate. The credit is allowable even though the gift tax is paid after the decedent's death and the amount of the gift tax is deductible from the gross estate as a debt of the decedent.

(b) *Limitations on credit.*—The credit for gift tax is limited to the smaller of the following amounts:

(1) The amount of gift tax paid on the gift, computed as set forth in paragraph (c) of this section, or

(2) The amount of the estate tax attributable to the inclusion of the gift in the gross estate, computed as set forth in paragraph (d) of this section.

When more than one gift is included in the gross estate, a separate computation of the two limitations on the credit is to be made for each gift.

(c) *"First limitation".*—The amount of the gift tax paid on the gift is the "first limitation." Thus, if only one gift was made during a certain calendar quarter or calendar year if the gift was made before January 1, 1971, and the gift is wholly included in the decedent's gross estate for the purpose of the estate tax, the credit with respect to the gift is limited to the amount of the gift tax paid for that calendar quarter or calendar year. On the other hand, if more than one gift was made during a certain calendar quarter or calendar year, the credit with respect to any such gift which is included in the decedent's gross estate is limited under section 2012(d) to an amount, A, which bears the same ratio to B (the total gift tax paid for that calendar quarter or calendar year) as C (the "amount of the gift," computed as described below) bears to D (the total taxable gifts for the calendar quarter or the calendar year, computed without deduction of the gift tax specific exemption). Stated algebraically, the "first limitation" (A) equals

$$\frac{\text{"amount of the gift" (C)}}{\text{total taxable gifts, plus specific exemption allowed (D)}} \times \text{total gift tax paid (B).}$$

For purposes of the ratio stated above, the "amount of the gift" referred to as factor "C" is the value of the gift reduced by any portion excluded or deducted under section 2503(b) (annual exclusion), 2522 (charitable deduction), or 2523 (marital deduction) of the Internal Revenue Code or corresponding provisions of prior law. In making the computations described in this paragraph, the values to be used are those finally determined for the purpose of the gift tax, irrespective of the values determined for the purpose of the estate tax. A similar computation is made in case only a portion of any gift is included in the decedent's gross estate. The application of this paragraph may be illustrated by the following example:

Example. The donor made gifts during the calendar year 1955 on which a gift tax was determined as shown below:

Gift of property to son on February 1 . . .	$13,000
Gift of property to wife on May 1	86,000
Gift of property to charitable organization on May 15	10,000
Total gifts	109,000
Less exclusions ($3,000 for each gift)	9,000
Total included amount of gifts	100,000

Marital deduction (for gift to wife)	$43,000	
Charitable deduction	7,000	
Specific exemption ($30,000 less $20,000 used in prior years)	10,000	
Total deductions		60,000
Taxable gifts		40,000
Total gift tax paid for calendar year 1955		$ 3,600

The donor's gift to his wife was made in contemplation of death and was thereafter included in his gross estate. Under the "first limitation," the credit with respect to that gift cannot exceed

$$\frac{\$86{,}000 - \$3{,}000 - \$43{,}000 \text{ (gift to wife, less annual exclusion and marital deduction)}}{\$40{,}000 + \$10{,}000 \text{ (taxable gifts, plus specific exemption allowed)}} \times \$3{,}600 \text{ (total gift tax paid)} = \$2{,}880.$$

(d) *"Second limitation"*.—(1) The amount of the estate tax attributable to the inclusion of the gift in the gross estate is the "second limitation". Thus, the credit with respect to any gift of property included in the gross estate is limited to an amount, E, which bears the same ratio to F (the gross estate tax, reduced by any credit for State death taxes under section 2011) as G (the "value of the gift," computed as described in subparagraph (2) of this paragraph) bears to H (the value of the entire gross estate, reduced by the total deductions allowed under sections 2055 or 2106(a)(2) (charitable deduction) and 2056 (marital deduction)). Stated algebraically, the "second limitation"

$$\text{(E) equals } \frac{\text{"value of the gift" (G)}}{\text{value of gross estate, less marital and charitable deductions (H)}} \times \text{gross estate tax, less credit for State death taxes (F).}$$

(2) For purposes of the ratio stated in subparagraph (1) of this paragraph, the "value of the gift" referred to as factor "G" is the value of the property transferred by gift and included in the gross estate, as determined for the purpose of the gift tax or for the purpose of the estate tax, whichever is lower, and adjusted as follows:

(i) The appropriate value is reduced by all or a portion of any annual exclusion allowed for gift tax purposes under section 2503(b) of the Internal Revenue Code or corresponding provisions of prior law. If the gift tax value is lower than the estate tax value, it is reduced by the entire amount of the exclusion. If the estate tax value is lower than the gift tax value, it is reduced by an amount which bears the same ratio to the estate tax value as the annual exclusion bears to the total value of the property as determined for gift tax purposes. To illustrate: In 1955, a donor, in contemplation of death, transferred certain property to his five children which was valued at $300,000 for the purpose of gift tax. Thereafter, the same property was included in his gross estate at a value of $270,000. In computing his gift tax, the donor was allowed annual exclusions totalling $15,000. The reduction provided for in this subdivision is

$$\frac{\$15{,}000 \text{ (annual exclusions allowed)}}{\$300{,}000 \text{ (value of transferred property for the purpose of the gift tax)}} \times \$270{,}000 \text{ (value of transferred property for the purpose of the estate tax)} = \$13{,}500.$$

(ii) The appropriate value is further reduced if any portion of the value of the property is allowed as a marital deduction under section 2056 or as a charitable deduction under section 2055 or section 2106(a)(2) (for estates of nonresidents not citizens). The amount of the reduction is an amount which bears the same ratio to the value determined under subdivision (i) of this subparagraph as the portion of the property allowed as a marital deduction or as a charitable deduction bears to the total value of the property as determined for the purpose of the estate tax. Thus, if a gift is made solely to the decedent's surviving spouse and is subsequently included in the decedent's gross estate as having been made in contemplation of death, but a marital deduction is allowed under section 2056 for the full value of the gift, no credit for gift tax on the gift will be allowed since the reduction under this subdivision together with the reduction under subdivision (i) of this subparagraph will have the effect of reducing the factor "G" of the ratio in subparagraph (1) of this paragraph to zero.

(e) *Credit for "split gifts"*.—If a decedent made a gift of property which is thereafter included in his gross estate, and, under the provisions of section 2513 of the Internal Revenue Code of 1954 or section 1000(f) of the Internal Revenue Code of 1939, the gift was considered as made one-half by the decedent and one-half by his spouse, credit against the estate tax is allowed for the gift tax paid with respect to both halves of the gift. The "first limitation" is to be separately computed with respect to each half of the gift in accordance with the principles stated in paragraph (c) of this section. The "second limitation" is to be computed with respect to the entire gift in accordance with the principles stated in paragraph (d) of this section. To illustrate: A donor, in contemplation of death, transferred property valued at $106,000 to his son on January 1, 1955, and he and his wife consented that the gift should be considered as made one-half by him and one-half by her. The property was thereafter included in the donor's gross estate. Under the "first limitation", the amount of the gift tax of the donor paid with respect to the one-half of the gift considered as made by him is determined to be $11,250, and the amount of the gift tax of his wife paid with respect to the one-half of the gift considered as made by her is determined to be $1,200. Under the "second limitation", the amount of the estate tax attributable to the property is determined to be $28,914. Therefore, the credit for gift tax allowed is $12,450 ($11,250 plus $1,200). [Reg. § 20.2012-1.]

□ [*T.D.* 6296, 6-23-58. *Amended by T.D.* 7238, 12-28-72 *and T.D.* 8522, 2-28-94.]

[Reg. § 20.2013-1]

§ 20.2013-1. Credit for tax on prior transfers.—(a) *In general.*—A credit is allowed under section 2013 against the Federal estate tax imposed on the present decedent's estate for Federal estate tax paid on the transfer of property to the present decedent from a transferor who died within ten years before, or within two years after, the present decedent's death. See § 20.2013-5 for definition of the terms "property" and "transfer." There is no requirement that the transferred property be identified in the estate of the present decedent or that the property be in existence at the time of the decedent's death. It is sufficient that the transfer of the property was subjected to Federal estate tax in the estate of the transferor and that the transferor died within the prescribed period of time. The executor must submit such proof as may be requested by the district director in order to establish the right of the estate to the credit.

(b) *Limitations on credit.*—The credit for tax on prior transfers is limited to the smaller of the following amounts:

(1) The amount of the Federal estate tax attributable to the transferred property in the transferor's estate, computed as set forth in § 20.2013-2; or

(2) The amount of the Federal estate tax attributable to the transferred property in the decedent's estate, computed as set forth in § 20.2013-3. Rules for valuing property for purposes of the credit are contained in § 20.2013-4.

(c) *Percentage reduction.*—If the transferor died within the two years before, or within the two years after, the present decedent's death, the credit is the smaller of the two limitations described in paragraph (b) of this section. If the transferor predeceased the present decedent by more than two years, the credit is a certain percentage of the smaller of the two limitations described in paragraph (b) of this section, determined as follows:

(1) 80 percent, if the transferor died within the third or fourth years preceding the present decedent's death;

(2) 60 percent, if the transferor died within the fifth or sixth years preceding the present decedent's death;

(3) 40 percent, if the transferor died within the seventh or eighth years preceding the present decedent's death; and

(4) 20 percent, if the transferor died within the ninth or tenth years preceding the present decedent's death.

The word "within" as used in this paragraph means "during". Therefore, if a death occurs on the second anniversary of another death, the first death is considered to have occurred within the two years before the second death. If the credit for tax on prior transfers relates to property received from two or more transferors, the provisions of this paragraph are to be applied separately with respect to the property received from each transferor. See paragraph (d) of example (2) in § 20.2013-6.

(d) *Examples.*—For illustrations of the application of this section, see examples (1) and (2) set forth in § 20.2013-6. [Reg. § 20.2013-1.]

□ [*T.D.* 6296, 6-23-58.]

[Reg. § 20.2013-2]

§ 20.2013-2. "First limitation.".—(a) The amount of the Federal estate tax attributable to the transferred property in the transferor's estate is the "first limitation." Thus, the credit is limited to an amount, A, which bears the same ratio to B (the "transferor's adjusted Federal estate tax," computed as described in paragraph (b) of this section) as C (the value of the property transferred (see § 20.2013-4)) bears to D (the "transferor's adjusted taxable estate," computed as described in paragraph (c) of this section). Stated algebraically, the "first limitation" (A) equals

$$\frac{\text{value of transferred property (C)}}{\text{"transferor's adjusted taxable estate" (D)}} \times \text{"transferor's adjusted Federal estate tax" (B).}$$

(b) For purposes of the ratio stated in paragraph (a) of this section, the "transferor's adjusted Federal estate tax" referred to as factor "B" is the amount of the Federal estate tax paid with respect to the transferor's estate plus:

(1) Any credit allowed the transferor's estate for gift tax under section 2012, or the corresponding provisions of prior law; and

(2) Any credit allowed the transferor's estate, under section 2013, for tax on prior transfers, but only if the transferor acquired property

from a person who died within 10 years before the death of the present decedent.

(c)(1) For purposes of the ratio stated in paragraph (a) of this section, the "transferor's adjusted taxable estate" referred to as factor "D" is the amount of the transferor's taxable estate (or net estate) decreased by the amount of any "death taxes" paid with respect to his gross estate and increased by the amount of the exemption allowed in computing his taxable estate (or net estate). The amount of the transferor's taxable estate (or net estate) is determined in accordance with the provisions of §20.2051-1 in the case of a citizen or resident of the United States or of §20.2106-1 in the case of a nonresident not a citizen of the United States (or the corresponding provisions of prior regulations). The term "death taxes" means the Federal estate tax plus all other estate, inheritance, legacy, succession, or similar death taxes imposed by, and paid to, any taxing authority, whether within or without the United States. However, only the net amount of such taxes paid is taken into consideration.

(2) The amount of the exemption depends upon the citizenship and residence of the transferor at the time of his death. Except in the case of a decedent described in section 2209 (relating to certain residents of possessions of the United States who are considered nonresidents not citizens), if the decedent was a citizen or resident of the United States, the exemption is the $60,000 authorized by section 2052 (or the corresponding provisions of prior law). If the decedent was a nonresident not a citizen of the United States, or is considered under section 2209 to have been such a nonresident, the exemption is the $30,000 or $2,000, as the case may be, authorized by section 2106(a)(3) (or the corresponding provisions of prior law), or such larger amount as is authorized by section 2106(a)(3)(B) or may have been allowed as an exemption pursuant to the prorated exemption provisions of an applicable death tax convention. See §20.2052-1 and paragraph (a)(3) of §20.2106-1.

(d) If the credit for tax on prior transfers relates to property received from two or more transferors, the provisions of this section are to be applied separately with respect to the property received from each transferor. See paragraph (b) of example (2) in §20.2013-6.

(e) For illustrations of the application of this section, see examples (1) and (2) set forth in §20.2013-6. [Reg. §20.2013-2.]

☐ [*T.D.* 6296, 6-23-58. *Amended by T.D.* 7296, 12-11-73.]

[Reg. §20.2013-3]

§20.2013-3. "Second limitation.".—(a) The amount of the Federal estate tax attributable to the transferred property in the present decedent's estate is the "second limitation." Thus, the credit is limited to the difference between—

(1) The net estate tax payable (see paragraph (b)(5) or (c), as the case may be, of §20.0-2) with respect to the present decedent's estate, determined without regard to any credit for tax on prior transfers under section 2013 or any credit for foreign death taxes claimed under the provisions of a death tax convention, and

(2) The net estate tax determined as provided in paragraph (1) of this section, but computed by subtracting from the present decedent's gross estate the value of the property transferred (see §20.2013-4), and by making only the adjustment indicated in paragraph (b) of this section if a charitable deduction is allowable to the estate of the present decedent.

(b) If a charitable deduction is allowable to the estate of the present decedent under the provisions of section 2055 or section 2106(a)(2) (for estates of nonresidents not citizens), for purposes of determining the tax described in paragraph (a)(2) of this section, the charitable deduction otherwise allowable is reduced by an amount, E, which bears the same ratio to F (the charitable deduction otherwise allowable) as G (the value of the transferred property (see §20.2013-4)) bears to H (the value of the present decedent's gross estate reduced by the amount of the deductions for expenses, indebtedness, taxes, losses, etc., allowed under the provisions of sections 2053 and 2054 or section 2106(a)(1) (for estates of nonresidents not citizens)). See paragraph (c)(2) of example (1) and paragraph (c)(2) of example (2) in §20.2013-6.

(c) If the credit for tax on prior transfers relates to property received from two or more transferors, the property received from all transferors is aggregated in determining the limitation on credit under this section (the "second limitation"). However, the limitation so determined is apportioned to the property received from each transferor in the ratio that the property received from each transferor bears to the total property received from all transferors. See paragraph (c) of example (2) in §20.2013-6.

(d) For illustrations of the application of this section, see examples (1) and (2) set forth in §20.2013-6. [Reg. §20.2013-3.]

☐ [*T.D.* 6296, 6-23-58. *Amended by T.D.* 7296, 12-11-73.]

[Reg. §20.2013-4]

§20.2013-4. Valuation of property transferred.—(a) For purposes of section 2013 and §§20.2013-1 to 20.2013-6, the value of the property transferred to the decedent is the value at which the property was included in the transferor's gross estate for the purpose of the Federal estate tax (see sections 2031, 2032, 2103, and 2107, and the regulations thereunder) reduced as indicated in paragraph (b) of this section. If the decedent received a life estate or a remainder or other limited interest in property that was included in a transferor decedent's gross estate, the value of the interest is determined as of the date of the transferor's death on the basis of recognized valuation principles (see §§20.2031-7 (or, for certain prior periods, §20.2031-7A) and 20.7520-1 through 20.7520-4). The application of this paragraph may be illustrated by the following examples:

Example (1). A died on January 1, 1953, leaving Blackacre to B. The property was included in A's gross estate at a value of $100,000. On January 1, 1955, B sold Blackacre to C for $150,000. B died on February 1, 1955. For purposes of computing the credit against the tax imposed on B's estate, the value of the property transferred to B is $100,000.

Example (2). A died on January 1, 1953, leaving Blackacre to B for life and, upon B's death, remainder to C. At the time of A's death, B was 56 years of age. The property was included in A's gross estate at a value of $100,000. The part of that value attributable to the life estate is $44,688 and the part of that value attributable to the remainder is $55,312 (see § 20.2031-7A(b)). B died on January 1, 1955, and C died on January 1, 1956. For purposes of computing the credit against the tax imposed on B's estate, the value of the property transferred to B is $44,688. For purposes of computing the credit against the tax imposed on C's estate, the value of the property transferred to C is $55,312.

(b) In arriving at the value of the property transferred to the decedent, the value at which the property was included in the transferor's gross estate (see paragraph (a) of this section) is reduced as follows:

(1) By the amount of the Federal estate tax and any other estate, inheritance, legacy, or succession taxes which were payable out of the property transferred to the decedent or which were payable by the decedent in connection with the property transferred to him. For example, if under the transferor's will or local law all death taxes are to be paid out of other property with the result that the decedent receives a bequest free and clear of all death taxes, no reduction is to be made under this subparagraph;

(2) By the amount of any marital deduction allowed the transferor's estate under section 2056 (or under section 812(e) of the Internal Revenue Code of 1939) if the decedent was the spouse of the transferor at the time of the transferor's death;

(3)(i) By the amount of administration expenses in accordance with the principles of § 20.2056(b)-4(d).

(ii) This paragraph (b)(3) applies to transfers from estates of decedents dying on or after December 3, 1999; and

(4)(i) By the amount of any encumbrance on the property or by the amount of any obligation imposed by the transferor and incurred by the decedent with respect to the property, to the extent such charges would be taken into account if the amount of a gift to the decedent of such property were being determined.

(ii) For purposes of this subparagraph, an obligation imposed by the transferor and incurred by the decedent with respect to the property includes a bequest, etc., in lieu of the interest of the surviving spouse under community property laws, unless the interest was, immediately prior to the transferor's death, a mere expectancy. However, an obligation imposed by the transferor and incurred by the decedent with respect to the property does not include a bequest, devise, or other transfer in lieu of dower, curtesy, or of a statutory estate created in lieu of dower or curtesy, or of other marital rights in the transferor's property or estate.

(iii) The application of this subparagraph may be illustrated by the following examples:

Example (1). The transferor devised to the decedent real estate subject to a mortgage. The value of the property transferred to the decedent does not include the amount of the mortgage. If, however, the transferor by his will directs the executor to pay off the mortgage, such payment constitutes an additional amount transferred to the decedent.

Example (2). The transferor bequeathed certain property to the decedent with a direction that the decedent pay $1,000 to X. The value of the property transferred to the decedent is the value of the property reduced by $1,000.

Example (3). The transferor bequeathed certain property to his wife, the decedent, in lieu of her interest in property held by them as community property under the law of the State of their residence. The wife elected to relinquish her community property interest and to take the bequest. The value of the property transferred to the decedent is the value of the property reduced by the value of the community property interest relinquished by the wife.

Example (4). The transferor bequeathed to the decedent his entire residuary estate, out of which certain claims were to be satisfied. The entire distributable income of the transferor's estate (during the period of its administration) was applied toward the satisfaction of these claims and the remaining portion of the claims was satisfied by the decedent out of his own funds. Thus, the decedent received a larger sum upon settlement of the transferor's estate than he was actually bequeathed. The value of the property transferred to the decedent is the value at which such property was included in the transferor's gross estate, reduced by the amount of the estate income and the decedent's own funds paid out in satisfaction of the claims. [Reg. § 20.2013-4.]

☐ [*T.D.* 6296, 6-23-58. *Amended by T.D.* 7077, 12-1-70; *T.D.* 7296, 12-11-73; *T.D.* 8522, 2-28-94; *T.D.* 8540, 6-9-94 *and T.D.* 8846, 12-2-99.]

[Reg. § 20.2013-5]

§ 20.2013-5. "Property" and "transfer" defined.—(a) For purposes of section 2013 and §§ 20.2013-1 through 20.2013-6, the term "property" means any beneficial interest in property, including a general power of appointment (as defined in section 2041) over property. Thus, the term does not include an interest in property consisting merely of a bare legal title, such as that of a trustee. Nor does the term include a power of appointment over property which is not a general power of appointment (as defined in section 2041). Examples of property, as described in this paragraph, are annuities, life estates, estates for terms of years, vested or contingent remainders and other future interests.

(b) In order to obtain the credit for tax on prior transfers, there must be a transfer of property described in paragraph (a) of this section by or from the transferor to the decedent. The term "transfer" of property by or from a transferor means any passing of property or an interest in property under circumstances which were such that the property or interest was included in the gross estate of the transferor. In this connection, if the decedent receives property as a result of the exercise or nonexercise of a power of appointment, the donee of the power (and not the creator) is deemed to be the transferor of the property if the property subject to the power is includible in the donee's gross estate under section 2041 (relating to powers of appointment). Thus, notwithstanding the designation by local law of the capacity in which the decedent takes, property received from the transferor includes interests in property held by or devolving upon the decedent: (1) as spouse under dower or curtesy laws or laws creating an estate in lieu of dower or curtesy; (2) as surviving tenant of a tenancy by the entirety or joint tenancy with survivorship rights; (3) as beneficiary of the proceeds of life insurance; (4) as survivor under an annuity contract; (5) as donee (possessor) of a general power of appointment (as defined in section 2041); (6) as appointee under the exercise of a general power of appointment (as defined in section 2041); or (7) as remainderman under the release or nonexercise of a power of appointment by reason of which the property is included in the gross estate of the donee of the power under section 2041.

(c) The application of this section may be illustrated by the following example:

Example. A devises Blackacre to B, as trustee, with directions to pay the income therefrom to C, his son, for life. Upon C's death, Blackacre is to be sold. C is given a general testamentary power to appoint one-third of the proceeds, and a testamentary power, which is not a general power, to appoint the remaining two-thirds of the proceeds, to such of the issue of his sister D as he should choose. D has a daughter, E, and a son, F. Upon his death, C exercised his general power by appointing one-third of the proceeds to D and his special power by appointing two-thirds of the proceeds to E. Since B's interest in Blackacre as a trustee is not a beneficial interest, no part of it is "property" for purpose of the credit in B's estate. On the other hand, C's life estate and his testamentary power over the one-third interest in the remainder constitute "property" received from A for purpose of the credit in C's estate. Likewise, D's one-third interest in the remainder received through the exercise of C's general power of appointment is "property" received from C for purpose of the credit in D's estate. No credit is allowed E's estate for the property which passed to her from C since the property was not included in C's gross estate. On the other hand, no credit is allowed in E's estate for property passing to her from A since her interest was not susceptible of valuation at the time of A's death (see § 20.2013-4). [Reg. § 20.2013-5.]

☐ [*T.D.* 6296, 6-23-58.]

[Reg. § 20.2013-6]

§ 20.2013-6. Examples.—The application of § § 20.2013-1 through 20.2013-5 may be further illustrated by the following examples:

Example (1). (a) A died December 1, 1953, leaving a gross estate of $1,000,000. Expenses, indebtedness, etc., amounted to $90,000. A bequeathed $200,000 to B, his wife, $100,000 of which qualifies for the marital deduction. B died November 1, 1954, leaving a gross estate of $500,000. Expenses, indebtedness, etc., amounted to $40,000. B bequeathed $150,000 to charity. A and B were both citizens of the United States. The estates of A and B both paid State death taxes equal to the maximum credit allowable for State death taxes. Death taxes were not a charge on the bequest to B.

(b) "First limitation" on credit for B's estate (§ 20.2013-2):

A's gross estate		$1,000,000.00
Expenses, indebtedness, etc.		90,000.00
A's adjusted gross estate		$910,000.00
Marital deduction	$100,000.00	
Exemption	60,000.00	160,000.00
A's taxable estate		750,000.00
A's gross estate tax		233,200.00
Credit for State death taxes		23,280.00
A's net estate tax payable		$209,920.00

"First limitation" = $209,920.00 (§ 20.2013-2(b)) × [($200,000.00 – $100,000.00) (§ 20.2013-4) ÷ ($750,000.00 – $209,920.00 – $23,280.00 + $60,000.00) (§ 20.2013-2(c))] = $36,393.90

(c) "Second limitation" on credit for B's estate (§ 20.2013-3):

(1) B's net estate tax payable as described in § 20.2013-3(a)(1) (previously taxed transfer included):

B's gross estate	$500,000.00
Expenses, indebtedness, etc.	$40,000.00
Charitable deduction	150,000.00

Exemption	60,000.00	250,000.00
B's taxable estate		$250,000.00
B's gross estate tax		$65,700.00
Credit for State death taxes		3,920.00
B's net estate tax payable		$61,780.00

(2) B's net estate tax payable as described in § 20.2013-3(a)(2) (previously taxed transfer excluded):

B's gross estate		$400,000.00
Expenses, indebtedness, etc.	$ 40,000.00	
Charitable deduction (§ 20.2013-3(b)) = $150,000.00 – [$150,000.00 × ($200,000.00 – $100,000.00 ÷ $500,000.00 – $ 40,000.00)] =	$117,391.30	
Exemption	60,000.00	217,391.30
B's taxable estate		$182,608.70
B's gross estate tax		$45,482.61
Credit for State death taxes		2,221.61
B's net estate tax payable		$43,260.00

(3) "Second limitation":

Subparagraph (1)	$61,780.00	
Less: Subparagraph (2)	43,260.00	$18,520.00

(d) Credit of B's estate for tax on prior transfers (§ 20.2013-1(c)):

Credit for tax on prior transfers = $18,520.00 (lower of paragraphs (b) and (c)) × 100% (percentage to be taken into account under § 20.2013-1(c))	$18,520.00

Example (2). (a) The facts are the same as those contained in example (1) of this paragraph with the following additions. C died December 1, 1950, leaving a gross estate of $250,000. Expenses, indebtedness, etc., amounted to $50,000. C bequeathed $50,000 to B. C was a citizen of the United States. His estate paid State death taxes equal to the maximum credit allowable for State death taxes. Death taxes were not a charge on the bequest to B.

(b) "First limitation" on credit for B's estate (§ 20.2013-2(d))—

(1) With respect to the property received from A:

"First limitation" = $36,393.90 (this computation is identical with the one contained in paragraph (b) of example (1) of this section).

(2) With respect to the property received from C:

C's gross estate		$250,000.00
Expenses, indebtedness, etc.	$50,000.00	
Exemption	60,000.00	110,000.00
C's taxable estate		$140,000.00
C's gross estate tax		$32,700.00
Credit for State death taxes		1,200.00
C's net estate tax payable		$31,500.00
"First limitation" = $31,500.00 (§ 20.2013-2(b)) × [$50,000.00 (§ 20.2013-4) ÷ ($140,000.00 – $31,500.00 – $1,200.00 + $60,000.00) (§ 20.2013-2(c))]	=	$9,414.23

(c) "Second limitation" on credit for B's estate (§ 20.2013-3(c)):

(1) B's net estate tax payable as described in § 20.2013-3(a)(1) (previously taxed transfers included) = $61,780.00 (this computation is identical with the one contained in paragraph (c)(1) of example (1) of this section).

(2) B's net estate tax payable as described in § 20.2013-3(a)(2) (previously taxed transfers excluded):

B's gross estate		$350,000.00
Expenses, indebtedness, etc.	$40,000.00	
Charitable deduction (§ 20.2013-3(b)) = $150,000.00 – [$150,000.00 × ($200,000.00 – $100,000.00 + $50,000.00) ÷ ($500,000.00 – $40,000.00)] =	101,086.96	
Exemption	60,000.00	201,086.96
B's taxable estate		$148,913.04
B's gross estate tax		$35,373.91
Credit for State death taxes		1,413.91
B's net estate tax payable		$33,960.00

(3) "Second limitation":

Subparagraph (1)	$61,780.00	
Less: Subparagraph (2)	33,960.00	$27,820.00

(4) Apportionment of "second limitation" on credit:

Transfer from A (§ 20.2013-4)	$100,000.00
Transfer from C (§ 20.2013-4)	50,000.00
Total	$150,000.00
Portion of "second limitation" attributable to transfer from A (100/150 of $27,820.00)	18,546.67
Portion of "second limitation" attributable to transfer from C (50/150 of $27,820.00)	9,273.33

(d) Credit of B's estate for tax on prior transfers (§ 20.2013-1(c)):

Credit for tax on transfer from A = $18,546.67 (lower of "first limitation" computed in paragraph (b)(1) and "second limitation" apportioned to A's transfer in paragraph (c)(4)) × 100% (percentage to be taken into account under § 20.2013-1(c))	$18,546.67
Credit for tax on transfer from C = $9,273.33 (lower of "first limitation" computed in paragraph (b)(2) and "second limitation" apportioned to B's transfer in paragraph (c)(4)) × 80% (percentage to be taken into account under § 20.2013-1(c))	7,418.66
Total credit for tax on prior transfers	$ 25,965.33

[Reg. § 20.2013-6.]

☐ [*T.D.* 6296, 6-23-58.]

[Reg. § 20.2014-1]

§ 20.2014-1. Credit for foreign death taxes.—(a) *In general.*—(1) A credit is allowed under section 2014 against the Federal estate tax for any estate, inheritance, legacy, or succession taxes actually paid to any foreign country (hereinafter referred to as "foreign death taxes"). The credit is allowed only for foreign death taxes paid (i) with respect to property situated within the country to which the tax is paid, (ii) with respect to property included in the decedent's gross estate, and (iii) with respect to the decedent's estate. The credit is allowable to the estate of a decedent who was a citizen of the United States at the time of his death. The credit is also allowable, as provided in paragraph (c) of this section, to the estate of a decedent who was a resident but not a citizen of the United States at the time of his death. The credit is not allowable to the estate of a decedent who was neither a citizen nor a resident of the United States at the time of his death. See paragraph(b)(1) of § 20.0-1 for the meaning of the term "resident" as applied to a decedent. The credit is allowable not only for death taxes paid to foreign countries which are states in the international sense, but also for death taxes paid to possessions or political subdivisions of foreign states. With respect to the estate of a decedent dying after September 2, 1958, the term "foreign country", as used in this section and §§ 20.2014-2 to 20.2014-6, includes a possession of the United States. See §§ 20.2011-1 and 20.2011-2 for the allowance of a credit for death taxes paid to a possession of the United States in the case of a decedent dying before September 3, 1958. No credit is allowable for interest or penalties paid in connection with foreign death taxes.

(2) In addition to the credit for foreign death taxes under section 2014, similar credits are allowed under death tax conventions with certain foreign countries. If credits against the Federal estate tax are allowable under section 2014, or under section 2014 and one or more death tax conventions, for death taxes paid to more than one country, the credits are combined and the aggregate amount is credited against the Federal estate tax, subject to the limitation provided for in paragraph (c) of § 20.2014-4. For application of the credit in cases involving a death tax convention, see § 20.2014-4.

(3) No credit is allowable under section 2014 in connection with property situated outside of the foreign country imposing the tax for which credit is claimed. However, such a credit may be allowable under certain death tax conventions. In the case of a tax imposed by a political subdivision of a foreign country, credit for the tax shall be allowed with respect to property having a situs in that foreign country, even though, under the principles described in this subparagraph, the property has a situs in a political subdivision different from the one imposing the tax. Whether or not particular property of a decedent is situated in the foreign country imposing the tax is determined in accordance with the same principles that would be applied in determining whether or not similar property of a nonresident decedent not a citizen of the United States is situated within the United States for Federal estate tax purposes. See §§ 20.2104-1 and 20.2105-1. For example, under § 20.2104-1 shares of stock are deemed to be situated in the United States only if issued by a domestic corporation. Thus, a share of corporate stock is regarded as situated in the foreign country imposing the tax only if the issuing corporation is incorporated in that country. Further, under § 20.2105-1 amounts receivable as insurance on the life of a nonresident not a citizen of the United States at the time of his death are not deemed situated in the United States. Therefore, in determining the credit under section 2014 in the case of a decedent who was a citizen or resident of the United States, amounts receivable as insurance on the life of the decedent and payable under a policy issued by a corporation incorporated in a foreign country are not deemed situated in such foreign country. In addition, under § 20.2105-1 in the case of an estate of a nonresident not a citizen of the United States who died on or after November 14, 1966, a debt obligation of a domestic corporation is not considered to be situated in the United States if any interest thereon would be treated under section 862(a)(1) as income from sources without the United States by reason of section 861(a)(1)(B) (relating to interest received from a domestic corporation less than 20 percent of whose gross income for a 3-year period was derived from sources within the United States). Accordingly, a debt obligation the primary obligor on which is a corporation incorporated in the foreign country imposing the tax is not considered to be situated in that country if, under circumstances corresponding to those described in § 20.2105-1 less than 20 percent of the gross income of the corporation for the 3-year period was derived from sources within that country. Further, under § 20.2104-1 in the case of an estate of a nonresident not a citizen of the United States who died before November 14, 1966, a bond for the payment of money is not situated within the United States unless it is physically located in the United States. Accordingly, in the case of the estate of a decedent dying before November 14, 1966, a bond is deemed situated in the foreign country imposing the tax only if it is physically located in that country. Finally, under § 20.2105-1 moneys deposited in the United States with any person carrying on the banking business by or for a nonresident not a citizen of the United States who died before November 14, 1966, and who was not engaged in business in the United States at the time of death are not deemed situated in the United States. Therefore, an account with a foreign bank in the foreign country imposing the tax is not considered to be situated in that country under corresponding circumstances.

(4) Where a deduction is allowed under section 2053(d) for foreign death taxes paid with respect to a charitable gift, the credit for foreign death taxes is subject to further limitations as explained in § 20.2014-7.

(b) *Limitations on credit.*—The credit for foreign death taxes is limited to the smaller of the following amounts:

(1) The amount of a particular foreign death tax attributable to property situated in the country imposing the tax and included in the decedent's gross estate for Federal estate tax purposes, computed as set forth in § 20.2014-2; or

(2) The amount of the Federal estate tax attributable to particular property situated in a foreign country, subjected to foreign death tax in that country, and included in the decedent's gross estate for Federal estate tax purposes, computed as set forth in § 20.2014-3.

(c) *Credit allowable to estate of resident not a citizen.*—(1) In the case of an estate of a decedent dying before November 14, 1966, who was a resident but not a citizen of the United States, a credit is allowed to the estate under section 2014 only if the foreign country of which the decedent was a citizen or subject, in imposing foreign death taxes, allows a similar credit to the estates of citizens of the United States who were resident in that foreign country at the time of death.

(2) In the case of an estate of a decedent dying on or after November 14, 1966, who was a resident but not a citizen of the United States, a credit is allowed to the estate under section 2014 without regard to the similar credit requirement of subparagraph (1) of this paragraph unless the decedent was a citizen or subject of a foreign country with respect to which there is in effect at the time of the decedent's death a Presidential proclamation, as authorized by section 2014(h), reinstating the similar credit requirement. In the case of an estate of a decedent who was a resi-

dent of the United States and a citizen or subject of a foreign country with respect to which such a proclamation has been made, and who dies while the proclamation is in effect, a credit is allowed under section 2014 only if that foreign country, in imposing foreign death taxes, allows a similar credit to the estates of citizens of the United States who were resident in that foreign country at the time of death. The proclamation authorized by section 2014(h) for the reinstatement of the similar credit requirement with respect to the estates of citizens or subjects of a specific foreign country may be made by the President whenever he finds that—

(i) The foreign country, in imposing foreign death taxes, does not allow a similar credit to the estates of citizens of the United States who were resident in the foreign country at the time of death,

(ii) The foreign country, after having been requested to do so, has not acted to provide a similar credit to the estates of such citizens, and

(iii) It is in the public interest to allow the credit under section 2014 to the estates of citizens or subjects of the foreign country only if the foreign country allows a similar credit to the estates of citizens of the United States who were resident in the foreign country at the time of death. The proclamation for the reinstatement of the similar credit requirement with respect to the estates of citizens or subjects of a specific foreign country may be revoked by the President. In that case, a credit is allowed under section 2014, to the estate of a decedent who was a citizen or subject of that foreign country and a resident of the United States at the time of death, without regard to the similar credit requirement if the decedent dies after the proclamation reinstating the similar credit requirement has been revoked. [Reg. § 20.2014-1.]

☐ [*T.D.* 6296, 6-23-58. *Amended by T.D.* 6526, 1-18-61, *T.D.* 6600, 5-28-62 *and T.D.* 7296, 12-11-73.]

[Reg. § 20.2014-2]

§ 20.2014-2. "First limitation".—(a) The amount of a particular foreign death tax attributable to property situated in the country imposing the tax and included in the decedent's gross estate for Federal estate tax purposes is the "first limitation." Thus, the credit for any foreign death tax is limited to an amount, A, which bears the same ratio to B (the amount of the foreign death tax without allowance of credit, if any, for Federal estate tax) as C (the value of the property situated in the country imposing the foreign death tax, subjected to the foreign death tax, included in the gross estate and for which a deduction is not allowed under section 2053(d)) bears to D (the value of all property subjected to the foreign death tax). Stated algebraically, the "first limitation"(A) equals

$$\frac{\text{Value of property in foreign country subjected to foreign death tax, in- cluded in gross estate and for which a deduction is not allowed under section 2053(d) (C)}}{\text{Value of all property subjected to foreign death tax (D)}} \times \text{Amount of foreign death tax (B)}$$

The values used in this proportion are the values determined for the purpose of the foreign death tax. The amount of the foreign death tax for which credit is allowable must be converted into United States money. The application of this paragraph may be illustrated by the following example:

Example. At the time of his death on June 1, 1966, the decedent, a citizen of the United States, owned stock in X Corp. (a corporation organized under the laws of Country Y) valued at $80,000. In addition, he owned bonds issued by Country Y valued at $80,000. The stock and bond certificates were in the United States. Decedent left by will $20,000 of the stock and $50,000 of the Country Y bonds to his surviving spouse. He left the rest of the stock and bonds to his son. Under the situs rules referred to in paragraph (a)(3) of § 20.2014-1 the stock is deemed situated in Country Y while the bonds are deemed to have their situs in the United States. (The bonds would be deemed to have their situs in Country Y if the decedent had died on or after November 14, 1966.) There is no death tax convention in existence between the United States and Country Y. The laws of Country Y provide for inheritance taxes computed as follows:

Inheritance tax of surviving spouse:	
Value of stock	$20,000
Value of bonds	50,000
Total value	70,000
Tax (16 percent rate)	$11,200
Inheritance tax of son:	
Value of stock	$60,000
Value of bonds	30,000
Total value	$90,000
Tax (16 percent rate)	$14,400

The "first limitation" on the credit for foreign death taxes is:

$$\frac{\$20{,}000 + \$60{,}000 \text{ (factor C of the ratio stated at § 20.2014-2(a))}}{\$70{,}000 + \$90{,}000 \text{ (factor D of the ratio stated at § 20.2014-2(a))}} \times (\$11{,}200 + \$14{,}400) \text{ (factor B of the ratio stated at § 20.2014-2(a))} = \$12{,}800$$

(b) If a foreign country imposes more than one kind of death tax or imposes taxes at different rates upon the several shares of an estate, or if a foreign country and a political subdivision or possession thereof each imposes a death tax, a "first limitation" is to be computed separately for each tax or rate and the results added in order to determine the total "first limitation." The application of this paragraph may be illustrated by the following example:

Example. The facts are the same as those contained in the example set forth in paragraph (a) of this section, except that the tax of the surviving spouse was computed at a 10-percent rate and amounted to $7,000, and the tax of the son was computed at a 20-percent rate and amounted to $18,000. In this case, the "first limitation" on the credit for foreign death taxes is computed as follows:

"First limitation" with respect to inheritance tax of surviving spouse =

$$\frac{\$20{,}000 \text{ (factor C of the ratio stated at § 20.2014-2(a))}}{\$70{,}000 \text{ (factor D of the ratio stated at § 20.2014-2(a))}} \times \$7{,}000 \text{ (factor B of the ratio stated at § 20.2014-2(a))} = \$2{,}000$$

"First limitation" with respect to inheritance tax of son =

$$\frac{\$60{,}000 \text{ (factor C of the ratio stated at § 20.2014-2(a))}}{\$90{,}000 \text{ (factor D of the ratio stated at § 20.2014-2(a))}} \times \$18{,}000 \text{ (factor B of the ratio stated at § 20.2014-2(a))} = \$12{,}000$$

Total "first limitation" on the credit for foreign death taxes $14,000

[Reg. § 20.2014-2.]

☐ [*T.D.* 6296, 6-23-58. *Amended by T.D.* 6600, 5-28-62; *T.D.* 6684, 10-23-63 *and T.D.* 7296, 12-11-73.]

[Reg. § 20.2014-3]

§ 20.2014-3. "Second limitation".—(a) The amount of the Federal estate tax attributable to particular property situated in a foreign country, subjected to foreign death tax in that country, and included in the decedent's gross estate for Federal estate tax purposes is the "second limitation." Thus, the credit is limited to an amount, E, which bears the same ratio to F (the gross Federal estate tax, reduced by any credit for State death taxes under section 2011 and by any credit for gift tax under section 2012) as G (the "adjusted value of the property situated in the foreign country, subjected to foreign death tax, and included in the gross estate," computed as described in paragraph (b) of this section) bears to H (the value of the entire gross estate, reduced by the total amount of the deductions allowed under sections 2055 (charitable deduction) and 2056 (marital deduction)). Stated algebraically, the "second limitation" (E) equals

$$\frac{\text{"adjusted value of the property situated in the foreign country, subjected to foreign death taxes, and included in the gross estate" (G)}}{\text{value of entire gross estate, less charitable and marital deductions (H)}} \times \text{gross Federal estate tax, less credits for State death taxes and gift tax (F).}$$

See p. 15 for regulations not amended to reflect law changes

The values used in this proportion are the values determined for the purpose of the Federal estate tax.

(b) Adjustment is required to factor "G" of the ratio stated in paragraph (a) of this section if a deduction for foreign death taxes under section 2053(d), a charitable deduction under section 2055, or a marital deduction under section 2056 is allowed with respect to the foreign property. If a deduction for foreign death taxes is allowed, the value of the property situated in the foreign country, subjected to foreign death tax, and included in the gross estate does not include the value of any property in respect of which the deduction for foreign death taxes is allowed. See § 20.2014-7. If a charitable deduction or a marital deduction is allowed, the value of such foreign property (after exclusion of the value of any property in respect of which the deduction for foreign death taxes is allowed) is reduced as follows:

(1) If a charitable deduction or a marital deduction is allowed to a decedent's estate with respect to any part of the foreign property, except foreign property in respect of which a deduction for foreign death taxes is allowed, specifically bequeathed, devised, or otherwise specifically passing to a charitable organization or to the decedent's spouse, the value of the foreign property is reduced by the amount of the charitable deduction or marital deduction allowed with respect to such specific transfer. See example (1) of paragraph (c) of this section.

(2) If a charitable deduction or a marital deduction is allowed to a decedent's estate with respect to a bequest, devise or other transfer of an interest in a group of assets including both the foreign property and other property, the value of the foreign property is reduced by an amount, I, which bears the same ratio to J (the amount of the charitable deduction or marital deduction allowed with respect to such transfer of an interest in a group of assets) as K (the value of the foreign property, except foreign property in respect of which a deduction for foreign death taxes is allowed, included in the group of assets) bears to L (the value of the entire group of assets). As used in this subparagraph, the term "group of assets" has reference to those assets which, under applicable law, are chargeable with the charitable or marital transfer. See example (2) of paragraph (c) of this section.

Any reduction described in paragraph (b)(1) or (b)(2) of this section on account of the marital deduction must proportionately take into account, if applicable, the limitation on the aggregate amount of the marital deduction contained in § 20.2056(a)-1(c). See § 20.2014-3(c), *Example 3.*

(c) The application of paragraphs (a) and (b) of this section may be illustrated by the following examples. In each case, the computations relate to the amount of credit under section 2014 without regard to the amount of credit which may be allowable under an applicable death tax convention.

Example (1). (i) Decedent, a citizen and resident of the United States at the time of his death on February 1, 1967, left a gross estate of $1,000,000 which includes the following: shares of stock issued by a domestic corporation, valued at $750,000; bonds issued in 1960 by the United States and physically located in foreign Country X, valued at $50,000; and shares of stock issued by a Country X corporation, valued at $200,000, with respect to which death taxes were paid to Country X. Expenses, indebtedness, etc., amounted to $60,000. Decedent specifically bequeathed $40,000 of the stock issued by the Country X corporation to a U. S. charity and left the residue of his estate, in equal shares, to his son and daughter. The gross Federal estate tax is $266,500, and the credit for State death taxes is $27,600. Under the situs rules referred to in paragraph (a)(3) of § 20.2014-1, the shares of stock issued by the Country X corporation comprise the only property deemed to be situated in Country X. (The bonds also would be deemed to have their situs in Country X if the decedent had died before November 14, 1966.)

(ii) The "second limitation" on the credit for foreign death taxes is

$$\frac{\text{\$200,000} - \text{\$40,000} \text{ (factor G of the ratio stated at § 20.2014-3(a); see also § 20.2014-3(b)(1))}}{\text{\$1,000,000} - \text{\$40,000} \text{ (factor H of the ratio stated at § 20.2014-3(a))}} \times (\text{\$266,500} - \text{\$27,600}) = \text{\$39,816.67} \text{ (factor F of the ratio stated at § 20.2014-3(a))}$$

The lesser of this amount and the amount of the "first limitation" (computed under § 20.2014-2) is the credit for foreign death taxes.

Example (2). (i) Decedent, a citizen and resident of the United States at the time of his death, left a gross estate of $1,000,000 which includes: shares of stock issued by a United States corporation, valued at $650,000; shares of stock issued by a Country X corporation, valued at $200,000; and life insurance, in the amount of $150,000, payable to a son. Expenses, indebtedness, etc., amounted to $40,000. The decedent made a specific bequest of $25,000 of the Country X corporation stock to Charity A and a general bequest of $100,000 to Charity B. The residue of his estate was left to his daughter. The gross Federal estate tax is $242,450 and the credit for State death taxes is $24,480. Under these facts and applicable law, neither the stock of the Country X corporation specifically bequeathed to Charity A nor the insurance payable to the son could be charged with satisfying the bequest to Charity B. Therefore, the "group of assets" which could be so charged is limited to stock of the Country X corporation valued at $175,000 and stock of the United States corporation valued at $650,000.

(ii) Factor "G" of the ratio which is used in determining the "second limitation" is computed as follows:

Value of property situated in Country X		$200,000.00
Less: Reduction described in § 20.2014-3(b)(1)	$25,000.00	
Reduction described in § 20.2014-3(b)(2) = [$175,000 (factor K of the ratio stated at § 20.2014-3(b)(2)) / $175,000 + $650,000 (factor L of the ratio stated at § 20.2014-3(b)(2))] × $100,000 = (factor J of the ratio stated at § 20.2014-3(b)(2))	21,212.12	46,212.12
Factor "G" of the ratio		$153,787.88

(iii) In this case, the "second limitation" on the credit for foreign death taxes is

$153,787.88 (factor G of the ratio stated at § 20.2014-3(a); see also subdivision (ii) above) / $1,000,000 − $125,000 (factor H of the ratio stated at § 20.2014-3(a)) × ($242,450 − $24,480) = $38,309.88 (factor F of the ratio stated at § 20.2014-3(a))

Example (3). (i) Decedent, a citizen and resident of the United States at the time of his death, left a gross estate of $850,000 which includes: shares of stock issued by United States corporations, valued at $440,000; real estate located in the United States, valued at $110,000; and shares of stock issued by Country X corporations, valued at $300,000. Expenses, indebtedness, etc., amounted to $50,000. Decedent devised $40,000 in real estate to a United States charity. In addition, he bequeathed to his wife $200,000 in United States stocks and $300,000 in Country X stocks. The residue of his estate passed to his children. The gross Federal estate tax is $81,700 and the credit for State death taxes is $5,520.

(ii) Decedent's adjusted gross estate is $800,000 (i.e., $850,000, gross estate less $50,000, expenses, indebtedness, etc.). Assume that the limitation imposed by section 2056(c), as in effect before 1982, is applicable so that the aggregate allowable marital deduction is limited to one-half the adjusted gross estate, or $400,000 (which is 50 percent of $800,000). Factor "G" of the ratio which is used in determining the "second limitation" is computed as follows:

Value of property situated in Country X		$300,000
Less: Reduction described in § 20.2014-3(b)(1) determined as follows (see also end of § 20.2014-3(b))—		
Total amount of bequests which qualify for the marital deduction:		
Specific bequest of Country X stock	$300,000	
Specific bequest of United States stock	200,000	
	500,000	
Limitation on aggregate marital deduction under section 2056(c)	$400,000	
Part of specific bequest of Country X stock with respect to which the marital deduction is allowed— $400,000 / $500,000 × $300,000		$240,000
Factor "G" of the ratio		60,000

(iii) Thus, the "second limitation" on the credit for foreign death taxes is

See p. 15 for regulations not amended to reflect law changes

$$\frac{\text{\$60,000 (factor G of the ratio stated at § 20.2014-3(a); see also subdivision (ii) above)}}{\text{\$850,000 – \$40,000 – \$400,000 (factor H of the ratio stated at § 20.2014-3(a))}} \times (\text{\$81,700 – \$5,520}) = \text{\$11,148.29. (factor F of the ratio stated at § 20.2014-3(a))}$$

(d) If the foreign country imposes more than one kind of death tax or imposes taxes at different rates upon the several shares of an estate, or if the foreign country and a political subdivision or possession thereof each imposes a death tax the "second limitation" is still computed by applying the ratio set forth in paragraph (a) of § 20.2014-3. Factor "G" of the ratio is determined by taking into consideration the combined value of the foreign property which is subjected to each different tax or different rate. The combined value, however, cannot exceed the value at which such property was included in the gross estate for Federal estate tax purposes. Thus, if Country X imposes a tax on the inheritance of a surviving spouse at a 10-percent rate and on the inheritance of a son at a 20-percent rate, the combined value of their inheritances is taken into consideration in determining factor "G" of the ratio, which is then used in computing the "second limitation." However, the "first limitation" is computed as provided in paragraph (b) of § 20.2014-2. The lesser of the "first limitation" and the "second limitation" is the credit for foreign death taxes. [Reg. § 20.2014-3.]

☐ [*T.D.* 6296, 6-23-58. *Amended by T.D.* 6600, 5-28-62; *T.D.* 7296, 12-11-73 *and T.D.* 8522, 2-28-94.]

[Reg. § 20.2014-4]

§ 20.2014-4. Application of credit in cases involving a death tax convention.—(a) *In general.*—(1) If credit for a particular foreign death tax is authorized by a death tax convention, there is allowed either the credit provided for by the convention or the credit provided for by section 2014, whichever is the more beneficial to the estate. For cases where credit may be taken under both the death tax convention and section 2014, see paragraph (b) of this section. The application of this paragraph may be illustrated by the following example:

Example. (i) Decedent, a citizen of the United States and a domiciliary of foreign Country X at the time of his death on December 1, 1966, left a gross estate of $1,000,000 which includes the following: shares of stock issued by a Country X corporation, valued at $400,000; bonds issued in 1962 by the United States and physically located in Country X, valued at $350,000; and real estate located in the United States, valued at $250,000. Expenses, indebtedness, etc., amounted to $50,000. Decedent left his entire estate to his son. There is in effect a death tax convention between the United States and Country X which provides for the allowance of credit by the United States for succession duties imposed by the national government of Country X. The gross Federal estate tax is $307,200, and the credit for State death taxes is $33,760. Country X imposed a net succession duty on the stocks and bonds of $180,000. Under the situs rules referred to in paragraph (a)(3) of § 20.2014-1, the shares of stock comprise the only property deemed to be situated in Country X. (If the decedent had died before November 14, 1966, the bonds also would be deemed to have their situs in Country X.) Under the convention, both the stocks and the bonds are deemed to be situated in Country X. In this example all figures are rounded to the nearest dollar.

(ii) *(a)* The credit authorized by the convention for death taxes imposed by Country X is computed as follows:

(1) Country X tax attributable to property situated in Country X and subjected to tax by both countries $\left(\frac{\$750{,}000}{\$750{,}000} \times \$180{,}000\right)$	$180,000
(2) Federal estate tax attributable to property situated in Country X and subjected to tax by both countries $\left(\frac{\$\ 750{,}000}{\$1{,}000{,}000} \times \$273{,}440\right)$	205,080
(3) Credit (subdivision *(1)* or *(2)*, whichever is less)	$180,000

(b) The credit authorized by section 2014 for death taxes imposed by Country X is computed as follows:

(1) "First limitation" computed under § 20.2014-2 $\left(\frac{\$400{,}000}{\$750{,}000} \times \$180{,}000\right)$	$96,000

(2) "Second limitation" computed under § 20.2014-3

$\frac{(\$400{,}000}{(\$1{,}000{,}000} \times \$273{,}440)$ 109,376

(3) Credit (subdivision *(1)* or *(2)*, whichever is less) $96,000

(iii) On the basis of the facts contained in this example, the credit of $180,000 authorized by the convention is the more beneficial to the estate.

(2) It should be noted that the greater of the treaty credit and the statutory credit is not necessarily the more beneficial to the estate. Such is the situation, for example, in those cases which involve both a foreign death tax credit and a credit under section 2013 for tax on prior transfers. The reason is that the amount of the credit for tax on prior transfers may differ depending upon whether the credit for foreign death tax is taken under the treaty or under the statute. Therefore, under certain circumstances, the advantage of taking the greater of the treaty credit and the statutory credit may be more than offset by a resultant smaller credit for tax on prior transfers. The solution is to compute the net estate tax payable first on the assumption that the treaty credit will be taken and then on the assumption that the statutory credit will be taken. Such computations will indicate whether the treaty credit or the statutory credit is in fact the more beneficial to the estate.

(b) *Taxes imposed by both a foreign country and a political subdivision thereof.*—If death taxes are imposed by both a foreign country with which the United States has entered into a death tax convention and one or more of its possessions or political subdivisions, there is allowed, against the tax imposed by section 2001—

(1) A credit for the combined death taxes paid to the foreign country and its political subdivisions or possessions as provided for by the convention, or

(2) A credit for the combined death taxes paid to the foreign country and its political subdivisions or possessions as determined under section 2014, or

(3)(i) A credit for that amount of the combined death taxes paid to the foreign country and its political subdivisions or possessions as is allowable under the convention, and

(ii) A credit under section 2014 for the death taxes paid to each political subdivision or possession, but only to the extent such death taxes are not directly or indirectly creditable under the convention, whichever is the most beneficial to the estate. The application of this paragraph may be illustrated by the following example:

Example. (1) Decedent, a citizen of the United States and a domiciliary of Province Y of foreign Country X at the time of his death on February 1, 1966, left a gross estate of $250,000 which includes the following: bonds issued by Country X physically located in Province Y, valued at $75,000; bonds issued by Province Z of Country X and physically located in the United States, valued at $50,000; and shares of stock issued by a domestic corporation, valued at $125,000. Decedent left his entire estate to his son. Expenses, indebtedness, etc., amounted to $26,000. The Federal estate tax after allowance of the credit for State death taxes is $38,124. Province Y imposed a death tax of 8 percent on the Country X bonds located therein which amounted to $6,000. No death tax was imposed by Province Z. Country X imposed a death tax of 15 percent on the Country X bonds and the Province Z bonds which amounted to $18,750 before allowance of any credit for the death tax of Province Y. Country X allows against its death taxes a credit for death taxes paid to any of its provinces on property which it also taxes, but only to the extent of one-half of the Country X death tax attributable to the property, or the amount of death taxes paid to its province, whichever is less. Country X, therefore, allowed a credit of $5,625 for the death taxes paid to Province Y. There is in effect a death tax convention between the United States and Country X which provides for allowance of credit by the United States for death taxes imposed by the national government of Country X. The death tax convention provides that in computing the "first limitation" for the credit under the convention, the tax of Country X is not to be reduced by the amount of the credit allowed for provincial taxes. Under the situs rules described in paragraph (a)(3) of § 20.2014-1, only the Country X bonds located in Province Y are deemed situated in Country X. (The bonds issued by Province Z also would be deemed to have their situs in Country X if the decedent had died on or after November 14, 1966.) Under the convention, both the Country X bonds and the Province Z bonds are deemed to be situated in Country X. In this example all figures are rounded to the nearest dollar.

(2)(i) The credit authorized by section 2014 for death taxes imposed by Country X (which includes death taxes imposed by Province Y according to § 20.2014-1(a)(1)) is computed as follows:

(a) "First limitation" with respect to tax imposed by national government of Country X (computed under paragraph (b) of § 20.2014-2)

(1) Gross Country X death tax attributable to Country X bonds (before allowance of provincial death taxes)

$\frac{\$75{,}000}{\$125{,}000} \times \$18{,}750$ $11,250

(2) Less credit for Province Y death taxes on such bonds 5,625

(3) Net Country X death tax attributable to such bonds 5,625

(*b*) "First limitation" with respect to tax imposed by Province Y (computed under paragraph (b) of § 20.2014-2)

$$\frac{\$75{,}000}{\$75{,}000} \times \$6{,}000 \quad \ldots\ldots \quad \$6{,}000$$

(*c*) Total "first limitation" . . 11,625

(*d*) "Second limitation" (computed under paragraph (d) of § 20.2014-3)

$$\frac{\$75{,}000}{\$250{,}000} \times \$38{,}124 \quad \ldots\ldots \quad \$11{,}437$$

(*e*) Credit (subdivision (*c*) or (*d*), whichever is less) . . 11,437

(ii) The credit authorized under the death tax convention between the United States and Country X is computed as follows:

(*a*) Country X tax attributable to property situated in Country X and subject to tax by both countries

$$\frac{\$125{,}000}{\$125{,}000} \times \$18{,}750 \quad \ldots\ldots \quad \$18{,}750$$

(*b*) Federal estate tax attributable to property situated in Country X and subjected to tax by both countries:

$$\frac{\$125{,}000}{\$250{,}000} \times \$38{,}124 \quad \ldots\ldots \quad \$19{,}062$$

(*c*) Credit (subdivision (*a*) or (*b*), whichever is less) $18,750

(3) If the estate takes a credit for death taxes under the convention, it would receive a credit of $18,750 which would include an indirect credit of $5,625 for death taxes paid to Province Y. The death tax of Province Y which was not directly or indirectly creditable under the convention is $375 ($6,000–$5,625). A credit for this tax would also be allowed under section 2014 but only to the extent of $187, as the amount of credit for the combined foreign death taxes is limited to the amount of Federal estate tax attributable to the property, determined in accordance with the rules prescribed for computing the "second limitation" under section 2014. In this case, the "second limitation" under section 2014 on the taxes attributable to the Country X bonds is $11,437 (see computation set forth in (2)(i) (*d*) of this example). The amount of credit under the convention for taxes attributable to Country X bonds is $11,250 ($75,000 ÷ $125,000 × $18,750). Inasmuch as the "second limitation" under section 2014 in respect of the Country X bonds ($11,437) exceeds the amount of the credit allowed under the convention in respect of the Country X bonds ($11,250) by $187, the additional credit allowable under section 2014 for the death taxes paid to Province Y not directly or indirectly creditable under the convention is limited to $187.

(c) *Taxes imposed by two foreign countries with respect to the same property.*—It is stated as a general rule in paragraph (a)(2) of § 20.2014-1 that if credits against the Federal estate tax are allowable under section 2014, or under section 2014 and one or more death tax conventions, for death taxes paid to more than one country, the credits are combined and the aggregate amount is credited against the Federal estate tax. This rule may result in credit being allowed for taxes imposed by two different countries upon the same item of property. If such is the case, the total amount of the credits with respect to such property is limited to the amount of the Federal estate tax attributable to the property, determined in accordance with the rules prescribed for computing the "second limitation" set forth in § 20.2014-3. The application of this section may be illustrated by the following example:

Example. The decedent, a citizen of the United States and a domiciliary of Country X at the time of his death on May 1, 1967, left a taxable estate which included bonds issued by Country Z and physically located in Country X. Each of the three countries involved imposed death taxes on the Country Z bonds. Assume that under the provisions of a treaty between the United States and Country X the estate is entitled to a credit against the Federal estate tax for death taxes imposed by Country X on the bonds in the maximum amount of $20,000. Assume, also, that since the decedent died after November 13, 1966, so that under the situs rules referred to in paragraph (a)(3) of § 20.2014-1 the bonds are deemed to have their situs in Country Z, the estate is entitled to a credit against the Federal estate tax for death taxes imposed by Country Z on the bonds in the maximum amount of $10,000. Finally, assume that the Federal estate tax attributable to the bonds is $25,000. Under these circumstances, the credit allowed the estate with respect to the bonds would be limited to $25,000. [Reg. § 20.2014-4.]

☐ [*T.D. 6296, 6-23-58. Amended by T.D. 6742, 6-22-64 and T.D. 7296, 12-11-73.*]

[Reg. § 20.2014-5]

§ 20.2014-5. Proof of credit.—(a) If the foreign death tax has not been determined and paid by the time the Federal estate tax return required by section 6018 is filed, credit may be claimed on the return in an estimated amount. However, before credit for the foreign death tax is finally allowed, satisfactory evidence, such as a statement by an authorized official of each country, possession or political subdivision thereof imposing the tax, must be submitted on Form 706CE certifying: (1) the full amount of the tax (exclusive of any interest or penalties), as computed before allowance of any credit, remission, or relief; (2) the amount of any credit, allowance, remission, or relief, and other pertinent information, including the nature of the allowance and a description of the property to which it pertains; (3) the net foreign death tax payable after any such allowance; (4) the date on which the death tax was paid, or if not all paid at one time, the date and amount of each partial payment; and (5) a list of the property situated in the foreign country and subjected to its tax, showing a description and the value of the property. Satisfactory evidence must also be submitted showing that no refund of the death tax is pending and none is authorized or, if any refund is pending or has been authorized, its amount and other pertinent information. See also section 2016 and § 20.2016-1 for requirements if foreign death taxes claimed as a credit are subsequently recovered.

(b) The following information must also be submitted whenever applicable:

(1) If any of the property subjected to the foreign death tax was situated outside of the country imposing the tax, the description of each item of such property and its value.

(2) If more than one inheritance or succession is involved with respect to which credit is claimed, or if the foreign country, possession or political subdivision thereof imposes more than one kind of death tax, or if both the foreign country and a possession or political subdivision thereof each imposes a death tax, a separate computation with respect to each inheritance or succession tax.

(c) In addition to the information required under paragraphs (a) and (b) of this section, the district director may require the submission of any further proof deemed necessary to establish the right to the credit. [Reg. § 20.2014-5.]

□ [*T.D.* 6296, 6-23-58.]

[Reg. § 20.2014-6]

§ 20.2014-6. Period of limitations on credit.—The credit for foreign death taxes under section 2014 is limited to those taxes which were actually paid and for which a credit was claimed within four years after the filing of the estate tax return for the decedent's estate. If, however, a petition has been filed with the The Tax Court of the United States for the redetermination of a deficiency within the time prescribed in section 6213(a), the credit is limited to those taxes which were actually paid and for which a credit was claimed within four years after the filing of the return, or before the expiration of 60 days after the decision of The Tax Court becomes final, whichever period is the last to expire. Similarly, if an extension of time has been granted under section 6161 for payment of the tax shown on the return, or of a deficiency, the credit is limited to those taxes which were actually paid and for which a credit was claimed within four years after the filing of the return, or before the date of the expiration of the period of the extension, whichever period is the last to expire. See section 2015 for the applicable period of limitations for credit for foreign death taxes on reversionary or remainder interests if an election is made under section 6163(a) to postpone payment of the estate tax attributable to reversionary or remainder interests. If a claim for refund based on the credit for foreign death taxes is filed within the applicable period described in this section, a refund may be made despite the general limitation provisions of sections 6511 and 6512. Any refund based on the credit for foreign death taxes shall be made without interest. [Reg. § 20.2014-6.]

□ [*T.D.* 6296, 6-23-58.]

[Reg. § 20.2014-7]

§ 20.2014-7. Limitation on credit if a deduction for foreign death taxes is allowed under section 2053(d).—If a deduction is allowed under section 2053(d) for foreign death taxes paid with respect to a charitable gift, the credit for foreign death taxes is subject to special limitations. In such a case the property described in subparagraphs(A), (B), and (C) of paragraphs (1) and (2) of section 2014(b) shall not include any property with respect to which a deduction is allowed under section 2053(d). The application of this section may be illustrated by the following example:

Example. The decedent, a citizen of the United States, died July 1, 1955, leaving a gross estate of $1,200,000 consisting of: Shares of stock issued by United States corporations, valued at $600,000; bonds issued by the United States Government physically located in the United States, valued at $300,000; and shares of stock issued by a Country X corporation, valued at $300,000. Expenses, indebtedness, etc., amounted to $40,000. The decedent made specific bequests of $400,000 of the United States corporation stock to a niece and $100,000 of the Country X corporation stock to a nephew. The residue of his estate was left to charity. There is no death tax convention in existence between the United States and Country X. The Country X tax imposed was at a 50-percent rate on all beneficiaries. A State inheritance tax of $20,000 was imposed on the niece and nephew. The decedent did not provide in his will for the payment of the death taxes, and under local law the Federal estate tax is payable from the general estate, the same as administration expenses.

Distribution of the Estate

Gross estate		$1,200,000.00
Debts and charges	$40,000.00	
Bequest of United States corporation stock to niece	400,000.00	
Bequest of Country X corporation stock to nephew	100,000.00	
Net Federal estate tax	136,917.88	$676,917.88
Residue before Country X tax		523,082.12
Country X succession tax on charity		100,000.00
Charitable deduction		$423,082.12

Taxable Estate and Federal Estate Tax

Gross estate		$1,200,000.00
Debts and charges	$40,000.00	
Deduction of foreign death tax under section 2053(d)	100,000.00	
Charitable deduction	423,082.12	
Exemption	60,000.00	623,082.12
Taxable estate		$576,917.88
Gross estate tax		$172,621.26
Credit for State death taxes		15,476.72
Gross estate tax less credit for State death taxes		$157,144.54
Credit for foreign death taxes		20,226.66
Net Federal estate tax		$136,917.88

Credit for Foreign Death Taxes

Country X tax	
Succession tax on nephew:	
Value of stock of Country X corporation	$100,000.00
Tax (50% rate)	50,000.00
Succession tax on charity:	
Value of stock of Country X corporation	200,000.00
Tax (50% rate)	100,000.00

Computation of exclusion under section 2014(b)

Value of property situated in Country X	$300,000.00
Value of property in respect of which a deduction is allowed under section 2053(d)	200,000.00
Value of property situated within Country X, subjected to tax, and included in gross estate as limited by section 2014(f)	$100,000.00

First limitation, § 20.2014-2(a)

$$\frac{\text{\$100,000 (factor C of the ratio stated at § 20.2014-2(a))}}{\text{\$100,000 + \$200,000 (factor D of the ratio stated at § 20.2014-2(a))}} \times \text{(\$50,000.00 + \$100,000.00) (factor B of the ratio stated at § 20.2014-2(a))} = \text{\$50,000.00}$$

Second limitation, § 20.2014-3(a)

$$\frac{\text{\$100,000 (factor G of the ratio stated at § 20.2014-3(a)) (as limited by section 2014(f))}}{\text{\$1,200,000} - \text{\$423,082.12 (factor H of the ratio stated at § 20.2014-3(a))}} \times \text{(\$172,621.26} - \text{\$15,476.72) (factor F of the ratio stated at § 20.2014-3(a))} = \text{\$20,226.66}$$

[Reg. § 20.2014-7.]

☐ [*T.D.* 6600, 5-28-62.]

[Reg. § 20.2015-1]

§ 20.2015-1. Credit for death taxes on remainders.—(a) If the executor of an estate elects under section 6163(a) to postpone the time for payment of any portion of the Federal estate tax attributable to a reversionary or remainder interest in property, credit is allowed under sections 2011 and 2014 against that portion of the Federal estate tax for State death taxes and foreign death taxes attributable to the reversionary or remainder interest if the State death taxes or foreign death taxes are paid and if credit therefor is claimed either—

(1) Within the time provided for in sections 2011 and 2014, or

(2) Within the time for payment of the tax imposed by section 2001 or 2101 as postponed under section 6163(a) and as extended under section 6163(b) (on account of undue hardship) or, if the precedent interest terminated before July 5, 1958, within 60 days after the termination of the preceding interest or interests in the property.

The allowance of credit, however, is subject to the other limitations contained in sections 2011 and 2014 and, in the case of the estate of a decedent who was a nonresident not a citizen of the United States, in section 2102(b).

(b) In applying the rule stated in paragraph (a) of this section, credit for State death taxes or foreign death taxes paid within the time provided in sections 2011 and 2014 is applied first to the portion of the Federal estate tax payment of which is not postponed, and any excess is applied to the balance of the Federal estate tax. However, credit for State death taxes or foreign death taxes not paid within the time provided in sections 2011 and 2014 is allowable only against the portion of the Federal estate tax attributable to the reversionary or remainder interest, and only for State or foreign death taxes attributable to that interest. If a State death tax or a foreign death tax is imposed upon both a reversionary or remainder interest and upon other property, without a definite apportionment of the tax, the amount of the tax deemed attributable to the reversionary or remainder interest is an amount which bears the same ratio to the total tax as the value of the reversionary or remainder interest bears to the value of the entire property with respect to which the tax was imposed. In applying this ratio, adjustments consistent with those required under paragraph (c) of § 20.6163-1 must be made.

(c) The application of this section may be illustrated by the following examples:

Example (1). One-third of the Federal estate tax was attributable to a remainder interest in real property located in State Y, and two-thirds of the Federal estate tax was attributable to other property located in State X. The payment of the tax attributable to the remainder interest was postponed under the provisions of section 6163(a). The maximum credit allowable for State death taxes under the provisions of section 2011 is $12,000. Therefore, of the maximum credit allowable, $4,000 is attributable to the remainder interest and $8,000 is attributable to the other property. Within the 4-year period provided for in section 2011, inheritance tax in the amount of $9,000 was paid to State X in connection with the other property. With respect to this $9,000, $8,000 (the maximum amount allowable) is allowed as a credit against the Federal estate tax attributable to the other property, and $1,000 is allowed as a credit against the postponed tax. The life estate or other precedent interest expired after July 4, 1958. After the expiration of the 4-year period but before the expiration of the period of postponement elected under section 6163(a) and of the period of extension granted under section 6163(b) for payment of the tax, inheritance tax in the amount of $5,000 was paid to State Y in connection with the remainder interest. As the maximum credit allowable with respect to the remainder interest is $4,000 and $1,000 has already been allowed as a credit, an additional $3,000 will be credited against the Federal estate tax attributable to the remainder interest. It should be noted that if the life estate or other precedent interest had expired after the expiration of the 4-year period but before July 5, 1958, the same result would be reached only if the inheritance tax had been paid to State Y before the expiration of 60 days after the termination of the life estate or other precedent interest.

Example (2). The facts are the same as in example (1), except that within the 4-year period inheritance tax in the amount of $2,500 was paid to State Y with respect to the remainder interest and inheritance tax in the amount of $7,500 was paid to State X with respect to the other property. The amount of $8,000 is allowed as a credit against the Federal estate tax attributable to the other property and the amount of $2,000 is allowed as a credit against the postponed tax. The life estate or other precedent interest expired after July 4, 1958. After the expiration of the 4-year period but before the expiration of the period of postponement elected under section 6163(a) and of the period of extension granted under section 6163(b) for payment of the tax, inheritance tax in the amount of $5,000 was paid to State Y in connection with the remainder interest. As the maximum credit allowable with respect to the remainder interest is $4,000 and $2,000 already has been allowed as a credit, an additional $2,000 will be credited against the Federal estate tax attributable to the remainder interest. It should be noted that if the life estate or other precedent interest had expired after the expiration of the 4-year period but before July 5, 1958, the same result would be reached only if the inheritance tax had been paid to State Y before the expiration of 60 days after the termination of the life estate or other precedent interest.

Example (3). The facts are the same as in example (2), except that no payment was made to State Y within the 4-year period. The amount of $7,500 is allowed as a credit against the Federal estate tax attributable to the other property. After termination of the life interest additional credit will be allowed in the amount of $4,000 against the Federal estate tax attributable to the remainder interest. Since the payment of $5,000 was made to State Y following the expiration of the 4-year period, no part of the payment may be allowed as a credit against the Federal estate tax attributable to the other property. [Reg. § 20.2015-1.]

☐ [*T.D. 6296, 6-23-58. Amended by T.D.* 6526, 1-18-61 *and T.D.* 7296, 12-11-73.]

[Reg. § 20.2016-1]

§ 20.2016-1. Recovery of death taxes claimed as credit.—In accordance with the provisions of section 2016, the executor (or any other person) receiving a refund of any State death taxes or foreign death taxes claimed as a credit under section 2011 or section 2014 shall notify the district director of the refund within 30 days of its receipt. The notice shall contain the following information:

(a) The name of the decedent;

(b) The date of the decedent's death;

(c) The property with respect to which the refund was made;

(d) The amount of the refund, exclusive of interest;

(e) The date of the refund; and

(f) The name and address of the person receiving the refund.

If the refund was in connection with foreign death taxes claimed as a credit under section 2014, the notice shall also contain a statement showing the amount of interest, if any, paid by the foreign country on the refund. Finally, the person filing the notice shall furnish the district director such additional information as he may request. Any Federal estate tax found to be due by reason of the refund is payable by the person or persons receiving it, upon notice and demand, even though the refund is received after the expiration of the period of limitations set forth in section 6501 (see section 6501(c)(5)). If the tax found to be due results from a refund of foreign death tax claimed as a credit under section 2014, such tax shall not bear interest for any period before the receipt of the refund, except to the extent that interest was paid by the foreign country on the refund. [Reg. § 20.2016-1.]

□ [*T.D.* 6296, 6-23-58.]

Gross Estate

[Reg. § 20.2031-0]

§ 20.2031-0. Table of contents.—This section lists the section headings and undesignated center headings that appear in the regulations under section 2031.

[Reg. § 20.2031-0.]

□ [*T.D.* 8540, 6-9-94. *Amended by T.D.* 8819, 4-29-99; *T.D.* 8886, 6-9-2000; *T.D.* 9448, 5-1-2009 *and T.D.* 9540, 8-9-2011.]

[Reg. § 20.2031-1]

§ 20.2031-1. Definition of gross estate; valuation of property.—(a) *Definition of gross estate.*—Except as otherwise provided in this paragraph the value of the gross estate of a decedent who was a citizen or resident of the United States at the time of his death is the total value of the interests described in sections 2033 through 2044. The gross estate of a decedent who died before October 17, 1962, does not include real property situated outside the United States (as defined in paragraph (b)(1) of § 20.0-1). Except as provided in paragraph (c) of this section (relating to the estates of decedents dying after October 16, 1962, and before July 1, 1964), in the case of a decedent dying after October 16, 1962, real property situated outside the United States which comes within the scope of sections 2033 through 2044 is included in the gross estate to the same extent as any other property coming within the scope of those sections. In arriving at the value of the gross estate the interests described in sections 2033 through 2044 are valued as described in this section, §§ 20.2031-2 through 20.2031-9 and § 20.2032-1. The contents of sections 2033 through 2044 are, in general, as follows:

(1) Sections 2033 and 2034 are concerned mainly with interests in property passing through the decedent's probate estate. Section 2033 includes in the decedent's gross estate any interest that the decedent has in property at the time of his death. Section 2034 provides that any interest of the decedent's surviving spouse in the decedent's property, such as dower or curtesy, does not prevent the inclusion of such property in the decedent's gross estate.

(2) Sections 2035 through 2038 deal with interests in property transferred by the decedent during his life under such circumstances as to bring the interests within the decedent's gross estate. Section 2035 includes in the decedent's gross estate property transferred in contemplation of death, even though the decedent had no interest in, or control over, the property at the time of his death. Section 2036 provides for the inclusion of transferred property with respect to which the decedent retained the income or the power to designate who shall enjoy the income. Section 2037 includes in the decedent's gross estate certain transfers under which the beneficial enjoyment of the property could be obtained only by surviving the decedent. Section 2038 provides for the inclusion of transferred property if the decedent had at the time of his death the power to change the beneficial enjoyment of the property. It should be noted that there is a considerable overlap in the application of sections 2036 through 2038 with respect to reserved powers, so that transferred property may be includible in the decedent's gross estate in varying degrees under more than one of those sections.

(3) Sections 2039 through 2042 deal with special kinds of property and powers. Sections 2039 and 2040 concern annuities and jointly held property, respectively. Section 2041 deals with powers held by the decedent over the beneficial enjoyment of property not originating with the decedent. Section 2042 concerns insurance under policies on the life of the decedent.

(4) Section 2043 concerns the sufficiency of consideration for transfers made by the decedent during his life. This has a bearing on the amount to be included in the decedent's gross estate under sections 2035 through 2038, and 2041. Section 2044 deals with retroactivity.

(b) *Valuation of property in general.*—The value of every item of property includible in a decedent's gross estate under sections 2031 through 2044 is its fair market value at the time of the decedent's death, except that if the executor elects the alternate valuation method under section 2032, it is the fair market value thereof at the date, and with the adjustments, prescribed in that section. The fair market value is the price at which the property would change hands between a willing buyer and a willing seller, neither being under any compulsion to buy or to sell and both having reasonable knowledge of relevant facts. The fair market value of a particular item of property includible in the decedent's gross estate is not to be determined by a forced sale price. Nor is the fair market value of an item of property to be determined by the sale price of the item in a market other than that in which such item is most commonly sold to the public, taking into account the location of the item wherever appropriate. Thus, in the case of an item of property includible in the decedent's gross estate, which is generally obtained by the public in the retail market, the fair market value of such an item of property is the price at which the item or a comparable item would be sold at retail. For example, the fair market value of an automobile (an article generally obtained by the public in the retail market) includible in the decedent's gross estate is the price for which an automobile of the same or approximately the same description, make, model, age, condition, etc., could be purchased by a member of the general public and not the price for which the particular automobile of the decedent would be purchased by a dealer in used automobiles. Examples of items of property which are generally sold to the public at retail may be found in § § 20.2031-6 and 20.2031-8. The value is generally to be determined by ascertaining as a basis the fair market value as of the applicable valuation date of each unit of property. For example, in the case of shares of stock or bonds, such unit of property is generally a share of stock or a bond. Livestock, farm machinery, harvested and growing crops must generally be itemized and the value of each item separately returned. Property shall not be returned at the value at which it is assessed for local tax purposes unless that value represents the fair market value as of the applicable valuation date. All relevant facts and elements of value as of the applicable valuation date shall be considered in every case. The value of items of property which were held by the decedent for sale in the course of a business generally should be reflected in the value of the business. For valuation of interests in businesses, see § 20.2031-3. See § 20.2031-2 and § § 20.2031-4 through 20.2031-8 for further information concerning the valuation of other particular kinds of property. For certain circumstances under which the sale of an item of property at a price below its fair market value may result in a deduction for the estate, see paragraph (d)(2) of § 20.2053-3.

(c) *Real property situated outside the United States; gross estate of decedent dying after October 16, 1962, and before July 1, 1964.*—(1) *In general.*—In the case of a decedent dying after October 16, 1962, and before July 1, 1964, the value of real property situated outside the United States (as defined in paragraph (b)(1) of § 20.0-1) is not included in the gross estate of the decedent—

(i) Under section 2033, 2034, 2035(a), 2036(a), 2037(a), or 2038(a) to the extent the real property, or the decedent's interest in it, was acquired by the decedent before February 1, 1962;

(ii) Under section 2040 to the extent such property or interest was acquired by the decedent before February 1, 1962, or was held by the decedent and the survivor in a joint tenancy or tenancy by the entirety before February 1, 1962; or

(iii) Under section 2041(a) to the extent that before February 1, 1962, such property or interest was subject to a general power of appointment (as defined in section 2041) possessed by the decedent.

(2) *Certain property treated as acquired before February 1, 1962.*—For purposes of this paragraph real property situated outside the United States (including property held by the decedent and the survivor in a joint tenancy or tenancy by the entirety), or an interest in such property or a general power of appointment in respect of such property, which was acquired by the decedent after January 31, 1962, is treated as acquired by the decedent before February 1, 1962, if

(i) Such property, interest, or power was acquired by the decedent by gift within the meaning of section 2511, or from a prior decedent by devise or inheritance, or by reason of death, form of ownership, or other conditions (including the exercise or nonexercise of a power of appointment); and

(ii) Before February 1, 1962, the donor or prior decedent had acquired the property or his interest therein or had possessed a power of appointment in respect thereof.

(3) *Certain property treated as acquired after January 31, 1962.*—For purposes of this paragraph that portion of capital additions or improvements made after January 31, 1962, to real property situated outside the United States is, to the extent that it materially increases the value of the property, treated as real property acquired after January 31, 1962. Accordingly, the gross estate may include the value of improvements on unimproved real property, such as office buildings, factories, houses, fences, drainage ditches, and other capital items, and the value of capital additions and improvements to existing improvements, placed on real property after January 31, 1962, whether or not the value of such real property or existing improvements is included in the gross estate. [Reg. § 20.2031-1.]

☐ [*T.D. 6296, 6-23-58. Amended by T.D. 6684, 10-23-63 and T.D. 6826, 6-14-65.*]

[Reg. § 20.2031-2]

§ 20.2031-2. Valuation of stocks and bonds.—(a) *In general.*—The value of stocks and bonds is the fair market value per share or bond on the applicable valuation date.

(b) *Based on selling prices.*—(1) In general, if there is a market for stocks or bonds, on a stock exchange, in an over-the-counter market, or otherwise, the mean between the highest and lowest quoted selling prices on the valuation date is the fair market value per share or bond. If there were no sales on the valuation date but there were sales on dates within a reasonable period both before and after the valuation date, the fair market value is determined by taking a weighted average of the means between the highest and lowest sales on the nearest date before and the nearest date after the valuation date. The average is to be weighted inversely by the respective numbers of trading days between the selling dates and the valuation date. If the stocks or bonds are listed on more than one exchange, the records of the exchange where the stocks or bonds are principally dealt in should be employed if such records are available in a generally available listing or publication of general circulation. In the event that such records are not so available and such stocks or bonds are listed on a composite listing of combined exchanges in a generally available listing or publication of general circulation, the records of such combined exchanges should be employed. In valuing listed securities, the executor should be careful to consult accurate records to obtain values as of the applicable valuation date. If quotations of unlisted securities are obtained from brokers, or evidence as to their sale is obtained from officers of the issuing companies, copies of the letters furnishing such quotations or evidence of sale should be attached to the return.

(2) If it is established with respect to bonds for which there is a market on a stock exchange, that the highest and lowest selling prices are not available for the valuation date in a generally available listing or publication of general circulation but that closing selling prices are so available, the fair market value per bond is the mean between the quoted closing selling price on the valuation date and the quoted closing selling price on the trading day before the valuation date. If there were no sales on the trading day before the valuation date but there were sales on a date within a reasonable period before the valuation date, the fair market value is determined by taking a weighted average of the quoted closing selling price on the valuation date and the quoted closing selling price on the nearest date before the valuation date. The closing selling price for the valuation date is to be weighted by the number of trading days between the previous selling date and the valuation date. If there were no sales within a reasonable period before the valuation date but there were sales on the valuation date, the fair market value is the closing selling price on such valuation date. If there were no sales on the valuation date but there were sales on dates within a reasonable period both before and after the valuation date, the fair market value is determined by taking a weighted average of the quoted closing selling prices on the nearest date before and the nearest date after the valuation date. The average is to be weighted inversely by the respective numbers of trading days between the selling dates and the valuation date. If the bonds are listed on more than one exchange, the records of the exchange where the bonds are principally dealt in should be employed. In valuing listed securities, the executor should be careful to consult accurate records to obtain values as of the applicable valuation date.

(3) The application of this paragraph may be illustrated by the following examples:

Example (1). Assume that sales of X Company common stock nearest the valuation date (Friday, June 15) occurred two trading days before (Wednesday, June 13) and three trading days after (Wednesday, June 20) and on these days the mean sale prices per share were $10 and $15, respectively. The price of $12 is taken as representing the fair market value of a share of X Company common stock as of the valuation date

$$\frac{(3 \times 10) + (2 \times 15)}{5}$$

Example (2). Assume the same facts as in example (1) except that the mean sale prices per share on June 13 and June 20 were $15 and $10, respectively. The price of $13 is taken as representing the fair market value of a share of X Company common stock as of the valuation date

$$\frac{(3 \times 15) + (2 \times 10)}{5}$$

Example (3). Assume the decedent died on Sunday, October 7, and that Saturday and Sunday were not trading days. If sales of X Company common stock occurred on Friday, October 5, at mean sale prices per share of $20 and on Monday, October 8, at mean sale prices per share of $23, the price of $21.50 is taken as representing the fair market value of a share of X Company common stock as of the valuation date

$$\frac{(1 \times 20) + (23 \times 1)}{2}$$

Example (4). Assume that on the valuation date (Tuesday, April 3, 1973) the closing selling price of a listed bond was $25 per bond and that the highest and lowest selling prices are not available in a generally available listing or publication of general circulation for that date. Assume further, that the closing selling price of the same listed bond was $21 per bond on the day before the valuation date (Monday, April 2, 1973). Thus, under paragraph (b)(2) of this section the price of $23 is taken as representing the fair market value per bond as of the valuation date

$$\frac{(25 + 21)}{2}$$

Example (5). Assume the same facts as in example (4) except that there were no sales on the day before the valuation date. Assume further, that there were sales on Thursday, March 29, 1973 and that the closing selling price on that day was $23. The price of $24.50 is taken as representing the fair market value per bond as of the valuation date

$$\frac{((1 \times 23) + (3 \times 25))}{4}$$

Example (6). Assume that no bonds were traded on the valuation date (Friday, April 20). Assume further, that sales of bonds nearest the valuation date occurred two trading days before (Wednesday, April 18) and three trading days after (Wednesday, April 25) the valuation date and that on these two days the closing selling prices per bond were $29 and $22, respectively. The highest and lowest selling prices are not available for these dates in a generally available listing or publication of general circulation. Thus, under paragraph (b)(2) of this section, the price of $26.20 is taken as representing the fair market value of a bond as of the valuation date

$$\frac{((3 \times 29) + (2 \times 22))}{5}$$

(c) *Based on bid and asked prices.*—If the provisions of paragraph (b) of this section are inapplicable because actual sales are not available during a reasonable period beginning before and ending after the valuation date, the fair market value may be determined by taking the mean between the bona fide bid and asked prices on the valuation date, or if none, by taking a weighted average of the means between the bona fide bid and asked prices on the nearest trading date before and the nearest trading date after the valuation date, if both such nearest dates are within a reasonable period. The average is to be determined in the manner described in paragraph (b) of this section.

(d) *Based on incomplete selling prices or bid and asked prices.*—If the provisions of paragraphs (b) and (c) of this section are inapplicable because no actual sale prices or bona fide bid and asked prices are available on a date within a reasonable period before the valuation date, but such prices are available on a date within a reasonable period after the valuation date, or vice versa, then the mean between the highest and lowest available sale prices or bid and asked prices may be taken as the value.

(e) *Where selling prices or bid and asked prices do not reflect fair market value.*—If it is established that the value of any bond or share of stock determined on the basis of selling or bid and asked prices as provided under paragraphs (b), (c), and (d) of this section does not reflect the fair market value thereof, then some reasonable modification of that basis or other relevant facts and elements of value are considered in determining the fair market value.

Where sales at or near the date of death are few or of a sporadic nature, such sales alone may not indicate fair market value. In certain exceptional cases, the size of the block of stock to be valued in relation to the number of shares changing hands in sales may be relevant in determining whether selling prices reflect the fair market value of the block of stock to be valued. If the executor can show that the block of stock to be valued is so large in relation to the actual sales on the existing market that it could not be liquidated in a reasonable time without depressing the market, the price at which the block could be sold as such outside the usual market, as through an underwriter, may be a more accurate indication of value than market quotations. Complete data in support of any allowance claimed due to the size of the block of stock being valued shall be submitted with the return. On the other hand, if the block of stock to be valued represents a controlling interest, either actual or effective, in a going business, the price at which other lots change hands may have little relation to its true value.

(f) *Where selling prices or bid and asked prices are unavailable.*—If the provisions of paragraphs (b), (c), and (d) of this section are inapplicable because actual sale prices and bona fide bid and asked prices are lacking, then the fair market value is to be determined by taking the following factors into consideration:

(1) In the case of corporate or other bonds, the soundness of the security, the interest yield, the date of maturity, and other relevant factors; and

(2) In the case of shares of stock, the company's net worth, prospective earning power and dividend-paying capacity, and other relevant factors.

Some of the "other relevant factors" referred to in subparagraphs (1) and (2) of this paragraph are: the good will of the business; the economic outlook in the particular industry; the company's position in the industry and its management; the degree of control of the business represented by the block of stock to be valued; and the values of securities of corporations engaged in the same or similar lines of business which are listed on a stock exchange. However, the weight to be accorded such comparisons or any other evidentiary factors considered in the determination of a value depends upon the facts of each case. In addition to the relevant factors described above, consideration shall also be given to nonoperating assets, including proceeds of life insurance policies payable to or for the benefit of the company, to the extent such nonoperating assets have not been taken into account in the determination of net worth, prospective earning power and dividend-earning capacity. Complete financial and other data upon which the valuation is based should be submitted with the return, including copies of reports of any examinations of the company made by accountants, engineers, or any technical experts as of or near the applicable valuation date.

(g) *Pledged securities.*—The full value of securities pledged to secure an indebtedness of the decedent is included in the gross estate. If the decedent had a trading account with a broker, all securities belonging to the decedent and held by the broker at the date of death must be included at their fair market value as of the applicable valuation date. Securities purchased on margin for the decedent's account and held by a broker must also be returned at their fair market value as of the applicable valuation date. The amount of the decedent's indebtedness to a broker or other person with whom securities were pledged is allowed as a deduction from the gross estate in accordance with the provisions of § 20.2053-1 or § 20.2106-1 (for estates of nonresidents not citizens).

(h) *Securities subject to an option or contract to purchase.*—Another person may hold an option or a contract to purchase securities owned by a decedent at the time of his death. The effect, if any, that is given to the option or contract price in determining the value of the securities for estate tax purposes depends upon the circumstances of the particular case. Little weight will be accorded a price contained in an option or contract under which the decedent is free to dispose of the underlying securities at any price he chooses during his lifetime. Such is the effect, for example, of an agreement on the part of a shareholder to purchase whatever shares of stock the decedent may own at the time of his death. Even if the decedent is not free to dispose of the underlying securities at other than the option or contract price, such price will be disregarded in determining the value of the securities unless it is determined under the circumstances of the particular case that the agreement represents a bona fide business arrangement and not a device to pass the decedent's shares to the natural objects of his bounty for less than an adequate and full consideration in money or money's worth. See section 2703 and the regulations at § 25.2703 of this chapter for special rules involving options and agreements (including contracts to purchase) entered into (or substantially modified after) October 8, 1990.

(i) *Stock sold "ex-dividend."*.—In any case where a dividend is declared on a share of stock before the decedent's death but payable to stockholders of record on a date after his death and the stock is selling "ex-dividend" on the date of the decedent's death, the amount of the dividend is added to the ex-dividend quotation in determining the fair market value of the stock as of the date of the decedent's death.

(j) *Application of chapter 14.*—See section 2701 and the regulations at § 25.2701 of this chapter for special rules for valuing the transfer of an interest in a corporation and for the treatment of unpaid qualified payments at the death of the transferor or an applicable family member. See section 2704(b) and the regulations at § 25.2704-2 of this chapter for special valuation rules involving certain restrictions on liquidation rights created after October 8, 1990. [Reg. § 20.2031-2]

☐ [*T.D.* 6296, 6-23-58. *Amended by T.D.* 6826, 6-14-65; *T.D.* 7312, 4-26-74; *T.D.* 7327, 9-30-74; *T.D.* 7432, 9-13-76 *and T.D.* 8395, 1-28-92.]

[Reg. § 20.2031-3]

§ 20.2031-3. Valuation of interests in businesses.—The fair market value of any interest of a decedent in a business, whether a partnership or a proprietorship, is the net amount which a willing purchaser, whether an individual or a corporation, would pay for the interest to a willing seller, neither being under any compulsion to buy or to sell and both having reasonable knowledge of relevant facts. The net value is determined on the basis of all relevant factors including—

(a) A fair appraisal as of the applicable valuation date of all the assets of the business, tangible and intangible, including good will;

(b) The demonstrated earning capacity of the business; and

(c) The other factors set forth in paragraphs (f) and (h) of § 20.2031-2 relating to the valuation of corporate stock, to the extent applicable.

Special attention should be given to determining an adequate value of the good will of the business in all cases in which the decedent has not agreed, for an adequate and full consideration in money or money's worth, that his interest passes at his death to, for example, his surviving partner or partners. Complete financial and other data upon which the valuation is based should be submitted with the return, including copies of reports of examinations of the business made by accountants, engineers, or any technical experts as of or near the applicable valuation date. See section 2701 and the regulations at § 25.2701 of this chapter for special rules for valuing the transfer of an interest in a partnership and for the treatment of unpaid qualified payments at the death of the transferor or an applicable family member. See section 2703 and the regulations at § 25.2703 of this chapter for special rules involving options and agreements (including contracts to purchase) entered into (or substantially modified after) October 8, 1990. See section 2704(b) and the regulations at § 25.2704-2 of this chapter for special valuation rules involving certain restrictions on liquidation rights created after October 8, 1990. [Reg. § 20.2031-3.]

☐ [*T.D.* 6296, 6-23-58. *Amended by T.D.* 8395, 1-28-92.]

[Reg. § 20.2031-4]

§ 20.2031-4. Valuation of notes.—The fair market value of notes, secured or unsecured, is presumed to be the amount of unpaid principal, plus interest accrued to the date of death, unless the executor establishes that the value is lower or that the notes are worthless. However, items of interest shall be separately stated on the estate tax return. If not returned at face value, plus accrued interest, satisfactory evidence must be submitted that the note is worth less than the unpaid amount (because of the interest rate, date of maturity, or other cause), or that the note is uncollectible, either in whole or in part (by reason of the insolvency of the party or parties liable, or for other cause), and that any property pledged or mortgaged as security is insufficient to satisfy the obligation. [Reg. § 20.2031-4.]

☐ [*T.D.* 6296, 6-23-58.]

[Reg. § 20.2031-5]

§ 20.2031-5. Valuation of cash on hand or on deposit.—The amount of cash belonging to the decedent at the date of his death, whether in his possession or in the possession of another, or deposited with a bank, is included in the decedent's gross estate. If bank checks outstanding at the time of the decedent's death and given in discharge of bona fide legal obligations of the decedent incurred for an adequate and full consideration in money or money's worth are subsequently honored by the bank and charged to the decedent's account, the balance remaining in the account may be returned, but only if the obligations are not claimed as deductions from the gross estate. [Reg. § 20.2031-5.]

☐ [*T.D.* 6926, 6-23-58.]

[Reg. § 20.2031-6]

§ 20.2031-6. Valuation of household and personal effects.—(a) *General rule.*—The fair market value of the decedent's household and personal effects is the price which a willing buyer would pay to a willing seller, neither being under any compulsion to buy or to sell and both having reasonable knowledge of relevant facts. A room by room itemization of household and personal effects is desirable. All the articles should be named specifically, except that a number of articles contained in the same room, none of which has a value in excess of $100, may be grouped. A separate value should be given for each article named. In lieu of an itemized list, the executor may furnish a written statement, containing a declaration that it is made under penalties of perjury, setting forth the aggregate value as appraised by a competent appraiser or appraisers of recognized standing and ability, or by a dealer or dealers in the class of personalty involved.

(b) *Special rule in cases involving a substantial amount of valuable articles.*—Notwithstanding the provisions of paragraph (a) of this section, if there are included among the household and personal effects articles having marked artistic or intrinsic value of a total value in excess of $3,000 (e.g., jewelry, furs, silverware, paintings, etchings, engravings, antiques, books, statuary, vases, oriental rugs, coin or stamp collections), the appraisal of an expert or experts, under oath, shall be filed with the return. The appraisal shall be accompanied by a written statement of the executor containing a declaration that it is made under the penalties of perjury as to the completeness of the itemized list of such property and as to the disinterested character and the qualifications of the appraiser or appraisers.

(c) *Disposition of household effects prior to investigation.*—If it is desired to effect distribution or sale of any portion of the household or personal effects of the decedent in advance of an investigation by an officer of the Internal Revenue Service, information to that effect shall be given to the district director. The statement to the district director shall be accompanied by an appraisal of such property, under oath, and by a written statement of the executor, containing a declaration that it is made under the penalties of perjury, regarding the completeness of the list of such property and the qualifications of the appraiser, as heretofore described. If a personal inspection by an officer of the Internal Revenue Service is not deemed necessary, the executor will be so advised. This procedure is designed to facilitate disposition of such property and to obviate future expense and inconvenience to the estate by affording the district director an opportunity to make an investigation should one be deemed necessary prior to sale or distribution.

(d) *Additional rules if an appraisal involved.*—If, pursuant to paragraphs (a), (b), and (c) of this section, expert appraisers are employed, care shall be taken to see that they are reputable and of recognized competency to appraise the particular class of property involved. In the appraisal, books in sets by standard authors shall be listed in separate groups. In listing paintings having artistic value, the size, subject, and artist's name shall be stated. In the case of oriental rugs, the size, make, and general condition shall be given. Sets of silverware shall be listed in separate groups. Groups or individual pieces of silverware shall be weighed and the weights given in troy ounces. In arriving at the value of silverware, the appraisers shall take into consideration its antiquity, utility, desirability, condition, and obsolescence. [Reg. § 20.2031-6.]

☐ [*T.D.* 6296, 6-23-58.]

[Reg. § 20.2031-7]

§ 20.2031-7. Valuation of annuities, interests for life or term of years, and remainder or reversionary interests.—(a) *In general.*—Except as otherwise provided in paragraph (b) of this section and § 20.7520-3(b) (pertaining to certain limitations on the use of prescribed tables), the fair market value of annuities, life estates, terms of years, remainders, and reversionary interests for estates of decedents is the present value of such interests, determined under paragraph (d) of this section. The regulations in this and in related sections provide tables with standard actuarial factors and examples that illustrate how to use the tables to compute the present value of ordinary annuity, life, and remainder interests in property. These sections also refer to standard and special actuarial factors that may be necessary to compute the present value of similar interests in more unusual fact situations.

(b) *Commercial annuities and insurance contracts.*—The value of annuities issued by companies regularly engaged in their sale, and of insurance policies on the lives of persons other than the decedent, is determined under

§ 20.2031-8. See § 20.2042-1 with respect to insurance policies on the decedent's life.

(c) *Actuarial valuations.*—The present value of annuities, life estates, terms of years, remainders, and reversions for estates of decedents for which the valuation date of the gross estate is on or after May 1, 2009, is determined under paragraph (d) of this section. The present value of annuities, life estates, terms of years, remainders, and reversions for estates of decedents for which the valuation date of the gross estate is before May 1, 2009, is determined under the following sections:

Valuation Date		*Applicable*
After	*Before*	*Regulations*
-	01-01-52	20.2031-7A(a)
12-31-51	01-01-71	20.2031-7A(b)
12-31-70	12-01-83	20.2031-7A(c)
11-30-83	05-01-89	20.2031-7A(d)
04-30-89	05-01-99	20.2031-7A(e)
04-30-99	05-01-09	20.2031-7A(f)

(d) *Actuarial valuations on or after May 1, 2009.*—(1) *In general.*—Except as otherwise provided in paragraph (b) of this section and § 20.7520-3(b) (pertaining to certain limitations on the use of prescribed tables), if the valuation date for the gross estate of the decedent is on or after May 1, 2009, the fair market value of annuities, life estates, terms of years, remainders, and reversionary interests is the present value determined by use of standard or special section 7520 actuarial factors. These factors are derived by using the appropriate section 7520 interest rate and, if applicable, the mortality component for the valuation date of the interest that is being valued. For purposes of the computations described in this section, the age of an individual is the age of that individual at the individual's nearest birthday. See §§ 20.7520-1 through 20.7520-4.

(2) *Specific interests.*—(i) *Charitable remainder trusts.*—The fair market value of a remainder interest in a pooled income fund, as defined in § 1.642(c)-5 of this chapter, is its value determined under § 1.642(c)-6(e). The fair market value of a remainder interest in a charitable remainder annuity trust, as defined in § 1.664-2(a), is the present value determined under § 1.664-2(c). The fair market value of a remainder interest in a charitable remainder unitrust, as defined in § 1.664-3, is its present value determined under § 1.664-4(e). The fair market value of a life interest or term of years in a charitable remainder unitrust is the fair market value of the property as of the date of valuation less the fair market value of the remainder interest on that date determined under § 1.664-4(e)(4) and (5).

(ii) *Ordinary remainder and reversionary interests.*—If the interest to be valued is to take effect after a definite number of years or after the death of one individual, the present value of the interest is computed by multiplying the value of the property by the appropriate remainder interest actuarial factor (that corresponds to the applicable section 7520 interest rate and remainder interest period) in Table B (for a term certain) or in Table S (for one measuring life), as the case may be. Table B is contained in paragraph (d)(6) of this section and Table S (for one measuring life when the valuation date is on or after May 1, 2009) is contained in paragraph (d)(7) of this section and in Internal Revenue Service Publication 1457. See § 20.2031-7A containing Table S for valuation of interests before May 1, 2009. For information about obtaining actuarial factors for other types of remainder interests, see paragraph (d)(4) of this section.

(iii) *Ordinary term-of-years and life interests.*—If the interest to be valued is the right of a person to receive the income of certain property, or to use certain nonincome-producing property, for a term of years or for the life of one individual, the present value of the interest is computed by multiplying the value of the property by the appropriate term-of-years or life interest actuarial factor (that corresponds to the applicable section 7520 interest rate and term-of-years or life interest period). Internal Revenue Service Publication 1457 includes actuarial factors for a remainder interest after a term of years in Table B and after the life of one individual in Table S (for one measuring life when the valuation date is on or after May 1, 2009). However, term-ofyears and life interest actuarial factors are not included in Table B in paragraph (d)(6) of this section or Table S in paragraph (d)(7) of this section (or in § 20.2031-7A). If Internal Revenue Service Publication 1457 (or any other reliable source of term-of-years and life interest actuarial factors) is not conveniently available, an actuarial factor for the interest may be derived mathematically. This actuarial factor may be derived by subtracting the correlative remainder factor (that corresponds to the applicable section 7520 interest rate and the term of years or the life) in Table B (for a term of years) in paragraph (d)(6) of this section or in Table S (for the life of one individual) in paragraph (d)(7) of this section, as the case may be, from 1.000000. For information about obtaining actuarial factors for other types of term-of-years and life interests, see paragraph (d)(4) of this section.

(iv) *Annuities.*—(A) If the interest to be valued is the right of a person to receive an annuity that is payable at the end of each year for a term of years or for the life of one individual, the present value of the interest is computed by multiplying the aggregate amount payable annually by the appropriate annuity actuarial factor (that corresponds to the applicable section

7520 interest rate and annuity period). Internal Revenue Publication 1457 includes actuarial factors for a remainder interest in Table B (after an annuity payable for a term of years) and in Table S (after an annuity payable for the life of one individual when the valuation date is on or after May 1, 2009). However, annuity actuarial factors are not included in Table B in paragraph (d)(6) of this section or Table S in paragraph (d)(7) of this section (or in §20.2031-7A). If Internal Revenue Service Publication 1457 (or any other reliable source of annuity actuarial factors) is not conveniently available, a required annuity factor for a term of years or for one life may be mathematically derived. This annuity factor may be derived by subtracting the applicable remainder factor (that corresponds to the applicable section 7520 interest rate and annuity period) in Table B (in the case of a term-of-years annuity) in paragraph (d)(6) of this section or in Table S (in the case of a one-life annuity when the valuation date is on or after May 1, 2009) in paragraph (d)(7) of this section, as the case may be, from 1.000000 and then dividing the result by the applicable section 7520 interest rate expressed as a decimal number.

(B) If the annuity is payable at the end of semiannual, quarterly, monthly, or weekly periods, the product obtained by multiplying the annuity factor by the aggregate amount payable annually is then multiplied by the applicable adjustment factor as contained in Table K in paragraph (d)(6) of this section for payments made at the end of the specified periods. The provisions of this paragraph (d)(2)(iv)(B) are illustrated by the following example:

Example. At the time of the decedent's death, the survivor/annuitant, age 72, is entitled to receive an annuity of $15,000 a year for life payable in equal monthly installments at the end of each period. The section 7520 rate for the month in which the decedent died is 5.6 percent. Under Table S in paragraph (d)(7) of this section, the remainder factor at 5.6 percent for an individual aged 72 is .53243. By converting the remainder factor to an annuity factor, as described above, the annuity factor at 5.6 percent for an individual aged 72 is 8.3495 (1.000000 minus .53243, divided by .056). Under Table K in paragraph (d)(6) of this section, the adjustment factor under the column for payments made at the end of each monthly period at the rate of 5.6 percent is 1.0254. The aggregate annual amount, $15,000, is multiplied by the factor 8.3495 and the product is multiplied by 1.0254. The present value of the annuity at the date of the decedent's death is, therefore, $128,423.66 ($15,000 x 8.3495 × 1.0254).

(C) If an annuity is payable at the beginning of annual, semiannual, quarterly, monthly, or weekly periods for a term of years, the value of the annuity is computed by multiplying the aggregate amount payable annually by the annuity factor described in paragraph (d)(2)(iv)(A) of this section, and the product so obtained is then multiplied by the adjustment factor in Table J in paragraph (d)(6) of this section at the appropriate interest rate component for payments made at the beginning of specified periods. If an annuity is payable at the beginning of annual, semiannual, quarterly, monthly, or weekly periods for one or more lives, the value of the annuity is the sum of the first payment plus the present value of a similar annuity, the first payment of which is not to be made until the end of the payment period, determined as provided in this paragraph (d)(2)(iv).

(v) *Annuity and unitrust interests for a term of years or until the prior death of an individual.*—See §25.2512-5(d)(2)(v) of this chapter for examples explaining how to compute the present value of an annuity or unitrust interest that is payable until the earlier of the lapse of a specific number of years or the death of an individual.

(3) *Transitional rule.*—(i) If a decedent dies on or after May 1, 2009, and if on May 1, 2009, the decedent was mentally incompetent so that the disposition of the decedent's property could not be changed, and the decedent dies without having regained competency to dispose of the decedent's property or dies within 90 days of the date on which the decedent first regains competency, the fair market value of annuities, life estates, terms for years, remainders, and reversions included in the gross estate of the decedent is their present value determined either under this section or under the corresponding section applicable at the time the decedent became mentally incompetent, at the option of the decedent's executor. For examples, see §20.2031-7A(d).

(ii) If a decedent dies on or after May 1, 2009, and before July 1, 2009, the fair market value of annuities, life estates, remainders, and reversions based on one or more measuring lives included in the gross estate of the decedent is their present value determined under this section by use of the section 7520 interest rate for the month in which the valuation date occurs (see §§20.7520-1(b) and 20.7520-2(a)(2)) and the appropriate actuarial tables under either paragraph (d)(7) of this section or §20.2031-7A(f)(4), at the option of the decedent's executor.

(iii) For purposes of paragraphs (d)(3)(i) and (d)(3)(ii) of this section, where the decedent's executor is given the option to use the appropriate actuarial tables under either paragraph (d)(7) of this section or §20.2031-7A(f)(4), the decedent's executor must use the same actuarial table with respect to each individual transaction and with respect to all transfers occurring on the valuation date. For example, gift and income tax charitable deductions with respect to the same transfer must be determined based on the same tables, and all assets includible in the gross estate and/or estate tax deductions claimed must be valued based on the same tables.

(4) *Publications and actuarial computations by the Internal Revenue Service.*—Many standard actuarial factors not included in paragraph (d)(6) or (d)(7) of this section are included in Internal Revenue Service Publication 1457, "Actuarial Valuations Version 3A" (2009). Publication 1457 also includes examples that illustrate how to compute many special factors for more unusual situations. This publication is available, at no charge, electronically via the Internal Revenue Service Internet site at *www.irs.gov*. If a special factor is required in the case of an actual decedent, the Internal Revenue Service may furnish the factor to the executor upon a request for a ruling. The request for a ruling must be accompanied by a recitation of the facts including a statement of the date of birth for each measuring life, the date of the decedent's death, any other applicable dates, and a copy of the will, trust, or other relevant documents. A request for a ruling must comply with the instructions for requesting a ruling published periodically in the Internal Revenue Bulletin (see §§601.201 and 601.601(d)(2)(ii)(b) of this chapter) and must include payment of the required user fee.

(5) *Examples.*—The provisions of this section are illustrated by the following examples:

Example 1. Remainder payable at an individual's death. The decedent, or the decedent's estate, was entitled to receive certain property worth $50,000 upon the death of A, to whom the income was bequeathed for life. At the time of the decedent's death, A was 47 years and 5 months old. In the month in which the decedent died, the section 7520 rate was 6.2 percent. Under Table S in paragraph (d)(7) of this section, the remainder factor at 6.2 percent for determining the present value of the remainder interest due at the death of a person aged 47, the number of years nearest A's actual age at the decedent's death, is .18672. The present value of the remainder interest at the date of the decedent's death is, therefore, $9,336.00 ($50,000 X .18672).

Example 2. Income payable for an individual's life. A's parent bequeathed an income interest in property to A for life, with the remainder interest passing to B at A's death. At the time of the parent's death, the value of the property was $50,000 and A was 30 years and 10 months old. The section 7520 rate at the time of the parent's death was 6.2 percent. Under Table S in paragraph (d)(7) of this section, the remainder factor at 6.2 percent for determining the present value of the remainder interest due at the death of a person aged 31, the number of years closest to A's age at the decedent's death, is .08697. Converting this remainder factor to an income factor, as described in paragraph (d)(2)(iii) of this section, the factor for determining the present value of an income interest for the life of a person aged 31 is .91303. The present value of A's interest at the time of the parent's death is, therefore, $45,651.50 ($50,000 X .91303).

Example 3. Annuity payable for an individual's life. A purchased an annuity for the benefit of both A and B. Under the terms of the annuity contract, at A's death, a survivor annuity of $10,000 per year payable in equal semiannual installments made at the end of each interval is payable to B for life. At A's death, B was 45 years and 7 months old. Also, at A's death, the section 7520 rate was 4.8 percent. Under Table S in paragraph (d)(7) of this section, the factor at 4.8 percent for determining the present value of the remainder interest at the death of a person age 46 (the number of years nearest B's actual age) is .24774. By converting the factor to an annuity factor, as described in paragraph (d)(2)(iv)(A) of this section, the factor for the present value of an annuity payable until the death of a person age 46 is 15.6721 (1.000000 minus .24774, divided by .048). The adjustment factor from Table K in paragraph (d)(6) of this section at an interest rate of 4.8 percent for semiannual annuity payments made at the end of the period is 1.0119. The present value of the annuity at the date of A's death is, therefore, $158,585.98 ($10,000 X 15.6721 X 1.0119).

Example 4. Annuity payable for a term of years. The decedent, or the decedent's estate, was entitled to receive an annuity of $10,000 per year payable in equal quarterly installments at the end of each quarter throughout a term certain. At the time of the decedent's death, the section 7520 rate was 9.8 percent. A quarterly payment had been made immediately prior to the decedent's death and payments were to continue for 5 more years. Under Table B in paragraph (d)(6) of this section for the interest rate of 9.8 percent, the factor for the present value of a remainder interest due after a term of 5 years is .626597. Converting the factor to an annuity factor, as described in paragraph (d)(2)(iv)(A) of this section, the factor for the present value of an annuity for a term of 5 years is 3.8102 (1.000000 minus .626597, divided by .098). The adjustment factor from Table K in paragraph (d)(6) of this section at an interest rate of 9.8 percent for quarterly annuity payments made at the end of the period is 1.0360. The present value of the annuity is, therefore, $39,473.67 ($10,000 X 3.8102 X 1.0360).

(6) *Actuarial Table B, Table J, and Table K where the valuation date is after April 30, 1989.*—Except as provided in §20.7520-3(b) (pertaining to certain limitations on prescribed tables), for determination of the present value of an interest that is dependent on a term of years, the tables in this paragraph (d)(6) must be used in the application of the provisions of this section when the section 7520 interest rate component is between 4.2 and 14 percent.

TABLE B
TERM CERTAIN REMAINDER FACTORS
APPLICABLE AFTER APRIL 30, 1989

	INTEREST RATE									
YEARS	*4.2%*	*4.4%*	*4.6%*	*4.8%*	*5.0%*	*5.2%*	*5.4%*	*5.6%*	*5.8%*	*6.0%*
1	.959693	.957854	.956023	.954198	.952381	.950570	.948767	.946970	.945180	.943396
2	.921010	.917485	.913980	.910495	.907029	.903584	.900158	.896752	.893364	.889996
3	.883887	.878817	.873786	.868793	.863838	.858920	.854040	.849197	.844390	.839619
4	.848260	.841779	.835359	.829001	.822702	.816464	.810285	.804163	.798100	.792094
5	.814069	.806302	.798623	.791031	.783526	.776106	.768771	.761518	.754348	.747258
6	.781257	.772320	.763501	.754801	.746215	.737744	.729384	.721135	.712994	.704961
7	.749766	.739770	.729925	.720230	.710681	.701277	.692015	.682893	.673908	.665057
8	.719545	.708592	.697825	.687242	.676839	.666613	.656561	.646679	.636964	.627412
9	.690543	.678728	.667137	.655765	.644609	.633663	.622923	.612385	.602045	.591898
10	.662709	.650122	.637798	.625730	.613913	.602341	.591009	.579910	.569041	.558395
11	.635997	.622722	.609750	.597071	.584679	.572568	.560729	.549157	.537846	.526788
12	.610362	.596477	.582935	.569724	.556837	.544266	.532001	.520035	.508361	.496969
13	.585760	.571339	.557299	.543630	.530321	.517363	.504745	.492458	.480492	.468839
14	.562150	.547259	.532790	.518731	.505068	.491790	.478885	.466343	.454151	.442301
15	.539491	.524195	.509360	.494972	.481017	.467481	.454350	.441612	.429255	.417265
16	.517746	.502102	.486960	.472302	.458112	.444374	.431072	.418194	.405723	.393646
17	.496877	.480941	.465545	.450670	.436297	.422408	.408987	.396017	.383481	.371364
18	.476849	.460671	.445071	.430028	.415521	.401529	.388033	.375016	.362458	.350344
19	.457629	.441256	.425498	.410332	.395734	.381681	.368153	.355129	.342588	.330513
20	.439183	.422659	.406786	.391538	.376889	.362815	.349291	.336296	.323807	.311805
21	.421481	.404846	.388897	.373605	.358942	.344881	.331396	.318462	.306056	.294155
22	.404492	.387783	.371794	.356494	.341850	.327834	.314417	.301574	.289278	.277505
23	.388188	.371440	.355444	.340166	.325571	.311629	.298309	.285581	.273420	.261797
24	.372542	.355785	.339813	.324586	.310068	.296225	.283025	.270437	.258431	.246979
25	.357526	.340791	.324869	.309719	.295303	.281583	.268525	.256096	.244263	.232999
26	.343115	.326428	.310582	.295533	.281241	.267664	.254768	.242515	.230873	.219810
27	.329285	.312670	.296923	.281998	.267848	.254434	.241715	.229654	.218216	.207368
28	.316012	.299493	.283866	.269082	.255094	.241857	.229331	.217475	.206253	.195630
29	.303275	.286870	.271382	.256757	.242946	.229902	.217582	.205943	.194947	.184557
30	.291051	.274780	.259447	.244997	.231377	.218538	.206434	.195021	.184260	.174110
31	.279319	.263199	.248038	.233776	.220359	.207736	.195858	.184679	.174158	.164255
32	.268061	.252106	.237130	.223069	.209866	.197468	.185823	.174886	.164611	.154957
33	.257256	.241481	.226702	.212852	.199873	.187707	.176303	.165612	.155587	.146186
34	.246887	.231304	.216732	.203103	.190355	.178429	.167270	.156829	.147058	.137912
35	.236935	.221556	.207201	.193801	.181290	.169609	.158701	.148512	.138996	.130105
36	.227385	.212218	.198089	.184924	.172657	.161225	.150570	.140637	.131376	.122741
37	.218220	.203274	.189377	.176454	.164436	.153256	.142856	.133179	.124174	.115793
38	.209424	.194707	.181049	.168373	.156605	.145681	.135537	.126116	.117367	.109239
39	.200983	.186501	.173087	.160661	.149148	.138480	.128593	.119428	.110933	.103056
40	.192882	.178641	.165475	.153302	.142046	.131635	.122004	.113095	.104851	.097222
41	.185107	.171112	.158198	.146281	.135282	.125128	.115754	.107098	.099103	.091719
42	.177646	.163900	.151241	.139581	.128840	.118943	.109823	.101418	.093670	.086527
43	.170486	.156992	.144590	.133188	.122704	.113064	.104197	.096040	.088535	.081630
44	.163614	.150376	.138231	.127088	.116861	.107475	.098858	.090947	.083682	.077009
45	.157019	.144038	.132152	.121267	.111297	.102163	.093793	.086124	.079094	.072650
46	.150690	.137968	.126340	.115713	.105997	.097113	.088988	.081557	.074758	.068538
47	.144616	.132153	.120784	.110413	.100949	.092312	.084429	.077232	.070660	.064658
48	.138787	.126583	.115473	.105356	.096142	.087749	.080103	.073136	.066786	.060998
49	.133193	.121248	.110395	.100530	.091564	.083412	.075999	.069258	.063125	.057546
50	.127824	.116138	.105540	.095926	.087204	.079289	.072106	.065585	.059665	.054288

See p. 15 for regulations not amended to reflect law changes

YEARS	4.2%	4.4%	4.6%	4.8%	5.0%	5.2%	5.4%	5.6%	5.8%	6.0%
51	.122672	.111243	.100898	.091532	.083051	.075370	.068411	.062107	.056394	.051215
52	.117728	.106555	.096461	.087340	.079096	.071644	.064907	.058813	.053302	.048316
53	.112982	.102064	.092219	.083340	.075330	.068103	.061581	.055695	.050380	.045582
54	.108428	.097763	.088164	.079523	.071743	.064737	.058426	.052741	.047618	.043001
55	.104058	.093642	.084286	.075880	.068326	.061537	.055433	.049944	.045008	.040567
56	.099864	.089696	.080580	.072405	.065073	.058495	.052593	.047296	.042541	.038271
57	.095839	.085916	.077036	.069089	.061974	.055604	.049898	.044787	.040208	.036105
58	.091976	.082295	.073648	.065924	.059023	.052855	.047342	.042412	.038004	.034061
59	.088268	.078826	.070409	.062905	.056212	.050243	.044916	.040163	.035921	.032133
60	.084710	.075504	.067313	.060024	.053536	.047759	.042615	.038033	.033952	.030314

TABLE B
TERM CERTAIN REMAINDER FACTORS
APPLICABLE AFTER APRIL 30, 1989

INTEREST RATE

YEARS	6.2%	6.4%	6.6%	6.8%	7.0%	7.2%	7.4%	7.6%	7.8%	8.0%
1	.941620	.939850	.938086	.936330	.934579	.932836	.931099	.929368	.927644	.925926
2	.886647	.883317	.880006	.876713	.873439	.870183	.866945	.863725	.860523	.857339
3	.834885	.830185	.825521	.820892	.816298	.811738	.807211	.802718	.798259	.793832
4	.786144	.780249	.774410	.768626	.762895	.757218	.751593	.746021	.740500	.735030
5	.740248	.733317	.726464	.719687	.712986	.706360	.699808	.693328	.686920	.680583
6	.697032	.689208	.681486	.673864	.666342	.658918	.651590	.644357	.637217	.630170
7	.656339	.647752	.639292	.630959	.622750	.614662	.606694	.598845	.591111	.583490
8	.618022	.608789	.599711	.590786	.582009	.573379	.564892	.556547	.548340	.540269
9	.581942	.572170	.562581	.553170	.543934	.534868	.525971	.517237	.508664	.500249
10	.547968	.537754	.527750	.517950	.508349	.498944	.489731	.480704	.471859	.463193
11	.515977	.505408	.495075	.484972	.475093	.465433	.455987	.446750	.437717	.428883
12	.485854	.475007	.464423	.454093	.444012	.434173	.424569	.415196	.406046	.397114
13	.457490	.446436	.435669	.425181	.414964	.405012	.395316	.385870	.376666	.367698
14	.430781	.419582	.408695	.398109	.387817	.377810	.368078	.358615	.349412	.340461
15	.405632	.394344	.383391	.372762	.362446	.352434	.342717	.333285	.324130	.315242
16	.381951	.370624	.359654	.349028	.338735	.328763	.319103	.309745	.300677	.291890
17	.359653	.348331	.337386	.326805	.316574	.306682	.297117	.287867	.278921	.270269
18	.338656	.327379	.316498	.305997	.295864	.286084	.276645	.267534	.258739	.250249
19	.318885	.307687	.296902	.286514	.276508	.266870	.257584	.248638	.240018	.231712
20	.300268	.289179	.278520	.268272	.258419	.248946	.239836	.231076	.222651	.214548
21	.282739	.271785	.261276	.251191	.241513	.232225	.223311	.214755	.206541	.198656
22	.266232	.255437	.245099	.235197	.225713	.216628	.207925	.199586	.191596	.183941
23	.250689	.240073	.229924	.220222	.210947	.202078	.193598	.185489	.177733	.170315
24	.236054	.225632	.215689	.206201	.197147	.188506	.180259	.172387	.164873	.157699
25	.222273	.212060	.202334	.193072	.184249	.175845	.167839	.160211	.152943	.146018
26	.209297	.199305	.189807	.180779	.172195	.164035	.156275	.148895	.141877	.135202
27	.197078	.187317	.178056	.169269	.160930	.153017	.145507	.138379	.131611	.125187
28	.185572	.176049	.167031	.158491	.150402	.142740	.135482	.128605	.122088	.115914
29	.174739	.165460	.156690	.148400	.140563	.133153	.126147	.119521	.113255	.107328
30	.164537	.155507	.146989	.138951	.131367	.124210	.117455	.111079	.105060	.099377
31	.154932	.146154	.137888	.130104	.122773	.115868	.109362	.103233	.097458	.092016
32	.145887	.137362	.129351	.121820	.114741	.108085	.101827	.095942	.090406	.085200
33	.137370	.129100	.121342	.114064	.107235	.100826	.094811	.089165	.083865	.078889
34	.129350	.121335	.113830	.106802	.100219	.094054	.088278	.082867	.077797	.073045
35	.121798	.114036	.106782	.100001	.093663	.087737	.082196	.077014	.072168	.067635
36	.114688	.107177	.100171	.093634	.087535	.081844	.076532	.071574	.066946	.062625
37	.107992	.100730	.093969	.087673	.081809	.076347	.071259	.066519	.062102	.057986
38	.101688	.094671	.088151	.082090	.076457	.071219	.066349	.061821	.057609	.053690
39	.095751	.088977	.082693	.076864	.071455	.066436	.061778	.057454	.053440	.049713
40	.090161	.083625	.077573	.071970	.066780	.061974	.057521	.053396	.049573	.046031
41	.084897	.078595	.072770	.067387	.062412	.057811	.053558	.049625	.045987	.042621
42	.079941	.073867	.068265	.063097	.058329	.053929	.049868	.046120	.042659	.039464
43	.075274	.069424	.064038	.059079	.054513	.050307	.046432	.042862	.039572	.036541
44	.070880	.065248	.060074	.055318	.050946	.046928	.043233	.039835	.036709	.033834
45	.066742	.061323	.056354	.051796	.047613	.043776	.040254	.037021	.034053	.031328
46	.062845	.057635	.052865	.048498	.044499	.040836	.037480	.034406	.031589	.029007
47	.059176	.054168	.049592	.045410	.041587	.038093	.034898	.031976	.029303	.026859
48	.055722	.050910	.046522	.042519	.038867	.035535	.032493	.029717	.027183	.024869
49	.052469	.047848	.043641	.039812	.036324	.033148	.030255	.027618	.025216	.023027
50	.049405	.044970	.040939	.037277	.033948	.030922	.028170	.025668	.023392	.021321
51	.046521	.042265	.038405	.034903	.031727	.028845	.026229	.023855	.021699	.019742

See p. 15 for regulations not amended to reflect law changes

YEARS	6.2%	6.4%	6.6%	6.8%	7.0%	7.2%	7.4%	7.6%	7.8%	8.0%
52	.043805	.039722	.036027	.032681	.029651	.026907	.024422	.022170	.020129	.018280
53	.041248	.037333	.033796	.030600	.027711	.025100	.022739	.020604	.018673	.016925
54	.038840	.035087	.031704	.028652	.025899	.023414	.021172	.019149	.017322	.015672
55	.036572	.032977	.029741	.026828	.024204	.021842	.019714	.017796	.016068	.014511
56	.034437	.030993	.027900	.025119	.022621	.020375	.018355	.016539	.014906	.013436
57	.032427	.029129	.026172	.023520	.021141	.019006	.017091	.015371	.013827	.012441
58	.030534	.027377	.024552	.022023	.019758	.017730	.015913	.014285	.012827	.011519
59	.028751	.025730	.023032	.020620	.018465	.016539	.014817	.013276	.011899	.010666
60	.027073	.024183	.021606	.019307	.017257	.015428	.013796	.012339	.011038	.009876

TABLE B
TERM CERTAIN REMAINDER FACTORS
APPLICABLE AFTER APRIL 30, 1989

	INTEREST RATE									
YEARS	*8.2%*	*8.4%*	*8.6%*	*8.8%*	*9.0%*	*9.2%*	*9.4%*	*9.6%*	*9.8%*	*10.0%*
1	.924214	.922509	.920810	.919118	.917431	.915751	.914077	.912409	.910747	.909091
2	.854172	.851023	.847892	.844777	.841680	.838600	.835536	.832490	.829460	.826446
3	.789438	.785077	.780747	.776450	.772183	.767948	.763744	.759571	.755428	.751315
4	.729610	.724241	.718920	.713649	.708425	.703250	.698121	.693039	.688003	.683013
5	.674316	.668119	.661989	.655927	.649931	.644001	.638136	.632335	.626597	.620921
6	.623213	.616346	.609566	.602874	.596267	.589745	.583305	.576948	.570671	.564474
7	.575982	.568585	.561295	.554112	.547034	.540059	.533186	.526412	.519737	.513158
8	.532331	.524524	.516846	.509294	.501866	.494560	.487373	.480303	.473349	.466507
9	.491988	.483879	.475917	.468101	.460428	.452894	.445496	.438233	.431101	.424098
10	.454703	.446383	.438230	.430240	.422411	.414738	.407218	.399848	.392624	.385543
11	.420243	.411792	.403526	.395441	.387533	.379797	.372228	.364824	.357581	.350494
12	.388394	.379882	.371571	.363457	.355535	.347799	.340245	.332869	.325666	.318631
13	.358960	.350445	.342147	.334060	.326179	.318497	.311010	.303713	.296599	.289664
14	.331756	.323288	.315052	.307040	.299246	.291664	.284287	.277110	.270127	.263331
15	.306613	.298236	.290103	.282206	.274538	.267092	.259860	.252838	.246017	.239392
16	.283376	.275126	.267130	.259381	.251870	.244589	.237532	.230691	.224059	.217629
17	.261901	.253806	.245976	.238401	.231073	.223983	.217123	.210485	204061	.197845
18	.242052	.234139	.226497	.219119	.211994	.205113	.198467	.192048	.185848	.179859
19	.223708	.215995	.208561	.201396	.194490	.187832	.181414	.175226	.169260	.163508
20	.206754	.199257	.192045	.185107	.178431	.172007	.165826	.159878	.154153	.148644
21	.191085	.183817	.176837	.170135	.163698	.157516	.151578	.145874	.140395	.135131
22	.176604	.169573	.162834	.156374	.150182	.144245	.138554	.133097	.127864	.122846
23	.163220	.156432	.149939	.143726	.137781	.132093	.126649	.121439	.116452	.111678
24	.150850	.144310	.138065	.132101	.126405	.120964	.115767	.110802	.106058	.101526
25	.139418	.133128	.127132	.121416	.115968	.110773	.105820	.101097	.096592	.092296
26	.128852	.122811	.117064	.111596	.106393	.101441	.096727	.092241	.087971	.083905
27	.119087	.113295	.107794	.102570	.097608	.092894	.088416	.084162	.080119	.076278
28	.110062	.104515	.099258	.094274	.089548	.085068	.080819	.076790	.072968	.069343
29	.101721	.096416	.091398	.086649	.082155	.077901	.073875	.070064	.066456	.063039
30	.094012	.088945	.084160	.079640	.075371	.071338	.067527	.063927	.060524	.057309
31	.086887	.082053	.077495	.073199	.069148	.065328	.061725	.058327	.055122	.052099
32	.080302	.075694	.071358	.067278	.063438	.059824	.056422	.053218	.050202	.047362
33	.074216	.069829	.065708	.061837	.058200	.054784	.051574	.048557	.045722	.043057
34	.068592	.064418	.060504	.056835	.053395	.050168	.047142	.044304	.041641	.039143
35	.063394	.059426	.055713	.052238	.048986	.045942	.043092	.040423	.037924	.035584
36	.058589	.054821	.051301	.048013	.044941	.042071	.039389	.036882	.034539	.032349
37	.054149	.050573	.047239	.044130	.041231	.038527	.036005	.033652	.031457	.029408
38	.050045	.046654	.043498	.040560	.037826	.035281	.032911	.030704	.028649	.026735
39	.046253	.043039	.040053	.037280	.034703	.032309	.030083	.028015	.026092	.024304
40	.042747	.039703	.036881	.034264	.031838	.029587	.027498	.025561	.023763	.022095
41	.039508	.036627	.033961	.031493	.029209	.027094	.025136	.023322	.021642	.020086
42	.036514	.033789	.031271	.028946	.026797	.024811	.022976	.021279	.019711	.018260
43	.033746	.031170	.028795	.026605	.024584	.022721	.021002	.019415	.017951	.016600
44	.031189	.028755	.026515	.024453	.022555	.020807	.019197	.017715	.016349	.015091
45	.028825	.026527	.024415	.022475	.020692	.019054	.017548	.016163	.014890	.013719
46	.026641	.024471	.022482	.020657	.018984	.017449	.016040	.014747	.013561	.012472
47	.024622	.022575	.020701	.018986	.017416	.015978	.014662	.013456	.012351	.011338
48	.022756	.020825	.019062	.017451	.015978	.014632	.013402	.012277	.011248	.010307
49	.021031	.019212	.017552	.016039	.014659	.013400	.012250	.011202	.010244	.009370
50	.019437	.017723	.016163	.014742	.013449	.012271	.011198	.010221	.009330	.008519

YEARS	8.2%	8.4%	8.6%	8.8%	9.0%	9.2%	9.4%	9.6%	9.8%	10.0%
51	.017964	.016350	.014883	.013550	.012338	.011237	.010236	.009325	.008497	.007744
52	.016603	.015083	.013704	.012454	.011319	.010290	.009356	.008508	.007739	.007040
53	.015345	.013914	.012619	.011446	.010385	.009423	.008552	.007763	.007048	.006400
54	.014182	.012836	.011620	.010521	.009527	.008629	.007817	.007083	.006419	.005818
55	.013107	.011841	.010699	.009670	.008741	.007902	.007146	.006463	.005846	.005289
56	.012114	.010923	.009852	.008888	.008019	.007237	.006532	.005897	.005324	.004809
57	.011196	.010077	.009072	.008169	.007357	.006627	.005971	.005380	.004849	.004371
58	.010347	.009296	.008354	.007508	.006749	.006069	.005458	.004909	.004416	.003974
59	.009563	.008576	.007692	.006901	.006192	.005557	.004989	.004479	.004022	.003613
60	.008838	.007911	.007083	.006343	.005681	.005089	.004560	.004087	.003663	.003284

TABLE B
TERM CERTAIN REMAINDER FACTORS
APPLICABLE AFTER APRIL 30, 1989

INTEREST RATE

YEARS	10.2%	10.4%	10.6%	10.8%	11.0%	11.2%	11.4%	11.6%	11.8%	12.0%
1	.907441	.905797	.904159	.902527	.900901	.899281	.897666	.896057	.894454	.892857
2	.823449	.820468	.817504	.814555	.811622	.808706	.805804	.802919	.800049	.797194
3	.747232	.743178	.739153	.735158	.731191	.727253	.723343	.719461	.715607	.711780
4	.678069	.673168	.668312	.663500	.658731	.654005	.649321	.644679	.640078	.635518
5	.615307	.609754	.604261	.598827	.593451	.588134	.582873	.577669	.572520	.567427
6	.558355	.552313	.546348	.540457	.534641	.528897	.523225	.517625	.512093	.506631
7	.506674	.500284	.493985	.487777	.481658	.475627	.469682	.463821	.458044	.452349
8	.459777	.453156	.446641	.440232	.433926	.427722	.421617	.415610	.409700	.403883
9	.417221	.410467	.403835	.397322	.390925	.384642	.378472	.372411	.366458	.360610
10	.378603	.371800	.365131	.358593	.352184	.345901	.339741	.333701	.327780	.321973
11	.343560	.336775	.330137	.323640	.317283	.311062	.304974	.299016	.293184	.287476
12	.311760	.305050	.298496	.292094	.285841	.279732	.273765	.267935	.262240	.256675
13	.282904	.276313	.269888	.263623	.257514	.251558	.245749	.240085	.234561	.229174
14	.256719	.250284	.244022	.237927	.231995	.226221	.220601	.215130	.209804	.204620
15	.232957	.226706	.220634	.214735	.209004	.203436	.198026	.192769	.187661	.182696
16	.211395	.205350	.199489	.193804	.188292	.182946	.177761	.172732	.167854	.163122
17	.191828	.186005	.180369	.174914	.169633	.164520	.159570	.154778	.150138	.145644
18	.174073	.168483	.163083	.157864	.152822	.147950	.143241	.138690	.134291	.130040
19	.157961	.152612	.147453	.142477	.137678	.133048	.128582	.124274	.120117	.116107
20	.143340	.138235	.133321	.128589	.124034	.119648	.115424	.111357	.107439	.103667
21	.130073	.125213	.120543	.116055	.111742	.107597	.103612	.099782	.096100	.092560
22	.118033	.113418	.108990	.104743	.100669	.096760	.093009	.089410	.085957	.082643
23	.107108	.102733	.098544	.094533	.090693	.087014	.083491	.080117	.076884	.073788
24	.097195	.093056	.089100	.085319	.081705	.078250	.074947	.071789	.068770	.065882
25	.088198	.084289	.080560	.077003	.073608	.070369	.067278	.064327	.061511	.058823
26	.080035	.076349	.072839	.069497	.066314	.063281	.060393	.057641	.055019	.052521
27	.072627	.069157	.065858	.062723	.059742	.056908	.054213	.051650	.049212	.046894
28	.065905	.062642	.059547	.056609	.053822	.051176	.048665	.046281	.044018	.041869
29	.059804	.056741	.053840	.051091	.048488	.046022	.043685	.041470	.039372	.037383
30	.054269	.051396	.048680	.046111	.043683	.041386	.039214	.037160	.035216	.033378
31	.049246	.046554	.044014	.041617	.039354	.037218	.035201	.033297	.031500	.029802
32	.044688	.042169	.039796	.037560	.035454	.033469	.031599	.029836	.028175	.026609
33	.040552	.038196	.035982	.033899	.031940	.030098	.028365	.026735	.025201	.023758
34	.036798	.034598	.032533	.030595	.028775	.027067	.025463	.023956	.022541	.021212
35	.033392	.031339	.029415	.027613	.025924	.024341	.022857	.021466	.020162	.018940
36	.030301	.028387	.026596	.024921	.023355	.021889	.020518	.019235	.018034	.016910
37	.027497	.025712	.024047	.022492	.021040	.019684	.018418	.017236	.016131	.015098
38	.024952	.023290	.021742	.020300	.018955	.017702	.016533	.015444	.014428	.013481
39	.022642	.021096	.019658	.018321	.017077	.015919	.014841	.013839	.012905	.012036
40	.020546	.019109	.017774	.016535	.015384	.014316	.013323	.012400	.011543	.010747
41	.018645	.017309	.016071	.014923	.013860	.012874	.011959	.011111	.010325	.009595
42	.016919	.015678	.014531	.013469	.012486	.011577	.010735	.009956	.009235	.008567
43	.015353	.014201	.013138	.012156	.011249	.010411	.009637	.008922	.008260	.007649
44	.013932	.012864	.011879	.010971	.010134	.009362	.008651	.007994	.007389	.006830
45	.012642	.011652	.010740	.009902	.009130	.008419	.007765	.007163	.006609	.006098
46	.011472	.010554	.009711	.008937	.008225	.007571	.006971	.006419	.005911	.005445
47	.010410	.009560	.008780	.008065	.007410	.006809	.006257	.005752	.005287	.004861
48	.009447	.008659	.007939	.007279	.006676	.006123	.005617	.005154	.004729	.004340
49	.008572	.007844	.007178	.006570	.006014	.005506	.005042	.004618	.004230	.003875
50	.007779	.007105	.006490	.005929	.005418	.004952	.004526	.004138	.003784	.003460

YEARS	10.2%	10.4%	10.6%	10.8%	11.0%	11.2%	11.4%	11.6%	11.8%	12.0%
51	.007059	.006435	.005868	.005351	.004881	.004453	.004063	.003708	.003384	.003089
52	.006406	.005829	.005306	.004830	.004397	.004005	.003647	.003322	.003027	.002758
53	.005813	.005280	.004797	.004359	.003962	.003601	.003274	.002977	.002708	.002463
54	.005275	.004783	.004337	.003934	.003569	.003238	.002939	.002668	.002422	.002199
55	.004786	.004332	.003922	.003551	.003215	.002912	.002638	.002390	.002166	.001963
56	.004343	.003924	.003546	.003205	.002897	.002619	.002368	.002142	.001938	.001753
57	.003941	.003554	.003206	.002892	.002610	.002355	.002126	.001919	.001733	.001565
58	.003577	.003220	.002899	.002610	.002351	.002118	.001908	.001720	.001550	.001398
59	.003246	.002916	.002621	.002356	.002118	.001905	.001713	.001541	.001387	.001248
60	.002945	.002642	.002370	.002126	.001908	.001713	.001538	.001381	.001240	.001114

TABLE B
TERM CERTAIN REMAINDER FACTORS
APPLICABLE AFTER APRIL 30, 1989

	INTEREST RATE									
YEARS	*12.2%*	*12.4%*	*12.6%*	*12.8%*	*13.0%*	*13.2%*	*13.4%*	*13.6%*	*13.8%*	*14.0%*
1	.891266	.889680	.888099	.886525	.884956	.883392	.881834	.880282	.878735	.877193
2	.794354	.791530	.788721	.785926	.783147	.780382	.777632	.774896	.772175	.769468
3	.707981	.704208	.700462	.696743	.693050	.689383	.685742	.682127	.678536	.674972
4	.630999	.626520	.622080	.617680	.613319	.608996	.604711	.600464	.596254	.592080
5	.562388	.557402	.552469	.547589	.542760	.537982	.533255	.528577	.523949	.519369
6	.501237	.495909	.490648	.485451	.480319	.475249	.470242	.465297	.460412	.455587
7	.446735	.441200	.435744	.430364	.425061	.419831	.414676	.409592	.404580	.399637
8	.398160	.392527	.386984	.381529	.376160	.370876	.365675	.360557	.355518	.350559
9	.354866	.349223	.343680	.338235	.332885	.327629	.322465	.317391	.312406	.307508
10	.316280	.310697	.305222	.299853	.294588	.289425	.284361	.279394	.274522	.269744
11	.281889	.276421	.271068	.265827	.260698	.255676	.250759	.245945	.241232	.236617
12	.251238	.245926	.240735	.235663	.230706	.225862	.221128	.216501	.211979	.207559
13	.223920	.218795	.213797	.208921	.204165	.199525	.194998	.190582	.186273	.182069
14	.199572	.194658	.189873	.185213	.180677	.176258	.171956	.167766	.163685	.159710
15	.177872	.173183	.168626	.164196	.159891	.155705	.151637	.147681	.143835	.140096
16	.158531	.154077	.149757	.145564	.141496	.137549	.133718	.130001	.126393	.122892
17	.141293	.137080	.132999	.129046	.125218	.121510	.117917	.114438	.111066	.107800
18	.125930	.121957	.118116	.114403	.110812	.107341	.103984	.100737	.097598	.094561
19	.112237	.108503	.104899	.101421	.098064	.094824	.091696	.088677	.085762	.082948
20	.100033	.096533	.093161	.089912	.086782	.083767	.080861	.078061	.075362	.072762
21	.089156	.085883	.082736	.079709	.076798	.073999	.071306	.068716	.066224	.063826
22	.079462	.076408	.073478	.070664	.067963	.065370	.062880	.060489	.058193	.055988
23	.070821	.067979	.065255	.062646	.060144	.057747	.055450	.053247	.051136	.049112
24	.063121	.060480	.057953	.055537	.053225	.051014	.048898	.046873	.044935	.043081
25	.056257	.053807	.051468	.049235	.047102	.045065	.043119	.041261	.039486	.037790
26	.050140	.047871	.045709	.043648	.041683	.039810	.038024	.036321	.034698	.033149
27	.044688	.042590	.040594	.038695	.036888	.035168	.033531	.031973	.030490	.029078
28	.039829	.037892	.036052	.034304	.032644	.031067	.029569	.028145	.026793	.025507
29	.035498	.033711	.032017	.030411	.028889	.027444	.026075	.024776	.023544	.022375
30	.031638	.029992	.028435	.026960	.025565	.024244	.022994	.021810	.020689	.019627
31	.028198	.026684	.025253	.023901	.022624	.021417	.020277	.019199	.018180	.017217
32	.025132	.023740	.022427	.021189	.020021	.018920	.017881	.016900	.015975	.015102
33	.022399	.021121	.019917	.018785	.017718	.016714	.015768	.014877	.014038	.013248
34	.019964	.018791	.017689	.016653	.015680	.014765	.013905	.013096	.012336	.011621
35	.017793	.016718	.015709	.014763	.013876	.013043	.012261	.011528	.010840	.010194
36	.015858	.014873	.013951	.013088	.012279	.011522	.010813	.010148	.009525	.008942
37	.014134	.013233	.012390	.011603	.010867	.010178	.009535	.008933	.008370	.007844
38	.012597	.011773	.011004	.010286	.009617	.008992	.008408	.007864	.007355	.006880
39	.011227	.010474	.009772	.009119	.008510	.007943	.007415	.006922	.006463	.006035
40	.010007	.009319	.008679	.008084	.007531	.007017	.006538	.006093	.005679	.005294
41	.008919	.008291	.007708	.007167	.006665	.006199	.005766	.005364	.004991	.004644
42	.007949	.007376	.006845	.006354	.005898	.005476	.005085	.004722	.004386	.004074
43	.007084	.006562	.006079	.005633	.005219	.004837	.004484	.004157	.003854	.003573
44	.006314	.005838	.005399	.004993	.004619	.004273	.003954	.003659	.003386	.003135
45	.005628	.005194	.004795	.004427	.004088	.003775	.003487	.003221	.002976	.002750
46	.005016	.004621	.004258	.003924	.003617	.003335	.003075	.002835	.002615	.002412
47	.004470	.004111	.003782	.003479	.003201	.002946	.002711	.002496	.002298	.002116
48	.003984	.003658	.003359	.003084	.002833	.002602	.002391	.002197	.002019	.001856
49	.003551	.003254	.002983	.002734	.002507	.002299	.002108	.001934	.001774	.001628
50	.003165	.002895	.002649	.002424	.002219	.002031	.001859	.001702	.001559	.001428

See p. 15 for regulations not amended to reflect law changes

YEARS	12.2%	12.4%	12.6%	12.8%	13.0%	13.2%	13.4%	13.6%	13.8%	14.0%
51	.002821	.002576	.002353	.002149	.001963	.001794	.001640	.001499	.001370	.001253
52	.002514	.002292	.002089	.001905	.001737	.001585	.001446	.001319	.001204	.001099
53	.002241	.002039	.001856	.001689	.001538	.001400	.001275	.001161	.001058	.000964
54	.001997	.001814	.001648	.001497	.001361	.001237	.001124	.001022	.000930	.000846
55	.001780	.001614	.001463	.001327	.001204	.001093	.000991	.000900	.000817	.000742
56	.001586	.001436	.001300	.001177	.001066	.000965	.000874	.000792	.000718	.000651
57	.001414	.001277	.001154	.001043	.000943	.000853	.000771	.000697	.000631	.000571
58	.001260	.001136	.001025	.000925	.000835	.000753	.000680	.000614	.000554	.000501
59	.001123	.001011	.000910	.000820	.000739	.000665	.000600	.000540	.000487	.000439
60	.001001	.000900	.000809	.000727	.000654	.000588	.000529	.000476	.000428	.000385

TABLE J
ADJUSTMENT FACTORS FOR TERM CERTAIN ANNUITIES
PAYABLE AT THE BEGINNING OF EACH INTERVAL
APPLICABLE AFTER APRIL 30, 1989
FREQUENCY OF PAYMENTS

INTEREST RATE	*ANNUALLY*	*SEMI ANNUALLY*	*QUARTERLY*	*MONTHLY*	*WEEKLY*
4.2	1.0420	1.0314	1.0261	1.0226	1.0213
4.4	1.0440	1.0329	1.0274	1.0237	1.0223
4.6	1.0460	1.0344	1.0286	1.0247	1.0233
4.8	1.0480	1.0359	1.0298	1.0258	1.0243
5.0	1.0500	1.0373	1.0311	1.0269	1.0253
5.2	1.0520	1.0388	1.0323	1.0279	1.0263
5.4	1.0540	1.0403	1.0335	1.0290	1.0273
5.6	1.0560	1.0418	1.0348	1.0301	1.0283
5.8	1.0580	1.0433	1.0360	1.0311	1.0293
6.0	1.0600	1.0448	1.0372	1.0322	1.0303
6.2	1.0620	1.0463	1.0385	1.0333	1.0313
6.4	1.0640	1.0478	1.0397	1.0343	1.0323
6.6	1.0660	1.0492	1.0409	1.0354	1.0333
6.8	1.0680	1.0507	1.0422	1.0365	1.0343
7.0	1.0700	1.0522	1.0434	1.0375	1.0353
7.2	1.0720	1.0537	1.0446	1.0386	1.0363
7.4	1.0740	1.0552	1.0458	1.0396	1.0373
7.6	1.0760	1.0567	1.0471	1.0407	1.0383
7.8	1.0780	1.0581	1.0483	1.0418	1.0393
8.0	1.0800	1.0596	1.0495	1.0428	1.0403
8.2	1.0820	1.0611	1.0507	1.0439	1.0413
8.4	1.0840	1.0626	1.0520	1.0449	1.0422
8.6	1.0860	1.0641	1.0532	1.0460	1.0432
8.8	1.0880	1.0655	1.0544	1.0471	1.0442
9.0	1.0900	1.0670	1.0556	1.0481	1.0452
9.2	1.0920	1.0685	1.0569	1.0492	1.0462
9.4	1.0940	1.0700	1.0581	1.0502	1.0472
9.6	1.0960	1.0715	1.0593	1.0513	1.0482
9.8	1.0980	1.0729	1.0605	1.0523	1.0492
10.0	1.1000	1.0744	1.0618	1.0534	1.0502
10.2	1.1020	1.0759	1.0630	1.0544	1.0512
10.4	1.1040	1.0774	1.0642	1.0555	1.0521
10.6	1.1060	1.0788	1.0654	1.0565	1.0531
10.8	1.1080	1.0803	1.0666	1.0576	1.0541
11.0	1.1100	1.0818	1.0679	1.0586	1.0551
11.2	1.1120	1.0833	1.0691	1.0597	1.0561
11.4	1.1140	1.0847	1.0703	1.0607	1.0571
11.6	1.1160	1.0862	1.0715	1.0618	1.0581
11.8	1.1180	1.0877	1.0727	1.0628	1.0590
12.0	1.1200	1.0892	1.0739	1.0639	1.0600
12.2	1.1220	1.0906	1.0752	1.0649	1.0610
12.4	1.1240	1.0921	1.0764	1.0660	1.0620
12.6	1.1260	1.0936	1.0776	1.0670	1.0630
12.8	1.1280	1.0950	1.0788	1.0681	1.0639
13.0	1.1300	1.0965	1.0800	1.0691	1.0649
13.2	1.1320	1.0980	1.0812	1.0701	1.0659
13.4	1.1340	1.0994	1.0824	1.0712	1.0669
13.6	1.1360	1.1009	1.0836	1.0722	1.0679
13.8	1.1380	1.1024	1.0849	1.0733	1.0688
14.0	1.1400	1.1039	1.0861	1.0743	1.0698

See p. 15 for regulations not amended to reflect law changes

TABLE K
ADJUSTMENT FACTORS FOR ANNUITIES
PAYABLE AT THE END OF EACH INTERVAL
APPLICABLE AFTER APRIL 30, 1989
FREQUENCY OF PAYMENTS

INTEREST RATE	*ANNUALLY*	*SEMI ANNUALLY*	*QUARTERLY*	*MONTHLY*	*WEEKLY*
4.2	1.0000	1.0104	1.0156	1.0191	1.0205
4.4	1.0000	1.0109	1.0164	1.0200	1.0214
4.6	1.0000	1.0114	1.0171	1.0209	1.0224
4.8	1.0000	1.0119	1.0178	1.0218	1.0234
5.0	1.0000	1.0123	1.0186	1.0227	1.0243
5.2	1.0000	1.0128	1.0193	1.0236	1.0253
5.4	1.0000	1.0133	1.0200	1.0245	1.0262
5.6	1.0000	1.0138	1.0208	1.0254	1.0272
5.8	1.0000	1.0143	1.0215	1.0263	1.0282
6.0	1.0000	1.0148	1.0222	1.0272	1.0291
6.2	1.0000	1.0153	1.0230	1.0281	1.0301
6.4	1.0000	1.0158	1.0237	1.0290	1.0311
6.6	1.0000	1.0162	1.0244	1.0299	1.0320
6.8	1.0000	1.0167	1.0252	1.0308	1.0330
7.0	1.0000	1.0172	1.0259	1.0317	1.0339
7.2	1.0000	1.0177	1.0266	1.0326	1.0349
7.4	1.0000	1.0182	1.0273	1.0335	1.0358
7.6	1.0000	1.0187	1.0281	1.0344	1.0368
7.8	1.0000	1.0191	1.0288	1.0353	1.0378
8.0	1.0000	1.0196	1.0295	1.0362	1.0387
8.2	1.0000	1.0201	1.0302	1.0370	1.0397
8.4	1.0000	1.0206	1.0310	1.0379	1.0406
8.6	1.0000	1.0211	1.0317	1.0388	1.0416
8.8	1.0000	1.0215	1.0324	1.0397	1.0425
9.0	1.0000	1.0220	1.0331	1.0406	1.0435
9.2	1.0000	1.0225	1.0339	1.0415	1.0444
9.4	1.0000	1.0230	1.0346	1.0424	1.0454
9.6	1.0000	1.0235	1.0353	1.0433	1.0463
9.8	1.0000	1.0239	1.0360	1.0442	1.0473
10.0	1.0000	1.0244	1.0368	1.0450	1.0482
10.2	1.0000	1.0249	1.0375	1.0459	1.0492
10.4	1.0000	1.0254	1.0382	1.0468	1.0501
10.6	1.0000	1.0258	1.0389	1.0477	1.0511
10.8	1.0000	1.0263	1.0396	1.0486	1.0520
11.0	1.0000	1.0268	1.0404	1.0495	1.0530
11.2	1.0000	1.0273	1.0411	1.0503	1.0539
11.4	1.0000	1.0277	1.0418	1.0512	1.0549
11.6	1.0000	1.0282	1.0425	1.0521	1.0558
11.8	1.0000	1.0287	1.0432	1.0530	1.0568
12.0	1.0000	1.0292	1.0439	1.0539	1.0577
12.2	1.0000	1.0296	1.0447	1.0548	1.0587
12.4	1.0000	1.0301	1.0454	1.0556	1.0596
12.6	1.0000	1.0306	1.0461	1.0565	1.0605
12.8	1.0000	1.0310	1.0468	1.0574	1.0615
13.0	1.0000	1.0315	1.0475	1.0583	1.0624
13.2	1.0000	1.0320	1.0482	1.0591	1.0634
13.4	1.0000	1.0324	1.0489	1.0600	1.0643
13.6	1.0000	1.0329	1.0496	1.0609	1.0652
13.8	1.0000	1.0334	1.0504	1.0618	1.0662
14.0	1.0000	1.0339	1.0511	1.0626	1.0671

(7) *Actuarial Table S and Table 2000CM where the valuation date is on or after May 1, 2009.*—Except as provided in § 20.7520-2(b) (pertaining to certain limitations on the use of prescribed tables), for determination of the present value of an interest that is dependent on the termination of a life interest, Table 2000CM and Table S (single life remainder factors applicable where the valuation date is on or after May 1, 2009) contained in this paragraph (d)(7) and Table J and Table K contained in paragraph (d)(6) of this section, must be used in the application of the provisions of this section when the section 7520 interest rate component is between 0.2 and 14 percent.

Table S
Based on Life Table 2000CM
Single Life Remainder Factors
Applicable On or After May 1, 2009

	Interest Rate									
AGE	0.2%	0.4%	0.6%	0.8%	1.0%	1.2%	1.4%	1.6%	1.8%	2.0%
0	.85816	.73751	.63478	.54723	.47252	.40872	.35416	.30747	.26745	.23313
1	.85889	.73863	.63604	.54844	.47355	.40948	.35459	.30752	.26711	.23239
2	.86054	.74145	.63968	.55260	.47802	.41409	.35922	.31209	.27155	.23664
3	.86221	.74433	.64339	.55687	.48263	.41887	.36404	.31685	.27619	.24112
4	.86390	.74725	.64716	.56121	.48733	.42374	.36898	.32175	.28098	.24575
5	.86560	.75018	.65097	.56561	.49209	.42871	.37401	.32675	.28588	.25050
6	.86731	.75314	.65482	.57006	.49692	.43375	.37913	.33186	.29090	.25538
7	.86902	.75611	.65868	.57454	.50180	.43885	.38432	.33704	.29601	.26035
8	.87073	.75909	.66258	.57907	.50674	.44403	.38960	.34233	.30122	.26544
9	.87246	.76209	.66651	.58364	.51173	.44928	.39497	.34771	.30654	.27064
10	.87419	.76511	.67046	.58826	.51679	.45459	.40042	.35319	.31197	.27596
11	.87592	.76814	.67445	.59291	.52190	.45998	.40596	.35876	.31750	.28139
12	.87766	.77119	.67845	.59761	.52706	.46544	.41157	.36443	.32313	.28693
13	.87939	.77424	.68247	.60232	.53225	.47094	.41723	.37015	.32884	.29255
14	.88112	.77728	.68649	.60704	.53746	.47646	.42293	.37592	.33460	.29823
15	.88284	.78031	.69050	.61176	.54267	.48199	.42865	.38172	.34038	.30394
16	.88455	.78333	.69449	.61647	.54788	.48752	.43437	.38752	.34619	.30968
17	.88625	.78633	.69848	.62117	.55309	.49307	.44012	.39336	.35203	.31546
18	.88795	.78933	.70246	.62588	.55830	.49863	.44589	.39923	.35791	.32129
19	.88964	.79232	.70644	.63059	.56354	.50422	.45170	.40514	.36385	.32719
20	.89132	.79532	.71044	.63534	.56882	.50987	.45757	.41114	.36987	.33317
21	.89301	.79832	.71445	.64010	.57413	.51555	.46350	.41719	.37597	.33925
22	.89470	.80133	.71847	.64488	.57947	.52129	.46948	.42332	.38216	.34541
23	.89639	.80434	.72251	.64970	.58486	.52708	.47554	.42954	.38844	.35168
24	.89808	.80737	.72658	.65456	.59031	.53295	.48169	.43586	.39484	.35809
25	.89978	.81042	.73068	.65947	.59583	.53890	.48795	.44230	.40137	.36464
26	.90149	.81349	.73482	.66443	.60141	.54494	.49430	.44886	.40804	.37134
27	.90320	.81657	.73899	.66944	.60707	.55107	.50076	.45554	.41484	.37819
28	.90492	.81968	.74319	.67450	.61278	.55728	.50733	.46233	.42178	.38520
29	.90665	.82279	.74741	.67960	.61856	.56356	.51398	.46924	.42884	.39233
30	.90837	.82591	.75165	.68473	.62438	.56990	.52070	.47623	.43601	.39959
31	.91010	.82904	.75592	.68989	.63024	.57631	.52751	.48333	.44329	.40698
32	.91182	.83218	.76020	.69509	.63616	.58278	.53440	.49052	.45068	.41449
33	.91355	.83532	.76449	.70031	.64212	.58931	.54137	.49780	.45818	.42213
34	.91527	.83847	.76880	.70556	.64811	.59589	.54839	.50516	.46578	.42988
35	.91700	.84162	.77312	.71082	.65414	.60253	.55549	.51261	.47347	.43774
36	.91872	.84477	.77744	.71611	.66021	.60921	.56266	.52014	.48127	.44572
37	.92043	.84792	.78178	.72142	.66631	.61594	.56989	.52774	.48916	.45381
38	.92215	.85107	.78613	.72675	.67244	.62272	.57718	.53544	.49715	.46201
39	.92386	.85422	.79048	.73210	.67860	.62955	.58453	.54320	.50523	.47032
40	.92557	.85736	.79483	.73746	.68479	.63641	.59194	.55104	.51340	.47873
41	.92727	.86050	.79918	.74283	.69100	.64331	.59940	.55894	.52165	.48724
42	.92896	.86364	.80354	.74820	.69723	.65024	.60690	.56691	.52998	.49585

See p. 15 for regulations not amended to reflect law changes

AGE	0.2%	0.4%	0.6%	0.8%	1.0%	1.2%	1.4%	1.6%	1.8%	2.0%
43	.93065	.86677	.80789	.75359	.70348	.65721	.61447	.57495	.53840	.50457
44	.93234	.86990	.81225	.75899	.70976	.66422	.62208	.58305	.54690	.51338
45	.93402	.87302	.81660	.76439	.71605	.67125	.62973	.59122	.55547	.52228
46	.93569	.87613	.82095	.76980	.72236	.67832	.63743	.59945	.56413	.53129
47	.93735	.87924	.82530	.77521	.72867	.68541	.64517	.60773	.57286	.54037
48	.93901	.88233	.82964	.78062	.73501	.69253	.65295	.61606	.58166	.54955
49	.94065	.88541	.83397	.78604	.74135	.69967	.66077	.62446	.59053	.55882
50	.94229	.88849	.83830	.79145	.74771	.70684	.66864	.63292	.59949	.56819
51	.94393	.89156	.84263	.79688	.75409	.71404	.67655	.64143	.60852	.57766
52	.94556	.89462	.84695	.80230	.76048	.72127	.68450	.65001	.61763	.58722
53	.94717	.89767	.85126	.80772	.76687	.72852	.69249	.65863	.62680	.59687
54	.94878	.90070	.85555	.81313	.77326	.73577	.70050	.66730	.63603	.60658
55	.95037	.90371	.85983	.81853	.77964	.74302	.70851	.67598	.64530	.61635
56	.95195	.90670	.86406	.82388	.78599	.75024	.71651	.68465	.65457	.62613
57	.95351	.90965	.86827	.82920	.79230	.75744	.72448	.69332	.66384	.63593
58	.95505	.91257	.87243	.83447	.79857	.76459	.73242	.70195	.67309	.64573
59	.95657	.91546	.87655	.83970	.80479	.77170	.74033	.71057	.68233	.65553
60	.95807	.91832	.88064	.84490	.81098	.77879	.74822	.71918	.69158	.66534
61	.95955	.92115	.88469	.85005	.81713	.78584	.75608	.72776	.70081	.67515
62	.96101	.92395	.88869	.85515	.82323	.79283	.76388	.73630	.71001	.68494
63	.96245	.92670	.89265	.86020	.82926	.79977	.77164	.74479	.71917	.69470
64	.96387	.92942	.89655	.86518	.83524	.80665	.77933	.75323	.72828	.70443
65	.96527	.93210	.90040	.87011	.84116	.81346	.78697	.76162	.73735	.71411
66	.96665	.93476	.90423	.87502	.84706	.82027	.79461	.77002	.74645	.72385
67	.96802	.93739	.90803	.87990	.85292	.82705	.80223	.77841	.75554	.73359
68	.96937	.93999	.91179	.88472	.85874	.83378	.80980	.78676	.76461	.74331
69	.97070	.94255	.91549	.88949	.86449	.84044	.81731	.79504	.77362	.75299
70	.97200	.94506	.91914	.89419	.87016	.84702	.82473	.80326	.78256	.76260
71	.97328	.94754	.92273	.89882	.87577	.85353	.83209	.81140	.79143	.77215
72	.97453	.94997	.92626	.90338	.88129	.85996	.83935	.81945	.80021	.78162
73	.97576	.95234	.92972	.90785	.88671	.86627	.84651	.82739	.80888	.79098
74	.97695	.95466	.93310	.91223	.89202	.87247	.85353	.83518	.81741	.80019
75	.97811	.95692	.93638	.91649	.89720	.87851	.86039	.84281	.82577	.80923
76	.97924	.95910	.93957	.92063	.90224	.88440	.86708	.85026	.83393	.81807
77	.98033	.96122	.94267	.92465	.90715	.89013	.87360	.85753	.84191	.82671
78	.98138	.96327	.94567	.92855	.91190	.89571	.87995	.86461	.84968	.83515
79	.98239	.96526	.94857	.93233	.91652	.90112	.88611	.87149	.85725	.84337
80	.98337	.96717	.95138	.93598	.92098	.90635	.89208	.87817	.86460	.85135
81	.98431	.96901	.95408	.93951	.92529	.91141	.89786	.88463	.87172	.85910
82	.98521	.97077	.95667	.94290	.92944	.91629	.90344	.89088	.87861	.86660
83	.98608	.97247	.95917	.94616	.93343	.92099	.90882	.89691	.88526	.87385
84	.98691	.97409	.96156	.94928	.93727	.92551	.91399	.90271	.89166	.88084
85	.98770	.97565	.96384	.95228	.94094	.92984	.91895	.90828	.89782	.88757
86	.98845	.97713	.96602	.95514	.94446	.93398	.92371	.91362	.90373	.89402
87	.98917	.97854	.96810	.95786	.94781	.93794	.92825	.91873	.90939	.90021
88	.98985	.97988	.97008	.96046	.95100	.94171	.93258	.92361	.91479	.90612
89	.99049	.98115	.97196	.96292	.95404	.94530	.93671	.92826	.91994	.91176
90	.99110	.98235	.97373	.96526	.95691	.94871	.94062	.93267	.92484	.91713
91	.99168	.98348	.97541	.96747	.95964	.95193	.94434	.93686	.92949	.92223
92	.99222	.98455	.97700	.96955	.96222	.95498	.94785	.94083	.93390	.92707
93	.99273	.98556	.97849	.97152	.96464	.95786	.95117	.94457	.93806	.93163
94	.99321	.98651	.97989	.97337	.96692	.96057	.95429	.94810	.94199	.93595
95	.99366	.98739	.98121	.97510	.96907	.96312	.95724	.95143	.94569	.94002
96	.99408	.98822	.98244	.97673	.97108	.96551	.95999	.95454	.94916	.94384
97	.99447	.98900	.98359	.97825	.97297	.96774	.96258	.95747	.95242	.94742

AGE	0.2%	0.4%	0.6%	0.8%	1.0%	1.2%	1.4%	1.6%	1.8%	2.0%
98	.99483	.98973	.98467	.97967	.97473	.96984	.96500	.96021	.95547	.95078
99	.99518	.99040	.98568	.98101	.97638	.97180	.96727	.96278	.95834	.95394
100	.99549	.99103	.98661	.98224	.97791	.97362	.96937	.96516	.96100	.95687
101	.99579	.99162	.98750	.98340	.97935	.97534	.97136	.96742	.96351	.95964
102	.99607	.99217	.98831	.98448	.98068	.97692	.97319	.96950	.96583	.96220
103	.99634	.99271	.98911	.98553	.98199	.97848	.97500	.97155	.96812	.96473
104	.99659	.99320	.98984	.98651	.98320	.97992	.97666	.97344	.97023	.96705
105	.99683	.99369	.99056	.98747	.98439	.98134	.97830	.97530	.97231	.96934
106	.99713	.99429	.99146	.98865	.98586	.98309	.98033	.97760	.97488	.97218
107	.99747	.99496	.99246	.98998	.98751	.98506	.98262	.98020	.97779	.97539
108	.99800	.99602	.99404	.99208	.99012	.98818	.98624	.98431	.98240	.98049
109	.99900	.99801	.99702	.99603	.99505	.99407	.99310	.99213	.99116	.99020

Table S
Based on Life Table 2000CM
Single Life Remainder Factors
Applicable On or After May 1, 2009

	Interest Rate									
AGE	2.2%	2.4%	2.6%	2.8%	3.0%	3.2%	3.4%	3.6%	3.8%	4.0%
0	.20365	.17830	.15648	.13767	.12144	.10741	.09528	.08476	.07564	.06772
1	.20251	.17677	.15458	.13542	.11885	.10451	.09209	.08131	.07194	.06379
2	.20656	.18060	.15817	.13877	.12197	.10740	.09476	.08376	.07420	.06586
3	.21084	.18466	.16200	.14236	.12533	.11054	.09767	.08647	.07670	.06817
4	.21527	.18888	.16600	.14613	.12887	.11385	.10076	.08935	.07938	.07066
5	.21984	.19324	.17013	.15004	.13255	.11730	.10399	.09237	.08220	.07329
6	.22454	.19773	.17440	.15408	.13636	.12089	.10736	.09553	.08515	.07605
7	.22933	.20233	.17879	.15824	.14030	.12460	.11085	.09880	.08822	.07892
8	.23425	.20705	.18330	.16254	.14436	.12844	.11447	.10221	.09142	.08193
9	.23930	.21191	.18795	.16697	.14857	.13243	.11824	.10576	.09476	.08507
10	.24446	.21689	.19273	.17153	.15292	.13655	.12214	.10945	.09824	.08835
11	.24975	.22200	.19764	.17623	.15740	.14081	.12619	.11328	.10187	.09177
12	.25515	.22724	.20268	.18107	.16202	.14521	.13037	.11724	.10563	.09533
13	.26064	.23256	.20782	.18600	.16674	.14972	.13466	.12132	.10949	.09900
14	.26620	.23796	.21303	.19101	.17154	.15430	.13903	.12547	.11344	.10273
15	.27179	.24340	.21829	.19607	.17639	.15894	.14344	.12968	.11743	.10652
16	.27742	.24887	.22358	.20117	.18128	.16361	.14790	.13391	.12145	.11034
17	.28309	.25439	.22893	.20632	.18622	.16834	.15241	.13821	.12554	.11421
18	.28881	.25997	.23434	.21154	.19123	.17314	.15699	.14258	.12969	.11815
19	.29461	.26563	.23983	.21684	.19633	.17803	.16167	.14703	.13393	.12218
20	.30050	.27139	.24543	.22226	.20156	.18304	.16646	.15161	.13829	.12633
21	.30649	.27726	.25114	.22779	.20689	.18817	.17138	.15631	.14277	.13060
22	.31259	.28323	.25697	.23344	.21235	.19342	.17642	.16114	.14739	.13500
23	.31879	.28934	.26293	.23923	.21795	.19882	.18161	.16612	.15215	.13955
24	.32515	.29559	.26904	.24519	.22372	.20440	.18699	.17128	.15710	.14429
25	.33166	.30201	.27534	.25133	.22969	.21018	.19256	.17665	.16226	.14924
26	.33833	.30861	.28182	.25767	.23586	.21616	.19835	.18224	.16764	.15440
27	.34517	.31538	.28849	.26420	.24224	.22236	.20436	.18804	.17324	.15980
28	.35217	.32233	.29535	.27093	.24882	.22877	.21058	.19407	.17907	.16542
29	.35932	.32944	.30237	.27784	.25558	.23537	.21701	.20031	.18511	.17126
30	.36661	.33670	.30956	.28492	.26253	.24216	.22362	.20674	.19135	.17730
31	.37403	.34411	.31691	.29217	.26965	.24914	.23044	.21338	.19779	.18355
32	.38160	.35167	.32442	.29960	.27697	.25631	.23745	.22022	.20445	.19002
33	.38930	.35939	.33211	.30721	.28447	.26368	.24467	.22727	.21133	.19671
34	.39713	.36724	.33993	.31497	.29213	.27123	.25207	.23451	.21839	.20360
35	.40509	.37523	.34792	.32290	.29998	.27896	.25967	.24195	.22567	.21070

AGE	2.2%	2.4%	2.6%	2.8%	3.0%	3.2%	3.4%	3.6%	3.8%	4.0%
36	.41318	.38337	.35606	.33100	.30800	.28688	.26746	.24961	.23317	.21803
37	.42139	.39165	.36435	.33927	.31621	.29499	.27546	.25746	.24087	.22557
38	.42974	.40008	.37281	.34771	.32460	.30330	.28366	.26554	.24880	.23334
39	.43821	.40864	.38141	.35631	.33316	.31179	.29205	.27381	.25694	.24133
40	.44679	.41734	.39016	.36507	.34189	.32046	.30064	.28229	.26529	.24954
41	.45549	.42616	.39906	.37399	.35080	.32932	.30942	.29097	.27386	.25797
42	.46430	.43511	.40809	.38307	.35987	.33836	.31840	.29986	.28264	.26662
43	.47324	.44421	.41729	.39232	.36913	.34760	.32758	.30897	.29165	.27552
44	.48229	.45343	.42663	.40172	.37857	.35702	.33697	.31829	.30088	.28465
45	.49144	.46277	.43611	.41128	.38817	.36663	.34655	.32782	.31033	.29400
46	.50072	.47225	.44574	.42101	.39796	.37644	.35634	.33757	.32002	.30360
47	.51009	.48185	.45550	.43089	.40791	.38642	.36633	.34753	.32992	.31343
48	.51958	.49158	.46540	.44093	.41803	.39660	.37652	.35770	.34006	.32351
49	.52917	.50143	.47545	.45113	.42833	.40696	.38691	.36810	.35043	.33383
50	.53888	.51141	.48566	.46150	.43883	.41754	.39754	.37874	.36106	.34442
51	.54871	.52153	.49602	.47204	.44951	.42832	.40838	.38961	.37194	.35528
52	.55865	.53179	.50653	.48276	.46038	.43931	.41945	.40073	.38307	.36641
53	.56869	.54217	.51718	.49363	.47143	.45050	.43074	.41208	.39446	.37781
54	.57882	.55265	.52796	.50465	.48265	.46186	.44222	.42364	.40607	.38945
55	.58902	.56322	.53884	.51579	.49400	.47338	.45387	.43540	.41789	.40131
56	.59926	.57383	.54978	.52701	.50544	.48501	.46565	.44729	.42987	.41335
57	.60951	.58449	.56078	.53830	.51698	.49675	.47755	.45932	.44201	.42555
58	.61978	.59517	.57182	.54964	.52858	.50858	.48956	.47147	.45427	.43790
59	.63007	.60589	.58290	.56105	.54027	.52050	.50167	.48375	.46668	.45041
60	.64039	.61665	.59405	.57254	.55205	.53253	.51392	.49617	.47925	.46310
61	.65072	.62743	.60524	.58409	.56390	.54465	.52627	.50872	.49196	.47595
62	.66104	.63822	.61645	.59566	.57581	.55683	.53870	.52136	.50478	.48892
63	.67133	.64900	.62766	.60726	.58774	.56907	.55120	.53409	.51770	.50200
64	.68161	.65977	.63887	.61887	.59970	.58134	.56375	.54688	.53071	.51519
65	.69186	.67053	.65009	.63049	.61170	.59367	.57637	.55976	.54381	.52849
66	.70216	.68136	.66140	.64223	.62383	.60615	.58916	.57283	.55713	.54203
67	.71250	.69224	.67277	.65405	.63605	.61874	.60208	.58605	.57062	.55575
68	.72283	.70312	.68416	.66590	.64833	.63140	.61509	.59938	.58423	.56963
69	.73312	.71398	.69553	.67776	.66062	.64409	.62815	.61277	.59793	.58360
70	.74335	.72479	.70688	.68959	.67291	.65680	.64124	.62621	.61168	.59764
71	.75353	.73556	.71819	.70141	.68519	.66951	.65434	.63968	.62549	.61176
72	.76364	.74626	.72945	.71318	.69744	.68220	.66745	.65317	.63933	.62593
73	.77365	.75686	.74061	.72487	.70962	.69484	.68051	.66662	.65315	.64009
74	.78350	.76733	.75164	.73643	.72167	.70735	.69346	.67997	.66688	.65417
75	.79318	.77761	.76249	.74781	.73355	.71971	.70625	.69318	.68048	.66813
76	.80266	.78769	.77314	.75899	.74524	.73187	.71886	.70621	.69390	.68192
77	.81194	.79756	.78358	.76997	.75672	.74382	.73127	.71904	.70713	.69553
78	.82100	.80722	.79380	.78072	.76798	.75556	.74346	.73166	.72016	.70894
79	.82984	.81664	.80378	.79124	.77900	.76706	.75542	.74405	.73296	.72213
80	.83843	.82582	.81351	.80149	.78976	.77830	.76711	.75618	.74550	.73507
81	.84678	.83474	.82298	.81148	.80025	.78927	.77853	.76803	.75777	.74773
82	.85487	.84339	.83217	.82119	.81045	.79994	.78966	.77959	.76974	.76009
83	.86269	.85177	.84107	.83060	.82035	.81030	.80047	.79083	.78139	.77214
84	.87024	.85986	.84968	.83970	.82993	.82035	.81095	.80174	.79271	.78385
85	.87751	.86765	.85798	.84849	.83919	.83005	.82110	.81230	.80368	.79521
86	.88450	.87515	.86597	.85696	.84811	.83942	.83089	.82251	.81428	.80619
87	.89119	.88234	.87363	.86508	.85668	.84843	.84031	.83234	.82450	.81679
88	.89760	.88922	.88099	.87289	.86492	.85708	.84938	.84180	.83434	.82700
89	.90372	.89580	.88801	.88034	.87280	.86537	.85806	.85087	.84378	.83681
90	.90954	.90207	.89471	.88746	.88032	.87329	.86637	.85954	.85282	.84620

AGE	2.2%	2.4%	2.6%	2.8%	3.0%	3.2%	3.4%	3.6%	3.8%	4.0%
91	.91508	.90803	.90109	.89424	.88750	.88085	.87429	.86783	.86146	.85518
92	.92033	.91369	.90714	.90068	.89432	.88803	.88184	.87572	.86969	.86374
93	.92530	.91904	.91287	.90678	.90078	.89484	.88899	.88321	.87751	.87188
94	.92999	.92411	.91830	.91256	.90690	.90130	.89578	.89032	.88493	.87961
95	.93442	.92889	.92342	.91802	.91269	.90741	.90220	.89706	.89197	.88694
96	.93858	.93338	.92824	.92316	.91813	.91316	.90825	.90340	.89859	.89385
97	.94248	.93759	.93276	.92798	.92325	.91857	.91395	.90937	.90484	.90036
98	.94614	.94155	.93701	.93252	.92807	.92367	.91931	.91500	.91073	.90650
99	.94959	.94528	.94101	.93679	.93260	.92846	.92436	.92030	.91628	.91229
100	.95278	.94874	.94473	.94075	.93682	.93292	.92906	.92523	.92144	.91769
101	.95581	.95201	.94824	.94451	.94081	.93715	.93352	.92992	.92635	.92281
102	.95860	.95503	.95149	.94798	.94450	.94105	.93763	.93424	.93088	.92754
103	.96136	.95802	.95470	.95142	.94816	.94492	.94171	.93853	.93538	.93224
104	.96390	.96077	.95766	.95458	.95152	.94848	.94547	.94248	.93951	.93657
105	.96640	.96347	.96057	.95769	.95483	.95199	.94917	.94637	.94359	.94083
106	.96950	.96684	.96420	.96157	.95896	.95636	.95379	.95123	.94868	.94616
107	.97301	.97064	.96829	.96595	.96362	.96131	.95901	.95672	.95445	.95219
108	.97859	.97670	.97482	.97295	.97109	.96923	.96739	.96555	.96373	.96191
109	.98924	.98828	.98733	.98638	.98544	.98450	.98356	.98263	.98170	.98077

Table S
Based on Life Table 2000CM
Single Life Remainder Factors
Applicable On or After May 1, 2009

Interest Rate

AGE	4.2%	4.4%	4.6%	4.8%	5.0%	5.2%	5.4%	5.6%	5.8%	6.0%
0	.06083	.05483	.04959	.04501	.04101	.03749	.03441	.03170	.02931	.02721
1	.05668	.05049	.04507	.04034	.03618	.03254	.02934	.02652	.02403	.02183
2	.05858	.05222	.04665	.04178	.03750	.03373	.03042	.02750	.02492	.02264
3	.06072	.05420	.04848	.04346	.03904	.03516	.03173	.02871	.02503	.02366
4	.06303	.05634	.05046	.04530	.04075	.03674	.03319	.03006	.02729	.02483
5	.06547	.05861	.05258	.04726	.04258	.03844	.03478	.03153	.02866	.02610
6	.06805	.06102	.05482	.04935	.04453	.04026	.03647	.03312	.03014	.02749
7	.07074	.06353	.05717	.05155	.04658	.04217	.03826	.03479	.03171	.02895
8	.07356	.06617	.05964	.05386	.04875	.04421	.04017	.03658	.03338	.03053
9	.07651	.06895	.06225	.05631	.05105	.04637	.04220	.03849	.03518	.03222
10	.07960	.07185	.06499	.05889	.05347	.04865	.04435	.04052	.03709	.03402
11	.08283	.07490	.06786	.06160	.05603	.05106	.04663	.04267	.03912	.03594
12	.08620	.07808	.07087	.06444	.05871	.05360	.04903	.04494	.04127	.03798
13	.08967	.08137	.07397	.06738	.06149	.05623	.05152	.04729	.04351	.04010
14	.09321	.08472	.07715	.07038	.06433	.05892	.05406	.04971	.04579	.04227
15	.09680	.08812	.08036	.07342	.06721	.06164	.05664	.05214	.04810	.04445
16	.10041	.09154	.08360	.07649	.07011	.06438	.05923	.05459	.05041	.04664
17	.10409	.09502	.08689	.07960	.07305	.06716	.06185	.05707	.05276	.04886
18	.10782	.09855	.09024	.08276	.07604	.06998	.06452	.05959	.05514	.05111
19	.11164	.10217	.09366	.08600	.07910	.07288	.06726	.06218	.05758	.05341
20	.11559	.10592	.09721	.08937	.08228	.07589	.07010	.06487	.06012	.05582
21	.11965	.10977	.10087	.09283	.08557	.07900	.07305	.06765	.06276	.05831
22	.12383	.11376	.10465	.09642	.08897	.08223	.07610	.07055	.06550	.06090
23	.12817	.11789	.10859	.10016	.09252	.08559	.07930	.07358	.06837	.06363
24	.13270	.12221	.11270	.10408	.09625	.08914	.08267	.07678	.07141	.06651
25	.13744	.12674	.11703	.10821	.10019	.09289	.08625	.08018	.07465	.06960
26	.14239	.13149	.12158	.11256	.10435	.09686	.09003	.08380	.07810	.07288
27	.14758	.13647	.12636	.11714	.10873	.10106	.09405	.08764	.08177	.07639
28	.15300	.14169	.13137	.12195	.11335	.10549	.09829	.09171	.08567	.08012
29	.15864	.14712	.13660	.12698	.11819	.11013	.10275	.09598	.08977	.08406

AGE	4.2%	4.4%	4.6%	4.8%	5.0%	5.2%	5.4%	5.6%	5.8%	6.0%
30	.16448	.15275	.14203	.13222	.12323	.11498	.10742	.10047	.09408	.08820
31	.17053	.15861	.14769	.13768	.12849	.12006	.11230	.10517	.09860	.09255
32	.17680	.16468	.15357	.14336	.13398	.12535	.11741	.11009	.10335	.09712
33	.18330	.17099	.15968	.14927	.13970	.13088	.12275	.11525	.10832	.10192
34	.19000	.17750	.16599	.15539	.14562	.13661	.12829	.12061	.11350	.10693
35	.19692	.18423	.17253	.16174	.15178	.14258	.13408	.12621	.11892	.11217
36	.20407	.19119	.17931	.16833	.15818	.14879	.14009	.13204	.12457	.11764
37	.21144	.19838	.18631	.17515	.16481	.15523	.14635	.13811	.13046	.12335
38	.21904	.20582	.19357	.18222	.17170	.16193	.15287	.14444	.13661	.12932
39	.22687	.21348	.20105	.18952	.17882	.16887	.15962	.15102	.14300	.13554
40	.23493	.22137	.20878	.19707	.18619	.17606	.16663	.15784	.14965	.14201
41	.24322	.22950	.21674	.20487	.19381	.18350	.17390	.16493	.15656	.14873
42	.25173	.23786	.22494	.21290	.20168	.19120	.18141	.17227	.16372	.15572
43	.26049	.24648	.23342	.22122	.20982	.19918	.18922	.17990	.17118	.16301
44	.26950	.25535	.24214	.22979	.21824	.20742	.19730	.18781	.17892	.17057
45	.27874	.26447	.25112	.23862	.22692	.21595	.20566	.19600	.18694	.17843
46	.28824	.27385	.26038	.24774	.23589	.22476	.21431	.20450	.19527	.18659
47	.29798	.28349	.26989	.25712	.24513	.23386	.22326	.21328	.20390	.19505
48	.30797	.29338	.27967	.26678	.25466	.24325	.23250	.22238	.21283	.20383
49	.31822	.30355	.28974	.27674	.26449	.25294	.24206	.23179	.22210	.21294
50	.32876	.31401	.30011	.28701	.27465	.26298	.25196	.24156	.23172	.22242
51	.33958	.32477	.31079	.29759	.28513	.27335	.26221	.25168	.24170	.23226
52	.35068	.33582	.32178	.30851	.29595	.28407	.27282	.26216	.25206	.24249
53	.36206	.34717	.33308	.31974	.30710	.29513	.28378	.27301	.26279	.25309
54	.37371	.35880	.34467	.33127	.31857	.30651	.29507	.28420	.27388	.26406
55	.38559	.37067	.35652	.34308	.33032	.31820	.30668	.29572	.28529	.27537
56	.39765	.38275	.36859	.35512	.34232	.33014	.31855	.30751	.29699	.28697
57	.40990	.39502	.38086	.36739	.35455	.34233	.33068	.31957	.30898	.29887
58	.42231	.40747	.39333	.37985	.36700	.35474	.34304	.33188	.32121	.31103
59	.43490	.42011	.40600	.39253	.37968	.36740	.35567	.34446	.33374	.32348
60	.44768	.43296	.41890	.40546	.39261	.38033	.36858	.35733	.34656	.33625
61	.46064	.44600	.43200	.41860	.40578	.39351	.38175	.37048	.35968	.34933
62	.47373	.45920	.44527	.43194	.41915	.40690	.39514	.38387	.37305	.36267
63	.48696	.47253	.45870	.44544	.43271	.42049	.40876	.39749	.38666	.37625
64	.50030	.48601	.47229	.45911	.44645	.43428	.42258	.41133	.40051	.39010
65	.51377	.49963	.48603	.47295	.46037	.44827	.43662	.42540	.41460	.40420
66	.52750	.51352	.50007	.48711	.47464	.46262	.45103	.43987	.42911	.41872
67	.54144	.52765	.51436	.50154	.48919	.47727	.46578	.45468	.44397	.43363
68	.55554	.54196	.52885	.51619	.50398	.49218	.48079	.46978	.45915	.44887
69	.56976	.55640	.54349	.53102	.51896	.50731	.49603	.48513	.47458	.46438
70	.58407	.57095	.55826	.54598	.53410	.52260	.51147	.50069	.49025	.48013
71	.59848	.58561	.57316	.56109	.54940	.53808	.52710	.51646	.50615	.49614
72	.61294	.60035	.58815	.57632	.56484	.55371	.54291	.53243	.52225	.51237
73	.62741	.61512	.60318	.59160	.58035	.56943	.55882	.54851	.53849	.52876
74	.64183	.62983	.61818	.60686	.59586	.58516	.57476	.56464	.55480	.54523
75	.65612	.64444	.63309	.62204	.61129	.60083	.59065	.58074	.57109	.56169
76	.67026	.65891	.64786	.63710	.62661	.61640	.60646	.59676	.58731	.57810
77	.68423	.67321	.66248	.65201	.64181	.63186	.62215	.61269	.60345	.59444
78	.69800	.68733	.67692	.66676	.65684	.64717	.63772	.62849	.61948	.61068
79	.71156	.70124	.69116	.68132	.67170	.66230	.65312	.64414	.63537	.62680
80	.72487	.71490	.70516	.69563	.68632	.67721	.66830	.65959	.65106	.64272
81	.73791	.72830	.71890	.70970	.70069	.69188	.68325	.67481	.66654	.65844
82	.75065	.74140	.73235	.72348	.71479	.70628	.69794	.68977	.68176	.67391
83	.76308	.75419	.74548	.73695	.72858	.72037	.71232	.70443	.69669	.68909
84	.77516	.76664	.75828	.75008	.74203	.73413	.72638	.71877	.71130	.70396

AGE	4.2%	4.4%	4.6%	4.8%	5.0%	5.2%	5.4%	5.6%	5.8%	6.0%
85	.78689	.77873	.77072	.76285	.75512	.74753	.74008	.73275	.72556	.71849
86	.79825	.79044	.78278	.77524	.76783	.76055	.75340	.74636	.73944	.73264
87	.80921	.80176	.79443	.78722	.78014	.77316	.76630	.75956	.75292	.74638
88	.81978	.81268	.80569	.79880	.79203	.78536	.77880	.77234	.76598	.75971
89	.82994	.82317	.81651	.80995	.80349	.79712	.79085	.78467	.77859	.77259
90	.83967	.83324	.82690	.82065	.81450	.80843	.80244	.79655	.79073	.78500
91	.84898	.84288	.83685	.83091	.82505	.81928	.81358	.80795	.80241	.79693
92	.85787	.85208	.84636	.84072	.83515	.82966	.82423	.81888	.81360	.80838
93	.86632	.86083	.85541	.85006	.84477	.83955	.83440	.82931	.82428	.81931
94	.87435	.86915	.86402	.85894	.85393	.84898	.84409	.83925	.83447	.82975
95	.88197	.87705	.87219	.86739	.86265	.85795	.85331	.84872	.84419	.83970
96	.88915	.88451	.87991	.87537	.87088	.86643	.86203	.85768	.85338	.84912
97	.89593	.89154	.88720	.88290	.87865	.87444	.87028	.86616	.86208	.85804
98	.90232	.89818	.89408	.89002	.88600	.88202	.87808	.87418	.87031	.86649
99	.90835	.90444	.90057	.89674	.89294	.88918	.88546	.88177	.87811	.87449
100	.91397	.91028	.90663	.90301	.89942	.89587	.89234	.88885	.88539	.88196
101	.91930	.91583	.91238	.90897	.90558	.90223	.89890	.89560	.89233	.88908
102	.92424	.92096	.91771	.91448	.91128	.90811	.90496	.90184	.89875	.89568
103	.92914	.92605	.92300	.91996	.91695	.91397	.91100	.90806	.90514	.90225
104	.93364	.93074	.92786	.92501	.92217	.91935	.91656	.91379	.91103	.90830
105	.93809	.93537	.93266	.92998	.92731	.92467	.92204	.91943	.91683	.91426
106	.94365	.94115	.93867	.93621	.93376	.93133	.92892	.92651	.92413	.92176
107	.94994	.94771	.94549	.94328	.94108	.93890	.93673	.93457	.93242	.93028
108	.96010	.95830	.95651	.95472	.95295	.95118	.94942	.94767	.94593	.94420
109	.97985	.97893	.97801	.97710	.97619	.97529	.97438	.97348	.97259	.97170

Table S
Based on Life Table 2000CM
Single Life Remainder Factors
Applicable On or After May 1, 2009

Interest Rate

AGE	6.2%	6.4%	6.6%	6.8%	7.0%	7.2%	7.4%	7.6%	7.8%	8.0%
0	.02534	.02370	.02223	.02093	.01978	.01874	.01782	.01699	.01625	.01559
1	.01989	.01817	.01664	.01528	.01406	.01298	.01202	.01115	.01037	.00967
2	.02061	.01882	.01722	.01580	.01454	.01340	.01239	.01148	.01066	.00993
3	.02156	.01969	.01802	.01654	.01521	.01403	.01297	.01201	.01115	.01038
4	.02264	.02069	.01896	.01741	.01602	.01478	.01367	.01267	.01176	.01095
5	.02383	.02180	.01999	.01838	.01693	.01563	.01446	.01341	.01246	.01161
6	.02512	.02301	.02113	.01944	.01793	.01657	.01535	.01424	.01325	.01235
7	.02650	.02430	.02234	.02058	.01900	.01758	.01630	.01514	.01410	.01315
8	.02798	.02570	.02365	.02182	.02017	.01868	.01734	.01613	.01503	.01404
9	.02957	.02720	.02507	.02316	.02143	.01988	.01848	.01721	.01606	.01502
10	.03128	.02881	.02659	.02460	.02280	.02118	.01971	.01838	.01718	.01608
11	.03309	.03053	.02823	.02615	.02428	.02258	.02105	.01966	.01839	.01725
12	.03503	.03237	.02997	.02781	.02585	.02408	.02248	.02103	.01971	.01850
13	.03704	.03428	.03179	.02954	.02750	.02565	.02398	.02246	.02108	.01982
14	.03909	.03623	.03364	.03130	.02918	.02726	.02551	.02392	.02248	.02116
15	.04117	.03820	.03551	.03308	.03087	.02886	.02704	.02538	.02387	.02249
16	.04324	.04016	.03737	.03484	.03254	.03046	.02855	.02682	.02524	.02379
17	.04533	.04214	.03924	.03661	.03422	.03205	.03007	.02826	.02661	.02509
18	.04746	.04415	.04114	.03841	.03592	.03366	.03159	.02970	.02798	.02639
19	.04963	.04620	.04309	.04025	.03766	.03530	.03315	.03117	.02937	.02772
20	.05191	.04835	.04512	.04217	.03948	.03702	.03478	.03272	.03083	.02910
21	.05427	.05058	.04723	.04416	.04137	.03881	.03647	.03432	.03235	.03054
22	.05672	.05291	.04943	.04625	.04334	.04067	.03823	.03599	.03394	.03205

See p. 15 for regulations not amended to reflect law changes

AGE	6.2%	6.4%	6.6%	6.8%	7.0%	7.2%	7.4%	7.6%	7.8%	8.0%
23	.05930	.05535	.05174	.04844	.04542	.04265	.04010	.03777	.03562	.03364
24	.06204	.05795	.05421	.05078	.04764	.04476	.04211	.03967	.03743	.03536
25	.06497	.06074	.05687	.05331	.05005	.04705	.04429	.04174	.03940	.03724
26	.06811	.06373	.05972	.05603	.05264	.04952	.04665	.04400	.04155	.03929
27	.07146	.06694	.06278	.05895	.05543	.05219	.04920	.04644	.04389	.04153
28	.07503	.07036	.06605	.06209	.05844	.05507	.05196	.04908	.04642	.04396
29	.07881	.07398	.06953	.06542	.06163	.05814	.05490	.05191	.04913	.04656
30	.08279	.07780	.07319	.06894	.06502	.06138	.05802	.05491	.05202	.04933
31	.08697	.08182	.07707	.07267	.06860	.06483	.06134	.05810	.05509	.05229
32	.09137	.08606	.08115	.07660	.07239	.06848	.06485	.06148	.05835	.05543
33	.09601	.09053	.08546	.08075	.07639	.07234	.06858	.06508	.06182	.05878
34	.10084	.09520	.08996	.08511	.08059	.07640	.07249	.06886	.06547	.06231
35	.10590	.10009	.09470	.08968	.08501	.08067	.07662	.07285	.06933	.06605
36	.11120	.10522	.09966	.09448	.08966	.08517	.08098	.07706	.07341	.06999
37	.11674	.11059	.10486	.09952	.09454	.08990	.08556	.08150	.07771	.07416
38	.12254	.11621	.11032	.10481	.09968	.09487	.09039	.08618	.08225	.07856
39	.12857	.12208	.11601	.11035	.10505	.10009	.09545	.09110	.08702	.08320
40	.13487	.12820	.12196	.11613	.11067	.10555	.10076	.09626	.09204	.08807
41	.14142	.13458	.12817	.12217	.11655	.11127	.10632	.10167	.09730	.09319
42	.14823	.14122	.13464	.12848	.12269	.11725	.11214	.10734	.10282	.09856
43	.15535	.14816	.14141	.13508	.12913	.12353	.11826	.11330	.10863	.10422
44	.16274	.15538	.14847	.14196	.13585	.13008	.12466	.11954	.11472	.11016
45	.17042	.16290	.15581	.14914	.14286	.13694	.13135	.12608	.12110	.11640
46	.17842	.17073	.16348	.15664	.15020	.14411	.13836	.13293	.12780	.12294
47	.18672	.17886	.17145	.16445	.15784	.15159	.14568	.14010	.13481	.12980
48	.19534	.18732	.17974	.17258	.16581	.15940	.15334	.14759	.14215	.13699
49	.20429	.19612	.18838	.18106	.17413	.16757	.16134	.15544	.14984	.14453
50	.21362	.20529	.19740	.18993	.18284	.17612	.16974	.16368	.15793	.15247
51	.22332	.21484	.20680	.19917	.19194	.18506	.17853	.17232	.16642	.16080
52	.23341	.22479	.21660	.20883	.20144	.19442	.18774	.18138	.17533	.16957
53	.24388	.23513	.22681	.21889	.21136	.20419	.19737	.19087	.18467	.17876
54	.25473	.24585	.23739	.22935	.22168	.21437	.20741	.20076	.19442	.18837
55	.26593	.25693	.24835	.24017	.23238	.22494	.21784	.21105	.20458	.19838
56	.27742	.26831	.25962	.25132	.24340	.23583	.22860	.22169	.21508	.20875
57	.28922	.28001	.27121	.26280	.25476	.24707	.23971	.23267	.22593	.21947
58	.30129	.29199	.28309	.27457	.26642	.25862	.25114	.24398	.23712	.23053
59	.31367	.30428	.29529	.28667	.27842	.27051	.26293	.25565	.24867	.24197
60	.32638	.31691	.30784	.29914	.29079	.28278	.27509	.26771	.26062	.25380
61	.33940	.32987	.32073	.31195	.30352	.29542	.28763	.28015	.27295	.26603
62	.35269	.34311	.33391	.32506	.31656	.30837	.30050	.29293	.28564	.27862
63	.36625	.35663	.34738	.33847	.32990	.32165	.31370	.30604	.29867	.29155
64	.38007	.37043	.36113	.35218	.34356	.33524	.32723	.31950	.31204	.30484
65	.39417	.38451	.37519	.36620	.35753	.34917	.34110	.33330	.32577	.31850
66	.40871	.39905	.38972	.38071	.37201	.36361	.35550	.34765	.34006	.33273
67	.42365	.41400	.40468	.39567	.38696	.37853	.37038	.36250	.35487	.34749
68	.43892	.42931	.42001	.41101	.40230	.39387	.38570	.37780	.37014	.36272
69	.45450	.44493	.43567	.42670	.41800	.40958	.40141	.39350	.38582	.37837
70	.47033	.46083	.45162	.44269	.43403	.42563	.41748	.40957	.40189	.39443
71	.48644	.47702	.46788	.45901	.45040	.44203	.43391	.42602	.41835	.41090
72	.50278	.49347	.48441	.47562	.46707	.45877	.45069	.44284	.43520	.42776
73	.51930	.51010	.50115	.49245	.48399	.47575	.46774	.45994	.45234	.44494
74	.53591	.52684	.51802	.50943	.50106	.49291	.48497	.47724	.46970	.46235
75	.55253	.54361	.53492	.52645	.51820	.51015	.50230	.49465	.48719	.47991
76	.56912	.56036	.55182	.54349	.53536	.52742	.51968	.51213	.50475	.49754
77	.58565	.57706	.56868	.56050	.55251	.54471	.53708	.52964	.52236	.51525

AGE	6.2%	6.4%	6.6%	6.8%	7.0%	7.2%	7.4%	7.6%	7.8%	8.0%
78	.60209	.59369	.58549	.57747	.56963	.56197	.55448	.54715	.53999	.53298
79	.61841	.61021	.60219	.59435	.58668	.57917	.57182	.56463	.55760	.55071
80	.63456	.62657	.61875	.61109	.60359	.59625	.58906	.58202	.57512	.56836
81	.65050	.64273	.63512	.62766	.62034	.61318	.60616	.59927	.59252	.58590
82	.66621	.65867	.65127	.64401	.63690	.62992	.62308	.61636	.60977	.60330
83	.68164	.67433	.66716	.66012	.65321	.64642	.63976	.63322	.62680	.62050
84	.69676	.68969	.68275	.67593	.66923	.66265	.65618	.64983	.64358	.63745
85	.71154	.70472	.69801	.69141	.68493	.67856	.67229	.66613	.66007	.65412
86	.72595	.71937	.71290	.70654	.70028	.69412	.68806	.68210	.67623	.67046
87	.73995	.73362	.72740	.72127	.71523	.70929	.70344	.69768	.69201	.68642
88	.75354	.74746	.74148	.73558	.72978	.72406	.71842	.71287	.70739	.70200
89	.76668	.76085	.75511	.74945	.74387	.73837	.73295	.72761	.72234	.71714
90	.77934	.77377	.76827	.76284	.75749	.75222	.74701	.74188	.73681	.73181
91	.79153	.78620	.78094	.77575	.77063	.76558	.76059	.75566	.75080	.74600
92	.80323	.79814	.79312	.78816	.78326	.77843	.77365	.76894	.76428	.75967
93	.81440	.80956	.80477	.80004	.79536	.79074	.78618	.78166	.77721	.77280
94	.82508	.82047	.81591	.81140	.80694	.80253	.79817	.79387	.78961	.78539
95	.83526	.83088	.82654	.82225	.81800	.81380	.80965	.80554	.80148	.79746
96	.84491	.84074	.83662	.83254	.82850	.82450	.82055	.81663	.81276	.80892
97	.85405	.85009	.84617	.84230	.83846	.83466	.83089	.82717	.82348	.81982
98	.86270	.85895	.85523	.85155	.84791	.84430	.84072	.83718	.83367	.83019
99	.87090	.86735	.86382	.86033	.85687	.85345	.85005	.84668	.84335	.84004
100	.87856	.87519	.87185	.86854	.86526	.86201	.85878	.85559	.85242	.84927
101	.88587	.88268	.87952	.87638	.87327	.87019	.86713	.86409	.86109	.85810
102	.89263	.88961	.88662	.88364	.88069	.87777	.87487	.87199	.86913	.86629
103	.89938	.89653	.89370	.89089	.88810	.88534	.88259	.87987	.87717	.87448
104	.90558	.90289	.90021	.89756	.89492	.89231	.88971	.88713	.88456	.88202
105	.91170	.90916	.90664	.90413	.90164	.89917	.89672	.89428	.89186	.88945
106	.91940	.91706	.91474	.91242	.91013	.90784	.90558	.90332	.90108	.89885
107	.92816	.92605	.92395	.92186	.91978	.91772	.91567	.91362	.91159	.90957
108	.94247	.94075	.93904	.93734	.93565	.93396	.93229	.93062	.92895	.92730
109	.97081	.96992	.96904	.96816	.96729	.96642	.96555	.96468	.96382	.96296

Table S
Based on Life Table 2000CM
Single Life Remainder Factors
Applicable On or After May 1, 2009

	Interest Rate									
AGE	8.2%	8.4%	8.6%	8.8%	9.0%	9.2%	9.4%	9.6%	9.8%	10.0%
0	.01498	.01444	.01395	.01351	.01310	.01273	.01240	.01209	.01181	.01155
1	.00904	.00847	.00796	.00749	.00707	.00668	.00633	.00601	.00572	.00545
2	.00926	.00866	.00812	.00763	.00718	.00677	.00640	.00606	.00575	.00547
3	.00968	.00905	.00848	.00796	.00748	.00705	.00666	.00630	.00597	.00567
4	.01021	.00955	.00894	.00839	.00789	.00744	.00702	.00664	.00629	.00597
5	.01083	.01013	.00949	.00891	.00839	.00790	.00746	.00706	.00669	.00635
6	.01153	.01080	.01012	.00951	.00895	.00844	.00798	.00755	.00715	.00679
7	.01229	.01151	.01081	.01016	.00957	.00903	.00854	.00808	.00767	.00728
8	.01314	.01232	.01157	.01089	.01026	.00969	.00917	.00869	.00825	.00784
9	.01407	.01321	.01242	.01170	.01104	.01044	.00989	.00938	.00891	.00848
10	.01509	.01418	.01335	.01259	.01190	.01126	.01068	.01014	.00965	.00919
11	.01620	.01525	.01437	.01358	.01285	.01218	.01156	.01099	.01047	.00998
12	.01740	.01640	.01549	.01465	.01388	.01317	.01252	.01192	.01137	.01086
13	.01867	.01762	.01665	.01577	.01496	.01422	.01353	.01290	.01231	.01177
14	.01995	.01885	.01784	.01691	.01606	.01527	.01455	.01389	.01327	.01270
15	.02123	.02007	.01901	.01803	.01714	.01632	.01556	.01485	.01420	.01360

AGE	8.2%	8.4%	8.6%	8.8%	9.0%	9.2%	9.4%	9.6%	9.8%	10.0%
16	.02247	.02126	.02015	.01913	.01818	.01732	.01652	.01578	.01509	.01446
17	.02371	.02244	.02127	.02020	.01921	.01830	.01746	.01668	.01596	.01529
18	.02494	.02361	.02239	.02126	.02022	.01926	.01838	.01756	.01680	.01610
19	.02620	.02480	.02352	.02234	.02125	.02024	.01931	.01844	.01764	.01690
20	.02751	.02605	.02471	.02346	.02232	.02126	.02028	.01937	.01853	.01775
21	.02888	.02735	.02593	.02463	.02343	.02231	.02128	.02032	.01944	.01861
22	.03030	.02870	.02722	.02585	.02458	.02341	.02233	.02132	.02038	.01951
23	.03181	.03013	.02858	.02714	.02581	.02458	.02344	.02237	.02139	.02047
24	.03345	.03169	.03006	.02855	.02715	.02586	.02465	.02353	.02249	.02152
25	.03524	.03340	.03169	.03010	.02863	.02727	.02600	.02482	.02373	.02270
26	.03720	.03527	.03348	.03181	.03027	.02884	.02750	.02626	.02510	.02402
27	.03934	.03732	.03544	.03370	.03208	.03057	.02916	.02786	.02664	.02549
28	.04167	.03955	.03759	.03576	.03406	.03247	.03099	.02962	.02833	.02713
29	.04417	.04196	.03990	.03798	.03619	.03453	.03298	.03153	.03017	.02890
30	.04684	.04452	.04237	.04036	.03848	.03674	.03510	.03358	.03215	.03081
31	.04969	.04727	.04501	.04291	.04094	.03911	.03739	.03579	.03428	.03287
32	.05272	.05019	.04783	.04563	.04357	.04165	.03984	.03816	.03657	.03509
33	.05595	.05331	.05085	.04854	.04639	.04437	.04248	.04070	.03904	.03748
34	.05936	.05661	.05403	.05162	.04936	.04725	.04527	.04341	.04166	.04001
35	.06297	.06010	.05741	.05489	.05253	.05032	.04824	.04629	.04445	.04272
36	.06679	.06380	.06100	.05837	.05590	.05358	.05140	.04935	.04742	.04561
37	.07083	.06771	.06479	.06204	.05947	.05704	.05476	.05261	.05059	.04868
38	.07511	.07186	.06881	.06595	.06326	.06072	.05834	.05609	.05397	.05196
39	.07961	.07623	.07306	.07007	.06726	.06462	.06212	.05977	.05754	.05544
40	.08434	.08083	.07753	.07442	.07149	.06873	.06612	.06366	.06133	.05913
41	.08932	.08568	.08225	.07901	.07596	.07308	.07035	.06778	.06534	.06304
42	.09455	.09077	.08720	.08384	.08066	.07766	.07481	.07213	.06958	.06717
43	.10007	.09615	.09245	.08895	.08564	.08251	.07955	.07674	.07408	.07156
44	.10586	.10180	.09796	.09433	.09089	.08763	.08454	.08162	.07884	.07621
45	.11195	.10774	.10376	.09999	.09642	.09303	.08982	.08677	.08387	.08112
46	.11835	.11400	.10987	.10596	.10225	.09873	.09539	.09222	.08920	.08633
47	.12505	.12055	.11629	.11224	.10839	.10474	.10126	.09796	.09482	.09182
48	.13209	.12745	.12303	.11884	.11485	.11106	.10746	.10402	.10075	.09764
49	.13948	.13469	.13013	.12579	.12167	.11774	.11400	.11043	.10703	.10379
50	.14727	.14233	.13762	.13314	.12887	.12481	.12093	.11723	.11370	.11033
51	.15546	.15037	.14551	.14089	.13648	.13228	.12826	.12443	.12077	.11726
52	.16407	.15884	.15384	.14907	.14452	.14018	.13603	.13206	.12826	.12463
53	.17312	.16774	.16260	.15769	.15300	.14852	.14423	.14012	.13620	.13243
54	.18259	.17707	.17179	.16674	.16191	.15729	.15286	.14862	.14456	.14067
55	.19247	.18680	.18139	.17620	.17123	.16648	.16192	.15755	.15335	.14933
56	.20270	.19690	.19135	.18602	.18092	.17603	.17134	.16684	.16251	.15836
57	.21329	.20736	.20167	.19622	.19099	.18596	.18114	.17650	.17205	.16777
58	.22422	.21816	.21235	.20677	.20140	.19625	.19130	.18653	.18195	.17754
59	.23553	.22935	.22341	.21770	.21221	.20693	.20185	.19696	.19225	.18772
60	.24725	.24095	.23489	.22906	.22345	.21805	.21285	.20783	.20300	.19834
61	.25937	.25296	.24679	.24084	.23511	.22959	.22427	.21914	.21419	.20941
62	.27185	.26534	.25906	.25300	.24716	.24153	.23609	.23084	.22577	.22088
63	.28469	.27808	.27169	.26553	.25959	.25384	.24830	.24294	.23776	.23275
64	.29789	.29119	.28471	.27845	.27240	.26656	.26091	.25544	.25016	.24504
65	.31148	.30468	.29812	.29177	.28563	.27969	.27394	.26837	.26299	.25777
66	.32564	.31877	.31213	.30570	.29948	.29345	.28761	.28195	.27647	.27115
67	.34034	.33341	.32671	.32021	.31391	.30780	.30188	.29614	.29057	.28517
68	.35552	.34855	.34179	.33523	.32887	.32270	.31671	.31089	.30524	.29976
69	.37115	.36414	.35734	.35073	.34432	.33809	.33204	.32616	.32045	.31489
70	.38719	.38016	.37332	.36668	.36023	.35396	.34786	.34193	.33616	.33054

AGE	8.2%	8.4%	8.6%	8.8%	9.0%	9.2%	9.4%	9.6%	9.8%	10.0%
71	.40366	.39662	.38977	.38311	.37663	.37032	.36419	.35821	.35240	.34674
72	.42053	.41350	.40665	.39998	.39349	.38716	.38100	.37500	.36916	.36346
73	.43774	.43073	.42389	.41723	.41074	.40441	.39824	.39222	.38636	.38063
74	.45519	.44821	.44140	.43476	.42829	.42197	.41580	.40979	.40391	.39818
75	.47280	.46587	.45910	.45250	.44605	.43975	.43360	.42759	.42173	.41599
76	.49051	.48364	.47693	.47037	.46396	.45770	.45158	.44560	.43975	.43403
77	.50830	.50150	.49486	.48836	.48201	.47580	.46972	.46377	.45795	.45225
78	.52613	.51942	.51286	.50644	.50015	.49400	.48797	.48208	.47630	.47064
79	.54396	.53736	.53089	.52456	.51835	.51227	.50632	.50048	.49476	.48915
80	.56174	.55525	.54888	.54265	.53653	.53054	.52466	.51890	.51325	.50770
81	.57941	.57305	.56681	.56068	.55467	.54878	.54299	.53731	.53174	.52627
82	.59696	.59073	.58461	.57861	.57272	.56693	.56125	.55566	.55018	.54480
83	.61430	.60822	.60224	.59637	.59061	.58494	.57937	.57389	.56851	.56322
84	.63142	.62549	.61966	.61393	.60830	.60276	.59731	.59196	.58669	.58150
85	.64825	.64249	.63682	.63124	.62575	.62035	.61503	.60980	.60465	.59958
86	.66477	.65918	.65367	.64825	.64291	.63765	.63248	.62738	.62236	.61741
87	.68092	.67550	.67016	.66490	.65972	.65462	.64959	.64463	.63975	.63493
88	.69669	.69145	.68628	.68119	.67618	.67123	.66635	.66154	.65680	.65212
89	.71201	.70696	.70198	.69706	.69221	.68742	.68270	.67805	.67345	.66892
90	.72688	.72201	.71721	.71246	.70779	.70317	.69861	.69411	.68966	.68528
91	.74126	.73658	.73196	.72739	.72289	.71844	.71404	.70970	.70541	.70117
92	.75513	.75063	.74620	.74181	.73748	.73320	.72897	.72479	.72066	.71657
93	.76844	.76414	.75988	.75568	.75152	.74741	.74334	.73932	.73535	.73142
94	.78123	.77711	.77303	.76901	.76502	.76108	.75718	.75332	.74951	.74573
95	.79348	.78954	.78565	.78179	.77798	.77421	.77047	.76677	.76312	.75950
96	.80513	.80137	.79765	.79397	.79032	.78671	.78314	.77960	.77610	.77263
97	.81621	.81262	.80908	.80556	.80208	.79864	.79522	.79184	.78849	.78517
98	.82674	.82333	.81995	.81660	.81328	.80999	.80673	.80351	.80031	.79713
99	.83677	.83352	.83030	.82711	.82395	.82082	.81771	.81463	.81158	.80855
100	.84616	.84307	.84001	.83697	.83396	.83097	.82801	.82507	.82216	.81927
101	.85514	.85221	.84930	.84641	.84355	.84070	.83788	.83509	.83231	.82956
102	.86348	.86069	.85792	.85517	.85245	.84974	.84706	.84439	.84175	.83912
103	.87182	.86918	.86655	.86395	.86136	.85880	.85625	.85372	.85121	.84872
104	.87950	.87699	.87450	.87203	.86957	.86713	.86471	.86231	.85992	.85755
105	.88706	.88468	.88232	.87998	.87765	.87534	.87304	.87076	.86849	.86624
106	.89664	.89444	.89225	.89008	.88792	.88577	.88364	.88152	.87941	.87731
107	.90756	.90557	.90358	.90160	.89964	.89768	.89574	.89380	.89188	.88997
108	.92565	.92401	.92238	.92075	.91914	.91753	.91592	.91433	.91274	.91116
109	.96211	.96125	.96041	.95956	.95872	.95788	.95704	.95620	.95537	.95455

Table S
Based on Life Table 2000CM
Single Life Remainder Factors
Applicable On or After May 1, 2009

					Interest Rate					
AGE	10.2%	10.4%	10.6%	10.8%	11.0%	11.2%	11.4%	11.6%	11.8%	12.0%
0	.01132	.01110	.01089	.01071	.01053	.01037	.01022	.01008	.00995	.00983
1	.00520	.00497	.00476	.00457	.00439	.00423	.00407	.00393	.00379	.00367
2	.00521	.00496	.00474	.00454	.00435	.00417	.00401	.00385	.00371	.00358
3	.00539	.00513	.00490	.00468	.00447	.00429	.00411	.00395	.00380	.00366
4	.00567	.00540	.00515	.00492	.00470	.00450	.00432	.00414	.00398	.00383
5	.00603	.00574	.00547	.00523	.00500	.00478	.00459	.00440	.00423	.00407
6	.00646	.00615	.00587	.00560	.00536	.00513	.00492	.00472	.00453	.00436
7	.00693	.00660	.00630	.00602	.00576	.00551	.00529	.00508	.00488	.00469
8	.00747	.00712	.00680	.00650	.00622	.00596	.00572	.00549	.00528	.00509
9	.00808	.00771	.00737	.00705	.00675	.00648	.00622	.00598	.00576	.00555

See p. 15 for regulations not amended to reflect law changes

AGE	10.2%	10.4%	10.6%	10.8%	11.0%	11.2%	11.4%	11.6%	11.8%	12.0%
10	.00877	.00838	.00801	.00767	.00736	.00707	.00679	.00654	.00630	.00608
11	.00954	.00912	.00873	.00838	.00804	.00773	.00744	.00717	.00692	.00668
12	.01038	.00994	.00953	.00915	.00880	.00847	.00816	.00788	.00761	.00735
13	.01127	.01081	.01038	.00998	.00960	.00925	.00893	.00862	.00833	.00806
14	.01217	.01168	.01122	.01080	.01040	.01003	.00969	.00937	.00906	.00878
15	.01305	.01253	.01205	.01160	.01118	.01079	.01042	.01008	.00976	.00946
16	.01387	.01333	.01282	.01234	.01190	.01149	.01110	.01074	.01040	.01009
17	.01467	.01409	.01356	.01306	.01259	.01216	.01175	.01137	.01101	.01067
18	.01544	.01484	.01427	.01374	.01325	.01279	.01236	.01195	.01157	.01122
19	.01621	.01557	.01497	.01442	.01390	.01341	.01295	.01253	.01213	.01175
20	.01702	.01634	.01571	.01512	.01457	.01406	.01357	.01312	.01270	.01230
21	.01784	.01713	.01646	.01584	.01526	.01471	.01420	.01372	.01327	.01285
22	.01870	.01794	.01724	.01658	.01596	.01539	.01485	.01434	.01386	.01342
23	.01961	.01881	.01807	.01737	.01672	.01611	.01554	.01500	.01449	.01402
24	.02062	.01977	.01899	.01825	.01756	.01691	.01630	.01573	.01520	.01469
25	.02175	.02085	.02002	.01924	.01851	.01782	.01718	.01657	.01600	.01547
26	.02301	.02207	.02119	.02036	.01958	.01886	.01817	.01753	.01692	.01635
27	.02443	.02343	.02250	.02162	.02080	.02003	.01930	.01862	.01798	.01737
28	.02600	.02495	.02396	.02303	.02216	.02134	.02057	.01985	.01916	.01852
29	.02771	.02660	.02555	.02457	.02365	.02278	.02197	.02120	.02047	.01979
30	.02956	.02838	.02728	.02624	.02526	.02434	.02348	.02266	.02189	.02116
31	.03155	.03031	.02914	.02804	.02701	.02604	.02512	.02425	.02344	.02266
32	.03370	.03239	.03115	.02999	.02890	.02787	.02690	.02598	.02511	.02429
33	.03601	.03463	.03333	.03210	.03095	.02985	.02883	.02785	.02693	.02606
34	.03847	.03701	.03564	.03434	.03312	.03197	.03088	.02985	.02887	.02795
35	.04109	.03956	.03811	.03675	.03546	.03424	.03308	.03199	.03096	.02998
36	.04390	.04228	.04076	.03932	.03795	.03667	.03545	.03429	.03320	.03216
37	.04688	.04518	.04358	.04206	.04062	.03926	.03798	.03676	.03560	.03450
38	.05007	.04829	.04660	.04500	.04349	.04205	.04069	.03940	.03818	.03701
39	.05346	.05158	.04981	.04812	.04653	.04502	.04358	.04222	.04092	.03969
40	.05705	.05508	.05321	.05144	.04976	.04817	.04666	.04522	.04385	.04255
41	.06086	.05879	.05683	.05497	.05320	.05152	.04993	.04841	.04697	.04559
42	.06488	.06271	.06066	.05870	.05684	.05508	.05340	.05180	.05028	.04882
43	.06917	.06690	.06474	.06269	.06074	.05888	.05711	.05543	.05382	.05229
44	.07370	.07132	.06906	.06691	.06486	.06291	.06105	.05928	.05759	.05598
45	.07850	.07602	.07365	.07139	.06924	.06719	.06524	.06338	.06160	.05990
46	.08360	.08100	.07852	.07616	.07390	.07176	.06970	.06775	.06587	.06409
47	.08897	.08626	.08367	.08120	.07884	.07659	.07443	.07238	.07041	.06853
48	.09466	.09183	.08912	.08654	.08407	.08172	.07946	.07730	.07524	.07326
49	.10069	.09774	.09492	.09222	.08964	.08717	.08481	.08255	.08038	.07831
50	.10711	.10403	.10109	.09827	.09558	.09300	.09053	.08816	.08589	.08371
51	.11392	.11072	.10765	.10472	.10191	.09921	.09663	.09415	.09178	.08950
52	.12116	.11783	.11464	.11159	.10866	.10585	.10315	.10057	.09808	.09569
53	.12883	.12538	.12206	.11889	.11584	.11291	.11010	.10740	.10481	.10231
54	.13694	.13336	.12992	.12662	.12345	.12041	.11748	.11467	.11196	.10936
55	.14547	.14176	.13820	.13478	.13149	.12832	.12528	.12235	.11953	.11682
56	.15437	.15054	.14685	.14330	.13989	.13661	.13345	.13040	.12747	.12464
57	.16365	.15969	.15588	.15221	.14868	.14527	.14199	.13883	.13578	.13284
58	.17330	.16921	.16528	.16149	.15783	.15431	.15091	.14763	.14447	.14141
59	.18335	.17914	.17508	.17117	.16739	.16375	.16023	.15684	.15356	.15039
60	.19385	.18952	.18534	.18131	.17741	.17365	.17001	.16650	.16311	.15982
61	.20480	.20035	.19605	.19189	.18788	.18400	.18025	.17662	.17311	.16971
62	.21615	.21158	.20717	.20290	.19877	.19477	.19090	.18716	.18354	.18003
63	.22791	.22323	.21870	.21431	.21007	.20596	.20198	.19812	.19439	.19077
64	.24009	.23530	.23066	.22616	.22181	.21758	.21349	.20953	.20568	.20195

AGE	10.2%	10.4%	10.6%	10.8%	11.0%	11.2%	11.4%	11.6%	11.8%	12.0%
65	.25271	.24781	.24306	.23846	.23400	.22967	.22547	.22139	.21744	.21360
66	.26600	.26100	.25615	.25145	.24688	.24245	.23814	.23396	.22990	.22596
67	.27992	.27483	.26989	.26509	.26043	.25590	.25150	.24722	.24306	.23901
68	.29443	.28926	.28423	.27934	.27459	.26997	.26548	.26110	.25685	.25271
69	.30950	.30424	.29914	.29417	.28934	.28463	.28005	.27559	.27125	.26703
70	.32508	.31976	.31459	.30955	.30464	.29986	.29520	.29067	.28625	.28194
71	.34122	.33585	.33062	.32552	.32054	.31570	.31097	.30637	.30187	.29749
72	.35790	.35249	.34721	.34205	.33703	.33213	.32734	.32268	.31812	.31367
73	.37505	.36960	.36428	.35909	.35403	.34908	.34425	.33953	.33492	.33042
74	.39258	.38711	.38177	.37655	.37145	.36647	.36160	.35684	.35219	.34764
75	.41039	.40491	.39956	.39432	.38921	.38420	.37931	.37452	.36983	.36525
76	.42843	.42296	.41760	.41236	.40724	.40222	.39731	.39250	.38779	.38318
77	.44668	.44122	.43588	.43065	.42552	.42050	.41559	.41077	.40605	.40143
78	.46510	.45967	.45435	.44914	.44403	.43902	.43411	.42930	.42458	.41995
79	.48365	.47826	.47298	.46780	.46271	.45773	.45284	.44804	.44333	.43871
80	.50226	.49693	.49169	.48655	.48150	.47655	.47169	.46692	.46224	.45763
81	.52090	.51562	.51044	.50536	.50036	.49546	.49064	.48590	.48125	.47668
82	.53951	.53431	.52920	.52418	.51924	.51439	.50963	.50494	.50033	.49580
83	.55802	.55291	.54788	.54294	.53808	.53329	.52859	.52396	.51941	.51493
84	.57640	.57139	.56645	.56159	.55681	.55210	.54747	.54291	.53843	.53401
85	.59459	.58968	.58484	.58008	.57539	.57077	.56623	.56175	.55733	.55298
86	.61254	.60774	.60302	.59836	.59377	.58925	.58479	.58040	.57607	.57180
87	.63019	.62551	.62090	.61635	.61187	.60745	.60309	.59880	.59456	.59038
88	.64751	.64296	.63847	.63405	.62968	.62537	.62112	.61693	.61279	.60871
89	.66444	.66003	.65567	.65137	.64712	.64293	.63880	.63471	.63068	.62670
90	.68094	.67667	.67244	.66827	.66415	.66009	.65607	.65210	.64818	.64431
91	.69699	.69285	.68877	.68473	.68074	.67680	.67291	.66906	.66526	.66150
92	.71254	.70855	.70460	.70071	.69685	.69304	.68928	.68555	.68187	.67823
93	.72753	.72369	.71989	.71613	.71242	.70874	.70510	.70150	.69794	.69442
94	.74200	.73830	.73464	.73103	.72745	.72390	.72040	.71693	.71350	.71010
95	.75591	.75236	.74885	.74538	.74194	.73853	.73516	.73182	.72851	.72524
96	.76920	.76580	.76243	.75909	.75579	.75252	.74928	.74607	.74289	.73974
97	.78188	.77863	.77540	.77220	.76904	.76590	.76279	.75971	.75665	.75363
98	.79399	.79088	.78779	.78473	.78170	.77869	.77571	.77276	.76983	.76693
99	.80555	.80257	.79962	.79670	.79380	.79092	.78807	.78525	.78244	.77966
100	.81641	.81357	.81075	.80796	.80518	.80243	.79971	.79700	.79432	.79165
101	.82683	.82412	.82144	.81877	.81612	.81350	.81089	.80831	.80574	.80320
102	.83652	.83394	.83137	.82882	.82630	.82379	.82130	.81883	.81637	.81394
103	.84624	.84379	.84135	.83892	.83652	.83413	.83176	.82941	.82707	.82475
104	.85519	.85285	.85053	.84822	.84593	.84365	.84139	.83915	.83692	.83470
105	.86400	.86178	.85957	.85737	.85519	.85302	.85087	.84873	.84660	.84449
106	.87523	.87316	.87110	.86905	.86702	.86500	.86299	.86099	.85900	.85703
107	.88806	.88617	.88429	.88242	.88055	.87870	.87686	.87502	.87320	.87139
108	.90958	.90802	.90646	.90490	.90336	.90182	.90028	.89876	.89724	.89573
109	.95372	.95290	.95208	.95126	.95045	.94964	.94883	.94803	.94723	.94643

Table S
Based on Life Table 2000CM
Single Life Remainder Factors
Applicable On or After May 1, 2009

Interest Rate

AGE	12.2%	12.4%	12.6%	12.8%	13.0%	13.2%	13.4%	13.6%	13.8%	14.0%
0	.00972	.00961	.00951	.00941	.00932	.00924	.00916	.00908	.00901	.00894
1	.00355	.00345	.00334	.00325	.00316	.00307	.00299	.00292	.00285	.00278
2	.00346	.00334	.00323	.00313	.00303	.00294	.00286	.00278	.00270	.00263

See p. 15 for regulations not amended to reflect law changes

AGE	12.2%	12.4%	12.6%	12.8%	13.0%	13.2%	13.4%	13.6%	13.8%	14.0%
3	.00353	.00340	.00329	.00318	.00307	.00298	.00289	.00280	.00272	.00264
4	.00369	.00356	.00343	.00332	.00321	.00310	.00300	.00291	.00283	.00274
5	.00392	.00377	.00364	.00352	.00340	.00329	.00318	.00308	.00299	.00290
6	.00420	.00405	.00391	.00377	.00365	.00353	.00342	.00331	.00321	.00311
7	.00452	.00436	.00421	.00406	.00393	.00380	.00368	.00357	.00346	.00336
8	.00490	.00473	.00457	.00441	.00427	.00413	.00400	.00388	.00376	.00365
9	.00535	.00517	.00499	.00483	.00467	.00453	.00439	.00426	.00413	.00402
10	.00587	.00567	.00548	.00531	.00514	.00499	.00484	.00470	.00456	.00444
11	.00645	.00624	.00605	.00586	.00568	.00551	.00536	.00521	.00506	.00493
12	.00711	.00689	.00668	.00648	.00629	.00611	.00595	.00579	.00563	.00549
13	.00781	.00757	.00735	.00714	.00694	.00675	.00657	.00640	.00624	.00609
14	.00851	.00826	.00802	.00780	.00759	.00739	.00720	.00702	.00684	.00668
15	.00918	.00891	.00866	.00842	.00820	.00799	.00779	.00759	.00741	.00724
16	.00979	.00950	.00924	.00899	.00875	.00853	.00832	.00811	.00792	.00774
17	.01035	.01006	.00978	.00951	.00926	.00902	.00880	.00859	.00838	.00819
18	.01088	.01057	.01027	.00999	.00973	.00948	.00924	.00901	.00880	.00860
19	.01139	.01106	.01075	.01045	.01017	.00990	.00965	.00942	.00919	.00898
20	.01192	.01157	.01124	.01092	.01063	.01035	.01008	.00983	.00959	.00936
21	.01245	.01208	.01173	.01139	.01108	.01078	.01050	.01023	.00998	.00974
22	.01300	.01260	.01222	.01187	.01154	.01122	.01092	.01064	.01037	.01011
23	.01357	.01315	.01275	.01238	.01202	.01168	.01137	.01106	.01078	.01051
24	.01422	.01377	.01334	.01294	.01257	.01221	.01187	.01155	.01124	.01095
25	.01496	.01448	.01403	.01361	.01320	.01282	.01246	.01212	.01180	.01149
26	.01582	.01531	.01483	.01438	.01395	.01354	.01316	.01279	.01244	.01211
27	.01680	.01626	.01575	.01527	.01481	.01437	.01396	.01357	.01320	.01285
28	.01791	.01734	.01679	.01628	.01579	.01533	.01489	.01447	.01408	.01370
29	.01914	.01853	.01795	.01740	.01688	.01639	.01592	.01548	.01505	.01465
30	.02048	.01982	.01921	.01862	.01807	.01754	.01704	.01657	.01612	.01569
31	.02193	.02124	.02058	.01996	.01937	.01881	.01828	.01777	.01729	.01683
32	.02351	.02278	.02208	.02142	.02079	.02019	.01962	.01908	.01857	.01808
33	.02523	.02445	.02371	.02300	.02234	.02170	.02109	.02052	.01997	.01944
34	.02707	.02624	.02545	.02470	.02399	.02331	.02267	.02205	.02146	.02091
35	.02905	.02817	.02733	.02653	.02577	.02505	.02436	.02371	.02308	.02249
36	.03117	.03024	.02935	.02850	.02769	.02693	.02619	.02550	.02483	.02419
37	.03345	.03246	.03151	.03061	.02976	.02894	.02816	.02742	.02671	.02603
38	.03590	.03485	.03385	.03289	.03198	.03112	.03029	.02950	.02874	.02802
39	.03852	.03740	.03634	.03533	.03436	.03344	.03256	.03172	.03092	.03015
40	.04131	.04013	.03900	.03793	.03690	.03593	.03499	.03410	.03324	.03242
41	.04428	.04303	.04184	.04070	.03962	.03858	.03759	.03664	.03573	.03486
42	.04744	.04612	.04486	.04366	.04250	.04140	.04035	.03934	.03838	.03745
43	.05083	.04943	.04810	.04683	.04561	.04444	.04333	.04226	.04123	.04025
44	.05443	.05296	.05155	.05021	.04892	.04768	.04650	.04537	.04428	.04324
45	.05827	.05672	.05523	.05381	.05245	.05114	.04989	.04869	.04754	.04643
46	.06237	.06074	.05917	.05767	.05623	.05485	.05352	.05225	.05103	.04986
47	.06673	.06500	.06335	.06177	.06025	.05879	.05739	.05605	.05475	.05351
48	.07137	.06955	.06781	.06614	.06454	.06300	.06152	.06010	.05874	.05742
49	.07632	.07441	.07258	.07082	.06913	.06750	.06595	.06444	.06300	.06161
50	.08162	.07962	.07769	.07584	.07407	.07236	.07071	.06913	.06760	.06614
51	.08731	.08520	.08318	.08124	.07937	.07757	.07583	.07416	.07256	.07101
52	.09340	.09119	.08907	.08703	.08507	.08317	.08135	.07959	.07790	.07627
53	.09991	.09760	.09538	.09324	.09118	.08919	.08728	.08543	.08365	.08193
54	.10685	.10443	.10211	.09987	.09771	.09562	.09361	.09167	.08980	.08799
55	.11420	.11168	.10925	.10690	.10464	.10246	.10035	.09832	.09635	.09445
56	.12191	.11928	.11675	.11430	.11193	.10965	.10745	.10531	.10325	.10126
57	.13001	.12727	.12462	.12207	.11960	.11721	.11491	.11268	.11052	.10843

AGE	12.2%	12.4%	12.6%	12.8%	13.0%	13.2%	13.4%	13.6%	13.8%	14.0%
58	.13846	.13561	.13286	.13020	.12762	.12513	.12273	.12040	.11814	.11595
59	.14732	.14436	.14150	.13873	.13605	.13346	.13095	.12851	.12616	.12388
60	.15665	.15358	.15060	.14772	.14494	.14224	.13962	.13709	.13463	.13225
61	.16642	.16324	.16016	.15717	.15428	.15147	.14875	.14611	.14355	.14107
62	.17663	.17333	.17014	.16704	.16404	.16113	.15830	.15556	.15290	.15031
63	.18726	.18385	.18055	.17734	.17423	.17121	.16828	.16544	.16267	.15999
64	.19833	.19481	.19140	.18809	.18487	.18175	.17871	.17576	.17289	.17010
65	.20987	.20624	.20273	.19931	.19598	.19275	.18961	.18656	.18358	.18069
66	.22213	.21840	.21478	.21125	.20783	.20449	.20125	.19809	.19501	.19202
67	.23508	.23125	.22753	.22390	.22037	.21694	.21360	.21034	.20716	.20407
68	.24868	.24476	.24094	.23722	.23359	.23006	.22662	.22327	.22000	.21681
69	.26291	.25889	.25498	.25117	.24745	.24383	.24030	.23685	.23349	.23020
70	.27773	.27364	.26964	.26574	.26194	.25823	.25461	.25107	.24762	.24425
71	.29321	.28904	.28496	.28099	.27710	.27331	.26961	.26599	.26246	.25900
72	.30933	.30508	.30094	.29689	.29294	.28907	.28530	.28160	.27799	.27446
73	.32602	.32171	.31751	.31340	.30938	.30545	.30160	.29784	.29416	.29056
74	.34319	.33884	.33458	.33042	.32634	.32236	.31845	.31463	.31089	.30723
75	.36076	.35637	.35207	.34786	.34374	.33970	.33575	.33188	.32808	.32437
76	.37867	.37425	.36991	.36567	.36151	.35744	.35344	.34953	.34569	.34192
77	.39690	.39245	.38810	.38383	.37964	.37554	.37151	.36756	.36369	.35989
78	.41541	.41096	.40659	.40231	.39811	.39398	.38993	.38596	.38206	.37823
79	.43418	.42973	.42536	.42107	.41686	.41272	.40866	.40467	.40075	.39691
80	.45311	.44868	.44432	.44003	.43582	.43169	.42763	.42363	.41971	.41585
81	.47219	.46777	.46343	.45916	.45497	.45084	.44679	.44280	.43888	.43502
82	.49135	.48696	.48265	.47841	.47424	.47014	.46610	.46213	.45822	.45437
83	.51052	.50618	.50191	.49771	.49357	.48950	.48549	.48154	.47766	.47383
84	.52966	.52537	.52115	.51700	.51291	.50887	.50490	.50099	.49714	.49334
85	.54870	.54448	.54032	.53622	.53218	.52820	.52428	.52041	.51660	.51284
86	.56759	.56344	.55935	.55532	.55135	.54742	.54356	.53974	.53598	.53227
87	.58626	.58219	.57818	.57422	.57031	.56646	.56266	.55891	.55521	.55155
88	.60468	.60070	.59677	.59290	.58907	.58529	.58157	.57788	.57425	.57066
89	.62277	.61888	.61505	.61126	.60753	.60383	.60018	.59658	.59302	.58950
90	.64048	.63670	.63296	.62927	.62563	.62202	.61846	.61494	.61146	.60803
91	.65778	.65411	.65048	.64689	.64334	.63983	.63636	.63293	.62954	.62619
92	.67462	.67106	.66754	.66406	.66061	.65720	.65383	.65050	.64720	.64393
93	.69094	.68749	.68408	.68071	.67737	.67406	.67079	.66756	.66435	.66118
94	.70673	.70340	.70011	.69685	.69362	.69042	.68725	.68412	.68102	.67794
95	.72199	.71878	.71560	.71246	.70934	.70625	.70319	.70016	.69716	.69419
96	.73662	.73353	.73047	.72743	.72443	.72145	.71850	.71557	.71268	.70981
97	.75063	.74766	.74471	.74180	.73890	.73604	.73319	.73038	.72758	.72482
98	.76405	.76120	.75837	.75557	.75279	.75003	.74730	.74459	.74190	.73923
99	.77690	.77417	.77146	.76877	.76610	.76345	.76083	.75822	.75564	.75308
100	.78901	.78639	.78379	.78121	.77866	.77612	.77360	.77110	.76862	.76616
101	.80067	.79816	.79568	.79321	.79076	.78832	.78591	.78351	.78114	.77877
102	.81152	.80912	.80674	.80438	.80203	.79970	.79738	.79508	.79280	.79054
103	.82245	.82016	.81789	.81563	.81339	.81116	.80895	.80676	.80458	.80241
104	.83250	.83031	.82814	.82599	.82384	.82171	.81960	.81750	.81541	.81334
105	.84239	.84030	.83823	.83617	.83412	.83209	.83006	.82806	.82606	.82407
106	.85507	.85311	.85117	.84924	.84733	.84542	.84352	.84164	.83976	.83790
107	.86958	.86779	.86600	.86422	.86246	.86070	.85895	.85721	.85548	.85376
108	.89422	.89272	.89123	.88974	.88826	.88679	.88533	.88386	.88241	.88096
109	.94563	.94484	.94405	.94326	.94248	.94170	.94092	.94014	.93937	.93860

Table 2000CM

Age x	l_x	Age x	l_x	Age x	l_x
0	100000	37	96921	74	66882
1	99305	38	96767	75	64561
2	99255	39	96600	76	62091
3	99222	40	96419	77	59476
4	99197	41	96223	78	56721
5	99176	42	96010	79	53833
6	99158	43	95782	80	50819
7	99140	44	95535	81	47694
8	99124	45	95268	82	44475
9	99110	46	94981	83	41181
10	99097	47	94670	84	37837
11	99085	48	94335	85	34471
12	99073	49	93975	86	31114
13	99057	50	93591	87	27799
14	99033	51	93180	88	24564
15	98998	52	92741	89	21443
16	98950	53	92270	90	18472
17	98891	54	91762	91	15685
18	98822	55	91211	92	13111
19	98745	56	90607	93	10773
20	98664	57	89947	94	8690
21	98577	58	89225	95	6871
22	98485	59	88441	96	5315
23	98390	60	87595	97	4016
24	98295	61	86681	98	2959
25	98202	62	85691	99	2122
26	98111	63	84620	100	1477
27	98022	64	83465	101	997
28	97934	65	82224	102	650
29	97844	66	80916	103	410
30	97750	67	79530	104	248
31	97652	68	78054	105	144
32	97549	69	76478	106	81
33	97441	70	74794	107	43
34	97324	71	73001	108	22
35	97199	72	71092	109	11
36	97065	73	69056	110	0

(e) *Effective/applicability dates.*—This section applies on and after May 1, 2009. [Reg. §20.2031-7.]

☐ [*T.D.* 8540, 6-10-94. *Amended by T.D.* 8819, 4-29-99; *T.D.* 8886, 6-9-2000; *T.D.* 9448, 5-1-2009 *and T.D.* 9540, 8-9-2011.]

[Reg. §20.2031-7A]

§20.2031-7A. Valuation of annuities, interests for life or term of years, and remainder or reversionary interests for estates of decedents for which the valuation date of the gross estate is before May 1, 2009.—(a) *Valuation of annuities, interests for life or term of years, and remainder or reversionary interests for estates of decedents for which the valuation date of the gross estate is before January 1, 1952.*—Except as otherwise provided in §20.2031-7(b), if the valuation date of the decedent's gross estate is before January 1, 1952, the present value of annuities, life estates, terms for years, remainders, and reversions is their present value determined under this section. If the valuation of the interest involved is dependent upon the continuation or termination of one or more lives or upon a term certain concurrent with one or more lives, the factor for the present value is computed on the basis of interest at the rate of 4 percent a year, compounded annually, and life contingencies as to each life involved from values that are based on the Actuaries' or Combined Experience Table of Mortality, as extended. This table and related factors are described in former §81.10 (as contained in the 26 CFR Part 81 edition revised as of April 1, 1958). The present value of an interest measured by a term of years is computed on the basis of interest at the rate of 4 percent a year.

(b) *Valuation of annuities, interests for life or term of years, and remainder or reversionary interests for estates of decedents for which the valuation date of the gross estate is after December 31, 1951, and before January 1, 1971.*—

Except as otherwise provided in § 20.2031-7(b), if the valuation date for the decedent's gross estate is after December 31, 1951, and before January 1, 1971, the present value of annuities, life estates, terms of years, remainders, and reversions is their present value determined under this section. If the valuation of the interest involved is dependent upon the continuation or termination of one or more lives, or upon a term certain concurrent with one or more lives, the factor for the present value is computed on the basis of interest at the rate of 3 1/2 percent a year, compounded annually, and life contingencies as to each life involved are taken from U.S. Life Table 38. This table and related factors are set forth in former § 20.2031-7 (as contained in the 26 CFR Part 20 edition revised as of April 1, 1984). Special factors involving one and two lives may be found in or computed with the use of tables contained in the publication entitled "Actuarial Values for Estate and Gift Tax," Internal Revenue Service Publication Number 11 (Rev. 5-59). This publication is no longer available for purchase from the Superintendent of Documents. However, it may be obtained by requesting a copy from: CC:DOM:CORP:T:R (IRS Publication 11), room 5228, Internal Revenue Service, POB 7604, Ben Franklin Station, Washington, DC 20044. The present value of an interest measured by a term of years is computed on the basis of interest at the rate of 3 1/2 percent a year.

(c) *Valuation of annuities, interests for life or term of years, and remainder or reversionary interests for estates of decedents for which the valuation date of the gross estate is after December 31, 1970, and before December 1, 1983.*—Except as otherwise provided in § 20.2031-7(b), if the valuation date of the decedent's gross estate is after December 31, 1970, and before December 1, 1983, the present value of annuities, life estates, terms of years, remainders, and reversions is their present value determined under this section. If the valuation of the interest involved is dependent upon the continuation of or termination of one or more lives or upon a term certain concurrent with one or more lives, the factor for the present value is computed on the basis of interest at the rate of 6 percent a year, compounded annually, and life contingencies are determined as to each male and female life involved, from values that are set forth in Table LN. Table LN contains values that are taken from the life table for total males and the life table for total females appearing as Tables 2 and 3, respectively, in United States Life Tables: 1959-1960, published by the Department of Health and Human Services, Public Health Service. Table LN and related factors are set forth in former § 20.2031-10 (as contained in the 26 CFR Part 20 edition revised as of April 1, 1994 (see FEGT ¶ 6435)). Special factors involving one and two lives may be found in or computed with the use of tables contained in Internal Revenue Service Publication 723, "Actuarial Values I: Valuation of Last Survivor Charitable Remainders," (12-70), and Internal Revenue Service Publication 723A, "Actuarial Values II: Factors at 6 Percent Involving One and Two Lives," (12-70). These publications are no longer available for purchase from the Superintendent of Documents. However, a copy of each may be obtained from: CC:DOM:CORP:T:R (IRS Publication 723/723A), room 5228, Internal Revenue Service, POB 7604, Ben Franklin Station, Washington, DC 20044.

(d) *Valuation of annuities, interests for life or term of years, and remainder or reversionary interests for estates of decedents for which the valuation date of the gross estate is after November 30, 1983, and before May 1, 1989.*—(1) MDULIn general.—(i) Except as otherwise provided in § 20.2031-7(b), if the decedent died after November 30, 1983, and the valuation date for the gross estate is before May 1, 1989, the fair market value of annuities, life estates, terms of years, remainders, and reversions is their present value determined under this section. If the decedent died after November 30, 1983, and before August 9, 1984, or, in cases where the valuation date of the decedent's gross estate is before May 1, 1989, if, on December 1, 1983, the decedent was mentally incompetent so that the disposition of the decedent's property could not be changed, and the decedent died on or after December 1, 1983, without having regained competency to dispose of the decedent's property, or if the decedent died within 90 days of the date on which the decedent first regained competency, the fair market value of annuities, life estates, terms for years, remainders, and reversions included in the gross estate of such decedent is their present value determined under either this section or § 20.2031-7A(c), at the option of the taxpayer. The value of annuities issued by companies regularly engaged in their sale, and of insurance policies on the lives of persons other than the decedent, is determined under § 20.2031-8. The fair market value of a remainder interest in a charitable remainder unitrust, as defined in § 1.664-3 of this chapter, is its present value determined under § 1.664-4 of this chapter. The fair market value of a life interest or term for years in a charitable remainder unitrust is the fair market value of the property as of the date of valuation less the fair market value of the remainder interest on such date determined under § 1.664-4 of this chapter. The fair market value of the interests in a pooled income fund, as defined in § 1.642(c)-5 of this chapter, is their value determined under § 1.642(c)-6 of this chapter.

(ii) The present value of an annuity, life estate, remainder, or reversion determined under this section which is dependent on the continuation or termination of the life of one person is computed by the use of Table A in paragraph (d)(6) of this section. The present value of an annuity, term for years, remainder, or reversion dependent on a term certain is computed by the use of Table B in paragraph (d)(6) of this section. If the interest to be valued is dependent upon more than one life or there is a term certain concurrent with one or more lives, see paragraph (d)(5) of this section. For purposes of the computations described in this section, the age of a person is to be taken as the age of that person at his or her nearest birthday.

(iii) In all examples set forth in this section, the decedent is assumed to have died on or after August 9, 1984, with the valuation date of the decedent's gross estate before May 1, 1989, and to have been competent to change the disposition of the property on December 1, 1983.

(2) *Annuities.*—(i) If an annuity is payable annually at the end of each year during the life of an individual (as for example if the first payment is due one year after the decedent's death), the amount payable annually is multiplied by the figure in column 2 of Table A opposite the number of years in column 1 nearest the age of the individual whose life measures the duration of the annuity. If the annuity is payable annually at the end of each year for a definite number of years, the amount payable annually is multiplied by the figure in column 2 of Table B opposite the number of years in column 1 representing the duration of the annuity. The application of this paragraph (d)(2)(i) may be illustrated by the following examples:

Example (1). The decedent received, under the terms of the decedent's father's will an annuity of $10,000 a year payable annually for the life of the decedent's elder brother. At the time the decedent died, an annual payment had just been made. The brother at the decedent's death was 40 years eight months old. By reference to Table A, the figure in column 2 opposite 41 years, the number nearest to the brother's actual age, is found to be 9.1030. The present value of the annuity at the date of the decedent's death is, therefore, $91,030 ($10,000 × 9.1030).

Example (2). The decedent was entitled to receive an annuity of $10,000 a year payable annually throughout a term certain. At the time the decedent died, the annual payment had just been made and five more annual payments were still to be made. By reference to Table B, it is found that the figure in column 2 opposite five years is 3.7908. The present value of the annuity is, therefore, $37,908 ($10,000 × 3.7908).

(ii) If an annuity is payable at the end of semiannual, quarterly, monthly, or weekly periods during the life of an individual (as for example if the first payment is due one month after the decedent's death), the aggregate amount to be paid within a year is first multiplied by the figure in column 2 of Table A opposite the number of years in column 1 nearest the age of the individual whose life measures the duration of the annuity. The product so obtained is then multiplied by whichever of the following factors is appropriate:

1.0244 for semiannual payments,

1.0368 for quarterly payments,

1.0450 for monthly payments,

1.0482 for weekly payments.

If the annuity is payable at the end of semiannual, quarterly, monthly or weekly periods for a definite number of years, the aggregate amount to be paid within a year is first multiplied by the figure in column 2 of Table B opposite the number of years in column 1 representing the duration of the annuity. The product so obtained is then multiplied by whichever of the above factors is appropriate. The application of this paragraph (d)(2)(ii) may be illustrated by the following example.

Example. The facts are the same as those contained in example (1) set forth in paragraph (d)(2)(i) of this section, except that the annuity is payable semiannually. The aggregate annual amount, $10,000, is multiplied by the factor 9.1030 and the product multiplied by 1.0244. The present value of the annuity at the date of the decedent's death is, therefore, $93,251.13 ($10,000 × 9.1030 × 1.0244).

(iii)(A) If the first payment of an annuity for the life of an individual is due at the beginning of the annual or other payment period rather than at the end (as for example if the first payment is to be made immediately after the decedent's death), the value of the annuity is the sum of (A) the first payment plus (B) the present value of a similar annuity, the first payment of which is not to be made until the end of the payment period, determined as provided in paragraphs (d)(2)(i) or (ii) of this section, the application of this paragraph (d)(2)(iii)(A) may be illustrated by the following example:

Example. The decedent was entitled to receive an annuity of $50 a month during the life of another person. The decedent died on the date the payment was due. At the date of the decedent's death, the person whose life measures the duration of the annuity was 50 years of age. The value of the annuity at the date of the decedent's death is $50 plus the product of $50 × 12 × 8.4743 (see Table A) × 1.0450 (See paragraph (d)(2)(ii) of this section). That is $50 plus $5,313.39, or $5,363.39.

(B) If the first payment of an annuity for a definite number of years is due at the beginning of the annual or other payment period, the applicable factor is the product of the factor shown in Table B multiplied by whichever of the following factors is appropriate:

1.1000 for annual payments,

1.0744 for semiannual payments,

1.0618 for quarterly payments,

1.0534 for monthly payments,

1.0502 for weekly payments.

The application of this paragraph (d)(2)(iii)(B) may be illustrated by the following example:

Example. The decedent was the beneficiary of an annuity of $50 a month. On the day a payment was due, the decedent died. There were 300 payments to be made, including the payment due. The value of the annuity as of the date of decedent's death is the product of $50 × 12 × 9.0770 (see Table B) × 1.0534, or $5,737.03.

(3) *Life estates and terms for years.*—If the interest to be valued is the right of a person for his or her life, or for the life of another person, to receive the income of certain property or to use nonincome-producing property, the value of the interest is the value of the property multiplied by the figure in column 3 of Table A opposite the number of years nearest to the actual age of the measuring life. If the interest to be valued is the right to receive income of property or to use nonincome-producing property for a term of years, column 3 of Table B is used. The application of this paragraph (d)(3) may be illustrated by the following example:

Example. The decedent or the decedent's estate was entitled to receive the income from a fund of $50,000 during the life of the decedent's elder brother. Upon the brother's death, the remainder is to go to B. The brother was 31 years, five months old at the time of the decedent's death. By reference to Table A the figure in column 3 opposite 31 years is found to be 0.95254. The present value of the decedent's interest is, therefore, $47,627 ($50,000 × 0.95254).

(4) *Remainders or reversionary interests.*—If a decedent had, at the time of the decedent's death, a remainder or a reversionary interest in property to take effect after an estate for the life of another, the present value of the decedent's interest is obtained by multiplying the value of the property by the figure in column 4 of Table A opposite the number of years nearest to the actual age of the person whose life measures the preceding estate. If the remainder or reversion is to take effect at the end of the term for years, column 4 of Table B is used. The application of this paragraph (d)(4) may be illustrated by the following example:

Example. The decedent was entitled to receive certain property worth $50,000 upon the death of the decedent's elder sister, to whom the income was bequeathed for life. At the time of the decedent's death, the elder sister was 31 years five months old. By reference to Table A the figure in column 4 opposite 31 years is found to be .04746. The present value of the remainder interest at the date of the decedent's death is, therefore, $2,373 ($50,000 × .04746).

(5) *Actuarial computation by the Internal Revenue Service.*—If the valuation of the interest involved is dependent upon the continuation or the termination of more than one life or upon a term certain concurrent with one or more lives a special factor must be used. The factor is to be computed on the basis of interest at the rate of 10 percent a year, compounded annually, and life contingencies determined, as to each person involved, from the values of 1x that are set forth in column 2 of Table LN of paragraph (d)(6). Table LN contains values of *lx* taken from the life table for the total population appearing as Table 1 of United States Life Tables: 1969-71, published by the Department of Health and Human Services, Public Health Service. Many special factors involving one and two lives may be found in or computed with the use of the tables contained in Internal Revenue Service Publication 723E, "Actuarial Values II: Factors at 10 Percent Involving One and Two Lives," (12-83). This publication is no longer available for purchase from the Superintendent of Documents. However, it may be obtained by requesting a copy from: CC:DOM:CORP:T:R (IRS Publication 723E), room 5228, Internal Revenue Service, POB 7604, Ben Franklin Station, Washington, DC 20044. However, if a special factor is required in the case of an actual decedent, the Commission will furnish the factor to the executor upon request. The request must be accompanied by a statement of the date of birth of each person, the duration of whose life may affect the value of the interest, and by copies of the relevant instruments. Special factors are not furnished for prospective transfers.

(6) *Tables.*—The following tables shall be used in the application of the provisions of this section:

See p. 15 for regulations not amended to reflect law changes

TABLE A

TABLE A—SINGLE LIFE, UNISEX, 10 PERCENT—TABLE SHOWING THE PRESENT WORTH OF AN ANNUITY, OF A LIFE ESTATE, AND A REMAINDER INTEREST—APPLICABLE FOR TRANSFERS AFTER NOVEMBER 30, 1983, AND BEFORE MAY 1, 1989

Age (1)	*Annuity* (2)	*Life Estate* (3)	*Remainder* (4)	*Age* (1)	*Annuity* (2)	*Life Estate* (3)	*Remainder* (4)
0	9.7188	.97188	.02812	55	8.0046	.80046	.19954
1	9.8988	.98988	.01012	56	7.9006	.79006	.20994
2	9.9017	.99017	.00983	57	7.7931	.77931	.22069
3	9.9008	.99008	.00992	58	7.6822	.76822	.23178
4	9.8981	.98981	.01019	59	7.5675	.75675	.24325
5	9.8938	.98938	.01062	60	7.4491	.74491	.25509
6	9.8884	.98884	.01116	61	7.3267	.73267	.26733
7	9.8822	.98822	.01178	62	7.2002	.72002	.27998
8	9.8748	.98748	.01252	63	7.0696	.70696	.29304
9	9.8663	.98663	.01337	64	6.9352	.69352	.30648
10	9.8565	.98565	.01435	65	6.7970	.67970	.32030
11	9.8453	.98453	.01547	66	6.6551	.66551	.33449
12	9.8329	.98329	.01671	67	6.5098	.65098	.34902
13	9.8198	.98198	.01802	68	6.3610	.63610	.36390
14	9.8066	.98066	.01934	69	6.2086	.62086	.37914
15	9.7937	.97937	.02063	70	6.0522	.60522	.39478
16	9.7815	.97815	.02185	71	5.8914	.58914	.41086
17	9.7700	.97700	.02300	72	5.7261	.57261	.42739
18	9.7590	.97590	.02410	73	5.5571	.55571	.44429
19	9.7480	.97480	.02520	74	5.3862	.53862	.46138
20	9.7365	.97365	.02635	75	5.2149	.52149	.47851
21	9.7245	.97245	.02755	76	5.0441	.50441	.49559
22	9.7120	.97120	.02880	77	4.8742	.48742	.51258
23	9.6986	.96986	.03014	78	4.7049	.47049	.52951
24	9.6841	.96841	.03159	79	4.5357	.45357	.54643
25	9.6678	.96678	.03322	80	4.3659	.43659	.56341
26	9.6495	.96495	.03505	81	4.1967	.41967	.58033
27	9.6290	.96290	.03710	82	4.0295	.40295	.59705
28	9.6062	.96062	.03938	83	3.8642	.38642	.61358
29	9.5813	.95813	.04187	84	3.6998	.36998	.63002
30	9.5543	.95543	.04457	85	3.5359	.35359	.64641
31	9.5254	.95254	.04746	86	3.3764	.33764	.66236
32	9.4942	.94942	.05058	87	3.2262	.32262	.67738
33	9.4608	.94608	.05392	88	3.0859	.30859	.69141
34	9.4250	.94250	.05750	89	2.9526	.29526	.70474
35	9.3868	.93868	.06132	90	2.8221	.28221	.71779
36	9.3460	.93460	.06540	91	2.6955	.26955	.73045
37	9.3026	.93026	.06974	92	2.5771	.25771	.74229
38	9.2567	.92567	.07433	93	2.4692	.24692	.75308
39	9.2083	.92083	.07917	94	2.3728	.23728	.76272
40	9.1571	.91571	.08429	95	2.2887	.22887	.77113
41	9.1030	.91030	.08970	96	2.2181	.22181	.77819
42	9.0457	.90457	.09543	97	2.1550	.21550	.78450
43	8.9855	.89855	.10145	98	2.1000	.21000	.79000
44	8.9221	.89221	.10779	99	2.0486	.20486	.79514
45	8.8558	.88558	.11442	100	1.9975	.19975	.80025
46	8.7863	.87863	.12137	101	1.9532	.19532	.80468
47	8.7137	.87137	.12863	102	1.9054	.19054	.80946
48	8.6374	.86374	.13626	103	1.8437	.18437	.81563
49	8.5578	.85578	.14422	104	1.7856	.17856	.82144
50	8.4743	.84743	.15257	105	1.6962	.16962	.83038
51	8.3874	.83874	.16126	106	1.5488	.15488	.84512
52	8.2969	.82969	.17031	107	1.3409	.13409	.86591
53	8.2028	.82028	.17972	108	1.0068	.10068	.89932
54	8.1054	.81054	.18946	109	0.4545	.04545	.95455

TABLE B

TABLE B—TERM CERTAIN, UNISEX, 10 PERCENT—TABLE SHOWING THE PRESENT WORTH OF AN ANNUITY FOR A TERM CERTAIN, OF AN INCOME INTEREST FOR A TERM CERTAIN, AND OF A REMAINDER INTEREST POSTPONED FOR A TERM CERTAIN—APPLICABLE FOR TRANSFERS AFTER NOVEMBER 30, 1983, AND BEFORE MAY 1, 1989

(1) Number of Years	*(2) Annuity*	*(3) Term Certain*	*(4) Remainder*	*(1) Number of Years*	*(2) Annuity*	*(3) Term Certain*	*(4) Remainder*
1	0.9091	.090909	.909091	31	9.4790	.947901	.052099
2	1.7355	.173554	.826446	32	9.5264	.952638	.047362
3	2.4869	.248685	.751315	33	9.5694	.956943	.043057
4	3.1699	.316987	.683013	34	9.6086	.960857	.039143
5	3.7908	.379079	.620921	35	9.6442	.964416	.035584
6	4.3553	.435526	.564474	36	9.6765	.967651	.032349
7	4.8684	.486842	.513158	37	9.7059	.970592	.029408
8	5.3349	.533493	.466507	38	9.7327	.973265	.026735
9	5.7590	.575902	.424098	39	9.7570	.975686	.024304
10	6.1446	.614457	.385543	40	9.7791	.977905	.022095
11	6.4951	.649506	.350494	41	9.7991	.979914	.020096
12	6.8137	.681369	.318631	42	9.8174	.981740	.018260
13	7.1034	.710336	.289664	43	9.8340	.983400	.016600
14	7.3667	.736669	.263331	44	9.8491	.984909	.015091
15	7.6061	.760608	.239392	45	9.8628	.986281	.013718
16	7.8237	.782371	.217629	46	9.8753	.987528	.012472
17	8.0216	.802155	.197845	47	9.8866	.988662	.011338
18	8.2014	.820141	.179859	48	9.8969	.989693	.010307
19	8.3649	.836492	.163508	49	9.9063	.990630	.009370
20	8.5136	.851356	.148644	50	9.9148	.991481	.008519
21	8.6487	.864869	.135131	51	9.9226	.992256	.007744
22	8.7715	.877154	.122846	52	9.9296	.992960	.007040
23	8.8832	.888322	.111678	53	9.9360	.993600	.006400
24	8.9847	.898474	.101526	54	9.9418	.994182	.005818
25	9.0770	.907704	.092296	55	9.9471	.994711	.005289
26	9.1609	.916095	.083905	56	9.9519	.995191	.004809
27	9.2372	.923722	.076278	57	9.9563	.995629	.004371
28	9.3066	.930657	.069343	58	9.9603	.996026	.003974
29	9.3696	.936961	.063039	59	9.9639	.996387	.003613
30	9.4269	.942691	.057309	60	9.9672	.996716	.003284

TABLE LN

TABLE LN—APPLICABLE FOR TRANSFERS AFTER NOVEMBER 30, 1983, AND BEFORE MAY 1, 1989

Age X (1)	*lx (2)*	*Age X (1)*	*lx (2)*	*Age X (1)*	*lx (2)*	*Age X (1)*	*lx (2)*	*Age X (1)*	*lx (2)*	*Age X (1)*	*lx (2)*
0	100000	19	96846	38	93843	57	83103	76	46946	95	2786
1	97998	20	96716	39	93593	58	81988	77	44101	96	2068
2	97876	21	96580	40	93322	59	80798	78	41192	97	1511
3	97792	22	96438	41	93028	60	79529	79	38245	98	1087
4	97724	23	96292	42	92712	61	78181	80	35285	99	772
5	97668	24	96145	43	92368	62	76751	81	32323	100	542
6	97619	25	96000	44	91995	63	75236	82	29375	101	375
7	97573	26	95859	45	91587	64	73631	83	26469	102	257
8	97531	27	95721	46	91144	65	71933	84	23638	103	175
9	97494	28	95586	47	90662	66	70139	85	20908	104	117
10	97460	29	95448	48	90142	67	68246	86	18282	105	78
11	97430	30	95307	49	89579	68	66254	87	15769	106	52
12	97401	31	95158	50	88972	69	64166	88	13407	107	34
13	97367	32	95003	51	88315	70	61984	89	11240	108	22
14	97322	33	94840	52	87605	71	59715	90	9297	109	14
15	97261	34	94666	53	86838	72	57360	91	7577	110	0
16	97181	35	94482	54	86007	73	54913	92	6070		
17	97083	36	94285	55	85110	74	52363	93	4773		
18	96970	37	94073	56	84142	75	49705	94	3682		

(e) *Valuation of annuities, interests for life or term of years, and remainder or reversionary interests for estates of decedents for which the valuation date of the gross estate is after April 30,1989, and before May 1, 1999.*—(1) *In general.*—Except as otherwise provided in § 20.2031-7(b) and § 20.7520-3(b) (pertaining to certain limitations on the use of prescribed tables), if the valuation date for the gross estate of the decedent is after April 30, 1989, and before May 1, 1999, the fair market value of annuities, life estates, terms of years, remainders, and reversionary interests is the present value of the interests determined by use of standard or special section 7520 actuarial factors and the valuation methodology described in § 20.2031-7(d). These factors are derived by using the appropriate section 7520 interest rate and, if applicable, the mortality component for the valuation date of the interest that is being valued. See § § 20.7520-1 through 20.7520-4. See paragraph (e)(4) of this section for determination of the appropriate table for use in valuing these interests.

(2) *Transitional rule.*—(i) If the valuation date is after April 30, 1989, and before June 10, 1994, a taxpayer can rely on Notice 89-24 (1989-1 C.B. 660), or Notice 89-60 (1989-1 C.B. 700). See § 601.601(d)(2)(ii)(*b*) of this chapter.

(ii) If a decedent dies after April 30, 1989, and if on May 1, 1989, the decedent was mentally incompetent so that the disposition of the decedent's property could not be changed, and the decedent dies without having regained competency to dispose of the decedent's property or dies within 90 days of the date on which the decedent first regains competency, the fair market value of annuities, life estates, terms for years, remainders, and reversions included in the gross estate of the decedent is their present value determined either under this section or under the corresponding section applicable at the time the decedent became mentally incompetent, at the option of the decedent's executor. For example, see paragraph (d) of this section.

(3) *Publications and actuarial computations by the Internal Revenue Service.*—Many standard actuarial factors not included in paragraph (e)(4) of this section or in § 20.2031-7(d)(6) are included in Internal Revenue Service Publication 1457, "Actuarial Values, Alpha Volume," (8-89). Publication 1457 also includes examples that illustrate how to compute many special factors for more unusual situations. Publication 1457 is no longer available for purchase from the Superintendent of Documents, United States Government Printing Office, Washington, DC 20402. However, pertinent factors in this publication may be obtained from: CC:DOM:CORP:R (IRS Publication 1457), room 5226, Internal Revenue Service, POB 7604, Ben Franklin Station, Washington, DC 20044. If a special factor is required in the case of an actual decedent, the Internal Revenue Service may furnish the factor to the executor upon a request for a ruling. The request for a ruling must be accompanied by a recitation of the facts including a statement of the date of birth for each measuring life, the date of the decedent's death, any other applicable dates, and a copy of the will, trust, or other relevant documents. A request for a ruling must comply with the instructions for requesting a ruling published periodically in the Internal Revenue Bulletin (see § § 601.201 and 601.601(d)(2)(ii)(*b*) of this chapter) and include payment of the required user fee.

(4) *Actuarial tables.*—Except as provided in § 20.7520-3(b) (pertaining to certain limitations on the use of prescribed tables), Life Table 80CNSMT and Table S (Single life remainder factors applicable where the valuation date is

after April 30, 1989, and before May 1, 1999), contained in this paragraph (e)(4), and Table B, Table J, and Table K set forth in § 20.2031-7(d)(6) must be used in the application of the provisions of this section when the section 7520 interest rate component is between 4.2 and 14 percent. Table S and Table 80CNSMT are as follows:

TABLE S
BASED ON LIFE TABLE 80CNSMT
SINGLE LIFE REMAINDER FACTORS
APPLICABLE AFTER APRIL 30, 1989,
AND BEFORE MAY 1, 1999
INTEREST RATE

AGE	*4.2%*	*4.4%*	*4.6%*	*4.8%*	*5.0%*	*5.2%*	*5.4%*	*5.6%*	*5.8%*	*6.0%*
0	.07389	.06749	.06188	.05695	.05261	.04879	.04541	.04243	.03978	.03744
1	.06494	.05832	.05250	.04738	.04287	.03889	.03537	.03226	.02950	.02705
2	.06678	.05999	.05401	.04874	.04410	.03999	.03636	.03314	.03028	.02773
3	.06897	.06200	.05587	.05045	.04567	.04143	.03768	.03435	.03139	.02875
4	.07139	.06425	.05796	.05239	.04746	.04310	.03922	.03578	.03271	.02998
5	.07401	.06669	.06023	.05451	.04944	.04494	.04094	.03738	.03421	.03137
6	.07677	.06928	.06265	.05677	.05156	.04692	.04279	.03911	.03583	.03289
7	.07968	.07201	.06521	.05918	.05381	.04903	.04477	.04097	.03757	.03453
8	.08274	.07489	.06792	.06172	.05621	.05129	.04689	.04297	.03945	.03630
9	.08597	.07794	.07079	.06443	.05876	.05370	.04917	.04511	.04148	.03821
10	.08936	.08115	.07383	.06730	.06147	.05626	.05159	.04741	.04365	.04027
11	.09293	.08453	.07704	.07035	.06436	.05900	.05419	.04988	.04599	.04250
12	.09666	.08807	.08040	.07354	.06739	.06188	.05693	.05248	.04847	.04486
13	.10049	.09172	.08387	.07684	.07053	.06487	.05977	.05518	.05104	.04731
14	.10437	.09541	.08738	.08017	.07370	.06788	.06263	.05791	.05364	.04978
15	.10827	.09912	.09090	.08352	.07688	.07090	.06551	.06064	.05623	.05225
16	.11220	.10285	.09445	.08689	.08008	.07394	.06839	.06337	.05883	.05472
17	.11615	.10661	.09802	.09028	.08330	.07699	.07129	.06612	.06144	.05719
18	.12017	.11043	.10165	.09373	.08656	.08009	.07422	.06890	.06408	.05969
19	.12428	.11434	.10537	.09726	.08992	.08327	.07724	.07177	.06679	.06226
20	.12850	.11836	.10919	.10089	.09337	.08654	.08035	.07471	.06959	.06492
21	.13282	.12248	.11311	.10462	.09692	.08991	.08355	.07775	.07247	.06765
22	.13728	.12673	.11717	.10848	.10059	.09341	.08686	.08090	.07546	.07049
23	.14188	.13113	.12136	.11248	.10440	.09703	.09032	.08418	.07858	.07345
24	.14667	.13572	.12575	.11667	.10839	.10084	.09395	.08764	.08187	.07659
25	.15167	.14051	.13034	.12106	.11259	.10486	.09778	.09130	.08536	.07991
26	.15690	.14554	.13517	.12569	.11703	.10910	.10184	.09518	.08907	.08346
27	.16237	.15081	.14024	.13056	.12171	.11359	.10614	.09930	.09302	.08724
28	.16808	.15632	.14555	.13567	.12662	.11831	.11068	.10366	.09720	.09125
29	.17404	.16208	.15110	.14104	.13179	.12329	.11547	.10827	.10163	.09551
30	.18025	.16808	.15692	.14665	.13721	.12852	.12051	.11313	.10631	.10002
31	.18672	.17436	.16300	.15255	.14291	.13403	.12584	.11827	.11127	.10480
32	.19344	.18090	.16935	.15870	.14888	.13980	.13142	.12367	.11650	.10985
33	.20044	.18772	.17598	.16514	.15513	.14587	.13730	.12936	.12201	.11519
34	.20770	.19480	.18287	.17185	.16165	.15221	.14345	.13533	.12780	.12080
35	.21522	.20215	.19005	.17884	.16846	.15883	.14989	.14159	.13388	.12670
36	.22299	.20974	.19747	.18609	.17552	.16571	.15660	.14812	.14022	.13287
37	.23101	.21760	.20516	.19360	.18286	.17288	.16358	.15492	.14685	.13933
38	.23928	.22572	.21311	.20139	.19048	.18032	.17085	.16201	.15377	.14607
39	.24780	.23409	.22133	.20945	.19837	.18804	.17840	.16939	.16097	.15310
40	.25658	.24273	.22982	.21778	.20654	.19605	.18624	.17706	.16847	.16043
41	.26560	.25163	.23858	.22639	.21499	.20434	.19436	.18502	.17627	.16806
42	.27486	.26076	.24758	.23525	.22370	.21289	.20276	.19326	.18434	.17597
43	.28435	.27013	.25683	.24436	.23268	.22172	.21143	.20177	.19270	.18416
44	.29407	.27975	.26633	.25373	.24191	.23081	.22038	.21057	.20134	.19265
45	.30402	.28961	.27608	.26337	.25142	.24019	.22962	.21966	.21028	.20144
46	.31420	.29970	.28608	.27326	.26120	.24983	.23913	.22904	.21951	.21053
47	.32460	.31004	.29632	.28341	.27123	.25975	.24892	.23870	.22904	.21991
48	.33521	.32058	.30679	.29379	.28151	.26992	.25897	.24862	.23883	.22957
49	.34599	.33132	.31746	.30438	.29201	.28032	.26926	.25879	.24888	.23949
50	.35695	.34224	.32833	.31518	.30273	.29094	.27978	.26921	.25918	.24966
51	.36809	.35335	.33940	.32619	.31367	.30180	.29055	.27987	.26973	.26010
52	.37944	.36468	.35070	.33744	.32486	.31292	.30158	.29081	.28057	.27083
53	.39098	.37622	.36222	.34892	.33629	.32429	.31288	.30203	.29170	.28186

See p. 15 for regulations not amended to reflect law changes

AGE	4.2%	4.4%	4.6%	4.8%	5.0%	5.2%	5.4%	5.6%	5.8%	6.0%
54	.40269	.38794	.37393	.36062	.34795	.33590	.32442	.31349	.30308	.29316
55	.41457	.39985	.38585	.37252	.35983	.34774	.33621	.32522	.31474	.30473
56	.42662	.41194	.39796	.38464	.37193	.35981	.34824	.33720	.32666	.31658
57	.43884	.42422	.41028	.39697	.38426	.37213	.36053	.34945	.33885	.32872
58	.45123	.43668	.42279	.40951	.39682	.38468	.37307	.36196	.35132	.34114
59	.46377	.44931	.43547	.42224	.40958	.39745	.38584	.37471	.36405	.35383
60	.47643	.46206	.44830	.43513	.42250	.41040	.39880	.38767	.37699	.36674
61	.48916	.47491	.46124	.44814	.43556	.42350	.41192	.40080	.39012	.37985
62	.50196	.48783	.47427	.46124	.44874	.43672	.42518	.41408	.40340	.39314
63	.51480	.50081	.48736	.47444	.46201	.45006	.43856	.42749	.41684	.40658
64	.52770	.51386	.50054	.48773	.47540	.46352	.45208	.44105	.43043	.42019
65	.54069	.52701	.51384	.50115	.48892	.47713	.46577	.45480	.44422	.43401
66	.55378	.54029	.52727	.51472	.50262	.49093	.47965	.46876	.45824	.44808
67	.56697	.55368	.54084	.52845	.51648	.50491	.49373	.48293	.47248	.46238
68	.58026	.56717	.55453	.54231	.53049	.51905	.50800	.49729	.48694	.47691
69	.59358	.58072	.56828	.55624	.54459	.53330	.52238	.51179	.50154	.49160
70	.60689	.59427	.58205	.57021	.55874	.54762	.53683	.52638	.51624	.50641
71	.62014	.60778	.59578	.58415	.57287	.56193	.55131	.54100	.53099	.52126
72	.63334	.62123	.60948	.59808	.58700	.57624	.56579	.55563	.54577	.53617
73	.64648	.63465	.62315	.61198	.60112	.59056	.58029	.57030	.56059	.55113
74	.65961	.64806	.63682	.62590	.61527	.60492	.59485	.58504	.57550	.56620
75	.67274	.66149	.65054	.63987	.62948	.61936	.60950	.59990	.59053	.58140
76	.68589	.67495	.66429	.65390	.64377	.63390	.62427	.61487	.60570	.59676
77	.69903	.68841	.67806	.66796	.65811	.64849	.63910	.62993	.62097	.61223
78	.71209	.70182	.69179	.68199	.67242	.66307	.65393	.64501	.63628	.62775
79	.72500	.71507	.70537	.69588	.68660	.67754	.66867	.65999	.65151	.64321
80	.73768	.72809	.71872	.70955	.70058	.69180	.68320	.67479	.66655	.65849
81	.75001	.74077	.73173	.72288	.71422	.70573	.69741	.68926	.68128	.67345
82	.76195	.75306	.74435	.73582	.72746	.71926	.71123	.70335	.69562	.68804
83	.77346	.76491	.75654	.74832	.74026	.73236	.72460	.71699	.70952	.70219
84	.78456	.77636	.76831	.76041	.75265	.74503	.73756	.73021	.72300	.71592
85	.79530	.78743	.77971	.77212	.76466	.75733	.75014	.74306	.73611	.72928
86	.80560	.79806	.79065	.78337	.77621	.76917	.76225	.75544	.74875	.74216
87	.81535	.80813	.80103	.79404	.78717	.78041	.77375	.76720	.76076	.75442
88	.82462	.81771	.81090	.80420	.79760	.79111	.78472	.77842	.77223	.76612
89	.83356	.82694	.82043	.81401	.80769	.80147	.79533	.78929	.78334	.77747
90	.84225	.83593	.82971	.82357	.81753	.81157	.80570	.79991	.79420	.78857
91	.85058	.84455	.83861	.83276	.82698	.82129	.81567	.81013	.80466	.79927
92	.85838	.85263	.84696	.84137	.83585	.83040	.82503	.81973	.81449	.80933
93	.86557	.86009	.85467	.84932	.84405	.83884	.83370	.82862	.82360	.81865
94	.87212	.86687	.86169	.85657	.85152	.84653	.84160	.83673	.83192	.82717
95	.87801	.87298	.86801	.86310	.85825	.85345	.84872	.84404	.83941	.83484
96	.88322	.87838	.87360	.86888	.86420	.85959	.85502	.85051	.84605	.84165
97	.88795	.88328	.87867	.87411	.86961	.86515	.86074	.85639	.85208	.84782
98	.89220	.88769	.88323	.87883	.87447	.87016	.86589	.86167	.85750	.85337
99	.89612	.89176	.88745	.88318	.87895	.87478	.87064	.86656	.86251	.85850
100	.89977	.89555	.89136	.88722	.88313	.87908	.87506	.87109	.86716	.86327
101	.90326	.89917	.89511	.89110	.88712	.88318	.87929	.87543	.87161	.86783
102	.90690	.90294	.89901	.89513	.89128	.88746	.88369	.87995	.87624	.87257
103	.91076	.90694	.90315	.89940	.89569	.89200	.88835	.88474	.88116	.87760
104	.91504	.91138	.90775	.90415	.90058	.89704	.89354	.89006	.88661	.88319
105	.92027	.91681	.91337	.90996	.90658	.90322	.89989	.89659	.89331	.89006
106	.92763	.92445	.92130	.91816	.91506	.91197	.90890	.90586	.90284	.89983
107	.93799	.93523	.93249	.92977	.92707	.92438	.92170	.91905	.91641	.91378
108	.95429	.95223	.95018	.94814	.94611	.94409	.94208	.94008	.93809	.93611
109	.97985	.97893	.97801	.97710	.97619	.97529	.97438	.97348	.97259	.97170

TABLE S
BASED ON LIFE TABLE 80CNSMT
SINGLE LIFE REMAINDER FACTORS
APPLICABLE AFTER APRIL 30, 1989,
AND BEFORE MAY 1, 1999
INTEREST RATE

AGE	*6.2%*	*6.4%*	*6.6%*	*6.8%*	*7.0%*	*7.2%*	*7.4%*	*7.6%*	*7.8%*	*8.0%*
0	.03535	.03349	.03183	.03035	.02902	.02783	.02676	.02579	.02492	.02413
1	.02486	.02292	.02119	.01963	.01824	.01699	.01587	.01486	.01395	.01312
2	.02547	.02345	.02164	.02002	.01857	.01727	.01609	.01504	.01408	.01321
3	.02640	.02429	.02241	.02073	.01921	.01785	.01662	.01552	.01451	.01361
4	.02753	.02535	.02339	.02163	.02005	.01863	.01735	.01619	.01514	.01418
5	.02883	.02656	.02453	.02269	.02105	.01956	.01822	.01700	.01590	.01490
6	.03026	.02790	.02578	.02387	.02215	.02060	.01919	.01792	.01677	.01572
7	.03180	.02935	.02714	.02515	.02336	.02174	.02027	.01894	.01773	.01664
8	.03347	.03092	.02863	.02656	.02469	.02300	.02146	.02007	.01881	.01766
9	.03528	.03263	.03025	.02810	.02615	.02438	.02278	.02133	.02000	.01880
10	.03723	.03449	.03201	.02977	.02774	.02590	.02423	.02271	.02133	.02006
11	.03935	.03650	.03393	.03160	.02949	.02757	.02583	.02424	.02279	.02147
12	.04160	.03865	.03598	.03356	.03136	.02936	.02755	.02589	.02438	.02299
13	.04394	.04088	.03811	.03560	.03331	.03123	.02934	.02761	.02603	.02458
14	.04629	.04312	.04025	.03764	.03527	.03311	.03113	.02933	.02768	.02617
15	.04864	.04536	.04238	.03968	.03721	.03496	.03290	.03103	.02930	.02773
16	.05099	.04759	.04451	.04170	.03913	.03679	.03466	.03270	.03090	.02926
17	.05333	.04982	.04662	.04370	.04104	.03861	.03638	.03434	.03247	.03075
18	.05570	.05207	.04875	.04573	.04296	.04044	.03812	.03599	.03404	.03225
19	.05814	.05438	.05095	.04781	.04494	.04231	.03990	.03769	.03565	.03378
20	.06065	.05677	.05321	.04996	.04698	.04424	.04173	.03943	.03731	.03535
21	.06325	.05922	.05554	.05217	.04907	.04623	.04362	.04122	.03901	.03697
22	.06594	.06178	.05797	.05447	.05126	.04831	.04559	.04309	.04078	.03865
23	.06876	.06446	.06051	.05688	.05355	.05048	.04766	.04505	.04265	.04042
24	.07174	.06729	.06321	.05945	.05599	.05281	.04987	.04715	.04465	.04233
25	.07491	.07031	.06609	.06219	.05861	.05530	.05224	.04941	.04680	.04438
26	.07830	.07355	.06918	.06515	.06142	.05799	.05481	.05187	.04915	.04662
27	.08192	.07702	.07250	.06832	.06446	.06090	.05759	.05454	.05170	.04906
28	.08577	.08071	.07603	.07171	.06772	.06402	.06059	.05740	.05445	.05170
29	.08986	.08464	.07981	.07534	.07120	.06736	.06380	.06049	.05742	.05456
30	.09420	.08882	.08383	.07921	.07492	.07095	.06725	.06381	.06061	.05763
31	.09881	.09327	.08812	.08335	.07891	.07479	.07095	.06738	.06405	.06095
32	.10369	.09797	.09267	.08774	.08315	.07888	.07491	.07120	.06774	.06451
33	.10885	.10297	.09750	.09241	.08767	.08325	.07913	.07529	.07170	.06834
34	.11430	.10824	.10261	.09736	.09246	.08790	.08363	.07964	.07592	.07243
35	.12002	.11380	.10800	.10259	.09754	.09282	.08841	.08428	.08041	.07679
36	.12602	.11963	.11366	.10809	.10288	.09800	.09344	.08917	.08516	.08140
37	.13230	.12574	.11961	.11387	.10850	.10347	.09876	.09433	.09018	.08628
38	.13887	.13214	.12584	.11994	.11441	.10922	.10436	.09978	.09549	.09145
39	.14573	.13883	.13237	.12630	.12061	.11527	.11025	.10553	.10109	.09690
40	.15290	.14583	.13920	.13297	.12712	.12162	.11644	.11157	.10698	.10266
41	.16036	.15312	.14633	.13994	.13393	.12827	.12294	.11792	.11318	.10871
42	.16810	.16071	.15375	.14720	.14103	.13522	.12973	.12456	.11967	.11505
43	.17614	.16858	.16146	.15475	.14842	.14245	.13682	.13149	.12645	.12169
44	.18447	.17675	.16948	.16261	.15613	.15000	.14421	.13873	.13355	.12864
45	.19310	.18524	.17780	.17078	.16414	.15787	.15192	.14630	.14096	.13591
46	.20204	.19402	.18644	.17926	.17247	.16604	.15995	.15418	.14870	.14350
47	.21128	.20311	.19538	.18806	.18112	.17454	.16830	.16238	.15676	.15141
48	.22080	.21249	.20462	.19716	.19007	.18335	.17696	.17090	.16513	.15964
49	.23059	.22214	.21413	.20653	.19930	.19244	.18591	.17970	.17379	.16816
50	.24063	.23206	.22391	.21617	.20881	.20180	.19514	.18879	.18274	.17697
51	.25095	.24225	.23398	.22610	.21861	.21147	.20466	.19818	.19199	.18609
52	.26157	.25275	.24436	.23636	.22874	.22147	.21453	.20791	.20159	.19556
53	.27249	.26357	.25505	.24694	.23919	.23180	.22474	.21799	.21154	.20537
54	.28369	.27466	.26604	.25782	.24995	.24244	.23526	.22839	.22181	.21552
55	.29518	.28605	.27734	.26900	.26103	.25341	.24611	.23912	.23243	.22601
56	.30695	.29774	.28893	.28050	.27242	.26469	.25728	.25019	.24338	.23685
57	.31902	.30973	.30084	.29232	.28415	.27632	.26881	.26161	.25469	.24805
58	.33138	.32203	.31306	.30446	.29621	.28829	.28069	.27339	.26637	.25962
59	.34402	.33461	.32558	.31691	.30859	.30059	.29290	.28550	.27839	.27155

AGE	6.2%	6.4%	6.6%	6.8%	7.0%	7.2%	7.4%	7.6%	7.8%	8.0%
60	.35690	.34745	.33836	.32963	.32124	.31317	.30540	.29792	.29073	.28379
61	.36999	.36050	.35137	.34259	.33414	.32601	.31817	.31062	.30334	.29633
62	.38325	.37374	.36458	.35576	.34726	.33907	.33117	.32356	.31621	.30912
63	.39669	.38717	.37799	.36913	.36060	.35236	.34441	.33674	.32933	.32217
64	.41031	.40078	.39159	.38272	.37415	.36588	.35789	.35016	.34270	.33548
65	.42416	.41464	.40545	.39656	.38798	.37968	.37166	.36390	.35639	.34912
66	.43825	.42876	.41958	.41070	.40211	.39380	.38576	.37797	.37043	.36312
67	.45260	.44315	.43399	.42513	.41655	.40824	.40019	.39238	.38482	.37749
68	.46720	.45779	.44868	.43985	.43129	.42299	.41494	.40713	.39956	.39221
69	.48197	.47263	.46357	.45478	.44625	.43798	.42995	.42215	.41458	.40722
70	.49686	.48760	.47861	.46988	.46140	.45316	.44516	.43738	.42983	.42248
71	.51182	.50265	.49374	.48508	.47666	.46847	.46051	.45276	.44523	.43790
72	.52685	.51778	.50896	.50038	.49203	.48390	.47599	.46829	.46079	.45349
73	.54194	.53298	.52426	.51578	.50751	.49946	.49161	.48397	.47652	.46926
74	.55714	.54832	.53972	.53134	.52317	.51520	.50744	.49986	.49247	.48527
75	.57250	.56382	.55536	.54710	.53904	.53118	.52351	.51601	.50870	.50156
76	.58803	.57951	.57120	.56308	.55515	.54740	.53984	.53245	.52522	.51817
77	.60369	.59535	.58720	.57923	.57144	.56383	.55639	.54912	.54200	.53504
78	.61942	.61126	.60329	.59549	.58787	.58040	.57310	.56596	.55896	.55212
79	.63508	.62713	.61935	.61174	.60428	.59698	.58983	.58283	.57597	.56925
80	.65059	.64285	.63527	.62785	.62058	.61345	.60646	.59961	.59290	.58632
81	.66579	.65827	.65090	.64368	.63659	.62965	.62283	.61615	.60959	.60316
82	.68061	.67332	.66616	.65914	.65226	.64550	.63886	.63235	.62595	.61968
83	.69499	.68793	.68099	.67418	.66749	.66092	.65447	.64813	.64191	.63579
84	.70896	.70213	.69541	.68881	.68233	.67595	.66969	.66353	.65748	.65153
85	.72256	.71596	.70947	.70308	.69681	.69063	.68456	.67859	.67271	.66693
86	.73569	.72931	.72305	.71688	.71081	.70484	.69896	.69318	.68748	.68188
87	.74818	.74204	.73599	.73003	.72417	.71839	.71271	.70711	.70159	.69616
88	.76011	.75419	.74836	.74261	.73695	.73137	.72588	.72046	.71512	.70986
89	.77169	.76599	.76037	.75484	.74938	.74400	.73870	.73347	.72831	.72323
90	.78302	.77755	.77215	.76683	.76158	.75640	.75129	.74625	.74128	.73638
91	.79395	.78870	.78352	.77842	.77337	.76840	.76349	.75864	.75385	.74913
92	.80423	.79920	.79423	.78933	.78449	.77971	.77499	.77033	.76572	.76118
93	.81377	.80894	.80417	.79946	.79481	.79022	.78568	.78120	.77677	.77239
94	.82247	.81784	.81325	.80873	.80425	.79983	.79547	.79115	.78688	.78266
95	.83033	.82586	.82145	.81709	.81278	.80852	.80431	.80014	.79602	.79195
96	.83729	.83298	.82872	.82451	.82034	.81622	.81215	.80812	.80414	.80019
97	.84361	.83944	.83532	.83124	.82721	.82322	.81927	.81537	.81151	.80769
98	.84929	.84525	.84126	.83730	.83339	.82952	.82569	.82190	.81815	.81443
99	.85454	.85062	.84674	.84290	.83910	.83534	.83161	.82792	.82427	.82066
100	.85942	.85561	.85184	.84810	.84440	.84074	.83711	.83352	.82997	.82644
101	.86408	.86037	.85670	.85306	.84946	.84589	.84236	.83886	.83539	.83196
102	.86894	.86534	.86177	.85823	.85473	.85126	.84782	.84442	.84104	.83770
103	.87408	.87060	.86714	.86371	.86032	.85695	.85362	.85031	.84703	.84378
104	.87980	.87644	.87311	.86980	.86653	.86328	.86005	.85686	.85369	.85054
105	.88684	.88363	.88046	.87731	.87418	.87108	.86800	.86494	.86191	.85890
106	.89685	.89389	.89095	.88804	.88514	.88226	.87940	.87656	.87374	.87094
107	.91117	.90858	.90600	.90344	.90089	.89836	.89584	.89334	.89085	.88838
108	.93414	.93217	.93022	.92828	.92634	.92442	.92250	.92060	.91870	.91681
109	.97081	.96992	.96904	.96816	.96729	.96642	.96555	.96468	.96382	.96296

See p. 15 for regulations not amended to reflect law changes

TABLE S
BASED ON LIFE TABLE 80CNSMT
SINGLE LIFE REMAINDER FACTORS
APPLICABLE AFTER APRIL 30, 1989,
AND BEFORE MAY 1, 1999
INTEREST RATE

AGE	8.2%	8.4%	8.6%	8.8%	9.0%	9.2%	9.4%	9.6%	9.8%	10.0%
0	.02341	.02276	.02217	.02163	.02114	.02069	.02027	.01989	.01954	.01922
1	.01237	.01170	.01108	.01052	.01000	.00953	.00910	.00871	.00834	.00801
2	.01243	.01172	.01107	.01048	.00994	.00944	.00899	.00857	.00819	.00784
3	.01278	.01203	.01135	.01073	.01016	.00964	.00916	.00872	.00832	.00795
4	.01332	.01253	.01182	.01116	.01056	.01001	.00951	.00904	.00862	.00822
5	.01400	.01317	.01241	.01172	.01109	.01051	.00998	.00949	.00904	.00862
6	.01477	.01390	.01310	.01238	.01171	.01110	.01054	.01002	.00954	.00910
7	.01563	.01472	.01389	.01312	.01242	.01178	.01118	.01064	.01013	.00966
8	.01660	.01564	.01477	.01396	.01322	.01254	.01192	.01134	.01081	.01031
9	.01770	.01669	.01577	.01492	.01414	.01342	.01276	.01216	.01159	.01107
10	.01891	.01785	.01688	.01599	.01517	.01442	.01372	.01308	.01249	.01194
11	.02026	.01915	.01814	.01720	.01634	.01555	.01481	.01414	.01351	.01293
12	.02173	.02056	.01950	.01852	.01761	.01678	.01601	.01529	.01463	.01402
13	.02326	.02204	.02092	.01989	.01895	.01807	.01726	.01651	.01582	.01517
14	.02478	.02351	.02234	.02126	.02027	.01935	.01850	.01771	.01698	.01630
15	.02628	.02495	.02372	.02259	.02155	.02058	.01969	.01886	.01810	.01738
16	.02774	.02635	.02507	.02388	.02279	.02178	.02084	.01997	.01917	.01842
17	.02917	.02772	.02637	.02513	.02399	.02293	.02194	.02103	.02018	.01940
18	.03059	.02907	.02767	.02637	.02517	.02406	.02302	.02207	.02118	.02035
19	.03205	.03046	.02899	.02763	.02637	.02521	.02412	.02312	.02218	.02131
20	.03355	.03188	.03035	.02892	.02760	.02638	.02524	.02419	.02320	.02229
21	.03509	.03334	.03173	.03024	.02886	.02758	.02638	.02527	.02424	.02328
22	.03669	.03487	.03318	.03162	.03017	.02882	.02757	.02640	.02532	.02430
23	.03837	.03646	.03470	.03306	.03154	.03013	.02881	.02759	.02644	.02538
24	.04018	.03819	.03634	.03463	.03303	.03155	.03016	.02888	.02767	.02655
25	.04214	.04006	.03812	.03633	.03465	.03309	.03164	.03029	.02902	.02784
26	.04428	.04210	.04008	.03820	.03644	.03481	.03328	.03186	.03052	.02928
27	.04662	.04434	.04223	.04025	.03841	.03670	.03509	.03360	.03219	.03088
28	.04915	.04677	.04456	.04249	.04056	.03876	.03708	.03550	.03403	.03264
29	.05189	.04941	.04709	.04493	.04291	.04102	.03925	.03760	.03604	.03458
30	.05485	.05226	.04984	.04757	.04546	.04348	.04162	.03988	.03825	.03671
31	.05805	.05535	.05282	.05045	.04824	.04616	.04421	.04238	.04067	.03905
32	.06149	.05867	.05603	.05356	.05124	.04906	.04702	.04510	.04329	.04160
33	.06520	.06226	.05950	.05692	.05449	.05221	.05007	.04806	.04616	.04438
34	.06916	.06609	.06322	.06052	.05799	.05560	.05336	.05125	.04926	.04738
35	.07339	.07020	.06720	.06439	.06174	.05925	.05690	.05469	.05260	.05063
36	.07787	.07455	.07143	.06850	.06573	.06313	.06068	.05836	.05617	.05411
37	.08262	.07917	.07593	.07287	.06999	.06727	.06470	.06228	.05999	.05783
38	.08765	.08407	.08069	.07751	.07451	.07167	.06899	.06646	.06407	.06180
39	.09296	.08925	.08574	.08243	.07931	.07635	.07356	.07092	.06841	.06604
40	.09858	.09472	.09109	.08765	.08440	.08132	.07841	.07565	.07303	.07055
41	.10449	.10050	.09673	.09316	.08978	.08658	.08355	.08067	.07794	.07535
42	.11069	.10656	.10265	.09895	.09544	.09212	.08896	.08596	.08312	.08041
43	.11718	.11291	.10887	.10503	.10140	.09794	.09466	.09154	.08858	.08576
44	.12399	.11958	.11540	.11143	.10766	.10407	.10067	.09743	.09434	.09141
45	.13111	.12656	.12224	.11814	.11423	.11052	.10699	.10362	.10042	.09736
46	.13856	.13387	.12941	.12516	.12113	.11728	.11362	.11013	.10680	.10363
47	.14633	.14150	.13690	.13252	.12835	.12438	.12059	.11697	.11352	.11022
48	.15442	.14945	.14471	.14020	.13589	.13179	.12787	.12412	.12055	.11713
49	.16280	.15769	.15281	.14816	.14373	.13949	.13544	.13157	.12787	.12433
50	.17147	.16622	.16121	.15643	.15186	.14749	.14331	.13931	.13548	.13182
51	.18045	.17507	.16993	.16501	.16030	.15580	.15150	.14737	.14342	.13963
52	.18979	.18427	.17899	.17394	.16911	.16448	.16004	.15579	.15172	.14780
53	.19947	.19383	.18842	.18324	.17828	.17352	.16896	.16458	.16038	.15635
54	.20950	.20372	.19819	.19288	.18779	.18291	.17822	.17372	.16940	.16524
55	.21986	.21397	.20831	.20288	.19767	.19266	.18785	.18322	.17878	.17450
56	.23058	.22457	.21879	.21324	.20791	.20278	.19785	.19310	.18854	.18414
57	.24167	.23554	.22965	.22399	.21854	.21329	.20824	.20338	.19870	.19419
58	.25314	.24690	.24090	.23512	.22956	.22420	.21904	.21407	.20927	.20464
59	.26497	.25863	.25252	.24664	.24097	.23550	.23023	.22515	.22024	.21551

See p. 15 for regulations not amended to reflect law changes

AGE	8.2%	8.4%	8.6%	8.8%	9.0%	9.2%	9.4%	9.6%	9.8%	10.0%
60	.27712	.27068	.26448	.25849	.25272	.24716	.24178	.23659	.23158	.22674
61	.28956	.28304	.27674	.27067	.26480	.25913	.25366	.24837	.24325	.23831
62	.30228	.29567	.28929	.28312	.27717	.27141	.26584	.26045	.25524	.25020
63	.31525	.30857	.30211	.29586	.28982	.28397	.27832	.27284	.26754	.26240
64	.32851	.32176	.31522	.30890	.30278	.29685	.29111	.28555	.28016	.27493
65	.34209	.33528	.32868	.32229	.31610	.31010	.30429	.29865	.29317	.28787
66	.35604	.34918	.34253	.33609	.32983	.32377	.31788	.31217	.30663	.30124
67	.37037	.36347	.35678	.35028	.34398	.33786	.33191	.32614	.32053	.31508
68	.38508	.37815	.37142	.36489	.35854	.35237	.34638	.34055	.33488	.32937
69	.40008	.39313	.38638	.37982	.37344	.36724	.36120	.35533	.34961	.34405
70	.41533	.40838	.40162	.39504	.38864	.38241	.37634	.37043	.36468	.35907
71	.43076	.42382	.41705	.41047	.40405	.39780	.39171	.38578	.38000	.37436
72	.44638	.43945	.43269	.42611	.41969	.41344	.40733	.40138	.39558	.38991
73	.46218	.45527	.44854	.44197	.43556	.42931	.42321	.41725	.41143	.40575
74	.47823	.47137	.46466	.45812	.45173	.44549	.43940	.43345	.42763	.42195
75	.49459	.48777	.48112	.47462	.46826	.46205	.45598	.45004	.44424	.43856
76	.51127	.50452	.49793	.49148	.48517	.47900	.47297	.46706	.46129	.45563
77	.52823	.52157	.51505	.50867	.50243	.49632	.49033	.48447	.47873	.47311
78	.54541	.53885	.53242	.52613	.51996	.51392	.50800	.50220	.49652	.49094
79	.56267	.55621	.54989	.54369	.53762	.53166	.52582	.52009	.51448	.50897
80	.57987	.57354	.56733	.56125	.55527	.54941	.54366	.53802	.53248	.52705
81	.59685	.59065	.58457	.57860	.57274	.56699	.56134	.55579	.55035	.54499
82	.61351	.60746	.60151	.59567	.58993	.58429	.57875	.57331	.56796	.56270
83	.62978	.62387	.61806	.61236	.60675	.60123	.59581	.59047	.58523	.58007
84	.64567	.63992	.63426	.62869	.62321	.61783	.61253	.60731	.60218	.59713
85	.66125	.65565	.65014	.64472	.63938	.63413	.62896	.62387	.61886	.61392
86	.67636	.67092	.66557	.66030	.65511	.65000	.64496	.64000	.63511	.63030
87	.69081	.68554	.68034	.67522	.67018	.66520	.66031	.65548	.65071	.64602
88	.70468	.69957	.69453	.68956	.68466	.67983	.67507	.67037	.66574	.66117
89	.71821	.71326	.70838	.70357	.69882	.69414	.68952	.68495	.68045	.67601
90	.73153	.72676	.72204	.71739	.71280	.70827	.70379	.69938	.69502	.69071
91	.74447	.73986	.73532	.73083	.72640	.72202	.71770	.71343	.70921	.70504
92	.75669	.75225	.74787	.74354	.73927	.73504	.73087	.72674	.72267	.71864
93	.76807	.76379	.75957	.75540	.75127	.74719	.74317	.73918	.73524	.73135
94	.77849	.77437	.77030	.76627	.76229	.75835	.75446	.75061	.74680	.74303
95	.78792	.78394	.78001	.77611	.77226	.76845	.76468	.76096	.75727	.75362
96	.79630	.79244	.78863	.78485	.78112	.77742	.77377	.77015	.76657	.76303
97	.80391	.80016	.79646	.79280	.78917	.78559	.78203	.77852	.77504	.77160
98	.81076	.80712	.80352	.79996	.79643	.79294	.78948	.78606	.78267	.77931
99	.81709	.81354	.81004	.80657	.80313	.79972	.79635	.79302	.78971	.78644
100	.82296	.81950	.81609	.81270	.80934	.80602	.80273	.79947	.79624	.79304
101	.82855	.82518	.82185	.81854	.81526	.81201	.80880	.80561	.80245	.79932
102	.83438	.83110	.82785	.82462	.82142	.81826	.81512	.81200	.80892	.80586
103	.84056	.83737	.83420	.83106	.82795	.82487	.82181	.81878	.81577	.81279
104	.84743	.84433	.84127	.83822	.83521	.83221	.82924	.82630	.82338	.82048
105	.85591	.85295	.85001	.84709	.84419	.84132	.83846	.83563	.83282	.83003
106	.86816	.86540	.86266	.85993	.85723	.85454	.85187	.84922	.84659	.84397
107	.88592	.88348	.88105	.87863	.87623	.87384	.87147	.86911	.86676	.86443
108	.91493	.91306	.91119	.90934	.90749	.90566	.90383	.90201	.90020	.89840
109	.96211	.96125	.96041	.95956	.95872	.95788	.95704	.95620	.95537	.95455

See p. 15 for regulations not amended to reflect law changes

TABLE S
BASED ON LIFE TABLE 80CNSMT
SINGLE LIFE REMAINDER FACTORS
APPLICABLE AFTER APRIL 30, 1989,
AND BEFORE MAY 1, 1999
INTEREST RATE

AGE	*10.2%*	*10.4%*	*10.6%*	*10.8%*	*11.0%*	*11.2%*	*11.4%*	*11.6%*	*11.8%*	*12.0%*
0	.01891	.01864	.01838	.01814	.01791	.01770	.01750	.01732	.01715	.01698
1	.00770	.00741	.00715	.00690	.00667	.00646	.00626	.00608	.00590	.00574
2	.00751	.00721	.00693	.00667	.00643	.00620	.00600	.00580	.00562	.00544
3	.00760	.00728	.00699	.00671	.00646	.00622	.00600	.00579	.00560	.00541
4	.00786	.00752	.00721	.00692	.00665	.00639	.00616	.00594	.00573	.00554
5	.00824	.00788	.00755	.00724	.00695	.00668	.00643	.00620	.00598	.00578
6	.00869	.00832	.00796	.00764	.00733	.00705	.00678	.00654	.00630	.00608
7	.00923	.00883	.00846	.00811	.00779	.00749	.00720	.00694	.00669	.00646
8	.00986	.00943	.00904	.00867	.00833	.00801	.00771	.00743	.00716	.00692
9	.01059	.01014	.00972	.00933	.00897	.00863	.00831	.00801	.00773	.00747
10	.01142	.01095	.01051	.01009	.00971	.00935	.00901	.00869	.00840	.00812
11	.01239	.01189	.01142	.01098	.01057	.01019	.00983	.00950	.00918	.00889
12	.01345	.01292	.01243	.01197	.01154	.01113	.01075	.01040	.01007	.00975
13	.01457	.01401	.01349	.01300	.01255	.01212	.01172	.01135	.01100	.01067
14	.01567	.01508	.01453	.01402	.01354	.01309	.01267	.01227	.01190	.01155
15	.01672	.01610	.01552	.01498	.01448	.01400	.01356	.01314	.01275	.01238
16	.01772	.01707	.01646	.01589	.01536	.01486	.01439	.01396	.01354	.01315
17	.01866	.01798	.01734	.01674	.01618	.01566	.01516	.01470	.01427	.01386
18	.01958	.01886	.01818	.01755	.01697	.01641	.01590	.01541	.01495	.01452
19	.02050	.01974	.01903	.01837	.01775	.01717	.01662	.01611	.01563	.01517
20	.02143	.02064	.01989	.01919	.01854	.01793	.01735	.01681	.01630	.01582
21	.02238	.02154	.02075	.02002	.01933	.01868	.01807	.01750	.01696	.01646
22	.02336	.02247	.02164	.02087	.02014	.01946	.01882	.01821	.01764	.01711
23	.02438	.02345	.02257	.02176	.02099	.02027	.01959	.01895	.01835	.01778
24	.02550	.02451	.02359	.02273	.02192	.02115	.02044	.01976	.01913	.01853
25	.02673	.02569	.02472	.02381	.02295	.02214	.02138	.02067	.01999	.01936
26	.02811	.02701	.02598	.02502	.02411	.02326	.02246	.02170	.02098	.02031
27	.02965	.02849	.02741	.02639	.02543	.02452	.02367	.02287	.02211	.02140
28	.03134	.03013	.02898	.02790	.02689	.02593	.02503	.02418	.02338	.02262
29	.03322	.03193	.03072	.02958	.02851	.02750	.02654	.02564	.02479	.02398
30	.03527	.03391	.03264	.03143	.03030	.02923	.02821	.02726	.02635	.02550
31	.03753	.03610	.03475	.03348	.03228	.03115	.03008	.02907	.02811	.02720
32	.04000	.03849	.03707	.03573	.03446	.03326	.03213	.03105	.03004	.02907
33	.04269	.04111	.03961	.03819	.03685	.03558	.03438	.03325	.03217	.03115
34	.04561	.04394	.04236	.04087	.03946	.03812	.03685	.03565	.03451	.03342
35	.04877	.04702	.04535	.04378	.04229	.04087	.03953	.03826	.03706	.03591
36	.05215	.05031	.04856	.04690	.04533	.04384	.04242	.04108	.03980	.03859
37	.05578	.05384	.05200	.05025	.04860	.04703	.04553	.04411	.04276	.04148
38	.05965	.05761	.05568	.05385	.05211	.05045	.04888	.04738	.04595	.04460
39	.06379	.06165	.05962	.05770	.05587	.05412	.05247	.05089	.04939	.04795
40	.06820	.06596	.06383	.06181	.05989	.05806	.05631	.05465	.05307	.05155
41	.07288	.07054	.06832	.06620	.06418	.06226	.06042	.05868	.05701	.05541
42	.07784	.07539	.07306	.07085	.06873	.06671	.06479	.06295	.06119	.05952
43	.08308	.08052	.07808	.07576	.07355	.07143	.06941	.06748	.06564	.06387
44	.08861	.08594	.08340	.08097	.07865	.07644	.07432	.07230	.07036	.06851
45	.09445	.09167	.08901	.08648	.08406	.08174	.07953	.07741	.07538	.07343
46	.10060	.09770	.09494	.09230	.08977	.08735	.08503	.08281	.08068	.07865
47	.10707	.10406	.10119	.09843	.09579	.09327	.09085	.08853	.08630	.08417
48	.11386	.11073	.10774	.10487	.10213	.09949	.09697	.09455	.09222	.08999
49	.12094	.11769	.11458	.11160	.10874	.10600	.10337	.10084	.09842	.09609
50	.12831	.12494	.12172	.11862	.11565	.11280	.11006	.10743	.10490	.10247
51	.13600	.13251	.12917	.12596	.12288	.11991	.11706	.11432	.11169	.10915
52	.14405	.14044	.13698	.13366	.13046	.12738	.12442	.12157	.11883	.11619
53	.15247	.14875	.14517	.14172	.13841	.13522	.13215	.12919	.12635	.12360
54	.16124	.15740	.15370	.15014	.14671	.14341	.14023	.13717	.13421	.13136
55	.17039	.16642	.16261	.15893	.15539	.15198	.14868	.14551	.14244	.13948
56	.17991	.17583	.17190	.16811	.16445	.16092	.15752	.15423	.15106	.14799
57	.18984	.18564	.18160	.17769	.17392	.17029	.16677	.16338	.16010	.15692
58	.20018	.19587	.19172	.18770	.18382	.18007	.17645	.17295	.16956	.16628
59	.21093	.20652	.20225	.19812	.19414	.19028	.18655	.18294	.17945	.17606

See p. 15 for regulations not amended to reflect law changes

AGE	*10.2%*	*10.4%*	*10.6%*	*10.8%*	*11.0%*	*11.2%*	*11.4%*	*11.6%*	*11.8%*	*12.0%*
60	.22206	.21753	.21316	.20893	.20483	.20087	.19703	.19332	.18972	.18624
61	.23353	.22890	.22442	.22009	.21589	.21182	.20788	.20407	.20037	.19678
62	.24532	.24059	.23601	.23158	.22728	.22311	.21907	.21515	.21135	.20767
63	.25742	.25260	.24793	.24339	.23900	.23473	.23060	.22658	.22268	.21890
64	.26987	.26495	.26019	.25556	.25107	.24671	.24248	.23837	.23438	.23050
65	.28271	.27771	.27286	.26815	.26357	.25912	.25480	.25059	.24651	.24254
66	.29601	.29093	.28600	.28120	.27654	.27200	.26760	.26331	.25913	.25507
67	.30978	.30462	.29961	.29474	.29000	.28539	.28090	.27653	.27227	.26813
68	.32401	.31879	.31371	.30877	.30396	.29927	.29471	.29027	.28593	.28171
69	.33863	.33336	.32822	.32322	.31835	.31359	.30896	.30445	.30005	.29576
70	.35361	.34829	.34310	.33804	.33311	.32830	.32361	.31903	.31457	.31021
71	.36886	.36349	.35826	.35316	.34818	.34332	.33858	.33394	.32942	.32500
72	.38439	.37899	.37373	.36858	.36356	.35866	.35387	.34919	.34461	.34015
73	.40021	.39479	.38950	.38432	.37927	.37433	.36950	.36478	.36016	.35565
74	.41639	.41096	.40565	.40046	.39538	.39042	.38556	.38081	.37616	.37161
75	.43301	.42758	.42226	.41706	.41198	.40699	.40212	.39734	.39267	.38809
76	.45009	.44467	.43937	.43417	.42908	.42410	.41921	.41443	.40974	.40514
77	.46761	.46221	.45693	.45175	.44667	.44170	.43682	.43203	.42734	.42274
78	.48548	.48013	.47488	.46973	.46468	.45972	.45486	.45009	.44541	.44082
79	.50356	.49826	.49306	.48795	.48294	.47802	.47319	.46845	.46379	.45922
80	.52171	.51647	.51133	.50628	.50132	.49644	.49166	.48695	.48233	.47779
81	.53974	.53457	.52950	.52451	.51961	.51479	.51006	.50541	.50083	.49633
82	.55753	.55245	.54745	.54254	.53771	.53296	.52828	.52369	.51917	.51472
83	.57500	.57001	.56510	.56026	.55551	.55083	.54623	.54170	.53724	.53285
84	.59216	.58726	.58245	.57770	.57304	.56844	.56391	.55945	.55506	.55074
85	.60906	.60428	.59956	.59492	.59034	.58583	.58139	.57702	.57270	.56845
86	.62555	.62088	.61627	.61173	.60725	.60284	.59849	.59420	.58997	.58580
87	.64139	.63683	.63233	.62790	.62352	.61921	.61495	.61076	.60661	.60253
88	.65666	.65221	.64783	.64350	.63923	.63502	.63086	.62675	.62270	.61871
89	.67163	.66730	.66304	.65882	.65466	.65055	.64650	.64249	.63854	.63463
90	.68646	.68226	.67812	.67402	.66998	.66599	.66204	.65814	.65430	.65049
91	.70093	.69686	.69285	.68888	.68496	.68108	.67725	.67347	.66973	.66604
92	.71466	.71073	.70684	.70300	.69920	.69545	.69173	.68806	.68444	.68085
93	.72750	.72370	.71994	.71622	.71254	.70890	.70530	.70174	.69822	.69474
94	.73931	.73562	.73198	.72838	.72481	.72129	.71780	.71434	.71093	.70755
95	.75001	.74644	.74291	.73941	.73595	.73253	.72914	.72579	.72247	.71919
96	.75953	.75606	.75262	.74923	.74586	.74253	.73924	.73598	.73275	.72955
97	.76819	.76481	.76147	.75816	.75489	.75165	.74844	.74526	.74211	.73899
98	.77599	.77270	.76944	.76621	.76302	.75986	.75672	.75362	.75054	.74750
99	.78319	.77998	.77680	.77365	.77053	.76744	.76437	.76134	.75833	.75535
100	.78987	.78673	.78362	.78054	.77748	.77446	.77146	.76849	.76555	.76263
101	.79622	.79315	.79010	.78708	.78409	.78113	.77819	.77528	.77239	.76953
102	.80283	.79983	.79685	.79390	.79097	.78807	.78519	.78234	.77951	.77671
103	.80983	.80690	.80399	.80111	.79825	.79541	.79260	.78981	.78705	.78430
104	.81760	.81475	.81192	.80912	.80633	.80357	.80083	.79810	.79541	.79273
105	.82726	.82451	.82178	.81907	.81638	.81371	.81106	.80843	.80582	.80322
106	.84137	.83879	.83623	.83368	.83115	.82863	.82614	.82366	.82119	.81874
107	.86211	.85981	.85751	.85523	.85297	.85071	.84847	.84624	.84403	.84182
108	.89660	.89481	.89304	.89127	.88950	.88775	.88601	.88427	.88254	.88081
109	.95372	.95290	.95208	.95126	.95045	.94964	.94883	.94803	.94723	.94643

TABLE S
BASED ON LIFE TABLE 80CNSMT
SINGLE LIFE REMAINDER FACTORS
APPLICABLE AFTER APRIL 30, 1989,
AND BEFORE MAY 1, 1999
INTEREST RATE

AGE	*12.2%*	*12.4%*	*12.6%*	*12.8%*	*13.0%*	*13.2%*	*13.4%*	*13.6%*	*13.8%*	*14.0%*
0	.01683	.01669	.01655	.01642	.01630	.01618	.01607	.01596	.01586	.01576
1	.00559	.00544	.00531	.00518	.00506	.00494	.00484	.00473	.00464	.00454
2	.00528	.00513	.00499	.00485	.00473	.00461	.00449	.00439	.00428	.00419
3	.00524	.00508	.00493	.00479	.00465	.00453	.00441	.00429	.00419	.00408
4	.00536	.00519	.00503	.00488	.00473	.00460	.00447	.00435	.00423	.00412
5	.00558	.00540	.00523	.00507	.00492	.00477	.00464	.00451	.00439	.00427
6	.00588	.00569	.00550	.00533	.00517	.00502	.00487	.00473	.00460	.00448
7	.00624	.00604	.00584	.00566	.00549	.00532	.00517	.00502	.00488	.00475
8	.00668	.00646	.00626	.00606	.00588	.00570	.00554	.00538	.00523	.00509
9	.00722	.00699	.00677	.00656	.00636	.00617	.00600	.00583	.00567	.00552
10	.00785	.00761	.00737	.00715	.00694	.00674	.00655	.00637	.00620	.00604
11	.00861	.00835	.00810	.00786	.00764	.00743	.00723	.00704	.00686	.00668
12	.00946	.00918	.00891	.00866	.00843	.00820	.00799	.00779	.00760	.00741
13	.01035	.01006	.00978	.00951	.00927	.00903	.00880	.00859	.00839	.00819
14	.01122	.01091	.01061	.01034	.01007	.00982	.00958	.00936	.00914	.00894
15	.01203	.01171	.01140	.01110	.01082	.01056	.01031	.01007	.00985	.00963
16	.01279	.01244	.01211	.01181	.01151	.01123	.01097	.01072	.01048	.01025
17	.01347	.01311	.01276	.01244	.01213	.01184	.01156	.01130	.01104	.01081
18	.01411	.01373	.01336	.01302	.01270	.01239	.01210	.01182	.01155	.01130
19	.01474	.01434	.01396	.01359	.01325	.01293	.01262	.01233	.01205	.01178
20	.01537	.01494	.01454	.01415	.01379	.01345	.01313	.01282	.01252	.01224
21	.01598	.01553	.01510	.01470	.01432	.01396	.01361	.01329	.01298	.01268
22	.01660	.01613	.01568	.01525	.01485	.01446	.01410	.01375	.01343	.01312
23	.01725	.01674	.01627	.01581	.01539	.01498	.01460	.01423	.01388	.01355
24	.01796	.01742	.01692	.01644	.01599	.01556	.01515	.01476	.01439	.01404
25	.01876	.01819	.01765	.01714	.01666	.01621	.01577	.01536	.01497	.01460
26	.01967	.01907	.01850	.01796	.01745	.01696	.01650	.01606	.01565	.01525
27	.02072	.02008	.01948	.01890	.01836	.01784	.01735	.01688	.01644	.01601
28	.02190	.02122	.02057	.01996	.01938	.01883	.01831	.01781	.01734	.01689
29	.02322	.02249	.02181	.02116	.02054	.01996	.01940	.01887	.01836	.01788
30	.02469	.02392	.02319	.02250	.02184	.02122	.02062	.02006	.01952	.01900
31	.02634	.02552	.02475	.02401	.02331	.02264	.02201	.02140	.02083	.02028
32	.02816	.02729	.02647	.02568	.02494	.02423	.02355	.02291	.02229	.02170
33	.03018	.02926	.02838	.02755	.02675	.02600	.02528	.02459	.02393	.02331
34	.03239	.03142	.03048	.02960	.02875	.02795	.02718	.02645	.02575	.02508
35	.03482	.03378	.03279	.03185	.03095	.03009	.02928	.02850	.02775	.02704
36	.03743	.03633	.03528	.03428	.03333	.03242	.03155	.03072	.02992	.02916
37	.04026	.03909	.03798	.03692	.03591	.03494	.03401	.03313	.03228	.03147
38	.04330	.04207	.04089	.03977	.03869	.03767	.03668	.03574	.03484	.03398
39	.04658	.04528	.04403	.04284	.04170	.04061	.03957	.03857	.03762	.03670
40	.05011	.04873	.04741	.04615	.04495	.04379	.04269	.04163	.04061	.03964
41	.05389	.05244	.05104	.04971	.04844	.04721	.04604	.04492	.04384	.04281
42	.05791	.05638	.05491	.05350	.05216	.05086	.04962	.04844	.04729	.04620
43	.06219	.06057	.05902	.05754	.05612	.05475	.05344	.05218	.05093	.04981
44	.06673	.06503	.06340	.06184	.06034	.05890	.05752	.05619	.05491	.05368
45	.07157	.06978	.06806	.06642	.06484	.06332	.06186	.06046	.05911	.05781
46	.07669	.07481	.07301	.07128	.06962	.06802	.06649	.06501	.06358	.06221
47	.08212	.08015	.07826	.07645	.07470	.07302	.07140	.06984	.06834	.06690
48	.08784	.08578	.08380	.08190	.08006	.07830	.07660	.07496	.07338	.07186
49	.09384	.09169	.08961	.08762	.08570	.08384	.08206	.08034	.07868	.07708
50	.10013	.09787	.09570	.09361	.09160	.08966	.08779	.08598	.08424	.08256
51	.10671	.10436	.10209	.09991	.09780	.09577	.09381	.09192	.09009	.08832
52	.11365	.11120	.10883	.10655	.10435	.10222	.10017	.09819	.09628	.09442
53	.12095	.11840	.11593	.11355	.11126	.10904	.10689	.10482	.10282	.10088
54	.12860	.12595	.12338	.12090	.11851	.11619	.11396	.11179	.10970	.10767
55	.13663	.13386	.13120	.12862	.12613	.12372	.12138	.11912	.11694	.11482
56	.14503	.14217	.13940	.13672	.13413	.13162	.12919	.12683	.12456	.12235
57	.15385	.15089	.14801	.14523	.14254	.13994	.13741	.13496	.13259	.13029
58	.16311	.16004	.15706	.15418	.15139	.14868	.14606	.14352	.14105	.13866
59	.17279	.16961	.16654	.16355	.16066	.15786	.15514	.15250	.14994	.14745

See p. 15 for regulations not amended to reflect law changes

AGE	*12.2%*	*12.4%*	*12.6%*	*12.8%*	*13.0%*	*13.2%*	*13.4%*	*13.6%*	*13.8%*	*14.0%*
60	.18286	.17958	.17640	.17332	.17033	.16743	.16462	.16188	.15922	.15664
61	.19330	.18992	.18665	.18347	.18038	.17738	.17447	.17164	.16889	.16622
62	.20409	.20061	.19724	.19396	.19078	.18768	.18467	.18175	.17891	.17614
63	.21522	.21165	.20818	.20480	.20152	.19833	.19523	.19221	.18928	.18642
64	.22672	.22306	.21949	.21602	.21265	.20937	.20617	.20306	.20003	.19708
65	.23867	.23491	.23125	.22769	.22423	.22085	.21757	.21437	.21125	.20821
66	.25112	.24727	.24353	.23988	.23632	.23286	.22948	.22619	.22299	.21986
67	.26409	.26016	.25633	.25260	.24896	.24541	.24195	.23857	.23528	.23206
68	.27760	.27359	.26968	.26586	.26214	.25851	.25497	.25151	.24814	.24484
69	.29157	.28748	.28350	.27961	.27581	.27211	.26849	.26495	.26150	.25812
70	.30596	.30181	.29775	.29379	.28992	.28614	.28245	.27884	.27532	.27187
71	.32069	.31648	.31236	.30833	.30440	.30055	.29679	.29312	.28952	.28600
72	.33578	.33151	.32733	.32325	.31925	.31535	.31152	.30778	.30412	.30054
73	.35123	.34691	.34269	.33855	.33450	.33054	.32666	.32286	.31914	.31550
74	.36715	.36279	.35852	.35434	.35024	.34623	.34230	.33845	.33468	.33098
75	.38360	.37921	.37491	.37069	.36656	.36250	.35853	.35464	.35082	.34708
76	.40064	.39623	.39190	.38765	.38349	.37941	.37540	.37148	.36762	.36384
77	.41823	.41381	.40947	.40521	.40103	.39692	.39290	.38895	.38507	.38126
78	.43632	.43189	.42755	.42329	.41910	.41499	.41095	.40698	.40309	.39926
79	.45473	.45032	.44599	.44173	.43755	.43344	.42940	.42543	.42153	.41770
80	.47333	.46894	.46463	.46040	.45623	.45213	.44811	.44414	.44025	.43642
81	.49191	.48755	.48328	.47907	.47493	.47085	.46684	.46290	.45902	.45520
82	.51034	.50603	.50179	.49762	.49351	.48947	.48549	.48157	.47772	.47392
83	.52852	.52427	.52008	.51595	.51189	.50788	.50394	.50006	.49623	.49246
84	.54648	.54228	.53815	.53407	.53006	.52610	.52221	.51836	.51458	.51084
85	.56426	.56013	.55606	.55205	.54810	.54420	.54035	.53656	.53282	.52913
86	.58169	.57764	.57364	.56970	.56581	.56197	.55818	.55445	.55076	.54713
87	.59850	.59452	.59060	.58673	.58291	.57913	.57541	.57174	.56811	.56453
88	.61476	.61086	.60702	.60322	.59947	.59577	.59212	.58851	.58494	.58142
89	.63078	.62697	.62321	.61950	.61583	.61220	.60862	.60508	.60159	.59813
90	.64674	.64302	.63935	.63573	.63215	.62861	.62511	.62165	.61823	.61485
91	.66238	.65877	.65520	.65167	.64819	.64474	.64133	.63795	.63462	.63132
92	.67730	.67379	.67032	.66689	.66350	.66014	.65682	.65354	.65029	.64708
93	.69130	.68789	.68452	.68119	.67789	.67463	.67140	.66820	.66504	.66191
94	.70421	.70090	.69762	.69438	.69118	.68800	.68486	.68175	.67867	.67563
95	.71594	.71272	.70954	.70639	.70326	.70017	.69712	.69409	.69109	.68812
96	.72638	.72325	.72014	.71707	.71403	.71101	.70803	.70507	.70215	.69925
97	.73590	.73285	.72982	.72682	.72385	.72090	.71799	.71510	.71224	.70941
98	.74448	.74149	.73853	.73560	.73269	.72981	.72696	.72414	.72134	.71856
99	.75240	.74948	.74658	.74371	.74086	.73805	.73525	.73248	.72974	.72702
100	.75974	.75687	.75403	.75121	.74842	.74566	.74292	.74020	.73751	.73484
101	.76669	.76388	.76109	.75833	.75559	.75287	.75018	.74751	.74486	.74223
102	.77393	.77117	.76844	.76573	.76304	.76037	.75773	.75511	.75251	.74993
103	.78158	.77888	.77620	.77355	.77091	.76830	.76571	.76313	.76058	.75805
104	.79007	.78743	.78482	.78222	.77964	.77709	.77455	.77203	.76953	.76705
105	.80065	.79809	.79556	.79304	.79054	.78805	.78559	.78314	.78071	.77829
106	.81631	.81389	.81149	.80911	.80674	.80438	.80204	.79972	.79741	.79511
107	.83963	.83745	.83529	.83313	.83099	.82886	.82674	.82463	.82254	.82045
108	.87910	.87739	.87569	.87400	.87232	.87064	.86897	.86731	.86566	.86401
109	.94563	.94484	.94405	.94326	.94248	.94170	.94092	.94014	.93937	.93860

TABLE 80CNSMT
APPLICABLE AFTER APRIL 30, 1989,
AND BEFORE MAY 1, 1999

Age x	1(x)	Age x	1(x)	Age x	1(x)
(1)	(2)	(1)	(2)	(1)	(2)
0	100000	37	95492	74	59279
1	98740	38	95317	75	56799
2	98648	39	95129	76	54239
3	98584	40	94926	77	51599
4	98535	41	94706	78	48878
5	98495	42	94465	79	46071
6	98459	43	94201	80	43180
7	98426	44	93913	81	40208
8	98396	45	93599	82	37172
9	98370	46	93256	83	34095
10	98347	47	92882	84	31012
11	98328	48	92472	85	27960
12	98309	49	92021	86	24961
13	98285	50	91526	87	22038
14	98248	51	90986	88	19235
15	98196	52	90402	89	16598
16	98129	53	89771	90	14154
17	98047	54	89087	91	11908
18	97953	55	88348	92	9863
19	97851	56	87551	93	8032
20	97741	57	86695	94	6424
21	97623	58	85776	95	5043
22	97499	59	84789	96	3884
23	97370	60	83726	97	2939
24	97240	61	82581	98	2185
25	97110	62	81348	99	1598
26	96982	63	80024	100	1150
27	96856	64	78609	101	815
28	96730	65	77107	102	570
29	96604	66	75520	103	393
30	96477	67	73846	104	267
31	96350	68	72082	105	179
32	96220	69	70218	106	119
33	96088	70	68248	107	78
34	95951	71	66165	108	51
35	95808	72	63972	109	33
36	95655	73	61673	110	0

(f) *Valuation of annuities, interests for life or term of years, and remainder or reversionary interests for estates of decedents for which the valuation date of the gross estate is after April 30,1999, and before May 1, 2009.*—(1) *In general.*—Except as otherwise provided in § 20.2031-7(b) and § 20.7520-3(b) (pertaining to certain limitations on the use of prescribed tables), if the valuation date for the gross estate of the decedent is after April 30, 1999, and before May 1, 2009, the fair market value of annuities, life estates, terms of years, remainders, and reversionary interests is the present value of the interests determined by use of standard or special section 7520 actuarial factors and the valuation methodology described in § 20.2031-7(d). These factors are derived by using the appropriate section 7520 interest rate and, if applicable, the mortality component for the valuation date of the interest that is being valued. See §§ 20.7520-1 through 20.7520-4. See paragraph (f)(4) of this section for determination of the appropriate table for use in valuing these interests.

(2) *Transitional rule.*—(i) If a decedent dies after April 30, 1999, and if on May 1, 1999, the decedent was mentally incompetent so that the disposition of the decedent's property could not be changed, and the decedent dies without having regained competency to dispose of the decedent's property or dies within 90 days of the date on which the decedent first regains competency, the fair market value of annuities, life estates, terms for years, remainders, and reversions included in the gross estate of the decedent is their present value determined either under this section or under the corresponding section applicable at the time the decedent became mentally incompetent, at the option of the decedent's executor. For example, see paragraph (d) of this section.

(ii) If a decedent dies after April 30, 1999, and before July 1, 1999, the fair market value of annuities, life estates, remainders, and reversions based on one or more measuring lives included in the gross estate of the decedent is their present value determined under this section by use of the section 7520 interest rate for the month in which the valuation date occurs (see §§ 20.7520-1(b) and 20.7520-2(a)(2) and the appropriate actuarial tables under either paragraph (e)(4) or paragraph (f)(4) of this section, at the option of the decedent's executor.

(iii) For purposes of paragraphs (f)(2)(i) and (f)(2)(ii) of this section, where the decedent's executor is given the option to use the appropriate actuarial tables under either paragraph (e)(4) or paragraph (f)(4) of this section, the decedent's executor must use the same actuarial table with respect to each individual transaction and with respect to all transfers occurring on the valuation date (for example, gift and income tax charitable deductions with respect to the same transfer must be determined based on the same tables, and all assets includible in the gross estate and/or estate tax deductions claimed must be valued based on the same tables).

(3) *Publications and actuarial computations by the Internal Revenue Service.*—Many standard actuarial factors not included in paragraph (f)(4) of this section or in § 20.2031-7(d)(6) are included in Internal Revenue Service Publication 1457, "Actuarial Values, Book Aleph," (7-99). Publication 1457 also includes examples that illustrate how to compute many special factors for more unusual situations. Publication 1457 is no longer available for purchase from the Superintendent of Documents, United States Government Printing Office. However, pertinent factors in this publication may be obtained from: CC:PA:LPD:PR (IRS Publication 1457), Room 5205, Internal Revenue Service, P.O.Box 7604, Ben Franklin Station, Washington, DC 20044. If a special factor is required in the case of an actual decedent, the Internal Revenue Service may furnish the factor to the executor upon a request for a ruling. The request for a ruling must be accompanied by a recitation of the facts including a statement of the date of birth for each measuring life, the date of the decedent's death, any other applicable dates, and a copy of the will, trust, or other relevant documents. A request for a ruling must comply with the instructions for requesting a ruling published periodically in the Internal Revenue Bulletin (see §§ 601.201 and 601.601(d)(2)(ii)(*b*)) and include payment of the required user fee.

(4) *Actuarial tables.*—Except as provided in § 20.7520-3(b) (pertaining to certain limitations on the use of prescribed tables), Life Table 90CM and Table S (Single life remainder factors applicable where the valuation date is after April 30, 1999, and before May 1, 2009), contained in this paragraph (f)(4), and Table B, Table J, and Table K set forth in § 20.2031-7(d)(6) must be used in the application of the provisions of this section when the section 7520 interest rate component is between 4.2 and 14 percent. Table S and Table 90CM are as follows:

TABLE S
BASED ON LIFE TABLE 90CM
SINGLE LIFE REMAINDER FACTORS
[APPLICABLE AFTER APRIL 30, 1999, AND BEFORE MAY 1, 2009]

	INTEREST RATE									
AGE	*4.2%*	*4.4%*	*4.6%*	*4.8%*	*5.0%*	*5.2%*	*5.4%*	*5.6%*	*5.8%*	*6.0%*
0	.06752	.06130	.05586	.05109	.04691	.04322	.03998	.03711	.03458	.03233
1	.06137	.05495	.04932	.04438	.04003	.03620	.03283	.02985	.02721	.02487
2	.06325	.05667	.05088	.04580	.04132	.03737	.03388	.03079	.02806	.02563
3	.06545	.05869	.05275	.04752	.04291	.03883	.03523	.03203	.02920	.02668
4	.06784	.06092	.05482	.04944	.04469	.04048	.03676	.03346	.03052	.02791
5	.07040	.06331	.05705	.05152	.04662	.04229	.03845	.03503	.03199	.02928
6	.07310	.06583	.05941	.05372	.04869	.04422	.04025	.03672	.03357	.03076
7	.07594	.06849	.06191	.05607	.05089	.04628	.04219	.03854	.03528	.03236
8	.07891	.07129	.06453	.05853	.05321	.04846	.04424	.04046	.03709	.03407
9	.08203	.07423	.06731	.06115	.05567	.05079	.04643	.04253	.03904	.03592
10	.08532	.07734	.07024	.06392	.05829	.05326	.04877	.04474	.04114	.03790
11	.08875	.08059	.07331	.06683	.06104	.05587	.05124	.04709	.04336	.04002
12	.09233	.08398	.07653	.06989	.06394	.05862	.05385	.04957	.04572	.04226
13	.09601	.08748	.07985	.07304	.06693	.06146	.05655	.05214	.04815	.04458
14	.09974	.09102	.08322	.07624	.06997	.06435	.05929	.05474	.05064	.04694
15	.10350	.09460	.08661	.07946	.07303	.06725	.06204	.05735	.05312	.04930
16	.10728	.09818	.09001	.08268	.07608	.07014	.06479	.05996	.05559	.05164
17	.11108	.10179	.09344	.08592	.07916	.07306	.06755	.06257	.05807	.05399
18	.11494	.10545	.09691	.08921	.08227	.07601	.07034	.06521	.06057	.05636
19	.11889	.10921	.10047	.09259	.08548	.07904	.07322	.06794	.06315	.05880
20	.12298	.11310	.10417	.09610	.08881	.08220	.07622	.07078	.06584	.06135
21	.12722	.11713	.10801	.09976	.09228	.08550	.07935	.07375	.06866	.06403
22	.13159	.12130	.11199	.10354	.09588	.08893	.08260	.07685	.07160	.06682
23	.13613	.12563	.11612	.10748	.09964	.09250	.08601	.08009	.07468	.06975
24	.14084	.13014	.12043	.11160	.10357	.09625	.08958	.08349	.07793	.07284
25	.14574	.13484	.12493	.11591	.10768	.10018	.09334	.08708	.08135	.07611
26	.15084	.13974	.12963	.12041	.11199	.10431	.09728	.09085	.08496	.07956
27	.15615	.14485	.13454	.12513	.11652	.10865	.10144	.09484	.08878	.08322
28	.16166	.15016	.13965	.13004	.12124	.11319	.10580	.09901	.09279	.08706
29	.16737	.15567	.14497	.13516	.12617	.11792	.11035	.10339	.09699	.09109
30	.17328	.16138	.15048	.14047	.13129	.12286	.11510	.10796	.10138	.09532
31	.17938	.16728	.15618	.14599	.13661	.12799	.12004	.11272	.10597	.09974
32	.18568	.17339	.16210	.15171	.14214	.13333	.12520	.11769	.11076	.10435
33	.19220	.17972	.16824	.15766	.14790	.13889	.13058	.12289	.11578	.10920
34	.19894	.18627	.17460	.16383	.15388	.14468	.13618	.12831	.12102	.11426
35	.20592	.19307	.18121	.17025	.16011	.15073	.14204	.13399	.12652	.11958
36	.21312	.20010	.18805	.17691	.16658	.15701	.14814	.13990	.13225	.12514
37	.22057	.20737	.19514	.18382	.17331	.16356	.15450	.14608	.13825	.13096
38	.22827	.21490	.20251	.19100	.18031	.17038	.16113	.15253	.14452	.13705
39	.23623	.22270	.21013	.19845	.18759	.17747	.16805	.15927	.15108	.14344
40	.24446	.23078	.21805	.20620	.19516	.18487	.17527	.16631	.15795	.15013
41	.25298	.23915	.22626	.21425	.20305	.19259	.18282	.17368	.16514	.15715
42	.26178	.24782	.23478	.22262	.21125	.20062	.19069	.18138	.17267	.16450
43	.27087	.25678	.24360	.23129	.21977	.20898	.19888	.18941	.18053	.17220
44	.28025	.26603	.25273	.24027	.22860	.21766	.20740	.19777	.18873	18023
45	.28987	.27555	.26212	.24953	.23772	.22664	.21622	.20644	.19724	.18858
46	.29976	.28533	.27179	.25908	.24714	.23591	.22536	.21542	.20606	.19725
47	.30987	.29535	.28171	.26889	.25682	.24546	.23476	.22468	.21518	.20621
48	.32023	.30563	.29190	.27897	.26678	.25530	.24447	.23425	.22460	.21549
49	.33082	.31615	.30234	.28931	.27702	.26543	.25447	.24412	.23434	.22509

See p. 15 for regulations not amended to reflect law changes

AGE	*4.2%*	*4.4%*	*4.6%*	*4.8%*	*5.0%*	*5.2%*	*5.4%*	*5.6%*	*5.8%*	*6.0%*
50	.34166	.32694	.31306	.29995	.28756	.27586	.26479	.25432	.24441	.23502
51	.35274	.33798	.32404	.31085	.29838	.28658	.27541	.26482	.25479	.24528
52	.36402	.34924	.33525	.32200	.30946	.29757	.28630	.27561	.26547	.25584
53	.37550	.36070	.34668	.33339	.32078	.30882	.29746	.28667	.27643	.26669
54	.38717	.37237	.35833	.34500	.33234	.32031	.30888	.29801	.28766	.27782
55	.39903	.38424	.37019	.35683	.34413	.33205	.32056	.30961	.29918	.28925
56	.41108	.39631	.38227	.36890	.35617	.34405	.33250	.32149	.31099	.30097
57	.42330	.40857	.39455	.38118	.36844	.35629	.34469	.33363	.32306	.31297
58	.43566	.42098	.40699	.39364	.38089	.36873	.35710	.34600	.33538	.32522
59	.44811	.43351	.41956	.40623	.39350	.38133	.36968	.35855	.34789	.33768
60	.46066	.44613	.43224	.41896	.40624	.39408	.38243	.37127	.36058	.35033
61	.47330	.45887	.44505	.43182	.41914	.40699	.39535	.38418	.37347	.36318
62	.48608	.47175	.45802	.44485	.43223	.42011	.40848	.39732	.38660	.37629
63	.49898	.48478	.47115	.45807	.44550	.43343	.42184	.41069	.39997	.38966
64	.51200	.49793	.48442	.47143	.45895	.44694	.43539	.42427	.41357	.40326
65	.52512	.51121	.49782	.48495	.47255	.46062	.44912	.43805	.42738	.41709
66	.53835	.52461	.51137	.49862	.48634	.47449	.46307	.45206	.44143	.43118
67	.55174	.53818	.52511	.51250	.50034	.48860	.47727	.46633	.45576	.44556
68	.56524	.55188	.53899	.52654	.51452	.50291	.49168	.48083	.47034	.46020
69	.57882	.56568	.55299	.54071	.52885	.51737	.50627	.49552	.48513	.47506
70	.59242	.57951	.56703	.55495	.54325	.53193	.52096	.51034	.50004	.49007
71	.60598	.59332	.58106	.56918	.55767	.54651	.53569	.52520	.51503	.50516
72	.61948	.60707	.59504	.58338	.57206	.56108	.55043	.54009	.53004	.52029
73	.63287	.62073	.60895	.59751	.58640	.57561	.56513	.55495	.54505	.53543
74	.64621	.63435	.62282	.61162	.60073	.59015	.57985	.56984	.56009	.55061
75	.65953	.64796	.63671	.62575	.61510	.60473	.59463	.58480	.57523	.56591
76	.67287	.66160	.65063	.63995	.62954	.61940	.60952	.59989	.59050	.58135
77	.68622	.67526	.66459	.65419	.64404	.63415	.62450	.61509	.60590	.59694
78	.69954	.68892	.67856	.66845	.65858	.64895	.63955	.63036	.62140	.61264
79	.71278	.70250	.69246	.68265	.67308	.66372	.65457	.64563	.63690	.62836
80	.72581	.71588	.70618	.69668	.68740	.67833	.66945	.66077	.65227	.64396
81	.73857	.72899	.71962	.71045	.70147	.69268	.68408	.67566	.66741	.65933
82	.75101	.74178	.73274	.72389	.71522	.70672	.69840	.69024	.68225	.67441
83	.76311	.75423	.74553	.73700	.72864	.72044	.71240	.70451	.69678	.68919
84	.77497	.76645	.75809	.74988	.74183	.73393	.72618	.71857	.71110	.70377
85	.78665	.77848	.77047	.76260	.75487	.74728	.73982	.73250	.72530	.71823
86	.79805	.79025	.78258	.77504	.76764	.76036	.75320	.74617	.73925	.73245
87	.80904	.80159	.79427	.78706	.77998	.77301	.76615	.75940	.75277	.74624
88	.81962	.81251	.80552	.79865	.79188	.78521	.77865	.77220	.76584	.75958
89	.82978	.82302	.81636	.80980	.80335	.79699	.79072	.78455	.77847	.77248
90	.83952	.83309	.82676	.82052	.81437	.80831	.80234	.79645	.79064	.78492
91	.84870	.84260	.83658	.83064	.82479	.81902	.81332	.80771	.80217	.79671
92	.85716	.85136	.84563	.83998	.83441	.82891	.82348	.81812	.81283	.80761
93	.86494	.85942	.85396	.84858	.84326	.83801	.83283	.82771	.82266	.81767
94	.87216	.86690	.86170	.85657	.85149	.84648	.84153	.83664	.83181	.82704
95	.87898	.87397	.86902	.86412	.85928	.85450	.84977	.84510	.84049	.83592
96	.88537	.88060	.87587	.87121	.86659	.86203	.85751	.85305	.84864	.84427
97	.89127	.88672	.88221	.87775	.87335	.86898	.86467	.86040	.85618	.85200
98	.89680	.89245	.88815	.88389	.87968	.87551	.87138	.86730	.86326	.85926
99	.90217	.89803	.89393	.88987	.88585	.88187	.87793	.87402	.87016	.86633
100	.90738	.90344	.89953	.89567	.89183	.88804	.88428	.88056	.87687	.87322
101	.91250	.90876	.90504	.90137	.89772	.89412	.89054	.88699	.88348	.88000
102	.91751	.91396	.91045	.90696	.90350	.90007	.89668	.89331	.88997	.88666
103	.92247	.91912	.91579	.91249	.90922	.90598	.90276	.89957	.89640	.89326
104	.92775	.92460	.92148	.91839	.91532	.91227	.90924	.90624	.90326	.90031

AGE	4.2%	4.4%	4.6%	4.8%	5.0%	5.2%	5.4%	5.6%	5.8%	6.0%
105	.93290	.92996	.92704	.92415	.92127	.91841	.91558	.91276	.90997	.90719
106	.93948	.93680	.93415	.93151	.92889	.92628	.92370	.92113	.91857	.91604
107	.94739	.94504	.94271	.94039	.93808	.93579	.93351	.93124	.92899	.92675
108	.95950	.95767	.95585	.95404	.95224	.95045	.94867	.94689	.94512	.94336
109	.97985	.97893	.97801	.97710	.97619	.97529	.97438	.97348	.97259	.97170

See p. 15 for regulations not amended to reflect law changes

TABLE S
BASED ON LIFE TABLE 90CM
SINGLE LIFE REMAINDER FACTORS
[APPLICABLE AFTER APRIL 30, 1999, AND BEFORE MAY 1, 2009]

	INTEREST RATE									
AGE	*6.2%*	*6.4%*	*6.6%*	*6.8%*	*7.0%*	*7.2%*	*7.4%*	*7.6%*	*7.8%*	*8.0%*
0	.03034	.02857	.02700	.02559	.02433	.02321	.02220	.02129	.02047	.01973
1	.02279	.02094	.01929	.01782	.01650	.01533	.01427	.01331	.01246	.01168
2	.02347	.02155	.01983	.01829	.01692	.01569	.01458	.01358	.01268	.01187
3	.02444	.02243	.02065	.01905	.01761	.01632	.01516	.01412	.01317	.01232
4	.02558	.02349	.02163	.01996	.01846	.01712	.01590	.01481	.01382	.01292
5	.02686	.02469	.02275	.02101	.01945	.01804	.01677	.01562	.01458	.01364
6	.02825	.02600	.02398	.02217	.02053	.01906	.01773	.01653	.01544	.01445
7	.02976	.02742	.02532	.02343	.02172	.02019	.01880	.01754	.01640	.01536
8	.03137	.02894	.02675	.02479	.02301	.02140	.01995	.01864	.01744	.01635
9	.03311	.03059	.02832	.02627	.02442	.02274	.02122	.01985	.01859	.01745
10	.03499	.03237	.03001	.02788	.02595	.02420	.02262	.02118	.01987	.01867
11	.03700	.03428	.03183	.02961	.02760	.02578	.02413	.02262	.02125	.02000
12	.03913	.03632	.03377	.03146	.02937	.02748	.02575	.02418	.02275	.02144
13	.04135	.03843	.03579	.03339	.03122	.02924	.02744	.02580	.02431	.02294
14	.04359	.04057	.03783	.03534	.03308	.03102	.02915	.02744	.02587	.02444
15	.04584	.04270	.03986	.03728	.03493	.03279	.03083	.02905	.02742	.02593
16	.04806	.04482	.04187	.03919	.03674	.03452	.03248	.03063	.02892	.02736
17	.05029	.04692	.04387	.04108	.03855	.03623	.03411	.03218	.03040	.02877
18	.05253	.04905	.04588	.04299	.04036	.03795	.03574	.03373	.03187	.03017
19	.05484	.05124	.04796	.04496	.04222	.03972	.03742	.03532	.03339	.03161
20	.05726	.05354	.05013	.04702	.04418	.04158	.03919	.03700	.03498	.03313
21	.05980	.05595	.05242	.04920	.04625	.04354	.04105	.03877	.03667	.03473
22	.06246	.05847	.05482	.05147	.04841	.04559	.04301	.04063	.03844	.03642
23	.06524	.06112	.05734	.05387	.05069	.04777	.04508	.04260	.04032	.03821
24	.06819	.06392	.06001	.05642	.05312	.05008	.04728	.04470	.04232	.04012
25	.07131	.06690	.06285	.05913	.05570	.05255	.04964	.04695	.04447	.04218
26	.07460	.07005	.06586	.06200	.05845	.05518	.05215	.04936	.04677	.04438
27	.07810	.07340	.06907	.06508	.06140	.05800	.05485	.05195	.04925	.04676
28	.08179	.07693	.07246	.06833	.06451	.06098	.05772	.05469	.05189	.04929
29	.08566	.08065	.07603	.07176	.06780	.06414	.06075	.05761	.05469	.05198
30	.08973	.08456	.07978	.07536	.07127	.06748	.06396	.06069	.05766	.05483
31	.09398	.08865	.08372	.07915	.07491	.07098	.06733	.06394	.06078	.05785
32	.09843	.09294	.08785	.08313	.07875	.07468	.07089	.06737	.06409	.06103
33	.10310	.09745	.09220	.08732	.08279	.07858	.07466	.07100	.06759	.06441
34	.10799	.10217	.09676	.09173	.08705	.08269	.07862	.07483	.07129	.06798
35	.11314	.10715	.10157	.09638	.09155	.08704	.08283	.07890	.07522	.07179
36	.11852	.11236	.10662	.10127	.09628	.09162	.08726	.08319	.07938	.07581
37	.12416	.11783	.11193	.10641	.10126	.09645	.09194	.08772	.08377	.08006
38	.13009	.12359	.11751	.11183	.10652	.10155	.09689	.09253	.08843	.08459
39	.13629	.12962	.12338	.11753	.11206	.10693	.10212	.09761	.09337	.08938
40	.14281	.13597	.12955	.12355	.11791	.11262	.10766	.10299	.09860	.09447
41	.14966	.14264	.13606	.12989	.12409	.11864	.11352	.10870	.10417	.09989
42	.15685	.14966	.14291	.13657	.13061	.12500	.11972	.11475	.11006	.10564
43	.16437	.15702	.15010	.14360	.13747	.13171	.12627	.12115	.11631	.11174
44	.17224	.16472	.15764	.15098	.14469	.13876	.13317	.12789	.12290	.11819
45	.18042	.17274	.16550	.15867	.15223	.14615	.14040	.13496	.12982	.12496
46	.18893	.18110	.17370	.16671	.16011	.15387	.14796	.14238	.13708	.13207
47	.19775	.18975	.18220	.17505	.16830	.16190	.15584	.15010	.14466	.13950
48	.20688	.19873	.19102	.18373	.17682	.17027	.16406	.15817	.15258	.14727
49	.21633	.20804	.20018	.19274	.18568	.17898	.17262	.16658	.16084	.15539

AGE	*6.2%*	*6.4%*	*6.6%*	*6.8%*	*7.0%*	*7.2%*	*7.4%*	*7.6%*	*7.8%*	*8.0%*
50	.22612	.21769	.20969	.20210	.19490	.18805	.18155	.17536	.16948	.16388
51	.23625	.22769	.21955	.21182	.20448	.19749	.19084	.18452	.17849	.17275
52	.24669	.23799	.22973	.22186	.21438	.20726	.20047	.19400	.18734	.18196
53	.25742	.24861	.24022	.23222	.22461	.21735	.21043	.20383	.19753	.19151
54	.26845	.25952	.25101	.24290	.23516	.22777	.22072	.21399	.20756	.20140
55	.27978	.27074	.26212	.25389	.24604	.23853	.23136	.22450	.21793	.21166
56	.29140	.28227	.27355	.26522	.25725	.24963	.24233	.23535	.22867	.22227
57	.30333	.29411	.28529	.27686	.26879	.26106	.25365	.24656	.23976	.23324
58	.31551	.30621	.29731	.28878	.28061	.27278	.26528	.25807	.25116	.24453
59	.32790	.31854	.30956	.30095	.29269	.28477	.27716	.26986	.26284	.25610
60	.34050	.33107	.32202	.31334	.30500	.29699	.28929	.28190	.27478	.26794
61	.35331	.34384	.33473	.32598	.31757	.30948	.30170	.29422	.28701	.28007
62	.36639	.35688	.34772	.33892	.33044	.32229	.31443	.30687	.29958	.29255
63	.37974	.37020	.36101	.35216	.34363	.33542	.32750	.31986	.31250	.30539
64	.39334	.38378	.37456	.36568	.35711	.34884	.34087	.33317	.32574	.31857
65	.40718	.39761	.38838	.37947	.37087	.36257	.35455	.34681	.33932	.33208
66	.42128	.41172	.40249	.39357	.38496	.37663	.36858	.36079	.35326	.34597
67	.43569	.42616	.41694	.40803	.39941	.39107	.38299	.37518	.36761	.36028
68	.45038	.44089	.43170	.42281	.41419	.40585	.39777	.38994	.38235	.37499
69	.46531	.45587	.44672	.43786	.42927	.42094	.41286	.40503	.39743	.39006
70	.48040	.47103	.46194	.45312	.44456	.43626	.42820	.42038	.41278	.40540
71	.49558	.48629	.47727	.46851	.46000	.45174	.44371	.43591	.42832	.42095
72	.51082	.50162	.49268	.48399	.47554	.46733	.45934	.45157	.44401	.43666
73	.52607	.51697	.50813	.49952	.49114	.48299	.47506	.46733	.45981	.45249
74	.54139	.53241	.52367	.51515	.50686	.49879	.49092	.48325	.47578	.46849
75	.55683	.54798	.53936	.53095	.52276	.51477	.50698	.49938	.49197	.48474
76	.57243	.56373	.55524	.54696	.53888	.53100	.52330	.51579	.50846	.50130
77	.58819	.57965	.57132	.56318	.55523	.54747	.53988	.53247	.52523	.51815
78	.60408	.59572	.58755	.57957	.57177	.56414	.55668	.54939	.54225	.53527
79	.62001	.61184	.60385	.59604	.58840	.58092	.57360	.56644	.55943	.55256
80	.63582	.62786	.62007	.61244	.60497	.59765	.59048	.58347	.57659	.56985
81	.65142	.64367	.63608	.62864	.62135	.61421	.60721	.60034	.59361	.58701
82	.66673	.65920	.65182	.64458	.63748	.63052	.62368	.61698	.61041	.60395
83	.68175	.67444	.66728	.66024	.65334	.64656	.63991	.63338	.62696	.62066
84	.69657	.68950	.68256	.67574	.66904	.66246	.65599	.64964	.64340	.63727
85	.71128	.70446	.69775	.69116	.68467	.67830	.67204	.66587	.65982	.65386
86	.72576	.71919	.71272	.70636	.70010	.69394	.68789	.68193	.67606	.67029
87	.73981	.73349	.72726	.72114	.71511	.70917	.70333	.69757	.69190	.68632
88	.75342	.74735	.74137	.73548	.72968	.72396	.71833	.71279	.70732	.70194
89	.76658	.76076	.75503	.74938	.74381	.73832	.73290	.72757	.72231	.71712
90	.77928	.77371	.76823	.76281	.75748	.75221	.74702	.74190	.73684	.73186
91	.79131	.78600	.78075	.77557	.77046	.76542	.76044	.75553	.75068	.74589
92	.80246	.79737	.79235	.78740	.78250	.77767	.77290	.76818	.76353	.75893
93	.81274	.80788	.80307	.79832	.79363	.78899	.78441	.77989	.77542	.77100
94	.82232	.81766	.81306	.80850	.80401	.79956	.79517	.79082	.78653	.78228
95	.83141	.82695	.82254	.81818	.81387	.80961	.80539	.80122	.79710	.79302
96	.83996	.83569	.83147	.82729	.82316	.81907	.81503	.81103	.80707	.80315
97	.84787	.84378	.83973	.83573	.83176	.82784	.82396	.82012	.81632	.81255
98	.85530	.85138	.84750	.84366	.83985	.83609	.83236	.82867	.82502	.82140
99	.86255	.85880	.85508	.85140	.84776	.84415	.84057	.83703	.83353	.83005
100	.86960	.86601	.86246	.85894	.85546	.85200	.84858	.84519	.84183	.83849
101	.87655	.87313	.86974	.86638	.86305	.85975	.85648	.85324	.85003	.84684
102	.88338	.88012	.87689	.87369	.87052	.86738	.86426	.86116	.85809	.85505
103	.89015	.88706	.88399	.88095	.87793	.87494	.87197	.86903	.86611	.86321
104	.89737	.89446	.89157	.88871	.88586	.88304	.88024	.87745	.87469	.87195

AGE	*6.2%*	*6.4%*	*6.6%*	*6.8%*	*7.0%*	*7.2%*	*7.4%*	*7.6%*	*7.8%*	*8.0%*
105	.90443	.90170	.89898	.89628	.89360	.89094	.88830	.88568	.88307	.88049
106	.91351	.91101	.90852	.90605	.90359	.90115	.89873	.89632	.89392	.89154
107	.92452	.92230	.92010	.91791	.91573	.91356	.91141	.90927	.90714	.90502
108	.94161	.93987	.93814	.93641	.93469	.93298	.93128	.92958	.92790	.92622
109	.97081	.96992	.96904	.96816	.96729	.96642	.96555	.96468	.96382	.96296

TABLE S
BASED ON LIFE TABLE 90CM
SINGLE LIFE REMAINDER FACTORS
[APPLICABLE AFTER APRIL 30, 1999, AND BEFORE MAY 1, 2009]

	INTEREST RATE									
AGE	*8.2%*	*8.4%*	*8.6%*	*8.8%*	*9.0%*	*9.2%*	*9.4%*	*9.6%*	*9.8%*	*10.0%*
0	.01906	.01845	.01790	.01740	.01694	.01652	.01613	.01578	.01546	.01516
1	.01098	.01034	.00977	.00924	.00876	.00833	.00793	.00756	.00722	.00691
2	.01113	.01046	.00986	.00930	.00880	.00834	.00791	.00753	.00717	.00684
3	.01155	.01084	.01020	.00962	.00909	.00860	.00816	.00775	.00737	.00702
4	.01211	.01137	.01069	.01008	.00952	.00900	.00853	.00810	.00770	.00733
5	.01279	.01201	.01130	.01065	.01006	.00952	.00902	.00856	.00814	.00775
6	.01356	.01274	.01199	.01131	.01068	.01011	.00959	.00910	.00865	.00824
7	.01442	.01356	.01277	.01205	.01140	.01079	.01023	.00972	.00925	.00881
8	.01536	.01446	.01363	.01287	.01218	.01154	.01096	.01041	.00991	.00945
9	.01641	.01546	.01460	.01380	.01307	.01240	.01178	.01120	.01068	.01019
10	.01758	.01659	.01567	.01484	.01407	.01336	.01270	.01210	.01154	.01103
11	.01886	.01781	.01686	.01598	.01517	.01442	.01373	.01310	.01251	.01196
12	.02024	.01915	.01814	.01721	.01636	.01558	.01485	.01419	.01357	.01299
13	.02168	.02054	.01948	.01851	.01762	.01679	.01603	.01533	.01467	.01407
14	.02313	.02193	.02083	.01981	.01887	.01801	.01721	.01646	.01578	.01514
15	.02456	.02330	.02214	.02107	.02009	.01918	.01834	.01756	.01684	.01617
16	.02593	.02462	.02340	.02229	.02126	.02030	.01942	.01860	.01785	.01714
17	.02728	.02590	.02463	.02346	.02238	.02138	.02046	.01960	.01880	.01806
18	.02861	.02717	.02584	.02462	.02348	.02243	.02146	.02056	.01972	.01894
19	.02998	.02847	.02708	.02580	.02461	.02351	.02249	.02154	.02066	.01984
20	.03142	.02984	.02839	.02704	.02580	.02465	.02357	.02258	.02165	.02079
21	.03295	.03130	.02978	.02837	.02706	.02585	.02473	.02368	.02271	.02180
22	.03455	.03283	.03124	.02976	.02839	.02712	.02594	.02484	.02382	.02286
23	.03626	.03446	.03279	.03124	.02981	.02847	.02723	.02608	.02500	.02400
24	.03809	.03620	.03446	.03283	.03133	.02993	.02863	.02741	.02628	.02522
25	.04005	.03808	.03625	.03456	.03298	.03151	.03014	.02887	.02768	.02656
26	.04216	.04010	.03819	.03641	.03476	.03322	.03178	.03044	.02919	.02802
27	.04444	.04229	.04029	.03843	.03670	.03508	.03357	.03217	.03085	.02962
28	.04687	.04463	.04254	.04059	.03877	.03708	.03550	.03402	.03263	.03133
29	.04946	.04712	.04493	.04289	.04099	.03922	.03756	.03600	.03455	.03318
30	.05221	.04976	.04748	.04534	.04335	.04149	.03975	.03812	.03659	.03515
31	.05511	.05255	.05017	.04794	.04585	.04390	.04208	.04037	.03876	.03725
32	.05818	.05551	.05302	.05069	.04851	.04647	.04455	.04276	.04107	.03948
33	.06144	.05866	.05606	.05363	.05135	.04921	.04720	.04532	.04355	.04188
34	.06489	.06200	.05928	.05674	.05436	.05212	.05002	.04805	.04619	.04444
35	.06857	.06555	.06273	.06007	.05758	.05524	.05304	.05097	.04902	.04718
36	.07246	.06932	.06638	.06361	.06101	.05856	.05626	.05409	.05205	.05012
37	.07659	.07332	.07025	.06737	.06466	.06210	.05969	.05742	.05528	.05325
38	.08098	.07758	.07439	.07138	.06855	.06588	.06336	.06099	.05874	.05662
39	.08563	.08210	.07878	.07565	.07270	.06992	.06729	.06480	.06245	.06023
40	.09059	.08692	.08347	.08021	.07714	.07423	.07149	.06889	.06643	.06411
41	.09586	.09206	.08848	.08509	.08189	.07886	.07600	.07329	.07072	.06828
42	.10147	.09753	.09381	.09029	.08696	.08381	.08083	.07800	.07531	.07277
43	.10742	.10334	.09948	.09583	.09237	.08909	.08598	.08304	.08024	.07758
44	.11373	.10950	.10551	.10172	.09813	.09472	.09148	.08841	.08549	.08272
45	.12035	.11599	.11185	.10792	.10420	.10066	.09730	.09410	.09106	.08817
46	.12732	.12281	.11853	.11447	.11061	.10694	.10345	.10013	.09696	.09395
47	.13460	.12995	.12553	.12133	.11733	.11353	.10991	.10646	.10317	.10004
48	.14223	.13743	.13287	.12853	.12439	.12046	.11671	.11313	.10972	.10646
49	.15020	.14526	.14056	.13608	.13181	.12774	.12385	.12015	.11661	.11322

AGE	8.2%	8.4%	8.6%	8.8%	9.0%	9.2%	9.4%	9.6%	9.8%	10.0%
50	.15855	.15347	.14862	.14401	.13960	.13540	.13138	.12754	.12388	.12037
51	.16727	.16205	.15707	.15232	.14777	.14344	.13929	.13532	.13153	.12789
52	.17634	.17098	.16587	.16097	.15630	.15183	.14755	.14345	.13953	.13577
53	.18576	.18027	.17501	.16999	.16518	.16057	.15616	.15194	.14789	.14400
54	.19552	.18990	.18451	.17935	.17441	.16968	.16514	.16078	.15661	.15260
55	.20564	.19989	.19437	.18908	.18402	.17915	.17449	.17001	.16571	.16157
56	.21613	.21025	.20461	.19919	.19400	.18901	.18422	.17962	.17519	.17093
57	.22698	.22098	.21522	.20968	.20436	.19925	.19434	.18961	.18507	.18069
58	.23816	.23204	.22616	.22051	.21507	.20984	.20481	.19996	.19530	.19080
59	.24962	.24339	.23740	.23163	.22608	.22073	.21558	.21062	.20584	.20123
60	.26136	.25502	.24892	.24304	.23738	.23192	.22666	.22158	.21669	.21196
61	.27339	.26695	.26075	.25477	.24900	.24343	.23806	.23288	.22787	.22304
62	.28578	.27925	.27295	.26687	.26100	.25533	.24985	.24456	.23945	.23451
63	.29854	.29192	.28553	.27935	.27339	.26762	.26205	.25666	.25145	.24641
64	.31164	.30494	.29846	.29221	.28615	.28030	.27463	.26915	.26384	.25870
65	.32508	.31831	.31177	.30543	.29930	.29336	.28761	.28203	.27663	.27140
66	.33891	.33208	.32547	.31906	.31285	.30684	.30101	.29536	.28987	.28456
67	.35318	.34630	.33963	.33316	.32689	.32081	.31491	.30918	.30363	.29823
68	.36785	.36093	.35422	.34770	.34138	.33524	.32928	.32349	.31787	.31240
69	.38290	.37595	.36920	.36265	.35628	.35009	.34408	.33824	.33256	.32703
70	.39823	.39127	.38450	.37791	.37151	.36529	.35924	.35335	.34762	.34204
71	.41378	.40681	.40003	.39343	.38701	.38076	.37467	.36875	.36298	.35736
72	.42950	.42253	.41575	.40914	.40271	.39644	.39034	.38438	.37858	.37293
73	.44535	.43840	.43162	.42502	.41858	.41231	.40619	.40022	.39440	.38872
74	.46139	.45446	.44771	.44112	.43469	.42842	.42230	.41632	.41049	.40479
75	.47769	.47080	.46408	.45752	.45111	.44485	.43874	.43277	.42693	.42123
76	.49430	.48747	.48079	.47427	.46790	.46167	.45558	.44963	.44380	.43811
77	.51123	.50447	.49786	.49139	.48506	.47888	.47282	.46690	.46111	.45543
78	.52845	.52177	.51523	.50884	.50257	.49645	.49044	.48457	.47881	.47317
79	.54584	.53926	.53282	.52650	.52032	.51426	.50833	.50251	.49681	.49122
80	.56325	.55678	.55044	.54423	.53813	.53216	.52630	.52056	.51492	.50939
81	.58054	.57419	.56797	.56186	.55587	.54999	.54422	.53856	.53300	.52754
82	.59762	.59140	.58530	.57931	.57343	.56766	.56198	.55641	.55094	.54557
83	.61448	.60840	.60243	.59657	.59081	.58515	.57958	.57411	.56874	.56346
84	.63124	.62531	.61949	.61376	.60813	.60259	.59715	.59179	.58652	.58134
85	.64800	.64224	.63657	.63099	.62550	.62010	.61478	.60955	.60441	.59934
86	.66461	.65902	.65351	.64810	.64276	.63751	.63233	.62724	.62222	.61728
87	.68083	.67541	.67008	.66483	.65965	.65455	.64953	.64458	.63970	.63489
88	.69663	.69140	.68624	.68116	.67615	.67121	.66634	.66154	.65680	.65213
89	.71201	.70696	.70199	.69708	.69224	.68747	.68276	.67811	.67353	.66900
90	.72694	.72209	.71730	.71257	.70791	.70330	.69876	.69427	.68984	.68547
91	.74117	.73650	.73190	.72735	.72286	.71842	.71404	.70972	.70545	.70123
92	.75439	.74991	.74548	.74110	.73678	.73251	.72829	.72412	.72000	.71593
93	.76664	.76233	.75806	.75385	.74969	.74557	.74150	.73748	.73350	.72957
94	.77809	.77394	.76983	.76578	.76177	.75780	.75388	.75000	.74616	.74237
95	.78899	.78500	.78106	.77715	.77329	.76947	.76569	.76195	.75826	.75460
96	.79928	.79544	.79165	.78790	.78418	.78050	.77686	.77326	.76970	.76617
97	.80883	.80514	.80149	.79787	.79430	.79075	.78725	.78377	.78033	.77693
98	.81781	.81427	.81075	.80727	.80382	.80041	.79703	.79368	.79036	.78708
99	.82661	.82320	.81982	.81648	.81316	.80988	.80662	.80340	.80020	.79704
100	.83519	.83192	.82868	.82547	.82228	.81913	.81600	.81290	.80982	.80678
101	.84368	.84055	.83744	.83437	.83131	.82829	.82529	.82231	.81936	.81643
102	.85203	.84904	.84607	.84313	.84021	.83731	.83444	.83159	.82876	.82596
103	.86034	.85748	.85465	.85184	.84906	.84629	.84355	.84082	.83812	.83544
104	.86923	.86653	.86385	.86119	.85855	.85593	.85333	.85074	.84818	.84563

AGE	8.2%	8.4%	8.6%	8.8%	9.0%	9.2%	9.4%	9.6%	9.8%	10.0%
105	.87792	.87537	.87283	.87032	.86782	.86534	.86287	.86042	.85799	.85557
106	.88918	.88683	.88450	.88218	.87987	.87758	.87530	.87304	.87079	.86855
107	.90291	.90082	.89873	.89666	.89460	.89255	.89051	.88849	.88647	.88447
108	.92455	.92288	.92123	.91958	.91794	.91630	.91468	.91306	.91145	.90984
109	.96211	.96125	.96041	.95956	.95872	.95788	.95704	.95620	.95537	.95455

TABLE S
BASED ON LIFE TABLE 90CM
SINGLE LIFE REMAINDER FACTORS
[APPLICABLE AFTER APRIL 30, 1999, AND BEFORE MAY 1, 2009]

	INTEREST RATE									
AGE	*10.2%*	*10.4%*	*10.6%*	*10.8%*	*11.0%*	*11.2%*	*11.4%*	*11.6%*	*11.8%*	*12.0%*
0	.01488	.01463	.01439	.01417	.01396	.01377	.01359	.01343	.01327	.01312
1	.00662	.00636	.00612	.00589	.00568	.00548	.00530	.00513	.00497	.00482
2	.00654	.00626	.00600	.00576	.00554	.00533	.00514	.00496	.00479	.00463
3	.00670	.00641	.00613	.00588	.00564	.00542	.00522	.00502	.00484	.00468
4	.00699	.00668	.00639	.00612	.00587	.00563	.00542	.00521	.00502	.00484
5	.00739	.00706	.00675	.00646	.00620	.00595	.00571	.00550	.00529	.00510
6	.00786	.00751	.00718	.00687	.00659	.00633	.00608	.00585	.00563	.00543
7	.00841	.00803	.00769	.00736	.00706	.00678	.00652	.00627	.00604	.00582
8	.00902	.00863	.00826	.00791	.00759	.00730	.00702	.00675	.00651	.00628
9	.00973	.00931	.00892	.00856	.00822	.00790	.00760	.00733	.00706	.00682
10	.01055	.01010	.00969	.00930	.00894	.00861	.00829	.00799	.00772	.00746
11	.01146	.01099	.01055	.01014	.00976	.00940	.00907	.00875	.00846	.00818
12	.01246	.01196	.01150	.01106	.01066	.01028	.00993	.00960	.00928	.00899
13	.01351	.01298	.01249	.01204	.01161	.01121	.01084	.01049	.01016	.00985
14	.01455	.01400	.01348	.01300	.01255	.01213	.01173	.01136	.01102	.01069
15	.01555	.01497	.01443	.01392	.01345	.01300	.01259	.01220	.01183	.01148
16	.01648	.01587	.01530	.01477	.01427	.01380	.01336	.01295	.01257	.01220
17	.01737	.01673	.01612	.01556	.01504	.01455	.01408	.01365	.01324	.01286
18	.01822	.01754	.01691	.01632	.01576	.01525	.01476	.01430	.01387	.01347
19	.01908	.01837	.01770	.01708	.01650	.01595	.01544	.01495	.01450	.01407
20	.01999	.01924	.01854	.01788	.01726	.01669	.01615	.01564	.01516	.01471
21	.02096	.02017	.01943	.01874	.01809	.01748	.01691	.01637	.01586	.01539
22	.02197	.02114	.02036	.01963	.01895	.01830	.01770	.01713	.01660	.01610
23	.02306	.02218	.02136	.02059	.01987	.01919	.01855	.01795	.01739	.01686
24	.02424	.02331	.02245	.02163	.02087	.02016	.01948	.01885	.01825	.01769
25	.02552	.02455	.02364	.02278	.02197	.02122	.02051	.01984	.01920	.01861
26	.02692	.02589	.02493	.02403	.02318	.02238	.02162	.02091	.02025	.01961
27	.02846	.02738	.02636	.02541	.02451	.02367	.02287	.02212	.02141	.02074
28	.03012	.02898	.02791	.02690	.02595	.02506	.02422	.02342	.02267	.02196
29	.03190	.03070	.02957	.02851	.02751	.02656	.02567	.02483	.02404	.02329
30	.03381	.03254	.03135	.03023	.02917	.02817	.02723	.02634	.02551	.02471
31	.03583	.03450	.03324	.03206	.03094	.02989	.02890	.02796	.02707	.02623
32	.03799	.03659	.03527	.03402	.03284	.03173	.03068	.02968	.02874	.02785
33	.04031	.03883	.03744	.03612	.03488	.03371	.03260	.03155	.03055	.02961
34	.04279	.04123	.03976	.03838	.03707	.03583	.03465	.03354	.03249	.03149
35	.04545	.04382	.04227	.04081	.03943	.03812	.03688	.03571	.03459	.03354
36	.04830	.04658	.04495	.04341	.04196	.04058	.03927	.03803	.03685	.03573
37	.05134	.04953	.04782	.04620	.04467	.04321	.04183	.04052	.03928	.03809
38	.05462	.05272	.05092	.04921	.04760	.04606	.04461	.04322	.04191	.04066
39	.05812	.05613	.05424	.05245	.05075	.04913	.04760	.04614	.04475	.04343
40	.06190	.05981	.05782	.05594	.05415	.05245	.05083	.04929	.04783	.04643
41	.06597	.06378	.06170	.05972	.05784	.05605	.05435	.05272	.05118	.04970
42	.07035	.06806	.06587	.06380	.06182	.05994	.05815	.05644	.05481	.05326
43	.07505	.07265	.07036	.06818	.06611	.06414	.06225	.06045	.05874	.05710
44	.08008	.07757	.07518	.07290	.07072	.06865	.06667	.06478	.06298	.06125
45	.08542	.08279	.08029	.07791	.07563	.07346	.07138	.06940	.06750	.06569
46	.09108	.08834	.08573	.08324	.08085	.07858	.07640	.07432	.07233	.07043
47	.09705	.09419	.09147	.08886	.08637	.08399	.08172	.07954	.07745	.07545
48	.10335	.10038	.09754	.09482	.09222	.08973	.08735	.08507	.08288	.08078
49	.10999	.10690	.10394	.10111	.09840	.09581	.09332	.09093	.08864	.08644

See p. 15 for regulations not amended to reflect law changes

AGE	10.2%	10.4%	10.6%	10.8%	11.0%	11.2%	11.4%	11.6%	11.8%	12.0%
50	.11701	.11380	.11073	.10778	.10496	.10225	.09965	.09716	.09477	.09247
51	.12441	.12108	.11789	.11482	.11189	.10907	.10636	.10376	.10126	.09886
52	.13217	.12871	.12540	.12222	.11916	.11623	.11341	.11071	.10810	.10560
53	.14028	.13670	.13327	.12997	.12680	.12375	.12082	.11801	.11529	.11268
54	.14875	.14505	.14150	.13808	.13480	.13163	.12859	.12566	.12284	.12012
55	.15760	.15378	.15011	.14657	.14317	.13989	.13674	.13370	.13077	.12794
56	.16684	.16290	.15911	.15546	.15194	.14855	.14528	.14213	.13909	.13615
57	.17648	.17242	.16851	.16474	.16111	.15760	.15422	.15096	.14781	.14477
58	.18647	.18229	.17827	.17438	.17064	.16702	.16353	.16015	.15689	.15374
59	.19678	.19249	.18835	.18435	.18049	.17676	.17316	.16968	.16631	.16305
60	.20740	.20300	.19875	.19464	.19066	.18682	.18311	.17952	.17604	.17268
61	.21837	.21385	.20949	.20527	.20119	.19724	.19341	.18971	.18613	.18266
62	.22973	.22511	.22064	.21631	.21212	.20807	.20414	.20033	.19664	.19306
63	.24152	.23680	.23222	.22779	.22350	.21934	.21530	.21139	.20760	.20392
64	.25372	.24890	.24422	.23969	.23529	.23103	.22690	.22289	.21899	.21521
65	.26633	.26141	.25664	.25201	.24752	.24316	.23893	.23482	.23083	.22695
66	.27940	.27439	.26953	.26481	.26023	.25577	.25145	.24724	.24316	.23918
67	.29299	.28790	.28296	.27815	.27348	.26894	.26453	.26024	.25606	.25200
68	.30709	.30193	.29691	.29202	.28728	.28265	.27816	.27378	.26952	.26537
69	.32166	.31643	.31134	.30639	.30157	.29687	.29230	.28785	.28351	.27928
70	.33661	.33133	.32618	.32116	.31628	.31152	.30688	.30235	.29794	.29364
71	.35188	.34654	.34134	.33627	.33133	.32651	.32181	.31722	.31275	.30838
72	.36742	.36204	.35679	.35168	.34668	.34181	.33706	.33241	.32788	.32345
73	.38317	.37776	.37248	.36733	.36229	.35738	.35257	.34788	.34330	.33882
74	.39923	.39380	.38849	.38330	.37823	.37328	.36844	.36370	.35908	.35455
75	.41566	.41021	.40489	.39968	.39459	.38961	.38474	.37997	.37531	.37074
76	.43254	.42709	.42176	.41655	.41144	.40645	.40156	.39677	.39208	.38749
77	.44988	.44444	.43912	.43391	.42880	.42380	.41891	.41411	.40940	.40479
78	.46765	.46224	.45694	.45174	.44665	.44166	.43677	.43197	.42726	.42265
79	.48574	.48037	.47510	.46993	.46487	.45990	.45502	.45024	.44554	.44094
80	.50397	.49865	.49343	.48830	.48327	.47834	.47349	.46873	.46406	.45947
81	.52219	.51693	.51176	.50669	.50171	.49682	.49201	.48729	.48265	.47809
82	.54029	.53510	.53000	.52499	.52007	.51523	.51047	.50580	.50120	.49667
83	.55826	.55315	.54813	.54319	.53834	.53356	.52886	.52424	.51969	.51522
84	.57624	.57123	.56629	.56144	.55666	.55195	.54732	.54277	.53828	.53386
85	.59435	.58944	.58460	.57984	.57516	.57054	.56599	.56151	.55710	.55275
86	.61241	.60762	.60289	.59824	.59365	.58913	.58468	.58029	.57596	.57170
87	.63015	.62548	.62087	.61633	.61185	.60744	.60309	.59880	.59456	.59039
88	.64753	.64299	.63851	.63409	.62973	.62543	.62118	.61700	.61287	.60879
89	.66454	.66013	.65579	.65150	.64726	.64308	.63895	.63488	.63086	.62689
90	.68115	.67689	.67268	.66853	.66442	.66037	.65637	.65241	.64851	.64465
91	.69706	.69294	.68887	.68486	.68089	.67696	.67309	.66925	.66547	.66173
92	.71190	.70792	.70399	.70011	.69627	.69247	.68872	.68501	.68134	.67771
93	.72569	.72184	.71804	.71429	.71057	.70689	.70326	.69967	.69611	.69259
94	.73861	.73490	.73123	.72759	.72400	.72044	.71692	.71344	.71000	.70659
95	.75097	.74739	.74384	.74033	.73686	.73342	.73002	.72665	.72331	.72001
96	.76267	.75922	.75579	.75240	.74905	.74572	.74243	.73917	.73595	.73275
97	.77356	.77022	.76691	.76363	.76039	.75718	.75399	.75084	.74772	.74463
98	.78382	.78059	.77740	.77423	.77110	.76799	.76491	.76186	.75884	.75584
99	.79390	.79079	.78771	.78465	.78162	.77862	.77565	.77270	.76978	.76688
100	.80376	.80076	.79779	.79485	.79193	.78904	.78617	.78333	.78051	.77771
101	.81353	.81066	.80780	.80497	.80217	.79938	.79662	.79388	.79117	.78847
102	.82318	.82042	.81768	.81496	.81227	.80960	.80694	.80431	.80170	.79911
103	.83278	.83014	.82752	.82491	.82233	.81977	.81723	.81470	.81220	.80971
104	.84310	.84059	.83810	.83563	.83317	.83073	.82831	.82591	.82352	.82115

AGE	*10.2%*	*10.4%*	*10.6%*	*10.8%*	*11.0%*	*11.2%*	*11.4%*	*11.6%*	*11.8%*	*12.0%*
105	.85318	.85079	.84843	.84607	.84374	.84142	.83911	.83682	.83455	.83229
106	.86633	.86413	.86193	.85975	.85758	.85543	.85329	.85116	.84904	.84694
107	.88247	.88049	.87852	.87656	.87460	.87266	.87073	.86881	.86690	.86500
108	.90825	.90666	.90507	.90350	.90193	.90037	.89881	.89727	.89572	.89419
109	.95372	.95290	.95208	.95126	.95045	.94964	.94883	.94803	.94723	.94643

TABLE S
BASED ON LIFE TABLE 90CM
SINGLE LIFE REMAINDER FACTORS
[APPLICABLE AFTER APRIL 30, 1999, AND BEFORE MAY 1, 2009]

	INTEREST RATE									
AGE	*12.2%*	*12.4%*	*12.6%*	*12.8%*	*13.0%*	*13.2%*	*13.4%*	*13.6%*	*13.8%*	*14.0%*
0	.01298	.01285	.01273	.01261	.01250	.01240	.01230	.01221	.01212	.01203
1	.00468	.00455	.00443	.00431	.00420	.00410	.00400	.00391	.00382	.00374
2	.00448	.00435	.00421	.00409	.00398	.00387	.00376	.00366	.00357	.00348
3	.00452	.00437	.00423	.00410	.00398	.00386	.00375	.00365	.00355	.00345
4	.00468	.00452	.00437	.00423	.00410	.00397	.00386	.00375	.00364	.00354
5	.00493	.00476	.00460	.00445	.00431	.00418	.00405	.00393	.00382	.00371
6	.00524	.00506	.00489	.00473	.00458	.00444	.00430	.00418	.00406	.00394
7	.00562	.00543	.00525	.00508	.00492	.00477	.00462	.00449	.00436	.00423
8	.00606	.00586	.00566	.00548	.00531	.00515	.00499	.00485	.00471	.00458
9	.00659	.00637	.00616	.00597	.00579	.00561	.00545	.00529	.00514	.00500
10	.00721	.00698	.00676	.00655	.00636	.00617	.00600	.00583	.00567	.00552
11	.00792	.00767	.00744	.00722	.00701	.00682	.00663	.00645	.00628	.00612
12	.00871	.00845	.00821	.00797	.00775	.00754	.00735	.00716	.00698	.00681
13	.00955	.00928	.00902	.00877	.00854	.00831	.00810	.00790	.00771	.00753
14	.01038	.01009	.00981	.00955	.00930	.00907	.00885	.00864	.00843	.00824
15	.01116	.01085	.01056	.01028	.01002	.00977	.00954	.00932	.00910	.00890
16	.01186	.01153	.01123	.01094	.01066	.01040	.01015	.00992	.00969	.00948
17	.01250	.01215	.01183	.01152	.01124	.01096	.01070	.01045	.01022	.00999
18	.01308	.01272	.01238	.01206	.01175	.01147	.01119	.01093	.01068	.01044
19	.01367	.01329	.01293	.01259	.01227	.01196	.01167	.01140	.01113	.01088
20	.01428	.01388	.01350	.01314	.01280	.01248	.01217	.01188	.01161	.01134
21	.01494	.01451	.01411	.01373	.01337	.01303	.01271	.01240	.01211	.01183
22	.01562	.01517	.01475	.01435	.01397	.01361	.01326	.01294	.01263	.01233
23	.01635	.01588	.01543	.01501	.01460	.01422	.01386	.01351	.01319	.01287
24	.01716	.01665	.01618	.01573	.01530	.01489	.01451	.01415	.01380	.01347
25	.01804	.01751	.01701	.01653	.01608	.01565	.01524	.01485	.01448	.01413
26	.01902	.01845	.01792	.01741	.01693	.01648	.01604	.01563	.01524	.01487
27	.02011	.01951	.01895	.01841	.01790	.01742	.01696	.01652	.01610	.01571
28	.02129	.02066	.02006	.01949	.01895	.01844	.01795	.01748	.01704	.01662
29	.02258	.02191	.02127	.02067	.02009	.01955	.01903	.01853	.01806	.01762
30	.02396	.02325	.02257	.02193	.02132	.02074	.02019	.01966	.01916	.01869
31	.02543	.02467	.02396	.02328	.02263	.02201	.02143	.02087	.02034	.01983
32	.02701	.02621	.02545	.02472	.02404	.02338	.02276	.02217	.02160	.02106
33	.02871	.02786	.02706	.02629	.02556	.02487	.02420	.02357	.02297	.02240
34	.03054	.02964	.02879	.02797	.02720	.02646	.02576	.02509	.02445	.02383
35	.03253	.03158	.03067	.02981	.02898	.02820	.02745	.02674	.02606	.02541
36	.03467	.03366	.03269	.03178	.03090	.03007	.02928	.02852	.02779	.02710
37	.03697	.03590	.03488	.03391	.03298	.03209	.03125	.03044	.02967	.02893
38	.03947	.03833	.03725	.03622	.03524	.03430	.03340	.03254	.03172	.03094
39	.04217	.04096	.03982	.03873	.03768	.03669	.03573	.03482	.03395	.03312
40	.04510	.04383	.04262	.04146	.04035	.03930	.03828	.03732	.03639	.03550
41	.04830	.04695	.04567	.04445	.04327	.04215	.04108	.04005	.03907	.03812
42	.05177	.05035	.04900	.04770	.04646	.04527	.04413	.04304	.04200	.04100
43	.05553	.05404	.05261	.05123	.04992	.04866	.04746	.04630	.04520	.04413
44	.05960	.05802	.05651	.05506	.05368	.05235	.05107	.04985	.04867	.04754
45	.06395	.06229	.06069	.05917	.05770	.05630	.05495	.05365	.05241	.05121
46	.06860	.06685	.06517	.06356	.06202	.06053	.05911	.05774	.05643	.05516
47	.07353	.07169	.06992	.06823	.06660	.06504	.06353	.06209	.06070	.05936
48	.07877	.07684	.07498	.07320	.07149	.06984	.06826	.06673	.06527	.06385
49	.08433	.08231	.08036	.07849	.07669	.07495	.07329	.07168	.07013	.06864

See p. 15 for regulations not amended to reflect law changes

AGE	*12.2%*	*12.4%*	*12.6%*	*12.8%*	*13.0%*	*13.2%*	*13.4%*	*13.6%*	*13.8%*	*14.0%*
50	.09026	.08814	.08609	.08413	.08224	.08042	.07867	.07698	.07535	.07378
51	.09655	.09433	.09219	.09013	.08815	.08624	.08440	.08262	.08091	.07926
52	.10318	.10086	.09863	.09647	.09439	.09239	.09046	.08860	.08680	.08506
53	.11017	.10774	.10541	.10315	.10098	.09888	.09686	.09491	.09302	.09120
54	.11750	.11498	.11254	.11019	.10792	.10572	.10361	.10156	.09958	.09767
55	.12522	.12258	.12005	.11759	.11522	.11294	.11072	.10859	.10652	.10451
56	.13332	.13059	.12794	.12539	.12292	.12054	.11823	.11599	.11383	.11174
57	.14183	.13899	.13624	.13359	.13102	.12853	.12613	.12380	.12154	.11936
58	.15070	.14775	.14490	.14215	.13948	.13689	.13439	.13197	.12962	.12734
59	.15990	.15685	.15389	.15103	.14826	.14558	.14298	.14046	.13801	.13564
60	.16942	.16626	.16321	.16024	.15737	.15459	.15189	.14927	.14673	.14426
61	.17929	.17603	.17287	.16981	.16684	.16395	.16115	.15844	.15580	.15324
62	.18960	.18623	.18297	.17980	.17673	.17375	.17085	.16803	.16530	.16264
63	.20035	.19688	.19352	.19025	.18708	.18400	.18100	.17809	.17525	.17250
64	.21154	.20797	.20451	.20114	.19787	.19469	.19159	.18859	.18566	.18281
65	.22318	.21951	.21595	.21249	.20912	.20584	.20265	.19955	.19652	.19358
66	.23532	.23156	.22790	.22434	.22088	.21751	.21422	.21102	.20791	.20487
67	.24804	.24419	.24044	.23679	.23324	.22977	.22640	.22311	.21990	.21678
68	.26133	.25740	.25356	.24983	.24618	.24263	.23917	.23579	.23250	.22929
69	.27516	.27114	.26723	.26341	.25969	.25605	.25251	.24905	.24567	.24237
70	.28945	.28536	.28137	.27747	.27367	.26996	.26633	.26279	.25934	.25596
71	.30412	.29996	.29590	.29193	.28806	.28427	.28057	.27696	.27343	.26998
72	.31913	.31491	.31078	.30675	.30281	.29895	.29519	.29150	.28790	.28438
73	.33444	.33016	.32597	.32188	.31788	.31396	.31013	.30638	.30271	.29913
74	.35012	.34579	.34155	.33741	.33335	.32938	.32549	.32168	.31795	.31430
75	.36628	.36190	.35762	.35343	.34932	.34530	.34136	.33750	.33372	.33001
76	.38299	.37858	.37427	.37004	.36589	.36183	.35784	.35394	.35011	.34636
77	.40028	.39585	.39151	.38725	.38307	.37898	.37496	.37103	.36716	.36337
78	.41812	.41368	.40933	.40506	.40086	.39675	.39271	.38874	.38485	.38103
79	.43641	.43198	.42762	.42334	.41914	.41502	.41096	.40698	.40308	.39924
80	.45496	.45054	.44619	.44192	.43772	.43360	.42954	.42556	.42164	.41779
81	.47360	.46920	.46487	.46061	.45643	.45231	.44827	.44429	.44038	.43653
82	.49223	.48785	.48355	.47932	.47516	.47106	.46703	.46307	.45916	.45532
83	.51081	.50648	.50221	.49802	.49388	.48982	.48581	.48187	.47799	.47416
84	.52951	.52523	.52101	.51686	.51277	.50874	.50477	.50086	.49701	.49321
85	.54847	.54425	.54009	.53600	.53196	.52798	.52406	.52019	.51638	.51262
86	.56749	.56335	.55926	.55523	.55126	.54734	.54348	.53966	.53591	.53220
87	.58627	.58221	.57820	.57425	.57035	.56650	.56270	.55895	.55526	.55161
88	.60477	.60079	.59688	.59301	.58919	.58542	.58170	.57802	.57439	.57081
89	.62297	.61909	.61527	.61149	.60776	.60408	.60044	.59685	.59330	.58979
90	.64084	.63707	.63335	.62968	.62604	.62246	.61891	.61540	.61194	.60851
91	.65803	.65437	.65076	.64719	.64366	.64017	.63672	.63330	.62993	.62659
92	.67412	.67058	.66707	.66360	.66017	.65678	.65342	.65010	.64682	.64357
93	.68911	.68567	.68227	.67890	.67557	.67227	.66901	.66578	.66258	.65942
94	.70321	.69988	.69657	.69330	.69006	.68686	.68369	.68055	.67744	.67437
95	.71674	.71351	.71031	.70713	.70399	.70088	.69781	.69476	.69174	.68875
96	.72959	.72646	.72335	.72028	.71724	.71422	.71123	.70828	.70534	.70244
97	.74156	.73853	.73552	.73254	.72959	.72666	.72376	.72089	.71804	.71522
98	.75287	.74993	.74702	.74413	.74126	.73842	.73561	.73282	.73006	.72732
99	.76401	.76117	.75834	.75555	.75277	.75002	.74730	.74459	.74191	.73926
100	.77494	.77219	.76946	.76676	.76408	.76142	.75878	.75616	.75357	.75099
101	.78580	.78315	.78052	.77791	.77532	.77275	.77021	.76768	.76517	.76268
102	.79654	.79399	.79146	.78894	.78645	.78397	.78152	.77908	.77666	.77426
103	.80724	.80479	.80236	.79994	.79755	.79517	.79280	.79046	.78813	.78582
104	.81879	.81646	.81413	.81183	.80954	.80726	.80501	.80276	.80054	.79832

AGE	12.2%	12.4%	12.6%	12.8%	13.0%	13.2%	13.4%	13.6%	13.8%	14.0%
105	.83005	.82782	.82560	.82340	.82121	.81904	.81688	.81474	.81260	.81049
106	.84485	.84277	.84071	.83866	.83662	.83459	.83257	.83057	.82857	.82659
107	.86311	.86124	.85937	.85751	.85566	.85382	.85199	.85017	.84835	.84655
108	.89266	.89114	.88963	.88812	.88662	.88513	.88364	.88216	.88068	.87922
109	.94563	.94484	.94405	.94326	.94248	.94170	.94092	.94014	.93937	.93860

See p. 15 for regulations not amended to reflect law changes

LIFE TABLE
TABLE 90CM
APPLICABLE AFTER APRIL 30, 1999, AND BEFORE MAY 1, 2009

Age x	*l(x)*	*Age x*	*l(x)*	*Age x*	*l(x)*
(1)	(2)	(1)	(2)	(1)	(2)
0	100000	37	95969	74	62852
1	99064	38	95780	75	60449
2	98992	39	95581	76	57955
3	98944	40	95373	77	55373
4	98907	41	95156	78	52704
5	98877	42	94928	79	49943
6	98850	43	94687	80	47084
7	98826	44	94431	81	44129
8	98803	45	94154	82	41091
9	98783	46	93855	83	37994
10	98766	47	93528	84	34876
11	98750	48	93173	85	31770
12	98734	49	92787	86	28687
13	98713	50	92370	87	25638
14	98681	51	91918	88	22658
15	98635	52	91424	89	19783
16	98573	53	90885	90	17046
17	98497	54	90297	91	14466
18	98409	55	89658	92	12066
19	98314	56	88965	93	9884
20	98215	57	88214	94	7951
21	98113	58	87397	95	6282
22	98006	59	86506	96	4868
23	97896	60	85537	97	3694
24	97784	61	84490	98	2745
25	97671	62	83368	99	1999
26	97556	63	82169	100	1424
27	97441	64	80887	101	991
28	97322	65	79519	102	672
29	97199	66	78066	103	443
30	97070	67	76531	104	284
31	96934	68	74907	105	175
32	96791	69	73186	106	105
33	96642	70	71357	107	60
34	96485	71	69411	108	33
35	96322	72	67344	109	17
36	96150	73	65154	110	0

(5) *Effective/applicability dates.*—Paragraphs (f)(1) through (f)(4) apply after April 30, 1999, and before May 1, 2009. [Reg. § 20.2031-7A.]

☐ [*T.D.* 6296, 6-23-58. *Amended by T.D.* 7077, 12-1-70 *and T.D.* 7955, 5-10-84. *Reg. § 20.2031-7 was redesignated Reg. § 20.2031-7A(d) and amended by T.D.* 8540, 6-9-94. *Amended by T.D.* 8819, 4-29-99 (*corrected* 6-21-99); *T.D.* 8886, 6-9-2000; *T.D.* 9448, 5-1-2009 *and T.D.* 9540, 8-9-2011.]

[Reg. § 20.2031-8]

§ 20.2031-8. Valuation of certain life insurance and annuity contracts; valuation of shares in an open-end investment company.—(a) *Valuation of certain life insurance and annuity contracts.*—(1) The value of a contract for the payment of an annuity, or an insurance policy on the life of a person other than the decedent, issued by a company regularly engaged in the selling of contracts of that character is established through the sale by that company of comparable contracts. An annuity payable under a combination annuity contract and life insurance policy on the decedent's life (e.g., a "retirement income" policy with death benefit) under which there was no insurance element at the time of the decedent's death (see paragraph (d) of § 20.2039-1) is treated like a contract for the payment of an annuity for purposes of this section.

(2) As valuation of an insurance policy through sale of comparable contracts is not readily ascertainable when, at the date of the decedent's death, the contract has been in force for some time and further premium payments are to be made, the value may be approximated by adding to the interpolated terminal reserve at the date of the decedent's death the proportionate part of the gross premium last paid before the date of the decedent's death which covers the period extending beyond that date. If, however, because of the unusual nature of the contract such an approximation is not reasonably close to the full value of the contract, this method may not be used.

(3) The application of this section may be illustrated by the following examples. In each case involving an insurance contract, it is as-

sumed that there are no accrued dividends or outstanding indebtedness on the contract.

Example (1). X purchased from a life insurance company a joint and survivor annuity contract under the terms of which X was to receive payments of $1,200 annually for his life and, upon X's death, his wife was to receive payments of $1,200 annually for her life. Five years after such purchase, when his wife was 50 years of age, X died. The value of the annuity contract at the date of X's death is the amount which the company would charge for an annuity providing for the payment of $1,200 annually for the life of a female 50 years of age.

Example (2). Y died holding the incidents of ownership in a life insurance policy on the life of his wife. The policy was one on which no further payments were to be made to the company (e.g., a single premium policy or a paid-up policy). The value of the insurance policy at the date of Y's death is the amount which the company would charge for a single premium contract of the same specified amount on the life of a person of the age of the insured.

Example (3). Z died holding the incidents of ownership in a life insurance policy on the life of his wife. The policy was an ordinary life policy issued nine years and four months prior to Z's death and at a time when Z's wife was 35 years of age. The gross annual premium is $2,811 and the decedent died four months after the last premium due date. The value of the insurance policy at the date of Z's death is computed as follows:

Terminal reserve at end of tenth year	$14,601.00
Terminal reserve at end of ninth year	12,965.00
Increase	$1,636.00
One-third of such increase (Z having died four months following the last preceding premium due date) is	$545.33
Terminal reserve at end of ninth year	12,965.00
Interpolated terminal reserve at date of Z's death	13,510.33
Two-thirds of gross premium (× $2,811)	1,874.00
Value of the insurance policy	$15,384.33

(b) *Valuation of shares in an open-end investment company.*—(1) The fair market value of a share in an open-end investment company (commonly known as a "mutual fund") is the public redemption price of a share. In the absence of an affirmative showing of the public redemption price in effect at the time of death, the last public redemption price quoted by the company for the date of death shall be presumed to be the applicable public redemption price. If the alternate valuation method under 2032 is elected, the last public redemption price quoted by the company for the alternate valuation date shall be the applicable redemption price. If there is no public redemption price quoted by the company for the applicable valuation date (e.g., the valuation date is a Saturday, Sunday, or holiday), the fair market value of the mutual fund share is the last public redemption price quoted by the company for the first day preceding the applicable valuation date for which there is a quotation. In any case where a dividend is declared on a share in an open-end investment company before the decedent's death but payable to shareholders of record on a date after his death and the share is quoted "ex-dividend" on the date of the decedent's death, the amount of the dividend is added to the ex-dividend quotation in determining the fair market value of the share as of the date of the decedent's death. As used in this paragraph, the term "open-end investment company" includes only a company which on the applicable valuation date was engaged in offering its shares to the public in the capacity of an open-end investment company.

(2) The provisions of this paragraph shall apply with respect to estates of decedents dying after August 16, 1954. [Reg. § 20.2031-8.]

☐ [*T.D.* 6296, 6-23-58. *Amended by T.D.* 6680, 10-9-63 *and T.D.* 7319, 7-22-74.]

[Reg. § 20.2031-9]

§ 20.2031-9. Valuation of other property.—The valuation of any property not specifically described in §§ 20.2031-2 through 20.2031-8 is made in accordance with the general principles set forth in § 20.2031-1. For example, a future interest in property not subject to valuation in accordance with the actuarial principles set forth in § 20.2031-7 is to be valued in accordance with the general principles set forth in § 20.2031-1. [Reg. § 20.2031-9.]

☐ [*T.D.* 6296, 6-23-58.]

[Reg. § 20.2032-1]

§ 20.2032-1. Alternate valuation.—(a) *In general.*—In general, section 2032 provides for the valuation of a decedent's gross estate at a date other than the date of the decedent's death. More specifically, if an executor elects the alternate valuation method under section 2032, the property included in the decedent's gross estate on the date of his death is valued as of whichever of the following dates is applicable:

(1) Any property distributed, sold, exchanged, or otherwise disposed of within 6 months (1 year, if the decedent died on or before December 31, 1970) after the decedent's death is valued as of the date on which it is first distributed, sold, exchanged, or otherwise disposed of;

(2) Any property not distributed, sold, exchanged, or otherwise disposed of within 6 months (1 year, if the decedent died on or before December 31, 1970) after the decedent's death is valued as of the date 6 months (1 year, if the

decedent died on or before December 31, 1970) after the date of the decedent's death;

(3) Any property, interest, or estate which is affected by mere lapse of time is valued as of the date of the decedent's death, but adjusted for any difference in its value not due to mere lapse of time as of the date 6 months (1 year, if the decedent died on or before December 31, 1970) after the decedent's death, or as of the date of its distribution, sale, exchange, or other disposition, whichever date first occurs.

(b) *Method and effect of election.*—(1) *In general.*—The election to use the alternate valuation method is made on the return of tax imposed by section 2001. For purposes of this paragraph (b), the term *return of tax imposed by section 2001* means the last estate tax return filed by the executor on or before the due date of the return (including extensions of time to file actually granted) or, if a timely return is not filed, the first estate tax return filed by the executor after the due date, provided the return is filed no later than 1 year after the due date (including extensions of time to file actually granted). Once the election is made, it is irrevocable, provided that an election may be revoked on a subsequent return filed on or before the due date of the return (including extensions of time to file actually granted). The election may be made only if it will decrease both the value of the gross estate and the sum (reduced by allowable credits) of the estate tax and the generation-skipping transfer tax payable by reason of the decedent's death with respect to the property includible in the decedent's gross estate. If the election is made, the alternate valuation method applies to all property included in the gross estate and cannot be applied to only a portion of the property.

(2) *Protective election.*—If, based on the return of tax as filed, use of the alternate valuation method would not result in a decrease in both the value of the gross estate and the sum (reduced by allowable credits) of the estate tax and the generation-skipping transfer tax liability payable by reason of the decedent's death with respect to the property includible in the decedent's gross estate, a protective election may be made to use the alternate valuation method if it is subsequently determined that such a decrease would occur. A protective election is made on the return of tax imposed by section 2001. The protective election is irrevocable as of the due date of the return (including extensions of time actually granted). The protective election becomes effective on the date on which it is determined that use of the alternate valuation method would result in a decrease in both the value of the gross estate and in the sum (reduced by allowable credits) of the estate tax and generation-skipping transfer tax liability payable by reason of the decedent's death with respect to the property includible in the decedent's gross estate.

(3) *Requests for extension of time to make the election.*—A request for an extension of time to make the election or protective election pursuant to §§301.9100-1 and 301.9100-3 of this chapter will not be granted unless the return of tax imposed by section 2001 is filed no later than 1 year after the due date of the return (including extensions of time actually granted).

(c) *Meaning of "distributed, sold, exchanged, or otherwise disposed of".*—(1) The phrase "distributed, sold, exchanged, or otherwise disposed of" comprehends all possible ways by which property ceases to form a part of the gross estate. For example, money on hand at the date of the decedent's death which is thereafter used in the payment of funeral expenses, or which is thereafter invested, falls within the term "otherwise disposed of." The term also includes the surrender of a stock certificate for corporate assets in complete or partial liquidation of a corporation pursuant to section 331. The term does not, however, extend to transactions which are mere changes in form. Thus, it does not include a transfer of assets to a corporation in exchange for its stock in a transaction with respect to which no gain or loss would be recognizable for income tax purposes under section 351. Nor does it include an exchange of stock or securities in a corporation for stock or securities in the same corporation or another corporation in a transaction, such as a merger, recapitalization, reorganization or other transaction described in section 368(a) or 355, with respect to which no gain or loss is recognizable for income tax purposes under section 354 or 355.

(2) Property may be "distributed" either by the executor, or by a trustee of property included in the gross estate under sections 2035 through 2038, or section 2041. Property is considered as "distributed" upon the first to occur of the following:

(i) The entry of an order or decree of distribution, if the order or decree subsequently becomes final;

(ii) The segregation or separation of the property from the estate or trust so that it becomes unqualifiedly subject to the demand or disposition of the distributee; or

(iii) The actual paying over or delivery of the property to the distributee.

(3) Property may be "sold, exchanged, or otherwise disposed of" by:

(i) The executor;

(ii) A trustee or other donee to whom the decedent during his lifetime transferred property included in his gross estate under sections 2035 through 2038, or section 2041;

(iii) An heir or devisee to whom title to property passes directly under local law;

(iv) A surviving joint tenant or tenant by the entirety; or

(v) Any other person.

If a binding contract for the sale, exchange, or other disposition of property is entered into, the property is considered as sold, exchanged, or otherwise disposed of on the effective date of the contract, unless the contract is not subsequently carried out substantially in accordance with its terms. The effective date of a contract is normally the date it is entered into (and not the date it is consummated, or the date legal title to the property passes) unless the contract specifies a different effective date.

(d) *"Included property" and "excluded property".*—If the executor elects the alternate valuation method under section 2032, all property interests existing at the date of decedent's death which form a part of his gross estate as determined under sections 2033 through 2044 are valued in accordance with the provisions of this section. Such property interests are referred to in this section as "included property". Furthermore, such property interests remain "included property" for the purpose of valuing the gross estate under the alternate valuation method even though they change in form during the alternate valuation period by being actually received, or disposed of, in whole or in part, by the estate. On the other hand, property earned or accrued (whether received or not) after the date of the decedent's death and during the alternate valuation period with respect to any property interest existing at the date of the decedent's death, which does not represent a form of "included property" itself or the receipt of "included property" is excluded in valuing the gross estate under the alternate valuation method. Such property is referred to in this section as "excluded property". Illustrations of "included property" and "excluded property" are contained in the subparagraphs (1) to (4) of this paragraph:

(1) *Interest-bearing obligations.*—Interest-bearing obligations, such as bonds or notes, may comprise two elements of "included property" at the date of the decedent's death, namely, (i) the principal of the obligation itself, and (ii) interest accrued to the date of death. Each of these elements is to be separately valued as of the applicable valuation date. Interest accrued after the date of death and before the subsequent valuation date constitutes "excluded property". However, any part payment of principal made between the date of death and the subsequent valuation date, or any advance payment of interest for a period after the subsequent valuation date made during the alternate valuation period which has the effect of reducing the value of the principal obligation as of the subsequent valuation date, will be included in the gross estate, and valued as of the date of such payment.

(2) *Leased property.*—The principles set forth in subparagraph (1) of this paragraph with respect to interest-bearing obligations also apply to leased realty or personalty which is included in the gross estate and with respect to which an obligation to pay rent has been reserved. Both the realty or personalty itself and the rents accrued to the date of death constitute "included property", and each is to be separately valued as of the applicable valuation date. Any rent accrued after the date of death and before the subsequent valuation date is "excluded property". Similarly, the principle applicable with respect to interest paid in advance is equally applicable with respect to advance payments of rent.

(3) *Noninterest-bearing obligations.*—In the case of noninterest-bearing obligations sold at a discount, such as savings bonds, the principal obligation and the discount amortized to the date of death are property interests existing at the date of death and constitute "included property". The obligation itself is to be valued at the subsequent valuation date without regard to any further increase in value due to amortized discount. The additional discount amortized after death and during the alternate valuation period is the equivalent of interest accruing during that period and is, therefore, not to be included in the gross estate under the alternate valuation method.

(4) *Stock of a corporation.*—Shares of stock in a corporation and dividends declared to stockholders of record on or before the date of the decedent's death and not collected at the date of death constitute "included property" of the estate. On the other hand, ordinary dividends out of earnings and profits (whether in cash, shares of the corporation, or other property) declared to stockholders of record after the date of the decedent's death are "excluded property" and are not to be valued under the alternate valuation method. If, however, dividends are declared to stockholders of record after the date of the decedent's death with the effect that the shares of stock at the subsequent valuation date do not reasonably represent the same "included property" of the gross estate as existed at the date of the decedent's death, the dividends are "included property", except to the extent that they are out of earnings of the corporation after the date of the decedent's death. For example, if a corporation makes a distribution in partial liquidation to stockholders of record during the alternate valuation period which is not accompanied by a surrender of a stock certificate for cancellation, the amount of the distribution received on stock included in the gross estate is itself "included property", except to the extent that the distribution was out of earnings and profits since the date of the decedent's death. Similarly, if a corporation, in which the decedent owned a substantial interest and which possessed at the date of the decedent's death accumulated earnings and profits equal to its paid-in capital, distributed all of its accumulated earnings and profits as a cash dividend to shareholders of record during the alternate valuation period, the amount of the dividends received on stock includible in the gross estate will be included in the gross estate under the alternate valuation method. Likewise, a stock dividend distributed under such circumstances is "included property".

(e) *Illustrations of "included property" and "excluded property".*—The application of paragraph (d) of this section may be further illustrated by the following example in which it is assumed that the decedent died on January 1, 1955:

Description	Subsequent valuation date	Alternate value	Value at date of death
Bond, par value $1,000, bearing interest at 4% payable quarterly on Feb. 1, May 1, Aug. 1, and Nov. 1. Bond distributed to legatee on Mar. 1, 1955	Mar. 1, 1955	$1,000.00	$1,000.00
Interest coupon of $10 attached to bond and not cashed at date of death although due and payable Nov. 1, 1954. Cashed by executor on Feb. 1, 1955	Feb. 1, 1955	10.00	10.00
Interest accrued from Nov. 1, 1954, to Jan. 1, 1955, collected on Feb. 1, 1955 . .	Feb. 1, 1955	6.67	6.67
Real estate, not disposed of within year following death. Rent of $300 due at the end of each quarter, Feb. 1, May 1, Aug. 1, and Nov. 1	Jan. 1, 1956	11,000.00	12,000.00
Rent due for quarter ending Nov. 1, 1954, but not collected until Feb. 1, 1955	Feb. 1, 1955	300.00	300.00
Rent accrued for November and December 1954, collected on Feb. 1, 1955	Feb. 1, 1955	200.00	200.00
Common stock, X Corporation, 500 shares, not disposed of within year following decedent's death	Jan. 1, 1956	47,500.00	50,000.00
Dividend of $2 per share declared Dec. 10, 1954, and paid on Jan. 10, 1955, to holders of record on Dec. 30, 1954	Jan. 10, 1955	$1,000.00	$1,000.00

(f) *Mere lapse of time.*—In order to eliminate changes in value due only to mere lapse of time, section 2032(a)(3) provides that any interest or estate "affected by mere lapse of time" is included in a decedent's gross estate under the alternate valuation method at its value as of the date of the decedent's death, but with adjustment for any difference in its value as of the subsequent valuation date not due to mere lapse of time. Properties, interests, or estates which are "affected by mere lapse of time" include patents, estates for the life of a person other than the decedent, remainders, reversions, and other like properties, interests, or estates. The phrase "affected by mere lapse of time" has no reference to obligations for the payment of money, whether or not interest-bearing, the value of which changes with the passing of time. However, such an obligation, like any other property, may become affected by lapse of time when made the subject of a bequest or transfer which itself is creative of an interest or estate so affected. The application of this paragraph is illustrated in subparagraphs (1) and (2) of this paragraph:

(1) [Reserved]. For guidance, see § 20.2032-1T(f)(1).

(2) *Patents.*—To illustrate the alternate valuation of a patent, assume that the decedent owned a patent which, on the date of the decedent's death, had an unexpired term of ten years and a value of $78,000. Six months after the date of the decedent's death, the patent was sold, because of lapse of time and other causes, for $60,000. The alternate value thereof would be obtained by dividing $60,000 by 0.95 (ratio of the remaining life of the patent at the alternate date to the remaining life of the patent at the date of the decedent's death), and would, therefore, be $63,157.89.

(g) *Effect of election on deductions.*—If the executor elects the alternate valuation method under section 2032, any deduction for administration expenses under section 2053(b) (pertaining to property not subject to claims) or losses under section 2054 (or section 2106(a)(1), relating to estates of nonresidents not citizens) is allowed only to the extent that it is not otherwise in effect allowed in determining the value of the gross estate. Furthermore, the amount of any charitable deduction under section 2055 (or section 2106(a)(2), relating to the estates of nonresidents not citizens) or the amount of any marital deduction under section 2056 is determined by the value of the property with respect to which the deduction is allowed as of the date of the decedent's death, adjusted, however, for any difference in its value as of the date 6 months (1 year, if the decedent died on or before December 31, 1970) after death, or as of the date of its distribution, sale, exchange, or other disposition, whichever first occurs. However, no such adjustment may take into account any difference in value due to lapse of time or to the occurrence or nonoccurrence of a contingency.

(h) *Effective date.*—Paragraph (b) of this section is applicable to decedents dying on or after January 4, 2005. However, pursuant to section 7805(b)(7), taxpayers may elect to apply paragraph (b) of this section retroactively if the period of limitations for filing a claim for a credit or refund of Federal estate or generation-skipping transfer tax under section 6511 has not expired. [Reg. § 20.2032-1.]

☐ [*T.D.* 6296, 6-23-58. *Amended by T.D.* 7238, 12-28-72, *T.D.* 7955, 5-10-84; *T.D.* 8540, 6-9-94; *T.D.* 8819, 4-29-99; *T.D.* 9172, 1-3-2005 *and T.D.* 9448, 5-1-2009 (*corrected* 6-5-2009).]

[Reg. § 20.2032-1T]

§ 20.2032-1T. Alternate Valuation (temporary).—(a) through (e) [Reserved]. For further guidance, see § 20.2032-1(a) through (e).

(f) [Reserved]. For further guidance, see § 20.2032-1(f).

(1) *Life estates, remainders, and similar interests.*—The values of life estates, remainders, and similar interests are to be obtained by applying the methods prescribed in § 20.2031-7, using (i) the age of each person, the duration of whose life may affect the value of the interest, as of the date of the decedent's death, and (ii) the value of the property as of the alternate valuation date. For example, assume that the decedent, or the decedent's estate, was entitled to receive certain property worth $50,000 upon the death of A, who was entitled to the income for life. At the time of the decedent's death, on or after May 1, 2009, A was 47 years and 5 months old. In the month in which the decedent died, the section 7520 rate was 6.2 percent. The value of the decedent's remainder interest at the date of the decedent's death would, as illustrated in *Example 1* of § 20.2031-7T(d)(5), be $9,336.00 ($50,000 × .18672). If, because of economic conditions, the property declined in value and was worth only $40,000 on the date that was 6 months after the date of the decedent's death, the value of the remainder interest would be $7,468.80 ($40,000 × .18672), even though A would be 48 years old on the alternate valuation date.

(f)(2) through (g) [Reserved]. For further guidance, see § 20.2032-1(f)(2) through (g).

(h) *Effective/applicability date.*—Paragraph (f)(1) applies on or after May 1, 2009.

(i) *Expiration date.*—Paragraph (f)(1) expires on or before May 1, 2012. [Temporary Reg. § 20.2032-1T.]

☐ [*T.D.* 9448, 5-1-2009.]

[Reg. § 20.2032A-3]

§ 20.2032A-3. Material participation requirements for valuation of certain farm and closely-held business real property.—(a) *In general.*—Under section 2032A, an executor may, for estate tax purposes, make a special election concerning valuation of qualified real property (as defined in section 2032A(b)) used as a farm for farming purposes or in another trade or business. If this election is made, the property will be valued on the basis of its value for its qualified use in farming or the other trade or business, rather than its fair market value determined on the basis of highest and best use (irrespective of whether its highest and best use is the use in farming or other business). For the special valuation rules of section 2032A to apply, the deceased owner and/or a member of the owner's family (as defined in section 2032A(e)(2)) must materially participate in the operation of the farm or other business. Whether the required material participation occurs is a factual determination, and the types of activities and financial risks which will support such a finding will vary with the mode of ownership of both the property itself and of any business in which it is used. Passively collecting rents, salaries, draws, dividends, or other income from the farm or other business is not sufficient for material participation, nor is merely advancing capital and reviewing a crop plan or other business proposal and financial reports each season or business year.

(b) *Types of qualified property.*—(1) *In general.*—Real property valued under section 2032A must pass from the decedent to a qualified heir or be acquired from the decedent by a qualified heir. The real property may be owned directly or may be owned indirectly through ownership of an interest in a corporation, a partnership, or a trust. Where the ownership is indirect, however, the decedent's interest in the business must, in addition to meeting the tests for qualification under section 2032A, qualify under the tests of section 6166(b)(1) as an interest in a closely-held business on the date of the decedent's death and for sufficient other time (combined with periods of direct ownership) to equal at least 5 years of the 8 year period preceding the death. All specially valued property must be used in a trade or business. Directly owned real property that is leased by a decedent to a separate closely held business is considered to be qualified real property, but only if the separate business qualifies as a closely held business under section 6166(b)(1) with respect to the decedent on the date of his or her death and for sufficient other time (combined with periods during which the property was operated as a proprietorship) to equal at least 5 years of the 8 year period preceding the death. For example, real property owned by the decedent and leased to a farming corporation or partnership owned and operated entirely by the decedent and fewer than 15 members of the decedent's family is eligible for special use valuation. Under section 2032A, the term trade or business applies only to an active business such as a manufacturing, mercantile, or service enterprise, or to the raising of agricultural or horticultural commodities, as distinguished from passive investment activities. The mere passive rental of property to a party other than a member of the decedent's family will not qualify. The decedent or a member of the decedent's family must own an equity interest in the farm operation. A trade or business is not necessarily present even though an office and regular hours are maintained for management of income producing assets, as the term "business" is not as broad under section 2032A as under section 162. Additionally, no trade or business is present in the case of activities not engaged in for profit. *See* section 183.

(2) *Structures and other real property improvements.*—Qualified real property includes residen-

tial buildings and other structures and real property improvements occupied or used on a regular basis by the owner or lessee of real property (or by employees of the owner or lessee) for the purpose of operating the farm or other closely held business. A farm residence occupied by the decedent owner of the specially valued property is considered to be occupied for the purpose of operating the farm even though a family member (not the decedent) was the person materially participating in the operation of the farm as required under section 2032A(b)(1)(C).

(c) *Period material participation must last.*—The required participation must last—

(1) For periods totalling 5 years or more during the 8 years immediately preceding the date of the decedent's death; and

(2) For periods totalling 5 years or more during any 8 year period ending after the date of the decedent's death (up to a maximum of 15 years after decedent's death, when the additional estate tax provisions of section 2032A(c) cease to apply).

In determining whether the material participation requirement is satisfied, no exception is made for periods during which real property is held by the decedent's estate. Additionally, contemporaneous material participation by 2 or more family members during a period totalling a year will not result in that year being counted as 2 or more years for purposes of satisfying the requirements of this paragraph (c). Death of a qualified heir (as defined in section 2032A(e)(1)) before the requisite time has passed ends any material participation requirement for that heir's portion of the property as to the original decedent's estate if the heir received a separate, joint or other undivided property interest from the decedent. If qualified heirs receive successive interests in specially valued property (e.g., life estate and remainder interests) from the decedent, the material participation requirement does not end with respect to any part of the property until the death of the last qualified heir (or, if earlier, the expiration of 15 years from the date of the decedent's death). The requirements of section 2032A will fully apply to an heir's estate if an election under this section is made for the same property by the heir's executor. In general, to determine whether the required participation has occurred, brief periods (*e. g.,* periods of 30 days or less) during which there was no material participation may be disregarded. This is so only if these periods were both preceded and followed by substantial periods (*e. g.,* periods of more than 120 days) in which there was uninterrupted material participation. *See* paragraph (e)(1) of this section which provides a special rule for periods when little or no activity is necessary to manage fully a farm.

(d) *Period property must be owned by decedent and family members.*—Only real property which is actually owned by any combination of the decedent, members of the decedent's family, and qualified closely held businesses for periods totalling at least 5 of the 8 years preceding the date of decedent's death may be valued under section 2032A. For example, replacement property acquired in [a] like-kind exchange under section 1031 is considered to be owned only from the date on which the replacement property is actually acquired. On the other hand, replacement property acquired as a result of an involuntary conversion in a transfer that would meet the requirements of section 2032A(h) if it occurred after the date of the decedent's death is considered to have been owned from the date in which the involuntarily converted property was acquired. Property transferred from a proprietorship to a corporation or a partnership during the 8-year period ending on the date of the decedent's death is considered to be continuously owned to the extent of the decedent's equity interest in the corporation or partnership if, (1) the transfer meets the requirements of section 351 or 721, respectively, and (2) the decedent's interest in the corporation or partnership meets the requirements for indirectly held property contained in paragraph (b)(1) of this section. Likewise, property transferred to a trust is considered to be continuously owned if the beneficial ownership of the trust property is such that the requirements of section 6166(b)(1)(C) would be so satisfied if the property were owned by a corporation and all beneficiaries having vested interests in the trust were shareholders in the corporation. Any periods following the transfer during which the interest in the corporation, partnership, or trust does not meet the requirements of section 6166(b)(1) may not be counted for purposes of satisfying the ownership requirement of this paragraph (d).

(e) *Required activities.*—(1) *In general.*—Actual employment of the decedent (or of a member of the decedent's family) on a substantially full-time basis (35 hours a week or more) or to any lesser extent necessary personally to manage fully the farm or business in which the real property to be valued under section 2032A is used constitutes material participation. For example, many farming operations require only seasonal activity. Material participation is present as long as all necessary functions are performed even though little or no actual activity occurs during nonproducing seasons. In the absence of this direct involvement in the farm or other business, the activities of either the decedent or family members must meet the standards prescribed in this paragraph and those prescribed in the regulations issued under section 1402(a)(1). Therefore, if the participant (or participants) is self-employed with respect to the farm or other trade or business, his or her income from the farm or other business must be earned income for purposes of the tax on self-employment income before the participant is considered to be materially participating under section 2032A. Payment of the self-employment tax is not conclusive as to the presence of material participation. If no self-employment taxes have been paid, however, material participation is presumed not to have occurred unless the executor demonstrates to the satisfaction of the Internal Revenue Service that material participation did in fact occur and informs the Service of the reason no such tax was paid. In addition, all such taxes (including interest and penalties) determined to be due must be paid. In determining whether the material participation requirement is satisfied, the activities of each participant are viewed separately from the activities of all other participants, and at any given time, the activities of at least one participant must be material. If the involvement is less than full-time, it must be pursuant to an arrangement providing for actual participation in the production or management of production where the land is used by any nonfamily member, or any trust or business entity, in farming or another business. The arrangement may be oral or written, but must be formalized in some manner capable of proof. Activities not contemplated by the arrangement will not support a finding of material participation under section 2032A, and activities of any agent or employee other than a family member may not be considered in determining the presence of material participation. Activities of family members are considered only if the family relationship existed at the time the activities occurred.

(2) *Factors considered.*—No single factor is determinative of the presence of material participation, but physical work and participation in management decisions are the principal factors to be considered. As a minimum, the decedent and/or a family member must regularly advise or consult with the other managing party on the operation of the business. While they need not make all final management decisions alone, the decedent and/or family members must participate in making a substantial number of these decisions. Additionally, production activities on the land should be inspected regularly by the family participant, and funds should be advanced and financial responsibility assumed for a substantial portion of the expense involved in the operation of the farm or other business in which the real property is used. In the case of a farm, the furnishing by the owner or other family members of a substantial portion of the machinery, implements, and livestock used in the production activities is an important factor to consider in finding material participation. With farms, hotels, or apartment buildings, the operation of which qualifies as a trade or business, the participating decedent or heir's maintaining his or her principal place of residence on the premises is a factor to consider in determining whether the overall participation is material. Retention of a professional farm manager will not by itself prevent satisfaction of the material participation requirement by the decedent and family members. However, the decedent and/or a family member must personally materially participate under the terms of arrangement with the professional farm manager to satisfy this requirement.

(f) *Special rules for corporations, partnerships, and trusts.*—(1) *Required arrangement.*—With indirectly owned property as with property that is directly owned, there must be an arrangement calling for material participation in the business by the decedent owner or a family member. Where the real property is indirectly owned, however, even full-time involvement must be pursuant to an arrangement between the entity and the decedent or family member specifying the services to be performed. Holding an office in which certain material functions are inherent may constitute the necessary arrangement for material participation. Where property is owned by a trust, the arrangement will generally be found in one or more of four situations. First, the arrangement may result from appointment as a trustee. Second, the arrangement may result from an employer-employee relationship in which the participant is employed by a qualified closely held business owned by the trust in a position requiring his or her material participation in its activities. Third, the participants may enter into a contract with the trustees to manage, or take part in managing, the real property for the trust. Fourth, where the trust agreement expressly grants the management rights to the beneficial owner, that grant is sufficient to constitute the arrangement required under this section.

(2) *Required activities.*—The same participation standards apply under section 2032A where property is owned by a qualified closely held business as where the property is directly owned. In the case of a corporation, a partnership, or a trust where the participating decedent and/or family members are employees and thereby not subject to self-employment income taxes, they are to be viewed as if they were self-employed, and their activities must be activities that would subject them to self-employment income taxes were they so. Where property is owned by a corporation, a partnership or a trust, participation in the management and operation of the real property itself as a component of the closely held business is the determinative factor. Nominally holding positions as a corporate officer or director and receiving a salary therefrom or merely being listed as a partner and sharing in profits and losses will not alone support a finding of material participation. This is so even though, as partners, the participants pay self-employment income taxes on their distributive shares of partnership earnings under § 1.1402(a)-2. Further, it is especially true for corporate directors in states where the board of directors need not be an actively functioning entity or need only act informally. Corporate offices held by an owner are, however, factors to be considered with all other relevant facts in judging the degree of participation. When real property is directly owned and is leased to a corporation or partnership in which the decedent owns an interest which qualifies as an interest in a trade or business within the meaning of section 6166(b)(1), the presence of material participation is determined by looking at the activities of the participant with regard to the property in whatever capacity rendered. During any periods when qualified real property is held by an estate, material participation is to be determined

in the same manner as if the property were owned by a trust.

(g) *Examples.*—The rules for determining material participation may be illustrated by the following examples. Additional illustrations may be found in examples (1) through (6) in § 1.1402(a)-4.

Example (1). A, the decedent, actively operated his 100-acre farm on a full-time basis for 20 years. He then leased it to B for the 10 years immediately preceding his death. By the terms of the lease, A was to consult with B on where crops were to be planted, to supervise marketing of the crop, and to share equally with B in expenses and earnings. A was present on the farm each spring for consultation; however, once planting was complete, he left for his retirement cottage where he remained until late summer, at which time he returned to the farm to supervise the marketing operations. A at all times maintained the farm home in which he had lived for the time he had owned the farm and lived there when at the farm. In light of his activities, assumption of risks, and valuable knowledge of proper techniques for the particular land gained over 20 years of full-time farming on the land involved, A is deemed to have materially participated in the farming business.

Example (2). D is the 70-year old widow of farmer C. She lives on a farm for which special valuation has been elected and has lived there for 20 years. D leases the land to E under an arrangement calling for her participation in the operation of the farm. D annually raises a vegetable garden, chickens, and hogs. She also inspects the tobacco fields (which produce approximately 50 percent of farm income) weekly and informs E if she finds any work that needs to be done. D and E share expenses and income equally. Other decisions such as what fields to plant and when to plant and harvest crops are left to E, but D does occasionally make suggestions. During the harvest season, D prepares and serves meals for all temporary farm help. D is deemed to participate materially in the farm operation based on her farm residence and her involvement with the main money crop.

Example (3). Assume that D in example (2) moved to a nursing home 1 year after her husband's death. E completely operated the farm for her for 6 years following her move. If E is not a member of D's family, material participation ceases when D moves; however, if E is a member of D's family, E's material participation will prevent disqualification even if D owns the property. Further, upon D's death, the section 2032A valuation could be elected for her estate if E were a member of her family and the other requirements of section 2032A were satisfied.

Example (4). F, a qualified heir, owned a specially valued farm. He contracted with G to manage the farm for him as F, a lawyer, lived and worked 15 miles away in a nearby town. F supplied all machinery and equipment and assumed financial responsibility for the expenses of the farm operation. The contract specified that G was to submit a crop plan and a list of expenses and earnings for F's approval. It also called for F to inspect the farm regularly and to approve all expenditures over $100. In practice, F visited the farm weekly during the growing season to inspect and discuss operations. He actively participated in making important management decisions such as what fields to plant or pasture and how to utilize the subsidy program. F is deemed to have materially participated in the farm operation as his personal involvement amounted to more than managing an investment. Had F not regularly inspected the farm and participated in management decisions, however, he would not be considered to be materially participating. This would be true even though F did assume financial responsibility for the operation and did review annual crop plans.

Example (5). Decedent I owned 90 percent of all outstanding stock of X Corporation, a qualified closely-held business which owns real property to be specially valued. I held no formal position in the corporation and there was no arrangement for him to participate in daily business operations. I regularly spent several hours each day at the corporate offices and made decisions on many routine matters. I is not deemed to have materially participated in the X Corporation despite his activity because there was no arrangement requiring him to act in the manner in which he did.

Example (6). Decedent J was a senior partner in the law firm of X, Y and Z, which is a qualified closely held business owning the building in which its offices are located. J ceased to practice law actively 5 years before his death in 1977; however, he remained a full partner and annually received a share of firm profits. J is not deemed to have materially participated under section 2032A even though he still may have reported his distributive share of partnership income for self-employment income tax purposes if the payments were not made pursuant to any retirement agreement. This is so because J does not meet the requirement of actual personal material participation.

Example (7). K, the decedent, owned a tree farm. He contracted with L, a professional forester, to manage the property for him as K, a doctor, lived and worked in a town 50 miles away. The activities of L are not considered in determining whether K materially participated in the tree farm operation. During the 5 years preceding K's death, there was no need for frequent inspections of the property or consultation concerning it, inasmuch as most of the land had been reforested and the trees were in the beginning stages of their growing cycle. However, once every year, L submitted for K's approval a proposed plan for the management of the property over the next year. K actively participated in making important management decisions, such as where and whether a pre-commercial thinning should be conducted, whether the timber was adequately protected from fire and disease, whether fire lines needed to be plowed around the new trees, and whether boundary lines were properly maintained around the property. K inspected the property at least twice every year and assumed financial responsibility for the expenses of the tree farm. K also reported his income from the tree farm as earned income for purposes of the tax on self-employment income. Over a period of several years, K had harvested and marketed timber from certain tracts of the tree farm and had supervised replanting of the areas where trees were removed. K's history of harvesting, marketing, and replanting of trees showed him to be in the business of tree farming rather than merely passively investing in timber land. If the history of K's tree farm did not show such an active business operation, however, the tree farm would not qualify for special use valuation. In light of all these facts, K is deemed to have materially participated in the farm as his personal involvement amounted to more than managing an investment.

Example (8). Decedent M died on January 1, 1978, owning a farm for which special use valuation under section 2032A has been elected. M owned the farm real property for 15 years before his death. During the 4 years preceding M's death (January 1, 1974 through December 31, 1977), the farm was rented to N, a non-family member, and neither M nor any member of his family materially participated in the farming operation. From January 1, 1970, until December 31, 1973, both M and his daughter, O, materially participated in the farming operation. The material participation requirement of section 2032A(b)(1)(C)(ii) is not satisfied because material participation did not occur for periods aggregating at least 5 different years of the 8 years preceding M's death. [Reg. § 20.2032A-3.]

☐ [*T.D.* 7710, 7-28-80. *Amended by T.D.* 7786, 8-25-81.]

[Reg. § 20.2032A-4]

§ 20.2032A-4. Method of valuing farm real property.—(a) *In general.*—Unless the executor of the decedent's estate elects otherwise under section 2032A(e)(7)(B)(ii) or fails to document comparable rented farm property meeting the requirements of this section, the value of the property which is used for farming purposes and which is subject to an election under section 2032A is determined by—

(1) Subtracting the average annual state and local real estate taxes on actual tracts of comparable real property in the same locality from the average annual gross cash rental for that same comparable property, and

(2) Dividing the results so obtained by the average annual effective interest rate charged on new Federal land bank loans.

The computation of each average annual amount is to be based on the 5 most recent calendar years ending before the date of the decedent's death.

(b) *Gross cash rental.*—(1) *Generally.*—Gross cash rental is the total amount of cash received for the use of actual tracts of comparable farm real property in the same locality as the property being specially valued during the period of one calendar year. This amount is not diminished by the amount of any expenses or liabilities associated with the farm operation or the lease. *See,* paragraph (d) of this section for a definition of comparable property and rules for property on which buildings or other improvements are located and farms including multiple property types. Only rentals from tracts of comparable farm property which are rented solely for an amount of cash which is not contingent upon production are acceptable for use in valuing real property under section 2032A(e)(7). The rentals considered must result from an arm's-length transaction as defined in this section. Additionally, rentals received under leases which provide for payment solely in cash are not acceptable as accurate measures of cash rental value if involvement by the lessor (or a member of the lessor's family who is other than a lessee) in the management or operation of the farm to an extent which amounts to material participation under the rules of section 2032A is contemplated or actually occurs. In general, therefore, rentals for any property which qualifies for special use valuation cannot be used to compute gross cash rentals under this section because the total amount received by the lessor does not reflect the true cash rental value of the real property.

(2) *Special rules.*—(i) *Documentation required of executor.*—The executor must identify to the Internal Revenue Service actual comparable property for all specially valued property and cash rentals from that property if the decedent's real property is valued under section 2032A(e)(7). If the executor does not identify such property and cash rentals, all specially valued real property must be valued under the rules of section 2032A(e)(8) if special use valuation has been elected. *See,* however, § 20.2032A-8(d) for a special rule for estates electing section 2032A treatment on or before August 30, 1980.

(ii) *Arm's-length transaction required.*—Only those cash rentals which result from a lease entered into in an arm's-length transaction are acceptable under section 2032A(e)(7). For these purposes, lands leased from the Federal government, or any state or local government, which are leased for less than the amount that would be demanded by a private individual leasing for profit are not leased in an arm's-length transaction. Additionally, leases between family members (as defined in section 2032A(e)(2)) which do not provide a return on the property commensurate with that received under leases between unrelated parties in the locality are not acceptable under this section.

(iii) *In-kind rents, statements of appraised rental value, and area averages.*—Rents which are paid wholly or partly in kind (*e.g.,* crop shares) may not be used to determine the value of real property under section 2032A(e)(7). Likewise, appraisals or other statements regarding rental value as well as area-wide averages of rentals (*i.e.,* those compiled by the United States Department of Agriculture) may not be used under section 2032A(e)(7) because they are not true measures of the actual cash rental value of comparable property in the same locality as the specially valued property.

(iv) *Period for which comparable real property must have been rented solely for cash.*—Comparable real property rented solely for cash must be identified for each of the five calendar years preceding the year of the decedent's death if section 2032A(e)(7) is used to value the decedent's real property. Rentals from the same tract of comparable property need not be used for each of these 5 years, however, provided an actual tract of property meeting the requirements of this section is identified for each year.

(v) *Leases under which rental of personal property is included.*—No adjustment to the rents actually received by the lessor is made for the use of any farm equipment or other personal property the use of which is included under a lease for comparable real property unless the lease specifies the amount of the total rental attributable to the personal property and that amount is reasonable under the circumstances.

(c) *State and local real estate taxes.*—For purposes of the farm valuation formula under section 2032A(e)(7) state and local taxes are taxes which are assessed by a state or local government and which are allowable deductions under section 164. However, only those taxes on the comparable real property from which cash rentals are determined may be used in the formula valuation.

(d) *Comparable real property defined.*—Comparable real property must be situated in the same locality as the specially valued property. This requirement is not to be viewed in terms of mileage or political divisions alone, but rather is to be judged according to generally accepted real property valuation rules. The determination of properties which are comparable is a factual one and must be based on numerous factors, no one of which is determinative. It will, therefore, frequently be necessary to value farm property in segments where there are different uses or land characteristics included in the specially valued farm. For example, if section 2032A(e)(7) is used, rented property on which comparable buildings or improvements are located must be identified for specially valued property on which buildings or other real property improvements are located. In cases involving multiple areas or land characteristics, actual comparable property for each segment must be used, and the rentals and taxes from all such properties combined (using generally accepted real property valuation rules) for use in the valuation formula given in this section. However, any premium or discount resulting from the presence of multiple uses or other characteristics in one farm is also to be reflected. All factors generally considered in real estate valuation are to be considered in determining comparability under section 2032A. While not intended as an exclusive list, the following factors are among those to be considered in determining comparability—

(1) Similarity of soil as determined by any objective means, including an official soil survey reflected in a soil productivity index;

(2) Whether the crops grown are such as would deplete the soil in a similar manner;

(3) The types of soil conservation techniques that have been practiced on the two properties;

(4) Whether the two properties are subject to flooding;

(5) The slope of the land;

(6) In the case of livestock operations, the carrying capacity of the land;

(7) Where the land is timbered, whether the timber is comparable to that on the subject property;

(8) Whether the property as a whole is unified or whether it is segmented, and where segmented, the availability of the means necessary for movement among the different segments;

(9) The number, types, and conditions of all buildings and other fixed improvements located on the properties and their location as it affects efficient management and use of property and value per se; and

(10) Availability of, and type of, transportation facilities in terms of costs and of proximity of the properties to local markets.

(e) *Effective interest rate defined.*—(1) *Generally.*—The annual effective interest rate on new Federal land bank loans is the average billing rate charged on new agricultural loans to farmers and ranchers in the farm credit district in which the real property to be valued under section 2032A is located, adjusted as provided in paragraph (e)(2) of this section. This rate is to be a single rate for each district covering the period of one calendar year and is to be computed to the nearest one-hundredth of one percent. In the event that the district billing rates of interest on such new agricultural loans change during a year, the rate for that year is to be weighted to reflect the portion of the year during which each such rate was charged. If a district's billing rate on such new agricultural loans varies according to the amount of the loan, the rate applicable to a loan in an amount resulting from dividing the total dollar amount of such loans closed during the year by the total number of the loans closed is to be used under section 2032A. Applicable rates may be obtained from the district director of internal revenue.

(2) *Adjustment to billing rate of interest.*—The billing rate of interest determined under this paragraph is to be adjusted to reflect the increased cost of borrowing resulting from the required purchase of land bank association stock. For section 2032A purposes, the rate of required stock investment is the average of the percentages of the face amount of new agricultural loans to farmers and ranchers required to be invested in such stock by the applicable district bank during the year. If this percentage changes during a year, the average is to be adjusted to reflect the period when each percentage requirement was effective. The percentage is viewed as a reduc-

tion in the loan proceeds actually received from the amount upon which interest is charged.

(3) *Example.*—The determination of the effective interest rate for any year may be illustrated as follows:

Example. District X of the Federal land bank system charged an 8 percent billed interest rate on new agricultural loans for 8 months of the year, 1976, and an 8.75 percent rate for 4 months of the year. The average billing rate was, therefore, 8.25 percent [(1.08 × 8/12) + (1.0875 × 4/12) = 1.0825]. The district required stock equal to 5 percent of the face amount of the loan to be purchased as a precondition to receiving a loan. Thus, the borrower only received 95 percent of the funds upon which he paid interest. The applicable annual interest rate for 1976 of 8.68 percent is computed as follows:

8.25 percent × 1.00 (total loan amount) = 8.25 percent (billed interest rate) divided by 0.95 (percent of loan proceeds received by borrower) = 8.68 percent (effective interest rate for 1976).

[Reg. § 20.2032A-4.]

☐ [*T.D.* 7710, 7-28-80.]

[Reg. § 20.2032A-8]

§ 20.2032A-8. Election and agreement to have certain property valued under section 2032A for estate tax purposes.—(a) *Election of special use valuation.*—(1) *In general.*—An election under section 2032A is made as prescribed in paragraph (a)(3) of this section and on Form 706, United States Estate Tax Return. Once made, this election is irrevocable; however, see paragraph(d) of this section for a special rule for estates for which elections are made on or before August 30, 1980. Under section 2032A(a)(2), special use valuation may not reduce the value of the decedent's estate by more than $500,000. This election is available only if, at the time of death, the decedent was a citizen or resident of the United States.

(2) *Elections to specially value less than all qualified real property included in an estate.*—An election under section 2032A need not include all real property included in an estate which is eligible for special use valuation, but sufficient property to satisfy the threshold requirements of section 2032A(b)(1)(B) must be specially valued under the election. If joint or undivided interests (e.g. interests as joint tenants or tenants in common) in the same property are received from a decedent by qualified heirs, an election with respect to one heir's joint or undivided interest need not include any other heir's interest in the same property if the electing heir's interest plus other property to be specially valued satisfy the requirements of section 2032A(b)(1)(B). If successive interests (e.g. life estates and remainder interests) are created by a decedent in otherwise qualified property, an election under section 2032A is available only with respect to that property (or portion thereof) in which qualified heirs of the decedent receive all of the successive interests, and such an election must include the interests of all of those heirs. For example, if a surviving spouse receives a life estate in otherwise qualified property and the spouse's brother receives a remainder interest in fee, no part of the property may be valued pursuant to an election under section 2032A. Where successive interests in specially valued property are created, remainder interests are treated as being received by qualified heirs only if such remainder interests are not contingent upon surviving a nonfamily member or are not subject to divestment in favor of a nonfamily member.

(3) *Time and manner of making election.*—An election under this section is made by attaching to a timely filed estate tax return the agreement described in paragraph (c)(1) of this section and a notice of election which contains the following information:

(i) The decedent's name and taxpayer identification number as they appear on the estate tax return;

(ii) The relevant qualified use;

(iii) The items of real property shown on the estate tax return to be specially valued pursuant to the election (identified by schedule and item number);

(iv) The fair market value of the real property to be specially valued under section 2032A and its value based on its qualified use (both values determined without regard to the adjustments provided by section 2032A(b)(3)(B));

(v) The adjusted value (as defined in section 2032A(b)(3)(B)) of all real property which is used in a qualified use and which passes from the decedent to a qualified heir and the adjusted value of all real property to be specially valued;

(vi) The items of personal property shown on the estate tax return that pass from the decedent to a qualified heir and are used in a qualified use under section 2032A (identified by schedule and item number) and the total value of such personal property adjusted as provided under section 2032A(b)(3)(B);

(vii) The adjusted value of the gross estate, as defined in section 2032A(b)(3)(A);

(viii) The method used in determining the special value based on use;

(ix) Copies of written appraisals of the fair market value of the real property;

(x) A statement that the decedent and/or a member of his or her family has owned all specially valued real property for at least 5 years of the 8 years immediately preceding the date of the decedent's death;

(xi) Any periods during the 8-year period preceding the date of the decedent's death during which the decedent or a member of his or her family did not own the property, use it in a qualified use, or materially participate in the operation of the farm or other business within the meaning of section 2032A(e)(6);

(xii) The name, address, taxpayer identification number, and relationship to the decedent of each person taking an interest in each item of specially valued property, and the value of the property interests passing to each such person based on both fair market value and qualified use;

(xiii) Affidavits describing the activities constituting material participation and the identity of the material participant or participants; and

(xiv) A legal description of the specially valued property.

If neither an election nor a protective election is timely made, special use valuation is not available to the estate. *See* sections 2032A(d)(1), 6075(a), and 6081(a).

(b) *Protective election.*—A protective election may be made to specially value qualified real property. The availability of special use valuation pursuant to this election is contingent upon values as finally determined (or agreed to following examination of a return) meeting the requirements of section 2032A. A protective election does not, however, extend the time for payment of any amount of tax. Rules for such extensions are contained in sections 6161, 6163, 6166, and 6166A. The protective election is to be made by a notice of election filed with a timely estate tax return stating that a protective election under section 2032A is being made pending final determination of values. This notice is to include the following information:

(1) The decedent's name and taxpayer identification number as they appear on the estate tax return;

(2) The relevant qualified use; and

(3) The items of real and personal property shown on the estate tax return which are used in a qualified use, and which pass to qualified heirs (identified by schedule and item number).

If it is found that the estate qualifies for special use valuation based upon values as finally determined (or agreed to following examination of a return), an additional notice of election must be filed within 60 days after the date of such determination. This notice must set forth the information required under paragraph (a)(3) of this section and is to be attached, together with the agreement described in paragraph (c)(1) of this section, to an amended estate tax return. The new return is to be filed with the Internal Revenue Service office where the original return was filed.

(c) *Agreement to special valuation by persons with an interest in property.*—(1) *In general.*—The agreement required under section 2032A(a)(1)(B) and (d)(2) must be executed by all parties who have any interest in the property being valued based on its qualified use as of the date of the decedent's death. In the case of a qualified heir, the agreement must express consent to personal liability under section 2032A(c) in the event of certain early dispositions of the property or early cessation of the qualified use. See section 2032A(c)(6). In the case of parties (other than qualified heirs) with interests in the property, the agreement must express consent to collection of any additional estate tax imposed under section 2032A(c) from the qualified property. The agreement is to be in a form that is binding on all parties having an interest in the property. It must designate an agent with satisfactory evidence of authority to act for the parties to the agreement in all dealings with the Internal Revenue Service on matters arising under section 2032A and must indicate the address of that agent.

(2) *Persons having an interest in designated property.*—An interest in property is an interest which, as of the date of the decedent's death, can be asserted under applicable local law so as to affect the disposition of the specially valued property by the estate. Any person in being at the death of the decedent who has any such interest in the property, whether present or future, or vested or contingent, must enter into the agreement. Included among such persons are owners of remainder and executory interests, the holders of general or special powers of appointment, beneficiaries of a gift over in default of exercise of any such power, co-tenants, joint tenants and holders of other undivided interests when the decedent held only a joint or undivided interest in the property or when only an undivided interest is specially valued, and trustees of trusts holding any interest in the property. An heir who has the power under local law to caveat (challenge) a will and thereby affect disposition of the property is not, however, considered to be a person with an interest in property under section 2032A solely by reason of that right. Likewise, creditors of an estate are not such persons solely by reason of their status as creditors.

(3) *Consent on behalf of interested party.*—If any person required to enter into the agreement provided for by paragraph (c)(1) either desires that an agent act for him or her or cannot legally bind himself or herself due to infancy or other incompetency, or to death before the election under section 2032A is timely exercised, a representative authorized under local law to bind such person in an agreement of this nature is permitted to sign the agreement on his or her behalf.

(4) *Duties of agent designated in agreement.*—The Internal Revenue Service will contact the agent designated in the agreement under paragraph (c)(1) on all matters relating to continued qualification under section 2032A of the specially valued real property and on all matters relating to the special lien arising under section 6324B. It is the duty of the agent as attorney-in-fact for the parties with interests in the specially valued property to furnish the Service with any requested information and to notify the Service of any disposition or cessation of qualified use of any part of the property.

(d) *Special rule for estates for which elections under section 2032A are made on or before August 30, 1980.*—An election to specially value real property under section 2032A that is made on or before August 30, 1980, may be revoked. To revoke an election, the executor must file a notice of revocation with the Internal Revenue Service office where the original estate tax return was filed on or before January 31, 1981 (or if earlier, the date on which the period of limitation for assessment expires). This notice of revocation must contain the decedent's name, date of death, and taxpayer identification number, and is to be accompanied by remittance of any additional amount of estate tax and interest determined to be due as a result of valuation of the qualified property based upon its fair market value. Elections that are made on or before August 30, 1980, that do not comply with this section as proposed on July 13, 1978 (43 FR 30070), and amended on December 21, 1978 (43 FR 59517), must be conformed to this final regulation by means of an amended return before the original estate tax return can be finally accepted by the Internal Revenue Service. [Reg. § 20.2032A-8.]

☐ [*T.D.* 7710, 7-28-80. *Amended by T.D.* 7786, 8-25-81.]

[Reg. § 22.0]

§ 22.0. Certain elections under the Economic Recovery Tax Act of 1981.—(a) *Election of special rules for woodlands.*

(1) *In general.*—This paragraph applies to the election of special rules for woodlands under section 2032A(e)(13) of the Code, as added by section 421(h) of the Economic Recovery Tax Act of 1981. The executor shall make this election for an estate by attaching to the estate tax return a statement that—

(i) Contains the decedent's name and taxpayer identification number as they appear on the estate tax return,

(ii) Identifies the election as an election under section 2032A(e)(13) of the Code,

(iii) Specifies the property with respect to which the election is made, and

(iv) Provides all information necessary to show that the executor is entitled to make the election.

(2) *Additional information required.*—If later regulations issued under section 2032A(e)(13) require the executor to furnish information in addition to that required under paragraph (a)(1) of this section and an office of the Internal Revenue Service requests the executor to furnish the additional information, the executor shall furnish the additional information in a statement filed with that office of the Internal Revenue Service within 60 days after the request is made. The statement shall also contain the information required by paragraph (a)(1)(i), (ii), and (iii) of this section. If the additional information is not provided within 60 days after the request is made, the election may, at the discretion of the Commissioner, be held invalid.

(b) *Election of special use valuation for qualified real property.*—This paragraph applies to the election of special use valuation for qualified real property under section 2032A(d)(1) of the Code, as amended by section 421(j)(3) of the Economic Recovery Tax Act of 1981. This election shall be made in the manner prescribed in § 20.2032A-8(a)(3), except that the election shall be valid even if the estate tax return is not timely filed.

(c) *Elections irrevocable.*—Elections to which this section applies may not be revoked.

(d) *Effective date.*—The elections described in this section are available with respect to the estate of decedents dying after 1981. [Temporary Reg. § 22.0.]

☐ [*T.D.* 7793, 10-29-81.]

[Reg. § 20.2033-1]

§ 20.2033-1. Property in which the decedent had an interest.—(a) *In general.*—The gross estate of a decedent who was a citizen or resident of the United States at the time of his death includes under section 2033 the value of all property, whether real or personal, tangible or intangible, and wherever situated, beneficially owned by the decedent at the time of his death. (For certain exceptions in the case of real property situated outside the United States, see paragraphs (a) and (c) of § 20.2031-1.) Real property is included whether it came into the possession and control of the executor or administrator or passed directly to heirs or devisees. Various statutory provisions which exempt bonds, notes, bills, and certificates of indebtedness of the Federal Government or its agencies and the interest thereon from taxation are generally not applicable to the estate tax, since such tax is an excise tax on the transfer of property at death and is not a tax on the property transferred.

(b) *Miscellaneous examples.*—A cemetery lot owned by the decedent is part of his gross estate, but its value is limited to the salable value of that part of the lot which is not designed for the interment of the decedent and the members of his family. Property subject to homestead or other exemptions under local law is included in the gross estate. Notes or other claims held by the decedent are likewise included even though they are cancelled by the decedent's will. Interest and rents accrued at the date of the decedent's death constitute a part of the gross estate. Similarly, dividends which are payable to the decedent or his estate by reason of the fact that on or before the date of the decedent's death he was a stockholder of record (but which have not been collected at death) constitute a part of the gross estate. [Reg. § 20.2033-1.]

☐ [*T.D.* 6296, 6-23-58. *Amended by T.D.* 6684, 10-23-63.]

[Reg. § 20.2034-1]

§ 20.2034-1. Dower or curtesy interests.—A decedent's gross estate includes under section 2034 any interest in property of the decedent's surviving spouse existing at the time of the decedent's death as dower or curtesy, or any interest created by statute in lieu thereof (although such other interest may differ in character from dower or curtesy). Thus, the full value of property is included in the decedent's gross estate, without deduction of such an interest of the surviving husband or wife, and without regard to when the right to such an interest arose. [Reg. § 20.2034-1.]

☐ [*T.D.* 6296, 6-23-58.]

[Reg. § 20.2036-1]

§ 20.2036-1. Transfers with retained life estate.—(a) *In general.*—A decedent's gross estate includes under section 2036 the value of any interest in property transferred by the decedent after March 3, 1931, whether in trust or otherwise, except to the extent that the transfer was for an adequate and full consideration in money or money's worth (see § 20.2043-1), if the decedent retained or reserved—

(1) For his life;

(2) For any period not ascertainable without reference to his death (if the transfer was made after June 6, 1932); or

(3) For any period which does not in fact end before his death:

(i) The use, possession, right to income, or other enjoyment of the transferred property.

(ii) The right, either alone or in conjunction with any other person or persons, to designate the person or persons who shall possess or enjoy the transferred property or its income (except that, if the transfer was made before June 7, 1932, the right to designate must be retained by or reserved to the decedent alone).

(b) *Meaning of terms.*—(1) A reservation by the decedent "for any period not ascertainable without reference to his death" may be illustrated by the following examples:

(i) A decedent reserved the right to receive the income from transferred property in quarterly payments, with the proviso that no part of the income between the last quarterly payment and the date of the decedent's death was to be received by the decedent or his estate; and

(ii) A decedent reserved the right to receive the income, annuity, or other payment from transferred property after the death of another person who was in fact enjoying the income, annuity, or other payment at the time of the decedent's death. In such a case, the amount to be included in the decedent's gross estate under this section does not include the value of the outstanding interest of the other person as determined in paragraphs (c)(1)(i) and (c)(2)(ii) of this section. See also, paragraphs (c)(1)(ii) *Example 1* and (c)(2)(iv) *Example 8* of this section. If the other person predeceased the decedent, the reservation by the decedent may be considered to be either for life, or for a period that does not in fact end before death.

(2) The "use, possession, right to the income, or other enjoyment of the transferred property" is considered as having been retained by or reserved to the decedent to the extent that the use, possession, right to the income, or other enjoyment is to be applied toward the discharge of a legal obligation of the decedent, or otherwise for his pecuniary benefit. The term "legal obligation" includes a legal obligation to support a dependent during the decedent's lifetime.

(3) The phrase "right . . . to designate the person or persons who shall possess or enjoy the transferred property or the income therefrom" includes a reserved power to designate the person or persons to receive the income from the transferred property, or to possess or enjoy nonincome-producing property, during the decedent's life or during any other period described in paragraph (a) of this section. With respect to such a power, it is immaterial (i) whether the power was exercisable alone or only in conjunction with another person or persons, whether or not having an adverse interest; (ii) in what capacity the power was exercisable by the decedent or by another person or persons in conjunction with the decedent; and (iii) whether the exercise of the power was subject to a contingency beyond the decedent's control which did not occur before his death (e.g., the death of another person during the decedent's lifetime). The phrase, however, does not include a power over the transferred property itself which does not affect the enjoyment of the income received or earned during the decedent's life. (See, however, section 2038 for the inclusion of property in the gross estate on account of such a power.) Nor does the phrase apply to a power held solely by a person other than the decedent. But, for example, if the decedent reserved the unrestricted power to remove or discharge a trustee at any time and appoint himself as trustee, the decedent is considered as having the powers of the trustee.

(c) *Retained or reserved interest.*—(1) *Amount included in gross estate.*—(i) *In general.*—If the decedent retained or reserved an interest or right with respect to all of the property transferred by him, the amount to be included in his gross estate under section 2036 is the value of the entire property, less only the value of any outstanding income interest which is not subject to the decedent's interest or right and which is actually being enjoyed by another person at the time of the decedent's death. If the decedent retained or reserved an interest or right with respect to a part only of the property transferred by him, the amount to be included in his gross estate under section 2036 is only a corresponding proportion of the amount described in the preceding sentence. An interest or right is treated as having been retained or reserved if at the time of the transfer there was an understanding, express or implied, that the interest or right would later be conferred. If this section applies to an interest retained by the decedent in a trust or otherwise and the terms of the trust or other governing instrument provide that, after the decedent's death, payments the decedent was receiving during life are to continue to be made to the decedent's estate for a specified period (as opposed to payments that were payable to the decedent prior to the decedent's death but were not actually paid until after the decedent's death), such payments that become payable after the decedent's death are not includible in the decedent's gross estate under section 2033 because they are properly reflected in the value of the trust corpus included under this section. Payments that become payable to the decedent prior to the decedent's date of death, but are not paid until after the decedent's date of death, are includible in the decedent's gross estate under section 2033.

(ii) *Examples.*—The application of paragraph (c)(1)(i) of this section is illustrated in the following examples:

Example 1. Decedent (D) creates an irrevocable inter vivos trust. The terms of the trust provide that all of the trust income is to be paid to D and D's child, C, in equal shares during their joint lives and, on the death of the first to die of D and C, all of the trust income is to be paid to the survivor. On the death of the survivor of D and C, the remainder is to be paid to another individual, F. Subsequently, D dies survived by C. Fifty percent of the value of the trust corpus is includible in D's gross estate under section 2036(a)(1) because, under the terms of the trust, D retained the right to receive one-half of the trust income for D's life. In addition, the excess (if any) of the value of the remaining 50 percent of the trust corpus, over the present value of C's outstanding life estate in that 50 percent of trust corpus, also is includible in D's gross estate under section 2036(a)(1), because D retained the right to receive all of the trust income for such time as D survived C. If C had predeceased D, then 100 percent of the trust corpus would have been includible in D's gross estate.

Example 2. D transferred D's personal residence to D's child (C), but retained the right to use the residence for a term of years. D dies during the term. At D's death, the fair market value of the personal residence is includible in D's gross estate under section 2036(a)(1) because D retained the right to use the residence for a period that did not in fact end before D's death.

(2) *Retained annuity, unitrust, and other income interests in trusts.*—(i) *In general.*—This paragraph (c)(2) applies to a grantor's retained use of an asset held in trust or a retained annuity, unitrust, or other interest in any trust (other than a trust constituting an employee benefit) including without limitation the following (collectively referred to in this paragraph (c)(2) as "trusts"): certain charitable remainder trusts (collectively CRTs) such as a charitable remainder annuity trust (CRAT) within the meaning of section 664(d)(1), a charitable remainder unitrust (CRUT) within the meaning of section 664(d)(2) or (d)(3), and any charitable remainder trust that does not qualify under section 664(d), whether because the CRT was created prior to 1969, there was a defect in the drafting of the CRT, there was no intention to qualify the CRT for the charitable deduction, or otherwise; other trusts established by a grantor (collectively GRTs) such as a grantor retained annuity trust (GRAT) paying out a qualified annuity interest within the meaning of § 25.2702-3(b) of this chapter, a grantor retained unitrust (GRUT) paying out a qualified unitrust interest within the meaning of § 25.2702-3(c) of this chapter; and various other forms of grantor retained income trusts (GRITs) whether or not the grantor's retained interest is a qualified interest as defined in section 2702(b), including without limitation a qualified personal residence trust (QPRT) within the meaning of § 25.2702-5(c) of this chapter and a personal residence trust (PRT) within the meaning of § 25.2702-5(b) of this chapter. If a decedent transferred property into such a trust and retained or reserved the right to use such property, or the right to an annuity, unitrust, or other interest in such trust with respect to the property decedent so transferred for decedent's life, any period not ascertainable without reference to the decedent's death, or for a period that does not in fact end before the decedent's death, then the decedent's right to use the property or the retained annuity, unitrust, or other interest (whether payable from income and/or principal) constitutes the retention of the possession or enjoyment of, or the right to the income from, the property for purposes of section 2036. The portion of the trust's corpus includible in the decedent's gross estate for Federal estate tax purposes is that portion of the trust corpus necessary to provide the decedent's retained use or retained annuity, unitrust, or other payment (without reducing or invading principal). In the case of a retained annuity or unitrust, the portion of the trust's corpus includible in the decedent's gross estate is that portion of the trust corpus necessary to generate sufficient income to satisfy the retained annuity or unitrust (without reducing or invading principal), using the interest rates provided in section 7520 and the adjustment factors prescribed in § 20.2031-7 (or § 20.2031-7A), if applicable. The computation is illustrated in paragraph (c)(2)(iv), *Examples 1, 2,* and *3* of this section. The portion of the trust's corpus includible in the decedent's gross estate under section 2036, however, shall not exceed the fair market value of the trust's corpus at the decedent's date of death.

(ii) *Decedent's retained annuity following a current annuity interest of another person.*—If the decedent retained the right to receive an annuity or other payment (rather than income) after the death of the current recipient of that interest, then the amount includible in the decedent's gross estate under this section is the amount of trust corpus required to produce sufficient income to satisfy the entire annuity or other payment the decedent would have been entitled to receive if the decedent had survived the current recipient (thus, also including the portion of that entire amount payable to the decedent before the current recipient's death), reduced by the present value of the current recipient's interest. However, the amount includible shall not be less than the amount of corpus required to produce sufficient income to satisfy the annuity or other payment the decedent was entitled, at the time of the decedent's death, to receive for each year. In addition, in no event shall the amount includible exceed the value of the trust corpus on the date of death. Finally, in calculating the present value of the current recipient's interest, the exhaustion of trust corpus test described in § 20.7520-3(b)(2) (exhaustion test) is not to be applied, even in cases where § 20.7520-3(b)(2) would otherwise require it to be applied. The following steps implement this computation.

(A) *Step 1*: Determine the fair market value of the trust corpus on the decedent's date of death.

(B) *Step 2*: Determine, in accordance with paragraph (c)(2)(i) of this section, the amount of corpus required to generate sufficient income to pay the annuity, unitrust, or other payment (determined on the date of the decedent's death) payable to the decedent for the trust year in which the decedent's death occurred.

(C) *Step 3*: Determine, in accordance with paragraph (c)(2)(i) of this section, the amount of corpus required to generate sufficient income to pay the annuity, unitrust, or other payment that the decedent would have been entitled to receive for each trust year if the decedent had survived the current recipient.

(D) *Step 4*: Determine the present value of the current recipient's annuity, unitrust, or other payment (without applying the exhaustion test).

(E) *Step 5*: Reduce the amount determined in Step 3 by the amount determined in Step 4, but not to below the amount determined in Step 2.

(F) *Step 6*: The amount includible in the decedent's gross estate under this section is the lesser of the amounts determined in Step 5 and Step 1.

(iii) *Graduated retained interests.*—(A) *In general.*—For purposes of this section, a *graduated retained interest* is the grantor's reservation of a right to receive an annuity, unitrust, or other payment as described in paragraph (c)(2)(i) of this section, payable at least annually, that increases (but does not decrease) over a period of time, not more often than annually.

(B) *Other definitions.*—*(1) Base amount.*—The *base amount* is the amount of corpus required to generate the annuity, unitrust, or other payment payable for the trust year in which the decedent's death occurs. See paragraph (c)(2)(i) of this section for the calculation of the base amount.

(2) Periodic addition.—The *periodic addition* in a graduated retained interest for each year after the year in which decedent's death occurs is the amount (if any) by which the annuity, unitrust, or other payment that would have been payable for that year if the decedent had survived exceeds the total amount of payments that would have been payable for the year immediately preceding that year. For example, assume the trust instrument provides that the grantor is to receive an annual annuity payable to the grantor or the grantor's estate for a 5-year term. The initial annual payment is $100,000, and each succeeding annual payment is to be 120 percent of the amount payable for the preceding year. Assuming the grantor dies in the second year of the trust (whether before or after the due date of the second annual payment), the periodic additions for years 3, 4, and 5 of the trust are as follows:

	(1) Annual Payment	(2) Prior Year Payment	(1 - 2) Periodic Addition
Year 3	144,000	120,000	24,000
Year 4	172,800	144,000	28,800
Year 5	207,360	172,800	34,560

(3) Corpus amount.—For each trust year in which a periodic addition occurs (increase year), the *corpus amount* is the amount of trust corpus which, starting from the decedent's date of death, is necessary to generate an amount of income sufficient to pay the periodic addition, beginning in the increase year and continuing in perpetuity, without reducing or invading principal. For each year with a periodic addition, the corpus amount required as of the decedent's date of death is the product of two factors: the first is the result of dividing the periodic addition (adjusted for payments made more frequently than annually, if applicable, and for payments due at the beginning, rather than the end, of a payment period (see Table K or J of § 20.2031-7(d)(6)) by the section 7520 rate (periodic addition / rate)); and the second is 1 divided by the sum of 1 and the section 7520 rate raised to the T power (1 / (1 + rate)^T). The second factor applies a present value discount to reflect the period beginning with the date of death and ending on the last day of the trust year immediately before the year for which the periodic addition is first payable.

(i) The corpus amount is determined as follows:

$$\frac{\text{(Periodic Addition)} \times \text{(Adjustment Factor)}}{\text{Section 7520 Rate}} \times \frac{1}{(1+ \text{Section 7520 Rate})^{T}}$$

(ii) The adjustment factor, if applicable, is the factor for payments made more frequently than annually and for payments due at the beginning, rather than the end, of a calendar period (see Table K or J of § 20.2031-7(d)(6)). T equals the time period in years from the decedent's date of death through the last day of the trust year immediately before the year for which the periodic addition is first payable.

(C) *Amount includible.*—The amount includible in the gross estate in the case of a graduated retained interest is the sum of the base amount and the corpus amount for each year for which a periodic addition is first payable. The sum of these amounts represents the amount of trust principal that would be necessary to generate the annual payments that would have been paid to the decedent if the decedent had survived and had continued to receive the graduated retained interest. The amount of trust corpus includible in a decedent's gross estate under this section, however, shall not exceed the fair market value of the trust corpus on the decedent's date of death. The provisions of this section also apply to graduated retained interests in transferred property not held in trust.

(iv) *Examples*.—The application of paragraphs (c)(2)(i), (c)(2)(ii), and (c)(2)(iii) of this section is illustrated in the following examples:

Example 1. (i) Decedent (D) transferred $100,000 to an inter vivos trust that qualifies as a CRAT under section 664(d)(1). The trust agreement provides for an annuity of $7,500 to be paid each year to D for D's life, then to D's child (C) for C's life, with the remainder to be distributed upon the survivor's death to N, a charitable organization described in sections 170(c), 2055(a), and 2522(a). The annuity is payable to D or C, as the case may be, annually on each December 31st. D dies in September 2006, survived by C who was then age 40. On D's death, the value of the trust assets was $300,000 and the section 7520 interest rate was 6 percent. D's executor does not elect to use the alternate valuation date.

(ii) The amount of corpus with respect to which D retained the right to the income, and thus the amount includible in D's gross estate under section 2036, is that amount of corpus necessary to yield the annual annuity payment to D (without reducing or invading principal). In this case, the formula for determining the amount of corpus necessary to yield the annual annuity payment to D is: annual annuity / section 7520 interest rate = amount includible under section 2036. The amount of corpus necessary to yield the annual annuity is $7,500 / .06 = $125,000. Therefore, $125,000 is includible in D's gross estate under section 2036(a)(1). (The result would be the same if D had retained an interest in the CRAT for a term of years and had died during the term. The result also would be the same if D had irrevocably relinquished D's annuity interest less than 3 years prior to D's death because of the application of section 2035.) If, instead, the trust agreement had provided that D could revoke C's annuity interest or change the identity of the charitable remainderman, see section 2038 with regard to the portion of the trust to be included in the gross estate on account of such a retained power to revoke. Under the facts presented, section 2039 does not apply to include any amount in D's gross estate by reason of this retained annuity. See § 20.2039-1(e).

Example 2. (i) D transferred $100,000 to a GRAT in which D's annuity is a qualified interest described in section 2702(b). The trust agreement provides for an annuity of $12,000 per year to be paid to D for a term of ten years or until D's earlier death. The annuity amount is payable in twelve equal installments at the end of each month. At the expiration of the term of years or on D's earlier death, the remainder is to be distributed to D's child (C). D dies prior to the expiration of the ten-year term. On the date of D's death, the value of the trust assets is $300,000 and the section 7520 interest rate is 6 percent. D's executor does not elect to use the alternate valuation date.

(ii) The amount of corpus with respect to which D retained the right to the income, and thus the amount includible in D's gross estate under section 2036, is that amount of corpus necessary to yield the annual annuity payment to D (without reducing or invading principal). In this case, the formula for determining the amount of corpus necessary to yield the annual annuity payment to D is: annual annuity (adjusted for monthly payments) / section 7520 interest rate = amount includible under section 2036. The Table K adjustment factor for monthly annuity payments in this case is 1.0272. Thus, the amount of corpus necessary to yield the annual annuity is ($12,000 × 1.0272) / .06 = $205,440. Therefore, $205,440 is includible in D's gross estate under section 2036(a)(1). If, instead, the trust agreement had provided that the annuity was to be paid to D during D's life and to D's estate for the balance of the 10-year term if D died during that term, then the portion of trust corpus includible in D's gross estate would still be as calculated in this paragraph. It is not material whether payments are made to D's estate after D's death. Under the facts presented, section 2039 does not apply to include any amount in D's gross estate by reason of this retained annuity. See § 20.2039-1(e).

Example 3. (i) In 2000, D created a CRUT within the meaning of section 664(d)(2). The trust instrument directs the trustee to hold, invest, and reinvest the corpus of the trust and to pay to D for D's life, and then to D's child (C) for C's life, in equal quarterly installments payable at the end of each calendar quarter, an amount equal to 6 percent of the fair market value of the trust as valued on December 15 of the prior taxable year of the trust. At the termination of the trust, the then-remaining corpus, together with any and all accrued income, is to be distributed to N, a charitable organization described in sections 170(c), 2055(a), and 2522(a). D dies in 2006, survived by C, who was then age 55. The value of the trust assets on D's death was $300,000. D's executor does not elect to use the alternate valuation date and, as a result, D's executor does not choose to use the section 7520 interest rate for either of the two months prior to D's death.

(ii) The amount of the corpus with respect to which D retained the right to the income, and thus the amount includible in D's gross estate under section 2036(a)(1), is that amount of corpus necessary to yield the unitrust payments. In this case, such amount of corpus is determined by dividing the trust's equivalent income interest rate by the section 7520 rate (which was 6 percent at the time of D's death). The equivalent income interest rate is determined by dividing the trust's adjusted payout rate by the excess of 1 over the adjusted payout rate. Based on § 1.664-4(e)(3) of this chapter, the appropriate adjusted payout rate for the trust at D's death is 5.786 percent (6 percent x .964365). Thus, the equivalent income interest rate is 6.141 percent (5.786 percent / (1 - 5.786 percent)). The ratio of the equivalent interest rate to the assumed interest rate under section 7520 is 102.35 percent (6.141 percent / 6 percent). Because this exceeds 100 percent, D's retained payout interest exceeds a full income interest in the trust, and D effectively retained the income from all the assets transferred to the trust. Accordingly, because D retained for life an interest at least equal to the right to all income from all the property transferred by D to the CRUT, the entire value of the corpus of the CRUT is includible in D's gross estate under section 2036(a)(1). (The result would be the same if D had retained, instead, an interest in the CRUT for a term of years and had died during the term.) Under the facts presented, section 2039 does not apply to include any amount in D's gross estate by reason of D's retained unitrust interest. See § 20.2039-1(e).

(iii) If, instead, D had retained the right to a unitrust amount having an adjusted payout for which the corresponding equivalent interest rate would have been less than the 6 percent assumed interest rate of section 7520, then a correspondingly reduced proportion of the trust corpus would be includible in D's gross estate under section 2036(a)(1). Alternatively, if the interest retained by D was instead only one-half of the 6 percent unitrust interest, then the amount included in D's estate would be the amount needed to produce a 3 percent unitrust interest. All of the results in this *Example 3* would be the same if the trust had been a GRUT instead of a CRUT.

Example 4. During life, D established a 15-year GRIT for the benefit of individuals who are not members of D's family within the meaning of section 2704(c)(2). D retained the right to receive all of the net income from the GRIT, payable annually, during the GRIT's term. D dies during the GRIT's term. D's executor does not elect to use the alternate valuation date. In this case, the GRIT's corpus is includible in D's gross estate under section 2036(a)(1) because D retained the right to receive all of the income from the GRIT for a period that did not in fact end before D's death. If, instead, D had retained the right to receive 60 percent of the GRIT's net income, then 60 percent of the GRIT's corpus would have been includible in D's gross estate under section 2036. Under the facts presented, section 2039 does not apply to include any amount in D's gross estate by reason of D's retained interest. See § 20.2039-1(e).

Example 5. In 2003, D transferred $10X to a pooled income fund that conforms to Rev. Proc. 88-53,1988-2 CB 712 (1988) in exchange for 1 unit in the fund. D is to receive all of the income from that 1 unit during D's life. Upon D's death, D's child (C), is to receive D's income interest for C's life. In 2008, D dies. D's executor does not elect to use the alternate valuation date. In this case, the fair market value of D's 1 unit in the pooled income fund is includible in D's gross estate under section 2036(a)(1) because D retained the right to receive all of the income from that unit for a period that did not in fact end before D's death. See § 601.601(d)(2)(ii)(b) of this chapter.

Example 6. D transferred D's personal residence to a trust that met the requirements of a qualified personal residence trust (QPRT) as set forth in § 25.2702- 5(c) of this chapter. Pursuant to the terms of the QPRT, D retained the right to use the residence for 10 years or until D's prior death. D dies before the end of the term. D's executor does not elect to use the alternate valuation date. In this case, the fair market value of the QPRT's assets on the date of D's death are includible in D's gross estate under section 2036(a)(1) because D retained the right to use the residence for a period that did not in fact end before D's death.

Example 7. (i) On November 1, year N, D transfers assets valued at $2,000,000 to a GRAT. Under the terms of the GRAT, the trustee is to pay to D an annuity for a 5-year term that is a qualified interest described in section 2702(b). The annuity amount is to be paid annually at the end of each trust year, on October 31st. The first annual payment is to be $100,000. Each succeeding payment is to be 120 percent of the amount paid in the preceding year. Income not distributed in any year is to be added to principal. If D dies during the 5-year term, the payments are to be made to D's estate for the balance of the GRAT term. At the end of the 5-year term, the trust is to terminate and the corpus is to be distributed to C, D's child. D dies on January 31st of the third year of the GRAT term. On the date of D's death, the value of the trust corpus is $3,200,000, the section 7520 interest rate is 6.8 percent, and the adjustment factor from Table K of § 20.2031-7 is 1.0000. D's executor does not elect to value the gross estate as of the alternate valuation date pursuant to section 2032.

(ii) The amount includible in D's gross estate under section 2036(a)(1) as described in paragraph (c)(2)(iii)(C) of this section is determined and illustrated as follows:

A	B	C	D	E	F	G
GRAT Year	Annual Annuity Payment	Periodic Addition	Required Principal: C × Adj. Factor / 0.068	Deferral Period: Death to GRAT Year	Present Value Factor: 1/(1+.068) E	Corpus or Base Amount At Death: D × F
3	144,000	n/a	2,117,647	n/a	n/a	2,117,647
4	172,800	28,800	423,529	0.747945	0.951985	403,193
5	207,360	34,560	508,235	1.747945	0.891372	453,026
					Total:	2,973,866

(iii) Specifically:

(A) *Column A.* First, determine the year of the trust term during which the decedent's death occurs, and the number of subsequent years remaining in the trust term for which the decedent retained or reserved an interest. In this example, D dies during year 3, with two additional years remaining in the term.

(B) *Column B.* Under the formula specified in the trust, the annuity payment to be made on October 31st of the 3rd year of the trust term is $144,000. Using that same formula, determine the annuity amounts for years 4 and 5.

(C) *Column C.* Determine the periodic addition for year 4 and year 5 by subtracting the annuity amount for the preceding year from the annuity amount for that year; the periodic addition for that year is the amount of the increase in the annuity amount for that year.

(D) *Columns D through G for year 3.* For the year of the decedent's death (year 3), determine the principal required to produce the annuity amount (Column D) by multiplying the annuity amount (Column B) by the adjustment factor (in this case 1.0000) and by dividing the product by the applicable interest rate under section 7520. Because this is the year of decedent's death and reflects the annuity amount payable to the decedent in that year, there is no deferral, so this is also the Base Amount (the amount of corpus required to produce the annuity for year 3) (Column G).

(E) *Columns D through G for years 4 and 5.* For each succeeding year of the trust term during which the periodic addition will not be payable until a year subsequent to the year of the decedent's death, determine the principal required to produce the periodic addition payable for that year (Column D) by multiplying the periodic addition (Column C) by the adjustment factor and by dividing the product by the applicable interest rate under section 7520. Compute the factors to reflect the length of the deferral period (Column E) and the present value (Column F) as described in paragraph (c)(2)(iii)(B)(3) of this section. Multiply the amount of corpus in Column D by the factors in Columns E and F to determine the Corpus Amount for that year (Column G).

(F) *Column G total.* The sum of the amounts in Column G represents the total amount includable in the gross estate (but not in excess of the fair market value of the trust on the decedent's date of death).

(iv) An illustration of the amount of trust corpus (as of the decedent's death) necessary to produce the scheduled payments is as follows:

		Year 3	*Year 4*	*Year 5*	*Corpus Amount*
2nd Periodic Addition	$34,560	*Deferral Period*		$453,026	$453,026
1st Periodic Addition	$28,800	*Deferral Period*	$403,193		$403,193
Annuity in year of death	$144,000	$2,117,647			$2,117,647
Total amount (sum) included in gross estate					$2,973,866

(v) A total corpus amount (as defined in paragraph (c)(2)(iii)(B)(3) of this section) of $2,973,866 constitutes the principal required as of decedent's date of death to produce (without reducing or invading principal) the annual payments that D would have received if D had survived and had continued to receive the retained annuity. Therefore, $2,973,866 of the trust corpus is includible in D's gross estate under section 2036(a)(1). The remaining $226,134 of the trust corpus is not includible in D's gross estate under section 2036(a)(1). The result would be the same if D's retained annuity instead had been payable to D for a term of 5 years, or until D's prior death, at which time the GRAT would have terminated and the trust corpus would have become payable to another.

(vi) If, instead, D's annuity was to have been paid on a monthly or quarterly basis, then the periodic addition would have to be adjusted as provided in paragraph (c)(2)(iii)(B)(3) of this section. Specifically, in Column D of the Table for years 4 and 5 in this example, the amount of the principal required would be computed by multiplying the periodic addition by the appropriate factor from Table K or J of § 20.2031-7(d)(6) before dividing as indicated and computing the amounts in Columns E through G. In addition, Column D in year 3 also would have to be so adjusted. Under the facts presented, section 2039 does not apply to include any amount in D's gross estate by reason of this retained interest. See § 20.2039-1(e).

Example 8. (i) D creates an irrevocable inter vivos trust. The terms of the trust provide that an annuity of $10,000 per year is to be paid to D and C, D's child, in equal shares during their joint lives. On the death of the first to die of D and C, the entire $10,000 annuity is to be paid to the survivor for life. On the death of the survivor of D and C, the remainder is to be paid to another individual, F. Subsequently, D dies survived by C. On D's date of death, the fair market value of the trust is $120,000 and the section 7520 rate is 7 percent. At the date of D's death, the amount of trust corpus needed to produce D's annuity interest ($5,000 per year) is $71,429 ($5,000/0.07). In addition, assume the present value of C's right to receive $5,000 annually for the remainder of C's life is $40,000. The portion of the trust corpus includible in D's gross estate under section 2036(a)(1) is $102,857, determined as follows:

(ii) *Step 1*: Fair market value of corpus.	$120,000
(iii) *Step 2*: Corpus required to produce D's date of death annuity ($5,000/0.07).	$71,429
(iv) *Step 3*: Corpus required to produce D's annuity if D had survived C ($10,000/0.07).	$142,857
(v) *Step 4*: Present value of C's interest.	$40,000
(vi) *Step 5*: The amount determined in Step 3, reduced by the amount determined in Step 4, but not to below the amount determined in Step 2 ($142,857 - $40,000, but not less than $71,429).	$102,857
(vii) *Step 6*: The lesser of the amounts determined in Steps 5 and 1 ($102,857 or $120,000).	$102,857.

(3) *Effective/applicability dates*.—Paragraphs (a) and (c)(1)(i) of this section are applicable to the estates of decedents dying after August 16, 1954. Paragraphs (c)(1)(ii) and (c)(2) of this section apply to the estates of decedents dying on or after July 14, 2008. All but the last two sentences at the end of paragraph (c)(1)(i) of this section are applicable to the estates of decedents dying after August 16, 1954. The first, second, and sixth sentences in paragraph (c)(2)(i) of this section and all but the introductory text, *Example 7*, and *Example 8* of paragraph (c)(2)(iv) of this section are applicable to the estates of decedent's dying on or after July 14, 2008. Paragraph (b)(1)(ii) of this section, the last two sentences at the end of paragraph (c)(1)(i) of this section, *Example 1* of paragraph (c)(1)(ii) of this section, the third, fourth, and fifth sentences in paragraph (c)(2)(i) of this section; paragraph (c)(2)(ii) of this section; paragraph (c)(2)(iii) of this section; and the introductory text, *Example 7*, and *Example 8* of paragraph (c)(2)(iv) of this section are applicable to the estates of decedents dying on or after November 8, 2011. [Reg. § 20.2036-1.]

☐ [*T.D.* 6296, 6-23-58. *Amended by T.D.* 6501, 11-15-60; *T.D.* 9414, 7-11-2008 (*corrected* 7-30-2008) *and T.D.* 9555, 11-7-2011.]

[Reg. § 20.2037-1]

§ 20.2037-1. Transfers taking effect at death.—(a) *In general*.—A decedent's gross estate includes under section 2037 the value of any interest in property transferred by the decedent after September 7, 1916, whether in trust or otherwise, except to the extent that the transfer was for an adequate and full consideration in money or money's worth (see § 20.2043-1), if—

(1) Possession or enjoyment of the property could, through ownership of the interest, have been obtained only by surviving the decedent,

(2) The decedent had retained a possibility (hereinafter referred to as a "reversionary interest") that the property, other than the income alone, would return to the decedent or his estate or would be subject to a power of disposition by him, and

(3) The value of the reversionary interest immediately before the decedent's death exceeded 5 percent of the value of the entire property.

However, if the transfer was made before October 8, 1949, section 2037 is applicable only if the reversionary interest arose by the express terms of the instrument of transfer and not by operation of law (see paragraph (f) of this section). See also paragraph (g) of this section with respect to transfers made between November 11, 1935, and January 29, 1940. The provisions of section 2037 do not apply to transfers made before September 8, 1916.

(b) *Condition of survivorship*.—As indicated in paragraph (a) of this section, the value of an interest in transferred property is not included in a decedent's gross estate under section 2037 unless possession or enjoyment of the property could, through ownership of such interest, have been obtained only by surviving the decedent. Thus, property is not included in the decedent's gross estate if, immediately before the decedent's death, possession or enjoyment of the property could have been obtained by any beneficiary either by surviving the decedent or through the occurrence of some other event such as the expiration of a term of years. However, if a consideration of the terms and circumstances of the transfer as a whole indicates that the "other event" is unreal and if the death of the decedent does, in fact, occur before the "other event," the beneficiary will be considered able to possess or enjoy the property only by surviving the decedent. Notwithstanding the foregoing, an interest in transferred property is not includible in a decedent's gross estate under section 2037 if possession or enjoyment of the property could have been obtained by any beneficiary during the decedent's life through the exercise of a general power of appointment (as defined in section 2041) which in fact was exercisable immediately before the decedent's death. See examples (5) and (6) in paragraph (e) of this section.

(c) *Retention of reversionary interest.*—(1) As indicated in paragraph (a) of this section, the value of an interest in transferred property is not included in a decedent's gross estate under section 2037 unless the decedent had retained a reversionary interest in the property, and the value of the reversionary interest immediately before the death of the decedent exceeded 5 percent of the value of the property.

(2) For purposes of section 2037, the term "reversionary interest" includes a possibility that property transferred by the decedent may return to him or his estate and a possibility that property transferred by the decedent may become subject to a power of disposition by him. The term is not used in a technical sense, but has reference to any reserved right under which the transferred property shall or may be returned to the grantor. Thus, it encompasses an interest arising either by the express terms of the instrument of transfer or by operation of law. (See, however, paragraph (f) of this section with respect to transfers made before October 8, 1949.) The term "reversionary interest" does not include rights to income only, such as the right to receive the income from a trust after the death of another person. (However, see section 2036 for the inclusion of property in the gross estate on account of such rights.) Nor does the term "reversionary interest" include the possibility that the decedent during his lifetime might have received back an interest in transferred property by inheritance through the estate of another person. Similarly, a statutory right of a spouse to receive a portion of whatever estate a decedent may leave at the time of his death is not a "reversionary interest".

(3) For purposes of this section, the value of the decedent's reversionary interest is computed as of the moment immediately before his death, without regard to whether or not the executor elects the alternate valuation method under section 2032 and without regard to the fact of the decedent's death. The value is ascertained in accordance with recognized valuation principles for determining the value for estate tax purposes of future or conditional interests in property. (See §§20.2031-1, 20.2031-7, and 20.2031-9.) For example, if the decedent's reversionary interest was subject to an outstanding life estate in his wife, his interest is valued according to the actuarial rules set forth in §20.2031-7. On the other hand, if the decedent's reversionary interest was contingent on the death of his wife without issue surviving and if it cannot be shown that his wife is incapable of having issue (so that his interest is not subject to valuation according to the actuarial rules in §20.2031-7), his interest is valued according to the general rules set forth in §20.2031-1. A possibility that the decedent may be able to dispose of property under certain conditions is considered to have the same value as a right of the decedent to the return of the property under those same conditions.

(4) In order to determine whether or not the decedent retained a reversionary interest in transferred property of a value in excess of 5 percent, the value of the reversionary interest is compared with the value of the transferred property, including interests therein which are not dependent upon survivorship of the decedent. For example, assume that the decedent, A, transferred property in trust with the income payable to B for life and with the remainder payable to C if A predeceases B, but with the property to revert to A if B predeceases A. Assume further that A does, in fact, predecease B. The value of A's reversionary interest immediately before his death is compared with the value of the trust corpus, without deduction of the value of B's outstanding life estate. If, in the above example, A had retained a reversionary interest in one-half only of the trust corpus, the value of his reversionary interest would be compared with the value of one-half of the trust corpus, again without deduction of any part of the value of B's outstanding life estate.

(d) *Transfers partly taking effect at death.*—If separate interests in property are transferred to one or more beneficiaries, paragraphs (a) through (c) of this section are to be separately applied with respect to each interest. For example, assume that the decedent transferred an interest in Blackacre to A which could be possessed or enjoyed only by surviving the decedent, and that the decedent transferred an interest in Blackacre to B which could be possessed or enjoyed only on the occurrence of some event unrelated to the decedent's death. Assume further that the decedent retained a reversionary interest in Blackacre of a value in excess of 5 percent. Only the value of the interest transferred to A is includible in the decedent's gross estate. Similar results would obtain if possession or enjoyment of the entire property could have been obtained only by surviving the decedent, but the decedent had retained a reversionary interest in a part only of such property.

(e) *Examples.*—The provisions of paragraphs (a) through (d) of this section may be further illustrated by the following examples. It is assumed that the transfers were made on or after October 8, 1949; for the significance of this date, see paragraphs (f) and (g) of this section:

Example (1). The decedent transferred property in trust with the income payable to his wife for life and, at her death, remainder to the decedent's then surviving children, or if none, to the decedent or his estate. Since each beneficiary can possess or enjoy the property without surviving the decedent, no part of the property is includible in the decedent's gross estate under section 2037, regardless of the value of the decedent's reversionary interest. (However, see section 2033 for inclusion of the value of the reversionary interest in the decedent's gross estate.)

Example (2). The decedent transferred property in trust with the income to be accumulated for the decedent's life, and at his death, principal and accumulated income to be paid to the decedent's then surviving issue, or, if none, to A or A's estate. Since the decedent retained no reversionary interest in the property, no part of the property is includible in the decedent's gross estate, even though possession or enjoy ment of the property could be obtained by the issue only by surviving the decedent.

Example (3). The decedent transferred property in trust with the income payable to his wife for life and with the remainder payable to the decedent or, if he is not living at his wife's death, to his daughter or her estate. The daughter cannot obtain possession or enjoyment of the property without surviving the decedent. Therefore, if the decedent's reversionary interest immediately before his death exceeded 5 percent of the value of the property, the value of the property, less the value of the wife's outstanding life estate, is includible in the decedent's gross estate.

Example (4). The decedent transferred property in trust with the income payable to his wife for life and with the remainder payable to his son or, if the son is not living at the wife's death, to the decedent or, if the decedent is not then living, to X or X's estate. Assume that the decedent was survived by his wife, his son, and X. Only X cannot obtain possession or enjoyment of the property without surviving the decedent. Therefore, if the decedent's reversionary interest immediately before his death exceeded 5 percent of the value of the property, the value of X's remainder interest (with reference to the time immediately after the decedent's death) is includible in the decedent's gross estate.

Example (5). The decedent transferred property in trust with the income to be accumulated for a period of 20 years or until the decedent's prior death, at which time the principal and accumulated income was to be paid to the decedent's son if then surviving. Assume that the decedent does, in fact, die before the expiration of the 20-year period. If, at the time of the transfer, the decedent was 30 years of age, in good health, etc., the son will be considered able to possess or enjoy the property without surviving the decedent. If, on the other hand, the decedent was 70 years of age at the time of the transfer, the son will not be considered able to possess or enjoy the property without surviving the decedent. In this latter case, if the value of the decedent's reversionary interest (arising by operation of law) immediately before his death exceeded 5 percent of the value of the property, the value of the property is includible in the decedent's gross estate.

Example (6). The decedent transferred property in trust with the income to be accumulated for his life and, at his death, the principal and accumulated income to be paid to the decedent's then surviving children. The decedent's wife was given the unrestricted power to alter, amend, or revoke the trust. Assume that the wife survived the decedent but did not, in fact, exercise her power during the decedent's lifetime. Since possession or enjoyment of the property could have been obtained by the wife during the decedent's lifetime under the exercise of a general power of appointment, which was, in fact, exercisable immediately before the decedent's death, no part of the property is includible in the decedent's gross estate.

(f) *Transfers made before October 8, 1949.*—(1) Notwithstanding any provisions to the contrary contained in paragraphs (a) to (e) of this section, the value of an interest in property transferred by a decedent before October 8, 1949, is included in his gross estate under section 2037 only if the decedent's reversionary interest arose by the express terms of the instrument and not by operation of law. For example, assume that the decedent, on January 1, 1947, transferred property in trust with the income payable to his wife for the decedent's life and, at his death, remainder to his then surviving descendants. Since no provision was made for the contingency that no descendants of the decedent might survive him, a reversion to the decedent's estate existed by operation of law. The descendants cannot obtain possession or enjoyment of the property without surviving the decedent. However, since the decedent's reversionary interest arose by operation of law, no part of the property is includible in the decedent's gross estate under section 2037. If, in the above example, the transfer had been made on or after October 8, 1949, and if the decedent's reversionary interest immediately before his death exceeded 5 percent of the value of the property, the value of the property would be includible in the decedent's gross estate.

(2) The decedent's reversionary interest will be considered to have arisen by the express terms of the instrument of transfer and not by operation of law if the instrument contains an express disposition which affirmatively creates the reversionary interest, even though the terms of the disposition do not refer to the decedent or his estate, as such. For example, where the disposition is, in its terms, to the next of kin of the decedent and such a disposition, under applicable local law, constitutes a reversionary interest in the decedent's estate, the decedent's reversionary interest will be considered to have arisen by the express terms of the instrument of transfer and not by operation of law.

(g) *Transfers made after November 11, 1935, and before January 29, 1940.*—The provisions of paragraphs (a) to (f) of this section are fully applicable to transfers made after November 11, 1935 (the date on which the Supreme Court decided *Helvering v. St. Louis Union Trust Co.* (296 U. S. 39) and *Becker v. St. Louis Union Trust Co.* (296 U. S. 48)), and before January 29, 1940 (the date on which the Supreme Court decided *Helvering v. Hallock* and companion cases (309 U. S. 106)), except that the value of an interest in property transferred between these dates is not included in a decedent's gross estate under section 2037 if—

(1) The Commissioner, whose determination shall be final, determines that the transfer is classifiable with the transfers involved in the *St. Louis Union Trust Co.* cases, rather than with the transfer involved in the case of *Klein v. United States* (283 U. S. 231), previously decided by the Supreme Court, and

(2) The transfer shall have been finally treated for all gift tax purposes, both as to the

calendar year of the transfer and as to subsequent calendar years, as a gift in an amount measured by the value of the property undiminished by reason of a provision in the instrument of transfer by which the property, in whole or in part, is to revert to the decedent should he survive the donee or another person, or the reversion is conditioned upon some other contingency terminable by the decedent's death. [Reg. § 20.2037-1.]

□ [*T.D.* 6296, 6-23-58.]

[Reg. § 20.2038-1]

§ 20.2038-1. Revocable transfers.—(a) *In general.*—A decedent's gross estate includes under section 2038 the value of any interest in property transferred by the decedent, whether in trust or otherwise, if the enjoyment of the interest was subject at the date of the decedent's death to any change through the exercise of a power by the decedent to alter, amend revoke, or terminate, or if the decedent relinquished such a power in contemplation of death. However, section 2038 does not apply—

(1) To the extent that the transfer was for an adequate and full consideration in money or money's worth (see § 20.2043-1);

(2) If the decedent's power could be exercised only with the consent of all parties having an interest (vested or contingent) in the transferred property, and if the power adds nothing to the rights of the parties under local law; or

(3) To a power held solely by a person other than the decedent. But, for example, if the decedent had the unrestricted power to remove or discharge a trustee at any time and appoint himself trustee, the decedent is considered as having the powers of the trustee. However, this result would not follow if he only had the power to appoint himself trustee under limited conditions which did not exist at the time of his death. (See last two sentences of paragraph (b) of this section.)

Except as provided in this paragraph, it is immaterial in what capacity the power was exercisable by the decedent or by another person or persons in conjunction with the decedent; whether the power was exercisable alone or only in conjunction with another person or persons, whether or not having an adverse interest (unless the transfer was made before June 2, 1924; see paragraph (d) of this section); and at what time or from what source the decedent acquired his power (unless the transfer was made before June 23, 1936; see paragraph (c) of this section). Section 2038 is applicable to any power affecting the time or manner of enjoyment of property or its income, even though the identity of the beneficiary is not affected. For example, section 2038 is applicable to a power reserved by the grantor of a trust to accumulate income or distribute it to A, and to distribute corpus to A, even though the remainder is vested in A or his estate, and no other person has any beneficial interest in the trust. However, only the value of an interest in property subject to a power to which section 2038 applies is included in the decedent's gross estate under section 2038.

(b) *Date of existence of power.*—A power to alter, amend, revoke, or terminate will be considered to have existed at the date of the decedent's death even though the exercise of the power was subject to a precedent giving of notice or even though the alteration, amendment, revocation, or termination would have taken effect only on the expiration of a stated period after the exercise of the power, whether or not on or before the date of the decedent's death notice had been given or the power had been exercised. In determining the value of the gross estate in such cases, the full value of the property transferred subject to the power is discounted for the period required to elapse between the date of the decedent's death and the date upon which the alteration, amendment, revocation, or termination could take effect. In this connection, see especially § 20.2031-7. However, section 2038 is not applicable to a power the exercise of which was subject to a contingency beyond the decedent's control which did not occur before his death (e.g., the death of another person during the decedent's life). See, however, section 2036(a)(2) for the inclusion of property in the decedent's gross estate on account of such a power.

(c) *Transfers made before June 23, 1936.*—Notwithstanding anything to the contrary in paragraphs (a) and (b) of this section, the value of an interest in property transferred by a decedent before June 23, 1936, is not included in his gross estate under section 2038 unless the power to alter, amend, revoke, or terminate was reserved at the time of the transfer. For purposes of this paragraph, the phrase "reserved at the time of the transfer" has reference to a power (arising either by the express terms of the instrument of transfer or by operation of law) to which the transfer was subject when made and which continued to the date of the decedent's death (see paragraph (b) of this section) to be exercisable by the decedent alone or by the decedent in conjunction with any other person or persons. The phrase also has reference to any understanding, express or implied, had in connection with the making of the transfer that the power would later be created or conferred.

(d) *Transfers made before June 2, 1924.*—Notwithstanding anything to the contrary in paragraphs (a) to (c) of this section, if an interest in property was transferred by a decedent before the enactment of the Revenue Act of 1924 (June 2, 1924, 4:01 p.m., eastern standard time), and if a power reserved by the decedent to alter, amend, revoke, or terminate was exercisable by the decedent only in conjunction with a person having a substantial adverse interest in the transferred property, or in conjunction with several persons some or all of whom held such an adverse interest, there is included in the decedent's gross estate only the value of any interest or interests held by a person or persons not required to join in the exercise of the power plus the value of any insubstantial adverse interest or interests of a person or persons required to join in the exercise of the power.

(e) *Powers relinquished in contemplation of death.*—(1) *In general.*—If a power to alter, amend, revoke, or terminate would have resulted in the inclusion of an interest in property in a decedent's gross estate under section 2038 if it had been held until the decedent's death, the relinquishment of the power in contemplation of the decedent's death within 3 years before his death results in the inclusion of the same interest in property in the decedent's gross estate, except to the extent that the power was relinquished for an adequate and full consideration in money or money's worth (see § 20.2043-1). For the meaning of the phrase "in contemplation of death", see paragraph (c) of § 20.2035-1.

(2) *Transfers before June 23, 1936.*—In the case of a transfer made before June 23, 1936, section 2038 applies only to a relinquishment made by the decedent. However, in the case of a transfer made after June 22, 1936, section 2038 also applies to a relinquishment made by a person or persons holding the power in conjunction with the decedent, if the relinquishment was made in contemplation of the decedent's death and had the effect of extinguishing the power.

(f) *Effect of disability to relinquish power in certain cases.*—Notwithstanding anything to the contrary in paragraphs (a) through (e) of this section the provisions of this section do not apply to a transfer if—

(1) The relinquishment on or after January 1, 1940, and on or before December 31, 1947, of the power would, by reason of section 1000(e), of the Internal Revenue Code of 1939, be deemed not a transfer of property for the purpose of the gift tax under chapter 4 of the Internal Revenue Code of 1939, and

(2) The decedent was, for a continuous period beginning on or before September 30, 1947, and ending with his death, after August 16, 1954, under a mental disability to relinquish a power.

For the purpose of the foregoing provision, the term "mental disability" means mental incompetence, in fact, to release the power whether or not there was an adjudication of incompetence. Such provision shall apply even though a guardian could have released the power for the decedent. No interest shall be allowed or paid on any overpayment allowable under section 2038(c) with respect to amounts paid before August 7, 1959. [Reg. § 20.2038-1.]

☐ [*T.D.* 6296, 6-23-58. *Amended by T.D.* 6600, 5-28-62.]

[Reg. § 20.2039-1]

§ 20.2039-1. Annuities.—(a) In general.—A decedent's gross estate includes under section 2039(a) and (b) the value of an annuity or other payment receivable by any beneficiary by reason of surviving the decedent under certain agreements or plans to the extent that the value of the annuity or other payment is attributable to contributions made by the decedent or his employer. Sections 2039(a) and (b), however, have no application to an amount which constitutes the proceeds of insurance under a policy on the decedent's life. Paragraph (b) of this section describes the agreements or plans to which section 2039(a) and (b) applies; paragraph (c) of this section provides rules for determining the amount includible in the decedent's gross estate; paragraph (d) of this section distinguishes proceeds of life insurance; and paragraph (e) of this section distinguishes annuity, unitrust, and other interests retained by a decedent in certain trusts. The fact that an annuity or other payment is not includible in a decedent's gross estate under section 2039(a) and (b) does not mean that it is not includible under some other section of part III of subchapter A of chapter 11. However, see section 2039(c) and (d) and § 20.2039-2 for rules relating to the exclusion from a decedent's gross estate of annuities and other payments under certain "qualified plans." Further, the fact that an annuity or other payment may be includible under section 2039(a) will not preclude the application of another section of chapter 11 with regard to that interest. For annuity interests in trust, see paragraph (e)(1) of this section.

(b) *Agreements or plans to which section 2039(a) and (b) applies.*—(1) Section 2039(a) and (b) applies to the value of an annuity or other payment receivable by any beneficiary under any form of contract or agreement entered into after March 3, 1931, under which—

(i) An annuity or other payment was payable to the decedent, either alone or in conjunction with another person or persons, for his life or for any period not ascertainable without reference to his death or for any period which does not in fact end before his death, or

(ii) The decedent possessed, for his life or for any period not ascertainable without reference to his death or for any period which does not in fact end before his death, the right to receive such an annuity or other payment, either alone or in conjunction with another person or persons.

The term "annuity or other payment" as used with respect to both the decedent and the beneficiary has reference to one or more payments extending over any period of time. The payments may be equal or unequal, conditional or unconditional, periodic or sporadic. The term "contract or agreement" includes any arrangement, understanding or plan, or any combination of arrangements, understandings or plans arising by reason of the decedent's employment. An annuity or other payment "was payable" to the decedent if, at the time of his death, the decedent was in fact receiving an annuity or other payment, whether or not he had an enforceable right to have payments continued. The decedent "possessed the right to receive" an annuity or other payment if, immediately before his death, the decedent had an enforceable right to receive payments at some time in the future, whether or not, at the time of his death, he had a present right to receive payments. In connection with the preceding sentence, the decedent will be regarded as having had "an enforceable right to receive payments at some time in the future" so long as he had complied with his obligations under the contract or agreement up to the time of his death. For the meaning of the phrase "for his life or for any period not ascertainable without reference to his death or for any period which does not in fact end before his death", see section 2036 and § 20.2036-1.

(2) The application of this paragraph is illustrated and more fully explained in the following examples. In each example: (i) It is assumed that all transactions occurred after March 3, 1931, and (ii) the amount stated to be includible in the decedent's gross estate is determined in accordance with the provisions of paragraph (c) of this section.

Example (1). The decedent purchased an annuity contract under the terms of which the issuing company agreed to pay an annuity to the decedent for his life and, upon his death, to pay a specified lump sum to his designated beneficiary. The decedent was drawing his annuity at the time of his death. The amount of the lump sum payment to the beneficiary is includible in the decedent's gross estate under section 2039(a) and (b).

Example (2). Pursuant to a retirement plan, the employer made contributions to a fund which was to provide the employee, upon his retirement at age 60, with an annuity for life, and which was to provide the employee's wife, upon his death after retirement, with a similar annuity for life. The benefits under the plan were completely forfeitable during the employee's life, but, upon his death after retirement, the benefits to the wife were forfeitable only upon her remarriage. The employee had no right originally to designate or ever to change the employer's designation of the surviving beneficiary. The retirement plan at no time met the requirements of section 401(a) (relating to qualified plans). Assume that the employee died at age 61 after the employer started payment of his annuity as described above. The value of the wife's annuity is includible in the decedent's gross estate under section 2039(a) and (b). Includibility in this case is based on the fact that the annuity to the decedent "was payable" at the time of his death. The fact that the decedent's annuity was forfeitable is of no consequence since, at the time of his death, he was in fact receiving payments under the plan. Nor is it important that the decedent had no right to choose the surviving beneficiary. The element of forfeitability in the wife's annuity may be taken into account only with respect to the valuation of the annuity in the decedent's gross estate.

Example (3). Pursuant to a retirement plan, the employer made contributions to a fund which was to provide the employee, upon his retirement at age 60, with an annuity of $100 per month for life, and which was to provide his designated beneficiary, upon the employee's death after retirement, with a similar annuity for life. The plan also provided that (a) upon the employee's separation from service before retirement, he would have a nonforfeitable right to receive a reduced annuity starting at age 60, and (b) upon the employee's death before retirement, a lump sum payment representing the amount of the employer's contributions credited to the employee's account would be paid to the designated beneficiary. The plan at no time met the requirements of section 401(a) (relating to qualified plans). Assume that the employee died at age 49 and that the designated beneficiary was paid the specified lump sum payment. Such amount is includible in the decedent's gross estate under section 2039(a) and (b). Since, immediately before his death, the employee had an enforceable right to receive an annuity commencing at age 60, he is considered to have "possessed the right to receive" an annuity as that term is used in section 2039(a). If, in this example, the employee would not be entitled to any benefits in the event of his separation from service before retirement for any reason other than death, the result would be the same so long as the decedent had complied with his obligations under the contract up to the time of his death. In such case, he is considered to have had, immediatley before his death, an enforceable right to receive an annuity commencing at age 60.

Example (4). Pursuant to a retirement plan, the employer made contributions to a fund which was to provide the employee, upon his retirement at age 60, with an annuity for life, and which was to provide his designated beneficiary, upon the employee's death after retirement, with a similar annuity for life. The plan provided, however, that no benefits were payable in the event of the employee's death before retirement. The retirement plan at no time met the requirements of section 401(a) (relating to qualified plans). Assume that the employee died at age 59 but that the employer nevertheless started payment of an annuity in a slightly reduced amount to the designated beneficiary. The value of the annuity is not includible in the decedent's gross estate under section 2039(a) and (b). Since the employee died before reaching the retirement age, the employer was under no obligation to pay the annuity to the employee's designated beneficiary. Therefore, the annuity was not paid under a "contract or agreement" as that term is used in section 2039(a). If, however, it can be established that the employer has consistently paid an annuity under such circumstances, the annuity will be considered as having been paid under a "contract or agreement."

Example (5). The employer made contributions to a retirement fund which were credited to the employee's individual account. Under the plan, the employee was to receive one-half the amount credited to his account upon his retirement at age 60, and his designated beneficiary was to receive the other one-half upon the employee's death after retirement. If the employee should die before reaching the retirement age, the entire amount credited to his account at such time was to be paid to the designated beneficiary. The retirement plan at no time met the requirements of section 401(a) (relating to qualified plans). Assume that the employee received one-half the amount credited to his account upon reaching the retirement age and that he died shortly thereafter. Since the employee received all that he was entitled to receive under the plan before his death, no amount was payable to him for his life or for any period not ascertainable without reference to his death, or for any period which did not in fact end before his death. Thus, the amount of the payment to the designated beneficiary is not includible in the decedent's gross estate under section 2039(a) and (b). If, in this example, the employee died before reaching the retirement age, the amount of the payment to the designated beneficiary would be includible in the decedent's gross estate under section 2039(a) and (b). In this latter case, the decedent possessed the right to receive a lump sum payment for a period which did not in fact end before his death.

Example (6). The employer made contributions to two different funds set up under two different plans. One plan was to provide the employee, upon his retirement at age 60, with an annuity for life, and the other plan was to provide the employee's designated beneficiary, upon the employee's death, with a similar annuity for life. Each plan was established at a different time and each plan was administered separately in every respect. Neither plan at any time met the requirements of section 401(a) (relating to qualified plans). The value of the designated beneficiary's annuity is includible in the employee's gross estate. All rights and benefits accruing to an employee and to others by reason of the employment (except rights and benefits accruing under certain plans meeting the requirements of section 401(a) (see § 20.2039-2)) are considered together in determining whether or not section 2039(a) and (b) applies. The scope of section 2039(a) and (b) cannot be limited by indirection.

(c) *Amount includible in the gross estate.*—The amount to be included in a decedent's gross estate under section 2039(a) and (b) is an amount which bears the same ratio to the value at the decedent's death of the annuity or other payment receivable by the beneficiary as the contribution made by the decedent, or made by his employer (or former employer) for any reason connected with his employment, to the cost of the contract or agreement bears to its total cost. In applying this ratio, the value at the decedent's death of the annuity or other payment is determined in accordance with the rules set forth in §§ 20.2031-1, 20.2031-7, 20.2031-8, and 20.2031-9. The application of this paragraph may be illustrated by the following examples:

Example (1). On January 1, 1945, the decedent and his wife each contributed $15,000 to the purchase price of an annuity contract under the terms of which the issuing company agreed to pay an annuity to the decedent and his wife for their joint lives and to continue the annuity to the survivor for his life. Assume that the value of the survivor's annuity at the decedent's death (computed under § 20.2031-8) is $20,000. Since the decedent contributed one-half of the cost of the contract, the amount to be included in his gross estate under section 2039(a) and (b) is $10,000.

Example (2). Under the terms of an employment contract entered into on January 1, 1945, the employer and the employee made contributions to a fund which was to provide the employee, upon his retirement at age 60, with an annuity for life, and which was to provide his designated beneficiary, upon the employee's death after retirement, with a similar annuity for life. The retirement fund at no time formed part of a plan meeting the requirements of section 401(a) (relating to qualified plans). Assume that the employer and the employee each contributed $5,000 to the retirement fund. Assume, further, that the employee died after retirement at which time the value of the survivor's annuity was $8,000. Since the employer's contributions were made by reason of the decedent's employment, the amount to be included in his gross estate under section 2039(a) and (b) is the entire $8,000. If, in the above example, only the employer made contributions to the fund, the amount to be included in the gross estate would still be $8,000.

(d) *Insurance under policies on the life of the decedent.*—If an annuity or other payment receivable by a beneficiary under a contract or agreement is in substance the proceeds of insurance under a policy on the life of the decedent, section 2039(a) and (b) does not apply. For the extent to which such an annuity or other payment is includible in a decedent's gross estate, see section 2042 and § 20.2042-1. A combination annuity contract and life insurance policy on the decedent's life (e. g., a "retirement income" policy with death benefits) which matured during the decedent's lifetime so that there was no longer an insurance element under the contract at the time of the decedent's death is subject to the provisions of section 2039(a) and (b). On the other hand, the treatment of a combination annuity contract and life insurance policy on the decedent's life which did not mature during the decedent's lifetime depends upon the nature of the contract at the time of the decedent's death. The nature of the contract is generally determined by the relation of the reserve value of the policy to the value of the death benefit at the time of the decedent's death. If the decedent dies before the reserve value equals the death benefit, there is still an insurance element under the contract. The contract is therefore considered, for estate tax purposes, to be an insurance policy subject to the provisions of section 2042. However, if the decedent dies after the reserve value equals the death benefit, there is no longer an insurance element under the contract. The contract is therefore considered to be a contract for an annuity or other payment subject to the provisions of section 2039(a) and (b) or some other section of part III of subchapter A of chapter 11. Notwithstanding the relation of the reserve value to the value of the death benefit, a contract under which the death benefit could never exceed the total premiums paid, plus interest, contains no insurance element.

Example. Pursuant to a retirement plan established January 1, 1945, the employer purchased a contract from an insurance company which was to provide the employee, upon his retirement at age 65, with an annuity of $100 per month for life, and which was to provide his designated beneficiary, upon the employee's death after retirement, with a similar annuity for life. The contract further provided that if the employee should die before reaching the retirement age, a lump sum payment of $20,000 would be paid to his designated beneficiary in lieu of the annuity described above. The plan at no time met the requirements of section 401(a) (relating to qualified plans). Assume that the reserve value of the contract at the retirement age would be $20,000. If the employee died after reaching the retirement age, the death benefit to the designated beneficiary would constitute an annuity, the value of which would be includible in the employee's gross estate under section 2039(a) and (b). If, on the other hand, the employee died before reaching his retirement age, the death benefit to the designated beneficiary would constitute insurance under a policy on the life of the decedent since the reserve value would be less than the death benefit. Accordingly, its includibility would depend upon section 2042 and § 20.2042-1.

(e) *No application to certain trusts.*—Section 2039 shall not be applied to include in a decedent's gross estate all or any portion of a trust (other than a trust constituting an employee benefit, but including those described in the following sentence) if the decedent retained a right to use property of the trust or retained an annuity, unitrust, or other interest in the trust, in either case as described in section 2036. Such trusts include without limitation the following (collectively referred to in this paragraph (e) as "trusts"): certain charitable remainder trusts (collectively CRTs) such as a charitable remainder annuity trust (CRAT) within the meaning of section 664(d)(1), a charitable remainder unitrust (CRUT) within the meaning of section 664(d)(2) or (d)(3), and any other charitable remainder trust that does not qualify under section 664(d), whether because the CRT was created prior to 1969, there was a defect in the drafting of the CRT, there was no intention to qualify the CRT for the charitable deduction, or otherwise; other trusts established by a grantor (collectively GRTs) such as a grantor retained annuity trust (GRAT) paying out a qualified annuity interest within the meaning of § 25.2702-3(b) of this chapter, a grantor retained unitrust (GRUT) paying out a qualified unitrust interest within the meaning of § 25.2702-3(c) of this chapter; and various forms of grantor retained income trusts (GRITs) whether or not the grantor's retained interest is a qualified interest as defined in section 2702(b), including without limitation a qualified personal residence trust (QPRT) within the meaning of § 25.2702-5(c) of this chapter and a personal residence trust (PRT) within the meaning of § 25.2702-5(b) of this chapter. For purposes of determining the extent to which a retained interest causes all or a portion of a trust to be included in a decedent's gross estate, see § 20.2036-1(c)(1), (2), and (3).

(f) *Effective/applicability dates.*—The first, second, and fourth sentences in paragraph (a) of this section are applicable to the estates of decedents dying after August 16, 1954. The fifth sentence of paragraph (a) of this section is applicable to the estates of decedents dying on or after October 27, 1972, and to the estates of decedents for which the period for filing a claim for credit or refund of an estate tax overpayment ends on or after October 27, 1972. The third, sixth, and seventh sentences of paragraph (a) of this section and all of paragraph (e) of this section are applicable to the estates of decedents dying on or after July 14, 2008. [Reg. § 20.2039-1.]

☐ [*T.D.* 6296, 6-23-58. *Amended by T.D.* 7416, 4-5-76 *and T.D.* 9414, 7-11-2008.]

[Reg. § 20.2039-1T]

§ 20.2039-1T. Limitations and repeal of estate tax exclusion for qualified plans and individual retirement plans (IRAs) (Temporary).

Q-1: Are there any exceptions to the general effective dates of the $100,000 limitation and the repeal of the estate tax exclusion for the value of interests under qualified plans and IRAs described in section 2039(c) and (e)?

A-1: (a) Yes. Section 245 of the Tax Equity and Fiscal Responsibility Act of 1982 (TEFRA) limited the estate tax exclusion to $100,000 for estates of decedents dying after December 31, 1982. Section 525 of the Tax Reform Act of 1984 (TRA of 1984) repealed the exclusion for estates of decedents dying after December 31, 1984.

(b) Section 525(b)(3) of the TRA of 1984 amended section 245 of TEFRA to provide that the $100,000 limitation on the exclusion for the value of a decedent's interest in a plan or IRA will not apply to the estate of any decedent dying after December 31, 1982, to the extent that the decedent-participant was in pay status on December 31, 1982, with respect to such interest and irrevocably elected the form of benefit payable under the plan or IRA (including the form of any survivor benefits) with respect to such interest before January 1, 1983.

(c) Similarly, the TRA of 1984 provides that the repeal of the estate tax exclusion for the value of a decedent's interest in a plan or IRA will not apply to the estate of a decedent dying after December 31, 1984, to the extent that the decedent-participant was in pay status on December 31, 1984, with respect to such interest and irrevocably elected the form of benefit payable under the plan or IRA (including the form of any survivor benefits) with respect to such interest before July 18, 1984.

Q-2: What is the meaning of "in pay status" on the applicable date?

A-2: A participant was in pay status on the applicable date with respect to a portion of his or her interest in a plan or IRA if such portion is to be paid in a benefit form that has been elected on or before such date and the participant has received, on or before such date, at least one payment under such benefit form.

Q-3: What is required for an election of the form of benefit payable under the plan to have been irrevocable as of any applicable date?

A-3: As of any applicable date, an election of the form of benefit payable under a plan is irrevocable if, as of such date, it was a written irrevocable election that, with respect to all payments to be received after such date, specified the form of distribution (e.g., lump sum, level dollar annuity, formula annuity) and the period over which the distribution would be made (e.g., single life, joint and survivor, term certain). An election is not irrevocable as of any applicable date if, on or after such date, the form or period of the distribution could be determined or altered by any person or persons. An election does not fail to be irrevocable as of an applicable date merely because the beneficiaries were not designated as of such date or could be changed after such date. If any interest in any IRA may not, by law or contract, be subject to an irrevocable election described in this section, any election of the form of benefit payable under the IRA does not satisfy the requirement that an irrevocable election have been made. [Temporary Reg. § 20.2039-1T.]

☐ [*T.D.* 8073, 1-29-86.]

[Reg. § 20.2039-2]

§ 20.2039-2. Annuities under "qualified plans" and section 403(b) annuity contracts.—(a) *Section 2039(c) exclusion.*—In general, in the case of a decedent dying after December 31, 1953, the value of an annuity or other payment receivable under a plan or annuity contract described in paragraph (b) of this section is excluded from the decedent's gross estate to the extent provided in paragraph (c) of this section. In the case of a plan described in paragraph (b) (1) or (2) of this section(a "qualified plan"), the exclusion is subject to the limitation described in § 20.2039-3 (relating to lump sum distributions paid with respect to a decedent dying after December 31, 1976, and before January 1, 1979) or § 20.2039-4 (relating to lump sum distributions paid with respect to a decedent dying after December 31, 1978).

(b) *Plans and annuity contracts to which section 2039(c) applies.*—Section 2039(c) excludes from a decedent's gross estate, to the extent provided in paragraph (c) of this section, the value of an annuity or other payment receivable by any beneficiary (except the value of an annuity or other payment receivable by or for the benefit of the decedent's estate) under—

(1) An employees' trust (or under a contract purchased by an employees' trust) forming part of a pension, stock bonus, or profit-sharing plan which, at the time of the decedent's separation from employment (whether by death or otherwise), or at the time of the earlier termination of the plan, met the requirements of section 401(a);

(2) A retirement annuity contract purchased by an employer (and not by an employees' trust) pursuant to a plan which, at the time of decedent's separation from employment (by death or otherwise), or at the time of the earlier termination of the plan, was described in section 403(a);

(3) In the case of a decedent dying after December 31, 1957, a retirement annuity contract purchased for an employee by an employer which, for its taxable year in which the purchase occurred, is an organization referred to in section 170(b)(1)(A)(ii) or (vi) or which is a religious organization (other than a trust), and is exempt from tax under section 501(a);

(4) In the case of a decedent dying after December 31, 1965, an annuity under chapter 73 of title 10 of the United States Code, (10 U. S. C. 1431, *et seq.*); or

(5) In the case of a decedent dying after December 31, 1962, a bond purchase plan described in section 405.

For the meaning of the term "annuity or other payment", see paragraph (b) of § 20.2039-1. For the meaning of the phrase "receivable by or for the benefit of the decedent's estate", see paragraph (b) of § 20.2042-1. The application of this paragraph may be illustrated by the following examples in each of which it is assumed that the amount stated to be excludable from the decedent's gross estate is determined in accordance with paragraph (c) of this section:

Example (1). Pursuant to a pension plan, the employer made contributions to a trust which was to provide the employee, upon his retirement at age 60, with an annuity for life, and which was to provide his wife, upon the employee's death after retirement, with a similar annuity for life. At the time of the employee's retirement, the pension trust formed part of a plan meeting the requirements of section 401(a). Assume that the employee died at age 61 after the trustee started payment of his annuity as described above. Since the wife's annuity was receivable under a qualified pension plan, no part of the value of such annuity is includible in the decedent's gross estate by reason of the provisions of section 2039(c). If, in this example, the employer provided other benefits under nonqualified plans, the result would be the same since the exclusion under section 2039(c) is confined to the benefits provided for under the qualified plan.

Example (2). Pursuant to a profit-sharing plan, the employer made contributions to a trust which were allocated to the employee's individual account. Under the plan, the employee would, upon retirement at age 60, receive a distribution of the entire amount credited to the account. If the employee should die before reaching retirement age, the amount credited to the account would be distributed to the employee's designated beneficiary. Assume that the employee died before reaching the retirement age and that at such time the plan met the requirements of section 401(a). Since the payment to the designated beneficiary is receivable under a qualified profit-sharing plan, the provisions of section 2039(c) apply. However, if the payment is a lump sum distribution to which § 20.2039-3 or § 20.2039-4 applies, the payment is excludable from the decedent's gross estate only as provided in such section.

Example (3). Pursuant to a pension plan, the employer made contributions to a trust which were used by the trustee to purchase a contract from an insurance company for the benefit of an employee. The contract was to provide the employee, upon retirement at age 65, with an annuity of $100 per month for life, and was to provide the employee's designated beneficiary upon the employee's death after retirement, with a similar annuity for life. The contract further provided that if the employee should die before reaching retirement age, a lump sum payment equal to the greater of (a) $10,000 or (b) the reserve value of the policy would be paid to the designated beneficiary in lieu of the annuity. Assume that the employee died before reaching the retirement age and that at such time the plan met the requirements of section 401(a). Since the payment to the designated beneficiary is receivable under a qualified pension plan, the provisions of section 2039(c) apply. However, if the payment is a lump sum distribution to which § 20.2039-3 or § 20.2039-4 applies, the payment is excludable from decedent's gross estate only as provided in such section. It should be noted that for purposes of the exclusion under section 2039(c) it is immaterial whether or not the payment constitutes the proceeds of life insurance under the principles set forth in § 20.2039-1(d).

Example (4). Pursuant to a profit-sharing plan, the employer made contributions to a trust which were allocated to the employee's individual account. Under the plan, the employee would, upon his retirement at age 60, be given the option to have the amount credited to his account (a) paid to him in a lump sum, (b) used to purchase a joint and survivor annuity for him and his designated beneficiary, or (c) left with the trustee under an arrangement whereby interest would be paid to him for his lifetime with the principal to be paid, at his death, to his designated beneficiary. The plan further provided that, if the third method of settlement were selected, the employee would retain the right to have the principal paid to himself in a lump sum up to the time of his death. At the time of the employee's retirement, the profit-sharing plan met the requirements of section 401(a). Assume that the employee, upon reaching his retirement age, elected to have the amount credited to his account left with the trustee under the interest arrangement. Assume, further, that the employee did not exercise his right to have such amount paid to him before his death. Under such circumstances, the employee is considered as having constructively received the amount credited to his account upon his retirement. Thus, such amount is not considered as receivable by the designated beneficiary under the profit-sharing plan and the exclusion of section 2039(c) is not applicable.

Example (5). An employer purchased a retirement annuity contract for an employee which was to provide the employee, upon his retirement at age 60, with an annuity for life and which was to provide his wife, upon the employee's death after retirement, with a similar annuity for life. The employer, for its taxable year in which the annuity contract was purchased, was an organization referred to in section 170(b)(1)(A)(ii), and was exempt from tax under section 501(a). The entire amount of the purchase price of the annuity contract was excluded from the employee's gross income under section 403(b). No part of the value of the survivor annuity payable after the employee's death is includible in the decedent's gross estate by reason of the provisions of section 2039(c).

(c) *Amounts excludable from the gross estate.*—(1) The amount to be excluded from a decedent's gross estate under section 2039(c) is an amount which bears the same ratio to the value at the decedent's death of an annuity or other payment receivable by the beneficiary as the employer's contribution (or a contribution made on the employer's behalf) on the employee's account to the plan or towards the purchase of the annuity contract bears to the total contributions on the employee's account to the plan or towards the purchase of the annuity contract. In applying this ratio—

(i) Payments or contributions made by or on behalf of the employer towards the purchase of an annuity contract described in paragraph (b)(3) of this section are considered to include only such payments or contributions as are, or were, excludable from the employee's gross income under section 403(b).

(ii) In the case of a decedent dying before January 1, 1977, payments or contributions made under a plan described in paragraph (b)(1), (2) or (5) of this section on behalf of the decedent for a period for which the decedent was self-employed, within the meaning of section 401(c)(1), with respect to the plan are considered payments or contributions made by the decedent and not by the employer.

(iii) In the case of a decedent dying after December 31, 1976, however, payments or contributions made under a plan described in paragraph (b)(1), (2) or (5) of this section on behalf of the decedent for a period for which the decedent was self-employed, within the meaning of section 401(c)(1), with respect to the plan are considered payments or contributions made by the employer to the extent the pay ments or contributions are, or were, deductible under section 404 or 405(c). Contributions or payments attributable to that period which are not, or were not, so deductible are considered made by the decedent.

(iv) In the case of a plan described in paragraph (b)(1) or (2) of this section, a rollover contribution described in section 402(a)(5), 403(a)(4), 408(d)(3)(A)(ii) or 409(b)(3)(C) is considered an amount contributed by the employer.

(v) In the case of an annuity contract described in paragraph (b)(3) of this section, a rollover contribution described in section 403(b)(8) is considered an amount contributed by the employer.

(vi) In the case of a plan described in paragraph (b)(1), (2) or (5) of this section, an amount includable in the gross income of an employer under section 1379(b) (relating to shareholder-employee beneficiaries under certain qualified plans) is considered an amount paid or contributed by the decedent.

(vii) Amounts payable under paragraph (b)(4) of this section are attributable to payments or contributions made by the decedent only to the extent of amounts deposited by the decedent pursuant to section 1438 or 1452(d) of Title 10 of the United States Code.

(viii) The value at the decedent's death of the annuity or other payment is determined under the rules of §§20.2031-1 and 20.2031-7 or, for certain prior periods, §20.2031-7A.

(2) In certain cases, the employer's contribution (or a contribution made on his behalf) to a plan on the employee's account and thus the total contributions to the plan on the employee's account cannot be readily ascertained. In order to apply the ratio stated in subparagraph (1) of this paragraph in such a case, the method outlined in the following two sentences must be used unless a more precise method is presented. In such a case, the total contributions to the plan on the employee's account is the value of any annuity or other payment payable to the decedent and his survivor computed as of the time the decedent's rights first mature (or as of the time the survivor's rights first mature if the decedent's rights never mature) and computed in accordance with the rules set forth in §§20.2031-1, 20.2031-7, 20.2031-8, and 20.2031.9. By subtracting from such value the amount of the employee's contribution to the plan, the amount of the employer's contribution to the plan on the employee's account may be obtained. The application of this paragraph may be illustrated by the following example:

Example. Pursuant to a pension plan, the employer and the employee contributed to a trust which was to provide the employee, upon his retirement at age 60, with an annuity for life, and which was to provide his wife, upon the employee's death after retirement, with a similar annuity for life. At the time of the employee's retirement, the pension trust formed part of a plan meeting the requirements of section 401(a). Assume the following: (i) that the employer's contributions to the fund were not credited to the accounts of individual employees; (ii) that the value of the employee's annuity and his wife's annuity, computed as of the time of the decedent's retirement, was $40,000; (iii) that the employee contributed $10,000 to the plan; and (iv) that the value at the decedent's death of the wife's annuity was $16,000. On the basis of these facts, the total contributions to the fund on the employee's account are presumed to be $40,000 and the employer's contribution to the plan on the employee's account is presumed to be $30,000 ($40,000 less $10,000). Since the wife's annuity was receivable under a qualified pension plan, that part of the value of such annuity which is attributable to the

$$\text{employer's contributions} \left(\frac{\$30{,}000}{\$40{,}000} \times \$16{,}000, \text{ or } \$12{,}000 \right) \text{ is excludable from}$$

the decedent's gross estate by reason of the provisions of section 2039(c). Compare this result with the results reached in the examples set forth in paragraph (b) of this section in which all contributions to the plans were made by the employer.

(d) *Exclusion of certain annuity interests created by community property laws.*—(1) In the case of an employee on whose behalf contributions or payments were made by his employer or former employer under an employees' trust forming part of a pension, stock bonus, or profit-sharing plan described in section 2039(c)(1), under an employee's retirement annuity contract described in section 2039(c)(2), or toward the purchase of an employee's retirement annuity contract described in section 2039(c)(3), which under section 2039(c) are not considered as contributed by the employee, if the spouse of such employee predeceases him, then, notwithstanding the provisions of section 2039 or of any other provision of law, there shall be excluded from the gross estate of such spouse the value of any interest of such spouse in such plan or trust or such contract, to the extent such interest—

(i) Is attributable to such contributions or payments, and

(ii) Arises solely by reason of such spouse's interest in community income under the community property laws of a State.

(2) Section 2039(d) and this paragraph do not provide any exclusion for such spouse's property interest in the plan, trust or contract to the extent it is attributable to the contributions of the employee spouse. Thus, the decedent's community property interest in the plan, trust, or contract which is attributable to contributions made by the employee spouse are includible in the decedent's gross estate. See paragraph (c) of this section.

(3) Section 2039(d) and this paragraph apply to the estate of a decedent who dies on or after October 27, 1972, and to the estate of a decedent who died before October 27, 1972, if the period for filing a claim for credit or refund of an overpayment of the estate tax ends on or after October 27, 1972. Interest will not be allowed or paid on any overpayment of tax resulting from the application of section 2039(d) and this paragraph for any period prior to April 26, 1973. [Reg. §20.2039-2.]

☐ [*T.D.* 6296, 6-23-58. *Amended by T.D.* 6526, 1-18-61, *T.D.* 6666, 7-15-63, *T.D.* 7043, 6-1-70, *T.D.* 7416, 4-5-76, *T.D.* 7428, 8-13-76, *T.D.* 7761, 1-21-81 *and T.D.* 8540, 6-9-94.]

[Reg. § 20.2039-3]

§ 20.2039-3. Lump sum distributions under "qualified plans"; decedents dying after December 31, 1976, and before January 1, 1979.—(a) *Limitation of section 2039(c) exclusion.*—This section applies in the case of a decedent dying after December 31, 1976, and before January 1, 1979. If a lump sum distribution is paid with respect to the decedent under a plan described in § 20.2039-2(b)(1) or (2) (a "qualified plan"), no amount payable with respect to the decedent under the plan is excludable from the decedent's gross estate under § 20.2039-2.

(b) *"Lump sum distribution" defined.*—For purposes of this section the term "lump sum distribution" means a lump sum distribution defined in section 402(e)(4)(A) that satisfies the requirements of section 402(e)(4)(C), relating to the aggregation of certain trusts and plans. The distribution of an annuity contract is not a lump sum distribution for purposes of this section, and § 20.2039-2 will apply with respect to the distribution of an annuity contract without regard to whether the contract is included in a distribution that is otherwise a lump sum distribution under this paragraph (b). A distribution is a lump sum distribution for purposes of this section without regard to the election described in section 402(e)(4)(B).

(c) *Amounts payable as a lump sum distribution.*—If on the date the estate tax return is filed, an amount under a qualified plan is payable with respect to the decedent as a lump sum distribution (whether at the election of a beneficiary or otherwise), for purposes of this section the amount is deemed paid as a lump sum distribution no later than on such date. Accordingly, no portion of the amount payable under the plan is excludable from the value of the decedent's gross estate under § 20.2039-2. If, however, the amount payable as a lump sum distribution is not, in fact, thereafter paid as a lump sum distribution, there shall be allowed a credit or refund of any tax paid which is attributable to treating such amount as a lump sum distribution under this paragraph. Any claim for credit or refund filed under this paragraph must be filed within the time prescribed by section 6511, and must provide satisfactory evidence that the amount originally payable as a lump sum distribution is no longer payable in such form.

(d) *Filing date.*—For purposes of paragraph (c) of this section, "the date the estate tax return is filed" means the earlier of—

(1) The date the estate tax return is actually filed, or

(2) The date nine months after the decedent's death, plus any extension of time for filing the estate tax return granted under section 6081. [Reg. § 20.2039-3.]

□ [*T.D.* 7761, 1-21-81.]

[Reg. § 20.2039-4]

§ 20.2039-4. Lump sum distributions from "qualified plans"; decedents dying after December 31, 1978.—(a) *Limitation on section 2039(c) exclusion.*—This section applies in the case of a decedent dying after December 31, 1978. If a lump sum distribution is paid or payable with respect to a decedent under a plan described in § 20.2039-2(b)(1) or (2) (a "qualified plan"), no amount paid or payable with respect to the decedent under the plan is excludable from the decedent's gross estate under § 20.2039-2, unless the recipient of the distribution makes the section 402(a)/403(a) taxation election described in paragraph(c) of this section. For purposes of this section, an amount is payable as a lump sum distribution under a plan if, as of the date the estate tax return is filed (as determined under § 20.2039-3(d)), it is payable as a lump sum distribution at the election of the recipient or otherwise.

(b) *"Lump sum distribution" defined; treatment of annuity contracts.*—For purposes of this section the term "lump sum distribution" means a lump sum distribution defined in section 402(e)(4)(A) that satisfies the requirements of section 402(e)(4)(C), relating to the aggregation of certain trusts and plans. A distribution is a lump sum distribution for purposes of this section without regard to the election described in section 402(e)(4)(B). The distribution of an annuity contract is not a lump sum distribution for purposes of this section, and the limitation described in this section does not apply to an annuity contract distributed under a plan. Accordingly, if the amount payable with respect to a decedent under a plan is paid to a recipient partly by the distribution of an annuity contract, and partly by the distribution of an amount that is a lump sum distribution within the meaning of this paragraph (b), § 20.2039-2 shall apply with respect to the annuity contract without regard to whether the recipient makes the section 402(a)/403(a) taxation election with respect to the remainder of the distribution.

(c) *Recipient's section 402(a)/403(a) taxation election.*—The section 402(a)/403(a) taxation election is the election by the recipient of a lump sum distribution to treat the distribution as—

(1) Taxable under section 402(a), without regard to section 402(a)(2), to the extent includable in gross income (in the case of a distribution under a qualified plan described in § 20.2039-2(b)(1)),

(2) Taxable under section 403(a), without regard to section 403(a)(2), to the extent includable in gross income (in the case of a distribution under a qualified annuity contract described in § 20.2039-2(b)(2)), or

(3) A rollover contribution, in whole or in part, under section 402(a)(7) (relating to rollovers by a decedent's surviving spouse).

Accordingly, if a recipient makes the election, no portion of the distribution is taxable to the recipient under the 10-year averaging provisions of section 402(e) or as long-term capital gain under section 402(a)(2). However, a recipient's election under this paragraph (c) does not preclude the application of section 402(e)(4)(J) to any securities of the employer corporation included in the distribution.

(d) *Method of election.*—(1) *General rule.*—The recipient of a lump sum distribution shall make the section 402(a)/403(a) taxation election by:

(i) Determining the income tax liability on the income tax return (or amended return) for the taxable year of the distribution in a manner consistent with paragraph (c)(1) or (2) of this section,

(ii) Rolling over all or any part of the distribution under section 402(a)(7), or

(iii) Filing a section 2039(f)(2) election statement described in paragraph (d)(2) of this section.

(2) *Election statement.*—A recipient may file a section 2039(f)(2) election statement indicating that the recipient elects to treat a lump sum distribution in the manner described in paragraph (c) of this section. The statement must be filed where the recipient would file the income tax return for the taxable year of the distribution. The statement must be signed by the recipient and include the individual's name, address, social security number, the name of the decedent, and a statement indicating the election is being made. A section 2039(f)(2) election statement may be filed at any time prior to making the election under paragraph (d)(1)(i) or (ii) of this section.

(3) *Effect on estate tax return.*—If the date the estate tax return is filed precedes the date on which the recipient makes the section 402(a)/403(a) taxation election with respect to a lump sum distribution, the estate tax return may not reflect the election. However, if after the estate tax return is filed, the recipient makes the section 402(a)/403(a) taxation election, the executor of the estate may file a claim for refund or credit of an overpayment of the Federal estate tax within the time prescribed in section 6511. See also, § 20.6081-1 for rules relating to obtaining an extension of time for filing the estate tax return.

(e) *Election irrevocable.*—If a recipient of a lump sum distribution files a section 2039(f)(2) election statement, an income tax return (or amended return) or makes a rollover contribution that constitutes the section 402(a)/403(a) taxation election described in paragraphs (c) and (d), the election may not be revoked. Accordingly, a subsequent and amended income tax return filed by the recipient that is inconsistent with the prior election will not be given effect for purposes of section 2039 and section 402 or 403.

(f) *Lump sum distribution to multiple recipients.*—In the case of a lump sum distribution paid or payable under a qualified plan with respect to the decedent to more than one recipient, the exclusion under § 20.2039-2 applies to so much of the distribution as is paid or payable to a recipient who makes the section 402(a)/403(a) taxation election.

(g) *Distributions of annuity contracts included multiple distributions.*—Notwithstanding that a recipient makes the section 402(a)/403(a) taxation election with respect to a lump sum distribution that includes the distribution of an annuity contract, the distribution of an annuity contract is to be taken into account by the recipient for purposes of the multiple distribution rules under section 402(e). [Reg. § 20.2039-4.]

☐ [*T.D.* 7761, 1-21-81. *Amended by T.D.* 7956, 5-11-84.]

[Reg. § 20.2039-5]

§ 20.2039-5. Annuities under individual retirement plans.—(a) *Section 2039(e) exclusion.*—(1) *In general.*—In the case of a decedent dying after December 31, 1976, section 2039(e) excludes from the decedent's gross estate, to the extent provided in paragraph (c) of this section, the value of a "qualifying annuity" receivable by a beneficiary under an individual retirement plan. The term "individual retirement plan" means—

(i) An individual retirement account described in section 408(a),

(ii) An individual retirement annuity described in section 408(b), or

(iii) A retirement bond described in section 409(a).

(2) *Limitations.*—(i) Section 2039(e) applies only with respect to the gross estate of a decedent on whose behalf the individual retirement plan was established. Accordingly, section 2039(e) does not apply with respect to the estate of a decedent who was only a beneficiary under the plan.

(ii) Section 2039(e) does not apply to an annuity receivable by or for the benefit of the decedent's estate. For the meaning of the term "receivable by or for the benefit of the decedent's estate," see § 20.2042-1(b).

(b) *Qualifying annuity.*—For purposes of this section, the term "qualifying annuity" means an annuity contract or other arrangement providing for a series of substantially equal periodic payments to be made to a beneficiary for the beneficiary's life or over a period ending at least 36 months after the decedent's death. The term "annuity contract" includes an annuity purchased for a beneficiary and distributed to the beneficiary, if under section 408 the contract is not included in the gross income of the beneficiary upon distribution. The term "other arrangement" includes any arrangement arising by reason of the decedent's participation in the program providing the individual retirement plan. Payments shall be considered "periodic" if under the arrangement or contract (including a distributed contract) payments are to be made to the beneficiary at regular intervals. If the contract or arrangement provides optional payment provisions, not all of which provide for periodic payments, payments shall be considered periodic only if an option providing periodic payments is elected not later than the date the estate tax return is filed (as determined under § 20.2039-3(d)). For this purpose, the right to surrender a contract (including a distributed contract) for a cash surrender value will not be considered an optional payment provision. Payments shall be considered "substantially equal" even though the amounts receivable by the beneficiary may vary. Payments shall not be considered substantially equal, however, if more than 40% of the total amount payable to the beneficiary under the individual retirement plan, determined as of the date of the decedent's death and excluding any postmortem increase, is payable to the beneficiary in any 12-month period.

(c) *Amount excludible from gross estate.*—(1) *In general.*—Except as otherwise described in this paragraph (c), the amount excluded from the decedent's gross estate under section 2039(e) is the entire value of the qualifying annuity (as determined under § § 20.2031-1 and 20.2031-7 or, for certain prior periods, § 20.2031-7A) payable under the individual retirement plan.

(2) *Excess contribution.*—In any case in which there exists, on the date of the decedent's death, an excess contribution (as defined in section 4973(b)) with respect to the individual retirement plan, the amount excluded from the value of the decedent's gross estate is determined under the following formula:

$$E = A - A \left(\frac{X}{C - R} \right)$$

Where:

E = the amount excluded from the decedent's gross estate under section 2039(e),

A = the value of the qualifying annuity at the decedent's death (as determined under § § 20.2031-1 and 20.2031-7 or, for certain prior periods, § 20.2031-7A),

X = the amount which is an excess contribution at the decedent's death (as determined under section 4973(b)),

C = the total amount contributed by or on behalf of the decedent to the individual retirement plan, and

R = the total of amounts paid or distributed from the individual retirement plan before the death of the decedent which were either includable in the gross income of the recipient under section 408(d)(1) and represented the payment or distribution of an excess contribution, or were payments or distributions described in section 408(d)(4) or (5) (relating to returned excess contributions).

(3) *Certain section 403(b)(8) rollover contributions.*—This subparagraph (3) applies if the decedent made a rollover contribution to the individual retirement plan under section 403(b)(8), and the contribution was attributable to a distribution under an annuity contract other than an annuity contract described in § 20.2039-2(b)(3). If such a rollover contribution was the only contribution made to the plan, no part of the value of the qualifying annuity payable under the plan is excluded from the decedent's gross estate under section 2039(e). If a contribution other than such a rollover contribution was made to the plan, the amount excluded from the decedent's gross estate is determined under the formula described in subparagraph (2) of this paragraph, except that for purposes of that formula, X includes the amount that was a rollover contribution under section 403(b)(8) attributable to a distribution under an annuity contract not described in § 20.2039-2(b)(3).

(4) *Surviving spouse's rollover contribution.*—This subparagraph (4) applies if the decedent made a rollover contribution to the individual retirement plan under section 402(a)(7), relating to rollovers by a surviving spouse. If the rollover contribution under section 402(a)(7) was the only contribution made by the decedent to the plan, no part of the value of the qualifying annuity payable under the plan is excluded from the decedent's gross estate under section 2039(e). If a contribution other than a rollover contribution under section 402(a)(7) was made by the decedent to the plan, the amount excluded from the decedent's gross estate is determined under the formula described in subparagraph (2) of this paragraph, except that for purposes of that formula, X includes the amount that was a rollover contribution under section 402(a)(7).

(5) *Election under § 1.408-2(b)(7)(ii).*—This subparagraph (5) applies if the decedent at any time made the election described in § 1.408-2(b)(7)(ii) with respect to an amount in the individual retirement plan. If this subparagraph (5) applies, the amount excluded from the decedent's gross estate is determined under the formula described in subparagraph (2), except that for purposes of that formula, X and C include the amount with respect to which the election was made.

(6) *Plan-to-plan rollovers.*—(i) This subparagraph (6) applies if the individual retirement plan is a transferee plan. A "transferee plan" is a plan that was the recipient of a contribution described in section 408(d)(3)(A)(i) or 409(b)(3)(C) (relating to rollovers from one individual retirement plan to another) made by the decedent. The amount of the contribution described in section 408(d)(3)(A)(i) or 409(b)(3)(C) is the "rollover amount." The plan from which the rollover amount was paid or distributed to the decedent is the "transferor plan."

(ii) If the decedent made a contribution described in subparagraph (3) or (4) to the transferor plan, the amount excluded from the decedent's gross estate with respect to the transferee plan is determined under the formula described in subparagraph (2), except that for purposes of that formula, X includes so much of the rollover amount as was attributable to the contribution to the transferor plan that was described in subparagraph (3) or (4). The extent to which a rollover amount is attributable to a contribution described in subparagraph (3) or (4) that was made to the transferor plan is determined by multiplying the rollover amount by a fraction, the numerator of which is the amount of such contribution, and the denominator of which is the sum of all amounts contributed by the decedent to the transferor plan (if not returned as described under R in subparagraph (2)), and any amount in the transferor plan to which the election described in subparagraph (5) applied.

(iii) If the decedent made the election described in subparagraph (5) with respect to an amount in the transferor plan, the amount excluded from the decedent's gross estate with respect to the transferee plan is determined under the formula described in subparagraph (2), except that for purposes of that formula, X includes so much of the rollover amount as was attributable to the amount in the transferor plan to which the election applied. The extent to which a rollover amount is attributable to an amount in the transferor plan to which the election applied is determined by multiplying the rollover amount by a fraction, the numerator of which is the amount to which the election applied, and the denominator of which is the sum of all amounts contributed by the decedent to the transferor plan (if not returned as described under R in subparagraph (2)), and the amount in the transferor plan to which the election applied.

(iv) If a transferor plan described in this subparagraph (6) was also a transferee plan, then the rules described in this subparagraph (6) are to be applied with respect to both the rollover amount paid to the plan and the rollover amount thereafter paid from the plan.

(d) *Examples.*—The provisions of this section are illustrated by the following examples:

Example (1). (1) A establishes an individual retirement account described in section 408(a) on January 1, 1976, when A is age 65. A's only contribution to the account is a rollover contribution described in section 402(a)(5). The trust agreement provides that A may at any time elect to have the balance in the account distributed in one of the following methods:

(i) A single sum payment of the account,

(ii) Equal or substantially equal semiannual payments over a period equal to A's life expectancy, or

(iii) Equal or substantially equal semiannual payments over a period equal to the life expectancy of A and A's spouse.

(2) The trust agreement further provides that although semiannual payments have commenced under option (ii) or (iii), A (or A's surviving spouse) may, by written notice to the trustee, receive all or a part of the balance remaining in the account. In addition, under option (ii), any balance remaining in the account at A's death is payable in a single sum to A's designated beneficiary. Under option (iii), any balance remaining in the account at the death of the survivor of A or A's spouse is payable in a single sum to a beneficiary designated by A or A's surviving spouse.

(3) A elects option (iii), and the first semiannual payment is made to A on July 1, 1976. On that date, A's life expectancy is 15 years, and that of A's spouse is 22 years. Under option (iii), the semiannual payments to A or A's surviving spouse will continue until July 1, 1998.

(4) A dies on November 20, 1978. On December 15, 1978, the trust agreement is modified so that A's surviving spouse no longer may elect to receive all or part of the balance remaining in the account. The value of the semiannual payments payable to A's spouse is excluded from A's gross estate under section 2039(e).

(5) A's spouse dies July 12, 1981, and the single sum payment payable on account of the death of A's spouse is paid to the designated beneficiary on August 1, 1981. Notwithstanding that the balance in the account was paid to the designated beneficiary within 36 months after A's death, the value of the semiannual payments payable to A's spouse are excluded from A's gross estate, since at A's death those semiannual payments were to be paid over a period extending beyond 36 months. Section 2039(e) does not apply to exclude any amount from the estate of A's spouse, because A's spouse was only a beneficiary and not the individual on whose behalf the account was established.

Example (2). Assume the same facts as in example (1), except that the trust agreement is not modified so that A's surviving spouse no longer may elect to receive all or part of the balance remaining in the account (see (2) and (4) in example (1)). Instead, the balance of the account is applied toward the purchase of a contract providing an immediate annuity, the contract is distributed to A's surviving spouse on December 15, 1978, and under section 408 the contract is not included in the gross income of the spouse upon its distribution. The value of the annuity contract is excluded from A's gross estate, if the contract provides for a series of substantially equal periodic payments (within the meaning of paragraph (b) of this section) to be made over the life of A's surviving spouse or over a period not ending before the date 36 months after A's death.

Example (3). (1) B establishes an individual retirement plan described in section 408(a) ("IRA B") on February 6, 1981, in order to receive a $220,000 rollover contribution from a qualified plan, as described in section 402(a)(5). B dies August 14, 1981. C, an individual, is the sole beneficiary under IRA B. The amount in IRA B ($238,000) is payable to C in whole or part as C may elect. Because the amount in IRA B is payable to C as other than a qualifying annuity, within the meaning of paragraph (b) of this section, no amount is excluded from B's gross estate under section 2039(e).

(2) On October 17, 1981, C contributes $1,500 on C's own behalf to IRA B. Under § 1.408-2(b)(7)(ii), C's contribution will cause IRA B to be treated as being maintained by and on behalf of C ("IRA C") and C's making the contribution constitutes an election to which paragraph (c)(5) of this section applies. The balance in IRA C immediately before C's contribution is $240,000. Accordingly, the amount with respect to which C made the election is $240,000.

(3) C dies January 19, 1982. E, an individual, is the sole beneficiary under the plan, and the amounts payable to E ($242,000) are payable as a qualifying annuity, within the meaning of paragraph (b) of this section.

(4) The rules described in section 2039(e) and this section are applied with respect to the gross estate of C without regard to whether amounts now payable under IRA C were or were not excluded from B's gross estate. Under paragraph (c) of this section, the amount not excluded from C's gross estate is the value of the qualifying annuity payable to E ($242,000), multiplied by the fraction $240,000/($240,000 + $1,500). Thus, the amount not excluded from C's gross estate is $240,497. [($242,000) ($240,000 ÷ ($240,000 + $1,500)) = $240,497.]The amount excluded is therefore $1,503 ($242,000 – $240,497).

Example (4). (1) F, an individual, establishes an individual retirement plan ("IRA F1") in 1977 and makes $1,250 annual contributions for 1977, 1978, 1979 and 1980 (4 × $1,250 = $5,000), each of which is deducted by F under section 219. In February 1980, F receives an $85,000 distribution on account of the death of G, F's spouse, from the qualified plan of G's former employer, and rolls it over into IRA F1, under section 402(a)(7). Because IRA F1 includes a rollover contribution under section 402(a)(7), paragraph (c)(4) of this section applies. In 1981, F's entire interest in IRA F1, $100,000, is paid to F and contributed to another individual retirement plan ("IRA F2") under section 408(d)(3)(A)(i). IRA F2 is a transferee plan to which paragraph (c)(6) of this section applies because of the rollover. F makes a $1,500 deductible contribution to IRA F2 for 1981.

(2) F dies in 1984. The balance in IRA F2 ($146,000) is payable to G, an individual, as a qualifying annuity, within the meaning of paragraph (b) of this section.

(3) Under paragraph (c) of this section, the amount *not* excluded from F's gross estate is the value of the qualifying annuity payable under IRA F2 multiplied by the fraction $96,700/$101,500. Accordingly, the amount not excluded is $139,096. [($146,000) ($96,700/$101,500) = $139,096.] The amount excluded is $6,904 ($146,000 – $139,096).

(4) The numerator of the fraction ($96,700) is determined by multiplying the amount rolled over from IRA F1 to IRA F2 ($100,000) by a fraction, the numerator of which is the amount of the rollover contribution to IRA F1 ($85,000), and the denominator of which is the total contributions to IRA F1 ($85,000 + $5,000 = $90,000). [($100,000) ($85,000/$90,000) = $96,700.]

(5) The denominator of the fraction ($101,500) is the sum of the contributions to IRA F2 (the $100,000 rollover contribution from IRA F1, and the $1,500 annual contribution to IRA F2). [Reg. § 20.2039-5.]

☐ [*T.D. 7761, 1-21-81. Amended by T.D. 8540, 6-9-94.*]

[Reg. § 20.2040-1]

§ 20.2040-1. Joint interests.—(a) *In general.*—A decedent's gross estate includes under section 2040 the value of property held jointly at the time of the decedent's death by the decedent and another person or persons with right of survivorship, as follows:

(1) To the extent that the property was acquired by the decedent and the other joint owner or owners by gift, devise, bequest, or inheritance, the decedent's fractional share of the property is included.

(2) In all other cases, the entire value of the property is included except such part of the entire value as is attributable to the amount of the consideration in money or money's worth furnished by the other joint owner or owners. See § 20.2043-1 with respect to adequacy of consideration. Such part of the entire value is that portion of the entire value of the property at the decedent's death (or at the alternate valuation date described in section 2032) which the consideration in money or money's worth furnished by the other joint owner or owners bears to the total cost of acquisition and capital additions. In determining the consideration furnished by the other joint owner or owners, there is taken into account only that portion of such consideration which is shown not to be attributable to money or other property acquired by the other joint owner or owners from the decedent for less than a full and adequate consideration in money or money's worth.

The entire value of jointly held property is included in a decedent's gross estate unless the executor submits facts sufficient to show that property was not acquired entirely with consideration furnished by the decedent, or was acquired by the decedent and the other joint owner or owners by gift, bequest, devise, or inheritance.

(b) *Meaning of "property held jointly."*.—Section 2040 specifically covers property held jointly by the decedent and any other person (or persons), property held by the decedent and spouse as tenants by the entirety, and a deposit of money, or a bond or other instrument, in the name of the decedent and any other person and payable to either or the survivor. The section applies to all classes of property, whether real or personal, and regardless of when the joint interests were created. Furthermore, it makes no difference that the survivor takes the entire interest in the property by right of survivorship and that no interest therein forms a part of the decedent's estate for purposes of administration. The section has no application to property held by the decedent and any other person (or persons) as tenants in common.

(c) *Examples.*—The application of this section may be explained in the following examples in each of which it is assumed that the other joint owner or owners survived the decedent:

(1) If the decedent furnished the entire purchase price of the jointly held property, the value of the entire property is included in his gross estate;

(2) If the decedent furnished only a part of the purchase price, only a corresponding portion of the value of the property is so included;

(3) If the decedent furnished no part of the purchase price, no part of the value of the property is so included;

(4) If the decedent, before the acquisition of the property by himself and the other joint owner, gave the latter a sum of money or other property which thereafter became the other joint owner's entire contribution to the purchase price then the value of the entire property is so included, notwithstanding the fact that the other property may have appreciated in value due to market conditions between the time of the gift and the time of the acquisition of the jointly held property;

(5) If the decedent, before the acquisition of the property by himself and the other joint owner, transferred to the latter for less than an adequate and full consideration in money or money's worth other income-producing property, the income from which belonged to and became the other joint owner's entire contribution to the purchase price, then the value of the jointly held property less that portion attributable to the income which the other joint owner did furnish is included in the decedent's gross estate;

(6) If the property originally belonged to the other joint owner and the decedent purchased his interest from the other joint owner, only that portion of the value of the property attributable to the consideration paid by the decedent is included;

(7) If the decedent and his spouse acquired the property by will or gift as tenants by the entirety, one-half of the value of the property is included in the decedent's gross estate; and

(8) If the decedent and his two brothers acquired the property by will or gift as joint tenants, one-third of the value of the property is so included. [Reg. § 20.2040-1.]

☐ [*T.D.* 6296, 6-23-58.]

[Reg. § 20.2041-1]

§ 20.2041-1. Powers of appointment; in general.—(a) *Introduction.*—A decedent's gross estate includes under section 2041 the value of property in respect of which the decedent possessed, exercised, or released certain powers of appointment. This section contains rules of general application; § 20.2041-2 contains rules specifically applicable to general powers of appointment created on or before October 21, 1942; and § 20.2041-3 sets forth specific rules applicable to powers of appointment created after October 21, 1942.

(b) *Definition of "power of appointment".*—(1) *In general.*—The term "power of appointment" includes all powers which are in substance and effect powers of appointment regardless of the nomenclature used in creating the power and regardless of local property law connotations. For example, if a trust instrument provides that the beneficiary may appropriate or consume the principal of the trust, the power to consume or appropriate is a power of appointment. Similarly, a power given to a decedent to affect the beneficial enjoyment of trust property or its income by altering, amending, or revoking the trust instrument or terminating the trust is a power of appointment. If the community property laws of a State confer upon the wife a power of testamentary disposition over property in which she does not have a vested interest she is considered as having a power of appointment. A power in a donee to remove or discharge a trustee and appoint himself may be a power of appointment. For example, if under the terms of a trust instrument, the trustee or his successor has the power to appoint the principal of the trust for the benefit of individuals including himself, and the decedent has the unrestricted power to remove or discharge the trustee at any time and appoint any other person including himself, the decedent is considered as having a power of appointment. However, the decedent is not considered to have a power of appointment if he only had the power to appoint a successor, including himself, under limited conditions which did not exist at the time of his death, without an accompanying unrestricted power of removal. Similarly, a power to amend only the administrative provisions of a trust instrument, which cannot substantially affect the beneficial enjoyment of the trust property or income, is not a power of appointment. The mere power of management, investment, custody of assets, or the power to allocate receipts and disbursements as between income and principal, exercisable in a fiduciary capacity, whereby the holder has no power to enlarge or shift any of the beneficial interests therein except as an incidental consequence of the discharge of such fiduciary duties is not a power of appointment. Further, the right in a beneficiary of a trust to assent to a periodic accounting, thereby relieving the trustee from further accountability, is not a power of appointment if the right of assent does not consist of any power or right to enlarge or shift the beneficial interest of any beneficiary therein.

(2) *Relation to other sections.*—For purposes of §§ 20.2041-1 to 20.2041-3, the term "power of appointment" does not include powers reserved by the decedent to himself within the concept of sections 2036 to 2038. (See §§ 20.2036-1 to 20.2038-1.) No provision of section 2041 or of §§ 20.2041-1 to 20.2041-3 is to be construed as in any way limiting the application of any other section of the Internal Revenue Code or of these regulations. The power of the owner of a property interest already possessed by him to dispose of his interest, and nothing more, is not a power of appointment, and the interest is includible in his gross estate to the extent it would be includible under section 2033 or some other provision of part III of subchapter A of chapter 11. For example, if a trust created by S provides for payment of the income to A for life with power in A to appoint the remainder by will and, in default of such appointment for payment of the income to A's widow, W, for her life and for payment of the remainder to A's estate, the value of A's interest in the remainder is includible in his gross estate under section 2033 regardless of its includibility under section 2041.

(3) *Powers over a portion of property.*—If a power of appointment exists as to part of an entire group of assets or only over a limited

interest in property, section 2041 applies only to such part or interest. For example, if a trust created by S provides for the payment of income to A for life, then to W for life, with power in A to appoint the remainder by will and in default of appointment for payment of the remainder to B or his estate, and if A dies before W, section 2041 applies only to the value of the remainder interest excluding W's life estate. If A dies after W, section 2041 would apply to the value of the entire property. If the power were only over one-half the remainder interest, section 2041 would apply only to one-half the value of the amounts described above.

(c) *Definition of "general power of appointment".*—(1) *In general.*—The term "general power of appointment" as defined in section 2041(b)(1) means any power of appointment exercisable in favor of the decedent, his estate, his creditors, or the creditors of his estate, except (i) joint powers, to the extent provided in §§20.2041-2 and 20.2041-3, and (ii) certain powers limited by an ascertainable standard, to the extent provided in subparagraph (2) of this paragraph. A power of appointment exercisable to meet the estate tax, or any other taxes, debts, or charges which are enforceable against the estate, is included within the meaning of a power of appointment exercisable in favor of the decedent's estate, his creditors, or the creditors of his estate. A power of appointment exercisable for the purpose of discharging a legal obligation of the decedent or for his pecuniary benefit is considered a power of appointment exercisable in favor of the decedent or his creditors. However, for purposes of §§20.2041-1 to 20.2041-3, a power of appointment not otherwise considered to be a general power of appointment is not treated as a general power of appointment merely by reason of the fact that an appointee may, in fact, be a creditor of the decedent or his estate. A power of appointment is not a general power if by its terms it is either—

(a) Exercisable only in favor of one or more designated persons or classes other than the decedent or his creditors, or the decedent's estate or the creditors of his estate, or

(b) Expressly not exercisable in favor of the decedent or his creditors, or the decedent's estate or the creditors of his estate.

A decedent may have two powers under the same instrument, one of which is a general power of appointment and the other of which is not. For example, a beneficiary may have a power to withdraw trust corpus during his life, and a testamentary power to appoint the corpus among his descendants. The testamentary power is not a general power of appointment.

(2) *Powers limited by an ascertainable standard.*—A power to consume, invade, or appropriate income or corpus, or both, for the benefit of the decedent which is limited by an ascertainable standard relating to the health, education, support, or maintenance of the decedent is, by reason of section 2041(b)(1)(A), not a general power of appointment. A power is limited by such a standard if the extent of the holder's duty to exercise and not to exercise the power is reasonably measurable in terms of his needs for health, education, or support (or any combination of them). As used in this subparagraph, the words "support" and "maintenance" are synonymous and their meaning is not limited to the bare necessities of life. A power to use property for the comfort, welfare, or happiness of the holder of the power is not limited by the requisite standard. Examples of powers which are limited by the requisite standard are powers exercisable for the holder's "support," "support in reasonable comfort," "maintenance in health and reasonable comfort" "support in his accustomed manner of living," "education, including college and professional education," "health," and "medical, dental, hospital and nursing expenses and expenses of invalidism." In determining whether a power is limited by an ascertainable standard, it is immaterial whether the beneficiary is required to exhaust his other income before the power can be exercised.

(3) *Certain powers under wills of decedents dying between January 1 and April 2, 1948.*—Section 210 of the Technical Changes Act of 1953 provides that if a decedent died after December 31, 1947, but before April 3, 1948, certain property interests described therein may, if the decedent's surviving spouse so elects, be accorded special treatment in the determination of the marital deduction to be allowed the decedent's estate under the provisions of section 812(e) of the Internal Revenue Code of 1939. See §81.47a(h) of Regulations 105 (26 CFR (1939) 81.47a(h)). The section further provides that property affected by the election shall, for the purpose of inclusion in the surviving spouse's gross estate, be considered property with respect to which she has a general power of appointment. Therefore, notwithstanding any other provision of law or of §§20.2041-1 to 20.2041-3, if the present decedent (in her capacity as surviving spouse of a prior decedent) has made an election under section 210 of the Technical Changes Act of 1953, the property which was the subject of the election shall be considered as property with respect to which the present decedent has a general power of appointment created after October 21, 1942, exercisable by deed or will, to the extent it was treated as an interest passing to the surviving spouse and not passing to any other person for the purpose of the marital deduction in the prior decedent's estate.

(d) *Definition of "exercise.".*—Whether a power of appointment is in fact exercised may depend upon local law. For example, the residuary clause of a will may be considered under local law as an exercise of a testamentary power of appointment in the absence of evidence of a contrary intention drawn from the whole of the testator's will. However, regardless of local law, a power of appointment is considered as exercised for purposes of section 2041 even though the exercise is in favor of the taker in default of appointment, and irrespective of whether the appointed interest and the interest in default of appointment are identical or whether the appointee renounces any right to take under the appointment. A power of appointment is also considered as exercised even though the disposition cannot take effect until the occurrence of an event after the exercise takes place, if the exercise is irrevocable and, as of the time of the exercise, the condition was not impossible of occurrence. For example, if property is left in trust to A for life, with a power in B to appoint the remainder by will, and B dies before A, exercising his power by appointing the remainder to C if C survives A, B is considered to have exercised his power if C is living at B's death. On the other hand, a testamentary power of appointment is not considered as exercised if it is exercised subject to the occurrence during the decedent's life of an express or implied condition which did not in fact occur. Thus, if in the preceding example, C dies before B, B's power of appointment would not be considered to have been exercised. Similarly, if a trust provides for income to A for life, remainder as A appoints by will, and A appoints a life estate in the property to B and does not otherwise exercise his power, but B dies before A, A's power is not considered to have been exercised.

(e) *Time of creation of power.*—A power of appointment created by will is, in general, considered as created on the date of the testator's death. However, section 2041(b)(3) provides that a power of appointment created by a will executed on or before October 21, 1942, is considered a power created on or before that date if the testator dies before July 1, 1949, without having republished the will, by codicil or otherwise, after October 21, 1942. A power of appointment created by an inter vivos instrument is considered as created on the date the instrument takes effect. Such a power is not considered as created at some future date merely because it is not exercisable on the date the instrument takes effect, or because it is revocable, or because the identity of its holders is not ascertainable until after the date the instrument takes effect. However, if the holder of a power exercises it by creating a second power, the second power is considered as created at the time of the exercise of the first. The application of this paragraph may be illustrated by the following examples:

Example (1). A created a revocable trust before October 22, 1942, providing for payment of income to B for life with remainder as B shall appoint by will. Even though A dies after October 21, 1942, without having exercised his power of revocation, B's power of appointment is considered a power created before October 22, 1942.

Example (2). C created an irrevocable inter vivos trust before October 22, 1942, naming T as trustee and providing for payment of income to D for life with remainder to E. T was given the power to pay corpus to D and the power to appoint a successor trustee. If T resigns after October 21, 1942, and appoints D as successor trustee, D is considered to have a power of appointment created before October 22, 1942.

Example (3). F created an irrevocable inter vivos trust before October 22, 1942, providing for payment of income to G for life with remainder as G shall appoint by will, but in default of appointment income to H for life with remainder as H shall appoint by will. If G died after October 21, 1942, without having exercised his power of appointment, H's power of appointment is considered a power created before October 22, 1942, even though it was only a contingent interest until G's death.

Example (4). If in example (3) above G had exercised his power of appointment by creating a similar power in J, J's power of appointment would be considered a power created after October 21, 1942. [Reg. § 20.2041-1.]

☐ [*T.D. 6296, 6-23-58. Amended by T.D. 6582, 12/11/61.*]

[Reg. § 20.2041-2]

§ 20.2041-2. Powers of appointment created on or before October 21, 1942.—(a) *In general.*—Property subject to a general power of appointment created on or before October 21, 1942, is includible in the gross estate of the holder of the power under section 2041 only if he exercised the power under specified circumstances. Section 2041(a)(1) requires that there be included in the gross estate of a decedent the value of property subject to such a power only if the power is exercised by the decedent either (1) by will, or (2) by a disposition which is of such nature that if it were a transfer of property owned by the decedent, the property would be includible in the decedent's gross estate under section 2035 (relating to transfers in contemplation of death), 2036 (relating to transfers with retained life estate), 2037 (relating to transfers taking effect at death), or 2038 (relating to revocable transfers). See paragraphs (b), (c), and (d) of § 20.2041-1 for the definition of various terms used in this section.

(b) *Joint powers created on or before October 21, 1942.*—Section 2041(b)(1)(B) provides that a power created on or before October 21, 1942, which at the time of the exercise is not exercisable by the decedent except in conjunction with another person, is not deemed a general power of appointment.

(c) *Exercise during life.*—The circumstances under which section 2041 applies to the exercise other than by will of a general power of appointment created on or before October 21, 1942, are set forth in paragraph (a) of this section. In this connection, the rules of sections 2035 through 2038 which are to be applied are those in effect on the date of the decedent's death which are applicable to transfers made on the date when the exercise of the power occurred. Those rules are to be applied in determining the extent to which and the conditions under which a disposition is considered a transfer of property. The application of this paragraph may be illustrated by the following examples:

Example (1). A decedent in 1951 exercised a general power of appointment created in 1940, reserving no interest in or power over the property subject to the general power. The decedent died in 1956. Since the exercise was not made within three years before the decedent's death, no part of the property is includible in his gross estate. See section 2035(b), relating to transfers in contemplation of death.

Example (2). S created a trust in 1930 to pay the income to A for life, remainder as B appoints by an instrument filed with the trustee during B's lifetime, and in default of appointment remainder to C. B exercised the power in 1955 by directing that after A's death the income be paid to himself for life with remainder to C. If B dies after A, the entire value of the trust property would be included in B's gross estate, since such a disposition if it were a transfer of property owned by B would cause the property to be included in his gross estate under section 2036(a)(1). If B dies before A, the value of the trust property less the value of A's life estate would be included in B's gross estate for the same reason.

Example (3). S created a trust in 1940 to pay the income to A for life, remainder as A appoints by an instrument filed with the trustee during A's lifetime. A exercised the power in 1955, five years before his death, reserving the right of revocation. The exercise, if not revoked before death, will cause the property subject to the power to be included in A's gross estate under section 2041(a)(1), since such a disposition if it were a transfer of property owned by A would cause the property to be included in his gross estate under section 2038. However, if the exercise were completely revoked, so that A died still possessed of the power, the property would not be included in A's gross estate for the reason that the power will not be treated as having been exercised.

Example (4). A decedent exercised a general power of appointment created in 1940 by making a disposition in trust under which possession or enjoyment of the property subject to the exercise could be obtained only by surviving the decedent and under which the decedent retained a reversionary interest in the property of a value of more than five percent. The exercise will cause the property subject to the power to be included in the decedent's gross estate, since such a disposition if it were a transfer of property owned by the decedent would cause the property to be included in his gross estate under section 2037.

(d) *Release or lapse.*—A failure to exercise a general power of appointment created on or before October 21, 1942, or a complete release of such a power is not considered to be an exercise of a general power of appointment. The phrase "a complete release" means a release of all powers over all or a portion of the property subject to a power of appointment, as distinguished from the reduction of a power of appointment to a lesser power. Thus, if the decedent completely relinquished all powers over one-half of the property subject to a power of appointment, the power is completely released as to that one-half. If at or before the time a power of appointment is relinquished, the holder of the power exercises the power in such a manner or to such an extent that the relinquishment results in the reduction, enlargement, or shift in a beneficial interest in property, the relinquishment will be considered to be an exercise and not a release of the power. For example, assume that A created a trust in 1940 providing for payment of the income to B for life and, upon B's death, remainder to C. Assume further that B was given the unlimited power to amend the trust instrument during his lifetime. If B amended the trust in 1948 by providing that upon his death the remainder was to be paid to D, and if he further amended the trust in 1950 by deleting his power to amend the trust, such relinquishment will be considered an exercise and not a release of a general power of appointment. On the other hand, if the 1948 amendment became ineffective before or at the time of the 1950 amendment, or if B in 1948 merely amended the trust by changing the purely ministerial powers of the trustee, his relinquishment of the power in 1950 will be considered as a release of a power of appointment.

(e) *Partial release.*—If a general power of appointment created on or before October 21, 1942, is partially released so that it is not thereafter a general power of appointment, a subsequent exercise of the partially released power is not an exercise of a general power of appointment if the partial release occurs before whichever is the later of the following dates:

(1) November 1, 1951, or

(2) If the decedent was under a legal disability to release the power on October 21, 1942, the day after the expiration of 6 months following the termination of such legal disability.

However, if a general power created on or before October 21, 1942, is partially released on or after the later of these dates, a subsequent exercise of the power will cause the property subject to the power to be included in the holder's gross estate, if the exercise is such that if it were a disposition of property owned by the decedent it would cause the property to be included in his gross estate. The legal disability referred to in this paragraph is determined under local law and may include the disability of an insane person, a minor, or an unborn child. The fact that the type of general power of appointment possessed by the decedent actually was not generally releasable under the local law does not place the decedent under a legal disability within the meaning of this paragraph. In general, however, it is assumed that all general powers of appointment are releasable, unless the local law on the subject is to the contrary, and it is presumed that the method employed to release the power is effective, unless it is not in accordance with the local law relating specifically to releases or, in the absence of such local law, is not in accordance with the local law relating to similar transactions.

(f) *Partial exercise.*—If a general power of appointment created on or before October 21, 1942, is exercised only as to a portion of the property subject to the power, section 2041 is applicable only to the value of that portion. For example, if a decedent had a general power of appointment exercisable by will created on or before October 21, 1942, over a trust fund valued at $200,000 at the date of his death, and if the decedent exercised his power either to the extent of directing the distribution of one-half of the trust property to B or of directing the payment of $100,000 to B, the trust property would be includible in the decedent's gross estate only to the extent of $100,000. [Reg. § 20.2041-2.]

☐ [*T. D.* 6296, 6/23/58.]

[Reg. § 20.2041-3]

§ 20.2041-3. Powers of appointment created after October 21, 1942.—(a) *In general.*—(1) Property subject to a power of appointment created after October 21, 1942, is includible in the gross estate of the holder of the power under varying conditions depending on whether the power is (i) general in nature, (ii) possessed at death, or (iii) exercised or released. See paragraphs (b), (c), and (d) of § 20.2041-1 for the definition of various terms used in this section. See paragraph (c) of this section for the rules applicable to determine the extent to which joint powers created after October 21, 1942, are to be treated as general powers of appointment.

(2) If the power is a general power of appointment, the value of an interest in property subject to such a power is includible in a decedent's gross estate under section 2041(a)(2) if either—

(i) The decedent has the power at the time of his death (and the interest exists at the time of his death), or

(ii) The decedent exercised or released the power, or the power lapsed, under the circumstances and to the extent described in paragraph (d) of this section.

(3) If the power is not a general power of appointment, the value of property subject to the power is includible in the holder's gross estate under section 2041(a)(3) only if it is exercised to create a further power under certain circumstances (see paragraph (e) of this section).

(b) *Existence of power at death.*—For purposes of section 2041(a)(2), a power of appointment is considered to exist on the date of a decedent's death even though the exercise of the power is subject to the precedent giving of notice, or even though the exercise of the power takes effect only on the expiration of a stated period after its exercise, whether or not on or before the decedent's death notice has been given or the power has been exercised. However, a power which by its terms is exercisable only upon the occurrence during the decedent's lifetime of an event or a contingency which did not in fact take place or occur during such time is not a power in existence on the date of the decedent's death. For example, if a decedent was given a general power of appointment exercisable only after he reached a certain age, only if he survived another person, or only if he died without descendants, the power would not be in existence on the date of the decedent's death if the condition precedent to its exercise had not occurred.

(c) *Joint powers created after October 21, 1942.*—The treatment of a power of appointment created after October 21, 1942, which is exercisable only in conjunction with another person is governed by section 2041(b)(1)(C), which provides as follows:

(1) Such a power is not considered a general power of appointment if it is not exercisable by the decedent except with the consent or joinder of the creator of the power.

(2) Such power is not considered a general power of appointment if it is not exercisable by the decedent except with the consent or joinder of a person having a substantial interest in the property subject to the power which is adverse to the exercise of the power in favor of the decedent, his estate, his creditors, or the creditors of his estate. An interest adverse to the exercise of a power is considered as substantial if its value in relation to the total value of the property subject to the power is not insignificant. For this purpose, the interest is to be valued in accordance with the actuarial principles set forth in § 20.2031-7 or, if it is not susceptible to valuation under those provisions, in accordance with the general principles set forth in § 20.2031-1. A taker in default of appointment under a power has an interest which is adverse to an exercise of the power. A coholder of the power has no adverse interest merely because of his joint possession of the power nor merely because he is a permissible appointee under a power. However, a coholder of a power is considered as having an adverse interest where he may possess the power after the decedent's death and may exercise it at that time in favor of himself, his estate, his creditors, or the creditors of his estate. Thus, for example, if X, Y, and Z held a power jointly to appoint among a group of persons which includes themselves and if on the death of X the power will pass to Y and Z jointly, then Y and Z are considered to have interests adverse to the exercise of the power in favor of X. Similarly, if on Y's death the power will pass to Z, Z is considered to have an interest adverse to the exercise of the power in favor of Y. The application of this subparagraph may be further illustrated by the following additional examples in each of which it is assumed that the value of the interest in question is substantial:

Example (1). The decedent and R were trustees of a trust under the terms of which the income was to be paid to the decedent for life and then to M for life, and the remainder was to be paid to R. The trustees had power to distribute corpus to the decedent. Since R's interest was substantially adverse to an exercise of the power in favor of the decedent the latter did not have a general power of appointment. If M and the decedent were the trustees, M's interest would likewise have been adverse.

Example (2). The decedent and L were trustees of a trust under the terms of which the income was to be paid to L for life and then to M for life, and the remainder was to be paid to the decedent. The trustees had power to distribute corpus to the decedent during L's life. Since L's interest was adverse to an exercise of the power in favor of the decedent, the decedent did not have a general power of appointment. If the decedent and M were the trustees, M's interest would likewise have been adverse.

Example (3). The decedent and L were trustees of a trust under the terms of which the income was to be paid to L for life. The trustees could designate whether corpus was to be distributed to the decedent or to A after L's death. L's interest was not adverse to an exercise of the power in favor of the decedent, and the decedent therefore had a general power of appointment.

(3) A power which is exercisable only in conjunction with another person, and which after application of the rules set forth in subparagraphs (1) and (2) of this paragraph constitutes a general power of appointment, will be treated as though the holders of the power who are permissible appointees of the property were joint owners of property subject to the power. The decedent, under this rule, will be treated as possessed of a general power of appointment over an aliquot share of the property to be determined with reference to the number of joint holders, including the decedent, who (or whose estates or creditors) are permissible appointees. Thus, for example, if X, Y, and Z hold an unlimited power jointly to appoint among a group of persons, including themselves, but on the death of X the power does not pass to Y and Z jointly, then Y and Z are not considered to have interests adverse to the exercise of the power in favor of X. In this case X is considered to possess a general power of appointment as to one-third of the property subject to the power.

(d) *Releases, lapses, and disclaimers of general powers of appointment.*—(1) Property subject to a general power of appointment created after October 21, 1942, is includible in the gross estate of a decedent under section 2041(a)(2) even though he does not have the power at the date of his death, if during his life he exercised or released the power under circumstances such that, if the property subject to the power had been owned and transferred by the decedent, the property would be includible in the decedent's gross estate under section 2035, 2036, 2037, or 2038. Further, section 2041(b)(2) provides that the lapse of a power of appointment is considered to be a release of the power to the extent set forth in subparagraph (3) of this paragraph. A release of a power of appointment need not be formal or express in character. The principles set forth in § 20.2041-2 for determining the application of the pertinent provisions of sections 2035 through 2038 to a particular exercise of a power of appointment are applicable for purposes of determining whether or not an exercise or release of a power of appointment created after October 21, 1942, causes the property to be included in a decedent's gross estate under section 2041(a)(2). If a general power of appointment created after October 21, 1942, is partially released, a subsequent exercise or release of the power under circumstances described in the first sentence of this subparagraph, or its possession at death, will nevertheless cause the property subject to the power to be included in the gross estate of the holder of the power.

(2) Section 2041(a)(2) is not applicable to the complete release of a general power of appointment created after October 21, 1942, whether exercisable during life or by will, if the release was not made in contemplation of death within the meaning of section 2035, and if after the release the holder of the power retained no interest in or control over the property subject to the power which would cause the property to be included in his gross estate under sections 2036 through 2038 if the property had been transferred by the holder.

(3) The failure to exercise a power of appointment created after October 21, 1942, within a specified time, so that the power lapses, constitutes a release of the power. However, section 2041(b)(2) provides that such a lapse of a power of appointment during any calendar year during the decedent's life is treated as a release for purposes of inclusion of property in the gross estate under section 2041(a)(2) only to the extent that the property which could have been appointed by exercise of the lapsed power exceeds the greater of (i) $5,000 or (ii) 5 percent of the aggregate value, at the time of the lapse, of the assets out of which, or the proceeds of which, the exercise of the lapsed power could have been satisfied. For example, assume that A transferred $200,000 worth of securities in trust providing for payment of income to B for life with remainder to B's issue. Assume further that B was given a non-cumulative right to withdraw $10,000 a year from the principal of the trust fund (which neither increased nor decreased in value prior to B's death). In such case, the failure of B to exercise his right of withdrawal will not result in estate tax with respect to the power to withdraw $10,000 which lapses each year before the year of B's death. At B's death there will be included in his gross estate the $10,000 which he was entitled to withdraw for the year in which his death occurs less any amount which he may have taken during that year. However, if in the above example B had possessed the right to withdraw $15,000 of the principal annually, the failure to exercise such power in any year will be considered a release of the power to the extent of the excess of the amount subject to withdrawal over 5 percent of the trust fund (in this example, $5,000, assuming that the trust fund is worth $200,000 at the time of the lapse). Since each lapse is treated as though B had exercised dominion over the trust property by making a transfer of principal reserving the income therefrom for his life, the value of the trust property (but only to the extent of the excess of the amount subject to withdrawal over 5 percent of the trust fund) is includible in B's gross estate (unless before B's death he has disposed of his right to the income under circumstances to which sections 2035 through 2038 would not be applicable). The extent to which the value of the trust property is included in the decedent's gross estate is determined as provided in subparagraph (4) of this paragraph.

(4) The purpose of section 2041(b)(2) is to provide a determination, as of the date of the lapse of the power, of the proportion of the property over which the power lapsed which is an exempt disposition for estate tax purposes and the proportion which, if the other requirements of sections 2035 through 2038 are satisfied, will be considered as a taxable disposition. Once the taxable proportion of any disposition at the date of lapse has been determined, the valuation of that proportion as of the date of the decedent's death (or, if the executor has elected the alternate valuation method under section 2032, the value as of the date therein provided), is to be ascertained in accordance with the principles which are applicable to the valuation of transfers of property by the decedent under the corresponding provisions of sections 2035 through 2038. For example, if the life beneficiary of a trust had a right exercisable only during one calendar year to draw down $50,000 from the corpus of a trust, which he did not exercise, and if at the end of the year the corpus was worth $800,000, the taxable portion over which the power lapsed is $10,000 (the excess of $50,000 over 5 percent of the corpus), or 1/80 of the total value. On the decedent's death, if the total value of the corpus of the trust (excluding income accumulated after the lapse of the power) on the applicable valuation date was $1,200,000, $15,000 (1/80 of $1,200,000) would be includible in the decedent's gross estate. However, if the total value was then $600,000, only $7,500 (1/80 of $600,000) would be includible.

(5) If the failure to exercise a power, such as a right of withdrawal, occurs in more than a single year, the proportion of the property over which the power lapsed which is treated as a taxable disposition will be determined separately for each such year. The aggregate of the taxable proportions for all such years, valued in accordance with the above principles, will be includible in the gross estate by reason of the lapse. The includible amount, however, shall not exceed the aggregate value of the assets out of which, or the proceeds of which, the exercise of the power could have been satisfied, valued as of the date of the decedent's death (or, if the executor has elected the alternate valuation method under section 2032, the value as of the date therein provided).

(6)(i) A disclaimer or renunciation of a general power of appointment created in a transfer made after December 31, 1976, is not considered to be the release of the power if the disclaimer or renunciation is a qualified disclaimer as described in section 2518 and the corresponding regulations. For rules relating to when the transfer creating the power occurs, see § 25.2518-2(c)(3) of this chapter. If the disclaimer or renunciation is not a qualified disclaimer, it is considered a release of the power by the disclaimant.

(ii) The disclaimer or renunciation of a general power of appointment created in a taxable transfer before January 1, 1977, in the person disclaiming is not considered to be a release of the power. The disclaimer or renunciation must be unequivocal and effective under local law. A disclaimer is a complete and unqualified refusal to accept the rights to which one is entitled. There can be no disclaimer or renunciation of a power after its acceptance. In the absence of facts to the contrary, the failure to renounce or disclaim within a reasonable time after learning of its existence will be presumed to constitute an acceptance of the power. In any case where a power is purported to be disclaimed or renounced as to only a portion of the property subject to the power, the determination as to whether or not there has been a complete and unqualified refusal to accept the rights to which one is entitled will depend on all the facts and circumstances of the particular case, taking into account the recognition and effectiveness of such a disclaimer under local law. Such rights refer to the incidents of the power and not to other interests of the decedent in the property. If effective under local law, the power may be disclaimed or renounced without disclaiming or renouncing such other interests.

(iii) The first and second sentences of paragraph (d)(6)(i) of this section are applicable for transfers creating the power to be disclaimed made on or after December 31, 1997.

(e) *Successive powers.*—(1) Property subject to a power of appointment created after October 21, 1942, which is not a general power, is includible in the gross estate of the holder of the power under section 2041(a)(3) if the power is exercised, and if both of the following conditions are met:

(i) If the exercise is *(a)* by will, or *(b)* by a disposition which is of such nature that if it were a transfer of property owned by the decedent, the property would be includible in the decedent's gross estate under sections 2035 through 2037; and

(ii) If the power is exercised by creating another power of appointment which, under the terms of the instruments creating and exercising the first power and under applicable local law, can be validly exercised so as to *(a)* postpone the vesting of any estate or interest in the property for a period ascertainable without regard to the date of the creation of the first power, or *(b)* (if the applicable rule against perpetuities is stated in terms of suspension of ownership or of the power of alienation, rather than of vesting) suspend the absolute ownership or the power of alienation of the property for a period ascertainable without regard to the date of the creation of the first power.

(2) For purposes of the application of section 2041(a)(3), the value of the property subject to the second power of appointment is considered to be its value unreduced by any precedent or subsequent interest which is not subject to the second power. Thus, if a decedent has a power to appoint by will $100,000 to a group of persons consisting of his children and grandchildren and exercises the power by making an outright appointment of $75,000 and by giving one appointee a power to appoint $25,000, no more

than $25,000 will be includible in the decedent's gross estate under section 2041(a)(3). If, however, the decedent appoints the income from the entire fund to a beneficiary for life with power in the beneficiary to appoint the remainder by will, the entire $100,000 will be includible in the decedent's gross estate under section 2041(a)(3) if the exercise of the second power can validly postpone the vesting of any estate or interest in the property or can suspend the absolute ownership or power of alienation of the property for a period ascertainable without regard to the date of the creation of the first power.

(f) *Examples.*—The application of this section may be further illustrated by the following examples, in each of which it is assumed, unless otherwise stated, that S has transferred property in trust after October 21, 1942, with the remainder payable to R at L's death, and that neither L nor R has any interest in or power over the enjoyment of the trust property except as is indicated separately in each example:

Example (1). Income is directed to be paid to L during his lifetime at the end of each year, if living. L has an unrestricted power during his lifetime to cause the income to be distributed to any other person, but no power to cause it to be accumulated. At L's death, no part of the trust property is includible in L's gross estate since L had a power to dispose of only his income interest, a right otherwise possessed by him.

Example (2). Income is directed to be accumulated during L's life but L has a noncumulative power to distribute $10,000 of each year's income to himself. Unless L's power is limited by an ascertainable standard (relating to his health, etc.), as defined in paragraph (c)(2) of § 20.2041-1, he has a general power of appointment over $10,000 of each year's income, the lapse of which may cause a portion of any income not distributed to be included in his gross estate under section 2041. See subparagraphs (3), (4), and (5) of paragraph (d) of this section. Thus, if the trust income during the year amounts to $20,000, L's failure to distribute any of the income to himself constitutes a lapse as to $5,000 (i.e., the amount by which $10,000 exceeds $5,000). If L's power were cumulative (i.e., if the power did not lapse at the end of each year but lapsed only by reason of L's death), the total accumulations which L chose not to distribute to himself immediately before his death would be includible in his gross estate under section 2041.

Example (3). L is entitled to all the income during his lifetime and has an unrestricted power to cause corpus to be distributed to himself. L had a general power of appointment over the corpus of the trust, and the entire corpus as of the time of his death is includible in his gross estate under section 2041.

Example (4). Income was payable to L during his lifetime. R has an unrestricted power to cause corpus to be distributed to L. R dies before L. In such case, R has only a power to dispose of his remainder interest, the value of which is includible in his gross estate under section 2033, and nothing in addition would be includible under section 2041. If in this example R's remainder were contingent on his surviving L, nothing would be includible in his gross estate under either section 2033 or 2041. While R would have a power of appointment, it would not be a general power.

Example (5). Income was payable to L during his lifetime. R has an unrestricted power to cause corpus to be distributed to himself. R dies before L. While the value of R's remainder interest is includible in his gross estate under section 2033, R also has a general power of appointment over the entire trust corpus. Under such circumstances, the entire value of the trust corpus is includible in R's gross estate under section 2041. [Reg. § 20.2041-3.]

☐ [*T.D.* 6296, 6-23-58. *Amended by T.D.* 8095, 8-6-86 *and T.D.* 8744, 12-30-97.]

[Reg. § 20.2042-1]

§ 20.2042-1. Proceeds of life insurance.—(a) *In general.*—(1) Section 2042 provides for the inclusion in a decedent's gross estate of the proceeds of insurance on the decedent's life (i) receivable by or for the benefit of the estate (see paragraph (b) of this section), and (ii) receivable by other beneficiaries(see paragraph (c) of this section). The term "insurance" refers to life insurance of every description, including death benefits paid by fraternal beneficial societies operating under the lodge system.

(2) Proceeds of life insurance which are not includible in the gross estate under section 2042 may, depending upon the facts of the particular case, be includible under some other section of part III of subchapter A of chapter 11. For example, if the decedent possessed incidents of ownership in an insurance policy on his life but gratuitously transferred all rights in the policy in contemplation of death, the proceeds would be includible under section 2035. Section 2042 has no application to the inclusion in the gross estate of the value of rights in an insurance policy on the life of a person other than the decedent, or the value of rights in a combination annuity contract and life insurance policy on the decedent's life (i.e., a "retirement income" policy with death benefit or an "endowment" policy) under which there was no insurance element at the time of the decedent's death (see paragraph (d) of § 20.2039-1).

(3) Except as provided in paragraph (c)(6), the amount to be included in the gross estate under section 2042 is the full amount receivable under the policy. If the proceeds of the policy are made payable to a beneficiary in the form of an annuity for life or for a term of years, the amount to be included in the gross estate is the one sum payable at death under an option which could have been exercised either by the insured or by the beneficiary, or if no option was granted, the sum used by the insurance company in determining the amount of the annuity.

(b) *Receivable by or for the benefit of the estate.*—(1) Section 2042 requires the inclusion in the gross estate of the proceeds of insurance on the decedent's life receivable by the executor or administrator, or payable to the decedent's estate. It makes no difference whether or not the estate is specifically named as the beneficiary under the terms of the policy. Thus, if under the terms of an insurance policy the proceeds are receivable by another beneficiary but are subject to an obligation, legally binding upon the other beneficiary, to pay taxes, debts, or other charges enforceable against the estate, then the amount of such proceeds required for the payment in full (to the extent of the beneficiary's obligation) of such taxes, debts, or other charges is includible in the gross estate. Similarly, if the decedent purchased an insurance policy in favor of another person or a corporation as collateral security for a loan or other accommodation, its proceeds are considered to be receivable for the benefit of the estate. The amount of the loan outstanding at the date of the decedent's death, with interest accrued to that date, will be deductible in determining the taxable estate. See § 20.2053-4.

(2) If the proceeds of an insurance policy made payable to the decedent's estate are community assets under the local community property law and, as a result, one-half of the proceeds belongs to the decedent's spouse, then only one-half of the proceeds is considered to be receivable by or for the benefit of the decedent's estate.

(c) *Receivable by other beneficiaries.*—(1) Section 2042 requires the inclusion in the gross estate of the proceeds of insurance on the decedent's life not receivable by or for the benefit of the estate if the decedent possessed at the date of his death any of the incidents of ownership in the policy, exercisable either alone or in conjunction with any other person. However, if the decedent did not possess any of such incidents of ownership at the time of his death nor transfer them in contemplation of death, no part of the proceeds would be includible in his gross estate under section 2042. Thus, if the decedent owned a policy of insurance on his life and, 4 years before his death, irrevocably assigned his entire interest in the policy to his wife retaining no reversionary interest therein (see subparagraph (3) of this paragraph), the proceeds of the policy would not be includible in his gross estate under section 2042.

(2) For purposes of this paragraph, the term "incidents of ownership" is not limited in its meaning to ownership of the policy in the technical legal sense. Generally speaking, the term has reference to the right of the insured or his estate to the economic benefits of the policy. Thus, it includes the power to change the beneficiary, to surrender or cancel the policy, to assign the policy, to revoke an assignment, to pledge the policy for a loan, or to obtain from the insurer a loan against the surrender value of the policy, etc. See subparagraph (6) of this paragraph for rules relating to the circumstances under which incidents of ownership held by a corporation are attributable to a decedent through his stock ownership.

(3) The term "incidents of ownership" also includes a reversionary interest in the policy or its proceeds, whether arising by the express terms of the policy or other instrument or by operation of law, but only if the value of the reversionary interest immediately before the death of the decedent exceeded 5 percent of the value of the policy. As used in this subparagraph, the term "reversionary interest" includes a possibility that the policy or its proceeds may return to the decedent or his estate and a possibility that the policy or its proceeds may become subject to a power of disposition by him. In order to determine whether or not the value of a reversionary interest immediately before the death of the decedent exceeded 5 percent of the value of the policy, the principles contained in paragraph (c)(3) and (4) of § 20.2037-1 insofar as applicable, shall be followed under this subparagraph. In that connection, there must be specifically taken into consideration any incidents of ownership held by others immediately before the decedent's death which would affect the value of the reversionary interest. For example, the decedent would not be considered to have a reversionary interest in the policy of a value in excess of 5 percent if the power to obtain the cash surrender value existed in some other person immediately before the decedent's death and was exercisable by such other person alone and in all events. The terms "reversionary interest" and "incidents of ownership" do not include the possibility that the decedent might receive a policy or its proceeds by inheritance through the estate of another person, or as a surviving spouse under a statutory right of election or a similar right.

(4) A decedent is considered to have an "incident of ownership" in an insurance policy on his life held in trust if, under the terms of the policy, the decedent (either alone or in conjunction with another person or persons) has the power (as trustee or otherwise) to change the beneficial ownership in the policy or its proceeds, or the time or manner of enjoyment thereof, even though the decedent has no beneficial interest in the trust. Moreover, assuming the decedent created the trust, such a power may result in the inclusion in the decedent's gross estate under section 2036 or 2038 of other property transferred by the decedent to the trust if, for example, the decedent has the power to surrender the insurance policy and if the income otherwise used to pay premiums on the policy would become currently payable to a beneficiary of the trust in the event that the policy were surrendered.

(5) As an additional step in determining whether or not a decedent possessed any incidents of ownership in a policy or any part of a policy, regard must be given to the effect of the State or other applicable law upon the terms of the policy. For example, assume that the decedent purchased a policy of insurance on his life with funds held by him and his surviving wife as community property, designating their son as beneficiary but retaining the right to surrender the policy. Under the local law, the proceeds upon surrender would have inured to the marital community. Assuming that the policy is not surrendered and that the son receives the pro-

ceeds on the decedent's death, the wife's transfer of her one-half interest in the policy was not considered absolute before the decedent's death. Upon the wife's prior death, one-half of the value of the policy would have been included in her gross estate. Under these circumstances, the power of surrender possessed by the decedent as agent for his wife with respect to one-half of the policy is not, for purposes of this section, an "incident of ownership", and the decedent is, therefore, deemed to possess an incident of ownership in only one-half of the policy.

(6) In the case of economic benefits of a life insurance policy on the decedent's life that are reserved to a corporation of which the decedent is the sole or controlling stockholder, the corporation's incidents of ownership will not be attributed to the decedent through his stock ownership to the extent the proceeds of the policy are payable to the corporation. Any proceeds payable to a third party for a valid business purpose, such as in satisfaction of a business debt of the corporation, so that the net worth of the corporation is increased by the amount of such proceeds, shall be deemed to be payable to the corporation for purposes of the preceding sentence. See § 20.2031-2(f) for a rule providing that the proceeds of certain life insurance policies shall be considered in determining the value of the decedent's stock. Except as hereinafter provided with respect to a group-term life insurance policy, if any part of the proceeds of the policy are not payable to or for the benefit of the corporation, and thus are not taken into account in valuing the decedent's stock holdings in the corporation for purposes of section 2031, any incidents of ownership held by the corporation as to that part of the proceeds will be attributed to the decedent through his stock ownership where the decedent is the sole or controlling stockholder. Thus, for example, if the decedent is the controlling stockholder in a corporation, and the corporation owns a life insurance policy on his life, the proceeds of which are payable to the decedent's spouse, the incidents of ownership held by the corporation will be attributed to the decedent through his stock ownership and the proceeds will be included in his gross estate under section 2042. If in this example the policy proceeds had been payable 40 percent to decedent's spouse and 60 percent to the corporation, only 40 percent of the proceeds would be included in decedent's gross estate under section 2042. For purposes of this subparagraph, the decedent will not be deemed to be the controlling stockholder of a corporation unless, at the time of his death, he owned stock possessing more than 50 percent of the total combined voting power of the corporation. Solely for purposes of the preceding sentence, a decedent shall be considered to be the owner of only the stock with respect to which legal title was held, at the time of his death, by (i) the decedent (or his agent or nominee); [(ii)] the decedent and another person jointly (but only the proportionate number of shares which corresponds to the portion of the total consideration which is considered to be furnished by the decedent for purposes of section 2040 and the regulations thereunder); and (iii) by a trustee of a voting trust (to the extent of the decedent's beneficial interest therein) or any other trust with respect to which the decedent was treated as an owner under subpart E, part I, subchapter J, chapter 1 of the Code immediately prior to his death. In the case of group-term life insurance, as defined the regulations under section 79, the power to surrender or cancel a policy held by a corporation shall not be attributed to any decedent through his stock ownership. [Reg. § 20.2042-1.]

☐ [*T.D.* 6296, 6-23-58. *Amended by T.D.* 7312, 4-26-74 *and T.D.* 7623, 5-14-79.]

[Reg. § 20.2043-1]

§ 20.2043-1. Transfers for insufficient consideration.—(a) *In general.*—The transfers, trusts, interests, rights or powers enumerated and described in sections 2035 through 2038 and section 2041 are not subject to the Federal estate tax if made, created, exercised, or relinquished in a transaction which constituted a bona fide sale for an adequate and full consideration in money or money's worth. To constitute a bona fide sale for an adequate and full consideration in money or money's worth, the transfer must have been made in good faith, and the price must have been an adequate and full equivalent reducible to a money value. If the price was less than such a consideration, only the excess of the fair market value of the property (as of the applicable valuation date) over the price received by the decedent is included in ascertaining the value of his gross estate.

(b) *Marital rights and support obligations.*—For purposes of chapter 11, a relinquishment or promised relinquishment of dower, curtesy, or of a statutory estate created in lieu of dower or curtesy, or of other marital rights in the decedent's property or estate, is not to support obligations. For purposes of chapter 11, a relinquishment or promised relinquishment of dower, curtesy, or of a statutory estate created in lieu of dower or curtesy, or of other marital rights in the decedent's property or estate, is not to any extent a consideration in "money or money's worth." [Reg. § 20.2043-1.]

☐ [*T.D.* 6296, 6-23-58.]

[Reg. § 20.2044-1]

§ 20.2044-1. Certain property for which marital deduction was previously allowed.—(a) *In general.*—Section 2044 generally provides for the inclusion in the gross estate of property in which the decedent had a qualifying income interest for life and for which a deduction was allowed under section 2056(b)(7) or 2523(f). The value of the property included in the gross estate under section 2044 is not reduced by the amount of any section 2503(b) exclusion that applied to the transfer creating the interest. See section 2207A, regarding the right of recovery against the persons receiving the property that is applicable in certain cases.

(b) *Passed from.*—For purposes of section 1014 and chapters 11 and 13 of subtitle B of the Internal Revenue Code, property included in a decedent's gross estate under section 2044 is considered to have been acquired from or to have passed from the decedent to the person receiving the property upon the decedent's death. Thus, for example, the property is treated as passing from the decedent for purposes of determining the availability of the charitable deduction under section 2055, the marital deduction under section 2056, and special use valuation under section 2032A. In addition, the tax imposed on property includible under section 2044 is eligible for the installment payment of estate tax under section 6166.

(c) *Presumption.*—Unless established to the contrary, section 2044 applies to the entire value of the trust at the surviving spouse's death. If a marital deduction is taken on either the estate or gift tax return with respect to the transfer which created the qualifying income interest, it is presumed that the deduction was allowed for purposes of section 2044. To avoid the inclusion of property in the decedent-spouse's gross estate under this section, the executor of the spouse's estate must establish that a deduction was not taken for the transfer which created the qualifying income interest. For example, to establish that a deduction was not taken, the executor may produce a copy of the estate or gift tax return filed with respect to the transfer by the first spouse or the first spouse's estate establishing that no deduction was taken under section 2523(f) or section 2056(b)(7). In addition, the executor may establish that no return was filed on the original transfer by the decedent because the value of the first spouse's gross estate was below the threshold requirement for filing under section 6018. Similarly, the executor could establish that the transfer creating the decedent's qualifying income interest for life was made before the effective date of section 2056(b)(7) or section 2523(f).

(d) *Amount included.*—(1) *In general.*—The amount included under this section is the value of the entire interest in which the decedent had a qualifying income interest for life, determined as of the date of the decedent's death (or the alternate valuation date, if applicable). If, in connection with the transfer of property that created the decedent's qualifying income interest for life, a deduction was allowed under section 2056(b)(7) or section 2523(f) for less than the entire interest in the property (i.e., for a fractional or percentage share of the entire interest in the transferred property), the amount includible in the decedent's gross estate under this section is equal to the fair market value of the entire interest in the property on the date of the decedent's death (or the alternate valuation date, if applicable) multiplied by the fractional or percentage share of the interest for which the deduction was taken.

(2) *Inclusion of income.*—If any income from the property for the period between the date of the transfer creating the decedent-spouse's interest and the date of the decedent-spouse's death has not been distributed before the decedent-spouse's death, the undistributed income is included in the decedent-spouse's gross estate under this section to the extent that the income is not so included under any other section of the Internal Revenue Code.

(3) *Reduction of includible share in certain cases.*—If only a fractional or percentage share is includible under this section, the includible share is appropriately reduced if—

(i) The decedent-spouse's interest was in a trust and distributions of principal were made to the spouse during the spouse's lifetime;

(ii) The trust provides that the distributions are to be made from the qualified terminable interest share of the trust; and

(iii) The executor of the decedent-spouse's estate can establish the reduction in that share based on the fair market value of the trust assets at the time of each distribution.

(4) *Interest in previously severed trust.*—If the decedent-spouse's interest was in a trust consisting of only qualified terminable interest property and the trust was severed (in compliance with § 20.2056(b)-7(b) or § 25.2523(f)-1(b) of this chapter) from a trust that, after the severance, held only property that was not qualified terminable interest property, only the value of the property in the severed portion of the trust is includible in the decedent-spouse's gross estate.

(e) *Examples.*—The following examples illustrate the principles in paragraphs (a) through (d) of this section, where the decedent, D, was survived by spouse, S.

Example 1. Inclusion of trust subject to election. Under D's will, assets valued at $800,000 in D's gross estate (net of debts, expenses and other charges, including death taxes, payable from the property) passed in trust with income payable to S for life. Upon S's death, the trust principal is to be distributed to D's children. D's executor elected under section 2056(b)(7) to treat the entire trust property as qualified terminable interest property and claimed a marital deduction of $800,000. S made no disposition of the income interest during S's lifetime under section 2519. On the date of S's death, the fair market value of the trust property was $740,000. S's executor did not elect the alternate valuation date. The amount included in S's gross estate pursuant to section 2044 is $740,000.

Example 2. Inclusion of trust subject to partial election. The facts are the same as in *Example 1,* except that D's executor elected under section 2056(b)(7) with respect to only 50 percent of the value of the trust ($400,000). Consequently, only the equivalent portion of the trust is included in S's gross estate; i.e., $370,000 (50 percent of $740,000).

Example 3. Spouse receives qualifying income interest in a fraction of trust income. Under D's will, assets valued at $800,000 in D's gross estate (net of debts, expenses and other charges, including death taxes, payable from the property) passed in trust with 20 percent of the trust income payable to S for S's life. The will provides that the trust principal is to be distributed to D's children upon S's death. D's executor elected to deduct, pursuant to section 2056(b)(7), 50 percent of the amount for which the election could be made; i.e., $80,000 (50 percent of 20 percent of $800,000). Consequently, on the death of S, only the equivalent portion of the trust is included in S's gross estate; i.e., $74,000 (50 percent of 20 percent of $740,000).

Example 4. Distribution of corpus during spouse's lifetime. The facts are the same as in *Example 3,* except that S was entitled to receive all the trust income but the executor of D's estate elected under section 2056(b)(7) with respect to only 50 percent of the value of the trust ($400,000). Pursuant to authority in the will, the trustee made a discretionary distribution of $100,000 of principal to S in 1995 and charged the entire distribution to the qualified terminable interest share. Immediately prior to the distribution, the fair market value of the trust property was $1,100,000 and the qualified terminable interest portion of the trust was 50 percent. Immediately after the distribution, the qualified terminable interest portion of the trust was 45 percent ($450,000 divided by $1,000,000). Provided S's executor can establish the relevant facts, the amount included in S's gross estate is $333,000 (45 percent of $740,000).

Example 5. Spouse assigns a portion of income interest during life. Under D's will, assets valued at $800,000 in D's gross estate (net of debts, expenses and other charges, including death taxes, payable from the property) passed in trust with all the income payable to S, for S's life. The will provides that the trust principal is to be distributed to D's children upon S's death. D's executor elected under section 2056(b)(7) to treat the entire trust property as qualified terminable interest property and claimed a marital deduction of $800,000. During the term of the trust, S transfers to C the right to 40 percent of the income from the trust for S's life. Because S is treated as transferring the entire remainder interest in the trust corpus under section 2519 (as well as 40 percent of the income interest under section 2511), no part of the trust is includible in S's gross estate under section 2044. However, if S retains until death an income interest in 60 percent of the trust corpus (which corpus is treated pursuant to section 2519 as having been transferred by S for both gift and estate tax purposes), 60 percent of the property will be includible in S's gross estate under section 2036(a) and a corresponding adjustment is made in S's adjusted taxable gifts.

Example 6. Inter vivos trust subject to election under section 2523(f). D transferred $800,000 to a trust providing that trust income is to be paid annually to S, for S's life. The trust provides that upon S's death, $100,000 of principal is to be paid to X charity and the remaining principal distributed to D's children. D elected to treat all of the property transferred to the trust as qualified terminable interest property under section 2523(f). At the time of S's death, the fair market value of the trust is $1,000,000. S's executor does not elect the alternate valuation date. The amount included in S's gross estate is $1,000,000; i.e., the fair market value at S's death of the entire trust property. The $100,000 that passes to X charity on S's death is treated as a transfer by S to X charity for purposes of section 2055. Therefore, S's estate is allowed a charitable deduction for the $100,000 transferred from the trust to the charity to the same extent that a deduction would be allowed by section 2055 for a bequest by S to X charity.

Example 7. Spousal interest in the form of an annuity. D died prior to October 24, 1992, the effective date of the Energy Policy Act of 1992 (Pub. L. 102-486). See § 20.2056(b)-7(e). Under D's will, assets valued at $500,000 in D's gross estate (net of debts, expenses and other charges, including death taxes, payable from the property) passed in trust pursuant to which an annuity of $20,000 a year was payable to S for S's life. Trust income not paid to S as an annuity is to be accumulated in the trust and may not be distributed during S's lifetime. D's estate deducted $200,000 under section 2056(b)(7) and § 20.2056(b)-7(e)(2). S did not assign any portion of S's interest during S's life. At the time of S's death, the value of the trust property is $800,000. S's executor does not elect the alternate valuation date. The amount included in S's gross estate pursuant to section 2044 is $320,000 ([$200,000/$500,000] × $800,000).

Example 8. Inclusion of trust property when surviving spouse dies before first decedent's estate tax return is filed. D dies on July 1, 1997. Under the terms of D's will, a trust is established for the benefit of D's spouse, S. The will provides that S is entitled to receive the income from that portion of the trust that the executor elects to treat as qualified terminable interest property. The remaining portion of the trust passes as of D's date of death to a trust for the benefit of C, D's child. The trust terms otherwise provide S with a qualifying income interest for life under section 2056(b)(7)(B)(ii). S dies on February 10, 1998. On April 1, 1998, D's executor files D's estate tax return on which an election is made to treat a portion of the trust as qualified terminable interest property under section 2056(b)(7). S's estate tax return is filed on November 10, 1998. The value on the date of S's death of the portion of the trust for which D's executor made a QTIP election is includible in S's gross estate under section 2044.

[Reg. § 20.2044-1.]

☐ [*T.D.* 8522, 2-28-94. *Amended by T.D.* 8779, 8-18-98.]

[Reg. § 20.2044-2]

§ 20.2044-2. Effective dates.—Except as specifically provided in *Example 7* of § 20.2044-1(e), the provisions of § 20.2044-1 are effective with respect to estates of a decedent-spouse dying after March 1, 1994. With respect to estates of decedent-spouses dying on or before such date, taxpayers may rely on any reasonable interpretation of the statutory provisions. For these purposes, the provisions of § 20.2044-1 (as well as project LR-211-76, 1984-1 C.B., page 598, see

§ 601.601(d)(2)(ii)(*b*) of this chapter) are considered a reasonable interpretation of the statutory provisions. [Reg. § 20.2044-2.]

☐ [*T.D.* 8522, 2-28-94.]

[Reg. § 20.2045-1]

§ 20.2045-1. Applicability to pre-existing transfers or interests.—Sections 2034 through 2042 are applicable regardless of when the interests and events referred to in those sections were created or took place, except as otherwise provided in those sections and the regulations thereunder. [Reg. § 20.2045-1.]

☐ [*T.D.* 6296, 6-23-58. *Redesignated by T.D.* 8522, 2-28-94.]

[Reg. § 20.2046-1]

§ 20.2046-1. Disclaimed property.—(a) This section shall apply to the disclaimer or renunciation of an interest in the person disclaiming by a transfer made after December 31, 1976. For rules relating to when the transfer creating the interest occurs, see § 25.2518-2(c)(3) and (c)(4) of this chapter. If a qualified disclaimer is made with respect to such a transfer, the Federal estate tax provisions are to apply with respect to the property interest disclaimed as if the interest had never been transferred to the person making the disclaimer. See section 2518 and the corresponding regulations for rules relating to a qualified disclaimer.

(b) The first and second sentences of this section are applicable for transfers creating the interest to be disclaimed made on or after December 31, 1997. [Reg. § 20.2046-1.]

☐ [*T.D.* 8095, 8-6-86. *Amended by T.D.* 8744, 12-30-97.]

Taxable Estate

[Reg. § 20.2051-1]

§ 20.2051-1. Definition of taxable estate.—(a) *General rule.*—The taxable estate of a decedent who was a citizen or resident (see § 20.0-1(b)(1)) of the United States at death is determined by subtracting the total amount of the deductions authorized by sections 2053 through 2058 from the total amount which must be included in the gross estate under sections 2031 through 2044. These deductions are in general as follows—

(1) Funeral and administration expenses and claims against the estate (including certain taxes and charitable pledges) (section 2053).

(2) Losses from casualty or theft during the administration of the estate (section 2054).

(3) Charitable transfers (section 2055).

(4) The marital deduction (section 2056).

(5) Qualified domestic trusts (section 2056A).

(6) Family-owned business interests (section 2057) to the extent applicable to estates of decedents.

(7) State death taxes (section 2058) to the extent applicable to estates of decedents.

(b) *Special rules.*—See section 2106 and the corresponding regulations for special rules regarding the computation of the taxable estate of a decedent who was not a citizen or resident of the United States. See also § 1.642(g)-1 of this chapter concerning the disallowance for income tax purposes of certain deductions allowed for estate tax purposes.

(c) *Effective/applicability date.*—This section applies to the estates of decedents dying on or after October 20, 2009. [Reg. § 20.2051-1.]

☐ [*T.D.* 6296, 6-23-58. *Amended by T.D.* 9468, 10-16-2009.]

[Reg. § 20.2053-1]

§ 20.2053-1. Deductions for expenses, indebtedness, and taxes; in general.—(a) *General rule.*—In determining the taxable estate of a decedent who was a citizen or resident of the United States at death, there are allowed as deductions under section 2053(a) and (b) amounts falling within the following two categories (subject to the limitations contained in this section and in § § 20.2053-2 through 20.2053-10)—

(1) *First category.*—Amounts which are payable out of property subject to claims and which are allowable by the law of the jurisdiction, whether within or without the United States, under which the estate is being administered for—

(i) Funeral expenses;

(ii) Administration expenses;

(iii) Claims against the estate (including taxes to the extent set forth in § 20.2053-6 and charitable pledges to the extent set forth in § 20.2053-5); and

(iv) Unpaid mortgages on, or any indebtedness in respect of, property, the value of the decedent's interest in which is included in the value of the gross estate undiminished by the mortgage or indebtedness.

As used in this subparagraph, the phrase "allowable by the law of the jurisdiction" means allowable by the law governing the administration of decedents' estates. The phrase has no reference to amounts allowable as deductions under a law which imposes a State death tax. See further § § 20.2053-2 through 20.2053-7.

(2) *Second category.*—Amounts representing expenses incurred in administering property which is included in the gross estate but which is not subject to claims and which—

(i) Would be allowed as deductions in the first category if the property being administered were subject to claims; and

(ii) Were paid before the expiration of the period of limitation for assessment provided in section 6501.

See further § 20.2053-8.

(b) *Provisions applicable to both categories.*—(1) *In general.*—If the item is not one of those described in paragraph (a) of this section, it is not deductible merely because payment is allowed by the local law. If the amount which may be expended for the particular purpose is limited by the local law, no deduction in excess of that limitation is permissible.

(2) *Bona fide requirement.*—(i) *In general.*—Amounts allowed as deductions under section 2053(a) and (b) must be expenses and claims that are bona fide in nature. No deduction is permissible to the extent it is founded on a transfer that is essentially donative in character (a mere cloak for a gift or bequest) except to the extent the deduction is for a claim that would be allowable as a deduction under section 2055 as a charitable bequest.

(ii) *Claims and expenses involving family members.*—Factors indicative (but not necessarily determinative) of the bona fide nature of a claim or expense involving a family member of a decedent, a related entity, or a beneficiary of a decedent's estate or revocable trust, in relevant instances, may include, but are not limited to, the following—

(A) The transaction underlying the claim or expense occurs in the ordinary course of business, is negotiated at arm's length, and is free from donative intent.

(B) The nature of the claim or expense is not related to an expectation or claim of inheritance.

(C) The claim or expense originates pursuant to an agreement between the decedent and the family member, related entity, or beneficiary, and the agreement is substantiated with contemporaneous evidence.

(D) Performance by the claimant is pursuant to the terms of an agreement between the decedent and the family member, related entity, or beneficiary and the performance and the agreement can be substantiated.

(E) All amounts paid in satisfaction or settlement of a claim or expense are reported by each party for Federal income and employment tax purposes, to the extent appropriate, in a manner that is consistent with the reported nature of the claim or expense.

(iii) *Definitions.*—The following definitions apply for purposes of this paragraph (b)(2):

(A) *Family members* include the spouse of the decedent; the grandparents, parents, siblings, and lineal descendants of the decedent or of the decedent's spouse; and the spouse and lineal descendants of any such grandparent, parent, and sibling. Family members include adopted individuals.

(B) A *related entity* is an entity in which the decedent, either directly or indirectly, had a beneficial ownership interest at the time of the decedent's death or at any time during the three-year period ending on the decedent's date of death. Such an entity, however, shall not include a publicly-traded entity nor shall it include a closely-held entity in which the combined beneficial interest, either direct or indirect, of the decedent and the decedent's family members, collectively, is less than 30 percent of the beneficial ownership interests (whether voting or nonvoting and whether an interest in stock, capital and/or profits), as determined at the time a claim described in this section is being asserted. Notwithstanding the foregoing, an entity in which the decedent, directly or indirectly, had any managing interest (for example, as a general partner of a partnership or as a managing member of a limited liability company) at the time of the decedent's death shall be considered a related entity.

(C) *Beneficiaries* of a decedent's estate include beneficiaries of a trust of the decedent.

(3) *Court decrees and settlements.*—(i) *Court decree.*—If a court of competent jurisdiction over the administration of an estate reviews and approves expenditures for funeral expenses, administration expenses, claims against the estate, or unpaid mortgages (referred to in this section as a "claim or expense"), a final judicial decision in that matter may be relied upon to establish the amount of a claim or expense that is otherwise deductible under section 2053 and these regulations provided that the court actually passes upon the facts on which deductibility depends. If the court does not pass upon those facts, its decree may not be relied upon to establish the amount of the claim or expense that is otherwise deductible under section 2053. It must appear that the court actually passed upon the merits of the claim. This will be presumed in all cases of an active and genuine contest. If the result reached appears to be unreasonable, this is some evidence that there was not such a contest, but it may be rebutted by proof to the contrary. Any amount meeting the requirements of this paragraph (b)(3)(i) is deductible to the extent it actually has been paid or will be paid, subject to any applicable limitations in this section.

(ii) *Claims and expenses where court approval not required under local law.*—A deduction for the amount of a claim or expense that is otherwise deductible under section 2053 and these regulations will not be denied under section 2053 solely because a local court decree has not been entered with respect to such amount, provided that no court decree is required under applicable law to determine the amount or allowability of the claim or expense.

(iii) *Consent decree.*—A local court decree rendered by consent may be relied on to establish the amount of a claim or expense that is otherwise deductible under section 2053 and these regulations provided that the consent resolves a bona fide issue in a genuine contest. Consent given by all parties having interests adverse to that of the claimant will be presumed to resolve a bona fide issue in a genuine contest. Any amount meeting the requirements of this paragraph (b)(3)(iii) is deductible to the extent it actually has been paid or will be paid, subject to any applicable limitations in this section.

(iv) *Settlements.*—A settlement may be relied on to establish the amount of a claim or expense (whether contingent or noncontingent) that is otherwise deductible under section 2053 and these regulations, provided that the settlement resolves a bona fide issue in a genuine contest and is the product of arm's-length negotiations by parties having adverse interests with respect to the claim or expense. A deduction will not be denied for a settlement amount paid by an estate if the estate can establish that the cost of defending or contesting the claim or expense, or the delay associated with litigating the claim or expense, would impose a higher burden on the estate than the payment of the amount paid to settle the claim or expense. Nevertheless, no deduction will be allowed for amounts paid in settlement of an unenforceable claim. For this purpose, to the extent a claim exceeds an applicable limit under local law, the claim is deemed to be unenforceable. However, as long as the enforceability of the claim is at issue in a bona fide dispute, the claim will not be deemed to be unenforceable for this purpose. Any amount meeting the requirements of this paragraph (b)(3)(iv) is deductible to the extent it actually has been paid or will be paid, subject to any applicable limitations in this section.

(v) *Additional rules*.—Notwithstanding paragraph (b)(3)(i) through (iv) of this section, additional rules may apply to the deductibility of certain claims and expenses. See § 20.2053-2 for additional rules regarding the deductibility of funeral expenses. See § 20.2053-3 for additional rules regarding the deductibility of administration expenses. See § 20.2053-4 for additional rules regarding the deductibility of claims against the estate. See § 20.2053-7 for additional rules regarding the deductibility of unpaid mortgages.

(4) *Examples*.—Unless otherwise provided, assume that the amount of any claim or expense is paid out of property subject to claims and is paid within the time prescribed for filing the "United States Estate (and Generation-Skipping Transfer) Tax Return," Form 706. The following examples illustrate the application of this paragraph (b):

Example 1. Consent decree at variance with the law of the State. Decedent's (D's) estate is probated in State. D's probate estate is valued at $100x. State law provides that the executor's commission shall not exceed 3 percent of the probate estate. A consent decree is entered allowing the executor's commission in the amount of $5x. The estate pays the executor's commission in the amount of $5x. For purposes of section 2053, the executor may deduct only $3x of the $5x expense paid for the executor's commission because the amount approved by the consent decree in excess of $3x is in excess of the applicable limit for executor's commissions under local law. Therefore, for purposes of section 2053, the consent decree may not be relied upon to establish the amount of the expense for the executor's commission.

Example 2. Decedent's (D's) estate is probated in State. State law grants authority to an executor to administer an estate without court approval, so long as notice of and a right to object to a proposed action is provided to interested persons. The executor of D's estate (E) proposes to sell property of the estate in order to pay the debts of D. E gives requisite notice to all interested parties and no interested person objects. E sells the real estate and pays a real estate commission of $20x to a professional real estate agent. The amount of the real estate commission paid does not exceed the applicable limit under State law. Provided that the sale of the property was necessary to pay D's debts, expenses of administration, or taxes, to preserve the estate, or to effect distribution, the executor may deduct the $20x expense for the real estate commission under section 2053 even though no court decree was entered approving the expense.

Example 3. Claim by family member. For a period of three years prior to D's death, D's niece (N) provides accounting and bookkeeping services on D's behalf. N is a CPA and provides similar accounting and bookkeeping services to unrelated clients. At the end of each month, N presents an itemized bill to D for services rendered. The fees charged by N conform to the prevailing market rate for the services rendered and are comparable to the fees N charges other clients for similar services. The amount due is timely paid each month by D and is properly reported for Federal income and employment tax purposes by N. In the six months prior to D's death, D's poor health prevents D from making payments to N for the amount due. After D's death, N asserts a claim against the estate for $25x, an amount representing the amount due for the sixmonth period prior to D's death. D's estate pays $25x to N in satisfaction of the claim before the return is timely filed and N properly reports the $25x received by E for income tax purposes. Barring any other relevant facts or circumstances, E may rely on the following factors to establish that the claim is bona fide: (1) N's claim for services rendered arose in the ordinary course of business, as N is a CPA performing similar services for other clients; (2) the fees charged were deemed to be negotiated at arm's length, as the fees were consistent with the fees N charged for similar services to unrelated clients; (3) the billing records and the records of D's timely payments to N constitute contemporaneous evidence of an agreement between D and N for N's bookkeeping services; and (4) the amount of the payments to N is properly reported by N for Federal income and employment tax purposes. E may deduct the amount paid to N in satisfaction of the claim.

(c) *Provision applicable to first category only*.—Deductions of the first category (described in paragraph (a)(1) of this section) are limited under section 2053(a) to amounts which would be properly allowable out of property subject to claims by the law of the jurisdiction under which the decedent's estate is being administered. Further, the total allowable amount of deductions of the first category is limited by section 2053(c)(2) to the sum of—

(1) The value of property included in the decedent's gross estate and subject to claims, plus

(2) Amounts paid, out of property not subject to claims against the decedent's estate, within 9 months (15 months in the case of the estate of a decedent dying before January 1, 1971) after the decedent's death (the period within which the estate tax return must be filed under section 6075), or within any extension of time for filing the return granted under section 6081. The term "property subject to claims" is defined in section 2053(c)(2) as meaning the property includible in the gross estate which, or the avails of which, under the applicable law, would bear the burden of the payment of these deductions in the final adjustment and settlement of the decedent's estate. However, for the purposes of this definition, the value of property subject to claims is first reduced by the amount of any deduction allowed under section 2054 for any losses from casualty or theft incurred during the settlement of the estate attributable to such property. The application of this paragraph may be illustrated by the following examples:

Example (1). The only item in the gross estate is real property valued at $250,000 which the decedent and his surviving spouse held as tenants by the entirety. Under the local law, this real property is not subject to claims. Funeral expenses of $1,200 and debts of the decedent in the amount of $1,500 are allowable under local law. Before the prescribed date for filing the estate tax return, the surviving spouse paid the funeral expenses and $1,000 of the debts. The remaining $500 of the debts was paid by her after the prescribed date for filing the return. The total amount allowable as deductions under section 2053 is limited to $2,200, the amount paid prior to the prescribed date for filing the return.

Example (2). The only two items in the gross estate were a bank deposit of $20,000 and insurance in the amount of $150,000. The insurance was payable to the decedent's surviving spouse and under local law was not subject to claims. Funeral expenses of $1,000 and debts in the amount of $29,000 were allowable under local law. A son was executor of the estate and before the prescribed date for filing the estate tax return he paid the funeral expenses and $9,000 of the debts, using therefor $5,000 of the bank deposit and $5,000 supplied by the surviving spouse. After the prescribed date for filing the return, the executor paid the remaining $20,000 of the debts, using for that purpose the $15,000 left in the bank account plus an additional $5,000 supplied by the surviving spouse. The total amount allowable as deductions under section 2053 is limited to $25,000 ($20,000 of property subject to claims plus the $5,000 additional amount which, before the prescribed date for filing the return, was paid out of property not subject to claims).

(d) *Amount deductible.*—(1) *General rule.*—To take into account properly events occurring after the date of a decedent's death in determining the amount deductible under section 2053 and these regulations, the deduction for any claim or expense described in paragraph (a) of this section is limited to the total amount actually paid in settlement or satisfaction of that item (subject to any applicable limitations in this section). However, see paragraph (d)(4) of this section for the rules for deducting certain ascertainable amounts; see § 20.2053-4(b) and (c) for the rules regarding the deductibility of certain claims against the estate; and see § 20.2053-7 for the rules regarding the deductibility of unpaid mortgages and other indebtedness.

(2) *Application of post-death events.*—In determining whether and to what extent a deduction under section 2053 is allowable, events occurring after the date of a decedent's death will be taken into consideration—

(i) Until the expiration of the applicable period of limitations on assessment prescribed in section 6501 (including without limitation at all times during which the running of the period of limitations is suspended); and

(ii) During subsequent periods, in determining the amount (if any) of an overpayment of estate tax due in connection with a claim for refund filed within the time prescribed in section 6511(a).

(3) *Reimbursements.*—A deduction is not allowed to the extent that a claim or expense described in paragraph (a) of this section is or could be compensated for by insurance or otherwise could be reimbursed. If the executor is able to establish that only a partial reimbursement could be collected, then only that portion of the potential reimbursement that reasonably could have been expected to be collected will reduce the estate's deductible portion of the total claim or expense. An executor may certify that the executor neither knows nor reasonably should have known of any available reimbursement for a claim or expense described in section 2053(a) or (b) on the estate's United States Estate (and Generation-Skipping Transfer) Tax Return (Form 706), in accordance with the instructions for that form. A potential reimbursement will not reduce the deductible amount of a claim or expense to the extent that the executor, on Form 706 and in accordance with the instructions for that form, provides a reasonable explanation for his or her reasonable determination that the burden of necessary collection efforts in pursuit of a right of reimbursement would outweigh the anticipated benefit from those efforts. Nevertheless, even if a reasonable explanation is provided, subsequent events (including without limitation an actual reimbursement) occurring within the period described in § 20.2053-1(d)(2) will be considered in determining the amount (if any) of a reduction under this paragraph (d)(3) in the deductible amount of a claim or expense.

(4) *Exception for certain ascertainable amounts.*—(i) *General rule.*—A deduction will be allowed for a claim or expense that satisfies all applicable requirements even though it is not yet paid, provided that the amount to be paid is ascertainable with reasonable certainty and will be paid. For example, executors' commissions

and attorneys' fees that are not yet paid, and that meet the requirements for deductibility under § 20.2053-3(b) and (c), respectively, are deemed to be ascertainable with reasonable certainty and may be deducted if such expenses will be paid. However, no deduction may be taken upon the basis of a vague or uncertain estimate. To the extent a claim or expense is contested or contingent, such a claim or expense cannot be ascertained with reasonable certainty.

(ii) *Effect of post-death events.*—A deduction under this paragraph (d)(4) will be allowed to the extent the Commissioner is reasonably satisfied that the amount to be paid is ascertainable with reasonable certainty and will be paid. In making this determination, the Commissioner will take into account events occurring after the date of a decedent's death. To the extent the amount for which a deduction was claimed does not satisfy the requirements of this paragraph (d)(4), and is not otherwise deductible, the deduction will be disallowed by the Commissioner. If a deduction is claimed on Form 706 for an amount that is not yet paid and the deduction is disallowed in whole or in part (or if no deduction is claimed on Form 706), then if the claim or expense subsequently satisfies the requirements of this paragraph (d)(4) or is paid, relief may be sought by filing a claim for refund. To preserve the estate's right to claim a refund for amounts becoming deductible after the expiration of the period of limitation for the filing of a claim for refund, a protective claim for refund may be filed in accordance with paragraph (d)(5) of this section.

(5) *Protective claim for refund.*—(i) *In general.*—A protective claim for refund under this section may be filed at any time before the expiration of the period of limitation prescribed in section 6511(a) for the filing of a claim for refund to preserve the estate's right to claim a refund by reason of claims or expenses that are not paid or do not otherwise meet the requirements of deductibility under section 2053 and these regulations until after the expiration of the period of limitation for filing a claim for refund. Such a protective claim shall be made in accordance with guidance that may be provided from time to time by publication in the Internal Revenue Bulletin (see § 601.601(d)(2)(ii)(*b*)). Although the protective claim need not state a particular dollar amount or demand an immediate refund, a protective claim must identify each outstanding claim or expense that would have been deductible under section 2053(a) or (b) if such item already had been paid and must describe the reasons and contingencies delaying the actual payment of the claim or expense. Action on protective claims will proceed after the executor has notified the Commissioner within a reasonable period that the contingency has been resolved and that the amount deductible under § 20.2053-1 has been established.

(ii) *Effect on marital and charitable deduction.*—To the extent that a protective claim for refund is filed with respect to a claim or expense that would have been deductible under section 2053(a) or (b) if such item already had been paid and that is payable out of a share that meets the requirements for a charitable deduction under section 2055 or a marital deduction under section 2056 or section 2056A, or from a combination thereof, neither the charitable deduction nor the marital deduction shall be reduced by the amount of such claim or expense until the amount is actually paid or meets the requirements of paragraph (d)(4) of this section for deducting certain ascertainable amounts or the requirements of § 20.2053-4(b) or (c) for deducting certain claims against the estate.

(6) [Reserved].

(7) *Examples.*—Assume that the amounts described in section 2053(a) are payable out of property subject to claims and are allowable by the law of the jurisdiction governing the administration of the estate, whether the applicable jurisdiction is within or outside of the United States. Assume that the claims against the estate are not deductible under § 20.2053-4(b) or (c). Also assume, unless otherwise provided, that none of the limitations on the amount of the deduction described in this section apply to the deduction claimed under section 2053. The following examples illustrate the application of this paragraph (d):

Example 1. Amount of expense ascertainable. Decedent's (D's) estate was probated in State. State law provides that the personal representative shall receive compensation equal to 2.5 percent of the value of the probate estate. The executor (E) may claim a deduction for estimated fees equal to 2.5 percent of D's probate estate on the Form 706 filed for D's estate under the rule for deducting certain ascertainable amounts set forth in paragraph (d)(4) of this section, provided that the estimated amount will be paid. However, the Commissioner will disallow the deduction upon examination of the estate's Form 706 to the extent that the amount for which a deduction was claimed no longer satisfies the requirements of paragraph (d)(4) of this section. If this occurs, E may file a protective claim for refund in accordance with paragraph (d)(5) of this section in order to preserve the estate's right to claim a refund for the amount of the fee that is subsequently paid or that subsequently meets the requirements of paragraph (d)(4) of this section for deducting certain ascertainable amounts.

Example 2. Amount of claim not ascertainable. Prior to death, Decedent (D) is sued by Claimant (C) for $100x in a tort proceeding and responds asserting affirmative defenses available to D under applicable local law. C and D are unrelated. D subsequently dies and D's Form 706 is due before a final judgment is entered in the case. The executor of D's estate (E) may not claim a deduction with respect to C's claim on D's Form 706 under the special rule contained in paragraph (d)(4) of this section because the deductible amount cannot be ascertained with reasonable certainty. However, E may file a timely protective claim for refund in accordance with paragraph (d)(5) of this section in order to preserve the estate's right to subsequently claim a refund at the time a final judgment is entered in the case and the claim is either paid or meets the requirements of paragraph (d)(4) of this section for deducting certain ascertainable amounts.

Example 3. Amount of claim payable out of property qualifying for marital deduction. The facts are the same as in *Example 2* except that the applicable credit amount, under section 2010, against the estate tax was fully consumed by D's lifetime gifts, D is survived by Spouse (S), and D's estate passes entirely to S in a bequest that qualifies for the marital deduction under section 2056. Even though any amount D's estate ultimately pays with respect to C's claim will be paid from the assets qualifying for the marital deduction, in filing Form 706, E need not reduce the amount of the marital deduction claimed on D's Form 706. Instead, pursuant to the protective claim for refund filed by E, the marital deduction will be reduced by the claim once a final judgment is entered in the case. At that time, a deduction will be allowed for the amount that is either paid or meets the requirements of paragraph (d)(4) of this section for deducting certain ascertainable amounts.

(e) *Disallowance of double deductions.*—See section 642(g) and § 1.642(g)-1 with respect to the disallowance for income tax purposes of certain deductions unless the right to take such deductions for estate tax purposes is waived.

(f) *Effective/applicability date.*—This section applies to the estates of decedents dying on or after October 20, 2009. [Reg. § 20.2053-1.]

☐ [*T.D.* 6296, 6-23-58. *Amended by T.D.* 7238, 12-28-72 *and T.D.* 9468, 10-16-2009 (*corrected* 11-24-2009).]

[Reg. § 20.2053-2]

§ 20.2053-2. Deduction for funeral expenses.—Such amounts for funeral expenses are allowed as deductions from a decedent's gross estate as (a) are actually expended, (b) would be properly allowable out of property subject to claims under the laws of the local jurisdiction, and (c) satisfy the requirements of paragraph (c) of § 20.2053-1. A reasonable expenditure for a tombstone, monument, or mausoleum, or for a burial lot, either for the decedent or his family, including a reasonable expenditure for its future care, may be deducted under this heading, provided such an expenditure is allowable by the local law. Included in funeral expenses is the cost of transportation of the person bringing the body to the place of burial. [Reg. § 20.2053-2.]

☐ [*T.D.* 6296, 6-23-58.]

[Reg. § 20.2053-3]

§ 20.2053-3. Deduction for expenses of administering estate.—(a) *In general.*—The amounts deductible from a decedent's gross estate as "administration expenses" of the first category (see paragraphs (a) and (c) of § 20.2053-1) are limited to such expenses as are actually and necessarily incurred in the administration of the decedent's estate; that is, in the collection of assets, payment of debts, and distribution of property to the persons entitled to it. The expenses contemplated in the law are such only as attend the settlement of an estate and the transfer of the property of the estate to individual beneficiaries or to a trustee, whether the trustee is the executor or some other person. Expenditures not essential to the proper settlement of the estate, but incurred for the individual benefit of the heirs, legatees, or devisees, may not be taken as deductions. Administration expenses include (1) executor's commissions; (2) attorney's fees; and (3) miscellaneous expenses. Each of these classes is considered separately in paragraphs (b) through (d) of this section.

(b) *Executor's commissions.*—(1) Executors' commissions are deductible to the extent permitted by § 20.2053-1 and this section, but no deduction may be taken if no commissions are to be paid. In addition, the amount of the commissions claimed as a deduction must be in accordance with the usually accepted standards and practice of allowing such an amount in estates of similar size and character in the jurisdiction in which the estate is being administered, or any deviation from the usually accepted standards or range of amounts (permissible under applicable local law) must be justified to the satisfaction of the Commissioner.

(2) A bequest or devise to the executor in lieu of commissions is not deductible. If, however, the terms of the will set forth the compensation payable to the executor for services to be rendered in the administration of the estate, a deduction may be taken to the extent that the amount so fixed does not exceed the compensation allowable by the local law or practice and to the extent permitted by § 20.2053-1.

(3) Except to the extent that a trustee is in fact performing services with respect to property subject to claims which would normally be performed by an executor, amounts paid as trustees' commissions do not constitute expenses of administration under the first category, and are only deductible as expenses of the second category to the extent provided in § 20.2053-8.

(c) *Attorney's fees.*—(1) Attorney's fees are deductible to the extent permitted by § 20.2053-1 and this section. Further, the amount of the fees claimed as a deduction may not exceed a reasonable remuneration for the services rendered, taking into account the size and character of the estate, the law and practice in the jurisdiction in which the estate is being administered, and the skill and expertise of the attorneys.

(2) A deduction for attorneys' fees incurred in contesting an asserted deficiency or in prosecuting a claim for refund should be claimed at the time the deficiency is contested or the refund claim is prosecuted. A deduction for reasonable attorney's fees actually incurred in contesting an asserted deficiency or in prosecuting a claim for refund will be allowed to the extent permitted by § 20.2053-1 even though the deduction, as such, was not claimed on the estate tax return or in the claim for refund. A deduction for these fees shall not be denied, and the sufficiency of a claim for

refund shall not be questioned, solely by reason of the fact that the amount of the fees to be paid was not established at the time that the right to the deduction was claimed.

(3) Attorneys' fees incurred by beneficiaries incident to litigation as to their respective interests are not deductible if the litigation is not essential to the proper settlement of the estate within the meaning of paragraph (a) of this section. An attorney's fee not meeting this test is not deductible as an administration expense under section 2053 and this section, even if it is approved by a probate court as an expense payable or reimbursable by the estate.

(d) *Miscellaneous administration expenses.*—(1) Miscellaneous administration expenses include such expenses as court costs, surrogates' fees, accountants' fees, appraisers' fees, clerk hire, etc. Expenses necessarily incurred in preserving and distributing the estate, including the cost of storing or maintaining property of the estate if it is impossible to effect immediate distribution to the beneficiaries, are deductible to the extent permitted by § 20.2053-1. Expenses for preserving and caring for the property may not include outlays for additions or improvements; nor will such expenses be allowed for a longer period than the executor is reasonably required to retain the property.

(2) Expenses for selling property of the estate are deductible to the extent permitted by § 20.2053-1 if the sale is necessary in order to pay the decedent's debts, expenses of administration, or taxes, to preserve the estate, or to effect distribution. The phrase "expenses for selling property" includes brokerage fees and other expenses attending the sale, such as the fees of an auctioneer if it is reasonably necessary to employ one. Where an item included in the gross estate is disposed of in a bona fide sale (including a redemption) to a dealer in such items at a price below its fair market value, for purposes of this paragraph there shall be treated as an expense for selling the item whichever of the following amounts is the lesser: (i) the amount by which the fair market value of the property on the applicable valuation date exceeds the proceeds of the sale, or (ii) the amount by which the fair market value of the property on the date of the sale exceeds the proceeds of the sale. The principles used in determining the value at which an item of property is included in the gross estate shall be followed in arriving at the fair market value of the property for purposes of this paragraph. See §§ 20.2031-1 through 20.2031-9.

(3) Expenses incurred in defending the estate against claims described in section 2053(a)(3) are deductible to the extent permitted by § 20.2053-1 if the expenses are incurred incident to the assertion of defenses to the claim available under the applicable law, even if the estate ultimately does not prevail. For purposes of this paragraph (d)(3), "expenses incurred in defending the estate against claims" include costs relating to the arbitration and mediation of contested issues, costs associated with defending the estate against claims (whether or not enforceable), and costs associated with reaching a negotiated settlement of the issues.

(e) *Effective/applicability date.*—This section applies to the estates of decedents dying on or after October 20, 2009. [Reg. § 20.2053-3.]

□ [*T.D.* 6296, 6-23-58. *Amended by T.D.* 6826, 6-14-65; *T.D.* 7612, 4-19-79 *and T.D.* 9468, 10-16-2009.]

[Reg. § 20.2053-4]

§ 20.2053-4. Deduction for claims against the estate.—(a) *In general.*—(1) *General rule.*—For purposes of this section, liabilities imposed by law or arising out of contracts or torts are deductible if they meet the applicable requirements set forth in § 20.2053-1 and this section. To be deductible, a claim against a decedent's estate must represent a personal obligation of the decedent existing at the time of the decedent's death. Except as otherwise provided in paragraphs (b) and (c) of this section and to the extent permitted by § 20.2053-1, the amounts that may be deducted as claims against a decedent's estate are limited to the amounts of bona fide claims that are enforceable against the decedent's estate (and are not unenforceable when paid) and claims that—

(i) Are actually paid by the estate in satisfaction of the claim; or

(ii) Meet the requirements of § 20.2053-1(d)(4) for deducting certain ascertainable amounts.

(2) *Effect of post-death events.*—Events occurring after the date of a decedent's death shall be considered in determining whether and to what extent a deduction is allowable under section 2053. See § 20.2053-1(d)(2).

(b) *Exception for claims and counterclaims in related matter.*—(1) *General rule.*—If a decedent's gross estate includes one or more claims or causes of action and there are one or more claims against the decedent's estate in the same or a substantiallyrelated matter, or, if a decedent's gross estate includes a particular asset and there are one or more claims against the decedent's estate integrally related to that particular asset, the executor may deduct on the estate's United States Estate (and Generation-Skipping Transfer) Tax Return (Form 706) the current value of the claim or claims against the estate, even though payment has not been made, provided that—

(i) Each such claim against the estate otherwise satisfies the applicable requirements set forth in § 20.2053-1;

(ii) Each such claim against the estate represents a personal obligation of the decedent existing at the time of the decedent's death;

(iii) Each such claim is enforceable against the decedent's estate (and is not unenforceable when paid);

(iv) The value of each such claim against the estate is determined from a "qualified appraisal" performed by a "qualified appraiser" within the meaning of section 170 of the Internal Revenue Code and the corresponding regulations;

(v) The value of each such claim against the estate is subject to adjustment for post-death events; and

(vi) The aggregate value of the related claims or assets included in the decedent's gross estate exceeds 10 percent of the decedent's gross estate.

(2) *Limitation on deduction.*—The deduction under this paragraph (b) is limited to the value of the related claims or particular assets included in decedent's gross estate.

(3) *Effect of post-death events.*—If, under this paragraph (b), a deduction is claimed on Form 706 for a claim against the estate and, during the period described in § 20.2053-1(d)(2), the claim is paid or meets the requirements of § 20.2053-1(d)(4) for deducting certain ascertainable amounts, the claimed deduction is subject to adjustment to reflect, and may not exceed, the amount paid on the claim or the amount meeting the requirements of § 20.2053-1(d)(4). If, under this paragraph (b), a deduction is claimed on Form 706 for a claim against the estate and, during the period described in § 20.2053-1(d)(2), the claim remains unpaid (and does not meet the requirements of § 20.2053-1(d)(4) for deducting certain ascertainable amounts), the claimed deduction is subject to adjustment to reflect, and may not exceed, the current valuation of the claim. A valuation of the claim will be considered current if it reflects events occurring after the decedent's death. With regard to any amount in excess of the amount deductible under this paragraph (b), an estate may preserve the estate's right to claim a refund for claims that are paid or that meet the requirements of § 20.2053-(1)(d)(4) after the expiration of the period of limitation for filing a claim for refund by filing a protective claim for refund in accordance with the rules in § 20.2053-1(d)(5).

(c) *Exception for claims totaling not more than $500,000.*—(1) *General rule.*—An executor may deduct on Form 706 the current value of one or more claims against the estate even though payment has not been made on the claim or claims to the extent that—

(i) Each such claim against the estate otherwise satisfies the applicable requirements for deductibility set forth in § 20.2053-1;

(ii) Each such claim against the estate represents a personal obligation of the decedent existing at the time of the decedent's death;

(iii) Each such claim is enforceable against the decedent's estate (and is not unenforceable when paid);

(iv) The value of each such claim against the estate is determined from a "qualified appraisal" performed by a "qualified appraiser" within the meaning of section 170 of the Internal Revenue Code and the corresponding regulations;

(v) The total amount deducted by the estate under this paragraph (c) does not exceed $500,000;

(vi) The full value of each claim, rather than just a portion of that amount, must be deductible under this paragraph (c) and, for this purpose, the full value of each such claim is deemed to be the unpaid amount of that claim that is not deductible after the application of §§ 20.2053-1 and 20.2053-4(b); and

(vii) The value of each claim deducted under this paragraph (c) is subject to adjustment for post-death events.

(2) *Effect of post-death events.*—If, under this paragraph (c), a deduction is claimed for a claim against the estate and, during the period described in § 20.2053-1(d)(2), the claim is paid or meets the requirements of § 20.2053-1(d)(4) for deducting certain ascertainable amounts, the amount of the allowable deduction for that claim is subject to adjustment to reflect, and may not exceed, the amount paid on the claim or the amount meeting the requirements of § 20.2053-1(d)(4). If, under this paragraph (c), a deduction is claimed for a claim against the estate and, during the period described in § 20.2053-1(d)(2), the claim remains unpaid (and does not meet the requirements of § 20.2053-1(d)(4) for deducting certain ascertainable amounts), the amount of the allowable deduction for that claim is subject to adjustment to reflect, and may not exceed, the current value of the claim. The value of the claim will be considered current if it reflects events occurring after the decedent's death. To claim a deduction for amounts in excess of the amount deductible under this paragraph (c), the estate may preserve the estate's right to claim a refund for claims that are not paid or that do not meet the requirements of § 20.2053-1(d)(4) until after the expiration of the period of limitation for the filing of a claim for refund by filing a protective claim for refund in accordance with the rules in § 20.2053-1(d)(5).

(3) *Examples.*—The following examples illustrate the application of this paragraph (c). Assume that the value of each claim is determined from a "qualified appraisal" performed by a "qualified appraiser" and reflects events occurring after the death of the decedent (D). Also assume that each claim represents a personal obligation of D that existed at D's death, that each claim is enforceable against the decedent's estate (and is not unenforceable when paid), and that each claim otherwise satisfies the requirements for deductibility of § 20.2053-1.

Example 1. There are three claims against the estate of the decedent (D) that are not paid and are not deductible under § 20.2053-1(d)(4) or paragraph (b) of this section: $25,000 of Claimant A, $35,000 of Claimant B, and $1,000,000 of Claimant C. The executor of D's estate (E) may not claim a deduction under this paragraph with respect to any portion of the claim of Claimant C because the value of that claim exceeds $500,000. E may claim a deduction under this paragraph for the total amount of the claims filed by Claimant A and Claimant B ($60,000) because the aggregate value of the full amount of those claims does not exceed $500,000.

Example 2. There are three claims against the estate of the decedent (D) that are not paid and are not deductible under § 20.2053-1(d)(4) or paragraph (b) of this section; specifically, a separate $200,000 claim of each of three claimants, A, B and C. The executor of D's estate (E) may claim a deduction under this paragraph for any two of these three claims because the aggregate value of the full amount of any two of the claims does not exceed $500,000. E may not deduct any part of the value of the remaining claim under this paragraph because the aggregate value of the full amount of all three claims would exceed $500,000.

Example 3. As a result of an automobile accident involving the decedent (D) and A, D's gross estate includes a claim against A that is valued at $750,000. In the same matter, A files a counterclaim against D's estate that is valued at $1,000,000. A's claim against D's estate is not paid and is not deductible under § 20.2053-1(d)(4). All other section 2053 claims and expenses of D's estate have been paid and are deductible. The executor of D's estate (E) deducts $750,000 of A's claim against the estate under § 20.2053-4(b). E may claim a deduction under this paragraph (c) for the total value of A's claim not deducted under § 20.2053-4(b), or $250,000. If, instead, the value of A's claim against D's estate is $1,500,000, so that the amount not deductible under § 20.2053-4(b) exceeds $500,000, no deduction is available under this paragraph (c).

(d) *Special rules.*—(1) *Potential and unmatured claims.*—Except as provided in § 20.2053-1(d)(4) and in paragraphs (b) and (c) of this section, no estate tax deduction may be taken for a claim against the decedent's estate while it remains a potential or unmatured claim. Claims that later mature may be deducted (to the extent permitted by § 20.2053-1) in connection with a timely claim for refund. To preserve the estate's right to claim a refund for claims that mature and become deductible after the expiration of the period of limitation for filing a claim for refund, a protective claim for refund may be filed in accordance with § 20.2053-1(d)(5). See § 20.2053-1(b)(3) for rules relating to the treatment of court decrees and settlements.

(2) *Contested claims.*—Except as provided in paragraphs (b) and (c) of this section, no estate tax deduction may be taken for a claim against the decedent's estate to the extent the estate is contesting the decedent's liability. Contested claims that later mature may be deducted (to the extent permitted by § 20.2053-1) in connection with a claim for refund filed within the time prescribed in section 6511(a). To preserve the estate's right to claim a refund for claims that mature and become deductible after the expiration of the period of limitation for the filing a claim for refund, a protective claim for refund may be filed in accordance with § 20.2053-1(d)(5). See § 20.2053-1(b)(3) for rules relating to the treatment of court decrees and settlements.

(3) *Claims against multiple parties.*—If the decedent or the decedent's estate is one of two or more parties against whom the claim is being asserted, the estate may deduct only the portion of the total claim due from and paid by the estate, reduced by the total of any reimbursement received from another party, insurance, or otherwise. The estate's deductible portion also will be reduced by the contribution or other amount the estate could have collected from another party or an insurer but which the estate declines or fails to attempt to collect. See further § 20.2053-1(d)(3).

(4) *Unenforceable claims.*—Claims that are unenforceable prior to or at the decedent's death are not deductible, even if they are actually paid. Claims that become unenforceable during the administration of the estate are not deductible to the extent that they are paid (or will be paid) after they become unenforceable. However, see § 20.2053-1(b)(3)(iv) regarding a claim whose enforceability is at issue.

(5) *Claims founded upon a promise.*—Except with regard to pledges or subscriptions (see § 20.2053-5), section 2053(c)(1)(A) provides that the deduction for a claim founded upon a promise or agreement is limited to the extent that the promise or agreement was bona fide and in exchange for adequate and full consideration in money or money's worth; that is, the promise or agreement must have been bargained for at arm's length and the price must have been an adequate and full equivalent reducible to a money value.

(6) *Recurring payments.*—(i) *Noncontingent obligations.*—If a decedent is obligated to make recurring payments on an enforceable and certain claim that satisfies the requirements for deductibility under this section and the payments are not subject to a contingency, the amount of the claim will be deemed ascertainable with reasonable certainty for purposes of the rule for deducting certain ascertainable amounts set forth in § 20.2053-1(d)(4). If the recurring payments will be paid, a deduction will be allowed under the rule for deducting certain ascertainable amounts set forth in § 20.2053-1(d)(4) (subject to any applicable limitations in § 20.2053-1). Recurring payments for purposes of this section exclude those payments made in connection with a mortgage or indebtedness described in and governed by § 20.2053-7. If a decedent's obligation to make a recurring payment is contingent on the death or remarriage of the claimant and otherwise satisfies the requirements of this paragraph (d)(6)(i), the amount of the claim (measured according to actuarial principles, using factors set forth in the transfer tax regulations or otherwise provided by the IRS) will be deemed ascertainable with reasonable certainty for purposes of the rule for deducting certain ascertainable amounts set forth in § 20.2053-1(d)(4).

(ii) *Contingent obligations.*—If a decedent has a recurring obligation to pay an enforceable and certain claim but the decedent's obligation is subject to a contingency or is not otherwise described in paragraph (d)(6)(i) of this section, the amount of the claim is not ascertainable with reasonable certainty for purposes of the rule for deducting certain ascertainable amounts set forth in § 20.2053-1(d)(4). Accordingly, the amount deductible is limited to amounts actually paid by the estate in satisfaction of the claim in accordance with § 20.2053-1(d)(1) (subject to any applicable limitations in § 20.2053-1).

(iii) *Purchase of commercial annuity to satisfy recurring obligation to pay.*—If a decedent has a recurring obligation (whether or not contingent) to pay an enforceable and certain claim and the estate purchases a commercial annuity from an unrelated dealer in commercial annuities in an arm's-length transaction to satisfy the obligation, the amount deductible by the estate (subject to any applicable limitations in § 20.2053-1) is the sum of—

(A) The amount paid for the commercial annuity, to the extent that the amount paid is not refunded, or expected to be refunded, to the estate;

(B) Any amount actually paid to the claimant by the estate prior to the purchase of the commercial annuity; and

(C) Any amount actually paid to the claimant by the estate in excess of the annuity amount as is necessary to satisfy the recurring obligation.

(7) *Examples.*—The following examples illustrate the application of paragraph (d) of this section. Except as is otherwise provided in the examples, assume—

(i) A claim satisfies the applicable requirements set forth in § 20.2053-1 and paragraph (a) of this section, is payable from property subject to claims, and the amount of the claim is not subject to any other applicable limitations in § 20.2053-1;

(ii) A claim is not deductible under paragraphs (b) or (c) of this section as an exception to the general rule contained in paragraph (a) of this section; and

(iii) The claimant (C) is not a family member, related entity or beneficiary of the estate of decedent (D) and is not the executor (E).

Example 1. Contested claim, single defendant, no decision. D is sued by C for $100x in a tort proceeding and responds asserting affirmative defenses available to D under applicable local law. D dies and E is substituted as defendant in the suit. D's Form 706 is due before a judgment is reached in the case. D's gross estate exceeds $100x. E may not take a deduction on Form 706 for the claim against the estate. However, E may claim a deduction under § 20.2053-3(c) or § 20.2053-3(d)(3) for expenses incurred in defending the estate against the claim if the expenses have been paid in accordance with § 20.2053-1(d)(1) or if the expenses meet the requirements of § 20.2053-1(d)(4) for deducting certain ascertainable amounts. E may file a protective claim for refund before the expiration of the period of limitation prescribed in section 6511(a) in order to preserve the estate's right to claim a refund, if the amount of the claim will not be paid or cannot be ascertained with reasonable certainty by the expiration of this limitation period. If payment is subsequently made pursuant to a court decision or a settlement, the payment, as well as expenses incurred incident to the claim and not previously deducted, may be deducted and relief may be sought in connection with a timely-filed claim for refund.

Example 2. Contested claim, single defendant, final court decree and payment. The facts are the same as in *Example 1* except that, before the Form 706 is timely filed, the court enters a decision in favor of C, no timely appeal is filed, and payment is made. E may claim a deduction on Form 706 for the amount paid in satisfaction of the claim against the estate pursuant to the final decision of the local court, including any interest accrued prior to D's death. In addition, E may claim a deduction under § 20.2053-3(c) or § 20.2053-3(d)(3) for expenses incurred in defending the estate against the claim and in processing payment of the claim if the expenses have been paid in accordance with § 20.2053-1(d)(1) or if the expenses meet the requirements of § 20.2053-1(d)(4) for deducting certain ascertainable amounts.

Example 3. Contested claim, single defendant, settlement and payment. The facts are the same as in *Example 1* except that a settlement is reached between E and C for $80x and payment is made before Form 706 is timely filed. E may claim a deduction on Form 706 for the amount paid to C ($80x) in satisfaction of the claim against the estate. In addition, E may claim a deduction under § 20.2053-3(c) or § 20.2053-3(d)(3) for expenses incurred in defending the estate, reaching a settlement, and processing payment of the claim if the expenses have been paid in accordance with § 20.2053-1(d)(1) or if the expenses meet the requirements of § 20.2053-1(d)(4) for deducting certain ascertainable amounts.

Example 4. Contested claim, multiple defendants. The facts are the same as in *Example 1* except that the suit filed by C lists D and an unrelated third-party (K) as defendants. If the claim against the estate is not resolved prior to the time the Form 706 is filed, E may not take a deduction for the claim on Form 706. If payment is subsequently made of D's share of the claim pursuant to a court decision holding D liable for 40 percent of the amount due and K liable for 60 percent of the amount due, then E may claim a deduction for the amount paid in satisfaction of the claim against the estate representing D's share of the liability as assigned by the court decree ($40x), plus any interest on that share accrued prior to D's death. If the court decision finds D and K jointly and severally liable for the entire $100x and D's estate pays the entire $100x but could have reasonably collected $50x from K in reimbursement, E may claim a deduction of $50x together with the interest on $50x accrued prior to D's death. In both instances, E also may claim a deduction under § 20.2053-3(c) or § 20.2053-3(d)(3) for expenses incurred and not previously deducted in defending the estate against the claim and processing payment of the amount due from D if the expenses have been paid in accordance with § 20.2053-1(d)(1) or if the expenses meet the requirements of § 20.2053-1(d)(4) for deducting certain ascertainable amounts.

Example 5. Contested claim, multiple defendants, settlement and payment. The facts are the same as in *Example 1* except that the suit filed by C lists D and an unrelated third-party (K) as defendants. D's estate settles with C for $10x and payment is made before Form 706 is timely filed. E may take a deduction on Form 706 for the amount paid to C ($10x) in satisfaction of the claim against the estate. In addition, E may claim a deduction under § 20.2053-3(c) or § 20.2053-3(d)(3) for expenses incurred in defending the estate, reaching a settlement, and processing payment of the claim if the expenses have been paid in accordance with § 20.2053-1(d)(1) or if the expenses meet the requirements of § 20.2053-1(d)(4) for deducting certain ascertainable amounts.

Example 6. Mixed claims. During life, D contracts with C to perform specific work on D's home for $75x. Under the contract, additional work must be approved in advance by D. C performs additional work and sues D for $100x for work completed including the $75x agreed to in the contract. D dies and D's Form 706 is due before a judgment is reached in the case. E accepts liability of $75x but contests liability of $25x. E may take a deduction of $75x on Form 706 if the amount has been paid or meets the requirements of § 20.2053-1(d)(4) for deducting certain ascertainable amounts. In addition, E may claim a deduction under § 20.2053-3(c) or § 20.2053-3(d)(3) for expenses incurred in defending the estate against the claim if the expenses have been paid or if the expenses meet the requirements of § 20.2053-1(d)(4) for deducting certain ascertainable amounts. E may file a protective claim for refund before the expiration of the period of limitation prescribed in section 6511(a) in order to preserve the estate's right to claim a refund for any amount in excess of $75x that is subsequently paid to resolve the claim against the estate. To the extent that any unpaid expenses incurred in defending the estate against the claim are not deducted as an ascertainable amount pursuant to § 20.2053-1(d)(4), they may be included in the protective claim for refund.

Example 7. Claim having issue of enforceability. D is sued by C for $100x in a tort proceeding in which there is an issue as to whether the claim is barred by the applicable period of limitations. After D's death but prior to the decision of the court, a settlement meeting the requirements of § 20.2053-1(b)(3)(iv) is reached between E and C in the amount of $50x. E pays C this amount before the Form 706 is timely filed. E may take a deduction on Form 706 for the amount paid to C ($50x) in satisfaction of the claim. If, subsequent to E's payment to C, facts develop to indicate that the claim was, in fact, unenforceable, the deduction will not be denied provided the enforceability of the claim was at issue in a bona dispute at the time of the payment. See § 20.2053-1(b)(3)(iv). A deduction may be available under § 20.2053-3(d)(3) for expenses incurred in defending the estate, reaching a settlement, and processing payment of the claim if the expenses have been paid in accordance with § 20.2053-1(d)(1) or if the expenses meet the requirements of § 20.2053-1(d)(4) for deducting certain ascertainable amounts.

Example 8. Noncontingent and recurring obligation to pay, binding on estate. D's property settlement agreement incident to D's divorce, signed three years prior to D's death, obligates D or D's estate to pay to S, D's former spouse, $20x per year until S's death or remarriage. Prior to D's death, D made payments in accordance with the agreement and, after D's death, E continues to make the payments in accordance with the agreement. D's obligation to pay S under the property settlement agreement is deemed to be a claim against the estate that is ascertainable with reasonable certainty for purposes of § 20.2053-1(d)(4). To the extent the obligation to make the recurring payment is a claim that will be paid, E may deduct the amount of the claim (measured according to actuarial principles, using factors set forth in the transfer tax regulations or otherwise provided by the IRS) under the rule for deducting certain ascertainable amounts set forth in § 20.2053-1(d)(4).

Example 9. Recurring obligation to pay, estate purchases a commercial annuity in satisfaction. D's settlement agreement with T, the claimant in a suit against D, signed three years prior to D's death, obligates D or D's estate to pay to T $20x per year for 10 years, provided that T does not reveal the details of the claim or of the settlement during that period. D dies in Year 1. In Year 2, D's estate purchases a commercial annuity from an unrelated issuer of commercial annuities, XYZ, to fund the obligation to T. E may deduct the entire amount paid to XYZ to obtain the annuity, even though the obligation to T was contingent.

(e) *Interest on claim.*—(1) Subject to any applicable limitations in § 20.2053-1, the interest on a deductible claim is itself deductible as a claim under section 2053 to the extent of the amount of interest accrued at the decedent's death (even if the executor elects the alternate valuation method under section 2032), but only to the extent of the amount of interest actually paid or meeting the requirements of § 20.2053-1(d)(4) for deducting certain ascertainable amounts.

(2) Post-death accrued interest may be deductible in appropriate circumstances either as an estate tax administration expense under section 2053 or as an income tax deduction.

(f) *Effective/applicability date.*—This section applies to the estates of decedents dying on or after October 20, 2009. [Reg. § 20.2053-4.]

□ [*T.D.* 6296, 6-23-58. *Amended by T.D.* 9468, 10-16-2009 (*corrected* 11-24-2009).]

[Reg. § 20.2053-5]

§ 20.2053-5. Deductions for charitable, etc., pledges or subscriptions.—(a) A pledge or a subscription, evidenced by a promissory note or otherwise, even though enforceable against the estate, is deductible (subject to any applicable limitations in § 20.2053-1) only to the extent that—

(1) Liability therefore was contracted bona fide and for an adequate and full consideration in cash or its equivalent, or

(2) It would have constituted an allowable deduction under section 2055 (relating to charitable, etc., deductions) if it had been a bequest.

(b) *Effective/applicability date.*—This section applies to the estates of decedents dying on or after October 20, 2009. [Reg. § 20.2053-5.]

□ [*T.D.* 6296, 6-23-58. *Amended by T.D.* 9468, 10-16-2009.]

[Reg. § 20.2053-6]

§ 20.2053-6. Deduction for taxes.—(a) *In general.*—(1) Taxes are deductible in computing a decedent's gross estate—

(i) Only as claims against the estate (except to the extent that excise taxes may be allowable as administration expenses);

(ii) Only to the extent not disallowed by section 2053(c)(1)(B) and this section; and

(iii) Subject to any applicable limitations in § 20.2053-1.

(2) See §§ 20.2053-9 and 20.2053-10 with respect to the deduction allowed for certain state and foreign death taxes.

(b) *Property taxes.*—Property taxes are not deductible unless they accrued before the decedent's death. However, they are not deductible merely because they have accrued in an accounting sense. Property taxes in order to be deductible must be an enforceable obligation of the decedent at the time of his death.

(c) *Death taxes.*—(1) For the estates of decedents dying on or before December 31, 2004, no estate, succession, legacy or inheritance tax payable by reason of the decedent's death is deductible, except as provided in §§ 20.2053-9 and 20.2053-10 with respect to certain state and foreign death taxes on transfers for charitable, etc., uses. However, see sections 2011 and 2014 and the corresponding regulations with respect to credits for death taxes.

(2) For the estates of decedents dying after December 31, 2004, see section 2058 to determine the deductibility of state death taxes.

(d) *Gift taxes.*—Unpaid gift taxes on gifts made by a decedent before his death are deductible. If a gift is considered as made one-half by the decedent and one-half by his spouse under section 2513, the entire amount of the gift tax, unpaid at the decedent's death, attributable to a gift in fact made by the decedent is deductible. No portion of the tax attributable to a gift in fact made by the decedent's spouse is deductible except to the extent that the obligation is enforced against the decedent's estate and his estate has no effective right of contribution against his spouse. (See section 2012 and § 20.2012-1 with respect to credit for gift taxes paid upon gifts of property included in a decedent's gross estate.)

(e) *Excise taxes.*—Excise taxes incurred in selling property of a decedent's estate are deductible as an expense of administration if the sale is necessary in order to (1) pay the decedent's debts, expenses of administration, or taxes, (2) preserve the estate, or (3) effect distribution. Excise taxes incurred in distributing property of the estate in kind are also deductible.

(f) *Income taxes.*—Unpaid income taxes are deductible if they are on income properly includible in an income tax return of the decedent for a period before his death. Taxes on income received after the decedent's death are not deductible. If income received by a decedent during his lifetime is included in a joint income tax return filed by the decedent and his spouse, or by the decedent's estate and his surviving spouse, the portion of the joint liability for the period covered by the return for which a deduction would be allowed is the amount for which the decedent's estate would be liable under local law, as between the decedent and his spouse, after enforcement of any effective right of reimbursement or contribution. In the absence of evidence to the contrary, the deductible amount is presumed to be an amount bearing the same ratio to the total joint tax liability for the period covered by the return that the amount of income tax for which the decedent would have been liable if he had filed a separate return for that period bears to the total of the amounts for which the decedent and his spouse would have been liable if they had both filed separate returns for that period. Thus, in the absence of evidence to the contrary, the deductible amount equals

$$\frac{\text{decedent's separate tax}}{\text{both separate taxes}} \times \text{joint tax.}$$

However, the deduction cannot in any event exceed the lesser of—

(1) The decedent's liability for the period (as determined in this paragraph) reduced by the amounts already contributed by the decedent toward payment of the joint liability, or

(2) If there is an enforceable agreement between the decedent and his spouse or between the executor and the spouse relative to the payment of the joint liability, the amount which pursuant to the agreement is to be contributed by the estate toward payment of the joint liability.

If the decedent's estate and his surviving spouse are entitled to a refund on account of an overpayment of a joint income tax liability, the overpayment is an asset includible in the decedent's gross estate under section 2033 in the amount to which the estate would be entitled under local law, as between the estate and the surviving spouse. In the absence of evidence to the contrary, the includible amount is presumed to be the amount by which the decedent's contributions toward payment of the joint tax exceeds his liability determined in accordance with the principles set forth in this paragraph (other than subparagraph (1) of this paragraph).

(g) *Post-death adjustments of deductible tax liability*.—Post-death adjustments increasing a tax liability accrued prior to the decedent's death, including increases of taxes deducted under this section, will increase the amount of the deduction available under section 2053(a)(3) for that tax liability. Similarly, any refund subsequently determined to be due to and received by the estate or its successor in interest with respect to taxes deducted by the estate under this section reduce the amount of the deduction taken for that tax liability under section 2053(a)(3). Expenses associated with defending the estate against the increase in tax liability or with obtaining the refund may be deductible under § 20.2053-3(d)(3). A protective claim for refund of estate taxes may be filed before the expiration of the period of limitation for filing a claim for refund in order to preserve the estate's right to claim a refund if the amount of a deductible tax liability may be affected by such an adjustment or refund. The application of this section may be illustrated by the following examples:

Example 1. Increase in tax due. After the decedent's death, the Internal Revenue Service examines the gift tax return filed by the decedent in the year before the decedent's death and asserts a deficiency of $100x. The estate pays attorney's fees of $30x in a non-frivolous defense against the increased deficiency. The final determination of the deficiency, in the amount of $90x, is paid by the estate prior to the expiration of the limitation period for filing a claim for refund. The estate may deduct $90x under section 2053(a)(3) and $30x under § 20.2053-3(c)(2) or (d)(3) in connection with a timely claim for refund.

Example 2. Refund of taxes paid. Decedent's estate timely files D's individual income tax return for the year in which the decedent died. The estate timely pays the entire amount of the tax due, $50x, as shown on that return. The entire $50x was attributable to income received prior to the decedent's death. Decedent's estate subsequently discovers an error on the income tax return and timely files a claim for refund of income tax. Decedent's estate receives a refund of $10x. The estate is allowed a deduction of only $40x under section 2053(a)(3) for the income tax liability accrued prior to the decedent's death. If D's estate had claimed a deduction of $50x on D's United States Estate (and Generation-Skipping Transfer) Tax Return (Form 706), the deduction claimed under section 2053(a)(3) will be allowed only to the extent of $40x upon examination by the Commissioner.

(h) *Effective/applicability date*.—This section applies to the estates of decedents dying on or after October 20, 2009. [Reg. § 20.2053-6.]

□ [*T.D. 6296, 6-23-58. Amended by T.D. 9468*, 10-16-2009.]

[Reg. § 20.2053-7]

§ 20.2053-7. Deduction for unpaid mortgages.—A deduction is allowed from a decedent's gross estate of the full unpaid amount of a mortgage upon, or of any other indebtedness in respect of, any property of the gross estate, including interest which had accrued thereon to the date of death, provided the value of the property, undiminished by the amount of the mortgage or indebtedness, is included in the value of the gross estate. If the decedent's estate is liable for the amount of the mortgage or indebtedness, the full value of the property subject to the mortgage or indebtedness must be included as part of the value of the gross estate; the amount of the mortgage or indebtedness being in such case allowed as a deduction. But if the decedent's estate is not so liable, only the value of the equity of redemption (or the value of the property, less the mortgage or indebtedness) need be returned as part of the value of the gross estate. In no case may the deduction on account of the mortgage or indebtedness exceed the liability therefor contracted bona fide and for an adequate and full consideration in money or money's worth. See § 20.2043-1. Only interest accrued to the date of the decedent's death is allowable even though the alternate valuation method under section 2032 is selected. In any case where real property situated outside the United States does not form a part of the gross estate, no deduction may be taken of any mortgage thereon or any other indebtedness in respect thereof. [Reg. § 20.2053-7.]

□ [*T.D. 6296, 6-23-58. Amended by T.D. 6684*, 10-23-63.]

[Reg. § 20.2053-8]

§ 20.2053-8. Deduction for expenses in administering property not subject to claims.—(a) Expenses incurred in administering property included in a decedent's gross estate but not subject to claims fall within the second category of deductions set forth in § 20.2053-1, and may be allowed as deductions if they—

(1) Would be allowed as deductions in the first category if the property being administered were subject to claims; and

(2) Were paid before the expiration of the period of limitation for assessment provided in section 6501.

Usually, these expenses are incurred in connection with the administration of a trust established by a decedent during his lifetime. They may also be incurred in connection with the collection of other assets or the transfer or clearance of title to other property included in a decedent's gross estate for estate tax purposes but not included in his probate estate.

(b) These expenses may be allowed as deductions only to the extent that they would be allowed as deductions under the first category if the property were subject to claims. See § 20.2053-3. The only expenses in administering property not subject to claims which are allowed as deductions are those occasioned by the decedent's death and incurred in settling the decedent's interest in the property or vesting good title to the property in the beneficiaries. Expenses not coming within the description in the preceding sentence but incurred on behalf of the transferees are not deductible.

(c) The principles set forth in paragraphs (b), (c), and (d) of § 20.2053-3 (relating to the allowance of executor's commissions, attorney's fees, and miscellaneous administration expenses of the first category) are applied in determining the extent to which trustee's commissions, attorney's and accountant's fees, and miscellaneous administration expenses are allowed in connection with the administration of property not subject to claims.

(d) The application of this section may be illustrated by the following examples:

Example (1). In 1940, the decedent made an irrevocable transfer of property to the X Trust Company, as trustee. The instrument of transfer provided that the trustee should pay the income from the property to the decedent for the duration of his life and, upon his death, distribute the corpus of the trust among designated beneficiaries. The property was included in the decedent's gross estate under the provisions of section 2036. Three months after the date of death, the trustee distributed the trust corpus among the beneficiaries, except for $6,000 which it withheld. The amount withheld represented $5,000 which it retained as trustee's commissions in connection with the termination of the trust and $1,000 which it had paid to an attorney for representing it in connection with the termination. Both the trustee's commissions and the attorney's fees were allowable under the law of the jurisdiction in which the trust was being administered, were reasonable in amount, and were in accord with local custom. Under these circumstances, the estate is allowed a deduction of $6,000.

Example (2). In 1945, the decedent made an irrevocable transfer of property to Y Trust Company, as trustee. The instrument of transfer provided that the trustee should pay the income from the property to the decedent during his life. If the decedent's wife survived him, the trust was to continue for the duration of her life, with Y Trust Company and the decedent's son as co-trustees, and with income payable to the decedent's wife for the duration of her life. Upon the death of both the decedent and his wife, the corpus is to be distributed among designated remaindermen. The decedent was survived by his wife. The property was included in the decedent's gross estate under the provisions of section 2036. In accordance with local custom, the trustee made an accounting to the court as of the date of the decedent's death. Following the death of the decedent, a controversy arose among the remaindermen as to their respective rights under the instrument of transfer, and a suit was brought in court to which the trustee was made a party. As a part of the accounting, the court approved the following expenses which the trustee had paid within 3 years following the date of death: $10,000, trustee's commissions; $5,000, accountant's fees; $25,000, attorney's fees; and $2,500, representing fees paid to the guardian of a remainderman who was a minor. The trustee's commissions and accountant's fees were for services in connection with the usual issues involved in a trust accounting as also were one-half of the attorney's and guardian's fees. The remainder of the attorney's and guardian's fees were for services performed in connection with the suit brought by the remaindermen. The amount allowed as a deduction is the $28,750 ($10,000, trustee's commissions; $5,000, accountant's fees; $12,500, attorney's fees; and $1,250, guardian's fees) incurred as expenses in connection with the usual issues involved in a trust accounting. The remaining expenses are not allowed as deductions since they were incurred on behalf of the transferees.

Example (3). Decedent in 1950 made an irrevocable transfer of property to the Z Trust Company, as trustee. The instrument of transfer provided that the trustee should pay the income from the property to the decedent's wife for the duration of her life. If the decedent survived his wife the trust corpus was to be returned to him but if he did not survive her, then upon the death of the wife, the trust corpus was to be distributed among their children. The decedent predeceased his wife and the transferred property, less the value of the wife's outstanding life estate, was included in his gross estate under the provisions of section 2037 since his reversionary interest therein immediately before his death was in excess of 5 percent of the value of the property. At the wife's request, the court ordered the trustee to render an accounting of the trust property as of the date of the decedent's death. No deduction will be allowed the decedent's estate for any of the expenses incurred in connection with the trust accounting, since the expenses were incurred on behalf of the wife.

Example (4). If, in the preceding example, the decedent died without other property and no executor or administrator of his estate was appointed, so that it was necessary for the trustee to prepare an estate tax return and participate in its audit, or if the trustee required accounting proceedings for its own protection in accordance with local custom, trustees', attorneys', and guardians' fees in connection with the estate tax or accounting proceedings would be deductible to the same extent that they would be deductible if the property were subject to claims. Deductions incurred under similar circumstances by a surviving joint tenant or the recipient of life insurance proceeds would also be deductible. [Reg. § 20.2053-8.]

☐ [*T.D.* 6296, 6-23-58.]

[Reg. § 20.2053-9]

§ 20.2053-9. Deduction for certain State death taxes.—(a) *General rule.*—A deduction is allowed a decedent's estate under section 2053(d) for the amount of any estate, succession, legacy, or inheritance tax imposed by a State, Territory, or the District of Columbia, or, in the case of a decedent dying before September 3, 1958, a possession of the United States upon a transfer by the decedent for charitable, etc., uses described in section 2055 or 2106(a)(2) (relating to the estates of nonresidents not citizens), but only if (1) the conditions stated in paragraph (b) of this section are met, and (2) an election is made in accordance with the provisions of paragraph (c) of this section. See section 2011(e) and §20.2011-2 for the effect which the allowance of this deduction has upon the credit for State death taxes. However, see section 2058 to determine the deductibility of state death taxes by estates to which section 2058 is applicable.

(b) *Condition for allowance of deduction.*—(1) The deduction is not allowed unless either—

(i) The entire decrease in the Federal estate tax resulting from the allowance of the deduction inures solely to the benefit of a charitable, etc., transferee described in section 2055 or 2106(a)(2), or

(ii) The Federal estate tax is equitably apportioned among all the transferees (including the decedent's surviving spouse and the charitable, etc., transferees) of property included in the decedent's gross estate.

For allowance of the credit, it is sufficient if either of these conditions is satisfied. Thus, in a case where the entire decrease in Federal estate tax inures to the benefit of a charitable transferee, the deduction is allowable even though the Federal estate tax is not equitably apportioned among all the transferees of property included in the decedent's gross estate. Similarly, if the Federal estate tax is equitably apportioned among all the transferees of property included in the decedent's gross estate, the deduction is allowable even though a noncharitable transferee receives some benefit from the allowance of the deduction.

(2) For purposes of this paragraph, the Federal estate tax is considered to be equitably apportioned among all the transferees (including the decedent's surviving spouse and the charitable, etc., transferees) of property included in the decedent's gross estate only if each transferee's share of the tax is based upon the net amount of his transfer subjected to the tax (taking into account any exemptions, credits, or deductions allowed by chapter 11). See examples (2) through (5) of paragraph (e) of this section.

(c) *Exercise of election.*—The election to take a deduction for a state death tax imposed upon a transfer for charitable, etc., uses shall be exercised by the executor by the filing of a written notification to that effect with the Commissioner. The notification shall be filed before the expiration of the period of limitation for assessment provided in section 6501 (usually 3 years from the last day for filing the return). The election may be revoked by the executor by the filing of a written notification to that effect with the Commissioner at any time before the expiration of such period.

(d) *Amount of State death tax imposed upon a transfer.*—If a State death tax is imposed upon the transfer of the decedent's entire estate and not upon the transfer of a particular share thereof, the State death tax imposed upon a transfer for charitable, etc., uses is deemed to be an amount, E, which bears the same ratio to F (the amount of the State death tax imposed with respect to the transfer of the entire estate) as G (the value of the charitable, etc., transfer, reduced as provided in the next sentence) bears to H (the total value of the properties, interests, and benefits subjected to the State death tax received by all persons interested in the estate, reduced as provided in the last sentence of this paragraph). In arriving at amount G of the ratio, the value of the charitable, etc., transfer is reduced by the amount of any deduction or exclusion allowed with respect to such property in determining the amount of the State death tax. In arriving at amount H of the ratio, the total value of the properties, interests, and benefits subjected to State death tax received by all persons interested in the estate is reduced by the amount of all deductions and exclusions allowed in determining the amount of the State death tax on account of the nature of a beneficiary or a beneficiary's relationship to the decedent.

(e) *Examples.*—The application of this section may be illustrated by the following examples:

Example (1). The decedent's gross estate was valued at $200,000. He bequeathed $90,000 to a newphew, $10,000 to Charity A, and the remainder of his estate to Charity B. State inheritance tax in the amount of $13,500 was imposed upon the bequest to the nephew, $1,500 upon the bequest to Charity A, and $15,000 upon the bequest to Charity B. Under the will and local law, each legatee is required to pay the State inheritance tax on his bequest, and the Federal estate tax is to be paid out of the residuary estate. Since the entire burden of paying the Federal estate tax falls on Charity B, it follows that the decrease in the Federal estate tax resulting from the allowance of deductions for State death taxes in the amounts of $1,500 and $15,000 would inure solely for the benefit of Charity B. Therefore, deductions of $1,500 and $15,000 are allowable under section 2053(d). If, in this example, the State death taxes as well as the Federal estate tax were to be paid out of the residuary estate, the result would be the same.

Example (2). The decedent's gross estate was valued at $350,000. Expenses, indebtedness, etc., amounted to $50,000. The entire estate was bequeathed in equal shares to a son, a daughter, and Charity C. State inheritance tax in the amount of $2,000 was imposed upon the bequest to the son, $2,000 upon the bequest to the daughter, and $5,000 upon the bequest to Charity C. Under the will and local law, each legatee is required to pay his own State inheritance tax and his proportionate share of the Federal estate tax determined by taking into consideration the net amount of his bequest subjected to the tax. Since each legatee's share of the Federal estate tax is based upon the net amount of his bequest subjected to the tax (note that the deductions under sections 2053(d) and 2055 will have the effect of reducing Charity C's proportionate share of the tax), the tax is considered to be equitably apportioned. Thus, a deduction of $5,000 is allowable under section 2053(d). This deduction together with a deduction of $95,000 under section 2055 (charitable deduction) will mean that none of Charity C's bequest is subjected to Federal estate tax. Hence, the son and the daughter will bear the entire estate tax.

Example (3). The decedent bequeathed his property in equal shares, after payment of all expenses, to a son, a daughter, and a charity. State inheritance tax of $2,000 was imposed upon the bequest to the son, $2,000 upon the bequest to the daughter, and $15,000 upon the bequest to the charity. Under the will and local law, each beneficiary pays the State inheritance tax on his bequest and the Federal estate tax is to be paid out of the estate as an administration expense. If the deduction for State death tax on the charitable bequest is allowed in this case, some portion of the decrease in the Federal estate tax would inure to the benefit of the son and the daughter. The Federal estate tax is not considered to be equitably apportioned in this case since each legatee's share of the Federal estate tax is not based upon the net amount of his bequest subjected to the tax (note that the deductions under sections 2053(d) and 2055 will not have the effect of reducing the charity's proportionate share of the tax). Inasmuch as some of the decrease in the Federal estate tax payable would inure to the benefit of the son and the daughter, and inasmuch as there is no equitable apportionment of the tax, no deduction is allowable under section 2053(d).

Example (4). The decedent bequeathed his entire residuary estate in trust to pay the income to X for life with remainder to charity. The State imposed inheritance taxes of $2,000 upon the bequest to X and $10,000 upon the bequest to charity. Under the will and local law, all State and Federal taxes are payable out of the residuary estate and therefore they would reduce the amount which would become the corpus of the trust. If the deduction for the State death tax on the charitable bequest is allowed in this case, some portion of the decrease in the Federal estate tax would inure to the benefit of X since the allowance of the deduction would increase the size of the corpus from which X is to receive the income for life. Also, the Federal estate tax is not considered to be equitably apportioned in this case since each legatee's share of the Federal estate tax is not based upon the net amount of his bequest subjected to the tax (note that the deductions under sections 2053(d) and 2055 will not have the effect of reducing the charity's proportionate share of the tax). Inasmuch as some of the decrease in the Federal estate tax payable would inure to the benefit of X, and inasmuch as there is no equitable apportionment of the tax, no deduction is allowable under section 2053(d).

Example (5). The decedent's gross estate was valued at $750,000. Expenses, indebtedness, etc., amounted to $50,000. The decedent bequeathed $350,000 of his estate to his surviving spouse and the remainder of his estate equally to his son and Charity D. State inheritance tax in the amount of $7,000 was imposed upon the bequest to the surviving spouse, $26,250 upon the bequest to the son, and $26,250 upon the bequest to Charity D. The will was silent concerning the payment of taxes. In such a case, the local law provides that each legatee shall pay his own State inheritance tax. The local law further provides for an apportionment of the Federal estate tax among the legatees of the estate. Under the apportionment provisions, the surviving spouse is not required to bear any part of the Federal estate tax with respect to her $350,000 bequest. It should be noted, however, that the marital deduction allowed to the decedent's estate by reason of the bequest to the surviving spouse is limited to $343,000 ($350,000 bequest less $7,000 State inheritance tax payable by the surviving spouse). Thus, the bequest to the surviving spouse is subjected to the Federal estate tax in the net amount of $7,000. If the deduction for State death tax on the charitable bequest is allowed in this case, some portion of the decrease in the Federal estate tax would inure to the benefit of the son. The Federal estate tax is not considered to be equitably apportioned in this case since each legatee's share of the Federal estate tax is not based upon the net amount of his bequest subjected to the tax (note that the surviving spouse is to pay no tax). Inasmuch as some of the decrease in the Federal estate tax payable would inure to the benefit of the son, and inasmuch as there is no equitable apportionment of the tax, no deduction is allowable under section 2053(d).

(f) *Effective/applicability date.*—(1) The last sentence of paragraph (a) of this section applies to the estates of decedents dying on or after October 20, 2009, to which section 2058 is applicable.

(2) The other provisions of this section apply to the estates of decedents dying on or after October 20, 2009, to which section 2058 is not applicable. [Reg. § 20.2053-9.]

☐ [*T.D.* 6296, 6-23-58. *Amended by T.D.* 6526, 1-18-61 *and T.D.* 9468, 10-16-2009.]

[Reg. § 20.2053-10]

§ 20.2053-10. Deduction for certain foreign death taxes.—(a) *General rule.*—A deduction is allowed the estate of a decedent dying on or after July 1, 1955, under section 2053(d) for the amount of any estate, succession, legacy, or inheritance tax imposed by and actually paid to any foreign country, in respect of any property situated within such foreign country and included in the gross estate of a citizen or resident of the United States, upon a transfer by the decedent for charitable, etc., uses described in section 2055, but only if (1) the conditions stated in paragraph (b) of this section are met, and (2) an election is made in accordance with the provisions of paragraph(c) of this section. The determination of the country within which property is situated is made in accordance with the rules contained in sections 2104 and 2105 in determining whether property is situated within or without the United States. See section 2014(f) and

§ 20.2014-7 for the effect which the allowance of this deduction has upon the credit for foreign death taxes.

(b) *Condition for allowance of deduction.*—(1) The deduction is not allowed unless either—

(i) The entire decrease in the Federal estate tax resulting from the allowance of the deduction inures solely to the benefit of a charitable, etc., transferee described in section 2055, or

(ii) The Federal estate tax is equitably apportioned among all the transferees (including the decedent's surviving spouse and the charitable, etc., transferees) of property included in the decedent's gross estate.

For allowance of the deduction, it is sufficient if either of these conditions is satisfied. Thus, in a case where the entire decrease in Federal estate tax inures to the benefit of a charitable transferee, the deduction is allowable even though the Federal estate tax is not equitably apportioned among all the transferees of property included in the decedent's gross estate. Similarly, if the Federal estate tax is equitably apportioned among all the transferees of property included in the decedent's gross estate, the deduction is allowable even though a noncharitable transferee receives some benefit from the allowance of the deduction.

(2) For purposes of this paragraph, the Federal estate tax is considered to be equitably apportioned among all the transferees (including the decedent's surviving spouse and the charitable, etc., transferees) of property included in the decedent's gross estate only if each transferee's share of the tax is based upon the net amount of his transfer subjected to the tax (taking into account any exemptions, credits, or deductions allowed by chapter 11). See examples (2) through (5) of paragraph (e) of § 20.2053-9.

(c) *Exercise of election.*—The election to take a deduction for a foreign death tax imposed upon a transfer for charitable, etc., uses shall be exercised by the executor by the filing of a written notification to that effect with the Commissioner of internal revenue in whose district the estate tax return for the decedent's estate was filed. An election to take the deduction for foreign death taxes is deemed to be a waiver of the right to claim a credit under a treaty with any foreign country for any tax or portion thereof claimed as a deduction under this section. The notification shall be filed before the expiration of the period of limitation for assessment provided in section 6501 (usually 3 years from the last day for filing the return). The election may be revoked by the executor by the filing of a written notification to that effect with the Commissioner at any time before the expiration of such period.

(d) *Amount of foreign death tax imposed upon a transfer.*—If a foreign death tax is imposed upon the transfer of the entire part of the decedent's estate subject to such tax and not upon the transfer of a particular share thereof, the foreign death tax imposed upon a transfer for charitable, etc., uses is deemed to be an amount, J, which bears the same ratio to K (the amount of the foreign death tax imposed with respect to the transfer of the entire part of the decedent's estate subject to such tax) as M (the value of the charitable, etc., transfer, reduced as provided in the next sentence) bears to N (the total value of the properties, interests, and benefits subjected to the foreign death tax received by all persons interested in the estate, reduced as provided in the last sentence of this paragraph). In arriving at amount M of the ratio, the value of the charitable, etc., transfer is reduced by the amount of any deduction or exclusion allowed with respect to such property in determining the amount of the foreign death tax. In arriving at amount N of the ratio, the total value of the properties, interests, and benefits subjected to foreign death tax received by all persons interested in the estate is reduced by the amount of all deductions and exclusions allowed in determining the amount of the foreign death tax on account of the nature of a beneficiary or a beneficiary's relationship to the decedent.

(e) *Effective/applicability date.*—This section applies to the estates of decedents dying on or after October 20, 2009. [Reg. § 20.2053-10.]

☐ [*T.D.* 6600, 5-28-62. *Amended by T.D.* 9468, 10-16-2009.]

[Reg. § 20.2054-1]

§ 20.2054-1. Deduction for losses from casualties or theft.—A deduction is allowed for losses incurred during the settlement of the estate arising from fires, storms, shipwrecks, or other casualties, or from theft, if the losses are not compensated for by insurance or otherwise. If the loss is partly compensated for, the excess of the loss over the compensation may be deducted. Losses which are not of the nature described are not deductible. In order to be deductible a loss must occur during the settlement of the estate. If a loss with respect to an asset occurs after its distribution to the distributee it may not be deducted. Notwithstanding the foregoing, no deduction is allowed under this section if the estate has waived its right to take such a deduction pursuant to the provisions of section 642(g) in order to permit its allowance for income tax purposes. See further § 1.642(g)-1. [Reg. § 20.2054-1.]

☐ [*T.D.* 6296, 6-23-58.]

[Reg. § 20.2055-1]

§ 20.2055-1. Deduction for transfers for public, charitable, and religious uses; in general.—(a) *General rule.*—A deduction is allowed under section 2055(a) from the gross estate of a decedent who was a citizen or resident of the United States at the time of his death for the value of property included in the decedent's gross estate and transferred by the decedent during his lifetime or by will—

(1) To or for the use of the United States, any State, Territory, any political subdivision thereof, or the District of Columbia, for exclusively public purposes;

(2) To or for the use of any corporation or association organized and operated exclusively for religious, charitable, scientific, literary, or educational purposes (including the encouragement of art and the prevention of cruelty to children or animals), if no part of the net earnings of the corporation or association inures to the benefit of any private stockholder or individual (other than as a legitimate object of such purposes), if the organization is not disqualified for tax exemption under section 501(c)(3) by reason of attempting to influence legislation, and if, in the case of transfers made after December 31, 1969, it does not participate in, or intervene in (including the publishing or distributing of statements), any political campaign on behalf of or in opposition to any candidate for public office;

(3) To a trustee or trustees, or a fraternal society, order, or association operating under the lodge system, if the transferred property is to be used exclusively for religious, charitable, scientific, literary, or educational purposes (or for the prevention of cruelty to children or animals), if no substantial part of the activities of such transferee is carrying on propaganda, or otherwise attempting, to influence legislation, and if, in the case of transfers made after December 31, 1969, such transferee does not participate in, or intervene in (including the publishing or distributing of statements), any political campaign on behalf of any candidate for public office; or

(4) To or for the use of any veterans' organization incorporated by act of Congress, or of any of its departments, local chapters, or posts, no part of the net earnings of which inures to the benefit of any private shareholder or individual.

The deduction is not limited, in the case of estates of citizens or residents of the United States, to transfers to domestic corporations or associations, or to trustees for use within the United States.

Nor is the deduction subject to percentage limitations such as are applicable to the charitable deduction under the income tax. An organization will not be considered to meet the requirements of subparagraph (2) or (3) of this paragraph if such organization engages in any activity which would cause it to be classified as an "action" organization under paragraph (c)(3) of § 1.501(c)(3)-1 of this chapter (Income Tax Regulations). See § 20.2055-4 and § 20.2055-5 for rules relating to the disallowance of deductions to trusts and organizations which engage in certain prohibited transactions or whose governing instruments do not contain certain specified requirements.

(b) *Powers of appointment.*—(1) *General rule.*—A deduction is allowable under section 2055(b) for the value of property passing to or for the use of a transferee described in paragraph (a) of this section by the exercise, failure to exercise, release or lapse of a power of appointment by reason of which the property is includible in the decedent's gross estate under section 2041.

(2) *Certain bequests subject to power of appointment.*—For the allowance of a deduction in the case of a bequest in trust where the decedent's surviving spouse (i) was over 80 years of age at the date of decedent's death, (ii) was entitled for life to all of the net income from the trust, and (iii) had a power of appointment over the corpus of the trust exercisable by will in favor of, among others, a charitable organization, see section 2055(b)(2). See also section 6503(e) for suspension of the period of limitations for assessment or collection of any deficiency attributable to the allowance of the deduction.

(c) *Submission of evidence.*—In establishing the right of the estate to the deduction authorized by section 2055, the executor should submit the following with the return:

(1) A copy of any instrument in writing by which the decedent made a transfer of property in his lifetime the value of which is required by statute to be included in his gross estate, for which a deduction under section 2055 is claimed. If the instrument is of record the copy should be certified, and if not of record, the copy should be verified.

(2) A written statement by the executor containing a declaration that it is made under penalties of perjury and stating whether any action has been instituted to construe or to contest the decedent's will or any provision thereof affecting the charitable deduction claimed and whether, according to his information and belief, any such action is designed or contemplated.

The executor shall also submit such other documents or evidence as may be requested by the district director.

(d) *Cross references.*—(1) See section 2055(f) for certain cross references relating to section 2055.

(2) For treatment of bequests accepted by the Secretary of State or the Secretary of Commerce, for the purpose of organizing and holding an international conference to negotiate a Patent Corporation Treaty, as bequests to or for the use of the United States, see section 3 of Joint Resolution of December 24, 1969 (P.L. 91-160, 83 Stat. 443).

(3) For treatment of bequests accepted by the Secretary of the Department of Housing and Urban Development, for the purpose of aiding or facilitating the work of the Department, as bequests to or for the use of the United States, see section 7(k) of the Department of Housing and Urban Development Act (42 U.S.C. 3535), as added by section 905 of P.L. 91-609 (84 Stat. 1809).

(4) For treatment of certain property accepted by the Chairman of the Administrative Conference of the United States, for the purpose of aiding and facilitating the work of the Conference, as a devise or bequest to the United States, see 5 U.S.C. 575(c)(12), as added by section 1(b) of the Act of October 21, 1972 (Public Law 92-526, 86 Stat. 1048).

(5) For treatment of the Board for International Broadcasting as a corporation described in section 2055(a)(2), see section 7 of the Board for International Broadcasting Act of 1973 (Public Law 93-129, 87 Stat. 459). [Reg. § 20.2055-1.]

☐ [*T.D.* 6296, 6-23-58. *Amended by T.D.* 7318, 7-10-74 *and T.D.* 8308, 8-30-90.]

[Reg. § 20.2055-2]

§ 20.2055-2. Transfers not exclusively for charitable purposes.—(a) *Remainders and similar interests.*—If a trust is created or property is transferred for both a charitable and a private purpose, deduction may be taken of the value of the charitable beneficial interest only insofar as that interest is presently ascertainable, and hence severable from the noncharitable interest. Thus, in the case of decedents dying before January 1, 1970, if money or property is placed in trust to pay the income to an individual during his life, or for a term of years, and then to pay the principal to a charitable organization, the present value of the remainder is deductible. See paragraph (e) of this section for limitations applicable to decedents dying after December 31, 1969. See paragraph (f) of this section for rules relating to valuation of partial interests in property passing for charitable purposes.

(b) *Transfers subject to a condition or a power.*—(1) If, as of the date of a decedent's death, a transfer for charitable purposes is dependent upon the performance of some act or the happening of a precedent event in order that it might become effective, no deduction is allowable unless the possibility that the charitable transfer will not become effective is so remote as to be negligible. If an estate or interest has passed to, or is vested in, charity at the time of a decedent's death and the estate or interest would be defeated by the subsequent performance of some act or the happening of some event, the possibility of occurrence of which appeared at the time of the decedent's death to be so remote as to be negligible, the deduction is allowable. If the legatee, devisee, donee, or trustee is empowered to divert the property or fund, in whole or in part, to a use or purpose which would have rendered it, to the extent that it is subject to such power, not deductible had it been directly so bequeathed, devised, or given by the decedent, the deduction will be limited to that portion, if any, of the property or fund which is exempt from an exercise of the power.

(2) The application of this paragraph may be illustrated by the following examples:

Example (1). In 1965, A dies leaving certain property in trust in which charity is to receive the income for the life of his widow. The assets placed in trust by the decedent consist of stock in a corporation the fiscal policies of which are controlled by the decedent and his family. The trustees of the trust and the remaindermen are members of the decedent's family, and the governing instrument contains no adequate guarantee of the requisite income to the charitable organization. Under such circumstances, no deduction will be allowed. Similarly, if the trustees are not members of the decedent's family but have no power to sell or otherwise dispose of the closely held stock, or otherwise insure the requisite enjoyment of income to the charitable organization, no deduction will be allowed.

Example (2). C dies leaving a tract of land to a city government for as long as the land is used by the city for a public park. If the city accepts the tract and if, on the date of C's death, the possibility that the city will not use the land for a public park is so remote as to be negligible, a deduction will be allowed.

(c) *Disclaimers.*—(1) *Decedents dying after December 31, 1976.*—In the case of a bequest, devise, or transfer made by a decedent dying after December 31, 1976, the amount of a bequest, devise or transfer for which a deduction is allowable under section 2055 includes an interest which falls into the bequest, devise or transfer as the result of either—

(i) A qualified disclaimer (see section 2518 and the corresponding regulations for rules relating to a qualified disclaimer), or

(ii) The complete termination of a power to consume, invade, or appropriate property for the benefit of an individual by reason of the death of such individual or for any other reason, if the termination occurs within the period of time (including extensions) for filing the decedent's Federal estate tax return and before such power has been exercised.

(2) *Decedents dying before January 1, 1977.*—In the case of a bequest, devise or transfer made by a decedent dying before January 1, 1977, the amount of a bequest, devise or transfer for which a deduction is allowable under section 2055 includes an interest which falls into the bequest, devise or transfer as a result of either—

(i) A disclaimer of a bequest, devise, transfer, or power, if the disclaimer is made within 9 months (15 months if the decedent died on or before December 31, 1970) after the decedent's death (the period of time within which the estate tax return must be filed under section 6075) or within any extension of time for filing the return granted pursuant to section 6081, and the disclaimer is irrevocable at the time the deduction is allowed, or

(ii) The complete termination of a power to consume, invade, or appropriate property for the benefit of an individual (whether the termination occurs by reason of the death of the individual, or otherwise) if the termination occurs within the period described in paragraph (c)(2)(i) of this section and before the power has been exercised. Ordinarily, a disclaimer made by a person not under any legal disability will be considered irrevocable when filed with the probate court. A disclaimer is a complete and unqualified refusal to accept the rights to which one is entitled. Thus, if a beneficiary uses these rights for his own purposes, as by receiving a consideration for his formal disclaimer, he has not refused the rights to which he was entitled. There can be no disclaimer after an acceptance of these rights, expressly or impliedly. The disclaimer of a power is to be distinguished from the release or exercise of a power. The release or exercise of a power by the donee of the power in favor of a person or object described in paragraph (a) of § 20.2055-1 does not result in any deduction under section 2055 in the estate of the donor of a power (but see paragraph (b)(1) of § 20.2055-1 with respect to the donee's estate).

(d) *Payments in compromise.*—If a charitable organization assigns or surrenders a part of a transfer to it pursuant to a compromise agreement in settlement of a controversy, the amount so assigned or surrendered is not deductible as a transfer to that charitable organization.

(e) *Limitation applicable to decedents dying after December 31, 1969.*—(1) *Disallowance of deduction.*—(i) *In general.*—In the case of decedents dying after December 31, 1969, where an interest in property passes or has passed from the decedent for charitable purposes and an interest (other than an interest which is extinguished upon the decedent's death) in the same property passes or has passed from the decedent for private purposes (for less than an adequate and full consideration in money or money's worth) after October 9, 1969, no deduction is allowed under section 2055 for the value of the interest which passes or has passed for charitable purposes unless the interest in property is a deductible interest described in subparagraph (2) of this paragraph. The principles of section 2056 and the regulations thereunder shall apply for purposes of determining under this subparagraph whether an interest in property passes or has passed from the decedent. If however, as of the date of a decedent's death, a transfer for a private purpose is dependent upon the performance of some act or the happening of a precedent event in order that it might become effective, an interest in property will be considered to pass for a private purpose unless the possibility of occurrence of such act or event is so remote as to be negligible. The application of this subparagraph may be illustrated by the following examples, in each of which it is assumed that the interest in property which passes for private purposes does not pass for an adequate and full consideration in money or money's worth:

Example (1). In 1973, H creates a trust which is to pay the income of the trust to W for her life, the reversionary interest in the trust being retained by H. H predeceases W in 1975. H's will provides that the residue of his estate (including the reversionary interest in the trust) is to be transferred to charity. For purposes of this paragraph (e)(1)(i), interests in the same property have passed from H for charitable purposes and for private purposes.

Example (2). In 1973, H creates a trust which is to pay the income of the trust to W for her life and upon termination of the life estate to transfer the remainder to S. S predeceases W in 1975. S's will provides that the residue of his estate (including the remainder interest in the trust) is to be transferred to charity. For purposes of this paragraph (e)(1)(i), interests in the same property have not passed from H or S for charitable purposes and for private purposes.

Example (3). H transfers Blackacre to A by gift, reserving the right to the rentals of Blackacre for a term of 20 years. H dies within the 20-year term, bequeathing the right to the remaining rentals to charity. For purposes of this paragraph (e)(1)(i) the term "property" refers to Blackacre, and the right to rentals from Blackacre consist of an interest in Blackacre. An interest in Blackacre has passed from H for charitable purposes and for private purposes.

Example (4). H bequeaths the residue of his estate in trust for the benefit of A and a charity. An annuity of $5,000 a year is to be paid to charity for 20 years. Upon termination of the 20-year term the corpus is to be distributed to A if living. However, if A should die during the 20-year term, the corpus is to be distributed to charity upon termination of the term. An interest in the residue of the estate has passed from H for charitable purposes. In addition, an interest in the residue of the estate has passed from H for private purposes, unless the possibility that A will survive the 20-year term is so remote as to be negligible.

Example (5). H bequeaths the residue of his estate in trust. Under the terms of the trust an annuity of $5,000 a year is to be paid to charity for 20 years. Upon termination of the term, the corpus is to pass to such of A's children and their issue as A may appoint. However, if A should die during the 20-year term without exercising the power of appointment, the corpus is to be distributed to charity upon termination of the term. Since the possible appointees include private persons, an interest in the residue of the estate is considered to have passed from H for private purposes.

Example (6). H devises Blackacre to X Charity. Under applicable local law, W, H's widow, is entitled to elect a dower interest in Blackacre. W elects to take her dower interest in Blackacre. For purposes of this paragraph (e)(1)(i), interests in the same property have passed from H for charitable purposes and for private purposes. If, however, W does not elect to take her dower interest in Blackacre, then, for purposes of this paragraph (e)(1)(i). interests in the same property have not passed from H for charitable purposes and for private purposes.

(ii) *Works of art and copyrights treated as separate properties.*—(*a*) *In general.*—For purposes of paragraphs (e)(1)(i) and (e)(2) of this section, in the case of decedents dying after December 31, 1981, if a decedent makes a qualified contribution of a work of art, the work of art and the copyright on such work of art shall be treated as separate properties. Thus, a deduction is allowable under section 2055 for a qualified contribution of a work of art, whether or not the related copyright is simultaneously transferred to a charitable organization.

(*b*) *Work of art defined.*—For purposes of paragraph (e)(1)(ii)(*a*) of this section, the term "work of art" means any tangible personal property with respect to which a copyright exists under Federal law.

(*c*) *Qualified contribution defined.*—For purposes of paragraph (e)(1)(ii)(*a*) of this section, the term "qualified contribution" means any transfer of property to a qualified organization (as defined in paragraph (e)(1)(ii)(*d*) of this section) if the use of the property by the organization is related to the purpose or function constituting the basis for its exemption under section 501. The rules contained in § 1.170A-4 (b)(3) shall apply in determining if the use of property by an organization is related to such purpose or function.

(*d*) *Qualified organization defined.*—For purposes of paragraph (e)(1)(ii)(*c*) of this section, the term "qualified organization" means any organization described in section 501(c)(3) other than a private foundation (as defined in section 509). A private operating foundation (as defined in section 4042(j)(3)) shall be considered a qualified organization under this paragraph.

(*e*) *Examples.*—The application of paragraphs (e)(1)(i) and (e)(1)(ii)(*a*) through (*d*) of this section may be illustrated by the following examples:

Example (1). A, an artist, died in 1983. A work of art created by A and the copyright interest in that work of art were included in A's estate. Under the terms of A's will, the work of art is transferred to X charity, the only charitable beneficiary under A's will. X has no suitable use for the work of art and sells it. It is determined under the rules of § 1.170A-4 (b)(3) that the property is put to an unrelated use by X charity. Therefore, the rule of paragraph (e)(1)(ii)(*a*), which treats works of art and their copyrights as separate properties, does not apply because the transfer of the work of art to X is not a qualified contribution. To determine whether paragraph (e)(1)(i) of this section applies to disallow a deduction under section 2055, it must be determined which interests are treated as passing to X under local law.

(i) If under local law A's will is treated as fully transferring both the work of art and the copyright interest to X, then paragraph (e)(1)(i) of this section does not apply to disallow a deduction under section 2055 for the value of the work of art and the copyright interest.

(ii) If under local law A's will is treated as transferring only the work of art to X, and the copyright interest is treated as part of the residue of the estate, no deduction is allowable under section 2055 to A's estate for the value of the work of art because the transfer of the work of art is not a qualified contribution and paragraph (e)(1)(i) of this section applies to disallow the deduction.

Example (2). B, a collector of art, purchased a work of art from an artist who retained the copyright interest. B died in 1983. Under the terms of B's will the work of art is given to Y charity. Since B did not own the copyright interest, paragraph (e)(1)(i) of this section does not apply to disallow a deduction under section 2055 for the value of the work of art, regardless of whether or not the contribution is a qualified contribution under paragraph (e)(1)(ii)(*c*) of this section.

(2) *Deductible interests.*—A deductible interest for purposes of subparagraph (1) of this paragraph is a charitable interest in property where—

(i) *Undivided portion of decedent's entire interest.*—The charitable interest is an undivided portion, not in trust, of the decedent's entire interest in property. An undivided portion of a decedent's entire interest in property must consist of a fraction or percentage of each and every substantial interest or right owned by the decedent in such property and must extend over the entire term of the decedent's interest in such property and in other property into which such property is converted. For example, if the decedent transferred a life estate in an office building to his wife for her life and retained a reversionary interest in the office building, the devise by the decedent of one-half of that reversionary interest to charity while his wife is still alive will not be considered the transfer of a deductible interest; because an interest in the same property has already passed from the decedent for private purposes, the reversionary interest will not be considered the decedent's entire interest in the property. If, on the other hand, the decedent had been given a life estate in Blackacre for the life of his wife and the decedent had no other interest in Blackacre at any time during his life, the devise by the decedent of one-half of that life estate to charity would be considered the transfer of a deductible interest; because the life estate would be considered the decedent's entire interest in the property, the devise would be of an undivided portion of such entire interest. An undivided portion of a decedent's entire interest in the property includes an interest in property whereby the charity is given the right, as a tenant in common with the decedent's devisee or legatee, to possession, dominion, and control of the property for a portion of each year appropriate to its interest in such property. However, except as provided in paragraphs (e)(2)(ii), (iii), and (iv) of this section, for purposes of this subdivision a charitable contribution of an interest in property not in trust where the decedent transfers some specific rights to one party and transfers other substantial rights to another party will not be considered a contribution of an undivided portion of the decedent's entire interest in property. A bequest to charity made on or before December 17, 1980, of an open space easement in gross in perpetuity shall be considered the transfer to charity of an undivided portion of the decedent's entire interest in the property. For the definition of an open space easement in gross in perpetuity, see § 1.170A-7(b)(1)(ii) of this chapter (Income Tax Regulations).

(ii) *Remainder interest in personal residence.*—The charitable interest is a remainder interest, not in trust, in a personal residence. Thus, for example, if the decedent devises to charity a remainder interest in a personal residence and bequeaths to his surviving spouse a life estate in such property, the value of the remainder interest is deductible under section 2055. For purposes of this subdivision, the term "personal residence" means any property which was used by the decedent as his personal residence even though it was not used as his principal residence. For example, a decedent's vacation home may be a personal residence for purposes of this subdivision. The term "personal residence" also includes stock owned by the decedent as a tenant-stockholder in a cooperative housing corporation (as those terms are defined in section 216(b)(1) and (2)) if the dwelling which the decedent was entitled to occupy as such stockholder was used by him as his personal residence.

(iii) *Remainder interest in a farm.*—The charitable interest is a remainder interest, not in trust, in a farm. Thus, for example, if the decedent devises to charity a remainder interest in a farm and bequeaths to his daughter a life estate in such property, the value of the remainder interest is deductible under section 2055. For purposes of this subdivision, the term "farm" means any land used by the decedent or his tenant for the production of crops, fruits, or other agricultural products or for the sustenance of livestock. The term "livestock" includes cattle, hogs, horses, mules, donkeys, sheep, goats, captive fur-bearing animals, chickens, turkeys, pigeons, and other poultry. A farm includes the improvements thereon.

(iv) *Qualified conservation contribution.*—The charitable interest is a qualified conservation contribution. For the definition of a qualified conservation contribution, see § 1.170A-14.

(v) *Charitable remainder trusts and pooled income funds.*—The charitable interest is a remainder interest in a trust which is a charitable remainder annuity trust, as defined in section 664(d)(1) and § 1.664-2 of this chapter; a charitable remainder unitrust, as defined in section 664(d)(2) and (3) and § 1.664-3 of this chapter; or a pooled income fund, as defined in section 642(c)(5) and § 1.642(c)-5 of this chapter. The charitable organization to or for the use of which the remainder interest passes must meet the requirements of both section 2055(a) and section 642(c)(5)(A), section 664(d)(1)(C), or section 664(d)(2)(C), whichever applies. For example, the charitable organization to which the remainder interest in a charitable remainder annuity trust passes may not be a foreign corporation.

(vi) *Guaranteed annuity interest.*—*(a)* The charitable interest is a guaranteed annuity interest, whether or not such interest is in trust. For purposes of this subdivision (vi), the term "guaranteed annuity interest" means the right pursuant to the instrument of transfer to receive a guaranteed annuity. A guaranteed annuity is an arrangement under which a determinable amount is paid periodically, but not less often than annually, for a specified term of years or for the life or lives of certain individuals, each of whom must be living at the date of death of the decedent and can be ascertained at such date. Only one or more of the following individuals may be used as measuring lives: the decedent's spouse, and an individual who, with respect to all remainder beneficiaries (other than charitable organizations described in section 170, 2055, or 2522), is either a lineal ancestor or the spouse of a lineal ancestor of those beneficiaries. A trust will satisfy the requirement that all noncharitable remainder beneficiaries are lineal descendants of the individual who is the measuring life, or that individual's spouse, if there is less than a 15% probability that individuals who are not lineal descendants will receive any trust corpus. This probability must be computed, based on the current applicable Life Table contained in § 20.2031-7, as of the date of the decedent's death taking into account the interests of all primary and contingent remainder beneficiaries who are living at that time. An interest payable for a specified term of years can qualify as a guaranteed annuity interest even if the governing instrument contains a savings clause intended to ensure compliance with a rule against perpetuities. The savings clause must utilize a period for vesting of 21 years after the deaths of measuring lives who are selected to maximize, rather than limit, the term of the trust. The rule in this paragraph that a charitable interest may be payable for the life or lives of only certain specified individuals does not apply in the case of a charitable guaranteed annuity interest payable under a charitable remainder trust described in section 664. An amount is determinable if the exact amount which must be paid under the conditions specified in the instrument of transfer can be ascertained as of the appropriate valuation date. For example, the amount to be paid may be a stated sum for a term of years, or for the life of the decedent's spouse, at the expiration of which it may be changed by a specified amount, but it may not be redetermined by reference to a fluctuating index such as the cost of living index. In further illustration, the amount to be paid may be expressed in terms of a fraction or a percentage of the net fair market value, as finally determined for Federal estate tax purposes, of the residue of the estate on the appropriate valuation date, or it may be expressed in terms of a fraction or percentage of the cost of living index on the appropriate valuation date.

(b) A charitable interest is a guaranteed annuity interest only if it is a guaranteed annuity interest in every respect. For example, if the charitable interest is the right to receive from a trust each year a payment equal to the lesser of a sum certain or a fixed percentage of the net fair market value of the trust assets, determined annually, such interest is not a guaranteed annuity interest.

(c) Where a charitable interest in the form of a guaranteed annuity interest is not in trust, the interest will be considered a guaranteed annuity interest only if it is to be paid by an insurance company or by an organization regularly engaged in issuing annuity contracts.

(d) Where a charitable interest in the form of a guaranteed annuity interest is in trust, the governing instrument of the trust may provide that income of the trust which is in excess of the amount required to pay the guaranteed annuity interest shall be paid to or for the use of a charity. Nevertheless, the amount of the deduc-

tion under section 2055 shall be limited to the fair market value of the guaranteed annuity interest as determined under paragraph (f)(2)(iv) of this section.

(e) Where a charitable interest in the form of a guaranteed annuity interest is in trust and the present value, on the appropriate valuation date, of all the income interests for a charitable purpose exceeds 60 percent of the aggregate fair market value of all amounts in such trust (after the payment of estate taxes and all other liabilities), the charitable interest will not be considered a guaranteed annuity interest unless the governing instrument of the trust prohibits both the acquisition and the retention of assets which would give rise to a tax under section 4944 if the trustee had acquired such assets.

(f) Where a charitable interest in the form of a guaranteed annuity interest is in trust, the charitable interest generally is not a guaranteed annuity interest if any amount may be paid by the trust for a private purpose before the expiration of all the charitable annuity interests. There are two exceptions to this general rule. First, the charitable interest is a guaranteed annuity interest if the amount payable for a private purpose is in the form of a guaranteed annuity interest and the trust's governing instrument does not provide for any preference or priority in the payment of the private annuity as opposed to the charitable annuity. Second, the charitable interest is a guaranteed annuity interest if under the trust's governing instrument the amount that may be paid for a private purpose is payable only from a group of assets that are devoted exclusively to private purposes and to which section 4947(a)(2) is inapplicable by reason of section 4947(a)(2)(B). For purposes of this paragraph (e)(2)(vi)*(f)*, an amount is not paid for a private purpose if it is paid for an adequate and full consideration in money or money's worth. See § 53.4947-1(c) of this chapter for rules relating to the inapplicability of section 4947(a)(2) to segregated amounts in a split-interest trust.

(g) Neither the requirement in *(e)* of this subdivision (v) for a prohibition in the governing instrument against the retention of assets which would give rise to a tax under section 4944 if the trustee had acquired the assets nor the provisions of *(f)* of this subdivision (vi) shall apply to—

(1) A trust executed on or before May 21, 1972, if—

(i) The trust is irrevocable on such date,

(ii) The trust is revocable on such date and the decedent dies within 3 years after such date without having amended any dispositive provision of the trust after such date, or

(iii) The trust is revocable on such date and no dispositive provision of the trust is amended within a period ending 3 years after such date and the decedent is, at the end of such 3-year period and at all times thereafter, under a mental disability (as defined in § 1.642(c)-2(b)(3)(ii) of this chapter) to amend the trust, or

(2) A will executed on or before May 21, 1972, if—

(i) The testator dies within 3 years after such date without having amended any dispositive provision of the will after such date, by codicil or otherwise,

(ii) The testator at no time after such date has the right to change the provisions of the will which pertain to the trust, or

(iii) No dispositive provision of the will is amended by the decedent, by codicil or otherwise, within a period ending 3 years after such date and the decedent is, at the end of such 3-year period and at all times thereafter, under a mental disability (as defined in § 1.642(c)-2(b)(3)(ii) of this chapter) to amend the will by codicil or otherwise.

(h) For purposes of this subdivision (vi) and paragraph (f) of this section, the term "appropriate valuation date" means the date of death or the alternate valuation date determined pursuant to an election under section 2032.

(i) For rules relating to certain governing instrument requirements and to the imposition of certain excise taxes where the guaranteed annuity interest is in trust and for rules governing payment of private income interests by split-interest trusts, see section 4947(a)(2) and (b)(3)(A), and the regulations thereunder.

(vii) *Unitrust interest.—(a)* The charitable interest is a unitrust interest, whether or not such interest is in trust. For purposes of this subdivision (vii), the term "unitrust interest" means the right pursuant to the instrument of transfer to receive payment, not less often than annually, of a fixed percentage of the net fair market value, determined annually, of the property which funds the unitrust interest. In computing the net fair market value of the property which funds the unitrust interest, all assets and liabilities shall be taken into account without regard to whether particular items are taken into account in determining the income from the property. The net fair market value of the property which funds the unitrust interest may be determined on any one date during the year or by taking the average of valuations made on more than one date during the year, provided that the same valuation date or dates and valuation methods are used each year. Where the charitable interest is a unitrust interest to be paid by a trust and the governing instrument of the trust does not specify the valuation date or dates, the trustee shall select such date or dates and shall indicate his selection on the first return on Form 1041 which the trust is required to file. Payments under a unitrust interest may be paid for a specified term of years or for the life or lives of certain individuals, each of whom must be living at the date of death of the decedent and can be ascertained at such date. Only one or more of the following individuals may be used as measuring lives: the decedent's spouse, and an individual who, with respect to all remainder beneficiaries (other than charitable organizations described in section 170, 2055, or 2522), is either a lineal ancestor or the spouse of a lineal ancestor of those beneficiaries. A trust will satisfy the requirement that all noncharitable remainder beneficiaries are lineal descendants of the individual who is the measuring life, or that individual's spouse, if there is less than a 15% probability that individuals who are not lineal descendants will receive any trust corpus. This probability must be computed, based on the current applicable Life Table contained in §20.2031-7, as of the date of the decedent's death taking into account the interests of all primary and contingent remainder beneficiaries who are living at that time. An interest payable for a specified term of years can qualify as a unitrust interest even if the governing instrument contains a savings clause intended to ensure compliance with a rule against perpetuities. The savings clause must utilize a period for vesting of 21 years after the deaths of measuring lives who are selected to maximize, rather than limit, the term of the trust. The rule in this paragraph that a charitable interest may be payable for the life or lives of only certain specified individuals does not apply in the case of a charitable unitrust interest payable under a charitable remainder trust described in section 664.

(*b*) A charitable interest is a unitrust interest only if it is a unitrust interest in every respect. For example, if the charitable interest is the right to receive from a trust each year a payment equal to the lesser of a sum certain or a fixed percentage of the net fair market value of the trust assets, determined annually, such interest is not a unitrust interest.

(*c*) Where a charitable interest in the form of a unitrust interest is not in trust, the interest will be considered a unitrust interest only if it is to be paid by an insurance company or by an organization regularly engaged in issuing interests otherwise meeting the requirements of a unitrust interest.

(*d*) Where a charitable interest in the form of a unitrust interest is in trust, the governing instrument of the trust may provide that income of the trust which is in excess of the amount required to pay the unitrust interest shall be paid to or for the use of a charity. Nevertheless, the amount of the deduction under section 2055 shall be limited to the fair market value of the unitrust interest as determined under paragraph (f)(2)(v) of this section.

(*e*) Where a charitable interest in the form of a unitrust interest is in trust, the charitable interest generally is not a unitrust interest if any amount may be paid by the trust for a private purpose before the expiration of all the charitable unitrust interests. There are two exceptions to this general rule. First, the charitable interest is a unitrust interest if the amount payable for a private purpose is in the form of a unitrust interest and the trust's governing instrument does not provide for any preference or priority in the payment of the private unitrust interest as opposed to the charitable unitrust interest. Second, the charitable interest is a unitrust interest if under the trust's governing instrument the amount that may be paid for a private purpose is payable only from a group of assets that are devoted exclusively to private purposes and to which section 4947(a)(2) is inapplicable by reason of section 4947(a)(2)(B). For purposes of this paragraph (e)(2)(vii)(*e*), an amount is not paid for a private purpose if it is paid for an adequate and full consideration in money or money's worth. See §53.4947-1(c) of this chapter for rules relating to the inapplicability of section 4947(a)(2) to segregated amounts in a split-interest trust.

(*f*) For rules relating to certain governing instrument requirements and to the imposition of certain excise taxes where the unitrust interest is in trust and for rules governing payment of private income interests by a split-interest trust, see section 4947(a)(2) and (b)(3)(A), and the regulations thereunder.

(3) *Effective/applicability date.*—The provisions of this paragraph apply only in the case of decedents dying after December 31, 1969, except that they do not apply—

(i) In the case of property passing under the terms of a will executed on or before October 9, 1969—

(*a*) If the decedent dies after October 9, 1969, but before October 9, 1972, without having amended any dispositive provision of the will after October 9, 1969, by codicil or otherwise,

(*b*) If the decedent dies after October 9, 1969, and at no time after that date had the right to change the portions of the will which pertain to the passing of the property to, or for the use of, an organization described in section 2055(a), or

(*c*) If no dispositive provision of the will is amended by the decedent, by codicil or otherwise, after October 9, 1969, and before October 9, 1972, and the decedent is on October 9, 1972, and at all times thereafter under a mental disability (as defined in §1.642(c)-2(b)(3)(ii) of this chapter (Income Tax Regulations)) to amend the will by codicil or otherwise, or

(ii) In the case of property transferred in trust on or before October 9, 1969—

(*a*) If the decedent dies after October 9, 1969, but before October 9, 1972, without having amended, after October 9, 1969, any dispositive provision of the instrument governing the disposition of the property,

(*b*) If the property transferred was an irrevocable interest to, or for the use of, an organization described in section 2055(a), or

(*c*) If no dispositive provision of the instrument governing the disposition of the property is amended by the decedent after October 9, 1969, and before October 9, 1972, and the decedent is on October 9, 1972, and at all times thereafter under a mental disability (as defined in §1.642(c)-2(b)(3)(ii) of this chapter) to change the disposition of the property, and

(iii) The rule in paragraphs (e)(2)(vi)(*a*) and (e)(2)(vii)(*a*) of this section that guaranteed annuity interests or unitrust interests, respectively, may be payable for a specified term of years or for the life or lives of only certain individuals is generally effective in the case of transfers pursuant to wills and revocable trusts when the decedent dies on or after April 4, 2000. Two exceptions from the application of this rule in paragraphs (e)(2)(vi)(*a*) and(e)(2)(vii)(*a*) of this section are provided in the case of transfers pursuant to a will or revocable trust executed before April 4, 2000. One exception is for a decedent who dies on or before July 5, 2001, without having republished the will (or amended the trust) by codicil or otherwise. The other exception is for a decedent who was on April 4, 2000, under a mental disability that prevented a change in the disposition of the decedent's property, and who either does not regain competence to dispose of such property before the date of death, or dies prior to the later of 90 days after the date on which the decedent first regains competence, or July 5, 2001, without having republished the will (or amended the trust) by codicil or otherwise. If a guaranteed annuity interest or unitrust interest created pursuant to a will or revocable trust of a decedent dying on or after April 4, 2000, uses an individual other than one permitted in paragraphs (e)(2)(vi)(*a*) and (e)(2)(vii)(*a*) of this section, and the interest does not qualify for this transitional relief, the interest may be reformed into a lead interest payable for a specified term of years. The term of years is determined by taking the factor for valuing the annuity or unitrust interest for the named individual measuring life and identifying the term of years (rounded up to the next whole year) that corresponds to the equivalent term of years factor for an annuity or unitrust interest. For example, in the case of an annuity interest payable for the life of an individual age 40 at the time of the transfer on or after May 1, 2009, assuming an interest rate of 7.4 percent under section 7520, the annuity factor from column 1 of Table S(7.4), contained in IRS Publication 1457, "Actuarial Valuations Version 3A", for the life of an individual age 40 is 12.1519 (1.000000 minus .10076, divided by .074). Based on Table B(7.4), contained in Publication 1457, "Actuarial Valuations Version 3A", the factor 12.1519 corresponds to a term of years between 32 and 33 years. Accordingly, the annuity interest must be reformed into an interest payable for a term of 33 years. A judicial reformation must be commenced prior to the later of July 5, 2001, or the date prescribed by section 2055(e)(3)(C)(iii). Any judicial reformation must be completed within a reasonable time after it is commenced. A non-judicial reformation is permitted if effective under state law, provided it is completed by the date on which a judicial reformation must be commenced. In the alternative, if a court, in a proceeding that is commenced on or before July 5, 2001, declares any transfer made pursuant to a will or revocable trust where the decedent dies on or after April 4, 2000, and on or before March 6, 2001, null and void ab initio, the Internal Revenue Service will treat such transfers in a manner similar to that described in section 2055(e)(3)(J).

(4) *Amendment of dispositive provisions.*—For purposes of subparagraphs (2) and (3) of this paragraph, an amendment shall generally be considered as one which amends the dispositive provisions of a will or trust if it results in a change in the persons to whom the funds are to be given or makes changes in the conditions under which the funds are given. Examples of amendments which do not amend the dispositive provisions of a will or trust include the substitution of one fiduciary for another to act in the capacity of executor or trustee and the change in the name of a legatee or beneficiary by reason of the legatee's or beneficiary's marriage. On the other hand, examples of amendments which do amend the dispositive provisions of a will or trust include an increase or decrease in the amount of a general bequest, an amendment which increases or decreases the power of a trustee to determine an allocation of income or corpus in such a way as to change the beneficiaries of the funds or a beneficiary's share of the funds, or a change in the allocation of, or in the right to allocate, receipts and expenditures between income and principal in such a way as to change the beneficiaries of the funds or a beneficiary's share of the funds.

(5) *Amendment of wills providing for pour-over into trusts.*—For purposes of subparagraphs (2) and (3) of this paragraph, an amendment of a dispositive provision of a trust to which assets are to be transferred under a will shall be considered a dispositive amendment of such will.

(f) *Valuation of charitable interest.*—(1) *In general.*—The amount of the deduction in the case of a contribution of a partial interest in property to which this section applies is the fair market value of the partial interest at the appropriate valuation date, as defined in paragraph (e)(2)(vi)(*h*) of this section. The fair market value of an annuity, life estate, term for years, remainder, reversion, or unitrust interest is its present value.

(2) *Certain decedents dying after July 31, 1969.*—In the case of a transfer of an interest described in subdivision (v), (vi), or (vii) of paragraph (e)(2) of this section by decedents dying after July 31, 1969, the present value of such interest is to be determined under the following rules:

(i) The present value of a remainder interest in a charitable remainder annuity trust is to be determined under § 1.664-2(c) of this chapter (Income Tax Regulations).

(ii) The present value of a remainder interest in a charitable remainder unitrust is to be determined under § 1.664-4 of this chapter.

(iii) The present value of a remainder interest in a pooled income fund is to be determined under § 1.642(c)-6 of this chapter.

(iv) The present value of a guaranteed annuity interest described in paragraph (e)(2)(vi) of this section is to be determined under § 20.2031-7 or, for certain prior periods, § 20.2031-7A, except that, if the annuity is issued by a company regularly engaged in the sale of annuities, the present value is to be determined under § 20.2031-8. If by reason of all the conditions and circumstances surrounding a transfer of an income interest in property in trust it appears that the charity may not receive the beneficial enjoyment of the interest, a deduction will be allowed under section 2055 only for the minimum amount it is evident the charity will receive.

Example (1). In 1975, B dies bequeathing $20,000 in trust with the requirement that a designated charity be paid a guaranteed annuity interest (as defined in paragraph (e)(2)(vi) of this section) of $4,100 a year, payable annually at the end of each year, for a period of 6 years and that the remainder be paid to his children. The fair market value of an annuity of $4,100 a year for a period of 6 years is $20,160.93 ($4,100 × 4.9173), as determined under Table B in § 20.2031-7A(d). The deduction with respect to the guaranteed annuity interest will be limited to $20,000, which is the minimum amount it is evident the charity will receive.

Example (2). In 1975, C dies bequeathing $40,000 in trust with the requirement that D, an individual, and X Charity be paid simultaneously guaranteed annuity interests (as defined in paragraph (e)(2)(vi) of this section) of $5,000 a year each, payable annually at the end of each year, for a period of 5 years and that the remainder be paid to C's children. The fair market value of two annuities of $5,000 each a year for a period of 5 years is $42,124 ([$5,000 × 4.2124] × 2), as determined under Table B in § 20.2031-7A(d). The trust instrument provides that in the event the trust fund is insufficient to pay both annuities in a given year, the trust fund will be evenly divided between the charitable and private annuitants. The deduction with respect to the charitable annuity will be limited to $20,000, which is the minimum amount it is evident the charity will receive.

Example (3). In 1975, D dies bequeathing $65,000 in trust with the requirement that a guaranteed annuity interest (as defined in paragraph (e)(2)(vi) of this section) of $5,000 a year, payable annually at the end of each year, be paid to Y Charity for a period of 10 years and that a guaranteed annuity interest (as defined in paragraph (e)(2)(vi) of this section) of $5,000 a year, payable annually at the end of each year, be paid to W, his widow, aged 62, for 10 years or until her prior death. The annuities are to be paid simultaneously, and the remainder is to be paid to D's children. The fair market value of the private annuity is $33,877 ($5,000 × 6.7754), as determined pursuant to § 20.2031-7A(c) and by the use of factors involving one life and a term of years as published in Publication 723A (12-70). The fair market value of the charitable annuity is $36,800.50 ($5,000 × 7.3601), as determined under Table B in § 20.2031-7A(d). It is not evident from the governing instrument of the trust or from local law that the trustee would be required to apportion the trust fund between the widow and charity in the event the fund were insufficient to pay both annuities in a given year. Accordingly, the deduction with respect to the charitable annuity will be limited to $31,123 ($65,000 less $33,877 [the value of the private annuity]), which is the minimum amount it is evident the charity will receive.

(v) The present value of a unitrust interest described in paragraph (e)(2)(vii) of this section is to be determined by subtracting the present value of all interests in the transferred property other than the unitrust interest from the fair market value of the transferred property.

(3) *Certain decedents dying before August 1, 1969.*—In the case of decedents dying before August 1, 1969, the present value of an interest described in subparagraph (2) of this paragraph is to be determined under § 20.2031-7 except that, if the interest is an annuity issued by a company regularly engaged in the sale of annuities, the present value is to be determined under § 20.2031-8.

(4) *Other decedents.*—The present value of an interest not described in paragraph (f)(2) of this section is to be determined under § 20.2031-7(d) in the case of decedents where the valuation date of the gross estate is on or after May 1, 2009, or under § 20.2031-7A in the case of decedents where the valuation date of the gross estate is before May 1, 2009.

(5) *Special computations.*—If the interest transferred is such that its present value is to be determined by a special computation, a request for a special factor, accompanied by a statement of the date of birth and sex of each individual the duration of whose life may affect the value of the interest, and by copies of the relevant instruments, may be submitted by the fiduciary to the Commissioner who may, if conditions permit, supply the factor requested. If the Commissioner furnishes the factor, a copy of the letter supplying the factor must be attached to the tax return in which the deduction is claimed. If the Commissioner does not furnish the factor, the claim for deduction must be supported by a full statement of the computation of the present value made in accordance with the principles set forth in this paragraph.

(6) *Effective/applicability date.*—Paragraphs (e)(3)(iii) and (f)(4) of this section apply on and after May 1, 2009. [Reg. § 20.2055-2.]

□ [*T.D.* 6296, 6-23-58. *Amended by T.D.* 7238, 12-28-72; *T.D.* 7318, 7-10-74; *T.D.* 7340, 1-6-75; *T.D.* 7955, 5-10-84; *T.D.* 7957, 5-16-84; *T.D.* 8069, 1-13-86; *T.D.* 8095, 8-6-86; *T.D.* 8540, 6-9-94; *T.D.* 8819, 4-29-99; *T.D.* 8886, 6-9-2000; *T.D.* 8923, 1-4-2001; *T.D.* 9068, 7-3-2003; *T.D.* 9448, 5-1-2009 *and T.D.* 9540, 8-9-2011.]

[Reg. § 20.2055-3]

§ 20.2055-3. Effect of death taxes and administration expenses.—(a) *Death taxes.*—(1) If under the terms of the will or other governing instrument, the law of the jurisdiction under which the estate is administered, or the law of the jurisdiction imposing the particular tax, the Federal estate tax, or any estate, succession, legacy, or inheritance tax is payable in whole or in part out of any property the transfer of which would otherwise be allowable as a deduction under section 2055, section 2055(c) provides that the sum deductible is the amount of the transferred property reduced by the amount of the tax. Section 2055(c) in effect provides that the deduction is based on the amount actually available for charitable uses, that is, the amount of the fund remaining after the payment of all death taxes. Thus, if $50,000 is bequeathed for a charitable purpose and is subjected to a State inheritance tax of $5,000, payable out of the $50,000, the amount deductible is $45,000. If a life estate is bequeathed to an individual with remainder over to a charitable organization, and by the local law the inheritance tax upon the life estate is paid out of the corpus with the result that the charitable organization will be entitled to receive only the amount of the fund less the tax, the deduction is limited to the present value, as of the date of the testator's death, of the remainder of the fund so reduced. If a testator bequeaths his residuary estate, or a portion of it, to charity, and his will contains a direction that certain inheritance taxes, otherwise payable from legacies upon which they were imposed, shall be payable out of the residuary estate, the deduction may not exceed the bequest to charity thus reduced pursuant to the direction of the will. If a residuary estate, or a portion of it, is bequeathed to charity, and by the local law the Federal estate tax is payable out of the residuary estate, the deduction may not exceed that portion of the residuary estate bequeathed to charity as reduced by the Federal estate tax. The return should fully disclose the computation of the amount to be deducted. If the amount to be deducted is dependent upon the amount of any death tax which has not been paid before the filing of the return, there should be submitted with the return a computation of that tax.

(2) It should be noted that if the Federal estate tax is payable out of a charitable transfer so that the amount of the transfer otherwise passing to charity is reduced by the amount of the tax, the resultant decrease in the amount passing to charity will further reduce the allowable deduction. In such a case, the amount of the charitable deduction can be obtained only by a series of trial-and-error computations, or by a formula. If, in addition, interdependent State and Federal taxes are involved, the computation becomes highly complicated. Examples of methods of computation of the charitable deduction and the marital deduction (with which similar problems are encountered) in various situations are contained in supplemental instructions to the estate tax return.

(3) For the allowance of a deduction to a decedent's estate for certain State death taxes imposed upon charitable transfers, see section 2053(d) and § 20.2053-9.

(b) *Administration expenses.*—(1) *Definitions.*—(i) *Management expenses.*—Estate management expenses are expenses that are incurred in connection with the investment of estate assets or with their preservation or maintenance during a reasonable period of administration. Examples of these expenses could include investment advisory fees, stock brokerage commissions, custodial fees, and interest.

(ii) *Transmission expenses.*—Estate transmission expenses are expenses that would not have been incurred but for the decedent's death and the consequent necessity of collecting the decedent's assets, paying the decedent's debts and death taxes, and distributing the decedent's property to those who are entitled to receive it. Estate transmission expenses include any administration expense that is not a management expense. Examples of these expenses could include executor commissions and attorney fees (except to the extent of commissions or fees specifically related to investment, preservation, or maintenance of the assets), probate fees, expenses incurred in construction proceedings and defending against will contests, and appraisal fees.

(iii) *Charitable share.*—The charitable share is the property or interest in property that passed from the decedent for which a deduction is allowable under section 2055(a) with respect to all or part of the property interest. The charitable share includes, for example, bequests to charitable organizations and bequests to a charitable lead unitrust or annuity trust, a charitable remainder unitrust or annuity trust, and a pooled income fund, described in section 2055(e)(2). The charitable share also includes the income produced by the property or interest in property during the period of administration if the income, under the terms of the governing instrument or applicable local law, is payable to the charitable organization or is to be added to the principal of the property interest passing in whole or in part to the charitable organization.

(2) *Effect of transmission expenses.*—For purposes of determining the charitable deduction, the value of the charitable share shall be reduced by the amount of the estate transmission expenses paid from the charitable share.

(3) *Effect of management expenses attributable to the charitable share.*—For purposes of determining the charitable deduction, the value of the charitable share shall not be reduced by the amount of the estate management expenses attributable to and paid from the charitable share. Pursuant to section 2056(b)(9), however, the amount of the allowable charitable deduction shall be reduced by the amount of any such management expenses that are deducted under section 2053 on the decedent's federal estate tax return.

(4) *Effect of management expenses not attributable to the charitable share.*—For purposes of determining the charitable deduction, the value of the charitable share shall be reduced by the amount of the estate management expenses paid from the charitable share but attributable to a property interest not included in the charitable share.

(5) *Example.*—The following example illustrates the application of this paragraph (b):

Example. The decedent, who dies in 2000, leaves his residuary estate, after the payment of debts, expenses, and estate taxes, to a charitable remainder unitrust that satisfies the requirements of section 664(d). During the period of administration, the estate incurs estate transmission expenses of $400,000. The residue of the estate (the charitable share) must be reduced by the $400,000 of transmission expenses and by the Federal and State estate taxes before the present value of the remainder interest passing to charity can be determined in accordance with the provisions of § 1.664-4 of this chapter. Because the estate taxes are payable out of the residue, the computation of the estate taxes and the allowable charitable deduction are interrelated. See paragraph (a)(2) of this section.

(6) *Cross reference.*—See § 20.2056(b)-4(d) for additional examples applicable to the treatment of administration expenses under this paragraph (b).

(7) *Effective date.*—The provisions of this paragraph (b) apply to estates of decedents dying on or after December 3, 1999. [Reg. § 20.2055-3.]

□ [*T.D.* 6296, 6-23-58. *Amended by T.D.* 8846, 12-2-99 (*corrected* 12-17-99).]

[Reg. § 20.2055-4]

§ 20.2055-4. Disallowance of charitable, etc., deductions because of "prohibited transactions" in the case of decedents dying before January 1, 1970.—(a) Sections 503(e) and 681(b)(5) provide that no deduction which would otherwise be allowable under section 2055 for the value of property transferred by the decedent during his lifetime or by will for religious, charitable, scientific, literary, or educational purposes (including the encouragement of art and the prevention of cruelty to children or animals) is allowed if (1) the transfer is made in trust, and, for income tax purposes for the taxable year of the trust in which the transfer is made, the deduction otherwise allowable to the trust under section 642(c) is limited by section 681(b)(1) by reason of the trust having engaged in a prohibited transaction described in section 681(b)(2), or (2) the transfer is made to a corporation, community chest, fund or foundation which, for its taxable year in which the transfer is made, is not exempt from income tax under section 501(a) by reason of having engaged in a prohibited transaction described in section 503(c).

(b) For purposes of section 681(b)(5) and section 503(e), the term "transfer" includes any gift, contribution, bequest, devise, legacy, or other disposition. In applying such sections for estate tax purposes, a transfer, whether made during the decedent's lifetime or by will, is considered as having been made at the moment of the decedent's death.

(c) The income tax regulations contain the rules for the determination of the taxable year of the trust for which the deduction under section 642(c) is limited by section 681(b) and for the determination of the taxable year of the organization for which an exemption is denied under section 503(a). Generally, such taxable year is a taxable year subsequent to the taxable year during which the trust or organization has been notified by the Commissioner of Internal Revenue that it has engaged in a prohibited transaction. However, if the trust or organization during or prior to the taxable year entered into the prohibited transaction for the purpose of diverting its corpus or income from the charitable or other purposes by reason of which it is entitled to a deduction or exemption, and the transaction involves a substantial part of the income or corpus, then the deduction of the trust under section 642(c) for such taxable year is limited by section 681(b), or exemption of the organization for such taxable year is denied under section 503(a), whether or not the organization has previously received notification by the Commissioner of Internal Revenue that it is engaged in a prohibited transaction. In certain cases, the limitation of sections 681 or 503 may be removed or the exemption may be reinstated for certain subsequent taxable years under the rules set forth in the income tax regulations under sections 681 and 503. In cases in which prior notification by the Commissioner of Internal Revenue is not required in order to limit the deduction of the trust under section 681(b) or to deny exemption of the organization under section 503, the deduction otherwise allowable under section 2055 is not disallowed in respect of transfers made during the same taxable year of the trust or organization in which a prohibited transaction occurred or in a prior taxable year unless the decedent or a member of his family was a party to the prohibited transaction. For the purpose of the preceding sentence, the members of the decedent's family include only his brothers and sisters, whether by whole or half blood, spouse, ancestors, and lineal descendants.

(d) This section applies only in the case of decedents dying before January 1, 1970. In the case of decedents dying after December 31, 1969, see § 20.2055-5. [Reg. § 20.2055-4.]

□ [*T.D.* 6296, 6-23-58. *Amended by T.D.* 7318, 7-10-74.]

[Reg. § 20.2055-5]

§ 20.2055-5. Disallowance of charitable, etc., deductions in the case of decedents dying after December 31, 1969.—(a) *Organizations subject to section 507(c) tax.*—Section 508(d)(1) provides that, in the case of decedents dying after December 31, 1969, a deduction which would otherwise be allowable under section 2055 for the value of property transferred by the decedent to or for the use of an organization upon which the tax provided by section 507(c) has been imposed shall not be allowed if the transfer is made by the decedent after notification is made under section 507(a) or if the decedent is a substantial contributor (as defined in section 507(d)(2)) who dies on or after the first day on which action is taken by such organization that culminates in the imposition of the tax under section 507(c). This paragraph does not apply if the entire amount of the unpaid portion of the tax imposed by section 507(c) is abated under section 507(g) by the Commissioner or his delegate.

(b) *Taxable private foundations, section 4947 trusts, etc.*—(1) *In general.*—Section 508(d)(2) provides that, in the case of decedents dying after December 31, 1969, a deduction which would otherwise be allowable under section 2055 for the value of property transferred by the decedent shall not be allowed if the transfer is made to or for the use of—

(i) A private foundation or a trust described in section 4947(a)(2) in a taxable year of such organization for which such organization fails to meet the governing instrument requirements of section 508(e) (determined without regard to section 508(e)(2)(B) and (C)), or

(ii) Any organization in a period for which it is not treated as an organization described in section 501(c)(3) by reason of its failure to give notification under section 508(a) of its status to the Commissioner.

For additional rules, see § 1.508-2(b)(1) of this chapter (Income Tax Regulations).

(2) *Transfers not covered by section 508(d)(2)(A).*—(i) *In general.*—Any deduction which would otherwise be allowable under section 2055 for the value of property transferred by a decedent dying after December 31, 1969, will not be disallowed under section 508(d)(2)(A) and subparagraph (1)(i) of this paragraph—

(a) In the case of property passing under the terms of a will executed on or before October 9, 1969—

(1) If the decedent dies after October 9, 1969, but before October 9, 1972, without having amended any dispositive provision of the will after October 9, 1969, by codicil or otherwise,

(2) If the decedent dies after October 9, 1969, and at no time after that date had the right to change the portions of the will which pertain to the passing of the property to, or for the use of, an organization described in section 2055(a), or

(3) If no dispositive provision of the will is amended by the decedent, by codicil or otherwise, after October 9, 1969, and before October 9, 1972, and the decedent is on October 9, 1972, and at all times thereafter under a mental disability (as defined in § 1.642(c)-2(b)(3)(ii) of this chapter) to amend the will by codicil or otherwise, or

(b) In the case of property transferred in trust on or before October 9, 1969—

(1) If the decedent dies after October 9, 1969, but before October 9, 1972, without having amended, after October 9, 1969, any dispositive provision of the instrument governing the disposition of the property,

(2) If the property transferred was an irrevocable interest to, or for the use of, an organization described in section 2055(a), or

(3) If no dispositive provision of the instrument governing the disposition of the property is amended by the decedent after October 9, 1969, and before October 9, 1972, and the decedent is on October 9, 1972, and at all times thereafter under a mental disability (as defined in § 1.642(c)-2(b)(3)(ii) of this chapter) to change the disposition of the property.

(ii) *Amendment of dispositive provisions.*—For purposes of subdivision (i) of this subparagraph, the provisions of paragraph (e)(4) and (5) of § 20.2055-2 shall apply in determining whether an amendment will be considered as one which amends the dispositive provisions of a will or trust.

(c) *Foreign organization with substantial support from foreign sources.*—Section 4948(c)(4) provides that, in the case of decedents dying after December 31, 1969, a deduction which would otherwise be allowable under section 2055 for the value of property transferred by the decedent to or for the use of a foreign organization which has received substantially all of its support (other than gross investment income) from sources without the United States shall not be allowed if the transfer is made (1) after the date on which the Commissioner has published notice that he has notified such organization that it has engaged in a prohibited transaction, or (2) in a taxable year of such organization for which it is not exempt from taxation under section 501(a) because it has engaged in a prohibited transaction after December 31, 1969. [Reg. § 20.2055-5.]

☐ [*T.D.* 7318, 7-10-74.]

[Reg. § 20.2055-6]

§ 20.2055-6. Disallowance of double deduction in the case of qualified terminable interest property.—No deduction is allowed from the decedent's gross estate under section 2055 for property with respect to which a deduction is allowed by reason of section 2056(b)(7). See section 2056(b)(9) and § 20.2056(b)-9. [Reg. § 20.2055-6.]

☐ [*T.D.* 8522, 2-28-94.]

[Reg. § 20.2056-0]

§ 20.2056-0. Table of contents.—This section lists the captions that appear in the regulations under §§ 20.2056(a)-1 through 20.2056(d)-2.

§ 20.2056(a)-1. Marital deduction; in general.

(a) In general.

(b) Requirements for marital deduction.

(1) In general.

(2) Burden of establishing requisite facts.

(c) Marital deduction; limitation on aggregate deductions.

(1) Estates of decedents dying before 1977.

(2) Estates of decedents dying after December 31, 1976, and before January 1, 1982.

(3) Estates of decedents dying after December 31, 1981.

§20.2056(c)-3. Marital deduction; definition of passed from the decedent to a person other than his surviving spouse.

§20.2056(d)-1. Marital deduction; special rules for marital deduction if surviving spouse is not a United States citizen.

§20.2056(d)-2. Marital deduction; effect of disclaimers of post-December 31,1976 transfers.

(a) Disclaimer by a surviving spouse.

(b) Disclaimer by a person other than a surviving spouse.

§20.2056(d)-3. Marital deduction; effect of disclaimers of pre-January 1, 1977 transfers.

(a) Disclaimers by a surviving spouse.

(b) Disclaimer by a person other than a surviving spouse.

(1) Decedents dying after October 3, 1966, and before January 1, 1977.

(2) Decedents dying after September 30, 1963, and before October 4, 1966.

(3) Decedents dying before October 4, 1966.

[Reg. §20.2056-0.]

☐ [*T.D.* 8522, 2-28-94. *Amended by T.D.* 8612, 8-21-95.]

[Reg. §20.2056(a)-1]

§20.2056(a)-1. Marital deduction; in general.—(a) *In general.*—A deduction is allowed under section 2056 from the gross estate of a decedent for the value of any property interest which passes from the decedent to the decedent's surviving spouse if the interest is a *deductible interest* as defined in §20.2056(a)-2. With respect to decedents dying in certain years, a deduction is allowed under section 2056 only to the extent that the total of the deductible interests does not exceed the applicable limitations set forth in paragraph(c) of this section. The deduction allowed under section 2056 is referred to as the *marital deduction*. See also sections 2056(d) and 2056A for special rules applicable in the case of decedents dying after November 10, 1988, if the decedent's surviving spouse is not a citizen of the United States at the time of the decedent's death. In such cases, the marital deduction may not be allowed unless the property passes to a qualified domestic trust as described in section 2056A(a).

(b) *Requirements for marital deduction.*—(1) *In general.*—To obtain the marital deduction with respect to any property interest, the executor must establish the following facts—

(i) The decedent was survived by a spouse (see §20.2056(c)-2(e));

(ii) The property interest passed from the decedent to the spouse (see §§20.2056(b)-5 through 20.2056(b)-8 and 20.2056(c)-1 through 20.2056(c)-3);

(iii) The property interest is a *deductible interest* (see §20.2056(a)-2); and

(iv) The value of the property interest (see §20.2056(b)-4).

(2) *Burden of establishing requisite facts.*—The executor must provide the facts relating to any applicable limitation on the amount of the allowable marital deduction under §20.2056(a)-1(c), and must submit proof necessary to establish any fact required under paragraph (b)(1), including any evidence requested by the district director.

(c) *Marital deduction; limitation on aggregate deductions.*—(1) *Estates of decedents dying before 1977.*—In the case of estates of decedents dying before January 1, 1977, the marital deduction is limited to one-half of the value of the *adjusted gross estate*, as that term was defined under section 2056(c)(2) prior to repeal by the Economic Recovery Tax Act of 1981.

(2) *Estates of decedents dying after December 31, 1976, and before January 1, 1982.*—Except as provided in §2002(d)(1) of the Tax Reform Act of 1976 (Pub. L. 94-455), in the case of decedents dying after December 31, 1976, and before January 1, 1982, the marital deduction is limited to the greater of—

(i) $250,000; or

(ii) One-half of the value of the decedent's adjusted gross estate, adjusted for intervivos gifts to the spouse as prescribed by section 2056(c)(1)(B) prior to repeal by the Economic Recovery Tax Act of 1981 (Pub. L. 97-34).

(3) *Estates of decedents dying after December 31, 1981.*—In the case of estates of decedents dying after December 31, 1981, the marital deduction is limited as prescribed in paragraph (c)(2) of this section if the provisions of section 403(e)(3) of Pub. L. 97-34 are satisfied. [Reg. §20.2056(a)-1.]

☐ [*T.D. 6296, 6-23-58. Amended by T.D. 8095, 8-6-86 and T.D.* 8522, 2-28-94.]

[Reg. §20.2056(a)-2]

§20.2056(a)-2. Marital deduction; deductible interests and nondeductible interests.—(a) *In general.*—Property interests which passed from a decedent to his surviving spouse fall within two general categories: (1) those with respect to which the marital deduction is authorized, and (2) those with respect to which the marital deduction is not authorized. These categories are referred to in this section and other sections of the regulations under section 2056 as "deductible interests" and "nondeductible interests," respectively (see paragraph (b) of this section). Subject to any applicable limitations set forth in §20.2056(a)-1(c), the amount of the marital deduction is the aggregate value of the *deductible interests*.

(b) *Deductible interests.*—An interest passing to a decedent's surviving spouse is a "deductible interest" if it does not fall within one of the following categories of "nondeductible interests":

(1) Any property interest which passed from the decedent to his surviving spouse is a "nondeductible interest" to the extent it is not included in the decedent's gross estate.

(2) If a deduction is allowed under section 2053 (relating to deductions for expenses and indebtedness) by reason of the passing of a property interest from the decedent to his surviving spouse, such interest is, to the extent of the deduction under section 2053, a "nondeductible interest." Thus, a property interest which passed from the decedent to his surviving spouse in satisfaction of a deductible claim of the spouse against the estate is, to the extent of the claim, a "nondeductible interest" (see § 20.2056(b)-4). Similarly, amounts deducted under section 2053(a)(2) for commissions allowed to the surviving spouse as executor are "nondeductible interests." As to the valuation, for the purpose of the marital deduction, of any property interest which passed from the decedent to his surviving spouse subject to a mortgage or other encumbrance, see § 20.2056(b)-4.

(3) If during settlement of the estate a loss deductible under section 2054 occurs with respect to a property interest, then that interest is, to the extent of the deductible loss, a "nondeductible interest" for the purpose of the marital deduction.

(4) A property interest passing to a decedent's surviving spouse which is a "terminable interest," as defined in § 20.2056(b)-1, is a "nondeductible interest" to the extent specified in that section. [Reg. § 20.2056(a)-2.]

☐ [*T.D.* 6296, 6-23-58. *Amended by T.D.* 8522, 2-28-94.]

[Reg. § 20.2056(b)-1]

§ 20.2056(b)-1. Marital deduction; limitation in case of life estate or other terminable interest.—(a) *In general.*—Section 2056(b) provides that no marital deduction is allowed with respect to certain property interests, referred to generally as "terminable interests," passing from a decedent to his surviving spouse. The phrase "terminable interest" is defined in paragraph (b) of this section. However, the fact that an interest in property passing to a decedent's surviving spouse is a "terminable interest" makes it nondeductible only (1) under the circumstances described in paragraph (c) of this section, and (2) if it does not come within one of the exceptions referred to in paragraph (d) of this section.

(b) *"Terminable interests."*—A "terminable interest" in property is an interest which will terminate or fail on the lapse of time or on the occurrence or the failure to occur of some contingency. Life estates, terms for years, annuities, patents, and copyrights are therefore terminable interests. However, a bond, note, or similar contractual obligation, the discharge of which would not have the effect of an annuity or a term for years, is not a terminable interest.

(c) *Nondeductible terminable interests.*—(1) A property interest which constitutes a terminable interest, as defined in paragraph (b) of this section, is nondeductible if—

(i) Another interest in the same property passed from the decedent to some other person for less than an adequate and full consideration in money or money's worth, and

(ii) By reason of its passing, the other person or his heirs or assigns may possess or enjoy any part of the property after the termination or failure of the spouse's interest.

(2) Even though a property interest which constitutes a terminable interest is not nondeductible by reason of the rules stated in subparagraph (1) of this paragraph, such an interest is nondeductible if—

(i) The decedent has directed his executor or a trustee to acquire such an interest for the decedent's surviving spouse (see further paragraph (f) of this section), or

(ii) Such an interest passing to the decedent's surviving spouse may be satisfied out of a group of assets which includes a nondeductible interest (see further § 20.2056(b)-2). In this case, however, full nondeductibility may not result.

(d) *Exceptions.*—A property interest passing to a decedent's surviving spouse is deductible (if it is not otherwise disqualified under § 20.2056(a)-2) even though it is a terminable interest, and even though an interest therein passed from the decedent to another person, if it is a terminable interest only because—

(1) It is conditioned on the spouse's surviving for a limited period, in the manner described in § 20.2056(b)-3;

(2) It is a right to income for life with a general power of appointment, meeting the requirements set forth in § 20.2056(b)-5;

(3) It consists of life insurance or annuity payments held by the insurer with a general power of appointment in the spouse, meeting the requirements set forth in § 20.2056(b)-6;

(4) It is qualified terminable interest property, meeting the requirements set forth in § 20.2056(b)-7; or

(5) It is an interest in a qualified charitable remainder trust in which the spouse is the only noncharitable beneficiary, meeting the requirements set forth in § 20.2056(b)-8.

(e) *Miscellaneous principles.*—(1) In determining whether an interest passed from the decedent to some other person, it is immaterial whether interests in the same property passed to the decedent's spouse and another person at the same time, or under the same instrument.

(2) In determining whether an interest in the same property passed from the decedent both to his surviving spouse and to some other person, a distinction is to be drawn between "property," as such term is used in section 2056, and an "interest in property." The term "property" refers to the underlying property in which various interests exist; each such interest is not for this purpose to be considered as "property."

(3) Whether or not an interest is nondeductible because it is a terminable interest is to be determined by reference to the property interests which actually passed from the decedent. Subsequent conversions of the property are immaterial for this purpose. Thus, where a decedent bequeathed his estate to his wife for life with re-

mainder to his children, the interest which passed to his wife is a nondeductible interest, even though the wife agrees with the children to take a fractional share of the estate in fee in lieu of the life interest in the whole, or sells the life estate for cash, or acquires the remainder interest of the children either by purchase or gift.

(4) The terms *passed from the decedent, passed from the decedent to his surviving spouse,* and *passed from the decedent to a person other than his surviving spouse* are defined in §§20.2056(c)-1 through 20.2056(c)-3.

(f) *Direction to acquire a terminable interest.*—No marital deduction is allowed with respect to a property interest which a decedent directs his executor or a trustee to convert after his death into a terminable interest for his surviving spouse. The marital deduction is not allowed even though no interest in the property subject to the terminable interest passes to another person and even though the interest would otherwise come within the exceptions described in §§20.2056(b)-5 and 20.2056(b)-6 (relating to life estates and life insurance and annuity payments with powers of appointment). However, a general investment power, authorizing investments in both terminable interests and other property, is not a direction to invest in a terminable interest.

(g) *Examples.*—The application of this section may be illustrated by the following examples. In each example, it is assumed that the executor made no election under section 2056(b)(7) (even if under the specific facts the election would have been available), that any property interest passing from the decedent to a person other than the surviving spouse passed for less than full and adequate consideration in money or money's worth, and that section 2056(b)(8) is inapplicable.

Example (1). H (the decedent) devised real property to W (his surviving wife) for life, with remainder to A and his heirs. The interest which passed from H to W is a nondeductible interest since it will terminate upon her death and A (or his heirs or assigns) will thereafter possess or enjoy the property.

Example (2). H bequeathed the residue of his estate in trust for the benefit of W and A. The trust income is to be paid to W for life, and upon her death the corpus is to be distributed to A or his issue. However, if A should die without issue, leaving W surviving, the corpus is then to be distributed to W. The interest which passed from H to W is a nondeductible interest since it will terminate in the event of her death if A or his issue survive, and A or his issue will thereafter possess or enjoy the property.

Example (3). H during his lifetime purchased an annuity contract providing for payments to himself for life and then to W for life if she should survive him. Upon the death of the survivor of H and W, the excess, if any, of the cost of the contract over the annuity payments theretofore made was to be refunded to A. The interest which passed from H to W is a nondeductible interest since A may possess or enjoy a part of the property following the termination of the interest of W. If, however, the contract provided for no refund upon the death of the survivor of H and W, or provided that any refund was to go to the estate of the survivor, then the interest which passed from H to W is (to the extent it is included in H's gross estate) a deductible interest.

Example (4). H, in contemplation of death, transferred a residence to A for life with remainder to W provided W survives A, but if W predeceases A, the property is to pass to B and his heirs. If it is assumed that H died during A's lifetime, and the value of the residence was included in determining the value of his gross estate, the interest which passed from H to W is a nondeductible interest since it will terminate if W predeceases A and the property will thereafter be possessed or enjoyed by B (or his heirs or assigns). This result is not affected by B's assignment of his interest during H's lifetime, whether made in favor of W or another person, since the term "assigns" (as used in section 2056(b)(1)(B)) includes such an assignee. However, if it is assumed that A predeceased H, the interest of B in the property was extinguished, and, viewed as of the time of the subsequent death of H, the interest which passed from him to W is the entire interest in the property and, therefore, a deductible interest.

Example (5). H transferred real property to A by gift, reserving the right to the rentals of the property for a term of 20 years. H died within the 20-year term, bequeathing the right to the remaining rentals to a trust for the benefit of W. The terms of the trust satisfy the five conditions stated in §20.2056(b)-5, so that the property interest which passed in trust is considered to have passed from H to W. However, the interest is a nondeductible interest since it will terminate upon the expiration of the term and A will thereafter possess or enjoy the property.

Example (6). H bequeathed a patent to W and A as tenants in common. In this case, the interest of W will terminate upon the expiration of the term of the patent, but possession or enjoyment of the property by A must necessarily cease at the same time. Therefore, since A's possession or enjoyment cannot outlast the termination of W's interest, the latter is a deductible interest.

Example (7). A decedent bequeathed $100,000 to his wife, subject to a direction to his executor to use the bequest for the purchase of an annuity for the wife. The bequest is a nondeductible interest.

Example (8). Assume that pursuant to local law an allowance for support is payable to the decedent's surviving spouse during the period of the administration of the decedent's estate, but that upon her death or remarriage during such period her right to any further allowance will terminate. Assume further that the surviving spouse is sole beneficiary of the decedent's estate. Under such circumstances, the allowance constitutes a deductible interest since any part of the allowance not receivable by the surviving spouse during her lifetime will pass to her estate under the terms of the decedent's will. If, in this example, the decedent bequeathed only one-third of his residuary estate to his surviving spouse, then two-thirds of the allowance for support would constitute a nondeductible terminable interest. [Reg. § 20.2056(b)-1.]

☐ [*T.D.* 6296, 6-23-58. *Amended by T.D.* 8522, 2-28-94.]

[Reg. § 20.2056(b)-2]

§ 20.2056(b)-2. Marital deduction; interest in unidentified assets.—(a) *In general.*—Section 2056(b)(2) provides that if an interest passing to a decedent's surviving spouse may be satisfied out of assets (or their proceeds) which include a particular asset that would be a nondeductible interest if it passed from the decedent to his spouse, the value of the interest passing to the spouse is reduced, for the purpose of the marital deduction, by the value of the particular asset.

(b) *Application of section 2056(b)(2).*—In order for section 2056(b)(2) to apply, two circumstances must coexist, as follows:

(1) The property interest which passed from the decedent to his surviving spouse must be payable out of a group of assets included in the gross estate. Examples of property interests payable out of a group of assets are a general legacy, a bequest of the residue of the decedent's estate or of a portion of the residue, and a right to a share of the corpus of a trust upon its termination.

(2) The group of assets out of which the property interest is payable must include one or more particular assets which, if passing specifically to the surviving spouse, would be nondeductible interests. Therefore, section 2056(b)(2) is not applicable merely because the group of assets includes a terminable interest, but would only be applicable if the terminable interest were nondeductible under the provisions of § 20.2056(b)-1.

(c) *Interest nondeductible if circumstances present.*—If both of the circumstances set forth in paragraph (b) of this section are present, the property interest payable out of the group of assets is (except as to any excess of its value over the aggregate value of the particular asset or assets which would not be deductible if passing specifically to the surviving spouse) a nondeductible interest.

(d) The application of this section may be illustrated by the following example:

Example. A decedent bequeathed one-third of the residue of his estate to his wife. The property passing under the decedent's will included a right to the rentals of an office building for a term of years, reserved by the decedent under a deed of the building by way of gift to his son. The decedent did not make a specific bequest of the right to such rentals. Such right, if passing specifically to the wife, would be a nondeductible interest (see example (5) of paragraph (g) of § 20.2056(b)-1). It is assumed that the value of the bequest of one-third of the residue of the estate to the wife was $85,000, and that the right to the rentals was included in the gross estate at a value of $60,000. If the decedent's executor had the right under the decedent's will or local law to assign the entire lease in satisfaction of the bequest, the bequest is a nondeductible interest to the extent of $60,000. If the executor could only assign a one-third interest in the lease in satisfaction of the bequest, the bequest is a nondeductible interest to the extent of $20,000. If the decedent's will provided that his wife's bequest could not be satisfied with a nondeductible interest, the entire bequest is a deductible interest. If, in this example, the asset in question had been foreign real estate not included in the decedent's gross estate, the results would be the same. [Reg. § 20.2056(b)-2.]

☐ [*T.D.* 6296, 6-23-58. *Amended by T.D.* 8522, 2-28-94.]

[Reg. § 20.2056(b)-3]

§ 20.2056(b)-3. Marital deduction; interest of spouse conditioned on survival for limited period.—(a) *In general.*—Generally, no marital deduction is allowable if the interest passing to the surviving spouse is a terminable interest as defined in paragraph (b) of § 20.2056(b)-1. However, section 2056(b)(3) provides an exception to this rule so as to allow a deduction if (1) the only condition under which it will terminate is the death of the surviving spouse within 6 months after the decedent's death, or her death as a result of a common disaster which also resulted in the decedent's death, and (2) the condition does not in fact occur.

(b) *Six months' survival.*—If the only condition which will cause the interest taken by the surviving spouse to terminate is the death of the surviving spouse and the condition is of such nature that it can occur only within 6 months following the decedent's death, the exception provided by section 2056(b)(3) will apply, provided the condition does not in fact occur. However, if the condition (unless it relates to death as a result of a common disaster) is one which may occur either within the 6-month period or thereafter, the exception provided by section 2056(b)(3) will not apply.

(c) *Common disaster.*—If a property interest passed from the decedent to his surviving spouse subject to the condition that she does not die as a result of a common disaster which also resulted in the decedent's death, the exception provided by section 2056(b)(3) will not be applied in the final audit of the return if there is still a possibility that the surviving spouse may be deprived of the property interest by operation of the common disaster provision as given effect by the local law.

(d) *Examples.*—The application of this section may be illustrated by the following examples:

Example (1). A decedent bequeathed his entire estate to his spouse on condition that she survive him by 6 months. In the event his spouse failed to survive him by 6 months, his estate was to go to his niece and her heirs. The decedent was survived by his spouse. It will be observed that, as of the time of the decedent's death, it was possible that the niece would, by reason of the interest which passed to her from the decedent, possess or enjoy the estate after the termination of the interest which passed to the spouse. Hence, under the general rule set forth in § 20.2056(b)-1, the interest which passed to the spouse would be regarded as a nondeductible interest. If the surviving spouse in fact died within 6 months after the decedent's death, that general rule is to be applied, and the interest which passed to the spouse is a nondeductible interest. However, if the spouse in fact survived the decedent by 6 months, thus extinguishing the interest of the niece, the case comes within the exception provided by section 2056(b)(3), and the interest which passed to the spouse is a deductible interest. (It is assumed for the purpose of this example that no other factor which would cause the interest to be nondeductible is present.)

Example (2). The facts are the same as in example (1) except that the will provided that the estate was to go to the niece either in case the decedent and his spouse should both die as a result of a common disaster, or in case the spouse should fail to survive the decedent by 3 months. It is assumed that the decedent was survived by his spouse. In this example, the interest which passed from the decedent to his surviving spouse is to be regarded as a nondeductible interest if the surviving spouse in fact died either within 3 months after the decedent's death or as a result of a common disaster which also resulted in the decedent's death. However, if the spouse in fact survived the decedent by 3 months, and did not thereafter die as a result of a common disaster which also resulted in the decedent's death, the exception provided under section 2056(b)(3) will apply and the interest will be deductible.

Example (3). The facts are the same as in example (1) except that the will provided that the estate was to go to the niece if the decedent and his spouse should both die as a result of a common disaster and if the spouse failed to survive the decedent by 3 months. If the spouse in fact survived the decedent by 3 months, the interest of the niece is extinguished, and the interest passing to the spouse is a deductible interest.

Example (4). A decedent devised and bequeathed his residuary estate to his wife if she was living on the date of distribution of his estate. The devise and bequest is a nondeductible interest even though distribution took place within 6 months after the decedent's death and the surviving spouse in fact survived the date of distribution. [Reg. § 20.2056(b)-3.]

☐ [*T.D.* 6296, 6-23-58.]

[Reg. § 20.2056(b)-4]

§ 20.2056(b)-4. Marital deduction; valuation of interest passing to surviving spouse.—(a) *In general.*—The value, for the purpose of the marital deduction, of any deductible interest which passed from the decedent to his surviving spouse is to be determined as of the date of the decedent's death, except that if the executor elects the alternate valuation method under section 2032 the valuation is to be determined as of the date of the decedent's death but with the adjustment described in paragraph (a)(3) of § 20.2032-1. The marital deduction may be taken only with respect to the net value of any deductible interest which passed from the decedent to his surviving spouse, the same principles being applicable as if the amount of a gift to the spouse were being determined.

(b) *Property interest subject to an encumbrance or obligation.*—If a property interest passed from the decedent to his surviving spouse subject to a mortgage or other encumbrance, or if an obligation is imposed upon the surviving spouse by the decedent in connection with the passing of a property interest, the value of the property interest is to be reduced by the amount of the mortgage, other encumbrance, or obligation. However, if under the terms of the decedent's will or under local law the executor is required to discharge, out of other assets of the decedent's estate, a mortgage or other encumbrance on property passing from the decedent to his surviving spouse, or is required to reimburse the surviving spouse for the amount of the mortgage or other encumbrance, the payment or reimbursement constitutes an additional interest passing to the surviving spouse. The passing of a property interest subject to the imposition of an obligation by the decedent does not include a bequest, devise, or transfer in lieu of dower, curtesy, or of a statutory estate created in lieu of dower or curtesy, or of other marital rights in the decedent's property or estate. The passing of a property interest subject to the imposition of an obligation by the decedent does, however, include a bequest, etc., in lieu of the interest of his surviving spouse under community property laws unless such interest was, immediately prior to the decedent's death, a mere expectancy. The following examples are illustrative of property interests which passed from the decedent to his surviving spouse subject to the imposition of an obligation by the decedent:

Example (1). A decedent devised a residence valued at $25,000 to his wife, with a direction that she pay $5,000 to his sister. For the purpose of the marital deduction, the value of the property interest passing to the wife is only $20,000.

Example (2). A decedent devised real property to his wife in satisfaction of a debt owing to her. The debt is a deductible claim under section 2053. Since the wife is obligated to relinquish the claim as a condition to acceptance of the devise, the value of the devise is, for the purpose of the marital deduction, to be reduced by the amount of the claim.

Example (3). A decedent bequeathed certain securities to his wife in lieu of her interest in property held by them as community property under the law of the State of their residence. The wife elected to relinquish her community property interest and to take the bequest. For the purpose of the marital deduction, the value of the bequest is to be reduced by the value of the community property interest relinquished by the wife.

(c) *Effect of death taxes.*—(1) In the determination of the value of any property interest which passed from the decedent to his surviving spouse, there must be taken into account the effect which the Federal estate tax, or any estate, succession, legacy, or inheritance tax, has upon the net value to the surviving spouse of the property interest.

(2) For example, assume that the only bequest to the surviving spouse is $100,000 and the spouse is required to pay a State inheritance tax in the amount of $1,500. If no other death taxes affect the net value of the bequest, the value, for the purpose of the marital deduction, is $98,500.

(3) As another example, assume that a decedent devised real property to his wife having a value for Federal estate tax purposes of $100,000 and also bequeathed to her a nondeductible interest for life under a trust. The State of residence valued the real property at $90,000 and the life interest at $30,000, and imposed an inheritance tax (at graduated rates) of $4,800 with respect to the two interests. If it is assumed that the inheritance tax on the devise is required to be paid by the wife, the amount of tax to be ascribed to the devise is

$$\frac{90{,}000}{120{,}000} \times \$4{,}800 = \$3{,}600.$$

Accordingly, if no other death taxes affect the net value of the bequest, the value, for the purpose of the marital deduction, is $100,000 less $3,600, or $96,400.

(4) If the decedent bequeaths his residuary estate, or a portion of it, to his surviving spouse, and his will contains a direction that all death taxes shall be payable out of the residuary estate, the value of the bequest, for the purpose of the marital deduction, is based upon the amount of the residue as reduced pursuant to such direction. If the residuary estate, or a portion of it, is bequeathed to the surviving spouse, and by the local law the Federal estate tax is payable out of the residuary estate, the value of the bequest, for the purpose of the marital deduction, may not exceed its value as reduced by the Federal estate tax. Methods of computing the deduction, under such circumstances, are set forth in supplemental instructions to the estate tax return.

(d) *Effect of administration expenses.*—(1) *Definitions.*—(i) *Management expenses.*—Estate management expenses are expenses that are incurred in connection with the investment of estate assets or with their preservation or maintenance during a reasonable period of administration. Examples of these expenses could include investment advisory fees, stock brokerage commissions, custodial fees, and interest.

(ii) *Transmission expenses.*—Estate transmission expenses are expenses that would not have been incurred but for the decedent's death and the consequent necessity of collecting the decedent's assets, paying the decedent's debts and death taxes, and distributing the decedent's property to those who are entitled to receive it. Estate transmission expenses include any administration expense that is not a management expense. Examples of these expenses could include executor commissions and attorney fees (except to the extent of commissions or fees specifically related to investment, preservation, or maintenance of the assets), probate fees, expenses incurred in construction proceedings and defending against will contests, and appraisal fees.

(iii) *Marital share.*—The marital share is the property or interest in property that passed from the decedent for which a deduction is allowable under section 2056(a). The marital share includes the income produced by the property or interest in property during the period of administration if the income, under the terms of the governing instrument or applicable local law, is payable to the surviving spouse or is to be added to the principal of the property interest passing to, or for the benefit of, the surviving spouse.

(2) *Effect of transmission expenses.*—For purposes of determining the marital deduction, the value of the marital share shall be reduced by the amount of the estate transmission expenses paid from the marital share.

(3) *Effect of management expenses attributable to the marital share.*—For purposes of determining the marital deduction, the value of the marital share shall not be reduced by the amount of the estate management expenses attributable to and paid from the marital share. Pursuant to section 2056(b)(9), however, the amount of the allowable marital deduction shall be reduced by the amount of any such management expenses that are deducted under section 2053 on the decedent's Federal estate tax return.

(4) *Effect of management expenses not attributable to the marital share.*—For purposes of determining the marital deduction, the value of the marital share shall be reduced by the amount of the estate management expenses paid from the marital share but attributable to a property interest not included in the marital share.

(5) *Examples.*—The following examples illustrate the application of this paragraph (d):

Example 1. The decedent dies after 2006 having made no lifetime gifts. The decedent makes a bequest of shares of ABC Corporation stock to the decedent's child. The bequest provides that the child is to receive the income from the shares from the date of the decedent's death. The value of the bequeathed shares on the decedent's date of death is $3,000,000. The residue of the estate is bequeathed to a trust for which the executor properly makes an election under section 2056(b)(7) to treat as qualified terminable interest property. The value of the residue on the decedent's date of death, before the payment of administration expenses and Federal and State estate taxes, is $6,000,000. Under applicable local law, the executor has the discretion to pay administration expenses from the income or principal of the residuary estate. All estate taxes are to be paid from the residue. The State estate tax equals the State death tax credit available under section 2011. During the period of administration, the estate incurs estate transmission expenses of $400,000, which the executor charges to the residue. For purposes of determining the marital deduction, the value of the residue is reduced by the Federal and State estate taxes and by the estate transmission expenses. If the transmission expenses are deducted on the Federal estate tax return, the marital deduction is $3,500,000 ($6,000,000 minus $400,000 transmission expenses and minus $2,100,000 Federal and State estate taxes). If the transmission expenses are deducted on the estate's Federal income tax return rather than on the estate tax return, the marital deduction is $3,011,111 ($6,000,000 minus $400,000 transmission expenses and minus $2,588,889 Federal and State estate taxes).

Example 2. The facts are the same as in *Example 1,* except that, instead of incurring estate transmission expenses, the estate incurs estate management expenses of $400,000 in connection with the residue property passing for the benefit of the spouse. The executor charges these management expenses to the residue. In determining the value of the residue passing to the spouse for marital deduction purposes, a reduction is made for Federal and State estate taxes payable from the residue but no reduction is made for the estate management expenses. If the management expenses are deducted on the estate's income tax return, the net value of the property passing to the spouse is $3,900,000 ($6,000,000 minus $2,100,000 Federal and State estate taxes). A marital deduction is claimed for that amount, and the taxable estate is $5,100,000.

Example 3. The facts are the same as in *Example 1,* except that the estate management expenses of $400,000 are incurred in connection with the bequest of ABC Corporation stock to the decedent's child. The executor charges these management expenses to the residue. For purposes of determining the marital deduction, the value of the residue is reduced by the Federal and State estate taxes and by the management expenses. The management expenses reduce the value of the residue because they are charged to the property passing to the spouse even though they were incurred with respect to stock passing to the child. If the management expenses are deducted on the estate's Federal income tax return, the marital deduction is $3,011,111 ($6,000,000 minus $400,000 management expenses and minus $2,588,889 Federal and State estate taxes). If the management expenses are deducted on the estate's Federal estate tax return, rather than on the estate's Federal income tax return, the marital deduction is $3,500,000 ($6,000,000 minus $400,000 management expenses and minus $2,100,000 in Federal and State estate taxes).

Example 4. The decedent, who dies in 2000, has a gross estate of $3,000,000. Included in the gross estate are proceeds of $150,000 from a policy insuring the decedent's life and payable to the decedent's child as beneficiary. The applicable credit amount against the tax was fully consumed by the decedent's lifetime gifts. Applicable State law requires the child to pay any estate taxes attributable to the life insurance policy. Pursuant to the decedent's will, the rest of the decedent's estate passes outright to the surviving spouse. During the period of administration, the estate incurs estate management expenses of $150,000 in connection with the property passing to the spouse. The value of the property passing to the spouse is $2,850,000 ($3,000,000 less the insurance proceeds of $150,000 passing to the child). For purposes of determining the marital deduction, if the management expenses are deducted on the estate's income tax return, the marital deduction is $2,850,000 ($3,000,000 less $150,000) and there is a resulting taxable estate of $150,000 ($3,000,000 less a marital deduction of $2,850,000). Suppose, instead, the management expenses of $150,000 are deducted on the estate's estate tax return under section 2053 as expenses of administration. In such a situation, claiming a marital deduction of $2,850,000 would be taking a deduction for the same $150,000 in property under both sections 2053 and 2056 and would shield from estate taxes the $150,000 in insurance proceeds passing to the decedent's child. Therefore, in accordance with section 2056(b)(9), the marital deduction is limited to $2,700,000, and the resulting taxable estate is $150,000.

Example 5. The decedent dies after 2006 having made no lifetime gifts. The value of the decedent's residuary estate on the decedent's date of death is $3,000,000, before the payment of administration expenses and Federal and State estate taxes. The decedent's will provides a formula for dividing the decedent's residuary estate between two trusts to reduce the estate's Federal estate taxes to zero. Under the formula, one trust, for the benefit of the decedent's child, is to be funded with that amount of property equal in value to so much of the applicable exclusion amount under section 2010 that would reduce the estate's Federal estate tax to zero. The other trust, for the benefit of the surviving spouse, satisfies the requirements of section 2056(b)(7) and is to be funded with the remaining property in the estate. The State estate tax equals the State death tax credit available under section 2011. During the period of administration, the estate incurs transmission expenses of $200,000. The transmission expenses of $200,000 reduce the value of the residue to $2,800,000. If the transmission expenses are deducted on the Federal estate tax return, then the formula divides the residue so that the value of the property passing to the child's trust is $1,000,000 and the value of the property passing to the marital trust is $1,800,000. The allowable marital deduction is $1,800,000. The applicable exclusion amount shields from Federal estate tax the entire $1,000,000 passing to the child's trust so that the amount of Federal and State estate taxes is zero. Alternatively, if the transmission expenses are deducted on the estate's Federal income tax return, the formula divides the residue so that the value of the property passing to the child's trust is $800,000 and the value of the property passing to the marital trust is $2,000,000. The allowable marital deduction is $2,000,000. The applicable exclusion amount shields from Federal estate tax the entire $800,000 passing to the child's trust so that the amount of Federal and State estate taxes remains zero.

Example 6. The facts are the same as in *Example 5*, except that the decedent's will provides that the child's trust is to be funded with that amount of property equal in value to the applicable exclusion amount under section 2010 allowable to the decedent's estate. The residue of the estate, after the payment of any debts, expenses, and Federal and State estate taxes, is to pass to the marital trust. The applicable exclusion amount in this case is $1,000,000, so the value of the property passing to the child's trust is $1,000,000. After deducting the $200,000 of transmission expenses, the residue of the estate is $1,800,000 less any estate taxes. If the transmission expenses are deducted on the Federal estate tax return, the allowable marital deduction is $1,800,000, the taxable estate is zero, and the Federal and State estate taxes are zero. Alternatively, if the transmission expenses are deducted on the estate's Federal income tax return, the net value of the property passing to the spouse is $1,657,874 ($1,800,000 minus $142,106 estate taxes). A marital deduction is claimed for that amount, the taxable estate is $1,342,106, and the Federal and State estate taxes total $142,106.

Example 7. The decedent, who dies in 2000, makes an outright pecuniary bequest of $3,000,000 to the decedent's surviving spouse, and the residue of the estate, after the payment of all debts, expenses, and Federal and State estate taxes, passes to the decedent's child. Under the terms of the governing instrument and applicable local law, a beneficiary of a pecuniary bequest is not entitled to any income on the bequest. During the period of administration, the estate pays estate transmission expenses from the income earned by the property that will be distributed to the surviving spouse in satisfaction of the pecuniary bequest. The income earned on this property is not part of the marital share. Therefore, the allowable marital deduction is $3,000,000, unreduced by the amount of the estate transmission expenses.

(6) *Effective date*.—The provisions of this paragraph (d) apply to estates of decedents dying on or after December 3, 1999.

(e) *Remainder interests*.—If the income from property is made payable to another individual for life, or for a term of years, with remainder absolutely to the surviving spouse or to her estate, the marital deduction is based upon the present value of the remainder. The present value of the remainder is to be determined in accordance with the rules stated in § 20.2031-7. For example, if the surviving spouse is to receive $50,000 upon the death of a person aged 31 years, the present value of the remainder is $14,466. If the remainder is such that its value is to be determined by a special computation (see paragraph (b) of § 20.2031-7), a request for a specific factor may be submitted to the Commissioner. The request should be accompanied by a statement of the date of birth of each person, the duration of whose life may affect the value of the remainder, and copies of the relevant instruments. The Commissioner may, if conditions permit, supply the factor requested. If the Commissioner does not furnish the factor, the claim for deduction must be supported by a full statement of the computation of the present value made in accordance with the principles set forth in the applicable paragraphs of § 20.2031-7. [Reg. § 20.2056(b)-4.]

☐ [*T.D.* 6296, 6-23-58. *Amended by T.D.* 8522, 2-28-94; *T.D.* 8540, 6-9-94 *and T.D.* 8846, 12-2-99 (*corrected* 12-17-99).]

[Reg. § 20.2056(b)-5]

§ 20.2056(b)-5. Marital deduction; life estate with power of appointment in surviving spouse.—(a) *In general*.—Section 2056(b)(5) provides that if an interest in property passes from the decedent to his surviving spouse (whether or not in trust) and the spouse is entitled for life to all the income from the entire interest or all the income from a specific portion of the entire interest, with a power in her to appoint the entire interest or the specific portion, the interest which passes to her is a deductible interest, to the extent that it satisfies all five of the conditions set forth below (see paragraph (b) of this section if one or more of the conditions is satisfied as to only a portion of the interest):

(1) The surviving spouse must be entitled for life to all of the income from the entire interest or a specific portion of the entire interest, or to a specific portion of all the income from the entire interest.

(2) The income payable to the surviving spouse must be payable annually or at more frequent intervals.

(3) The surviving spouse must have the power to appoint the entire interest or the specific portion to either herself or her estate.

(4) The power in the surviving spouse must be exercisable by her alone and (whether exercisable by will or during life) must be exercisable in all events.

(5) The entire interest or the specific portion must not be subject to a power in any other person to appoint any part to any person other than the surviving spouse.

(b) *Specific portion; deductible amount*.—If either the right to income or the power of appointment passing to the surviving spouse pertains only to a specific portion of a property interest passing from the decedent, the marital deduction is allowed only to the extent that the rights in the surviving spouse meet all of the five conditions described in paragraph (a) of this section. While the rights over the income and the power must coexist as to the same interest in property, it is not necessary that the rights over the income or the power as to such interest be in the same proportion. However, if the rights over income meeting the required conditions set forth in paragraph (a)(1) and (2) of this section extend over a smaller share of the property interest than the share with respect to which the power of appointment requirements set forth in paragraph (a)(3) through (5) of this section are satisfied, the deductible interest is limited to the smaller share. Correspondingly, if a power of appointment meeting all the requirements extends to a smaller portion of the property interest than the portion over which the income rights pertain, the deductible interest cannot exceed the value of the portion to which such power of appointment applies. Thus, if the decedent leaves to his surviving spouse the right to receive annually all of the income from a particular property interest and a power of appointment meeting the specifications prescribed in paragraph (a)(3) through (5) of this section as to only one-half of the property interest, then only one-half of the property interest is treated as a deductible interest. Correspondingly, if the income interest of the spouse satisfying the requirements extends to only one-fourth of the property interest and a testamentary power of appointment satisfying the requirements extends to all of the property interest, then only one-fourth of the interest in the spouse qualifies as a deductible interest. Further, if the surviving spouse has no right to income from a specific portion of a property interest but a testamentary power of appointment which meets the necessary conditions over the entire interest, then none of the interest qualifies for the deduction. In addition, if, from the time of the decedent's death, the surviving spouse has a power of appointment meeting all of the required conditions over three-fourths of the entire property interest and the prescribed income rights over the entire interest, but with a power in another person to appoint one-half of the entire interest, the value of the interest in the surviving spouse over only one-half of the property interest will qualify as a deductible interest.

(c) *Meaning of specific portion.*—(1) *In general.*—Except as provided in paragraphs (c)(2) and (c)(3) of this section, a partial interest in property is not treated as a specific portion of the entire interest. In addition, any specific portion of an entire interest in property is nondeductible to the extent the specific portion is subject to invasion for the benefit of any person other than the surviving spouse, except in the case of a deduction allowable under section 2056(b)(5), relating to the exercise of a general power of appointment by the surviving spouse.

(2) *Fraction or percentage share.*—Under section 2056(b)(10), a partial interest in property is treated as a specific portion of the entire interest if the rights of the surviving spouse in income, and the required rights as to the power described in § 20.2056(b)-5(a), constitute a fractional or percentage share of the entire property interest, so that the surviving spouse's interest reflects its proportionate share of the increase or decrease in the value of the entire property interest to which the income rights and the power relate. Thus, if the spouse's right to income and the spouse's power extend to a specified fraction or percentage of the property, or the equivalent, the interest is in a specific portion of the property. In accordance with paragraph (b) of this section, if the spouse has the right to receive the income from a specific portion of the trust property (after applying paragraph (c)(3) of this section) but has a power of appointment over a different specific portion of the property (after applying paragraph (c)(3) of this section), the marital deduction is limited to the lesser specific portion.

(3) *Special rule in the case of estates of decedents dying on or before October 24, 1992, and certain decedents dying after October 24, 1992, with wills or revocable trusts executed on or prior to that date.*

(i) In the case of estates of decedents within the purview of the effective date and transitional rules contained in paragraphs (c)(3)(ii) and (iii) of this section:

(A) A specific sum payable annually, or at more frequent intervals, out of the property and its income that is not limited by the income of the property is treated as the right to receive the income from a specific portion of the property. The specific portion, for purposes of paragraph (c)(2) of this section, is the portion of the property that, assuming the interest rate generally applicable for the valuation of annuities at the time of the decedent's death, would produce income equal to such payments. However, a pecuniary amount payable annually to a surviving spouse is not treated as a right to the income from a specific portion of the trust property for purposes of this paragraph (c)(3)(i)(A) if any person other than the surviving spouse may receive, during the surviving spouse's lifetime, any distribution of the property. To determine the applicable interest rate for valuing annuities, see sections 2031 and 7520 and the regulations under those sections.

(B) The right to appoint a pecuniary amount out of a larger fund (or trust corpus) is considered the right to appoint a specific portion of such fund or trust for purposes of paragraph (c)(2) in an amount equal to such pecuniary amount.

(ii) The rules contained in paragraphs (c)(3)(i)(A) and (B) of this section apply with respect to estates of decedents dying on or before October 24, 1992.

(iii) The rules contained in paragraphs (c)(3)(i)(A) and (B) of this section apply in the case of decedents dying after October 24, 1992, if property passes to the spouse pursuant to a will or revocable trust agreement executed on or before October 24, 1992, and either—

(A) On that date, the decedent was under a mental disability to change the disposition of the property and did not regain competence to dispose of such property before the date of death; or

(B) The decedent dies prior to October 24, 1995.

(iv) Notwithstanding paragraph (c)(3)(iii) of this section, paragraphs (c)(3)(i)(A) and (B) of this section do not apply if the will or revocable trust is amended after October 24, 1992, in any respect that increases the amount of the transfer qualifying for the marital deduction or alters the terms by which the interest so passes to the surviving spouse of the decedent.

(4) *Local law.*—A partial interest in property is treated as a specific portion of the entire interest if it is shown that the surviving spouse has rights under local law that are identical to those the surviving spouse would have acquired had the partial interest been expressed in terms satisfying the requirements of paragraph (c)(2) (or paragraph (c)(3) if applicable) of this section.

(5) *Examples.*—The following examples illustrate the application of paragraphs (a) through (c)(4) of this section:

Example 1. Spouse entitled to the lesser of an annuity or a fraction of trust income. The decedent, D, died prior to October 24, 1992. D bequeathed in trust 500 identical shares of X company stock, valued for estate tax purposes at $500,000. The trust provides that during the lifetime of D's spouse, S, the trustee is to pay annually to S the lesser of one-half of the trust income or $20,000. Any trust income not paid to S is to be accumulated in the trust and may not be distributed during S's lifetime. S has a testamentary general power of appointment over the entire trust principal. The applicable interest rate for valuing annuities as of D's date of death under section 7520 is 10 percent. For purposes of paragraphs (a) through (c) of this section, S is treated as receiving all of the income from the lesser of—

(i) One half of the stock ($250,000); or

(ii) $200,000, the specific portion of the stock which, as determined in accordance with § 20.2056(b)-5(c)(3)(i)(A), would produce annual income of $20,000 (20,000/.10). Accordingly, the marital deduction is limited to $200,000 (200,000/500,000 or 2/5th of the value of the trust).

Example 2. Spouse possesses power and income interest over different specific portions of trust. The facts are the same as in *Example 1* except that S's testamentary general power of appointment is exercisable over only 1/4th of the trust principal. Consequently, under section 2056(b)(5), the marital deduction is allowable only for the value of 1/4th of the trust ($125,000); i.e., the lesser of the value of the portion with respect to which S is deemed to be entitled to all of the income (2/5th of the trust or $200,000), or the value of the portion with respect to which S possesses the requisite power of appointment (1/4th of the trust or $125,000).

Example 3. Power of appointment over pecuniary amount. The decedent, D, died prior to October 24, 1992. D bequeathed property valued at $400,000 for estate tax purposes in trust. The trustee is to pay annually to D's spouse, S, one-fourth of the trust income. Any trust income not paid to S is to be accumulated in the trust and may not be distributed during S's lifetime. The will gives S a testamentary general power of appointment over the sum of $160,000. Because D died prior to October 24, 1992, S's power of appointment over $160,000 is treated as a power of appointment over a specific portion of the entire trust interest. The marital deduction allowable under section 2056(b)(5) is limited to $100,000; that is, the lesser of—

(1) The value of the trust corpus ($400,000);

(2) The value of the trust corpus over which S has a power of appointment ($160,000); or

(3) That specific portion of the trust with respect to which S is entitled to all the income ($100,000).

Example 4. Power of appointment over shares of stock constitutes a power over a specific portion. Under D's will, 250 shares of Y company stock were bequeathed in trust pursuant to which all trust income was payable annually to S, D's spouse, for life. S was given a testamentary general power of appointment over 100 shares of stock. The trust provides that if the trustee sells the Y company stock, S's general power of appointment is exercisable with respect to the sale proceeds or the property in which the proceeds are reinvested. Because the amount of property represented by a single share of stock would be altered if the corporation split its stock, issued stock dividends, made a distribution of capital, etc., a power to appoint 100 shares at the time of S's death is not necessarily a power to appoint the entire interest that the 100 shares represented on the date of D's death. If it is shown that, under local law, S has a general power to appoint not only the 100 shares designated by D but also 100/250 of any distributions by the corporation that are included in trust principal, the requirements of paragraph (c)(2) of this section are satisfied and S is treated as having a general power to appoint 100/250 of the entire interest in the 250 shares. In that case, the marital deduction is limited to 40 percent of the trust principal. If local law does not give S that power, the 100 shares would not constitute a specific portion under § 20.2056(b)-5(c) (including § 20.2056(b)-5(c)(3)(i)(B)). The nature of the asset is such that a change in the capitalization of the corporation could cause an alteration in the original value represented by the shares at the time of D's death and, thus, it does not represent a specific portion of the trust.

(d) *Meaning of entire interest.*—Because a marital deduction is allowed for each separate qualifying interest in property passing from the decedent to the decedent's surviving spouse (subject to any applicable limitations in § 20.2056(a)-1(c)), for purposes of paragraphs (a) and (b) of this section, each property interest with respect to which the surviving spouse received any rights is considered separately in determining whether the surviving spouse's rights extend to the entire interest or to a specific portion of the entire interest. A property interest which consists of several identical units of property (such as a block of 250 shares of stock, whether the ownership is evidenced by one or several certificates) is considered one property interest, unless certain of the units are to be segregated and accorded different treatment, in which case each segregated group of items is considered a separate property interest. The bequest of a specified sum of money constitutes the bequest of a separate property interest if immediately following distribution by the executor and thenceforth it, and the investments made with it, must be so segregated or accounted for as to permit its identification as a separate item of property. The application of this paragraph may be illustrated by the following examples:

Example (1). The decedent transferred to a trustee three adjoining farms, Blackacre, Whiteacre, and Greenacre. His will provided that during the lifetime of the surviving spouse the trustee should pay her all of the income from the trust. Upon her death, all of Blackacre, a one-half interest in Whiteacre, and a one-third interest in Greenacre were to be distributed to the person or persons appointed by her in her will. The surviving spouse is considered as being entitled to all of the income from the entire interest in Blackacre, all of the income from the entire interest in Whiteacre, and all of the income from the entire interest in Greenacre. She also is considered as having a power of appointment over the entire interest in Blackacre, over one-half of the entire interest in Whiteacre, and over one-third of the entire interest in Greenacre.

Example (2). The decedent bequeathed $250,000 to C, as trustee. C is to invest the money and pay all of the income from the investments to W, the decedent's surviving spouse, annually. W was given a general power, exercisable by will, to appoint one-half of the corpus of the trust. Here, immediately following distribution by the executor the $250,000 will be sufficiently segregated to permit its identification as a separate item, and the $250,000 will constitute an entire property interest. Therefore, W has a right to income and a power of appointment such that one-half of the entire interest is a deductible interest.

Example (3). The decedent bequeathed 100 shares of Z Corporation stock to D, as trustee. W, the decedent's surviving spouse, is to receive all of the income of the trust annually and is given a general power, exercisable by will, to appoint out of the trust corpus the sum of $25,000. In this case the $25,000 is not, immediately following distribution, sufficiently segregated to permit its identification as a separate item of property in which the surviving spouse has the entire interest. Therefore, the $25,000 does not constitute the entire interest in a property for the purpose of paragraphs (a) and (b) of this section.

(e) *Application of local law.*—In determining whether or not the conditions set forth in paragraph (a)(1) through (5) of this section are satisfied by the instrument of transfer, regard is to be had to the applicable provisions of the law of the jurisdiction under which the interest passes and, if the transfer is in trust, the applicable provisions of the law governing the administration of the trust. For example, silence of a trust instrument as to the frequency of payment will not be regarded as a failure to satisfy the condition set forth in paragraph (a)(2) of this section that income must be payable to the surviving spouse annually or more frequently unless the applicable law permits payment to be made less frequently than annually. The principles outlined in this paragraph and paragraphs (f) and (g) of this section which are applied in determining whether transfers in trust meet such conditions are equally applicable in ascertaining whether, in the case of interests not in trust, the surviving spouse has the equivalent in rights over income and over the property.

(f) *Right to income.*—(1) If an interest is transferred in trust, the surviving spouse is "entitled for life to all of the income from the entire interest or a specific portion of the entire interest," for the purpose of the condition set forth in paragraph (a)(1) of this section, if the effect of the trust is to give her substantially that degree of beneficial enjoyment of the trust property during her life which the principles of the law of trusts accord to a person who is unqualifiedly designated as the life beneficiary of a trust. Such degree of enjoyment is given only if it was the decedent's intention, as manifested by the terms of the trust instrument and the surrounding circumstances, that the trust should produce for the surviving spouse during her life such an income, or that the spouse should have such use of the trust property as is consistent with the value of the trust corpus and with its preservation. The designation of the spouse as sole income beneficiary for life of the entire interest or a specific portion of the entire interest will be sufficient to qualify the trust unless the terms of the trust and the surrounding circumstances considered as a whole evidence an intention to deprive the spouse of the requisite degree of enjoyment. In determining whether a trust evidences that intention, the treatment required or permitted with respect to individual items must be considered in relation to the entire system provided for the administration of the trust. In addition, the surviving spouse's interest shall meet the condition set forth in paragraph (a)(1) of this section if the spouse is entitled to income as determined by applicable local law that provides for a reasonable apportionment between the income and remainder beneficiaries of the total return of the trust and that meets the requirements of § 1.643(b)-1 of this chapter.

(2) If the over-all effect of a trust is to give to the surviving spouse such enforceable rights as will preserve to her the requisite degree of enjoyment, it is immaterial whether that result is effected by rules specifically stated in the trust instrument, or, in their absence, by the rules for the management of the trust property and the allocation of receipts and expenditures supplied by the State law. For example, a provision in the trust instrument for amortization of bond premium by appropriate periodic charges to interest will not disqualify the interest passing in trust even though there is no State law specifically authorizing amortization, or there is a State law denying amortization which is applicable only in the absence of such a provision in the trust instrument.

(3) In the case of a trust, the rules to be applied by the trustee in allocation of receipts and expenses between income and corpus must be considered in relation to the nature and expected productivity of the assets passing in trust, the nature and frequency of occurrence of the expected receipts, and any provisions as to change in the form of investments. If it is evident from the nature of the trust assets and the rules provided for management of the trust that the allocation to income of such receipts as rents, ordinary cash dividends, and interest will give to the spouse the substantial enjoyment during life required by the statute, provisions that such receipts as stock dividends and proceeds from the conversion of trust assets shall be treated as corpus will not disqualify the interest passing in trust. Similarly, provision for a depletion charge against income in the case of trust assets which are subject to depletion will not disqualify the interest passing in trust, unless the effect is to deprive the spouse of the requisite beneficial enjoyment. The same principle is applicable in the case of deprecia tion, trustees' commissions, and other charges.

(4) Provisions granting administrative powers to the trustee will not have the effect of disqualifying an interest passing in trust unless the grant of powers evidences the intention to deprive the surviving spouse of the beneficial enjoyment required by the statute. Such an intention will not be considered to exist if the entire terms of the instrument are such that the local courts will impose reasonable limitations upon the exercise of the powers. Among the powers which if subject to reasonable limitations will not disqualify the interest passing in trust are the power to determine the allocation or apportionment of receipts and disbursements between income and corpus, the power to apply the income or corpus for the benefit of the spouse, and the power to retain the assets passing to the trust. For example, a power to retain trust assets which consist substantially of unproductive property will not disqualify the interest if the applicable rules for the administration of the trust require, or permit the spouse to require, that the trustee either make the property productive or convert it within a reasonable time. Nor will such a power disqualify the interest if the applicable rules for administration of the trust require the trustee to use the degree of judgment and care in the exercise of the power which a prudent man would use if he were owner of the trust assets. Further, a power to retain a residence or other property for the personal use of the spouse will not disqualify the interest passing in trust.

(5) An interest passing in trust will not satisfy the condition set forth in paragraph (a)(1) of this section that the surviving spouse be entitled to all the income if the primary purpose of the trust is to safeguard property without providing the spouse with the required beneficial enjoyment. Such trusts include not only trusts which expressly provide for the accumulation of the income but also trusts which indirectly accomplish a similar purpose. For example, assume that the corpus of a trust consists substantially of property which is not likely to be income producing during the life of the surviving spouse and that the spouse cannot compel the trustee to convert or otherwise deal with the property as described in subparagraph (4) of this paragraph. An interest passing to such a trust will not qualify unless the applicable rules for the administration require, or permit the spouse to require, that the trustee provide the required beneficial enjoyment, such as by payments to the spouse out of other assets of the trust.

(6) If a trust is created during the decedent's life, it is immaterial whether or not the interest passing in trust satisfied the conditions set forth in paragraph (a)(1) through (5) of this section prior to the decedent's death. If a trust may be terminated during the life of the surviving spouse, under her exercise of a power of appointment or by distribution of the corpus to her, the interest passing in trust satisfies the condition set forth in paragraph (a)(1) of this section (that the spouse be entitled to all the income) if she (i) is entitled to the income until the trust terminates, or (ii) has the right, exercisable in all events, to have the corpus distributed to her at any time during her life.

(7) An interest passing in trust fails to satisfy the condition set forth in paragraph (a)(1) of this section, that the spouse be entitled to all the income, to the extent that the income is required to be accumulated in whole or in part or may be accumulated in the discretion of any person other than the surviving spouse; to the extent that the consent of any person other than the surviving spouse is required as a condition precedent to distribution of the income; or to the extent that any person other than the surviving spouse has the power to alter the terms of the trust so as to deprive her of her right to the income. An interest passing in trust will not fail to satisfy the condition that the spouse be entitled to all the income merely because its terms provide that the right of the surviving spouse to the income shall not be subject to assignment, alienation, pledge, attachment or claims of creditors.

(8) In the case of an interest passing in trust, the terms "entitled for life" and "payable annually or at more frequent intervals", as used in the conditions set forth in paragraph (a)(1) and (2) of this section, require that under the terms of the trust the income referred to must be currently (at least annually; see paragraph (e) of this section) distributable to the spouse or that she must have such command over the income that it is virtually hers. Thus, the conditions in paragraph (a)(1) and (2) of this section are satisfied in this respect if, under the terms of the trust instrument, the spouse has the right exercisable annually (or more frequently) to require distribution to herself of the trust income, and otherwise the trust income is to be accumulated and added to corpus. Similarly, as respects the income for the period between the last distribution date and the date of the spouse's death, it is sufficient if that income is subject to the spouse's power to appoint. Thus, if the trust instrument provides that

income accrued or undistributed on the date of the spouse's death is to be disposed of as if it had been received after her death, and if the spouse has a power of appointment over the trust corpus, the power necessarily extends to the undistributed income.

(9) An interest is not to be regarded as failing to satisfy the conditions set forth in paragraph (a)(1) and (2) of this section (that the spouse be entitled to all the income and that it be payable annually or more frequently) merely because the spouse is not entitled to the income from estate assets for the period before distribution of those assets by the executor, unless the executor is, by the decedent's will, authorized or directed to delay distribution beyond the period reasonably required for administration of the decedent's estate. As to the valuation of the property interest passing to the spouse in trust where the right to income is expressly postponed, see § 20.2056(b)-4.

(g) *Power of appointment in surviving spouse.*—(1) The conditions set forth in paragraph (a)(3) and (4) of this section, that is, that the surviving spouse must have a power of appointment exercisable in favor of herself or her estate and exercisable alone and in all events, are not met unless the power of the surviving spouse to appoint the entire interest or a specific portion of it falls within one of the following categories:

(i) A power so to appoint fully exercisable in her own favor at any time following the decedent's death (as, for example, an unlimited power to invade); or

(ii) A power so to appoint exercisable in favor of her estate. Such a power, if exercisable during life, must be fully exercisable at any time during life, or, if exercisable by will, must be fully exercisable irrespective of the time of her death (subject in either case to the provisions of § 20.2056(b)-3, relating to interests condi tioned on survival for a limited period); or

(iii) A combination of the powers described under subparagraphs (i) and (ii) of this subparagraph. For example, the surviving spouse may, until she attains the age of 50 years, have a power to appoint to herself and thereafter have a power to appoint to her estate. However, the condition that the spouse's power must be exercisable in all events is not satisfied unless irrespective of when the surviving spouse may die the entire interest or a specific portion of it will at the time of her death be subject to one power or the other (subject to the exception in § 20.2056(b)-3, relating to interests contingent on survival for a limited period).

(2) The power of the surviving spouse must be a power to appoint the entire interest or a specific portion of it as unqualified owner (and free of the trust if a trust is involved, or free of the joint tenancy if a joint tenancy is involved) or to appoint the entire interest or a specific portion of it as a part of her estate (and free of the trust if a trust is involved), that is, in effect, to dispose of it to whomsoever she pleases. Thus, if the decedent devised property to a son and the surviving spouse as joint tenants with right of survivorship and under local law the surviving spouse has a power of severance exercisable without consent of the other joint tenant, and by exercising this power could acquire a one-half interest in the property as a tenant in common, her power of severance will satisfy the condition set forth in paragraph (a)(3) of this section that she have a power of appointment in favor of herself or her estate. However, if the surviving spouse entered into a binding agreement with the decedent to exercise the power only in favor of their issue, that condition is not met. An interest passing in trust will not be regarded as failing to satisfy the condition merely because takers in default of the surviving spouse's exercise of the power are designated by the decedent. The decedent may provide that, in default of exercise of the power, the trust shall continue for an additional period.

(3) A power is not considered to be a power exercisable by a surviving spouse alone and in all events as required by paragraph (a)(4) of this section if the exercise of the power in the surviving spouse to appoint the entire interest or a specific portion of it to herself or to her estate requires the joinder or consent of any other person. The power is not "exercisable in all events", if it can be terminated during the life of the surviving spouse by any event other than her complete exercise or release of it. Further, a power is not "exercisable in all events" if it may be exercised for a limited purpose only. For example, a power which is not exercisable in the event of the spouse's remarriage is not exercisable in all events. Likewise, if there are any restrictions, either by the terms of the instrument or under applicable local law, on the exercise of a power to consume property (whether or not held in trust) for the benefit of the spouse, the power is not exercisable in all events. Thus, if a power of invasion is exercisable only for the spouse's support, or only for her limited use, the power is not exercisable in all events. In order for a power of invasion to be exercisable in all events, the surviving spouse must have the unrestricted power exercisable at any time during her life to use all or any part of the property subject to the power, and to dispose of it in any manner, including the power to dispose of it by gift (whether or not she has power to dispose of it by will).

(4) The power in the surviving spouse is exercisable in all events only if it exists immediately following the decedent's death. For example, if the power given to the surviving spouse is exercisable during life, but cannot be effectively exercised before distribution of the assets by the executor, the power is not exercisable in all events. Similarly, if the power is exercisable by will, but cannot be effectively exercised in the event the surviving spouse dies before distribution of the assets by the executor, the power is not exercisable in all events. However, an interest will not be disqualified by the mere fact that, in the event the power is exercised during administration of the estate, distribution of the property to the appointee will be delayed for the period of administration. If the power is in existence at all times following the decedent's death,

limitations of a formal nature will not disqualify an interest. Examples of formal limitations on a power exercisable during life are requirements that an exercise must be in a particular form, that it must be filed with a trustee during the spouse's life, that reasonable notice must be given, or that reasonable intervals must elapse between successive partial exercises. Examples of formal limitations on a power exercisable by will are that it must be exercised by a will executed by the surviving spouse after the decedent's death or that exercise must be by specific reference to the power.

(5) If the surviving spouse has the requisite power to appoint to herself or her estate, it is immaterial that she also has one or more lesser powers. Thus, if she has a testamentary power to appoint to her estate, she may also have a limited power of withdrawal or of appointment during her life. Similarly, if she has an unlimited power of withdrawal, she may have a limited testamentary power.

(h) *Requirement of survival for a limited period.*—A power of appointment in the surviving spouse will not be treated as failing to meet the requirements of paragraph (a)(3) of this section even though the power may terminate, if the only conditions which would cause the termination are those described in paragraph (a) of § 20.2056(b)-3, and if those conditions do not in fact occur. Thus, the entire interest or a specific portion of it will not be disqualified by reason of the fact that the exercise of the power in the spouse is subject to a condition of survivorship described in § 20.2056(b)-3 if the terms of the condition, that is, the survivorship of the surviving spouse, or the failure to die in a common disaster, are fulfilled.

(i) [Reserved].

(j) *Existence of a power in another.*—Paragraph (a)(5) of this section provides that a transfer described in paragraph (a) is nondeductible to the extent that the decedent created a power in the trustee or in any other person to appoint a part of the interest to any person other than the surviving spouse. However, only powers in other persons which are in opposition to that of the surviving spouse will cause a portion of the interest to fail to satisfy the condition set forth in paragraph (a)(5) of this section. Thus, a power in a trustee to distribute corpus to or for the benefit of a surviving spouse will not disqualify the trust. Similarly, a power to distribute corpus to the spouse for the support of minor children will not disqualify the trust if she is legally obligated to support such children. The application of this paragraph may be illustrated by the following examples:

Example (1). Assume that a decedent created a trust, designating his surviving spouse as income beneficiary for life with an unrestricted power in the spouse to appoint the corpus during her life. The decedent further provided that in the event the surviving spouse should die without having exercised the power, the trust should continue for the life of his son with a power in the son to appoint the corpus. Since the power in the son could become exercisable only after the death of the surviving spouse, the interest is not regarded as failing to satisfy the condition set forth in paragraph (a)(5) of this section.

Example (2). Assume that the decedent created a trust, designating his surviving spouse as income beneficiary for life and as donee of a power to appoint by will the entire corpus. The decedent further provided that the trustee could distribute 30 percent of the corpus to the decedent's son when he reached the age of 35 years. Since the trustee has a power to appoint 30 percent of the entire interest for the benefit of a person other than the surviving spouse, only 70 percent of the interest placed in trust satisfied the condition set forth in paragraph (a)(5) of this section. If, in this case, the surviving spouse had a power, exercisable by her will, to appoint only one-half of the corpus as it was constituted at the time of her death, it should be noted that only 35 percent of the interest placed in the trust would satisfy the condition set forth in paragraph (a)(3) of this section. [Reg. § 20.2056(b)-5.]

☐ [*T.D.* 6296, 6-23-58. *Amended by T.D.* 8522, 2-28-94 *and T.D.* 9102, 12-30-2003.]

[Reg. § 20.2056(b)-6]

§ 20.2056(b)-6. Marital deduction; life insurance or annuity payments with power of appointment in surviving spouse.—(a) *In general.*—Section 2056(b)(6) provides that an interest in property passing from a decedent to his surviving spouse, which consists of proceeds held by an insurer under the terms of a life insurance, endowment, or annuity contract, is a "deductible interest" to the extent that it satisfied all five of the following conditions (see paragraph (b) of this section if one or more of the conditions is satisfied as to only a portion of the proceeds):

(1) The proceeds, or a specific portion of the proceeds, must be held by the insurer subject to an agreement either to pay the entire proceeds or a specific portion thereof in installments, or to pay interest thereon, and all or a specific portion of the installments or interest payable during the life of the surviving spouse must be payable only to her.

(2) The installments or interest payable to the surviving spouse must be payable annually, or more frequently, commencing not later than 13 months after the decedent's death.

(3) The surviving spouse must have the power to appoint all or a specific portion of the amounts so held by the insurer to either herself or her estate.

(4) The power in the surviving spouse must be exercisable by her alone and (whether exercisable by will or during life) must be exercisable in all events.

(5) The amounts or the specific portion of the amounts payable under such contract must not be subject to a power in any other person to appoint any part thereof to any person other than the surviving spouse.

(b) *Specific portion; deductible interest.*—If the right to receive interest or installment payments or the power of appointment passing to the surviving spouse pertains only to a specific portion of the proceeds held by the insurer, the marital deduction is allowed only to the extent that the rights of the surviving spouse in the specific portion meet the five conditions described in paragraph (a) of this section. While the rights to interest, or to receive payment in installments, and the power must coexist as to the proceeds of the same contract, it is not necessary that the rights to each be in the same proportion. If the rights to interest meeting the required conditions set forth in paragraph (a)(1) and (2) of this section extend over a smaller share of the proceeds than the share with respect to which the power of appointment requirements set forth in paragraph (a)(3) through (5) of this section are satisfied, the deductible interest is limited to the smaller share. Similarly, if the portion of the proceeds payable in installments is a smaller portion of the proceeds than the portion to which the power of appointment meeting such requirements relates, the deduction is limited to the smaller portion. In addition, if a power of appointment meeting all the requirements extends to a smaller portion of the proceeds than the portion over which the interest or installment rights pertain, the deductible interest cannot exceed the value of the portion to which such power of appointment applies. Thus, if the contract provides that the insurer is to retain the entire proceeds and pay all of the interest thereon annually to the surviving spouse and if the surviving spouse has a power of appointment meeting the specifications prescribed in paragraph (a)(3) through (5) of this section, as to only one-half of the proceeds held, then only one-half of the proceeds may be treated as a deductible interest. Correspondingly, if the rights of the spouse to receive installment payments or interest satisfying the requirements extend to only one-fourth of the proceeds and a testamentary power of appointment satisfying the requirements of paragraph (a)(3) through (5) of this section extends to all of the proceeds, then only one-fourth of the proceeds qualifies as a deductible interest. Further, if the surviving spouse has no right to installment payments (or interest) over any portion of the proceeds but a testamentary power of appointment which meets the necessary conditions over the entire remaining proceeds, then none of the proceeds qualifies for the deduction. In addition, if, from the time of the decedent's death, the surviving spouse has a power of appointment meeting all of the required conditions over three-fourths of the proceeds and the right to receive interest from the entire proceeds, but with a power in another person to appoint one-half of the entire proceeds, the value of the interest in the surviving spouse over only one-half of the proceeds will qualify as a deductible interest.

(c) *Applicable principles.*—(1) The principles set forth in paragraph (c) of §20.2056(b)-5 for determining what constitutes a "specific portion of the entire interest" for the purpose of section 2056(b)(5) are applicable in determining what constitutes a "specific portion of all such amounts" for the purpose of section 2056(b)(6). However, the interest in the proceeds passing to the surviving spouse will not be disqualified by the fact that the installment payments or interest to which the spouse is entitled or the amount of the proceeds over which the power of appointment is exercisable may be expressed in terms of a specific sum rather than a fraction or a percentage of the proceeds provided it is shown that such sums are a definite or fixed percentage or fraction of the total proceeds.

(2) The provisions of paragraph (a) of this section are applicable with respect to a property interest which passed from the decedent in the form of proceeds of a policy of insurance upon the decedent's life, a policy of insurance upon the life of a person who predeceased the decedent, a matured endowment policy, or an annuity contract, but only in case the proceeds are to be held by the insurer. With respect to proceeds under any such contract which are to be held by a trustee, with power of appointment in the surviving spouse, see §20.2056(b)-5. As to the treatment of proceeds not meeting the requirements of §20.2056(b)-5 or of this section, see §20.2056(a)-2.

(3) In the case of a contract under which payments by the insurer commenced during the decedent's life, it is immaterial whether or not the conditions in subparagraphs (1) through (5) of paragraph (a) of this section were satisfied prior to the decedent's death.

(d) *Payments of installments or interest.*—The conditions in subparagraphs (1) and (2) of paragraph (a) of this section relative to the payments of installments or interest to the surviving spouse are satisfied if, under the terms of the contract, the spouse has the right exercisable annually (or more frequently) to require distribution to herself of installments of the proceeds or a specific portion thereof, as the case may be, and otherwise such proceeds or interest are to be accumulated and held by the insurer pursuant to the terms of the contract. A contract which otherwise requires the insurer to make annual or more frequent payments to the surviving spouse following the decedent's death, will not be disqualified merely because the surviving spouse must comply with certain formalities in order to obtain the first payment. For example, the contract may satisfy the conditions in subparagraphs (1) and (2) of paragraph (a) of this section even though it requires the surviving spouse to furnish proof of death before the first payment is made. The condition in paragraph (a)(1) of this section is satisfied where interest on the proceeds or a specific portion thereof is payable, annually or more frequently, for a term, or until the occurrence of a specified event, following which the proceeds or a specific portion thereof are to be paid in annual or more frequent installments.

(e) *Powers of appointment.*—(1) In determining whether the terms of the contract satisfy the conditions in subparagraph (3), (4), or (5) of paragraph (a) of this section relating to a power of appointment in the surviving spouse or any other person, the principles stated in § 20.2056(b)-5 are applicable. As stated in § 20.2056(b)-5, the surviving spouse's power to appoint is "exercisable in all events" only if it is in existence immediately following the decedent's death, subject, however, to the operation of § 20.2056(b)-3 relating to interests conditioned on survival for a limited period.

(2) For examples of formal limitations on the power which will not disqualify the contract, see paragraph (g)(4) of § 20.2056(b)-5. If the power is exercisable from the moment of the decedent's death, the contract is not disqualified merely because the insurer may require proof of the decedent's death as a condition to making payment to the appointee. If the submission of proof of the decedent's death is a condition to the exercise of the power, the power will not be considered "exercisable in all events" unless in the event the surviving spouse had died immediately following the decedent, her power to appoint would have been considered to exist at the time of her death, within the meaning of section 2041(a)(2). See paragraph (b) of § 20.2041-3.

(3) It is sufficient for the purposes of the condition in paragraph (a)(3) of this section that the surviving spouse have the power to appoint amounts held by the insurer to herself or her estate if the surviving spouse has the unqualified power, exercisable in favor of herself or her estate, to appoint amounts held by the insurer which are payable after her death. Such power to appoint need not extend to installments or interest which will be paid to the spouse during her life. Further, the power to appoint need not be a power to require payment in a single sum. For example, if the proceeds of a policy are payable in installments, and if the surviving spouse has the power to direct that all installments payable after her death be paid to her estate, she has the requisite power.

(4) It is not necessary that the phrase "power to appoint" be used in the contract. For example, the condition in paragraph (a)(3) of this section that the surviving spouse have the power to appoint amounts held by the insurer to herself or her estate is satisfied by terms of a contract which give the surviving spouse a right which is, in substance and effect, a power to appoint to herself or her estate, such as a right to withdraw the amount remaining in the fund held by the insurer, or a right to direct that any amount held by the insurer under the contract at her death shall be paid to her estate. [Reg. § 20.2056(b)-6.]

□ [*T.D.* 6296, 6-23-58.]

[Reg. § 20.2056(b)-7]

§ 20.2056(b)-7. Election with respect to life estate for surviving spouse.—(a) *In general.*—Subject to section 2056(d), a marital deduction is allowed under section 2056(b)(7) with respect to estates of decedents dying after December 31, 1981, for qualified terminable interest property as defined in paragraph (b) of this section. All of the property for which a deduction is allowed under this paragraph (a) is treated as passing to the surviving spouse (for purposes of § 20.2056(a)-1), and no part of the property is treated as passing to any person other than the surviving spouse (for purposes of § 20.2056(b)-1).

(b) *Qualified terminable interest property.*—(1) *In general.*—Section 2056(b)(7)(B)(i) provides the definition of *qualified terminable interest property.*

(i) Terminable interests described in section 2056(b)(1)(C) cannot qualify as qualified terminable interest property. Thus, if the decedent directs the executor to purchase a terminable interest with estate assets, the terminable interest acquired will not qualify as qualified terminable interest property.

(ii) For purposes of section 2056(b)(7)(B)(i), the term *property* generally means the *entire interest in property* (within the meaning of § 20.2056(b)-5(d)) or a *specific portion of the entire interest* (within the meaning of § 20.2056(b)-5(c)).

(2) *Property for which an election may be made.*—(i) *In general.*—The election may relate to all or any part of property that meets the requirements of section 2056(b)(7)(B)(i), provided that any partial election must be made with respect to a fractional or percentage share of the property so that the elective portion reflects its proportionate share of the increase or decrease in value of the entire property for purposes of applying sections 2044 or 2519. The fraction or percentage may be defined by formula.

(ii) *Division of trusts.*—(A) *In general.*—A trust may be divided into separate trusts to reflect a partial election that has been made, or is to be made, if authorized under the governing instrument or otherwise permissible under local law. Any such division must be accomplished no later than the end of the period of estate administration. If, at the time of the filing of the estate tax return, the trust has not yet been divided, the intent to divide the trust must be unequivocally signified on the estate tax return.

(B) *Manner of dividing and funding trust.*—The division of the trust must be done on a fractional or percentage basis to reflect the partial election. However, the separate trusts do not have to be funded with a pro rata portion of each asset held by the undivided trust.

(C) *Local law.*—A trust may be divided only if the fiduciary is required, either by applicable local law or by the express or implied provisions of the governing instrument, to divide the trust on the basis of the fair market value of the assets of the trust at the time of the division.

(3) *Persons permitted to make the election.*—The election referred to in section 2056(b)(7)(B)(i)(III) must be made by the executor that is appointed, qualified, and acting within the United States, within the meaning of section 2203, regardless of whether the property with respect to which the election is to be made is in the executor's possession. If there is no executor appointed, qualified, and acting within

the United States, the election may be made by any person with respect to property in the actual or constructive possession of that person and may also be made by that person with respect to other property not in the actual or constructive possession of that person if the person in actual or constructive possession of such other property does not make the election. For example, in the absence of an appointed executor, the trustee of an intervivos trust (that is included in the gross estate of the decedent) can make the election.

(4) *Manner and time of making the election.*—(i) *In general.*—The election referred to in section 2056(b)(7)(B)(i)(III) and (v) is made on the return of tax imposed by section 2001 (or section 2101). For purposes of this paragraph, the term *return of tax imposed by section 2001* means the last estate tax return filed by the executor on or before the due date of the return, including extensions or, if a timely return is not filed, the first estate tax return filed by the executor after the due date.

(ii) *Election irrevocable.*—The election, once made, is irrevocable, provided that an election may be revoked or modified on a subsequent return filed on or before the due date of the return, including extensions actually granted. If an executor appointed under local law has made an election on the return of tax imposed by section 2001 (or section 2101) with respect to one or more properties, no subsequent election may be made with respect to other properties included in the gross estate after the return of tax imposed by section 2001 is filed. An election under section 2056(b)(7)(B)(v) is separate from any elections made under section 2056A(a)(3).

(c) *Protective elections.*—(1) *In general.*—A protective election may be made to treat property as qualified terminable interest property only if, at the time the federal estate tax return is filed, the executor of the decedent's estate reasonably believes that there is a bona fide issue that concerns whether an asset is includible in the decedent's gross estate, or the amount or nature of the property the surviving spouse is entitled to receive, i.e., whether property that is includible is eligible for the qualified terminable interest property election. The protective election must identify either the specific asset, group of assets, or trust to which the election applies and the specific basis for the protective election.

(2) *Protective election irrevocable.*—The protective election, once made on the return of tax imposed by section 2001, cannot be revoked. For example, if a protective election is made on the basis that a bona fide question exists regarding the inclusion of a trust corpus in the gross estate and it is later determined that the trust corpus is so includible, the protective election becomes effective with respect to the trust corpus and cannot thereafter be revoked.

(d) *Qualifying income interest for life.*—(1) *In general.*—Section 2056(b)(7)(B)(ii) provides the definition of *qualifying income interest for life*. For purposes of section 2056(b)(7)(B)(ii)(II), the surviving spouse is included within the prohibited class of powerholders referred to therein. A power under applicable local law that permits the trustee to adjust between income and principal to fulfill the trustee's duty of impartiality between the income and remainder beneficiaries that meets the requirements of § 1.643(b)-1 of this chapter will not be considered a power to appoint trust property to a person other than the surviving spouse.

(2) *Entitled for life to all income.*—The principles of § 20.2056(b)-5(f), relating to whether the spouse is entitled for life to all of the income from the entire interest, or a specific portion of the entire interest, apply in determining whether the surviving spouse is entitled for life to all of the income from the property regardless of whether the interest passing to the spouse is in trust.

(3) *Contingent income interests.*—(i) An income interest for a term of years, or a life estate subject to termination upon the occurrence of a specified event (e.g., remarriage), is not a qualifying income interest for life. However, a qualifying income interest for life that is contingent upon the executor's election under section 2056(b)(7)(B)(v) will not fail to be a qualifying income interest for life because of such contingency or because the portion of the property for which the election is not made passes to or for the benefit of persons other than the surviving spouse. This paragraph (d)(3)(i) applies with respect to estates of decedents whose estate tax returns are due after February 18, 1997. This paragraph (d)(3)(i) also applies to estates of decedents whose estate tax returns were due on or before February 18, 1997, that meet the requirements of paragraph (d)(3)(ii) of this section.

(ii) Estates of decedents whose estate tax returns were due on or before February 18, 1997, that did not make the election under section 2056(b)(7)(B)(v) because the surviving spouse's income interest in the property was contingent upon the election or because the nonelected portion of the property was to pass to a beneficiary other than the surviving spouse are granted an extension of time to make the QTIP election if the following requirements are satisfied:

(A) The period of limitations on filing a claim for credit or refund under section 6511(a) has not expired.

(B) A claim for credit or refund is filed on Form 843 with a revised Recapitulation and Schedule M, Form 706 (or 706NA) that signifies the QTIP election. Reference to this section should be made on the Form 843.

(C) The following statement is included with the Form 843: "The undersigned certifies that the property with respect to which the QTIP election is being made will be included in the gross estate of the surviving spouse as provided in section 2044 of the Internal Revenue Code, in determining the federal estate tax liability on the spouse's death." The statement must be signed, under penalties of perjury, by the surviving spouse, the surviving spouse's legal representative (if the surviving spouse is legally incompetent), or the surviving spouse's executor (if the surviving spouse is deceased).

(4) *Income between last distribution date and date of spouse's death.*—An income interest does not fail to constitute a qualifying income interest for life solely because income between the last distribution date and the date of the surviving spouse's death is not required to be distributed to the surviving spouse or to the estate of the surviving spouse. See § 20.2044-1 relating to the inclusion of such undistributed income in the gross estate of the surviving spouse.

(5) *Pooled income funds.*—An income interest in a pooled income fund described in section 642(c)(5) constitutes a qualifying income interest for life for purposes of section 2056(b)(7)(B)(ii).

(6) *Power to distribute principal to spouse.*—An income interest in a trust will not fail to constitute a qualifying income interest for life solely because the trustee has a power to distribute principal to or for the benefit of the surviving spouse. The fact that property distributed to a surviving spouse may be transferred by the spouse to another person does not result in a failure to satisfy the requirement of section 2056(b)(7)(B)(ii)(II). However, if the surviving spouse is legally bound to transfer the distributed property to another person without full and adequate consideration in money or money's worth, the requirement of section 2056(b)(7)(B)(ii)(II) is not satisfied.

(e) *Annuities payable from trusts in the case of estates of decedents dying on or before October 24, 1992, and certain decedents dying after October 24, 1992, with wills or revocable trusts executed on or prior to that date.*—(1) *In general.*—In the case of estates of decedents within the purview of the effective date and transitional rules contained in § 20.2056(b)-7(e)(5), a surviving spouse's lifetime annuity interest payable from a trust or other group of assets passing from the decedent is treated as a qualifying income interest for life for purposes of section 2056(b)(7)(B)(ii).

(2) *Deductible interest.*—The deductible interest, for purposes of § 20.2056(a)-2(b), is the specific portion of the property that, assuming the applicable interest rate for valuing annuities, would produce income equal to the minimum amount payable annually to the surviving spouse. If, based on the applicable interest rate, the entire property from which the annuity may be satisfied is insufficient to produce income equal to the minimum annual payment, the value of the deductible interest is the entire value of the property. The value of the deductible interest may not exceed the value of the property from which the annuity is payable. If the annual payment may increase, the increased amount is not taken into account in valuing the deductible interest.

(3) *Distributions permissible only to surviving spouse.*—An annuity interest is not treated as a qualifying income interest for life for purposes of section 2056(b)(7)(B)(ii) if any person other than the surviving spouse may receive, during the surviving spouse's lifetime, any distribution of the property or its income (including any distribution under an annuity contract) from which the annuity is payable.

(4) *Applicable interest rate.*—To determine the applicable interest rate for valuing annuities, see sections 2031 and 7520 and the regulations under those sections.

(5) *Effective dates.*—(i) The rules contained in § 20.2056(b)-7(e) apply with respect to estates of decedents dying on or before October 24, 1992.

(ii) The rules contained in § 20.2056(b)-7(e) apply in the case of decedents dying after October 24, 1992, if property passes to the spouse pursuant to a will or revocable trust executed on or before October 24, 1992, and either—

(A) On that date, the decedent was under a mental disability to change the disposition of his property and did not regain his competence to dispose of such property before the date of death; or

(B) The decedent dies prior to October 24, 1995.

(iii) Notwithstanding the foregoing, the rules contained in § 20.2056(b)-7(e) do not apply if the will or revocable trust is amended after October 24, 1992, in any respect that increases the amount of the transfer qualifying for the marital deduction or alters the terms by which the interest so passes to the surviving spouse.

(f) *Joint and survivor annuities.*—[Reserved]

(g) *Application of local law.*—The provisions of local law are taken into account in determining whether the conditions of section 2056(b)(7)(B)(ii)(I) are satisfied. For example, silence of a trust instrument as to the frequency of payment is not regarded as a failure to satisfy the requirement that the income must be payable to the surviving spouse annually or more frequently unless applicable local law permits payments less frequently.

(h) *Examples.*—The following examples illustrate the application of paragraphs (a) through (g) of this section. In each example, it is assumed that the decedent, D, was survived by S, D's spouse and that, unless stated otherwise, S is not the trustee of any trust established for S's benefit.

Example 1. Life estate in residence. D owned a personal residence valued at $250,000 for estate tax purposes. Under D's will, the exclusive and unrestricted right to use the residence (including the right to continue to occupy the property as a personal residence or to rent the property and receive the income) passes to S for life. At S's death, the property passes to D's children. Under applicable local law, S must consent to any sale of the property. If the executor elects to treat all of the personal residence as qualified terminable interest property, the deductible interest is $250,000, the value of the residence for estate tax purposes.

Example 2. Power to make property productive. D's will established a trust funded with property valued for estate tax purposes at $500,000. The assets include both income producing assets and non-productive assets. S was given the power, exercisable annually, to require distribution of all of the trust income to herself. No trust property may be distributed during S's lifetime to any person other than S. Applicable local law permits S to require that the trustee either make the trust property productive or sell the property and reinvest in productive property within a reasonable time after D's death. If the executor elects to treat all of the trust as qualified terminable interest property, the deductible interest is $500,000. If the executor elects to treat only 20 percent of the trust as qualified terminable interest property, the deductible interest is $100,000, i.e., 20 percent of $500,000.

Example 3. Power of distribution over fraction of trust income. The facts are the same as in *Example 2* except that S is given the right exercisable annually for S's lifetime to require distribution to herself of only 50 percent of the trust income for life. The remaining trust income is to be accumulated or distributed among S and the decedent's children in the trustee's discretion. The maximum amount that D's executor may elect to treat as qualified terminable interest property is $250,000; i.e., the estate tax value of the trust ($500,000) multiplied by the percentage of the trust in which S has a qualifying income interest for life (50 percent). If D's executor elects to treat only 20 percent of the portion of the trust in which S has a qualifying income interest as qualified terminable interest property, the deductible interest is $50,000, i.e., 20 percent of $250,000.

Example 4. Power to distribute trust corpus to other beneficiaries. D's will established a trust providing that S is entitled to receive at least annually all the trust income. The trustee is given the power to use annually during S's lifetime $5,000 from the trust for the maintenance and support of S's minor child, C. Any such distribution does not necessarily relieve S of S's obligation to support and maintain C. S does not have a qualifying income interest for life in any portion of the trust because the bequest fails to satisfy the condition that no person have a power, other than a power the exercise of which takes effect only at or after S's death, to appoint any part of the property to any person other than S. The trust would also be nondeductible under section 2056(b)(7) if S, rather than the trustee, held the power to appoint a portion of the principal to C. However, in the latter case, if S made a qualified disclaimer (within the meaning of section 2518) of the power to appoint to C, the trust could qualify for the marital deduction pursuant to section 2056(b)(7), assuming that the power is personal to S and S's disclaimer terminates the power. Similarly, in either case, if C made a qualified disclaimer of C's right to receive distributions from the trust, the trust would qualify under section 2056(b)(7), assuming that C's disclaimer effectively negates the trustee's power under local law.

Example 5. Spouse's income interest terminable on remarriage. D's will established a trust providing that all of the trust income is payable at least annually to S for S's lifetime, provided that, if S remarries, S's interest in the trust will pass to X. The trust is not deductible under section 2056(b)(7). S's income interest is not a *qualifying income interest for life* because it is not for life but, rather, is terminable upon S's remarriage.

Example 6. Spouse's qualifying income interest for life contingent on executor's election. D's will established a trust providing that S is entitled to receive the income, payable at least annually, from that portion of the trust that the executor elects to treat as qualified terminable interest property. The portion of the trust which the executor does not elect to treat as qualified terminable interest property passes as of D's date of death to a trust for the benefit of C, D's child. Under these facts, the executor is not considered to have a power to appoint any part of the trust property to any person other than S during S's life.

Example 7. Formula partial election. D's will established a trust funded with the residue of D's estate. Trust income is to be paid annually to S for life, and the principal is to be distributed to D's children upon S's death. S has the power to require that all the trust property be made productive. There is no power to distribute trust property during S's lifetime to any person other than S. D's executor elects to deduct a fractional share of the residuary estate under section 2056(b)(7). The election specifies that the numerator of the fraction is the amount of deduction necessary to reduce the Federal estate tax to zero (taking into account final estate tax values) and the denominator of the fraction is the final estate tax value of the residuary estate (taking into account any specific bequests or liabilities of the estate paid out of the residuary estate). The formula election is of a fractional share. The value of the share qualifies for the marital deduction even though the executor's determinations to claim administration expenses as estate or income tax deductions and the final estate tax values will affect the size of the fractional share.

Example 8. Formula partial election. The facts are the same as in *Example 7* except that, rather than defining a fraction, the executor's formula states: "I elect to treat as qualified terminable interest property that portion of the residuary trust, up to 100 percent, necessary to reduce the Federal estate tax to zero, after taking into account the available unified credit, final estate tax values and any liabilities and specific bequests paid from the residuary estate." The formula election is of a fractional share. The share is equivalent to the fractional share determined in *Example 7*.

Example 9. Severance of QTIP trust. D's will established a trust funded with the residue of D's estate. Trust income is to be paid annually to S for life, and the principal is to be distributed to D's children upon S's death. S has the power to require that all of the trust property be made productive. There is no power to distribute trust property during S's lifetime to any person other than S. D's will authorizes the executor to make the election under section 2056(b)(7) only with respect to the minimum amount of property necessary to reduce estate taxes on D's estate to zero, authorizes the executor to divide the residuary estate into two separate trusts to reflect the election, and authorizes the executor to charge any payment of principal to S to the qualified terminable interest trust. S is the sole beneficiary of both trusts during S's lifetime. The authorizations in the will do not adversely affect the allowance of the marital deduction. Only the property remaining in the marital deduction trust, after payment of principal to S, is subject to inclusion in S's gross estate under section 2044 or subject to gift tax under section 2519.

Example 10. Payments to spouse from individual retirement account. S is the life beneficiary of sixteen remaining annual installments payable from D's individual retirement account. The terms of the account provide for the payment of the account balance in nineteen annual installments that commenced when D reached age 70 1/2. Each installment is equal to all the income earned on the remaining principal in the account plus a share of the remaining principal equal to 1/19 in the first year, 1/18 in the second year, 1/17 in the third year, etc. Under the terms of the account, S has no right to withdraw any other amounts from the account. Any payments remaining after S's death pass to D's children. S's interest in the account qualifies as a qualifying income interest for life under section 2056(b)(7)(B)(ii), without regard to the provisions of section 2056(b)(7)(C).

Example 11. Spouse's interest in trust in the form of an annuity. D died prior to October 24, 1992. D's will established a trust funded with income producing property valued at $500,000 for estate tax purposes. The trustee is required by the trust instrument to pay $20,000 a year to S for life. Trust income in excess of the annuity amount is to be accumulated in the trust and may not be distributed during S's lifetime. S's lifetime annuity interest is treated as a qualifying income interest for life. If the executor elects to treat the entire portion of the trust in which S has a qualifying income interest as qualified terminable interest property, the value of the deductible interest is (assuming that 10 percent is the applicable interest rate under section 7520 for valuing annuities on the appropriate valuation date) $200,000, because that amount would yield an income to S of $20,000 a year.

Example 12. Value of spouse's annuity exceeds value of trust corpus. The facts are the same as in *Example 11* except that the trustee is required to pay S $70,000 a year for life. If the executor elects to treat the entire portion of the trust in which S has a qualifying income interest as qualified terminable interest property, the value of the deductible interest is $500,000, which is the lesser of the entire value of the property ($500,000), or the amount of property that (assuming a 10 percent interest rate) would yield an income to S of $70,000 a year ($700,000).

Example 13. Pooled income fund. D's will provides for a bequest of $200,000 to a pooled income fund described in section 642(c)(5), designating S as the income beneficiary for life. If D's executor elects to treat the entire $200,000 as qualified terminable interest property, the deductible interest is $200,000.

Example 14. Funding severed QTIP trusts. D's will established a trust satisfying the requirements of section 2056(b)(7). Pursuant to the authority in D's will and § 20.2056(b)-7(b)(2)(ii), D's executor indicates on the Federal estate tax return that an election under section 2056(b)(7) is being made with respect to 50 percent of the trust, and that the trust will subsequently be divided to reflect the partial election on the basis of the fair market value of the property at the time of the division. D's executor funds the trust at the end of the period of estate administration. At that time, the property available to fund the trusts consists of 100 shares of X Corporation stock with a current value of $400,000 and 200 shares of Y Corporation stock with a current value of $400,000. D may fund each trust with the stock of either or both corporations, in any combination, provided that the aggregate value of the stock allocated to each trust is $400,000. [Reg. § 20.2056(b)-7.]

☐ [*T.D.* 8522, 2-28-94. *Amended by T.D.* 8779, 8-18-98 *and T.D.* 9102, 12-30-2003.]

[Reg. § 20.2056(b)-8]

§ 20.2056(b)-8. Special rule for charitable remainder trusts.—(a) *In general.*—(1) *Surviving spouse only noncharitable beneficiary.*—With respect to estates of decedents dying after December 31, 1981, subject to section 2056(d), if the surviving spouse of the decedent is the only noncharitable beneficiary of a charitable remainder annuity trust or a charitable remainder unitrust described in section 664 (qualified charitable remainder trust), section 2056(b)(1) does not apply to the interest in the trust that is transferred to the surviving spouse. Thus, the value of the annuity or unitrust interest passing to the spouse qualifies for a marital deduction under section 2056(b)(8) and the value of the remainder interest qualifies for a charitable deduction under section 2055. If an interest in property qualifies for a marital deduction under section 2056(b)(8), no election may be made with respect to the property under section 2056(b)(7). For purposes of this section, the term *noncharitable beneficiary* means any beneficiary of the qualified charitable remainder trust other than an organization described in section 170(c).

(2) *Interest for life or term of years.*—The surviving spouse's interest need not be an interest for life to qualify for a marital deduction under section 2056(b)(8). However, for purposes of section 664, an annuity or unitrust interest payable to the spouse for a term of years cannot be payable for a term that exceeds 20 years.

(3) *Payment of state death taxes.*—A deduction is allowed under section 2056(b)(8) even if the transfer to the surviving spouse is conditioned on the spouse's payment of state death taxes, if any, attributable to the qualified charitable remainder trust. See § 20.2056(b)-4(c) for the

effect of such a condition on the amount of the deduction allowable.

(b) *Charitable remainder trusts where the surviving spouse is not the only noncharitable beneficiary.*—In the case of a charitable remainder trust where the decedent's spouse is not the only noncharitable beneficiary (for example, where the noncharitable interest is payable to the decedent's spouse for life and then to another individual for life), the qualification of the interest as qualified terminable interest property is determined solely under section 2056(b)(7) and not under section 2056(b)(8). Accordingly, if the decedent died on or before October 24, 1992, or the trust otherwise comes within the purview of the transitional rules contained in § 20.2056(b)-7(e)(5), the spousal annuity or unitrust interest may qualify under § 20.2056(b)-(7)(e) as a qualifying income interest for life. [Reg. § 20.2056(b)-8.]

☐ [*T.D.* 8522, 2-28-94.]

[Reg. § 20.2056(b)-9]

§ 20.2056(b)-9. Denial of double deduction.—The value of an interest in property may not be deducted for Federal estate tax purposes more than once with respect to the same decedent. For example, where a decedent transfers a life estate in a farm to the spouse with a remainder to charity, the entire property is, pursuant to the executor's election under section 2056(b)(7), treated as passing to the spouse. The entire value of the property qualifies for the marital deduction. No part of the value of the property qualifies for a charitable deduction under section 2055 in the decedent's estate. [Reg. § 20.2056(b)-9.]

☐ [*T.D.* 8522, 2-28-94.]

[Reg. § 20.2056(b)-10]

§ 20.2056(b)-10. Effective dates.—Except as specifically provided in §§ 20.2056(b)-5(c)(3)(ii) and (iii), 20.2056(b)-7(d)(3), 20.2056(b)-7(e)(5), and 20.2056(b)-8(b), the provisions of §§ 20.2056(b)-5(c), 20.2056(b)-7, 20.2056(b)-8, and 20.2056(b)-9 are applicable with respect to estates of decedents dying after March 1, 1994. With respect to decedents dying on or before such date, the executor of the decedent's estate may rely on any reasonable interpretation of the statutory provisions. In addition, the rule in the last sentence of § 20.2056(b)-5(f)(1) and the rule in the last sentence of § 20.2056(b)-7(d)(1) regarding the effect on the spouse's right to income if applicable local law provides for the reasonable apportionment between the income and remainder beneficiaries of the total return of the trust are applicable with respect to trusts for taxable years ending after January 2, 2004. [Reg. § 20.2056(b)-10.]

☐ [*T.D.* 8522, 2-28-94. *Amended by T.D.* 8779, 8-18-98 *and T.D.* 9102, 12-30-2003.]

[Reg. § 20.2056(c)-1]

§ 20.2056(c)-1. Marital deduction; definition of "passed from the decedent".—(a) *In general.*—The following rules are applicable in determining the person to whom any property interest "passed from the decedent":

(1) Property interests devolving upon any person (or persons) as surviving co-owner with the decedent under any form of joint ownership under which the right of survivorship existed are considered as having passed from the decedent to such person (or persons).

(2) Property interests at any time subject to the decedent's power to appoint (whether alone or in conjunction with any person) are considered as having passed from the decedent to the appointee under his exercise of the power, or, in case of the lapse, release or nonexercise of the power, as having passed from the decedent to the taker in default of exercise.

(3) The dower or curtesy interest (or statutory interest in lieu thereof) of the decedent's surviving spouse is considered as having passed from the decedent to his spouse.

(4) The proceeds of insurance upon the life of the decedent are considered as having passed from the decedent to the person who, at the time of the decedent's death, was entitled to receive the proceeds.

(5) Any property interest transferred during life, bequeathed or devised by the decedent, or inherited from the decedent, is considered as having passed to the person to whom he transferred, bequeathed, or devised the interest, or to the person who inherited the interest from him.

(6) The survivor's interest in an annuity or other payment described in section 2039 (see §§ 20.2039-1 and 20.2039-2) is considered as having passed from the decedent to the survivor only to the extent that the value of such interest is included in the decedent's gross estate under that section. If only a portion of the entire annuity or other payment is included in the decedent's gross estate and the annuity or other payment is payable to more than one beneficiary, then the value of the interest considered to have passed to each beneficiary is that portion of the amount payable to each beneficiary that the amount of the annuity or other payment included in the decedent's gross estate bears to the total value of the annuity or other payment payable to all beneficiaries.

(b) *Expectant interest in property under community property laws.*—If before the decedent's death the decedent's surviving spouse had merely an expectant interest in property held by her and the decedent under community property laws, that interest is considered as having passed from the decedent to the spouse. [Reg. § 20.2056(c)-1.]

☐ [*T.D.* 6296, 6-23-58. *Redesignated and amended by T.D.* 8522, 2-28-94.]

[Reg. § 20.2056(c)-2]

§ 20.2056(c)-2. Marital deduction; definition of "passed from the decedent to his surviving spouse".—(a) *In general.*—In general, the definition stated in § 20.2056(c)-1 is applicable in determining the property interests which "passed from the decedent to his surviving spouse." Special rules are provided, however, for the following:

(1) In the case of certain interests with income for life to the surviving spouse with power of appointment in her (see § 20.2056(b)-5);

(2) In the case of certain interests with income for life to the surviving spouse that the executor elects to treat as qualified terminable interest property (see § 20.2056(b)-7);

(3) In the case of proceeds held by the insurer under a life insurance, endowment, or annuity contract with power of appointment in the surviving spouse (see § 20.2056(b)-6);

(4) In case of the disclaimer of an interest by the surviving spouse or by any other person (see § 20.2056(d)-1);

(5) In case of an election by the surviving spouse (see paragraph (c) of this section); and

(6) In case of a controversy involving the decedent's will, see paragraph (d) of this section.

A property interest is considered as passing to the surviving spouse only if it passes to the spouse as beneficial owner, except to the extent otherwise provided in §§ 20.2056(b)-5 through 20.2056(b)-7 in the case of certain life estates and insurance and annuity contracts with powers of appointment. For this purpose, where a property interest passed from the decedent in trust, such interest is considered to have passed from him to his surviving spouse to the extent of her beneficial interest therein. The deduction may not be taken with respect to a property interest which passed to such spouse merely as trustee, or subject to a binding agreement by the spouse to dispose of the interest in favor of a third person. An allowance or award paid to a surviving spouse pursuant to local law for her support during the administration of the decedent's estate constitutes a property interest passing from the decedent to his surviving spouse. In determining whether or not such an interest is deductible, however, see generally the terminable interest rules of § 20.2056(b)-1 and especially example (8) of paragraph (g) of that section.

(b) *Examples.*—The following illustrate the provisions of paragraph (a) of this section:

(1) A property interest bequeathed in trust by H (the decedent) is considered as having passed from him to W (his surviving spouse)—

(i) If the trust income is payable to W for life and upon her death the corpus is distributable to her executors or administrators;

(ii) If W is entitled to the trust income for a term of years following which the corpus is to be paid to W or her estate;

(iii) If the trust income is to be accumulated for a term of years or for W's life and the augmented fund paid to W or her estate; or

(iv) If the terms of the transfer satisfy the requirements of § 20.2056(b)-5 or 20.2056(b)-7.

(2) If H devised property—

(i) To A for life with remainder absolutely to W or her estate, the remainder interest is considered to have passed from H to W;

(ii) To W for life with remainder to her estate, the entire property is considered as having passed from H to W; or

(iii) Under conditions which satisfy the provisions of § 20.2056(b)-5 or 20.2056(b)-7, the entire property is considered as having passed from H to W.

(3) Proceeds of insurance upon the life of H are considered as having passed from H to W if the terms of the contract—

(i) Meet the requirements of § 20.2056(b)-6;

(ii) Provide that the proceeds are payable to W in a lump sum;

(iii) Provide that the proceeds are payable in installments to W for life and after her death any remaining installments are payable to her estate;

(iv) Provide that interest on the proceeds is payable to W for life and upon her death the principal amount is payable to her estate; or

(v) Provide that the proceeds are payable to a trustee under an arrangement whereby the requirements of § 2056 (b)(5) or 20.2056(b)-7 are satisfied.

(c) *Effect of election by surviving spouse.*—This paragraph contains rules applicable if the surviving spouse may elect between a property interest offered to her under the decedent's will or other instrument and a property interest to which she is otherwise entitled (such as dower, a right in the decedent's estate, or her interest under community property laws) of which adverse disposition was attempted by the decedent under the will or other instrument. If the surviving spouse elects to take against the will or other instrument, then the property interests offered thereunder are not considered as having "passed from the decedent to his surviving spouse" and the dower or other property interest retained by her is considered as having so passed (if it otherwise so qualifies under this section). If the surviving spouse elects to take under the will or other instrument, then the dower or other property interest relinquished by her is not considered as having "passed from the decedent to his surviving spouse" (irrespective of whether it otherwise comes within the definition stated in paragraph (a) of this section) and the interest taken under the will or other instrument is considered as having so passed (if it otherwise so qualifies). As to the valuation of the property interest taken under the will or other instrument, see paragraph (b) of § 20.2056(b)-4.

(d) *Will contests.*—(1) If as a result of a controversy involving the decedent's will, or involving any bequest or devise thereunder, his surviving spouse assigns or surrenders a property interest in settlement of the controversy, the interest so assigned or surrendered is not considered as having "passed from the decedent to his surviving spouse."

(2) If as a result of the controversy involving the decedent's will, or involving any bequest or devise thereunder, a property interest is assigned or surrendered to the surviving spouse, the interest so acquired will be regarded as having "passed from the decedent to his surviving spouse" only if the assignment or surrender was

a bona fide recognition of enforceable rights of the surviving spouse in the decedent's estate. Such a bona fide recognition will be presumed where the assignment or surrender was pursuant to a decision of a local court upon the merits in an adversary proceeding following a genuine and active contest. However, such a decree will be accepted only to the extent that the court passed upon the facts upon which deductibility of the property interests depends. If the assignment or surrender was pursuant to a decree rendered by consent, or pursuant to an agreement not to contest the will or not to probate the will, it will not necessarily be accepted as a bona fide evaluation of the rights of the spouse.

(e) *Survivorship*.—If the order of deaths of the decedent and his spouse cannot be established by proof, a presumption (whether supplied by local law, the decedent's will, or otherwise) that the decedent was survived by his spouse will be recognized as satisfying paragraph (b)(1) of §20.2056(a)-1, but only to the extent that it has the effect of giving to the spouse an interest in property includible in her gross estate under part III of subchapter A of chapter 11. Under these circumstances, if an estate tax return is required to be filed for the estate of the decedent's spouse, the marital deduction will not be allowed in the final audit of the estate tax return of the decedent's estate with respect to any property interest which has not been finally determined to be includible in the gross estate of his spouse. [Reg. §20.2056(c)-2.]

□ [*T.D.* 6296, 6-23-58. *Redesignated and amended by T.D.* 8522, 2-28-94.]

[Reg. §20.2056(c)-3]

§20.2056(c)-3. Marital deduction; definition of "passed from the decedent to a person other than his surviving spouse".—The expression "passed from the decedent to a person other than his surviving spouse" refers to any property interest which, under the definition stated in §20.2056(c)-1 is considered as having "passed from the decedent" and which under the rules referred to in §20.2056(c)-2 is not considered as having "passed from the decedent to his surviving spouse." Interests which passed to a person other than the surviving spouse include interests so passing under the decedent's exercise, release, or nonexercise of a nontaxable power to appoint. It is immaterial whether the property interest which passed from the decedent to a person other than his surviving spouse is included in the decedent's gross estate. The term "person other than his surviving spouse" includes the possible unascertained takers of a property interest, as, for example, the members of a class to be ascertained in the future. As another example, assume that the decedent created a power of appointment over a property interest, which does not come within the purview of §20.2056(b)-5 or §20.2056(b)-6. In such a case, the term "person other than his surviving spouse" refers to the possible appointees and possible takers in default (other than the spouse) of such property interest. Whether or not there is a possibility that the "person other than his surviving spouse" (or the heirs or assigns of such person) may possess or enjoy the property following termination or failure of the interest therein which passed from the decedent to his surviving spouse is to be determined as of the time of the decedent's death. [Reg. §20.2056(c)-3.]

□ [*T.D.* 6296, 6-23-58. *Redesignated and amended by T.D.* 8522, 2-28-94.]

[Reg. §20.2056(d)-1]

§20.2056(d)-1. Marital deduction; special rules for marital deduction if surviving spouse is not a United States citizen.—Rules pertaining to the application of section 2056(d), including certain transition rules, are contained in §§20.2056A-1 through 20.2056A-13. [Reg. §20.2056(d)-1.]

□ [*T.D.* 8612, 8-21-95.]

[Reg. §20.2056(d)-2]

§20.2056(d)-2. Marital deduction; effect of disclaimers of post-December 31, 1976 transfers.—(a) *Disclaimer by a surviving spouse*.—If a surviving spouse disclaims an interest in property passing to such spouse from the decedent, which interest was created in a transfer made after December 31, 1976, the effectiveness of the disclaimer will be determined by section 2518 and the corresponding regulations. For rules relating to when the transfer creating the interest occurs, see §25.2518-2(c)(3) and (c)(4) of this chapter. If a qualified disclaimer is determined to have been made by the surviving spouse, the property interest disclaimed is treated as if such interest had never been transferred to the surviving spouse.

(b) *Disclaimer by a person other than a surviving spouse*.—If an interest in property passes from a decedent to a person other than the surviving spouse, and the interest is created in a transfer made after December 31, 1976, and—

(1) The person other than the surviving spouse makes a qualified disclaimer with respect to such interest; and

(2) The surviving spouse is entitled to such interest in property as a result of such disclaimer, the disclaimed interest is treated as passing directly from the decedent to the surviving spouse. For rules relating to when the transfer creating the interest occurs, see §25.2518-2(c)(3) and (c)(4) of this chapter.

(c) *Effective date*.—The first and second sentences of paragraphs (a) and (b) of this section are applicable for transfers creating the interest to be disclaimed made on or after December 31, 1997. [Reg. §20.2056(d)-2.]

□ [*T.D.* 6296, 6-23-58. *Amended by T.D.* 8095, 8-6-86. *Redesignated by T.D.* 8612, 8-21-95. *Amended by T.D.* 8744, 12-30-97.]

[Reg. §20.2056(d)-3]

§20.2056(d)-3. Marital deduction; effect of disclaimers of pre-January 1, 1977 transfers.—(a) *Disclaimer by a surviving spouse*.—If an interest in property passes to a decedent's surviving spouse in a taxable transfer made by a decedent dying before January 1, 1977, and the decedent's surviving spouse makes a disclaimer of this property interest, the disclaimed interest is considered as passing from the decedent to the person or persons entitled to receive the interest as a result of the disclaimer. A disclaimer is a complete and unqualified refusal to accept the rights to which one is entitled. It is, therefore, necessary to distinguish between the surviving spouse's disclaimer of a property interest and such surviving spouse's acceptance and subsequent disposal of a property interest. For example, if proceeds of insurance are payable to the surviving spouse and the proceeds are refused so that they consequently pass to an alternate beneficiary designated by the decedent, the proceeds are considered as having passed from the decedent to the alternate beneficiary. On the other hand, if the insurance company is directed by the surviving spouse to hold the proceeds at interest during such spouse's life and, upon this spouse's death, to pay the principal sum to another person designated by the surviving spouse, thus effecting a transfer of a remainder interest, the proceeds are considered as having passed from the decedent to the surviving spouse. See paragraph(c) of § 20.2056(e)-2 with respect to a spouse's exercise or failure to exercise a right to take against a decedent's will.

(b) *Disclaimer by a person other than a surviving spouse.*—(1) *Decedents dying after October 3, 1966 and before January 1, 1977.*—This paragraph (b)(1) applies in the case of a disclaimer of property passing to one other than the surviving spouse from a decedent dying after October 3, 1966 and before January 1, 1977. If a surviving spouse is entitled to receive property from the decedent as a result of the timely disclaimer made by the disclaimant, the property received by the surviving spouse is to be treated as passing to the surviving spouse from the decedent. Both a disclaimer of property passing by the laws of intestacy or otherwise, as by insurance or by trust, and a disclaimer of bequests and devises under the will of a decedent are to be fully effective for purposes of computing the marital deduction under section 2056. A disclaimer is a complete and unqualified refusal to accept some or all of the rights to which one is entitled. It must be a valid refusal under State law and must be made without consideration. For example, a disclaimer for the benefit of a surviving spouse who promises to give or bequeath property to a child of the person who disclaims is not a disclaimer within the meaning of this paragraph (b)(1). The disclaimer must be made before the person disclaiming accepts any property under the disclaimed interest. In the case of property transferred by a decedent dying after December 31, 1970, and before January 1, 1977, the disclaimer must be made within 9 months after the decedent's death (or within any extension of time for filing the estate tax return granted pursuant to section 6081). In the case of property transferred by a decedent dying after October 3, 1966, and before January 1, 1971, the disclaimer must be made within 15 months after the decedent's death (or within any extension of time for filing the estate's tax return granted pursuant to section 6081). If the disclaimer does not satisfy the requirements of this paragraph (b)(1), for the purpose of the marital deduction, the property is considered as passing from the decedent to the person who made the disclaimer as if the disclaimer had not been made.

(2) *Decedents dying after September 30, 1963 and before October 4, 1966.*—This paragraph (b)(2) applies in the case of a disclaimer of property passing to one other than the surviving spouse from a decedent dying after September 30, 1963 and before October 4, 1966. If, as a result of the disclaimer by the disclaimant, the surviving spouse is entitled to receive the disclaimed property interest, then such interest shall, for the purposes of this paragraph (b)(2), be considered as passing from the decedent to the surviving spouse if the following conditions are met. First, the interest disclaimed was bequeathed or devised to the disclaimant. Second, the disclaimant disclaimed all bequests and devises under the will before the date prescribed for the filing of the estate tax return. Third, the disclaimant did not accept any property under the bequest or devise before making the disclaimer. The interests passing by disclaimer to the surviving spouse under this paragraph (b)(2) are to qualify for the marital deduction only to the extent that, when added to any other allowable marital deduction without regard to this paragraph (b)(2), they do not exceed the greater of the deductions which would be allowable for the marital deduction without regard to the disclaimer if the surviving spouse exercised the election under State law to take against the will, or an amount equal to one-third of the decedent's adjusted gross estate. If the disclaimer does not satisfy the requirements of this paragraph (b)(2), the property is treated as passing from the decedent to the person who made the disclaimer, in the same manner as if the disclaimer had not been made.

(3) *Decedents dying before October 4, 1966.*—Unless the rule of paragraph (b)(2) of this section applies, this paragraph (b)(3) applies in the case of a disclaimer of property passing to one other than the surviving spouse from a decedent dying before October 4, 1966. For the purpose of these transfers, it is unnecessary to distinguish for the purpose of the marital deduction between a disclaimer by a person other than the surviving spouse and a transfer by such person. If the surviving spouse becomes entitled to receive an interest in property from the decedent as a result of a disclaimer made by some other person, the interest is, nevertheless, considered as having passed from the decedent, not to the surviving spouse, but to the person who made the disclaimer, as though the disclaimer had not been made. If, as a result of a disclaimer made by a person other than the surviving spouse, a property interest passes to the surviving spouse under circumstances which meet the conditions set forth in § 20.2056(b)-5 (relating to a life estate

with a power of appointment), the rule stated in the preceding sentence applies, not only with respect to the portion of the interest which beneficially vests in the surviving spouse, but also with respect to the portion over which such spouse acquires a power to appoint. The rule applies also in the case of proceeds under a life insurance, endowment, or annuity contract which, as a result of a disclaimer made by a person other than the surviving spouse, are held by the insurer subject to the conditions set forth in § 20.2056(b)-6. [Reg. § 20.2056(d)-3.]

☐ [*T.D. 8095, 8-6-86. Redesignated by T.D. 8612, 8-21-95.*]

[Reg. § 20.2056A-0]

§ 20.2056A-0. Table of contents.—This section lists the captions that appear in the final regulations under § § 20.2056A-1 through 20.2056A-13.

§ 20.2056A-1. Restrictions on allowance of marital deduction if surviving spouse is not a United States citizen.

(a) General rule.

(b) Marital deduction allowed if resident spouse becomes citizen.

(c) Special rules in the case of certain transfers subject to estate and gift tax treaties.

§ 20.2056A-2. Requirements for qualified domestic trust.

(a) In general.

(b) Qualified marital interest requirements.

(1) Property passing to QDOT.

(2) Property passing outright to spouse.

(3) Property passing under a nontransferable plan or arrangement.

(c) Statutory requirements.

(d) Additional requirements to ensure collection of the section 2056A estate tax.

(1) Security and other arrangements for payment of estate tax imposed under section 2056A(b)(1).

(2) Individual trustees.

(3) Annual reporting requirements.

(4) Request for alternate arrangement or waiver.

(5) Adjustment of dollar threshold and exclusion.

(6) Effective date and special rules.

§ 20.2056A-3. QDOT election.

(a) General rule.

(b) No partial elections.

(c) Protective elections.

(d) Manner of election.

§ 20.2056A-4. Procedures for conforming marital trusts and nontrust marital transfers to the requirements of a qualified domestic trust.

(a) Marital trusts.

(1) In general.

(2) Judicial reformations.

(3) Tolling of statutory assessment period.

(b) Nontrust marital transfers.

(1) In general.

(2) Form of transfer or assignment.

(3) Assets eligible for transfer or assignment.

(4) Pecuniary assignment - special rules.

(5) Transfer tax treatment of transfer or assignment.

(6) Period for completion of transfer.

(7) Retirement accounts and annuities.

(8) Protective assignment.

(c) Nonassignable annuities and other arrangements.

(1) Definition and general rule.

(2) Agreement to remit section 2056A estate tax on corpus portion of each annuity payment.

(3) Agreement to roll over corpus portion of annuity payment to QDOT.

(4) Determination of corpus portion.

(5) Information Statement.

(6) Agreement to pay section 2056A estate tax.

(7) Agreement to roll over annuity payments.

(d) Examples.

§ 20.2056A-5. Imposition of section 2056A estate tax.

(a) In general.

(b) Amounts subject to tax.

(1) Distribution of principal during the spouse's lifetime.

(2) Death of surviving spouse.

(3) Trust ceases to qualify as QDOT.

(c) Distributions and dispositions not subject to tax.

(1) Distributions of principal on account of hardship.

(2) Distributions of income to the surviving spouse.

(3) Certain miscellaneous distributions and dispositions.

§ 20.2056A-6. Amount of tax.

(a) Definition of tax.

(b) Benefits allowed in determining amount of section 2056A estate tax.

(1) General rule.

(2) Treatment as resident.

(3) Special rule in the case of trusts described in section 2056(b)(8).

(4) Credit for state and foreign death taxes.

(5) Alternate valuation and special use valuation.

(c) Miscellaneous rules.

(d) Examples.

§ 20.2056A-7. Allowance of prior transfer credit under section 2013.

(a) Property subject to QDOT election.

(b) Property not subject to QDOT election.

(c) Example.

§ 20.2056A-8. Special rules for joint property.

(a) Inclusion in gross estate.

(1) General rule.

(2) Consideration furnished by surviving spouse.

(3) Amount allowed to be transferred to QDOT.

(b) Surviving spouse becomes citizen.

(c) Examples.

§ 20.2056A-9. Designated Filer.

§ 20.2056A-10. Surviving spouse becomes citizen after QDOT established.

(a) Section 2056A estate tax no longer imposed under certain circumstances.

(b) Special election by spouse.

§ 20.2056A-11. Filing requirements and payment of the section 2056A estate tax.

(a) Distributions during surviving spouse's life.

(b) Tax at death of surviving spouse.

(c) Extension of time for paying section 2056A estate tax.

(1) Extension of time for paying tax under section 6161(a)(2).

(2) Extension of time for paying tax under section 6161(a)(1).

(d) Liability for tax.

§ 20.2056A-12. Increased basis for section 2056A estate tax paid with respect to distribution from a QDOT.

§ 20.2056A-13. Effective date.

[Reg. § 20.2056A-0.]

☐ [*T.D.* 8612, 8-21-95. *Amended by T.D.* 8686, 11-27-96.]

[Reg. § 20.2056A-1]

§ 20.2056A-1. Restrictions on allowance of marital deduction if surviving spouse is not a United States citizen.—(a) *General rule.*—Subject to the special rules provided in section 7815(d)(14) of the Omnibus Budget Reconciliation Act of 1989 (Pub. L. 101-239; 103 Stat. 2106), in the case of a decedent dying after November 10, 1988, the federal estate tax marital deduction is not allowed for property passing to or for the benefit of a surviving spouse who is not a United States citizen at the date of the decedent's death (whether or not the surviving spouse is a resident of the United States) unless—

(1) The property passes from the decedent to (or pursuant to)—

(i) A qualified domestic trust (QDOT) described in section 2056A and § 20.2056A-2;

(ii) A trust that, although not meeting all of the requirements for a QDOT, is reformed after the decedent's death to meet the requirements of a QDOT (see § 20.2056A-4(a));

(iii) The surviving spouse not in trust (e.g., by outright bequest or devise, by operation of law, or pursuant to the terms of an annuity or other similar plan or arrangement) and, prior to the date that the estate tax return is filed and on or before the last date prescribed by law that the QDOT election may be made (no more than one year after the time prescribed by law, including extensions, for filing the return), the surviving spouse either actually transfers the property to a QDOT or irrevocably assigns the property to a QDOT (see § 20.2056A-4(b)); or

(iv) A plan or other arrangement that would have qualified for the marital deduction but for section 2056(d)(1)(A), and whose payments are not assignable or transferable to a QDOT, if the requirements of § 20.2056A-4(c) are met; and

(2) The executor makes a timely QDOT election under § 20.2056A-3.

(b) *Marital deduction allowed if resident spouse becomes citizen.*—For purposes of section 2056(d)(1) and paragraph (a) of this section, the surviving spouse is treated as a citizen of the United States at the date of the decedent's death if the requirements of section 2056(d)(4) are satisfied. For purposes of section 2056(d)(4)(A) and notwithstanding § 20.2056A-3(a), a return filed prior to the due date (including extensions) is considered filed on the last date that the return is required to be filed (including extensions), and a late return filed at any time after the due date is considered filed on the date that it is actually filed. A surviving spouse is a resident only if the spouse is a resident under chapter 11 of the Internal Revenue Code. See § 20.0-1(b)(1). The status of the spouse as a resident under section 7701(b) is not relevant to this determination except to the extent that the income tax residency of the spouse is pertinent in applying § 20.0-1(b)(1).

(c) *Special rules in the case of certain transfers subject to estate and gift tax treaties.*—Under section 7815(d)(14) of the Omnibus Budget Reconciliation Act of 1989 (Pub. L. 101-239, 103 Stat. 2106) certain special rules apply in the case of transfers governed by certain estate and gift tax treaties to which the United States is a party. In the case of the estate of, or gift by, an individual who was not a citizen or resident of the United States but was a resident of a foreign country with which the United States has a tax treaty with respect to estate, inheritance, or gift taxes, the amendments made by section 5033 of the Technical and Miscellaneous Revenue Act of 1988 (Pub. L. 100-647, 102 Stat. 3342) do not apply to the extent such amendments would be inconsistent with the provisions of such treaty relating to estate, inheritance, or gift tax marital deductions. Under this rule, the estate may choose either the statutory deduction under section 2056A or the marital deduction allowed under the treaty. Thus, the estate may not avail itself of both the marital deduction under the treaty and the marital deduction under the QDOT provisions of section 2056A and chapter 11 of the Internal Revenue Code with respect to the remainder of the marital property that is not deductible under the treaty. [Reg. § 20.2056A-1.]

☐ [*T.D.* 8612, 8-21-95.]

[Reg. § 20.2056A-2]

§ 20.2056A-2. Requirements for qualified domestic trust.—(a) *In general.*—In order to qualify as a qualified domestic trust (QDOT), the requirements of paragraphs (b) and (c) of this section, and the requirements of § 20.2056A-2T(d), must be satisfied. The executor of the decedent's estate and the U.S. Trustee shall establish in such manner as may be prescribed by the Commissioner on the estate tax return and applicable instructions that these requirements have been satisfied or are being complied with. In order to constitute a QDOT, the trust must be maintained under the laws of a state of the United States or the District of Columbia, and the administration of the trust must be governed by the laws of a particular state of the United States or the District of Columbia. For purposes of this paragraph, a trust is maintained under the laws of a state of the United States or the District of Columbia if the records of the trust (or copies thereof) are kept in that state (or the District of Columbia). The trust may be established pursuant to an instrument executed under either the laws of a state of the United States or the District of Columbia or pursuant to an instrument executed under the laws of a foreign jurisdiction, such as a foreign will or trust, provided that such foreign instrument designates the law of a particular state of the United States or the District of Columbia as governing the administration of the trust, and such designation is effective under the law of the designated jurisdiction. In addition, the trust must constitute an ordinary trust, as defined in § 301.7701-4(a) of this chapter, and not any other type of entity. For purposes of this paragraph (a), a trust will not fail to constitute an ordinary trust solely because of the nature of the assets transferred to that trust, regardless of its classification under §§ 301.7701-2 through 301.7701-4 of this chapter.

(b) *Qualified marital interest requirements.*—(1) *Property passing to QDOT.*—If property passes from a decedent to a QDOT, the trust must qualify for the federal estate tax marital deduction under section 2056(b)(5) (life estate with power of appointment), section 2056(b)(7) (qualified terminable interest property, including joint and survivor annuities under section 2056(b)(7)(C)), or section 2056(b)(8) (surviving spouse is the only noncharitable beneficiary of a charitable remainder trust), or meet the requirements of an estate trust as defined in § 20.2056(c)-2(b)(1)(i) through (iii).

(2) *Property passing outright to spouse.*—If property does not pass from a decedent to a QDOT, but passes to a noncitizen surviving spouse in a form that meets the requirements for a marital deduction without regard to section 2056(d)(1)(A), and that is not described in paragraph (b)(1) of this section, the surviving spouse must either actually transfer the property, or irrevocably assign the property, to a trust (whether created by the decedent, the decedent's executor or by the surviving spouse) that meets the requirements of paragraph (c) of this section and the requirements of § 20.2056A-2T(d) (pertaining, respectively, to statutory requirements and regulatory requirements imposed to ensure collection of tax) prior to the filing of the estate tax return for the decedent's estate and on or before the last date prescribed by law that the QDOT election may be made (see § 20.2056A-3(a)).

(3) *Property passing under a nontransferable plan or arrangement.*—If property does not pass from a decedent to a QDOT, but passes under a plan or other arrangement that meets the requirements for a marital deduction without regard to section 2056(d)(1)(A) and whose payments are not assignable or transferable (see § 20.2056A-4(c)), the property is treated as meeting the requirements of this section, and the requirements of § 20.2056A-2T(d), if the requirements of § 20.2056A-4(c) are satisfied. In addition, where an annuity or similar arrangement is described above except that it is assignable or transferable, see § 20.2056A-4(b)(7).

(c) *Statutory requirements.*—The requirements of section 2056A(a)(1)(A) and (B) must be satisfied. For purposes of that section, a domestic corporation is a corporation that is created or organized under the laws of the United States or under the laws of any state of the United States or the District of Columbia. The trustee required under that section is referred to herein as the "U.S. Trustee".

(d) *Additional requirements to ensure collection of the section 2056A estate tax.*—(1) *Security and other arrangements for payment of estate tax imposed under section 2056A(b)(1).*—(i) *QDOTs with assets in excess of $2 million.*—If the fair market value of the assets passing, treated, or deemed to have passed to the QDOT (or in the form of a QDOT), determined without reduction for any indebtedness with respect to the assets, as finally determined for federal estate tax purposes, exceeds $2 million as of the date of the decedent's death or, if applicable, the alternate valuation date (adjusted as provided in paragraph (d)(1)(iii) of this section), the trust instrument must meet the requirements of either paragraph (d)(1)(i)(A), (B), or (C) of this section at all times during the term of the QDOT. The QDOT may alternate between any of the arrangements provided in paragraphs (d)(1)(i)(A), (B), and (C) of this section provided that, at any given time, one of the arrangements must be operative. See paragraph (d)(1)(iii) of this section for the definition of finally determined. The QDOT may provide that the trustee has the discretion to use any one of the security arrangements or may provide that the trustee is limited to using only one or two of the arrangements specified in the trust instrument. A trust instrument that specifically states that the trust must be administered in compliance with paragraph (d)(1)(i)(A), (B), or (C) of this section is treated as meeting the requirements of paragraphs (d)(1)(i)(A), (B), or (C) for purposes of paragraphs (d)(1)(i) and, if applicable, (d)(1)(ii) of this section.

(A) *Bank Trustee.*—Except as otherwise provided in paragraph (d)(6)(ii) or (iii) of this section, the trust instrument must provide that whenever the Bank Trustee security alternative is used for the QDOT, at least one U.S. Trustee must be a bank as defined in section 581. Alternatively, except as otherwise provided in paragraph (d)(6)(ii) or (iii) of this section, at least one trustee must be a United States branch of a foreign bank, provided that, in such cases, during the entire term of the QDOT a U.S. Trustee must act as a trustee with the foreign bank trustee.

(B) *Bond.*—Except as otherwise provided in paragraph (d)(6)(ii) or (iii) of this section, the trust instrument must provide that whenever the bond security arrangement alternative is used for the QDOT, the U.S. Trustee must furnish a bond in favor of the Internal Revenue Service in an amount equal to 65 percent of the fair market value of the trust assets (determined without regard to any indebtedness with respect to the assets) as of the date of the decedent's death (or alternate valuation date, if applicable), as finally determined for federal estate tax purposes (and as further adjusted as provided in paragraph (d)(1)(iv) of this section). If, after examination of the estate tax return, the fair market value of the trust assets, as originally reported on the estate tax return, is adjusted (pursuant to a judicial proceeding or otherwise) resulting in a final determination of the value of the assets as reported on the return, the U.S. Trustee has a reasonable period of time (not exceeding sixty days after the conclusion of the proceeding or other action resulting in a final determination of the value of the assets) to adjust the amount of the bond accordingly. But see, paragraph (d)(1)(i)(D) of this section for a special rule in the case of a substantial undervaluation of QDOT assets. Unless an alternate arrangement under paragraph (d)(1)(i)(A), (B), or (C) of this section, or an arrangement prescribed under paragraph (d)(4) of this section, is provided, or the trust is otherwise no longer subject to the requirements of section 2056A pursuant to section 2056A(b)(12), the bond must remain in effect until the trust ceases to function as a QDOT and any tax liability finally determined to be due under section 2056A(b) is paid, or is finally determined to be zero.

(1) Requirements for the bond.—The bond must be with a satisfactory surety, as prescribed under section 7101 and § 301.7101-1 of this chapter (Regulations on Procedure and Administration), and is subject to Internal Revenue Service review as may be prescribed by the Commissioner. The bond may not be cancelled. The bond must be for a term of at least one year and must be automatically renewable at the end of that term, on an annual basis thereafter, unless notice of failure to renew is mailed to the U.S. Trustee and the Internal Revenue Service at least 60 days prior to the end of the term, including periods of automatic extensions. Any notice of failure to renew required to be sent to the Internal Revenue Service must be sent to the Estate and Gift Tax Group in the District Office of the Internal Revenue Service that has examination jurisdiction over the decedent's estate (Internal Revenue Service, District Director, *[specify location]* District Office, Estate and Gift Tax Examination Group, [specify Street Address, City, State, Zip Code]) (or in the case of noncitizen decedents and United States citizens who die domiciled outside the United States, Estate Tax Group, Assistant Commissioner (International), 950 L'Enfant Plaza, CP:IN:D:C:EX:HQ:1114, Washington, DC 20024). The Internal Revenue Service will not draw on the bond if, within 30 days of receipt of the notice of failure to renew, the U.S. Trustee notifies the Internal Revenue Service (at the same address to which notice of failure to renew is to be sent) that an alternate arrangement under paragraph (d)(1)(i)(A), (B), or (C) or (d)(4) of this section, has been secured and that the arrangement will take effect immediately prior to or upon expiration of the bond.

(2) Form of bond.—The bond must be in the following form (or in a form that is the same as the following form in all material respects), or in such alternative form as the Commissioner may prescribe by guidance published in the Internal Revenue Bulletin (see § 601.601(d)(2) of this chapter):

Bond in Favor of the Internal Revenue Service To Secure Payment of Section 2056A Estate Tax Imposed Under Section 2056A(b) of the Internal Revenue Code.

KNOW ALL PERSONS BY THESE PRESENTS, That the undersigned, _____, the SURETY, and ______, the PRINCIPAL, are irrevocably held and firmly bound to pay the Internal Revenue Service upon written demand that amount of any tax up to $ *[amount determined under paragraph (d)(1)(i)(B) of this section]*, imposed under section 2056A(b)(1) of the Internal Revenue Code (including penalties and interest on said tax) determined by the Internal Revenue Service to be payable with respect to the principal as trustee for: *[Identify trust and governing instrument, name and address of trustee]*, a qualified domestic trust as defined in section 2056A(a) of the Internal Revenue Code, for the payment of which the said Principal and said Surety, bind themselves, their heirs, executors, administrators, successors and assigns, jointly and severally, firmly by these presents.

WHEREAS, The Internal Revenue Service may demand payment under this bond at any time if the Internal Revenue Service in its sole discretion determines that a taxable event with respect to the trust has occurred; the trust no longer qualifies as a qualified domestic trust as described in section 2056A(a) of the Internal Revenue Code and the regulations promulgated thereunder, or a distribution subject to the tax imposed under section 2056A(b)(1) has been made. Demand by the Internal Revenue Service for payment may be made whether or not the tax and tax return (Form 706-QDT) with respect to the taxable event is due at the time of such demand, or an assessment has been made by the Internal Revenue Service with respect to the tax.

NOW THEREFORE, The condition of this obligation is such that it must not be cancelled and, if payment of all tax liability finally determined to be imposed under section 2056A(b) is made, then this obligation is null and void; otherwise, this obligation is to remain in full force and effect for one year from its effective date and is to be automatically renewable on an annual basis unless, at least 60 days prior to the expiration date, including periods of automatic renewals, the surety mails to the U.S. Trustee and the Internal Revenue Service by Registered or Certified Mail, return receipt requested, notice of the failure to renew. Receipt of this notice of failure to renew by the Internal Revenue Service may be considered a taxable event. The Internal Revenue Service will not draw upon the bond if, within 30 days of receipt of the notice of failure to renew, the trustee notifies the Internal Revenue Service that an alternate security arrangement has been secured and that the arrangement will take effect immediately prior to or upon expiration of the bond. The surety remains liable for all taxable events occurring prior to the date of expiration. All notices required to be sent to the Internal Revenue Service under this instrument should be sent to District Director, *[specify location]* District Office, Estate and Gift Tax Examination Group, Street Address, City, State, Zip Code. (In the case of nonresident noncitizen decedents and United States citizens who die domiciled outside the United States, all notices should be sent to Estate Tax Group, Assistant Commissioner (International), 950 L'Enfant Plaza, CP:IN:D:C:EX:HQ:1114, Washington, DC 20024).

This bond shall be effective as of ____.

Principal ____________________

Date ____________________

Surety ____________________

Date ____________________

(3) Additional governing instrument requirements.—The trust instrument must provide that in the event the Internal Revenue Service draws on the bond, in accordance with its terms, neither the U.S. Trustee nor any other person will seek a return of any part of the remittance until after April 15th of the calendar year following the year in which the bond is drawn upon. After that date, any such remittance will be treated as a deposit and returned (without interest) upon request of the U.S. Trustee, unless it is determined that assessment or collection of the tax imposed by section 2056A(b)(1) is in jeopardy, within the meaning of section 6861. If an assessment under section 6861 is made, the remittance will first be credited to any tax liability reported on the Form 706-QDT, then to any unpaid balance of a section 2056A(b)(1)(A) tax liability (plus interest and penalties) for any prior taxable years, and any balance will then be returned to the U.S. Trustee.

(4) Procedure.—The bond is to be filed with the decedent's federal estate tax return, Form 706 or 706NA (unless an extension for filing the bond is granted under § 301.9100 of this chapter). The U.S. Trustee must provide a written statement with the bond that provides a list of the assets that will be used to fund the QDOT and the respective values of the assets. The written statement must also indicate whether any exclusions under paragraph (d)(1)(iv) of this section are claimed.

(C) *Letter of credit.*—Except as otherwise provided in paragraph (d)(6)(ii) or (iii) of this section, the trust instrument must provide that whenever the letter of credit security arrangement is used for the QDOT, the U.S. Trustee must furnish an irrevocable letter of credit issued by a bank as defined in section 581, a United States branch of a foreign bank, or a foreign bank with a confirmation by a bank as defined in section 581. The letter of credit must be for an amount equal to 65 percent of the fair market value of the trust assets (determined without regard to any indebtedness with respect to the assets) as of the date of the decedent's death (or alternate valuation date, if applicable), as finally determined for federal estate tax purposes (and as further adjusted as provided in paragraph (d)(1)(iv) of this section). If, after examination of the estate tax return, the fair market value of the trust assets, as originally reported on the estate tax return, is adjusted (pursuant to a judicial proceeding or otherwise) resulting in a final determination of the value of the assets as reported on the return, the U.S. Trustee has a reasonable period of time (not exceeding 60 days after the conclusion of the proceeding or other action resulting in a final determination of the value of the assets) to adjust the amount of the letter of credit accordingly. But see, paragraph (d)(1)(i)(D) of this section for a special rule in the case of a substantial undervaluation of QDOT assets. Unless an alternate arrangement under paragraph (d)(1)(i)(A), (B), or (C) of this section, or an arrangement prescribed under paragraph (d)(4) of this section, is provided, or the trust is otherwise no longer subject to the requirements of section 2056A pursuant to section 2056A(b)(12), the letter of credit must remain in effect until the trust ceases to function as a QDOT and any tax liability finally determined to be due under section 2056A(b) is paid or is finally determined to be zero.

(1) Requirements for the letter of credit.—The letter of credit must be irrevocable and provide for sight payment. The letter of credit must have a term of at least one year and must be automatically renewable at the end of the term, at least on an annual basis, unless notice of failure to renew is mailed to the U.S. Trustee and the Internal Revenue Service at least sixty days prior to the end of the term, including periods of automatic renewals. If the letter of credit is issued by the U.S. branch of a foreign bank and the U.S. branch is closing, the branch (or foreign bank) must notify the U.S. Trustee and the Internal Revenue Service of the closure and the notice of closure must be mailed at least 60 days prior to the date of closure. Any notice of failure to renew or closure of a U.S. branch of a foreign bank required to be sent to the Internal Revenue Service must be sent to the Estate and Gift Tax Group in the District Office of the Internal Revenue Service that has examination jurisdiction over the decedent's estate (Internal Revenue Service, District Director, *[specify location]* District Office, Estate and Gift Tax Examination Group, [Street Address, City State, Zip Code]) (or in the case of noncitizen decedents and United States citizens who die domiciled outside the United States, Estate Tax, Assistant

Commissioner (International), 950 L'Enfant Plaza, CP:IN:D:C:EX:HQ:1114, Washington, DC 20024). The Internal Revenue Service will not draw on the letter of credit if, within 30 days of receipt of the notice of failure to renew or closure of the U.S. branch of a foreign bank, the U.S. Trustee notifies the Internal Revenue Service (at the same address to which notice is to be sent) that an alternate arrangement under paragraph (d)(1)(i)(A), (B), or (C), or (d)(4) of this section, has been secured and that the arrangement will take effect immediately prior to or upon expiration of the letter of credit or closure of the U.S. branch of the foreign bank.

(2) *Form of letter of credit.*—The letter of credit must be made in the following form (or in a form that is the same as the following form in all material respects), or an alternative form that the Commissioner prescribes by guidance published in the Internal Revenue Bulletin (see § 601.601(d)(2) of this chapter):

[Issue Date]

To: Internal Revenue Service

Attention: District Director, *[specify location]* District Office

Estate and Gift Tax Examination Group

[Street Address, City, State, ZIP Code]

[Or in the case of nonresident noncitizen decedents and United States citizens who die domiciled outside the United States,

To: Estate Tax Group,
Assistant Commissioner (International)
950 L'Enfant Plaza
CP:IN:D:C:EX:HQ:1114
Washington, DC 20024].

Dear Sirs:

We hereby establish our irrevocable Letter of Credit No.—in your favor for drawings up to U.S. $ *[Applicant should provide bank with amount which Applicant determined under paragraph (d)(1)(i)(C)]* effective immediately. This Letter of Credit is issued, presentable and payable at our office at ______ and expires at 3:00 p.m. [EDT, EST, CDT, CST, MDT, MST, PDT, PST]on ______ at said office.

For information and reference only, we are informed that this Letter of Credit relates to *[Applicant should provide bank with the identity of qualified domestic trust and governing instrument]*, and the name, address, and identifying number of the trustee is *[Applicant should provide bank with the trustee name, address and the QDOT's TIN number, if any]*.

Drawings on this Letter of Credit are available upon presentation of the following documents:

1. Your draft drawn at sight on us bearing our Letter of Credit No. ______; and

2. Your signed statement as follows:

The amount of the accompanying draft is payable under *[identify bank]* irrevocable Letter of Credit No. ______ pursuant to section 2056A of the Internal Revenue Code and the regulations promulgated thereunder, because the Internal Revenue Service in its sole discretion has determined that a "taxable event" with respect to the trust has occurred; e.g., the trust no longer qualifies as a qualified domestic trust as described in section 2056A of the Internal Revenue Code and regulations promulgated thereunder, or a distribution subject to the tax imposed under section 2056A(b)(1) of the Internal Revenue Code has been made.

Except as expressly stated herein, this undertaking is not subject to any agreement, requirement or qualification. The obligation of *[Name of Issuing Bank]* under this Letter of Credit is the individual obligation of *[Name of Issuing Bank]* and is in no way contingent upon reimbursement with respect thereto.

It is a condition of this Letter of Credit that it is deemed to be automatically extended without amendment for a period of one year from the expiration date hereof, or any future expiration date, unless at least 60 days prior to any expiration date, we mail to you and to the U.S. Trustee notice by Registered Mail or Certified Mail, return receipt requested, or by courier to your and the trustee's address indicated above, that we elect not to consider this Letter of Credit renewed for any such additional period. Upon receipt of this notice, you may draw hereunder on or before the then current expiration date, by presentation of your draft and statement as stipulated above.

[In the case of a letter of credit issued by a U.S. branch of a foreign bank the following language must be added]. It is a further condition of this Letter of Credit that if the U.S. branch of *[name of foreign bank]* is to be closed, that at least sixty days prior to closing, we mail to you and the U.S. Trustee notice by Registered Mail or Certified Mail, return receipt requested, or by courier to your and the U.S. Trustee's address indicated above, that this branch will be closing. This notice will specify the actual date of closing. Upon receipt of the notice, you may draw hereunder on or before the date of closure, by presentation of your draft and statement as stipulated above.

Except where otherwise stated herein, this Letter of Credit is subject to the Uniform Customs and Practice for Documentary Credits, 1993 Revision, ICC Publication No. 500. If we notify you of our election not to consider this Letter of Credit renewed and the expiration date occurs during an interruption of business described in Article 17 of said Publication 500, unless you had consented to cancellation prior to the expiration date, the bank hereby specifically agrees to effect payment if this Letter of Credit is drawn against within 30 days after the resumption of business.

Except as stated herein, this Letter of Credit cannot be modified or revoked without your consent.

Authorized Signature ______

Date ______

(3) *Form of confirmation.*—If the requirements of this paragraph (d)(1)(i)(C) are satisfied by the issuance of a letter of credit by a foreign bank with confirmation by a bank as

defined in section 581, the confirmation must be made in the following form (or in a form that is the same as the following form in all material respects), or an alternative form as the Commissioner prescribes by guidance published in the Internal Revenue Bulletin (see § 602.101(d)(2) of this chapter):

[Issue Date]

To: Internal Revenue Service

Attention: District Director, *[specify location]* District Office

Estate and Gift Tax Examination Group

[State Address, City, State, ZIP Code]

[or in the case of nonresident noncitizen decedents and United States citizens who die domiciled outside the United States,

To: Estate Tax Group,
Assistant Commissioner (International)
950 L'Enfant Plaza
CP:IN:D:C:EX:HQ:1114
Washington, DC 20024].

Dear Sirs:

We hereby confirm the enclosed irrevocable Letter of Credit No. ______, and amendments thereto, if any, in your favor by ______ [Issuing Bank] for drawings up to U.S. $ [same amount as in initial Letter of Credit] effective immediately. This confirmation is issued, presentable and payable at our office at ______ and expires at 3:00 p.m. [EDT, EST, CDT, CST, MDT, MST, PDT, PST]on ______ at said office.

For information and reference only, we are informed that this Confirmation relates to [Applicant should provide bank with the identity of qualified domestic trust and governing instrument], and the name, address, and identifying number of the trustee is [Applicant should provide bank with the trustee name, address and the QDOT's TIN number, if any].

We hereby undertake to honor your sight draft(s) drawn as specified in the Letter of Credit.

Except as expressly stated herein, this undertaking is not subject to any agreement, condition or qualification. The obligation of *[Name of Confirming Bank]* under this Confirmation is the individual obligation of *[Name of Confirming Bank]* and is in no way contingent upon reimbursement with respect thereto.

It is a condition of this Confirmation that it is deemed to be automatically extended without amendment for a period of one year from the expiry date hereof, or any future expiration date, unless at least sixty days prior to the expiration date, we send to you and to the U.S. Trustee notice by Registered Mail or Certified Mail, return receipt requested, or by courier to your and the trustee's addresses, respectively, indicated above, that we elect not to consider this Confirmation renewed for any additional period. Upon receipt of this notice by you, you may draw hereunder on or before the then current expiration date, by presentation of your draft and statement as stipulated above.

Except where otherwise stated herein, this Confirmation is subject to the Uniform Customs and Practice for Documentary Credits, 1993 Revision, ICC Publication No. 500. If we notify you of our election not to consider this Confirmation renewed and the expiration date occurs during an interruption of business described in Article 17 of said Publication 500, unless you had consented to cancellation prior to the expiration date, the bank hereby specifically agrees to effect payment if this Confirmation is drawn against within 30 days after the resumption of business.

Except as stated herein, this Confirmation cannot be modified or revoked without your consent.

Authorized Signature ______________

Date ______________

(4) Additional governing instrument requirements.—The trust instrument must provide that if the Internal Revenue Service draws on the letter of credit (or confirmation) in accordance with its terms, neither the U.S. Trustee nor any other person will seek a return of any part of the remittance until April 15th of the calendar year following the year in which the letter of credit (or confirmation) is drawn upon. After that date, any such remittance will be treated as a deposit and returned (without interest) upon request of the U.S. Trustee after the date specified above, unless it is determined that assessment or collection of the tax imposed by section 2056A(b)(1) is in jeopardy, within the meaning of section 6861. If an assessment under section 6861 is made, the remittance will first be credited to any tax liability reported on the Form 706-QDT, then to any unpaid balance of a section 2056A(b)(1)(A) tax liability (plus interest and penalties) for any prior taxable years, and any balance will then be returned to the U.S. Trustee.

(5) Procedure.—The letter of credit (and confirmation, if applicable) is to be filed with the decedent's federal estate tax return, Form 706 or 706NA (unless an extension for filing the letter of credit is granted under § 301.9100 of this chapter). The U.S. Trustee must provide a written statement with the letter of credit that provides a list of the assets that will be used to fund the QDOT and the respective values of the assets. The written statement must also indicate whether any exclusions under paragraph (d)(1)(iv) of this section are claimed.

(D) *Disallowance of marital deduction for substantial undervaluation of QDOT property in certain situations.*—*(1)* If either—

(i) The bond or letter of credit security arrangement under paragraph (d)(1)(i)(B) or (C) of this section is chosen by the U.S. Trustee; or

(ii) The QDOT property as originally reported on the decedent's estate tax return is valued at $2 million or less but, as finally determined for federal estate tax purposes, the QDOT property is determined to be in excess of $2 million, then the marital deduction will be disallowed in its entirety for failure to comply

with the requirements of section 2056A if the value of the QDOT property reported on the estate tax return is 50 percent or less of the amount finally determined to be the correct value of the property for federal estate tax purposes.

(2) The preceding sentence does not apply if—

(i) There was reasonable cause for the undervaluation; and

(ii) The fiduciary of the estate acted in good faith with respect to the undervaluation. For this purpose, § 1.6664-4(b) of this chapter applies, to the extent applicable, with respect to the facts and circumstances to be taken into account in making this determination.

(ii) *QDOTs with assets of $2 million or less.*—If the fair market value of the assets passing, treated, or deemed to have passed to the QDOT (or in the form of a QDOT), determined without reduction for any indebtedness with respect to the assets, as finally determined for federal estate tax purposes, is $2 million or less as of the date of the decedent's death or, if applicable, the alternate valuation date (adjusted as provided in paragraph (d)(1)(iv) of this section), the trust instrument must provide that either no more than 35 percent of the fair market value of the trust assets, determined annually on the last day of the taxable year of the trust (or on the last day of the calendar year if the QDOT does not have a taxable year), will consist of real property located outside of the United States, or the trust will meet the requirements prescribed by paragraph (d)(1)(i)(A), (B), or (C) of this section. See paragraph (d)(1)(ii)(D) of this section for special rules in the case of principal distributions from a QDOT, fluctuations in the value of foreign real property held by a QDOT due to changes in value of foreign currency, and fluctuations in the fair market value of assets held by the QDOT. See paragraph (d)(1)(iv) of this section for a special rule for personal residences. If the fair market value, as originally reported on the decedent's estate tax return, of the assets passing or deemed to have passed to the QDOT (determined without reduction for any indebtedness with respect to the assets) is $2 million or less, but the fair market value of the assets as finally determined for federal estate tax purposes is more than $2 million, the U.S. Trustee has a reasonable period of time (not exceeding sixty days after the conclusion of the proceeding or other action resulting in a final determination of the value of the assets) to meet the requirements prescribed by paragraph (d)(1)(i)(A), (B), or (C) of this section. However, see paragraph (d)(1)(i)(D) of this section in the case of a substantial undervaluation of QDOT assets. See § 20.2056A-2(d)(1)(iii) for the definition of finally determined.

(A) *Multiple QDOTs.*—For purposes of this paragraph (d)(1)(ii), if more than one QDOT is established for the benefit of the surviving spouse, the fair market value of all the QDOTs are aggregated in determining whether the $2 million threshold under this paragraph (d)(1)(ii) is exceeded.

(B) *Look-through rule.*—For purposes of determining whether no more than 35 percent of the fair market value of the QDOT assets consists of foreign real property, if the QDOT owns more than 20% of the voting stock or value in a corporation with 15 or fewer shareholders, or more than 20% of the capital interest of a partnership with 15 or fewer partners, then all assets owned by the corporation or partnership are deemed to be owned directly by the QDOT to the extent of the QDOT's pro rata share of the assets of that corporation or partnership. For a partnership, the QDOT partner's pro rata share is based on the greater of its interest in the capital or profits of the partnership. For purposes of this paragraph, all stock in the corporation or interests in the partnership, as the case may be, owned by or held for the benefit of the surviving spouse, or any members of the surviving spouse's family (within the meaning of section 267(c)(4)), are treated as owned by the QDOT solely for purposes of determining the number of partners or shareholders in the entity and the QDOT's percentage voting interest or value in the corporation or capital interest in the partnership, but not for the purpose of determining the QDOT's pro rata share of the assets of the entity.

(C) *Interests in other entities.*—Interests owned by the QDOT in other entities (such as an interest in a trust) are accorded treatment consistent with that described in paragraph (d)(1)(ii)(B) of this section.

(D) *Special rule for foreign real property.*—For purposes of this paragraph (d)(1)(ii), if, on the last day of any taxable year during the term of the QDOT (or the last day of the calendar year if the QDOT does not have a taxable year), the value of foreign real property owned by the QDOT exceeds 35 percent of the fair market value of the trust assets due to: distributions of QDOT principal during that year; fluctuations in the value of the foreign currency in the jurisdiction where the real estate is located; or fluctuations in the fair market value of any assets held in the QDOT, then the QDOT will not be treated as failing to meet the requirements of this paragraph (d)(1). Accordingly, the QDOT will not cease to be a QDOT within the meaning of § 20.2056A-5(b)(3) if, by the end of the taxable year (or the last day of the calendar year if the QDOT does not have a taxable year) of the QDOT immediately following the year in which the 35 percent limit was exceeded, the value of the foreign real property held by the QDOT does not exceed 35 percent of the fair market value of the trust assets or, alternatively, the QDOT meets the requirements of either paragraph (d)(1)(i)(A), (B), or (C) of this section on or before the close of that succeeding year.

(iii) *Definition of finally determined.*—For purposes of § 20.2056A-2(d)(1)(i) and (ii), the fair market value of assets will be treated as finally determined on the earliest to occur of—

(A) The entry of a decision, judgment, decree, or other order by any court of competent jurisdiction that has become final;

(B) The execution of a closing agreement made under section 7121;

(C) Any final disposition by the Internal Revenue Service of a claim for refund;

(D) The issuance of an estate tax closing letter (Form L-154 or equivalent) if no claim for refund is filed; or

(E) The expiration of the period of assessment.

(iv) *Special rules for personal residence and related personal effects.*—(A) *Two million dollar threshold.*—For purposes of determining whether the $2 million threshold under paragraphs (d)(1)(i) and (ii) of this section has been exceeded, the executor of the estate may elect to exclude up to $600,000 in value attributable to real property (and related furnishings) owned directly by the QDOT that is used by, or held for the use of the surviving spouse as a personal residence and that passes, or is treated as passing, to the QDOT under section 2056(d). The election may be made regardless of whether the real property is situated within or without the United States. The election is made by attaching to the estate tax return on which the QDOT election is made a written statement claiming the exclusion. The statement must clearly identify the property or properties (i.e. address and location) for which the election is being made.

(B) *Security requirement.*—For purposes of determining the amount of the bond or letter of credit required when paragraph (d)(1)(i)(B) or (C) of this section applies, the executor of the estate may elect to exclude, during the term of the QDOT, up to $600,000 in value attributable to real property (and related furnishings) owned directly by the QDOT that is used by, or held for the use of the surviving spouse as a personal residence and that passes, or is treated as passing, to the QDOT under section 2056(d). The election may be made regardless of whether the real property is situated within or without the United States. The election is made by attaching to the estate tax return on which the QDOT election is made a written statement claiming the exclusion. If an election is not made on the decedent's estate tax return, the election may be made, prospectively, at any time, during the term of the QDOT, by attaching to the Form 706-QDT a written statement claiming the exclusion. A statement may also be attached to the Form 706-QDT that cancels a prior election of the personal residence exclusion that was made under this paragraph, either on the decedent's estate tax return or on a Form 706-QDT.

(C) *Foreign real property limitation.*—The special rules of this paragraph (d)(1)(iv) do not apply for purposes of determining whether more than 35 percent of the QDOT assets consist of foreign real property under paragraph (d)(1)(ii) of this section.

(D) *Personal residence.*—For purposes of this paragraph (d)(1)(iv), a *personal residence* is either the principal residence of the surviving spouse within the meaning of section 1034 or one other residence of the surviving spouse. In order to be used by or held for the use of the spouse as a personal residence, the residence must be available at all times for use by the surviving spouse. The residence may not be rented to another party, even when not occupied by the spouse. A personal residence may include appurtenant structures used by the surviving spouse for residential purposes and adjacent land not in excess of that which is reasonably appropriate for residential purposes (taking into account the residence's size and location).

(E) *Related furnishings.*—The term *related furnishings* means furniture and commonly included items such as appliances, fixtures, decorative items and china, that are not beyond the value associated with normal household and decorative use. Rare artwork, valuable antiques, and automobiles of any kind or class are not within the meaning of this term.

(F) *Required statement.*—If one or both of the exclusions provided in paragraph (d)(1)(iv)(A) or (B) of this section are elected by the executor of the estate and the personal residence is later sold or ceases to be used, or held for use as a personal residence, the U.S. Trustee must file the statement that is required under paragraph (d)(3) of this section at the time and in the manner provided in paragraphs (d)(3)(ii) and (iii) of this section.

(G) *Cessation of use.*—Except as provided in this paragraph (d)(1)(iv)(G), if the residence ceases to be used by, or held for the use of, the spouse as a personal residence of the spouse, or if the residence is sold during the term of the QDOT, the exclusions provided in paragraphs (d)(1)(iv)(A) and (B) of this section cease to apply. However, if the residence is sold, the exclusion continues to apply if, within 12 months of the date of sale, the amount of the adjusted sales price (as defined in section 1034(b)(1)) is reinvested to purchase a new personal residence for the spouse. If less than the amount of the adjusted sales price is reinvested, the amount of the exclusion equals the amount reinvested in the new residence plus any amount previously allocated to a residence that continues to qualify for the exclusion, up to a total of $600,000. If the QDOT ceases to qualify for all or any portion of the initially claimed exclusions, paragraph (d)(1)(i) of this section, if applicable (determined as if the portion of the exclusions disallowed had not been initially claimed by the QDOT), must be complied with no later than 120 days after the effective date of the cessation. In addition, if a residence ceases to be used by, or held for the use of the spouse as a personal residence of the spouse or if the personal residence is sold during the term of the QDOT, the personal residence exclusion may be allocated to another residence that is held in either the same QDOT or in another QDOT that is established for the surviving spouse, if the other residence qualifies as being used by, or held for the use of the spouse as a personal residence. The trustee may allocate up to $600,000 to the new personal residence (less the amount previously allocated to a residence that continues to qualify for the exclusion) even if the entire $600,000 exclusion was not previously utilized with respect to the original personal residence(s).

(v) *Anti-abuse rule.*—Regardless of whether the QDOT designates a bank as the U.S. Trustee under paragraph (d)(1)(i)(A) of this section (or otherwise complies with paragraph (d)(1)(i)(A) of this section by naming a foreign bank with a United States branch as a trustee to serve with the U.S. Trustee), complies with paragraph (d)(1)(i)(B) or (C) of this section, or is subject to and complies with the foreign real property requirements of paragraph (d)(1)(ii) of this section, the trust immediately ceases to qualify as a QDOT if the trust utilizes any device or arrangement that has, as a principal purpose, the avoidance of liability for the estate tax imposed under section 2056A(b)(1), or the prevention of the collection of the tax. For example, the trust may become subject to this paragraph (d)(1)(v) if the U.S. Trustee that is selected is a domestic corporation established with insubstantial capitalization by the surviving spouse or members of the spouse's family.

(2) *Individual trustees.*—If the U.S. Trustee is an individual United States citizen, the individual must have a tax home (as defined in section 911(d)(3)) in the United States.

(3) *Annual reporting requirements.*—(i) *In general.*—The U.S. Trustee must file a written statement described in paragraph (d)(3)(iii) of this section, if the QDOT satisfies any one of the following criteria for the applicable reporting years—

(A) The QDOT directly owns any foreign real property on the last day of its taxable year (or the last day of the calendar year if it has no taxable year), and the QDOT does not satisfy the requirements of paragraph (d)(1)(i)(A), (B), or (C) or (d)(4) of this section by employing a bank as trustee or providing security; or

(B) The personal residence previously subject to the exclusion under paragraph (d)(1)(iv) of this section is sold, or that personal residence ceases to be used, or held for use, as a personal residence, during the taxable year (or during the calendar year if the QDOT does not have a taxable year); or

(C) After the application of the look-through rule contained in paragraph (d)(1)(ii)(B) of this section, the QDOT is treated as owning any foreign real property on the last day of the taxable year (or the last day of the calendar year if the QDOT has no taxable year), and the QDOT does not satisfy the requirements of paragraph (d)(1)(A), (B), (C) or (d)(4) of this section by employing a bank as trustee or providing security.

(ii) *Time and manner of filing.*—The written statement, containing the information described in paragraph (d)(3)(iii) of this section, is to be filed for the taxable year of the QDOT (calendar year if the QDOT does not have a taxable year) for which any of the events or conditions requiring the filing of a statement under paragraph (d)(3)(i) of this section have occurred or have been satisfied. The written statement is to be submitted to the Internal Revenue Service by filing a Form 706-QDT, with the statement attached, no later than April 15th of the calendar year following the calendar year in which or with which the taxable year of the QDOT ends (or by April 15th of the following year if the QDOT has no taxable year), unless an extension of time is obtained under § 20.2056A-11(a). The Form 706-QDT, with attached statement, must be filed regardless of whether the Form 706-QDT is otherwise required to be filed under the provisions of this chapter. Failure to file timely the statement may subject the QDOT to the rules of paragraph (d)(1)(v) of this section.

(iii) *Contents of statement.*—The written statement must contain the following information—

(A) The name, address, and taxpayer identification number, if any, of the U.S. Trustee and the QDOT; and

(B) A list summarizing the assets held by the QDOT, together with the fair market value of each listed QDOT asset, determined as of the last day of the taxable year (December 31 if the QDOT does not have a taxable year) for which the written statement is filed. If the look-through rule contained in paragraph (d)(1)(ii)(B) of this section applies, then the partnership, corporation, trust or other entity must be identified and the QDOT's pro rata share of the foreign real property and other assets owned by that entity must be listed on the statement as if directly owned by the QDOT; and

(C) If a personal residence previously subject to the exclusion under paragraph (d)(1)(iv) of this section is sold during the taxable year (or during the calendar year if the QDOT does not have a taxable year), the statement must provide the date of sale, the adjusted sales price (as defined in section 1034(b)(1)), the extent to which the amount of the adjusted sales price has been or will be used to purchase a new personal residence and, if not timely reinvested, the steps that will or have been taken to comply with paragraph (d)(1)(i) of this section, if applicable; and

(D) If the personal residence ceases to be used, or held for use, as a personal residence by the surviving spouse during the taxable year (or during the calendar year if the QDOT does not have a taxable year), the written statement must describe the steps that will or have been taken to comply with paragraph (d)(1)(i) of this section, if applicable.

(4) *Request for alternate arrangement or waiver.*—If the Commissioner provides guidance published in the Internal Revenue Bulletin (see § 601.601(d)(2) of this chapter) pursuant to which a testator, executor, or the U.S. Trustee may adopt an alternate plan or arrangement to assure collection of the section 2056A estate tax, and if

the alternate plan or arrangement is adopted in accordance with the published guidance, then the QDOT will be treated, subject to paragraph (d)(1)(v) of this section, as meeting the requirements of paragraph (d)(1) of this section. Until this guidance is published in the Internal Revenue Bulletin (see § 601.601(d)(2) of this chapter), taxpayers may submit a request for a private letter ruling for the approval of an alternate plan or arrangement proposed to be adopted to assure collection of the section 2056A estate tax in lieu of the requirements prescribed in this paragraph (d)(4).

(5) *Adjustment of dollar threshold and exclusion.*—The Commissioner may increase or decrease the dollar amounts referred to in paragraph (d)(1)(i), (ii) or (iv) of this section in accordance with guidance published in the Internal Revenue Bulletin (see § 601.601(d)(2) of this chapter).

(6) *Effective date and special rules.*—(i) This paragraph (d) is effective for estates of decedents dying after February 19, 1996.

(ii) *Special rule in the case of incompetency.*—A revocable trust or a trust created under the terms of a will is deemed to meet the governing instrument requirements of this paragraph (d) notwithstanding that the requirements are not contained in the governing instrument (or otherwise incorporated by reference) if the trust instrument (or will) was executed on or before November 20, 1995, and—

(A) The testator or settlor dies after February 19, 1996;

(B) The testator or settlor is, on November 20, 1995, and at all times thereafter, under a legal disability to amend the will or trust instrument;

(C) The will or trust instrument does not provide the executor or the U.S. Trustee with a power to amend the instrument in order to meet the requirements of section 2056A; and

(D) The U.S. Trustee provides a written statement with the federal estate tax return (Form 706 or 706NA) that the trust is being administered (or will be administered) so as to be in actual compliance with the requirements of this paragraph (d) and will continue to be administered so as to be in actual compliance with this paragraph (d) for the duration of the trust. This statement must be binding on all successor trustees.

(iii) *Special rule in the case of certain irrevocable trusts.*—An irrevocable trust is deemed to meet the governing instrument requirements of this paragraph (d) notwithstanding that the requirements are not contained in the governing instrument (or otherwise incorporated by reference) if the trust was executed on or before November 20, 1995, and:

(A) The settlor dies after February 19, 1996;

(B) The trust instrument does not provide the U.S. Trustee with a power to amend the trust instrument in order to meet the requirements of section 2056A; and

(C) The U.S. Trustee provides a written statement with the decedent's federal estate tax return (Form 706 or 706NA) that the trust is being administered in actual compliance with the requirements of this paragraph (d) and will continue to be administered so as to be in actual compliance with this paragraph (d) for the duration of the trust. This statement must be binding on all successor trustees. [Reg. § 20.2056A-2.]

☐ [*T.D.* 8612, 8-21-95. *Amended by T.D.* 8686, 11-27-96.]

[Reg. § 20.2056A-3]

§ 20.2056A-3. QDOT election.—(a) *General rule.*—Subject to the time period prescribed in section 2056A(d), the election to treat a trust as a QDOT must be made on the last federal estate tax return filed before the due date (including extensions of time to file actually granted) or, if a timely return is not filed, on the first federal estate tax return filed after the due date. The election, once made, is irrevocable.

(b) *No partial elections.*—An election to treat a trust as a QDOT may not be made with respect to a specific portion of an entire trust that would otherwise qualify for the marital deduction but for the application of section 2056(d). However, if the trust is actually severed in accordance with the applicable requirements of § 20.2056(b)-7(b)(2)(ii) prior to the due date for the election, a QDOT election may be made for any one or more of the severed trusts.

(c) *Protective elections.*—A protective election may be made to treat a trust as a QDOT only if at the time the federal estate tax return is filed, the executor of the decedent's estate reasonably believes that there is a bona fide issue that concerns either the residency or citizenship of the decedent, the citizenship of the surviving spouse, whether an asset is includible in the decedent's gross estate, or the amount or nature of the property the surviving spouse is entitled to receive. For example, if at the time the federal estate tax return is filed either the estate is involved in a bona fide will contest, there is uncertainty regarding the inclusion in the gross estate of an asset which, if includible, would be eligible for the QDOT election, or there is uncertainty regarding the status of the decedent as a resident alien or a nonresident alien for estate tax purposes, or a similar uncertainty regarding the citizenship status of the surviving spouse, a protective QDOT election may be made. The protective election is in addition to, and is not in lieu of, the requirements set forth in § 20.2056A-4. The protective QDOT election must be made on a written statement signed by the executor under penalties of perjury and must be attached to the return described in paragraph (a) of this section, and must identify the specific assets to which the protective election refers and the specific basis for the protective election. However, the protective election may otherwise be defined by means of a formula (such as the minimum amount necessary to reduce the estate tax to zero). Once made, the protective election is irrevocable. For example, if a protective election is made because a bona fide question exists as to the includibility of an asset in the decedent's gross estate and it is later finally determined that the asset is so includible, the protective election becomes effective with respect to the asset and cannot thereafter be revoked.

(d) *Manner of election.*—The QDOT election under paragraph (a) of this section is made in the form and manner set forth in the decedent's estate tax return, including applicable instructions. [Reg. § 20.2056A-3.]

☐ [*T.D.* 8612, 8-21-95.]

[Reg. § 20.2056A-4]

§ 20.2056A-4. Procedures for conforming marital trusts and nontrust marital transfers to the requirements of a qualified domestic trust.—(a) *Marital trusts.*—(1) *In general.*—If an interest in property passes from the decedent to a trust for the benefit of a noncitizen surviving spouse and if the trust otherwise qualifies for a marital deduction but for the provisions of section 2056(d)(1)(A), the property interest is treated as passing to the surviving spouse in a QDOT if the trust is reformed, either in accordance with the terms of the decedent's will or trust agreement or pursuant to a judicial proceeding, to meet the requirements of a QDOT. For this purpose, the requirements of a QDOT include all of the applicable requirements set forth in § 20.2056A-2, and the requirements of § 20.2056A-2T(d). A reformation pursuant to the terms of the decedent's will or trust instrument must be completed by the time prescribed (including extensions) for filing the decedent's estate tax return. For purposes of this paragraph (a), a return filed prior to the due date (including extensions) is considered filed on the last date that the return is required to be filed (including extensions), and a late return filed at any time after the due date is considered filed on the date that it is actually filed.

(2) *Judicial reformations.*—In general, a reformation pursuant to a judicial proceeding is permitted under this section if the reformation is commenced on or before the due date (determined with regard to extensions actually granted) for filing the return of tax imposed by chapter 11 of the Internal Revenue Code, regardless of the date that the return is actually filed. The reformation (either pursuant to a judicial proceeding or otherwise) must result in a trust that is effective under local law. The reformed trust may be revocable by the spouse, or otherwise be subject to the spouse's general power of appointment, provided that no person (including the spouse) has the power to amend the trust during the continued existence of the trust such that it would no longer qualify as a QDOT. Prior to the time that the judicial reformation is completed, the trust must be treated as a QDOT. Thus, the trustee of the trust is responsible for filing the Form 706-QDT, paying any section 2056A estate tax that becomes due, and filing the annual statement required under § 20.2056A-2T(d)(3), if applicable. Failure to comply with these requirements may cause the trust to be subject to the anti-abuse rule under § 20.2056A-2T(d)(1)(iv). In addition, if the judicial reformation is terminated prior to the time that the reformation is completed, the estate of the decedent is required to pay the increased estate tax imposed on the decedent's estate (plus interest and any applicable penalties) that becomes due at the time of such termination as a result of the failure of the trust to comply with section 2056(d). See section 6511 as to applicable time periods for credit or refund of tax.

(3) *Tolling of statutory assessment period.*—For the tolling of the statute of limitations in the case of a judicial reformation, see section 2056(d)(5)(B).

(b) *Nontrust marital transfers.*—(1) *In general.*—Under section 2056(d)(2)(B), if an interest in property passes outright from a decedent to a noncitizen surviving spouse either by testamentary bequest or devise, by operation of law, or pursuant to an annuity or other similar plan or arrangement, and such property interest otherwise qualifies for a marital deduction except that it does not pass in a QDOT, solely for purposes of section 2056(d)(2)(A), the property is treated as passing to the surviving spouse in a QDOT if the property interest is either actually transferred to a QDOT before the estate tax return is filed and on or before the last date prescribed by law that the QDOT election may be made, or is assigned to a QDOT under an enforceable and irrevocable written assignment made on or before the date on which the return is filed and on or before the last date prescribed by law that the QDOT election may be made. The transfer or assignment of property to a QDOT may be made by the surviving spouse, the surviving spouse's legal representative (if the surviving spouse is incompetent), or the personal representative of the surviving spouse's estate (if the surviving spouse has died). The QDOT to which the property is transferred may be created by the decedent (during life or by will), by the surviving spouse, or by the executor. For purposes of section 2056(d)(2)(B), if no property other than the property passing to the surviving spouse from the decedent is transferred to the QDOT, the transferee QDOT need not be in a form such that the property transferred to the QDOT would qualify for a marital deduction under section 2056(a). However, if other property is or has been transferred to the QDOT, 100 percent of the value of the transferee QDOT must qualify for the marital deduction under section 2056. For example, if the decedent, a U.S. citizen, bequeaths property to a trust that does not satisfy the requirements of section 2056(b)(5) or (7), or to a trust that does not qualify as an estate trust under § 20.2056(c)-2(b)(1)(i)-(iii), that trust cannot be used as a transferee QDOT by the surviving spouse, since after that trust is fully funded the portion of the value of the trust attributable to property bequeathed to the trust by the decedent will not qualify for a marital deduction under section 2056. Similarly, if the decedent, a nonresident not a citizen of the United States, bequeaths foreign situs assets to a trust created under his will, the surviving spouse may not transfer U.S. situs assets passing to the spouse outside of the will to that trust under this paragraph. See § 20.2056A-3(c) with respect to protective elections. See § 20.2056A-3(a) with respect to the time limitations for making the QDOT election.

(2) *Form of transfer or assignment.*—A transfer or assignment of property to a QDOT must be in writing and otherwise be in accordance with all local law requirements for such assignment or transfer. The transfer or assignment may be of a specific asset or a group of assets, or a fractional share of either, or may be of a pecuniary amount. A transfer or assignment of less than an entire interest in an asset or a group of assets may be expressed by means of a formula (such as the minimum amount necessary to reduce the estate tax to zero). In the case of a transfer, a copy of the trust instrument evidencing the transfer must be submitted with the decedent's estate tax return. In the case of an assignment, a copy of the assignment must be submitted with the decedent's estate tax return.

(3) *Assets eligible for transfer or assignment.*—If a transfer or assignment is of a specific asset or group of assets, only assets included in the decedent's gross estate and passing from the decedent to the spouse (or the proceeds from the sale, exchange or conversion of such assets) may be transferred or assigned to the QDOT. The noncitizen surviving spouse may not transfer or assign to the QDOT property owned by the surviving spouse at the time of the decedent's death in lieu of property included in the decedent's gross estate that passes to the spouse (or in lieu of the proceeds from the sale, exchange or conversion of such includible assets). In addition, if only a portion of an asset is includible in the decedent's gross estate, the spouse may only transfer the portion that is so includible to the transferee trust under this paragraph (b)(3).

(4) *Pecuniary assignment—special rules.*—If the assignment is expressed in the form of a pecuniary amount (such as a fixed dollar amount or a formula designed to reduce the decedent's estate tax to zero), the assignment must specify that—

(i) Assets actually transferred to the QDOT in satisfaction of the assignment have an aggregate fair market value on the date of actual transfer to the QDOT amounting to no less than the amount of the pecuniary transfer or assignment; or

(ii) The assets actually transferred to the QDOT be fairly representative of appreciation or depreciation in the value of all property available for transfer to the QDOT between the valuation date and the date of actual transfer to the QDOT, if the assignment is to be satisfied by accounting for the assets on the basis of their fair market value as of some date before the date of actual transfer to the QDOT.

(5) *Transfer tax treatment of transfer or assignment.*—Property assigned or transferred to a QDOT pursuant to section 2056(d)(2)(B) is treated as passing from the decedent to a QDOT solely for purposes of section 2056(d)(2)(A). For all other purposes (e.g., income, gift, estate, generation-skipping transfer tax, and section 1491 excise tax), the surviving spouse is treated as the transferor of the property to the QDOT. However, the spouse is not considered the transferor of property to a QDOT if the transfer by the spouse constitutes a transfer that satisfies the requirements of section 2518(c)(3). For a special exception to the valuation rules of section 2702 in the case of a transfer by the surviving spouse to a QDOT, see § 25.2702-1(c)(8) of this chapter.

(6) *Period for completion of transfer.*—Property irrevocably assigned but not actually transferred to the QDOT before the estate tax return is filed must actually be conveyed and transferred to the QDOT under applicable local law before the administration of the decedent's estate is completed. If there is no administration of the decedent's estate (because for example, none of the decedent's assets are subject to probate under local law), the conveyance must be made on or before the date that is one year after the due date (including extensions) for filing the decedent's estate tax return. If an actual transfer to the QDOT is not timely made, section 2056(d)(1)(A) applies and the marital deduction is not allowed. The executor of the decedent's estate (or other authorized legal representative) may request a private letter ruling from the Internal Revenue Service requesting an extension of the time for completing the conveyance or waiving the actual conveyance under specified circumstances under § 301.9100-1(a) of this chapter.

(7) *Retirement accounts and annuities.*—(i) *In general.*—An assignment otherwise in compliance with this paragraph (b) of rights under annuities or other similar arrangements that are assignable and thus, are not described in paragraph (c) of this section, is treated as a transfer of such property to the QDOT regardless of the method of payment actually elected under such annuity or plan.

(ii) *Individual retirement annuities.*—Individual retirement annuities described in section 408(b) are not assignable pursuant to section 408(b)(1) and thus, do not come within the purview of this paragraph (b)(7). See the procedures provided in paragragh (c) of this section.

(iii) *Individual retirement accounts.*—Unless the terms of the account provide otherwise, individual retirement accounts described in section 408(a) are assignable and subject to the provisions of this paragraph (b)(7). However, under paragraph (c) of this section, the surviving spouse may treat an individual retirement account as nonassignable and, therefore, eligible for the procedures in paragraph (c) of this section if the spouse timely complies with the requirements in paragraph (c) of this section.

(iv) *Other effects of assignment.*—The provisions of this paragraph (b)(7) apply solely for purposes of qualifying the annuity or account under the rules of § 20.2056A-2 and this section. See, for example, section 408(d) and 4980A regarding the consequences of an assignment for purposes other than this paragraph (b)(7).

(8) *Protective assignment.*—A protective assignment of property to a QDOT may be made only if, at the time the federal estate tax return is filed, the executor of the decedent's estate reasonably believes that there is a bona fide issue that concerns either the residency or citizenship of the decedent, the citizenship of the surviving spouse, whether all or a portion of an asset is includible in the decedent's gross estate, or the amount or nature of the property the surviving spouse is entitled to receive. For example, if at the time the federal estate tax return is filed, either the estate is involved in a bona fide will contest, there is uncertainty regarding the inclusion in the gross estate of an asset which, if includible, would be eligible for the QDOT election, or there is uncertainty regarding the status of the decedent as a resident alien or a nonresident alien for estate tax purposes, or a similar uncertainty regarding the citizenship status of the surviving spouse, a protective assignment may be made. The protective assignment must be made on a written statement signed by the assignor under penalties of perjury on or before the date prescribed under paragraph (b)(1) of this section, and must identify the specific assets to which the assignment refers and the specific basis for the protective assignment. However, the protective assignment may otherwise be defined by means of a formula (such as the minimum amount necessary to reduce the estate tax to zero). Once made, the protective assignment cannot be revoked. For example, if a protective assignment is made because a bona fide question exists as to the includibility of an asset in the decedent's gross estate and it is later finally determined that the asset is so includible, the protective assignment becomes effective with respect to the asset and cannot thereafter be revoked. Protective assignments are, in all events, subject to paragraph (b)(6) of this section. A copy of the protective assignment must be submitted with the decedent's estate tax return.

(c) *Nonassignable annuities and other arrangements.*—(1) *Definition and general rule.*—For purposes of this section, a *nonassignable annuity or other arrangement* means a plan, annuity, or other arrangement (whether qualified or not qualified under part I of subchapter D of chapter 1 of subtitle A of the Internal Revenue Code) that qualifies for the marital deduction but for section 2056(d)(1)(A), and whose payments are not assignable or transferable to the QDOT under either federal law (see, e.g., section 401(a)(13)), state law, foreign law, or the terms of the plan or arrangement itself. For purposes of this paragraph (c), a surviving spouse's interest as beneficiary of an individual retirement annuity described in section 408(b) is a nonassignable annuity or other arrangement. See section 408(b)(1). For purposes of this paragraph (c), a surviving spouse's interest as beneficiary of an individual retirement account described in section 408(a), although assignable under that section, is considered to be a nonassignable annuity or other arrangement eligible for the procedures contained in this paragraph (c), at the option of the surviving spouse, if the requirements of this paragraph are otherwise satisfied. See paragraph (b)(7) of this section if the spouse elects to treat the account as assignable. In the case of a plan, annuity, or other arrangement which is not assignable or transferable (or is treated as such), the property passing under the plan from the decedent is treated as meeting the requirements § 20.2056A-2, and the requirements of § 20.2056A-2T(d) (pertaining, respectively, to general requirements, qualified marital interest requirements, statutory requirements, and requirements to ensure collection of the tax) if the requirements of either paragraph (c)(2) or (3) of this section are satisfied. Thus, the property will be treated as passing in the form of a QDOT, notwithstanding that the spouse does not irrevocably transfer or assign the annuity or other payment to the QDOT as provided in paragraph (b) of this section. The Commissioner will prescribe by administrative guidance the extent, if any, to which the provisions of this paragraph (c) apply to a rollover from a qualified trust to an eligible retirement plan within the meaning of section 402(c) or a distribution from an individual retirement account or an individual retirement annuity that is paid into an individual retirement account or an individual retirement annuity within the meaning of section 408(d)(3).

(2) *Agreement to remit section 2056A estate tax on corpus portion of each annuity payment.*—The requirements of this paragraph (c)(2) are satisfied if—

(i) The noncitizen surviving spouse agrees to pay on an annual basis, as described in paragraph (c)(6)(i) of this section, the estate tax imposed under section 2056A(b)(1) due on the corpus portion, as defined in paragraph (c)(4) of this section, of each nonassignable annuity or other payment received under the plan or arrangement. However, for purposes of this paragraph (c)(2), if the financial circumstances of the spouse are such that an amount equal to all or a portion of the corpus portion of a nonassignable annuity payment received by the spouse would be subject to a hardship exemption (as defined in § 20.2056A-5(c)) if paid from a QDOT, then all or a corresponding part of the corpus portion will be exempt from the tax payment requirement under this paragraph (c)(2);

(ii) The executor of the decedent's estate files with the estate tax return the Information Statement described in paragraph (c)(5) of this section;

(iii) The executor files with the estate tax return the Agreement To Pay Section 2056A Estate Tax described in paragraph (c)(6) of this section; and

(iv) The executor makes the election under § 20.2056A-3 with respect to the nonassignable annuity or other payment.

(3) *Agreement to roll over corpus portion of annuity payment to QDOT.*—The requirements of this paragraph (c)(3) are satisfied if—

(i) The noncitizen surviving spouse agrees to roll over and transfer, within the time prescribed under paragraph (c)(7)(i) of this section, the corpus portion of each annuity payment to a QDOT, whether the QDOT is created by the decedent's will, the executor of the decedent's estate, or the surviving spouse. However, for purposes of this section, if the financial circumstances of the spouse are such that an amount equal to all or a portion of the corpus portion of a nonassignable annuity payment received by the spouse would be subject to a hardship exemption (as defined in § 20.2056A-5(c)) if paid from a QDOT, then all or a corresponding part of the corpus portion will be exempt from the rollover requirement under this paragraph (c)(3);

(ii) A QDOT for the benefit of the surviving spouse is established prior to the date that the estate tax return is filed and on or prior to the last date prescribed by law that the QDOT election may be made;

(iii) The executor of the decedent's estate files with the estate tax return the Information Statement described in paragraph (c)(5) of this section;

(iv) The executor files with the estate tax return the Agreement To Roll Over Annuity Payments described in paragraph (c)(7) of this section; and

(v) The executor makes the election under § 20.2056A-3 with respect to the nonassignable annuity or other payment. See § 20.2056A-5(c)(3)(iv)(A), regarding distributions from the QDOT reimbursing the spouse for income taxes paid (either by actual payment or withholding) by the spouse with respect to amounts transferred to the QDOT pursuant to this paragraph (c)(3).

(4) *Determination of corpus portion.*—(i) *Corpus portion.*—For purposes of this paragraph (c), the corpus portion of each nonassignable annuity or other payment is the corpus amount of the annual payment divided by the total annual payment.

(ii) *Corpus amount.*—(A) The corpus amount of the annual payment is determined in accordance with the following formula:

$$\text{Corpus Amount} = \frac{\text{Total present value of annuity or other payment}}{\text{Expected annuity term}}$$

(B) The total present value of the annuity or other payment is the present value of the nonassignable annuity or other payment as of the date of the decedent's death, determined in accordance with the interest rates and mortality data prescribed by section 7520. The expected annuity term is the number of years that would be required for the scheduled payments to exhaust a hypothetical fund equal to the present value of the scheduled payments. This is determined by first dividing the total present value of the payments by the annual payment. From the quotient so obtained, the expected annuity term is derived by identifying the term of years that corresponds to the annuity factor equal to the quotient. This is determined by using column 1 of Table B, for the applicable interest rate, contained in Publication 1457, "Actuarial Valuations Version 3A". A copy of this publication is available, at no charge, electronically via the IRS Internet site at *www.irs.gov*. If the quotient obtained falls between two terms, the longer term is used.

(5) *Information Statement.*—(i) *In general.*—In order for a nonassignable annuity or other payment described in this paragraph (c) to qualify under either paragraph (c)(2) or (3) of this section, the Information Statement described in paragraph (c)(5)(ii) of this section must be filed with the decedent's federal estate tax return. The Information Statement must be signed under penalties of perjury by both the executor of the decedent's estate and by the surviving spouse of the decedent (or by the legal representative of the surviving spouse if the surviving spouse is legally incompetent to sign the statement). The Statement must contain all of the information prescribed by this paragraph (c)(5).

(ii) *Annuity source information.*—(A) *Employment-related annuity.*—If the nonassignable annuity or other payment is employment-related, the following information must be provided—

(1) The name and address of the employer;

(2) The date of retirement or other separation from employment of the decedent;

(3) The name and address of the pension fund, insurance company, or other obligor that is paying the annuity (or similar payment); and

(4) The identification number, if any, that the obligor has assigned to the annuity or other payment.

(B) *Annuity not employment-related.*—If the nonassignable annuity or other payment is not employment-related, the following information must be provided—

(1) The name and address of the person or entity paying the nonassignable annuity or other payment;

(2) The date of acquisition of the nonassignable annuity contract by the decedent or by the decedent and the surviving spouse; and

(3) The identification number, if any, that the obligor has assigned to the nonassignable annuity or other payment.

(iii) *The total annuity amount payable each year.*—The total amount payable annually under the nonassignable annuity or other arrangement, including a description of whether the annuity is payable monthly, quarterly, or at some other interval, and a description of any scheduled changes in the annuity payout amount.

(iv) *The duration of the annuity.*—A description of the term of the nonassignable annuity or other payment in years, if it is determined by a term certain, and the name, address, and birthdate of any measuring life if the nonassignable annuity or other payment is determined by one or more lives.

(v) *The market interest rate under section 7520.*—The applicable interest rate as determined under section 7520.

(vi) *Determination of corpus portion of each payment (in accordance with paragraph (c)(4) of this section).*—The following items are required in order to determine the corpus portion of each payment—

(A) The present value of the nonassignable annuity or other payment as of the decedent's death;

(B) The expected annuity term;

(C) The corpus amount of the annual annuity payments (paragraph (c)(5)(vi)(A) of this section divided by paragraph (c)(5)(vi)(B) of this section); and

(D) The corpus portion of the annual payments (paragraph (c)(5)(vi)(C) of this section divided by the total amount payable annually).

(vii) *Recipient QDOT.*—In the case of an agreement to rollover under paragraph (c)(3) of this section, the following must be provided—

(A) The name and address of the trustee of the QDOT who is the U.S. Trustee; and

(B) The name and taxpayer identification number of the QDOT.

(viii) *Certification statement.*—The executor of the decedent's estate and the surviving spouse of the decedent (or the legal representative of the surviving spouse if the surviving spouse is legally incompetent to so certify) must each sign a Certification Statement as follows:

Under penalties of perjury, I hereby certify that, to the best of my knowledge and belief, the information reported in this Information Statement is true, correct and complete.

(6) *Agreement to pay section 2056A estate tax.*—(i) *Payment of section 2056A estate tax.*—The tax payable under paragraph (c)(2) of this section is payable on an annual basis, commencing in the calendar year following the calendar year of the receipt by the surviving spouse of the spouse's first annuity payment. Form 706QDT and the payment are due on April 15th of each year following the calendar year in which an annuity payment is received except that, in the year of the deceased spouse's death, the Form 706-QDT and the payment are not due prior to the due date, including extensions, for filing the deceased spouse's estate tax return, or if no return is filed, no later than 9 months from the date of the deceased spouse's death; and, in the year of the surviving spouse's death, the Form 706-QDT must be filed and the payment made no later than 9 months from the date of the surviving spouse's death. See § 20.2056A-11 for extensions of time for filing Form 706-QDT and paying the section 2056A estate tax.

(ii) *Agreement.*—In order for a nonassignable annuity or other payment described in this paragraph (c) to qualify under paragraph (c)(2) of this section, the executor of the decedent's estate must file with the estate tax return the following Agreement To Pay Section 2056A Estate Tax, which must be signed by the surviving spouse of the decedent (or by the surviving spouse's legal representative if the surviving spouse is legally incompetent to sign the agreement):

I [*name*] hereby agree that I will report all annuity payments received under the [*name of plan or arrangement*]on Form 706-QDT for the calendar year and remit, on an annual basis, to the Internal Revenue Service the estate tax that is imposed under section 2056A(b)(1) of the Internal Revenue Code on the corpus portion of each annuity payment (as defined in § 20.2056A-4(c)(4) of the Estate Tax Regulations) received under the plan during the calendar year. I also agree that Form 706-QDT is to be filed no later than April 15th of the year following the calendar year in which any annuity payments are received except that: in the case of annuity payments received in the year of my spouse's death, Form 706-QDT and the payment shall not be due prior to the due date, including extensions, for filing my spouse's estate tax return or, if no return is filed, no later than 9 months from the date of my spouse's death (except if I am granted an extension of time to file Form 706-QDT under the provisions of § 20.2056A-11); and in the year of my death, the Form 706-QDT must be filed and the payment made no later than the date my estate tax return is filed (or if no return is filed, no later than 9 months from the date of my death). I further agree that if I fail to timely file Form 706-QDT or to timely pay the tax imposed on the corpus portion of any annuity payment (determined after any extensions of time to pay granted to me under the provisions of § 20.2056A-11), I may become immediately liable to pay the amount of the tax determined by application of section 2056A(b)(1) on the entire remaining present value of the annuity, calculated as of the beginning of the year in which the payment was received with respect to which I failed to timely pay the tax or failed to timely file the return. However, I may make an application for relief under § 301.9100-1 of the Procedure and Administration Regualations, from the consequences of failing to timely file the Form 706-QDT or failing to timely pay the tax on the corpus portion. [The following sentence is applicable only in cases where the plan or arrangement is established and administered by a person or an entity that is located outside of the United States.] I agree, at the request of the District Director, [or the Assistant Commissioner (International) in the case of a surviving spouse of a nonresident noncitizen decedent or a surviving spouse of a United States citizen who died domiciled outside the United States] to enter into a security agreement to secure my undertakings under this agreement.

(7) *Agreement to roll over annuity payments.*—(i) *Roll over of corpus portion.*—Beginning in the calendar year of the receipt by the surviving spouse of the spouse's first annuity payment, the corpus portion of each annuity payment, as determined under paragraph (c)(4) of this section, must, within 60 days of receipt, be transferred to a QDOT. In addition, all annuity payments received during the calendar year must be reported on Form 706-QDT no later than April 15th of the year following the year in which the annuity payments are received, except that in the year of the surviving spouse's death, the Form 706-QDT must be filed no later than the date the estate tax return is filed (or if no return is filed, no later than 9 months from the date of the surviving spouse's death). See § 20.2056A-11 for extensions of time for filing Form 706-QDT.

(ii) *Agreement.*—In order for a nonassignable annuity or other payment described in this paragraph (c) to qualify under paragraph (c)(3) of this section, the executor of the decedent's estate must file with the estate tax return the following Agreement To Roll Over Annuity Payments, which must be signed by the surviving spouse of the decedent (or by the legal representative of the surviving spouse if the surviving spouse is legally incompetent to sign the agreement):

I [*name*] hereby agree that within 60 days of receipt of each annuity payment paid under the [*name of plan or arrangement*], I will transfer an amount equal to percent (the corpus portion determined under § 20.2056A-4(c)(4) of the Estate Tax Regulations) of each annuity payment to [*identify the QDOT*]. Further, I will report all annuity payments received during the calendar year under the [*name of plan or arrangement*]on Form 706-QDT including a schedule of transfers to the [*identify the QDOT*]. I also agree that Form 706-QDT is to be filed no later than April 15th of the year following the year in which any annuity payments are received except that: in the case of annuity payments received in the year of my spouse's death, Form 706-QDT shall not be due prior to the due date, including extensions, for filing my spouse's estate tax return, or, if no return is filed, no later than 9 months from the date of my spouse's death (except if I am granted an extension of time to file Form 706-QDT under the provisions of § 20.2056A-11); and in the year of my death, the Form 706-QDT must be filed no later than the date my estate tax return is filed (or if no return is filed, no later than 9 months from the date of my death), and except if I am granted an extension of time to file Form 706-QDT under the provisions of § 20.2056A-11. I further agree that if I fail to timely transfer any required amount with respect to any annuity payment, or fail to timely file Form 706-QDT reporting the transfers for any year, I may become immediately liable to pay the amount of the tax determined by application of section 2056A(b)(1) on the entire remaining present value of the annuity, calculated as of the beginning of the year in which the payment was received with respect to which I failed to make the timely transfer or timely file a return. However, I may make an application for relief under § 301.9100-1 of the Procedure and Administration Regulations, from the consequences of failing to timely file Form 706-QDT or failing to timely transfer the corpus portion of any annuity payment to the QDOT. [The following sentence is applicable only in cases where the plan or arrangement is established and administered by a person or an entity that is located outside of the United States.] I agree, at the request of the District Director [or the Assistant Commissioner (International) in the case of a surviving spouse of a nonresident noncitizen decedent or a surviving spouse of a United States citizen who died domiciled outside the United States] to enter into a security agreement to secure my undertakings under this agreement.

(d) *Examples.*—The provisions of this section are illustrated by the following examples. In each of the following examples the decedent, *D*, a citizen of the United States, died after August 22, 1995, and *D*'s surviving spouse, *S*, is not a United States citizen at the time of *D*'s death.

Example 1. Transfer and assignment of probate and nonprobate property to QDOT.—(i) *S* is the beneficiary of the following probate and nonprobate assets included in *D*'s gross estate:

Pecuniary bequest under will	$400,000
Proceeds of life insurance	200,000
D's interest in property owned jointly with S includible in the gross estate under § 2040(a)	300,000
Devise of real property under will	100,000
Total	$1,000,000

(ii) Before the estate tax return for *D*'s estate is filed and before the date that the QDOT election must be made, *S* creates a QDOT pursuant to which all income is payable to *S* for life and the remainder is distributable to *S*'s children. *S* retains a power of appointment over the disposition of the remainder to ensure that *S* does not make an immediate gift of the remainder of the trust. Also, before the estate tax return is filed and before the date that the QDOT election must be made, *S* transfers the life insurance proceeds and the specifically devised real property to the QDOT. *S* decides not to transfer the property that had been jointly owned to the QDOT. Because *S* has not received distribution of the pecuniary bequest before *D*'s estate tax return is filed and before the date that the QDOT election must be made, *S* irrevocably assigns the interest in the pecuniary bequest to the QDOT. Assume that the pecuniary bequest is in fact transferred by *S* to the QDOT before the estate administration is concluded. *D*'s executor makes a QDOT election on the estate tax return for the $700,000 in property that *S* has transferred and assigned to the QDOT. A marital deduction of $700,000 is allowed to *D*'s estate assuming the estate tax return is filed and the QDOT election is made within the time limitation prescribed in § 20.2056A-3(a). No marital deduction is allowed for the $300,000 interest in jointly-owned property not transferred to the QDOT.

Example 2. Formula assignment. Under the terms of *D*'s will, the entire probate estate passes outright to *S*. Prior to the date *D*'s estate tax return is filed and before the date that the QDOT election must be made, *S* establishes a QDOT and *S* executes an irrevocable assignment in which *S* assigns to the QDOT, "that portion of the gross estate necessary to reduce the estate tax to zero, taking into account all available credits and deductions." The assignment meets the requirements of paragraph (b) of this section, assuming that the QDOT is funded by the time that administration of *D*'s estate is completed.

Example 3. Jointly owned property. At the time of *D*'s death, *D* and *S* hold real property as joint tenants with right of survivorship. In accordance with section 2056(d)(1)(B), section 2040(a), and § 20.2056A-8(a), 60 percent of the value of the property is included in *D*'s gross estate. *S* establishes a QDOT and, prior to the date the estate tax return is filed and before the date that the QDOT election must be made, *S* transfers a 60 percent interest in the real property to the QDOT. The transfer satisfies the requirements of paragraph (b) of this section.

Example 4. Computation of corpus portion of annuity payment. (i) At the time of D's death on or after May 1, 2009, D is a participant in an employees' pension plan described in section 401(a). On D's death, D's spouse S, a resident of the United States, becomes entitled to receive a survivor's annuity of $72,000 per year, payable monthly, for life. At the time of D's death, S is age 60. Assume that under section 7520, the appropriate discount rate to be used for valuing annuities in the case of this decedent is 6.0 percent. The annuity factor at 6.0 percent for a person age 60 is 11.0625 (1.000000 minus .33625, divided by .06). The adjustment factor at 6.0 percent in Table K for monthly payments is 1.0272. Accordingly, the right to receive $72,000 per year on a monthly basis is equal to the right to receive $73,958.40 ($72,000 × 1.0272) on an annual basis.

(ii) The corpus portion of each annuity payment received by S is determined as follows. The first step is to determine the annuity factor for the number of years that would be required to exhaust a hypothetical fund that has a present value and a payout corresponding to S's interest in the payments under the plan, determined as follows:

(A) Present value of S's annuity: $73,958.40 × 11.0625 = $818,164.80.

(B) Annuity Factor for Expected Annuity Term: $818,164.80 / $73,958.40 = 11.0625.

(iii) The second step is to determine the number of years that would be required for S 's annuity to exhaust a hypothetical fund of $818,164.80. The term certain annuity factor of 11.0625 falls between the annuity factors for 18 and 19 years in a 6.0 percent term certain annuity table (Column 1 of Table B, Publication 1457 Actuarial Valuations Version 3A, which may be obtained on the IRS Internet site). Accordingly, the expected annuity term is 19 years.

(iv) The third step is to determine the corpus amount by dividing the expected term of 19 years into the present value of the hypothetical fund as follows:

(A) Corpus amount of annual payment: $818,164.80/19 = $43,061.31.

(B) [Reserved].

(v) In the fourth step, the corpus portion of each annuity payment is determined by dividing the corpus amount of each annual payment by the annual annuity payment (adjusted for payments more frequently than annually as in (i) of this *Example 4*) as follows:

(A) Corpus portion of each annuity payment: $43,061.31/$73,958.40 = .58.

(B) [Reserved].

(vi) Accordingly, 58 percent of each payment to S is deemed to be a distribution of corpus. A marital deduction is allowed for $818,164.80, the present value of the annuity as of D's date of death, if either: S agrees to roll over the corpus portion of each payment to a QDOT and the executor files the Information Statement described in paragraph (c)(5) of this section and the Roll Over Agreement described in paragraph (c)(7) of this section; or S agrees to pay the tax due on the corpus portion of each payment and the executor files the Information Statement described in paragraph (c)(5) of this section and the Payment Agreement described in paragraph (c)(6) of this section.

Example 5. Transfer to QDOT subject to gift tax. *D*'s will bequeaths $700,000 outright to *S*. The bequest qualifies for a marital deduction under section 2056(a) except that it does not pass in a QDOT. *S* creates an irrevocable trust that meets the requirements for a QDOT and transfers the $700,000 to the QDOT. The QDOT instrument provides that *S* is entitled to all the income from the QDOT payable at least annually and that, upon the death of *S*, the property remaining in the QDOT is to be distributed to the grandchildren of *D* and *S* in equal shares. The trust instrument contains all other provisions required to qualify as a QDOT. On *D*'s estate tax return, *D*'s executor makes a QDOT election under section 2056A(a)(3). Solely for purposes of the marital deduction, the property is deemed to pass from *D* to the QDOT. *D*'s estate is entitled to a marital deduction for the $700,000 value of the property passing from *D* to *S*. *S*'s transfer of property to the QDOT is treated as a gift of the remainder interest for gift tax purposes because *S*'s transfer creates a vested remainder interest in the grandchildren of *D* and *S*. Accordingly, as of the date that *S* transfers the property to the QDOT, a gift tax is imposed on the present value of the remainder interest. See § 25.2702-1(c)(8) of this chapter exempting *S*'s transfer from the special valuation rules contained in section 2702. At *S*'s death, *S* is treated as the transferor of the property into the trust for estate tax and generation-skipping transfer tax purposes. See, e.g., sections 2036 and 2652(a)(1). The trust is not eligible for a reverse QTIP election by *D*'s estate under section 2652(a)(3) because a QTIP election cannot be made for the QDOT. This is so because the marital deduction is allowed under section 2056(a) for the outright bequest to the spouse and the spouse is then separately treated as the transferor of the property to the QDOT.

(e) *Effective/applicability date.*—Paragraph (c)(4)(ii)(B) and *Example 4* in paragraph (d) of this section are applicable with respect to decedents dying on or after May 1, 2009. [Reg. § 20.2056A-4.]

☐ [*T.D.* 8612, 8-21-95. *Amended by T.D.* 8819, 4-29-99; *T.D.* 9448, 5-1-2009; *and T.D.* 9540, 8-9-2011.]

[Reg. § 20.2056A-5]

§ 20.2056A-5. Imposition of section 2056A estate tax.—(a) *In general.*—An estate tax is imposed under section 2056A(b)(1) on the occurrence of a taxable event, as defined in section 2056A(b)(9). The tax is generally equal to the amount of estate tax that would have been imposed if the amount involved in the taxable event had been included in the decedent's taxable estate and had not been deductible under section 2056. See section 2056A(b)(3) and paragraph (c) of this section for certain exceptions from taxable events.

(b) *Amounts subject to tax.*—(1) *Distribution of principal during the spouse's lifetime.*—If a taxable event occurs during the noncitizen surviving spouse's lifetime, the amount on which the section 2056A estate tax is imposed is the amount of money and the fair market value of the property that is the subject of the distribution (including property distributed from the trust pursuant to the exercise of a power of appointment), including any amount withheld from the distribution by the U.S. Trustee to pay the tax. If, however, the tax is not withheld by the U.S. Trustee but is paid by the U.S. Trustee out of other assets of the QDOT, an amount equal to the tax so paid is treated as an additional distribution to the spouse in the year that the tax is paid.

(2) *Death of surviving spouse.*—If a taxable event occurs as a result of the death of the surviving spouse, the amount subject to tax is the fair market value of the trust assets on the date of the spouse's death (or alternate valuation date if applicable). See also section 2032A. Any corpus portion amounts, within the meaning of § 20.2056A-4(c)(4)(i), remaining in a QDOT upon the surviving spouse's death, are subject to tax under section 2056A(b)(1)(B), as well as any residual payments resulting from a nonassignable plan or arrangement that, upon the surviving spouse's death, are payable to the spouse's estate or to successor beneficiaries.

(3) *Trust ceases to qualify as QDOT.*—If a taxable event occurs as a result of the trust ceasing to qualify as a QDOT (for example, the trust ceases to have at least one U.S. Trustee), the amount subject to tax is the fair market value of the trust assets on the date of disqualification.

(c) *Distributions and dispositions not subject to tax.*—(1) *Distributions of principal on account of hardship.*—Section 2056A(b)(3)(B) provides an exemption from the section 2056A estate tax for distributions to the surviving spouse on account of hardship. A distribution of principal is treated as made on account of hardship if the distribution is made to the spouse from the QDOT in response to an immediate and substantial financial need relating to the spouse's health, maintenance, education, or support, or the health, maintenance, education, or support of any person that the surviving spouse is legally obligated to support. A distribution is not treated as made on account of hardship if the amount distributed may be obtained from other sources that are reasonably available to the surviving spouse; e.g., the sale by the surviving spouse of personally owned, publicly traded stock or the cashing in of a certificate of deposit owned by the surviving spouse. Assets such as closely held business interests, real estate and tangible personalty are not considered sources that are reasonably available to the surviving spouse. Although a hardship distribution of principal is exempt from the section 2056A estate tax, it must be reported on Form 706-QDT even if it is the only distribution that occurred during the filing period. See § 20.2056A-11 regarding filing requirements for Form 706-QDT.

(2) *Distributions of income to the surviving spouse.*—Section 2056A(b)(3)(A) provides an exemption from the section 2056A estate tax for distributions of income to the surviving spouse. In general, for purposes of section 2056A(b)(3)(A), the term *income* has the same meaning as is provided in section 643(b), except that income does not include capital gains. In addition, income does not include any other item that would be allocated to corpus under applicable local law governing the administration of trusts irrespective of any specific trust provision to the contrary. However, distributions made to the surviving spouse as the income beneficiary in conformance with applicable local law that defines the term income as a unitrust amount (or permits a right to income to be satisfied by such an amount), or that permits the trustee to adjust between principal and income to fulfill the trustee's duty of impartiality between income and principal beneficiaries, will be considered distributions of trust income if applicable local law provides for a reasonable apportionment between the income and remainder beneficiaries of the total return of the trust and meets the requirements of § 1.643(b)-1 of this chapter. In

cases where there is no specific statutory or case law regarding the allocation of such items under the law governing the administration of the QDOT, the allocation under this paragraph (c)(2) will be governed by general principles of law (including but not limited to any uniform state acts, such as the Uniform Principal and Income Act, or any Restatements of applicable law). Further, except as provided in this paragraph (c)(2) or in administrative guidance published by the Internal Revenue Service, income does not include items constituting income in respect of a decedent (IRD) under section 691. However, in cases where a QDOT is designated by the decedent as a beneficiary of a pension or profit sharing plan described in section 401(a) or an individual retirement account or annuity described in section 408, the proceeds of which are payable to the QDOT in the form of an annuity, any payments received by the QDOT may be allocated between income and corpus using the method prescribed under § 20.2056A-4(c) for determining the corpus and income portion of an annuity payment.

(3) *Certain miscellaneous distributions and dispositions.*—Certain miscellaneous distributions and dispositions of trust assets are exempt from the section 2056A estate tax, including but not limited to the following—

(i) Payments for ordinary and necessary expenses of the QDOT (including bond premiums and letter of credit fees);

(ii) Payments to applicable governmental authorities for income tax or any other applicable tax imposed on the QDOT (other than a payment of the section 2056A estate tax due on the occurrence of a taxable event as described in paragraph (b) of this section);

(iii) Dispositions of trust assets by the trustees (such as sales, exchanges, or pledging as collateral) for full and adequate consideration in money or money's worth; and

(iv) Pursuant to section 2056A(b)(15), amounts paid from the QDOT to reimburse the surviving spouse for any tax imposed on the spouse under Subtitle A of the Internal Revenue Code on any item of income of the QDOT to which the surviving spouse is not entitled under the terms of the trust. Such distributions include (but are not limited to) amounts paid from the QDOT to reimburse the spouse for income taxes paid by the spouse (either by actual payment or through withholding) with respect to amounts received from a nonassignable annuity or other arrangement that are transferred by the spouse to a QDOT pursuant to § 20.2056A-4(c)(3); and income taxes paid by the spouse (either by actual payment or through withholding) with respect to amounts received in a lump sum distribution from a qualified plan if the lump sum distribution is assigned by the surviving spouse to a QDOT. For purposes of this paragraph (c)(3)(iv), the amount of attributable tax eligible for reimbursement is the difference between the actual income tax liability of the spouse and the spouse's income tax liability determined as if the item had not been included in the spouse's gross income in the applicable taxable year. [Reg. § 20.2056A-5.]

☐ [*T.D.* 8612, 8-21-95. *Amended by T.D.* 9102, 12-30-2003.]

[Reg. § 20.2056A-6]

§ 20.2056A-6. Amount of tax.—(a) *Definition of tax.*—Section 2056A(b)(2) provides for the computation of the section 2056A estate tax. For purposes of sections 2056A(b)(2)(A)(i) and (ii), in determining the tax that would have been imposed under section 2001 on the estate of the first decedent, the rates in effect on the date of the first decedent's death are used. For this purpose, the provisions of section 2001(c)(2) (pertaining to phaseout of graduated rates and unified credit) apply. In addition, for purposes of sections 2056A(b)(2)(A)(i) and (ii), *the tax which would have been imposed by section 2001 on the estate of the decedent* means the net tax determined under section 2001 or 2101, as the case may be, after allowance of any allowable credits, including the unified credit allowable under section 2010, the credit for state death taxes under section 2011, the credit for tax on prior transfers under section 2013, and the credit for foreign death taxes under section 2014. See paragraph (b)(4) of this section regarding the application of the credits under sections 2011 and 2014. In the case of a decedent nonresident not a citizen of the United States, the applicable credits are determined under section 2102. The estate tax (net of any applicable credits) imposed under section 2056A(b)(1) constitutes an estate tax for purposes of section 691(c)(2)(A).

(b) *Benefits allowed in determining amount of section 2056A estate tax.*—(1) *General rule.*—Section 2056A(b)(10) provides for the allowance of certain benefits in computing the section 2056A estate tax. Except as provided in this section, the rules of each of the credit, deduction and deferral provisions, as provided in the Internal Revenue Code must be complied with.

(2) *Treatment as resident.*—For purposes of section 2056A(b)(10)(A), a noncitizen spouse is treated as a resident of the United States for purposes of determining whether the QDOT property is includible in the spouse's gross estate under chapter 11 of the Internal Revenue Code, and for purposes of determining whether any of the credits, deductions or deferral provisions are allowable with respect to the QDOT property to the estate of the spouse.

(3) *Special rule in the case of trusts described in section 2056(b)(8).*—In the case of a QDOT in which the spouse's interest qualifies for a marital deduction under section 2056(b)(8), the provisions of section 2056A(b)(10)(A) apply in determining the allowance of a charitable deduction in computing the section 2056A estate tax, notwithstanding that the QDOT is not includible in the spouse's gross estate.

(4) *Credit for state and foreign death taxes.*—If the assets of the QDOT are included in the surviving spouse's gross estate for federal estate tax purposes, or would have been so includible if

the spouse had been a United States resident, and state or foreign death taxes are paid by the spouse's estate with respect to the QDOT, the taxes paid by the spouse's estate with respect to the QDOT are creditable, to the extent allowable under section 2011 or 2014, as applicable, in computing the section 2056A estate tax. In addition, state or foreign death taxes previously paid by the decedent/transferor's estate are also creditable in computing the section 2056A estate tax to the extent allowable under sections 2011 and 2014. Specifically, the tax that would have been imposed on the decedent's estate if the taxable estate had been increased by the value of the QDOT assets on the spouse's death plus the amount involved in prior taxable events (section 2056A(b)(2)(A)(i)), is determined after allowance of a credit equal to the lesser of the state or foreign death tax previously paid by the decedent's estate, or the amount prescribed under section 2011(b) or 2014(b) computed based on a taxable estate increased by such amounts. Similarly, the tax that would have been imposed on the decedent's estate if the taxable estate had been increased only by the amount involved in prior taxable events (section 2056A(b)(2)(A)(ii)) is determined after allowance of a credit equal to the lesser of the state or foreign death tax previously paid by the decedent's estate, or the amount prescribed under section 2011(b) or 2014(b) computed based on a taxable estate increased by the amount involved in such prior taxable events. See paragraph (d), *Example* 2, of this section.

(5) *Alternate valuation and special use valuation.*—(i) *In general.*—In order to claim the benefits of alternate valuation under section 2032, or special use valuation under section 2032A, for purposes of computing the section 2056A estate tax, an election must be made on the Form 706-QDT that is filed with respect to the balance remaining in the QDOT upon the death of the surviving spouse. In addition, the separate requirements for making the section 2032 and/or section 2032A elections under those sections and the regulations thereunder must be complied with except that, for this purpose, the surviving spouse is treated as a resident of the United States regardless of the surviving spouse's actual residency status. Solely for purposes of this paragraph (b)(5), the citizenship of the first decedent is immaterial.

(ii) *Alternate valuation.*—For purposes of the alternate valuation election under section 2032, the election may not be made unless the election decreases both the value of the property remaining in the QDOT upon the death of the surviving spouse and the net amount of section 2056A estate tax due. Once made, the election is irrevocable.

(iii) *Special use valuation.*—For purposes of section 2032A, the Designated Filer (in the case of multiple QDOTs) or the U.S. Trustee may elect to value certain farm and closely held business real property at its farm or business use value, rather than its fair market value, if all of the requirements under section 2032A and the applicable regulations are met, except that, for this purpose, the surviving spouse is treated as a resident of the United States regardless of the spouse's actual residency status. The total value of property valued under section 2032A in the QDOT cannot be decreased from fair market value by more than $750,000.

(c) *Miscellaneous rules.*—See sections 2056A(b)(2)(B)(i) and 2056A(b)(2)(C) for special rules regarding the appropriate rate of tax. See section 2056A(b)(2)(B)(ii) for provisions regarding a credit or refund with respect to the section 2056A estate tax.

(d) *Examples.*—The rules of this section are illustrated by the following examples.

Example 1. (i) *D*, a United States citizen, dies in 1995 a resident of State X, with a gross estate of $1,200,000. Under *D*'s will, a pecuniary bequest of $700,000 passes to a QDOT for the benefit of *D*'s spouse *S*, who is a resident but not a citizen of the United States. *D*'s estate tax is computed as follows:

Gross estate	$1,200,000	
Marital Deduction	(700,000)	
Taxable Estate	$500,000	
Gross Tax		$155,800
Less: Unified Credit		(155,800)
Net Tax		0

(ii) *S* dies in 1997 at which time *S* is still a resident of the United States and the value of the assets of the QDOT is $700,000. Assuming there were no taxable events during *S*'s lifetime with respect to the QDOT, the estate tax imposed under section 2056A(b)(1)(B) is $235,000, computed as follows:

D's actual taxable estate	$500,000	
QDOT property	700,000	
Total	$1,200,000	
Gross Tax		$427,800
Less: Unified Credit		(192,800)
Net Tax		$235,000
Less: Tax that would have been imposed on D's actual taxable estate of $500,000		0
Section 2056A Estate Tax		$235,000

Example 2. (i) The facts are the same as in *Example 1,* except that *D's* gross estate was $2,000,000 and *D's* estate paid $70,000 in state death taxes to State X. *D's* estate tax is computed as follows:

Gross Estate	$2,000,000	
Marital Deduction	(700,000)	
Taxable Estate	$1,300,000	
Gross Tax		$469,800
Less: Unified Credit	192,800	
State Death Tax Credit Limitation (lesser of $51,600 or $70,000 tax paid)	51,600	(244,400)
Estate Tax		$225,400

(ii) *S* dies in 1997 at which time *S* is still a resident of the United States and the value of the assets of the QDOT is $800,000. *S's* estate pays $40,000 in State X death taxes with respect to the inclusion of the QDOT in *S's* gross estate for state death tax purposes. Assuming there were no taxable events during *S's* lifetime with respect to the QDOT, the estate tax imposed under section 2056A(b)(1)(B) is $ 304,800 computed as follows:

D's Actual Taxable Estate	$1,300,000	
QDOT Property	800,000	
Total	$2,100,000	
Gross Tax		$829,800
Less: Unified Credit		(192,800)
Pre-2011 section 2056A estate tax		$637,000
(A) State Death Tax Credit Computation:		
(1) State death tax paid by *S's* estate with respect to the QDOT [$40,000] plus state death tax previously paid by *D's* estate [$70,000] = $110,000.		
(2) Credit limit under section 2011(b) (based on *D's* adjusted taxable estate of $ 2,040,000 under sections 2056A(b)(2)(A) and 2011(b)) = $106,800.		
(B) State death tax credit allowable against section 2056A estate tax (lesser of paragraph (ii)(A)(1) or (2) of this *Example 2*		(106,800)
Net Tax		$530,200
Less: Tax that would have been imposed on D's taxable estate of $1,300,000		225,400
Section 2056A Estate Tax		$304,800

[Reg. § 20.2056A-6.]

☐ [*T.D.* 8612, 8-21-95.]

[Reg. § 20.2056A-7]

§ 20.2056A-7. Allowance of prior transfer credit under section 2013.—(a) *Property subject to QDOT election.*—Section 2056(d)(3) provides special rules for computing the section 2013 credit allowed with respect to property subject to a QDOT election. In computing the credit under section 2013, the amount of the credit is determined under section 2013 and the regulations thereunder, except that—

(1) The first limitation as described in section 2013(b) and § 20.2013-2 is the amount of the estate tax imposed under section 2056A(b)(1)(A), with respect to distributions during the spouse's life, and under section 2056A(b)(1)(B), with respect to the value of the QDOT assets on the spouse's death;

(2) In computing the second limitation as described in section 2013(c) and § 20.2013-3, the value of the property transferred to the decedent (as defined in section 2013(d) and § 20.2013-4) is deemed to be the value of the QDOT assets on the date of death of the surviving spouse. The value as so determined is not reduced by the section 2056A estate tax imposed at the time of the spouse's death; and

(3) The amount of the credit is determined without regard to the percentage limitations contained in section 2013(a).

(b) *Property not subject to QDOT election.*—If property includible in a decedent's gross estate passes to a noncitizen surviving spouse (the transferee) and no deduction is allowed to the decedent's estate for that interest in property under section 2056(a) solely because the requirements of section 2056(d)(2) are not satisfied, and the transferee spouse dies with an estate that is subject to tax under section 2001 or 2101, as the case may be, any credit for tax on prior transfers allowable to the estate of the transferee spouse under section 2013 with respect to such interest in property is determined in accordance with the rules of section 2013 and the regulations thereunder, except that the amount of the credit is determined without regard to the percentage limitations contained in section 2013(a).

(c) *Example.*—The application of this section may be illustrated by the following example:

Example. The facts are the same as in § 20.2056A-6, *Example* 2(ii). *D*, a United States citizen, dies in 1994, a resident of State X, with a gross estate of $2,000,000. Under *D*'s will, a pecuniary bequest of $700,000 passes to a QDOT for the benefit of *D*'s spouse *S*, who is a resident but not a citizen of the United States. *S* dies in 1997 at which time *S* is still a resident of the United States and the value of the assets of the QDOT is $800,000. There were no taxable events during *S*'s lifetime. An estate tax of $304,800 is imposed under section 2056A(b)(1)(B). *S*'s taxable estate, including the value of the QDOT ($800,000), is $1,500,000.

(i) Under paragraph (a)(1) of this section, the first limitation for purposes of section 2013(b) is $304,800, the amount of the section 2056A estate tax.

(ii) Under paragraph (a)(2) of this section, the second limitation for purposes of section 2013(c) is computed as follows:

(A) *S*'s net estate tax payable under § 20.2013-3(a)(1), as modified under paragraph (a)(2) of this section, is computed as follows:

Taxable estate		$1,500,000
Gross estate tax		555,800
Less: Unified credit	$192,800	
Credit for state death taxes	64,400	257,200
Pre-2013 net estate tax payable		$298,600

(B) *S*'s net estate tax payable under § 20.2013-3(a)(2), as modified under paragraph (a)(2) of this section, is computed as follows:

Taxable estate		$700,000
Gross estate tax		229,800
Less: Unified credit	$192,800	
Credit for state death taxes	18,000	210,800
Net tax payable		$19,000
(C) *Second Limitation:*		
Paragraph (ii)(A) of this *Example*	$298,600	
Less: Paragraph (ii)(B) of this *Example*	19,000	$279,600

(iii) Credit for tax on prior transfers = $279,600 (lesser of paragraphs (i) or (ii) of this *Example*. [Reg. § 20.2056A-7.]

☐ [*T.D.* 8612, 8-21-95.]

[Reg. § 20.2056A-8]

§ 20.2056A-8. Special rules for joint property.—(a) *Inclusion in gross estate.*—(1) *General rule.*—If property is held by the decedent and the surviving spouse of the decedent as joint tenants with right of survivorship, or as tenants by the entirety, and the surviving spouse is not a United States citizen (or treated as a United States citizen) at the time of the decedent's death, the property is subject to inclusion in the decedent's gross estate in accordance with the rules of section 2040(a) (general rule for includibility of joint interests), and section 2040(b) (special rule for includibility of certain joint interests of husbands and wives) does not apply. Accordingly, the rules contained in section 2040(a) and § 20.2040-1 govern the extent to which such joint interests are includible in the gross estate of a decedent who was a citizen or resident of the United States. Under § 20.2040-1(a)(2), the entire value of jointly held property is included in the decedent's gross estate unless the executor submits facts sufficient to show that property was not entirely acquired with consideration furnished by the decedent, or was acquired by the decedent and the other joint owner by gift, bequest, devise or inheritance. If the decedent is a nonresident not a citizen of the United States, the rules of this paragraph (a)(1) apply pursuant to sections 2103, 2031, 2040(a), and 2056(d)(1)(B).

(2) *Consideration furnished by surviving spouse.*—For purposes of applying section 2040(a), in determining the amount of consideration furnished by the surviving spouse, any consideration furnished by the decedent with respect to the property before July 14, 1988, is treated as consideration furnished by the surviving spouse to the extent that the consideration was treated as a gift to the spouse under section 2511, or to the extent that the decedent elected to treat the transfer as a gift to the spouse under section 2515 (to the extent applicable). For purposes of determining whether the consideration was a gift by the decedent under section 2511, it is presumed that the decedent was a citizen of the United States at the time the consideration was so furnished to the spouse. The special rule of this paragraph (a)(2) is applicable only if the donor spouse predeceases the donee spouse and not if the donee spouse predeceases the donor spouse. In cases where the donee spouse predeceases the donor spouse, any portion of the consideration treated as a gift to the donee spouse/decedent on the creation of the tenancy (or subsequently thereafter), regardless of the date the tenancy was created, is not treated as consideration furnished by the donee spouse/decedent for purposes of section 2040(a).

(3) *Amount allowed to be transferred to QDOT.*—If, as a result of the application of the rules described above, only a portion of the

value of a jointly-held property interest is includible in a decedent's gross estate, only that portion that is so includible may be transferred to a QDOT under section 2056(d)(2). See §20.2056A-4(b)(1) and (d), *Example 3*.

(b) *Surviving spouse becomes citizen.*—Paragraph (a) of this section does not apply if the surviving spouse meets the requirements of section 2056(d)(4). For the definition of resident in applying section 2056(d)(4), see §20.0-1(b).

(c) *Examples.*—The provisions of this section are illustrated by the following examples:

Example 1. In 1987, *D*, a United States citizen, purchases real property and takes title in the names of *D* and *S*, *D*'s spouse (a noncitizen, but a United States resident), as joint tenants with right of survivorship. In accordance with §25.2511-1(h)(5) of this chapter, one-half of the value of the property is a gift to *S*. *D* dies in 1995. Because *S* is not a United States citizen, the provisions of section 2040(a) are determinative of the extent to which the real property is includible in *D*'s gross estate. Because the joint tenancy was established before July 14, 1988, and under the applicable provisions of the Internal Revenue Code and regulations the transfer was treated as a gift of one-half of the property, one-half of the value of the property is deemed attributable to consideration furnished by *S* for purposes of section 2040(a). Accordingly, only one-half of the value of the property is includible in *D*'s gross estate under section 2040(a).

Example 2. The facts are the same as in *Example 1*, except that *S* dies in 1995 survived by *D* who is not a citizen of the United States. For purposes of applying section 2040(a), *D*'s gift to *S* on the creation of the tenancy is not treated as consideration furnished by *S* toward the acquisition of the property. Accordingly, since *S* made no other contributions with respect to the property, no portion of the property is includible in *S*'s gross estate.

Example 3. The facts are the same as in *Example 1*, except that *D* and *S* purchase real property in 1990 making the down payment with funds from a joint bank account. All subsequent mortgage payments and improvements are paid from the joint bank account. The only funds deposited in the joint bank account are the earnings of *D* and *S*. It is established that *D* earned approximately 60% of the funds and *S* earned approximately 40% of the funds. *D* dies in 1995. The establishment of *S*'s contribution to the joint bank account is sufficient to show that *S* contributed 40% of the consideration for the property. Thus, under paragraph §20.2040-1(a)(2), 60% of the value of the property is includible in *D*'s gross estate. [Reg. §20.2056A-8.]

☐ [*T.D.* 8612, 8-21-95.]

[Reg. §20.2056A-9]

§20.2056A-9. Designated Filer.—Section 2056A(b)(2)(C) provides special rules where more than one QDOT is established with respect to a decedent. The designation of a person responsible for filing a return under section 2056A(b)(2)(C)(i) (the Designated Filer) must be made on the decedent's federal estate tax return, or on the first Form 706-QDT that is due and is filed by its prescribed date, including extensions. The Designated Filer must be a U.S. Trustee. If the U.S. Trustee is an individual, that individual must have a tax home (as defined in section 911(d)(3)) in the United States. At least sixty days before the due date for filing the tax returns for all of the QDOTs, the U.S. Trustee(s) of each of the QDOTs must provide to the Designated Filer all of the necessary information relating to distributions from their respective QDOTs. The section 2056A estate tax due from each QDOT is allocated on a pro rata basis (based on the ratio of the amount of each respective distribution constituting a taxable event to the amount of all such distributions), unless a different allocation is required under the terms of the governing instrument or under local law. Unless the decedent has provided for a successor Designated Filer, if the Designated Filer ceases to qualify as a U.S. Trustee, or otherwise becomes unable to serve as the Designated Filer, the remaining trustees of each QDOT must select a qualifying successor Designated Filer (who is also a U.S. Trustee) prior to the due date for the filing of Form 706-QDT (including extensions). The selection is to be indicated on the Form 706-QDT. Failure to select a successor Designated Filer will result in the application of section 2056A(b)(2)(C). [Reg. §20.2056A-9.]

☐ [*T.D.* 8612, 8-21-95.]

[Reg. §20.2056A-10]

§20.2056A-10. Surviving spouse becomes citizen after QDOT established.—(a) *Section 2056A estate tax no longer imposed under certain circumstances.*—Section 2056A(b)(12) provides that a QDOT is no longer subject to the imposition of the section 2056A estate tax if the surviving spouse becomes a citizen of the United States and the following conditions are satisfied—

(1) The spouse either was a United States resident (for the definition of resident for this purpose, see §20.2056A-1(b)) at all times after the death of the decedent and before becoming a United States citizen, or no taxable distributions are made from the QDOT before the spouse becomes a United States citizen (regardless of the residency status of the spouse); and

(2) The U.S. Trustee(s) of the QDOT notifies the Internal Revenue Service and certifies in writing that the surviving spouse has become a United States citizen. Notice is to be made by filing a final Form 706-QDT on or before April 15th of the calendar year following the year in which the surviving spouse becomes a United States citizen, unless an extension of time for filing is granted under section 6081.

(b) *Special election by spouse.*—If the surviving spouse becomes a United States citizen and the spouse is not a United States resident at all times after the death of the decedent and before becoming a United States citizen, and a tax was previously imposed under section 2056A(b)(1)(A) with respect to any distribution from the QDOT before the surviving spouse becomes a United States citizen, the estate tax imposed under section 2056A(b)(1) does not apply to distributions after the spouse becomes a citizen if—

(1) The spouse elects to treat any taxable distribution from the QDOT prior to the spouse's election as a taxable gift made by the spouse for purposes of section 2001(b)(1)(B) (referring to adjusted taxable gifts), and for purposes of determining the amount of the tax imposed by section 2501 on actual taxable gifts made by the spouse during the year in which the spouse becomes a citizen or in any subsequent year;

(2) The spouse elects to treat any previous reduction in the section 2056A estate tax by reason of the decedent's unified credit (under either section 2010 or section 2102(c)) as a reduction in the spouse's unified credit under section 2505 for purposes of determining the amount of the credit allowable with respect to taxable gifts made by the surviving spouse during the taxable year in which the spouse becomes a citizen, or in any subsequent year; and

(3) The elections referred to in this paragraph (b) are made by timely filing a Form 706-QDT on or before April 15th of the year following the year in which the surviving spouse becomes a citizen (unless an extension of time for filing is granted under section 6081) and attaching notification of the election to the return. [Reg. § 20.2056A-10.]

☐ [*T.D.* 8612, 8-21-95.]

[Reg. § 20.2056A-11]

§ 20.2056A-11. Filing requirements and payment of the section 2056A estate tax.—(a) *Distributions during surviving spouse's life.*—Section 2056A(b)(5)(A) provides the due date for payment of the section 2056A estate tax imposed on distributions during the spouse's lifetime. An extension of not more than 6 months may be obtained for the filing of Form 706-QDT under section 6081(a) if the conditions specified therein are satisfied. See also § 20.2056A-5(c)(1) regarding the requirements for filing a Form 706-QDT in the case of a distribution to the surviving spouse on account of hardship, and § 20.2056A-2T(d)(3) regarding the requirements for filing Form 706-QDT in the case of the required annual statement.

(b) *Tax at death of surviving spouse.*—Section 2056A(b)(5)(B) provides the due date for payment of the section 2056A estate tax imposed on the death of the spouse under section 2056A(b)(1)(B). An extension of not more than 6 months may be obtained for the filing of the Form 706-QDT under section 6081(a), if the conditions specified therein are satisfied. The obtaining of an extension of time to file under section 6081(a) does not extend the time to pay the section 2056A estate tax as prescribed under section 2056A(b)(5)(B).

(c) *Extension of time for paying section 2056A estate tax.*—(1) *Extension of time for paying tax under section 6161(a)(2).*—Pursuant to sections 2056A(b)(10)(C) and 6161(a)(2), upon a showing of reasonable cause, an extension of time for a reasonable period beyond the due date may be granted to pay any part of the estate tax that is imposed upon the surviving spouse's death under section 2056A(b)(1)(B) and shown on the final Form 706-QDT, or any part of any installments of such tax payable under section 6166 (including any part of a deficiency prorated to any installment under such section). The extension may not exceed 10 years from the date prescribed for payment of the tax (or in the case of an installment or part of a deficiency prorated to an installment, if later, not beyond the date that is 12 months after the due date for the last installment). Such extension may be granted by the district director or the director of the service center where the Form 706-QDT is filed.

(2) *Extension of time for paying tax under section 6161(a)(1).*—An extension of time beyond the due date to pay any part of the estate tax imposed on lifetime distributions under section 2056A(b)(1)(A), or imposed at the death of the surviving spouse under section 2056A(b)(1)(B), may be granted for a reasonable period of time, not to exceed 6 months (12 months in the case of the estate tax imposed under section 2056A(b)(1)(B) at the surviving spouse's death), by the district director or the director of the service center where the Form 706-QDT is filed.

(d) *Liability for tax.*—Under section 2056A(b)(6), each trustee (and not solely the U.S. Trustee(s)) of a QDOT is personally liable for the amount of the estate tax imposed in the case of any taxable event under section 2056A(b)(1). In the case of multiple QDOTs with respect to the same decedent, each trustee of a QDOT is personally liable for the amount of the section 2056A estate tax imposed on any taxable event with respect to that trustee's QDOT, but is not personally liable for tax imposed with respect to taxable events involving QDOTs of which that person is not a trustee. However, the assets of any QDOT are subject to collection by the Internal Revenue Service for any tax resulting from a taxable event with respect to any other QDOT established with respect to the same decedent. The trustee may also be personally liable as a withholding agent under section 1461 or other applicable provisions of the Internal Revenue Code. [Reg. § 20.2056A-11.]

☐ [*T.D.* 8612, 8-21-95.]

[Reg. § 20.2056A-12]

§ 20.2056A-12. Increased basis for section 2056A estate tax paid with respect to distribution from a QDOT.—Under section 2056A(b)(13), in the case of any distribution from a QDOT on which an estate tax is imposed under section 2056A(b)(1)(A), the distribution is treated as a transfer by gift for purposes of section 1015, and any estate tax paid under section 2056A(b)(1)(A) is treated as a gift tax. See § 1.1015-5(c)(4) and (5) of this chapter for rules for determining the amount by which the basis of the distributed property is increased. [Reg. § 20.2056A-12.]

☐ [*T.D.* 8612, 8-21-95.]

[Reg. § 20.2056A-13]

§ 20.2056A-13. Effective date.—Except as provided in this section, the provisions of §§ 20.2056A-1 through 20.2056A-12 are applicable with respect to estates of decedents dying after August 22, 1995. The rule in the fourth sentence of § 20.2056A-5(c)(2) regarding unitrusts and distributions of income to the surviving spouse in conformance with applicable local law is applicable to trusts for taxable years ending after January 2, 2004. [Reg. § 20.2056A-13.]

☐ [*T.D.* 8612, 8-21-95. *Amended by T.D.* 9102, 12-30-2003.]

Estates of Nonresidents Not Citizens

[Reg. § 20.2101-1]

§ 20.2101-1. Estates of nonresidents not citizens; tax imposed.—(a) *Imposition of tax.*—Section 2101 imposes a tax on the transfer of the taxable estate of a nonresident who is not a citizen of the United States at the time of death. In the case of estates of decedents dying after November 10, 1988, the tax is computed at the same rates as the tax that is imposed on the transfer of the taxable estate of a citizen or resident of the United States in accordance with the provisions of sections 2101(b) and (c). For the meaning of the terms *resident, nonresident,* and *United States,* as applied to a decedent for purposes of the estate tax, see § 20.0-1(b)(1) and (2). For the liability of the executor for the payment of the tax, see section 2002. For special rules as to the phaseout of the graduated rates and unified credit, see sections 2001(c)(2) and 2101(b).

(b) *Special rates in the case of certain decedents.*—In the case of an estate of a nonresident who was not a citizen of the United States and who died after December 31, 1976, and on or before November 10, 1988, the tax on the nonresident's taxable estate is computed using the formula provided under section 2101(b), except that the rate schedule in paragraph (c) of this section is to be used in lieu of the rate schedule in section 2001(c).

(c) *Rate schedule for decedents dying after December 31, 1976 and on or before November 10, 1988.*

If the amount for which the tentative tax to be computed is:	The tentative tax is:
Not over $100,000	6% of such amount.
Over $100,000 but not over $500,000	$6,000, plus 12% of excess over $100,000.
Over $500,000 but not over $1,000,000	$54,000, plus 18% of excess over $500,000.
Over $1,000,000 but not over $2,000,000	$144,000, plus 24% of excess over $1,000,000
Over $2,000,000	$384,000, plus 30% of excess over $2,000,000.

[Reg. § 20.2101-1.]

☐ [*T.D.* 6296, 6-23-58. *Amended by T.D.* 7296, 12-11-73 *and T.D.* 8612, 8-21-95.]

[Reg. § 20.2102-1]

§ 20.2102-1. Estates of nonresidents not citizens; credits against tax.—(a) *In general.*—In arriving at the net estate tax payable with respect to the transfer of an estate of a nonresident who was not a citizen of the United States at the time of his death, the following credits are subtracted from the tax imposed by section 2101:

(1) The State death tax credit under section 2011, to the extent permitted by section 2102(b) and paragraph (b) of this section;

(2) The gift tax credit under section 2012; and

(3) The credit under section 2013 for tax on prior transfers.

Except as provided in section 2102(b) and paragraph (b) of this section (relating to a special limitation on the amount of the credit for State death taxes), the amount of each of these credits is determined in the same manner as that prescribed for its determination in the case of estates of citizens or residents of the United States. See §§ 20.2011 through 20.2013-6. Subject to the additional special limitation contained in section 2102(b) in the case of section 2015, the provisions of sections 2015 and 2016, relating respectively to the credit for death taxes on remainders and the recovery of taxes claimed as a credit, are applicable with respect to the credit for State death taxes in the case of the estates of nonresidents not citizens. However, no credit is allowed under section 2014 for foreign death taxes.

(b) *Special limitation.*—(1) *In general.*—In the case of estates of decedents dying on or after November 14, 1966, other than estates the estate tax treatment of which is subject to a Presidential proclamation made pursuant to section 2108(a), the maximum credit allowable under section 2011 for State death taxes against the tax imposed by section 2101 on the transfer of estates of nonresidents not citizens of the United States is an amount which bears the same ratio to the maximum credit computed as provided in section 2011(b) (and without regard to this special limitation) as the value of the property (determined in the same manner as that prescribed in paragraph (b) of § 20.2031-1 for the estates of citizens or residents of the United States) in respect of which a State death tax was actually paid and which is included in the gross estate under section 2103 or, if applicable, section 2107(b) bears to the value (as so determined) of the total gross estate under section 2103 or 2107(b). For purposes of this special limitation, the term "State death taxes" means the taxes described in section 2011(a) and paragraph (a) of § 20.2011-1.

(2) *Illustrations*.—The application of this paragraph may be illustrated by the following examples:

Example (1). A, a nonresident not a citizen of the United States, died on February 15, 1967, owning real property in State Z valued at $50,000 and stock in various domestic corporations valued at $100,000 and not subject to death taxes in any State. State Z's inheritance tax actually paid with respect to the real property in State Z is $2,000. A's taxable estate for Federal estate tax purposes is $110,000, in respect of which the maximum credit under section 2011 would be $720 in the absence of the special limitation contained in section 2102(b). However, under section 2102(b) and this paragraph the amount of the maximum credit allowable in respect to A's estate for State death taxes is limited to the amount which bears the same ratio to $720 (the maximum credit computed as provided in section 2011(b)) as $50,000 (the value of the property in respect of which a State death tax was actually paid and which is included in A's gross estate under section 2103) bears to $150,000 (the value of A's total gross estate under section 2103). Accordingly, the maximum credit allowable under section 2102 and this section for all State death taxes actually paid is $240 ($720 × $50,000/$150,000).

Example (2). B, a nonresident not a citizen of the United States, died on January 15, 1967, owning real property in State X valued at $100,000, real property in State Y valued at $200,000, and stock in various domestic corporations valued at $300,000 and not subject to death taxes in any State. States X and Y both impose inheritance taxes. State X has, in addition to its inheritance tax, an estate tax equal to the amount by which the maximum State death tax credit allowable to an estate against its Federal estate tax exceeds the amount of the inheritance tax imposed by State X plus the amount of death taxes paid to other States. State Y has no estate tax. The amount of the inheritance tax actually paid to State X with respect to the real property situated in State X is $4,000; the amount of the inheritance tax actually paid to State Y with respect to the real property situated in State Y is $9,000. B's taxable estate for Federal estate tax purposes is $550,000, in respect of which the maximum credit under section 2011 would be $14,400 in the absence of the special limitation contained in section 2102(b). However, under section 2102(b) and this paragraph the amount of the maximum credit allowable in respect of B's estate for State death taxes is limited to the amount which bears the same ratio to $14,400 (the maximum credit computed as provided in section 2011(b)) as $300,000 (the value of the property in respect of which a State death tax was actually paid and which is included in B's gross estate under section 2103) bears to $600,000 (the value of B's total gross estate under section 2103). Accordingly, the maximum credit allowable under section 2102 and this section for all State death taxes actually paid is $7,200 ($14,400 × $300,000/$600,000), and the estate tax of State X is not applicable to B's estate.

(c) *Unified credit*.—(1) *In general*.—Subject to paragraph (c)(2) of this section, in the case of estates of decedents dying after November 10, 1988, a unified credit of $13,000 is allowed against the tax imposed by section 2101 subject to the limitations of section 2102(c).

(2) *When treaty is applicable*.—To the extent required under any treaty obligation of the United States, the estate of a nonresident not a citizen of the United States is allowed the unified credit permitted to a United States citizen or resident of $192,800, multiplied by the proportion that the total gross estate of the decedent situated in the United States bears to the decedent's total gross estate wherever situated.

(3) *Certain residents of possessions*.—In the case of a decedent who is considered to be a nonresident not a citizen of the United States under section 2209, there is allowed a unified credit equal to the greater of $13,000, or $46,800 multiplied by the proportion that the decedent's gross estate situated in the United States bears to the total gross estate of the decedent wherever situated. [Reg. § 20.2102-1.]

☐ [*T.D.* 6296, 6-23-58. *Amended by T.D.* 7296, 12-11-73 *and T.D.* 8612, 8-21-95.]

[Reg. § 20.2103-1]

§ 20.2103-1. Estates of nonresidents not citizens; "entire gross estate".—The "entire gross estate" wherever situated of a nonresident who was not a citizen of the United States at the time of his death is made up in the same way as the "gross estate" of a citizen or resident of the United States. See §§ 20.2031 through 20.2044-1. See paragraphs (a) and (c) of § 20.2031-1 for the circumstances under which real property situated outside the United States is excluded from the gross estate of a citizen or resident of the United States. However, except as provided in section 2107(b) with respect to the estates of certain expatriates, in the case of a nonresident not a citizen, only that part of the entire gross estate which on the date of the decedent's death is situated in the United States is included in his taxable estate. In fact, property situated outside the United States need not be disclosed on the return unless section 2107 is applicable, certain deductions are claimed, or information is specifically requested. See §§ 20.2106-1, 20.2106-2, and 20.2107-1. For a description of property considered to be situated in the United States, see § 20.2104-1. For a description of property considered to be situated outside the United States, see § 20.2105-1. [Reg. § 20.2103-1.]

☐ [*T.D.* 6296, 6-23-58. *Amended by T.D.* 6684, 10-23-63 *and T.D.* 7296, 12-11-73.]

[Reg. § 20.2104-1]

§ 20.2104-1. Estates of nonresidents not citizens; property within the United States.—(a) *In general.*—Property of a nonresident who was not a citizen of the United States at the time of his death is considered to be situated in the United States if it is—

(1) Real property located in the United States.

(2) Tangible personal property located in the United States, except certain works of art on loan for exhibition (see paragraph (b) of § 20.2105-1).

(3) In the case of an estate of a decedent dying before November 14, 1966, written evidence of intangible personal property which is treated as being the property itself, such as a bond for the payment of money, if it is physically located in the United States; except that this subparagraph shall not apply to obligations of the United States (but not its instrumentalities) issued before March 1, 1941, if the decedent was not engaged in business in the United States at the time of his death. See section 2106(c).

(4) Except as specifically provided otherwise in this section or in § 20.2105-1 (which specific exceptions, in the case of estates of decedents dying on or after November 14, 1966, cause this subparagraph to have relatively limited applicability), intangible personal property the written evidence of which is not treated as being the property itself, if it is issued by or enforceable against a resident of the United States or a domestic corporation or governmental unit.

(5) Shares of stock issued by a domestic corporation, irrespective of the location of the certificates (see, however, paragraph (i) of § 20.2105-1 for a special rule with respect to certain withdrawable accounts in savings and loan or similar associations).

(6) In the case of an estate of a decedent dying before November 14, 1966, moneys deposited in the United States by or for the decedent with any person carrying on the banking business, if the decedent was engaged in business in the United States at the time of his death.

(7) In the case of an estate of a decedent dying on or after November 14, 1966, except as specifically provided otherwise in paragraph (d), (i), (j), (l), or (m) of § 20.2105-1, any debt obligation, including a bank deposit, the primary obligor of which is—

(i) A United States person (as defined in section 7701(a)(30)), or

(ii) The United States, a State or any political subdivision thereof, the District of Columbia, or any agency or instrumentality of any such government.

This subparagraph applies irrespective of whether the written evidence of the debt obligation is treated as being the property itself or whether the decedent was engaged in business in the United States at the time of his death. For purposes of this subparagraph and paragraphs (k), (l), and (m) of § 20.2105-1, a debt obligation on which there are two or more primary obligors shall be apportioned among such obligors, taking into account to the extent appropriate under all the facts and circumstances any choate or inchoate rights of contribution existing among such obligors with respect to the indebtedness. The term "agency or instrumentality", as used in subdivision (ii) of this subparagraph, does not include a possession of the United States or an agency or instrumentality of a possession. Currency is not a debt obligation for purposes of this subparagraph.

(8) In the case of an estate of a decedent dying on or after January 1, 1970, except as specifically provided otherwise in paragraph (i) or (l) of § 20.2105-1, deposits with a branch in the United States of a foreign corporation, if the branch is engaged in the commercial banking business, whether or not the decedent was engaged in business in the United States at the time of his death.

(b) *Transfers.*—Property of which the decedent has made a transfer taxable under sections 2035 through 2038 is deemed to be situated in the United States if it is determined, under the provisions of paragraph (a) of this section, to be so situated either at the time of the transfer or at the time of the decedent's death. See §§ 20.2035-1 through 20.2038-1.

(c) *Death tax convention.*—It should be noted that the situs rules described in this section may be modified for various purposes under the provisions of an applicable death tax convention with a foreign country. [Reg. § 20.2104-1.]

☐ [*T.D.* 6296, 6-23-58. *Amended by T.D.* 7296, 12-11-73 *and T.D.* 7321, 8-15-74.]

[Reg. § 20.2105-1]

§ 20.2105-1. Estates of nonresidents not citizens; property without the United States.—Property of a nonresident who was not a citizen of the United States at the time of his death is considered to be situated outside the United States if it is—

(a)(1) Real property located outside the United States, except to the extent excludable from the entire gross estate wherever situated under § 20.2103-1.

(2) Tangible personal property located outside the United States.

(b) Works of art owned by the decedent if they were—

(1) Imported into the United States solely for exhibition purposes,

(2) Loaned for those purposes to a public gallery or museum, no part of the net earnings of which inures to the benefit of any private shareholder or individual, and

(3) At the time of the death of the owner, on exhibition, or en route to or from exhibition, in such a public gallery or museum.

(c) In the case of an estate of a decedent dying before November 14, 1966, written evidence of intangible personal property which is treated as being the property itself, such as a bond for the payment of money, if it is not physically located in the United States.

(d) Obligations of the United States issued before March 1, 1941, even though physically located in the United States, if the decedent was not engaged in business in the United States at the time of his death.

(e) Except as specifically provided otherwise in this section or in § 20.2104-1, intangible personal property the written evidence of which is not treated as being the property itself, if it is not issued by or enforceable against a resident of the United States or a domestic corporation or governmental unit.

(f) Shares of stock issued by a corporation which is not a domestic corporation, regardless of the location of the certificates.

(g) Amounts receivable as insurance on the decedent's life.

(h) In the case of an estate of a decedent dying before November 14, 1966, moneys deposited in the United States by or for the decedent with any person carrying on the banking business, if the decedent was not engaged in business in the United States at the time of his death.

(i) In the case of an estate of a decedent dying on or after November 14, 1966, and before January 1, 1976, any amount deposited in the United States which is described in section 861(c) (relating to certain bank deposits, withdrawable accounts, and amounts held by an insurance company under an agreement to pay interest), if any interest thereon, were such interest received by the decedent at the time of his death, would be treated under section 862(a)(1) as income from sources without the United States by reason of section 861(a)(1)(A) (relating to interest on amounts described in section 861(c) which is not effectively connected with the conduct of a trade or business within the United States) and the regulations thereunder. If such interest would be treated by reason of those provisions as income from sources without the United States only in part, the amount described in section 861(c) shall be considered situated outside the United States in the same proportion as the part of the interest which would be treated as income from sources without the United States bears to the total amount of the interest. This paragraph applies whether or not the decedent was engaged in business in the United States at the time of his death, and, except with respect to amounts described in section 861(c)(3) (relating to amounts held by an insurance company under an agreement to pay interest), whether or not the deposit or other amount is in fact interest bearing.

(j) In the case of an estate of a decedent dying on or after November 14, 1966, deposits with a branch outside of the United States of a domestic corporation or domestic partnership, if the branch is engaged in the commercial banking business. This paragraph applies whether or not the decedent was engaged in business in the United States at the time of his death, and whether or not the deposits, upon withdrawal, are payable in currency of the United States.

(k) In the case of an estate of a decedent dying on or after November 14, 1966, except as specifically provided otherwise in paragraph (a)(8) of § 20.2104-1 with respect to estates of decedents dying on or after January 1, 1970, any debt obligation, including a bank deposit, the primary obligor of which is neither—

(1) A United States person (as defined in section 7701(a)(30)), nor

(2) The United States, a State or any political subdivision thereof, the District of Columbia, or any agency or instrumentality of any such government.

This paragraph applies irrespective of whether the written evidence of the debt obligation is treated as being the property itself or whether the decedent was engaged in business in the United States at the time of his death. See paragraph (a)(7) of § 20.2104-1 for the treatment of a debt obligation on which there are two or more primary obligors. The term "agency or instrumentality", as used in subparagraph (2) of this paragraph, does not include a possession of the United States or an agency or instrumentality of a possession. Currency is not a debt obligation for purposes of this paragraph.

(l) In the case of an estate of a decedent dying on or after November 14, 1966, any debt obligation to the extent that the primary obligor on the debt obligation is a domestic corporation, if any interest thereon, were the interest received from such obligor by the decedent at the time of his death, would be treated under section 862(a)(1) as income from sources without the United States by reason of section 861(a)(1)(B) (relating to interest received from a domestic corporation less than 20 percent of whose gross income for a 3-year period was derived from sources within the United States) and the regulations thereunder. For such purposes the 3-year period referred to in section 861(a)(1)(B) is the period of 3 years ending with the close of the domestic corporation's last taxable year terminating before the decedent's death. This paragraph applies whether or not (1) the obligation is in fact interest-bearing, (2) the written evidence of the debt obligation is treated as being the property itself, or (3) the decedent was engaged in business in the United States at the time of his death. See paragraph (a)(7) of § 20.2104-1 for the treatment of a debt obligation on which there are two or more primary obligors.

(m)(1) In the case of an estate of a decedent dying after December 31, 1972, except as otherwise provided in subparagraph (2) of this paragraph, any debt obligation to the extent that the primary obligor on the debt obligation is a domestic corporation or domestic partnership, if any interest thereon, were the interest received from such obligor by the decedent at the time of his death, would be treated under section 862(a)(1) as income from sources without the United States by reason of section 861(a)(1)(G) (relating to interest received on certain debt obligations with respect to which elections have been made under section 4912(c)) and the regulations thereunder. This paragraph applies whether or not (i) the obligation is in fact interest bearing, (ii) the written evidence of the debt obligation is treated as being the property itself, or (iii) the decedent was engaged in business in the United States at the time of his death. See paragraph (a)(7) of § 20.2104-1 for the treatment of a debt obligation on which there are two or more primary obligors.

(2) In the case of an estate of a decedent dying before January 1, 1974, this paragraph does not apply to any debt obligation of a foreign corporation assumed by a domestic corporation which is treated under section 4912(c)(2) as issued by such domestic corporation during 1973. [Reg. § 20.2105-1.]

□ [*T.D.* 6296, 6-23-58. *Amended by T.D.* 6684, 10-23-63; *T.D.* 7296, 12-11-73; *and T.D.* 7321, 8-15-74.]

[Reg. § 20.2106-1]

§ 20.2106-1. Estates of nonresidents not citizens; taxable estate; deductions in general.—(a) The taxable estate of a nonresident who was not a citizen of the United States at the time of his death is determined by adding the value of that part of his gross estate which, at the time of his death, is situated in the United States and, in the case of an estate to which section 2107 (relating to expatriation to avoid taxes) applies, any amounts includible in his gross estate under section 2107(b), and then subtracting from the sum thereof the total amount of the following deductions:

(1) The deductions allowed in the case of estates of decedents who were citizens or residents of the United States under sections 2053 and 2054 (see §§ 20.2053-1 through 20.2053-9 and § 20.2054-1) for expenses, indebtedness and taxes, and for losses, to the extent provided in § 20.2106-2.

(2) A deduction computed in the same manner as the one allowed under section 2055 (see §§ 20.2055-1 through 20.2055-5) for charitable, etc., transfers, except—

(i) That the deduction is allowed only for transfers to corporations and associations created or organized in the United States, and to trustees for use within the United States, and

(ii) That the provisions contained in paragraph (c)(2) of § 20.2055-2 relating to termination of a power to consume are not applicable.

(3) Subject to the special rules set forth at § 20.2056A-1(c), the amount which would be deductible with respect to property situated in the United States at the time of the decedent's death under the principles of section 2056. Thus, if the surviving spouse of the decedent is a citizen of the United States at the time of the decedent's death, a marital deduction is allowed with respect to the estate of the decedent if all other applicable requirements of section 2056 are satisfied. If the surviving spouse of the decedent is not a citizen of the United States at the time of the decedent's death, the provisions of section 2056, including specifically the provisions of section 2056(d) and (unless section 2056(d)(4) applies) the provisions of section 2056A (QDOTs) must be satisfied.

(b) Section 2106(b) provides that no deduction is allowed under paragraph (a)(1) or (2) of this section unless the executor discloses in the estate tax return the value of that part of the gross estate not situated in the United States. See § 20.2105-1. Such part must be valued as of the date of the decedent's death, or if the alternate valuation method under section 2032 is elected, as of the applicable valuation date. [Reg. § 20.2106-1.]

□ [*T.D.* 6296, 6-23-58. *Amended by T.D.* 6526, 1-18-61; *T.D.* 7296, 12-11-73; *T.D.* 7318, 7-10-74 *and T.D.* 8612, 8-21-95.]

[Reg. § 20.2106-2]

§ 20.2106-2. Estates of nonresidents not citizens; deductions for expenses, losses, etc.—(a) In computing the taxable estate of a nonresident who was not a citizen of the United States at the time of his death, deductions are allowed under sections 2053 and 2054 for expenses, indebtedness and taxes, and for losses, to the following extent:

(1) A pledge or subscription is deductible if it is an enforceable claim against the estate and if it would constitute an allowable deduction under paragraph (a)(2) of § 20.2106-1, relating to charitable, etc., transfers, if it had been a bequest.

(2) That proportion of other deductions under sections 2053 and 2054 is allowed which the value of that part of the decedent's gross estate situated in the United States at the time of his death bears to the value of the decedent's entire gross estate wherever situated. It is immaterial whether the amounts to be deducted were incurred or expended within or without the United States. For purposes of this subparagraph, an amount which is includible in the decedent's gross estate under section 2107(b) with respect to stock in a foreign corporation shall be included in the value of the decedent's gross estate situated in the United States.

No deduction is allowed under this paragraph unless the value of the decedent's entire gross estate is disclosed in the estate tax return. See paragraph (b) of § 20.2106-1.

(b) In order that the Internal Revenue Service may properly pass upon the items claimed as deductions, the executor should submit a certified copy of the schedule of liabilities, claims against the estate, and expenses of administration filed under any applicable foreign death duty act. If no such schedule was filed, the executor should submit a certified copy of the schedule of these liabilities, claims and expenses filed with the foreign court in which administration was had. If the items of deduction allowable under section 2106(a)(1) were not included in either such schedule, or if no such schedules were filed, then there should be submitted a written statement of the foreign executor containing a declaration that it is made under the penalties of perjury setting forth the facts relied upon as entitling the estate to the benefit of the particular deduction or deductions.

(c) [Reserved][Reg. § 20.2106-2.]

☐ [*T.D.* 6296, 6-23-58. *Amended by T.D.* 7296, 12-11-73 *and T.D.* 8612, 8-21-95.]

[Reg. § 20.2107-1]

§ 20.2107-1. Expatriation to avoid tax.—(a) *Rate of tax.*—The tax imposed by section 2107(a) on the transfer of the taxable estates of certain nonresident expatriate decedents who were formerly citizens of the United States is computed in accordance with the table contained in section 2001, relating to the rate of the tax imposed on the transfer of the taxable estates of decedents who were citizens or residents of the United States. Except for any amounts included in the gross estate solely by reason of section 2107(b) and paragraph (b)(1)(ii) and (iii) of this section, the value of the taxable estate to be used in this computation is determined as provided in section 2106 and § 20.2106-1. The decedents to which section 2107(a) and this section apply are described in paragraph (d) of this section.

(b) *Gross estate.*—(1) *Determination of value.*—(i) *General rule.*—Except as provided in subdivision (ii) of this subparagraph with respect to stock in certain foreign corporations, for purposes of the tax imposed by section 2107(a) the value of the gross estate of every estate the transfer of which is subject to the tax imposed by that section is determined as provided in section 2103 and § 20.2103-1.

(ii) *Amount includible with respect to stock in certain foreign corporations.*—If at the time of his death a nonresident expatriate decedent the transfer of whose estate is subject to the tax imposed by section 2107(a)—

(*a*) Owned (within the meaning of section 958(a) and the regulations thereunder) 10 percent or more of the total combined voting power of all classes of stock entitled to vote in a foreign corporation, and

(*b*) Owned (within the meaning of section 958(a) and the regulations thereunder), or is considered to have owned (by applying the ownership rules of section 958(b) and the regulations thereunder), more than 50 percent of the total combined voting power of all classes of stock entitled to vote in such foreign corporation, then section 2107(b) requires the inclusion in the decedent's gross estate, in addition to amounts otherwise includible therein under subdivision (i) of this subparagraph, of an amount equal to that proportion of the fair market value (determined at the time of the decedent's death or, if so elected by the executor of the decedent's estate, on the alternate valuation date as provided in section 2032) of the stock in such foreign corporation owned (within the meaning of section 958(a) and the regulations thereunder) by the decedent at the time of his death, which the fair market value of any assets owned by such foreign corporation and situated in the United States, at the time of his death, bears to the total fair market value of all assets owned by such foreign corporation at the time of his death.

(iii) *Rules of application.*—(*a*) In determining the proportion of the fair market value of the stock which is includible in the gross estate under subdivision (ii) of this subparagraph, the fair market value of the foreign corporation's assets situated in the United States and of its total assets shall be determined without reduction for any outstanding liabilities of the corporation.

(*b*) For purposes of subdivision (ii) of this subparagraph, the foreign corporation's assets which are situated in the United States shall be all its property which, by applying the provisions of sections 2104, 2105, and §§ 20.2104-1 and 20.2105-1, would be considered to be situated in the United States if such property were property of a nonresident who was not a citizen of the United States.

(*c*) For purposes of subdivision (ii) (*a*) of this subparagraph, a decedent is treated as owning stock in a foreign corporation at the time of his death to the extent he owned (within the meaning of section 958(a) and the regulations thereunder) the stock at the time he made a transfer of the stock in a transfer described in sections 2035 to 2038, inclusive (relating respectively to transfers made in contemplation of death, transfers with a retained life estate, transfers taking effect at death, and revocable transfers). For purposes of subdivision (ii) (*b*) of this subparagraph, a decedent is treated as owning stock in a foreign corporation at the time of his death to the extent he owned (within the meaning of section 958(a) and the regulations thereunder), or is considered to have owned (by applying the ownership rules of section 958(b) and the regulations thereunder), the stock at the time he made a transfer of the stock in a transfer described in sections 2035 to 2038, inclusive. In applying the proportion rule of section 2107(b) and subdivision (ii) of this subparagraph where a decedent is treated as owning stock in a foreign corporation at the time of his death by reason of having transferred his interest in such stock in a transfer described in sections 2035 to 2038, inclusive, the proportionate value of the interest includible in his gross estate is based upon the value as of the applicable valuation date described in section 2031 or 2032 of the amount, determined as of the date of transfer, of his interest in the stock. See example (2) in subparagraph (2) of this paragraph.

(*d*) For purposes of applying subdivision (ii) (*b*) of this subparagraph, the same shares of stock may not be counted more than once. See example (2) in subparagraph (2) of this paragraph.

(*e*) The principles applied in paragraph (b) of § 1.957-1 of this chapter (Income Tax Regulations) for determining what constitutes total combined voting power of all classes of stock entitled to vote in a foreign corporation for purposes of section 957(a) shall be applied in determining what constitutes total combined voting power of all classes of stock entitled to vote in a foreign corporation for purposes of section 2107(b) and subdivision (ii) of this subparagraph. In applying such principles under this paragraph changes in language shall be made, where necessary, in order to treat the nonresident expatriate decedent, rather than U. S. shareholders, as owning such total combined voting power.

(2) *Illustrations.*—The application of this paragraph may be illustrated by the following examples:

Example (1). (a) At the time of his death, H, a nonresident expatriate decedent the transfer of whose estate is subject to the tax imposed by section 2107(a), owned a 60-percent interest in M Company, a foreign partnership, which in turn owned stock issued by N Corporation, a foreign corporation. The stock in N Corporation held by M Company, which constituted 50 percent of the total combined voting power of all classes of stock entitled to vote in N Corporation, was valued at $50,000 at the time of H's death. In addition, W, H's wife, also a nonresident not a citizen of the United States, owned at the time of H's death stock in N Corporation constituting 25 percent of the total combined voting power of all classes of stock entitled to vote in that corporation. The fair market value of the assets of N Corporation which, at the time of H's death, were situated in the United States constituted 40 percent of the fair market value of all assets of that corporation. It is assumed for purposes of this example that the executor of H's estate has not elected to value the estate on the alternate valuation date provided in section 2032.

(b) The test contained in subparagraph (1)(ii) *(a)* of this paragraph is met since at the time of his death H indirectly owned (within the meaning of section 958(a) and the regulations thereunder) 30 percent (60% of 50%) of the total combined voting power of all classes of stock entitled to vote in N Corporation; and the test contained in subparagraph (1)(ii) *(b)* of this paragraph is met since at such time H owned or is considered to have owned (within the meaning of section 958(a) and (b) and the regulations thereunder) 55 percent of the total combined voting power of all classes of stock entitled to vote in N Corporation (having constructive ownership of his wife's 25 percent, in addition to his own indirect ownership of 30 percent, of the total combined voting power). Accordingly, $12,000 is included in H's gross estate by reason of section 2107(b) and this paragraph. This $12,000 is the amount which is equal to 40 percent (the percentage of the fair market value of N Corporation's assets which were situated within the United States at H's death) of $30,000 (the fair market value of the stock then owned by H within the meaning of section 958(a) and the regulations thereunder, *i. e.,* H's 60-percent interest in the $50,000 fair market value of stock held by M Company).

Example (2). (a) Assume the same facts as those given in example (1) except that H made a transfer to W in contemplation of his death (within the meaning of section 2035) of his 60-percent interest in M Company, that on the date of the transfer M Company held stock in N Corporation constituting 80 percent of the total combined voting power of all classes of stock entitled to vote in that corporation (rather than the 50 percent of total combined voting power held by M Company on the date of H's death), and that the 80 percent of total combined voting power owned by M Company on the date of the transfer is valued at $70,000 on that date and at $85,000 at the time of H's death. It is assumed for purposes of this example that the 60-percent interest in M Company was held by W at the time of H's death.

(b) The test contained in subparagraph (1)(ii) *(a)* of this paragraph is met since, under subparagraph (1)(iii) *(c)* of this paragraph, H is treated as owning (within the meaning of section 958(a) and the regulations thereunder), at the time of his death, the 48 percent (60% of 80%) of the total combined voting power of all classes of stock entitled to vote in N Corporation represented by his transferred interest in M Company; and the test contained in subparagraph (1)(ii) *(b)* of this paragraph is met since, under that subparagraph and subparagraph (1)(iii) *(c)* of this paragraph, H is treated as owning (within the meaning of section 958(a) or (b)), at the time of his death, 73 percent (48% plus 25%) of the total combined voting power of all classes of stock entitled to vote in N Corporation. Accordingly, $20,400 is included in H's gross estate by reason of section 2107(b) and this paragraph. This $20,400 is the amount which is equal to 40 percent (the percentage of the fair market value of N Corporation's assets which were situated within the United States at H's death) of $51,000 (the fair market value at the time of H's death of the transferred interest which under subparagraph (1)(iii) *(c)* of this paragraph H is considered to own within the meaning of section 958(a) and the regulations thereunder at that time, *i. e.,* the 60-percent interest in the $85,000 fair market value at that time of the 80-percent total combined voting power held by M Company on the date of transfer).

(c) The fact that the stock in N Corporation owned by M Company is considered under subparagraph (1)(ii) *(b)* of this paragraph to be owned by H for two independent reasons (*i. e.,* under section 958(a) and the regulations thereunder, because H transferred his 60-percent interest in M Company to W in contemplation of death, and under section 958(b) and the regulations thereunder, because H is considered to own the stock in N Corporation indirectly owned by his wife, W, by reason of her ownership of such transferred interest) does not cause the shares of stock represented by the transferred interest in M Company to be counted twice in determining whether the test contained in that subparagraph is met. See subparagraph (1)(iii) *(d)* of this paragraph.

Example (3). (a) At the time of his death, H, a nonresident expatriate decedent the transfer of whose estate is subject to the tax imposed by section 2107(a), owned a 40-percent beneficial interest in a domestic trust; at that time he also directly owned stock in P Corporation, a foreign corporation, constituting 15 percent of the total combined voting power of all classes of stock entitled to vote in that corporation. The trust owned stock in P Corporation constituting 51 percent of the total combined voting power of all classes of stock entitled to vote in that corporation. The stock in P Corporation owned directly by H was valued at $20,000 on the alternate valuation date determined pursuant to an election under section 2032. The fair market value of the assets of P Corporation which, at the time of H's death, were situated in the United States constituted 20 percent of the fair market value of all assets of that corporation.

(b) By reason of section 958(b)(2) and the regulations thereunder, the trust is considered to own all the stock entitled to vote in P Corporation since it owns more than 50 percent of the total combined voting power of all classes of stock entitled to vote in that corporation. The test contained in subparagraph (1)(ii) *(a)* of this paragraph is met since at the time of his death H owned (within the meaning of section 958(a) and the regulations thereunder) 15 percent of the total combined voting power of all classes of stock entitled to vote in P Corporation; the stock in P Corporation owned by the trust is not considered to have been owned by H under section 958(a)(2) since the trust is not a foreign trust. In addition, the test contained in subparagraph (1)(ii) *(b)* of this paragraph is met since at the time of his death H owned or is considered to have owned (within the meaning of section 958(a) and (b) and the regulations thereunder) 55 percent of the total combined voting power of all classes of stock entitled to vote in that corporation (his 15 percent directly owned plus his 40 percent (40% of 100%) considered to be owned). Accordingly, $4,000 is included in H's gross estate by reason of section 2107(b) of this paragraph. This $4,000 is the amount which is equal to 20 percent (the percentage of the fair market value of P Corporation's assets which were situated within the United States at H's death) of $20,000 (the fair market value of the stock then owned by H within the meaning of section 958(a) and the regulations thereunder). In addition, the value of H's interest in the domestic trust is included in his gross estate under section 2103 to the extent it constitutes property having a situs in the United States.

(c) *Credits.*—Credits against the tax imposed by section 2107(a) are allowed for any amounts determined in accordance with section 2102 and § 20.2102-1 (relating to credits against the estate tax for State death taxes, gift tax, and tax on prior transfers). In computing the special limitation on the credit for State death taxes contained in section 2102(b) and paragraph (b) of § 20.2102-1, amounts included in the gross estate under section 2107(b) and paragraph (b)(1) of this section are to be taken into account.

(d) *Decedents to whom the tax imposed by section 2107(a) applies.*—(1) *General rule.*—The tax imposed by section 2107(a) applies to the transfer of the taxable estate of every decedent nonresident not a citizen of the United States dying on or after November 14, 1966, who lost his U. S. citizenship after March 8, 1965, and within the 10-year period ending with the date of his death, except in the case of the estate of a decedent whose loss of U. S. citizenship either—

(i) Resulted from the application of section 301(b), 350, or 355 of the Immigration and Nationality Act, as amended (8 U. S. C. 1401(b), 1482, or 1487); or

(ii) Did not have for one of its principal purposes (but not necessarily its only principal purpose) the avoidance of Federal income, estate, or gift tax.

Section 301(b) of the Immigration and Nationality Act provides generally that a U. S. citizen, who is born outside the United States of parents one of whom is an alien and the other is a U. S. citizen who was physically present in the United States for a specified period, shall lose his U. S. citizenship if, within a specified period preceding the age of 28 years, he fails to be continuously physically present in the United States for at least 5 years. Section 350 of that Act provides that under certain circumstances a person, who at birth acquired the nationality of the United States and of a foreign country and who has voluntarily sought or claimed benefits of the nationality of any foreign country, shall lose his U. S. nationality if, after attaining the age of 22 years, he has a continuous residence for 3 years in the foreign country of which he is a national by birth. Section 355 of that Act provides that a person having U. S. nationality, who is under 21 years of age and whose residence is in a foreign country with or under the legal custody of a parent who loses his U. S. nationality under specified circumstances, shall lose his U. S. nationality if he has or acquires the nationality of that foreign country and attains the age of 25 years without having established his residence in the United States. Section 2107 and this section do not apply to the transfer of any estate the estate tax treatment of which is subject to a Presidential proclamation made pursuant to section 2108(a) (relating to the application of pre-1967 estate tax provisions in the case of a foreign country which imposes a more burdensome tax than the United States).

(2) *Burden of proof.*—(i) *General rule.*—In determining for purposes of subparagraph (1)(ii) of this paragraph whether a principal purpose for the loss of U. S. citizenship by a decedent was the avoidance of Federal income, estate, or gift tax, the Commissioner must first establish that it is reasonable to believe that the decedent's loss of U. S. citizenship would, but for section 2107 and this section, result in a substantial reduction in the sum of *(a)* the Federal estate tax and *(b)* all estate, inheritance, legacy, and succession taxes imposed by foreign countries and political subdivisions thereof, in respect of the transfer of the decedent's estate. Once the Commissioner has so established, the burden of proving that the loss of citizenship by the decedent did not have for one of its principal purposes the avoidance of

Federal income, estate, or gift tax shall be on the executor of the decedent's estate.

(ii) *Tentative determination of substantial reduction in Federal and foreign death taxes.*—In the absence of complete factual information, the Commissioner may make a tentative determination, based on the information available, that the decedent's loss of U. S. citizenship would, but for section 2107 and this section, result in a substantial reduction in the sum of the Federal and foreign death taxes described in subdivision (i) *(a)* and *(b)* of this subparagraph. This tentative determination may be based upon the fact that the laws of the foreign country of which the decedent became a citizen and the laws of the foreign country of which the decedent was a resident at the time of his death, including the laws of any political subdivisions of those foreign countries, would ordinarily result, in the case of an estate of a nonexpatriate decedent having the same citizenship and residence as the decedent, in liability for total death taxes under such laws substantially lower than the amount of the Federal estate tax which would be imposed on the transfer of a comparable estate of a citizen of the United States. In the absence of a preponderance of evidence to the contrary, this tenative determination shall be sufficient to establish that it is reasonable to believe that the decedent's loss of U. S. citizenship would, but for section 2107 and this section, result in a substantial reduction in the sum of the Federal and foreign death taxes described in subdivision (i) *(a)* and *(b)* of this subparagraph. [Reg. § 20.2107-1.]

☐ [*T.D.* 7296, 12-11-73.]

Miscellaneous

[Reg. § 20.2203-1]

§ 20.2203-1. Definition of executor.—The term "executor" means the executor or administrator of the decedent's estate. However, if there is no executor or administrator appointed, qualified and acting within the United States, the term means any person in actual or constructive possession of any property of the decedent. The term "person in actual or constructive possession of any property of the decedent" includes, among others, the decedent's agents and representatives; safe-deposit companies, warehouse companies, and other custodians of property in this country; brokers holding, as collateral, securities belonging to the decedent; and debtors of the decedent in this country. [Reg. § 20.2203-1.]

☐ [*T.D.* 6296, 6-23-58.]

[Reg. § 20.2204-1]

§ 20.2204-1. Discharge of executor from personal liability.—(a) *General rule.*—The executor of a decedent's estate may make written application to the applicable internal revenue officer with whom the estate tax return is required to be filed, as provided in § 20.6091-1, for a determination of the Federal estate tax and for a discharge of personal liability therefrom. Within 9 months after receipt of the application, or if the application is made before the return is filed then within 9 months after the return is filed, the executor will be notified of the amount of the tax and, upon payment thereof, he will be discharged from personal liability for any deficiency in the tax thereafter found to be due. If no such notification is received, the executor is discharged at the end of such 9-month period from personal liability for any deficiency thereafter found to be due. The discharge of the executor from personal liability under this section applies only to him in his personal capacity and to his personal assets. The discharge is not applicable to his liability as executor to the extent of the assets of the estate in his possession or control. Further, the discharge is not to operate as a release of any part of the gross estate from the lien for estate tax for any deficiency that may thereafter be determined to be due.

(b) *Special rule in the case of extension of time for payment of tax.*—In addition to the provisions of paragraph (a) of this section, an executor of the estate of a decedent dying after December 31, 1970, may make written application to be discharged from personal liability for the amount of Federal estate tax for which the time for payment has been extended under section 6161, 6163, or 6166. In such a case, the executor will be notified of the amount of bond, if any, to be furnished within 9 months after receipt of the application, or, if the application is made before the return is filed, within 9 months after the return is filed. The amount of any bond required under the provisions of this paragraph shall not exceed the amount of tax the payment of which has been extended. Upon furnishing the bond in the form required under § 301.7101-1 of this chapter (Regulations on Procedure and Administration), or upon receipt of the notification that no bond is required, the executor will be discharged from personal liability for the tax the payment of which has been extended. If no notification is received, the executor is discharged at the end of such 9-month period from personal liability for the tax the payment of which has been extended. [Reg. § 20.2204-1.]

☐ [*T.D.* 6296, 6-23-58. *Amended by T.D.* 7238, 12-28-72, *and T.D.* 7941, 2-6-84.]

[Reg. § 20.2204-2]

§ 20.2204-2. Discharge of fiduciary other than executor from personal liability.—(a) A fiduciary (not including a fiduciary of the estate of a nonresident decedent), other than the executor, who as a fiduciary holds, or has held at any time since the decedent's death, property transferred to the fiduciary from a decedent dying after December 31, 1970, or his estate, may make written application to the applicable internal revenue officer with whom the estate tax return is required to be filed, as provided in § 20.6091-1, for a determination of the Federal estate tax liability with respect to such property and for a discharge of personal liability therefrom. The application must be accompanied by a copy of the instrument, if any, under which the fiduciary is acting, a description of all the property transferred to the fiduciary from the decedent or his estate, and any other information that would be relevant to a determination of the fiduciary's tax liability.

(b) Upon the discharge of the executor from personal liability under §20.2204-1, or, if later, within 6 months after the receipt of the application filed by a fiduciary pursuant to the provisions of paragraph (a) of this section, such fiduciary will be notified either (1) of the amount of tax for which it has been determined the fiduciary is liable, or (2) that it has been determined that the fiduciary is not liable for any such tax. The fiduciary will also be notified of the amount of bond, if any, to be furnished for any Federal estate tax for which the time for payment has been extended under section 6161, 6163, or 6166. The amount of any bond required under the provisions of this paragraph shall not exceed the amount of tax the payment of which has been so extended. Upon payment of the amount for which it has been determined the fiduciary is liable, and upon furnishing any bond required under this paragraph in the form specified under §301.7101-1 of this chapter (Regulations on Procedure and Administration), or upon receipt by the fiduciary of notification of a determination that he is not liable for such tax or that a bond is not required, the fiduciary will be discharged from personal liability for any deficiency in the tax thereafter found to be due. If no such notification is received, the fiduciary is discharged at the end of such 6 months (or upon discharge of the executor, if later) from personal liability for any deficiency thereafter found to be due. The discharge of the fiduciary from personal liability under this section applies only to him in his personal capacity and to his personal assets. The discharge is not applicable to his liability as a fiduciary (such as a trustee) to the extent of the assets of the estate in his possession or control. Further, the discharge is not to operate as a release of any part of the gross estate from the lien for estate tax for any deficiency that may thereafter be determined to be due. [Reg. §20.2204-2.]

☐ [*T.D.* 7238, 12-28-72.]

[Reg. §20.2204-3]

§20.2204-3. Special rules for estates of decedents dying after December 31, 1976; special lien under section 6324A.—For purposes of §§20.2204-1(b) and 20.2204-2(b), in the case of a decedent dying after December 31, 1976, if the executor elects a special lien in favor of the United States under section 6324A, relating to special lien for estate taxes deferred under section 6166 or 6166A (as in effect prior to its repeal by the Economic Recovery Tax Act of 1981), such lien shall be treated as the furnishing of a bond with respect to the amount for which the time for payment has been extended under section 6166. If an election has been made under section 6324A, the executor may not thereafter substitute a bond pursuant to section 2204 in lieu of that lien. If a bond has been supplied under section 2204, however, the executor may, by filing a proper notice of election and agreement, substitute a lien under section 6324A for any part or all of such bond. See §§20.6324A-1 and 301.6324A-1 for rules relating to a special lien under section 6324A. [Reg. §20.2204-3.]

☐ [*T.D.* 7941, 2-6-84.]

[Reg. §20.2205-1]

§20.2205-1. Reimbursement out of estate.—If any portion of the tax is paid by or collected out of that part of the estate passing to, or in the possession of, any person other than the duly qualified executor or administrator, that person may be entitled to reimbursement, either out of the undistributed estate or by contribution from other beneficiaries whose shares or interests in the estate would have been reduced had the tax been paid before distribution of the estate, or whose shares or interests are subject either to an equal or prior liability for the payment of taxes, debts, or other charges against the estate. For specific provisions giving the executor the right to reimbursement from life insurance beneficiaries and from recipients of property over which the decedent had a power of appointment, see sections 2206 and 2207. These provisions, however, are not designed to curtail the right of the district director to collect the tax from any person, or out of any property, liable for its payment. The district director cannot be required to apportion the tax among the persons liable nor to enforce any right of reimbursement or contribution. [Reg. §20.2205-1.]

☐ [*T.D.* 6296, 6-23-58.]

[Reg. §20.2206-1]

§20.2206-1. Liability of life insurance beneficiaries.—With respect to the right of the district director to collect the tax without regard to the provisions of section 2206, see §20.2205-1. [Reg. §20.2206-1.]

☐ [*T.D.* 6296, 6-23-58.]

[Reg. §20.2207-1]

§20.2207-1. Liability of recipient of property over which decedent had power of appointment.—With respect to the right of the district director to collect the tax without regard to the provisions of section 2207, see §20.2205-1. [Reg. §20.2207-1.]

☐ [*T.D.* 6296, 6-23-58.]

[Reg. §20.2207A-1]

§20.2207A-1. Right of recovery of estate taxes in the case of certain marital deduction property.—(a) *In general.*—(1) *Right of recovery from person receiving the property.*—If the gross estate includes the value of property that is includible by reason of section 2044 (relating to certain property in which the decedent had a qualifying income interest for life under sections 2056(b)(7) or 2523(f)), the estate of the surviving spouse is entitled to recover from the *person receiving the property* (as defined in paragraph (d) of this section) the amount of Federal estate tax attributable to that property. The right of recovery arises when the Federal estate tax with respect to the property includible in the gross estate by reason of section 2044 is paid by the estate. There is no right of recovery from any person for the property received by that person for which a deduction was allowed from the gross estate if no tax is attributable to that property.

(2) *Failure to exercise right of recovery.*—Failure of an estate to exercise a right of recovery under this section upon a transfer subject to section 2044 is treated as a transfer for Federal gift tax purposes of the unrecovered amounts from the persons who would benefit from the recovery to the persons from whom the recovery could have been obtained. See § 25.2511-1 of this chapter. The transfer is considered made when the right of recovery is no longer enforceable under applicable law. A delay in the exercise of the right of recovery without payment of sufficient interest is a below-market loan. Section 1.7872-5T of the Temporary Income Tax regulations describes factors that are used to determine, based on the facts and circumstances of a particular case, whether a loan otherwise subject to imputation under section 7872 (relating to the treatment of below-market loans) is exempted from its provisions.

(3) *Waiver of right of recovery.*—The provisions of § 20.2207A-1(a)(2) do not apply to the extent that the surviving spouse's will provides that a recovery shall not be made or to the extent that the beneficiaries cannot otherwise compel recovery. Thus, e.g., if the surviving spouse gives the executor of the estate discretion to waive the right of recovery and the executor waives the right, no gift occurs under § 25.2511-1 of this chapter if the persons who would benefit from the recovery cannot compel the executor to exercise the right of recovery.

(b) *Amount of estate tax attributable to property includible under section 2044.*—The amount of Federal estate tax attributable to property includible in the gross estate under section 2044 is the amount by which the total Federal estate tax (including penalties and interest attributable to the tax) under chapter 11 of the Internal Revenue Code that has been paid, exceeds the total Federal estate tax (including penalties and interest attributable to the tax) under chapter 11 of the Internal Revenue Code that would have been paid if the value of the property includible in the gross estate by reason of section 2044 had not been so included.

(c) *Amount of estate tax attributable to a particular property.*—An estate's right of recovery with respect to a particular property is an amount equal to the amount determined in paragraph (b) of this section multiplied by a fraction. The numerator of the fraction is the value for Federal estate tax purposes of the particular property included in the gross estate by reason of section 2044, less any deduction allowed with respect to the property. The denominator of the fraction is the total value of all properties included in the gross estate by reason of section 2044, less any deductions allowed with respect to those properties.

(d) *Person receiving the property.*—If the property is in a trust at the time of the decedent's death, the *person receiving the property* is the trustee and any person who has received a distribution of the property prior to the expiration of the right of recovery if the property does not remain in trust. This paragraph (d) does not affect the right, if any, under local law, of any person with an interest in property to reimbursement or contribution from another person with an interest in the property.

(e) *Example.*—The following example illustrates the application of paragraphs (a) through (d) of this section.

Example. D died in 1994. D's will created a trust funded with certain income producing assets included in D's gross estate at $1,000,000. The trust provides that all the income is payable to D's wife, S, for life, remainder to be divided equally among their four children. In computing D's taxable estate, D's executor deducted, pursuant to section 2056(b)(7), $1,000,000. Assume that S received no other property from D and that S died in 1996. Assume further that S made no section 2519 disposition of the property, that the property was included in S's gross estate at a value of $1,080,000, and that S's will contained no provision regarding section 2207A(a). The tax attributable to the property is equal to the amount by which the total Federal estate tax (including penalties and interest) paid by S's estate exceeds the Federal estate tax (including penalties and interest) that would have been paid if S's gross estate had been reduced by $1,080,000. That amount of tax may be recovered by S's estate from the trust. If, at the time S's estate seeks reimbursement, the trust has been distributed to the four children, S's estate is also entitled to recover the tax from the children. [Reg. § 20.2207A-1.]

☐ [*T.D.* 8522, 2-28-94. *Amended by T.D.* 9077, 7-17-2003.]

[Reg. § 20.2207A-2]

§ 20.2207A-2. Effective date.—The provisions of § 20.2207A-1 are effective with respect to estates of decedents dying after March 1, 1994. With respect to estates of decedent dying on or before such date, the executor of the decedent's estate may rely on any reasonable interpretation of the statutory provisions. For these purposes, the provisions of § 20.2207A-1 (as well as project LR-211-76, 1984-1 C.B., page 598, see § 601.601(d)(2)(ii)(*b*) of this chapter), are considered a reasonable interpretation of the statutory provisions. [Reg. § 20.2207A-2.]

☐ [*T.D.* 8522, 2-28-94.]

[Reg. § 20.2208-1]

§ 20.2208-1. Certain residents of possessions considered citizens of the United States.—As used in this part, the term "citizen of the United States" is considered to include a decedent dying after September 2, 1958, who, at the time of his death, was domiciled in a possession of the United States and was a United States citizen, and who did not acquire his United States citizenship solely by reason of his being a citizen of such possession or by reason of his birth or residence within such possession. The estate of such a decedent is, therefore, subject to the tax imposed by section 2001. See paragraph (a)(2) of § 20.0-1 and § 20.2209-1 for further information relating to the application of the Federal estate tax to the estates of decedents who were residents of possessions of the United States. The application of this section may be illustrated by the following example and the examples set forth in § 20.2209-1:

Example. A, a citizen of the United States by reason of his birth in the United States at San Francisco, established residence in Puerto Rico and acquired a Puerto Rican citizenship. A died on September 4, 1958, while a citizen and domiciliary of Puerto Rico. A's estate is, by reason of the provisions of section 2208, subject to the tax imposed by section 2001 inasmuch as his United States citizenship is based on birth in the United States and is not based solely on being a citizen of a possession or solely on birth or residence in a possession. [Reg. § 20.2208-1.]

☐ [*T.D.* 6526, 1-18-61.]

[Reg. § 20.2209-1]

§ 20.2209-1. Certain residents of possessions considered nonresidents not citizens of the United States.—As used in this part, the term "nonresident not a citizen of the United States" is considered to include a decedent dying after September 14, 1960, who, at the time of his death, was domiciled in a possession of the United States and was a United States citizen, and who acquired his United States citizenship solely by reason of his being a citizen of such possession or by reason of his birth or residence within such possession. The estate of such a decedent is, therefore, subject to the tax imposed by section 2101 which is the tax applicable in the case of a "nonresident not a citizen of the United States." See paragraph (a)(2) of § 20.0-1 and § 20.2208-1 for further information relating to the application of the Federal estate tax to the estates of decedents who were residents of possessions of the United States. The application of this section may be illustrated by the following examples and the example set forth in § 20.2208-1. In each of the following examples the decedent is deemed a "nonresident not a citizen of the United States" and his estate is subject to the tax imposed by section 2101 since the decedent died after September 14, 1960, but would not have been so deemed and subject to such tax if the decedent had died on or before September 14, 1960.

Example (1). C, who acquired his United States citizenship under section 5 of the Act of March 2, 1917 (39 Stat. 953), by reason of being a citizen of Puerto Rico, died in Puerto Rico on October 1, 1960, while domiciled therein. C is considered to have acquired his United States citizenship solely by reason of his being a citizen of Puerto Rico.

Example (2). E, whose parents were United States citizens by reason of their birth in Boston, was born in the Virgin Islands on March 1, 1927. On September 30, 1960, he died in the Virgin Islands while domiciled therein. E is considered to have acquired his United States citizenship solely by reason of his birth in the Virgin Islands (section 306 of the Immigration and Nationality Act (66 Stat. 237, 8 U. S. C. 1406)).

Example (3). N, who acquired United States citizenship by reason of being a native of the Virgin Islands and a resident thereof on June 28, 1932 (section 306 of the Immigration and Nationality Act (66 Stat. 237, 8 U. S. C. 1406)), died on October 1, 1960, while domiciled in the Virgin Islands. N is considered to have acquired his United States citizenship solely by reason of his birth or residence in the Virgin Islands.

Example (4). P, a former Danish citizen, who on January 17, 1917, resided in the Virgin Islands, made the declaration to preserve his Danish citizenship required by Article 6 of the treaty entered into on August 4, 1916, between the United States and Denmark. Subsequently P acquired United States citizenship when he renounced such declaration before a court of record (section 306 of the Immigration and Nationality Act (66 Stat. 237, 8 U. S. C. 1406)). P died on October 1,

1960, while domiciled in the Virgin Islands. P is considered to have acquired his United States citizenship solely by reason of his birth or residence in the Virgin Islands.

Example (5). R, a former French citizen, acquired his United States citizenship through naturalization proceedings in a court located in the Virgin Islands after having qualified for citizenship by residing in the Virgin Islands for 5 years. R died on October 1, 1960, while domiciled in the Virgin Islands. R is considered to have acquired his United States citizenship solely by reason of his birth or residence within the Virgin Islands. [Reg. § 20.2209-1.]

☐ [*T.D.* 6526, 1-18-61.]

Gift Tax

See p. 15 for regulations not amended to reflect law changes

DETERMINATION OF TAX LIABILITY

[Reg. § 25.0-1]

§ 25.0-1. Introduction.—(a) *In general.*—(1) The regulations in this part are designated "Gift Tax Regulations." These regulations pertain to (i) the gift tax imposed by chapter 12 of subtitle B of the Internal Revenue Code on the transfer of property by gift by individuals in the calendar year 1955, in subsequent calendar years beginning before the calendar year 1971, in calendar quarters beginning with the first calendar quarter of calendar year 1971 through the last calendar quarter of the calendar year 1981, and in calendar years beginning with the calendar year 1982, and (ii) certain related administrative provisions of subtitle F of the Code. It should be noted that the application of some of the provisions of these regulations may be affected by the provisions of an applicable gift tax convention with a foreign country. Unless otherwise indicated, references in these regulations to the "Internal Revenue Code" or the "Code" are references to the Internal Revenue Code of 1954, as amended, and references to a section or other provision of law are references to a section or other provision of the Internal Revenue Code of 1954, as amended. The Gift Tax Regulations are applicable to the transfer of property by gift by individuals in calendar years 1955 through 1970, in calendar quarters beginning with the first calendar quarter of calendar year 1971 through the last calendar quarter of the calendar year 1981, and in calendar years beginning with the calendar year 1982, and supersede the regulations contained in Part 86, Subchapter B, Chapter 1, Title 26, Code of Federal Regulations (1939) (Regulations 108, Gift Tax (8 F. R. 10858)), as prescribed and made applicable to the Internal Revenue Code of 1954 by Treasury Decision 6091, signed August 16, 1954 (19 F. R. 5167, Aug. 17, 1954).

(2) Section 2501(b) makes the provisions of chapter 12 of the Code apply in the case of gifts made after September 2, 1958, by certain citizens of the United States who were residents of a possession thereof at the time the gifts were made. Section 2501(c) makes the provisions of chapter 12 apply in the case of gifts made after September 14, 1960, by certain other citizens of the United States who were residents of a possession thereof at the time the gifts were made. See paragraphs (c) and (d) of § 25.2501-1. Except as otherwise provided in paragraphs (c) and (d) of § 25.2501-1, the provisions of these regulations do not apply to the making of gifts by such citizens.

(b) *Nature of tax.*—The gift tax is not a property tax. It is a tax imposed upon the transfer of property by individuals. It is not applicable to transfers by corporations or persons other than individuals. However, see paragraph (h)(1) of § 25.2511-1 with respect to the extent to which a transfer by or to a corporation is considered a transfer by or to its shareholders.

(c) *Scope of regulations.*—(1) *Determination of tax liability.*—Subchapter A of chapter 12 of the Code pertains to the determination of tax liability. The regulations pursuant to subchapter A are set forth in §§ 25.2501-1 through 25.2504-2 of this part. Sections 25.2701-5 and 25.2702-6 contain rules that provide additional adjustments to mitigate double taxation where the amount of the transferor's property was previously determined under the special valuation provisions of sections 2701 and 2702.

(2) *Transfer.*—Subchapter B of chapter 12 and chapter 14 of the Internal Revenue Code pertain to the transfers which constitute the making of gifts and the valuation of those transfers. The regulations pursuant to subchapter B are set forth in §§ 25.2511-1 through 25.2518-3. The regulations pursuant to chapter 14 are set forth in §§ 25.2701-1 through 25.2704-3.

(3) *Deductions.*—Subchapter C of chapter 12 of the Code pertains to the deductions which are allowed in determining the amount of taxable gifts. The regulations pursuant to subchapter C are set forth in §§ 25.2521-1 through 25.2524-1 of this part.

(4) *Procedure and administration provisions.*—Subtitle F of the Internal Revenue Code contains some sections which are applicable to the gift tax. The regulations pursuant to those sections are set forth in §§ 25.6001-1 through 25.7101-1. Such regulations do not purport to be all the regulations on procedure and administration which are pertinent to gift tax matters. For the remainder of the regulations on procedure and administration which are pertinent to gift tax matters, see part 301 of this chapter (Regulations on Procedure and Administration).

(d) *Arrangement and numbering.*—Each section of the regulations in this part (other than this section) is designated by a number composed of the part number followed by a decimal point (25.); the section of the Internal Revenue Code which it interprets; a hyphen (-); and a number identifying the section. By use of these designations one can ascertain the sections of the regulations relating to a provision of the Code. For example, the regulations pertaining to section 2521 of the Code are designated § 25.2521-1. [Reg. § 25.0-1.]

☐ [*T.D.* 6334, 11-14-58. *Amended by T.D.* 6542, 1-19-61; *T.D.* 7238, 12-28-72; *T.D.* 7296, 12-11-73; *T.D.* 7665, 1-24-80; *T.D.* 7910, 9-6-83 *and T.D.* 8395, 1-28-92.]

[Reg. § 25.2207A-1]

§ 25.2207A-1. Right of recovery of gift taxes in the case of certain marital deduction property.—(a) *In general.*—If an individual is treated as transferring an interest in property by reason of section 2519, the individual or the individual's estate is entitled to recover from the *person receiving the property* (as defined in paragraph (e) of this section) the amount of gift tax attributable to that property. The value of property to which this paragraph (a) applies is the value of all interests in the property other than the qualifying income interest. There is no right of recovery from any person for the property received by that person for which a deduction was allowed from the total amount of gifts, if no Federal gift tax is attributable to the property. The right of recovery arises at the time the Federal gift tax is actually paid by the transferor subject to section 2519.

(b) *Failure of a person to exercise the right of recovery.*—(1) The failure of a person to exercise a right of recovery provided by section 2207A(b) upon a lifetime transfer subject to section 2519 is treated as a transfer for Federal gift tax purposes of the unrecovered amounts to the person(s) from whom the recovery could have been obtained. See § 25.2511-1. The transfer is considered to be made when the right to recovery is no longer enforceable under applicable law and is treated as a gift even if recovery is impossible. A delay in the exercise of the right of recovery without payment of sufficient interest is a below-market loan. Section 1.7872-5T of this chapter describes factors that are used to determine, based on the facts and circumstances of a particular case, whether a loan otherwise subject to imputation under section 7872 (relating to the treatment of below-market loans) is exempted from its provisions.

(2) The transferor subject to section 2519 may execute a written waiver of the right of recovery arising under section 2207A before that right of recovery becomes unenforceable. If a waiver is executed, the transfer of the unrecovered amounts by the transferor is considered to be made on the later of—

(i) The date of the valid and irrevocable waiver rendering the right of recovery no longer enforceable; or

(ii) The date of the payment of the tax by the transferor.

(c) *Amount of gift tax attributable to all properties.*—The amount of Federal gift tax attributable to all properties includible in the total amount of gifts under section 2519 made during the calendar year is the amount by which the total Federal gift tax for the calendar year (including penalties and interest attributable to the tax) under chapter 12 of the Internal Revenue Code which has been paid, exceeds the total Federal gift tax for the calendar year (including penalties and interest attributable to the tax) under chapter 12 of the Internal Revenue Code which would have been paid if the value of the properties includible in the total amount of gifts by reason of section 2519 had not been included.

(d) *Amount of gift tax attributable to a particular property.*—A person's right of recovery with respect to a particular property is an amount equal to the amount determined in paragraph (c) of this section multiplied by a fraction. The numerator of the fraction is the value of the particular property included in the total amount of gifts made during the calendar year by reason of section 2519, less any deduction allowed with respect to the property. The denominator of the fraction is the total value of all properties included in the total amount of gifts made during the calendar year by reason of section 2519, less any deductions allowed with respect to those properties.

(e) *Person receiving the property.*—If the property is in a trust at the time of the transfer, the *person receiving the property* is the trustee, and any person who has received a distribution of the property prior to the expiration of the right of recovery if the property does not remain in trust. This paragraph (e) does not affect the right, if any, under local law, of any person with an interest in property to reimbursement or contribution from another person with an interest in the property.

(f) *Example.*—The following example illustrates the application of paragraphs (a) through (e) of this section.

Example. D created an inter vivos trust during 1994 with certain income producing assets valued at $1,000,000. The trust provides that all income is payable to D's wife, S, for S's life, with the remainder at S's death to be divided equally among their four children. In computing taxable gifts during calendar year 1994, D deducted, pursuant to section 2523(f), $1,000,000 from the total amount of gifts made. In addition, assume that S received no other transfers from D and that S made a gift during 1996 of the entire life interest to one of the children, at which time the value of trust assets was $1,080,000 and the value of S's life interest was $400,000. Although the entire value of the trust assets ($1,080,000) is, pursuant to sections 2511 and 2519, included in the total amount of S's gifts for calendar year 1996, S is only entitled to reimbursement for the Federal gift tax attributable to the value of the remainder interest, that is, the Federal gift tax attributable to $680,000 ($1,080,000 less $400,000). The Federal gift tax attributable to $680,000 is equal to the amount by which the total Federal gift tax (including penalties and interest) paid for the calendar year exceeds the federal gift tax (including penalties and interest) that would have been paid if the total amount of gifts during 1996 had been reduced by $680,000. That amount of tax may be recovered by S from the trust. [Reg. § 25.2207A-1.]

☐ [*T.D.* 8522, 2-28-94. *Amended by T.D.* 9077, 7-17-2003.]

[Reg. § 25.2207A-2]

§ 25.2207A-2. Effective date.—The provisions of § 25.2207A-1 are effective with respect to dispositions made after March 1, 1994. With respect to gifts made on or before such date, the donor may rely on any reasonable interpretation of the statutory provisions. For these purposes, the provisions of § 25.2207A-1 (as well as project LR-211-76, 1984-1 C.B., page 598, see § 601.601(d)(2)(ii)(*b*) of this chapter), are considered a reasonable interpretation of the statutory provisions. [Reg. § 25.2207A-2.]

☐ [*T.D.* 8522, 2-28-94.]

[Reg. § 25.2501-1]

§ 25.2501-1. Imposition of tax.—(a) *In general.*—(1) The tax applies to all transfers by gift of property, wherever situated, by an individual who is a citizen or resident of the United States, to the extent the value of the transfers exceeds the amount of the exclusions authorized by section 2503 and the deductions authorized by sections 2521 (as in effect prior to its repeal by the Tax Reform Act of 1976), 2522, and 2523. For each "calendar period" (as defined in § 25.2502-1(c)(1)), the tax described in this paragraph (a) is imposed on the transfer of property by gift during such calendar quarter. For calendar years after 1954 and before 1971, the tax described in this subparagraph is imposed on the transfer of property by gift during such calendar period. For gift tax rules related to an ABLE account established under section 529A, see § 1.529A-4 of this chapter.

(2) The tax does not apply to a transfer by gift of intangible property before January 1, 1967, by a nonresident not a citizen of the United States, unless the donor was engaged in business in the United States during the calendar year in which the transfer was made.

(3)(i) The tax does not apply to any transfer by gift of intangible property on or after January 1, 1967, by a nonresident not a citizen of the United States (whether or not he was engaged in business in the United States), unless the donor is an expatriate who lost his U. S. citizenship after March 8, 1965, and within the 10-year period ending with the date of transfer, and the loss of citizenship—

(a) Did not result from the application of section 301(b), 350, or 355 of the Immigration and Nationality Act, as amended (8 U. S. C. 1401(b), 1482, or 1487) (For a summary of these sections, see paragraph (d)(1) of § 20.2107-1 of this chapter (Estate Tax Regulations)), and

(b) Had for one of its principal purposes (but not necessarily its only principal purpose) the avoidance of Federal income, estate, or gift tax.

(ii) In determining for purposes of subdivision (i)*(b)* of this subparagraph whether a principal purpose for the loss of U. S. citizenship by a donor was the avoidance of Federal income, estate, or gift tax, the Commissioner must first establish that it is reasonable to believe that the donor's loss of U. S. citizenship would, but for section 2501(a)(3) and this subparagraph, result in a substantial reduction for the "calendar period" (as defined in § 25.2502-1(c)(1)), in the sum of *(a)* the Federal gift tax and *(b)* all gift taxes imposed by foreign countries and political subdivisions thereof, in respect of the transfer of property by gift. Once the Commissioner has so established, the burden of proving that the loss of citizenship by the donor did not have for one of its principal purposes the avoidance of Federal income, estate, or gift tax shall be on the donor. In the absence of complete factual information, the Commissioner may make a tentative determination, based on the information available, that the donor's loss of U. S. citizenship would, but for section 2501(a)(3) and this subparagraph, result in a substantial reduction for the calendar period in the sum of the Federal and foreign gift taxes described in *(a)* and *(b)* of this subdivision on the transfer of property by gift. This tentative determination may be based upon the fact that the laws of the foreign country of which the donor became a citizen and the laws of the foreign country of which the donor was a resident at the time of the transfer, including the laws of any political subdivision of those foreign countries, would ordinarily result, in the case of a nonexpatriate donor having the same citizenship and residence as the donor, in liability for total gift taxes under such laws for the calendar period substantially lower than the amount of the Federal gift tax which would be imposed for such period on an amount of comparable gifts by a citizen of the United States. In the absence of a preponderance of evidence to the contrary, this tentative determination shall be sufficient to establish that it is reasonable to believe that the donor's loss of U. S. citizenship would, but for section 2501(a)(3) and this subparagraph, result in a substantial reduction for the calendar period in the sum of the Federal and foreign gift taxes described in *(a)* and *(b)* of this subdivision on the transfer of property by gift.

(4) For additional rules relating to the application of the tax to transfers by nonresidents not citizens of the United States, see section 2511 and § 25.2511-3.

(5) The general rule of this paragraph (a) shall not apply to a transfer after May 7, 1974, of money or other property to a political organization for the use of that organization. However, this exception to the general rule applies solely to a transfer to a political organization as defined in section 527(e)(1) and including a newsletter fund to the extent provided under section 527(g). The general rule governs a transfer of property to an organization other than a political organization as so defined.

(b) *Resident.*—A resident is an individual who has his domicile in the United States at the time of the gift. For this purpose the United States includes the States and the District of Columbia. The term also includes the Territories of Alaska and Hawaii prior to admission as a State. See section 7701(a)(9). All other individuals are nonresidents. A person acquires a domicile in a place by living there, for even a brief period of time, with no definite present intention of moving therefrom. Residence without the requisite intention to remain indefinitely will not constitute domicile, nor will intention to change domicile effect such a change unless accompanied by actual removal.

(c) *Certain residents of possessions considered citizens of the United States.*—As used in this part, the term "citizen of the United States" includes a person who makes a gift after September 2, 1958 and who, at the time of making the gift, was domiciled in a possession of the United States and was a United States citizen, and who did not acquire his United States citizenship solely by reason of his being a citizen of such possession or by reason of his birth or residence within such possession. The gift of such a person is, therefore, subject to the tax imposed by section 2501 in the same manner in which a gift made by a resident of the United States is subject to the tax. See paragraph (a) of § 25.01 and paragraph (d) of this section for further information relating to the application of the Federal gift tax to gifts made by persons who were residents of possessions of the United States. The application of this paragraph may be illustrated by the following example and the examples set forth in paragraph (d) of this section:

Example. A, a citizen of the United States by reason of his birth in the United States at San Francisco, established residence in Puerto Rico and acquired Puerto Rican citizenship. A makes a gift of stock of a Spanish corporation on September 4, 1958, while a citizen and domiciliary of Puerto Rico. A's gift is, by reason of the provisions of section 2501(b) subject to the tax imposed by section 2501 inasmuch as his United States citizenship is based on birth in the United States and is not based solely on being a citizen of a possession or solely on birth or residence in a possession.

(d) *Certain residents of possessions considered nonresidents not citizens of the United States.*—As used in this part, the term "nonresident not a citizen of the United States" includes a person who makes a gift after September 14, 1960, and who at the time of making the gift, was domiciled in a possession of the United States and was a United States citizen, and who acquired his United States citizenship solely by reason of his being a citizen of such possession or by reason of his birth or residence within such possession. The gift of such a person is, therefore, subject to the tax imposed by section 2501 in the same manner in which a gift is subject to the tax when made by a donor who is a "nonresident not a citizen of the United States." See paragraph (a) of § 25.01 and paragraph (c) of this section for further information relating to the application of the Federal gift tax to gifts made by persons who were residents of possessions of the United States. The application of this paragraph may be illustrated by the following examples and the example set forth in paragraph (c) of this section. In each of the following examples the person who makes the gift is deemed a "nonresident not a citizen of the United States" and his gift is subject to the tax imposed by section 2501 in the same manner in which a gift is subject to the tax when made by a donor who is a nonresident not a citizen of the United States, since he made the gift after September 14, 1960, but would not have been so deemed and subject to such tax if the person who made the gift had made it on or before September 14, 1960.

Example (1). C, who acquired his United States citizenship under section 5 of the Act of March 2, 1917 (39 Stat. 953), by reason of being a citizen of Puerto Rico, while domiciled in Puerto Rico makes a gift on October 1, 1960, of real estate located in New York. C is considered to have acquired his United States citizenship solely by reason of his being a citizen of Puerto Rico.

Example (2). E, whose parents were United States citizens by reason of their birth in Boston, was born in the Virgin Islands on March 1, 1927. On September 30, 1960, while domiciled in the Virgin Islands, he made a gift of tangible personal property situated in Kansas. E is considered to have acquired his United States citizenship solely by reason of his birth in the Virgin Islands (section 306 of the Immigration and Nationality Act (66 Stat. 237, 8 U. S. C. 1406)).

Example (3). N, who acquired United States citizenship by reason of being a native of the Virgin Islands and a resident thereof on June 28, 1932 (section 306 of the Immigration and Nationality Act (66 Stat. 237, 8 U. S. C. 1406)), made a gift on October 1, 1960, at which time he was domiciled in the Virgin Islands, of tangible personal property situated in Wisconsin. N is considered to have acquired his United States citizenship solely by reason of his birth or residence in the Virgin Islands.

Example (4). P, a former Danish citizen, who on January 17, 1917 resided in the Virgin Islands, made the declaration to preserve his Danish citizenship required by Article 6 of the treaty entered into on August 14, 1916, between the United States and Denmark. Subsequently P acquired United States citizenship when he renounced such declaration before a court of record (section 306 of the Immigration and Nationality Act (66 Stat. 237, 8 U. S. C. 1406)). P, while domiciled in the Virgin Islands, made a gift on October 1, 1960, of tangible personal property situated in California. P is considered to have acquired his United States citizenship solely by reason of his birth or residence in the Virgin Islands.

Example (5). R, a former French citizen, acquired his United States citizenship through naturalization proceedings in a court located in the Virgin Islands after having qualified for citizenship by residing in the Virgin Islands for 5 years. R, while domiciled in the Virgin Islands, made a gift of tangible personal property situated in Hawaii on October 1, 1960. R is considered to have acquired his United States citizenship solely by reason of his birth or residence within the Virgin Islands. [Reg. § 25.2501-1.]

☐ [*T.D.* 6334, 11-14-58. *Amended by T.D.* 6542, 1-19-61; *T.D.* 7238, 12-28-72; *T.D.* 7296, 12-11-73; *T.D.* 7671, 2-5-80, *T.D.* 7910, 9-6-83 *and T.D.* 9923, 11-18-2020.]

[Reg. § 25.2502-1]

§ 25.2502-1. Rate of tax.—(a) *Computation of tax.*—The rate of tax is determined by the total of all gifts made by the donor during the calendar period and all the preceding calendar periods since June 6, 1932. See § 25.2502-1(c)(1) for the definition of "calendar period" and § 25.2502-1(c)(2) for the definition of "preceding calendar periods." The following six steps are to be followed in computing the tax:

(1) *First step.*—Ascertain the amount of the "taxable gifts" (as defined in § 25.2503-1) for the calendar period for which the return is being prepared.

(2) *Second step.*—Ascertain "the aggregate sum of the taxable gifts for each of the preceding "calendar periods" (as defined in § 25.2504-1), considering only those gifts made after June 6, 1932.

(3) *Third step.*—Ascertain the total amount of the taxable gifts, which is the sum of the amounts determined in the first and second steps. See § 25.2702-6 for an adjustment to the total amount of an individual's taxable gifts where the individual's current taxable gifts include the transfer of certain interests in trust that were previously valued under the provisions of section 2702.

(4) *Fourth step.*—Compute the tentative tax on the total amount of taxable gifts (as determined in the third step) using the rate schedule in effect at the time the gift (for which the return is being filed) is made.

(5) *Fifth step.*—Compute the tentative tax on the aggregate sum of the taxable gifts for each of the preceding calendar periods (as determined in the second step), using the same rate schedule set forth in the fourth step of this paragraph (a).

(6) *Sixth step.*—Subtract the amount determined in the fifth step from the amount determined in the fourth step. The amount remaining is the gift tax for the calendar period for which the return is being prepared.

(b) *Rate of tax.*—The tax is computed in accordance with the rate schedule in effect at the time the gift was made as set forth in section 2001(c) or corresponding provisions of prior law.

(c) *Definitions.*—(1) The term "calendar period" means:

(i) Each calendar year for the calendar years 1932 (but only that portion of such year after June 6, 1932) through 1970;

(ii) Each calendar quarter for the first calendar quarter of the calendar year 1971 through the last calendar quarter of calendar year 1981; or

(iii) Each calendar year for the calendar year 1982 and each succeeding calendar year.

(2) The term "preceding calendar periods" means all calendar periods ending prior to the calendar period for which the tax is being computed.

(d) *Examples.*—The following examples illustrate the application of this section with respect to gifts made by citizens or residents of the United States:

Example (1). Assume that in 1955 the donor made taxable gifts, as ascertained under the first step (paragraph (a)(2) of this section), of $62,500 and that there were no taxable gifts for prior years, with the result that the amount ascertainable under the third step is $62,500. Under the fourth step a tax is computed on this amount. Reference to the tax rate schedule in effect in the year 1955 discloses that the tax on this amount is $7,650.

Example (2). A donor makes gifts (other than gifts of future interests in property) during the calendar year 1955 of $30,000 to A and $33,000 to B. Two exclusions of $3,000 each are allowable, in accordance with the provisions of section 2503(b), which results in included gifts for 1955 of $57,000. Specific exemption was claimed and allowed in a total amount of $50,000 in the donor's gift tax returns for the calendar years 1934 and 1935 so there remains no specific exemption available for the donor to claim for 1955. The total amount of gifts made by the donor during preceding years, after excluding $5,000 for each donee for each calendar year in accordance with the provisions of section 1003(b)(1) of the 1939 Code, is computed as follows:

Calendar year 1934	$120,000
Calendar year 1935	25,000
Total amount of included gifts for preceding calendar years	$145,000

The aggregate sum of the taxable gifts for preceding calendar years is $115,000, which is determined by deducting a specific exemption of $30,000 from $145,000, the total amount of included gifts for preceding calendar years. The deduction from the 1934 and 1935 gifts for the specific exemption cannot exceed $30,000 for purposes of computing the tax on the 1955 gifts even though a specific exemption in a total amount of $50,000 was allowed in computing the donor's gift tax liability for 1934 and 1935. See paragraph (b) of § 25.2504-1. The computation of the tax for the calendar year 1955 (following the steps set forth in paragraph (a) of this section) is shown below:

(1)	Amount of taxable gifts for year	$57,000
(2)	Total amount of taxable gifts for preceding years	$115,000
(3)	Total taxable gifts	$172,000
(4)	Tax computed on item 3 in accordance with the rate schedule in effect for the year 1955	$31,725
(5)	Tax computed on item 2 (using same rate schedule)	18,900
(6)	Tax for year 1955 (item 4 minus item 5)	$12,825

Example (3). (i) *Facts.* During the calendar year 1955, H makes the following gifts of present interests:

To his daughter	$ 40,000
To his son	5,000
To W, his wife	5,000
To a charitable organization	10,000

The gifts to W qualify for the marital deduction, and, pursuant to the provisions of section 2513 (see § 25.2513-1), H and W consent to treat the gifts to third parties as having been made one-half by each spouse. The amount of H's taxable gifts for preceding years is $50,000. Only $25,000 of H's specific exemption provided under section 2521, which was in effect at the time, was claimed and allowed in preceding years. H's remaining specific exemption of $5,000 is claimed for the calendar year 1955. See § 25.2521-1. W made no gifts during the calendar year 1955 nor during any preceding calendar year. W claims sufficient specific exemption on her return to eliminate tax liability.

(ii) *Computation of H's tax for the calendar year 1955—(a) H's taxable gifts for year*

Total gifts of H		$60,000
Less: Portion of items to be reported by spouse (one-half of total gifts to daughter, son and charity)		27,500
Balance		$32,500
Less: Exclusions (three of $3,000 each for daughter, wife and charity and one of $2,500 for son)		11,500
Total included amount of gifts for year		$21,000
Less: Deductions:		
Charity	$2,000	
Marital	2,000	
Specific exemption	5,000	
Total deductions		9,000
Amount of taxable gifts for year		$12,000

(b) *Computation of tax.* The steps set forth in paragraph (a) of this section are followed.

(1)	Amount of taxable gifts for year	$12,000
(2)	Total taxable gifts for preceding years	50,000
(3)	Total taxable gifts (item *(1)* plus item *(2)*)	$62,000
(4)	Tax computed on item 3 in accordance with the rate schedule in effect for the year 1955	$7,545
(5)	Tax computed on item 2 in accordance with the rate schedule in effect for the year 1955	5,250
(6)	Tax for calendar year (item *(4)* minus item *(5)*)	$2,295

(iii) *Computation of W's tax for calendar year 1955—(a) W's taxable gifts for year*

Total gifts of W		$0
Less: Portion of items to be reported by spouse		0
Balance		$0
Gifts of spouse to be included		27,500
Total gifts for year		$27,500
Less: Exclusions (two of $3,000 each for daughter and charity and one of $2,500 for son)		8,500
Balance		$19,000
Less: Deductions:		
Charity	$ 2,000	
Marital	0	
Specific exemption	17,000	
Total deductions		19,000
Amount of taxable gifts for year		$ 0

(b) *Computation of tax.*—Since W had no "taxable gifts" during the year, there is no tax.

Example (4). (i) *Facts.* The facts are the same as in example (3) except that W made outright gifts of $10,000 to her niece and $20,000 to H at various times during the year. The amount of taxable gifts made by W in preceding calendar years is $75,000, and only $20,000 of her specific exemption provided under section 2521, which was in effect at the time, was claimed and allowed for preceding years. See § 25.2521-1. The remaining specific exemption of $10,000 is claimed for the calendar year 1955.

(ii) *Computation of H's tax for the calendar year 1955—(a) H's taxable gifts for year.*

Total gifts of H		$60,000
Less: Portion of items to be reported by spouse		27,500
Balance		$32,500
Gifts of spouse to be included		5,000
Total gifts for year		$37,500
Less: Exclusions ($11,500) as shown in example (3) plus $3,000 exclusion for gift to niece)		14,500
Total included amount of gifts for year		$23,000
Deductions:		
Charity	$2,000	
Marital	2,000	
Specific exemption	5,000	
Total deductions		9,000
Amount of taxable gifts for year		$14,000

(b) *Computation of tax.*

(1)	Amount of taxable gifts for year	$14,000
(2)	Total taxable gifts for preceding years	50,000
(3)	Total taxable gifts (item (1) plus item (2))	$64,000
(4)	Tax computed on item 3	$7,965
(5)	Tax computed on item 2	$5,250
(6)	Tax for year (item (4) minus item (5))	$2,715

(iii) *Computation of W's tax for the calendar year 1955—(a) W's taxable gifts for year*

Total gifts of W		$30,000
Less: Portion of items to be reported by spouse (one-half of gift to niece)		5,000
Balance		$25,000
Gifts of spouse to be included		27,500
Total gifts for year		$52,500
Less: Exclusions (four of $3,000 each for daughter, husband, niece and charity, and one of $2,500 for son)		14,500
Total included amount of gifts for year		$38,000
Deductions:		
Charity	$2,000	
Marital	10,000	
Specific exemption	10,000	
Total deductions		22,000
Amount of taxable gifts for year		$16,000

(b) *Computation of tax.*

(1)	Amount of taxable gifts for year	$16,000
(2)	Total taxable gifts for preceding years	75,000
(3)	Total taxable gifts	$91,000
(4)	Tax computed on item 3	13,635
(5)	Tax computed on item 2	10,275
(6)	Tax for year (item 4 minus item 5)	$ 3,360

Example (5). A makes gifts (other than gifts of future interests in property) to B in the first quarter of 1971 of $43,000 and in the second quarter of 1971 of $60,000. A gave to C in the second quarter of 1971 land valued at $11,000. The full amount of A's specific exemption provided under section 2521 was claimed and allowed in 1956. In 1966, A made taxable gifts totaling $21,000 on which gift tax was timely paid and no other taxable gifts were made by A in any other year preceding 1971. The gift tax return due for the first calendar quarter of 1971 was timely filed and the tax paid. With respect to the gifts made to B in 1971, the $3,000 annual gift tax exclusion provided by section 2503(b) is applied in its entirety against the $43,000 gift made to B in the first quarter and therefore is not available to offset the $60,000 gift made to B in the second quarter. (See § 25.2503-2(b).) A further $3,000 annual gift tax exclusion is available, however, to offset the $11,000 gift made to C in the second quarter of 1971. The computation of the gift tax for the second calendar quarter of 1971 due on August 15, 1971 (following the steps set forth in paragraph (a) of this section) is shown below:

(1)	Amount of taxable gifts for the second calendar quarter of 1971 ($60,000 + $11,000 – $3,000)	$ 68,000
(2)	Total amount of taxable gifts for preceding calendar periods ($43,000 – $3,000 + $21,000)	61,000
(3)	Total taxable gifts	$129,000
(4)	Tax computed on item 3 in accordance with rate schedule in effect for the year 1971	$ 22,050
(5)	Tax computed on item 2 (using same rate schedule)	$ 7,335
(6)	Tax for second calendar quarter of 1971 (item 4 minus item 5)	$ 14,715

Example (6). A makes gifts (other than gifts of future interests in property) during the calendar year 1982 of $160,000 to B and $100,000 to C. Two exclusions of $10,000 each are allowable, in accordance with the provisions of section 2503(b), which results in taxable gifts for 1982 of $240,000. In the first calendar quarter of 1978, A made taxable gifts totaling $100,000 on which gift tax was paid. For the calendar year 1969, A made taxable gifts totaling $50,000. The full amount of A's specific exemption provided under section 2521, which was in effect at the time, was claimed and allowed in 1968. The computation of the gift tax for the calendar period 1982 (following the steps set forth in paragraph (a) of this section) is shown below.

(1) Amount of taxable gifts for the calendar year 1982, $240,000.

(2) Total amount of taxable gifts for preceding calendar periods ($100,000 + $50,000), $150,000.

(3) Total taxable gifts, $390,000.

(4) Tax computed on item 3 (in accordance with the rate schedule in effect for the year 1982), $118,400.

(5) Tax computed on item 2 (using same rate schedule), $38,800.

(6) Tax for year 1982 (Item 4 minus item 5), $79,600.

[Reg. § 25.2502-1.]

☐ [*T.D.* 6334, 11-14-58. *Amended by T.D.* 7238, 12-28-72; *T.D.* 7910, 9-6-83 *and T.D.* 8395, 1-28-92.]

[Reg. § 25.2502-2]

§ 25.2502-2. Donor primarily liable for tax.—Section 2502(d) provides that the donor shall pay the tax. If the donor dies before the tax is paid the amount of the tax is a debt due the United States from the decedent's estate and his executor or administrator is responsible for its payment out of the estate. (See § 25.6151-1 for the time and place for paying the tax.) If there is no duly qualified executor or administrator, the heirs, legatees, devisees and distributees are liable for and required to pay the tax to the extent of the value of their inheritances, bequests, devises or distributive shares of the donor's estate. If a husband and wife effectively signify consent, under section 2513, to have gifts made to a third party during any "calendar period" (as defined in § 25.2502-1(c)(1)) considered as made one-half by each, the liability with respect to the gift tax of each spouse for that calendar period is joint and several (see § 25.2513-4). As to the personal liability of the donee, see paragraph (b) of § 301.6324-1 of this chapter (Regulations on Procedure and Administration). As to the personal liability of the executor or administrator, see section 3467 of the Revised Statutes (31 U. S. C. 192), which reads as follows:

Every executor, administrator, or assignee, or other person, who pays, in whole or in part, any debt due by the person or estate for whom or for which he acts before he satisfies and pays the debts due to the United States from such person or estate, shall become answerable in his own person and estate to the extent of such payments for the debts so due to the United States, or for so much thereof as may remain due and unpaid.

As used in such section 3467, the word "debt" includes a beneficiary's distributive share of an estate. Thus if an executor pays a debt due by the estate which is being administered by him or distributes any portion of the estate before there is paid all of the gift tax which he has a duty to pay, the executor is personally liable, to the extent of the payment or distribution, for so much of the gift tax as remains due and unpaid. [Reg. § 25.2502-2.]

☐ [*T.D.* 6334, 11-14-58. *Amended by T.D.* 7238, 12-38-72 *and T.D*, 7910, 9-6-83.]

[Reg. § 25.2503-1]

§ 25.2503-1. General definitions of "taxable gifts" and of "total amount of gifts".—The term "taxable gifts" means the "total amount of gifts" made by the donor during the "calendar period" (as defined in § 25.2502-1(c)(1)) less the deductions provided for in sections 2521 (as in effect before its repeal by the Tax Reform Act of 1976), 2522, and 2523 (specific exemption, charitable, etc., gifts and the marital deduction, respectively). The term "total amount of gifts" means the sum of the values of the gifts made during the calendar period less the amounts excludable under section 2503(b). See § 25.2503-2. The entire value of any gift of a future interest in property must be included in the total amount of gifts for the calendar period in which the gift is made. See § 25.2503-3. [Reg. § 25.2503-1.]

☐ [*T.D.* 6334, 11-14-58. *Amended by T.D.* 7238, 12-28-72 *and T.D.* 7910, 9-6-83.]

[Reg. § 25.2503-2]

§ 25.2503-2. Exclusions from gifts.—(a) *Gifts made after December 31, 1981.*—Except as provided in paragraph (f) of this section (involving gifts to a noncitizen spouse), the first $10,000 of gifts made to any one donee during the calendar year 1982 or any calendar year thereafter, except gifts of future interests in property as defined in §§ 25.2503-3 and 25.2503-4, is excluded in determining the total amount of gifts for the calendar year. In the case of a gift in trust the beneficiary of the trust is the donee.

(b) *Gifts made after December 31, 1970 and before January 1, 1982.*—In computing taxable gifts for the calendar quarter, in the case of gifts (other than gifts of future interests in property) made to any person by the donor during any calendar quarter of the calendar year 1971 or any subsequent calendar year, $3,000 of such gifts to such person less the aggregate of the amounts of such gifts to such person during all preceding calendar quarters of any such calendar year shall not be included in the total amount of gifts made during such quarter. Thus, the first $3,000 of gifts made to any one donee during the calendar year 1971 or any calendar year thereafter, except gifts of future interests in property as defined in §§ 25.2503-3 and 25.2503-4, is excluded in determining the total amount of gifts for a calendar quarter. In the case of a gift in trust the beneficiary of the trust is the donee. The application of this paragraph may be illustrated by the following examples:

Example (1). A made a gift of $3,000 to B on January 8, 1971, and on April 20, 1971, gave B an additional gift of $10,000. A made no other gifts in 1971. The total amount of gifts made by A during the second quarter of 1971 is $10,000 because the $3,000 exclusion provided by section 2503(b) is first applied to the January 8 gift.

Example (2). A gave $2,000 to B on January 8, 1971, and on April 20, 1971, gave him $10,000. The total amount of gifts made by A during the second quarter of 1971 is $9,000 because only $2,000 of the $3,000 exclusion provided by section 2503(b) was applied against the January 8 gift; $1,000 was available to offset other gifts (except gifts of a future interest) made to B during 1971.

(c) *Gifts made before January 1, 1971.*—The first $3,000 of gifts made to any one donee during the calendar year 1955, or 1970, or any calendar year intervening between calendar year 1955 and calendar year 1970, except gifts of future interests in property as defined in §§ 25.2503-3 and 25.2503-4, is excluded in determining the total amount of gifts for the calendar year. In the case of a gift in trust the beneficiary of the trust is the donee.

(d) *Transitional rule.*—The increased annual gift tax exclusion as defined in section 2503(b) shall not apply to any gift subject to a power of appointment granted under an instrument executed before September 12, 1981, and not amended on or after that date, provided that: (1) The power is exercisable after December 31, 1981, (2) the power is expressly defined in terms of, or by reference to, the amount of the gift tax exclusion under section 2503(b) (or the corresponding provision of prior law), and (3) there is not enacted a State law applicable to such instrument which construes the power of appointment as referring to the increased annual gift tax exclusion provided by the Economic Recovery Tax Act of 1981.

(e) *Examples.*—The provisions of paragraph (d) of this section may be illustrated by the following examples:

Example (1). A executed an instrument to create a trust for the benefit of B on July 2, 1981. The trust granted to B the power, for a period of 90 days after any transfer of cash to the trust, to withdraw from the trust the lesser of the amount of the transferred cash or the amount equal to the section 2503(b) annual gift tax exclusion. The trust was not amended on or after September 12, 1981. No state statute has been enacted which construes the power of appointment as referring to the increased annual gift tax exclusion provided by the Economic Recovery Tax Act of 1981. Accordingly, the maximum annual gift tax exclusion applicable to any gift subject to the exercise of the power of appointment is $3,000.

Example (2). Assume the same facts as in example (1) except that the power of appointment granted in the trust refers to section 2503(b) as amended at any time. The maximum annual gift tax exclusion applicable to any gift subject to the exercise of the power of appointment is $10,000.

(f) *Special rule in the case of gifts made on or after July 14, 1988, to a spouse who is not a United States citizen.*—(1) *In general.*—Subject to the special rules set forth at § 20.2056A-1(c) of this chapter, in the case of gifts made on or after July 14, 1988, if the donee of the gift is the donor's spouse and the donee spouse is not a citizen of the United States at the time of the gift, the first $100,000 of gifts made during the calendar year to the donee spouse (except gifts of future interests) is excluded in determining the total amount of gifts for the calendar year. The rule of this paragraph (f) applies regardless of whether the donor is a citizen or resident of the United States for purposes of chapter 12 of the Internal Revenue Code.

(2) *Gifts made after June 29, 1989.*—In the case of gifts made after June 29, 1989, the $100,000 exclusion provided in paragraph (f)(1) of this section applies only if the gift in excess of the otherwise applicable annual exclusion is in a form that qualifies for the gift tax marital deduction under section 2523(a) but for the provisions of section 2523(i)(1) (disallowing the marital deduction if the donee spouse is not a United States citizen.) See § 25.2523(i)-1(d), *Example 4*.

(3) *Effective date.*—This paragraph (f) is effective with respect to gifts made after August 22, 1995. [Reg. § 25.2503-2.]

☐ [*T.D.* 6334, 11-14-58. *Amended by T.D.* 7238, 12-28-72; *T.D.* 7910, 9-6-83; *T.D.* 7978, 9-28-84 *and T.D.* 8612, 8-21-95.]

[Reg. § 25.2503-3]

§ 25.2503-3. Future interests in property.—(a) No part of the value of a gift of a future interest may be excluded in determining the total amount of gifts made during the "calendar period"(as defined § 25.2502-1(c)(1)). "Future interest" is a legal term, and includes reversions, remainders, and other interests or estates, whether vested or contingent, and whether or not supported by a particular interest or estate, which are limited to commence in use, possession, or enjoyment at some future date or time. The term has no reference to such contractual rights as exist in a bond, note (though bearing no interest until maturity), or in a policy of life insurance, the obligations of which are to be discharged by payments in the future. But a future interest or interests in such contractual obligations may be created by the limitations contained in a trust or other instrument of transfer used in effecting a gift. A contribution to an ABLE account established under section 529A is not a future interest.

(b) An unrestricted right to the immediate use, possession, or enjoyment of property or the income from property (such as a life estate or term certain) is a present interest in property. An exclusion is allowable with respect to a gift of such an interest (but not in excess of the value of the interest). If a donee has received a present interest in property, the possibility that such interest may be diminished by the transfer of a greater interest in the same property to the donee through the exercise of a power is disregarded in computing the value of the present interest, to the extent that no part of such interest will at any time pass to any other person (see example (4) of paragraph (c) of this section). For an exception to the rule disallowing an exclusion for gifts of future interests in the case of certain gifts to minors, see § 25.2503-4.

(c) The operation of this section may be illustrated by the following examples:

Example (1). Under the terms of a trust created by A the trustee is directed to pay the net income to B, so long as B shall live. The trustee is authorized in his discretion to withhold payments of income during any period he deems advisable and add such income to the trust corpus. Since B's right to receive the income payments is subject to the trustee's discretion, it is not a present interest and no exclusion is allowable with respect to the transfer in trust.

Example (2). C transfers certain insurance policies on his own life to a trust created for the benefit of D. Upon C's death the proceeds of the policies are to be invested and the net income therefrom paid to D during his lifetime. Since the income payments to D will not begin until after C's death the transfer in trust represents a gift of a future interest in property against which no exclusion is allowable.

Example (3). Under the terms of a trust created by E the net income is to be distributed to E's three children in such shares as the trustee, in his uncontrolled discretion, deems advisable. While the terms of the trust provide that all of the net income is to be distributed, the amount of income any one of the three beneficiaries will receive rests entirely within the trustee's discretion and cannot be presently ascertained. Accordingly, no exclusions are allowable with respect to the transfers to the trust.

Example (4). Under the terms of a trust the net income is to be paid to F for life, with the remainder payable to G on F's death. The trustee has the uncontrolled power to pay over the corpus to F at any time. Although F's present right to receive the income may be terminated, no other person has the right to such income interest. Accordingly, the power in the trustee is disregarded in determining the value of F's present interest. The power would not be disregarded to the extent that the trustee during F's life could distribute corpus to persons other than F.

Example (5). The corpus of a trust created by J consists of certain real property, subject to a mortgage. The terms of the trust provide that the net income from the property is to be used to pay the mortgage. After the mortgage is paid in full the net income is to be paid to K during his lifetime. Since K's right to receive the income payments will not begin until after the mortgage is paid in full the transfer in trust represents a gift of a future interest in property against which no exclusion is allowable.

Example (6). L pays premiums on a policy of insurance on his life. All the incidents of ownership in the policy (including the right to surrender the policy) are vested in M. The payment of premiums by L constitutes a gift of a present interest in property. [Reg. § 25.2503-3.]

☐ [*T.D.* 6334, 11-14-58. *Amended by T.D.* 7238, 12-28-72, *T.D.* 7910, 9-6-83 *and T.D.* 9923, 11-18-2020.]

[Reg. §25.2503-4]

§25.2503-4. Transfer for the benefit of a minor.—(a) Section 2503(c) provides that no part of a transfer for the benefit of a donee who has not attained the age of 21 years on the date of the gift will be considered a gift of a future interest in property if the terms of the transfer satisfy all of the following conditions:

(1) Both the property itself and its income may be expended by or for the benefit of the donee before he attains the age of 21 years;

(2) Any portion of the property and its income not disposed of under (1) will pass to the donee when he attains the age of 21 years; and

(3) Any portion of the property and its income not disposed of under (1) will be payable either to the estate of the donee or as he may appoint under a general power of appointment as defined in section 2514(c) if he dies before attaining the age of 21 years.

(b) Either a power of appointment exercisable by the donee by will or a power of appointment exercisable by the donee during his lifetime will satisfy the conditions set forth in paragraph (a)(3) of this section. However, if the transfer is to qualify for the exclusion under this section, there must be no restrictions of substance (as distinguished from formal restrictions of the type described in paragraph (g)(4) of §25.2523(e)-1) by the terms of the instrument of transfer on the exercise of the power by the donee. However, if the minor is given a power of appointment exercisable during lifetime or is given a power of appointment exercisable by will, the fact that under the local law a minor is under a disability to exercise an inter vivos power or to execute a will does not cause the transfer to fail to satisfy the conditions of section 2503(c). Further, a transfer does not fail to satisfy the conditions of section 2503(c) by reason of the mere fact that—

(1) There is left to the discretion of a trustee the determination of the amounts, if any, of the income or property to be expended for the benefit of the minor and the purpose for which the expenditure is to be made, provided there are no substantial restrictions under the terms of the trust instrument on the exercise of such discretion;

(2) The donee, upon reaching age 21, has the right to extend the term of the trust; or

(3) The governing instrument contains a disposition of the property or income not expended during the donee's minority to persons other than the donee's estate in the event of the default of appointment by the donee.

(c) A gift to a minor which does not satisfy the requirements of section 2503(c) may be either a present or a future interest under the general rules of §25.2503-3. Thus, for example, a transfer of property in trust with income required to be paid annually to a minor beneficiary and corpus to be distributed to him upon his attaining the age of 25 is a gift of a present interest with respect to the right to income but is a gift of a future interest with respect to the right to corpus. [Reg. §25.2503-4.]

☐ [*T.D.* 6334, 11-14-58.]

[Reg. §25.2503-6]

§25.2503-6. Exclusion for certain qualified transfer for tuition or medical expenses.—(a) *In general.*—Section 2503(e) provides that any qualified transfer after December 31, 1981, shall not be treated as a transfer of property by gift for purposes of chapter 12 of subtitle B of the Code. Thus, a qualified transfer on behalf of any individual is excluded in determining the total amount of gifts in calendar year 1982 and subsequent years. This exclusion is available in addition to the $10,000 annual gift tax exclusion. Furthermore, an exclusion for a qualified transfer is permitted without regard to the relationship between the donor and the donee. A contribution to an ABLE account established under section 529A is not a qualified transfer.

(b) *Qualified transfers.*—(1) *Definition.*—For purposes of this paragraph, the term "qualified transfer" means any amount paid on behalf of an individual—

(i) As tuition to a qualifying educational organization for the education or training of that individual, or

(ii) To any person who provides medical care with respect to that individual as payment for the qualifying medical expenses arising from such medical care.

(2) *Tuition expenses.*—For purposes of paragraph (b)(1)(i) of this section, a qualifying educational organization is one which normally maintains a regular faculty and curriculum and normally has a regularly enrolled body of pupils or students in attendance at the place where its educational activities are regularly carried on. See section 170(b)(1)(A)(ii) and the regulations thereunder. The unlimited exclusion is permitted for tuition expenses of full-time or part-time students paid directly to the qualifying educational organization providing the education. No unlimited exclusion is permitted for amounts paid for books, supplies, dormitory fees, board, or other similar expenses which do not constitute direct tuition costs.

(3) *Medical expenses.*—For purposes of paragraph (b)(1)(ii) of this section, qualifying medical expenses are limited to those expenses defined in section 213(d) (section 213(e) prior to January 1, 1984) and include expenses incurred for the diagnosis, cure, mitigation, treatment or prevention of disease, or for the purpose of affecting any structure or function of the body or for transportation primarily for and essential to medical care. In addition, the unlimited exclusion from the gift tax includes amounts paid for medical insurance on behalf of any individual. The unlimited exclusion from the gift tax does not apply to amounts paid for medical care that are reimbursed by the donee's insurance. Thus, if payment for a medical expense is reimbursed by the donee's insurance company, the donor's pay-

ment for that expense, to the extent of the reimbursed amount, is not eligible for the unlimited exclusion from the gift tax and the gift is treated as having been made on the date the reimbursement is received by the donee.

(c) *Examples.*—The provisions of paragraph (b) of this section may be illustrated by the following examples.

Example (1). In 1982, A made a tuition payment directly to a foreign univerity on behalf of B. A had no legal obligation to make this payment. The foreign university is described in section 170(b)(1)(A)(ii) of the Code. A's tuition payment is exempt from the gift tax under section 2503(e) of the Code.

Example (2). A transfers $100,000 to a trust the provisions of which state that the funds are to be used for tuition expenses incurred by A's grandchildren. A's transfer to the trust is a completed gift for Federal gift tax purposes and is not a direct transfer to an educational organization as provided in paragraph (b)(2) of this section and does not qualify for the unlimited exclusion from gift tax under section 2503(e).

Example (3). C was seriously injured in an automobile accident in 1982. D, who is unrelated to C, paid C's various medical expenses by checks made payable to the physician. D also paid the hospital for C's hospital bills. These medical and hospital expenses were types described in section 213 of the Code and were not reimbursed by insurance or otherwise. Because the medical and hospital bills paid in 1982 for C were medical expenses within the meaning of section 213 of the Code, and since they were paid directly by D to the person rendering the medical care, they are not treated as transfers subject to the gift tax.

Example (4). Assume the same facts as in example (2) except that instead of making the payments directly to the medical service provider, D reimbursed C for the medical expenses which C had previously paid. The payments made by D to C do not qualify for the exclusion under section 2503(e) of the Code and are subject to the gift tax on the date the reimbursement is received by C to the extent the reimbursement and all other gifts from D to C during the year of the reimbursement exceed the $10,000 annual exclusion provided in section 2503(b). [Reg. §25.2503-6.]

☐ [*T.D.* 7978, 9-28-84. *Amended by T.D.* 9923, 11-18-2020.]

[Reg. §25.2504-1]

§25.2504-1. Taxable gifts for preceding calendar periods.—(a) In order to determine the correct gift tax liability for any calendar period it is necessary to ascertain the correct amount, if any, of the aggregate sum of the taxable gifts for each of the "preceding calendar periods" (as defined in §25.2502-1(c)(2)). See paragraph (a) of §25.2502-1. The term aggregate sum of the taxable gifts for each of the preceding calendar periods means the correct aggregate of such gifts, not necessarily that returned for those calendar periods and in respect of which tax was paid. All transfers that constituted gifts in prior calendar periods under the laws, including the provisions of law relating to exclusions from gifts, in effect at the time the transfers were made are included in determining the amount of taxable gifts for preceding calendar periods. The deductions other than for the specific exemption (see paragraph (b) of this section) allowed by the laws in effect at the time the transfers were made also are taken into account in determining the aggregate sum of the taxable gifts for preceding calendar periods. (The allowable exclusion from a gift is $5,000 for years before 1939, $4,000 for the calendar years 1939 through 1942, $3,000 for the calendar years 1943 through 1981, and $10,000 thereafter.)

(b) In determining the aggregate sum of the taxable gifts for the "preceding calendar periods" (as defined in §25.2502-1(c)(2)), the total of the amounts allowed as deductions for the specific exemption, under section 2521 (as in effect prior to its repeal by the Tax Reform Act of 1976) and the corresponding provisions of prior laws, shall not exceed $30,000. Thus, if the only prior gifts by a donor were made in 1940 and 1941 (at which time the specific exemption allowable was $40,000), and if in the donor's returns for those years the donor claimed deductions totaling $40,000 for the specific exemption and reported taxable gifts totaling $110,000, then in determining the aggregate sum of the taxable gifts for the preceding calendar period: the deductions for the specific exemption cannot exceed $30,000, and the donor's taxable gifts for such periods will be $120,000 (instead of the $110,000 reported on his returns). (The allowable deduction for the specific exemption was $50,000 for calendar years before 1936, $40,000 for calendar years 1936 through 1942, and $30,000 for 1943 through 1976.)

(c) If the donor and the donor's spouse consented to have gifts made to third parties considered as made one-half by each spouse, pursuant to the provisions of section 2513 or section 1000(f) of the Internal Revenue Code of 1939 (which corresponds to section 2513), these provisions shall be taken into account in determining the aggregate sum of the taxable gifts for the preceding calendar periods (under paragraph (a) of this section).

(d) If interpretations of the gift tax law in preceding calendar periods resulted in the erroneous inclusion of property for gift tax purposes that should have been excluded, or the erroneous exclusion of property that should have been included, adjustments must be made in order to arrive at the correct aggregate of taxable gifts for the preceding calendar periods (under paragraph (a) of this section). However, see §25.2504-2(b) regarding certain gifts made after August 5, 1997. [Reg. §25.2504-1.]

☐ [*T.D.* 6334, 11-14-58. *Amended by T.D.* 7238, 12-28-72; *T.D.* 7910, 9-6-83 *and T.D.* 8845, 12-2-99.]

[Reg. § 25.2504-2]

§ 25.2504-2. Determination of gifts for preceding calendar periods.—(a) *Gifts made before August 6, 1997.*—If the time has expired within which a tax may be assessed under chapter 12 of the Internal Revenue Code (or under corresponding provisions of prior laws) on the transfer of property by gift made during a preceding calendar period, as defined in § 25.2502-1(c)(2), the gift was made prior to August 6, 1997, and a tax has been assessed or paid for such prior calendar period, the value of the gift, for purposes of arriving at the correct amount of the taxable gifts for the preceding calendar periods (as defined under § 25.2504-1(a)), is the value used in computing the tax for the last preceding calendar period for which a tax was assessed or paid under chapter 12 of the Internal Revenue Code or the corresponding provisions of prior laws. However, this rule does not apply where no tax was paid or assessed for the prior calendar period. Furthermore, this rule does not apply to adjustments involving issues other than valuation. See § 25.2504-1(d).

(b) *Gifts made or section 2701(d) taxable events occurring after August 5, 1997.*—If the time has expired under section 6501 within which a gift tax may be assessed under chapter 12 of the Internal Revenue Code (or under corresponding provisions of prior laws) on the transfer of property by gift made during a preceding calendar period, as defined in § 25.2502-1(c)(2), or with respect to an increase in taxable gifts required under section 2701(d) and § 25.2701-4, and the gift was made, or the section 2701(d) taxable event occurred, after August 5, 1997, the amount of the taxable gift or the amount of the increase in taxable gifts, for purposes of determining the correct amount of taxable gifts for the preceding calendar periods (as defined in § 25.2504-1(a)), is the amount that is finally determined for gift tax purposes (within the meaning of § 20.2001-1(c) of this chapter) and such amount may not be thereafter adjusted. The rule of this paragraph (b) applies to adjustments involving all issues relating to the gift including valuation issues and legal issues involving the interpretation of the gift tax law. For purposes of determining if the time has expired within which a gift tax may be assessed, see § 301.6501(c)-1(e) and (f) of this chapter.

(c) *Examples.*—The following examples illustrate the rules of paragraphs (a) and (b) of this section:

Example 1. (i) *Facts.* In 1996, A transferred closely-held stock in trust for the benefit of B, A's child. A timely filed a Federal gift tax return reporting the 1996 transfer to B. No gift tax was assessed or paid as a result of the gift tax annual exclusion and the application of A's available unified credit. In 2001, A transferred additional closely-held stock to the trust. A's Federal gift tax return reporting the 2001 transfer was timely filed and the transfer was adequately disclosed under § 301.6501(c)-1(f)(2) of this chapter. In computing the amount of taxable gifts, A claimed annual exclusions with respect to the transfers in 1996 and 2001. In 2003, A transfers additional property to B and timely files a Federal gift tax return reporting the gift.

(ii) *Application of the rule limiting adjustments to prior gifts.* Under section 2504(c), in determining A's 2003 gift tax liability, the amount of A's 1996 gift can be adjusted for purposes of computing prior taxable gifts, since that gift was made prior to August 6, 1997, and therefore, the provisions of paragraph (a) of this section apply. Adjustments can be made with respect to the valuation of the gift and legal issues presented (for example, the availability of the annual exclusion with respect to the gift). However, A's 2001 transfer was adequately disclosed on a timely filed gift tax return and, thus, under paragraph (b) of this section, the amount of the 2001 taxable gift by A may not be adjusted (either with respect to the valuation of the gift or any legal issue) for purposes of computing prior taxable gifts in determining A's 2003 gift tax liability.

Example 2. (i) *Facts.* In 1996, A transferred closely-held stock to B, A's child. A timely filed a Federal gift tax return reporting the 1996 transfer to B and paid gift tax on the value of the gift reported on the return. On August 1, 1997, A transferred additional closely-held stock to B in exchange for a promissory note signed by B. Also, on September 10, 1997, A transferred closely-held stock to C, A's other child. On April 15, 1998, A timely filed a gift tax return for 1997 reporting the September 10, 1997, transfer to C and, under § 301.6501(c)-1(f)(2) of this chapter, adequately disclosed that transfer and paid gift tax with respect to the transfer. However, A believed that the transfer to B on August 1, 1997, was for full and adequate consideration and A did not report the transfer to B on the 1997 Federal gift tax return. In 2002, A transfers additional property to B and timely files a Federal gift tax return reporting the gift.

(ii) *Application of the rule limiting adjustments to prior gifts.* Under section 2504(c), in determining A's 2002 gift tax liability, the value of A's 1996 gift cannot be adjusted for purposes of computing the value of prior taxable gifts, since that gift was made prior to August 6, 1997, and a timely filed Federal gift tax return was filed on which a gift tax was assessed and paid. However, A's prior taxable gifts can be adjusted to reflect the August 1, 1997, transfer because, although a gift tax return for 1997 was timely filed and gift tax was paid, under § 301.6501(c)-1(f) of this chapter the period for assessing gift tax with respect to the August 1, 1997, transfer did not commence to run since that transfer was not adequately disclosed on the 1997 gift tax return. Accordingly, a gift tax may be assessed with respect to the August 1, 1997, transfer and the amount of the gift would be reflected in prior taxable gifts for purposes of computing A's gift tax liability for 2002. A's September 10, 1997, transfer to C was adequately disclosed on a timely filed gift tax return and, thus, under paragraph (b) of this section, the amount of the September 10, 1997, taxable gift by A may not be adjusted for purposes of computing prior taxable gifts in determining A's 2002 gift tax liability.

Example 3. (i) *Facts.* In 1994, A transferred closely-held stock to B and C, A's children. A timely filed a Federal gift tax return reporting the 1994 transfers to B and C and paid gift tax on the value of the gifts reported on the return. Also in 1994, A transferred closely-held stock to B in exchange for a bona fide promissory note signed by B. A believed that the transfer to B in exchange for the promissory note was for full and adequate consideration and A did not report that transfer to B on the 1994 Federal gift tax return. In 2002, A transfers additional property to B and timely files a Federal gift tax return reporting the gift.

(ii) *Application of the rule limiting adjustments to prior gifts.* Under section 2504(c), in determining A's 2002 gift tax liability, the value of A's 1994 gifts cannot be adjusted for purposes of computing prior taxable gifts because those gifts were made prior to August 6, 1997, and a timely filed Federal gift tax return was filed with respect to which a gift tax was assessed and paid, and the period of limitations on assessment has expired. The provisions of paragraph (a) of this section apply to the 1994 transfers. However, for purposes of determining A's adjusted taxable gifts in computing A's estate tax liability, the gifts may be adjusted. See § 20.2001-1(a) of this chapter.

(d) *Effective dates.*—Paragraph (a) of this section applies to transfers of property by gift made prior to August 6, 1997. Paragraphs (b) and (c) of this section apply to transfers of property by gift made after August 5, 1997, if the gift tax return for the calendar period in which the transfer is reported is filed after December 3, 1999. [Reg. § 25.2504-2.]

☐ [*T.D.* 6334, 11-14-58. *Amended by T.D.* 7238, 12-28-72; *T.D.* 7910, 9-6-83 *and T.D.* 8845, 12-2-99.]

[Reg. § 25.2505-0]

§ 25.2505-0. Table of contents.—This section lists the table of contents for §§ 25.2505-1 and 25.2505-2.

[Reg. § 25.2505-0.]

☐ [*T.D.* 9725, 6-12-2015.]

[Reg. § 25.2505-1]

§ 25.2505-1. Unified credit against gift tax; in general.—(a) *General rule.*—Section 2505(a) allows a citizen or resident of the United States a credit against the tax imposed by section 2501 for each calendar year. The allowable credit is the applicable credit amount in effect under section 2010(c) that would apply if the donor died as of the end of the calendar year, reduced by the sum of the amounts allowable as a credit against the gift tax due for all preceding calendar periods. See §§ 25.2505-2, 20.2010-1, and 20.2010-2 for additional rules and definitions related to determining the applicable credit amount in effect under section 2010(c).

(b) *Applicable rate of tax.*—In determining the amounts allowable as a credit against the gift tax due for all preceding calendar periods, the unified rate schedule under section 2001(c) in effect for such calendar year applies instead of the rates of tax actually in effect for preceding calendar periods. See sections 2505(a) and 2502(a)(2).

(c) *Special rule in case of certain gifts made before 1977.*—The applicable credit amount allowable under paragraph (a) of this section must be reduced by an amount equal to 20 percent of the aggregate amount allowed as a specific exemption under section 2521 (as in effect before its repeal by the Tax Reform Act of 1976) for gifts made by the decedent after September 8, 1976, and before January 1, 1977.

(d) *Credit limitation.*—The applicable credit amount allowed under paragraph (a) of this section for any calendar year shall not exceed the amount of the tax imposed by section 2501 for such calendar year.

(e) *Effective/applicability date.*—This section applies to gifts made on or after June 12, 2015. See 26 CFR 25.2505-1T, as contained in 26 CFR part 25, revised as of April 1, 2015, for the rules applicable to gifts made on or after January 1, 2011, and before June 12, 2015. [Reg. § 25.2505-1.]

☐ [*T.D.* 9725, 6-12-2015.]

[Reg. § 25.2505-2]

§ 25.2505-2. Gifts made by a surviving spouse having a DSUE amount available.—(a) *Donor who is surviving spouse is limited to DSUE amount of last deceased spouse.*—(1) *In general.*—In computing a surviving spouse's gift tax liability with regard to a transfer subject to the tax imposed by section 2501 (taxable gift), a deceased spousal unused exclusion (DSUE) amount of a decedent, computed under § 20.2010-2(c), is included in determining the surviving spouse's applicable exclusion amount under section 2010(c)(2), provided:

(i) Such decedent is the last deceased spouse of such surviving spouse within the meaning of § 20.2010-1(e)(5) at the time of the surviving spouse's taxable gift; and

(ii) The executor of the decedent's estate elected portability (see § 20.2010-2(a) and (b) for applicable requirements).

(2) *No DSUE amount available from last deceased spouse.*—If on the date of the surviving spouse's taxable gift the last deceased spouse of such surviving spouse had no DSUE amount or if the executor of the estate of such last deceased spouse did not elect portability, the surviving spouse has no DSUE amount (except as and to the extent provided in paragraph (c)(1)(ii) of this section) to be included in determining his or her applicable exclusion amount, even if the surviving spouse previously had a DSUE amount available from another decedent who, prior to the death of the last deceased spouse, was the last deceased spouse of such surviving spouse. See paragraph (c) of this section for a special rule in the case of multiple deceased spouses.

(3) *Identity of last deceased spouse unchanged by subsequent marriage or divorce.*—A decedent is the last deceased spouse (as defined in § 20.2010-1(e)(5)) of a surviving spouse even if, on the date of the surviving spouse's taxable gift, the surviving spouse is married to another (then-living) individual. If a surviving spouse marries again and that marriage ends in divorce or an annulment, the subsequent death of the divorced spouse does not end the status of the prior deceased spouse as the last deceased spouse of the surviving spouse. The divorced spouse, not being married to the surviving spouse at death, is not the last deceased spouse as that term is defined in § 20.2010-1(e)(5).

(b) *Manner in which DSUE amount is applied.*—If a donor who is a surviving spouse makes a taxable gift and a DSUE amount is included in determining the surviving spouse's applicable exclusion amount under section 2010(c)(2), such surviving spouse will be considered to apply such DSUE amount to the taxable gift before the surviving spouse's own basic exclusion amount.

(c) *Special rule in case of multiple deceased spouses and previously-applied DSUE amount.*—(1) *In general.*—A special rule applies to compute the DSUE amount included in the applicable exclusion amount of a surviving spouse who previously has applied the DSUE amount of one or more deceased spouses. If a surviving spouse applied the DSUE amount of one or more (successive) last deceased spouses to the surviving spouse's previous lifetime transfers, and if any of those last deceased spouses is different from the surviving spouse's last deceased spouse as defined in § 20.2010-1(e)(5) at the time of the current taxable gift by the surviving spouse, then the DSUE amount to be included in determining the applicable exclusion amount of the surviving spouse that will be applicable at the time of the current taxable gift is the sum of—

(i) The DSUE amount of the surviving spouse's last deceased spouse as described in paragraph (a)(1) of this section; and

(ii) The DSUE amount of each other deceased spouse of the surviving spouse to the extent that such amount was applied to one or more previous taxable gifts of the surviving spouse.

(2) *Example.*—The following example, in which all described individuals are U.S. citizens, illustrates the application of this paragraph (c):

Example. (i) *Facts.* Husband 1 (H1) dies in 2011, survived by Wife (W). Neither has made any taxable gifts during H1's lifetime. H1's executor elects portability of H1's deceased spousal unused exclusion (DSUE) amount. The DSUE amount of H1 as computed on the estate tax return filed on behalf of H1's estate is $5,000,000. In 2012, W makes taxable gifts to her children valued at $2,000,000. W reports the gifts on a timely filed gift tax return. W is considered to have applied $2,000,000 of H1's DSUE amount to the 2012 taxable gifts, in accordance with paragraph (b) of this section, and, therefore, W owes no gift tax. W is considered to have an applicable exclusion amount remaining in the amount of $8,120,000 ($3,000,000 of H1's remaining DSUE amount plus W's own $5,120,000 basic exclusion amount). In 2013, W marries Husband 2 (H2). H2 dies on June 30, 2015. H2's executor elects portability of H2's DSUE amount, which is properly computed on H2's estate tax return to be $2,000,000.

(ii) *Application.* The DSUE amount to be included in determining the applicable exclusion amount available to W for gifts during the second half of 2015 is $4,000,000, determined by adding the $2,000,000 DSUE amount of H2 and the $2,000,000 DSUE amount of H1 that was applied by W to W's 2012 taxable gifts. Thus, W's applicable exclusion amount during the balance of 2015 is $9,430,000 ($4,000,000 DSUE plus $5,430,000 basic exclusion amount for 2015).

(d) *Date DSUE amount taken into consideration by donor who is a surviving spouse.*—(1) *General rule.*—A portability election made by an executor of a decedent's estate (see § 20.2010-2(a) and (b) for applicable requirements) generally applies as of the date of such decedent's death. Thus, the decedent's DSUE amount is included in the applicable exclusion amount of the decedent's surviving spouse under section 2010(c)(2) and will be applicable to transfers made by the surviving spouse after the decedent's death (subject to the limitations in paragraph (a) of this section). However, such decedent's DSUE amount will not be included in the applicable exclusion amount of the surviving spouse, even if the surviving spouse had made a taxable gift in reliance on the availability or computation of the decedent's DSUE amount:

(i) If the executor of the decedent's estate supersedes the portability election by filing a subsequent estate tax return in accordance with § 20.2010-2(a)(4);

(ii) To the extent that the DSUE amount subsequently is reduced by a valuation adjustment or the correction of an error in calculation; or

(iii) To the extent that the DSUE amount claimed on the decedent's return cannot be determined.

(2) *Exception when surviving spouse not a U.S. citizen on date of deceased spouse's death.*—If a surviving spouse becomes a citizen of the United States after the death of the surviving spouse's last deceased spouse, the DSUE amount of the surviving spouse's last deceased spouse becomes available to the surviving spouse on the date the surviving spouse becomes a citizen of the United States (subject to the limitations in paragraph (a) of this section). However, when the special rule regarding qualified domestic trusts in paragraph (d)(3) of this section applies, the earliest date on which a decedent's DSUE amount may be included in the applicable exclusion amount of such decedent's surviving spouse who becomes a U.S. citizen is as provided in paragraph (d)(3) of this section.

(3) *Special rule when property passes to surviving spouse in a qualified domestic trust.*—(i) *In general.*—When property passes from a decedent for the benefit of the decedent's surviving spouse in one or more qualified domestic trusts (QDOT) as defined in section 2056A(a) and the decedent's executor elects portability, the DSUE amount available to be included in the applicable exclusion amount of the surviving spouse under section 2010(c)(2) is the DSUE amount of the decedent as redetermined in accordance with § 20.2010-2(c)(4) (subject to the limitations in paragraph (a) of this section). The earliest date on which such decedent's DSUE amount may be included in the applicable exclusion amount of the surviving spouse under section 2010(c)(2) is the date of the occurrence of the final QDOT distribution or final other event (generally, the termination of all QDOTs created by or funded with assets passing from the decedent or the death of the surviving spouse) on which tax under section 2056A is imposed. However, the decedent's DSUE amount as redetermined in accordance with § 20.2010-2(c)(4) may be applied to the surviving spouse's taxable gifts made in the year of the surviving spouse's death or, if the terminating event occurs prior to the surviving spouse's death, then in the year of that terminating event and/or in any subsequent year during the surviving spouse's life.

(ii) *Surviving spouse becomes a U.S. citizen.*—If a surviving spouse for whom property has passed from a decedent in one or more QDOTs becomes a citizen of the United States and the requirements in section 2056A(b)(12) and the corresponding regulations are satisfied, then the date on which such decedent's DSUE amount may be included in the applicable exclusion amount of the surviving spouse under section 2010(c)(2) (subject to the limitations in paragraph (a) of this section) is the date on which the surviving spouse becomes a citizen of the United States. See § 20.2010-2(c)(4) for the rules for computing the decedent's DSUE amount in the case of a qualified domestic trust.

(iii) *Example.*—The following example illustrates the application of this paragraph (d)(3):

Example. (i) *Facts.* Husband (H), a U.S. citizen, dies in 2011 having made no taxable gifts during his lifetime. H's gross estate is $3,000,000. H's wife (W) is not a citizen of the United States and, under H's will, a pecuniary bequest of $2,000,000 passes to a QDOT for the benefit of W. H's executor timely files an estate tax return and makes the QDOT election for the property passing to the QDOT, and H's estate is allowed a marital deduction of $2,000,000 under section 2056(d) for the value of that property. H's taxable estate is $1,000,000. On H's estate tax return, H's executor computes H's preliminary DSUE amount to be $4,000,000. No taxable events within the meaning of section 2056A occur during W's lifetime with respect to the QDOT, and W resides in the United States at all times after H's death. W makes a taxable gift of $1,000,000 to X in 2012 and a taxable gift of $1,000,000 to Y in January 2015, in each case from W's own assets rather than from the QDOT. W dies in September 2015, not having married again, when the value of the assets of the QDOT is $2,200,000.

(ii) *Application.* H's DSUE amount is redetermined to be $1,800,000 (the lesser of the $5,000,000 basic exclusion amount for 2011, or the excess of H's $5,000,000 applicable exclusion amount over $3,200,000 (the sum of the $1,000,000 taxable estate augmented by the $2,200,000 of QDOT assets)). On W's gift tax return filed for 2012, W cannot apply any DSUE amount to the gift made to X. However, because W's gift to Y was made in the year that W died, W's executor will apply $1,000,000 of H's redetermined DSUE amount to the gift on W's gift tax return filed for 2015. The remaining $800,000 of H's redetermined DSUE amount is included in W's applicable exclusion amount to be used in computing W's estate tax liability.

(e) *Authority to examine returns of deceased spouses.*—For the purpose of determining the DSUE amount to be included in the applicable exclusion amount of a surviving spouse, the Internal Revenue Service (IRS) may examine returns of each of the surviving spouse's deceased spouses whose DSUE amount is claimed to be included in the surviving spouse's applicable exclusion amount, regardless of whether the period of limitations on assessment has expired for any such return. The IRS's authority to examine returns of a deceased spouse applies with respect to each transfer by the surviving spouse to which a DSUE amount is or has been applied. Upon examination, the IRS may adjust or eliminate the DSUE amount reported on such a return of a deceased spouse; however, the IRS may assess additional tax on that return only if that tax is assessed within the period of limitations on assessment under section 6501 applicable to the tax shown on that return. See also section 7602 for the IRS's authority, when ascertaining the correctness of any return, to examine any returns that may be relevant or material to such inquiry.

(f) *Availability of DSUE amount for nonresidents who are not citizens.*—A nonresident surviving spouse who was not a citizen of the United States at the time of making a transfer subject to tax under chapter 12 of the Internal Revenue Code shall not take into account the DSUE amount of any deceased spouse except to the extent allowed under any applicable treaty obligation of the United States. See section 2102(b)(3).

(g) *Effective/applicability date.*—This section applies to gifts made on or after June 12, 2015. See 26 CFR 25.2505-2T, as contained in 26 CFR part 25, revised as of April 1, 2015, for the rules applicable to gifts made on or after January 1, 2011, and before June 12, 2015. [Reg. § 25.2505-2.]

□ [*T.D.* 9725, 6-12-2015 (*corrected* 2-5-2020).]

TRANSFERS

[Reg. § 25.2511-1]

§ 25.2511-1. Transfers in general.—(a) The gift tax applies to a transfer by way of gift whether the transfer is in trust or otherwise, whether the gift is direct or indirect, and whether the property is real or personal, tangible or intangible. For example, a taxable transfer may be effected by the creation of a trust, the forgiving of a debt, the assignment of a judgment, the assignment of the benefits of an insurance policy, or the transfer of cash, certificates of deposit, or Federal, State or municipal bonds. Statutory provisions which exempt bonds, notes, bills and certificates of indebtedness of the Federal Government or its agencies and the interest thereon from taxation are not applicable to the gift tax, since the gift tax is an excise tax on the transfer, and is not a tax on the subject of the gift.

(b) In the case of a gift by a nonresident not a citizen of the United States—

(1) If the gift was made on or after January 1, 1967, by a donor who was not an expatriate to whom section 2501(a)(2) was inapplicable on the date of the gift by reason of section 2501(a)(3) and paragraph (a)(3) of § 25.2501-1, or

(2) If the gift was made before January 1, 1967, by a donor who was not engaged in business in the United States during the calendar year in which the gift was made,

the gift tax applies only if the gift consisted of real property or tangible personal property situated within the United States at the time of the transfer. See § § 25.2501-1 and 25.2511-3.

(c)(1) The gift tax also applies to gifts indirectly made. Thus, any transaction in which an interest in property is gratuitously passed or conferred upon another, regardless of the means or device employed, constitutes a gift subject to tax. See further § 25.2512-8 relating to transfers for insufficient consideration. However, in the case of a transfer creating an interest in property (within the meaning of § 25.2518-2(c)(3) and (c)(4)) made after December 31, 1976, this paragraph (c)(1) shall not apply to the donee if, as a result of a qualified disclaimer by the donee, the interest passes to a different donee. Nor shall it apply to a donor if, as a result of a qualified disclaimer by the donee, a completed transfer of an interest in property is not effected. See section 2518 and the corresponding regulations for rules relating to a qualified disclaimer.

(2) In the case of taxable transfers creating an interest in the person disclaiming made before January 1, 1977, where the law governing the administration of the decedent's estate gives a beneficiary, heir, or next-of-kin a right completely and unqualifiedly to refuse to accept ownership of property transferred from a decedent (whether the transfer is effected by the decedent's will or by the law of descent and distribution), a refusal to accept ownership does not constitute the making of a gift if the refusal is made within a reasonable time after knowledge of the existence of the transfer. The refusal must be unequivocal and effective under the local law. There can be no refusal of ownership of property after its acceptance. In the absence of the facts to the contrary, if a person fails to refuse to accept a transfer to him of ownership of a decedent's property within a reasonable time after learning of the existence of the transfer, he will be presumed to have accepted the property. Where the local law does not permit such a refusal, any disposition by the beneficiary, heir, or next-of-kin whereby ownership is transferred gratuitously to another constitutes the making of a gift by the beneficiary, heir, or next-of-kin. In any case where a refusal is purported to relate to only a part of the property, the determination of whether or not there has been a complete and unqualified refusal to accept ownership will depend on all of the facts and circumstances in each particular case, taking into account the recognition and effectiveness of such a purported refusal under the local law. In illustration, if Blackacre was devised to A under the decedent's will (which also provided that all lapsed legacies and devises shall go to B, the residuary beneficiary), and under the local law A could refuse to accept ownership in which case title would be

considered as never having passed to A, A's refusal to accept Blackacre within a reasonable time of learning of the devise will not constitute the making of a gift by A to B. However, if a decedent who owned Greenacre died intestate with C and D as his only heirs, and under local law the heir of a decedent cannot, by refusal to accept, prevent himself from becoming an owner of intestate property, any gratuitous disposition by C (by whatever term it is known) whereby he gives up his ownership of a portion of Greenacre and D acquires the whole thereof constitutes the making of a gift by C to D.

(3) The fourth sentence of paragraph (c)(1) of this section is applicable for transfers creating an interest to be disclaimed made on or after December 31, 1997.

(d) If a joint income tax return is filed by a husband and wife for a taxable year, the payment by one spouse of all or part of the income tax liability for such year is not treated as resulting in a transfer which is subject to gift tax. The same rule is applicable to the payment of gift tax for a "calendar period" (as defined in §25.2502-1(c)(1)) in the case of a husband and wife who have consented to have the gifts made considered as made half by each of them in accordance with the provisions of section 2513.

(e) If a donor transfers by gift less than his entire interest in property, the gift tax is applicable to the interest transferred. The tax is applicable, for example, to the transfer of an undivided half interest in property, or to the transfer of a life estate when the grantor retains the remainder interest, or vice versa. However, if the donor's retained interest is not susceptible of measurement on the basis of generally accepted valuation principles, the gift tax is applicable to the entire value of the property subject to the gift. Thus, if a donor, aged 65 years, transfers a life estate in property to A, aged 25 years, with remainder to A's issue, or in default of issue, with reversion to the donor, the gift tax will normally be applicable to the entire value of the property.

(f) If a donor is the owner of only a limited interest in property, and transfers his entire interest, the interest is in every case to be valued by the rules set forth in §§25.2512-1 through 25.2512-7. If the interest is a remainder or reversion or other future interest, it is to be valued on the basis of actuarial principles set forth in §25.2512-5, or if it is not susceptible of valuation in that manner, in accordance with the principles set forth in §25.2512-1.

(g)(1) Donative intent on the part of the transferor is not an essential element in the application of the gift tax to the transfer. The application of the tax is based on the objective facts of the transfer and the circumstances under which it is made, rather than on the subjective motives of the donor. However, there are certain types of transfers to which the tax is not applicable. It is applicable only to a transfer of a beneficial interest in property. It is not applicable to a transfer of bare legal title to a trustee. A transfer by a trustee of trust property in which he has no beneficial interest does not constitute a gift by the trustee (but such a transfer may constitute a gift by the creator of the trust, if until the transfer he had the power to change the beneficiaries by amending or revoking the trust). The gift tax is not applicable to a transfer for a full and adequate consideration in money or money's worth, or to ordinary business transactions, described in §25.2512-8.

(2) If a trustee has a beneficial interest in trust property, a transfer of the property by the trustee is not a taxable transfer if it is made pursuant to a fiduciary power the exercise or nonexercise of which is limited by a reasonably fixed or ascertainable standard which is set forth in the trust instrument. A clearly measurable standard under which the holder of a power is legally accountable is such a standard for this purpose. For instance, a power to distribute corpus for the education, support, maintenance, or health of the beneficiary; for his reasonable support and comfort; to enable him to maintain his accustomed standard of living; or to meet an emergency, would be such a standard. However, a power to distribute corpus for the pleasure, desire, or happiness of a beneficiary is not such a standard. The entire context of a provision of a trust instrument granting a power must be considered in determining whether the power is limited by a reasonably definite standard. For example, if a trust instrument provides that the determination of the trustee shall be conclusive with respect to the exercise or nonexercise of a power, the power is not limited by a reasonably definite standard. However, the fact that the governing instrument is phrased in discretionary terms is not in itself an indication that no such a standard exists.

(h) The following are examples of transactions resulting in taxable gifts and in each case it is assumed that the transfers were not made for an adequate and full consideration in money or money's worth:

(1) A transfer of property by a corporation to B is a gift to B from the stockholders of the corporation. If B himself is a stockholder, the transfer is a gift to him from the other stockholders but only to the extent it exceeds B's own interest in such amount as a shareholder. A transfer of property by B to a corporation generally represents gifts by B to the other individual shareholders of the corporation to the extent of their proportionate interests in the corporation. However, there may be an exception to this rule, such as a transfer made by an individual to a charitable, public, political or similar organization which may constitute a gift to the organization as a single entity, depending upon the facts and circumstances in the particular case.

(2) The transfer of property to B if there is imposed upon B the obligation of paying a commensurate annuity to C is a gift to C.

(3) The payment of money or the transfer of property to B in consideration of B's promise to render a service to C is a gift to C, or to both B

and C, depending on whether the service to be rendered to C is or is not an adequate and full consideration in money or money's worth for that which is received by B. See section 2512(b) and the regulations thereunder.

(4) If A creates a joint bank account for himself and B (or a similar type of ownership by which A can regain the entire fund without B's consent), there is a gift to B when B draws upon the account for his own benefit, to the extent of the amount drawn without any obligation to account for a part of the proceeds to A. Similarly, if A purchases a United States savings bond, registered as payable to "A or B," there is a gift to B when B surrenders the bond for cash without any obligation to account for a part of the proceeds to A.

(5) If A with his own funds purchases property and has the title conveyed to himself and B as joint owners, with rights of survivorship (other than a joint ownership described in example (4)) but which rights may be defeated by either party severing his interest, there is a gift to B in the amount of half the value of the property. However, see § 25.2515-1 relative to the creation of a joint tenancy (or tenancy by the entirety) between husband and wife in real property with rights of survivorship which, unless the donor elects otherwise, is not considered as a transfer includible for Federal gift tax purposes at the time of the creation of the joint tenancy. See § 25.2515-2 with respect to determining the extent to which the creation of a tenancy by the entirety constitutes a taxable gift if the donor elects to have the creation of the tenancy so treated. See also § 25.2523(d)-1 with respect to the marital deduction allowed in the case of the creation of a joint tenancy or a tenancy by the entirety.

(6) If A is possessed of a vested remainder interest in property, subject to being divested only in the event he should fail to survive one or more individuals or the happening of some other event, an irrevocable assignment of all or any part of his interest would result in a transfer includible for Federal gift tax purposes. See especially § 25.2512-5 for the valuation of an interest of this type.

(7) If A, without retaining a power to revoke the trust or to change the beneficial interests therein, transfers property in trust whereby B is to receive the income for life and at his death the trust is to terminate and the corpus is to be returned to A, provided A survives, but if A predeceases B the corpus is to pass to C, A has made a gift equal to the total value of the property less the value of his retained interest. See § 25.2512-5 for the valuation of the donor's retained interest.

(8) If the insured purchases a life insurance policy, or pays a premium on a previously issued policy, the proceeds of which are payable to a beneficiary or beneficiaries other than his estate, and with respect to which the insured retains no reversionary interest in himself or his estate and no power to revest the economic benefits in himself or his estate or to change the beneficiaries or their proportionate benefits (or if the insured relinquishes by assignment, by designation of a new beneficiary or otherwise, every such power that was retained in a previously issued policy), the insured has made a gift of the value of the policy, or to the extent of the premium paid, even though the right of the assignee or beneficiary to receive the benefits is conditioned upon his surviving the insured. For the valuation of life insurance policies see § 25.2512-6.

(9) Where property held by a husband and wife as community property is used to purchase insurance upon the husband's life and a third person is revocably designated as beneficiary and under the State law the husband's death is considered to make absolute the transfer by the wife, there is a gift by the wife at the time of the husband's death of half the amount of the proceeds of such insurance.

(10) If under a pension plan (pursuant to which he has an unqualified right to an annuity) an employee has an option to take either a retirement annuity for himself alone or a smaller annuity for himself with a survivorship annuity payable to his wife, an irrevocable election by the employee to take the reduced annuity in order that an annuity may be paid, after the employee's death, to his wife results in the making of a gift. However, see section 2517 and the regulations thereunder for the exemption from gift tax of amounts attributable to employers' contributions under qualified plans and certain other contracts. [Reg. § 25.2511-1.]

☐ [*T.D.* 6334, 11-14-58. *Amended by T.D.* 6542, 1-19-61; *T.D.* 7150, 12-1-71; *T.D.* 7238, 12-28-72; *T.D.* 7296, 12-11-73; *T.D.* 7910, 9-6-83; *T.D.* 8095, 8-6-86; *T.D.* 8540, 6-9-94 *and T.D.* 8744, 12-30-97.]

[Reg. § 25.2511-2]

§ 25.2511-2. Cessation of donor's dominion and control.—(a) The gift tax is not imposed upon the receipt of the property by the donee, nor is it necessarily determined by the measure of enrichment resulting to the donee from the transfer, nor is it conditioned upon ability to identify the donee at the time of the transfer. On the contrary, the tax is a primary and personal liability of the donor, is an excise upon his act of making the transfer, is measured by the value of the property passing from the donor, and attaches regardless of the fact that the identity of the donee may not then be known or ascertainable. For gift tax rules related to an ABLE account established under section 529A, see § 1.529A-4 of this chapter.

(b) As to any property, or part thereof or interest therein, of which the donor has so parted with dominion and control as to leave in him no power to change its disposition, whether for his own benefit or for the benefit of another, the gift is complete. But if upon a transfer of property (whether in trust or otherwise) the donor reserves any power over its disposition, the gift may be wholly incomplete, or may be partially complete and partially incomplete, depending upon all the facts in the particular case. Accordingly, in every case of a transfer of property subject to a reserved power, the terms of the power must be examined and its scope determined. For example, if a donor transfers property to another in trust to pay the income to the donor or accumulate it in the discretion of the trustee, and the donor retains a testamentary power to appoint the remainder among his descendants, no portion of the transfer is a completed gift. On the other hand, if the donor had not retained the testamentary power of appointment, but instead provided that the remainder should go to X or his heirs, the entire transfer would be a completed gift. However, if the exercise of the trustee's power in favor of the grantor is limited by a fixed or ascertainable standard (see paragraph (g)(2) of § 25.2511-1), enforceable by or on behalf of the grantor, then the gift is incomplete to the extent of the ascertainable value of any rights thus retained by the grantor.

(c) A gift is incomplete in every instance in which a donor reserves the power to revest the beneficial title to the property in himself. A gift is also incomplete if and to the extent that a reserved power gives the donor the power to name new beneficiaries or to change the interests of the beneficiaries as between themselves unless the power is a fiduciary power limited by a fixed or ascertainable standard. Thus, if an estate for life is transferred but, by an exercise of a power, the estate may be terminated or cut down by the donor to one of less value, and without restriction upon the extent to which the estate may be so cut down, the transfer constitutes an incomplete gift. If in this example the power was confined to the right to cut down the estate for life to one for a term of five years, the certainty of an estate for not less than that term results in a gift to that extent complete.

(d) A gift is not considered incomplete, however, merely because the donor reserves the power to change the manner or time of enjoyment. Thus, the creation of a trust the income of which is to be paid annually to the donee for a period of years, the corpus being distributable to him at the end of the period, and the power reserved by the donor being limited to a right to require that, instead of the income being so payable, it should be accumulated and distributed with the corpus to the donee at the termination of the period, constitutes a completed gift.

(e) A donor is considered as himself having a power if it is exercisable by him in conjunction with any person not having a substantial adverse interest in the disposition of the transferred property or the income therefrom. A trustee, as such, is not a person having an adverse interest in the disposition of the trust property or its income.

(f) The relinquishment or termination of a power to change the beneficiaries of transferred property, occurring otherwise than by the death of the donor (the statute being confined to transfers by living donors), is regarded as the event which completes the gift and causes the tax to apply. For example, if A transfers property in trust for the benefit of B and C but reserves the power as trustee to change the proportionate interests of B and C, and if A thereafter has another person appointed trustee in place of himself, such later relinquishment of the power by A to the new trustee completes the gift of the transferred property, whether or not the new trustee has a substantial adverse interest. The receipt of income or of other enjoyment of the transferred property by the transferee or by the beneficiary (other than by the donor himself) during the interim between the making of the initial transfer and the relinquishment or termination of the power operates to free such income or other enjoyment from the power, and constitutes a gift of such income or of such other enjoyment taxable as of the "calendar period" (as defined in § 25.2502-1(c)(1). If property is transferred in trust to pay the income to A for life with remainder to B, powers to distribute corpus to A, and to withhold income from A for future distribution to B, are powers to change the beneficiaries of the transferred property.

(g) If a donor transfers property to himself as trustee (or to himself and some other person, not possessing a substantial adverse interest, as trustees), and retains no beneficial interest in the trust property and no power over it except fiduciary powers, the exercise or nonexercise of which is limited by a fixed or ascertainable standard, to change the beneficiaries of the transferred property, the donor has made a completed gift and the entire value of the transferred property is subject to the gift tax.

(h) If a donor delivers a properly indorsed stock certificate to the donee or the donee's agent, the gift is completed for gift tax purposes on the date of delivery. If the donor delivers the certificate to his bank or broker as his agent, or to the issuing corporation or its transfer agent, for transfer into the name of the donee, the gift is completed on the date the stock is transferred on the books of the corporation.

(i) [Reserved]

(j) If the donor contends that a power is of such nature as to render the gift incomplete, and hence not subject to the tax as of the calendar period (as defined in § 25.2502-1(c)(1)) of the initial transfer, see § 301.6501(c)-1(f)(5) of this chapter. [Reg. § 25.2511-2.]

☐ [*T.D.* 6334, 11-14-58. *Amended by T.D.* 7238, 12-28-72; *T.D.* 7910, 9-6-83, *T.D.* 8845, 12-2-99 *and T.D.* 9923, 11-18-2020.]

[Reg. § 25.2511-3]

§ 25.2511-3. Transfers by nonresidents not citizens.—(a) *In general.*—Sections 2501 and 2511 contain rules relating to the taxation of transfers of property by gift by a donor who is a nonresident not a citizen of the United States. (See paragraph(b) of § 25.2501-1 for the definition of the term "resident" for purposes of the gift tax.) As combined these rules are:

(1) The gift tax applies only to the transfer of real property and tangible personal property

situated in the United States at the time of the transfer if either—

(i) The gift was made on or after January 1, 1967, by a nonresident not a citizen of the United States who was not an expatriate to whom section 2501(a)(2) was inapplicable on the date of the gift by reason of section 2501(a)(3) and paragraph (a)(3) of § 25.2501-1, or

(ii) The gift was made before January 1, 1967, by a nonresident not a citizen of the United States who was not engaged in business in the United States during the calendar year in which the gift was made.

(2) The gift tax applies to the transfer of all property (whether real or personal, tangible or intangible) situated in the United States at the time of the transfer if either—

(i) The gift was made on or after January 1, 1967, by a nonresident not a citizen of the United States who was an expatriate to whom section 2501(a)(2) was inapplicable on the date of the gift by reason of section 2501(a)(3) and paragraph (a)(3) of § 25.2501-1, or

(ii) The gift was made before January 1, 1967, by a nonresident not a citizen of the United States who was engaged in business in the United States during the calendar year in which the gift was made.

(b) *Situs of property.*—For purposes of applying the gift tax to the transfer of property owned and held by a nonresident not a citizen of the United States at the time of the transfer—

(1) *Real property and tangible personal property.*—Real property and tangible personal property constitute property within the United States only if they are physically situated therein.

(2) *Intangible personal property.*—Except as provided otherwise in subparagraphs (3) and (4) of this paragraph, intangible personal property constitutes property within the United States if it consists of a property right issued by or enforceable against a resident of the United States or a domestic corporation (public or private), irrespective of where the written evidence of the property is physically located at the time of the transfer.

(3) *Shares of stock.*—Irrespective of where the stock certificates are physically located at the time of the transfer—

(i) Shares of stock issued by a domestic corporation constitute property within the United States, and

(ii) Shares of stock issued by a corporation which is not a domestic corporation constitute property situated outside the United States.

(4) *Debt obligations.*—(i) In the case of gifts made on or after January 1, 1967, a debt obligation, including a bank deposit, the primary obligor of which is a United States person (as defined in section 7701(a)(30)), the United States, a State, or any political subdivision thereof, the District of Columbia, or any agency or instrumentality of any such government constitutes property situated within the United States. This subdivision applies—

(a) In the case of a debt obligation of a domestic corporation, whether or not any interest on the obligation would be treated under section 862(a)(1) as income from sources without the United States by reason of section 861(a)(1)(B) (relating to interest received from a domestic corporation less than 20 percent of whose gross income for a 3-year period was derived from sources within the United States) and the regulations thereunder;

(b) In the case of an amount described in section 861(c) (relating to certain bank deposits, withdrawable accounts, and amounts held by an insurance company under an agreement to pay interest), whether or not any interest thereon would be treated under section 862(a)(1) as income from sources without the United States, by reason of section 861(a)(1)(A) (relating to interest on amounts described in section 861(c) which is not effectively connected with the conduct of a trade or business within the United States) and the regulations thereunder;

(c) In the case of a deposit with a domestic corporation or domestic partnership, whether or not the deposit is with a foreign branch thereof engaged in the commercial banking business; and

(d) Irrespective of where the written evidence of the debt obligation is physically located at the time of the transfer.

For purposes of this subdivision, a debt obligation on which there are two or more primary obligors shall be apportioned among such obligors, taking into account to the extent appropriate under all the facts and circumstances any choate or inchoate rights of contribution existing among such obligors with respect to the indebtedness. The term "agency or instrumentality," as used in this subdivision, does not include a possession of the United States or an agency or instrumentality of a possession.

(ii) In the case of gifts made on or after January 1, 1967, a debt obligation, including a bank deposit, not deemed under subdivision (i) of this subparagraph to be situated within the United States, constitutes property situated outside the United States.

(iii) In the case of gifts made before January 1, 1967, a debt obligation the written evidence of which is treated as being the property itself constitutes property situated within the United States if the written evidence of the obligation is physically located in the United States at the time of the transfer, irrespective of who is the primary obligor on the debt. If the written evidence of the obligation is physically located outside the United States, the debt obligation constitutes property situated outside the United States.

(iv) Currency is not a debt obligation for purposes of this subparagraph. [Reg. § 25.2511-3.]

☐ [*T.D.* 6334, 11-14-58. *Amended by T.D.* 6542, 1-19-61; *T.D.* 7238, 12-28-72 *and T.D.* 7296, 12-11-73.]

[Reg. § 25.2512-0]

§ 25.2512-0. Table of contents.—This section lists the section headings that appear in the regulations under section 2512.

[Reg. § 25.2512-0.]

☐ [*T.D.* 8540, 6-9-94. *Amended by T.D.* 8819, 4-29-99; *T.D.* 8886, 6-9-2000; *T.D.* 9448, 5-1-2009 *and T.D.* 9540, 8-9-2011.]

[Reg. § 25.2512-1]

§ 25.2512-1. Valuation of property; in general.—Section 2512 provides that if a gift is made in property, its value at the date of the gift shall be considered the amount of the gift. The value of the property is the price at which such property would change hands between a willing buyer and a willing seller, neither being under any compulsion to buy or to sell, and both having reasonable knowledge of relevant facts. The value of a particular kind of property is not the price that a forced sale of the property would produce. Nor is the fair market value of an item of property the sale price in a market other than that in which such item is most commonly sold to the public, taking into account, the location of the item wherever appropriate. Thus, in the case of an item of property made the subject of a gift, which is generally obtained by the public in the retail market, the fair market value of such an item of property is the price at which the item or a comparable item would be sold at retail. For example, the value of an automobile (an article generally obtained by the public in the retail market) which is the subject of a gift, is the price for which an automobile of the same or approximately the same description, make, model, age, condition, etc., could be purchased by a member of the general public and not the price for which the particular automobile of the donor would be purchased by a dealer in used automobiles. Examples of items of property which are generally sold to the public at retail may be found in § 25.2512-6. The value is generally to be determined by ascertaining as a basis the fair market value at the time of the gift of each unit of the property. For example, in the case of shares of stocks or bonds, such unit of property is generally a share or a bond. Property shall not be returned at the value at which it is assessed for local tax purposes unless that value represents the fair market value thereof on the date of the gift. All relevant facts and elements of value as of the time of the gift shall be considered. Where the subject of a gift is an interest in a business, the value of items of property in the inventory of the business generally should be reflected in the value of the business. For valuation of interests in businesses, see § 25.2512-3. See § 25.2512-2 and §§ 25.2512-4 through 25.2512-6 for further information concerning the valuation of other particular kinds of property. See section 2701 and the regulations at § 25.2701 for special rules for valuing transfers of an interest in a corporation or a partnership and for the treatment of unpaid qualified payments at the subsequent transfer of an applicable retained interest by the transferor or by an applicable family member. See section 2704(b) and the regulations at § 25.2704-2 for special valuation rules where an interest in property is subject to an applicable restriction. [Reg. § 25.2512-1.]

☐ [*T.D.* 6334, 11-14-58. *Amended by T.D.* 6826, 6-14-65 *and T.D.* 8395, 1-28-92.]

[Reg. § 25.2512-2]

§ 25.2512-2. Stocks and bonds.—(a) *In general.*—The value of stocks and bonds is the fair market value per share or bond on the date of the gift.

(b) *Based on selling prices.*—(1) In general, if there is a market for stocks or bonds, on a stock exchange, in an over-the-counter market or otherwise, the mean between the highest and lowest quoted selling prices on the date of the gift is the fair market value per share or bond. If there were no sales on the date of the gift but there were sales on dates within a reasonable period both before and after the date of the gift, the fair market value is determined by taking a weighted average of the means between the highest and lowest sales on the nearest date before and the nearest date after the date of the gift. The average is to be weighted inversely by the respective numbers of trading days between the selling dates and the date of the gift. If the stocks or bonds are listed on more than one exchange, the records of the exchange where the stocks or bonds are principally dealt in should be employed if such records are available in a generally available listing or publication of general circulation. In the event such records are not so available and such stocks or bonds are listed on a composite listing of combined exchanges available in a generally available listing or publication of general circulation, the records of such combined exchanges should be employed. In valuing listed securities, the donor should be careful to consult accurate records to obtain values as of the date of the gift. If quotations of unlisted securities are obtained from brokers, or evidence as to their sale is obtained from the officers of the issuing companies, copies of letters furnishing such quotations or evidence of sale should be attached to the return.

(2) If it is established with respect to bonds for which there is a market on a stock exchange, that the highest and lowest selling prices are not available for the date of the gift in a generally available listing or publication of general circulation but that closing prices are so available, the fair market value per bond is the mean between the quoted closing selling price on the date of the gift and the quoted closing selling price on the trading day before the date of the gift. If there were no sales on the trading day before the date of the gift but there were sales on dates within a reasonable period before the date of the gift, the fair market value is determined by taking a weighted average of the quoted closing selling prices on the date of the gift and the nearest date before the date of the gift. The closing selling price for the date of the gift is to be weighted by the respective number of trading days between the previous selling date and the date of the gift. If there were no sales within a reasonable period before the date of the gift but there were sales on the date of the gift, the fair market value is the closing selling price on the date of the gift. If there were no sales on the date of the gift but there were sales within a reasonable period both before and after the date of the gift, the fair market value is determined by taking a weighted average of the quoted closing selling prices on the nearest date before and the nearest date after the date of the gift. The average is to be weighted inversely by the respective numbers of trading days between the selling dates and the date of the gift. If the bonds are listed on more than one exchange, the records of the exchange where the bonds are principally dealt in should be employed. In valuing listed securities, the donor should be careful to consult accurate records to obtain values as of the date of the gift.

(3) The application of this paragraph may be illustrated by the following examples:

Example (1). Assume that sales of stock nearest the date of the gift (Friday, June 15) occurred two trading days before (Wednesday, June 13) and three trading days after (Wednesday, June 20) and on these days the mean sale prices per share were $10 and $15, respectively. The price of $12 is taken as representing the fair market value of a share of stock as of the date of the gift

$$\frac{((3 \times 10) + (2 \times 15)).}{5}$$

Example (2). Assume the same facts as in example 1 except that the mean sale prices per share on June 13 and June 20 were $15 and $10 respectively. The price of $13 is taken as representing the fair market value of a share of stock as of the date of the gift

$$\frac{(3 \times 15) + (2 \times 10).}{5}$$

Example (3). Assume that on the date of the gift (Tuesday, April 3, 1973) the closing selling price of certain listed bonds was $25 per bond and that the highest and lowest selling prices are not available in a generally available listing or publication of general circulation for that date. Assume further, that the closing selling price of such bonds was $21 per bond on the day before the date of the gift (Monday, April 2, 1973). Thus, under paragraph (b)(2) of this section, the price of $23 is taken as representing the fair market value per bond as of the date of the gift

$$\frac{(25 + 21).}{2}$$

Example (4). Assume the same facts as in example 3 except that there were no sales on the day before the date of the gift. Assume further, that there were sales on Thursday, March 29, 1973, and that the closing selling price on that day was $23. The price of $24.50 is taken as representing the fair market value per bond as of the date of the gift

$$\frac{((1 \times 23) + (3 \times 25)).}{4}$$

Example (5). Assume that no bonds were traded on the date of the gift (Friday, April 20). Assume further, that sales of bonds nearest the date of the gift occurred two trading days before (Wednesday, April 18) and three trading days after (Wednesday, April 25) the date of the gift and that on these two days the closing selling prices per bond were $29 and $22, respectively. The highest and lowest selling prices are not available for these dates in a generally available listing or publication of general circulation. Thus, under paragraph (b)(2) of this section the price of $26.20 is taken as representing the fair market value of a bond as of the date of the gift

$$\frac{((3 \times 29) + (2 \times 22)).}{5}$$

(c) *Based on bid and asked prices.*—If the provisions of paragraph (b) of this section are inapplicable because actual sales are not available during a reasonable period beginning before and ending after the date of the gift, the fair market value may be determined by taking the mean between the bona fide bid and asked prices on the date of the gift, or if none, by taking a weighted average of the means between the bona fide bid and asked prices on the nearest trading date before and the nearest trading date after the date of the gift, if both such nearest dates are within a reasonable period. The average is to be determined in the manner described in paragraph (b) of this section.

(d) *Where selling prices and bid and asked prices are not available for dates both before and after the date of gift.*—If the provisions of paragraphs (b) and (c) of this section are inapplicable because no actual sale prices or quoted bona fide bid and asked prices are available on a date within a reasonable period before the date of the gift, but such prices are available on a date within a reasonable period after the date of the gift, or vice versa, then the mean between the highest and lowest available sale prices or bid and asked prices may be taken as the value.

(e) *Where selling prices or bid and asked prices do not represent fair market value.*—In cases in which it is established that the value per bond or share of any security determined on the basis of the selling or bid and asked prices as provided under paragraphs (b), (c), and (d) of this section does not represent the fair market value thereof, then some reasonable modification of the value determined on that basis or other relevant facts and elements of value shall be considered in determining fair market value. Where sales at or near the date of the gift are few or of a sporadic nature, such sales alone may not indicate fair market value. In certain exceptional cases, the size of the block of securities made the subject of each separate gift in relation to the number of shares changing hands in sales may be relevant in determining whether selling prices reflect the fair market value of the block of stock to be valued. If the donor can show that the block of stock to be valued, with reference to each separate gift, is so large in relation to the actual sales on the existing market that it could not be liquidated in a reasonable time without depressing the market, the price at which the block could be sold as such outside the usual market, as through an underwriter, may be a more accurate indication of value than market quotations. Complete data in support of any allowance claimed due to the size of the block of stock being valued should be submitted with the return. On the other hand, if the block of stock to be valued represents a controlling interest, either actual or effective, in a going business, the price at which other lots change hands may have little relation to its true value.

(f) *Where selling prices or bid and asked prices are unavailable.*—If the provisions of paragraphs (b), (c), and (d) of this section are inapplicable because actual sale prices and bona fide bid and asked prices are lacking, then the fair market value is to be determined by taking the following factors into consideration:

(1) In the case of corporate or other bonds, the soundness of the security, the interest yield, the date of maturity, and other relevant factors; and

(2) In the case of shares of stock, the company's net worth, prospective earning power and dividend-paying capacity, and other relevant factors.

Some of the "other relevant factors" referred to in subparagraphs (1) and (2) of this paragraph are: the good will of the business; the economic outlook in the particular industry; the company's position in the industry and its management; the degree of control of the business represented by the block of stock to be valued; and the values of securities of corporations engaged in the same or similar lines of business which are listed on a stock exchange. However, the weight to be accorded such comparisons or any other evidentiary factors considered in the determination of a value depends upon the facts of each case. Complete financial and other data upon which the valuation is based should be submitted with the return, including copies of reports of any examinations of the company have been made by accountants, engineers, or any technical experts as of or near the date of the gift. [Reg. §25.2512-2.]

☐ [*T.D.* 6334, 11-14-58. *Amended by T.D.* 7327, 9-30-74 *and by T.D.* 7432, 9-10-76.]

[Reg. §25.2512-3]

§25.2512-3. Valuation of interests in businesses.—(a) Care should be taken to arrive at an accurate valuation of any interest in a business which the donor transfers without an adequate and full consideration in money or money's worth. The fair market value of any interest in a business, whether a partnership or a proprietorship, is the net amount which a willing purchaser, whether an individual or a corporation, would pay for the interest to a willing seller, neither being under any compulsion to buy or to sell and both having reasonable knowledge of the relevant facts. The net value is determined on the basis of all relevant factors including—

(1) A fair appraisal as of the date of the gift of all the assets of the business, tangible and intangible, including good will;

(2) The demonstrated earning capacity of the business; and

(3) The other factors set forth in paragraph (f) of §25.2512-2 relating to the valuation of corporate stock, to the extent applicable.

Special attention should be given to determining an adequate value of the good will of the business. Complete financial and other data upon which the valuation is based should be submitted with the return, including copies of reports of examinations of the business made by accountants, engineers, or any technical experts as of or near the date of the gift. [Reg. §25.2512-3.]

☐ [*T.D.* 6334, 11-14-58.]

[Reg. §25.2512-4]

§25.2512-4. Valuation of notes.—The fair market value of notes, secured or unsecured, is presumed to be the amount of unpaid principal, plus accrued interest to the date of the gift, unless the donor establishes a lower value. Unless returned at face value, plus accrued interest, it must be shown by satisfactory evidence that the note is worth less than the unpaid amount (because of the interest rate, or date of maturity, or other cause), or that the note is uncollectible in part (by reason of the insolvency of the party or parties liable, or for other cause), and that the property, if any, pledged or mortgaged as security is insufficient to satisfy it. [Reg. §25.2512-4.]

☐ [*T.D.* 6334, 11-14-58.]

[Reg. §25.2512-5]

§25.2512-5. Valuation of annuities, unitrust interests, interests for life or term of years, and remainder or reversionary interests.—(a) *In general.*—Except as otherwise provided in paragraph(b) of this section and §25.7520-3(b), the fair market value of annuities, unitrust interests, life estates, terms of years, remainders, and reversions transferred by gift is the present value of the interests determined under paragraph (d) of this section. Section 20.2031-7 of this chapter (Estate Tax Regulations) and related sections provide tables with standard actuarial factors and examples that illustrate how to use the tables to compute the present value of ordinary annuity, life, and remainder interests in property. These sections also refer to standard and special actuarial factors that may be necessary to compute the present value of similar interests in more unusual fact situations. These factors and examples are also generally applicable for gift tax purposes in computing the values of taxable gifts.

(b) *Commercial annuities and insurance contracts.*—The value of life insurance contracts and contracts for the payment of annuities issued by companies regularly engaged in their sale is determined under §25.2512-6.

(c) *Actuarial valuations.*—The present value of annuities, unitrust interests, life estates, terms of years, remainders, and reversions transferred by gift on or after May 1, 2009, is determined under paragraph (d) of this section. The present value of annuities, unitrust interests, life estates, terms of years, remainders, and reversions transferred by gift before May 1, 2009, is determined under the following sections:

Transfers After	Transfers Before	Applicable Regulations
-	01-01-52	25.2512-5A(a)
12-31-51	01-01-71	25.2512-5A(b)
12-31-70	12-01-83	25.2512-5A(c)
11-30-83	05-01-89	25.2512-5A(d)
04-30-89	05-01-99	25.2512-5A(e)
04-30-99	05-01-09	25.2512-5A(f)

(d) *Actuarial valuations on or after May 1, 2009.*—(1) *In general.*—Except as otherwise provided in paragraph (b) of this section and §25.7520-3(b) (relating to exceptions to the use of prescribed tables under certain circumstances), if the valuation date for the gift is on or after May 1, 2009, the fair market value of annuities, life estates, terms of years, remainders, and reversions transferred on or after May 1, 2009, is the present value of such interests determined under paragraph (d)(2) of this section and by use of standard or special section 7520 actuarial factors. These factors are derived by using the appropriate section 7520 interest rate and, if applicable, the mortality component for the valuation date of the interest that is being valued. See §§25.7520-1 through 25.7520-4. The fair market value of a qualified annuity interest described in section 2702(b)(1) and a qualified unitrust interest described in section 2702(b)(2) is the present value of such interests determined under §25.7520-1(c).

(2) *Specific interests.*—When the donor transfers property in trust or otherwise and retains an interest therein, generally, the value of the gift is the value of the property transferred less the value of the donor's retained interest. However, if the donor transfers property after October 8, 1990, to or for the benefit of a member of the donor's family, the value of the gift is the value of the property transferred less the value of the donor's retained interest as determined under section 2702. If the donor assigns or relinquishes an annuity, life estate, remainder, or reversion that the donor holds by virtue of a transfer previously made by the donor or another, the value of the gift is the value of the interest transferred. However, see section 2519 for a special rule in the case of the assignment of an income interest by a person who received the interest from a spouse.

(i) *Charitable remainder trusts.*—The fair market value of a remainder interest in a pooled income fund, as defined in §1.642(c)-5 of this chapter, is its value determined under §1.642(c)-6(e) (see §1.642(c)-6A for certain prior periods). The fair market value of a remainder interest in a charitable remainder annuity trust, as described in §1.664-2(a), is its present value determined under §1.664-2(c). The fair market value of a remainder interest in a charitable remainder unitrust, as defined in §1.664-3, is its present value determined under §1.664-4(e). The fair market value of a life interest or term for years in a charitable remainder unitrust is the fair market value of the property as of the date of transfer less the fair market value of the remainder interest, determined under §1.664-4(e)(4) and (e)(5).

(ii) *Ordinary remainder and reversionary interests.*—If the interest to be valued is to take effect after a definite number of years or after the death of one individual, the present value of the interest is computed by multiplying the value of the property by the appropriate remainder interest actuarial factor (that corresponds to the applicable section 7520 interest rate and remainder interest period) in Table B (for a term certain) or in Table S (for one measuring life), as the case may be. Table B is contained in §20.2031-7(d)(6) of this chapter and Table S (for one measuring life when the valuation date is on or after May 1, 2009) is included in §20.2031-7(d)(7) and Internal

Revenue Service Publication 1457. See § 20.2031-7A containing Table S for valuation of interests before May 1, 2009. For information about obtaining actuarial factors for other types of remainder interests, see paragraph (d)(4) of this section.

(iii) *Ordinary term-of-years and life interests.*—If the interest to be valued is the right of a person to receive the income of certain property, or to use certain nonincome-producing property, for a term of years or for the life of one individual, the present value of the interest is computed by multiplying the value of the property by the appropriate term-of-years or life interest actuarial factor (that corresponds to the applicable section 7520 interest rate and term-of-years or life interest period). Internal Revenue Service Publication 1457 includes actuarial factors for a remainder interest after a term of years in Table B and after the life of one individual in Table S (for one measuring life when the valuation date is on or after May 1, 2009). However, term-ofyears and life interest actuarial factors are not included in Table B in § 20.2031-7(d)(6) of this chapter or Table S in § 20.2031-7(d)(7) (or in § 20.2031-7A). If Internal Revenue Service Publication 1457 (or any other reliable source of term-of-years and life interest actuarial factors) is not conveniently available, an actuarial factor for the interest may be derived mathematically. This actuarial factor may be derived by subtracting the correlative remainder factor (that corresponds to the applicable section 7520 interest rate) in Table B (for a term of years) in § 20.2031-7(d)(6) or in Table S (for the life of one individual) in § 20.2031-7(d)(7), as the case may be, from 1.000000. For information about obtaining actuarial factors for other types of term-of-years and life interests, see paragraph (d)(4) of this section.

(iv) *Annuities.*—(A) If the interest to be valued is the right of a person to receive an annuity that is payable at the end of each year for a term of years or for the life of one individual, the present value of the interest is computed by multiplying the aggregate amount payable annually by the appropriate annuity actuarial factor (that corresponds to the applicable section 7520 interest rate and annuity period). Internal Revenue Service Publication 1457 includes actuarial factors in Table B (for a remainder interest after an annuity payable for a term of years) and in Table S (for a remainder interest after an annuity payable for the life of one individual when the valuation date is on or after May 1, 2009). However, annuity actuarial factors are not included in Table B in § 20.2031-7(d)(6) of this chapter or Table S in § 20.2031-7(d)(7) (or in § 20.2031-7A). If Internal Revenue Service Publication 1457 (or any other reliable source of annuity actuarial factors) is not conveniently available, an annuity factor for a term of years or for one life may be derived mathematically. This annuity factor may be derived by subtracting the applicable remainder factor (that corresponds to the applicable section 7520 interest rate and annuity period) in Table B (in the case of a term-of-years annuity) in § 20.2031-7(d)(6) or in Table S (in the case of a one-life annuity) in § 20.2031-7(d)(7), as the case may be, from 1.000000 and then dividing the result by the applicable section 7520 interest rate expressed as a decimal number. See § 20.2031-7(d)(2)(iv) for an example that illustrates the computation of the present value of an annuity.

(B) If the annuity is payable at the end of semiannual, quarterly, monthly, or weekly periods, the product obtained by multiplying the annuity factor by the aggregate amount payable annually is then multiplied by the applicable adjustment factor set forth in Table K in § 20.2031-7(d)(6) at the appropriate interest rate component for payments made at the end of the specified periods. The provisions of this paragraph (d)(2)(iv)(B) are illustrated by the following example:

Example. In July of a year after 2009 but before 2019, the donor agreed to pay the annuitant the sum of $10,000 per year, payable in equal semiannual installments at the end of each period. The semiannual installments are to be made on each December 31st and June 30th. The annuity is payable until the annuitant's death. On the date of the agreement, the annuitant is 68 years and 5 months old. The donee annuitant's age is treated as 68 for purposes of computing the present value of the annuity. The section 7520 rate on the date of the agreement is 6.6 percent. Under Table S in § 20.2031-7(d)(7), the factor at 6.6 percent for determining the present value of a remainder interest payable at the death of an individual aged 68 is .42001. Converting the remainder factor to an annuity factor, as described above, the annuity factor for determining the present value of an annuity transferred to an individual age 68 is 8.7877 (1.000000 minus .42001 divided by .066). The adjustment factor from Table K in § 20.2031-7(d)(6) in the column for payments made at the end of each semiannual period at the rate of 6.6 percent is 1.0162. The aggregate annual amount of the annuity, $10,000, is multiplied by the factor 8.7877 and the product is multiplied by 1.0162. The present value of the donee's annuity is, therefore, $89,300.61 ($10,000 × 8.7877 × 1.0162).

(C) If an annuity is payable at the beginning of annual, semiannual, quarterly, monthly, or weekly periods for a term of years, the value of the annuity is computed by multiplying the aggregate amount payable annually by the annuity factor described in paragraph (d)(2)(iv)(A) of this section; and the product so obtained is then multiplied by the adjustment factor in Table J in § 20.2031-7(d)(6) of this chapter at the appropriate interest rate component for payments made at the beginning of specified periods. If an annuity is payable at the beginning of annual, semiannual, quarterly, monthly, or weekly periods for one or more lives, the value of the annuity is the sum of the first payment and the present value of a similar annuity, the first payment of which is not to be made until the end of the payment period, determined as provided in paragraph (d)(2)(iv)(B) of this section.

(v) *Annuity and unitrust interests for a term of years or until the prior death of an individual.*—

(A) *Annuity interests.*—The present value of an annuity interest that is payable until the earlier to occur of the lapse of a specific number of years or the death of an individual may be computed with values from the tables in §§ 20.2031-7(d)(6) and 20.2031-7(d)(7) of this chapter as described in the following example:

Example. The donor transfers $100,000 into a trust early in 2010, and retains the right to receive an annuity from the trust in the amount of $6,000 per year, payable in equal semiannual installments at the end of each period. The semiannual installments are to be made on each June 30th and December 31st.

The annuity is payable for 10 years or until the donor's prior death. At the time of the transfer, the donor is 59 years and 6 months old. The donor's age is deemed to be 60 for purposes of computing the present value of the retained annuity. If the section 7520 rate for the month in which the transfer occurs is 5.8 percent, the present value of the donor's retained interest would be $42,575.65, determined as follows:

TABLE S value at 5.8 percent, age 60	.34656
TABLE S value at 5.8 percent, age 70	.49025
TABLE 2000CM value at age 70	74794
TABLE 2000CM value at age 60	87595
TABLE B value at 5.8 percent, 10 years	.569041
TABLE K value at 5.8 percent	1.0143

Factor for donor's retained interest at 5.8 percent:

$$\frac{(1.00000 - .34656) - (.569041 \times (74794/87595) \times (1.00000 - .49025))}{.058} = 6.9959$$

Present value of donor's retained interest:

($6,000 × 6.9959 × 1.0143) $42,575.65

(B) *Unitrust interests.*—The present value of a unitrust interest that is payable until the earlier to occur of the lapse of a specific number of years or the death of an individual may be computed with values from the tables in §§ 1.664-4(e)(6) and 1.664-4(e)(7) of this chapter as described in the following example:

Example. The donor who, as of the nearest birthday, is 60 years old, transfers $100,000 to a unitrust on January 1st of a year after 2009 but before 2019. The trust instrument requires that each year the trust pay to the donor, in equal semiannual installments on June 30th and December 31st, 6 percent of the fair market value of the trust assets, valued as of January 1st each year, for 10 years or until the prior death of the donor. The section 7520 rate for the January in which the transfer occurs is 6.6 percent. Under Table F(6.6) in § 1.664-4(e)(6), the appropriate adjustment factor is .953317 for semiannual payments payable at the end of the semiannual period. The adjusted payout rate is 5.720 percent (6% × .953317). The present value of the donor's retained interest is $41,920.00 determined as follows:

TABLE U(1) value at 5.6 percent, age 60	.33970
TABLE U(1) value at 5.6 percent, age 70	.48352
TABLE 2000CM value at age 70	74794
TABLE 2000CM value at age 60	87595
TABLE D value at 5.6 percent, 10 years	.561979

Factor for donor's retained interest at 5.6 percent:

$$(1.000000 - .33970) - (.561979 \times (74794/87595) \times (1.000000 - .48352)) = .41247$$

TABLE U(1) value at 5.8 percent, age 60	.32846
TABLE U(1) value at 5.8 percent, age 70	.47241
TABLE 2000CM value at age 70	74794
TABLE 2000CM value at age 60	87595
TABLE D value at 5.8 percent, 10 years	.550185

Factor for donor's retained interest at 5.8 percent:

(1.000000 – .32846) – (.550185 × (74974/87595) × (1.000000 – .47241)) = .42369
Difference .... .01122

Interpolation adjustment:

$$\frac{5.720\% - 5.6\%}{0.2\%} = \frac{x}{.01122}$$

x = .00673

Factor at 5.6 percent, age 60	.41247
Plus: Interpolation adjustment	.00673
Interpolated Factor	.41920

Present value of donor's retained interest:

($100,000 × .41920) $41,920.00

(3) *Transitional rule.*—If the valuation date of a transfer of property by gift is on or after May 1, 2009, and before July 1, 2009, the fair market value of the interest transferred is determined by use of the section 7520 interest rate for the month in which the valuation date occurs (see §§25.7520-1(b) and 25.7520-2(a)(2)) and the appropriate actuarial tables under either §20.2031-7(d)(7) or §20.2031-7A(f)(4) of this chapter, at the option of the donor. However, with respect to each individual transaction and with respect to all transfers occurring on the valuation date, the donor must use the same actuarial tables (for example, gift and income tax charitable deductions with respect to the same transfer must be determined based on the same tables, and all transfers made on the same date must be valued based on the same tables).

(4) *Publications and actuarial computations by the Internal Revenue Service.*—Many standard actuarial factors not included in §20.2031-7(d)(6) or §20.2031-7(d)(7) of this chapter are included in Internal Revenue Service Publication 1457, "Actuarial Valuations Version 3A" (2009). Internal Revenue Service Publication 1457 also includes examples that illustrate how to compute many special factors for more unusual situations. A copy of this publication is available, at no charge, electronically via the IRS Internet site at *www.irs.gov.* If a special factor is required in the case of a completed gift, the Internal Revenue Service may furnish the factor to the donor upon a request for a ruling. The request for a ruling must be accompanied by a recitation of the facts including a statement of the date of birth for each measuring life, the date of the gift, any other applicable dates, and a copy of the will, trust, or other relevant documents. A request for a ruling must comply with the instructions for requesting a ruling published periodically in the Internal Revenue Bulletin (see §§601.201 and 601.601(d)(2)(ii)(b) of this chapter) and include payment of the required user fee.

(e) *Effective/applicability dates.*—This section applies on and after May 1, 2009. [Reg. §25.2512-5.]

☐ [*T.D.* 8540, 6-9-94. *Amended by T.D.* 8819, 4-29-99; *T.D.* 8886, 6-9-2000 (*corrected* 9-27-2000); *T.D.* 9448-5-1-2009 *and T.D.* 9540, 8-9-2011.]

[Reg. §25.2512-5A]

§25.2512-5A. Valuation of annuities, unitrust interests, interests for life or term of years, and remainder or reversionary interests transferred before May 1, 2009.—(a) *Valuation of annuities, interests for life or term of years, and remainder or reversionary interests transferred before January 1, 1952.*—Except as otherwise provided in §25.2512-5(b), if the transfer was made before January 1, 1952, the present value of annuities, life estates, terms of years, remainders, and reversions is their present value determined under this section. If the valuation of the interest involved is dependent upon the continuation or termination of one or more lives or upon a term certain concurrent with one or more lives, the factor for the present value is computed on the basis of interest at the rate of 4 percent a year, compounded annually, and life contingencies for each life involved from values that are based upon the "Actuaries' or Combined Experience Table of Mortality, as extended." This table and many additional factors are described in former §86.19 (as contained in the 26 CFR Part 81 edition revised as of April 1, 1958). The present value of an interest measured by a term of years is computed on the basis of interest at the rate of 4 percent a year.

(b) *Valuation of annuities, interests for life or term of years, and remainder or reversionary interests transferred after December 31, 1951, and before January 1, 1971.*—Except as otherwise provided in §25.2512-5(b), the present value of annuities, life estates, terms of years, remainders, and reversions transferred after December 31, 1951, and before January 1, 1971, is the present value of such interests determined under this section. If the value of the interest involved is dependent upon the continuation or termination of one or more lives, the factor for the present value is computed on the basis of interest at the rate of $3^1/_2$ percent a year, compounded annually, and life contingencies for each life involved from U.S.

Life Table 38. This table and many accompanying factors are set forth in former §25.2512-5 (as contained in the 26 CFR Part 25 edition revised as of April 1, 1984). Special factors involving one and two lives may be found in or computed with the use of tables contained in Internal Revenue Service Publication Number 11, "Actuarial Values for Estate and Gift Tax," (Rev. 5-59). This publication is no longer available for purchase from the Superintendent of Documents. However, it may be obtained by requesting a copy from: CC:DOM:CORP:T:R (IRS Publication 11), room 5228, Internal Revenue Service, POB 7604, Ben Franklin Station, Washington, DC 20044. The present value of an interest measured by a term of years is computed on the basis of interest at the rate of 3$^1/_2$ percent a year.

(c) *Valuation of annuities, interests for life or term of years, and remainder or reversionary interests transferred after December 31, 1970, and before December 1, 1983.*—Except as otherwise provided in §25.2512-5(b), the present value of annuities, life estates, terms of years, remainders, and reversions transferred after December 31, 1970, and before December 1, 1983, is the present value of such interests determined under this section. If the interest to be valued is dependent upon the continuation or termination of one or more lives or upon a term certain concurrent with one or more lives, the factor for the present value is computed on the basis of interest at the rate of 6 percent a year, compounded annually, and life contingencies determined for each male and female life involved, from the values that are set forth in Table LN. Table LN contains values that are taken from the life table for total males and the life table for total females appearing as Tables 2 and 3, respectively, in United States Life Tables: 1959-61, published by the Department of Health and Human Services, Public Health Service. Table LN and accompanying factors are set forth in former §25.2512-9 (as contained in the 26 CFR Part 25 edition revised as of April 1, 1994). Special factors involving one and two lives may be found in or computed with the use of tables contained in Internal Revenue Service Publication 723, entitled "Actuarial Values I: Valuation of Last Survivor Charitable Remainders" (12-70), and Internal Revenue Service Publication 723A, entitled "Actuarial Values II: Factors at 6 Percent Involving One and Two Lives" (12-70). These publications are no longer available for purchase from the Superintendent of Documents. However, a copy of each may be obtained from: CC:DOM:CORP:T:R (IRS Publication 723/723A), room 5228, Internal Revenue Service, POB 7604, Ben Franklin Station, Washington, DC 20044. The present value of an interest measured by a term of years is computed on the basis of interest at the rate of 6 percent a year.

(d) *Valuation of annuities, interests for life or term of years, and remainder or reversionary interests transferred after November 30, 1983, and before May 1, 1989.*—(1) *In general.*—(i)(A) Except as otherwise provided in §25.2512-5(b) and in this paragraph (d)(1)(i)(A), the fair market value of annuities, life estates, terms of years, remainders, and reversions transferred after November 30, 1983, and before May 1, 1989, is the present value of such interests determined under this section. The value of annuities issued by companies regularly engaged in their sale and of insurance policies issued by companies regularly engaged in their sale is determined under §25.2512-6. The fair market value of a remainder interest in a charitable remainder unitrust, as defined in §1.664-3, is its present value determined under §1.664-4. The fair market value of a life interest or term for years in a charitable remainder unitrust is the fair market value of the property as of the date of transfer less the fair market value of the remainder interest on such date determined under §1.664-4. The fair market value of interests in a pooled income fund, as defined in §1.642(c)-5, is their value determined under §1.642(c)-6. Where the donor transfers property in trust or otherwise and retains an interest therein, the value of the gift is the value of the property transferred less the value of the donor's retained interest. See section 2702 and the regulations at §25.2702 for special rules for valuing transfers of interests in trust after October 8, 1990. See §25.2512-9 with respect to the valuation of annuities, life estates, terms for years, remainders, and reversions transferred after December 31, 1970, and before December 1, 1983.

(B) If the donor transfers in December of 1983, either—

(1) A remainder or a reversion subject to a life interest or a term for years where the life interest or term for years was transferred by the donor after December 31, 1982, and before December 1, 1983, or

(2) A life interest or term for years, the remainder interest of which was transferred by the donor after December 31, 1982, and before December 1, 1983,

the donor shall make an election. The donor may elect to value both interests transferred in 1983 under §25.2512-5A(c) as if such section applied to all transfers made before January 1, 1984, or the donor may elect to have both interests transferred valued under this section. The donor shall indicate the election being made in a statement attached to the donor's gift tax return for 1983.

(C) If the donor transfers in calendar year 1984, either—

(1) A remainder on [or] a reversion subject to a life interest or a term for years where the life interest or term for years was transferred by the donor in the first eleven months of 1983, or

(2) A life interest or term for years, the remainder interest of which was transferred by the donor in the first eleven months of 1983,

the donor shall make an election. The donor may elect to value the interest transferred in 1984 under §25.2512-5A(c) as if such section applied to all transfers made before January 1, 1985, or the donor may elect to have the transfer valued under this section. If the donor elects to value the interest transferred in 1984 under § 25.2512-5A(c), the donor shall indicate that the election is being made by attaching a statement to the donor's gift tax return for 1984. If the donor elects to value the interest transferred in 1984 under this section the election shall not be effective unless the donor declares, in a statement attached to the donor's gift tax return for 1984, that the donor has filed an amended gift tax return for 1983, in which the donor has revalued the transfers made in the first eleven months of 1983 under this section as if this section applied to transfers made after December 31, 1982.

(ii) The present value of an annuity, life estate, remainder, or reversion determined under this section which is dependent on the continuation or termination of the life of one person is computed by the use of Table A in paragraph (d)(6) of this section. The present value of an annuity, term for years, remainder, or reversion dependent on a term certain is computed by the use of Table B in paragraph (d)(6) of this section. If the interest to be valued is dependent upon more than one life or there is a term certain concurrent with one or more lives, see paragraph (d)(5) of this section. For purposes of the computations described in this section, the age of the person is to be taken at his or her nearest birthday.

(iii) In all examples set forth in this section, the interest is assumed to have been transferred after November 30, 1983 and before May 1, 1989.

(2) *Annuities.*—(i) If an annuity is payable annually at the end of each year during the life of an individual (as for example if the first payment is due one year after the date of the gift), the amount payable annually is multiplied by the figure in column 2 of Table A opposite the number of years in column 1 nearest the age of the individual whose life measures the duration of the annuity. If the annuity is payable annually at the end of each year for a definite number of years, the amount payable annually is multiplied by the figure in column 2 of Table B opposite the number of years in column 1 representing the duration of the annuity.

The application of this paragraph (d)(2)(i) may be illustrated by the following examples:

Example (1). The donor assigns an annuity of $10,000 a year payable annually during the donor's life immediately after an annual payment has been made. The age of the donor on the date of assignment is 40 years and eight months. By reference to Table A, it is found that the figure in column 2 opposite 41 years is 9.1030. The value of the gift is, therefore, $91,030 ($10,000 multiplied by 9.1030).

Example (2). The donor was entitled to receive an annuity of $10,000 a year payable annually at the end of annual periods throughout a term of 20 years. The donor, when 15 years have elapsed, makes a gift thereof to the donor's son. By reference to Table B, it is found that the figure in column 2 opposite five years, the unexpired portion of the 20-year period, is 3.7906. The present value of the annuity is, therefore, $37,908 ($10,000 multiplied by 3.7908).

(ii) If an annuity is payable at the end of semiannual, quarterly, monthly, or weekly periods during the life of an individual (as for example if the first payment is due one month after the date of the gift), the aggregate amount to be paid within a year is first multiplied by the figure in column 2 of Table A opposite the number of years in column 1 nearest the age of the individual whose life measures the duration of the annuity. The product so obtained is then multiplied by whichever of the following factors is appropriate:

1.0244 for semiannual payments,
1.0368 for quarterly payments,
1.0450 for monthly payments,
1.0482 for weekly payments.

If the annuity is payable at the end of semiannual, quarterly, monthly, or weekly periods for a definite number of years the aggregate amount to be paid within a year is first multiplied by the figure in column 2 of Table B opposite the number of years in column 1 representing the duration of the annuity. The product so obtained is then multiplied by whichever of the above factors is appropriate. The application of this paragraph (d)(2)(ii) may be illustrated by the following example:

Example. The facts are the same as those contained in example (1) set forth in paragraph (d)(2)(i) above, except that the annuity is payable semiannually. The aggregate annual amount, $10,000[,] is multiplied by the factor 9.1030, and the product multiplied by 1.0244. The value of the gift is, therefore, $93,251.13 ($10,000 × 9.1030 × 1.0244).

(iii)(A) If the first payment of an annuity for the life of an individual is due at the beginning of the annual or other payment period rather than at the end (as for example if the first payment is to be made immediately after the date of the gift), the value of the annuity is the sum of (A) the first payment plus (B) the present value of a similar annuity, the first payment of which is not to be made until the end of the payment period, determined as provided in paragraphs (d)(2)(i) or (ii) of this section. The application of this paragraph (d)(2)(iii)(A) may be illustrated by the following example:

Example. The donee is made the beneficiary for life of an annuity of $50 a month from the income of a trust, subject to the right reserved by the donor to cause the annuity to be paid for the donor's own benefit or for the benefit of another. On the day a payment is due, the donor relinquishes the reserved power. The donee is then 50 years of age. The value of the gift is $50 plus the product of $50 × 12 × 8.4743 (see Table A) × 1:0450. That is, $50 plus $5,313.39, or $5,363.39.

(B) If the first payment of an annuity for a definite number of years is due at the beginning of the annual or other payment period, the applicable factor is the product of the factor shown in Table B multiplied by whichever of the following factors is appropriate:

1.1000 for annual payments,
1.0744 for semiannual payments,
1.0618 for quarterly payments,
1.0534 for monthly payments,or
1.0502 for weekly payments.

The application of this paragraph (d)(2)(iii)(B) may be illustrated by the following example:

Example. The donee is the beneficiary of an annuity of $50 a month, subject to a reserved right in the donor to cause the annuity or the cash value thereof to be paid for the donor's own benefit or the benefit of another. On the day a payment is due, the donor relinquishes the power. There are 308 payments to be made covering a period of 25 years, including the payment due. The value of the gift is the product of $50 × 12 × 9.0770 (factor for 25 years Table B) × 1.0534, or $5,737.03.

(3) *Life estates and terms for years.*—If the interest to be valued is the right of a person for his or her life, or for the life of another person, to receive the income of certain property or to use non-income-producing property, the value of the interest is the value of the property multiplied by the figure in column 3 of Table A opposite the number of years nearest to the actual age of the measuring life. If the interest to be valued is the right to receive income of property or to use non-income-producing property for a term of years, column 3 of Table B is used. The application of this paragraph (c) may be illustrated by the following example:

Example. The donor who during the donor's life is entitled to receive the income from property worth $50,000, makes a gift of such interest. The donor is 31 years old on the date of the gift. The value of the gift is $47,627 ($50,000 × .95254).

(4) *Remainders or reversionary interests.*—If the interest to be valued is a remainder or reversionary interest subject to a life estate, the value of the interest should be obtained by multiplying the value of the property at the date of the gift by the figure in column 4 of Table A opposite the number of years nearest the age of the life tenant. If the remainder or reversion is to take effect at the end of a term for years, column 4 of Table B should be used. The application of this paragraph (d) may be illustrated by the following example:

Example. The donor transfers by gift a remainder interest in property worth $50,000, subject to the donor's sister's right to receive the income therefrom for her life. The sister at the date of the gift is 31 years of age. By reference to Table A it is found that the figure in column 4 opposite age 31 is .04746. The value of the gift is, therefore, $2,373 ($50,000 × .04746).

(5) *Actuarial computations by the Internal Revenue Service.*—If the interest to be valued is dependent upon the continuation or termination of more than one life, or there is a term certain concurrent with one or more lives, or if the retained interest of the donor is conditioned upon survivorship, a special factor is necessary. The factor is to be computed on the basis of interest at the rate of 10 percent a year, compounded annually, and life contingencies are determined for each person involved from the values of *lx* that are set forth in column 2 of Table LN in § 20.2031-7A(d)(6) of this chapter. Table LN contains values of *lx* taken from the life table for the total population appearing as Table 1 in United States Life Tables: 1969-71, published by the Department of Health and Human Services, Public Health Service. A copy of the publication containing many such special factors, may be purchased from the Superintendent of Documents, United States Government Printing Office, Washington, D.C. 20402. However, if a special factor is required in the case of an actual gift, the Commissioner will furnish the factor to the donor upon request. The request must be accompanied by a statement of the date of birth of each person the duration of whose life may affect the value of the interest, and by copies of the relevant instruments. Special factors are not furnished for prospective transfers.

(6) *Tables.*—(i) For actuarial factors showing the present worth at 10 percent of a single life annuity, a life interest, and a remainder interest postponed for a single life, see § 20.2031-7A(d)(6) of this chapter, Table A, of the Estate Tax Regulations.

(ii) For actuarial factors showing the present worth at 10 percent of an annuity for a term certain, an income interest for a term certain, and a remainder interest postponed for a term certain, see § 20.2031-7A(d)(6) of this chapter, Table B, of the Estate Tax Regulations.

(e) *Valuation of annuities, unitrust interests, interests for life or term of years, and remainder or reversionary interests transferred after April 30, 1989, and before May 1, 1999.*—(1) *In general.*—Except as otherwise provided in §§ 25.2512-5(b) and 25.7520-3(b) (pertaining to certain limitations on the use of prescribed tables), if the valuation date of the transferred interest is after April 30, 1989, and before May 1, 1999, the fair market value of annuities, unitrust interests, life estates, terms of years, remainders, and reversions transferred by gift is the present value of the interests determined by use of standard or special section 7520 actuarial factors and the valuation methodology described in § 25.2512-5(d). Sections 20.2031-7(d)(6) and 20.2031-7A(e)(4) of this chapter and related sections provide tables with standard actuarial factors and examples that illustrate how to use the tables to compute the present value of ordinary annuity, life, and remainder interests in property. These sections also refer to standard and special actuarial factors that may be necessary to compute the present value of similar interests in more unusual fact situations. These factors and examples are also generally applicable for gift tax purposes in computing the values of taxable gifts.

(2) *Transitional rule.*—(i) If the valuation date of a transfer of an interest in property by gift is after April 30, 1989, and before June 10,

1994, a donor can rely on Notice 89-24 (1989-1 C.B. 660), or Notice 89-60 (1989-1 C.B. 700), in valuing the transferred interest. (See § 601.601(d)(2)(ii)(*b*) of this chapter.)

(ii) If a donor transferred an interest in property by gift after December 31, 1988, and before May 1, 1989, retaining an interest in the same property, and after April 30, 1989, and before January 1, 1990, transferred the retained interest in property, the donor may, at the option of the donor, value the transfer of the retained interest under this paragraph (e) or paragraph (d) of this section.

(3) *Publications and actuarial computations by the Internal Revenue Service.*—Many standard actuarial factors not included in § § 20.2031-7(d)(6) and 20.2031-7A(e)(4) of this chapter are included in Internal Revenue Service Publication 1457, "Actuarial Values, Alpha Volume," (8-89). Internal Revenue Service Publication 1457 also includes examples that illustrate how to compute many special factors for more unusual situations. Publication 1457 is no longer available for purchase from the Superintendent of Documents, United States Government Printing Office, Washington, DC 20402. However, pertinent factors in this publication may be obtained from: CC:DOM:CORP:R (IRS Publication 1457), room 5226, Internal Revenue Service, POB 7604, Ben Franklin Station, Washington, DC 20044. If a special factor is required in the case of a completed gift, the Internal Revenue Service may furnish the factor to the donor upon a request for a ruling. The request for a ruling must be accompanied by a recitation of the facts including a statement of the date of birth for each measuring life, the date of the gift, any other applicable dates, and a copy of the will, trust, or other relevant documents. A request for a ruling must comply with the instructions for requesting a ruling published periodically in the Internal Revenue Bulletin (see § § 601.201 and 601.601(d)(2)(ii)(*b*) of this chapter) and include payment of the required user fee.

(f) *Valuation of annuities, unitrust interests, interests for life or term of years, and remainder or reversionary interests transferred after April 30, 1999, and before May 1, 2009.*—(1) *In general.*—Except as otherwise provided in § § 25.2512-5(b) and 25.7520-3(b) (pertaining to certain limitations on the use of prescribed tables), if the valuation date of the transferred interest is after April 30, 1999, and before May 1, 2009, the fair market value of annuities, unitrust interests, life estates, terms of years, remainders, and reversions transferred by gift is the present value of the interests determined by use of standard or special section 7520 actuarial factors and the valuation methodology described in § 25.2512-5(d). Sections 20.2031-7(d)(6) and 20.2031-7A(f)(4) and related sections provide tables with standard actuarial factors and examples that illustrate how to use the tables to compute the present value of ordinary annuity, life, and remainder interests in property. These sections also refer to standard and special actuarial factors that may be necessary to compute the present value of similar interests in more unusual fact situations. These factors and examples are also generally applicable for gift tax purposes in computing the values of taxable gifts.

(2) *Transitional rule.*—If the valuation date of a transfer of property by gift is after April 30, 1999, and before July 1, 1999, the fair market value of the interest transferred is determined by use of the section 7520 interest rate for the month in which the valuation date occurs (see § § 25.7520-1(b) and 25.7520-2(a)(2) and the appropriate actuarial tables under either § 20.2031-7A(e)(4) or § 20.2031-7A(f)(4), at the option of the donor. However, with respect to each individual transaction and with respect to all transfers occurring on the valuation date, the donor must use the same actuarial tables (for example, gift and income tax charitable deductions with respect to the same transfer must be determined based on the same tables, and all transfers made on the same date must be valued based on the same tables).

(3) *Publications and actuarial computations by the Internal Revenue Service.*—Many standard actuarial factors not included in § § 20.2031-7(d)(6) and 20.2031-7A(f)(4) are included in Internal Revenue Service Publication 1457, "Actuarial Values, Book Aleph," (7-99). Internal Revenue Service Publication 1457 also includes examples that illustrate how to compute many special factors for more unusual situations. Publication 1457 is no longer available for purchase from the Superintendent of Documents, United States Government Printing Office. However, pertinent factors in this publication may be obtained from: CC:PA:LPD:PR (IRS Publication 1457), Room 5205, Internal Revenue Service, P.O.Box 7604, Ben Franklin Station, Washington, DC 20044. If a special factor is required in the case of a completed gift, the Internal Revenue Service may furnish the factor to the donor upon a request for a ruling. The request for a ruling must be accompanied by a recitation of the facts including a statement of the date of birth for each measuring life, the date of the gift, any other applicable dates, and a copy of the will, trust, or other relevant documents. A request for a ruling must comply with the instructions for requesting a ruling published periodically in the Internal Revenue Bulletin (see § § 601.201 and 601.601(d)(2)(ii)(*b*)) and include payment of the required user fee.

(4) *Effective/applicability dates.*—Paragraphs (f)(1) through (f)(3) apply after April 30, 1999, and before May 1, 2009. [Reg. § 25.2512-5A.]

☐ [*T.D.* 6334, 11-14-58. *Amended by T.D.* 7955, 5-10-84, *T.D.* 8395, 1-28-92. *Reg. § 25.2512-5 was redesignated Reg. § 25.2512-5A(d) and amended by T.D.* 8540, 6-9-94. *Amended by T.D.* 8819, 4-29-99; *T.D.* 8886, 6-9-2000; *T.D.* 9448, 5-1-2009 *and T.D.* 9540, 8-9-2011.]

[Reg. §25.2512-6]

§25.2512-6. Valuation of certain life insurance and annuity contracts; valuation of shares in an open-end investment company.—(a) *Valuation of certain life insurance and annuity contracts.*—The value of a life insurance contract or of a contract for the payment of an annuity issued by a company regularly engaged in the selling of contracts of that character is established through the sale of the particular contract by the company, or through the sale by the company of comparable contracts. As valuation of an insurance policy through sale of comparable contracts is not readily ascertainable when the gift is of a contract which has been in force for some time and on which further premium payments are to be made, the value may be approximated by adding to the interpolated terminal reserve at the date of the gift the proportionate part of the gross premium last paid before the date of the gift which covers the period extending beyond that date. If, however, because of the unusual nature of the contract such approximation is not reasonably close to the full value, this method may not be used.

The following examples, so far as relating to life insurance contracts, are of gifts of such contracts on which there are no accrued dividends or outstanding indebtedness.

Example (1). A donor purchases from a life insurance company for the benefit of another a life insurance contract or a contract for the payment of an annuity. The value of the gift is the cost of the contract.

Example (2). An annuitant purchased from a life insurance company a single payment annuity contract by the terms of which he was entitled to receive payments of $1,200 annually for the duration of his life. Five years subsequent to such purchase, and when the age of 50 years, he gratuitously assigns the contract. The value of the gift is the amount which the company would charge for an annuity contract providing for the payment of $1,200 annually for the life of a person 50 years of age.

Example (3). A donor owning a life insurance policy on which no further payments are to be made to the company (e.g., a single premium policy or paid-up policy) makes a gift of the contract. The value of the gift is the amount which the company would charge for a single premium contract of the same specified amount on the life of a person of the age of the insured.

Example (4). A gift is made four months after the last premium due date of an ordinary life insurance policy issued nine years and four months prior to the gift thereof by the insured, who was 35 years of age at date of issue. The gross annual premium is $2,811. The computation follows:

Terminal reserve at end of tenth year	$14,601.00
Terminal reserve at end of ninth year	12,965.00
Increase	$1,636.00
One-third of such increase (the gift having been made four months following the last preceding premium due date), is	$545.33
Terminal reserve at end of ninth year	12,965.00
Interpolated terminal reserve at the date of gift	$13,510.33
Two-thirds of gross premium ($2,811)	1,874.00
Value of the gift	$15,384.33

Example (5). A donor purchases from a life insurance company for $15,198 a joint and survivor annuity contract which provides for the payment of $60 a month to the donor during his lifetime, and then to his sister for such time as she may survive him. The premium which would have been charged by the company for an annuity of $60 monthly payable during the life of the donor alone is $10,690. The value of the gift is $4,508 ($15,198 less $10,690).

(b) *Valuation of shares in an open-end investment company.*—(1) The fair market value of a share in an open-end investment company (commonly known as a "mutual fund") is the public redemption price of a share. In the absence of an affirmative showing of the public redemption price in effect at the time of the gift, the last public redemption price quoted by the company for the date of the gift shall be presumed to be the applicable public redemption price. If there is no public redemption price quoted by the company for the date of the gift (e.g., the date of the gift is a Saturday, Sunday, or holiday), the fair market value of the mutual fund share is the last public redemption price quoted by the company for the first day preceding the date of the gift for which there is a quotation. As used in this paragraph the term "open-end investment company" includes only a company which on the date of the gift was engaged in offering its shares to the public in the capacity of an open-end investment company.

(2) The provisions of this paragraph shall apply with respect to gifts made after December 31, 1954. [Reg. § 25.2512-6.]

☐ [*T.D.* 6334, 11-14-58. *Amended by T.D.* 6542, 1-19-61; *T.D.* 6680, 10-9-63 *and T.D.* 7319, 7-22-74.]

[Reg. §25.2512-7]

§25.2512-7. Effect of excise tax.—If jewelry, furs or other property, the purchase of which is subject to an excise tax, is purchased at retail by a taxpayer and made the subject of gifts within a reasonable time after purchase, the purchase price, including the excise tax, is considered to be the fair market value of the property on the date of the gift, in the absence of evidence that the market price of similar articles has increased or decreased in the meantime. Under other circumstances, the excise tax is taken into account in determining the fair market value of property to the extent, and only to the extent, that it affects the price at which the property would change hands between a willing buyer and a willing seller, as provided in § 25.2512-1. [Reg. § 25.2512-7.]

☐ [*T.D.* 6334, 11-14-58.]

[Reg. § 25.2512-8]

§ 25.2512-8. Transfers for insufficient consideration.—Transfers reached by the gift tax are not confined to those only which, being without a valuable consideration, accord with the common law concept of gifts, but embrace as well sales, exchanges, and other dispositions of property for a consideration to the extent that the value of the property transferred by the donor exceeds the value in money or money's worth of the consideration given therefor. However, a sale, exchange, or other transfer of property made in the ordinary course of business (a transaction which is bona fide, at arm's length, and free from any donative intent), will be considered as made for an adequate and full consideration in money or money's worth. A consideration not reducible to a value in money or money's worth, as love and affection, promise of marriage, etc., is to be wholly disregarded, and the entire value of the property transferred constitutes the amount of the gift. Similarly, a relinquishment or promised relinquishment of dower or curtesy, or of a statutory estate created in lieu of dower or curtesy, or of other marital rights in the spouse's property or estate, shall not be considered to any extent a consideration "in money or money's worth." See, however, section 2516 and the regulations thereunder with respect to certain transfers incident to a divorce. See also sections 2701, 2702, 2703 and 2704 and the regulations at §§ 25.2701-0 through 25.2704-3 for special rules for valuing transfers of business interests, transfers in trust, and transfers pursuant to options and purchase agreements. [Reg. § 25.2512-8.]

☐ [*T.D.* 6334, 11-14-58. *Amended by T.D.* 8395, 1-28-92.]

[Reg. § 25.2513-1]

§ 25.2513-1. Gifts by husband or wife to third party considered as made one-half by each.—(a) A gift made by one spouse to a person other than his (or her) spouse may, for the purpose of the gift tax, be considered as made one-half by him and one-half by his spouse, but only if at the time of the gift each spouse was a citizen or resident of the United States. For purposes of this section, an individual is to be considered as the spouse of another individual only if he was married to such individual at the time of the gift and does not remarry during the remainder of the "calendar period" (as defined in § 25.2502-1(c)(1)).

(b) The provisions of this section will apply to gifts made during a particular "calendar period" (as defined in § 25.2502-1(c)(1)) only if both spouses signify their consent to treat all gifts made to third parties during that calendar period by both spouses while married to each other as having been made one-half by each spouse. As to the manner and time for signifying consent, see § 25.2513-2. Such consent, if signified with respect to any calendar period, is effective with respect to all gifts made to third parties during such calendar period except as follows:

(1) If the consenting spouses were not married to each other during a portion of the calendar period, the consent is not effective with respect to any gifts made during such portion of the calendar period. Where the consent is signified by an executor or administrator of a deceased spouse, the consent is not effective with respect to gifts made by the surviving spouse during the portion of the calendar period that his spouse was deceased.

(2) If either spouse was a nonresident not a citizen of the United States during any portion of the calendar period, the consent is not effective with respect to any gift made during that portion of the calendar year.

(3) The consent is not effective with respect to a gift by one spouse of a property interest over which he created in his spouse a general power of appointment (as defined in section 2514(c)).

(4) If one spouse transferred property in part to his spouse and in part to third parties, the consent is effective with respect to the interest transferred to third parties only insofar as such interest is ascertainable at the time of the gift and hence severable from the interest transferred to his spouse. See § 25.2512-5 for the principles to be applied in the valuation of annuities, life estates, terms for years, remainders and reversions.

(5) The consent applies alike to gifts made by one spouse alone and to gifts made partly by each spouse, provided such gifts were to third parties and do not fall within any of the exceptions set forth in subparagraphs (1) through (4) of this paragraph. The consent may not be applied only to a portion of the property interest constituting such gifts. For example, a wife may not treat gifts made by her spouse from his separate property to third parties as having been made one-half by her if her spouse does not consent to treat gifts made by her to third parties during the same calendar period as having been made one-half by him. If the consent is effectively signified on either the husband's return or the wife's return, all gifts made by the spouses to third parties (except as described in subparagraphs (1) through (4) of this paragraph), during the calendar period will be treated as having been made one-half by each spouse.

(c) If a husband and wife consent to have the gifts made to third party donees considered as made one-half by each spouse, and only one spouse makes gifts during the "calendar period" (as defined in § 25.2502-1(c)(1)), the other spouse is not required to file a gift tax return provided: (1) The total value of the gifts made to each third party donee since the beginning of the calendar year is not in excess of $20,000 ($6,000 for calendar years prior to 1982), and (2) no portion of the property transferred constitutes a gift of a future interest. If a transfer made by either spouse during the calendar period to a third party represents a gift of a future interest in property and the spouses consent to have the gifts considered as made one-half by each, a gift tax return for such calendar period must be filed by each spouse regardless of the value of the transfer. (See § 25.2503-3 for the definition of a future interest.)

(d) The following examples illustrate the application of this section relative to the requirements for the filing of a return, assuming that a consent was effectively signified:

(1) A husband made gifts valued at $7,000 during the second quarter of 1971 to a third party and his wife made no gifts during this time. Each spouse is required to file a return for the second calendar quarter of 1971.

(2) A husband made gifts valued at $5,000 to each of two third parties during the year 1970 and his wife made no gifts. Only the husband is required to file a return. (See § 25.6019-2.)

(3) During the third quarter of 1971, a husband made gifts valued at $5,000 to a third party, and his wife made gifts valued at $2,000 to the same third party. Each spouse is required to file a return for the third calendar quarter of 1971.

(4) A husband made gifts valued at $5,000 to a third party and his wife made gifts valued at $3,000 to another third party during the year 1970. Only the husband is required to file a return for the calendar year 1970. (See § 25.6019-2.)

(5) A husband made gifts valued at $2,000 during the first quarter of 1971 to third parties which represented gifts of future interests in property (see § 25.2503-3), and his wife made no gifts during such calendar quarter. Each spouse is required to file a return for the first calendar quarter of 1971. [Reg. § 25.2513-1.]

☐ [*T.D.* 6334, 11-14-58. *Amended by T.D.* 7238, 12-28-72 *and T.D.* 7910, 9-6-83.]

[Reg. § 25.2513-2]

§ 25.2513-2. Manner and time of signifying consent.—(a)(1) Consent to the application of the provisions of section 2513 with respect to a "calendar period" (as defined in § 25.2502-1(c)(1)) shall, in order to be effective, be signified by both spouses. If both spouses file gift tax returns within the time for signifying consent, it is sufficient if—

(i) The consent of the husband is signified on the wife's return, and the consent of the wife is signified on the husband's return;

(ii) The consent of each spouse is signified on his own return; or

(iii) The consent of both spouses is signified on one of the returns.

If only one spouse files a gift tax return within the time provided for signifying consent, the consent of both spouses shall be signified on that return. However, wherever possible, the notice of the consent is to be shown on both returns and it is preferred that the notice be executed in the manner described in subdivision (i) of this subparagraph. The consent may be revoked only as provided in § 25.2513-3. If one spouse files more than one gift tax return for a calendar period on or before the due date of the return, the last return so filed shall, for the purpose of determining whether a consent has been signified, be considered as the return. (See § § 25.6075-1 and 25.6075-2 for the due date of a gift tax return.)

(2) For gifts made after December 31, 1970, and before January 1, 1982, subject to the limitations of paragraph (b) of this section, the consent signified on a return filed for a calendar quarter will be effective for a previous calendar quarter of the same calendar year for which no return was filed because the gifts made during such previous calendar quarter did not exceed the annual exclusion provided by section 2503(b), if the gifts in such previous calendar quarter are listed on that return. Thus, for example, if A gave $2,000 to his son in the first quarter of 1972 (and filed no return because of section 2503(b)) and gave a further $4,000 to such son in the last quarter of the year, A and his spouse could signify consent to the application of section 2513 on the return filed for the fourth quarter and have it apply to the first quarter as well, provided that the $2,000 gift is listed on such return.

(b)(1) With respect to gifts made after December 31, 1981, or before January 1, 1971, the consent may be signified at any time following the close of the calendar year, subject to the following limitations:

(i) The consent may not be signified after the 15th day of April following the close of the calendar year, unless before such 15th day, no return has been filed for the year by either spouse, in which case the consent may not be signified after a return for the year is filed by either spouse; and

(ii) The consent may not be signified for a calendar year after a notice of deficiency in gift tax for that year has been sent to either spouse in accordance with section 6212(a).

(2) With respect to gifts made after December 31, 1970 and before January 1, 1982, the consent may be signified at any time following the close of the calendar quarter in which the gift was made, subject to the following limitations:

(i) The consent may not be signified after the 15th day of the second month following the close of the calendar quarter, unless before such 15th day, no return has been filed for such quarter by either spouse, in which case the consent may not be signified after a return for such calendar quarter is filed by either spouse; and

(ii) The consent may not be signified after a notice of deficiency with respect to the tax for such calendar quarter has been sent to either spouse in accordance with section 6212(a).

(c) The executor or administrator of a deceased spouse, or the guardian or committee of a legally incompetent spouse, as the case may be, may signify the consent.

(d) If the donor and spouse consent to the application of section 2513, the return or returns for the "calendar period" [as defined in § 25.2502-1(c)(1)] must set forth, to the extent provided thereon, information relative to the transfers made by each spouse. [Reg. § 25.2513-2.]

☐ [*T.D.* 6334, 11-14-58. *Amended by T.D.* 7238, 12-28-72 *and T.D.* 7910, 9-6-83.]

[Reg. § 25.2513-3]

§ 25.2513-3. Revocation of consent.—(a)(1) With respect to gifts made after December 31, 1981, or before January 1, 1971, if the consent to the application of the provisions of section 2513 for a calendar year was effectively signified on or before the 15th day of April following the close of the calendar year, either spouse may revoke the consent by filing in duplicate a signed statement of revocation, but only if the statement is filed on or before such 15th day of April. Therefore, a consent that was not effectively signified until after the 15th day of April following the close of the calendar year to which it applies may not be revoked.

(2) With respect to gifts made after December 31, 1970, and before January 1, 1982, if the consent to the application of the provisions of section 2513 for a calendar quarter was effectively signified on or before the 15th day of the second month following the close of such calendar quarter, either spouse may revoke the consent by filing in duplicate a signed statement of revocation, but only if the statement is filed on or before such 15th day of the second month following the close of such calendar quarter. Therefore, a consent that was not effectively signified until after the 15th day of the second month following the close of the calendar quarter to which it applies may not be revoked.

(b) Except as provided in paragraph (b) of § 301.6091-1 of this chapter (relating to hand-carried documents), the statement referred to in paragraph (a) of this section shall be filed with the internal revenue officer with whom the gift tax return is required to be filed, or with whom the gift tax return would be required to be filed if a return were required. [Reg. § 25.2513-3.]

☐ [*T.D.* 6334, 11-14-58. *Amended by T.D.* 7012, 5-14-64; *T.D.* 7238, 12-28-72 *and T.D.* 7910, 9-6-83.]

[Reg. § 25.2513-4]

§ 25.2513-4. Joint and several liability for tax.—If consent to the application of the provisions of section 2513 is signified as provided in § 25.2513-2, and not revoked as provided in § 25.2513-3, the liability with respect to the entire gift tax of each spouse for such "calendar period" (as defined in § 25.2502-1(c)(1)) is joint and several. See paragraph (d) of § 25.2511-1. [Reg. § 25.2513-4.]

☐ [*T.D.* 6334, 11-14-58. *Amended by T.D.* 7238, 12-28-72 *and T.D.* 7910, 9-6-83.]

[Reg. § 25.2514-1]

§ 25.2514-1. Transfers under power of appointment.—(a) *Introductory.*—(1) Section 2514 treats the exercise of a general power of appointment created on or before October 21, 1942, as a transfer of property for purposes of the gift tax. The section also treats as a transfer of property the exercise or complete release of a general power of appointment created after October 21, 1942, and under certain circumstances the exercise of a power of appointment (not a general power of appointment) created after October 21, 1942, by the creation of another power of appointment. See paragraph (d) of § 25.2514-3. Under certain circumstances, also, the failure to exercise a power of appointment created after October 21, 1942, within a specified time, so that the power lapses, constitutes a transfer of property. Paragraphs (b) through (e) of this section contain definitions of certain terms used in §§ 25.2514-2 and 25.2514-3. See § 25.2514-2 for specific rules applicable to certain powers created on or before October 21, 1942. See § 25.2514-3 for specific rules applicable to powers created after October 21, 1942.

(b) *Definition of "power of appointment".*—(1) *In general.*—The term "power of appointment" includes all powers which are in substance and effect powers of appointment received by the donee of the power from another person, regardless of the nomenclature used in creating the power and regardless of local property law connotations. For example, if a trust instrument provides that the beneficiary may appropriate or consume the principal of the trust, the power to consume or appropriate is a power of appointment. Similarly, a power given to a donee to affect the beneficial enjoyment of a trust property or its income by altering, amending or revoking the trust instrument or terminating the trust is a power of appointment. A power in a donee to remove or discharge a trustee and appoint himself may be a power of appointment. For example, if under the terms of a trust instrument, the trustee or his successor has the power to appoint the principal of the trust for the benefit of individuals including himself, and A, another person, has the unrestricted power to remove or discharge the trustee at any time and appoint any other person including himself, A is considered as having a power of appointment. However, he would not be considered to have a power of appointment if he only had the power to appoint a successor, including himself, under limited conditions which did not exist at the time of exercise, release or lapse of the trustee's power, without an accompanying unrestricted power of removal. Similarly, a power to amend only the administrative provisions of a trust instrument, which cannot substantially affect the beneficial enjoyment of the trust property or income, is not a power of appointment. The mere power of management, investment, custody of assets, or the power to allocate receipts and disbursements as between income and principal, exercisable in a fiduciary capacity, whereby the holder has no power to enlarge or shift any of the beneficial interests therein except as an incidental consequence of the discharge of such fiduciary duties is not a power of appointment. Further, the right in a beneficiary of a trust to assent to a periodic accounting, thereby relieving the trustee from further accountability, is not a power of appointment if the right of assent does not consist of any power or right to enlarge or shift the beneficial interest of any beneficiary therein.

(2) *Relation to other sections.*—For purposes of §§25.2514-1 through 25.2514-3, the term "power of appointment" does not include powers reserved by a donor to himself. No provision of section 2514 or of §§25.2514-1 through 25.2514-3 is to be construed as in any way limiting the application of any other section of the Internal Revenue Code or of these regulations. The power of the owner of a property interest already possessed by him to dispose of his interest, and nothing more, is not a power of appointment, and the interest is includible in the amount of his gifts to the extent it would be includible under section 2511 or other provisions of the Internal Revenue Code. For example, if a trust created by S provides for payment of the income to A for life with power in A to appoint the entire trust property by deed during her lifetime to a class consisting of her children, and a further power to dispose of the entire corpus by will to anyone, including her estate, and A exercises the inter vivos power in favor of her children, she has necessarily made a transfer of her income interest which constitutes a taxable gift under section 2511(a), without regard to section 2514. This transfer also results in a relinquishment of her general power to appoint by will, which constitutes a transfer under section 2514 if the power was created after October 21, 1942.

(3) *Powers over a portion of property.*—If a power of appointment exists as to part of an entire group of assets or only over a limited interest in property, section 2514 applies only to such part or interest.

(c) *Definition of "general power of appointment".*—(1) *In general.*—The term "general power of appointment" as defined in section 2514(c) means any power of appointment exercisable in favor of the person possessing the power (referred to as the "possessor"), his estate, his creditors, or the creditors of his estate, except (i) joint powers, to the extent provided in §§25.2514-2 and 25.2514-3 and (ii) certain powers limited by an ascertainable standard, to the extent provided in subparagraph (2) of this paragraph. A power of appointment exercisable to meet the estate tax, or any other taxes, debts, or charges which are enforceable against the possessor or his estate, is included within the meaning of a power of appointment exercisable in favor of the possessor, his estate, his creditors, or the creditors of his estate. A power of appointment exercisable for the purpose of discharging a legal obligation of the possessor for his pecuniary benefit is considered a power of appointment exercisable in favor of the possessor or his creditors. However, for purposes of §§25.2514-1 through 25.2514-3, a power of appointment not otherwise considered to be a general power of appointment is not treated as a general power of appointment merely by reason of the fact that an appointee may, in fact, be a creditor of the possessor or his estate. A power of appointment is not a general power if by its terms it is either—

(*a*) Exercisable only in favor of one or more designated persons or classes other than the possessor or his creditors, or the possessor's estate or the creditors of his estate, or

(*b*) Expressly not exercisable in favor of the possessor or his creditors, the possessor's estate or the creditors of his estate.

A beneficiary may have two powers under the same instrument, one of which is a general power of appointment and the other of which is not. For example, a beneficiary may have a general power to withdraw a limited portion of trust corpus during his life, and a further power exercisable during his lifetime to appoint the corpus among his children. The latter power is not a general power of appointment (but its exercise may result in the exercise of the former power; see paragraph (d) of this section).

(2) *Powers limited by an ascertainable standard.*—A power to consume, invade, or appropriate income or corpus, or both, for the benefit of the possessor which is limited by an ascertainable standard relating to the health, education, support, or maintenance of the possessor is, by reason of section 2514(c)(1), not a general power of appointment. A power is limited by such a standard if the extent of the possessor's duty to exercise and not to exercise the power is reasonably measurable in terms of his needs for health, education, or support (or any combination of them). As used in this subparagraph, the words "support" and "maintenance" are synonymous and their meaning is not limited to the bare necessities of life. A power to use property for the comfort, welfare, or happiness of the holder of the power is not limited by the requisite standard. Examples of powers which are limited by the requisite standard are powers exercisable for the holder's "support," "support in reasonable comfort," "maintenance in health and reasonable comfort," "support in his accustomed manner of living," "education, including college and professional education," "health," and "medical, dental, hospital and nursing expenses and expenses of invalidism." In determining whether a power is limited by an ascertainable standard, it is immaterial whether the beneficiary is required to exhaust his other income before the power can be exercised.

(3) *Certain powers under wills of decedents dying between January 1 and April 2, 1948.*—Section 210 of the Technical Changes Act of 1953 provides that if a decedent died after December 31,

1947, but before April 3, 1948, certain property interests described therein may, if the decedent's surviving spouse so elects, be accorded special treatment in the determination of the marital deduction to be allowed the decedent's estate under the provisions of section 812(e) of the Internal Revenue Code of 1939. See paragraph (h) of § 81.47a of Regulations 105 (26 CFR (1939) 81.47a(h)). The section further provides that property affected by the election shall be considered property with respect to which the surviving spouse has a general power of appointment. Therefore, notwithstanding any other provision of law or of § § 25.2514-1 through 25.2514-3, if the surviving spouse has made an election under section 210 of the Technical Changes Act of 1953, the property which was the subject of the election shall be considered as property with respect to which she has a general power of appointment created after October 21, 1942, exercisable by deed or will, to the extent it was treated as an interest passing to the surviving spouse and not passing to any other person for the purpose of the marital deduction in the prior decedent's estate.

(d) *Definition of "exercise."*.—Whether a power of appointment is in fact exercised may depend upon local law. However, regardless of local law, a power of appointment is considered as exercised for purposes of section 2514 even though the exercise is in favor of the taker in default of appointment, and irrespective of whether the appointed interest and the interest in default of appointment are identical or whether the appointee renounces any right to take under the appointment. A power of appointment is also considered as exercised even though the disposition cannot take effect until the occurrence of an event after the exercise takes place, if the exercise is irrevocable and, as of the time of the exercise, the condition was not impossible of occurrence. For example, if property is left in trust to A for life, with a power in A to appoint the remainder by an instrument filed with the trustee during his life, and A exercises his power by appointing the remainder to B in the event that B survives A, A is considered to have exercised his power if the exercise was irrevocable. Furthermore, if a person holds both a presently exercisable general power of appointment and a presently exercisable nongeneral power of appointment over the same property, the exercise of the nongeneral power is considered the exercise of the general power only to the extent that immediately after the exercise of the nongeneral power the amount of money or property subject to being transferred by the exercise of the general power is decreased. For example, assume A has a noncumulative annual power to withdraw the greater of $5,000 or 5 percent of the value of a trust having a value of $300,000 and a lifetime nongeneral power to appoint all or a portion of the trust corpus to A's child or grandchildren. If A exercises the nongeneral power by appointing $150,000 to A's child, the exercise of the nongeneral power is treated as the exercise of the general power to the extent of $7,500 (maximum exercise of general power before the exercise of the nongeneral power, 5% of $300,000 or $15,000, less maximum exercise of the general power after the exercise of the nongeneral power, 5% of $150,000 or $7,500).

(e) *Time of creation of power.*—A power of appointment created by will is, in general, considered as created on the date of the testator's death. However, section 2514(f) provides that a power of appointment created by a will executed on or before October 21, 1942, is considered a power created on or before that date if the testator dies before July 1, 1949, without having republished the will, by codicil or otherwise, after October 21, 1942. A power of appointment created by an inter vivos instrument is considered as created on the date the instrument takes effect. Such a power is not considered as created at some future date merely because it is not exercisable on the date the instrument takes effect, or because it is revocable, or because the identity of its holders is not ascertainable until after the date the instrument takes effect. However, if the holder of a power exercises it by creating a second power, the second power is considered as created at the time of the exercise of the first. The application of this paragraph may be illustrated by the following examples:

Example (1). A created a revocable trust before October 22, 1942, providing for payment of income to B for life with remainder as B shall appoint by deed or will. Even though A dies after October 21, 1942, without having exercised his power of revocation, B's power of appointment is considered a power created before October 22, 1942.

Example (2). C created an irrevocable inter vivos trust before October 22, 1942, naming T as trustee and providing for payment of income to D for life with remainder to E. T was given the power to pay corpus to D and the power to appoint a successor trustee. If T resigns after October 21, 1942, and appoints D as successor trustee, D is considered to have a power of appointment created before October 22, 1942.

Example (3). F created an irrevocable inter vivos trust before October 22, 1942, providing for payment of income to G for life with remainder as G shall appoint by deed or will, but in default of appointment income to H for life with remainder as H shall appoint by deed or will. If G died after October 21, 1942, without having exercised his power of appointment, H's power of appointment is considered a power created before October 22, 1942, even though it was only a contingent interest until G's death.

Example (4). If in example (3) above G had exercised by will his power of appointment, by creating a similar power in J, J's power of appointment would be considered a power created after October 21, 1942. [Reg. § 25.2514-1.]

□ [*T.D.* 6334, 11-14-58. *Amended by T.D.* 6582, 12-11-61 *and T.D.* 7757, 1-16-81.]

[Reg. § 25.2514-2]

§ 25.2514-2. Powers of appointment created on or before October 21, 1942.—(a) *In general.*—The exercise of a general power of appointment created on or before October 21, 1942, is deemed to be a transfer of property by the individual possessing the power.

(b) *Joint powers created on or before October 21, 1942.*—Section 2514(c)(2) provides that a power created on or before October 21, 1942, which at the time of the exercise is not exercisable by the possessor except in conjunction with another person, is not deemed a general power of appointment.

(c) *Release or lapse.*—A failure to exercise a general power of appointment created on or before October 21, 1942, or a complete release of such a power is not considered to be an exercise of a general power of appointment. The phrase "a complete release" means a release of all powers over all or a portion of the property subject to a power of appointment, as distinguished from the reduction of a power of appointment to a lesser power. Thus, if the possessor completely relinquished all powers over one-half of the property subject to a power of appointment, the power is completely released as to that one-half. If at or before the time a power of appointment is relinquished, the holder of the power exercises the power in such a manner or to such an extent that the relinquishment results in the reduction, enlargement, or shift in a beneficial interest in property, the relinquishment will be considered to be an exercise and not a release of the power. For example, assume that A created a trust in 1940 providing for payment of the income to B for life with the power in B to amend the trust, and for payment of the remainder to such persons as B shall appoint or, upon default of appointment, to C. If B amended the trust in 1948 by providing that upon his death the remainder was to be paid to D, and if he further amended the trust in 1955 by deleting his power to amend the trust, such relinquishment will be considered an exercise and not a release of a general power of appointment. On the other hand, if the 1948 amendment became ineffective before or at the time of the 1955 amendment, or if B in 1948 merely amended the trust by changing the purely ministerial powers of the trustee, his relinquishment of the power in 1955 will be considered as release of a power of appointment.

(d) *Partial release.*—If a general power of appointment created on or before October 21, 1942, is partially released so that it is not thereafter a general power of appointment, a subsequent exercise of the partially released power is not an exercise of a general power of appointment if the partial release occurs before whichever is the later of the following dates:

(1) November 1, 1951; or

(2) If the possessor was under a legal disability to release the power on October 21, 1942, the day after the expiration of 6 months following the termination of such legal disability.

However, if a general power created on or before October 21, 1942, is partially released on or after the later of those dates, a subsequent exercise of the power will constitute an exercise of a general power of appointment. The legal disability referred to in this paragraph is determined under local law and may include the disability of an insane person, a minor, or an unborn child. The fact that the type of general power of appointment possessed by the holder actually was not generally releasable under the local law does not place the holder under a legal disability within the meaning of this paragraph. In general, however, it is assumed that all general powers of appointment are releasable, unless the local law on the subject is to the contrary, and it is presumed that the method employed to release the power is effective, unless it is not in accordance with the local law relating specifically to releases or, in the absence of such local law, is not in accordance with the local law relating to similar transactions.

(e) *Partial exercise.*—If a general power of appointment created on or before October 21, 1942, is exercised only as to a portion of the property subject to the power, the exercise is considered to be a transfer only as to the value of that portion. [Reg. § 25.2514-2.]

☐ [*T.D.* 6334, 11-14-58.]

[Reg. § 25.2514-3]

§ 25.2514-3. Powers of appointment created after October 21, 1942.—(a) *In general.*—The exercise, release, or lapse (except as provided in paragraph(c) of this section) of a general power of appointment created after October 21, 1942, is deemed to be a transfer of property by the individual possessing the power. The exercise of a power of appointment that is not a general power is considered to be a transfer if it is exercised to create a further power under certain circumstances(see paragraph (d) of this section). See paragraph (c) of § 25.2514-1 for the definition of various terms used in this section. See paragraph (b) of this section for the rules applicable to determine the extent to which joint powers created after October 21, 1942, are to be treated as general powers of appointment.

(b) *Joint powers created after October 21, 1942.*—The treatment of a power of appointment created after October 21, 1942, which is exercisable only in conjunction with another person is governed by section 2514(c)(3), which provides as follows:

(1) Such a power is not considered as a general power of appointment if it is not exercisable by the possessor except with the consent or joinder of the creator of the power.

(2) Such power is not considered as a general power of appointment if it is not exercisable by the possessor except with the consent or joinder of a person having a substantial interest in the property subject to the power which is adverse to the exercise of the power in favor of the possessor, his estate, his creditors, or the creditors of his estate. An interest adverse to the

exercise of a power is considered as substantial if its value in relation to the total value of the property subject to the power is not insignificant. For this purpose, the interest is to be valued in accordance with the actuarial principles set forth in § 25.2512-5 or, if it is not susceptible to valuation under those provisions, in accordance with the general principles set forth in § 25.2512-1. A taker in default of appointment under a power has an interest which is adverse to an exercise of the power. A coholder of the power has no adverse interest merely because of his joint possession of the power nor merely because he is a permissible appointee under a power. However, a coholder of a power is considered as having an adverse interest where he may possess the power after the possessor's death and may exercise it at that time in favor of himself, his estate, his creditors, or the creditors of his estate. Thus, for example, if X, Y, and Z held a power jointly to appoint among a group of persons which includes themselves and if on the death of X the power will pass to Y and Z jointly, then Y and Z are considered to have interests adverse to the exercise of the power in favor of X. Similarly, if on Y's death the power will pass to Z, Z is considered to have an interest adverse to the exercise of the power in favor of Y. The application of this subparagraph may be further illustrated by the following examples in each of which it is assumed that the value of the interest in question is substantial:

Example (1). The taxpayer and R are trustees of a trust under which the income is to be paid to the taxpayer for life and then to M for life, and R is remainderman. The trustees have power to distribute corpus to the taxpayer. Since R's interest is substantially adverse to an exercise of the power in favor of the taxpayer, the latter does not have a general power of appointment. If M and the taxpayer were trustees, M's interest would likewise be adverse.

Example (2). The taxpayer and L are trustees of a trust under which the income is to be paid to L for life and then to M for life, and the taxpayer is remainderman. The trustees have power to distribute corpus to the taxpayer during L's life. Since L's interest is adverse to an exercise of the power in favor of the taxpayer, the taxpayer does not have a general power of appointment. If the taxpayer and M were trustees, M's interest would likewise be adverse.

Example (3). The taxpayer and L are trustees of a trust under which the income is to be paid to L for life. The trustees can designate whether corpus is to be distributed to the taxpayer or to A after L's death. L's interest is not adverse to an exercise of the power in favor of the taxpayer, and the taxpayer therefore has a general power of appointment.

(3) A power which is exercisable only in conjunction with another person, and which after application of the rules set forth in subparagraphs (1) and (2) of this paragraph, constitutes a general power of appointment, will be treated as though the holders of the power who are permissible appointees of the property were joint owners of property subject to the power. The possessor, under this rule, will be treated as possessed of a general power of appointment over an aliquot share of the property to be determined with reference to the number of joint holders, including the possessor, who (or whose estates or creditors) are permissible appointees. Thus, for example, if X, Y, and Z hold an unlimited power jointly to appoint among a group of persons, including themselves, but on the death of X the power does not pass to Y and Z jointly, then Y and Z are not considered to have interests adverse to the exercise of the power in favor of X. In this case, X is considered to possess a general power of appointment as to one-third of the property subject to the power.

(c) *Partial releases, lapses and disclaimers of general powers of appointment created after October 21, 1942.*—(1) *Partial release of power.*—The general principles set forth in § 25.2511-2 for determining whether a donor of property (or of a property right or interest) has divested himself of all or any portion of his interest therein to the extent necessary to effect a completed gift are applicable in determining whether a partial release of a power of appointment constitutes a taxable gift. Thus, if a general power of appointment is partially released so that thereafter the donor may still appoint among a limited class of persons not including himself the partial release does not effect a complete gift, since the possessor of the power has retained the right to designate the ultimate beneficiaries of the property over which he holds the power and since it is only the termination of such control which completes a gift.

(2) *Power partially released before June 1, 1951.*—If a general power of appointment created after October 21, 1942, was partially released prior to June 1, 1951, so that it no longer represented a general power of appointment, as defined in paragraph (c) of § 25.2514-1, the subsequent exercise, release, or lapse of the partially released power at any time thereafter will not constitute the exercise or release of a general power of appointment. For example, assume that A created a trust in 1943 under which B possessed a general power of appointment. By an instrument executed in 1948 such general power of appointment was reduced in scope by B to an excepted power. The inter vivos exercise in 1955, or in any "calendar period" (as defined in § 25.2502-1(c)(1)) thereafter, of such excepted power is not considered an exercise or release of a general power of appointment for purposes of the gift tax.

(3) *Power partially released after May 31, 1951.*—If a general power of appointment created after October 21, 1942, was partially released after May 31, 1951, the subsequent exercise, release or a lapse of the power at any time thereafter, will constitute the exercise or release of a general power of appointment for gift tax purposes.

(4) *Release or lapse of power.*—A release of a power of appointment need not be formal or express in character. For example, the failure to exercise a general power of appointment created after October 21, 1942, within a specified time so that the power lapses, constitutes a release of the power. In any case where the possessor of a general power of appointment is incapable of validly exercising or releasing a power, by reason of minority, or otherwise, and the power may not be validly exercised or released on his behalf, the failure to exercise or release the power is not a lapse of the power. If a trustee has in his capacity as trustee a power which is considered as a general power of appointment, his resignation or removal as trustee will cause a lapse of his power. However, section 2514(e) provides that a lapse during any calendar year is considered as a release so as to be subject to the gift tax only to the extent that the property which could have been appointed by exercise of the lapsed power of appointment exceeds the greater of (i) $5,000, or (ii) 5 percent of the aggregate value, at the time of the lapse, of the assets out of which, or the proceeds of which, the exercise of the lapsed power could be satisfied. For example, if an individual has a noncumulative right to withdraw $10,000 a year from the principal of a trust fund, the failure to exercise this right of withdrawal in a particular year will not constitute a gift if the fund at the end of the year equals or exceeds $200,000. If, however, at the end of the particular year the fund should be worth only $100,000, the failure to exercise the power will be considered a gift to the extent of $5,000, the excess of $10,000 over 5 percent of a fund of $100,000. Where the failure to exercise the power, such as the right of withdrawal, occurs in more than a single year, the value of the taxable transfer will be determined separately for each year.

(5) *Disclaimer of power created after December 31, 1976.*—A disclaimer or renunciation of a general power of appointment created in a transfer made after December 31, 1976, is not considered a release of the power for gift tax purposes if the disclaimer or renunciation is a qualified disclaimer as described in section 2518 and the corresponding regulations. For rules relating to when a transfer creating the power occurs, see § 25.2518-2(c)(3). If the disclaimer or renunciation is not a qualified disclaimer, it is considered a release of the power.

(6) *Disclaimer of power created before January 1, 1977.*—A disclaimer or renunciation of a general power of appointment created in a taxable transfer before January 1, 1977, in the person disclaiming is not considered a release of the power. The disclaimer or renunciation must be unequivocal and effective under local law. A disclaimer is a complete and unqualified refusal to accept the rights to which one is entitled. There can be no disclaimer or renunciation of a power after its acceptance. In the absence of facts to the contrary, the failure to renounce or disclaim within a reasonable time after learning of the existence of a power shall be presumed to constitute an acceptance of the power. In any case where a power is purported to be disclaimed or renounced as to only a portion of the property subject to the power, the determination as to whether there has been a complete and unqualified refusal to accept the rights to which one is entitled will depend on all the facts and circumstances of the particular case, taking into account the recognition and effectiveness of such a disclaimer under local law. Such rights refer to the incidents of the power and not to other interests of the possessor of the power in the property. If effective under local law, the power may be disclaimed or renounced without disclaiming or renouncing such other interests.

(7) The first and second sentences of paragraph (c)(5) of this section are applicable for transfers creating the power to be disclaimed made on or after December 31, 1997.

(d) *Creation of another power in certain cases.*—Paragraph (d) of section 2514 provides that there is a transfer for purposes of the gift tax of the value of property (or of property rights or interests) with respect to which a power of appointment, which is not a general power of appointment, created after October 21, 1942, is exercised by creating another power of appointment, which under the terms of the instruments creating and exercising the first power and under applicable local law, can be validly exercised so as to (1) postpone the vesting of any estate or interest in the property for a period ascertainable without regard to the date of the creation of the first power, or (2) (if the applicable rule against perpetuities is stated in terms of suspension of ownership or of the power of alienation, rather than of vesting) suspend the absolute ownership or the power of alienation of the property for a period ascertainable without regard to the date of the creation of the first power. For the purpose of section 2514(d), the value of the property subject to the second power of appointment is considered to be its value unreduced by any precedent or subsequent interest which is not subject to the second power. Thus, if a donor has a power to appoint $100,000 among a group consisting of his children or grandchildren and during his lifetime exercises the power by making an outright appointment of $75,000 and by giving one appointee a power to appoint $25,000, no more than $25,000 will be considered a gift under section 2514(d). If, however, the donor appoints the income from the entire fund to a beneficiary for life with power in the beneficiary to appoint the remainder, the entire $100,000 will be considered a gift under section 2514(d), if the exercise of the second power can validly postpone the vesting of any estate or interest in the property or can suspend the absolute ownership or power of alienation of the property for a period ascertainable without regard to the date of the creation of the first power.

(e) *Examples.*—The application of this section may be further illustrated by the following examples in each of which it is assumed, unless otherwise stated, that S has transferred property in trust after October 21, 1942, with the remainder payable to R at L's death, and that neither L nor R has any interest in or power over the enjoyment of the trust property except as is indicated separately in each example:

Example (1). The income is payable to L for life. L has the power to cause the income to be paid to R. The exercise of the right constitutes the making of a transfer of property under section 2511. L's power does not constitute a power of appointment since it is only a power to dispose of his income interest, a right otherwise possessed by him.

Example (2). The income is to be accumulated during L's life. L has the power to have the income distributed to himself. If L's power is limited by an ascertainable standard (relating to health, etc.) as defined in paragraph (c)(2) of §25.2514-1, the lapse of such power will not constitute a transfer of property for gift tax purposes. If L's power is not so limited, its lapse or release during L's lifetime may constitute a transfer of property for gift tax purposes. See especially paragraph (c)(4) of §25.2514-3.

Example (3). The income is to be paid to L for life. L has a power, exercisable at any time, to cause corpus to be distributed to himself. L has a general power of appointment over the remainder interest, the release of which constitutes a transfer for gift tax purposes of the remainder interest. If in this example L had a power to cause the corpus to be distributed only to X, L would have a power of appointment which is not a general power of appointment, the exercise or release of which would not constitute a transfer of property for purposes of the gift tax. Although the exercise or release of the nongeneral power is not taxable under this section, see §25.2514-1(b)(2) for the gift tax consequences of the transfer of the life income interest.

Example (4). The income is payable to L for life. R has the right to cause the corpus to be distributed to L at any time. R's power is not a power of appointment, but merely a right to dispose of his remainder interest, a right already possessed by him. In such a case, the exercise of the right constitutes the making of a transfer of property under section 2511 of the value, if any, of his remainder interest. See paragraph (e) of §25.2511-1.

Example (5). The income is to be paid to L. R has the right to appoint the corpus to himself at any time. R's general power of appointment over the corpus includes a general power to dispose of L's income interest therein. The lapse or release of R's general power over the income interest during his life may constitute the making of a transfer of property. See especially paragraph (c)(4) of §25.2514-3. [Reg. §25.2514-3.]

☐ [*T.D.* 6334, 11-14-68. *Amended by T.D.* 7238, 12-28-72, *T.D.* 7776, 5-20-81; *T.D.* 7910, 9-6-83; *T.D.* 8095, 8-6-86 *and T.D.* 8744, 12-30-97.]

[Reg. §25.2515-1]

§25.2515-1. Tenancies by the entirety; in general.—(a) *Scope.*—(1) *In general.*—This section and §§25.2515-2 through 25.2515-4 do not apply to the creation of a tenancy by the entirety after December 31, 1981, and do not reflect changes made to the Internal Revenue Code by sections 702(k)(1)(A) of the Revenue Act of 1978, or section 2002(c)(2) of the Tax Reform Act of 1976.

(2) *Special rule in the case of tenancies created after July 13, 1988, if the donee spouse is not a United States citizen.*—Under section 2523(i)(3), applicable (subject to the special treaty rule contained in Pub. L. 101-239, section 7815(d)(14)) in the case of tenancies by the entirety and joint tenancies created between spouses after July 13, 1988, if the donee spouse is not a citizen of the United States, the principles contained in section 2515 and §§25.2515-1 through 25.2515-4 apply in determining the gift tax consequences with respect to the creation and termination of the tenancy, except that the election provided in section 2515(a) (prior to repeal by the Economic Recovery Tax Act of 1981) and §25.2515-2 (relating to the donor's election to treat the creation of the tenancy as a transfer for gift tax purposes) does not apply.

(3) *Nature of.*—An estate by the entirety in real property is essentially a joint tenancy between husband and wife with the right of survivorship. As used in this section and §§25.2515-2 through 25.2515-4, the term "tenancy by the entirety" includes a joint tenancy between husband and wife in real property with right of survivorship, or a tenancy which accords to the spouses rights equivalent thereto regardless of the term by which such a tenancy is described in local property law.

(b) *Gift upon creation of tenancy by the entirety; in general.*—During calendar years prior to 1955 the contribution made by a husband or wife in the creation of a tenancy by the entirety constituted a gift to the extent that the consideration furnished by either spouse exceeded the value of the rights retained by that spouse. The contribution made by either or both spouses in the creation of such a tenancy during the calendar year 1955, any calendar year beginning before January 1, 1971, or any calendar quarter beginning after December 31, 1970, is not deemed a gift by either spouse, regardless of the proportion of the total consideration furnished by either spouse, unless the donor spouse elects (see §25.2515-2) under section 2515(c) to treat such transaction as a gift in the calendar quarter or calendar year in which the transaction is effected. See §25.2502-1(c)(1) for the definition of calendar quarter. However, there is a gift upon the termination of such a tenancy, other than by the death of a spouse, if the proceeds received by one spouse on termination of the tenancy are larger than the proceeds allocable to the consideration furnished by that spouse to the tenancy. The creation of a tenancy by the entirety takes place if (1) a husband or his wife purchases property and causes the title thereto to be conveyed to themselves as tenants by the entirety, (2) both join in such a purchase, or (3) either or both cause to be created such a tenancy in property already owned by either or both of them. The rule prescribed herein with respect to the creation of a tenancy by the entirety applies also to contributions made in the making of additions to the value of such a tenancy (in the form of improvements, reductions in the indebtedness, or otherwise), regardless of the proportion of the consideration furnished by each spouse. See § 25.2516-1 for transfers made pursuant to a property settlement agreement incident to divorce.

(c) *Consideration*.—(1) *In general*.—(i) The consideration furnished by a person in the creation of a tenancy by the entirety or the making of additions to the value thereof is the amount contributed by him in connection therewith. The contribution may be made by either spouse or by a third party. It may be furnished in the form of money, other property, or an interest in property. If it is furnished in the form of other property or an interest in property, the amount of the contribution is the fair market value of the property or interest at the time it was transferred to the tenancy or was exchanged for the property which became the subject of the tenancy. For example, if a decedent devised real property to the spouses as tenants by the entirety and the fair market value of the property was $30,000 at the time of the decedent's death, the amount of the decedent's contribution to the creation of the tenancy was $30,000. As another example, assume that in 1950 the husband purchased real property for $25,000, taking it in his own name as sole owner, and that in 1956 when the property had a fair market value of $40,000 he caused it to be transferred to himself and his wife as tenants by the entirety. Here, the amount of the husband's contribution to the creation of the tenancy was $40,000 (the fair market value of the property at the time it was transferred to the tenancy). Similarly, assume that in 1950 the husband purchased, as sole owner, corporate shares for $25,000 and in 1956, when the shares had a fair market value of $35,000, he exchanged them for real property which was transferred to the husband and his wife as tenants by the entirety. The amount of the husband's contribution to the creation of the tenancy was $35,000 (the fair market value of the shares at the time he exchanged them for the real property which became the subject of the tenancy).

(ii) Whether consideration derived from third-party sources is deemed to have been furnished by a third party or to have been furnished by the spouses will depend upon the terms under which the transfer is made. If a decedent devises real property to the spouses as tenants by the entirety, the decedent, and not the spouses, is the person who furnished the consideration for the creation of the tenancy. Likewise, if a decedent in his will directs his executor to discharge an indebtedness of the tenancy, the decedent, and not the spouses, is the person who furnished the consideration for the addition to the value of the tenancy. However, if the decedent bequeathed a general legacy to the husband and the wife and they used the legacy to discharge an indebtedness of the tenancy, the spouses, and not the decedent, are the persons who furnished the consideration for the addition to the value of the tenancy. The principles set forth in this subdivision with respect to transfers by decedents apply equally well to inter vivos transfers by third parties.

(iii) Where a tenancy is terminated in part (*e.g.*, where a portion of the property subject to the tenancy is sold to a third party, or where the original property is disposed of and in its place there is substituted other property of lesser value acquired through reinvestment under circumstances which satisfy the requirements of paragraph (d)(2)(ii) of this section), the proportionate contribution of each person to the remaining tenancy is in general the same as his proportionate contribution to the original tenancy, and the character of his contribution remains the same. These proportions are applied to the cost of the remaining or substituted property. Thus, if the total contribution to the cost of the property was $20,000 and a fourth of the property was sold, the contribution to the remaining portion of the tenancy is normally $15,000. However, if it is shown that at the time of the contribution more or less than one-fourth thereof was attributable to the portion sold, the contribution is divided between the portion sold and the portion retained in the proper proportion. If the portion sold was acquired as a separate tract, it is treated as a separate tenancy. As another example of the application of this subdivision, assume that in 1950 X (a third party) gave to H and W (H's wife), as tenants by the entirety, real property then having a value of $15,000. In 1955, H spent $5,000 thereon in improvements and under section 2515(c) elected to treat his contribution as a gift. In 1956, W spent $10,000 in improving the property but did not elect to treat her contribution as a gift. Between 1957 and 1960 the property appreciated in value by $30,000. In 1960, the property was sold for $60,000, and $45,000 of the proceeds of the sale were, under circumstances that satisfy the requirements of paragraph (d)(2)(ii) of this section, reinvested in other real property. Since X contributed one-half of the total consideration for the original property and the additions to its value, he is considered as having furnished $22,500 (one-half of $45,000) toward the creation of the remaining portion of the tenancy and the making of additions to the value thereof. Similarly, H is considered as having furnished $7,500 (one-sixth of $45,000) which was treated as a gift in the year furnished, and W is considered as having furnished $15,000 (one-third of $45,000) which was not treated as a gift in the year furnished.

(2) *Proportion of consideration attributable to appreciation*.—Any general appreciation (appreciation due to fluctuations in market value) in the

value of the property occurring between two successive contribution dates which can readily be measured and which can be determined with reasonable certainty to be allocable to any particular contribution or contributions previously furnished is to be treated, for the purpose of the computations in §§25.2515-3 and 25.2515-4, as though it were additional consideration furnished by the person who furnished the prior consideration. Any general depreciation in value is treated in a comparable manner. For the purpose of the first sentence of this subparagraph, successive contribution dates are the two consecutive dates on which any contributions to the tenancy are made, not necessarily by the same party. Further, appreciation allocable to the prior consideration falls in the same class as the prior consideration to which it relates. The application of this subparagraph may be illustrated by the following examples:

Example (1). In 1940, H purchased real property for $15,000 which he caused to be transferred to himself and W (his wife) as tenants by the entirety. In 1956 when the fair market value of the property was $30,000, W made $5,000 improvements to the property. In 1957 the property was sold for $35,000. The general appreciation of $15,000 which occurred between the date of purchase and the date of W's improvements to the property constitutes an additional contribution by H, having the same characteristics as his original contribution of $15,000.

Example (2). In 1955 real property was purchased by H and W and conveyed to them as tenants by the entirety. The purchase price of the property was $15,000 of which H contributed $10,000 and W, $5,000. In 1960 when the fair market value of the property is $21,000, W makes improvements thereto of $5,000. The property then is sold for $26,000. The appreciation in value of $6,000 results in an additional contribution of $4,000 (10,000/15,000 × $6,000) by H, and an additional contribution by W of $2,000 (5,000/15,000 × $6,000). H's total contribution to the tenancy is $14,000 ($10,000 + $4,000) and W's total contribution is $12,000 ($5,000 + $2,000 + $5,000).

Example (3). In 1956 real property was purchased by H and W and conveyed to them as tenants by the entirety. The purchase price of the property was $15,000, on which a down payment of $3,000 was made. The remaining $12,000 was to be paid in monthly installments over a period of 15 years. H furnished $2,000 of the down payment and W, $1,000. H paid all the monthly installments. During the period 1956 to 1971 the property gradually appreciates in value to $24,000. Here, the appreciation is so gradual and the contributions so numerous that the amount allocable to any particular contribution cannot be ascertained with any reasonable certainty. Accordingly, in such a case the appreciation in value may be disregarded in determining the amount of consideration furnished in making the computations provided for in §§25.2515-3 and 25.2515-4.

(d) *Gift upon termination of tenancy by the entirety.*—(1) *In general.*—Upon the termination of the tenancy, whether created before, during, or subsequent to the calendar year 1955, a gift may result, depending upon the disposition made of the proceeds of the termination (whether the proceeds be in the form of cash, property, or interests in property). A gift may result notwithstanding the fact that the contribution of either spouse to the tenancy was treated as a gift. See §25.2515-3 for the method of determining the amount of any gift that may result from the termination of the tenancy in those cases in which no portion of the consideration contributed was treated as a gift by the spouses in the calendar quarter or calendar year in which it was furnished. See §25.2515-4 for the method of determining the amount of any gift that may result from the termination of the tenancy in those cases in which all or a portion of the consideration contributed was treated as constituting a gift by the spouses in the calendar quarter or calendar year in which it was furnished. See §25.2515-2 for the procedure to be followed by a donor who elects under section 2515(c) to treat the creation of a tenancy by the entirety (or the making of additions to its value) as a transfer subject to the gift tax in the calendar quarter (calendar year with respect to such transfers made before January 1, 1971) in which the transfer is made, and for the method of determining the amount of the gift. See §25.2502-1(c)(1) for the definition of calendar quarter.

(2) *Termination.*—(i) *In general.*—Except as indicated in subdivision (ii) of this subparagraph, a termination of a tenancy is effected when all or a portion of the property so held by the spouses is sold, exchanged, or otherwise disposed of, by gift or in any other manner, or when the spouses through any form of conveyance or agreement become tenants in common of the property or otherwise alter the nature of their respective interests in the property formerly held by them as tenants by the entirety. In general, any increase in the indebtedness on a tenancy constitutes a termination of the tenancy to the extent of the increase in the indebtedness. However, such an increase will not constitute a termination of the tenancy to the extent that the increase is offset by additions to the tenancy within a reasonable time after such increase. Such additions (to the extent of the increase in the indebtedness) shall not be treated by the spouses as contributions within the meaning of paragraph (c) of this section.

(ii) *Exchange or reinvestment.*—A termination is not considered as effected to the extent that the property subject to the tenancy is exchanged for other real property, the title of which is held by the spouses in an identical tenancy. For this purpose, a tenancy is considered identical if the proportionate values of the spouses' respective rights (other than any change in the proportionate values resulting solely from the passing of time) are identical to those held in the property which was sold. In addition the sale, exchange (other than an exchange described above), or other disposition of property held as tenants by the entirety is not considered as a termination if all three of the following conditions are satisfied:

(a) There is no division of the proceeds of the sale, exchange or other disposition of the property held as tenants by the entirety;

(b) On or before the due date for the filing of a gift tax return for the calendar quarter or calendar year (see § 25.6075-1 for the time for filing gift tax returns) in which the property held as tenants by the entirety was sold, exchanged, or otherwise disposed of, the spouses enter into a binding contract for the purchase of other real property; and

(c) After the sale, exchange or other disposition of the former property and within a reasonable time after the date of the contract referred to in (b) of this subdivision, such other real property actually is acquired by the spouses and held by them in an identical tenancy.

To the extent that all three of the conditions set forth in this subdivision are not met (whether by reason of the death of one of the spouses or for any other reason), the provisions of the preceding sentence shall not apply, and the sale, exchange or other disposition of the property will constitute a termination of the tenancy. As used in subdivision (c) the expression "a reasonable time" means the time which, under the particular facts in each case, is needed for those matters which are incident to the acquisition of the other property (*i.e.*, perfecting of title, arranging for financing, construction, etc.). The fact that proceeds of a sale are deposited in the name of one tenant or of both tenants separately or jointly as a convenience does not constitute a division within the meaning of subdivision (a) if the other requirements of this subdivision are met. The proceeds of a sale, exchange or other disposition of the property held as tenants by the entirety will be deemed to have been used for the purchase of other real property if applied to the purchase or construction of improvements which themselves constitute real property and which are additions to other real property held by the spouses in a tenancy identical to that in which they held the property which was sold, exchanged, or otherwise disposed of.

(3) *Proceeds of termination.*—(i) The proceeds of termination may be received by a spouse in the form of money, property, or an interest in property. Where the proceeds are received in the form of property (other than money) or an interest in property, the value of the proceeds received by that spouse is the fair market value, on the date of termination of the tenancy by the entirety, of the property or interest received. Thus, if a tenancy by the entirety is terminated so that thereafter each spouse owns an undivided half interest in the property as tenant in common, the value of the proceeds of termination received by each spouse is one-half the value of the property at the time of the termination of the tenancy by the entirety. If under local law one spouse, without the consent of the other, can bring about a severance of his or her interest in a tenancy by the entirety and does so by making a gift of his or her interest to a third party, that spouse is considered as having received proceeds of termination in the amount of the fair market value, at the time of the termination, of his severable interest determined in accordance with the rules prescribed in § 25.2512-5. He has, in addition, made a gift to the third party of the fair market value of the interest conveyed to the third party. In such a case, the other spouse also is considered as having received as proceeds of termination the fair market value, at the time of termination, of the interest which she thereafter holds in the property as tenant in common with the third party. However, since section 2515(b) contemplates that the spouses may divide the proceeds of termination in some proportion other than that represented by the values of their respective legal interests in the property, if both spouses join together in making a gift to a third party of property held by them as tenants by the entirety, the value of the proceeds of termination which will be treated as received by each is the amount which each reports (on his or her gift tax return filed for the calendar quarter or calendar year in which the termination occurs) as the value of his or her gift to the third party. This amount is the amount which each reports without regard to whether the spouses elect under section 2513 to treat the gifts as made one-half by each. For example, assume that H and W (his wife) hold real property as tenants by the entirety; that in the first calendar quarter of 1972, when the property has a fair market value of $60,000, they give it to their son; and that on their gift tax returns for such calendar quarter, H reports himself as having made a gift to the son of $36,000 and W reports herself as having made a gift to the son of $24,000. Under these circumstances, H is considered as having received proceeds of termination valued at $36,000, and W is considered as having received proceeds of termination valued at $24,000.

(ii) Except as provided otherwise in subparagraph (2)(ii) of this paragraph (under which certain tenancies by the entirety are considered not to be terminated), where the proceeds of a sale, exchange, or other disposition of the property are not actually divided between the spouses but are held (whether in a bank account or otherwise) in their joint names or in the name of one spouse as custodian or trustee for their joint interests, each spouse is presumed, in the absence of a showing to the contrary, to have received, as of the date of termination, proceeds of termination equal in value to the value of his or her enforceable property rights in respect of the proceeds. [Reg. § 25.2515-1.]

☐ [*T.D.* 6334, 11-15-58. *Amended by T.D.* 7238, 12-29-72 *and T.D.* 8522, 2-28-94.]

[Reg. § 25.2515-2]

§ 25.2515-2. Tenancies by the entirety; transfers treated as gifts; manner of election and valuation.—(a) The election to treat the creation of a tenancy by the entirety in real property, or additions made to its value, as constituting a gift in the calendar quarter or calendar year in which effected, shall be exercised by including the value of such gifts in the gift tax return of the donor for such calendar quarter or calendar year in which the tenancy was created, or the additions in value were made to the property. See section 6019 and the regulations thereunder. The election may be exercised only in a return filed within the time prescribed by law, or before the expiration of any extension of time granted pursuant to law for the filing of the return. See section 6075 for the time for filing the gift tax return and section 6081 for extensions of time for filing the return, together with the regulations thereunder. In order to make the election, a gift tax return must be filed for the calendar quarter or calendar year in which the tenancy was created, or additions in value thereto made, even though the value of the gift involved does not exceed the amount of the exclusion provided by section 2503(b). See § 25.2502-1(c)(1) for the definition of calendar quarter.

(b) If the donor spouse exercises the election as provided in paragraph (a) of this section, the amount of the gift at the creation of the tenancy is the amount of his contribution to the tenancy less the value of his retained interest in it, determined as follows:

(1) If under the law of the jurisdiction governing the rights of the spouses, either spouse, acting alone, can bring about a severance of his or her interest in the property, the value of the donor's retained interest is one-half the value of the property.

(2) If, under the law of the jurisdiction governing the rights of the spouses each is entitled to share in the income or other enjoyment of the property but neither, acting alone, may defeat the right of the survivor of them to the whole of the property, the amount of retained interest of the donor is determined by use of the appropriate actuarial factors for the spouses at their respective attained ages at the time the transaction is effected.

(c) Factors representing the respective interests of the spouses, under a tenancy by the entirety, at their attained ages at the time of the transaction may be readily computed based on the method described in § 25.2512-5. State law may provide that the husband only is entitled to all of the income or other enjoyment of the real property held as tenants by the entirety, and the wife's interest consists only of the right of survivorship with no right of severance. In such a case, a special factor may be needed to determine the value of the interests of the respective spouses. See § 25.2512-5(d)(4) for the procedure for obtaining special factors from the Internal Revenue Service in appropriate cases.

(d) The application of this paragraph may be illustrated by the following example:

Example. A husband with his own funds acquires real property valued at $10,000 and has it conveyed to himself and his wife as tenants by the entirety. Under the law of the jurisdiction governing the rights of the parties, each spouse is entitled to share in the income from the property but neither spouse acting alone could bring about a severance of his or her interest. The husband elects to treat the transfer as a gift in the year in which effected. At the time of transfer, the ages of the husband and wife are 45 and 40, respectively, on their birthdays nearest to the date of transfer. The value of the gift to the wife is $5,502.90, computed as follows:

Value of property transferred	$10,000.00
Less $10,000 × 0.44971 (factor for value of donor's retained rights) . . .	4,497.10
Value of gift	5,502.90

[Reg. § 25.2515-2.]

☐ [*T.D.* 6334, 11-15-58. *Amended by T.D.* 7150, 12-2-71, *T.D.* 7238, 12-29-72 *and T.D.* 8540, 6-9-94.]

[Reg. § 25.2515-3]

§ 25.2515-3. Termination of tenancy by the entirety; cases in which entire value of gift is determined under section 2515(b).—(a) *In any case in which.*—(1) The creation of a tenancy by the entirety (including additions in value thereto) was not treated as a gift, and

(2) The entire consideration for the creation of the tenancy, and any additions in value thereto, was furnished solely by the spouses (see paragraph (c)(1)(ii) of § 25.2515-1),

the termination of the tenancy (other than by the death of a spouse) always results in the making of a gift by a spouse who receives a smaller share of the proceeds of the termination (whether received in cash, property or interests in property) than the share of the proceeds attributable to the total consideration furnished by him. See paragraph (c) of § 25.2515-1 for a discussion of what constitutes consideration and the value thereof. Thus, a gift is effected at the time of termination of the tenancy by the spouse receiving less than one-half of the proceeds of termination if such spouse (regardless of age) furnished one-half or more of the total consideration for the purchase and improvements, if any, of the property held in the tenancy. Also, if one spouse furnished the entire consideration, a gift is made by such spouse to the extent that the other spouse receives any portion of the proceeds of termination. See § 25.2515-4 for determination of the amount of the gift, if any, in cases in which the creation of the tenancy was treated as a gift or a portion of the consideration was furnished by a third person. See paragraph (d)(2) of § 25.2515-1 as to the acts which effect a termination of the tenancy.

(b) In computing the value of the gift under the circumstances described in paragraph (a) of this section, it is first necessary to determine the spouse's share of the proceeds attributable to the consideration furnished by him. This share is computed by multiplying the total value of the proceeds of the termination by a fraction, the numerator of which is the total consideration furnished by the donor spouse and the denominator of which is the total consideration furnished by both spouses. From this amount there is subtracted the value of the proceeds of termination received by the donor spouse. The amount remaining is the value of the gift. In arriving at the "total consideration furnished by the donor spouse" and the "total consideration furnished by both spouses", for purposes of the computation provided for in this paragraph, the consideration furnished (see paragraph (c) of § 25.2515-1) is not reduced by any amounts which otherwise would have been excludable under section 2503(b) in determining the amounts of taxable gifts for calendar quarters or calendar years in which the consideration was furnished. (See § 25.2502-1(c)(1) for the definition of calendar quarter.) As an example assume that in 1955, real property was purchased for $30,000, the husband and wife each contributing $12,000 and the remaining $6,000 being obtained through a mortgage on the property. In each of the years 1956 and 1957, the husband paid $3,000 on the principal of the indebtedness, but did not disclose the value of these transfers on his gift tax returns for those years. The total consideration furnished by the husband is $18,000, the total consideration furnished by the wife is $12,000, and the total consideration furnished by both spouses is $30,000.

(c) The application of this section may be illustrated by the following examples:

Example (1). In 1956 the husband furnished $30,000 and his wife furnished $10,000 of the consideration for the purchase and subsequent improvement of real property held by them as tenants by the entirety. The husband did not elect to treat the consideration furnished as a gift. The property later is sold for $60,000, the husband receiving $35,000 and his wife receiving $25,000 of the proceeds of the termination. The termination of the tenancy results in a gift of $10,000 by the husband to his wife, computed as follows:

[$30,000 (consideration furnished by husband) ÷ $40,000 (total consideration furnished by both spouses)] × $60,000 (proceeds of termination) = $45,000

$45,000 – $35,000 (proceeds received by husband) = $10,000 gift by husband to wife.

Example (2). In 1950 the husband purchased shares of X Company for $10,000. In 1955 when those shares had a fair market value of $30,000, he and his wife purchased real property from A and had it conveyed to them as tenants by the entirety. In payment for the real property, the husband transferred his shares of X Company to A and the wife paid A the sum of $10,000. They later sold the real property for $60,000, divided $24,000 (each taking $12,000) and reinvested the remaining $36,000 in other real property under circumstances that satisfied the conditions set forth in paragraph (d)(2)(ii) of § 25.2515-1. The tenancy was terminated only with respect to the $24,000 divided between them. This termination of the tenancy resulted in a gift of $6,000 by the husband to the wife, computed as follows:

[$30,000 (consideration furnished by husband) ÷ $40,000 (total consideration furnished by both spouses)] × $24,000 (proceeds of termination) = $18,000

$18,000 – $12,000 (proceeds received by husband) = $6,000 gift by husband to wife.

Since the tenancy was terminated only in part, with respect to the remaining portion of the tenancy each spouse is considered as having furnished that proportion of the total consideration for the remaining portion of the tenancy as the consideration furnished by him before the sale bears to the total consideration furnished by both spouses before the sale. See paragraph (c) of § 25.2515-1. The consideration furnished by the husband for the reduced tenancy is $27,000, computed as follows:

[$30,000 (consideration furnished by husband before sale) ÷ $40,000 (total consideration furnished by both spouses before sale)]× $36,000 (consideration for reduced tenancy) = $27,000

The consideration furnished by the wife is $9,000, computed in a similar manner. [Reg. § 25.2515-3.]

□ [*T.D.* 6334, 11-15-58. *Amended by T.D.* 7238, 12-29-72.]

[Reg. § 25.2515-4]

§ 25.2515-4. Termination of tenancy by entirety; cases in which none, or a portion only, of value of gift is determined under section 2515(b).—(a) *In general.*—The rules provided in section 2515(b) (see § 25.2515-3) are not applied in determining whether a gift has been made at the termination of a tenancy to the extent that the consideration furnished for the creation of the tenancy was treated as a gift or if the consideration for the creation of the tenancy was furnished by a third party. Consideration furnished for the creation of the tenancy was treated as a gift if it was furnished either (1) during calendar years prior to 1955, or (2) during the calendar year 1955 and subsequent calendar years and calendar quarters and the donor spouse exercised the election to treat the furnishing of consideration as a gift. (For the definition of calendar quarter see § 25.2502-1(c)(1).) See paragraph (b) of this section for the manner of computing the value of gifts resulting from the termination of the tenancy under these circumstances. See paragraph (c) of this section for the rules to be applied where part of the total consideration for the creation of the tenancy and additions to the value thereof was not treated as a gift and part either was treated as a gift or was furnished by a third party.

(b) *Value of gift when entire consideration is of the type described in paragraph (a) of this section.*—If the entire consideration for the creation of a tenancy by the entirety was treated as a gift or contributed by a third party, the determination of the amount, if any, of a gift made at the termination of the tenancy will be made by the application of the general principles set forth in § 25.2511-1. Under those principles, when a spouse surrenders a property interest in a tenancy, the creation of which was treated as a gift, and in return receives an amount (whether in the form of cash, property, or an interest in property) less than the value of the property interest surrendered, that spouse is deemed to have made a gift in an amount equal to the difference between the value at the time of termination, of the property interest surrendered by such spouse and the amount received in exchange. Thus, if the husband's interest in such a tenancy at the time of termination is worth $44,971 and the wife's interest therein at the time is worth $55,029, the property is sold for $100,000, and each spouse received $50,000 out of the proceeds of the sale, the wife has made a gift to the husband of $5,029. The principles applied in paragraph (c) of § 25.2515-2 for the method of determining the value of the respective interests of the spouses at the time of the creation of a tenancy by the entirety are equally applicable in determining the value of each spouse's interest in the tenancy at termination, except that the actuarial factors to be applied are those for the respective spouses at the ages attained at the date of termination.

(c) *Valuation of gift where both types of consideration are involved.*—If the consideration furnished consists in part of the type described in paragraph (a) of § 25.2515-3 (consideration furnished by the spouses after 1954, and not treated as a gift in the calendar quarter or calendar year in which it was furnished) and in part of the type described in paragraph (a) of this section (consideration furnished by the spouses and treated as a gift or furnished by a third party), the amount of the gift is determined as follows:

(1) By applying the principles set forth in paragraph (b) of § 25.2515-3 to that portion of the total proceeds of termination which the consideration described in paragraph (a) of § 25.2515-3 bears to the total consideration furnished;

(2) By applying the principles set forth in paragraph (b) of this section to the remaining portion of the total proceeds of termination; and

(3) By subtracting the proceeds of termination received by the donor from the total of the amounts which under the principles referred to in subparagraphs (1) and (2) of this paragraph are to be compared with the proceeds of termination received by a spouse in determining whether a gift was made by that spouse. For example, assume that consideration of $30,000 was furnished by the husband in 1954. Assume also that on February 1, 1955, the husband contributed $12,000 and the wife $8,000, the husband's contribution not being treated as a gift (see paragraph (b) of § 25.2515-1). Assume further that between 1957 and 1965 the property appreciated in value by $40,000 and was sold in 1965 for $90,000 (of which the husband received $40,000 and the wife $50,000). The principles set forth in paragraph (b) of § 25.2515-3 are applied to $36,000 (20,000/50,000 × $90,000) in arriving at the amount which is compared with the proceeds of termination received by a spouse. Applying the principles set forth in paragraph (b) of § 25.2515-3, this amount in the case of the husband is $21,600 (12,000/20,000 × $36,000). Similarly, the principles set forth in paragraph (b) of this section are applied to $54,000 ($90,000 − 36,000), the remaining portion of the proceeds of termination, in arriving at the amount which is compared with the proceeds of termination received by a spouse. If in this case either spouse, without the consent of the other spouse, can bring about a severance of his interest in the tenancy, the amount determined under paragraph (b) of this section in the case of the husband would be $27,000 (1/2 of $54,000). The total of the two amounts which are to be compared with the proceeds of termination received by the husband is $48,600 ($21,600 + 27,000). This sum of $48,600 is then compared with the $40,000 proceeds received by the husband, and the termination of the tenancy has resulted, for gift tax purposes, in a transfer of $8,600 by the husband to his wife in 1965. See paragraph (d) of this section for an additional example illustrating the application of this paragraph.

(d) The application of paragraph (c) of this section may further be illustrated by the following example:

Example. X died in 1948 and devised real property to Y and Z (Y's wife) as tenant by the entirety. Under the law of the jurisdiction, both spouses are entitled to share equally in the income from, or the enjoyment of, the property, but neither spouse, acting along, may defeat the right of the survivor of them to the whole of the property. The fair market value of the property at the time of X's death was $100,000 and this amount is the consideration which X furnished toward the creation of the tenancy. In 1955, at which time the fair market value of the property was the same as at the time of X's death, improvements of $50,000 were made to the property, of which Y furnished $40,000 out of his own funds and Z furnished $10,000 out of her own funds. Y did not elect to treat his transfer to the tenancy as resulting in the making of a gift in 1955. In 1956 the property was sold for $300,000 and Y and Z each received $150,000 of the proceeds. At the time the property was sold Y and Z were 45 and 40 years of age, respectively, on their birthdays nearest the date of sale. The value of the gift made by Y to Z is $19,942, computed as follows:

Amount determined under principles set forth in § 25.2515-3:
$50,000 (consideration not treated as gift in year furnished) ÷ $150,000 (total consideration furnished) × $300,000 (proceeds of termination) = $100,000 (proceeds of termination to which principles set forth in § 25.2515-3 apply)

$40,000 (consideration furnished by H and not treated as gift) ÷ $50,000 (total consideration not treated as gift) × $100,000 = $80,000
Amount determined under principles set forth in paragraph (b) of this section:
$300,000 (total proceeds of termination) − $100,000 (proceeds to which principles set forth in § 25.2515-3 apply) = $200,000 (proceeds to which principles set forth in paragraph (b) apply) 0.44971 (factor for Y's latest) × $200,000 = $89,942

Amount of gift:	
Amount determined under § 25.2515-3	$80,000
Amount determined under paragraph (b)	89,942
Total	169,942
Less: Proceeds received by Y	150,000
Amount of gift made by Y to Z	19,942

[Reg. § 25.2515-4.]

☐ [*T.D.* 6334, 11-15-58. *Amended by T.D.* 7238, 12-29-72.]

[Reg. § 25.2516-1]

§ 25.2516-1. Certain property settlements.—(a) Section 2516 provides that transfers of property or interests in property made under the terms of a written agreement between spouses in settlement of their marital or property rights are deemed to be for an adequate and full consideration in money or money's worth and, therefore, exempt from the gift tax (whether or not such agreement is approved by a divorce decree), if the spouses obtain a final decree of divorce from each other within two years after entering into the agreement.

(b) See paragraph (b) of § 25.6019-3 for the circumstances under which information relating to property settlements must be disclosed on the transferor's gift tax return for the "calendar period" (as defined in § 25.2502-1(c)(1)) in which the agreement becomes effective. [Reg. § 25.2516-1.]

☐ [*T.D.* 6334, 11-14-58. *Amended by T.D.* 7238, 12-28-72 *and T.D.* 7910, 9-6-83.]

[Reg. § 25.2516-2]

§ 25.2516-2. Transfers in settlement of support obligations.—Transfers to provide a reasonable allowance for the support of children (including legally adopted children) of a marriage during minority are not subject to the gift tax if made pursuant to an agreement which satisfies the requirements of section 2516. [Reg. § 25.2516-2.]

☐ [*T.D.* 6334, 11-14-58.]

[Reg. § 25.2518-1]

§ 25.2518-1. Qualified disclaimers of property; In general.—(a) *Applicability.*—(1) *In general.*—The rules described in this section, § 25.2518-2, and § 25.2518-3 apply to the qualified disclaimer of an interest in property which is created in the person disclaiming by a transfer made after December 31, 1976. In general, a qualified disclaimer is an irrevocable and unqualified refusal to accept the ownership of an interest in property. For rules relating to the determination of when a transfer creating an interest occurs, see § 25.2518-2(c)(3) and (4).

(2) *Example.*—The provisions of paragraph (a)(1) of this section may be illustrated by the following example:

Example. W creates an irrevocable trust on December 10, 1968, and retains the right to receive the income for life. Upon the death of W, which occurs after December 31, 1976, the trust property is distributable to W's surviving issue, *per stirpes.* The transfer creating the remainder interest in the trust occurred in 1968. See § 25.2511-1(c)(2). Therefore, section 2518 does not apply to the disclaimer of the remainder interest because the transfer creating the interest was made prior to January 1, 1977. If, however, W had caused the gift to be incomplete by also retaining the power to designate the person or persons to receive the trust principal at death, and, as a result, no transfer (within the meaning of § 25.2511-1(c)(2)) of the remainder interest was made at the time of the creation of the trust, section 2518 would apply to any disclaimer made after W's death with respect to an interest in the trust property.

(3) Paragraph (a)(1) of this section is applicable for transfers creating the interest to be disclaimed made on or after December 31, 1997.

(b) *Effect of a qualified disclaimer.*—If a person makes a qualified disclaimer as described in section 2518(b) and § 25.2518-2, for purposes of the Federal estate, gift, and generation-skipping transfer tax provisions, the disclaimed interest in property is treated as if it had never been transferred to the person making the qualified disclaimer. Instead, it is considered as passing directly from the transferor of the property to the person entitled to receive the property as a result of the disclaimer. Accordingly, a person making a qualified disclaimer is not treated as making a gift. Similarly, the value of a decedent's gross estate for purposes of the Federal estate tax does not include the value of property with respect to which the decedent, or the decedent's executor or administrator on behalf of the decedent, has made a qualified disclaimer. If the disclaimer is not a qualified disclaimer, for the purposes of the Federal estate, gift, and generation-skipping transfer tax provisions, the disclaimer is disregarded and the disclaimant is treated as having received the interest.

(c) *Effect of local law.*—(1) *In general.*—(i) *Interests created before 1982.*—A disclaimer of an interest created in a taxable transfer before 1982 which otherwise meets the requirements of a qualified disclaimer under section 2518 and the corresponding regulations but which, by itself, is not effective under applicable local law to divest ownership of the disclaimed property from the disclaimant and vest it in another, is nevertheless treated as a qualified disclaimer under section

2518 if, under applicable local law, the disclaimed interest in property is transferred, as a result of attempting the disclaimer, to another person without any direction on the part of the disclaimant. An interest in property will not be considered to be transferred without any direction on the part of the disclaimant if, under applicable local law, the disclaimant has any discretion (whether or not such discretion is exercised) to determine who will receive such interest. Actions by the disclaimant which are required under local law merely to divest ownership of the property from the disclaimant and vest ownership in another person will not disqualify the disclaimer for purposes of section 2518(a). See § 25.2518-2(d)(1) for rules relating to the immediate vesting of title in the disclaimant.

(ii) *Interests created after 1981.*—[Reserved].

(2) *Creditor's claims.*—The fact that a disclaimer is voidable by the disclaimant's creditors has no effect on the determination of whether such disclaimer constitutes a qualified disclaimer. However, a disclaimer that is wholly void or that is voided by the disclaimant's creditors cannot be a qualified disclaimer.

(3) *Examples.*—The provisions of paragraphs (c)(1) and (2) of this section may be illustrated by the following examples:

Example (1). F dies testate in State Y on June 17, 1978. G and H are beneficiaries under the will. The will provides that any disclaimed property is to pass to the residuary estate. H has no interest in the residuary estate. Under the applicable laws of State Y, a disclaimer must be made within 6 months of the death of the testator. Seven months after F's death, H disclaimed the real property H received under the will. The disclaimer statute of State Y has a provision stating that an untimely disclaimer will be treated as an assignment of the interest disclaimed to those persons who would have taken had the disclaimer been valid. Pursuant to this provision, the disclaimed property became part of the residuary estate. Assuming the remaining requirements of section 2518 are met, H has made a qualified disclaimer for purposes of section 2518(a).

Example (2). Assume the same facts as in example (1) except that the law of State Y does not treat an ineffective disclaimer as a transfer to alternative takers. H assigns the disclaimed interest by deed to those who would have taken had the disclaimer been valid. Under these circumstances, H has not made a qualified disclaimer for purposes of section 2518(a) because the disclaimant directed who would receive the property.

Example (3). Assume the same facts as in example (1) except that the law of State Y requires H to pay a transfer tax in order to effectuate the transfer under the ineffective disclaimer provision. H pays the transfer tax. H has made a qualified disclaimer for purposes of section 2518(a).

(d) *Cross-reference.*—For rules relating to the effect of qualified disclaimers on the estate tax charitable and marital deductions, see §§ 20.2055-2(c) and 20.2056(d)-1 respectively. For rules relating to the effect of a qualified disclaimer of a general power of appointment, see § 20.2041-3(d). [Reg. § 25.2518-1.]

□ [*T.D.* 8095, 8-6-89. *Amended by T.D.* 8744, 12-30-97.]

[Reg § 25.2518-2]

§ 25.2518-2. Requirements for a qualified disclaimer.—(a) *In general.*—For the purposes of section 2518(a), a disclaimer shall be a qualified disclaimer only if it satisfies the requirements of this section. In general, to be a qualified disclaimer—

(1) The disclaimer must be irrevocable and unqualified;

(2) The disclaimer must be in writing;

(3) The writing must be delivered to the person specified in paragraph (b)(2) of this section within the time limitations specified in paragraph (c)(1) of this section;

(4) The disclaimant must not have accepted the interest disclaimed or any of its benefits; and

(5) The interest disclaimed must pass either to the spouse of the decedent or to a person other than the disclaimant without any direction on the part of the person making the disclaimer.

(b) *Writing.*—(1) *Requirements.*—A disclaimer is a qualified disclaimer only if it is in writing. The writing must identify the interest in property disclaimed and be signed either by the disclaimant or by the disclaimant's legal representative.

(2) *Delivery.*—The writing described in paragraph (b)(1) of this section must be delivered to the transferor of the interest, the transferor's legal representative, the holder of the legal title to the property to which the interest relates, or the person in possession of such property.

(c) *Time limit.*—(1) *In general.*—A disclaimer is a qualified disclaimer only if the writing described in paragraph (b)(1) of this section is delivered to the persons described in paragraph (b)(2) of this section no later than the date which is 9 months after the later of—

(i) The date on which the transfer creating the interest in the disclaimant is made, or

(ii) The day on which the disclaimant attains age 21.

(2) *A timely mailing of a disclaimer treated as a timely delivery.*—Although section 7502 and the regulations under that section apply only to documents to be filed with the Service, a timely mailing of a disclaimer to the person described in paragraph (b)(2) of this section is treated as a timely delivery if the mailing requirements under paragraphs (c)(1), (c)(2) and (d) of § 301.7502-1 are met. Further, if the last day of the period specified in paragraph (c)(1) of this section falls on Saturday, Sunday or a legal holiday (as defined in paragraph (b) of § 301.7503-1),

then the delivery of the writing described in paragraph (b)(1) of this section shall be considered timely if delivery is made on the first succeeding day which is not Saturday, Sunday or a legal holiday. See paragraph (d)(3) of this section for rules applicable to the exception for individuals under 21 years of age.

(3) *Transfer*.—(i) For purposes of the time limitation described in paragraph (c)(1)(i) of this section, the 9-month period for making a disclaimer generally is to be determined with reference to the transfer creating the interest in the disclaimant. With respect to inter vivos transfers, a transfer creating an interest occurs when there is a completed gift for Federal gift tax purposes regardless of whether a gift tax is imposed on the completed gift. Thus, gifts qualifying for the gift tax annual exclusion under section 2503(b) are regarded as transfers creating an interest for this purpose. With respect to transfers made by a decedent at death or transfers that become irrevocable at death, the transfer creating the interest occurs on the date of the decedent's death, even if an estate tax is not imposed on the transfer. For example, a bequest of foreign-situs property by a nonresident alien decedent is regarded as a transfer creating an interest in property even if the transfer would not be subject to estate tax. If there is a transfer creating an interest in property during the transferor's lifetime and such interest is later included in the transferor's gross estate for estate tax purposes (or would have been included if such interest were subject to estate tax), the 9-month period for making the qualified disclaimer is determined with reference to the earlier transfer creating the interest. In the case of a general power of appointment, the holder of the power has a 9-month period after the transfer creating the power in which to disclaim. If a person to whom any interest in property passes by reason of the exercise, release, or lapse of a general power desires to make a qualified disclaimer, the disclaimer must be made within a 9-month period after the exercise, release, or lapse regardless of whether the exercise, release, or lapse is subject to estate or gift tax. In the case of a nongeneral power of appointment, the holder of the power, permissible appointees, or takers in default of appointment must disclaim within a 9-month period after the original transfer that created or authorized the creation of the power. If the transfer is for the life of an income beneficiary with succeeding interests to other persons, both the life tenant and the other remaindermen, whether their interests are vested or contingent, must disclaim no later than 9 months after the original transfer creating an interest. In the case of a remainder interest in property which an executor elects to treat as qualified terminable interest property under section 2056(b)(7), the remainderman must disclaim within 9 months of the transfer creating the interest, rather than 9 months from the date such interest is subject to tax under section 2044 or 2519. A person who receives an interest in property as the result of a qualified disclaimer of the interest must disclaim the previously disclaimed interest no later than 9 months after the date of the transfer creating the interest in the preceding disclaimant. Thus, if A were to make a qualified disclaimer of a specific bequest and as a result of the qualified disclaimer the property passed as part of the residue, the beneficiary of the residue could make a qualified disclaimer no later than 9 months after the date of the testator's death. See paragraph (d)(3) of this section for the time limitation rule with reference to recipients who are under 21 years of age.

(ii) Sentences 1 through 10 and 12 of paragraph (c)(3)(i) of this section are applicable for transfers creating the interest to be disclaimed made on or after December 31, 1997.

(4) *Joint property*.—(i) *Interests in joint tenancy with right of survivorship or tenancies by the entirety*.—Except as provided in paragraph (c)(4)(iii) of this section (with respect to joint bank, brokerage, and other investment accounts), in the case of an interest in a joint tenancy with right of survivorship or a tenancy by the entirety, a qualified disclaimer of the interest to which the disclaimant succeeds upon creation of the tenancy must be made no later than 9 months after the creation of the tenancy regardless of whether such interest can be unilaterally severed under local law. A qualified disclaimer of the survivorship interest to which the survivor succeeds by operation of law upon the death of the first joint tenant to die must be made no later than 9 months after the death of the first joint tenant to die regardless of whether such interest can be unilaterally severed under local law and, except as provided in paragraph (c)(4)(ii) of this section (with respect to certain tenancies created on or after July 14, 1988), such interest is deemed to be a one-half interest in the property. (See, however, section 2518(b)(2)(B) for a special rule in the case of disclaimers by persons under age 21.) This is the case regardless of the portion of the property attributable to consideration furnished by the disclaimant and regardless of the portion of the property that is included in the decedent's gross estate under section 2040 and regardless of whether the interest can be unilaterally severed under local law. See paragraph (c)(5), Examples *(7)* and *(8)*, of this section.

(ii) *Certain tenancies in real property between spouses created on or after July 14, 1988*.—In the case of a joint tenancy between spouses or a tenancy by the entirety in real property created on or after July 14, 1988, to which section 2523(i)(3) applies (relating to the creation of a tenancy where the spouse of the donor is not a United States citizen), the surviving spouse may disclaim any portion of the joint interest that is includible in the decedent's gross estate under section 2040. See paragraph (c)(5), *Example (9)*, of this section.

(iii) *Special rule for joint bank, brokerage, and other investment accounts (e.g., accounts held at mutual funds) established between spouses or between persons other than husband and wife.*—In the case of a transfer to a joint bank, brokerage, or other investment account (e.g., an account held at a mutual fund), if a transferor may unilaterally regain the transferor's own contributions to the account without the consent of the other cotenant, such that the transfer is not a completed gift under § 25.2511-1(h)(4), the transfer creating the survivor's interest in the decedent's share of the account occurs on the death of the deceased cotenant. Accordingly, if a surviving joint tenant desires to make a qualified disclaimer with respect to funds contributed by a deceased cotenant, the disclaimer must be made within 9 months of the cotenant's death. The surviving joint tenant may not disclaim any portion of the joint account attributable to consideration furnished by that surviving joint tenant. See paragraph (c)(5), *Examples(12), (13),* and *(14),* of this section, regarding the treatment of disclaimed interests under sections 2518, 2033 and 2040.

(iv) *Effective date.*—This paragraph (c)(4) is applicable for disclaimers made on or after December 31, 1997.

(5) *Examples.*—The provisions of paragraphs (c)(1) through (c)(4) of this section may be illustrated by the following examples. For purposes of the following examples, assume that all beneficiaries are over 21 years of age.

Example (1). On May 13, 1978, in a transfer which constitutes a completed gift for Federal gift tax purposes, A creates a trust in which B is given a lifetime interest in the income from the trust. B is also given a nongeneral testamentary power of appointment over the corpus of the trust. The power of appointment may be exercised in favor of any of the issue of A and B. If there are no surviving issue at B's death or if the power is not exercised, the corpus is to pass to E. On May 13, 1978, A and B have two surviving children, C and D. If A, B, C or D wishes to make a qualified disclaimer, the disclaimer must be made no later than 9 months after May 13, 1978.

Example (2). Assume the same facts as in example (1) except that B is given a general power of appointment over the corpus of the trust. B exercises the general power of appointment in favor of C upon B's death on June 17, 1989. C may make a qualified disclaimer no later than 9 months after June 17, 1989. If B had died without exercising the general power of appointment, E could have made a qualified disclaimer no later than 9 months after June 17, 1989.

Example (3). F creates a trust on April 1, 1978, in which F's child G is to receive the income from the trust for life. Upon G's death, the corpus of the trust is to pass to G's child H. If either G or H wishes to make a qualified disclaimer, it must be made no later than 9 months after April 1, 1978.

Example (4). A creates a trust on February 15, 1978, in which B is named the income beneficiary for life. The trust further provides that upon B's death the proceeds of the trust are to pass to C, if then living. If C predeceases D, the proceeds shall pass to D or D's estate. To have timely disclaimers for purposes of section 2518, B, C, and D must disclaim their respective interests no later than 9 months after February 15, 1978.

Example (5). A, a resident of State Q, dies on January 10, 1979, devising certain real property to B. The disclaimer laws of State Q require that a disclaimer be made within a reasonable time after a transfer. B disclaims the entire interest in real property on November 10, 1979. Although B's disclaimer may be effective under State Q law, it is not a qualified disclaimer under section 2518 because the disclaimer was made later than 9 months after the taxable transfer to B.

Example (6). A creates a revocable trust on June 1, 1980, in which B and C are given the income interest for life. Upon the death of the last income beneficiary, the remainder interest is to pass to D. The creation of the trust is not a completed gift for Federal gift tax purposes, but each distribution of trust income to B and C is a completed gift at the date of distribution. B and C must disclaim each income distribution no later than 9 months after the date of the particular distribution. In order to disclaim an income distribution in the form of a check, the recipient must return the check to the trustee uncashed along with a written disclaimer. A dies on September 1, 1982, causing the trust to become irrevocable, and the trust corpus is includible in A's gross estate for Federal estate tax purposes under section 2038. If B or C wishes to make a qualified disclaimer of his income interest, he must do so no later than 9 months after September 1, 1982. If D wishes to make a qualified disclaimer of his remainder interest, he must do so no later than 9 months after September 1, 1982.

Example (7). On February 1, 1990, A purchased real property with A's funds. Title to the property was conveyed to "A and B, as joint tenants with right of survivorship." Under applicable state law, the joint interest is unilaterally severable by either tenant. B dies on May 1, 1998, and is survived by A. On January 1, 1999, A disclaims the one-half survivorship interest in the property to which A succeeds as a result of B's death. Assuming that the other requirements of section 2518(b) are satisfied, A has made a qualified disclaimer of the one-half survivorship interest (but not the interest retained by A upon the creation of the tenancy, which may not be disclaimed by A). The result is the same whether or not A and B are married and regardless of the proportion of consideration furnished by A and B in purchasing the property.

Example (8). Assume the same facts as in *Example (7)* except that A and B are married and title to the property was conveyed to "A and B, as tenants by the entirety." Under applicable state law, the tenancy cannot be unilaterally severed by either tenant. Assuming that the other requirements of section 2518(b) are satisfied, A has made a qualified disclaimer of the one-half survivorship interest (but not the interest retained by A upon the creation of the tenancy, which may not be disclaimed by A). The result is the same regardless of the proportion of consideration furnished by A and B in purchasing the property.

Example (9). On March 1, 1989, H and W purchase a tract of vacant land which is conveyed to them as tenants by the entirety. The entire consideration is paid by H. W is not a United States citizen. H dies on June 1, 1998. W can disclaim the entire joint interest because this is the interest includible in H's gross estate under section 2040(a). Assuming that W's disclaimer is received by the executor of H's estate no later than 9 months after June 1, 1998, and the other requirements of section 2518(b) are satisfied, W's disclaimer of the property would be a qualified disclaimer. The result would be the same if the property was held in joint tenancy with right of survivorship that was unilaterally severable under local law.

Example (10). In 1986, spouses A and B purchased a personal residence taking title as tenants by the entirety. B dies on July 10, 1998. A wishes to disclaim the one-half undivided interest to which A would succeed by right of survivorship. If A makes the disclaimer, the property interest would pass under B's will to their child C. C, an adult, and A resided in the residence at B's death and will continue to reside there in the future. A continues to own a one-half undivided interest in the property. Assuming that the other requirements of section 2518(b) are satisfied, A may make a qualified disclaimer with respect to the one-half undivided survivorship interest in the residence if A delivers the written disclaimer to the personal representative of B's estate by April 10, 1999, since A is not deemed to have accepted the interest or any of its benefits prior to that time and A's occupancy of the residence after B's death is consistent with A's retained undivided ownership interest. The result would be the same if the property was held in joint tenancy with right of survivorship that was unilaterally severable under local law.

Example (11). H and W, husband and wife, reside in state X, a community property state. On April 1, 1978, H and W purchase real property with community funds. The property is not held by H and W as jointly owned property with rights of survivorship. H and W hold the property until January 3, 1985, when H dies. H devises his portion of the property to W. On March 15, 1985, W disclaims the portion of the property devised to her by H. Assuming all the other requirements of section 2518(b) have been met, W has made a qualified disclaimer of the interest devised to her by H. However, W could not disclaim the interest in the property that she acquired on April 1, 1978.

Example (12). On July 1, 1990, A opens a bank account that is held jointly with B, A's spouse, and transfers $50,000 of A's money to the account. A and B are United States citizens. A can regain the entire account without B's consent, such that the transfer is not a completed gift under § 25.2511-1(h)(4). A dies on August 15, 1998, and B disclaims the entire amount in the bank account on October 15, 1998. Assuming that the remaining requirements of section 2518(b) are satisfied, B made a qualified disclaimer under section 2518(a) because the disclaimer was made within 9 months after A's death at which time B had succeeded to full dominion and control over the account. Under state law, B is treated as predeceasing A with respect to the disclaimed interest. The disclaimed account balance passes through A's probate estate and is no longer joint property includible in A's gross estate under section 2040. The entire account is, instead, includible in A's gross estate under section 2033. The result would be the same if A and B were not married.

Example (13). The facts are the same as *Example (12)*, except that B, rather than A, dies on August 15, 1998. A may not make a qualified disclaimer with respect to any of the funds in the bank account, because A furnished the funds for the entire account and A did not relinquish dominion and control over the funds.

Example (14). The facts are the same as *Example (12)*, except that B disclaims 40 percent of the funds in the account. Since, under state law, B is treated as predeceasing A with respect to the disclaimed interest, the 40 percent portion of the account balance that was disclaimed passes as part of A's probate estate, and is no longer characterized as joint property. This 40 percent portion of the account balance is, therefore, includible in A's gross estate under section 2033. The remaining 60 percent of the account balance that was not disclaimed retains its character as joint property and, therefore, is includible in A's gross estate as provided in section 2040(b). Therefore, 30 percent (1/2 x 60 percent) of the account balance is includible in A's gross estate under section 2040(b), and a total of 70 percent of the aggregate account balance is includible in A's gross estate. If A and B were not married, then the 40 percent portion of the account subject to the disclaimer would be includible in A's gross estate as provided in section 2033 and the 60 percent portion of the account not subject to the disclaimer would be includible in A's gross estate as provided in section 2040(a), because A furnished all of the funds with respect to the account.

(d) *No acceptance of benefits.*—(1) *Acceptance.*— A qualified disclaimer cannot be made with respect to an interest in property if the disclaimant has accepted the interest or any of its benefits, expressly or impliedly, prior to making the disclaimer. Acceptance is manifested by an affirmative act which is consistent with ownership of the interest in property. Acts indicative of acceptance include using the property or the interest in property; accepting dividends, interest, or rents from the property; and directing others to act with respect to the property or interest in property. However, merely taking delivery of an instrument of title, without more, does not constitute acceptance. Moreover, a disclaimant is not considered to have accepted property merely because under applicable local law title to the property vests immediately in the disclaimant upon the death of a decedent. The acceptance of one interest in property will not, by itself, constitute an acceptance of any other separate interests created by the transferor and held by the disclaimant in the same property. In the case of residential property, held in joint tenancy by some or all of the residents, a joint tenant will not be considered to have accepted the joint interest merely because the tenant resided on the property prior to disclaiming his interest in the property. The exercise of a power of appointment to any extent by the donee of the power is an acceptance of its benefits. In addition, the acceptance of any consideration in return for making the disclaimer is an acceptance of the benefits of the entire interest disclaimed.

(2) *Fiduciaries.*—If a beneficiary who disclaims an interest in property is also a fiduciary, actions taken by such person in the exercise of fiduciary powers to preserve or maintain the disclaimed property shall not be treated as an acceptance of such property or any of its benefits. Under this rule, for example, an executor who is also a beneficiary may direct the harvesting of a crop or the general maintenance of a home. A fiduciary, however, cannot retain a wholly discretionary power to direct the enjoyment of the disclaimed interest. For example, a fiduciary's disclaimer of a beneficial interest does not meet the requirements of a qualified disclaimer if the fiduciary exercised or retains a discretionary power to allocate enjoyment of that interest among members of a designated class. See paragraph (e) of this section for rules relating to the effect of directing the redistribution of disclaimed property.

(3) *Under 21 years of age.*—A beneficiary who is under 21 years of age has until 9 months after his twenty-first birthday in which to make a qualified disclaimer of his interest in property. Any actions taken with regard to an interest in property by a beneficiary or a custodian prior to the beneficiary's twenty-first birthday will not be an acceptance by the beneficiary of the interest.

(4) *Examples.*—The provisions of paragraphs (d)(1), (2) and (3) of this section may be illustrated by the following examples:

Example (1). On April 9, 1977, A established a trust for the benefit of B, then age 22. Under the terms of the trust, the current income of the trust is to be paid quarterly to B. Additionally, one half the principal is to be distributed to B when B attains the age of 30 years. The balance of the principal is to be distributed to B when B attains the age of 40 years. Pursuant to the terms of the trust, B received a distribution of income on June 30, 1977. On August 1, 1977, B disclaimed B's right to receive both the income from the trust and the principal of the trust. B's disclaimer of the income interest is not a qualified disclaimer for purposes of section 2518(a) because B accepted income prior to making the disclaimer. B's disclaimer of the principal, however, does satisfy section 2518(b)(3). See also § 25.2518-3 for rules relating to the disclaimer of less than an entire interest in property.

Example (2). B is the recipient of certain property devised to B under the will of A. The will stated that any disclaimed property was to pass to C. B and C entered into negotiations in which it was decided that B would disclaim all interest in the real property that was devised to B. In exchange, C promised to let B live in the family home for life. B's disclaimer is not a qualified disclaimer for purposes of section 2518(a) because B accepted consideration for making the disclaimer.

Example (3). A received a gift of Blackacre on December 25, 1978. A never resided on Blackacre but when property taxes on Blackacre became due on July 1, 1979, A paid them out of personal funds. On August 15, 1979, A disclaimed the gift of Blackacre. Assuming all the requirements of section 2518(b) have been met, A has made a qualified disclaimer of Blackacre. Merely paying the property taxes does not constitute an acceptance of Blackacre even though A's personal funds were used to pay the taxes.

Example (4). A died on February 15, 1978. Pursuant to A's will, B received a farm in State Z. B requested the executor to sell the farm and to give the proceeds to B. The executor then sold the farm pursuant to B's request. B then disclaimed $50,000 of the proceeds from the sale of the farm. B's disclaimer is not a qualified disclaimer. By requesting the executor to sell the farm B accepted the farm even though the executor may not have been legally obligated to comply with B's request. See also § 25.2518-3 for rules relating to the disclaimer of less than an entire interest in property.

Example (5). Assume the same facts as in example (4) except that instead of requesting the executor to sell the farm, B pledged the farm as security for a short-term loan which was paid off prior to distribution of the estate. B then disclaimed his interest in the farm. B's disclaimer is not a qualified disclaimer. By pledging the farm as security for the loan, B accepted the farm.

Example (6). A delivered 1,000 shares of stock in Corporation X to B as a gift on February 1, 1980. A had the shares registered in B's name on that date. On April 1, 1980, B disclaimed the interest in the 1,000 shares. Prior to making the disclaimer, B did not pledge the shares, accept any dividends or otherwise commit any acts indicative of acceptance. Assuming the remaining requirements of section 2518 are satisfied, B's disclaimer is a qualified disclaimer.

Example (7). On January 1, 1980, A created an irrevocable trust in which B was given a testamentary general power of appointment over the trust's corpus. B executed a will on June 1, 1980, in which B provided for the exercise of the power of appointment. On September 1, 1980, B disclaimed the testamentary power of appointment. Assuming the remaining requirements of section 2518(b) are satisfied, B's disclaimer of the testamentary power of appointment is a qualified disclaimer.

Example (8). H and W reside in X, a community property state. On January 1, 1981, H and W purchase a residence with community funds. They continue to reside in the house until H dies testate on February 1, 1990. Although H could devise his portion of the residence to any person, H devised his portion of the residence to W. On September 1, 1990, W disclaims the portion of the residence devised to her pursuant to H's will but continues to live in the residence. Assuming the remaining requirements of section 2518(b) are satisfied, W's disclaimer is a qualified disclaimer under section 2518(a). W's continued occupancy of the house prior to making the disclaimer will not by itself be treated as an acceptance of the benefits of the portion of the residence devised to her by H.

Example (9). In 1979, D established a trust for the benefit of D's minor children E and F. Under the terms of the trust, the trustee is given the power to make discretionary distributions of current income and corpus to both children. The corpus of the trust is to be distributed equally between E and F when E becomes 35 years of age. Prior to attaining the age of 21 years on April 8, 1982, E receives several distributions of income from the trust. E receives no distributions of income between April 8, 1982 and August 15, 1982, which is the date on which E disclaims all interest in the income from the trust. As a result of the disclaimer the income will be distributed to F. If the remaining requirements of section 2518 are met, E's disclaimer is a qualified disclaimer under section 2518(a). To have a qualified disclaimer of the interest in corpus, E must disclaim the interest no later than 9 months after April 8, 1982, E's 21st birthday.

Example (10). Assume the same facts as in example (9) except that E accepted a distribution of income on May 13, 1982. E's disclaimer is not a qualified disclaimer under section 2518 because by accepting an income distribution after attaining the age of 21, E accepted benefits from the income interest.

Example (11). F made a gift of 10 shares of stock to G as custodian for H under the State X Uniform Gifts to Minors Act. At the time of the gift, H was 15 years old. At age 18, the local age of majority, the 10 shares were delivered to and registered in the name of H. Between the receipt of the shares and H's 21st birthday, H received dividends from the shares. Within 9 months of attaining age 21, H disclaimed the 10 shares. Assuming H did not accept any dividends from the shares after attaining age 21, the disclaimer by H is a qualified disclaimer under section 2518.

(e) *Passage without direction by the disclaimant of beneficial enjoyment of disclaimed interest.*—(1) *In general.*—A disclaimer is not a qualified disclaimer unless the disclaimed interest passes without any direction on the part of the disclaimant to a person other than the disclaimant (except as provided in paragraph (e)(2) of this section). If there is an express or implied agreement that the disclaimed interest in property is to be given or bequeathed to a person specified by the disclaimant, the disclaimant shall be treated as directing the transfer of the property interest. The requirements of a qualified disclaimer under section 2518 are not satisfied if—

(i) The disclaimant, either alone or in conjunction with another, directs the redistribution or transfer of the property or interest in property to another person (or has the power to direct the redistribution or transfer of the property or interest in property to another person unless such power is limited by an ascertainable standard); or

(ii) The disclaimed property or interest in property passes to or for the benefit of the disclaimant as a result of the disclaimer (except as provided in paragraph (e)(2) of this section).

If a power of appointment is disclaimed, the requirements of this paragraph (e)(1) are satisfied so long as there is no direction on the part of the disclaimant with respect to the transfer of the interest subject to the power or with respect to the transfer of the power to another person. A person may make a qualified disclaimer of a beneficial interest in property even if after such disclaimer the disclaimant has a fiduciary power to distribute to designated beneficiaries, but only if the power is subject to an ascertainable standard. See examples (11) and (12) of paragraph (e)(5) of this section.

(2) *Disclaimer by surviving spouse.*—In the case of a disclaimer made by a decedent's surviving spouse with respect to property transferred by the decedent, the disclaimer satisfies the requirements of this paragraph (e)(2) if the interest passes as a result of the disclaimer without direction on the part of the surviving spouse either to the surviving spouse or to another person. If the surviving spouse, however, retains the right to direct the beneficial enjoyment of the disclaimed property in a transfer that is not subject to Federal estate and gift tax (whether as trustee or otherwise), such spouse will be treated as directing the beneficial enjoyment of the disclaimed property, unless such power is limited by an ascertainable standard. See examples (4), (5), and (6) in paragraph (e)(5) of this section.

(3) *Partial failure of disclaimer.*—If a disclaimer made by a person other than the surviving spouse is not effective to pass completely an interest in property to a person other than the disclaimant because—

(i) The disclaimant also has a right to receive such property as an heir at law, residuary beneficiary, or by any other means; and

(ii) The disclaimant does not effectively disclaim these rights,

the disclaimer is not a qualified disclaimer with respect to the portion of the disclaimed property which the disclaimant has a right to receive. If the portion of the disclaimed interest in property which the disclaimant has a right to receive is not severable property or an undivided portion of the property, then the disclaimer is not a qualified disclaimer with respect to any portion of the property. Thus, for example, if a disclaimant who is not a surviving spouse receives a specific bequest of a fee simple interest in property and as a result of the disclaimer of the entire interest, the property passes to a trust in which the disclaimant has a remainder interest, then the disclaimer will not be a qualified disclaimer unless the remainder interest in the property is also disclaimed. See §25.2518-3(a)(1)(ii) for the definition of severable property.

(4) *Effect of precatory language*.—Precatory language in a disclaimer naming takers of disclaimed property will not be considered as directing the redistribution or transfer of the property or interest in property to such persons if the applicable State law gives the language no legal effect.

(5) *Examples*.—The provisions of this paragraph (e) may be illustrated by the following examples:

Example (1). A, a resident of State X, died on July 30, 1978. Pursuant to A's will, B, A's son and heir at law, received the family home. In addition, B and C each received 50 percent of A's residuary estate. B disclaimed the home. A's will made no provision for the distribution of property in the case of a beneficiary's disclaimer. Therefore, pursuant to the disclaimer laws of State X, the disclaimed property became part of the residuary estate. Because B's 50 percent share of the residuary estate will be increased by 50 percent of the value of the family home, the disclaimed property will not pass solely to another person. Consequently, B's disclaimer of the family home is a qualified disclaimer only with respect to the 50 percent portion ($60,000) that passes solely to C. Had B also disclaimed B's 50 percent interest in the residuary estate, the disclaimer would have been a qualified disclaimer under section 2518 of the entire interest in the home (assuming the remaining requirements of a qualified disclaimer were satisfied). Similarly, if under the laws of State X, the disclaimer has the effect of divesting B of all interest in the home, both as devisee and as a beneficiary of the residuary estate, including any property resulting from its sale, the disclaimer would be a qualified disclaimer of B's entire interest in the home.

Example (2). D, a resident of State Y, died testate on June 30, 1978. E, an heir at law of D, received specific bequests of certain severable personal property from D. E disclaimed the property transferred by D under the will. The will had no residuary clause and made no provision for the distribution of property in the case of a beneficiary's disclaimer. The disclaimer laws of State Y provide that such property shall pass to the decedent's heirs at law in the same manner as if the disclaiming beneficiary had died immediately before the testator's death. Because State Y's law treats E as predeceasing D, the property disclaimed by E does not pass to E as an heir at law or otherwise. Consequently, if the remaining requirements of section 2518(b) are satisfied, E's disclaimer is a qualified disclaimer under section 2518(a).

Example (3). Assume the same facts as in example (2) except that State Y has no provision treating the disclaimant as predeceasing the testator. E's disclaimer satisfies section 2518(b)(4) only to the extent that E does not have a right to receive the property as an heir at law. Had E disclaimed both the share E received under D's will and E's intestate share, the requirement of section 2518(b)(4) would have been satisfied.

Example (4). B died testate on February 13, 1980. B's will established both a marital trust and a nonmarital trust. The decedent's surviving spouse, A, is an income beneficiary of the marital trust and has a testamentary general power of appointment over its assets. A is also an income beneficiary of the nonmarital trust, but has no power to appoint or invade the corpus. The provisions of the will specify that any portion of the marital trust disclaimed is to be added to the nonmarital trust. A disclaimed 30 percent of the marital trust. (See §25.2518-3(b) for rules relating to the disclaimer of an undivided portion of an interest in property.) Pursuant to the will, this portion of the marital trust property was transferred to the nonmarital trust without any direction on the part of A. This disclaimer by A satisfies section 2518(b)(4).

Example (5). Assume the same facts as in example (4) except that A, the surviving spouse, has both an income interest in the nonmarital trust and a testamentary nongeneral power to appoint among designated beneficiaries. This power is not limited by an ascertainable standard. The requirements of section 2518(b)(4) are not satisfied unless A also disclaims the nongeneral power to appoint the portion of the trust corpus that is attributable to the property that passed to the nonmarital trust as a result of A's disclaimer. Assuming that the fair market value of the disclaimed property on the date of the disclaimer is $250,000 and that the fair market value of the nonmarital trust (including the disclaimed property) immediately after the disclaimer is $750,000, A must disclaim the power to appoint one-third of the nonmarital trust's corpus. The result is the same regardless of whether the nongeneral power is testamentary or inter vivos.

Example (6). Assume the same facts as in example (4) except that A has both an income interest in the nonmarital trust and a power to invade corpus if needed for A's health or maintenance. In addition, an independent trustee has power to distribute to A any portion of the corpus which the trustee determines to be desirable for A's happiness. Assuming the other requirements of section 2518 are satisfied, A may make a qualified disclaimer of interests in the marital trust without disclaiming any of A's interests in the nonmarital trust.

Example (7). B died testate on June 1, 1980. B's will created both a marital trust and a nonmarital trust. The decedent's surviving spouse, C, is an income beneficiary of the marital trust and has a testamentary general power of appointment over its assets. C is an income beneficiary of the nonmarital trust, and additionally has the noncumulative right to withdraw yearly the greater of $5,000 or 5 percent of the aggregate value of the principal. The provisions of the will specify that any portion of the marital trust disclaimed is to be added to the nonmarital trust. C disclaims 50 percent of the marital trust corpus. Pursuant to the will, this amount is transferred to the nonmarital trust. Assuming the remaining requirements of section 2518(b) are satisfied, C's disclaimer is a qualified disclaimer.

Example (8). A, a resident of State X, died on July 19, 1979. A was survived by a spouse B, and three children, C, D, and E. Pursuant to A's will, B received one-half of A's estate and the children received equal shares of the remaining one-half of the estate. B disclaimed the entire interest B had received. The will made no provisions for the distribution of property in the case of a beneficiary's disclaimer. The disclaimer laws of State X provide that under these circumstances disclaimed property passes to the decedent's heirs at law in the same manner as if the disclaiming beneficiary had died immediately before the testator's death. As a result, C, D, and E are A's only remaining heirs at law, and will divide the disclaimed property equally among themselves. B's disclaimer includes language stating that "it is my intention that C, D, and E will share equally in the division of this property as a result of my disclaimer." State X considers these to be precatory words and gives them no legal effect. B's disclaimer meets all other requirements imposed by State X on disclaimers, and is considered an effective disclaimer under which the property will vest solely in C, D, and E in equal shares without any further action required by B. Therefore, B is not treated as directing the redistribution or transfer of the property. If the remaining requirements of section 2518 are met, B's disclaimer is a qualified disclaimer.

Example (9). C died testate on January 1, 1979. According to C's will, D was to receive 1/3 of the residuary estate with any disclaimed property going to E. D was also to receive a second 1/3 of the residuary estate with any disclaimed property going to F. Finally, D was to receive a final 1/3 of the residuary estate with any disclaimed property going to G. D specifically states that he is disclaiming the interest in which the disclaimed property is designated to pass to E. D has effectively directed that the disclaimed property will pass to E and therefore D's disclaimer is not a qualified disclaimer under section 2518(a).

Example (10). Assume the same facts as in example (9) except that C's will also states that D was to receive Blackacre and Whiteacre. C's will further provides that if D disclaimed Blackacre then such property was to pass to E and that if D disclaimed Whiteacre then Whiteacre was to pass to F. D specifically disclaims Blackacre with the intention that it pass to E. Assuming the other requirements of section 2518 are met, D has made a qualified disclaimer of Blackacre. Alternatively, D could disclaim an undivided portion of both Blackacre and Whiteacre. Assuming the other requirements of section 2518 are met, this would also be a qualified disclaimer.

Example (11). G creates an irrevocable trust on February 16, 1983, naming H, I and J as the income beneficiaries for life and F as the remainderman. F is also named the trustee and as trustee has the discretionary power to invade the corpus and make discretionary distributions to H, I or J during their lives. F disclaims the remainder interest on August 8, 1983, but retains his discretionary power to invade the corpus. F has not made a qualified disclaimer because F retains the power to direct enjoyment of the corpus and the retained fiduciary power is not limited by an ascertainable standard.

Example (12). Assume the same facts as in example (11) except that F may only invade the corpus to make distributions for the health, maintenance or support of H, I or J during their lives. If the other requirements of section 2518(b) are met, F has made a qualified disclaimer of the remainder interest because the retained fiduciary power is limited by an ascertainable standard.
[Reg. § 25.2518-2.]

☐ [*T.D.* 8095, 8-6-86. *Amended by T.D.* 8744, 12-30-97.]

[Reg. § 25.2518-3]

§ 25.2518-3. Disclaimer of less than an entire interest.—(a) *Disclaimer of a partial interest.*—(1) *In general.*—(i) *Interest.*—If the requirements of this section are met, the disclaimer of all or an undivided portion of any separate interest in property may be a qualified disclaimer even if the disclaimant has another interest in the same property. In general, each interest in property that is separately created by the transferor is treated as a separate interest. For example, if an income interest in securities is bequeathed to A for life, then to B for life, with the remainder interest in such securities bequeathed to A's estate, and if the remaining requirements of section 2518(b) are met, A could make a qualified disclaimer of either the income interest or the remainder, or an undivided portion of either interest. A could not, however, make a qualified disclaimer of the income interest for a certain number of years. Further, where local law merges interests separately created by the transferor, a qualified disclaimer will be allowed only if there is a disclaimer of the entire merged interest or an undivided portion of such merged interest. See example (12) in paragraph(d) of this section. See § 25.2518-3(b) for rules relating to the disclaimer of an undivided portion. Where the merger of separate interests would occur but for the creation by the transferor of a nominal interest (as defined in paragraph (a)(1)(iv) of this section), a qualified disclaimer will be allowed only if there is a disclaimer of all the separate interests, or an undivided portion of all such interests, which would have merged but for the nominal interest.

(ii) *Severable property.*—A disclaimant shall be treated as making a qualified disclaimer of a separate interest in property if the disclaimer relates to severable property and the disclaimant makes a disclaimer which would be a qualified disclaimer if such property were the only property in which the disclaimant had an interest. If applicable local law does not recognize a purported disclaimer of severable property, the disclaimant must comply with the requirements of paragraph (c)(1) of § 25.2518-1 in order to make a qualified disclaimer of the severable property. Severable property is property which can be divided into separate parts each of which, after severance, maintains a complete and independent existence. For example, a legatee of shares of corporate stock may accept some shares of the stock and make a qualified disclaimer of the remaining shares.

(iii) *Powers of appointment.*—A power of appointment with respect to property is treated as a separate interest in such property and such power of appointment with respect to all or an undivided portion of such property may be disclaimed independently from any other interests separately created by the transferor in the property if the requirements of section 2518(b) are met. See example (21) of paragraph (d) of this section. Further, a disclaimer of a power of appointment with respect to property is a qualified disclaimer only if any right to direct the beneficial enjoyment of the property which is retained by the disclaimant is limited by an ascertainable standard. See example (9) of paragraph (d) of this section.

(iv) *Nominal interest.*—A nominal interest is an interest in property created by the transferor that—

(A) Has an actuarial value (as determined under § 20.2031-7) of less than 5 percent of the total value of the property at the time of the taxable transfer creating the interest,

(B) Prevents the merger under local law of two or more other interests created by the transferor, and

(C) Can be clearly shown from all the facts and circumstances to have been created primarily for the purpose of preventing the merger of such other interests.

Factors to be considered in determining whether an interest is created primarily for the purpose of preventing merger include (but are not limited to) the following: the relationship between the transferor and the interest holder; the age difference between the interest holder and the beneficiary whose interests would have merged; the interest holder's state of health at the time of the taxable transfer; and, in the case of a contingent remainder, any other factors which indicate that the possibility of the interest vesting as a fee simple is so remote as to be negligible.

(2) *In trust.*—A disclaimer is not a qualified disclaimer under section 2518 if the beneficiary disclaims income derived from specific property transferred in trust while continuing to accept income derived from the remaining properties in the same trust unless the disclaimer results in such property being removed from the trust and passing, without any direction on the part of the disclaimant, to persons other than the disclaimant or to the spouse of the decedent. Moreover, a disclaimer of both an income interest and a remainder interest in specific trust assets is not a qualified disclaimer if the beneficiary retains interests in other trust property unless, as a result of the disclaimer, such assets are removed from the trust and pass, without any direction on the part of the disclaimant, to persons other than the disclaimant or to the spouse of the decedent. The disclaimer of an undivided portion of an interest in a trust may be a qualified disclaimer. See also paragraph (b) of this section for rules relating to the disclaimer of an undivided portion of an interest in property.

(b) *Disclaimer of undivided portion.*—A disclaimer of an undivided portion of a separate interest in property which meets the other requirements of a qualified disclaimer under section 2518(b) and the corresponding regulations is a qualified disclaimer. An undivided portion of a disclaimant's separate interest in property must consist of a fraction or percentage of each and every substantial interest or right owned by the disclaimant in such property and must extend over the entire term of the disclaimant's interest in such property and in other property into which such property is converted. A disclaimer of some specific rights while retaining other rights with respect to an interest in the property is not a qualified disclaimer of an undivided portion of the disclaimant's interest in property. Thus, for example, a disclaimer made by the devisee of a fee simple interest in Blackacre is not a qualified disclaimer if the disclaimant disclaims a remainder interest in Blackacre but retains a life estate.

(c) *Disclaimer of a pecuniary amount.*—A disclaimer of a specific pecuniary amount out of a pecuniary or nonpecuniary bequest or gift which satisfies the other requirements of a qualified disclaimer under section 2518(b) and the corresponding regulations is a qualified disclaimer provided that no income or other benefit of the disclaimed amount inures to the benefit of the disclaimant either prior to or subsequent to the disclaimer. Thus, following the disclaimer of a specific pecuniary amount from a bequest or gift, the amount disclaimed and any income attributable to such amount must be segregated from the portion of the gift or bequest that was not disclaimed. Such a segregation of assets making up the disclaimer of a pecuniary amount must be made on the basis of the fair market value of the assets on the date of the disclaimer or on a basis that is fairly representative of value changes that may have occurred between the date of transfer and the date of the disclaimer. A pecuniary amount distributed to the disclaimant from the bequest or gift prior to the disclaimer shall be treated as a distribution of corpus from the bequest or gift. However, the acceptance of a distribution from the gift or bequest shall also be considered to be an acceptance of a proportionate amount of income earned by the bequest or gift. The proportionate share of income considered to be accepted by the disclaimant shall be determined at the time of the disclaimer according to the following formula:

$$\frac{\text{total amount of distributions received by the disclaimant out of the gift or bequest}}{\text{total value of the gift or bequest on the date of transfer}} \times \text{total amount of income earned by the gift or bequest between date of transfer and date of disclaimer.}$$

See examples (17), (18), and (19) in §25.2518-3 (d) for illustrations of the rules set forth in this paragraph (c).

(d) *Examples.*—The provisions of this section may be illustrated by the following examples:

Example (1). A, resident of State Q, died on August 1, 1978. A's will included specific bequests of 100 shares of stock in X corporation; 200 shares of stock in Y corporation; 500 shares of stock in Z corporation; personal effects consisting of paintings, home furnishings, jewelry, and silver; and a 500 acre farm consisting of a residence, various outbuildings, and 500 head of cattle. The laws of State Q provide that a disclaimed interest passes in the same manner as if the disclaiming beneficiary had died immediately before the testator's death. Pursuant to A's will, B was to receive both the personal effects and the farm. C was to receive all the shares of stock in Corporation X and Y and D was to receive all the shares of stock in Corporation Z. B disclaimed 2 of the paintings and all the jewelry, C disclaimed 50 shares of Y corporation stock, and D disclaimed 100 shares of Z corporation stock. If the remaining requirements of section 2518(b) and the corresponding regulations are met, each of these disclaimers is a qualified disclaimer for purposes of section 2518(a).

Example (2). Assume the same facts as in example (1) except that D disclaimed the income interest in the shares of Z corporation stock while retaining the remainder interest in such shares. D's disclaimer is not a qualified disclaimer.

Example (3). Assume the same facts as in example (1) except that B disclaimed 300 identified acres of the 500 acres. Assuming that B's disclaimer meets the remaining requirements of section 2518(b), it is a qualified disclaimer.

Example (4). Assume the same facts as in example (1) except that A devised the income from the farm to B for life and the remainder interest to C. B disclaimed 40 percent of the income from the farm. Assuming that it meets the remaining requirements of section 2518(b), B's disclaimer of an undivided portion of the income is a qualified disclaimer.

Example (5). E died on September 13, 1978. Under the provisions of E's will, E's shares of stock in X, Y, and Z corporations were to be transferred to a trust. The trust provides that all income is to be distributed currently to F and G in equal parts until F attains the age of 45 years. At that time the corpus of the trust is to be divided equally between F and G. F disclaimed the income arising from the shares of X stock. G disclaimed 20 percent of G's interest in the trust. F's disclaimer is not a qualified disclaimer because the X stock remains in the trust. If the remaining requirements of section 2518(b) are met, G's disclaimer is a qualified disclaimer.

Example (6). Assume the same facts as in example (5) except that F disclaimed both the income interest and the remainder interest in the shares of X stock. F's disclaimer results in the X stock being transferred out of the trust to G without any direction on F's part. F's disclaimer is a qualified disclaimer under section 2518(b).

Example (7). Assume the same facts as in example (5) except that F is only an income beneficiary of the trust. The X stock remains in the trust after F's disclaimer of the income arising from the shares of X stock. F's disclaimer is not a qualified disclaimer under section 2518.

Example (8). Assume the same facts as in example (5) except that F disclaimed the entire income interest in the trust while retaining the interest F has in corpus. Alternatively, assume that G disclaimed G's entire corpus interest while retaining G's interest in the income from the trust. If the remaining requirements of section 2518(b) are met, either disclaimer will be a qualified disclaimer.

Example (9). G creates an irrevocable trust on May 13, 1980, with H, I, and J as the income beneficiaries. In addition, H, who is the trustee, holds the power to invade corpus for H's health, maintenance, support and happiness and a testamentary power of appointment over the corpus. In the absence of the exercise of the power of appointment, the property passes to I and J in equal shares. H disclaimed the power to invade corpus for H's health, maintenance, support and happiness. Because H retained the testamentary power to appoint the property in the corpus, H's disclaimer is not a qualified disclaimer. If H also disclaimed the testamentary power of appointment, H's disclaimer would have been a qualified disclaimer.

Example (10). E creates an irrevocable trust on May 1, 1980, in which D is the income beneficiary for life. Subject to the trustee's discretion, E's children, A, B, and C, have the right to receive corpus during D's lifetime. The remainder passes to D if D survives A, B, C, and all their issue. D also holds an inter vivos power to appoint the trust corpus to A, B, and C. On September 1, 1980, D disclaimed the remainder interest. D's disclaimer is not a qualified disclaimer because D retained the power to direct the use and enjoyment of corpus during D's life.

Example (11). Under H's will, a trust is created from which W is to receive all of the income for life. The trustee has the power to invade the trust corpus for the support or maintenance of D during the life of W. The trust is to terminate at W's death, at which time the trust property is to be distributed to D. D makes a timely disclaimer of the right to corpus during W's lifetime, but does not disclaim the remainder interest. D's disclaimer is a qualified disclaimer assuming the remaining requirements of section 2518 are met.

Example (12). Under the provisions of G's will A received a life estate in a farm, and was the sole beneficiary of property in the residuary estate. The will also provided that the remainder interest in the farm pass to the residuary estate. Under local law A's interests merged to give A a fee simple in the farm. A made a timely disclaimer of the life estate. A's disclaimer of a partial interest is not a qualified disclaimer under section 2518(a). If A makes a disclaimer of the entire merged interest in the farm or an undivided portion of such merged interest then A would be making a qualified disclaimer assuming all the other requirements of section 2518(b) are met.

Example (13). A, a resident of State Z, dies on September 3, 1980. Under A's will, Blackacre is devised to C for life, then to D for 1 month, remainder to C. Had A not created D's interest, State Z law would have merged C's life estate and the remainder to C to create a fee simple interest in C. Assume that the actuarial value of D's interest is less than 5 percent of the total value of Blackacre on the date of A's death. Further assume that facts and circumstances (particularly the duration of D's interest) clearly indicate that D's interest was created primarily for the purpose of preventing the merger of C's two interests in Blackacre. D's interest in Blackacre is a nominal interest and C's two interests will, for purposes of making a qualified disclaimer, be considered to have merged. Thus, C cannot make a qualified disclaimer of his remainder while retaining the life estate. C can, however, make a qualified disclaimer of both of these interests entirely or an undivided portion of both.

Example (14). A, a resident of State X, dies on October 12, 1978. Under A's will, Blackacre was devised to B for life, then to C for life if C survives B, remainder to B's estate. On the date of A's death, B and C are both 8 year old grandchildren of A. In addition, C is in good health. The actual value of C's interest is less than 5 percent of the total value of Blackacre on the date of A's death. No facts are present which would indicate that the possibility of C's contingent interest vesting is so remote as to be negligible. Had C's contingent life estate not been created, B's life estate and remainder interests would have merged under local law to give B a fee simple interest in Blackacre. Although C's interest prevents the merger of B's two interests and has an actual value of less than 5 percent, C's interest is not a nominal interest within the meaning of § 25.2518-3(a)(1)(iv) because the facts and circumstances do not clearly indicate that the interest was created primarily for the purpose of preventing the merger of other interests in the property. Assuming all the other requirements of section 2518(b) are met, B can make a qualified disclaimer of the remainder while retaining his life estate.

Example (15). In 1981, A transfers $60,000 to a trust created for the benefit of B who was given the income interest for life and who also has a testamentary nongeneral power of appointment over the corpus. A transfers an additional $25,000 to the trust on June 1, 1984. At that time the trust corpus (exclusive of the $25,000 transfer) has a fair market value of $75,000. On January 1, 1985, B disclaims the right to receive income attributable to 25 percent of the corpus

$$\frac{\$25{,}000 \text{ (1984 transfer)}}{\$100{,}000 \text{ (Fair market value of corpus immediately after the 1984 transfer)}} = 25\%.$$

Assuming that no distributions were made to B attributable to the $25,000, B's disclaimer is a qualified disclaimer for purposes of section 2518(a) if all the remaining requirements of section 2518(b) are met.

Example (16). Under the provisions of B's will, A is left an outright cash legacy of $50,000 and has no other interest in B's estate. A timely disclaimer by A of any stated dollar amount is a qualified disclaimer under section 2518(a).

Example (17). D bequeaths his brokerage account to E. The account consists of stocks and bonds and a cash amount earning interest. The total value of the cash and assets in the account on the date of D's death is $100,000. Four months after D's death, E makes a withdrawal of cash from the account for personal use amounting to $40,000. Eight months after D's death, E disclaims $60,000 of the account without specifying any particular assets or cash. The cumulative fair market value of the stocks and bonds in the account on the date of the disclaimer is equal to the value of such stocks and bonds on the date of D's death. The income earned by the account between the date of D's death and the date of E's disclaimer was $20,000. The amount of income earned by the account that E accepted by withdrawing $40,000 from the account prior to the disclaimer is determined by applying the formula set forth in § 25.2518-3(c) as follows:

$$\frac{\$40{,}000}{\$100{,}000} \times \$20{,}000 = \$8{,}000$$

E is considered to have accepted $8,000 of the income earned by the account. If (i) the $60,000 disclaimed by E and the $12,000 of income earned prior to the disclaimer which is attributable to that amount are segregated from the $8,000 of income E is considered to have accepted, (ii) E does not accept any benefits of the $72,000 so segregated, and (iii) the other requirements of section 2518(b) are met, then E's disclaimer of $60,000 from the account is a qualified disclaimer.

Example (18). A bequeathed his residuary estate to B. The residuary estate had a value of $1 million on the date of A's death. Six months later, B disclaimed $200,000 out of this bequest. B received distributions of all the income from the entire estate during the period of administration. When the estate was distributed, B received the entire residuary estate except for $200,000 in cash. B did not make a qualified disclaimer since he accepted the benefits of the $200,000 during the period of estate administration.

Example (19). Assume the same facts as in example (18) except that no income was paid to B and the value of the residuary estate on the date of the disclaimer (including interest earned from date of death) was $1.5 million. In addition, as soon as B's disclaimer was made, the executor of A's estate set aside assets worth $300,000

$$\frac{\$200{,}000}{\$1{,}000{,}000} \times \$1{,}500{,}000$$

and the interest earned after the disclaimer on that amount in a separate fund so that none of the income was paid to B. B's disclaimer is a qualified disclaimer under section 2518(a).

Example (20). A bequeathed his residuary estate to B. B disclaims a fractional share of the residuary estate. Any disclaimed property will pass to A's surviving spouse, W. The numerator of the fraction disclaimed is the smallest amount which will allow A's estate to pass free of Federal estate tax and the denominator is the value of the residuary estate. B's disclaimer is a qualified disclaimer.

Example (21). A created a trust on July 1, 1979. The trust provides that all current income is to be distributed equally between B and C for the life of B. B also is given a testamentary general power of appointment over the corpus. If the power is not exercised, the corpus passes to C or C's heirs. B disclaimed the testamentary power to appoint an undivided one-half of the trust corpus. Assuming the remaining requirements of section 2518(b) are satisfied, B's disclaimer is a qualified disclaimer under section 2518(a). [Reg. § 25.2518-3.]

☐ [*T.D.* 8095, 8-6-86. *Amended by T.D.* 8540, 6-9-94.]

[Reg. § 25.2519-1]

§ 25.2519-1. Dispositions of certain life estates.—(a) *In general.*—If a donee spouse makes a disposition of all or part of a qualifying income interest for life in any property for which a deduction was allowed under section 2056(b)(7) or section 2523(f) for the transfer creating the qualifying income interest, the donee spouse is treated for purposes of chapters 11 and 12 of subtitle B of the Internal Revenue Code as transferring all interests in property other than the qualifying income interest. For example, if the donee spouse makes a disposition of part of a qualifying income interest for life in trust corpus, the spouse is treated under section 2519 as making a transfer subject to chapters 11 and 12 of the entire trust other than the qualifying income interest for life. Therefore, the donee spouse is treated as making a gift under section 2519 of the entire trust less the qualifying income interest, and is treated for purposes of section 2036 as having transferred the entire trust corpus, including that portion of the trust corpus from which the retained income interest is payable. A transfer of all or a portion of the income interest of the spouse is a transfer by the spouse under section 2511. See also section 2702 for special rules applicable in valuing the gift made by the spouse under section 2519.

(b) *Presumption.*—Unless the donee spouse establishes to the contrary, section 2519 applies to the entire trust at the time of the disposition. If a deduction is taken on either the estate or gift tax return with respect to the transfer which created the qualifying income interest, it is presumed that the deduction was allowed for purposes of section 2519. To avoid the application of section 2519 upon a transfer of all or part of the donee spouse's income interest, the donee spouse must establish that a deduction was not taken for the transfer of property which created the qualifying income interest. For example, to establish that a deduction was not taken, the donee spouse may produce a copy of the estate or gift tax return filed with respect to the transfer creating the qualifying income interest for life establishing that no deduction was taken under section 2056(b)(7) or section 2523(f). In addition, the donee spouse may establish that no return was filed on the original transfer by the donor spouse because the value of the first spouse's gross estate was below the threshold requirement for filing under section 6018. Similarly, the donee spouse could establish that the transfer creating the qualifying income interest for life was made before the effective date of section 2056(b)(7) or section 2523(f), whichever is applicable.

(c) *Amount treated as a transfer.*—(1) *In general.*—The amount treated as a transfer under this section upon a disposition of all or part of a qualifying income interest for life in qualified terminable interest property is equal to the fair market value of the entire property subject to the qualifying income interest, determined on the date of the disposition (including any accumulated income and not reduced by any amount excluded from total gifts under section 2503(b) with respect to the transfer creating the interest), less the value of the qualifying income interest in the property on the date of the disposition. The gift tax consequences of the disposition of the qualifying income interest are determined separately under § 25.2511-2. See paragraph (c)(4) of this section for the effect of gift tax that the donee spouse is entitled to recover under section 2207A.

(2) *Disposition of interest in property with respect to which a partial election was made.*—If, in connection with the transfer of property that created the spouse's qualifying income interest for life, a deduction was allowed under section 2056(b)(7) or section 2523(f) for less than the entire interest in the property (i.e., for a fractional or percentage share of the entire interest in the transferred property) the amount treated as a

transfer by the donee spouse under this section is equal to the fair market value of the entire property subject to the qualifying income interest on the date of the disposition, less the value of the qualifying income interest for life, multiplied by the fractional or percentage share of the interest for which the deduction was taken.

(3) *Reduction for distributions charged to nonelective portion of trust.*—The amount determined under paragraph (c)(2) of this section (if applicable) is appropriately reduced if—

(i) The donee spouse's interest is in a trust and distributions of principal have been made to the donee spouse;

(ii) The trust provides that distributions of principal are made first from the qualified terminable interest share of the trust; and

(iii) The donee spouse establishes the reduction in that share based on the fair market value of the trust assets at the time of each distribution.

(4) *Effect of gift tax entitled to be recovered under section 2207A on the amount of the transfer.*—The amount treated as a transfer under paragraph (c)(1) of this section is further reduced by the amount the donee spouse is entitled to recover under section 2207A(b) (relating to the right to recover gift tax attributable to the remainder interest). If the donee spouse is entitled to recover gift tax under section 2207A(b), the amount of gift tax recoverable and the value of the remainder interest treated as transferred under section 2519 are determined by using the same interrelated computation applicable for other transfers in which the transferee assumes the gift tax liability. The gift tax consequences of failing to exercise the right of recovery are determined separately under § 25.2207A-1(b).

(5) *Interest in previously severed trust.*—If the donee spouse's interest is in a trust consisting of only qualified terminable interest property, and the trust was previously severed (in compliance with § 20.2056(b)-7(b)(2)(ii) of this chapter or § 25.2523(f)-1(b)(3)(ii) from a trust that, after the severance, held only property that was not qualified terminable interest property, only the value of the property in the severed portion of the trust at the time of the disposition is treated as transferred under this section.

(d) *Identification of property transferred.*—If only part of the property in which a donee spouse has a qualifying income interest for life is qualified terminable interest property, the donee spouse is, in the case of a disposition of all or part of the income interest within the meaning of section 2519, deemed to have transferred a pro rata portion of the entire qualified terminable interest property for purposes of this section.

(e) *Exercise of power of appointment.*—The exercise by any person of a power to appoint qualified terminable interest property to the donee spouse is not treated as a disposition under section 2519, even though the donee spouse subsequently disposes of the appointed property.

(f) *Conversion of qualified terminable interest property.*—The conversion of qualified terminable interest property into other property in which the donee spouse has a qualifying income interest for life is not, for purposes of this section, treated as a disposition of the qualifying income interest. Thus, the sale and reinvestment of assets of a trust holding qualified terminable interest property is not a disposition of the qualifying income interest, provided that the donee spouse continues to have a qualifying income interest for life in the trust after the sale and reinvestment. Similarly, the sale of real property in which the spouse possesses a legal life estate and thus meets the requirements of qualified terminable interest property, followed by the transfer of the proceeds into a trust which also meets the requirements of qualified terminable interest property, or by the reinvestment of the proceeds in income producing property in which the donee spouse has a qualifying income interest for life, is not considered a disposition of the qualifying income interest. On the other hand, the sale of qualified terminable interest property, followed by the payment to the donee spouse of a portion of the proceeds equal to the value of the donee spouse's income interest, is considered a disposition of the qualifying income interest.

(g) *Examples.*—The following examples illustrate the application of paragraphs (a) through (f) of this section. Except as provided otherwise in the examples, assume that the decedent, D, was survived by spouse, S, that in each example the section 2503(b) exclusion has already been fully utilized for each year with respect to the donee in question, that section 2503(e) is not applicable to the amount deemed transferred, and that the gift taxes on the amount treated as transferred under paragraph (c) are offset by S's unified credit. The examples are as follows:

Example 1. Transfer of the spouse's life estate in residence. Under D's will, a personal residence valued for estate tax purposes at $250,000 passes to S for life, and after S's death to D's children. D's executor made a valid election to treat the property as qualified terminable interest property. During 1995, when the fair market value of the property is $300,000 and the value of S's life interest in the property is $100,000, S makes a gift of S's entire interest in the property to D's children. Pursuant to section 2519, S makes a gift in the amount of $200,000 (i.e., the fair market value of the qualified terminable interest property of $300,000 less the fair market value of S's qualifying income interest in the property of $100,000). In addition, under section 2511, S makes a gift of $100,000 (i.e., the fair market value of S's income interest in the property). See § 25.2511-2.

Example 2. Sale of spouse's life estate. The facts are the same as in *Example 1* except that during 1995, S sells S's interest in the property to D's children for $100,000. Pursuant to section 2519, S makes a gift of $200,000 ($300,000 less $100,000 value of the qualifying income interest in the property). S does not make a gift of the income interest under section 2511, because the consideration received for S's income interest is equal to the value of the income interest.

Example 3. Transfer of income interest in trust subject to partial election. D's will established a trust valued for estate tax purposes at $500,000, all of the income of which is payable annually to S for life. After S's death, the principal of the trust is to be distributed to D's children. Assume that only 50 percent of the trust was treated as qualified terminable interest property. During 1995, S makes a gift of all of S's interest in the trust to D's children at which time the fair market value of the trust is $400,000 and the fair market value of S's life income interest in the trust is $100,000. Pursuant to section 2519, S makes a gift of $150,000 (the fair market value of the qualified terminable interest property, 50 percent of $400,000, less the $50,000 income interest in the qualified terminable interest property). S also makes a gift pursuant to section 2511 of $100,000 (i.e., the fair market value of S's life income interest).

Example 4. Transfer of a portion of income interest in trust subject to a partial election. The facts are the same as in *Example 3* except that S makes a gift of only 40 percent of S's interest in the trust. Pursuant to section 2519, S makes a gift of $150,000 (i.e., the fair market value of the qualified terminable interest property, 50 percent of $400,000, less the $50,000 value of S's qualified income interest in the qualified terminable interest property). S also makes a gift pursuant to section 2511 of $40,000 (i.e., the fair market value of 40 percent of S's life income interest). See also section 2702 for additional rules that may affect the value of the total amount of S's gift under section 2519 to take into account the fact that S's 30 percent retained income interest attributable to the qualifying income interest is valued at zero under that section, thereby increasing the value of S's section 2519 gift to $180,000. In addition, under § 25.2519-1(d), S's disposition of 40 percent of the income interest is deemed to be a transfer of a pro rata portion of the qualified terminable interest property. Thus, assuming no further lifetime dispositions by S, 30 percent (60 percent of 50 percent) of the trust property is included in S's gross estate under section 2036 and an adjustment is made to S's adjusted taxable gifts under section 2001(b)(1)(B). If S later disposes of all or a portion of the retained income interest, see § 25.2702-6.

Example 5. Transfer of a portion of spouse's interest in a trust from which corpus was previously distributed to the spouse. D's will established a trust valued for estate tax purposes at $500,000, all of the income of which is payable annually to S for life. The trustee is granted the discretion to distribute trust principal to S. All appointments of principal must be made from the portion of the trust subject to the section 2056(b)(7) election. After S's death, the principal of the trust is to be distributed to D's children. The executor makes the section 2056(b)(7) election with respect to 50 percent of the trust. In 1994, pursuant to the terms of D's will, the trustee distributed $50,000 of principal to S and charged the entire distribution to the qualified terminable interest portion of the trust. Immediately prior to the distribution, the value of the entire trust was $550,000 and the value of the qualified terminable interest portion was $275,000 (50 percent of $550,000). Provided S can establish the above facts, the qualified terminable interest portion of the trust immediately after the distribution is $225,000 or 45 percent of the value of the trust ($225,000/$500,000). In 1996, when the value of the trust is $400,000 and the value of S's income interest is $100,000, S makes a transfer of 40 percent of S's income interest. S's gift under section 2519 is $135,000; i.e., the fair market value of the qualified terminable interest property, 45 percent of $400,000 ($180,000), less the value of the income interest in the qualified terminable interest property, $45,000 (45 percent of $100,000). S also makes a gift under section 2511 of $40,000; i.e., the fair market value of 40 percent of S's income interest. S's disposition of 40 percent of the income interest is deemed to be a transfer under section 2519 of the entire 45 percent portion of the remainder subject to the section 2056(b)(7) election. Since S retained 60 percent of the income interest, 27 percent (60 percent of 45 percent) of the trust property is includible in S's gross estate under section 2036. See also section 2702 and *Example 4* as to the principles applicable in valuing S's gift under section 2702 and adjusted taxable gifts upon S's subsequent death.

Example 6. Transfer of Spousal Annuity Payable From Trust. D died prior to October 24, 1992. D's will established a trust valued for estate tax purposes at $500,000. The trust instrument required the trustee to pay an annuity to S of $20,000 a year for life. All the trust income other than the amounts paid to S as an annuity are to be accumulated in the trust and may not be distributed during S's lifetime to any person other than S. After S's death, the principal of the trust is to be distributed to D's children. Because D died prior to the effective date of section 1941 of the Energy Policy Act of 1992, S's annuity interest qualifies as a qualifying income interest for life. Under § 20.2056(b)-7(e) of this chapter, based on an applicable 10 percent interest rate, 40 percent of the property, or $200,000, is the value of the deductible interest. During 1996, S makes a gift of the annuity interest to D's children at which time the fair market value of the trust is $800,000 and the fair market value of S's annuity interest in the trust is $100,000. Pursuant to section 2519, S is treated as making a gift of $220,000 (the fair market value of the qualified terminable interest property, 40 percent of $800,000 ($320,000), less the $100,000 annuity interest in the qualified terminable interest property). S is also treated pursuant to section 2511 as making a gift of $100,000 (the fair market value of S's annuity interest). [Reg. § 25.2519-1.]

☐ [*T.D.* 8522, 2-28-94. *Amended by T.D.* 9077, 7-17-2003.]

[Reg. § 25.2519-2]

§ 25.2519-2. Effective date.—Except as specifically provided in § 25.2519-1(g), *Example 6*, the provisions of § 25.2519-1 are effective with respect to gifts made after March 1, 1994. With respect to gifts made on or before such date, the donee spouse of a section 2056(b)(7) or section 2523(f) transfer may rely on any reasonable interpretation of the statutory provisions. For these purposes, the provisions of § 25.2519-1 (as well as project LR-211-76, 1984-1 C.B., page 598, see § 601.601(d)(2)(ii)(*b*) of this chapter), are considered a reasonable interpretation of the statutory provisions. [Reg. § 25.2519-2.]

☐ [*T.D.* 8522, 2-28-94.]

DEDUCTIONS

[Reg. § 25.2522(a)-1]

§ 25.2522(a)-1. Charitable and similar gifts; citizens or residents.—(a) In determining the amount of taxable gifts for the "calendar period" (as defined in § 25.2502-1(c)(1)) there may be deducted, in the case of a donor who was a citizen or resident of the United States at the time the gifts were made, all gifts included in the "total amount of gifts" made by the donor during the calendar period (see section 2503 and the regulations thereunder) and made to or for the use of:

(1) The United States, any State, Territory, or any political subdivision thereof, or the District of Columbia, for exclusively public purposes.

(2) Any corporation, trust, community chest, fund, or foundation organized and operated exclusively for religious, charitable, scientific, literary, or educational purposes, including the encouragement of art and the prevention of cruelty to children or animals, if no part of the net earnings of the organization inures to the benefit of any private shareholder or individual, if it is not disqualified for tax exemption under section 501(c)(3) by reason of attempting to influence legislation, and if, in the case of gifts made after December 31, 1969, it does not participate in, or intervene in (including the publishing or distributing of statements), any political campaign on behalf of or in opposition to any candidate for public office.

(3) A fraternal society, order, or association, operating under the lodge system, provided the gifts are to be used by the society, order or association exclusively for one or more of the purposes set forth in subparagraph (2) of this paragraph.

(4) Any post or organization of war veterans or auxiliary unit or society thereof, if organized in the United States or any of its possessions, and if no part of its net earnings inures to the benefit of any private shareholder or individual.

The deduction is not limited to gifts for use within the United States or to gifts to or for the use of domestic corporations, trusts, community chests, funds, or foundations, or fraternal societies, orders, or associations operating under the lodge system. An organization will not be considered to meet the requirements of subparagraph (2) of this paragraph, or of paragraph (b)(2) or (3) of this section, if such organization engages in any activity which would cause it to be classified as an "action" organization under paragraph (c)(3) of § 1.501(c)(3)-1 of this chapter (Income Tax Regulations). For the deductions for charitable and similar gifts made by a nonresident who was not a citizen of the United States at the time the gifts were made, see § 25.2522(b)-1. See § 25.2522(c)-1 and § 25.2522(c)-2 for rules relating to the disallowance of deductions to trusts and organizations which engage in certain prohibited transactions or whose governing instruments do not contain certain specified requirements.

(b) The deduction under section 2522 is not allowed for a transfer to a corporation, trust, community chest, fund, or foundation unless the organization or trust meets the following four tests:

(1) It must be organized and operated exclusively for one or more of the specified purposes.

(2) It must not be disqualified for tax exemption under section 501(c)(3) by reason of attempting to influence legislation.

(3) In the case of gifts made after December 31, 1969, it must not participate in, or intervene in (including the publishing or distributing of statements), any political campaign on behalf of any candidate for public office.

(4) Its net earnings must not inure in whole or in part to the benefit of private shareholders or individuals other than as legitimate objects of the exempt purposes.

(c) In order to prove the right to the charitable, etc., deduction provided by section 2522, the donor must submit such data as may be requested by the Internal Revenue Service. As to the extent the deductions provided by this section are allowable, see section 2524. [Reg. § 25.2522(a)-1.]

☐ [*T.D.* 6334, 11-14-58. *Amended by T.D.* 7012, 5-14-69; *T.D.* 7238, 12-28-72; *T.D.* 7318, 7-10-74; *T.D.* 7910, 9-6-83 *and T.D.* 8308, 8-30-90.]

[Reg. § 25.2522(b)-1]

§ 25.2522(b)-1. Charitable and similar gifts; nonresidents not citizens.—(a) The deduction for charitable and similar gifts in the case of a nonresident who was not a citizen of the United States at the time he made the gifts is governed by the same rules as those applying to gifts by citizens or residents, subject, however, to the following exceptions:

(1) If the gifts are made to or for the use of a corporation, the corporation must be one created

or organized under the laws of the United States or of any State or Territory thereof.

(2) If the gifts are made to or for the use of a trust, community chest, fund or foundation, or a fraternal society, order or association operating under the lodge system, the gifts must be for use within the United States exclusively for religious, charitable, scientific, literary or educational purposes, including encouragement of art and the prevention of cruelty to children or animals. [Reg. § 25.2522(b)-1.]

☐ [*T.D.* 6334, 11-14-58.]

[Reg. § 25.2522(c)-1]

§ 25.2522(c)-1. Disallowance of charitable, etc., deductions because of "prohibited transactions" in the case of gifts made before January 1, 1970.—(a) Sections 503(e) and 681(b)(5) provide that no deduction which would otherwise be allowable under section 2522 for a gift for religious, charitable, scientific, literary or educational purposes, including the encouragement of art and the prevention of cruelty to children or animals, is allowed if—

(1) The gift is made in trust and, for income tax purposes for the taxable year of the trust in which the gift is made, the deduction otherwise allowable to the trust under section 642(c) is limited by section 681(b)(1) by reason of the trust having engaged in a prohibited transaction described in section 681(b)(2); or

(2) The gift is made to any corporation, community chest, fund or foundation which, for its taxable year in which the gift is made, is not exempt from income tax under section 501(a) by reason of having engaged in a prohibited transaction described in section 503(c).

(b) For purposes of section 503(e) and section 681(b)(5), the term "gift" includes any gift, contribution, or transfer without adequate consideration.

(c) Regulations relating to the income tax contain the rules for the determination of the taxable year of the trust for which the deduction under section 642(c) is limited by section 681(b), and for the determination of the taxable year of the organization for which an exemption is denied under section 503(a). Generally, such taxable year is a taxable year subsequent to the taxable year during which the trust or organization has been notified by the Internal Revenue Service that it has engaged in a prohibited transaction. However, if the trust or organization during or prior to the taxable year entered into the prohibited transaction for the purpose of diverting its corpus or income from the charitable or other purposes by reason of which it is entitled to a deduction or exemption, and the transaction involves a substantial part of such income or corpus, then the deduction of the trust under section 642(c) for such taxable year is limited by section 681(b), or the exemption of the organization for such taxable year is denied under section 503(a), whether or not the organization has previously received notification by the Internal Revenue Service that it has engaged in a prohibited transaction. In certain cases, the limitation of section 503 or 681 may be removed or the exemption may be reinstated for certain subsequent taxable years under the rules set forth in the income tax regulations under sections 503 and 681.

(d) In cases in which prior notification by the Internal Revenue Service is not required in order to limit the deduction of the trust under section 681(b), or to deny exemption of the organization under section 503, the deduction otherwise allowable under § 25.2522(a)-1 is not disallowed with respect to gifts made during the same taxable year of the trust or organization in which a prohibited transaction occurred, or in a prior taxable year, unless the donor or a member of his family was a party to the prohibited transaction. For purposes of the preceding sentence, the members of the donor's family include only his brothers and sisters (whether by whole or half blood), spouse, ancestors, and lineal descendants.

(e) This section applies only to gifts made before January 1, 1970. In the case of gifts made after December 31, 1969, see § 25.2522(c)-2. [Reg. § 25.2522(c)-1.]

☐ [*T.D.* 6334, 11-14-58. *Amended by T.D.* 7318, 7-10-74.]

[Reg. § 25.2522(c)-2]

§ 25.2522(c)-2. Disallowance of charitable, etc., deductions in the case of gifts made after December 31, 1969.—(a) *Organizations subject to section 507(c) tax.*—Section 508(d)(1) provides that, in the case of gifts made after December 31, 1969, a deduction which would otherwise be allowable under section 2522 for a gift to or for the use of an organization upon which the tax provided by section 507(c) has been imposed shall not be allowed if the gift is made by the donor after notification is made under section 507(a) or if the donor is a substantial contributor (as defined in section 507(d)(2)) who makes such gift in his taxable year (as defined in section 441) which includes the first day on which action is taken by such organization that culminates in the imposition of the tax under section 507(c) and any subsequent taxable year. This paragraph does not apply if the entire amount of the unpaid portion of the tax imposed by section 507(c) is abated under section 507(g) by the Commissioner or his delegate.

(b) *Taxable private foundations, section 4947 trusts, etc.*—Section 508(d)(2) provides that, in the case of gifts made after December 31, 1969, a deduction which would otherwise be allowable under section 2522 shall not be allowed if the gift is made to or for the use of—

(1) A private foundation or a trust described in section 4947(a)(2) in a taxable year of such organization for which such organization fails to meet the governing instrument requirements of section 508(e) (determined without regard to section 508(e)(2)(B) and (C)), or

(2) Any organization in a period for which it is not treated as an organization described in

section 501(c)(3) by reason of its failure to give notification under section 508(a) of its status to the Commissioner.

For additional rules, see § 1.508-2(b)(1) of this chapter (Income Tax Regulations).

(c) *Foreign organizations with substantial support from foreign sources.*—Section 4948(c)(4) provides that, in the case of gifts made after December 31, 1969, a deduction which would otherwise be allowable under section 2522 for a gift to or for the use of a foreign organization which has received substantially all of its support (other than gross investment income) from sources without the United States shall not be allowed if the gift is made (1) after the date on which the Commissioner has published notice that he has notified such organization that it has engaged in a prohibited transaction or (2) in a taxable year of such organization for which it is not exempt from taxation under section 501(a) because it has engaged in a prohibited transaction after December 31, 1969. [Reg. § 25.2522(c)-2.]

□ [*T.D.* 7318, 6-10-74.]

[Reg. § 25.2522(c)-3]

§ 25.2522(c)-3. Transfers not exclusively for charitable, etc., purposes in the case of gifts made after July 31, 1969.—(a) *Remainders and similar interests.*—If a trust is created or property is transferred for both a charitable and a private purpose, deduction may be taken of the value of the charitable beneficial interest only insofar as that interest is presently ascertainable, and hence severable from the noncharitable interest.

(b) *Transfers subject to a condition or a power.*—(1) If, as of the date of the gift, a transfer for charitable purposes is dependent upon the performance of some act or the happening of a precedent event in order that it might become effective, no deduction is allowable unless the possibility that the charitable transfer will not become effective is so remote as to be negligible. If an estate or interest has passed to, or is vested in, charity on the date of the gift and the estate or interest would be defeated by the performance of some act or the happening of some event, the possibility of occurrence of which appeared on such date to be so remote as to be negligible, the deduction is allowable. If the donee or trustee is empowered to divert the property or fund, in whole or in part, to a use or purpose which would have rendered it, to the extent that it is subject to such power, not deductible had it been directly so given by the donor, the deduction will be limited to that portion, if any, of the property or fund which is exempt from an exercise of the power.

(2) The application of this paragraph may be illustrated by the following examples:

Example (1). In 1965, A transfers certain property in trust in which charity is to receive the income for his life. The assets placed in trust by the donor consist of stock in a corporation the fiscal policies of which are controlled by the donor and his family. The trustees of the trust and the remainderman are members of the donor's family and the governing instrument contains no adequate guarantee of the requisite income to the charitable organization. Under such circumstances, no deduction will be allowed. Similarly, if the trustees are not members of the donor's family but have no power to sell or otherwise dispose of the closely held stock, or otherwise insure the requisite enjoyment of income to the charitable organization, no deduction will be allowed.

Example (2). C transfers a tract of land to a city government for as long as the land is used by the city for a public park. If on the date of gift the city does plan to use the land for a public park and the possibility that the city will not use the land for a public park is so remote as to be negligible, a deduction will be allowed.

(c) *Transfers of partial interests in property.*—(1) *Disallowance of deduction.*—(i) *In general.*—If a donor transfers an interest in property after July 31, 1969, for charitable purposes and an interest in the same property is retained by the donor, or is transferred or has been transferred for private purposes after such date (for less than an adequate and full consideration in money or money's worth), no deduction is allowed under section 2522 for the value of the interest which is transferred or has been transferred for charitable purposes unless the interest in property is a deductible interest described in subparagraph (2) of this paragraph. The principles that are used in applying section 2523 and the regulations thereunder shall apply for purposes of determining under this subparagraph whether an interest in property is retained by the donor, or is transferred or has been transferred by the donor. If, however, as of the date of the gift, a retention of an interest by a donor, or a transfer for a private purpose, is dependent upon the performance of some act or the happening of a precedent event in order that it may become effective, an interest in property will be considered retained by the donor, or transferred for a private purpose, unless the possibility of occurrence of such act or event is so remote as to be negligible. The application of this subparagraph may be illustrated by the following examples, in each of which it is assumed that the property interest which is transferred for private purposes is not transferred for an adequate and full consideration in money or money's worth:

Example (1). In 1973, H creates a trust which is to pay the income of the trust to W for her life, the reversionary interest in the trust being retained by H. In 1975, H gives the reversionary interest to charity, while W is still living. For purposes of this paragraph (c)(1)(i), interests in the same property have been transferred by H for charitable purposes and for private purposes.

Example (2). In 1973, H creates a trust which is to pay the income of the trust to W for her life and upon termination of the life estate to transfer the remainder to S. In 1975, S gives his remainder interest to charity, while W is still living. For purposes of this paragraph (c)(1)(i), interests in the same property have not been transferred by H or S for charitable purposes and for private purposes.

Example (3). H transfers Blackacre to A by gift, reserving the right to the rentals of Blackacre for a term of 20 years. After 4 years H transfers the right to the remaining rentals to charity. For purposes of this paragraph (c)(1)(i) the term "property" refers to Blackacre, and the right to rentals from Blackacre consists of an interest in Blackacre. An interest in Blackacre has been transferred by H for charitable purposes and for private purposes.

Example (4). H transfers property in trust for the benefit of A and a charity. An annuity of $5,000 a year is to be paid to charity for 20 years. Upon termination of the 20-year term the corpus is to be distributed to A if living. However, if A should die during the 20-year term, the corpus is to be distributed to charity upon termination of the term. An interest in property has been transferred by H for charitable purposes. In addition, an interest in the same property has been transferred by H for private purposes unless the possibility that A will survive the 20-year term is so remote as to be negligible.

Example (5). H transfers property in trust, under the terms of which an annuity of $5,000 a year is to be paid to charity for 20 years. Upon termination of the term, the corpus is to pass to such of A's children and their issue as A may appoint. However, if A should die during the 20-year term without exercising the power of appointment, the corpus is to be distributed to charity upon termination of the term. Since the possible appointees include private persons, an interest in the corpus of the trust is considered to have been transferred by H for private purposes.

(ii) *Works of art and copyright treated as separate properties.*—For purposes of paragraphs (c)(1)(i) and (c)(2) of this section, rules similar to the rules in § 20.2055-2(e)(1)(ii) shall apply in the case of transfers made after December 31, 1981.

(2) *Deductible interests.*—A deductible interest for purposes of subparagraph (i) of this paragraph is a charitable interest in property where—

(i) *Undivided portion of donor's entire interest.*—The charitable interest is an undivided portion, not in trust, of the donor's entire interest in property. An undivided portion of a donor's entire interest in property must consist of a fraction or percentage of each and every substantial interest or right owned by the donor in such property and must extend over the entire term of the donor's interest in such property and in other property into which such property is converted. For example, if the donor gave a life estate in an office building to his wife for her life and retained a reversionary interest in the office building, the gift by the donor of one-half of that reversionary interest to charity while his wife is still alive will not be considered the transfer of a deductible interest; because an interest in the same property has already passed from the donor for private purposes, the reversionary interest will not be considered the donor's entire interest in the property. If, on the other hand, the donor had been given a life estate in Blackacre for the life of his wife and the donor had no other interest in Blackacre on or before the time of gift, the gift by the donor of one-half of that life estate to charity would be considered the transfer of a deductible interest; because the life estate would be considered the donor's entire interest in the property, the gift would be of an undivided portion of such entire interest. An undivided portion of a donor's entire interest in property includes an interest in property whereby the charity is given the right, as a tenant in common with the donor, to possession, dominion, and control of the property for a portion of each year appropriate to its interest in such property. However, except as provided in paragraphs (c)(2)(ii), (iii), and (iv) of this section, for purposes of this subdivision a charitable contribution of an interest in property not in trust where the decedent transfers some specific rights to one party and transfers other substantial rights to another party will not be considered a contribution of an undivided portion of the decedent's entire interest in property. A gift of an open space easement in gross in perpetuity shall be considered a gift of an undivided portion of the donor's entire interest in property. A gift to charity made on or before December 17, 1980, of an open space easement in gross in perpetuity shall be considered the transfer to charity of an undivided portion of the donor's entire interest in property.

(ii) *Remainder interest in a personal residence.*—The charitable interest is an irrevocable remainder interest, not in trust, in a personal residence. Thus, for example, if the donor gives to charity a remainder interest in a personal residence and retains an estate in such property for life or a term of years the value of such remainder interest is deductible under section 2522. For purposes of this subdivision, the term "personal residence" means any property which is used by the donor as his personal residence even though it is not used as his principal residence. For example, a donor's vacation home may be a personal residence for purposes of this subdivision. The term "personal residence" also includes stock owned by the donor on the date of gift as a tenant-stockholder in a cooperative housing corporation (as those terms are defined in section 216(b)(1) and (2)) if the dwelling which the donor is entitled to occupy as such stockholder is used by him as his personal residence.

(iii) *Remainder interest in a farm.*—The charitable interest is an irrevocable remainder interest, not in trust, in a farm. Thus, for example, if the donor gives to charity a remainder interest in a farm and retains an estate in such property for life or a term of years, the value of such remainder interest is deductible under section 2522. For purposes of this subdivision, the term "farm" means any land used by the donor or his tenant for the production of crops, fruits, or other agricultural products or for the sustenance of livestock. The term "livestock" includes cattle, hogs, horses, mules, donkeys, sheep, goats, captive fur-bearing animals, chickens, turkeys, pigeons, and other poultry. A farm includes the improvements thereon.

(iv) *Qualified conservation contribution.*—The charitable interest is a qualified conservation contribution. For the definition of a qualified conservation contribution, see § 1.170A-14.

(v) *Charitable remainder trust and pooled income funds.*—The charitable interest is a remainder interest in a trust which is a charitable remainder annuity trust, as defined in section 664(d)(1) and § 1.664-2 of this chapter; a charitable remainder unitrust, as defined in section 664(d)(2) and (3) and § 1.664-3 of this chapter; or a pooled income fund, as defined in section 642(c)(5) and § 1.642(c)-5 of this chapter. The charitable organization to or for the use of which the remainder interest is transferred must meet the requirements of both section 2522(a) or (b) and section 642(c)(5)(A), section 664(d)(1)(C), or section 664(d)(2)(C), whichever applies. For example, the charitable organization to which the remainder interest in a charitable remainder annuity trust is transferred may not be a foreign corporation.

(vi) *Guaranteed annuity interest.*—*(a)* The charitable interest is a guaranteed annuity interest, whether or not such interest is in trust. For purposes of this paragraph (c)(2)(vi), the term "guaranteed annuity interest" means an irrevocable right pursuant to the instrument of transfer to receive a guaranteed annuity. A guaranteed annuity is an arrangement under which a determinable amount is paid periodically, but not less often than annually, for a specified term of years or for the life or lives of certain individuals, each of whom must be living at the date of the gift and can be ascertained at such date. Only one or more of the following individuals may be used as measuring lives: the donor, the donor's spouse, and an individual who, with respect to all remainder beneficiaries (other than charitable organizations described in section 170, 2055, or 2522), is either a lineal ancestor or the spouse of a lineal ancestor of those beneficiaries. A trust will satisfy the requirement that all noncharitable remainder beneficiaries are lineal descendants of the individual who is the measuring life, or that individual's spouse, if there is less than a 15% probability that individuals who are not lineal descendants will receive any trust corpus. This probability must be computed, based on the current applicable Life Table contained in § 20.2031-7, at the time property is transferred to the trust taking into account the interests of all primary and contingent remainder beneficiaries who are living at that time. An interest payable for a specified term of years can qualify as a guaranteed annuity interest even if the governing instrument contains a savings clause intended to ensure compliance with a rule against perpetuities. The savings clause must utilize a period for vesting of 21 years after the deaths of measuring lives who are selected to maximize, rather than limit, the term of the trust. The rule in this paragraph that a charitable interest may be payable for the life or lives of only certain specified individuals does not apply in the case of a charitable guaranteed annuity interest payable under a charitable remainder trust described in section 664. An amount is determinable if the exact amount which must be paid under the conditions specified in the instrument of transfer can be ascertained as of the date of gift. For example, the amount to be paid may be a stated sum for a term of years, or for the life of the donor, at the expiration of which it may be changed by a specified amount, but it may not be redetermined by reference to a fluctuating index such as the cost of living index. In further illustration, the amount to be paid may be expressed as a fraction or percentage of the cost of living index on the date of gift.

(b) A charitable interest is a guaranteed annuity interest only if it is a guaranteed annuity interest in every respect. For example, if the charitable interest is the right to receive from a trust each year a payment equal to the lesser of a sum certain or a fixed percentage of the net fair market value of the trust assets, determined annually, such interest is not a guaranteed annuity interest.

(c) Where a charitable interest in the form of a guaranteed annuity interest is not in trust, the interest will be considered a guaranteed annuity interest only if it is to be paid by an insurance company or by an organization regularly engaged in issuing annuity contracts.

(d) Where a charitable interest in the form of a guaranteed annuity interest is in trust, the governing instrument of the trust may provide that income of the trust which is in excess of the amount required to pay the guaranteed annuity interest shall be paid to or for the use of a charity. Nevertheless, the amount of the deduction under section 2522 shall be limited to the fair market value of the guaranteed annuity interest as determined under paragraph (d)(2)(iv) of this section.

(e) Where a charitable interest in the form of a guaranteed annuity interest is in trust and the present value on the date of gift of all income interests for a charitable purpose exceeds 60 percent of the aggregate fair market value of all amounts in such trust (after the payment of liabilities), the charitable interest will not be considered a guaranteed annuity interest unless the governing instrument of the trust prohibits both the acquisition and the retention of assets which would give rise to a tax under section 4944 if the trustee had acquired such assets. The requirement in this *(e)* for a prohibition in the governing instrument against the retention of assets which would give rise to a tax under section 4944 if the trustee had acquired the assets shall not apply to a gift made on or before May 21, 1972.

(f) Where a charitable interest in the form of a guaranteed annuity interest is in trust, and the gift of such interest is made after May

21, 1972, the charitable interest generally is not a guaranteed annuity interest if any amount may be paid by the trust for a private purpose before the expiration of all the charitable annuity interests. There are two exceptions to this general rule. First, the charitable interest is a guaranteed annuity interest if the amount payable for a private purpose is in the form of a guaranteed annuity interest and the trust's governing instrument does not provide for any preference or priority in the payment of the private annuity as opposed to the charitable annuity. Second, the charitable interest is a guaranteed annuity interest if under the trust's governing instrument the amount that may be paid for a private purpose is payable only from a group of assets that are devoted exclusively to private purposes and to which section 4947(a)(2) is inapplicable by reason of section 4947(a)(2)(B). For purposes of this paragraph (c)(2)(vi)(*f*), an amount is not paid for a private purpose if it is paid for an adequate and full consideration in money or money's worth. See §53.4947-1(c) of this chapter for rules relating to the inapplicability of section 4947(a)(2) to segregated amounts in a split-interest trust.

(*g*) For rules relating to certain governing instrument requirements and to the imposition of certain excise taxes where the guaranteed annuity interest is in trust and for rules governing payment of private income interests by a split-interest trust, see section 4947(a)(2) and (b)(3)(A), and the regulations thereunder.

(vii) *Unitrust interest.*—(*a*) The charitable interest is a unitrust interest, whether or not such interest is in trust. For purposes of this paragraph (c)(2)(vii), the term "unitrust interest" means an irrevocable right pursuant to the instrument of transfer to receive payment, not less often than annually, of a fixed percentage of the net fair market value, determined annually, of the property which funds the unitrust interest. In computing the net fair market value of the property which funds the unitrust interest, all assets and liabilities shall be taken into account without regard to whether particular items are taken into account in determining the income from the property. The net fair market value of the property which funds the unitrust interest may be determined on any one date during the year or by taking the average of valuations made on more than one date during the year, provided that the same valuation date or dates and valuation methods are used each year. Where the charitable interest is a unitrust interest to be paid by a trust and the governing instrument of the trust does not specify the valuation date or dates, the trustee shall select such date or dates and shall indicate his selection on the first return on Form 1041 which the trust is required to file. Payments under a unitrust interest may be paid for a specified term of years or for the life or lives of certain individuals, each of whom must be living at the date of the gift and can be ascertained at such date. Only one or more of the following individuals may be used as measuring lives: the donor, the donor's spouse, and an individual who, with respect to all remainder beneficiaries (other than charitable organizations described in section 170, 2055, or 2522), is either a lineal ancestor or the spouse of a lineal ancestor of those beneficiaries. A trust will satisfy the requirement that all noncharitable remainder beneficiaries are lineal descendants of the individual who is the measuring life, or that individual's spouse, if there is less than a 15% probability that individuals who are not lineal descendants will receive any trust corpus. This probability must be computed, based on the current applicable Life Table contained in §20.2031-7, at the time property is transferred to the trust taking into account the interests of all primary and contingent remainder beneficiaries who are living at that time. An interest payable for a specified term of years can qualify as a unitrust interest even if the governing instrument contains a savings clause intended to ensure compliance with a rule against perpetuities. The savings clause must utilize a period for vesting of 21 years after the deaths of measuring lives who are selected to maximize, rather than limit, the term of the trust. The rule in this paragraph that a charitable interest may be payable for the life or lives of only certain specified individuals does not apply in the case of a charitable unitrust interest payable under a charitable remainder trust described in section 664.

(*b*) A charitable interest is a unitrust interest only if it is a unitrust interest in every respect. For example, if the charitable interest is the right to receive from a trust each year a payment equal to the lesser of a sum certain or a fixed percentage of the net fair market value of the trust assets, determined annually, such interest is not a unitrust interest.

(*c*) Where a charitable interest in the form of a unitrust interest is not in trust, the interest will be considered a unitrust interest only if it is to be paid by an insurance company or by an organization regularly engaged in issuing interests otherwise meeting the requirements of a unitrust interest.

(*d*) Where a charitable interest in the form of a unitrust interest is in trust, the governing instrument of the trust may provide that income of the trust which is in excess of the amount required to pay the unitrust interest shall be paid to or for the use of a charity. Nevertheless, the amount of the deduction under section 2522 shall be limited to the fair market value of the unitrust interest as determined under paragraph (d)(2)(v) of this section.

(*e*) Where a charitable interest in the form of a unitrust interest is in trust, the charitable interest generally is not a unitrust interest if any amount may be paid by the trust for a private purpose before the expiration of all the charitable unitrust interests. There are two exceptions to this general rule. First, the charitable interest is a unitrust interest if the amount payable for a private purpose is in the form of a unitrust interest and the trust's governing instrument does not provide for any preference or priority in the payment of the private unitrust interest as opposed to the charitable unitrust interest. Second, the charitable interest is a unitrust interest if under the trust's governing instrument the amount that may be paid for a private purpose is payable only from a group of assets that are devoted exclusively to private purposes and to which section 4947(a)(2) is inapplicable by reason of section 4947(a)(2)(B). For purposes of this paragraph (c)(2)(vii)(*e*), an amount is not paid for a private purpose if it is paid for an adequate and full consideration in money or money's worth. See § 53.4947-1(c) of this chapter for rules relating to the inapplicability of section 4947(a)(2) to segregated amounts in a split-interest trust.

(*f*) For rules relating to certain governing instrument requirements and to the imposition of certain excise taxes where the unitrust interest is in trust and for rules governing payment of private income interests by a split-interest trust, see sections 4947(a)(2) and (b)(3)(A), and the regulations thereunder.

(d) *Valuation of charitable interest.*—(1) *In general.*—The amount of the deduction in the case of a contribution of a partial interest in property to which this section applies is the fair market value of the partial interest on the date of gift. The fair market value of an annuity, life estate, term for years, remainder, reversion or unitrust interest is its present value.

(2) *Certain transfers after July 31, 1969.*—In the case of a transfer after July 31, 1969, of an interest described in paragraph (c)(2)(v), (vi), or (vii) of this section, the present value of such interest is to be determined under the following rules:

(i) The present value of a remainder interest in a charitable remainder annuity trust is to be determined under § 1.664-2(c) of this chapter (Income Tax Regulations).

(ii) The present value of a remainder interest in a charitable remainder unitrust is to be determined under § 1.664-4 of this chapter.

(iii) The present value of a remainder interest in a pooled income fund is to be determined under § 1.642(c)-6 of this chapter.

(iv) The present value of a guaranteed annuity interest described in paragraph (c)(2)(vi) of this section is to be determined under § 25.2512-5 except that, if the annuity is issued by a company regularly engaged in the sale of annuities, the present value is to be determined under § 25.2512-6. If by reason of all the conditions and circumstances surrounding a transfer of an income interest in property in trust it appears that the charity may not receive the beneficial enjoyment of the interest, a deduction will be allowed under section 2522 only for the minimum amount it is evident the charity will receive.

Example (1). In 1975, B transfers $20,000 in trust with the requirement that a designated charity be paid a guaranteed annuity interest (as defined in paragraph (c)(2)(vi) of this section) of $4,100 a year, payable annually at the end of each year for a period of 6 years and that the remainder be paid to his children. The fair market value of an annuity of $4,100 a year for a period of 6 years is $20,160.93 ($4,100 × 4.9173), as determined under § 25.2512-5A(c). The deduction with respect to the guaranteed annuity interest will be limited to $20,000, which is the minimum amount it is evident the charity will receive.

Example (2). In 1975, C transfers $40,000 in trust with the requirement that D, an individual, and X Charity be paid simultaneously guaranteed annuity interests (as defined in paragraph (c)(2)(vi) of this section) of $5,000 a year each, payable annually at the end of each year, for a period of 5 years and that the remainder be paid to C's children. The fair market value of two annuities of $5,000 each a year for a period of 5 years is $42,124 ([$5,000 × 4.2124] × 2), as determined under § 25.2512-5A(c). The trust instrument provides that in the event the trust fund is insufficient to pay both annuities in a given year, the trust fund will be evenly divided between the charitable and private annuitants. The deduction with respect to the charitable annuity will be limited to $20,000, which is the minimum amount it is evident the charity will receive.

Example (3). In 1975, D transfers $65,000 in trust with the requirement that a guaranteed annuity interest (as defined in paragraph (c)(2)(vi) of this section) of $5,000 a year, payable annually at the end of each year, be paid to Y Charity for a period of 10 years and that a guaranteed annuity interest (as defined in paragraph (c)(2)(vi) of this section) of $5,000 a year, payable annually at the end of each year, be paid to W, his wife, aged 62[,]for 10 years or until her prior death. The annuities are to be paid simultaneously, and the remainder is to be paid to D's children. The fair market value of the private annuity is $33,877 ($5,000 × 6.7754), as determined pursuant to § 25.2512-5A(c) and by the use of factors involving one life and a term of years as published in Publication 723A (12-70). The fair market value of the charitable annuity is $36,800.50 ($5,000 × 7.3601), as determined under § 25.2512-5A(c). It is not evident from the governing instrument of the trust or from local law that the trustee would be required to apportion the trust fund between the wife and charity in the event the fund were insufficient to pay both annuities in a given year. Accordingly, the deduction with respect to the charitable annuity will be limited to $31,123 ($65,000 less $33,877 [the value of the private annuity]), which is the minimum amount it is evident the charity will receive.

(v) The present value of a unitrust interest described in paragraph (c)(2)(vii) of this section is to be determined by subtracting the present value of all interests in the transferred property other than the unitrust interest from the fair market value of the transferred property.

(3) *Other transfers.*—The present value of an interest not described in paragraph (d)(2) of this section is to be determined under §25.2512-5.

(4) *Special computations.*—If the interest transferred is such that its present value is to be determined by a special computation, a request for a special factor, accompanied by a statement of the date of birth and sex of each individual the duration of whose life may affect the value of the interest, and by copies of the relevant instruments, may be submitted by the donor to the Commissioner who may, if conditions permit, supply the factor requested. If the Commissioner furnishes the factor, a copy of the letter supplying the factor must be attached to the tax return in which the deduction is claimed. If the Commissioner does not furnish the factor, the claim for deduction must be supported by a full statement of the computation of the present value made in accordance with the principles set forth in this paragraph.

(e) *Effective/applicability date.*—This section applies only to gifts made after July 31, 1969. In addition, the rule in paragraphs (c)(2)(vi)(a) and (c)(2)(vii)(a) of this section that guaranteed annuity interests or unitrust interests, respectively, may be payable for a specified term of years or for the life or lives of only certain individuals applies to transfers made on or after April 4, 2000. If a transfer is made on or after April 4, 2000, that uses an individual other than one permitted in paragraphs (c)(2)(vi)(a) and (c)(2)(vii)(a) of this section, the interest may be reformed into a lead interest payable for a specified term of years. The term of years is determined by taking the factor for valuing the annuity or unitrust interest for the named individual measuring life and identifying the term of years (rounded up to the next whole year) that corresponds to the equivalent term of years factor for an annuity or unitrust interest. For example, in the case of an annuity interest payable for the life of an individual age 40 at the time of the transfer on or after May 1, 2009 (the effective date of Table S), assuming an interest rate of 7.4 percent under section 7520, the annuity factor from column 1 of Table S(7.4), contained in IRS Publication 1457, Actuarial Valuations Version 3A, for the life of an individual age 40 is 12.1519 (1 − .10076 / .074). Based on Table B(7.4), contained in Publication 1457, "Actuarial Valuations Version 3A", the factor 12.1519 corresponds to a term of years between 32 and 33 years. Accordingly, the annuity interest must be reformed into an interest payable for a term of 33 years. A judicial reformation must be commenced prior to October 15th of the year following the year in which the transfer is made and must be completed within a reasonable time after it is commenced. A non-judicial reformation is permitted if effective under state law, provided it is completed by the date on which a judicial reformation must be commenced. In the alternative, if a court, in a proceeding that is commenced on or before July 5, 2001, declares any transfer, made on or after April 4, 2000, and on or before March 6, 2001, null and void ab initio, the Internal Revenue Service will treat such transfers in a manner similar to that described in section 2055(e)(3)(J). [Reg. §25.2522(c)-3.]

□ [*T.D.* 7318, 7-10-74. *Amended by T.D.* 7340, 1-6-75; *T.D.* 7955, 5-10-84; *T.D.* 7957, 5-16-84; *T.D.* 8069, 1-13-86, *T.D.* 8540, 6-9-94; *T.D.* 8630, 12-12-95; *T.D.* 8923, 1-4-2001; *T.D.* 9068, 7-3-2003; *T.D.* 9448, 5-1-2009 *and T.D.* 9540, 8-9-2011.]

[Reg. §25.2522(c)-4]

§25.2522(c)-4. Disallowance of double deduction in the case of qualified terminable interest property.—No deduction is allowed under section 2522 for the transfer of an interest in property if a deduction is taken from the *total amount of gifts* with respect to that property by reason of section 2523(f). See §25.2523(h)-1. [Reg. §25.2522(c)-4.]

□ [*T.D.* 8522, 2-28-94.]

[Reg. §25.2522(d)-1]

§25.2522(d)-1. Additional cross references.—(a) See section 14 of the Wild and Scenic Rivers Act (Public Law 90-542, 82 Stat. 918) for provisions relating to the claim and allowance of the value of certain easements as a gift under section 2522.

(b) For treatment of gifts accepted by the Secretary of State or the Secretary of Commerce, for the purpose of organizing and holding an international conference to negotiate a Patent Corporation Treaty, as gifts to or for the use of the United States, see section 3 of Joint Resolution of December 24, 1969 (Public Law 91-160, 83 Stat. 443).

(c) For treatment of gifts accepted by the Secretary of the Department of Housing and Urban Development, for the purpose of aiding or facilitating the work of the Department, as gifts to or for the use of the United States, see section 7(k) of the Department of Housing and Urban Development Act (42 U. S. C. 3535), as added by section 905 of Public Law 91-609 (84 Stat. 1809).

(d) For treatment of certain property accepted by the Chairman of the Administrative Conference of the United States, for the purpose of aiding and facilitating the work of the Conference, as gifts to the United States, see 5 U. S. C. 575(c)(12), as added by section 1(b) of the Act of October 21, 1972 (Public Law 92-526, 86 Stat. 1048).

(e) For treatment of the Board for International Broadcasting as a corporation described in section 2522(a)(2), see section 7 of the Board for International Broadcasting Act of 1973 (Public Law 93-129, 87 Stat. 459). [Reg. §25.2522(d)-1.]

□ [*T.D.* 7318, 6-10-74.]

[Reg. §25.2523(a)-1]

§25.2523(a)-1. Gift to spouse; in general.—(a) *In general.*—In determining the amount of taxable gifts for the calendar quarter (with respect to gifts made after December 31, 1970, and before January 1, 1982), or calendar year (with respect to gifts made before January 1, 1971, or after December 31, 1981), a donor may deduct the value of any property interest transferred by gift to a donee who at the time of the gift is the donor's spouse, except as limited by paragraphs (b) and (c) of this section. See § 25.2502-1(c)(1) for the definition of calendar quarter. This deduction is referred to as the *marital deduction*. In the case of gifts made prior to July 14, 1988, no marital deduction is allowed with respect to a gift if, at the time of the gift, the donor is a nonresident not a citizen of the United States. Further, in the case of gifts made on or after July 14, 1988, no marital deduction is allowed (regardless of the donor's citizenship or residence) for transfers to a spouse who is not a citizen of the United States at the time of the transfer. However, for certain special rules applicable in the case of estate and gift tax treaties, see section 7815(d)(14) of Pub. L. 101-239. The donor must submit any evidence necessary to establish the donor's right to the marital deduction.

(b) *Deductible interests and nondeductible interests.*—(1) *In general.*—The property interests transferred by a donor to his spouse consist of either transfers with respect to which the marital deduction is authorized (as described in subparagraph (2) of this paragraph) or transfers with respect to which the marital deduction is not authorized (as described in subparagraph (3) of this paragraph). These transfers are referred to in this section and in § § 25.2523(b)-1 through 25.2523(f)-1 as *deductible interests* and *nondeductible interests*, respectively.

(2) *Deductible interest.*—A property interest transferred by a donor to his spouse is a *deductible interest* if it does not fall within either class of *nondeductible interests* described in subparagraph (3) of this paragraph.

(3) *Nondeductible interests.*—(i) A property interest transferred by a donor to his spouse which is a *terminable interest*, as defined in § 25.2523(b)-1, is a *nondeductible interest* to the extent specified in that section.

(ii) Any property interest transferred by a donor to the donor's spouse is a *nondeductible interest* to the extent it is not required to be included in a gift tax return for a calendar quarter (for gifts made after December 31, 1970, and before January 1, 1982) or calendar year (for gifts made before January 1, 1971, or after December 31, 1981).

(c) *Computation.*—(1) *In general.*—The amount of the marital deduction depends upon when the interspousal gifts are made, whether the gifts are terminable interests, whether the limitations of § 25.2523(f)-1A (relating to gifts of community property before January 1, 1982) are applicable, and whether § 25.2523(f)-1 (relating to the election with respect to life estates) is applicable, and (with respect to gifts made on or after July 14, 1988) whether the donee spouse is a citizen of the United States (see section 2523(i)).

(2) *Gifts prior to January 1, 1977.*—Generally, with respect to gifts made during a calendar quarter prior to January 1, 1977, the marital deduction allowable under section 2523 is 50 percent of the aggregate value of the deductible interests. See section 2524 for an additional limitation on the amount of the allowable deduction.

(3) *Gifts after December 31, 1976, and before January 1, 1982.*—Generally, with respect to gifts made during a calendar quarter beginning after December 31, 1976, and ending prior to January 1, 1982, the marital deduction allowable under section 2523 is computed as a percentage of the deductible interests in those gifts. If the aggregate amount of deductions for such gifts is $100,000 or less, a deduction is allowed for 100 percent of the deductible interests. No deduction is allowed for otherwise deductible interests in an aggregate amount that exceeds $100,000 and is equal to or less than $200,000. For deductible interests in excess of $200,000, the deduction is limited to 50 percent of such deductible interests. If a donor remarries, the computations in this paragraph (c)(3) are made on the basis of aggregate gifts to all persons who at the time of the gifts are the donor's spouse. See section 2524 for an additional limitation on the amount of the allowable deduction.

(4) *Gifts after December 31, 1981.*—Generally, with respect to gifts made during a calendar year beginning after December 31, 1981 (other than gifts made on or after July 14, 1988, to a spouse who is not a United States citizen on the date of the transfer), the marital deduction allowable under section 2523 is 100 percent of the aggregate value of the deductible interests. See section 2524 for an additional limitation on the amount of the allowable deduction, and section 2523(i) regarding disallowance of the marital deduction for gifts to a spouse who is not a United States citizen.

(d) *Examples.*—The following examples (in which it is assumed that the donors have previously utilized any specific exemptions provided by section 2521 for gifts prior to January 1, 1977) illustrate the application of paragraph (c) of this section and the interrelationship of sections 2523 and 2503. Generally, the marital deduction is equal to one-half of the aggregate value of the "deductible interests." The following examples (in each of which it is assumed that the donor has previously utilized his entire $30,000 specific exemption provided by section 2521) illustrate the marital deduction computation and the interrelationship of sections 2503(b) and 2523(a):

Example 1. A donor made a transfer by gift of $6,000 cash to his spouse on December 25, 1971. The donor made no other transfers during 1971. The amount of the marital deduction for the fourth calendar quarter of 1971 is $3,000 (one-half of $6,000); the amount of the annual exclusion under § 2503(b) is $3,000; and the amount of taxable gifts is zero ($6,000 – $3,000 (annual exclusion) – $3,000 (marital deduction)).

Example 2. A donor made transfers by gift to his spouse of $3,000 cash on January 1, 1971, and $3,000 cash on May 1, 1971. The donor made no other transfers during 1971. For the first calendar quarter of 1971 the marital deduction is zero because the amount excluded under section 2503(b) is $3,000, and the amount of taxable gifts is also zero. For the second calendar quarter of 1971 the marital deduction is $1,500 (one-half of $3,000), and the amount of taxable gifts is $1,500 ($3,000 – $1,500 (marital deduction)). Under section 2503(b) no amount of the second $3,000 gift may be excluded because the entire $3,000 annual exclusion was applied against the gift made in the first calendar quarter of 1971.

Example 3. A donor made a transfer by gift to his spouse of $10,000 cash on April 1, 1972. The donor made no other transfers during 1972. For the second calendar quarter of 1972 the amount of the marital deduction is $5,000 (one-half of $10,000); the amount excluded under section 2503(b) is $3,000; the amount of taxable gifts is $2,000 ($10,000 – $3,000 (annual exclusion) – $5,000 (marital deduction)).

Example 4. A donor made transfers by gift to his spouse of $2,000 cash on January 1, 1971, $2,000 cash on April 5, 1971, and $10,000 cash on December 1, 1971. The donor made no other transfers during 1971. For the first calendar quarter of 1971 the marital deduction is zero because the amount excluded under section 2503(b) is $2,000, and the amount of taxable gifts is also zero. For the second calendar quarter of 1971 the marital deduction is $1,000 (one-half of $2,000) (see section 2524); the amount excluded under section 2503(b) is $1,000 because $2,000 of the $3,000 annual exclusion was applied against the gift made in the first calendar quarter of 1971; and the amount of taxable gifts is zero ($2,000 – $1,000 (annual exclusion) – $1,000 (marital deduction)). For the fourth calendar quarter of 1971, the marital deduction is $5,000 (one-half of $10,000); the amount excluded under section 2503(b) is zero because the entire $3,000 annual exclusion was applied against the gifts made in the first and second calendar quarters of 1971; and the amount of taxable gifts is $5,000 ($10,000 – $5,000 (marital deduction)).

Example 5. A donor made transfers by gift to his spouse of $2,000 cash on January 10, 1972, $2,000 cash on May 1, 1972, and a remainder interest valued at $16,000 on June 1, 1972. The donor made no other transfers during 1972. For the first calendar quarter of 1972, the marital deduction is zero because $2,000 is excluded under section 2503(b), and the amount of taxable gifts is also zero. For the second calendar quarter of 1972 the marital deduction is $9,000 (one-half of $16,000 plus one-half of $2,000); the amount excluded under section 2503(b) is $1,000 because $2,000 of the $3,000 annual exclusion was applied against the gift made in the first calendar quarter of 1971 [1972]; and the amount of taxable gifts is $8,000 ($18,000 – $1,000 (annual exclusion) – $9,000 (marital deduction)).

Example 6. A donor made transfers by gift to his spouse of $2,000 cash on January 1, 1972, a remainder interest valued at $16,000 on January 5, 1972, and $2,000 cash on April 30, 1972. The donor made no other transfers during 1972. For the first calendar quarter of 1972, the marital deduction is $9,000 (one-half of $16,000 plus one-half of $2,000); the amount excluded under section 2503(b) is $2,000; and the amount of taxable gifts is $7,000 ($18,000 – $2,000 (annual exclusion) – $9,000 (marital deduction)). For the second calendar quarter of 1972 the marital deduction is $1,000 (one-half of $2,000); the amount excluded under section 2503(b) is $1,000 because $2,000 of the $3,000 annual exclusion was applied against the gift of the present interest in the first calendar quarter of 1971 [1972]; and the amount of taxable gifts is zero ($2,000 – $1,000 (annual exclusion) – $1,000 (marital deduction)).

Example 7. A donor made a transfer by gift to his spouse of $12,000 cash on July 17, 1955. The donor made no other transfers during 1955. For the calendar year 1955 the amount of the marital deduction is $6,000 (one-half of $12,000); the amount excluded under section 2503(b) is $3,000; and the amount of taxable gifts is $3,000 ($12,000 – $3,000 (annual exclusion) – $6,000 (marital deduction)).

Example 8. A donor made a transfer by gift to the donor's spouse, a United States citizen, of $200,000 cash on January 1, 1995. The donor made no other transfers during 1995. For calendar year 1995, the amount excluded under section 2503(b) is $10,000; the marital deduction is $190,000; and the amount of taxable gifts is zero ($200,000 – $10,000 (annual exclusion) – $190,000 (marital deduction)).

(e) *Valuation.*—If the income from property is made payable to the donor or another individual for life or for a term of years, with remainder to the donor's spouse or to the estate of the donor's spouse, the marital deduction is computed (pursuant to § 25.2523(a)-1(c)) with respect to the present value of the remainder, determined under section 7520. The present value of the remainder (that is, its value as of the date of gift) is to be determined in accordance with the rules stated in § 25.2512-5 or, for certain periods, § 25.2512-5A. See the example in paragraph (d) of § 25.2512-5. If the remainder is such that its value is to be determined by a special computation, a request for a specific factor, accompanied by a statement of the dates of birth of each person, the duration of whose life may affect the value of the remainder, and by copies of the relevant instruments may be submitted by the donor to the Commissioner who, if conditions permit, may supply the factor requested. If the Commissioner does not furnish the factor, the claim for deduction must be supported by a full statement of the computation of the present value, made in accordance with the principles set forth in § 25.2512-5(d) or, for certain periods, § 25.2512-5A. [Reg. § 25.2523(a)-1.]

☐ [*T.D.* 6334, 11-14-58. *Amended by T.D.* 7012, 5-14-69; *T.D.* 7238, 12-28-72; *T.D.* 7955, 5-10-84; *T.D.* 8522, 2-28-94 *and T.D.* 8540, 6-9-94.]

See p. 15 for regulations not amended to reflect law changes

[Reg. § 25.2523(b)-1]

§ 25.2523(b)-1. Life estate or other terminable interest.—(a) *In general.*—(1) The provisions of section 2523(b) generally disallow a marital deduction with respect to certain property interests (referred to generally as *terminable interests* and defined in paragraph (a)(3) of this section) transferred to the donee spouse under the circumstances described in paragraph (a)(2) of this section, unless the transfer comes within the purview of one of the exceptions set forth in § 25.2523(d)-1 (relating to certain joint interests); § 25.2523(e)-1 (relating to certain life estates with powers of appointment); § 25.2523(f)-1 (relating to certain qualified terminable interest property); or § 25.2523(g)-1 (relating to certain qualified charitable remainder trusts).

(2) If a donor transfers a terminable interest in property to the donee spouse, the marital deduction is disallowed with respect to the transfer if the donor spouse also—

(i) Transferred an interest in the same property to another donee (see paragraph (b) of this section), or

(ii) Retained an interest in the same property in himself (see paragraph (c) of this section), or

(iii) Retained a power to appoint an interest in the same property (see paragraph (d) of this section).

Notwithstanding the preceding sentence, the marital deduction is disallowed under these circumstances only if the other donee, the donor, or the possible appointee, may, by reason of the transfer or retention, possess or enjoy any part of the property after the termination or failure of the interest therein transferred to the donee spouse.

(3) For purposes of this section, a distinction is to be drawn between "property," as such term is used in section 2523, and an "interest in property." The "property" referred to is the underlying property in which various interests exist; each such interest is not, for this purpose, to be considered as "property." A "terminable interest" in property is an interest which will terminate or fail on the lapse of time or on the occurrence or failure to occur of some contingency. Life estates, terms for years, annuities, patents, and copyrights are therefore terminable interests. However, a bond, note, or similar contractual obligation, the discharge of which would not have the effect of an annuity or term for years, is not a terminable interest.

(b) *Interest in property which another donee may possess or enjoy.*—(1) Section 2523(b) provides that no marital deduction shall be allowed with respect to the transfer to the donee spouse of a "terminable interest" in property, in case—

(i) The donor transferred (for less than an adequate and full consideration in money or money's worth) an interest in the same property to any person other than the donee spouse (or the estate of such spouse), and,

(ii) By reason of such transfer, such person (or his heirs or assigns) may possess or enjoy any part of such property after the termination or failure of the interest therein transferred to the donee spouse.

(2) In determining whether the donor transferred an interest in property to any person other than the donee spouse, it is immaterial whether the transfer to the person other than the donee spouse was made at the same time as the transfer to such spouse, or at any earlier time.

(3) Except as provided in § 25.2523(e)-1 or 25.2523(f)-1, if at the time of the transfer it is impossible to ascertain the particular person or persons who may receive a property interest transferred by the donor, such interest is considered as transferred to a person other than the donee spouse for the purpose of section 2523(b). This rule is particularly applicable in the case of the transfer of a property interest by the donor subject to a reserved power. See § 25.2511-2. Under this rule, any property interest over which the donor reserved a power to revest the beneficial title in himself, or over which the donor reserved the power to name new beneficiaries or to change the interests of the beneficiaries as between themselves, is for the purpose of section 2523(b), considered as transferred to a "person other than the donee spouse." The following examples, in which it is assumed that the donor did not make an election under sections 2523(f)(2)(C) and (f)(4), illustrate the application of the provisions of this paragraph (b)(3):

Example 1. If a donor transferred property in trust, naming his wife as the irrevocable income beneficiary for 10 years, and providing that, upon the expiration of that term, the corpus should be distributed among his wife and children in such proportions as the trustee should determine, the right to the corpus, for the purpose of the marital deduction, is considered as transferred to a "person other than the donee spouse."

Example 2. If, in the above example, the donor had provided that, upon the expiration of the 10-year term, the corpus was to be paid to his wife, but also reserved the power to revest such corpus in himself, the right to corpus, for the purpose of the marital deduction, is considered as transferred to a "person other than the donee spouse."

(4) The term "person other than the donee spouse" includes the possible unascertained takers of a property interest, as, for example, the members of a class to be ascertained in the future. As another example, assume that the donor created a power of appointment over a property interest, which does not come within the purview of § 25.2523(e)-1. In such a case, the term "person other than the donee spouse" refers to the possible appointees and takers in default (other than the spouse) of such property interest.

(5) An exercise or release at any time by the donor (either alone or in conjunction with any person) of a power to appoint an interest in property, even though not otherwise a transfer

by him is considered as a transfer by him in determining, for the purpose of section 2523(b), whether he transferred an interest in such property to a person other than the donee spouse.

(6) The following examples illustrate the application of this paragraph. In each example, it is assumed that the donor made no election under sections 2523(f)(2)(C) and (f)(4) and that the property interest that the donor transferred to a person other than the donee spouse is not transferred for adequate and full consideration in money or money's worth:

Example 1. H (the donor) transferred real property to W (his wife) for life, with remainder to A and his heirs. No marital deduction may be taken with respect to the interest transferred to W, since it will terminate upon her death and A (or his heirs or assigns) will thereafter possess or enjoy the property.

Example 2. H transferred property for the benefit of W and A. The income was payable to W for life and upon her death the principal was to be distributed to A or his issue. However, if A should die without issue, leaving W surviving, the principal was then to be distributed to W. No marital deduction may be taken with respect to the interest transferred to W, since it will terminate in the event of her death if A or his issue survive, and A or his issue will thereafter possess or enjoy the property.

Example 3. H purchased for $100,000 a life annuity for W. If the annuity payments made during the life of W should be less than $100,000, further payments were to be made to A. No marital deduction may be taken with respect to the interest transferred to W, since A may possess or enjoy a part of the property following the termination of W's interest. If, however, the contract provided for no continuation of payments, and provided for no refund upon the death of W, or provided that any refund was to go to the estate of W, then a marital deduction may be taken with respect to the gift.

Example 4. H transferred property to A for life with remainder to W provided W survives A, but if W predeceases A, the property is to pass to B and his heirs. No marital deduction may be taken with respect to the interest transferred to W.

Example 5. H transferred real property to A, reserving the right to the rentals of the property for a term of 20 years. H later transferred the right to the remaining rentals to W. No marital deduction may be taken with respect to the interest since it will terminate upon the expiration of the balance of the 20-year term and A will thereafter possess or enjoy the property.

Example 6. H transferred a patent to W and A as tenants in common. In this case, the interest of W will terminate upon the expiration of the term of the patent, but possession and enjoyment of the property by A must necessarily cease at the same time. Therefore, since A's possession or enjoyment cannot outlast the termination of W's interest, the provisions of section 2523(b) do not disallow the marital deduction with respect to the interest.

(c) *Interest in property which the donor may possess or enjoy.*—(1) Section 2523(b) provides that no marital deduction is allowed with respect to the transfer to the donee spouse of a "terminable interest" in property, if—

(i) The donor retained in himself an interest in the same property, and

(ii) By reason of such retention, the donor (or his heirs or assigns) may possess or enjoy any part of the property after the termination or failure of the interest transferred to the donee spouse. However, as to a transfer to the donee spouse as sole joint tenant with the donor or as tenant by the entirety, see § 25.2523(d)-1.

(2) In general, the principles illustrated by the examples under paragraph (b) of this section are applicable in determining whether the marital deduction may be taken with respect to a property interest transferred to the donee spouse subject to the retention by the donor of an interest in the same property. The application of this paragraph may be further illustrated by the following example, in which it is assumed that the donor made no election under sections 2523(f)(2)(C) and (f)(4):

Example. The donor purchased three annuity contracts for the benefit of his wife and himself. The first contract provided for payments to the wife for life, with refund to the donor in case the aggregate payments made to the wife were less than the cost of the contract. The second contract provided for payments to the donor for life, and then to the wife for life if she survived the donor. The third contract provided for payments to the donor and his wife for their joint lives and then to the survivor of them for life. No marital deduction may be taken with respect to the gifts resulting from the purchases of the contracts since, in the case of each contract, the donor may possess or enjoy a part of the property after the termination or failure of the interest transferred to the wife.

(d) *Interest in property over which the donor retained a power to appoint.*—(1) Section 2523(b) provides that no marital deduction is allowed with respect to the transfer to the donee spouse of a "terminable interest" in property if—

(i) The donor had, immediately after the transfer, a power to appoint an interest in the same property, and

(ii) The donor's power was exercisable (either alone or in conjunction with any person) in such manner that the appointee may possess or enjoy any part of the property after the termination or failure of the interest transferred to the donee spouse.

(2) For the purposes of section 2523(b), the donor is to be considered as having, immediately after the transfer to the donee spouse, such a power to appoint even though the power cannot be exercised until after the lapse of time, upon the occurrence of an event or contingency, or upon the failure of an event or contingency to

occur. It is immaterial whether the power retained by the donor was a taxable power of appointment under section 2514.

(3) The principles illustrated by the examples under paragraph (b) of this section are generally applicable in determining whether the marital deduction may be taken with respect to a property interest transferred to the donee spouse subject to retention by the donor of a power to appoint an interest in the same property. The application of this paragraph may be further illustrated by the following example:

Example. The donor, having a power of appointment over certain property, appointed a life estate to his spouse. No marital deduction may be taken with respect to such transfer, since, if the retained power to appoint the remainder interest is exercised, the appointee thereunder may possess or enjoy the property after the termination or failure of the interest taken by the donee spouse. [Reg. § 25.2523(b)-1.]

☐ [*T.D.* 6334, 11-14-58. *Amended by T.D.* 8522, 2-28-94.]

[Reg. § 25.2523(c)-1]

§ 25.2523(c)-1. Interest in unidentified assets.—(a) Section 2523(c) provides that if an interest passing to a donee spouse may be satisfied out of a group of assets (or their proceeds) which include a particular asset that would be a nondeductible interest if it passed from the donor to his spouse, the value of the interest passing to the spouse is reduced, for the purpose of the marital deduction, by the value of the particular asset.

(b) In order for this section to apply, two circumstances must coexist, as follows:

(1) The property interest transferred to the donee spouse must be payable out of a group of assets. An example of a property interest payable out of a group of assets is a right to a share of the corpus of a trust upon its termination.

(2) The group of assets out of which the property interest is payable must include one or more particular assets which, if transferred by the donor to the donee spouse, would not qualify for the marital deduction. Therefore, section 2523(c) is not applicable merely because a group of assets includes a terminable interest, but would only be applicable if the terminable interest were nondeductible under the provisions of § 25.2523(b)-1.

(c) If both of the circumstances set forth in paragraph (b) of this section exist, only a portion of the property interest passing to the spouse is a deductible interest. The portion qualifying as a deductible interest is an amount equal to the excess, if any, of the value of the property interest passing to the spouse over the aggregate value of the asset (or assets) that if transferred to the spouse would not qualify for the marital deduction. See paragraph (c) of § 25.2523(a)-1 to determine the percentage of the deductible interest allowable as a marital deduction. The application of this section may be illustrated by the following example:

Example. H was absolute owner of a rental property and on July 1, 1950, transferred it to A by gift, reserving the income for a period of 20 years. On July 1, 1955, he created a trust to last for a period of 10 years. H was to receive the income from the trust and at the termination of the trust the trustee is to turn over to H's wife, W, property having a value of $100,000. The trustee has absolute discretion in deciding which properties in the corpus he shall turn over to W in satisfaction of the gift to her. The trustee received two items of property from H. Item (1) consisted of shares of corporate stock. Item (2) consisted of the right to receive the income from the rental property during the unexpired portion of the 20-year term. Assume that at the termination of the trust on July 1, 1965, the value of the right to the rental income from the then unexpired term of 5 years (item 2) will be $30,000. Since item (2) is a nondeductible interest and the trustee can turn it over to W in partial satisfaction of her gift, only $70,000 of the $100,000 receivable by her on July 1, 1965, will be considered as property with respect to which a marital deduction is allowable. The present value on July 1, 1955, of the right to receive $70,000 at the end of 10 years is $49,624.33 as determined under § 25.2512-5A(c). The value of the property qualifying for the marital deduction, therefore, is $49,624.33 and a marital deduction is allowed for one-half of that amount, or $24,812.17. [Reg. § 25.2523(c)-1.]

☐ [*T.D.* 6334, 11-14-58. *Amended by T.D.* 8522, 2-28-94 *and T.D.* 8540, 6-9-94.]

[Reg. § 25.2523(d)-1]

§ 25.2523(d)-1. Joint interests.—Section 2523(d) provides that if a property interest is transferred to the donee spouse as sole joint tenant with the donor or as a tenant by the entirety, the interest of the donor in the property which exists solely by reason of the possibility that the donor may survive the donee spouse, or that there may occur a severance of the tenancy, is not for the purposes of section 2523(b), to be considered as an interest retained by the donor in himself. Under this provision, the fact that the donor may, as surviving tenant, possess or enjoy the property after the termination of the interest transferred to the donee spouse does not preclude the allowance of the marital deduction with respect to the latter interest. Thus, if the donor purchased real property in the name of the donor and the donor's spouse as tenants by the entirety or as joint tenants with rights of survivorship, a marital deduction is allowable with respect to the value of the interest of the donee spouse in the property (subject to the limitations set forth in § 25.2523(a)-1). See paragraph (c) of § 25.2523(b)-1 and section 2524. [Reg. § 25.2523(d)-1.]

☐ [*T.D.* 6334, 11-14-58. *Amended by T.D.* 7238, 12-28-72 *and T.D.* 8522, 2-28-94.]

[Reg. §25.2523(e)-1]

§25.2523(e)-1. Marital deduction; life estate with power of appointment in donee spouse.—(a) *In general.*—Section 2523(e) provides that if an interest in property is transferred by a donor to his spouse (whether or not in trust) and the spouse is entitled for life to all the income from the entire interest or all the income from a specific portion of the entire interest, with a power in her to appoint the entire interest or the specific portion, the interest transferred to her is a deductible interest, to the extent that it satisfies all five of the conditions set forth below (see paragraph (b) of this section if one or more of the conditions is satisfied as to only a portion of the interest):

(1) The donee spouse must be entitled for life to all of the income from the entire interest or a specific portion of the entire interest, or to a specific portion of all the income from the entire interest.

(2) The income payable to the donee spouse must be payable annually or at more frequent intervals.

(3) The donee spouse must have the power to appoint the entire interest or the specific portion to either herself or her estate.

(4) The power in the donee spouse must be exercisable by her alone and (whether exercisable by will or during life) must be exercisable in all events.

(5) The entire interest or the specific portion must not be subject to a power in any other person to appoint any part to any person other than the donee spouse.

(b) *Specific portion; deductible amount.*—If either the right to income or the power of appointment given to the donee spouse pertains only to a specific portion of a property interest, the portion of the interest which qualifies as a deductible interest is limited to the extent that the rights in the donee spouse meet all of the five conditions described in paragraph (a) of this section. While the rights over the income and the power must coexist as to the same interest in property, it is not necessary that the rights over the income or the power as to such interest be in the same proportion. However, if the rights over income meeting the required conditions set forth in paragraph (a)(1) and (2) of this section extend over a small share of the property interest than the share with respect to which the power of appointment requirements set forth in paragraph (a)(3) through (5) of this section are satisfied, the deductible interest is limited to the smaller share. Conversely, if a power of appointment meeting all the requirements extends to a smaller portion of the property interest than the portion over which the income rights pertain, the deductible interest cannot exceed the value of the portion to which such power of appointment applies. Thus, if the donor gives to the donee spouse the right to receive annually all of the income from a particular property interest and a power of appointment meeting the specifications prescribed in paragraph (a)(3) through (5) of this section as to only one-half of the property interest, then only one-half of the property interest is treated as a deductible interest. Correspondingly, if the income interest of the spouse satisfying the requirements extends to only one-fourth of the property interest and a testamentary power of appointment satisfying the requirements extends to all of the property interest, then only one-fourth of the interest in the spouse qualifies as a deductible interest. Further, if the donee spouse has no right to income from a specific portion of a property interest but a testamentary power of appointment which meets the necessary conditions over the entire interest, then none of the interest qualifies for the deduction. In addition, if, from the time of the transfer, the donee spouse has a power of appointment meeting all of the required conditions over three-fourths of the entire property interest and the prescribed income rights over the entire interest, but with a power in another person to appoint one-half of the entire interest, the value of the interest in the donee spouse over only one-half of the property interest will qualify as a deductible interest.

(c) *Meaning of specific portion.*—(1) *In general.*—Except as provided in paragraphs (c)(2) and (c)(3) of this section, a partial interest in property is not treated as a *specific portion* of the entire interest. In addition, any specific portion of an entire interest in property is nondeductible to the extent the specific portion is subject to invasion for the benefit of any person other than the donee spouse, except in the case of a deduction allowable under section 2523(e), relating to the exercise of a general power of appointment by the donee spouse.

(2) *Fraction or percentage share.*—Under section 2523(e), a partial interest in property is treated as a specific portion of the entire interest if the rights of the donee spouse in income, and the required rights as to the power described in §25.2523(e)-1(a), constitute a fractional or percentage share of the entire property interest, so that the donee spouse's interest reflects its proportionate share of the increase or decrease in the value of the entire property interest to which the income rights and the power relate. Thus, if the spouse's right to income and the spouse's power extend to a specified fraction or percentage of the property, or its equivalent, the interest is in a specific portion of the property. In accordance with paragraph (b) of this section, if the spouse has the right to receive the income from a specific portion of the trust property (after applying paragraph (c)(3) of this section) but has a power of appointment over a different specific portion of the property (after applying paragraph (c)(3) of this section), the marital deduction is limited to the lesser specific portion.

(3) *Special rule in the case of gifts made on or before October 24, 1992.*—In the case of gifts within the purview of the effective date rule contained in paragraph (c)(3)(iii) of this section:

(i) A specific sum payable annually, or at more frequent intervals, out of the property and its income that is not limited by the income of the property is treated as the right to receive the income from a specific portion of the property. The specific portion, for purposes of paragraph (c)(2) of this section, is the portion of the property that, assuming the interest rate generally applicable for the valuation of annuities at the time of the donor's gift, would produce income equal to such payments. However, a pecuniary amount payable annually to a donee spouse is not treated as a right to the income from a specific portion of trust property for purposes of this paragraph (c)(3)(i) if any person other than the donee spouse may receive, during the donee spouse's lifetime, any distribution of the property. To determine the applicable interest rate for valuing annuities, see sections 2512 and 7520 and the regulations under those sections.

(ii) The right to appoint a pecuniary amount out of a larger fund (or trust corpus) is considered the right to appoint a specific portion of such fund or trust in an amount equal to such pecuniary amount.

(iii) The rules contained in paragraphs(c)(3)(i) and (ii) of this section apply with respect to gifts made on or before October 24, 1992.

(4) *Local law.*—A partial interest in property is treated as a specific portion of the entire interest if it is shown that the donee spouse has rights under local law that are identical to those the donee spouse would have acquired had the partial interest been expressed in terms satisfying the requirements of paragraph (c)(2) of this section (or paragraph (c)(3) of this section if applicable).

(5) *Examples.*—The following examples illustrate the application of paragraphs (b) and (c) of this section, where D, the donor, transfers property to D's spouse, S:

Example 1. Spouse entitled to the lesser of an annuity or a fraction of trust income. Prior to October 24, 1992, D transferred in trust 500 identical shares of X Company stock, valued for gift tax purposes at $500,000. The trust provided that during the lifetime of D's spouse, S, the trustee is to pay annually to S the lesser of one-half of the trust income or $20,000. Any trust income not paid to S is to be accumulated in the trust and may not be distributed during S's lifetime. S has a testamentary general power of appointment over the entire trust principal. The applicable interest rate for valuing annuities as of the date of D's gift under section 7520 is 10 percent. For purposes of paragraphs (a) through (c) of this section, S is treated as receiving all of the income from the lesser of one-half of the stock ($250,000), or $200,000, the specific portion of the stock which, as determined in accordance with § 25.2523(e)-1(c)(3)(i) of this chapter, would produce annual income of $20,000 (20,000÷.10). Accordingly, the marital deduction is limited to $200,000 (200,000÷500,000 or 2/5th of the value of the trust.)

Example 2. Spouse possesses power and income interest over different specific portions of trust. The facts are the same as in *Example 1* except that S's testamentary general power of appointment is exercisable over only 1/4th of the trust principal. Consequently, under section 2523(e), the marital deduction is allowable only for the value of 1/4th of the trust ($125,000); i.e., the lesser of the value of the portion with respect to which S is deemed to be entitled to all of the income (2/5th of the trust or $200,000), or the value of the portion with respect to which S possesses the requisite power of appointment (1/4th of the trust or $125,000).

Example 3. Power of appointment over shares of stock constitutes a power over a specific portion. D transferred 250 identical shares of Y company stock to a trust under the terms of which trust income is to be paid annually to S, during S's lifetime. S was given a testamentary general power of appointment over 100 shares of stock. The trust provides that if the trustee sells the Y company stock, S's general power of appointment is exercisable with respect to the sale proceeds or the property in which the proceeds are reinvested. Because the amount of property represented by a single share of stock would be altered if the corporation split its stock, issued stock dividends, made a distribution of capital, etc., a power to appoint 100 shares at the time of S's death is not necessarily a power to appoint the entire interest that the 100 shares represented on the date of D's gift. If it is shown that, under local law, S has a general power to appoint not only the 100 shares designated by D but also 100/250 of any distributions by the corporation that are included in trust principal, the requirements of paragraph (c)(2) of this section are satisfied and S is treated as having a general power to appoint 100/250 of the entire interest in the 250 shares. In that case, the marital deduction is limited to 40 percent of the trust principal. If local law does not give S that power, the 100 shares would not constitute a specific portion under § 25.2523(e)-1(c) (including § 25.2523(e)-1(c)(3)(ii)). The nature of the asset is such that a change in the capitalization of the corporation could cause an alteration in the original value represented by the shares at the time of the transfer and is thus not a specific portion of the trust.

(d) *Definition of "entire interest".*—Since a marital deduction is allowed for each qualifying separate interest in property transferred by the donor to the donee spouse, for purposes of paragraphs (a) and (b) of this section, each property interest with respect to which the donee spouse received some rights is considered separately in determining whether her rights extend to the entire interest or to a specific portion of the entire interest. A property interest which consists of several identical units of property (such as a block of 250 shares of stock, whether the ownership is evidenced by one or several certificates) is considered one property interest, unless certain of the units are to be segregated and accorded different treatment, in which case each segregated group of items is considered a separate property interest. The bequest of a specified sum of money constitutes the bequest of a separate property interest if immediately following the transfer and thenceforth it, and the investments made with it, must be so segregated or accounted for as to permit its identification as a separate item of property. The application of this paragraph may be illustrated by the following examples:

Example (1). The donor transferred to a trustee three adjoining farms, Blackacre, Whiteacre, and Greenacre. The trust instrument provided that during the lifetime of the donee spouse the trustee should pay her all of the income from the trust. Upon her death, all of Blackacre, a one-half interest in Whiteacre, and a one-third interest in Greenacre were to be distributed to the person or persons appointed by her in her will. The donee spouse is considered as being entitled to all of the income from the entire interest in Blackacre, all of the income from the entire interest in Whiteacre, and all of the income from the entire interest in Greenacre. She also is considered as having a power of appointment over the entire interest in Blackacre, over one-half of the entire interest in Whiteacre, and over one-third of the entire interest in Greenacre.

Example (2). The donor transferred $250,000 to C, as trustee. C is to invest the money and pay all of the income from the investments to W, the donor's spouse, annually. W was given a general power, exercisable by will, to appoint one-half of the corpus of the trust. Here, immediately following establishment of the trust, the $250,000 will be sufficiently segregated to permit its identification as a separate item, and the $250,000 will constitute an entire property interest. Therefore, W has a right to income and a power of appointment such that one-half of the entire interest is a deductible interest.

Example (3). The donor transferred 100 shares of Z Corporation stock to D, as trustee. W, the donor's spouse, is to receive all of the income of the trust annually and is given a general power, exercisable by will, to appoint out of the trust corpus the sum of $25,000. In this case the $25,000 is not, immediately following establishment of the trust, sufficiently segregated to permit its identification as a separate item of property in which the donee spouse has the entire interest. Therefore, the $25,000 does not constitute the entire interest in a property for the purpose of paragraphs (a) and (b) of this section.

(e) *Application of local law.*—In determining whether or not the conditions set forth in paragraph (a)(1) through (5) of this section are satisfied by the instrument of transfer, regard is to be had to the applicable provisions of the law of the jurisdiction under which the interest passes and, if the transfer is in trust, the applicable provisions of the law governing the administration of the trust. For example, silence of a trust instrument as to the frequency of payment will not be regarded as a failure to satisfy the condition set forth in paragraph (a)(2) of this section that income must be payable to the donee spouse annually or more frequently unless the applicable law permits payment to be made less frequently than annually. The principles outlined in this paragraph and paragraphs (f) and (g) of this section which are applied in determining whether transfers in trust meet such conditions are equally applicable in ascertaining whether, in the case of interests not in trust, the donee spouse has the equivalent in rights over income and over the property.

(f) *Right to income.*—(1) If an interest is transferred in trust, the donee spouse is "entitled for life to all of the income from the entire interest or a specific portion of the entire interest," for the purpose of the condition set forth in paragraph (a)(1) of this section, if the effect of the trust is to give her substantially that degree of beneficial enjoyment of the trust property during her life which the principles of the law of trusts accord to a person who is unqualifiedly designated as the life beneficiary of a trust. Such degree of enjoyment is given only if it was the donor's intention, as manifested by the terms of the trust instrument and the surrounding circumstances, that the trust should produce for the donee spouse during her life such an income, or that the spouse should have such use of the trust property as is consistent with the value of the trust corpus and with its preservation. The designation of the spouse as sole income beneficiary for life of the entire interest or a specific portion of the entire interest will be sufficient to qualify the trust unless the terms of the trust and the surrounding circumstances considered as a whole evidence an intention to deprive the spouse of the requisite degree of enjoyment. In determining whether a trust evidences that intention, the treatment required or permitted with respect to individual items must be considered in relation to the entire system provided for the administration of the trust. In addition, the spouse's interest shall meet the condition set forth in paragraph (a)(1) of this section if the spouse is entitled to income as defined or determined by applicable local law that provides for a reasonable apportionment between the income and remainder beneficiaries of the total return of the trust and that meets the requirements of § 1.643(b)-1 of this chapter.

(2) If the over-all effect of a trust is to give to the donee spouse such enforceable rights as will preserve to her the requisite degree of enjoyment, it is immaterial whether that result is effected by rules specifically stated in the trust instrument, or, in their absence, by the rules for the management of the trust property and the allocation of receipts and expenditures supplied by the State law. For example, a provision in the trust instrument for amortization of bond premium by appropriate periodic charges to interest will not disqualify the interest transferred in trust even though there is no State law specifically authorizing amortization or there is a State law denying amortization which is applicable

only in the absence of such a provision in the trust instrument.

(3) In the case of a trust, the rules to be applied by the trustee in allocation of receipts and expenses between income and corpus must be considered in relation to the nature and expected productivity of the assets transferred in trust, the nature and frequency of occurrence of the expected receipts, and any provisions as to change in the form of investments. If it is evident from the nature of the trust assets and the rules provided for management of the trust that the allocation to income of such receipts as rents, ordinary cash dividends and interest will give to the spouse the substantial enjoyment during life required by the statute, provisions that such receipts as stock dividends and proceeds from the conversion of trust assets shall be treated as corpus will not disqualify the interest transferred in trust. Similarly, provision for a depletion charge against income in the case of trust assets which are subject to depletion will not disqualify the interest transferred in trust, unless the effect is to deprive the spouse of the requisite beneficial enjoyment. The same principle is applicable in the case of depreciation, trustees' commissions, and other charges.

(4) Provisions granting administrative powers to the trustees will not have the effect of disqualifying an interest transferred in trust unless the grant of powers evidences the intention to deprive the donee spouse of the beneficial enjoyment required by the statute. Such an intention will not be considered to exist if the entire terms of the instrument are such that the local courts will impose reasonable limitations upon the exercise of the powers. Among the powers which if subject to reasonable limitations will not disqualify the interest transferred in trust are the power to determine the allocation or apportionment of receipts and disbursements between income and corpus, the power to apply the income or corpus for the benefit of the spouse, and the power to retain the assets transferred to the trust. For example, a power to retain trust assets which consist substantially of unproductive property will not disqualify the interest if the applicable rules for the administration of the trust require, or permit the spouse to require, that the trustee either make the property productive or convert it within a reasonable time. Nor will such a power disqualify the interest if the applicable rules for administration of the trust require the trustee to use the degree of judgment and care in the exercise of the power which a prudent man would use if he were owner of the trust assets. Further, a power to retain a residence for the spouse or other property for the personal use of the spouse will not disqualify the interest transferred in trust.

(5) An interest transferred in trust will not satisfy the condition set forth in paragraph (a)(1) of this section that the donee spouse be entitled to all the income if the primary purpose of the trust is to safeguard property without providing the spouse with the required beneficial enjoyment. Such trusts include not only trusts which expressly provide for the accumulation of the income but also trusts which indirectly accomplish a similar purpose. For example, assume that the corpus of a trust consists substantially of property which is not likely to be income producing during the life of the donee spouse and that the spouse cannot compel the trustee to convert or otherwise deal with the property as described in subparagraph (4) of this paragraph. An interest transferred to such a trust will not qualify unless the applicable rules for the administration require, or permit the spouse to require, that the trustee provide the required beneficial enjoyment, such as by payments to the spouse out of other assets of the trust.

(6) If a trust may be terminated during the life of the donee spouse, under her exercise of a power of appointment or by distribution of the corpus to her, the interest transferred in trust satisfies the condition set forth in paragraph (a)(1) of this section (that the spouse be entitled to all the income) if she (i) is entitled to the income until the trust terminates, or (ii) has the right, exercisable in all events, to have the corpus distributed to her at any time during her life.

(7) An interest transferred in trust fails to satisfy the condition set forth in paragraph (a)(1) of this section, that the spouse be entitled to all the income, to the extent that the income is required to be accumulated in whole or in part or may be accumulated in the discretion of any person other than the donee spouse; to the extent that the consent of any person other than the donee spouse is required as a condition precedent to distribution of the income; or to the extent that any person other than the donee spouse has the power to alter the terms of the trust so as to deprive her of her right to the income. An interest transferred in trust will not fail to satisfy the condition that the spouse be entitled to all the income merely because its terms provide that the right of the donee spouse to the income shall not be subject to assignment, alienation, pledge, attachment or claims of creditors.

(8) In the case of an interest transferred in trust, the terms "entitled for life" and "payable annually or at more frequent intervals", as used in the conditions set forth in paragraph (a)(1) and (2) of this section, require that under the terms of the trust the income referred to must be currently (at least annually; see paragraph (e) of this section) distributable to the spouse or that she must have such command over the income that it is virtually hers. Thus, the conditions in paragraph (a)(1) and (2) of this section are satisfied in this respect if, under the terms of the trust instrument, the donee spouse has the right exercisable annually (or more frequently) to require distribution to herself of the trust income, and otherwise the trust income is to be accumulated and added to corpus. Similarly, as respects the income for the period between the last distribution date and the date of the spouse's death, it is sufficient if that income is subject to the spouse's power to appoint. Thus, if the trust instrument provides that income accrued or undistributed

on the date of the spouse's death is to be disposed of as if it had been received after her death, and if the spouse has a power of appointment over the trust corpus, the power necessarily extends to the undistributed income.

(g) *Power of appointment in donee spouse.*—(1) The conditions set forth in paragraph (a)(3) and (4) of this section, that is, that the donee spouse must have a power of appointment exercisable in favor of herself or her estate and exercisable alone and in all events, are not met unless the power of the donee spouse to appoint the entire interest or a specific portion of it falls within one of the following categories:

(i) A power so to appoint fully exercisable in her own favor at any time during her life (as, for example, an unlimited power to invade); or

(ii) A power so to appoint exercisable in favor of her estate. Such a power, if exercisable during life, must be fully exercisable at any time during life, or, if exercisable by will, must be fully exercisable irrespective of the time of her death; or

(iii) A combination of the powers described under subdivisions (i) and (ii) of this subparagraph. For example, the donee spouse may, until she attains the age of 50 years, have a power to appoint to herself and thereafter have a power to appoint to her estate. However, the condition that the spouse's power must be exercisable in all events is not satisfied unless irrespective of when the donee spouse may die the entire interest or a specific portion of it will at the time of her death be subject to one power or the other.

(2) The power of the donee spouse must be a power to appoint the entire interest or a specific portion of it as unqualified owner (and free of the trust if a trust is involved, or free of the joint tenancy if a joint tenancy is involved) or to appoint the entire interest or a specific portion of it as a part of her estate (and free of the trust if a trust is involved), that is, in effect, to dispose of it to whomsoever she pleases. Thus, if the donor transferred property to a son and the donee spouse as joint tenants with right of survivorship and under local law the donee spouse has a power of severance exercisable without consent of the other joint tenant, and by exercising this power could acquire a one-half interest in the property as a tenant in common, her power of severance will satisfy the condition set forth in paragraph (a)(3) of this section that she have a power of appointment in favor of herself or her estate. However, if the donee spouse entered into a binding agreement with the donor to exercise the power only in favor of their issue, that condition is not met. An interest transferred in trust will not be regarded as failing to satisfy the condition merely because takers in default of the donee spouse's exercise of the power are designated by the donor. The donor may provide that, in default of exercise of the power, the trust shall continue for an additional period.

(3) A power is not considered to be a power exercisable by a donee spouse alone and in all events as required by paragraph (a)(4) of this section if the exercise of the power in the donee spouse to appoint the entire interest or a specific portion of it to herself or to her estate requires the joinder or consent of any other person. The power is not "exercisable in all events" if it can be terminated during the life of the donee spouse by any event other than her complete exercise or release of it. Further, a power is not "exercisable in all events" if it may be exercised for a limited purpose only. For example, a power which is not exercisable in the event of the spouse's remarriage is not exercisable in all events. Likewise, if there are any restrictions, either by the terms of the instrument or under applicable local law, on the exercise of a power to consume property (whether or not held in trust) for the benefit of the spouse, the power is not exercisable in all events. Thus, if a power of invasion is exercisable only for the spouse's support, or only for her limited use, the power is not exercisable in all events. In order for a power of invasion to be exercisable in all events, the donee spouse must have the unrestricted power exercisable at any time during her life to use all or any part of the property subject to the power, and to dispose of it in any manner, including the power to dispose of it by gift (whether or not she has power to dispose of it by will).

(4) If the power is in existence at all times following the transfer of the interest, limitations of a formal nature will not disqualify the interest. Examples of formal limitations on a power exercisable during life are requirements that an exercise must be in a particular form, that it must be filed with a trustee during the spouse's life, that reasonable notice must be given, or that reasonable intervals must elapse between successive partial exercises. Examples of formal limitations on a power exercisable by will are that it must be exercised by a will executed by the donee spouse after the making of the gift or that exercise must be by specific reference to the power.

(5) If the donee spouse has the requisite power to appoint to herself or her estate, it is immaterial that she also has one or more lesser powers. Thus, if she has a testamentary power to appoint to her estate, she may also have a limited power of withdrawal or of appointment during her life. Similarly, if she has an unlimited power of withdrawal, she may have a limited testamentary power.

(h) *Existence of a power in another.*—Paragraph (a)(5) of this section provides that a transfer described in paragraph (a) is nondeductible to the extent that the donor created a power in the trustee or in any other person to appoint a part of the interest to any person other than the donee spouse. However, only powers in other persons which are in opposition to that of the donee spouse will cause a portion of the interest to fail to satisfy the condition set forth in paragraph (a)(5) of this section. Thus, a power in a trustee to distribute corpus to or for the benefit of the donee spouse will not disqualify the trust. Similarly, a power to distribute corpus to the spouse for the support of minor children will not disqualify the trust if she is legally obligated to support such children. The application of this paragraph may be illustrated by the following examples:

Example (1). Assume that a donor created a trust, designating his spouse as income beneficiary for life with an unrestricted power in the spouse to appoint the corpus during her life. The donor further provided that in the event the donee spouse should die without having exercised the power, the trust should continue for the life of his son with a power in the son to appoint the corpus. Since the power in the son could become exercisable only after the death of the donee spouse, the interest is not regarded as failing to satisfy the condition set forth in paragraph (a)(5) of this section.

Example (2). Assume that the donor created a trust, designating his spouse as income beneficiary for life and as donee of a power to appoint by will the entire corpus. The donor further provided that the trustee could distribute 30 percent of the corpus to the donor's son when he reached the age of 35 years. Since the trustee has a power to appoint 30 percent of the entire interest for the benefit of a person other than the donee spouse, only 70 percent of the interest placed in trust satisfied the condition set forth in paragraph (a)(5) of this section. If, in this case, the donee spouse had a power, exercisable by her will, to appoint only one-half of the corpus as it was constituted at the time of her death, it should be noted that only 35 percent of the interest placed in the trust would satisfy the condition set forth in paragraph (a)(3) of this section. [Reg. § 25.2523(e)-1.]

☐ [*T.D.* 6334, 11-14-58. *Amended by T.D.* 6542, 1-19-61; *T.D.* 8522, 2-28-94 *and T.D.* 9102, 12-30-2003.]

[Reg. § 25.2523(f)-1A]

§ 25.2523(f)-1A. Special rule applicable to community property transferred prior to January 1, 1982.—(a) *In general.*—With respect to gifts made prior to January 1, 1982, the marital deduction is allowable with respect to any transfer by a donor to the donor's spouse only to the extent that the transfer is shown to represent a gift of property that was not, at the time of the gift, held as *community property,* as defined in paragraph (b) of this section.

(b) *Definition of "community property".*—(1) For the purpose of paragraph (a) of this section, the term "community property" is considered to include—

(i) Any property held by the donor and his spouse as community property under the law of any State, Territory, or possession of the United States, or of any foreign country, except property in which the donee spouse had at the time of the gift merely an expectant interest. The donee spouse is regarded as having, at any particular time, merely an expectant interest in property held at that time by the donor and herself as community property under the law of any State, Territory, or possession of the United States, or of any foreign country, if, in case such property were transferred by gift into the separate property of the donee spouse, the entire value of such property (and not merely one-half of it), would be treated as the amount of the gift.

(ii) Separate property acquired by the donor as a result of a "conversion," after December 31, 1941, of property held by him and the donee spouse as community property under the law of any State, Territory, or possession of the United States, or of any foreign country (except such property in which the donee spouse had at the time of the "conversion" merely an expectant interest), into their separate property, subject to the limitation with respect to value contained in subparagraph (5) of this paragraph.

(iii) Property acquired by the donor in exchange (by one exchange or a series of exchanges) for separate property resulting from such "conversion."

(2) The characteristics of property which acquired a noncommunity instead of a community status by reason of an agreement (whether antenuptial or postnuptial) are such that section 2523(f) classifies the property as community property of the donor and his spouse in the computation of the marital deduction. In distinguishing property which thus acquired a noncommunity status from property which acquired such a status solely by operation of the community property law, section 2523(f) refers to the former category of property as "separate property" acquired as a result of a "conversion" of "property held as such community property." As used in section 2523(f) the phrase "property held as such community property" is used to denote the body of property comprehended within the community property system; the expression "separate property" includes any noncommunity property, whether held in joint tenancy, tenancy by the entirety, tenancy in common, or otherwise; and the term "conversion" includes any transaction or agreement which transforms property from a community status into a noncommunity status.

(3) The separate property which section 2523(f) classifies as community property is not limited to that which was in existence at the time of the conversion. The following are illustrative of the scope of section 2523(f):

(i) A partition of community property between husband and wife, whereby a portion of the property became the separate property of each, is a conversion of community property.

(ii) A transfer of community property into some other form of coownership, such as a joint tenancy, is a conversion of the property.

(iii) An agreement (whether made before or after marriage) that future earnings and gains which would otherwise be community property shall be shared by the spouses as separate property effects a conversion of such earnings and gains.

(iv) A change in the form of ownership of property which causes future rentals, which would otherwise have been acquired as community property, to be acquired as separate property effects a conversion of the rentals.

(4) The rules of section 2523(f) are applicable, however, only if the conversion took place after December 31, 1941, and only to the extent stated in this section.

(5) If the value of the separate property acquired by the donor as a result of a conversion did not exceed the value of the separate property thus acquired by the donee spouse, the entire separate property thus acquired by the donor is to be considered, for the purposes of this section, as held by him and the donee spouse as community property. If the value (at the time of conversion) of the separate property so acquired by the donor exceeded the value (at that time) of the separate property so acquired by the donee spouse, only a part of the separate property so acquired by the donor (and only the same fractional part of property acquired by him in exchange for such separate property) is to be considered, for purposes of this section, as held by him and the donee spouse as community property. The part of such separate property (or property acquired in exchange for it) which is considered as so held is the same proportion of it which the value (at the time of the conversion) of the separate property so acquired by the donee spouse is of the value (at the time) of the separate property so acquired by the donor. The following example illustrates the application of the provisions of this paragraph:

Example. During 1942 the donor and his spouse partitioned certain real property held by them under community property laws. The real property then had a value of $224,000. A portion of the property, then having a value of $160,000, was converted into the donor's separate property, and the remaining portion, then having a value of $64,000, was converted into his spouse's separate property. In 1955 the donor made a gift to his spouse of the property acquired by him as a result of the partition, which property then had a value of $200,000. The portion of the property transferred by gift which is considered as community property is

$$\frac{\$64{,}000 \text{ (value of property acquired by donee spouse)}}{\$160{,}000 \text{ (value of property acquired by donor spouse)}} \times \$200{,}000 = \$80{,}000$$

The marital deduction with respect to the gift is, therefore, limited to one-half of $120,000 (the difference between $200,000, the value of the gift, and $80,000, the portion of the gift considered to have been of "community property"). The marital deduction with respect to the gift is, therefore, $60,000. [Reg. § 25.2523(f)-1A.]

☐ [*T.D.* 6334, 11-14-58. *Redesignated and amended by T.D.* 8522, 2-28-94.]

[Reg. § 25.2523(f)-1]

§ 25.2523(f)-1. Election with respect to life estate transferred to donee spouse.—(a) *In general.*—(1) With respect to gifts made after December 31, 1981, subject to section 2523(i), a marital deduction is allowed under section 2523(a) for transfers of *qualified terminable interest property.* Qualified terminable interest property is terminable interest property described in section 2523(b)(1) that satisfies the requirements of section 2523(f)(2) and this section. Terminable interests that are described in section 2523(b)(2) cannot qualify as qualified terminable interest property. Thus, if the donor retains a power described in section 2523(b)(2) to appoint an interest in qualified terminable interest property, no deduction is allowable under section 2523(a) for the property.

(2) All of the property for which a deduction is allowed under this paragraph (a) is treated as passing to the donee spouse (for purposes of § 25.2523(a)-1), and no part of the property is treated as retained by the donor or as passing to any person other than the donee spouse (for purposes of § 25.2523(b)-1(b)).

(b) *Qualified terminable interest property.*—(1) *Definition.*—Section 2523(f)(2) provides the definition of *qualified terminable interest property.*

(2) *Meaning of property.*—For purposes of section 2523(f)(2), the term *property* generally means an *entire interest in property* (within the meaning of § 25.2523(e)-1(d)) or a *specific portion of the entire interest* (within the meaning of § 25.2523(e)-1(c)).

(3) *Property for which the election may be made.*—(i) *In general.*—The election may relate to all or any part of property that meets the requirements of section 2523(f)(2)(A) and (B), provided that any partial election must be made with respect to a fractional or percentage share of the property so that the elective portion reflects its proportionate share of the increase or decrease in the entire property for purposes of applying sections 2044 or 2519. Thus, if the interest of the donee spouse in a trust (or other property in which the spouse has a qualifying income interest) meets the requirements of this section, the election may be made under section 2523(f)(2)(C) with respect to a part of the trust (or other property) only if the election relates to a defined fraction or percentage of the entire trust (or other property) or specific portion thereof within the meaning of § 25.2523(e)-1(c). The fraction or percentage may be defined by formula.

(ii) *Division of trusts.*—If the interest of the donee spouse in a trust meets the requirements of this section, the trust may be divided into separate trusts to reflect a partial election that has been made, if authorized under the terms of the governing instrument or otherwise permissible under local law. A trust may be divided only if the fiduciary is required, either by applicable local law or by the express or implied provisions of the governing instrument, to divide the trust according to the fair market value of the assets of the trust at the time of the division. The division of the trusts must be done on a fractional or percentage basis to reflect the partial election. However, the separate trusts do not have to be funded with a pro rata portion of each asset held by the undivided trust.

(4) *Manner and time of making election.*—(i) An election under section 2523(f)(2)(C) (other than a deemed election with respect to a joint and survivor annuity as described in section 2523(f)(6)), is made on a gift tax return for the calendar year in which the interest is transferred. The return must be filed within the time prescribed by section 6075(b) (determined without regard to section 6019(a)(2)), including any extensions authorized under section 6075(b)(2) (relating to an automatic extension of time for filing a gift tax return where the donor is granted an extension of time to file the income tax return).

(ii) If the election is made on a return for the calendar year that includes the date of death of the donor, the return (as prescribed by section 6075(b)(3)) must be filed no later than the time (including extensions) for filing the estate tax return. The election, once made, is irrevocable.

(c) *Qualifying income interest for life.*—(1) *In general.*—For purposes of this section, the term *qualifying income interest for life* is defined as provided in section 2056(b)(7)(B)(ii) and § 20.2056(b)-7(d)(1).

(i) *Entitled for life to all the income.*—The principles outlined in § 25.2523(e)-1(f) (relating to whether the spouse is entitled for life to all of the income from the entire interest or a specific portion of the entire interest) apply in determining whether the donee spouse is entitled for life to all the income from the property, regardless of whether the interest passing to the donee spouse is in trust. An income interest granted for a term of years, or a life estate subject to termination upon the occurrence of a specified event (e.g., divorce) is not a qualifying income interest for life.

(ii) *Income between last distribution date and date of spouse's death.*—An income interest does not fail to constitute a qualifying income interest for life solely because income for the period between the last distribution date and the date of the donee spouse's death is not required to be distributed to the estate of the donee spouse. See § 20.2044-1 of this chapter relating to the inclusion of such undistributed income in the gross estate of the donee spouse.

(iii) *Pooled income funds.*—An income interest in a pooled income fund described in section 642(c)(5) constitutes a qualifying income interest for life for purposes of this section.

(iv) *Distribution of principal for the benefit of the donee spouse.*—An income interest does not fail to constitute a qualifying income interest for life solely because the trustee has a power to distribute principal to or for the benefit of the donee spouse. The fact that property distributed to a donee spouse may be transferred by the spouse to another person does not result in a failure to satisfy the requirement of section 2056(b)(7)(B)(ii)(II). However, if the governing instrument requires the donee spouse to transfer the distributed property to another person without full and adequate consideration in money or money's worth, the requirement of section 2056(b)(7)(B)(ii)(II) is not satisfied.

(2) *Immediate right to income.*—In order to constitute a qualifying income interest for life, the donee spouse must be granted the immediate right to receive the income from the property. Thus, an income interest does not constitute a qualifying income interest for life if the donee spouse receives the right to trust income commencing at some time in the future, e.g., on the termination of a preceding life income interest of the donor spouse.

(3) *Annuities payable from trusts in the case of gifts made on or before October 24, 1992.*—(i) In the case of gifts made on or before October 24, 1992, a donee spouse's lifetime annuity interest payable from a trust or other group of assets passing from the donor is treated as a qualifying income interest for life for purposes of section 2523(f)(2)(B). The deductible interest, for purposes of § 25.2523(a)-1(b), is the specific portion of the property that, assuming the applicable interest rate for valuing annuities at the time the annuity interest is transferred, would produce income equal to the minimum amount payable annually to the donee spouse. If, based on the applicable interest rate, the entire property from which the annuity may be satisfied is insufficient to produce income equal to the minimum annual payment, the value of the deductible interest is the entire value of the property. The value of the deductible interest may not exceed the value of the property from which the annuity is payable. If the annual payment may increase, the increased amount is not taken into account in valuing the deductible interest.

(ii) An annuity interest is not treated as a qualifying income interest for life for purposes of section 2523(f)(2)(B) if any person other than the donee spouse may receive during the donee spouse's lifetime, any distribution of the property or its income from which the annuity is payable.

(iii) To determine the applicable interest rate for valuing annuities, see sections 2512 and 7520 and the regulations under those sections.

(4) *Joint and survivor annuities.*—[Reserved]

(d) *Treatment of interest retained by the donor spouse.*—(1) *In general.*—Under section 2523(f)(5)(A), if a donor spouse retains an interest in qualified terminable interest property, any subsequent transfer by the donor spouse of the retained interest in the property is not treated as a transfer for gift tax purposes. Further, the retention of the interest until the donor spouse's death does not cause the property subject to the retained interest to be includible in the gross estate of the donor spouse.

(2) *Exception.*—Under section 2523(f)(5)(B), the rule contained in paragraph (d)(1) of this section does not apply to any property after the donee spouse is treated as having transferred the property under section 2519, or after the property is includible in the gross estate of the donee spouse under section 2044.

(e) *Application of local law.*—The provisions of local law are taken into account in determining whether or not the conditions of section 2523(f)(2)(A) and (B), and the conditions of paragraph (c) of this section, are satisfied. For example, silence of a trust instrument on the frequency of payment is not regarded as a failure to satisfy the requirement that the income must be payable to the donee spouse annually or more frequently unless applicable local law permits payments less frequently to the donee spouse.

(f) *Examples.*—The following examples illustrate the application of this section, where D, the donor, transfers property to D's spouse, S. Unless stated otherwise, it is assumed that S is not the trustee of any trust established for S's benefit:

Example 1. Life estate in residence. D transfers by gift a personal residence valued at $250,000 on the date of the gift to S and D's children, giving S the exclusive and unrestricted right to use the property (including the right to continue to occupy the property as a personal residence or rent the property and receive the income for her lifetime). After S's death, the property is to pass to D's children. Under applicable local law, S's consent is required for any sale of the property. If D elects to treat all of the transferred property as qualified terminable interest property, the deductible interest is $250,000, the value of the property for gift tax purposes.

Example 2. Power to make property productive. D transfers assets having a fair market value of $500,000 to a trust pursuant to which S is given the right exercisable annually to require distribution of all the trust income to S. No trust property may be distributed during S's lifetime to any person other than S. The assets used to fund the trust include both income producing assets and nonproductive assets. Applicable local law permits S to require that the trustee either make the trust property productive or sell the property and reinvest the proceeds in productive property within a reasonable time after the transfer. If D elects to treat the entire trust as qualified terminable interest property, the deductible interest is $500,000. If D elects to treat only 20 percent of the trust as qualified terminable interest property, the deductible interest is $100,000; i.e., 20 percent of $500,000.

Example 3. Power of distribution over fraction of trust income. The facts are the same as in *Example 2* except that S is given the power exercisable annually to require distribution to S of only 50 percent of the trust income for life. The remaining trust income may be accumulated or distributed among D's children and S in the trustee's discretion. The maximum amount that D may elect to treat as qualified terminable interest property is $250,000; i.e., the value of the trust for gift tax purposes ($500,000) multiplied by the percentage of the trust in which S has a qualifying income interest for life (50 percent). If D elects to treat only 20 percent of the portion of the trust in which S has a qualifying income interest as qualified terminable interest property, the deductible interest is $50,000; i.e., 20 percent of $250,000.

Example 4. Power to distribute trust corpus to other beneficiaries. D transfers $500,000 to a trust providing that all the trust income is to be paid to D's spouse, S, during S's lifetime. The trustee is given the power to use annually $5,000 from the trust for the maintenance and support of S's minor child, C. Any such distribution does not necessarily relieve S of S's obligation to support and maintain C. S does not have a qualifying income interest for life in any portion of the trust because the gift fails to satisfy the condition in sections 2523(f)(3) and 2056(b)(7)(B)(ii)(II) that no person have a power, other than a power the exercise of which takes effect only at or after S's death, to appoint any part of the property to any person other than S. The trust would also be nondeductible under section 2523(f) if S, rather than the trustee, were given the power to appoint a portion of the principal to C. However, in the latter case, if S made a qualified disclaimer (within the meaning of section 2518) of the power to appoint to C, the trust could qualify for the marital deduction pursuant to section 2523(f), assuming that the power was personal to S and S's disclaimer terminates the power. Similarly, if C made a qualified disclaimer of the right to receive distributions from the trust, the trust would qualify under section 2523(f) assuming that C's disclaimer effectively negates the trustee's power under local law.

Example 5. Spouse's interest terminable on divorce. The facts are the same as in *Example 3* except that if S and D divorce, S's interest in the trust will pass to C. S's income interest is not a qualifying income interest for life because it is terminable upon S's divorce. Therefore, no portion of the trust is deductible under section 2523(f).

Example 6. Spouse's interest in trust in the form of an annuity. Prior to October 24, 1992, D established a trust funded with income producing property valued for gift tax purposes at $800,000. The trustee is required by the trust instrument to pay $40,000 a year to S for life. Any income in excess of the annuity amount is to be accumulated in the trust and may not be distributed during S's lifetime. S's lifetime annuity interest is treated as a qualifying income interest for life. If D elects to treat the entire portion of the trust in which S has a qualifying income interest as qualified terminable interest property, the value of the deductible interest is $400,000, because that amount would yield an income to S of $40,000 a year (assuming a 10 percent interest rate applies in valuing annuities at the time of the transfer).

Example 7. Value of spouse's annuity exceeds value of trust corpus. The facts are the same as in *Example 6*, except that the trustee is required to pay S $100,000 a year for S's life. If D elects to treat the entire portion of the trust in which S has a qualifying income interest for life as qualified terminable interest property, the value of the deductible interest is $800,000, which is the lesser of the entire value of the property ($800,000) or the amount of property that (assuming a 10 percent interest rate) would yield an income to S of $100,000 a year ($1,000,000).

Example 8. Transfer to pooled income fund. D transfers $200,000 on June 1, 1994, to a pooled income fund (described in section 642(c)(5)) designating S as the only life income beneficiary. If D elects to treat the entire $200,000 as qualified terminable interest property, the deductible interest is $200,000.

Example 9. Retention by donor spouse of income interest in property. On October 1, 1994, D transfers property to an irrevocable trust under the terms of which trust income is to be paid to D for life, then to S for life and, on S's death, the trust corpus is to be paid to D's children. Because S does not possess an immediate right to receive trust income, S's interest does not qualify as a qualifying income interest for life under section 2523(f)(2). Further, under section 2702(a)(2) and § 25.2702-2(b), D is treated for gift tax purposes as making a gift with a value equal to the entire value of the property. If D dies in 1996 survived by S, the trust corpus will be includible in D's gross estate under section 2036. However, in computing D's estate tax liability, D's adjusted taxable gifts under section 2001(b)(1)(B) are adjusted to reflect the inclusion of the gifted property in D's gross estate. In addition, if S survives D, the trust property is eligible for treatment as qualified terminable interest property under section 2056(b)(7) in D's estate.

Example 10. Retention by donor spouse of income interest in property. On October 1, 1994, D transfers property to an irrevocable trust under the terms of which trust income is to be paid to S for life, then to D for life and, on D's death, the trust corpus is to be paid to D's children. D elects under section 2523(f) to treat the property as qualified terminable interest property. D dies in 1996, survived by S. S subsequently dies in 1998. Under § 2523(f)-1(d)(1), because D elected to treat the transfer as qualified terminable interest property, no part of the trust corpus is includible in D's gross estate because of D's retained interest in the trust corpus. On S's subsequent death in 1998, the trust corpus is includible in S's gross estate under section 2044.

Example 11. Retention by donor spouse of income interest in property. The facts are the same as in *Example 10*, except that S dies in 1996 survived by D, who subsequently dies in 1998. Because D made an election under section 2523(f) with respect to the trust, on S's death the trust corpus is includible in S's gross estate under section 2044. Accordingly, under section 2044(c), S is treated as the transferor of the property for estate and gift tax purposes. Upon D's subsequent death in 1998, because the property was subject to inclusion in S's gross estate under section 2044, the exclusion rule in § 25.2523(f)-1(d)(1) does not apply under § 25.2523(f)-1(d)(2). However, because S is treated as the transferor of the property, the property is not subject to inclusion in D's gross estate under section 2036 or section 2038. If the executor of S's estate made a section 2056(b)(7) election with respect to the trust, the trust is includible in D's gross estate under section 2044 upon D's later death. [Reg. § 25.2523(f)-1.]

☐ [*T.D.* 8522, 2-28-94.]

[Reg. § 25.2523(g)-1]

§ 25.2523(g)-1. Special rule for charitable remainder trusts.—(a) *In general.*—(1) With respect to gifts made after December 31, 1981, subject to section 2523(i), if the donor's spouse is the only noncharitable beneficiary (other than the donor) of a charitable remainder annuity trust or charitable remainder unitrust described in section 664 (qualified charitable remainder trust), section 2523(b) does not apply to the interest in the trust transferred to the donee spouse. Thus, the value of the annuity or unitrust interest passing to the spouse qualifies for a marital deduction under section 2523(g) and the value of the remainder interest qualifies for a charitable deduction under section 2522.

(2) A marital deduction for the value of the donee spouse's annuity or unitrust interest in a qualified charitable remainder trust to which section 2523(g) applies is allowable only under section 2523(g). Therefore, if an interest in property qualifies for a marital deduction under section 2523(g), no election may be made with respect to the property under section 2523(f).

(3) The donee spouse's interest need not be an interest for life to qualify for a marital deduction under section 2523(g). However, for purposes of section 664, an annuity or unitrust interest payable to the spouse for a term of years cannot be payable for a term that exceeds 20 years or the trust does not qualify under section 2523(g).

(4) A deduction is allowed under section 2523(g) even if the transfer to the donee spouse is conditioned on the donee spouse's payment of state death taxes, if any, attributable to the qualified charitable remainder trust.

(5) For purposes of this section, the term *noncharitable beneficiary* means any beneficiary of the qualified charitable remainder trust other than an organization described in section 170(c).

(b) *Charitable remainder trusts where the donee spouse and the donor are not the only noncharitable beneficiaries.*—In the case of a charitable remainder trust where the donor and the donor's spouse are not the only noncharitable beneficiaries (for example, where the noncharitable interest is payable to the donor's spouse for life and then to another individual (other than the donor) for life), the qualification of the interest as qualified terminable interest property is determined solely under section 2523(f) and not under section 2523(g). Accordingly, if the transfer to the trust is made prior to October 24, 1992, the spousal annuity or unitrust interest may qualify under § 25.2523(f)-(1)(c)(3) as a qualifying income interest for life. [Reg. § 25.2523(g)-1.]

☐ [*T.D.* 8522, 2-28-94.]

[Reg. § 25.2523(h)-1]

§ 25.2523(h)-1. Denial of double deduction.—The value of an interest in property may not be deducted for Federal gift tax purposes more than once with respect to the same donor. For example, assume that D, a donor, transferred a life estate in a farm to D's spouse, S, with a remainder to charity and that D elects to treat the property as qualified terminable interest property. The entire value of the property is deductible under section 2523(f). No part of the value of the property qualifies for a charitable deduction under section 2522 for gift tax purposes. [Reg. § 25.2523(h)-1.]

☐ [*T.D.* 8522, 2-28-94.]

[Reg. § 25.2523(h)-2]

§ 25.2523(h)-2. Effective Dates.—Except as specifically provided, in §§ 25.2523(e)-1(c)(3), 25.2523(f)-1(c)(3), and 25.2523(g)-1(b), the provisions of §§ 25.2523(e)-1(c), 25.2523(f)-1, 25.2523(g)-1, and 25.2523(h)-1 are effective with respect to gifts made after March 1, 1994. With respect to gifts made on or before such date, donors may rely on any reasonable interpretation of the statutory provisions. For these purposes, the provisions of §§ 25.2523(e)-1(c), 25.2523(f)-1, 25.2523(g)-1, and 25.2523(h)-1, (as well as project LR-211-76, 1984-1 C.B., page 598, see § 601.601(d)(2)(ii)(*b*) of this chapter), are considered a reasonable interpretation of the statutory provisions. In addition, the rule in the last sentence of § 25.2523(e)-1 (f)(1) regarding the determination of income under applicable local law applies to trusts for taxable years ending after January 2, 2004. [Reg. § 25.2523(h)-2.]

☐ [*T.D.* 8522, 2-28-94. *Amended by T.D.* 9102, 12-30-2003.]

[Reg. § 25.2523(i)-1]

§ 25.2523(i)-1. Disallowance of marital deduction when spouse is not a United States citizen.—(a) *In general.*—Subject to § 20.2056A-1(c) of this chapter, section 2523(i)(1) disallows the marital deduction if the spouse of the donor is not a citizen of the United States at the time of the gift. If the spouse of the donor is a citizen of the United States at the time of the gift, the gift tax marital deduction under section 2523(a) is allowed regardless of whether the donor is a citizen or resident of the United States at the time of the gift, subject to the otherwise applicable rules of section 2523.

(b) *Exception for certain joint and survivor annuities.*—Paragraph (a) does not apply to disallow the marital deduction with respect to any transfer resulting in the acquisition of rights by a noncitizen spouse under a joint and survivor annuity described in section 2523(f)(6).

(c) *Increased annual exclusion.*—(1) *In general.*—In the case of gifts made from a donor to the donor's spouse for which a marital deduction is not allowable under this section, if the gift otherwise qualifies for the gift tax annual exclusion under section 2503(b), the amount of the annual exclusion under section 2503(b) is $100,000 in lieu of $10,000. However, in the case of gifts made after June 29, 1989, in order for the increased annual exclusion to apply, the gift in excess of the otherwise applicable annual exclusion under section 2503(b) must be in a form that qualifies for the marital deduction but for the disallowance provision of section 2523(i)(1). See paragraph (d), *Example 4*, of this section.

(2) *Status of donor.*—The $100,000 annual exclusion for gifts to a noncitizen spouse is available regardless of the status of the donor. Accordingly, it is immaterial whether the donor is a citizen, resident or a nonresident not a citizen of the United States, as long as the spouse of the donor is not a citizen of the United States at the time of the gift and the conditions for allowance of the increased annual exclusion have been satisfied. See § 25.2503-2(f).

(d) *Examples.*—The principles outlined in this section are illustrated in the following examples. Assume in each of the examples that the donee, *S*, is *D*'s spouse and is not a United States citizen at the time of the gift.

Example 1. Outright transfer of present interest. In 1995, *D*, a United States citizen, transfers to *S*, outright, 100 shares of *X* corporation stock valued for federal gift tax purposes at $130,000. The transfer is a gift of a present interest in property under section 2503(b). Additionally, the gift qualifies for the gift tax marital deduction except for the disallowance provision of section 2523(i)(1). Accordingly, $100,000 of the $130,000 gift is excluded from the total amount of gifts made during the calendar year by *D* for gift tax purposes.

Example 2. Transfer of survivor benefits. In 1995, *D*, a United States citizen, retires from employment in the United States and elects to receive a reduced retirement annuity in order to provide *S* with a survivor annuity upon *D*'s death. The transfer of rights to *S* in the joint and survivor annuity is a gift by *D* for gift tax purposes. However, under paragraph (b) of this section, the gift qualifies for the gift tax marital deduction even though *S* is not a United States citizen.

Example 3. Transfer of present interest in trust property. In 1995, *D*, a resident alien, transfers property valued at $500,000 in trust to *S*, who is also a resident alien. The trust instrument provides that the trust income is payable to *S* at least quarterly and *S* has a testamentary general power to appoint the trust corpus. The transfer to *S* qualifies for the marital deduction under section 2523 but for the provisions of section 2523(i)(1). Because *S* has a life income interest in the trust, *S* has a present interest in a portion of the trust. Accordingly, *D* may exclude the present value of *S*'s income interest (up to $100,000) from *D*'s total 1995 calendar year gifts.

Example 4. Transfer of present interest in trust property. The facts are the same as in *Example 3*, except that *S* does not have a testamentary general power to appoint the trust corpus. Instead, *D*'s child, *C*, has a remainder interest in the trust. If *S* were a United States citizen, the transfer would qualify for the gift tax marital deduction if a qualified terminable interest property election was made under section 2523(f)(4). However, because *S* is not a U.S. citizen, *D* may not make a qualified terminable interest property election. Accordingly, the gift does not qualify for the gift tax marital deduction but for the disallowance provision of section 2523(i)(1). The $100,000 annual exclusion under section 2523(i)(2) is not available with respect to *D*'s transfer in trust and *D* may not exclude the present value of *S*'s income interest in excess of $10,000 from *D*'s total 1995 calendar year gifts.

Example 5. Spouse becomes citizen after transfer. *D*, a United States citizen, transfers a residence valued at $350,000 on December 20, 1995, to *D*'s spouse, *S*, a resident alien. On January 31, 1996, *S* becomes a naturalized United States citizen. On *D*'s federal gift tax return for 1995, *D* must include $250,000 as a gift ($350,000 transfer less $100,000 exclusion). Although *S* becomes a citizen in January, 1996, *S* is not a citizen of the United States at the time the transfer is made. Therefore, no gift tax marital deduction is allowable. However, the transfer does qualify for the $100,000 annual exclusion. [Reg. § 25.2523(i)-1.]

□ [*T.D.* 8612, 8-21-95.]

[Reg. § 25.2523(i)-2]

§ 25.2523(i)-2. Treatment of spousal joint tenancy property where one spouse is not a United States citizen.—(a) *In general.*—In the case of a joint tenancy with right of survivorship between spouses, or a tenancy by the entirety, where the donee spouse is not a United States citizen, the gift tax treatment of the creation and termination of the tenancy (regardless of whether the donor is a citizen, resident or nonresident not a citizen of the United States at such time), is governed by the principles of sections 2515 and 2515A (as such sections were in effect before their repeal by the Economic Recovery Tax Act of 1981). However, in applying these principles, the donor spouse may not elect to treat the creation of a tenancy in real property as a gift, as provided in section 2515(c) (prior to its repeal by the Economic Recovery Tax Act of 1981, Pub. L. 97-34, 95 Stat. 172).

(b) *Tenancies by the entirety and joint tenancies in real property.*—(1) *Creation of the tenancy on or after July 14, 1988.*—Under the principles of section 2515 (without regard to section 2515(c)), the creation of a tenancy by the entirety (or joint tenancy) in real property (either by one spouse alone or by both spouses), and any additions to the value of the tenancy in the form of improvements, reductions in indebtedness thereon, or otherwise, is not deemed to be a transfer of property for purposes of the gift tax, regardless of the proportion of the consideration furnished by each spouse, but only if the creation of the tenancy would otherwise be a gift to the donee spouse who is not a citizen of the United States at the time of the gift.

(2) *Termination.*—(i) *Tenancies created after December 31, 1954 and before January 1,1982 not subject to an election under section 2515(c), and tenancies created on or after July 14, 1988.*—When a tenancy to which this paragraph (b) applies is terminated on or after July 14, 1988, other than by reason of the death of a spouse, then, under the principles of section 2515, a spouse is deemed to have made a gift to the extent that the proportion of the total consideration furnished by the spouse, multiplied by the proceeds of the termination (whether in the form of cash, property, or interests in property), exceeds the value of the proceeds of termination received by the spouse. See section 2523(i), and § 25.2523(i)-1 and § 25.2503-2(f) as to certain of the tax consequences that may result upon termination of the tenancy. This paragraph (b)(2)(i) applies to tenancies created after December 31, 1954, and before January 1, 1982, not subject to an election under section 2515(c), and to tenancies created on or after July 14, 1988.

(ii) *Tenancies created after December 31, 1954 and before January 1, 1982 subject to an election under section 2515(c) and tenancies created after December 31, 1981 and before July 14, 1988.*—When a tenancy to which this paragraph (a) applies is terminated on or after July 14, 1988, other than by reason of the death of a spouse, then, under the principles of section 2515, a spouse is deemed to have made a gift to the extent that the proportion of the total consideration furnished by the spouse, multiplied by the proceeds of the termination (whether in the form of cash, property, or interests in property), exceeds the value of the proceeds of termination received by the spouse. See section 2523(i), and §§ 25.2523(i)-1 and 25.2503-2(f) as to certain of the tax consequences that may result upon termination of the tenancy. In the case of tenancies to which this paragraph applies, if the creation of the tenancy was treated as a gift to the noncitizen donee spouse under section 2515(c) (in the case of tenancies created prior to 1982) or section 2511 (in the case of tenancies created after December 31, 1981 and before July 14, 1988), then, upon termination of the tenancy, for purposes of applying the principles of section 2515 and the regulations thereunder, the amount treated as a gift on creation of the tenancy is treated as consideration originally belonging to the noncitizen spouse and never acquired by the noncitizen spouse from the donor spouse. This paragraph (b)(2)(ii) applies to tenancies created after December 31, 1954, and before January 1, 1982, subject to an election under section 2515(c), and to tenancies created after December 31, 1981, and before July 14, 1988.

(3) *Miscellaneous provisions.*—(i) *Tenancy by the entirety.*—For purposes of this section, *tenancy*

by the entirety includes a joint tenancy between husband and wife with right of survivorship.

(ii) *No election to treat as gift.*—The regulations under section 2515 that relate to the election to treat the creation of a tenancy by the entirety as constituting a gift and the consequences of such an election upon termination of the tenancy (§ § 25.2515-2 and 25.2515-4) do not apply for purposes of section 2523(i)(3).

(4) *Examples.*—The application of this section may be illustrated by the following examples:

Example 1. In 1992, *A*, a United States citizen, furnished $200,000 and *A*'s spouse *B*, a resident alien, furnished $50,000 for the purchase and subsequent improvement of real property held by them as tenants by the entirety. The property is sold in 1998 for $300,000. *A* receives $225,000 and *B* receives $75,000 of the sales proceeds. The termination results in a gift of $15,000 by *A* to *B*, computed as follows:

$$\frac{\$200{,}000 \text{ (consideration furnished by A)}}{\$250{,}000 \text{ (total consideration furnished by both spouses)}} \times$$

$300,000 (proceeds of termination) = $240,000 (Proceeds of termination attributable to *A*.)
$240,000 – $225,000 (proceeds received by *A*) = $15,000 gift by *A* to *B*.

Example 2. In 1986, *A* purchased real property for $300,000 and took title in the names of *A* and *B*, *A*'s spouse, as joint tenants. Under section 2511 and § 25.2511-1(h)(1) of the regulations, *A* was treated as making a gift of one-half of the value of the property ($150,000) to *B*. In 1995, the real property is sold for $400,000 and *B* receives the entire proceeds of sale. For purposes of determining the amount of the gift on termination of the tenancy under the principles of section 2515 and the regulations thereunder, the amount treated as a gift to *B* on creation of the tenancy under section 2511 is treated as *B*'s contribution towards the purchase of the property. Accordingly, the termination of the tenancy results in a gift of $200,000 from *A* to *B* determined as follows:

$$\frac{\$150{,}000 \text{ (consideration furnished by A)}}{\$300{,}000 \text{ (total consideration deemed furnished by both spouses)}} \times$$

$400,000 (proceeds of termination) = $200,000 (Proceeds of termination attributable to *A*.)
$200,000 – 0 (proceeds received by *A*) = $200,000 gift by *A* to *B*.

(c) *Tenancies by the entirety in personal property where one spouse is not a United States citizen.*—(1) *In general.*—In the case of the creation (either by one spouse alone or by both spouses where at least one of the spouses is not a United States citizen) of a joint interest in personal property with right of survivorship, or additions to the value thereof in the form of improvements, reductions in the indebtedness thereof, or otherwise, the retained interest of each spouse, solely for purposes of determining whether there has been a gift by the donor to the spouse who is not a citizen of the United States at the time of the gift, is treated as one-half of the value of the joint interest. See section 2523(i) and § § 25.2523(i)-1 and 25.2503-2(f) as to certain of the tax consequences that may result upon creation and termination of the tenancy.

(2) *Exception.*—The rule provided in paragraph (c)(1) of this section does not apply with respect to any joint interest in property if the fair market value of the interest in property (determined as if each spouse had a right to sever) cannot reasonably be ascertained except by reference to the life expectancy of one or both spouses. In these cases, actuarial principles may need to be resorted to in determining the gift tax consequences of the transaction. [Reg. § 25.2523(i)-2.]

□ [*T.D.* 8612, 8-21-95.]

[Reg. § 25.2523(i)-3]

§ 25.2523(i)-3. Effective date.—The provisions of § § 25.2523(i)-1 and 25.2523(i)-2 are effective in the case of gifts made after August 22, 1995. [Reg. § 25.2523(i)-3.]

□ [*T.D.* 8612, 8-21-95.]

[Reg. § 25.2524-1]

§ 25.2524-1. Extent of deductions.—Under the provisions of section 2524, the charitable deduction provided for in section 2522 and the marital deduction provided for in section 2523 are allowable only to the extent that the gifts, with respect to which those deductions are authorized, are included in the "total amount of gifts" made during the "calendar period" (as defined in § 25.2502-1(c)(1)), computed as provided in section 2503 and § 25.2503-1 (i.e., the total gifts less exclusions). The following examples (in both of which it is assumed that the donor has previously utilized his entire $30,000 specific exemption provided by section 2521 which was in effect at the time) illustrate the application of the provisions of this section:

Example (1). A donor made transfers by gift to his spouse of $5,000 cash on January 1, 1971, and $1,000 cash on April 5, 1971. The donor made no other transfers during 1971. The first $3,000 of such gifts for the calendar year is excluded under the provisions of section 2503(b) in determining the "total amount of gifts" made during the first calendar quarter of 1971. The marital deduction for the first calendar quarter of $2,500 (one-half of $5,000) otherwise allowable is limited by section 2524 to $2,000. The amount of taxable gifts is zero ($5,000 – $3,000 (annual exclusion) – $2,000 (marital deduction)). For the second calendar quarter of 1971, the marital deduction is $500 (one-half of $1,000); the amount excluded under section 2503(b) is zero because the entire $3,000 annual exclusion was applied against the gift in the first calendar quarter of 1971; and the amount of taxable gifts is $500 ($1,000 – $500 (marital deduction)).

Example (2). The only gifts made by a donor to his spouse during calendar year 1969 were a gift of $2,400 in May and a gift of $3,000 in August. The first $3,000 of such gifts is excluded under the provisions of section 2503(b) in determining the "total amount of gifts" made during the calendar year. The marital deduction for 1969 of $2,700 (one-half of $2,400 plus one-half of $3,000) otherwise allowable is limited by section 2524 to $2,400. The amount of taxable gifts is zero ($5,400 – $3,000 (annual exclusion) – $2,400 (marital deduction)). [Reg. § 25.2524-1.]

☐ [*T.D.* 6334, 11-14-58. *Amended by T.D.* 7238, 12-28-72 *and T.D.* 7910, 9-6-83.]

Tax on Generation-Skipping Transfers

See p. 15 for regulations not amended to reflect law changes

TAX IMPOSED

[Reg. § 26.2600-1]

§ 26.2600-1. Table of contents.—*§ 26.2601-1. Effective dates.*

☐ [*T.D.* 8644, 12-26-95. *Amended by T.D.* 8912, 12-19-2000; *T.D.* 9208, 6-28-2005; *T.D.* 9214, 7-15-2005; *T.D.* 9348, 8-1-2007 *and T.D.* 9421, 7-30-2008.]

[Reg. § 26.2601-1]

§ 26.2601-1. Effective dates.—(a) *Transfers subject to the generation-skipping transfer tax.*—(1) *In general.*—Except as otherwise provided in this section, the provisions of chapter 13 of the Internal Revenue Code of 1986 (Code) apply to any generation-skipping transfer (as defined in section 2611) made after October 22, 1986.

(2) *Certain transfers treated as if made after October 22, 1986.*—Solely for purposes of chapter 13, an inter vivos transfer is treated as if it were made on October 23, 1986, if it was—

(i) Subject to chapter 12 (regardless of whether a tax was actually incurred or paid); and

(ii) Made after September 25, 1985, but before October 23, 1986. For purposes of this paragraph, the value of the property transferred shall be the value of the property on the date the property was transferred.

(3) *Certain trust events treated as if occurring after October 22, 1986.*—For purposes of chapter 13, if an inter vivos transfer is made to a trust after September 25, 1985, but before October 23, 1986, any subsequent distribution from the trust or termination of an interest in the trust that occurred before October 23, 1986, is treated as occurring immediately after the deemed transfer on October 23, 1986. If more than one distribution or termination occurs with respect to a trust, the events are treated as if they occurred on October 23, 1986, in the same order as they occurred. See paragraph (b)(1)(iv)(B) of this section for rules determining the portion of distributions and terminations subject to tax under chapter 13. This paragraph (a)(3) does not apply to transfers to trusts not subject to chapter 13 by reason of the transition rules in paragraphs (b)(2) and (3) of this section. The provisions of this paragraph (a)(3) do not apply in determining the value of the property under chapter 13.

(4) *Example.*—The following example illustrates the principle that paragraph (a)(2) of this section is not applicable to transfers under a revocable trust that became irrevocable by reason of the transferor's death after September 25, 1985, but before October 23, 1986:

Example. T created a revocable trust on September 30, 1985, that became irrevocable when T died on October 10, 1986. Although the trust terminated in favor of a grandchild of T, the transfer to the grandchild is not treated as occurring on October 23, 1986, pursuant to paragraph (a)(2) of this section because it is not an inter vivos transfer subject to chapter 12. The transfer is not subject to chapter 13 because it is in the nature of a testamentary transfer that occurred prior to October 23, 1986.

(b) *Exceptions.*—(1) *Irrevocable trusts.*—(i) *In general.*—The provisions of chapter 13 do not apply to any generation-skipping transfer under a trust (as defined in section 2652(b)) that was irrevocable on September 25, 1985. The rule of the preceding sentence does not apply to a pro rata portion of any generation-skipping transfer under an irrevocable trust if additions are made to the trust after September 25, 1985. See paragraph (b)(1)(iv) of this section for rules for determining the portion of the trust that is subject to the provisions of chapter 13. Further, the rule in the first sentence of this paragraph (b)(1)(i) does not apply to a transfer of property pursuant to the exercise, release, or lapse of a general power of appointment that is treated as a taxable transfer under chapter 11 or chapter 12. The transfer is made by the person holding the power at the time the exercise, release, or lapse of the power becomes effective, and is not considered a transfer under a trust that was irrevocable on September 25, 1985. See paragraph (b)(1)(v)(B) of this section regarding the treatment of the release, exercise, or lapse of a power of appointment that will result in a constructive addition to a trust. See §26.2652-1(a) for the definition of a transferor.

(ii) *Irrevocable trust defined.*—(A) *In general.*—Unless otherwise provided in either paragraph (b)(1)(ii)(B) or (C) of this section, any trust (as defined in section 2652(b)) in existence on September 25, 1985, is considered an irrevocable trust.

(B) *Property includible in the gross estate under section 2038.*—For purposes of this chapter a trust is not an irrevocable trust to the extent that, on September 25, 1985, the settlor held a power with respect to such trust that would have caused the value of the trust to be included in the settlor's gross estate for Federal estate tax purposes by reason of section 2038 (without regard to powers relinquished before September 25, 1985) if the settlor had died on September 25, 1985. A trust is considered subject to a power on September 25, 1985, even though the exercise of the power was subject to the precedent giving of notice, or even though the exercise could take effect only on the expiration of a stated period, whether or not on or before September 25, 1985, notice had been given or the power had been exercised. A trust is not considered subject to a power if the power is, by its terms, exercisable only on the occurrence of an event or contingency not subject to the settlor's control (other than the death of the settlor) and if the event or contingency had not in fact taken place on September 25, 1985.

(C) *Property includible in the gross estate under section 2042.*—A policy of insurance on an individual's life that is treated as a trust under section 2652(b) is not considered an irrevocable trust to the extent that, on September 25, 1985, the insured possessed any incident of ownership (as defined in §20.2042-1(c) of this chapter, and without regard to any incidents of ownership relinquished before September 25, 1985), that would have caused the value of the trust, (i.e., the insurance proceeds) to be included in the insured's gross estate for Federal estate tax purposes by reason of section 2042, if the insured had died on September 25, 1985.

(D) *Examples.*—The following examples illustrate the application of this paragraph (b)(1):

Example 1. Section 2038 applicable. On September 25, 1985, T, the settlor of a trust that was created before September 25, 1985, held a testamentary power to add new beneficiaries to the trust. T held no other powers over any portion of the trust. The testamentary power held by T would have caused the trust to be included in T's gross estate under section 2038 if T had died on September 25, 1985. Therefore, the trust is not an irrevocable trust for purposes of this section.

Example 2. Section 2038 not applicable when power held by a person other than settlor. On September 25, 1985, S, the spouse of the settlor of a trust in existence on that date, had an annual right to withdraw a portion of the principal of the trust. The trust was otherwise irrevocable on that date. Because the power was not held by the settlor of the trust, it is not a power described in section 2038. Thus, the trust is considered an irrevocable trust for purposes of this section.

Example 3. Section 2038 not applicable. In 1984, T created a trust and retained the right to expand the class of remaindermen to include any of T's afterborn grandchildren. As of September 25, 1985, all of T's grandchildren were named remaindermen of the trust. Since the exercise of T's power was dependent on there being afterborn grandchildren who were not members of the class of remaindermen, a contingency that did not exist on September 25, 1985, the trust is not considered subject to the power on September 25, 1985, and is an irrevocable trust for purposes of this section. The result is not changed even if grandchildren are born after September 25, 1985, whether or not T exercises the power to expand the class of remaindermen.

Example 4. Section 2042 applicable. On September 25, 1985, T purchased an insurance policy on T's own life and designated child, C, and grandchild, GC, as the beneficiaries. T retained the power to obtain from the insurer a loan against the surrender value of the policy. T's insurance policy is a trust (as defined in section 2652(b)) for chapter 13 purposes. The trust is not considered an irrevocable trust because, on September 25, 1985, T possessed an incident of ownership that would have caused the value of the policy to be included in T's gross estate under section 2042 if T had died on that date.

Example 5. Trust partially irrevocable. In 1984, T created a trust naming T's grandchildren as the income and remainder beneficiaries. T retained the power to revoke the trust as to one-half of the principal at any time prior to T's death. T retained no other powers over the trust principal. T did not die before September 25, 1985, and did not exercise or release the power before that date. The half of the trust not subject to T's power to revoke is an irrevocable trust for purposes of this section.

(iii) *Trust containing qualified terminable interest property.*—(A) *In general.*—For purposes of chapter 13, a trust described in paragraph (b)(1)(ii) of this section that holds qualified terminable interest property by reason of an election under section 2056(b)(7) or section 2523(f) (made either on, before or after September 25, 1985) is treated in the same manner as if the decedent spouse or the donor spouse (as the case may be) had made an election under section 2652(a)(3). Thus, transfers from such trusts are not subject to chapter 13, and the decedent spouse or the donor spouse (as the case may be) is treated as the transferor of such property. The rule of this paragraph (b)(1)(iii) does not apply to that portion of the trust that is subject to chapter 13 by reason of an addition to the trust occurring after September 25, 1985. See §26.2652-2(a) for rules where an election under section 2652(a)(3) is made. See §26.2652-2(c) for rules where a portion of a trust is subject to an election under section 2652(a)(3).

(B) *Examples.*—The following examples illustrate the application of this paragraph (b)(1)(iii):

Example 1. QTIP election made after September 25, 1985. On March 28, 1985, T established a trust. The trust instrument provided that the trustee must distribute all income annually to T's spouse, S, during S's life. Upon S's death, the remainder is to be distributed to GC, the grandchild of T and S. On April 15, 1986, T elected under section 2523(f) to treat the property in the trust as qualified terminable interest property. On December 1, 1987, S died and soon thereafter the trust assets were distributed to GC. Because the trust was irrevocable on September 25, 1985, the transfer to GC is not subject to tax under chapter 13. T is treated as the transferor with respect to the transfer of the trust assets to GC in the same manner as if T had made an election under section 2652(a)(3) to reverse the effect of the section 2523(f) election for chapter 13 purposes.

Example 2. Section 2652(a)(3) election deemed to have been made. Assume the same facts as in *Example 1*, except the trust instrument provides that after S's death all income is to be paid annually to C, the child of T and S. Upon C's death, the remainder is to be distributed to GC. C died on October 1, 1992, and soon thereafter the trust assets are distributed to GC. Because the trust was irrevocable on September 25, 1985, the termination of C's interest is not subject to chapter 13.

(iv) *Additions to irrevocable trusts.*—(A) *In general.*—If an addition is made after September 25, 1985, to an irrevocable trust which is excluded from chapter 13 by reason of paragraph (b)(1) of this section, a pro rata portion of subsequent distributions from (and terminations of interests in property held in) the trust is subject to the provisions of chapter 13. If an addition is made, the trust is thereafter deemed to consist of two portions, a portion not subject to chapter 13 (the non-chapter 13 portion) and a portion subject to chapter 13 (the chapter 13 portion), each with a separate inclusion ratio (as defined in section 2642(a)). The non-chapter 13 portion represents the value of the assets of the trust as it existed on September 25, 1985. The applicable fraction (as defined in section 2642(a)(2)) for the non-chapter 13 portion is deemed to be 1 and the inclusion ratio for such portion is 0. The chapter 13 portion of the trust represents the value of all additions made to the trust after September 25,

1985. The inclusion ratio for the chapter 13 portion is determined under section 2642. This paragraph (b)(1)(iv)(A) requires separate portions of one trust only for purposes of determining inclusion ratios. For purposes of chapter 13, a constructive addition under paragraph (b)(1)(v) of this section is treated as an addition. See paragraph (b)(4) of this section for exceptions to the additions rule of this paragraph (b)(1)(iv). See § 26.2654-1(a)(2) for rules treating additions to a trust by an individual other than the initial transferor as a separate trust for purposes of chapter 13.

(B) *Terminations of interests in and distributions from trusts.*—Where a termination or distribution described in section 2612 occurs with respect to a trust to which an addition has been made, the portion of such termination or distribution allocable to the chapter 13 portion is determined by reference to the allocation fraction, as defined in paragraph (b)(1)(iv)(C) of this section. In the case of a termination described in section 2612(a) with respect to a trust, the portion of such termination that is subject to chapter 13 is the product of the allocation fraction and the value of the trust (to the extent of the terminated interest therein). In the case of a distribution described in section 2612(b) from a trust, the portion of such distribution that is subject to chapter 13 is the product of the allocation fraction and the value of the property distributed.

(C) *Allocation fraction.*—*(1) In general.*—The allocation fraction allocates appreciation and accumulated income between the chapter 13 and non-chapter 13 portions of a trust. The numerator of the allocation fraction is the amount of the addition (valued as of the date the addition is made), determined without regard to whether any part of the transfer is subject to tax under chapter 11 or chapter 12, but reduced by the amount of any Federal or state estate or gift tax imposed and subsequently paid by the recipient trust with respect to the addition. The denominator of the allocation fraction is the total value of the entire trust immediately after the addition. For purposes of this paragraph (b)(1)(iv)(C), the total value of the entire trust is the fair market value of the property held in trust (determined under the rules of section 2031), reduced by any amount attributable to or paid by the trust and attributable to the transfer to the trust that is similar to an amount that would be allowable as a deduction under section 2053 if the addition had occurred at the death of the transferor, and further reduced by the same amount that the numerator was reduced to reflect Federal or state estate or gift tax incurred by and subsequently paid by the recipient trust with respect to the addition. Where there is more than one addition to principal after September 25, 1985, the portion of the trust subject to chapter 13 after each such addition is determined pursuant to a revised fraction. In each case, the numerator of the revised fraction is the sum of the value of the chapter 13 portion of the trust immediately before the latest addition, and the amount of the latest addition. The denominator of the revised fraction is the total value of the entire trust immediately after the addition. If the transfer to the trust is a generation-skipping transfer, the numerator and denominator are reduced by the amount of the generation-skipping transfer tax, if any, that is imposed by chapter 13 on the transfer and actually recovered from the trust. The allocation fraction is rounded off to five decimal places (.00001).

(2) Examples.—The following examples illustrate the application of paragraph (b)(1)(iv) of this section. In each of the examples, assume that the recipient trust does not pay any Federal or state transfer tax by reason of the addition.

Example 1. Post September 25, 1985, addition to trust. (i) On August 16, 1980, T established an irrevocable trust. Under the trust instrument, the trustee is required to distribute the entire income annually to T's child, C, for life, then to T's grandchild, GC, for life. Upon GC's death, the remainder is to be paid to GC's issue. On October 1, 1986, when the total value of the entire trust is $400,000, T transfers $100,000 to the trust. The allocation fraction is computed as follows:

$$\frac{\text{Value of addition}}{\text{Total value of trust}} = \frac{\$100{,}000}{\$400{,}000 + \$100{,}000} = .2$$

(ii) Thus, immediately after the transfer, 20 percent of the value of future generation-skipping transfers under the trust will be subject to chapter 13.

Example 2. Effect of expenses. Assume the same facts as in *Example 1*, except immediately prior to the transfer on October 1, 1986, the fair market value of the individual assets in the trust totaled $400,000. Also, assume that the trust had accrued and unpaid debts, expenses, and taxes totaling $300,000. Assume further that the entire $300,000 represented amounts that would be deductible under section 2053 if the trust were includible in the transferor's gross estate. The numerator of the allocation fraction is $100,000 and the denominator of the allocation fraction is $200,000 (($400,000 - $300,000) + $100,000). Thus, the allocation fraction is .5 ($100,000/$200,000) and 50 percent of the value of future generation-skipping transfers will be subject to chapter 13.

Example 3. Multiple additions. (i) Assume the same facts as in *Example 1*, except on January 30, 1988, when the total value of the entire trust is $600,000, T transfers an additional $40,000 to the trust. Before the transfer, the value of the portion of the trust that was attributable to the prior addition was $120,000 ($600,000 x .2). The new allocation fraction is computed as follows:

$$\frac{\text{Total value of additions}}{\text{Total value of trust}} = \frac{\$120{,}000 + \$40{,}000}{\$600{,}000 + \$40{,}000} = \frac{\$160{,}000}{\$640{,}000} = .25$$

(ii) Thus, immediately after the transfer, 25 percent of the value of future generation-skipping transfers under the trust will be subject to chapter 13.

Example 4. Allocation fraction at time of generation-skipping transfer. Assume the same facts as in *Example 3*, except on March 1, 1989, when the value of the trust is $800,000, C dies. A generation-skipping transfer occurs at C's death because of the termination of C's life estate. Therefore, $200,000 ($800,000 x .25) is subject to tax under chapter 13.

(v) *Constructive additions*.—(A) *Powers of Appointment*.—Except as provided in paragraph (b)(1)(v)(B) of this section, where any portion of a trust remains in the trust after the post-September 25, 1985, release, exercise, or lapse of a power of appointment over that portion of the trust, and the release, exercise, or lapse is treated to any extent as a taxable transfer under chapter 11 or chapter 12, the value of the entire portion of the trust subject to the power that was released, exercised, or lapsed is treated as if that portion had been withdrawn and immediately retransferred to the trust at the time of the release, exercise, or lapse. The creator of the power will be considered the transferor of the addition except to the extent that the release, exercise, or lapse of the power is treated as a taxable transfer under chapter 11 or chapter 12. See § 26.2652-1 for rules for determining the identity of the transferor of property for purposes of chapter 13.

(B) *Special rule for certain powers of appointment*.—The release, exercise, or lapse of a power of appointment (other than a general power of appointment as defined in § 2041(b)) is not treated as an addition to a trust if—

(1) Such power of appointment was created in an irrevocable trust that is not subject to chapter 13 under paragraph (b)(1) of this section; and

(2) In the case of an exercise, the power of appointment is not exercised in a manner that may postpone or suspend the vesting, absolute ownership or power of alienation of an interest in property for a period, measured from the date of creation of the trust, extending beyond any life in being at the date of creation of the trust plus a period of 21 years plus, if necessary, a reasonable period of gestation (the perpetuities period). For purposes of this paragraph (b)(1)(v)(B)(2), the exercise of a power of appointment that validly postpones or suspends the vesting, absolute ownership or power of alienation of an interest in property for a term of years that will not exceed 90 years (measured from the date of creation of the trust) will not be considered an exercise that postpones or suspends vesting, absolute ownership or the power of alienation beyond the perpetuities period. If a power is exercised by creating another power, it is deemed to be exercised to whatever extent the second power may be exercised.

(C) *Constructive addition if liability is not paid out of trust principal*.—Where a trust described in paragraph (b)(1) of this section is relieved of any liability properly payable out of the assets of such trust, the person or entity who actually satisfies the liability is considered to have made a constructive addition to the trust in an amount equal to the liability. The constructive addition occurs when the trust is relieved of liability (e.g., when the right of recovery is no longer enforceable). But see § 26.2652-1(a)(3) for rules involving the application of section 2207A in the case of an election under section 2652(a)(3).

(D) *Examples*.—The following examples illustrate the application of this paragraph (b)(1)(v):

Example 1. Lapse of a power of appointment. On June 19, 1980, T established an irrevocable trust with a corpus of $500,000. The trust instrument provides that the trustee shall distribute the entire income from the trust annually to T's spouse, S, during S's life. At S's death, the remainder is to be distributed to T and S's grandchild, GC. T also gave S a general power of appointment over one-half of the trust assets. On December 21, 1989, when the value of the trust corpus is $1,500,000, S died without having exercised the general power of appointment. The value of one-half of the trust corpus, $750,000 ($1,500,000 x .5) is included in S's gross estate under section 2041(a) and is subject to tax under Chapter 11. Because the value of one-half of the trust corpus is subject to tax under Chapter 11 with respect to S's estate, S is treated as the transferor of that property for purposes of Chapter 13 (see section 2652(a)(1)(A)). For purposes of the generation-skipping transfer tax, the lapse of S's power of appointment is treated as if $750,000 ($1,500,000 x .5) had been distributed to S and then transferred back to the trust. Thus, S is considered to have added $750,000 ($1,500,000 x .5) to the trust at the date of S's death. Because this constructive addition occurred after September 25, 1985, 50 percent of the corpus of the trust became subject to Chapter 13 at S's death.

Example 2. Multiple actual additions. On June 19, 1980, T established an irrevocable trust with a principal of $500,000. The trust instrument provides that the trustee shall distribute the entire income from the trust annually to T's spouse, S, during S's life. At S's death, the remainder is to be distributed to GC, the grandchild of T and S. On October 1, 1985, when the trust assets were valued at $800,000, T added $200,000 to the trust. After the transfer on October 1, 1985, the allocation fraction was .2 ($200,000/$1,000,000). On December 21, 1989, when the value of the trust principal is

$1,000,000, T adds $1,000,000 to the trust. After this addition, the new allocation fraction is 0.6 ($1,200,000/$2,000,000). The numerator of the fraction is the value of that portion of trust assets that were subject to chapter 13 immediately prior to the addition (by reason of the first addition), $200,000 (.2 x $1,000,000), plus the value of the second transfer, $1,000,000, which equals $1,200,000. The denominator of the fraction, $2,000,000, is the total value of the trust assets immediately after the second transfer. Thus, 60 percent of the principal of the trust becomes subject to chapter 13.

Example 3. Entire portion of trust subject to lapsed power is treated as an addition. On September 25, 1985, B possessed a general power of appointment over the assets of an irrevocable trust that had been created by T in 1980. Under the terms of the trust, B's power lapsed on July 20, 1987. For Federal gift tax purposes, B is treated as making a gift of ninety-five percent (100% - 5%) of the value of the principal (see section 2514). However, because the entire trust was subject to the power of appointment, 100 percent (that portion of the trust subject to the power) of the assets of the trust are treated as a constructive addition. Thus, the entire amount of all generation-skipping transfers occurring pursuant to the trust instrument after July 20, 1987, are subject to chapter 13.

Example 4. Exercise of power of appointment in favor of another trust. On March 1, 1985, T established an irrevocable trust as defined in paragraph (b)(1)(ii) of this section. Under the terms of the trust instrument, the trustee is required to distribute the entire income annually to T's child, C, for life, then to T's grandchild, GC, for life. GC has the power to appoint any or all of the trust assets to Trust 2 which is an irrevocable trust (as defined in paragraph (b)(1)(ii) of this section) that was established on August 1, 1985. The terms of Trust 2's governing instrument provide that the trustee shall pay income to T's great grandchild, GGC, for life. Upon GGC's death, the remainder is to be paid to GGC's issue. GGC was alive on March 1, 1985, when Trust 1 was created. C died on April 1, 1986. On July 1, 1987, GC exercised the power of appointment. The exercise of GC's power does not subject future transfers from Trust 2 to tax under chapter 13 because the exercise of the power in favor of Trust 2 does not suspend the vesting, absolute ownership, or power of alienation of an interest in property for a period, measured from the date of creation of Trust 1, extending beyond the life of GGC (a beneficiary under Trust 2 who was in being at the date of creation of Trust 1) plus a period of 21 years. The result would be the same if Trust 2 had been created after the effective date of chapter 13.

Example 5. Exercise of power of appointment in favor of another trust. Assume the same facts as in *Example 4*, except that GGC was born on March 28, 1986. The valid exercise of GC's power in favor of Trust 2 causes the principal of Trust 1 to be subject to chapter 13, because GGC was not born until after the creation of Trust 1. Thus, such exercise may suspend the vesting, absolute ownership, or power of alienation of an interest in the trust principal for a period, measured from the date of creation of Trust 1, extending beyond the life of GGC (a beneficiary under Trust 2 who was not a life in being at the date of creation of Trust 1).

Example 6. Extension for the longer of two periods. Prior to the effective date of chapter 13, GP established an irrevocable trust under which the trust income was to be paid to GP's child, C, for life. C was given a testamentary power to appoint the remainder in further trust for the benefit of C's issue. In default of C's exercise of the power, the remainder was to pass to charity. C died on February 3, 1995, survived by a child who was alive when GP established the trust. C exercised the power in a manner that validly extends the trust in favor of C's issue until the later of May 15, 2064 (80 years from the date the trust was created), or the death of C's child plus 21 years. C's exercise of the power is a constructive addition to the trust because the exercise may extend the trust for a period longer than the permissible periods of either the life of C's child (a life in being at the creation of the trust) plus 21 years or a term not more than 90 years measured from the creation of the trust. On the other hand, if C's exercise of the power could extend the trust based only on the life of C's child plus 21 years or only for a term of 80 years from the creation of the trust (but not the later of the two periods) then the exercise of the power would not have been a constructive addition to the trust.

Example 7. Extension for the longer of two periods. The facts are the same as in *Example 6* except local law provides that the effect of C's exercise is to extend the term of the trust until May 15, 2064, whether or not C's child predeceases that date by more than 21 years. C's exercise is not a constructive addition to the trust because C exercised the power in a manner that cannot postpone or suspend vesting, absolute ownership, or power of alienation for a term of years that will exceed 90 years. The result would be the same if the effect of C's exercise is either to extend the term of the trust until 21 years after the death of C's child or to extend the term of the trust until the first to occur of May 15, 2064 or 21 years after the death of C's child.

(vi) *Appreciation and income.*—Except to the extent that the provisions of paragraphs (b)(1)(iv) and (v) of this section allocate subsequent appreciation and accumulated income between the original trust and additions thereto, appreciation in the value of the trust and undistributed income added thereto are not considered an addition to the principal of a trust.

(2) *Transition rule for wills or revocable trusts executed before October 22, 1986.*—(i) *In general.*—The provisions of chapter 13 do not apply to any generation-skipping transfer under a will or revocable trust executed before October 22, 1986, provided that—

(A) The document in existence on October 21, 1986, is not amended at any time after October 21, 1986, in any respect which results in the creation of, or an increase in the amount of, a generation-skipping transfer;

(B) In the case of a revocable trust, no addition is made to the revocable trust after October 21, 1986, that results in the creation of, or an increase in the amount of, a generation-skipping transfer; and

(C) The decedent dies before January 1, 1987.

(ii) *Revocable trust defined.*—For purposes of this section, the term *revocable trust* means any trust (as defined in section 2652(b)) except to the extent that, on October 22, 1986, the trust—

(A) Was an irrevocable trust described in paragraph (b)(1) of this section; or

(B) Would have been an irrevocable trust described in paragraph (b)(1) of this section had it not been created or become irrevocable after September 25, 1985, and before October 22, 1986.

(iii) *Will or revocable trust containing qualified terminable interest property.*—The rules contained in paragraph (b)(1)(iii) of this section apply to any will or revocable trust within the scope of the transition rule of this paragraph (b)(2).

(iv) *Amendments to will or revocable trust.*—For purposes of this paragraph (b)(2), an amendment to a will or a revocable trust in existence on October 21, 1986, is not considered to result in the creation of, or an increase in the amount of, a generation-skipping transfer where the amendment is—

(A) Basically administrative or clarifying in nature and only incidentally increases the amount transferred; or

(B) Designed to ensure that an existing bequest or transfer qualifies for the applicable marital or charitable deduction for estate, gift, or generation-skipping transfer tax purposes and only incidentally increases the amount transferred to a skip person or to a generation-skipping trust.

(v) *Creation of, or increase in the amount of, a GST.*—In determining whether a particular amendment to a will or revocable trust creates, or increases the amount of, a generation-skipping transfer for purposes of this paragraph (b)(2), the effect of the instrument(s) in existence on October 21, 1986, is measured against the effect of the instrument(s) in existence on the date of death of the decedent or on the date of any prior generation-skipping transfer. If the effect of an amendment cannot be immediately determined, it is deemed to create, or increase the amount of, a generation-skipping transfer until a determination can be made.

(vi) *Additions to revocable trusts.*—Any addition made after October 21, 1986, but before the death of the settlor, to a revocable trust subjects all subsequent generation-skipping transfers under the trust to the provisions of chapter 13. Any addition made to a revocable trust after the death of the settlor (if the settlor dies before January 1, 1987) is treated as an addition to an irrevocable trust. See paragraph (b)(1)(v) of this section for rules involving constructive additions to trusts. See paragraph (b)(1)(v)(B) of this section for rules providing that certain transfers to trusts are not treated as additions for purposes of this section.

(vii) *Examples.*—The following examples illustrate the application of paragraph (b)(2)(iv) of this section:

(A) *Facts applicable to Examples 1 through 5.*—In each of *Examples 1* through *5* assume that T executed a will prior to October 22, 1986, and that T dies on December 31, 1986.

Example 1. Administrative change. On November 1, 1986, T executes a codicil to T's will removing one of the co-executors named in the will. Although the codicil may have the effect of lowering administrative costs and thus increasing the amount transferred, it is considered administrative in nature and thus does not cause generation-skipping transfers under the will to be subject to chapter 13.

Example 2. Effect of amendment not immediately determinable. On November 1, 1986, T executes a codicil to T's will revoking a bequest of $100,000 to C, a non-skip person (as defined under section 2613(b)) and causing that amount to be added to a residuary trust held for a skip person. The amendment is deemed to increase the amount of a generation-skipping transfer and prevents any transfers under the will from qualifying under paragraph (b)(2)(i) of this section. If, however, C dies before T and under local law the property would have been added to the residue in any event because the bequest would have lapsed, the codicil is not considered an amendment that increases the amount of a generation-skipping transfer.

Example 3. Refund of tax paid because of amendment. T's will provided that an amount equal to the maximum allowable marital deduction would pass to T's spouse with the residue of the estate passing to a trust established for the benefit of skip persons. On October 23, 1986, the will is amended to provide that the marital share passing to T's spouse shall be the lesser of the maximum allowable marital deduction or the minimum amount that will result in no estate tax liability for T's estate. The amendment may increase the amount of a generation-skipping transfer. Therefore, any generation-skipping transfers under the will are subject to tax under chapter 13. If it becomes apparent that the amendment does not increase the amount of a generation-skipping transfer, a claim for refund may be filed with respect to any generation-skipping transfer tax that was paid within the period set forth in section 6511. For example, it would become apparent that the amendment did not result in an increase in the residue if it is subsequently determined that the maximum marital deduction and the minimum amount that will result in no estate tax liability are equal in amount.

Example 4. An amendment that increases a generation-skipping transfer causes complete loss of exempt status. T's will provided for the creation of two trusts for the benefit of skip persons. On November 1, 1986, T executed a codicil to the will specifically increasing the amount of a generation-skipping transfer under the will. All transfers made pursuant to the will or either of the trusts created thereunder are precluded from qualifying under the transition rule of paragraph (b)(2)(i) of this section and are subject to tax under chapter 13.

Example 5. Corrective action effective. Assume that T in *Example 4* later executes a second codicil deleting the increase to the generation-skipping transfer. Because the provision increasing a generation-skipping transfer does not become effective, it is not considered an amendment to a will in existence on October 22, 1986.

(B) *Facts applicable to Examples 6 through 8.*—T created a trust on September 30, 1985, in which T retained the power to revoke the transfer at any time prior to T's death. The trust provided that, upon the death of T, the income was to be paid to T's spouse, W, for life and then to A, B, and C, the children of T's sibling, S, in equal shares for life, with one-third of the principal to be distributed per stirpes to each child's surviving issue upon the death of the child. The trustee has the power to make discretionary distributions of trust principal to T's sibling, S.

Example 6. Amendment that affects only a person who is not a skip person. A became disabled, and T modified the trust on December 1, 1986, to increase A's share of the income. Since the amendment does not result in the creation of, or increase in the amount of, a generation-skipping transfer, transfers pursuant to the trust are not subject to chapter 13.

Example 7. Amendment that adds a skip person. Assume that T amends the trust to add T's grandchild, D, as an income beneficiary. The trust will be subject to the provisions of chapter 13 because the amendment creates a generation-skipping transfer.

Example 8. Refund of tax paid during interim period when effect of amendment is not determinable. Assume that T amends the trust to provide that the issue of S are to take a one-fourth share of the principal per stirpes upon S's death. Because the distribution to be made upon S's death may involve skip persons, the amendment is considered an amendment that creates or increases the amount of a generation-skipping transfer until a determination can be made. Accordingly, any distributions from (or terminations of interests in) such trust are subject to chapter 13 until it is determined that no skip person has been added to the trust. At that time, a claim for refund may be filed within the period set forth in section 6511 with respect to any generation-skipping transfer tax that was paid.

(3) *Transition rule in the case of mental incompetency.*—(i) *In general.*—If an individual was under a mental disability to change the disposition of his or her property continuously from October 22, 1986, until the date of his or her death, the provisions of chapter 13 do not apply to any generation-skipping transfer—

(A) Under a trust (as defined in section 2652(b)) to the extent such trust consists of property, or the proceeds of property, the value of which was included in the gross estate of the individual (other than property transferred by or on behalf of the individual during the individual's life after October 22, 1986); or

(B) Which is a direct skip (other than a direct skip from a trust) that occurs by reason of the death of the individual.

(ii) *Mental disability defined.*—For purposes of this paragraph (b)(2), the term *mental disability* means mental incompetence to execute an instrument governing the disposition of the individual's property, whether or not there was an adjudication of incompetence and regardless of whether there has been an appointment of a guardian, fiduciary, or other person charged with either the care of the individual or the care of the individual's property.

(iii) *Decedent who has not been adjudged mentally incompetent.*—(A) If there has not been a court adjudication that the decedent was mentally incompetent on or before October 22, 1986, the executor must file, with Form 706, either—

(1) A certification from a qualified physician stating that the decedent was—

(i) mentally incompetent at all times on and after October 22, 1986; and

(ii) did not regain competence to modify or revoke the terms of the trust or will prior to his or her death; or

(2) Sufficient other evidence demonstrating that the decedent was mentally incompetent at all times on and after October 22, 1986, as well as a statement explaining why no certification is available from a physician; and

(3) Any judgement or decree relating to the decedent's incompetency that was made after October 22, 1986.

(B) Such items in paragraphs (b)(3)(iii)(A), (*1*), (*2*), and (*3*) of this section will be considered relevant, but not determinative, in establishing the decedent's state of competency.

(iv) *Decedent who has been adjudged mentally incompetent.*—If the decedent has been adjudged mentally incompetent on or before October 22, 1986, a copy of the judgment or decree, and any modification thereof, must be filed with the Form 706.

(v) *Rule applies even if another person has power to change trust terms.*—In the case of a transfer from a trust, this paragraph (b)(3) applies even though a person charged with the care of the decedent or the decedent's property has the power to revoke or modify the terms of the trust, provided that the power is not exercised after October 22, 1986, in a manner that creates, or increases the amount of, a generation-skipping transfer. See paragraph (b)(2)(iv) of this section for rules concerning amendments that create or increase the amount of a generation-skipping transfer.

(vi) *Example.*—The following example illustrates the application of paragraph (b)(3)(v) of this section:

Example. T was mentally incompetent on October 22, 1986, and remained so until death in 1993. Prior to becoming incompetent, T created a revocable generation-skipping trust that was includible in T's gross estate. Prior to October 22, 1986, the appropriate court issued an order under which P, who was thereby charged with the care of T's property, had the power to modify or revoke the revocable trust. Although P exercised the power after October 22, 1986, and while T was incompetent, the power was not exercised in a manner that created, or increased the amount of, a generation-skipping transfer. Thus, the existence and exercise of P's power did not cause the trust to lose its exempt status under paragraph (b)(3) of this section. The result would be the same if the court order was issued after October 22, 1986.

(4) *Retention of trust's exempt status in the case of modifications, etc.*—(i) *In general.*—This paragraph (b)(4) provides rules for determining when a modification, judicial construction, settlement agreement, or trustee action with respect to a trust that is exempt from the generation-skipping transfer tax under paragraph (b)(1), (2), or (3) of this section (hereinafter referred to as an exempt trust) will not cause the trust to lose its exempt status. In general, unless specifically provided otherwise, the rules contained in this paragraph are applicable only for purposes of determining whether an exempt trust retains its exempt status for generation-skipping transfer tax purposes. Thus (unless specifically noted), the rules do not apply in determining, for example, whether the transaction results in a gift subject to gift tax, or may cause the trust to be included in the gross estate of a beneficiary, or may result in the realization of gain for purposes of section 1001.

(A) *Discretionary powers.*—The distribution of trust principal from an exempt trust to a new trust or retention of trust principal in a continuing trust will not cause the new or continuing trust to be subject to the provisions of chapter 13, if—

(1) Either—

(i) The terms of the governing instrument of the exempt trust authorize distributions to the new trust or the retention of trust principal in a continuing trust, without the consent or approval of any beneficiary or court; or

(ii) at the time the exempt trust became irrevocable, state law authorized distributions to the new trust or retention of principal in the continuing trust, without the consent or approval of any beneficiary or court; and

(2) The terms of the governing instrument of the new or continuing trust do not extend the time for vesting of any beneficial interest in the trust in a manner that may postpone or suspend the vesting, absolute ownership, or power of alienation of an interest in property for a period, measured from the date the original trust became irrevocable, extending beyond any life in being at the date the original trust became irrevocable plus a period of 21 years, plus if necessary, a reasonable period of gestation. For purposes of this paragraph (b)(4)(i)(A), the exercise of a trustee's distributive power that validly postpones or suspends the vesting, absolute ownership, or power of alienation of an interest in property for a term of years that will not exceed 90 years (measured from the date the original trust became irrevocable) will not be considered an exercise that postpones or suspends vesting, absolute ownership, or the power of alienation beyond the perpetuities period. If a distributive power is exercised by creating another power, it is deemed to be exercised to whatever extent the second power may be exercised.

(B) *Settlement.*—A court-approved settlement of a bona fide issue regarding the administration of the trust or the construction of terms of the governing instrument will not cause an exempt trust to be subject to the provisions of chapter 13, if—

(1) The settlement is the product of arm's length negotiations; and

(2) The settlement is within the range of reasonable outcomes under the governing instrument and applicable state law addressing the issues resolved by the settlement. A settlement that results in a compromise between the positions of the litigating parties and reflects the parties' assessments of the relative strengths of their positions is a settlement that is within the range of reasonable outcomes.

(C) *Judicial construction.*—A judicial construction of a governing instrument to resolve an ambiguity in the terms of the instrument or to correct a scrivener's error will not cause an exempt trust to be subject to the provisions of chapter 13, if—

(1) The judicial action involves a bona fide issue; and

(2) The construction is consistent with applicable state law that would be applied by the highest court of the state.

(D) *Other changes.*—*(1)* A modification of the governing instrument of an exempt trust (including a trustee distribution, settlement, or construction that does not satisfy paragraph (b)(4)(i)(A), (B), or (C) of this section) by judicial reformation, or nonjudicial reformation that is valid under applicable state law, will not cause an exempt trust to be subject to the provisions of chapter 13, if the modification does not shift a beneficial interest in the trust to any beneficiary who occupies a lower generation (as defined in section 2651) than the person or persons who held the beneficial interest prior to the modification, and the modification does not extend the time for vesting of any beneficial interest in the trust beyond the period provided for in the original trust.

(2) For purposes of this section, a modification of an exempt trust will result in a shift in beneficial interest to a lower generation beneficiary if the modification can result in either an increase in the amount of a GST transfer or the creation of a new GST transfer. To determine whether a modification of an irrevocable trust will shift a beneficial interest in a trust to a beneficiary who occupies a lower generation, the effect of the instrument on the date of the modification is measured against the effect of the instrument in existence immediately before the modification. If the effect of the modification cannot be immediately determined, it is deemed to shift a beneficial interest in the trust to a beneficiary who occupies a lower generation (as defined in section 2651) than the person or persons who held the beneficial interest prior to the modification. A modification that is administrative in nature that only indirectly increases the amount transferred (for example, by lowering administrative costs or income taxes) will not be considered to shift a beneficial interest in the trust. In addition, administration of a trust in conformance with applicable local law that defines the term income as a unitrust amount (or permits a right to income to be satisfied by such an amount) or that permits the trustee to adjust between principal and income to fulfill the trustee's duty of impartiality between income and principal beneficiaries will not be considered to shift a beneficial interest in the trust, if applicable local law provides for a reasonable apportionment between the income and remainder beneficiaries of the total return of the trust and meets the requirements of § 1.643(b)-1 of this chapter.

(E) *Examples.*—The following examples illustrate the application of this paragraph (b)(4). In each example, assume that the trust established in 1980 was irrevocable for purposes of paragraph (b)(1)(ii) of this section and that there have been no additions to any trust after September 25, 1985. The examples are as follows:

Example 1. Trustee's power to distribute principal authorized under trust instrument. In 1980, Grantor established an irrevocable trust (Trust) for the benefit of Grantor's child, *A*, *A*'s spouse, and *A*'s issue. At the time Trust was established, *A* had two children, *B* and *C*. A corporate fiduciary was designated as trustee. Under the terms of Trust, the trustee has the discretion to distribute all or part of the trust income to one or more of the group consisting of *A*, *A*'s spouse or *A*'s issue. The trustee is also authorized to distribute all or part of the trust principal to one or more trusts for the benefit of *A*, *A*'s spouse, or *A*'s issue under terms specified by the trustee in the trustee's discretion. Any trust established under Trust, however, must terminate 21 years after the death of the last child of *A* to die who was alive at the time Trust was executed. Trust will terminate on the death of *A*, at which time the remaining principal will be distributed to *A*'s issue, per stirpes. In 2002, the trustee distributes part of Trust's principal to a new trust for the benefit of *B* and *C* and their issue. The new trust will terminate 21 years after the death of the survivor of *B* and *C*, at which time the trust principal will be distributed to the issue of B and C, per stirpes. The terms of the governing instrument of Trust authorize the trustee to make the distribution to a new trust without the consent or approval of any beneficiary or court. In addition, the terms of the governing instrument of the new trust do not extend the time for vesting of any beneficial interest in a manner that may postpone or suspend the vesting, absolute ownership or power of alienation of an interest in property for a period, measured from the date of creation of Trust, extending beyond any life in being at the date of creation of Trust plus a period of 21 years, plus if necessary, a reasonable period of gestation. Therefore, neither Trust nor the new trust will be subject to the provisions of chapter 13 of the Internal Revenue Code.

Example 2. Trustee's power to distribute principal pursuant to state statute. In 1980, Grantor established an irrevocable trust (Trust) for the benefit of Grantor's child, *A*, *A*'s spouse, and *A*'s issue. At the time Trust was established, *A* had two children, *B* and *C*. A corporate fiduciary was designated as trustee. Under the terms of Trust, the trustee has the discretion to distribute all or part of the trust income or principal to one or more of the group consisting of *A*, *A*'s spouse or *A*'s issue. Trust will terminate on the death of *A*, at which time, the trust principal will be distributed to *A*'s issue, per stirpes. Under a state statute enacted after 1980 that is applicable to Trust, a trustee who has the absolute discretion under the terms of a testamentary instrument or irrevocable inter vivos trust agreement to invade the principal of a trust for the benefit of the income beneficiaries of the trust, may exercise the discretion by appointing so much or all of the principal of the trust in favor of a trustee of a trust under an instrument other than that under which the power to invade is created, or under the same instrument. The trustee may take the action either with consent of all the persons interested in the trust but without prior court approval, or with court approval, upon notice to all of the parties. The exercise of the discretion, however, must not reduce any fixed income interest of any income beneficiary of the trust and must be in favor of the beneficiaries of the trust. Under state law prior to the enactment of the state statute, the trustee did not have the authority to make distributions in trust. In 2002, the trustee distributes one-half of Trust's principal to a new trust that provides for the payment of trust income to *A* for life and further provides that, at *A*'s death, one-half of the trust remainder will pass to *B* or *B*'s issue and one-half of the trust will pass to *C* or *C*'s issue. Because the state statute was enacted after Trust was created and requires the consent of all of the parties, the transaction constitutes a modification of Trust. However, the modification does not shift any beneficial interest in Trust to a beneficiary or beneficiaries who occupy a lower generation than the person or persons who held the beneficial interest prior to the modification. In addition, the modification does not extend the time for vesting of any beneficial interest in Trust beyond the period provided for in the original trust. The new trust will terminate at the same date provided under Trust. Therefore, neither Trust nor the new trust will be subject to the provisions of chapter 13 of the Internal Revenue Code.

Example 3. Construction of an ambiguous term in the instrument. In 1980, Grantor established an irrevocable trust for the benefit of Grantor's children, *A* and *B*, and their issue. The trust is to terminate on the death of the last to die of *A* and *B*, at which time the principal is to be distributed to their issue. However, the provision governing the termination of the trust is ambiguous regarding whether the trust principal is to be distributed per stirpes, only to the children of *A* and *B*, or per capita among the children, grandchildren, and more remote issue of *A* and *B*. In 2002, the trustee files a construction suit with the appropriate local court to resolve the ambiguity. The court issues an order construing the instrument to provide for per capita distributions to the children, grandchildren, and more remote issue of *A* and *B* living at the time the trust terminates. The court's construction resolves a bona fide issue regarding the proper interpretation of the instrument and is consistent with applicable state law as it would be interpreted by the highest court of the state. Therefore, the trust will not be subject to the provisions of chapter 13 of the Internal Revenue Code.

Example 4. Change in trust situs. In 1980, Grantor, who was domiciled in State X, executed an irrevocable trust for the benefit of Grantor's issue, naming a State *X* bank as trustee. Under the terms of the trust, the trust is to terminate, in all events, no later than 21 years after the death of the last to die of certain designated individuals living at the time the trust was executed. The provisions of the trust do not specify that any particular state law is to govern the administration and construction of the trust. In State *X*, the common law rule against perpetuities applies to trusts. In 2002, a State *Y* bank is named as sole trustee. The effect of changing trustees is that the situs of the trust changes to State *Y*, and the laws of State *Y* govern the administration and construction of the trust. State *Y* law contains no rule against perpetuities. In this case, however, in view of the terms of the trust instrument, the trust will terminate at the same time before and after the change in situs. Accordingly, the change in situs does not shift any beneficial interest in the trust to a beneficiary who occupies a lower generation (as defined in section 2651) than the person or persons who held the beneficial interest prior to the transfer. Furthermore, the change in situs does not extend the time for vesting of any beneficial interest in the trust beyond that provided for in the original trust. Therefore, the trust will not be subject to the provisions of chapter 13 of the Internal Revenue Code. If, in this example, as a result of the change in situs, State *Y* law governed such that the time for vesting was extended beyond the period prescribed under the terms of the original trust instrument, the trust would not retain exempt status.

Example 5. Division of a trust. In 1980, Grantor established an irrevocable trust for the benefit of his two children, *A* and *B*, and their issue. Under the terms of the trust, the trustee has the discretion to distribute income and principal to *A*, *B*, and their issue in such amounts as the trustee deems appropriate. On the death of the last to die of *A* and *B*, the trust principal is to be distributed to the living issue of *A* and *B*, per stirpes. In 2002, the appropriate local court approved the division of the trust into two equal trusts, one for the benefit of *A* and *A*'s issue and one for the benefit of *B* and *B*'s issue. The trust for *A* and *A*'s issue provides that the trustee has the discretion to distribute trust income and principal to *A* and *A*'s issue in such amounts as the trustee deems appropriate. On *A*'s death, the trust principal is to be distributed equally to *A*'s issue, per stirpes. If *A* dies with no living descendants, the principal will be added to the trust for *B* and *B*'s issue. The trust for *B* and *B*'s issue is identical (except for the beneficiaries), and terminates at *B*'s death at which time the trust principal is to be distributed equally to *B*'s issue, per stirpes. If *B* dies with no living descendants, principal will be added to the trust for *A* and *A*'s issue. The division of the trust into two trusts does not shift any beneficial interest in the trust to a beneficiary who occupies a lower generation (as defined in section 2651) than the person or persons who held the beneficial interest prior to the division. In addition, the division does not extend the time for vesting of any beneficial interest in the trust beyond the period provided for in the original trust. Therefore, the two partitioned trusts resulting from the division will not be subject to the provisions of chapter 13 of the Internal Revenue Code.

Example 6. Merger of two trusts. In 1980, Grantor established an irrevocable trust for Grantor's child and the child's issue. In 1983, Grantor's spouse also established a separate irrevocable trust for the benefit of the same child and issue. The terms of the spouse's trust and Grantor's trust are identical. In 2002, the appropriate local court approved the merger of the two trusts into one trust to save administrative costs and enhance the management of the investments. The merger of the two trusts does not shift any beneficial interest in the trust to a beneficiary who occupies a lower generation (as defined in section 2651) than the person or persons who held the beneficial interest prior to the merger. In addition, the merger does not extend the time for vesting of any beneficial interest in the trust beyond the period provided for in the original trust. Therefore, the trust that resulted from the merger will not be subject to the provisions of chapter 13 of the Internal Revenue Code.

Example 7. Modification that does not shift an interest to a lower generation. In 1980, Grantor established an irrevocable trust for the benefit of Grantor's grandchildren, *A*, *B*, and *C*. The trust provides that income is to be paid to *A*, *B*, and *C*, in equal shares for life. The trust further provides that, upon the death of the first grandchild to die, one-third of the principal is to be distributed to that grandchild's issue, per stirpes. Upon the death of the second grandchild to die, one-half of the remaining trust principal is to be distributed to that grandchild's issue, per stirpes, and upon the death of the last grandchild to die, the remaining principal is to be distributed to that grandchild's issue, per stirpes. In 2002, *A* became disabled. Subsequently, the trustee, with the consent of *B* and *C*, petitioned the appropriate local court and the court approved a modification of the trust that increased *A*'s share of trust income. The modification does not shift a beneficial interest to a lower generation beneficiary because the modification does not increase the amount of a GST transfer under the original trust or create the possibility that new GST transfers not contemplated in the original trust may be made. In this case, the modification will increase the amount payable to *A* who is a member of the same generation as *B* and *C*. In addition, the modification does not extend the time for vesting of any beneficial interest in the trust beyond the period provided for in the original trust. Therefore, the trust as modified will not be subject to the provisions of chapter 13 of the Internal Revenue Code. However, the modification increasing *A*'s share of trust income is a transfer by *B* and *C* to *A* for Federal gift tax purposes.

Example 8. Conversion of income interest into unitrust interest. In 1980, Grantor established an irrevocable trust under the terms of which trust income is payable to *A* for life and, upon *A*'s death, the remainder is to pass to *A*'s issue, per stirpes. In 2002, the appropriate local court approves a modification to the trust that converts *A*'s income interest into the right to receive the greater of the entire income of the trust or a fixed percentage of the trust assets valued annually (unitrust interest) to be paid each year to *A* for life. The modification does not result in a shift in beneficial interest to a beneficiary who occupies a lower generation (as defined in section 2651) than the person or persons who held the beneficial interest prior to the modification. In this case, the modification can only operate to increase the amount distributable to A and decrease the amount distributable to *A*'s issue. In addition, the modification does not extend the time for vesting of any beneficial interest in the trust beyond the period provided for in the original trust. Therefore, the trust will not be subject to the provisions of chapter 13 of the Internal Revenue Code.

Example 9. Allocation of capital gain to income. In 1980, Grantor established an irrevocable trust under the terms of which trust income is payable to Grantor's child, *A*, for life, and upon *A*'s death, the remainder is to pass to *A*'s issue, per stirpes. Under applicable state law, unless the governing instrument provides otherwise, capital gain is allocated to principal. In 2002, the trust is modified to allow the trustee to allocate capital gain to the income. The modification does not shift any beneficial interest in the trust to a beneficiary who occupies a lower generation (as defined in section 2651) than the person or persons who held the beneficial interest prior to the modification. In this case, the modification can only have the effect of increasing the amount distributable to *A*, and decreasing the amount distributable to *A*'s issue. In addition, the modification does not extend the time for vesting of any beneficial interest in the trust beyond the period provided for in the original trust. Therefore, the trust will not be subject to the provisions of chapter 13 of the Internal Revenue Code.

Example 10. Administrative change to terms of a trust. In 1980, Grantor executed an irrevocable trust for the benefit of Grantor's issue, naming a bank and five other individuals as trustees. In 2002, the appropriate local court approves a modification of the trust that decreases the number of trustees which results in lower administrative costs. The modification pertains to the administration of the trust and does not shift a beneficial interest in the trust to any beneficiary who occupies a lower generation (as defined in section 2651) than the person or persons who held the beneficial interest prior to the modification. In addition, the modification does not extend the time for vesting of any beneficial interest in the trust beyond the period provided for in the original trust. Therefore, the trust will not be subject to the provisions of chapter 13 of the Internal Revenue Code.

Example 11. Conversion of income interest to unitrust interest under state statute. In 1980, Grantor, a resident of State X, established an irrevocable trust for the benefit of Grantor's child, A, and A's issue. The trust provides that trust income is payable to A for life and upon A's death the remainder is to pass to A's issue, per stirpes. In 2002, State X amends its income and principal statute to define income as a unitrust amount of 4% of the fair market value of the trust assets valued annually. For a trust established prior to 2002, the statute provides that the new definition of income will apply only if all the beneficiaries who have an interest in the trust consent to the change within two years after the effective date of the statute. The statute provides specific procedures to establish the consent of the beneficiaries. A and A's issue consent to the change in the definition of income within the time period, and in accordance with the procedures, prescribed by the state statute. The administration of the trust, in accordance with the state statute defining income to be a 4% unitrust amount, will not be considered to shift any beneficial interest in the trust. Therefore, the trust will not be subject to the provisions of chapter 13 of the Internal Revenue Code. Further, under these facts, no trust beneficiary will be treated as having made a gift for federal gift tax purposes, and neither the trust nor any trust beneficiary will be treated as having made a taxable exchange for federal income tax purposes. Similarly, the conclusions in this example would be the same if the beneficiaries' consent was not required, or, if the change in administration of the trust occurred because the situs of the trust was changed to State X from a state whose statute does not define income as a unitrust amount or if the situs was changed to such a state from State X.

Example 12. Equitable adjustments under state statute. The facts are the same as in *Example 11*, except that in 2002, State X amends its income and principal statute to permit the trustee to make adjustments between income and principal when the trustee invests and manages the trust assets under the state's prudent investor standard, the trust describes the amount that shall or must be distributed to a beneficiary by referring to the trust's income, and the trustee after applying the state statutory rules regarding allocation of receipts between income and principal is unable to administer the trust impartially. The provision permitting the trustees to make these adjustments is effective in 2002 for trusts created at any time. The trustee invests and manages the trust assets under the state's prudent investor standard, and pursuant to authorization in the state statute, the trustee allocates receipts between the income and principal accounts in a manner to ensure the impartial administration of the trust. The administration of the trust in accordance with the state statute will not be considered to shift any beneficial interest in the trust. Therefore, the trust will not be subject to the provisions of chapter 13 of the Internal Revenue Code. Further, under these facts, no trust beneficiary will be treated as having made a gift for federal gift tax purposes, and neither the trust nor any trust beneficiary will be treated as having made a taxable exchange for federal income tax purposes. Similarly, the conclusions in this example would be the same if the change in administration of the trust occurred because the situs of the trust was changed to State X from a state whose statute does not authorize the trustee to make adjustments between income and principal or if the situs was changed to such a state from State X.

(ii) *Effective dates.*—The rules in this paragraph (b)(4) are generally applicable on and after December 20, 2000. However, the rule in the last sentence of paragraph (b)(4)(i)(D)(2) of this section and *Example 11* and *Example 12* in paragraph (b)(4)(i)(E) of this section regarding the administration of a trust and the determination of income in conformance with applicable state law applies to trusts for taxable years ending after January 2, 2004.

(5) *Exceptions to additions rule.*—(i) *In general.*—Any addition to a trust made pursuant to an instrument or arrangement covered by the transition rules in paragraph (b)(1), (2) or (3) of this section is not treated as an addition for purposes of this section. Moreover, any property transferred inter vivos to a trust is not treated as an addition if the same property would have been added to the trust pursuant to an instrument covered by the transition rules in paragraph (b)(2) or (3) of this section.

(ii) *Examples.*—The following examples illustrate the application of paragraph (b)(4)(i) of this section:

Example 1. Addition pursuant to terms of exempt instrument. On December 31, 1980, T created an irrevocable trust having a principal of $100,000. Under the terms of the trust, the principal was to be held for the benefit of T's grandchild, GC. Pursuant to the terms of T's will, a document entitled to relief under the transition rule of paragraph (b)(2) of this section, the residue of the estate was paid to the trust. Because the addition to the trust was paid pursuant to the terms of an instrument (T's will) that is not subject to the provisions of chapter 13 because of paragraph (b)(2) of this section, the payment to the trust is not considered an addition to the principal of the trust. Thus, distributions to or for the benefit of GC, are not subject to the provisions of chapter 13.

Example 2. Property transferred inter vivos that would have been transferred to the same trust by the transferor's will. T is the grantor of a trust that was irrevocable on September 25, 1985. T's will, which was executed before October 22, 1986, and not amended thereafter, provides that, upon T's death, the entire estate will pour over into T's trust. On October 1, 1985, T transfers $100,000 to the trust. While T's will otherwise qualifies for relief under the transition rule in paragraph (b)(2) of this section, the transition rule is not applicable unless T dies prior to January 1, 1987. Thus, if T dies after December 31, 1986, the transfer is treated as an addition to the trust for purposes of any distribution made from the trust after the transfer to the trust on October 1, 1985. If T dies before January 1, 1987, the entire trust (as well as any distributions from or terminations of interests in the trust prior to T's death) is exempt, under paragraph (b)(2) of this section, from chapter 13 because the $100,000 would have been added to the trust under a will that would have qualified under paragraph (b)(2) of this section. In either case, for any generation-skipping transfers made after the transfer to the trust on October 1, 1985, but before T's death, the $100,000 is treated as an addition to the trust and a proportionate amount of the trust is subject to chapter 13.

Example 3. Pour over to a revocable trust. T and S are the settlors of separate revocable trusts with equal values. Both trusts were established for the benefit of skip persons (as defined in section 2613). S dies on December 1, 1985, and under the provisions of S's trust, the principal pours over into T's trust. If T dies before January 1, 1987, the entire trust is excluded under paragraph (b)(2) of this section from the operation of chapter 13. If T dies after December 31, 1986, the entire trust is subject to the generation-skipping transfer tax provisions because T's trust is not a trust described in paragraph (b)(1) or (2) of this section. In the latter case, the fact that S died before January 1, 1987, is irrelevant because the principal of S's trust was added to a trust that never qualified under the transition rules of paragraph (b)(1) or (2) of this section.

Example 4. Pour over to exempt trust. Assume the same facts as in *Example 3*, except upon the death of S on December 1, 1985, S's trust continues as an irrevocable trust and that the principal of T's trust is to be paid over upon T's death to S's trust. Again, if T dies before January 1, 1987, S's entire trust falls within the provisions of paragraph (b)(2) of this section. However, if T dies after December 31, 1986, the pour-over is considered an addition to the trust. Therefore, S's trust is not a trust excluded under paragraph (b)(2) of this section because an addition is made to the trust.

Example 5. Lapse of a general power of appointment. S, the spouse of the settlor of an irrevocable trust that was created in 1980, had, on September 25, 1985, a general power of appointment over the trust assets. The trust provides that should S fail to exercise the power of appointment the property is to remain in the trust. On October 21, 1986, S executed a will under which S failed to exercise the power of appointment. If S dies before January 1, 1987, without having exercised the power in a manner which results in the creation of, or increase in the amount of, a generation-skipping transfer (or amended the will in a manner that results in the creation of, or increase in the amount of, a generation-skipping transfer), transfers pursuant to the trust or the will are not subject to chapter 13 because the trust is an irrevocable trust and the will qualifies under paragraph (b)(2) of this section.

Example 6. Lapse of general power of appointment held by intestate decedent. Assume the same facts as in *Example 5*, except on October 22, 1986, S did not have a will and that S dies after that date. Upon S's death, or upon the prior exercise or release of the power, the value of the entire trust is treated as having been distributed to S, and S is treated as having made an addition to the trust in the amount of the entire principal. Any distribution or termination pursuant to the trust occurring after S's death is subject to chapter 13. It is immaterial whether S's death occurs before January 1, 1987, since paragraph (b)(2) of this section is only applicable where a will or revocable trust was executed before October 22, 1986.

(c) *Additional effective dates.*—Except as otherwise provided, the regulations under §§26.2611-1, 26.2612-1, 26.2613-1, 26.2632-1, 26.2641-1, 26.2642-1, 26.2642-2, 26.2642-3, 26.2642-4, 26.2642-5, 26.2652-1, 26.2652-2, 26.2653-1, 26.2654-1, 26.2663-1, and 26.2663-2 are effective with respect to generation-skipping transfers as defined in §26.2611-1 made on or after December 27, 1995. However, taxpayers may, at their option, rely on these regulations in the case of generation-skipping transfers made, and trusts that became irrevocable, after December 23, 1992, and before December 27, 1995. The last four sentences in paragraph (b)(1)(i) of this section are applicable on and after November 18, 1999. [Reg. §26.2601-1.]

□ [*T.D.* 8644, 12-26-95. *Amended by T.D.* 8912, 12-19-2000 (*corrected* 2-21-2001) *and T.D.* 9102, 12-30-2003.]

GENERATION-SKIPPING TRANSFERS

[Reg. §26.2611-1]

§26.2611-1. Generation-skipping transfer defined.—A generation-skipping transfer (GST) is an event that is either a direct skip, a taxable distribution, or a taxable termination. See §26.2612-1 for the definition of these terms. The determination as to whether an event is a GST is made by reference to the most recent transfer subject to the estate or gift tax. See §26.2652-1(a)(2) for determining whether a transfer is subject to Federal estate or gift tax. [Reg. §26.2611-1.]

□ [*T.D.* 8644, 12-26-95.]

[Reg. §26.2612-1]

§26.2612-1. Definitions.—(a) *Direct skip.*—A direct skip is a transfer to a skip person that is subject to Federal estate or gift tax. If property is transferred to a trust, the transfer is a direct skip only if the trust is a skip person. Only one direct skip occurs when a single transfer of property skips two or more generations. See paragraph (d) of this section for the definition of skip person. See §26.2652-1(b) for the definition of trust. See §26.2632-1(c)(4) for the time that a direct skip occurs if the transferred property is subject to an estate tax inclusion period.

(b) *Taxable termination.*—(1) *In general.*—Except as otherwise provided in this paragraph (b), a taxable termination is a termination (occurring for any reason) of an interest in trust unless—

(i) A transfer subject to Federal estate or gift tax occurs with respect to the property held in the trust at the time of the termination;

(ii) Immediately after the termination, a person who is not a skip person has an interest in the trust; or

(iii) At no time after the termination may a distribution, other than a distribution the probability of which occurring is so remote as to be negligible (including a distribution at the termination of the trust) be made from the trust to a skip person. For this purpose, the probability that a distribution will occur is so remote as to be negligible only if it can be ascertained by actuarial standards that there is less than a 5 percent probability that the distribution will occur.

(2) *Partial termination.*—If a distribution of a portion of trust property is made to a skip per-

son by reason of a termination occurring on the death of a lineal descendant of the transferor, the termination is a taxable termination with respect to the distributed property.

(3) *Simultaneous terminations.*—A simultaneous termination of two or more interests creates only one taxable termination.

(c) *Taxable distribution.*—(1) *In general.*—A taxable distribution is a distribution of income or principal from a trust to a skip person unless the distribution is a taxable termination or a direct skip. If any portion of GST tax (including penalties and interest thereon) imposed on a distributee is paid from the distributing trust, the payment is an additional taxable distribution to the distributee. For purposes of chapter 13, the additional distribution is treated as having been made on the last day of the calendar year in which the original taxable distribution is made. If Federal estate or gift tax is imposed on any individual with respect to an interest in property held by a trust, the interest in property is treated as having been distributed to the individual to the extent that the value of the interest is subject to Federal estate or gift tax. See § 26.2652-1(a)(6) *Example 5*, regarding the treatment of the lapse of a power of appointment as a transfer to a trust.

(2) *Look-through rule not to apply.*—Solely for purposes of determining whether any transfer from a trust to another trust is a taxable distribution, the rules of section 2651(e)(2) do not apply. If the transferring trust and the recipient trust have the same transferor, see § 26.2642-4(a)(1) and (2) for rules for recomputing the applicable fraction of the recipient trust.

(d) *Skip person.*—A skip person is—

(1) An individual assigned to a generation more than one generation below that of the transferor (determined under the rules of section 2651); or

(2) A trust if—

(i) All interests in the trust are held by skip persons; or

(ii) No person holds an interest in the trust and no distributions, other than a distribution the probability of which occurring is so remote as to be negligible (including distributions at the termination of the trust), may be made after the transfer to a person other than a skip person. For this purpose, the probability that a distribution will occur is so remote as to be negligible only if it can be ascertained by actuarial standards that there is less than a 5 percent probability that the distribution will occur.

(e) *Interest in trust.*—(1) *In general.*—An interest in trust is an interest in property held in trust as defined in section 2652(c) and these regulations. An interest in trust exists if a person—

(i) Has a present right to receive trust principal or income;

(ii) Is a permissible current recipient of trust principal or income and is not described in section 2055(a); or

(iii) Is described in section 2055(a) and the trust is a charitable remainder annuity trust or unitrust (as defined in section 664(d)) or a pooled income fund (as defined in section 642(c)(5)).

(2) *Exceptions.*—(i) *Support obligations.*—In general, an individual has a present right to receive trust income or principal if trust income or principal may be used to satisfy the individual's support obligations. However, an individual does not have an interest in a trust merely because a support obligation of that individual may be satisfied by a distribution that is either within the discretion of a fiduciary or pursuant to provisions of local law substantially equivalent to the Uniform Gifts (Transfers) to Minors Act.

(ii) *Certain interests disregarded.*—An interest which is used primarily to postpone or avoid the GST tax is disregarded for purposes of chapter 13. An interest is considered as used primarily to postpone or avoid the GST tax if a significant purpose for the creation of the interest is to postpone or avoid the tax.

(3) *Disclaimers.*—An interest does not exist to the extent it is disclaimed pursuant to a disclaimer that constitutes a qualified disclaimer under section 2518.

(f) *Examples.*—The following examples illustrate the provisions of this section.

Example 1. Direct skip. T gratuitously conveys Blackacre to T's grandchild. Because the transfer is a transfer to a skip person of property subject to Federal gift tax, it is a direct skip.

Example 2. Direct skip of more than one generation. T gratuitously conveys Blackacre to T's great-grandchild. The transfer is a direct skip. Only one GST tax is imposed on the direct skip although two generations are skipped by the transfer.

Example 3. Withdrawal power in trust. T transfers $50,000 to a new trust providing that trust income is to be paid to T's child, C, for life and, on C's death, the trust principal is to be paid to T's descendants. Under the terms of the trust, T grants four grandchildren the right to withdraw $10,000 from the trust for a 60 day period following the transfer. Since C, who is not a skip person, has an interest in the trust, the trust is not a skip person. T's transfer to the trust is not a direct skip.

Example 4. Taxable termination. T establishes an irrevocable trust under which the income is to be paid to T's child, C, for life. On the death of C, the trust principal is to be paid to T's grandchild, GC. Since C has an interest in the trust, the trust is not a skip person and the transfer to the trust is not a direct skip. If C dies survived by GC, a taxable termination occurs at C's death because C's interest in the trust terminates and thereafter the trust property is held by a skip person who occupies a lower generation than C.

Example 5. Direct skip of property held in trust. T establishes a testamentary trust under which the income is to be paid to T's surviving spouse, S, for life and the remainder is to be paid to a grandchild of T and S. T's executor elects to treat the trust as qualified terminable interest property under section 2056(b)(7). The transfer to the trust is not a direct skip because S, a person who is not a skip person, holds a present right to receive income from the trust. Upon S's death, the trust property is included in S's gross estate under section 2044 and passes directly to a skip person. The GST occurring at that time is a direct skip because it is a transfer subject to chapter 11. The fact that the interest created by T is terminated at S's death is immaterial because S becomes the transferor at the time of the transfer subject to chapter 11.

Example 6. Taxable termination. T establishes an irrevocable trust for the benefit of T's child, C, T's grandchild, GC, and T's great-grandchild, GGC. Under the terms of the trust, income and principal may be distributed to any or all of the living beneficiaries at the discretion of the trustee. Upon the death of the second beneficiary to die, the trust principal is to be paid to the survivor. C dies first. A taxable termination occurs at that time because, immediately after C's interest terminates, all interests in the trust are held by skip persons (GC and GGC).

Example 7. Taxable termination resulting from distribution. The facts are the same as in *Example 6*, except twenty years after C's death the trustee exercises its discretionary power and distributes the entire principal to GGC. The distribution results in a taxable termination because GC's interest in the trust terminates as a result of the distribution of the entire trust property to GGC, a skip person. The result would be the same if the trustee retained sufficient funds to pay the GST tax due by reason of the taxable termination, as well as any expenses of winding up the trust.

Example 8. Simultaneous termination of interests of more than one beneficiary. T establishes an irrevocable trust for the benefit of T's child, C, T's grandchild, GC, and T's great-grandchild, GGC. Under the terms of the trust, income and principal may be distributed to any or all of the living beneficiaries at the discretion of the trustee. Upon the death of C, the trust property is to be distributed to GGC if then living. If C is survived by both GC and GGC, both C's and GC's interests in the trust will terminate on C's death. However, because both interests will terminate at the same time and as a result of one event, only one taxable termination occurs.

Example 9. Partial taxable termination. T creates an irrevocable trust providing that trust income is to be paid to T's children, A and B, in such proportions as the trustee determines for their joint lives. On the death of the first child to die, one-half of the trust principal is to be paid to T's then living grandchildren. The balance of the trust principal is to be paid to T's grandchildren on the death of the survivor of A and B. If A predeceases B, the distribution occurring on the termination of A's interest in the trust is a taxable termination and not a taxable distribution. It is a taxable termination because the distribution is a distribution of a portion of the trust that occurs as a result of the death of A, a lineal descendant of T. It is immaterial that a portion of the trust continues and that B, a person other than a skip person, thereafter holds an interest in the trust.

Example 10. Taxable distribution. T establishes an irrevocable trust under which the trust income is payable to T's child, C, for life. When T's grandchild, GC, attains 35 years of age, GC is to receive one-half of the principal. The remaining one-half of the principal is to be distributed to GC on C's death. Assume that C survives until GC attains age 35. When the trustee distributes one-half of the principal to GC on GC's 35th birthday, the distribution is a taxable distribution because it is a distribution to a skip person and is neither a taxable termination nor a direct skip.

Example 11. Exercise of withdrawal right as taxable distribution. The facts are the same as in *Example 10*, except GC holds a continuing right to withdraw trust principal and after one year GC withdraws $10,000. The withdrawal by GC is not a taxable termination because the withdrawal does not terminate C's interest in the trust. The withdrawal by GC is a taxable distribution to GC.

Example 12. Interest in trust. T establishes an irrevocable trust under which the income is to be paid to T's child, C, for life. On the death of C, the trust principal is to be paid to T's grandchild, GC. Because C has a present right to receive income from the trust, C has an interest in the trust. Because GC cannot currently receive distributions from the trust, GC does not have an interest in the trust.

Example 13. Support obligation. T establishes an irrevocable trust for the benefit of T's grandchild, GC. The trustee has discretion to distribute property for GC's support without regard to the duty or ability of GC's parent, C, to support GC. Because GC is a permissible current recipient of trust property, GC has an interest in the trust. C does not have an interest in the trust because the potential use of the trust property to satisfy C's support obligation is within the discretion of a fiduciary. C would be treated as having an interest in the trust if the trustee was required to distribute trust property for GC's support. [Reg. § 26.2612-1.]

☐ [*T.D.* 8644, 12-26-95. *Amended by T.D.* 9214, 7-15-2005.]

[Reg. § 26.2613-1]

§ 26.2613-1. Skip person.—For the definition of *skip person* see § 26.2612-1(d). [Reg. § 26.2613-1.]

☐ [*T.D.* 8644, 12-26-95.]

GST EXEMPTION

[Reg. §26.2632-1]

§26.2632-1. Allocation of GST exemption.—(a) *General rule*.—Except as otherwise provided in this section, an individual or the individual's executor may allocate the individual's $1 million GST exemption at any time from the date of the transfer through the date for filing the individual's Federal estate tax return (including any extensions for filing that have been actually granted). If no estate tax return is required to be filed, the GST exemption may be allocated at any time through the date a Federal estate tax return would be due if a return were required to be filed (including any extensions actually granted). If property is held in trust, the allocation of GST exemption is made to the entire trust rather than to specific trust assets. If a transfer is a direct skip to a trust, the allocation of GST exemption to the transferred property is also treated as an allocation of GST exemption to the trust for purposes of future GSTs with respect to the trust by the same transferor.

(b) *Lifetime allocations*.—(1) *Automatic allocation to direct skips*.—(i) *In general*.—If a direct skip occurs during the transferor's lifetime, the transferor's GST exemption not previously allocated (unused GST exemption) is automatically allocated to the transferred property (but not in excess of the fair market value of the property on the date of the transfer). The transferor may prevent the automatic allocation of GST exemption by describing on a timely-filed United States Gift (and Generation-Skipping Transfer) Tax Return (Form 709) the transfer and the extent to which the automatic allocation is not to apply. In addition, a timely-filed Form 709 accompanied by payment of the GST tax (as shown on the return with respect to the direct skip) is sufficient to prevent an automatic allocation of GST exemption with respect to the transferred property. See paragraph (c)(4) of this section for special rules in the case of direct skips treated as occurring at the termination of an estate tax inclusion period.

(ii) *Time for filing Form 709*.—A Form 709 is timely filed if it is filed on or before the date required for reporting the transfer if it were a taxable gift (i.e., the date prescribed by section 6075(b), including any extensions to file actually granted (the due date)). Except as provided in paragraph (b)(1)(iii) of this section, the automatic allocation of GST exemption (or the election to prevent the allocation, if made) is irrevocable after the due date. An automatic allocation of GST exemption is effective as of the date of the transfer to which it relates. Except as provided above, a Form 709 need not be filed to report an automatic allocation.

(iii) *Transitional rule*.—An election to prevent an automatic allocation of GST exemption filed on or before January 26, 1996, becomes irrevocable on July 24, 1996.

(2) *Automatic allocation to indirect skips made after December 31, 2000*.—(i) *In general*.—An indirect skip is a transfer of property to a GST trust as defined in section 2632(c)(3)(B) provided that the transfer is subject to gift tax and does not qualify as a direct skip. In the case of an indirect skip made after December 31, 2000, to which section 2642(f) (relating to transfers subject to an estate tax inclusion period (ETIP)) does not apply, the transferor's unused GST exemption is automatically allocated to the property transferred (but not in excess of the fair market value of the property on the date of the transfer). The automatic allocation pursuant to this paragraph is effective whether or not a Form 709 is filed reporting the transfer, and is effective as of the date of the transfer to which it relates. An automatic allocation is irrevocable after the due date of the Form 709 for the calendar year in which the transfer is made. In the case of an indirect skip to which section 2642(f) does apply, the indirect skip is deemed to be made at the close of the ETIP and the GST exemption is deemed to be allocated at that time. In either case, except as otherwise provided in paragraph (b)(2)(ii) of this section, the automatic allocation of exemption applies even if an allocation of exemption is made to the indirect skip in accordance with section 2632(a).

(ii) *Prevention of automatic allocation*.—Except as otherwise provided in forms or other guidance published by the Service, the transferor may prevent the automatic allocation of GST exemption with regard to an indirect skip (including indirect skips to which section 2642(f) may apply) by making an election, as provided in paragraph (b)(2)(iii) of this section. Notwithstanding paragraph (b)(2)(iii)(B) of this section, the transferor may also prevent the automatic allocation of GST exemption with regard to an indirect skip by making an affirmative allocation of GST exemption on a Form 709 filed at any time on or before the due date for timely filing (within the meaning of paragraph (b)(1)(ii) of this section) of an amount that is less than (but not equal to) the value of the property transferred as reported on that return, in accordance with the provisions of paragraph (b)(4) of this section. See paragraph (b)(4)(iii) *Example 6* of this section. Any election out of the automatic allocation rules under this section has no effect on the application of the automatic allocation rules applicable after the transferor's death under section 2632(e) and paragraph (d) of this section.

(iii) *Election to have automatic allocation rules not apply*.—(A) *In general*.—A transferor may prevent the automatic allocation of GST exemption (elect out) with respect to any transfer or transfers constituting an indirect skip made to a trust or to one or more separate shares that are treated as separate trusts under §26.2654-1(a)(1) (collectively referred to hereinafter as a trust). In the case of a transfer treated under section 2513 as made one-half by the transferor and one-half by the transferor's spouse, each spouse shall be treated as a separate transferor who must satisfy separately the requirements of paragraph (b)(2)(iii)(B) to elect out with respect to the transfer. A transferor may elect out with respect to—

(1) One or more prior-year transfers subject to section 2642(f) (regarding ETIPs) made by the transferor to a specified trust or trusts;

(2) One or more (or all) current-year transfers made by the transferor to a specified trust or trusts;

(3) One or more (or all) future transfers made by the transferor to a specified trust or trusts;

(4) All future transfers made by the transferor to all trusts (whether or not in existence at the time of the election out); or

(5) Any combination of paragraphs (b)(2)(iii)(A)(*1*) through (*4*) of this section.

(B) *Manner of making an election out.*—Except as otherwise provided in forms or other guidance published by the IRS, an election out is made as described in this paragraph (b)(2)(iii)(B). To elect out, the transferor must attach a statement (election out statement) to a Form 709 filed within the time period provided in paragraph (b)(2)(iii)(C) of this section (whether or not any transfer was made in the calendar year for which the Form 709 was filed, and whether or not a Form 709 otherwise would be required to be filed for that year). See paragraph (b)(4)(iv) *Example 7* of this section. The election out statement must identify the trust (except for an election out under paragraph (b)(2)(iii)(A)(4) of this section), and specifically must provide that the transferor is electing out of the automatic allocation of GST exemption with respect to the described transfer or transfers. Prior-year transfers that are subject to section 2642(f), and to which the election out is to apply, must be specifically described or otherwise identified in the election out statement. Further, unless the election out is made for all transfers made to the trust in the current year and/or in all future years, the current-year transfers and/or future transfers to which the election out is to apply must be specifically described or otherwise identified in the election out statement.

(C) *Time for making an election out.*—To elect out, the Form 709 with the attached election out statement must be filed on or before the due date for timely filing (within the meaning of paragraph (b)(1)(ii) of this section) of the Form 709 for the calendar year in which—

(1) For a transfer subject to section 2642(f), the ETIP closes; or

(2) For all other elections out, the first transfer to be covered by the election out was made.

(D) *Effect of election out.*—An election out does not affect the automatic allocation of GST exemption to any transfer not covered by the election out statement. Except for elections out for transfers described in paragraph (b)(2)(iii)(A)(*1*) of this section that are specifically described in an election out statement, an election out does not apply to any prior-year transfer to a trust, including any transfer subject to an ETIP (even if the ETIP closes after the election is made). An election out does not prevent the transferor from allocating the transferor's available GST exemption to any transfer covered by the election out, either on a timely filed Form 709 reporting the transfer or at a later date in accordance with the provisions of paragraph (b)(4) of this section. An election out with respect to future transfers remains in effect unless and until terminated. Once an election out with respect to future transfers is made, a transferor need not file a Form 709 in future years solely to prevent the automatic allocation of the GST exemption to any future transfer covered by the election out.

(E) *Termination of election out.*—Except as otherwise provided in forms or other guidance published by the IRS, an election out may be terminated as described in this paragraph (b)(2)(iii)(E). Pursuant to this section, a transferor may terminate an election out made on a Form 709 for a prior year, to the extent that election out applied to future transfers or to a transfer subject to section 2642(f). To terminate an election out, the transferor must attach a statement (termination statement) to a Form 709 filed on or before the due date of the Form 709 for the calendar year in which is made the first transfer to which the election out is not to apply (whether or not any transfer was made in the calendar year for which the Form 709 was filed, and whether or not a Form 709 otherwise would be required to be filed for that year). The termination statement must identify the trust (if applicable), describe the prior election out that is being terminated, specifically provide that the prior election out is being terminated, and either describe the extent to which the prior election out is being terminated or describe any current-year transfers to which the election out is not to apply. Consequently, the automatic allocation rules contained in section 2632(c)(1) will apply to any current-year transfer described on the termination statement and, except as otherwise provided in this paragraph, to all future transfers that otherwise would have been covered by the election out. The termination of an election out does not affect any transfer, or any election out, that is not described in the termination statement. The termination of an election out will not revoke the election out for any prior-year transfer, except for a prior-year transfer subject to section 2642(f) for which the election out is revoked on a timely filed Form 709 for the calendar year in which the ETIP closes or for any prior calendar year. The termination of an election out does not preclude the transferor from making another election out in the same or any subsequent year.

(3) *Election to treat trust as a GST trust.*—(i) *In general.*—A transferor may elect to treat any trust as a GST trust (GST trust election), without regard to whether the trust is subject to section 2642(f), with respect to—

(A) Any current-year transfer (or any or all current-year transfers) by the electing transferor to the trust;

(B) Any selected future transfers by the electing transferor to the trust;

(C) All future transfers by the electing transferor to the trust; or

(D) Any combination of paragraphs (b)(3)(i)(A) through (C) of this section.

(ii) *Time and Manner of making GST trust election.*—Except as otherwise provided in forms or other guidance published by the Internal Revenue Service, a GST trust election is made as described in this paragraph (b)(3)(ii). To make a GST trust election, the transferor must attach a statement (GST trust election statement) to a Form 709 filed on or before the due date for timely filing (within the meaning of paragraph (b)(1)(ii) of this section) of the Form 709 for the calendar year in which the first transfer to be covered by the GST trust election is made (whether or not any transfer was made in the calendar year for which the Form 709 was filed, and whether or not a Form 709 otherwise would be required to be filed for that year). The GST trust election statement must identify the trust, specifically describe or otherwise clearly identify the transfers to be covered by the election, and specifically provide that the transferor is electing to have the trust treated as a GST trust with respect to the covered transfers.

(iii) *Effect of GST trust election.*—Except as otherwise provided in this paragraph, a GST trust election will cause all transfers made by the electing transferor to the trust that are subject to the election to be deemed to be made to a GST trust as defined in section 2632(c)(3)(B). Thus, the electing transferor's unused GST exemption may be allocated automatically to such transfers in accordance with paragraph (b)(2) of this section. A transferor may prevent the automatic allocation of GST exemption to future transfers to the trust either by terminating the GST trust election in accordance with paragraph (b)(3)(iv) of this section (in the case of trusts that would not otherwise be treated as GST trusts) or by electing out of the automatic allocation of GST exemption in accordance with paragraph (b)(2) of this section.

(iv) *Termination of GST trust election.*—Except as otherwise provided in forms or other guidance published by the Service, a GST trust election may be terminated as described in this paragraph (b)(3)(iv). A transferor may terminate a GST trust election made on a Form 709 for a prior year, to the extent that election applied to future transfers or to a transfer subject to section 2642(f). To terminate a GST trust election, the transferor must attach a statement (termination statement) to a Form 709 filed on or before the due date for timely filing (within the meaning of paragraph (b)(1)(ii) of this section) a Form 709 for the calendar year: in which is made the electing transferor's first transfer to which the GST trust election is not to apply; or that is the first calendar year for which the GST trust election is not to apply, even if no transfer is made to the trust during that year. The termination statement must identify the trust, describe the current-year transfer (if any), and provide that the prior GST trust election is terminated. Accordingly, if the trust otherwise does not satisfy the definition of a GST trust, the automatic allocation rules contained in section 2632(c)(1) will not apply to the described current-year transfer or to any future transfers made by the transferor to the trust, unless and until another election under this paragraph (b)(3) is made.

(4) *Allocation to other transfers.*—(i) *In general.*—An allocation of GST exemption to property transferred during the transferor's lifetime, other than in a direct skip, is made on Form 709. The allocation must clearly identify the trust to which the allocation is being made, the amount of GST exemption allocated to it, and if the allocation is late or if an inclusion ratio greater than zero is claimed, the value of the trust assets at the effective date of the allocation. See paragraph (b)(4)(ii) of this section. The allocation should also state the inclusion ratio of the trust after the allocation. Except as otherwise provided in this paragraph, an allocation of GST exemption may be made by a formula; e.g., the allocation may be expressed in terms of the amount necessary to produce an inclusion ratio of zero. However, formula allocations made with respect to charitable lead annuity trusts are not valid except to the extent they are dependent on values as finally determined for Federal estate or gift tax purposes. With respect to a timely allocation, an allocation of GST exemption becomes irrevocable after the due date of the return. Except as provided in § 26.2642-3 (relating to charitable lead annuity trusts), an allocation of GST exemption to a trust is void to the extent the amount allocated exceeds the amount necessary to obtain an inclusion ratio of zero with respect to the trust. See § 26.2642-1 for the definition of inclusion ratio. An allocation is also void if the allocation is made with respect to a trust that has no GST potential with respect to the transferor making the allocation, at the time of the allocation. For this purpose, a trust has GST potential even if the possibility of a GST is so remote as to be negligible.

(ii) *Effective date of allocation.*—(A) *In general.*—*(1)* Except as otherwise provided, an allocation of GST exemption is effective as of the date of any transfer as to which the Form 709 on which it is made is a timely filed return (a timely allocation). If more than one timely allocation is made, the earlier allocation is modified only if the later allocation clearly identifies the transfer and the nature and extent of the modification. Except as provided in paragraph (d)(1) of this section, an allocation to a trust made on a Form 709 filed after the due date for reporting a transfer to the trust (a late allocation) is effective on the date the Form 709 is filed and is deemed to precede in point of time any taxable event occurring on such date. For purposes of this paragraph (b)(4)(ii), the Form 709 is deemed filed on the date it is postmarked to the Internal Revenue Service address as directed in forms or other guidance published by the Service. See § 26.2642-2 regarding the effect of a late allocation in determining the inclusion ratio, etc. See paragraph (c)(1) of this section regarding allocation of GST exemption to property subject to an estate tax inclusion period. If it is unclear whether an allocation of GST exemption on a Form 709 is a late or a timely allocation to a trust, the allocation is effective in the following order—

(i) To any transfer to the trust disclosed on the return as to which the return is a timely return;

(ii) As a late allocation; and

(iii) To any transfer to the trust not disclosed on the return as to which the return would be a timely return.

(2) A late allocation to a trust may be made on a Form 709 that is timely filed with respect to another transfer. A late allocation is irrevocable when made.

(B) *Amount of allocation.*—If other transfers exist with respect to which GST exemption could be allocated under paragraphs (b)(4)(ii)(A)(*1*)(*ii*) and (*iii*), any GST exemption allocated under paragraph (b)(4)(ii)(A)(*1*)(*i*) of this section is allocated in an amount equal to the value of the transferred property as reported on the Form 709. Thus, if the GST exemption allocated on the Form 709 exceeds the value of the transfers reported on that return that have generation-skipping potential, the initial allocation under paragraph (b)(4)(ii)(A)(*1*)(*i*) of this section is in the amount of the value of those transfers as reported on that return. Any remaining amount of GST exemption allocated on that return is then allocated pursuant to paragraphs (b)(4)(ii)(A)(*1*)(*ii*) and (*iii*) of this section, notwithstanding any subsequent upward adjustment in value of the transfers reported on the return.

(iii) *Examples.*—The following examples illustrate the provisions of this paragraph (b):

Example 1. Modification of allocation of GST exemption. On December 1, 2003, T transfers $100,000 to an irrevocable GST trust described in section 2632(c)(3)(B). The transfer to the trust is not a direct skip. The date prescribed for filing the gift tax return reporting the taxable gift is April 15, 2004. On February 10, 2004, T files a Form 709 on which T properly elects out of the automatic allocation rules contained in section 2632(c)(1) with respect to the transfer in accordance with paragraph (b)(2)(iii) of this section, and allocates $50,000 of GST exemption to the trust. On April 13th of the same year, T files an additional Form 709 on which T confirms the election out of the automatic allocation rules contained in section 2632(c)(1) and allocates $100,000 of GST exemption to the trust in a manner that clearly indicates the intention to modify and supersede the prior allocation with respect to the 2003 transfer. The allocation made on the April 13 return supersedes the prior allocation because it is made on a timely-filed Form 709 that clearly identifies the trust and the nature and extent of the modification of GST exemption allocation. The allocation of $100,000 of GST exemption to the trust is effective as of December 1, 2003. The result would be the same if the amended Form 709 decreased the amount of the GST exemption allocated to the trust.

Example 2. Modification of allocation of GST exemption. The facts are the same as in *Example 1* except, on July 8, 2004, T files a Form 709 attempting to reduce the earlier allocation. The return filed on July 8, 2004, is not a timely filed return. The $100,000 GST exemption allocated to the trust, as amended on April 13, 2004, remains in effect because an allocation, once made, is irrevocable and may not be modified after the last date on which a timely filed Form 709 may be filed.

Example 3. Effective date of late allocation of GST exemption. On November 15, 2003, T transfers $100,000 to an irrevocable GST trust described in section 2632(c)(3)(B). The transfer to the trust is not a direct skip. The date prescribed for filing the gift tax return reporting the taxable gift is April 15, 2004. On February 10, 2004, T files a Form 709 on which T properly elects out of the automatic allocation rules contained in section 2632(c)(1) in accordance with paragraph (b)(2)(iii) of this section with respect to that transfer. On December 1, 2004, T files a Form 709 and allocates $50,000 to the trust. The allocation is effective as of December 1, 2004.

Example 4. Effective date of late allocation of GST exemption. T transfers $100,000 to an irrevocable GST trust on December 1, 2003, in a transfer that is not a direct skip. On April 15, 2004, T files a Form 709 on which T properly elects out of the automatic allocation rules contained in section 2632(c)(1) with respect to the entire transfer in accordance with paragraph (b)(2)(iii) of this section and T does not make an allocation of any GST exemption on the Form 709. On September 1, 2004, the trustee makes a taxable distribution from the trust to T's grandchild in the amount of $30,000. Immediately prior to the distribution, the value of the trust assets was $150,000. On the same date, T allocates GST exemption to the trust in the amount of $50,000. The allocation of GST exemption on the date of the transfer is treated as preceding in point of time the taxable distribution. At the time of the GST, the trust has an inclusion ratio of .6667 (1 - (50,000/150,000)).

Example 5. Automatic allocation to split-gift. On December 1, 2003, T transfers $50,000 to an irrevocable GST Trust described in section 2632(c)(3)(B). The transfer to the trust is not a direct skip. On April 30, 2004, T and T's spouse, S, each files an initial gift tax return for 2003, on which they consent, pursuant to section 2513, to have the gift treated as if one-half had been made by each. In spite of being made on a late-filed gift tax return for 2003, the election under section 2513 is valid because neither spouse had filed a timely gift tax return for that year. Previously, neither T nor S filed a timely gift tax return electing out of the automatic allocation rules contained in section 2632(c)(1). As a result of the election under section 2513, which is retroactive to the date of T's transfer, T and S are each treated as the transferor of one-half of the property transferred in the indirect skip. Thus, $25,000 of T's unused GST exemption and $25,000 of S's unused GST exemption is automatically allocated to the trust. Both allocations are effective on and after the date that T made the transfer. The result would be the same if T's transfer constituted a direct skip subject to the automatic allocation rules contained in section 2632(b).

Example 6. Partial allocation of GST exemption. On December 1, 2003, T transfers $100,000 to an irrevocable GST trust described in section 2632(c)(3)(B). The transfer to the trust is not a direct skip. The date prescribed for filing the gift tax return reporting the taxable gift is April 15, 2004. On February 10, 2004, T files a Form 709 on which T allocates $40,000 of GST exemption to the trust. By filing a timely Form 709 on which a partial allocation is made of $40,000, T effectively elected out of the automatic allocation rules for the remaining value of the transfer for which T did not allocate GST exemption.

(iv) *Example.*—The following example illustrates language that may be used in the statement required under paragraph (b)(2)(iii) of this section to elect out of the automatic allocation rules under various scenarios:

Example 1. On March 1, 2006, T transfers $100,000 to Trust B, a GST trust described in section 2632(c)(3)(B). Subsequently, on September 15, 2006, T transfers an additional $75,000 to Trust B. No other transfers are made to Trust B in 2006. T attaches an election out statement to a timely filed Form 709 for calendar year 2006. Except with regard to paragraph (v) of this *Example 1*, the election out statement identifies Trust B as required under paragraph (b)(2)(iii)(B) of this section, and contains the following alternative election statements:

(i) "T hereby elects that the automatic allocation rules will not apply to the $100,000 transferred to Trust B on March 1, 2006." The election out of the automatic allocation rules will be effective only for T's March 1, 2006, transfer and will not apply to T's $75,000 transfer made on September 15, 2006.

(ii) "T hereby elects that the automatic allocation rules will not apply to any transfers to Trust B in 2006." The election out of the automatic allocation rules will be effective for T's transfers to Trust B made on March 1, 2006, and September 15, 2006.

(iii) "T hereby elects that the automatic allocation rules will not apply to any transfers to Trust B made by T in 2006 or to any additional transfers T may make to Trust B in subsequent years." The election out of the automatic allocation rules will be effective for T's transfers to Trust B in 2006 and for all future transfers to be made by T to Trust B, unless and until T terminates the election out of the automatic allocation rules.

(iv) "T hereby elects that the automatic allocation rules will not apply to any transfers T has made or will make to Trust B in the years 2006 through 2008." The election out of the automatic allocation rules will be effective for T's transfers to Trust B in 2006 through 2008. T's transfers to Trust B after 2008 will be subject to the automatic allocation rules, unless T elects out of those rules for one or more years after 2008. T may terminate the election out of the automatic allocation rules for 2007, 2008, or both in accordance with the termination rules of paragraph (b)(2)(iii)(E) of this section. T may terminate the election out for one or more of the transfers made in 2006 only on a later but still timely filed Form 709 for calendar year 2006.

(v) "T hereby elects that the automatic allocation rules will not apply to any current or future transfer that T may make to any trust." The election out of the automatic allocation rules will be effective for all of T's transfers (current-year and future) to Trust B and to any and all other trusts (whether such trusts exist in 2006 or are created in a later year), unless and until T terminates the election out of the automatic allocation rules. T may terminate the election out with regard to one or more (or all) of the transfers covered by the election out in accordance with the termination rules of paragraph (b)(2)(iii)(E) of this section.

(c) *Special rules during an estate tax inclusion period.*—(1) *In general.*—(i) *Automatic allocations with respect to direct skips and indirect skips.*—A direct skip or an indirect skip that is subject to an estate tax inclusion period (ETIP) is deemed to have been made only at the close of the ETIP. The transferor may prevent the automatic allocation of GST exemption to a direct skip or an indirect skip by electing out of the automatic allocation rules at any time prior to the due date of the Form 709 for the calendar year in which the close of the ETIP occurs (whether or not any transfer was made in the calendar year for which the Form 709 was filed, and whether or not a Form 709 otherwise would be required to be filed for that year). See paragraph (b)(2)(i) of this section regarding the automatic allocation of GST exemption to an indirect skip subject to an ETIP.

(ii) *Other allocations.*—An affirmative allocation of GST exemption cannot be revoked, but becomes effective as of (and no earlier than) the date of the close of the ETIP with respect to the trust. If an allocation has not been made prior to the close of the ETIP, an allocation of exemption is effective as of the close of the ETIP during the transferor's lifetime if made by the due date for filing the Form 709 for the calendar year in which the close of the ETIP occurs (timely ETIP return). An allocation of exemption is effective in the case of the close of the ETIP by reason of the death of the transferor as provided in paragraph (d) of this section.

(iii) *Portion of trust subject to ETIP.*—If any part of a trust is subject to an ETIP, the entire trust is subject to the ETIP. See § 26.2642-1(b)(2) for rules determining the inclusion ratio applicable in the case of GSTs during an ETIP.

(2) *Estate tax inclusion period defined.*—(i) *In general.*—An ETIP is the period during which, should death occur, the value of transferred property would be includible (other than by reason of section 2035) in the gross estate of—

(A) The transferor; or

(B) The spouse of the transferor.

(ii) *Exceptions.*—(A) For purposes of paragraph (c)(2) of this section, the value of transferred property is not considered as being subject to inclusion in the gross estate of the transferor or the spouse of the transferor if the possibility that the property will be included is so remote as to be negligible. A possibility is so remote as to be negligible if it can be ascertained by actuarial standards that there is less than a 5 percent probability that the property will be included in the gross estate.

(B) For purposes of paragraph (c)(2) of this section, the value of transferred property is not considered as being subject to inclusion in the gross estate of the spouse of the transferor, if the spouse possesses with respect to any transfer to the trust, a right to withdraw no more than the greater of $5,000 or 5 percent of the trust corpus, and such withdrawal right terminates no later than 60 days after the transfer to the trust.

(C) The rules of this paragraph (c)(2) do not apply to qualified terminable interest property with respect to which the special election under § 26.2652-2 has been made.

(3) *Termination of an ETIP.*—An ETIP terminates on the first to occur of—

(i) The death of the transferor;

(ii) The time at which no portion of the property is includible in the transferor's gross estate (other than by reason of section 2035) or, in the case of an individual who is a transferor solely by reason of an election under section 2513, the time at which no portion would be includible in the gross estate of the individual's spouse (other than by reason of section 2035);

(iii) The time of a GST, but only with respect to the property involved in the GST; or

(iv) In the case of an ETIP arising by reason of an interest or power held by the transferor's spouse under subsection (c)(2)(i)(B) of this section, at the first to occur of—

(A) The death of the spouse; or

(B) The time at which no portion of the property would be includible in the spouse's gross estate (other than by reason of section 2035).

(4) *Treatment of direct skips.*—If property transferred to a skip person is subject to an ETIP, the direct skip is treated as occurring on the termination of the ETIP.

(5) *Examples.*—The following examples illustrate the rules of this section as they apply to the termination of an ETIP during the lifetime of the transferor. In each example assume that T transfers $100,000 to an irrevocable trust:

Example 1. Allocation of GST exemption during ETIP. The trust instrument provides that trust income is to be paid to T for 9 years or until T's prior death. The trust principal is to be paid to T's grandchild on the termination of T's income interest. If T dies within the 9-year period, the value of the trust principal is includible in T's gross estate under section 2036(a). Thus, the trust is subject to an ETIP. T files a timely Form 709 reporting the transfer and allocating $100,000 of GST exemption to the trust. The allocation of GST exemption to the trust is not effective until the termination of the ETIP.

Example 2. Effect of prior allocation on termination of ETIP. The facts are the same as in *Example 1*, except the trustee has the power to invade trust principal on behalf of T's grandchild, GC, during the term of T's income interest. In year 4, when the value of the trust is $200,000, the trustee distributes $15,000 to GC. The distribution is a taxable distribution. The ETIP with respect to the property distributed to GC terminates at the time of the taxable distribution. See paragraph (c)(3)(iii) of this section. Solely for purposes of determining the trust's inclusion ratio with respect to the taxable distribution, the prior $100,000 allocation of GST exemption (as well as any additional allocation made on a timely ETIP return) is effective immediately prior to the taxable distribution. See § 26.2642-1(b)(2). The trust's inclusion ratio with respect to the taxable distribution is therefore .50 (1-(100,000/200,000)).

Example 3. Split-gift transfers subject to ETIP. The trust instrument provides that trust income is to be paid to T for 9 years or until T's prior death. The trust principal is to be paid to T's grandchild on the termination of T's income interest. T files a timely Form 709 reporting the transfer. T's spouse, S, consents to have the gift treated as made one-half by S under section 2513. Because S is treated as transferring one-half of the property to T's grandchild, S becomes the transferor of one-half of the trust for purposes of chapter 13. Because the value of the trust would be includible in T's gross estate if T died immediately after the transfer, S's transfer is subject to an ETIP. If S should die prior to the termination of the trust, S's executor may allocate S's GST exemption to the trust, but only to the portion of the trust for which S is treated as the transferor. However, the allocation does not become effective until the earlier of the expiration of T's income interest or T's death.

Example 4. Transfer of retained interest as ETIP termination. The trust instrument provides that trust income is to be paid to T for 9 years or until T's prior death. The trust principal is to be paid to T's grandchild on the termination of T's income interest. Four years after the initial transfer, T transfers the income interest to T's sibling. The ETIP with respect to the trust terminates on T's transfer of the income interest because, after

See p. 15 for regulations not amended to reflect law changes

the transfer, the trust property would not be includible in T's gross estate (other than by reason of section 2035) if T died at that time.

Example 5. Election out of automatic allocation of GST exemption for trust subject to an ETIP. On December 1, 2003, T transfers $100,000 to Trust A, an irrevocable GST trust described in section 2632(c)(3) that is subject to an estate tax inclusion period (ETIP). T made no other gifts in 2003. The ETIP terminates on December 31, 2008. T timely files a gift tax return (Form 709) reporting the gift on April 15, 2004. On May 15, 2006, T files a Form 709 on which T properly elects out of the automatic allocation rules contained in section 2632(c)(1) with respect to the December 1, 2003, transfer to Trust A in accordance with paragraph (b)(2)(iii) of this section. Because the indirect skip is not deemed to occur until December 31, 2008, T's election out of automatic GST allocation filed on May 15, 2006, is timely, and will be effective as of December 31, 2008 (unless revoked on a Form 709 filed on or before the due date of a Form 709 for calendar year 2008).

(d) *Allocations after the transferor's death.*—(1) *Allocation by executor.*—Except as otherwise provided in this paragraph (d), an allocation of a decedent's unused GST exemption by the executor of the decedent's estate is made on the appropriate United States Estate (and Generation-Skipping Transfer) Tax Return (Form 706 or Form 706NA) filed on or before the date prescribed for filing the return by section 6075(a) (including any extensions actually granted (the due date)). An allocation of GST exemption with respect to property included in the gross estate of a decedent is effective as of the date of death. A timely allocation of GST exemption by an executor with respect to a lifetime transfer of property that is not included in the transferor's gross estate is made on a Form 709. A late allocation of GST exemption by an executor, other than an allocation that is deemed to be made under section 2632(b)(1) or (c)(1), with respect to a lifetime transfer of property is made on Form 706, Form 706NA, or Form 709 (filed on or before the due date of the transferor's estate tax return) and applies as of the date the allocation is filed. An allocation of GST exemption to a trust (whether or not funded at the time the Form 706 or Form 706NA is filed) is effective if the notice of allocation clearly identifies the trust and the amount of the decedent's GST exemption allocated to the trust. An executor may allocate the decedent's GST exemption by use of a formula. For purposes of this section, an allocation is void if the allocation is made for a trust that has no GST potential with respect to the transferor for whom the allocation is being made, as of the date of the transferor's death. For this purpose, a trust has GST potential even if the possibility of a GST is so remote as to be negligible.

(2) *Automatic allocation after death.*—A decedent's unused GST exemption is automatically allocated on the due date for filing Form 706 or Form 706NA to the extent not otherwise allocated by the decedent's executor on or before that date. The automatic allocation occurs whether or not a return is actually required to be filed. Unused GST exemption is allocated pro rata (subject to the rules of § 26.2642-2(b)), on the basis of the value of the property as finally determined for purposes of chapter 11 (chapter 11 value), first to direct skips treated as occurring at the transferor's death. The balance, if any, of unused GST exemption is allocated pro rata (subject to the rules of § 26.2642-2(b)) on the basis of the chapter 11 value of the nonexempt portion of the trust property (or in the case of trusts that are not included in the gross estate, on the basis of the date of death value of the trust) to trusts with respect to which a taxable termination may occur or from which a taxable distribution may be made. The automatic allocation of GST exemption is irrevocable, and an allocation made by the executor after the automatic allocation is made is ineffective. No automatic allocation of GST exemption is made to a trust that will have a new transferor with respect to the entire trust prior to the occurrence of any GST with respect to the trust. In addition, no automatic allocation of GST exemption is made to a trust if, during the nine month period ending immediately after the death of the transferor—

(i) No GST has occurred with respect to the trust; and

(ii) At the end of such period no future GST can occur with respect to the trust.

(e) *Effective dates.*—This section is applicable as provided in § 26.2601-1(c), with the following exceptions:

(1) Paragraphs (b)(2) and (b)(3), the third sentence of paragraph (b)(4)(i), the fourth sentence of paragraph (b)(4)(ii)(A)(1), paragraphs (b)(4)(iii) and (b)(4)(iv), and the fourth sentence of paragraph (d)(1) of this section, which will apply to elections made on or after July 13, 2004; and

(2) Paragraph (c)(1), and *Example 5* of paragraph (c)(5), which will apply to elections made on or after June 29, 2005. [Reg. § 26.2632-1.]

☐ [*T.D.* 8644, 12-26-95. *Amended by T.D.* 9208, 6-28-2005.]

APPLICABLE RATE; INCLUSION RATIO

[Reg. § 26.2641-1]

§ 26.2641-1. Applicable rate of tax.—The rate of tax applicable to any GST (applicable rate) is determined by multiplying the maximum Federal estate tax rate in effect at the time of the GST by the inclusion ratio (as defined in § 26.2642-1). For this purpose, the maximum Federal estate tax rate is the maximum rate set forth under section 2001(c) (without regard to section 2001(c)(2)). [Reg. § 26.2641-1.]

☐ [*T.D.* 8644, 12-26-95.]

[Reg. § 26.2642-1]

§ 26.2642-1. Inclusion ratio.—(a) *In general.*—Except as otherwise provided in this section, the inclusion ratio is determined by subtracting the applicable fraction (rounded to the nearest one-thousandth (.001)) from 1. In rounding the applicable fraction to the nearest one-thousandth, any amount that is midway between one one-thousandth and another one-thousandth is rounded up to the higher of those two amounts. For generation-skipping transfer tax rules related to an ABLE account established under section 529A, see § 1.529A-4 of this chapter.

(b) *Numerator of applicable fraction.*—(1) *In general.*—Except as otherwise provided in this paragraph (b), and in §§ 26.2642-3 (providing a special rule for charitable lead annuity trusts) and 26.2642-4 (providing rules for the redetermination of the applicable fraction), the numerator of the applicable fraction is the amount of GST exemption allocated to the trust (or to the transferred property in the case of a direct skip not in trust).

(2) *GSTs occurring during an ETIP.*—(i) *In general.*—For purposes of determining the inclusion ratio with respect to a taxable termination or a taxable distribution that occurs during an ETIP, the numerator of the applicable fraction is the sum of—

(A) The GST exemption previously allocated to the trust (including any allocation made to the trust prior to any taxable termination or distribution) reduced (but not below zero) by the nontax amount of any prior GSTs with respect to the trust; and

(B) Any GST exemption allocated to the trust on a timely ETIP return filed after the termination of the ETIP. See § 26.2632-1(c)(5) *Example 2.*

(ii) *Nontax amount of a prior GST.*—*(1)* The nontax amount of a prior GST with respect to the trust is the amount of the GST multiplied by the applicable fraction attributable to the trust at the time of the prior GST.

(2) For rules regarding the allocation of GST exemption to property during an ETIP, see § 26.2632-1(c).

(c) *Denominator of applicable fraction.*—(1) *In general.*—Except as otherwise provided in this paragraph (c) and in §§ 26.2642-3 and 26.2642-4, the denominator of the applicable fraction is the value of the property transferred to the trust (or transferred in a direct skip not in trust) (as determined under § 26.2642-2) reduced by the sum of—

(i) Any Federal estate tax and any State death tax incurred by reason of the transfer that is chargeable to the trust and is actually recovered from the trust;

(ii) The amount of any charitable deduction allowed under section 2055, 2106, or 2522 with respect to the transfer; and

(iii) In the case of a direct skip, the value of the portion of the transfer that is a nontaxable gift. See paragraph (c)(3) of this section for the definition of nontaxable gift.

(2) *Zero denominator.*—If the denominator of the applicable fraction is zero, the inclusion ratio is zero.

(3) *Nontaxable gifts.*—Generally, for purposes of chapter 13, a transfer is a nontaxable gift to the extent the transfer is excluded from taxable gifts by reason of section 2503(b) (after application of section 2513) or section 2503(e). However, a transfer to a trust for the benefit of an individual is not a nontaxable gift for purposes of this section unless—

(i) Trust principal or income may, during the individual's lifetime, be distributed only to or for the benefit of the individual; and

(ii) The assets of the trust will be includible in the gross estate of the individual if the individual dies before the trust terminates.

(d) *Examples.*—The following examples illustrate the provisions of this section. See § 26.2652-2(d) *Examples 2* and *3* for illustrations of the computation of the inclusion ratio where the special (reverse QTIP) election may be applicable.

Example 1. Computation of the inclusion ratio. T transfers $100,000 to a newly-created irrevocable trust providing that income is to be accumulated for 10 years. At the end of 10 years, the accumulated income is to be distributed to T's child, C, and the trust principal is to be paid to T's grandchild. T allocates $40,000 of T's GST exemption to the trust on a timely-filed gift tax return. The applicable fraction with respect to the trust is .40 ($40,000 (the amount of GST exemption allocated to the trust) over $100,000 (the value of the property transferred to the trust)). The inclusion ratio is .60 (1 – .40). If the maximum Federal estate tax rate is 55 percent at the time of a GST, the rate of tax applicable to the transfer (applicable rate) will be .333 (55 percent (the maximum estate tax rate) x .60 (the inclusion ratio)).

Example 2. Gift entirely nontaxable. On December 1, 1996, T transfers $10,000 to an irrevocable trust for the benefit of T's grandchild, GC. GC possesses a right to withdraw any contributions to the trust such that the entire transfer qualifies for the annual exclusion under section 2503(b). Under the terms of the trust, the income is to be paid to GC for 10 years or until GC's prior death. Upon the expiration of GC's income interest, the trust principal is payable to GC or GC's estate. The transfer to the trust is a direct skip. T made no prior gifts to or for the benefit of GC during 1996. The entire $10,000 transfer is a nontaxable transfer. For purposes of computing the tax on the direct skip, the denominator of the applicable fraction is zero, and thus, the inclusion ratio is zero.

Example 3. Gift nontaxable in part. T transfers $12,000 to an irrevocable trust for the benefit of T's grandchild, GC. Under the terms of the trust, the income is to be paid to GC for 10 years or until GC's prior death. Upon the expiration of

GC's income interest, the trust principal is payable to GC or GC's estate. Further, GC has the right to withdraw $10,000 of any contribution to the trust such that $10,000 of the transfer qualifies for the annual exclusion under section 2503(b). The amount of the nontaxable transfer is $10,000. Solely for purposes of computing the tax on the direct skip, T's transfer is divided into two portions. One portion is equal to the amount of the nontaxable transfer ($10,000) and has a zero inclusion ratio; the other portion is $2,000 ($12,000 - $10,000). With respect to the $2,000 portion, the denominator of the applicable fraction is $2,000. Assuming that T has sufficient GST exemption available, the numerator of the applicable fraction is $2,000 (unless T elects to have the automatic allocation provisions not apply). Thus, assuming T does not elect to have the automatic allocation not apply, the applicable fraction is one ($2,000/$2,000 = 1) and the inclusion ratio is zero (1 - 1 = 0).

Example 4. Gift nontaxable in part. Assume the same facts as in *Example 3*, except T files a timely Form 709 electing that the automatic allocation of GST exemption not apply to the $12,000 transferred in the direct skip. T's transfer is divided into two portions, a $10,000 portion with a zero inclusion ratio and a $2,000 portion with an applicable fraction of zero (0/$2,000 = 0) and an inclusion ratio of one (1 - 0 = 1). [Reg. § 26.2642-1.]

□ [*T.D.* 8644, 12-26-95. *Amended by T.D.* 9923, 11-18-2020.]

[Reg. § 26.2642-2]

§ 26.2642-2. Valuation.—(a) *Lifetime transfers.*—(1) *In general.*—For purposes of determining the denominator of the applicable fraction, the value of property transferred during life is its fair market value on the effective date of the allocation of GST exemption. In the case of a timely allocation under § 26.2632-1(b)(2)(ii), the denominator of the applicable fraction is the fair market value of the property as finally determined for purposes of chapter 12.

(2) *Special rule for late allocations during life.*—If a transferor makes a late allocation of GST exemption to a trust, the value of the property transferred to the trust is the fair market value of the trust assets determined on the effective date of the allocation of GST exemption. Except as otherwise provided in this paragraph (a)(2), if a transferor makes a late allocation of GST exemption to a trust, the transferor may, solely for purposes of determining the fair market value of the trust assets, elect to treat the allocation as having been made on the first day of the month during which the late allocation is made (valuation date). An election under this paragraph (a)(2) is not effective with respect to a life insurance policy or a trust holding a life insurance policy, if the insured individual has died. An allocation subject to the election contained in this paragraph (a)(2) is not effective until it is actually filed with the Internal Revenue Service. The election is made by stating on the Form 709 on which the allocation is made—

(i) That the election is being made;

(ii) The applicable valuation date; and

(iii) The fair market value of the trust assets on the valuation date.

(b) *Transfers at death.*—(1) *In general.*—Except as provided in paragraphs (b)(2) and (3) of this section, in determining the denominator of the applicable fraction, the value of property included in the decedent's gross estate is its value for purposes of chapter 11. In the case of qualified real property with respect to which the election under section 2032A is made, the value of the property is the value determined under section 2032A provided the recapture agreement described in section 2032A(d)(2) filed with the Internal Revenue Service specifically provides for the signatories' consent to the imposition of, and personal liability for, additional GST tax in the event an additional estate tax is imposed under section 2032A(c). See § 26.2642-4(a)(4). If the recapture agreement does not contain these provisions, the value of qualified real property as to which the election under section 2032A is made is the fair market value of the property determined without regard to the provisions of section 2032A.

(2) *Special rule for pecuniary payments.*—(i) *In general.*—If a pecuniary payment is satisfied with cash, the denominator of the applicable fraction is the pecuniary amount. If property other than cash is used to satisfy a pecuniary payment, the denominator of the applicable fraction is the pecuniary amount only if payment must be made with property on the basis of the value of the property on—

(A) The date of distribution; or

(B) A date other than the date of distribution, but only if the pecuniary payment must be satisfied on a basis that fairly reflects net appreciation and depreciation (occurring between the valuation date and the date of distribution) in all of the assets from which the distribution could have been made.

(ii) *Other pecuniary amounts payable in kind.*—The denominator of the applicable fraction with respect to any property used to satisfy any other pecuniary payment payable in kind is the date of distribution value of the property.

(3) *Special rule for residual transfers after payment of a pecuniary payment.*—(i) *In general.*—Except as otherwise provided in this paragraph (b)(3), the denominator of the applicable fraction with respect to a residual transfer of property after the satisfaction of a pecuniary payment is the estate tax value of the assets available to satisfy the pecuniary payment reduced, if the pecuniary payment carries appropriate interest (as defined in paragraph (b)(4) of this section), by the pecuniary amount. The denominator of the applicable fraction with respect to a residual transfer of property after the satisfaction of a pecuniary payment that does not carry appropri-

ate interest is the estate tax value of the assets available to satisfy the pecuniary payment reduced by the present value of the pecuniary payment. For purposes of this paragraph (b)(3)(i), the present value of the pecuniary payment is determined by using—

(A) The interest rate applicable under section 7520 at the death of the transferor; and

(B) The period between the date of the transferor's death and the date the pecuniary amount is paid.

(ii) *Special rule for residual transfers after pecuniary payments payable in kind.*—The denominator of the applicable fraction with respect to any residual transfer after satisfaction of a pecuniary payment payable in kind is the date of distribution value of the property distributed in satisfaction of the residual transfer, unless the pecuniary payment must be satisfied on the basis of the value of the property on—

(A) The date of distribution; or

(B) A date other than the date of distribution, but only if the pecuniary payment must be satisfied on a basis that fairly reflects net appreciation and depreciation (occurring between the valuation date and the date of distribution) in all of the assets from which the distribution could have been made.

(4) *Appropriate interest.*—(i) *In general.*—For purposes of this section and §26.2654-1 (relating to certain trusts treated as separate trusts), appropriate interest means that interest must be payable from the date of death of the transferor (or from the date specified under applicable State law requiring the payment of interest) to the date of payment at a rate—

(A) At least equal to—

(1) The statutory rate of interest, if any, applicable to pecuniary bequests under the law of the State whose law governs the administration of the estate or trust; or

(2) If no such rate is indicated under applicable State law, 80 percent of the rate that is applicable under section 7520 at the death of the transferor; and

(B) Not in excess of the greater of—

(1) The statutory rate of interest, if any, applicable to pecuniary bequests under the law of the State whose law governs the administration of the trust; or

(2) 120 percent of the rate that is applicable under section 7520 at the death of the transferor.

(ii) *Pecuniary payments deemed to carry appropriate interest.*—For purposes of this paragraph (b)(4), if a pecuniary payment does not carry appropriate interest, the pecuniary payment is considered to carry appropriate interest to the extent—

(A) The entire payment is made or property is irrevocably set aside to satisfy the entire pecuniary payment within 15 months of the transferor's death; or

(B) The governing instrument or applicable local law specifically requires the executor or trustee to allocate to the pecuniary payment a pro rata share of the income earned by the fund from which the pecuniary payment is to be made between the date of death of the transferor and the date of payment. For purposes of paragraph (b)(4)(ii)(A) of this section, property is irrevocably set aside if it is segregated and held in a separate account pending distribution.

(c) *Examples.*—The following examples illustrate the provisions of this section:

Example 1. T transfers $100,000 to a newly-created irrevocable trust on December 15, 1996. The trust provides that income is to be paid to T's child for 10 years. At the end of the 10-year period, the trust principal is to be paid to T's grandchild. T does not allocate any GST exemption to the trust on the gift tax return reporting the transfer. On November 15, 1997, T files a Form 709 allocating $50,000 of GST exemption to the trust. Because the allocation was made on a late filed return, the value of the property transferred to the trust is determined on the date the allocation is filed (unless an election is made pursuant to paragraph (a)(2) of this section to value the trust property as of the first day of the month in which the allocation document is filed with the Internal Revenue Service). On November 15, 1997, the value of the trust property is $150,000. Effective as of November 15, 1997, the applicable fraction with respect to the trust is .333 ($50,000 (the amount of GST exemption allocated to the trust) over $150,000 (the value of the trust principal on the effective date of the GST exemption allocation)), and the inclusion ratio is .667 (1.0 - .333).

Example 2. The facts are the same as in *Example 1*, except the value of the trust property is $80,000 on November 15, 1997. The applicable fraction is .625 ($50,000 over $80,000) and the inclusion ratio is .375 (1.0 - .625).

Example 3. T transfers $100,000 to a newly-created irrevocable trust on December 15, 1996. The trust provides that income is to be paid to T's child for 10 years. At the end of the 10-year period, the trust principal is to be paid to T's grandchild. T does not allocate any GST exemption to the trust on the gift tax return reporting the transfer. On November 15, 1997, T files a Form 709 allocating $50,000 of GST exemption to the trust. T elects to value the trust principal on the first day of the month in which the allocation is made pursuant to the election provided in paragraph (a)(2) of this section. Because the late allocation is made in November, the value of the trust is determined as of November 1, 1997. [Reg. §26.2642-2.]

☐ [*T.D.* 8644, 12-26-95.]

[Reg. §26.2642-3]

§26.2642-3. Special rule for charitable lead annuity trusts.—(a) *In general.*—In determining the applicable fraction with respect to a charitable lead annuity trust—

(1) The numerator is the adjusted generation-skipping transfer tax exemption (adjusted GST exemption); and

(2) The denominator is the value of all property in the trust immediately after the termination of the charitable lead annuity.

(b) *Adjusted GST exemption defined.*—The adjusted GST exemption is the amount of GST exemption allocated to the trust increased by an amount equal to the interest that would accrue if an amount equal to the allocated GST exemption were invested at the rate used to determine the amount of the estate or gift tax charitable deduction, compounded annually, for the actual period of the charitable lead annuity. If a late allocation is made to a charitable lead annuity trust, the adjusted GST exemption is the amount of GST exemption allocated to the trust increased by the interest that would accrue if invested at such rate for the period beginning on the date of the late allocation and extending for the balance of the actual period of the charitable lead annuity. The amount of GST exemption allocated to a charitable lead annuity trust is not reduced even though it is ultimately determined that the allocation of a lesser amount of GST exemption would have resulted in an inclusion ratio of zero. For purposes of chapter 13, a charitable lead annuity trust is any trust providing an interest in the form of a guaranteed annuity described in § 25.2522(c)-3(c)(2)(vi) of this chapter for which the transferor is allowed a charitable deduction for Federal estate or gift tax purposes.

(c) *Example.*—The following example illustrates the provisions of this section:

Example. T creates a charitable lead annuity trust for a 10-year term with the remainder payable to T's grandchild. T timely allocates an amount of GST exemption to the trust which T expects will ultimately result in a zero inclusion ratio. However, at the end of the charitable lead interest, because the property has not appreciated to the extent T anticipated, the numerator of the applicable fraction is greater than the denominator. The inclusion ratio for the trust is zero. No portion of the GST exemption allocated to the trust is restored to T or to T's estate. [Reg. § 26.2642-3.]

□ [*T.D.* 8644, 12-26-95.]

[Reg. § 26.2642-4]

§ 26.2642-4. Redetermination of applicable fraction.—(a) *In general.*—The applicable fraction for a trust is redetermined whenever additional exemption is allocated to the trust or when certain changes occur with respect to the principal of the trust. Except as otherwise provided in this paragraph(a), the numerator of the redetermined applicable fraction is the sum of the amount of GST exemption currently being allocated to the trust (if any) plus the value of the nontax portion of the trust, and the denominator of the redetermined applicable fraction is the value of the trust principal immediately after the event occurs. The nontax portion of a trust is determined by multiplying the value of the trust assets, determined immediately prior to the event, by the then applicable fraction.

(1) *Multiple transfers to a single trust.*—If property is added to an existing trust, the denominator of the redetermined applicable fraction is the value of the trust immediately after the addition reduced as provided in § 26.2642-1(c).

(2) *Consolidation of separate trusts.*—If separate trusts created by one transferor are consolidated, a single applicable fraction for the consolidated trust is determined. The numerator of the redetermined applicable fraction is the sum of the nontax portions of each trust immediately prior to the consolidation.

(3) *Property included in transferor's gross estate.*—If the value of property held in a trust created by the transferor, with respect to which an allocation was made at a time that the trust was not subject to an ETIP, is included in the transferor's gross estate, the applicable fraction is redetermined if additional GST exemption is allocated to the property. The numerator of the redetermined applicable fraction is an amount equal to the nontax portion of the property immediately after the death of the transferor increased by the amount of GST exemption allocated by the executor of the transferor's estate to the trust. If additional GST exemption is not allocated to the trust, then, except as provided in this paragraph (a)(3), the applicable fraction immediately before death is not changed, if the trust was not subject to an ETIP at the time GST exemption was allocated to the trust. In any event, the denominator of the applicable fraction is reduced to reflect any federal or state, estate or inheritance taxes paid from the trust.

(4) *Imposition of recapture tax under section 2032A.*—(i) If an additional estate tax is imposed under section 2032A and if the section 2032A election was effective (under § 26.2642-2(b)) for purposes of the GST tax, the applicable fraction with respect to the property is redetermined as of the date of death of the transferor. In making the redetermination, any available GST exemption not allocated at the death of the transferor (or at a prior recapture event) is automatically allocated to the property. The denominator of the applicable fraction is the fair market value of the property at the date of the transferor's death reduced as provided in § 26.2642-1(c) and further reduced by the amount of the additional GST tax actually recovered from the trust.

(ii) The GST tax imposed with respect to any taxable termination, taxable distribution, or direct skip occurring prior to the recapture event is recomputed based on the applicable fraction as redetermined. Any additional GST tax as recomputed is due and payable on the date that is six months after the event that causes the imposition of the additional estate tax under section 2032A. The additional GST tax is remitted with Form 706-A and is reported by attaching a statement to Form 706-A showing the computation of the additional GST tax.

(iii) The applicable fraction, as redetermined under this section, is also used in determining any GST tax imposed with respect to GSTs occurring after the date of the recapture event.

(b) *Examples.*—The following examples illustrate the principles of this section:

Example 1. Allocation of additional exemption. T transfers $200,000 to an irrevocable trust under which the income is payable to T's child, C, for life. Upon the termination of the trust, the remainder is payable to T's grandchild, GC. At a time when no ETIP exists with respect to the trust property, T makes a timely allocation of $100,000 of GST exemption, resulting in an inclusion ratio of .50. Subsequently, when the entire trust property is valued at $500,000, T allocates an additional $100,000 of T's unused GST exemption to the trust. The inclusion ratio of the trust is recomputed at that time. The numerator of the applicable fraction is $350,000 ($250,000 (the nontax portion as of the date of the allocation) plus $100,000 (the GST exemption currently being allocated)). The denominator is $500,000 (the date of allocation fair market value of the trust). The inclusion ratio is .30 (1 - .70).

Example 2. Multiple transfers to a trust, allocation both timely and late. On December 10, 1993, T transfers $10,000 to an irrevocable trust that does not satisfy the requirements of section 2642(c)(2). T makes identical transfers to the trust on December 10, 1994, 1995, 1996, and on January 15, 1997. Immediately after the transfer on January 15, 1997, the value of the trust principal is $40,000. On January 14, 1998, when the value of the trust principal is $50,000, T allocates $30,000 of GST exemption to the trust. T discloses the 1997 transfer on the Form 709 filed on January 14, 1998. Thus, T's allocation is a timely allocation with respect to the transfer in 1997, $10,000 of the allocation is effective as of the date of that transfer, and, on and after January 15, 1997, the inclusion ratio of the trust is .75 (1 - ($10,000/$40,000)). The balance of the allocation is a late allocation with respect to prior transfers to the trust and is effective as of January 14, 1998. In redetermining the inclusion ratio as of that date, the numerator of the redetermined applicable fraction is $32,500 ($12,500 (.25 x $50,000), the nontax portion of the trust on January 14, 1998) plus $20,000 (the amount of GST exemption allocated late to the trust). The denominator of the new applicable fraction is $50,000 (the value of the trust principal at the time of the late allocation).

Example 3. Excess allocation. (i) T creates an irrevocable trust for the benefit of T's child and grandchild in 1996 transferring $50,000 to the trust on the date of creation. T allocates no GST exemption to the trust on the Form 709 reporting the transfer. On July 1, 1997 (when the value of the trust property is $60,000), T transfers an additional $40,000 to the trust.

(ii) On April 15, 1998, when the value of the trust is $150,000, T files a Form 709 reporting the 1997 transfer and allocating $150,000 of GST exemption to the trust. The allocation is a timely allocation of $40,000 with respect to the 1997 transfer and is effective as of that date. Thus, the applicable fraction for the trust as of July 1, 1997 is .40 ($40,000/$100,000 ($40,000 + $60,000)).

(iii) The allocation is also a late allocation of $90,000, the amount necessary to attain a zero inclusion ratio on April 15, 1998, computed as follows: $60,000 (the nontax portion immediately prior to the allocation (.40 X $150,000)) plus $90,000 (the additional allocation necessary to produce a zero inclusion ratio based on a denominator of $150,000)/$150,000 equals one and, thus, an inclusion ratio of zero. The balance of the allocation, $20,000 ($150,000 less the timely allocation of $40,000 less the late allocation of $90,000) is void.

Example 4. Undisclosed transfer. (i) The facts are the same as in *Example 3*, except that on February 1, 1998 (when the value of the trust is $150,000), T transfers an additional $50,000 to the trust and the value of the entire trust corpus on April 15, 1998 is $220,000. The Form 709 filed on April 15, 1998 does not disclose the 1998 transfer. Under the rule in § 26.2632-1(b)(2)(ii), the allocation is effective first as a timely allocation to the 1997 transfer; second, as a late allocation to the trust as of April 15, 1998; and, finally as a timely allocation to the February 1, 1998 transfer. As of April 15, 1998, $55,000, a pro rata portion of the trust assets, is considered to be the property transferred to the trust on February 1, 1998 (($50,000/$200,000) X $220,000). The balance of the trust, $165,000, represents prior transfers to the trust.

(ii) As in *Example 3*, the allocation is a timely allocation as to the 1997 transfer (and the applicable fraction as of July 1, 1997 is .40) and a late allocation as of 1998. The amount of the late allocation is $99,000, computed as follows: (.40 X $165,000 plus $99,000)/$165,000 = one.

(iii) The balance of the allocation, $11,000 ($150,000 less the timely allocation of $40,000 less the late allocation of $99,000) is a timely allocation as of February 1, 1998. The applicable fraction with respect to the trust, as of February 1, 1998, is .355, computed as follows: $60,000 (the nontax portion of the trust immediately prior to the February 1, 1998 transfer (.40 X $150,000)) plus $11,000 (the amount of the timely allocation to the 1998 transfer)/$200,000 (the value of the trust on February 1, 1998, after the transfer on that date) = $71,000/$200,000 = .355.

(iv) The applicable fraction with respect to the trust, as of April 15, 1998, is .805 computed as follows: $78,100 (the nontax portion immediately prior to the allocation (.355 X $220,000)) plus $99,000 (the amount of the late allocation)/ $220,000 = $177,100/$220,000 = .805.

Example 5. Redetermination of inclusion ratio on ETIP termination. (i) T transfers $100,000 to an irrevocable trust. The trust instrument provides that trust income is to be paid to T for 9 years or until T's prior death. The trust principal is to be paid to T's grandchild, GC, on the termination of T's income interest. The trustee has the power to invade trust principal for the benefit of GC during the term of T's income interest. The trust is subject to an ETIP while T holds the retained income interest. T files a timely Form 709 reporting the transfer and allocates $100,000 of GST exemption to the trust. In year 4, when the value of the trust is $200,000, the trustee distributes $15,000 to GC. The distribution is a taxable distribution. Because of the existence of the ETIP, the inclusion ratio with respect to the taxable distribution is determined immediately prior to the occurrence of the GST. Thus, the inclusion ratio applicable to the year 4 GST is .50 (1 - ($100,000/$200,000)).

(ii) In year 5, when the value of the trust is again $200,000, the trustee distributes another $15,000 to GC. Because the trust is still subject to the ETIP in year 5, the inclusion ratio with respect to the year 5 GST is again computed immediately prior to the GST. In computing the new inclusion ratio, the numerator of the applicable fraction is reduced by the nontax portion of prior GSTs occurring during the ETIP. Thus, the numerator of the applicable fraction with respect to the GST in year 5 is $92,500 ($100,000 - (.50 X $15,000)) and the inclusion ratio applicable with respect to the GST in year 5 is .537 (1 - ($92,500/$200,000) = .463). Any additional GST exemption allocated on a timely ETIP return with respect to the GST in year 5 is effective immediately prior to the transfer. [Reg. § 26.2642-4.]

□ [*T.D.* 8644, 12-26-95.]

[Reg. § 26.2642-5]

§ 26.2642-5. Finality of inclusion ratio.—(a) *Direct skips.*—The inclusion ratio applicable to a direct skip becomes final when no additional GST tax (including additional GST tax payable as a result of a cessation, etc. of qualified use under section 2032A(c)) may be assessed with respect to the direct skip.

(b) *Other GSTs.*—With respect to taxable distributions and taxable terminations, the inclusion ratio for a trust becomes final, on the later of—

(1) The expiration of the period for assessment with respect to the first GST tax return filed using that inclusion ratio (unless the trust is subject to an election under section 2032A in which case the applicable date under this subsection is the expiration of the period of assessment of any additional GST tax due as a result of a cessation, etc. of qualified use under section 2032A); or

(2) The expiration of the period for assessment of Federal estate tax with respect to the estate of the transferor. For purposes of this paragraph (b)(2), if an estate tax return is not required to be filed, the period for assessment is determined as if a return were required to be filed and as if the return were timely filed within the period prescribed by section 6075(a). [Reg. § 26.2642-5.]

□ [*T.D.* 8644, 12-26-95.]

[Reg. § 26.2642-6]

§ 26.2642-6. Qualified severance.—(a) *In general.*—If a trust is divided in a qualified severance into two or more trusts, the separate trusts resulting from the severance will be treated as separate trusts for generation-skipping transfer (GST) tax purposes and the inclusion ratio of each new resulting trust may differ from the inclusion ratio of the original trust. Because the post-severance resulting trusts are treated as separate trusts for GST tax purposes, certain actions with respect to one resulting trust will generally have no GST tax impact with respect to the other resulting trust(s). For example, GST exemption allocated to one resulting trust will not impact on the inclusion ratio of the other resulting trust(s); a GST tax election made with respect to one resulting trust will not apply to the other resulting trust(s); the occurrence of a taxable distribution or termination with regard to a particular resulting trust will not have any GST tax impact on any other trust resulting from that severance. In general, the rules in this section are applicable only for purposes of the GST tax and are not applicable in determining, for example, whether the resulting trusts may file separate income tax returns or whether the severance may result in a gift subject to gift tax, may cause any trust to be included in the gross estate of a beneficiary, or may result in a realization of gain for purposes of section 1001. See § 1.1001-1(h) of this chapter for rules relating to whether a qualified severance will constitute an exchange of property for other property differing materially either in kind or in extent.

(b) *Qualified severance defined.*—A qualified severance is a division of a trust (other than a division described in § 26.2654-1(b)) into two or more separate trusts that meets each of the requirements in paragraph (d) of this section.

(c) *Effective date of qualified severance.*—A qualified severance is applicable as of the date of the severance, as defined in § 26.2642-6(d)(3), and the resulting trusts are treated as separate trusts for GST tax purposes as of that date.

(d) *Requirements for a qualified severance.*—For purposes of this section, a qualified severance must satisfy each of the following requirements:

(1) The single trust is severed pursuant to the terms of the governing instrument, or pursuant to applicable local law.

(2) The severance is effective under local law.

(3) The date of severance is either the date selected by the trustee as of which the trust assets are to be valued in order to determine the funding of the resulting trusts, or the court-imposed date of funding in the case of an order of the local court with jurisdiction over the trust ordering the trustee to fund the resulting trusts on or as of a specific date. For a date to satisfy the definition in the preceding sentence, however, the funding must be commenced immedi-

ately upon, and funding must occur within a reasonable time (but in no event more than 90 days) after, the selected valuation date.

(4) The single trust (original trust) is severed on a fractional basis, such that each new trust (resulting trust) is funded with a fraction or percentage of the original trust, and the sum of those fractions or percentages is one or one hundred percent, respectively. For this purpose, the fraction or percentage may be determined by means of a formula (for example, that fraction of the trust the numerator of which is equal to the transferor's unused GST tax exemption, and the denominator of which is the fair market value of the original trust's assets on the date of severance). The severance of a trust based on a pecuniary amount does not satisfy this requirement. For example, the severance of a trust is not a qualified severance if the trust is divided into two trusts, with one trust to be funded with $1,500,000 and the other trust to be funded with the balance of the original trust's assets. With respect to the particular assets to be distributed to each separate trust resulting from the severance, each such trust may be funded with the appropriate fraction or percentage (pro rata portion) of each asset held by the original trust. Alternatively, the assets may be divided among the resulting trusts on a non-pro rata basis, based on the fair market value of the assets on the date of severance. However, if a resulting trust is funded on a non-pro rata basis, each asset received by a resulting trust must be valued, solely for funding purposes, by multiplying the fair market value of the asset held in the original trust as of the date of severance by the fraction or percentage of that asset received by that resulting trust. Thus, the assets must be valued without taking into account any discount or premium arising from the severance, for example, any valuation discounts that might arise because the resulting trust receives less than the entire interest held by the original trust. See paragraph (j), *Example 6* of this section.

(5) The terms of the resulting trusts must provide, in the aggregate, for the same succession of interests of beneficiaries as are provided in the original trust. This requirement is satisfied if the beneficiaries of the separate resulting trusts and the interests of the beneficiaries with respect to the separate trusts, when the separate trusts are viewed collectively, are the same as the beneficiaries and their respective beneficial interests with respect to the original trust before severance. With respect to trusts from which discretionary distributions may be made to any one or more beneficiaries on a non-pro rata basis, this requirement is satisfied if—

(i) The terms of each of the resulting trusts are the same as the terms of the original trust (even though each permissible distributee of the original trust is not a beneficiary of all of the resulting trusts);

(ii) Each beneficiary's interest in the resulting trusts (collectively) equals the beneficiary's interest in the original trust, determined by the terms of the trust instrument or, if none, on a per-capita basis. For example, in the case of the severance of a discretionary trust established for the benefit of A, B, and C and their descendants with the remainder to be divided equally among those three families, this requirement is satisfied if the trust is divided into three separate trusts of equal value with one trust established for the benefit of A and A's descendants, one trust for the benefit of B and B's descendants, and one trust for the benefit of C and C's descendants;

(iii) The severance does not shift a beneficial interest in the trust to any beneficiary in a lower generation (as determined under section 2651) than the person or persons who held the beneficial interest in the original trust; and

(iv) The severance does not extend the time for the vesting of any beneficial interest in the trust beyond the period provided for in (or applicable to) the original trust.

(6) In the case of a qualified severance of a trust with an inclusion ratio as defined in § 26.2642-1 of either one or zero, each trust resulting from the severance will have an inclusion ratio equal to the inclusion ratio of the original trust.

(7)(i) In the case of a qualified severance occurring after GST tax exemption has been allocated to the trust (whether by an affirmative allocation, a deemed allocation, or an automatic allocation pursuant to the rules contained in section 2632), if the trust has an inclusion ratio as defined in § 26.2642-1 that is greater than zero and less than one, then either paragraph (d)(7)(ii) or (iii) of this section must be satisfied.

(ii) The trust is severed initially into only two resulting trusts. One resulting trust must receive that fractional share of the total value of the original trust as of the date of severance that is equal to the applicable fraction, as defined in § 26.2642-1(b) and (c), used to determine the inclusion ratio of the original trust immediately before the severance. The other resulting trust must receive that fractional share of the total value of the original trust as of the date of severance that is equal to the excess of one over the fractional share described in the preceding sentence. The trust receiving the fractional share equal to the applicable fraction shall have an inclusion ratio of zero, and the other trust shall have an inclusion ratio of one. If the applicable fraction with respect to the original trust is .50, then, with respect to the two equal trusts resulting from the severance, the trustee may designate which of the resulting trusts will have an inclusion ratio of zero and which will have an inclusion ratio of one. Each separate trust resulting from the severance then may be further divided in accordance with the rules of this section. See paragraph (j), *Example 7*, of this section.

(iii) The trust is severed initially into more than two resulting trusts. One or more of the resulting trusts in the aggregate must receive that fractional share of the total value of the original trust as of the date of severance that is equal to the applicable fraction used to determine the inclusion ratio of the original trust immediately before the severance. The trust or trusts receiving such fractional share shall have an inclusion ratio of zero, and each of the other resulting trust or trusts shall have an inclusion ratio of one. (If, however, two or more of the resulting trusts each receives the fractional share of the total value of the original trust equal to the applicable fraction, the trustee may designate which of those resulting trusts will have an inclusion ratio of zero and which will have an inclusion ratio of one.) The resulting trust or trusts with an inclusion ratio of one must receive in the aggregate that fractional share of the total value of the original trust as of the date of severance that is equal to the excess of one over the fractional share described in the second sentence of this paragraph. See paragraph (j), *Example 9*, of this section.

(e) *Reporting a qualified severance.*—(1) *In general.*—A qualified severance is reported by filing Form 706-GS(T), "Generation-Skipping Transfer Tax Return for Terminations," (or such other form as may be provided from time to time by the Internal Revenue Service (IRS) for the purpose of reporting a qualified severance). Unless otherwise provided in the applicable form or instructions, the IRS requests that the filer write "Qualified Severance" at the top of the form and attach a Notice of Qualified Severance (Notice). The return and attached Notice should be filed by April 15th of the year immediately following the year during which the severance occurred or by the last day of the period covered by an extension of time, if an extension of time is granted, to file such form.

(2) *Information concerning the original trust.*—The Notice should provide, with respect to the original trust that was severed—

(i) The name of the transferor;

(ii) The name and date of creation of the original trust;

(iii) The tax identification number of the original trust; and

(iv) The inclusion ratio before the severance.

(3) *Information concerning each new trust.*—The Notice should provide, with respect to each of the resulting trusts created by the severance—

(i) The name and tax identification number of the trust;

(ii) The date of severance (within the meaning of paragraph (c) of this section);

(iii) The fraction of the total assets of the original trust received by the resulting trust;

(iv) Other details explaining the basis for the funding of the resulting trust (a fraction of the total fair market value of the assets on the date of severance, or a fraction of each asset); and

(v) The inclusion ratio.

(f) *Time for making a qualified severance.*—(1) A qualified severance of a trust may occur at any time prior to the termination of the trust. Thus, provided that the separate resulting trusts continue in existence after the severance, a qualified severance may occur either before or after—

(i) GST tax exemption has been allocated to the trust;

(ii) A taxable event has occurred with respect to the trust; or

(iii) An addition has been made to the trust.

(2) Because a qualified severance is effective as of the date of severance, a qualified severance has no effect on a taxable termination as defined in section 2612(a) or a taxable distribution as defined in section 2612(b) that occurred prior to the date of severance. A qualified severance shall be deemed to occur before a taxable termination or a taxable distribution that occurs by reason of the qualified severance. See paragraph (j) *Example 8* of this section.

(g) *Trusts that were irrevocable on September 25, 1985.*—(1) *In general.*—See § 26.2601-1(b)(4) for rules regarding severances and other actions with respect to trusts that were irrevocable on September 25, 1985.

(2) *Trusts in receipt of a post-September 25, 1985, addition.*—A trust described in § 26.2601-1(b)(1)(iv)(A) that is deemed for GST tax purposes to consist of one separate share not subject to GST tax (the non-chapter 13 portion) with an inclusion ratio of zero, and one separate share subject to GST tax (the chapter 13 portion) with an inclusion ratio determined under section 2642, may be severed into two trusts in accordance with § 26.2654-1(a)(3). One resulting trust will hold the non-chapter 13 portion of the original trust (the non-chapter 13 trust) and will not be subject to GST tax, and the other resulting trust will hold the chapter 13 portion of the original trust (the chapter 13 trust) and will have the same inclusion ratio as the chapter 13 portion immediately prior to the severance. The chapter 13 trust may be further divided in a qualified severance in accordance with the rules of this section. The non-chapter 13 trust may be further divided in accordance with the rules of § 26.2601-1(b)(4).

(h) *Treatment of trusts resulting from a severance that is not a qualified severance.*—Trusts resulting from a severance (other than a severance recognized for GST tax purposes under § 26.2654-1) that does not meet the requirements of a qualified severance under paragraph (b) of this section will be treated, after the date of severance, as separate trusts for purposes of the GST tax, provided that the trusts resulting from such severance are recognized as separate trusts under applicable state law. The post-severance treatment of the resulting trusts as separate trusts for GST tax purposes generally permits the allocation of GST tax exemption, the making of various elections permitted for GST tax purposes, and the occurrence of a taxable distribution or termination with regard to a particular resulting trust, with no GST tax impact on any other trust resulting from that severance. Each trust resulting from a severance described in this paragraph (h), however, will have the same inclusion ratio immediately after the severance as that of the original trust immediately before the severance. (See § 26.2654-1 for the inclusion ratio of each trust resulting from a severance described in that section.) Further, any trust resulting from a nonqualified severance may be severed subsequently, pursuant to a qualified severance described in this § 26.2642-6.

(i) [Reserved].

(j) *Examples*.—The rules of this section are illustrated by the following examples:

Example 1. Succession of interests. T dies in 2006. T's will establishes a testamentary trust (Trust) providing that income is to be paid to T's sister, S, for her life. On S's death, one-half of the corpus is to be paid to T's child, C (or to C's estate if C fails to survive S), and one-half of the corpus is to be paid to T's grandchild, GC (or to GC's estate if GC fails to survive S). On the Form 706, "United States Estate (and Generation-Skipping Transfer) Tax Return," filed for T's estate, T's executor allocates all of T's available GST tax exemption to other transfers and trusts, such that Trust's inclusion ratio is 1. Subsequent to filing the Form 706 in 2007 and in accordance with applicable state law, the trustee divides Trust into two separate trusts, Trust 1 and Trust 2, with each trust receiving 50 percent of the value of the assets of the original trust as of the date of severance. Trust 1 provides that trust income is to be paid to S for life with remainder to C or C's estate, and Trust 2 provides that trust income is to be paid to S for life with remainder to GC or GC's estate. Because Trust 1 and Trust 2 provide for the same succession of interests in the aggregate as provided in the original trust, the severance constitutes a qualified severance, provided that all other requirements of section 2642(a)(3) and this section are satisfied.

Example 2. Succession of interests in discretionary trust. In 2006, T establishes Trust, an irrevocable trust providing that income may be paid from time to time in such amounts as the trustee deems advisable to any one or more members of the group consisting of T's children (A and B) and their respective descendants. In addition, the trustee may distribute corpus to any trust beneficiary in such amounts as the trustee deems advisable. On the death of the last to die of A and B, the trust is to terminate and the corpus is to be distributed in two equal shares, one share to the then-living descendants of each child, per stirpes. T elects, under section 2632(c)(5), to not have the automatic allocation rules contained in section 2632(c) apply with respect to T's transfers to Trust, and T does not otherwise allocate GST tax exemption with respect to Trust. As a result, Trust has an inclusion ratio of one. In 2008, the trustee of Trust, pursuant to applicable state law, divides Trust into two equal but separate trusts, Trust 1 and Trust 2, each of which has terms identical to the terms of Trust except for the identity of the beneficiaries. Trust 1 and Trust 2 each has an inclusion ratio of one. Trust 1 provides that income is to be paid in such amounts as the trustee deems advisable to A and A's descendants. In addition, the trustee may distribute corpus to any trust beneficiary in such amounts as the trustee deems advisable. On the death of A, Trust 1 is to terminate and the corpus is to be distributed to the then-living descendants of A, per stirpes, but, if A dies with no living descendants, the principal will be added to Trust 2. Trust 2 contains identical provisions, except that B and B's descendants are the trust beneficiaries and, if B dies with no living descendants, the principal will be added to Trust 1. Trust 1 and Trust 2 in the aggregate provide for the same beneficiaries and the same succession of interests as provided in Trust, and the severance does not shift any beneficial interest to a beneficiary who occupies a lower generation than the person or persons who held the beneficial interest in Trust. Accordingly, the severance constitutes a qualified severance, provided that all other requirements of section 2642(a)(3) and this section are satisfied.

Example 3. Severance based on actuarial value of beneficial interests. In 2004, T establishes Trust, an irrevocable trust providing that income is to be paid to T's child C during C's lifetime. Upon C's death, Trust is to terminate and the assets of Trust are to be paid to GC, C's child, if living, or, if GC is not then living, to GC's estate. T properly elects, under section 2632(c)(5). not to have the automatic allocation rules contained in section 2632(c) apply with respect to T's transfers to Trust, and T does not otherwise allocate GST tax exemption with respect to Trust. Thus, Trust has an inclusion ratio of one. In 2009, the trustee of Trust, pursuant to applicable state law, divides Trust into two separate trusts, Trust 1 for the benefit of C (and on C's death to C's estate), and Trust 2 for the benefit of GC (and on GC's death to GC's estate). The document severing Trust directs that Trust 1 is to be funded with an amount equal to the actuarial value of C's interest in Trust prior to the severance, determined under section 7520 of the Internal Revenue Code. Similarly, Trust 2 is to be funded with an amount equal to the actuarial value of GC's interest in Trust prior to the severance, determined under section 7520. Trust 1 and Trust 2 do not provide for the same succession of interests as provided under the terms of the original trust. Therefore, the severance is not a qualified severance. Furthermore, because the severance results in no non-skip person having an interest in Trust 2, Trust 2 constitutes a skip person under section 2613 and, therefore, the severance results in a taxable termination subject to GST tax.

Example 4. Severance of a trust with a 50% inclusion ratio. On September 1, 2006, T transfers $100,000 to a trust for the benefit of T's grandchild, GC. On a timely filed Form 709, "United States Gift (and Generation-Skipping Transfer) Tax Return," reporting the transfer, T allocates all of T's remaining GST tax exemption ($50,000) to the trust. As a result of the allocation, the applicable fraction with respect to the trust is .50 [$50,000 (the amount of GST tax exemption allocated to the trust) divided by $100,000 (the value of the property transferred to the trust)]. The inclusion ratio with respect to the trust is .50 [1 - .50]. In 2007, pursuant to authority granted under applicable state law, the trustee severs the trust into two trusts, Trust 1 and Trust 2, each of which is identical to the original trust and each of which receives a 50 percent fractional share of the total value of the original trust, valued as of the date of severance. Because the applicable fraction with respect to the original trust is .50 and the trust is severed into two equal trusts, the trustee may designate which resulting trust has an inclusion ratio of one, and which resulting trust has an inclusion ratio of zero. Accordingly, in the Notice of Qualified Severance reporting the severance, the trustee designates Trust 1 as having an inclusion ratio of zero, and Trust 2 as having an inclusion ratio of one. The severance constitutes a qualified severance, provided that all other requirements of section 2642(a)(3) and this section are satisfied.

Example 5. Funding of severed trusts on a non-pro rata basis. T's will establishes a testamentary trust (Trust) for the benefit of T's descendants, to be funded with T's stock in Corporation A and Corporation B, both publicly traded stocks. T dies on May 1, 2004, at which time the Corporation A stock included in T's gross estate has a fair market value of $100,000 and the stock of Corporation B included in T's gross estate has a fair market value of $200,000. On a timely filed Form 706, T's executor allocates all of T's remaining GST tax exemption ($270,000) to Trust. As a result of the allocation, the applicable fraction with respect to Trust is .90 [$270,000 (the amount of GST tax exemption allocated to the trust) divided by $300,000 (the value of the property transferred to the trust)]. The inclusion ratio with respect to Trust is .10 [1 - .90]. On August 1, 2008, in accordance with applicable local law, the trustee executes a document severing Trust into two trusts, Trust 1 and Trust 2, each of which is identical to Trust. The instrument designates August 3, 2008, as the date of severance (within the meaning of paragraph (d)(3) of this section). The terms of the instrument severing Trust provide that Trust 1 is to be funded on a non-pro rata basis with assets having a fair market value on the date of severance equal to 90% of the value of Trust's assets on that date, and Trust 2 is to be funded with assets having a fair market value on the date of severance equal to 10% of the value of Trust's assets on that date. On August 3, 2008, the value of the Trust assets totals $500,000, consisting of Corporation A stock worth $450,000 and Corporation B stock worth $50,000. On August 4, 2008, the trustee takes all action necessary to transfer all of the Corporation A stock to Trust 1 and to transfer all of the Corporation B stock to Trust 2. On August 6, 2008, the stock transfers are completed and the stock is received by the appropriate resulting trust. Accordingly, Trust 1 is funded with assets having a value equal to 90% of the value of Trust as of the date of severance, August 3, 2008, and Trust 2 is funded with assets having a value equal to 10% of the value of Trust as of the date of severance. Therefore, the severance constitutes a qualified severance, provided that all other requirements of section 2642(a)(3) and this section are satisfied. Trust 1 will have an inclusion ratio of zero and Trust 2 will have an inclusion ratio of one.

Example 6. Funding of severed trusts on a non-pro rata basis. (i) T's will establishes an irrevocable trust (Trust) for the benefit of T's descendants. As a result of the allocation of GST tax exemption, the applicable fraction with respect to Trust is .60 and Trust's inclusion ratio is .40 [1 - .60]. Pursuant to authority granted under applicable state law, on August 1, 2008, the trustee executes a document severing Trust into two trusts, Trust 1 and Trust 2, each of which is identical to Trust. The instrument of severance provides that the severance is intended to qualify as a qualified severance within the meaning of section 2642(a)(3) and designates August 3, 2008, as the date of severance (within the meaning of paragraph (d)(3) of this section). The instrument further provides that Trust 1 and Trust 2 are to be funded on a non-pro rata basis with Trust 1 funded with assets having a fair market value on the date of severance equal to 40% of the value of Trust's assets on that date and Trust 2 funded with assets having a fair market value equal to 60% of the value of Trust's assets on that date. The fair market value of the assets used to fund each trust is to be determined in compliance with the requirements of paragraph (d)(4) of this section.

(ii) On August 3, 2008, the fair market value of the Trust assets totals $4,000,000, consisting of 52% of the outstanding common stock in Company, a closelyheld corporation, valued at $3,000,000 and $1,000,000 in cash and marketable securities. Trustee proposes to divide the Company stock equally between Trust 1 and Trust 2, and thus transfer 26% of the Company stock to Trust 1 and 26% of the stock to Trust 2. In addition, the appropriate amount of cash and marketable securities will be distributed to each trust. In accordance with paragraph (d)(4) of this section, for funding purposes, the interest in the Company stock distributed to each trust is valued as a pro rata portion of the value of the 52% interest in Company held by Trust before severance, without taking into account, for example, any valuation discount that might otherwise apply in valuing the noncontrolling interest distributed to each resulting trust.

(iii) Accordingly, for funding purposes, each 26% interest in Company stock distributed to Trust 1 and Trust 2 is valued at $1,500,000 (.5 × $3,000,000). Therefore, Trust 1, which is to be funded with $1,600,000 (.40 × $4,000,000), receives $100,000 in cash and marketable securities valued as of August 3, 2008, in addition to the Company stock, and Trust 2, which is to be funded with $2,400,000 (.60 × $4,000,000), receives $900,000 in cash and marketable securities in addition to the Company stock. Therefore, the severance is a qualified severance, provided that all other requirements of section 2642(a)(3) and this section are satisfied.

Example 7. Statutory qualified severance. T dies on October 1, 2004. T's will establishes a testamentary trust (Trust) to be funded with $1,000,000. Trust income is to be paid to T's child, S, for S's life. The trustee may also distribute trust corpus from time to time, in equal or unequal shares, for the benefit of any one or more members of the group consisting of S and T's three grandchildren (GC1, GC2, and GC3). On S's death, Trust is to terminate and the assets are to be divided equally among GC1, GC2, and GC3 (or their respective then-living descendants, per stirpes). On a timely filed Form 706, T's executor allocates all of T's remaining GST tax exemption ($300,000) to Trust. As a result of the allocation, the applicable fraction with respect to the trust is .30 [$300,000 (the amount of GST tax exemption allocated to the trust) divided by $1,000,000 (the value of the property transferred to the trust)]. The inclusion ratio with respect to the trust is .70 [1 - .30]. On June 1, 2007, the trustee determines that it is in the best interest of the beneficiaries to sever Trust to provide a separate trust for each of T's three grandchildren and their respective families. The trustee severs Trust into two trusts, Trust 1 and Trust 2, each with terms and beneficiaries identical to Trust and thus each providing that trust income is to be paid to S for life, trust principal may be distributed for the benefit of any or all members of the group consisting of S and T's grandchildren, and, on S's death, the trust is to terminate and the assets are to be divided equally among GC1, GC2, and GC3 (or their respective then-living descendants, per stirpes). The instrument severing Trust provides that Trust 1 is to receive 30% of Trust's assets and Trust 2 is to receive 70% of Trust's assets. Further, each such trust is to be funded with a pro rata portion of each asset held in Trust. The trustee then severs Trust 1 into three equal trusts, Trust GC1, Trust GC2, and Trust GC3. Each trust is named for a grandchild of T and provides that trust income is to be paid to S for life, trust principal may be distributed for the benefit of S and T's grandchild for whom the trust is named, and, on S's death, the trust is to terminate and the trust proceeds distributed to the respective grandchild for whom the trust is named. If that grandchild has predeceased the termination date, the trust proceeds are to be distributed to that grandchild's then-living descendants, per stirpes, or, if none, then equally to the other two trusts resulting from the severance of Trust 1. Each such resulting trust is to be funded with a pro rata portion of each Trust 1 asset. The trustee also severs Trust 2 in a similar manner, into Trust GC1(2), Trust GC2(2), and Trust GC3(2). The severance of Trust into Trust 1 and Trust 2, the severance of Trust 1 into Trust GC1, Trust GC2, Trust GC3, and the severance of Trust 2 into Trust GC1(2), Trust GC2(2) and Trust GC3(2), constitute qualified severances, provided that all other requirements of section 2642(a)(3) and this section are satisfied with respect to each severance. Trust GC1, Trust GC2, Trust GC3 will each have an inclusion ratio of zero and Trust GC1(2), Trust GC2(2), and Trust GC3(2) will each have an inclusion ratio of one.

Example 8. Qualified severance deemed to precede a taxable termination. In 2004, T establishes an inter vivos irrevocable trust (Trust) for a term of 10 years providing that Trust income is to be paid annually in equal shares to T's child C and T's grandchild GC (the child of another then-living child of T). If either C or GC dies prior to the expiration of the 10-year term, the deceased beneficiary's share of Trust's income is to be paid to that beneficiary's then-living descendants, per stirpes, for the balance of the trust term. At the expiration of the 10-year trust term, the corpus is to be distributed equally to C and GC; if either C or GC is not then living, then such decedent's share is to be distributed instead to such decedent's then-living descendants, per stirpes. T allocates T's GST tax exemption to Trust such that Trust's applicable fraction is .50 and Trust's inclusion ratio is .50 [1-.50]. In 2006. pursuant to applicable state law, the trustee severs the trust into two equal trusts, Trust 1 and Trust 2. The instrument severing Trust provides that Trust 1 is to receive 50% of the Trust assets, and Trust 2 is to receive 50% of Trust's assets. Both resulting trusts are identical to Trust, except that each has different beneficiaries: C and C's descendants are designated as the beneficiaries of Trust 1, and GC and GC's descendants are designated as the beneficiaries of Trust 2. The severance constitutes a qualified severance, provided all other requirements of section 2642(a)(3) and this section are satisfied. Because the applicable fraction with respect to Trust is .50 and Trust was severed into two equal trusts, the trustee may designate which resulting trust has an inclusion ratio of one, and which has an inclusion ratio of zero. Accordingly, in the Notice of Qualified Severance reporting the severance, the trustee designates Trust 1 as having an inclusion ratio of one, and Trust 2 as having an inclusion ratio of zero. Because Trust 2 is a skip person under section 2613, the severance of Trust resulting in the distribution of 50% of Trust's corpus to Trust 2 would constitute a taxable termination or distribution (as described in section 2612(a)) of that 50% of Trust for GST tax purposes, but for the rule that a qualified severance is deemed to precede a taxable termination that is caused by the qualified severance. Thus, no GST tax will be due with regard to the creation and funding of Trust 2 because the inclusion ratio of Trust 2 is zero.

Example 9. Regulatory qualified severance. (i) In 2004, T establishes an inter vivos irrevocable trust (Trust) providing that trust income is to be paid annually in equal shares to T's children, A and B, for 10 years. Trust provides that the trustee has discretion to make additional distributions of principal to A and B during the 10-year term without adjustments to their shares of income or the trust remainder. If either (or both) dies prior to the expiration of the 10-year term, the deceased child's share of trust income is to be paid to the child's then living descendants, per stirpes, for the balance of the trust term. At the expiration of the 10-year term, the corpus is to be distributed equally to A and B; if A and B (or either or them) is not then living, then such decedent's share is to be distributed instead to such decedent's then living descendants, per stirpes. T allocates GST tax exemption to Trust such that Trust's applicable fraction is .25 and its inclusion ratio is .75.

(ii) In 2006, pursuant to applicable state law, the trustee severs the trust into three trusts: Trust 1, Trust 2, and Trust 3. The instrument severing Trust provides that Trust 1 is to receive 50% of Trust's assets, Trust 2 is to receive 25% of Trust's assets, and Trust 3 is to receive 25% of Trust's assets. All three resulting trusts are identical to Trust, except that each has different beneficiaries: A and A's issue are designated as the beneficiaries of Trust 1, and B and B's issue are designated as the beneficiaries of Trust 2 and Trust 3. The severance constitutes a qualified severance, provided that all other requirements of section 2642(a)(3) and this section are satisfied. Trust 1 will have an inclusion ratio of 1. Because both Trust 2 and Trust 3 have each received the fractional share of Trust's assets equal to Trust's applicable fraction of .25, trustee designates that Trust 2 will have an inclusion ratio of one and that Trust 3 will have an inclusion ratio of zero.

Example 10. Beneficiary's interest dependent on inclusion ratio. On August 8, 2006, T transfers $1,000,000 to Trust and timely allocates $400,000 of T's remaining GST tax exemption to Trust. As a result of the allocation, the applicable fraction with respect to Trust is .40 [$400,000 divided by $1,000,000]and Trust's inclusion ratio is .60 [1 - .40]. Trust provides that all income of Trust will be paid annually to C, T's child, for life. On C's death, the corpus is to pass in accordance with C's exercise of a testamentary limited power to appoint the corpus of Trust to C's lineal descendants. However, Trust provides that if, at the time of C's death, Trust's inclusion ratio is greater than zero, then C may also appoint that fraction of the trust corpus equal to the inclusion ratio to the creditors of C's estate. On May 3, 2008, pursuant to authority granted under applicable state law, the trustee severs Trust into two trusts. Trust 1 is funded with 40% of Trust's assets, and Trust 2 is funded with 60% of Trust's assets in accordance with the requirements of this section. Both Trust 1 and Trust 2 provide that all income of Trust will be paid annually to C during C's life. On C's death, Trust 1 corpus is to pass in accordance with C's exercise of a testamentary limited power to appoint the corpus to C's lineal descendants. Trust 2 is to pass in accordance with C's exercise of a testamentary power to appoint the corpus of Trust to C's lineal descendants and to the creditors of C's estate. The severance constitutes a qualified severance, provided that all other requirements of section 2642(a)(3) and this section are satisfied. No additional contribution or allocation of GST tax exemption is made to either Trust 1 or Trust 2 prior to C's death. Accordingly, the inclusion ratio with respect to Trust 1 is zero. The inclusion ratio with respect to Trust 2 is one until C's death, at which time C will become the transferor of Trust 2 for GST tax purposes. (Some or all of C's GST tax exemption may be allocated to Trust 2 upon C's death.)

Example 11. Date of severance. Trust is an irrevocable trust that has both skip person and non-skip person beneficiaries. Trust holds two parcels of real estate, Property A and Property B, stock in Company X, a publicly traded company, and cash. On June 16, 2008, the local court with jurisdiction over Trust issues an order, pursuant to the trustee's petition authorized under state law, severing Trust into two resulting trusts of equal value, Trust 1 and Trust 2. The court order directs that Property A will be distributed to Trust 1 and Property B will be distributed to Trust 2, and that an appropriate amount of stock and cash will be distributed to each trust such that the total value of property distributed to each trust as of the date of severance will be equal. The court order does not mandate a particular date of funding. Trustee receives notice of the court order on June 24, and selects July 16, 2008, as the date of severance. On June 26, 2008, Trustee commences the process of transferring title to Property A and Property B to the appropriate resulting trust(s), which process is completed on July 8, 2008. Also on June 26, the Trustee hires a professional appraiser to value Property A and Property B as of the date of severance and receives the appraisal report on Friday, October 3, 2008. On Monday, October 6, 2008, Trustee commences the process of transferring to Trust 1 and Trust 2 the appropriate amount of Company X stock valued as of July 16, 2008, and that transfer (as well as the transfer of Trust's cash) is completed by October 9, 2008. Under the facts presented, the funding of Trust 1 and Trust 2 occurred within 90 days of the date of severance selected by the trustee, and within a reasonable time after the date of severance taking into account the nature of the assets involved and the need to obtain an appraisal. Accordingly, the date of severance for purposes of this section is July 16, 2008, the resulting trusts are to be funded based on the value of the original trust assets as of that date, and the severance is a qualified severance assuming that all other requirements of section 2642(a)(3) and this section are met. (However, if Trust had contained only marketable securities and cash, then in order to satisfy the reasonable time requirement, the stock transfer would have to have been commenced, and generally completed, immediately after the date of severance, and the cash distribution would have to have been made at the same time.)

Example 12. Other severance that does not meet the requirements of a qualified severance. (i) In 2004, T establishes an irrevocable inter vivos trust (Trust) providing that Trust income is to be paid to T's children, A and B, in equal shares for their joint lives. Upon the death of the first to die of A and B, all Trust income will be paid to the survivor of A and B. At the death of the survivor, the corpus is to be distributed in equal shares to T's grandchildren, W and X (with any then-deceased grandchild's share being paid in accordance with that grandchild's testamentary general power of appointment). W is A's child and X is B's child. T elects under section 2632(c)(5) not to have the automatic allocation rules contained in section 2632(c) apply with respect to T's transfers to Trust, but T allocates GST tax exemption to Trust resulting in Trust having an inclusion ratio of .30.

(ii) In 2009, the trustee of Trust, as permitted by applicable state law, divides Trust into two separate trusts, Trust 1 and Trust 2. Trust 1 provides that trust income is to be paid to A for life and, on A's death, the remainder is to be distributed to W (or pursuant to W's testamentary general power of appointment). Trust 2 provides that trust income is to be paid to B for life and, on B's death, the remainder is to be distributed to X (or pursuant to X's testamentary general power of appointment). Because Trust 1 and Trust 2 do not provide A and B with the contingent survivor income interests that were provided to A and B under the terms of Trust, Trust 1 and Trust 2 do not provide for the same succession of interests in the aggregate as provided by Trust. Therefore, the severance does not satisfy the requirements of this section and is not a qualified severance. Provided that Trust 1 and Trust 2 are recognized as separate trusts under applicable state law, Trust 1 and Trust 2 will be recognized as separate trusts for GST tax purposes pursuant to paragraph (h) of this section, prospectively from the date of the severance. However, Trust 1 and Trust 2 each have an inclusion ratio of .30 immediately after the severance, the same as the inclusion ratio of Trust prior to severance.

Example 13. Qualified severance following a non-qualified severance. Assume the same facts as in *Example 12*, except that, as of November 4, 2010, the trustee of Trust 1 severs Trust 1 into two trusts, Trust 3 and Trust 4, in accordance with applicable local law. The instrument severing Trust 1 provides that both resulting trusts have provisions identical to Trust 1. The terms of the instrument severing Trust 1 further provide that Trust 3 is to be funded on a pro rata basis with assets having a fair market value as of the date of severance equal to 70% of the value of Trust 1's assets on that date, and Trust 4 is to be funded with assets having a fair market value as of the date of severance equal to 30% of the value of Trust 1's assets on that date. The severance constitutes a qualified severance, provided that all other requirements of section 2642(a)(3) and this section are satisfied. Trust 3 will have an inclusion ratio of zero and Trust 4 will have an inclusion ratio of one.

(k) *Effective/applicability date.*—(1) *In general.*—Except as otherwise provided in this paragraph (k), this section applies to severances occurring on or after August 2, 2007. Paragraph (d)(7)(iii), paragraph (h), and *Examples 9, 12* and *13* of paragraph (j) of this section apply to severances occurring on or after September 2, 2008.

(2) *Transition rule.*—In the case of a qualified severance occurring after December 31, 2000, and before August 2, 2007, taxpayers may rely on any reasonable interpretation of section 2642(a)(3) as long as reasonable notice concerning the qualified severance and identification of the trusts involved has been given to the IRS. For this purpose, the proposed regulations (69 FR 51967) are treated as a reasonable interpretation of the statute. For purposes of the reporting provisions of § 26.2642-6(e), notice to the IRS should be mailed by the due date of the gift tax return (including extensions granted) for gifts made during the year in which the severance occurred. If no gift tax return is filed, notice to the IRS should be mailed by April 15th of the year immediately following the year during which the severance occurred. For severances occurring between December 31, 2000, and January 1, 2007, notification should be mailed to the IRS as soon as reasonably practicable after August 2, 2007, if sufficient notice has not already been given. [Reg. § 26.2642-6.]

☐ [*T.D.* 9348, 8-1-2007. *Amended by T.D.* 9421, 7-30-2008.]

[Reg. § 26.2651-1]

§ 26.2651-1. Generation assignment.—(a) *Special rule for persons with a deceased parent.*—(1) *In general.*—This paragraph (a) applies for purposes of determining whether a transfer to or for the benefit of an individual who is a descendant of a parent of the transferor (or the transferor's spouse or former spouse) is a generation-skipping transfer. If that individual's parent, who is a lineal descendant of the parent of the transferor (or the transferor's spouse or former spouse), is deceased at the time the transfer (from which an interest of such individual is established or derived) is subject to the tax imposed on the transferor by chapter 11 or 12 of the Internal Revenue Code, the individual is treated as if that individual were a member of the generation that is one generation below the lower of—

(i) The transferor's generation; or

(ii) The generation assignment of the individual's youngest living lineal ancestor who is also a descendant of the parent of the transferor (or the transferor's spouse or former spouse).

(2) *Special rules.*—(i) *Corresponding generation adjustment.*—If an individual's generation assignment is adjusted with respect to a transfer in accordance with paragraph (a)(1) of this section, a corresponding adjustment with respect to that transfer is made to the generation assignment of each—

(A) Spouse or former spouse of that individual;

(B) Descendant of that individual; and

(C) Spouse or former spouse of each descendant of that individual.

(ii) *Continued application of generation assignment.*—If a transfer to a trust would be a generation-skipping transfer but for paragraph (a)(1) of this section, any generation assignment determined under this paragraph (a) continues to apply in determining whether any subsequent distribution from (or termination of an interest in) the portion of the trust attributable to that transfer is a generation-skipping transfer.

(iii) *Ninety-day rule.*—For purposes of paragraph (a)(1) of this section, any individual who dies no later than 90 days after a transfer occurring by reason of the death of the transferor is treated as having predeceased the transferor.

(iv) *Local law.*—A living person is not treated as having predeceased the transferor solely by reason of a provision of applicable local law; e.g., an individual who disclaims is not treated as a predeceased parent solely because state law treats a disclaimant as having predeceased the transferor for purposes of determining the disposition of the disclaimed property.

(3) *Established or derived.*—For purposes of section 2651(e) and paragraph (a)(1) of this section, an individual's interest is established or derived at the time the transferor is subject to transfer tax on the property. See § 26.2652-1(a) for the definition of a transferor. If the same transferor, on more than one occasion, is subject to transfer tax imposed by either chapter 11 or 12 of the Internal Revenue Code on the property so transferred (whether the same property, reinvestments thereof, income thereon, or any or all of these), then the relevant time for determining whether paragraph (a)(1) of this section applies is the earliest time at which the transferor is subject to the tax imposed by either chapter 11 or 12 of the Internal Revenue Code. For purposes of section 2651(e) and paragraph (a)(1) of this section, the interest of a remainder beneficiary of a trust for which an election under section 2523(f) or section 2056(b)(7) (QTIP election) has been made will be deemed to have been established or derived, to the extent of the QTIP election, on the date as of which the value of the trust corpus is first subject to tax under section 2519 or section 2044. The preceding sentence does not apply to a trust, however, to the extent that an election under section 2652(a)(3) (reverse QTIP election) has been made for the trust because, to the extent of a reverse QTIP election, the spouse who established the trust will remain the transferor of the trust for generation-skipping transfer tax purposes.

(4) *Special rule in the case of additional contributions to a trust.*—If a transferor referred to in paragraph (a)(1) of this section contributes additional property to a trust that existed before the application of paragraph (a)(1), then the additional property is treated as being held in a separate trust for purposes of chapter 13 of the Internal Revenue Code. The provisions of § 26.2654-1(a)(2), regarding treatment as separate trusts, apply as if different transferors had contributed to the separate portions of the single trust. Additional subsequent contributions from that transferor will be added to the new share that is treated as a separate trust.

(b) *Limited application to collateral heirs.*—Paragraph (a) of this section does not apply in the case of a transfer to any individual who is not a lineal descendant of the transferor (or the transferor's spouse or former spouse) if the transferor has any living lineal descendant at the time of the transfer.

(c) *Examples.*—The following examples illustrate the provisions of this section:

Example 1. T establishes an irrevocable trust, Trust, providing that trust income is to be paid to T's grandchild, GC, for 5 years. At the end of the 5-year period or on GC's prior death, Trust is to terminate and the principal is to be distributed to GC if GC is living or to GC's children if GC has died. The transfer that occurred on the creation of the trust is subject to the tax imposed by chapter 12 of the Internal Revenue Code and, at the time of the transfer, T's child, C, who is a parent of GC, is deceased. GC is treated as a member of the generation that is one generation below T's generation. As a result, GC is not a skip person and Trust is not a skip person. Therefore, the transfer to Trust is not a direct skip. Similarly, distributions to GC during the term of Trust and at the termination of Trust will not be GSTs.

Example 2. On January 1, 2004, T transfers $100,000 to an irrevocable inter vivos trust that provides T with an annuity payable for four years or until T's prior death. The annuity satisfies the definition of a qualified interest under section 2702(b). When the trust terminates, the corpus is to be paid to T's grandchild, GC. The transfer is subject to the tax imposed by chapter 12 of the Internal Revenue Code and, at the time of the transfer, T's child, C, who is a parent of GC, is living. C dies in 2006. In this case, C was alive at the time the transfer by T was subject to the tax imposed by chapter 12 of the Internal Revenue Code. Therefore, section 2651(e) and paragraph (a)(1) of this section do not apply. When the trust subsequently terminates, the distribution to GC is a taxable termination that is subject to the GST tax to the extent the trust has an inclusion ratio greater than zero. See section 2642(a).

Example 3. T dies testate in 2002, survived by T's spouse, S, their children, C1 and C2, and C1's child, GC. Under the terms of T's will, a trust is established for the benefit of S and of T and S's descendants. Under the terms of the trust, all income is payable to S during S's lifetime and the trustee may distribute trust corpus for S's health, support and maintenance. At S's death, the corpus is to be distributed, outright, to C1 and C2. If either C1 or C2 has predeceased S, the deceased child's share of the corpus is to be distributed to that child's then-living descendants, per stirpes. The executor of T's estate makes the election under section 2056(b)(7) to treat the trust property as qualified terminable interest property (QTIP) but does not make the election under section 2652(a)(3) (reverse QTIP election). In 2003, C1 dies survived by S and GC. In 2004, S dies, and the trust terminates. The full fair market value of the trust is includible in S's gross estate under section 2044 and S becomes the transferor of the trust under section

See p. 15 for regulations not amended to reflect law changes

2652(a)(1)(A). GC's interest is considered established or derived at S's death, and because C1 is deceased at that time, GC is treated as a member of the generation that is one generation below the generation of the transferor, S. As a result, GC is not a skip person and the transfer to GC is not a direct skip.

Example 4. The facts are the same as in *Example 3.* However, the executor of T's estate makes the election under section 2652(a)(3) (reverse QTIP election) for the entire trust. Therefore, T remains the transferor because, for purposes of chapter 13 of the Internal Revenue Code, the election to be treated as qualified terminable interest property is treated as if it had not been made. In this case, GC's interest is established or derived on T's death in 2002. Because C1 was living at the time of T's death, the predeceased parent rule under section 2651(e) does not apply, even though C1 was deceased at the time the transfer from S to GC was subject to the tax under chapter 11 of the Internal Revenue Code. When the trust terminates, the distribution to GC is a taxable termination that is subject to the GST tax to the extent the trust has an inclusion ratio greater than zero. See section 2642(a).

Example 5. T establishes an irrevocable trust providing that trust income is to be paid to T's grandniece, GN, for 5 years or until GN's prior death. At the end of the 5-year period or on GN's prior death, the trust is to terminate and the principal is to be distributed to GN if living, or if GN has died, to GN's then-living descendants, per stirpes. S is a sibling of T and the parent of N. N is the parent of GN. At the time of the transfer, T has no living lineal descendant, S is living, N is deceased, and the transfer is subject to the gift tax imposed by chapter 12 of the Internal Revenue Code. GN is treated as a member of the generation that is one generation below T's generation because S, GN's youngest living lineal ancestor who is also a descendant of T's parent, is in T's generation. As a result, GN is not a skip person and the transfer to the trust is not a direct skip. In addition, distributions to GN during the term of the trust and at the termination of the trust will not be GSTs.

Example 6. On January 1, 2004, T transfers $50,000 to a great-grandniece, GGN, who is the great-grandchild of B, a brother of T. At the time of the transfer, T has no living lineal descendants and B's grandchild, GN, who is a parent of GGN and a child of B's living child, N, is deceased. GGN will be treated as a member of the generation that is one generation below the lower of T's generation or the generation assignment of GGN's youngest living lineal ancestor who is also a descendant of the parent of the transferor. In this case, N is GGN's youngest living lineal ancestor who is also a descendant of the parent of T. Because N's generation assignment is lower than T's generation, GGN will be treated as a member of the generation that is one generation below N's generation assignment (i.e., GGN will be treated as a member of her parent's generation). As a result, GGN remains a skip person and the transfer to GGN is a direct skip.

Example 7. T has a child, C. C and C's spouse, S, have a 20-year-old child, GC. C dies and S subsequently marries S2. S2 legally adopts GC. T transfers $100,000 to GC. Under section 2651(b)(1), GC is assigned to the generation that is two generations below T. However, since GC's parent, C, is deceased at the time of the transfer, GC will be treated as a member of the generation that is one generation below T. As a result, GC is not a skip person and the transfer to GC is not a direct skip.

[Reg. § 26.2651-1.]

☐ [*T.D.* 9214, 7-15-2005.]

[Reg. § 26.2651-2]

§ 26.2651-2. Individual assigned to more than 1 generation.—(a) *In general.*—Except as provided in paragraph (b) or (c) of this section, an individual who would be assigned to more than 1 generation is assigned to the youngest of the generations to which that individual would be assigned.

(b) *Exception.*—Notwithstanding paragraph (a) of this section, an adopted individual (as defined in this paragraph) will be treated as a member of the generation that is one generation below the adoptive parent for purposes of determining whether a transfer to the adopted individual from the adoptive parent (or the spouse or former spouse of the adoptive parent, or a lineal descendant of a grandparent of the adoptive parent) is subject to chapter 13 of the Internal Revenue Code. For purposes of this paragraph (b), an adopted individual is an individual who is—

(1) Legally adopted by the adoptive parent;

(2) A descendant of a parent of the adoptive parent (or the spouse or former spouse of the adoptive parent);

(3) Under the age of 18 at the time of the adoption; and

(4) Not adopted primarily for the purpose of avoiding GST tax. The determination of whether an adoption is primarily for GST tax-avoidance purposes is made based upon all of the facts and circumstances. The most significant factor is whether there is a bona fide parent/child relationship between the adoptive parent and the adopted individual, in which the adoptive parent has fully assumed all significant responsibilities for the care and raising of the adopted child. Other factors may include (but are not limited to), at the time of the adoption—

(i) The age of the adopted individual (for example, the younger the age of the adopted individual, or the age of the youngest of siblings who are all adopted together, the more likely the adoption will not be considered primarily for GST tax-avoidance purposes); and

(ii) The relationship between the adopted individual and the individual's parents (for example, objective evidence of the absence or incapacity of the parents may indicate that the adoption is not primarily for GST tax-avoidance purposes).

(c) *Special rules.*—(1) *Corresponding generation adjustment.*—If an individual's generation assignment is adjusted with respect to a transfer in accordance with paragraph (b) of this section, a corresponding adjustment with respect to that transfer is made to the generation assignment of each—

(i) Spouse or former spouse of that individual;

(ii) Descendant of that individual; and

(iii) Spouse or former spouse of each descendant of that individual.

(2) *Continued application of generation assignment.*—If a transfer to a trust would be a generation-skipping transfer but for paragraph (b) of this section, any generation assignment determined under paragraph (b) or (c) of this section continues to apply in determining whether any subsequent distribution from (or termination of an interest in) the portion of the trust attributable to that transfer is a generation-skipping transfer.

(d) *Example.*—The following example illustrates the provisions of this section:

Example. T has a child, C. C has a 20-year-old child, GC. T legally adopts GC and transfers $100,000 to GC. GC's generation assignment is determined by section 2651(b)(1) and GC is assigned to the generation that is two generations below T. In addition, because T has legally adopted GC, GC is generally treated as a child of T under state law. Under these circumstances, GC is an individual who is assigned to more than one generation and the exception in §26.2651-2(b) does not apply. Thus, the special rule under section 2651(f)(1) applies and GC is assigned to the generation that is two generations below T. GC remains a skip person with respect to T and the transfer to GC is a direct skip.

[Reg. §26.2651-2.]

□ [*T.D.* 9214, 7-15-2005.]

[Reg. §26.2651-3]

§26.2651-3. Effective dates.—(a) *In general.*—The rules of §§ 26.2651-1 and 26.2651-2 are applicable for terminations, distributions, and transfers occurring on or after July 18, 2005.

(b) *Transition rule.*—In the case of transfers occurring after December 31, 1997, and before July 18, 2005, taxpayers may rely on any reasonable interpretation of section 2651(e). For this purpose, these final regulations, as well as the proposed regulations issued on September 3, 2004 (69 FR 53862), are treated as a reasonable interpretation of the statute. [Reg. §26.2651-3.]

□ [*T.D.* 9214, 7-15-2005.]

OTHER DEFINITIONS AND SPECIAL RULES

[Reg. §26.2652-1]

§26.2652-1. Transferor defined; other definitions.—(a) *Transferor defined.*—(1) *In general.*—Except as otherwise provided in paragraph (a)(3) of this section, the individual with respect to whom property was most recently subject to Federal estate or gift tax is the transferor of that property for purposes of chapter 13. An individual is treated as transferring any property with respect to which the individual is the transferor. Thus, an individual may be a transferor even though there is no transfer of property under local law at the time the Federal estate or gift tax applies. For purposes of this paragraph, a surviving spouse is the transferor of a qualified domestic trust created by the deceased spouse that is included in the surviving spouse's gross estate, provided the trust is not subject to the election described in §26.2652-2 (reverse QTIP election). A surviving spouse is also the transferor of a qualified domestic trust created by the surviving spouse pursuant to section 2056(d)(2)(B). For generation-skipping transfer tax rules related to an ABLE account established under section 529A, see §1.529A-4 of this chapter.

(2) *Transfers subject to Federal estate or gift tax.*—For purposes of this chapter, a transfer is subject to Federal gift tax if a gift tax is imposed under section 2501(a) (without regard to exemptions, exclusions, deductions, and credits). A transfer is subject to Federal estate tax if the value of the property is includible in the decedent's gross estate as determined under section 2031 or section 2103.

(3) *Special rule for certain QTIP trusts.*—Solely for purposes of chapter 13, if a transferor of qualified terminable interest property (QTIP) elects under §26.2652-2(a) to treat the property as if the QTIP election had not been made (reverse QTIP election), the identity of the transferor of the property is determined without regard to the application of sections 2044, 2207A, and 2519.

(4) *Split-gift transfers.*—In the case of a transfer with respect to which the donor's spouse makes an election under section 2513 to treat the gift as made one-half by the spouse, the electing spouse is treated as the transferor of one-half of the entire value of the property transferred by the donor, regardless of the interest the electing spouse is actually deemed to have transferred under section 2513. The donor is treated as the transferor of one-half of the value of the entire property. See §26.2632-1(c)(5) *Example 3*, regarding allocation of GST exemption with respect to split-gift transfers subject to an ETIP.

(5) *Examples.*—The following examples illustrate the principles of this paragraph (a):

Example 1. Identity of transferor. T transfers $100,000 to a trust for the sole benefit of T's grandchild. The transfer is subject to Federal gift tax because a gift tax is imposed under section 2501(a) (without regard to exemptions, deductions, and credits). Thus, for purposes of chapter 13, T is the transferor of the $100,000. It is immaterial that a portion of the transfer is excluded from the total amount of T's taxable gift by reason of section 2503(b).

Example 2. Gift splitting and identity of transferor. The facts are the same as in *Example 1,* except T's spouse, S, consents under section 2513 to split the gift with T. For purposes of chapter 13, S and T are each treated as a transferor of $50,000 to the trust.

Example 3. Change of transferor on subsequent transfer tax event. T transfers $100,000 to a trust providing that all the net trust income is to be paid to T's spouse, S, for S's lifetime. T elects under section 2523(f) to treat the transfer as a transfer of qualified terminable interest property, and T does not make the reverse QTIP election under section 2652(a)(3). On S's death, the trust property is included in S's gross estate under section 2044. Thus, S becomes the transferor at the time of S's death.

Example 4. Effect of transfer of an interest in trust on identity of the transferor. T transfers $100,000 to a trust providing that all of the net income is to be paid to T's child, C, for C's lifetime. At C's death, the trust property is to be paid to T's grandchild. C transfers the income interest to X, an unrelated party, in a transfer that is a completed transfer for Federal gift tax purposes. Because C's transfer is a transfer of a term interest in the trust that does not affect the rights of other parties with respect to the trust property, T remains the transferor with respect to the trust.

Example 5. Effect of lapse of withdrawal right on identity of transferor. T transfers $10,000 to a new trust providing that the trust income is to be paid to T's child, C, for C's life and, on the death of C, the trust principal is to be paid to T's grandchild, GC. The trustee has discretion to distribute principal for GC's benefit during C's lifetime. C has a right to withdraw $10,000 from the trust for a 60-day period following the transfer. Thereafter, the power lapses. C does not exercise the withdrawal right. The transfer by T is subject to Federal gift tax because a gift tax is imposed under section 2501 (without regard to exemptions, deductions, and credits) and, thus, T is treated as having transferred the entire $10,000 to the trust. On the lapse of the withdrawal right, C becomes a transferor to the extent C is treated as having made a completed transfer for purposes of chapter 12. Therefore, except to the extent that the amount with respect to which the power of withdrawal lapses exceeds the greater of $5,000 or 5% of the value of the trust property, T remains the transferor of the trust property for purposes of chapter 13.

Example 6. Effect of reverse QTIP election on identity of the transferor. T establishes a testamentary trust having a principal of $500,000. Under the terms of the trust, all trust income is payable to T's surviving spouse, S, during S's lifetime. T's executor makes an election to treat the trust property as qualified terminable interest property and also makes the reverse QTIP election. For purposes of chapter 13, T is the transferor with respect to the trust. On S's death, the then full fair market value of the trust is includible in S's gross estate under section 2044. However, because of the reverse QTIP election, S does not become the transferor with respect to the trust; T continues to be the transferor.

Example 7. Effect of reverse QTIP election on constructive additions. The facts are the same as in *Example 6,* except the inclusion of the QTIP trust in S's gross estate increased the Federal estate tax liability of S's estate by $200,000. The estate does not exercise the right of recovery from the trust granted under section 2207A. Under local law, the beneficiaries of S's residuary estate (which bears all estate taxes under the will) could compel the executor to exercise the right of recovery but do not do so. Solely for purposes of chapter 13, the beneficiaries of the residuary estate are not treated as having made an addition to the trust by reason of their failure to exercise their right of recovery. Because of the reverse QTIP election, for GST purposes, the trust property is not treated as includible in S's gross estate and, under those circumstances, no right of recovery exists.

Example 8. Effect of reverse QTIP election on constructive additions. S, the surviving spouse of T, dies testate. At the time of S's death, S was the beneficiary of a trust with respect to which T's executor made a QTIP election under section 2056(b)(7). Thus, the trust is includible in S's gross estate under section 2044. T's executor also made the reverse QTIP election with respect to the trust. S's will provides that all death taxes payable with respect to the trust are payable from S's residuary estate. Since the transferor of the property is determined without regard to section 2044 and section 2207A, S is not treated as making a constructive addition to the trust by reason of the tax apportionment clause in S's will.

Example 9. Split-gift transfers. T transfers $100,000 to an inter vivos trust that provides T with an annuity payable for ten years or until T's prior death. The annuity satisfies the definition of a qualified interest under section 2702(b). When the trust terminates, the corpus is to be paid to T's grandchild, GC. T's spouse, S, consents under section 2513 to have the gift treated as made one-half by S. Under section 2513, only the actuarial value of the gift to GC is eligible to be treated as made one-half by S. However, because S is treated as the donor of one-half of the gift to GC, S becomes the transferor of one-half of the entire trust ($50,000) for purposes of Chapter 13.

(b) *Trust defined.*—(1) *In general.*—A trust includes any arrangement (other than an estate) that has substantially the same effect as a trust. Thus, for example, arrangements involving life estates and remainders, estates for years, and insurance and annuity contracts are trusts. Generally, a transfer as to which the identity of the transferee is contingent upon the occurrence of an event is a transfer in trust; however, a transfer of property included in the transferor's gross estate, as to which the identity of the transferee is contingent upon an event that must occur within 6 months of the transferor's death, is not considered a transfer in trust solely by reason of the existence of the contingency.

(2) *Examples.*—The following examples illustrate the provisions of this paragraph (b):

Example 1. Uniform gifts to minors transfers. T transfers cash to an account in the name of T's child, C, as custodian for C's child, GC (who is a minor), under a state statute substantially similar to the Uniform Gifts to Minors Act. For purposes of chapter 13, the transfer to the custodial account is treated as a transfer to a trust.

Example 2. Contingent transfers. T bequeaths $200,000 to T's child, C, provided that if C does not survive T by more than 6 months, the bequest is payable to T's grandchild, GC. C dies 4 months after T. The bequest is not a transfer in trust because the contingency that determines the recipient of the bequest must occur within 6 months of T's death. The bequest to GC is a direct skip.

Example 3. Contingent transfers. The facts are the same as in *Example 2,* except C must survive T by 18 months to take the bequest. The bequest is a transfer in trust for purposes of chapter 13, and the death of C is a taxable termination.

(c) *Trustee defined.*—The trustee of a trust is the person designated as trustee under local law or, if no such person is so designated, the person in actual or constructive possession of property held in trust.

(d) *Executor defined.*—For purposes of chapter 13, the executor is the executor or administrator of the decedent's estate. However, if no executor or administrator is appointed, qualified or acting within the United States, the executor is the fiduciary who is primarily responsible for payment of the decedent's debts and expenses. If there is no such executor, administrator or fiduciary, the executor is the person in actual or constructive possession of the largest portion of the value of the decedent's gross estate.

(e) *Interest in trust.*—See § 26.2612-1(e) for the definition of *interest in trust.* [Reg. § 26.2652-1.]

☐ [*T.D.* 8644, 12-26-95. *Amended by T.D.* 8720, 5-19-97 *and T.D.* 9923, 11-18-2020.]

[Reg. § 26.2652-2]

§ 26.2652-2. Special election for qualified terminable interest property.—(a) *In general.*—If an election is made to treat property as qualified terminable interest property (QTIP) under section 2523(f) or section 2056(b)(7), the person making the election may, for purposes of chapter 13, elect to treat the property as if the QTIP election had not been made (reverse QTIP election). An election under this section is irrevocable. An election under this section is not effective unless it is made with respect to all of the property in the trust to which the QTIP election applies. See, however, § 26.2654-1(b)(1). Property that qualifies for a deduction under section 2056(b)(5) is not eligible for the election under this section.

(b) *Time and manner of making election.*—An election under this section is made on the return on which the QTIP election is made. If a protective QTIP election is made, no election under this section is effective unless a protective reverse QTIP election is also made.

(c) *Transitional rule.*—If a reverse QTIP election is made with respect to a trust prior to December 27, 1995, and GST exemption has been allocated to that trust, the transferor (or the transferor's executor) may elect to treat the trust as two separate trusts, one of which has a zero inclusion ratio by reason of the transferor's GST exemption previously allocated to the trust. The separate trust with the zero inclusion ratio consists of that fractional share of the value of the entire trust equal to the value of the nontax portion of the trust under § 26.2642-4(a). The reverse QTIP election is treated as applying only to the trust with the zero inclusion ratio. An election under this paragraph (c) is made by attaching a statement to a copy of the return on which the reverse QTIP election was made under section 2652(a)(3). The statement must indicate that an election is being made to treat the trust as two separate trusts and must identify the values of the two separate trusts. The statement is to be filed in the same place in which the original return was filed and must be filed before June 24, 1996. A trust subject to the election described in this paragraph is treated as a trust that was created by two transferors. See § 26.2654-1(a)(2) for special rules involving trusts with multiple transferors.

(d) *Examples.*—The following examples illustrate the provisions of this section:

Example 1. Special (reverse QTIP) election under section 2652(a)(3). T transfers $1,000,000 to a trust providing that all trust income is to be paid to T's spouse, S, for S's lifetime. On S's death, the trust principal is payable to GC, a grandchild of S and T. T elects to treat all of the transfer as a transfer of QTIP and also makes the reverse QTIP election for all of the property. Because of the reverse QTIP election, T continues to be treated as the transferor of the property after S's death for purposes of chapter 13. A taxable termination rather than a direct skip occurs on S's death.

Example 2. Election under transition rule. In 1994, T died leaving $4 million in trust for the benefit of T's surviving spouse, S. On January 16, 1995, T's executor filed T's Form 706 on which the executor elects to treat the entire trust as qualified terminable interest property. The executor also makes a reverse QTIP election. The reverse QTIP election is effective with respect to the entire trust even though T's executor could allocate only $1 million of GST exemption to the trust. T's executor may elect to treat the trust as two separate trusts, one having a value of 25% of the value of the single trust and an inclusion ratio of zero, but only if the election is made prior to June 24, 1996. If the executor makes the transitional election, the other separate trust, having a value of 75% of the value of the single trust and an inclusion ratio of one, is not treated as subject to the reverse QTIP election.

Example 3. Denominator of the applicable fraction of QTIP trust. T bequeaths $1,500,000 to a trust in which T's surviving spouse, S, receives an income interest for life. Upon the death of S, the property is to remain in trust for the benefit of C, the child of T and S. Upon C's death, the trust is to terminate and the trust property paid to the descendants of C. The bequest qualifies for the estate tax marital deduction under section 2056(b)(7) as QTIP. The executor does not make the reverse QTIP election under section 2652(a)(3). As a result, S becomes the transferor of the trust at S's death when the value of the property in the QTIP trust is included in S's gross estate under section 2044. For purposes of computing the applicable fraction with respect to the QTIP trust upon S's death, the denominator of the fraction is reduced by any Federal estate tax (whether imposed under section 2001, 2101 or 2056A(b)) and State death tax attributable to the trust property that is actually recovered from the trust. [Reg. § 26.2652-2.]

☐ [*T.D.* 8644, 12-26-95.]

[Reg. § 26.2653-1]

§ 26.2653-1. Taxation of multiple skips.—(a) *General rule.*—If property is held in trust immediately after a GST, solely for purposes of determining whether future events involve a skip person, the transferor is thereafter deemed to occupy the generation immediately above the highest generation of any person holding an interest in the trust immediately after the transfer. If no person holds an interest in the trust immediately after the GST, the transferor is treated as occupying the generation above the highest generation of any person in existence at the time of the GST who then occupies the highest generation level of any person who may subsequently hold an interest in the trust. See § 26.2612-1(e) for rules determining when a person has an interest in property held in trust.

(b) *Examples.*—The following examples illustrate the provisions of this section:

Example 1. T transfers property to an irrevocable trust for the benefit of T's grandchild, GC, and great-grandchild, GGC. During GC's life, the trust income may be distributed to GC and GGC in the trustee's absolute discretion. At GC's death, the trust property passes to GGC. Both GC and GGC have an interest in the trust for purposes of chapter 13. The transfer by T to the trust is a direct skip, and the property is held in trust immediately after the transfer. After the direct skip, the transferor is treated as being one generation above GC, the highest generation individual having an interest in the trust. Therefore, GC is no longer a skip person and distributions to GC are not taxable distributions. However, because GGC occupies a generation that is two generations below the deemed generation of T, GGC is a skip person and distributions of trust income to GGC are taxable distributions.

Example 2. T transfers property to an irrevocable trust providing that the income is to be paid to T's child, C, for life. At C's death, the trust income is to be accumulated for 10 years and added to principal. At the end of the 10-year accumulation period, the trust income is to be paid to T's grandchild, GC, for life. Upon GC's death, the trust property is to be paid to T's great-grandchild, GGC, or to GGC's estate. A GST occurs at C's death. Immediately after C's death and during the 10-year accumulation period, no person has an interest in the trust within the meaning of section 2652(c) and § 26.2612-1(e) because no one can receive current distributions of income or principal. Immediately after C's death, T is treated as occupying the generation above the generation of GC (the trust beneficiary in existence at the time of the GST who then occupies the highest generation level of any person who may subsequently hold an interest in the trust). Thus, subsequent income distributions to GC are not taxable distributions. [Reg. § 26.2653-1.]

☐ [*T.D.* 8644, 12-26-95.]

[Reg. § 26.2654-1]

§ 26.2654-1. Certain trusts treated as separate trusts.—(a) *Single trust treated as separate trusts.*—(1) *Substantially separate and independent shares.*—(i) *In general.*—If a single trust consists solely of substantially separate and independent shares for different beneficiaries, the share attributable to each beneficiary (or group of beneficiaries) is treated as a separate trust for purposes of Chapter 13. The phrase "substantially separate and independent shares" generally has the same meaning as provided in § 1.663(c)-3. However, except as provided in paragraph (a)(1)(iii) of this section, a portion of a trust is not a separate share unless such share exists from and at all times after the creation of the trust. For purposes of this paragraph (a)(1), a trust is treated as created at the date of death of the grantor if the trust is includible in its entirety in the grantor's gross estate for Federal estate tax purposes. Further, except with respect to shares or trusts that are treated as separate trusts under local law, treatment of a single trust as separate trusts under this paragraph (a)(1) does not permit treatment of those portions as separate trusts for purposes of filing returns and payment of tax or for purposes of computing any other tax imposed under the Internal Revenue Code. Also, additions to, and distributions from, such trusts are allocated pro rata among the separate trusts, unless the governing instrument expressly provides otherwise. See § 26.2642-6 and paragraph (b) of this section regarding the treatment, for purposes of Chapter 13, of separate trusts resulting from the discretionary severance of a single trust.

(ii) *Certain pecuniary amounts.*—For purposes of this section, if a person holds the current right to receive a mandatory (i.e., nondiscretionary and noncontingent) payment of a pecuniary amount at the death of the transferor from an inter vivos trust that is includible in the transferor's gross estate, or a testamentary trust, the pecuniary amount is a separate and independent share if—

(A) The trustee is required to pay appropriate interest (as defined in § 26.2642-2(b)(4)(i) and (ii)) to the person; and

(B) If the pecuniary amount is payable in kind on the basis of value other than the date of distribution value of the assets, the trustee is required to allocate assets to the pecuniary payment in a manner that fairly reflects net appreciation or depreciation in the value of the assets in the fund available to pay the pecuniary amount measured from the valuation date to the date of payment.

(iii) *Mandatory severances.*—For purposes of this section, if the governing instrument of a trust requires the division or severance of a single trust into separate trusts upon the future occurrence of a particular event not within the discretion of the trustee or any other person, and if the trusts resulting from such a division or severance are recognized as separate trusts under applicable state law, then each resulting trust is treated as a separate trust for purposes of Chapter 13. For this purpose, the rules of paragraph (b)(1)(ii)(C) of this section apply with respect to the severance and funding of the trusts. Similarly, if the governing instrument requires the division of a single trust into separate shares under the circumstances described in this paragraph, each such share is treated as a separate trust for purposes of Chapter 13. The post-severance treatment of the resulting shares or trusts as separate trusts for GST tax purposes generally permits the allocation of GST tax exemption, the making of various elections permitted for GST tax purposes, and the occurrence of a taxable distribution or termination with regard to a particular resulting share or trust, with no GST tax impact on any other trust or share resulting from that severance. The treatment of a single trust as separate trusts under this paragraph (a)(1), however, does not permit treatment of those portions as separate trusts for purposes of filing returns and payment of tax or for purposes of computing any other tax imposed under the Internal Revenue Code, if those portions are not treated as separate trusts under local law. Also, additions to, and distributions from, such trusts are allocated pro rata among the separate trusts, unless the governing instrument expressly provides otherwise. Each separate share and each trust resulting from a mandatory division or severance described in this paragraph will have the same inclusion ratio immediately after the severance as that of the original trust immediately before the division or severance.

(2) *Multiple transferors with respect to single trust.*—(i) *In general.*—If there is more than one transferor with respect to a trust, the portions of the trust attributable to the different transferors are treated as separate trusts for purposes of chapter 13. Treatment of a single trust as separate trusts under this paragraph (a)(2) does not permit treatment of those portions as separate trusts for purposes of filing returns and payment of tax or for purposes of computing any other tax imposed under the Internal Revenue Code. Also, additions to, and distributions from, such trusts are allocated pro rata among the separate trusts unless otherwise expressly provided in the governing instrument.

(ii) *Addition by a transferor.*—If an individual makes an addition to a trust of which the individual is not the sole transferor, the portion of the single trust attributable to each separate trust is determined by multiplying the fair market value of the single trust immediately after the contribution by a fraction. The numerator of the fraction is the value of the separate trust immediately after the contribution. The denominator of the fraction is the fair market value of all the property in the single trust immediately after the transfer.

(3) *Severance of a single trust.*—A single trust treated as separate trusts under paragraphs (a)(1) or (2) of this section may be divided at any time into separate trusts to reflect that treatment. For this purpose, the rules of paragraph (b)(1)(ii)(C) of this section apply with respect to the severance and funding of the severed trusts.

(4) *Allocation of exemption.*—(i) *In general.*—With respect to a separate share treated as a separate trust under paragraph (a)(1) or (2) of this section, an individual's GST exemption is allocated to the separate trust. See § 26.2632-1 for rules concerning the allocation of GST exemption.

(ii) *Automatic allocation to direct skips.*—If the transfer is a direct skip to a trust that occurs during the transferor's lifetime and is treated as a transfer to separate trusts under paragraphs (a)(1) or (a)(2) of this section, the transferor's GST exemption not previously allocated is automatically allocated on a pro rata basis among the separate trusts. The transferor may prevent an automatic allocation of GST exemption to a separate share of a single trust by describing on a timely-filed United States Gift (and Generation-Skipping Transfer) Tax Return (Form 709) the transfer and the extent to which the automatic allocation is not to apply to a particular share. See § 26.2632-1(b) for rules for avoiding the automatic allocation of GST exemption.

(5) *Examples.*—The following examples illustrate the principles of this section (a):

Example 1. Separate shares as separate trusts. T transfers $100,000 to a trust under which income is to be paid in equal shares for 10 years to T's child, C, and T's grandchild, GC (or their respective estates). The trust does not permit distributions of principal during the term of the trust. At the end of the 10-year term, the trust principal is to be distributed to C and GC in equal shares. The shares of C and GC in the trust are separate and independent and, therefore, are treated as separate trusts. The result would not be the same if the trust permitted distributions of principal unless the distributions could only be made from a one-half separate share of the initial trust principal and the distributee's future rights with respect to the trust are correspondingly reduced. T may allocate part of T's GST exemption under section 2632(a) to the share held for the benefit of GC.

Example 2. Separate share rule inapplicable. The facts are the same as in *Example 1,* except the trustee holds the discretionary power to distribute the income in any proportion between C and GC during the last year of the trust. The shares of C and GC in the trust are not separate and independent shares throughout the entire term of the trust and, therefore, are not treated as separate trusts for purposes of chapter 13.

Example 3. Pecuniary payment as separate share. T creates a lifetime revocable trust providing that on T's death $500,000 is payable to T's spouse, S, with the balance of the principal to be held for the benefit of T's grandchildren. The value of the trust is includible in T's gross estate upon T's death. Under the terms of the trust, the payment to S is required to be made in cash, and under local law S is entitled to receive interest on the payment at an annual rate of 6 percent, commencing immediately upon T's death. For purposes of chapter 13, the trust is treated as created at T's death, and the $500,000 payable to S from the trust is treated as a separate share. The result would be the same if the payment to S could be satisfied using noncash assets at their value on the date of distribution. Further, the result would be the same if the decedent's probate estate poured over to the revocable trust on the decedent's death and was then distributed in accordance with the terms of the trust.

Example 4. Pecuniary payment not treated as separate share. The facts are the same as in *Example 3,* except the bequest to S is to be paid in noncash assets valued at their values as finally determined for Federal estate tax purposes. Neither the trust instrument nor local law requires that the assets distributed in satisfaction of the bequest fairly reflect net appreciation or depreciation in all the assets from which the bequest may be funded. S's $500,000 bequest is not treated as a separate share and the trust is treated as a single trust for purposes of chapter 13.

Example 5. Multiple transferors to single trust. A transfers $100,000 to an irrevocable generation-skipping trust; B simultaneously transfers $50,000 to the same trust. As of the time of the transfers, the single trust is treated as two trusts for purposes of chapter 13. Because A contributed 2/3 of the value of the initial corpus, 2/3 of the single trust principal is treated as a separate trust created by A. Similarly, because B contributed 1/3 of the value of the initial corpus, 1/3 of the single trust is treated as a separate trust created by B. A or B may allocate their GST exemption under section 2632(a) to the respective separate trusts.

Example 6. Additional contributions. A transfers $100,000 to an irrevocable generation-skipping trust; B simultaneously transfers $50,000 to the same trust. When the value of the single trust has increased to $180,000, A contributes an additional $60,000 to the trust. At the time of the additional contribution, the portion of the single trust attributable to each grantor's separate trust must be redetermined. The portion of the single trust attributable to A's separate trust immediately after the contribution is 3/4 (((2/3 x $180,000) + $60,000)/$240,000). The portion attributable to B's separate trust after A's addition is 1/4.

Example 7. Distributions from a separate share. The facts are the same as in *Example 6,* except that, after A's second contribution, $50,000 is distributed to a beneficiary of the trust. Absent a provision in the trust instrument that charges the distribution against the contribution of either A or B, 3/4 of the distribution is treated as made from the separate trust of which A is the transferor and 1/4 from the separate trust of which B is the transferor.

Example 8. Subsequent mandatory division into separate trusts. T creates an irrevocable trust that provides the trustee with the discretionary power to distribute income or corpus to T's children and grandchildren. The trust provides that, when T's youngest child reaches age 21, the trust will be divided into separate shares, one share for each child of T. The income from a respective child's share will be paid to the child during the child's life, with the remainder passing on the child's death to such child's children (grandchildren of T). The separate shares that come into existence when the youngest child reaches age 21 will be recognized as of that date as separate trusts for purposes of Chapter 13. The inclusion ratio of the separate trusts will be identical to the inclusion ratio of the trust before the severance. Any allocation of GST tax exemption to the trust after T's youngest child reaches age 21 may be made to any one or more of the separate shares. The result would be the same if the trust instrument provided that the trust was to be divided into separate trusts when T's youngest child reached age 21, provided that the severance and funding of the separate trusts meets the requirements of this section.

(b) *Division of a trust included in the gross estate.*—(1) *In general.*—The severance of a trust that is included in the transferor's gross estate (or created under the transferor's will) into two or more trusts is recognized for purposes of chapter 13 if—

(i) The trust is severed pursuant to a direction in the governing instrument providing that the trust is to be divided upon the death of the transferor; or

(ii) The governing instrument does not require or otherwise direct severance but the trust is severed pursuant to discretionary authority granted either under the governing instrument or under local law; and

(A) The terms of the new trusts provide in the aggregate for the same succession of interests and beneficiaries as are provided in the original trust;

(B) The severance occurs (or a reformation proceeding, if required, is commenced) prior to the date prescribed for filing the Federal estate tax return (including extensions actually granted) for the estate of the transferor; and

(C) Either—

(1) The new trusts are severed on a fractional basis. If severed on a fractional basis, the separate trusts need not be funded with a pro rata portion of each asset held by the undivided trust. The trusts may be funded on a nonpro rata basis provided funding is based on either the fair market value of the assets on the date of funding or in a manner that fairly reflects the net appreciation or depreciation in the value of the assets measured from the valuation date to the date of funding; or

(2) If the severance is required (by the terms of the governing instrument) to be made on the basis of a pecuniary amount, the pecuniary payment is satisfied in a manner that would meet the requirements of paragraph (a)(1)(ii) of this section if it were paid to an individual.

(2) *Special rule*.—If a court order severing the trust has not been issued at the time the Federal estate tax return is filed, the executor must indicate on a statement attached to the return that a proceeding has been commenced to sever the trust and describe the manner in which the trust is proposed to be severed. A copy of the petition or other instrument used to commence the proceeding must also be attached to the return. If the governing instrument of a trust or local law authorizes the severance of the trust, a severance pursuant to that authorization is treated as meeting the requirement of paragraph (b)(1)(ii)(B) of this section if the executor indicates on the Federal estate tax return that separate trusts will be created (or funded) and clearly sets forth the manner in which the trust is to be severed and the separate trusts funded.

(3) *Allocation of exemption*.—An individual's GST exemption under § 2632 may be allocated to the separate trusts created pursuant to this section at the discretion of the executor or trustee.

(4) *Examples*.—The following examples illustrate the provisions of this section (b):

Example 1. Severance of single trust. T's will establishes a testamentary trust providing that income is to be paid to T's spouse for life. At the spouse's death, one-half of the corpus is to be paid to T's child, C, or C's estate (if C fails to survive the spouse) and one-half of the corpus is to be paid to T's grandchild, GC, or GC's estate (if GC fails to survive the spouse). If the requirements of paragraph (b) of this section are otherwise satisfied, T's executor may divide the testamentary trust equally into two separate trusts, one trust providing an income interest to spouse for life with remainder to C, and the other trust with an income interest to spouse for life with remainder to GC. Furthermore, if the requirements of paragraph (b) of this section are satisfied, the executor or trustee may further divide the trust for the benefit of GC. GST exemption may be allocated to any of the divided trusts.

Example 2. Severance of revocable trust. T creates an inter vivos revocable trust providing that, at T's death and after payment of all taxes and administration expenses, the remaining corpus will be divided into two trusts. One trust, for the benefit of T's spouse, is to be funded with the smallest amount that, if qualifying for the marital deduction, will reduce the estate tax to zero. The other trust, for the benefit of T's descendants, is to be funded with the balance of the revocable trust corpus. The trust corpus is includible in T's gross estate. Each trust is recognized as a separate trust for purposes of chapter 13.

Example 3. Formula severance. T's will establishes a testamentary marital trust (Trust) that meets the requirements of qualified terminable interest property (QTIP) if an election under section 2056(b)(7) is made. Trust provides that all trust income is to be paid to T's spouse for life. On the spouse's death, the trust corpus is to be held in further trust for the benefit of T's then-living descendants. On T's date of death in January of 2004, T's unused GST tax exemption is $1,200,000, and T's will includes $200,000 of bequests to T's grandchildren. Prior to the due date for filing the Form 706, "United States Estate (and Generation-Skipping Transfer) Tax Return," for T's estate, T's executor, pursuant to applicable state law, divides Trust into two separate trusts, Trust 1 and Trust 2. Trust 1 is to be funded with that fraction of the Trust assets, the numerator of which is $1,000,000, and the denominator of which is the value of the Trust assets as finally determined for federal estate tax purposes. Trust 2 is to be funded with that fraction of the Trust assets, the numerator of which is the excess of the Trust assets over $1,000,000, and the denominator of which is the value of the Trust assets as finally determined for federal estate tax purposes. On the Form 706 filed for the estate, T's executor makes a QTIP election under section 2056(b)(7) with respect to Trust 1 and Trust 2 and a "reverse" QTIP election under section 2652(a)(3) with respect to Trust 1. Further, T's executor allocates $200,000 of T's available GST tax exemption to the bequests to T's grandchildren, and the balance of T's exemption ($1,000,000) to Trust 1. If the requirements of paragraph (b) of this section are otherwise satisfied, Trust 1 and Trust 2 are recognized as separate trusts for GST tax purposes. Accordingly, the "reverse" QTIP election and allocation of GST tax exemption with respect to Trust 1 are recognized and effective for generation-skipping transfer tax purposes.

(c) *Cross reference*.—For rules applicable to the qualified severance of trusts (whether or not includible in the transferor's gross estate), see § 26.2642-6.

(d) *Effective date.*—Paragraph (a)(1)(i), paragraph (a)(1)(iii), and *Example* 8 of paragraph (a)(5) apply to severances occurring on or after September 2, 2008. [Reg. § 26.2654-1.]

☐ [*T.D.* 8644, 12-26-95. *Amended by T.D.* 9348, 8-1-2007 *and T.D.* 9421, 7-30-2008.]

ADMINISTRATION

[Reg. § 26.2662-1]

§ 26.2662-1. Generation-skipping transfer tax return requirements.—(a) *In general.*—Chapter 13 imposes a tax on generation-skipping transfers(as defined in section 2611). The requirements relating to the return of tax depend on the type of generation-skipping transfer involved. This section contains rules for filing the required tax return. Paragraph (c)(2) of this section provides special rules concerning the return requirements for generation-skipping transfers pursuant to certain trust arrangements (as defined in paragraph (c)(2)(ii) of this section), such as life insurance policies and annuities.

(b) *Form of return.*—(1) *Taxable distributions.*—Form 706GS(D) must be filed in accordance with its instructions for any taxable distribution (as defined in section 2612(b)). The trust involved in a transfer described in the preceding sentence must file Form 706GS(D-1) in accordance with its instructions. A copy of Form 706GS(D-1) shall be sent to each distributee.

(2) *Taxable terminations.*—Form 706GS(T) must be filed in accordance with its instructions for any taxable termination (as defined in section 2612(a)).

(3) *Direct skip.*—(i) *Inter vivos direct skips.*—Form 709 must be filed in accordance with its instructions for any direct skip (as defined in section 2612(c)) that is subject to chapter 12 and occurs during the life of the transferor.

(ii) *Direct skips occurring at death.*—(A) *In general.*—Form 706 or Form 706NA must be filed in accordance with its instructions for any direct skips (as defined in section 2612(c)) that are subject to chapter 11 and occur at the death of the decedent.

(B) *Direct skips payable from a trust.*—Schedule R-1 of Form 706 must be filed in accordance with its instructions for any direct skip from a trust if such direct skip is subject to chapter 11. See paragraph (c)(2) of this section for special rules relating to the person liable for tax and required to make the return under certain circumstances.

(c) *Person liable for tax and required to make return.*—(1) *In general.*—Except as otherwise provided in this section, the following person is liable for the tax imposed by section 2601 and must make the required tax return—

(i) The transferee in a taxable distribution (as defined in section 2612(b));

(ii) The trustee in the case of a taxable termination (as defined in section 2612(a));

(iii) The transferor (as defined in section 2652(a)(1)(B)) in the case of an inter vivos direct skip (as defined in section 2612(c));

(iv) The trustee in the case of a direct skip from a trust or with respect to property that continues to be held in trust; or

(v) The executor in the case of a direct skip (other than a direct skip described in paragraph (c)(1)(iv) of this section) if the transfer is subject to chapter 11. See paragraph (c)(2) of this section for special rules relating to direct skips to or from certain trust arrangements (as defined in paragraph (c)(2)(ii) of this section).

(2) *Special rule for direct skips occurring at death with respect to property held in trust arrangements.*—(i) *In general.*—In the case of certain property held in a trust arrangement (as defined in paragraph (c)(2)(ii) of this section) at the date of death of the transferor, the person who is required to make the return and who is liable for the tax imposed by chapter 13 is determined under paragraphs (c)(2)(iii) and (iv) of this section.

(ii) *Trust arrangement defined.*—For purposes of this section, the term *trust arrangement* includes any arrangement (other than an estate) which, although not an explicit trust, has the same effect as an explicit trust. For purposes of this section, the term "explicit trust" means a trust described in § 301.7701-4(a).

(iii) *Executor's liability in the case of transfers with respect to decedents dying on or after June 24, 1996, if the transfer is less than $250,000.*—In the case of a direct skip occurring at death, the executor of the decedent's estate is liable for the tax imposed on that direct skip by chapter 13 and is required to file Form 706 or Form 706NA (and not Schedule R-1 of Form 706) if, at the date of the decedent's death—

(A) The property involved in the direct skip is held in a trust arrangement; and

(B) The total value of the property involved in direct skips with respect to the trustee of that trust arrangement is less than $250,000.

(iv) *Executor's liability in the case of transfers with respect to decedents dying prior to June 24, 1996, if the transfer is less than $100,000.*—In the case of a direct skip occurring at death with respect to a decedent dying prior to June 24, 1996, the rule in paragraph (c)(2)(iii) of this section that imposes liability upon the executor applies only if the property involved in the direct skip with respect to the trustee of the trust arrangement, in the aggregate, is less than $100,000.

(v) *Executor's right of recovery.*—In cases where the rules of paragraphs (c)(2)(iii) and (iv) of this section impose liability for the generation-skipping transfer tax on the executor, the executor is entitled to recover from the trustee (if the property continues to be held in trust) or from the recipient of the property (in the case of a transfer from a trust), the generation-skipping transfer tax attributable to the transfer.

(vi) *Examples.*—The following examples illustrate the application of this paragraph (c)(2) with respect to decedents dying on or after June 24, 1996:

Example 1. Insurance proceeds less than $250,000. On August 1, 1997, T, the insured under an insurance policy, died. The proceeds ($200,000) were includible in T's gross estate for Federal estate tax purposes. T's grandchild, GC, was named the sole beneficiary of the policy. The insurance policy is treated as a trust under section 2652(b)(1), and the payment of the proceeds to GC is a transfer from a trust for purposes of chapter 13. Therefore, the payment of the proceeds to GC is a direct skip. Since the proceeds from the policy ($200,000) are less than $250,000, the executor is liable for the tax imposed by chapter 13 and is required to file Form 706.

Example 2. Aggregate insurance proceeds of $250,000 or more. Assume the same facts as in *Example 1*, except T is the insured under two insurance policies issued by the same insurance company. The proceeds ($150,000) from each policy are includible in T's gross estate for Federal estate tax purposes. T's grandchild, GC1, was named the sole beneficiary of Policy 1, and T's other grandchild, GC2, was named the sole beneficiary of Policy 2. GC1 and GC2 are skip persons (as defined in section 2613). Therefore, the payments of the proceeds are direct skips. Since the total value of the policies ($300,000) exceeds $250,000, the insurance company is liable for the tax imposed by chapter 13 and is required to file Schedule R-1 of Form 706.

Example 3. Insurance proceeds of $250,000 or more held by insurance company. On August 1, 1997, T, the insured under an insurance policy, dies. The policy provides that the insurance company shall make monthly payments of $750 to GC, T's grandchild, for life with the remainder payable to T's great grandchild, GGC. The face value of the policy is $300,000. Since the proceeds continue to be held by the insurance company (the trustee), the proceeds are treated as if they were transferred to a trust for purposes of chapter 13. The trust is a skip person (as defined in section 2613(a)(2)) and the transfer is a direct skip. Since the total value of the policy ($300,000) exceeds $250,000, the insurance company is liable for the tax imposed by chapter 13 and is required to file Schedule R-1 of Form 706.

Example 4. Insurance proceeds less than $250,000 held by insurance company. Assume the same facts as in *Example 3*, except the policy provides that the insurance company shall make monthly payments of $500 to GC and that the face value of the policy is $200,000. The transfer is a transfer to a trust for purposes of chapter 13. However, since the total value of the policy ($200,000) is less than $250,000, the executor is liable for the tax imposed by chapter 13 and is required to file Form 706.

Example 5. On August 1, 1997, A, the insured under a life insurance policy, dies. The insurance proceeds on A's life that are payable under policies issued by Company X are in the aggregate amount of $200,000 and are includible in A's gross estate. Because the proceeds are includible in A's gross estate, the generation-skipping transfer that occurs upon A's death, if any, will be a direct skip rather than a taxable distribution or a taxable termination. Accordingly, because the aggregate amount of insurance proceeds with respect to Company X is less than $250,000, Company X may pay the proceeds without regard to whether the beneficiary is a skip person in relation to the decedent-transferor.

(3) *Limitation on personal liability of trustee.*—Except as provided in paragraph (c)(3)(iii) of this section, a trustee is not personally liable for any increases in the tax imposed by section 2601 which is attributable to the fact that—

(i) A transfer is made to the trust during the life of the transferor for which a gift tax return is not filed; or

(ii) The inclusion ratio with respect to the trust, determined by reference to the transferor's gift tax return, is erroneous, the actual inclusion ratio being greater than the reported inclusion ratio.

(iii) This paragraph (c)(3) does not apply if the trustee has or is deemed to have knowledge of facts sufficient to reasonably conclude that a gift tax return was required to be filed or that the inclusion ratio is erroneous. A trustee is deemed to have knowledge of such facts if the trustee's agent, employee, partner, or co-trustee has knowledge of such facts.

(4) *Exceptions.*—(i) *Legal or mental incapacity.*—If a distributee is legally or mentally incapable of making a return, the return may be made for the distributee by the distributee's guardian or, if no guardian has been appointed, by a person charged with the care of the distributee's person or property.

(ii) *Returns made by fiduciaries.*—See section 6012(b) for a fiduciary's responsibilities regarding the returns of decedents, returns of persons under a disability, returns of estates and trusts, and returns made by joint fiduciaries.

(d) *Time and manner of filing return.*—(1) *In general.*—Forms 706, 706NA, 706GS(D), 706GS(D-1), 706GS(T), 709, and Schedule R-1 of Form 706 must be filed with the Internal Revenue Service office with which an estate or gift tax return of the transferor must be filed. The return shall be filed—

(i) *Direct skip.*—In the case of a direct skip, on or before the date on which an estate or gift tax return is required to be filed with respect to the transfer (see section 6075(b)(3)); and

(ii) *Other transfers.*—In all other cases, on or before the 15th day of the 4th month after the close of the calendar year in which such transfer occurs. See paragraph (d)(2) of this section for an exception to this rule when an election is made under section 2624(c) to value property included in certain taxable terminations in accordance with section 2032.

(2) *Exception for alternative valuation of taxable termination.*—In the case of a taxable termination with respect to which an election is made under section 2624(c) to value property in accordance with section 2032, a Form 706GS(T) must be filed on or before the 15th day of the 4th month after the close of the calendar year in which the taxable termination occurred, or on or before the 10th month following the month in which the death that resulted in the taxable termination occurred, whichever is later.

(e) *Place for filing returns.*—See section 6091 for the place for filing any return, declaration, statement, or other document, or copies thereof, required by chapter 13.

(f) *Lien on property.*—The liens imposed under sections 6324, 6324A, and 6324B are applicable with respect to the tax imposed under chapter 13. Thus, a lien under section 6324 is imposed in the amount of the tax imposed by section 2601 on all property transferred in a generation-skipping transfer until the tax is fully paid or becomes uncollectible by reason of lapse of time. The lien attaches at the time of the generation-skipping transfer and is in addition to the lien for taxes under section 6321. [Reg. § 26.2662-1.]

☐ [*T.D.* 8644, 12-26-95.]

[Reg. § 26.2663-1]

§ 26.2663-1. Recapture tax under section 2032A.—See § 26.2642-4(a)(4) for rules relating to the recomputation of the applicable fraction and the imposition of additional GST tax, if additional estate tax is imposed under section 2032A. [Reg. § 26.2663-1.]

☐ [*T.D.* 8644, 12-26-95.]

[Reg. § 26.2663-2]

§ 26.2663-2. Application of chapter 13 to transfers by nonresidents not citizens of the United States.—(a) *In general.*—This section provides rules for applying chapter 13 of the Internal Revenue Code to transfers by a transferor who is a nonresident not a citizen of the United States (NRA transferor). For purposes of this section, an individual is a resident or citizen of the United States if that individual is a resident or citizen of the United States under the rules of chapter 11 or 12 of the Internal Revenue Code, as the case may be. Every NRA transferor is allowed a GST exemption of $1,000,000. See § 26.2632-1 regarding the allocation of the exemption.

(b) *Transfers subject to chapter 13.*—(1) *Direct skips.*—A transfer by a NRA transferor is a direct skip subject to chapter 13 only to the extent that the transfer is subject to the Federal estate or gift tax within the meaning of § 26.2652-1(a)(2). See § 26.2612-1(a) for the definition of *direct skip*.

(2) *Taxable distributions and taxable terminations.*—Chapter 13 applies to a taxable distribution or a taxable termination to the extent that the initial transfer of property to the trust by a NRA transferor, whether during life or at death, was subject to the Federal estate or gift tax within the meaning of § 26.2652-1(a)(2). See § 26.2612-1(b) for the definition of a *taxable termination* and § 26.2612-1(c) for the definition of a *taxable distribution*.

(c) *Trusts funded in part with property subject to chapter 13 and in part with property not subject to chapter 13.*—(1) *In general.*—If a single trust created by a NRA transferor is in part subject to chapter 13 under the rules of paragraph (b) of this section and in part not subject to chapter 13, the applicable fraction with respect to the trust is determined as of the date of the transfer, except as provided in paragraph (c)(3) of this section.

(i) *Numerator of applicable fraction.*—The numerator of the applicable fraction is the sum of the amount of GST exemption allocated to the trust (if any) plus the value of the nontax portion of the trust.

(ii) *Denominator of applicable fraction.*—The denominator of the applicable fraction is the value of the property transferred to the trust reduced as provided in § 26.2642-1(c).

(2) *Nontax portion of the trust.*—The nontax portion of a trust is a fraction, the numerator of which is the value of property not subject to chapter 13 determined as of the date of the initial completed transfer to the trust, and the denominator of which is the value of the entire trust. For example, T, a NRA transferor, transfers property that has a value of $1,000 to a generation-skipping trust. Of the property transferred to the trust, property having a value of $200 is subject to chapter 13 and property having a value of $800 is not subject to chapter 13. The nontax portion is .8 ($800 (the value of the property not subject to chapter 13) over $1,000 (the total value of the property transferred to the trust)).

(3) *Special rule with respect to the estate tax inclusion period.*—For purposes of this section, the provisions of § 26.2632-1(c), providing rules applicable in the case of an estate tax inclusion period (ETIP), apply only if the property transferred by the NRA transferor is subsequently included in the transferor's gross estate. If the property is not subsequently included in the gross estate, then the nontax portion of the trust and the applicable fraction are determined as of the date of the initial transfer. If the property is subsequently included in the gross estate, then the nontax portion and the applicable fraction are determined as of the date of death.

(d) *Examples.*—The following examples illustrate the provisions of this section. In each example T, a NRA, is the transferor; C is T's child; and GC is C's child and a grandchild of T:

Example 1. Direct transfer to skip person. T transfers property to GC in a transfer that is subject to Federal gift tax under chapter 12 within the meaning of § 26.2652-1(a)(2). At the time of the transfer, C and GC are NRAs. T's transfer is subject to chapter 13 because the transfer is subject to gift tax under chapter 12.

Example 2. Transfers of both U.S. and foreign situs property. (i) T's will established a testamentary trust for the benefit of C and GC. The trust was funded with stock in a publicly traded U.S. corporation having a value on the date of T's death of $100,000, and property not situated in the United States (and therefore not subject to estate tax) having a value on the date of T's death of $400,000.

(ii) On a timely filed estate tax return (Form 706NA), the executor of T's estate allocates $50,000 of GST exemption under section 2632(a) to the trust. The numerator of the applicable fraction is $450,000, the sum of $50,000 (the amount of exemption allocated to the trust) plus $400,000 (the value of the nontax portion of the trust (4/5 x $500,000)). The denominator is $500,000. Hence, the applicable fraction with respect to the trust is .9 ($450,000/$500,000), and the inclusion ratio is .1 (1 - 9/10).

Example 3. Inter vivos transfer of U.S. and foreign situs property to a trust and a timely allocation of GST exemption. T establishes a trust providing that trust income is payable to T's child for life and the remainder is to be paid to T's grandchild. T transfers property to the trust that has a value of $100,000 and is subject to chapter 13. T also transfers property to the trust that has a value of $300,000 but is not subject to chapter 13. T allocates $100,000 of exemption to the trust on a timely filed United States Gift (and Generation-Skipping Transfer) Tax Return (Form 709). The applicable fraction with respect to the trust is 1, determined as follows: $300,000 (the value of the nontax portion of the trust) plus $100,000 (the exemption allocated to the trust)/$400,000 (the total value of the property transferred to the trust).

Example 4. Inter vivos transfer of U.S. and foreign situs property to a trust and a late allocation of GST exemption. (i) In 1996, T transfers $500,000 of property to an inter vivos trust the terms of which provide that income is payable to C, for life, with the remainder to GC. The property transferred to the trust consists of property subject to chapter 13 that has a value of $400,000 on the date of the transfer and property not subject to chapter 13 that has a value of $100,000. T does not allocate GST exemption to the trust. On the transfer date, the nontax portion of the trust is .2 ($100,000/$500,000) and the applicable fraction is also .2 determined as follows: $100,000 (the value of the nontax portion of the trust)/ $500,000 (the value of the property transferred to the trust).

(ii) In 1999, when the value of the trust is $800,000, T allocates $100,000 of GST exemption to the trust. The applicable fraction of the trust must be recomputed. The numerator of the applicable fraction is $260,000 ($100,000 (the amount of GST exemption allocated to the trust)) plus $160,000 (the value of the nontax portion of the trust as of the date of allocation (.2 x $800,000)). The denominator of the applicable fraction is $800,000. Accordingly, the applicable fraction with respect to the trust after the allocation is .325 ($260,000/$800,000) and the inclusion ratio is .675 (1 - .325).

Example 5. Taxable termination. The facts are the same as in *Example 4* except that, in 2006, when the value of the property is $1,200,000, C dies and the trust corpus is distributed to GC. The termination is a taxable termination. If no further GST exemption has been allocated to the trust, the applicable fraction remains .325 and the inclusion ratio remains .675.

Example 6. Estate Tax Inclusion Period. (i) T transferred property to an inter vivos trust the terms of which provided T with an annuity payable for 10 years or until T's prior death. The annuity satisfies the definition of a qualified interest under section 2702(b). The trust also provided that, at the end of the trust term, the remainder will pass to GC or GC's estate. The property transferred to the trust consisted of property subject to chapter 13 that has a value of $100,000 and property not subject to chapter 13 that has a value of $400,000. T allocated $100,000 of GST exemption to the trust. If T dies within the 10 year period, the value of the trust principal will be subject to inclusion in T's gross estate to the extent provided in sections 2103 and 2104(b). Accordingly, the ETIP rule under paragraph (c)(3) of this section applies.

(ii) In year 6 of the trust term, T died. At T's death, the trust corpus had a value of $800,000, and $500,000 was includible in T's gross estate as provided in sections 2103 and 2104(b). Thus, $500,000 of the trust corpus is subject to chapter 13 and $300,000 is not subject to chapter 13. The $100,000 GST exemption allocation is effective as of T's date of death. Also, the nontax portion of the trust and the applicable fraction are determined as of T's date of death. In this case, the nontax portion of the trust is .375, determined as follows: $300,000 (the value of the trust not subject to chapter 13)/$800,000 (the value of the trust). The numerator of the applicable fraction is $400,000, determined as follows: $100,000 (GST exemption previously allocated to the trust) plus $300,000 (the value of the nontax portion of the trust). The denominator of the applicable fraction is $800,000. Thus, the applicable fraction with respect to the trust is .50, unless additional exemption is allocated to the trust by T's executor or the automatic allocation rules of § 26.2632-1(d)(2) apply.

Example 7. The facts are the same as in *Example 6* except that T survives the termination date of T's retained annuity and the trust corpus is distributed to GC. Since the trust was not included in T's gross estate, the ETIP rules do not apply.

Accordingly, the nontax portion of the trust and the applicable fraction are determined as of the date of the transfer to the trust. The nontax portion of the trust is .80 ($400,000/$500,000). The numerator of the applicable fraction is $500,000 determined as follows: $100,000 (GST exemption allocated to the trust) plus $400,000 (the value of the nontax portion of the trust). Accordingly, the applicable fraction is 1, and the inclusion ratio is zero.

(e) *Transitional rule for allocations for transfers made before December 27, 1995.*—If a NRA made a GST (inter vivos or testamentary) after December 23, 1992, and before December 27, 1995, that is subject to chapter 13 (within the meaning of § 26.2663-2), the NRA will be treated as having made a timely allocation of GST exemption to the transfer in a calendar year in the order prescribed in section 2632(c). Thus, a NRA's unused GST exemption will initially be treated as allocated to any direct skips made during the calendar year and then to any trusts with respect to which the NRA made transfers during the same calendar year and from which a taxable distribution or a taxable termination may occur. Allocations within the above categories are made in the order in which the transfers occur. Allocations among simultaneous transfers within the same category are made pursuant to the principles of section 2632(c)(2). This transitional allocation rule will not apply if the NRA transferor, or the executor of the NRA's estate, as the case may be, elected to have an automatic allocation of GST exemption not apply by describing on a timely-filed Form 709 for the year of the transfer, or a timely filed Form 706NA, the details of the transfer and the extent to which the allocation was not to apply. [Reg. § 26.2663-2.]

☐ [*T.D.* 8644, 12-26-95.]

Special Valuation Rules

See p. 15 for regulations not amended to reflect law changes

[Reg. § 25.2701-0]

§ 25.2701-0. Table of contents.—This section lists the major paragraphs contained in §§ 25.2701-1 through 25.2701-8.

§25.2701-6. Indirect holding of interests.

(a) In general.

(1) Attribution to individuals.

(2) Corporations.

(3) Partnerships.

(4) Estates, trusts, and other entities.

(5) Multiple attribution.

(b) Examples.

§25.2701-7. Separate interests.

§25.2701-8. Effective dates.

[Reg. §25.2701-0.]

☐ [*T.D.* 8395, 1-28-92. *Amended by T.D.* 8536, 5-4-94.]

[Reg. §25.2701-1]

§25.2701-1. Special valuation rules in the case of transfers of certain interests in corporations and partnerships.—(a) *In general.*—(1) *Scope of section 2701.*—Section 2701 provides special valuation rules to determine the amount of the gift when an individual transfers an equity interest in a corporation or partnership to a member of the individual's family. For section 2701 to apply, the transferor or an applicable family member (as defined in paragraph (d)(2) of this section) must, immediately after the transfer, hold an applicable retained interest (a type of equity interest defined in §25.2701-2(b)(1)). If certain subsequent payments with respect to the applicable retained interest do not conform to the assumptions used in valuing the interest at the time of the initial transfer, §25.2701-4 provides a special rule to increase the individual's later taxable gifts or taxable estate. Section 25.2701-5 provides an adjustment to mitigate the effects of double taxation when an applicable retained interest is subsequently transferred.

(2) *Effect of section 2701.*—If section 2701 applies to a transfer, the amount of the transferor's gift, if any, is determined using a subtraction method of valuation (described in §25.2701-3). Under this method, the amount of the gift is determined by subtracting the value of any family-held applicable retained interests and other non-transferred equity interests from the aggregate value of family-held interests in the corporation or partnership (the "entity"). Generally, in determining the value of any applicable retained interest held by the transferor or an applicable family member—

(i) Any put, call, or conversion right, any right to compel liquidation, or any similar right is valued at zero if the right is an "extraordinary payment right" (as defined in §25.2701-2(b)(2));

(ii) Any distribution right in a controlled entity (*e.g.*, a right to receive dividends) is valued at zero unless the right is a "qualified payment right" (as defined in §25.2701-2(b)(6)); and

(iii) Any other right (including a qualified payment right) is valued as if any right valued at zero did not exist but otherwise without regard to section 2701.

(3) *Example.*—The following example illustrates rules of this paragraph (a).

Example. A, an individual, holds all the outstanding stock of S Corporation. A exchanges A's shares in S for 100 shares of 10-percent cumulative preferred stock and 100 shares of voting common stock. A transfers the common stock to A's child. Section 2701 applies to the transfer because A has transferred an equity interest (the common stock) to a member of A's family, and immediately thereafter holds an applicable retained interest (the preferred stock). A's preferred stock is valued under the rules of section 2701. A's gift is determined under the subtraction method by subtracting the value of A's preferred stock from the value of A's interest in S immediately prior to the transfer.

(b) *Transfers and other triggering events.*—(1) *Completed transfers.*—Section 2701 applies to determine the existence and amount of any gift, whether or not the transfer would otherwise be a taxable gift under chapter 12 of the Internal Revenue Code. For example, section 2701 applies to a transfer that would not otherwise be a gift under chapter 12 because it was a transfer for full and adequate consideration.

(2) *Transactions treated as transfers.*—(i) *In general.*—Except as provided in paragraph (b)(3) of this section, for purposes of section 2701, transfer includes the following transactions:

(A) A contribution to the capital of a new or existing entity;

(B) A redemption, recapitalization, or other change in the capital structure of an entity (a "capital structure transaction"), if—

(1) The transferor or an applicable family member receives an applicable retained interest in the capital structure transaction;

(2) The transferor or an applicable family member holding an applicable retained interest before the capital structure transaction surrenders an equity interest that is junior to the applicable retained interest (a "subordinate interest") and receives property other than an applicable retained interest; or

(3) The transferor or an applicable family member holding an applicable retained interest before the capital structure transaction surrenders an equity interest in the entity (other than a subordinate interest) and the fair market value of the applicable retained interest is increased; or

(C) The termination of an indirect holding in an entity (as defined in §25.2701-6) (or a contribution to capital by an entity to the extent an individual indirectly holds an interest in the entity), if—

(1) The property is held in a trust as to which the indirect holder is treated as the owner under subchapter J of chapter 1 of the Internal Revenue Code; or

(2) If the termination (or contribution) is not treated as a transfer under paragraph (b)(2)(i)(C)(*1*) of this section, to the extent the value of the indirectly-held interest would have been included in the value of the indirect holder's gross estate for Federal estate tax pur-

poses if the indirect holder died immediately prior to the termination.

(ii) *Multiple attribution.*—For purposes of paragraph (b)(2)(i)(C) of this section, if the transfer of an indirect holding in property is treated as a transfer with respect to more than one indirect holder, the transfer is attributed in the following order:

(A) First, to the indirect holder(s) who transferred the interest to the entity (without regard to section 2513);

(B) Second, to the indirect holder(s) possessing a presently exercisable power to designate the person who shall possess or enjoy the property;

(C) Third, to the indirect holder(s) presently entitled to receive the income from the interest;

(D) Fourth, to the indirect holder(s) specifically entitled to receive the interest at a future date; and

(E) Last, to any other indirect holder(s) proportionally.

(3) *Excluded transactions.*—For purposes of section 2701, a transfer does not include the following transactions:

(i) A capital structure transaction, if the transferor, each applicable family member, and each member of the transferor's family holds substantially the same interest after the transaction as that individual held before the transaction. For this purpose, common stock with non-lapsing voting rights and nonvoting common stock are interests that are substantially the same;

(ii) A shift of rights occurring upon the execution of a qualified disclaimer described in section 2518; and

(iii) A shift of rights occurring upon the release, exercise, or lapse of a power of appointment other than a general power of appointment described in section 2514, except to the extent the release, exercise, or lapse would otherwise be a transfer under chapter 12.

(c) *Circumstances in which section 2701 does not apply.*—To the extent provided, section 2701 does not apply in the following cases:

(1) *Marketable transferred interests.*—Section 2701 does not apply if there are readily available market quotations on an established securities market for the value of the transferred interests.

(2) *Marketable retained interests.*—Section 25.2701-2 does not apply to any applicable retained interest if there are readily available market quotations on an established securities market for the value of the applicable retained interests.

(3) *Interests of the same class.*—Section 2701 does not apply if the retained interest is of the same class of equity as the transferred interest or if the retained interest is of a class that is proportional to the class of the transferred interest. A class is the same class as is (or is proportional to the class of) the transferred interest if the rights are identical (or proportional) to the rights of the transferred interest, except for non-lapsing differences in voting rights (or, for a partnership, non-lapsing differences with respect to management and limitations on liability). For purposes of this section, non-lapsing provisions necessary to comply with partnership allocation requirements of the Internal Revenue Code (*e.g.*, section 704(b)) are non-lapsing differences with respect to limitations on liability. A right that lapses by reason of Federal or State law is treated as a non-lapsing right unless the Secretary determines, by regulation or by published revenue ruling, that it is necessary to treat such a right as a lapsing right to accomplish the purposes of section 2701. An interest in a partnership is not an interest in the same class as the transferred interest if the transferor or applicable family members have the right to alter the liability of the transferee.

(4) *Proportionate transfers.*—Section 2701 does not apply to a transfer by an individual to a member of the individual's family of equity interests to the extent the transfer by that individual results in a proportionate reduction of each class of equity interest held by the individual and all applicable family members in the aggregate immediately before the transfer. Thus, for example, section 2701 does not apply if P owns 50 percent of each class of equity interest in a corporation and transfers a portion of each class to P's child in a manner that reduces each interest held by P and any applicable family members, in the aggregate, by 10 percent even if the transfer does not proportionately reduce P's interest in each class. See § 25.2701-6 regarding indirect holding of interests.

(d) *Family definitions.*—(1) *Member of the family.*—A member of the family is, with respect to any transferor—

(i) The transferor's spouse;

(ii) Any lineal descendant of the transferor or the transferor's spouse; and

(iii) The spouse of any such lineal descendant.

(2) *Applicable family member.*—An applicable family member is, with respect to any transferor—

(i) The transferor's spouse;

(ii) Any ancestor of the transferor or the transferor's spouse; and

(iii) The spouse of any such ancestor.

(3) *Relationship by adoption.*—For purposes of section 2701, any relationship by legal adoption is the same as a relationship by blood.

(e) *Examples.*—The following examples illustrate provisions of this section:

Example 1. P, an individual, holds all the outstanding stock of X Corporation. Assume the fair market value of P's interest in X immediately prior to the transfer is $1.5 million. X is recapitalized so that P holds 1,000 shares of $1,000 par value preferred stock bearing an annual cumulative dividend of $100 per share (the aggregate fair market value of which is assumed to be $1 million) and 1,000 shares of voting common stock. P transfers the common stock to P's child. Section 2701 applies to the transfer because P has transferred an equity interest (the common stock) to a member of P's family and immediately thereafter holds an applicable retained interest (the preferred stock). P's right to receive annual cumulative dividends is a qualified payment right and is valued for purposes of section 2701 at its fair market value of $1,000,000. The amount of P's gift, determined using the subtraction method of § 25.2701-3, is $500,000 ($1,500,000 minus $1,000,000).

Example 2. The facts are the same as in *Example 1*, except that the preferred dividend right is noncumulative. Under § 25.2701-2, P's preferred dividend right is valued at zero because it is a distribution right in a controlled entity, but is not a qualified payment right. All of P's other rights in the preferred stock are valued as if P's dividend right does not exist but otherwise without regard to section 2701. The amount of P's gift, determined using the subtraction method, is $1,500,000 ($1,500,000 minus $0). P may elect, however, to treat the dividend right as a qualified payment right as provided in § 25.2701-2(c)(2). [Reg. § 25.2701-1.]

☐ [*T.D.* 8395, 1-28-92. *Amended by T.D.* 8536, 5-4-94.]

[Reg. § 25.2701-2]

§ 25.2701-2. Special valuation rules for applicable retained interests.—(a) *In general*.—In determining the amount of a gift under § 25.2701-3, the value of any applicable retained interest (as defined in paragraph (b)(1) of this section) held by the transferor or by an applicable family member is determined using the rules of chapter 12, with the modifications prescribed by this section. See § 25.2701-6 regarding the indirect holding of interests.

(1) *Valuing an extraordinary payment right*.—Any extraordinary payment right (as defined in paragraph (b)(2) of this section) is valued at zero.

(2) *Valuing a distribution right*.—Any distribution right (as defined in paragraph (b)(3) of this section) in a controlled entity is valued at zero, unless it is a qualified payment right (as defined in paragraph (b)(6) of this section). Controlled entity is defined in paragraph (b)(5) of this section.

(3) *Special rule for valuing a qualified payment right held in conjunction with an extraordinary payment right*.—If an applicable retained interest confers a qualified payment right and one or more extraordinary payment rights, the value of all these rights is determined by assuming that each extraordinary payment right is exercised in a manner that results in the lowest total value being determined for all the rights, using a consistent set of assumptions and giving due regard to the entity's net worth, prospective earning power, and other relevant factors (the "lower of" valuation rule). See § § 20.2031-2(f) and 20.2031-3 for rules relating to the valuation of business interests generally.

(4) *Valuing other rights*.—Any other right (including a qualified payment right not subject to the prior paragraph) is valued as if any right valued at zero does not exist and as if any right valued under the lower of rule is exercised in a manner consistent with the assumptions of that rule but otherwise without regard to section 2701. Thus, if an applicable retained interest carries no rights that are valued at zero or under the lower of rule, the value of the interest for purposes of section 2701 is its fair market value.

(5) *Example*.—The following example illustrates rules of this paragraph (a).

Example. P, an individual, holds all 1,000 shares of X Corporation's $1,000 par value preferred stock bearing an annual cumulative dividend of $100 per share and holds all 1,000 shares of X's voting common stock. P has the right to put all the preferred stock to X at any time for $900,000. P transfers the common stock to P's child and immediately thereafter holds the preferred stock. Assume that at the time of the transfer, the fair market value of X is $1,500,000, and the fair market value of P's annual cumulative dividend right is $1,000,000. Because the preferred stock confers both an extraordinary payment right (the put right) and a qualified payment right (*i.e.,* the right to receive cumulative dividends), the lower of rule applies and the value of these rights is determined as if the put right will be exercised in a manner that results in the lowest total value being determined for the rights (in this case, by assuming that the put will be exercised immediately). The value of P's preferred stock is $900,000 (the lower of $1,000,000 or $900,000). The amount of the gift is $600,000 ($1,500,000 minus $900,000).

(b) *Definitions*.—(1) *Applicable retained interest*.—An applicable retained interest is any equity interest in a corporation or partnership with respect to which there is either—

(i) An extraordinary payment right (as defined in paragraph (b)(2) of this section), or

(ii) In the case of a controlled entity (as defined in paragraph (b)(5) of this section), a distribution right (as defined in paragraph (b)(3) of this section).

(2) *Extraordinary payment right*.—Except as provided in paragraph (b)(4) of this section, an extraordinary payment right is any put, call, or conversion right, any right to compel liquidation, or any similar right, the exercise or nonexercise of which affects the value of the transferred interest. A call right includes any warrant, option, or other right to acquire one or more equity interests.

(3) *Distribution right*.—A distribution right is the right to receive distributions with respect to an equity interest. A distribution right does not include—

(i) Any right to receive distributions with respect to an interest that is of the same class as, or a class that is subordinate to, the transferred interest;

(ii) Any extraordinary payment right; or

(iii) Any right described in paragraph (b)(4) of this section.

(4) *Rights that are not extraordinary payment rights or distribution rights.*—Mandatory payment rights, liquidation participation rights, rights to guaranteed payments of a fixed amount under section 707(c), and non-lapsing conversion rights are neither extraordinary payment rights nor distribution rights.

(i) *Mandatory payment right.*—A mandatory payment right is a right to receive a payment required to be made at a specific time for a specific amount. For example, a mandatory redemption right in preferred stock requiring that the stock be redeemed at its fixed par value on a date certain is a mandatory payment right and therefore not an extraordinary payment right or a distribution right. A right to receive a specific amount on the death of the holder is a mandatory payment right.

(ii) *Liquidation participation rights.*—A liquidation participation right is a right to participate in a liquidating distribution. If the transferor, members of the transferor's family, or applicable family members have the ability to compel liquidation, the liquidation participation right is valued as if the ability to compel liquidation—

(A) Did not exist, or

(B) If the lower of rule applies, is exercised in a manner that is consistent with that rule.

(iii) *Right to a guaranteed payment of a fixed amount under section 707(c).*—The right to a guaranteed payment of a fixed amount under section 707(c) is the right to a guaranteed payment (within the meaning of section 707(c)) the amount of which is determined at a fixed rate (including a rate that bears a fixed relationship to a specified market interest rate). A payment that is contingent as to time or amount is not a guaranteed payment of a fixed amount.

(iv) *Non-lapsing conversion right.*—(A) *Corporations.*—A non-lapsing conversion right, in the case of a corporation, is a non-lapsing right to convert an equity interest in a corporation into a fixed number or a fixed percentage of shares of the same class as the transferred interest (or into an interest that would be of the same class but for non-lapsing differences in voting rights), that is subject to proportionate adjustments for changes in the equity ownership of the corporation and to adjustments similar to those provided in section 2701(d) for unpaid payments.

(B) *Partnerships.*—A non-lapsing conversion right, in the case of a partnership, is a non-lapsing right to convert an equity interest in a partnership into a specified interest (other than an interest represented by a fixed dollar amount) of the same class as the transferred interest (or into an interest that would be of the same class but for non-lapsing differences in management rights or limitations on liability) that is subject to proportionate adjustments for changes in the equity ownership of the partnership and to adjustments similar to those provided in section 2701(d) for unpaid payments.

(C) *Proportionate adjustments in equity ownership.*—For purposes of this paragraph (b)(4), an equity interest is subject to proportionate adjustments for changes in equity ownership if, in the case of a corporation, proportionate adjustments are required to be made for splits, combinations, reclassifications, and similar changes in capital stock, or, in the case of a partnership, the equity interest is protected from dilution resulting from changes in the partnership structure.

(D) *Adjustments for unpaid payments.*—For purposes of this paragraph (b)(4), an equity interest is subject to adjustments similar to those provided in section 2701(d) if it provides for—

(1) Cumulative payments;

(2) Compounding of any unpaid payments at the rate specified in § 25.2701-4(c)(2); and

(3) Adjustment of the number or percentage of shares or the size of the interest into which it is convertible to take account of accumulated but unpaid payments.

(5) *Controlled entity.*—(i) *In general.*—For purposes of section 2701, a controlled entity is a corporation or partnership controlled, immediately before a transfer, by the transferor, applicable family members, and any lineal descendants of the parents of the transferor or the transferor's spouse. See § 25.2701-6 regarding indirect holding of interests.

(ii) *Corporations.*—(A) *In general.*—In the case of a corporation, control means the holding of at least 50 percent of the total voting power or total fair market value of the equity interests in the corporation.

(B) *Voting rights.*—Equity interests that carry no right to vote other than on liquidation, merger, or a similar event are not considered to have voting rights for purposes of this paragraph (b)(5)(ii). Generally, a voting right is considered held by an individual to the extent that the individual, either alone or in conjunction with any other person, is entitled to exercise (or direct the exercise of) the right. However, if an equity interest carrying voting rights is held in a fiduciary capacity, the voting rights are not considered held by the fiduciary, but instead are considered held by each beneficial owner of the interest and by each individual who is a permissible recipient of the income from the interest. A voting right does not include a right to vote that is subject to a contingency that has not occurred, other than a contingency that is within the control of the individual holding the right.

(iii) *Partnerships.*—In the case of any partnership, control means the holding of at least 50 percent of either the capital interest or the profits interest in the partnership. Any right to a guaranteed payment under section 707(c) of a fixed amount is disregarded in making this determination. In addition, in the case of a limited partnership, control means the holding of any equity interest as a general partner. See § 25.2701-2(b)(4)(iii) for the definition of a right to a guaranteed payment of a fixed amount under section 707(c).

(6) *Qualified payment right.*—(i) *In general.*—A qualified payment right is a right to receive qualified payments. A qualified payment is a distribution that is—

(A) A dividend payable on a periodic basis (at least annually) under any cumulative preferred stock, to the extent such dividend is determined at a fixed rate;

(B) Any other cumulative distribution payable on a periodic basis (at least annually) with respect to an equity interest, to the extent determined at a fixed rate or as a fixed amount; or

(C) Any distribution right for which an election has been made pursuant to paragraph (c)(2) of this section.

(ii) *Fixed rate.*—For purposes of this section, a payment rate that bears a fixed relationship to a specified market interest rate is a payment determined at a fixed rate.

(c) *Qualified payment elections.*—(1) *Election to treat a qualified payment right as other than a qualified payment right.*—Any transferor holding a qualified payment right may elect to treat all rights held by the transferor of the same class as rights that are not qualified payment rights. An election may be a partial election, in which case the election must be exercised with respect to a consistent portion of each payment right in the class as to which the election has been made.

(2) *Election to treat other distribution rights as qualified payment rights.*—Any individual may elect to treat a distribution right held by that individual in a controlled entity as a qualified payment right. An election may be a partial election, in which case the election must be exercised with respect to a consistent portion of each payment right in the class as to which the election has been made. An election under this paragraph (c)(2) will not cause the value of the applicable retained interest conferring the distribution right to exceed the fair market value of the applicable retained interest (determined without regard to section 2701). The election is effective only to the extent—

(i) Specified in the election, and

(ii) That the payments elected are permissible under the legal instrument giving rise to the right and are consistent with the legal right of the entity to make the payment.

(3) *Elections irrevocable.*—Any election under paragraph (c)(1) or (c)(2) of this section is revocable only with the consent of the Commissioner.

(4) *Treatment of certain payments to applicable family members.*—Any payment right described in paragraph (b)(6) of this section held by an applicable family member is treated as a payment right that is not a qualified payment right unless the applicable family member elects (pursuant to paragraph (c)(2) of this section) to treat the payment right as a qualified payment right. An election may be a partial election, in which case the election must be exercised with respect to a consistent portion of each payment right in the class as to which the election has been made.

(5) *Time and manner of elections.*—Any election under paragraph (c)(1) or (c)(2) of this section is made by attaching a statement to the Form 709, Federal Gift Tax Return, filed by the transferor on which the transfer is reported. An election filed after the time of the filing of the Form 709 reporting the transfer is not a valid election. An election filed as of March 28, 1992, for transfers made prior to its publication is effective. The statement must—

(i) Set forth the name, address, and taxpayer identification number of the electing individual and of the transferor, if different;

(ii) If the electing individual is not the transferor filing the return, state the relationship between the individual and the transferor;

(iii) Specifically identify the transfer disclosed on the return to which the election applies;

(iv) Describe in detail the distribution right to which the election applies;

(v) State the provision of the regulation under which the election is being made; and

(vi) If the election is being made under paragraph (c)(2) of this section—

(A) State the amounts that the election assumes will be paid, and the times that the election assumes the payments will be made;

(B) Contain a statement, signed by the electing individual, in which the electing individual agrees that—

(1) If payments are not made as provided in the election, the individual's subsequent taxable gifts or taxable estate will, upon the occurrence of a taxable event (as defined in § 25.2701-4(b)), be increased by an amount determined under § 25.2701-4(c), and

(2) The individual will be personally liable for any increase in tax attributable thereto.

(d) *Examples.*—The following examples illustrate provisions of this section:

Example 1. On March 30, 1991, P transfers nonvoting common stock of X Corporation to P's child, while retaining $100 par value voting preferred stock bearing a cumulative annual dividend of $10. Immediately before the transfer, P held 100 percent of the stock. Because X is a controlled entity (within the meaning of paragraph (b)(5) of this section), P's dividend right is a distribution right that is subject to section 2701. See § 25.2701-2(b)(3). Because the distribution right is an annual cumulative dividend, it is a qualified payment right. See § 25.2701-2(b)(6).

Example 2. The facts are the same as in *Example 1*, except that the dividend right is non-cumulative. P's dividend right is a distribution right in a controlled entity, but is not a qualified payment right because the dividend is non-cumulative. Therefore, the non-cumulative dividend right is valued at zero under § 25.2701-2(a)(2). If the corporation were not a controlled entity, P's dividend right would be valued without regard to section 2701.

Example 3. The facts are the same as in *Example 1*. Because P holds sufficient voting power to compel liquidation of X, P's right to participate in liquidation is an extraordinary payment right under paragraph (b)(2) of this section. Because P holds an extraordinary payment right in conjunction with a qualified payment right (the right to receive cumulative dividends), the lower of rule applies.

Example 4. The facts are the same as in *Example 1*, except that immediately before the transfer, P, applicable family members of P, and members of P's family, hold 60 percent of the voting rights in X. Assume that 80 percent of the vote is required to compel liquidation of any interest in X. P's right to participate in liquidation is not an extraordinary payment right under paragraph (b)(2) of this section, because P and P's family cannot compel liquidation of X. P's preferred stock is an applicable retained interest that carries no rights that are valued under the special valuation rules of section 2701. Thus, in applying the valuation method of § 25.2701-3, the value of P's preferred stock is its fair market value determined without regard to section 2701.

Example 5. L holds 10-percent non-cumulative preferred stock and common stock in a corporation that is a controlled entity. L transfers the common stock to L's child. L holds no extraordinary payment rights with respect to the preferred stock. L elects under paragraph (c)(2) of this section to treat the noncumulative dividend right as a qualified payment right consisting of the right to receive a cumulative annual dividend of 5 percent. Under § 25.2701-2(c)(2), the value of the distribution right pursuant to the election is the lesser of—

(A) The fair market value of the right to receive a cumulative 5-percent dividend from the corporation, giving due regard to the corporation's net worth, prospective earning power, and dividend-paying capacity; or

(B) The value of the distribution right determined without regard to section 2701 and without regard to the terms of the qualified payment election. [Reg. § 25.2701-2.]

☐ [*T.D.* 8395, 1-28-92.]

[Reg. § 25.2701-3]

§ 25.2701-3. Determination of amount of gift.—(a) *Overview*.—(1) *In general*.—The amount of the gift resulting from any transfer to which section 2701 applies is determined by a subtraction method of valuation. Under this method, the amount of the transfer is determined by subtracting the values of all family-held senior equity interests from the fair market value of all family-held interests in the entity determined immediately before the transfer. The values of the senior equity interests held by the transferor and applicable family members generally are determined under section 2701. Other family-held senior equity interests are valued at their fair market value. The balance is then appropriately allocated among the transferred interests and other family-held subordinate equity interests. Finally, certain discounts and other appropriate reductions are provided, but only to the extent permitted by this section.

(2) *Definitions*.—The following definitions apply for purposes of this section.

(i) *Family-held*.—Family-held means held (directly or indirectly) by an individual described in § 25.2701-2(b)(5)(i).

(ii) *Senior equity interest*.—Senior equity interest means an equity interest in the entity that carries a right to distributions of income or capital that is preferred as to the rights of the transferred interest.

(iii) *Subordinate equity interest*.—Subordinate equity interest means an equity interest in the entity as to which an applicable retained interest is a senior equity interest.

(b) *Valuation methodology*.—The following methodology is used to determine the amount of the gift when section 2701 applies.

(1) *Step 1—Valuation of family-held interests*.—(i) *In general*.—Except as provided in paragraph (b)(1)(ii) of this section[,] determine the fair market value of all family-held equity interests in the entity immediately after the transfer. The fair market value is determined by assuming that the interests are held by one individual, using a consistent set of assumptions.

(ii) *Special rule for contributions to capital*.—In the case of a contribution to capital, determine the fair market value of the contribution.

(2) *Step 2—Subtract the value of senior equity interests*.—*In general*.—If the amount determined in *Step 1* of paragraph (b)(1) of this section is not determined under the special rule for contributions to capital, from that value subtract the following amounts:

(A) An amount equal to the sum of the fair market value of all family-held senior equity interests, (other than applicable retained interests held by the transferor or applicable family members) and the fair market value of any family-held equity interests of the same class or a subordinate class to the transferred interests held by persons other than the transferor, members of the transferor's family, and applicable family members of the transferor. The fair market value of an interest is its pro rata share of the fair market value of all family-held senior equity interests of the same class (determined, immediately after the transfer, as is [if] all family-held senior equity interests were held by one individual); and

(B) The value of all applicable retained interests held by the transferor or applicable family members (other than an interest received as consideration for the transfer) determined under § 25.2701-2, taking into account the adjustment described in paragraph (b)(5) of this section.

(ii) *Special rule for contributions to capital.*—If the value determined in *Step 1* of paragraph (b)(1) of this section is determined under the special rule for contributions to capital, subtract the value of any applicable retained interest received in exchange for the contribution to capital determined under § 25.2701-2.

(3) *Step 3—Allocate the remaining value among the transferred interests and other family-held subordinate equity interests.*—The value remaining after Step 2 is allocated among the transferred interests and other subordinate equity interests held by the transferor, applicable family members, and members of the transferor's family. If more than one class of family-held subordinate equity interest exists, the value remaining after Step 2 is allocated, beginning with the most senior class of subordinate equity interest, in the manner that would most fairly approximate their value if all rights valued under section 2701 at zero did not exist (or would be exercised in a manner consistent with the assumptions of the rule of § 25.2702-2(a)(4), if applicable). If there is no clearly appropriate method of allocating the remaining value pursuant to the preceding sentence, the remaining value (or the portion remaining after any partial allocation pursuant to the preceding sentence) is allocated to the interests in proportion to their fair market values determined without regard to section 2701.

(4) *Step 4—Determine the amount of the gift.*—(i) *In general.*—The amount allocated to the transferred interests in step 3 is reduced by the amounts determined under this paragraph (b)(4).

(ii) *Reduction for minority or similar discounts.*—Except as provided in § 25.2701-3(c), if the value of the transferred interest (determined without regard to section 2701) would be determined after application of a minority or similar discount with respect to the transferred interest, the amount of the gift determined under section 2701 is reduced by the excess, if any, of—

(A) A pro rata portion of the fair market value of the family-held interests of the same class (determined as if all voting rights conferred by family-held equity interests were held by one person who had no interest in the entity other than the family-held interests of the same class, but otherwise without regard to section 2701), over

(B) The value of the transferred interest (without regard to section 2701).

(iii) *Adjustment for transfers with a retained interest.*—If the value of the transferor's gift (determined without regard to section 2701) would be reduced under section 2702 to reflect the value of a retained interest, the value determined under section 2701 is reduced by the same amount.

(iv) *Reduction for consideration.*—The amount of the transfer (determined under section 2701) is reduced by the amount of consideration in money or money's worth received by the transferor, but not in excess of the amount of the gift (determined without regard to section 2701). The value of consideration received by the transferor in the form of an applicable retained interest in the entity is determined under section 2701 except that, in the case of a contribution to capital, the Step 4 value of such an interest is zero.

(5) *Adjustment in Step 2.*—(i) *In general.*—For purposes of paragraph (b)(2) of this section, if the percentage of any class of applicable retained interest held by the transferor and by applicable family members (including any interest received as consideration for the transfer) exceeds the family interest percentage, the excess is treated as a family-held interest that is not held by the transferor or an applicable family member.

(ii) *Family interest percentage.*—The family interest percentage is the highest ownership percentage (determined on the basis of relative fair market values) of family-held interests in—

(A) Any class of subordinate equity interest; or

(B) All subordinate equity interests, valued in the aggregate.

(c) *Minimum value rule.*—(1) *In general.*—If section 2701 applies to the transfer of an interest in an entity, the value of a junior equity interest is not less than its pro-rata portion of 10 percent of the sum of—

(i) The total value of all equity interests in the entity, and

(ii) The total amount of any indebtedness of the entity owed to the transferor and applicable family members.

(2) *Junior equity interest.*—For purposes of paragraph (c)(1) of this section, junior equity interest means common stock or, in the case of a partnership, any partnership interest under which the rights to income and capital are junior to the rights of all other classes of partnership interests. Common stock means the class or classes of stock that, under the facts and circumstances, are entitled to share in the reasonably anticipated residual growth in the entity.

(3) *Indebtedness.*—(i) *In general.*—For purposes of paragraph (c)(1) of this section, indebtedness owed to the transferor (or an applicable family member) does not include—

(A) Short-term indebtedness incurred with respect to the current conduct of the entity's trade or business (such as amounts payable for current services);

(B) Indebtedness owed to a third party solely because it is guaranteed by the transferor or an applicable family member; or

(C) Amounts permanently set aside in a qualified deferred compensation arrangement, to the extent the amounts are unavailable for use by the entity.

(ii) *Leases.*—A lease of property is not indebtedness, without regard to the length of the lease term, if the lease payments represent full and adequate consideration for use of the property. Lease payments are considered full and adequate consideration if a good faith effort is made to determine the fair rental value under the lease and the terms of the lease conform to the value so determined. Arrearages with respect to a lease are indebtedness.

(d) *Examples.*—The application of the subtraction method described in this section is illustrated by the following examples:

Example 1. Corporation X has outstanding 1,000 shares of $1,000 par value voting preferred stock, each share of which carries a cumulative annual dividend of 8 percent and a right to put the stock to X for its par value at any time. In addition, there are outstanding 1,000 shares of non-voting common stock. A holds 600 shares of the preferred stock and 750 shares of the common stock. The balance of the preferred and common stock is held by B, a person unrelated to A. Because the preferred stock confers both a qualified payment right and an extraordinary payment right, A's rights are valued under the "lower of" rule of § 25.2701-2(a)(3). Assume that A's rights in the preferred stock are valued at $800 per share under the "lower of" rule (taking account of A's voting rights). A transfers all of A's common stock to A's child. The method for determining the amount of A's gift is as follows—

Step 1: Assume the fair market value of all the family-held interests in X, taking account of A's control of the corporation, is determined to be $1 million.

Step 2: From the amount determined under Step 1, subtract $480,000 (600 shares × $800 (the section 2701 value of A's preferred stock, computed under the "lower of" rule of § 25.2701-2(a)(3))).

Step 3: The result of Step 2 is a balance of $520,000. This amount is fully allocated to the 750 shares of family-held common stock.

Step 4: Because no consideration was furnished for the transfer, the adjustment under Step 4 is limited to the amount of any appropriate minority or similar discount. Before the application of Step 4 the amount of A's gift is $520,000.

Example 2. The facts are the same as in *Example 1,* except that prior to the transfer A holds only 50 percent of the common stock and B holds the remaining 50 percent. Assume that the fair market value of A's 600 shares of preferred stock is $600,000.

Step 1: Assume that the result of this step (determining the value of the family-held interest) is $980,000.

Step 2: From the amount determined under Step 1, subtract $500,000 ($400,000, the value of 500 shares of A's preferred stock determined under section 2701 plus $100,000, the fair market value of A's other 100 shares of preferred stock determined without regard to section 2701 pursuant to the valuation adjustment determined under paragraph (b)(5) of this section). The adjustment in Step 2 applies in this example because A's percentage ownership of the preferred stock (60 percent) exceeds the family interest percentage of the common stock (50 percent). Therefore, 100 shares of A's preferred stock are valued at fair market value, or $100,000 (100 × $1,000). The balance of A's preferred stock is valued under section 2701 at $400,000 (500 shares × $800). The value of A's preferred stock for purposes of section 2701 equals $500,000 ($100,000 plus $400,000).

Step 3: The result of Step 2 is $480,000 ($980,000 minus $500,000) which is allocated to the family-held common stock. Because A transferred all of the family-held subordinate equity interests, all of the value determined under Step 2 is allocated to the transferred shares.

Step 4: The adjustment under Step 4 is the same as in *Example 1.* Thus, the amount of the gift is $480,000.

Example 3. Corporation X has outstanding 1,000 shares of $1,000 par value non-voting preferred stock, each share of which carries a cumulative annual dividend of 8 percent and a right to put the stock to X for its par value at any time. In addition, there are outstanding 1,000 shares of voting common stock. A holds 600 shares of the preferred stock and 750 shares of the common stock. The balance of the preferred and common stock is held by B, a person unrelated to A. Assume further that steps one through three, as in *Example 1,* result in $520,000 being allocated to the family-held common stock and that A transfers only 75 shares of A's common stock. The transfer fragments A's voting interest. Under Step 4, an adjustment is appropriate to reflect the fragmentation of A's voting rights. The amount of the adjustment is the difference between 10 percent (75/750) of the fair market value of A's common shares and the fair market value of the transferred shares, each determined as if the holder thereof had no other interest in the corporation.

Example 4. On December 31, 1990, the capital structure of Y corporation consists of 1,000 shares of voting common stock held three-fourths by A and one-fourth by A's child, B. On January 15, 1991, A transfers 250 shares of common stock to Y in exchange for 300 shares of nonvoting, noncumulative 8% preferred stock with a section 2701 value of zero. Assume that the fair market value of Y is $1,000,000 at the time of the exchange and that the exchange by A is for full and adequate consideration in moneys' worth. However, for purposes of section 2701, if a subordinate equity interest is transferred in exchange for an applicable retained interest, consideration in the exchange is determined with reference to the section 2701 value of the senior interest. Thus, A is treated as transferring the common stock to the corporation for no consideration. Immediately after the transfer, B is treated as holding one-third (250/750) of the common stock and A is treated as holding two-thirds (500/750). The amount of the gift is determined as follows:

Step 1. Because Y is held exclusively by A and B, the Step 1 value is $1,000,000.

Step 2. The result of Step 2 is $1,000,000 ($1,000,000 – 0).

Step 3. The amount allocated to the transferred common stock is $250,000 (250/1,000 × $1,000,000). That amount is further allocated in proportion to the respective holdings of A and B in the common stock ($166,667 and $83,333, respectively).

Step 4. There is no Step 4 adjustment because the section 2701 value of the consideration received by A was zero and no minority discount would have been involved in the exchange. Thus, the amount of the gift is $83,333. If the section 2701 value of the applicable retained interests were $100,000, the Step 4 adjustment would have been a $33,333 reduction for consideration received ((250/750) × $100,000).

Example 5. The facts are the same as in *Example 4*, except that on January 6, 1992, when the fair market value of Y is still $1,000,000, A transfers A's remaining 500 shares of common stock to Y in exchange for 2500 shares of preferred stock. The second transfer is also for full and adequate consideration in money or money's worth. The result of Step 2 is the same—$1,000,000.

Step 3. The amount allocated to the common stock is $666,667 (500/750 × $1,000,000). Since A holds no common stock immediately after the transfer, A is treated as transferring the entire interest to the other shareholder (B). Thus, the amount of the gift is $666,667.

Step 4. There is no Step 4 adjustment because the section 2701 value of the consideration received by A was zero and no minority discount would have been involved in the exchange. Thus, the amount of the gift is the difference between $666,667 and the fair market value of B's shares immediately prior to the transfer to which section 2701 applied. [Reg. § 25.2701-3.]

☐ [*T.D.* 8395, 1-28-92.]

[Reg. § 25.2701-4]

§ 25.2701-4. Accumulated qualified payments.—(a) *In general.*—If a taxable event occurs with respect to any applicable retained interest conferring a distribution right that was previously valued as a qualified payment right (a "qualified payment interest"), the taxable estate or taxable gifts of the individual holding the interest are increased by the amount determined under paragraph(c) of this section.

(b) *Taxable event.*—(1) *In general.*—Except as otherwise provided in this section, taxable event means the transfer of a qualified payment interest, either during life or at death, by the individual in whose hands the interest was originally valued under section 2701 (the "interest holder") or by any individual treated pursuant to paragraph (b)(3) of this section in the same manner as the interest holder. Except as provided in paragraph (a)(2) of this section, any termination of an individual's rights with respect to a qualified payment interest is a taxable event. Thus, for example, if an individual is treated as indirectly holding a qualified payment interest held by a trust, a taxable event occurs on the earlier of—

(i) The termination of the individual's interest in the trust (whether by death or otherwise), or

(ii) The termination of the trust's interest in the qualified payment interest (whether by disposition or otherwise).

(2) *Exception.*—If, at the time of a termination of an individual's rights with respect to a qualified payment interest, the value of the property would be includible in the individual's gross estate for Federal estate tax purposes if the individual died immediately after the termination, a taxable transfer does not occur until the earlier of—

(i) The time the property would no longer be includible in the individual's gross estate (other than by reason of section 2035), or

(ii) The death of the individual.

(3) *Individual treated as interest holder.*—(i) *In general.*—If a taxable event involves the transfer of a qualified payment interest by the interest holder (or an individual treated as the interest holder) to an applicable family member of the individual who made the transfer to which section 2701 applied (other than the spouse of the individual transferring the qualified payment interest), the transferee applicable family member is treated in the same manner as the interest holder with respect to late or unpaid qualified payments first due after the taxable event. Thus, for example, if an interest holder transfers during life a qualified payment interest to an applicable family member, that transfer is a taxable event with respect to the interest holder whose taxable gifts are increased for the year of the transfer as provided in paragraph (c) of this section. The transferee is treated thereafter in the same manner as the interest holder with respect to late or unpaid qualified payments first due after the taxable event.

(ii) *Transfers to spouse.*—(A) *In general.*—If an interest holder (or an individual treated as the interest holder) transfers a qualified payment interest, the transfer is not a taxable event to the extent a marital deduction is allowed with respect to the transfer under sections 2056, 2106(a)(3), or 2523 or, in the case of a transfer during the individual's lifetime, to the extent the spouse furnishes consideration for the transfer. If this exception applies, the transferee spouse is treated as if he or she were the holder of the interest from the date the transferor spouse acquired the interest. If the deduction for a transfer to a spouse is allowable under section 2056(b)(8) or 2523(g) (relating to charitable remainder trusts), the transferee spouse is treated as the holder of the entire interest passing to the trust.

(B) *Marital bequests.*—If the selection of property with which a marital bequest is funded is discretionary, a transfer of a qualified payment interest will not be considered a transfer to the surviving spouse unless—

(1) The marital bequest is funded with the qualified payment interest before the due date for filing the decedent's Federal estate tax return (including extensions actually granted) (the "due date"), or

(2) The executor—

(i) Files a statement with the return indicating the extent to which the marital bequest will be funded with the qualified payment interest, and

(ii) Before the date that is one year prior to the expiration of the period of limitations on assessment of the Federal estate tax, notifies the District Director having jurisdiction over the return of the extent to which the bequest was funded with the qualified payment interest (or the extent to which the qualified payment interest has been permanently set aside for that purpose).

(C) *Purchase by the surviving spouse.*—For purposes of this section, the purchase (before the date prescribed for filing the decedent's estate tax return, including extensions actually granted) by the surviving spouse (or a trust described in section 2056(b)(7)) of a qualified payment interest held (directly or indirectly) by the decedent immediately before death is considered a transfer with respect to which a deduction is allowable under section 2056 or section 2106(a)(3), but only to the extent that the deduction is allowed to the estate. For example, assume that A bequeaths $50,000 to A's surviving spouse, B, in a manner that qualifies for deduction under section 2056, and that subsequent to A's death B purchases a qualified payment interest from A's estate for $200,000, its fair market value. The economic effect of the transaction is the equivalent of a bequest by A to B of the qualified payment interest, one-fourth of which qualifies for the marital deduction. Therefore, for purposes of this section, one-fourth of the qualified payment interest purchased by B ($50,000 ÷ $200,000) is considered a transfer of an interest with respect to which a deduction is allowed under [section] 2056. If the purchase by the surviving spouse is not made before the due date of the decedent's return, the purchase of the qualified payment interest will not be considered a bequest for which a marital deduction is allowed unless the executor—

(1) Files a statement with the return indicating the qualified payment interests to be purchased by the surviving spouse (or a trust described in section 2056(b)(7)), and

(2) Before the date that is one year prior to the expiration of the period of limitations on assessment of the Federal estate tax, notifies the District Director having jurisdiction over the return that the purchase of the qualified payment interest has been made (or that the funds necessary to purchase the qualified payment interest have been permanently set aside for that purpose).

(c) *Amount of increase.*—(1) *In general.*—Except as limited by paragraph (c)(6) of this section, the amount of the increase to an individual's taxable estate or taxable gifts is the excess, if any, of—

(i) The sum of—

(A) The amount of qualified payments payable during the period beginning on the date of the transfer to which section 2701 applied (or, in the case of an individual treated as the interest holder, on the date the interest of the prior interest holder terminated) and ending on the date of the taxable event; and

(B) The earnings on those payments, determined hypothetically as if each payment were paid on its due date and reinvested as of that date at a yield equal to the appropriate discount rate (as defined below); over

(ii) The sum of—

(A) The amount of the qualified payments actually paid during the same period;

(B) The earnings on those payments, determined hypothetically as if each payment were reinvested as of the date actually paid at a yield equal to the appropriate discount rate; and

(C) To the extent required to prevent double inclusion, by an amount equal to the sum of—

(1) The portion of the fair market value of the qualified payment interest solely attributable to any right to receive unpaid qualified payments determined as of the date of the taxable event;

(2) The fair market value of any equity interest in the entity received by the individual in lieu of qualified payments and held by the individual at the taxable event; and

(3) The amount by which the individual's aggregate taxable gifts were increased by reason of the failure of the individual to enforce the right to receive qualified payments.

(2) *Due date of qualified payments.*—With respect to any qualified payment, the "due date" is that date specified in the governing instrument as the date on which payment is to be made. If no date is specified in the governing instrument, the due date is the last day of each calendar year.

(3) *Appropriate discount rate.*—The appropriate discount rate is the discount rate that was applied in determining the value of the qualified payment right at the time of the transfer to which section 2701 applied.

(4) *Application of payments.*—For purposes of this section, any payment of an unpaid qualified

payment is applied in satisfaction of unpaid qualified payments beginning with the earliest unpaid qualified payment. Any payment in excess of the total of all unpaid qualified payments is treated as a prepayment of future qualified payments.

(5) *Payment.*—For purposes of this paragraph (c), the transfer of a debt obligation bearing compound interest from the due date of the payment at a rate not less than the appropriate discount rate is a qualified payment if the term of the obligation (including extensions) does not exceed four years from the date issued. A payment in the form of an equity interest in the entity is not a qualified payment. Any payment of a qualified payment made (or treated as made) either before or during the four-year period beginning on the due date of the payment but before the date of the taxable event is treated as having been made on the due date.

(6) *Limitation.*—(i) *In general.*—The amount of the increase to an individual's taxable estate or taxable gifts is limited to the applicable percentage of the excess, if any, of—

(A) The sum of—

(1) The fair market value of all outstanding equity interests in the entity that are subordinate to the applicable retained interest, determined as of the date of the taxable event without regard to any accrued liability attributable to unpaid qualified payments; and

(2) Any amounts expended by the entity to redeem or otherwise acquire any such subordinate interest during the period beginning on the date of the transfer to which section 2701 applied (or, in the case of an individual treated as an interest holder, on the date the interest of the prior interest holder terminated) and ending on the date of the taxable event (reduced by any amounts received on the resale or issuance of any such subordinate interest during the same period); over

(B) The fair market value of all outstanding equity interests in the entity that are subordinate to the applicable retained interest, determined as of the date of the transfer to which section 2701 applied (or, in the case of an individual treated as an interest holder, on the date the interest of the prior interest holder terminated).

(ii) *Computation of limitation.*—For purposes of computing the limitation applicable under this paragraph (c)(6), the aggregate fair market value of the subordinate interests in the entity are determined without regard to §25.2701-3(c).

(iii) *Applicable percentage.*—The applicable percentage is determined by dividing the number of shares or units of the applicable retained interest held by the interest holder (or an individual treated as the interest holder) on the date of the taxable event by the total number of such shares or units outstanding on the same date. If an individual holds applicable retained interests in two or more classes of interests, the applicable percentage is equal to the largest applicable percentage determined with respect to any class. For example, if T retains 40 percent of the class A preferred and 60 percent of the class B preferred in a corporation, the applicable percentage with respect to T's holdings is 60 percent.

(d) *Taxpayer election.*—(1) *In general.*—An interest holder (or individual treated as an interest holder) may elect to treat as a taxable event the payment of an unpaid qualified payment occurring more than four years after its due date. Under this election, the increase under paragraph (c) of this section is determined only with respect to that payment and all previous payments for which an election was available but not made. Payments for which an election applies are treated as having been paid on their due dates for purposes of subsequent taxable events. The election is revocable only with the consent of the Commissioner.

(2) *Limitation not applicable.*—If a taxable event occurs by reason of an election described in paragraph (d)(1) of this section, the limitation described in paragraph (c)(6) of this section does not apply.

(3) *Time and manner of election.*—(i) *Timely-filed returns.*—The election may be made by attaching a statement to a Form 709, Federal Gift Tax Return, filed by the recipient of the qualified payment on a timely basis for the year in which the qualified payment is received. In that case, the taxable event is deemed to occur on the date the qualified payment is received.

(ii) *Election on late returns.*—The election may be made by attaching a statement to a Form 709, Federal Gift Tax Return, filed by the recipient of the qualified payment other than on a timely basis for the year in which the qualified payment is received. In that case, the taxable event is deemed to occur on the first day of the month immediately preceding the month in which the return is filed. If an election, other than an election on a timely return, is made after the death of the interest holder, the taxable event with respect to the decedent is deemed to occur on the later of—

(A) The date of the recipient's death, or

(B) The first day of the month immediately preceding the month in which the return is filed.

(iii) *Requirements of statement.*—The statement must—

(A) Provide the name, address, and taxpayer identification number of the electing individual and the interest holder, if different;

(B) Indicate that a taxable event election is being made under paragraph (d) of this section;

(C) Disclose the nature of the qualified payment right to which the election applies, including the due dates of the payments, the dates the payments were made, and the amounts of the payments;

(D) State the name of the transferor, the date of the transfer to which section 2701 applied, and the discount rate used in valuing the qualified payment right; and

(E) State the resulting amount of increase in taxable gifts.

(4) *Example.*—The following example illustrates the rules of this paragraph (d).

Example. A holds cumulative preferred stock that A retained in a transfer to which section 2701 applied. No dividends were paid in years 1 through 5 following the transfer. In year 6, A received a qualified payment that, pursuant to paragraph (c)(3) of this section, is considered to be in satisfaction of the unpaid qualified payment for year 1. No election was made to treat that payment as a taxable event. In year 7, A receives a qualified payment that, pursuant to paragraph (c)(4) of this section, is considered to be in satisfaction of the unpaid qualified payment for year 2. A elects to treat the payment in year 7 as a taxable event. The election increases A's taxable gifts in year 7 by the amount computed under paragraph (c) of this section with respect to the payments due in both year 1 and year 2. For purposes of any future taxable events, the payments with respect to years 1 and 2 are treated as having been made on their due dates. [Reg. § 25.2701-4.]

☐ [*T.D.* 8395, 1-28-92.]

[Reg. § 25.2701-5]

§ 25.2701-5. Adjustments to mitigate double taxation.—(a) *Reduction of transfer tax base.*—(1) *In general.*—This section provides rules under which an individual (the initial transferor) making a transfer subject to section 2701 (the initial transfer) is entitled to reduce his or her taxable gifts or adjusted taxable gifts (the reduction). The amount of the reduction is determined under paragraph(b) of this section. See paragraph (e) of this section if section 2513 (split gifts) applied to the initial transfer.

(2) *Federal gift tax modification.*—If, during the lifetime of the initial transferor, the holder of a section 2701 interest (as defined in paragraph (a)(4) of this section) transfers the interest to or for the benefit of an individual other than the initial transferor or an applicable family member of the initial transferor in a transfer subject to Federal estate or gift tax, the initial transferor may reduce the amount on which the initial transferor's tentative tax is computed under section 2502(a). The reduction is first applied on any gift tax return required to be filed for the calendar year in which the section 2701 interest is transferred; any excess reduction is carried forward and applied in each succeeding calendar year until the reduction is exhausted. The amount of the reduction that is used in a calendar year is the amount of the initial transferor's taxable gifts for that year. Any excess reduction remaining at the death of the initial transferor may be applied by the executor of the initial transferor's estate as provided under paragraph (a)(3) of this section. See paragraph (a)(4) of this section for the definition of a section 2701 interest. See § 25.2701-6 for rules relating to indirect ownership of equity interests transferred to trusts and other entities.

(3) *Federal estate tax modification.*—Except as otherwise provided in this paragraph (a)(3), in determining the Federal estate tax with respect to an initial transferor, the executor of the initial transferor's estate may reduce the amount on which the decedent's tentative tax is computed under section 2001(b) (or section 2101(b)) by the amount of the reduction (including any excess reduction carried forward under paragraph (a)(2) of this section). The amount of the reduction under this paragraph (a)(3) is limited to the amount that results in zero Federal estate tax with respect to the estate of the initial transferor.

(4) *Section 2701 interest.*—A section 2701 interest is an applicable retained interest that was valued using the special valuation rules of section 2701 at the time of the initial transfer. However, an interest is a section 2701 interest only to the extent the transfer of that interest effectively reduces the aggregate ownership of such class of interest by the initial transferor and applicable family members of the initial transferor below that held by such persons at the time of the initial transfer (or the remaining portion thereof).

(b) *Amount of reduction.*—Except as otherwise provided in paragraphs (c)(3)(iv) (pertaining to transfers of partial interests) and (e) (pertaining to initial split gifts) of this section, the amount of the reduction is the lesser of—

(1) The amount by which the initial transferor's taxable gifts were increased as a result of the application of section 2701 to the initial transfer; or

(2) The amount (determined under paragraph (c) of this section) duplicated in the transfer tax base at the time of the transfer of the section 2701 interest (the duplicated amount).

(c) *Duplicated amount.*—(1) *In general.*—The duplicated amount is the amount by which the transfer tax value of the section 2701 interest at the time of the subsequent transfer exceeds the value of that interest determined under section 2701 at the time of the initial transfer. If, at the time of the initial transfer, the amount allocated to the transferred interest under § 25.2701-3(b)(3) (*Step 3* of the valuation methodology) is less than the entire amount available for allocation at that time, the duplicated amount is a fraction of the amount described in the preceding sentence. The numerator of the fraction is the amount allocated to the transferred interest at the time of the initial transfer (pursuant to § 25.2701-3(b)(3)) and the denominator of the fraction is the amount available for allocation at the time of the initial transfer (determined after application of § 25.2701-3(b)(2)).

(2) *Transfer tax value—in general.*—Except as provided in paragraph (c)(3) of this section, for purposes of paragraph (c)(1) of this section the

transfer tax value of a section 2701 interest is the value of that interest as finally determined for Federal transfer tax purposes under chapter 11 or chapter 12, as the case may be (including the right to receive any distributions thereon (other than qualified payments)), reduced by the amount of any deduction allowed with respect to the section 2701 interest to the extent that the deduction would not have been allowed if the section 2701 interest were not included in the transferor's total amount of gifts for the calendar year or the transferor's gross estate, as the case may be. Rules similar to the rules of section 691(c)(2)(C) are applicable to determine the extent that a deduction would not be allowed if the section 2701 interest were not so included.

(3) *Special transfer tax value rules.*—(i) *Transfers for consideration.*—Except as provided in paragraph (c)(3)(iii) of this section, if, during the life of the initial transferor, a section 2701 interest is transferred to or for the benefit of an individual other than the initial transferor or an applicable family member of the initial transferor for consideration in money or money's worth, or in a transfer that is treated as a transfer for consideration in money or money's worth, the transfer of the section 2701 interest is deemed to occur at the death of the initial transferor. In this case, the estate of the initial transferor is entitled to a reduction in the same manner as if the initial transferor's gross estate included a section 2701 interest having a chapter 11 value equal to the amount of consideration in money or money's worth received in the exchange (determined as of the time of the exchange).

(ii) *Interests held by applicable family members at date of initial transferor's death.*—If a section 2701 interest in existence on the date of the initial transferor's death is held by an applicable family member and, therefore, is not included in the gross estate of the initial transferor, the section 2701 interest is deemed to be transferred at the death of the initial transferor to or for the benefit of an individual other than the initial transferor or an applicable family member of the initial transferor. In this case, the transfer tax value of that interest is the value that the executor of the initial transferor's estate can demonstrate would be determined under chapter 12 if the interest were transferred immediately prior to the death of the initial transferor.

(iii) *Nonrecognition transactions.*—If an individual exchanges a section 2701 interest in a nonrecognition transaction (within the meaning of section 7701(a)(45)), the exchange is not treated as a transfer of a section 2701 interest and the transfer tax value of that interest is determined as if the interest received in exchange is the section 2701 interest.

(iv) *Transfer of less than the entire section 2701 interest.*—If a transfer is a transfer of less than the entire section 2701 interest, the amount of the reduction under paragraph (a)(2) or (a)(3) of this section is reduced proportionately.

(v) *Multiple classes of section 2701 interest.*—For purposes of paragraph (b) of this section, if more than one class of section 2701 interest exists, the amount of the reduction is determined separately with respect to each such class.

(vi) *Multiple initial transfers.*—If an initial transferor has made more than one initial transfer, the amount of the reduction with respect to any section 2701 interest is the sum of the reductions computed under paragraph (b) of this section with respect to each such initial transfer.

(d) *Examples.*—The following examples illustrate the provisions of paragraphs (a) through (c) of this section.

Facts. (1) *In general.* (i) P, an individual, holds 1,500 shares of $1,000 par value preferred stock of X corporation (bearing an annual noncumulative dividend of $100 per share that may be put to X at any time for par value) and 1,000 shares of voting common stock of X. There is no other outstanding common stock of X.

(ii) On January 15, 1991, when the aggregate fair market value of the preferred stock is $1,500,000 and the aggregate fair market value of the common stock is $500,000, P transfers common stock to P's child. The fair market value of P's interest in X (common and preferred) immediately prior to the transfer is $2,000,000, and the section 2701 value of the preferred stock (the section 2701 interest) is zero. Neither P nor P's spouse, S, made gifts prior to 1991.

(2) *Additional facts applicable to Examples 1 through 3.* P's transfer consists of all 1,000 shares of P's common stock. With respect to the initial transfer, the amount remaining after Step 2 of the subtraction method of § 25.2701-3 is $2,000,000 ($2,000,000 minus zero), all of which is allocated to the transferred stock. P's aggregate taxable gifts for 1991 (including the section 2701 transfer) equal $2,500,000.

(3) *Additional facts applicable to Examples 4 and 5.* P's initial transfer consists of one-half of P's common stock. With respect to the initial transfer in this case, only $1,000,000 (one-half of the amount remaining after Step 2 of the subtraction method of § 25.2701-3) is allocated to the transferred stock. P's aggregate taxable gifts for 1991 (the section 2701 transfer and P's other transfers) equal $2,500,000.

Example 1. Inter vivos transfer of entire section 2701 interest. (i) On October 1, 1994, at a time when the value of P's preferred stock is $1,400,000, P transfers all of the preferred stock to P's child. In computing P's 1994 gift tax, P, as the initial transferor, is entitled to reduce the amount on which P's tentative tax is computed under section 2502(a) by $1,400,000.

(ii) The amount of the reduction computed under paragraph (b) of this section is the lesser of $1,500,000 (the amount by which the initial transferor's taxable gifts were increased as a result of the application of section 2701 to the initial transfer) or $1,400,000 (the duplicated amount). The duplicated amount is 100 percent (the portion of the section 2701 interest subsequently transferred) times $1,400,000 (the amount by which the gift tax value of the preferred stock ($1,400,000 at the time of the subsequent transfer) exceeds zero (the section 2701 value of the preferred stock at the time of the initial transfer)).

(iii) The result would be the same if the preferred stock had been held by P's parent, GM, and GM had, on October 1, 1994, transferred the preferred stock to or for the benefit of an individual other than P or an applicable family member of P. In that case, in computing the tax on P's 1994 and subsequent transfers, P would be entitled to reduce the amount on which P's tentative tax is computed under section 2502(a) by $1,400,000. If the value of P's 1994 gifts is less than $1,400,000, P is entitled to claim the excess adjustment in computing the tax with respect to P's subsequent transfers.

Example 2. Transfer of section 2701 interest at death of initial transferor. (i) P continues to hold the preferred stock until P's death. The chapter 11 value of the preferred stock at the date of P's death is the same as the fair market value of the preferred stock at the time of the initial transfer. In computing the Federal estate tax with respect to P's estate, P's executor is entitled to a reduction of $1,500,000 under paragraph (a)(3) of this section.

(ii) The result would be the same if P had sold the preferred stock to any individual other than an applicable family member at a time when the value of the preferred stock was $1,500,000. In that case, the amount of the reduction is computed as if the preferred stock were included in P's gross estate at a fair market value equal to the sales price. If the value of P's taxable estate is less than $1,500,000, the amount of the adjustment available to P's executor is limited to the actual value of P's taxable estate.

(iii) The result would also be the same if the preferred stock had been held by P's parent, GM, and at the time of P's death, GM had not transferred the preferred stock.

Example 3. Transfer of after-acquired preferred stock. On September 1, 1992, P purchases 100 shares of X preferred stock from an unrelated party. On October 1, 1994, P transfers 100 shares of X preferred stock to P's child. In computing P's 1994 gift tax, P is not entitled to reduce the amount on which P's tentative tax is computed under section 2502(a) because the 1994 transfer does not reduce P's preferred stock holding below that held at the time of the initial transfer. See paragraph (a)(4) of this section.

Example 4. Inter vivos transfer of entire section 2701 interest. (i) On October 1, 1994, at a time when the value of P's preferred stock is $1,400,000, P transfers all of the preferred stock to P's child. In computing P's 1994 gift tax, P, as the initial transferor, is entitled to reduce the amount on which P's tentative tax is computed under section 2502(a) by $700,000.

(ii) The amount of the reduction computed under paragraph (b) of this section is the lesser of $750,000 (($1,500,000 × .5 ($1,000,000 over $2,000,000)) the amount by which the initial transferor's taxable gifts were increased as a result of the application of section 2701 to the initial transfer) or $700,000 (($1,400,000 × .5) the duplicated amount). The duplicated amount is 100 percent (the portion of the section 2701 interest subsequently transferred) times $700,000; e.g., one-half (the fraction representing the portion of the common stock transferred in the initial transfer ($1,000,000/$2,000,000)) of the amount by which the gift tax value of the preferred stock at the time of the subsequent transfer ($1,400,000) exceeds zero (the section 2701 value of the preferred stock at the time of the initial transfer).

Example 5. Subsequent transfer of less than the entire section 2701 interest. On October 1, 1994, at a time when the value of P's preferred stock is $1,400,000, P transfers only 250 of P's 1,000 shares of preferred stock to P's child. In this case, the amount of the reduction computed under paragraph (b) is $175,000 (one-fourth (250/1,000) of the amount of the reduction available if P had transferred all 1,000 shares of preferred stock.

(e) *Computation of reduction if initial transfer is split under section 2513.*—(1) *In general.*—If section 2513 applies to the initial transfer (a split initial transfer), the special rules of this paragraph (e) apply.

(2) *Transfers during joint lives.*—If there is a split initial transfer and the corresponding section 2701 interest is transferred during the joint lives of the donor and the consenting spouse, for purposes of determining the reduction under paragraph (a)(2) of this section each spouse is treated as if the spouse was the initial transferor of one-half of the split initial transfer.

(3) *Transfers at or after death of either spouse.*—(i) *In general.*—If there is a split initial transfer and the corresponding section 2701 interest is transferred at or after the death of the first spouse to die, the reduction under paragraph (a)(2) or (a)(3) of this section is determined as if the donor spouse was the initial transferor of the entire initial transfer.

(ii) *Death of donor spouse.*—Except as provided in paragraph (e)(3)(iv) of this section, the executor of the estate of the donor spouse in a split initial transfer is entitled to compute the reduction as if the donor spouse was the initial transferor of the section 2701 interest otherwise attributable to the consenting spouse. In this case, if the consenting spouse survives the donor spouse—

(A) The consenting spouse's aggregate sum of taxable gifts used in computing each tentative tax under section 2502(a) (and, therefore, adjusted taxable gifts under section 2001(b)(1)(B) (or section 2101(b)(1)(B)) and the tax payable on the consenting spouse's prior taxable gifts under section 2001(b)(2) (or section 2101(b)(2))) is reduced to eliminate the remaining effect of the section 2701 interest; and

(B) Except with respect to any excess reduction carried forward under paragraph (a)(2) of this section, the consenting spouse ceases to be treated as the initial transferor of the section 2701 interest.

(iii) *Death of consenting spouse.*—If the consenting spouse predeceases the donor spouse, except for any excess reduction carried forward under paragraph (a)(2) of this section, the reduction with respect to any section 2701 interest in the split initial transfer is not available to the estate of the consenting spouse (regardless of whether the interest is included in the consenting spouse's gross estate). Similarly, if the consenting spouse predeceases the donor spouse, no reduction is available to the consenting spouse's adjusted taxable gifts under section 2001(b)(1)(B) (or section 2101(b)(1)(B)) or to the consenting spouse's gift tax payable under section 2001(b)(2) (or section 2101(b)(2)). See paragraph (a)(2) of this section for rules involving transfers by an applicable family member during the life of the initial transferor.

(iv) *Additional limitation on reduction.*—If the donor spouse (or the estate of the donor spouse) is treated under this paragraph (e) as the initial transferor of the section 2701 interest otherwise attributable to the consenting spouse, the amount of additional reduction determined under paragraph (b) of this section is the amount determined under that paragraph with respect to the consenting spouse. If a reduction was previously available to the consenting spouse under this paragraph (e), the amount determined under this paragraph (e)(3)(iv) with respect to the consenting spouse is determined as if the consenting spouse's taxable gifts in the split initial transfer had been increased only by that portion of the increase that corresponds to the remaining portion of the section 2701 interest. The amount of the additional reduction (i.e., the amount determined with respect to the consenting spouse) is limited to the amount that results in a reduction in the donor spouse's Federal transfer tax no greater than the amount of the increase in the consenting spouse's gift tax incurred by reason of the section 2701 interest (or the remaining portion thereof).

(f) *Examples.*—The following examples illustrate the provisions of paragraph (e) of this section. The examples assume the facts set out in this paragraph (f).

Facts. (1) In each example assume that P, an individual, holds 1,500 shares of $1,000 par value preferred stock of X corporation (bearing an annual noncumulative dividend of $100 per share that may be put to X at any time for par value) and 1,000 shares of voting common stock of X. There is no other outstanding stock of X. The annual exclusion under section 2503 is not allowable with respect to any gift.

(2) On January 15, 1991, when the aggregate fair market value of the preferred stock is $1,500,000 and the aggregate fair market value of the common stock is $500,000, P transfers all 1,000 shares of the common stock to P's child. Section 2701 applies to the initial transfer because P transferred an equity interest (the common stock) to a member of P's family and immediately thereafter held an applicable retained interest (the preferred stock). The fair market value of P's interest in X immediately prior to the transfer is $2,000,000 and the section 2701 value of the preferred stock (the section 2701 interest) is zero. With respect to the initial transfer, the amount remaining after Step 2 of the subtraction method of § 25.2701-3 was $2,000,000 ($2,000,000 minus zero), all of which is allocated to the transferred stock. P had made no gifts prior to 1991. The sum of P's aggregate taxable gifts for the calendar year 1991 (including the section 2701 transfer) is $2,500,000. P's spouse, S, made no gifts prior to 1991.

(3) P and S elected pursuant to section 2513 to treat one-half of their 1991 gifts as having been made by each spouse. Without the application of section 2701, P and S's aggregate gifts would have been $500,000 and each spouse would have paid no gift tax because of the application of the unified credit under section 2505. However, because of the application of section 2701, both P and S are each treated as the initial transferor of aggregate taxable gifts in the amount of $1,250,000 and, after the application of the unified credit under section 2505, each paid $255,500 in gift tax with respect to their 1991 transfers. On October 1, 1994, at a time when the value of the preferred stock is the same as at the time of the initial transfer, P transfers the preferred stock (the section 2701 interest) to P's child.

Example 1. Inter vivos transfer of entire section 2701 interest. P transfers all of the preferred stock to P's child. P and S are each entitled to a reduction of $750,000 in computing their 1994 gift tax. P is entitled to the reduction because P subsequently transferred the one-half share of the section 2701 interest as to which P was the initial transferor to an individual who was not an applicable family member of P. S is entitled to the reduction because P, an applicable family member with respect to S, transferred the one-half share of the section 2701 interest as to which S was the initial transferor to an individual other than S or an applicable family member of S. S may claim the reduction against S's 1994 gifts. If S's 1994 taxable gifts are less than $750,000, S may claim the remaining amount of the reduction against S's next succeeding lifetime transfers.

Example 2. Inter vivos transfer of portion of section 2701 interest. P transfers one-fourth of the preferred stock to P's child. In this case, P and S are each entitled to a reduction of $187,500, the corresponding portion of the reduction otherwise available to each spouse (one-fourth of $750,000).

Example 3. Transfer at death of donor spouse. P, the donor spouse in the section 2513 election, dies on October 1, 1994, while holding all of the preferred stock. The executor of P's estate is entitled to a reduction in the computation of the tentative tax under section 2001(b). Since no reduction had been previously available with respect to the section 2701 interest, P's estate is entitled to a full reduction of $750,000 with respect to the one-half share of the preferred stock as to which P was the initial transferor. In addition, P's estate is entitled to an additional reduction of up to $750,000 for the remaining section 2701 interest as to which S was the initial transferor. The reduction for the consenting spouse's remaining section 2701 interest is limited to that amount that will produce a tax saving in P's Federal estate tax of $255,500, the amount of gift tax incurred by S by reason of the application of section 2701 to the split initial transfer.

Example 4. Transfer after death of donor spouse. The facts are the same as in *Example 3,* except that S acquires the preferred stock from P's estate and subsequently transfers the preferred stock to S's child. S is not entitled to a reduction because S ceased to be an initial transferor upon P's death (and S's prior taxable gifts were automatically adjusted at that time to the level that would have existed had the split initial transfer not been subject to section 2701).

Example 5. Death of donor spouse after inter vivos transfer. (i) P transfers one-fourth of the preferred stock to P's child. In this case, P and S are each entitled to a reduction of $187,500, the corresponding portion of the reduction otherwise available to each spouse (one-fourth of $750,000). S may claim the reduction against S's 1994 or subsequent transfers. P dies on November 1, 1994.

(ii) P's executor is entitled to include, in computing the reduction available to P's estate, the remaining reduction to which P is entitled and an additional amount of up to $562,500 ($750,000 minus $187,500, the amount of the remaining reduction attributable to the consenting spouse determined immediately prior to P's death). The amount of additional reduction available to P's estate cannot exceed the amount that will reduce P's estate tax by $178,625, the amount that S's 1991 gift tax would have been increased if the application of section 2701 had increased S's taxable gifts by only $562,500 ($750,000 – $187,500).

(g) *Double taxation otherwise avoided.*—No reduction is available under this section if—

(1) Double taxation is otherwise avoided in the computation of the estate tax under section 2001 (or section 2101); or

(2) A reduction was previously taken under the provisions of section 2701(e)(6) with respect to the same section 2701 interest and the same initial transfer.

(h) *Effective date.*—This section is effective for transfers of section 2701 interests after May 4, 1994. If the transfer of a section 2701 interest occurred on or before May 4, 1994, the initial transferor may rely on either this section, project PS-30-91 (1991-2 C.B. 1118, and 1992-1 C.B. 1239 (see § 601.601(d)(2)(ii)(*b*) of this chapter)) or any other reasonable interpretation of the statute. [Reg. § 25.2701-5.]

□ *T.D.* 8536, 5-4-94.]

[Reg. § 25.2701-6]

§ 25.2701-6. Indirect holding of interests.—(a) *In general.*—(1) *Attribution to individuals.*—For purposes of section 2701, an individual is treated as holding an equity interest to the extent the interest is held indirectly through a corporation, partnership, estate, trust, or other entity. If an equity interest is treated as held by a particular individual in more than one capacity, the interest is treated as held by the individual in the manner that attributes the largest total ownership of the equity interest. An equity interest held by a lower-tier entity is attributed to higher-tier entities in accordance with the rules of this section. For example, if an individual is a 50-percent beneficiary of a trust that holds 50 percent of the preferred stock of a corporation, 25 percent of the preferred stock is considered held by the individual under these rules.

(2) *Corporations.*—A person is considered to hold an equity interest held by or for a corporation in the proportion that the fair market value of the stock the person holds bears to the fair market value of all the stock in the corporation (determined as if each class of stock were held separately by one individual). This paragraph applies to any entity classified as a corporation or as an association taxable as a corporation for federal income tax purposes.

(3) *Partnerships.*—A person is considered to hold an equity interest held by or for a partnership in the proportion that the fair market value of the larger of the person's profits interest or capital interest in the partnership bears to the total fair market value of the corresponding profits interests or capital interests in the partnership, as the case may be (determined as if each class were held by one individual). This paragraph applies to any entity classified as a partnership for federal income tax purposes.

(4) *Estates, trusts and other entities.*—(i) *In general.*—A person is considered to hold an equity interest held by or for an estate or trust to the extent the person's beneficial interest therein may be satisfied by the equity interest held by the estate or trust, or the income or proceeds thereof, assuming the maximum exercise of discretion in favor of the person. A beneficiary of an estate or trust who cannot receive any distribution with respect to an equity interest held by the estate or trust, including the income therefrom or the proceeds from the disposition thereof, is not considered the holder of the equity interest. Thus, if stock held by a decedent's estate has been specifically bequeathed to one beneficiary and the residue of the estate has been bequeathed to other beneficiaries, the stock is considered held only by the beneficiary to whom it was specifically bequeathed. However, any person who may receive distributions from a trust is considered to hold an equity interest held by the trust if the distributions may be made from current or accumulated income from or the proceeds from the disposition of the equity interest, even though under the terms of the trust the

interest can never be distributed to that person. This paragraph applies to any entity that is not classified as a corporation, an association taxable as a corporation, or a partnership for federal income tax purposes.

(ii) *Special rules.*—(A) Property is held by a decedent's estate if the property is subject to claims against the estate and expenses of administration.

(B) A person holds a beneficial interest in a trust or an estate so long as the person may receive distributions from the trust or the estate other than payments for full and adequate consideration.

(C) An individual holds an equity interest held by or for a trust if the individual is considered an owner of the trust (a "grantor trust") under subpart E, part 1, subchapter J of the Internal Revenue Code (relating to grantors and others treated as substantial owners). However, if an individual is treated as the owner of only a fractional share of a grantor trust because there are multiple grantors, the individual holds each equity interest held by the trust, except to the extent that the fair market value of the interest exceeds the fair market value of the fractional share.

(5) *Multiple attribution.*—(i) *Applicable retained interests.*—If this section attributes an applicable retained interest to more than one individual in a class consisting of the transferor and one or more applicable family members, the interest is attributed within that class in the following order—

(A) If the interest is held in a grantor trust, to the individual treated as the holder thereof;

(B) To the transferor;

(C) To the transferor's spouse; or

(D) To each applicable family member on a pro rata basis.

(ii) *Subordinate equity interests.*—If this section attributes a subordinate equity interest to more than one individual in a class consisting of the transferor, applicable family members, and members of the transferor's family, the interest is attributed within that class in the following order—

(A) To the transferee;

(B) To each member of the transferor's family on a pro rata basis;

(C) If the interest is held in a grantor trust, to the individual treated as the holder thereof;

(D) To the transferor;

(E) To the transferor's spouse; or

(F) To each applicable family member on a pro rata basis.

(b) *Examples.*—The following examples illustrate the provisions of this section:

Example 1. A, an individual, holds 25 percent by value of each class of stock of Y Corporation. Persons unrelated to A hold the remaining stock. Y holds 50 percent of the stock of Corporation X. Under paragraph (a)(2) of this section, Y's interests in X are attributed proportionately to the shareholders of Y. Accordingly, A is considered to hold a 12.5 percent (25 percent × 50 percent) interest in X.

Example 2. Z Bank's authorized capital consists of 100 shares of common stock and 100 shares of preferred stock. A holds 60 shares of each (common and preferred) and A's child, B, holds 40 shares of common stock. Z holds the balance of its own preferred stock, 30 shares as part of a common trust fund it maintains and 10 shares permanently set aside to satisfy a deferred obligation. For purposes of section 2701, A holds 60 shares of common stock and 66 shares of preferred stock in Z, 60 shares of each class directly and 6 shares of preferred stock indirectly (60 percent of the 10 shares set aside to fund the deferred obligation).

Example 3. An irrevocable trust holds a 10-percent general partnership interest in Partnership Q. One-half of the trust income is required to be distributed to O Charity. The other one-half of the income is to be distributed to D during D's life and thereafter to E for such time as E survives D. D holds one-half of the trust's interest in Q by reason of D's present right to receive one-half of the trust's income, and E holds one-half of the trust's interest in Q by reason of E's future right to receive one-half of the trust's income. Nevertheless, no family member is treated as holding more than one-half of the trust's interest in Q because at no time will either D or E actually hold, in the aggregate, any right with respect to income or corpus greater than one-half.

Example 4. An irrevocable trust holds a 10-percent general partnership interest in partnership M. One-half of the trust income is to be paid to D for D's life. The remaining income may, in the trustee's discretion, be accumulated or paid to or for the benefit of a class that includes D's child F, in such amounts as the trustee determines. On the death of the survivor of D and F, the trust corpus is required to be distributed to O Charity. The trust's interest in M is held by the trust's beneficiaries to the extent that present and future income or corpus may be distributed to them. Accordingly, D holds one-half of the trust's interest in M because D is entitled to receive one-half of the trust income currently. F holds the entire value of the interest because F is a member of the class eligible to receive the entire trust income for such time as F survives D. See paragraph (a)(5) of this section for rules applicable in the case of multiple attribution.

Example 5. The facts are the same as in *Example 4,* except that all the income is required to be paid to O Charity for the trust's initial year. The result is the same as in *Example 4.* [Reg. § 25.2701-6.]

☐ [*T.D.* 8395, 1-28-92.]

[Reg. § 25.2701-7]

§ 25.2701-7. Separate interests.—The Secretary may, by regulation, revenue ruling, notice, or other document of general application, prescribe rules under which an applicable retained interest is treated as two or more separate interests for purposes of section 2701. In addition, the Commissioner may, by ruling issued to a taxpayer upon request, treat any applicable retained interest as two or more separate interests as may be necessary and appropriate to carry out the purposes of section 2701. [Reg. § 25.2701-7.]

☐ [*T.D.* 8395, 1-28-92.]

[Reg. § 25.2701-8]

§ 25.2701-8. Effective dates.—Sections 25.2701-1 through 25.2701-4 and § § 25.2701-6 and 25.2701-7 are effective as of January 28, 1992. For transfers made prior to January 28, 1992, taxpayers may rely on any reasonable interpretation of the statutory provisions. For these purposes, the provisions of the proposed regulations and the final regulations are considered a reasonable interpretation of the statutory provisions. [Reg. § 25.2701-8.]

☐ [*T.D.* 8395, 1-28-92.]

[Reg. § 25.2702-0]

§ 25.2702-0. Table of contents.—This section lists the major paragraphs contained in § § 25.2702-1 through 25.2702-7.

[Reg. §25.2702-0.]

☐ [*T.D.* 8395, 1-28-92. *Amended by T.D.* 9181, 2-24-2005.]

[Reg. §25.2702-1]

§25.2702-1. Special valuation rules in the case of transfers of interests in trust.—(a) *Scope of section 2702.*—Section 2702 provides special rules to determine the amount of the gift when an individual makes a transfer in trust to (or for the benefit of) a member of the individual's family and the individual or an applicable family member retains an interest in the trust. Section 25.2702-4 treats certain transfers of property as transfers in trust. Certain transfers, including transfers to a personal residence trust, are not subject to section 2702. See paragraph (c) of this section. Member of the family is defined in §25.2702-2(a)(1). Applicable family member is defined in §25.2701-1(d)(2).

(b) *Effect of section 2702.*—If section 2702 applies to a transfer, the value of any interest in the trust retained by the transferor or any applicable family member is determined under §25.2702-2(b). The amount of the gift, if any, is then determined by subtracting the value of the interests retained by the transferor or any applicable family member from the value of the transferred property. If the retained interest is not a qualified interest (as defined in §25.2702-3), the retained interest is generally valued at zero, and the amount of the gift is the entire value of the property.

(c) *Exceptions to section 2702.*—Section 2702 does not apply to the following transfers.

(1) *Incomplete gift.*—A transfer no portion of which would be treated as a completed gift without regard to any consideration received by the transferor. If a transfer is wholly incomplete as to an undivided fractional share of the property transferred (without regard to any consideration received by the transferor), for purposes of this paragraph the transfer is treated as incomplete as to that share.

(2) *Personal residence trust.*—A transfer in trust that meets the requirements of §25.2702-5.

(3) *Charitable remainder trust.*—(i) For transfers made on or after May 19, 1997, a transfer to a pooled income fund described in section 642(c)(5); a transfer to a charitable remainder annuity trust described in section 664(d)(1); a transfer to a charitable remainder unitrust described in section 664(d)(2) if under the terms of the governing instrument the unitrust amount can be computed only under section 664(d)(2)(A); and a transfer to a charitable remainder unitrust if under the terms of the governing instrument the unitrust amount can be computed under section 664(d)(2) and (3) and either there are only two consecutive noncharitable beneficial interests and the transferor holds the second of the two interests, or the only permissible recipients of the unitrust amount are the transferor, the transferor's U.S. citizen spouse, or both the transferor and the transferor's U.S. citizen spouse.

(ii) For transfers made before May 19, 1997, a transfer in trust if the remainder interest in the trust qualifies for a deduction under section 2522.

(4) *Pooled income fund.*—A transfer of property to a pooled income fund (as defined in section 642(c)(5)).

(5) *Charitable lead trust.*—A transfer in trust if the only interest in the trust, other than the remainder interest or a qualified annuity or unitrust interest, is an interest that qualifies for deduction under section 2522.

(6) *Certain assignments of remainder interests.*—The assignment of a remainder interest if the only retained interest of the transferor or an applicable family member is as the permissible recipient of distributions of income in the sole discretion of an independent trustee (as defined in section 674(c)).

(7) *Certain property settlements.*—A transfer in trust if the transfer of an interest to a spouse is deemed to be for full and adequate consideration by reason of section 2516 (relating to certain property settlements) and the remaining interests in the trust are retained by the other spouse.

(8) *Transfer or assignment to a Qualified Domestic Trust.*—A transfer or assignment (as described in section 2056(d)(2)(B)) by a noncitizen surviving spouse of property to a Qualified Domestic Trust under the circumstances described in §20.2056A-4(b) of this chapter, where the surviving spouse retains an interest in the transferred property that is not a qualified interest and the transfer is not described in section 2702(a)(3)(A)(ii) or 2702(c)(4). [Reg. §25.2702-1.]

☐ [*T.D.* 8395, 1-28-92. *Amended by T.D.* 8612, 8-21-95 *and T.D.* 8791, 12-9-98.]

[Reg. §25.2702-2]

§25.2702-2. Definitions and valuation rules.—(a) *Definitions.*—The following definitions apply for purposes of section 2702 and the regulations thereunder.

(1) *Member of the family.*—With respect to any individual, member of the family means the individual's spouse, any ancestor or lineal descendant of the individual or the individual's spouse, any brother or sister of the individual, and any spouse of the foregoing.

(2) *Transfer in trust.*—A transfer in trust includes a transfer to a new or existing trust and an assignment of an interest in an existing trust. Transfer in trust does not include—

(i) The exercise, release or lapse of a power of appointment over trust property that is not a transfer under chapter 12; or

(ii) The execution of a qualified disclaimer (as defined in section 2518).

(3) *Retained.*—Retained means held by the same individual both before and after the transfer in trust. In the case of the creation of a term interest, any interest in the property held by the transferor immediately after the transfer is treated as held both before and after the transfer.

(4) *Interest.*—An interest in trust includes a power with respect to a trust if the existence of the power would cause any portion of a transfer to be treated as an incomplete gift under chapter 12.

(5) *Holder.*—The holder is the person to whom the annuity or unitrust interest is payable during the fixed term of that interest. References to holder shall also include the estate of that person.

(6) *Qualified interest.*—Qualified interest means a qualified annuity interest, a qualified unitrust interest, or a qualified remainder interest. If a transferor retains a power to revoke a qualified annuity interest or qualified unitrust interest of the transferor's spouse, then the revocable qualified annuity or unitrust interest of the transferor's spouse is treated as a retained qualified interest of the transferor. In order for the transferor to be treated as having retained a qualified interest under the preceding sentence, the interest of the transferor's spouse (the successor holder) must be an interest that meets the requirements of a qualified annuity interest in accordance with § 25.2702-3(b) and (d), or a qualified unitrust interest in accordance with § 25.2702-3(c) and (d), but for the transferor's retained power to revoke the interest.

(7) *Qualified annuity interest.*—Qualified annuity interest means an interest that meets all the requirements of § 25.2702-3(b) and (d).

(8) *Qualified unitrust interest.*—Qualified unitrust interest means an interest that meets all the requirements of § 25.2702-3(c) and (d).

(9) *Qualified remainder interest.*—Qualified remainder interest means an interest that meets all the requirements of § 25.2702-3(f).

(10) *Governing instrument.*—Governing instrument means the instrument or instruments creating and governing the operation of the trust arrangement.

(b) *Valuation of retained interests.*—(1) *In general.*—Except as provided in paragraphs (b)(2) and (c) of this section, the value of any interest retained by the transferor or an applicable family member is zero.

(2) *Qualified interest.*—The value[s] of a qualified annuity interest and a qualified remainder interest following a qualified annuity interest are determined under section 7520. The value[s] of a qualified unitrust interest and a qualified remainder interest following a qualified unitrust interest are determined as if they were interests described in section 664.

(c) *Valuation of a term interest in certain tangible property.*—(1) *In general.*—If section 2702 applies to a transfer in trust of tangible property described in paragraph (c)(2) of this section ("tangible property"), the value of a retained term interest (other than a qualified interest) is not determined under section 7520 but is the amount the transferor establishes as the amount a willing buyer would pay a willing seller for the interest, each having reasonable knowledge of the relevant facts and neither being under any compulsion to buy or sell. If the transferor cannot reasonably establish the value of the term interest pursuant to this paragraph (c)(1), the interest is valued at zero.

(2) *Tangible property subject to rule.*—(i) *In general.*—Except as provided in paragraph (c)(2)(ii) of this section, paragraph (c)(1) of this section applies only to tangible property—

(A) For which no deduction for depreciation or depletion would be allowable if the property were used in a trade or business or held for the production of income; and

(B) As to which the failure to exercise any rights under the term interest would not increase the value of the property passing at the end of the term interest.

(ii) *Exception for de minimis amounts of depreciable property.*—In determining whether property meets the requirements of this paragraph (c)(2) at the time of the transfer in trust, improvements that would otherwise cause the property not to qualify are ignored if the fair market value of the improvements, in the aggregate, do [sic] not exceed 5 percent of the fair market value of the entire property.

(3) *Evidence of value of property*—The best evidence of the value of any term interest to which this paragraph (c) applies is actual sales or rentals that are comparable both as to the nature and character of the property and the duration of the term interest. Little weight is accorded appraisals in the absence of such evidence. Amounts determined under section 7520 are not evidence of what a willing buyer would pay a willing seller for the interest.

(4) *Conversion of property.*—(i) *In general.*—Except as provided in paragraph (c)(4)(iii) of this section, if a term interest in property is valued under paragraph (c)(1) of this section, and during the term the property is converted into property a term interest in which would not qualify for valuation under paragraph (c)(1) of this section, the conversion is treated as a transfer for no consideration for purposes of chapter 12 of the value of the unexpired portion of the term interest.

(ii) *Value of unexpired portion of term interest.*—For purposes of paragraph (c)(4)(i) of this section, the value of the unexpired portion of a term interest is the amount that bears the same relation to the value of the term interest as of the date of conversion (determined under section 7520 using the rate in effect under section 7520 on the date of the original transfer and the fair market value of the property as of the date of the original transfer) as the value of the term interest as of the date of the original transfer (determined under paragraph (c)(1) of this section) bears to the value of the term interest as of the date of the original transfer (determined under section 7520).

(iii) *Conversion to qualified annuity interest.*—The conversion of tangible property previously valued under paragraph (c)(1) of this section into property a term interest in which would not qualify for valuation under paragraph (c)(1) of this section is not a transfer of the value of the unexpired portion of the term interest if the interest thereafter meets the requirements of a qualified annuity interest. The rules of § 25.2702-5(d)(8) (including governing instrument requirements) apply for purposes of determining the amount of the annuity payment required to be made and the determination of whether the interest meets the requirements of a qualified annuity interest.

(5) *Additions or improvements to property.*—(i) *Additions or improvements substantially affecting nature of property.*—If an addition or improvement is made to property a term interest in which was valued under paragraph (c)(1) of this section, and the addition or improvement affects the nature of the property to such an extent that the property would not be treated as property meeting the requirements of paragraph (c)(2) of this section if the property had included the addition or improvement at the time it was transferred, the entire property is deemed, for purposes of paragraph (c)(4) of this section, to convert (effective as of the date the addition or improvement is commenced) into property a term interest in which would not qualify for valuation under paragraph (c)(1) of this section.

(ii) *Other additions or improvements.*—If an addition or improvement is made to property, a term interest in which was valued under paragraph (c)(1) of this section, and the addition or improvement does not affect the nature of the property to such an extent that the property would not be treated as property meeting the requirements of paragraph (c)(2) of this section if the property had included the addition or improvement at the time it was transferred, the addition or improvement is treated as an additional transfer (effective as of the date the addition or improvement is commenced) subject to § 25.2702-2(b)(1).

(d) *Examples.*—(1) The following examples illustrate the rules of § 25.2702-1 and § 25.2702-2. Each example assumes that all applicable requirements of those sections not specifically described in the example are met.

Example 1. A transfers property to an irrevocable trust, retaining the right to receive the income of the trust for 10 years. On the expiration of the 10-year term, the trust is to terminate and the trust corpus is to be paid to A's child. However, if A dies during the 10-year term, the entire trust corpus is to be paid to A's estate. Each retained interest is valued at zero because it is not a qualified interest. Thus, the amount of A's gift is the fair market value of the property transferred to the trust.

Example 2. A transfers property to an irrevocable trust, retaining a 10-year annuity interest that meets the requirements set forth in § 25.2702-3 for a qualified annuity interest. Upon expiration of the 10-year term, the trust is to terminate and the trust corpus is to be paid to A's child. The amount of A's gift is the fair market value of the property transferred to the trust less the value of the retained qualified annuity interest determined under section 7520.

Example 3. D transfers property to an irrevocable trust under which the income is payable to D's spouse for life. Upon the death of D's spouse, the trust is to terminate and the trust corpus is to be paid to D's child. D retains no interest in the trust. Although the spouse is an applicable family member of D under section 2702, the spouse has not retained an interest in the trust because the spouse did not hold the interest both before and after the transfer. Section 2702 does not apply because neither the transferor nor an applicable family member has retained an interest in the trust. The result is the same whether or not D elects to treat the transfer as a transfer of qualified terminable interest property under section 2056(b)(7).

Example 4. A transfers property to an irrevocable trust, under which the income is to be paid to A for life. Upon termination of the trust, the trust corpus is to be distributed to A's child. A also retains certain powers over principal that cause the transfer to be wholly incomplete for federal gift tax purposes. Section 2702 does not apply because no portion of the transfer would be treated as a completed gift.

Example 5. The facts are the same as in *Example 4*, except that the trust is divided into separate fractional shares and A's retained powers apply to only one of the shares. Section 2702 applies except with respect to the share of the trust as to which A's retained powers cause the transfer to be an incomplete gift.

(2) The following facts apply for *Examples 6* through *8*(examples illustrating § 25.2702-2(c)—tangible property exception):

Facts. A transfers a painting having a fair market value of $2,000,000 to A's child, B, retaining the use of the painting for 10 years. The painting does not possess an ascertainable useful life. Assume that the painting would not be depreciable if it were used in a trade or business or held for the production of income. Assume that the value of A's term interest, determined under section 7520, is $1,220,000, and that A establishes that a willing buyer of A's interest would pay $500,000 for the interest.

Example 6. A's term interest is not a qualified interest under § 25.2702-3. However, because of the nature of the property, A's failure to exercise A's rights with regard to the painting would not be expected to cause the value of the painting to be higher than it would otherwise be at the time it passes to B. Accordingly, A's interest is valued under § 25.2702-2(c)(1) at $500,000. The amount of A's gift is $1,500,000, the difference between the fair market value of the painting and the amount determined under § 25.2702-2(c)(1).

Example 7. Assume that the only evidence produced by A to establish the value of A's 10-year term interest is the amount paid by a museum for the right to use a comparable painting for 1 year. A asserts that the value of the 10-year term is 10 times the value of the 1-year term. A has not established the value of the 10-year term interest because a series of short-term rentals the aggregate duration of which equals the duration of the actual term interest does not establish what a willing buyer would pay a willing seller for the 10-year term interest. However, the value of the 10-year term interest is not less than the value of the 1-year term because it can be assumed that a willing buyer would pay no less for a 10-year term interest than a 1-year term interest.

Example 8. Assume that after 24 months A and B sell the painting for $2,000,000 and invest the proceeds in a portfolio of securities. A continues to hold an income interest in the securities for the duration of the 10-year term. Under § 25.2702-2(c)(4) the conversion of the painting into a type of property a term interest in which would not qualify for valuation under § 25.2702-2(c)(1) is treated as a transfer by A of the value of the unexpired portion of A's original term interest, unless the property is thereafter held in a trust meeting the requirements of a qualified annuity interest. Assume that the value of A's remaining term interest in $2,000,000 (determined under section 7520 using the section 7520 rate in effect on the date of the original transfer) is $1,060,000. The value of the unexpired portion of A's interest is $434,426, the amount that bears the same relation to $1,060,000 as $500,000 (the value of A's interest as of the date of the original transfer determined under paragraph (c)(1) of this section) bears to $1,220,000 (the value of A's interest as of the date of the original transfer determined under section 7520). [Reg. § 25.2702-2.]

☐ [*T.D.* 8395, 1-28-92. *Amended by T.D.* 9181, 2-24-2005.]

[Reg. § 25.2702-3]

§ 25.2702-3. Qualified interests.—(a) *In general.*—This section provides rules for determining if an interest is a qualified annuity interest, a qualified unitrust interest, or a qualified remainder interest.

(b) *Special rules for qualified annuity interests.*—An interest is a qualified annuity interest only if it meets the requirements of this paragraph and paragraph (d) of this section.

(1) *Payment of annuity amount.*—(i) *In general.*—A qualified annuity interest is an irrevocable right to receive a fixed amount. The annuity amount must be payable to (or for the benefit of) the holder of the annuity interest at least annually. A right of withdrawal, whether or not cumulative, is not a qualified annuity interest. Issuance of a note, other debt instrument, option, or other similar financial arrangement, directly or indirectly, in satisfaction of the annuity amount does not constitute payment of the annuity amount.

(ii) *Fixed amount.*—A fixed amount means—

(A) A stated dollar amount payable periodically, but not less frequently than annually, but only to the extent the amount does not exceed 120 percent of the stated dollar amount payable in the preceding year; or

(B) A fixed fraction or percentage of the initial fair market value of the property transferred to the trust, as finally determined for federal tax purposes, payable periodically but not less frequently than annually, but only to the extent the fraction or percentage does not exceed 120 percent of the fixed fraction or percentage payable in the preceding year.

(iii) *Income in excess of the annuity amount.*—An annuity interest does not fail to be a qualified annuity interest merely because the trust permits income in excess of the amount required to pay the annuity amount to be paid to or for the benefit of the holder of the qualified annuity interest. Nevertheless, the right to receive the excess income is not a qualified interest and is not taken into account in valuing the qualified annuity interest.

(2) *Incorrect valuations of trust property.*—If the annuity is stated in terms of a fraction or percentage of the initial fair market value of the trust property, the governing instrument must contain provisions meeting the requirements of § § 1.664-2(a)(1)(iii) of this chapter (relating to adjustments for any incorrect determination of the fair market value of the property in the trust).

(3) *Period for payment of annuity amount.*—The annuity amount may be payable based on either the anniversary date of the creation of the trust or the taxable year of the trust. In either situation, the annuity amount may be paid annually or more frequently, such as semi-annually, quarterly, or monthly. If the payment is made based on the anniversary date, proration of the annuity amount is required only if the last period during which the annuity is payable to the grantor is a period of less than 12 months. If the payment is made based on the taxable year, proration of the annuity amount is required for each short taxable year of the trust during the grantor's term. The prorated amount is the annual annuity amount multiplied by a fraction, the numerator of which is the number of days in the short period and the denominator of which is 365 (366 if February 29 is a day included in the numerator).

(4) *Payment of the annuity amount in certain circumstances.*—An annuity amount payable based on the anniversary date of the creation of the trust must be paid no later than 105 days after the anniversary date. An annuity amount payable based on the taxable year of the trust may be paid after the close of the taxable year, provided the payment is made no later than the date by which the trustee is required to file the Federal income tax return of the trust for the taxable year (without regard to extensions). If the trustee reports for the taxable year pursuant to § 1.671-4(b) of this chapter, the annuity payment must be made no later than the date by which the trustee would have been required to file the Federal income tax return of the trust for the taxable year (without regard to extensions) had the trustee reported pursuant to § 1.671-4(a) of this chapter.

(5) *Additional contributions prohibited.*—The governing instrument must prohibit additional contributions to the trust.

(c) *Special rules for qualified unitrust interests.*—An interest is a qualified unitrust interest only if it meets the requirements of this paragraph and paragraph (d) of this section.

(1) *Payment of unitrust amount.*—(i) *In general.*—A qualified unitrust interest is an irrevocable right to receive payment periodically, but not less frequently than annually, of a fixed percentage of the net fair market value of the trust assets, determined annually. For rules relating to computation of the net fair market value of the trust assets see § 25.2522(c)-3(c)(2)(vii). The unitrust amount must be payable to (or for the benefit of) the holder of the unitrust interest at least annually. A right of withdrawal, whether or not cumulative, is not a qualified unitrust interest. Issuance of a note, other debt instrument, option, or other similar financial arrangement, directly or indirectly, in satisfaction of the unitrust amount does not constitute payment of the unitrust amount.

(ii) *Fixed percentage.*—A fixed percentage is a fraction or percentage of the net fair market value of the trust assets, determined annually, payable periodically but not less frequently than annually, but only to the extent the fraction or percentage does not exceed 120 percent of the fixed fraction or percentage payable in the preceding year.

(iii) *Income in excess of unitrust amount.*—A unitrust interest does not fail to be a qualified unitrust interest merely because the trust permits income in excess of the amount required to pay the unitrust amount to be paid to or for the benefit of the holder of the qualified unitrust interest. Nevertheless, the right to receive the excess income is not a qualified interest and is not taken into account in valuing the qualified unitrust interest.

(2) *Incorrect valuations of trust property.*—The governing instrument must contain provisions meeting the requirements of § 1.664-3(a)(1)(iii) of this chapter (relating to the incorrect determination of the fair market value of the property in the trust).

(3) *Period for payment of unitrust amount.*—The unitrust amount may be payable based on either the anniversary date of the creation of the trust or the taxable year of the trust. In either situation, the unitrust amount may be paid annually or more frequently, such as semi-annually, quarterly, or monthly. If the payment is made based on the anniversary date, proration of the unitrust amount is required only if the last period during which the annuity is payable to the grantor is a period of less than 12 months. If the payment is made based on the taxable year, proration of the unitrust amount is required for each short taxable year of the trust during the grantor's term. The prorated amount is the annual unitrust amount multiplied by a fraction, the numerator of which is the number of days in the short period and the denominator of which is 365 (366 if February 29 is a day included in the numerator).

(4) *Payment of the unitrust amount in certain circumstances.*—A unitrust amount payable based on the anniversary date of the creation of the trust must be paid no later than 105 days after the anniversary date. A unitrust amount payable based on the taxable year of the trust may be paid after the close of the taxable year, provided the payment is made no later than the date by which the trustee is required to file the Federal income tax return of the trust for the taxable year (without regard to extensions). If the trustee reports for the taxable year pursuant to § 1.671-4(b) of this chapter, the unitrust payment must be made no later than the date by which the trustee would have been required to file the Federal income tax return of the trust for the taxable year (without regard to extensions) had the trustee reported pursuant to § 1.671-4(a) of this chapter.

(d) *Requirements applicable to qualified annuity interests and qualified unitrust interests.*—(1) *In general.*—To be a qualified annuity or unitrust interest, an interest must be a qualified annuity interest in every respect or a qualified unitrust interest in every respect. For example, if the interest consists of the right to receive each year a payment equal to the lesser of a fixed amount of the initial trust assets or a fixed percentage of the annual value of the trust assets, the interest is not a qualified interest. If, however, the interest consists of the right to receive each year a payment equal to the greater of a stated dollar amount or a fixed percentage of the initial trust assets or a fixed percentage of the annual value of the trust assets, the interest is a qualified interest that is valued at the greater of the two values. To be a qualified interest, the interest must meet the definition of and function exclusively as a qualified interest from the creation of the trust.

(2) *Contingencies.*—A holder's qualified interest must be payable in any event to or for the benefit of the holder for the fixed term of that

interest. Thus, payment of the interest cannot be subject to any contingency other than either the survival of the holder until the commencement, or throughout the term, of that holder's interest, or, in the case of a revocable interest described in § 25.2702-2(a)(6), the transferor's right to revoke the qualified interest of that transferor's spouse.

(3) *Amounts payable to other persons.*—The governing instrument must prohibit distributions from the trust to or for the benefit of any person other than the holder of the qualified annuity or unitrust interest during the term of the qualified interest.

(4) *Term of the annuity or unitrust interest.*—The governing instrument must fix the term of the annuity or unitrust and the term of the interest must be fixed and ascertainable at the creation of the trust. The term must be for the life of the holder, for a specified term of years, or for the shorter (but not the longer) of those periods. Successive term interests for the benefit of the same individual are treated as the same term interest.

(5) *Commutation.*—The governing instrument must prohibit commutation (prepayment) of the interest of the holder.

(6) *Use of debt obligations to satisfy the annuity or unitrust payment obligation.*—(i) *In general.*—In the case of a trust created on or after September 20, 1999, the trust instrument must prohibit the trustee from issuing a note, other debt instrument, option, or other similar financial arrangement in satisfaction of the annuity or unitrust payment obligation.

(ii) *Special rule in the case of a trust created prior to September 20, 1999.*—In the case of a trust created prior to September 20, 1999, the interest will be treated as a qualified interest under section 2702(b) if—

(A) Notes, other debt instruments, options, or similar financial arrangements are not issued after September 20, 1999, to satisfy the annuity or unitrust payment obligation; and

(B) Any notes or any other debt instruments that were issued to satisfy the annual payment obligation on or prior to September 20, 1999, are paid in full by December 31, 1999, and any option or similar financial arrangement issued to satisfy the annual payment obligation is terminated by December 31, 1999, such that the grantor receives cash or other trust assets in satisfaction of the payment obligation. For purposes of the preceding sentence, an option will be considered terminated only if the grantor receives cash or other trust assets equal in value to the greater of the required annuity or unitrust payment plus interest computed under section 7520 of the Internal Revenue Code, or the fair market value of the option.

(e) *Examples.*—The following examples illustrate the rules of paragraphs (b), (c), and (d) of this section. Each example assumes that all applicable requirements for a qualified interest are met unless otherwise specifically stated.

Example 1. A transfers property to an irrevocable trust, retaining the right to receive the greater of $10,000 or the trust income in each year for a term of 10 years. Upon expiration of the 10-year term, the trust is to terminate and the entire trust corpus is to be paid to A's child, provided that if A dies within the 10-year term the trust corpus is to be paid to A's estate. A's annual payment right is a qualified annuity interest to the extent of the right to receive $10,000 per year for 10 years or until A's prior death, and is valued under section 7520 without regard to the right to receive any income in excess of $10,000 per year. The contingent reversion is valued at zero. The amount of A's gift is the fair market value of the property transferred to the trust less the value of the qualified annuity interest.

Example 2. U transfers property to an irrevocable trust, retaining the right to receive $10,000 in each of years 1 through 3, $12,000 in each of years 4 through 6, and $15,000 in each of years 7 through 10. The interest is a qualified annuity interest to the extent of U's right to receive $10,000 per year in years 1 through 3, $12,000 in years 4 through 6, $14,400 in year 7, and $15,000 in years 8 through 10, because those amounts represent the lower of the amount actually payable each year or an amount that does not exceed 120 percent of the stated dollar amount for the preceding year.

Example 3. S transfers property to an irrevocable trust, retaining the right to receive $50,000 in each of years 1 through 3 and $10,000 in each of years 4 through 10. S's entire retained interest is a qualified annuity interest.

Example 4. R transfers property to an irrevocable trust retaining the right to receive annually an amount equal to the lesser of 8 percent of the initial fair market value of the trust property or the trust income for the year. R's annual payment right is not a qualified annuity interest to any extent because R does not have the irrevocable right to receive a fixed amount for each year of the term.

Example 5. A transfers property to an irrevocable trust, retaining the right to receive 5 percent of the net fair market value of the trust property, valued annually, for 10 years. If A dies within the 10-year term, the unitrust amount is to be paid to A's estate for the balance of the term. The interest of A (and A's estate) to receive the unitrust amount for the specified term of 10 years in all events is a qualified unitrust interest for a term of 10 years.

Example 6. The facts are the same as in *Example 5*, except that if A dies within the 10-year term the unitrust amount will be paid to A's estate for an additional 35 years. As in *Example 5*, the interest of A (and A's estate) to receive the unitrust amount for a specified term of 10 years in all events is a qualified unitrust interest for a term of 10 years. However, the right of A's estate to continue to receive the unitrust amount after the expiration of the 10-year term if A dies within that 10-year period is not fixed and ascertainable at the creation of the interest and is not a qualified unitrust interest.

Example 7. B transfers property to an irrevocable trust retaining the right to receive annually an amount equal to 8 percent of the initial fair market value of the trust property for 10 years. Upon expiration of the 10-year term, the trust is to terminate and the entire trust corpus is to be paid to B's child. The governing instrument provides that income in excess of the annuity amount may be paid to B's child in the trustee's discretion. B's interest is not a qualified annuity interest to any extent because a person other than the individual holding the term interest may receive distributions from the trust during the term.

Example 8. A transfers property to an irrevocable trust, retaining the right to receive an annuity equal to 6 percent of the initial net fair market value of the trust property for 10 years, or until A's prior death. At the expiration of the 10-year term, or on A's death prior to the expiration of the 10-year term, the annuity is to be paid to B, A's spouse, if then living, for 10 years or until B's prior death. A retains an inter vivos and testamentary power to revoke B's interest during the initial 10-year term. If not exercised by A during the initial 10-year term (whether during A's life or on A's death), A's right to revoke B's interest will lapse upon either A's death during the 10-year term, or the expiration of A's 10-year term (assuming A survives the term). Upon expiration of B's interest (or on the expiration of A's interest if A revokes B's interest or if B predeceases A), the trust terminates and the trust corpus is payable to A's child. Because A has made a completed gift of the remainder interest, the transfer of property to the trust is not incomplete as to all interests in the property and section 2702 applies. A's annuity interest (A's right to receive the annuity for 10 years, or until A's prior death) is a retained interest that is a qualified annuity interest under paragraphs (b) and (d) of this section. In addition, because A has retained the power to revoke B's interest, B's interest is treated as an interest retained by A for purposes of section 2702. B's successive annuity interest otherwise satisfies the requirements for a qualified interest contained in paragraph (d) of this section, but for A's power to revoke. The term of B's interest is specified in the governing instrument and is fixed and ascertainable at the creation of the trust, and B's right to receive the annuity is contingent only on B's survival, and A's power to revoke. Following the expiration of A's interest, the annuity is to be paid for a 10-year term or for B's (the successor holder's) life, whichever is shorter. Accordingly, A is treated as retaining B's revocable qualified annuity interest pursuant to § 25.2702-2(a)(6). Because both A's interest and B's interest are treated as qualified interests retained by A, the value of the gift is the value of the property transferred to the trust less the value of both A's qualified interest and B's qualified interest (subject to A's power to revoke), each valued as a single-life annuity. If A survives the 10-year term without having revoked B's interest, then A's power to revoke lapses and A will make a completed gift to B at that time. Further, if A revokes B's interest prior to the commencement of that interest, A is treated as making an additional completed gift at that time to A's child. In either case, the amount of the gift would be the present value of B's interest determined under section 7520 and the applicable regulations, as of the date the revocation power lapses or the interest is revoked. See § 25.2511-2(f).

Example 9. (i) A transfers property to an irrevocable trust, retaining the right to receive 6 percent of the initial net fair market value of the trust property for 10 years, or until A's prior death. If A survives the 10-year term, the trust terminates and the trust corpus is payable to A's child. If A dies prior to the expiration of the 10-year term, the annuity is payable to B, A's spouse, if then living, for the balance of the 10-year term, or until B's prior death. A retains the right to revoke B's interest. Upon expiration of B's interest (or upon A's death if A revokes B's interest or if B predeceases A), the trust terminates and the trust corpus is payable to A's child. As is the case in *Example 8*, A's retained annuity interest (A's right to receive the annuity for 10 years, or until A's prior death) is a qualified annuity interest under paragraphs (b) and (d) of this section. However, B's interest does not meet the requirements of paragraph (d) of this section. The term of B's annuity is not fixed and ascertainable at the creation of the trust, because it is not payable for the life of B, a specified term of years, or for the shorter of those periods. Rather, B's annuity is payable for an unspecified period that will depend upon the number of years left in the original term after A's death. Further, B's annuity is payable only if A dies prior to the expiration of the 10-year term. Thus, payment of B's annuity is not dependent solely on B's survival, but rather is dependent on A's failure to survive.

(ii) Accordingly, the amount of the gift is the fair market value of the property transferred to the trust reduced by the value of A's qualified interest (A's right to receive the stated annuity for 10 years or until A's prior death). B's interest is not a qualified interest and is thus valued at zero under section 2702.

(f) *Qualified remainder interest.*—(1) *Requirements.*—An interest is a qualified remainder interest only if it meets all of the following requirements:

(i) It is a qualified remainder interest in every respect.

(ii) It meets the definition of and functions exclusively as a qualified interest from the creation of the interest.

(iii) It is non-contingent. For this purpose, an interest is non-contingent only if it is payable to the beneficiary or the beneficiary's estate in all events.

(iv) All interests in the trust, other than non-contingent remainder interests, are qualified annuity interests or qualified unitrust interests.

Thus, an interest is a qualified remainder interest only if the governing instrument does not permit payment of income in excess of the annuity or unitrust amount to the holder of the qualified annuity or unitrust interest.

(2) *Remainder interest.*—Remainder interest is the right to receive all or a fractional share of the trust property on termination of all or a fractional share of the trust. Remainder interest includes a reversion. A transferor's right to receive an amount that is a stated or pecuniary amount is not a remainder interest. Thus, the right to receive the original value of the trust corpus (or a fractional share) is not a remainder interest.

(3) *Examples.*—The following examples illustrate rules of this paragraph (f). Each example assumes that all applicable requirements of a qualified interest are met unless otherwise specifically stated.

Example 1. A transfers property to an irrevocable trust. The income of the trust is payable to A's child for life. On the death of A's child, the trust is to terminate and the trust corpus is to be paid to A. A's remainder interest is not a qualified remainder interest because the interest of A's child is neither a qualified annuity interest nor a qualified unitrust interest.

Example 2. The facts are the same as in *Example 1*, except that A's child has the right to receive the greater of the income of the trust or $10,000 per year. A's remainder interest is not a qualified remainder interest because the right of A's child to receive income in excess of the annuity amount is not a qualified interest.

Example 3. A transfers property to an irrevocable trust. The trust provides a qualified annuity interest to A's child for 12 years. An amount equal to the initial value of the trust corpus is to be paid to A at the end of that period and the balance is to be paid to A's grandchild. A's interest is not a qualified remainder interest because the amount A is to receive is not a fractional share of the trust property.

Example 4. U transfers property to an irrevocable trust. The trust provides a qualified unitrust interest to U's child for 15 years, at which time the trust terminates and the trust corpus is paid to U or, if U is not then living, to U's child. Because U's remainder interest is contingent, it is not a qualified remainder interest. [Reg. § 25.2702-3.]

☐ [*T.D.* 8395, 1-28-92. *Amended by T.D.* 8536, 5-4-94; *T.D.* 8633, 12-20-95; *T.D.* 8899, 9-1-2000 (*corrected* 11-27-2000) *and T.D.* 9181, 2-24-2005.]

[Reg. § 25.2702-4]

§ 25.2702-4. Certain property treated as held in trust.—(a) *In general.*—For purposes of section 2702, a transfer of an interest in property with respect to which there are one or more term interests is treated as a transfer in trust. A term interest is one of a series of successive (as contrasted with concurrent) interests. Thus, a life interest in property or an interest in property for a term of years is a term interest. However, a term interest does not include a fee interest in property merely because it is held as a tenant in common, a tenant by the entireties, or a joint tenant with right of survivorship.

(b) *Leases.*—A leasehold interest in property is not a term interest to the extent the lease is for full and adequate consideration (without regard to section 2702). A lease will be considered for full and adequate consideration if, under all the facts and circumstances as of the time the lease is entered into or extended, a good faith effort is made to determine the fair rental value of the property and the terms of the lease conform to the value so determined.

(c) *Joint purchases.*—Solely for purposes of section 2702, if an individual acquires a term interest in property and, in the same transaction or series of transactions, one or more members of the individual's family acquire an interest in the same property, the individual acquiring the term interest is treated as acquiring the entire property so acquired, and transferring to each of those family members the interests acquired by that family member in exchange for any consideration paid by that family member. For purposes of this paragraph (c), the amount of the individual's gift will not exceed the amount of consideration furnished by that individual for all interests in the property.

(d) *Examples.*—The following examples illustrate rules of this section:

Example 1. A purchases a 20-year term interest in an apartment building and A's child purchases the remainder interest in the property. A and A's child each provide the portion of the purchase price equal to the value of their respective interests in the property determined under section 7520. Solely for purposes of section 2702, A is treated as acquiring the entire property and transferring the remainder interest to A's child in exchange for the portion of the purchase price provided by A's child. In determining the amount of A's gift, A's retained interest is valued at zero because it is not a qualified interest.

Example 2. K holds rental real estate valued at $100,000. K sells a remainder interest in the property to K's child, retaining the right to receive the income from the property for 20 years. Assume the purchase price paid by K's child for the remainder interest is equal to the value of the interest determined under section 7520. K's retained interest is not a qualified interest and is therefore valued at zero. K has made a gift in the amount of $100,000 less the consideration received from K's child.

Example 3. G and G's child each acquire a fifty percent undivided interest as tenants in common in an office building. The interests of G and G's child are not term interests to which section 2702 applies.

Example 4. B purchases a life estate in property from R, B's grandparent, for $100 and B's child purchases the remainder interest for $50. Assume that the value of the property is $300, the value of the life estate determined under section 7520 is $250 and the value of the remainder interest is $50. B is treated as acquiring the entire property and transferring the remainder interest to B's child. However, the amount of B's gift is $100, the amount of consideration ($100) furnished by B for B's interest.

Example 5. H and W enter into a written agreement relative to their marital and property rights that requires W to transfer property to an irrevocable trust, the terms of which provide that the income of the trust will be paid to H for 10 years. On the expiration of the 10-year term, the trust is to terminate and the trust corpus is to be paid to W. H and W divorce within two years after the agreement is entered into. Pursuant to section 2516, the transfer to H would otherwise be deemed to be for full and adequate consideration. Section 2702 does not apply to the acquisition of the term interest by H because no member of H's family acquired an interest in the property in the same transaction or series of transactions. The result would not be the same if, on the termination of H's interest in the trust, the trust corpus were distributable to the children of H and W rather than W. [Reg. § 25.2702-4.]

□ [*T.D.* 8395, 1-28-92.]

[Reg. § 25.2702-5]

§ 25.2702-5. Personal residence trusts.—(a)(1) *In general.*—Section 2702 does not apply to a transfer in trust meeting the requirements of this section. A transfer in trust meets the requirements of this section only if the trust is a personal residence trust (as defined in paragraph (b) of this section). A trust meeting the requirements of a qualified personal residence trust (as defined in paragraph (c) of this section) is treated as a personal residence trust. A trust of which the term holder is the grantor that otherwise meets the requirements of a personal residence trust (or a qualified personal residence trust) is not a personal residence trust (or a qualified personal residence trust) if, at the time of transfer, the term holder of the trust already holds term interests in two trusts that are personal residence trusts (or qualified personal residence trusts) of which the term holder was the grantor. For this purpose, trusts holding fractional interests in the same residence are treated as one trust.

(2) *Modification of trust.*—A trust that does not comply with one or more of the regulatory requirements under paragraph (b) or (c) of this section will, nonetheless, be treated as satisfying these requirements if the trust is modified, by judicial reformation (or nonjudicial reformation if effective under state law), to comply with the requirements. In the case of a trust created after December 31, 1996, the reformation must be commenced within 90 days after the due date (including extensions) for the filing of the gift tax return reporting the transfer of the residence under section 6075 and must be completed within a reasonable time after commencement. If the reformation is not completed by the due date (including extensions) for filing the gift tax return, the grantor or grantor's spouse must attach a statement to the gift tax return stating that the reformation has been commenced or will be commenced within the 90-day period. In the case of a trust created before January 1, 1997, the reformation must be commenced within 90 days after December 23, 1997, and must be completed within a reasonable time after commencement.

(b) *Personal residence trust.*—(1) *In general.*—A personal residence trust is a trust the governing instrument of which prohibits the trust from holding, for the original duration of the term interest, any asset other than one residence to be used or held for use as a personal residence of the term holder and qualified proceeds (as defined in paragraph (b)(3) of this section). A residence is held for use as a personal residence of the term holder so long as the residence is not occupied by any other person (other than the spouse or a dependent of the term holder) and is available at all times for use by the term holder as a personal residence. A trust does not meet the requirements of this section if, during the original duration of the term interest, the residence may be sold or otherwise transferred by the trust or may be used for a purpose other than as a personal residence of the term holder. In addition, the trust does not meet the requirements of this section unless the governing instrument prohibits the trust from selling or transferring the residence, directly or indirectly, to the grantor, the grantor's spouse, or an entity controlled by the grantor or the grantor's spouse, at any time after the original duration of the term interest during which the trust is a grantor trust. For purposes of the preceding sentence, a sale or transfer to another grantor trust of the grantor or the grantor's spouse is considered a sale or transfer to the grantor or the grantor's spouse; however, a distribution (for no consideration) upon or after the expiration of the original duration of the term interest to another grantor trust of the grantor or the grantor's spouse pursuant to the express terms of the trust will not be considered a sale or transfer to the grantor or the grantor's spouse if such other grantor trust prohibits the sale or transfer of the property to the grantor, the grantor's spouse, or an entity controlled by the grantor or the grantor's spouse. In the event the grantor dies prior to the expiration of the original duration of the term interest, this paragraph (b)(1) does not apply to the distribution (for no consideration) of the residence to any person (including the grantor's estate) pursuant to the express terms of the trust or pursuant to the exercise of a power retained by the grantor under the terms of the trust. Further, this paragraph (b)(1) does not apply to any outright distribution (for no consideration) of the residence to the grantor's spouse after the expiration of the original duration of the term interest pursuant to the express terms of the trust. For purposes of this paragraph (b)(1), a *grantor trust* is a trust treated as owned in whole or in part by the grantor or the grantor's spouse pursuant to sections 671 through 678, and *control* is defined in § 25.2701-2(b)(5)(ii) and (iii). Expenses of the trust whether or not attributable to trust principal may be paid directly by the term holder of the trust.

(2) *Personal residence.*—(i) *In general.*—For purposes of this paragraph (b), a personal residence of a term holder is either—

(A) The principal residence of the term holder (within the meaning of section 1034);

(B) One other residence of the term holder (within the meaning of section 280A(d)(1) but without regard to section 280A(d)(2)); or

(C) An undivided fractional interest in either.

(ii) *Additional property.*—A personal residence may include appurtenant structures used by the term holder for residential purposes and adjacent land not in excess of that which is reasonably appropriate for residential purposes (taking into account the residence's size and location). The fact that a residence is subject to a mortgage does not affect its status as a personal residence. The term personal residence does not include any personal property (*e.g.*, household furnishings).

(iii) *Use of residence.*—A residence is a personal residence only if its primary use is as a residence of the term holder when occupied by the term holder. The principal residence of the term holder will not fail to meet the requirements of the preceding sentence merely because a portion of the residence is used in an activity meeting the requirements of section 280A(c)(1) or (4) (relating to deductibility of expenses related to certain uses), provided that such use is secondary to use of the residence as a residence. A residence is not used primarily as a residence if it is used to provide transient lodging and substantial services are provided in connection with the provision of lodging (*e.g.* a hotel or a bed and breakfast). A residence is not a personal residence if, during any period not occupied by the term holder, its primary use is other than as a residence.

(iv) *Interests of spouses in the same residence.*—If spouses hold interests in the same residence (including community property interests), the spouses may transfer their interests in the residence (or a fractional portion of their interests in the residence) to the same personal residence trust, provided that the governing instrument prohibits any person other than one of the spouses from holding a term interest in the trust concurrently with the other spouse.

(3) *Qualified proceeds.*—Qualified proceeds means the proceeds payable as a result of damage to, or destruction or involuntary conversion (within the meaning of section 1033) of, the residence held by a personal residence trust, provided that the governing instrument requires that the proceeds (including any income thereon) be reinvested in a personal residence within two years from the date on which the proceeds are received.

(c) *Qualified personal residence trust.*—(1) *In general.*—A qualified personal residence trust is a trust meeting all the requirements of this paragraph (c). These requirements must be met by provisions in the governing instrument, and these governing instrument provisions must by their terms continue in effect during the existence of any term interest in the trust.

(2) *Personal residence.*—(i) *In general.*—For purposes of this paragraph (c), a personal residence of a term holder is either—

(A) The principal residence of the term holder (within the meaning of section 1034);

(B) One other residence of the term holder (within the meaning of section 280A(d)(1) but without regard to section 280A(d)(2)); or

(C) An undivided fractional interest in either.

(ii) *Additional property.*—A personal residence may include appurtenant structures used by the term holder for residential purposes and adjacent land not in excess of that which is reasonably appropriate for residential purposes (taking into account the residence's size and location). The fact that a residence is subject to a mortgage does not affect its status as a personal residence. The term personal residence does not include any personal property (*e.g.*, household furnishings).

(iii) *Use of residence.*—A residence is a personal residence only if its primary use is as a residence of the term holder when occupied by the term holder. The principal residence of the term holder will not fail to meet the requirements of the preceding sentence merely because a portion of the residence is used in an activity meeting the requirements of section 280A(c)(1) or (4) (relating to deductibility of expenses related to certain uses), provided that such use is secondary to use of the residence as a residence. A residence is not used primarily as a residence if it is used to provide transient lodging and substantial services are provided in connection with the provision of lodging (*e.g.* a hotel or a bed and breakfast). A residence is not a personal residence if, during any period not occupied by the term holder, its primary use is other than as a residence.

(iv) *Interests of spouses in the same residence.*—If spouses hold interests in the same residence (including community property interests), the spouses may transfer their interests in the residence (or a fractional portion of their interests in the residence) to the same qualified personal residence trust, provided that the governing instrument prohibits any person other than one of the spouses from holding a term interest in the trust concurrently with the other spouse.

(3) *Income of the trust.*—The governing instrument must require that any income of the

trust be distributed to the term holder not less frequently than annually.

(4) *Distributions from the trust to other persons.*—The governing instrument must prohibit distributions of corpus to any beneficiary other than the transferor prior to the expiration of the retained term interest.

(5) *Assets of the trust.*—(i) *In general.*—Except as otherwise provided in paragraphs (c)(5)(ii) and (c)(8) of this section, the governing instrument must prohibit the trust from holding, for the entire term of the trust, any asset other than one residence to be used or held for use (within the meaning of paragraph (c)(7)(i) of this section) as a personal residence of the term holder (the "residence").

(ii) *Assets other than personal residence.*—Except as otherwise provided, the governing instrument may permit a qualified personal residence trust to hold the following assets (in addition to the residence) in the amounts and in the manner described in this paragraph (c)(5)(ii):

(A) *Additions of cash for payment of expenses, etc.*—*(1) Additions.*—The governing instrument may permit additions of cash to the trust, and may permit the trust to hold additions of cash in a separate account, in an amount which, when added to the cash already held in the account for such purposes, does not exceed the amount required:

(i) For payment of trust expenses (including mortgage payments) already incurred or reasonably expected to be paid by the trust within six months from the date the addition is made;

(ii) For improvements to the residence to be paid by the trust within six months from the date the addition is made; and

(iii) For purchase by the trust of the initial residence, within three months of the date the trust is created, provided that no addition may be made for this purpose, and the trust may not hold any such addition, unless the trustee has previously entered into a contract to purchase that residence; and

(iv) For purchase by the trust of a residence to replace another residence, within three months of the date the addition is made, provided that no addition may be made for this purpose, and the trust may not hold any such addition, unless the trustee has previously entered into a contract to purchase that residence.

(2) Distributions of excess cash.—If the governing instrument permits additions of cash to the trust pursuant to paragraph (c)(5)(ii)(A)(*1*) of this section, the governing instrument must require that the trustee determine, not less frequently than quarterly, the amounts held by the trust for payment of expenses in excess of the amounts permitted by that paragraph and must require that those amounts be distributed immediately thereafter to the term holder. In addition, the governing instrument must require, upon termination of the term holder's interest in the trust, any amounts held by the trust for the purposes permitted by paragraph (c)(5)(ii)(A)(*1*) of this section that are not used to pay trust expenses due and payable on the date of termination (including expenses directly related to termination) be distributed outright to the term holder within 30 days of termination.

(B) *Improvements.*—The governing instrument may permit improvements to the residence to be added to the trust and may permit the trust to hold such improvements, provided that the residence, as improved, meets the requirements of a personal residence.

(C) *Sale proceeds.*—The governing instrument may permit the sale of the residence (except as set forth in paragraph (c)(9) of this section) and may permit the trust to hold proceeds from the sale of the residence, in a separate account.

(D) *Insurance and insurance proceeds.*—The governing instrument may permit the trust to hold one or more policies of insurance on the residence. In addition, the governing instrument may permit the trust to hold, in a separate account, proceeds of insurance payable to the trust as a result of damage to or destruction of the residence. For purposes of this paragraph, amounts (other than insurance proceeds payable to the trust as a result of damage to or destruction of the residence) received as a result of the involuntary conversion (within the meaning of section 1033) of the residence are treated as proceeds of insurance.

(6) *Commutation.*—The governing instrument must prohibit commutation (prepayment) of the term holder's interest.

(7) *Cessation of use as a personal residence.*—(i) *In general.*—The governing instrument must provide that a trust ceases to be a qualified personal residence trust if the residence ceases to be used or held for use as a personal residence of the term holder. A residence is held for use as a personal residence of the term holder so long as the residence is not occupied by any other person (other than the spouse or a dependent of the term holder) and is available at all times for use by the term holder as a personal residence. See §25.2702-5(c)(8) for rules governing disposition of assets of a trust as to which the trust has ceased to be a qualified personal residence trust.

(ii) *Sale of personal residence.*—The governing instrument must provide that the trust ceases to be a qualified personal residence trust upon sale of the residence if the governing instrument does not permit the trust to hold proceeds of sale of the residence pursuant to paragraph (c)(5)(ii)(C) of this section. If the governing instrument permits the trust to hold proceeds of sale pursuant to that paragraph, the governing instrument must provide that the trust ceases to be a qualified personal residence trust with respect to all proceeds of sale held by the trust not later than the earlier of—

(A) The date that is two years after the date of sale;

(B) The termination of the term holder's interest in the trust; or

(C) The date on which a new residence is acquired by the trust.

(iii) *Damage to or destruction of personal residence.*—(A) *In general.*—The governing instrument must provide that, if damage or destruction renders the residence unusable as a residence, the trust ceases to be a qualified personal residence trust on the date that is two years after the date of damage or destruction (or the date of termination of the term holder's interest in the trust, if earlier) unless, prior to such date—

(1) Replacement of or repairs to the residence are completed; or

(2) A new residence is acquired by the trust.

(B) *Insurance proceeds.*—For purposes of this paragraph (C)(7)(iii), if the governing instrument permits the trust to hold proceeds of insurance received as a result of damage to or destruction of the residence pursuant to paragraph (c)(5)(ii)(D) of this section, the governing instrument must contain provisions similar to those required by paragraph (c)(7)(ii) of this section.

(8) *Disposition of trust assets on cessation as personal residence trust.*—(i) *In general.*—The governing instrument must provide that, within 30 days after the date on which the trust has ceased to be a qualified personal residence trust with respect to certain assets, either—

(A) The assets be distributed outright to the term holder;

(B) The assets be converted to and held for the balance of the term holder's term in a separate share of the trust meeting the requirements of a qualified annuity interest; or

(C) In the trustee's sole discretion, the trustee may elect to comply with either paragraph (C)(8)(i)(A) or (B) of this section pursuant to their terms.

(ii) *Requirements for conversion to a qualified annuity interest.*—(A) *Governing instrument requirements.*—For assets subject to this paragraph (c)(8) to be converted to and held as a qualified annuity interest, the governing instrument must contain all provisions required by §25.2702-3 with respect to a qualified annuity interest.

(B) *Effective date of annuity.*—The governing instrument must provide that the right of the term holder to receive the annuity amount begins on the date of sale of the residence, the date of damage to or destruction of the residence, or the date on which the residence ceases to be used or held for use as a personal residence, as the case may be ("the cessation date"). Notwithstanding the preceding sentence, the governing instrument may provide that the trustee may defer payment of any annuity amount otherwise payable after the cessation date until the date that is 30 days after the assets are converted to a qualified annuity interest under paragraph (c)(8)(i)(B) of this section ("the conversion date"); provided that any deferred payment must bear interest from the cessation date at a rate not less than the section 7520 rate in effect on the cessation date. The governing instrument may permit the trustee to reduce aggregate deferred annuity payments by the amount of income actually distributed by the trust to the term holder during the deferral period.

(C) *Determination of annuity amount.*—*(1) In general.*—The governing instrument must require that the annuity amount be no less than the amount determined under this paragraph (C).

(2) Entire trust ceases to be a qualified personal residence trust.—If, on the conversion date, the assets of the trust do not include a residence used or held for use as a personal residence, the annuity may not be less than an amount determined by dividing the lesser of the value of all interests retained by the term holder (as of the date of the original transfer or transfers) or the value of all the trust assets (as of the conversion date) by an annuity factor determined—

(i) For the original term of the term holder's interest; and

(ii) At the rate used in valuing the retained interest at the time of the original transfer.

(3) Portion of trust continues as qualified personal residence trust.—If, on the conversion date, the assets of the trust include a residence used or held for use as a personal residence, the annuity must not be less than the amount determined under paragraph (c)(8)(ii)(C)(2) of this section multiplied by a fraction. The numerator of the fraction is the excess of the fair market value of the trust assets on the conversion date over the fair market value of the assets as to which the trust continues as a qualified personal residence trust, and the denominator of the fraction is the fair market value of the trust assets on the conversion date.

(9) *Sale of residence to grantor, grantor's spouse, or entity controlled by grantor or grantor's spouse.*—The governing instrument must prohibit the trust from selling or transferring the residence, directly or indirectly, to the grantor, the grantor's spouse, or an entity controlled by the grantor or the grantor's spouse during the retained term interest of the trust, or at any time after the retained term interest that the trust is a grantor trust. For purposes of the preceding sentence, a sale or transfer to another grantor trust of the grantor or the grantor's spouse is considered a sale or transfer to the grantor or the grantor's spouse; however, a distribution (for no consideration) upon or after the expiration of the retained term interest to another grantor trust of the grantor or the grantor's spouse pursuant to the express terms of the trust will not be considered a sale or transfer to the grantor or the

grantor's spouse if such other grantor trust prohibits the sale or transfer of the property to the grantor, the grantor's spouse, or an entity controlled by the grantor or the grantor's spouse. In the event the grantor dies prior to the expiration of the retained term interest, this paragraph (c)(9) does not apply to the distribution (for no consideration) of the residence to any person (including the grantor's estate) pursuant to the express terms of the trust or pursuant to the exercise of a power retained by the grantor under the terms of the trust. Further, this paragraph (c)(9) does not apply to an outright distribution (for no consideration) of the residence to the grantor's spouse after the expiration of the retained trust term pursuant to the express terms of the trust. For purposes of this paragraph (c)(9), a *grantor trust* is a trust treated as owned in whole or in part by the grantor or the grantor's spouse pursuant to sections 671 through 678, and *control* is defined in § 25.2701-2(b)(5)(ii) and (iii).

(d) *Examples.*—The following examples illustrate rules of this section. Each example assumes that all applicable requirements of a personal residence trust (or qualified personal residence trust) are met unless otherwise stated.

Example 1. C maintains C's principal place of business in one room of C's principal residence. The room meets the requirements of section 280A(c)(1) for deductibility of expenses related to such use. The residence is a personal residence.

Example 2. L owns a vacation condominium that L rents out for six months of the year, but which is treated as L's residence under section 280A(d)(1) because L occupies it for at least 18 days per year. L provides no substantial services in connection with the rental of the condominium. L transfers the condominium to an irrevocable trust, the terms of which meet the requirements of a qualified personal residence trust. L retains the right to use the condominium during L's lifetime. The trust is a qualified personal residence trust.

Example 3. W owns a 200-acre farm. The farm includes a house, barns, equipment buildings, a silo, and enclosures for confinement of farm animals. W transfers the farm to an irrevocable trust, retaining the use of the farm for 20 years, with the remainder to W's child. The trust is not a personal residence trust because the farm includes assets not meeting the requirements of a personal residence.

Example 4. A transfers A's principal residence to an irrevocable trust, retaining the right to use the residence for a 20-year term. The governing instrument of the trust does not prohibit the trust from holding personal property. The trust is not a qualified personal residence trust.

Example 5. T transfers a personal residence to a trust that meets the requirements of a qualified personal residence trust, retaining a term interest in the trust for 10 years. During the period of T's retained term interest, T is forced for health reasons to move to a nursing home. T's spouse continues to occupy the residence. If the residence is available at all times for T's use as a residence during the term (without regard to T's ability to actually use the residence), the residence continues to be held for T's use and the trust does not cease to be a qualified personal residence trust. The residence would cease to be held for use as a personal residence of T if the trustee rented the residence to an unrelated party, because the residence would no longer be available for T's use at all times.

Example 6. T transfers T's personal residence to a trust that meets the requirements of a qualified personal residence trust, retaining the right to use the residence for 12 years. On the date the residence is transferred to the trust, the fair market value of the residence is $100,000. After 6 years, the trustee sells the residence, receiving net proceeds of $250,000, and invests the proceeds of sale in common stock. After an additional eighteen months, the common stock has paid $15,000 in dividends and has a fair market value of $260,000. On that date, the trustee purchases a new residence for $200,000. On the purchase of the new residence, the trust ceases to be a qualified personal residence trust with respect to any amount not reinvested in the new residence. The governing instrument of the trust provides that the trustee, in the trustee's sole discretion, may elect either to distribute the excess proceeds or to convert the proceeds into a qualified annuity interest. The trustee elects the latter option. The amount of the annuity is the amount of the annuity that would be payable if no portion of the sale proceeds had been reinvested in a personal residence multiplied by a fraction. The numerator of the fraction is $60,000 (the amount remaining after reinvestment) and the denominator of the fraction is $260,000 (the fair market value of the trust assets on the conversion date). The obligation to pay the annuity commences on the date of sale, but payment of the annuity that otherwise would have been payable during the period between the date of sale and the date on which the trust ceased to be a qualified personal residence trust with respect to the excess proceeds may be deferred until 30 days after the date on which the new residence is purchased. Any amount deferred must bear compound interest from the date the annuity is payable at the section 7520 rate in effect on the date of sale. The $15,000 of income distributed to the term holder during that period may be used to reduce the annuity amount payable with respect to that period if the governing instrument so provides and thus reduce the amount on which compound interest is computed. [Reg. § 25.2702-5.]

☐ [*T.D.* 8395, 1-28-92. *Amended by T.D.* 8743, 12-22-97.]

[Reg. § 25.2702-6]

§ 25.2702-6. Reduction in taxable gifts.—(a) *Transfers of retained interests in trust.*—(1) *Inter vivos transfers.*—If an individual subsequently transfers by gift an interest in trust previously valued (when held by that individual) under § 25.2702-2(b)(1) or (c), the individual is entitled to a reduction in aggregate taxable gifts. The amount of the reduction is determined under paragraph(b) of this section. Thus, for example, if an individual transferred property to an irrevocable trust, retaining an interest in the trust that was valued at zero under § 25.2702-2(b)(1), and the individual later transfers the retained interest by gift, the individual is entitled to a reduction in aggregate taxable gifts on the subsequent transfer. For purposes of this section, aggregate taxable gifts means the aggregate sum of the individual's taxable gifts for the calendar year determined under section 2502(a)(1).

(2) *Testamentary transfers.*—If either—

(i) A term interest in trust is included in an individual's gross estate solely by reason of section 2033, or

(ii) A remainder interest in trust is included in an individual's gross estate,

and the interest was previously valued (when held by that individual) under § 25.2702-2(b)(1) or (c), the individual's estate is entitled to a reduction in the individual's adjusted taxable gifts in computing the Federal estate tax payable under section 2001. The amount of the reduction is determined under paragraph (b) of this section.

(3) *Gift splitting on subsequent transfer.*—If an individual who is entitled to a reduction in aggregate taxable gifts (or adjusted taxable gifts) subsequently transfers the interest in a transfer treated as made one-half by the individual's spouse under section 2513, the individual may assign one-half of the amount of the reduction to the consenting spouse. The assignment must be attached to the Form 709 on which the consenting spouse reports the split gift.

(b) *Amount of reduction.*—(1) *In general.*—The amount of the reduction in aggregate taxable gifts (or adjusted taxable gifts) is the lesser of—

(i) The increase in the individual's taxable gifts resulting from the interest being valued at the time of the initial transfer under § 25.2702-2(b)(1) or (c); or

(ii) The increase in the individual's taxable gifts (or gross estate) resulting from the subsequent transfer of the interest.

(2) *Treatment of annual exclusion.*—For purposes of determining the amount under paragraph (b)(1)(ii) of this section, the exclusion under section 2503(b) applies first to transfers in that year other than the transfer of the interest previously valued under § 25.2702-2(b)(1) or (c).

(3) *Overlap with section 2001.*—Notwithstanding paragraph (b)(1) of this section, the amount of the reduction is reduced to the extent section 2001 would apply to reduce the amount of an individual's adjusted taxable gifts with respect to the same interest to which paragraph (b)(1) of this section would otherwise apply.

(c) *Examples.*—The rules of this section are illustrated by the following examples. The following facts apply for *Examples 1-4:*

Facts. In 1992, X transferred property to an irrevocable trust retaining the right to receive the trust income for life. On the death of X, the trust is to terminate and the trust corpus is to be paid to X's child, C. X's income interest had a value under section 7520 of $40,000 at the time of the transfer; however, because X's retained interest was not a qualified interest, it was valued at zero under § 25.2702-2(b)(1) for purposes of determining the amount of X's gift. X's taxable gifts in 1992 were therefore increased by $40,000. In 1993, X transfers the income interest to C for no consideration.

Example 1. Assume that the value under section 7520 of the income interest on the subsequent transfer to C is $30,000. If X makes no other gifts to C in 1993, X is entitled to a reduction in aggregate taxable gifts of $20,000, the lesser of the amount by which X's taxable gifts were increased as a result of the income interest being valued at zero on the initial transfer ($40,000) or the amount by which X's taxable gifts are increased as a result of the subsequent transfer of the income interest ($30,000 minus $10,000 annual exclusion).

Example 2. Assume that in 1993, 4 months after X transferred the income interest to C, X transferred $5,000 cash to C. In determining the increase in taxable gifts occurring on the subsequent transfer, the annual exclusion under section 2503(b) is first applied to the cash gift. X is entitled to a reduction in aggregate taxable gifts of $25,000, the lesser of the amount by which X's taxable gifts were increased as a result of the income interest being valued at zero on the initial transfer ($40,000) or the amount by which X's taxable gifts are increased as a result of the subsequent transfer of the income interest ($25,000 (($30,000 + $5,000) – $10,000 annual exclusion).

Example 3. Assume that the value under section 7520 of the income interest on the subsequent transfer to C is $55,000. X is entitled to reduce aggregate taxable gifts by $40,000, the lesser of the amount by which X's taxable gifts were increased as a result of the income interest being valued at zero on the initial transfer ($40,000) or the amount by which X's taxable gifts are increased as a result of the subsequent transfer of the income interest ($55,000 minus $10,000 annual exclusion = $45,000).

Example 4. Assume that X and X's spouse, S, split the subsequent gift to C. X is entitled to assign one-half the reduction to S. If the assignment is made, each is entitled to reduce aggregate taxable gifts by $17,500, the lesser of their portion of the increase in taxable gifts on the initial transfer by reason of the application of section 2702 ($20,000) and their portion of the increase in taxable gifts on the subsequent transfer of the retained interest ($27,500 – $10,000 annual exclusion).

Example 5. In 1992, A transfers property to an irrevocable trust, retaining the right to receive the trust income for 10 years. On the expiration of the 10-year term, the trust is to terminate and the trust corpus is to be paid to A's child, B. Assume that A's term interest has a value under section 7520 of $20,000 at the time of the transfer; however, because A's retained interest was not a qualified interest, it was valued at zero under § 25.2702-2(b)(1) for purposes of determining the amount of A's gift. Assume also that A and A's spouse, S, split the gift of the remainder interest under section 2513. In 1993, A transfers A's term interest to D, A's other child, for no consideration. A is entitled to reduce A's aggregate taxable gifts on the transfer. Assume that A and S also split the subsequent gift to D, and that A dies one month after making the subsequent transfer of the term interest and S dies six months later. The gift of the term interest is included in A's gross estate under section 2035(d)(2). To the extent S's taxable gifts are reduced pursuant to section 2001(e), S is entitled to no reduction in aggregate or adjusted taxable gifts under this section.

Example 6. T transfers property to an irrevocable trust retaining the power to direct the distribution of trust income for 10 years among T's descendants in whatever shares T deems appropriate. On the expiration of the 10-year period, the trust corpus is to be paid in equal shares to T's children. T's transfer of the remainder interest is a completed gift. Because T's retained interest is not a qualified interest, it is valued at zero under § 25.2702-2(b)(1) and the amount of T's gift is the fair market value of the property transferred to the trust. The distribution of income each year is not a transfer of a retained interest in trust. Therefore, T is not entitled to reduce aggregate taxable gifts as a result of the distributions of income from the trust.

Example 7. The facts are the same as in *Example 6*, except that after 3 years T exercises the right to direct the distribution of trust income by assigning the right to the income for the balance of the term to T's child, C. The exercise is a transfer of a retained interest in trust for purposes of this section. T is entitled to reduce aggregate taxable gifts by the lesser of the increase in taxable gifts resulting from the application of section 2702 to the initial transfer or the increase in taxable gifts resulting from the transfer of the retained interest in trust.

Example 8. In 1992, V purchases an income interest for 10 years in property in the same transaction or series of transactions in which G, V's child, purchases the remainder interest in the same property. V dies in 1997 still holding the term interest, the value of which is includible in V's gross estate under section 2033. V's estate would be entitled to a reduction in adjusted taxable gifts in the amount determined under paragraph (b) of this section. [Reg. § 25.2702-6.]

☐ [*T.D.* 8395, 1-28-92.]

[Reg. § 25.2702-7]

§ 25.2702-7. Effective dates.—Except as provided in this section, §§ 25.2702-1 through 25.2702-6 apply as of January 28, 1992. With respect to transfers to which section 2702 applied made prior to January 28, 1992, taxpayers may rely on any reasonable interpretation of the statutory provisions. For these purposes, the provisions of the proposed regulations and the final regulations are considered a reasonable interpretation of the statutory provisions. The fourth through eighth sentences of § 25.2702-5(b)(1) and § 25.2702-5(c)(9) apply with respect to trusts created after May 16, 1996. Section 25.2702-2(a)(5), the second and third sentences of § 25.2702-2(a)(6), § 25.2702-3(d)(2), the first two sentences of § 25.2702-3(d)(4), the last sentence of § 25.2702-3(e), *Example 5*, the last two sentences of § 25.2702-3(e), *Example 6*, and § 25.2702-3(e), *Examples 8* and *9*, apply for trusts created on or after July 26, 2004. However, the Internal Revenue Service will not challenge any prior application of the changes to *Examples 5* and *6* in § 25.2702-3(e). [Reg. § 25.2702-7.]

☐ [*T.D.* 8395, 1-28-92. *Amended by T.D.* 8743, 12-22-97 *and T.D.* 9181, 2-24-2005.]

[Reg. § 25.2703-1]

§ 25.2703-1. Property subject to restrictive arrangements.—(a) *Disregard of rights or restrictions.*—(1) *In general.*—For purposes of subtitle B (relating to estate, gift, and generation-skipping transfer taxes), the value of any property is determined without regard to any right or restriction relating to the property.

(2) *Right or restriction.*—For purposes of this section, right or restriction means—

(i) Any option, agreement, or other right to acquire or use the property at a price less than fair market value (determined without regard to the option, agreement, or right); or

(ii) Any restriction on the right to sell or use the property.

(3) *Agreements, etc., containing rights or restrictions.*—A right or restriction may be contained in a partnership agreement, articles of incorporation, corporate bylaws, a shareholders' agreement, or any other agreement. A right or restriction may be implicit in the capital structure of an entity.

(4) *Qualified easements.*—A perpetual restriction on the use of real property that qualified for a charitable deduction under either section 2522(d) or section 2055(f) of the Internal Revenue Code is not treated as a right or restriction.

(b) *Exceptions.*—(1) *In general.*—This section does not apply to any right or restriction satisfying the following three requirements—

(i) The right or restriction is a bona fide business arrangement;

(ii) The right or restriction is not a device to transfer property to the natural objects of the transferor's bounty for less than full and adequate consideration in money or money's worth; and

(iii) At the time the right or restriction is created, the terms of the right or restriction are comparable to similar arrangements entered into by persons in an arm's length transaction.

(2) *Separate requirements.*—Each of the three requirements described in paragraph (b)(1) of this section must be independently satisfied for a right or restriction to meet this exception. Thus, for example, the mere showing that a right or restriction is a bona fide business arrangement is not sufficient to establish that the right or restriction is not a device to transfer property for less than full and adequate consideration.

(3) *Exception for certain rights or restrictions.*—A right or restriction is considered to meet each of the three requirements described in paragraph (b)(1) of this section if more than 50 percent by value of the property subject to the right or restriction is owned directly or indirectly (within the meaning of § 25.2701-6) by individuals who are not members of the transferor's family. In order to meet this exception, the property owned by those individuals must be subject to the right or restriction to the same extent as the property owned by the transferor. For purposes of this section, members of the transferor's family include the persons described in § 25.2701-2(b)(5) and any other individual who is a natural object of the transferor's bounty. Any property held by a member of the transferor's family under the rules of § 25.2701-6 (without regard to § 25.2701-6(a)(5)) is treated as held only by a member of the transferor's family.

(4) *Similar arrangement.*—(i) *In general.*—A right or restriction is treated as comparable to similar arrangements entered into by persons in an arm's length transaction if the right or restriction is one that could have been obtained in a fair bargain among unrelated parties in the same business dealing with each other at arm's length. A right or restriction is considered a fair bargain among unrelated parties in the same business if it conforms with the general practice of unrelated parties under negotiated agreements in the same business. This determination generally will entail consideration of such factors as the expected term of the agreement, the current fair market value of the property, anticipated changes in value during the term of the arrangement, and the adequacy of any consideration given in exchange for the rights granted.

(ii) *Evidence of general business practice.*—Evidence of general business practice is not met by showing isolated comparables. If more than one valuation method is commonly used in a business, a right or restriction does not fail to evidence general business practice merely because it uses only one of the recognized methods. It is not necessary that the terms of a right or restriction parallel the terms of any particular agreement. If comparables are difficult to find because the business is unique, comparables from similar businesses may be used.

(5) *Multiple rights or restrictions.*—If property is subject to more than one right or restriction described in paragraph (a)(2) of this section, the failure of a right or restriction to satisfy the requirements of paragraph (b)(1) of this section does not cause any other right or restriction to fail to satisfy those requirements if the right or restriction otherwise meets those requirements. Whether separate provisions are separate rights or restrictions, or are integral parts of a single right or restriction, depends on all the facts and circumstances.

(c) *Substantial modification of a right or restriction.*—(1) *In general.*—A right or restriction that is substantially modified is treated as a right or restriction created on the date of the modification. Any discretionary modification of a right or restriction, whether or not authorized by the terms of the agreement, that results in other than a *de minimis* change to the quality, value, or timing of the rights of any party with respect to property that is subject to the right or restriction is a substantial modification. If the terms of the right or restriction require periodic updating, the failure to update is presumed to substantially modify the right or restriction unless it can be shown that updating would not have resulted in a substantial modification. The addition of any family member as a party to a right or restriction (including by reason of a transfer of property that subjects the transferee family member to a right or restriction with respect to the transferred property) is considered a substantial modification unless the addition is mandatory under the terms of the right or restriction or the added family member is assigned to a generation (determined under the rules of section 2651 of the Internal Revenue Code) no lower than the lowest generation occupied by individuals already party to the right or restriction).

(2) *Exceptions.*—A substantial modification does not include—

(i) A modification required by the terms of a right or restriction;

(ii) A discretionary modification of an agreement conferring a right or restriction if the modification does not change the right or restriction;

(iii) A modification of a capitalization rate used with respect to a right or restriction if the rate is modified in a manner that bears a fixed relationship to a specified market interest rate; and

(iv) A modification that results in an option price that more closely approximates fair market value.

(d) *Examples.*—The following examples illustrate the provisions of this section:

Example 1. T dies in 1992 owning title to Blackacre. In 1991, T and T's child entered into a lease with respect to Blackacre. At the time the lease was entered into, the terms of the lease were not comparable to leases of similar property entered into among unrelated parties. The lease is a restriction on the use of the property that is disregarded in valuing the property for Federal estate tax purposes.

Example 2. T and T's child, C, each own 50 percent of the outstanding stock of X corporation. T and C enter into an agreement in 1987 providing for the disposition of stock held by the first to die at the time of death. The agreement also provides certain restrictions with respect to lifetime transfers. In 1992, as permitted (but not required) under the agreement, T transfers one-half of T's stock to T's spouse, S. S becomes a party to the agreement between T and C by reason of the transfer. The transfer is the addition of a family member to the right or restriction. However, it is not a substantial modification of the right or restriction because the added family member would be assigned to a generation under section 2651 of the Internal Revenue Code no lower than the generation occupied by C.

Example 3. The facts are the same as in *Example* 2. In 1993, the agreement is amended to reflect a change in the company's name and a change of address for the company's registered agent. These changes are not a substantial modification of the agreement conferring the right or restriction because the right or restriction has not changed. [Reg. § 25.2703-1.]

☐ [*T.D.* 8395, 1-28-92.]

[Reg. § 25.2703-2]

§ 25.2703-2. Effective date.—Section 25.2703-1 applies to any right or restriction created or substantially modified after October 8, 1990, and is effective as of January 28, 1992. With respect to transfers occurring prior to January 28, 1992, and for purposes of determining whether an event occurring prior to January 28, 1992 constitutes a substantial modification, taxpayers may rely on any reasonable interpretation of the statutory provisions. For these purposes, the provisions of the proposed regulations and the final regulations are considered a reasonable interpretation of the statutory provisions. [Reg. § 25.2703-2.]

☐ [*T.D.* 8395, 1-28-92.]

[Reg. § 25.2704-1]

§ 25.2704-1. Lapse of certain rights.—(a) *Lapse treated as transfer.*—(1) *In general.*—The lapse of a voting right or a liquidation right in a corporation or partnership (an "entity") is a transfer by the individual directly or indirectly holding the right immediately prior to its lapse (the "holder") to the extent provided in paragraphs (b) and (c) of this section. This section applies only if the entity is controlled by the holder and members of the holder's family immediately before and after the lapse. The amount of the transfer is determined under paragraph (d) of this section. If the lapse of a voting right or a liquidation right occurs during the holder's lifetime, the lapse is a transfer by gift. If the lapse occurs at the holder's death, the lapse is a transfer includible in the holder's gross estate.

(2) *Definitions.*—The following definitions apply for purposes of this section.

(i) *Control.*—Control has the meaning given it in § 25.2701-2(b)(5).

(ii) *Member of the family.*—Member of the family has the meaning given it in § 25.2702-2(a)(1).

(iii) *Directly or indirectly held.*—An interest is directly or indirectly held only to the extent the value of the interest would have been includible in the gross estate of the individual if the individual had died immediately prior to the lapse.

(iv) *Voting right.*—Voting right means a right to vote with respect to any matter of the entity. In the case of a partnership, the right of a general partner to participate in partnership management is a voting right. The right to compel the entity to acquire all or a portion of the holder's equity interest in the entity by reason of aggregate voting power is treated as a liquidation right and is not treated as a voting right.

(v) *Liquidation right.*—Liquidation right means a right or ability to compel the entity to acquire all or a portion of the holder's equity interest in the entity, including by reason of aggregate voting power, whether or not its exercise would result in the complete liquidation of the entity.

(vi) *Subordinate.*—Subordinate has the meaning given it in § 25.2701-3(a)(2)(iii).

(3) *Certain temporary lapses.*—If a lapsed right may be restored only upon the occurrence of a future event not within the control of the holder or members of the holder's family, the lapse is deemed to occur at the time the lapse becomes permanent with respect to the holder, *i.e.* either by a transfer of the interest or otherwise.

(4) *Source of right or lapse.*—A voting right or a liquidation right may be conferred by and may lapse by reason of a State law, the corporate charter or bylaws, an agreement, or other means.

(b) *Lapse of voting right.*—A lapse of a voting right occurs at the time a presently exercisable voting right is restricted or eliminated.

(c) *Lapse of liquidation right.*—(1) *In general.*—A lapse of a liquidation right occurs at the time a presently exercisable liquidation right is restricted or eliminated. Except as otherwise provided, a transfer of an interest that results in the lapse of a liquidation right is not subject to this section if the rights with respect to the transferred interest are not restricted or eliminated. However, a transfer that results in the elimination of the transferor's right or ability to compel the entity to acquire an interest retained by the transferor that is subordinate to the transferred interest is a lapse of a liquidation right with respect to the subordinate interest.

(2) *Exceptions.*—Section 2704(a) does not apply to the lapse of a liquidation right under the following circumstances.

(i) *Family cannot obtain liquidation value.*—(A) *In general.*—Section 2704(a) does not apply to the lapse of a liquidation right to the extent the holder (or the holder's estate) and members of the holder's family cannot immediately after the lapse liquidate an interest that the holder held directly or indirectly and could have liquidated prior to the lapse.

(B) *Ability to liquidate.*—Whether an interest can be liquidated immediately after the lapse is determined under the State law generally applicable to the entity, as modified by the governing instruments of the entity, but without regard to any restriction described in section 2704(b). Thus, if, after any restriction described in section 2704(b) is disregarded, the remaining requirements for liquidation under the governing instruments are less restrictive than the State law that would apply in the absence of the governing instruments, the ability to liquidate is determined by reference to the governing instruments.

(ii) *Rights valued under section 2701.*—Section 2704(a) does not apply to the lapse of a liquidation right previously valued under section 2701 to the extent necessary to prevent double taxation (taking into account any adjustment available under § 25.2701-5).

(iii) *Certain changes in State law.*—Section 2704(a) does not apply to the lapse of a liquidation right that occurs solely by reason of a change in State law. For purposes of this paragraph, a change in the governing instrument of an entity is not a change in State law.

(d) *Amount of transfer.*—The amount of the transfer is the excess, if any, of—

(1) The value of all interests in the entity owned by the holder immediately before the lapse (determined immediately after the lapse as if the lapsed right was nonlapsing); over

(2) The value of the interests described in the preceding paragraph immediately after the lapse (determined as if all such interests were held by one individual).

(e) *Application to similar rights.*—[RESERVED]

(f) *Examples.*—The following examples illustrate the provisions of this section:

Example 1. Prior to D's death, D owned all the preferred stock of Corporation Y and D's children owned all the common stock. At that time, the preferred stock had 60 percent of the total voting power and the common stock had 40 percent. Under the corporate by-laws, the voting rights of the preferred stock terminated on D's death. The value of D's interest immediately prior to D's death (determined as if the voting rights were non-lapsing) was $100X. The value of that interest immediately after death would have been $90X if the voting rights had been non-lapsing. The decrease in value reflects the loss in value resulting from the death of D (whose involvement in Y was a key factor in Y's profitability). Section 2704(a) applies to the lapse of voting rights on D's death. D's gross estate includes an amount equal to the excess, if any, of $90X over the fair market value of the preferred stock determined after the lapse of the voting rights.

Example 2. Prior to D's death, D owned all the preferred stock of Corporation Y. The preferred stock and the common stock each carried 50 percent of the total voting power of Y. D's children owned 40 percent of the common stock and unrelated parties own the remaining 60 percent. Under the corporate by-laws, the voting rights of the preferred stock terminate on D's death. Section 2704(a) does not apply to the lapse of D's voting rights because members of D's family do not control Y after the lapse.

Example 3. The by-laws of Corporation Y provide that the voting rights of any transferred shares of the single outstanding class of stock are reduced to $^1/_2$ vote per share after the transfer but are fully restored to the transferred shares after 5 years. D owned 60 percent of the shares prior to death and members of D's family owned the balance. On D's death, D's shares pass to D's children and the voting rights are reduced pursuant to the by-laws. Section 2704(a) applies to the lapse of D's voting rights. D's gross estate includes an amount equal to the excess, if any, of the fair market value of D's stock (determined immediately after D's death as though the voting rights had not been reduced and would not be reduced) over the stock's fair market value immediately after D's death.

Example 4. D owns 84 percent of the single outstanding class of stock of Corporation Y. The by-laws require at least 70 percent of the vote to liquidate Y. D gives one-half of D's stock in equal shares to D's three children (14 percent to each). Section 2704(a) does not apply to the loss of D's ability to liquidate Y, because the voting rights with respect to the corporation are not restricted or eliminated by reason of the transfer.

Example 5. D and D's two children, A and B, are partners in Partnership X. Each has a 3 $^1/_3$ percent general partnership interest and a 30 percent limited partnership interest. Under State law, a general partner has the right to participate in partnership management. The partnership agreement provides that when a general partner withdraws or dies, X must redeem the general partnership interest for its liquidation value. Also, under the agreement any general partner can liquidate the partnership. A limited partner cannot liquidate the partnership and a limited partner's capital interest will be returned only when the partnership is liquidated. A deceased limited partner's interest continues as a limited partnership interest. D dies, leaving his limited partnership interest to D's spouse. Because of a general partner's right to dissolve the partnership, a limited partnership interest has a greater fair market value when held in conjunction with a general partnership interest than when held alone. Section 2704(a) applies to the lapse of D's liquidation right because after the lapse, members of D's family could liquidate D's limited partnership interest. D's gross estate includes an amount equal to the excess of the value of all D's interests in X immediately before D's death (determined immediately after D's death but as though the liquidation right had not lapsed and would not lapse) over the fair market value of all D's interests in X immediately after D's death.

Example 6. The facts are the same as in *Example 5,* except that under the partnership agreement D is the only general partner who holds a unilateral liquidation right. Assume further that the partnership agreement contains a restriction described in section 2704(b) that prevents D's family members from liquidating D's limited partnership interest immediately after D's death. Under State law, in the absence of the restriction in the partnership agreement, D's family members could liquidate the partnership. The restriction on the family's ability to liquidate is disregarded and the amount of D's gross estate is increased by reason of the lapse of D's liquidation right.

Example 7. D owns all the stock of Corporation X, consisting of 100 shares of non-voting preferred stock and 100 shares of voting common stock. Under the by-laws, X can only be liquidated with the consent of at least 80 percent of the voting shares. D transfers 30 shares of common stock to D's child. The transfer is not a lapse of a liquidation right with respect to the common stock because the voting rights that enabled D to liquidate prior to the transfer are not restricted or eliminated. The transfer is not a lapse of a liquidation right with respect to the retained preferred stock because the preferred stock is not subordinate to the transferred common stock.

Example 8. D owns all of the single class of stock of Corporation Y. D recapitalizes Y, exchanging D's common stock for voting common stock and non-voting, non-cumulative preferred stock. The preferred stock carries a right to put the stock for its par value at any time during the next 10 years. D transfers the common stock to D's grandchild in a transfer subject to section 2701. In determining the amount of D's gift under section 2701, D's retained put right is valued at zero. D's child, C, owns the preferred stock when the put right lapses. Section 2704(a) applies to the lapse, without regard to the application of section 2701, because the put right was not valued under section 2701 in the hands of C.

Example 9. A and A's two children are equal general and limited partners in Partnership Y. Under the partnership agreement, each general partner has a right to liquidate the partnership at any time. Under State law that would apply in the absence of contrary provisions in the partnership agreement, the death or incompetency of a general partner terminates the partnership. However, the partnership agreement provides that the partnership does not terminate on the incompetence or death of a general partner, but that an incompetent partner cannot exercise rights as a general partner during any period of incompetency. A partner's full rights as general partner are restored if the partner regains competency. A becomes incompetent. The lapse of A's voting right on becoming incompetent is not subject to section 2704(a) because it may be restored to A in the future. However, if A dies while incompetent, a lapse subject to section 2704(a) is deemed to occur at that time because the lapsed right cannot thereafter be restored to A. [Reg. § 25.2704-1.]

□ [*T.D.* 8395, 1-28-92.]

[Reg. § 25.2704-2]

§ 25.2704-2. Transfers subject to applicable restrictions.—(a) *In general.*—If an interest in a corporation or partnership (an "entity") is transferred to or for the benefit of a member of the transferor's family, any applicable restriction is disregarded in valuing the transferred interest. This section applies only if the transferor and members of the transferor's family control the entity immediately before the transfer. For the definition of control, see § 25.2701-2(b)(5). For the definition of member of the family, see § 25.2702-2(a)(1).

(b) *Applicable restriction defined.*—An applicable restriction is a limitation on the ability to liquidate the entity (in whole or in part) that is more restrictive than the limitations that would apply under the State law generally applicable to the entity in the absence of the restriction. A restriction is an applicable restriction only to the extent that either the restriction by its terms will lapse at any time after the transfer, or the transferor (or the transferor's estate) and any members of the transferor's family can remove the restriction immediately after the transfer. Ability to remove the restriction is determined by reference to the State law that would apply but for a more restrictive rule in the governing instruments of the entity. See § 25.2704-1(c)(1)(B) for a discussion of the term "State law." An applicable restriction does not include a commercially reasonable restriction on liquidation imposed by an unrelated person providing capital to the entity for the entity's trade or business operations whether in the form of debt or equity. An unrelated person is any person whose relationship to the transferor, the transferee, or any member of the family of either is not described in section 267(b) of the Internal Revenue Code, provided that for purposes of this section the term "fiduciary of a trust" as used in section 267(b) does not include a bank as defined in section 581 of the Internal Revenue Code. A restriction imposed or required to be imposed by Federal or State law is not an applicable restriction. An option, right to use property, or agreement that is subject to section 2703 is not an applicable restriction.

(c) *Effect of disregarding an applicable restriction.*—If an applicable restriction is disregarded under this section, the transferred interest is valued as if the restriction does not exist and as if the rights of the transferor are determined under the State law that would apply but for the restriction. For example, an applicable restriction with respect to preferred stock will be disregarded in determining the amount of a transfer of common stock under section 2701.

(d) *Examples.*—The following examples illustrate the provisions of this section:

Example 1. D owns a 76 percent interest and each of D's children, A and B, owns a 12 percent interest in General Partnership X. The partnership agreement requires the consent of all the partners to liquidate the partnership. Under the State law that would apply in the absence of the restriction in the partnership agreement, the consent of partners owning 70 percent of the total partnership interests would be required to liquidate X. On D's death, D's partnership interest passes to D's child, C. The requirement that all the partners consent to liquidation is an applicable restriction. Because A, B and C (all members of D's family), acting together after the transfer, can remove the restriction on liquidation, D's interest is valued without regard to the restriction; *i.e.,* as though D's interest is sufficient to liquidate the partnership.

Example 2. D owns all the preferred stock in Corporation X. The preferred stock carries a right to liquidate X that cannot be exercised until 1999. D's children, A and B, own all the common stock of X. The common stock is the only voting stock. In 1994, D transfers the preferred stock to D's child, A. The restriction on D's right to liquidate is an applicable restriction that is disregarded. Therefore, the preferred stock is valued as though the right to liquidate were presently exercisable.

Example 3. D owns 60 percent of the stock of Corporation X. The corporate by-laws provide that the corporation cannot be liquidated for 10 years after which time liquidation requires approval by 60 percent of the voting interests. In the absence of the provision in the by-laws, State law would require approval by 80 percent of the voting interests to liquidate X. D transfers the stock to a trust for the benefit of D's child, A, during the 10-year period. The 10-year restriction is an applicable restriction and is disregarded. Therefore, the value of the stock is determined as if the transferred block could currently liquidate X.

Example 4. D and D's children, A and B, are partners in Limited Partnership Y. Each has a 3.33 percent general partnership interest and a 30 percent limited partnership interest. Any general partner has the right to liquidate the partnership at any time. As part of a loan agreement with a lender who is related to D, each of the partners agree that the partnership may not be liquidated without the lender's consent while any portion of the loan remains outstanding. During the term of the loan agreement, D transfers one-half of both D's partnership interests to each of A and B. Because the lender is a related party, the requirement that the lender consent to liquidation is an applicable restriction and the transfers of D's interests are valued as if such consent were not required.

Example 5. D owns 60 percent of the preferred and 70 percent of the common stock in Corporation X. The remaining stock is owned by individuals unrelated to D. The preferred stock carries a put right that cannot be exercised until 1999. In 1995, D transfers the common stock to D's child in a transfer that is subject to section 2701. The restriction on D's right to liquidate is an applicable restriction that is disregarded in determining the amount of the gift under section 2701. [Reg. § 25.2704-2.]

☐ [*T.D.* 8395, 1-28-92.]

[Reg. § 25.2704-3]

§ 25.2704-3. Effective date.—Section 25.2704-1 applies to lapses occurring after January 28, 1992, of rights created after October 8, 1990. Section 25.2704-2 applies to transfers occurring after January 28, 1992, of property subject to applicable restrictions created after October 8, 1990. In determining whether a voting right or a liquidation right has lapsed prior to that date, and for purposes of determining whether the lapse is subject to section 2704(a), taxpayers may rely on any reasonable interpretation of the statutory provisions. For transfers of interests occurring before January 28, 1992, taxpayers may rely on any reasonable interpretation of the statutory provisions in determining whether a restriction is an applicable restriction that must be disregarded in determining the value of the transferred interest. For these purposes, the provisions of the proposed regulations and the final regulations are considered a reasonable interpretation of the statutory provisions. [Reg. § 25.2704-3.]

☐ [*T.D.* 8395, 1-28-92.]

Procedure and Administration

See p. 15 for regulations not amended to reflect law changes

[SELECTED REGULATIONS]

[Reg. § 1.6001-1]

§ 1.6001-1. Records.—(a) *In general.*—Except as provided in paragraph (b) of this section, any person subject to tax under subtitle A of the Code (including a qualified State individual income tax which is treated pursuant to section 6361(a) as if it were imposed by chapter 1 of subtitle A), or any person required to file a return of information with respect to income, shall keep such permanent books of account or records, including inventories, as are sufficient to establish the amount of gross income, deductions, credits, or other matters required to be shown by such person in any return of such tax or information.

(b) *Farmers and wage-earners.*—Individuals deriving gross income from the business of farming, and individuals whose gross income includes salaries, wages, or similar compensation for personal services rendered, are required with respect to such income to keep such records as will enable the district director to determine the correct amount of income subject to the tax. It is not necessary, however, that with respect to such income individuals keep the books of account or records required by paragraph (a) of this section. For rules with respect to the records to be kept in substantiation of traveling and other business expenses of employees, see § 1.162-17.

(c) *Exempt organizations.*—In addition to such permanent books and records as are required by paragraph (a) of this section with respect to the tax imposed by section 511 on unrelated business income of certain exempt organizations, every organization exempt from tax under section 501(a) shall keep such permanent books of account or records, including inventories, as are sufficient to show specifically the items of gross income, receipts and disbursements. Such organizations shall also keep such books and records as are required to substantiate the information required by section 6033. See section 6033 and §§ 1.6033-1 through -3.

(d) *Notice by district director requiring returns, statements, or the keeping of records.*—The district director may require any person, by notice served upon him, to make such returns, render such statements, or keep such specific records as will enable the district director to determine whether or not such person is liable for tax under subtitle A of the Code, including qualified State individual income taxes, which are treated pursuant to section 6361(a) as if they were imposed by chapter 1 of subtitle A.

(e) *Retention of records.*—The books or records required by this section shall be kept at all times available for inspection by authorized internal revenue officers or employees, and shall be retained so long as the contents thereof may become material in the administration of any internal revenue law [Reg. § 1.6001-1.]

□ [*T.D.* 6364, 2-13-59. *Amended by T.D.* 7122, 6-7-71; *T.D.* 7577, 12-19-78 *and T.D.* 8308, 8-30-90.]

[Reg. § 20.6001-1]

§ 20.6001-1. Persons required to keep records and render statements.—(a) It is the duty of the executor to keep such complete and detailed records of the affairs of the estate for which he acts as will enable the district director to determine accurately the amount of the estate tax liability. All documents and vouchers used in preparing the estate tax return (§ 20.6018-1) shall be retained by the executor so as to be available for inspection whenever required.

(b) In addition to filing an estate tax return (see § 20.6018-1) and, if applicable, a preliminary notice (see § 20.6036-1), the executor shall furnish such supplemental data as may be necessary to establish the correct estate tax. It is therefore the duty of the executor (1) to furnish, upon requests, copies of any documents in his possession (or on file in any court having jurisdiction over the estate) relating to the estate, appraisal lists of any items included in the gross estate, copies of balance sheets or other financial statements obtainable by him relating to the value of stock, and any other information obtainable by him that may be found necessary in the determination of the tax, and (2) to render any written statement, containing a declaration that it is made under penalties of perjury, of facts within his knowledge which the district director may require for the purpose of determining whether a tax liability exists and, if so, the extent thereof. Failure to comply with such a request will render the executor liable to penalties (see section 7269), and proceedings may be instituted in the proper court of the United States to secure compliance therewith (see section 7604).

(c) Persons having possession or control of any records or documents containing or supposed to contain any information concerning the estate, or having knowledge of or information about any fact or facts which have a material bearing upon the liability, or the extent of liability, of the estate for the estate tax, shall, upon request of the district director, make disclosure thereof. Failure on the part of any person to comply with such request will render him liable to penalties (section 7269), and compliance with the request may be enforced in the proper court of the United States (section 7604).

(d) Upon notification from the Internal Revenue Service, a corporation (organized or created in the United States) or its transfer agent is required to furnish the following information pertaining to stocks or bonds registered in the name of a nonresident decedent (regardless of citizenship): (1) The name of the decedent as registered;

(2) the date of the decedent's death; (3) the decedent's residence and his place of death; (4) the names and addresses of executors, attorneys, or other representatives of the estate, within and without the United States; and (5) a description of the securities, the number of shares or bonds and the par values thereof. [Reg. § 20.6001-1.]

☐ [*T.D.* 6296, 6-23-58. *Amended by T.D.* 7238, 12-28-72.]

[Reg. § 25.6001-1]

§ 25.6001-1. Records required to be kept.—(a) *In general.*—Every person subject to taxation under chapter 12 of the Internal Revenue Code of 1954 shall for the purpose of determining the total amount of his gifts, keep such permanent books of account or records as are necessary to establish the amount of his total gifts (limited as provided by section 2503(b)), together with the deductions allowable in determining the amount of his taxable gifts, and the other information required to be shown in a gift tax return. All documents and vouchers used in preparing the gift tax return (see § 25.6019-1) shall be retained by the donor so as to be available for inspection whenever required.

(b) *Supplemental data.*—In order that the Internal Revenue Service may determine the correct tax the donor shall furnish such supplemental data as may be deemed necessary by the Internal Revenue Service. It is, therefore, the duty of the donor to furnish, upon request, copies of all documents relating to his gift or gifts, appraisal lists of any items included in the total amount of gifts, copies of balance sheets or other financial statements obtainable by him relating to the value of stock constituting the gift, and any other information obtainable by him that may be necessary in the determination of the tax. See section 2512 and the regulations issued thereunder. For every policy of life insurance listed on the return, the donor must procure a statement from the insurance company on Form 712 and file it with the internal revenue officer with whom the return is filed. If specifically requested by an internal revenue officer, the insurance company shall file this statement direct with the internal revenue officer. [Reg. § 25.6001-1.]

☐ [*T.D.* 6334, 11-14-58. *Amended by T.D.* 7012, 5-14-69 *and T.D.* 7517, 11-11-77.]

[Reg. § 20.6011-1]

§ 20.6011-1. General requirement of return, statement, or list.—(a) *General rule.*—Every person made liable for any tax imposed by subtitle B of the Code shall make such returns or statements as are required by the regulations in this part. The return or statement shall include therein the information required by the applicable regulations or forms.

(b) *Use of prescribed forms.*—Copies of the forms prescribed by §§ 20.6018-1 and 20.6036-1 may be obtained from district directors. The fact that an executor has not been furnished with copies of these forms will not excuse him from making a return or, if applicable, from filing a preliminary notice. Application for a form shall be made to the district director in ample time for the executor to have the form prepared, verified, and filed with the appropriate internal revenue office on or before the date prescribed for the filing thereof (see §§ 20.6071-1 and 20.6075-1). The executor shall carefully prepare the return and, if applicable, the preliminary notice so as to set forth fully and clearly the data called for therein. A return or, if applicable, a preliminary notice which has not been so prepared will not be accepted as meeting the requirements of §§ 20.6018-1 through 20.6018-4 and § 20.6036-1. [Reg. § 20.6011-1.]

☐ [*T.D.* 6296, 6-23-58. *Amended by T.D.* 7238, 12-28-72.]

[Reg. § 25.6011-1]

§ 25.6011-1. General requirement of return, statement, or list.—(a) *General rule.*—Every person made liable for any tax imposed by chapter 12 of the Code shall make such returns or statements as are required by the regulations in this part. The return or statement shall include therein the information required by the applicable regulations or forms.

(b) *Use of prescribed forms.*—Copies of the forms prescribed by paragraph (b) of § 25.6001-1 and § 25.6019-1 may be obtained from district directors and directors of service centers. The fact that a person required to file a form has not been furnished with copies of a form will not excuse him from the making of a gift tax return, or from the furnishing of the evidence for which the forms are to be used. Application for a form should be made to the district director or director of a service center in ample time to enable the person whose duty it is to file the form to have the form prepared, verified, and filed on or before the date prescribed for the filing thereof. [Reg. § 25.6011-1.]

☐ [*T.D.* 6334, 11-14-58. *Amended by T.D.* 7012, 5-14-69.]

[Reg. § 301.6011-2]

§ 301.6011-2. Required use of electronic form.—(a) *Meaning of terms.*—The following definitions apply for purposes of this section:

(1) *Magnetic media or electronic form.*—The terms *magnetic media or electronic form* mean any media or form permitted under applicable regulations, revenue procedures or publications, or, in the case of returns filed with the Social Security Administration, Social Security Administration publications. These generally include electronic filing, as well as magnetic tape, tape cartridge, diskette, and other media specifically permitted under the applicable regulations, procedures, or publications.

(2) *Machine-readable paper form.*—The term "machine-readable paper form" means—

(i) Optical-scan paper form; or

(ii) Any other machine-readable paper form permitted under applicable regulations, revenue procedures, or Social Security Administration publications.

(3) *Person.*—The term "person" includes any person that is required to file a return that is described in paragraph (b) of this section. Thus, the term "person" includes the United States, a State, the District of Columbia, a foreign government, a political subdivision of a State or of a foreign government, or an international organization. In addition, in the case of an affiliated group of corporations filing a consolidated return, each member of the affiliated group is a separate person.

(b) *Returns required electronically.*—(1) If the use of Form 1042–S, Form 1094 series, Form 1095–B, Form 1095–C, Form 1097-BTC, Form 1098, Form 1098-C, Form 1098–E, Form 1098-Q, Form 1098–T, Form 1099 series, Form 3921, Form 3922, Form 5498 series, Form 8027, or Form W–2G is required by the applicable regulations or revenue procedures for the purpose of making an information return, the information required by the form must be submitted electronically, except as otherwise provided in paragraph (c) of this section. Returns filed electronically must be made in accordance with applicable revenue procedures, publications, forms, or instructions.

(2) If the use of Form W–2 (Wage and Tax Statement), Form 499R–2/W–2PR (Withholding Statement (Puerto Rico)), Form W–2VI (U.S. Virgin Islands Wage and Tax Statement), Form W–2GU (Guam Wage and Tax Statement), or Form W–2AS (American Samoa Wage and Tax Statement) is required for the purpose of making an information return, the information required by the form must be submitted electronically, except as otherwise provided in paragraph (c) of this section. Returns described in this paragraph (b)(2) must be made in accordance with applicable Social Security Administration procedures or publications (which may be obtained from the local office of the Social Security Administration).

(3) If a person is required to make a return for the purpose of section 6050I, and such person is required to file returns described in paragraphs (b)(1) and (2) of this section electronically, then such person must also file the information required by section 6050I electronically. Returns described in this paragraph (b)(3) must be made in accordance with applicable IRS revenue procedures, publications, forms, instructions, or other guidance, including postings to the *IRS.gov* website, as well as instructions and guidance on the *FinCEN.gov* website.

(4) The Commissioner may exempt certain returns from the electronic requirements of this section through revenue procedures, publications, forms, instructions, or other guidance, including postings to the *IRS.gov* website.

(c) *Electronic-filing threshold.*—(1) *In general.*—No person is required to file information returns electronically in a calendar year unless the person is required to file at least 10 returns during that calendar year. Persons required to file fewer than 10 returns during the calendar year may make the returns on the prescribed paper form or, alternatively, electronically in accordance with paragraph (b) of this section.

(2) *Machine-readable forms.*—Returns made on a paper form under paragraph (c)(1) of this section must be machine-readable, as described in paragraph (a)(2) of this section, if applicable revenue procedures provide for a machine-readable paper form.

(3) *Special rule for partnerships.*—Notwithstanding paragraph (c)(1) of this section, a partnership with more than 100 partners is required to file its information returns covered under paragraph (b) of this section electronically.

(4) *Calculating the number of returns.*—(i) *Aggregation of returns.*—In calculating whether a person is required to file at least 10 returns under paragraph (c)(1) of this section, all the information returns described in paragraphs (b)(1) and (2) of this section required to be filed during the calendar year are counted in the aggregate. Neither corrected information returns, information returns described in paragraph (b)(3) of this section, nor returns other than those described in paragraphs (b)(1) and (2) of this section are taken into account in calculating whether a person is required to file at least 10 returns.

(ii) *Corrected returns.*—(A) If an original information return covered by paragraph (b) of this section is required to be filed electronically, any corrected information return corresponding to that original return must also be filed electronically.

(B) If an original information return is permitted to be filed on paper and is filed on paper, any corrected information return corresponding to that original return must be filed on paper.

(5) *Examples.*—The provisions of paragraphs (c)(3) and (4) of this section are illustrated by the following examples:

(i) *Example 1.*—During the 2024 calendar year, Company W, is required to file five Forms 1099-INT, *Interest Income*, and five Forms 1099-DIV, *Dividends and Distributions*, for a total of 10 returns covered by paragraphs (b)(1) and (2) of this section. Because Company W is required to file 10 returns as calculated under paragraph (c)(4) of this section during the 2024 calendar year, Company W must file all its 2023 Forms 1099-INT and 1099-DIV electronically.

(ii) *Example 2.*—Same facts as paragraph (c)(5)(i) of this section *(Example 1)*, except after electronically filing its 10 Forms 1099-DIV and 1099-INT, Company W files two corrected Forms 1099-DIV and four corrected Forms 1099-INT. Because Company W electronically filed its original 2023 Forms 1099-DIV and 1099-INT, Company W must electronically file its corrected 2023 Forms 1099-DIV and 1099-INT.

(iii) *Example 3.*—Same facts as paragraph (c)(5)(i) of this section *(Example 1)*, except on May 16, 2024, Company W received cash in excess of $10,000 and must file a Form 8300 by May 31, 2024. Because Company W is required to file information returns covered under paragraphs (b)(1) and (2) of this section electronically during the 2024 calendar year, Company W must also file all its Forms 8300 electronically during the 2024 calendar year.

(iv) *Example 4.*—Same facts as paragraph (c)(5)(i) of this section *(Example 1)*, except Company W is not required to file any Forms 1099-INT during calendar year 2024. On December 19, 2023, Company W receives cash in excess of $10,000 and must file a Form 8300 by January 3, 2024. Because Company W is not required to file information returns covered under paragraphs (b)(1) and (2) of this section electronically during the 2024 calendar year, Company W is not required to file this Form 8300 electronically.

(v) *Example 5.*—During the 2024 calendar year, Partnership P, a partnership with 15 partners, is required to file eight Forms 1099-MISC, *Miscellaneous Information*, and five Forms 1099-INT. Because Partnership P is required to file at least 10 returns covered by paragraphs (b)(1) and (2) of this section during the 2024 calendar year, Partnership P must electronically file all its 2022 Forms 1099-MISC and 1099-INT.

(6) *Exclusions from electronic-filing requirements.*—(i) *Waivers.*—The Commissioner may grant waivers of the requirements of this section in cases of undue hardship. One principal factor in determining hardship will be the amount, if any, by which the cost of filing the return electronically in accordance with this section exceeds the cost of filing the return on paper. A request for a waiver must be made in accordance with applicable IRS revenue procedures, publications, forms, instructions, or other guidance, including postings to the *IRS.gov* website. The waiver request will specify the type of filing (that is, a return required under paragraph (b) of this section) and the period to which it applies. For purposes of paragraph (b)(3) of this section, a waiver granted for a return under paragraph (b)(1) or (2) will be deemed to have waived the electronic-filing requirement for any returns required to be filed under section 6050I.

(ii) *Exemptions.*—The Commissioner may provide exemptions from the requirements of this section to promote effective and efficient tax administration. An exemption will be allowed for filers for whom using the technology required to file in electronic form conflicts with their religious beliefs. A submission claiming an exemption must be made in accordance with applicable IRS revenue procedures, publications, forms, instructions, or other guidance, including postings to the *IRS.gov* website.

(iii) *Additional Exclusion.*—If an employer is required to make a final return on Form 941, or a variation thereof, and expedited filing of Forms W-2, Forms 499R-2/W-2PR, Forms W-2VI, Forms W-2GU, or Form W-2AS is required, if the IRS's systems do not support electronic filing, taxpayers will not be required to file electronically (see § 31.6071(a)-1(a)(3)(ii) of this chapter).

(d) *Paper form returns.*—Returns submitted on paper forms (whether or not machine-readable) permitted under paragraph (c) of this section shall be in accordance with applicable Internal Revenue Service or Social Security Administration procedures.

(e) *Applicability of current procedures.*—Until procedures are prescribed which further implement the mandatory filing on magnetic media provided by this section, a return to which this section applies shall be made in the manner and shall be subject to the requirements and conditions (including the requirement of applying for consent to the magnetic medium) prescribed in the regulations, revenue procedures and Social Security Administration publications relating to the filing of such return on magnetic media.

(f) *Failure to file.*—If a person fails to file an information return on magnetic media when required to do so by this section, the person is deemed to have failed to file the return. In addition, if a person making returns on a paper form under paragraph (c) of this section fails to file a return on machine-readable paper form when required to do so by this section, the person is deemed to have failed to file the return. See sections 6652, 6693, and 6721 for penalties for failure to file certain returns. See also section 6724 and the regulations under section 6721 for the specific rules and limitations regarding the penalty imposed under section 6721 for failure to file on magnetic media.

(g) *Applicability date.*—The rules of this section apply to information returns required to be filed during calendar years beginning after December 31, 2023. [Reg. § 301.6011-2.]

☐ [*T.D.* 8081, 3-20-86. *Amended by T.D.* 8097, 8-25-86; *T.D.* 8140, 5-15-87; *T.D.* 8636, 12-20-95; *T.D.* 8772, 6-29-98; *T.D.* 8992, 4-26-2002; *T.D.* 9029, 12-18-2002, *T.D.* 9660, 3-5-2014, *T.D.* 9804, 12-14-2016, *T.D.* 9923, 11-18-2020 *and T.D.* 9972, 2-21-2023.]

[Reg. § 1.6011-4]

§ 1.6011-4. Requirement of statement disclosing participation in certain transactions by taxpayers.—(a) *In general.*—Every taxpayer that has participated, as described in paragraph (c)(3) of this section, in a reportable transaction within the meaning of paragraph (b) of this section and who is required to file a tax return must file within the time prescribed in paragraph (e) of this section a disclosure statement in the form prescribed by paragraph (d) of this section. The fact that a transaction is a reportable transaction shall not affect the legal determination of whether the taxpayer's treatment of the transaction is proper.

(b) *Reportable transactions.*—(1) *In general.*—A reportable transaction is a transaction described in any of the paragraphs (b)(2) through (7) of this section. The term transaction includes all of the factual elements relevant to the expected tax treatment of any investment, entity, plan, or arrangement, and includes any series of steps carried out as part of a plan.

(2) *Listed transactions.*—A listed transaction is a transaction that is the same as or substantially similar to one of the types of transactions that the Internal Revenue Service (IRS) has determined to be a tax avoidance transaction and identified by notice, regulation, or other form of published guidance as a listed transaction.

(3) *Confidential transactions.*—(i) *In general.*—A confidential transaction is a transaction that is offered to a taxpayer under conditions of confidentiality and for which the taxpayer has paid an advisor a minimum fee.

(ii) *Conditions of confidentiality.*—A transaction is considered to be offered to a taxpayer under conditions of confidentiality if the advisor who is paid the minimum fee places a limitation on disclosure by the taxpayer of the tax treatment or tax structure of the transaction and the limitation on disclosure protects the confidentiality of that advisor's tax strategies. A transaction is treated as confidential even if the conditions of confidentiality are not legally binding on the taxpayer. A claim that a transaction is proprietary or exclusive is not treated as a limitation on disclosure if the advisor confirms to the taxpayer that there is no limitation on disclosure of the tax treatment or tax structure of the transaction.

(iii) *Minimum fee.*—For purposes of this paragraph (b)(3), the minimum fee is—

(A) $250,000 for a transaction if the taxpayer is a corporation;

(B) $50,000 for all other transactions unless the taxpayer is a partnership or trust, all of the owners or beneficiaries of which are corporations (looking through any partners or beneficiaries that are themselves partnerships or trusts), in which case the minimum fee is $250,000.

(iv) *Determination of minimum fee.*—For purposes of this paragraph (b)(3), in determining the minimum fee, all fees for a tax strategy or for services for advice (whether or not tax advice) or for the implementation of a transaction are taken into account. Fees include consideration in whatever form paid, whether in cash or in kind, for services to analyze the transaction (whether or not related to the tax consequences of the transaction), for services to implement the transaction, for services to document the transaction, and for services to prepare tax returns to the extent return preparation fees are unreasonable in light of the facts and circumstances. For purposes of this paragraph (b)(3), a taxpayer also is treated as paying fees to an advisor if the taxpayer knows or should know that the amount it pays will be paid indirectly to the advisor, such as through a referral fee or fee-sharing arrangement. A fee does not include amounts paid to a person, including an advisor, in that person's capacity as a party to the transaction. For example, a fee does not include reasonable charges for the use of capital or the sale or use of property. The IRS will scrutinize carefully all of the facts and circumstances in determining whether consideration received in connection with a confidential transaction constitutes fees.

(v) *Related parties.*—For purposes of this paragraph (b)(3), persons who bear a relationship to each other as described in section 267(b) or 707(b) will be treated as the same person.

(4) *Transactions with contractual protection.*—(i) *In general.*—A transaction with contractual protection is a transaction for which the taxpayer or a related party (as described in section 267(b) or 707(b)) has the right to a full or partial refund of fees (as described in paragraph (b)(4)(ii) of this section) if all or part of the intended tax consequences from the transaction are not sustained. A transaction with contractual protection also is a transaction for which fees (as described in paragraph (b)(4)(ii) of this section) are contingent on the taxpayer's realization of tax benefits from the transaction. All the facts and circumstances relating to the transaction will be considered when determining whether a fee is refundable or contingent, including the right to reimbursements of amounts that the parties to the transaction have not designated as fees or any agreement to provide services without reasonable compensation.

(ii) *Fees.*—Paragraph (b)(4)(i) of this section only applies with respect to fees paid by or on behalf of the taxpayer or a related party to any person who makes or provides a statement, oral or written, to the taxpayer or related party (or for whose benefit a statement is made or provided to the taxpayer or related party) as to the potential tax consequences that may result from the transaction.

(iii) *Exceptions.*—(A) *Termination of transaction.*—A transaction is not considered to have contractual protection solely because a party to the transaction has the right to terminate the transaction upon the happening of an event affecting the taxation of one or more parties to the transaction.

(B) *Previously reported transaction.*—If a person makes or provides a statement to a taxpayer as to the potential tax consequences that may result from a transaction only after the taxpayer has entered into the transaction and reported the consequences of the transaction on a filed tax return, and the person has not previously received fees from the taxpayer relating to the transaction, then any refundable or contingent fees are not taken into account in determining whether the transaction has contractual protection. This paragraph (b)(4) does not provide any substantive rules regarding when a person may charge refundable or contingent fees with respect to a transaction. See Circular 230, 31 CFR Part 10, for the regulations governing practice before the IRS.

(5) *Loss transactions.*—(i) *In general.*—A loss transaction is any transaction resulting in the taxpayer claiming a loss under section 165 of at least—

(A) $10 million in any single taxable year or $20 million in any combination of taxable years for corporations;

(B) $10 million in any single taxable year or $20 million in any combination of taxable years for partnerships that have only corporations as partners (looking through any partners that are themselves partnerships), whether or not any losses flow through to one or more partners; or

(C) $2 million in any single taxable year or $4 million in any combination of taxable years for all other partnerships, whether or not any losses flow through to one or more partners;

(D) $2 million in any single taxable year or $4 million in any combination of taxable years for individuals, S corporations, or trusts, whether or not any losses flow through to one or more shareholders or beneficiaries; or

(E) $50,000 in any single taxable year for individuals or trusts, whether or not the loss flows through from an S corporation or partnership, if the loss arises with respect to a section 988 transaction (as defined in section 988(c)(1) relating to foreign currency transactions).

(ii) *Cumulative losses.*—In determining whether a transaction results in a taxpayer claiming a loss that meets the threshold amounts over a combination of taxable years as described in paragraph (b)(5)(i) of this section, only losses claimed in the taxable year that the transaction is entered into and the five succeeding taxable years are combined.

(iii) *Section 165 loss.*—(A) For purposes of this section, in determining the thresholds in paragraph (b)(5)(i) of this section, the amount of a section 165 loss is adjusted for any salvage value and for any insurance or other compensation received. See § 1.165-1(c)(4). However, a section 165 loss does not take into account offsetting gains, or other income or limitations. For example, a section 165 loss does not take into account the limitation in section 165(d) (relating to wagering losses) or the limitations in sections 165(f), 1211, and 1212 (relating to capital losses). The full amount of a section 165 loss is taken into account for the year in which the loss is sustained, regardless of whether all or part of the loss enters into the computation of a net operating loss under section 172 or a net capital loss under section 1212 that is a carryback or carryover to another year. A section 165 loss does not include any portion of a loss, attributable to a capital loss carryback or carryover from another year, that is treated as a deemed capital loss under section 1212.

(B) For purposes of this section, a section 165 loss includes an amount deductible pursuant to a provision that treats a transaction as a sale or other disposition, or otherwise results in a deduction under section 165. A section 165 loss includes, for example, a loss resulting from a sale or exchange of a partnership interest under section 741 and a loss resulting from a section 988 transaction.

(6) *Transactions of interest.*—A transaction of interest is a transaction that is the same as or substantially similar to one of the types of transactions that the IRS has identified by notice, regulation, or other form of published guidance as a transaction of interest.

(7) *[Reserved].*

(8) *Exceptions.*—(i) *In general.*—A transaction will not be considered a reportable transaction, or will be excluded from any individual category of reportable transaction under paragraphs (b)(3) through (7) of this section, if the Commissioner makes a determination by published guidance that the transaction is not subject to the reporting requirements of this section. The Commissioner may make a determination by individual letter ruling under paragraph (f) of this section that an individual letter ruling request on a specific transaction satisfies the reporting requirements of this section with regard to that transaction for the taxpayer who requests the individual letter ruling.

(ii) *Special rule for RICs.*—For purposes of this section, a regulated investment company (RIC) as defined in section 851 or an investment vehicle that is owned 95 percent or more by one or more RICs at all times during the course of the transaction is not required to disclose a transaction that is described in any of paragraphs (b)(3) through (5) and (b)(7) of this section unless the transaction is also a listed transaction or a transaction of interest.

(c) *Definitions.*—For purposes of this section, the following definitions apply:

(1) *Taxpayer.*—The term *taxpayer* means any person described in section 7701(a)(1), including S corporations. Except as otherwise specifically provided in this section, the term *taxpayer* also includes an affiliated group of corporations that joins in the filing of a consolidated return under section 1501.

(2) *Corporation.*—When used specifically in this section, the term *corporation* means an entity that is required to file a return for a taxable year on any 1120 series form, or successor form, excluding S corporations.

(3) *Participation.*—(i) *In general.*—(A) *Listed transactions.*—A taxpayer has participated in a listed transaction if the taxpayer's tax return reflects tax consequences or a tax strategy described in the published guidance that lists the transaction under paragraph (b)(2) of this section. A taxpayer also has participated in a listed transaction if the taxpayer knows or has reason to know that the taxpayer's tax benefits are derived directly or indirectly from tax consequences or a tax strategy described in published guidance that lists a transaction under paragraph (b)(2) of this section. Published guidance may identify other types or classes of persons that will be treated as participants in a listed transaction. Published guidance also may identify types or classes of persons that will not be treated as participants in a listed transaction.

(B) *Confidential transactions.*—A taxpayer has participated in a confidential transaction if the taxpayer's tax return reflects a tax benefit from the transaction and the taxpayer's disclosure of the tax treatment or tax structure of the transaction is limited in the manner described in paragraph (b)(3) of this section. If a partnership's, S corporation's or trust's disclosure is limited, and the partner's, shareholder's, or beneficiary's disclosure is not limited, then the partnership, S corporation, or trust, and not the partner, shareholder, or beneficiary, has participated in the confidential transaction.

(C) *Transactions with contractual protection.*—A taxpayer has participated in a transaction with contractual protection if the taxpayer's tax return reflects a tax benefit from the transaction and, as described in paragraph (b)(4) of this section, the taxpayer has the right to the full or partial refund of fees or the fees are contingent. If a partnership, S corporation, or trust has the right to a full or partial refund of fees or has a contingent fee arrangement, and the partner, shareholder, or beneficiary does not individually have the right to the refund of fees or a contingent fee arrangement, then the partnership, S corporation, or trust, and not the partner, shareholder, or beneficiary, has participated in the transaction with contractual protection.

(D) *Loss transactions.*—A taxpayer has participated in a loss transaction if the taxpayer's tax return reflects a section 165 loss and the amount of the section 165 loss equals or exceeds the threshold amount applicable to the taxpayer as described in paragraph (b)(5)(i) of this section. If a taxpayer is a partner in a partnership, shareholder in an S corporation, or beneficiary of a trust and a section 165 loss as described in paragraph (b)(5) of this section flows through the entity to the taxpayer (disregarding netting at the entity level), the taxpayer has participated in a loss transaction if the taxpayer's tax return reflects a section 165 loss and the amount of the section 165 loss that flows through to the taxpayer equals or exceeds the threshold amounts applicable to the taxpayer as described in paragraph (b)(5)(i) of this section. For this purpose, a tax return is deemed to reflect the full amount of a section 165 loss described in paragraph (b)(5) of this section allocable to the taxpayer under this paragraph (c)(3)(i)(D), regardless of whether all or part of the loss enters into the computation of a net operating loss under section 172 or net capital loss under section 1212 that the taxpayer may carry back or carry over to another year.

(E) *Transactions of interest.*—A taxpayer has participated in a transaction of interest if the taxpayer is one of the types or classes of persons identified as participants in the transaction in the published guidance describing the transaction of interest.

(F) *[Reserved].*

(G) *Shareholders of foreign corporations.*—*(1) In general.*—A reporting shareholder of a foreign corporation participates in a transaction described in paragraphs (b)(2) through (5) and (b)(7) of this section if the foreign corporation would be considered to participate in the transaction under the rules of this paragraph (c)(3) if it were a domestic corporation filing a tax return that reflects the items from the transaction. A reporting shareholder of a foreign corporation participates in a transaction described in paragraph (b)(6) of this section only if the published guidance identifying the transaction includes the reporting shareholder among the types or classes of persons identified as participants. A reporting shareholder (and any successor in interest) is considered to participate in a transaction under this paragraph (c)(3)(i)(G) only for its first taxable year with or within which ends the first taxable year of the foreign corporation in which the foreign corporation participates in the transaction, and for the reporting shareholder's five succeeding taxable years.

(2) Reporting shareholder.—The term *reporting shareholder* means a United States shareholder (as defined in section 951(b)) in a controlled foreign corporation (as defined in section 957) or a 10 percent shareholder (by vote or value) of a qualified electing fund (as defined in section 1295).

(ii) *Examples.*—The following examples illustrate the provisions of paragraph (c)(3)(i) of this section:

Example 1. Notice 2003-55 (2003-2 CB 395), which modified and superseded Notice 95-53 (1995-2 CB 334) (see § 601.601(d)(2) of this chapter), describes a lease stripping transaction in which one party (the transferor) assigns the right to receive future payments under a lease of tangible property and treats the amount realized from the assignment as its current income. The transferor later transfers the property subject to the lease in a transaction intended to qualify as a transferred basis transaction, for example, a transaction described in section 351. The transferee corporation claims the deductions associated with the high basis property subject to the lease. The transferor's and transferee corporation's tax returns reflect tax positions described in Notice 2003-55. Therefore, the transferor and transferee corporation have participated in the listed transaction. In the section 351 transaction, the transferor will have received stock with low value and high basis from the transferee corporation. If the transferor subsequently transfers the high basis/low value stock to a taxpayer in another transaction intended to qualify as a transferred basis transaction and the taxpayer uses the stock to generate a loss, and if the taxpayer knows or has reason to know that the tax loss claimed was derived indirectly from the lease stripping transaction, then the taxpayer has participated in the listed transaction. Accordingly, the taxpayer must disclose the transaction and the manner of the taxpayer's participation in the transaction under the rules of this section. For purposes of this example, if a bank lends money to the transferor, transferee corporation, or taxpayer for use in their transactions, the bank has not participated in the listed transaction because the bank's tax return does not reflect tax consequences or a tax strategy described in the listing notice (nor does the bank's tax return reflect a tax benefit derived from tax consequences or a tax strategy described in the listing notice) nor is the bank described as a participant in the listing notice.

Example 2. XYZ is a limited liability company treated as a partnership for tax purposes. X, Y, and Z are members of XYZ. X is an individual, Y is an S corporation, and Z is a partnership. XYZ enters into a confidential transaction under paragraph (b)(3) of this section. XYZ and X are bound by the confidentiality agreement, but Y and Z are not bound by the agreement. As a result of the transaction, XYZ, X, Y, and Z all reflect a tax benefit on their tax returns. Because XYZ's and X's disclosure of the tax treatment and tax structure are limited in the manner described in paragraph (b)(3) of this section and their tax returns reflect a tax benefit from the transaction, both XYZ and X have participated in the confidential transaction. Neither Y nor Z has participated in the confidential transaction because they are not subject to the confidentiality agreement.

Example 3. P, a corporation, has an 80% partnership interest in PS, and S, an individual, has a 20% partnership interest in PS. P, S, and PS are calendar year taxpayers. In 2006, PS enters into a transaction and incurs a section 165 loss (that does not meet any of the exceptions to a section 165 loss identified in published guidance) of $12 million and offsetting gain of $3 million. On PS' 2006 tax return, PS includes the section 165 loss and the corresponding gain. PS must disclose the transaction under this section because PS' section 165 loss of $12 million is equal to or greater than $2 million. P is allocated $9.6 million of the section 165 loss and $2.4 million of the offsetting gain. P does not have to disclose the transaction under this section because P's section 165 loss of $9.6 million is not equal to or greater than $10 million. S is allocated $2.4 million of the section 165 loss and $600,000 of the offsetting gain. S must disclose the transaction under this section because S's section 165 loss of $2.4 million is equal to or greater than $2 million.

(4) *Substantially similar.*—The term *substantially similar* includes any transaction that is expected to obtain the same or similar types of tax consequences and that is either factually similar or based on the same or similar tax strategy. Receipt of an opinion regarding the tax consequences of the transaction is not relevant to the determination of whether the transaction is the same as or substantially similar to another transaction. Further, the term *substantially similar* must be broadly construed in favor of disclosure. For example, a transaction may be substantially similar to a listed transaction even though it involves different entities or uses different Internal Revenue Code provisions. (See for example, Notice 2003-54 (2003-2 CB 363), describing a transaction substantially similar to the transactions in Notice 2002-50 (2002-2 CB 98), and Notice 2002-65 (2002-2 CB 690).) The following examples illustrate situations where a transaction is the same as or substantially similar to a listed transaction under paragraph (b)(2) of this section. (Such transactions may also be reportable transactions under paragraphs (b)(3) through (7) of this section.) See § 601.601(d)(2)(ii)(*b*) of this chapter. The following examples illustrate the provisions of this paragraph (c)(4):

Example 1. Notice 2000-44 (2000-2 CB 255) (see § 601.601(d)(2)(ii)(*b*) of this chapter), sets forth a listed transaction involving offsetting options transferred to a partnership where the taxpayer claims basis in the partnership for the cost of the purchased options but does not adjust basis under section 752 as a result of the partnership's assumption of the taxpayer's obligation with respect to the options. Transactions using short sales, futures, derivatives or any other type of offsetting obligations to inflate basis in a partnership interest would be the same as or substantially similar to the transaction described in Notice 2000-44. Moreover, use of the inflated basis in the partnership interest to diminish gain that would otherwise be recognized on the transfer of a partnership asset would also be the same as or substantially similar to the transaction described in Notice 2000-44. See § 601.601(d)(2)(ii)(b).

Example 2. Notice 2001-16 (2001-1 CB 730) (see § 601.601(d)(2)(ii)(*b*) of this chapter), sets forth a listed transaction involving a seller (X) who desires to sell stock of a corporation (T), an intermediary corporation (M), and a buyer (Y) who desires to purchase the assets (and not the stock) of T. M agrees to facilitate the sale to prevent the recognition of the gain that T would otherwise report. Notice 2001-16 describes M as a member of a consolidated group that has a loss within the group or as a party not subject to tax. Transactions utilizing different intermediaries to prevent the recognition of gain would be the same as or substantially similar to the transaction described in Notice 2001-16. An example is a transaction in which M is a corporation that does not file a consolidated return but which buys T stock, liquidates T, sells assets of T to Y, and offsets the gain on the sale of those assets with currently generated losses. See § 601.601(d)(2)(ii)(*b*).

(5) *Tax.*—The term *tax* means Federal income tax.

(6) *Tax benefit.*—A tax benefit includes deductions, exclusions from gross income, nonrecognition of gain, tax credits, adjustments (or the absence of adjustments) to the basis of property, status as an entity exempt from Federal income taxation, and any other tax consequences that may reduce a taxpayer's Federal income tax liability by affecting the amount, timing, character, or source of any item of income, gain, expense, loss, or credit.

(7) *Tax return.*—The term *tax return* means a Federal income tax return and a Federal information return.

(8) *Tax treatment.*—The tax treatment of a transaction is the purported or claimed Federal income tax treatment of the transaction.

(9) *Tax structure.*—The tax structure of a transaction is any fact that may be relevant to understanding the purported or claimed Federal income tax treatment of the transaction.

(d) *Form and content of disclosure statement.*—A taxpayer required to file a disclosure statement under this section must file a completed Form 8886, "Reportable Transaction Disclosure Statement" (or a successor form), in accordance with this paragraph (d) and the instructions to the form. The Form 8886 (or a successor form) is the disclosure statement required under this section. The form must be attached to the appropriate tax return(s) as provided in paragraph (e) of this section. If a copy of a disclosure statement is required to be sent to the Office of Tax Shelter Analysis (OTSA) under paragraph (e) of this section, it must be sent in accordance with the instructions to the form. To be considered complete, the information provided on the form must describe the expected tax treatment and all potential tax benefits expected to result from the transaction, describe any tax result protection (as defined in § 301.6111-3(c)(12) of this chapter) with respect to the transaction, and identify and describe the transaction in sufficient detail for the IRS to be able to understand the tax structure of the reportable transaction and the identity of all parties involved in the transaction. An incomplete Form 8886 (or a successor form) containing a statement that information will be provided upon request is not considered a complete disclosure statement. If the form is not completed in accordance with the provisions in this paragraph (d) and the instructions to the form, the taxpayer will not be considered to have complied with the disclosure requirements of this section. If a taxpayer receives one or more reportable transaction numbers for a reportable transaction, the taxpayer must include the reportable transaction number(s) on the Form 8886 (or a successor form). See § 301.6111-3(d)(2) of this chapter.

(e) *Time of providing disclosure.*—(1) *In general.*—The disclosure statement for a reportable transaction must be attached to the taxpayer's tax return for each taxable year for which a taxpayer participates in a reportable transaction. In addition, a disclosure statement for a reportable transaction must be attached to each amended return that reflects a taxpayer's participation in a reportable transaction. A copy of the disclosure statement must be sent to OTSA at the same time that any disclosure statement is first filed by the taxpayer pertaining to a particular reportable transaction. If a reportable transaction results in a loss which is carried back to a prior year, the disclosure statement for the reportable transaction must be attached to the taxpayer's application for tentative refund or amended tax return for that prior year. In the case of a taxpayer that is a partnership, an S corporation, or a trust, the disclosure statement for a reportable transaction must be attached to the partnership, S corporation, or trust's tax return for each taxable year in which the partnership, S corporation, or trust participates in the transaction under the rules of paragraph (c)(3)(i) of this section. If a taxpayer who is a partner in a partnership, a shareholder in an S corporation, or a beneficiary of a trust receives a timely Schedule K-1 less than 10 calendar days before the due date of the taxpayer's return (including extensions) and, based on receipt of the timely Schedule K-1, the taxpayer determines that the taxpayer participated in a reportable transaction within the meaning of paragraph (c)(3) of this section, the disclosure statement will not be considered late if the taxpayer discloses the reportable transaction by filing a disclosure statement with OTSA within 60 calendar days after the due date of the taxpayer's return (including extensions). The Commissioner in his discretion may issue in published guidance other provisions for disclosure under § 1.6011-4.

(2) *Special rules.*—(i) *Listed transactions and transactions of interest.*—In general, if a transaction becomes a listed transaction or a transaction of interest after the filing of a taxpayer's tax return (including an amended return) reflecting the taxpayer's participation in the listed transaction or transaction of interest and before the end of the period of limitations for assessment of tax for any taxable year in which the taxpayer participated in the listed transaction or transaction of interest, then a disclosure statement must be filed, regardless of whether the taxpayer participated in the transaction in the year the transaction became a listed transaction or a transaction of interest, with OTSA within 90 calendar days after the date on which the transaction became a listed transaction or a transaction of interest. The Commissioner also may determine the time for disclosure of listed transactions and transactions of interest in the published guidance identifying the transaction.

(ii) *Loss transactions.*—If a transaction becomes a loss transaction because the losses equal or exceed the threshold amounts as described in paragraph (b)(5)(i) of this section, a disclosure statement must be filed as an attachment to the taxpayer=s tax return for the first taxable year in which the threshold amount is reached and to any subsequent tax return that reflects any amount of section 165 loss from the transaction.

(3) *Multiple disclosures.*—The taxpayer must disclose the transaction in the time and manner provided for under the provisions of this section regardless of whether the taxpayer also plans to disclose the transaction under other published guidance, for example, § 1.6662-3(c)(2).

(4) *Example.*—The following example illustrates the application of this paragraph (e):

Example. In January of 2008, F, a calendar year taxpayer, enters into a transaction that at the time is not a listed transaction and is not a transaction described in any of the paragraphs (b)(3) through (7) of this section. All the tax benefits from the transaction are reported on F's 2008 tax return filed timely in April 2009. On May 2, 2011, the IRS publishes a notice identifying the transaction as a listed transaction described in paragraph (b)(2) of this section. Upon issuance of the May 2, 2011 notice, the transaction becomes a reportable transaction described in paragraph (b) of this section. The period of limitations on assessment for F's 2008 taxable year is still open. F is required to file Form 8886 for the transaction with OTSA within 90 calendar days after May 2, 2011.

(f) *Rulings and protective disclosures.*—(1) *Rulings.*—If a taxpayer requests a ruling on the merits of a specific transaction on or before the date that disclosure would otherwise be required under this section, and receives a favorable ruling as to the transaction, the disclosure rules under this section will be deemed to have been satisfied by that taxpayer with regard to that transaction, so long as the request fully discloses all relevant facts relating to the transaction which would otherwise be required to be disclosed under this section. If a taxpayer requests a ruling as to whether a specific transaction is a reportable transaction on or before the date that disclosure would otherwise be required under this section, the Commissioner in his discretion may determine that the submission satisfies the disclosure rules under this section for the taxpayer requesting the ruling for that transaction if the request fully discloses all relevant facts relating to the transaction which would otherwise be required to be disclosed under this section. The potential obligation of the taxpayer to disclose the transaction under this section will not be suspended during the period that the ruling request is pending.

(2) *Protective disclosures.*—If a taxpayer is uncertain whether a transaction must be disclosed under this section, the taxpayer may disclose the transaction in accordance with the requirements of this section and comply with all the provisions of this section, and indicate on the disclosure statement that the disclosure statement is being filed on a protective basis. The IRS will not treat disclosure statements filed on a protective basis any differently than other disclosure statements filed under this section. For a protective disclosure to be effective, the taxpayer must comply with these disclosure regulations by providing to the IRS all information requested by the IRS under this section.

(g) *Retention of documents.*—(1) In accordance with the instructions to Form 8886 (or a successor form), the taxpayer must retain a copy of all documents and other records related to a transaction subject to disclosure under this section that are material to an understanding of the tax treatment or tax structure of the transaction. The documents must be retained until the expiration of the statute of limitations applicable to the final taxable year for which disclosure of the transaction was required under this section. (This document retention requirement is in addition to any document retention requirements that section 6001 generally imposes on the taxpayer.) The documents may include the following:

(i) Marketing materials related to the transaction;

(ii) Written analyses used in decision-making related to the transaction;

(iii) Correspondence and agreements between the taxpayer and any advisor, lender, or other party to the reportable transaction that relate to the transaction;

(iv) Documents discussing, referring to, or demonstrating the purported or claimed tax benefits arising from the reportable transaction; and documents, if any, referring to the business purposes for the reportable transaction.

(2) A taxpayer is not required to retain earlier drafts of a document if the taxpayer retains a copy of the final document (or, if there is no final document, the most recent draft of the document) and the final document (or most recent draft) contains all the information in the earlier drafts of the document that is material to an understanding of the purported tax treatment or tax structure of the transaction.

(h) *Effective/applicability date.*—(1) *In general.*—This section applies to transactions entered into on or after August 3, 2007. However, this section applies to transactions of interest entered into on or after November 2, 2006. Paragraph (f)(1) of this section applies to ruling requests received on or after November 1, 2006. Otherwise, the rules that apply with respect to transactions entered into before August 3, 2007, are contained in § 1.6011-4 in effect prior to August 3, 2007. (See 26 CFR part 1 revised as of April 1, 2007).

(2) *[Reserved].*

[Reg. § 1.6011-4.]

☐ [*T.D.* 9046, 2-28-2003. *Amended by T.D.* 9108, 12-29-2003; *T.D.* 9295, 11-1-2006 *and T.D.* 9350, 7-31-2007 (*corrected* 5-10-2010).]

[Reg. § 20.6011-4]

§ 20.6011-4. Requirement of statement disclosing participation in certain transactions by taxpayers.—(a) *In general.*—If a transaction is identified as a *listed transaction* or a *transaction of interest* as defined in § 1.6011-4 of this chapter by the Commissioner in published guidance (see § 601.601(d)(2)(ii)(*b*) of this chapter), and the listed transaction or transaction of interest involves an estate tax under chapter 11 of subtitle B of the Internal Revenue Code, the transaction must be disclosed in the manner stated in such published guidance.

(b) *Effective/applicability date.*—This section applies to listed transactions entered into on or after January 1, 2003. This section applies to transactions of interest entered into on or after November 2, 2006. [Reg. § 20.6011-4.]

☐ [*T.D.* 9046, 2-28-2003. *Amended by T.D.* 9350, 7-31-2007.]

[Reg. § 25.6011-4]

§ 25.6011-4. Requirement of statement disclosing participation in certain transactions by taxpayers.—(a) *In general.*—If a transaction is identified as a *listed transaction* or a *transaction of interest* as defined in § 1.6011-4 of this chapter by the Commissioner in published guidance (see § 601.601(d)(2)(ii)(*b*) of this chapter), and the listed transaction or transaction of interest involves a gift tax under chapter 12 of subtitle B of the Internal Revenue Code, the transaction must be disclosed in the manner stated in such published guidance.

(b) *Effective/applicability date.*—This section applies to listed transactions entered into on or after January 1, 2003. This section applies to transactions of interest entered into on or after November 2, 2006. [Reg. § 25.6011-4.]

☐ [*T.D.* 9046, 2-28-2003. *Amended by T.D.* 9350, 7-31-2007.]

[Reg. § 26.6011-4]

§ 26.6011-4. Requirement of statement disclosing participation in certain transactions by taxpayers.—(a) *In general.*—If a transaction is identified as a *listed transaction* or a *transaction of interest* as defined in § 1.6011-4 of this chapter by the Commissioner in published guidance, and the listed transaction or transaction of interest involves a tax on generation-skipping transfers under chapter 13 of subtitle B of the Internal Revenue Code, the transaction must be disclosed in the manner stated in such published guidance.

(b) *Effective/applicability date.*—This section applies to listed transactions and transactions of interest entered into on or after November 14, 2011. [Reg. § 26.6011-4.]

☐ [*T.D.* 9556, 11-10-2011.]

[Reg. § 1.6012-3]

§ 1.6012-3. Returns by fiduciaries.—(a) *For estates and trusts.*—(1) *In general.*—Every fiduciary, or at least one of the joint fiduciaries, must make a return of income on form 1041 (or by use of a composite return pursuant to § 1.6012-5) and attach the required form if the estate or trust has items of tax preference (as defined in section 57 and the regulations thereunder) in any amount—

(i) For each estate for which he acts if the gross income of such estate for the taxable year is $600 or more;

(ii) For each trust for which he acts, except a trust exempt under section 501(a), if such trust has for the taxable year any taxable income, or has for the taxable year gross income of $600 or more regardless of the amount of taxable income; and

(iii) For each estate and each trust for which he acts, except a trust exempt under section 501(a), regardless of the amount of income for the taxable year, if any beneficiary of such estate or trust is a nonresident alien.

(iv) For each trust electing to be taxed as, or as part of, an estate under section 645 for which a trustee acts, and for each related estate joining in a section 645 election for which an executor acts, if the aggregate gross income of the electing trust(s) and related estate, if any, joining in the election for the taxable year is $600 or more. (For the respective filing requirements of the trustee of each electing trust and executor of any related estate, see § 1.645-1).

(2) *Wills and trust instruments.*—At the request of the Internal Revenue Service, a copy of the will or trust instrument (including any amendments), accompanied by a written declaration of the fiduciary under the penalties of perjury that it is a true and complete copy, shall be filed together with a statement by the fiduciary indicating the provisions of the will or trust instrument (including any amendments) which, in the fiduciary's opinion, determine the extent to which the income of the estate or trust is taxable to the estate or trust, the beneficiaries, or the grantor, respectively.

(3) *Domiciliary and ancillary representatives.*—In the case of an estate required to file a return under subparagraph (1) of this paragraph, having both domiciliary and ancillary representatives, the domiciliary and ancillary representatives must each file a return on Form 1041. The domiciliary representative is required to include in the return rendered by him as such domiciliary representative the entire income of the estate. The return of the ancillary representative shall be filed with the district director for his internal revenue district and shall show the name and address of the domiciliary representative, the amount of gross income received by the ancillary representative, and the deductions to be claimed against such income, including any amount of income properly paid or credited by the ancillary representative to any legatee, heir, or other beneficiary. If the ancillary representative for the estate of a nonresident alien is a citizen or resident of the United States, and the domiciliary representative is a nonresident alien, such ancillary representative is required to render the return otherwise required of the domiciliary representative.

(4) *Two or more trusts.*—A trustee of two or more trusts must make a separate return for each trust, even though such trusts were created by the same grantor for the same beneficiary or beneficiaries.

(5) *Trusts with unrelated business income.*—Every fiduciary for a trust described in section 511(b)(2) which is subject to the tax on its unrelated business taxable income by section 511(b)(1) shall make a return on Form 990-T for each taxable year if the trust has gross income, included in computing unrelated business taxable income for such taxable year, of $1,000 or more. The filing of a return of unrelated business income does not relieve the fiduciary of such trusts from the duty of filing other required returns.

(6) *Charitable remainder trusts.*—Every fiduciary for a charitable remainder annuity trust (as defined in § 1.664-2) or a charitable remainder unitrust (as defined in § 1.664-3) shall make a return on Form 1041-B for each taxable year of the trust even though it is nonexempt because it has unrelated business taxable income. The return on Form 1041-B shall be made in accordance with the instructions for the form and shall be filed with the designated Internal Revenue office on or before the 15th day of the fourth month following the close of the taxable year of the trust. A copy of the instrument governing the trust, accompanied by a written declaration of

the fiduciary under the penalties of perjury that it is a true and complete copy, shall be attached to the return for the first taxable year of the trust.

(7) *Certain trusts described in section 4947(a)(1).*—For taxable years beginning after December 31, 1980, in the case of a trust described in section 4947(a)(1) which has no taxable income for a taxable year, the filing requirements of Section 6012 and this section shall be satisfied by the filing, pursuant to § 53.6011-1 of this chapter (Foundation Excise Tax Regulations) and § 1.6033-2(a), by the fiduciary of such trust of—

(i) Form 990-PF if such trust is treated as a private foundation, or

(ii) Form 990 if such trust is not treated as a private foundation.

When the provisions of this paragraph (7) are met, the fiduciary shall not be required to file Form 1041.

(8) *Estates and trusts liable for qualified tax.*—In the case of an estate or trust which is liable for one or more qualified State individual income taxes, as defined in section 6362, for a taxable year, see paragraph (b) of § 301.6361-1 of this chapter (Regulations on Procedure and Administration) for rules relating to returns required to be made.

(9) *A trust any portion of which is treated as owned by the grantor or another person pursuant to sections 671 through 678.*—In the case of a trust any portion of which is treated as owned by the grantor or another person under the provisions of subpart E (section 671 and following) part I, subchapter J, chapter 1 of the Internal Revenue Code see § 1.671-4.

(10) *Hospital organizations organized as trusts with noncompliant hospital facilities.*—Every fiduciary for a hospital organization (as defined in § 1.501(r)-1(b)(18)) organized as a trust described in section 511(b)(2) that is subject to the tax imposed by § 1.501(r)-2(d) shall make a return on Form 990-T. The filing of a return to pay the tax described in § 1.501(r)-2(d) does not relieve the organization of the duty of filing other required returns.

(b) *For other persons.*—(1) *Decedents.*—The executor or administrator of the estate of a decedent, or other person charged with the property of a decedent, shall make the return of income required in respect of such decedent. For the decedent's taxable year which ends with the date of his death, the return shall cover the period during which he was alive. For the filing of returns of income for citizens and alien residents of the United States, and alien residents of Puerto Rico, see paragraph (a) of § 1.6012-1. For the filing of a joint return after death of spouse, see paragraph (d) of § 1.6013-1.

(2) *Nonresident alien individuals.*—(i) *In general.*—A resident or domestic fiduciary or other person charged with the care of the person or property of a nonresident alien individual shall make a return for that individual and pay the tax unless—

(*a*) The nonresident alien individual makes a return of, and pays the tax on, his income for the taxable year,

(*b*) A responsible representative or agent in the United States of the nonresident alien individual makes a return of, and pays the tax on, the income of such alien individual for the taxable year, or

(*c*) The nonresident alien individual has appointed a person in the United States to act as his agent for the purpose of making a return of income and, if such fiduciary is required to file a Form 1041 for an estate or trust of which such alien individual is a beneficiary, such fiduciary attaches a copy of the agency appointment to his return on Form 1041.

(ii) *Income to be returned.*—A return of income shall be required under this subparagraph only if the nonresident alien individual is otherwise required to make a return in accordance with paragraph (b) of § 1.6012-1. The provisions of that paragraph shall apply in determining the form of return to be used and the income to be returned.

(iii) *Disallowance of deductions and credits.*—For provisions disallowing deductions and credits when a return of income has not been filed by or on behalf of a nonresident alien individual, see section 874 and the regulations thereunder.

(iv) *Alien resident of Puerto Rico.*—This subparagraph shall not apply to the return of a nonresident alien individual who is a bona fide resident of Puerto Rico during the entire taxable year. See § 1.876-1.

(v) *Cross reference.*—For requirements of withholding tax at source on nonresident alien individuals and of returns with respect to such withheld taxes, see §§ 1.1441-1 to 1.1465-1, inclusive.

(3) *Persons under a disability.*—A fiduciary acting as the guardian of a minor, or as the guardian or committee of an insane person, must make the return of income required in respect of such person unless, in the case of a minor, the minor himself makes the return or causes it to be made.

(4) *Corporations.*—A receiver, trustee in dissolution, trustee in bankruptcy, or assignee, who, by order of a court of competent jurisdiction, by operation of law or otherwise, has possession of or holds title to all or substantially all the property or business of a corporation, shall make the return of income for such corporation in the same manner and form as corporations are required to make such returns. Such return shall be filed whether or not the receiver, trustee, or assignee is operating the property or business of the corporation. A receiver in charge of only a small part of the property of a corporation, such as a receiver in mortgage foreclosure proceedings involving merely a small portion of its property, need not make the return of income. See also § 1.6041-1, relating to returns regarding information at source; §§ 1.6042-1 to 1.6042-3, in-

clusive, relating to returns regarding payments of dividends; §§1.6044-1 to 1.6044-4, inclusive, relating to returns regarding payments of patronage dividends; §§1.6049-1 and 1.6049-2, relating to returns regarding certain payments of interest.

(5) *Individuals in receivership.*—A receiver who stands in the place of an individual must make the return of income required in respect of such individual. A receiver of only part of the property of an individual need not file a return, and the individual must make his own return.

(c) *Joint fiduciaries.*—In the case of joint fiduciaries, a return is required to be made by only one of such fiduciaries. A return made by one of joint fiduciaries shall contain a statement that the fiduciary has sufficient knowledge of the affairs of the person for whom the return is made to enable him to make the return, and that the return is, to the best of his knowledge and belief, true and correct.

(d) *Other provisions.*—For the definition of the term "fiduciary", see section 7701(a)(6) and the regulations thereunder. For information returns required to be made by fiduciaries under section 6041, see §1.6041-1. As to further duties and liabilities of fiduciaries, see section 6903 and §301.6903-1 of this chapter (Regulations on Procedure and Administration). [Reg. §1.6012-3.]

☐ [*T.D.* 6031, 7-8-58 *and T.D.* 6364, 2-13-59. *Amended by T.D.* 6628, 12-27-62; *T.D.* 6972, 9-11-68; *T.D.* 7200, 8-15-72; *T.D.* 7202, 8-22-72; *T.D.* 7332, 12-20-74; *T.D.* 7407, 3-3-76; *T.D.* 7564, 9-11-78; *T.D.* 7577, 12-19-78; *T.D.* 7608, 4-3-79; *T.D.* 7796, 11-23-81; *T.D.* 7838, 10-5-82; *T.D.* 8026, 5-17-85; *T.D.* 8633, 12-20-95; *T.D.* 9032, 12-23-2002 *and T.D.* 9708, 12-29-2014.]

[Reg. §20.6018-1]

§20.6018-1. Returns.—(a) *Estates of citizens or residents.*—A return must be filed on Form 706 for the estate of every citizen or resident of the United States whose gross estate exceeded $60,000 in value on the date of his death. The value of the gross estate at the date of death governs with respect to the filing of the return regardless of whether the value of the gross estate is, at the executor's election, finally determined as of a date subsequent to the date of death pursuant to the provisions of section 2032. Duplicate copies of the return are not required to be filed. For the contents of the return, see §20.6018-3.

(b) *Estates of nonresidents not citizens.*—(1) *In general.*—Except as provided in subparagraph (2) of this paragraph, a return must be filed on Form 706 or Form 706NA for the estate of every nonresident not a citizen of the United States if the value of that part of the gross estate situated in the United States on the date of his death exceeded $30,000 in the case of a decedent dying on or after November 14, 1966, or $2,000 in the case of a decedent dying before November 14, 1966. Under certain conditions the return may be made only on Form 706. See the instructions on Form 706NA for circumstances under which that form may not be used. Duplicate copies of the return are not required to be filed. For the contents of the return, see §20.6018-3. For the determination of the gross estate situated in the United States, see §§20.2103-1 and 20.2104-1.

(2) *Certain estates of decedents dying on or after November 14, 1966.*—In the case of an estate of a nonresident not a citizen of the United States dying on or after November 14, 1966—

(i) *Transfers subject to the tax imposed by section 2107(a).*—If the transfer of the estate is subject to the tax imposed by section 2107(a) (relating to expatriation to avoid tax), any amounts includible in the decedent's gross estate under section 2107(b) are to be added to the value on the date of his death of that part of his gross estate situated in the United States, for purposes of determining under subparagraph (1) of this paragraph whether his gross estate exceeded $30,000 on the date of his death.

(ii) *Transfers subject to a Presidential proclamation.*—If the transfer of the estate is subject to tax pursuant to a Presidential proclamation made under section 2108(a) (relating to Presidential proclamations of the application of pre-1967 estate tax provisions), the return must be filed on Form 706 or Form 706NA if the value on the date of the decedent's death of that part of his gross estate situated in the United States exceeded $2,000.

(c) *Place for filing.*—See §20.6091-1 for the place where the return shall be filed.

(d) *Time for filing.*—See §20.6075-1 for the time for filing the return. [Reg. §20.6018-1.]

☐ [*T.D.* 7296, 12-11-73.]

[Reg. §20.6018-2]

§20.6018-2. Returns; person required to file return.—It is required that the duly qualified executor or administrator shall file the return. If there is more than one executor or administrator, the return must be made jointly by all. If there is no executor or administrator appointed, qualified and acting within the United States, every person in actual or constructive possession of any property of the decedent situated in the United States is constituted an executor for purposes of the tax (see §20.2203-1), and is required to make and file a return. If in any case the executor is unable to make a complete return as to any part of the gross estate, he is required to give all the information he has as to such property, including a full description, and the name of every person holding a legal or beneficial interest in the property. If the executor is unable to make a return as to any property, every person holding a legal or beneficial interest therein shall, upon notice from the district director, make a return as to that part of the gross estate. For delinquency penalty for failure to file return, see section 6651 and §301.6651-1 of this chapter (Regulations on Procedure and Administration). For criminal penalties for failure to file a return and filing a false or fraudulent return, see sections 7203, 7206, 7207, and 7269. [Reg. §20.6018-2.]

☐ [*T.D.* 6296, 6-23-58.]

[Reg. §20.6018-3]

§20.6018-3. Returns; contents of returns.—(a) *Citizens or residents*.—The return of an estate of a decedent who was a citizen or resident of the United States at the time of his death must contain an itemized inventory by schedule of the property constituting the gross estate and lists of the deductions under the proper schedules. The return shall set forth (1) the value of the gross estate (see §§20.2031-1 through 20.2044-1), (2) the deductions claimed (see §§20.2052-1 through 20.2056(e)-3), (3) the taxable estate (see §20.2051-1), and (4) the gross estate tax, reduced by any credits (see §§20.2011-1 through 20.2014-6) against the tax. In listing upon the return the property constituting the gross estate (other than household and personal effects for which see §20.2031-6), the description of it shall be such that the property may be readily identified for the purpose of verifying the value placed on it by the executor.

(b) *Nonresidents not citizens*.—The return of an estate of a decedent who was not a citizen or resident of the United States at the time of his death must contain the following information: (1) An itemized list of that part of the gross estate situated in the United States (see §§20.2103-1 and 20.2104-1); (2) in the case of an estate the transfer of which is subject to the tax imposed by section 2107(a) (relating to expatriation to avoid tax), a list of any amounts with respect to stock in a foreign corporation which are includible in the gross estate under section 2107(b), together with an explanation of how the amounts were determined; (3) an itemized list of any deductions claimed (see §§20.2106-1 and 20.2106-2); (4) the amount of the taxable estate (see §20.2106-1); and (5) the gross estate tax, reduced by any credits against the tax (see §20.2102-1). For the disallowance of certain deductions if the return does not disclose that part of the gross estate not situated in the United States, see §§20.2106-1 and 20.2106-2.

(c) *Provisions applicable to returns described in paragraphs (a) and (b) of this section*.—(1) A legal description shall be given of each parcel of real estate, and, if located in a city, the name of the street and number, its area, and, if improved, a short statement of the character of the improvements.

(2) A description of bonds shall include the number held, principal amount, name of obligor, date of maturity, rate of interest, date or dates on which interest is payable, series number if there is more than one issue, and the principal exchange upon which listed, or the principal business office of the obligor, if unlisted. A description of stocks, shall include number of shares, whether common or preferred, and, if preferred, what issue, par value, quotation at which returned, exact name of corporation, and, if the stock is unlisted, the location of the principal business office and State in which incorporated and the date of incorporation, or if the stock is listed, the principal exchange upon which sold. A description of notes shall include name of maker, date on which given, date of maturity, amount of principal, amount of principal unpaid, rate of interest and whether simple or compound, date to which interest has been paid and amount of unpaid interest. A description of the seller's interest in land contracts shall include name of buyer, date of contract, description of property, sale price, initial payment, amounts of installment payments, unpaid balance of principal and accrued interest, interest rate and date prior to decedent's death to which interest had been paid.

(3) A description of bank accounts shall disclose the name and address of depository, amount on deposit, whether a checking, savings, or a time-deposit account, rate of interest, if any payable, amount of interest accrued and payable, and serial number. A description of life insurance shall give the name of the insurer, number of policy, name of the beneficiary, and the amount of the proceeds.

(4) In describing an annuity, the name and address of the grantor of the annuity shall be given, or, if the annuity is payable out of a trust or other funds, such a description as will fully identify it. If the annuity is payable for a term of years, the duration of the term and the date on which it began shall be given, and if payable for the life of a person other than the decedent, the date of birth of such person shall be stated. If the executor has not included in the gross estate the full value of an annuity or other payment described in section 2039, he shall nevertheless fully describe the annuity and state its total purchase price and the amount of the contribution made by each person (including the decedent's employer) toward the purchase price. If the executor believes that any part of the annuity or other payment is excludable from the gross estate under the provisions of section 2039, or for any other reason, he shall state in the return the reason for his belief.

(5) Judgments should be described by giving the title of the cause and the name of the court in which rendered, date of judgment, name and address of the judgment debtor, amount of judgment, and rate of interest to which subject, and by stating whether any payments have been made thereon, and, if so, when and in what amounts.

(6) If, pursuant to section 2032, the executor elects to have the estate valued at a date or dates subsequent to the time of the decedent's death, there must be set forth on the return: (i) An itemized description of all property included in the gross estate on the date of the decedent's death, together with the value of each item as of that date; (ii) an itemized disclosure of all distributions, sales, exchanges, and other dispositions of any property during the 6-month (1 year, if the decedent died on or before December 31, 1970) period after the date of the decedent's death, together with the dates thereof; and (iii) the value of each item of property in accordance

with the provisions of section 2032 (see § 20.2032-1). Interest and rents accrued at the date of the decedent's death and dividends declared to stockholders of record on or before the date of the decedent's death and not collected at that date are to be shown separately. (See also paragraph (e) of § 20.6018-4 with respect to documents required to be filed with the return.)

(7) All transfers made by the decedent within 3 years before the date of his death of a value of $1,000 or more and all transfers (other than outright transfers not in trust) made by the decedent at any time during his life of a value of $5,000 or more, except bona fide sales for an adequate and full consideration in money or money's worth, must be disclosed in the return, whether or not the executor regards the transfers as subject to the tax. If the executor believes that such a transfer is not subject to the tax, a brief statement of the pertinent facts shall be made. [Reg. § 20.6018-3.]

□ [*T.D.* 7238, 12-28-72 *and T.D.* 7295, 12-11-73.]

[Reg. § 20.6018-4]

§ 20.6018-4. Returns; documents to accompany the return.—(a) A certified copy of the will, if the decedent died testate, must be submitted with the return, together with copies of such other documents as are required in Form 706 and in the applicable sections of these regulations. There may also be filed copies of any documents which the executor may desire to submit in explanation of the return.

(b) In the case of an estate of a nonresident citizen, the executor shall also file the following documents with the return: (1) A copy of any inventory of property and schedule of liabilities, claims against the estate and expenses of administration filed with the foreign court of probate jurisdiction, certified by a proper official of the court; and (2) a copy of any return filed under any applicable foreign inheritance, estate, legacy, or succession tax act, certified by a proper official of the foreign tax department.

(c) In the case of an estate of a nonresident not a citizen of the United States, the executor must also file with the return, but only if deductions are claimed or the transfer of the estate is subject to the tax imposed by section 2107(a) (relating to expatriation to avoid tax), a copy of the inventory of property filed under the foreign death duty act; or, if no such inventory was filed, a certified copy of the inventory filed with the foreign court of probate jurisdiction.

(d) For every policy of life insurance listed on the return, the executor must procure a statement, on Form 712, by the company issuing the policy and file it with the return.

(e) If, pursuant to section 2032, the executor elects to have the estate valued at a date or dates subsequent to the time of the decedent's death, the executor shall file with the return evidence in support of any statements made by him in the return as to distributions, sales, exchanges, or other dispositions of property during the 6-month (1 year, if the decedent died on or before December 31, 1970) period which followed the decedent's death. If the court having jurisdiction over the estate makes an order or decree of distribution during that period, a certified copy thereof must be submitted as part of the evidence. The district director, or the director of a service center, may require the submission of such additional evidence as is deemed necessary.

(f) In any case where a transfer, by trust or otherwise, was made by a written instrument, a copy thereof shall be filed with the return if (1) the property is included in the gross estate, or (2) the executor pursuant to the provisions of paragraph (c)(7) of § 20.6018-3 has made a disclosure of the transfer on the return but has not included its value in the gross estate in the belief that it is not so includible. If the written instrument is of public record, the copy shall be certified, or if it is not of record, the copy shall be verified. If the decedent was a nonresident not a citizen at the time of his death, the copy may be either certified or verified.

(g) If the executor contends that the value of property transferred by the decedent within a period of three years ending with the date of the decedent's death should not be included in the gross estate because he considers that the transfer was not made in contemplation of death, he shall file with the return (1) a copy of the death certificate, and (2) a statement, containing a declaration that it is made under the penalties of perjury, of all the material facts and circumstances, including those directly or indirectly indicating the decedent's motive in making the transfer and his mental and physical condition at that time. However, this data need not be furnished with respect to transfers of less than $1,000 in value unless requested by the district director. [Reg. § 20.6018-4.]

□ [*T.D.* 6296, 6-23-58. *Amended by T.D.* 7238, 12-28-72 *and T.D.* 7296, 12-11-73.]

[Reg. § 25.6019-1]

§ 25.6019-1. Persons required to file returns.—(a) *Gifts made after December 31, 1981.*—Subject to section 2523(i)(2), an individual citizen or resident of the United States who in any calendar year beginning after December 31, 1981, makes any transfer by gift other than a transfer that, under section 2503(b) or (e) (relating, respectively, to certain gifts of $10,000 per donee and the exclusion for payment of certain educational and medical expenses), is not included in the total amount of gifts for that year, or a transfer of an interest with respect to which a marital deduction is allowed for the value of the entire interest under section 2523 (other than a marital deduction allowed by reason of section 2523(f), regarding qualified terminable interest property for which a return must be filed in order to make the election under that section), must file a gift tax return on Form 709 for that calendar year.

(b) *Gifts made after December 31, 1976, and before January 1, 1982.*—An individual citizen or resident of the United States who makes a transfer by gift within any calendar year beginning after December 31, 1976, and before January 1, 1982, must file a gift tax return on Form 709 for any calendar quarter in which the sum of the taxable gifts made during that calendar quarter, plus all other taxable gifts made during the year (for which a return has not yet been required to be filed), exceeds $25,000. If the aggregate transfers made in a calendar year after 1976 and before 1982 that must be reported do not exceed $25,000, only one return must be filed for the calendar year and it must be filed by the due date for a fourth quarter gift tax return (April 15).

(c) *Gifts made after December 31, 1970, and before January 1, 1977.*—An individual citizen or resident of the United States who makes a transfer by gift within any calendar year beginning after December 31, 1970, and before January 1, 1977, must file a gift tax return on Form 709 for the calendar quarter in which any portion of the value of the gift, or any portion of the sum of the values of the gifts to such donee during that calendar year, is not excluded from the total amount of taxable gifts for that year, and must also make a return for any subsequent quarter within the same taxable year in which any additional gift is made to the same donee.

(d) *Gifts by nonresident alien donors.*—The rules contained in paragraphs (a) through (c) of this section also apply to a nonresident not a citizen of the United States provided that, under section 2501(a)(1) and § 25.2511-3, the transfer is subject to the gift tax.

(e) *Miscellaneous provisions.*—Only individuals are required to file returns and not trusts, estates, partnerships, or corporations. Duplicate copies of the return are not required to be filed. See § § 25.6075-1 and 25.6091-1 for the time and place for filing the gift tax return. For delinquency penalties for failure to file or pay the tax, see section 6651 and § 301.6651-1 of this chapter (Procedure and Administration Regulations). For criminal penalties for failure to file a return and filing a false or fraudulent return, see sections 7203, 7206, and 7207.

(f) *Return required even if no tax due.*—The return is required even though, because of the deduction authorized by section 2522 (charitable deduction) or the unified credit under section 2505, no tax may be payable on the transfer.

(g) *Deceased donor.*—If the donor dies before filing his return, the executor of his will or the administrator of his estate shall file the return. If the donor becomes legally incompetent before filing his return, his guardian or committee shall file the return.

(h) *Ratification of return.*—The return shall not be made by an agent unless by reason of illness, absence, or nonresidence, the person liable for the return is unable to make it within the time prescribed. Mere convenience is not sufficient reason for authorizing an agent to make the return. If by reason of illness, absence or nonresidence, a return is made by an agent, the return must be ratified by the donor or other person liable for its filing within a reasonable time after such person becomes able to do so. If the return filed by the agent is not so ratified, it will not be considered the return required by the statute. Supplemental data may be submitted at the time of ratification. The ratification may be in the form of a statement executed under the penalties of perjury and filed with the internal revenue officer with whom the return was filed, showing specifically that the return made by the agent has been carefully examined and that the person signing ratifies the return as the donor's. If a return is signed by an agent, a statement fully explaining the inability of the donor must accompany the return. [Reg. § 25.6019-1.]

☐ [*T.D.* 6334, 11-14-58. *Amended by T.D.* 7012, 5-14-69; *T.D.* 7238, 12-28-72 *and T.D.* 8522, 2-28-94.]

[Reg. § 25.6019-2]

§ 25.6019-2. Returns required in case of consent under section 2513.—Except as otherwise provided in this section, the provisions of § 25.6019-1 (other than paragraph (d) of § 25.6019-1) apply with respect to the filing of a gift tax return or returns in the case of a husband and wife who consent (see § 25.2513-1) to the application of section 2513. If both spouses are (without regard to the provisions of section 2513) required under the provisions of § 25.6019-1 to file returns, returns must be filed by both spouses. If only one of the consenting spouses is (without regard to the provisions of section 2513) required under § 25.6019-1 to file a return, a return must be filed by that spouse. In the latter case if, after giving effect to the provisions of section 2513, the other spouse is considered to have made a gift not excluded from the total amount of such other spouse's gifts for the taxable year by reason of section 2503(b) or (e) (relating, respectively, to certain gifts of $10,000 per donee and the exclusion for certain educational or medical expenses), a return must also be filed by such other spouse. Thus, if during a calendar year beginning after December 31, 1981, the first spouse made a gift of $18,000 to a child (the gift not being either a future interest in property or an amount excluded under section 2503(e)) and the other spouse made no gifts, only the first spouse is required to file a return for that calendar year. However, if the other spouse had made a gift in excess of $2,000 to the same child during the same calendar year or if the gift made by the first spouse had amounted to $21,000, each spouse would be required to file a return if the consent is signified as provided in section 2513. [Reg. § 25.6019-2.]

☐ [*T.D.* 6334, 11-14-58. *Amended by T.D.* 7238, 12-28-72 *and T.D.* 8522, 2-28-94.]

[Reg. § 25.6019-3]

§ 25.6019-3. Contents of return.—(a) *In general.*—The return must set forth each gift made during the calendar year (or calendar quarter with respect to gifts made after December 31, 1970, and before January 1, 1982) that under sections 2511 through 2515 is to be included in computing taxable gifts; the deductions claimed and allowable under sections 2521 through 2524; and the taxable gifts made for each of the preceding reporting periods. (See § 25.2504-1.) In addition the return shall set forth the fair market value of all gifts not made in money, including gifts resulting from sales and exchanges of property made for less than full and adequate consideration in money or money's worth, giving, as of the date of the sale or exchange, both the fair market value of the property sold or exchanged and the fair market value of the consideration received by the donor. If a donor contends that his retained power over property renders the gift incomplete(see § 25.2511-2) and hence not subject to tax as of the calendar quarter or calendar year of the initial transfer, the transaction should be disclosed in the return for the calendar quarter or calendar year of the initial transfer and evidence showing all relevant facts, including a copy of the instrument of transfer, shall be submitted with the return. The instructions printed on the return should be carefully followed. A certified or verified copy of each document required by the instructions printed on the return form shall be filed with the return. Any additional documents the donor may desire to submit may be submitted with the return.

(b) *Disclosure of transfers coming within provisions of section 2516.*—Section 2516 provides that certain transfers of property pursuant to written property settlements between husband and wife are deemed to be transfers for full and adequate consideration in money or money's worth if divorce occurs within 2 years. In any case where a husband and wife enter into a written agreement of the type contemplated by section 2516 and the final decree of divorce is not granted on or before the due date for the filing of a gift tax return for the calendar year (or calendar quarter with respect to periods beginning after December 31, 1970, and ending before January 1, 1982) in which the agreement became effective (see § 25.6075-1), then, except to the extent § 25.6019-1 provides otherwise, the transfer must be disclosed by the transferor upon a gift tax return filed for the calendar year (or calendar quarter) in which the agreement becomes effective, and a copy of the agreement must be attached to the return. In addition, a certified copy of the final divorce decree shall be furnished the internal revenue officer with whom the return was filed not later than 60 days after the divorce is granted. Pending receipt of evidence that the final decree of divorce has been granted (but in no event for a period of more than 2 years from the effective date of the agreement), the transfer will tentatively be treated as made for a full and adequate consideration in money or money's worth. [Reg. § 25.6019-3.]

□ [*T.D.* 6334, 11-14-58. *Amended by T.D.* 7012, 5-14-69; *T.D.* 7238, 12-28-72 *and T.D.* 8522, 2-28-94.]

[Reg. § 25.6019-4]

§ 25.6019-4. Description of property listed on return.—The properties comprising the gifts made during the calendar year (or calendar quarter with respect to gifts made after December 31, 1970, and before January 1, 1982) must be listed on the return and described in a manner that they may be readily identified. Thus, there should be given for each parcel of real estate a legal description, its area, a short statement of the character of any improvements, and, if located in a city, the name of the street and number. Description of bonds shall include the number transferred, principal amount, name of obligor, date of maturity, rate of interest, date or dates on which interest is payable, series number where there is more than one issue, and the principal exchange upon which listed, or the principal business office of the obligor, if unlisted. Description of stocks shall include number of shares, whether common or preferred, and, if preferred, what issue thereof, par value, quotation at which returned, exact name of corporation, and, if the stock is unlisted, the location of the principal business office, the State in which incorporated and the date of incorporation, or if the stock is listed, the principal exchange upon which sold. Description of notes shall include name of maker, date on which given, date of maturity, amount of principal, amount of principal unpaid, rate of interest and whether simple or compound, and date to which interest has been paid. If the gift or property includes accrued income thereon to the date of the gift, the amount of such accrued income shall be separately set forth. Description of the seller's interest in land contracts transferred shall include name of buyer, date of contract, description of property, sale price, initial payment, amounts of installment payments, unpaid balance of principal, interest rate, and date prior to gift to which interest has been paid. Description of life insurance policies shall show the name of the insurer and the number of the policy. In describing an annuity, the name and address of the issuing company shall be given, or, if payable out of a trust or other fund, such a description as will fully identify the trust or fund. If the annuity is payable for a term of years, the duration of the term and the date on which it began shall be given, and if payable for the life of any person, the date of birth of that person shall be stated. Judgments shall be described by giving the title of the cause and the name of the court in which rendered, date of judgment, name and address of judgment debtor, amount of judgment, rate of interest to which subject, and by stating whether any payments have been made thereon, and, if so, when and in what amounts. [Reg. § 25.6019-4.]

□ [*T.D.* 6334, 11-14-58. *Amended by T.D.* 7238, 12-28-72 *and T.D.* 8522, 2-28-94.]

[Reg. § 1.6034-1]

§ 1.6034-1. Information returns required of trusts described in section 4947(a) or claiming charitable or other deductions under section 642(c).—(a) *In general.*—Every trust (other than a trust described in paragraph (b) of this section) claiming a charitable or other deduction under section 642(c) for the taxable year shall file, with respect to such taxable year, a return of information on Form 1041-A. In addition, for taxable years beginning after December 31, 1969, every trust (other than a trust described in paragraph (b) of this section) described in section 4947(a)(2) (including trusts described in section 664) shall file such return for each taxable year, unless all transfers in trust occurred before May 27, 1969. The return shall set forth the name and address of the trust and the following information concerning the trust in such detail as is prescribed by the form or in the instructions issued with respect to such form:

(1) The amount of the charitable or other deduction taken under section 642(c) for the taxable year (and, for taxable years beginning prior to January 1, 1970, showing separately for each class of activity for which disbursements were made (or amounts were permanently set aside) the amounts which, during such year, were paid out (or which were permanently set aside) for charitable or other purposes under section 642(c));

(2) The amount paid out during the taxable year which represents amounts permanently set aside in prior years for which charitable or other deductions have been taken under section 642(c), and separately listing for each class of activity, for which disbursements were made, the total amount paid out;

(3) The amount for which charitable or other deductions have been taken in prior years under section 642(c) and which had not been paid out at the beginning of the taxable year;

(4)(i) The amount paid out of principal in the taxable year for charitable, etc., purposes, and separately listing for each such class of activity, for which disbursements were made, the total amount paid out;

(ii) The total amount paid out of principal in prior years for charitable, etc., purposes;

(5) The gross income of the trust for the taxable year and the expenses attributable thereto, in sufficient detail to show the different categories of income and of expense; and

(6) A balance sheet showing the assets, liabilities, and net worth of the trust as of the beginning of the taxable year.

(b) *Exceptions.*—(1) *In general.*—A trust is not required to file a Form 1041-A for any taxable year with respect to which the trustee is required by the terms of the governing instrument and applicable local law to distribute currently all of the income of the trust. For this purpose, the income of the trust shall be determined in accordance with section 643(b) and §§1.643(b)-1 and 1.643(b)-2.

(2) *Trusts described in section 4947(a)(1).*—For taxable years beginning after December 31, 1980, a trust described in section 4947(a)(1) is not required to file a Form 1041-A.

(c) *Time and place for filing return.*—The return on Form 1041-A shall be filed on or before the 15th day of the 4th month following the close of the taxable year of the trust, with the internal revenue officer designated by the instructions applicable to such form. For extensions of time for filing returns under this section, see §1.6081-1.

(d) *Other provisions.*—For publicity of information on Form 1041-A, see section 6104 and the regulations thereunder in Part 301 of this chapter. For provisions relating to penalties for failure to file a return required by this section, see section 6652(d). For the criminal penalties for a willful failure to file a return and filing a false or fraudulent return, see sections 7203, 7206, and 7207. [Reg. §1.6034-1.]

□ [*T.D. 6364, 2-13-59. Amended by T.D. 7012, 5-14-69; T.D. 7563, 9-8-78 and T.D. 8026, 5-17-85.*]

[Reg. §1.6035-1]

§1.6035-1. [Reserved].

□ [*T.D. 6364, 2-13-59. Amended by T.D. 7322, 8-23-74; T.D. 7517, 11-11-77; T.D. 7557, 8-4-78; T.D. 8028, 6-3-85 and T.D. 8573, 12-13-94. Removed and reserved by T.D. 9849, 3-11-2019.*]

[Reg. §1.6035-2]

§1.6035-2. Transitional relief.—(a) *Statements due before June 30, 2016.*—Executors and other persons required to file or furnish a statement under section 6035(a)(1) or (2) after July 31, 2015 and before June 30, 2016, need not have done so until June 30, 2016.

(b) *Applicability Date.*—This section is applicable to executors and other persons who file a return required by section 6018(a) or (b) after July 31, 2015. [Reg. §1.6035-2.]

□ [*T.D. 6364, 2-13-59. Amended by T.D. 7322, 8-23-74, T.D. 8028, 6-3-85 and T.D. 9797, 12-1-2016.*]

[Reg. §20.6036-1]

§20.6036-1. Notice of qualification as executor.—(a) *Preliminary notice for estates of decedents dying before January 1, 1971.*—(1) A preliminary notice must be filed on Form 704 for the estate of every citizen or resident of the United States whose gross estate exceeded $60,000 in value on the date of his death.

(2) In the case of a nonresident not a citizen of the United States dying on or after November 14, 1966—

(i) Subject to the provisions of subdivisions (ii) and (iii) of this subparagraph, a preliminary notice must be filed on Form 705 if that part of the decedent's gross estate situated in the United States exceeded $30,000 in value on the date of his death (see §§20.2103-1 and 20.2104-1).

(ii) If the transfer of the estate is subject to the tax imposed by section 2107(a) (relating to expatriation to avoid tax), any amounts includible in the decedent's gross estate under section 2107(b) are to be added to the value on the date of his death of that part of his gross estate situated in the United States, for purposes of determining under subdivision (i) of this subparagraph whether his gross estate exceeded $30,000 in value on the date of his death.

(iii) If the transfer of the estate is subject to tax pursuant to a Presiden tial proclamation made under section 2108(a) (relating to Presidential proclamations of the application of pre-1967 estate tax provisions), a preliminary notice must be filed on Form 705 if the value on the date of the decedent's death of that part of his gross estate situated in the United States exceeded $2,000.

(3) A preliminary notice must be filed on Form 705 for the estate of every nonresident not a citizen of the United States dying before November 14, 1966, if the value on the date of his death of that part of his gross estate situated in the United States exceeded $2,000.

(4) The value of the gross estate on the date of death governs with respect to the requirement for filing the preliminary notice irrespective of whether the value of the gross estate is, at the executor's election, finally determined pursuant to the provisions of section 2032 as of a date subsequent to the date of death. If there is doubt as to whether the gross estate exceeds $60,000, $30,000, or $2,000, as the case may be, the notice shall be filed as a matter of precaution in order to avoid the possibility of penalties attaching.

(5) The primary purpose of the preliminary notice is to advise the Internal Revenue Service of the existence of taxable estates, and filing shall not be delayed beyond the period provided for in § 20.6071-1 merely because of uncertainty as to the exact value of the assets. The estimate of the gross estate called for by the notice shall be the best approximation of value which can be made within the time allowed. Duplicate copies of the preliminary notice are not required to be filed.

(6) For criminal penalties for failure to file a notice and filing a false or fraudulent notice, see sections 7203, 7207, and 7269. See § 20.6091-1 for the place for filing the notice. See § 20.6071-1 for the time for filing the notice.

(b) *Persons required to file.*—In the case of an estate of a citizen or resident of the United States described in paragraph (a) of this section, the preliminary notice must be filed by the duly qualified executor or administrator, or if none qualifies within 2 months after the decedent's death, by every person in actual or constructive possession of any property of the decedent at or after the time of the decedent's death. The signature of one executor or administrator on the preliminary notice is sufficient. In the case of a nonresident not a citizen, the notice must be filed by every duly qualified executor or administrator within the United States, or if none qualifies within 2 months after the decedent's death, by every person in actual or constructive possession of any property of the decedent at or after the time of the decedent's death. [Reg. § 20.6036-1.]

□ [*T.D.* 6296, 6-23-58. *Amended by T.D.* 7238, 12-28-72 *and T.D.* 7296, 12-11-73.]

[Reg. § 301.6036-1]

§ 301.6036-1. Notice required of executor or of receiver or other like fiduciary.—(a) *Receivers and other like fiduciaries.*—(1) *Exemption for bankruptcy proceedings.*—(i) A bankruptcy trustee, debtor in possession or other like fiduciary in a bankruptcy proceeding is not required by this section to give notice of appointment, qualification or authorization to act to the Secretary or his delegate. (However, see the notice requirements under the Bankruptcy Rules.)

(ii) Paragraph (a)(1)(i) of this section is effective for appointments, qualifications and authorizations to act made on or after January 29, 1988. For appointments, qualifications and authorizations to act made before the foregoing date, 26 CFR 301.6036-1(a)(1) and (4)(i) (revised as of April 1, 1986) apply.

(2) *Proceedings other than bankruptcy.*—A receiver in a receivership proceeding or a similar fiduciary in any proceeding (including a fiduciary in aid of foreclosure), designated by order of any court of the United States or of any State or Territory or of the District of Columbia as in control of all or substantially all the assets of a debtor or other party to such proceeding shall, on, or within 10 days of, the date of his appointment or authorization to act, give notice thereof in writing to the district director for the internal revenue district in which the debtor, or such other party, is or was required to make returns. Moreover, any fiduciary in aid of foreclosure not appointed by order of any such court, if he takes possession of all or substantially all the assets of the debtor, shall, on, or within 10 days of, the date of his taking possession, give notice thereof in writing to such district director.

(3) *Assignment for benefit of creditors.*—An assignee for the benefit of a creditor or creditors shall, on, or within 10 days of, the date of an assignment, give notice thereof in writing to the district director for the internal revenue district in which the debtor is or was required to make returns. For purposes of this subparagraph, an assignee for the benefit of creditors shall be any person who, by authority of law, by the order of any court, by oral or written agreement, or in any other manner acquires control or possession of or title to all or substantially all the assets of a debtor, and who under such acquisition is authorized to use, reassign, sell, or in any manner dispose of such assets so that the proceeds from the use, sale, or other disposition may be paid to or may inure directly or indirectly to the benefit of a creditor or creditors of such debtor.

(4) *Contents of notice.*—(i) *Proceedings other than bankruptcy.*—The written notice required under paragraph (a)(2) of this section shall contain—

(*a*) The name and address of the person making such notice and the date of his appointment or of his taking possession of the assets of the debtor or other person whose assets are controlled,

(*b*) The name, address, and, for notices filed after December 20, 1972, the taxpayer identification number of the debtor or other person whose assets are controlled, and

(*c*) In the case of a court proceeding—

(*1*) The name and location of the court in which the proceedings are pending,

(*2*) The date on which such proceedings were instituted,

(3) The number under which such proceedings are docketed, and

(4) When possible, the date, time, and place of any hearing, meeting of creditors, or other scheduled action with respect to such proceedings.

(ii) *Assignment for benefit of creditors.*—The written notice required under subparagraph (3) of this paragraph shall contain—

(a) The name and address of, and the date the asset or assets were assigned to, the assignee,

(b) The name, address, and, for notices filed after December 20, 1972, the taxpayer identification number of the debtor whose assets were assigned,

(c) A brief description of the assets assigned,

(d) An explanation of the action expected to be taken with respect to such assets, and

(e) When possible, the date, time, and place of any hearing, meeting of creditors, sale, or other scheduled action with respect to such assets.

(iii) The notice required by this section shall be sent to the attention of the Chief, Special Procedures Staff, of the District office to which it is required to be sent.

(b) *Executors, administrators, and persons in possession of property of decedent.*—For provisions relating to the requirement of filing, by an executor, administrator, or person in possession of property of a decedent, of a preliminary notice in the case of the estate of a decedent dying before January 1, 1971, see §20.6036-1 of this chapter (Estate Tax Regulations).

(c) *Notice of fiduciary relationship.*—When a notice is required under §301.6903-1 of a person acting in fiduciary capacity and is also required of such person under this section, notice given in accordance with the provisions of this section shall be considered as complying with both sections.

(d) *Suspension of period on assessment.*—For suspension of the running of the period of limitations on the making of assessments from the date a proceeding is instituted to a date 30 days after receipt of notice from a fiduciary in any proceeding under the Bankruptcy Act or from a receiver in any other court proceeding, see section 6872 and §301.6872-1.

(e) *Applicability.*—Except as provided in paragraph (a)(1)(ii) of this section, the provisions of this section shall apply to those persons referred to in this section whose appointments, authorizations, or assignments occur on or after the date of the publication of these regulations in the Federal Register as a Treasury decision.

(f) *Cross references.*—(1) For criminal penalty for willful failure to supply information, see section 7203.

(2) For criminal penalties for willfully making false or fraudulent statements, see sections 7206 and 7207.

(3) For time for performance of acts where the last day falls on a Saturday, Sunday, or legal holiday, see section 7503 and §301.7503-1 [Reg. §301.6036-1.]

☐ [*T.D.* 6517, 12-20-60. *Amended by T.D.* 7222, 11-20-72; *T.D.* 7238, 12-28-72 *and T.D.* 8172, 1-28-88.]

[Reg. §20.6036-2]

§20.6036-2. Notice of qualification as executor of estate of decedent dying after 1970.—In the case of the estate of a decedent dying after December 31, 1970, no special notice of qualification as executor of an estate is required to be filed. The requirement of section 6036 for notification of qualification as executor of an estate shall be satisfied by the filing of the estate tax return required by section 6018 and the regulations thereunder. [Reg. §20.6036-2.]

☐ [*T.D.* 7238, 12-28-72.]

[Reg. §1.6060-1]

§1.6060-1. Reporting requirements for tax return preparers.—(a) *In general.*—(1) Each person who employs one or more signing tax return preparers to prepare any return of tax or claim for refund of tax, other than for the person, at any time during a return period shall satisfy the requirements of section 6060 of the Internal Revenue Code by—

(i) Retaining a record of the name, taxpayer identification number, and principal place of work during the return period of each tax return preparer employed by the person at any time during that period; and

(ii) Making that record available for inspection upon request by the Commissioner.

(2) The record described in this paragraph (a) must be retained and kept available for inspection for the 3-year period following the close of the return period to which that record relates.

(3) The person may choose any form of documentation to be used under this section as a record of the signing tax return preparers employed during a return period. The record, however, must disclose on its face which individuals were employed as tax return preparers during that period.

(4) For the definition of the term "signing tax return preparer", see §301.7701-15(b)(1) of this chapter. For the definition of the term "return period", see paragraph (b) of this section.

(5)(i) For purposes of this section, any individual who, in acting as a signing tax return preparer, is not employed by another tax return preparer shall be treated as his or her own employer. Thus, a sole proprietor shall retain and make available a record with respect to himself (or herself) as provided in this section.

(ii) A partnership shall, for purposes of this section, be treated as the employer of the partners of the partnership and shall retain and make available a record with respect to the partners and others employed by the partnership as provided in this section.

(b) *Return period defined.*—For purposes of this section, the term "return period" means the 12-month period beginning on July 1 of each year.

(c) *Penalty.*—For the civil penalty for failure to retain and make available a record of the tax return preparers employed during a return period as required under this section, or for failure to include an item in the record required to be retained and made available under this section, see § 1.6695-1(e).

(d) *Effective/applicability date.*—This section is applicable to returns and claims for refund filed after December 31, 2008. [Reg. § 1.6060-1.]

☐ [*T.D.* 7519, 11-17-77. *Amended by T.D.* 7640, 8-22-79 *and T.D.* 9436, 12-15-2008.]

[Reg. § 20.6060-1]

§ 20.6060-1. Reporting requirements for tax return preparers.—(a) *In general.*—A person that employs one or more tax return preparers to prepare a return or claim for refund of estate tax under chapter 11 of subtitle B of the Internal Revenue Code, other than for the person, at any time during a return period, shall satisfy the recordkeeping and inspection requirements in the manner stated in § 1.6060-1 of this chapter.

(b) *Effective/applicability date.*—This section is applicable to returns and claims for refund filed after December 31, 2008. [Reg. § 20.6060-1.]

☐ [*T.D.* 9436, 12-15-2008.]

[Reg. § 25.6060-1]

§ 25.6060-1. Reporting requirements for tax return preparers.—(a) *In general.*—A person that employs one or more tax return preparers to prepare a return or claim for refund of gift tax under chapter 12 of subtitle B of the Internal Revenue Code, other than for the person, at any time during a return period, shall satisfy the record keeping and inspection requirements in the manner stated in § 1.6060-1 of this chapter.

(b) *Effective/applicability date.*—This section is applicable to returns and claims for refund filed after December 31, 2008. [Reg. § 25.6060-1.]

☐ [*T.D.* 9436, 12-15-2008.]

[Reg. § 26.6060-1]

§ 26.6060-1. Reporting requirements for tax return preparers.—(a) *In general.*—A person that employs one or more tax return preparers to prepare a return or claim for refund of generation-skipping transfer tax under chapter 13 of subtitle B of the Internal Revenue Code, other than for the person, at any time during a return period, shall satisfy the record keeping and inspection requirements in the manner stated in § 1.6060-1 of this chapter.

(b) *Effective/applicability date.*—This section is applicable to returns and claims for refund filed after December 31, 2008. [Reg. § 26.6060-1.]

☐ [*T.D.* 9436, 12-15-2008.]

[Reg. § 1.6061-1]

§ 1.6061-1. Signing of returns and other documents by individuals.—(a) *Requirement.*—Each individual (including a fiduciary) shall sign the income tax return required to be made by him, except that the return may be signed for the taxpayer by an agent who is duly authorized in accordance with paragraph (a)(5) or (b) of § 1.6012-1 to make such return. Other returns, statements, or documents required under the provisions of subtitle A or F of the Code or of the regulations thereunder to be made by any person with respect to any tax imposed by subtitle A of the Code shall be signed in accordance with any regulations contained in this chapter, or any instructions, issued with respect to such returns, statements, or other documents.

(b) *Cross references.*—For provisions relating to the signing of returns, statements, or other documents required to be made by corporations and partnerships with respect to any tax imposed by subtitle A of the Code, see §§ 1.6062-1 and 1.6063-1, respectively. For provisions relating to the making of returns by agents, see paragraphs (a)(5) and (b) of § 1.6012-1; and to the making of returns for minors and persons under a disability, see paragraph (a)(4) of § 1.6012-1 and paragraph (b) of § 1.6012-3. [Reg. § 1.6061-1.]

☐ [*T.D.* 6364, 2-13-59. *Amended by T.D.* 7332, 12-20-74.]

[Reg. § 20.6061-1]

§ 20.6061-1. Signing of returns and other documents.—Any return, statement, or other document required to be made under any provision of chapter 11 or subtitle F of the Code or regulations prescribed thereunder with respect to any tax imposed by chapter 11 of the Code shall be signed by the executor, administrator or other person required or duly authorized to sign in accordance with the regulations, forms or instructions prescribed with respect to such return, statement, or other document. See § 20.2203 for definition of executor, administrator, etc. The person required or duly authorized to make the return may incur liability for the penalties provided for erroneous, false, or fraudulent returns. For criminal penalties see sections 7201, 7203, 7206, 7207, and 7269. [Reg. § 20.6061-1.]

☐ [*T.D.* 6600, 5-28-62.]

[Reg. § 25.6061-1]

§ 25.6061-1. Signing of returns and other documents.—Any return, statement, or other document required to be made under any provision of chapter 12 or subtitle F of the Code or regulations prescribed thereunder with respect to any tax imposed by chapter 12 of the Code shall be signed by the donor or other person required or duly authorized to sign in accordance with the regulations, forms or instructions prescribed with respect to such return, statement, or other document. The person required or duly authorized to make the return may incur liability for the penalties provided for erroneous, false, or fraudulent returns. For criminal penalties see sections 7201, 7203, 7206, 7207, and 7269. [Reg. § 25.6061-1.]

☐ [*T.D.* 6600, 5-28-62.]

[Reg. § 31.6061-1]

§ 31.6061-1. Signing of returns.—Each return required under the regulations in this subpart shall, if signature is called for by the form or instructions relating to the return, be signed by (a) the individual, if the person required to make the return is an individual; (b) the president, vice president, or other principal officer, if the person required to make the return is a corporation; (c) a responsible and duly authorized member or officer having knowledge of its affairs, if the person required to make the return is a partnership or other unincorporated organization; or (d) the fiduciary, if the person required to make the return is a trust or estate. The return may be signed for the taxpayer by an agent who is duly authorized in accordance with § 31.6011(a)-7 to make such return. [Reg. § 31.6061-1.]

☐ [*T.D.* 6472, 6-22-60.]

[Reg. § 301.6064-1]

§ 301.6064-1. Signature presumed authentic.—An individual's name signed to a return, statement, or other document shall be prima facie evidence for all purposes that the return, statement, or other document was actually signed by him. [Reg. § 301.6064-1.]

☐ [*T.D.* 6498, 10-24-60.]

[Reg. § 1.6065-1]

§ 1.6065-1. Verification of returns.—(a) *Persons signing returns.*—If a return, declaration, statement, or other document made under the provisions of subtitle A or F of the Code, or the regulation thereunder, with respect to any tax imposed by subtitle A of the Code is required by the regulations contained in this chapter, or the form and instructions, issued with respect to such return, declaration, statement, or other document, to contain or be verified by a written declaration that it is made under the penalties of perjury, such return, declaration, statement, or other document shall be so verified by the person signing it.

(b) *Persons preparing returns.*—(1) *In general.*—Except as provided in subparagraph (2) of this paragraph, if a return, declaration, statement, or other document is prepared for a taxpayer by another person for compensation or as an incident to the performance of other services for which such person receives compensation, and the return, declaration, statement, or other document requires that it shall contain or be verified by a written declaration that it is prepared under the penalties of perjury, the preparer must so verify the return, declaration, statement, or other document. A person who renders mere mechanical assistance in the preparation of a return, declaration, statement, or other document as, for example, a stenographer or typist, is not considered as preparing the return, declaration, statement, or other document.

(2) *Exception.*—The verification required by subparagraph (1) of this paragraph is not required on returns, declarations, statements, or other documents which are prepared—

(i) For an employee either by his employer or by an employee designated for such purpose by the employer, or

(ii) For an employer as a usual incident of the employment of one regularly or continuously employed by such employer. [Reg. § 1.6065-1.]

☐ [*T.D.* 6364, 2-13-59.]

[Reg. § 20.6065-1]

§ 20.6065-1. Verification of returns.—(a) *Penalties of perjury.*—If a return, statement, or other document made under the provisions of chapter 11 or subtitle F of the Code or the regulations thereunder with respect to any tax imposed by chapter 11 of the Code, or the form and instructions issued with respect to such return, statement, or other document, requires that it shall contain or be verified by a written declaration that it is made under the penalties of perjury, it must be so verified by the person or persons required to sign such return, statement or other document. In addition, any other statement or document submitted under any provision of chapter 11 or subtitle F of the Code or regulations thereunder with respect to any tax imposed by chapter 11 of the Code may be required to contain or be verified by a written declaration that it is made under the penalties of perjury.

(b) *Oath.*—Any return, statement, or other document required to be submitted under chapter 11 or subtitle F of the Code or regulations prescribed thereunder with respect to any tax imposed by chapter 11 of the Code may be required to be verified by an oath. [Reg. § 20.6065-1.]

☐ [*T.D.* 6600, 5-28-62.]

[Reg. § 25.6065-1]

§ 25.6065-1. Verification of returns.—(a) *Penalties of perjury.*—If a return, statement, or other document made under the provisions of chapter 12 or subtitle F of the Code or the regulations thereunder with respect to any tax imposed by chapter 12 of the Code, or the form and instructions issued with respect to such return, statement, or other document, requires that it shall contain or be verified by a written declaration that it is made under the penalties of perjury, it must be so verified by the person or persons required to sign such return, statement, or other document. In addition, any other statement or document submitted under any provision of chapter 12 or subtitle F of the Code or regulations thereunder with respect to any tax imposed by chapter 12 of the Code may be required to contain or be verified by a written declaration that it is made under the penalties of perjury.

(b) *Oath.*—Any return, statement, or other document required to be submitted under chapter 12 or subtitle F of the Code or regulations prescribed thereunder with respect to any tax imposed by chapter 12 of the Code may be required to be verified by an oath. [Reg. § 25.6065-1.]

☐ [*T.D.* 6600, 5-28-62.]

[Reg. § 1.6071-1]

§ 1.6071-1. Time for filing returns and other documents.—(a) *In general.*—Whenever a return, statement, or other document is required to be made under the provisions of subtitle A or F of the Code, or the regulations thereunder, with respect to any tax imposed by subtitle A of the Code, and the time for filing such return, statement, or other document is not provided for by the Code, it shall be filed at the time prescribed by the regulations contained in this chapter with respect to such return, statement, or other document.

(b) *Return for a short period.*—In the case of a return with respect to tax under subtitle A of the Code for a short period (as defined in section 443), the district director or director of the Internal Revenue Service Center may, upon a showing by the taxpayer of unusual circumstances, prescribe a time for filing the return for such period later than the time when such return would otherwise be due. However, the district director or director of the Internal Revenue Service Center may not extend the time when the return for a DISC (as defined in Section 992(a)(1)) must be filed, as specified in section 6072(b).

(c) *Time for filing certain information returns.*—(1) For provisions relating to the time for filing returns of partnership income, see paragraph (e)(2) of § 1.6031-1.

(2) For provisions relating to the time for filing information returns by banks with respect to common trust funds, see § 1.6032-1.

(3) For provisions relating to the time for filing information returns by certain organizations exempt from taxation under section 501(a), see paragraph (e) of § 1.6033-1.

(4) For provisions relating to the time for filing returns by trusts claiming charitable deductions under section 642(c), see paragraph (c) of § 1.6034-1.

(5) [Reserved].

(6) For provisions relating to the time for filing information returns with respect to certain stock option transactions, see paragraph (c) of § 1.6039-1.

(7) For provisions relating to the time for filing information returns by persons making certain payments, see § 1.6041-2(a)(3) and § 1.6041-6.

(8) For provisions relating to the time for filing information returns regarding payments of dividends, see § 1.6042-2(c).

(9) For provisions relating to the time for filing information returns by corporations with respect to contemplated dissolution or liquidations, see paragraph (a) of § 1.6043-1.

(10) For provisions relating to the time for filing information returns by corporations with respect to distributions in liquidation, see paragraph (a) of § 1.6043-2.

(11) For provisions relating to the time for filing information returns with respect to payments of patronage dividends, see § 1.6044-2(d).

(12) For provisions relating to the time for filing information returns with respect to formation or reorganization of foreign corporations, see § 1.6046-1.

(13) For provisions relating to the time for filing information returns regarding certain payments of interest, see § 1.6049-4(g).

(14) For provisions relating to the time for filing information returns with respect to payment of wages in the form of group-term life insurance, see paragraph (b) of § 1.6052-1.

(15) For provisions relating to the time for filing an annual information return on Form 1042-S, "Foreign Person's U.S. Source Income subject to Withholding," or Form 8805, "Foreign Partner's Information Statement of Section 1446 Withholding Tax," for any tax withheld under chapter 3 of the Internal Revenue Code (relating to withholding of tax on nonresident aliens and foreign corporations and tax-free covenant bonds), see § 1.1461-1(c) and § 1.1446-3(d).

(16) for provisions relating to the time for filing annual information returns on Form 1042S of the tax withheld under chapter 3 of the Code (relating to withholding of tax on nonresident aliens and foreign corporations and tax-free covenant bonds), see paragraph (c) of § 1.1461-2.

(d) *Effective/Applicability date.*—The references to Form 8805 and § 1.1446-3(d) in paragraph (c)(15) of this section shall apply to partnership taxable years beginning after April 29, 2008. [Reg. § 1.6071-1.]

☐ [*T.D.* 6364, 2-13-59. *Amended by T.D.* 6628, 12-27-62; *T.D.* 6887, 6-23-66; *T.D.* 6908, 12-30-66; *T.D.* 7284, 8-2-73; *T.D.* 7533, 2-14-78; *T.D.* 8734, 10-6-97 (T.D. 8804 delayed the effective date of T.D. 8734 from January 1, 1999, to January 1, 2000; T.D. 8856 further delayed the effective date of T.D. 8734 until January 1, 2001) *T.D.* 9394, 4-28-2008 *and T.D.* 9849, 3-11-2019.]

[Reg. § 20.6071-1]

§ 20.6071-1. Time for filing preliminary notice required by § 20.6036-1.—In the case of the estate of a decedent dying before January 1, 1971, if a duly qualified executor or administrator of the estate of such a decedent who was a resident or a citizen of the United States qualifies within 2 months after a decedent's death, or if a duly qualified executor or administrator of the estate of such a decedent who was a nonresident not a citizen qualifies within the United States within 2 months after the decedent's death, the preliminary notice required by § 20.6036-1 must be filed within 2 months after his qualification. If no such executor or administrator qualifies within that period, the preliminary notice must be filed within 2 months of the decedent's death. [Reg. § 20.6071-1.]

☐ [*T.D.* 7238, 12-28-72.]

[Reg. § 1.6072-1]

§ 1.6072-1. Time for filing returns of individuals, estates, and trusts.—(a) *In general.*—(1) *Returns of income for individuals, estates and trusts.*—Except as provided in paragraphs (b) and (c) of this section, returns of income required under sections 6012, 6013, 6014, and 6017 of individuals, estates, domestic trusts, and foreign trusts having an office or place of business in the United States (including unrelated business tax returns of such trusts referred to in section 511(b)(2)) shall be filed on or before the fifteenth day of the fourth month following the close of the taxable year.

(2) *Return of trust, or portion of a trust, treated as owned by a decedent.*—(i) *In general.*—In the case of a return of a trust, or portion of a trust, that was treated as owned by a decedent under subpart E (section 671 and following), part I, subchapter J, chapter 1 of the Internal Revenue Code as of the date of the decedent's death that is filed in accordance with § 1.671-4(a) for the fractional part of the year ending with the date of the decedent's death, the due date of such return shall be the fifteenth day of the fourth month following the close of the 12-month period which began with the first day of the decedent's taxable year.

(ii) *Effective date.*—This paragraph (a)(2) applies to taxable years ending on or after December 24, 2002.

(b) *Decedents.*—In the case of a final return of a decedent for a fractional part of a year, the due date of such return shall be the fifteenth day of the fourth month following the close of the 12-month period which began with the first day of such fractional part of the year.

(c) *Nonresident alien individuals and foreign trusts.*—The income tax return of a nonresident alien individual (other than one treated as a resident under section 6013(g) or (h)) and of a foreign trust which does not have an office or place of business in the United States (including unrelated business tax returns of such trusts referred to in section 511(b)(2)) shall be filed on or before the fifteenth day of the sixth month following the close of the taxable year. However, a nonresident alien individual who for the taxable year has wages subject to withholding under chapter 24 of the Code shall file his income tax return on or before the fifteenth day of the fourth month following the close of the taxable year.

(d) *Last day for filing return.*—For provisions relating to the time for filing a return where the last day for filing falls on Saturday, Sunday, or a legal holiday, see section 7503 and § 301.7503-1 of this chapter (Regulations on Procedure and Administration). [Reg. § 1.6072-1.]

□ [*T.D.* 6364, 2-13-59. *Amended by T.D.* 7426, 8-6-76; *T.D.* 7670, 1-30-80 *and T.D.* 9032, 12-23-2002.]

[Reg. § 20.6075-1]

§ 20.6075-1. Returns; time for filing estate tax return.—The estate tax return required by section 6018 must be filed on or before the due date. The due date is the date on or before which the return is required to be filed in accordance with the provisions of section 6075(a) or the last day of the period covered by an extension of time as provided in § 20.6081-1. The due date, for a decedent dying after December 31, 1970, is, unless an extension of time for filing has been obtained, the day of the ninth calendar month after the decedent's death numerically corresponding to the day of the calendar month on which death occurred. However, if there is no numerically corresponding day in the ninth month, the last day of the ninth month is the due date. For example, if the decedent dies on July 31, 2000, the estate tax return and tax payment must be made on or before April 30, 2001. When the due date falls on Saturday, Sunday, or a legal holiday, the due date for filing the return is the next succeeding day that is not Saturday, Sunday, or a legal holiday. For the definition of a legal holiday, see section 7503 and § 301.7503-1 of this chapter. As to additions to the tax in the case of failure to file the return or pay the tax within the prescribed time, see section 6651 and § 301.6651-1 of this chapter. For rules with respect to the right to elect to have the property valued as of a date or dates subsequent to the decedent's death, see section 2032 and § 20.2032-1, and section 7502 and § 301.7502-1 of this chapter. This section applies to estates of decedents dying after August 16, 1954. [Reg. § 20.6075-1.]

□ [*T.D.* 7238, 12-28-72. *Amended by T.D.* 8957, 7-24-2001.]

[Reg. § 25.6075-1]

§ 25.6075-1. Returns, time for filing gift tax returns for gifts made after December 31, 1981.—(a) *In general.*—Except as provided in paragraphs (b)(1) and (2) of this section, a return required to be filed under section 6019 for gifts made after December 31, 1981, must be filed on or before the 15th day of April following the close of the calendar year in which the gift was made.

(b) *Special rules.*—(1) *Extensions.*—Except as provided in paragraph (b)(2) of this section, if a taxpayer files an income tax return on the calendar year basis and the taxpayer is granted an extension of time for filing the return of income tax imposed by Subtitle A of the Internal Revenue Code, then such taxpayer shall also be deemed to have been granted an extension of time for filing the gift tax return under section 6019 for such calendar year equal to the extension of time granted for filing the income tax return. See section 6081 and the regulations thereunder for rules relating to extension of time for filing returns.

(2) *Death of donor.*—Where a gift is made during the calendar year in which the donor dies, the time for filing the return made under

section 6019 shall not be later than the time (including extensions) for filing the return made under section 6018 (relating to estate tax returns) with respect to such donor. In addition, should the time for filing the estate tax return fall later than the 15th day of April following the close of the calendar year, the time for filing the gift tax return shall be on or before the 15th day of April following the close of the calendar year, unless an extension (not extending beyond the time for filing the estate tax return) was granted for filing the gift tax return. If no estate tax return is required to be filed, the time for filing the gift tax return shall be on or before the 15th day of April following the close of the calendar year, unless an extension was granted for filing the gift tax return.

(c) Paragraphs (a) and (b) may be illustrated by the following examples.

Example (1). Donor makes a taxable gift on April 1, 1982, for which a return must be made under section 6019. Donor files the income tax return on the calendar year basis. The donor was granted a 4-month extension from April 15, 1983 to August 15, 1983, in which to file the 1982 income tax return. Under these circumstances, the donor is not required to file the gift tax return prior to August 15, 1983. See paragraph (b)(1) of this section.

Example (2). Donor makes a taxable gift on April 1, 1982, for which a return must be made under section 6019. The donor dies on May 1, 1982. Under these circumstances, since the due date for filing the estate tax return, February 1, 1983 (assuming an estate tax return under 6018 was required to be filed), falls prior to the due date for the gift tax return (as specified in section 6075(b)(1)), the last day for filing the gift tax return is February 1, 1983. See paragraph (b)(2) of this section.

Example (3). The facts are the same as in example (2), except the donor dies on November 30, 1982. Although the estate tax return if [is] due on or before August 30, 1983, the last day for filing the gift tax return is April 15, 1983. See paragraph (b) of this section.

Example (4). The facts are the same as in example (3), except that the executor receives a 4-month extension for filing the decedent's income tax return. Under these circumstances, the last day for filing the gift tax return is August 15, 1983. See paragraphs (b)(1) and (2) of this section.

Example (5). The facts are the same as in example (3), except that the donor-decedent receives an extension of 6 months for filing the gift tax return. See section 6081 and §25.6081-1. Since section 6075(b)(3) and §25.6075-2(b) provide that the time for filing the gift tax return made under section 6019 shall not be later than the time (including extensions) for filing the estate tax return made under section 6018, the last day for filing the gift tax return is August 30, 1983.

(d) See section 7503 and §301.7503-1 concerning the timely filing of a return that falls due on a Saturday, Sunday of [or] legal holiday. As to additions to the tax for failure to file the return within the prescribed time, see section 6651 and §301.6651-1. [Reg. §25.6075-1.]

☐ [*T.D.* 7910, 9-6-83.]

[Reg. §25.6075-2]

§25.6075-2. Returns, time for filing gift tax returns for gifts made after December 31, 1976, and before January 1, 1982.—(a) *Due date for filing quarterly gift tax returns.*—(1) Except as provided in paragraph (b) of this section, a return required to be filed under section 6019 for the first, second, or third calendar quarter of any calendar year must be filed on or before the 15th day of the second month following the close of the calendar quarter in which the taxable gift was made.

(2) If a return is required to be filed under section 6019 for the fourth calendar quarter, then—

(i) For gifts made after December 31, 1976 and before January 1, 1979, the return must be filed on or before February 15th following the close of the fourth calendar quarter, or

(ii) For gifts made after December 31, 1978, and before January 1, 1982, the return must be filed on or before April 15th following the close of the fourth calendar quarter.

(b) *Special rule.*—(1) If the total amount of taxable gifts (determined after the application of paragraph (c)(1) of this section, relating to split gifts) made by a person during a calendar quarter is $25,000 or less, the return required under section 6019 for that quarter must be filed on or before the date prescribed in paragraph (a)(1) of this section for filing the return for gifts made in the first subsequent calendar quarter (unless the first subsequent calendar quarter is the fourth calendar quarter in which case see paragraph (b)(2) of this section) in the calendar year in which the sum of—

(i) The taxable gifts made during such subsequent calendar quarter, plus

(ii) All other taxable gifts made in prior quarters of the calendar year for which no return has yet been required to be filed, exceeds $25,000.

The return must include transfers by gift (as required by section 6019 and the regulations under that section) made during such subsequent and prior quarters of the calendar year for which no return has yet been required to be filed and identify in which quarter such transfers were made. The return must meet all the requirements for a separate return as if a separate return had been made for each quarter in which a transfer by gift was made. This return will be treated as a separate return for each of the quarters identified on the return.

(2) If a return is not required to be filed under paragraph (b)(1) of this section, then—

(i) For gifts made after December 31, 1976 and before January 1, 1979, the return must be filed on or before February 15th following the close of the fourth calendar quarter, or

(ii) For gifts made after December 31, 1978, and before January 1, 1982, the return must be filed on or before April 15th following the close of the fourth calendar quarter.

The return must include all transfers by gift (as required under section 6019 and the regulations under that section) made during the calendar year for which no return has yet been required to be filed and identify in which quarter such transfers were made. The return must meet all the requirements for a separate return as if a separate return had been made for each quarter in which a transfer by gift was made. This return will be treated as a separate return for each of the quarters identified on the return.

(3) Under section 6075(b)(3), any extension of time granted a taxpayer for filing the return of income taxes imposed by subtitle A for any taxable year which is a calendar year shall be treated as an extension of time granted the taxpayer for filing any return under section 6019 which is due (under paragraphs (a)(2)(ii) and (b)(2)(ii) of this section) on or before April 15th following the close of the fourth calendar quarter. See also section 6081 and § 25.6081-1 for other rules relating to extensions of time for filing returns.

(4) See section 7503 and § 301.7503-1 for the due date of a return that falls on a Saturday, Sunday, or a legal holiday. As to additions to the tax for failure to file the return within the prescribed time, see section 6651 and § 301.6651-1.

(c) *Effect of section 2513.*—(1) In determining whether taxable gifts made during any calendar quarter exceed $25,000, and in determining whether taxable gifts made in the current calendar quarter and the preceding calendar quarters of the calendar year for which no return has yet been required to be filed exceed $25,000, the effect of section 2513 is not taken into account for any gifts made in the current or previous quarters for which a return is now being filed unless an irrevocable consent was made by either spouse on a return that was required to be filed prior to the due date of the current return. See § 25.2513-3 for the rules relating to when a consent becomes irrevocable.

(2) Paragraph (c)(1) of this section may be illustrated by the following examples:

Example (1). During the first quarter of 1980 A made taxable gifts of $17,000 ($20,000—$3,000 annual exclusion under section 2503(b)) to D. During the second quarter A made another taxable gift of $10,000 to D. A's taxable gifts for the first two quarters are $27,000. Therefore, A is required to file a return for the first and second quarters on or before August 15, 1980. On that return A's wife, B, consented to the application of section 2513 (relating to split gifts) for the second quarter. Even though A split the second quarter gift with his wife, A's return is nevertheless required to be filed on or before August 15, 1980 because in determining whether taxable gifts exceed $25,000, the effect of section 2513 is only taken into account for the quarter in which an irrevocable consent was made on a return required to be filed before August 15, 1980.

Example (2). Assume the same facts as in Example (1). In addition, during the third quarter A made another taxable gift of $20,000 to D, and B made a taxable gift of $24,000 to D. B is required to file a return reporting the taxable gifts made during the second and third quarters on or before November 15, 1980 because B's total taxable gifts exceed $25,000 (second quarter gifts after taking section 2513 into account = 1/2 ($10,000) – $3,000 (annual exclusion under section 2503(b)) = $2,000 plus a $24,000 gift in the third quarter). Even if A and B had consented to the application of section 2513 for the third quarter, B's return would nevertheless be due on or before November 15, 1980, because an irrevocable consent was not made on a return that was required to be filed prior to November 15, 1980. However, the effect of section 2513 is taken into account for the second quarter because an irrevocable consent was made on a return that was required to be filed prior to November 15, 1980.

Example (3). During the first quarter of 1980 A made taxable gifts of $27,000 to F ($30,000 – $3,000 annual exclusion under section 2503(b)). A is required to file a return on or before May 15, 1980. A fails to file a return until August 1, 1980. On that return B, A's spouse, consented to the application of section 2513. The consent on that return is irrevocable under § 25.2513-3. During the second quarter B made taxable gifts of $14,000 to F. A and B made no other gifts during 1980. B has made total taxable gifts of $26,000 ($12,000 for the first quarter and $14,000 for the second quarter). Therefore, B is required to file a return on or before August 15, 1980. Even if A and B had consented to the application of section 2513 for the second quarter, B's return is nevertheless due on or before August 15, 1980. Assuming no other gifts were made during the year, A's return reporting the second quarter split gift would be due on or before April 15, 1981.

Example (4). During the first quarter of 1980 A made taxable gifts of $20,000 to G. B, A's spouse, files a gift tax return on June 15, 1980 reporting that gift and both A and B signify their consent to the application of section 2513 on that return. In determining whether either spouse has exceeded the $25,000 amount for the remainder of 1980, the effect of section 2513 will be taken into account for the transfer by gift made in the first quarter.

(d) *Nonresident not citizens of the United States.*—In the case of a donor who is a nonresident not a citizen of the United States, paragraphs (a) and (b) of this section shall be applied by substituting "$12,500" for "$25,000" each place it appears. For rules relating to whether certain residents of possessions are considered nonresidents not citizens of the United States, see section 2501(c) and § 25.2501-1(d).

(e) *Effective date.*—This section is effective for gifts made after December 31, 1976, and before January 1, 1982. [Reg. § 25.6075-2.]

□ [*Amended by T.D.* 7012, 5-14-69, *T.D.* 7238, 12-28-72 *and T.D.* 7757, 1-16-81. *Redesignated and amended by T.D.* 7910, 9-6-83.]

[Reg. § 1.6081-1]

§ 1.6081-1. Extension of time for filing returns.—(a) *In general.*—The Commissioner is authorized to grant a reasonable extension of time for filing any return, declaration, statement, or other document that relates to any tax imposed by subtitle A of the Internal Revenue Code (Code) and that is required under the provisions of subtitle A or F of the Code. However, other than in the case of taxpayers who are abroad or as specified in section 6081(b), such extensions of time shall not be granted for more than six months, and the extension of time for filing the return of a DISC (as defined in section 992(a)), as specified in section 6072(b), shall not be granted. Except in the case of an extension of time pursuant to § 1.6081-5, an extension of time for filing an income tax return shall not operate to extend the time for the payment of the tax unless specified to the contrary in the extension. For rules relating to extensions of time for paying tax, see § 1.6161-1.

(b) *Application for extension of time.*—(1) *In general.*—Under other sections in this chapter, certain taxpayers may request an automatic extension of time to file certain returns. Except in undue hardship cases, no extension of time to file a return will be allowed under this section until an automatic extension of time to file the return has been allowed under the applicable section. No extension of time to file a return will be granted under this section for a period of time greater than that provided for by automatic extension. A taxpayer desiring an extension of the time for filing a return, statement, or other document shall submit an application for extension on or before the due date of such return, statement, or other document. If a form exists for the application for an extension, the taxpayer should use the form; however, taxpayers may apply for an extension in a letter that includes the information required by this paragraph. Except as provided in § 301.6091-1(b) of this chapter (relating to hand-carried documents), the taxpayer should make the application for extension to the Internal Revenue Service office where such return, statement, or other document is required to be filed. Except for requests for automatic extensions of time to file certain returns provided for elsewhere in this chapter, the application must be in writing, signed by the taxpayer or his duly authorized agent, and must clearly set forth—

(i) The particular tax return, information return, statement, or other document, including the taxable year or period thereof, for which the taxpayer requests an extension; and

(ii) An explanation of the reasons for requesting the extension to aid the internal revenue officer in determining whether to grant the request.

(2) *Taxpayer unable to sign.*—In any case in which a taxpayer is unable, by reason of illness, absence, or other good cause, to sign a request for an extension, any person standing in close personal or business relationship to the taxpayer may sign the request on his behalf, and shall be considered as a duly authorized agent for this purpose, provided the request sets forth the reasons for a signature other than the taxpayer's and the relationship existing between the taxpayer and the signer.

(c) *Applicability date.*—This section applies to requests for extension of time to file returns on or after January 30, 2020. Section 1.6081-1T (as contained in 26 CFR part 1, revised April 2019) applies to requests for extension of time to file returns before January 30, 2020. [Reg. § 1.6081-1.]

☐ [*T.D.* 6364, 2-13-59. *Amended by T.D.* 6371, 4-6-59; *T.D.* 6436, 12-30-59; *T.D.* 6581, 12-5-61; *T.D.* 6950, 4-3-68; *T.D.* 7133, 7-21-71; *T.D.* 7160, 2-1-72; *T.D.* 7260, 2-9-73; *T.D.* 7533, 2-14-78; *T.D.* 7651, 10-25-79; *T.D.* 8241, 2-22-89; *T.D.* 9163, 12-6-2004, *T.D.* 9407, 6-30-2008, *T.D.* 9821, 7-18-2017 *and T.D.* 9892, 1-29-2020.]

[Reg. § 20.6081-1]

§ 20.6081-1. Extension of time for filing the return.—(a) *Procedures for requesting an extension of time for filing the return.*—A request for an extension of time to file the return required by section 6018 must be made by filing Form 4768, "Application for Extension of Time To File a Return and/or Pay U. S. Estate (and Generation-Skipping Transfer) Taxes." Form 4768 must be filed with the Internal Revenue Service office designated in the application's instructions (except as provided in § 301.6091-1(b) of this chapter for hand-carried documents). Form 4768 must include an estimate of the amounts of estate and generation-skipping transfer tax liabilities with respect to the estate.

(b) *Automatic extension.*—An estate will be allowed an automatic 6-month extension of time beyond the date prescribed in section 6075(a) to file Form 706, "United States Estate (and Generation-Skipping Transfer) Tax Return," if Form 4768 is filed on or before the due date for filing Form 706 and in accordance with the procedures under paragraph (a) of this section.

(c) *Extension for good cause shown.*—In its discretion, the Internal Revenue Service may, upon the showing of good and sufficient cause, grant an extension of time to file the return required by section 6018 in certain situations. Such an extension may be granted to an estate that did not request an automatic extension of time to file Form 706 prior to the due date under paragraph (b) of this section, to an estate or person that is required to file forms other than Form 706, or to an executor who is abroad and is requesting an additional extension of time to file Form 706 beyond the 6-month automatic extension. Unless the executor is abroad, the extension of time may not be for more than 6 months beyond the filing date prescribed in section 6075(a). To obtain such an extension, Form 4768 must be filed in accordance with the procedures under paragraph (a) of this section and must contain a detailed explanation of why it is impossible or impractical to file a reasonably complete return by the due date. Form 4768 should be filed sufficiently early to permit the Internal Revenue Service time to consider the matter and reply before what otherwise would be the due date of the return. Failure to file Form 4768 before that due date may indicate negligence and constitute sufficient cause for denial of the extension. If an estate did not request an automatic extension of time to file Form 706 under paragraph (b) of this section, Form 4768 must also contain an explanation showing good cause for not requesting the automatic extension.

(d) *Filing the return.*—A return as complete as possible must be filed before the expiration of the extension period. The return thus filed will be the return required by section 6018(a), and any tax shown on the return will be the amount determined by the executor as the tax referred to in section 6161(a)(2), or the amount shown as the tax by the taxpayer upon the taxpayer's return referred to in section 6211(a)(1)(A). The return cannot be amended after the expiration of the extension period although supplemental information may subsequently be filed that may result in a finally determined tax different from the amount shown as the tax on the return.

(e) *Payment of the tax.*—An extension of time for filing a return does not operate to extend the time for payment of the tax. See §20.6151-1 for the time for payment of the tax, and §§20.6161-1 and 20.6163-1 for extensions of time for payment of the tax. If an extension of time to file a return is obtained, but no extension of time for payment of the tax is granted, interest will be due on the tax not paid by the due date and the estate will be subject to all applicable late payment penalties.

(f) *Effective date.*—This section applies to estates of decedents dying after August 16, 1954, except for paragraph (b) of this section which applies to estate tax returns due after July 25, 2001. [Reg. §20.6081-1.]

☐ [*T.D.* 6296, 6-23-58. *Amended by T.D.* 6711, 3-23-64; *T.D.* 7238, 12-28-72; *T.D.* 7710, 7-28-80 *and T.D.* 8957, 7-24-2001.]

[Reg. §25.6081-1]

§25.6081-1. Automatic extension of time for filing gift tax returns.—(a) *In general.*—Under section 6075(b)(2), an automatic six-month extension of time granted to a donor to file the donor's return of income under §1.6081-4 of this chapter shall be deemed also to be a six-month extension of time granted to file a return on Form 709, "United States Gift (and Generation-Skipping Transfer) Tax Return." If a donor does not obtain an extension of time to file the donor's return of income under §1.6081-4 of this chapter, the donor will be allowed an automatic 6-month extension of time to file Form 709 after the date prescribed for filing if the donor files an application under this section in accordance with paragraph (b) of this section. In the case of an individual described in §1.6081-5(a)(5) or (6) of this chapter, the automatic 6-month extension of time to file Form 709 will run concurrently with the extension of time to file granted pursuant to §1.6081-5 of this chapter.

(b) *Requirements.*—To satisfy this paragraph (b), a donor must—

(1) Submit a complete application on Form 8892, "Payment of Gift/GST Tax and/or Application for Extension of Time To File Form 709," or in any other manner prescribed by the Commissioner;

(2) File the application on or before the later of—

(i) The date prescribed for filing the return; or

(ii) The expiration of any extension of time to file granted pursuant to §1.6081-5 of this chapter; and

(3) File the application with the Internal Revenue Service office designated in the application's instructions.

(c) *No extension of time for the payment of tax.*—An automatic extension of time for filing a return granted under paragraph (a) of this section will not extend the time for payment of any tax due on such return.

(d) *Termination of automatic extension.*—The Commissioner may terminate an extension at any time by mailing to the donor a notice of termination at least 10 days prior to the termination date designated in such notice. The Commissioner must mail the notice of termination to the address shown on the Form 8892, or to the donor's last known address. For further guidance regarding the definition of last known address, see §301.6212-2 of this chapter.

(e) *Penalties.*—See section 6651 for failure to file a gift tax return or failure to pay the amount shown as tax on the return.

(f) *Effective/applicability dates.*—This section is applicable for applications for an extension of time to file Form 709 filed after July 1, 2008. [Reg. §25.6081-1.]

☐ [*T.D.* 9407, 6-30-2008.]

[Reg. §26.6081-1]

§26.6081-1. Automatic extension of time for filing generation-skipping transfer tax returns.—(a) *In general.*—A skip person distributee required to file a return on Form 706-GS(D), "Generation-Skipping Transfer Tax Return for Distributions," or a trustee required to file a return on Form 706-GS(T), "Generation-Skipping Transfer Tax Return for Terminations," will be allowed an automatic 6-month extension of time to file the return after the date prescribed for filing if the skip person distributee or trustee files an application under this section in accordance with paragraph (b) of this section.

(b) *Requirements.*—To satisfy this paragraph (b), a skip person distributee or trustee must—

(1) Submit a complete application on Form 7004, "Application for Automatic Extension of Time to File Certain Business Income Tax, Information, and Other Returns," or in any other manner prescribed by the Commissioner;

(2) File the application on or before the date prescribed for filing the return with the Internal

Revenue Service office designated in the application's instructions; and

(3) Remit the amount of the properly estimated unpaid tax liability on or before the date prescribed for payment.

(c) *No extension of time for the payment of tax.*—An automatic extension of time for filing a return granted under paragraph (a) of this section will not extend the time for payment of any tax due on such return.

(d) *Termination of automatic extension.*—The Commissioner may terminate an automatic extension at any time by mailing to the skip person distributee or trustee a notice of termination at least 10 days prior to the termination date designated in such notice. The Commissioner must mail the notice of termination to the address shown on the Form 7004 or to the skip person distributee or trustee's last known address. For further guidance regarding the definition of last known address, see § 301.6212-2 of this chapter.

(e) *Penalties.*—See section 6651 for failure to file a generation-skipping transfer tax return or failure to pay the amount shown as tax on the return.

(f) *Effective/applicability dates.*—This section is applicable for applications for an automatic extension of time to file a generation-skipping transfer tax return filed after July 1, 2008. [Reg. § 26.6081-1.]

☐ [*T.D.* 9407, 6-30-2008.]

[Reg. § 1.6081-6]

§ 1.6081-6. Automatic extension of time to file estate or trust income tax return.—(a) *In general.*—(1) Except as provided in paragraph (a)(2) of this section, any estate, including but not limited to an estate defined in section 2031, or trust required to file an income tax return on Form 1041, "U.S. Income Tax Return for Estates and Trusts," will be allowed an automatic five and one-half month extension of time to file the return after the date prescribed for filing the return if the estate or trust files an application under this section in accordance with paragraph (b) of this section. No additional extension will be allowed pursuant to § 1.6081-1(b) beyond the automatic five and one-half month extension provided by this section.

(2) A bankruptcy estate that is created when an individual debtor files a petition under either chapter 7 or chapter 11 of Title 11 of the U.S. Code that is required to file an income tax return on Form 1041, "U.S. Income Tax Return for Estates and Trusts," and an estate or trust required to file an income tax return on Form 1041-N, "U.S. Income Tax Return for Electing Alaska Native Settlement," or Form 1041-QFT, "U.S. Income Tax Return for Qualified Funeral Trusts" for any taxable year will be allowed an automatic 6-month extension of time to file the return after the date prescribed for filing the return if the estate files an application under this section in accordance with paragraph (b) of this section.

(b) *Requirements.*—To satisfy this paragraph (b), an estate or trust must—

(1) Submit a complete application on Form 7004, "Application for Automatic Extension of Time to File Certain Business Income Tax, Information, and Other Returns," or in any other manner prescribed by the Commissioner;

(2) File the application on or before the date prescribed for filing the return with the Internal Revenue Service office designated in the application's instructions; and

(3) Show the amount properly estimated as tax for the estate or trust for the taxable year.

(c) *No extension of time for the payment of tax.*—An automatic extension of time for filing a return granted under paragraph (a) of this section will not extend the time for payment of any tax due on such return.

(d) *Effect of extension on beneficiary.*—An automatic extension of time to file an estate or trust income tax return under this section will not extend the time for filing the income tax return of a beneficiary of the estate or trust or the time for the payment of any tax due on the beneficiary's income tax return.

(e) *Termination of automatic extension.*—The Commissioner may terminate an automatic extension at any time by mailing to the estate or trust a notice of termination at least 10 days prior to the termination date designated in such notice. The Commissioner must mail the notice of termination to the address shown on the Form 7004 or to the estate or trust's last known address. For further guidance regarding the definition of last known address, see § 301.6212-2 of this chapter.

(f) *Penalties.*—*See* section 6651 for failure to file an estate or trust income tax return or failure to pay the amount shown as tax on the return.

(g) *Applicability date.*—This section applies to applications for an automatic extension of time to file an estate or trust income tax return on or after January 30, 2020. Section 1.6081-6T (as contained in 26 CFR part 1, revised April 2019) applies to applications for an automatic extension of time to file a return before January 30, 2020. [Reg. § 1.6081-6.]

☐ [*T.D.* 9531, 6-23-2011. *Amended by T.D.* 9821, 7-18-2017 *and T.D.* 9892, 1-29-2020.]

[Reg. § 20.6091-1]

§ 20.6091-1. Place for filing returns or other documents.—(a) *General rule.*—If the decedent was domiciled in the United States at the time of his death, the preliminary notice required by § 20.6036-1 in the case of the estate of a decedent dying before January 1, 1971, and the estate tax return required by § 20.6018-1 shall be filed with:

(1) The service center serving the location in which the decedent was domiciled at the time of his death, if the instructions applicable to the estate tax return provide that the return shall be filed with a service center, or

(2) Any person assigned the responsibility to receive returns in the local Internal Revenue

Service office serving the location in which the decedent was domiciled at the time of his death, if paragraph (1) does not apply.

(b) *Non-U.S. domiciliaries.*—If the decedent was not domiciled in the United States at the time of his death, the preliminary notice required by § 20.6036-1 in the case of the estate of a decedent dying before January 1, 1971, and the estate tax return required by § 20.6018-1 shall be filed with the Internal Revenue Service Center, Philadelphia, Pennsylvania, or as designated on the return form or in the instructions issued with respect to such form. This paragraph applies whether or not the decedent was a citizen of the United States and whether or not the return is made by hand-carrying. [Reg. § 20.6091-1.]

☐ [*T.D.* 6600, 5-28-62; *T.D.* 7238, 12-28-72; *T.D.* 7302, 1-24-74; *T.D.* 7495, 6-29-77 *and T.D.* 9156, 9-15-2004.]

[Reg. § 25.6091-1]

§ 25.6091-1. Place for filing returns and other documents.—(a) *In general.*—If the donor is a resident of the United States, the gift tax return required by section 6019 shall be filed with any person assigned the responsibility to receive returns in the local Internal Revenue Service office that serves the legal residence or principal place of business of the donor. If the donor is a nonresident (whether or not a citizen), and his principal place of business is served by a local Internal Revenue Service office, the gift tax return shall be filed with any person assigned the responsibility to receive returns in that office.

(b) *Returns filed with service centers.*—Notwithstanding paragraph (a) of this section, unless a return is filed by hand-carrying, whenever instructions applicable to gift tax returns provide that the returns be filed with a service center, the returns must be so filed in accordance with the instructions. Returns which are filed by hand carrying shall be filed with any person assigned the responsibility to receive hand-carried returns in the local Internal Revenue Service office in accordance with paragraph (a) of this section.

(c) *Returns of certain nonresidents.*—If the donor is a nonresident (whether or not a citizen), and he does not have a principal place of business in the United States, the gift tax return required by section 6019, whether or not such return is made by hand carrying, shall be filed with the Internal Revenue Service Center, Philadelphia, Pennsylvania, or as designated on the return form or in the instructions issued with respect to such form. [Reg. § 25.6091-1.]

☐ [*Amended by T.D.* 7012, 5-14-69; *T.D.* 7238, 12-28-72; *T.D.* 7302, 1-2-74; *T.D.* 7495, 6-29-77 *and T.D.* 9156, 9-15-2004.]

[Reg. § 1.6091-2]

§ 1.6091-2. Place for filing income tax returns.—Except as provided in § 1.6091-3 (relating to certain international income tax returns) and § 1.6091-4 (relating to exceptional cases)—

(a) *Individuals, estates, and trusts.*—(1) Except as provided in paragraph (c) of this section, income tax returns of individuals, estates, and trusts shall be filed with any person assigned the responsibility to receive returns at the local Internal Revenue Service office that serves the legal residence or principal place of business of the person required to make the return.

(2) An individual employed on a salary or commission basis who is not also engaged in conducting a commercial or professional enterprise for profit on his own account does not have a "principal place of business" within the meaning of this section.

(b) *Corporations.*—Except as provided in paragraph (c) of this section, income tax returns of corporations shall be filed with any person assigned the responsibility to receive returns in the local Internal Revenue Service office that serves the principal place of business or principal office or agency of the corporation.

(c) *Returns filed with service centers.*—Notwithstanding paragraphs (a) and (b) of this section, whenever instructions applicable to income tax returns provide that the returns be filed with a service center, the returns must be so filed in accordance with the instructions.

(d) *Hand-carried returns.*—Notwithstanding paragraphs (1) and (2) of section 6091(b) and paragraph (c) of this section—

(1) *Persons other than corporations.*—Returns of persons other than corporations which are filed by hand carrying shall be filed with any person assigned the responsibility to receive hand-carried returns in the local Internal Revenue Service office as provided in paragraph (a) of this section.

(2) *Corporations.*—Returns of corporations which are filed by hand carrying shall be filed with any person assigned the responsibility to receive hand-carried returns in the local Internal Revenue Service office as provided in paragraph (b) of this section.

See § 301.6091-1 of this chapter (Regulations on Procedure and Administration) for provisions relating to the definition of hand carried.

(e) *Amended returns.*—In the case of amended returns filed after April 14, 1968, except as provided in paragraph (d) of this section—

(1) *Persons other than corporations.*—Amended returns of persons other than corporations shall be filed with the service center serving the legal residence or principal place of business of the person required to make the return.

(2) *Corporations.*—Amended returns of corporations shall be filed with the service center serving the principal place of business or principal office or agency of the corporation.

(f) *Returns of persons subject to a termination assessment.*—Notwithstanding paragraph (c) of this section—

(1) *Persons other than corporations.*—Returns of persons other than corporations with respect to whom an assessment was made under section

6851(a) with respect to the taxable year shall be filed with any person assigned the responsibility to receive returns in the local Internal Revenue Service office as provided in paragraph (a) of this section.

(2) *Corporations.*—Returns of corporations with respect to whom an assessment was made under section 6851(a) with respect to the taxable year shall be filed with any person assigned the responsibility to receive returns in the local Internal Revenue Service office as provided in paragraph (b) of this section.

(g) *Returns of persons subject to a termination assessment.*—Notwithstanding paragraph (c) of this section, income tax returns of persons with respect to whom an income tax assessment was made under section 6852(a) with respect to the taxable year must be filed with any person assigned the responsibility to receive returns in the local Internal Revenue Service office as provided in paragraphs (a) and (b) of this section. [Reg. § 1.6091-2.]

☐ [*T.D.* 6364, 2-13-59. *Amended by T.D.* 6950, 4-3-68; *T.D.* 7012, 5-14-69; *T.D.* 7495, 6-2-77; *T.D.* 7575, 12-15-78; *T.D.* 8628, 12-4-95 *and T.D.* 9156, 9-15-2004.]

[Reg. § 20.6091-2]

§ 20.6091-2. Exceptional cases.—Notwithstanding the provisions of § 20.6091-1 the Commissioner may permit the filing of the preliminary notice required by § 20.6036-1 and the estate tax return required by § 20.6018-1 in any local Internal Revenue Service office. [Reg. § 20.6091-2.]

☐ [*T.D.* 6600, 5-28-62. *Amended by T.D.* 9156, 9-15-2004.]

[Reg. § 25.6091-2]

§ 25.6091-2. Exceptional cases.—Notwithstanding the provisions of § 25.6091-1 the Commissioner may permit the filing of the gift tax return required by section 6019 in any local Internal Revenue Service office. [Reg. § 25.6091-2.]

☐ [*T.D.* 6600, 5-28-62. *Amended by T.D.* 9156, 9-15-2004.]

[Reg. § 301.6102-1]

§ 301.6102-1. Computations on returns or other documents.—(a) *Amounts shown on forms.*—To the extent permitted by any internal revenue form or instructions prescribed for use with respect to any internal revenue return, declaration, statement, other document, or supporting schedules, any amount required to be reported on such form shall be entered at the nearest whole dollar amount. The extent to which, and the conditions under which, such whole dollar amounts shall be entered on any form will be set forth in the instructions issued with respect to such form. For the purpose of the computation to the nearest dollar, a fractional part of a dollar shall be disregarded unless it amounts to one-half dollar or more, in which case the amount (determined without regard to the fractional part of a dollar) shall be increased by $1. The following illustrates the application of this paragraph:

Exact amount	To be reported as—
$18.49	$18
18.50	19
18.51	19

(b) *Election not to use whole dollar amounts.*—(1) *Method of election.*—Where any internal revenue form, or the instructions issued with respect to such form, provide that whole dollar amounts shall be reported, any person making a return, declaration, statement, or other document on such form may elect not to use whole dollar amounts by reporting thereon all amounts in full, including cents.

(2) *Time of election.*—The election not to use whole dollar amounts must be made at the time of filing the return, declaration, statement, or other document. Such election may not be revoked after the time prescribed for filing such return, declaration, statement, or other document, including extensions of time granted for such filing. Such election may be made on any return, declaration, statement, or other document which is filed after the time prescribed for filing (including extensions of time), and such an election is irrevocable.

(3) *Effect of election.*—The taxpayer's election shall be binding only on the return, declaration, statement, or other document filed for a taxable year or period, and a new election may be made on the return, declaration, statement, or other document filed for a subsequent taxable year or period. An election by either a husband or a wife not to report whole dollar amounts on a separate income tax return shall be binding on any subsequent joint return filed under the provisions of section 6013(b).

(4) *Fractional part of a cent.*—For treatment of the fractional part of a cent in the payment of taxes, see section 6313 and § 301.6313-1.

(c) *Inapplicability to computation of amount.*—The provisions of paragraph (a) of this section apply only to amounts required to be reported on a return, declaration, statement, or other document. They do not apply to items which must be taken into account in making the computations necessary to determine such amounts. For example, each item of receipt must be taken into account at its exact amount, including cents, in computing the amount of total receipts required to be reported on an income tax return or supporting schedule. It is the amount of total receipts, so computed, which is to be reported at the nearest whole dollar on the return or supporting schedule.

(d) *Effect on accounting method.*—Section 6102 and this section have no effect on any authorized accounting method. [Reg. § 301.6102-1.]

☐ [*T.D.* 6142, 9-2-55. *Amended by T.D.* 6498, 10-24-60.]

[Reg. §1.6107-1]

§1.6107-1. Tax return preparer must furnish copy of return or claim for refund to taxpayer and must retain a copy or record.—(a) *Furnishing copy to taxpayer.*—(1) A person who is a signing tax return preparer of any return of tax or claim for refund of tax under the Internal Revenue Code shall furnish a completed copy of the return or claim for refund to the taxpayer (or nontaxable entity) not later than the time the return or claim for refund is presented for the signature of the taxpayer (or nontaxable entity). The signing tax return preparer may, at its option, request a receipt or other evidence from the taxpayer (or nontaxable entity) sufficient to show satisfaction of the requirement of this paragraph (a).

(2) The tax return preparer must provide a complete copy of the return or claim for refund filed with the IRS to the taxpayer in any media, including electronic media, that is acceptable to both the taxpayer and the tax return preparer. In the case of an electronically filed return, a complete copy of a taxpayer's return or claim for refund consists of the electronic portion of the return or claim for refund, including all schedules, forms, pdf attachments, and jurats, that was filed with the IRS. The copy provided to the taxpayer must include all information submitted to the IRS to enable the taxpayer to determine what schedules, forms, electronic files, and other supporting materials have been filed with the return. The copy, however, need not contain the identification number of the paid tax return preparer. The electronic portion of the return or claim for refund may be contained on a replica of an official form or on an unofficial form. On an unofficial form, however, data entries must reference the line numbers or descriptions on an official form.

(3) For electronically filed Forms 1040EZ, "Income Tax Return for Single Filers and Joint Filers With No Dependents," and Form 1040A, "U.S. Individual Income Tax Return," filed for the 2009, 2010 and 2011 taxable years, the information may be provided on a replica of a Form 1040, "U.S. Individual Income Tax Return", that provides all of the information. For other electronically filed returns, the information may be provided on a replica of an official form that provides all of the information.

(b) *Copy or record to be retained.*—(1) A person who is a signing tax return preparer of any return or claim for refund shall—

(i)(A) Retain a completed copy of the return or claim for refund; or

(B) Retain a record, by list, card file, or otherwise of the name, taxpayer identification number, and taxable year of the taxpayer (or nontaxable entity) for whom the return or claim for refund was prepared, and the type of return or claim for refund prepared;

(ii) Retain a record, by retention of a copy of the return or claim for refund, maintenance of a list, card file, or otherwise, for each return or claim for refund presented to the taxpayer (or nontaxable entity), of the name of the individual tax return preparer required to sign the return or claim for refund pursuant to §1.6695-1(b); and

(iii) Make the copy or record of returns and claims for refund and record of the individuals required to sign available for inspection upon request by the Commissioner.

(2) The material described in this paragraph (b) shall be retained and kept available for inspection for the 3-year period following the close of the return period during which the return or claim for refund was presented for signature to the taxpayer (or nontaxable entity). In the case of a return that becomes due (with extensions, if any) during a return period following the return period during which the return was presented for signature, the material shall be retained and kept available for inspection for the 3-year period following the close of the later return period in which the return became due. For the definition of "return period," see section 6060(c). If the person subject to the record retention requirement of this paragraph (b) is a corporation or a partnership that is dissolved before completion of the 3-year period, then all persons who are responsible for the winding up of the affairs of the corporation or partnership under state law shall be subject, on behalf of the corporation or partnership, to these record retention requirements until completion of the 3-year period. If state law does not specify any person or persons as responsible for winding up, then, collectively, the directors or general partners shall be subject, on behalf of the corporation or partnership, to the record retention requirements of this paragraph (b). For purposes of the penalty imposed by section 6695(d), such designated persons shall be deemed to be the tax return preparer and will be jointly and severally liable for each failure.

(c) *Tax return preparer.*—For the definition of "signing tax return preparer," see §301.7701-15(b)(1) of this chapter. For purposes of applying this section, a corporation, partnership or other organization that employs a signing tax return preparer to prepare for compensation (or in which a signing tax return preparer is compensated as a partner or member to prepare) a return of tax or claim for refund shall be treated as the sole signing tax return preparer.

(d) *Penalties.*—(1) For the civil penalty for failure to furnish a copy of the return or claim for refund to the taxpayers (or nontaxable entity) as required under paragraph (a) of this section, see section 6695(a) and §1.6695-1(a).

(2) For the civil penalty for failure to retain a copy of the return or claim for refund, or to retain a record as required under paragraph (b) of this section, see section 6695(d) and §1.6695-1(d).

(e) *Effective/applicability date.*—This section is applicable to returns and claims for refund filed after December 31, 2008. [Reg. §1.6107-1.]

☐ [*T.D.* 7519, 11-17-77. *Amended by T.D.* 7640, 8-22-79; *T.D.* 7948, 3-7-84 *and T.D.* 9436, 12-15-2008 (*corrected* 1-28-2009).]

[Reg. § 20.6107-1]

§ 20.6107-1. Tax return preparer must furnish copy of return to taxpayer and must retain a copy or record.—(a) *In general.*—A person who is a signing tax return preparer of any return or claim for refund of estate tax under chapter 11 of subtitle B of the Internal Revenue Code shall furnish a completed copy of the return or claim for refund to the taxpayer and retain a completed copy or record in the manner stated in § 1.6107-1 of this chapter.

(b) *Effective/applicability date.*—This section is applicable to returns and claims for refund filed after December 31, 2008. [Reg. § 20.6107-1.]

☐ [*T.D.* 9436, 12-15-2008.]

[Reg. § 25.6107-1]

§ 25.6107-1. Tax return preparer must furnish copy of return to taxpayer and must retain a copy or record.—(a) *In general.*—A person who is a signing tax return preparer of any return or claim for refund of gift tax under chapter 12 of subtitle B of the Internal Revenue Code shall furnish a completed copy of the return or claim for refund to the taxpayer, and retain a completed copy or record in the manner stated in § 1.6107-1 of this chapter.

(b) *Effective/applicability date.*—This section is applicable to returns and claims for refund filed after December 31, 2008. [Reg. § 25.6107-1.]

☐ [*T.D.* 9436, 12-15-2008.]

[Reg. § 26.6107-1]

§ 26.6107-1. Tax return preparer must furnish copy of return to taxpayer and must retain a copy or record.—(a) *In general.*—A person who is a signing tax return preparer of any return or claim for refund of generation-skipping transfer tax under chapter 13 of subtitle B of the Internal Revenue Code shall furnish a completed copy of the return or claim for refund to the taxpayer, and retain a completed copy or record in the manner stated in § 1.6107-1 of this chapter.

(b) *Effective/applicability date.*—This section is applicable to returns and claims for refund filed after December 31, 2008. [Reg. § 26.6107-1.]

☐ [*T.D.* 9436, 12-15-2008.]

[Reg. § 20.6109-1]

§ 20.6109-1. Tax return preparers furnishing identifying numbers for returns or claims for refund.—(a) *In general.*—Each estate tax return or claim for refund prepared by one or more signing tax return preparers must include the identifying number of the preparer required by § 1.6695-1(b) of this chapter to sign the return or claim for refund in the manner stated in § 1.6109-2 of this chapter.

(b) *Effective/applicability date.*—Paragraph (a) of this section is applicable to returns and claims for refund filed after December 31, 2008. [Reg. § 20.6109-1.]

☐ [*T.D.* 9436, 12-15-2008.]

[Reg. § 25.6109-1]

§ 25.6109-1. Tax return preparers furnishing identifying numbers for returns or claims for refund.—(a) *In general.*—Each gift tax return or claim for refund prepared by one or more signing tax return preparers must include the identifying number of the preparer required by § 1.6695-1(b) of this chapter to sign the return or claim for refund in the manner stated in § 1.6109-2 of this chapter.

(b) *Effective/applicability date.*—Paragraph (a) of this section is applicable to returns and claims for refund filed after December 31, 2008. [Reg. § 25.6109-1.]

☐ [*T.D.* 9436, 12-15-2008.]

[Reg. § 26.6109-1]

§ 26.6109-1. Tax return preparers furnishing identifying numbers for returns or claims for refund.—(a) *In general.*—Each generation-skipping transfer tax return or claim for refund prepared by one or more signing tax return preparers must include the identifying number of the preparer required by § 1.6695-1(b) of this chapter to sign the return or claim for refund in the manner stated in § 1.6109-2 of this chapter.

(b) *Effective/applicability date.*—Paragraph (a) of this section is applicable to returns and claims for refund filed after December 31, 2008. [Reg. § 26.6109-1.]

☐ [*T.D.* 9436, 12-15-2008.]

[Reg. § 301.6109-1]

§ 301.6109-1. Identifying numbers.—(a) *In general.*—(1) *Taxpayer identifying numbers.*—(i) *Principal types.*—There are several types of taxpayer identifying numbers that include the following: social security numbers, Internal Revenue Service (IRS) individual taxpayer identification numbers, IRS adoption taxpayer identification numbers, and employer identification numbers. Social security numbers take the form 000-00-0000. IRS individual taxpayer identification numbers and IRS adoption taxpayer identification numbers also take the form 000-00-0000 but include a specific number or numbers designated by the IRS. Employer identification numbers take the form 00-0000000.

(ii) *Uses.*—Social security numbers, IRS individual taxpayer identification numbers, and IRS adoption taxpayer identification numbers are used to identify individual persons. Employer identification numbers are used to identify employers. For the definition of social security number and employer identification number, see §§ 301.7701-11 and 301.7701-12, respectively. For the definition of IRS individual taxpayer identification number, see paragraph (d)(3) of this section. For the definition of IRS adoption taxpayer identification number, see § 301.6109-3(a). Except as otherwise provided in applicable regulations under this chapter or on a return, statement, or other document, and related instructions, taxpayer identifying numbers must be used as follows:

* * *

(C) Any person other than an individual (such as corporations, partnerships, nonprofit associations, trusts, estates, and similar nonindividual persons) that is required to furnish a taxpayer identifying number must use an employer identification number.

* * *

(2) *A trust that is treated as owned by one or more persons pursuant to sections 671 through 678.*—(i) *Obtaining a taxpayer identification number.*—(A) *General rule.*—Unless the exception in paragraph (a)(2)(i)(B) of this section applies, a trust that is treated as owned by one or more persons under sections 671 through 678 must obtain a taxpayer identification number as provided in paragraph (d)(2) of this section.

(B) *Exception for a trust all of which is treated as owned by one grantor or one other person and that reports under §1.671-4(b)(2)(i)(A) of this chapter.*—A trust that is treated as owned by one grantor or one other person under sections 671 through 678 need not obtain a taxpayer identification number, provided the trust reports pursuant to §1.671-4(b)(2)(i)(A) of this chapter. The trustee must obtain a taxpayer identification number as provided in paragraph (d)(2) of this section for the first taxable year that the trust is no longer owned by one grantor or one other person or for the first taxable year that the trust does not report pursuant to §1.671-4(b)(2)(i)(A) of this chapter.

(ii) *Obligations of persons who make payments to certain trusts.*—Any payor that is required to file an information return with respect to payments of income or proceeds to a trust must show the name and taxpayer identification number that the trustee has furnished to the payor on the return. Regardless of whether the trustee furnishes to the payor the name and taxpayer identification number of the grantor or other person treated as an owner of the trust, or the name and taxpayer identification number of the trust, the payor must furnish a statement to recipients to the trustee of the trust, rather than to the grantor or other person treated as the owner of the trust. Under these circumstances, the payor satisfies the obligation to show the name and taxpayer identification number of the payee on the information return and to furnish a statement to recipients to the person whose taxpayer identification number is required to be shown on the form.

(3) *Obtaining a taxpayer identification number for a trust, or portion of a trust, following the death of the individual treated as the owner.*—(i) *In general.*—(A) *A trust all of which was treated as owned by a decedent.*—In general, a trust all of which is treated as owned by a decedent under subpart E (section 671 and following), part I, subchapter J, chapter 1 of the Internal Revenue Code as of the date of the decedent's death must obtain a new taxpayer identification number following the death of the decedent if the trust will continue after the death of the decedent.

(B) *Taxpayer identification number of trust with multiple owners.*—With respect to a portion of a trust treated as owned under subpart E (section 671 and following), part I, subchapter J, chapter 1 (subpart E) of the Internal Revenue Code by a decedent as of the date of the decedent's death, if, following the death of the decedent, the portion treated as owned by the decedent remains part of the original trust and the other portion (or portions) of the trust continues to be treated as owned under subpart E by a grantor(s) or other person(s), the trust reports under the taxpayer identification number assigned to the trust prior to the decedent's death and the portion of the trust treated as owned by the decedent prior to the decedent's death (assuming the decedent's portion of the trust is not treated as terminating upon the decedent's death) continues to report under the taxpayer identification number used for reporting by the other portion (or portions) of the trust. For example, if a trust, reporting under §1.671-4(a) of this chapter, is treated as owned by three persons and one of them dies, the trust, including the portion of the trust no longer treated as owned by a grantor or other person, continues to report under the tax identification number assigned to the trust prior to the death of that person. See §1.671-4(a) of this chapter regarding rules for filing the Form 1041, "U.S. Income Tax Return for Estates and Trusts," where only a portion of the trust is treated as owned by one or more persons under subpart E.

(ii) *Furnishing correct taxpayer identification number to payors following the death of the decedent.*—If the trust continues after the death of the decedent and is required to obtain a new taxpayer identification number under paragraph (a)(3)(i)(A) of this section, the trustee must furnish payors with a new Form W-9, "Request for Taxpayer Identification Number and Certification," or an acceptable substitute Form W-9, containing the new taxpayer identification number required under paragraph (a)(3)(i)(A) of this section, the name of the trust, and the address of the trustee.

(4) *Taxpayer identification number to be used by a trust upon termination of a section 645 election.*—(i) *If there is an executor.*—Upon the termination of the section 645 election period, if there is an executor, the trustee of the former electing trust may need to obtain a taxpayer identification number. If §1.645-1(g) of this chapter regarding the appointment of an executor after a section 645 election is made applies to the electing trust, the electing trust must obtain a new TIN upon termination of the election period. See the instructions to the Form 1041 for whether a new taxpayer identification number is required for other former electing trusts.

(ii) *If there is no executor.*—Upon termination of the section 645 election period, if there is no executor, the trustee of the former electing trust must obtain a new taxpayer identification number.

(iii) *Requirement to provide taxpayer identification number to payors.*—If the trustee is required to obtain a new taxpayer identification number for a former electing trust pursuant to this paragraph (a)(4), or pursuant to the instructions to the Form 1041, the trustee must furnish all payors of the trust with a completed Form W-9 or acceptable substitute Form W-9 signed under penalties of perjury by the trustee providing each payor with the name of the trust, the new taxpayer identification number, and the address of the trustee.

(5) *Persons treated as payors.*—For purposes of paragraphs (a)(2), (3), and (4) of this section, a *payor* is a person described in § § 1.671-4(b)(4) of this chapter.

(6) *Effective date.*—Paragraphs (a)(3), (4), and (5) of this section apply to trusts of decedents dying on or after December 24, 2002.

* * *

(d) *Obtaining a taxpayer identifying number.*—

* * *

(2) *Employer identification number.*—(i) *In general.*—Any person required to furnish an employer identification number must apply for one, if not done so previously, on Form SS-4. A Form SS-4 may be obtained from any office of the Internal Revenue Service, U.S. consular office abroad, or from an acceptance agent described in paragraph (d)(3)(iv) of this section. The person must make such application far enough in advance of the first required use of the employer identification number to permit issuance of the number in time for compliance with such requirement. The form, together with any supplementary statement, must be prepared and filed in accordance with the form, accompanying instructions, and relevant regulations, and must set forth fully and clearly the requested data.

(ii) *Updating of application information.*—(A) *Requirements.*—Persons issued employer identification numbers in accordance with the application process set forth in paragraph (d)(2)(i) of this section must provide to the Internal Revenue Service any updated application information in the manner and frequency required by forms, instructions, or other appropriate guidance.

(B) *Effective/applicability date.*—Paragraph (d)(2)(ii)(A) of this section applies to all persons possessing an employer identification number on or after January 1, 2014.

* * *

(3) *IRS individual taxpayer identification number.*—(i) *Definition.*—The term *IRS individual taxpayer identification number* means a taxpayer identifying number issued to an alien individual by the Internal Revenue Service, upon application, for use in connection with filing requirements under this title. The term *IRS individual taxpayer identification number* does not refer to a social security number or an account number for use in employment for wages. For purposes of this section, the term *alien individual* means an individual who is not a citizen or national of the United States.

(ii) *General rule for obtaining number.*—Any individual who is not eligible to obtain a social security number and is required to furnish a taxpayer identifying number must apply for an IRS individual taxpayer identification number on Form W-7, Application for IRS Individual Taxpayer Identification Number, or such other form as may be prescribed by the Internal Revenue Service. Form W-7 may be obtained from any office of the Internal Revenue Service, U.S. consular office abroad, or any acceptance agent described in paragraph (d)(3)(iv) of this section. The individual shall furnish the information required by the form and accompanying instructions, including the individual's name, address, foreign tax identification number (if any), and specific reason for obtaining an IRS individual taxpayer identification number. The individual must make such application far enough in advance of the first required use of the IRS individual taxpayer identification number to permit issuance of the number in time for compliance with such requirement. The application form, together with any supplementary statement and documentation, must be prepared and filed in accordance with the form, accompanying instructions, and relevant regulations, and must set forth fully and clearly the requested data.

(iii) *General rule for assigning number.*—Under procedures issued by the Internal Revenue Service, an IRS individual taxpayer identification number will be assigned to an individual upon the basis of information reported on Form W-7 (or/such other form as may be prescribed by the Internal Revenue Service) and any such accompanying documentation that may be required by the Internal Revenue Service. An applicant for an IRS individual taxpayer identification number must submit such documentary evidence as the Internal Revenue Service may prescribe in order to establish alien status and identity. Examples of acceptable documentary evidence for this purpose may include items such as an original (or a certified copy of the original) passport, driver's license, birth certificate, identity card, or immigration documentation.

(iv) *Acceptance agents.*—(A) *Agreements with acceptance agents.*—A person described in paragraph (d)(3)(iv)(B) of this section will be accepted by the Internal Revenue Service to act as an acceptance agent for purposes of the regulations under this section upon entering into an agreement with the Internal Revenue Service, under which the acceptance agent will be authorized to act on behalf of taxpayers seeking to obtain a taxpayer identifying number from the Internal Revenue Service. The agreement must contain such terms and conditions as are necessary to insure proper administration of the process by which the Internal Revenue Service issues taxpayer identifying numbers to foreign persons, including proof of their identity and foreign status. In particular, the agreement may contain—

(1) Procedures for providing Form SS-4 and Form W-7, or such other necessary form to applicants for obtaining a taxpayer identifying number;

(2) Procedures for providing assistance to applicants in completing the application form or completing it for them;

(3) Procedures for collecting, reviewing, and maintaining; in the normal course of business, a record of the required documentation for assignment of a taxpayer identifying number;

(4) Procedures for submitting the application form and required documentation to the Internal Revenue Service, or if permitted under the agreement, submitting the application form together with a certification that the acceptance agent has reviewed the required documentation and that it has no actual knowledge or reason to know that the documentation is not complete or accurate;

(5) Procedures for assisting taxpayers with notification procedures described in paragraph (g)(2) of this section in the event of change of foreign status;

(6) Procedures for making all documentation or other records furnished by persons applying for a taxpayer identifying number promptly available for review by the Internal Revenue Service, upon request; and

(7) Provisions that the agreement may be terminated in the event of a material failure to comply with the agreement, including failure to exercise due diligence under the agreement.

(B) *Persons who may be acceptance agents.*—An acceptance agent may include any financial institution as defined in section 265(b)(5) or §1.165-12(c)(1)(v) of this chapter, any college or university that is an educational organization as defined in §1.501(c)(3)-1(d)(3)(i) of this chapter, any federal agency as defined in section 6402(f) or any other person or categories of persons that may be authorized by regulations or Internal Revenue Service procedures. A person described in this paragraph (d)(3)(iv)(B) that seeks to qualify as an acceptance agent must have an employer identification number for use in any communication with the Internal Revenue Service. In addition, it must establish to the satisfaction of the Internal Revenue Service that it has adequate resources and procedures in place to comply with the terms of the agreement described in paragraph (d)(3)(iv)(A) of this section.

(4) *Coordination of taxpayer identifying numbers.*—(i) *Social security number.*—Any individual who is duly assigned a social security number or who is entitled to a social security number will not be issued an IRS individual taxpayer identification number. The individual can use the social security number for all tax purposes under this title, even though the individual is, or later becomes, a nonresident alien individual. Further, any individual who has an application pending with the Social Security Administration will be issued an IRS individual taxpayer identification number only after the Social Security Administration has notified the individual that a social security number cannot be issued. Any alien individual duly issued an IRS individual taxpayer identification number who later becomes a U.S. citizen, or an alien lawfully permitted to enter the United States either for permanent residence or under authority of law permitting U.S. employment, will be required to obtain a social security number. Any individual who has an IRS individual taxpayer identification number and a social security number, due to the circumstances described in the preceding sentence, must notify the Internal Revenue Service of the acquisition of the social security number and must use the newly-issued social security number as the taxpayer identifying number on all future returns, statements, or other documents filed under this title.

(ii) *Employer identification number.*—Any individual with both a social security number (or an IRS individual taxpayer identification number) and an employer identification number may use the social security number (or the IRS individual taxpayer identification number) for individual taxes, and the employer identification number for business taxes as required by returns, statements, and other documents and their related instructions. Any alien individual duly assigned an IRS individual taxpayer identification number who also is required to obtain an employer identification number must furnish the previously-assigned IRS individual taxpayer identification number to the Internal Revenue Service on Form SS-4 at the time of application for the employer identification number. Similarly, where an alien individual has an employer identification number and is required to obtain an IRS individual taxpayer identification number, the Individual must furnish the previously-assigned employer identification number to the Internal Revenue Service on Form W-7, or such other form as may be prescribed by the Internal Revenue Service, at the time of application for the IRS individual taxpayer identification number.

(e) *Banks, and brokers and dealers in securities.*—For additional requirements relating to deposits, share accounts, and brokerage accounts, see 31 CFR 103.34 and 103.35.

(f) *Penalty.*—For penalties for failure to supply taxpayer identifying numbers, see sections 6721 through 6724.

(g) *Special rules for taxpayer identifying numbers issued to foreign persons.*—(1) *General rule.*—(i) *Social security number.*—A social security number is generally identified in the records and database of the Internal Revenue Service as a number belonging to a U.S. citizen or resident alien individual. A person may establish a different status for the number by providing proof of foreign status with the Internal Revenue Service under such procedures as the Internal Revenue Service shall prescribe, including the use of a form as the Internal Revenue Service may specify. Upon accepting an individual as a nonresident alien individual, the Internal Revenue Service will assign this status to the individuals social security number.

(ii) *Employer identification number*.—An employer identification number is generally identified in the records and database of the Internal Revenue Service as a number belonging to a U.S. person. However, the Internal Revenue Service may establish a separate class of employer identification numbers solely dedicated to foreign persons which will be identified as such in the records and database of the Internal Revenue Service. A person may establish a different status for the number either at the time of application or subsequently by providing proof of U.S. or foreign status with the Internal Revenue Service under such procedures as the Internal Revenue Service shall prescribe, including the use of a form as the Internal Revenue Service may specify. The Internal Revenue Service may require a person to apply for the type of employer identification number that reflects the status of that person as a U.S. or foreign person.

(iii) *IRS individual taxpayer identification number*.—An IRS individual taxpayer identification number is generally identified in the records and database of the Internal Revenue Service as a number belonging to a nonresident alien individual. If the Internal Revenue Service determines at the time of application or subsequently, that an individual is not a nonresident alien individual, the Internal Revenue Service may require that the individual apply for a social security number. If a social security number is not available, the Internal Revenue Service may accept that the individual use an IRS individual taxpayer identification number, which the Internal Revenue Service will identify as a number belonging to a U.S. resident alien.

(2) *Change of foreign status*.—Once a taxpayer identifying number is identified in the records and database of the Internal Revenue Service as a number belonging to a U.S. or foreign person, the status of the number is permanent until the circumstances of the taxpayer change. A taxpayer whose status changes (for example, a nonresident alien individual with a social security number becomes a U.S. resident alien) must notify the Internal Revenue Service of the change of status under such procedures as the Internal Revenue Service shall prescribe, including the use of a form as the Internal Revenue Service may specify.

(3) *Waiver of prohibition to disclose taxpayer information when acceptance agent acts*.—As part of its request for an IRS individual taxpayer identification number or submission of proof of foreign status with respect to any taxpayer identifying number, where the foreign person acts through an acceptance agent, the foreign person will agree to waive the limitations in section 6103 regarding the disclosure of certain taxpayer information. However, the waiver will apply only for purposes of permitting the Internal Revenue Service and the acceptance agent to communicate with each other regarding matters related to the assignment of a taxpayer identifying number, including disclosure of any taxpayer identifying number previously issued to the foreign person, and change of foreign status. This paragraph (g)(3) applies to payments made after December 31, 2001.

* * *

(j) *Effective date*.—(1) *General rule*.—Except as otherwise provided in this paragraph (j), the provisions of this section are generally effective for information that must be furnished after April 15, 1974. However, the provisions relating to IRS individual taxpayer identification numbers apply on and after May 29, 1996. An application for an IRS individual taxpayer identification number (Form W-7) may be filed at any time on or after July 1, 1996.

(2) *Special rules*.—(i) *Employer identification number of an estate*.—The requirement under paragraph (a)(1)(ii)(C) of this section that an estate obtain an employer identification number applies on and after January 1, 1984.

* * *

□ [*T.D.* 6606, 8-24-62. *Amended by T.D.* 7306, 3-14-74; *T.D.* 7670, 1-30-80; *T.D.* 7796, 11-23-81; *T.D.* 8633, 12-20-95; *T.D.* 8637, 12-20-95; *T.D.* 8671, 5-23-96; *T.D.* 8697, 12-17-96; *T.D.* 8717, 5-8-97; *T.D.* 8734, 10-6-97 (T.D. 8804 delayed the effective date of T.D. 8734 from January 1, 1999, to January 1, 2000; T.D. 8856 further delayed the effective date of T.D. 8734 until January 1, 2001); *T.D.* 8739, 11-21-97; *T.D.* 8839, 9-21-99; *T.D.* 8844, 11-26-99; *T.D.* 8869, 1-20-2000; *T.D.* 8977, 1-16-2002; *T.D.* 9023, 11-21-2002; *T.D.* 9032, 12-23-2002; *T.D.* 9082, 8-4-2003; *T.D.* 9200, 5-13-2005; *T.D.* 9241, 1-23-2006 *and T.D.* 9617, 5-3-2013.]

[Reg. § 1.6109-2]

§ 1.6109-2. Tax return preparers furnishing identifying numbers for returns or claims for refund and related requirements.—(a) *Furnishing identifying number*.—(1) Each filed return of tax or claim for refund of tax under the Internal Revenue Code prepared by one or more tax return preparers must include the identifying number of the tax return preparer required by § 1.6695-1(b) to sign the return or claim for refund. In addition, if there is an employment arrangement or association between the individual tax return preparer and another person (except to the extent the return prepared is for the person), the identifying number of the other person must also appear on the filed return or claim for refund. For the definition of the term "tax return preparer," see section 7701(a)(36) and § 301.7701-15 of this chapter.

(2)(i) For tax returns or claims for refund filed on or before December 31, 2010, the identifying number of an individual tax return preparer is that individual's social security number or such alternative number as may be prescribed by the Internal Revenue Service in forms, instructions, or other appropriate guidance.

(ii) For tax returns or claims for refund filed after December 31, 2010, the identifying number of a tax return preparer is the individual's preparer tax identification number or such other number prescribed by the Internal Revenue Service in forms, instructions, or other appropriate guidance.

(3) The identifying number of a person (whether an individual or entity) who employs or associates with an individual tax return preparer described in paragraph (a)(2) of this section to prepare the return or claim for refund (other than a return prepared for the person) is the person's employer identification number.

(b) and (c) [Reserved]. For further guidance, see §1.6109-2A(b) and (c).

(d) Beginning after December 31, 2010, all tax return preparers must have a preparer tax identification number or other prescribed identifying number that was applied for and received at the time and in the manner, including the payment of a user fee, as may be prescribed by the Internal Revenue Service in forms, instructions, or other appropriate guidance. Except as provided in paragraph (h) of this section, beginning after December 31, 2010, to obtain a preparer tax identification number or other prescribed identifying number, a tax return preparer must be an attorney, certified public accountant, enrolled agent, or registered tax return preparer authorized to practice before the Internal Revenue Service under 31 U.S.C. 330 and the regulations thereunder.

(e) The Internal Revenue Service may designate an expiration date for any preparer tax identification number or other prescribed identifying number and may further prescribe the time and manner for renewing a preparer tax identification number or other prescribed identifying number, including the payment of a user fee, as set forth in forms, instructions, or other appropriate guidance. The Internal Revenue Service may provide that any identifying number issued by the Internal Revenue Service prior to the effective date of this regulation will expire on December 31, 2010, unless properly renewed as set forth in forms, instructions, or other appropriate guidance, including these regulations.

(f) As may be prescribed in forms, instructions, or other appropriate guidance, the IRS may conduct a Federal tax compliance check on a tax return preparer who applies for or renews a preparer tax identification number or other prescribed identifying number.

(g) Only for purposes of paragraphs (d), (e), and (f) of this section, the term *tax return preparer* means any individual who is compensated for preparing, or assisting in the preparation of, all or substantially all of a tax return or claim for refund of tax. Factors to consider in determining whether an individual is a tax return preparer under this paragraph (g) include, but are not limited to, the complexity of the work performed by the individual relative to the overall complexity of the tax return or claim for refund of tax; the amount of the items of income, deductions, or losses attributable to the work performed by the individual relative to the total amount of income, deductions, or losses required to be correctly reported on the tax return or claim for refund of tax; and the amount of tax or credit attributable to the work performed by the individual relative to the total tax liability required to be correctly reported on the tax return or claim for refund of tax. The preparation of a form, statement, or schedule, such as Schedule EIC (Form 1040), "Earned Income Credit," may constitute the preparation of all or substantially all of a tax return or claim for refund based on the application of the foregoing factors. A tax return preparer does not include an individual who is not otherwise a tax return preparer as that term is defined in §301.7701-15(b)(2), or who is an individual described in §301.7701-15(f). The provisions of this paragraph (g) are illustrated by the following examples:

Example 1. Employee A, an individual employed by Tax Return Preparer B, assists Tax Return Preparer B in answering telephone calls, making copies, inputting client tax information gathered by B into the data fields of tax preparation software on a computer, and using the computer to file electronic returns of tax prepared by B. Although Employee A must exercise judgment regarding which data fields in the tax preparation software to use, A does not exercise any discretion or independent judgment as to the clients' underlying tax positions. Employee A, therefore, merely provides clerical assistance or incidental services and is not a tax return preparer required to apply for a PTIN or other identifying number as the Internal Revenue Service may prescribe in forms, instructions, or other appropriate guidance.

Example 2. The facts are the same as in *Example 1*, except that Employee A also interviews B's clients and obtains from them information needed for the preparation of tax returns. Employee A determines the amount and character of entries on the returns and whether the information provided is sufficient for purposes of preparing the returns. For at least some of B's clients, A obtains information and makes determinations that constitute all or substantially all of the tax return. Employee A is a tax return preparer required to apply for a PTIN or other identifying number as the Internal Revenue Service may prescribe in forms, instructions, or other appropriate guidance. Employee A is a tax return preparer even if Employee A relies on tax preparation software to prepare the return.

Example 3. C is an employee of a firm that prepares tax returns and claims for refund of tax for compensation. C is responsible for preparing a Form 1040, "U.S. Individual Income Tax Return," for a client. C obtains the information necessary for the preparation of the tax return during a meeting with the client, and makes determinations with respect to the proper application of the tax laws to the information in order to determine the client's tax liability. C completes the tax return and sends the completed return to employee D, who reviews the return for accuracy before signing it. Both C and D are tax return preparers required to apply for a PTIN or other identifying number as the Internal Revenue Service may prescribe in forms, instructions, or other appropriate guidance.

Example 4. E is an employee at a firm which prepares tax returns and claims for refund of tax for compensation. The firm is engaged by a corporation to prepare its Federal income tax return on Form 1120, "U.S. Corporation Income Tax Return." Among the documentation that the corporation provides to E in connection with the preparation of the tax return is documentation relating to the corporation's potential eligibility to claim a recently enacted tax credit for the taxable year. In preparing the return, and specifically for purposes of the new tax credit, E (with the corporation's consent) obtains advice from F, a subject matter expert on this and similar credits. F advises E as to the corporation's entitlement to the credit and provides his calculation of the amount of the credit. Based on this advice from F, E prepares the corporation's Form 1120 claiming the tax credit in the amount recommended by F. The additional credit is one of many tax credits and deductions claimed on the tax return, and determining the credit amount does not constitute preparation of all or substantially all of the corporation's tax return under this paragraph (g). F will not be considered to have prepared all or substantially all of the corporation's tax return, and F is not a tax return preparer required to apply for a PTIN or other identifying number as the Internal Revenue Service may prescribe in forms, instructions, or other appropriate guidance. The analysis is the same whether or not the tax credit is a substantial portion of the return under §301.7701-15 of this chapter (as opposed to substantially all of the return), and whether or not F is in the same firm with E. E is a tax return preparer required to apply for a PTIN or other identifying number as the Internal Revenue Service may prescribe in forms, instructions, or other appropriate guidance.

(h) The Internal Revenue Service, through forms, instructions, or other appropriate guidance, may prescribe exceptions to the requirements of this section, including the requirement that an individual be authorized to practice before the Internal Revenue Service before receiving a preparer tax identification number or other prescribed identifying number, as necessary in the interest of effective tax administration. The Internal Revenue Service, through other appropriate guidance, may also specify specific returns, schedules, and other forms that qualify as tax returns or claims for refund for purposes of these regulations.

(i) *Effective/applicability date.*—Paragraph (a)(1) of this section is applicable to tax returns and claims for refund filed after December 31, 2008. Paragraph (a)(2)(i) of this section is applicable to tax returns and claims for refund filed on or before December 31, 2010. Paragraph (a)(2)(ii) of this section is applicable to tax returns and claims for refund filed after December 31, 2010. Paragraph (d) of this section is applicable to tax return preparers after December 31, 2010. Paragraphs (e) through (h) of this section are effective after September 30, 2010. [Reg. §1.6109-2.]

□ [*T.D.* 9014, 8-12-2002. *Amended by T.D.* 9436, 12-15-2008 *and T.D.* 9501, 9-28-2010.]

[Reg. §301.6114-1]

§301.6114-1. Treaty-based return positions.—(a) *Reporting requirement.*—(1) *General rule.*—(i) Except as provided in paragraph (c) of this section, if a taxpayer takes a return position that any treaty of the United States (including, but not limited to, an income tax treaty, estate and gift tax treaty, or friendship, commerce and navigation treaty) overrules or modifies any provision of the Internal Revenue Code and thereby effects (or potentially effects) a reduction of any tax incurred at any time, the taxpayer shall disclose such return position on a statement (in the form required in paragraph (d) of this section) attached to such return.

(ii) If a return of tax would not otherwise be required to be filed, a return must nevertheless be filed for purposes of making the disclosure required by this section. For this purpose, such return need include only the taxpayer's name, address, taxpayer identifying number, and be signed under penalties of perjury (as well as the subject disclosure). Also, the taxpayer's taxable year shall be deemed to be the calendar year (unless the taxpayer has previously established, or timely chooses for this purpose to establish, a different taxable year). In the case of a disclosable return position relating solely to income subject to withholding (as defined in §1.1441-2(a) of this chapter), however, the statement required to be filed in paragraph (d) of this section must instead be filed at times and in accordance with procedures published by the Internal Revenue Service.

(2) *Application.*—(i) A taxpayer is considered to adopt a return position when the taxpayer determines its tax liability with respect to a particular item of income, deduction or credit. A taxpayer may be considered to adopt a return position whether or not a return is actually filed. To determine whether a return position is a "treaty-based return position" so that reporting is required under this paragraph (a), the taxpayer must compare:

(A) The tax liability (including credits, carrybacks, carryovers, and other tax consequences or attributes for the current year as well as for any other affected tax years) to be reported on a return of the taxpayer, and

(B) The tax liability (including such credits, carrybacks, carryovers, and other tax consequences or attributes) that would be reported if the relevant treaty provision did not exist.

If there is a difference (or potential difference) in these two amounts, the position taken on a return is a treaty-based return position that must be reported.

(ii) In the event a taxpayer's return position is based on a conclusion that a treaty provision is consistent with a Code provision, but the effect of the treaty provision is to alter the scope of the Code provision from the scope that it would have in the absence of the treaty, then the return position is a treaty-based return position that must be reported.

(iii) A return position is a treaty-based return position unless the taxpayer's conclusion that no reporting is required under paragraphs (a)(2)(i) and (ii) of this section has a substantial probability of successful defense if challenged.

(3) *Examples.*—The application of section 6114 and paragraph (a)(2) of this section may be illustrated by the following examples:

Example (1). X, a Country A corporation, claims the benefit of a provision of the income tax treaty between the United States and Country A that modifies a provision of the Code. This position does not result in a change of X's U.S. tax liability for the current tax year but does give rise to, or increases, a net operating loss which may be carried back (or forward) such that X's tax liability in the carryback (or forward) year may be affected by the position taken by X in the current year. X must disclose this treaty-based return position with its tax return for the current tax year.

Example (2). Z, a domestic corporation, is engaged in a trade or business in Country B. Country B imposes a tax on the income from certain of Z's petroleum activities at a rate significantly greater than the rate applicable to income from other activities. Z claims a foreign tax credit for this tax on its tax return. The tax imposed on Z is specifically listed as a creditable tax in the income tax treaty between the United States and Country B; however, there is no specific authority that such tax would otherwise be a creditable tax for U.S. purposes under sections 901 or 903 of the Code. Therefore, in the absence of the treaty, the creditability of this petroleum tax would lack a substantial probability of successful defense if challenged, and Z must disclose this treaty-based return position (see also paragraph (b)(7) of this section).

(b) *Reporting specifically required.*—Reporting is required under this section except as expressly waived under paragraph (c) of this section. The following list is not a list of all positions for which reporting is required under this section but is a list of particular positions for which reporting is specifically required. These positions are as follows:

(1) That a nondiscrimination provision of a treaty precludes the application of any otherwise applicable Code provision, other than with respect to the making of or the effect of an election under section 897(i);

(2) That a treaty reduces or modifies the taxation of gain or loss from the disposition of a United States real property interest;

(3) That a treaty exempts a foreign corporation from (or reduces the amount of tax with respect to) the branch profits tax (section 884(a)) or the tax on excess interest (section 884(f)(1)(B));

(4) That, notwithstanding paragraph (c)(1)(i) of this section,

(i) A treaty exempts from tax, or reduces the rate of tax on, interest or dividends paid by a foreign corporation that are from sources within the United States by reason of section 861(a)(2)(B) or section 884(f)(1)(A); or

(ii) A treaty exempts from tax, or reduces the rate of tax on, fixed or determinable annual or periodical income subject to withholding under section 1441 or 1442 that a foreign person receives from a U.S. person, but only if described in paragraphs (b)(4)(ii)(A) and (B) of this section, or in paragraph (b)(4)(ii)(C) or (D) of this section as follows—

(A) The payment is not properly reported to the Service on a Form 1042S; and

(B) The foreign person is any of the following:

(1) A controlled foreign corporation (as defined in section 957) in which the U.S. person is a U.S. shareholder within the meaning of section 951(b);

(2) A foreign corporation that is controlled within the meaning of section 6038 by the U.S. person;

(3) A foreign shareholder of the U.S. person that, in the case of tax years beginning on or before July 10, 1989, is controlled within the meaning of section 6038A by the foreign shareholder, or, in the case of tax years beginning after July 10, 1989, is 25-percent owned within the meaning of section 6038A by the foreign shareholder; or

(4) With respect to payments made after October 10, 1990, a foreign related party, as defined in section 6038A(c)(2)(B), to the U.S. person; or

(C) For payments made after December 31, 2000, with respect to a treaty that contains a limitation on benefits article, that—

(1) The treaty exempts from tax, or reduces the rate of tax on income subject to withholding (as defined in § 1.1441-2(a) of this chapter) that is received by a foreign person (other than a State, including a political subdivision or local authority) that is the beneficial owner of the income and the beneficial owner is related to the person obligated to pay the income within the meaning of sections 267(b) and 707(b), and the income exceeds $500,000; and

(2) A foreign person (other than an individual or a State, including a political subdivision or local authority) meets the requirements of the limitation on benefits article of the treaty; or

(D) For payments made after December 31, 2000, with respect to a treaty that imposes any other conditions for the entitlement of treaty benefits, for example as a part of the interest, dividends, or royalty article, that such conditions are met;

(5) That, notwithstanding paragraph (c)(1)(i) of this section, under a treaty—

(i) Income that is effectively connected with a U.S. trade or business of a foreign corporation or a nonresident alien is not attributable to a permanent establishment or a fixed base of operations in the United States and, thus, is not subject to taxation on a net basis, or that

(ii) Expenses are allowable in determining net business income so attributable, notwithstanding an inconsistent provision of the Code;

(6) Except as provided in paragraph (c)(1)(iv) of this section, that a treaty alters the source of any item of income or deduction;

(7) That a treaty grants a credit for a specific foreign tax for which a foreign tax credit would not be allowed by the Code; or

(8) For returns relating to taxable years for which the due date for filing returns (without extensions) is after December 15, 1997, that residency of an individual is determined under a treaty and apart from the Internal Revenue Code.

(c) *Reporting requirement waived.*—(1) Pursuant to the authority contained in section 6114(b), reporting is waived under this section with respect to any of the following return positions taken by the taxpayer:

(i) For amounts received on or after January 1, 2001, reporting under paragraph (b)(4)(ii) is waived, unless reporting is specifically required under paragraphs (b)(4)(ii)(A) and (B) of this section, paragraph (b)(4)(ii)(C) of this section, or paragraph (b)(4)(ii)(D) of this section;

(ii) Notwithstanding paragraph (b)(4) or (5) of this section, that a treaty has reduced the rate of withholding tax otherwise applicable to a particular type of fixed or determinable annual or periodical income subject to withholding under section 1441 or 1442, such as dividends, interest, rents, or royalties to the extent such income is beneficially owned by an individual or a State (including a political subdivision or local authority);

(iii) For returns relating to taxable years for which the due date for filing returns (without extensions) is on or before December 15, 1997, that residency of an individual is determined under a treaty and apart from the Internal Revenue Code.

(iv) That a treaty reduces or modifies the taxation of income derived from dependent personal services, pensions, annuities, social security and other public pensions, or income derived by artistes, athletes, students, trainees or teachers;

(v) That income of an individual is resourced (for purposes of applying the foreign tax credit limitation) under a treaty provision relating to elimination of double taxation;

(vi) That a nondiscrimination provision of a treaty allows the making of an election under section 897(i);

(vii) That a Social Security Totalization Agreement or a Diplomatic or Consular Agreement reduces or modifies the taxation of income derived by the taxpayer; or

(viii) That a treaty exempts the taxpayer from the excise tax imposed by section 4371, but only if:

(A) The person claiming such treaty-based return position is an insured, as defined in section 4372(d) (without the limitation therein referring to section 4371(1)), or a U.S. or foreign broker of insurance risks,

(B) Reporting under this section that would otherwise be required to be made by foreign insurers or reinsurers on a Form 720 on a quarterly basis is made on an annual basis on a Form 720 by a date no later than the date on which the return is due for the first quarter after the end of the calendar year, or

(C) A closing agreement relating to entitlement to the exemption from the excise tax has been entered into with the Service by the foreign insurance company that is the beneficial recipient of the premium that is subject to the excise tax.

(ix) Notwithstanding paragraph (b)(1) of this section, that a nondiscrimination provision of a qualified income tax treaty, as defined in Treas. Reg. § 1.5000C-1(c)(13), exempts a payment from tax under section 5000C, but only if the foreign person claiming such relief has provided a Section 5000C Certificate (such as Form W-14, "Certificate of Foreign Contracting Party Receiving Federal Procurement Payments") to the acquiring agency in accordance with section 5000C and the regulations thereunder.

(2) Reporting is waived for an individual if payments or income items otherwise reportable under this section (other than by reason of paragraph (b)(8) of this section), received by the individual during the course of the taxable year do not exceed $10,000 in the aggregate or, in the case of payments or income items reportable only by reason of paragraph (b)(8) of this section, do not exceed $100,000 in the aggregate.

(3) Reporting with respect to payments or income items the treatment of which is mandated by the terms of a closing agreement with the Internal Revenue Service, and that would otherwise be subject to the reporting requirements of this section, is also waived.

(4) If a partnership, trust, or estate that has the taxpayer as a partner or beneficiary discloses on its information return a position for which reporting is otherwise required by the taxpayer, the taxpayer (partner or beneficiary) is then excused from disclosing that position on a return.

(5) This section does not apply to a withholding agent with respect to the performance of its withholding functions.

(6)(i) For taxable years ending after December 31, 2004, except as provided in paragraph (c)(6)(ii) of this section, reporting under paragraph (b)(4)(ii) of this section is waived for amounts received by a related party, within the meaning of section 6038A(c)(2), from a withholding agent that is a reporting corporation, within the meaning of section 6038A(a), and that are properly reported on Form 1042-S.

(ii) Paragraph (c)(6)(i) of this section does not apply to any amounts for which reporting is specifically required under the instructions to Form 8833.

(7)(i) For taxable years ending after December 31, 2004, except as provided in paragraph (c)(7)(iv) of this section, reporting under paragraph (b)(4)(ii) of this section is waived for amounts properly reported on Form 1042-S (on either a specific payee or pooled basis) by a withholding agent described in paragraph (c)(7)(ii) of this section if the beneficial owner is described in paragraph (c)(7)(iii) of this section.

(ii) A withholding agent described in this paragraph (c)(7)(ii) is a U.S. financial institution, as defined in § 1.1441-1(c)(5) of this chapter, a qualified intermediary, as defined in § 1.1441-1(e)(5)(ii) of this chapter, a withholding foreign partnership, as defined § 1.1441-5(c)(2)(i) of this chapter, or a withholding foreign trust, as defined in § 1.1441-5(e)(5)(v) of this chapter.

(iii) A beneficial owner described in this paragraph (c)(7)(iii) of this section is a direct account holder of a U.S. financial institution or qualified intermediary, a direct partner of a withholding foreign partnership, or a direct beneficiary or owner of a simple or grantor trust that is a withholding foreign trust. A beneficial owner described in this paragraph (c)(7)(iii) also includes an account holder to which a qualified intermediary has applied section 4A.01 or 4A.02 of the qualified intermediary agreement, contained in Revenue Procedure 2000-12 (2000-1 C.B. 387), (as amended by Revenue Procedure 2003-64, (2003-2 C.B. 306); Revenue Procedure 2004-21 (2004-1 C.B. 702); Revenue Procedure 2005-77 (2005-51 I.R.B. 1176) (see § 601.601(b)(2) of this chapter) a partner to which a withholding foreign partnership has applied section 10.01 or 10.02 of the withholding foreign partnership agreement, and a beneficiary or owner to which a withholding foreign trust has applied section 10.01 or 10.02 of the withholding foreign trust agreement, contained in Revenue Procedure 2003-64, (2003-2 C.B. 306), (as amended by Revenue Procedure 2004-21 (2004-1 C.B. 702); Revenue Procedure 2005-77 (2005-51 I.R.B. 1176); (see § 601.601(b)(2) of this chapter).

(iv) Paragraph (c)(7)(i) of this section does not apply to any amounts for which reporting is specifically required under the instructions to Form 8833.

(8)(i) For taxable years ending after December 31, 2004, except as provided in paragraph (c)(8)(ii) of this section, reporting under paragraph (b)(4)(ii) of this section is waived for taxpayers that are not individuals or States and that receive amounts of income that have been properly reported on Form 1042-S, that do not exceed $500,000 in the aggregate for the taxable year and that are not received through an account with an intermediary, as defined in § 1.1441-1(c)(13), or with respect to interest in a flow-through entity, as defined in § 1.1441-1(c)(23),

(ii) The exception contained in paragraph (c)(8)(i) of this section does not apply to any amounts for which reporting is specifically required under the instructions to Form 8833.

(d) *Information to be reported.*—(1) *Returns due after December 15, 1997.*—When reporting is required under this section for a return relating to a taxable year for which the due date (without extensions) is after December 15, 1997, the taxpayer must furnish, in accordance with paragraph (a) of this section, as an attachment to the return, a fully completed Form 8833 (Treaty-Based Return Position Disclosure Under Section 6114 or 7701(b)) or appropriate successor form.

(2) *Earlier returns.*—For returns relating to taxable years for which the due date for filing returns (without extensions) is on or before December 15, 1997, the taxpayer must furnish information in accordance with paragraph (d) of this section in effect prior to December 15, 1997 (see § 301.6114-1(d) as contained in 26 CFR part 301, revised April 1, 1997).

(3) *In general.*—(i) *Permanent establishment.*—For purposes of determining the nature and amount (or reasonable estimate thereof) of gross receipts, if a taxpayer takes a position that it does not have a permanent establishment or a fixed base in the United States and properly discloses that position, it need not separately report its payment of actual or deemed dividends or interest exempt from tax by reason of a treaty (or any liability for tax imposed by reason of section 884).

(ii) *Single income item.*—For purposes of the statement of facts relied upon to support each separate Treaty-Based Return Position taken, a taxpayer may treat payments or income items of the same type (e.g., interest items) received from the same ultimate payor (e.g., the obligor on a note) as a single separate payment or income item.

(iii) *Foreign source effectively connected income.*—If a taxpayer takes the return position that, under the treaty, income that would be income effectively connected with a U.S. trade or business is not subject to U.S. taxation because it is income treated as derived from sources outside the United States, the taxpayer may treat payments or income items of the same type (e.g., interest items) as a single separate payment or income item.

(iv) *Sales or services income.*—Income from separate sales or services, whether or not made or preformed by an agent (independent or dependent), to different U.S. customers on behalf of a foreign corporation not having a permanent establishment in the United States may be treated as a single payment or income item.

(v) *Foreign insurers or reinsurers.*—For purposes of reporting by foreign insurers or reinsurers, as described in paragraph (c)(1)(vii)(B) of this section, such reporting must separately set forth premiums paid with respect to casualty insurance and indemnity bonds (subject to section 4371(1)); life insurance, sickness and accident policies, and annuity contracts (subject to section 4371(2)); and reinsurance (subject to section 4371(3)). All premiums paid with respect to each of these three categories may be treated as a single payment or income item within that category. For reports first due before May 1, 1991, the report may disclose, for each of the three categories, the total amount of premiums derived by the foreign insurer or reinsurer in U.S. dollars (even if a portion of these premiums relate to risks that are not U.S. situs). Reasonable estimates of the amounts required to be disclosed will satisfy these reporting requirements.

(e) *Effective/applicability date.*—(1) *In general.*—This section is effective for taxable years of the taxpayer for which the due date for filing returns (without extensions) occurs after December 31, 1988. However, if—

(i) A taxpayer has filed a return for such a taxable year, without complying with the reporting requirement of this section, before November 13, 1989, or

(ii) A taxpayer is not otherwise than by paragraph (a) of this section required to file a return for a taxable year before November 13, 1989, such taxpayer must file (apart from any earlier filed return) the statement required by paragraph (d) of this section before June 12, 1990, by mailing the required statement to the Internal Revenue Service, P.O. Box 21086, Philadelphia, PA 19114. Any such statement filed apart from a return must be dated, signed and sworn to by the taxpayer under the penalties of perjury. In addition, with respect to any return due (without extensions) on or before March 10, 1990, the reporting required by paragraph (a) of this section must be made no later than June 12, 1990. If a taxpayer files or has filed a return on or before November 13, 1989, that provides substantially the same information required by paragraph (d) of this section, no additional submission will be required. Foreign insurers and reinsurers subject to reporting described in paragraph (c)(7)(ii) of this section must so report for calendar years 1988 and 1989 no later than August 15, 1990.

(2) *Section 5000C.*—Paragraph (c)(1)(ix) of this section applies to payments made on and after November 16, 2016 pursuant to contracts entered into on and after January 2, 2011. However, a taxpayer that receives payments exempt from tax under section 5000C by reason of a qualified income tax treaty before November 16, 2016 is not required to disclose this position on Form 8833, provided it has properly relied on Notice 2015-35, I.R.B. 2016-14, 533, in claiming the exemption.

(f) *Cross reference.*—For the provisions concerning penalties for failure to disclose a treaty-based return position, see section 6712 and § 301.6712-1. [Reg. § 301.6114-1.]

☐ [*T.D.* 8292, 3-13-90. *Amended by T.D.* 8305, 7-11-90; *T.D.* 8733, 10-6-97; *T.D.* 8734, 10-6-97; *T.D.* 8804, 12-30-98; *T.D.* 8856, 12-29-99, *T.D.* 9253, 3-13-2006 *and T.D.* 9782, 8-17-2016.]

[Reg. § 20.6151-1]

§ 20.6151-1. Time and place for paying tax shown on the return.—(a) *General rule.*—The tax shown on the estate tax return is to be paid at the time and place fixed for filing the return (determined without regard to any extension of time for filing the return). For provisions relating to the time and place for filing the return, see §§ 20.6075-1 and 20.6091-1. For the duty of the executor to pay the tax, see § 20.2002-1.

(b) *Extension of time for paying.*—(1) *In general.*—For general provisions relating to extension of time for paying the tax, see § 20.6161-1.

(2) *Reversionary or remainder interests.*—For provisions relating to extension of time for payment of estate tax on the value of a reversionary or remainder interest in property, see § 20.6163-1.

(c) *Payment with obligations of the United States.*—Treasury bonds of certain issues which were owned by the decedent at the time of his death or which were treated as part of his gross estate under the rules contained in § 306.28 of Treasury Department Circular No. 300, Revised (31 CFR Part 306), may be redeemed at par plus accrued interest for the purpose of payment of the estate tax, as provided in said section. Whether bonds of particular issues may be redeemed for this purpose will depend on the terms of the offering circulars cited on the face of the bonds. A current list of eligible issues may be obtained from any Federal reserve bank or branch, or from the Bureau of Public Debt, Washington, D.C. See section 6312 and §§ 301.6312-1 and 301.6312-2 of this chapter (Regulations on Procedure and Administration) for provisions relating to the payment of taxes with United States Treasury obligations.

(d) *Receipt for payment.*—For provisions relating to duplicate receipts for payment of the tax, see § 20.6314-1. [Reg. § 20.6151-1.]

☐ [*T.D.* 6296, 6-23-58.]

[Reg. § 25.6151-1]

§ 25.6151-1. Time and place for paying tax shown on return.—The tax shown on the gift tax return is to be paid by the donor at the time and place fixed for filing the return (determined without regard to any extension of time for filing the return), unless the time for paying the tax is extended in accordance with the provisions of section 6161. However, for provisions relating to certain cases in which the time for paying the gift tax is postponed by reason of an individual serving in, or in support of, the Armed Forces of the United States in a combat zone, see section 7508. For provisions relating to the time and place for filing the return, see §§ 25.6075-1 and 25.6091-1. [Reg. § 25.6151-1.]

☐ [*T.D.* 6334, 11-14-58.]

[Reg. § 300.0]

§ 300.0. User fees; in general.—(a) *In general.*—The regulations in this part 300 are designated the User Fee Regulations and provide rules relating to user fees under 31 U.S.C. 9701.

(b) *Applicability.*—User fees are imposed on the following services:

(1) Entering into an installment agreement.

(2) Restructuring or reinstating an installment agreement.

(3) Processing an offer to compromise.

(4) Taking the special enrollment examination to become an enrolled agent.

(5) Enrolling an enrolled agent.

(6) Renewing the enrollment of an enrolled agent.

(7) Enrolling an enrolled actuary.

(8) Renewing the enrollment of an enrolled actuary.

(9) Renewing the enrollment of an enrolled retirement plan agent.

(10) Taking the registered tax return preparer competency examination.

(11) Applying for a preparer tax identification number.

(12) Requesting an estate tax closing letter. [Reg. § 300.0.]

☐ [*T.D.* 8589, 2-10-95. *Amended by T.D.* 9086, 8-14-2003; *T.D.* 9288, 10-3-2006; *T.D.* 9306, 12-27-2006; *T.D.* 9370, 12-18-2007; *T.D.* 9503, 9-28-2010; *T.D.* 9523, 4-14-2011, *T.D.* 9559, 11-22-2011 *T.D.* 9858, 5-10-2019 *T.D.* 9957, 9-27-2021 *and T.D.* 9962, 2-25-2022.]

[Reg. § 300.1]

§ 300.1. Installment agreement fee.—(a) *Applicability*.—This section applies to installment agreements under section 6159 of the Internal Revenue Code.

(b) *Fee*.—The fee for entering into an installment agreement before January 1, 2017, is $120. The fee for entering into an installment agreement on or after January 1, 2017, is $225. A reduced fee applies in the following situations:

(1) For installment agreements entered into before January 1, 2017, the fee is $52 when the taxpayer pays by way of a direct debit from the taxpayer's bank account. The fee is $107 when the taxpayer pays by way of a direct debit from the taxpayer's bank account for installment agreements entered into on or after January 1, 2017;

(2) For online payment agreements entered into before January 1, 2017, the fee is $120, except that the fee is $52 when the taxpayer pays by way of a direct debit from the taxpayer's bank account. The fee is $149 for entering into online payment agreements on or after January 1, 2017, except that the fee is $31 when the taxpayer pays by way of a direct debit from the taxpayer's bank account; and

(3) Notwithstanding the type of installment agreement and method of payment, the fee is $43 if the taxpayer is a low-income taxpayer, that is, an individual who falls at or below 250 percent of the dollar criteria established by the poverty guidelines updated annually in the **Federal Register** by the U.S. Department of Health and Human Services under authority of section 673(2) of the Omnibus Budget Reconciliation Act of 1981 (95 Stat. 357, 511), or such other measure that is adopted by the Secretary, except that the fee is $31 when the taxpayer pays by way of a direct debit from the taxpayer's bank account with respect to online payment agreements entered into on or after January 1, 2017;

(c) *Person liable for fee*.—The person liable for the installment agreement fee is the taxpayer entering into an installment agreement.

(d) *Applicability date*.—This section is applicable beginning January 1, 2017. [Reg. § 300.1.]

☐ [*T.D.* 8589, 2-10-95. *Amended by T.D.* 9306, 12-27-2006; *T.D.* 9503, 9-28-2010, *T.D.* 9647, 11-29-2013 *and T.D.* 9798, 11-29-2016.]

[Reg. § 300.2]

§ 300.2. Restructuring or reinstatement of installment agreement fee.—(a) *Applicability*.—This section applies to installment agreements under section 6159 of the Internal Revenue Code that are in default. An installment agreement is deemed to be in default when a taxpayer fails to meet any of the conditions of the installment agreement.

(b) *Fee*.—The fee for restructuring or reinstating an installment agreement before January 1, 2017, is $50. The fee for restructuring or reinstating an installment agreement on or after January 1, 2017, is $89. If the taxpayer is a low-income taxpayer, that is, an individual who falls at or below 250 percent of the dollar criteria established by the poverty guidelines updated annually in the **Federal Register** by the U.S. Department of Health and Human Services under authority of section 673(2) of the Omnibus Budget Reconciliation Act of 1981 (95 Stat. 357, 511), or such other measure that is adopted by the Secretary, then the fee for restructuring or reinstating an installment agreement on or after January 1, 2017 is $43.

(c) *Person liable for fee*.—The person liable for the restructuring or reinstatement fee is the taxpayer that has an installment agreement restructured or reinstated.

(d) *Applicability date*.—This section is applicable beginning January 1, 2017. [Reg. § 300.2.]

☐ [*T.D.* 8589, 2-10-95. *Amended by T.D.* 9306, 12-27-2006; *T.D.* 9503, 9-28-2010, *T.D.* 9647, 11-29-2013 *and T.D.* 9798, 11-29-2016.]

[Reg. § 300.3]

§ 300.3. Offer to compromise fee.—(a) *Applicability*.—This section applies to the processing of offers to compromise tax liabilities pursuant to § 301.7122-1 of this chapter. Except as provided in this section, this fee applies to all offers to compromise accepted for processing.

(b) *Fee*.—(1) The fee for processing an offer to compromise submitted before April 27, 2020, is $186. The fee for processing an offer to compromise submitted on or after April 27, 2020, is $205. No fee will be charged if an offer is—

(i) Based solely on doubt as to liability as defined in § 301.7122-1(b)(1) of this chapter;

(ii) Made by a low-income taxpayer, that is, an individual whose income falls at or below the dollar criteria established by the poverty guidelines updated annually in the **Federal Register** by the U.S. Department of Health and Human Services under authority of section 673(2) of the Omnibus Budget Reconciliation Act of 1981 (95 Stat. 357, 511) or such other measure that is adopted by the Secretary; or

(iii) Made by a low-income taxpayer, as described in section 7122(c)(3) of the Internal Revenue Code, and submitted after July 1, 2019.

(2) The fee will be applied against the amount of the offer, unless the taxpayer requests that it be refunded, if the offer is—

(i) Accepted to promote effective tax administration pursuant to § 301.7122-1(b)(3) of this chapter; or

(ii) Accepted based on doubt as to collectibility and a determination that collection of an amount greater than the amount offered would create economic hardship within the meaning of § 301.6343-1 of this chapter.

(3) Except as otherwise provided in this paragraph (b), the fee will not be refunded to the taxpayer if the offer is accepted, rejected, withdrawn, or returned as nonprocessable after acceptance for processing.

(4) No additional fee will be charged if a taxpayer resubmits an offer the Secretary determines to have been rejected in error or returned in error after acceptance for processing.

(c) *Person liable for the fee.*—The person liable for the processing fee is the taxpayer whose tax liabilities are the subject of the offer.

(d) *Applicability date.*—This section is applicable beginning April 27, 2020. [Reg. § 300.3.]

☐ [*T.D.* 9086, 8-14-2003. *Amended by T.D.* 9503, 9-28-2010, *T.D.* 9647, 11-29-2013 *and T.D.* 9894, 3-12-2020.]

[Reg. § 300.4]

§ 300.4. Enrolled agent special enrollment examination fee.—(a) *Applicability.*—This section applies to the special enrollment examination to become an enrolled agent pursuant to 31 CFR 10.4(a).

(b) *Fee.*—The fee for taking the enrolled agent special enrollment examination is $99 per part, which is the cost to the government for overseeing the development and administration of the examination and is in addition to the fees charged by the administrator of the examination.

(c) *Person liable for the fee.*—The person liable for the special enrollment examination fee is the applicant taking the examination.

(d) *Applicability date.*—This section applies to registrations for the enrolled agent special enrollment examination that occur on or after March 31, 2022. [Reg. § 300.4.]

☐ [*T.D.* 9288, 10-3-2006. *Amended by T.D.* 9503, 9-28-2010, *T.D.* 9523, 4-14-2011 *T.D.* 9820, 7-18-2017 *and T.D.* 9962, 2-25-2022.]

[Reg. § 300.5]

§ 300.5. Enrollment of enrolled agent fee.—(a) *Applicability.*—This section applies to the initial enrollment of enrolled agents with the IRS Office of Professional Responsibility pursuant to 31 CFR 10.5(b).

(b) *Fee.*—The fee for initially enrolling as an enrolled agent with the IRS is $140.

(c) *Person liable for the fee.*—The person liable for the enrollment fee is the applicant filing for enrollment as an enrolled agent with the IRS Office of Professional Responsibility.

(d) *Applicability date.*—This section is applicable beginning October 31, 2022. [Reg. § 300.5.]

☐ [*T.D.* 9288, 10-3-2006. *Amended by T.D.* 9503, 9-28-2010, *T.D.* 9523, 4-14-2011, *T.D.* 9858, 5-10-2019 *and T.D.* 9966, 9-27-2022.]

[Reg. § 300.6]

§ 300.6. Renewal of enrollment of enrolled agent fee.—(a) *Applicability.*—This section applies to the renewal of enrollment of enrolled agents with the IRS Office of Professional Responsibility pursuant to 31 CFR 10.6(d)(6).

(b) *Fee.*—The fee for renewal of enrollment as an enrolled agent with the IRS is $140.

(c) *Person liable for the fee.*—The person liable for the renewal of enrollment fee is the person renewing their enrollment as an enrolled agent with the IRS Office of. Professional Responsibility.

(d) *Applicability date.*—This section is applicable beginning October 31, 2022. [Reg. § 300.6.]

☐ [*T.D.* 9288, 10-3-2006. *Amended by T.D.* 9503, 9-28-2010, *T.D.* 9523, 4-14-2011, *T.D.* 9858, 5-10-2019 *and T.D.* 9966, 9-27-2022.]

[Reg. § 300.7]

§ 300.7. Enrollment of enrolled actuary fee.—(a) *Applicability.*—This section applies to the initial enrollment of enrolled actuaries with the Joint Board for the Enrollment of Actuaries pursuant to 20 CFR Part 901.

(b) *Fee.*—The fee for initially enrolling as an enrolled actuary with the Joint Board for the Enrollment of Actuaries is $250.00.

(c) *Person liable for the fee.*—The person liable for the enrollment fee is the applicant filing for enrollment as an enrolled actuary with the Joint Board for the Enrollment of Actuaries.

(d) *Effective/applicability date.*—This section is applicable beginning January 22, 2008. [Reg. § 300.7.]

☐ [*T.D.* 9370, 12-18-2007. *Amended by T.D.* 9503, 9-28-2010.]

[Reg. § 300.8]

§ 300.8. Renewal of enrollment of enrolled actuary fee.—(a) *Applicability.*—This section applies to the renewal of enrollment of enrolled actuaries with the Joint Board for the Enrollment of Actuaries pursuant to 20 CFR Part 901.

(b) *Fee.*—The fee for renewal of enrollment as an enrolled actuary with the Joint Board for the Enrollment of Actuaries is $250.00.

(c) *Person liable for the fee.*—The person liable for the renewal of enrollment fee is the person renewing their enrollment as an enrolled actuary with the Joint Board for the Enrollment of Actuaries.

(d) *Effective/applicability date.*—This section is applicable beginning January 22, 2008. [Reg. §300.8.]

☐ [*T.D.* 9370, 12-18-2007. *Amended by T.D.* 9503, 9-28-2010.]

[Reg. §300.9]

§300.9. Renewal of enrollment of enrolled retirement plan agent fee.—(a) *Applicability.*—This section applies to the renewal of enrollment of enrolled retirement plan agents with the IRS pursuant to 31 CFR 10.5(b).

(b) *Fee.*—The fee for renewal of enrollment as an enrolled retirement plan agent with the IRS is $140.

(c) *Person liable for the fee.*—The person liable for the renewal of enrollment fee is the person renewing enrollment as an enrolled retirement plan agent with the IRS.

(d) *Applicability date.*—This section is applicable beginning October 31, 2022. [Reg. §300.9.]

☐ [*T.D.* 9523, 4-14-2011. *Redesignated and amended by T.D.* 9858, 5-10-2019 *and redesignated by T.D.* 9962, 2-25-2022. *Amended by T.D.* 9966, 9-27-2022.]

[Reg. §300.10]

§300.10. Registered tax return preparer competency examination fee.—(a) *Applicability.*—This section applies to the competency examination to become a registered tax return preparer pursuant to 31 CFR 10.4(c).

(b) *Fee.*—The fee for taking the registered tax return preparer competency examination is $27, which is the government cost for overseeing the examination and does not include any fees charged by the administrator of the examination.

(c) *Person liable for the fee.*—The person liable for the competency examination fee is the applicant taking the examination.

(d) *Effective/applicability date.*—This section is applicable beginning November 25, 2011. [Reg. §300.10.]

☐ [*T.D.* 9559, 11-22-2011. *Redesignated by T.D.* 9858, 5-10-2019 *and by T.D.* 9962, 2-25-2022.]

[Reg. §300.11]

§300.11. Fee for obtaining a preparer tax identification number.—(a) *Applicability.*—This section applies to the application for and renewal of a preparer tax identification number pursuant to 26 CFR 1.6109-2(d).

(b) *Fee.*—The fee to apply for or renew a preparer tax identification number is $21 per year and is in addition to the fee charged by the contractor.

(c) *Person liable for the fee.*—The individual liable for the application or renewal fee is the individual applying for and renewing a preparer tax identification number from the IRS.

(d) *Applicability date.*—This section applies to applications for or renewal of a preparer tax identification number filed on or after August 17, 2020. [Reg. §300.11.]

☐ [*T.D.* 9503, 9-28-2010. *Redesignated by T.D.* 9523, 4-14-2011. *Amended by T.D.* 9559, 11-22-2011, *T.D.* 9742, 10-29-2015 and *T.D.* 9781, 8-9-2016. *Redesignated by T.D.* 9858, 5-10-2019. *Amended by T.D.* 9903, 7-15-2020. *Redesignated by T.D.* 9962, 2-25-2022.]

[Reg. §300.12]

§300.12. Fee for estate tax closing letter.—(a) *Applicability.*—This section applies to the request by a person described in paragraph (c) of this section for an estate tax closing letter from the IRS.

(b) *Fee.*—The fee for issuing an estate tax closing letter is $67.

(c) *Person liable for the fee.*—The person liable for the fee is the estate of the decedent or other person requesting, in accordance with applicable procedures and policies, an estate tax closing letter to be issued with respect to the estate.

(d) *Applicability date.*—This section applies to requests for estate tax closing letters received by the IRS on or after October 28, 2021. [Reg. §300.12.]

☐ [*T.D.* 9957, 9-27-2021. *Redesignated by T.D.* 9962, 2-25-2022.]

[Reg. §301.6159-0]

§301.6159-0. Table of contents.—

 [Reg. §301.6159-0.]

☐ [*T.D.* 9473, 11-24-2009.]

[Reg. §301.6159-1]

§301.6159-1. Agreements for payment of tax liability in installments.—(a) *Authority.*—The Commissioner may enter into a written agreement with a taxpayer that allows the taxpayer to make scheduled periodic payments of any tax liability if the Commissioner determines that such agreement will facilitate full or partial collection of the tax liability.

(b) *Procedures for submission and consideration of proposed installment agreements.*—(1) *In general.*—

A proposed installment agreement must be submitted according to the procedures, and in the form and manner, prescribed by the Commissioner.

(2) *When a proposed installment agreement becomes pending.*—A proposed installment agreement becomes pending when it is accepted for processing. The Internal Revenue Service (IRS) may not accept a proposed installment agreement for processing following reference of a case involving the liability that is the subject of the proposed installment agreement to the Department of Justice for prosecution or defense. The proposed installment agreement remains pending until the IRS accepts the proposal, the IRS notifies the taxpayer that the proposal has been rejected, or the proposal is withdrawn by the taxpayer. If a proposed installment agreement that has been accepted for processing does not contain sufficient information to permit the IRS to evaluate whether the proposal should be accepted, the IRS will request the taxpayer to provide the needed additional information. If the taxpayer does not submit the additional information that the IRS has requested within a reasonable time period after such a request, the IRS may reject the proposed installment agreement.

(3) *Revised proposals of installment agreements submitted following rejection.*—If, following the rejection of a proposed installment agreement, the IRS determines that the taxpayer made a good faith revision of the proposal and submitted the revision within 30 days of the date of rejection, the provisions of this section shall apply to that revised proposal. If, however, the IRS determines that a revision was not made in good faith, the provisions of this section do not apply to the revision and the appeal period in paragraph (d)(3) of this section continues to run from the date of the original rejection.

(c) *Acceptance, form, and terms of installment agreements.*—(1) *Acceptance of an installment agreement.*—(i) *In general.*—A proposed installment agreement has not been accepted until the IRS notifies the taxpayer or the taxpayer's representative of the acceptance. Except as provided in paragraph (c)(1)(iii) of this section, the Commissioner has the discretion to accept or reject any proposed installment agreement.

(ii) *Acceptance does not reduce liabilities.*—The acceptance of an installment agreement by the IRS does not reduce the amount of taxes, interest, or penalties owed. (However, penalties may continue to accrue at a reduced rate pursuant to section 6651(h).)

(iii) *Guaranteed installment agreements.*—In the case of a liability of an individual for income tax, the Commissioner shall accept a proposed installment agreement if, as of the date the individual proposes the installment agreement—

(A) The aggregate amount of the liability (not including interest, penalties, additions to tax, and additional amounts) does not exceed $10,000;

(B) The taxpayer (and, if the liability relates to a joint return, the taxpayer's spouse) has not, during any of the preceding five taxable years—

(1) Failed to file any income tax return;

(2) Failed to pay any required income tax; or

(3) Entered into an installment agreement for the payment of any income tax;

(C) The Commissioner determines that the taxpayer is financially unable to pay the liability in full when due (and the taxpayer submits any information the Commissioner requires to make that determination);

(D) The installment agreement requires full payment of the liability within three years; and

(E) The taxpayer agrees to comply with the provisions of the Internal Revenue Code for the period the agreement is in effect.

(2) *Form of installment agreements.*—An installment agreement must be in writing. A written installment agreement may take the form of a document signed by the taxpayer and the Commissioner or a written confirmation of an agreement entered into by the taxpayer and the Commissioner that is mailed or personally delivered to the taxpayer.

(3) *Terms of installment agreements.*—(i) Except as otherwise provided in this section, an installment agreement is effective from the date the IRS notifies the taxpayer or the taxpayer's representative of its acceptance until the date the agreement ends by its terms or until it is superseded by a new installment agreement.

(ii) By its terms, an installment agreement may end upon the expiration of the period of limitations on collection in section 6502 and § 301.6502-1, or at some prior date.

(iii) As a condition to entering into an installment agreement with a taxpayer, the Commissioner may require that—

(A) The taxpayer agree to a reasonable extension of the period of limitations on collection; and

(B) The agreement contain terms that protect the interests of the Government.

(iv) Except as otherwise provided in an installment agreement, all payments made under the installment agreement will be applied in the best interests of the Government.

(v) While an installment agreement is in effect, the Commissioner may request, and the taxpayer must provide, a financial condition update at any time.

(vi) At any time after entering into an installment agreement, the Commissioner and the taxpayer may agree to modify or terminate an installment agreement or may agree to a new installment agreement that supersedes the existing agreement.

(d) *Rejection of a proposed installment agreement.*—(1) *When a proposed installment agreement becomes rejected.*—A proposed installment agreement has not been rejected until the IRS notifies the taxpayer or the taxpayer's representative of the rejection, the reason(s) for rejection, and the right to an appeal.

(2) *Independent administrative review.*—The IRS may not notify a taxpayer or taxpayer's representative of the rejection of an installment agreement until an independent administrative review of the proposed rejection is completed.

(3) *Appeal of rejection of a proposed installment agreement.*—The taxpayer may administratively appeal a rejection of a proposed installment agreement to the IRS Office of Appeals (Appeals) if, within the 30-day period commencing the day after the taxpayer is notified of the rejection, the taxpayer requests an appeal in the manner provided by the Commissioner.

(e) *Modification or termination of installment agreements by the Internal Revenue Service.*—(1) *Inadequate information or jeopardy.*—The Commissioner may terminate an installment agreement if the Commissioner determines that—

(i) Information which was provided to the IRS by the taxpayer or the taxpayer's representative in connection with either the granting of the installment agreement or a request for a financial update was inaccurate or incomplete in any material respect; or

(ii) Collection of any liability to which the installment agreement applies is in jeopardy.

(2) *Change in financial condition, failure to timely pay an installment or another Federal tax liability, or failure to provide requested financial information.*—The Commissioner may modify or terminate an installment agreement if—

(i) The Commissioner determines that the financial condition of a taxpayer that is party to the agreement has significantly changed; or

(ii) A taxpayer that is party to the installment agreement fails to—

(A) Timely pay an installment in accordance with the terms of the installment agreement;

(B) Pay any other Federal tax liability when the liability becomes due; or

(C) Provide a financial condition update requested by the Commissioner.

(3) *Request by taxpayer.*—Upon request by a taxpayer that is a party to the installment agreement, the Commissioner may terminate or modify the terms of an installment agreement if the Commissioner determines that the financial condition of the taxpayer has significantly changed. The taxpayer's request will not suspend the statute of limitations under section 6502 for collection of any liability. While the Commissioner is considering the request, the taxpayer shall comply with the terms of the existing installment agreement.

(4) *Notice.*—Unless the Commissioner determines that collection of the tax is in jeopardy, the Commissioner will notify the taxpayer in writing at least 30 days prior to modifying or terminating an installment agreement pursuant to paragraph (e)(1) or (2) of this section. The notice provided pursuant to this section must briefly describe the reason for the intended modification or termination. Upon receiving notice, the taxpayer may provide information showing that the reason for the proposed modification or termination is incorrect.

(5) *Appeal of modification or termination of an installment agreement.*—The taxpayer may administratively appeal the modification or termination of an installment agreement to Appeals if, following issuance of the notice required by paragraph (e)(4) of this section and prior to the expiration of the 30-day period commencing the day after the modification or termination is to take effect, the taxpayer requests an appeal in the manner provided by the Commissioner.

(f) *Effect of installment agreement or pending installment agreement on collection activity.*—(1) *In general.*—No levy may be made to collect a tax liability that is the subject of an installment agreement during the period that a proposed installment agreement is pending with the IRS, for 30 days immediately following the rejection of a proposed installment agreement, during the period that an installment agreement is in effect, and for 30 days immediately following the termination of an installment agreement. If, prior to the expiration of the 30-day period following the rejection or termination of an installment agreement, the taxpayer appeals the rejection or termination decision, no levy may be made while the rejection or termination is being considered by Appeals. This section will not prohibit levy to collect the liability of any person other than the person or persons named in the installment agreement.

(2) *Exceptions.*—Paragraph (f)(1) of this section shall not prohibit levy if the taxpayer files a written notice with the IRS that waives the restriction on levy imposed by this section, the IRS determines that the proposed installment agreement was submitted solely to delay collection, or the IRS determines that collection of the tax to which the installment agreement or proposed installment agreement relates is in jeopardy.

(3) *Other actions by the IRS while levy is prohibited.*—(i) *In general.*—The IRS may take actions other than levy to protect the interests of the Government with regard to the liability identified in an installment agreement or proposed installment agreement. Those actions include, for example—

(A) Crediting an overpayment against the liability pursuant to section 6402;

(B) Filing or refiling notices of Federal tax lien; and

(C) Taking action to collect from any person who is not named in the installment agreement or proposed installment agreement but who is liable for the tax to which the installment agreement relates.

(ii) *Proceedings in court.*—Except as otherwise provided in this paragraph (f)(3)(ii), the IRS will not refer a case to the Department of Justice for the commencement of a proceeding in court, against a person named in an installment agreement or proposed installment agreement, if levy to collect the liability is prohibited by paragraph (f)(1) of this section. Without regard to whether a person is named in an installment agreement or proposed installment agreement, however, the IRS may authorize the Department of Justice to file a counterclaim or third-party complaint in a refund action or to join that person in any other proceeding in which liability for the tax that is the subject of the installment agreement or proposed installment agreement may be established or disputed, including a suit against the United States under 28 U.S.C. 2410. In addition, the United States may file a claim in any bankruptcy proceeding or insolvency action brought by or against such person. If a person named in an installment agreement is joined in a proceeding, the United States obtains a judgment against that person, and the case is referred back to the IRS for collection, collection will continue to occur pursuant to the terms of the installment agreement. Notwithstanding the installment agreement, any claim or suit permitted will be for the full amount of the liabilities owed.

(g) *Suspension of the statute of limitations on collection.*—The statute of limitations under section 6502 for collection of any liability shall be suspended during the period that a proposed installment agreement relating to that liability is pending with the IRS, for 30 days immediately following the rejection of a proposed installment agreement, and for 30 days immediately following the termination of an installment agreement. If, within the 30 days following the rejection or termination of an installment agreement, the taxpayer files an appeal with Appeals, the statute of limitations for collection shall be suspended while the rejection or termination is being considered by Appeals. The statute of limitations for collection shall continue to run if an exception under paragraph (f)(2) of this section applies and levy is not prohibited with respect to the taxpayer.

(h) *Annual statement.*—The Commissioner shall provide each taxpayer who is party to an installment agreement under this section with an annual statement setting forth the initial balance owed at the beginning of the year, the payments made during the year, and the remaining balance as of the end of the year.

(i) *Biennial review of partial payment installment agreements.*—The Commissioner shall perform a review of the taxpayer's financial condition in the case of a partial payment installment agreement at least once every two years. The purpose of this review is to determine whether the taxpayer's financial condition has significantly changed so as to warrant an increase in the value of the payments being made or termination of the agreement.

(j) *Cross reference.*—Pursuant to section 6601(b)(1), the last day prescribed for payment is determined without regard to any installment agreement, including for purposes of computing penalties and interest provided by the Internal Revenue Code. For special rules regarding the computation of the failure to pay penalty while certain installment agreements are in effect, see section 6651(h) and §301.6651-1(a)(4).

(k) *Effective/applicability date.*—This section is applicable on November 25, 2009. [Reg. §301.6159-1.]

☐ [*T.D.* 8583, 12-22-94. *Amended by T.D.* 9473, 11-24-2009.]

[Reg. §20.6161-1]

§20.6161-1. Extension of time for paying tax shown on the return.—(a) *Basis for granting an extension of time.*—(1) *Reasonable cause.*—With respect to the estate of a decedent dying after December 31, 1970, an extension of time beyond the due date to pay any part of the tax shown on the estate tax return may be granted for a reasonable period of time, not to exceed 12 months, by the district director or the director of a service center, at the request of the executor, if an examination of all the facts and circumstances discloses that such request is based upon reasonable cause. (See paragraph (b) of this section for rules relating to application for extension.) The following examples illustrate cases involving reasonable cause for granting an extension of time pursuant to this paragraph:

Example (1). An estate includes sufficient liquid assets to pay the estate tax when otherwise due. The liquid assets, however, are located in several jurisdictions and are not immediately subject to the control of the executor. Consequently, such assets cannot readily be marshalled by the executor, even with the exercise of due diligence.

Example (2). An estate is comprised in substantial part of assets consisting of rights to receive payments in the future (i.e., annuities, copyright royalties, contingent fees, or accounts receivable). These assets provide insufficient present cash with which to pay the estate tax when otherwise due and the estate cannot borrow against these assets except upon terms which would inflict loss upon the estate.

Example (3). An estate includes a claim to substantial assets which cannot be collected without litigation. Consequently, the size of the gross estate is unascertainable as of the time the tax is otherwise due.

Example (4). An estate does not have sufficient funds (without borrowing at a rate of interest higher than that generally available) with which to pay the entire estate tax when otherwise due, to provide a reasonable allowance during the remaining period of administration of the estate for the decedent's widow and dependent children, and to satisfy claims against the estate that are due and payable. Furthermore, the executor has made a reasonable effort to convert assets in his possession (other than an interest in a closely held business to which §6166 applies) into cash.

(2) *Undue hardship.*—(i) *General rule.*—In any case where the district director finds that

See p. 15 for regulations not amended to reflect law changes

payment on the due date of any part of the tax shown on the return, or payment of any part of an installment under section 6166 (including any part of a deficiency prorated to an installment the date for payment of which had not arrived) on the date fixed for payment thereof, would impose undue hardship upon the estate, he may extend the time for payment for a period or periods not to exceed one year for any one period and for all periods not to exceed 10 years from the date prescribed in section 6151(a) for payment of the tax. See paragraph (a) of § 20.6151-1. In addition, if the district director finds that payment upon notice and demand of any part of a deficiency prorated under the provisions of section 6166 to installments the date for payment of which had arrived would impose undue hardship upon the estate, he may extend the time for payment for a similar period or periods.

(ii) *Definition of "undue hardship"*.—The extension provided under this subparagraph on the basis of undue hardship to the estate will not be granted upon a general statement of hardship or merely upon a showing of reasonable cause. The term "undue hardship" means more than an inconvenience to the estate. A sale of property at a price equal to its current fair market value, where a market exists, is not ordinarily considered as resulting in an undue hardship to the estate. The following examples illustrate cases in which an extension of time will be granted based on undue hardship pursuant to this paragraph:

Example (1). A farm (or other closely held business) comprises a significant portion of an estate, but the percentage requirements of section 6166(a) (relating to an extension where the estate includes a closely held business) are not satisfied and, therefore, that section does not apply. Sufficient funds for the payment of the estate tax when otherwise due are not readily available. The farm (or closely held business) could be sold to unrelated persons at a price equal to its fair market value, but the executor seeks an extension of time to facilitate the raising of funds from other sources for the payment of the estate tax.

Example (2). The assets in the gross estate which must be liquidated to pay the estate tax can only be sold at a sacrifice price or in a depressed market if the tax is to be paid when otherwise due.

(b) *Application for extension*.—An application containing a request for an extension of time for paying the tax shown on the return shall be in writing, shall state the period of the extension requested, and shall include a declaration that it is made under penalties of perjury. If the application is based upon reasonable cause (see paragraph (a)(1) of this section), a statement of such reasonable cause shall be included in the application. If the application is based upon undue hardship to the estate (see paragraph (a)(2) of this section), the application shall include a statement explaining in detail the undue hardship to the estate that would result if the requested extension were refused. At the option of the executor, an application for an extension of time based upon undue hardship may contain an alternative request for an extension based upon reasonable cause if the application for an extension based upon undue hardship is denied. However, an application for an extension of time based solely upon reasonable cause will be treated as such even though an examination of all the facts and circumstances discloses that an application for an extension of time based upon undue hardship might have been granted had such an application therefor been made. If the application is based solely on reasonable cause, it shall be filed with the internal revenue officer with whom the estate tax return is required to be filed under the provisions of § 20.6091-1(a). If the application is based on undue hardship (including an application in which the executor makes an alternative request for an extension based on reasonable cause), it shall be filed with the appropriate district director referred to in paragraph (a)(2) of § 20.6091-1 whether or not the return is to be filed with, or the tax is to be paid to, such district director. An application for an extension of time relating to the estate of a decedent who was not domiciled in the United States at the time of death shall be filed with the Director of International Operations, Internal Revenue Service, Washington, D. C. 20225. When received, the application will be examined, and, if possible, within 30 days will be denied, granted, or tentatively granted subject to certain conditions of which the executor will be notified. An application for an extension of time for payment of the tax, or of an installment under section 6166 (including any part of a deficiency prorated to an installment the date for payment of which had not arrived), will not be considered unless the extension is applied for on or before the date fixed for payment of the tax or installment. Similarly, an application for such extension of time for payment of any part of a deficiency prorated under the provisions of section 6166 to installments the date for payment of which had arrived, will not be considered unless the extension is applied for on or before the date prescribed for payment of the deficiency as shown by the notice and demand from the district director. If the executor desires to obtain an additional extension of time for payment of any part of the tax shown on the return, or any part of an installment under section 6166 (including any part of a deficiency prorated to installment), it must be applied for on or before the date of the expiration of the previous extension. The granting of the extension of time for paying the tax is discretionary with the appropriate internal revenue officer and his authority will be exercised under such conditions as he may deem advisable. However, if a request for an extension of time for payment of estate tax under this section is denied by a district director or a director of a service center, a written appeal may be made, by registered or certified mail or hand delivery, to the regional commissioner with authority over such district director or service center director within 10 days after the denial is mailed to the executor. The provisions of sections 7502 (relating to timely mailing treated as timely filing) and 7503 (relating to time for performance of acts where the last day falls on Saturday, Sunday, or a legal holiday) apply in the case of appeals filed under this paragraph. When received, the appeal will be examined, and if possible, within 30 days will be denied, granted, or tentatively granted subject to certain conditions of which the executor will be notified. If in the mistaken belief that an estate satisfies the requirements of section 6166 the executor, within the time prescribed in paragraph (e) of § 20.6166-1, files a notification of election to pay estate tax in installments, the notification of election to pay tax in installments will be treated as a timely filed application for an extension, under section 6161, of time for payment of the tax if the executor so requests, in writing, within a reasonable time after being notified by the district director that the estate does not satisfy the requirements of section 6166. A request that the election under section 6166 be treated as a timely filed application for an extension under section 6161 must contain, or be supported by the same information required by this paragraph with respect to an application for such an extension.

(c) *Special rules.*—(1) *Payment pursuant to extension.*—The amount of the tax for which an extension is granted, with the additions thereto, shall be paid on or before the expiration of the period of extension without the necessity of notice and demand from the district director.

(2) *Interest.*—The granting of an extension of the time for payment of the tax will not relieve the estate from liability for the payment of interest thereon during the period of the extension. See section 6601.

(3) *Duty to file timely return.*—The granting of an extension of time for paying the tax will not relieve the executor from the duty of filing the return on or before the date provided for in § 20.6075-1.

(4) *Credit for taxes.*—An extension of time to pay the tax may extend the period within which State and foreign death taxes allowed as a credit under sections 2011 and 2014 are required to be paid and the credit therefor claimed. See paragraph (c) of § § 20.2011-1 and 20.2014-6.

(d) *Cross references.*—For provisions requiring the furnishing of security for the payment of the tax for which an extension is granted, see paragraph (a) of § 20.6165-1. For provisions relating to extensions of time for payment of tax on the value of a reversionary or remainder interest in property, see § 20.6163-1. [Reg. § 20.6161-1.]

□ [*Amended by T.D.* 6711, 3-23-64, *T.D.* 7238, 12-28-72 *and T.D.* 7384, 10-21-75.]

[Reg. § 25.6161-1]

§ 25.6161-1. Extension of time for paying tax or deficiency.—(a) *In general.*—(1) *Tax shown on return.*—A reasonable extension of time to pay the amount of tax shown on the return may be granted by the district director at the request of the donor. The period of such extension shall not be in excess of six months from the date fixed for the payment of the tax, except that if the taxpayer is abroad the period of extension may be in excess of six months.

(2) *Deficiency.*—The time for payment of any amount determined as a deficiency in respect of tax imposed by chapter 12 of the Code, or for payment of any part thereof may be extended by the district director at the request of the donor for a period not to exceed 18 months from the date fixed for the payment of the deficiency, as shown on the notice and demand from the district director, and, in exceptional cases, for a further period not in excess of 12 months. No extension of time for the payment of a deficiency shall be granted if the deficiency is due to negligence, to intentional disregard of rules and regulations, or to fraud with intent to evade tax.

(3) *Extension of time for filing distinguished.*—The granting of an extension of time for filing a return does not operate to extend the time for the payment of the tax or any part thereof, unless so specified in the extension.

(b) *Undue hardship required for extension.*—An extension of the time for payment shall be granted only upon a satisfactory showing that payment on the due date of the amount with respect to which the extension is desired will result in an undue hardship. The extension will not be granted upon a general statement of hardship. The term "undue hardship" means more than an inconvenience to the taxpayer. It must appear that substantial financial loss, for example, loss due to the sale of property at a sacrifice price, will result to the donor from making payment on the due date of the amount with respect to which the extension is desired. If a market exists, the sale of the property at the current market price is not ordinarily considered as resulting in an undue hardship.

(c) *Application for extension.*—An application for an extension of the time for payment of the tax shown on the return, or for the payment of any amount determined as a deficiency, shall be in writing and shall be accompanied by evidence showing the undue hardship that would result to the donor if the extension were refused. The application shall also be accompanied by a statement of the assets and liabilities of the donor and an itemized statement showing all receipts and disbursements for each of the three months immediately preceding the due date of the amount to which the application relates. The application, with supporting documents, must be filed with the applicable district director referred to in paragraph (a) of § 25.6091-1 regardless of whether the return is to be filed with, or the tax is to be paid to, such district director on or before the date prescribed for payment of the amount with respect to which the extension is desired. The application will be examined by the district director, and within 30 days, if possible, will be denied, granted, or tentatively granted subject to certain conditions of which the donor will be notified. If an additional extension is desired, the request therefor must be made to the district director on or before the expiration of the period for which the prior extension is granted.

(d) *Payment pursuant to extension.*—If an extension of time for payment is granted, the amount the time for payment of which is so extended shall be paid on or before the expiration of the period of the extension without the necessity of notice and demand from the district director. The granting of an extension of the time for payment of the tax or deficiency does not relieve the donor from liability for the payment of interest thereon during the period of the extension. See section 6601 and §301.6601-1 of this chapter (Regulations on Procedure and Administration). [Reg. §25.6161-1.]

☐ [*T.D.* 6334, 11-14-58. *Amended by T.D.* 7012, 5-14-69.]

[Reg. §20.6161-2]

§20.6161-2. Extension of time for paying deficiency in tax.—(a) In any case in which the district director finds that payment, on the date prescribed therefor, of any part of a deficiency would impose undue hardship upon the estate, he may extend the time for payment for a period or periods not to exceed one year for any one period and for all periods not to exceed four years from the date prescribed for payment thereof. However, see §20.6161-1 for extensions of time for payment of the part of a deficiency which is prorated to installments under the provisions of section 6166.

(b) The extension will not be granted upon a general statement of hardship. The term "undue hardship" means more than an inconvenience to the estate. It must appear that a substantial financial loss, for example, due to the sale of property at a sacrifice price, will result to the estate from making payment of the deficiency at the date prescribed therefor. If a market exists, a sale of property at the current market price is not ordinarily considered as resulting in an undue hardship. No extension will be granted if the deficiency is due to negligence or intentional disregard of rules and regulations or to fraud with intent to evade the tax.

(c) An application for such an extension must be in writing and must contain, or be supported by, information in a written statement declaring that it is made under penalties of perjury showing the undue hardship that would result to the estate if the extension were refused. The application, with the supporting information, must be filed with the district director. When received, it will be examined, and, if possible, within thirty days will be denied, granted, or tentatively granted subject to certain conditions of which the executor will be notified. The district director will not consider an application for such an extension unless it is applied for on or before the date prescribed for payment of the deficiency, as shown by the notice and demand from the district director. If the executor desires to obtain an additional extension, it must be applied for on or before the date of the expiration of the previous extension. The granting of the extension of time for paying the deficiency is discretionary with the district director.

(d) The amount of the deficiency for which an extension is granted, with the additions thereto, shall be paid on or before the expiration of the period of extension without the necessity of notice and demand from the district director.

(e) The granting of an extension of time for paying the deficiency will not operate to prevent the running of interest. See section 6601. An extension of time to pay the deficiency may extend the period within which State and foreign death taxes allowed as a credit under sections 2011 and 2014 are required to be paid and the credit therefor claimed. See paragraph (c) of §20.2011-1 and §20.2014-6.

(f) For provisions requiring the furnishing of security for the payment of the deficiency for which an extension is granted, see §20.6165-1. [Reg. §20.6161-2.]

☐ [*T.D.* 6296, 6-23-58. *Amended by T.D.* 6522, 12-28-60.]

[Reg. §20.6163-1]

§20.6163-1. Extension of time for payment of estate tax on value of reversionary or remainder interest in property.—(a)(1) In case there is included in the gross estate a reversionary or remainder interest in property, the payment of the part of the tax attributable to that interest may, at the election of the executor, be postponed until six months after the termination of the precedent interest or interests in the property. The provisions of this section are limited to cases in which the reversionary or remainder interest is included in the decedent's gross estate as such and do not extend to cases in which the decedent creates future interests by his own testamentary act.

(2) If the district director finds that the payment of the tax at the expiration of the period of postponement described in subparagraph (1) of this paragraph would result in undue hardship to the estate, he may—

(i) After September 2, 1958, and before February 27, 1964, extend the time for payment for a reasonable period or periods not to exceed in all 2 years from the expiration of the period of postponement, but only if the precedent interest or interests in the property terminated after March 2, 1958, or

(ii) After February 26, 1964, extend the time for payment for a reasonable period or periods not to exceed in all 3 years from the expiration of the period of postponement, but only if the time for payment of the tax, including any extensions thereof, did not expire before February 26, 1964.

See paragraph (a)(2)(ii) of §20.6161-1 for the meaning of the term "undue hardship". An example of undue hardship is a case where, by reason of the time required to settle the complex issues involved in a trust, the decedent's heirs or beneficiaries cannot reasonably expect to receive the decedent's remainder interest in the trust before the expiration of the period of postponement. The extension will be granted only in the manner provided in paragraph (b) of § 20.6161-1, and the amount of the tax for which the extension is granted, with the additions thereto, shall be paid on or before the expiration of the period of extension without the necessity of notice and demand from the district director.

(b) Notice of the exercise of the election to postpone the payment of the tax attributable to a reversionary or remainder interest should be filed with the district director before the date prescribed for payment of the tax. The notice of election may be made in the form of a letter addressed to the district director. There shall be filed with the notice of election a certified copy of the will or other instrument under which the reversionary or remainder interest was created, or a copy verified by the executor if the instrument is not filed of record. The district director may require the submission of such additional proof as he deems necessary to disclose the complete facts. If the duration of the precedent interest is dependent upon the life of any person, the notice of election must show the date of birth of that person.

(c) If the decedent's gross estate consists of both a reversionary or remainder interest in property and other property, the tax attributable to the reversionary or remainder interest, within the meaning of this section, is an amount which bears the same ratio to the total tax as the value of the reversionary or remainder interest (reduced as provided in the following sentence) bears to the entire gross estate (reduced as provided in the last sentence of this paragraph). In applying this ratio, the value of the reversionary or remainder interest is reduced by (1) the amount of claims, mortgages, and indebtedness which is a lien upon such interest; (2) losses in respect of such interest during the settlement of the estate which are deductible under the provisions of section 2054 or section 2106(a)(1); (3) any amount deductible in respect of such interest under section 2055 or 2106(a)(2) for charitable, etc., transfers; and (4) the portion of the marital deduction allowed under the provisions of section 2056 on account of bequests, etc., of such interests to the decedent's surviving spouse. Likewise, in applying the ratio, the value of the gross estate is reduced by such deductions having similar relationship to the items comprising the gross estate.

(d) For provisions requiring the payment of interest during the period of the extension occurring before July 1, 1975, see section 6601(b) prior to its amendment by section 7(d)(1) of the Act of Jan. 3, 1975 (Pub. L. 93-625, 88 Stat. 2115). For provisions requiring the furnishing of security for the payment of the tax for which the extension is granted, see paragraph (b) of § 20.6165-1. For provisions concerning the time within which credit for State and foreign death taxes on such a reversionary or remainder interest may be taken, see section 2015 and the regulations thereunder. [Reg. § 20.6163-1.]

☐ [*T.D.* 6296, 6-23-58. *Amended by T.D.* 6526, 1-18-61, *T.D.* 6716, 3-25-64, *T.D.* 6736, 5-27-64, *T.D.* 7238, 12-28-72, *and T.D.* 7384, 10-21-75.]

[Reg. § 20.6165-1]

§ 20.6165-1. Bonds where time to pay tax or deficiency has been extended.—(a) *Extensions under sections 6161 and 6163(b) of time to pay tax or deficiency.*—If an extension of time for payment of tax or deficiency is granted under section 6161 or 6163(b), the district director may, if he deems it necessary, require the executor to furnish a bond for the payment of the amount in respect of which the extension is granted in accordance with the terms of the extension. However, such bond shall not exceed double the amount with respect to which the extension is granted. For other provisions relating to bonds required where extensions of time to pay estate taxes or deficiencies are granted under sections 6161 and 6163(b), see the regulations under section 7101 contained in Part 301 of this chapter (Regulations on Procedure and Administration).

(b) *Extensions under section 6163 of time to pay estate tax attributable to reversionary or remainder interests.*—As a prerequisite to the postponement of the payment of the tax attributable to a reversionary or remainder interest as provided in § 20.6163-1, a bond equal to double the amount of the tax and interest for the estimated duration of the precedent interest must be furnished conditioned upon the payment of the tax and interest accrued thereon within six months after the termination of the precedent interest. If after the acceptance of a bond it is determined that the amount of the tax attributable to the reversionary or remainder interest was understated in the bond, a new bond or a supplemental bond may be required, or the tax, to the extent of the understatement, may be collected. The bond must be conditioned upon the principal or surety promptly notifying the district director when the precedent interest terminates and upon the principal or surety notifying the district director during the month of September of each year as to the continuance of the precedent interest, if the duration of the precedent interest is dependent upon the life or lives of any person or persons, or is otherwise indefinite. For other provisions relating to bonds where an extension of time has been granted for paying the tax, see the regulations under section 7101 contained in Part 301 of this chapter (Regulations on Procedure and Administration). [Reg. § 20.6165-1.]

☐ [*T.D.* 6296, 6-23-58. *Amended by T.D.* 6526, 1-18-61, *T.D.* 6600, 5-28-62.]

[Reg. § 25.6165-1]

§ 25.6165-1. Bonds where time to pay tax or deficiency has been extended.—If an extension of time for payment of tax or deficiency is granted under section 6161, the district director may, if he deems it necessary, require a bond for the payment of the amount in respect of which the extension is granted in accordance with the terms of the extension. However, such bond shall not exceed double the amount with respect to which the extension is granted. For provisions relating to form of bonds, see the regulations under section 7101 contained in Part 301 of this chapter (Regulations on Procedure and Administration). [Reg. § 25.6165-1.]

□ [*T.D.* 6334, 11-14-58. *Amended by T.D.* 6600, 5-28-62.]

[Reg. § 20.6166-1]

§ 20.6166-1. Election of alternate extension of time for payment of estate tax where estate consists largely of interest in closely held business.—(a) *In general.*—Section 6166 allows an executor to elect to extend payment of part or all of the portion of the estate tax which is attributable to a closely held business interest (as defined in section 6166(b)(1)). If it is made at the time the estate tax return is filed, the election is applicable both to the tax originally determined to be due and to certain deficiencies. If no election is made when the estate tax return is filed, up to the full amount of certain later deficiencies (but not any tax originally determined to be due) may be paid in installments.

(b) *Time and manner of election.*—The election provided under section 6166(a) is made by attaching to a timely filed estate tax return a notice of election containing the following information:

(1) The decedent's name and taxpayer identification number as they appear on the estate tax return;

(2) The amount of tax which is to be paid in installments;

(3) The date selected for payment of the first installment;

(4) The number of annual installments, including the first installment, in which the tax is to be paid;

(5) The properties shown on the estate tax return which constitute the closely held business interest (identified by schedule and item number); and

(6) The facts which formed the basis for the executor's conclusion that the estate qualifies for payment of the estate tax in installments. In the absence of a statement in the notice of election as to the amount of tax to be paid in installments, the date selected for payment of the first installment, or the number of installments, the election is presumed to be for the maximum amount so payable and for payment thereof in 10 equal installments, the first of which is due on the date which is 5 years after the date prescribed in section 6151(a) for payment of estate tax.

(c) *Treatment of certain deficiencies.*—(1) *No election before assessment of deficiency.*—Where a deficiency is assessed and no election, including a protective election, has been made under section 6166(a) to pay any tax in installments, the executor may elect under section 6166(h) to pay the portion of the deficiency attributable to the closely held business interest in installments. However, this is true only if the estate qualifies under section 6166 based upon values as finally determined (or agreed to following examination of a return). Such an election is exercised by filing a notice of election with the Internal Revenue Service office where the estate tax return was filed. The notice of election must be filed within 60 days after issuance of notice and demand for payment of the deficiency, and it must contain the same information as is required under paragraph (b) of this section. The notice of election is to be accompanied by payment of the amount of tax and interest, the date for payment of which has arrived as determined under paragraphs (e) and (f) of this section, plus any amount of unpaid tax and interest which is not attributable to the closely held business interest and which is not eligible for further extension (or currently extended) under another section (other than section 6166A).

(2) *Election made with estate tax return.*—If the executor makes an election under section 6166(a) (other than a protective election) at the time the estate tax return is filed and a deficiency is later assessed, the portion of the deficiency which is attributable to the closely held business interest (but not any accrued interest thereon) will be prorated to the installments payable pursuant to the original section 6166(a) election. Any part of the deficiency prorated to an installment, the date for payment of which has arrived, is due upon notice and demand. Interest for any such period, including the deferral period, is payable upon notice and demand.

(3) *Portion of deficiency attributable to closely held business interest.*—Only that portion of any deficiency which is attributable to a closely held business interest may be paid in installments under section 6166. The amount of any deficiency which is so attributable is the difference between the amount of tax which the executor has previously elected to pay in installments under section 6166 and the maximum amount of tax which the executor could have elected to pay in installments on the basis of a return which reflects the adjustments that resulted in the deficiency.

(d) *Protective election.*—A protective election may be made to defer payment of any portion of tax remaining unpaid at the time values are finally determined (or agreed to following examination of a return) and any deficiencies attributable to the closely held business interest (within the meaning of paragraph (c)(3) of this section). Extension of tax payments pursuant to this election is contingent upon final values meeting the requirements of section 6166. A protective election does not, however, extend the time for payment of any amount of tax. Rules for such extensions are contained in sections 6161, 6163, and 6166A. A protective election is made by filing a notice of election with a timely filed estate tax return stating that the election is being made. Within 60 days after values are finally determined (or agreed to following examination of a return), a final notice of election which sets forth the information required under paragraph (b) of this section must be filed with the Internal Revenue Service office where the original estate tax return was filed. That notice of final election is to be accompanied by payment of any amount of previously unpaid tax and interest, the date for payment of which has arrived as determined under paragraphs (e) and (f) of this section, plus any amount of unpaid tax and interest which is not attributable to the closely held business interest and which is not eligible for further extension (or currently extended) under another section (other than section 6166A).

(e) *Special rules.*—(1) *Effect of deficiencies and protective elections upon payment.*—Upon election to extend the time for payment of a deficiency or upon final determination of values following a protective election, the executor must prorate the tax or deficiency attributable to the closely held business interest among all installments. All amounts attributed to installments which would have been due had the election been made at the time the tax was due to be paid under section 6151(a) and all accrued interest must be paid at the time the election is made.

(2) *Determination of date for payment of first installment.*—The executor may defer payment of tax (but not interest) for any period up to 5 years from the date determined under section 6151(a) for payment of the estate tax. The date chosen for payment of the first installment of tax is not required to be on an annual anniversary of the original due date of the tax; however, it must be the date within any month which corresponds to the day of the month determined under section 6151(a).

(f) *Rule for computing interest.*—Section 6601(j) provides a special 4 percent interest rate for the amount of tax (including deficiencies) which is to be paid in installments under section 6166. This special interest rate applies only to that amount of tax which is to be paid in installments and which does not exceed the limitation of section 6601(j)(2). Where payment of a greater amount of tax than is subject to section 6601(j)(2) is extended under section 6166, each installment is deemed to be comprised of both tax subject to the 4 percent interest rate and tax subject to the rate otherwise prescribed by section 6621. The percentage of any installment subject to the special 4 percent rate is equal to the percentage of the total tax payable in installments which is subject to the 4 percent rate. Where an election is made under the provisions of paragraphs (b) or (c)(1) of this section, the 4 percent rate applies from the date on which the estate tax was originally due to be paid. If only a protective election is made, section 6601(j) applies to the amount which is to be paid in installments, limited to the amount of any deficiency, from the due date for payment of estate tax. After the date upon which the section 6166 election is made final, section 6601(j) applies to the entire amount to be paid in installments.

(g) *Relation of section 6166 and 6166A.*—No election may be made under section 6166 if an election under section 6166A applies with respect to an estate. For example, no election can be made under section 6166(h) where an executor has made an election under section 6166A. If an election is timely made under either section 6166 or section 6166A, however, a protective election can be made under the other section at the same time. If the executor then files a timely notice of final election under the section protectively elected and pays any amounts determined to be due currently following final determination of (or agreement as to) estate tax values, the original election under the other provision will be deemed never to have applied to the estate.

(h) *Special rule for estates for which elections under section 6166 are made on or before August 30, 1980.*—An election to extend payment of estate tax under section 6166 that is made on or before August 30, 1980 may be revoked. To revoke an election, the executor must file a notice of revocation with the Internal Revenue Service office where the original estate tax return was filed on or before January 31, 1981 (or if earlier, the date on which the period of limitation on assessment expires). This notice of revocation must contain the decedent's name, date of death, and taxpayer identification number, and is to be accompanied by remittance of any additional amount of estate tax and interest determined to be due.

(i) *Examples.*—The provisions of this section may be illustrated by the following examples:

Example (1)—(i). Based upon values shown on decedent A's timely filed estate tax return, 60 percent of the value of A's adjusted gross estate consisted of a farm which was a closely held business within the meaning of section 6166. A's executor, B, made a protective election under section 6166 when he filed A's estate tax return. B also applied for an extension of time under section 6161 to pay $15,000 of the $30,000 of estate tax shown due on the return. The requested extension was granted and was renewed at the end of 1 year. Eighteen months after the return was filed and after examination of A's estate tax return, the value of the farm was found to constitute 67 percent of the adjusted gross estate. B entered into an agreement consenting to the values as established on examination and to a deficiency of $5,000. B then filed a final notice of election under section 6166, choosing a 5-year deferral followed by 10 annual installment payments and thereby terminated his extension under section 6161 because that amount of tax was then included under the section 6166 election. B could have extended payment of 67 percent of the total estate tax, or $23,450. $23,450 is eligible for installment payments under section 6166 and the section 6166 election is considered to be for that amount. B is considered to have prepaid $3,450 of tax since only $20,000 of tax remained unpaid. The $3,450 is attributed to the first installment of $2,345 and to $1,105 of the second installment which would have been payable under the section 6166 election.

(ii) Had B been granted an extension of time under section 6161 to pay $20,000 of tax, $25,000 would remain unpaid when the final section 6166 election is made. Payment of the full $23,450 (67 percent) of tax which is attributable to the closely held business interest is included under the section 6166 election. The balance of unpaid tax ($1,550) is due upon expiration of the estate's section 6161 extension.

(iii) Assume the facts under example (1)(i). B must pay all unpaid accrued interest with his notice of final election. Since only 18 months have passed, no installments of tax are due. Interest on the $5,000 deficiency is computed at 4 percent per annum for the entire 18 months, and interest for 12 months of that period is currently due to be paid. Interest for the remaining 6 months is due at the next succeeding date for payment of interest. Interest on the $15,000 of tax extended under section 6161 is computed at the rate determined under section 6621 until the date of the final section 6166 election and is due upon termination of the section 6161 extension. After that date, the interest on the $15,000 will also accrue at 4 percent per annum.

Example (2). Assume the facts as in example (1), except B initially made an election under section 6166A and made no protective election under section 6166. Following final determination of values, B is not permitted to make any election under section 6166; however, had B protectively elected section 6166 at the time he made the section 6166A election, he could have terminated the section 6166A election and finally elected under section 6166. In such a case, the full $23,450 of tax attributable to the farm would have been eligible for extension under section 6166. The 4 percent interest rate would apply to the $5,000 deficiency from the original due date of the tax, and, as with the extension under section 6161, it would apply to the amounts extended under section 6166A only from the date on which the election under section 6166 was finalized.

Example (3). C died in 1977. His estate owes Federal estate taxes of $750,000, $500,000 of which is attributable to a closely held business interest. Payment of the $500,000 was extended under section 6166. A 5-year deferral followed by 10 annual installment payments was chosen by C's executor. Under paragraph (f) of this section, only 63.16 percent of each installment will be subject to the special 4 percent interest rate and the remainder will be subject to the rate determined under section 6621. The same rule applies in computing interest for the 5 years during which payment of tax is deferred. (This is so because the 4 percent interest rate applies only to a maximum of $345,800 of tax less the $30,000 of credit allowable under section 2010(a) rather than to the entire $500,000 extended amount.) [Reg. § 20.6166-1.]

☐ [*T.D.* 7710, 7-28-80.]

[Reg. § 20.6166A-1]

§ 20.6166A-1. Extension of time for payment of estate tax where estate consists largely of interest in closely held business.—(a) *In general.*—Section 6166 provides that where the value of an interest in a closely held business, which is included in the gross estate of a decedent who was a citizen or resident of the United States at the time of his death, exceeds either (1) 35 percent of the value of the gross estate, or (2) 50 percent of the taxable estate, the executor may elect to pay part or all of the Federal estate tax in installments. The election to pay the tax in installments applies to deficiencies in tax as well as to the tax shown on the return, unless the deficiency is due to negligence, to intentional disregard of rules and regulations, or to fraud with intent to evade tax. Except as otherwise provided in section 6166(i) and § 20.6166-4, the provisions of section 6166 and this section apply only if the due date of the return is after September 2, 1958. See § 20.6166-4 for special rules applicable where the decedent died after August 16, 1954, and the due date of the return was on or before September 2, 1958. See also § 20.6075-1 for the due date of the return, and § 20.6166-2 for definition of the term "interest in a closely held business." Since the election must be made on or before the due date of the return, the provisions of section 6166 will not apply to a deficiency in a case where, for whatever reason, no election was made to pay in installments the tax shown on the return. However, see paragraph (e)(3) of this section concerning a protective election. The general administrative provisions of subtitle F of the Code are applicable in connection with an election by the executor to pay the estate tax in installments in the same manner in which they are applied in a case where an extension of time under section 6161 is granted for payment of the tax. See paragraph(a) of § 20.6165-1 for provisions requiring the furnishing of security for the payment of the tax in cases where an extension is granted under section 6161.

(b) *Limitation on amount of tax payable in installments.*—The amount of estate tax which the executor may elect to pay in installments is limited to an amount A, which bears the same ratio to B (the gross Federal estate tax, reduced by the credits authorized by sections 2011 through 2014 and any death tax convention) as C (the value of the interest in a closely held business which is included in the gross estate) bears to D (the value of the gross estate). Stated algebraically, the limitation (A) equals

$$\frac{\text{value of interest in a closely held business which is included in the gross estate (C)}}{\text{value of gross estate (D)}} \times \text{gross Federal estate tax, reduced by the credits authorized by sections 2011 through 2014 and any death tax convention (B).}$$

The executor may elect to pay in installments an amount less than the amount computed under the limitation in this paragraph. For example, if the total estate tax payable is $100,000 and the amount computed under the limitation in this paragraph is $60,000, the executor may elect to pay in installments some lesser sum such as $30,000, in which event the executor must pay $73,000 to the district director on or before the date prescribed by section 6151(a) for payment of the tax. Of such payment, $70,000 represents tax which the executor either could not elect to pay in installments or did not choose to so elect, and $3,000 represents a payment of the first installment of the tax which the executor elected to pay in installments.

(c) *Number of installments and dates for payment.*—The executor may elect to pay part or all of the tax (determined after application of the limitation contained in paragraph (b) of this section) in two or more, but not exceeding 10, equal annual installments. The first installment shall be paid on or before the date prescribed by section 6151(a) for payment of the tax (see paragraph (a) of § 20.6151-1), and each succeeding installment shall be paid on or before the date which is one year after the date prescribed for the payment of the preceding installment. See § 20.6166-3 for the circumstances under which the privilege of paying the tax in installments will terminate.

(d) *Deficiencies.*—The amount of a deficiency which may be paid in installments shall not exceed the difference between the amount of tax which the executor elected to pay in installments and the maximum amount of tax (determined under paragraph (b) of this section) which the executor could have elected to pay in installments on the basis of a return which reflects the adjustments which resulted in the deficiency. This amount is then prorated to the installments in which the executor elected to pay the tax. The part of the deficiency prorated to installments not yet due shall be paid at the same time as, and as a part of, such installments. The part of the deficiency prorated to installments already paid or due shall be paid upon notice and demand from the district director. At the time the executor receives such notice and demand he may, of course, prepay the portions of the deficiency which have been prorated to installments not yet due. See paragraph (h) of this section.

(e) *Notice of election.*—(1) *Filing of notice.*—The notice of election to pay the estate tax in installments shall be filed with the district director on or before the due date of the return. However, if the due date of the return is after September 2, 1958, but before November 3, 1958, the election will be considered as timely made if the notice is filed with the district director on or before November 3, 1958. See § 20.6075-1 for the due date of the return.

(2) *Form of notice.*—The notice of election to pay the estate tax in installments may be in the form of a letter addressed to the district director. The executor shall state in the notice the amount of tax which he elects to pay in installments, and the total number of installments (including the installment due 9 months (15 months, in the case of a decedent dying before January 1, 1971) after the date of the decedent's death) in which he elects to pay the tax. The properties in the gross estate which constitute the decedent's interest in a closely held business should be listed in the notice, and identified by the schedule and item number at which they appear on the estate tax return. The notice should set forth the facts which formed the basis for the executor's conclusion that the estate qualifies for the payment of the estate tax in installments.

(3) *Protective election.*—In a case where the estate does not qualify under section 6166(a) on the basis of the values as returned, or where the return shows no tax as due, an election may be made, contingent upon the values as finally determined meeting the percentage requirements set forth in section 6166(a), to pay in installments any portion of the estate tax, including a deficiency, which may be unpaid at the time of such final determination and which does not exceed the limitation provided in section 6166(b). The protective election must be made on or before the due date of the return and should state that it is a protective election. In the absence of a statement in the protective election as to the amount of tax to be paid in installments and the number of installments, the election will be presumed to be made for the maximum amount so payable and for the payment thereof in 10 equal annual installments, the first of which would have been due on the date prescribed in section 6151(a) for payment of the tax. The unpaid portion of the tax which may be paid in installments is prorated to the installments which would have been due if the provisions of section 6166(a) had applied to the tax, if any, shown on the return. The part of the unpaid portion of the tax so prorated to installments the date for payment of which would not have arrived before the deficiency is assessed shall be paid at the time such installments would have been due. The part of the unpaid portion of the tax so prorated to any installment the date for payment of which would have arrived before the deficiency is assessed shall be paid upon receipt of notice and demand from the district director. At the time the executor receives such notice and demand he may, of course, prepay the unpaid portions of the tax which have been prorated to installments not yet due. See paragraph (h) of this section.

(f) *Time for paying interest.*—Under the provisions of section 6601, interest at the annual rate referred to in the regulations under section 6621 shall be paid on the unpaid balance of the estate tax which the executor has elected to pay in installments, and on the unpaid balance of any deficiency prorated to the installments. Interest on such unpaid balance of estate tax shall be paid annually at the same time as, and as a part of, each installment of the tax. Accordingly, interest is computed on the entire unpaid balance for the period from the preceding installment date to the current installment date, and is paid with the current installment. In making such a computation, proper adjustment shall be made for any advance payments made during the period, whether the advance payments are voluntary or are brought about by the operation of section 6166(h)(2). In computing the annual interest payment, the portion of any deficiency which is prorated to installments the date for payment of which has not arrived shall be added to the unpaid balance at the beginning of the annual period during which the assessment of the deficiency occurs. Interest on such portion of the deficiency for the period from the original due date of the tax to the date fixed for the payment of the last installment preceding the date of assessment of a deficiency shall be paid upon notice and demand from the district director. Any extension of time under section 6161(a)(2) (on account of undue hardship to the estate) for payment of an installment will not extend the time for payment of the interest which is due on the installment date.

(g) *Extensions of time for payment in hardship cases.*—The provisions of section 6161, under which extensions of time may be granted for payment of estate tax in cases involving undue hardship, apply to both the portion of the tax which may be paid in installments under section 6166 and the portion of the tax which is not so payable. Therefore, in a case involving undue hardship, the executor may elect under section 6166 to pay in installments the portion of the tax which is attributable to the interest in the closely held business and, in addition, may file an application under section 6161 for an extension of time to pay both the portion of the tax which is not attributable to the interest in the closely held business and such of the installments as are payable within the period of the requested extension. If an executor files a notice of election to pay the tax in installments and thereafter it is determined that the estate does not qualify for the privilege of paying the tax in installments, the executor is not deprived of the right to request an extension under section 6161 of time for payment of the tax to which the purported election applied. See §20.6161-1 for the circumstances under which a timely filed election to pay the tax in installments will be treated as a timely filed application for an extension of time to pay the tax on account of undue hardship to the estate.

(h) *Prepayments.*—Voluntary prepayment may be made at any time of all, or of any part, of the unpaid portion of the tax (including deficiencies) payable in installments. Voluntary prepayments shall be applied in payment of such installments, installment, or part of an installment as the person making the prepayment shall designate. For purposes of this paragraph, a payment described in paragraph (d)(2) of §20.6166-3 of tax in an amount not less than the amount of money or other property distributed in a section 303 redemption is considered to be a voluntary prepayment to the extent paid before the date prescribed for payment of the first installment after the redemption or, if paid on the date prescribed for payment of such installment, to the extent it exceeds the amount due on the installment. See paragraph (b)(3) of §20.6166-3 for the application to be made of the prepayment required by section 6166(h)(2). [Reg. §20.6166A-1.]

☐ [*T.D.* 6522, 12-28-60. *Amended by T.D.* 7238, 12-28-72 *and T.D.* 7384, 10-21-75. *Redesignated by T.D.* 7710, 7-28-80.]

[Reg. §20.6166A-2]

§20.6166A-2. Definition of an interest in a closely held business.—(a) *In general.*—For purposes of §§20.6166-1, 20.6166-3, and 20.6166-4, the term "interest in a closely held business" means

(1) An interest as a proprietor in a trade or business carried on as a proprietorship.

(2) An interest as a partner in a partnership carrying on a trade or business if 20 percent or more of the total capital interest in the partnership is included in determining the decedent's gross estate or if the partnership had 10 or less partners.

(3) Stock in a corporation carrying on a trade or business if 20 percent or more in value of the voting stock of the corporation is included in determining the decedent's gross estate or if the corporation had 10 or less shareholders.

(b) *Number of partners or shareholders.*—The number of partners of the partnership or shareholders of the corporation is determined as of the time immediately before the decedent's death. Where an interest in a partnership, or stock in a corporation, is the community property of husband and wife, both the husband and the wife are counted as partners or shareholders in arriving at the number of partners or shareholders. Similarly, if stock is held by co-owners, tenants in common, tenants by the entirety, or joint tenants, each co-owner, tenant in common, tenant by the entirety, or joint tenant is counted as a shareholder.

(c) *Carrying on a trade or business.*—(1) In order for the interest in a partnership or the stock of a corporation to qualify as an interest in a closely held business it is necessary that the partnership or the corporation be engaged in carrying on a trade or business at the time of the decedent's death. However, it is not necessary that all the assets of the partnership or the corporation be utilized in the carrying on of the trade or business.

(2) In the case of a trade or business carried on as a proprietorship, the interest in the closely held business includes only those assets of the decedent which were actually utilized by him in the trade or business. Thus, if a building was used by the decedent in part as a personal residence and in part for the carrying on of a mercantile business, the part of the building used as a residence does not form any part of the interest in the closely held business. Whether an asset will be considered as used in the trade or business will depend on the facts and circumstances of the particular case. For example, if a bank account was held by the decedent in his individual name (as distinguished from the trade or business name) and it can be clearly shown that the amount on deposit represents working capital of the business as well as nonbusiness funds (e.g., receipts from investments, such as dividends and interest), then that part of the amount on deposit which represents working capital of the business will constitute a part of the interest in the closely held business. On the other hand, if a bank account is held by the decedent in the trade or business name and it can be shown that the amount represents nonbusiness funds as well

as working capital, then only that part of the amount on deposit which represents working capital of the business will constitute a part of the interest in the closely held business. In a case where an interest in a partnership or stock of a corporation qualifies as an interest in a closely held business, the decedent's entire interest in the partnership, or the decedent's entire holding of stock in the corporation, constitutes an interest in a closely held business even though a portion of the partnership or corporate assets is used for a purpose other than the carrying on of a trade or business.

(d) *Interests in two or more closely held businesses.*—For purposes of paragraphs (a) and (b) of §20.6166-1 and paragraphs (d) and (e) of §20.6166-3, interests in two or more closely held businesses shall be treated as an interest in a single closely held business if more than 50 percent of the total value of each such business is included in determining the value of the decedent's gross estate. For the purpose of the 50 percent requirement set forth in the preceding sentence, an interest in a closely held business which represents the surviving spouse's interest in community property shall be considered as having been included in determining the value of the decedent's gross estate. [Reg. §20.6166A-2.]

□ [*T.D.* 6522, 12-28-60. *Redesignated by T.D.* 7710, 7-28-80.]

[Reg. §20.6166A-3]

§20.6166A-3. Acceleration of payment.—(a) *In general.*—Under the circumstances described in this section all or a part of the tax which the executor has elected to pay in installments shall be paid before the dates fixed for payment of the installments. Upon an estate's having undistributed net income described in paragraph (b) of this section for any taxable year after its fourth taxable year, the executor shall pay an amount equal to such undistributed net income in liquidation of the unpaid portion of the tax payable in installments. Upon the happening of any of the events described in paragraphs (c), (d), and (e) of this section, any unpaid portion of the tax payable in installments shall be paid upon notice and demand from the district director.

(b) *Undistributed net income of estate.*—(1) If an estate has undistributed net income for any taxable year after its fourth taxable year, the executor shall pay an amount equal to such undistributed net income in liquidation of the unpaid portion of the tax payable in installments. The amount shall be paid to the district director on or before the time prescribed for the filing of the estate's income tax return for such taxable year. For this purpose extensions of time granted for the filing of the income tax return are taken into consideration in determining the time prescribed for filing the return and making such payment. In determining the number of taxable years, a short taxable year is counted as if it were a full taxable year.

(2) The term "undistributed net income" of the estate for any taxable year for purposes of this section is the amount by which the distributable net income of the estate, as defined in section 643, exceeds the sum of—

(i) The amount for such year specified in section 661(a)(1) and (2),

(ii) The amount of the Federal income tax imposed on the estate for such taxable year under chapter 1 of the Code, and

(iii) The amount of the Federal estate tax, including interest thereon, paid for the estate during such taxable year (other than any amount paid by reason of the application of this acceleration rule).

(3) The payment described in subparagraph (1) of this paragraph shall be applied against the total unpaid portion of the tax which the executor elected to pay in installments, and shall be divided equally among the installments due after the date of such payment. The application of this subparagraph may be illustrated by the following example:

Example. The decedent died on January 1, 1959. The executor elects under section 6166 to pay tax in the amount of $100,000 in 10 installments of $10,000. The first installment is due on April 1, 1960. The estate files its income tax returns on a calendar year basis. For its fifth taxable year (calendar year 1963) it has undistributed net income of $6,000. If the prepayment of $6,000 required by section 6166(h)(2)(A), and due on or before April 15, 1964, is paid before the fifth installment (due April 1, 1964), the $6,000 is apportioned equally among installments 5 through 10, leaving $9,000 as the amount due on each of such installments. However, if the prepayment of $6,000 is paid after the fifth installment, it is apportioned equally among installments 6 through 10, leaving $8,800 as the amount due on each of such installments.

(c) *Failure to pay installment on or before due date.*—If any installment of tax is not paid on or before the date fixed for its payment (including any extension of time for the payment thereof), the whole of the unpaid portion of the tax which is payable in installments becomes due and shall be paid upon notice and demand from the district director. See paragraph (c) of §20.6166-1 for the dates fixed for the payment of installments. See also §20.6161-1 for the circumstances under which an extension of time for the payment of an installment will be granted.

(d) *Withdrawal of funds from business.*—(1) In any case where money or other property is withdrawn from the trade or business and the aggregate withdrawals of money or other property equal or exceed 50 percent of the value of the trade or business, the privilege of paying the tax in installments terminates and the whole of the unpaid portion of the tax which is payable in installments becomes due and shall be paid upon notice and demand from the district director. The withdrawals of money or other property from the trade or business must be in connection with the interest therein included in the gross estate, and must equal or exceed 50 percent of the value of the entire trade or business (and not just 50 percent of the value of the interest therein included in the gross estate). The withdrawal must be a withdrawal of money or other property which constitutes "included property" within the meaning of that term as used in paragraph (d) of § 20.2032-1. The provisions of this section do not apply to the withdrawal of money or other property which constitutes "excluded property" within the meaning of that term as used in such paragraph (d).

(2) If a distribution in redemption of stock is (by reason of the provisions of section 303 or so much of section 304 as relates to section 303) treated for income tax purposes as a distribution in full payment in exchange for the stock so redeemed, the amount of such distribution is not counted as a withdrawal of money or other property made with respect to the decedent's interest in the trade or business for purposes of determining whether the withdrawals of money or other property made with respect to the decedent's interest in the trade or business for purposes of determining whether the withdrawals of money or other property made with respect to the decedent's interest in the trade or business equal or exceed 50 percent of the value of the trade or business. However, in the case described in the preceding sentence the value of the trade or business for purposes of applying the rule set forth in subparagraph (1) of this paragraph is the value thereof reduced by the proportionate part thereof which such distribution represents. The proportionate part of the value of the trade or business which the distribution represents is determined at the time of the distribution, but the reduction in the value of the trade or business represented by it relates back to the time of the decedent's death, or the alternate valuation date if an election is made under section 2032, for purposes of determining whether other withdrawals with respect to the decedent's interest in the trade or business constitute withdrawals equaling or exceeding 50 percent of the value of the trade or business. See example (3) of paragraph (e)(6) of this section for illustration of this principle. The rule stated in the first sentence of this subparagraph does not apply unless after the redemption, but on or before the date prescribed for payment of the first installment which becomes due after the redemption, there is paid an amount of estate tax not less than the amount of money or other property distributed. Where there are a series of section 303 redemptions, each redemption is treated separately and the failure of one redemption to qualify under the rule stated in the first sentence of this subparagraph does not necessarily mean that another redemption will not qualify.

(3) The application of this paragraph may be illustrated by the following examples, in each of which the executor elected to pay the estate tax in installments:

Example (1). A, who died on July 1, 1957, owned an 80 percent interest in a partnership which qualified as an interest in a closely held business. B owned the other 20 percent interest in the partnership. On the date of A's death the value of the business was $200,000 and the value of A's interest therein was included in his gross estate at $160,000. On October 1, 1958, when the value of the business was the same as at A's death, the executor withdrew $80,000 from the business. On December 1, 1958, when the value of the remaining portion of the business was $160,000, the executor withdrew $20,000 from the business and B withdrew $10,000. On February 1, 1959, when the value of the then remaining portion of the business was $150,000 the executor withdrew $15,000. The withdrawals of money or other property from the trade or business with respect to the interest therein included in the gross estate are considered as not having equaled or exceeded 50 percent of the value of the trade or business until February 1, 1959. The executor is considered as having withdrawn 40 percent of the value of the trade or business on October 1, 1958, computed as follows:

$$\frac{\text{\$80,000 (withdrawal)}}{\text{\$200,000 (value of trade or business at time of withdrawal)}} \times 100 \text{ percent} = 40 \text{ percent}$$

Immediately following the October withdrawal the remaining portion of the business represents 60 percent of the value of the trade or business in existence at the time of A's death (100 percent less 40 percent withdrawn). The executor is considered as having withdrawn 7.5 percent of the value of the trade or business on December 1, 1958, and B as having withdrawn 3.75 percent of the value thereof at that time, computed as follows:

Executor's withdrawal—

$$\frac{\text{\$20,000 (withdrawal)}}{\text{\$160,000 (value of trade or business at time of withdrawal)}} \times 60 \text{ percent} = 7.5 \text{ percent}$$

B's withdrawal—

$$\frac{\text{\$10,000 (withdrawal)}}{\text{\$160,000 (value of trade or business at time of withdrawal)}} \times 60 \text{ percent} = 3.75 \text{ percent}$$

Immediately following the December withdrawal the then remaining portion of the business represented 48.75 percent of the value of the trade or business in existence at the time of A's death (100 percent less 40 percent withdrawn by executor in October, 7.5 percent withdrawn by executor in December, and 3.75 percent withdrawn by B in December). It should be noted that while at this point the total withdrawals by the executor and B from the trade or business exceed 50 percent of the value thereof, the aggregate of the withdrawals by the executor were less than 50 percent of the value of the trade or business. Also it should be noted that while the total withdrawals by the executor exceeded 50 percent of the value of A's interest in the trade or business, they did not exceed 50 percent of the value of the entire trade or business. The executor is considered as having withdrawn 4.875 percent of the value of the trade or business on February 1, 1959, computed as follows:

$$\frac{\$15{,}000 \text{ (withdrawal)}}{\$150{,}000 \text{ (value of trade or business at time of withdrawal)}} \times 48.75 \text{ percent} = 4.875 \text{ percent}$$

As of February 1, 1959, the total withdrawals from the trade or business made with respect to A's interest therein was 52.375 percent of the value of the trade or business.

Example (2). The decedent's 40 percent interest in the XYZ partnership constituted an interest in a closely held business. Since the decedent's interest in the closely held business amounted to less than 50 percent of the value of the business, money or other property equaling or exceeding 50 percent of the value of the business could not be withdrawn from the decedent's interest in the business. Therefore, withdrawals of money or other property from this trade or business never would accelerate the payment of the tax under the provisions of this paragraph.

Example (3). The decedent died on September 1, 1957. He owned 100 shares of B Corporation (the total number of shares outstanding at the time of his death) and a 75 percent interest in a partnership of which C was the other partner. The B Corporation stock and the interest in the partnership together make up the interest in the closely held business which was included in the decedent's gross estate. The B Corporation stock was included in the gross estate at a value of $400,000 and the interest in the partnership was included at a value of $300,000. On November 1, 1957, at which time the value of the corporation's assets had not changed, in a section 303 redemption the executor surrendered 26 shares of B Corporation stock for $104,000. On December 1, 1957, at which time the value of the partnership's assets had not changed, the partners withdrew 90 percent of the assets of the partnership, with the executor receiving $270,000 and C receiving $90,000. The estate tax amounts to $240,000, of which the executor elected under section 6166 to pay $140,000 in 10 installments of $14,000 each. On December 1, 1958, the due date for paying the estate tax which was not payable in installments and for paying the first installment under section 6166, the executor paid estate tax of $114,000, of which $100,000 represented the tax not payable in installments and $14,000 represented the first installment. Inasmuch as after the section 303 distribution and on or before the due date of the first installment (December 1, 1958) after the section 303 distribution the executor paid as estate tax an amount not less than the amount of the distribution, the section 303 distribution does not constitute a withdrawal of money or other property from the business for purposes of section 6166(h)(1). Therefore, the value of the trade or business is reduced by the amount of the section 303 distribution. Accordingly, the value of the entire trade or business is $696,000, of which $400,000 represents the value of the partnership and $296,000 represents the value of the B Corporation stock. Since the executor is considered as having withdrawn only $270,000 (the withdrawal from the partnership) from the trade or business, the withdrawal of money or other property from the trade or business made with respect to the decedent's interest therein was 270,000/696,000 of the value of the entire trade or business, or less than 50 percent thereof.

(e) *Disposition of interest in business.*—(1) In any case where in the aggregate 50 percent or more of the decedent's interest in a closely held business has been distributed, sold, exchanged, or otherwise disposed of, the privilege of paying the tax in installments terminates and the whole of the unpaid portion of the tax which is payable in installments becomes due and shall be paid upon notice and demand from the district director. A transfer by the executor of an interest in a closely held business to a beneficiary or trustee named in the decedent's will or to an heir who is entitled to receive it under the applicable intestacy law does not constitute a distribution thereof for purposes of determining whether 50 percent or more of an interest in a closely held business has been distributed, sold, exchanged, or otherwise disposed of. However, a subsequent transfer of the interest by the beneficiary, trustee, or heir will constitute a distribution, sale, exchange, or other disposition thereof for such purposes. The disposition must be a disposition of an interest which constitutes "included property" within the meaning of that term as used in paragraph (d) of § 20.2032-1. The provisions of this section do not apply to the disposition of an interest which constitutes "excluded property" within the meaning of that term as used in such paragraph (d).

(2) The phrase "distributed, sold, exchanged, or otherwise disposed of" comprehends all possible ways by which an interest in a closely held business ceases to form a part of the gross estate. The term includes the surrender of a

stock certificate for corporate assets in complete or partial liquidation of a corporation pursuant to section 331. The term also includes the surrender of stock for stock pursuant to a transaction described in subparagraphs (A), (B), or (C) of section 368(a)(1). In general the term does not, however, extend to transactions which are mere changes in form. It does not include a transfer of assets to a corporation in exchange for its stock in a transaction with respect to which no gain or loss would be recognizable for income tax purposes under section 351. It does not include an exchange of stock in a corporation for stock in the same corporation or another corporation pursuant to a plan of reorganization described in subparagraphs (D), (E), or (F) of section 368(a)(1), nor to an exchange to which section 355 (or so much of section 356 as relates to section 355) applies. However, any stock received in an exchange to which the two preceding sentences apply shall for purposes of this paragraph be treated as an interest in a closely held business.

(3) An interest in a closely held business may be "distributed" by either a trustee who received it from the executor, or a trustee of an interest which is included in the gross estate under sections 2035 through 2038, or section 2041. See subparagraph (1) of this paragraph relative to the distribution of an interest by the executor to the person entitled to receive it under the decedent's will or an intestacy law.

(4) An interest in a closely held business may be "sold, exchanged, or otherwise disposed of" by (i) the executor; (ii) a trustee or other donee to whom the decedent in his lifetime transferred the interest included in his gross estate under sections 2035 through 2038, or section 2041; (iii) a beneficiary, trustee, or heir entitled to receive the property from the executor under the decedent's will or under the applicable law of descent and distribution, or to whom title to the interest passed directly under local law; (iv) a surviving joint tenant or tenant by the entirety; or (v) any other person.

(5) If a distribution in redemption of stock is (by reason of the provisions of section 303 or so much of section 304 as relates to section 303) treated for income tax purposes as a distribution in full payment in exchange for the stock redeemed, the stock so redeemed is not counted as distributed, sold, exchanged, or otherwise disposed of for purposes of determining whether 50 percent or more of the decedent's interest in a closely held business has been distributed, sold, exchanged, or otherwise disposed of. However, in the case described in the preceding sentence the interest in the closely held business for purposes of applying the rule set forth in subparagraph (1) of this paragraph is such interest reduced by the proportionate part thereof which the redeemed stock represents. The proportionate part of the interest which the redeemed stock represents is determined at the time of the redemption, but the reduction in the interest represented by it relates back to the time of the decedent's death, or the alternate valuation date if an election is made under section 2032, for purposes of determining whether other distributions, sales, exchanges, and dispositions of the decedent's interest in the closely held business equal or exceed in the aggregate 50 percent of such interest. See example (3) of subparagraph (6) of this paragraph for illustration of this principle. The rule stated in the first sentence of this subparagraph does not apply unless after the redemption, but on or before the date prescribed for payment of the first installment which becomes due after the redemption, there is paid an amount of estate tax not less than the amount of money or other property distributed. Where there are a series of section 303 redemptions, each redemption is treated separately and the failure of one redemption to qualify under the rule stated in the first sentence of this subparagraph does not necessarily mean that another redemption will not qualify.

(6) The application of this paragraph may be illustrated by the following examples, in each of which the executor elected to pay the tax in installments:

Example (1). The decedent died on October 1, 1957. He owned 8,000 of the 12,000 shares of D Corporation outstanding at the time of his death and 3,000 of the 5,000 shares of E Corporation outstanding at that time. The D Corporation stock was included in the gross estate at $50 per share, or a total of $400,000. The E Corporation stock was included in the gross estate at $100 per share, or a total of $300,000. On November 1, 1958, the executor sold the 3,000 shares of E Corporation and on February 1, 1959, he sold 1,000 shares of D Corporation. Since the decedent's shares of D Corporation and E Corporation together constituted the interest in a closely held business, the value of such interest was $700,000 ($400,000 plus $300,000) and the D Corporation stock represented 400,000/700,000 thereof and the E Corporation stock represented 300,000/700,000 thereof. While the sale of 3,000 shares of E Corporation on November 1, 1958, was a sale of the decedent's entire interest in E Corporation and a sale of more than 50 percent of the outstanding stock of E Corporation, nevertheless it constituted a sale of only 300,000/700,000 of the interest in the closely held business. The sale of 1,000 shares of D Corporation stock on February 1, 1959, represented a sale of 50,000/700,000 of the interest in the closely held business. The numerator of $50,000 is determined as follows:

$$\frac{\text{1,000 (shares sold)}}{\text{8,000 (shares owned)}} \times \$400{,}000 \quad \text{(value of shares owned, as included in gross estate)}$$

Taken together the two sales represented a sale of 50 percent (350,000/700,000) of the interest in the closely held business. Therefore, as of February 1, 1959 (the date of the sale of 1,000 shares of

E Corporation), 50 percent or more in value of the interest in the closely held business is considered as distributed, sold, exchanged, or otherwise disposed of.

Example (2). The decedent died on September 1, 1958. The interest owned by him in a closely held business consisted of 100 shares of the M Corporation. On February 1, 1959, in a section 303 redemption, 20 shares were redeemed for cash and an amount equivalent to the proceeds was paid on the Federal estate tax before the date of the next installment. On July 1, 1959, the executor sold 40 of the remaining shares of the stock. The section 303 redemption is not considered to be a distribution, sale, exchange, or other disposition of the portion of the interest represented by the 20 shares redeemed. As a result of the section 303 redemption the remaining 80 shares represent the decedent's entire interest in the closely held business for purposes of determining whether in the aggregate 50 percent or more of the interest in the closely held business has been distributed, sold, exchanged, or otherwise disposed of. The sale on July 1, 1959, of the 40 shares represents a sale of 50 percent of the interest in the closely held business.

Example (3). The facts are the same as in example (2) except that the 40 shares were sold on December 1, 1958 (before the section 303 redemption was made) instead of on July 1, 1959 (after the section 303 redemption was made). The sale of the 40 shares in December represents, as of that date, a sale of 40 percent of the interest in the closely held business. However, the section 303 redemption of 20 shares does not count as a distribution, sale, exchange, or other disposition of the interest, but it does reduce the interest to 80 shares (100 shares less 20 shares redeemed) for purposes of determining whether other distributions, sales, exchanges, and dispositions in the aggregate equal or exceed 50 percent of the interest in the closely held business. Since the reduction of the interest to 80 shares relates back to the time of the decedent's death, or the alternate valuation date if an election is made under section 2032, the sale of the 40 shares, as recomputed represents a sale of 50 percent of the interest. However, since the sale of the 40 shares did not represent a sale of 50 percent of the interest until the section 303 distribution was made, February 1, 1959 (the date of the section 303 distribution) is considered the date on which 50 percent of the interest was distributed, sold, exchanged, or otherwise disposed of.

(f) *Information to be furnished by executor.*—(1) If the executor acquires knowledge of the happening of any transaction described in paragraph (d) or (e) of this section which, in his opinion, standing alone or when taken together with other transactions of which he has knowledge, would result in

(i) Aggregate withdrawals of money or other property from the trade or business equal to or exceeding 50 percent of the value of the entire trade or business, or

(ii) Aggregate distributions, sales, exchanges, and other dispositions equal to or exceeding 50 percent of the interest in the closely held business which was included in the gross estate,

the executor shall so notify the district director, in writing, within 30 days of acquiring such knowledge.

(2) On the date fixed for payment of each installment of tax (determined without regard to any extension of time for the payment thereof), other than the final installment, the executor shall furnish the district director, in writing, with either

(i) A complete disclosure of all transactions described in paragraphs (d) and (e) of this section of which he has knowledge and which have not previously been made known by him to the district director, or

(ii) A statement that to the best knowledge of the executor all transactions described in paragraphs (d) and (e) of this section which have occurred have not produced a result described in subparagraph (1)(i) or (ii) of this paragraph.

(3) The district director may require the submission of such additional information as is deemed necessary to establish the estate's right to continue payment of the tax in installments. [Reg. § 20.6166A-3.]

☐ [*T.D.* 6522, 12-28-60. *Redesignated by T.D.* 7710, 7-28-80.]

[Reg. § 301.6211-1]

§ 301.6211-1. Deficiency defined.—(a) In the case of the income tax imposed by subtitle A of the Code, the estate tax imposed by chapter 11, subtitle B, of the Code, the gift tax imposed by chapter 12, subtitle B, of the Code, and any excise tax imposed by chapter 41, 42, 43, or 44 of the Code, the term "deficiency" means the excess of the tax (income, estate, gift, or excise tax as the case may be) over the sum of the amount shown as such tax by the taxpayer upon his return and the amounts previously assessed (or collected without assessment) as a deficiency; but such sum shall first be reduced by the amount of rebates made. If no return is made, or if the return (except a return of income tax pursuant to sec. 6014) does not show any tax, for the purpose of the definition "the amount shown as the tax by the taxpayer upon his return" shall be considered as zero. Accordingly, in any such case, if no deficiencies with respect to the tax have been assessed, or collected without assessment, and no rebates with respect to the tax have been made, the deficiency is the amount of the income tax imposed by subtitle A, the estate tax imposed by chapter 11, the gift tax imposed by chapter 12, or any excise tax imposed by chapter 41, 42, 43, or 44. Any amount shown as additional tax on an "amended return," so-called (other than amounts of additional tax which such return clearly indicates the taxpayer is protesting rather than admitting) filed after the due date of the return, shall be treated as an amount shown by the taxpayer "upon his return" for purposes of computing the amount of a deficiency.

* * *

(f) As used in section 6211, the term "rebate" means so much of an abatement, credit, refund, or other repayment as is made on the ground that the income tax imposed by subtitle A, the estate tax imposed by chapter 11, the gift tax imposed by chapter 12, or the excise tax imposed by chapter 41, 42, 43, or 44, is less than the excess of (1) the amount shown as the tax by the taxpayer upon the return increased by the amount previously assessed (or collected without assessment) as a deficiency over (2) the amount of rebates previously made. For example, assume that the amount of income tax shown by the taxpayer upon his return for the taxable year is $600 and the amount claimed as a credit under section 31 for income tax withheld at the source is $900. If the district director determines that the tax imposed by subtitle A is $600 and makes a refund of $300, no part of such refund constitutes a "rebate" since the refund is not made on the ground that the tax imposed by subtitle A is less than the tax shown on the return. If, however, the district director determines that the tax imposed by subtitle A is $500 and refunds $400, the amount of $100 of such refund would constitute a rebate since it is made on the ground that the tax imposed by subtitle A ($500) is less than the tax shown on the return ($600). The amount of such rebate ($100) would be taken into account in arriving at the amount of any deficiency subsequently determined. [Reg. § 301.6211-1.]

☐ [*T.D.* 6119, 12-31-54. *Amended by T.D.* 6498, 10-24-60; *T.D.* 7102, 3-23-71; *T.D.* 7498, 7-12-77; *T.D.* 7575, 12-15-78; *T.D.* 7838, 10-5-82 *and T.D.* 8628, 12-4-95.]

[Reg. § 301.6212-1]

§ 301.6212-1. Notice of deficiency.—(a) *General rule.*—If a district director or director of a service center (or regional director of appeals), determines that there is a deficiency in respect of income, estate, or gift tax imposed by subtitle A or B, or excise tax imposed by chapter 41, 42, 43, or 44, of the Code, such official is authorized to notify the taxpayer of the deficiency by either registered or certified mail.

(b) *Address for notice of deficiency.*—(1) *Income, gift, and chapter 41, 42, 43, and 44 taxes.*—Unless the district director for the district in which the return in question was filed has been notified under the provisions of section 6903 as to the existence of a fiduciary relationship, notice of a deficiency in respect of income tax, gift tax, or tax imposed by chapter 41, 42, 43, or 44 shall be sufficient if mailed to the taxpayer at his last known address, even though such taxpayer is deceased, or is under a legal disability, or, in the case of a corporation, has terminated its existence.

(2) *Joint income tax returns.*—If a joint income tax return has been filed by husband and wife, the district director (or assistant regional commissioner, appellate) may, unless the district director for the district in which such joint return was filed has been notified by either spouse that a separate residence has been established, send either a joint or separate notice of deficiency to the taxpayers at their last known address. If, however, the proper district director has been so notified, a separate notice of deficiency, that is, a duplicate original of the joint notice, must be sent by registered mail prior to September 3, 1958, and by either registered or certified mail on and after September 3, 1958, to each spouse at his or her last known address. The notice of separate residences should be addressed to the district director for the district in which the joint return was filed.

(3) *Estate tax.*—In the absence of notice, under the provisions of section 6903 as to the existence of a fiduciary relationship, to the district director for the district in which the estate tax return was filed, notice of a deficiency in respect of the estate tax imposed by chapter 11 of subtitle B shall be sufficient if addressed in the name of the decedent or other person subject to liability and mailed to his last known address.

(c) *Further deficiency letters restricted.*—If the district director or director of a service center (or regional director of appeals) mails to the taxpayer notice of a deficiency, and the taxpayer files a petition with the Tax Court within the prescribed period, no additional deficiency may be determined with respect to income tax for the same taxable year, gift tax for the same "calendar period" (as defined in § 25.2502-1(c)(1)), estate tax with respect to the taxable estate of the same decedent, chapter 41, 43, or 44 tax of the taxpayer for the same taxable year, section 4940 tax for the same taxable year, or chapter 42 tax of the taxpayer (other than under section 4940) with respect to the same act (or failure to act) to which such petition relates. This restriction shall not apply in the case of fraud, assertion of deficiencies with respect to any qualified tax (as defined in paragraph (b) of § 301.6361-4) in respect of which no deficiency was asserted for the taxable year in the notice, assertion of deficiencies with respect to the Federal tax when deficiencies with respect to only a qualified tax (and not the Federal tax) were asserted for the taxable year in the notice, assertion of greater deficiencies before the Tax Court as provided in section 6214(a), mathematical errors as provided in section 6213(b)(1), termination assessments in section 6851 or 6852, or jeopardy assessments as provided in section 6961(c). Solely for purposes of applying the restriction of section 6212(c), a notice of deficiency with respect to second tier tax under chapter 43 shall be deemed to be a notice of deficiency for the taxable year in which the taxable event occurs. See § 53.4963-1(e)(7)(iii) or (iv) for the date on which the taxable event occurs. [Reg. § 301.6212-1.]

☐ [*T.D.* 6119, 12-31-54. *Amended by T.D.* 6425, 11-10-59; *T.D.* 6498, 10-24-60; *T.D.* 7238, 12-28-72; *T.D.* 7577, 12-19-78; *T.D.* 7838, 10-5-82; *T.D.* 7910, 9-6-83; *T.D.* 8084, 5-1-86 *and T.D.* 8628, 12-4-95.]

[Reg. § 301.6213-1]

§ 301.6213-1. Restrictions applicable to deficiencies; petition to Tax Court.—(a) *Time for filing petition and restrictions on assessment.*—

(1) *Time for filing petition.*—Within 90 days after notice of the deficiency is mailed (or within 150 days after mailing in the case of such notice addressed to a person outside the States of the Union and the District of Columbia), as provided in section 6212, a petition may be filed with the Tax Court of the United States for a redetermination of the deficiency. In determining such 90-day or 150-day period, Saturday, Sunday, or a legal holiday in the District of Columbia is not counted as the 90th or 150th day. In determining the time for filing a petition with the Tax Court in the case of a notice of deficiency mailed to a resident of Alaska prior to 12:01 p.m., e.s.t., January 3, 1959, and in the case of a notice of deficiency mailed to a resident of Hawaii prior to 4:00 p.m. e.d.s.t., August 21, 1959, the term "States of the Union" does not include Alaska or Hawaii, respectively, and the 150-day period applies. In determining the time within which a petition to the Tax Court may be filed in the case of a notice of deficiency mailed to a resident of Alaska after 12:01 p.m., e.s.t., January 3, 1959, and in the case of a notice of deficiency mailed to a resident of Hawaii after 4:00 p.m., e.d.s.t., August 21, 1959, the term "States of the Union" includes Alaska and Hawaii, respectively, and the 90-day period applies.

(2) *Restrictions on assessment.*—Except as otherwise provided by this section, by sections 6851, 6852, and 6861(a) (relating to termination and jeopardy assessments), by section 6871(a) (relating to immediate assessment of claims for income, estate, and gift taxes in bankruptcy and receivership cases), or by section 7485 (in case taxpayer petitions for a review of a Tax Court decision without filing bond), no assessment of a deficiency in respect to a tax imposed by subtitle A or B or chapter 41, 42, 43, or 44 of the Code and no levy or proceeding in court for its collection shall be made until notice of deficiency has been mailed to the taxpayer, nor until the expiration of the 90-day or 150-day period within which a petition may be filed with the Tax Court, nor, if a petition has been filed with the Tax Court, until the decision of the Tax Court has become final. As to the date on which a decision of the Tax Court becomes final, see section 7481. Notwithstanding the provisions of section 7421(a), the making of an assessment or the beginning of a proceeding or levy which is forbidden by this paragraph may be enjoined by a proceeding in the proper court. In any case where the running of the time prescribed for filing a petition in the Tax Court with respect to a tax imposed by chapter 42 or 43 is suspended under section 6213(e), no assessment of a deficiency in respect of such tax shall be made until expiration of the entire period for filing the petition.

(b) *Exceptions to restrictions on assessment of deficiencies.*—(1) *Mathematical errors.*—If a taxpayer is notified of an additional amount of tax due on account of a mathematical error appearing upon the return, such notice is not deemed a notice of deficiency, and the taxpayer has no right to file a petition with the Tax Court upon the basis of such notice, nor is the assessment of such additional amount prohibited by section 6213(a).

(2) *Tentative carryback adjustments.*—(i) If the district director or the director of the regional service center determines that any amount applied, credited, or refunded under section 6411(b) with respect to an application for a tentative carryback adjustment is in excess of the overassessment properly attributable to the carryback upon which such application was based, the district director or the director of the regional service center may assess the amount of the excess as a deficiency as if such deficiency were due to a mathematical error appearing on the return. That is, the district director or the director of the regional service center may assess an amount equal to the excess, and such amount may be collected, without regard to the restrictions on assessment and collection imposed by section 6213(a). Thus, the district director or the director of the regional service center may assess such amount without regard to whether the taxpayer has been mailed a prior notice of deficiency. Either before or after assessing such an amount, the district director or the director of the regional service center will notify the taxpayer that such assessment has been or will be made. Such notice will not constitute a notice of deficiency, and the taxpayer may not file a petition with the Tax Court of the United States based on such notice. However, the taxpayer within the applicable period of limitation, may file a regular claim for credit or refund based on the carryback, if he has not already filed such a claim, and may maintain a suit based on such claim if it is disallowed or if it is not acted upon by the Internal Revenue Service within 6 months from the date the claim was filed.

(ii) The method provided in subdivision (i) of this subparagraph to recover any amount applied, credited, or refunded in respect of an application for a tentative carryback adjustment which should not have been so applied, credited, or refunded is not an exclusive method. Two other methods are available to recover such amount: (*a*) By way of a deficiency notice under section 6212; or (*b*) by a suit to recover an erroneous refund under section 7405. Any one or more of the three available methods may be used to recover any amount which was improperly applied, credited, or refunded in respect of an application for a tentative carryback adjustment.

(3) *Assessment of amount paid.*—Any payment made after the mailing of a notice of deficiency which is made by the taxpayer as a payment with respect to the proposed deficiency may be assessed without regard to the restrictions on assessment and collection imposed by section 6213(a) even though the taxpayer has not filed a waiver of restrictions on assessment as provided in section 6213(d). A payment of all or part of the deficiency asserted in the notice together with the assessment of the amount so paid will not affect the jurisdiction of the Tax Court. If any payment is made before the mailing of a notice of deficiency, the district director or the director of the regional service center is

not prohibited by section 6213(a) from assessing such amount, and such amount may be assessed if such action is deemed to be proper. If such amount is assessed, the assessment is taken into account in determining whether or not there is a deficiency for which a notice of deficiency must be issued. Thus, if such a payment satisfies the taxpayer's tax liability, no notice of deficiency will be mailed and the Tax Court will have no jurisdiction over the matter. In any case in which there is a controversy as to the correct amount of the tax liability, the assessment of any amount pursuant to the provisions of section 6213(b)(3) shall in no way be considered to be the acceptance of an offer by the taxpayer to settle such controversy.

(4) *Jeopardy*.—If the district director believes that the assessment or collection of a deficiency will be jeopardized by delay, such deficiency shall be assessed immediately, as provided in section 6861(a).

(c) *Failure to file petition*.—If no petition is filed with the Tax Court within the period prescribed in section 6213(a), the district director or the director of the regional service center shall assess the amount determined as the deficiency and of which the taxpayer was notified by registered or certified mail and the taxpayer shall pay the same upon notice and demand therefor. In such case the district director will not be precluded from determining a further deficiency and notifying the taxpayer thereof by registered or certified mail. If a petition is filed with the Tax Court the taxpayer should notify the district director who issued the notice of deficiency that the petition has been filed in order to prevent an assessment of the amount determined to be the deficiency.

(d) *Waiver of restrictions*.—The taxpayer may at any time by a signed notice in writing filed with the district director waive the restrictions on the assessment and collection of the whole or any part of the deficiency. The notice must in all cases be filed with the district director or other authorized official under whose jurisdiction the audit or other consideration of the return in question is being conducted. The filing of such notice with the Tax Court does not constitute filing with the district director within the meaning of the Internal Revenue Code. After such waiver has been acted upon by the district director and the assessment has been made in accordance with its terms, the waiver cannot be withdrawn.

(e) *Suspension of filing period for certain chapter 42 and chapter 43 taxes*.—The period prescribed by section 6213(a) for filing a petition in the Tax Court with respect to the taxes imposed by section 4941, 4942, 4943, 4944, 4945, 4951, 4952, 4955, 4958, 4971, or 4975, shall be suspended for any other period which the Commissioner has allowed for making correction under §53.4963-1(e)(3). Where the time for filing a petition with the Tax Court has been suspended under the authority of this paragraph (e), the extension shall not be reduced as a result of the correction being made prior to expiration of the period allowed for making correction. [Reg. §301.6213-1.]

☐ [*T.D.* 6119, 12-31-54. *Amended by T.D.* 6425, 11-10-59; *T.D.* 6498, 10-24-60; *T.D.* 6585, 12-27-61; *T.D.* 7838, 10-5-82; *T.D.* 8084, 5-1-86; *T.D.* 8628, 12-4-95 *and T.D.* 8920, 1-9-2001.]

[Reg. §20.6302-1]

§20.6302-1. Voluntary payments of estate taxes by electronic funds transfer.—Any person may voluntarily remit by electronic funds transfer any payment of tax to which this part 20 applies. Such payment must be made in accordance with procedures prescribed by the Commissioner. [Reg. §20.6302-1.]

☐ [*T.D.* 8828, 7-12-99.]

[Reg. §25.6302-1]

§25.6302-1. Voluntary payments of gift taxes by electronic funds transfer.—Any person may voluntarily remit by electronic funds transfer any payment of tax to which this part 25 applies. Such payment must be made in accordance with procedures prescribed by the Commissioner. [Reg. §25.6302-1.]

☐ [*T.D.* 8828, 7-12-99.]

[Reg. §20.6314-1]

§20.6314-1. Duplicate receipts for payments of estate taxes.—The internal revenue officer with whom the estate tax return is filed will, upon request, give to the person paying the tax duplicate receipts, either of which will be sufficient evidence of such payment and entitle the executor to be credited with the amount by any court having jurisdiction to audit or settle his accounts. [Reg. §20.6314-1.]

☐ [*T.D.* 6296, 6-23-58. *Amended by T.D.* 7238, 12-28-72.]

[Reg. §20.6321-1]

§20.6321-1. Lien for taxes.—For regulations concerning the lien for taxes, see §301.6321-1 of this chapter (Regulations on Procedure and Administration). [Reg. §20.6321-1.]

☐ [*T.D.* 6296, 6-23-58.]

[Reg. §25.6321-1]

§25.6321-1. Lien for taxes.—For regulations concerning the lien for taxes, see §301.6321-1 of this chapter (Regulations on Procedure and Administration). [Reg. §25.6321-1.]

☐ [*T.D.* 6334, 10-14-58.]

[Reg. §301.6321-1]

§301.6321-1. Lien for taxes.—If any person liable to pay any tax neglects or refuses to pay the same after demand, the amount (including any interest, additional amount, addition to tax, or assessable penalty, together with any costs that may accrue in addition thereto) shall be a lien in favor of the United States upon all property and rights to property, whether real or personal, tangible or intangible, belonging to such person. For purposes of section 6321 and this section, the term "any tax" shall include a State individual income tax which is a "qualified tax", as defined in paragraph(b) of § 301.6361-4. The lien attaches to all property and rights to property belonging to such person at any time during the period of the lien, including any property or rights to property acquired by such person after the lien arises. Solely for purposes of sections 6321 and 6331, any interest in restricted land held in trust by the United States for an individual noncompetent Indian (and not for a tribe) shall not be deemed to be property, or a right to property, belonging to such Indian. For the method of allocating amounts collected pursuant to a lien between the Federal Government and a State or States imposing a qualified tax with respect to which the lien attached, see paragraph (f) of § 301.6361-1. For the special lien for estate and gift taxes, see section 6324 and § 301.6324-1. [Reg. § 301.6321-1.]

□ [*T.D.* 6119, 12-31-54. *Amended by T.D.* 7139, 8-11-71 *and T.D.* 7577, 12-19-78.]

[Reg. § 20.6323-1]

§ 20.6323-1. Validity and priority against certain persons.—For regulations concerning the validity of the lien imposed by section 6321 against certain persons, see §§ 301.6323(a)-1 through 301.6323(i)-1 of this chapter (Regulations on Procedure and Administration). [Reg. § 20.6323-1.]

□ [*T.D.* 6296, 6-23-58. *Amended by T.D.* 7429, 8-20-76.]

[Reg. § 25.6323-1]

§ 25.6323-1. Validity and priority against certain persons.—For regulations concerning the validity of the lien imposed by section 6321 against certain persons, see §§ 301.6323(a)-1 through 301.6323(i)-1 of this chapter (Regulations on Procedure and Administration). [Reg. § 25.6323-1.]

□ [*T.D.* 6334, 10-14-58. *Amended by T.D.* 7429, 8-20-76.]

[Reg. § 20.6324-1]

§ 20.6324-1. Special lien for estate tax.—For regulations concerning the special lien for the estate tax, see § 301.6324-1 of this chapter (Regulations on Procedure and Administration). [Reg. § 20.6324-1.]

□ [*T.D.* 6296, 6-23-58.]

[Reg. § 25.6324-1]

§ 25.6324-1. Special lien for gift tax.—For regulations concerning the special lien for the gift tax, see § 301.6324-1 of this chapter (Regulations on Procedure and Administration). [Reg. § 25.6324-1.]

□ [*T.D.* 6334, 10-14-58.]

[Reg. § 301.6324-1]

§ 301.6324-1. Special liens for estate and gift taxes; personal liability of transferees and others.—(a) *Estate tax.*—(1) The lien imposed by section 6324(a) attaches at the date of the decedent's death to every part of the gross estate, whether or not the property comes into the possession of the duly qualified executor or administrator. The lien attaches to the extent of the tax shown to be due by the return and of any deficiency in tax found to be due upon review and audit. If the estate tax is not paid when due, then the spouse, transferee, trustee (except the trustee of an employee's trust which meets the requirements of section 401(a)), surviving tenant, person in possession of the property by reason of the exercise, nonexercise, or release of a power of appointment, or beneficiary, who receives, or has on the date of the decedent's death, property included in the gross estate under sections 2034 to 2042, inclusive, shall be personally liable for the tax to the extent of the value, at the time of the decedent's death, of the property.

(2) Unless the tax is paid in full or becomes unenforceable by reason of lapse of time, and except as otherwise provided in paragraph (c) of this section, the lien upon the entire property constituting the gross estate continues for a period of 10 years after the decedent's death, except that the lien shall be divested with respect to—

(i) The portion of the gross estate used for the payment of charges against the estate and expenses of its administration allowed by any court having jurisdiction thereof;

(ii) Property included in the gross estate under sections 2034 to 2042, inclusive, which is transferred by (or transferred by the transferee of) the spouse, transferee, trustee, surviving tenant, person in possession of the property by reason of the exercise, nonexercise, or release of a power of appointment, or beneficiary to a purchaser or holder of a security interest. In such case a like lien attaches to all the property of the spouse, transferee, trustee, surviving tenant, person in possession, beneficiary, or transferee of any such person, except the part which is transferred to a purchaser or a holder of a security interest. See section 6323(h)(1) and (6) and the regulations thereunder, respectively, for the definitions of "security interest" and "purchaser";

(iii) The portion of the gross estate (or any interest therein) which has been transferred to a purchaser or holder of a security interest if payment is made of the full amount of tax determined by the district director pursuant to a request of the fiduciary (executor, in the case of the estate of a decedent dying before January 1, 1971) for discharge from personal liability as authorized by section 2204 (relating to discharge of fiduciary from personal liability) but there is substituted a like lien upon the consideration received from the purchaser or holder of a security interest; and

(iv) Property as to which the district director has issued a certificate releasing a lien under section 6325(a) and the regulations thereunder.

(b) *Lien for gift tax.*—Except as provided in paragraph (c) of this section, a lien attaches upon all gifts made during the period for which the return was filed (see § 25.6019-1 of this chapter) for the amount of tax imposed upon the gifts made during such period. The lien extends for a period of 10 years from the time the gifts are made, unless the tax is sooner paid in full or becomes unenforceable by reason of lapse of time. If the tax is not paid when due, the donee of any gift becomes personally liable for the tax to the extent of the value of his gift. Any part of the property comprised in the gift transferred by the donee (or by a transferee of the donee) to a purchaser or holder of a security interest is divested of the lien, but a like lien, to the extent of the value of the gift, attaches to all the property (including after-acquired property) of the donee (or the transferee) except any part transferred to a purchaser or holder of a security interest. See section 6323(h)(1) and (6) and the regulations thereunder, respectively, for the definitions of "security interest" and "purchaser."

(c) *Exceptions.*—(1) A lien described in either paragraph (a) or paragraph (b) of this section is not valid against a mechanic's lienor (as defined in section 6323(h)(2) and the regulations thereunder) and, subject to the conditions set forth under section 6323(b) (relating to protection for certain interests even though notice filed), is not valid with respect to any lien or interest described in section 6323(b) and the regulations thereunder.

(2) If a lien described in either paragraph (a) or paragraph (b) of this section is not valid against a lien or security interest (as defined in section 6323(h)(1) and the regulations thereunder), the priority of the lien or security interest extends to any item described in section 6323(e) (relating to priority of interest and expenses) to the extent that, under local law, the item has the same priority as the lien or security interest to which it relates.

(d) *Application of lien imposed by section 6321.*—The general lien under section 6321 and the special lien under subsection (a) or (b) of section 6324 for the estate or gift tax are not exclusive of each other, but are cumulative. Each lien will arise when the conditions precedent to the creation of such lien are met and will continue in accordance with the provisions applicable to the particular lien. Thus, the special lien may exist without the general lien being in force, or the general lien may exist without the special lien being in force, or the general lien and the special lien may exist simultaneously, depending upon the facts and pertinent statutory provisions applicable to the respective liens. [Reg. §301.6324-1.]

□ [*T.D.* 6119, 12-31-54. *Amended by T.D.* 6498, 10-24-60 *and T.D.* 7238, 12-28-72.]

[Reg. §20.6324A-1]

§20.6324A-1. Special lien for estate tax deferred under section 6166 or 6166A.—(a) *In general.*—If the executor of an estate of a decedent dying after December 31, 1976, makes an election under section 6166 or 6166A (as in effect prior to its repeal by the Economic Recovery Tax Act of 1981) to defer the payment of estate tax, the executor may make an election under section 6324A. An election under section 6324A will cause a lien in favor of the United States to attach to the estate's section 6166 lien property, as defined in paragraph (b)(1) of this section. This lien is in lieu of the bonds required by sections 2204 and 6165 and in lieu of any lien under section 6324 on the same property with respect to the same estate. The value of the property which the district director may require under section 6324A as section 6166 lien property may not exceed the sum of the deferred amount (as defined in paragraph (e)(1) of this section) and the required interest amount (as defined in paragraph (e)(2) of this section). The unpaid portion of the deferred amount (plus any unpaid interest, additional amount, addition to tax, assessable penalty, and cost attributable to the deferred amount) shall be a lien in favor of the United States on the section 6166 lien property. See §301.6324A-1 of this chapter (Regulations on Procedure and Administration) for provisions relating to the election of and agreement to the special lien for estate tax deferred under section 6166 or 6166A (as in effect prior to its repeal by the Economic Recovery Tax Act of 1981).

(b) *Section 6166 lien property.*—(1) *In general.*—Section 6166 lien property consists of those interests in real and personal property designated in the agreement referred to in section 6324A(c) (see paragraph (b) of §301.6324A-1 of this chapter). An interest in property may be designated as section 6166 lien property only to the extent such interest can be expected to survive the deferral period (as defined in paragraph (e)(3) of this section). Property designated, however, need not be property included in the decedent's estate.

(2) *Maximum value of required property.*—The fair market value of the property required by the district director to be designated as section 6166 lien property with respect to any estate shall not be greater than the sum of the deferred amount and the required interest amount, as these terms are defined in paragraphs (e)(1) and (2) of this section. However, the parties to the agreement referred to in section 6324A(c) may voluntarily designate property having a fair market value in excess of that sum. The fair market value of the section 6166 lien property shall be determined as of the date prescribed in section 6151(a) (without regard to any extension) for payment of the estate tax. Such value must take into account any encumbrance on the property (such as a mortgage or a lien under section 6324B).

(3) *Additional lien property may be required.*—If, at any time, the unpaid portion of the deferred amount and the required interest amount exceeds the fair market value of the section 6166 lien property, the district director may require the addition of property to the agreement in an amount up to such excess. When additional property is required, the district director shall make notice and demand upon the agent designated in the agreement setting forth the amount of additional property required. Property having the required value (or other security equal to the required value) must be added to the agreement

within 90 days after notice and demand from the district director. Failure to comply with the demand within the 90-day period shall be treated as an act accelerating payment of installments under section 6166(g) or 6166A(h) (as in effect prior to its repeal by the Economic Recovery Tax Act of 1981).

(4) *Partial substitution of bond.*—See paragraph (c) of § 301.6324A-1 of this chapter for rules relating to the partial substitution of a bond for the lien where the value of property designated as section 6166 lien property is less than the amount of unpaid estate tax plus interest.

(c) *Special rules.*—(1) *Period of lien.*—The lien under section 6324A arises at the earlier of the date—

(i) The executor is discharged from liability under section 2204; or

(ii) Notice of lien is filed in accordance with § 301.6323(f)-1 of this chapter.

The section 6324A lien continues until the liability for the deferred amount is satisfied or becomes unenforceable by reason of lapse of time. The provisions of § 301.6325-1(c), relating to release of lien or discharge of property, shall apply to this paragraph (c)(1).

(2) *Requirement that lien be filed.*—The lien imposed by section 6324A is not valid against a purchaser (as defined in paragraph (f) of § 301.6323(h)-1), holder of a security interest (as defined in paragraph (a) of § 301.6323(h)-1), mechanic's lienor (as defined in paragraph (b) of § 301.6323(h)-1), or judgment lien creditor (as defined in paragraph (g) of § 301.6323(h)-1) until notice of the lien is filed. Once filed, the notice of lien remains effective without being refiled.

(3) *Priorities.*—Although a notice of lien under section 6324A has been properly filed, that lien is not valid—

(i) To the extent provided in section 6323(b)(6), relating to real property tax and special assessment liens, regardless of whether such liens came into existence before or after the filing of the notice of Federal tax lien;

(ii) In the case of any real property subject to a lien for repair or improvement, as against a mechanic's lienor, whether or not such lien came into existence before or after the notice of tax lien was filed; and

(iii) As against any security interest set forth in section 6323(c)(3), relating to real property construction or improvement financing agreements, regardless whether such security interest came into existence before or after the filing of the notice of tax lien.

However, paragraphs (c)(3)(ii) and (iii) of this section shall not apply to any security interest that came into existence after the date of filing of notice (in a manner similar to a notice filed under section 6323(f)) that payment of the deferred amount has been accelerated under section 6166(g) or 6166A(h) (as in effect prior to its repeal by the Economic Recovery Tax Act of 1981).

(d) *Release or discharge of lien.*—For rules relating to release of the lien imposed by section 6324A or discharge of the section 6166 lien property, see section 6325 and § 301.6325-1 of this chapter.

(e) *Definitions.*—For purposes of section 6324A of this section—

(1) *Deferred amount.*—The deferred amount is the aggregate amount of estate tax deferred under section 6166 or 6166A (as in effect prior to its repeal by the Economic Recovery Tax Act of 1981) determined as of the date prescribed by section 6151(a) for payment of the estate tax.

(2) *Required interest amount.*—The required interest amount is the aggregate amount of interest payable over the first four years of the deferral period. For purposes of computing the required interest amount, the interest rate prescribed by section 6621 in effect on the date prescribed by section 6151(a) for payment of the estate tax shall be used for computing the interest for the first four years of the deferral period. The 4-percent interest rate prescribed by section 6601(j) shall apply to the extent provided in that section. For purposes of computing interest during deferral periods beginning after December 31, 1982, interest shall be compounded daily.

(3) *Deferral period.*—The deferral period is the period for which the payment of tax is deferred pursuant to the election under section 6166 or 6166A (as in effect prior to its repeal by the Economic Recovery Tax Act of 1981).

(4) *Application of definitions.*—In the case of a deficiency, a separate deferred amount, required interest amount, and deferral period shall be determined as of the due date of the first installment after the deficiency is prorated to installments under section 6166 or 6166A (as in effect prior to its repeal by the Economic Recovery Tax Act of 1981). [Reg. § 20.6324A-1.]

□ [*T.D. 7710, 7-28-80. Amended by T.D. 7941, 2-6-84.*]

[Reg. § 301.6324A-1]

§ 301.6324A-1. Election of and agreement to special lien for estate tax deferred under section 6166 or 6166A.—(a) *Election of lien.*—If payment of a portion of the estate tax is deferred under section 6166 or 6166A (as in effect prior to its repeal by [the] Economic Recovery Tax Act of 1981), an executor of a decedent's estate who seeks to be discharged from personal liability may elect a lien in favor of the United States in lieu of the bonds required by sections 2204 and 6165. This election is made by applying to the Internal Revenue Service office where the estate tax return is filed at any time prior to payment of the full amount of estate tax and interest due. The application is to be a notice of election requesting the special lien provided by section 6324A and is to be accompanied by the agreement described in paragraph(b)(1) of this section.

(b) *Agreement to lien.*—(1) *In general.*—A lien under this section will not arise unless all parties having any interest in all property designated in the notice of election as property to which the lien is to attach sign an agreement in which they consent to the creation of the lien. (Property so designated need not be property included in the decedent's estate.) The agreement is to be attached to the notice in which the lien under section 6324A is elected. It must be in a form that is binding on all parties having any interest on the property and must contain the following:

(i) The decedent's name and taxpayer identification number as they appear on the estate tax return;

(ii) The amount of the lien;

(iii) The fair market value of the property to be subject to the lien as of the date of the decedent's death and the date of the election under this section;

(iv) The amount, as of the date of the decedent's death and the date of the election, of all encumbrances on the property, including mortgages and any lien under section 6324B;

(v) A clear description of the property which is to be subject to the lien, and in the case of property other than land, a statement of its estimated remaining useful life; and

(vi) Designation of an agent (including the agent's address) for the beneficiaries of the estate and the consenting parties to the lien for all dealings with the Internal Revenue Service on matters arising under section 6166 or 6166A (as in effect prior to its repeal by [the] Economic Recovery Tax Act of 1981), or under section 6324A.

(2) *Persons having an interest in designated property.*—An interest in property is any interest which as of the date of the election can be asserted under applicable local law so as to affect the disposition of any property designated in the agreement required under this section. Any person in being at the date of the election who has any such interest in the property, whether present or future, or vested or contingent, must enter into the agreement. Included among such persons are owners of remainder and executory interests, the holders of general or special powers of appointment, beneficiaries of a gift over in default of exercise of any such power, co-tenants, joint tenants, and holders of other undivided interests when the decedent held a joint or undivided interest in the property, and trustees of trusts holding any interest in the property. An heir who has the power under local law to caveat (challenge) a will and thereby affect disposition of the property is not, however, considered to be a person with an interest in property under section 6324A solely by reason of that right. Likewise, creditors of an estate are not such persons solely by reason of their status as creditors.

(3) *Consent on behalf of interested party.*—If any person required to enter into the agreement provided for by this paragraph either desires that an agent act for him or her or cannot legally bind himself or herself due to infancy or other incompetency, a representative authorized under local law to bind the interested party in an agreement of this nature is permitted to sign the agreement on his or her behalf.

(4) *Duties of agent designated in agreement.*—The Internal Revenue Service will contact the agent designated in the agreement under paragraph (b)(1) on all matters relating to continued qualification of the estate under section 6166 or 6166A (as in effect prior to its repeal by [the] Economic Recovery Tax Act of 1981) and on all matters relating to the special lien arising under section 6324A. It is the duty of the agent as attorney-in-fact for the parties with interests in the property subject to the lien under section 6324A to furnish the Service with any requested information and to notify the Service of any event giving rise to acceleration of the deferred amount of tax.

(c) *Partial substitution of bond for lien.*—If the amount of unpaid estate tax plus interest exceeds the value (determined for purposes of section 6324A(b)(2)) of property listed in the agreement under paragraph (b) of this section, the Internal Revenue Service may condition the release from personal liability upon the executor's submitting an agreement listing additional property or furnishing an acceptable bond in the amount of such excess.

(d) *Relation of sections 6324A and 2204.*—The lien under section 6324A is deemed to be a bond under section 2204 for purposes of determining an executor's release from personal liability. If an election has been made under section 6324A, the executor may not substitute a bond pursuant to section 2204 in lieu of that lien. If a bond has been supplied under section 2204, however, the executor may, by filing a proper notice of election and agreement, substitute a lien under section 6324A for any part or all of such bond.

(e) *Relation of sections 6324A and 6324.*—If there is a lien under this section on any property with respect to an estate, that lien is in lieu of the lien provided by section 6324 on such property with respect to the same estate.

(f) *Section 6324A lien to be in lieu of bond under section 6165.*—The lien under section 6324A is in lieu of any bond otherwise required under section 6165 with respect to tax to be paid in installments under section 6166 or section 6166A (as in effect prior to its repeal by [the] Economic Recovery Tax Act of 1981).

(g) *Special rule for estates for which elections under section 6324A are made on or before August 30, 1980.*—If a lien is elected under section 6324A on or before August 30, 1980, the original election may be revoked. To revoke an election, the executor must file a notice of revocation containing the decedent's name, date of death, and taxpayer identification number with the Internal Revenue Service office where the original estate tax return for the decedent was filed. The notice must be filed on or before January 31, 1981 (or if earlier, the date on which the period of limitation for assessment expires). [Reg. § 301.6324A-1.]

□ [*T.D.* 7710, 7-28-80. *Amended by T.D.* 7941, 2-6-84.]

[Reg. § 20.6324B-1]

§ 20.6324B-1. Special lien for additional estate tax attributable to farm, etc., valuation.—(a) *General rule.*—In the case of an estate of a decedent dying after December 31, 1976, which includes any interest in qualified real property, if the executor elects to value part or all of such property pursuant to section 2032A, a lien arises in favor of the United States on the property to which the election applies. The lien is in the amount equal to the adjusted tax difference attributable to such interest (as defined by section 2032A(c)(2)(B)). The term "qualified real property" means qualified real property as defined in section 2032A(b), qualified replacement property within the meaning of section 2032A(h)(3)(B), and qualified exchange property within the meaning of section 2032A(i)(3). The rules set forth in the regulations under section 2032A shall apply in determining whether this section is applicable to otherwise qualified real property held by a partnership, corporation or trust.

(b) *Period of lien.*—The lien shall arise at the time the executor files an election under section 2032A. It shall remain in effect until one of the following occurs:

(1) The liability for the additional estate tax under section 2032A(c) with respect to such interest has been satisfied; or

(2) Such liability has become unenforceable by reason of lapse of time; or

(3) The district director is satisfied that no further liability for additional estate tax with respect to such interest may arise under section 2032A(c), i.e., the required time period has elapsed since the decedent's death without the occurrence of an event described in section 2032A(c)(1), or the qualified heir (as defined in section 2032A(e)(1)) has died.

For procedures regarding the release or subordination of liens or discharge of property from liens, see § 301.6325-1 of this chapter (Regulations on Procedure and Administration).

(c) *Substitution of security for lien.*—The district director may, upon written application of the qualified heir (as defined in section 2032A(e)(1)) acquiring any interest in qualified real property to which a lien imposed by section 6324B attaches, issue a certificate of discharge of any or all property subject to such lien, after receiving a bond or other security in an amount or value determined by the district director as sufficient security for the maximum potential liability for additional estate tax with respect to such interest. Any bond shall be in the form and with the security prescribed in § 301.7101-1 of this chapter.

(d) *Special rules.*—The rules set forth in section 6324A(d)(1), (3), and (4), and the regulations thereunder, shall apply with respect to a lien imposed by section 6324B as if it were a lien imposed by section 6324A. [Reg. § 20.6324B-1.]

□ [*T.D.* 7847, 11-9-82.]

[Reg. § 20.6325-1]

§ 20.6325-1. Release of lien or partial discharge of property; transfer certificates in nonresident estates.—(a) A transfer certificate is a certificate permitting the transfer of property of a nonresident decedent without liability. Except as provided in paragraph (b) of this section, no domestic corporation or its transfer agent should transfer stock registered in the name of a nonresident decedent (regardless of citizenship) except such shares which have been submitted for transfer by a duly qualified executor or administrator who has been appointed and is acting in the United States, without first requiring a transfer certificate covering all of the decedent's stock of the corporation and showing that the transfer may be made without liability. Corporations, transfer agents of domestic corporations, transfer agents of foreign corporations (except as to shares held in the name of a nonresident decedent not a citizen of the United States), banks, trust companies, or other custodians in actual or constructive possession of property, of such a decedent can insure avoidance of liability for taxes and penalties only by demanding and receiving transfer certificates before transfer of property of nonresident decedents.

(b)(1) Subject to the provisions of paragraph (b)(2) of this section—

(i) In the case of a nonresident not a citizen of the United States dying on or after January 1, 1977, a transfer certificate is not required with respect to the transfer of any property of the decedent if the value on the date of death of that part of the decedent's gross estate situated in the United States did not exceed the lesser of $60,000 or $60,000 reduced by the adjustments, if any, required by section 6018(a)(4) for certain taxable gifts made by the decedent and for the aggregate amount of certain specific exemptions.

(ii) In the case of a nonresident not a citizen of the United States dying on or after November 14, 1966, a transfer certificate is not required with respect to the transfer before June 24, 1981, of any property of the decedent if the value on the date of death of that part of the decedent's gross estate situated in the United States did not exceed $30,000.

(2)(i) If the transfer of the estate is subject to the tax imposed by section 2107(a) (relating to expatriation to avoid tax), any amounts which are includible in the decedent's gross estate under section 2107(b) must be added to the date of death value of the decedent's gross estate situated in the United States to determine the value on the date of death of the decedent's gross estate for purposes of paragraph (b)(1) of this section.

(ii) If the transfer of the estate is subject to tax pursuant to a Presidential proclamation made under section 2108(a) (relating to Presidential proclamations of the application of pre-1967 estate tax provisions), a transfer certificate is not required with respect to the transfer of any property of the decedent if the value on the date of death of that part of the decedent's gross estate

See p. 15 for regulations not amended to reflect law changes

situated in the United States did not exceed $2,000.

(3) A corporation, transfer agent, bank, trust company, or other custodian will not incur liability for a transfer of the decedent's property without a transfer certificate if the corporation or other person, having no information to the contrary, first receives from the executor or other responsible person, who may be reasonably regarded as in possession of the pertinent facts, a statement of the facts relating to the estate showing that the sum of the value on the date of the decedent's death of that part of his gross estate situated in the United States, and, if applicable, any amounts includible in his gross estate under section 2107(b), is such an amount that, pursuant to the provisions of paragraph (b)(1) or (b)(2) of this section, a transfer certificate is not required.

(4) For the determination of the gross estate situated in the United States, see §§20.2103-1 and 20.2104-1.

(c) A transfer certificate will be issued by the service center director or the district director when he is satisfied that the tax imposed upon the estate, if any, has been fully discharged or provided for. The tax will be considered fully discharged for purposes of the issuance of a transfer certificate only when investigation has been completed and payment of the tax, including any deficiency finally determined, has been made. If the tax liability has not been fully discharged, transfer certificates may be issued permitting the transfer of particular items of property without liability upon the filing with the district director of such security as he may require. No transfer certificate is required in an estate of a resident decedent. Further, in the case of an estate of a nonresident decedent (regardless of citizenship) a transfer certificate is not required with respect to property which is being administered by an executor or administrator appointed, qualified, and acting within the United States. For additional regulations under section 6325, see §301.6325-1 of this chapter (Regulations on Procedure and Administration). [Reg. §20.6325-1.]

☐ [*T.D.* 6296, 6-23-58. *Amended by T.D.* 7296, 12-11-73, *T.D.* 7302, 1-2-74 *and T.D.* 7825, 8-12-82.]

[Reg. §301.6325-1]

§301.6325-1. Release of lien or discharge of property.—(a) *Release of lien.*—(1) *Liability satisfied or unenforceable.*—The appropriate official shall issue a certificate of release for a filed notice of Federal tax lien, no later than 30 days after the date on which he finds that the entire tax liability listed in such notice of Federal tax lien either has been fully satisfied (as defined in paragraph (a)(4) of this section) or has become legally unenforceable. In all cases, the liability for the payment of the tax continues until satisfaction of the tax in full or until the expiration of the statutory period for collection, including such extension of the period for collection as is agreed to.

(2) *Bond accepted.*—The appropriate official shall issue a certificate of release of any tax lien if he is furnished and accepts a bond that is conditioned upon the payment of the amount assessed (together with all interest in respect thereof), within the time agreed upon in the bond, but not later than 6 months before the expiration of the statutory period for collection, including any agreed upon extensions. For provisions relating to bonds, see sections 7101 and 7102 and §§301.7101-1 and 301.7102-1.

(3) *Certificate of release for a lien which has become legally unenforceable.*—The appropriate official shall have the authority to file a notice of Federal tax lien which also contains a certificate of release pertaining to those liens which become legally unenforceable. Such release will become effective as a release as of a date prescribed in the document containing the notice of Federal tax lien and certificate of release.

(4) *Satisfaction of tax liability.*—For purposes of paragraph (a)(1) of this section, satisfaction of the tax liability occurs when—

(i) The appropriate official determines that the entire tax liability listed in a notice of Federal tax lien has been fully satisfied. Such determination will be made as soon as practicable after tender of payment; or

(ii) The taxpayer provides the appropriate official with proof of full payment (as defined in paragraph (a)(5) of this section) with respect to the entire tax liability listed in a notice of Federal tax lien together with the information and documents set forth in paragraph (a)(7) of this section. See paragraph (a)(6) of this section if more than one tax liability is listed in a notice of Federal tax lien.

(5) *Proof of full payment.*—As used in paragraph (a)(4)(ii) of this section, the term *proof of full payment* means—

(i) An internal revenue cashier's receipt reflecting full payment of the tax liability in question;

(ii) A canceled check in an amount sufficient to satisfy the tax liability for which the release is being sought;

(iii) A record, made in accordance with procedures prescribed by the Commissioner, of proper payment of the tax liability by credit or debit card or by electronic funds transfer; or

(iv) Any other manner of proof acceptable to the appropriate official.

(6) *Notice of a Federal tax lien which lists multiple liabilities.*—When a notice of Federal tax lien lists multiple tax liabilities, the appropriate official shall issue a certificate of release when all of the tax liabilities listed in the notice of Federal tax lien have been fully satisfied or have become legally unenforceable. In addition, if the taxpayer requests that a certificate of release be issued with respect to one or more tax liabilities listed in the notice of Federal tax lien and such liability has been fully satisfied or has become legally unenforceable, the appropriate official shall issue a certificate of release. For example, if a notice of Federal tax lien lists two separate liabilities and one of the liabilities is satisfied, the

taxpayer may request the issuance of a certificate of release with respect to the satisfied tax liability and the appropriate official shall issue a release.

(7) *Taxpayer requests.*—A request for a certificate of release with respect to a notice of Federal tax lien shall be submitted in writing to the appropriate official. The request shall contain the information required in the appropriate IRS Publication.

(b) *Discharge of specific property from the lien.*—(1) *Property double the amount of the liability.*—(i) The appropriate official may, in his discretion, issue a certificate of discharge of any part of the property subject to a Federal tax lien imposed under chapter 64 of the Internal Revenue Code if he determines that the fair market value of that part of the property remaining subject to the Federal tax lien is at least double the sum of the amount of the unsatisfied liability secured by the Federal tax lien and of the amount of all other liens upon the property which have priority over the Federal tax lien. In general, fair market value is that amount which one ready and willing but not compelled to buy would pay to another ready and willing but not compelled to sell the property.

(ii) The following example illustrates a case in which a certificate of discharge may not be given under this subparagraph:

Example. The Federal tax liability secured by a lien is $1,000. The fair market value of all property which after the discharge will continue to be subject to the Federal tax lien is $10,000. There is a prior mortgage on the property of $5,000, including interest, and the property is subject to a prior lien of $100 for real estate taxes. Accordingly, the taxpayer's equity in the property over and above the amount of the mortgage and real estate taxes is $4,900, or nearly five times the amount required to pay the assessed tax on which the Federal tax lien is based. Nevertheless, a discharge under this subparagraph is not permissible. In the illustration, the sum of the amount of the Federal tax liability ($1,000) and of the amount of the prior mortgage and the lien for real estate taxes ($5,000 + $100 = $5,100) is $6,100. Double the sum is $12,200, but the fair market value of the remaining property is only $10,000. Hence, a discharge of the property is not permissible under this subparagraph, since the Code requires that the fair market value of the remaining property be at least double the sum of two amounts, one amount being the outstanding Federal tax liability and the other amount being all prior liens upon such property. In order that the discharge may be issued, it would be necessary that the remaining property be worth not less than $12,200.

(2) *Part payment; interest of United States valueless.*—(i) *Part payment.*—The appropriate official may, in his discretion, issue a certificate of discharge of any part of the property subject to a Federal tax lien imposed under chapter 64 of the Internal Revenue Code if there is paid over to him in partial satisfaction of the liability secured by the Federal tax lien an amount determined by him to be not less than the value of the interest of the United States in the property to be so discharged. In determining the amount to be paid, the appropriate official will take into consideration all the facts and circumstances of the case, including the expenses to which the government has been put in the matter. In no case shall the amount to be paid be less than the value of the interest of the United States in the property with respect to which the certificate of discharge is to be issued.

(ii) *Interest of the United States valueless.*—The appropriate official may, in his discretion, issue a certificate of discharge of any part of the property subject to the Federal tax lien if he determines that the interest of the United States in the property to be so discharged has no value.

(3) *Discharge of property by substitution of proceeds of sale.*—The appropriate official may, in his discretion, issue a certificate of discharge of any part of the property subject to a Federal tax lien imposed under chapter 64 of the Internal Revenue Code if such part of the property is sold and, pursuant to a written agreement with the appropriate official, the proceeds of the sale are held, as a fund subject to the Federal tax liens and claims of the United States, in the same manner and with the same priority as the Federal tax liens or claims had with respect to the discharged property. This paragraph does not apply unless the sale divests the taxpayer of all right, title, and interest in the property sought to be discharged. Any reasonable and necessary expenses incurred in connection with the sale of the property and the administration of the sale proceeds shall be paid by the applicant or from the proceeds of the sale before satisfaction of any Federal tax liens or claims of the United States.

(4) *Right of substitution of value.*—(i) *Issuance of certificate of discharge to property owner who is not the taxpayer.*—If an owner of property subject to a Federal tax lien imposed under chapter 64 of the Internal Revenue Code submits an application for a certificate of discharge pursuant to paragraph (b)(5) of this section, the appropriate official shall issue a certificate of discharge of such property after the owner either deposits with the appropriate official an amount equal to the value of the interest of the United States in the property, as determined by the appropriate official pursuant to paragraph (b)(6) of this section, or furnishes an acceptable bond in a like amount. This paragraph does not apply if the person seeking the discharge is the person whose unsatisfied liability gave rise to the Federal tax lien. Thus, if the property is owned by both the taxpayer and another person, the other person may obtain a certificate of discharge of the property under this paragraph, but the taxpayer may not.

(ii) *Refund of deposit and release of bond.*—The appropriate official may, in his discretion, determine that either the entire unsatisfied tax liability listed on the notice of Federal tax lien can be satisfied from a source other than the property sought to be discharged, or the value of the interest of the United States is less than the prior determination of such value. The appropriate official shall refund the amount deposited with interest at the overpayment rate determined under section 6621 or release the bond furnished to the extent that he makes this determination.

(iii) *Refund request.*—If a property owner desires an administrative refund of his deposit or release of the bond, the owner shall file a request in writing with the appropriate official. The request shall contain such information as the appropriate IRS Publication may require. The request must be filed within 120 days after the date the certificate of discharge is issued. A refund request made under this paragraph neither is required nor is effective to extend the period for filing an action in court under section 7426(a)(4).

(iv) *Internal Revenue Service's use of deposit if court action not filed.*—If no action is filed under section 7426(a)(4) for refund of the deposit or release of the bond within the 120-day period specified therein, the appropriate official shall, within 60 days after the expiration of the 120-day period, apply the amount deposited or collect on such bond to the extent necessary to satisfy the liability listed on the notice of Federal tax lien, and shall refund, with interest at the overpayment rate determined under section 6621, any portion of the amount deposited that is not used to satisfy the liability. If the appropriate official has not completed the application of the deposit to the unsatisfied liability before the end of the 60-day period, the deposit will be deemed to have been applied to the unsatisfied liability as of the 60th day.

(5) *Application for certificate of discharge.*—Any person desiring a certificate of discharge under this paragraph (b) shall submit an application in writing to the appropriate official. The application shall contain the information required by the appropriate IRS Publication. For purposes of this paragraph (b), any application for certificate of discharge made by a property owner who is not the taxpayer, and any amount submitted pursuant to the application, will be treated as an application for discharge and a deposit under section 6325(b)(4) unless the owner of the property submits a statement, in writing, that the application is being submitted under another paragraph of section 6325 and not under section 6325(b)(4), and the owner in writing waives the rights afforded under paragraph (b)(4), including the right to seek judicial review.

(6) *Valuation of interest of United States.*—For purposes of paragraphs (b)(2) and (b)(4) of this section, in determining the value of the interest of the United States in the property, or any part thereof, with respect to which the certificate of discharge is to be issued, the appropriate official shall give consideration to the value of the property and the amount of all liens and encumbrances thereon having priority over the Federal tax lien. In determining the value of the property, the appropriate official may, in his discretion, give consideration to the forced sale value of the property in appropriate cases.

(c) *Estate or gift tax liability fully satisfied or provided for.*—(1) *Certificate of discharge.*—If the appropriate official determines that the tax liability for estate or gift tax has been fully satisfied, he may issue a certificate of discharge of any or all property from the lien imposed thereon. If the appropriate official determines that the tax liability for estate or gift tax has been adequately provided for, he may issue a certificate discharging particular items of property from the lien. If a lien has arisen under section 6324B (relating to special lien for additional estate tax attributable to farm, etc., valuation) and the appropriate official determines that the liability for additional estate tax has been fully secured in accordance with § 20.6324B-1(c) of this chapter, the appropriate official may issue a certificate of discharge of the real property from the section 6324B lien. The issuance of such a certificate is a matter resting within the discretion of the appropriate official, and a certificate will be issued only in case there is actual need therefor. The primary purpose of such discharge is not to evidence payment or satisfaction of the tax, but to permit the transfer of property free from the lien in case it is necessary to clear title. The tax will be considered fully satisfied only when investigation has been completed and payment of the tax, including any deficiency determined, has been made.

(2) *Application for certificate of discharge.*—An application for a certificate of discharge of property from the lien for estate or gift tax should be filed with the appropriate official responsible for the collection of the tax. It should be made in writing under penalties of perjury and should explain the circumstances that require the discharge, and should fully describe the particular items for which the discharge is desired. Where realty is involved each parcel sought to be discharged from the lien should be described on a separate page and each such description submitted in duplicate. In the case of an estate tax lien, the application should show the applicant's relationship to the estate, such as executor, heir, devisee, legatee, beneficiary, transferee, or purchaser. If the estate or gift tax return has not been filed, a statement under penalties of perjury may be required showing (i) the value of the property to be discharged, (ii) the basis for such valuation, (iii) in the case of the estate tax, the approximate value of the gross estate and the approximate value of the total real property included in the gross estate, (iv) in the case of the gift tax, the total amount of gifts made during the calendar year and the prior calendar years subsequent to the enactment of the Revenue Act of 1932 and the approximate value of all real estate subject to the gift tax lien, and (v) if the property is to be sold or otherwise transferred, the name and address of the purchaser or transferee and the consideration, if any, paid or to be paid by him.

(d) *Subordination of lien.*—(1) *By payment of the amount subordinated.*—The appropriate official may, in his discretion, issue a certificate of subordination of a lien imposed under chapter 64 of the Internal Revenue Code upon any part of the property subject to the lien if there is paid over to the appropriate official an amount equal to the amount of the lien or interest to which the certificate subordinates the lien of the United States. For this purpose, the tax lien may be subordinated to another lien or interest on a dollar-for-dollar basis. For example, if a notice of a Federal tax lien is filed and a delinquent taxpayer secures a mortgage loan on a part of the property subject to the tax lien and pays over the proceeds of the loan to the appropriate official after an application for a certificate of subordination is approved, the appropriate official will issue a certificate of subordination. This certificate will have the effect of subordinating the tax lien to the mortgage.

(2) *To facilitate tax collection.*—(i) *In general.*—The appropriate official may, in his discretion, issue a certificate of subordination of a lien imposed under chapter 64 of the Internal Revenue Code upon any part of the property subject to the lien if the appropriate official believes that the subordination of the lien will ultimately result in an increase in the amount realized by the United States from the property subject to the lien and will facilitate the ultimate collection of the tax liability.

(ii) *Examples.*—The provisions of this subparagraph may be illustrated by the following examples:

Example (1). A, a farmer, needs money in order to harvest his crop. A Federal tax lien, notice of which has been filed, is outstanding with respect to A's property. B, a lending institution, is willing to make the necessary loan if the loan is secured by a first mortgage on the farm which is prior to the Federal tax lien. Upon examination, the appropriate official believes that ultimately the amount realizable from A's property will be increased and the collection of the tax liability will be facilitated by the availability of cash when the crop is harvested and sold. In this case, the appropriate official may, in his discretion, subordinate the tax lien on the farm to the mortgage securing the crop harvesting loan.

Example (2). C owns a commercial building which is deteriorating and in unsalable condition. Because of outstanding Federal tax liens, notices of which have been filed, C is unable to finance the repair and rehabilitation of the building. D, a contractor, is willing to do the work if his mechanic's lien on the property is superior to the Federal tax liens. Upon examination, the appropriate official believes that ultimately the amount realizable from C's property will be increased and the collection of the tax liability will be facilitated by arresting deterioration of the property and restoring it to salable condition. In this case, the appropriate official may, in his discretion, subordinate the tax lien on the building to the mechanic's lien.

Example (3). E, a manufacturer of electronic equipment, obtains financing from F, a lending institution, pursuant to a security agreement, with respect to which a financing statement was duly filed under the Uniform Commercial Code on June 1, 1970. On April 15, 1971, F gains actual notice or knowledge that notice of a Federal tax lien had been filed against E on March 31, 1971, and F refuses to make further advances unless its security interest is assured of priority over the Federal tax lien. Upon examination, the appropriate official believes that ultimately the amount realizable from E's property will be increased and the collection of the tax liability will be facilitated if the work in process can be completed and the equipment sold. In this case, the appropriate official may, in his discretion, subordinate the tax lien to F's security interest for the further advances required to complete the work.

Example (4). Suit is brought against G by H, who claims ownership of property the legal title to which is held by G. A Federal tax lien against G, notice of which has previously been filed, will be enforceable against the property if G's title is confirmed. Because section 6323(b)(8) is inapplicable, J, an attorney, is unwilling to defend the case for G unless he is granted a contractual lien on the property, superior to the Federal tax lien. Upon examination, the appropriate official believes that the successful defense of the case by G will increase the amount ultimately realizable from G's property and will facilitate collection of the tax liability. In this case, the appropriate official may, in his discretion, subordinate the tax lien to J's contractual lien on the disputed property to secure J's reasonable fees and expenses.

(3) *Subordination of section 6324B lien.*—The appropriate official may issue a certificate of subordination with respect to a lien imposed by section 6324B if the appropriate official determines that the interests of the United States will be adequately secured after such subordination. For example, *A*, a qualified heir of qualified real property, needs to borrow money for farming purposes. If the current fair market value of the real property is $150,000, the amount of the claim to which the special lien is to be subordinated is $40,000, the potential liability for additional tax (as defined in section 2032A(c)) is less than $55,000, and there are no other facts to indicate that the interest of the United States will not be adequately secured, the appropriate official may issue a certificate of subordination. The result would be the same if the loan were for bona fide purposes other than farming.

(4) *Application for certificate of subordination.*—Any person desiring a certificate of subordination under this paragraph shall submit an application therefor in writing to the appropriate official responsible for the collection of the tax. The application shall contain such information as the appropriate official may require.

(e) *Nonattachment of lien.*—If the appropriate official determines that, because of confusion of names or otherwise, any person (other than the person against whom the tax was assessed) is or may be injured by the appearance that a notice of lien filed in accordance with § 301.6323(f)-1 refers to such person, the appropriate official may issue a certificate of nonattachment. Such certificate shall state that the lien, notice of which has been filed, does not attach to the property of such person. Any person desiring a certificate of nonattachment under this paragraph shall submit an application therefor in writing to the appropriate official responsible for the collection of the tax. The application shall c ontain such information as the appropriate official may require.

(f) *Effect of certificate.*—(1) *Conclusiveness.*—Except as provided in subparagraphs (2) and (3) of this paragraph, if a certificate is issued under section 6325 by the appropriate official and the certificate is filed in the same office as the notice of lien to which it relates (if the notice of lien has been filed), the certificate shall have the following effect—

(i) In the case of a certificate of release issued under paragraph (a) of this section, the certificate shall be conclusive that the tax lien referred to in the certificate is extinguished;

(ii) In the case of a certificate of discharge issued under paragraph (b) or (c) of this section, the certificate shall be conclusive that the property covered by the certificate is discharged from the tax lien;

(iii) In the case of a certificate of subordination issued under paragraph (d) of this section, the certificate shall be conclusive that the lien or interest to which the Federal tax lien is subordinated is superior to the tax lien; and

(iv) In the case of a certificate of nonattachment issued under paragraph (e), the certificate shall be conclusive that the lien of the United States does not attach to the property of the person referred to in the certificate.

(2) *Revocation of certificate of release or nonattachment.*—(i) *In general.*—If the appropriate official determines that either—

(a) A certificate of release or a certificate of nonattachment of the general tax lien imposed by section 6321 was issued erroneously or improvidently, or

(b) A certificate of release of such lien was issued in connection with a compromise agreement under section 7122 which has been breached,

and if the period of limitation on collection after assessment of the tax liability has not expired, the appropriate official may revoke the certificate and reinstate the tax lien. The provisions of this subparagraph do not apply in the case of the lien imposed by section 6324 relating to estate and gift taxes.

(ii) *Method of revocation and reinstatement.*—The revocation and reinstatement described in subdivision (i) of this subparagraph is accomplished by—

(a) Mailing notice of the revocation to the taxpayer at his last known address (see § 301.6212-2 for further guidance regarding the definition of last known address); and

(b) Filing notice of the revocation of the certificate in the same office in which the notice of lien to which it relates was filed (if the notice of lien has been filed).

(iii) *Effect of reinstatement.*—*(a) Effective date.*—A tax lien reinstated in accordance with the provisions of this subparagraph is effective on and after the date the notice of revocation is mailed to the taxpayer in accordance with the provisions of subdivision (ii)*(a)* of this subparagraph, but the reinstated lien is not effective before the filing of notice of revocation, in accordance with the provisions of subdivision (ii)*(b)* of this subparagraph, if the filing is required by reason of the fact that a notice of the lien had been filed.

(b) Treatment of reinstated lien.—As of the effective date of reinstatement, a reinstated lien has the same force and effect as a general tax lien imposed by section 6321 which arises upon assessment of a tax liability. The reinstated lien continues in existence until the expiration of the period of limitation on collection after assessment of the tax liability to which it relates. The reinstatement of the lien does not retroactively reinstate a previously filed notice of lien. The reinstated lien is not valid against any holder of a lien or interest described in § 301.6323(a)-1 until notice of the reinstated lien has been filed in accordance with the provisions of § 301.6323(f)-1 subsequent to or concurrent with the time the reinstated lien became effective.

(iv) *Example.*—The provisions of this subparagraph may be illustrated by the following example:

Example. On March 1, 1967, an assessment of an unpaid Federal tax liability is made against A. On March 1, 1968, notice of the Federal tax lien, which arose at the time of assessment, is filed. On April 1, 1968, A executes a bona fide mortgage on property belonging to him to B. On May 1, 1968, a certificate of release of the tax lien is erroneously issued and is filed by A in the same office in which the notice of lien was filed. On June 3, 1968, the lien is reinstated in accordance with the provisions of this subparagraph. On July 1, 1968, A executes a bona fide mortgage on property belonging to him to C. On August 1, 1968, a notice of the lien which was reinstated is properly filed in accordance with the provisions of § 301.6323(f)-1. The mortgages of both B and C will have priority over the rights of the United States with respect to the tax liability in question. Because a reinstated lien continues in existence only until the expiration of the period of limitation on collection after assessment of the tax liability to which the lien relates, in the absence of any extension or suspension of the period of limitation on collection after assessment, the reinstated lien will become unenforceable by reason of lapse of time after February 28, 1973.

(3) *Certificates void under certain conditions.*—Notwithstanding any other provisions of subtitle F of the Internal Revenue Code, any lien for Federal taxes attaches to any property with respect to which a certificate of discharge has been

issued if the person liable for the tax reacquires the property after the certificate has been issued. Thus, if property subject to a Federal tax lien is discharged therefrom and is later reacquired by the delinquent taxpayer at a time when the lien is still in existence, the tax lien attaches to the reacquired property and is enforceable against it as in the case of after-acquired property generally.

(g) *Filing of certificates and notices.*—If a certificate or notice described in this section may not be filed in the office designated by State law in which the notice of lien imposed by section 6321 (to which the certificate or notice relates) is filed, the certificate or notice is effective if filed in the office of the clerk of the United States district court for the judicial district in which the State office where the notice of lien is filed is situated.

(h) As used in this section, the term *appropriate official* means either the official or office identified in the relevant IRS Publication or, if such official or office is not so identified, the Secretary or his delegate.

(i) *Effective/applicability date.*—This section applies to any release of lien or discharge of property that is requested after January 31, 2008. [Reg. § 301.6325-1.]

☐ [*T.D.* 6119, 12-31-54. *Amended by T.D.* 6425, 11-10-59; *T.D.* 6498, 10-24-60; *T.D.* 6700, 1-6-64; *T.D.* 7429, 8-20-76; *T.D.* 7847, 11-9-82; *T.D.* 8939, 1-11-2001 *and T.D.* 9378, 1-30-2008 (*corrected* 2-21-2008).]

[Reg. § 301.6402-1]

§ 301.6402-1. Authority to make credits or refunds.—The Commissioner, within the applicable period of limitations, may credit any overpayment of tax, including interest thereon, against any outstanding liability for any tax (or for any interest, additional amount, addition to the tax, or assessable penalty) owed by the person making the overpayment and the balance, if any, shall be refunded, subject to section 6402(c) and (d) and the regulations thereunder, to that person by the Commissioner. [Reg. § 301.6402-1.]

☐ [*T.D.* 6119, 12-31-54. *Amended by T.D.* 7808, 2-3-82 *and T.D.* 8053, 9-27-85.]

[Reg. § 301.6402-2]

§ 301.6402-2. Claims for credit or refund.—(a) *Requirement that claim be filed.*—(1) Credits or refunds of overpayments may not be allowed or made after the expiration of the statutory period of limitation properly applicable unless, before the expiration of such period, a claim therefor has been filed by the taxpayer. Furthermore, under section 7422, a civil action for refund may not be instituted unless a claim has been filed within the properly applicable period of limitation.

(2) Except as provided in paragraph (b) of § 301.6091-1 (relating to hand-carried documents), if a taxpayer is required to file a claim for credit or refund using a particular form, then the claim, together with appropriate supporting evidence, shall be filed in a manner consistent with such form, form instructions, publications, or other guidance found on the IRS.gov website. If a taxpayer is filing a claim in response to an IRS notice or correspondence, then the claim must be filed in accordance with the specific instructions contained in the notice or correspondence regarding the manner of filing. Any other claim not described in the preceding sentences generally must be filed with the service center at which the taxpayer currently would be required to file a tax return for the type of tax to which the claim relates or via the appropriate electronic portal. For rules relating to interest in the case of credits or refunds, see section 6611. For rules treating timely mailing as timely filing, see section 7502. For rules relating to the time for filing a claim when the last day falls on Saturday, Sunday, or a legal holiday, see section 7503.

(b) *Grounds set forth in claim.*—(1) No refund or credit will be allowed after the expiration of the statutory period of limitation applicable to the filing of a claim therefor except upon one or more of the grounds set forth in a claim filed before the expiration of such period. The claim must set forth in detail each ground upon which a credit or refund is claimed and facts sufficient to apprise the Commissioner of the exact basis thereof. The statement of the grounds and facts must be verified by a written declaration that it is made under the penalties of perjury. A claim which does not comply with this paragraph will not be considered for any purpose as a claim for refund or credit.

(2) The IRS does not have the authority to refund on equitable grounds penalties or other amounts legally collected.

(c) *Form for filing claim.*—If a particular form is prescribed on which the claim must be made, then the claim must be made on the form so prescribed. For special rules applicable to refunds of income taxes, see § 301.6402-3. For provisions relating to credits and refunds of taxes other than income tax, see the regulations relating to the particular tax. All claims by taxpayers for the refund of taxes, interest, penalties, and additions to tax that are not otherwise provided for must be made on Form 843, "Claim for Refund and Request for Abatement."

(d) *Separate claims for separate taxable periods.*—In the case of income and gift taxes, income tax withheld, taxes under the Federal Insurance Contributions Act, taxes under the Railroad Retirement Tax Act, and taxes under the Federal Unemployment Tax Act, a separate claim must be made for each return for each taxable period.

(e) *Proof of representative capacity.*—If a return is filed by an individual and, after his death, a refund claim is filed by his legal representative, certified copies of the letters testamentary, letters of administration, or other similar evidence must be annexed to the claim, to show the authority of the legal representative to file the claim. If an executor, administrator, guardian, trustee, receiver, or other fiduciary files a return and thereafter a refund claim is filed by the same fiduciary, documentary evidence to establish the legal authority of the fiduciary need not accompany the claim, provided a statement is made in the claim showing that the return was filed by the fiduciary and that the latter is still acting. In such cases, if a refund is to be paid, letters testamentary, letters of administration, or other evidence may be required, but should be submitted only upon the receipt of a specific request therefor. If a claim is filed by a fiduciary other than the one by whom the return was filed, the necessary documentary evidence should accompany the claim. A claim may be executed by an agent of the person assessed, but in such case a power of attorney must accompany the claim.

(f) *Mailing of refund check.*—(1) Checks in payment of claims allowed will be drawn in the names of the persons entitled to the money and, except as provided in subparagraph (2) of this paragraph, the checks may be sent direct to the claimant or to such person in care of an attorney or agent who has filed a power of attorney specifically authorizing him to receive such checks.

(2) Checks in payment of claims which have either been reduced to judgment or settled in the course or as a result of litigation will be drawn in the name of the person or persons entitled to the money and will be sent to the Assistant Attorney General, Tax Division, Department of Justice, for delivery to the taxpayer or the counsel of record in the court proceeding.

(3) For restrictions on the assignment of claims, see sections 3477 of the Revised Statutes (31 U.S.C. 203).

(g) *Misdirected direct deposit refund.*—(1) *Definition.*—The term *misdirected direct deposit refund* includes any refund of an overpayment of tax that is disbursed as a direct deposit but is not deposited into the account designated on the claim for refund to receive the direct deposit refund.

(2) *Procedures for reporting a misdirected direct deposit refund.*—(i) *In general.*—A taxpayer or a taxpayer's authorized representative may report to the IRS that the taxpayer never received a direct deposit refund and request a replacement refund. The report must include the name of the taxpayer who requested the refund, the taxpayer identification number of the taxpayer, the taxpayer's mailing address, the type of return to which the refund is related, the account number and routing number that the taxpayer requested the refund be directly deposited into, and any other information necessary to locate the misdirected direct deposit refund.

(ii) *How to report a misdirected direct deposit refund.*—A reporting described in paragraph (g)(2)(i) of this section may be made in the following ways:

(A) By calling the IRS;

(B) On the form prescribed by the IRS and in accordance with the applicable publications, instructions, or other appropriate guidance;

(C) By contacting the Office of the Taxpayer Advocate by telephone, by mail, facsimile, or in person; or

(D) By submitting the appropriate form in person at a Taxpayer Assistance Center.

(3) *Procedures for coordination with financial institutions.*—(i) *Identification of the account that received the misdirected direct deposit refund.*—If the IRS receives a report described in paragraph (g)(2)(ii) of this section, the IRS will confirm that the overpayment was issued as a direct deposit. The IRS will confirm that the overpayment was not credited or offset pursuant to the law in effect immediately prior to the direct deposit being disbursed. If the direct deposit described in the report was issued, the IRS will initiate a refund trace to request the assistance of the Department of the Treasury's Bureau of the Fiscal Service. In accordance with its own procedures, the Bureau of the Fiscal Service coordinates with the financial institution that holds directly or indirectly the deposit account into which the refund was made, requesting from the financial institution such information as is necessary to identify whether the financial institution received the refund; whether the financial institution returned, or will return, the refund to the IRS, or if no funds are available for return; whether a deposit was made into the account designated on the claim for refund; and the identity of the deposit account owner to whom the deposit was disbursed.

(ii) *Coordination to recover the amounts transferred.*—Recovery of the misdirected direct deposit refund from a financial institution shall follow the procedures established by the Bureau of the Fiscal Service. The Bureau of the Fiscal Service shall request the return of the misdirected direct deposit refund from the financial institution that received it. The IRS may contact the financial institution directly to recover the misdirected direct deposit refund.

(4) *Issuance of replacement refund.*—When the IRS has determined that a misdirected direct deposit refund has occurred, the IRS will issue a replacement refund in the full amount of the refund that was misdirected. The replacement refund may be issued as a direct deposit or as a paper check sent to the taxpayer's last known address.

(5) *Applicability of this paragraph (g) to missing refunds.*—The provisions of paragraphs (g)(2) through (g)(3)(i) of this section should be used for any refund that was disbursed as a direct deposit and that the taxpayer reports as missing. For example, although a refund that was deposited into an incorrect bank account because the taxpayer transposed two digits in their bank account number is not considered to be a misdirected direct deposit refund, the provisions of paragraphs (g)(2) through (g)(3)(i) of this section should be used. If the application of these procedures results in an amount recovered by the IRS, the recovered amount will be refunded or credited as allowed by law.

(h) *Applicability dates.*—Paragraphs (a)(2), (b)(2), (c), and (d) of this section apply to claims for credit or refund filed on or after July 24, 2015.

Paragraphs (a)(1), (b)(1), (e), and (f) of this section apply to claims for credit or refund filed before, on or after July 24, 2015. Paragraph (g) of this section applies to reports described in paragraph (g)(2)(ii) of this section made after December 22, 2020. [Reg. § 301.6402-2.]

□ [*T.D.* 6119, 12-31-54. *Amended by T.D.* 6292, 4-18-58; *T.D.* 6498, 10-24-60; *T.D.* 6585, 12-27-61; *T.D.* 6950, 4-3-68; *T.D.* 7008, 2-28-69; *T.D.* 7188, 6-28-72; *T.D.* 7410, 3-15-76, *T.D.* 7484, 4-29-77, *T.D.* 9727, 7-23-2015 *and T.D.* 9940, 12-18-2020.]

[Reg. § 301.6402-3]

§ 301.6402-3. Special rules applicable to income tax.—(a) The following rules apply to a claim for credit or refund of income tax:—

(1) In general, in the case of an overpayment of income taxes, a claim for credit or refund of such overpayment shall be made on the appropriate income tax return.

(2) In the case of an overpayment of income taxes for a taxable year of an individual for which a Form 1040 or 1040A has been filed, a claim for refund shall be made on Form 1040X ("Amended U.S. Individual Income Tax Return").

(3) In the case of an overpayment of income taxes for a taxable year of a corporation for which a Form 1120 has been filed, a claim for refund shall be made on Form 1120X ("Amended U.S. Corporation Income Tax Return").

(4) In the case of an overpayment of income taxes for a taxable year for which a form other than Form 1040, 1040A, or 1120 was filed (such as Form 1041 (U.S. Fiduciary Income Tax Return) or Form 990T (Exempt Organization Business Income Tax Return)), a claim for credit or refund shall be made on the appropriate amended income tax return.

(5) A properly executed individual, fiduciary, or corporation original income tax return or an amended return (on 1040X or 1120X if applicable) shall constitute a claim for refund or credit within the meaning of section 6402 and section 6511 for the amount of the overpayment disclosed by such return (or amended return). For purposes of section 6511, such claim shall be considered as filed on the date on which such return (or amended return) is considered as filed, except that if the requirements of § 301.7502-1, relating to timely mailing treated as timely filing are met, the claim shall be considered to be filed on the date of the postmark stamped on the cover in which the return (or amended return) was mailed. A return or amended return shall constitute a claim for refund or credit if it contains a statement setting forth the amount determined as an overpayment and advising whether such amount shall be refunded to the taxpayer or shall be applied as a credit against the taxpayer's estimated income tax for the taxable year immediately succeeding the taxable year for which such return (or amended return) is filed. If the taxpayer indicates on its return (or amended return) that all or part of the overpayment shown by its return (or amended return) is to be applied to its estimated income tax for its succeeding taxable year, such indication shall constitute an election to so apply such overpayment, and no interest shall be allowed on such portion of the overpayment credited and such amount shall be applied as a payment on account of the estimated income tax for such year or the installments thereof.

(6) Notwithstanding paragraph (a)(5) of this section, the Internal Revenue Service, within the applicable period of limitations, may credit any overpayment of individual, fiduciary, or corporation income tax, including interest thereon, against—

(i) First, any outstanding liability for any tax (or for any interest, additional amount, additions to the tax, or assessable penalty) owed by the taxpayer making the overpayment;

(ii) Second, in the case of an individual taxpayer, amounts of past-due support assigned to a State under section 402(a)(26) or 471(a)(17) of the Social Security Act under procedures set forth in the regulations under section 6402(c);

(iii) Third, past-due and legally enforceable debt under procedures set forth in the regulations under section 6402(d); and

(iv) Fourth, qualifying amounts of past-due support not assigned to a State under procedures set forth in the regulations under section 6402(c).

Only the balance, if any, of the overpayment remaining after credits described in this paragraph (a)(6) shall be treated in the manner so elected.

(b) [Reserved]

(c) If the taxpayer is not required to show the tax on the form (see section 6014 and the accompanying regulations), the IRS will treat a properly filed income tax return as a claim for refund and such return will constitute a claim for refund within the meaning of section 6402 and section 6511 for the amount of the overpayment shown by the computation of the tax made by the IRS on the basis of the return. For purposes of the limitations period of section 6511, such claim will be treated as filed on the date the return is treated as filed.

(d) In any case in which a taxpayer elects to have an overpayment refunded to him he may not thereafter change his election to have the overpayment applied as a payment on account of his estimated income tax.

(e) In the case of a nonresident alien individual or foreign corporation, the appropriate income tax return on which the claim for refund or credit is made must contain the tax identification number of the taxpayer required pursuant to section 6109 and the entire amount of income of the taxpayer subject to tax, even if the tax liability for that income was fully satisfied at source through withholding under chapters 3 or 4 of the Internal Revenue Code (Code). Also, if the overpayment of tax resulted from the withholding of tax at source under chapter 3 or 4 of the Code, a copy of the Form 1042-S, "Foreign Person's U.S. Source Income subject to Withholding," Form 8805, "Foreign Partner's Information Statement of Section 1446 Withholding Tax," or other statement (required under § 1.1446-3(d)(2) of this chapter) required to be provided to the beneficial owner or partner pursuant to § 1.1461-1(c)(1)(i), § 1.1474-1(d)(1)(i), or § 1.1446-3(d) of this chapter must be attached to the return. For purposes of claiming a refund, the Form 8805 or other statement must include the taxpayer identification number of the beneficial owner or partner even if not otherwise required. No claim for refund or credit under chapter 65 of the Code may be made by the taxpayer for any amount that the payor has repaid to the taxpayer pursuant to reimbursement or set-off procedures (described in § 1.1461-2(a)(2), (3) or § 1.1474-2(a)(3), (4) of this chapter). In addition, no claim for refund or credit may be made by a taxpayer for any amount that has been repaid to a qualified intermediary (as described in § 1.1441-1(e)(5)(ii)) or a participating FFI (as described in § 1.1471-1(b)(91)) pursuant to a collective refund filed by such entity on behalf of the taxpayer. See § 1.1441-1(e)(5)(iii) (describing a qualified intermediary agreement) and § 1.1471-4(h) (describing a collective refund). Upon request, a taxpayer must also submit such documentation as the IRS, may require establishing that the taxpayer is the beneficial owner of the income for which a claim for refund or credit is being made and verifying the grounds and facts set forth in taxpayer's claim as required by § 301.6402-2(b)(1). See § 1.1474-5 for additional requirements that may apply in the case of a refund of tax withheld under chapter 4.

(f) *Effective/applicability date.*—(1) Except as provided in paragraph (f)(2) of this section, this section applies on or after January 6, 2017. (For payments made after June 30, 2014, and before January 6, 2017, see this section as in effect and contained in 26 CFR part 1, revised April 1, 2016.)

(2) References in paragraph (e) of this section to Form 8805 or other statements required under § 1.1446-3(d)(2) shall apply to partnership taxable years beginning after April 29, 2008. References in paragraph (e) of this section to amounts withheld under chapter 4 of the Code and claims made with respect to amounts withheld under chapter 4 of the Code shall apply to withholdable payments made after June 30, 2014. [Reg. § 301.6402-3.]

□ [*T.D.* 6119, 12-31-54. *Amended by T.D.* 6292, 4-18-58; *T.D.* 6425, 11-10-59; *T.D.* 6498, 10-24-60; *T.D.* 6585, 12-27-61; *T.D.* 7057, 9-2-70; *T.D.* 7102, 3-23-71; *T.D.* 7234, 12-20-72; *T.D.* 7269, 4-12-73; *T.D.* 7293, 11-27-73; *T.D.* 7298, 12-21-73; *T.D.* 7410, 3-15-76; *T.D.* 7808, 2-3-82; *T.D.* 8053, 9-27-85; *T.D.* 8734, 10-6-97 (T.D. 8804 delayed the effective date of T.D. 8734 from January 1, 1999, to January 1, 2000; T.D. 8856 further delayed the effective date of T.D. 8734 until January 1, 2001); *T.D.* 9394, 4-28-2008, *T.D.* 9658, 2-28-2014, *T.D.* 9727, 7-23-2015 *and T.D.* 9808, 12-30-2016.]

[Reg. § 301.6402-4]

§ 301.6402-4. Payments in excess of amounts shown on return.—(a) If the IRS determines that the payments by the taxpayer that are made within the period prescribed for payment and before the filing of the return exceed the amount of tax shown on the return (for example, excessive estimated income tax payments or excessive withholding), the IRS may credit or refund such overpayment without awaiting examination of the completed return and without awaiting the filing of a claim for refund. The provisions of §§ 301.6402-2 and 301.6402-3 are applicable to such overpayment, and taxpayers should submit claims for refund (if the income tax return is not itself a claim for refund, as provided in § 301.6402-3) to protect themselves in the event the IRS fails to make such determination and credit or refund. The provisions of section 6405 (relating to reports of refunds in excess of the statutorily prescribed threshold referral amount to the Joint Committee on Taxation) do not apply to the overpayments described in this section.

(b) *Effective/applicability date.*—The rules of this section apply to payments made on or after July 24, 2015. [Reg. § 301.6402-4.]

□ [*T.D.* 6119, 12-31-54. *Amended by T.D.* 6585, 12-27-61 *and T.D.* 9727, 7-23-2015.]

[Reg. § 301.6404-2]

§ 301.6404-2. Abatement of interest.—(a) *In general.*—(1) Section 6404(e)(1) provides that the Commissioner may (in the Commissioner's discretion) abate the assessment of all or any part of interest on any—

(i) Deficiency (as defined in section 6211(a), relating to income, estate, gift, generation-skipping, and certain excise taxes) attributable in whole or in part to any unreasonable error or delay by an officer or employee of the Internal Revenue Service (IRS) (acting in an official capacity) in performing a ministerial or managerial act; or

(ii) Payment of any tax described in section 6212(a) (relating to income, estate, gift, generation-skipping, and certain excise taxes) to the extent that any unreasonable error or delay in payment is attributable to an officer or employee of the IRS (acting in an official capacity) being erroneous or dilatory in performing a ministerial or managerial act.

(2) An error or delay in performing a ministerial or managerial act will be taken into account only if no significant aspect of the error or delay is attributable to the taxpayer involved or to a person related to the taxpayer within the meaning of section 267(b) or section 707(b)(1). Moreover, an error or delay in performing a ministerial or managerial act will be taken into account only if it occurs after the IRS has contacted the taxpayer in writing with respect to the deficiency or payment. For purposes of this paragraph (a)(2), no significant aspect of the error or delay is attributable to the taxpayer merely because the taxpayer consents to extend the period of limitations.

(b) *Definitions.*—(1) *Managerial act.*—means an administrative act that occurs during the processing of a taxpayer's case involving the temporary or permanent loss of records or the exercise of judgment or discretion relating to management of personnel. A decision concerning the proper application of federal tax law (or other federal or state law) is not a managerial act. Further, a general administrative decision, such as the IRS's decision on how to organize the processing of tax returns or its delay in implementing an improved computer system, is not a managerial act for which interest can be abated under paragraph (a) of this section.

(2) *Ministerial act.*—means a procedural or mechanical act that does not involve the exercise of judgment or discretion, and that occurs during the processing of a taxpayer's case after all prerequisites to the act, such as conferences and review by supervisors, have taken place. A decision concerning the proper application of federal tax law (or other federal or state law) is not a ministerial act.

(c) *Examples.*—The following examples illustrate the provisions of paragraphs (b)(1) and (2) of this section. Unless otherwise stated, for purposes of the examples, no significant aspect of any error or delay is attributable to the taxpayer, and the IRS has contacted the taxpayer in writing with respect to the deficiency or payment. The examples are as follows:

Example 1. A taxpayer moves from one state to another before the IRS selects the taxpayer's income tax return for examination. A letter explaining that the return has been selected for examination is sent to the taxpayer's old address and then forwarded to the new address. The taxpayer timely responds, asking that the audit be transferred to the IRS's district office that is nearest the new address. The group manager timely approves the request. After the request for transfer has been approved, the transfer of the case is a ministerial act. The Commissioner may (in the Commissioner's discretion) abate interest attributable to any unreasonable delay in transferring the case.

Example 2. An examination of a taxpayer's income tax return reveals a deficiency with respect to which a notice of deficiency will be issued. The taxpayer and the IRS identify all agreed and unagreed issues, the notice is prepared and reviewed (including review by District Counsel, if necessary), and any other relevant prerequisites are completed. The issuance of the notice of deficiency is a ministerial act. The Commissioner may (in the Commissioner's discretion) abate interest attributable to any unreasonable delay in issuing the notice.

Example 3. A revenue agent is sent to a training course for an extended period of time, and the agent's supervisor decides not to reassign the agent's cases. During the training course, no work is done on the cases assigned to the agent. The decision to send the revenue agent to the training course and the decision not to reassign the agent's cases are not ministerial acts; however, both decisions are managerial acts. The Commissioner may (in the Commissioner's discretion) abate interest attributable to any unreasonable delay resulting from these decisions.

Example 4. A taxpayer appears for an office audit and submits all necessary documentation and information. The auditor tells the taxpayer that the taxpayer will receive a copy of the audit report. However, before the report is prepared, the auditor is permanently reassigned to another group. An extended period of time passes before the auditor's cases are reassigned. The decision to reassign the auditor and the decision not to reassign the auditor's cases are not ministerial acts; however, they are managerial acts. The Commissioner may (in the Commissioner's discretion) abate interest attributable to any unreasonable delay resulting from these decisions.

Example 5. A taxpayer is notified that the IRS intends to audit the taxpayer's income tax return. The agent assigned to the case is granted sick leave for an extended period of time, and the taxpayer's case is not reassigned. The decision to grant sick leave and the decision not to reassign the taxpayer's case to another agent are not ministerial acts; however, they are managerial acts. The Commissioner may (in the Commissioner's discretion) abate interest attributable to any unreasonable delay caused by these decisions.

Example 6. A revenue agent has completed an examination of the income tax return of a taxpayer. There are issues that are not agreed upon between the taxpayer and the IRS. Before the notice of deficiency is prepared and reviewed, a clerical employee misplaces the taxpayer's case file. The act of misplacing the case file is a managerial act. The Commissioner may (in the Commissioner's discretion) abate interest attributable to any unreasonable delay resulting from the file being misplaced.

Example 7. A taxpayer invests in a tax shelter and reports a loss from the tax shelter on the taxpayer's income tax return. IRS personnel conduct an extensive examination of the tax shelter, and the processing of the taxpayer's case is delayed because of that examination. The decision to delay the processing of the taxpayer's case until the completion of the examination of the tax shelter is a decision on how to organize the processing of tax returns. This is a general administrative decision. Consequently, interest attributable to a delay caused by this decision cannot be abated under paragraph (a) of this section.

Example 8. A taxpayer claims a loss on the taxpayer's income tax return and is notified that the IRS intends to examine the return. However, a decision is made not to commence the examination of the taxpayer's return until the processing of another return, for which the statute of limitations is about to expire, is completed. The decision on how to prioritize the processing of returns based on the expiration of the statute of limitations is a general administrative decision. Consequently, interest attributable to a delay caused by this decision cannot be abated under paragraph (a) of this section.

Example 9. During the examination of an income tax return, there is disagreement between the taxpayer and the revenue agent regarding certain itemized deductions claimed by the taxpayer on the return. To resolve the issue, advice is requested in a timely manner from the Office of Chief Counsel on a substantive issue of federal tax law. The decision to request advice is a decision concerning the proper application of federal tax law; it is neither a ministerial nor a managerial act. Consequently, interest attributable to a delay resulting from the decision to request advice cannot be abated under paragraph (a) of this section.

Example 10. The facts are the same as in *Example 9* except the attorney who is assigned to respond to the request for advice is granted leave for an extended period of time. The case is not reassigned during the attorney's absence. The decision to grant leave and the decision not to reassign the taxpayer's case to another attorney are not ministerial acts; however, they are managerial acts. The Commissioner may (in the Commissioner's discretion) abate interest attributable to any unreasonable delay caused by these decisions.

Example 11. A taxpayer contacts an IRS employee and requests information with respect to the amount due to satisfy the taxpayer's income tax liability for a particular taxable year. Because the employee fails to access the most recent data, the employee gives the taxpayer an incorrect amount due. As a result, the taxpayer pays less than the amount required to satisfy the tax liability. Accessing the most recent data is a ministerial act. The Commissioner may (in the Commissioner's discretion) abate interest attributable to any unreasonable error or delay arising from giving the taxpayer an incorrect amount due to satisfy the taxpayer's income tax liability.

Example 12. A taxpayer contacts an IRS employee and requests information with respect to the amount due to satisfy the taxpayer's income tax liability for a particular taxable year. To determine the current amount due, the employee must interpret complex provisions of federal tax law involving net operating loss carrybacks and foreign tax credits. Because the employee incorrectly interprets these provisions, the employee gives the taxpayer an incorrect amount due. As a result, the taxpayer pays less than the amount required to satisfy the tax liability. Interpreting complex provisions of federal tax law is neither a ministerial nor a managerial act. Consequently, interest attributable to an error or delay arising from giving the taxpayer an incorrect amount due to satisfy the taxpayer's income tax liability in this situation cannot be abated under paragraph (a) of this section.

Example 13. A taxpayer moves from one state to another after the IRS has undertaken an examination of the taxpayer's income tax return. The taxpayer asks that the audit be transferred to the IRS's district office that is nearest the new address. The group manager approves the request, and the case is transferred. Thereafter, the taxpayer moves to yet another state, and once again asks that the audit be transferred to the IRS's district office that is nearest that new address. The group manager approves the request, and the case is again transferred. The agent then assigned to the case is granted sick leave for an extended period of time, and the taxpayer's case is not reassigned. The taxpayer's repeated moves result in a delay in the completion of the examination. Under paragraph (a)(2) of this section, interest attributable to this delay cannot be abated because a significant aspect of this delay is attributable to the taxpayer. However, as in *Example 5*, the Commissioner may (in the Commissioner's discretion) abate interest attributable to any unreasonable delay caused by the managerial decisions to grant sick leave and not to reassign the taxpayer's case to another agent.

(d) *Effective dates.*—(1) *In general.*—Except as provided in paragraph (d)(2) of this section, the provisions of this section apply to interest accruing with respect to deficiencies or payments of any tax described in section 6212(a) for taxable years beginning after July 30, 1996.

(2) *Special rules.*—(i) *Estate tax.*—The provisions of this section apply to interest accruing with respect to deficiencies or payments of—

(A) Estate tax imposed under section 2001 on estates of decedents dying after July 30, 1996;

(B) The additional estate tax imposed under sections 2032A(c) and 2056A(b)(1)(B) in the case of taxable events occurring after July 30, 1996; and

(C) The additional estate tax imposed under section 2056A(b)(1)(A) in the case of taxable events occurring after December 31, 1996.

(ii) *Gift tax.*—The provisions of this section apply to interest accruing with respect to deficiencies or payments of gift tax imposed under chapter 12 on gifts made after December 31, 1996.

(iii) *Generation-skipping transfer tax.*—The provisions of this section apply to interest accruing with respect to deficiencies or payments of generation-skipping transfer tax imposed under chapter 13—

(A) On direct skips occurring at death, if the transferor dies after July 30, 1996; and

(B) On inter vivos direct skips, and all taxable terminations and taxable distributions occurring after December 31, 1996. [Reg. § 301.6404-2.]

□ [*T.D.* 8789, 12-17-98.]

[Reg. § 301.6501(a)-1]

§ 301.6501(a)-1. Period of limitations upon assessment and collection.—(a) The amount of any tax imposed by the Internal Revenue Code (other than a tax collected by means of stamps) shall be assessed within 3 years after the return was filed. For rules applicable in cases where the return is filed prior to the due date thereof, see section 6501(b). In the case of taxes payable by stamp, assessment shall be made at any time after the tax became due and before the expiration of 3 years after the date on which any part of the tax was paid. For exceptions and additional rules, see subsections (b) to (g) of section

6501, and for cross references to other provisions relating to limitations on assessment and collection, see sections 6501(h) and 6504.

(b) No proceeding in court without assessment for the collection of any tax shall be begun after the expiration of the applicable period for the assessment of such tax. [Reg. § 301.6501(a)-1.]

☐ [*T.D.* 6172, 5-2-56. *Amended by T.D.* 6425, 11-10-59 *and T.D.* 6498, 10-24-60.]

[Reg. § 301.6501(b)-1]

§ 301.6501(b)-1. Time return deemed filed for purposes of determining limitations.—(a) *Early return.*—Any return, other than a return of tax referred to in paragraph (b) of this section, filed before the last day prescribed by law or regulations for the filing thereof (determined without regard to any extension of time for filing) shall be considered as filed on such last day.

(b) *Returns of social security tax and of income tax withholding.*—If a return on or after November 13, 1966, of tax imposed by chapter 3 of the Code (relating to withholding of tax on nonresident aliens and foreign corporations and tax-free covenant bonds), or if a return of tax imposed by chapter 21 of the Code (relating to the Federal Insurance Contributions Act) or by chapter 24 of the Code (relating to collection of income tax at source on wages), for any period ending with or within a calendar year is filed before April 15 of the succeeding calendar year, such return shall be deemed filed on April 15 of such succeeding calendar year. For example, if quarterly returns of the tax imposed by chapter 24 of the Code are filed for the four quarters of 1955 on April 30, July 31, and October 31, 1955, and on January 31, 1956, the period of limitation for assessment with respect to the tax required to be reported on such return is measured from April 15, 1956. However, if any of such returns is filed after April 15, 1956, the period of limitation for assessment of the tax required to be reported on that return is measured from the date it is in fact filed.

(c) *Returns executed by district directors or other internal revenue officers.*—The execution of a return by a district director or other authorized internal revenue officer or employee under the authority of section 6020(b) shall not start the running of the statutory period of limitations on assessment and collection. [Reg. § 301.6501(b)-1.]

☐ [*T.D.* 6172, 5-2-56. *Amended by T.D.* 6498, 10-24-60 *and T.D.* 6922, 6-16-67.]

[Reg. § 301.6501(c)-1]

§ 301.6501(c)-1. Exceptions to general period of limitations on assessment and collection.—(a) *False return.*—In the case of a false or fraudulent return with intent to evade any tax, the tax may be assessed, or a proceeding in court for the collection of such tax may be begun without assessment, at any time after such false or fraudulent return is filed.

(b) *Willful attempt to evade tax.*—In the case of a willful attempt in any manner to defeat or evade any tax imposed by the Code (other than a tax imposed by subtitle A or B, relating to income, estate, or gift taxes), the tax may be assessed, or a proceeding in court for the collection of such tax may be begun without assessment, at any time.

(c) *No return.*—In the case of a failure to file a return, the tax may be assessed, or a proceeding in court for the collection of such tax may be begun without assesment, at any time after the date prescribed for filing the return. For special rules relating to filing a return for chapter 42 and similar taxes, see §§ 301.6501(n)-1, 301.6501(n)-2, and 301.6501(n)-3.

(d) *Extension by agreement.*—The time prescribed by section 6501 for the assessment of any tax (other than the estate tax imposed by chapter 11 of the Code) may, prior to the expiration of such time, be extended for any period of time agreed upon in writing by the taxpayer and the district director or an assistant regional commissioner. The extension shall become effective when the agreement has been executed by both parties. The period agreed upon may be extended by subsequent agreements in writing made before the expiration of the period previously agreed upon.

(e) *Gifts subject to chapter 14 of the Internal Revenue Code not adequately disclosed on the return.*—(1) *In general.*—If any transfer of property subject to the special valuation rules of section 2701 or section 2702, or if the occurrence of any taxable event described in section § 25.2701-4 of this chapter, is not adequately shown on a return of tax imposed by chapter 12 of subtitle B of the Internal Revenue Code (without regard to section 2503(b)), any tax imposed by chapter 12 of subtitle B of the Code on the transfer or resulting from the taxable event may be assessed, or a proceeding in court for the collection of the appropriate tax may be begun without assessment, at any time.

(2) *Adequately shown.*—A transfer of property valued under the rules of section 2701 or section 2702 or any taxable event described in § 25.2701-4 of this chapter will be considered adequately shown on a return of tax imposed by chapter 12 of subtitle B of the Internal Revenue Code only if, with respect to the entire transaction or series of transactions (including any transaction that affected the transferred interest) of which the transfer (or taxable event) was a part, the return provides:

(i) A description of the transactions, including a description of transferred and retained interests and the method (or methods) used to value each;

(ii) The identity of, and relationship between, the transferor, transferee, all other persons participating in the transactions, and all parties related to the transferor holding an equity interest in any entity involved in the transaction; and

(iii) A detailed description (including all actuarial factors and discount rates used) of the method used to determine the amount of the gift arising from the transfer (or taxable event), including, in the case of an equity interest that is not actively traded, the financial and other data used in determining value. Financial data should generally include balance sheets and statements of net earnings, operating results, and dividends paid for each of the 5 years immediately before the valuation date.

(3) *Effective date.*—The provisions of this paragraph (e) are effective as of January 28, 1992. In determining whether a transfer or taxable event is adequately shown on a gift tax return filed prior to that date, taxpayers may rely on any reasonable interpretation of the statutory provisions. For these purposes, the provisions of the proposed regulations and the final regulations are considered a reasonable interpretation of the statutory provisions.

(f) *Gifts made after December 31, 1996, not adequately disclosed on the return.*—(1) *In general.*—If a transfer of property, other than a transfer described in paragraph (e) of this section, is not adequately disclosed on a gift tax return (Form 709, "United States Gift (and Generation-Skipping Transfer) Tax Return"), or in a statement attached to the return, filed for the calendar period in which the transfer occurs, then any gift tax imposed by chapter 12 of subtitle B of the Internal Revenue Code on the transfer may be assessed, or a proceeding in court for the collection of the appropriate tax may be begun without assessment, at any time.

(2) *Adequate disclosure of transfers of property reported as gifts.*—A transfer will be adequately disclosed on the return only if it is reported in a manner adequate to apprise the Internal Revenue Service of the nature of the gift and the basis for the value so reported. Transfers reported on the gift tax return as transfers of property by gift will be considered adequately disclosed under this paragraph (f)(2) if the return (or a statement attached to the return) provides the following information—

(i) A description of the transferred property and any consideration received by the transferor;

(ii) The identity of, and relationship between, the transferor and each transferee;

(iii) If the property is transferred in trust, the trust's tax identification number and a brief description of the terms of the trust, or in lieu of a brief description of the trust terms, a copy of the trust instrument;

(iv) Except as provided in § 301.6501-1(f)(3), a detailed description of the method used to determine the fair market value of property transferred, including any financial data (for example, balance sheets, etc. with explanations of any adjustments) that were utilized in determining the value of the interest, any restrictions on the transferred property that were considered in determining the fair market value of the property, and a description of any discounts, such as discounts for blockage, minority or fractional interests, and lack of marketability, claimed in valuing the property. In the case of a transfer of an interest that is actively traded on an established exchange, such as the New York Stock Exchange, the American Stock Exchange, the NASDAQ National Market, or a regional exchange in which quotations are published on a daily basis, including recognized foreign exchanges, recitation of the exchange where the interest is listed, the CUSIP number of the security, and the mean between the highest and lowest quoted selling prices on the applicable valuation date will satisfy all of the requirements of this paragraph (f)(2)(iv). In the case of the transfer of an interest in an entity (for example, a corporation or partnership) that is not actively traded, a description must be provided of any discount claimed in valuing the interests in the entity or any assets owned by such entity. In addition, if the value of the entity or of the interests in the entity is properly determined based on the net value of the assets held by the entity, a statement must be provided regarding the fair market value of 100 percent of the entity (determined without regard to any discounts in valuing the entity or any assets owned by the entity), the pro rata portion of the entity subject to the transfer, and the fair market value of the transferred interest as reported on the return. If 100 percent of the value of the entity is not disclosed, the taxpayer bears the burden of demonstrating that the fair market value of the entity is properly determined by a method other than a method based on the net value of the assets held by the entity. If the entity that is the subject of the transfer owns an interest in another non-actively traded entity (either directly or through ownership of an entity), the information required in this paragraph (f)(2)(iv) must be provided for each entity if the information is relevant and material in determining the value of the interest; and

(v) A statement describing any position taken that is contrary to any proposed, temporary or final Treasury regulations or revenue rulings published at the time of the transfer (see § 601.601(d)(2) of this chapter).

(3) *Submission of appraisals in lieu of the information required under paragraph (f)(2)(iv) of this section.*—The requirements of paragraph (f)(2)(iv) of this section will be satisfied if the donor submits an appraisal of the transferred property that meets the following requirements—

(i) The appraisal is prepared by an appraiser who satisfies all of the following requirements:

(A) The appraiser is an individual who holds himself or herself out to the public as an appraiser or performs appraisals on a regular basis.

(B) Because of the appraiser's qualifications, as described in the appraisal that details the appraiser's background, experience, education, and membership, if any, in professional appraisal associations, the appraiser is qualified to make appraisals of the type of property being valued.

(C) The appraiser is not the donor or the donee of the property or a member of the family of the donor or donee, as defined in section 2032A(e)(2), or any person employed by the donor, the donee, or a member of the family of either; and

(ii) The appraisal contains all of the following:

(A) The date of the transfer, the date on which the transferred property was appraised, and the purpose of the appraisal.

(B) A description of the property.

(C) A description of the appraisal process employed.

(D) A description of the assumptions, hypothetical conditions, and any limiting conditions and restrictions on the transferred property that affect the analyses, opinions, and conclusions.

(E) The information considered in determining the appraised value, including in the case of an ownership interest in a business, all financial data that was used in determining the value of the interest that is sufficiently detailed so that another person can replicate the process and arrive at the appraised value.

(F) The appraisal procedures followed, and the reasoning that supports the analyses, opinions, and conclusions.

(G) The valuation method utilized, the rationale for the valuation method, and the procedure used in determining the fair market value of the asset transferred.

(H) The specific basis for the valuation, such as specific comparable sales or transactions, sales of similar interests, asset-based approaches, merger-acquisition transactions, etc.

(4) *Adequate disclosure of non-gift completed transfers or transactions.*—Completed transfers to members of the transferor's family, as defined in section 2032A(e)(2), that are made in the ordinary course of operating a business are deemed to be adequately disclosed under paragraph (f)(2) of this section, even if the transfer is not reported on a gift tax return, provided the transfer is properly reported by all parties for income tax purposes. For example, in the case of salary paid to a family member employed in a family owned business, the transfer will be treated as adequately disclosed for gift tax purposes if the item is properly reported by the business and the family member on their income tax returns. For purposes of this paragraph (f)(4), any other completed transfer that is reported, in its entirety, as not constituting a transfer by gift will be considered adequately disclosed under paragraph (f)(2) of this section only if the following information is provided on, or attached to, the return—

(i) The information required for adequate disclosure under paragraphs (f)(2)(i), (ii), (iii) and (v) of this section; and

(ii) An explanation as to why the transfer is not a transfer by gift under chapter 12 of the Internal Revenue Code.

(5) *Adequate disclosure of incomplete transfers.*—Adequate disclosure of a transfer that is reported as a completed gift on the gift tax return will commence the running of the period of limitations for assessment of gift tax on the transfer, even if the transfer is ultimately determined to be an incomplete gift for purposes of §25.2511-2 of this chapter. For example, if an incomplete gift is reported as a completed gift on the gift tax return and is adequately disclosed, the period for assessment of the gift tax will begin to run when the return is filed, as determined under section 6501(b). Further, once the period of assessment for gift tax expires, the transfer will be subject to inclusion in the donor's gross estate for estate tax purposes only to the extent that a completed gift would be so included. On the other hand, if the transfer is reported as an incomplete gift whether or not adequately disclosed, the period for assessing a gift tax with respect to the transfer will not commence to run even if the transfer is ultimately determined to be a completed gift. In that situation, the gift tax with respect to the transfer may be assessed at any time, up until three years after the donor files a return reporting the transfer as a completed gift with adequate disclosure.

(6) *Treatment of split gifts.*—If a husband and wife elect under section 2513 to treat a gift made to a third party as made one-half by each spouse, the requirements of this paragraph (f) will be satisfied with respect to the gift deemed made by the consenting spouse if the return filed by the donor spouse (the spouse that transferred the property) satisfies the requirements of this paragraph (f) with respect to that gift.

(7) *Examples.*—The following examples illustrate the rules of this paragraph (f):

Example 1. (i) *Facts.* In 2001, A transfers 100 shares of common stock of XYZ Corporation to A's child. The common stock of XYZ Corporation is actively traded on a major stock exchange. For gift tax purposes, the fair market value of one share of XYZ common stock on the date of the transfer, determined in accordance with §25.2512-2(b) of this chapter (based on the mean between the highest and lowest quoted selling prices), is $150.00. On A's Federal gift tax return, Form 709, for the 2001 calendar year, A reports the gift to A's child of 100 shares of common stock of XYZ Corporation with a value for gift tax purposes of $15,000. A specifies the date of the transfer, recites that the stock is publicly traded, identifies the stock exchange on which the stock is traded, lists the stock's CUSIP number, and lists the mean between the highest and lowest quoted selling prices for the date of transfer.

(ii) *Application of the adequate disclosure standard.* A has adequately disclosed the transfer. Therefore, the period of assessment for the transfer under section 6501 will run from the time the return is filed (as determined under section 6501(b)).

Example 2. (i) *Facts.* On December 30, 2001, A transfers closely-held stock to B, A's child. A determined that the value of the transferred stock, on December 30, 2001, was $9,000. A made no other transfers to B, or any other donee, during 2001. On A's Federal gift tax return, Form 709, for the 2001 calendar year, A provides the

See p. 15 for regulations not amended to reflect law changes

information required under paragraph (f)(2) of this section such that the transfer is adequately disclosed. A claims an annual exclusion under section 2503(b) for the transfer.

(ii) *Application of the adequate disclosure standard*. Because the transfer is adequately disclosed under paragraph (f)(2) of this section, the period of assessment for the transfer will expire as prescribed by section 6501(b), notwithstanding that if A's valuation of the closely-held stock was correct, A was not required to file a gift tax return reporting the transfer under section 6019. After the period of assessment has expired on the transfer, the Internal Revenue Service is precluded from redetermining the amount of the gift for purposes of assessing gift tax or for purposes of determining the estate tax liability. Therefore, the amount of the gift as reported on A's 2001 Federal gift tax return may not be redetermined for purposes of determining A's prior taxable gifts (for gift tax purposes) or A's adjusted taxable gifts (for estate tax purposes).

Example 3. (i) *Facts*. A owns 100 percent of the common stock of X, a closely-held corporation. X does not hold an interest in any other entity that is not actively traded. In 2001, A transfers 20 percent of the X stock to B and C, A's children, in a transfer that is not subject to the special valuation rules of section 2701. The transfer is made outright with no restrictions on ownership rights, including voting rights and the right to transfer the stock. Based on generally applicable valuation principles, the value of X would be determined based on the net value of the assets owned by X. The reported value of the transferred stock incorporates the use of minority discounts and lack of marketability discounts. No other discounts were used in arriving at the fair market value of the transferred stock or any assets owned by X. On A's Federal gift tax return, Form 709, for the 2001 calendar year, A provides the information required under paragraph (f)(2) of this section including a statement reporting the fair market value of 100 percent of X (before taking into account any discounts), the pro rata portion of X subject to the transfer, and the reported value of the transfer. A also attaches a statement regarding the determination of value that includes a discussion of the discounts claimed and how the discounts were determined.

(ii) *Application of the adequate disclosure standard*. A has provided sufficient information such that the transfer will be considered adequately disclosed and the period of assessment for the transfer under section 6501 will run from the time the return is filed (as determined under section 6501(b)).

Example 4. (i) *Facts*. A owns a 70 percent limited partnership interest in PS. PS owns 40 percent of the stock in X, a closely-held corporation. The assets of X include a 50 percent general partnership interest in PB. PB owns an interest in commercial real property. None of the entities (PS, X, or PB) is actively traded and, based on generally applicable valuation principles, the value of each entity would be determined based on the net value of the assets owned by each entity. In 2001, A transfers a 25 percent limited partnership interest in PS to B, A's child. On the Federal gift tax return, Form 709, for the 2001 calendar year, A reports the transfer of the 25 percent limited partnership interest in PS and that the fair market value of 100 percent of PS is $y and that the value of 25 percent of PS is $z, reflecting marketability and minority discounts with respect to the 25 percent interest. However, A does not disclose that PS owns 40 percent of X, and that X owns 50 percent of PB and that, in arriving at the $y fair market value of 100 percent of PS, discounts were claimed in valuing PS's interest in X, X's interest in PB, and PB's interest in the commercial real property.

(ii) *Application of the adequate disclosure standard*. The information on the lower tiered entities is relevant and material in determining the value of the transferred interest in PS. Accordingly, because A has failed to comply with requirements of paragraph (f)(2)(iv) of this section regarding PS's interest in X, X's interest in PB, and PB's interest in the commercial real property, the transfer will not be considered adequately disclosed and the period of assessment for the transfer under section 6501 will remain open indefinitely.

Example 5. The facts are the same as in *Example 4* except that A submits, with the Federal tax return, an appraisal of the 25 percent limited partnership interest in PS that satisfies the requirements of paragraph (f)(3) of this section in lieu of the information required in paragraph (f)(2)(iv) of this section. Assuming the other requirements of paragraph (f)(2) of this section are satisfied, the transfer is considered adequately disclosed and the period for assessment for the transfer under section 6501 will run from the time the return is filed (as determined under section 6501(b) of this chapter).

Example 6. A owns 100 percent of the stock of X Corporation, a company actively engaged in a manufacturing business. B, A's child, is an employee of X and receives an annual salary paid in the ordinary course of operating X Corporation. B reports the annual salary as income on B's income tax returns. In 2001, A transfers property to family members and files a Federal gift tax return reporting the transfers. However, A does not disclose the 2001 salary payments made to B. Because the salary payments were reported as income on B's income tax return, the salary payments are deemed to be adequately disclosed. The transfer of property to family members, other than the salary payments to B, reported on the gift tax return must satisfy the adequate disclosure requirements under paragraph (f)(2) of this section in order for the period of assessment under section 6501 to commence to run with respect to those transfers.

(8) *Effective date*.—This paragraph (f) is applicable to gifts made after December 31, 1996, for which the gift tax return for such calendar year is filed after December 3, 1999.

(g) *Listed transactions*.—(1) *In general*.—If a taxpayer is required to disclose a listed transaction under section 6011 and the regulations thereunder and does not do so in the time and manner required, then the time to assess any tax attributable to that listed transaction for the taxable year(s) to which the failure to disclose relates (as defined in paragraph (g)(3)(iii) of this section) will not expire before the earlier of one year after the date on which the taxpayer makes the disclosure described in paragraph (g)(5) of this section or one year after the date on which a material advisor makes a disclosure described in paragraph (g)(6) of this section. In no case will the operation of this paragraph (g) cause the period of limitations on assessment to expire any earlier than the period that would have otherwise applied under this section determined without regard to this paragraph (g)(1).

(2) *Limitations period if paragraph (g)(5) or (g)(6) is satisfied.*—If one of the disclosure provisions described in paragraphs (g)(5) or (6) of this section is satisfied, then the tax attributable to the listed transaction may be assessed at any time before the expiration of the limitations period that would have otherwise applied under this section (determined without regard to paragraph (g)(1) of this section) or the period ending one year after the date that one of the disclosure provisions described in paragraphs (g)(5) or (6) of this section was satisfied, whichever is later. If both disclosure provisions are satisfied, the one-year period will begin on the earlier of the dates on which the provisions were satisfied. Paragraph (g)(1) of this section does not apply to any period of limitations on assessment that expired before the date on which the failure to disclose the listed transaction under section 6011 occurred.

(3) *Definitions.*—(i) *Listed transaction.*—The term *listed transaction* means a transaction described in section 6707A(c)(2) of the Code and § 1.6011-4(b)(2) of this chapter.

(ii) *Material advisor.*—The term *material advisor* means a person described in section 6111(b)(1) of the Code and § 301.6111-3(b) of this chapter.

(iii) *Taxable year(s) to which the failure to disclose relates.*—The *taxable year(s) to which the failure to disclose relates* are each taxable year that the taxpayer participated (as defined under section 6011 and the regulations thereunder) in a transaction that was identified as a listed transaction and the taxpayer failed to disclose the listed transaction as required under section 6011. If the taxable year in which the taxpayer participated in the listed transaction is different from the taxable year in which the taxpayer is required to disclose the listed transaction under section 6011, the taxable year(s) to which the failure to disclose relates are each taxable year that the taxpayer participated in the transaction.

(4) *Application of paragraph with respect to pass-through entities.*—In the case of taxpayers who are partners in partnerships, shareholders in S corporations, or beneficiaries of trusts and are required to disclose a listed transaction under section 6011 and the regulations thereunder, paragraph (g)(1) of this section will apply to a particular partner, shareholder, or beneficiary if that particular partner, shareholder, or beneficiary does not disclose within the time and in the form and manner provided by section 6011 and § 1.6011-4(d) and (e), regardless of whether the partnership, S corporation, or trust or another partner, shareholder, or beneficiary discloses in accordance with section 6011 and the regulations thereunder. Similarly, because paragraph (g)(1) of this section applies on a taxpayer-by-taxpayer basis, the failure of a partnership, S corporation, or trust that has a disclosure obligation under section 6011 and that does not disclose within the time or in the form and manner provided by § 1.6011-4(d) and (e) will not cause paragraph (g)(1) of this section to apply to a partner, shareholder or beneficiary of the entity. Instead, the application of paragraph (g)(1) of this section to a partner, shareholder, or beneficiary will be determined based on whether the particular partner, shareholder, or beneficiary satisfied their disclosure obligation under section 6011 and the regulations thereunder.

(5) *Taxpayer's disclosure of a listed transaction that the taxpayer did not properly disclose under section 6011.*—(i) *In general.*—(A) *Method of disclosure.*—The taxpayer must complete the most current version of Form 8886, "Reportable Transaction Disclosure Statement" (or successor form), available on the date the taxpayer attempts to satisfy this paragraph (g)(5) in accordance with § 1.6011-4(d) and the instructions to the Form in effect on that date. The taxpayer must indicate on the Form 8886 that the form is being submitted for purposes of section 6501(c)(10) and the tax return(s) and taxable year(s) for which the taxpayer is making a section 6501(c)(10) disclosure. Disclosure under this paragraph (g)(5) will only be effective for the tax return(s) and taxable year(s) that the taxpayer specifies on the Form 8886 that he or she is attempting to disclose for purposes of section 6501(c)(10). If the Form 8886 contains a line for this purpose, then the taxpayer must complete the line in accordance with the instructions to that form. Otherwise, the taxpayer must include on the top of Page 1 of the Form 8886, and each copy of the form, the following statement: "*Section 6501(c)(10) Disclosure*" followed by the tax return(s) and taxable year(s) for which the taxpayer is making a section 6501(c)(10) disclosure. For example, if the taxpayer did not properly disclose its participation in a listed transaction the tax consequences of which were reflected on the taxpayer's Form 1040 for the 2005 taxable year, the taxpayer must include the following statement: "*Section 6501(c)(10) Disclosure; 2005 Form 1040*" on the form. The taxpayer must submit the properly completed Form 8886 and a cover letter, which must be completed in accordance with the requirements set forth in paragraph (g)(5)(i)(B) of this section, to the Office of Tax Shelter Analysis (OTSA). The taxpayer is permitted, but not required, to file an amended return with the Form 8886 and cover letter. Separate Forms 8886 and

separate cover letters must be submitted for each listed transaction the taxpayer did not properly disclose under section 6011. If the taxpayer participated in one listed transaction over multiple years, the taxpayer may submit one Form 8886 (or successor form) and cover letter and indicate on that form all of the tax returns and taxable years for which the taxpayer is making a section 6501(c)(10) disclosure. If a taxpayer participated in more than one listed transaction, then the taxpayer must submit separate Forms 8886 (or successor form) for each listed transaction, unless the listed transactions are the same or substantially similar, in which case all the listed transactions may be reported on one Form 8886.

(B) *Cover letter.*—*(1)* A cover letter to which a Form 8886 is to be attached must identify the tax return(s) and taxable year(s) for which the taxpayer is making a section 6501(c)(10) disclosure and include the following statement signed under penalties of perjury by the taxpayer:

> Under penalties of perjury, I declare that I have examined this reportable transaction disclosure statement and, to the best of my knowledge and belief, this reportable transaction disclosure statement is true, correct, and complete.

(2) If the Form 8886 is prepared by a paid preparer, in addition to the statement under penalties of perjury signed by the taxpayer, the Form 8886 must also include the following statement signed under penalties of perjury by the paid preparer.

> Under penalties of perjury, I declare that I have examined this reportable transaction disclosure statement and, to the best of my knowledge and belief, this reportable transaction disclosure statement is true, correct, and complete. This declaration is based on all information of which I, as paid preparer, have any knowledge.

(C) *Taxpayer under examination or Appeals consideration.*—A taxpayer making a disclosure under paragraph (g)(5) of this section with respect to a taxable year under examination or Appeals consideration by the IRS must satisfy the requirements of paragraphs (g)(5)(i)(A) and (B) of this section and also submit a copy of the submission to the IRS examiner or Appeals officer examining or considering the taxable year(s) to which the disclosure under this paragraph (g) relates.

(D) *Date the one-year period will begin to run if paragraph (g)(5) satisfied.*—Unless an earlier expiration is provided for in paragraph (g)(6) of this section, the time to assess tax under this paragraph (g) will not expire before one year after the date on which the Secretary is furnished the information from the taxpayer that satisfies all of the requirements of paragraphs (g)(5)(i)(A) and (B) of this section and, if applicable, paragraph (g)(5)(i)(C) of this section. If the taxpayer does not satisfy all of the requirements on the same date, the one-year period will begin on the date that the IRS is furnished the information that, together with prior disclosures of information, satisfies the requirements of this paragraph (g)(5). For purposes of this paragraph (g)(5), the information is deemed furnished on the date the IRS receives the information.

(ii) *Exception for returns other than annual returns.*—The IRS may prescribe alternative procedures to satisfy the requirements of this paragraph (g)(5) in a revenue procedure, notice, or other guidance published in the Internal Revenue Bulletin for circumstances involving returns other than annual returns.

(6) *Material advisor's disclosure of a listed transaction not properly disclosed by a taxpayer under section 6011.*—(i) *In general.*—In response to a written request of the IRS under section 6112, a material advisor with respect to a listed transaction must furnish to the IRS the information described in section 6112 and § 301.6112-1(b) in the form and manner prescribed by section 6112 and § 301.6112-1(e). If the information the material advisor furnishes identifies the taxpayer as a person who entered into the listed transaction, regardless of whether the material advisor provides the information before or after the taxpayer's failure to disclose the listed transaction under section 6011, then the requirements of this paragraph (g)(6) will be satisfied for that taxpayer. The requirements of this paragraph (g)(6) will be considered satisfied even if the material advisor furnishes the information required under section 6112 to the IRS after the date prescribed in section 6708 or published guidance relating to section 6708.

(ii) *Paragraph (g)(6) not satisfied.*—(A) *Information not furnished by a material advisor or a person permitted to act on behalf of the material advisor.*—The requirements of this paragraph (g)(6) are not satisfied for a taxpayer unless the information is furnished by—

(1) A person who is a material advisor (as defined in paragraph (g)(3)(ii) of this section) with respect to the taxpayer,

(2) A person who is providing the information pursuant to § 301.6112-1(d) on behalf of a dissolved or liquidated material advisor with respect to the taxpayer, or

(3) a person who is providing the information on behalf of a material advisor with respect to the taxpayer under a designation agreement in accordance with § 301.6112-1(f).

(B) *No written request by IRS.*—The requirements of this paragraph (g)(6) are not satisfied unless the information is furnished in response to a written request made by the IRS to the material advisor under section 6112 (except as provided in § 301.6112-1(d) with respect to a list furnished to OTSA within 60 days after dissolution or liquidation of a material advisor).

(C) *Information furnished does not identify the taxpayer.*—The requirements of this paragraph (g)(6) are not satisfied for a taxpayer unless the information furnished identifies the taxpayer as a person who entered into the listed transaction.

(iii) *Date the one-year period will begin if paragraph (g)(6) is satisfied.*—Unless an earlier expiration is provided for in paragraph (g)(5) of this section, the time to assess tax under this paragraph (g) will expire one year after the date on which the material advisor satisfies the requirements of paragraph (g)(6)(i) of this section with respect to the taxpayer. For purposes of this paragraph (g)(6), information is deemed to be furnished on the date that, in response to a request under section 6112, the IRS receives the information from a material advisor that satisfies the requirements of paragraph (g)(6)(i) of this section with respect to the taxpayer.

(7) *Tax assessable under this section.*—If the period of limitations on assessment for a taxable year remains open under this section, the Secretary has authority to assess any tax with respect to the listed transaction in that year. This includes, but is not limited to, adjustments made to the tax consequences claimed on the return plus interest, additions to tax, additional amounts, and penalties that are related to the listed transaction or adjustments made to the tax consequences. This also includes any item to the extent the item is affected by the listed transaction even if it is unrelated to the listed transaction. An example of an item affected by, but unrelated to, a listed transaction is the threshold for the medical expense deduction under section 213 that varies if there is a change in an individual's adjusted gross income. An example of a penalty related to the listed transaction is the penalty under section 6707A for failure to file the disclosure statement reporting the taxpayer's participation in the listed transaction. Examples of penalties related to the adjustments made to the tax consequences are the accuracy-related penalties under sections 6662 and 6662A.

(8) *Examples.*—The rules of this paragraph (g) are illustrated by the following examples:

Example 1. No requirement to disclose under section 6011. P, an individual, is a partner in a partnership that entered into a transaction in 2001 that was the same as or substantially similar to the transaction identified as a listed transaction in Notice 2000-44 (2000-2 CB 255). P claimed a loss from the transaction on his Form 1040 for the tax year 2001. P filed the Form 1040 prior to June 14, 2002. P did not disclose his participation in the listed transaction because P was not required to disclose the transaction under the applicable section 6011 regulations (TD 8961), which were effective for any transaction entered into before January 1, 2001 and any transaction entered into on or after January 1, 2001 that was reported on a return of the taxpayer filed on or before June 14, 2002. Although the transaction was a listed transaction and P did not disclose the transaction, P had no obligation to include on any return or statement any information with respect to a listed transaction within the meaning of section 6501(c)(10) because TD 8961 only applied to corporations, not individuals. Accordingly, section 6501(c)(10) does not apply.

Example 2. Taxable year to which the failure to disclose relates when transaction is identified as a listed transaction after first year of participation and the transaction must be disclosed with the return next filed. (i) On December 30, 2003, Y, a corporation, enters into a transaction that at the time is not a reportable transaction. On March 15, 2004, Y timely files its 2003 Form 1120, reporting the tax consequences from the transaction. On April 1, 2004, the IRS issues Notice 2004-31 that identifies the transaction as a listed transaction. Y also reports tax consequences from the transaction on its 2004 Form 1120, which it timely filed on March 15, 2005. Y did not attach a completed Form 8886 to its 2004 Form 1120 and did not send a copy of the form to OTSA. The general three-year period of limitations on assessment for Y's 2003 and 2004 taxable years would expire on March 15, 2007, and March 17, 2008, respectively.

(ii) The period of limitations on assessment for Y's 2003 taxable year was open on the date the transaction was identified as a listed transaction. Under the applicable section 6011 regulations (TD 9108), which were effective for transactions entered into before August 3, 2007, Y should have disclosed its participation in the transaction with its next filed return, which was its 2004 Form 1120, but Y did not disclose its participation. Y's failure to disclose with the 2004 Form 1120 relates to taxable years 2003 and 2004. Section 6501(c)(10) operates to keep the period of limitations on assessment open for the 2003 and 2004 taxable years with respect to the listed transaction until at least one year after the date Y satisfies the requirements of paragraph (g)(5) of this section or a material advisor satisfies the requirements of paragraph (g)(6) of this section with respect to Y.

Example 3. Taxable year to which the failure to disclose relates when transaction is identified as a listed transaction after the first year of participation and the transaction must be disclosed 90 days after the transaction became a listed transaction. (i) In January 2015, A, a calendar year taxpayer, enters into a transaction that at the time is not a listed transaction. A reports the tax consequences from the transaction on its individual income tax return for 2015 timely filed on April 15, 2016. The time for the IRS to assess tax against A under the general three-year period of limitations for A's 2015 taxable year would expire on April 15, 2019. A only participated in the transaction in 2015. On March 7, 2017, the IRS identifies the transaction as a listed transaction. A does not file the Form 8886 with OTSA by June 5, 2017.

(ii) The period of limitations on assessment for A's 2015 taxable year was open on the date the transaction was identified as a listed transaction. Under the current section 6011 regulations (TD 9350) which are effective for transactions entered into on or after August 3, 2007, A must disclose its participation in the transaction by filing a completed Form 8886 with OTSA on or before June 5, 2017, which is 90 days after the date the transaction became a listed transaction. A did not disclose the transaction as required. A's failure to disclose relates to taxable year 2015 even though the obligation to disclose did not arise until 2017. Section 6501(c)(10) operates to keep the period of limitations on assessment open for the 2015 taxable year with respect to the listed transaction until at least one year after the date A satisfies the requirements of paragraph (g)(5) of this section or a material advisor satisfies the requirements of paragraph (g)(6) of this section with respect to A.

Example 4. Requirements of paragraph (g)(6) satisfied. Same facts as *Example 3*, except that on April 5, 2019, the IRS hand delivers to Advisor J, who is a material advisor, a section 6112 request related to the listed transaction. Advisor J furnishes the required list with all the information required by section 6112 and § 301.6112-1, including all the information required with respect to A, to the IRS on May 8, 2019. The submission satisfies the requirements of paragraph (g)(6) even though Advisor J furnishes the information outside of the 20-business-day period provided in section 6708. Accordingly, under section 6501(c)(10), the period of limitations with respect to A's taxable year 2015 will end on May 8, 2020, one year after the IRS received the required information, unless the period of limitations remains open under another exception. Any tax for the 2015 taxable year not attributable to the listed transaction must be assessed by April 15, 2019.

Example 5. Requirements of paragraph (g)(5) also satisfied. Same facts as *Examples 3 and 4*, except that on May 23, 2019, A files a properly completed Form 8886 and signed cover letter with OTSA both identifying that the section 6501(c)(10) disclosure relates to A's Form 1040 for 2015. A satisfied the requirements of paragraph (g)(5) of this section as of May 23, 2019. Because the requirements of paragraph (g)(6) were satisfied first as described in *Example 4*, under section 6501(c)(10) the period of limitations will end on May 8, 2020 (one year after the requirements of paragraph (g)(6) were satisfied) instead of May 23, 2020 (one year after the requirements of paragraph (g)(5) were satisfied). Any tax for the 2015 taxable year not attributable to the listed transaction must be assessed by April 15, 2019.

Example 6. Period to assess tax remains open under another exception. Same facts as *Examples 3, 4, and 5*, except that on April 1, 2019, A signed Form 872, consenting to extend, without restriction, its period of limitations on assessment for taxable year 2015 under section 6501(c)(4) until July 15, 2020. In that case, although under section 6501(c)(10) the period of limitations would otherwise expire on May 8, 2020, the IRS may assess tax with respect to the listed transaction (as well as any other item on the return covered by the Form 872 extension) at any time up to and including July 15, 2020, pursuant to section 6501(c)(4). Section 6501(c)(10) operates to extend the assessment period but not to shorten any other applicable assessment period.

Example 7. Requirements of (g)(5) not satisfied. In 2015, X, a corporation, enters into a listed transaction. On March 15, 2016, X timely files its 2015 Form 1120, reporting the tax consequences from the transaction. X does not disclose the transaction as required under section 6011 when it files its 2015 return. The failure to disclose relates to taxable year 2015. On February 13, 2017, X completes and files a Form 8886 with respect to the listed transaction with OTSA but does not submit a cover letter, as required. The requirements of paragraph (g)(5) of this section have not been satisfied. Therefore, the time to assess tax against X with respect to the transaction for taxable year 2015 remains open under section 6501(c)(10).

Example 8. Section 6501(c)(10) applies to keep one partner's period of limitations on assessment open. T and S are partners in a partnership, TS, that enters into a listed transaction in 2015. T and S each receive a Schedule K-1 from TS on April 11, 2016. On April 15, 2016, TS, T and S each file their 2015 returns. Under the applicable section 6011 regulations, TS, T, and S each are required to disclose the transaction. TS attaches a completed Form 8886 to its 2015 Form 1065 and sends a copy of Form 8886 to OTSA. Neither T nor S files a disclosure statement with their respective returns nor sends a copy to OTSA on April 15, 2016. On May 17, 2016, T timely files a completed Form 8886 with OTSA pursuant to § 1.6011-4(e)(1). T's disclosure is timely because T received the Schedule K-1 within 10 calendar days before the due date of the return and, thus, T had 60 calendar days to file Form 8886 with OTSA. TS and T properly disclosed the transaction in accordance with the applicable regulations under section 6011, but S did not. S's failure to disclose relates to taxable year 2015. The time to assess tax with respect to the transaction against S for 2015 remains open under section 6501(c)(10) even though TS and T disclosed the transaction.

Example 9. Section 6501(c)(10) satisfied before expiration of three-year period of limitations under section 6501(a). Same facts as *Example 8*, except that on August 26, 2016, S satisfies the requirements of paragraph (g)(5) of this section. No material advisor satisfied the requirements of paragraph (g)(6) of this section with respect to S on a date earlier than August 26, 2016. Under section 6501(c)(10), the period of time in which the IRS may assess tax against S with respect to the listed transaction would expire no earlier than August 26, 2017, one year after the date S satisfied the requirements of paragraph (g)(5). As the general three-year period of limitations on assessment under section 6501(a) does not expire until April 15, 2019, the IRS will have until that date to assess any tax with respect to the listed transaction.

Example 10. No section 6112 request. B, a calendar year taxpayer, entered into a listed transaction in 2015. B did not comply with the applicable disclosure requirements under section 6011 for taxable year 2015; therefore, section 6501(c)(10) applies to keep the period of limitations on assessment open with respect to the tax related to the transaction until at least one year after B satisfies the requirements of paragraph (g)(5) of this section or a material advisor satisfies the requirements of paragraph (g)(6) of this section with respect to B. In June 2016, the IRS conducts a section 6700 investigation of Advisor K, who is a material advisor to B with respect to the listed transaction. During the course of the investigation, the IRS obtains the name, address, and TIN of all of Advisor K's clients who engaged in the transaction, including B. The information provided does not satisfy the requirements of paragraph (g)(6) with respect to B because the information was not provided pursuant to a section 6112 request. Therefore, the time to assess tax against B with respect to the transaction for taxable year 2015 remains open under section 6501(c)(10).

Example 11. Section 6112 request but the requirements of paragraph (g)(6) are not satisfied with respect to B. Same facts as *Example 10*, except that on January 9, 2017, the IRS sends by certified mail a section 6112 request to Advisor L, who is another material advisor to B with respect to the listed transaction. Advisor L furnishes some of the information required under section 6112 and §301.6112-1 to the IRS for inspection on January 17, 2017. The list includes information with respect to many clients of Advisor L, but it does not include any information with respect to B. The submission does not satisfy the requirements of paragraph (g)(6) of this section with respect to B. Therefore, the time to assess tax against B with respect to the transaction for taxable year 2015 remains open under section 6501(c)(10).

Example 12. Section 6112 submission made before taxpayer failed to disclose a listed transaction. Advisor M, who is a material advisor, advises C, an individual, in 2015 with respect to a transaction that is not a reportable transaction at that time. C files its return claiming the tax consequences of the transaction on April 15, 2016. The time for the IRS to assess tax against C under the general three-year period of limitations for C's 2015 taxable year would expire on April 15, 2019. The IRS identifies the transaction as a listed transaction on November 3, 2017. On December 7, 2017, the IRS hand delivers to Advisor M a section 6112 request related to the transaction. Advisor M furnishes the information to the IRS on December 29, 2017. The information contains all the required information with respect to Advisor M's clients, including C. C does not disclose the transaction on or before February 1, 2018, as required under section 6011 and the regulations under section 6011. Advisor M's submission under section 6112 satisfies the requirements of paragraph (g)(6) of this section even though it occurred prior to C's failure to disclose the listed transaction. Thus, under section 6501(c)(10), the period of limitations to assess tax against C with respect to the listed transaction will end on December 29, 2018 (one year after the requirements of paragraph (g)(6) of this section were satisfied), unless the period of limitations remains open under another exception.

Example 13. Transaction removed from the category of listed transactions after taxpayer failed to disclose. D, a calendar year taxpayer, entered into a listed transaction in 2015. D did not comply with the applicable disclosure requirements under section 6011 for taxable year 2015; therefore, section 6501(c)(10) applies to keep the period of limitations on assessment open with respect to the tax related to the transaction until at least one year after D satisfies the requirements of paragraph (g)(5) of this section or a material advisor satisfies the requirements of paragraph (g)(6) of this section with respect to D. In 2017, the IRS removes the transaction from the category of listed transactions because of a change in law. Section 6501(c)(10) continues to apply to keep the period of limitations on assessment open for D's taxable year 2015.

Example 14. Taxes assessed with respect to the listed transaction. (i) F, an individual, enters into a listed transaction in 2015. F files its 2015 Form 1040 on April 15, 2016, but does not disclose his participation in the listed transaction in accordance with section 6011 and the regulations under section 6011. F's failure to disclose relates to taxable year 2015. Thus, section 6501(c)(10) applies to keep the period of limitations on assessment open with respect to the tax related to the listed transaction for taxable year 2015 until at least one year after the date F satisfies the requirements of paragraph (g)(5) of this section or a material advisor satisfies the requirements of paragraph (g)(6) of this section with respect to F.

(ii) On July 2, 2020, the IRS completes an examination of F's 2015 taxable year and disallows the tax consequences claimed as a result of the listed transaction. The disallowance of a loss increased F's adjusted gross income. Due to the increase of F's adjusted gross income, certain credits, such as the child tax credit, and exemption deductions were disallowed or reduced because of limitations based on adjusted gross income. In addition, F now is liable for the alternative minimum tax. The examination also uncovered that F claimed two deductions on Schedule C to which F was not entitled. Under section 6501(c)(10), the IRS can timely issue a statutory notice of deficiency (and assess in due course) against F for the deficiency resulting from (1) disallowing the loss, (2) disallowing the credits and exemptions to which F was not entitled based on F's increased adjusted gross income, and (3) being liable for the alternative minimum tax. In addition, the IRS can assess any interest and applicable penalties related to those adjustments, such as the accuracy-related penalty under sections 6662 and 6662A and the penalty under section 6707A for F's failure to disclose the transaction as required under section 6011 and the regulations under section 6011. The IRS cannot, however, pursuant to section 6501(c)(10), assess the increase in tax that would result from disallowing the two deductions on F's Schedule C because those deductions are not related to, or affected by, the adjustments concerning the listed transaction.

(9) *Effective/applicability date.*—The rules of this paragraph (g) apply to taxable years with respect to which the period of limitations on assessment under section 6501 (including subsection (c)(10)) did not expire before March 31, 2015. [Reg. § 301.6501(c)-1.]

☐ [*T.D.* 6172, 5-2-56. *Amended by T.D.* 6498, 10-24-60; *T.D.* 7838, 10-5-82; *T.D.* 8395, 1-28-92; *T.D.* 8845, 12-2-99 (*corrected* 1-6-2000) *and T.D.* 9718, 3-30-15 (*corrected* 4-27-2015).]

[Reg. § 301.6501(d)-1]

§ 301.6501(d)-1. Request for prompt assessment.—(a) Except as otherwise provided in section 6501(c), (e), or (f), any tax for which a return is required and for which:

(1) A decedent or an estate of a decedent may be liable, other than the estate tax imposed by chapter 11 of the Code, or

(2) A corporation which is contemplating dissolution, is in the process of dissolution, or has been dissolved, may be liable,

shall be assessed, or a proceeding in court without assessment for the collection of such tax shall be begun, within 18 months after the receipt of a written request for prompt assessment thereof.

(b) The executor, administrator, or other fiduciary representing the estate of the decedent, or the corporation, or the fiduciary representing the dissolved corporation, as the case may be, shall, after the return in question has been filed, file the request for prompt assessment in writing with the district director for the internal revenue district in which such return was filed. The request, in order to be effective, must be transmitted separately from any other document, must set forth the classes of tax and the taxable periods for which the prompt assessment is requested, and must clearly indicate that it is a request for prompt assessment under the provisions of section 6501(d). The effect of such a request is to limit the time in which an assessment of tax may be made, or a proceeding in court without assessment for collection of tax may be begun, to a period of 18 months from the date the request is filed with the proper district director. The request does not extend the time within which an assessment may be made, or a proceeding in court without assessment may be begun, beyond 3 years from the date the return was filed. This special period of limitations will not apply to any return filed after a request for prompt assessment has been made unless an additional request is filed in the manner provided herein.

(c) In the case of a corporation the 18-month period shall not apply unless:

(1) The written request notifies the district director that the corporation contemplates dissolution at or before the expiration of such 18-month period; the dissolution is in good faith begun before the expiration of such 18-month period; and the dissolution so begun is completed either before or after the expiration of such 18-month period; or

(2) The written request notifies the district director that a dissolution has in good faith been begun, and the dissolution is completed either before or after the expiration of such 18-month period; or

(3) A dissolution has been completed at the time the written request is made. [Reg. § 301.6501(d)-1.]

☐ [*T.D.* 6172, 5-2-56. *Amended by T.D.* 6425, 11-10-59 *and T.D.* 6498, 10-24-60.]

[Reg. § 301.6501(e)-1]

§ 301.6501(e)-1. Omission from return.—(a) *Income taxes.*—(1) *General rule.*—(i) If a taxpayer omits from the gross income stated in the return of a tax imposed by subtitle A of the Internal Revenue Code an amount properly includible therein that is in excess of 25 percent of the gross income so stated, the tax may be assessed, or a proceeding in court for the collection of that tax may be begun without assessment, at any time within 6 years after the return was filed.

(ii) For purposes of paragraph (a)(1)(i) of this section, the term *gross income,* as it relates to a trade or business, means the total of the amounts received or accrued from the sale of goods or services, to the extent required to be shown on the return, without reduction for the cost of those goods or services.

(iii) For purposes of paragraph (a)(1)(i) of this section, the term *gross income,* as it relates to any income other than from the sale of goods or services in a trade or business, has the same meaning as provided under section 61(a), and includes the total of the amounts received or accrued, to the extent required to be shown on the return. In the case of amounts received or accrued that relate to the disposition of property, and except as provided in paragraph (a)(1)(ii) of this section, *gross income* means the excess of the amount realized from the disposition of the property over the unrecovered cost or other basis of the property. Consequently, except as provided in paragraph (a)(1)(ii) of this section, an understated amount of gross income resulting from an overstatement of unrecovered cost or other basis constitutes an omission from gross income for purposes of section 6501(e)(1)(A)(i).

(iv) An amount shall not be considered as omitted from gross income if information sufficient to apprise the Commissioner of the nature and amount of the item is disclosed in the return, including any schedule or statement attached to the return.

(2) [Reserved]

(b) *Estate and gift taxes.*—(1) If the taxpayer omits from the gross estate as stated in the estate tax return, or from the total amount of the gifts made during the period for which the gift tax return was filed (see § 25.6019-1 of this chapter) as stated in the gift tax return, an item or items properly includible therein the amount of which is in excess of 25 percent of the gross estate as stated in the estate tax return, or 25 percent of the total amount of the gifts as stated in the gift tax return, the tax may be assessed, or a proceeding in court for the collection thereof may be begun without assessment, at any time within 6 years after the estate tax or gift tax return, as applicable, was filed.

(2) For purposes of this paragraph (b), an item disclosed in the return or in any schedule or statement attached to the return in a manner sufficient to apprise the Commissioner of the nature and amount thereof shall not be taken into account in determining items omitted from the gross estate or total gifts, as the case may be. Further, there shall not be taken into account in computing the 25 percent omission from the gross estate stated in the estate tax return or from the total gifts stated in the gift tax return, any increases in the valuation of assets disclosed on the return.

(c) *Excise taxes.*—(1) *In general.*—If the taxpayer omits from a return of a tax imposed under a provision of subtitle D an amount properly includible thereon, which amount is in excess of 25 percent of the amount of tax reported thereon, the tax may be assessed or a proceeding in court for the collection thereof may be begun without assessment, at any time within 6 years after the return was filed. For special rules relating to chapter 41, 42, 43 and 44 taxes, see paragraphs (c)(2), (3), (4), and (5) of this section.

(2) *Chapter 41 excise taxes.*—If an organization discloses an expenditure in its return (or in a schedule or statement attached thereto) in a manner sufficient to apprise the Commissioner of the existence and nature of the expenditure, the three-year limitation on assessment and collection described in section 6501(a) shall apply with respect to any tax under chapter 41 arising from the expenditure. If a taxpayer fails to so disclose an expenditure in its return (or in a schedule or statement attached thereto), the tax arising from the expenditure not so disclosed may be assessed, or a proceeding in court for the collection of the tax may be begun without assessment, at any time within 6 years after the return was filed.

(3) *Chapter 42 excise taxes.*—(i) If a private foundation omits from its annual return with respect to the tax imposed by section 4940 an amount of tax properly includible therein that is in excess of 25 percent of the amount of tax imposed by section 4940 that is reported on the return, the tax may be assessed, or a proceeding in court for the collection of the tax may be begun without assessment, at any time within 6 years after the return was filed. If a private foundation discloses in its return (or in a schedule or statement attached thereto) the nature, source, and amount of any income giving rise to any omitted tax, the tax arising from the income shall be counted as reported on the return in computing whether the foundation has omitted more than 25 percent of the tax reported on its return.

(ii) If a private foundation, trust, or other organization (as the case may be) discloses an item in its return (or in a schedule or statement attached thereto) in a manner sufficient to apprise the Commissioner of the existence and nature of the item, the three-year limitation on assessment and collection described in section 6501(a) shall apply with respect to any tax imposed under sections 4941(a), 4942(a), 4943(a), 4944(a), 4945(a), 4951(a), 4952(a), 4953 and 4958, arising from any transaction disclosed by the item. If a private foundation, trust, or other organization (as the case may be) fails to so disclose an item in its return (or in a schedule or statement attached thereto), the tax arising from any transaction not so disclosed may be assessed or a proceeding in court for the collection of the tax may be begun without assessment, at any time within 6 years after the return was filed.

(4) *Chapter 43 excise taxes.*—If a taxpayer discloses an item in its return (or in a schedule or statement attached thereto) in a manner sufficient to apprise the Commissioner of the existence and nature of the item, the three-year limitation on assessment and collection described in section 6501(a) shall apply with respect to any tax imposed under sections 4971(a), 4972, 4973,4974 and 4975(a), arising from any transaction disclosed by the item. If a taxpayer fails to so disclose an item in its return (or in a schedule or statement attached thereto), the tax arising from any transaction not so disclosed may be assessed, or a proceeding in court for the collection of the tax may be begun without assessment, at any time within 6 years after the return was filed. The applicable return for the tax under sections 4971, 4972, 4973 and 4974, is the return designated by the Commissioner for reporting the respective tax. The applicable return for the tax under section 4975 is the return filed by the plan used to report the act giving rise to the tax.

(5) *Chapter 44 excise taxes.*—If a real estate investment trust omits from its annual return with respect to the tax imposed by section 4981 an amount of tax properly includible therein that is in excess of 25 percent of the amount of tax imposed by section 4981 that is reported on the return, the tax may be assessed, or a proceeding in court for the collection of the tax may be begun without assessment, at any time within 6 years after the return was filed. If a real estate investment trust discloses in its return (or in a schedule or statement attached thereto) the nature, source, and amount of any income giving rise to any omitted tax, the tax arising from the income shall be counted as reported on the return in computing whether the trust has omitted more than 25 percent of the tax reported on its return.

(d) *Exception.*—The provisions of this section do not limit the application of section 6501(c).

(e) *Effective/applicability date.*—(1) *Income taxes.*—Paragraph (a) of this section applies to taxable years with respect to which the period for assessing tax was open on or after September 24, 2009.

(2) *Estate, gift and excise taxes.*—Paragraphs (b) through (d) of this section continue to apply as they did prior to being removed inadvertently on September 28, 2009. Specifically, paragraph (b) of this section applies to returns filed on or after May 2, 1956, except for the amendment to paragraph (b)(1) of this section that applies to returns filed on or after December 29, 1972. Paragraph (c) of this section applies to returns filed on or after October 7, 1982, except for the amendment to paragraph (c)(3)(ii) of this section that applies to returns filed on or after January 10, 2001. Paragraph (d) of this section applies to returns filed on or after May 2, 1956. [Reg. §301.6501(e)-1.]

☐ [*T.D.* 9511, 12-14-2010.]

[Reg. §301.6502-1]

§301.6502-1. Collection after assessment.—(a) *General rule.*—In any case in which a tax has been assessed within the applicable statutory period of limitations on assessment, a proceeding in court to collect the tax may be commenced, or a levy to collect the tax may be made, within 10 years after the date of assessment.

(b) *Agreement to extend the period of limitations on collection.*—The Secretary may enter into an agreement with a taxpayer to extend the period of limitations on collection in the following circumstances:

(1) *Extension agreement entered into in connection with an installment agreement.*—If the Secretary and the taxpayer enter into an installment agreement for the tax liability prior to the expiration of the period of limitations on collection, the Secretary and the taxpayer, at the time the installment agreement is entered into, may enter into a written agreement to extend the period of limitations on collection to a date certain. A written extension agreement entered into under this paragraph shall extend the period of limitations on collection until the 89th day after the date agreed upon in the written agreement.

(2) *Extension agreement entered into in connection with the release of a levy under section 6343.*—If the Secretary has levied on any part of the taxpayer's property prior to the expiration of the period of limitations on collection and the levy is subsequently released pursuant to section 6343 after the expiration of the period of limitations on collection, the Secretary and the taxpayer, prior to the release of the levy, may enter into a written agreement to extend the period of limitations on collection to a date certain. A written extension agreement entered into under this paragraph shall extend the period of limitations on collection until the date agreed upon in the extension agreement.

(c) *Proceeding in court for the collection of the tax.*—If a proceeding in court for the collection of a tax is begun within the period provided in paragraph (a) of this section (or within any extended period as provided in paragraph (b) of this section), the period during which the tax may be collected by levy is extended until the liability for the tax or a judgment against the taxpayer arising from the liability is satisfied or becomes unenforceable.

(d) *Effect of statutory suspensions of the period of limitations on collection if executed collection extension agreement is in effect.*—(1) Any statutory suspension of the period of limitations on collection tolls the running of the period of limitations on collection, as extended pursuant to an executed extension agreement under paragraph (b) of this section, for the amount of time set forth in the relevant statute.

(2) The following example illustrates the principle set forth in this paragraph (d):

Example. In June of 2003, the Internal Revenue Service (IRS) enters into an installment agreement with the taxpayer to provide for periodic payments of the taxpayer's timely assessed tax liabilities. At the time the installment agreement is entered into, the taxpayer and the IRS execute a written agreement to extend the period of limitations on collection. The extension agreement executed in connection with the installment agreement operates to extend the period of limitations on collection to the date agreed upon in the extension agreement, plus 89 days. Subsequently, and prior to the expiration of the extended period of limitations on collection, the taxpayer files a bankruptcy petition under chapter 7 of the Bankruptcy Code and receives a discharge from bankruptcy a few months later. Assuming the tax is not discharged in the bankruptcy, section 6503(h) of the Internal Revenue Code operates to suspend the running of the previously extended period of limitations on collection for the period of time the IRS is prohibited from collecting due to the bankruptcy proceeding, and for 6 months thereafter. The new expiration date for the IRS to collect the tax is the date agreed upon in the previously executed extension agreement, plus 89 days, plus the period during which the IRS is prohibited from collecting due to the bankruptcy proceeding, plus 6 months.

(e) *Date when levy is considered made.*—The date on which a levy on property or rights to property is considered made is the date on which the notice of seizure required under section 6335(a) is given.

(f) *Effective date.*—This section is applicable on September 6, 2006. [Reg. §301.6502-1.]

☐ [*T.D.* 6172, 5-2-56. *Amended by T.D.* 7305, 3-14-74; *T.D.* 8391, 2-10-92 *and T.D.* 9284, 9-5-2006.]

[Reg. §301.6503(d)-1]

§301.6503(d)-1. Suspension of running of period of limitation; extension of time for payment of estate tax.—Where an estate is granted an extension of time as provided in section 6161(a)(2) or (b)(2), or under the provisions of section 6166, for payment of any estate tax, the running of the period of limitations for collection of such tax is suspended for the period of time for which the extension is granted. [Reg. § 301.6503(d)-1.]

☐ [*T.D.* 6172, 5-2-56. *Amended by T.D.* 6425, 11-10-59 *and T.D.* 6498, 10-24-60.]

[Reg. § 301.6511(a)-1]

§ 301.6511(a)-1. Period of limitation on filing claim.—(a) In the case of any tax (other than a tax payable by stamp):

(1) If a return is filed, a claim for credit or refund of an overpayment must be filed by the taxpayer within 3 years from the time the return was filed or within 2 years from the time the tax was paid, whichever of such periods expires the later.

(2) If no return is filed, the claim for credit or refund of an overpayment must be filed by the taxpayer within 2 years from the time the tax was paid.

(b) In the case of any tax payable by means of a stamp, a claim for credit or refund of an overpayment of such tax must be filed by the taxpayer within 3 years from the time the tax was paid. For provisions relating to redemption of unused stamps, see section 6805.

(c) For limitations on allowance of credit or refund, special rules, and exceptions, see subsections (b) through (e) of section 6511. For limitations in the case of a petition to the Tax Court, see section 6512. For rules as to time return is deemed filed and tax considered paid, see section 6513. [Reg. § 301.6511(a)-1.]

☐ [*T.D.* 6172, 5-2-56. *Amended by T.D.* 6425, 11-10-59.]

[Reg. § 301.6511(b)-1]

§ 301.6511(b)-1. Limitations on allowance of credits and refunds.—(a) *Effect of filing claim.*—Unless a claim for credit or refund of an overpayment is filed within the period of limitation prescribed in section 6511(a), no credit or refund shall be allowed or made after the expiration of such period.

(b) *Limit on amount to be credited or refunded.*—(1) In the case of any tax (other than a tax payable by stamp):

(i) If a return was filed, and a claim is filed within 3 years from the time the return was filed, the amount of the credit or refund shall not exceed the portion of the tax paid within the period, immediately preceding the filing of the claim, equal to 3 years plus the period of any extension of time for filing the return.

(ii) If a return was filed, and a claim is filed after the 3-year period described in subdivision (i) of this subparagraph but within 2 years from the time the tax was paid, the amount of the credit or refund shall not exceed the portion of the tax paid within the 2 years immediately preceding the filing of the claim.

(iii) If no return was filed, but a claim is filed, the amount of the credit or refund shall not exceed the portion of the tax paid within the 2 years immediately preceding the filing of the claim.

(iv) If no claim is filed, the amount of the credit or refund allowed or made by the district director or the director of the regional service center shall not exceed the amount that would have been allowable under the preceding subdivisions of this subparagraph if a claim had been filed on the date the credit or refund is allowed.

(2) In the case of a tax payable by stamp—

(i) If a claim is filed, the amount of the credit or refund shall not exceed the portion of the tax paid within the 3 years immediately preceding the filing of the claim.

(ii) If no claim is filed, the amount of the credit or refund allowed or made by the district director or the director of the regional service center shall not exceed the portion of the tax paid within the 3 years immediately preceding the allowance of the credit or refund. [Reg. § 301.6511(b)-1.]

☐ [*T.D.* 6172, 5-2-56. *Amended by T.D.* 6425, 11-10-59, *T.D.* 6498, 10-24-60 *and T.D.* 6585, 12-27-61.]

[Reg. § 301.6511(c)-1]

§ 301.6511(c)-1. Special rules applicable in case of extension of time by agreement.—(a) *Scope.*—If, within the period prescribed in section 6511(a) for the filing of a claim for credit or refund, an agreement extending the period of assessment of a tax has been made in accordance with the provisions of section 6501(c)(4), the special rules provided in this section become applicable. This section shall not apply to any claim filed, or credit or refund allowed if no claim is filed, either (1) prior to the execution of an agreement extending the period in which assessment may be made, or (2) more than 6 months after the expiration of the period within which an assessment may be made pursuant to the agreement or any extension thereof.

(b) *Period in which claim may be filed.*—Claim for credit or refund of an overpayment may be filed, or credit or refund may be allowed if no claim is filed, at any time within which an assessment may be made pursuant to an agreement, or any extension thereof, under section 6501(c)(4), and for 6 months thereafter.

(c) *Limit on amount to be credited or refunded.*—(1) If a claim is filed within the time prescribed in paragraph (b) of this section, the amount of the credit or refund allowed or made shall not exceed the portion of the tax paid after the execution of the agreement and before the filing of the claim, plus the amount that could have been properly credited or refunded under the provisions of section 6511(b)(2) if a claim had been filed on the date of the execution of the agreement.

(2) If no claim is filed, the amount of credit or refund allowed or made within the time prescribed in paragraph (b) of this section shall not exceed the portion of the tax paid after the execution of the agreement and before the making of the credit or refund, plus the amount that could have been properly credited or refunded under the provisions of section 6511(b)(2) if a

claim had been filed on the date of the execution of the agreement.

(d) *Effective date of agreement.*—The agreement referred to in this section shall become effective when signed by the taxpayer and the district director or an assistant regional commissioner. [Reg. § 301.6511(c)-1.]

☐ [*T.D.* 6172, 5-2-56. *Amended by T.D.* 6498, 10-24-60.]

[Reg. § 301.6512-1]

§ 301.6512-1. Limitations in case of petition to Tax Court.—(a) *Effect of petition to Tax Court.*—(1) *General rule.*—If a person having a right to file a petition with the Tax Court with respect to a deficiency in income, estate, gift, or excise tax imposed by subtitle A or B, or chapter 41, 42, 43, or 44 of the Code has filed such petition within the time prescribed in section 6213(a), no credit or refund of income tax for the same taxable year, of gift tax for the same calendar year or calendar quarter, of estate tax in respect of the taxable estate of the same decedent, or of tax imposed by chapter 41, 42, 43, or 44 with respect to any act (or failure to act) to which such petition relates, in respect of which a district director or director of a service center (or a regional director of appeals) has determined the deficiency, shall be allowed or made, and no suit in any court for the recovery of any part of such tax shall be instituted by the taxpayer, except as to items set forth in paragraph (a)(2) of this section.

(2) *Exceptions.*—The exceptions to the rule stated in subparagraph (1) of this paragraph are as follows:

(i) An overpayment determined by a decision of the Tax Court which has become final;

(ii) Any amount collected in excess of an amount computed in accordance with the decision of the Tax Court which has become final; and

(iii) Any amount collected after the expiration of the period of limitation upon levying or beginning a proceeding in court for collection.

(b) *Overpayment determined by Tax Court.*—If the Tax Court finds that there is no deficiency and further finds that the taxpayer has made an overpayment of income tax for the same taxable year, of gift tax for the same calendar year or calendar quarter, of estate tax in respect of the taxable estate of the same decedent, or of tax imposed by chapter 41, 42, 43, or 44 with respect to any act (or failure to act) to which such petition relates, in respect of which a district director, or director of a service center (or a regional director of appeals) has determined the deficiency, or finds that there is a deficiency but that the taxpayer had made an overpayment of such tax, the overpayment determined by the Tax Court shall be credited or refunded to the taxpayer when the decision of the Tax Court has become final. (See section 7481, relating to the date when a Tax Court decision becomes final.) No such credit or refund shall be allowed or made of any portion of the tax unless the Tax Court determines as part of its decision that such portion was paid—

(1) After the mailing of the notice of deficiency, or

(2) Within the period which would be applicable under section 6511(b)(2), (c), (d), or (g) (see §§ 301.6511(b)-1, 301.6511(c)-1, 301.6511(d)-1, 301.6511(d)-2, and 301.6511(d)-3), if on the date of the mailing of the notice of deficiency a claim had been filed (whether or not filed) stating the grounds upon which the Tax Court finds that there is an overpayment.

(c) *Jeopardy assessments.*—In the case of a jeopardy assessment made under section 6861(a), if the amount which should have been assessed as determined by a decision of the Tax Court which has become final is less than the amount already collected, the excess payment shall be credited or refunded subject to a determination being made by the Tax Court with respect to the time of payment as stated in paragraph (b) of this section.

(d) *Disallowance of deficiency by reviewing court.*—If the amount of the deficiency determined by the Tax Court (in a case where collection has not been stayed by the filing of a bond) is disallowed in whole or in part by the reviewing court, then the overpayment resulting from such disallowance shall be credited or refunded without the making of claim therefor, subject to a determination being made by the Tax Court with respect to the time of payment as stated in paragraph (b) of this section. (See section 7481, relating to date Tax Court decision becomes final.)

(e) *Collection in excess of amount determined by Tax Court.*—Where the amount collected is in excess of the amount computed in accordance with the decision of the Tax Court which has become final, the excess payment shall be credited or refunded within the period of limitation provided in section 6511.

(f) *Collection after expiration of statutory period.*—Where an amount is collected after the statutory period of limitation upon the beginning of levy or a proceeding in court for collection has expired (see section 6502, relating to collection after assessment), the taxpayer may file a claim for refund of the amount so collected within the period of limitation provided in section 6511. In any such case, the decision of the Tax Court as to whether the statutory period upon collection of the tax expired before notice of the deficiency was mailed shall, when the decision becomes final, be conclusive. [Reg. § 301.6512-1.]

☐ [*T.D.* 6172, 5-2-56. *Amended by T.D.* 7238, 12-28-72 *and T.D.* 7838, 10-5-82.]

[Reg. § 301.6513-1]

§ 301.6513-1. Time return deemed filed and tax considered paid.—(a) *Early return or advance payment of tax.*—For purposes of section 6511, a return filed before the last day prescribed by law or regulations for the filing thereof shall be considered as filed on such last day. For purposes of section 6511(b)(2) and (c) and section 6512, payment of any portion of the tax made before the last day prescribed for payment shall be considered made on such last day. An extension of time for filing a return or for paying any tax, or an election to pay any tax in installments, shall not be given any effect in determining under this section the last day prescribed for filing a return or paying any tax.

* * *

[Reg. 301.6513-1]

☐ [*T.D.* 6172, 5-2-56. *Amended by T.D.* 6498, 10-24-60 *and T.D.* 6922, 6-16-67.]

[Reg. § 20.6601-1]

§ 20.6601-1. Interest on underpayment, nonpayment, or extensions of time for payment, of tax.—For regulations concerning interest on underpayments, etc., see § 301.6601-1 of this chapter (Regulations on Procedure and Administration). [Reg. § 20.6601-1.]

☐ [*T.D.* 6296, 6-23-58.]

[Reg. § 25.6601-1]

§ 25.6601-1. Interest on underpayment, nonpayment, or extensions of time for payment, of tax.—For regulations concerning interest on underpayment, nonpayment, or extensions of time for payment of tax, see § 301.6601-1 of this chapter(Regulations on Procedure and Administration). [Reg. § 25.6601-1.]

☐ [*T.D.* 6334, 10-14-58.]

[Reg. § 301.6601-1]

§ 301.6601-1. Interest on underpayments.—(a) *General rule.*—(1) Interest at the annual rate referred to in the regulations under section 6621 shall be paid on any unpaid amount of tax from the last date prescribed for payment of the tax (determined without regard to any extension of time for payment) to the date on which payment is received.

(2) For provisions requiring the payment of interest during the period occurring before July 1, 1975, see section 6601(a) prior to its amendment by section 7 of the Act of Jan. 3, 1975 (Pub. L. 93-625, 88 Stat. 2115).

(b) *Satisfaction by credits made after December 31, 1957.*—(1) *In general.*—If any portion of a tax is satisfied by the credit of an overpayment after December 31, 1957, interest shall not be imposed under section 6601 on such portion of the tax for any period during which interest on the overpayment would have been allowable if the overpayment had been refunded.

(2) *Examples.*—The provisions of this paragraph may be illustrated by the following examples:

Example (1). An examination of A's income tax returns for the calendar years 1955 and 1956 discloses an underpayment of $800 for 1955 and an overpayment of $500 for 1956. Interest under section 6601(a) ordinarily accrues on the underpayment of $800 from April 15, 1956, to the date of payment. However, the 1956 overpayment of $500 is credited after December 31, 1957, against the underpayment in accordance with the provisions of section 6402(a) and § 301.6402-1. Under such circumstances interest on the $800 underpayment runs from April 15, 1956, the last date prescribed for payment of the 1955 tax, to April 15, 1957, the date the overpayment of $500 was made. Since interest would have been allowed on the overpayment, if refunded, from April 15, 1957, to a date not more than 30 days prior to the date of the refund check, no interest is imposed after April 15, 1957, on $500, the portion of the underpayment satisfied by credit. Interest continues to run, however, on $300 (the $800 underpayment for 1955 less the $500 overpayment for 1956) to the date of payment.

Example (2). An examination of A's income tax returns for the calendar years 1956 and 1957 discloses an overpayment, occurring on April 15, 1957, of $700 for 1956 and an underpayment of $400 for 1957. After April 15, 1958, the last date prescribed for payment of the 1957 tax, the district director credits $400 of the overpayment against the underpayment. In such a case, interest will accrue upon the overpayment of $700 from April 15, 1957, to April 15, 1958, the due date of the amount against which the credit is taken. Interest will also accrue under section 6611 upon $300 ($700 overpayment less $400 underpayment) from April 15, 1958, to a date not more than 30 days prior to the date of the refund check. Since a refund of the portion of the overpayment credited against the underpayment would have resulted in interest running upon such portion from April 15, 1958, to a date not more than 30 days prior to the date of the refund check, no interest is imposed upon the underpayment.

(c) *Last date prescribed for payment.*—(1) In determining the last date prescribed for payment, any extension of time granted for payment of tax (including any postponement elected under section 6163(a)) shall be disregarded. The granting of an extension of time for the payment of tax does not relieve the taxpayer from liability for the payment of interest thereon during the period of the extension. Thus, except as provided in paragraph (b) of this section, interest at the annual rate referred to in the regulations under section 6621 is payable on any unpaid portion of the tax for the period during which such portion remains unpaid by reason of an extension of time for the payment thereof.

(2)(i) If a tax or portion thereof is payable in installments in accordance with an election made under section 6152(a) or 6156(a), the last date prescribed for payment of any installment of such tax or portion thereof shall be determined under the provisions of section 6152(b) or 6156(b), as the case may be, and interest shall run on any unpaid installment from such last date to the date on which payment is received. However in the event installment privileges are terminated for failure to pay an installment when due as provided by section 6152(d) and the time for the payment of any remaining installment is accelerated by the issuance of a notice and demand therefor, interest shall run on such unpaid installment from the date of the notice and demand to the date on which payment is received. But see section 6601(e)(4).

(ii) If the tax shown on a return is payable in installments, interest will run on any tax not shown on the return from the last date prescribed for payment of the first installment. If a deficiency is prorated to any unpaid installments, in accordance with section 6152(c), interest shall run on such prorated amounts from the date prescribed for the payment of the first installment to the date on which payment is received.

(3) If, by reason of jeopardy, a notice and demand for payment of any tax is issued before the last date otherwise prescribed for payment, such last date shall nevertheless be used for the purpose of the interest computation, and no interest shall be imposed for the period commencing with the date of the issuance of the notice and demand and ending on such last date. If the tax is not paid on or before such last date, interest will automatically accrue from such last date to the date on which payment is received.

(4) In the case of taxes payable by stamp and in all other cases where the last date for payment of the tax is not otherwise prescribed, such last date for the purpose of the interest computation shall be deemed to be the date on which the liability for the tax arose. However, such last date shall in no event be later than the date of issuance of a notice and demand for the tax.

(d) *Suspension of interest; waiver of restrictions on assessment.*—In the case of a deficiency determined by a district director (or an assistant regional commissioner, appellate) with respect to any income, estate, gift, or chapter 41, 42, 43, or 44 tax, if the taxpayer files with such internal revenue officer an agreement waiving the restrictions on assessment of such deficiency, and if notice and demand for payment of such deficiency is not made within 30 days after the filing of such waiver, no interest shall be imposed on the deficiency for the period beginning immediately after such 30th day and ending on the date notice and demand is made. In the case of an agreement with respect to a portion of the deficiency, the rules as set forth in this paragraph are applicable only to that portion of the deficiency to which the agreement relates.

(e) *Income tax reduced by carryback.*—(1) The carryback of a net operating loss, net capital loss, investment credit, or a work incentive program (WIN) credit shall not affect the computation of interest on any income tax for the period commencing with the last day prescribed for the payment of such tax and ending with the last day of the taxable year in which the loss or credit arises. For example, if the carryback of a net operating loss, a net capital loss, an investment credit, or a WIN credit to a prior taxable period eliminates or reduces a deficiency in income tax for that period, the full amount of the deficiency will nevertheless bear interest at the annual rate referred to in the regulations under section 6621 from the last date prescribed for payment of such tax until the last day of the taxable year in which the loss or credit arose. Interest will continue to run beyond such last day on any portion of the deficiency which is not eliminated by the carryback. With respect to any portion of an investment credit carryback or a WIN credit carryback from a taxable year attributable to a net operating loss carryback or a capital loss carryback from a subsequent taxable year, such investment credit carryback or WIN credit carryback shall not affect the computation of interest on any income tax for the period commencing with the last day prescribed for the payment of such tax and ending with the last day of such subsequent taxable year.

(2) Where an extension of time for payment of income tax has been granted under section 6164 to a corporation expecting a net operating loss carryback or a net capital loss carryback, interest is payable at the annual rate established under section 6621 on the amount of such unpaid tax from the last date prescribed for payment thereof without regard to such extension.

(3) Where there has been an allowance of an overpayment attributable to a net operating loss carryback, a capital loss carryback, or an investment credit carryback and all or part of such allowance is later determined to be excessive, interest shall be computed on the excessive amount from the last day of the year in which the net operating loss, net capital loss, or investment credit arose until the date on which the repayment of such excessive amount is received. Where there has been an allowance of an overpayment with respect to any portion of an investment credit carryback from a taxable year attributable to a net operating loss carryback or a capital loss carryback from a subsequent taxable year and all or part of such allowance is later determined to be excessive, interest shall be computed on the excessive amount from the last day of such subsequent taxable year until the date on which the repayment of such excessive amount is received.

(f) *Applicable rules.*—(1) Any interest prescribed by section 6601 shall be assessed and collected in the same manner as tax and shall be paid upon notice and demand by the district director or the director of the regional service center. Any reference in the Code (except in subchapter B, chapter 63, relating to deficiency procedures) to any tax imposed by the Code shall be deemed also to refer to the interest imposed by section 6601 on such tax. Interest on a tax may be assessed and collected at any time within the period of limitation on collection after assessment of the tax to which it relates. For rules relating to the period of limitation on collection after assessment, see section 6502.

(2) No interest under section 6601 shall be payable on any interest provided by such section. This paragraph (f)(2) shall not apply after December 31, 1982, with respect to interest accruing after such date, or accrued but unpaid on such date. See § 301.6622-1.

(3) Interest will not be imposed on any assessable penalty, addition to the tax (other than

an addition to tax described in section 6601(e)(2)(B)), or additional amount if the amount is paid within 21 calendar days (10 business days if the amount assessed and shown on the notice and demand equals or exceeds $100,000) from the date of the notice and demand. If interest is imposed, it will be imposed only for the period from the date of the notice and demand to the date on which payment is received. This paragraph (f)(3) is applicable with respect to any notice and demand made after December 31, 1996.

(4) If notice and demand is made after December 31, 1996, for any amount and the amount is paid within 21 calendar days (10 business days if the amount assessed and shown on the notice and demand equals or exceeds $100,000) from the date of the notice and demand, interest will not be imposed for the period after the date of the notice and demand.

(5) For purposes of paragraphs (f)(3) and (4) of this section—

(i) The term *business day* means any day other than a Saturday, Sunday, legal holiday in the District of Columbia, or a statewide legal holiday in the state where the taxpayer resides or where the taxpayer's principal place of business is located. With respect to the tenth business day (after taking into account the first sentence of this paragraph (f)(5)(i)), see section 7503 relating to time for performance of acts where the last day falls on a statewide legal holiday in the state where the act is required to be performed.

(ii) The term *calendar day* means any day. With respect to the twenty-first calendar day, see section 7503 relating to time for performance of acts where the last day falls on a Saturday, Sunday, or legal holiday.

(6) No interest shall be imposed for failure to pay estimated tax as required by section 59 of the Internal Revenue Code of 1939 or section 6153 or 6154 of the Internal Revenue Code of 1954. [Reg. § 301.6601-1.]

☐ [*T.D.* 6234, 5-21-57. *Amended by T.D.* 6425, 11-10-59, *T.D.* 6498, 10-24-60, *T.D.* 6585, 12-27-61, *T.D.* 6730, 5-7-64, *T.D.* 7238, 12-28-72, *T.D.* 7301, 1-3-74, *T.D.* 7384, 10-21-75, *T.D.* 7838, 10-5-82; *T.D.* 7907, 8-22-83 *and T.D.* 8725, 7-21-97.]

[Reg. § 301.6621-1]

§ 301.6621-1. Interest rate.—(a) *In general.*—The interest rate established under section 6621 shall be—

(1) On amounts outstanding before July 1, 1975, 6 percent per annum (or 4 percent in the case of certain extensions of time for payment of taxes as provided in sections 6601(b) and (j) prior to amendment by section 7(b) of the Act of Jan. 3, 1975 (Pub. L. 93-625, 88 Stat. 2115), and certain overpayments of the unrelated business income tax as provided in section 514(b)(3)(D), prior to its amendment by such Act).

(2) On amounts outstanding—

After	*And before*	*Rate per annum (percent)*
June 30, 1975	February 1, 1976	9 percent
January 31, 1976	February 1, 1978	7 percent
January 31, 1978	February 1, 1980	6 percent
January 31, 1980	February 1, 1982	12 percent
January 31, 1982	January 1, 1983	20 percent

(3) On amounts outstanding after December 31, 1982, the adjusted rate established by the Commissioner under section 6621(b). This adjusted rate shall be published by the Commissioner in a Revenue Ruling. See § 301.6622-1 for application of daily compounding in determining interest accruing after December 31, 1982. Because interest accruing after December 31, 1982, accrues at the prescribed rate per annum compounded daily, the effective annual percentage rate of interest will exceed the prescribed rate of interest.

(b) [Reserved]

(c) *Applicability of interest rate.*—(1) *Computation.*—Interest and additions to tax on any amount outstanding on a specific day shall be computed at the annual rate applicable on such day.

(2) *Additions to tax.*—Additions to tax under any section of the Code that refers to the annual rate established under this section, including sections 644(a)(2)(B), 4497(c)(2), 6654(a), and 6655(a) and (g), shall be computed at the same rate per annum as the interest rate set forth under paragraph (a) of this section.

(3) *Interest.*—Interest provided for under any section of the Code that refers to the annual rate established under this section, including sections 47(d)(3)(G), 167(q), 6332(c)(1), 6343(c), 6601(a), 6602, 6611(a), 7426(g), and section 1961(c)(1) or 2411 of Title 28 of the United States Code, shall be computed at the rate per annum set forth under paragraph (a) of this section.

(d) *Examples.*—The provisions of this section may be illustrated by the following examples. Example (6) illustrates the computation of interest for interest accruing after December 31, 1982.

Example (1). A, an individual, files an income tax return for the calendar year 1974 on April 15, 1975, showing a tax due of $1,000. A pays the $1,000 on September 1, 1975. Pursuant to section 6601(a), interest on the underpayment of $1,000 is computed at the rate of 6 percent per annum from April 15, 1975, to June 30, 1975, a total of 76 days. Interest for 63 days, from June 30, 1975, to September 1, 1975, shall be computed at the rate of 9 percent per annum.

Example (2). An executor of an estate is granted, in accordance with section 6161(a)(2)(A), a two-year extension of time for payment of the estate tax shown on the estate tax return, which tax was otherwise due on January

15, 1974. The tax is paid on January 15, 1976. Interest on the underpayment shall be computed at the rate of 4 percent per annum from January 15, 1974, to June 30, 1975, and at the rate of 9 percent per annum from June 30, 1975, to January 15, 1976.

Example (3). X, a corporation, files its 1973 corporate income tax return on March 15, 1974, and pays the balance of tax due shown thereon. On August 1, 1975, an assessment of a deficiency is made against X with respect to such tax. The deficiency is paid on October 1, 1975. Interest at the rate of 6 percent per annum is due on the deficiency from March 15, 1974, the due date of the return, to June 30, 1975, and at the rate of 9 percent per annum from June 30, 1975, to October 1, 1975.

Example (4). Y, an individual, files an amended individual income tax return on October 1, 1975, for the refund of an overpayment of income tax Y made on April 15, 1975. Interest is allowed on the overpayment to December 1, 1975. Pursuant to section 6611(a), interest is computed at the rate of 6 percent per annum from April 15, 1975, the date of overpayment, to June 30, 1975. Interest from June 30, 1975, to December 1, 1975, shall be computed at the rate of 9 percent per annum.

Example (5). A, an individual, is liable for an addition to tax under section 6654 for the underpayment of estimated tax from April 15, 1975 until January 15, 1976. The addition to tax shall be computed at the annual rate of 6 percent per annum from April 15, 1975, to June 30, 1975, and at the annual rate of 9 percent per annum from June 30, 1975, to January 15, 1976.

Example (6). B, an individual, files an income tax return for calendar year 1980 on April 15, 1981, showing a tax due of $1,000. B pays the $1,000 on March 1, 1983. Under section 6601(a), interest on the $1,000 underpayment is due from April 15, 1981, to March 1, 1983. Such interest is computed at the rate of 12 percent per annum, simple interest, from April 15, 1981, to January 31, 1982, and at the rate of 20 percent per annum, simple interest, from January 31, 1982, to December 31, 1982, and at the rate of 16 percent per annum, compounded daily, from December 31, 1982, to March 1, 1983. The total simple interest accrued but unpaid at the end of December 31, 1982, is combined with the $1,000 underpayment for purposes of determining the amount of daily compounded interest to be charged from December 31, 1982, to March 1, 1983. [Reg. § 301.6621-1.]

□ [*T.D.* 7384, 10-21-75. *Amended by T.D.* 7907, 8-22-83.]

[Reg. § 301.6622-1]

§ 301.6622-1. Interest compounded daily.—(a) *General rule.*—Effective for interest accruing after December 31, 1982, in computing the amount of any interest required to be paid under the Internal Revenue Code of 1954 or sections 1961(c)(1) or 2411 of Title 28, United States Code, by the Commissioner or by the taxpayer, or in computing any other amount determined by reference to such amount of interest, or by reference to the interest rate established under section 6621, such interest or such other amount shall be compounded daily by dividing such rate of interest by 365 (366 in a leap year) and compounding such daily interest rate each day.

(b) *Exception.*—Paragraph (a) of this section shall not apply for purposes of determining the amount of any addition to tax under sections 6654 or 6655 (relating to failure to pay estimated income tax).

(c) *Applicability to unpaid amounts on December 31, 1982.*—(1) *In general.*—The unpaid interest (or other amount) that shall be compounded daily includes the interest (or other amount) accrued but unpaid on December 31, 1982.

(2) *Illustration.*—The provisions of this (c) may be illustrated by the following example.

Example. Individual A files a tax return for calendar year 1981 on April 15, 1982, showing a tax due of $10,000. A pays $10,000 on December 31, 1982, but A does not pay any interest with respect to this underpayment until March 1, 1983, on which date A paid all amounts of interest with respect to the $10,000 underpayment of tax. On December 31, 1982, A's unsatisfied interest liability was $1,424.66 ($10,000 × 20 percent × 260/365 days). Interest, compounded daily, accrues on this unsatisfied interest obligation beginning on January 1, 1983, until March 1, 1983, the date the total interest obligation is satisfied. On March 1, 1983, the total interest obligation is $1,462.62, computed as follows:

Item	*Amount*
Unpaid tax at December 31, 1982	—0—
Unpaid interest at December 31, 1982	$1,424.66
Total unsatisfied obligation at December 31, 1982	$1,424.66
Interest from December 31, 1982, to March 1, 1983, at 16 percent per year compounded daily	$37.96
Total due, March 1, 1983	$1,462.62

[Reg. § 301.6622-1.]

□ [*T.D.* 7907, 8-22-83.]

[Reg. § 301.6651-1]

§ 301.6651-1. Failure to file tax return or to pay tax.—(a) *Addition to the tax.*—(1) *Failure to file tax return.*—In case of failure to file a return required under authority of—

(i) Subchapter A, chapter 61 of the Code, relating to returns and records (other than sections 6015 and 6016, relating to declarations of estimated tax, and part III thereof, relating to information returns);

(ii) Subchapter A, chapter 51 of the Code, relating to distilled spirits, wines, and beer;

(iii) Subchapter A, chapter 52 of the Code, relating to cigars, cigarettes, and cigarette papers and tubes; or

(iv) Subchapter A, chapter 53 of the Code, relating to machine guns, destructive devices, and certain other firearms; and

The regulations thereunder, on or before the date prescribed for filing (determined with regard to any extension of time for such filing), there shall be added to the tax required to be shown on the return the amount specified below unless the failure to file the return within the prescribed time is shown to the satisfaction of the district director, the director of the service center, or, as provided in paragraph (c) of this section, the Assistant Regional Commissioner (Alcohol, Tobacco and Firearms), to be due to reasonable cause and not to willful neglect. The amount to be added to the tax is 5 percent thereof if the failure is for not more than 1 month, with an additional 5 percent for each additional month or fraction thereof during which the failure continues, but not to exceed 25 percent in the aggregate. The amount of any addition under this subparagraph shall be reduced by the amount of the addition under subparagraph (2) of this paragraph for any month to which an addition to tax applies under both subparagraphs (1) and (2) of this paragraph (a).

(2) *Failure to pay tax shown on return.*—In case of failure to pay the amount shown as tax on any return (required to be filed after December 31, 1969, without regard to any extension of time for filing thereof) specified in subparagraph (1) of this paragraph on or before the date prescribed for payment of such tax (determined with regard to any extension of time for payment), there shall be added to the tax shown on the return the amount specified below unless the failure to pay the tax within the prescribed time is shown to the satisfaction of the district director or the director of the service center to be due to reasonable cause and not to willful neglect. Except as provided in paragraph (a)(4) of this section, the amount to be added to the tax is 0.5 percent of the amount of tax shown on the return if the failure is for not more than 1 month, with an additional 0.5 percent for each additional month or fraction thereof during which the failure continues, but not to exceed 25 percent in the aggregate.

(3) *Failure to pay tax not shown on return.*—In the case of failure to pay any amount of any tax required to be shown on a return specified in paragraph (a)(1) of this section that is not so shown (including an assessment made pursuant to section 6213(b)) within 21 calendar days from the date of the notice and demand (10 business days if the amount assessed and shown on the notice and demand equals or exceeds $100,000) with respect to any notice and demand made after December 31, 1996, there will be added to the amount stated in the notice and demand the amount specified below unless the failure to pay the tax within the prescribed time is shown to the satisfaction of the district director or the director of the service center to be due to reasonable cause and not to willful neglect. Except as provided in paragraph (a)(4) of this section, the amount to be added to the tax is 0.5 percent of the amount stated in the notice and demand if the failure is for not more than 1 month, with an additional 0.5 percent for each additional month or fraction thereof during which the failure continues, but not to exceed 25 percent in the aggregate. For purposes of this paragraph (a)(3), see § 301.6601-1(f)(5) for the definition of *calendar day* and *business day*.

(4) *Reduction of failure to pay penalty during the period an installment agreement is in effect.*—(i) *In general.*—In the case of a return filed by an individual on or before the due date for the return (including extensions)—

(A) The amount added to tax for a month or fraction thereof is determined by using 0.25 percent instead of 0.5 percent under paragraph (a)(2) of this section if at any time during the month an installment agreement under section 6159 is in effect for the payment of such tax; and

(B) The amount added to tax for a month or fraction thereof is determined by using 0.25 percent instead of 0.5 percent under paragraph (a)(3) of this section if at any time during the month an installment agreement under section 6159 is in effect for the payment of such tax.

(ii) *Effective date.*—This paragraph (a)(4) applies for purposes of determining additions to tax for months beginning after December 31, 1999.

(b) *Month defined.*—(1) If the date prescribed for filing the return or paying tax is the last day of a calendar month, each succeeding calendar month or fraction thereof during which the failure to file or pay tax continues shall constitute a month for purposes of section 6651.

(2) If the date prescribed for filing the return or paying tax is a date other than the last day of a calendar month, the period which terminates with the date numerically corresponding thereto in the succeeding calendar month and each such successive period shall constitute a month for purposes of section 6651. If, in the month of February, there is no date corresponding to the date prescribed for filing the return or paying tax, the period from such date in January through the last day of February shall constitute a month for purposes of section 6651. Thus, if a return is due on January 30, the first month shall end on February 28 (or 29 if a leap year), and the succeeding months shall end on March 30, April 30, etc.

(3) If a return is not timely filed or tax is not timely paid, the fact that the date prescribed for filing the return or paying tax, or the corresponding date in any succeeding calendar month, falls on a Saturday, Sunday, or a legal holiday is immaterial in determining the number of months for which the addition to the tax under section 6651 applies.

(c) *Showing of reasonable cause.*—(1) Except as provided in subparagraphs (3) and (4) of this paragraph, a taxpayer who wishes to avoid the addition to the tax for failure to file a tax return or pay tax must make an affirmative showing of all facts alleged as a reasonable cause for his failure to file such return or pay such tax on time in the form of a written statement containing a declaration that it is made under penalties of perjury. Such statement should be filed with the district director or the director of the service center with whom the return is required to be filed; *Provided,* That where special tax return of liquor dealers are delivered to an alcohol, tobacco and firearms officer working under the supervision of the Regional Director, Bureau of Alcohol, Tobacco and Firearms, such statement may be delivered with the return. If the district director, the director of the service center, or, where applicable, the Regional Director, Bureau of Alcohol, Tobacco and Firearms, determines that the delinquency was due to a reasonable cause and not to willful neglect, the addition to the tax will not be assessed. If the taxpayer exercised ordinary business care and prudence and was nevertheless unable to file the return within the prescribed time, then the delay is due to a reasonable cause. A failure to pay will be considered to be due to reasonable cause to the extent that the taxpayer has made a satisfactory showing that he exercised ordinary business care and prudence in providing for payment of his tax liability and was nevertheless either unable to pay the tax or would suffer an undue hardship (as described in § 1.6161-1(b) of this chapter) if he paid on the due date. In determining whether the taxpayer was unable to pay the tax in spite of the exercise of ordinary business care and prudence in providing for payment of his tax liability, consideration will be given to all the facts and circumstances of the taxpayer's financial situation, including the amount and nature of the taxpayer's expenditures in light of the income (or other amounts) he could, at the time of such expenditures, reasonably expect to receive prior to the date prescribed for the payment of the tax. Thus, for example, a taxpayer who incurs lavish or extravagant living expenses in an amount such that the remainder of his assets and anticipated income will be insufficient to pay his tax, has not exercised ordinary business care and prudence in providing for the payment of his tax liability. Further, a taxpayer who invests funds in speculative or illiquid assets has not exercised ordinary business care and prudence in providing for the payment of his tax liability unless, at the time of the investment, the remainder of the taxpayer's assets and estimated income will be sufficient to pay his tax or it can be reasonably foreseen that the speculative or illiquid investment made by the taxpayer can be utilized (by sale or as security for a loan) to realize sufficient funds to satisfy the tax liability. A taxpayer will be considered to have exercised ordinary business care and prudence if he made reasonable efforts to conserve sufficient assets in marketable form to satisfy his tax liability and nevertheless was unable to pay all or a portion of the tax when it became due.

(2) In determining if the taxpayer exercised ordinary business care and prudence in providing for the payment of his tax liability, consideration will be given to the nature of the tax which the taxpayer has failed to pay. Thus, for example, facts and circumstances which, because of the taxpayer's efforts to conserve assets in marketable form, may constitute reasonable cause for nonpayment of income taxes may not constitute reasonable cause for failure to pay over taxes described in section 7501 that are collected or withheld from any other person.

(3) If, for a taxable year ending on or after December 31, 1995, an individual taxpayer satisfies the requirement of § 1.6081-4(a) of this chapter (relating to automatic extension of time for filing an individual income tax return), reasonable cause will be presumed, for the period of the extension of time to file, with respect to any underpayment of tax if—

(i) The excess of the amount of tax shown on the individual income tax return over the amount of tax paid on or before the regular due date of the return (by virtue of tax withheld by the employer, estimated tax payments, and any payment with an application for extension of time to file pursuant to § 1.6081-4 of this chapter) is no greater than 10 percent of the amount of tax shown on the individual income tax return; and

(ii) Any balance due shown on the individual income tax return is remitted with the return.

(4) If, for a taxable year ending on or after December 31, 1972, a corporate taxpayer satisfies the requirements of § 1.6081-3(a) (relating to an automatic extension of time for filing a corporation income tax return), reasonable cause shall be presumed, for the period of the extension of time to file, with respect to any underpayment of tax if—

(i) The amount of tax (determined without regard to any pre-payment thereof) shown on Form 7004, or the amount of tax paid on or before the regular due date of the return, is at least 90 percent of the amount of tax shown on the taxpayer's Form 1120, and

(ii) Any balance due shown on the Form 1120 is paid on, or before the due date of the return, including any extensions of time for filing.

(d) *Penalty imposed on net amount due.*—(1) *Credits against the tax.*—The amount of tax required to be shown on the return for purposes of section 6651(a)(1) and the amount shown as tax on the return for purposes of section 6651(a)(2) shall be reduced by the amount of any part of the tax which is paid on or before the date prescribed for payment of the tax and by the amount of any credit against the tax which may be claimed on the return.

(2) *Partial payments.*—(i) The amount of tax required to be shown on the return for purposes of section 6651(a)(2) shall, for the purpose of computing the addition for any month, be reduced by the amount of any part of the tax which is paid after the date prescribed for payment and on or before the first day of such month.

(ii) The amount of tax stated in the notice and demand for purposes of section 6651(a)(3) shall, for the purpose of computing the addition for any month, be reduced by the amount of any part of the tax which is paid before the first day of such month.

(e) *No addition to tax if fraud penalty assessed.*—No addition to the tax under section 6651 shall be assessed with respect to an underpayment of tax if a 50-percent addition to the tax for fraud is assessed with respect to the same underpayment under section 6653(b). See section 6653(d).

(f) *Examples.*—The provisions of this section may be illustrated by the following examples:

Example (1). (a) Under section 6072(a), income tax returns of individuals on a calendar year basis must be filed on or before the 15th day of April following the close of the calendar year. Assume an individual filed his income tax return for the calendar year 1969 on July 20, 1970, and the failure to file on or before the prescribed date is not due to reasonable cause. The tax shown on the return is $800 and a deficiency of $200 is subsequently assessed, making the tax required to be shown on the return, $1,000. Of this amount, $300 has been paid by withholding from wages and $400 has been paid as estimated tax. The balance due as shown on the return of $100 ($800 shown as tax on the return less $700 previously paid) is paid on August 21, 1970. The failure to pay on or before the prescribed date is not due to reasonable cause. There will be imposed, in addition to interest, an additional amount under section 6651(a)(2) of $2.50, which is 2.5 percent (2% for the 4 months from April 16 through August 15, and 0.5% for the fractional part of the month from August 16 through August 21) of the net amount due as shown on the return of $100 ($800 shown on the return less $700 paid on or before April 15). There will also be imposed an additional amount under section 6651(a)(1) of $58, determined as follows:

20 percent (5% per month for the 3 months from April 16 through July 15 and 5% for the fractional part of the month from July 16 through July 20) of the net amount due of $300 ($1,000 required to be shown on the return less $700 paid on or before April 15)	$60
Reduced by the amount of the addition imposed under section 6651(a)(2) for those months	2
Addition to tax under section 6651(a)(1)	$58

(b) A notice and demand for the $200 deficiency is issued on January 8, 1971, but the taxpayer does not pay the deficiency until December 23, 1971. In addition to interest there will be imposed an additional amount under section 6651(a)(3) of $10, determined as follows:

Addition computed without regard to limitation:		
6 percent ($5^1/_2$% for the 11 months from January 19, 1971, through December 18, 1971, and 0.5% for the fractional part of the month from December 19 through December 23) of the amount stated in the notice and demand ($200)		$12
Limitation on addition:		
25 percent of the amount stated in the notice and demand ($200)	$50	
Reduced by the part of the addition under section 6651(a)(1) for failure to file attributable to the $200 deficiency (20% of $200)	$40	
Maximum amount of the addition under section 6651(a)(3)		$10

Example (2). An individual files his income tax return for the calendar year 1969 on December 2, 1970, and such delinquency is not due to reasonable cause. The balance due, as shown on the return, of $500 is paid when the return is filed on December 2, 1970. In addition to interest and the addition for failure to pay under section 6651(a)(2) of $20, (8 months at 0.5% per month, 4%) there will also be imposed an additional amount under section 6651(a)(1) of $112.50, determined as follows:

Penalty at 5% for maximum of 5 months, 25% of $500	$125.00
Less reduction for the amount of the addition under section 6651(a)(2):	
Amount imposed under section 6651(a)(2) for failure to pay for the months in which there is also an addition for failure to file—$2^1/_2$ percent for the 5 months April 16 through September 15 of the net amount due ($500)	$12.50
Addition to tax under section 6651(a)(1)	$112.50

(g) *Treatment of returns prepared by the Secretary.*—(1) *In general.*—A return prepared by the Secretary under section 6020(b) will be disregarded for purposes of determining the amount of the addition to tax for failure to file any return pursuant to paragraph (a)(1) of this section. However, the return prepared by the Secretary will be treated as a return filed by the taxpayer for purposes of determining the amount of the addition to tax for failure to pay the tax shown on any return and for failure to pay the tax required to be shown on a return that is not so shown pursuant to paragraphs (a)(2) and (3) of this section, respectively.

(2) *Effective date.*—This paragraph (g) applies to returns the due date for which (determined without regard to extensions) is after July 30, 1996. [Reg. § 301.6651-1.]

□ [*T.D.* 6268, 11-15-75. *Amended by T.D.* 6498, 10-24-60; *T.D.* 6585, 7-21-71; *T.D.* 7160, 2-1-72; *T.D.* 7260, 2-9-73; *T.D.* 8651, 1-3-96; *T.D.* 8703, 12-30-96; *T.D.* 8725, 7-21-97; *T.D.* 8895, 8-17-2000 *and T.D.* 9163, 12-6-2004.]

[Reg. § 1.6662-0]

§ 1.6662-0. Table of contents.—This section lists the captions that appear in §§ 1.6662-1 through 1.6662-7.

§1.6662-1. Overview of the accuracy-related penalty.

§1.6662-2. Accuracy-related penalty.

(a) In general.

(b) Amount of penalty.

(1) In general.

(2) Increase in penalty for gross valuation misstatement.

(c) No stacking of accuracy-related penalty components.

(d) Effective dates.

(1) Returns due before January 1, 1994.

(2) Returns due after December 31, 1993.

(3) Special rules for tax shelter items.

(4) Special rule for reasonable basis.

(5) Returns filed after December 31, 2002.

§1.6662-3. Negligence or disregard of rules or regulations.

(a) In general.

(b) Definitions and rules.

(1) Negligence.

(2) Disregard of rules or regulations.

(3) Reasonable basis.

(c) Exception for adequate disclosure.

(1) In general.

(2) Method of disclosure.

(d) Special rules in the case of carrybacks and carryovers.

(1) In general.

(2) Transition rule for carrybacks to pre-1990 years.

(3) Example.

§1.6662-4. Substantial understatement of income tax.

(a) In general.

(b) Definitions and computational rules.

(1) Substantial.

(2) Understatement.

(3) Amount of the tax required to be shown on the return.

(4) Amount of the tax imposed which is shown on the return.

(5) Rebate.

(6) Examples.

(c) Special rules in the case of carrybacks and carryovers.

(1) In general.

(2) Understatements for carryback years not reduced by amount of carrybacks.

(3) Tainted items defined.

(i) In general.

(ii) Tax shelter items.

(4) Transition rule for carrybacks to pre-1990 years.

(5) Examples.

(d) Substantial authority.

(1) Effect of having substantial authority.

(2) Substantial authority standard.

(3) Determination of whether substantial authority is present.

(i) Evaluation of authorities.

(ii) Nature of analysis.

(iii) Types of authority.

(iv) Special rules.

(A) Written determinations.

(B) Taxpayer's jurisdiction.

(C) When substantial authority determined.

(v) Substantial authority for tax returns due before January 1, 1990.

(e) Disclosure of certain information.

(1) Effect of adequate disclosure.

(2) Circumstances where disclosure will not have an effect.

(3) Restriction for corporations.

(f) Method of making adequate disclosure.

(1) Disclosure statement.

(2) Disclosure on return.

(3) Recurring item.

(4) Carrybacks and carryovers.

(5) Pass-through entities.

(g) Items relating to tax shelters.

(1) In general.

(i) Noncorporate taxpayers.

(ii) Corporate taxpayers.

(A) In general.

(B) Special rule for transactions occurring prior to December 9, 1994.

(iii) Disclosure irrelevant.

(iv) Cross-reference.

(2) Tax shelter.

(i) In general.

(ii) Principal purpose.

(3) Tax shelter item.

(4) Reasonable belief.

(i) In general.

(ii) Facts and circumstances; reliance on professional tax advisor.

(5) Pass-through entities.

§1.6662-5. Substantial and gross valuation misstatements under chapter 1.

(a) In general.

(b) Dollar limitation.

(c) Special rules in the case of carrybacks and carryovers.

(1) In general.

(2) Transition rule for carrybacks to pre-1990 years.

(d) Examples.

(e) Definitions.

(1) Substantial valuation misstatement.

(2) Gross valuation misstatement.

(3) Property.

(f) Multiple valuation misstatements on a return.

(1) Determination of whether valuation misstatements are substantial or gross.

(2) Application of dollar limitation.

(g) Property with a value or adjusted basis of zero.

(h) Pass-through entities.

(1) In general.

(2) Example.

(i) [Reserved]

(j) Transactions between persons described in section 482 and net section 482 transfer price adjustments. [Reserved]

(k) Returns affected.

§ 1.6662-5T. Substantial and gross valuation misstatements under chapter 1 (Temporary).

(a) through (e)(3) [Reserved].

(e)(4) Tests related to section 482.

(i) Substantial valuation misstatement.

(ii) Gross valuation misstatement.

(iii) Property.

(f) through (i) [Reserved].

(j) Transactions between persons described in section 482 and net section 482 transfer price adjustments.

§ 1.6662-6. Transactions between persons described in section 482 and net section 482 transfer price adjustments.

(a) In general.

(1) Purpose and scope.

(2) Reported results.

(3) Identical terms used in the section 482 regulations.

(b) The transactional penalty.

(1) Substantial valuation misstatement.

(2) Gross valuation misstatement.

(3) Reasonable cause and good faith.

(c) Net adjustment penalty.

(1) Net section 482 adjustment.

(2) Substantial valuation misstatement.

(3) Gross valuation misstatement.

(4) Setoff allocation rule.

(5) Gross receipts.

(6) Coordination with reasonable cause exception under section 6664(c).

(7) Examples.

(d) Amounts excluded from net section 482 adjustments.

(1) In general.

(2) Application of a specified section 482 method.

(i) In general.

(ii) Specified method requirement.

(iii) Documentation requirement.

(A) In general.

(B) Principal documents.

(C) Background documents.

(3) Application of an unspecified method.

(i) In general.

(ii) Unspecified method requirement.

(A) In general.

(B) Specified method potentially applicable.

(C) No specified method applicable.

(iii) Documentation requirement.

(A) In general.

(B) Principal and background documents.

(4) Certain foreign to foreign transactions.

(5) Special rule.

(6) Examples.

(e) Special rules in the case of carrybacks and carryovers.

(f) Rules for coordinating between the transactional penalty and the net adjustment penalty.

(1) Coordination of a net section 482 adjustment subject to the net adjustment penalty and a gross valuation misstatement subject to the transactional penalty.

(2) Coordination of net section 482 adjustment subject to the net adjustment penalty and substantial valuation misstatements subject to the transactional penalty.

(3) Examples.

(g) Effective date.

§ 1.6662-7. Omnibus Budget Reconciliation Act of 1993 changes to the accuracy-related penalty.

(a) Scope.

(b) No disclosure exception for negligence penalty.

(c) Disclosure standard for other penalties is reasonable basis.

(d) Reasonable basis.

[Reg. § 1.6662-0.]

☐ [*T.D.* 8381, 12-30-91. *Amended by T.D.* 8519, 1-27-94; *T.D.* 8533, 3-14-94; *T.D.* 8551, 7-5-94; *T.D.* 8617, 8-31-95; *T.D.* 8656, 2-8-96; *T.D.* 8790, 12-1-98 *and T.D.* 9109, 12-29-2003.]

[Reg. § 1.6662-1]

§ 1.6662-1. Overview of the accuracy-related penalty.—Section 6662 imposes an accuracy-related penalty on any portion of an underpayment of tax required to be shown on a return that is attributable to one or more of the following:

(a) Negligence or disregard of rules or regulations;

(b) Any substantial understatement of income tax;

(c) Any substantial valuation misstatement under chapter 1;

(d) Any substantial overstatement of pension liabilities; or

(e) Any substantial estate or gift tax valuation understatement.

Sections 1.6662-1 through 1.6662-5 address only the first three components of the accuracy-related penalty, *i.e.,* the penalties for negligence or disregard of rules or regulations, substantial understatements of income tax, and substantial (or gross) valuation misstatements under chapter 1. The penalties for disregard of rules or regulations and for a substantial understatement of income tax may be avoided by adequately disclosing certain information as provided in § 1.6662-3(c) and §§ 1.6662-4(e) and (f), respectively. The penalties for negligence and for a substantial (or gross) valuation misstatement under chapter 1 may not be avoided by disclosure. No accuracy-related penalty may be imposed on any portion of an underpayment if there was reasonable cause for, and the taxpayer acted in good faith with respect to, such portion. The reasonable cause and good faith exception to the accuracy-related penalty is set forth in § 1.6664-4. [Reg. § 1.6662-1.]

☐ [*T.D.* 8381, 12-30-91. *Amended by T.D.* 8617, 8-31-95.]

[Reg. § 1.6662-2]

§ 1.6662-2. Accuracy-related penalty.—(a) *In general.*—Section 6662(a) imposes an accuracy-related penalty on any portion of an underpayment of tax (as defined in section 6664(a) and § 1.6664-2) required to be shown on a return if such portion is attributable to one or more of the following types of misconduct:

(1) Negligence or disregard of rules or regulations (see § 1.6662-3);

(2) Any substantial understatement of income tax (see § 1.6662-4); or

(3) Any substantial (or gross) valuation misstatement under chapter 1 ("substantial valuation misstatement" or "gross valuation misstatement"), provided the applicable dollar limitation set forth in section 6662(e)(2) is satisfied (see § 1.6662-5).

The accuracy-related penalty applies only in cases in which a return of tax is filed, except that the penalty does not apply in the case of a return prepared by the Secretary under the authority of section 6020(b). The accuracy-related penalty under section 6662 and the penalty under section 6651 for failure to timely file a return of tax may both be imposed on the same portion of an underpayment if a return is filed, but is filed late. The fact that a return is filed late, however, is not taken into account in determining whether an accuracy-related penalty should be imposed. No accuracy-related penalty may be imposed on any portion of an underpayment of tax on which the fraud penalty set forth in section 6663 is imposed.

(b) *Amount of penalty.*—(1) *In general.*—The amount of the accuracy-related penalty is 20 percent of the portion of an underpayment of tax required to be shown on a return that is attributable to any of the types of misconduct listed in paragraphs (a)(1) through (a)(3) of this section, except as provided in paragraph (b)(2) of this section.

(2) *Increase in penalty for gross valuation misstatement.*—In the case of a gross valuation misstatement, as defined in section 6662(h)(2) and § 1.6662-5(e)(2), the amount of the accuracy-related penalty is 40 percent of the portion of an underpayment of tax required to be shown on a return that is attributable to the gross valuation misstatement, provided the applicable dollar limitation set forth in section 6662(e)(2) is satisfied.

(c) *No stacking of accuracy-related penalty components.*—The maximum accuracy-related penalty imposed on a portion of an underpayment may not exceed 20 percent of such portion (40 percent of the portion attributable to a gross valuation misstatement), notwithstanding that such portion is attributable to more than one of the types of misconduct described in paragraph (a) of this section. For example, if a portion of an underpayment of tax required to be shown on a return is attributable both to negligence and a substantial understatement of income tax, the maximum accuracy-related penalty is 20 percent of such portion. Similarly, the maximum accuracy-related penalty imposed on any portion of an underpayment that is attributable both to negligence and a gross valuation misstatement is 40 percent of such portion.

(d) *Effective dates.*—(1) *Returns due before January 1, 1994.*—Section 1.6662-3(c) and §§ 1.6662-4(e) and (f) (relating to methods of making adequate disclosure) (as contained in 26 CFR part 1 revised April 1, 1995) apply to returns the due date of which (determined without regard to extensions of time for filing) is after December 31, 1991, but before January 1, 1994. Except as provided in the preceding sentence and in paragraphs (d)(2), (3), and (4) of this section, §§ 1.6662-1 through 1.6662-5 apply to returns the due date of which (determined without regard to extensions of time for filing) is after December 31, 1989, but before January 1, 1994. To the extent the provisions of these regulations were not reflected in the statute as amended by the Omnibus Budget Reconciliation Act of 1989 (OBRA 1989), in Notice 90-20, 1990-1 C.B. 328, or in rules and regulations in effect prior to March 4, 1991 (to the extent not inconsistent with the statute as amended by OBRA 1989), these regulations will not be adversely applied to a taxpayer who took a position based upon such prior rules on a return filed before January 1, 1992.

(2) *Returns due after December 31, 1993.*—Except as provided in paragraphs (d)(3), (4) and (5) of this section and the last sentence of this paragraph (d)(2), the provisions of §§ 1.6662-1 through 1.6662-4 and § 1.6662-7 (as revised to reflect the changes made to the accuracy-related penalty by the Omnibus Budget Reconciliation Act of 1993) and of § 1.6662-5 apply to returns the due date of which (determined without regard to extensions of time for filing) is after December 31, 1993. These changes include raising the disclosure standard for the penalties for disregarding rules or regulations and for a substantial understatement of income tax from not frivolous to reasonable basis, eliminating the disclosure exception for the negligence penalty, and providing guidance on the meaning of reasonable basis. The Omnibus Budget Reconciliation Act of 1993 changes relating to the penalties for negligence or disregard of rules or regulations will not apply to returns (including qualified amended returns) that are filed on or before March 14, 1994, but the provisions of §§ 1.6662-1 through 1.6662-3 (as contained in 26 CFR part 1 revised April 1, 1995) relating to those penalties will apply to such returns.

(3) *Special rules for tax shelter items.*—Sections 1.6662-4(g)(1) and 1.6662-4(g)(4) apply to returns the due date of which (determined without regard to extensions of time for filing) is after September 1, 1995. Except as provided in the last sentence of this paragraph (d)(3), §§ 1.6662-4(g)(1) and 1.6662-4(g)(4) (as contained in 26 CFR part 1 revised April 1, 1995) apply to returns the due date of which (determined without regard to extensions of time for filing) is on or before September 1, 1995, and after December

31, 1989. For transactions occurring after December 8, 1994, §§1.6662-4(g)(1) and 1.6662-4(g)(2) (as contained in 26 CFR part 1 revised April 1, 1995) are applied taking into account the changes made to section 6662(d)(2)(C) (relating to the substantial understatement penalty for tax shelter items of corporations) by section 744 of Title VII of the Uruguay Round Agreements Act, Pub. L. 103-465 (108 Stat. 4809).

(4) *Special rules for reasonable basis.*—Section 1.6662-3(b)(3) applies to returns filed on or after December 2, 1998.

(5) *For returns filed after December 31, 2002.*—Sections 1.6662-3(a), 1.6662-3(b)(2) and 1.6662-3(c)(1) (relating to adequate disclosure) apply to returns filed after December 31, 2002, with respect to transactions entered into on or after January 1, 2003. Except as provided in paragraph (d)(1) of this section, §§1.6662-3(a), 1.6662-3(b)(2) and 1.6662-3(c)(1) (as contained in 26 CFR part 1 revised April 1, 2003) apply to returns filed with respect to transactions entered into prior to January 1, 2003. [Reg. §1.6662-2.]

[☐ *T.D.* 8381, 12-30-91. *Amended by T.D.* 8617, 8-31-95; *T.D.* 8790, 12-1-98 *and T.D.* 9109, 12-29-2003.]

[Reg. §1.6662-3]

§1.6662-3. Negligence or disregard of rules or regulations.—(a) *In general.*—If any portion of an underpayment, as defined in section 6664(a) and §1.6664-2, of any income tax imposed under subtitle A of the Internal Revenue Code that is required to be shown on a return is attributable to negligence or disregard of rules or regulations, there is added to the tax an amount equal to 20 percent of such portion. The penalty for disregarding rules or regulations does not apply, however, if the requirements of paragraph (c)(1) of this section are satisfied and the position in question is adequately disclosed as provided in paragraph (c)(2) of this section (and, if the position relates to a reportable transaction as defined in §1.6011-4(b) (or §1.6011-4T(b), as applicable), the transaction is disclosed in accordance with §1.6011-4 (or §1.6011-4T, as applicable)), or to the extent that the reasonable cause and good faith exception to this penalty set forth in §1.6664-4 applies. In addition, if a position with respect to an item (other than with respect to a reportable transaction, as defined in §1.6011-4(b) or §1.6011-4T(b), as applicable) is contrary to a revenue ruling or notice (other than a notice of proposed rulemaking) issued by the Internal Revenue Service and published in the Internal Revenue Bulletin (see §601.601(d)(2) of this chapter), this penalty does not apply if the position has a realistic possibility of being sustained on its merits. See §1.6694-2(b) of the income tax return preparer penalty regulations for a description of the realistic possibility standard.

(b) *Definitions and rules.*—(1) *Negligence.*—The term "negligence" includes any failure to make a reasonable attempt to comply with the provisions of the internal revenue laws or to exercise ordinary and reasonable care in the preparation of a tax return. "Negligence" also includes any failure by the taxpayer to keep adequate books and records or to substantiate items properly. A return position that has a reasonable basis as defined in paragraph (b)(3) of this section is not attributable to negligence. Negligence is strongly indicated where—

(i) A taxpayer fails to include on an income tax return an amount of income shown on an information return, as defined in section 6724(d)(1);

(ii) A taxpayer fails to make a reasonable attempt to ascertain the correctness of a deduction, credit or exclusion on a return which would seem to a reasonable and prudent person to be "too good to be true" under the circumstances;

(iii) A partner fails to comply with the requirements of section 6222, which requires that a partner treat partnership items on its return in a manner that is consistent with the treatment of such items on the partnership return (or notify the Secretary of the inconsistency); or

(iv) A shareholder fails to comply with the requirements of section 6242, which requires that an S corporation shareholder treat subchapter S items on its return in a manner that is consistent with the treatment of such items on the corporation's return (or notify the Secretary of the inconsistency).

(2) *Disregard of rules or regulations.*—The term "disregard" includes any careless, reckless or intentional disregard of rules or regulations. The term "rules or regulations" includes the provisions of the Internal Revenue Code, temporary or final Treasury regulations issued under the Code, and revenue rulings or notices (other than notices of proposed rulemaking) issued by the Internal Revenue Service and published in the Internal Revenue Bulletin. A disregard of rules or regulations is "careless" if the taxpayer does not exercise reasonable diligence to determine the correctness of a return position that is contrary to the rule or regulation. A disregard is "reckless" if the taxpayer makes little or no effort to determine whether a rule or regulation exists, under circumstances which demonstrate a substantial deviation from the standard of conduct that a reasonable person would observe. A disregard is "intentional" if the taxpayer knows of the rule or regulation that is disregarded. Nevertheless, a taxpayer who takes a position (other than with respect to a reportable transaction, as defined in §1.6011-4(b) or §1.6011-4T(b), as applicable) contrary to a revenue ruling or notice has not disregarded the ruling or notice if the contrary position has a realistic possibility of being sustained on its merits.

(3) *Reasonable basis.*—Reasonable basis is a relatively high standard of tax reporting, that is, significantly higher than not frivolous or not patently improper. The reasonable basis standard is not satisfied by a return position that is merely arguable or that is merely a colorable claim. If a return position is reasonably based on one or more of the authorities set forth in §1.6662-4(d)(3)(iii) (taking into account the rele-

vance and persuasiveness of the authorities, and subsequent developments), the return position will generally satisfy the reasonable basis standard even though it may not satisfy the substantial authority standard as defined in § 1.6662-4(d)(2). (See § 1.6662-4(d)(3)(ii) for rules with respect to relevance, persuasiveness, subsequent developments, and use of a well-reasoned construction of an applicable statutory provision for purposes of the substantial understatement penalty.) In addition, the reasonable cause and good faith exception in § 1.6664-4 may provide relief from the penalty for negligence or disregard of rules or regulations, even if a return position does not satisfy the reasonable basis standard.

(c) *Exception for adequate disclosure.*—(1) *In general.*—No penalty under section 6662(b)(1) may be imposed on any portion of an underpayment that is attributable to a position contrary to a rule or regulation if the position is disclosed in accordance with the rules of paragraph (c)(2) of this section (and, if the position relates to a reportable transaction as defined in § 1.6011-4(b) (or § 1.6011-4T(b), as applicable), the transaction is disclosed in accordance with § 1.6011-4 (or § 1.6011-4T, as applicable)) and, in case of a position contrary to a regulation, the position represents a good faith challenge to the validity of the regulation. This disclosure exception does not apply, however, in the case of a position that does not have a reasonable basis or where the taxpayer fails to keep adequate books and records or to substantiate items properly.

(2) *Method of disclosure.*—Disclosure is adequate for purposes of the penalty for disregarding rules or regulations if made in accordance with the provisions of §§ 1.6662-4(f)(1), (3), (4) and (5), which permit disclosure on a properly completed and filed Form 8275 or 8275-R, as appropriate. In addition, the statutory or regulatory provision or ruling in question must be adequately identified on the Form 8275 or 8275-R, as appropriate. The provisions of § 1.6662-4(f)(2), which permit disclosure in accordance with an annual revenue procedure for purposes of the substantial understatement penalty, do not apply for purposes of this section.

(d) *Special rules in the case of carrybacks and carryovers—.*—(1) *In general.*—The penalty for negligence or disregard of rules or regulations applies to any portion of an underpayment for a year to which a loss, deduction or credit is carried, which portion is attributable to negligence or disregard of rules or regulations in the year in which the carryback or carryover of the loss, deduction or credit arises (the "loss or credit year").

(2) *Transition rule for carrybacks to pre-1990 years.*—A 20 percent penalty under section 6662(b)(1) is imposed on any portion of an underpayment for a carryback year, the return for which is due (without regard to extensions) before January 1, 1990, if—

(i) That portion is attributable to negligence or disregard of rules or regulations in a loss or credit year; and

(ii) The return for the loss or credit year is due (without regard to extensions) after December 31, 1989.

(3) *Example.*—The following example illustrates the provisions of paragraph (d) of this section. This example does not take into account the reasonable cause exception under § 1.6664-4.

Example. Corporation M is a C corporation. In 1990, M had a loss of $200,000 before taking into account a deduction of $350,000 that M claimed as an expense in careless disregard of the capitalization requirements of section 263 of the Code. M failed to make adequate disclosure of the item for 1990. M reported a $550,000 loss for 1990 and carried back the loss to 1987 and 1988. M had reported taxable income of $400,000 for 1987 and $200,000 for 1988, before application of the carryback. The carryback eliminated all of M's taxable income for 1987 and $150,000 of taxable income for 1988. After disallowance of the $350,000 expense deduction and allowance of a $35,000 depreciation deduction with respect to the capitalized amount, the correct loss for 1990 was determined to be $235,000. Because there is no underpayment for 1990, the penalty for negligence or disregard of rules or regulations does not apply for 1990. However, as a result of the 1990 adjustments, the loss carried back to 1987 is reduced from $550,000 to $235,000. After application of the $235,000 carryback, M has taxable income of $165,000 for 1987 and $200,000 for 1988. This adjustment results in underpayments for 1987 and 1988 that are attributable to the disregard of rules or regulations on the 1990 return. Therefore, the 20 percent penalty rate applies to the 1987 and 1988 underpayments attributable to the disallowed carryback. [Reg. § 1.6662-3.]

☐ [*T.D.* 8381, 12-30-91. *Amended by T.D.* 8617, 8-31-95; *T.D.* 8790, 12-1-98 *and T.D.* 9109, 12-29-2003.]

[Reg. § 1.6662-4]

§ 1.6662-4. Substantial understatement of income tax.—(a) *In general.*—If any portion of an underpayment, as defined in section 6664(a) and § 1.6664-2, of any income tax imposed under subtitle A of the Code that is required to be shown on a return is attributable to a substantial understatement of such income tax, there is added to the tax an amount equal to 20 percent of such portion. Except in the case of any item attributable to a tax shelter (as defined in paragraph (g)(2) of this section), an understatement is reduced by the portion of the understatement that is attributable to the tax treatment of an item for which there is substantial authority, or with respect to which there is adequate disclosure. General rules for determining the amount of an understatement are set forth in paragraph (b) of this section and more specific rules in the case of carrybacks and carryovers are set forth in paragraph (c) of this section. The rules for determining when substantial authority exists are set forth in § 1.6662-4(d). The rules for determining when there is adequate disclosure are set forth in § 1.6662-4(e) and (f). This penalty does not apply to the extent that the reasonable cause and good faith exception to this penalty set forth in § 1.6664-4 applies.

(b) *Definitions and computational rules.*—(1) *Substantial.*—An understatement (as defined in paragraph (b)(2) of this section) is "substantial" if it exceeds the greater of—

(i) 10 percent of the tax required to be shown on the return for the taxable year (as defined in paragraph (b)(3) of this section); or

(ii) $5,000 ($10,000 in the case of a corporation other than an S corporation (as defined in section 1361(a)(1)) or a personal holding company (as defined in section 542)).

(2) *Understatement.*—Except as provided in paragraph (c)(2) of this section (relating to special rules for carrybacks), the term "understatement" means the excess of—

(i) The amount of the tax required to be shown on the return for the taxable year (as defined in paragraph (b)(3) of this section), over

(ii) The amount of the tax imposed which is shown on the return for the taxable year (as defined in paragraph (b)(4) of this section), reduced by any rebate (as defined in paragraph (b)(5) of this section).

The definition of understatement also may be expressed as—

$$Understatement = X - (Y - Z)$$

where X = the amount of the tax required to be shown on the return; Y = the amount of the tax imposed which is shown on the return; and Z = any rebate.

(3) *Amount of the tax required to be shown on the return.*—The "amount of the tax required to be shown on the return" for the taxable year has the same meaning as the "amount of income tax imposed" as defined in § 1.6664-2(b).

(4) *Amount of the tax imposed which is shown on the return.*—The "amount of the tax imposed which is shown on the return" for the taxable year has the same meaning as the "amount shown as the tax by the taxpayer on his return," as defined in § 1.6664-2(c), except that—

(i) There is no reduction for the excess of the amount described in § 1.6664-2(c)(1)(i) over the amount described in § 1.6664-2(c)(1)(ii), and

(ii) The tax liability shown by the taxpayer on his return is recomputed as if the following items had been reported properly:

(A) Items (other than tax shelter items as defined in § 1.6662-4(g)(3)) for which there is substantial authority for the treatment claimed (as provided in § 1.6662-4(d)).

(B) Items (other than tax shelter items as defined in § 1.6662-4(g)(3)) with respect to which there is adequate disclosure (as provided in § 1.6662-4(e) and (f)).

(C) Tax shelter items (as defined in § 1.6662-4(g)(3)) for which there is substantial authority for the treatment claimed (as provided in § 1.6662-4(d)), and with respect to which the taxpayer reasonably believed that the tax treatment of the items was more likely than not the proper tax treatment (as provided in § 1.6662-4(g)(4)).

(5) *Rebate.*—The term "rebate" has the meaning set forth in § 1.6664-2(e), except that—

(i) "Amounts not so shown previously assessed (or collected without assessment)" includes only amounts not so shown previously assessed (or collected without assessment) as a deficiency, and

(ii) The amount of the rebate is determined as if any items to which the rebate is attributable that are described in paragraph (b)(4) of this section had received the proper tax treatment.

(6) *Examples.*—The following examples illustrate the provisions of paragraph (b) of this section. These examples do not take into account the reasonable cause exception under § 1.6664-4:

Example 1. In 1990, Individual A, a calendar year taxpayer, files a return for 1989, which shows taxable income of $18,200 and tax liability of $2,734. Subsequent adjustments on audit for 1989 increase taxable income to $51,500 and tax liability to $12,339. There was substantial authority for an item resulting in an adjustment that increases taxable income by $5,300. The item is not a tax shelter item. In computing the amount of the understatement, the amount of tax shown on A's return is determined as if the item for which there was substantial authority had been given the proper tax treatment. Thus, the amount of tax that is treated as shown on A's return is $4,176, i.e., the tax on $23,500 ($18,200 taxable income actually shown on A's return plus $5,300, the amount of the adjustment for which there was substantial authority). The amount of the understatement is $8,163, i.e., $12,339 (the amount of tax required to be shown) less $4,176 (the amount of tax treated as shown on A's return after adjustment for the item for which there was substantial authority). Because the $8,163 understatement exceeds the greater of 10 percent of the tax required to be shown on the return for the year, i.e., $1,234 ($12,339 × .10) or $5,000, A has a substantial understatement of income tax for the year.

Example 2. Individual B, a calendar year taxpayer, files a return for 1990 that fails to include income reported on an information return, Form 1099, that was furnished to B. The Service detects this omission through its document matching program and assesses $3,000 in unreported tax liability. B's return is later examined and as a result of the examination the Service makes an adjustment to B's return of $4,000 in additional tax liability. Assuming there was neither substantial authority nor adequate disclosure with respect to the items adjusted, there is an understatement of $7,000 with respect to B's return. There is also an underpayment of $7,000. (See § 1.6664-2.) The amount of the understatement is not reduced by imposition of a negligence penalty on the $3,000 portion of the underpayment that is attributable to the unreported income. However, if the Service does impose the negligence penalty on this $3,000 portion, the Service may only impose the substantial understatement penalty on the remaining $4,000 portion of the underpayment. (See § 1.6662-2(c), which prohibits stacking of accuracy-related penalty components.)

(c) *Special rules in the case of carrybacks and carryovers.*—(1) *In general.*—The penalty for a substantial understatement of income tax applies to any portion of an underpayment for a year to which a loss, deduction or credit is carried that is attributable to a "tainted item" for the year in which the carryback or carryover of the loss, deduction or credit arises (the "loss or credit year"). The determination of whether an understatement is substantial for a carryback or carryover year is made with respect to the return of the carryback or carryover year. "Tainted items" are taken into account with items arising in a carryback or carryover year to determine whether the understatement is substantial for that year.

(2) *Understatements for carryback years not reduced by amount of carrybacks.*—The amount of an understatement for a carryback year is not reduced on account of a carryback of a loss, deduction or credit to that year.

(3) *Tainted items defined.*—(i) *In general.*—Except in the case of a tax shelter item (as defined in paragraph (g)(3) of this section), a "tainted item" is any item for which there is neither substantial authority nor adequate disclosure with respect to the loss or credit year.

(ii) *Tax shelter items.*—In the case of a tax shelter item (as defined in paragraph (g)(3) of this section), a "tainted item" is any item for which there is not, with respect to the loss or credit year, both substantial authority and a reasonable belief that the tax treatment is more likely than not the proper treatment.

(4) *Transition rule for carrybacks to pre-1990 years.*—A 20 percent penalty under section 6662(b)(2) is imposed on any portion of an underpayment for a carryback year, the return for which is due (without regard to extensions) before January 1, 1990, if—

(i) That portion is attributable to one or more "tainted items" (as defined in paragraph (c)(3) of this section) arising in a loss or credit year; and

(ii) The return for the loss or credit year is due (without regard to extensions) after December 31, 1989.

The preceding sentence applies only if the understatement in the carryback year is substantial. See *Example 2* in paragraph (c)(5) of this section.

(5) *Examples.*—The following examples illustrate the rules of paragraph (c) of this section regarding carrybacks and carryovers. These examples do not take into account the reasonable cause exception under § 1.6664-4.

Example 1. (i) Corporation N, a calendar year taxpayer, is a C corporation. N was formed on January 1, 1987, and timely filed the following income tax returns:

Tax Year	*1987*	*1988*	*1989*	*1990*
Taxable Income	$30,000	$100,000	($300,000)	$50,000 (Before NOLCO)
Tax Liability	$4,575	$22,250	–0–	$ 7,500 (Before NOLCO)

(ii) During 1990, N files Form 1139, Corporation Application for Tentative Refund, to carry back the NOL generated in 1989 (NOLCB). N received refunds of $4,575 for 1987 and $22,250 for 1988.

(iii) For tax year 1990, N carries over $50,000 of the 1989 loss to offset $50,000 of income earned in 1990 and reduce taxable income to zero. N would have reported $7,500 of tax liability for 1990 if it were not for use of the net operating loss carryover (NOLCO). N assumes there is a remaining NOLCO of $120,000 to be applied for tax year 1991.

(iv) In June 1991, the Service completes its examination of the 1989 loss year return and makes the following adjustment:

Taxable income per 1989 return		($300,000)
Adjustment: Unreported income		310,000
Corrected taxable income		$ 10,000
Corrected tax liability	$1,500	

(v) There was not substantial authority for N's treatment of the items comprising the 1989 adjustment and N did not make adequate disclosure.

(vi) As a result of the adjustment to the 1989 return, N had an understatement of $4,575 for tax year 1987; an understatement of $22,250 for tax year 1988; an understatement of $1,500 for tax year 1989; and an understatement of $7,500 for tax year 1990. Only the $22,250 understatement for 1988 is a substantial understatement, i.e., it exceeds the greater of (a) $2,225 (10 percent of the tax required to be shown on the return for the taxable year (.10 × $22,250)) or (b) $10,000. The underpayment for 1988 is subject to a penalty rate of 20 percent.

Example 2. The facts are the same as in *Example 1,* except that in addition to examining the 1989 return, the Service also examines the 1987 return and makes an adjustment that results in an understatement. (This adjustment is unrelated to the adjustment on the 1987 return for the disallowance of the NOLCB from 1989.) If the understatement resulting from the adjustment to the 1987 return, when combined with the understatement resulting from the disallowance of the NOLCB from 1989, exceeds the greater of (a) 10 percent of the tax required to be shown on the return for 1987 or (b) $10,000, the underpayment for 1987 will also be subject to a substantial understatement penalty. The portion of the underpayment attributable to the adjustment unrelated to the disallowance of the NOLCB will be subject to a penalty rate of 25 percent under former section 6661. The portion of the underpayment attributable to the disallowance of the NOLCB will be subject to a penalty rate of 20 percent under section 6662.

Example 3. Individual P, a calendar year single taxpayer, files his 1990 return reporting taxable income of $10,000 and a tax liability of $1,504. An examination of the 1990 return results in an adjustment for unreported income of $25,000. There was not substantial authority for P's failure to report the income, and P did not make adequate disclosure with respect to the unreported income. P's correct tax liability for 1990 is determined to be $7,279, resulting in an understatement of $5,775 (the difference between the amount of tax required to be shown on the return ($7,279) and the tax shown on the return ($1,504)). Because the understatement exceeds the greater of (a) $728 (10 percent of the tax required to be shown on the return (.10 × $7,279)) or (b) $5,000, the understatement is substantial. Subsequently, P files his 1993 return showing a net operating loss. The loss is carried back to his 1990 return, reducing his taxable income for 1990 to zero. However, the amount of the understatement for 1990 is not reduced on account of the NOLCB to that year. P is subject to the 20 percent penalty rate under section 6662 on the underpayment attributable to the substantial understatement for 1990, notwithstanding that the tax required to be shown on the return for that year, after application of the NOLCB, is zero.

(d) *Substantial authority.*—(1) *Effect of having substantial authority.*—If there is substantial authority for the tax treatment of an item, the item is treated as if it were shown properly on the return for the taxable year in computing the amount of the tax shown on the return. Thus, for purposes of section 6662(d), the tax attributable to the item is not included in the understatement for that year. (For special rules relating to tax shelter items see § 1.6662-4(g).)

(2) *Substantial authority standard.*—The substantial authority standard is an objective standard involving an analysis of the law and application of the law to relevant facts. The substantial authority standard is less stringent than the more likely than not standard (the standard that is met when there is a greater than 50-percent likelihood of the position being upheld), but more stringent than the reasonable basis standard as defined in § 1.6662-3(b)(3). The possibility that a return will not be audited or, if audited, that an item will not be raised on audit, is not relevant in determining whether the substantial authority standard (or the reasonable basis standard) is satisfied.

(3) *Determination of whether substantial authority is present.*—(i) *Evaluation of authorities.*—There is substantial authority for the tax treatment of an item only if the weight of the authorities supporting the treatment is substantial in relation to the weight of authorities supporting contrary treatment. All authorities relevant to the tax treatment of an item, including the authorities contrary to the treatment, are taken into account in determining whether substantial authority exists. The weight of authorities is determined in light of the pertinent facts and circumstances in the manner prescribed by paragraph (d)(3)(ii) of this section. There may be substantial authority for more than one position with respect to the same item. Because the substantial authority standard is an objective standard, the taxpayer's belief that there is substantial authority for the tax treatment of an item is not relevant in determining whether there is substantial authority for that treatment.

(ii) *Nature of analysis.*—The weight accorded an authority depends on its relevance and persuasiveness, and the type of document providing the authority. For example, a case or revenue ruling having some facts in common with the tax treatment at issue is not particularly relevant if the authority is materially distinguishable on its facts, or is otherwise inapplicable to the tax treatment at issue. An authority that merely states a conclusion ordinarily is less persuasive than one that reaches its conclusion by cogently relating the applicable law to pertinent facts. The weight of an authority from which information has been deleted, such as a private letter ruling, is diminished to the extent that the deleted information may have affected the authority's conclusions. The type of document also must be considered. For example, a revenue ruling is accorded greater weight than a private letter ruling addressing the same issue. An older private letter ruling, technical advice memorandum, general counsel memorandum or action on decision generally must be accorded less weight than a more recent one. Any document described in the preceding sentence that is more than 10 years old generally is accorded very little weight. However, the persuasiveness and relevance of a document, viewed in light of subsequent developments, should be taken into account along with the age of the document. There may be substantial authority for the tax treatment of an item despite the absence of certain types of authority. Thus, a taxpayer may have substantial authority for a position that is supported only by a well-reasoned construction of the applicable statutory provision.

(iii) *Types of authority.*—Except in cases described in paragraph (d)(3)(iv) of this section concerning written determinations, only the following are authority for purposes of determining whether there is substantial authority for the tax treatment of an item: applicable provisions of the Internal Revenue Code and other statutory provisions; proposed, temporary and final regulations construing such statutes; revenue rulings and revenue procedures; tax treaties and regulations thereunder, and Treasury Department and other official explanations of such treaties; court cases; congressional intent as reflected in committee reports, joint explanatory statements of managers included in conference committee reports, and floor statements made prior to enactment by one of a bill's managers; General Explanations of tax legislation prepared by the Joint Committee on Taxation (the Blue Book); private letter rulings and technical advice memoranda issued after October 31, 1976; actions on decisions and general counsel memoranda issued after March 12, 1981 (as well as general counsel memoranda published in pre-1955 volumes of the Cumulative Bulletin); Internal Revenue Service information or press releases; and notices, announcements and other administrative pronouncements published by the Service in the Internal Revenue Bulletin. Conclusions reached in treatises, legal periodicals, legal opinions or opinions rendered by tax professionals are not authority. The authorities underlying such expressions of opinion where applicable to the facts of a particular case, however, may give rise to substantial authority for the tax treatment of an item. Notwithstanding the preceding list of authorities, an authority does not continue to be an authority to the extent it is overruled or modified, implicitly or explicitly, by a body with the power to overrule or modify the earlier authority. In the case of court decisions, for example, a district court opinion on an issue is not an authority if overruled or reversed by the United States Court of Appeals for such district. However, a Tax Court opinion is not considered to be overruled or modified by a court of appeals to which a taxpayer does not have a right of appeal, unless the Tax Court adopts the holding of the court of appeals. Similarly, a private letter ruling is not authority if revoked or if inconsistent with a subsequent proposed regulation, revenue ruling or other administrative pronouncement published in the Internal Revenue Bulletin.

(iv) *Special rules.*—(A) *Written determinations.*—There is substantial authority for the tax treatment of an item by a taxpayer if the treatment is supported by the conclusion of a ruling or a determination letter (as defined in §301.6110-2(d) and (e)) issued to the taxpayer, by the conclusion of a technical advice memorandum in which the taxpayer is named, or by an affirmative statement in a revenue agent's report with respect to a prior taxable year of the taxpayer ("written determinations"). The preceding sentence does not apply, however, if—

(1) There was a misstatement or omission of a material fact or the facts that subsequently develop are materially different from the facts on which the written determination was based, or

(2) The written determination was modified or revoked after the date of issuance by—

(i) A notice to the taxpayer to whom the written determination was issued,

(ii) The enactment of legislation or ratification of a tax treaty,

(iii) A decision of the United States Supreme Court,

(iv) The issuance of temporary or final regulations, or

(v) The issuance of a revenue ruling, revenue procedure, or other statement published in the Internal Revenue Bulletin.

Except in the case of a written determination that is modified or revoked on account of §1.6662-4(d)(3)(iv)(A)(*1*), a written determination that is modified or revoked as described in §1.6662-4(d)(3)(iv)(A)(*2*) ceases to be authority on the date, and to the extent, it is so modified or revoked. See section 6404(f) for rules which require the Secretary to abate a penalty that is attributable to erroneous written advice furnished to a taxpayer by an officer or employee of the Internal Revenue Service.

(B) *Taxpayer's jurisdiction.*—The applicability of court cases to the taxpayer by reason of the taxpayer's residence in a particular jurisdiction is not taken into account in determining whether there is substantial authority for the tax treatment of an item. Notwithstanding the preceding sentence, there is substantial authority for the tax treatment of an item if the treatment is supported by controlling precedent of a United States Court of Appeals to which the taxpayer has a right of appeal with respect to the item.

(C) *When substantial authority determined.*—There is substantial authority for the tax treatment of an item if there is substantial authority at the time the return containing the item is filed or there was substantial authority on the last day of the taxable year to which the return relates.

(v) *Substantial authority for tax returns due before January 1, 1990.*—There is substantial authority for the tax treatment of an item on a return that is due (without regard to extensions) after December 31, 1982 and before January 1, 1990, if there is substantial authority for such treatment under either the provisions of paragraph (d)(3)(iii) of this section (which set forth an expanded list of authorities) or of §1.6661-3(b)(2) (which set forth a narrower list of authorities). Under either list of authorities, authorities both for and against the position must be taken into account.

(e) *Disclosure of certain information.*—(1) *Effect of adequate disclosure.*—Items for which there is adequate disclosure as provided in this paragraph (e) and in paragraph (f) of this section are treated as if such items were shown properly on the return for the taxable year in computing the amount of the tax shown on the return. Thus, for purposes of section 6662(d), the tax attributable to such items is not included in the understatement for that year.

(2) *Circumstances where disclosure will not have an effect.*—The rules of paragraph (e)(1) of this section do not apply where the item or position on the return —

(i) Does not have a reasonable basis (as defined in § 1.6662-3(b)(3));

(ii) Is attributable to a tax shelter (as defined in section 6662(d)(2)(C)(iii) and paragraph (g)(2) of this section); or

(iii) Is not properly substantiated, or the taxpayer failed to keep adequate books and records with respect to the item or position.

(3) *Restriction for corporations.*—For purposes of paragraph (e)(2)(i) of this section, a corporation will not be treated as having a reasonable basis for its tax treatment of an item attributable to a multi-party financing transaction entered into after August 5, 1997, if the treatment does not clearly reflect the income of the corporation.

(f) *Method of making adequate disclosure.*—(1) *Disclosure statement.*—Disclosure is adequate with respect to an item (or group of similar items, such as amounts paid or incurred for supplies by a taxpayer engaged in business) or a position on a return if the disclosure is made on a properly completed form attached to the return or to a qualified amended return (as defined in § 1.6664-2(c)(3)) for the taxable year. In the case of an item or position other than one that is contrary to a regulation, disclosure must be made on Form 8275 (Disclosure Statement); in the case of a position contrary to a regulation, disclosure must be made on Form 8275-R (Regulation Disclosure Statement).

(2) *Disclosure on return.*—The Commissioner may by annual revenue procedure (or otherwise) prescribe the circumstances under which disclosure of information on a return (or qualified amended return) in accordance with applicable forms and instructions is adequate. If the revenue procedure does not include an item, disclosure is adequate with respect to that item only if made on a properly completed Form 8275 or 8275-R, as appropriate, attached to the return for the year or to a qualified amended return.

(3) *Recurring item.*—Disclosure with respect to a recurring item, such as the basis of recovery property, must be made for each taxable year in which the item is taken into account.

(4) *Carrybacks and carryovers.*—Disclosure is adequate with respect to an item which is included in any loss, deduction or credit that is carried to another year only if made in connection with the return (or qualified amended return) for the taxable year in which the carryback or carryover arises (the "loss or credit year"). Disclosure is not also required in connection with the return for the taxable year in which the carryback or carryover is taken into account.

(5) *Pass-through entities.*—Disclosure in the case of items attributable to a pass-through entity (pass-through items) is made with respect to the return of the entity, except as provided in this paragraph (f)(5). Thus, disclosure in the case of pass-through items must be made on a Form 8275 or 8275-R, as appropriate, attached to the return (or qualified amended return) of the entity, or on the entity's return in accordance with the revenue procedure described in paragraph (f)(2) of this section, if applicable. A taxpayer (i.e., partner, shareholder, beneficiary, or holder of a residual interest in a REMIC) also may make adequate disclosure with respect to a pass-through item, however, if the taxpayer files a properly completed Form 8275 or 8275-R, as appropriate, in duplicate, one copy attached to the taxpayer's return (or qualified amended return) and the other copy filed with the Internal Revenue Service Center with which the return of the entity is required to be filed. Each Form 8275 or 8275-R, as appropriate, filed by the taxpayer should relate to the pass-through items of only one entity. For purposes of this paragraph (f)(5), a pass-through entity is a partnership, S corporation (as defined in section 1361(a)(1)), estate, trust, regulated investment company (as defined in section 851(a)), real estate investment trust (as defined in section 856(a)), or real estate mortgage investment conduit ("REMIC") (as defined in section 860D(a)).

(g) *Items relating to tax shelters.*—(1) *In general.*—(i) *Noncorporate taxpayers.*—Tax shelter items (as defined in paragraph (g)(3) of this section) of a taxpayer other than a corporation are treated for purposes of this section as if such items were shown properly on the return for a taxable year in computing the amount of the tax shown on the return, and thus the tax attributable to such items is not included in the understatement for the year, if—

(A) There is substantial authority (as provided in paragraph (d) of this section) for the tax treatment of that item; and

(B) The taxpayer reasonably believed at the time the return was filed that the tax treatment of that item was more likely than not the proper treatment.

(ii) *Corporate taxpayers.*—(A) *In general.*—Except as provided in paragraph (g)(1)(ii)(B) of this section, all tax shelter items (as defined in paragraph (g)(3) of this section) of a corporation are taken into account in computing the amount of any understatement.

(B) *Special rule for transactions occurring prior to December 9, 1994.*—The tax shelter items of a corporation arising in connection with transactions occurring prior to December 9, 1994 are treated for purposes of this section as if such items were shown properly on the return if the requirements of paragraph (g)(1)(i) are satisfied with respect to such items.

(iii) *Disclosure irrelevant.*—Disclosure made with respect to a tax shelter item of either a corporate or noncorporate taxpayer does not affect the amount of an understatement.

(iv) *Cross-reference.*—See § 1.6664-4(f) for certain rules regarding the availability of the reasonable cause and good faith exception to the substantial understatement penalty with respect to tax shelter items of corporations.

(2) *Tax shelter.*—(i) *In general.*—For purposes of section 6662(d), the term "tax shelter" means—

(A) A partnership or other entity (such as a corporation or trust),

(B) An investment plan or arrangement, or

(C) Any other plan or arrangement,

if the principal purpose of the entity, plan or arrangement, based on objective evidence, is to avoid or evade Federal income tax. The principal purpose of an entity, plan or arrangement is to avoid or evade Federal income tax if that purpose exceeds any other purpose. Typical of tax shelters are transactions structured with little or no motive for the realization of economic gain, and transactions that utilize the mismatching of income and deductions, overvalued assets or assets with values subject to substantial uncertainty, certain nonrecourse financing, financing techniques that do not conform to standard commercial business practices, or the mischaracterization of the substance of the transaction. The existence of economic substance does not of itself establish that a transaction is not a tax shelter if the transaction includes other characteristics that indicate it is a tax shelter.

(ii) *Principal purpose.*—The principal purpose of an entity, plan or arrangement is not to avoid or evade Federal income tax if the entity, plan or arrangement has as its purpose the claiming of exclusions from income, accelerated deductions or other tax benefits in a manner consistent with the statute and Congressional purpose. For example, an entity, plan or arrangement does not have as its principal purpose the avoidance or evasion of Federal income tax solely as a result of the following uses of tax benefits provided by the Internal Revenue Code: the purchasing or holding of an obligation bearing interest that is excluded from gross income under section 103; taking an accelerated depreciation allowance under section 168; taking the percentage depletion allowance under section 613 or section 613A; deducting intangible drilling and development costs as expenses under section 263(c); establishing a qualified retirement plan under sections 401-409; claiming the possession tax credit under section 936; or claiming tax benefits available by reason of an election under section 992 to be taxed as a domestic international sales corporation ("DISC"), under section 927(f)(1) to be taxed as a foreign sales corporation ("FSC"), or under section 1362 to be taxed as an S corporation.

(3) *Tax shelter item.*—An item of income, gain, loss, deduction or credit is a "tax shelter item" if the item is directly or indirectly attributable to the principal purpose of a tax shelter to avoid or evade Federal income tax. Thus, if a partnership is established for the principal purpose of avoiding or evading Federal income tax by acquiring and overstating the basis of property for purposes of claiming accelerated depreciation, the depreciation with respect to the property is a tax shelter item. However, a deduction claimed in connection with a separate transaction carried on by the same partnership is not a tax shelter item if the transaction does not constitute a plan or arrangement the principal purpose of which is to avoid or evade tax.

(4) *Reasonable belief.*—(i) *In general.*—For purposes of section 6662(d) and paragraph (g)(1)(i)(B) of this section (pertaining to tax shelter items of noncorporate taxpayers), a taxpayer is considered reasonably to believe that the tax treatment of an item is more likely than not the proper tax treatment if (without taking into account the possibility that a return will not be audited, that an issue will not be raised on audit, or that an issue will be settled)—

(A) The taxpayer analyzes the pertinent facts and authorities in the manner described in paragraph (d)(3)(ii) of this section, and in reliance upon that analysis, reasonably concludes in good faith that there is a greater than 50-percent likelihood that the tax treatment of the item will be upheld if challenged by the Internal Revenue Service; or

(B) The taxpayer reasonably relies in good faith on the opinion of a professional tax advisor, if the opinion is based on the tax advisor's analysis of the pertinent facts and authorities in the manner described in paragraph (d)(3)(ii) of this section and unambiguously states that the tax advisor concludes that there is a greater than 50-percent likelihood that the tax treatment of the item will be upheld if challenged by the Internal Revenue Service.

(ii) *Facts and circumstances; reliance on professional tax advisor.*—All facts and circumstances must be taken into account in determining whether a taxpayer satisfies the requirements of paragraph (g)(4)(i) of this section. However, in no event will a taxpayer be considered to have reasonably relied in good faith on the opinion of a professional tax advisor for purposes of paragraph (g)(4)(i)(B) of this section unless the requirements of § 1.6664-4(c)(1) are met. The fact that the requirements of § 1.6664-4(c)(1) are satisfied will not necessarily establish that the taxpayer reasonably relied on the opinion in good faith. For example, reliance may not be reasonable or in good faith if the taxpayer knew, or should have known, that the advisor lacked knowledge in the relevant aspects of Federal tax law.

(5) *Pass-through entities.*—In the case of tax shelter items attributable to a pass-through entity, the actions described in paragraphs (g)(4)(i)(A) and (B) of this section, if taken by the entity, are deemed to have been taken by the taxpayer and are considered in determining whether the taxpayer reasonably believed that the tax treatment of an item was more likely than not the proper tax treatment. [Reg. § 1.6662-4.]

☐ [*T.D.* 8381, 12-30-91. *Amended by T.D.* 8617, 8-31-95; *T.D.* 8790, 12-1-98 *and T.D.* 9109, 12-29-2003.]

[Reg. § 1.6662-5]

§ 1.6662-5. Substantial and gross valuation misstatements under chapter 1.—(a) *In general.*—If any portion of an underpayment, as defined in section 6664(a) and § 1.6664-2, of any income tax imposed under chapter 1 of subtitle A of the Code that is required to be shown on a return is attributable to a substantial valuation misstatement under chapter 1 ("substantial valuation misstatement"), there is added to the tax an amount equal to 20 percent of such portion. Section 6662(h) increases the penalty to 40 percent in the case of a gross valuation misstatement under chapter 1 ("gross valuation misstatement"). No penalty under section 6662(b)(3) is imposed, however, on a portion of an underpayment that is attributable to a substantial or gross valuation misstatement unless the aggregate of all portions of the underpayment attributable to substantial or gross valuation misstatements exceeds the applicable dollar limitation ($5,000 or $10,000), as provided in section 6662(e)(2) and paragraphs (b) and (f)(2) of this section. This penalty also does not apply to the extent that the reasonable cause and good faith exception to this penalty set forth in § 1.6664-4 applies. There is no disclosure exception to this penalty.

(b) *Dollar limitation.*—No penalty may be imposed under section 6662(b)(3) for a taxable year unless the portion of the underpayment for that year that is attributable to substantial or gross valuation misstatements exceeds $5,000 ($10,000 in the case of a corporation other than an S corporation (as defined in section 1361(a)(1)) or a personal holding company (as defined in section 542)). This limitation is applied separately to each taxable year for which there is a substantial or gross valuation misstatement.

(c) *Special rules in the case of carrybacks and carryovers.*—(1) *In general.*—The penalty for a substantial or gross valuation misstatement applies to any portion of an underpayment for a year to which a loss, deduction or credit is carried that is attributable to a substantial or gross valuation misstatement for the year in which the carryback or carryover of the loss, deduction or credit arises (the "loss or credit year"), provided that the applicable dollar limitation set forth in section 6662(e)(2) is satisfied in the carryback or carryover year.

(2) *Transition rule for carrybacks to pre-1990 years.*—The penalty under section 6662(b)(3) is imposed on any portion of an underpayment for a carryback year, the return for which is due (without regard to extensions) before January 1, 1990, if—

(i) That portion is attributable to a substantial or gross valuation misstatement for a loss or credit year; and

(ii) The return for the loss or credit year is due (without regard to extensions) after December 31, 1989.

The preceding sentence applies only if the underpayment for the carryback year exceeds the applicable dollar limitation ($5,000, or $10,000 for most corporations). See *Example 3* in paragraph (d) of this section.

(d) *Examples.*—The following examples illustrate the provisions of paragraphs (b) and (c) of this section. These examples do not take into account the reasonable cause exception under § 1.6664-4.

Example 1. Corporation Q is a C corporation. In 1990, the first year of its existence, Q had taxable income of $200,000 without considering depreciation of a particular asset. On its calendar year 1990 return, Q overstated its basis in this asset by an amount that caused a substantial valuation misstatement. The overstated basis resulted in depreciation claimed of $350,000, which was $250,000 more than the $100,000 allowable. Thus, on its 1990 return, Q showed a loss of $150,000. In 1991, Q had taxable income of $450,000 before application of the loss carryover, and Q claimed a carryover loss deduction under section 172 of $150,000, resulting in taxable income of $300,000 for 1991. Upon audit of the 1990 return, the basis of the asset was corrected, resulting in an adjustment of $250,000. For 1990, the underpayment resulting from the $100,000 taxable income (–$150,000 + $250,000) is attributable to the valuation misstatement. Assuming the underpayment resulting from the $100,000 taxable income exceeds the $10,000 limitation, the penalty will be imposed in 1990. For 1991, the elimination of the loss carryover results in additional taxable income of $150,000. The underpayment for 1991 resulting from that adjustment is also attributable to the substantial valuation misstatement on the 1990 return. Assuming the underpayment resulting from the $150,000 additional taxable income for 1991 exceeds the $10,000 limitation, the substantial valuation misstatement penalty also will be imposed for that year.

Example 2. (i) Corporation T is a C corporation. In 1990, the first year of its existence, T had a loss of $3,000,000 without considering depreciation of its major asset. On its calendar year 1990 return, T overstated its basis in this asset in an amount that caused a substantial valuation misstatement. This overstatement resulted in depreciation claimed of $3,500,000, which was $2,500,000 more than the $1,000,000 allowable. Thus, on its 1990 return, T showed a loss of $6,500,000. In 1991, T had taxable income of $4,500,000 before application of the carryover loss, but claimed a carryover loss deduction under section 172 in the amount of $4,500,000, resulting in taxable income of zero for that year and leaving a $2,000,000 carryover available. Upon audit of the 1990 return, the basis of the asset was corrected, resulting in an adjustment of $2,500,000.

(ii) For 1990, the underpayment is still zero (–$6,500,000 + $2,500,000 = – $4,000,000). Thus, the penalty does not apply in 1990. The loss for 1990 is reduced to $4,000,000.

(iii) For 1991, there is additional taxable income of $500,000 as a result of the reduction of the carryover loss ($4,500,000 reported income before carryover loss minus corrected carryover loss of $4,000,000 = $500,000). The underpayment for 1991 resulting from reduction of the carryover loss is attributable to the valuation misstatement on the 1990 return. Assuming the underpayment resulting from the $500,000 additional taxable income exceeds the $10,000 limitation, the substantial valuation misstatement penalty will be imposed in 1991.

Example 3. Corporation V is a C corporation. In 1990, V had a loss of $100,000 without considering depreciation of a particular asset which it had fully depreciated in earlier years. V had a depreciable basis in the asset of zero, but on its 1990 calendar year return erroneously claimed a basis in the asset of $1,250,000 and depreciation of $250,000. V reported a $350,000 loss for the year 1990, and carried back the loss to the 1987 and 1988 tax years. V had reported taxable income of $300,000 in 1987 and $200,000 in 1988, before application of the carryback. The $350,000 carryback eliminated all taxable income for 1987, and $50,000 of the taxable income for 1988. After disallowance of the $250,000 depreciation deduction for 1990, V still had a loss of $100,000. Because there is no underpayment for 1990, no valuation misstatement penalty is imposed for 1990. However, as a result of the 1990 depreciation adjustment, the carryback to 1987 is reduced from $350,000 to $100,000. After absorption of the $100,000 carryback, V has taxable income of $200,000 for 1987. This adjustment results in an underpayment for 1987 that is attributable to the valuation misstatement on the 1990 return. The valuation misstatement for 1990 is a gross valuation misstatement because the correct adjusted basis of the depreciated asset was zero. (See paragraph (e)(2) of this section.) Therefore, the 40 percent penalty rate applies to the 1987 underpayment attributable to the 1990 misstatement, provided that this underpayment exceeds $10,000. The adjustment also results in the elimination of any loss carryback to 1988 resulting in an increase in taxable income for 1988 of $50,000. Assuming the underpayment resulting from this additional $50,000 of income exceeds $10,000, the gross valuation misstatement penalty is imposed on the underpayment for 1988.

(e) *Definitions.*—(1) *Substantial valuation misstatement.*—There is a substantial valuation misstatement if the value or adjusted basis of any property claimed on a return of tax imposed under chapter 1 is 200 percent or more of the correct amount.

(2) *Gross valuation misstatement.*—There is a gross valuation misstatement if the value or adjusted basis of any property claimed on a return of tax imposed under chapter 1 is 400 percent or more of the correct amount.

(3) *Property.*—For purposes of this section, the term "property" refers to both tangible and intangible property. Tangible property includes property such as land, buildings, fixtures and inventory. Intangible property includes property such as goodwill, covenants not to compete, leaseholds, patents, contract rights, debts and choses in action.

(f) *Multiple valuation misstatements on a return.*—(1) *Determination of whether valuation misstatements are substantial or gross.*—The determination of whether there is a substantial or gross valuation misstatement on a return is made on a property-by-property basis. Assume, for example, that property A has a value of 60 but a taxpayer claims a value of 110, and that property B has a value of 40 but the taxpayer claims a value of 100. Because the claimed and correct values are compared on a property-by-property basis, there is a substantial valuation misstatement with respect to property B, but not with respect to property A, even though the claimed values (210) are 200 percent or more of the correct values (100) when compared on an aggregate basis.

(2) *Application of dollar limitation.*—For purposes of applying the dollar limitation set forth in section 6662(e)(2), the determination of the portion of an underpayment that is attributable to a substantial or gross valuation misstatement is made by aggregating all portions of the underpayment attributable to substantial or gross valuation misstatements. Assume, for example, that the value claimed for property C on a return is 250 percent of the correct value, and that the value claimed for property D on the return is 400 percent of the correct value. Because the portions of an underpayment that are attributable to a substantial or gross valuation misstatement on a return are aggregated in applying the dollar limitation, the dollar limitation is satisfied if the portion of the underpayment that is attributable to the misstatement of the value of property C, when aggregated with the portion of the underpayment that is attributable to the misstatement of the value of property D, exceeds $5,000 ($10,000 in the case of most corporations).

(g) *Property with a value or adjusted basis of zero.*—The value or adjusted basis claimed on a return of any property with a correct value or adjusted basis of zero is considered to be 400 percent or more of the correct amount. There is a gross valuation misstatement with respect to such property, therefore, and the applicable penalty rate is 40 percent.

(h) *Pass-through entities.*—(1) *In general.*—The determination of whether there is a substantial or gross valuation misstatement in the case of a return of a pass-through entity (as defined in § 1.6662-4(f)(5)) is made at the entity level. However, the dollar limitation ($5,000 or $10,000, as the case may be) is applied at the taxpayer level (*i.e.*, with respect to the return of the shareholder, partner, beneficiary, or holder of a residual interest in a REMIC).

(2) *Example.*—The rules of paragraph (h)(1) of this section may be illustrated by the following example.

Example. Partnership P has two partners, individuals A and B. P claims a $40,000 basis in a depreciable asset which, in fact, has a basis of $15,000. The determination that there is a substantial valuation misstatement is made solely with reference to P by comparing the $40,000 basis claimed by P with P's correct basis of $15,000. However, the determination of whether the $5,000 threshold for application of the penalty has been reached is made separately for each partner. With respect to partner A, the penalty will apply if the portion of A's underpayment attributable to the passthrough of the depreciation deduction, when aggregated with any other portions of A's underpayment also attributable to substantial or gross valuation misstatements, exceeds $5,000 (assuming there is not reasonable cause for the misstatements (*see* § 1.6664-4(c)).

(i) [Reserved]

(j) *Transactions between persons described in section 482 and net section 482 transfer price adjustments.*—[Reserved]

(k) *Returns affected.*—Except in the case of rules relating to transactions between persons described in section 482 and net section 482 transfer price adjustments, the provisions of section 6662(b)(3) apply to returns due (without regard to extensions of time to file) after December 31, 1989, notwithstanding that the original substantial or gross valuation misstatement occurred on a return that was due (without regard to extensions) before January 1, 1990. Assume, for example, that a calendar year corporation claimed a deduction on its 1990 return for depreciation of an asset with a basis of X. Also assume that it had reported the same basis for computing depreciation on its returns for the preceding 5 years and that the basis shown on the return each year was 200 percent or more of the correct basis. The corporation may be subject to a penalty for substantial valuation misstatements on its 1989 and 1990 returns, even though the original misstatement occurred prior to the effective date of sections 6662(b)(3) and (e). [Reg. § 1.6662-5.]

□ [*T.D.* 8381, 12-30-91.]

[Reg. § 1.6662-5T]

§ 1.6662-5T. Substantial and gross valuation misstatements under chapter 1 (Temporary).—(a) through (e)(3) [Reserved]. For further information, see § 1.6662-5(a) through (e)(3).

(e)(4) *Tests related to section 482.*—(i) *Substantial valuation misstatement.*—There is a substantial valuation misstatement if there is a misstatement described in § 1.6662-6(b)(1) or (c)(1) (concerning substantial valuation misstatements pertaining to transactions between related persons).

(ii) *Gross valuation misstatement.*—There is a gross valuation misstatement if there is a misstatement described in § 1.6662-6(b)(2) or (c)(2) (concerning gross valuation misstatements pertaining to transactions between related persons).

(iii) *Property.*—For purposes of this section, the term *property* refers to both tangible and intangible property. Tangible property includes property such as money, land, buildings, fixtures and inventory. Intangible property includes property such as goodwill, covenants not to compete, leaseholds, patents, contract rights, debts, choses in action, and any other item of intangible property described in § 1.482-4(b).

(f) through (h) [Reserved] For further information, see § 1.6662-5(f) through (h).

(i) [Reserved].

(j) *Transactions between persons described in section 482 and net section 482 transfer price adjustments.*—For rules relating to the penalty imposed with respect to a substantial or gross valuation misstatement arising from a section 482 allocation, see § 1.6662-6. [Temporary Reg. § 1.6662-5T.]

□ [*T.D.* 8519, 1-27-94. *Amended by T.D.* 8656, 2-8-96.]

[Reg. § 1.6662-6]

§ 1.6662-6. Transactions between persons described in section 482 and net section 482 transfer price adjustments.—(a) *In general.*—(1) *Purpose and scope.*—Pursuant to section 6662(e) a penalty is imposed on any underpayment attributable to a substantial valuation misstatement pertaining to either a transaction between persons described in section 482 (the transactional penalty) or a net section 482 transfer price adjustment (the net adjustment penalty). The penalty is equal to 20 percent of the underpayment of tax attributable to that substantial valuation misstatement. Pursuant to section 6662(h) the penalty is increased to 40 percent of the underpayment in the case of a gross valuation misstatement with respect to either penalty. Paragraph(b) of this section provides specific rules related to the transactional penalty. Paragraph (c) of this section provides specific rules related to the net adjustment penalty, and paragraph (d) of this section describes amounts that will be excluded for purposes of calculating the net adjustment penalty. Paragraph (e) of this section sets forth special rules in the case of carrybacks and carryovers. Paragraph (f) of this section provides coordination rules between penalties. Paragraph (g) of this section provides the effective date of this section.

(2) *Reported results.*—Whether an underpayment is attributable to a substantial or gross valuation misstatement must be determined from the results of controlled transactions that are reported on an income tax return, regardless of whether the amount reported differs from the transaction price initially reflected in the taxpayer's books and records. The results of controlled transactions that are reported on an amended return will be used only if the amended return is filed before the Internal Revenue Service has contacted the taxpayer regarding the corresponding original return. A written statement furnished by a taxpayer subject to the Coordinated Examination Program or a written statement furnished by the taxpayer when elect-

ing Accelerated Issue Resolution or similar procedures will be considered an amended return for purposes of this section if it satisfies either the requirements of a qualified amended return for purposes of § 1.6664-2(c)(3) or such requirements as the Commissioner may prescribe by revenue procedure. In the case of a taxpayer that is a member of a consolidated group, the rules of this paragraph (a)(2) apply to the consolidated income tax return of the group.

(3) *Identical terms used in the section 482 regulations.*—For purposes of this section, the terms used in this section shall have the same meaning as identical terms used in regulations under section 482.

(b) *The transactional penalty.*—(1) *Substantial valuation misstatement.*—In the case of any transaction between related persons, there is a substantial valuation misstatement if the price for any property or services (or for the use of property) claimed on any return is 200 percent or more (or 50 percent or less) of the amount determined under section 482 to be the correct price.

(2) *Gross valuation misstatement.*—In the case of any transaction between related persons, there is a gross valuation misstatement if the price for any property or services (or for the use of property) claimed on any return is 400 percent or more (or 25 percent or less) of the amount determined under section 482 to be the correct price.

(3) *Reasonable cause and good faith.*—Pursuant to section 6664(c), the transactional penalty will not be imposed on any portion of an underpayment with respect to which the requirements of § 1.6664-4 are met. In applying the provisions of § 1.6664-4 in a case in which the taxpayer has relied on professional analysis in determining its transfer pricing, whether the professional is an employee of, or related to, the taxpayer is not determinative in evaluating whether the taxpayer reasonably relied in good faith on advice. A taxpayer that meets the requirements of paragraph (d) of this section with respect to an allocation under section 482 will be treated as having established that there was reasonable cause and good faith with respect to that item for purposes of § 1.6664-4. If a substantial or gross valuation misstatement under the transactional penalty also constitutes (or is part of) a substantial or gross valuation misstatement under the net adjustment penalty, then the rules of paragraph (d) of this section (and not the rules of § 1.6664-4) will be applied to determine whether the adjustment is excluded from calculation of the net section 482 adjustment.

(c) *Net adjustment penalty.*—(1) *Net section 482 adjustment.*—For purposes of this section, the term *net section 482 adjustment* means the sum of all increases in the taxable income of a taxpayer for a taxable year resulting from allocations under section 482 (determined without regard to any amount carried to such taxable year from another taxable year) less any decreases in taxable income attributable to collateral adjustments as described in § 1.482-1(g). For purposes of this section, amounts that meet the requirements of paragraph (d) of this section will be excluded from the calculation of the net section 482 adjustment. Substantial and gross valuation misstatements that are subject to the transactional penalty under paragraph (b)(1) or (2) of this section are included in determining the amount of the net section 482 adjustment. See paragraph (f) of this section for coordination rules between penalties.

(2) *Substantial valuation misstatement.*—There is a substantial valuation misstatement if a net section 482 adjustment is greater than the lesser of 5 million dollars or ten percent of gross receipts.

(3) *Gross valuation misstatement.*—There is a gross valuation misstatement if a net section 482 adjustment is greater than the lesser of 20 million dollars or twenty percent of gross receipts.

(4) *Setoff allocation rule.*—If a taxpayer meets the requirements of paragraph (d) of this section with respect to some, but not all of the allocations made under section 482, then for purposes of determining the net section 482 adjustment, setoffs, as taken into account under § 1.482-1(g)(4), must be applied ratably against all such allocations. The following example illustrates the principle of this paragraph (c)(4):

Example. (i) The Internal Revenue Service makes the following section 482 adjustments for the taxable year:

(1)	Attributable to an increase in gross income because of an increase in royalty payments	$9,000,000
(2)	Attributable to an increase in sales proceeds due to a decrease in the profit margin of a related buyer . . .	6,000,000
(3)	Because of a setoff under § 1.482-1(g)(4)	(5,000,000)
	Total section 482 adjustments	10,000,000

(ii) The taxpayer meets the requirements of paragraph (d) with respect to adjustment number one, but not with respect to adjustment number two. The five million dollar setoff will be allocated ratably against the nine million dollar adjustment ($9,000,000/$15,000,000 x $5,000,000 = $3,000,000) and the six million dollar adjustment ($6,000,000/$15,000,000 x $5,000,000 = $2,000,000). Accordingly, in determining the net section 482 adjustment, the nine million dollar adjustment is reduced to six million dollars ($9,000,000 - $3,000,000) and the six million dollar adjustment is reduced to four million dollars ($6,000,000 - $2,000,000). Therefore, the net section 482 adjustment equals four million dollars.

(5) *Gross receipts.*—For purposes of this section, gross receipts must be computed pursuant to the rules contained in § 1.448-1T(f)(2)(iv), as adjusted to reflect allocations under section 482.

(6) *Coordination with reasonable cause exception under section 6664(c).*—Pursuant to section 6662(e)(3)(D), a taxpayer will be treated as having reasonable cause under section 6664(c) for any portion of an underpayment attributable to a net section 482 adjustment only if the taxpayer

meets the requirements of paragraph (d) of this section with respect to that portion.

(7) *Examples.*—The principles of this paragraph (c) are illustrated by the following examples:

Example 1. (i) The Internal Revenue Service makes the following section 482 adjustments for the taxable year:

(1) Attributable to an increase in gross income because of an increase in royalty payments .	$2,000,000
(2) Attributable to an increase in sales proceeds due to a decrease in the profit margin of a related buyer	2,500,000
(3) Attributable to a decrease in the cost of goods sold because of a decrease in the cost plus mark-up of a related seller	2,000,000
Total section 482 adjustments .	6,500,000

(ii) None of the adjustments are excluded under paragraph (d) of this section. The net section 482 adjustment ($6.5 million) is greater than five million dollars. Therefore, there is a substantial valuation misstatement.

Example 2. (i) The Internal Revenue Service makes the following section 482 adjustments for the taxable year:

(1) Attributable to an increase in gross income because of an increase in royalty payments .	$11,000,000
(2) Attributable to an increase in sales proceeds due to a decrease in the profit margin of a related buyer	2,000,000
(3) Because of a setoff under § 1.482-1(g)(4)	(9,000,000)
Total section 482 adjustments .	4,000,000

(ii) The taxpayer has gross receipts of sixty million dollars after taking into account all section 482 adjustments. None of the adjustments are excluded under paragraph (d) of this section. The net section 482 adjustment ($4 million) is less than the lesser of five million dollars or ten percent of gross receipts ($60 million × 10% = $6 million). Therefore, there is no substantial valuation misstatement.

Example 3. (i) The Internal Revenue Service makes the following section 482 adjustments to the income of an affiliated group that files a consolidated return for the taxable year:

(1) Attributable to Member A . . .	$1,500,000
(2) Attributable to Member B . . .	1,000,000
(3) Attributable to Member C . . .	2,000,000
Total section 482 adjustments .	4,500,000

(ii) Members A, B, and C have gross receipts of 20 million dollars, 12 million dollars, and 11 million dollars, respectively. Thus, the total gross receipts are 43 million dollars. None of the adjustments are excluded under paragraph (d) of this section. The net section 482 adjustment ($4.5 million) is greater than the lesser of five million dollars or ten percent of gross receipts ($43 million x 10% = $4.3 million). Therefore, there is a substantial valuation misstatement.

Example 4. (i) The Internal Revenue Service makes the following section 482 adjustments to the income of an affiliated group that files a consolidated return for the taxable year:

(1) Attributable to Member A	$1,500,000
(2) Attributable to Member B	3,000,000
(3) Attributable to Member C	2,500,000
Total section 482 adjustments	7,000,000

(ii) Members A, B, and C have gross receipts of 20 million dollars, 35 million dollars, and 40 million dollars, respectively. Thus, the total gross receipts are 95 million dollars. None of the adjustments are excluded under paragraph (d) of this section. The net section 482 adjustment (7 million dollars) is greater than the lesser of five million dollars or ten percent of gross receipts ($95 million × 10% = $9.5 million). Therefore, there is a substantial valuation misstatement.

Example 5. (i) The Internal Revenue Service makes the following section 482 adjustments to the income of an affiliated group that files a consolidated return for the taxable year:

(1) Attributable to Member A . . .	$2,000,000
(2) Attributable to Member B . . .	1,000,000
(3) Attributable to Member C . . .	1,500,000
Total section 482 adjustments .	4,500,000

(ii) Members A, B, and C have gross receipts of 10 million dollars, 35 million dollars, and 40 million dollars, respectively. Thus, the total gross receipts are 85 million dollars. None of the adjustments are excluded under paragraph (d) of this section. The net section 482 adjustment ($4.5 million) is less than the lesser of five million dollars or ten percent of gross receipts ($85 million x 10% = $8.5 million). Therefore, there is no substantial valuation misstatement even though individual member A's adjustment ($2 million) is greater than ten percent of its individual gross receipts ($10 million x 10% = $1 million).

(d) *Amounts excluded from net section 482 adjustments.*—(1) *In general.*—An amount is excluded from the calculation of a net section 482 adjustment if the requirements of paragraph (d)(2), (3), or (4) of this section are met with respect to that amount.

(2) *Application of a specified section 482 method.*—(i) *In general.*—An amount is excluded from the calculation of a net section 482 adjustment if the taxpayer establishes that both the specified method and documentation requirements of this paragraph (d)(2) are met with respect to that amount. For purposes of this paragraph (d), a method will be considered a specified method if it is described in the regulations under section 482 and the method applies to transactions of the type under review. An unspecified method is not considered a specified method. See §§ 1.482-3(e) and 1.482-4(d).

(ii) *Specified method requirement.*—(A) The specified method requirement is met if the taxpayer selects and applies a specified method in a reasonable manner. The taxpayer's selection and application of a specified method is reasonable only if, given the available data and the applicable pricing methods, the taxpayer reasonably concluded that the method (and its application of that method) provided the most reliable measure of an arm's length result under the principles of the best method rule of § 1.482-1(c). A taxpayer can reasonably conclude that a specified method provided the most reliable measure of an arm's length result only if it has made a reasonable effort to evaluate the potential applicability of the other specified methods in a manner consistent with the principles of the best method rule. The extent of this evaluation generally will depend on the nature of the available data, and it may vary from case to case and from method to method. This evaluation may not entail an exhaustive analysis or detailed application of each method. Rather, after a reasonably thorough search for relevant data, the taxpayer should consider which method would provide the most reliable measure of an arm's length result given that data. The nature of the available data may enable the taxpayer to conclude reasonably that a particular specified method provides a more reliable measure of an arm's length result than one or more of the other specified methods, and accordingly no further consideration of such other specified methods is needed. Further, it is not necessary for a taxpayer to conclude that the selected specified method provides a more reliable measure of an arm's length result than any unspecified method. For examples illustrating the selection of a specified method consistent with this paragraph (d)(2)(ii), see § 1.482-8. Whether the taxpayer's conclusion was reasonable must be determined from all the facts and circumstances. The factors relevant to this determination include the following:

(1) The experience and knowledge of the taxpayer, including all members of the taxpayer's controlled group.

(2) The extent to which reliable data was available and the data was analyzed in a reasonable manner. A taxpayer must engage in a reasonably thorough search for the data necessary to determine which method should be selected and how it should be applied. In determining the scope of a reasonably thorough search for data, the expense of additional efforts to locate new data may be weighed against the likelihood of finding additional data that would improve the reliability of the results and the amount by which any new data would change the taxpayer's taxable income. Furthermore, a taxpayer must use the most current reliable data that is available before the end of the taxable year in question. Although the taxpayer is not required to search for relevant data after the end of the taxable year, the taxpayer must maintain as a principal document described in paragraph (d)(2)(iii)(B)*(9)* of this section any relevant data it obtains after the end of the taxable year but before the return is filed, if that data would help determine whether the taxpayer has reported its true taxable income.

(3) The extent to which the taxpayer followed the relevant requirements set forth in regulations under section 482 with respect to the application of the method.

(4) The extent to which the taxpayer reasonably relied on a study or other analysis performed by a professional qualified to conduct such a study or analysis, including an attorney, accountant, or economist. Whether the professional is an employee of, or related to, the taxpayer is not determinative in evaluating the reliability of that study or analysis, as long as the study or analysis is objective, thorough, and well reasoned. Such reliance is reasonable only if the taxpayer disclosed to the professional all relevant information regarding the controlled transactions at issue. A study or analysis that was reasonably relied upon in a prior year may reasonably be relied upon in the current year if the relevant facts and circumstances have not changed or if the study or analysis has been appropriately modified to reflect any change in facts and circumstances.

(5) If the taxpayer attempted to determine an arm's length result by using more than one uncontrolled comparable, whether the taxpayer arbitrarily selected a result that corresponds to an extreme point in the range of results derived from the uncontrolled comparables. Such a result generally would not likely be closest to an arm's length result. If the uncontrolled comparables that the taxpayer uses to determine an arm's length result are described in § 1.482-1(e)(2)(iii)(B), one reasonable method of selecting a point in the range would be that provided in § 1.482-1(e)(3).

(6) The extent to which the taxpayer relied on a transfer pricing methodology developed and applied pursuant to an Advance Pricing Agreement for a prior taxable year, or specifically approved by the Internal Revenue Service pursuant to a transfer pricing audit of the transactions at issue for a prior taxable year, provided that the taxpayer applied the approved method reasonably and consistently with its prior application, and the facts and circumstances surrounding the use of the method have not materially changed since the time of the IRS's action, or if the facts and circumstances have changed in a way that materially affects the reliability of the results, the taxpayer makes appropriate adjustments to reflect such changes.

(7) The size of a net transfer pricing adjustment in relation to the size of the controlled transaction out of which the adjustment arose.

(B) *Services cost method.*—A taxpayer's selection of the services cost method for certain services, described in § 1.482-9(b), and its application of that method to a controlled services transaction will be considered reasonable for purposes of the specified method requirement only if the taxpayer reasonably allocated and apportioned costs in accordance with § 1.482-9(k), and reasonably concluded that the controlled services transaction satisfies the requirements described in § 1.482-9(b)(2). Whether the taxpayer's conclusion was reasonable must be determined from all the facts and circumstances. The factors relevant to this determination include those described in paragraph (d)(2)(ii)(A) of this section, to the extent applicable.

(iii) *Documentation requirement.*—(A) *In general.*—The documentation requirement of this paragraph (d)(2)(iii) is met if the taxpayer maintains sufficient documentation to establish that the taxpayer reasonably concluded that, given the available data and the applicable pricing methods, the method (and its application of that method) provided the most reliable measure of an arm's length result under the principles of the best method rule in § 1.482-1(c), and provides that documentation to the Internal Revenue Service within 30 days of a request for it in connection with an examination of the taxable year to which the documentation relates. With the exception of the documentation described in paragraphs (d)(2)(iii)(B)(*9*) and (*10*) of this section, that documentation must be in existence when the return is filed. The district director may, in his discretion, excuse a minor or inadvertent failure to provide required documents, but only if the taxpayer has made a good faith effort to comply, and the taxpayer promptly remedies the failure when it becomes known. The required documentation is divided into two categories, principal documents and background documents as described in paragraphs (d)(2)(iii)(B) and (C) of this section.

(B) *Principal documents.*—The principal documents should accurately and completely describe the basic transfer pricing analysis conducted by the taxpayer. The documentation must include the following—

(*1*) An overview of the taxpayer's business, including an analysis of the economic and legal factors that affect the pricing of its property or services;

(*2*) A description of the taxpayer's organizational structure (including an organization chart) covering all related parties engaged in transactions potentially relevant under section 482, including foreign affiliates whose transactions directly or indirectly affect the pricing of property or services in the United States;

(*3*) Any documentation explicitly required by the regulations under section 482;

(*4*) A description of the method selected and an explanation of why that method was selected, including an evaluation of whether the regulatory conditions and requirements for application of that method, if any, were met;

(*5*) A description of the alternative methods that were considered and an explanation of why they were not selected;

(*6*) A description of the controlled transactions (including the terms of sale) and any internal data used to analyze those transactions. For example, if a profit split method is applied, the documentation must include a schedule providing the total income, costs, and assets (with adjustments for different accounting practices and currencies) for each controlled taxpayer participating in the relevant business activity and detailing the allocations of such items to that activity. Similarly, if a cost-based method (such as the cost plus method, the services cost method for certain services, or a comparable profits method with a cost-based profit level indicator) is applied, the documentation must include a description of the manner in which relevant costs are determined and are allocated and apportioned to the relevant controlled transaction.

(*7*) A description of the comparables that were used, how comparability was evaluated, and what (if any) adjustments were made;

(*8*) An explanation of the economic analysis and projections relied upon in developing the method. For example, if a profit split method is applied, the taxpayer must provide an explanation of the analysis undertaken to determine how the profits would be split;

(*9*) A description or summary of any relevant data that the taxpayer obtains after the end of the tax year and before filing a tax return, which would help determine if a taxpayer selected and applied a specified method in a reasonable manner; and

(*10*) A general index of the principal and background documents and a description of the recordkeeping system used for cataloging and accessing those documents.

(C) *Background documents.*—The assumptions, conclusions, and positions contained in principal documents ordinarily will be based on, and supported by, additional background documents. Documents that support the principal documentation may include the documents listed in § 1.6038A-3(c) that are not otherwise described in paragraph (d)(2)(iii)(B) of this section. Every document listed in those regulations may not be relevant to pricing determinations under the taxpayer's specific facts and circumstances and, therefore, each of those documents need not be maintained in all circumstances. Moreover, other documents not listed in those regulations may be necessary to establish that the taxpayer's method was selected and applied in the way that provided the most reliable measure of an arm's length result under the principles of the best method rule in § 1.482-1(c). Background documents need not be provided to the Internal Revenue Service in response to a request for principal documents. If the Internal Revenue Service subsequently requests background documents, a taxpayer must provide that documentation to the Internal Revenue Service within 30 days of the request. However, the district director may, in his discretion, extend the period for producing the background documentation.

(D) Satisfaction of the documentation requirements described in § 1.482-7(k)(2) for the purpose of complying with the rules for CSAs under § 1.482-7 also satisfies all of the documentation requirements listed in paragraph (d)(2)(iii)(B) of this section, except the requirements listed in paragraphs (d)(2)(iii)(B)(2) and (10) of this section, with respect to CSTs and PCTs described in § 1.482-7(b)(1)(i) and (ii), provided that the documentation also satisfies the requirements of paragraph (d)(2)(iii)(A) of this section.

(3) *Application of an unspecified method.*—(i) *In general.*—An adjustment is excluded from the calculation of a net section 482 adjustment if the taxpayer establishes that both the unspecified method and documentation requirements of this paragraph (d)(3) are met with respect to that amount.

(ii) *Unspecified method requirement.*—(A) *In general.*—If a method other than a specified method was applied, the unspecified method requirement is met if the requirements of paragraph (d)(3)(ii)(B) or (C) of this section, as appropriate, are met.

(B) *Specified method potentially applicable.*—If the transaction is of a type for which methods are specified in the regulations under section 482, then a taxpayer will be considered to have met the unspecified method requirement if the taxpayer reasonably concludes, given the available data, that none of the specified methods was likely to provide a reliable measure of an arm's length result, and that it selected and applied an unspecified method in a way that would likely provide a reliable measure of an arm's length result. A taxpayer can reasonably conclude that no specified method was likely to provide a reliable measure of an arm's length result only if it has made a reasonable effort to evaluate the potential applicability of the specified methods in a manner consistent with the principles of the best method rule. However, it is not necessary for a taxpayer to conclude that the selected method provides a more reliable measure of an arm's length result than any other unspecified method. Whether the taxpayer's conclusion was reasonable must be determined from all the facts and circumstances. The factors relevant to this conclusion include those set forth in paragraph (d)(2)(ii) of this section.

(C) *No specified method applicable.*—If the transaction is of a type for which no methods are specified in the regulations under section 482, then a taxpayer will be considered to have met the unspecified method requirement if it selected and applied an unspecified method in a reasonable manner. For purposes of this paragraph (d)(3)(ii)(C), a taxpayer's selection and application is reasonable if the taxpayer reasonably concludes that the method (and its application of that method) provided the most reliable measure of an arm's length result under the principles of the best method rule in § 1.482-1(c). However, it is not necessary for a taxpayer to conclude that the selected method provides a more reliable measure of an arm's length result than any other unspecified method. Whether the taxpayer's conclusion was reasonable must be determined from all the facts and circumstances. The factors relevant to this conclusion include those set forth in paragraph (d)(2)(ii) of this section.

(iii) *Documentation requirement.*—(A) *In general.*—The documentation requirement of this paragraph (d)(3) is met if the taxpayer maintains sufficient documentation to establish that the unspecified method requirement of paragraph (d)(3)(ii) of this section is met and provides that documentation to the Internal Revenue Service within 30 days of a request for it. That documentation must be in existence when the return is filed. The district director may, in his discretion, excuse a minor or inadvertent failure to provide required documents, but only if the taxpayer has made a good faith effort to comply, and the taxpayer promptly remedies the failure when it becomes known.

(B) *Principal and background documents.*—See paragraphs (d)(2)(iii)(B) and (C) of this section for rules regarding these two categories of required documentation.

(4) *Certain foreign to foreign transactions.*—For purposes of calculating a net section 482 adjustment, any increase in taxable income resulting from an allocation under section 482 that is attributable to any controlled transaction solely between foreign corporations will be excluded unless the treatment of that transaction affects the determination of either corporation's income from sources within the United States or taxable income effectively connected with the conduct of a trade or business within the United States.

(5) *Special rule.*—If the regular tax (as defined in section 55(c)) imposed on the taxpayer is determined by reference to an amount other than taxable income, that amount shall be treated as the taxable income of the taxpayer for purposes of section 6662(e)(3). Accordingly, for taxpayers whose regular tax is determined by reference to an amount other than taxable income, the increase in that amount resulting from section 482 allocations is the taxpayer's net section 482 adjustment.

(6) *Examples.*—The principles of this paragraph (d) are illustrated by the following examples:

Example 1. (i) The Internal Revenue Service makes the following section 482 adjustments for the taxable year:

(1) Attributable to an increase in gross income because of an increase in royalty payments .	$9,000,000
(2) Not a 200 percent or 400 percent adjustment	2,000,000
(3) Attributable to a decrease in the cost of goods sold because of a decrease in the cost plus mark-up of a realted seller	9,000,000
Total section 482 adjustments .	20,000,000

(ii) The taxpayer has gross receipts of 75 million dollars after all section 482 adjustments. The taxpayer establishes that for adjustments number one and three, it applied a transfer pricing method specified in section 482, the selection and application of the method was reasonable, it documented the pricing analysis, and turned that documentation over to the IRS within 30 days of a request. Accordingly, eighteen million dollars is excluded from the calculation of the net section 482 adjustment. Because the net section 482 adjustment is two million dollars, there is no substantial valuation misstatement.

Example 2. (i) The Internal Revenue Service makes the following section 482 adjustments for the taxable year:

(1) Attributable to an increase in gross income because of an increase in royalty payments .	$9,000,000
(2) Attributable to an adjustment that is 200 percent or more of the correct section 482 price . .	2,000,000
(3) Attributable to a decrease in the cost of goods sold because of a decrease in the cost plus mark-up of a related seller	9,000,000
Total section 482 adjustments .	20,000,000

(ii) The taxpayer has gross receipts of 75 million dollars after all section 482 adjustments. The taxpayer establishes that for adjustments number one and three it applied a transfer pricing method specified in section 482, the selection and application of the method was reasonable, it documented that analysis, and turned the documentation over to the IRS within 30 days. Accordingly, eighteen million dollars is excluded from the calculation of the section 482 transfer pricing adjustments for purposes of applying the five million dollar or 10% of gross receipts test. Because the net section 482 adjustment is only two million dollars, the taxpayer is not subject to the net adjustment penalty. However, the taxpayer may be subject to the transactional penalty on the underpayment of tax attributable to the two million dollar adjustment.

Example 3. CFC1 and CFC2 are controlled foreign corporations within the meaning of section 957. Applying section 482, the IRS disallows a deduction for 25 million dollars of the interest that CFC1 paid to CFC2, which results in CFC1's U.S. shareholder having a subpart F inclusion in excess of five million dollars. No other adjustments under section 482 are made with respect to the controlled taxpayers. However, the increase has no effect upon the determination of CFC1's or CFC2's income from sources within the United States or taxable income effectively connected with the conduct of a trade or business within the United States. Accordingly, there is no substantial valuation misstatement.

(e) *Special rules in the case of carrybacks and carryovers.*—If there is a substantial or gross valuation misstatement for a taxable year that gives rise to a loss, deduction or credit that is carried to another taxable year, the transactional penalty and the net adjustment penalty will be imposed on any resulting underpayment of tax in that other taxable year. In determining whether there is a substantial or gross valuation misstatement for a taxable year, no amount carried from another taxable year shall be included. The following example illustrates the principle of this paragraph (e):

Example. The Internal Revenue Service makes a section 482 adjustment of six million dollars in taxable year 1, no portion of which is excluded under paragraph (d) of this section. The taxpayer's income tax return for year 1 reported a loss of three million dollars, which was carried to taxpayer's year 2 income tax return and used to reduce income taxes otherwise due with respect to year 2. A determination is made that the six million dollar allocation constitutes a substantial valuation misstatement, and a penalty is imposed on the underpayment of tax in year 1 attributable to the substantial valuation misstatement and on the underpayment of tax in year 2 attributable to the disallowance of the net operating loss in year 2. For purposes of determining whether there is a substantial or gross valuation misstatement for year 2, the three million dollar reduction of the net operating loss will not be added to any section 482 adjustments made with respect to year 2.

(f) *Rules for coordinating between the transactional penalty and the net adjustment penalty.*—(1) *Coordination of a net section 482 adjustment subject to the net adjustment penalty and a gross valuation misstatement subject to the transactional penalty.*—In determining whether a net section 482 adjustment exceeds five million dollars or 10 percent of gross receipts, an adjustment attributable to a substantial or gross valuation misstatement that is subject to the transactional penalty will be taken into account. If the net section 482 adjustment exceeds five million dollars or ten percent of gross receipts, any portion of such amount that is attributable to a gross valuation misstatement will be subject to the transactional penalty at the forty percent rate, but will not also be subject to net adjustment penalty at a twenty percent rate. The remaining amount is subject to the net adjustment penalty at the twenty percent rate, even if such amount is less than the lesser of five million dollars or ten percent of gross receipts.

(2) *Coordination of net section 482 adjustment subject to the net adjustment penalty and substantial valuation misstatements subject to the transactional penalty.*—If the net section 482 adjustment exceeds twenty million dollars or 20 percent of gross receipts, the entire amount of the adjustment is subject to the net adjustment penalty at a forty percent rate. No portion of the adjustment is subject to the transactional penalty at a twenty percent rate.

(3) *Examples.*—The following examples illustrate the principles of this paragraph (f):

Example 1. (i) Applying section 482, the Internal Revenue Service makes the following adjustments for the taxable year:

(1) Attributable to an adjustment that is 400 percent or more of the correct section 482 arm's length result	$2,000,000
(2) Not a 200 or 400 percent adjustment	2,500,000
Total	4,500,000

(ii) The taxpayer has gross receipts of 75 million dollars after all section 482 adjustments. None of the adjustments is excluded under paragraph (d) (Amounts excluded from net section 482 adjustments) of this section, in determining the five million dollar or 10% of gross receipts test under section 6662(e)(1)(B)(ii). The net section 482 adjustment (4.5 million dollars) is less than the lesser of five million dollars or ten percent of gross receipts ($75 million × 10% = $7.5 million). Thus, there is no substantial valuation misstatement. However, the two million dollar adjustment is attributable to a gross valuation misstatement. Accordingly, the taxpayer may be subject to a penalty, under section 6662(h), equal to 40 percent of the underpayment of tax attributable to the gross valuation misstatement of two million dollars. The 2.5 million dollar adjustment is not subject to a penalty under section 6662(b)(3).

Example 2. The facts are the same as in *Example 1,* except the taxpayer has gross receipts of 40 million dollars. The net section 482 adjustment ($4.5 million) is greater than the lesser of five million dollars or ten percent of gross receipts ($40 million × 10% = $4 million). Thus, the five million dollar or 10% of gross receipts test has been met. The two million dollar adjustment is attributable to a gross valuation misstatement. Accordingly, the taxpayer is subject to a penalty, under section 6662(h), equal to 40 percent of the underpayment of tax attributable to the gross valuation misstatement of two million dollars. The 2.5 million dollar adjustment is subject to a penalty under sections 6662(a) and 6662(b)(3), equal to 20 percent of the underpayment of tax attributable to the substantial valuation misstatement.

Example 3. (i) Applying section 482, the Internal Revenue Service makes the following transfer pricing adjustments for the taxable year:

(1) Attributable to an adjustment that is 400 percent or more of the correct section 482 arm's length result	$6,000,000
(2) Not a 200 or 400 percent adjustment	15,000,000
Total	21,000,000

(ii) None of the adjustments are excluded under paragraph (d) (Amounts excluded from net section 482 adjustments) in determining the twenty million dollar or 20% of gross receipts test under section 6662(h). The net section 482 adjustment (21 million dollars) is greater than twenty million dollars and thus constitutes a gross valuation misstatement. Accordingly, the total adjustment is subject to the net adjustment penalty equal to 40 percent of the underpayment of tax attributable to the 21 million dollar gross valuation misstatement. The six million dollar adjustment will not be separately included for purposes of any additional penalty under section 6662.

(g) *Effective/applicability date.*—(1) *In general.*—This section is generally applicable on February 9, 1996. However, taxpayers may elect to apply this section to all open taxable years beginning after December 31, 1993.

(2) *Special rules.*—The provisions of paragraphs (d)(2)(ii)(B), (d)(2)(iii)(B)(*4*) and (d)(2)(iii)(B)(*6*) of this section are applicable for taxable years beginning after July 31, 2009. However, taxpayers may elect to apply the provisions of paragraphs (d)(2)(ii)(B), (d)(2)(iii)(B)(*4*) and (d)(2)(iii)(B)(*6*) of this section to earlier taxable years in accordance with the rules set forth in § 1.482-9(n)(2). [Reg. § 1.6662-6.]

☐ [*T.D.* 8656, 2-8-96. *Amended by T.D.* 9278, 7-31-2006; *T.D.* 9441, 12-31-2008; *T.D.* 9456, 7-31-2009 *and T.D.* 9568, 12-16-2011.]

[Reg. § 1.6662-7]

§ 1.6662-7. Omnibus Budget Reconciliation Act of 1993 changes to the accuracy-related penalty.—(a) *Scope.*—The Omnibus Budget Reconciliation Act of 1993 made certain changes to the accuracy-related penalty in section 6662. This section provides rules reflecting those changes.

(b) *No disclosure exception for negligence penalty.*—The penalty for negligence in section 6662(b)(1) may not be avoided by disclosure of a return position.

(c) *Disclosure standard for other penalties is reasonable basis.*—The penalties for disregarding rules or regulations in section 6662(b)(1) and for a substantial understatement of income tax in section 6662(b)(2) may be avoided by adequate disclosure of a return position only if the position has at least a reasonable basis. See § 1.6662-3(c) and § § 1.6662-4(e) and (f) for other applicable disclosure rules.

(d) *Reasonable basis.*—For purposes of § § 1.6662-3(c) and 1.6662-4(e) and (f) (relating to methods of making adequate disclosure), the provisions of § 1.6662-3(b)(3) apply in determining whether a return position has a reasonable basis. [Reg. § 1.6662-7.]

☐ [*T.D.* 8617, 8-31-95. *Amended by T.D.* 8790, 12-1-98.]

[Reg. § 1.6664-0]

§ 1.6664-0. Table of contents.—This section lists the captions in § § 1.6664-1 through 1.6664-4T.

(4) Special rules.
(5) Examples.
(d) Amounts not so shown previously assessed (or collected without assessment).
(e) Rebates.
(f) Underpayments for certain carryback years not reduced by amount of carrybacks.
(g) Examples.

§1.6664-3. Ordering rules for determining the total amount of penalties imposed.
(a) In general.
(b) Order in which adjustments are taken into account.
(c) Manner in which unclaimed prepayment credits are allocated.
(d) Examples.

§1.6664-4. Reasonable cause and good faith exception to section 6662 penalties.
(a) In general.
(b) Facts and circumstances taken into account.
(1) In general.
(2) Examples.
(c) Reliance on opinion or advice.
(1) Fact and circumstances; minimum requirements.
(i) All facts and circumstances considered.
(ii) No unreasonable assumptions.
(iii) Reliance on the invalidity of a regulation.
(2) Advice defined.
(3) Cross-reference.
(d) Underpayments attributable to reportable transactions.
(e) Pass-through items.
(f) Special rules for substantial understatement penalty attributable to the tax shelter items of corporations.
(1) In general; facts and circumstances.
(2) Reasonable cause based on legal justification.
(i) Minimum requirements.
(A) Authority requirement.
(B) Belief requirement.
(ii) Legal justification defined.
(3) Minimum requirements not dispositive.
(4) Other factors.
(g) Transactions between persons described in section 482 and net section 482 transfer price adjustments. [Reserved]
(h) Valuation misstatements of charitable deduction property.
(1) In general.
(2) Definitions.
(3) Special rules.
(i) Charitable deduction property.
(ii) Qualified appraisal.
(iii) Qualified appraiser.

§1.6664-4T. Reasonable cause and good faith exception to section 6662 penalties.
(a) through (c) [Reserved]
(d) Transactions between persons described in section 482 and net section 482 transfer price adjustments.
[Reg. §1.6664-0.]

☐ [*T.D.* 8381, 12-30-91. *Amended by T.D.* 8519, 1-27-94; *T.D.* 8617, 8-31-95; *T.D.* 8656, 2-8-96; *T.D.* 8790, 12-1-98; *T.D.* 9109, 12-29-2003, *and T.D.* 9309, 1-8-2007.]

[Reg. §1.6664-1]

§1.6664-1. Accuracy-related and fraud penalties; definitions, effective date and and special rules.—(a) *In general.*—Section 6664(a) defines the term "underpayment" for purposes of the accuracy-related penalty under section 6662 and the fraud penalty under section 6663. The definition of "underpayment" of income taxes imposed under subtitle A is set forth in §1.6664-2. Ordering rules for computing the total amount of accuracy-related and fraud penalties imposed with respect to a return are set forth in §1.6664-3. Section 6664(c) provides a reasonable cause and good faith exception to the accuracy-related penalty. Rules relating to the reasonable cause and good faith exception are set forth in §1.6664-4.

(b) *Effective date.*—(1) *In general.*—Sections 1.6664-1 through 1.6664-3 apply to returns the due date of which (determined without regard to extensions of time for filing) is after December 31, 1989.

(2) *Reasonable cause and good faith exception to section 6662 penalties.*—(i) *For returns due after September 1, 1995.*—Section 1.6664-4 applies to returns the due date of which (determined without regard to extensions of time for filing) is after September 1, 1995. Except as provided in the last sentence of this paragraph (b)(2), §1.6664-4 (as contained in 26 CFR part 1 revised April 1, 1995) applies to returns the due date of which (determined without regard to extensions of time for filing) is on or before September 1, 1995, and after December 31, 1989. For transactions occurring after December 8, 1994, §1.6664-4 (as contained in 26 CFR part 1 revised April 1, 1995) is applied taking into account the changes made to section 6662(d)(2)(C) (relating to the substantial understatement penalty for tax shelter items of corporations) by section 744 of Title VII of the Uruguay Round Agreements Act, Pub. L. 103-465 (108 Stat. 4809).

(ii) *For returns filed after December 31, 2002.*—Sections 1.6664-4(c) (relating to relying on opinion or advice) and (d) (relating to underpayments attributable to reportable transactions) apply to returns filed after December 31, 2002, with respect to transactions entered into on or after January 1, 2003. Except as provided in paragraph (b)(2)(i) of this section, §1.6664-4 (as contained in 26 CFR part 1 revised April 1, 2003) applies to returns filed with respect to transactions entered into before January 1, 2003.

(3) *Qualified amended returns.*—Sections 1.6664-2(c)(1), (c) (2), (c) (3) (i) (A), (c) (3) (i) (B), (c) (3) (i) (C), (c) (3) (i) (D) (2), (c)(3)(i)(E), and (c)(4) are applicable for amended returns and requests for administrative adjustment filed on

or after March 2, 2005. Sections 1.6664-2(c)(3)(i)(D)(1) and (c)(3)(ii)(B) and (C) are applicable for amended returns and requests for administrative adjustment filed on or after April 30, 2004. The applicability date for §1.6664-2(c)(3)(ii)(A) varies depending upon which event occurs under §1.6664-2(c)(3)(i). For purposes of §1.6664-2(c)(3)(ii)(A), the date described in §1.6664-2(c)(3)(i)(D)(1) is applicable for amended returns and requests for administrative adjustment filed on or after April 30, 2004. For purposes of §1.6664-2(c)(3)(ii)(A), the dates described in §1.6664-2(c)(3)(i)(A), (B), (C), (D)(2), and (E) are applicable for amended returns and requests for administrative adjustment filed on or after March 2, 2005. Section 1.6664-2(c)(1) through (c)(3), as contained in 26 CFR part 1 revised as of April 1, 2004 and as modified by Notice 2004-38, 2004-1 C.B. 949, applies with respect to returns and requests for administrative adjustment filed on or after April 30, 2004 and before March 2, 2005. Section 1.6664-2(c)(1) through (3), as contained in 26 CFR part 1 revised as of April 30, 2004, applies with respect to returns and requests for administrative adjustment filed before April 30, 2004. [Reg. §1.6664-1.]

□ [*T.D.* 8381, 12-30-91. *Amended by T.D.* 8617, 8-31-95; *T.D.* 9109, 12-29-2003 *and T.D.* 9309, 1-8-2007.]

[Reg. §1.6664-2]

§1.6664-2. Underpayment.— (a) *Underpayment defined.*—In the case of income taxes imposed under subtitle A, an underpayment for purposes of section 6662, relating to the accuracy-related penalty, and section 6663, relating to the fraud penalty, means the amount by which any income tax imposed under this subtitle (as defined in paragraph (b) of the section) exceeds the excess of—

(1) The sum of—

(i) The amount shown as the tax by the taxpayer on his return (as defined in paragraph (c) of this section), plus

(ii) Amounts not so shown previously assessed (or collected without assessment) (as defined in paragraph (d) of this section), over

(2) The amount of rebates made (as defined in paragraph (e) of this section).

The definition of underpayment also may be expressed as—

Underpayment $= W - (X + Y - Z)$,

where W = the amount of income tax imposed; X = the amount shown as the tax by the taxpayer on his return; Y = amounts not so shown previously assessed (or collected without assessment); and Z = the amount of rebates made.

(b) *Amount of income tax imposed.*—For purposes of paragraph (a) of this section, the "amount of income tax imposed" is the amount of tax imposed on the taxpayer under subtitle A for the taxable year, determined without regard to—

(1) The credits for tax withheld under sections 31 (relating to tax withheld on wages) and 33 (relating to tax withheld at source on nonresident aliens and foreign corporations);

(2) Payments of tax or estimated tax by the taxpayer;

(3) Any credit resulting from the collection of amounts assessed under section 6851 as the result of a termination assessment, or section 6861 as the result of a jeopardy assessment; and

(4) Any tax that the taxpayer is not required to assess on the return (such as the tax imposed by section 531 on the accumulated taxable income of a corporation).

(c) *Amount shown as the tax by the taxpayer on his return.*—(1) *Defined.*—For purposes of paragraph (a) of this section, the amount shown as the tax by the taxpayer on his return is the tax liability shown by the taxpayer on his return, determined without regard to the items listed in paragraphs (b)(1), (2), and (3) of this section, except that it is reduced by the excess of—

(i) The amounts shown by the taxpayer on his return as credits for tax withheld under section 31 (relating to tax withheld on wages) and section 33 (relating to tax withheld at source on nonresident aliens and foreign corporations), as payments of estimated tax, or as any other payments made by the taxpayer with respect to a taxable year before filing the return for such taxable year, over

(ii) The amounts actually withheld, actually paid as estimated tax, or actually paid with respect to a taxable year before the return is filed for such taxable year.

(2) *Effect of qualified amended return.*—The amount shown as the tax by the taxpayer on his return includes an amount shown as additional tax on a qualified amended return (as defined in paragraph (c)(3) of this section), except that such amount is not included if it relates to a fraudulent position on the original return.

(3) *Qualified amended return defined.*—(i) *General rule.*—A qualified amended return is an amended return, or a timely request for an administrative adjustment under section 6227, filed after the due date of the return for the taxable year (determined with regard to extensions of time to file) and before the earliest of—

(A) The date the taxpayer is first contacted by the Internal Revenue Service (IRS) concerning any examination (including a criminal investigation) with respect to the return;

(B) The date any person is first contacted by the IRS concerning an examination of that person under section 6700 (relating to the penalty for promoting abusive tax shelters) for an activity with respect to which the taxpayer claimed any tax benefit on the return directly or indirectly through the entity, plan or arrangement described in section 6700(a)(1)(A);

(C) In the case of a pass-through item (as defined in §1.6662-4(f)(5)), the date the pass-through entity (as defined in §1.6662-4(f)(5)) is first contacted by the IRS in connection with an examination of the return to which the pass-through item relates;

(D)*(1)* The date on which the IRS serves a summons described in section 7609(f) relating to the tax liability of a person, group, or class that includes the taxpayer (or pass-through entity of which the taxpayer is a partner, shareholder, beneficiary, or holder of a residual interest in a REMIC) with respect to an activity for which the taxpayer claimed any tax benefit on the return directly or indirectly.

(2) The rule in paragraph (c)(3)(i)(D)(1) of this section applies to any return on which the taxpayer claimed a direct or indirect tax benefit from the type of activity that is the subject of the summons, regardless of whether the summons seeks the production of information for the taxable period covered by such return; and

(E) The date on which the Commissioner announces by revenue ruling, revenue procedure, notice, or announcement, to be published in the Internal Revenue Bulletin (see § 601.601(d)(2) of this chapter), a settlement initiative to compromise or waive penalties, in whole or in part, with respect to a listed transaction. This rule applies only to a taxpayer who participated in the listed transaction and for the taxable year(s) in which the taxpayer claimed any direct or indirect tax benefits from the listed transaction. The Commissioner may waive the requirements of this paragraph or identify a later date by which a taxpayer who participated in the listed transaction must file a qualified amended return in the published guidance announcing the listed transaction settlement initiative.

(ii) *Undisclosed listed transactions.*—An undisclosed listed transaction is a transaction that is the same as, or substantially similar to, a listed transaction within the meaning of § 1.6011-4(b)(2) (regardless of whether § 1.6011-4 requires the taxpayer to disclose the transaction) and was neither previously disclosed by the taxpayer within the meaning of § 1.6011-4 or § 1.6011-4T, nor disclosed under Announcement 2002-2 (2002-1 C.B. 304), (see § 601.601(d)(2)(ii) of this chapter) by the deadline therein. In the case of an undisclosed listed transaction for which a taxpayer claims any direct or indirect tax benefits on its return (regardless of whether the transaction was a listed transaction at the time the return was filed), an amended return or request for administrative adjustment under section 6227 will not be a qualified amended return if filed on or after the earliest of—

(A) The dates described in paragraph (c)(3)(i) of this section;

(B) The date on which the IRS first contacts any person regarding an examination of that person's liability under section 6707(a) with respect to the undisclosed listed transaction of the taxpayer; or

(C) The date on which the IRS requests, from any person who made a tax statement to or for the benefit of the taxpayer or from any person who gave the taxpayer material aid, assistance, or advice as described in section 6111(b)(1)(A)(i) with respect to the taxpayer, the information required to be included on a list under section 6112 relating to a transaction that was the same as, or substantially similar to, the undisclosed listed transaction, regardless of whether the taxpayer's information is required to be included on that list.

(4) *Special rules.*—(i) A qualified amended return includes an amended return that is filed to disclose information pursuant to § 1.6662-3(c) or § 1.6662-4(e) and (f) even though it does not report any additional tax liability. See § 1.6662-3(c), § 1.6662-4(f), and § 1.6664-4(c) for rules relating to adequate disclosure.

(ii) The Commissioner may by revenue procedure prescribe the manner in which the rules of paragraph (c) of this section regarding qualified amended returns apply to particular classes of taxpayers.

(5) *Examples.* The following examples illustrate the provisions of paragraphs (c)(3) and (c)(4) of this section:

Example 1. T, an individual taxpayer, claimed tax benefits on its 2002 Federal income tax return from a transaction that is substantially similar to the transaction identified as a listed transaction in Notice 2002-65, 2002-2 C.B. 690 (Partnership Entity Straddle Tax Shelter). T did not disclose his participation in this transaction on a Form 8886, "Reportable Transaction Disclosure Statement," as required by § 1.6011-4. On June 30, 2004, the IRS requested from P, T's material advisor, an investor list required to be maintained under section 6112. The section 6112 request, however, related to the type of transaction described in Notice 2003-81, 2003-2 C.B. 1223 (Tax Avoidance Using Offsetting Foreign Currency Option Contracts). T did not participate in (within the meaning of § 1.6011-4(c)) a transaction described in Notice 2003-81. T may file a qualified amended return relating to the transaction described in Notice 2002-65 because T did not claim a tax benefit with respect to the listed transaction described in Notice 2003-81, which is the subject of the section 6112 request.

Example 2. The facts are the same as in *Example 1,* except that T's 2002 Federal income tax return reflected T's participation in the transaction described in Notice 2003-81. As of June 30, 2004, T may not file a qualified amended return for the 2002 tax year.

Example 3. (i) Corporation X claimed tax benefits from a transaction on its 2002 Federal income tax return. In October 2004, the IRS and Treasury Department identified the transaction as a listed transaction. In December 2004, the IRS contacted P concerning an examination of P's liability under section 6707(a) (as in effect prior to the amendment to section 6707 by section 816 of the American Jobs Creation Act of 2004 (the Jobs Act), Public Law 108-357 (118 Stat. 1418)). P is the organizer of a section 6111 tax shelter (as in effect prior to the amendment to section 6111 by section 815 of the Jobs Act) who provided representations to X regarding tax benefits from the transaction, and the IRS has contacted P about the failure to register that transaction. Three days later, X filed an amended return.

See p. 15 for regulations not amended to reflect law changes

(ii) X's amended return is not a qualified amended return, because X did not disclose the transaction before the IRS contacted P. X's amended return would have been a qualified amended return if it was submitted prior to the date on which the IRS contacted P.

Example 4. The facts are the same as in *Example 3* except that, instead of contacting P concerning an examination under section 6707(a), in December 2004, the IRS served P with a John Doe summons described in section 7609(f) relating to the tax liability of participants in the type of transaction for which X claimed tax benefits on its return. X cannot file a qualified amended return after the John Doe summons has been served regardless of when, or whether, the transaction becomes a listed transaction.

Example 5. On November 30, 2003, the IRS served a John Doe summons described in section 7609(f) on Corporation Y, a credit card company. The summons requested the identity of, and information concerning, United States taxpayers who, during the taxable years 2001 and 2002, had signature authority over Corporation Y's credit cards issued by, through, or on behalf of certain offshore financial institutions. Corporation Y complied with the summons, and identified, among others, Taxpayer B. On May 31, 2004, before the IRS first contacted Taxpayer B concerning an examination of Taxpayer B's Federal income tax return for the taxable year 2002, Taxpayer B filed an amended return for that taxable year, that showed an increase in Taxpayer B's Federal income tax liability. Under paragraph (c)(3)(i)(D) of this section, the amended return is not a qualified amended return because it was not filed before the John Doe summons was served on Corporation Y.

Example 6. The facts are the same as in *Example 5.* Taxpayer B continued to maintain the offshore credit card account through 2003 and filed an original tax return for the 2003 taxable year claiming tax benefits attributable to the existence of the account. On March 21, 2005, Taxpayer B filed an amended return for the taxable year 2003, that showed an increase in Taxpayer B's Federal income tax liability. Under paragraph (c)(3)(i)(D) of this section, the amended return is not a qualified amended return because it was not filed before the John Doe summons for 2001 and 2002 was served on Corporation Y, and the return reflects benefits from the type of activity that is the subject of the John Doe summons.

Example 7. (i) On November 30, 2003, the IRS served a John Doe summons described in section 7609(f) on Corporation Y, a credit card company. The summons requested the identity of, and information concerning, United States taxpayers who, during the taxable years 2001 and 2002, had signature authority over Corporation Y's credit cards issued by, through, or on behalf of certain offshore financial institutions. Taxpayer C did not have signature authority over any of Corporation Y's credit cards during either 2001 or 2002 and, therefore, was not a person described in the John Doe summons.

(ii) In 2003, Taxpayer C first acquired signature authority over a Corporation Y credit card issued by an offshore financial institution. Because Taxpayer C did not have signature authority during 2001 or 2002 over a Corporation Y credit card issued by an offshore financial institution, and was therefore not covered by the John Doe summons served on November 30, 2003, Taxpayer C's ability to file a qualified amended return for the 2003 taxable year is not limited by paragraph (c)(3)(i)(D) of this section.

(d) *Amounts not so shown previously assessed (or collected without assessment).*—For purposes of paragraph (a) of this section, "amounts not so shown previously assessed" means only amounts assessed before the return is filed that were not shown on the return, such as termination assessments under section 6851 and jeopardy assessments under section 6861 made prior to the filing of the return for the taxable year. For purposes of paragraph (a) of this section, the amount "collected without assessment" is the amount by which the total of the credits allowable under section 31 (relating to tax withheld on wages) and section 33 (relating to tax withheld at source on nonresident aliens and foreign corporations), estimated tax payments, and other payments in satisfaction of tax liability made before the return is filed, exceed the tax shown on the return (provided such excess has not been refunded or allowed as a credit to the taxpayer).

(e) *Rebates.*—The term "rebate" means so much of an abatement credit, refund or other repayment, as was made on the ground that the tax imposed was less than the excess of—

(1) The sum of—

(i) The amount shown as the tax by the taxpayer on his return, plus

(ii) Amounts not so shown previously assessed (or collected without assessment), over

(2) Rebates previously made.

(f) *Underpayments for certain carryback years not reduced by amount of carrybacks.*—The amount of an underpayment for a taxable year that is attributable to conduct proscribed by sections 6662 or 6663 is not reduced on account of a carryback of a loss, deduction or credit to that year. Such conduct includes negligence or disregard of rules or regulations; a substantial understatement of income tax; and a substantial (or gross) valuation misstatement under chapter 1, provided that the applicable dollar limitation is satisfied for the carryback year.

(g) *Examples.*—The following examples illustrate this section:

Example 1. Taxpayer's 1990 return showed a tax liability of $18,000. Taxpayer had no amounts previously assessed (or collected without assessment) and received no rebates of tax. Taxpayer claimed a credit in the amount of $23,000 for income tax withheld under section 3402, which resulted in a refund received of $5,000. It is later determined that the taxpayer should have reported additional income and that the correct tax for the taxable year is $25,500. There is an underpayment of $7,500, determined as follows:

Tax imposed under subtitle A		$25,500
Tax shown on return	$18,000	
Tax previously assessed (or collected without assessment)	None	
Amount of rebates made	None	
Balance		$18,000
Underpayment		$7,500

Example 2. The facts are the same as in *Example 1* except that the taxpayer failed to claim on the return a credit of $1,500 for income tax withheld. This $1,500 constitutes an amount collected without assessment as defined in paragraph (d) of this section. The underpayment is $6,000, determined as follows:

Tax imposed under subtitle A		$25,500
Tax shown on return	$18,000	
Tax previously assessed (or collected without assessment)	1,500	
Amount of rebates made	None	
Balance		$19,500
Underpayment		$6,000

Example 3. On Form 1040 filed for tax year 1990, taxpayer reported a tax liability of $10,000, estimated tax payments of $15,000, and received a refund of $5,000. Estimated tax payments actually made with respect to tax year 1990 were only $7,000. For purposes of determining the amount of underpayment subject to a penalty under section 6662 or section 6663, the tax shown on the return is $2,000 (reported tax liability of $10,000 reduced by the overstated estimated tax of $8,000 ($15,000 – $7,000)). The underpayment is $8,000, determined as follows:

Tax imposed under subtitle A		$10,000
Tax shown on return	$2,000	
Tax previously assessed (or collected without assessment)	None	
Amount of rebates made	None	
Balance		$2,000
Underpayment		$8,000

[Reg. § 1.6664-2.]

□ [*T.D.* 8381, 12-30-91. *Amended by T.D.* 9186, 3-1-2005 *and T.D.* 9309, 1-8-2007.]

[Reg. § 1.6664-3]

§ 1.6664-3. Ordering rules for determining the total amount of penalties imposed.—(a) *In general.*—This section provides rules for determining the order in which adjustments to a return are taken into account for the purpose of computing the total amount of penalties imposed under sections 6662 and 6663, where—

(1) There is at least one adjustment with respect to which no penalty has been imposed and at least one with respect to which a penalty has been imposed, or

(2) There are at least two adjustments with respect to which penalties have been imposed and they have been imposed at different rates.

This section also provides rules for allocating unclaimed prepayment credits to adjustments to a return.

(b) *Order in which adjustments are taken into account.*—In computing the portions of an underpayment subject to penalties imposed under sections 6662 and 6663, adjustments to a return are considered made in the following order:

(1) Those with respect to which no penalties have been imposed.

(2) Those with respect to which a penalty has been imposed at a 20 percent rate (*i.e.,* a penalty for negligence or disregard of rules or regulations, substantial understatement of income tax, or substantial valuation misstatement, under sections 6662(b)(1) through 6662(b)(3), respectively).

(3) Those with respect to which a penalty has been imposed at a 40 percent rate (*i.e.,* a penalty for a gross valuation misstatement under sections 6662(b)(3) and (h)).

(4) Those with respect to which a penalty has been imposed at a 75 percent rate (*i.e.,* a penalty for fraud under section 6663).

(c) *Manner in which unclaimed prepayment credits are allocated.*—Any income tax withholding or other payment made before a return was filed, that was neither claimed on the return nor previously allowed as a credit against the tax liability for the taxable year (an "unclaimed prepayment credit"), is allocated as follows—

(1) If an unclaimed prepayment credit is allocable to a particular adjustment, such credit is applied in full in determining the amount of the underpayment resulting from such adjustment.

(2) If an unclaimed prepayment credit is not allocable to a particular adjustment, such credit is applied in accordance with the ordering rules set forth in paragraph (b) of this section.

(d) *Examples.*—The following examples illustrate the rules of this § 1.6664-3. These examples do not take into account the reasonable cause exception to the accuracy-related penalty under § 1.6664-4.

Example 1. A and B, husband and wife, filed a joint federal income tax return for calendar year 1989, reporting taxable income of $15,800 and a tax liability of $2,374. A and B had no amounts previously assessed (or collected without assessment) and no rebates had been made. Subsequently, the return was examined and the following adjustments and penalties were agreed to:

Adjustment #1 (No penalty imposed)		$1,000
Adjustment #2 (Substantial understatement penalty imposed)		40,000
Adjustment # 3 (Civil fraud penalty imposed)		45,000
Total adjustments		$86,000
Taxable income shown on return		15,800
Taxable income as corrected		$101,800
Computation of underpayment:		
Tax imposed by subtitle A		$25,828
Tax shown on return	$2,374	
Previous assessments	None	
Rebates	None	
Balance		$2,374
Underpayment		$23,454

Computation of the portions of the underpayment on which penalties under section 6662(b)(2) and section 6663 are imposed:

Step 1 Determine the portion, if any, of the underpayment on which no accuracy-related or fraud penalty is imposed:

Taxable income shown on return . . .	$15,800
Adjustment #1	1,000
"Adjusted" taxable income	$16,800
Tax on "adjusted" taxable income . .	$2,524
Tax shown on return	2,374
Portion of underpayment on which no penalty is imposed	$150

Step 2 Determine the portion, if any, of the underpayment on which a penalty of 20 percent is imposed:

"Adjusted" taxable income from step 1	$16,800
Adjustment #2	40,000
"Adjusted" taxable income	$56,800
Tax on "adjusted" taxable income . . .	$11,880
Tax on "adjusted" taxable income from step 1	2,524
Portion of underpayment on which 20 percent penalty is imposed	$9,356

Step 3 Determine the portion, if any, of the underpayment on which a penalty of 75 percent is imposed:

Total underpayment		$23,454
Less the sum of the portions of such underpayment determined in:		
Step 1	$150	
Step 2	$9,356	
Total		$9,506
Portion of underpayment on which 75 percent penalty is imposed		$13,948

Example 2. The facts are the same as in *Example 1* except that the taxpayers failed to claim on their return a credit of $1,500 for income tax withheld on unreported additional income that resulted in Adjustment #2. Because the unclaimed prepayment credit is allocable to Adjustment #2, the portion of the underpayment attributable to that adjustment is $7,856 ($9,356 – $1,500). The portions of the underpayment attributable to Adjustments #1 and #3 remain the same.

Example 3. The facts are the same as in *Example 1* except that the taxpayers made a timely estimated tax payment of $1,500 for 1989 which they failed to claim (and which the Service had not previously allowed). This unclaimed prepayment credit is not allocable to any particular adjustment. Therefore, the credit is allocated first to the portion of the underpayment on which no penalty is imposed ($150). The remaining amount ($1,350) is allocated next to the 20 percent penalty portion of the underpayment ($9,356). Thus, the portion of the underpayment that is not penalized is zero ($150 – $150), the portion subject to a 20 percent penalty is $8,006 ($9,356 – $1,350) and the portion subject to a 75 percent penalty is unchanged at $13,948. [Reg. § 1.6664-3.]

☐ [*T.D.* 8381, 12-30-91.]

[Reg. § 1.6664-4]

§ 1.6664-4. Reasonable cause and good faith exception to section 6662 penalties.—(a) *In general.*—No penalty may be imposed under section 6662 with respect to any portion of an underpayment upon a showing by the taxpayer that there was reasonable cause for, and the taxpayer acted in good faith with respect to, such portion. Rules for determining whether the reasonable cause and good faith exception applies are set forth in paragraphs (b) through (h) of this section.

(b) *Facts and circumstances taken into account.*—(1) *In general.*—The determination of whether a taxpayer acted with reasonable cause and in good faith is made on a case-by-case basis, taking into account all pertinent facts and circumstances. (See paragraph (e) of this section for certain rules relating to a substantial understatement penalty attributable to tax shelter items of corporations.) Generally, the most important factor is the extent of the taxpayer's effort to assess the taxpayer's proper tax liability. Circumstances that may indicate reasonable cause and good faith include an honest misunderstanding of fact or law that is reasonable in light of all of the facts and circumstances, including the experience, knowledge, and education of the taxpayer. An isolated computational or transcriptional error generally is not inconsistent with reasonable cause and good faith. Reliance on an information return or on the advice of a professional tax advisor or an appraiser does not necessarily demonstrate reasonable cause and good faith. Similarly, reasonable cause and good faith is not necessarily indicated by reliance on facts that, unknown to the taxpayer, are incorrect. Reliance on an information return, professional advice, or other facts, however, constitutes reasonable cause and good faith if, under all the circumstances, such reliance was reasonable and the taxpayer acted in good faith. (See paragraph (c) of this section for certain rules relating to reliance on the advice of others.) For example, reliance on erroneous information (such as an error relating to the cost or adjusted basis of property, the date property was placed in service, or the amount of opening or closing inventory) inadvertently included in data compiled by the various divisions of a multidivisional corporation or in financial books and records prepared by those divisions generally indicates reasonable cause and good faith, provided the corporation employed internal controls and procedures, reasonable under the circumstances, that were designed to identify such factual errors. Reasonable cause and good faith ordinarily is not indicated by the mere fact that there is an appraisal of the value of property. Other factors to consider include the methodology and assumptions underlying the appraisal, the appraised value, the relationship between appraised value and purchase price, the circumstances under which the appraisal was obtained, and the appraiser's relationship to the taxpayer or to the activity in which the property is used. (See paragraph (g) of this section for certain rules relating to appraisals for charitable deduction property.) A taxpayer's reliance on erroneous information reported on a Form W-2, Form 1099, or other information return indicates reasonable cause and good faith, provided the taxpayer did not know or have reason to know that the information was incorrect. Generally, a taxpayer knows, or has reason to know, that the information on an information return is incorrect if such information is inconsistent with other information reported or otherwise furnished to the taxpayer, or with the taxpayer's knowledge of the transaction. This knowledge includes, for example, the taxpayer's knowledge of the terms of his employment relationship or of the rate of return on a payor's obligation.

(2) *Examples.*—The following examples illustrate this paragraph (b). They do not involve tax shelter items. (See paragraph (e) of this section for certain rules relating to the substantial understatement penalty attributable to the tax shelter items of corporations.)

Example 1. A, an individual calendar year taxpayer, engages B, a professional tax advisor, to give A advice concerning the deductibility of certain state and local taxes. A provides B with full details concerning the taxes at issue. B advises A that the taxes are fully deductible. A, in preparing his own tax return, claims a deduction for the taxes. Absent other facts, and assuming the facts and circumstances surrounding B's advice and A's reliance on such advice satisfy the requirements of paragraph (c) of this section, A is considered to have demonstrated good faith by seeking the advice of a professional tax advisor, and to have shown reasonable cause for any underpayment attributable to the deduction claimed for the taxes. However, if A had sought advice from someone that A knew, or should have known, lacked knowledge in the relevant aspects of Federal tax law, or if other facts demonstrate that A failed to act reasonably or in good faith, A would not be considered to have shown reasonable cause or to have acted in good faith.

Example 2. C, an individual, sought advice from D, a friend who was not a tax professional, as to how C might reduce his Federal tax obligations. D advised C that, for a nominal investment in Corporation X, D had received certain tax benefits which virtually eliminated D's Federal tax liability. D also named other investors who had received similar benefits. Without further inquiry, C invested in X and claimed the benefits that he had been assured by D were due him. In this case, C did not make any good faith attempt to ascertain the correctness of what D had advised him concerning his tax matters, and is not considered to have reasonable cause for the underpayment attributable to the benefits claimed.

Example 3. E, an individual, worked for Company X doing odd jobs and filling in for other employees when necessary. E worked irregular hours and was paid by the hour. The amount of E's pay check differed from week to week. The Form W-2 furnished to E reflected wages for 1990 in the amount of $29,729. It did not, however, include compensation of $1,467 paid for some hours E worked. Relying on the Form W-2, E filed a return reporting wages of $29,729. E had no reason to know that the amount reported on the Form W-2 was incorrect. Under the circumstances, E is considered to have acted in good faith in relying on the Form W-2 and to have reasonable cause for the underpayment attributable to the unreported wages.

Example 4. H, an individual, did not enjoy preparing his tax returns and procrastinated in doing so until April 15th. On April 15th, H hurriedly gathered together his tax records and materials, prepared a return, and mailed it before midnight. The return contained numerous errors, some of which were in H's favor and some of which were not. The net result of all the adjustments, however, was an underpayment of tax by H. Under these circumstances, H is not considered to have reasonable cause for the underpayment or to have acted in good faith in attempting to file an accurate return.

(c) *Reliance on opinion or advice.*—(1) *Facts and circumstances; minimum requirements.*—All facts and circumstances must be taken into account in determining whether a taxpayer has reasonably relied in good faith on advice (including the opinion of a professional tax advisor) as to the treatment of the taxpayer (or any entity, plan, or arrangement) under Federal tax law. For example, the taxpayer's education, sophistication and business experience will be relevant in determining whether the taxpayer's reliance on tax advice was reasonable and made in good faith. In no event will a taxpayer be considered to have reasonably relied in good faith on advice (including an opinion) unless the requirements of this paragraph (c)(1) are satisfied. The fact that these requirements are satisfied, however, will not necessarily establish that the taxpayer reasonably relied on the advice (including the opinion of a tax advisor) in good faith. For example, reliance may not be reasonable or in good faith if the taxpayer knew, or reasonably should have known, that the advisor lacked knowledge in the relevant aspects of Federal tax law.

(i) *All facts and circumstances considered.*—The advice must be based upon all pertinent facts and circumstances and the law as it relates to those facts and circumstances. For example, the advice must take into account the taxpayer's purposes (and the relative weight of such purposes) for entering into a transaction and for structuring a transaction in a particular manner. In addition, the requirements of this paragraph (c)(1) are not satisfied if the taxpayer fails to disclose a fact that it knows, or reasonably should know, to be relevant to the proper tax treatment of an item.

(ii) *No unreasonable assumptions.*—The advice must not be based on unreasonable factual or legal assumptions (including assumptions as to future events) and must not unreasonably rely on the representations, statements, findings, or agreements of the taxpayer or any other person. For example, the advice must not be based upon a representation or assumption which the taxpayer knows, or has reason to know, is unlikely to be true, such as an inaccurate representation or assumption as to the taxpayer's purposes for entering into a transaction or for structuring a transaction in a particular manner.

(iii) *Reliance on the invalidity of a regulation.*—A taxpayer may not rely on an opinion or advice that a regulation is invalid to establish that the taxpayer acted with reasonable cause and good faith unless the taxpayer adequately disclosed, in accordance with § 1.6662-3(c)(2), the position that the regulation in question is invalid.

(2) *Advice defined.*—Advice is any communication, including the opinion of a professional tax advisor, setting forth the analysis or conclusion of a person, other than the taxpayer, provided to (or for the benefit of) the taxpayer and on which the taxpayer relies, directly or indirectly, with respect to the imposition of the section 6662 accuracy-related penalty. Advice does not have to be in any particular form.

(3) *Cross-reference.*—For rules applicable to advisors, see e.g., § § 1.6694-1 through 1.6694-3 (regarding preparer penalties), 31 CFR 10.22 (regarding diligence as to accuracy), 31 CFR 10.33 (regarding tax shelter opinions), and 31 CFR 10.34 (regarding standards for advising with respect to tax return positions and for preparing or signing returns).

(d) *Underpayments attributable to reportable transactions.*—If any portion of an underpayment is attributable to a reportable transaction, as defined in § 1.6011-4(b) (or § 1.6011-4T(b), as applicable), then failure by the taxpayer to disclose the transaction in accordance with § 1.6011-4 (or § 1.6011-4T, as applicable) is a strong indication that the taxpayer did not act in good faith with respect to the portion of the underpayment attributable to the reportable transaction.

(e) *Pass-through items.*—The determination of whether a taxpayer acted with reasonable cause and in good faith with respect to an underpayment that is related to an item reflected on the return of a pass-through entity is made on the basis of all pertinent facts and circumstances, including the taxpayer's own actions, as well as the actions of the pass-through entity.

(f) *Special rules for substantial understatement penalty attributable to tax shelter items of corporations.*—(1) *In general; facts and circumstances.*—The determination of whether a corporation acted with reasonable cause and in good faith in its treatment of a tax shelter item (as defined in § 1.6662-4(g)(3)) is based on all pertinent facts and circumstances. Paragraphs (f)(2), (3), and (4) of this section set forth rules that apply, in the case of a penalty attributable to a substantial understatement of income tax (within the meaning of section 6662(d)), in determining whether a corporation acted with reasonable cause and in good faith with respect to a tax shelter item.

(2) *Reasonable cause based on legal justification.*—(i) *Minimum requirements.*—A corporation's legal justification (as defined in paragraph (f)(2)(ii) of this section) may be taken into account, as appropriate, in establishing that the corporation acted with reasonable cause and in good faith in its treatment of a tax shelter item only if the authority requirement of paragraph (f)(2)(i)(A) of this section and the belief requirement of paragraph (f)(2)(i)(B) of this section are satisfied (the minimum requirements). Thus, a failure to satisfy the minimum requirements will preclude a finding of reasonable cause and good faith based (in whole or in part) on the corporation's legal justification.

(A) *Authority requirement.*—The authority requirement is satisfied only if there is substantial authority (within the meaning of § 1.6662-4(d)) for the tax treatment of the item.

(B) *Belief requirement.*—The belief requirement is satisfied only if, based on all facts and circumstances, the corporation reasonably believed, at the time the return was filed, that the tax treatment of the item was more likely than not the proper treatment. For purposes of the preceding sentence, a corporation is considered reasonably to believe that the tax treatment of an item is more likely than not the proper-tax treatment if (without taking into account the possibility that a return will not be audited, that an issue will not be raised on audit, or that an issue will be settled)—

(1) The corporation analyzes the pertinent facts and authorities in the manner described in § 1.6662-4(d)(3)(ii), and in reliance upon that analysis, reasonably concludes in good faith that there is a greater than 50-percent likelihood that the tax treatment of the item will be upheld if challenged by the Internal Revenue Service; or

(2) The corporation reasonably relies in good faith on the opinion of a professional tax advisor, if the opinion is based on the tax advisor's analysis of the pertinent facts and authorities in the manner described in § 1.6662-4(d)(3)(ii) and unambiguously states that the tax advisor concludes that there is a greater than 50-percent likelihood that the tax treatment of the item will be upheld if challenged by the Internal Revenue Service. (For this purpose, the requirements of paragraph (c) of this section must be met with respect to the opinion of a professional tax advisor.)

(ii) *Legal justification defined.*—For purposes of this paragraph (f), *legal justification* includes any justification relating to the treatment or characterization under the Federal tax law of the tax shelter item or of the entity, plan, or arrangement that gave rise to the item. Thus, a taxpayer's belief (whether independently formed or based on the advice of others) as to the merits of the taxpayer's underlying position is a legal justification.

(3) *Minimum requirements not dispositive.*—Satisfaction of the minimum requirements of paragraph (f)(2) of this section is an important factor to be considered in determining whether a corporate taxpayer acted with reasonable cause and in good faith, but is not necessarily dispositive. For example, depending on the circumstances, satisfaction of the minimum requirements may not be dispositive if the taxpayer's participation in the tax shelter lacked significant business purpose, if the taxpayer claimed tax benefits that are unreasonable in comparison to the taxpayer's investment in the tax shelter, or if the taxpayer agreed with the organizer or promoter of the tax shelter that the taxpayer would protect the confidentiality of the tax aspects of the structure of the tax shelter.

(4) *Other factors.*—Facts and circumstances other than a corporation's legal justification may be taken into account, as appropriate, in determining whether the corporation acted with reasonable cause and in good faith with respect to a tax shelter item regardless of whether the minimum requirements of paragraph (f)(2) of this section are satisfied.

(g) *Transactions between persons described in section 482 and net section 482 transfer price adjustments.*—[Reserved]

(h) *Valuation misstatements of charitable deduction property.*—(1) *In general.*—There may be reasonable cause and good faith with respect to a portion of an underpayment that is attributable to a substantial (or gross) valuation misstatement of charitable deduction property (as defined in paragraph (h)(2) of this section) only if—

(i) The claimed value of the property was based on a qualified appraisal (as defined in paragraph (h)(2) of this section) by a qualified appraiser (as defined in paragraph (h)(2) of this section); and

(ii) In addition to obtaining a qualified appraisal, the taxpayer made a good faith investigation of the value of the contributed property.

(2) *Definitions.*—For purposes of this paragraph (h):

Charitable deduction property means any property (other than money or publicly traded securities, as defined in § 1.170A-13(c)(7)(xi)) contributed by the taxpayer in a contribution for which a deduction was claimed under section 170.

Qualified appraisal means a qualified appraisal as defined in § 1.170A-13(c)(3).

Qualified appraiser means a qualified appraiser as defined in § 1.170A-13(c)(5).

(3) *Special rules.*—The rules of this paragraph (h) apply regardless of whether § 1.170A-13 permits a taxpayer to claim a charitable contribution deduction for the property without obtaining a qualified appraisal. The rules of this paragraph (h) apply in addition to the generally applicable rules concerning reasonable cause and good faith. [Reg. § 1.6664-4.]

☐ [*T.D.* 8381, 12-30-91. *Amended by T.D.* 8617, 8-31-95; *T.D.* 8790, 12-1-98 *and T.D.* 9109, 12-29-2003.]

[Reg. § 1.6664-4T]

§ 1.6664-4T. Reasonable cause and good faith exception to section 6662 penalties.—(a) through (e) [Reserved].

(f) *Transactions between persons described in section 482 and net section 482 transfer price adjustments.*—For purposes of applying the reasonable cause and good faith exception of section 6664(c) to net section 482 adjustments, the rules of § 1.6662-6(d) apply. A taxpayer that does not satisfy the rules of § 1.6662-6(d) for a net section 482 adjustment cannot satisfy the reasonable cause and good faith exception under section 6664(c). The rules of this section apply to underpayments subject to the transactional penalty in § 1.6662-6(b). If the standards of the net section 482 penalty exclusion provisions under § 1.6662-6(d) are met with respect to such underpayments, then the taxpayer will be considered to have acted with reasonable cause and good faith for purposes of this section. [Temporary Reg. § 1.6664-4T.]

☐ [*T.D.* 8519, 1-27-94. *Amended by T.D.* 8656, 2-8-96.]

[Reg. § 1.6694-0]

§ 1.6694-0. Table of contents.—This section lists the captions that appear in §§ 1.6694-1 through 1.6694-4.

§ 1.6694-1 Section 6694 penalties applicable to tax return preparers.

(iv) Reduction of compensation.
(3) Individual and firm allocation.
(4) Examples.
(g) Effective/applicability date.
§1.6694-2 Penalty for understatement due to an unreasonable position.
(a) In general.
(1) Proscribed conduct.
(2) Special rule for corporations, partnerships, and other firms.
(b) Reasonable to believe that the position would more likely than not be sustained on its merits.
(1) In general.
(2) Authorities.
(3) Written determinations.
(4) Taxpayer's jurisdiction.
(5) When "more likely than not" standard must be satisfied.
(c) Substantial authority.
(d) Exception for adequate disclosure of positions with a reasonable basis.
(1) In general.
(2) Reasonable basis.
(3) Adequate disclosure.
(i) Signing tax return preparers.
(ii) Nonsigning tax return preparers.
(A) Advice to taxpayers.
(B) Advice to another tax return preparer.
(iii) Requirements for advice.
(iv) Pass-through entities.
(v) Examples.
(e) Exception for reasonable cause and good faith.
(1) Nature of the error causing the understatement.
(2) Frequency of errors.
(3) Materiality of errors.
(4) Tax return preparer's normal office practice.
(5) Reliance on advice of others.
(6) Reliance on generally accepted administrative or industry practice.
(f) Effective/applicability date.
§1.6694-3 Penalty for understatement due to willful, reckless, or intentional conduct.
(a) In general.
(1) Proscribed conduct.
(2) Special rule for corporations, partnerships, and other firms.
(b) Willful attempt to understate liability.
(c) Reckless or intentional disregard.
(d) Examples.
(e) Rules or regulations.
(f) Section 6694(b) penalty reduced by section 6694(a) penalty.
(g) Effective/applicability date.
§1.6694-4 Extension of period of collection when tax return preparer pays 15 percent of a penalty for understatement of taxpayer's liability and certain other procedural matters.
(a) In general.
(b) Tax return preparer must bring suit in district court to determine liability for penalty.
(c) Suspension of running of period of limitations on collection.
(d) Effective/applicability date.
[Reg. §1.6694-0.]

☐ *T.D.* 8382, 12-30-91. *Amended by T.D.* 9436, 12-15-2008.]

[Reg. §1.6694-1]

§1.6694-1. Section 6694 penalties applicable to tax return preparers.—(a) *Overview.*—(1) *In general.*—Sections 6694(a) and (b) impose penalties on tax return preparers for conduct giving rise to certain understatements of liability on a return (including an amended or adjusted return) or claim for refund. For positions other than those with respect to tax shelters (as defined in section 6662(d)(2)(C)(ii)) and reportable transactions to which section 6662A applies, the section 6694(a) penalty is imposed in an amount equal to the greater of $1,000 or 50 percent of the income derived (or to be derived) by the tax return preparer for an understatement of tax liability that is due to an undisclosed position for which the tax return preparer did not have substantial authority or due to a disclosed position for which there is no reasonable basis. For positions with respect to tax shelters (as defined in section 6662(d)(2)(C)(ii)) or reportable transactions to which section 6662A applies, the section 6694(a) penalty is imposed in an amount equal to the greater of $1,000 or 50 percent of the income derived (or to be derived) by the tax return preparer for an understatement of tax liability for which it is not reasonable to believe that the position would more likely than not be sustained on its merits. The section 6694(b) penalty is imposed in an amount equal to the greater of $5,000 or 50 percent of the income derived (or to be derived) by the tax return preparer for an understatement of liability with respect to tax that is due to a willful attempt to understate tax liability or that is due to reckless or intentional disregard of rules or regulations. Refer to §1.6694-2 for rules relating to the penalty under section 6694(a). Refer to §1.6694-3 for rules relating to the penalty under section 6694(b).

(2) *Date return is deemed prepared.*—For purposes of the penalties under section 6694, a return or claim for refund is deemed prepared on the date it is signed by the tax return preparer. If a signing tax return preparer within the meaning of §301.7701-15(b)(1) of this chapter fails to sign the return, the return or claim for refund is deemed prepared on the date the return or claim is filed. See §1.6695-1 of this section. In the case of a nonsigning tax return preparer within the meaning of §301.7701-15(b)(2) of this chapter, the relevant date is the date the nonsigning tax return preparer provides the tax advice with respect to the position giving rise to the understatement. This date will be determined based on all the facts and circumstances.

(b) *Tax return preparer.*—(1) *In general.*—For purposes of this section, "tax return preparer" means any person who is a tax return preparer within the meaning of section 7701(a)(36) and §301.7701-15 of this chapter. An individual is a tax return preparer subject to section 6694 if the individual is primarily responsible for the position(s) on the return or claim for refund giving rise to an understatement. See §301.7701-15(b)(3). There is only one individual within a firm who is primarily responsible for each position on the return or claim for refund giving rise to an understatement. In the course of identifying the individual who is primarily responsible for the position, the Internal Revenue Service (IRS) may advise multiple individuals within the firm that it may be concluded that they are the individual within the firm who is primarily responsible. In some circumstances, there may be more than one tax return preparer who is primarily responsible for the position(s) giving rise to an understatement if multiple tax return preparers are employed by, or associated with, different firms.

(2) *Responsibility of signing tax return preparer.*—If there is a signing tax return preparer within the meaning of §301.7701-15(b)(1) of this chapter within a firm, the signing tax return preparer generally will be considered the person who is primarily responsible for all of the positions on the return or claim for refund giving rise to an understatement unless, based upon credible information from any source, it is concluded that the signing tax return preparer is not primarily responsible for the position(s) on the return or claim for refund giving rise to an understatement. In that case, a nonsigning tax return preparer within the signing tax return preparer's firm (as determined in paragraph (b)(3) of this section) will be considered the tax return preparer who is primarily responsible for the position(s) on the return or claim for refund giving rise to an understatement.

(3) *Responsibility of nonsigning tax return preparer.*—If there is no signing tax return preparer within the meaning of §301.7701-15(b)(1) of this chapter for the return or claim for refund within the firm or if, after the application of paragraph (b)(2) of this section, it is concluded that the signing tax return preparer is not primarily responsible for the position, the nonsigning tax return preparer within the meaning of §301.7701-15(b)(2) of this chapter within the firm with overall supervisory responsibility for the position(s) giving rise to the understatement generally will be considered the tax return preparer who is primarily responsible for the position for purposes of section 6694 unless, based upon credible information from any source, it is concluded that another nonsigning tax return preparer within that firm is primarily responsible for the position(s) on the return or claim for refund giving rise to the understatement.

(4) *Responsibility of signing and nonsigning tax return preparer.*—If the information presented would support a finding that, within a firm, either the signing tax return preparer or a nonsigning tax return preparer is primarily responsible for the position(s) giving rise to the understatement, the penalty may be assessed against either one of the individuals, but not both, as the primarily responsible tax return preparer.

(5) *Tax return preparer and firm responsibility.*—To the extent provided in §§1.6694-2(a)(2) and 1.6694-3(a)(2), an individual and the firm that employs the individual, or the firm of which the individual is a partner, member, shareholder, or other equity holder, both may be subject to penalty under section 6694 with respect to the position(s) on the return or claim for refund giving rise to an understatement. If an individual (other than the sole proprietor) who is employed by a sole proprietorship is subject to penalty under section 6694, the sole proprietorship is considered a "firm" for purposes of this paragraph (b).

(6) *Examples.*—The provisions of paragraph (b) of this section are illustrated by the following examples:

Example 1. Attorney A provides advice to Client C concerning the proper treatment of an item with respect to which all events have occurred on C's tax return. In preparation for providing that advice, A seeks advice regarding the proper treatment of the item from Attorney B, who is within the same firm as A, but A is the attorney who signs C's return as a tax return preparer. B provides advice on the treatment of the item upon which A relies. B's advice is reflected on C's tax return but no disclosure was made in accordance with §1.6694-2(d)(3). The advice constitutes preparation of a substantial portion of the return within the meaning of §301.7701-15(b)(3). The IRS later challenges the position taken on the tax return, giving rise to an understatement of liability. For purposes of the regulations under section 6694, A is initially considered the tax return preparer with respect to C's return, and the IRS advises A that A may be subject to the penalty under section 6694 with respect to C's return. Based upon information received from A or another source, it may be concluded that B, rather than A, had primary responsibility for the position taken on the return that gave rise to the understatement and may be subject to penalty under section 6694 instead of A.

Example 2. Same as *Example 1,* except that neither Attorney A nor any other source produce credible information that Attorney B had primary responsibility for the position on the return giving rise to an understatement. Attorney A is the tax return preparer who may be subject to penalty under section 6694 with respect to C's return.

Example 3. Same as *Example 1,* except that neither Attorney A nor any other attorney within A's firm signs Client C's return as a tax return preparer. Attorney B is the nonsigning tax return preparer within the firm with overall supervisory responsibility for the position giving rise to an understatement. Accordingly, B is the tax return preparer who is primarily responsible for the position on C's return giving rise to an understatement and may be subject to penalty under section 6694.

Example 4. Same as *Example 1,* except Attorney D, who works for a different firm than A, also provides advice on the same position upon which A relies. It may be concluded that D is also primarily responsible for the position on the return and may be subject to penalty under section 6694.

Example 5. Same as *Example 1,* except Attorney B is able to present credible information that A is also responsible for the position on C's return giving rise to an understatement. The IRS may conclude between A and B, the two responsible persons for the position, who is primarily responsible and may assess a section 6694 penalty against A or B, but not both, as the primarily responsible tax return preparer.

(c) *Understatement of liability.*—For purposes of this section, an "understatement of liability" exists if, viewing the return or claim for refund as a whole, there is an understatement of the net amount payable with respect to any tax imposed by the Internal Revenue Code (Code), or an overstatement of the net amount creditable or refundable with respect to any tax imposed by the Code. The net amount payable in a taxable year with respect to the return for which the tax return preparer engaged in conduct proscribed by section 6694 is not reduced by any carryback. Tax imposed by the Code does not include additions to the tax, additional amounts, and assessable penalties imposed by subchapter 68 of the Code. Except as provided in paragraph (d) of this section, the determination of whether an understatement of liability exists may be made in a proceeding involving the tax return preparer that is separate and apart from any proceeding involving the taxpayer.

(d) *Abatement of penalty where taxpayer's liability not understated.*—If a penalty under section 6694(a) or (b) concerning a return or claim for refund has been assessed against one or more tax return preparers, and if it is established at any time in a final administrative determination or a final judicial decision that there was no understatement of liability relating to the position(s) on the return or claim for refund, then—

(1) The assessment shall be abated; and

(2) If any amount of the penalty was paid, that amount shall be refunded to the person or persons who so paid, as if the payment were an overpayment of tax, without consideration of any period of limitations.

(e) *Verification of information furnished by taxpayer or other party.*—(1) *In general.*—For purposes of sections 6694(a) and (b) (including demonstrating that a position complied with relevant standards under section 6694(a) and demonstrating reasonable cause and good faith under § 1.6694-2(e)), the tax return preparer generally may rely in good faith without verification upon information furnished by the taxpayer. A tax return preparer also may rely in good faith and without verification upon information and advice furnished by another advisor, another tax return preparer or other party (including another advisor or tax return preparer at the tax return preparer's firm). The tax return preparer is not required to audit, examine or review books and records, business operations, documents, or other evidence to verify independently information provided by the taxpayer, advisor, other tax return preparer, or other party. The tax return preparer, however, may not ignore the implications of information furnished to the tax return preparer or actually known by the tax return preparer. The tax return preparer must make reasonable inquiries if the information as furnished appears to be incorrect or incomplete. Additionally, some provisions of the Code or regulations require that specific facts and circumstances exist (for example, that the taxpayer maintain specific documents) before a deduction or credit may be claimed. The tax return preparer must make appropriate inquiries to determine the existence of facts and circumstances required by a Code section or regulation as a condition of the claiming of a deduction or credit.

(2) *Verification of information on previously filed returns.*—For purposes of section 6694(a) and (b) (including meeting the reasonable to believe that the position would more likely than not be sustained on its merits and reasonable basis standards in §§ 1.6694-2(b) and (d)(2), and demonstrating reasonable cause and good faith under § 1.6694-2(e)), a tax return preparer may rely in good faith without verification upon a tax return that has been previously prepared by a taxpayer or another tax return preparer and filed with the IRS. For example, a tax return preparer who prepares an amended return (including a claim for refund) need not verify the positions on the original return. The tax return preparer, however, may not ignore the implications of information furnished to the tax return preparer or actually known by the tax return preparer. The tax return preparer must make reasonable inquiries if the information as furnished appears to be incorrect or incomplete. The tax return preparer must confirm that the position being relied upon has not been adjusted by examination or otherwise.

(3) *Examples.*—The provisions of this paragraph (e) are illustrated by the following examples:

Example 1. During an interview conducted by Preparer E, a taxpayer stated that he had made a charitable contribution of real estate in the amount of $50,000 during the tax year, when in fact he had not made this charitable contribution. E did not inquire about the existence of a qualified appraisal or complete a Form 8283, Noncash Charitable Contributions, in accordance with the reporting and substantiation requirements under section 170(f)(11). E reported a deduction on the tax return for the charitable contribution, which resulted in an understatement of liability for tax, and signed the tax return as the tax return preparer. E is subject to a penalty under section 6694.

Example 2. While preparing the 2008 tax return for an individual taxpayer, Preparer F realizes that the taxpayer did not provide a Form 1099-INT, "Interest Income", for a bank account that produced significant taxable income in 2007. When F inquired about any other income, the taxpayer furnished the Form 1099-INT to F for use in preparation of the 2008 tax return. F did not know that the taxpayer owned an additional bank account that generated taxable income for 2008, and the taxpayer did not reveal this information to the tax return preparer notwithstanding F's general inquiry about any other income. F signed the taxpayer's return as the tax return preparer. F is not subject to a penalty under section 6694.

Example 3. In preparing a tax return, for purposes of determining the deductibility of a contribution by an employer for a qualified pension plan, Accountant G relies on a computation of the section 404 limit on deductible amounts made by the enrolled actuary for the plan. On the basis of this calculation, G completed and signed the tax return. It is later determined that there is an understatement of liability for tax that resulted from the overstatement of the section 404 limit on deductible amounts made by the actuary. G had no reason to believe that the actuary's calculation of the limit on deductible contributions was incorrect or incomplete, and the calculation appeared reasonable on its face. G was also not aware at the time the return was prepared of any reason why the actuary did not know all of the relevant facts or that the calculation of the limit on deductible contributions was no longer reliable due to developments in the law since the time the calculation was given. G is not subject to a penalty under section 6694. The actuary, however, may be subject to penalty under section 6694 if the calculation provided by the actuary constitutes a substantial portion of the tax return within the meaning of §301.7701-15(b)(3) of this chapter.

(f) *Income derived (or to be derived) with respect to the return or claim for refund.*—(1) *In general.*—For purposes of sections 6694(a) and (b), *income derived (or to be derived)* means all compensation the tax return preparer receives or expects to receive with respect to the engagement of preparing the return or claim for refund or providing tax advice (including research and consultation) with respect to the position(s) taken on the return or claim for refund that gave rise to the understatement. In the situation of a tax return preparer who is not compensated directly by the taxpayer, but rather by a firm that employs the tax return preparer or with which the tax return preparer is associated, *income derived (or to be derived)* means all compensation the tax return preparer receives from the firm that can be reasonably allocated to the engagement of preparing the return or claim for refund or providing tax advice (including research and consultation) with respect to the position(s) taken on the return or claim for refund that gave rise to the understatement. In the situation where a firm that employs the individual tax return preparer (or the firm of which the individual tax return preparer is a partner, member, shareholder, or other equity holder) is subject to a penalty under section 6694(a) or (b) pursuant to the provisions in §§1.6694-2(a)(2) or 1.6694-3(a)(2), *income derived (or to be derived)* means all compensation the firm receives or expects to receive with respect to the engagement of preparing the return or claim for refund or providing tax advice (including research and consultation) with respect to the position(s) taken on the return or claim for refund that gave rise to the understatement.

(2) *Compensation.*—(i) *Multiple engagements.*—For purposes of applying paragraph (f)(1) of this section, if the tax return preparer or the tax return preparer's firm has multiple engagements related to the same return or claim for refund, only those engagements relating to the position(s) taken on the return or claim for refund that gave rise to the understatement are considered for purposes of calculating the income derived (or to be derived) with respect to the return or claim for refund.

(ii) *Reasonable allocation.*—For purposes of applying paragraph (f)(1) of this section, only compensation for tax advice that is given with respect to events that have occurred at the time the advice is rendered and that relates to the position(s) giving rise to the understatement will be taken into account for purposes of calculating the section 6694(a) and (b) penalties. If a lump sum fee is received that includes amounts not taken into account under the preceding sentence, the amount of income derived will be based on a reasonable allocation of the lump sum fee between the tax advice giving rise to the penalty and the advice that does not give rise to the penalty.

(iii) *Fee refunds.*—For purposes of applying paragraph (f)(1) of this section, a refund to the taxpayer of all or part of the amount paid to the tax return preparer or the tax return preparer's firm will not reduce the amount of the section 6694 penalty assessed. A refund in this context does not include a discounted fee or alternative billing arrangement for the services provided.

(iv) *Reduction of compensation.*—For purposes of applying paragraph (f)(1) of this section, it may be concluded based upon information provided by the tax return preparer or the tax return preparer's firm that an appropriate allocation of compensation attributable to the position(s) giving rise to the understatement on the return or claim for refund is less than the total amount of compensation associated with the engagement. For example, the number of hours of the engagement spent on the position(s) giving rise to the understatement may be less than the total hours associated with the engagement. If this is concluded, the amount of the penalty will be calculated based upon the compensation attributable to the position(s) giving rise to the understatement. Otherwise, the total amount of compensation from the engagement will be the amount of income derived for purposes of calculating the penalty under section 6694.

(3) *Individual and firm allocation.*—If both an individual within a firm and a firm that employs the individual (or the firm of which the individual is a partner, member, shareholder, or other equity holder) are subject to a penalty under section 6694(a) or (b) pursuant to the provisions in §§1.6694-2(a)(2) or 1.6694-3(a)(2), the amount of penalties assessed against the individual and the firm shall not exceed 50 percent of the income derived (or to be derived) by the firm from the engagement of preparing the return or claim for refund or providing tax advice (including research and consultation) with respect to the position(s) taken on the return or claim for refund that gave rise to the understatement. The portion of the total amount of the penalty assessed against the individual tax return preparer shall not exceed 50 percent of the individual's compensation as determined under paragraphs (f)(1) and (2) of this section.

(4) *Examples.*—The provisions of this paragraph (f) are illustrated by the following examples:

Example 1. Signing Tax Return Preparer H is engaged by a taxpayer and paid a total of $21,000. Of this amount, $20,000 relates to research and consultation regarding a transaction that is later reported on a return, and $1,000 is for the activities relating to the preparation of the return. Based on H's hourly rates, a reasonable allocation of the amount of compensation related to the advice rendered prior to the occurrence of events that are the subject of the advice is $5,000. The remaining compensation of $16,000 is considered to be compensation related to the advice rendered after the occurrence of events that are the subject of the advice and return preparation. The income derived by H with respect to the return for purposes of computing the penalty under section 6694(a) is $16,000, and the amount of the penalty imposed under section 6694(a) is $8,000.

Example 2. Accountants I, J, and K are employed by Firm L. I is a principal manager of Firm L and provides corporate tax advice for the taxpayer after all events have occurred subject to an engagement for corporate tax advice. J provides international tax advice for the taxpayer after all events have occurred subject to a different engagement for international tax advice. K prepares and signs the taxpayer's return under a general tax services engagement. I's advice is the source of an understatement on the return and the advice constitutes preparation of a substantial portion of the return within the meaning of §301.7701-15(b) of this chapter. I is the nonsigning tax return preparer within the firm with overall supervisory responsibility for the position on the taxpayer's return giving rise to an understatement. Thus, I is the tax return preparer who is primarily responsible for the position on the taxpayer's return giving rise to the understatement. Because K's signature as the signing tax return preparer is on the return, the IRS advises K that K may be subject to the section 6694(a) penalty. K provides credible information that I is the tax return preparer with primary responsibility for the position that gave rise to the understatement. The IRS, therefore, assesses the section 6694 penalty against I. The portion of the total amount of the penalty allocable to I does not exceed 50 percent of that part of I's compensation that is attributable to the corporate tax advice engagement. In the event that Firm L is also liable under the provisions in §1.6694-2(a)(2), the IRS assesses the section 6694 penalty in an amount not exceeding 50 percent of Firm L's firm compensation based on the engagement relating to the corporate tax advice services provided by I where there is no applicable reduction in compensation pursuant to §1.6694-1(f)(2)(iii).

Example 3. Same facts as *Example 2,* except that I provides the advice on the corporate matter when the events have not yet occurred. I's advice is the cause of an understatement position on the return, but I is not a tax return preparer pursuant to §301.7701-15(b)(2) or (3) of this chapter. K is not limited to reliance on persons who provide post-transactional advice if such reliance is reasonable and in good faith. Further, K has reasonable cause because K relied on I for the advice on the corporate tax matter. I, K and Firm L are not liable for the section 6694 penalty.

Example 4. Attorney M is an employee of Firm N with a salary of $75,000 per year. M performs tax preparation work for Client O. Client O's return contains a position that results in an understatement subject to the section 6694 penalty. M spent 100 hours on the position (out of a total 2,000 billed during the year). The total fees earned by Firm N with respect to the position reflected on Client O's return are $50,000. If M is subject to the penalty, the penalty amount computed under the 50 percent of income standard is .5 × (100/2000) × $75,000 = $1,875. If Firm N is subject to the penalty, the penalty amount computed under the 50% of income standard is .5 × $50,000 = $25,000, less any penalty amount imposed against M. If a penalty of $1,875 was assessed against M and Firm N was subject to the penalty, a penalty of $23,125 would be the amount of penalty assessed against Firm N.

(g) *Effective/applicability date.*—This section is applicable to returns and claims for refund filed, and advice provided, after December 31, 2008. [Reg. §1.6694-1.]

☐ [*T.D.* 7519. *Amended by T.D.* 7572, 11-15-78; *T.D.* 8382, 12-30-91 *and T.D.* 9436, 12-15-2008 (*corrected* 1-28-2009).]

[Reg. §20.6694-1]

§20.6694-1. Section 6694 penalties applicable to tax return preparer.—(a) *In general.*—For general definitions regarding section 6694 penalties applicable to preparers of estate tax returns or claims for refund, see §1.6694-1 of this chapter.

(b) *Effective/applicability date.*—Paragraph (a) of this section is applicable to returns and claims for refund filed, and advice provided, after December 31, 2008. [Reg. § 20.6694-1.]

☐ [*T.D.* 9436, 12-15-2008 (*corrected* 1-28-2009).]

[Reg. § 25.6694-1]

§ 25.6694-1. Section 6694 penalties applicable to tax return preparer.—(a) *In general.*—For general definitions regarding section 6694 penalties applicable to preparers of gift tax returns or claims for refund, see § 1.6694-1 of this chapter.

(b) *Effective/applicability date.*—Paragraph (a) of this section is applicable to returns and claims for refund filed, and advice provided, after December 31, 2008. [Reg. § 25.6694-1.]

☐ [*T.D.* 9436, 12-15-2008 (*corrected* 1-28-2009).]

[Reg. § 26.6694-1]

§ 26.6694-1. Section 6694 penalties applicable to tax return preparer.—(a) *In general.*—For general definitions regarding section 6694 penalties applicable to preparers of generation-skipping transfer tax returns or claims for refund, see § 1.6694-1 of this chapter.

(b) *Effective/applicability date.*—Paragraph (a) of this section is applicable to returns and claims for refund filed, and advice provided, after December 31, 2008. [Reg. § 26.6694-1.]

☐ [*T.D.* 9436, 12-15-2008 (*corrected* 1-28-2009).]

[Reg. § 1.6694-2]

§ 1.6694-2. Penalty for understatement due to an unreasonable position.—(a) *In general.*—(1) *Proscribed conduct.*—Except as otherwise provided in this section, a tax return preparer is liable for a penalty under section 6694(a) equal to the greater of $1,000 or 50 percent of the income derived (or to be derived) by the tax return preparer for any return or claim for refund that it prepares that results in an understatement of liability due to a position if the tax return preparer knew (or reasonably should have known) of the position and either—

(i) The position is with respect to a tax shelter (as defined in section 6662(d)(2)(C)(ii)) or a reportable transaction to which section 6662A applies, and it was not reasonable to believe that the position would more likely than not be sustained on its merits;

(ii) The position was not disclosed as provided in this section, the position is not with respect to a tax shelter (as defined in section 6662(d)(2)(C)(ii)) or a reportable transaction to which section 6662A applies, and there was not substantial authority for the position; or

(iii) The position (other than a position with respect to a tax shelter or a reportable transaction to which section 6662A applies) was disclosed as provided in this section but there was no reasonable basis for the position.

(2) *Special rule for corporations, partnerships, and other firms.*—A firm that employs a tax return preparer subject to a penalty under section 6694(a) (or a firm of which the individual tax return preparer is a partner, member, shareholder or other equity holder) is also subject to penalty if, and only if—

(i) One or more members of the principal management (or principal officers) of the firm or a branch office participated in or knew of the conduct proscribed by section 6694(a);

(ii) The corporation, partnership, or other firm entity failed to provide reasonable and appropriate procedures for review of the position for which the penalty is imposed; or

(iii) The corporation, partnership, or other firm entity disregarded its reasonable and appropriate review procedures through willfulness, recklessness, or gross indifference (including ignoring facts that would lead a person of reasonable prudence and competence to investigate or ascertain) in the formulation of the advice, or the preparation of the return or claim for refund, that included the position for which the penalty is imposed.

(b) *Reasonable to believe that the position would more likely than not be sustained on its merits.*—(1) *In general.*—If a position is with respect to a tax shelter (as defined in section 6662(d)(2)(C)(ii)) or a reportable transaction to which section 6662A applies, it is "reasonable to believe that a position would more likely than not be sustained on its merits" if the tax return preparer analyzes the pertinent facts and authorities and, in reliance upon that analysis, reasonably concludes in good faith that the position has a greater than 50 percent likelihood of being sustained on its merits. In reaching this conclusion, the possibility that the position will not be challenged by the Internal Revenue Service (IRS) (for example, because the taxpayer's return may not be audited or because the issue may not be raised on audit) is not to be taken into account. The analysis prescribed by § 1.6662-4(d)(3)(ii) (or any successor provision) for purposes of determining whether substantial authority is present applies for purposes of determining whether the more likely than not standard is satisfied. Whether a tax return preparer meets this standard will be determined based upon all facts and circumstances, including the tax return preparer's diligence. In determining the level of diligence in a particular situation, the tax return preparer's experience with the area of Federal tax law and familiarity with the taxpayer's affairs, as well as the complexity of the issues and facts, will be taken into account. A tax return preparer may reasonably believe that a position more likely than not would be sustained on its merits despite the absence of other types of authority if the position is supported by a well-reasoned construction of the applicable statutory provision. For purposes of determining whether it is reasonable to believe that the position would more likely than not be sustained on the merits, a tax return preparer may rely in good faith without verification upon information furnished by the taxpayer and information and advice furnished by another advisor, another tax return preparer, or other party (including another advisor or tax return preparer at the tax return preparer's firm), as provided in §§ 1.6694-1(e) and 1.6694-2(e)(5).

(2) *Authorities.*—The authorities considered in determining whether a position satisfies the more likely than not standard are those authorities provided in § 1.6662-4(d)(3)(iii) (or any successor provision).

(3) *Written determinations.*—The tax return preparer may avoid the section 6694(a) penalty by taking the position that the tax return preparer reasonably believed that the taxpayer's position satisfies the "more likely than not" standard if the taxpayer is the subject of a "written determination" as provided in § 1.6662-4(d)(3)(iv)(A).

(4) *Taxpayer's jurisdiction.*—The applicability of court cases to the taxpayer by reason of the taxpayer's residence in a particular jurisdiction is not taken into account in determining whether it is reasonable to believe that the position would more likely than not be sustained on the merits. Notwithstanding the preceding sentence, the tax return preparer may reasonably believe that the position would more likely than not be sustained on the merits if the position is supported by controlling precedent of a United States Court of Appeals to which the taxpayer has a right of appeal with respect to the item.

(5) *When "more likely than not" standard must be satisfied.*—For purposes of this section, the requirement that a position satisfies the "more likely than not" standard must be satisfied on the date the return is deemed prepared, as prescribed by § 1.6694-1(a)(2).

(c) [Reserved].

(d) *Exception for adequate disclosure of positions with a reasonable basis.*—(1) *In general.*—The section 6694(a) penalty will not be imposed on a tax return preparer if the position taken (other than a position with respect to a tax shelter or a reportable transaction to which section 6662A applies) has a reasonable basis and is adequately disclosed within the meaning of paragraph (c)(3) of this section. For an exception to the section 6694(a) penalty for reasonable cause and good faith, see paragraph (e) of this section.

(2) *Reasonable basis.*—For purposes of this section, "reasonable basis" has the same meaning as in § 1.6662-3(b)(3) or any successor provision of the accuracy-related penalty regulations. For purposes of determining whether the tax return preparer has a reasonable basis for a position, a tax return preparer may rely in good faith without verification upon information furnished by the taxpayer and information and advice furnished by another advisor, another tax return preparer, or other party (including another advisor or tax return preparer at the tax return preparer's firm), as provided in §§ 1.6694-1(e) and 1.6694-2(e)(5).

(3) *Adequate disclosure.*—(i) *Signing tax return preparers.*—In the case of a signing tax return preparer within the meaning of § 301.7701-15(b)(1) of this chapter, disclosure of a position (other than a position with respect to a tax shelter or a reportable transaction to which section 6662A applies) for which there is a reasonable basis but for which there is not substantial authority is adequate if the tax return preparer meets any of the following standards:

(A) The position is disclosed in accordance with § 1.6662-4(f) (which permits disclosure on a properly completed and filed Form 8275, "Disclosure Statement," or Form 8275-R, "Regulation Disclosure Statement," as appropriate, or on the tax return in accordance with the annual revenue procedure described in § 1.6662-4(f)(2));

(B) The tax return preparer provides the taxpayer with the prepared tax return that includes the disclosure in accordance with § 1.6662-4(f); or

(C) For returns or claims for refund that are subject to penalties pursuant to section 6662 other than the accuracy-related penalty attributable to a substantial understatement of income tax under section 6662(b)(2) and (d), the tax return preparer advises the taxpayer of the penalty standards applicable to the taxpayer under section 6662. The tax return preparer must also contemporaneously document the advice in the tax return preparer's files.

(ii) *Nonsigning tax return preparers.*—In the case of a nonsigning tax return preparer within the meaning of § 301.7701-15(b)(2) of this chapter, disclosure of a position (other than a position with respect to a tax shelter or a reportable transaction to which section 6662A applies) that satisfies the reasonable basis standard but does not satisfy the substantial authority standard is adequate if the position is disclosed in accordance with § 1.6662-4(f) (which permits disclosure on a properly completed and filed Form 8275 or Form 8275-R, as applicable, or on the return in accordance with an annual revenue procedure described in § 1.6662-4(f)(2)). In addition, disclosure of a position is adequate in the case of a nonsigning tax return preparer if, with respect to that position, the tax return preparer complies with the provisions of paragraph (d)(3)(ii)(A) or (B) of this section, whichever is applicable.

(A) *Advice to taxpayers.*—If a nonsigning tax return preparer provides advice to the taxpayer with respect to a position (other than a position with respect to a tax shelter or a reportable transaction to which section 6662A applies) for which there is a reasonable basis but for which there is not substantial authority, disclosure of that position is adequate if the tax return preparer advises the taxpayer of any opportunity to avoid penalties under section 6662 that could apply to the position, if relevant, and of the standards for disclosure to the extent applicable. The tax return preparer must also contemporaneously document the advice in the tax return preparer's files. The contemporaneous documentation should reflect that the affected taxpayer has been advised by a tax return preparer in the firm of the potential penalties and the opportunity to avoid penalty through disclosure.

(B) *Advice to another tax return preparer.*—If a nonsigning tax return preparer provides advice to another tax return preparer with respect to a position (other than a position with respect to a tax shelter or a reportable transaction to which section 6662A applies) for which there is a reasonable basis but for which there is not substantial authority, disclosure of that position is adequate if the tax return preparer advises the other tax return preparer that disclosure under section 6694(a) may be required. The tax return preparer must also contemporaneously document the advice in the tax return preparer's files. The contemporaneous documentation should reflect that the tax return preparer outside the firm has been advised that disclosure under section 6694(a) may be required. If the advice is to another nonsigning tax return preparer within the same firm, contemporaneous documentation is satisfied if there is a single instance of contemporaneous documentation within the firm.

(iii) *Requirements for advice.*—For purposes of satisfying the disclosure standards of paragraphs (d)(3)(i)(C) and (ii) of this section, each return position for which there is a reasonable basis but for which there is not substantial authority must be addressed by the tax return preparer. The advice to the taxpayer with respect to each position, therefore, must be particular to the taxpayer and tailored to the taxpayer's facts and circumstances. The tax return preparer is required to contemporaneously document the fact that the advice was provided. There is no general pro forma language or special format required for a tax return preparer to comply with these rules. A general disclaimer will not satisfy the requirement that the tax return preparer provide and contemporaneously document advice regarding the likelihood that a position will be sustained on the merits and the potential application of penalties as a result of that position. Tax return preparers, however, may rely on established forms or templates in advising clients regarding the operation of the penalty provisions of the Internal Revenue Code. A tax return preparer may choose to comply with the documentation standard in one document addressing each position or in multiple documents addressing all of the positions.

(iv) *Pass-through entities.*—Disclosure in the case of items attributable to a pass-through entity is adequate if made at the entity level in accordance with the rules in § 1.6662-4(f)(5) or at the entity level in accordance with the rules in paragraphs (d)(3)(i) or (ii) of this section.

(v) *Examples.*—The provisions of paragraph (d)(3) of this section are illustrated by the following examples:

Example 1. An individual taxpayer hires Accountant R to prepare its income tax return. A particular position taken on the tax return does not have substantial authority although there is a reasonable basis for the position. The position is not with respect to a tax shelter or a reportable transaction to which section 6662A applies. R prepares and signs the tax return and provides the taxpayer with the prepared tax return that includes the Form 8275, "Disclosure Statement," disclosing the position taken on the tax return. The individual taxpayer signs and files the tax return without disclosing the position. The IRS later challenges the position taken on the tax return, resulting in an understatement of liability. R is not subject to a penalty under section 6694.

Example 2. Attorney S advises a large corporate taxpayer concerning the proper treatment of complex entries on the corporate taxpayer's tax return. S has reason to know that the tax attributable to the entries is a substantial portion of the tax required to be shown on the tax return within the meaning of § 301.7701-15(b)(3). When providing the advice, S concludes that one position does not have substantial authority, although the position meets the reasonable basis standard. The position is not with respect to a tax shelter or a reportable transaction to which section 6662A applies. S advises the corporate taxpayer that the position lacks substantial authority and the taxpayer may be subject to an accuracy-related penalty under section 6662 unless the position is disclosed in a disclosure statement included in the return. S also documents the fact that this advice was contemporaneously provided to the corporate taxpayer at the time the advice was provided. Neither S nor any other attorney within S's firm signs the corporate taxpayer's return as a tax return preparer, but the advice by S constitutes preparation of a substantial portion of the tax return, and S is the individual with overall supervisory responsibility for the position giving rise to the understatement. Thus, S is a tax return preparer for purposes of section 6694. S, however, will not be subject to a penalty under section 6694.

(e) *Exception for reasonable cause and good faith.*—The penalty under section 6694(a) will not be imposed if, considering all the facts and circumstances, it is determined that the understatement was due to reasonable cause and that the tax return preparer acted in good faith. Factors to consider include:

(1) *Nature of the error causing the understatement.*—The error resulted from a provision that was complex, uncommon, or highly technical, and a competent tax return preparer of tax returns or claims for refund of the type at issue reasonably could have made the error. The reasonable cause and good faith exception, however, does not apply to an error that would have been apparent from a general review of the return or claim for refund by the tax return preparer.

(2) *Frequency of errors.*—The understatement was the result of an isolated error (such as an inadvertent mathematical or clerical error) rather than a number of errors. Although the reasonable cause and good faith exception generally applies to an isolated error, it does not apply if the isolated error is so obvious, flagrant, or material that it should have been discovered during a review of the return or claim for refund. Furthermore, the reasonable cause and good faith exception does not apply if there is a pattern of errors

on a return or claim for refund even though any one error, in isolation, would have qualified for the reasonable cause and good faith exception.

(3) *Materiality of errors.*—The understatement was not material in relation to the correct tax liability. The reasonable cause and good faith exception generally applies if the understatement is of a relatively immaterial amount. Nevertheless, even an immaterial understatement may not qualify for the reasonable cause and good faith exception if the error or errors creating the understatement are sufficiently obvious or numerous.

(4) *Tax return preparer's normal office practice.*—The tax return preparer's normal office practice, when considered together with other facts and circumstances, such as the knowledge of the tax return preparer, indicates that the error in question would occur rarely and the normal office practice was followed in preparing the return or claim for refund in question. Such a normal office practice must be a system for promoting accuracy and consistency in the preparation of returns or claims for refund and generally would include, in the case of a signing tax return preparer, checklists, methods for obtaining necessary information from the taxpayer, a review of the prior year's return, and review procedures. Notwithstanding these rules, the reasonable cause and good faith exception does not apply if there is a flagrant error on a return or claim for refund, a pattern of errors on a return or claim for refund, or a repetition of the same or similar errors on numerous returns or claims for refund.

(5) *Reliance on advice of others.*—For purposes of demonstrating reasonable cause and good faith, a tax return preparer may rely without verification upon advice and information furnished by the taxpayer and information and advice furnished by another advisor, another tax return preparer or other party, as provided in § 1.6694-1(e). The tax return preparer may rely in good faith on the advice of, or schedules or other documents prepared by, the taxpayer, another advisor, another tax return preparer, or other party (including another advisor or tax return preparer at the tax return preparer's firm), who the tax return preparer had reason to believe was competent to render the advice or other information. The advice or information may be written or oral, but in either case the burden of establishing that the advice or information was received is on the tax return preparer. A tax return preparer is not considered to have relied in good faith if—

(i) The advice or information is unreasonable on its face;

(ii) The tax return preparer knew or should have known that the other party providing the advice or information was not aware of all relevant facts; or

(iii) The tax return preparer knew or should have known (given the nature of the tax return preparer's practice), at the time the return or claim for refund was prepared, that the advice or information was no longer reliable due to developments in the law since the time the advice was given.

(6) *Reliance on generally accepted administrative or industry practice.*—The tax return preparer reasonably relied in good faith on generally accepted administrative or industry practice in taking the position that resulted in the understatement. A tax return preparer is not considered to have relied in good faith if the tax return preparer knew or should have known (given the nature of the tax return preparer's practice), at the time the return or claim for refund was prepared, that the administrative or industry practice was no longer reliable due to developments in the law or IRS administrative practice since the time the practice was developed.

(f) *Effective/applicability date.*—This section is applicable to returns and claims for refund filed, and advice provided, after December 31, 2008. [Reg. § 1.6694-2.]

☐ [*T.D.* 7519, 11-17-77. *Amended by T.D.* 8382, 12-30-91 *and T.D.* 9436, 12-15-2008 (*corrected* 1-28-2009).]

[Reg. § 20.6694-2]

§ 20.6694-2. Penalties for understatement due to an unreasonable position.—(a) *In general.*—A person who is a tax return preparer of any return or claim for refund of estate tax under chapter 11 of subtitle B of the Internal Revenue Code (Code) shall be subject to penalties under section 6694(a) of the Code in the manner stated in § 1.6694-2 of this chapter.

(b) *Effective/applicability date.*—This section is applicable to returns and claims for refund filed, and advice provided, after December 31, 2008. [Reg. § 20.6694-2.]

☐ [*T.D.* 9436, 12-15-2008.]

[Reg. § 25.6694-2]

§ 25.6694-2. Penalties for understatement due to an unreasonable position.—(a) *In general.*—A person who is a tax return preparer of any return or claim for refund of gift tax under chapter 12 of subtitle B of the Internal Revenue Code (Code) shall be subject to penalties under section 6694(a) of the Code in the manner stated in § 1.6694-2 of this chapter.

(b) *Effective/applicability date.*—This section is applicable to returns and claims for refund filed, and advice provided, after December 31, 2008. [Reg. § 25.6694-2.]

☐ [*T.D.* 9436, 12-15-2008.]

[Reg. § 26.6694-2]

§ 26.6694-2. Penalties for understatement due to an unreasonable position.—(a) *In general.*—A person who is a tax return preparer of any return or claim for refund of generationskipping transfer tax under chapter 13 of subtitle B of the Internal Revenue Code (Code) shall be subject to penalties under section 6694(a) of the Code in the manner stated in § 1.6694-2 of this chapter.

(b) *Effective/applicability date.*—This section is applicable to returns and claims for refund filed, and advice provided, after December 31, 2008. [Reg. § 26.6694-2.]

☐ [*T.D.* 9436, 12-15-2008.]

[Reg. § 1.6694-3]

§ 1.6694-3. Penalty for understatement due to willful, reckless, or intentional conduct.—(a) *In general.*—(1) *Proscribed conduct.*—A tax return preparer is liable for a penalty under section 6694(b) equal to the greater of $5,000 or 50 percent of the income derived (or to be derived) by the tax return preparer if any part of an understatement of liability for a return or claim for refund that is prepared is due to—

(i) A willful attempt by a tax return preparer to understate in any manner the liability for tax on the return or claim for refund; or

(ii) Any reckless or intentional disregard of rules or regulations by a tax return preparer.

(2) *Special rule for corporations, partnerships, and other firms.*—A firm that employs a tax return preparer subject to a penalty under section 6694(b) (or a firm of which the individual tax return preparer is a partner, member, shareholder or other equity holder) is also subject to penalty if, and only if—

(i) One or more members of the principal management (or principal officers) of the firm or a branch office participated in or knew of the conduct proscribed by section 6694(b);

(ii) The corporation, partnership, or other firm entity failed to provide reasonable and appropriate procedures for review of the position for which the penalty is imposed; or

(iii) The corporation, partnership, or other firm entity disregarded its reasonable and appropriate review procedures through willfulness, recklessness, or gross indifference (including ignoring facts that would lead a person of reasonable prudence and competence to investigate or ascertain) in the formulation of the advice, or the preparation of the return or claim for refund, that included the position for which the penalty is imposed.

(b) *Willful attempt to understate liability.*—A preparer is considered to have willfully attempted to understate liability if the preparer disregards, in an attempt wrongfully to reduce the tax liability of the taxpayer, information furnished by the taxpayer or other persons. For example, if a preparer disregards information concerning certain items of taxable income furnished by the taxpayer or other persons, the preparer is subject to the penalty. Similarly, if a taxpayer states to a preparer that the taxpayer has only two dependents, and the preparer reports six dependents on the return, the preparer is subject to the penalty.

(c) *Reckless or intentional disregard.*—(1) Except as provided in paragraphs (c)(2) and (c)(3) of this section, a preparer is considered to have recklessly or intentionally disregarded a rule or regulation if the preparer takes a position on the return or claim for refund that is contrary to a rule or regulation (as defined in paragraph (f) of this section) and the preparer knows of, or is reckless in not knowing of, the rule or regulation in question. A preparer is reckless in not knowing of a rule or regulation if the preparer makes little or no effort to determine whether a rule or regulation exists, under circumstances which demonstrate a substantial deviation from the standard of conduct that a reasonable preparer would observe in the situation.

(2) A tax return preparer is not considered to have recklessly or intentionally disregarded a rule or regulation if the position contrary to the rule or regulation has a reasonable basis as defined in § 1.6694-2(d)(2) and is adequately disclosed in accordance with §§ 1.6694-2(d)(3)(i)(A) or (C) or 1.6694-2(d)(3)(ii). In the case of a position contrary to a regulation, the position must represent a good faith challenge to the validity of the regulation and, when disclosed in accordance with §§ 1.6694-2(d)(3)(i)(A) or (C) or 1.6694-2(d)(3)(ii), the tax return preparer must identify the regulation being challenged. For purposes of this section, disclosure on the return in accordance with an annual revenue procedure under § 1.6662-4(f)(2) is not applicable.

(3) In the case of a position contrary to a revenue ruling or notice (other than a notice of proposed rulemaking) published by the Internal Revenue Service in the Internal Revenue Bulletin, a tax return preparer also is not considered to have recklessly or intentionally disregarded the ruling or notice if the position meets the substantial authority standard described in § 1.6662-4(d) and is not with respect to a reportable transaction to which section 6662A applies.

(d) *Examples.*—The provisions of paragraphs (b) and (c) of this section are illustrated by the following examples:

Example 1. A taxpayer provided Preparer T with detailed check registers reflecting personal and business expenses. One of the expenses was for domestic help, and this expense was identified as personal on the check register. T knowingly deducted the expenses of the taxpayer's domestic help as wages paid in the taxpayer's business. T is subject to the penalty under section 6694(b).

Example 2. A taxpayer provided Preparer U with detailed check registers to compute the taxpayer's expenses. U, however, knowingly overstated the expenses on the return. After adjustments by the examiner, the tax liability increased significantly. Because U disregarded information provided in the check registers, U is subject to the penalty under section 6694(b).

Example 3. Preparer V prepares a taxpayer's return in 2009 and encounters certain expenses incurred in the purchase of a business. Final regulations provide that such expenses incurred in the purchase of a business must be capitalized. One U.S. Tax Court case decided in 2006 has expressly invalidated that portion of the regulations. There are no courts that ruled favorably with respect to the validity of that portion of the regulations and there are no other authorities existing on the issue. Under these facts, V will have a reasonable basis for the position as defined in § 1.6694-2(d)(2) and will not be subject to the section 6694(b) penalty if the position is adequately disclosed in accordance with paragraph (c)(2) of this section because the position represents a good faith challenge to the validity of the regulations.

(e) *Rules or regulations.*—The term *rules or regulations* includes the provisions of the Internal Revenue Code (Code), temporary or final Treasury regulations issued under the Code, and revenue rulings or notices (other than notices of proposed rulemaking) issued by the Internal Revenue Service and published in the Internal Revenue Bulletin.

(f) *Section 6694(b) penalty reduced by section 6694(a) penalty.*—The amount of any penalty to which a tax return preparer may be subject under section 6694(b) for a return or claim for refund is reduced by any amount assessed and collected against the tax return preparer under section 6694(a) for the same position on a return or claim for refund.

(g) *Effective/applicability date.*—This section is applicable to returns and claims for refund filed, and advice provided, after December 31, 2008.

(h) *Burden of proof.*—In any proceeding with respect to the penalty imposed by section 6694(b), the Government bears the burden of proof on the issue of whether the preparer willfully attempted to understate the liability for tax. See section 7427. The preparer bears the burden of proof on such other issues as whether—

(1) The preparer recklessly or intentionally disregarded a rule or regulation;

(2) A position contrary to a regulation represents a good faith challenge to the validity of the regulation; and

(3) Disclosure was adequately made in accordance with paragraph (e) of this section. [Reg. § 1.6694-3.]

☐ [*T.D.* 8382, 12-30-91. *Amended by T.D.* 9436, 12-15-2008 (*corrected* 1-28-2009).]

[Reg. § 20.6694-3]

§ 20.6694-3. Penalty for understatement due to willful, reckless, or intentional conduct.—(a) *In general.*—A person who is a tax return preparer of any return or claim for refund of estate tax under chapter 11 of subtitle B of the Internal Revenue Code (Code) shall be subject to penalties under section 6694(b) of the Code in the manner stated in § 1.6694-3 of this chapter.

(b) *Effective/applicability date.*—This section is applicable to returns and claims for refund filed, and advice provided, after December 31, 2008. [Reg. § 20.6694-3.]

☐ [*T.D.* 9436, 12-15-2008.]

[Reg. § 25.6694-3]

§ 25.6694-3. Penalty for understatement due to willful, reckless, or intentional conduct.—(a) *In general.*—A person who is a tax return preparer of any return or claim for refund of gift tax under chapter 12 of subtitle B of the Internal Revenue Code (Code) shall be subject to penalties under section 6694(b) of the Code in the manner stated in § 1.6694-3 of this chapter.

(b) *Effective/applicability date.*—This section is applicable to returns and claims for refund filed, and advice provided, after December 31, 2008. [Reg. § 25.6694-3.]

☐ [*T.D.* 9436, 12-15-2008.]

[Reg. § 26.6694-3]

§ 26.6694-3. Penalty for understatement due to willful, reckless, or intentional conduct.—(a) *In general.*—A person who is a tax return preparer of any return or claim for refund of generation-skipping transfer tax under chapter 13 of subtitle B of the Internal Revenue Code (Code) shall be subject to penalties under section 6694(b) of the Code in the manner stated in § 1.6694-3 of this chapter.

(b) *Effective/applicability date.*—This section is applicable to returns and claims for refund filed, and advice provided, after December 31, 2008. [Reg. § 26.6694-3.]

☐ [*T.D.* 9436, 12-15-2008.]

[Reg. § 1.6694-4]

§ 1.6694-4. Extension of period of collection when tax return preparer pays 15 percent of a penalty for understatement of taxpayer's liability and certain other procedural matters.—(a) *In general.*—(1) The Internal Revenue Service (IRS) will investigate the preparation by a tax return preparer of a return of tax under the Internal Revenue Code (Code) or claim for refund of tax under the Code as described in § 301.7701-15(b)(4) of this chapter, and will send a report of the examination to the tax return preparer before the assessment of either—

(i) A penalty for understating tax liability due to a position for which either it was not reasonable to believe that the position would more likely than not be sustained on its merits under section 6694(a) or no substantial authority, as applicable (or not a reasonable basis for disclosed positions); or

(ii) A penalty for willful understatement of liability or reckless or intentional disregard of rules or regulations under section 6694(b).

(2) Unless the period of limitations (if any) under section 6696(d) may expire without adequate opportunity for assessment, the IRS will also send, before assessment of either penalty, a 30-day letter to the tax return preparer notifying him of the proposed penalty or penalties and offering an opportunity to the tax return preparer to request further administrative consideration and a final administrative determination by the IRS concerning the assessment. If the tax return preparer then makes a timely request, assessment may not be made until the IRS makes a final administrative determination adverse to the tax return preparer.

(3) If the IRS assesses either of the two penalties described in section 6694(a) and section 6694(b), it will send to the tax return preparer a statement of notice and demand, separate from

any notice of a tax deficiency, for payment of the amount assessed.

(4) Within 30 days after the day on which notice and demand of either of the two penalties described in section 6694(a) and section 6694(b) is made against the tax return preparer, the tax return preparer must either—

(i) Pay the entire amount assessed (and may file a claim for refund of the amount paid at any time not later than 3 years after the date of payment); or

(ii) Pay an amount which is not less than 15 percent of the entire amount assessed with respect to each return or claim for refund and file a claim for refund of the amount paid.

(5) If the tax return preparer pays an amount and files a claim for refund under paragraph (a)(4)(ii) of this section, the IRS may not make, begin, or prosecute a levy or proceeding in court for collection of the unpaid remainder of the amount assessed until the later of—

(i) A date which is more than 30 days after the earlier of—

(A) The day on which the tax return preparer's claim for refund is denied; or

(B) The expiration of 6 months after the day on which the tax return preparer filed the claim for refund; and

(ii) Final resolution of any proceeding begun as provided in paragraph (b) of this section.

(6) The IRS may counterclaim in any proceeding begun as provided in paragraph (b) of this section for the unpaid remainder of the amount assessed. Final resolution of a proceeding includes any settlement between the IRS and the tax return preparer, any final determination by a court (for which the period for appeal, if any, has expired) and, generally, the types of determinations provided under section 1313(a) (relating to taxpayer deficiencies). Notwithstanding section 7421(a) (relating to suits to restrain assessment or collection), the beginning of a levy or proceeding in court by the IRS in contravention of paragraph (a)(5) of this section may be enjoined by a proceeding in the proper court.

(b) *Preparer must bring suit in district court to determine liability for penalty.*—The IRS may proceed with collection of the amount of the penalty not paid under paragraph (a)(4)(ii) of this section if the preparer fails to begin a proceeding for refund in the appropriate United States district court within 30 days after the earlier of—

(1) The day on which the preparer's claim for refund filed under paragraph (a)(4)(ii) of this section is denied; or

(2) The expiration of 6 months after the day on which the preparer filed the claim for refund.

(c) *Suspension of running of period of limitations on collection.*—The running of the period of limitations provided in section 6502 on the collection by levy or by a proceeding in court of the unpaid amount of a penalty or penalties described in section 6694(a) or section 6694(b) is suspended for the period during which the IRS, under paragraph (a)(5) of this section, may not collect the unpaid amount of the penalty or penalties by levy or a proceeding in court.

(d) *Effective/applicability date.*—This section is applicable to returns and claims for refund filed, and advice provided, after December 31, 2008. [Reg. § 1.6694-4.]

□ [*T.D.* 8382, 12-30-91. *Amended by T.D.* 9436, 12-15-2008.]

[Reg. § 20.6694-4]

§ 20.6694-4. Extension of period of collection when preparer pays 15 percent of a penalty for understatement of taxpayer's liability and certain other procedural matters.—(a) *In general.*—For rules relating to the extension of the period of collection when a tax return preparer who prepared a return or claim for refund for estate tax under chapter 11 of subtitle B of the Internal Revenue Code pays 15 percent of a penalty for understatement of the taxpayer's liability, and procedural matters relating to the investigation, assessment and collection of the penalties under sections 6694(a) and (b), the rules under § 1.6694-4 of this chapter will apply.

(b) *Effective/applicability date.*—This section is applicable to returns and claims for refund filed, and advice provided, after December 31, 2008. [Reg. § 20.6694-4.]

□ [*T.D.* 9436, 12-15-2008.]

[Reg. § 25.6694-4]

§ 25.6694-4. Extension of period of collection when tax return preparer pays 15 percent of a penalty for understatement of taxpayer's liability and certain other procedural matters.—(a) *In general.*—For rules for the extension of period of collection when a tax return preparer who prepared a return or claim for refund for gift tax under chapter 12 of subtitle B of the Internal Revenue Code pays 15 percent of a penalty for understatement of taxpayer's liability, and procedural matters relating to the investigation, assessment and collection of the penalties under section 6694(a) and (b), the rules under § 1.6694-4 of this chapter will apply.

(b) *Effective/applicability date.*—This section is applicable to returns and claims for refund filed, and advice provided, after December 31, 2008. [Reg. § 25.6694-4.]

□ [*T.D.* 9436, 12-15-2008.]

[Reg. § 26.6694-4]

§ 26.6694-4. Extension of period of collection when preparer pays 15 percent of a penalty for understatement of taxpayer's liability and certain other procedural matters.—(a) *In general.*—For rules relating to the extension of period of collection when a tax return preparer who prepared a return or claim for refund for generation-skipping transfer tax under chapter 13 of subtitle B of the Internal Revenue Code pays 15 percent of a penalty for understatement of taxpayer's liability, and procedural matters relating to the investigation, assessment and collection of the penalties under section 6694(a) and (b), the rules under § 1.6694-4 of this chapter will apply.

See p. 15 for regulations not amended to reflect law changes

(b) *Effective/applicability date.*—This section is applicable to returns and claims for refund filed, and advice provided, after December 31, 2008. [Reg. § 26.6694-4.]

☐ [*T.D.* 9436, 12-15-2008.]

[Reg. § 1.6695-1]

§ 1.6695-1. Other assessable penalties with respect to the preparation of tax returns for other persons.—(a) *Failure to furnish copy to taxpayer.*—(1) A person who is a signing tax return preparer as described in § 301.7701-15(b)(1) of this chapter of any return of tax or claim for refund of tax under the Internal Revenue Code (Code), and who fails to satisfy the requirements imposed by section 6107(a) and § 1.6107-1(a) to furnish a copy of the return or claim for refund to the taxpayer (or nontaxable entity), shall be subject to a penalty of $50 for such failure, with a maximum penalty of $25,000 per person imposed with respect to each calendar year, unless it is shown that the failure is due to reasonable cause and not due to willful neglect.

(2) No penalty may be imposed under section 6695(a) and paragraph (a)(1) of this section upon a tax return preparer who furnishes a copy of the return or claim for refund to taxpayers who—

(i) Hold an elected or politically appointed position with the government of the United States or a state or political subdivision thereof; and

(ii) In order faithfully to carry out their official duties, have so arranged their affairs that they have less than full knowledge of the property that they hold or of the debts for which they are responsible, if information is deleted from the copy in order to preserve or maintain this arrangement.

(b) *Failure to sign return.*—(1) An individual who is a signing tax return preparer as described in § 301.7701-15(b)(1) of this chapter with respect to a return of tax or claim for refund of tax under the Code as described in § 301.7701-15(b)(4) that is not signed electronically shall sign the return or claim for refund after it is completed and before it is presented to the taxpayer (or nontaxable entity) for signature. For rules covering electronically signed returns, see paragraph (b)(2) of this section. If the signing tax return preparer is unavailable for signature, another tax return preparer shall review the entire preparation of the return or claim for refund, and then shall sign the return or claim for refund. The tax return preparer shall sign the return in the manner prescribed by the Commissioner in forms, instructions, or other appropriate guidance.

(2) In the case of electronically signed tax returns, the signing tax return preparer need not sign the return prior to presenting a completed copy of the return to the taxpayer. The signing tax return preparer, however, must furnish all of the information that will be transmitted as the electronically signed tax return to the taxpayer contemporaneously with furnishing the Form 8879, "IRS e-file Signature Authorization," or other similar Internal Revenue Service (IRS) e-file signature form. The information may be furnished on a replica of an official form. The signing tax return preparer shall electronically sign the return in the manner prescribed by the Commissioner in forms, instructions, or other appropriate guidance.

(3) An individual required by this paragraph (b) to sign a return or claim for refund shall be subject to a penalty of $50 for each failure to sign, with a maximum of $25,000 per person imposed with respect to each calendar year, unless it is shown that the failure is due to reasonable cause and not due to willful neglect. If the tax return preparer asserts reasonable cause for failure to sign, the IRS will require a written statement to substantiate the tax return preparer's claim of reasonable cause. For purposes of this paragraph (b), reasonable cause is a cause that arises despite ordinary care and prudence exercised by the individual tax return preparer.

(4) *Examples.*—The application of this paragraph (b) is illustrated by the following examples:

Example 1. Law Firm A employs B, a lawyer, to prepare for compensation estate tax returns and claims for refund of taxes. Firm A is engaged by C to prepare a Federal estate tax return. Firm A assigns B to prepare the return. B obtains the information necessary for completing the return from C and makes determinations with respect to the proper application of the tax laws to such information in order to determine the estate's tax liability. B then forwards such information to D, a computer tax service that performs the mathematical computations and prints the return by means of computer processing. D then sends the completed estate tax return to B who reviews the accuracy of the return. B is the individual tax return preparer who is primarily responsible for the overall accuracy of the estate tax return. B must sign the return as tax return preparer in order to not be subject to the section 6695(b) penalty.

Example 2. Partnership E is a national accounting firm that prepares returns and claims for refund of taxes for compensation. F and G, employees of Partnership E, are involved in preparing the Form 990-T, Exempt Organization Business Income Tax Return, for H, a tax exempt organization. After they complete the return, including the gathering of the necessary information, analyzing the proper application of the tax laws to such information, and the performance of the necessary mathematical computations, I, a supervisory employee of Partnership E, reviews the return. As part of this review, I reviews the information provided and the application of the tax laws to this information. The mathematical computations and carriedforward amounts are reviewed by J, an employee of Partnership E. The policies and practices of Partnership E require that K, a partner, finally review the return. The scope of K's review includes reviewing the information provided and applying to this information his knowledge of H's affairs, observing that Partnership E's policies and practices have been followed, and making the final determination with respect to the proper application of the tax laws to determine H's tax liability. K may or may not exercise these responsibilities, or may exercise them to a greater or lesser extent, depending on the degree of complexity of the return, his confidence in I (or F and G), and other factors. K is the individual tax return preparer who is primarily responsible for the overall accuracy of H's return. K must sign the return as tax return preparer in order to not be subject to the section 6695(b) penalty.

Example 3. L corporation maintains an office in Seattle, Washington, for the purpose of preparing partnership returns for compensation. L makes compensatory arrangements with individuals (but provides no working facilities) in several states to collect information from partners of a partnership and to make decisions with respect to the proper application of the tax laws to the information in order to prepare the partnership return and calculate the partnership's distributive items. M, an individual, who has such an arrangement in Los Angeles with L, collects information from N, the general partner of a partnership, and completes a worksheet kit supplied by L that is stamped with M's name and an identification number assigned to M by L. In this process, M classifies this information in appropriate categories for the preparation of the partnership return. The completed worksheet kit signed by M is then mailed to L. O, an employee in L's office, reviews the worksheet kit to make sure it was properly completed. O does not review the information obtained from N for its validity or accuracy. O may, but did not, make the final decision with respect to the proper application of tax laws to the information provided. The data from the worksheet is entered into a computer and the return form is completed. The return is prepared for submission to N with filing instructions. M is the individual tax return preparer primarily responsible for the overall accuracy of the partnership return. M must sign the return as tax return preparer in order to not be subject to the section 6695(b) penalty.

Example 4. P employs R, S, and T to prepare gift tax returns for taxpayers. After R and S have collected the information from a taxpayer and applied the tax laws to the information, the return form is completed by a computer service. On the day the returns prepared by R and S are ready for their signatures, R is away from the city for 1 week on another assignment and S is on detail to another office in the same city for the day. T may sign the gift tax returns prepared by R, provided that T reviews the information obtained by R relative to the taxpayer, and T reviews the preparation of each return prepared by R. T may not sign the returns prepared by S because S is available.

(5) *Effective/applicability date.*—This paragraph (b) is applicable to returns and claims for refund filed after December 31, 2008.

(c) *Failure to furnish identifying number.*—(1) A person who is a signing tax return preparer as described in § 301.7701-15(b)(1) of this chapter of any return of tax under the Code or claim for refund of tax under the Code, and who fails to satisfy the requirement of section 6109(a)(4) and § 1.6109-2(a) to furnish one or more identifying numbers of signing tax return preparers or persons employing the signing tax return preparer (or with which the signing tax return preparer is associated) on a return or claim for refund after it is completed and before it is presented to the taxpayer (or nontaxable entity) for signature shall be subject to a penalty of $50 for each failure, with a maximum of $25,000 per person imposed with respect to each calendar year, unless it is shown that the failure is due to reasonable cause and not due to willful neglect.

(2) No more than one penalty of $50 may be imposed under section 6695(c) and paragraph (c)(1) of this section with respect to a single return or claim for refund.

(d) *Failure to retain copy or record.*—(1) A person who is a signing tax return preparer as described in § 301.7701-15(b)(1) of this chapter of any return of tax under the Code or claim for refund of tax under the Code, and who fails to satisfy the requirements imposed upon him or her by section 6107(b) and § 1.6107-1(b) and (c) (other than the record requirement described in both § 1.6107-1(b)(2) and (3)) to retain and make available for inspection a copy of the return or claim for refund, or to include the return or claim for refund in a record of returns and claims for refund and make the record available for inspection, shall be subject to a penalty of $50 for the failure, unless it is shown that the failure is due to reasonable cause and not due to willful neglect.

(2) A person may not, for returns or claims for refund presented to the taxpayers (or nontaxable entities) during each calendar year, be subject to more than $25,000 in penalties under section 6695(d) and paragraph (d)(1) of this section.

(e) *Failure to file correct information returns.*—A person who is subject to the reporting requirements of section 6060 and § 1.6060-1 and who fails to satisfy these requirements shall pay a penalty of $50 for each such failure, with a maximum of $25,000 per person imposed for each calendar year, unless such failure was due to reasonable cause and not due to willful neglect.

(f) *Negotiation of check.*—(1) No person who is a tax return preparer as described in § 301.7701-15 of this chapter may endorse or otherwise negotiate, directly or through an agent, a check (including an electronic version of a check) for the refund of tax under the Code that is issued to a taxpayer other than the tax return preparer if the person was a tax return preparer of the return or claim for refund which gave rise to the refund check. A tax return preparer will not be considered to have endorsed or otherwise negotiated a check for purposes of this paragraph (f)(1) solely as a result of having affixed the taxpayer's name to a refund check for the purpose of depositing the check into an account in the name of the taxpayer or in the joint names of the taxpayer and one or more other persons (excluding the tax return preparer) if authorized by the taxpayer or the taxpayer's recognized representative.

(2) Section 6695(f) and paragraphs (f)(1) and (3) of this section do not apply to a tax return preparer-bank that—

(i) Cashes a refund check and remits all of the cash to the taxpayer or accepts a refund check for deposit in full to a taxpayer's account, so long as the bank does not initially endorse or negotiate the check (unless the bank has made a loan to the taxpayer on the basis of the anticipated refund); or

(ii) Endorses a refund check for deposit in full to a taxpayer's account pursuant to a written authorization of the taxpayer (unless the bank has made a loan to the taxpayer on the basis of the anticipated refund).

(3) A tax return preparer-bank may also subsequently endorse or negotiate a refund check as a part of the checkclearing process through the financial system after initial endorsement or negotiation.

(4) The tax return preparer shall be subject to a penalty of $500 for each endorsement or negotiation of a check prohibited under section 6695(f) and paragraph (f)(1) of this section.

(g) *Effective/applicability date.*—This section is applicable to returns and claims for refund filed after December 31, 2008. [Reg. § 1.6695-1.]

☐ [*T.D.* 7519, 11-17-77. *Amended by T.D.* 7640, 8-21-79; *T.D.* 8549, 6-28-94; *T.D.* 8689, 12-11-96; *T.D.* 8803, 12-30-98; *T.D.* 8893, 7-17-2000; *T.D.* 9053, 4-23-2003; *T.D.* 9119, 3-24-2004 *and T.D.* 9436, 12-15-2008 (*corrected* 1-28-2009).]

[Reg. § 20.6695-1]

§ 20.6695-1. Other assessable penalties with respect to the preparation of tax returns for other persons.—(a) *In general.*—A person who is a tax return preparer of any return or claim for refund of estate tax under chapter 11 of subtitle B of the Internal Revenue Code (Code) shall be subject to penalties for failure to furnish a copy to the taxpayer under section 6695(a) of the Code, failure to sign the return under section 6695(b) of the Code, failure to furnish an identification number under section 6695(c) of the Code, failure to retain a copy or list under section 6695(d) of the Code, failure to file a correct information return under section 6695(e) of the Code, and negotiation of a check under section 6695(f) of the Code, in the manner stated in § 1.6695-1 of this chapter.

(b) *Effective/applicability date.*—This section is applicable to returns and claims for refund filed after December 31, 2008. [Reg. § 20.6695-1.]

☐ [*T.D.* 9436, 12-15-2008.]

[Reg. § 25.6695-1]

§ 25.6695-1. Other assessable penalties with respect to the preparation of tax returns for other persons.—(a) *In general.*—A person who is a tax return preparer of any return or claim for refund of gift tax under chapter 12 of subtitle B of the Internal Revenue Code (Code) shall be subject to penalties for failure to furnish a copy to the taxpayer under section 6695(a) of the Code, failure to sign the return under section 6695(b) of the Code, failure to furnish an identification number under section 6695(c) of the Code, failure to retain a copy or list under section 6695(d) of the Code, failure to file a correct information return under section 6695(e) of the Code, and negotiation of a check under section 6695(f) of the Code, in the manner stated in § 1.6695-1 of this chapter.

(b) *Effective/applicability date.*—This section is applicable to returns and claims for refund filed after December 31, 2008. [Reg. § 25.6695-1.]

☐ [*T.D.* 9436, 12-15-2008.]

[Reg. § 26.6695-1]

§ 26.6695-1. Other assessable penalties with respect to the preparation of tax returns for other persons.—(a) *In general.*—A person who is a tax return preparer of any return or claim for refund of generation-skipping transfer tax under chapter 13 of subtitle B of the Internal Revenue Code (Code) shall be subject to penalties for failure to furnish a copy to the taxpayer under section 6695(a) of the Code, failure to sign the return under section 6695(b) of the Code, failure to furnish an identification number under section 6695(c) of the Code, failure to retain a copy or list under section 6695(d) of the Code, failure to file a correct information return under section 6695(e) of the Code, and negotiation of a check under section 6695(f) of the Code, in the manner stated in § 1.6695-1 of this chapter.

(b) *Effective/applicability date.*—This section is applicable to returns and claims for refund filed after December 31, 2008. [Reg. § 26.6695-1.]

☐ [*T.D.* 9436, 12-15-2008.]

[Reg. § 1.6696-1]

§ 1.6696-1. Claims for credit or refund by tax return preparers or appraisers.—(a) *Notice and demand.*—(1) The Internal Revenue Service (IRS) shall issue to each tax return preparer or appraiser one or more statements of notice and demand for payment for all penalties assessed against the tax return preparer or appraiser under section 6694 and § 1.6694-1, under section 6695 and § 1.6695-1, or under section 6695A (and any subsequently issued regulations).

(2) For the definition of the term "tax return preparer", see section 7701(a)(36) and § 301.7701-15 of this chapter. A person who prepares a claim for credit or refund under this section for another person, however, is not, with respect to that preparation, a tax return preparer as defined in section 7701(a)(36) and § 301.7701-15 of this chapter.

(b) *Claim filed by tax return preparer or appraiser.*—A claim for credit or refund of a penalty (or penalties) assessed against a tax return preparer or appraiser under section 6694 and § 1.6694-1, under section 6695 and § 1.6695-1, or under section 6695A (and any subsequently issued regulations) may be filed under this section only by the tax return preparer or the appraiser (or the tax return preparer's or appraiser's estate) against whom the penalty (or penalties) is assessed and not by, for example, the tax return preparer's or appraiser's employer. This paragraph (b) is not intended, however, to impose any restrictions on the preparation of this claim for credit or refund. The claim may be prepared by the tax return preparer's or appraiser's employer or by other persons. In all cases, however, the claim for credit or refund shall contain the information specified in paragraph (d) of this section and, as required by paragraph (d) of this section, shall be verified by a written declaration by the tax return preparer or appraiser that the information is provided under penalty of perjury.

(c) *Separation and consolidation of claims.*—(1) Unless paragraph (c)(2) of this section applies, a tax return preparer shall file a separate claim for each penalty assessed in each statement of notice and demand issued to the tax return preparer.

(2) A tax return preparer may file one or more consolidated claims for any or all penalties imposed on the tax return preparer by a single IRS campus or office under section 6695(a) and § 1.6695-1(a) (relating to failure to furnish copy of return to taxpayer), section 6695(b) and § 1.6695-1(b) (relating to failure to sign), section 6695(c) and § 1.6695-1(c) (relating to failure to furnish identifying number), or under section 6695(d) and § 1.6695-1(d) (relating to failure to retain copy of return or record), whether the penalties are asserted on a single or on separate statements of notice and demand. In addition, a tax return preparer may file one consolidated claim for any or all penalties imposed on the tax return preparer by a single IRS campus or office under section 6695(e) and § 1.6695-1(e) (relating to failure to file correct information return), which are asserted on a single statement of notice and demand.

(d) *Content of claim.*—Each claim for credit or refund for any penalty (or penalties) paid by a tax return preparer under section 6694 and § 1.6694-1, or under section 6695 and § 1.6695-1, or paid by an appraiser under section 6695A (and any subsequently issued regulations) shall include the following information, verified by a written declaration by the tax return preparer or appraiser that the information is provided under penalty of perjury:

(1) The tax return preparer's or appraiser's name.

(2) The tax return preparer's or appraiser's identification number. If the tax return preparer or appraiser is—

(i) An individual (not described in paragraph (d)(2)(iii) of this section) who is a citizen or resident of the United States, the tax return preparer's or appraiser's social security account number (or such alternative number as may be prescribed by the IRS in forms, instructions, or other appropriate guidance) shall be provided;

(ii) An individual who is not a citizen or resident of the United States and also was not employed by another tax return preparer or appraiser to prepare the document (or documents) with respect to which the penalty (or penalties) was assessed, the tax return preparer's or appraiser's employer identification number shall be provided; or

(iii) A person (whether an individual, corporation, or partnership) that employed one or more persons to prepare the document (or documents) with respect to which the penalty (or penalties) was assessed, the tax return preparer's or appraiser's employer identification number shall be provided.

(3) The tax return preparer's or appraiser's address where the IRS mailed the statement (or statements) of notice and demand and, if different, the tax return preparer's or appraiser's address shown on the document (or documents) with respect to which the penalty (or penalties) was assessed.

(4)(i) The address of the IRS campus or office that issued the statement (or statements) of notice and demand for payment of the penalty (or penalties).

(ii) The date (or dates) and identifying number (or numbers) of the statement (or statements) of notice and demand.

(5)(i) The identification, by amount, type, and document to which related, of each penalty included in the claim. Each document referred to in the preceding sentence shall be identified by the form title or number, by the taxpayer's (or nontaxable entity's) name and taxpayer identification number, and by the taxable year to which the document relates.

(ii) The date (or dates) of payment of the amount (or amounts) of the penalty (or penalties) included in the claim.

(iii) The total amount claimed.

(6) A statement setting forth in detail—

(i) Each ground upon which each penalty overpayment claim is based; and

(ii) Facts sufficient to apprise the IRS of the exact basis of each such claim.

(e) *Form for filing claim.*—Notwithstanding § 301.6402-2(c) of this chapter, Form 6118, "Claim for Refund of Tax Return Preparer and Promoter Penalties," is the form prescribed for making a claim as provided in this section with respect to penalties under sections 6694 and 6695. Form 843, Claim for Refund and Request for Abatement, is the form prescribed for making a claim as provided in this section with respect to a penalty under section 6695A.

(f) *Place for filing claim.*—A claim filed under this section shall be filed with the IRS campus or office that issued to the tax return preparer or appraiser the statement (or statements) of notice and demand for payment of the penalty (or penalties) included in the claim.

(g) *Time for filing claim.*—(1)(i) Except as provided in section 6694(c)(1) and § 1.6694-4(a)(4)(ii) and (5), and in section 6694(d) and § 1.6694-1(d):

(A) A claim for a penalty paid by a tax return preparer under section 6694 and § 1.6694-1, or under section 6695 and § 1.6695-1, or by an appraiser under section 6695A (and any subsequently issued regulations) shall be filed within three years from the date the payment was made.

(B) A consolidated claim, permitted under paragraph (c)(2) of this section, shall be filed within three years from the first date of payment of any penalty included in the claim.

(ii) For purposes of this paragraph (g)(1), payment is considered made on the date payment is received by the IRS or, if applicable, on the date an amount is credited in satisfaction of the penalty.

(2) For purposes of determining whether a claim is timely filed, the rules under sections 7502 and 7503 and the provisions of §§ 1.7502-1, 1.7502-2, and 1.7503-1 apply.

(h) *Application of refund to outstanding liability of tax return preparer or appraiser.*—The IRS may, within the applicable period of limitations, credit any amount of an overpayment by a tax return preparer or appraiser of a penalty (or penalties) paid under section 6694 and § 1.6694-1, under section 6695 and § 1.6695-1, or under section 6695A (and any subsequently issued regulations) against any outstanding liability for any tax (or for any interest, additional amount, addition to the tax, or assessable penalty) owed by the tax return preparer or appraiser making the overpayment. If a portion of an overpayment is so credited, only the balance will be refunded to the tax return preparer or appraiser.

(i) *Interest.*—(1) Section 6611 and § 301.6611-1 of this chapter apply to the payment by the IRS of interest on an overpayment by a tax return preparer or appraiser of a penalty (or penalties) paid under section 6694 and § 1.6694-1, under section 6695 and § 1.6695-1, or under section 6695A (and any subsequently issued regulations).

(2) Section 6601 and § 301.6601-1 of this chapter apply to the payment of interest by a tax return preparer or appraiser to the IRS on any penalty (or penalties) assessed against the tax return preparer under section 6694 and § 1.6694-1, under section 6695 and § 1.6695-1, or under section 6695A (and any subsequently issued regulations).

(j) *Suits for refund of penalty.*—(1) A tax return preparer or appraiser may not maintain a civil action for the recovery of any penalty paid under section 6694 and § 1.6694-1, under section 6695 and § 1.6695-1, or under section 6695A(and any subsequently issued regulations), unless the tax return preparer or appraiser has previously filed a claim for credit or refund of the penalty as provided in this section (and the court has jurisdiction of the proceeding). See sections 6694(c) and 7422.

(2)(i) Except as provided in section 6694(c)(2) and § 1.6694-4(b), the periods of limitation contained in section 6532 and § 301.6532-1 of this chapter apply to a tax return preparer's or appraiser's suit for the recovery of any penalty paid under section 6694 and § 1.6694-1, under section 6695 and § 1.6695-1, or under section 6695A (and any subsequently issued regulations).

(ii) The rules under section 7503 and § 301.7503-1 of this chapter apply to the timely commencement by a tax return preparer or appraiser of a suit for the recovery of any penalty paid under section 6694 and § 1.6694-1, under section 6695 and § 1.6695-1, or under section 6695A (and any subsequently issued regulations).

(k) *Effective/applicability date.*—This section is applicable to returns and claims for refund filed, and advice provided, after December 31, 2008. [Reg. § 1.6696-1.]

☐ [*T.D.* 7621, 5-11-79. *Amended by T.D.* 9436, 12-15-2008 (*corrected* 1-28-2009).]

[Reg. § 20.6696-1]

§ 20.6696-1. Claims for credit or refund by tax return preparers or appraisers.—(a) *In general.*—For rules for claims for credit or refund by a tax return preparer who prepared a return or claim for refund for estate tax under chapter 11 of subtitle B of the Internal Revenue Code, or by an appraiser that prepared an appraisal in connection with such a return or claim for refund under section 6695A, the rules under § 1.6696-1 of this chapter will apply.

(b) *Effective/applicability date.*—This section is applicable to returns and claims for refund filed, and advice provided, after December 31, 2008. [Reg. § 20.6696-1.]

☐ [*T.D.* 9436, 12-15-2008.]

[Reg. § 25.6696-1]

§ 25.6696-1. Claims for credit or refund by tax return preparers.—(a) *In general.*—For rules for claims for credit or refund by a tax return preparer who prepared a return or claim for refund for gift tax under chapter 12 of subtitle B of the Internal Revenue Code, or by an appraiser that prepared an appraisal in connection with such a return or claim for refund under section 6695A, the rules under § 1.6696-1 of this chapter will apply.

(b) *Effective/applicability date.*—This section is applicable to returns and claims for refund filed, and advice provided, after December 31, 2008. [Reg. § 25.6696-1.]

☐ [*T.D.* 9436, 12-15-2008.]

[Reg. § 26.6696-1]

§ 26.6696-1. Claims for credit or refund by tax return preparers.—(a) *In general.*—For rules for claims for credit or refund by a tax return preparer who prepared a return or claim for refund for generation-skipping transfer tax under chapter 13 of subtitle B of the Internal Revenue Code, or by an appraiser that prepared an appraisal in connection with such a return or claim for refund under section 6695A, the rules under § 1.6696-1 of this chapter will apply.

(b) *Effective/applicability date.*—This section is applicable to returns and claims for refund filed, and advice provided, after December 31, 2008. [Reg. § 26.6696-1.]

☐ [*T.D.* 9436, 12-15-2008.]

[Reg. § 301.6721-1]

§ 301.6721-1. Failure to file correct information returns.—(a) *Imposition of penalty.*—(1) *General rule.*—A penalty of $50 is imposed for each information return (as defined in section 6724(d)(1) and paragraph (g) of this section) with respect to which a failure (as defined in section 6721(a)(2) and paragraph (a)(2) of this section) occurs. No more than one penalty will be imposed under this paragraph (a)(1) with respect to a single information return even though there may be more than one failure with respect to such return. The total amount imposed on any person for all failures during any calendar year with respect to all information returns shall not exceed $250,000. See paragraph (b) of this section for a reduction in the penalty when the failures are corrected within specified periods. See paragraph (c) of this section for an exception to the penalty for inconsequential errors or omissions. See paragraph(d) of this section for an exception to the penalty for a *de minimis* number of failures. See paragraph (e) of this section for lower limitations to the $250,000 maximum penalty. See paragraph (f) of this section for higher penalties when a failure is due to intentional disregard of the requirement to file timely correct information returns. See paragraph (a)(1) of § 301.6724-1 for waiver of the penalty for a failure that is due to reasonable cause.

(2) *Failures subject to the penalty.*—The failures to which section 6721(a) and paragraph (a)(1) of this section apply are—

(i) A failure to file an information return on or before the required filing date ("failure to file timely"), and

(ii) A failure to include all the information required to be shown on the return or including incorrect information (failure to include correct information). A failure to file timely includes a failure to file in the required manner, for example, electronically or in other machine-readable form as provided under section 6011(e). However, no penalty is imposed under paragraph (a)(1) of this section solely by reason of any failure to comply with the requirements of section 6011(e)(2), except to the extent that the failure occurs with respect to more than 10 returns, or with respect to a return described in section 6011(e)(4). If a partnership return under section 6031(a) is required to be filed electronically, each schedule required to be included with such return with respect to each partner will be treated as a separate information return for purposes of this section. See section 6724(e). Filers who are required to file information returns electronically and who file those information returns electronically are considered to have satisfied the electronic-filing requirement. Except as provided in paragraph (c)(1) or (e)(1) of this section, a failure to include correct information encompasses a failure to include the information required by applicable information-reporting statutes or by any administrative pronouncements (such as regulations, revenue rulings, revenue procedures, or information-reporting forms, and form instructions). A failure to include information in the correct format may be either a failure to file timely an information return or a failure to include correct information on an information return. For example, an error on an electronic submission to the Internal Revenue Service that prevents processing by the Internal Revenue Service may constitute a failure to file timely. However, if information is set forth on the wrong field of the electronic submission, that error may constitute a failure to file timely or a failure to include correct information, depending upon the extent of the failure. For purposes of paragraph (b) of this section, a failure to file corrected information returns in the format required under § 301.6011-2(c)(4)(ii) is a failure to correct the corresponding original information returns.

(b) *Reduction in the penalty when a correction is made within specified periods.*—(1) *Correction within 30 days.*—The penalty imposed under section 6721(a) for a failure to file timely or for a failure to include correct information shall be $15 in lieu of $50 if the failure is corrected on or before the 30th day after the required filing date ("within 30 days"). The total amount imposed on a person for all failures during any calendar year that are corrected within 30 days shall not exceed $75,000.

(2) *Correction after 30 days but on or before August 1.*—The penalty imposed under section 6721(a) for a failure to file timely or for a failure to include correct information shall be $30 in lieu of $50 if the failure is corrected after the 30-day period described in paragraph (b)(1) of this section but on or before August 1 of the year in which the required filing date occurs ("after 30 days but on or before August 1"). (See paragraph (b)(6) of this section for an exception to the provisions of this paragraph (b)(2) for returns that are not due on February 28 or March 15.) The total amount imposed on a person for all failures during any calendar year corrected after 30 days but on or before August 1 shall not exceed $150,000.

(3) *Required filing date defined.*—The term "required filing date" means the date prescribed for filing an information return with the Internal Revenue Service (or the Social Security Administration in the case of Forms W-2) determined with regard to any extension of time for filing.

(4) *Penalty amount for return with multiple failures.*—If a return is subject to a penalty for more than one failure, and the penalty amounts for the failures differ, the higher penalty amount will be imposed.

(5) *Examples.*—The provisions of paragraphs (a) and (b)(1) through (4) of this section may be illustrated by the following examples. These examples do not take into account

any possible application of the *de minimis* exception under paragraph (d) of this section, the lower small-business limitations under paragraph (e) of this section, the penalty for intentional disregard under paragraph (f) of this section, adjustments for inflation under section 6721(f), or the reasonable-cause waiver under § 301.6724-1(a):

(i) *Example 1.*—Corporation R fails to file timely 11,000 Forms 1099-MISC (relating to miscellaneous income) for the 1990 calendar year. Five thousand of these returns are filed with correct information within 30 days, and 6,000 after 30 days but on or before August 1, 1991. For the same year R fails to file timely 400 Forms 1099-INT (relating to payments of interest) which R eventually files on September 28, 1991, after the period for reduction of the penalty has elapsed. R is subject to a penalty of $20,000 for the 400 forms which were not filed by August 1 ($50 × 400 = $20,000), $150,000 for the 6,000 forms filed after 30 days ($30 × 6,000 = $180,000, limited to $150,000 under paragraph (b)(2) of this section), and $75,000 for the 5,000 forms filed within 30 days ($15 × 5,000 = $75,000), for a total penalty of $245,000.

(ii) *Example 2.*—Corporation T fails to file timely 6,000 Forms 1099-MISC for the 1990 calendar year. T files the 6000 Forms 1099-MISC on September 1, 1991. Because T does not correct the failure by August 1, 1991, T is subject to a penalty of $250,000, the maximum penalty under paragraph (a) of this section. Without the limitation of paragraph (a), T would be subject to a $300,000 penalty ($50 × 6,000 = $300,000).

(iii) *Example 3.*—In calendar year 2024, Corporation U timely files on paper 12 Forms 1099–MISC for the 2023 calendar year with correct information. Under § 301.6011-2, a person required to file at least 10 returns during calendar year 2024 must file those returns electronically. Corporation U does not correct its failures to file these returns electronically by August 1, 2024. See section 6721(b)(2). Corporation U is therefore subject to a penalty for a failure to file timely under paragraph (a)(2) of this section. However, under section 6724(c) and paragraph (a)(2) of this section, the penalty for a failure to file timely electronically applies only to the extent the number of returns exceeds 10. As Corporation U was required to file 12 returns electronically, it is subject to a penalty of $500 for two returns ($250 x 2 = $500).

(iv) *Example 4.*—In calendar year 2024, Corporation W timely electronically files 25 Forms 1099-B (relating to proceeds from broker and barter exchange transactions) with incorrect information. On August 1, 2024, Corporation W discovers the errors and files 25 corrected Forms 1099-B on paper. Under § 301.6011-2(c)(4)(ii)(A), a person required to file an original information return covered by § 301.6011-2(b) electronically must file any corrected information return corresponding to that original return electronically. Under paragraph (a)(2)(ii) of this section, a failure to file a corrected information return electronically when required to do so is a failure to correct the corresponding original information return. As Corporation W was required to file its 25 corrected information returns electronically, it has failed to correct the original information returns and is subject to a penalty of $6,250 for failure to include correct information on its 25 original Forms 1099-B ($250 x 25 = $6,250), without any reductions for correcting the information on or before August 1.

(v) *Example 5.*—During the 2024 calendar year, Corporation V files 25 Forms 1099-B (relating to proceeds from broker and barter exchange transactions) on paper. The forms were filed on March 15, 2024, rather than on the required filing date of February 28, 2024. Under § 301.6011-2, a person required to file at least 10 returns during calendar years 2024 and after must file those returns electronically. Corporation V does not correctly file these returns electronically by August 1, 2024. See section 6721(b)(2). Corporation V is subject to a penalty of $500 for filing 10 of the returns late, but within 30 days after the required filing date ($50 x 10). In addition, Corporation V is subject to a penalty of $3,750 for failing to file 15 returns electronically ($250 x 15).

(vi) *Example 6.*—Partnership X has 120 partners in calendar year 2023. In calendar year 2024, it timely filed on paper its 2023 Form 1065 and 230 accompanying Schedules K-1 and Schedules K-3 (120 Schedules K-1 and 110 Schedules K-3). Partnership X filed no other returns during calendar year 2024. Under § 301.6011-3(a)(1)(ii), a partnership with more than 100 partners must electronically file its partnership return, including Schedules K-1 and K-3. Under section 6724(e), Schedules K-1 and K-3 are treated as separate information returns for purposes of penalties under section 6721, even though they are not listed under § 301.6011-2(b) as information returns required to be filed electronically and are not defined as information returns under section 6724(d). Under section 6724(c) and paragraph (a)(2) of this section, the penalty for a failure to file timely electronically applies only to the extent the number of returns exceeds 10. Partnership X would be subject to a penalty of $55,000 for failing to electronically file 220 Schedules K-1 and K-3 required to be included with the partnership return: the 11th through the 230th of the required schedules ($250 x 220 = $55,000). See section 6698 for the penalty for the failure to file the partnership return.

(6) *Application to returns not due on February 28 or March 15.*—For returns that are not due on February 28 or March 15 (for example, Forms 8300 reporting certain cash payments of $10,000 or more), the penalty is $15 if the failure is corrected within 30 days. If the failure is corrected after 30 days, the penalty is $50 rather than $30. There is no period during which the penalty is reduced to $30 under paragraph (b)(2) of this section.

(c) *Exception for inconsequential errors or omissions.*—(1) *In general.*—An inconsequential error or omission is not considered a failure to include correct information. For purposes of this paragraph (c)(1), the term "inconsequential error or omission" means any failure that does not prevent or hinder the Internal Revenue Service from processing the return, from correlating the information required to be shown on the return with the information shown on the payee's tax return, or from otherwise putting the return to its intended use. See paragraph (g)(5) of this section for the definition of "payee."

(2) *Errors or omissions that are never inconsequential.*—Errors or omissions relating to the following are never inconsequential—

(i) A taxpayer identification number;

(ii) A surname of a payee (*i.e.*, the person required to be furnished a copy of the information set forth on an information return); and

(iii) Any monetary amounts.

The Internal Revenue Service may, by administrative pronouncement, specify other types of errors or omissions that are never inconsequential.

(3) *Examples.*—The provisions of this paragraph (c) may be illustrated by the following examples, which do not take into account any possible application of the penalty for intentional disregard under paragraph (f) of this section or the reasonable cause waiver under paragraph (a) of § 301.6724-1:

Example 1. A filer files a Form 1099-MISC (relating to miscellaneous income) with the Internal Revenue Service. The Form 1099-MISC is complete and correct except that the word "street" is misspelled in the payee's address. The error does not prevent or hinder the Internal Revenue Service from processing the return, from correlating the information required to be shown on the return with the information shown on the payee's tax return, or from otherwise putting the return to its intended use. Therefore, no penalty is imposed under paragraph (a) of this section.

Example 2. A filer files a Form 1099-MISC with the Internal Revenue Service. The Form 1099-MISC is complete and correct except that the payee's first name, William, is misspelled as "Willaim." The error does not prevent or hinder the Internal Revenue Service from processing the return, from correlating the information required to be shown on the return with the information shown on the payee's tax return, or from otherwise putting the return to its intended use. See paragraph (c)(2) of this section. Therefore, no penalty is imposed under paragraph (a) of this section.

Example 3. A filer files a Form 1099-MISC with the Internal Revenue Service. The Form 1099-MISC is complete and correct except that the payee's name, "John Doe," is misspelled as "John Ode." Under paragraph (c)(2) of this section, supplying an incorrect surname for a payee is never considered an inconsequential error. Therefore, a penalty is imposed under paragraph (a) of this section.

(d) *Exception for a de minimis number of failures.*—(1) *Requirements.*—The penalty under paragraph (a) of this section is not imposed for a *de minimis* number of failures to include correct information if the filer corrects such failures on or before August 1 of the year in which the required filing date occurs. (See paragraph (d)(4) of this section for special rules relating to returns that are not due on February 28 or March 15.)

(2) *Calculation of the de minimis exception.*—The number of returns to which the *de minimis* exception applies for any calendar year shall not exceed the greater of 10 or one-half of one percent of the total number of all information returns the filer is required to file during the year. If the number of returns on which the filer fails to include correct information exceeds the number of returns to which the *de minimis* exception applies, the *de minimis* exception applies to those returns that will afford the filer the greatest reduction in penalty. The *de minimis* exception applies to failures to include correct information that exist after the application (if any) of the waiver for reasonable cause under section 6724(a) and § 301.6724-1. Returns to which the *de minimis* exception applies are treated as having been originally filed with correct information.

(3) *Examples.*—The provisions of this paragraph (d) may be illustrated by the following examples. In each of the examples, the failures to file and to include correct information are subject to penalty under paragraph (a) of this section. The examples do not take into account any possible application of paragraph (f) of this section or the reasonable cause waiver under paragraph (a) of § 301.6724-1 of this section.

Example 1. Corporation T files timely 10,000 Forms 1099-INT (relating to payments of interest) for 1990 by February 28, 1991. The 10,000 returns are all the information returns that T is required to file during the 1991 calendar year. Of the returns filed, 70 contained incorrect information. T corrects the failures on July 12, 1991. No penalty is imposed for 50 of the failures (i.e., the greater of 10 or .005 × 10,000 = 50) even though the total failures, 70, exceed the number to which the *de minimis* exception may apply. The $30 penalty under paragraph (b)(2) of this section is imposed, in lieu of $50, for the remaining 20 failures, which were corrected after 30 days but on or before August 1, resulting in a total penalty of $600 ($30 × 20 = $600).

Example 2. Corporation U files timely 9,500 Forms 1099-INT for 1990 by February 28, 1991, the required filing date. Fifty of these returns contain incorrect information with respect to which U files correct information on August 1, 1991. U also files 500 Forms 1099-INT for 1990 on August 30, 1991, after the required filing date. The 10,000 returns are all the information returns that U is required to file during the 1991 calendar year. The calculation of the *de minimis* exception is based on the 10,000 returns required to be filed during the 1991 calendar year even though 500 of the returns filed during the year were not filed timely. Therefore, the number of failures for which the *de minimis* exception applies is 50, and accordingly no penalty is imposed for the 50 Forms 1099-INT that were corrected on August 1, 1991. However, the $50 penalty under paragraph (a)(1) of this section is imposed for each failure to file timely, resulting in a total penalty of $25,000 ($50 × 500 = $25,000).

Example 3. Corporation V files timely 9,950 Forms 1099-INT for 1990 by February 28, 1991. However, V fails to file timely 50 of its Forms 1099-INT. The 10,000 returns are all the information returns that V is required to file during the 1991 calendar year. Upon discovering the error, V files the 50 returns within 30 days of February 28, 1991. The 50 returns are complete and correct except that V fails to include the taxpayer identification numbers of the payees on the returns. V files corrected returns on August 1, 1991. Absent application of the *de minimis* exception, the penalty imposed for the failure to include correct information would be $1,500 ($30 × 50 = $1,500). Because the incorrect returns are corrected on August 1, the 50 forms are treated under the *de minimis* exception as originally filed with correct information, and therefore no penalty is imposed under paragraph (a) of this section for the failure to include correct information. Nevertheless, the penalty under paragraph (a) of this section is imposed for the failure to file timely the 50 returns because the *de minimis* exception does not apply to the penalty for the failure to file timely. Hence, a penalty of $750 ($15 × 50 = $750) is imposed.

Example 4. Corporation W files timely 100 Forms 1099-DIV and files an additional 50 Forms 1099-DIV late, but within 30 days of February 28, 1991. These are all the information returns that W was required to file during the 1991 calendar year. W discovers errors on 10 of the returns that were filed timely, and on 5 of the returns that were filed late. W corrects all the errors on August 1. The *de minimis* exception applies to 10 of the corrected returns. The exception will be allocated to the 10 returns that were filed timely with incorrect information because that allocation is most favorable to W (*i.e.*, applying the exception to a return filed late with incorrect information would save W $15, by reducing the penalty on that return from $30 to $15, but applying the exception to a return filed timely would save W $30, by reducing the penalty on that return from $30 to $0). (See paragraph (b)(4) of this section.)

(4) *Nonapplication to returns not due on February 28 or March 15.*—The exception for a *de minimis* number of failures provided in paragraph (d)(1) of this section does not apply to failures with respect to returns that are not due on February 28 or March 15 (for example, Forms 8300 reporting certain cash payments of $10,000 or more). Nevertheless, the returns that are not due on February 28 or March 15 are included in the total number of all information returns that the filer is required to file during a year for purposes of calculating the number of the returns subject to the *de minimis* exception under paragraph (d)(2) of this section.

(e) *Lower limitations on the $250,000 maximum penalty amount with respect to persons with gross receipts of not more than $5,000,000.*—(1) *In general.*—If a person meets the gross receipts test (as defined in paragraph (e)(2) of this section) for any calendar year, the total amount of the penalty imposed on such person for all failures described in section 6721(a)(2) and paragraph (a)(2) of this section during such calendar year shall not exceed $100,000. The total amount of the penalty imposed under paragraph (b)(1) of this section for failures corrected within 30 days shall not exceed $25,000 for such calendar year. The total amount of the penalty imposed under paragraph (b)(2) of this section for failures corrected after 30 days but on or before August 1 shall not exceed $50,000 for such calendar year.

(2) *Gross receipts test.*—A person meets the gross receipts test for any calendar year if the average annual gross receipts for such person for the three most recent taxable years ending before such calendar year do not exceed $5,000,000. For purposes of determining the amount of gross receipts during the three most recent taxable years, the rules of section 448(c)(2) and (3) shall apply.

(f) *Higher penalty for intentional disregard of requirement to file timely correct information returns.*—(1) *Application of section 6721(e).*—If a failure is due to intentional disregard of the requirement to file timely or to include correct information on a return as described in paragraph (g) of this section, the amount of the penalty imposed under paragraph (a) of this section shall be determined under paragraph (f)(4) of this section.

(2) *Meaning of "intentional disregard."*—A failure is due to intentional disregard if it is a knowing or willful—

(i) Failure to file timely, or

(ii) Failure to include correct information.

Whether a person knowingly or willfully fails to file timely or fails to include correct information is determined on the basis of all the facts and circumstances in the particular case.

(3) *Facts and circumstances considered.*—The facts and circumstances that are considered in determining whether a failure is due to intentional disregard include, but are not limited to—

(i) Whether the failure to file timely or the failure to include correct information is part of a pattern of conduct by the person who filed the return of repeatedly failing to file timely or repeatedly failing to include correct information;

(ii) Whether correction was promptly made upon discovery of the failure;

(iii) Whether the filer corrects a failure to file or a failure to include correct information within 30 days after the date of any written request from the Internal Revenue Service to file or to correct; and

(iv) Whether the amount of the information reporting penalties is less than the cost of complying with the requirement to file timely or to include correct information on an information return.

(4) *Amount of the penalty.*—If one or more failures to file timely or to include correct information are due to intentional disregard of the requirement to file timely or to include correct information, then, with respect to each such failure determined under this paragraph (f)—

(i) Paragraphs (b), (d), and (e) of this section shall not apply;

(ii) The $250,000 limitation under paragraph (a) of this section shall not apply, and the penalty under this paragraph (f) shall not be taken into account in applying the $250,000 limitation (or any similar limitation under paragraph (b) or (e) of this section) to penalties not determined under this paragraph (f);

(iii) The penalty imposed under paragraph (a) of this section shall be $100 or, if greater, the statutory percentage; and

(iv) The term "statutory percentage" means—

(A) In the case of a return other than a return required under section 6045(a), 6041A(b), 6050H, 6050I (for amounts received after November 5, 1990), 6050J, 6050K, or 6050L, 10 percent of the aggregate dollar amount of the items required to be reported correctly,

(B) In the case of a return required to be filed by section 6045(a), 6050K, or 6050L, 5 percent of the aggregate dollar amount of the items required to be reported correctly, or

(C) In the case of a return required to be filed under section 6050I(a) with respect to amounts received after November 5, 1990, for any transaction (or related transactions), the greater of $25,000 or the amount of cash (within the meaning of section 6050I(d)) received in such transaction to the extent the amount of such cash does not exceed $100,000.

(5) *Computation of the penalty; aggregate dollar amount of the items required to be reported correctly.*—The aggregate dollar amount used in computing the penalty under this paragraph (f) is the amount that is not reported or is reported incorrectly. If the intentional disregard relates to a dollar amount, the statutory percentage is applied to the difference between the dollar amount reported and the amount required to be reported correctly. If the intentional disregard relates to any other item on the return, the statutory percentage is applied to the aggregate amount of items required to be reported correctly. In determining the aggregate amount of items required to be reported correctly, no item shall be taken into account more than once. For example, if a filer willfully fails to file a Form 1099-INT on which $800 of interest and $160 of Federal income tax withheld (*i.e.*, backup withholding) is required to be reported, only the $800 amount is taken into account in computing the penalty.

(6) *Examples.*—The provisions of this paragraph (f) may be illustrated by the following examples:

Example 1. On December 1, 1990, Automobile dealer P receives $55,000 from an individual for the purchase of an automobile in a transaction subject to reporting under section 6050I. The individual presents documents to P that identify him as "John Doe." However, P completes the Form 8300 (relating to cash received in a trade or business) and reflects the name of a cartoon character as the payor. Because P knew at the time of filing the Form 8300 that the payor's name was not the name of the cartoon character, he willfully failed to include correct information as described under paragraph (f)(2) of this section. Therefore, the penalty under paragraph (f)(4) of this section is imposed for the intentional disregard of the requirement to include correct information. The amount used in computing the penalty under paragraph (f)(5) of this section is $55,000 (*i.e.*, the amount required to be reported on the return with respect to which the payee is not correctly identified). The amount of the penalty determined under paragraph (f)(4)(ii)(C) of this section is $55,000 (*i.e.*, the greater of $25,000 or the amount of cash received in the transaction up to $100,000).

Example 2. On December 1, 1990, Individual B contacts his agent, F, to act as his intermediary in the purchase of an automobile. B gives F $20,000 and requests F to purchase the automobile in F's name, which F does. F prepares the Form 8300 as required under section 6050I, but in the area designated for the name of the payor, F writes "confidential." Because F knew at the time the return was filed that it contained incomplete information, the penalty under paragraph (f)(4) of this section is imposed for the intentional disregard of the requirement to include correct information. The amount used in computing the penalty under paragraph (f)(5) of this section is $20,000 (*i.e.*, the amount required to be reported on the return with respect to which the payee is not correctly identified). The amount of the penalty determined under paragraph (f)(4)(ii)(C) of this section is $25,000 (*i.e.*, the greater of $25,000 or the amount of cash received in the transaction up to $100,000).

Example 3. Corporation M deliberately does not include $5,000 of dividends on a Form 1099-DIV (relating to payments of dividends) on which a total of $200,000 (including the $5,000 dividends) is required to be reported under section 6042(a). Because the failure was deliberate, Corporation M's failure is due to intentional disregard of the requirement to include correct information. Accordingly, the amount of the penalty imposed under paragraph (a) is determined under paragraph (f)(4) of this section. Because the Form 1099-DIV is required to be filed under section 6042(a), under paragraph (f)(4)(ii)(A) the amount of the penalty with respect to such failure is 10 percent of the aggregate dollar amount of the items that were required to be but that were not reported correctly. Under paragraph (f)(5) of this section, $5,000 is the difference between the dollar amount reported and the amount required to be reported correctly. Therefore, the amount of the penalty is $500 ($5,000 × .10 = $500).

Example 4. Form 8027 requires certain large food and beverage establishments to report certain information with respect to tips. The form requires (among other things) that the establishment report its gross receipts from food and beverage operations. Establishment A, in intentional disregard of the information reporting requirement, reported gross receipts of $1,000,000, when the correct amount was $1,500,000. The significance of the gross receipts reporting requirement is that section 6053(c)(3)(A) requires an establishment to allocate as tips among its employees the excess of 8 percent of its gross receipts over the aggregate amount reported by employees to the establishment as tips under section 6053(a). A's misstatement of its gross receipts caused A to show $80,000 on the Form 8027 as 8 percent of its gross receipts, rather than the correct amount of $120,000. A correctly reported the amount of tips reported to it by employees under section 6053(a) as $80,000. Thus A reported the excess of 8 percent of its gross receipts over tips reported to it as zero, rather than as the correct amount of $40,000. The requirement of reporting gross receipts is considered merely a step in the computation of the excess of 8 percent of gross receipts over tips reported to A under section 6053(a), so that the penalty for intentional disregard will be $4,000 (*i.e.*, 10 percent of the difference between the $40,000 required to be reported as the excess of 8 percent of gross receipts over tips reported under section 6053(a), and the zero amount actually reported).

(g) *Definitions*.—(1) *Information return*.—For purposes of this section the term "information return" means any statement described in paragraph (g)(2) of this section, any return described in paragraph (g)(3) of this section, and any other items described in paragraph (g)(4) of this section.

(2) *Statements*.—The statements subject to this section are the statements required by—

(i) Section 6041(a) or (b) (relating to certain information at source, generally reported on Form 1099-MISC, "Miscellaneous Income"; Form W-2, "Wage and Tax Statement"; Form W-2G, "Certain Gambling Winnings"; and Form 1099-INT, "Interest Income");

(ii) Section 6042(a)(1) (relating to payments of dividends, generally reported on Form 1099-DIV, "Dividends and Distributions");

(iii) Section 6044(a)(1) (relating to payments of patronage dividends, generally reported on Form 1099-PATR, "Taxable Distributions Received From Cooperatives");

(iv) Section 6049(a) (relating to payments of interest, generally reported on Form 1099-INT or Form 1099-OID, "Original Issue Discount");

(v) Section 6050A(a) (relating to reporting requirements of certain fishing boat operators, generally reported on Form 1099-MISC);

(vi) Section 6050N(a) (relating to payments of royalties, generally reported on Form 1099-MISC);

(vii) Section 6051(d) (relating to information returns with respect to income tax withheld, generally reported on Form W-2);

(viii) Section 6050R (relating to returns relating to certain purchases of fish, generally reported on Form 1099-MISC);

(ix) Section 110(d) (relating to qualified lessee construction allowances for shortterm leases, generally reported by attaching a statement to an income tax return);

(x) Section 408(i) (relating to reports with respect to individual retirement accounts or annuities on Form 1099-R, "Distributions From Pensions, Annuities, Retirement or Profit-Sharing Plans, IRAs, Insurance Contracts, etc."); or

(xi) Section 6047(d) (relating to reports by employers, plan administrators, etc., on Form 1099-R).

(3) *Returns*.—The returns subject to this section are the returns required by—

(i) Section 6041A(a) or (b) (relating to returns of direct sellers, generally reported on Form 1099-MISC);

(ii) Section 6043A(a) (relating to returns relating to taxable mergers and acquisitions);

(iii) Section 6045(a) or (d) (relating to returns of brokers, generally reported on Form 1099-B, "Proceeds From Broker and Barter Exchange Transactions," for broker transactions; Form 1099-S, "Proceeds From Real Estate Transactions," for gross proceeds from the sale or exchange of real estate; and Form 1099-MISC for certain substitute payments and payments to attorneys);

(iv) Section 6045B(a) (relating to returns relating to actions affecting basis of specified securities);

(v) Section 6050H(a) or (h)(1) (relating to mortgage interest received in trade or business from individuals, generally reported on Form 1098, "Mortgage Interest Statement");

(vi) Section 6050I(a) or (g)(1) (relating to cash received in trade or business, etc., generally reported on Form 8300, "Report of Cash Payments Over $10,000 Received In a Trade or Business");

(vii) Section 6050J(a) (relating to foreclosures and abandonments of security, generally reported on Form 1099-A, "Acquisition or Abandonment of Secured Property");

(viii) Section 6050K(a) (relating to exchanges of certain partnership interests, generally reported on Form 8308, "Report of a Sale or Exchange of Certain Partnership Interests");

(ix) Section 6050L(a) (relating to returns relating to certain dispositions of donated property, generally reported on Form 8282, "Donee Information Return");

(x) Section 6050P (relating to returns relating to the cancellation of indebtedness by certain financial entities, generally reported on Form 1099-C, "Cancellation of Debt");

(xi) Section 6050Q (relating to certain long-term care benefits, generally reported on Form 1099-LTC, "Long-Term Care and Accelerated Death Benefits");

(xii) Section 6050S (relating to returns relating to payments for qualified tuition and related expenses, generally reported on Form 1098-E, "Student Loan Interest Statement," or Form 1098-T, "Tuition Statement");

(xiii) Section 6050T (relating to returns relating to credit for health insurance costs of eligible individuals, generally reported on Form 1099-H, "Health Coverage Tax Credit (HCTC) Advance Payments");

(xiv) Section 6052(a) (relating to reporting payment of wages in the form of group-life insurance, generally reported on Form W-2);

(xv) Section 6050V (relating to returns relating to applicable insurance contracts in which certain exempt organizations hold interests, generally reported on Form 8921, "Applicable Insurance Contract Information Return");

(xvi) Section 6053(c)(1) (relating to reporting with respect to certain tips, generally reported on Form 8027, "Employer's Annual Information Return of Tip Income and Allocated Tips");

(xvii) Section 1060(b) (relating to reporting requirements of transferors and transferees in certain asset acquisitions, generally reported on Form 8594, "Asset Acquisition Statement"), or section 1060(e) (relating to information required in the case of certain transfers of interests in entities (effective for acquisitions after October 9, 1990, except any acquisition pursuant to a written binding contract in effect on October 9, 1990, and at all times thereafter before such acquisition));

(xviii) Section 4101(d) (relating to information reporting with respect to fuel oils (effective for information returns required to be filed after November 30, 1990));

(xix) Section 338(h)(10)(C) (relating to information required to be furnished to the Secretary in case of elective recognition of gain or loss (effective for acquisitions after October 9, 1990, except any acquisition pursuant to a written binding contract in effect on October 9, 1990, and at all times thereafter before such acquisition));

(xx) Section 264(f)(5)(A)(iv) (relating to reporting with respect to certain life insurance and annuity contracts);

(xxi) Section 6050U (relating to charges or payments for qualified long-term care insurance contracts under combined arrangements, generally reported on Form 1099-R);

(xxii) Section 6039(a) (relating to returns required with respect to certain options);

(xxiii) Section 6050W (relating to information returns with respect to payments made in settlement of payment card and third party network transactions);

(xxiv) Section 6055 (relating to information returns reporting minimum essential coverage); or

(xxv) Section 6056 (relating to information returns reporting on offers of health insurance coverage by applicable large employer members).

(4) *Other items.*—The term *information return* also includes any form, statement, or schedule required to be filed with the Internal Revenue Service with respect to any amount from which tax is required to be deducted and withheld under chapter 3 of the Internal Revenue Code (or from which tax would be required to be so deducted and withheld but for an exemption under the Internal Revenue Code or any treaty obligation of the United States), generally Forms 1042-S, "Foreign Person's U.S. Source Income Subject to Withholding," and 8805, "Foreign Partner's Information Statement of Section 1446 Withholding Tax." The provisions of this paragraph (g)(4) referring to Form 8805, shall apply to partnership taxable years beginning after May 18, 2005, or such earlier time as the regulations under §§1.1446-1 through 1.1446-5 of this chapter apply by reason of an election under §1.1446-7 of this chapter.

(5) *Payee.*—For purposes of section 6721 the term "payee" means any person who is required to receive a copy of the information set forth on an information return by the filer of the return as defined in section 6724(d)(1).

(6) *Filer.*—For purposes of this section the term "filer" means a person that is required to file an information return as defined in paragraph (g)(1) of this section under the applicable information reporting section described in paragraph (g)(2) through (4) of this section.

(h) *Applicability date.*—The rules of paragraph (a)(2)(ii) of this section apply to information returns required to be filed during calendar years beginning after December 31, 2023. For the rules that apply under paragraph (a)(2)(i) of this section to information returns required to be filed during calendar years beginning before January 1, 2024, see 26 CFR part 301, revised as of April 1, 2022. [Reg. §301.6721-1.]

☐ [*T.D.* 8386, 12-27-91. *Amended by T.D.* 8843, 11-10-99; *T.D.* 9200, 5-13-2005; *T.D.* 9496, 8-13-2010; *T.D.* 9504, 10-12-2010, *T.D.* 9660, 3-5-2014 *and T.D.* 9972, 2-21-2023.]

[Reg. §301.6722-1]

§301.6722-1. Failure to furnish correct payee statements.—(a) *Imposition of penalty.*—(1) *General rule.*—A penalty of $50 is imposed for each payee statement (as defined in section 6724(d)(2)) with respect to which a failure (as defined in section 6722(a) and paragraph (a)(2) of this section) occurs. No more than one penalty will be imposed under this paragraph (a) with respect to a single payee statement even though there may be more than one failure with respect to such statement. However, the penalty shall apply to failures on composite substitute payee statements as though each type of payment and other required information were furnished on separate statements. A "composite substitute payee statement" is a single document created by a filer to reflect several types of payments made to the same payee. The total amount imposed on any person for all failures during any calendar year with respect to all payee statements shall not exceed $100,000. See section 6722(c) and paragraph(c) of this section for higher penalties when a failure is due to intentional disregard of the requirement to furnish timely correct payee statements. See paragraph (a)(1) of § 301.6724-1 for a waiver of the penalty for a failure that is due to reasonable cause.

(2) *Failures subject to the penalty*.—The failures to which section 6722(a) and paragraph (a)(1) of this section apply are—

(i) A failure to furnish a payee statement on or before the prescribed date therefor to the person to whom such statement is required to be furnished ("failure to furnish timely"), and

(ii) A failure to include all of the information required to be shown on a payee statement or the inclusion of incorrect information ("failure to include correct information").

A failure to furnish timely includes a failure to furnish a written statement to the payee in a statement mailing as required under sections 6042(c), 6044(e), 6049(c), and 6050N(b), as well as a failure to furnish the statement on a form acceptable to the Internal Revenue Service. Except as provided in paragraph (b) of this section, a failure to include correct information encompasses a failure to include the information required by applicable information reporting statutes or by any administrative pronouncements issued thereunder (such as regulations, revenue rulings, revenue procedures, or information reporting forms).

(b) *Exception for inconsequential errors or omissions*.—(1) *In general*.—An inconsequential error or omission is not considered a failure to include correct information. For purposes of this paragraph (b), the term "inconsequential error or omission" means any failure that cannot reasonably be expected to prevent or hinder the payee from timely receiving correct information and reporting it on his or her return or from otherwise putting the statement to its intended use.

(2) *Errors or omissions that are never inconsequential*.—Errors or omissions relating to the following are never inconsequential:

(i) A dollar amount,

(ii) The significant items in the address of a payee, which is the address provided by the payee to the filer,

(iii) The appropriate form for the information provided (*i.e.*, whether or not the form is an acceptable substitute for an official form of the Internal Revenue Service), and

(iv) The manner of furnishing a statement required under sections 6042(c), 6044(e), 6049(e), and 6050N(b).

The Internal Revenue Service may, by administrative pronouncement, specify other types of errors or omissions that are never inconsequential.

(3) *Examples*.—The provisions of this paragraph (b) may be illustrated by the following examples which do not take into account any possible application of the penalty for intentional disregard under paragraph (c) of this section or the reasonable cause waiver under paragraph (a) of § 301.6724-1:

Example 1. A payor furnishes a statement with respect to a Form 1099-MISC (relating to miscellaneous income). The payee statement is complete and correct, except the word "boulevard" is misspelled in the payee's address. The error cannot reasonably be expected to prevent or hinder the payee from timely receiving correct information and reporting it on his or her tax return or from otherwise putting the statement to its intended use. Therefore, no penalty is imposed under paragraph (a) of this section.

Example 2. Assume the same facts as in *Example 1*, except that the only error on the payee statement is that the payee's street address, 4821 Grant Boulevard, is reported incorrectly as 8421 Grant Boulevard. A penalty is imposed under paragraph (a) of this section with respect to the payee statement because the error can reasonably be expected to prevent or hinder the payee from timely receiving correct information and reporting it on his or her tax return or from otherwise putting the statement to its intended use.

(c) *Higher penalty for intentional disregard of requirement to furnish timely correct payee statements*.—(1) *Application of section 6722(c)*.—If a failure is due to intentional disregard of the requirement to furnish timely correct payee statements, the amount of the penalty shall be determined under paragraph (c)(2) of this section. Whether a failure is due to intentional disregard of the requirement to furnish timely correct payee statements is based upon the facts and circumstances surrounding the failure. The facts and circumstances considered include those under § 301.6721-1(f)(3), which shall apply in determining whether a failure under this section is due to intentional disregard.

(2) *Amount of the penalty*.—If one or more failures under paragraph (a) of this section are due to intentional disregard of the requirement to furnish timely payee statements or of the requirement to include correct information, then, with respect to each such failure determined under this paragraph (c)(2)—

(i) The $100,000 limitation under paragraph (a) of this section shall not apply and the penalty under this paragraph (c)(2) shall not be taken into account in applying the $100,000 limitation to penalties not determined under this paragraph (c)(2);

(ii) The penalty imposed under paragraph (a) of this section shall be $100 or, if greater, the statutory percentage; and

(iii) The term "statutory percentage" means—

(A) In the case of a payee statement other than a statement required under section 6045(b), 6041A(e) (in respect of a return required under section 6041A(b)), 6050H(d), 6050J(e), 6050K(b), or 6050L(c), 10 percent of the aggregate dollar amount of the items required to be reported correctly, or

(B) In the case of a payee statement required under section 6045(b), 6050K(b), or 6050L(c), 5 percent of the aggregate dollar amount of the items required to be reported correctly.

(3) *Computation of the penalty; aggregate dollar amount of items required to be shown correctly.*—The aggregate dollar amount used in computing the penalty under this paragraph (c) is the amount that is not reported or is reported incorrectly. If the intentional disregard relates to a dollar amount, the statutory percentage is applied to the difference between the dollar amount reported and the amount required to be reported correctly. If the intentional disregard relates to any other item on the return, the statutory percentage is applied to the aggregate amount of items required to be reported correctly. In determining such amount the same item shall be counted only once. For example, if a filer willfully fails to furnish a Form 1099-INT on which $800 of interest and $160 of Federal income tax withheld (*i.e.*, backup withholding) is required to be shown, only the $800 amount is taken into account in computing the penalty.

(d) *Definitions.*—(1) *Payee.*—See § 301.6721-1(g)(5) for the definition of "payee."

(2) *Payee statement.*—The term *payee statement* means any statement required to be furnished under—

(i) Section 6031(b) or (c), 6034A, or 6037(b) (relating to statements furnished by certain pass-thru entities, generally a Schedule K-1 (Form 1065), "Partner's Share of Income, Deductions, Credits, etc.," for section 6031(b) or (c), a copy of the Schedule K-1 (Form 1041), "Beneficiary's Share of Income, Deductions, Credits, etc.," for section 6034A, and a copy of Schedule K-1 (Form 1120S), "Shareholder's Share of Income, Deductions, Credits, etc.," for section 6037(b));

(ii) Section 6039(b) (relating to information required in connection with certain options);

(iii) Section 6041(d) (relating to information at source, generally the recipient copy of Form 1099-MISC, "Miscellaneous Income"; Form W-2, "Wage and Tax Statement"; Form 1099-INT, "Interest Income"; and the winner's copies of Form W-2G, "Certain Gambling Winnings");

(iv) Section 6041A(e) (relating to returns regarding payments of remuneration for services and direct sales, generally the recipient copy of Form 1099-MISC);

(v) Section 6042(c) (relating to returns regarding payments of dividends and corporate earnings and profits, generally the recipient copy of Form 1099-DIV, "Dividends and Distributions");

(vi) Section 6043A(b) or (d) (relating to returns relating to taxable mergers and acquisitions);

(vii) Section 6044(e) (relating to returns regarding payments of patronage dividends, generally the recipient copy of Form 1099-PATR, "Taxable Distributions Received From Cooperatives");

(viii) Section 6045(b) or (d) (relating to returns of brokers, generally the recipient copy of Form 1099-B, "Proceeds From Broker and Barter Exchange Transactions," for broker transactions; the transferor copy of Form 1099-S, "Proceeds From Real Estate Transactions," for reporting proceeds from real estate transactions; and the recipient copy of Form 1099-MISC for certain substitute payments and payments to attorneys);

(ix) Section 6045A (relating to information required in connection with transfers of covered securities to brokers);

(x) Section 6045B(c) or (e) (relating to returns relating to actions affecting basis of specified securities);

(xi) Section 6049(c) (relating to returns regarding payments of interest, generally the recipient copy of Form 1099-INT or Form 1099-OID, "Original Issue Discount");

(xii) Section 6050A(b) (relating to reporting requirements of certain fishing boat operators, generally the recipient copy of Form 1099-MISC);

(xiii) Section 6050H(d) or (h)(2) (relating to returns relating to mortgage interest received in trade or business from individuals, generally the payor copy of Form 1098, "Mortgage Interest Statement");

(xiv) Section 6050I(e), (g)(4), or (g)(5) (relating to returns relating to cash received in trade or business, etc., generally a copy of Form 8300, "Report of Cash Payments Over $10,000 Received In a Trade or Business");

(xv) Section 6050J(e) (relating to returns relating to foreclosures and abandonments of security, generally the borrower copy of Form 1099-A, "Acquisition or Abandonment of Secured Property");

(xvi) Section 6050K(b) (relating to returns relating to exchanges of certain partnership interests, generally a copy of Form 8308, "Report of a Sale or Exchange of Certain Partnership Interests");

(xvii) Section 6050L(c) (relating to returns relating to certain dispositions of donated property, generally a copy of Form 8282, "Donee Information Return");

(xviii) Section 6050N(b) (relating to returns regarding payments of royalties, generally the recipient copy of Form 1099-MISC);

(xix) Section 6050P(d) (relating to returns relating to the cancellation of indebtedness by certain financial entities, generally the recipient copy of Form 1099-C, "Cancellation of Debt");

(xx) Section 6050Q(b) (relating to certain long-term care benefits, generally the policyholder and insured copies of Form 1099-LTC, "Long-Term Care and Accelerated Death Benefits");

(xxi) Section 6050R(c) (relating to returns relating to certain purchases of fish, generally the recipient copy of Form 1099-MISC);

(xxii) Section 6051 (relating to receipts for employees, generally the employee copy of Form W-2);

(xxiii) Section 6052(b) (relating to returns regarding payment of wages in the form of group-term life insurance, generally the employee copy of Form W-2);

(xxiv) Section 6053(b) or (c) (relating to reports of tips, generally the employee copy of Form W-2);

(xxv) Section 6048(b)(1)(B) (relating to foreign trust reporting requirements, generally copies of the owner and beneficiary statements of Form 3520-A, "Annual Information Return of Foreign Trust With a U.S. Owner");

(xxvi) Section 408(i) (relating to reports with respect to individual retirement plans on the recipient copies of Form 1099-R, "Distributions From Pensions, Annuities, Retirement or Profit-Sharing Plans, IRAs, Insurance Contracts, etc.");

(xxvii) Section 6047(d) (relating to reports by plan administrators on the recipient copies of Form 1099-R);

(xxviii) Section 6050S(d) (relating to returns relating to qualified tuition and related expenses, generally the borrower copy of Form 1098-E, "Student Loan Interest Statement," or the student copy of Form 1098-T, "Tuition Statement");

(xxix) Section 264(f)(5)(A)(iv) (relating to reporting with respect to certain life insurance and annuity contracts);

(xxx) Section 6050T (relating to returns relating to credit for health insurance costs of eligible individuals, generally the recipient copy of Form 1099-H, "Health Coverage Tax Credit (HCTC) Advance Payments");

(xxxi) Section 6050U (relating to charges or payments for qualified long-term care insurance contracts under combined arrangements, generally the recipient copy of Form 1099-R);

(xxxii) Section 6050W (relating to information returns with respect to payments made in settlement of payment card and third party network transactions);

(xxxiii) Section 6055 (relating to information returns reporting minimum essential coverage); or

(xxxiv) Section 6056 (relating to information returns reporting on offers of health insurance coverage by applicable large employer members).

(3) *Other items.*—The term *payee statement* also includes any form, statement, or schedule required to be furnished to the recipient of any amount from which tax is required to be deducted and withheld under chapter 3 of the Internal Revenue Code (or from which tax would be required to be so deducted and withheld but for an exemption under the Internal Revenue Code or any treaty obligation of the United States) (generally the recipient copy of Form 1042-S, "Foreign Person's U.S. Source Income subject to Withholding," or Form 8805, "Foreign Partner's Information Statement of Section 1446 Withholding Tax.")

(e) *Effective/Applicability date.*—The reference in paragraph (d)(3) of this section to Form 8805 shall apply to partnership taxable years beginning after April 29, 2008. [Reg. § 301.6722-1.]

☐ [*T.D.* 8386, 12-27-91. *Amended by T.D.* 9394, 4-28-2008; *T.D.* 9496, 8-13-2010; *T.D.* 9504, 10-12-2010 *and T.D.* 9660, 3-5-2014.]

[Reg. § 301.6901-1]

§ 301.6901-1. Procedure in the case of transferred assets.—(a) *Method of collection.*—(1) *Income, estate, and gift taxes.*—The amount for which a transferee of property of—

(i) A taxpayer, in the case of a tax imposed by subtitle A (relating to income taxes),

(ii) A decedent, in the case of the estate tax imposed by chapter 11 of the Code, or

(iii) A donor, in the case of the gift tax imposed by chapter 12 of the Code, is liable, at law or in equity, and the amount of the personal liability of a fiduciary under section 3467 of the Revised Statutes, as amended (31 U.S.C. 192), in respect of the payment of such taxes, whether shown on the return of the taxpayer or determined as a deficiency in the tax, shall be assessed against such transferee or fiduciary and paid and collected in the same manner and subject to the same provisions and limitations as in the case of a deficiency in the tax with respect to which such liability is incurred, except as hereinafter provided.

(2) *Other taxes.*—The liability, at law or in equity, of a transferee of property of any person liable in respect of any other tax, in any case where the liability of the transferee arises on the liquidation of a corporation or partnership, or a corporate reorganization within the meaning of section 368(a), shall be assessed against such transferee and paid and collected in the same manner and subject to the same provisions and limitations as in the case of the tax with respect to which such liability is incurred, except as hereinafter provided.

(3) *Applicable provisions.*—The provisions of the Code made applicable by section 6901(a) to the liability of a transferee or fiduciary referred to in subparagraphs (1) and (2) of this paragraph include the provisions relating to:

(i) Delinquency in payment after notice and demand and the amount of interest attaching because of such delinquency;

(ii) The authorization of distraint and proceedings in court for collection;

(iii) The prohibition of claims and suits for refund; and

(iv) In any instance in which the liability of a transferee or fiduciary is one referred to in subparagraph (1) of this paragraph, the filing of a petition with the Tax Court of the United States and the filing of a petition for review of the Tax Court's decision.

For detailed provisions relating to assessments, collections, and refunds, see chapters 63, 64, and 65 of the Code, respectively.

(b) *Definition of transferee.*—As used in this section, the term "transferee" includes an heir, legatee, devisee, distributee of an estate of a deceased person, the shareholder of a dissolved corporation, the assignee or donee of an insolvent person, the successor of a corporation, a party to a reorganization as defined in section 368, and all other classes of distributees. Such term also includes, with respect to the gift tax, a donee (without regard to the solvency of the donor) and, with respect to the estate tax, any person who, under section 6324(a)(2), is personally liable for any part of such tax.

(c) *Period of limitation on assessment.*—The period of limitation for assessment of the liability of a transferee or of a fiduciary is as follows:

(1) *Initial transferee.*—In the case of the liability of an initial transferee, one year after the expiration of the period of limitation for assessment against the taxpayer in the case of a tax imposed by subtitle A (relating to income taxes), the executor in the case of the estate tax imposed by Chapter 11, or the donor in the case of the gift tax imposed by Chapter 12, each of which for purposes of this section is referred to as the "taxpayer" (see subchapter A of Chapter 66 of the Code).

(2) *Transferee of transferee.*—In the case of the liability of a transferee of a transferee, one year after the expiration of the period of limitation for assessment against the preceding transferee, or three years after the expiration of the period of limitation for assessment against the taxpayer, whichever of such periods first expires.

(3) *Court proceeding against taxpayer or last preceding transferee.*—If, before the expiration of the period specified in subparagraph (1) or subparagraph (2) of this paragraph (whichever is applicable), a court proceeding against the taxpayer or last preceding transferee for the collection of the tax or liability in respect thereof, respectively, has been begun within the period of limitation for the commencement of such proceeding, then within one year after the return of execution in such proceeding.

(4) *Fiduciary.*—In the case of the liability of a fiduciary, not later than one year after the liability arises or not later than the expiration of the period for collection of the tax in respect of which such liability arises, whichever is the later.

(d) *Extension by agreement.*—(1) *Extension of time for assessment.*—The time prescribed by section 6901 for the assessment of the liability of a transferee or fiduciary may, prior to the expiration of such time, be extended for any period of time agreed upon in writing by the transferee or fiduciary and the district director or an assistant regional commissioner. The extension shall become effective when the agreement has been executed by both parties. The period agreed upon may be extended by subsequent agreements in writing made before the expiration of the period previously agreed upon.

(2) *Extension of time for credit or refund.*—(i) For the purpose of determining the period of limitation on credit or refund to the transferee or fiduciary of overpayments made by such transferee or fiduciary or overpayments made by the taxpayer to which such transferee or fiduciary may be legally entitled to credit or refund, an agreement and any extension thereof referred to in subparagraph (1) of this paragraph shall be deemed an agreement and extension thereof for purposes of section 6511(c) (relating to limitations on credit or refund in case of extension of time by agreement).

(ii) For the purpose of determining the limit specified in section 6511(c)(2) on the amount of the credit or refund, if the agreement is executed after the expiration of the period of limitation for assessment against the taxpayer with reference to whom the liability of such transferee or fiduciary arises, the periods specified in section 6511(b)(2) shall be increased by the period from the date of such expiration to the date the agreement is executed. The application of this subdivision may be illustrated by the following example:

Example. Assume that Corporation A files its income tax return on March 15, 1955, for the calendar year 1954, showing a liability of $100,000 which is paid with the return. The period within which an assessment may be made against Corporation A expires on March 15, 1958. Corporation B is a transferee of Corporation A. An agreement is executed on October 9, 1958, extending beyond its normal expiration date of March 15, 1959, the period within which an assessment may be made against Corporation B. Under section 6511(c)(2) and section 6511(b)(2)(A) the portion of an overpayment, paid before the execution of an agreement extending the period for assessment, may not be credited or refunded unless paid within three years prior to the date on which the agreement is executed. However, as applied to Corporation B such 3-year period is increased under section 6901(d)(2) to include the period from March 15, 1958, to October 9, 1958, the date on which the agreement was executed.

(e) *Period of assessment against taxpayer.*—For the purpose of determining the period of limitation for assessment against a transferee or a fiduciary, if the taxpayer is deceased, or, in the case of a corporation, has terminated its existence, the period of limitation for assessment against the taxpayer shall be the period that would be in effect had the death or termination of existence not occurred.

(f) *Suspension of running of period of limitations.*—In the cases of the income, estate, and gift taxes, if a notice of the liability of a transferee or the liability of a fiduciary has been mailed to such transferee or to such fiduciary under the provisions of section 6212, then the running of the statute of limitations shall be suspended for the period during which assessment is prohibited in respect of the liability of the transferee or fiduciary (and in any event, if a proceeding in respect of the liability is placed on the docket of the Tax Court, until the decision of the Tax Court becomes final), and for 60 days thereafter. [Reg. § 301.6901-1.]

☐ [*T.D.* 6246, 8-2-57. *Amended by T.D.* 6498, 10-24-60 *and T.D.* 6585, 12-27-61.]

[Reg. §301.6903-1]

§301.6903-1. Notice of fiduciary relationship.—(a) *Rights and obligations of fiduciary.*—Every person acting for another person in a fiduciary capacity shall give notice thereof to the district director in writing. As soon as such notice is filed with the district director such fiduciary must, except as otherwise specifically provided, assume the powers, rights, duties, and privileges of the taxpayer with respect to the taxes imposed by the Code. If the person is acting as a fiduciary for a transferee or other person subject to the liability specified in section 6901, such fiduciary is required to assume the powers, rights, duties, and privileges of the transferee or other person under that section. The amount of the tax or liability is ordinarily not collectible from the personal estate of the fiduciary but is collectible from the estate of the taxpayer or from the estate of the transferee or other person subject to the liability specified in section 6901.

(b) *Manner of notice.*—(1) *Notices filed before April 24, 2002.*—This paragraph (b)(1) applies to notices filed before April 24, 2002. The notice shall be signed by the fiduciary, and shall be filed with the Internal Revenue Service office where the return of the person for whom the fiduciary is acting is required to be filed. The notice must state the name and address of the person for whom the fiduciary is acting, and the nature of the liability of such person; that is, whether it is a liability for tax, and, if so, the type of tax, the year or years involved, or a liability at law or in equity of a transferee of property of a taxpayer, or a liability of a fiduciary under section 3467 of the Revised Statutes, as amended (31 U.S.C. 192) in respect of the payment of any tax from the estate of the taxpayer. Satisfactory evidence of the authority of the fiduciary to act for any other person in a fiduciary capacity must be filed with and made a part of the notice. If the fiduciary capacity exists by order of court, a certified copy of the order may be regarded as satisfactory evidence. When the fiduciary capacity has terminated, the fiduciary, in order to be relieved of any further duty or liability as such, must file with the Internal Revenue Service office with whom the notice of fiduciary relationship was filed written notice that the fiduciary capacity has terminated as to him, accompanied by satisfactory evidence of the termination of the fiduciary capacity. The notice of termination should state the name and address of the person, if any, who has been substituted as fiduciary. Any written notice disclosing a fiduciary relationship which has been filed with the Commissioner under the Internal Revenue Code of 1939 or any prior revenue law shall be considered as sufficient notice within the meaning of section 6903. Any satisfactory evidence of the authority of the fiduciary to act for another person already filed with the Commissioner or district director need not be resubmitted.

(2) *Notices filed on or after April 24, 2002.*—This paragraph (b)(2) applies to notices filed on or after April 24, 2002. The notice shall be signed by the fiduciary, and shall be filed with the Internal Revenue Service Center where the return of the person for whom the fiduciary is acting is required to be filed. The notice must state the name and address of the person for whom the fiduciary is acting, and the nature of the liability of such person; that is, whether it is a liability for tax, and if so, the type of tax, the year or years involved, or a liability at law or in equity of a transferee of property of a taxpayer, or a liability of a fiduciary under 31 U.S.C. 3713(b), in respect of the payment of any tax from the estate of the taxpayer. The fiduciary must retain satisfactory evidence of his or her authority to act for any other person in a fiduciary capacity as long as the evidence may become material in the administration of any internal revenue law.

(c) *Where notice is not filed.*—If the notice of the fiduciary capacity described in paragraph (b) of this section is not filed with the district director before the sending of notice of a deficiency by registered mail or certified mail to the last known address of the taxpayer (see section 6212), or the last known address of the transferee or other person subject to liability (see section 6901(g)), no notice of the deficiency will be sent to the fiduciary. For further guidance regarding the definition of last known address, see §301.6212-2. In such a case the sending of the notice to the last known address of the taxpayer, transferee, or other person, as the case may be, will be a sufficient compliance with the requirements of the Code, even though such taxpayer, transferee, or other person is deceased, or is under a legal disability, or, in the case of a corporation, has terminated its existence. Under such circumstances, if no petition is filed with the Tax Court of the United States within 90 days after the mailing of the notice (or within 150 days after mailing in the case of such a notice addressed to a person outside the States of the Union and the District of Columbia) to the taxpayer, transferee, or other person, the tax, or liability under section 6901, will be assessed immediately upon the expiration of such 90-day or 150-day period, and demand for payment will be made. See paragraph (a) of §301.6213-1 with respect to the expiration of such 90-day or 150-day period.

(d) *Definition of fiduciary.*—The term "fiduciary" is defined in section 7701(a)(6) to mean a guardian, trustee, executor, administrator, receiver, conservator, or any person acting in any fiduciary capacity for any person.

(e) *Applicability of other provisions.*—This section, relating to the provisions of section 6903, shall not be taken to abridge in any way the powers and duties of fiduciaries provided for in other sections of the Code. [Reg. §301.6903-1.]

□ [*T.D.* 6246, 8-2-57. *Amended by T.D.* 6498, 10-24-60; *T.D.* 6585, 12-27-61; *T.D.* 8939, 1-11-2001; *T.D.* 8989, 4-23-2002 *and T.D.* 9040, 1-30-2003.]

[Reg. § 20.6905-1]

§ 20.6905-1. Discharge of executor from personal liability for decedent's income and gift taxes.—For regulations concerning the discharge of an executor from personal liability for a decedent's income and gift taxes, see § 301.6905-1 of this chapter (Regulations on Procedure and Administration). [Reg. § 20.6905-1.]

☐ [*T.D.* 7238, 12-28-72.]

[Reg. § 25.6905-1]

§ 25.6905-1. Discharge of executor from personal liability for decedent's income and gift taxes.—For regulations concerning the discharge of an executor from personal liability for a decedent's income and gift taxes, see § 301.6905-1 of this chapter (Regulations on Procedure and Administration). [Reg. § 25.6905-1.]

☐ [*T.D.* 7238, 12-28-72.]

[Reg. § 301.6905-1]

§ 301.6905-1. Discharge of executor from personal liability for decedent's income and gift taxes.—(a) *Discharge of liability.*—With respect to decedents dying after December 31, 1970, the executor of a decedent's estate may make written application to the applicable internal revenue officer with whom the estate tax return is required to be filed, as provided in § 20.6091-1 of this chapter, for a determination of the income or gift taxes imposed upon the decedent by subtitle A or by chapter 12 of the Code, and for a discharge of personal liability therefrom. If no estate tax return is required to be filed, then such application should be filed where the decedent's final income tax return is required to be filed. The application must be filed after the return with respect to such income or gift taxes is filed. Within 9 months (1 year with respect to the estate of a decedent dying before January 1, 1974) after receipt of the application, the executor shall be notified of the amount of the income or gift tax and, upon payment thereof, he will be discharged from personal liability for any deficiency in income or gift tax thereafter found to be due. If no such notification is received, the executor is discharged at the end of such 9-month (1 year with respect to the estate of a decedent dying before January 1, 1974) period from personal liability for any deficiency thereafter found to be due. The discharge of the executor under this section from personal liability applies only to him in his personal capacity and to his personal assets. The discharge is not applicable to his liability as executor to the extent of the assets of the estate in his possession or control. Further, the discharge does not operate as a release of any part of the property from the lien provided under section 6321 or the special lien provided under subsection (a) or (b) of section 6324.

(b) *Definition of "executor."*.—For purposes of this section, the term "executor" means the executor or administrator of the decedent appointed, qualified, and acting within the United States.

(c) *Cross reference.*—For provisions concerning the discharge of the executor from personal liability for estate taxes imposed by chapter 11 of the Code, see section 2204 and the regulations thereunder. [Reg. § 301.6905-1.]

☐ [*T.D.* 7238, 12-28-72.]

[Reg. § 20.7101-1]

§ 20.7101-1. Form of bonds.—See paragraph (b) of § 20.6165-1 for provisions relating to the bond required in any case in which the payment of the tax attributable to a reversionary or remainder interest has been postponed under the provisions of § 20.6163-1. For further provisions relating to bonds, see § 20.6165-1 of these regulations and the regulations under section 7101 contained in Part 301 of this chapter (Regulations on Procedure and Administration). **[Reg. § 20.7101-1.]**

☐ [*T.D.* 6296, 6-23-58. *Amended by T.D.* 6600, 5-28-62.]

[Reg. § 25.7101-1]

§ 25.7101-1. Form of bonds.—For provisions relating to form of bonds, see the regulations under section 7101 contained in Part 301 of this chapter (Regulations on Procedure and Administration). **[Reg. § 25.7101-1.]**

☐ [*T.D.* 6334, 10-14-58. *Amended by T.D.* 6600, 5-28-62.]

[Reg. § 301.7101-1]

§ 301.7101-1. Form of bond and surety required.—(a) *In general.*—Any person required to furnish a bond under the provisions of the Code (other than section 6803(a)(1), relating to bonds required of certain postmasters before June 6, 1972, and section 7485, relating to bonds to stay assessment and collection of a deficiency pending review of a Tax Court decision), or under any rules or regulations prescribed under the Code, shall (except as provided in paragraph (d) of this section) execute such bond;

(1) On the appropriate form prescribed by the Internal Revenue Service (which may be obtained from the district director), and

(2) With satisfactory surety.

For provisions as to what will be considered "satisfactory surety", see paragraph (b) of this section. The bonds referred to in this paragraph shall be drawn in favor of the United States.

(b) *Satisfactory surety.*—(1) *Approved surety company or bonds or notes of the United States.*—For purposes of paragraph (a) of this section, a bond shall be considered executed with satisfactory surety if:

(i) It is executed by a surety company holding a certificate of authority from the Secretary as an acceptable surety on Federal bonds; or

(ii) It is secured by bonds or notes of the United States as provided in 6 U.S.C. 15 (see 31 CFR Part 225).

(2) *Other surety acceptable in discretion of district director.*—Unless otherwise expressly provided in the Code, or the regulations thereunder, a bond may, in the discretion of the district

director, be considered executed with satisfactory surety if, in lieu of being executed or secured as provided in subparagraph (1) of this paragraph, it is—

(i) Executed by a corporate surety (other than a surety company), provided such corporate surety establishes that it is within its corporate powers to act as surety for another corporation or an individual;

(ii) Executed by two or more individual sureties, provided such individual sureties meet the conditions contained in subparagraph (3) of this paragraph;

(iii) Secured by a mortgage on real or personal property;

(iv) Secured by a certified, cashier's, or treasurer's check drawn on any bank or trust company incorporated under the laws of the United States or any State, Territory, or possession of the United States, or by a United States postal, bank, express, or telegraph money order;

(v) Secured by corporate bonds or stocks, or by bonds issued by a State or political subdivision thereof, of recognized stability; or

(vi) Secured by any other acceptable collateral.

Collateral shall be deposited with the district director or, in his discretion, with a responsible financial institution acting as escrow agent.

(3) *Conditions to be met by individual sureties.*—If a bond is executed by two or more individual sureties, the following conditions must be met by each such individual surety:

(i) He must reside within the State in which the principal place of business or legal residence of the primary obligor is located;

(ii) He must have property subject to execution of a current market value, above all encumbrances, equal to at least the penalty of the bond;

(iii) All real property which he offers as security must be located in the State in which the principal place of business or legal residence of the primary obligor is located;

(iv) He must agree not to mortgage, or otherwise encumber, any property offered as security while the bond continues in effect without first securing the permission of the district director; and

(v) He must file with the bond, and annually thereafter so long as the bond continues in effect, an affidavit as to the adequacy of his security, executed on the appropriate form furnished by the district director.

Partners may not act as sureties upon bonds of their partnership. Stockholders of a corporate principal may be accepted as sureties provided their qualifications as such are independent of their holding of the stock of the corporation.

(4) *Adequacy of surety.*—No surety or security shall be accepted if it does not adequately protect the interest of the United States.

(c) *Bonds required by Internal Revenue Code of 1939.*—This section shall also apply in the case of bonds required under the Internal Revenue Code of 1939 (other than sections 1423(b) and 1145) or under the regulations under such Code.

(d) *Bonds required under subtitle E and chapter 75 of the Internal Revenue Code of 1954.*—Bonds required under subtitle E and chapter 75, subtitle F, of the Internal Revenue Code of 1954 (or under the corresponding provisions of the Internal Revenue Code of 1939) shall be in such form and with such surety or sureties as are prescribed in the regulations in Subchapter E of this Chapter (Alcohol, Tobacco, and other Excise Taxes). [Reg. § 301.7101-1.]

☐ [*T.D.* 6443, 1-7-60. *Amended by T.D.* 6498, 10-24-60 *and T.D.* 7239, 12-27-72.]

[Reg. § 301.7269-1]

§ 301.7269-1. Failure to produce records.—Whoever fails to comply with any duty imposed upon him by section 6018, 6036 (in the case of an executor), or 6075(a), or, having in his possession or control any record, file, or paper, containing or supposed to contain any information concerning the estate or the decedent, or, having in his possession or control any property comprised in the gross estate of the decedent, fails to exhibit the same upon request of any officer or employee of the Internal Revenue Service who desires to examine the same in the performance of his duties under chapter 11 of the Code (relating to estate taxes) shall be liable to a penalty of not exceeding $500, to be recovered with costs of suit, in a civil action in the name of the United States. [Reg. § 301.7269-1.]

☐ [*T.D.* 6498, 10-24-60.]

[Reg. § 301.7430-0]

§ 301.7430-0. Table of contents.—This section lists the captions that appear in §§ 301.7430-1 through 301.7430-6.

(iv) Reasonable administrative costs.
(v) Prevailing party.
(vi) Not unreasonably protracted.
(vii) Procedural requirements.
(2) Determination by court.
(c) Procedure for recovering reasonable administrative costs.
(1) In general.
(2) Where request must be filed.
(3) Contents of request.
(i) Statements.
(ii) Affidavit or affidavits.
(iii) Documentation and information.
(4) Form of request.
(5) Period for requesting costs from the Internal Revenue Service.
(6) Notice.
(7) Appeal to Tax Court.
(d) Unreasonable protraction of administrative proceeding.
(e) Examples.

§ 301.7430-3 Administrative proceeding and administrative proceeding date.

(a) Administrative proceeding.
(b) Collection action.
(c) Administrative proceeding date.
(1) General rule.
(2) Notice of the decision of the Internal Revenue Service Office of Appeals.
(3) Notice of deficiency.
(4) First letter of proposed deficiency that allows the taxpayer an opportunity for administrative review in the Office of Appeals.
(d) Examples.

§ 301.7430-4 Reasonable administrative costs.

(a) In general.
(b) Costs described.
(1) In general.
(2) Representative and specially qualified representative.
(i) Representative.
(ii) Specially qualified representative.
(3) Limitation on fees for a representative.
(i) In general.
(ii) Cost of living adjustment.
(iii) Special factor adjustment.
(A) In general.
(B) Special factor.
(C) Limited availability.
(D) Local availability of tax expertise.
(E) Difficulty of the issues.
(F) Example.
(c) Certain costs excluded.
(1) Costs not incurred in an administrative proceeding.
(2) Costs incurred in an administrative proceeding but not reasonable.
(i) In general.
(ii) Special rule for expert witness' fees on issue of prevailing market rates.
(3) Litigation costs.
(4) Examples.
(d) Pro bono representation.
(1) In general.
(2) Requirements.
(3) Nominal fee.
(4) Payment when representation provided for a nominal fee.
(5) Requirements.
(6) Hourly rate.
(7) Examples.

§ 301.7430-5 Prevailing party.

(a) In general.
(b) Position of the Internal Revenue Service.
(c) Examples.
(d) Substantially justified.
(1) In general.
(2) Position in courts of appeal.
(3) Examples.
(4) Included costs.
(5) Examples.
(6) Exception.
(7) Presumption.
(e) Amount in controversy.
(f) Most significant issue or set of issues presented.
(1) In general.
(2) Example.
(g) Net worth and size limitations.
(1) Individuals.
(2) Estates and trusts.
(3) Others.
(4) Special rule for charitable organizations and certain cooperatives.
(5) Special rule for TEFRA partnerships.
(6) Determining net worth.
(h) Determination of prevailing party.
(i) Examples.

§ 301.7430-6 Effective/applicability dates.

§ 301.7430-7 Qualified offers.

(a) In general.
(b) Requirements for treatment as a prevailing party based upon having made a qualified offer.
(1) In general.
(2) Liability under the last qualified offer.
(3) Liability pursuant to the judgment.
(c) Qualified offer.
(1) In general.
(2) To the United States.
(3) Specifies the offered amount.
(4) Designated at the time it is made as a qualified offer.
(5) Remains open.
(6) Last qualified offer.
(7) Qualified offer period.
(8) Interest as a contested issue
(d) [Reserved].
(e) Examples.
(f) Effective date.

§ 301.7430-8 Administrative costs incurred in damage actions for violations of section 362 or 524 of the Bankruptcy Code.

(a) In general.
(b) Prevailing party.

(c) Administrative proceeding.

(d) Costs incurred after filing of bankruptcy petition.

(e) Time for filing claim for administrative costs.

(f) Effective date.

[Reg. § 301.7430-0.]

☐ [*T.D.* 8542, 6-6-94. *Amended by T.D.* 8725, 7-21-97 *and T.D.* 9756, 2-29-2016.]

[Reg. § 301.7430-1]

§ 301.7430-1. Exhaustion of administrative remedies.—(a) *In general.*—Section 7430(b)(1) provides that a court shall not award reasonable litigation costs in any civil tax proceeding under section 7430(a) unless the court determines that the prevailing party has exhausted the administrative remedies available to the party within the Internal Revenue Service. This section sets forth the circumstances in which such administrative remedies shall be deemed to have been exhausted.

(b) *Requirements.*—(1) *In general.*—A party has not exhausted the administrative remedies available within the Internal Revenue Service with respect to any tax matter for which an Appeals office conference is available under §§ 601.105 and 601.106 of this chapter (other than a tax matter described in paragraph (c) of this section) unless—

(i) The party, prior to filing a petition in the Tax Court or a civil action for refund in a court of the United States (including the Court of Federal Claims), participates, either in person or through a qualified representative described in § 601.502 of this chapter, in an Appeals office conference; or

(ii) If no Appeals office conference is granted, the party, prior to the issuance of a statutory notice in the case of a petition in the Tax Court or the issuance of a notice of disallowance in the case of a civil action for refund in a court of the United States (including the Court of Federal Claims)—

(A) Requests an Appeals office conference in accordance with §§ 601.105 and 601.106 of this chapter or any successor published guidance; and

(B) Files a written protest if a written protest is required to obtain an Appeals office conference.

(2) *Participates.*—For purposes of this section, a party or qualified representative of the party described in § 601.502 of this chapter participates in an Appeals office conference if the party or qualified representative discloses to the Appeals office all relevant information regarding the party's tax matter to the extent such information and its relevance were known or should have been known to the party or qualified representative at the time of such conference.

(3) *Tax matter.*—For purposes of this section, "tax matter" means a matter in connection with the determination, collection or refund of any tax, interest, penalty, addition to tax or additional amount under the Internal Revenue Code.

(4) *Failure to agree to extension of time for assessments.*—Any failure by the prevailing party to agree to an extension of the time for the assessment of any tax will not be taken into account for purposes of determining whether the prevailing party has exhausted the administrative remedies available to the party within the Internal Rrevenue Service.

(c) *Revocation of a determination that an organization is described in section 501(c)(3).*—A party has not exhausted the administrative remedies available within the Internal Revenue Service with respect to a revocation of a determination that it is an organization described in section 501(c)(3) unless, prior to filing a declaratory judgment action under section 7428, the party has exhausted its administrative remedies in accordance with section 7428, and any regulations, rules, and revenue procedures thereunder.

(d) *Actions involving summonses, levies, liens, jeopardy and termination assessments, etc.*—(1) A party has not exhausted the administrative remedies available within the Internal Revenue Service with respect to a matter other than one to which paragraph (b) or (c) of this section applies (including summonses, levies, liens, and jeopardy and termination assessments) unless, prior to filing an action in a court of the United States (including the Tax Court and the Court of Federal Claims)—

(i) The party follows all applicable Internal Revenue Service procedures for contesting the matter (including filing a written protest or claim, requesting an administrative appeal, and participating in an administrative hearing or conference); or

(ii) If there are no applicable Internal Revenue Service procedures, the party submits to the Area Director of the area having jurisdiction over the dispute a written claim for relief reciting facts and circumstances sufficient to show the nature of the relief requested and that the party is entitled to the requested relief, and the Area Director denies the claim for relief in writing or fails to act on the claim within a reasonable period after the claim is received by the Area Director.

(2) For purposes of paragraph (d)(1)(ii) of this section, a *reasonable period* is—

(i) The 5-day period preceding the filing of a petition to quash an administrative summons issued under section 7609;

(ii) The 5-day period preceding the filing of a wrongful levy action in which a demand for the return of property is made;

(iii) The period expressly provided for administrative review of the party's claim by an applicable provision of the Internal Revenue Code that expressly provides for the pursuit of administrative remedies (such as the 16-day period provided under section 7429(b)(1)(B) relating to review of jeopardy assessment procedures); or

(iv) The 60-day period following receipt of the claim for relief in all other cases.

(e) *Actions involving willful violations of the automatic stay under section 362 or the discharge provisions under section 524 of the Bankruptcy Code.*—(1) *Section 7433 claims.*—A party has not exhausted administrative remedies within the Internal Revenue Service with respect to asserted violations of the automatic stay under section 362 of the Bankruptcy Code or the discharge provisions under section 524 of the Bankruptcy Code unless it files an administrative claim for damages or for relief from a violation of section 362 or 524 of the Bankruptcy Code with the Chief, Local Insolvency Unit, for the judicial district in which the bankruptcy petition that is the basis for the asserted automatic stay or discharge violation was filed pursuant to § 301.7433-2(e) and satisfies the other conditions set forth in § 301.7433-2(d) prior to filing a petition under section 7433.

(2) *Section 362(h) claims.*—A party has not exhausted administrative remedies within the Internal Revenue Service with respect to asserted violations of the automatic stay under section 362 of the Bankruptcy Code unless it files an administrative claim for relief from a violation of section 362 of the Bankruptcy Code with the Chief, Local Insolvency Unit, for the judicial district in which the bankruptcy petition that is the basis for the asserted automatic stay violation was filed pursuant to § 301.7433-2(e) and satisfies the other conditions set forth in § 301.7433-2(d) prior to filing a petition under section 362(h) of the Bankruptcy Code.

(f) *Exception to requirement that party pursue administrative remedies.*—If the conditions set forth in paragraph (f)(1), (f)(2), (f)(3), or (f)(4) of this section are satisfied, a party's administrative remedies within the Internal Revenue Service shall be deemed to have been exhausted for purposes of section 7430.

(1) The Internal Revenue Service notifies the party in writing that the pursuit of administrative remedies in accordance with paragraphs (b), (c), and (d) of this section is unnecessary.

(2) In the case of a petition in the Tax Court—

(i) The party did not receive a notice of proposed deficiency (30-day letter) prior to the issuance of the statutory notice and the failure to receive such notice was not due to actions of the party (such as a failure to supply requested information or a current mailing address to the Internal Revenue Service office or service center having jurisdiction over the tax matter); and

(ii) The party does not refuse to participate in an Appeals office conference while the case is in docketed status.

(3) In the case of a civil action for refund involving a tax matter other than a tax matter described in paragraph (e)[(f)](4) of this section, the party—

(i) Participates in an Appeals office conference with respect to the tax matter prior to issuance of a statutory notice of deficiency with respect to such tax matter; or

(ii) Did not receive written notification that an Appeals office conference was available prior to issuance of a notice of disallowance and the failure to receive such a notification was not due to the actions of the party (such as the failure to supply requested information or a current mailing address to the Internal Revenue Service office or service center having jurisdiction over the tax matter); or

(iii) Did not receive either written or oral notification that an Appeals office conference had been granted within six months from the date of the filing of the claim for refund and the failure to receive such notice was not due to actions of the party (such as the failure to supply requested information or a current mailing address to the Internal Revenue Service office or service center having jurisdiction over the tax matter).

(4) In the case of a civil action for refund involving a tax matter under sections 6703 or 6694—

(i) The party did not receive a notice of proposed disallowance prior to issuance of a notice of disallowance and the failure to receive such notice was not due to actions of the party (such as the failure to supply requested information or a current mailing address to the Internal Revenue Service office or service center having jurisdiction over the tax matter); or

(ii) During the six-month period following the day on which the party's claim for refund is filed, the party's claim for refund is not denied, and the Internal Revenue Service has failed to process the claim with due diligence.

(g) *Examples.*—The provisions of this section may be illustrated by the following examples:

Example 1. Taxpayer A exchanges property held for investment for similar property and claims that the gain on the exchange is not recognized under section 1031. The Internal Revenue Service conducts a field examination and determines that there has not been a like-kind exchange. No agreement is reached on the matter and a notice of proposed deficiency (30-day letter) is sent to A. A does not file a request for an Appeals office conference. A pays the amount of the proposed deficiency and files a claim for refund. A notice of proposed disallowance is issued by the Internal Revenue Service. A does not request an Appeals office conference and, instead, files a civil action for refund in a United States District Court. A has not exhausted the administrative remedies available within the Internal Revenue Service.

Example 2. Assume the same facts as in *Example 1* except that, after receiving the notice of proposed deficiency (30-day letter), A files a request for an Appeals office conference. No agreement is reached at the conference. A pays the amount of the proposed deficiency and files a claim for refund. A notice of proposed disallowance is issued by the Internal Revenue Service. A does not request an Appeals office conference and files a civil action for refund in a United States District Court. A has exhausted the administrative remedies available within the Internal Revenue Service.

Example 3. Assume the same facts as in *Example 1* except A first requests an Appeals office conference after A's receipt of the notice of proposed disallowance. A is granted an Appeals office conference and A participates in such conference. A has exhausted the administrative remedies available within the Internal Revenue Service.

Example 4. Taxpayer B receives a notice of proposed deficiency (30-day letter) after completion of a field examination. B provided to the Internal Revenue Service during the examination all relevant information under the taxpayer's control and all relevant legal arguments supporting the taxpayer's position. B properly requests an Appeals office conference. The Appeals office, to obtain an additional period of time to consider the tax matter, requests that B sign Form 872 to extend the time for an assessment of tax, but B declines. Appeals then denies the request for a conference and issues a notice of deficiency. B has exhausted the administrative remedies available within the Internal Revenue Service.

Example 5. Taxpayer C receives a notice of proposed deficiency (30-day letter) and a written statement that C need not file a written protest or request an Appeals office conference since a conference will not be granted. C files a petition in the Tax Court after receiving the statutory notice of deficiency. C's administrative remedies within the Internal Revenue Service are deemed to have been exhausted.

Example 6. On January 2, the Internal Revenue Service serves a summons issued under section 7609 on third-party recordkeeper D to produce records of taxpayer E. On January 5, notice of the summons is given to E. The last day on which E may file a petition in a court of the United States to quash the summons is January 25. Thereafter, E files a written claim for relief with the Internal Revenue Service office having jurisdiction over the matter together with a copy of the summons. The claim and copy are received by the Internal Revenue Service office on January 20. On January 25, E files a petition to quash the summons. E has exhausted the administrative remedies available within the Internal Revenue Service.

Example 7. A notice of Federal tax lien is filed in County M on March 3, in the name of F. On April 2, F pays the entire liability thereby satisfying the lien. On May 2, F files a written claim with the Internal Revenue Service office having jurisdiction over the tax matter demanding a certificate of release of lien. Thereafter, F provides the Internal Revenue Service office with a copy of the notice of Federal tax lien and a copy of the cancelled check in satisfaction of the lien, which are received by the district director on May 15. F's claim is deemed to have been filed on May 15. Accordingly, F must wait until after July 14 (60 days following the filing of the claim for relief on May 15) to commence an action, in order to have exhausted the administrative remedies available within the Internal Revenue Service.

Example 8. A revenue officer seizes an automobile to effect collection of G's liability on January 10. On January 22, H submits a written claim to the Internal Revenue Service office having jurisdiction over the tax matter claiming that H purchased the automobile from G for an adequate consideration before the tax lien against G arose, and demands immediate return of the automobile. A copy of the title certificate and H's cancelled check are submitted with the claim. The claim is received by the Internal Revenue Service office on January 25. On January 30, H brings a wrongful levy action. H has exhausted the administrative remedies available within the Internal Revenue Service.

Example 9. The Internal Revenue Service issues a revenue ruling which holds that ear piercing does not affect a function or structure of the body within the meaning of section 213 and therefore is not deductible. Taxpayer I deducts the costs of ear piercing and, following an examination, receives a notice of proposed deficiency (30-day letter) disallowing the treatment of these costs. Because of the revenue ruling, I believes a conference would not aid in the resolution of the tax dispute. Accordingly, I does not request an Appeals office conference. After receiving a statutory notice of deficiency, I files a petition in the Tax Court. I has not exhausted the administrative remedies available within the Internal Revenue Service. The issuance of a revenue ruling covering the same fact situation but taking a contrary position does not constitute notification by the Internal Revenue Service to I that the pursuit of administrative remedies is unnecessary. Similarly, the issuance to I of a private letter ruling or technical advice does not constitute notification by the Internal Revenue Service that the pursuit of administrative remedies is unnecessary.

Example 10. Taxpayer J is assessed a penalty under section 6701 for aiding in the understatement of the tax liability of another person. J pays 15% of the penalty in accordance with section 6703 and files a claim for refund on June 15. J is not issued a notice of proposed disallowance and thus cannot participate in an Appeals office conference within six months of the filing of the claim for refund. J brings an action on December 23. J has exhausted the administrative remedies available within the Internal Revenue Service.

Example 11. Taxpayer K receives a notice of proposed deficiency (30-day letter) and neither requests nor participates in an Appeals office conference. The Service then issues a statutory notice of deficiency (90-day letter). Upon receiving the statutory notice, and after filing a petition with the Tax Court, K requests an Appeals office conference. K has not exhausted the administrative remedies available within the Internal Revenue Service because the request for an Appeals office conference was made after the issuance of the statutory notice.

(h) *Effective date.*—This section applies to court proceedings described in section 7430 filed in a court of the United States (including the Tax

Court and the Court of Federal Claims) after May 7, 1992. [Reg. § 301.7430-1.]

☐ [*T.D. 7950, 4-16-83. Amended by T.D. 8543, 6-6-94; T.D. 8725, 7-21-97 T.D. 9050, 3-24-2003 and T.D. 9756, 2-29-2016.*]

[Reg. § 301.7430-2]

§ 301.7430-2. Requirements and procedures for recovery of reasonable administrative costs.—(a) *Introduction.*—Section 7430(a)(1) provides for the recovery, under certain circumstances, of reasonable administrative costs incurred in connection with an administrative proceeding before the Internal Revenue Service. Paragraph (b) of this section lists the requirements that a taxpayer must meet to be entitled to an award of reasonable administrative costs from the Internal Revenue Service. Paragraph (c) of this section describes the procedures that a taxpayer must follow to recover reasonable administrative costs. Paragraphs (b) and (c) apply to requests for administrative costs regarding all administrative proceedings within the Internal Revenue Service.

(b) *Requirements for recovery.*—(1) *Determination by the Internal Revenue Service.*—The Internal Revenue Service will grant a taxpayer's request for recovery of reasonable administrative costs incurred in connection with an administrative proceeding under section 7430 and this section only if—

(i) *Jurisdiction.*—The underlying substantive issues or the issue of reasonable administrative costs are not, and have never been, before any court of the United States (including the Tax Court or United States Court of Federal Claims) with jurisdiction over those issues;

(ii) *Administrative proceeding.*—The costs were incurred in connection with an administrative proceeding as defined in § 301.7430-3(a);

(iii) *Administrative proceeding date.*—The costs were incurred on or after the administrative proceeding date as defined in § 301.7430-3(c);

(iv) *Reasonable administrative costs.*—The costs were reasonable administrative costs as defined in § 301.7430-4;

(v) *Prevailing party.*—The taxpayer is a prevailing party as defined in § 301.7430-5;

(vi) *Not unreasonably protracted.*—The administrative proceeding was not unreasonably protracted by the taxpayer as discussed in paragraph (d) of this section; and

(vii) *Procedural requirements.*—The taxpayer follows the procedures set forth in paragraph (c) of this section.

(2) *Determination by court.*—Although the Internal Revenue Service will not grant a request for reasonable administrative costs where the requirements of paragraph (b)(1)(i) of this section are not met, a taxpayer may file a claim for reasonable administrative costs with the court with jurisdiction over the judicial proceeding. The court may award the taxpayer reasonable administrative costs under section 7430(a). Under section 7430(c)(4)(C)(ii), where the final determination with respect to the tax, interest, or penalty at issue is made by a court, the court determines whether the taxpayer qualifies as a prevailing party. Thus, where the requirements of paragraph (b)(1)(i) of this section are not met, the taxpayer's only possibility of obtaining an award of reasonable administrative costs is to obtain an award of these costs from the court. In the event the court awards reasonable administrative costs, it may also award litigation costs for the reasonable costs of pursuing the claim for reasonable administrative costs, provided the requirements under section 7430 regarding an award of reasonable administrative costs are satisfied with respect to these costs. A claim filed with the court should be made in accordance with the rules of the court.

(c) *Procedure for recovering reasonable administrative costs.*—(1) *In general.*—The Internal Revenue Service will not award administrative costs under section 7430 unless the taxpayer files a written request to recover reasonable administrative costs in accordance with the provisions of this section.

(2) *Where request must be filed.*—A request required by paragraph (c)(1) of this section must be filed with the Internal Revenue Service personnel who have jurisdiction over the tax matter underlying the claim for the costs, except that requests with respect to administrative proceedings defined by § 301.7430-8(c) should be made to the Chief, Local Insolvency Unit. However, if those persons are unknown to the taxpayer making the request, the taxpayer may send the request to the Internal Revenue Service office that considered the underlying matter.

(3) *Contents of request.*—The request must be in writing and must contain the following statements, affidavits, documentation, and information with regard to the taxpayer's administrative proceeding—

(i) *Statements*—

(A) A statement that the underlying substantive issues or the issue of reasonable administrative costs are not, and have never been, before any court of the United States (including the Tax Court or United States Court of Federal Claims) with jurisdiction over those issues;

(B) A clear and concise statement of the reasons why the taxpayer alleges that the position of the Internal Revenue Service in the administrative proceeding was not substantially justified. For administrative proceedings commenced after July 30, 1996, if the taxpayer alleges that the Internal Revenue Service did not follow any applicable published guidance, the statement must identify all applicable published guidance that the taxpayer alleges that the Internal Revenue Service did not follow. For purposes of this paragraph (c)(3)(i)(B), the term applicable published guidance means final or temporary regulations, revenue rulings, revenue procedures, information releases, notices, announcements, and, if issued to the taxpayer, private letter rulings, technical advice memoranda, and determination letters. Also, for purposes of this paragraph (c)(3)(i)(B), the term administrative proceeding includes only those administrative proceedings or portions of administrative proceedings occurring on or after the administrative proceeding date as defined in § 301.7430-3(c). For costs incurred after January 18, 1999, if the taxpayer alleges that the United States has lost in courts of appeal for other circuits on substantially similar issues, the taxpayer must provide, for each such case, the full name of the case, volume and pages of the reporter in which the opinion appears, the circuit in which the case was decided, and the year of the opinion;

(C) A statement sufficient to demonstrate that the taxpayer has substantially prevailed as to the amount in controversy or with respect to the most significant issue or set of issues presented in the proceeding;

(D) A statement that the taxpayer has not unreasonably protracted the portion of the administrative proceeding for which the taxpayer is requesting costs; and

(E) A statement supported by a detailed affidavit executed by the taxpayer or the taxpayer's representative that sets forth the nature and amount of each specific item of reasonable administrative costs for which the taxpayer is seeking recovery. This statement must identify whether the representation is on a pro bono basis as defined in § 301.7430-4(d) and, if so, to whom payment should be made. Specifically, the statement must direct whether payment should be made to the taxpayer's representative or to the representative's employer.

(ii) *Affidavit or affidavits*—

(A) An affidavit executed by the taxpayer stating that the taxpayer meets the net worth and size limitations of § 301.7430-5(f);

(B) An affidavit supporting the statement described in paragraph (c)(3)(i)(E) of this section; and

(C) For costs incurred after January 18, 1999, if more than $125 per hour (as adjusted for an increase in the cost of living pursuant to § 301.7430-4(b)(3)) is claimed for the fees of a representative in connection with the administrative proceeding, an affidavit is necessary stating that a special factor described in § 301.7430-4(b)(3) is applicable, such as the difficulty of the issues presented in the case or the lack of local availability of tax expertise. If a special factor is claimed based on specialized skills and distinctive knowledge as described in § 301.7430-4(b)(2)(ii), the affidavit should state—

(1) Why the specialized skills and distinctive knowledge were necessary in the representation;

(2) That there is a limited availability of representatives possessing these specialized skills and distinctive knowledge; and

(3) How the representative's education and experience qualifies the representative as someone with the necessary specialized skills and distinctive knowledge.

(iii) *Documentation and information*—

(A) A copy of the billing records of the representative for the requested fees; and

(B) An address at which the taxpayer wishes to receive notice of the determination of the Internal Revenue Service with regard to the request for reasonable administrative costs.

(C) In cases of pro bono representation, time records similar to billing records, detailing the time spent and work completed, must be submitted for the requested fees.

(4) *Form of Request*.—No specific form is required for the request other than one that satisfies the requirements of paragraph (c)(3) of this section. Where practicable the required statements may be included in a single document. Similarly, where practicable, the required affidavits may be combined in a single affidavit to the extent they are to be executed by the same person.

(5) *Period for requesting costs from the Internal Revenue Service*.—To recover reasonable administrative costs pursuant to section 7430 and this section, the taxpayer must file a written request for costs within 90 days after the date the final adverse decision of the Internal Revenue Service with respect to all tax, additions to tax, interest, and penalties at issue in the administrative proceeding is mailed or otherwise furnished to the taxpayer. For purposes of this section, *interest* means the interest that is specifically at issue in the administrative proceeding independent of the taxpayer's objections to the underlying tax, additions to tax, and penalties imposed. The final decision of the Internal Revenue Service for purposes of this section is the document that resolves the taxpayer's liability with regard to all tax, additions to tax, interest, and penalties at issue in the administrative proceeding (such as a Form 870 or closing agreement), or a notice of assessment for that liability (such as the notice and demand under section 6303), whichever is earlier mailed or otherwise furnished to the taxpayer. For purposes of this section, if the 90th day falls on a Saturday, Sunday, or a legal holiday, the 90-day period shall end on the next succeeding day that is not a Saturday, Sunday, or a legal holiday as defined by section 7503.

(6) *Notice*.—The Internal Revenue Service is authorized, but not required, to notify the taxpayer of its decision to grant or deny (in whole or in part) an award for reasonable administrative costs under section 7430 and this section by certified mail or registered mail. If the Internal Revenue Service does not respond on the merits to a request by the taxpayer for an award of reasonable administrative costs filed under paragraph (c)(1) of this section within 6 months after the request is filed, the Internal Revenue Service's failure to respond may be considered by the taxpayer as a decision of the Internal Revenue Service denying an award for reasonable administrative costs.

(7) *Appeal to Tax Court*.—A taxpayer may appeal a decision by the Internal Revenue Service denying (in whole or in part) a request for

reasonable administrative costs under section 7430 and this section by filing a petition for reasonable administrative costs with the Tax Court. The petition must be in accordance with the Tax Court's Rules of Practice and Procedure and must be filed with the Tax Court after the Internal Revenue Service denies (in whole or in part) the taxpayer's request for reasonable administrative costs. Once a notice of decision denying (in whole or in part) an award for reasonable administrative costs is mailed by the Internal Revenue Service via certified mail or registered mail as required by paragraph (c)(6) of this section, a taxpayer may obtain judicial review of that decision by filing a petition for review with the Tax Court prior to the 91st day after the mailing of the notice of decision.

(d) *Unreasonable protraction of administrative proceeding.*—An award of reasonable administrative costs will not be made where the taxpayer unreasonably protracted the administrative proceeding. However, a taxpayer that unreasonably protracted only a portion of the administrative proceeding, but not other portions of the administrative proceeding, may recover reasonable administrative costs for the portion(s) of the administrative proceeding that the taxpayer did not unreasonably protract, if the requirements of paragraph (b)(1) of this section are otherwise satisfied.

(e) The following examples primarily illustrate paragraph (a) of this section:

Example 1. Taxpayer A receives a notice of proposed deficiency (30-day letter). A requests and is granted Appeals office consideration. The administrative file contains certain documents provided by A as substantiation for the tax matters at issue. Appeals determines that the information submitted is insufficient. Appeals then issues a notice of deficiency. After receiving the notice of deficiency but before the 90-day period for filing a petition with the Tax Court has expired, and before filing a petition with the Tax Court, A convinces Appeals that the information previously submitted and reviewed by Appeals is sufficient and, therefore, the notice of deficiency is incorrect and A owes no additional tax. Pursuant to section 6212(d), the notice of deficiency is rescinded. Appeals then closes the case showing a zero deficiency and mails A a notice to this effect. Assuming that Appeals did not rely on any new information provided by A in rescinding the notice of deficiency and that all of the other requirements of section 7430 are satisfied, A may recover reasonable administrative costs incurred after the date of the 30-day letter (the administrative proceeding date as defined in Treas. Reg. § 301.7430-3(c)). To recover these costs, A must file a request for administrative costs with the Appeals office personnel who settled A's tax matter, or if that person is unknown to A, with the Area Director of the area that considered the underlying matter, within 90 days after the date of mailing of the Office of Appeals' final decision that A owes no additional tax.

Example 2. Taxpayer B files a request for an abatement of interest pursuant to section 6404 and the regulations thereunder. The Area Director issues a notice of proposed disallowance of the abatement request (akin to a 30-day letter). B requests and is granted Appeals office consideration. No agreement is reached with Appeals and the Office of Appeals issues a notice of disallowance of the abatement request. B does not file suit in the Tax Court, but instead contacts the Appeals office within 180 days after the mailing date of the notice of disallowance of the abatement request to attempt to reverse the decision. B convinces the Appeals office that the notice of disallowance is in error. The Appeals office agrees to abate the interest and mails the taxpayer a notification of this decision. The mailing date of the notification from Appeals of the decision to abate interest commences the 90-day period from which the taxpayer may request administrative costs. Assuming that Appeals did not rely on any new information provided by B in reversing its notice of disallowance, and that all of the other requirements of section 7430 are satisfied, B may recover reasonable administrative costs incurred after the date the Area Director issued the notice of proposed disallowance of the abatement request (the administrative proceeding date as defined in Treas. Reg. § 301.7430-3(c)). To recover these costs, B must file a request for costs with the Appeals office personnel who settled B's tax matter, or if that person is unknown to B, with the Area Director of the area that considered the underlying matter within 90 days after the date of mailing of the Office of Appeals' final decision that B is entitled to abatement of interest.

Example 3. Taxpayer C receives a notice of proposed adjustment and employment tax 30-day letter. C requests and is granted Appeals office consideration. The administrative file contains certain documents provided by C to support C's position in the tax matters at issue. Appeals determines that the documents submitted are insufficient. Appeals then issues a notice of determination of worker classification. After receiving the notice of determination of worker classification but before the 90-day period for filing a petition with the Tax Court has expired, C convinces Appeals that the documents previously submitted and reviewed by Appeals adequately support its position and, therefore, C owes no additional employment tax. Appeals then closes the case showing a zero tax adjustment and mails C a no-change letter. Assuming that Appeals did not rely on any new information provided by C in reversing its notice of determination of worker classification, and that all of the other requirements of section 7430 are satisfied, C may recover reasonable administrative costs incurred after the date of the notice of proposed adjustment and 30-day letter (the administrative proceeding date as defined in Treas. Reg. § 301.7430-3(c)). To recover these costs, C must file a request for administrative costs with the Appeals office personnel who settled C's tax matter, or if that person is unknown to C, with the Area Director of the area that considered the underlying matter, within 90 days after the date of mailing of the Office of Appeals' final decision that C owes no additional tax. [Reg. § 301.7430-2.]

☐ [*T.D.* 8542, 6-6-94. *Amended by T.D.* 8725, 7-21-97 *T.D.* 9050, 3-24-2003 *and T.D.* 9756, 2-29-2016.]

[Reg. § 301.7430-3]

§ 301.7430-3. Administrative proceeding and administrative proceeding date.—(a) *Administrative proceeding*.—For purposes of section 7430, an administrative proceeding generally means any procedure or other action before the Internal Revenue Service that is commenced after November 10, 1988. However, an administrative proceeding does not include—

(1) Proceedings involving matters of general application, including hearings on regulations, comments on forms, or proceedings involving revenue rulings or revenue procedures;

(2) Proceedings involving requests for private letter rulings or similar determinations;

(3) Proceedings involving technical advice memoranda, except those submitted after the administrative proceeding date (as defined in paragraph (c) of this section); and

(4) Proceedings in connection with collection actions (as defined in paragraph (b) of this section), including proceedings under section 7432 or 7433, except proceedings brought under section 7433(e) and § 301.7433-2 or proceedings otherwise described in § 301.7430-8(c). See § 301.7430-8.

(b) *Collection action*.—A collection action generally includes any action taken by the Internal Revenue Service to collect a tax (or any interest, additional amount, addition to tax, or penalty, together with any costs in addition to the tax) or any action taken by a taxpayer in response to the Internal Revenue Service's act or failure to act in connection with the collection of a tax (including any interest, additional amount, addition to tax, or penalty, together with any costs in addition to the tax). A collection action for purposes of section 7430 and this section includes any action taken by the Internal Revenue Service under Chapter 64 of Subtitle F to collect a tax. Collection actions also include collection due process hearings under sections 6320 and 6330 (unless the underlying tax liability is properly at issue), and those actions taken by a taxpayer to remedy the Internal Revenue Service's failure to release a lien under section 6325 or to remedy any unauthorized collection action as described by section 7433, except those collection actions described by section 7433(e). An action or procedure directly relating to a claim for refund after payment of an assessed tax is not a collection action.

(c) *Administrative proceeding date*.—(1) *General rule*.—For purposes of section 7430 and the regulations thereunder, the term *administrative proceeding date* means the earlier of—

(i) The date of the receipt by the taxpayer of the notice of the decision of the Internal Revenue Service Office of Appeals;

(ii) The date of the notice of deficiency; or

(iii) The date on which the first letter of proposed deficiency that allows the taxpayer an opportunity for administrative review in the Internal Revenue Service Office of Appeals is sent.

(2) *Notice of the decision of the Internal Revenue Service Office of Appeals*.—For purposes of section 7430 and the regulations thereunder, a notice of the decision of the Internal Revenue Service Office of Appeals is the final written document, mailed or delivered to the taxpayer, that is signed by an individual in the Office of Appeals who has been delegated the authority to settle the dispute on behalf of the Commissioner, and states or indicates that the notice is the final determination of the entire case. A notice of claim disallowance issued by the Office of Appeals is a notice of the decision of the Internal Revenue Service Office of Appeals. Solely for purposes of determining the administrative proceeding date, a notice of deficiency issued by the Office of Appeals is not a notice of the decision of the Internal Revenue Service Office of Appeals.

(3) *Notice of deficiency*.—A notice of deficiency is a notice described in section 6212(a), including a notice rescinded pursuant to section 6212(d). For purposes of determining reasonable administrative costs under section 7430 and the regulations thereunder, the following will be treated as a notice of deficiency:

(i) A notice of final partnership administrative adjustment described in section 6223(a)(2).

(ii) A notice of determination of worker classification issued pursuant to section 7436.

(iii) A final notice of determination denying innocent spouse relief issued pursuant to section 6015.

(4) *First letter of proposed deficiency that allows the taxpayer an opportunity for administrative review in the Office of Appeals*.—Generally, the first letter of proposed deficiency that allows the taxpayer an opportunity for administrative review in the Office of Appeals is the first letter issued to the taxpayer that describes the proposed adjustments and advises the taxpayer of the opportunity to contact the Office of Appeals. It also may be a claim disallowance or the first letter of determination that allows the taxpayer an opportunity for administrative review in the Office of Appeals.

(d) *Examples*.—The provisions of this section are illustrated by the following examples:

Example 1. Taxpayer A receives a notice of proposed deficiency (30-day letter). A files a request for and is granted an Appeals office conference. At the Appeals conference no agreement is reached on the tax matters at issue. The Office of Appeals then issues a notice of deficiency. Upon receiving the notice of deficiency, A does not file a petition with the Tax Court. Instead, A pays the deficiency and files a claim for refund. The claim for refund is considered by the Internal Revenue Service and the Area Director issues a notice of proposed claim disallowance. A requests and is granted Appeals office consideration. A convinces Appeals that A's claim is correct and Appeals allows A's claim. A may recover reasonable administrative costs incurred on or after the date of the notice of proposed deficiency (30-day letter), but only if the other requirements of section 7430 and the regulations thereunder are satisfied. A cannot recover costs incurred prior to the date of the 30-day letter because these costs were incurred before the administrative proceeding date.

Example 2. Taxpayer B files an individual income tax return showing a balance due. No payment is made with the return and the Internal Revenue Service assesses the amount shown on the return. The Internal Revenue Service issues a Notice Of Intent to Levy And Notice Of Your Right To A Hearing pursuant to sections 6330(a) and 6331(d). B timely requests and is granted a Collection Due Process (CDP) hearing. In connection with the CDP hearing, B enters into an installment agreement as a collection alternative. The costs that B incurred in connection with the CDP hearing were not incurred in an administrative proceeding, but rather in a collection action. Accordingly, B may not recover those costs as reasonable administrative costs under section 7430 and the regulations thereunder. [Reg. § 301.7430-3.]

☐ [*T.D.* 8542, 6-6-94. *Amended by T.D.* 9050, 3-24-2003 *and T.D.* 9756, 2-29-2016.]

[Reg. § 301.7430-4]

§ 301.7430-4. Reasonable administrative costs.—(a) *In general.*—For purposes of section 7430 and the regulations thereunder, reasonable administrative costs are any costs described in paragraph (b) of this section that are incurred in connection with an administrative proceeding (as defined in § 301.7430-3(a)) and incurred on or after the administrative proceeding date (as defined in § 301.7430-3(c)).

(b) *Costs described.*—(1) *In general.*—The costs described in this paragraph are the reasonable and necessary amount of costs incurred by the taxpayer to present the taxpayer's position with respect to the merits of the tax controversy or the recovery of reasonable administrative costs. These costs include—

(i) Any administrative fees or similar charges imposed by the Internal Revenue Service;

(ii) Reasonable expenses of expert witnesses;

(iii) Reasonable costs of any study, analysis, engineering report, test or project that is necessary for, and incurred in preparation of, the taxpayer's case; and

(iv) Reasonable fees paid or incurred for the services of a representative (as defined in paragraph (b)(2) of this section) in connection with the administrative proceeding.

(2) *Representative and specially qualified representative.*—(i) *Representative.*—A representative is a person compensated for services rendered in connection with the administrative proceeding, who is authorized to practice before the Internal Revenue Service or the Tax Court.

(ii) *Specially qualified representative.*—For purposes of paragraphs (b)(3)(iii) and (c)(2)(ii) of this section, a specially qualified representative is a representative (as defined in paragraph (b)(2)(i) of this section) possessing a distinctive knowledge or a unique and specialized skill that is necessary to adequately represent the taxpayer in the proceeding. Examples of a unique and specialized skill or distinctive knowledge would be an identifiable practice specialty such as patent law or knowledge of a foreign law or language where that specialty or knowledge is necessary to adequately represent the taxpayer in the proceeding. For purposes of this paragraph, neither knowledge of tax law nor experience in representing taxpayers before the Internal Revenue Service is considered distinctive knowledge or a unique and specialized skill. An extraordinary level of general representational knowledge and ability that is useful in all proceedings is not considered, in and of itself, distinctive knowledge or a unique and specialized skill. Specially qualified representatives also do not include those who have a distinctive knowledge of the underlying subject matter of the controversy in circumstances where that distinctive knowledge could reasonably be supplied through the use of an expert, or could readily be obtained through literature pertaining to the subject.

(3) *Limitation on fees for a representative.*—(i) *In general.*—Except as otherwise provided in this section, fees incurred after January 18, 1999, and described in paragraph (b)(1)(iv) of this section that are recoverable under section 7430 and the regulations thereunder as reasonable administrative costs may not exceed $125 per hour (as adjusted for an increase in the cost of living and, if appropriate, a special factor adjustment).

(ii) *Cost of living adjustment.*—The Internal Revenue Service will make a cost of living adjustment to the $125 per hour limitation for fees incurred in any calendar year beginning after December 31, 1996. The cost of living adjustment will be an amount equal to $125 multiplied by the cost of living adjustment determined under section 1(f)(3) for the calendar year (substituting "calendar year 1995" for "calendar year 1992" in section 1(f)(3)(B)). If the dollar limitation as adjusted by this cost of living increase is not a multiple of $10, the dollar amount will be rounded to the nearest multiple of $10 (rounding up if the amount is a multiple of $5).

(iii) *Special factor adjustment.*—(A) *In general.*—If the presence of a special factor is demonstrated by the taxpayer, the amount reimbursable is the amount of reasonable fees paid or incurred by the taxpayer in connection with the proceeding for the services of a representative as defined in paragraph (b)(2)(i) of this section.

(B) *Special factor.*—A *special factor* is a factor, other than an increase in the cost of living, that justifies an increase in the $125 per hour limitation of section 7430(c)(1)(B)(iii). The undesirability of the case, the work and the ability of counsel, the results obtained, and customary fees and awards in other cases, are factors applicable to a broad spectrum of litigation and do not constitute special factors for the purpose of increasing the $125 per hour limitation. By contrast, the limited availability of a specially qualified representative for the proceeding, the limited local availability of tax expertise, and the difficulty of the issues are special factors justifying an increase in the $125 per hour limitation.

(C) *Limited availability.*—Limited availability of a specially qualified representative is established by demonstrating that a specially qualified representative for the proceeding is not available at the $125 per hour rate (as adjusted for an increase in the cost of living). The representative's special qualification must be based on nontax expertise. Initially, this showing may be made by submission of an affidavit signed by the taxpayer or by the taxpayer's counsel, that in a case similar to the taxpayer's, a specially qualified representative that practices within a reasonable distance from the taxpayer's principal residence or principal office would normally charge a client similar to the taxpayer at a rate in excess of this amount. If the Internal Revenue Service challenges this initial showing, the taxpayer may submit additional evidence to establish the limited availability of a specially qualified representative at the rate specified above.

(D) *Limited local availability of tax expertise.*—Limited local availability of tax expertise is established by demonstrating that a representative possessing tax expertise is not available in the taxpayer's geographical area. Initially, this showing may be made by submission of an affidavit signed by the taxpayer, or by the taxpayer's counsel, that no representative possessing tax expertise practices within a reasonable distance from the taxpayer's principal residence or principal office. The hourly rate charged by representatives in the geographical area is not relevant in determining whether tax expertise is locally available. If the Internal Revenue Service challenges this initial showing, the taxpayer may submit additional evidence to establish the limited local availability of a representative possessing tax expertise.

(E) *Difficulty of the issues.*—In determining whether the difficulty of the issues justifies an increase in the $125 per hour limitation on the applicable hourly rate, the Internal Revenue Service will consider the following factors:

(1) The number of different provisions of law involved in each issue.

(2) The complexity of the particular provision or provisions of law involved in each issue.

(3) The number of factual issues present in the proceeding.

(4) The complexity of the factual issues present in the proceeding.

(F) *Example.*—The provisions of this section are illustrated by the following example:

Example. Taxpayer A is represented by B, a CPA and attorney with a LL.M. Degree in Taxation with Highest Honors who regularly handles cases dealing with TEFRA partnership issues. B represents A in an administrative proceeding involving TEFRA partnership issues that is subject to the provisions of this section. Assuming A qualifies for an award of reasonable administrative costs by meeting the requirements of section 7430, the amount of the award attributable to the fees of B may not exceed the $125 per hour limitation (as adjusted for an increase in the cost of living), absent a special factor. B is not a specially qualified representative because extraordinary knowledge of the tax laws does not constitute distinctive knowledge or a unique and specialized skill constituting a special factor. A higher rate may be justified by another special factor, that is, the limited local availability of tax expertise or the difficulty of the issues.

(c) *Certain costs excluded.*—(1) *Costs not incurred in an administrative proceeding.*—Costs that are not reasonable administrative costs for purposes of section 7430 include any costs incurred in connection with a proceeding that is not an administrative proceeding within the meaning of § 301.7430-3.

(2) *Costs incurred in an administrative proceeding but not reasonable.*—(i) *In general.*—Costs incurred in an administrative proceeding that are incurred on or after the administrative proceeding date, and that are otherwise described in paragraph (b) of this section, are not recoverable unless they are reasonable in both nature and amount. For example, costs normally included in the hourly rate of the representative by the custom and usage of the representative's profession, when billed separately, are not recoverable separate and apart from the representative's hourly rate. These costs typically include costs such as secretarial and overhead expenses. In contrast, costs that are normally billed separately may be reasonable administrative costs that may be recoverable in addition to the representative's hourly rate. Therefore, necessary costs incurred for travel; expedited mail delivery; messenger service; expenses while on travel; long distance telephone calls; and necessary copying fees imposed by the Internal Revenue Service, any court, bank or other third party, when normally billed separately from the representative's hourly rate, may be reasonable administrative costs.

(ii) *Special Rule for Expert Witness' Fees on Issue of Prevailing Market Rates.*—Under paragraph (b)(3)(iii)(C) of this section, the taxpayer may initially establish a limited availability of specially qualified representatives for the proceeding by submission of an affidavit signed by the taxpayer or by the taxpayer's representative. The Internal Revenue Service may endeavor to rebut the affidavit submitted on this issue by demonstrating either that a specially qualified representative was not necessary to represent the taxpayer in the proceeding, that the taxpayer's representative is not a specially qualified representative or that the prevailing rate for specially qualified representatives does not exceed $125 per hour (as adjusted for an increase in the cost of living). Unless the Internal Revenue Service endeavors to demonstrate that the prevailing rate for specially qualified representatives does not exceed $125 per hour (as adjusted for an increase in the cost of living), fees for expert witnesses used to establish prevailing market rates are not included in the term reasonable administrative costs.

(3) *Litigation costs.*—Litigation costs are not reasonable administrative costs because they are not incurred in connection with an administrative proceeding. Litigation costs include—

(i) Costs incurred in connection with the preparation and filing of a petition with the United States Tax Court or in connection with the commencement of any other court proceeding; and

(ii) Costs incurred after the filing of a petition with the United States Tax Court or after the commencement of any other court proceeding.

(4) *Examples.*—The provisions of this section are illustrated by the following examples:

Example 1. After incurring fees for representation during the Internal Revenue Service's examination of A's income tax return, A receives a notice of proposed deficiency (30-day letter). A files a request for and is granted an Appeals office conference. At the conference no agreement is reached on the tax matters at issue. The Internal Revenue Service then issues a notice of deficiency. Upon receiving the notice of deficiency, A discontinues A's administrative efforts and files a petition with the Tax Court. A's costs incurred before the date of the mailing of the 30-day letter are not reasonable administrative costs because they were incurred before the administrative proceeding date. Similarly, A's costs incurred in connection with the preparation and filing of a petition with the Tax Court are litigation costs and not reasonable administrative costs.

Example 2. Assume the same facts as in *Example 1* except that after A receives the notice of deficiency, in addition to petitioning the Tax Court, A recontacts Appeals and A convinces Appeals that the information previously submitted during the review by Appeals is sufficient and, therefore, the notice of deficiency is incorrect and A owes no additional tax. The Internal Revenue Service and A agree to a stipulated decision in the Tax Court case to reflect Appeals' decision. The Tax Court enters the decision. If A seeks administrative costs, A may recover costs incurred after the date of the mailing of the 30-day letter, costs incurred in recontacting Appeals after the issuance of the notice of deficiency, and costs incurred up to the time the Tax Court petition was filed, as reasonable administrative costs, but only if the other requirements of section 7430 and the regulations thereunder are satisfied. The costs incurred before the date of the mailing of the 30-day letter are not reasonable administrative costs because they were incurred before the administrative proceeding date, as set forth in §301.7430-3(c)(1)(iii). A's costs incurred in connection with the filing of a petition with the Tax Court are not reasonable administrative costs because those costs are litigation costs. Similarly, A's costs incurred after the filing of the petition are not reasonable administrative costs, as they are litigation costs.

(d) *Pro bono representation.*—(1) *In general.*—Fees recoverable under section 7430 and the regulations thereunder as reasonable administrative costs may exceed the attorneys' fees paid or incurred by the prevailing party if such fees are less than the reasonable attorneys' fees because an individual is representing the prevailing party on a pro bono basis. In addition to attorneys' fees, reasonable costs incurred or paid by the individual providing the pro bono representation that are normally billed separately also may be recovered under this section. The Treasury Department and the Internal Revenue Service may, in revenue rulings, notices, or other guidance published in the Internal Revenue Bulletin, provide for additional rules that apply for awards of costs for pro bono representation for purposes of this paragraph (d).

(2) *Requirements.*—Pro bono representation is established by demonstrating—

(i) Representation was provided for no fee or for a fee that (taking into account all the facts and circumstances) constitutes a nominal fee;

(ii) The representative intended to provide representation for no fee or for a nominal fee from the commencement of the representation. Intent to provide representation for no fee or for a nominal fee may be demonstrated through documentation such as a retainer agreement. An individual will not be considered to have represented a client on a pro bono basis if the facts demonstrate that the individual anticipated a fee greater than a nominal fee or provided representation on a contingency fee basis. The fact that the representative intended to seek recovery of fees under section 7430 will not prevent the representative from satisfying this requirement.

(3) *Nominal fee.*—A *nominal fee* is defined as a fee that is insignificantly small or minimal. A nominal fee is a trivial payment, bearing no relation to the value of the representation provided, taking into account all the facts and circumstances.

(4) *Payment when representation provided at no charge or for a nominal fee.*—A prevailing party who receives representation at no charge or for a nominal fee and who satisfies the requirements under this section is eligible to receive reasonable fees in excess of the fees actually paid or

incurred. Payment will be made to the representative or the representative's employer.

(5) *Recordkeeping.*—Contemporaneous records must be maintained, demonstrating the work performed and the time allocated to each task. These records should contain similar information to billing records.

(6) *Examples.*—The provisions of this section are illustrated by the following example:

Example 1. Taxpayer A, an attorney, files a petition with the Tax Court and pays a $60 filing fee. A appears pro se in the court proceeding. If A prevails, he will not be entitled to an award of reasonable litigation costs for his services. A is rendering services on his own behalf, not providing pro bono representation. His lost opportunity costs are not compensable under section 7430. A may recover the filing fee as a litigation cost, but only if the other requirements of section 7430 and the regulations thereunder are satisfied. [Reg. §301.7430-4.]

☐ [*T.D.* 8542, 6-6-94. *Amended by T.D.* 8725, 7-21-97 *and T.D.* 9756, 2-29-2016.]

[Reg. §301.7430-5]

§301.7430-5. Prevailing party.—(a) *In general.*—For purposes of an award of reasonable administrative costs under section 7430 in the case of administrative proceedings commenced after July 30, 1996, a taxpayer is a prevailing party (other than by reason of section 7430(c)(4)(E)) only if—

(1) At least one issue (other than recovery of administrative costs) remains in dispute as of the date that the Internal Revenue Service takes a position in the administrative proceeding, as described in paragraph (b) of this section;

(2) The position of the Internal Revenue Service was not substantially justified;

(3) The taxpayer substantially prevails as to the amount in controversy or with respect to the most significant issue or set of issues presented; and

(4) The taxpayer satisfies the net worth and size limitations referenced in paragraph (f) of this section.

(b) *Position of the Internal Revenue Service.*—The position of the Internal Revenue Service in an administrative proceeding is the position taken by the Internal Revenue Service as of the earlier of—

(1) The date of the receipt by the taxpayer of the notice of the decision of the Internal Revenue Service Office of Appeals; or

(2) The date of the notice of deficiency or any date thereafter.

(c) *Examples.*—The provisions of this section may be illustrated by the following examples:

Example 1. Taxpayer A receives a notice of proposed deficiency (30-day letter). A pays the amount of the proposed deficiency and files a claim for refund. A's claim is considered and a notice of proposed claim disallowance is issued by the Area Director. A does not request an Appeals office conference and the Area Director issues a notice of claim disallowance. A then files suit in a United States District Court. A cannot recover reasonable administrative costs because the notice of claim disallowance is not a notice of the decision of the Internal Revenue Service Office of Appeals or a notice of deficiency. Accordingly, the Internal Revenue Service has not taken a position in the administrative proceeding pursuant to section 7430(c)(7)(B).

Example 2. Taxpayer B receives a notice of proposed deficiency (30-day letter). B disputes the proposed adjustments and requests an Appeals office conference. The Appeals office determines that B has no additional tax liability. B requests administrative costs from the date of the 30-day letter. B is not the prevailing party and may not recover administrative costs because all of the proposed adjustments in the case were resolved as of the date that the Internal Revenue Service took a position in the administrative proceeding.

(d) *Substantially justified.*—(1) *In general.*—The position of the Internal Revenue Service is substantially justified if it has a reasonable basis in both fact and law. A significant factor in determining whether the position of the Internal Revenue Service is substantially justified as of a given date is whether, on or before that date, the taxpayer has presented all relevant information under the taxpayer's control and relevant legal arguments supporting the taxpayer's position to the appropriate Internal Revenue Service personnel. The appropriate Internal Revenue Service personnel are personnel responsible for reviewing the information or arguments, or personnel who would transfer the information or arguments in the normal course of procedure and administration to the personnel who are responsible.

(2) *Position in courts of appeal.*—Whether the United States has won or lost an issue substantially similar to the one in the taxpayer's case in courts of appeal for circuits other than the one to which the taxpayer's case would be appealable should be taken into consideration in determining whether the Internal Revenue Service's position was substantially justified.

(3) *Example.*—The provisions of this section (d) are illustrated by the following example:

Example. The Internal Revenue Service, in the conduct of a correspondence examination of taxpayer A's individual income tax return, requests substantiation from A of claimed medical expenses. A does not respond to the request and the Internal Revenue Service issues a notice of deficiency. After receiving the notice of deficiency, A presents sufficient information and arguments to convince a tax compliance officer that the notice of deficiency is incorrect and that A owes no tax. The revenue agent then closes the case showing no deficiency. Although A incurred costs after the issuance of the notice of deficiency, A is unable to recover these costs because, as of the date these costs were incurred, A had not presented relevant information under A's control and relevant legal arguments supporting A's position to the appropriate Internal

Revenue Service personnel. Accordingly, the position of the Internal Revenue Service was substantially justified at the time the costs were incurred.

(4) *Included costs.*—(i) An award of reasonable administrative costs shall only include costs incurred on or after the administrative proceeding date as defined in section 301.7430-3(c) of this chapter.

(ii) If the Internal Revenue Service takes a position in an administrative proceeding, as defined in paragraph (b) of this section, and the position is not substantially justified, the taxpayer may be permitted to recover costs incurred before the position was taken, but not before the dates set forth in this paragraph (d)(4).

(5) *Examples.*—The provisions of this section may be illustrated by the following examples:

Example 1. Pursuant to section 6672, taxpayer D receives from the Area Director Collection Operations (Collection) a proposed assessment of trust fund taxes (Trust Fund Recovery Penalty). D requests and is granted Appeals office consideration. Appeals considers the issues and decides to uphold Collection's recommended assessment. Appeals notifies D of this decision in writing. Collection then assesses the tax and notice and demand is made. D timely pays the minimum amount required to commence a court proceeding, files a claim for refund, and furnishes the required bond. Collection disallows the claim, but Appeals, on reconsideration, reverses its original position, thus upholding D's position. If Appeals' initial determination was not substantially justified, D may recover administrative costs incurred on or after the mailing of the proposed assessment of trust fund taxes, because the proposed assessment is the first determination letter that allows the taxpayer an opportunity for administrative review in the Internal Revenue Service Office of Appeals.

Example 2. Taxpayer E receives a notice of proposed deficiency (30-day letter). E pays the amount of the proposed deficiency and files a claim for refund. E's claim is considered and a notice of proposed disallowance is issued by the Area Director. E requests and is granted Appeals office consideration. No agreement is reached with Appeals and the Office of Appeals issues a notice of claim disallowance. E does not file suit in a United States District Court but instead contacts the Appeals office to attempt to reverse the decision. E convinces the Appeals officer that the notice of claim disallowance is in error. The Appeals officer then abates the assessment. E may recover reasonable administrative costs if the position taken in the notice of claim disallowance issued by the Office of Appeals was not substantially justified and the other requirements of section 7430 and the regulations thereunder are satisfied. If so, E may recover administrative costs incurred from the mailing date of the 30-day letter because the requirements of paragraph (c)(2) of this section are met. E cannot recover the costs incurred prior to the mailing of the 30-day letter because they were incurred before the administrative proceeding date.

(6) *Exception.*—If the position of the Internal Revenue Service was substantially justified with respect to some issues in the proceeding and not substantially justified with respect to the remaining issues, any award of reasonable administrative costs to the taxpayer may be limited to only reasonable administrative costs attributable to those issues with respect to which the position of the Internal Revenue Service was not substantially justified. If the position of the Internal Revenue Service was substantially justified for only a portion of the period of the proceeding and not substantially justified for the remaining portion of the proceeding, any award of reasonable administrative costs to the taxpayer may be limited to only reasonable administrative costs attributable to that portion during which the position of the Internal Revenue Service was not substantially justified. Where an award of reasonable administrative costs is limited to that portion of the administrative proceeding during which the position of the Internal Revenue Service was not substantially justified, whether the position of the Internal Revenue Service was substantially justified is determined as of the date any cost is incurred.

(7) *Presumption.*—If the Internal Revenue Service did not follow any applicable published guidance in an administrative proceeding commenced after July 30, 1996, the position of the Internal Revenue Service, on those issues to which the guidance applies and for all periods during which the guidance was not followed, will be presumed not to be substantially justified. This presumption may be rebutted. For purposes of this paragraph (d)(7), the term *applicable published guidance* means final or temporary regulations, revenue rulings, revenue procedures, information releases, notices, and announcements published in the Internal Revenue Bulletin and, if issued to or with respect to the taxpayer, private letter rulings, technical advice memoranda, and determination letters (§ 601.601(d)(2) of this chapter). Also, for purposes of this paragraph (d)(7), the term administrative proceeding includes only those administrative proceedings or portions of administrative proceedings occurring on or after the administrative proceeding date as defined in § 301.7430-3(c).

(e) *Amount in controversy.*—The amount in controversy shall include the amount in issue as of the administrative proceeding date as increased by any amounts subsequently placed in issue by any party. The amount in controversy is determined without increasing or reducing the amount in controversy for amounts of loss, deduction, or credit carried over from years not in issue.

(f) *Most significant issue or set of issues presented.*—(1) *In general.*—Where the taxpayer has not substantially prevailed with respect to the amount in controversy the taxpayer may nonetheless be a prevailing party if the taxpayer substantially prevails with respect to the most significant issue or set of issues presented. The issues presented include those raised as of the administrative proceeding date and those raised subsequently. Only in a multiple issue proceeding can a most significant issue or set of issues presented exist. However, not all multiple issue proceedings contain a most significant issue or set of issues presented. An issue or set of issues constitutes the most significant issue or set of issues presented if, despite involving a lesser dollar amount in the proceeding than the other issue or issues, it objectively represents the most significant issue or set of issues for the taxpayer or the Internal Revenue Service. This may occur because of the effect of the issue or set of issues on other transactions or other taxable years of the taxpayer or related parties.

(2) *Example.*—The provisions of this section may be illustrated by the following example:

Example. In the purchase of an ongoing business, Taxpayer F obtains from the previous owner of the business a covenant not to compete for a period of five years. On audit of F's individual income tax return for the year in which the business was acquired, the Internal Revenue Service challenges the basis assigned to the covenant not to compete and a deduction taken as a business expense for a seminar attended by F. Both parties agree that the covenant not to compete is amortizable over a period of five years; however, the Internal Revenue Service asserts that the proper basis of the covenant is $25,000, while F asserts the basis is $50,000 and claims a deduction of $10,000 in the year in which the business was acquired. F deducted $12,000 for the seminar. The Internal Revenue Service determines that the deduction for the seminar should be disallowed entirely. In the notice of deficiency, the Internal Revenue Service adjusts the amortization deduction to reflect the change to the basis of the covenant not to compete, and disallows the seminar expense. Thus, of the two adjustments determined for the year under audit, the adjustment attributable to the disallowance of the seminar is larger than that attributable to the covenant not to compete. Due to the impact on the next succeeding four years, however, the covenant not to compete adjustment is the most significant issue to both F and the Internal Revenue Service.

(g) *Net worth and size limitations.*—(1) *Individuals.*—A taxpayer who is a natural person meets the net worth and size limitations of this paragraph if the taxpayer's net worth does not exceed two million dollars. For purposes of determining net worth, individuals filing a joint return, and jointly incurring administrative or litigation costs shall have their net worth determined jointly, with all assets and liabilities treated as joint for purposes of the net worth evaluation, and applying a joint cap of four million dollars. Individuals who file a joint return, but incur separate administrative or litigation costs, by retaining separate representation, and/or seeking individual administrative review or petitioning the court individually, such as under section 6015, shall have their net worth determined separately, with only those assets and liabilities reasonably attributable to each spouse considered against separate caps of two million dollars per spouse.

(2) *Estates and trusts.*—An estate or a trust meets the net worth and size limitations of this paragraph if the estate or trust's net worth does not exceed two million dollars. The net worth of an estate shall be determined as of the date of the decedent's death provided the date of death is prior to the date the court proceeding is commenced. The net worth of a trust shall be determined as of the last day of the last taxable year involved in the proceeding.

(3) *Others.*—(i) A taxpayer that is a partnership, corporation, association, unit of local government, or organization (other than an organization described in paragraph (g)(4) of this section) meets the net worth and size limitations of this paragraph if, as of the administrative proceeding date:

(A) The taxpayer's net worth does not exceed seven million dollars; and

(B) The taxpayer does not have more than 500 employees.

(ii) A taxpayer who is a natural person and owns an unincorporated business is subject to the net worth and size limitations contained in paragraph (g)(3)(i) of this section if the tax at issue (or any interest, additional amount, addition to tax, or penalty, together with any costs in addition to the tax) relates directly to the business activities of the unincorporated business.

(4) *Special rule for charitable organizations and certain cooperatives.*—An organization described in section 501(c)(3) exempt from taxation under section 501(a), or a cooperative association as defined in section 15(a) of the Agricultural Marketing Act, 12 U.S.C. 1141j(a) (as in effect on October 22, 1986), meets the net worth and size limitations of this paragraph if, as of the administrative proceeding date, the organization or cooperative association does not have more than 500 employees.

(5) *Special rule for TEFRA partnership proceedings.*—(i) In cases involving partnerships subject to the unified audit and litigation procedures of subchapter C of chapter 63 of the Internal Revenue Code (TEFRA partnership cases), the TEFRA partnership meets the net worth and size limitations requirements of this paragraph (g) if, on the administrative proceeding date—

(A) The partnership's net worth does not exceed seven million dollars; and

(B) The partnership does not have more than 500 employees.

(ii) In addition, each partner requesting fees pursuant to section 7430 must meet the appropriate net worth and size limitations set forth in paragraph (g)(1), (g)(2), or (g)(3) of this section. For example, if a partner is an individual, his or her net worth must not exceed two million dollars as of the administrative proceeding date. If the partner is a corporation, its net worth must not exceed seven million dollars and it must not have more than 500 employees.

(6) *Determining net worth.*—For purposes of determining net worth under this paragraph (g), assets are valued based on the cost of their acquisition.

(h) *Determination of prevailing party.*—If the final decision with respect to the tax, interest, or penalty is made at the administrative level, the determination of whether a taxpayer is a prevailing party shall be made by agreement of the parties, or absent an agreement, by the Internal Revenue Service. See § 301.7430-2(c)(7) regarding the right to appeal the decision of the Internal Revenue Service denying (in whole or in part) a request for reasonable administrative costs to the Tax Court. [Reg. § 301.7430-5.]

☐ [*T.D.* 8542, 6-6-94. *Amended by T.D.* 8725, 7-21-97 *and T.D.* 9756, 2-29-2016.]

[Reg. § 301.7430-6]

§ 301.7430-6. Effective/applicability dates.—Sections 301.7430-2 through 301.7430-6, other than § § 301.7430-2(b)(2), (c)(3)(i)(B), (c)(3)(i)(E), (c)(3)(ii)(C), (c)(3)(iii)(C), (c)(5), (c)(7), and (e); § § 301.7430-3(c)(1), (c)(3), (c)(4), and (d); § § 301.7430-4(b)(3)(i), (b)(3)(ii), (b)(3)(iii)(B), (b)(3)(iii)(C), (b)(3)(iii)(D), (b)(3)(iii)(E), (b)(3)(iii)(F), (c)(2)(ii), (c)(4), and (d); and § § 301.7430-5(a), (b), (c)(3), (d)(2), (d)(3), (d)(4), (d)(5), (d)(7), (f)(2), (g)(1), (g)(2), (g)(3), (g)(5), and (g)(6) apply to claims for reasonable administrative costs filed with the Internal Revenue Service after December 23, 1992, with respect to costs incurred in administrative proceedings commenced after November 10, 1988. Section 301.7430-2(c)(5) is applicable to costs incurred and services performed in cases in which the petition was filed on or after March 1, 2016, except for the last two sentences, which are applicable March 23, 1993. Sections 301.7430-2(b)(2), and (c)(3)(i)(B) (except the last sentence); 301.7430-4(b)(3)(ii), (b)(3)(iii)(C) (except the first two sentences), and (c)(2)(ii) (except for references to the statutory cap as $125); and 301.7430-5(a) (except the parenthetical of 5(a) and all of 5(a)(1)), and the first and last sentence of (d)(7) are applicable for administrative proceedings commenced after July 30, 1996. Sections 301.7430-1(e), 301.7430-2(c)(2), 7430-3(a)(4) and (b) are applicable with respect to actions taken by the Internal Revenue Service after July 22, 1998. The last sentence of § 301.7430-2(c)(3)(i)(B), the first two sentences of § 301.7430-2(b)(3)(iii)(C), § § 301.7430-2(c)(3)(i)(E), (c)(3)(ii)(C), (c)(3)(iii)(C), (c)(7), (e); 301.7430-3(c)(1), (c)(3), (c)(4), (d); Reg. § 301.7430-4(b)(3)(i),(b)(3)(iii)(B), (b)(3)(iii)(E), (b)(3)(iii)(F), (c)(2)(ii)(to the extent it references the statutory cap as $125), (c)(4), (d); the parenthetical of § 301.7430-5(a) and § § 301.7430-5(a)(1), (b), (d)(2), (d)(3), (d)(4), (d)(5), (d)(7), except the first and last sentences, (f)(2), (g)(1), (g)(2), (g)(3), (g)(5), and (g)(6)apply to costs incurred and services performed in cases in which the petition was filed on or after March 1, 2016. [Reg. § 301.7430-6.]

☐ [*T.D.* 8542, 6-6-94. *Amended by T.D.* 8725, 7-21-97, *T.D.* 9050, 3-24-2003 *and T.D.* 9756, 2-29-2016.]

[Reg. § 301.7430-7]

§ 301.7430-7. Qualified offers.—(a) *In general.*—Section 7430(c)(4)(E) (the qualified offer rule) provides that a party to a court proceeding satisfying the timely filing and net worth requirements of section 7430(c)(4)(A)(ii) shall be treated as the prevailing party if the liability of the taxpayer pursuant to the judgment in the proceeding (determined without regard to interest) is equal to or less than the liability of the taxpayer which would have been so determined if the United States had accepted the last qualified offer of the party as defined in section 7430(g). For purposes of this section, the term *judgment* means the cumulative determinations of the court concerning the adjustments at issue and litigated to a determination in the court proceeding. In making the comparison between the liability under the qualified offer and the liability under the judgment, the taxpayer's liability under the judgment is further modified by the provisions of paragraph (b)(3) of this section. The provisions of the qualified offer rule do not apply if the taxpayer's liability under the judgment, as modified by the provisions of paragraph (b)(3) of this section, is determined exclusively pursuant to a settlement, or to any proceeding in which the amount of tax liability is not in issue, including any declaratory judgment proceeding, any proceeding to enforce or quash any summons issued pursuant to the Internal Revenue Code (Code), and any action to restrain disclosure under section 6110(f). If the qualified offer rule applies to the court proceeding, the determination of whether the liability under the qualified offer would have equaled or exceeded the liability pursuant to the judgment is made by reference to the last qualified offer made with respect to the tax liability at issue in the administrative or court proceeding. An award of reasonable administrative and litigation costs under the qualified offer rule only includes those costs incurred on or after the date of the last qualified offer and is limited to those costs attributable to the adjustments at issue at the time the last qualified offer was made that were included in the court's judgment other than by reason of settlement. The qualified offer rule is inapplicable to reasonable administrative or litigation costs otherwise awarded to a taxpayer who is a prevailing party under any other provision of section 7430(c)(4). This section sets forth the requirements to be satisfied for a taxpayer to be treated as a prevailing party by reason of the taxpayer making a qualified offer, as well as the circumstances leading to the application of the exceptions, special rules, and coordination provisions of the qualified offer rule. Furthermore, this section sets forth the elements necessary for an offer to be treated as a qualified offer under section 7430(g).

(b) *Requirements for treatment as a prevailing party based upon having made a qualified offer.*—

(1) *In general.*—In order to be treated as a prevailing party by reason of having made a qualified offer, the liability of the taxpayer for the type or types of tax and the taxable year or years at issue in the proceeding (as calculated pursuant to paragraph (b)(2) of this section), based on the last qualified offer (as defined in paragraph (c) of this section) made by the taxpayer in the court or administrative proceeding, must equal or exceed the liability of the taxpayer pursuant to the judgment by the court for the same type or types of tax and the same taxable year or years (as calculated pursuant to paragraph (b)(3) of this section). Furthermore, the taxpayer must meet the timely filing and net worth requirements of section 7430(c)(4)(A)(ii). If all of the adjustments subject to the last qualified offer are settled prior to the entry of the judgment by the court, the taxpayer is not a prevailing party by reason of having made a qualified offer. The taxpayer may, however, still qualify as a prevailing party if the requirements of section 7430(c)(4)(A) are met. If one or more adjustments covered by a qualified offer (see paragraph (c)(3)) are settled following a ruling by the court that substantially resolves those adjustments, then those adjustments will not be treated as having been settled prior to the entry of the judgment by the court and instead will be treated as amounts included in the judgment as a result of the court's determinations. For purposes of the preceding sentence, rulings relating to discovery, admissibility of evidence, and burden of proof are not rulings that substantially resolve adjustments covered by a qualified offer.

(2) *Liability under the last qualified offer.*—For purposes of paragraph (b)(1) of this section, the taxpayer's liability under the last qualified offer is the change in the taxpayer's liability that would have resulted if the United States had accepted the taxpayer's last qualified offer on all of the adjustments that were at issue in the administrative or court proceeding at the time that the offer was made compared to the amount shown on the return or returns (or as previously adjusted). The portion of a taxpayer's liability that is attributable to adjustments raised by either party after the making of the last qualified offer is not included in the calculation of the liability under that offer. The taxpayer's liability under the last qualified offer is calculated without regard to adjustments that the parties have stipulated will be resolved in accordance with the outcome of a separate pending Federal, state, or other judicial or administrative proceeding. For example, the parties may stipulate that the taxpayer's liability will be resolved in accordance with the outcome of an alternative dispute resolution proceeding or a separate court proceeding, such as a probate, tort liability, or trademark action. Furthermore, the taxpayer's liability under the last qualified offer is calculated without regard to interest, unless the taxpayer's liability for, or entitlement to, interest is a contested issue in the administrative or court proceeding and is one of the adjustments included in the last qualified offer.

(3) *Liability pursuant to the judgment.*—For purposes of paragraph (b)(1) of this section, the taxpayer's liability pursuant to the judgment is the change in the taxpayer's liability resulting from amounts contained in the judgment as a result of the court's determinations, and amounts contained in settlements not included in the judgment, that are attributable to all adjustments that were included in the last qualified offer compared to the amount shown on the return or returns (or as previously adjusted). This liability includes amounts attributable to adjustments included in the last qualified offer and settled by the parties prior to the entry of judgment regardless of whether those amounts are actually included in the judgment entered by the court. The taxpayer's liability pursuant to the judgment does not include amounts attributable to adjustments that are not included in the last qualified offer, even if those amounts are actually included in the judgment entered by the court. The taxpayer's liability under the judgment is calculated without regard to adjustments that the parties have stipulated will be resolved in accordance with the outcome of a separate pending Federal, state, or other judicial or administrative proceeding. Furthermore, the taxpayer's liability pursuant to the judgment is calculated without regard to interest, unless the taxpayer's liability for, or entitlement to, interest is a contested issue in the administrative or court proceeding and is one of the adjustments included in the last qualified offer. Where adjustments raised by either party subsequent to the making of the last qualified offer are included in the judgment entered by the court, or are settled prior to the court proceeding, the taxpayer's liability pursuant to the judgment is calculated by treating the subsequently raised adjustments as if they had never been raised.

(c) *Qualified offer.*—(1) *In general.*—A qualified offer is defined in section 7430(g) to mean a written offer which—

(i) Is made by the taxpayer to the United States during the qualified offer period;

(ii) Specifies the offered amount of the taxpayer's liability (determined without regard to interest, unless interest is a contested issue in the proceeding);

(iii) Is designated at the time it is made as a qualified offer for purposes of section 7430(g); and

(iv) By its terms, remains open during the period beginning on the date it is made and ending on the earliest of the date the offer is rejected, the date the trial begins, or the 90th day after the date the offer is made.

(2) *To the United States.*—(i) A qualified offer is made to the United States when it is delivered to the office or personnel within the Internal Revenue Service, Office of Appeals, Office of Chief Counsel (including field personnel) or Department of Justice that has jurisdiction over the tax matter at issue in the administrative or court proceeding. If those offices or persons are unknown to the taxpayer making the qualified of-

fer, the taxpayer may deliver the offer to the appropriate office, as follows:

(A) If the taxpayer's initial pleading in a court proceeding has been answered, the taxpayer may deliver the offer to the office that filed the answer.

(B) If the taxpayer's petition in the Tax Court has not yet been answered, the taxpayer may deliver the offer to the Office of Chief Counsel, 1111 Constitution Avenue, NW., Washington, DC 20224.

(C) If the taxpayer's initial pleading in any Federal court, other than the Tax Court, has not yet been answered, the taxpayer may deliver the offer to the Attorney General of the United States, 950 Pennsylvania Ave., NW., Washington, DC 20530-0001. For a suit brought in a United States district court, a copy of the offer should also be delivered to the United States Attorney for the district in which the suit was brought.

(D) In any other situation, the taxpayer may deliver the offer to the office that sent the taxpayer the first letter of proposed deficiency which allows the taxpayer an opportunity for administrative review in the Internal Revenue Service Office of Appeals.

(ii) Until an offer is received by the appropriate personnel or office under this paragraph (c)(2), it is not considered to have been made, with the following exception. If the offer is deposited in the United States mail, in an envelope or other appropriate wrapper, postage prepaid, properly addressed to the appropriate personnel or office under this paragraph (c)(2), the date of the United States postmark stamped on the cover in which the offer is mailed shall be deemed to be the date of receipt of that offer by the addressee. If any offer is deposited with a designated delivery service, as defined in section 7502(f)(2), in lieu of the United States mail, the provisions of section 7502(f)(1) shall apply in determining whether that offer qualifies for this exception.

(3) *Specifies the offered amount.*—A qualified offer specifies the offered amount if it clearly specifies the amount for the liability of the taxpayer, calculated as set forth in paragraph (b)(2) of this section. The offer may be a specific dollar amount of the total liability or a percentage of the adjustments at issue in the proceeding at the time the offer is made. This amount must be with respect to all of the adjustments at issue in the administrative or court proceeding at the time the offer is made and only those adjustments. The specified amount must be an amount, the acceptance of which by the United States will fully resolve the taxpayer's liability, and only that liability (determined without regard to adjustments that the parties have stipulated will be resolved in accordance with the outcome of a separate pending Federal, state, or other judicial or administrative proceeding, or interest, unless interest is a contested issue in the proceeding) for the type or types of tax and the taxable year or years at issue in the proceeding. In cases involving multiple tax years, if adjustments in different tax years arise from separate and distinct issues such that the resolution of issues in one or more tax years will not affect the taxpayer's liability in one or more of the other tax years in the proceeding, then a qualified offer may be made for less than all of the tax years involved. A qualified offer, however, must resolve all of the issues for the tax years covered by the offer and also must cover all tax years in the proceeding affected by those issues. A tax year (affected year) is affected by an issue if the treatment of the issue in another tax year involved in the proceeding necessarily affects the treatment of the issue in the affected year.

(4) *Designated at the time it is made as a qualified offer.*—An offer is not a qualified offer unless it designates in writing at the time it is made that it is a qualified offer for purposes of section 7430(g). An offer made at a time when one or more adjustments not included in the first letter of proposed deficiency which allows the taxpayer an opportunity for administrative review in the Internal Revenue Service Office of Appeals have been raised by the taxpayer and remain unresolved, is not considered to be a qualified offer unless contemporaneously or prior to the making of the offer, the taxpayer has provided the United States with the substantiation and legal and factual arguments necessary to allow for informed consideration of the merits of those adjustments. For example, a taxpayer will be considered to have provided the United States with the necessary substantiation and legal and factual arguments if the taxpayer (or a recognized representative of the taxpayer described in § 601.502 of this chapter) participates in an Appeals office conference, participates in an Area Counsel conference, or confers with the Department of Justice, and at that time, discloses all relevant information. All relevant information includes, but is not limited to, the legal and factual arguments supporting the taxpayer's position on any adjustments raised by the taxpayer after the issuance of the first letter of proposed deficiency which allows the taxpayer an opportunity for administrative review in the Internal Revenue Service Office of Appeals. A taxpayer has disclosed all relevant information if the taxpayer has supplied sufficient information to allow informed consideration of the taxpayer's tax matter to the extent the information and its relevance were known or should have been known to the taxpayer at the time of the conference.

(5) *Remains open.*—A qualified offer must, by its terms, remain open for acceptance by the United States from the date it is made, as defined in paragraph (c)(2)(ii) of this section, until the earliest of the date it is rejected in writing by a person with authority to reject the offer, the date the trial begins, or the 90th day after being received by the United States. The offer, by its written terms, may remain open after the occurrence of one or more of the above-referenced events. Once made, the period during which a qualified offer remains open may be extended by the taxpayer prior to its expiration, but an extension cannot be used to make an offer meet the

minimum period for remaining open required by this paragraph (c)(5).

(6) *Last qualified offer*.—A taxpayer may make multiple qualified offers during the qualified offer period. For purposes of the comparison under paragraph (b) of this section, the making of a qualified offer supersedes any previously made qualified offers. In making the comparison described in paragraph (b) of this section, only the qualified offer made most closely in time to the end of the qualified offer period is compared to the taxpayer's liability under the judgment.

(7) *Qualified offer period*.—To constitute a qualified offer, an offer must be made during the qualified offer period. The qualified offer period begins on the date on which the first letter of proposed deficiency which allows the taxpayer an opportunity for administrative review in the Internal Revenue Service Office of Appeals is sent to the taxpayer. For this purpose, the date of the notice of claim disallowance will begin the qualified offer period in a refund case. If there has been no notice of claim disallowance in a refund case, the qualified offer period begins on the date on which the answer or other responsive pleading is filed with the court. The qualified offer period ends on the date which is thirty days before the date the case is first set for trial. In determining when the qualified offer period ends for cases in the Tax Court and other Federal courts using calendars for trial, a case will be considered set for trial on the date scheduled for the calendar call. A case may be removed from a trial calendar at any time. Thus, a case may be removed from a trial calendar before the date that precedes by thirty days the date scheduled for that trial calendar. The qualified offer period does not end until the case remains on a trial calendar on the date that precedes by 30 days the scheduled date of the calendar call for that trial session. The qualified offer period may not be extended beyond the periods set forth in this paragraph (c)(7), although the period during which a qualified offer remains open may extend beyond the end of the qualified offer period.

(8) *Interest as a contested issue*.—To constitute a qualified offer, an offer must specify the offered amount of the taxpayer's liability (determined without regard to interest, unless interest is a contested issue in the proceeding), as provided in paragraphs (c)(1)(ii) and (c)(3) of this section. Therefore, a qualified offer generally may only include an offer to compromise tax, penalties, additions to the tax, and additional amounts. Interest may only be included in a qualified offer if interest is a contested issue in the proceeding. For purposes of this section, interest is a contested issue in the proceeding only if the court in which the proceeding could be brought would have jurisdiction to determine the amount of interest due on the underlying tax, penalties, additions to the tax, and additional amounts. Examples of proceedings in which interest might be a contested issue include proceedings in which the increased interest rate for large corporate underpayments under section 6621(c) is imposed by the Internal Revenue Service and interest abatement proceedings brought under section 6404. Interest is not a contested issue in the proceeding if the court that would have jurisdiction over the proceeding would not have jurisdiction to determine the amount or rate of interest, regardless of whether the taxpayer attempts to raise interest as an issue in the proceeding. Consequently, interest will not be a contested issue in the vast majority of tax cases because they merely involve the straightforward application of statutory interest under section 6601. Accordingly, in those cases, interest may not be included in the offer.

(d) [Reserved].

(e) *Examples*.—The following examples illustrate the provisions of this section:

Example 1. Definition of a judgment. The Internal Revenue Service (IRS) audits Taxpayer A for year X and issues a notice of proposed deficiency (30-day letter) proposing to disallow deductions 1, 2, 3, and 4. A files a protest and participates in a conference with the Internal Revenue Service Office of Appeals (Appeals). Appeals allows deduction 1, and issues a statutory notice of deficiency for deductions 2, 3, and 4. A's petition to the United States Tax Court for year X never mentions deduction 2. Prior to trial, A concedes deduction 3. After the trial, the Tax Court issues an opinion allowing A to deduct a portion of deduction 4. As used in paragraph (a) of this section, the term judgment means the cumulative determinations of the court concerning the adjustments at issue in the court proceeding. Thus, the term judgment does not include deduction 1 because it was never at issue in the court proceeding. Similarly, the term judgment does not include deduction 2 because it was not placed at issue by A in the court proceeding. Although deduction 3 was at issue in the court proceeding, it is not included in the term judgment because it was not determined by the court, but rather by concession or settlement. For purposes of section 7430(c)(4)(E), the term judgment only includes the portion of deduction 4 disallowed by the Tax Court.

Example 2. Liability under the offer and liability under the judgment. Assume the same facts as in *Example 1* except that A makes a qualified offer after the Appeals conference, which is not accepted by the IRS. A's offer is with respect to all adjustments at issue at that time. Those adjustments are deductions 2, 3, and 4. At the conclusion of the litigation, A's entitlement to an award based upon the qualified offer will depend, among other things, on a comparison of the change in A's liability for income tax for year X resulting from the judgment of the Tax Court with the change that would have resulted had the IRS accepted A's qualified offer. In making this comparison, the term judgment (as discussed in *Example 1*) is modified by including the amounts of settled or conceded adjustments that were at issue at the time the qualified offer was made. Any settled or conceded adjustments that were not at issue at the time the qualified offer was made, either because the settlement or concession occurred before the offer or because the adjustment was not raised until after the offer, are not included in the comparison. Thus, A's offer on deductions 2, 3, and 4 is compared with the change in A's liability resulting from the Tax Court's determination of deduction 4, and the concessions of issues 2 and 3 by A.

Example 3. Offer must resolve full liability. Assume the same facts as in *Example 2* except that A's offer after the Appeals conference explicitly states that it is only with respect to adjustments 2 and 3 and not with respect to adjustment 4. Even if A's liability pursuant to the judgment, calculated under paragraph (b)(3) of this section as illustrated in *Example 2*, is equal to or less than it would have been had the IRS accepted A's offer after the Appeals conference, A is not a prevailing party under section 7430(c)(4)(E). A qualified offer must include all adjustments at issue at the time the offer is made. Since A's offer excluded adjustment 4, which was an adjustment at issue at the time the offer was made, it does not constitute a qualified offer pursuant to paragraph (b)(2) of this section.

Example 4. Offer must resolve full liability. Assume the same facts as in *Example 1*, except that A makes a qualified offer that is accepted by the IRS. After the offer is accepted, A attempts to reduce the amount A will pay pursuant to the offer by applying net operating loss carryovers to the years in issue. Because the net operating losses were not at issue when the offer was made, A's offer was a qualified offer. Whether A is entitled to apply net operating losses to reduce the amount stated in the offer will depend upon the application of contract principles, local court rules, and, because net operating losses are at issue, section 6511(d) and related provisions.

Example 5. Qualified offer rule for multiple tax years, partial resolution offer is a qualified offer. Taxpayer B receives a notice of deficiency for taxable years 2001, 2002, and 2003. For 2001, the statutory notice disallows business deductions. For 2002, the statutory notice increases income for unreported lottery winnings. For 2003, the statutory notice disallows a child care credit. B submits a qualified offer only with respect to 2002. Since the adjustments for the three tax years are separate and distinct, B may submit a qualified offer for a single year. If B's liability under the judgment is equal to or less than the qualified offer with respect to 2002, irrespective of 2001 and 2003, B is a prevailing party for 2002 for purposes of section 7430(g). Assuming B satisfies the remaining requirements of section 7430, B may recover reasonable administrative and litigation costs that are attributable to 2002 from the date of the qualified offer. To qualify for any costs with respect to 2001 or 2003, B must satisfy the requirements of section 7430(c)(4).

Example 6. Qualified offer rule for multiple tax years, partial resolution offer is not a qualified offer. Assume the same facts as in *Example 5* except that with respect to 2002, in addition to increasing B's income for the unreported lottery winnings, the statutory notice also disallows a charitable contribution deduction. B submits a settlement offer that purports to be a qualified offer, but only covers the unreported lottery winnings. B's offer is not a qualified offer because it does not address the charitable contribution issue, and thus, does not fully resolve B's liability for 2002.

Example 7. Qualified offer rule for multiple tax years, partial resolution offer is not a qualified offer. Taxpayer C receives a notice of deficiency for taxable years 2001, 2002, and 2003 adjusting the amount of a depreciation deduction due to the Internal Revenue Service's increase to the recovery period. C submits a settlement offer relating only to 2003 that purports to be a qualified offer. C's offer is not a qualified offer because the issue in the three tax years is not separable given that the treatment of the issue in one of the years necessarily affects the treatment of the issue in the other years, and C's offer only applies to one of the years in the proceeding. In cases involving multiple tax years with nonseparable tax issues affecting all tax years, an offer is not a qualified offer unless it resolves the liability for all tax years at issue in the administrative or judicial proceeding.

Example 8. Qualified offer rule inapplicable when all issues settled. Taxpayer D receives a notice of proposed deficiency (30-day letter) proposing to disallow both a personal interest deduction in the amount of $10,000 (Adjustment 1), and a charitable contribution deduction in the amount of $2,000 (Adjustment 2), and to include in income $4,000 of unreported interest income (Adjustment 3). D timely files a protest with Appeals. At the Appeals conference, D presents substantiation for the charitable contribution and presents arguments that the interest paid was deductible mortgage interest and that the interest received was held in trust for Taxpayer E. At the conference, D also provides the Appeals officer assigned to D's case a written offer to settle the case for a deficiency of $2,000, exclusive of interest. The offer states that it is a qualified offer for purposes of section 7430(g) and that it will remain open for acceptance by the IRS for a period in excess of 90 days. After considering D's substantiation and arguments, the Appeals Officer accepts the $2,000 offer to settle the case in full. Although D's offer is a qualified offer, because all three adjustments contained in the qualified offer were settled, the qualified offer rule is inapplicable.

Example 9. Qualified offer rule inapplicable when all issues contained in the qualified offer are settled; subsequently raised adjustments ignored. Assume the same facts as in *Example 8* except that D's qualified offer was for a deficiency of $1,800 and the IRS rejected that offer. Subsequently, the IRS issued a statutory notice of deficiency disallowing the three adjustments contained in *Example 8*, and, in addition, disallowing a home office expense in the amount of $5,000 (Adjustment 4). After petitioning the Tax Court, D presents the field attorney assigned to the case with a written offer, which is not designated as a qualified offer for purposes of section 7430(g), to settle the three adjustments that had been the subject of the qualified offer, plus adjustment 4, for a total deficiency of $2,500. After negotiating with D, a settlement is reached on the three adjustments that were the subject of the rejected qualified offer, for a deficiency of $1,800. Adjustment 4 is litigated in the Tax Court and the court determines that D is entitled to the full $5,000 deduction for that adjustment. Consequently, a decision is entered by the Tax Court reflecting the $1,800 settlement amount, which matches exactly the amount of D's only qualified offer in the case. Although the determined liability for adjustments 1, 2, and 3, equals that of the rejected qualified offer, because all three adjustments contained in the qualified offer were settled, the qualified offer rule is inapplicable.

Example 10. Exclusion of adjustments made after the qualified offer is made. Assume the same facts as in *Example 9* except the settlement is reached only on adjustments 1 and 2, for a liability of $1,500. Adjustments 3 and 4 are tried in the Tax Court and in accordance with the court's opinion, the taxpayer has a $300 deficiency attributable to Adjustment 3, and a $1,550 deficiency attributable to adjustment 4. Consequently, a decision is entered reflecting the $1,500 settled amount, the $300 liability on adjustment 3, and the $1,550 liability on adjustment 4. The $3,350 deficiency reflected in the Tax Court's decision exceeds the last (and only) qualified offer made by D. For purposes of determining whether D is a prevailing party as a result of having made a qualified offer in the proceeding, the liability attributable to adjustment 4, which was raised after the last qualified offer was made, is not included in the comparison of D's liability under the judgment with D's offered liability under the last qualified offer. Thus, D's $1,800 liability under the judgment, as modified for purposes of the qualified offer rule comparison, is equal to D's offered liability under the last qualified offer. Because D's liability under the last qualified offer equals or exceeds D's liability under the judgment, as calculated under paragraph (b)(3) of this section, D is a prevailing party for purposes of section 7430. Assuming D satisfies the remaining requirements of section 7430, D may recover those reasonable administrative and litigation costs attributable to adjustment 3. To qualify for any further award of reasonable administrative and litigation costs, D must satisfy the requirements of section 7430(c)(4)(A).

Example 11. Qualified offer in a refund case. Taxpayer E timely files an amended return claiming a refund of $1,000. This refund claim results from several omitted deductions which, if allowed, would reduce E's tax liability from $10,000 to $9,000. E receives a notice of claim disallowance and files a complaint with the appropriate United States District Court. Subsequently, E makes a qualified offer for a refund of $500. The offer is rejected and after trial the court finds E is entitled to a refund of $700. The change in E's liability from the tax shown on the return that would have resulted from the acceptance of E's qualified offer is a reduction in that liability of $500. The change in E's liability from the tax shown on the return resulting from the judgment of the court is a reduction in that liability of $700. Because E's liability under the qualified offer exceeds E's liability under the judgment, E is a prevailing party for purposes of section 7430. Assuming E satisfies the remaining requirements of section 7430, E may recover those reasonable litigation costs incurred on or after the date of the qualified offer. To qualify for any further award of reasonable administrative and litigation costs E must satisfy the requirements of section 7430(c)(4)(A).

Example 12. End of qualified offer period when case is removed from Tax Court trial calendar more than 30 days before scheduled trial calendar. Taxpayer F has petitioned the Tax Court in response to the issuance of a notice of deficiency. F receives notice that the case will be heard on the July trial session in F's city of residence. The scheduled date for the calendar call for that trial session is July 1st. On May 15th, F's motion to remove the case from the July trial session and place it on the October trial session for that city is granted. The scheduled date for the calendar call for the October trial session is October 1st. On May 31st, F delivers a qualified offer to the field attorney assigned to the case. On August 31st, F delivers a revised qualified offer to the field attorney assigned to the case. Neither offer is accepted. The case is tried during the October trial session, and at some time thereafter, a decision is entered by the court. Assume the judgment in the case, as calculated under paragraph (b)(3) of this section, is greater than the amount offered, as calculated under paragraph (b)(2) of this section, in the qualified offer delivered on May 31st, but less than the amount offered, as similarly calculated, in the qualified offer delivered on August 31st. Because the qualified offer period did not end until September 1st, and the offer of August 31st otherwise satisfied the requirements of paragraph (c) of this section, the offer delivered on August 31st is a qualified offer. Furthermore, because the August 31st qualified offer is closer in time to the end of the qualified offer period than the May 31st qualified offer, the August 31st qualified offer is the last qualified offer made by F. Consequently, the August 31st offer is the qualified offer that is compared to the judgment for purposes of determining whether F is a prevailing party under section 7430(c)(4)(E). Because F's liability under the August 31st qualified offer equals or exceeds F's liability under the judgment as calculated under paragraph (b)(3) of this section, F is a prevailing party for purposes of section 7430.

Example 13. End of qualified offer period when case is removed from Tax Court trial calendar less than 30 days before scheduled trial calendar. Assume the same facts as in *Example 12* except that F's motion was granted on June 15th. Because the qualified offer period ended on June 1st when the case remained on the July trial session on the date that preceded by 30 days the scheduled date of the calendar call for that trial session, the offer delivered on May 31st was F's last qualified offer. The August 31st offer is not a qualified offer for purposes of this rule. Consequently, F is not a prevailing party under the qualified offer rule. Therefore, F must satisfy the requirements of section 7430(c)(4)(A) to qualify for any award of reasonable administrative and litigation costs.

Example 14. When a qualified offer can be made and to whom it must be made. During the examination of Taxpayer G's return, the IRS issues a notice of deficiency without having first issued a 30-day letter. After receiving the notice of deficiency G timely petitions the Tax Court. The next day G mails an offer to the office that issued the notice of deficiency, which offer satisfies the requirements of paragraphs (c)(3) through (6) of this section. This is the only written offer made by G during the administrative or court proceeding, and by its terms it is to remain open for a period in excess of 90 days after the date of mailing to the office issuing the notice of deficiency. The office that issued the notice of deficiency transmitted the offer to the field attorney with jurisdiction over the Tax Court case. After answering the case, the field attorney refers the case to Appeals pursuant to Rev. Proc. 87-24 (1987-1 C.B. 720). See § 601.601(d)(2)(ii)(*b*) of this chapter. After careful consideration, Appeals rejects the offer and holds a conference with G during which some adjustments are settled. The remainder of the adjustments are tried in the Tax Court and G's liability resulting from the Tax Court's determinations, when added to G's liability resulting from the settled adjustments, is less than G's liability would have been under the offer rejected by Appeals. Because the Tax Court case had not yet been answered when the offer was sent, G properly mailed the offer to the office that issued the notice of deficiency. Thus, G's offer satisfied the requirements of paragraph (c)(2) of this section. Furthermore, even though G did not receive a 30-day letter, G's offer was made after the beginning of the qualified offer period, satisfying the requirements of paragraph (c)(7) of this section, because the issuance of the statutory notice provided G with notice of the IRS's determination of a deficiency, and the docketing of the case provided G with an opportunity for administrative review in the Internal Revenue Service Office of Appeals under Rev. Proc. 87-24. See § 601.601(d)(2)(ii)(*b*) of this chapter. Because G's offer satisfied all of the requirements of paragraph (c) of this section, the offer was a qualified offer and G is a prevailing party.

Example 15. Substitution of parties permitted under last qualified offer. Taxpayer H receives a 30-day letter and participates in a conference with the Office of Appeals but no agreement is reached. Subsequently, H receives a notice of deficiency and petitions the Tax Court. Upon receiving the Internal Revenue Service's answer to the petition, H sends a qualified offer to the field attorney who signed the answer, by United States mail. The qualified offer stated that it would remain open for more than 90 days. Thirty days after making the offer, H dies and, on motion under Rule 63(a) of the Tax Court's Rules of Practice and Procedure by H's personal representative, I is substituted for H as a party in the Tax Court proceeding. I makes no qualified offers to settle the case and the case proceeds to trial, with the Tax Court issuing an opinion partially in favor of I. Even though I was not a party when the qualified offer was made by H, that offer constitutes a qualified offer because by its terms, when made, it was to remain open until at least the earlier of the date it is rejected, the date of trial, or 90 days. If the liability of I under the qualified offer, as determined under paragraph (b)(2) of this section, equals or exceeds the liability under the judgment of the Tax Court, as determined under paragraph (b)(3) of this section, I will be a prevailing party for purposes of an award of reasonable litigation costs under section 7430.

Example 16. Qualified offer may not compromise interest unless it is a contested issue. Taxpayer J receives a notice of deficiency making an adjustment resulting in a deficiency in tax of $6,500 plus a penalty of $500. Interest is not a contested issue in the proceeding. Within the qualified offer period, J submits a written offer to settle the case for a deficiency of $1,000, including all taxes, penalties, and interest. The offer states that it is a qualified offer for purposes of section 7430(g) and that it will remain open for acceptance by the Internal Revenue Service for a period of 90 days. Section 7430(g)(2)(B) and paragraph (c)(3) of this section state that the amount of a qualified offer must be without regard to interest unless interest is at issue in the proceeding. Since J's offer attempts to compromise interest, which is not a contested issue in the proceeding, it is not a qualified offer.

Example 17. Qualified offer based on new defense or legal theory. Taxpayers K and L received a statutory notice of deficiency for tax year 2005, a tax year when they were married and filed a joint income tax return. Taxpayer K files a separate petition claiming innocent spouse relief and simultaneously submits an offer purporting to be a qualified offer. The offer states that K is entitled to innocent spouse relief and offers to settle the 2005 deficiency as to K. K's innocent spouse claim was not raised during K and L's audit, nor was it raised during their appeals conference. Additionally, at no time prior to or contemporaneously with submitting the offer did K file with the Internal Revenue Service a Form 8857, Request for Innocent Spouse Relief, or otherwise provide the information specified in § 1.6015-5(a) of this chapter. K's offer is not a qualified offer because K did not file a Form 8857 or otherwise provide substantiation or legal and factual arguments necessary to allow for informed consideration of the merits of the innocent spouse claim as required by paragraph (c)(4) of this section, contemporaneously with the offer or prior to making the offer.

(f) *Effective/applicability date.*—This section is applicable with respect to qualified offers made in administrative or court proceedings described in section 7430 after December 24, 2003, except that paragraph (c)(8) is effective as of March 1, 2016. [Reg. § 301.7430-7.]

☐ [*T.D.* 9106, 12-24-2003 (*corrected* 1-27-2004). *Amended by T.D.* 9756, 2-29-2016.]

See p. 15 for regulations not amended to reflect law changes

[Reg. §301.7477-1]

§301.7477-1. Declaratory judgments relating to the value of certain gifts for gift tax purposes.—(a) *In general.*—If the adjustment(s) proposed by the Internal Revenue Service (IRS) will not result in any deficiency in or refund of the donor's gift tax liability for the calendar year, and if the requirements contained in paragraph (d) of this section are satisfied, then the declaratory judgment procedure under section 7477 is available to the donor for determining the amount of one or more of the donor's gifts during that calendar year for Federal gift tax purposes.

(b) *Declaratory judgment procedure.*—(1) *In general.*—If a donor does not resolve a dispute with the IRS concerning the value of a transfer for gift tax purposes at the Examination level, the donor will be sent a notice of preliminary determination of value (Letter 950-G or such other document as may be utilized by the IRS for this purpose from time to time, but referred to in this section as Letter 950-G), inviting the donor to file a formal protest and to request consideration by the appropriate IRS Appeals office. See §§601.105 and 601.106 of this chapter. Subsequently, the donor will be sent a notice of determination of value (Letter 3569, or such other document as may be utilized from time to time by the IRS for this purpose in cases where no deficiency or refund would result, but referred to in this section as Letter 3569) if—

(i) The donor requests Appeals consideration in writing within 30 calendar days after the mailing date of the Letter 950-G, or by such later date as determined pursuant to IRS procedures, and the matter is not resolved by Appeals;

(ii) The donor does not request Appeals consideration within the time provided in paragraph (b)(1)(i) of this section; or

(iii) The IRS does not issue a Letter 950-G in circumstances described in paragraph (d)(4)(iv) of this section.

(2) *Notice of determination of value.*—The Letter 3569 will notify the donor of the adjustment(s) proposed by the IRS, and will advise the donor that the donor may contest the determination made by the IRS by filing a petition with the Tax Court before the 91st day after the date on which the Letter 3569 was mailed to the donor by the IRS.

(3) *Tax Court petition.*—If the donor does not file a timely petition with the Tax Court, the IRS determination as set forth in the Letter 3569 will be considered the final determination of value, as defined in sections 2504(c) and 2001(f). If the donor files a timely petition with the Tax Court, the Tax Court will determine whether the donor has exhausted available administrative remedies. Under section 7477, the Tax Court is not authorized to issue a declaratory judgment unless the Tax Court finds that the donor has exhausted all administrative remedies within the IRS. See paragraph (d)(4) of this section regarding the exhaustion of administrative remedies.

(c) *Adjustments subject to declaratory judgment procedure.*—The declaratory judgment procedures set forth in this section apply to adjustments involving all issues relating to the transfer, including without limitation valuation issues and legal issues involving the interpretation and application of the gift tax law.

(d) *Requirements for declaratory judgment procedure.*—(1) *In general.*—The declaratory judgment procedure provided in this section is available to a donor with respect to a transfer only if all the requirements of paragraphs (d)(2) through (5) of this section with regard to that transfer are satisfied.

(2) *Reporting.*—The transfer is shown or disclosed on the return of tax imposed by chapter 12 for the calendar year during which the transfer was made or on a statement attached to such return. For purposes of this paragraph (d)(2), the term *return of tax imposed by chapter 12* means the last gift tax return (Form 709, "United States Gift (and Generation-Skipping Transfer) Tax Return" or such other form as may be utilized for this purpose from time to time by the IRS) for the calendar year filed on or before the due date of the return, including extensions granted if any, or, if a timely return is not filed, the first gift tax return for that calendar year filed after the due date. For purposes of satisfying this requirement, the transfer need not be reported in a manner that constitutes adequate disclosure within the meaning of §301.6501(c)-1(e) or (f) (and thus for which, under §§20.2001-1(b) and 25.2504-2(b) of this chapter, the period during which the IRS may adjust the value of the gift will not expire). The issuance of a Letter 3569 with regard to a transfer disclosed on a return does not constitute a determination by the IRS that the transfer was adequately disclosed, or otherwise cause the period of limitations on assessment to commence to run with respect to that transfer. In addition, in the case of a transfer that is shown on the return, the IRS may in its discretion defer until a later time making a determination with regard to such transfer. If the IRS exercises its discretion to defer such determination in that case, the transfer will not be addressed in the Letter 3569 (if any) sent to the donor currently, and the donor is not yet eligible for a declaratory judgment with regard to that transfer under section 7477.

(3) *IRS determination and actual controversy.*—The IRS makes a determination regarding the gift tax treatment of the transfer that results in an actual controversy. The IRS makes a determination that results in an actual controversy with respect to a transfer by mailing a Letter 3569 to the donor, thereby notifying the donor of the adjustment(s) proposed by the IRS with regard to that transfer and of the donor's rights under section 7477.

(4) *Exhaustion of administrative remedies.*—(i) *In general.*—The Tax Court determines whether the donor has exhausted all administrative remedies available within the IRS for resolving the controversy.

(ii) *Appeals office consideration.*—For purposes of this section, the IRS will consider a donor to have exhausted all administrative remedies if, prior to filing a petition in Tax Court (except as provided in paragraphs (d)(4)(iii) and (iv) of this section), the donor, or a qualified representative of the donor described in § 601.502 of this chapter, timely requests consideration by Appeals and participates fully (within the meaning of paragraph (d)(4)(vi) of this section) in the Appeals consideration process. A timely request for consideration by Appeals is a written request from the donor for Appeals consideration made within 30 days after the mailing date of the Letter 950-G, or by such later date for responding to the Letter 950-G as is agreed to between the donor and the IRS.

(iii) *Request for Appeals office consideration not granted.*—If the donor, or a qualified representative of the donor described in § 601.502 of this chapter, timely requests consideration by Appeals and Appeals does not grant that request, the IRS nevertheless will consider the donor to have exhausted all administrative remedies within the IRS for purposes of section 7477 upon the issuance of the Letter 3569, provided that the donor, or a qualified representative of the donor described in § 601.502 of this chapter, after the filing of a petition in Tax Court for a declaratory judgment pursuant to section 7477, participates fully (within the meaning of paragraph (d)(4)(vi) of this section) in the Appeals office consideration if offered by the IRS while the case is in docketed status.

(iv) *No Letter 950-G issued.*—If the IRS does not issue a Letter 950-G to the donor prior to the issuance of Letter 3569, the IRS nevertheless will consider the donor to have exhausted all administrative remedies within the IRS for purposes of section 7477 upon the issuance of the Letter 3569, provided that—

(A) The IRS decision not to issue the Letter 950-G was not due to actions or inactions of the donor (such as a failure to supply requested information or a current mailing address to the Area Director having jurisdiction over the tax matter); and

(B) The donor, or a qualified representative of the donor described in § 601.502 of this chapter, after the filing of a petition in Tax Court for a declaratory judgment pursuant to section 7477, participates fully (within the meaning of paragraph (d)(4)(vi) of this section) in the Appeals office consideration if offered by the IRS while the case is in docketed status.

(v) *Failure to agree to extension of time for assessment.*—For purposes of section 7477, the donor's refusal to agree to an extension of the time under section 6501 within which gift tax with respect to the transfer at issue (if any) may be assessed will not be considered by the IRS to constitute a failure by the donor to exhaust all administrative remedies available to the donor within the IRS.

(vi) *Participation in Appeals consideration process.*—For purposes of this section, the donor or a qualified representative of the donor described in § 601.502 of this chapter participates fully in the Appeals consideration process if the donor or the qualified representative timely submits all information related to the transfer that is requested by the IRS in connection with the Appeals consideration and discloses to the Appeals office all relevant information regarding the controversy to the extent such information and its relevance is known or should be known by the donor or the qualified representative during the time the issue is under consideration by Appeals.

(5) *Timely petition in Tax Court.*—The donor files a pleading with the Tax Court requesting a declaratory judgment under section 7477. This pleading must be filed with the Tax Court before the 91st day after the date of mailing of the Letter 3569 by the IRS to the donor. The pleading must be in the form of a petition subject to Tax Court Rule 211(d).

(e) *Examples.*—The following examples illustrate the provisions of this section, and assume that in each case the Tax Court petition is filed on or after September 9, 2009. These examples, however, do not address any other situations that might affect the Tax Court's jurisdiction over the proceeding:

Example 1. Exhaustion of administrative remedies. The donor (D) timely files a Form 709, "United States Gift (and Generation-Skipping Transfer) Tax Return," on which D reports D's completed gift of closely held stock. After conducting an examination, the IRS concludes that the value of the stock on the date of the gift is greater than the value reported on the return. Because the amount of D's available applicable credit amount under section 2505 is sufficient to cover any resulting tax liability, no gift tax deficiency will result from the adjustment. D is unable to resolve the matter with the IRS examiner. The IRS sends a Letter 950-G to D informing D of the proposed adjustment. D, within 30 calendar days after the mailing date of the letter, submits a written request for Appeals consideration. During the Appeals process, D provides to the Appeals office all additional information (if any) requested by Appeals relevant to the determination of the value of the stock in a timely fashion. The Appeals office and D are unable to reach an agreement regarding the value of the stock as of the date of the gift. The Appeals office sends D a notice of determination of value (Letter 3569). For purposes of section 7477, the IRS will consider D to have exhausted all available administrative remedies within the IRS, and thus will not contest the allegation in D's petition that D has exhausted all such administrative remedies.

Example 2. Exhaustion of administrative remedies. Assume the same facts as in *Example 1*, except that D does not timely request consideration by Appeals after receiving the Letter 950-G. A Letter 3569 is mailed to D more than 30 days after the mailing of the Letter 950-G and prior to the expiration of the period of limitations for assessment of gift tax. D timely files a petition in Tax Court pursuant to section 7477. After the case is docketed, D requests Appeals consideration. In this situation, because D did not respond timely to the Letter 950-G with a written request for Appeals consideration, the IRS will not consider D to have exhausted all administrative remedies available within the IRS for purposes of section 7477 prior to filing the petition in Tax Court, and thus may contest any allegation in D's petition that D has exhausted all such administrative remedies.

Example 3. Exhaustion of administrative remedies. D timely files a Form 709 on which D reports D's completed gifts of interests in a family limited partnership. After conducting an examination, the IRS proposes to adjust the value of the gifts as reported on the return. No gift tax deficiency will result from the adjustments, however, because D has a sufficient amount of available applicable credit amount under section 2505. D declines to consent to extend the time for the assessment of gift tax with respect to the gifts at issue. Because of the pending expiration of the period of limitation on assessment within which a gift tax, if any, could be assessed, the IRS determines that there is not adequate time for Appeals consideration. Accordingly, the IRS mails to D a Letter 3569, even though a Letter 950-G had not first been issued to D. D timely files a petition in Tax Court pursuant to section 7477. After the case is docketed in Tax Court, D is offered the opportunity for Appeals to consider any dispute regarding the determination and participates fully in the Appeals consideration process. However, the Appeals office and D are unable to resolve the issue. The IRS will consider D to have exhausted all administrative remedies available within the IRS, and thus will not assert that D has not exhausted all such administrative remedies.

Example 4. Legal issue. D transfers nonvested stock options to a trust for the benefit of D's child. D timely files a Form 709 reporting the transfer as a completed gift for Federal gift tax purposes and complies with the adequate disclosure requirements for purposes of triggering the commencement of the applicable statute of limitations. Pursuant to § 301.6501(c)-1(f)(5), adequate disclosure of a transfer that is reported as a completed gift on the Form 709 will commence the running of the period of limitations for assessment of gift tax on D, even if the transfer is ultimately determined to be an incomplete gift for purposes of § 25.2511-2 of this chapter. After conducting an examination, the IRS concurs with the reported valuation of the stock options, but concludes that the reported transfer is not a completed gift for Federal gift tax purposes. D is unable to resolve the matter with the IRS examiner. The IRS sends a Letter 950-G to D, who timely mails a written request for Appeals consideration. Assuming that the IRS mails to D a Letter 3569 with regard to this transfer, and that D complies with the administrative procedures set forth in this section, including the exhaustion of all administrative remedies available within the IRS, then D may file a petition for declaratory judgment with the Tax Court pursuant to section 7477.

Example 5. Transfers in controversy. On April 16, 2007, D timely files a Form 709 on which D reports gifts made in 2006 of fractional interests in certain real property and of interests in a family limited partnership (FLP). However, although the gifts are disclosed on the return, the return does not contain information sufficient to constitute adequate disclosure under § 301.6501(c)-1(e) or (f) for purposes of the application of the statute of limitations on assessment of gift tax with respect to the reported gifts. The IRS conducts an examination and concludes that the value of both the interests in the real property and the FLP interests on the date(s) of the transfers are greater than the values reported on the return. No gift tax deficiency will result from the adjustments because D has a sufficient amount of remaining applicable credit amount under section 2505. However, D does not agree with the adjustments. The IRS sends a Letter 950-G to D informing D of the proposed adjustments in the value of the reported gifts. D, within 30 calendar days after the mailing date of the letter, submits a written request for Appeals consideration. The Appeals office and D are unable to reach an agreement regarding the value of any of the gifts. In the exercise of its discretion, the IRS decides to resolve currently only the value of the real property interests, and to defer the resolution of the value of the FLP interests. On May 28, 2009, the Appeals office sends D a Letter 3569 addressing only the value of the gifts of interests in the real property. Because none of the gifts reported on the return filed on April 16, 2007, were adequately disclosed for purposes of § 301.6501(c)-1(e) or (f), the period of limitations during which the IRS may adjust the value of those gifts has not begun to run. Accordingly, the Letter 3569 is timely mailed. If D timely files a petition in Tax Court pursuant to section 7477 with regard to the value of the interests in the real property, then, assuming the other requirements of section 7477 are satisfied with regard to those interests, the Tax Court's declaratory judgment, once it becomes final, will determine the value of the gifts of the interests in the real property. Because the IRS has not yet put the gift tax value of the interests in the FLP into controversy, the procedure under section 7477 is not yet available with regard to those gifts.

(f) *Effective/applicability date.*—This section applies to civil proceedings described in section 7477 filed in the United States Tax Court on or after September 9, 2009. [Reg. § 301.7477-1.]

☐ [*T.D. 7596, 2-22-79. Amended by T.D. 7954, 5-7-84 and T.D. 9460, 9-8-2009 (corrected 10-26-2009).*]

[Reg. § 301.7502-1]

§ 301.7502-1. Timely mailing of documents and payments treated as timely filing and paying.—(a) *General rule.*—Section 7502 provides that, if the requirements of that section are met, a document or payment is deemed to be filed or paid on the date of the postmark stamped on the envelope or other appropriate wrapper (envelope) in which the document or payment was mailed. Thus, if the envelope that contains the document or payment has a timely postmark, the document or payment is considered timely filed or paid even if it is received after the last date, or the last day of the period, prescribed for filing the document or making the payment. Section 7502 does not apply in determining whether a failure to file a return or pay a tax has continued for an additional month or fraction thereof for purposes of computing the penalties and additions to tax imposed by section 6651. Except as provided in section 7502(e) and § 301.7502-2, relating to the timely mailing of deposits, and paragraph (d) of this section, relating to electronically filed documents, section 7502 is applicable only to those documents or payments as defined in paragraph (b) of this section and only if the document or payment is mailed in accordance with paragraph (c) of this section and is delivered in accordance with paragraph (e) of this section.

(b) *Definitions.*—(1) *Document defined.*—(i) The term *document*, as used in this section, means any return, claim, statement, or other document required to be filed within a prescribed period or on or before a prescribed date under authority of any provision of the internal revenue laws, except as provided in paragraph (b) (1) (ii), (iii), or (iv) of this section.

(ii) The term does not include returns, claims, statements, or other documents that are required under any provision of the internal revenue laws or the regulations thereunder to be delivered by any method other than mailing.

(iii) The term does not include any document filed in any court other than the Tax Court, but the term does include any document filed with the Tax Court, including a petition and a notice of appeal of a decision of the Tax Court.

(iv) The term does not include any document that is mailed to an authorized financial institution under section 6302. However, see § 301.7502-2 for special rules relating to the timeliness of deposits and documents required to be filed with deposits.

(2) *Claims for refund.*—(i) *In general.*—In the case of certain taxes, a return may constitute a claim for credit or refund. Section 7502 is applicable to the determination of whether a claim for credit or refund is timely filed for purposes of section 6511(a) if the conditions of section 7502 are met, irrespective of whether the claim is also a return. For rules regarding claims for refund on late filed tax returns, see paragraph (f) of this section. Section 7502 is also applicable when a claim for credit or refund is delivered after the last day of the period specified in section 6511(b)(2)(A) or in any other corresponding provision of law relating to the limit on the amount of credit or refund that is allowable.

(ii) *Example.*—The rules of paragraph (b)(2)(i) of this section are illustrated by the following example:

Example. (A) Taxpayer A, an individual, mailed his 2004 Form 1040, "U.S. Individual Income Tax Return," on May 10, 2005, but no tax was paid at that time because the tax liability disclosed by the return had been completely satisfied by the income tax that had been withheld on A's wages. On April 15, 2008, A mails, in accordance with the requirements of this section, a Form 1040X, "Amended U.S. Individual Income Tax Return," claiming a refund of a portion of the tax that had been paid through withholding during 2004. The date of the postmark on the envelope containing the claim for refund is April 15, 2008. The claim is received by the IRS on April 18, 2008.

(B) Under section 6511(a), A's claim for refund is timely if filed within three years from May 10, 2005, the date on which A's 2004 return was filed. As a result of the limitations of section 6511(b)(2)(A), if A's claim is not filed within three years after April 15, 2005, the date on which A is deemed under section 6513 to have paid his 2004 tax, A is not entitled to any refund. Because A's claim for refund is postmarked and mailed in accordance with the requirements of this section and is delivered after the last day of the period specified in section 6511(b)(2)(A), section 7502 is applicable and the claim is deemed to have been filed on April 15, 2008.

(3) *Payment defined.*—(i) The term *payment*, as used in this section, means any payment required to be made within a prescribed period or on or before a prescribed date under the authority of any provision of the internal revenue laws, except as provided in paragraph(b)(3)(ii), (iii), (iv), or (v) of this section.

(ii) The term does not include any payment that is required under any provision of the internal revenue laws or the regulations thereunder to be delivered by any method other than mailing. See, for example, section 6302(h) and the regulations thereunder regarding electronic funds transfer.

(iii) The term does not include any payment, whether it is made in the form of currency or other medium of payment, unless it is actually received and accounted for. For example, if a check is used as the form of payment, this section does not apply unless the check is honored upon presentation.

(iv) The term does not include any payment to any court other than the Tax Court.

(v) The term does not include any deposit that is required to be made with an authorized financial institution under section 6302. However, see § 301.7502-2 for rules relating to the timeliness of deposits.

(4) *Last date or last day prescribed.*—As used in this section, the term *the last date, or the last day of the period, prescribed for filing the document or making the payment* includes any extension of time granted for that action. When the last date, or the last day of the period, prescribed for filing the document or making the payment falls on a Saturday, Sunday or legal holiday, section 7503 applies. Therefore, in applying the rules of this paragraph (b)(4), the next succeeding day that is not a Saturday, Sunday, or legal holiday is treated as the last date, or the last day of the

See p. 15 for regulations not amended to reflect law changes

period, prescribed for filing the document or making the payment. Also, when the last date, or the last day of the period, prescribed for filing the document or making the payment falls within a period disregarded under section 7508 or section 7508A, the next succeeding day after the expiration of the section 7508 period or section 7508A period that is not a Saturday, Sunday, or legal holiday is treated as the last date, or the last day of the period, prescribed for filing the document or making the payment.

(c) *Mailing requirements.*—(1) *In general.*—Section 7502 does not apply unless the document or payment is mailed in accordance with the following requirements:

(i) *Envelope and address.*—The document or payment must be contained in an envelope, properly addressed to the agency, officer, or office with which the document is required to be filed or to which the payment is required to be made.

(ii) *Timely deposited in U.S. mail.*—The document or payment must be deposited within the prescribed time in the mail in the United States with sufficient postage prepaid. For this purpose, a document or payment is deposited in the mail in the United States when it is deposited with the domestic mail service of the U.S. Postal Service. The domestic mail service of the U.S. Postal Service, as defined by the Domestic Mail Manual as incorporated by reference in the postal regulations, includes mail transmitted within, among, and between the United States of America, its territories and possessions, and Army post offices (APO), fleet post offices (FPO), and the United Nations, NY. (See Domestic Mail Manual, section G011.2.1, as incorporated by reference in 39 CFR 111.1.) Section 7502 does not apply to any document or payment that is deposited with the mail service of any other country.

(iii) *Postmark.*—(A) *U.S. Postal Service postmark.*—If the postmark on the envelope is made by the U.S. Postal Service, the postmark must bear a date on or before the last date, or the last day of the period, prescribed for filing the document or making the payment. If the postmark does not bear a date on or before the last date, or the last day of the period, prescribed for filing the document or making the payment, the document or payment is considered not to be timely filed or paid, regardless of when the document or payment is deposited in the mail. Accordingly, the sender who relies upon the applicability of section 7502 assumes the risk that the postmark will bear a date on or before the last date, or the last day of the period, prescribed for filing the document or making the payment. See, however, paragraph (c)(2) of this section with respect to the use of registered mail or certified mail to avoid this risk. If the postmark on the envelope is made by the U.S. Postal Service but is not legible, the person who is required to file the document or make the payment has the burden of proving the date that the postmark was made. Furthermore, if the envelope that contains a document or payment has a timely postmark made by the U.S. Postal Service, but it is received after the time when a document or payment postmarked and mailed at that time would ordinarily be received, the sender may be required to prove that it was timely mailed.

(B) *Postmark made by other than U.S. Postal Service.*—*(1) In general.*—If the postmark on the envelope is made other than by the U.S. Postal Service—

(i) The postmark so made must bear a legible date on or before the last date, or the last day of the period, prescribed for filing the document or making the payment; and

(ii) The document or payment must be received by the agency, officer, or office with which it is required to be filed not later than the time when a document or payment contained in an envelope that is properly addressed, mailed, and sent by the same class of mail would ordinarily be received if it were postmarked at the same point of origin by the U.S. Postal Service on the last date, or the last day of the period, prescribed for filing the document or making the payment.

(2) Document or payment received late.—If a document or payment described in paragraph (c)(1)(iii)(B)*(1)* is received after the time when a document or payment so mailed and so postmarked by the U.S. Postal Service would ordinarily be received, the document or payment is treated as having been received at the time when a document or payment so mailed and so postmarked would ordinarily be received if the person who is required to file the document or make the payment establishes—

(i) That it was actually deposited in the U.S. mail before the last collection of mail from the place of deposit that was postmarked (except for the metered mail) by the U.S. Postal Service on or before the last date, or the last day of the period, prescribed for filing the document or making the payment;

(ii) That the delay in receiving the document or payment was due to a delay in the transmission of the U.S. mail; and

(iii) The cause of the delay.

(3) U.S. and non-U.S. postmarks.—If the envelope has a postmark made by the U.S. Postal Service in addition to a postmark not so made, the postmark that was not made by the U.S. Postal Service is disregarded, and whether the envelope was mailed in accordance with this paragraph (c)(1)(iii)(B) will be determined solely by applying the rule of paragraph (c)(1)(iii)(A) of this section.

(2) *Registered or certified mail.*—If the document or payment is sent by U.S. registered mail, the date of registration of the document or payment is treated as the postmark date. If the document or payment is sent by U.S. certified mail and the sender's receipt is postmarked by the postal employee to whom the document or payment is presented, the date of the U.S. postmark on the receipt is treated as the postmark date of the document or payment. Accordingly, the risk

that the document or payment will not be postmarked on the day that it is deposited in the mail may be eliminated by the use of registered or certified mail.

(3) *Private delivery services.*—Under section 7502(f)(1), a service of a private delivery service (PDS) may be treated as an equivalent to United States mail for purposes of the postmark rule if the Commissioner determines that the service satisfies the conditions of section 7502(f)(2). Thus, the Commissioner may, in guidance published in the Internal Revenue Bulletin (see § 601.601(d)(2)(ii)(b) of this chapter), prescribe procedures and additional rules to designate a service of a PDS for purposes of the postmark rule of section 7502(a).

(d) *Electronically filed documents.*—(1) *In general.*—A document filed electronically with an electronic return transmitter (as defined in paragraph (d)(3)(i) of this section and authorized pursuant to paragraph (d)(2) of this section) in the manner and time prescribed by the Commissioner is deemed to be filed on the date of the electronic postmark (as defined in paragraph (d)(3)(ii) of this section) given by the authorized electronic return transmitter. Thus, if the electronic postmark is timely, the document is considered filed timely although it is received by the agency, officer, or office after the last date, or the last day of the period, prescribed for filing such document.

(2) *Authorized electronic return transmitters.*—The Commissioner may enter into an agreement with an electronic return transmitter or prescribe in forms, instructions, or other appropriate guidance the procedures under which the electronic return transmitter is authorized to provide taxpayers with an electronic postmark to acknowledge the date and time that the electronic return transmitter received the electronically filed document.

(3) *Definitions.*—(i) *Electronic return transmitter.*—For purposes of this paragraph (d), the term *electronic return transmitter* has the same meaning as contained in section 3.01(4) of Rev. Proc. 2000-31 (2000-31 I.R.B. 146 (July 31, 2000)) (see § 601.601(d)(2) of this chapter) or in procedures prescribed by the Commissioner.

(ii) *Electronic postmark.*—For purposes of this paragraph (d), the term *electronic postmark* means a record of the date and time (in a particular time zone) that an authorized electronic return transmitter receives the transmission of a taxpayer's electronically filed document on its host system. However, if the taxpayer and the electronic return transmitter are located in different time zones, it is the taxpayer's time zone that controls the timeliness of the electronically filed document.

(e) *Delivery.*—(1) *General rule.*—Except as provided in section 7502(f) and paragraphs (c)(3) and (d) of this section, section 7502 is not applicable unless the document or payment is delivered by U.S. mail to the agency, officer, or office with which the document is required to be filed or to which payment is required to be made.

(2) *Exceptions to actual delivery.*—(i) *Registered and certified mail.*—In the case of a document (but not a payment) sent by registered or certified mail, proof that the document was properly registered or that a postmarked certified mail sender's receipt was properly issued and that the envelope was properly addressed to the agency, officer, or office constitutes prima facie evidence that the document was delivered to the agency, officer, or office. Other than direct proof of actual delivery, proof of proper use of registered or certified mail, and proof of proper use of a duly designated PDS as provided for by paragraph (e)(2)(ii) of this section, are the exclusive means to establish prima facie evidence of delivery of a document to the agency, officer, or office with which the document is required to be filed. No other evidence of a postmark or of mailing will be prima facie evidence of delivery or raise a presumption that the document was delivered.

(ii) *Equivalents of registered and certified mail.*—Under section 7502(f)(3), the Secretary may extend the prima facie evidence of delivery rule of section 7502(c)(1)(A) to a service of a designated PDS, which is substantially equivalent to United States registered or certified mail. Thus, the Commissioner may, in guidance published in the Internal Revenue Bulletin (see § 601.601(d)(2)(ii)(b) of this chapter), prescribe procedures and additional rules to designate a service of a PDS for purposes of demonstrating prima facie evidence of delivery of a document pursuant to section 7502(c).

(f) *Claim for credit or refund on late filed tax return.*—(1) *In general.*—Generally, an original income tax return may constitute a claim for credit or refund of income tax. See § 301.6402-3(a)(5). Other original tax returns can also be considered claims for credit or refund if the liability disclosed on the return is less than the amount of tax that has been paid. If section 7502 would not apply to a return (but for the operation of paragraph (f)(2) of this section) that is also considered a claim for credit or refund because the envelope that contains the return does not have a postmark dated on or before the due date of the return, section 7502 will apply separately to the claim for credit or refund if—

(i) The date of the postmark on the envelope is within the period that is three years (plus the period of any extension of time to file) from the day the tax is paid or considered paid (see section 6513), and the claim for credit or refund is delivered after this three-year period; and

(ii) The conditions of section 7502 are otherwise met.

(2) *Filing date of late filed return.*—If the conditions of paragraph (f)(1) of this section are met, the late filed return will be deemed filed on the postmark date.

(3) *Example.*—The rules of this paragraph (f) are illustrated by the following example

Example. (i) Taxpayer A, an individual, mailed his 2001 Form 1040, "U.S. Individual Income Tax Return," on April 15, 2005, claiming a refund of amounts paid through withholding during 2001. The date of the postmark on the envelope containing the return and claim for refund is April 15, 2005. The return and claim for refund are received by the Internal Revenue Service (IRS) on April 18, 2005. Amounts withheld in 2001 exceeded A's tax liability for 2001 and are treated as paid on April 15, 2002, pursuant to section 6513.

(ii) Even though the date of the postmark on the envelope is after the due date of the return, the claim for refund and the late filed return are treated as filed on the postmark date for purposes of this paragraph (f). Accordingly, the return will be treated as filed on April 15, 2005. In addition, the claim for refund will be treated as timely filed on April 15, 2005. Further, the entire amount of the refund attributable to withholding is allowable as a refund under section 6511(b)(2)(A).

(g) *Effective date*.—(1) *In general*.—Except as provided in paragraphs (g) (2) and (3) of this section, the rules of this section apply to any payment or document mailed and delivered in accordance with the requirements of this section in an envelope bearing a postmark dated after January 11, 2001.

(2) *Claim for credit or refund on late filed tax return*.—Paragraph (f) of this section applies to any claim for credit or refund on a late filed tax return described in paragraph (f) (1) of this section except for those claims for credit or refund which (without regard to paragraph (f) of this section) were barred by the operation of section 6532(a) or any other law or rule of law (including res judicata) as of January 11, 2001.

(3) *Electronically filed documents*.—This section applies to any electronically filed return, claim, statement, or other document transmitted to an electronic return transmitter that is authorized to provide an electronic postmark pursuant to paragraph (d) (2) of this section after January 11, 2001.

(4) *Registered or certified mail as the means to prove delivery of a document*.—Section 301.7502-1(e)(2) will apply to all documents mailed after September 21, 2004. [Reg. § 301.7502-1.]

☐ [*T.D.* 6232, 5-2-57. *Amended by T.D.* 6292, 4-18-58; *T.D.* 6444, 1-14-60; *T.D.* 6498, 10-24-60; *T.D.* 8807, 1-14-99; *T.D.* 8932, 1-10-2001 *and T.D.* 9543, 8-22-2011.]

[Reg. § 301.7508A-1]

§ 301.7508A-1. Postponement of certain tax-related deadlines by reasons of a federally declared disaster or terroristic or military action.—(a) *Scope*.—This section provides rules by which the Internal Revenue Service (IRS) may postpone deadlines for performing certain acts with respect to taxes other than taxes not administered by the IRS such as firearms tax (chapter 32, section 4181); harbor maintenance tax (chapter 36, section 4461); and alcohol and tobacco taxes (subtitle E).

(b) *Postponed deadlines*.—(1) *In general*.—In the case of a taxpayer determined by the Secretary to be affected by a federally declared disaster (as defined in section 1033(h)(3)) or a terroristic or military action (as defined in section 692(c)(2)), the Secretary may specify a postponement period (as defined in paragraph (d)(1) of this section) of up to one year that may be disregarded in determining under the internal revenue laws, in respect of any tax liability of the affected taxpayer (as defined in paragraph (d)(1) of this section)—

(i) Whether any or all of the acts described in paragraph (c) of this section were performed within the time prescribed;

(ii) The amount of interest, penalty, additional amount, or addition to the tax; and

(iii) The amount of credit or refund.

(2) *Effect of postponement period*.—When an affected taxpayer is required to perform a tax-related act by a due date that falls within the postponement period, the affected taxpayer is eligible for postponement of time to perform the act until the last day of the period. The affected taxpayer is eligible for relief from interest, penalties, additional amounts, or additions to tax during the postponement period.

(3) *Interaction between postponement period and extensions of time to file or pay*.—(i) *In general*.—The postponement period under section 7508A runs concurrently with extensions of time to file and pay, if any, under other sections of the Internal Revenue Code.

(ii) *Original due date prior to, but extended due date within, the postponement period*.—When the original due date precedes the first day of the postponement period and the extended due date falls within the postponement period, the following rules apply. If an affected taxpayer received an extension of time to file, filing will be timely on or before the last day of the postponement period, and the taxpayer is eligible for relief from penalties or additions to tax related to the failure to file during the postponement period. Similarly, if an affected taxpayer received an extension of time to pay, payment will be timely on or before the last day of the postponement period, and the taxpayer is eligible for relief from interest, penalties, additions to tax, or additional amounts related to the failure to pay during the postponement period.

(4) *Due date not extended*.—The postponement of the deadline of a tax-related act does not extend the due date for the act, but merely allows the IRS to disregard a time period of up to one year for performance of the act. To the extent that other statutes may rely on the date a return is due to be filed, the postponement period will not change the due date of the return.

(5) *Additional relief*.—The rules of this paragraph (b) demonstrate how the IRS generally implements section 7508A. The IRS may determine, however, that additional relief to taxpay-

ers is appropriate and may provide additional relief to the extent allowed under section 7508A. To the extent that the IRS grants additional relief, the IRS will provide specific guidance on the scope of relief in the manner provided in paragraph (e) of this section.

(c) *Acts for which a period may be disregarded.*—(1) *Acts performed by taxpayers.*—Paragraph (b) of this section applies to the following acts performed by affected taxpayers (as defined in paragraph (d)(1) of this section)—

(i) Filing any return of income tax, estate tax, gift tax, generation-skipping transfer tax, excise tax (other than firearms tax (chapter 32, section 4181); harbor maintenance tax (chapter 36, section 4461); and alcohol and tobacco taxes (subtitle E)), or employment tax (including income tax withheld at source and income tax imposed by subtitle C or any law superseded thereby);

(ii) Paying any income tax, estate tax, gift tax, generation-skipping transfer tax, excise tax (other than firearms tax (chapter 32, section 4181); harbor maintenance tax (chapter 36, section 4461); and alcohol and tobacco taxes (subtitle E)), employment tax (including income tax withheld at source and income tax imposed by subtitle C or any law superseded thereby), any installment of those taxes (including payment under section 6159 relating to installment agreements), or of any other liability to the United States in respect thereof, but not including deposits of taxes pursuant to section 6302 and the regulations under section 6302;

(iii) Making contributions to a qualified retirement plan (within the meaning of section 4974(c)) under section 219(f)(3), 404(a)(6), 404(h)(1)(B), or 404(m)(2); making distributions under section 408(d)(4); recharacterizing contributions under section 408A(d)(6); or making a rollover under section 402(c), 403(a)(4), 403(b)(8), or 408(d)(3);

(iv) Filing a petition with the Tax Court, or for review of a decision rendered by the Tax Court;

(v) Filing a claim for credit or refund of any tax;

(vi) Bringing suit upon a claim for credit or refund of any tax; and

(vii) Any other act specified in a revenue ruling, revenue procedure, notice, announcement, news release, or other guidance published in the Internal Revenue Bulletin (see § 601.601(d)(2) of this chapter).

(2) *Acts performed by the government.*—Paragraph (b) of this section applies to the following acts performed by the government—

(i) Assessing any tax;

(ii) Giving or making any notice or demand for the payment of any tax, or with respect to any liability to the United States in respect of any tax;

(iii) Collecting by the Secretary, by levy or otherwise, of the amount of any liability in respect of any tax;

(iv) Bringing suit by the United States, or any officer on its behalf, in respect of any liability in respect of any tax;

(v) Allowing a credit or refund of any tax; and

(vi) Any other act specified in a revenue ruling, revenue procedure, notice, or other guidance published in the Internal Revenue Bulletin (see § 601.601(d)(2) of this chapter).

(d) *Definitions.*—(1) *Affected taxpayer* means—

(i) Any individual whose principal residence (for purposes of section 1033(h)(4)) is located in a covered disaster area;

(ii) Any business entity or sole proprietor whose principal place of business is located in a covered disaster area;

(iii) Any individual who is a relief worker affiliated with a recognized government or philanthropic organization and who is assisting in a covered disaster area;

(iv) Any individual whose principal residence (for purposes of section 1033(h)(4)), or any business entity or sole proprietor whose principal place of business is not located in a covered disaster area, but whose records necessary to meet a deadline for an act specified in paragraph (c) of this section are maintained in a covered disaster area;

(v) Any estate or trust that has tax records necessary to meet a deadline for an act specified in paragraph (c) of this section and that are maintained in a covered disaster area;

(vi) The spouse of an affected taxpayer, solely with regard to a joint return of the husband and wife; or

(vii) Any individual, business entity, or sole proprietorship not located in a covered disaster area, but whose records necessary to meet a deadline for an act specified in paragraph (c) of this section are located in the covered disaster area;

(viii) Any individual visiting the covered disaster area who was killed or injured as a result of the disaster; or

(ix) Any other person determined by the IRS to be affected by a federally declared disaster (within the meaning of section 1033(h)(3)).

(2) *Covered disaster area* means an area of a federally declared disaster (within the meaning of section 1033(h)(3)) to which the IRS has determined paragraph (b) of this section applies.

(3) *Postponement period* means the period of time (up to one year) that the IRS postpones deadlines for performing tax-related acts under section 7508A.

(e) *Notice of postponement of certain acts.*—If a tax-related deadline is postponed under section 7508A and this section, the IRS will publish a revenue ruling, revenue procedure, notice, announcement, news release, or other guidance (see § 601.601(d)(2) of this chapter) describing the acts postponed, the postponement period, and the location of the covered disaster area. Guidance under this paragraph (e) will be published as soon as practicable after the occurrence

See p. 15 for regulations not amended to reflect law changes

of a terroristic or military action or declaration of a federally declared disaster.

(f) *Examples*.—The rules of this section are illustrated by the following examples:

Example 1. (i) Corporation X, a calendar year taxpayer, has its principal place of business in County M in State W. Pursuant to a timely filed request for extension of time to file, Corporation X's 2008 Form 1120, "U.S. Corporation Income Tax Return," is due on September 15, 2009. Also due on September 15, 2009, is Corporation X's third quarter estimated tax payment for 2009. Corporation X's 2009 third quarter Form 720, "Quarterly Federal Excise Tax Return," and third quarter Form 941, "Employer's Quarterly Federal Tax Return," are due on October 31, 2009. In addition, Corporation X has an employment tax deposit due on September 15, 2009.

(ii) On September 1, 2009, a hurricane strikes County M in State W. On September 7, 2009, certain counties in State W (including County M) are determined to be disaster areas within the meaning of section 1033(h)(3) that are eligible for assistance by the Federal government under the Stafford Act. Also on September 7, 2009, the IRS determines that County M in State W is a covered disaster area and publishes guidance announcing that the time period for affected taxpayers to file returns, pay taxes, and perform other time-sensitive acts falling on or after September 1, 2009, and on or before November 30, 2009, has been postponed to November 30, 2009, pursuant to section 7508A.

(iii) Because Corporation X's principal place of business is in County M, Corporation X is an affected taxpayer. Accordingly, Corporation X's 2008 Form 1120 will be timely if filed on or before November 30, 2009. Corporation X's 2009 third quarter estimated tax payment will be timely if made on or before November 30, 2009. In addition, pursuant to paragraph (c) of this section, Corporation X's 2009 third quarter Form 720 and third quarter Form 941 will be timely if filed on or before November 30, 2009. However, because deposits of taxes are excluded from the scope of paragraph (c) of this section, Corporation X's employment tax deposit is due on September 15, 2009. In addition, Corporation X's deposits relating to the third quarter Form 720 are not postponed. Absent reasonable cause, Corporation X is subject to the failure to deposit penalty under section 6656 and accrual of interest.

Example 2. The facts are the same as in *Example 1*, except that because of the severity of the hurricane, the IRS determines that postponement of government acts is necessary. During 2009, Corporation X's 2005 Form 1120 is being examined by the IRS. Pursuant to a timely filed request for extension of time to file, Corporation X timely filed its 2005 Form 1120 on September 15, 2006. Without application of this section, the statute of limitation on assessment for the 2005 income tax year will expire on September 15, 2009. However, pursuant to paragraph (c) of this section, assessment of tax is one of the government acts for which up to one year may be disregarded. Because September 15, 2009, falls within the period in which government acts are postponed, the statute of limitation on assessment for Corporation X's 2005 income tax will expire on November 30, 2009. Because Corporation X did not timely file an extension of time to pay, payment of its 2005 income tax was due on March 15, 2006. As such, Corporation X will be subject to the failure to pay penalty and related interest beginning on March 15, 2006. The due date for payment of Corporation X's 2005 income tax preceded the postponement period. Therefore, Corporation X is not entitled to the suspension of interest or penalties during the disaster period with respect to its 2005 income tax liability.

Example 3. The facts are the same as in *Example 2*, except that the examination of the 2005 taxable year was completed earlier in 2009, and on July 28, 2009, the IRS mailed a statutory notice of deficiency to Corporation X. Without application of this section, Corporation X has 90 days (or until October 26, 2009) to file a petition with the Tax Court. However, pursuant to paragraph (c) of this section, filing a petition with the Tax Court is one of the taxpayer acts for which a period of up to one year may be disregarded. Because Corporation X is an affected taxpayer, Corporation X's petition to the Tax Court will be timely if filed on or before November 30, 2009, the last day of the postponement period.

Example 4. (i) H and W, individual calendar year taxpayers, intend to file a joint Form 1040, "U.S. Individual Income Tax Return," for the 2008 taxable year and are required to file a Schedule H, "Household Employment Taxes." The joint return is due on April 15, 2009. H and W's principal residence is in County M in State Q.

(ii) On April 2, 2009, a severe ice storm strikes County M. On April 5, 2009, certain counties in State Q (including County M) are determined to be disaster areas within the meaning of section 1033(h)(3) that are eligible for assistance by the Federal government under the Stafford Act. Also on April 5, 2009, the IRS determines that County M in State Q is a covered disaster area and publishes guidance announcing that the time period for affected taxpayers to file returns, pay taxes, and perform other time-sensitive acts falling on or after April 2, 2009, and on or before June 2, 2009, has been postponed to June 2, 2009.

(iii) Because H and W's principal residence is in County M, H and W are affected taxpayers. April 15, 2009, the due date for the filing of H and W's 2008 Form 1040 and Schedule H, falls within the postponement period described in the IRS published guidance. Thus, H and W's return will be timely if filed on or before June 2, 2009. If H and W request an extension of time to file under section 6081 on or before June 2, 2009, the extension is deemed to have been filed by April 15, 2009. Thus, H and W's return will be timely if filed on or before October 15, 2009.

(iv) April 15, 2009, is also the due date for the payment due on the return. This date falls within the postponement period described in the IRS published guidance. Thus, the payment of tax due with the return will be timely if paid on or before June 2, 2009, the last day of the postponement period. If H and W fail to pay the tax due on the 2008 Form 1040 by June 2, 2009, and do not receive an extension of time to pay under section 6161, H and W will be subject to failure to pay penalties and accrual of interest beginning on June 3, 2009.

Example 5. (i) H and W, residents of County D in State G, intend to file an amended return to request a refund of 2008 taxes. H and W timely filed their 2008 income tax return on April 15, 2009. Under section 6511(a), H and W's amended 2008 tax return must be filed on or before April 16, 2012 (because April 15, 2012, falls on a Sunday, H and W's amended return was due to be filed on April 16, 2012).

(ii) On April 2, 2012, an earthquake strikes County D. On April 6, 2012, certain counties in State G (including County D) are determined to be disaster areas within the meaning of section 1033(h)(3) that are eligible for assistance by the Federal government under the Stafford Act. Also on April 6, 2012, the IRS determines that County D in State G is a covered disaster area and publishes guidance announcing that the time period for affected taxpayers to file returns, pay taxes, and perform other time-sensitive acts falling on or after April 2, 2012, and on or before October 2, 2012, has been postponed to October 2, 2012.

(iii) Under paragraph (c) of this section, filing a claim for refund of tax is one of the taxpayer acts for which the IRS may disregard a period of up to one year. The postponement period for this disaster begins on April 2, 2012, and ends on October 2, 2012. Accordingly, H and W's claim for refund for 2008 taxes will be timely if filed on or before October 2, 2012. Moreover, in applying the lookback period in section 6511(b)(2)(A), which limits the amount of the allowable refund, the period from October 2, 2012, back to April 2, 2012, is disregarded under paragraph (b)(1)(iii) of this section. Thus, if the claim is filed on or before October 2, 2012, amounts deemed paid on April 15, 2009, under section 6513(b), such as estimated tax and tax withheld from wages, will have been paid within the lookback period of section 6511(b)(2)(A).

Example 6. (i) A is an unmarried, calendar year taxpayer whose principal residence is located in County W in State Q. A intends to file a Form 1040 for the 2008 taxable year. The return is due on April 15, 2009. A timely files Form 4868, "Application for Automatic Extension of Time to File U.S. Individual Income Tax Return." Due to A's timely filing of Form 4868, the extended filing deadline for A's 2008 tax return is October 15, 2009. Because A timely requested an extension of time to file, A will not be subject to the failure to file penalty under section 6651(a)(1), if A files the 2008 Form 1040 on or before October 15, 2009. However, A failed to pay the tax due on the return by April 15, 2009, and did not receive an extension of time to pay under section 6161. Absent reasonable cause, A is subject to the failure to pay penalty under section 6651(a)(2) and accrual of interest.

(ii) On September 30, 2009, a blizzard strikes County W. On October 5, 2009, certain counties in State Q (including County W) are determined to be disaster areas within the meaning of section 1033(h)(3) that are eligible for assistance by the Federal government under the Stafford Act. Also on October 5, 2009, the IRS determines that County W in State Q is a covered disaster area and announces that the time period for affected taxpayers to file returns, pay taxes, and perform other time-sensitive acts falling on or after September 30, 2009, and on or before December 2, 2009, has been postponed to December 2, 2009.

(iii) Because A's principal residence is in County W, A is an affected taxpayer. Because October 15, 2009, the extended due date to file A's 2008 Form 1040, falls within the postponement period described in the IRS's published guidance, A's return is timely if filed on or before December 2, 2009. However, the payment due date, April 15, 2009, preceded the postponement period. Thus, A will continue to be subject to failure to pay penalties and accrual of interest during the postponement period.

Example 7. (i) H and W, individual calendar year taxpayers, intend to file a joint Form 1040 for the 2008 taxable year. The joint return is due on April 15, 2009. After credits for taxes withheld on wages and estimated tax payments, H and W owe tax for the 2008 taxable year. H and W's principal residence is in County J in State W.

(ii) On March 3, 2009, severe flooding strikes County J. On March 6, 2009, certain counties in State W (including County J) are determined to be disaster areas within the meaning of section 1033(h)(3) that are eligible for assistance by the Federal government under the Stafford Act. Also on March 6, 2009, the IRS determines that County J in State W is a covered disaster area and publishes guidance announcing that the time period for affected taxpayers to file returns, pay taxes, and perform other time-sensitive acts falling on or after March 3, 2009, and on or before June 1, 2009, has been postponed to June 1, 2009.

(iii) Because H and W's principal residence is in County J, H and W are affected taxpayers. April 15, 2009, the due date for filing the 2008 joint return, falls within the postponement period described in the IRS published guidance. Therefore, H and W's joint return without extension will be timely if filed on or before June 1, 2009. Similarly, H and W's 2008 income taxes will be timely paid if paid on or before June 1, 2009.

(iv) On April 30, 2009, H and W timely file Form 4868, "Application for Automatic Extension of Time to File U.S. Individual Income Tax Return." H and W's extension will be deemed to have been filed on April 15, 2009. Thus, H and W's 2008 income tax return will be timely if filed on or before October 15, 2009.

(v) H and W did not request or receive an extension of time to pay. Therefore, the payment of tax due with the 2008 joint return will be timely if paid on or before June 1, 2009. If H and W fail to pay the tax due on the 2008 joint return

See p. 15 for regulations not amended to reflect law changes

by June 1, 2009, H and W will be subject to failure to pay penalties and accrual of interest beginning on June 2, 2009.

Example 8. (i) H and W, individual calendar year taxpayers, entered into an installment agreement with respect to their 2006 tax liabilities. H and W's installment agreement required H and W to make regularly scheduled installment payments on the 15th day of the month for the next 60 months. H and W's principal residence is in County K in State X.

(ii) On May 1, 2009, severe flooding strikes County K. On May 5, 2009, certain counties in State X including County K) are determined by the Federal government to be disaster areas within the meaning of section 1033(h)(3), and are eligible for assistance under the Stafford Act. Also on May 5, 2009, the IRS determines that County K in State X is a covered disaster area and publishes guidance announcing that the time period for affected taxpayers to file returns, pay taxes, and perform other time-sensitive acts falling on or after May 1, 2009, and on or before July 1, 2009, has been postponed to July 1, 2009.

(iii) Because H and W's principal residence is in County K, H and W are affected taxpayers. Pursuant to the IRS's grant of relief under section 7508A, H and W's installment agreement payments that become due during the postponement period are suspended until after the postponement period has ended. H and W will be required to resume payments no later than August 15, 2009. Skipped payments will be tacked on at the end of the installment payment period. Because the installment agreement pertains to prior year tax liabilities, interest and penalties will continue to accrue. H and W may, however, be entitled to abatement of the failure to pay penalties incurred during the postponement period upon establishing reasonable cause.

(g) *Mandatory 60-day postponement.*—(1) *In general.*—In addition to (or concurrent with) the postponement period specified by the Secretary in an exercise of the authority under section 7508A(a) to postpone time-sensitive acts by reason of a federally declared disaster, qualified taxpayers (as defined in section 7508A(d)(2)) are entitled to a mandatory 60-day postponement period during which the time to perform those time-sensitive acts is disregarded in the same manner as under section 7508A(a). The rules of this paragraph (g)(1) apply with respect to a postponement period specified by the Secretary under section 7508A(b), to postpone acts as provided in section 7508A(d)(4). Except for the acts set forth in paragraph (g)(2) of this section, section 7508A(d) does not apply to postpone any acts.

(2) *Acts postponed.*—The time-sensitive acts that are postponed for the mandatory 60-day postponement period are the acts determined to be postponed by the Secretary's exercise of authority under section 7508A(a) or (b). In addition, in the case of any person described in section 7508A(b), the time-sensitive acts postponed for the mandatory 60-day postponement period include those described in section 7508A(d)(4):

(i) Making contributions to a qualified retirement plan (within the meaning of section 4974(c)) under section 219(f)(3), 404(a)(6), 404(h)(1)(B), or 404(m)(2);

(ii) Making distributions under section 408(d)(4);

(iii) Recharacterizing contributions under section 408A(d)(6); and

(iv) Making a rollover under section 402(c), 403(a)(4), 403(b)(8), or 408(d)(3).

(3) *Calculation of mandatory 60-day postponement period.*—(i) *In general.*—The mandatory 60-day postponement period begins on the earliest incident date specified in a disaster declaration for a federally declared disaster and ends on the date that is 60 days after the latest incident date specified in the disaster declaration. In accordance with section 7508A(d)(5), the mandatory 60-day postponement period under section 7508A(d) runs concurrently with the postponement period determined by the Secretary in exercising discretion under section 7508A(a) or (b) if the period determined by the Secretary is equal to or longer than 60 days after the latest incident date. If the period determined by the Secretary in exercising discretion under section 7508A(a) or (b) ends prior to 60 days after the latest incident date, in accordance with section 7508A(d)(5), the mandatory 60-day postponement period will run concurrently for the length of the period determined by the Secretary under section 7508A(a) or (b) and then continue running in addition to the period determined by the Secretary under section 7508A(a) or (b).

(ii) *Limitations on the mandatory 60-day postponement period.*—(A) In no event will the mandatory 60-day postponement period be calculated to exceed one year.

(B) In the event the Secretary determines to postpone time-sensitive acts pursuant to a declaration establishing a federally declared disaster for purposes of section 7508A that does not specify an incident date, there is no mandatory postponement period under section 7508A(d). In such cases, the only postponement period will be the period determined by the Secretary under section 7508A(a) or (b).

(4) *Examples.*—The rules of this paragraph (g) are illustrated by the following examples:

(i) *Example (1).*—Individual A lives in a state that experienced severe but isolated tornado damage on March 15. On March 20, FEMA issued a Federal Register Notice announcing a major disaster declaration approved by the President for the state where Individual A lives, describing the incident date for the tornado as March 15. Based upon that major disaster declaration, the IRS published a news release identifying the taxpayers (by county) affected by the disaster for purposes of section 7508A and specifying the time-sensitive acts that are postponed and a period of postponement from March 15 through July 31, pursuant to section 7508A(a). The county where Individual A lives was included in the news release. Under section 7508A(d), the mandatory 60-day postponement period that Individual A is entitled to begins on March 15 and ends 60 days after March 15, on May 14. The mandatory postponement period applies to the same time-sensitive acts and runs concurrently with the relief the IRS provided to Individual A under section 7508A(a).

(ii) *Example (2)*.—Individual B lives in a coastal state which experienced harmful effects from a hurricane that began to affect the weather in his state on August 15 and ceased to be a weather factor in his state on August 19. On August 22, FEMA issued a Federal Register Notice announcing a major disaster declaration approved by the President, determining that the coastline counties in the state, including the county where Individual B lives, were severely affected and that these counties were entitled to both individual assistance and public assistance. The major disaster declaration specified the earliest incident date for the hurricane in the state where Individual B lives as August 15 and the latest incident date as August 19. Based upon that major disaster declaration, the IRS published a news release identifying the taxpayers affected by the disaster for purposes of section 7508A and specifying the time-sensitive acts that are postponed and a period of postponement from August 15 through December 31, pursuant to section 7508A(a). Under section 7508A(d), the mandatory 60-day postponement period that Individual B is entitled to begins on August 15 and ends 60 days after August 19, on October 18. The mandatory postponement period applies to the same time-sensitive acts and runs concurrently with the relief the IRS provided to Individual B under section 7508A(a).

(iii) *Example (3)*.—Individual C lives in a county of a state that is experiencing ongoing wildfires. On August 14, FEMA issued a Federal Register Notice announcing an emergency declaration approved by the President to make public assistance available under the Stafford Act to local governments to fight the wildfires. This declaration specified an earliest incident date of August 14 and no latest incident date. On August 17, FEMA issued a Federal Register Notice announcing a major disaster declaration approved by the President for the same wildfires incident, announcing that the residents of the county where Individual C lives were eligible to receive individual assistance under the Stafford Act. This declaration specified August 15 as the earliest incident date and described the incident period as ongoing. Based upon that major disaster declaration, the IRS exercised its discretion under section 7508A(a) to publish a news release identifying the taxpayers (by county) affected by the wildfires disaster for purposes of section 7508A and specifying both the time-sensitive acts that are postponed and a period of postponement from August 15 through December 15. Following the initial news release, the wildfires disaster remained ongoing, with no ending incident date specified, for several months. The IRS published a second news release postponing the time-sensitive acts through January 15. FEMA subsequently amended the major disaster declaration to specify the latest incident date of November 19. Because the IRS acted in its discretion to provide relief in response to the major disaster declaration, and not to provide relief in response to the emergency declaration, the mandatory 60-day postponement period that Individual C is entitled to under section 7508A(d) begins on August 15, the earliest incident date specified in the major disaster declaration, and ends 60 days after the latest incident date of November 19. The mandatory postponement period applies to the same time-sensitive acts and runs concurrently with the relief the IRS provided to Individual C under section 7508A(a), and ends on January 18, which is 60 days after the latest incident date and three days beyond the postponement period specified by the IRS under section 7508A(a) in its news release.

(iv) *Example (4)*.—Individual D lives in the United States, which is experiencing a nationwide emergency as a result of its residents being exposed to a highly infectious and dangerous pandemic disease. On March 13, the President declared a nationwide emergency under section 501(b) of the Stafford Act. The pandemic became a federally declared disaster for purposes of section 7508A on March 13, however, no incident date was specified in the President's emergency declaration. Pursuant to the President's March 13 emergency declaration, the IRS published several notices identifying the taxpayers affected by the disaster for purposes of section 7508A and specifying the time-sensitive acts that are postponed and a period of postponement that generally ran from April 1 through July 15, pursuant to section 7508A(a). Because, in this circumstance, the emergency declaration pursuant to which the notices were published did not specify an incident date, there is no mandatory postponement period under section 7508A(d). The only postponement period is the period determined by the Secretary pursuant to the discretionary authority under section 7508A(a).

(h) *Applicability dates*.—(1) *In general*.—Except as provided in paragraph (h)(2) of this section, this section applies to disasters declared after January 15, 2009.

(2) *Paragraph (g) of this section*.—Paragraph (g) of this section applies to disasters declared on or after December 21, 2019. [Reg. § 301.7508A-1.]

☐ [*T.D.* 8911, 12-14-2000 (*corrected* 2-14-2001). *Amended by T.D.* 9443, 1-14-2009 (*corrected* 12-16-2009). *and T.D.* 9950, 6-10-2021.]

[Reg. § 20.7520-1]

§ 20.7520-1. Valuation of annuities, unitrust interests, interests for life or terms of years, and remainder or reversionary interests.—(a) *General actuarial valuations*.—(1) Except as otherwise provided in this section and in § 20.7520-3 (relating to exceptions to the use of prescribed tables under certain circumstances),

See p. 15 for regulations not amended to reflect law changes

in the case of estates of decedents with valuation dates after April 30, 1989, the fair market value of annuities, interests for life or for a term of years (including unitrust interests), remainders, and reversions is their present value determined under this section. See §20.2031-7(d) (and, for periods prior to May 1, 2009, §20.2031-7A) for the computation of the value of annuities, unitrust interests, life estates, terms for years, remainders, and reversions, other than interests described in paragraphs (a)(2) and (a)(3) of this section.

(2) In the case of a transfer to a pooled income fund, see §1.642(c)-6(e) of this chapter (or, for periods prior to May 1, 2009, §1.642(c)-6A) with respect to the valuation of the remainder interest.

(3) In the case of a transfer to a charitable remainder annuity trust with a valuation date after April 30, 1989, see §1.664-2 of this chapter with respect to the valuation of the remainder interest. See §1.664-4 of this chapter with respect to the valuation of the remainder interest in property transferred to a charitable remainder unitrust.

(b) *Components of valuation.*—(1) *Interest rate component.*—(i) *Section 7520 Interest rate.*—The section 7520 interest rate is the rate of return, rounded to the nearest two-tenths of one percent, that is equal to 120 percent of the applicable Federal mid-term rate, compounded annually, for purposes of section 1274(d)(1), for the month in which the valuation date falls. In rounding the rate to the nearest two-tenths of a percent, any rate that is midway between one two-tenths of a percent and another is rounded up to the higher of those two rates. For example, if 120 percent of the applicable Federal mid-term rate is 10.30, the section 7520 interest rate component is 10.4. The section 7520 interest rate is published monthly by the Internal Revenue Service in the Internal Revenue Bulletin (See §601.601(d)(2)(ii)(*b*) of this chapter).

(ii) *Valuation date.*—Generally, the valuation date is the date on which the transfer takes place. For estate tax purposes, the valuation date is the date of the decedent's death, unless the executor elects the alternate valuation date in accordance with section 2032, in which event, and under the limitations prescribed in section 2032 and the regulations thereunder, the valuation date is the alternate valuation date. For special rules in the case of charitable transfers, see §20.7520-2.

(2) *Mortality component.*—The mortality component reflects the mortality data most recently available from the United States census. As new mortality data becomes available after each decennial census, the mortality component described in this section will be revised and the revised mortality component tables will be published in the regulations at that time. For decedent's estates with valuation dates on or after May 1, 2009, the mortality component table (Table 2000CM) is contained in §20.2031-7(d)(7). See §20.2031-7A for mortality component tables applicable to decedent's estates with valuation dates before May 1, 2009.

(c) *Tables.*—The present value on the valuation date of an annuity, life estate, term of years, remainder, or reversion is computed by using the section 7520 interest rate component that is described in paragraph (b)(1) of this section and the mortality component that is described in paragraph (b)(2) of this section. Actuarial factors for determining these present values are included in tables in these regulations and in publications by the Internal Revenue Service. If a special factor is required in order to value an interest, the Internal Revenue Service will furnish the factor upon a request for a ruling. The request for a ruling must be accompanied by a recitation of the facts, including the date of birth for each measuring life and copies of relevant instruments. A request for a ruling must comply with the instructions for requesting a ruling published periodically in the Internal Revenue Bulletin (see Rev. Proc. 94-1, 1994-1 I.R.B. 10, and the first Rev. Proc. published each year, and §§601.201 and 601.601(d)(2)(ii)(*b*) of this chapter) and include payment of the required user fee.

(1) *Regulation sections containing tables with interest rates between 0.2 and 14 percent for valuation dates on or after May 1, 2009.*—Section 1.642(c)-6(e)(6) of this chapter contains Table S used for determining the present value of a single life remainder interest in a pooled income fund as defined in §1.642(c)-5. See §1.642(c)-6A for single life remainder factors applicable to valuation dates before May 1, 2009. Section 1.664-4(e)(6) contains Table F (payout factors) and Table D (actuarial factors used in determining the present value of a remainder interest postponed for a term of years). Section 1.664-4(e)(7) contains Table U(1) (unitrust single life remainder factors). These tables are used in determining the present value of a remainder interest in a charitable remainder unitrust as defined in §1.664-3. See §1.664-4A for unitrust single life remainder factors applicable to valuation dates before May 1, 2009. Section 20.2031-7(d)(6) contains Table B (actuarial factors used in determining the present value of an interest for a term of years), Table K (annuity end-of-interval adjustment factors), and Table J (term certain annuity beginning-of-interval adjustment factors). Section 20.2031-7(d)(7) contains Table S (single life remainder factors), and Table 2000CM (mortality components). These tables are used in determining the present value of annuities, life estates, remainders, and reversions. See §20.2031-7A for single life remainder factors applicable to valuation dates before May 1, 2009.

(2) *Internal Revenue Service publications containing tables with interest rates between 0.2 and 22 percent for valuation dates on or after May 1, 2009.*—The following documents are available, at no charge, electronically via the IRS Internet site at *www.irs.gov*:

(i) Internal Revenue Service Publication 1457, "Actuarial Valuations Version 3A" (2009). This publication includes tables of valuation factors, as well as examples that show how to compute other valuation factors, for determining the present value of annuities, life estates, terms of years, remainders, and reversions, measured by one or two lives. These factors may also be used in the valuation of interests in a charitable remainder annuity trust as defined in § 1.664-2 of this chapter and a pooled income fund as defined in § 1.642(c)-5.

(ii) Internal Revenue Service Publication 1458, "Actuarial Valuations Version 3B" (2009). This publication includes term certain tables and tables of one and two life valuation factors for determining the present value of remainder interests in a charitable remainder unitrust as defined in § 1.664-3 of this chapter.

(iii) Internal Revenue Service Publication 1459, "Actuarial Valuations Version 3C" (2009). This publication includes tables for computing depreciation adjustment factors. See § 1.170A-12 of this chapter.

(d) *Effective/applicability dates.*—This section applies on and after May 1, 2009. [Reg. § 20.7520-1.]

☐ [*T.D.* 8540, 6-9-94. *Amended by T.D.* 8819, 4-29-99; *T.D.* 8886, 6-9-2000; *T.D.* 9448, 5-1-2009; *and T.D.* 9540, 8-9-2011.]

[Reg. § 25.7520-1]

§ 25.7520-1. Valuation of annuities, unitrust interests, interests for life or terms of years, and remainder or reversionary interests.—(a) *General actuarial valuations.*—(1) Except as otherwise provided in this section and in § 25.7520-3(b) (relating to exceptions to the use of prescribed tables under certain circumstances), in the case of certain gifts after April 30, 1989, the fair market value of annuities, interests for life or for a term of years (including unitrust interests), remainders, and reversions is their present value determined under this section. See § 20.2031-7(d) of this chapter (and, for periods prior to May 1, 2009, § 20.2031-7A) for the computation of the value of annuities, unitrust interests, life estates, terms for years, remainders, and reversions, other than interests described in paragraphs (a)(2) and (a)(3) of this section.

(2) In the case of a gift to a beneficiary of a pooled income fund, see § 1.642(c)-6(e) of this chapter (or, for periods prior to May 1, 2009, § 1.642(c)-6A) with respect to the valuation of the remainder interest.

(3) In the case of a gift to a beneficiary of a charitable remainder annuity trust after April 30, 1989, see § 1.664-2 of this chapter with respect to the valuation of the remainder interest. See § 1.664-4 of this chapter (Income Tax Regulations) with respect to the valuation of the remainder interest in property transferred to a charitable remainder unitrust.

(b) *Components of valuation.*—(1) *Interest rate component.*—(i) *Section 7520 interest rate.*—The section 7520 interest rate is the rate of return, rounded to the nearest two-tenths of one percent, that is equal to 120 percent of the applicable Federal mid-term rate, compounded annually, for purposes of section 1274(d)(1), for the month in which the valuation date falls. In rounding the rate to the nearest two-tenths of a percent, any rate that is midway between one two-tenths of a percent and another is rounded up to the higher of those two rates. For example, if 120 percent of the applicable Federal mid-term rate is 10.30, the section 7520 interest rate component is 10.4. The section 7520 interest rate is published monthly by the Internal Revenue Service in the Internal Revenue Bulletin (See § 601.601(d)(2)(ii)(*b*) of this chapter).

(ii) *Valuation date.*—Generally, the valuation date is the date on which the gift is made. For gift tax purposes, the valuation date is the date on which the gift is complete under § 25.2511-2. For special rules in the case of charitable transfers, see § 25.7520-2.

(2) *Mortality component.*—The mortality component reflects the mortality data most recently available from the United States census. As new mortality data becomes available after each decennial census, the mortality component described in this section will be revised and the revised mortality component tables will be published in the regulations at that time. For gifts with valuation dates on or after May 1, 2009, the mortality component table (Table 2000CM) is contained in § 20.2031-7(d)(7). See § 20.2031-7A of this chapter for mortality component tables applicable to gifts for which the valuation date falls before May 1, 2009.

(c) *Tables.*—The present value on the valuation date of an annuity, life estate, term of years, remainder, or reversion is computed by using the section 7520 interest rate component that is described in paragraph (b)(1) of this section and the mortality component that is described in paragraph (b)(2) of this section. Actuarial factors for determining these present values are included in tables in these regulations and in publications by the Internal Revenue Service. If a special factor is required in order to value an interest, the Internal Revenue Service will furnish the factor upon a request for a ruling. The request for a ruling must be accompanied by a recitation of the facts, including the date of birth for each measuring life and copies of relevant instruments. A request for a ruling must comply with the instructions for requesting a ruling published periodically in the Internal Revenue Bulletin (see Rev. Proc. 94-1, 1994-1 I.R.B. 10, and subsequent updates, and §§ 601.201 and 601.601(d)(2)(ii)(*b*) of this chapter) and include payment of the required user fee.

(1) *Regulation sections containing tables with interest rates between 0.2 and 14 percent for valuation dates on or after May 1, 2009.*—Section 1.642(c)-6(e)(6) of this chapter contains Table S used for determining the present value of a single life remainder interest in a pooled income fund as defined in § 1.642(c)-5. See § 1.642(c)-6A for single life remainder factors applicable to valuation dates before May 1, 2009. Section 1.664-4(e)(6) contains Table F (payout factors) and Table D (actuarial factors used in determin-

ing the present value of a remainder interest postponed for a term of years). Section 1.664-4(e)(7) contains Table U(1) (unitrust single life remainder factors). These tables are used in determining the present value of a remainder interest in a charitable remainder unitrust as defined in § 1.664-3. See § 1.664-4A for unitrust single life remainder factors applicable to valuation dates before May 1, 2009. Section 20.2031-7(d)(6) of this chapter contains Table B (actuarial factors used in determining the present value of an interest for a term of years), Table K (annuity end-of-interval adjustment factors), and Table J (term certain annuity beginning-of-interval adjustment factors). Section 20.2031-7(d)(7) contains Table S (single life remainder factors), and Table 2000CM (mortality components). These tables are used in determining the present value of annuities, life estates, remainders, and reversions. See § 20.2031-7A for single life remainder factors and mortality components applicable to valuation dates before May 1, 2009.

(2) *Internal Revenue Service publications containing tables with interest rates between 0.2 and 22 percent for valuation dates on or after May 1, 2009.*—The following documents are available, at no charge, electronically via the IRS Internet site at *www.irs.gov*:

(i) Internal Revenue Service Publication 1457, "Actuarial Valuations Version 3A" (2009). This publication includes tables of valuation factors, as well as examples that show how to compute other valuation factors, for determining the present value of annuities, life estates, terms of years, remainders, and reversions, measured by one or two lives. These factors may also be used in the valuation of interests in a charitable remainder annuity trust as defined in § 1.664-2 and a pooled income fund as defined in § 1.642(c)-5 of this chapter.

(ii) Internal Revenue Service Publication 1458, "Actuarial Valuations Version 3B" (2009). This publication includes term certain tables and tables of one and two life valuation factors for determining the present value of remainder interests in a charitable remainder unitrust as defined in § 1.664-3 of this chapter.

(iii) Internal Revenue Service Publication 1459, "Actuarial Valuations Version 3C" (2009). This publication includes tables for computing depreciation adjustment factors. See § 1.170A-12 of this chapter.

(d) *Effective/applicability dates.*—This section applies on and after May 1, 2009. [Reg. § 25.7520-1.]

☐ [*T.D.* 8540, 6-9-94. *Amended by T.D.* 8819, 4-29-99 (corrected 6-21-99); *T.D.* 8886, 6-9-2000; *T.D.* 9448, 5-1-2009 *and T.D.* 9540, 8-9-2011.]

[Reg. § 20.7520-2]

§ 20.7520-2. Valuation of charitable interests.—(a) *In general.*—(1) *Valuation.*—Except as otherwise provided in this section and in § 20.7520-3 (relating to exceptions to the use of prescribed tables under certain circumstances), the fair market value of annuities, interests for life or for a term of years, remainders, and reversions for which an estate tax charitable deduction is allowable is the present value of such interests determined under § 20.7520-1.

(2) *Prior-month election rule.*—If any part of the property interest transferred qualifies for an estate tax charitable deduction under section 2055 or 2106, the executor may compute the present value of the transferred interest by use of the section 7520 interest rate for the month during which the interest is transferred or the section 7520 interest rate for either of the 2 months preceding the month during which the interest is transferred. Paragraph (b) of this section explains how a prior-month election is made. The interest rate for the month so elected is the applicable section 7520 interest rate. If the executor elects the alternate valuation date under section 2032 and also elects to use the section 7520 interest rate for either of the 2 months preceding the month in which the interest is transferred, the month so elected (either of the 2 months preceding the month in which the alternate valuation date falls) is the valuation date. If the actuarial factor for either or both of the 2 months preceding the month during which the interest is transferred is based on a mortality experience that is different from the mortality experience at the date of the transfer and if the executor elects to use the section 7520 rate for a prior month with the different mortality experience, the executor must use the actuarial factor derived from the mortality experience in effect during the month of the section 7520 rate elected. All actuarial computations relating to the transfer must be made by applying the interest rate component and the mortality component of the month elected by the executor.

(3) *Transfers of more than one interest in the same property.*—If a decedent's estate includes the transfer of more than one interest in the same property, the executor must, for purposes of valuing the transferred interests, use the same interest rate and mortality components for each interest in the property transferred.

(4) *Information required with tax return.*—The following information must be attached to the estate tax return (or be filed subsequently as supplemental information to the return) if the estate claims a charitable deduction for the present value of a temporary or remainder interest in property—

(i) A complete description of the interest that is transferred, including a copy of the instrument of transfer;

(ii) The valuation date of the transfer;

(iii) The names and identification numbers of the beneficiaries of the transferred interest;

(iv) The names and birthdates of any measuring lives, a description of any relevant terminal illness condition of any measuring life, and (if applicable) an explanation of how any terminal illness condition was taken into account in valuing the interest; and

(v) A computation of the deduction showing the applicable section 7520 interest rate that is used to value the transferred interest.

(5) *Place for filing returns.*—See section 6091 of the Internal Revenue Code and the regulations thereunder for the place for filing the return or other document required by this section.

(b) *Election of interest rate component.*—(1) *Time for making election.*—An executor makes a prior-month election under paragraph (a)(2) of this section by attaching the information described in paragraph (b)(2) of this section to the decedent's estate tax return or by filing a supplemental statement of the election information within 24 months after the later of the date the original estate tax return was filed or the due date for filing the return.

(2) *Manner of making election.*—A statement that the prior-month election under section 7520(a) of the Internal Revenue Code is being made and that identifies the elected month must be attached to the estate tax return (or by subsequently filing the statement as supplemental information to the return).

(3) *Revocability.*—The prior-month election may be revoked by filing a statement of supplemental information within 24 months after the later of the date the original return of tax for the decedent's estate was filed or the due date for filing the return. The revocation must be filed in the place referred to in paragraph (a)(5) of this section.

(c) *Effective dates.*—Paragraph (a) of this section is effective as of May 1, 1989. Paragraph (b) of this section is effective for elections made after June 10, 1994. [Reg. § 20.7520-2.]

☐ [*T.D.* 8540, 6-9-94.]

[Reg. § 25.7520-2]

§ 25.7520-2. Valuation of charitable interests.—(a) *In general.*—(1) *Valuation.*—Except as otherwise provided in this section and in § 25.7520-3 (relating to exceptions to the use of prescribed tables under certain circumstances), the fair market value of annuities, interests for life or for a term for years, remainders, and reversions for which a gift tax charitable deduction is allowable is the present value of such interests determined under § 25.7520-1.

(2) *Prior-month election rule.*—If any part of the property interest transferred qualifies for a gift tax charitable deduction under section 2522, the donor may elect to compute the present value of the interest transferred by use of the section 7520 interest rate for the month during which the gift is made or the section 7520 interest rate for either of the 2 months preceding the month during which the gift is made. Paragraph (b) of this section explains how a prior-month election is made. The interest rate for the month so elected is the applicable section 7520 interest rate. If the actuarial factor for either or both of the 2 months preceding the month during which the gift is made is based on a mortality experience that is different from the mortality experience at the date of the gift and if the donor elects to use the section 7520 rate for a prior month with the different mortality experience, the donor must use the actuarial factor derived from the mortality experience in effect during the month of the section 7520 rate elected. All actuarial computations relating to the gift must be made by applying the interest rate component and the mortality component of the month elected by the donor.

(3) *Gifts of more than one interest in the same property.*—If a donor makes a gift of more than one interest in the same property at the same time, the donor must, for purposes of valuing the gifts, use the same interest rate and mortality components for the gift of each interest in the property. If the donor has made gifts of more than one interest in the same property at different times, the donor must determine the value of the gift by the use of the interest rate component and mortality component in effect during the month of that gift or, if applicable under paragraph (a)(2) of this section, either of the two months preceding the month of the gift.

(4) *Information required with tax return.*—The following information must be attached to the gift tax return (or to the amended return) if the donor claims a charitable deduction for the present value of a temporary or remainder interest in property—

(i) A complete description of the interest that is transferred, including a copy of the instrument of transfer;

(ii) The valuation date of the transfer;

(iii) The names and identification numbers of the beneficiaries of the transferred interest;

(iv) The names and birthdates of any measuring lives, a description of any relevant terminal illness condition of any measuring life, and (if applicable) an explanation of how any terminal illness condition was taken into account in valuing the interest; and

(v) A computation of the deduction showing the applicable section 7520 interest rate that is used to value the transferred interest.

(5) *Place for filing returns.*—See section 6091 of the Internal Revenue Code and the regulations thereunder for the place for filing the return or other document required by this section.

(b) *Election of interest rate component.*—(1) *Time for making election.*—A taxpayer makes a prior-month election under paragraph (a)(2) of this section by attaching the information described in paragraph (b)(2) of this section to the donor's gift tax return or to an amended return for that year that is filed within 24 months after the later of the date the original return for the year was filed or the due date for filing the return.

(2) *Manner of making election.*—A statement that the prior-month election under section 7520(a) of the Internal Revenue Code is being made and that identifies the elected month must be attached to the gift tax return (or to the amended return).

(3) *Revocability.*—The prior-month election may be revoked by filing an amended return within 24 months after the later of the date the original return of tax for that year was filed or the due date for filing the return. The revocation must be filed in the place referred to in paragraph (a)(5) of this section.

(c) *Effective dates.*—Paragraph (a) of this section is effective as of May 1, 1989. Paragraph (b) of this section is effective for elections made after June 10, 1994. [Reg. § 25.7520-2.]

☐ [*T.D.* 8540, 6-9-94.]

[Reg. § 20.7520-3]

§ 20.7520-3. Limitation on the application of section 7520.—(a) *Internal Revenue Code sections to which section 7520 does not apply.*—Section 7520 of the Internal Revenue Code does not apply for purposes of—

(1) Part I, subchapter D of subtitle A (section 401 et. seq.), relating to the income tax treatment of certain qualified plans. (However, section 7520 does apply to the estate and gift tax treatment of certain qualified plans and for purposes of determining excess accumulations under section 4980A);

(2) Sections 72 and 101(b), relating to the income taxation of life insurance, endowment, and annuity contracts, unless otherwise provided for in the regulations under sections 72, 101, and 1011 (see, particularly, § § 1.101-2(e)(1)(iii)(*b*)(2), and 1.1011-2(c), *Example 8*);

(3) Sections 83 and 451, unless otherwise provided for in the regulations under those sections;

(4) Section 457, relating to the valuation of deferred compensation, unless otherwise provided for in the regulations under section 457;

(5) Sections 3121(v) and 3306(r), relating to the valuation of deferred amounts, unless otherwise provided for in the regulations under those sections;

(6) Section 6058, relating to valuation statements evidencing compliance with qualified plan requirements, unless otherwise provided for in the regulations under section 6058;

(7) Section 7872, relating to income and gift taxation of interest-free loans and loans with below-market interest rates, unless otherwise provided for in the regulations under section 7872; or

(8) Section 2702(a)(2)(A), relating to the value of a nonqualified retained interest upon a transfer of an interest in trust to or for the benefit of a member of the transferor's family; and

(9) Any other sections of the Internal Revenue Code to the extent provided by the Internal Revenue Service in revenue rulings or revenue procedures. (See § § 601.201 and 601.601 of this chapter).

(b) *Other limitations on the application of section 7520.*—(1) *In general.*—(i) *Ordinary beneficial interests.*—For purposes of this section:

(A) An *ordinary annuity interest* is the right to receive a fixed dollar amount at the end of each year during one or more measuring lives or for some other defined period. A standard section 7520 annuity factor for an ordinary annuity interest represents the present worth of the right to receive $1.00 per year for a defined period, using the interest rate prescribed under section 7520 for the appropriate month. If an annuity interest is payable more often than annually or is payable at the beginning of each period, a special adjustment must be made in any computation with a standard section 7520 annuity factor.

(B) An *ordinary income interest* is the right to receive the income from or the use of property during one or more measuring lives or for some other defined period. A standard section 7520 income factor for an ordinary income interest represents the present worth of the right to receive the use of $1.00 for a defined period, using the interest rate prescribed under section 7520 for the appropriate month.

(C) An *ordinary remainder or reversionary interest* is the right to receive an interest in property at the end of one or more measuring lives or some other defined period. A standard section 7520 remainder factor for an ordinary remainder or reversionary interest represents the present worth of the right to receive $1.00 at the end of a defined period, using the interest rate prescribed under section 7520 for the appropriate month.

(ii) *Certain restricted beneficial interests.*—A *restricted beneficial interest* is an annuity, income, remainder, or reversionary interest that is subject to any contingency, power, or other restriction, whether the restriction is provided for by the terms of the trust, will, or other governing instrument or is caused by other circumstances. In general, a standard section 7520 annuity, income, or remainder factor may not be used to value a restricted beneficial interest. However, a special section 7520 annuity, income, or remainder factor may be used to value a restricted beneficial interest under some circumstances. See paragraphs (b)(2)(v) *Example 4* and (b)(4) *Example 1* of this section, which illustrate situations where special section 7520 actuarial factors are needed to take into account limitations on beneficial interests. See § 20.7520-1(c) for requesting a special factor from the Internal Revenue Service.

(iii) *Other beneficial interests.*—If, under the provisions of this paragraph (b), the interest rate and mortality components prescribed under section 7520 are not applicable in determining the value of any annuity, income, remainder, or reversionary interest, the actual fair market value of the interest (determined without regard to section 7520) is based on all of the facts and circumstances if and to the extent permitted by the Internal Revenue Code provision applicable to the property interest.

(2) *Provisions of governing instrument and other limitations on source of payment.*—(i) *Annuities.*—A standard section 7520 annuity factor may not be used to determine the present value of an annuity for a specified term of years or the life of one or more individuals unless the

effect of the trust, will, or other governing instrument is to ensure that the annuity will be paid for the entire defined period. In the case of an annuity payable from a trust or other limited fund, the annuity is not considered payable for the entire defined period if, considering the applicable section 7520 interest rate at the valuation date of the transfer, the annuity is expected to exhaust the fund before the last possible annuity payment is made in full. For this purpose, it must be assumed that it is possible for each measuring life to survive until age 110. For example, for a fixed annuity payable annually at the end of each year, if the amount of the annuity payment (expressed as a percentage of the initial corpus) is less than or equal to the applicable section 7520 interest rate at the date of the transfer, the corpus is assumed to be sufficient to make all payments. If the percentage exceeds the applicable section 7520 interest rate and the annuity is for a definite term of years, multiply the annual annuity amount by the Table B term certain annuity factor, as described in § 20.7520-1(c)(1), for the number of years of the defined period. If the percentage exceeds the applicable section 7520 interest rate and the annuity is payable for the life of one or more individuals, multiply the annual annuity amount by the Table B annuity factor for 110 years minus the age of the youngest individual. If the result exceeds the limited fund, the annuity may exhaust the fund, and it will be necessary to calculate a special section 7520 annuity factor that takes into account the exhaustion of the trust or fund. This computation would be modified, if appropriate, to take into account annuities with different payment terms. See § 25.7520-3(b)(2)(v) *Example 5* of this chapter, which provides an illustration involving an annuity trust that is subject to exhaustion.

(ii) *Income and similar interests.*—(A) *Beneficial enjoyment.*—A standard section 7520 income factor for an ordinary income interest may not be used to determine the present value of an income or similar interest in trust for a term of years, or for the life of one or more individuals, unless the effect of the trust, will, or other governing instrument is to provide the income beneficiary with that degree of beneficial enjoyment of the property during the term of the income interest that the principles of the law of trusts accord to a person who is unqualifiedly designated as the income beneficiary of a trust for a similar period of time. This degree of beneficial enjoyment is provided only if it was the transferor's intent, as manifested by the provisions of the governing instrument and the surrounding circumstances, that the trust provide an income interest for the income beneficiary during the specified period of time that is consistent with the value of the trust corpus and with its preservation. In determining whether a trust arrangement evidences that intention, the treatment required or permitted with respect to individual items must be considered in relation to the entire system provided for in the administration of the subject trust. Similarly, in determining the present value of the right to use tangible property (whether or not in trust) for one or more measuring lives or for some other specified period of time, the interest rate component prescribed under section 7520 and § 1.7520-1 of this chapter may not be used unless, during the specified period, the effect of the trust, will or other governing instrument is to provide the beneficiary with that degree of use, possession, and enjoyment of the property during the term of interest that applicable state law accords to a person who is unqualifiedly designated as a life tenant or term holder for a similar period of time.

(B) *Diversions of income and corpus.*—A standard section 7520 income factor for an ordinary income interest may not be used to value an income interest or similar interest in property for a term of years, or for one or more measuring lives, if—

(1) The trust, will, or other governing instrument requires or permits the beneficiary's income or other enjoyment to be withheld, diverted, or accumulated for another person's benefit without the consent of the income beneficiary; or

(2) The governing instrument requires or permits trust corpus to be withdrawn from the trust for another person's benefit without the consent of the income beneficiary during the income beneficiary's term of enjoyment and without accountability to the income beneficiary for such diversion.

(iii) *Remainder and reversionary interests.*—A standard section 7520 remainder interest factor for an ordinary remainder or reversionary interest may not be used to determine the present value of a remainder or reversionary interest (whether in trust or otherwise) unless, consistent with the preservation and protection that the law of trusts would provide for a person who is unqualifiedly designated as the remainder beneficiary of a trust for a similar duration, the effect of the administrative and dispositive provisions for the interest or interests that precede the remainder or reversionary interest is to assure that the property will be adequately preserved and protected (e.g., from erosion, invasion, depletion, or damage) until the remainder or reversionary interest takes effect in possession and enjoyment. This degree of preservation and protection is provided only if it was the transferor's intent, as manifested by the provisions of the arrangement and the surrounding circumstances, that the entire disposition provide the remainder or reversionary beneficiary with an undiminished interest in the property transferred at the time of the termination of the prior interest.

(iv) *Pooled income fund interests.*—In general, pooled income funds are created and administered to achieve a special rate of return. A beneficial interest in a pooled income fund is not ordinarily valued using a standard section 7520 income or remainder interest factor. The present value of a beneficial interest in a pooled income fund is determined according to rules and special remainder factors prescribed in § 1.642(c)-6 of this chapter and, when applicable, the rules set forth under paragraph (b)(3) of this section if the individual who is the measuring life is terminally ill at the time of the transfer.

(v) *Examples*.—The provisions of this paragraph (b)(2) are illustrated by the following examples:

Example 1. Unproductive property. A died, survived by B and C. B died two years after A. A's will provided for a bequest of corporation stock in trust under the terms of which all of the trust income was paid to B for life. After the death of B, the trust terminated and the trust property was distributed to C. The trust specifically authorized, but did not require, the trustee to retain the shares of stock. The corporation paid no dividends on this stock during the 5 years before A's death and the 2 years before B's death. There was no indication that this policy would change after A's death. Under applicable state law, the corporation is considered to be a sound investment that satisfies fiduciary standards. The facts and circumstances, including applicable state law, indicate that B did not have the legal right to compel the trustee to make the trust corpus productive in conformity with the requirements for a lifetime trust income interest under applicable local law. Therefore, B's life income interest in this case is considered nonproductive. Consequently, B's income interest may not be valued actuarially under this section.

Example 2. Beneficiary's right to make trust productive. The facts are the same as in *Example 1*, except that the trustee is not specifically authorized to retain the shares of stock. Further, the terms of the trust specifically provide that B, the life income beneficiary, may require the trustee to make the trust corpus productive consistent with income yield standards for trusts under applicable state law. Under that law, the minimum rate of income that a productive trust may produce is substantially below the section 7520 interest rate for the month of A's death. In this case, because B has the right to compel the trustee to make the trust productive for purposes of applicable local law during the beneficiary's lifetime, the income interest is considered an ordinary income interest for purposes of this paragraph, and the standard section 7520 life income interest factor may be used to determine the present value of B's income interest.

Example 3. Discretionary invasion of corpus. The decedent, A, transferred property to a trust under the terms of which all of the trust income is to be paid to A's child for life and the remainder of the trust is to be distributed to a grandchild. The trust authorizes the trustee without restriction to distribute corpus to A's surviving spouse for the spouse's comfort and happiness. In this case, because the trustee's power to invade trust corpus is unrestricted, the exercise of the power could result in the termination of the income interest at any time. Consequently, the income interest is not considered an ordinary income interest for purposes of this paragraph, and may not be valued actuarially under this section.

Example 4. Limited invasion of corpus. The decedent, A, bequeathed property to a trust under the terms of which all of the trust income is to be paid to A's child for life and the remainder is to be distributed to A's grandchild. The trust authorizes the child to withdraw up to $5,000 per year from the trust corpus. In this case, the child's power to invade trust corpus is limited to an ascertainable amount each year. Annual invasions of any amount would be expected to progressively diminish the property from which the child's income is paid. Consequently, the income interest is not considered an ordinary income interest for purposes of this paragraph, and the standard section 7520 income interest factor may not be used to determine the present value of the income interest. Nevertheless, the present value of the child's income interest is ascertainable by making a special actuarial calculation that would take into account not only the initial value of the trust corpus, the section 7520 interest rate for the month of the transfer, and the mortality component for the child's age, but also the assumption that the trust corpus will decline at the rate of $5,000 each year during the child's lifetime. The child's right to receive an amount not in excess of $5,000 per year may be separately valued in this instance and, assuming the trust corpus would not exhaust before the child would attain age 110, would be considered an ordinary annuity interest.

Example 5. Power to consume. The decedent, A, devised a life estate in 3 parcels of real estate to A's surviving spouse with the remainder to a child, or, if the child doesn't survive, to the child's estate. A also conferred upon the spouse an unrestricted power to consume the property, which includes the right to sell part or all of the property and to use the proceeds for the spouse's support, comfort, happiness, and other purposes. Any portion of the property or its sale proceeds remaining at the death of the surviving spouse is to vest by operation of law in the child at that time. The child predeceased the surviving spouse. In this case, the surviving spouse's power to consume the corpus is unrestricted, and the exercise of the power could entirely exhaust the remainder interest during the life of the spouse. Consequently, the remainder interest that is includible in the child's estate is not considered an ordinary remainder interest for purposes of this paragraph and may not be valued actuarially under this section.

(3) *Mortality component*.—(i) *Terminal illness*.—Except as provided in paragraph (b)(3)(ii) of this section, the mortality component prescribed under section 7520 may not be used to determine the present value of an annuity, income interest, remainder interest, or reversionary interest if an individual who is a measuring life is terminally ill at the time of the decedent's death. For purposes of this paragraph (b)(3), an individual who is known to have an incurable illness or other deteriorating physical condition

is considered terminally ill if there is at least a 50 percent probability that the individual will die within 1 year. However, if the individual survives for eighteen months or longer after the date of the decedent's death, that individual shall be presumed to have not been terminally ill at the date of death unless the contrary is established by clear and convincing evidence.

(ii) *Terminal illness exceptions.*—In the case of the allowance of the credit for tax on a prior transfer under section 2013, if a final determination of the federal estate tax liability of the transferor's estate has been made under circumstances that required valuation of the life interest received by the transferee, the value of the property transferred, for purposes of the credit allowable to the transferee's estate, shall be the value determined previously in the transferor's estate. Otherwise, for purposes of section 2013, the provisions of paragraph (b)(3)(i) of this section shall govern in valuing the property transferred. The value of a decedent's reversionary interest under sections 2037(b) and 2042(2) shall be determined without regard to the physical condition, immediately before the decedent's death, of the individual who is the measuring life.

(iii) *Death resulting from common accidents.*—The mortality component prescribed under section 7520 may not be used to determine the present value of an annuity, income interest, remainder interest, or reversionary interest if the decedent, and the individual who is the measuring life, die as a result of a common accident or other occurrence.

(4) *Examples.*—The provisions of paragraph (b)(3) of this section are illustrated by the following examples:

Example 1. Terminal illness. The decedent bequeaths $1,000,000 to a trust under the terms of which the trustee is to pay $103,000 per year to a charitable organization during the life of the decedent's child. Upon the death of the child, the remainder in the trust is to be distributed to the decedent's grandchild. The child, who is age 60, has been diagnosed with an incurable illness, and there is at least a 50 percent probability of the child dying within 1 year. Assuming the presumption provided for in paragraph (b)(3)(i) of this section does not apply, the standard life annuity factor for a person age 60 may not be used to determine the present value of the charitable organization's annuity interest because there is at least a 50 percent probability that the child, who is the measuring life, will die within 1 year. Instead, a special section 7520 annuity factor must be computed that takes into account the projection of the child's actual life expectancy.

Example 2. Deaths resulting from common accidents, etc. The decedent's will establishes a trust to pay income to the decedent's surviving spouse for life. The will provides that, upon the spouse's death or, if the spouse fails to survive the decedent, upon the decedent's death the trust property is to pass to the decedent's children. The decedent and the decedent's spouse die simultaneously in an accident under circumstances in which it was impossible to determine who survived the other. Even if the terms of the will and applicable state law presume that the decedent died first with the result that the property interest is considered to have passed in trust for the benefit of the spouse for life, after which the remainder is to be distributed to the decedent's children, the spouse's life income interest may not be valued by use of the mortality component described under section 7520. The result would be the same even if it was established that the spouse survived the decedent.

(5) *Additional limitations.*—Section 7520 does not apply to the extent as may otherwise be provided by the Commissioner.

(c) *Effective date.*—Section § 20.7520-3(a) is effective as of May 1, 1989. The provisions of paragraph (b) of this section are effective with respect to estates of decedents dying after December 13, 1995. [Reg. § 20.7520-3.]

☐ [*T.D.* 8540, 6-9-94. *Amended by T.D.* 8630, 12-12-95.]

[Reg. § 25.7520-3]

§ 25.7520-3. Limitation on the application of section 7520.—(a) *Internal Revenue Code sections to which section 7520 does not apply.*—Section 7520 of the Internal Revenue Code does not apply for purposes of—

(1) Part I, subchapter D of subtitle A (section 401 et. seq.), relating to the income tax treatment of certain qualified plans. (However, section 7520 does apply to the estate and gift tax treatment of certain qualified plans and for purposes of determining excess accumulations under section 4980A);

(2) Sections 72 and 101(b), relating to the income taxation of life insurance, endowment, and annuity contracts, unless otherwise provided for in the regulations under sections 72, 101, and 1011 (see, particularly, § § 1.101-2(e)(1)(iii)(*b*)(2), and 1.1011-2(c), *Example 8*);

(3) Sections 83 and 451, unless otherwise provided for in the regulations under those sections;

(4) Section 457, relating to the valuation of deferred compensation, unless otherwise provided for in the regulations under section 457;

(5) Sections 3121(v) and 3306(r), relating to the valuation of deferred amounts, unless otherwise provided for in the regulations under those sections;

(6) Section 6058, relating to valuation statements evidencing compliance with qualified plan requirements, unless otherwise provided for in the regulations under section 6058;

(7) Section 7872, relating to income and gift taxation of interest-free loans and loans with below-market interest rates, unless otherwise provided for in the regulations under section 7872; or

(8) Section 2702(a)(2)(A), relating to the value of a nonqualified retained interest upon a

transfer of an interest in trust to or for the benefit of a member of the transferor's family; and

(9) Any other section of the Internal Revenue Code to the extent provided by the Internal Revenue Service in revenue rulings or revenue procedures. (See §§601.201 and 601.601 of this chapter).

(b) *Other limitations on the application of section 7520.*—(1) *In general.*—(i) *Ordinary beneficial interests.*—For purposes of this section:

(A) An *ordinary annuity interest* is the right to receive a fixed dollar amount at the end of each year during one or more measuring lives or for some other defined period. A standard section 7520 annuity factor for an ordinary annuity interest represents the present worth of the right to receive $1.00 per year for a defined period, using the interest rate prescribed under section 7520 for the appropriate month. If an annuity interest is payable more often than annually or is payable at the beginning of each period, a special adjustment must be made in any computation with a standard section 7520 annuity factor.

(B) An *ordinary income interest* is the right to receive the income from or the use of property during one or more measuring lives or for some other defined period. A standard section 7520 income factor for an ordinary income interest represents the present worth of the right to receive the use of $1.00 for a defined period, using the interest rate prescribed under section 7520 for the appropriate month. However, in the case of certain gifts made after October 8, 1990, if the donor does not retain a qualified annuity, unitrust, or reversionary interest, the value of any interest retained by the donor is considered to be zero if the remainder beneficiary is a member of the donor's family. See §25.2702-2.

(C) An *ordinary remainder or reversionary interest* is the right to receive an interest in property at the end of one or more measuring lives or some other defined period. A standard section 7520 remainder factor for an ordinary remainder or reversionary interest represents the present worth of the right to receive $1.00 at the end of a defined period, using the interest rate prescribed under section 7520 for the appropriate month.

(ii) *Certain restricted beneficial interests.*—A *restricted beneficial interest* is an annuity, income, remainder, or reversionary interest that is subject to any contingency, power, or other restriction, whether the restriction is provided for by the terms of the trust, will, or other governing instrument or is caused by other circumstances. In general, a standard section 7520 annuity, income, or remainder factor may not be used to value a restricted beneficial interest. However, a special section 7520 annuity, income, or remainder factor may be used to value a restricted beneficial interest under some circumstances. See paragraphs (b)(2)(v) *Example 5* and (b)(4) of this section, which illustrate situations in which special section 7520 actuarial factors are needed to take into account limitations on beneficial interests. See §25.7520-1(c) for requesting a special factor from the Internal Revenue Service.

(iii) *Other beneficial interests.*—If, under the provisions of this paragraph (b), the interest rate and mortality components prescribed under section 7520 are not applicable in determining the value of any annuity, income, remainder, or reversionary interest, the actual fair market value of the interest (determined without regard to section 7520) is based on all of the facts and circumstances if and to the extent permitted by the Internal Revenue Code provision applicable to the property interest.

(2) *Provisions of governing instrument and other limitations on source of payment.*—(i) *Annuities.*—A standard section 7520 annuity factor may not be used to determine the present value of an annuity for a specified term of years or the life of one or more individuals unless the effect of the trust, will, or other governing instrument is to ensure that the annuity will be paid for the entire defined period. In the case of an annuity payable from a trust or other limited fund, the annuity is not considered payable for the entire defined period if, considering the applicable section 7520 interest rate on the valuation date of the transfer, the annuity is expected to exhaust the fund before the last possible annuity payment is made in full. For this purpose, it must be assumed that it is possible for each measuring life to survive until age 110. For example, for a fixed annuity payable annually at the end of each year, if the amount of the annuity payment (expressed as a percentage of the initial corpus) is less than or equal to the applicable section 7520 interest rate at the date of the transfer, the corpus is assumed to be sufficient to make all payments. If the percentage exceeds the applicable section 7520 interest rate and the annuity is for a definite term of years, multiply the annual annuity amount by the Table B term certain annuity factor, as described in §25.7520-1(c)(1), for the number of years of the defined period. If the percentage exceeds the applicable section 7520 interest rate and the annuity is payable for the life of one or more individuals, multiply the annual annuity amount by the Table B annuity factor for 110 years minus the age of the youngest individual. If the result exceeds the limited fund, the annuity may exhaust the fund, and it will be necessary to calculate a special section 7520 annuity factor that takes into account the exhaustion of the trust or fund. This computation would be modified, if appropriate, to take into account annuities with different payment terms.

(ii) *Income and similar interests.*—(A) *Beneficial enjoyment.*—A standard section 7520 income factor for an ordinary income interest is not to be used to determine the present value of an income or similar interest in trust for a term of years or for the life of one or more individuals unless the effect of the trust, will, or other governing instrument is to provide the income beneficiary with that degree of beneficial enjoyment of the property during the term of the income interest that the principles of the law of trusts accord to a person who is unqualifiedly designated as the income beneficiary of a trust for a similar period of time. This degree of beneficial enjoyment is provided only if it was the transferor's intent, as manifested by the provisions of the governing instrument and the surrounding circumstances, that the trust provide an income interest for the income beneficiary during the specified period of time that is consistent with the value of the trust corpus and with its preservation. In determining whether a trust arrangement evidences that intention, the treatment required or permitted with respect to individual items must be considered in relation to the entire system provided for in the administration of the subject trust. Similarly, in determining the present value of the right to use tangible property (whether or not in trust) for one or more measuring lives or for some other specified period of time, the interest rate component prescribed under section 7520 and § 1.7520-1 of this chapter may not be used unless, during the specified period, the effect of the trust, will or other governing instrument is to provide the beneficiary with that degree of use, possession, and enjoyment of the property during the term of interest that applicable state law accords to a person who is unqualifiedly designated as a life tenant or term holder for a similar period of time.

(B) *Diversions of income and corpus.*—A standard section 7520 income factor for an ordinary income interest may not be used to value an income interest or similar interest in property for a term of years, or for one or more measuring lives, if—

(1) The trust, will, or other governing instrument requires or permits the beneficiary's income or other enjoyment to be withheld, diverted, or accumulated for another person's benefit without the consent of the income beneficiary; or

(2) The governing instrument requires or permits trust corpus to be withdrawn from the trust for another person's benefit without the consent of the income beneficiary during the income beneficiary's term of enjoyment and without accountability to the income beneficiary for such diversion.

(iii) *Remainder and reversionary interests.*—A standard section 7520 remainder interest factor for an ordinary remainder or reversionary interest may not be used to determine the present value of a remainder or reversionary interest (whether in trust or otherwise) unless, consistent with the preservation and protection that the law of trusts would provide for a person who is unqualifiedly designated as the remainder beneficiary of a trust for a similar duration, the effect of the administrative and dispositive provisions for the interest or interests that precede the remainder or reversionary interest is to assure that the property will be adequately preserved and protected (e.g., from erosion, invasion, depletion, or damage) until the remainder or reversionary interest takes effect in possession and enjoyment. This degree of preservation and protection is provided only if it was the transferor's intent, as manifested by the provisions of the arrangement and the surrounding circumstances, that the entire disposition provide the remainder or reversionary beneficiary with an undiminished interest in the property transferred at the time of the termination of the prior interest.

(iv) *Pooled income fund interests.*—In general, pooled income funds are created and administered to achieve a special rate of return. A beneficial interest in a pooled income fund is not ordinarily valued using a standard section 7520 income or remainder interest factor. The present value of a beneficial interest in a pooled income fund is determined according to rules and special remainder factors prescribed in § 1.642(c)-6 of this chapter and, when applicable, the rules set forth under paragraph (b)(3) of this section if the individual who is the measuring life is terminally ill at the time of the transfer.

(v) *Examples.*—The provisions of this paragraph (b)(2) are illustrated by the following examples:

Example 1. Unproductive property. The donor transfers corporation stock to a trust under the terms of which all of the trust income is payable to A for life. Considering the applicable federal rate under section 7520 and the appropriate life estate factor for a person A's age, the value of A's income interest, if valued under this section, would be $10,000. After A's death, the trust is to terminate and the trust property is to be distributed to B. The trust specifically authorizes, but does not require, the trustee to retain the shares of stock. The corporation has paid no dividends on this stock during the past 5 years, and there is no indication that this policy will change in the near future. Under applicable state law, the corporation is considered to be a sound investment that satisfies fiduciary standards. The facts and circumstances, including applicable state law, indicate that the income beneficiary would not have the legal right to compel the trustee to make the trust corpus productive in conformity with the requirements for a lifetime trust income interest under applicable local law. Therefore, the life income interest in this case is considered nonproductive. Consequently, A's income interest may not be valued actuarially under this section.

Example 2. Beneficiary's right to make trust productive. The facts are the same as in *Example 1*, except that the trustee is not specifically authorized to retain the shares of corporation stock. Further, the terms of the trust specifically provide that the life income beneficiary may require the trustee to make the trust corpus productive consistent with income yield standards for trusts under applicable state law. Under that law, the minimum rate of income that a productive trust may produce is substantially below the section 7520 interest rate on the valuation date. In this case, because A, the income beneficiary, has the right to compel the trustee to make the trust productive for purposes of applicable local law during A's lifetime, the income interest is considered an ordinary income interest for purposes of this paragraph, and the standard section 7520 life income factor may be used to determine the value of A's income interest. However, in the case of gifts made after October 8, 1990, if the donor was the life income beneficiary, the value of the income interest would be considered to be zero in this situation. See § 25.2702-2.

Example 3. Annuity trust funded with unproductive property. The donor, who is age 60, transfers corporation stock worth $1,000,000 to a trust. The trust will pay a 6 percent ($60,000 per year) annuity in cash or other property to the donor for 10 years or until the donor's prior death. Upon the termination of the trust, the trust property is to be distributed to the donor's child. The section 7520 rate for the month of the transfer is 8.2 percent. The corporation has paid no dividends on the stock during the past 5 years, and there is no indication that this policy will change in the near future. Under applicable state law, the corporation is considered to be a sound investment that satisfies fiduciary standards. Therefore, the trust's sole investment in this corporation is not expected to adversely affect the interest of either the annuity beneficiary or the remainder beneficiary. Considering the 6 percent annuity payout rate and the 8.2 percent section 7520 interest rate, the trust corpus is considered sufficient to pay this annuity for the entire 10-year term of the trust, or even indefinitely. The trust specifically authorizes, but does not require, the trustee to retain the shares of stock. Although it appears that neither beneficiary would be able to compel the trustee to make the trust corpus produce investment income, the annuity interest in this case is considered to be an ordinary annuity interest, and a section 7520 annuity factor may be used to determine the present value of the annuity. In this case, the section 7520 annuity factor would represent the right to receive $1.00 per year for a term of 10 years or the prior death of a person age 60.

Example 4. Unitrust funded with unproductive property. The facts are the same as in *Example* 3, except that the donor has retained a unitrust interest equal to 7 percent of the value of the trust property, valued as of the beginning of each year. Although the trust corpus is nonincome-producing, the present value of the donor's retained unitrust interest may be determined by using the section 7520 unitrust factor for a term of years or a prior death.

Example 5. Eroding corpus in an annuity trust. (i) The donor, who is age 60 and in normal health, transfers property worth $1,000,000 to a trust on or after May 1, 2009, but before 2019. The trust will pay a 10 percent ($100,000 per year) annuity to a charitable organization for the life of the donor, payable annually at the end of each period, and the remainder then will be distributed to the donor's child. The section 7520 rate for the month of the transfer is 6.8 percent. First, it is necessary to determine whether the annuity may exhaust the corpus before all annuity payments are made. Because it is assumed that any measuring life may survive until age 110, any life annuity could require payments until the measuring life reaches age 110. Based on a section 7520 interest rate of 6.8 percent, the determination of whether the annuity may exhaust the corpus before the termination of the annuity interest is made as follows:

Age to which life annuity may continue	110
less: Age of measuring life at date of transfer	60
Number of years annuity may continue	50
Annual annuity payment	$100,000.00
times: Annuity factor for 50 years derived from Table B (1 - .037277 / .068)	14.1577
Present value of term certain annuity	$1,415,770.00

(ii) Because the present value of an annuity for a term of 50 years exceeds the corpus, the annuity may exhaust the trust before all payments are made. Consequently, the annuity must be valued as an annuity payable for a term of years or until the prior death of the annuitant, with the term of years determined by when the fund will be exhausted by the annuity payments.

(iii) The annuity factor for a term of years at 6.8 percent is derived by subtracting the applicable remainder factor in Table B (see § 20.2031-7(d)(6)) from 1.000000 and then dividing the result by .068. An annuity of $100,000 payable at the end of each year for a period that has an annuity factor of 10.0 would have a present value exactly equal to the principal available to pay the annuity over the term. The annuity factor for 17 years is 9.8999 and the annuity factor for 18 years is 10.2059. Thus, it is determined that the $1,000,000 initial transfer will be sufficient to make 17 annual payments of $100,000, but not to make the entire 18th payment. The present value of an annuity of $100,000 payable at the end of each year for 17 years is $100,000 times 9.8999 or $989,990. The remaining amount is $10,010.00. Of the initial corpus amount, $10,010.00 is not needed to make payments for 17 years, so this amount, as accumulated for 18 years, will be available for the final payment. The 18-year accumulation factor is $(1 + 0.068)^{18}$ or 3.268004, so the amount available in 18 years is $10,010.00 times 3.268004 or $32,712.72. Therefore, for purposes of analysis, the annuity payments are considered to be composed of two distinct annuity components. The two annuity components taken together must equal the total annual amount of $100,000. The first annuity component is the exact amount that the trust will have available for the final payment, $32,712.72. The second annuity component then must be $100,000 minus $32,712.72, or $67,287.28. Specifically, the initial corpus will be able to make payments of $67,287.28 per year for 17 years plus payments of $32,712.72 per year for

18 years. The total annuity is valued by adding the value of the two separate annuity components.

(iv) Based on Table H of Publication 1457, Actuarial Valuations Version 3A, which may be obtained from the IRS Internet site, the present value of an annuity of $67,287.28 per year payable for 17 years or until the prior death of a person aged 60 is $597,013.12 ($67,287.28 X 8.8726). The present value of an annuity of $32,712.72 per year payable for 18 years or until the prior death of a person aged 60 is $296,887.56 ($32,712.72 X 9.0756). Thus, the present value of the charitable annuity interest is $893,900.68 ($597,013.12 + $296,887.56).

(3) *Mortality component*.—The mortality component prescribed under section 7520 may not be used to determine the present value of an annuity, income interest, remainder interest, or reversionary interest if an individual who is a measuring life dies or is terminally ill at the time the gift is completed. For purposes of this paragraph (b)(3), an individual who is known to have an incurable illness or other deteriorating physical condition is considered terminally ill if there is at least a 50 percent probability that the individual will die within 1 year. However, if the individual survives for eighteen months or longer after the date the gift is completed, that individual shall be presumed to have not been terminally ill at the date the gift was completed unless the contrary is established by clear and convincing evidence.

(4) *Example*.—The provisions of paragraph (b)(3) of this section are illustrated by the following example:

Example. Terminal illness. The donor transfers property worth $1,000,000 to a child on or after May 1, 2009 but before 2019, in exchange for the child's promise to pay the donor $80,000 per year for the donor's life, payable annually at the end of each period. The donor is age 75 but has been diagnosed with an incurable illness and has at least a 50 percent probability of dying within 1 year. The section 7520 interest rate for the month of the transfer is 7.6 percent, and the standard annuity factor at that interest rate for a person age 75 in normal health is 6.6493 (1 - .49465 / .076). Thus, if the donor were not terminally ill, the present value of the annuity would be $531,944.00 ($80,000 X 6.6493). Assuming the presumption provided in paragraph (b)(3) of this section does not apply, because there is at least a 50 percent probability that the donor will die within 1 year, the standard section 7520 annuity factor may not be used to determine the present value of the donor's annuity interest. Instead, a special section 7520 annuity factor must be computed that takes into account the projection of the donor's actual life expectancy.

(5) *Additional limitations*.—Section 7520 does not apply to the extent as may otherwise be provided by the Commissioner.

(c) *Effective/applicability dates*.—Section 25.7520-3(a) is effective as of May 1, 1989. The provisions of paragraph (b) of this section, except *Example 5* in paragraph (b)(2)(v) and paragraph (b)(4), are effective with respect to gifts made after December 13, 1995. *Example 5* in paragraph (b)(2)(v) and paragraph (b)(4) are effective with respect to gifts made on or after May 1, 2009. [Reg. § 25.7520-3.]

☐ [*T.D.* 8540, 6-9-94. *Amended by T.D.* 8630, 12-12-95; *T.D.* 8819, 4-29-99; *T.D.* 8886, 6-9-2000; *T.D.* 9448, 5-1-2009 *and T.D.* 9540, 8-9-2011.]

[Reg. § 20.7520-4]

§ 20.7520-4. Transitional rules.—(a) *Reliance*.—If the valuation date is after April 30, 1989, and before June 10, 1994, an executor can rely on Notice 89-24, 1989-1 C.B. 660, or Notice 89-60, 1989-1 C.B. 700 (See § 601.601(d)(2)(ii)(*b*) of this chapter), in valuing the transferred interest.

(b) *Effective date*.—This section is effective as of May 1, 1989. [Reg. § 20.7520-4.]

☐ [*T.D.* 8540, 6-9-94.]

[Reg. § 25.7520-4]

§ 25.7520-4. Transitional rules.—(a) *Reliance*.—If the valuation date is after April 30, 1989, and before June 10, 1994, a donor can rely on Notice 89-24, 1989-1 C.B. 660, or Notice 89-60, 1989-1 C.B. 700 (See § 601.601(d)(2)(ii)(*b*) of this chapter), in valuing the transferred interest.

(b) *Transfers in 1989*.—If a donor transferred an interest in property by gift after December 31, 1988, and before May 1, 1989, retaining an interest in the same property and, after April 30, 1989, and before January 1, 1990, transferred the retained interest in the property, the donor may, at the donor's option, value the transfer of the retained interest under either § 25.2512-5(d) or § 25.2512-5A(d).

(c) *Effective date*.—This section is effective as of May 1, 1989. [Reg. § 25.7520-4.]

☐ [*T.D.* 8540, 6-9-94.]

[Reg. § 301.7602-1]

§ 301.7602-1. Examination of books and witnesses.—(a) *In general*.—For the purpose of ascertaining the correctness of any return, making a return where none has been made, determining the liability of any person for any internal revenue tax (including any interest, additional amount, addition to the tax, or civil penalty) or the liability at law or in equity of any transferee or fiduciary of any person in respect of any internal revenue tax, collecting any such liability or inquiring into any offense connected with the administration or enforcement of the internal revenue laws, any authorized officer or employee of the Internal Revenue Service may examine any books, papers, records or other data which may be relevant or material to such inquiry; and take such testimony of the person concerned, under oath, as may be relevant to such inquiry.

(b) *Summons*.—(1) *In general*.—For the purposes described in § 301.7602-1(a), the Commissioner is authorized to summon the person liable for tax or required to perform the act, or any officer or employee of such person or any person having possession, custody, or care of books of accounts containing entries relating to the business of the person liable for tax or required to perform the act, or any other person deemed proper, to appear before one or more officers or employees of the Internal Revenue Service at a time and place named in the summons and to produce such books, papers, records, or other data, and to give such testimony, under oath, as may be relevant or material to such inquiry; and take such testimony of the person concerned, under oath, as may be relevant or material to such inquiry. This summons power may be used in an investigation of either civil or criminal tax-related liability. The Commissioner may designate one or more officers or employees of the IRS as the individuals before whom a person summoned pursuant to section 6420(e)(2), 6421(g)(2), 6427(j)(2), or 7602 shall appear. Any such officer or employee is authorized to take testimony under oath of the person summoned and to receive and examine books, papers, records, or other data produced in compliance with the summons.

(2) *Officer or employee of the IRS.*—For purposes of this paragraph (b), officer or employee of the IRS means all officers and employees of the United States, who are engaged in the administration and enforcement of the internal revenue laws or any other laws administered by the IRS, and who are appointed or employed by, or subject to the directions, instructions, or orders of the Secretary of the Treasury or the Secretary's delegate (Secretary). An officer or employee of the IRS, for purposes of this paragraph (b), shall include an officer or employee of the Office of Chief Counsel.

(3) *Participation of a person described in section 6103(n).*—(i) *IRS contractor access to books and records obtained by the IRS administratively.*—(A) *In general.*—The Secretary may not, under the authority of section 6103(n), provide any books, papers, records, or other data obtained pursuant to section 7602 to any person authorized under section 6103(n), except when such person requires such information for the sole purpose of providing expert evaluation and assistance to the IRS.

(B) *Persons providing expert evaluation and assistance.*—For the purposes of paragraph (b)(3)(i)(A) of this section, persons providing expert evaluation and assistance may include, but are not limited to, the following:

(1) Persons with specialized expertise in certain substantive areas, including, but not limited to, economists, engineers, attorneys specializing in an area relevant to an issue in the examination (such as patent law, property law, environmental law, or foreign, state, or local law (including foreign, state, or local tax law)), industry experts, or other subject-matter experts;

(2) Persons providing support as ancillary service contractors including, but not limited to, court reporters, translators or interpreters, photocopy services, providers of data processing programs or equipment, litigation support services, or other similar contractors; and

(3) Whistleblower-related contractors described in § 301.6103(n)-2.

(C) *Hiring of certain non-government attorneys.*—The IRS may not hire an attorney as a contractor to assist in an examination under section 7602 unless the attorney is hired by the IRS as a specialist in foreign, state, or local law (including foreign, state, or local tax law), or in non-tax substantive law that is relevant to an issue in the examination, such as patent law, property law, or environmental law, or is hired for knowledge, skills, or abilities other than providing legal services as an attorney.

(ii) *IRS contractor participation in an IRS summons interview.*—(A) *In general.*—No person other than an officer or employee of the IRS or its Office of Chief Counsel may, on behalf of the Secretary, question a witness under oath whose testimony was obtained pursuant to section 7602. Persons authorized by section 6103(n) and with whom the Secretary may provide books, papers, records, or other data obtained pursuant to section 7602 may also attend a summons interview and provide assistance to the IRS or Office of Chief Counsel employees in attendance, but may not question the summoned witness under oath or ask a summoned person's representative to clarify an objection or assertion of privilege.

(B) *Court reporters, translators, and interpreters are not barred from asking questions.*—Court reporters who are hired as contractors by the IRS to make a record of an IRS summons interview are permitted to ask typical housekeeping questions of a summoned witness. Examples of such questions include, but are not limited to, asking whether the witness swears to tell the truth, asking the witness to spell a word or phrase, and asking whether the witness can speak up or speak rather than gesture an answer. Translators and interpreters who are hired as contractors by the IRS to assist in the interview of a summoned witness are permitted to translate any of the questions that are asked of the witness by an IRS or Office of Chief Counsel officer or employee and to ask questions which may be necessary to clarify the translation.

(c) *Proscription on issuing of administrative summons when a Justice Department referral is in effect.*—(1) *In general.*—The Commissioner may neither issue a summons under this title nor initiate a proceeding to enforce a previously issued summons by way of section 7604 with respect to any person whose tax liability is in issue, if a Justice Department referral is in effect with respect to that person for that liability.

(2) *Justice Department referral in effect.*—A Justice Department referral is in effect with respect to any person when:

(i) The Secretary recommends, within the meaning of this paragraph, that the Attorney General either commence a grand jury investigation of or criminal prosecution of such person for any alleged offense connected with the administration or enforcement of the internal revenue laws, or

(ii) The Attorney General (or Deputy Attorney General or Assistant Attorney General) under section 6103(h)(3)(B) requests in writing that the Secretary disclose a return of, or return information relating to, such person. The request must set forth that the need for disclosure is for the purpose of a grand jury investigation of or potential or pending criminal prosecution of such person for any alleged offense connected with the administration or enforcement of the internal revenue laws.

The referral is effective at the time the document recommending criminal prosecution or grand jury investigation is signed by the Secretary or upon the Secretary's receipt of the section 6103(h)(3)(B) request.

(3) *Cessation of Justice Department referral.*—A Justice Department referral ceases to be in effect with respect to a person:

(i) When the Secretary receives written notification from the Attorney General that the Justice Department:

(A) Will not prosecute that person for any offense connected with the administration or enforcement of the internal revenue laws that gave rise to the referral under paragraph (2)(i) of this section, or

(B) Will not authorize a grand jury investigation of that person with respect to such offense, or

(C) Will discontinue any grand jury investigation of that person with respect to such offense;

(ii) When a final disposition with respect to a criminal proceeding brought against that person has been made; or

(iii) When the Secretary receives written notification from the Attorney General, Deputy Attorney General, or an Assistant Attorney General, that the Justice Department will not prosecute such person for any offense connected with the administration or enforcement of the internal revenue laws, based upon a previous request for disclosure under section 6103(h)(3)(B).

(4) *Taxable years and taxes imposed by separate chapters of the Code treated separately.*—(i) *In general.*—For purposes of this section, each taxable period (or, if there is no taxable period, each taxable event) and each tax imposed by a separate chapter of the Code is treated separately.

(ii) *Examples.*—The following examples illustrate the application of this paragraph (c)(4):

Example (1). A Justice Department referral is in effect for D's criminal evasion of income tax for the taxable year 1979. The Commissioner may issue a summons respecting D's 1980 criminal and/or civil tax liability. The Commissioner may not issue a summons respecting D's 1979 income tax liability.

Example (2). A referral has been made to the Department of Justice for the criminal prosecution of F with regard to F's income tax liability for the taxable year 1978. The Commissioner may issue a summons respecting F's gift tax liability for the taxable year 1978.

Example (3). A referral has been made to the Department of Justice for a grand jury investigation respecting G's 1980 income tax liability. The Commissioner may issue a summons related to an investigation of G's liability for Federal Insurance Contribution Act (FICA) taxes for the taxable year 1980.

Example (4). A referral has been made to the Department of Justice respecting J's criminal evasion of windfall profit tax for all quarters of the calendar year 1982. The Commissioner may issue a summons respecting J's liability for highway motor vehicle use tax covering the same periods.

Example (5). A referral has been made to the Department of Justice for a grand jury investigation respecting L's 1983 income tax liability. The Commissioner may issue a summons related to the investigation of L's liability under sections 6700 (abusive tax shelter promoter penalty) and 7408 of the Code for his conduct during 1983.

(d) *Applicability date.*—This section is applicable after September 3, 1982, except for paragraphs (b)(1) and (2) of this section, which are applicable on and after April 1, 2005, and paragraph (b)(3) of this section, which applies to examinations begun or administrative summonses served by the IRS on or after August 6, 2020. For rules under paragraphs (b)(1) and (2) of this section that are applicable to summonses issued on or after September 10, 2002 or under paragraph (b)(3) of this section that are applicable to summons interviews conducted on or after June 18, 2014 and before July 14, 2016, see 26 CFR 301.7602-1T (revised as of April 1, 2016). For rules under paragraph (b)(3) of this section that are applicable to administrative summonses served by the IRS before August 6, 2020, see 26 CFR 301.7602-1 (revised as of April 1, 2020). [Reg. § 301.7602-1.]

☐ [*T.D.* 6421, 10-23-59. *Amended by T.D.* 6498, 10-24-60, *T.D.* 7188, 6-28-72, *T.D.* 7297, 12-18-73; *T.D.* 8091, 6-24-86; *T.D.* 9015, 9-9-2002, *T.D.* 9195, 3-31-2005, *T.D.* 9778, 7-12-2016 *and T.D.* 9952, 9-2-2021.]

[Reg. § 20.7701-1]

§ 20.7701-1. Tax return preparer.—(a) *In general.*—For the definition of a tax return preparer, see § 301.7701-15 of this chapter.

(b) *Effective/applicability date.*—This section is applicable to returns and claims for refund filed, and advice provided, after December 31, 2008. [Reg. § 20.7701-1.]

☐ [*T.D.* 9436, 12-15-2008.]

[Reg. § 25.7701-1]

§ 25.7701-1. Tax return preparer.—(a) *In general.*—For the definition of a tax return preparer, see § 301.7701-15 of this chapter.

(b) *Effective/applicability date.*—This section is applicable to returns and claims for refund filed, and advice provided, after December 31, 2008. [Reg. § 25.7701-1.]

☐ [*T.D.* 9436, 12-15-2008.]

[Reg. § 26.7701-1]

§ 26.7701-1. Tax return preparer.—(a) *In general.*—For the definition of a tax return preparer, see § 301.7701-15 of this chapter.

(b) *Effective/applicability date.*—This section is applicable to returns and claims for refund filed, and advice provided, after December 31, 2008. [Reg. § 26.7701-1.]

☐ [*T.D.* 9436, 12-15-2008.]

[Reg. § 20.7701-2]

§ 20.7701-2. Definitions; spouse, husband and wife, husband, wife, marriage.—(a) *In general.*—For the definition of the terms spouse, husband and wife, husband, wife, and marriage, see § 301.7701-18 of this chapter.

(b) *Applicability date.*—The rules of this section apply to taxable years ending on or after September 2, 2016. [Reg. § 20.7701-2.]

☐ [*T.D.* 9785, 8-31-2016.]

[Reg. § 25.7701-2]

§ 25.7701-2. Definitions; spouse, husband and wife, husband, wife, marriage.—(a) *In general.*—For the definition of the terms spouse, husband and wife, husband, wife, and marriage, see § 301.7701-18 of this chapter.

(b) *Applicability date.*—The rules of this section apply to taxable years ending on or after September 2, 2016. [Reg. § 25.7701-2.]

☐ [*T.D.* 9785, 8-31-2016.]

[Reg. § 26.7701-2]

§ 26.7701-2. Definitions; spouse, husband and wife, husband, wife, marriage.—(a) *In general.*—For the definition of the terms spouse, husband and wife, husband, wife, and marriage, see § 301.7701-18 of this chapter.

(b) *Applicability date.*—The rules of this section apply to taxable years ending on or after September 2, 2016. [Reg. § 26.7701-2.]

☐ [*T.D.* 9785, 8-31-2016.]

[Reg. § 301.7701-4]

§ 301.7701-4. Trusts.—(a) *Ordinary trusts.*—In general, the term "trust" as used in the Internal Revenue Code refers to an arrangement created either by a will or by an inter vivos declaration whereby trustees take title to property for the purpose of protecting or conserving it for the beneficiaries under the ordinary rules applied in chancery or probate courts. Usually the beneficiaries of such a trust do no more than accept the benefits thereof and are not the voluntary planners or creators of the trust arrangement. However, the beneficiaries of such a trust may be the persons who create it and it will be recognized as a trust under the Internal Revenue Code if it was created for the purpose of protecting or conserving the trust property for beneficiaries who stand in the same relation to the trust as they would if the trust had been created by others for them. Generally speaking, an arrangement will be treated as a trust under the Internal Revenue Code if it can be shown that the purpose of the arrangement is to vest in trustees responsibility for the protection and conservation of property for beneficiaries who cannot share in the discharge of this responsibility and, therefore, are not associates in a joint enterprise for the conduct of business for profit.

(b) *Business trusts.*—There are other arrangements which are known as trusts because the legal title to property is conveyed to trustees for the benefit of beneficiaries, but which are not classified as trusts for purposes of the Internal Revenue Code because they are not simply arrangements to protect or conserve the property for the beneficiaries. These trusts, which are often known as business or commercial trusts, generally are created by the beneficiaries simply as a device to carry on a profit-making business which normally would have been carried on through business organizations that are classified as corporations or partnerships under the Internal Revenue Code. However, the fact that the corpus of the trust is not supplied by the beneficiaries is not sufficient reason in itself for classifying the arrangement as an ordinary trust rather than as an association or partnership. The fact that any organization is technically cast in the trust form, by conveying title to property to trustees for the benefit of persons designated as beneficiaries, will not change the real character of the organization if the organization is more properly classified as a business entity under § 301.7701-2.

(c) *Certain investment trusts.*—(1) An "investment" trust will not be classified as a trust if there is a power under the trust agreement to vary the investment of the certificate holders. *See Commissioner v. North American Bond Trust,* 122 F. 2d 545 [41-2 USTC ¶ 9644](2d Cir. 1941), *cert. denied,* 314 U.S. 701 (1942). An investment trust with a single class of ownership interests, representing undivided beneficial interests in the assets of the trust, will be classified as a trust if there is no power under the trust agreement to vary the investment of the certificate holders. An investment trust with multiple classes of ownership interests ordinarily will be classified as a business entity under § 301.7701-2; however, an investment trust with multiple classes of ownership interests, in which there is no power under the trust agreement to vary the investment of the certificate holders, will be classified as a trust if the trust is formed to facilitate direct investment in the assets of the trust and the existence of multiple classes of ownership interests is incidental to that purpose. See § 1.1001-6(f) of this chapter for additional rules that may apply to an investment trust that holds one or more contracts that provide for a rate referencing a discontinued IBOR, as defined in § 1.1001-6(h)(4) of this chapter, and for additional rules that may apply to an investment trust with one or more ownership interests that reference a discontinued IBOR.

(2) The provisions of paragraph (c)(1) of this section may be illustrated by the following examples:

Example (1): A corporation purchases a portfolio of residential mortgages and transfers the mortgages to a bank under a trust agreement. At the same time, the bank as trustee delivers to the corporation certificates evidencing rights to payments from the pooled mortgages; the corporation sells the certificates to the public. The trustee holds legal title to the mortgages in the pool for the benefit of the certificate holders but has no power to reinvest proceeds attributable to the mortgages in the pool or to vary investments in the pool in any other manner. There are two classes of certificates. Holders of class A certificates are entitled to all payments of mortgage principal, both scheduled and prepaid, until their certificates are retired; holders of class B certificates receive payments of principal only after all class A certificates have been retired. The different rights of the class A and class B certificates serve to shift to the holders of the class A certificates, in addition to the earlier scheduled payments of principal, the risk that mortgages in the pool will be prepaid so that the holders of the class B certificates will have "call protection" (freedom from premature termination of their interests on account of prepayments). The trust thus serves to create investment interests with respect to the mortgages held by the trust that differ significantly from direct investment in the mortgages. As a consequence, the existence of multiple classes of trust ownership is not incidental to any purpose of the trust to facilitate direct investment, and, accordingly, the trust is classified as a business entity under § 301.7701-2.

Example (2): Corporation M is the originator of a portfolio of residential mortgages and transfers the mortgages to a bank under a trust agreement. At the same time, the bank as trustee delivers to M certificates evidencing rights to payments from the pooled mortgages. The trustee holds legal title to the mortgages in the pool for the benefit of the certificate holders, but has no power to reinvest proceeds attributable to the mortgages in the pool or to vary investments in the pool in any other manner. There are two classes of certificates. Holders of class C certificates are entitled to receive 90 percent of the payments of principal and interest on the mortgages; class D certificate holders are entitled to receive the other ten percent. The two classes of certificates are identical except that, in the event of a default on the underlying mortgages, the payment rights of class D certificate holders are subordinated to the rights of class C certificate holders. M sells the class C certificates to investors and retains the class D certificates. The trust has multiple classes of ownership interests, given the greater security provided to holders of class C certificates. The interests of certificate holders, however, are substantially equivalent to undivided interests in the pool of mortgages, coupled with a limited recourse guarantee running from M to the holders of class C certificates. In such circumstances, the existence of multiple classes of ownership interests is incidental to the trust's purpose of facilitating direct investment in the assets of the trust. Accordingly, the trust is classified as a trust.

Example (3): A promoter forms a trust in which shareholders of a publicly traded corporation can deposit their stock. For each share of stock deposited with the trust, the participant receives two certificates that are initially attached, but may be separated and traded independently of each other. One certificate represents the right to dividends and the value of the underlying stock up to a specified amount; the other certificate represents the right to appreciation in the stock's value above the specified amount. The separate certificates represent two different classes of ownership interest in the trust, which effectively separate dividend rights on the stock held by the trust from a portion of the right to appreciation in the value of such stock. The multiple classes of ownership interests are designed to permit investors, by transferring one of the certificates and retaining the other, to fulfill their varying investment objectives of seeking primarily either dividend income or capital appreciation from the stock held by the trust. Given that the trust serves to create investment interests with respect to the stock held by the trust that differ significantly from direct investment in such stock, the trust is not formed to facilitate direct investment in the assets of the trust. Accordingly, the trust is classified as a business entity under § 301.7701-2.

Example (4): Corporation N purchases a portfolio of bonds and transfers the bonds to a bank under a trust agreement. At the same time, the trustee delivers to N certificates evidencing interests in the bonds. These certificates are sold to public investors. Each certificate represents the right to receive a particular payment with respect to a specific bond. Under section 1286, stripped coupons and stripped bonds are treated as separate bonds for federal income tax purposes. Although the interest of each certificate holder is different from that of each other certificate holder, and the trust thus has multiple classes of ownership, the multiple classes simply provide each certificate holder with a direct interest in what is treated under section 1286 as a separate bond. Given the similarity of the interests acquired by the certificate holders to the interests that could be acquired by direct investment, the multiple classes of trust interests merely facilitate direct investment in the assets held by the trust. Accordingly, the trust is classified as a trust.

(d) *Liquidating trusts.*—Certain organizations which are commonly known as liquidating trusts are treated as trusts for purposes of the Internal Revenue Code. An organization will be considered a liquidating trust if it is organized for the primary purpose of liquidating and distributing the assets transferred to it, and if its activities are all reasonably necessary to, and consistent with, the accomplishment of that purpose. A liquidating trust is treated as a trust for purposes of the Internal Revenue Code because it is formed with

See p. 15 for regulations not amended to reflect law changes

the objective of liquidating particular assets and not as an organization having as its purpose the carrying on of a profit-making business which normally would be conducted through business organizations classified as corporations or partnerships. However, if the liquidation is unreasonably prolonged or if the liquidation purpose becomes so obscured by business activities that the declared purpose of liquidation can be said to be lost or abandoned, the status of the organization will no longer be that of a liquidating trust. Bondholders' protective committees, voting trusts, and other agencies formed to protect the interests of security holders during insolvency, bankruptcy, or corporate reorganization proceedings are analogous to liquidating trusts but if subsequently utilized to further the control or profitable operation of a going business on a permanent continuing basis, they will lose their classification as trusts for purposes of the Internal Revenue Code.

(e) *Environmental remediation trusts.*—(1) An environmental remediation trust is considered a trust for purposes of the Internal Revenue Code. For purposes of this paragraph (e), an organization is an environmental remediation trust if the organization is organized under state law as a trust; the primary purpose of the trust is collecting and disbursing amounts for environmental remediation of an existing waste site to resolve, satisfy, mitigate, address, or prevent the liability or potential liability of persons imposed by federal, state, or local environmental laws; all contributors to the trust have (at the time of contribution and thereafter) actual or potential liability or a reasonable expectation of liability under federal, state, or local environmental laws for environmental remediation of the waste site; and the trust is not a qualified settlement fund within the meaning of § 1.468B-1(a) of this chapter. An environmental remediation trust is classified as a trust because its primary purpose is environmental remediation of an existing waste site and not the carrying on of a profit-making business that normally would be conducted through business organizations classified as corporations or partnerships. However, if the remedial purpose is altered or becomes so obscured by business or investment activities that the declared remedial purpose is no longer controlling, the organization will no longer be classified as a trust. For purposes of this paragraph (e), environmental remediation includes the costs of assessing environmental conditions, remedying and removing environmental contamination, monitoring remedial activities and the release of substances, preventing future releases of substances, and collecting amounts from persons liable or potentially liable for the costs of these activities. For purposes of this paragraph (e), persons have potential liability or a reasonable expectation of liability under federal, state, or local environmental laws for remediation of the existing waste site if there is authority under a federal, state, or local law that requires or could reasonably be expected to require such persons to satisfy all or a portion of the costs of the environmental remediation.

(2) Each contributor (grantor) to the trust is treated as the owner of the portion of the trust contributed by that grantor under rules provided in section 677 and § 1.677(a)-1(d) of this chapter. Section 677 and § 1.677(a)-1(d) of this chapter provide rules regarding the treatment of a grantor as the owner of a portion of a trust applied in discharge of the grantor's legal obligation. Items of income, deduction, and credit attributable to an environmental remediation trust are not reported by the trust on Form 1041, but are shown on a separate statement to be attached to that form. See § 1.671-4(a) of this chapter. The trustee must also furnish to each grantor a statement that shows all items of income, deduction, and credit of the trust for the grantor's taxable year attributable to the portion of the trust treated as owned by the grantor. The statement must provide the grantor with the information necessary to take the items into account in computing the grantor's taxable income, including information necessary to determine the federal tax treatment of the items (for example, whether an item is a deductible expense under section 162(a) or a capital expenditure under section 263(a)) and how the item should be taken into account under the economic performance rules of section 461(h) and the regulations thereunder. See § 1.461-4 of this chapter for rules relating to economic performance.

(3) All amounts contributed to an environmental remediation trust by a grantor (cash-out grantor) who, pursuant to an agreement with the other grantors, contributes a fixed amount to the trust and is relieved by the other grantors of any further obligation to make contributions to the trust, but remains liable or potentially liable under the applicable environmental laws, will be considered amounts contributed for remediation. An environmental remediation trust agreement may direct the trustee to expend amounts contributed by a cash-out grantor (and the earnings thereon) before expending amounts contributed by other grantors (and the earnings thereon). A cash-out grantor will cease to be treated as an owner of a portion of the trust when the grantor's portion is fully expended by the trust.

(4) The provisions of this paragraph (e) may be illustrated by the following example:

Example. (a) *X*, *Y*, and *Z* are calendar year corporations that are liable for the remediation of an existing waste site under applicable federal environmental laws. On June 1, 1996, pursuant to an agreement with the governing federal agency, *X*, *Y*, and *Z* create an environmental remediation trust within the meaning of paragraph (e)(1) of this section to collect funds contributed to the trust by *X*, *Y*, and *Z* and to carry out the remediation of the waste site to the satisfaction of the federal agency. *X*, *Y*, and *Z* are jointly and severally liable under the federal environmental laws for the remediation of the waste site, and the federal agency will not release *X*, *Y*, or *Z* from liability until the waste site is remediated to the satisfaction of the agency.

(b) The estimated cost of the remediation is $20,000,000. *X*, *Y*, and *Z* agree that, if *Z* contributes $1,000,000 to the trust, *Z* will not be required to make any additional contributions to the trust, and *X* and *Y* will complete the remediation of the waste site and make additional contributions if necessary.

(c) On June 1, 1996, *X*, *Y*, and *Z* each contribute $1,000,000 to the trust. The trust agreement directs the trustee to spend *Z*'s contributions to the trust and the income allocable to *Z*'s portion before spending *X*'s and *Y*'s portions. On November 30, 1996, the trustee disburses $2,000,000 for remediation work performed from June 1, 1996, through September 30, 1996. For the six-month period ending November 30, 1996, the interest earned on the funds in the trust was $75,000, which is allocated in equal shares of $25,000 to *X*'s, *Y*'s, and *Z*'s portions of the trust.

(d) *Z* made no further contributions to the trust. Pursuant to the trust agreement, the trustee expended *Z*'s portion of the trust before expending *X*'s and *Y*'s portion. Therefore, *Z*'s share of the remediation disbursement made in 1996 is $1,025,000 ($1,000,000 contribution by *Z* plus $25,000 of interest allocated to *Z*'s portion of the trust). *Z* takes the $1,025,000 disbursement into account under the appropriate federal tax accounting rules. In addition, *X*'s share of the remediation disbursement made in 1996 is $487,500, and *Y*'s share of the remediation disbursement made in 1996 is $487,500. *X* and *Y* take their respective shares of the disbursement into account under the appropriate federal tax accounting rules.

(e) The trustee made no further remediation disbursements in 1996, and *X* and *Y* made no further contributions in 1996. From December 1, 1996, to December 31, 1996, the interest earned on the funds remaining in the trust was $5,000, which is allocated $2,500 to *X*'s portion and $2,500 to *Y*'s portion. Accordingly, for 1996, *X* and *Y* each had interest income of $27,500 from the trust and *Z* had interest income of $25,000 from the trust.

(5) This paragraph (e) is applicable to trusts meeting the requirements of paragraph (e)(1) of this section that are formed on or after May 1, 1996. This paragraph (e) may be relied on by trusts formed before May 1, 1996, if the trust has at all times met all requirements of this paragraph (e) and the grantors have reported items of income and deduction consistent with this paragraph (e) on original or amended returns. For trusts formed before May 1, 1996, that are not described in the preceding sentence, the Commissioner may permit by letter ruling, in appropriate circumstances, this paragraph (e) to be applied subject to appropriate terms and conditions.

(f) *Effective date*.—The rules of this section generally apply to taxable years beginning after December 31, 1960. Paragraph (e)(5) of this section contains rules of applicability for paragraph (e) of this section. In addition, the last sentences of paragraphs (b), (c)(1), and (c)(2) *Example 1* and *Example 3* of this section are effective as of January 1, 1997. [Reg. § 301.7701-4.]

☐ [*T.D.* 6503, 11-15-60. *Amended by T.D.* 8080, 3-21-86; *T.D.* 8668, 4-30-96, *T.D.* 8697, 12-17-96 *and T.D.* 9961, 12-30-2021.]

[Reg. § 301.7701-6]

§ 301.7701-6. Definitions; person, fiduciary.—(a) *Person*.—The term *person* includes an individual, a corporation, a partnership, a trust or estate, a joint-stock company, an association, or a syndicate, group, pool, joint venture, or other unincorporated organization or group. The term also includes a guardian, committee, trustee, executor, administrator, trustee in bankruptcy, receiver, assignee for the benefit of creditors, conservator, or any person acting in a fiduciary capacity.

(b) *Fiduciary*.—(1) *In general*.—Fiduciary is a term that applies to persons who occupy positions of peculiar confidence toward others, such as trustees, executors, and administrators. A fiduciary is a person who holds in trust an estate to which another has a beneficial interest, or receives and controls income of another, as in the case of receivers. A committee or guardian of the property of an incompetent person is a fiduciary.

(2) *Fiduciary distinguished from agent*.—There may be a fiduciary relationship between an agent and a principal, but the word agent does not denote a fiduciary. An agent having entire charge of property, with authority to effect and execute leases with tenants entirely on his own responsibility and without consulting his principal, merely turning over the net profits from the property periodically to his principal by virtue of authority conferred upon him by a power of attorney, is not a fiduciary within the meaning of the Internal Revenue Code. In cases when no legal trust has been created in the estate controlled by the agent and attorney, the liability to make a return rests with the principal.

(c) *Effective date*.—The rules of this section are effective as of January 1, 1997. [Reg. § 301.7701-6.]

☐ [*T.D.* 6503, 11-15-60. *Amended by T.D.* 8697, 12-17-96.]

[Reg. § 301.7701-7]

§ 301.7701-7. Trusts—domestic and foreign.—(a) *In general*.—(1) A trust is a United States person if—

(i) A court within the United States is able to exercise primary supervision over the administration of the trust (court test), and

(ii) One or more United States persons have the authority to control all substantial decisions of the trust (control test).

(2) A trust is a United States person for purposes of the Internal Revenue Code (Code) on any day that the trust meets both the court test and the control test. For purposes of the regulations in this chapter, the term *domestic trust* means a trust that is a United States person. The term *foreign trust* means any trust other than a domestic trust.

See p. 15 for regulations not amended to reflect law changes

(3) Except as otherwise provided in part I, subchapter J, chapter 1 of the Code, the taxable income of a foreign trust is computed in the same manner as the taxable income of a nonresident alien individual who is not present in the United States at any time. Section 641(b). Section 7701(b) is not applicable to trusts because it only applies to individuals. In addition, a foreign trust is not considered to be present in the United States at any time for purposes of section 871(a)(2), which deals with capital gains of nonresident aliens present in the United States for 183 days or more.

(b) *Applicable law.*—The terms of the trust instrument and applicable law must be applied to determine whether the court test and the control test are met.

(c) *The court test.*—(1) *Safe harbor.*—A trust satisfies the court test if–

(i) The trust instrument does not direct that the trust be administered outside of the United States;

(ii) The trust in fact is administered exclusively in the United States; and

(iii) The trust is not subject to an automatic migration provision described in paragraph (c)(4)(ii) of this section.

(2) *Example.*—The following example illustrates the rule of paragraph (c)(1) of this section:

Example. A creates a trust for the equal benefit of *A*'s two children, *B* and *C*. The trust instrument provides that *DC*, a State *Y* corporation, is the trustee of the trust. State *Y* is a state within the United States. *DC* administers the trust exclusively in State *Y* and the trust instrument is silent as to where the trust is to be administered. The trust is not subject to an automatic migration provision described in paragraph (c)(4)(ii) of this section. The trust satisfies the safe harbor of paragraph (c)(1) of this section and the court test.

(3) *Definitions.*—The following definitions apply for purposes of this section:

(i) *Court.*—The term *court* includes any federal, state, or local court.

(ii) *The United States.*—The term *the United States* is used in this section in a geographical sense. Thus, for purposes of the court test, the United States includes only the States and the District of Columbia. See section 7701(a)(9). Accordingly, a court within a territory or possession of the United States or within a foreign country is not a court within the United States.

(iii) *Is able to exercise.*—The term *is able to exercise* means that a court has or would have the authority under applicable law to render orders or judgments resolving issues concerning administration of the trust.

(iv) *Primary supervision.*—The term *primary supervision* means that a court has or would have the authority to determine substantially all issues regarding the administration of the entire trust. A court may have primary supervision under this paragraph (c)(3)(iv) notwithstanding the fact that another court has jurisdiction over a trustee, a beneficiary, or trust property.

(v) *Administration.*—The term *administration* of the trust means the carrying out of the duties imposed by the terms of the trust instrument and applicable law, including maintaining the books and records of the trust, filing tax returns, managing and investing the assets of the trust, defending the trust from suits by creditors, and determining the amount and timing of distributions.

(4) *Situations that cause a trust to satisfy or fail to satisfy the court test.*—(i) Except as provided in paragraph (c)(4)(ii) of this section, paragraphs (c)(4)(i)(A) through (D) of this section set forth some specific situations in which a trust satisfies the court test. The four situations described are not intended to be an exclusive list.

(A) *Uniform Probate Code.*—A trust meets the court test if the trust is registered by an authorized fiduciary or fiduciaries of the trust in a court within the United States pursuant to a state statute that has provisions substantially similar to Article VII, *Trust Administration*, of the Uniform Probate Code, 8 Uniform Laws Annotated 1 (West Supp. 1998), available from the National Conference of Commissioners on Uniform State Laws, 676 North St. Clair Street, Suite 1700, Chicago, Illinois 60611.

(B) *Testamentary trust.*—In the case of a trust created pursuant to the terms of a will probated within the United States (other than an ancillary probate), if all fiduciaries of the trust have been qualified as trustees of the trust by a court within the United States, the trust meets the court test.

(C) *Inter vivos trust.*—In the case of a trust other than a testamentary trust, if the fiduciaries and/or beneficiaries take steps with a court within the United States that cause the administration of the trust to be subject to the primary supervision of the court, the trust meets the court test.

(D) *A United States court and a foreign court are able to exercise primary supervision over the administration of the trust.*—If both a United States court and a foreign court are able to exercise primary supervision over the administration of the trust, the trust meets the court test.

(ii) *Automatic migration provisions.*—Notwithstanding any other provision in this section, a court within the United States is not considered to have primary supervision over the administration of the trust if the trust instrument provides that a United States court's attempt to assert jurisdiction or otherwise supervise the administration of the trust directly or indirectly would cause the trust to migrate from the United States. However, this paragraph (c)(4)(ii) will not apply if the trust instrument provides that the trust will migrate from the United States only in the case of foreign invasion of the United States or widespread confiscation or nationalization of property in the United States.

(5) *Examples.*—The following examples illustrate the rules of this paragraph (c):

Example 1. A, a United States citizen, creates a trust for the equal benefit of *A*'s two children, both of whom are United States citizens. The trust instrument provides that *DC*, a domestic corporation, is to act as trustee of the trust and that the trust is to be administered in Country *X*, a foreign country. *DC* maintains a branch office in Country *X* with personnel authorized to act as trustees in Country *X*. The trust instrument provides that the law of State *Y*, a state within the United States, is to govern the interpretation of the trust. Under the law of Country *X*, a court within Country *X* is able to exercise primary supervision over the administration of the trust. Pursuant to the trust instrument, the Country *X* court applies the law of State *Y* to the trust. Under the terms of the trust instrument the trust is administered in Country *X*. No court within the United States is able to exercise primary supervision over the administration of the trust. The trust fails to satisfy the court test and therefore is a foreign trust.

Example 2. A, a United States citizen, creates a trust for *A*'s own benefit and the benefit of *A*'s spouse, *B*, a United States citizen. The trust instrument provides that the trust is to be administered in State *Y*, a state within the United States, by *DC*, a State *Y* corporation. The trust instrument further provides that in the event that a creditor sues the trustee in a United States court, the trust will automatically migrate from State *Y* to Country *Z*, a foreign country, so that no United States court will have jurisdiction over the trust. A court within the United States is not able to exercise primary supervision over the administration of the trust because the United States court's jurisdiction over the administration of the trust is automatically terminated in the event the court attempts to assert jurisdiction. Therefore, the trust fails to satisfy the court test from the time of its creation and is a foreign trust.

(d) *Control test.*—(1) *Definitions.*—(i) *United States person.*—The term *United States person* means a United States person within the meaning of section 7701(a)(30). For example, a domestic corporation is a United States person, regardless of whether its shareholders are United States persons.

(ii) *Substantial decisions.*—The term *substantial decisions* means those decisions that persons are authorized or required to make under the terms of the trust instrument and applicable law and that are not ministerial. Decisions that are ministerial include decisions regarding details such as the bookkeeping, the collection of rents, and the execution of investment decisions. Substantial decisions include, but are not limited to, decisions concerning—

(A) Whether and when to distribute income or corpus;

(B) The amount of any distributions;

(C) The selection of a beneficiary;

(D) Whether a receipt is allocable to income or principal;

(E) Whether to terminate the trust;

(F) Whether to compromise, arbitrate, or abandon claims of the trust;

(G) Whether to sue on behalf of the trust or to defend suits against the trust;

(H) Whether to remove, add, or replace a trustee;

(I) Whether to appoint a successor trustee to succeed a trustee who has died, resigned, or otherwise ceased to act as a trustee, even if the power to make such a decision is not accompanied by an unrestricted power to remove a trustee, unless the power to make such a decision is limited such that it cannot be exercised in a manner that would change the trust's residency from foreign to domestic, or vice versa; and

(J) Investment decisions; however, if a United States person under section 7701(a)(30) hires an investment advisor for the trust, investment decisions made by the investment advisor will be considered substantial decisions controlled by the United States person if the United States person can terminate the investment advisor's power to make investment decisions at will.

(iii) *Control.*—The term *control* means having the power, by vote or otherwise, to make all of the substantial decisions of the trust, with no other person having the power to veto any of the substantial decisions. To determine whether United States persons have control, it is necessary to consider all persons who have authority to make a substantial decision of the trust, not only the trust fiduciaries.

(iv) *Safe harbor for certain employee benefit trusts and investment trusts.*—Notwithstanding the provisions of this paragraph (d), the trusts listed in this paragraph (d)(1)(iv) are deemed to satisfy the control test set forth in paragraph (a)(1)(ii) of this section, provided that United States trustees control all of the substantial decisions made by the trustees of the trust—

(A) A qualified trust described in section 401(a);

(B) A trust described in section 457(g);

(C) A trust that is an individual retirement account described in section 408(a);

(D) A trust that is an individual retirement account described in section 408(k) or 408(p);

(E) A trust that is a Roth IRA described in section 408A;

(F) A trust that is an education individual retirement account described in section 530;

(G) A trust that is a voluntary employees' beneficiary association described in section 501(c)(9);

(H) A group trust described in Rev. Rul. 81-100 (1981-1 C.B. 326) (See § 601.601(d)(2) of this chapter);

(I) An investment trust classified as a trust under § 301.7701-4(c), provided that the following conditions are satisfied—

(1) All trustees are United States persons and at least one of the trustees is a bank, as defined in section 581, or a United States Government-owned agency or United States Government-sponsored enterprise;

(2) All sponsors (persons who exchange investment assets for beneficial interests with a view to selling the beneficial interests) are United States persons; and

(3) The beneficial interests are widely offered for sale primarily in the United States to United States persons;

(J) Such additional categories of trusts as the Commissioner may designate in revenue procedures, notices, or other guidance published in the Internal Revenue Bulletin (see § 601.601(d)(2)(ii)(*b*)).

(v) *Examples*.—The following examples illustrate the rules of paragraph (d)(1) of this section:

Example 1. Trust is a testamentary trust with three fiduciaries, *A*, *B*, and *C*. *A* and *B* are United States citizens, and *C* is a nonresident alien. No persons except the fiduciaries have authority to make any decisions of the trust. The trust instrument provides that no substantial decisions of the trust can be made unless there is unanimity among the fiduciaries. The control test is not satisfied because United States persons do not control all the substantial decisions of the trust. No substantial decisions can be made without *C*'s agreement.

Example 2. Assume the same facts as in *Example 1*, except that the trust instrument provides that all substantial decisions of the trust are to be decided by a majority vote among the fiduciaries. The control test is satisfied because a majority of the fiduciaries are United States persons and therefore United States persons control all the substantial decisions of the trust.

Example 3. Assume the same facts as in *Example 2*, except that the trust instrument directs that *C* is to make all of the trust's investment decisions, but that *A* and *B* may veto *C*'s investment decisions. *A* and *B* cannot act to make the investment decisions on their own. The control test is not satisfied because the United States persons, *A* and *B*, do not have the power to make all of the substantial decisions of the trust.

Example 4. Assume the same facts as in *Example 3*, except *A* and *B* may accept or veto *C*'s investment decisions and can make investments that *C* has not recommended. The control test is satisfied because the United States persons control all substantial decisions of the trust.

Example 5. *X*, a foreign corporation, conducts business in the United States through various branch operations. *X* has United States employees and has established a trust as part of a qualified employee benefit plan under section 401(a) for these employees. The trust is established under the laws of State *A*, and the trustee of the trust is *B*, a United States bank governed by the laws of State *A*. *B* holds legal title to the trust assets for the benefit of the trust beneficiaries. A plan committee makes decisions with respect to the plan and the trust. The plan committee can direct *B*'s actions with regard to those decisions and under the governing documents *B* is not liable for those decisions. Members of the plan committee consist of United States persons and nonresident aliens, but nonresident aliens make up a majority of the plan committee. Decisions of the plan committee are made by majority vote. In addition, *X* retains the power to terminate the trust and to replace the United States trustee or to appoint additional trustees. This trust is deemed to satisfy the control test under paragraph (d)(1)(iv) of this section because *B*, a United States person, is the trust's only trustee. Any powers held by the plan committee or *X* are not considered under the safe harbor of paragraph (d)(1)(iv) of this section. In the event that *X* appoints additional trustees including foreign trustees, any powers held by such trustees must be considered in determining whether United States trustees control all substantial decisions made by the trustees of the trust.

(2) *Replacement of any person who had authority to make a substantial decision of the trust.*—(i) *Replacement within 12 months.*—In the event of an inadvertent change in any person that has the power to make a substantial decision of the trust that would cause the domestic or foreign residency of the trust to change, the trust is allowed 12 months from the date of the change to make necessary changes either with respect to the persons who control the substantial decisions or with respect to the residence of such persons to avoid a change in the trust's residency. For purposes of this section, an inadvertent change means the death, incapacity, resignation, change in residency or other change with respect to a person that has a power to make a substantial decision of the trust that would cause a change to the residency of the trust but that was not intended to change the residency of the trust. If the necessary change is made within 12 months, the trust is treated as retaining its pre-change residency during the 12-month period. If the necessary change is not made within 12 months, the trust's residency changes as of the date of the inadvertent change.

(ii) *Request for extension of time.*—If reasonable actions have been taken to make the necessary change to prevent a change in trust residency, but due to circumstances beyond the trust's control the trust is unable to make the modification within 12 months, the trust may provide a written statement to the district director having jurisdiction over the trust's return setting forth the reasons for failing to make the necessary change within the required time period. If the district director determines that the failure was due to reasonable cause, the district director may grant the trust an extension of time to make the necessary change. Whether an extension of time is granted is in the sole discretion of the district director and, if granted, may contain such terms with respect to assessment as may be necessary to ensure that the correct amount of tax will be collected from the trust, its owners, and its beneficiaries. If the district director does not grant an extension, the trust's residency changes as of the date of the inadvertent change.

(iii) *Examples.*—The following examples illustrate the rules of paragraphs (d)(2)(i) and (ii) of this section:

Example 1. A trust that satisfies the court test has three fiduciaries, *A, B,* and *C. A* and *B* are United States citizens and *C* is a nonresident alien. All decisions of the trust are made by majority vote of the fiduciaries. The trust instrument provides that upon the death or resignation of any of the fiduciaries, *D,* is the successor fiduciary. *A* dies and *D* automatically becomes a fiduciary of the trust. When *D* becomes a fiduciary of the trust, *D* is a nonresident alien. Two months after *A* dies, *B* replaces *D* with *E,* a United States person. Because *D* was replaced with *E* within 12 months after the date of *A*'s death, during the period after *A*'s death and before *E* begins to serve, the trust satisfies the control test and remains a domestic trust.

Example 2. Assume the same facts as in *Example 1* except that at the end of the 12-month period after *A*'s death, *D* has not been replaced and remains a fiduciary of the trust. The trust becomes a foreign trust on the date *A* died unless the district director grants an extension of the time period to make the necessary change.

(3) *Automatic migration provisions.*—Notwithstanding any other provision in this section, United States persons are not considered to control all substantial decisions of the trust if an attempt by any governmental agency or creditor to collect information from or assert a claim against the trust would cause one or more substantial decisions of the trust to no longer be controlled by United States persons.

(4) *Examples.*—The following examples illustrate the rules of this paragraph (d):

Example 1. A, a nonresident alien individual, is the grantor and, during *A*'s lifetime, the sole beneficiary of a trust that qualifies as an individual retirement account (IRA). *A* has the exclusive power to make decisions regarding withdrawals from the IRA and to direct its investments. The IRA's sole trustee is a United States person within the meaning of section 7701(a)(30). The control test is satisfied with respect to this trust because the special rule of paragraph (d)(1)(iv) of this section applies.

Example 2. A, a nonresident alien individual, is the grantor of a trust and has the power to revoke the trust, in whole or in part, and revest assets in *A. A* is treated as the owner of the trust under sections 672(f) and 676. *A* is not a fiduciary of the trust. The trust has one trustee, *B,* a United States person, and the trust has one beneficiary, *C. B* has the discretion to distribute corpus or income to *C.* In this case, decisions exercisable by *A* to have trust assets distributed to *A* are substantial decisions. Therefore, the trust is a foreign trust because *B* does not control all substantial decisions of the trust.

Example 3. A trust, Trust *T,* has two fiduciaries, *A* and *B.* Both *A* and *B* are United States persons. *A* and *B* hire *C,* an investment advisor who is a foreign person, and may terminate *C*'s employment at will. The investment advisor makes the investment decisions for the trust. *A* and *B* control all other decisions of the trust. Although *C* has the power to make investment decisions, *A* and *B* are treated as controlling these decisions. Therefore, the control test is satisfied.

Example 4. G, a United States citizen, creates a trust. The trust provides for income to *A* and *B* for life, remainder to *A*'s and *B*'s descendants. *A* is a nonresident alien and *B* is a United States person. The trustee of the trust is a United States person. The trust instrument authorizes *A* to replace the trustee. The power to replace the trustee is a substantial decision. Because *A,* a nonresident alien, controls a substantial decision, the control test is not satisfied.

(e) *Effective date.*—(1) *General rule.*—Except for the election to remain a domestic trust provided in paragraph (f) of this section and except as provided in paragraph (e)(3) of this section, this section is applicable to taxable years ending after February 2, 1999. This section may be relied on by trusts for taxable years beginning after December 31, 1996, and also may be relied on by trusts whose trustees have elected to apply sections 7701(a)(30) and (31) to the trusts for taxable years ending after August 20, 1996, under section 1907(a)(3)(B) of the Small Business Job Protection Act of 1996, (the SBJP Act) Public Law 104-188, 110 Stat. 1755 (26 U.S.C. 7701 note).

(2) *Trusts created after August 19, 1996.*—If a trust is created after August 19, 1996, and before April 5, 1999, and the trust satisfies the control test set forth in the regulations project REG-251703-96 published under section 7701(a)(30) and (31) (1997-1 C.B. 795) (See § 601.601(d)(2) of this chapter), but does not satisfy the control test set forth in paragraph (d) of this section, the trust may be modified to satisfy the control test of paragraph (d) by December 31, 1999. If the modification is completed by December 31, 1999, the trust will be treated as satisfying the control test of paragraph (d) for taxable years beginning after December 31, 1996, (and for taxable years ending after August 20, 1996, if the election under section 1907(a)(3)(B) of the SBJP Act has been made for the trust).

(3) *Effective date of safe harbor for certain employee benefit trusts and investment trusts.*—Paragraphs (d)(1)(iv) and (v) *Examples 1* and *5* of this section apply to trusts for taxable years ending on or after August 9, 2001. Paragraphs (d)(1)(iv) and (v) *Examples 1* and *5* of this section may be relied on by trusts for taxable years beginning after December 31, 1996, and also may be relied on by trusts whose trustees have elected to apply sections 7701(a)(30) and (31) to the trusts for taxable years ending after August 20, 1996, under section 1907(a)(3)(B) of the SBJP Act.

(f) *Election to remain a domestic trust.*—(1) *Trusts eligible to make the election to remain domestic.*—A trust that was in existence on August 20, 1996, and that was treated as a domestic trust on August 19, 1996, as provided in paragraph (f)(2) of this section, may elect to continue treatment as a domestic trust notwithstanding section 7701(a)(30)(E). This election is not available to a trust that was wholly-owned by its grantor under subpart E, part I, subchapter J, chapter 1, of the Code on August 20, 1996. The election is available to a trust if only a portion of the trust was treated as owned by the grantor under subpart E on August 20, 1996. If a partially-owned grantor trust makes the election, the election is effective for the entire trust. Also, a trust may not make the election if the trust has made an election pursuant to section 1907(a)(3)(B) of the SBJP Act to apply the new trust criteria to the first taxable year of the trust ending after August 20, 1996, because that election, once made, is irrevocable.

(2) *Determining whether a trust was treated as a domestic trust on August 19, 1996.*—(i) *Trusts filing Form 1041 for the taxable year that includes August 19, 1996.*—For purposes of the election, a trust is considered to have been treated as a domestic trust on August 19, 1996, if: the trustee filed a Form 1041, "U.S. Income Tax Return for Estates and Trusts," for the trust for the period that includes August 19, 1996 (and did not file a Form 1040NR, "U.S. Nonresident Alien Income Tax Return," for that year); and the trust had a reasonable basis (within the meaning of section 6662) under section 7701(a)(30) prior to amendment by the SBJP Act (prior law) for reporting as a domestic trust for that period.

(ii) *Trusts not filing a Form 1041.*—Some domestic trusts are not required to file Form 1041. For example, certain group trusts described in Rev. Rul. 81-100 (1981-1 C.B. 326) (See § 601.601(d)(2) of this chapter) consisting of trusts that are parts of qualified retirement plans and individual retirement accounts are not required to file Form 1041. Also, a domestic trust whose gross income for the taxable year is less than the amount required for filing an income tax return and that has no taxable income is not required to file a Form 1041. Section 6012(a)(4). For purposes of the election, a trust that filed neither a Form 1041 nor a Form 1040NR for the period that includes August 19, 1996, will be considered to have been treated as a domestic trust on August 19, 1996, if the trust had a reasonable basis (within the meaning of section 6662) under prior law for being treated as a domestic trust for that period and for filing neither a Form 1041 nor a Form 1040NR for that period.

(3) *Procedure for making the election to remain domestic.*—(i) *Required Statement.*—To make the election, a statement must be filed with the Internal Revenue Service in the manner and time described in this section. The statement must be entitled "Election to Remain a Domestic Trust under Section 1161 of the Taxpayer Relief Act of 1997," be signed under penalties of perjury by at least one trustee of the trust, and contain the following information—

(A) A statement that the trust is electing to continue to be treated as a domestic trust under section 1161 of the Taxpayer Relief Act of 1997;

(B) A statement that the trustee had a reasonable basis (within the meaning of section 6662) under prior law for treating the trust as a domestic trust on August 19, 1996. (The trustee need not explain the reasonable basis on the election statement.);

(C) A statement either that the trust filed a Form 1041 treating the trust as a domestic trust for the period that includes August 19, 1996, (and that the trust did not file a Form 1040NR for that period), or that the trust was not required to file a Form 1041 or a Form 1040NR for the period that includes August 19, 1996, with an accompanying brief explanation as to why a Form 1041 was not required to be filed; and

(D) The name, address, and employer identification number of the trust.

(ii) *Filing the required statement with the Internal Revenue Service.*—(A) Except as provided in paragraphs (f)(3)(ii)(E) through (G) of this section, the trust must attach the statement to a Form 1041. The statement may be attached to either the Form 1041 that is filed for the first taxable year of the trust beginning after December 31, 1996 (1997 taxable year), or to the Form 1041 filed for the first taxable year of the trust beginning after December 31, 1997 (1998 taxable year). The statement, however, must be filed no later than the due date for filing a Form 1041 for the 1998 taxable year, plus extensions. The election will be effective for the 1997 taxable year, and thereafter, until revoked or terminated. If the trust filed a Form 1041 for the 1997 taxable year without the statement attached, the statement should be attached to the Form 1041 filed for the 1998 taxable year.

(B) If the trust has insufficient gross income and no taxable income for its 1997 or 1998 taxable year, or both, and therefore is not required to file a Form 1041 for either or both years, the trust must make the election by filing a Form 1041 for either the 1997 or 1998 taxable year with the statement attached (even though not otherwise required to file a Form 1041 for that year). The trust should only provide on the Form 1041 the trust's name, name and title of fiduciary, address, employer identification number, date created, and type of entity. The statement must be attached to a Form 1041 that is filed no later than October 15, 1999.

(C) If the trust files a Form 1040NR for the 1997 taxable year based on application of new section 7701(a)(30)(E) to the trust, and satisfies paragraph (f)(1) of this section, in order for the trust to make the election the trust must file an amended Form 1040NR return for the 1997 taxable year. The trust must note on the amended Form 1040NR that it is making an election under section 1161 of the Taxpayer Relief Act of 1997. The trust must attach to the amended Form 1040NR the statement required by paragraph (f)(3)(i) of this section and a completed Form 1041 for the 1997 taxable year. The items of income, deduction and credit of the trust must be excluded from the amended Form 1040NR and reported on the Form 1041. The amended Form 1040NR for the 1997 taxable year, with the statement and the Form 1041 attached, must be filed with the Philadelphia Service Center no later than the due date, plus extensions, for filing a Form 1041 for the 1998 taxable year.

(D) If a trust has made estimated tax payments as a foreign trust based on application of section 7701(a)(30)(E) to the trust, but has not yet filed a Form 1040NR for the 1997 taxable year, when the trust files its Form 1041 for the 1997 taxable year it must note on its Form 1041 that it made estimated tax payments based on treatment as a foreign trust. The Form 1041 must be filed with the Philadelphia Service Center (and not with the service center where the trust ordinarily would file its Form 1041).

(E) If a trust forms part of a qualified stock bonus, pension, or profit sharing plan, the election provided by this paragraph (f) must be made by attaching the statement to the plan's annual return required under section 6058 (information return) for the first plan year beginning after December 31, 1996, or to the plan's information return for the first plan year beginning after December 31, 1997. The statement must be attached to the plan's information return that is filed no later than the due date for filing the plan's information return for the first plan year beginning after December 31, 1997, plus extensions. The election will be effective for the first plan year beginning after December 31, 1996, and thereafter, until revoked or terminated.

(F) Any other type of trust that is not required to file a Form 1041 for the taxable year, but that is required to file an information return (for example, Form 5227) for the 1997 or 1998 taxable year must attach the statement to the trust's information return for the 1997 or 1998 taxable year. However, the statement must be attached to an information return that is filed no later than the due date for filing the trust's information return for the 1998 taxable year, plus extensions. The election will be effective for the 1997 taxable year, and thereafter, until revoked or terminated.

(G) A group trust described in Rev. Rul. 81-100 consisting of trusts that are parts of qualified retirement plans and individual retirement accounts (and any other trust that is not described above and that is not required to file a Form 1041 or an information return) need not attach the statement to any return and should file the statement with the Philadelphia Service Center. The trust must make the election provided by this paragraph (f) by filing the statement by October 15, 1999. The election will be effective for the 1997 taxable year, and thereafter, until revoked or terminated.

(iii) *Failure to file the statement in the required manner and time.*—If a trust fails to file the statement in the manner or time provided in paragraphs (f)(3)(i) and (ii) of this section, the trustee may provide a written statement to the district director having jurisdiction over the trust setting forth the reasons for failing to file the statement in the required manner or time. If the district director determines that the failure to file the statement in the required manner or time was due to reasonable cause, the district director may grant the trust an extension of time to file the statement. Whether an extension of time is granted shall be in the sole discretion of the district director. However, the relief provided by this paragraph (f)(3)(iii) is not ordinarily available if the statute of limitations for the trust's 1997 taxable year has expired. Additionally, if the district director grants an extension of time, it may contain terms with respect to assessment as may be necessary to ensure that the correct amount of tax will be collected from the trust, its owners, and its beneficiaries.

(4) *Revocation or termination of the election.*—(i) *Revocation of election.*—The election provided by this paragraph (f) to be treated as a domestic trust may only be revoked with the consent of the Commissioner. See sections 684, 6048, and 6677 for the federal tax consequences and reporting requirements related to the change in trust residence.

(ii) *Termination of the election.*—An election under this paragraph (f) to remain a domestic trust terminates if changes are made to the trust subsequent to the effective date of the election that result in the trust no longer having any reasonable basis (within the meaning of section 6662) for being treated as a domestic trust under section 7701(a)(30) prior to its amendment by the SBJP Act. The termination of the election will result in the trust changing its residency from a domestic trust to a foreign trust on the effective date of the termination of the election. See sections 684, 6048, and 6677 for the federal tax consequences and reporting requirements related to the change in trust residence.

(5) *Effective date.*—This paragraph (f) is applicable beginning on February 2, 1999. [Reg. § 301.7701-7.]

☐ [*T.D.* 8813, 2-1-99. *Amended by T.D.* 8962, 8-8-2001.]

[Reg. § 301.7701-8]

§ 301.7701-8. Military or naval forces and Armed Forces of the United States.—The term "military or naval forces of the United States" and the term "Armed Forces of the United States" each includes all regular and reserve components of the uniformed services which are subject to the jurisdiction of the Secretary of Defense, the Secretary of the Army, the Secretary of the Navy, or the Secretary of the Air Force. The terms also include the Coast Guard. The members of such forces include commissioned officers and the personnel below the grade of commissioned officer in such forces. [Reg. § 301.7701-8.]

☐ [*T.D.* 6503, 11-15-60.]

[Reg. § 301.7701-15]

§ 301.7701-15. Tax return preparer.—(a) *In general.*—A *tax return preparer* is any person who prepares for compensation, or who employs one or more persons to prepare for compensation, all or a substantial portion of any return of tax or any claim for refund of tax under the Internal Revenue Code (Code).

(b) *Definitions.*—(1) *Signing tax return preparer..*—A *signing tax return preparer* is the individual tax return preparer who has the primary responsibility for the overall substantive accuracy of the preparation of such return or claim for refund.

(2) *Nonsigning tax return preparer.*—(i) *In general.*—A *nonsigning tax return preparer* is any tax return preparer who is not a signing tax return preparer but who prepares all or a substantial portion of a return or claim for refund within the meaning of paragraph (b)(3) of this section with respect to events that have occurred at the time the advice is rendered. In determining whether an individual is a nonsigning tax return preparer, time spent on advice that is given after events have occurred that represents less than 5 percent of the aggregate time incurred by such individual with respect to the position(s) giving rise to the understatement shall not be taken into account. Notwithstanding the preceding sentence, time spent on advice before the events have occurred will be taken into account if all facts and circumstances show that the position(s) giving rise to the understatement is primarily attributable to the advice, the advice was substantially given before events occurred primarily to avoid treating the person giving the advice as a tax return preparer, and the advice given before events occurred was confirmed after events had occurred for purposes of preparing a tax return. Examples of nonsigning tax return preparers are tax return preparers who provide advice (written or oral) to a taxpayer (or to another tax return preparer) when that advice leads to a position or entry that constitutes a substantial portion of the return within the meaning of paragraph(b)(3) of this section.

(ii) *Examples.*—The provisions of this paragraph (b)(2) are illustrated by the following examples:

Example 1. Attorney A, an attorney in a law firm, provides legal advice to a large corporate taxpayer regarding a completed corporate transaction. The advice provided by A is directly relevant to the determination of an entry on the taxpayer's return, and this advice leads to a position(s) or entry that constitutes a substantial portion of the return. A, however, does not prepare any other portion of the taxpayer's return and is not the signing tax return preparer of this return. A is considered a nonsigning tax return preparer.

Example 2. Attorney B, an attorney in a law firm, provides legal advice to a large corporate taxpayer regarding the tax consequences of a proposed corporate transaction. Based upon this advice, the corporate taxpayer enters into the transaction. Once the transaction is completed, the corporate taxpayer does not receive any additional advice from B with respect to the transaction. B did not provide advice with respect to events that have occurred and is not considered a tax return preparer.

Example 3. The facts are the same as *Example 2*, except that Attorney B provides supplemental advice to the corporate taxpayer on a phone call after the transaction is completed. Attorney B did not provide advice before the corporate transaction occurred with the primary intent to avoid being treated as a tax return preparer. The time incurred on this supplemental advice by B represented less than 5 percent of the aggregate amount of time spent by B providing tax advice on the position. B is not considered a tax return preparer.

(3) *Substantial portion.*—(i) Only a person who prepares all or a substantial portion of a return or claim for refund shall be considered to be a tax return preparer of the return or claim for refund. A person who renders tax advice on a position that is directly relevant to the determination of the existence, characterization, or amount of an entry on a return or claim for refund will be regarded as having prepared that entry. Whether a schedule, entry, or other portion of a return or claim for refund is a substantial portion is determined based upon whether the person knows or reasonably should know that the tax attributable to the schedule, entry, or other portion of a return or claim for refund is a substantial portion of the tax required to be shown on the return or claim for refund. A single tax entry may constitute a substantial portion of the tax required to be shown on a return. Factors to consider in determining whether a schedule, entry, or other portion of a return or claim for refund is a substantial portion include but are not limited to—

(A) the size and complexity of the item relative to the taxpayer's gross income; and

(B) the size of the understatement attributable to the item compared to the taxpayer's reported tax liability.

(ii)(A) For purposes of applying the rules of paragraph (b)(3)(i) of this section to a nonsigning tax return preparer within the meaning of paragraph (b)(2) of this section only, the schedule or other portion is not considered to be a substantial portion if the schedule, entry, or other portion of the return or claim for refund involves amounts of gross income, amounts of deductions, or amounts on the basis of which credits are determined that are—

(1) Less than $10,000; or

(2) Less than $400,000 and also less than 20 percent of the gross income as shown on the return or claim for refund (or, for an individual, the individual's adjusted gross income).

(B) If more than one schedule, entry or other portion is involved, all schedules, entries or other portions shall be aggregated in applying the de minimis rule in paragraph (b)(3)(ii)(A) of this section.

(C) The de minimis rule in paragraph (b)(3)(ii)(A) of this section shall not apply to a signing tax return preparer within the meaning of paragraph (b)(1) of this section.

(iii) A tax return preparer with respect to one return is not considered to be a tax return preparer of another return merely because an entry or entries reported on the first return may affect an entry reported on the other return, unless the entry or entries reported on the first return are directly reflected on the other return and constitute a substantial portion of the other return. For example, the sole preparer of a partnership return of income or small business corporation income tax return is considered a tax return preparer of a partner's or a shareholder's return if the entry or entries on the partnership or small business corporation return reportable on the partner's or shareholder's return constitute a substantial portion of the partner's or shareholder's return.

(iv) *Examples.*—The provisions of this paragraph (b)(3) are illustrated by the following examples:

Example 1. Accountant C prepares a Form 8886, "Reportable Transaction Disclosure Statement", that is used to disclose reportable transactions. C does not prepare the tax return or advise the taxpayer regarding the tax return reporting position of the transaction to which the Form 8886 relates. The preparation of the Form 8886 is not directly relevant to the determination of the existence, characterization, or amount of an entry on a tax return or claim for refund. Rather, the Form 8886 is prepared by C to disclose a reportable transaction. C has not prepared a substantial portion of the tax return and is not considered a tax return preparer under section 6694.

Example 2. Accountant D prepares a schedule for an individual taxpayer's Form 1040, "U.S. Individual Income Tax Return", reporting $4,000 in dividend income and gives oral or written advice about Schedule A, which results in a claim of a medical expense deduction totaling $5,000, but does not sign the tax return. D is not a nonsigning tax return preparer because the total aggregate amount of the deductions is less than $10,000.

(4) *Return and claim for refund.*—(i) *Return.*—For purposes of this section, a return of tax is a return (including an amended or adjusted return) filed by or on behalf of a taxpayer reporting the liability of the taxpayer for tax under the Code, if the type of return is identified in published guidance in the Internal Revenue Bulletin. A return of tax also includes any information return or other document identified in published guidance in the Internal Revenue Bulletin and that reports information that is or may be reported on another taxpayer's return under the Code if the information reported on the information return or other document constitutes a substantial portion of the taxpayer's return within the meaning of paragraph (b)(3) of this section.

(ii) *Claim for refund.*—For purposes of this section, a claim for refund of tax includes a claim for credit against any tax that is included in published guidance in the Internal Revenue Bulletin. A claim for refund also includes a claim for payment under section 6420, 6421, or 6427.

(c) *Mechanical or clerical assistance.*—A person who furnishes to a taxpayer or other tax return preparer sufficient information and advice so that completion of the return or claim for refund is largely a mechanical or clerical matter is considered a tax return preparer, even though that person does not actually place or review placement of information on the return or claim for refund. See also paragraph (b)(3) of this section.

(d) *Qualifications.*—A person may be a tax return preparer without regard to educational qualifications and professional status requirements.

(e) *Outside the United States.*—A person who prepares a return or claim for refund outside the United States is a tax return preparer, regardless of the person's nationality, residence, or the location of the person's place of business, if the person otherwise satisfies the definition of *tax return preparer*. Notwithstanding the provisions of § 301.6109-1(g), the person shall secure an employer identification number if the person is an employer of another tax return preparer, is a partnership in which one or more of the general partners is a tax return preparer, is a firm in which one or more of the equity holders is a tax return preparer, or is an individual not employed by another tax return preparer.

(f) *Persons who are not tax return preparers.*—(1) The following persons are not tax return preparers:

(i) An official or employee of the Internal Revenue Service (IRS) performing official duties.

(ii) Any individual who provides tax assistance under a Volunteer Income Tax Assistance (VITA) program established by the IRS, but only with respect to those returns prepared as part of the VITA program.

(iii) Any organization sponsoring or administering a VITA program established by the IRS, but only with respect to that sponsorship or administration.

(iv) Any individual who provides tax counseling for the elderly under a program established pursuant to section 163 of the Revenue Act of 1978, but only with respect to those returns prepared as part of that program.

(v) Any organization sponsoring or administering a program to provide tax counseling for the elderly established pursuant to section 163 of the Revenue Act of 1978, but only with respect to that sponsorship or administration.

(vi) Any individual who provides tax assistance as part of a qualified Low-Income Taxpayer Clinic (LITC), as defined by section 7526, subject to the requirements of paragraphs (f)(2) and (3) of this section, but only with respect to those returns and claims for refund prepared as part of the LITC program.

(vii) Any organization that is a qualified LITC, as defined by section 7526, subject to the requirements of paragraphs (f)(2) and (3) of this section.

(viii) An individual providing only typing, reproduction, or other mechanical assistance in the preparation of a return or claim for refund.

(ix) An individual preparing a return or claim for refund of a taxpayer, or an officer, a general partner, member, shareholder, or employee of a taxpayer, by whom the individual is regularly and continuously employed or compensated or in which the individual is a general partner.

(x) An individual preparing a return or claim for refund for a trust, estate, or other entity of which the individual either is a fiduciary or is an officer, general partner, or employee of the fiduciary.

(xi) An individual preparing a claim for refund for a taxpayer in response to—

(A) A notice of deficiency issued to the taxpayer; or

(B) A waiver of restriction on assessment after initiation of an audit of the taxpayer or another taxpayer if a determination in the audit of the other taxpayer affects, directly or indirectly, the liability of the taxpayer for tax.

(xii) A person who prepares a return or claim for refund for a taxpayer with no explicit or implicit agreement for compensation, even if the person receives an insubstantial gift, return service, or favor.

(2) Paragraphs (f)(1)(vi) and (vii) of this section apply only if any assistance with a return of tax or claim for refund is directly related to a controversy with the IRS for which the qualified LITC is providing assistance or is an ancillary part of a LITC program to inform individuals for whom English is a second language about their rights and responsibilities under the Code.

(3) Notwithstanding paragraph (f)(2) of this section, paragraphs (f)(1)(vi) and (f)(1)(vii) of this section do not apply if an LITC charges a separate fee or varies a fee based on whether the LITC provides assistance with a return of tax or claim for refund under the Code or if the LITC charges more than a nominal fee for its services.

(4) For purposes of paragraph (f)(1)(ix) of this section, the employee of a corporation owning more than 50 percent of the voting power of another corporation, or the employee of a corporation more than 50 percent of the voting power of which is owned by another corporation, is considered the employee of the other corporation as well.

(5) For purposes of paragraph (f)(1)(x) of this section, an estate, guardianship, conservatorship, committee, or any similar arrangement for a taxpayer under a legal disability (such as a minor, an incompetent, or an infirm individual) is considered a trust or estate.

(6) *Examples.*—The mechanical assistance exception described in paragraph (f)(1)(viii) of this section is illustrated by the following examples:

Example 1. A reporting agent received employment tax information from a client from the client's business records. The reporting agent did not render any tax advice to the client or exercise any discretion or independent judgment on the client's underlying tax positions. The reporting agent processed the client's information, signed the return as authorized by the client pursuant to Form 8655, Reporting Agent Authorization, and filed the client's return using the information supplied by the client. The reporting agent is not a tax return preparer.

Example 2. A reporting agent rendered tax advice to a client on determining whether its workers are employees or independent contractors for Federal tax purposes. For compensation, the reporting agent received employment tax information from the client, processed the client's information and filed the client's return using the information supplied by the client. The reporting agent is a tax return preparer.

(g) *Effective/applicability date.*—This section is applicable to returns and claims for refund filed, and advice provided, after December 31, 2008. [Reg. § 301.7701-15.]

☐ [*T.D.* 7519, 11-17-77. *Amended by T.D.* 7675, 2-20-80; *T.D.* 9026, 12-17-2002 *and T.D.* 9436, 12-15-2008 (*corrected* 1-28-2009).]

[Reg. § 301.7701-18]

§ 301.7701-18. Definitions; spouse, husband and wife, husband, wife, marriage.—(a) *In general.*—For federal tax purposes, the terms *spouse, husband,* and *wife* mean an individual lawfully married to another individual. The term *husband and wife* means two individuals lawfully married to each other.

(b) *Persons who are lawfully married for federal tax purposes.*—(1) *In general.*—Except as provided in paragraph (b)(2) of this section regarding marriages entered into under the laws of a foreign jurisdiction, a marriage of two individuals is recognized for federal tax purposes if the marriage is recognized by the state, possession, or territory of the United States in which the marriage is entered into, regardless of domicile.

(2) *Foreign marriages.*—Two individuals who enter into a relationship denominated as marriage under the laws of a foreign jurisdiction are recognized as married for federal tax purposes if the relationship would be recognized as marriage under the laws of at least one state, possession, or territory of the United States, regardless of domicile.

(c) *Persons who are not lawfully married for federal tax purposes.*—The terms *spouse, husband,* and *wife* do not include individuals who have entered into a registered domestic partnership, civil union, or other similar formal relationship not denominated as a marriage under the law of the state, possession, or territory of the United States where such relationship was entered into, regardless of domicile. The term *husband and wife* does not include couples who have entered into such a formal relationship, and the term *marriage* does not include such formal relationships.

(d) *Applicability date.*—The rules of this section apply to taxable years ending on or after September 2, 2016. [Reg. § 301.7701-18.]

☐ [*T.D.* 9785, 8-31-2016.]

[Reg. § 305.7871-1]

§ 305.7871-1. Indian tribal governments treated as States for certain purposes (Temporary).—(a) *In general.*—An Indian tribal government, as defined in section 7701(a)(40) and the regulations thereunder, shall be treated as a State, and a subdivision of an Indian tribal government, as determined under section 7871(d) and paragraph(e) of this section, shall be treated as a political subdivision of a State, under the following sections and regulations thereunder—

(1) Section 170 (relating to income tax deductions for charitable, etc., contributions and gifts), sections 2055 and 2106(a)(2) (relating to estate tax deductions for transfers of public, charitable and religious uses), and section 2522 (relating to gift tax deductions for charitable and similar gifts), for purposes of determining whether and in what amount any contribution or transfer to or for the use of an Indian tribal government (or subdivision thereof) is deductible;

(2) Section 164 (relating to deductions for taxes);

(3) Section 511 (a)(2)(B) (relating to the taxation of colleges and universities which are agencies or instrumentalities of governments or their political subdivisions);

(4) Section 37(e)(9)(A) (relating to certain public retirement systems);

(5) Section 41(c)(4) (defining "State" for purposes of credit for contributions to candidates for public offices);

(6) Section 117(b)(2)(A) (relating to scholarships and fellowship grants);

(7) Section 403(b)(1)(A)(ii) (relating to the taxation of contributions of certain employers for employee annuities);

(8) Chapter 41 of the Code (relating to tax on excess expenditures to influence legislation); and

(9) Subchapter A of chapter 42 of the Code (relating to private foundations).

(b) *Special rule for excise tax provisions.*—An Indian tribal government shall be treated as a State, and a subdivision of an Indian tribal government shall be treated as a political subdivision of a State, for purposes of any exemption from, credit or refund of, or payment with respect to, an excise tax imposed on a transaction under—

(1) Chapter 31 of the Code (relating to tax on special fuels);

(2) Chapter 32 of the Code (relating to manufacturers excise taxes);

(3) Subchapter B of chapter 33 of the Code (relating to communications excise tax); and

(4) Subchapter D of chapter 36 of the Code (relating to tax on use of certain highway vehicles),

if, in addition to satisfying all requirements applicable to a similar transaction involving a State (or political subdivision thereof) under the Code, the transaction involves the exercise of an essential governmental function of the Indian tribal government, as defined in paragraph (d) of this section.

(c) *Special rule for tax-exempt bonds.*—An Indian tribal government shall be treated as a State and a subdivision of an Indian tribal government shall be treated as a political subdivision of a State for purposes of any obligation issued by such government or subdivision under section 103 (relating to interest on certain governmental obligations) if such obligation is part of an issue substantially all of the proceeds of which are to be used in the exercise of an essential governmental function, as defined in paragraph (d) of this section. For purposes of section 7871 and this section, the "substantially all" test is the same as that provided in § 1.103-8(a)(1)(i). An Indian tribal government shall not be treated as a State and a subdivision of an Indian tribal government shall not be treated as a political subdivision of a State, however, for issues of the following private activity bonds—

(1) An industrial development bond (as defined in section 103(b)(2));

(2) An obligation described in section 103(l)(1)(A) (relating to scholarship bonds); or

(3) A mortgage subsidy bond (as defined in section 103A(b)(1), without regard to section 103A(b)(2)).

(d) *Essential governmental function.*—For purposes of section 7871 and this section, an essential governmental function of an Indian tribal government (or portion thereof) is a function of a type which is—

(1) Eligible for funding under 25 U.S.C. 13 and the regulations thereunder;

(2) Eligible for grants or contracts under 25 U.S.C. 450(f), (g), and (h) and the regulations thereunder; or

(3) An essential governmental function under section 115 and the regulations thereunder when conducted by a State or political subdivision thereof.

(e) *Treatment of subdivisions of Indian tribal governments as political subdivisions.*—A subdivision of an Indian tribal government shall be treated as a political subdivision of a State for purposes of section 7871 and this section if the Internal Revenue Service determines that the subdivision has been delegated the right to exercise one or more of the substantial governmental functions of the Indian tribal government. Designation of a subdivision of an Indian tribal government as a political subdivision of a State will be by revenue procedure. If a subdivision of an Indian tribal government is not currently designated by the applicable revenue procedure as a political subdivision of a State, and such subdivision believes that it qualifies for such designation, the subdivision may apply for a ruling from the Internal Revenue Service. In order to qualify as a political subdivision of a State, for purposes of section

7871 and this section, such subdivision must receive a favorable ruling from the Internal Revenue Service. The request for a ruling shall be made in accordance with all applicable procedural rules set forth in the Statement of Procedural Rules (26 CFR Part 601) and any applicable revenue procedures relating to submission of ruling requests. The request shall be submitted to the Internal Revenue Service, Associate Chief Counsel (Technical), Attention: CC:IND:S, Room 6545, 1111 Constitution Ave., N.W., Washington, D.C. 20224.

(f) *Effective dates.*—(1) *In general.*—Except as provided in paragraph (f)(2) of this section, the provisions of this section are effective after December 31, 1982.

(2) *Specific effective dates.*—Specific provisions of this section are effective as follows:

(i) Provisions relating to Chapter 1 of the Internal Revenue Code of 1954 (other than section 103 and section 37(e)(9)(A)) shall apply to taxable years beginning after December 31, 1982, and before January 1, 1985;

(ii) Provisions relating to section 37(e)(9)(A) shall apply to taxable years beginning after December 31, 1982, and before January 1, 1984;

(iii) Provisions relating to section 103 shall apply to obligations issued after December 31, 1982, and before January 1, 1985;

(iv) Provisions relating to chapter 11 of the Code shall apply to estates of decedents dying after December 31, 1982, and before January 1, 1985;

(v) Provisions relating to chapter 12 of the Code shall apply to gifts made after December 31, 1982, and before January 1, 1985; and

(vi) Provisions relating to taxes imposed by subtitle D of the Code shall take effect on January 1, 1983 and shall cease to apply at the close of December 31, 1984. [Temporary Reg. § 305.7871-1.]

□ [*T.D.* 7952, 5-4-84.]

[Reg. § 1.7872-5]

§ 1.7872-5. Exempted loans.—(a) *In general.*—(1) *General rule.*—Except as provided in paragraph (a)(2) of this section, notwithstanding any other provision of section 7872 and the regulations under that section, section 7872 does not apply to the loans listed in paragraph (b) of this section because the interest arrangements do not have a significant effect on the Federal tax liability of the borrower or the lender.

(2) *No exemption for tax avoidance loans.*—If a taxpayer structures a transaction to be a loan described in paragraph (b) of this section and one of the principal purposes of so structuring the transaction is the avoidance of Federal tax, then the transaction will be recharacterized as a tax avoidance loan as defined in section 7872(c)(1)(D).

(b) *List of exemptions.*—Except as provided in paragraph (a) of this section, the following transactions are exempt from section 7872:

(1) through (15) [Reserved]. For further guidance, see § 1.7872-5T(b)(1) through (15).

(16) An exchange facilitator loan (within the meaning of § 1.468B-6(c)(1)) if the amount of the exchange funds (as defined in § 1.468B-6(b)(2)) treated as loaned does not exceed $2,000,000 and the duration of the loan is 6 months or less. The Commissioner may increase this $2,000,000 loan exemption amount in published guidance of general applicability, see § 601.601(d)(2) of this chapter.

(c) [Reserved]. For further guidance, see § 1.7872-5T(c).

(d) *Effective/applicability date.*—This section applies to exchange facilitator loans issued on or after October 8, 2008. [Reg. § 1.7872-5.]

□ [*T.D.* 9413, 7-9-2008.]

[Reg. § 1.7872-5T]

§ 1.7872-5T. Exempted loans (temporary).—(a) *In general.*—(1) *General rule.*—Except as provided in paragraph (a) (2) of this section, notwithstanding any other provision of section 7872 and the regulations thereunder, section 7872 does not apply to the loans listed in paragraph (b) of this section because the interest arrangements do not have a significant effect on the Federal tax liability of the borrower or the lender.

(2) *No exemption for tax avoidance loans.*—If a taxpayer structures a transaction to be a loan described in paragraph (b) of this section and one of the principal purposes of so structuring the transaction is the avoidance of Federal tax, then the transaction will be recharacterized as a tax avoidance loan as defined in section 7872(c)(1)(D).

(b) *List of exemptions.*—Except as provided in paragraph (a) of this section, the following transactions are exempt from section 7872:

(1) Loans which are made available by the lender to the general public on the same terms and conditions and which are consistent with the lender's customary business practice;

(2) Accounts or withdrawable shares with a bank (as defined in section 581), or an institution to which section 591 applies, or a credit union, made in the ordinary course of its business;

(3) Acquisitions of publicly traded debt obligations for an amount equal to the public trading price at the time of acquisition;

(4) Loans made by a life insurance company (as defined in section 816(a)), in the ordinary course of its business, to an insured, under a loan right contained in a life insurance policy and in which the cash surrender values are used as collateral for the loans;

(5) Loans subsidized by the Federal, State (including the District of Columbia), or Municipal government (or any agency or instrumentality thereof), and which are made available under a program of general application to the public;

(6) Employee-relocation loans that meet the requirements of paragraph (c)(1) of this section;

(7) Obligations the interest on which is excluded from gross income under section 103;

(8) Obligations of the United States government;

(9) Gift loans to a charitable organization (described in section 170(c)), but only if at no time during the taxable year will the aggregate outstanding amount of loans by the lender to that organization exceed $250,000. Charitable organizations which are effectively controlled, within the meaning of section 1.482-1(a)(1), by the same person or persons shall be considered one charitable organization for purposes of this limitation.

(10) Loans made to or from a foreign person that meet the requirements of paragraph (c)(2) of this section;

(11) Loans made by a private foundation or other organization described in section 170(c), the primary purpose of which is to accomplish one or more of the purposes described in section 170(c)(2)(B);

(12) Indebtedness subject to section 482, but such indebtedness is exempt from the application of section 7872 only during the interest-free period, if any, determined under § 1.482-2(a)(1)(iii) with respect to intercompany trade receivables described in § 1.482-2(a)(1)(ii)(A)(*ii*). See also § 1.482-2(a)(3);

(13) All money, securities, and property—

(i) Received by a futures commission merchant or registered broker/dealer or by a clearing organization (A) to margin, guarantee or secure contracts for future delivery on or subject to the rules of a qualified board or exchange (as defined in section 1256(g)(7)), or (B) to purchase, margin, guarantee or secure options contracts traded on or subject to the rules of a qualified board or exchange, so long as the amounts so received to purchase, margin, guarantee or secure such contracts for future delivery or such options contracts are reasonably necessary for such purposes and so long as any commissions received by the futures commission merchant, registered broker/dealer, or clearing organization are not reduced for those making deposits of money, and all money accruing to account holders as the result of such futures and options contracts or

(ii) Received by a clearing organization from a member thereof as a required deposit to a clearing fund, guaranty fund, or similar fund maintained by the clearing organization to protect it against defaults by members.

(14) Loans the interest arrangements of which the taxpayer is able to show have no significant effect of any Federal tax liability of the lender or the borrower, as described in paragraph (c)(3) of this section; and

(15) Loans, described in revenue rulings or revenue procedures issued under section 7872(g)(1)(C), if the Commissioner finds that the factors justifying an exemption for such loans are sufficiently similar to the factors justifying the exemptions contained in this section.

(c) *Special rules.*—(1) *Employee-relocation loans.*—(i) *Mortgage loans.*—In the case of a compensation-related loan to an employee, where such loan is secured by a mortgage on the new principal residence (within the meaning of section 217 and the regulations thereunder) of the employee, acquired in connection with the transfer of that employee to a new principal place of work (which meets the requirements in section 217(c) and the regulations thereunder), the loan will be exempt from section 7872 if the following conditions are satisfied:

(A) The loan is a demand loan or is a term loan the benefits of the interest arrangements of which are not transferable by the employee and are conditioned on the future performance of substantial services by the employee;

(B) The employee certifies to the employer that the employee reasonably expects to be entitled to and will itemize deductions for each year the loan is outstanding; and

(C) The loan agreement requires that the loan proceeds be used only to purchase the new principal residence of the employee.

(ii) *Bridge loans.*—In the case of a compensation-related loan to an employee which is not described in paragraph (c)(1)(i) of this section, and which is used to purchase a new principal residence (within the meaning of section 217 and the regulations thereunder) of the employee acquired in connection with the transfer of that employee to a new principal place of work (which meets the requirements in section 217(c) and the regulations thereunder), the loan will be exempt from section 7872 if the following conditions are satisfied:

(A) The conditions contained in paragraphs (c)(1)(i)(A), (B), and (C) of this section;

(B) The loan agreement provides that the loan is payable in full within 15 days after the date of the sale of the employee's immediately former principal residence;

(C) The aggregate principal amount of all outstanding loans described in this paragraph (c)(1)(ii) to an employee is no greater than the employer's reasonable estimate of the amount of the equity of the employee and the employee's spouse in the employee's immediately former principal residence; and

(D) The employee's immediately former principal residence is not converted to business or investment use.

(2) *Below-market loans involving foreign persons.*—(i) Section 7872 shall not apply to a below-market loan (other than a compensation-related loan or a corporation-shareholder loan where the borrower is a shareholder that is not a C corporation as defined in section 1361(a)(2)) if the lender is a foreign person and the borrower is a U.S. person unless the interest income imputed to the foreign lender (without regard to this paragraph) would be effectively connected with the conduct of a U.S. trade or business within the meaning of section 864(c) and the regulations thereunder and not exempt from U.S. income taxation under an applicable income tax treaty.

(ii) Section 7872 shall not apply to a below-market loan where both the lender and the borrower are foreign persons unless the interest income imputed to the lender (without regard to this paragraph) would be effectively connected with the conduct of a U.S. trade or business within the meaning of section 864(c) and the regulations thereunder and not exempt from U.S. income taxation under an applicable income tax treaty.

(iii) For purposes of this section, the term "foreign person" means any person that is not a U.S. person.

(3) *Loans without significant tax effect.*—Whether a loan will be considered to be a loan the interest arrangements of which have a significant effect on any Federal tax liability of the lender or the borrower will be determined according to all of the facts and circumstances. Among the factors to be considered are—

(i) whether items of income and deduction generated by the loan offset each other;

(ii) the amount of such items;

(iii) the cost to the taxpayer of complying with the provisions of section 7872 if such section were applied; and

(iv) any non-tax reasons for deciding to structure the transaction as a below-market loan rather than a loan with interest at a rate equal to or greater than the applicable Federal rate and a payment by the lender to the borrower. [Temporary Reg. § 1.7872-5T.]

☐ [*T.D.* 8045, 8-15-85. *Amended by T.D.* 8093, 7-9-86 *and T.D.* 8204, 5-20-88.]

[Reg. § 1.7872-15]

§ 1.7872-15. Split-dollar loans.—(a) *General rules.*—(1) *Introduction.*—This section applies to split-dollar loans as defined in paragraph (b)(1) of this section. If a split-dollar loan is not a below-market loan, then, except as provided in this section, the loan is governed by the general rules for debt instruments (including the rules for original issue discount (OID) under sections 1271 through 1275 and the regulations thereunder). If a split-dollar loan is a below-market loan, then, except as provided in this section, the loan is governed by section 7872. The timing, amount, and characterization of the imputed transfers between the lender and borrower of a below-market split-dollar loan depend upon the relationship between the parties and upon whether the loan is a demand loan or a term loan. For additional rules relating to the treatment of split-dollar life insurance arrangements, see § 1.61-22.

(2) *Loan treatment.*—(i) *General rule.*—A payment made pursuant to a split-dollar life insurance arrangement is treated as a loan for Federal tax purposes, and the owner and non-owner are treated, respectively, as the borrower and the lender, if—

(A) The payment is made either directly or indirectly by the non-owner to the owner (including a premium payment made by the non-owner directly or indirectly to the insurance company with respect to the policy held by the owner);

(B) The payment is a loan under general principles of Federal tax law or, if it is not a loan under general principles of Federal tax law (for example, because of the nonrecourse nature of the obligation or otherwise), a reasonable person nevertheless would expect the payment to be repaid in full to the non-owner (whether with or without interest); and

(C) The repayment is to be made from, or is secured by, the policy's death benefit proceeds, the policy's cash surrender value, or both.

(ii) *Payments that are only partially repayable.*—For purposes of § 1.61-22 and this section, if a non-owner makes a payment pursuant to a split-dollar life insurance arrangement and the non-owner is entitled to repayment of some but not all of the payment, the payment is treated as two payments: one that is repayable and one that is not. Thus, paragraph (a)(2)(i) of this section refers to the repayable payment.

(iii) *Treatment of payments that are not split-dollar loans.*—See § 1.61-22(b)(5) for the treatment of payments by a non-owner that are not split-dollar loans.

(iv) *Examples.*—The provisions of this paragraph (a)(2) are illustrated by the following examples:

Example 1. Assume an employee owns a life insurance policy under a split-dollar life insurance arrangement, the employer makes premium payments on this policy, there is a reasonable expectation that the payments will be repaid, and the repayments are secured by the policy. Under paragraph (a)(2)(i) of this section, each premium payment is a loan for Federal tax purposes.

Example 2. (i) Assume an employee owns a life insurance policy under a split-dollar life insurance arrangement and the employer makes premium payments on this policy. The employer is entitled to be repaid 80 percent of each premium payment, and the repayments are secured by the policy. Under paragraph (a)(2)(ii) of this section, the taxation of 20 percent of each premium payment is governed by § 1.61-22(b)(5). If there is a reasonable expectation that the remaining 80 percent of a payment will be repaid in full, then, under paragraph (a)(2)(i) of this section, the 80 percent is a loan for Federal tax purposes.

(ii) If less than 80 percent of a premium payment is reasonably expected to be repaid, then this paragraph (a)(2) does not cause any of the payment to be a loan for Federal tax purposes. If the payment is not a loan under general principles of Federal tax law, the taxation of the entire premium payment is governed by § 1.61-22(b)(5).

(3) *No de minimis exceptions.*—For purposes of this section, section 7872 is applied to a split-dollar loan without regard to the de minimis exceptions in section 7872(c)(2) and (3).

(4) *Certain interest provisions disregarded.*—(i) *In general.*—If a split-dollar loan provides for the payment of interest and all or a portion of the interest is to be paid directly or indirectly by the lender (or a person related to the lender), then the requirement to pay the interest (or portion thereof) is disregarded for purposes of this section. All of the facts and circumstances determine whether a payment to be made by the lender (or a person related to the lender) is sufficiently independent from the split-dollar loan for the payment to not be an indirect payment of the interest (or a portion thereof) by the lender (or a person related to the lender).

(ii) *Examples.*—The provisions of this paragraph (a)(4) are illustrated by the following examples:

Example 1—(i) On January 1, 2009, Employee *B* issues a split-dollar term loan to Employer *Y*. The split-dollar term loan provides for five percent interest, compounded annually. Interest and principal on the split-dollar term loan are due at maturity. On January 1, 2009, *B* and *Y* also enter into a fully vested non-qualified deferred compensation arrangement that will provide a payment to *B* in an amount equal to the accrued but unpaid interest due at the maturity of the split-dollar term loan.

(ii) Under paragraph (a)(4)(i) of this section, *B*'s requirement to pay interest on the split-dollar term loan is disregarded for purposes of this section, and the split-dollar term loan is treated as a loan that does not provide for interest for purposes of this section.

Example 2—(i) On January 1, 2004, Employee *B* and Employer *Y* enter into a fully vested non-qualified deferred compensation arrangement that will provide a payment to *B* equal to *B*'s salary in the three years preceding the retirement of *B*. On January 1, 2009, *B* and *Y* enter into a split-dollar life insurance arrangement and, under the arrangement, *B* issues a split-dollar term loan to *Y* on that date. The split-dollar term loan provides for five percent interest, compounded annually. Interest and principal on the split-dollar term loan are due at maturity. Over the period in which the non-qualified deferred compensation arrangement is effective, the terms and conditions of *B*'s non-qualified deferred compensation arrangement do not change in a way that indicates that the payment of the non-qualified deferred compensation is related to *B*'s requirement to pay interest on the split-dollar term loan. No other facts and circumstances exist to indicate that the payment of the non-qualified deferred compensation is related to *B*'s requirement to pay interest on the split-dollar term loan.

(ii) The facts and circumstances indicate that the payment by *Y* of non-qualified deferred compensation is independent from *B*'s requirement to pay interest under the split-dollar term loan. Under paragraph (a)(4)(i) of this section, the fully vested non-qualified deferred compensation does not cause *B*'s requirement to pay interest on the split-dollar term loan to be disregarded for purposes of this section. For purposes of this section, the split-dollar term loan is treated as a loan that provides for stated interest of five percent, compounded annually.

(b) *Definitions.*—For purposes of this section, the terms *split-dollar life insurance arrangement*, *owner*, and *non-owner* have the same meanings as provided in §1.61-22(b) and (c). In addition, the following definitions apply for purposes of this section:

(1) A *split-dollar loan* is a loan described in paragraph (a)(2)(i) of this section.

(2) A *split-dollar demand loan* is any split-dollar loan that is payable in full at any time on the demand of the lender (or within a reasonable time after the lender's demand).

(3) A *split-dollar term loan* is any split-dollar loan other than a split-dollar demand loan. See paragraph (e)(5) of this section for special rules regarding certain split-dollar term loans payable on the death of an individual, certain split-dollar term loans conditioned on the future performance of substantial services by an individual, and gift split-dollar term loans.

(c) *Interest deductions for split-dollar loans.*—The borrower may not deduct any qualified stated interest, OID, or imputed interest on a split-dollar loan. See sections 163(h) and 264(a). In certain circumstances, an indirect participant may be allowed to deduct qualified stated interest, OID, or imputed interest on a deemed loan. See paragraph (e)(2)(iii) of this section (relating to indirect loans).

(d) *Treatment of split-dollar loans providing for nonrecourse payments.*—(1) *In general.*—Except as provided in paragraph (d)(2) of this section, if a payment on a split-dollar loan is nonrecourse to the borrower, the payment is a contingent payment for purposes of this section. See paragraph (j) of this section for the treatment of a split-dollar loan that provides for one or more contingent payments.

(2) *Exception for certain loans with respect to which the parties to the split-dollar life insurance arrangement make a representation.*—(i) *Requirement.*—An otherwise noncontingent payment on a split-dollar loan that is nonrecourse to the borrower is not a contingent payment under this section if the parties to the split-dollar life insurance arrangement represent in writing that a reasonable person would expect that all payments under the loan will be made.

(ii) *Time and manner for providing written representation.*—The Commissioner may prescribe the time and manner for providing the written representation required by paragraph (d)(2)(i) of this section. Until the Commissioner prescribes otherwise, the written representation that is required by paragraph (d)(2)(i) of this section must meet the requirements of this paragraph (d)(2)(ii). Both the borrower and the lender must sign the representation not later than the last day (including extensions) for filing the Federal income tax return of the borrower or lender, whichever is earlier, for the taxable year in which the lender makes the first split-dollar loan under the split-dollar life insurance arrangement. This representation must include the names, addresses, and taxpayer identification numbers of the borrower, lender, and any indirect participants. Unless otherwise stated therein, this representation applies to all subsequent split-dollar loans made pursuant to the split-dollar life insurance arrangement. Each party should retain an original of the representation as part of its books and records and should attach a copy of this representation to its Federal income tax return for any taxable year in which the lender makes a loan to which the representation applies.

(e) *Below-market split-dollar loans.*—(1) *Scope.*—(i) *In general.*—This paragraph (e) applies to below-market split-dollar loans enumerated under section 7872(c)(1), which include gift loans, compensation-related loans, and corporation-shareholder loans. The characterization of a split-dollar loan under section 7872(c)(1) and of the imputed transfers under section 7872(a)(1) and (b)(1) depends upon the relationship between the lender and the borrower or the lender, borrower, and any indirect participant. For example, if the lender is the borrower's employer, the split-dollar loan is generally a compensation-related loan, and any imputed transfer from the lender to the borrower is generally a payment of compensation. The loans covered by this paragraph (e) include indirect loans between the parties. See paragraph (e)(2) of this section for the treatment of certain indirect split-dollar loans. See paragraph (f) of this section for the treatment of any stated interest or OID on split-dollar loans. See paragraph (j) of this section for additional rules that apply to a split-dollar loan that provides for one or more contingent payments.

(ii) *Significant-effect split-dollar loans.*—If a direct or indirect below-market split-dollar loan is not enumerated in section 7872(c)(1)(A), (B), or (C), the loan is a significanteffect loan under section 7872(c)(1)(E).

(2) *Indirect split-dollar loans.*—(i) *In general.*—If, based on all the facts and circumstances, including the relationship between the borrower or lender and some third person (the indirect participant), the effect of a below-market split-dollar loan is to transfer value from the lender to the indirect participant and from the indirect participant to the borrower, then the below-market split-dollar loan is restructured as two or more successive below-market loans (the deemed loans) as provided in this paragraph (e)(2). The transfers of value described in the preceding sentence include (but are not limited to) a gift, compensation, a capital contribution, and a distribution under section 301 (or, in the case of an S corporation, under section 1368). The deemed loans are—

(A) A deemed below-market split-dollar loan made by the lender to the indirect participant; and

(B) A deemed below-market split-dollar loan made by the indirect participant to the borrower.

(ii) *Application.*—Each deemed loan is treated as having the same provisions as the original loan between the lender and borrower, and section 7872 is applied to each deemed loan. Thus, for example, if, under a split-dollar life insurance arrangement, an employer (lender) makes an interest-free split-dollar loan to an employee's child (borrower), the loan is restructured as a deemed compensation-related below-market split-dollar loan from the lender to the employee (the indirect participant) and a second deemed gift below-market split-dollar loan from the employee to the employee's child. In appropriate circumstances, section 7872(d)(1) may limit the interest that accrues on a deemed loan for Federal income tax purposes. For loan arrangements between husband and wife, see section 7872(f)(7).

(iii) *Limitations on investment interest for purposes of section 163(d).*—For purposes of section 163(d), the imputed interest from the indirect participant to the lender that is taken into account by the indirect participant under this paragraph (e)(2) is not investment interest to the extent of the excess, if any, of—

(A) The imputed interest from the indirect participant to the lender that is taken into account by the indirect participant; over

(B) The imputed interest to the indirect participant from the borrower that is recognized by the indirect participant.

(iv) *Examples.*—The provisions of this paragraph (e)(2) are illustrated by the following examples:

Example 1. (i) On January 1, 2009, Employer *X* and Individual *A* enter into a split-dollar life insurance arrangement under which *A* is named as the policy owner. *A* is the child of *B*, an employee of *X*. On January 1, 2009, *X* makes a $30,000 premium payment, repayable upon demand without interest. Repayment of the premium payment is fully recourse to *A*. The payment is a below-market split-dollar demand loan. *A*'s net investment income for 2009 is $1,100, and there are no other outstanding loans between *A* and *B*. Assume that the blended annual rate for 2009 is 5 percent, compounded annually.

(ii) Based on the relationships among the parties, the effect of the below-market split-dollar loan from *X* to *A* is to transfer value from *X* to *B* and then to transfer value from *B* to *A*. Under paragraph (e)(2) of this section, the below-market split-dollar loan from *X* to *A* is restructured as two deemed below-market split-dollar demand loans: a compensation-related below-market split-dollar loan between *X* and *B* and a gift below-market split-dollar loan between *B* and *A*. Each of the deemed loans has the same terms and conditions as the original loan.

(iii) Under paragraph (e)(3) of this section, the amount of forgone interest deemed paid to *B* by *A* in 2009 is $1,500 ([$30,000 × 0.05] – 0). Under section 7872(d)(1), however, the amount of forgone interest deemed paid to *B* by *A* is limited to $1,100 (*A*'s net investment income for the year). Under paragraph (e)(2)(iii) of this section, *B*'s deduction under section 163(d) in 2009 for interest deemed paid on *B*'s deemed loan from *X* is limited to $1,100 (the interest deemed received from *A*).

Example 2. (i) The facts are the same as the facts in *Example 1*, except that *T*, an irrevocable life insurance trust established for the benefit of *A* (*B*'s child), is named as the policy owner. *T* is not a grantor trust.

(ii) Based on the relationships among the parties, the effect of the below-market split-dollar loan from X to *T* is to transfer value from *X* to *B* and then to transfer value from *B* to *T*. Under paragraph (e)(2) of this section, the below-market split-dollar loan from *X* to *T* is restructured as two deemed below-market split-dollar demand loans: a compensation-related below-market split-dollar loan between *X* and *B* and a gift below-market split-dollar loan between *B* and *T*. Each of the deemed loans has the same terms and conditions as the original loan.

(iii) Under paragraph (e)(3) of this section, the amount of forgone interest deemed paid to *B* by *T* in 2009 is $1,500 ([$30,000 × 0.05] − 0). Section 7872(d)(1) does not apply because *T* is not an individual. The amount of forgone interest deemed paid to *B* by *T* is $1,500. Under paragraph (e)(2)(iii) of this section, *B*'s deduction under section 163(d) in 2009 for interest deemed paid on *B*'s deemed loan from *X* is $1,500 (the interest deemed received from *T*).

(3) *Split-dollar demand loans.*—(i) *In general.*—This paragraph (e)(3) provides rules for testing split-dollar demand loans for sufficient interest, and, if the loans do not provide for sufficient interest, rules for the calculation and treatment of forgone interest on these loans. See paragraph (g) of this section for additional rules that apply to a split-dollar loan providing for certain variable rates of interest.

(ii) *Testing for sufficient interest.*—Each calendar year that a split-dollar demand loan is outstanding, the loan is tested to determine if the loan provides for sufficient interest. A split-dollar demand loan provides for sufficient interest for the calendar year if the rate (based on annual compounding) at which interest accrues on the loan's adjusted issue price during the year is no lower than the blended annual rate for the year. (The Internal Revenue Service publishes the blended annual rate in the Internal Revenue Bulletin in July of each year (see § 601.601(d)(2)(ii) of this chapter).) If the loan does not provide for sufficient interest, the loan is a below-market split-dollar demand loan for that calendar year. See paragraph (e)(3)(iii) of this section to determine the amount and treatment of forgone interest for each calendar year the loan is below-market.

(iii) *Imputations.*—(A) *Amount of forgone interest.*—For each calendar year, the amount of forgone interest on a split-dollar demand loan is treated as transferred by the lender to the borrower and as retransferred as interest by the borrower to the lender. This amount is the excess of—

(1) The amount of interest that would have been payable on the loan for the calendar year if interest accrued on the loan's adjusted issue price at the blended annual rate (determined in paragraph (e)(3)(ii) of this section) and were payable annually on the day referred to in paragraph (e)(3)(iii)(B) of this section; over

(2) Any interest that accrues on the loan during the year.

(B) *Timing of transfers of forgone interest.*—*(1) In general.*—Except as provided in paragraphs (e)(3)(iii)(B)(*2*) and (*3*) of this section, the forgone interest (as determined under paragraph (e)(3)(iii)(A) of this section) that is attributable to a calendar year is treated as transferred by the lender to the borrower (and retransferred as interest by the borrower to the lender) on the last day of the calendar year and is accounted for by each party to the split-dollar loan in a manner consistent with that party's method of accounting.

(2) Exception for death, liquidation, or termination of the borrower.—In the taxable year in which the borrower dies (in the case of a borrower who is a natural person) or is liquidated or otherwise terminated (in the case of a borrower other than a natural person), any forgone interest is treated, for both the lender and the borrower, as transferred and retransferred on the last day of the borrower's final taxable year.

(3) Exception for repayment of below-market split-dollar loan.—Any forgone interest is treated, for both the lender and the borrower, as transferred and retransferred on the day the split-dollar loan is repaid in full.

(4) *Split-dollar term loans.*—(i) *In general.*—Except as provided in paragraph (e)(5) of this section, this paragraph (e)(4) provides rules for testing split-dollar term loans for sufficient interest and, if the loans do not provide for sufficient interest, rules for imputing payments on these loans. See paragraph (g) of this section for additional rules that apply to a split-dollar loan providing for certain variable rates of interest.

(ii) *Testing a split-dollar term loan for sufficient interest.*—A split-dollar term loan is tested on the day the loan is made to determine if the loan provides for sufficient interest. A split-dollar term loan provides for sufficient interest if the imputed loan amount equals or exceeds the amount loaned. The imputed loan amount is the present value of all payments due under the loan, determined as of the date the loan is made, using a discount rate equal to the AFR in effect on that date. The AFR used for purposes of the preceding sentence must be appropriate for the loan's term (short-term, mid-term, or long-term) and for the compounding period used in computing the present value. See section 1274(d)(1). If the split-dollar loan does not provide for sufficient interest, the loan is a below-market split-dollar term loan subject to paragraph (e)(4)(iv) of this section.

(iii) *Determining loan term.*—This paragraph (e)(4)(iii) provides rules to determine the term of a split-dollar term loan for purposes of paragraph (e)(4)(ii) of this section. The term of the loan determined under this paragraph (e)(4)(iii) (other than paragraph (e)(4)(iii)(C) of this section) applies to determine the split-dollar loan's term, payment schedule, and yield for all purposes of this section.

(A) *In general.*—Except as provided in paragraph (e)(4)(iii)(B), (C), (D) or (E) of this section, the term of a split-dollar term loan is based on the period from the date the loan is made until the loan's stated maturity date.

(B) *Special rules for certain options.*—*(1) Payment schedule that minimizes yield.*—If a split-dollar term loan is subject to one or more unconditional options that are exercisable at one or more times during the term of the loan and that, if exercised, require payments to be made on the split-dollar loan on an alternative payment schedule (for example, an option to extend or an option to call a split-dollar loan), then the rules of this paragraph (e)(4)(iii)(B)(*1*) determine the term of the loan. However, this paragraph (e)(4)(iii)(B)(*1*) applies only if the timing and amounts of the payments that comprise each payment schedule are known as of the issue date. For purposes of determining a split-dollar loan's term, the borrower is projected to exercise or not exercise an option or combination of options in a manner that minimizes the loan's overall yield. Similarly, the lender is projected to exercise or not exercise an option or combination of options in a manner that minimizes the loan's overall yield. If different projected patterns of exercise or non-exercise produce the same minimum yield, the parties are projected to exercise or not exercise an option or combination of options in a manner that produces the longest term.

(2) Change in circumstances.—If the borrower (or lender) does or does not exercise the option as projected under paragraph (e)(4)(iii)(B)(*1*) of this section, the split-dollar loan is treated for purposes of this section as retired and reissued on the date the option is or is not exercised for an amount of cash equal to the loan's adjusted issue price on that date. The reissued loan must be retested using the appropriate AFR in effect on the date of reissuance to determine whether it is a below-market loan.

(3) Examples.—The following examples illustrate the rules of this paragraph (e)(4)(iii)(B):

Example 1. Employee *B* issues a 10-year split-dollar term loan to Employer *Y*. *B* has the right to prepay the loan at the end of year 5. Interest is payable on the split-dollar loan at 1 percent for the first 5 years and at 10 percent for the remaining 5 years. Under paragraph (e)(4)(iii)(B)(*1*) of this section, this arrangement is treated as a 5-year split-dollar term loan from *Y* to *B*, with interest payable at 1 percent.

Example 2. The facts are the same as the facts in *Example 1*, except that *B* does not in fact prepay the split-dollar loan at the end of year 5. Under paragraph (e)(4)(iii)(B)(*2*) of this section, the first loan is treated as retired at the end of year 5 and a new 5-year split-dollar term loan is issued at that time, with interest payable at 10 percent.

Example 3. Employee *A* issues a 10-year split-dollar term loan on which the lender, Employer *X*, has the right to demand payment at the end of year 2. Interest is payable on the split-dollar loan at 7 percent each year that the loan is outstanding. Under paragraph (e)(4)(iii)(B)(*1*) of this section, this arrangement is treated as a 10-year split-dollar term loan because the exercise of *X*'s put option would not reduce the yield of the loan (the yield of the loan is 7 percent, compounded annually, whether or not *X* demands payment).

(C) *Split-dollar term loans providing for certain variable rates of interest.*—If a split-dollar term loan is subject to paragraph (g) of this section (a split-dollar loan that provides for certain variable rates of interest), the term of the loan for purposes of paragraph (e)(4)(ii) of this section is determined under paragraph (g)(3)(ii) of this section.

(D) *Split-dollar loans payable upon the death of an individual.*—If a split-dollar term loan is described in paragraph (e)(5)(ii)(A) or (v)(A) of this section, the term of the loan for purposes of paragraph (e)(4)(ii) of this section is determined under paragraph (e)(5)(ii)(C) or (v)(B)(*2*) of this section, whichever is applicable.

(E) *Split-dollar loans conditioned on the future performance of substantial services by an individual.*—If a split-dollar term loan is described in paragraph (e)(5)(iii)(A)(*1*) or (v)(A) of this section, the term of the loan for purposes of paragraph (e)(4)(ii) of this section is determined under paragraph (e)(5)(iii)(C) or (v)(B)(*2*) of this section, whichever is applicable.

(iv) *Timing and amount of imputed transfer in connection with below-market split-dollar term loans.*—If a split-dollar term loan is a below-market loan, then the rules applicable to below-market term loans under section 7872 apply. In general, the loan is recharacterized as consisting of two portions: an imputed loan amount (as defined in paragraph (e)(4)(ii) of this section) and an imputed transfer from the lender to the borrower. The imputed transfer occurs at the time the loan is made (for example, when the lender makes a premium payment on a life insurance policy) and is equal to the excess of the amount loaned over the imputed loan amount.

(v) *Amount treated as OID.*—In the case of any below-market split-dollar term loan described in this paragraph (e)(4), for purposes of applying sections 1271 through 1275 and the regulations thereunder, the issue price of the loan is the amount determined under § 1.1273-2, reduced by the amount of the imputed transfer described in paragraph (e)(4)(iv) of this section.

Thus, the loan is generally treated as having OID in an amount equal to the amount of the imputed transfer described in paragraph (e)(4)(iv) of this section, in addition to any other OID on the loan (determined without regard to section 7872(b)(2)(A) or this paragraph (e)(4)).

(vi) *Example.*—The provisions of this paragraph (e)(4) are illustrated by the following example:

Example. (i) On July 1, 2009, Corporation Z and Shareholder *A* enter into a split-dollar life insurance arrangement under which *A* is named as the policy owner. On July 1, 2009, *Z* makes a $100,000 premium payment, repayable without interest in 15 years. Repayment of the premium payment is fully recourse to *A*. The premium payment is a split-dollar term loan. Assume the long-term AFR (based on annual compounding) at the time the loan is made is 7 percent.

(ii) Based on a 15-year term and a discount rate of 7 percent, compounded annually (the long-term AFR), the present value of the payments under the loan is $36,244.60, determined as follows: $100,000/[1+(0.07/1)]^{15}. This loan is a below-market split-dollar term loan because the imputed loan amount of $36,244.60 (the present value of the amount required to be repaid to Z) is less than the amount loaned ($100,000).

(iii) In accordance with section 7872(b)(1) and paragraph (e)(4)(iv) of this section, on the date that the loan is made, *Z* is treated as transferring to *A* $63,755.40 (the excess of $100,000 (amount loaned) over $36,244.60 (imputed loan amount)). Under section 7872 and paragraph (e)(1)(i) of this section, *Z* is treated as making a section 301 distribution to *A* on July 1, 2009, of $63,755.40. *Z* must take into account as OID an amount equal to the imputed transfer. See § 1.1272-1 for the treatment of OID.

(5) *Special rules for certain split-dollar term loans.*—(i) *In general.*—This paragraph (e)(5) provides rules for split-dollar loans payable on the death of an individual, split-dollar loans conditioned on the future performance of substantial services by an individual, and gift term loans. These split-dollar loans are split-dollar term loans for purposes of determining whether the loan provides for sufficient interest. If, however, the loan is a below-market split-dollar loan, then, except as provided in paragraph (e)(5)(v) of this section, forgone interest is determined annually, similar to a demand loan, but using an AFR that is appropriate for the loan's term and that is determined when the loan is issued.

(ii) *Split-dollar loans payable not later than the death of an individual.*—(A) *Applicability.*—This paragraph (e)(5)(ii) applies to a split-dollar term loan payable not later than the death of an individual.

(B) *Treatment of loan.*—A split-dollar loan described in paragraph (e)(5)(ii)(A) of this section is tested under paragraph (e)(4)(ii) of this section to determine if the loan provides for sufficient interest. If the loan provides for sufficient interest, then section 7872 does not apply to the loan, and the interest on the loan is taken into account under paragraph (f) of this section. If the loan does not provide for sufficient interest, then section 7872 applies to the loan, and the loan is treated as a below-market demand loan subject to paragraph (e)(3)(iii) of this section. For each year that the loan is outstanding, however, the rate used in the determination of forgone interest under paragraph (e)(3)(iii) of this section is not the blended annual rate but rather is the AFR (based on annual compounding) appropriate for the loan's term as of the month in which the loan is made. See paragraph (e)(5)(ii)(C) of this section to determine the loan's term.

(C) *Term of loan.*—For purposes of paragraph (e)(5)(ii)(B) of this section, the term of a split-dollar loan payable on the death of an individual (including the death of the last survivor of a group of individuals) is the individual's life expectancy as determined under the appropriate table in § 1.72-9 on the day the loan is made. If a split-dollar loan is payable on the earlier of the individual's death or another term determined under paragraph (e)(4)(iii) of this section, the term of the loan is whichever term is shorter.

(D) *Retirement and reissuance of loan.*—If a split-dollar loan described in paragraph (e)(5)(ii)(A) of this section remains outstanding longer than the term determined under paragraph (e)(5)(ii)(C) of this section because the individual outlived his or her life expectancy, the split-dollar loan is treated for purposes of this section as retired and reissued as a split-dollar demand loan at that time for an amount of cash equal to the loan's adjusted issue price on that date. However, the loan is not retested at that time to determine whether the loan provides for sufficient interest. For purposes of determining forgone interest under paragraph (e)(5)(ii)(B) of this section, the appropriate AFR for the reissued loan is the AFR determined under paragraph (e)(5)(ii)(B) of this section on the day the loan was originally made.

(iii) *Split-dollar loans conditioned on the future performance of substantial services by an individual.*—(A) *Applicability.*—*(1) In general.*—This paragraph (e)(5)(iii) applies to a split-dollar term loan if the benefits of the interest arrangements of the loan are not transferable and are conditioned on the future performance of substantial services (within the meaning of section 83) by an individual.

(2) Exception.—Notwithstanding paragraph (e)(5)(iii)(A)(*1*) of this section, this paragraph (e)(5)(iii) does not apply to a split-dollar loan described in paragraph (e)(5)(v)(A) of this section (regarding a split-dollar loan that is payable on the later of a term certain and the date on which the condition to perform substantial future services by an individual ends).

(B) *Treatment of loan.*—A split-dollar loan described in paragraph (e)(5)(iii)(A)(*1*) of this section is tested under paragraph (e)(4)(ii) of this section to determine if the loan provides for sufficient interest. Except as provided in paragraph (e)(5)(iii)(D) of this section, if the loan provides for sufficient interest, then section 7872 does not apply to the loan and the interest on the loan is taken into account under paragraph (f) of this section. If the loan does not provide for sufficient interest, then section 7872 applies to the loan and the loan is treated as a below-market demand loan subject to paragraph (e)(3)(iii) of this section. For each year that the loan is outstanding, however, the rate used in the determination of forgone interest under paragraph (e)(3)(iii) of this section is not the blended annual rate but rather is the AFR (based on annual compounding) appropriate for the loan's term as of the month in which the loan is made. See paragraph (e)(5)(iii)(C) of this section to determine the loan's term.

(C) *Term of loan.*—The term of a split-dollar loan described in paragraph (e)(5)(iii)(A)(*1)* of this section is based on the period from the date the loan is made until the loan's stated maturity date. However, if a split-dollar loan described in paragraph (e)(5)(iii)(A)(*1*) of this section does not have a stated maturity date, the term of the loan is presumed to be seven years.

(D) *Retirement and reissuance of loan.*—If a split-dollar loan described in paragraph (e)(5)(iii)(A)(*1*) of this section remains outstanding longer than the term determined under paragraph (e)(5)(iii)(C) of this section because of the continued performance of substantial services, the split-dollar loan is treated for purposes of this section as retired and reissued as a split-dollar demand loan at that time for an amount of cash equal to the loan's adjusted issue price on that date. The loan is retested at that time to determine whether the loan provides for sufficient interest.

(iv) *Gift split-dollar term loans.*—(A) *Applicability.*—This paragraph (e)(5)(iv) applies to gift split-dollar term loans.

(B) *Treatment of loan.*—A split-dollar loan described in paragraph (e)(5)(iv)(A) of this section is tested under paragraph (e)(4)(ii) of this section to determine if the loan provides for sufficient interest. If the loan provides for sufficient interest, then section 7872 does not apply to the loan and the interest on the loan is taken into account under paragraph (f) of this section. If the loan does not provide for sufficient interest, then section 7872 applies to the loan and the loan is treated as a below-market demand loan subject to paragraph (e)(3)(iii) of this section. For each year that the loan is outstanding, however, the rate used in the determination of forgone interest under paragraph (e)(3)(iii) of this section is not the blended annual rate but rather is the AFR (based on annual compounding) appropriate for the loan's term as of the month in which the loan is made. See paragraph (e)(5)(iv)(C) of this section to determine the loan's term.

(C) *Term of loan.*—For purposes of paragraph (e)(5)(iv)(B) of this section, the term of a gift split-dollar term loan is the term determined under paragraph (e)(4)(iii) of this section.

(D) *Limited application for gift split-dollar term loans.*—The rules of paragraph (e)(5)(iv)(B) of this section apply to a gift split-dollar term loan only for Federal income tax purposes. For purposes of Chapter 12 of the Internal Revenue Code (relating to the gift tax), gift below-market split-dollar term loans are treated as term loans under section 7872(b) and paragraph (e)(4) of this section. See section 7872(d)(2).

(v) *Split-dollar loans payable on the later of a term certain and another specified date.*—(A) *Applicability.*—This paragraph (e)(5)(v) applies to any split-dollar term loan payable upon the later of a term certain or—

(1) The death of an individual; or

(2) For a loan described in paragraph (e)(5)(iii)(A)(*1*) of this section, the date on which the condition to perform substantial future services by an individual ends.

(B) *Treatment of loan.*—*(1) In general.*—A split-dollar loan described in paragraph (e)(5)(v)(A) of this section is a split-dollar term loan, subject to paragraph (e)(4) of this section.

(2) Term of the loan.—The term of a split-dollar loan described in paragraph (e)(5)(v)(A) of this section is the term certain.

(3) Appropriate AFR.—The appropriate AFR for a split-dollar loan described in paragraph (e)(5)(v)(A) of this section is based on a term of the longer of the term certain or the loan's expected term as determined under either paragraph (e)(5)(ii) or (iii) of this section, whichever is applicable.

(C) *Retirement and reissuance.*—If a split-dollar loan described in paragraph (e)(5)(v)(A) of this section remains outstanding longer than the term certain, the split-dollar loan is treated for purposes of this section as retired and reissued at the end of the term certain for an amount of cash equal to the loan's adjusted issue price on that date. The reissued loan is subject to paragraph (e)(5)(ii) or (iii) of this section, whichever is applicable. However, the loan is not retested at that time to determine whether the loan provides for sufficient interest. For purposes of paragraph (e)(3)(iii) of this section, the appropriate AFR for the reissued loan is the AFR determined under paragraph (e)(5)(v)(B)(*3*) of this section on the day the loan was originally made.

(vi) *Example.*—The provisions of this paragraph (e)(5) are illustrated by the following example:

Example. (i) On January 1, 2009, Corporation *Y* and Shareholder *B*, a 65 year-old male, enter into a split-dollar life insurance arrangement under which *B* is named as the policy owner. On January 1, 2009, *Y* makes a $100,000 premium payment, repayable, without interest, from the death benefits of the underlying contract upon *B*'s death. The premium payment is a split-dollar term loan. Repayment of the premium payment is fully recourse to *B*. Assume the long-term AFR (based on annual compounding) at the time of the loan is 7 percent.

Both *Y* and *B* use the calendar year as their taxable years.

(ii) Based on Table 1 in § 1.72-9, the expected term of the loan is 15 years. Under paragraph (e)(5)(ii)(C) of this section, the long-term AFR (based on annual compounding) is the appropriate test rate. Based on a 15-year term and a discount rate of 7 percent, compounded annually (the long-term AFR), the present value of the payments under the loan is $36,244.60, determined as follows: $100,000/[1+(0.07/1)]^{15}$. Under paragraph (e)(5)(ii)(B) of this section, this loan is a below-market split-dollar term loan because the imputed loan amount of $36,244.60 (the present value of the amount required to be repaid to *Y*) is less than the amount loaned ($100,000).

(iii) Under paragraph (e)(5)(ii)(B) of this section, the amount of forgone interest for 2009 (and each subsequent full calendar year that the loan remains outstanding) is $7,000, which is the amount of interest that would have been payable on the loan for the calendar year if interest accrued on the loan's adjusted issue price ($100,000) at the long-term AFR (7 percent, compounded annually). Under section 7872 and paragraph (e)(1)(i) of this section, on December 31, 2009, *Y* is treated as making a section 301 distribution to *B* of $7,000. In addition, *Y* has $7,000 of imputed interest income for 2009.

(f) *Treatment of stated interest and OID for split-dollar loans.*—(1) *In general.*—If a split-dollar loan provides for stated interest or OID, the loan is subject to this paragraph (f), regardless of whether the split-dollar loan has sufficient interest. Except as otherwise provided in this section, split-dollar loans are subject to the same Internal Revenue Code and regulatory provisions for stated interest and OID as other loans. For example, the lender of a split-dollar loan that provides for stated interest must account for any qualified stated interest (as defined in § 1.1273-1(c)) under its regular method of accounting (for example, an accrual method or the cash receipts and disbursements method). See § 1.446-2 to determine the amount of qualified stated interest that accrues during an accrual period. In addition, the lender must account under § 1.1272-1 for any OID on a split-dollar loan. However, § 1.1272-1(c) does not apply to any split-dollar loan. See paragraph (h) of this section for a subsequent waiver, cancellation, or forgiveness of stated interest on a split-dollar loan.

(2) *Term, payment schedule, and yield.*—The term of a split-dollar term loan determined under paragraph (e)(4)(iii) of this section (other than paragraph (e)(4)(iii)(C) of this section) applies to determine the split-dollar loan's term, payment schedule, and yield for all purposes of this section.

(g) *Certain variable rates of interest.*—(1) *In general.*—This paragraph (g) provides rules for a split-dollar loan that provides for certain variable rates of interest. If this paragraph (g) does not apply to a variable rate split-dollar loan, the loan is subject to the rules in paragraph (j) of this section for split-dollar loans that provide for one or more contingent payments.

(2) *Applicability.*—(i) *In general.*—Except as provided in paragraph (g)(2)(ii) of this section, this paragraph (g) applies to a split-dollar loan that is a variable rate debt instrument (within the meaning of § 1.1275-5) and that provides for stated interest at a qualified floating rate (or rates).

(ii) *Interest rate restrictions.*—This paragraph (g) does not apply to a split-dollar loan if, as a result of interest rate restrictions (such as an interest rate cap), the expected yield of the loan taking the restrictions into account is significantly less than the expected yield of the loan without regard to the restrictions. Conversely, if reasonably symmetric interest rate caps and floors or reasonably symmetric governors are fixed throughout the term of the loan, these restrictions generally do not prevent this paragraph (g) from applying to the loan.

(3) *Testing for sufficient interest.*—(i) *Demand loan.*—For purposes of paragraph (e)(3)(ii) of this section (regarding testing a split-dollar demand loan for sufficient interest), a split-dollar demand loan is treated as if it provided for a fixed rate of interest for each accrual period to which a qualified floating rate applies. The projected fixed rate for each accrual period is the value of the qualified floating rate as of the beginning of the calendar year that contains the last day of the accrual period.

(ii) *Term loan.*—For purposes of paragraph (e)(4)(ii) of this section (regarding testing a split-dollar term loan for sufficient interest), a split-dollar term loan subject to this paragraph (g) is treated as if it provided for a fixed rate of interest for each accrual period to which a qualified floating rate applies. The projected fixed rate for each accrual period is the value of the qualified floating rate on the date the split-dollar term loan is made. The term of a split-dollar loan that is subject to this paragraph (g)(3)(ii) is determined using the rules in § 1.1274-4(c)(2). For example, if the loan provides for interest at a qualified floating rate that adjusts at varying intervals, the term of the loan is determined by reference to the longest interval between interest adjustment dates. See paragraph (e)(5) of this section for special rules relating to certain split-dollar term loans, such as a split-dollar term loan payable not later than the death of an individual.

(4) *Interest accruals and imputed transfers.*—For purposes of paragraphs (e) and (f) of this section, the projected fixed rate or rates determined under paragraph (g)(3) of this section are used for purposes of determining the accrual of interest each period and the amount of any imputed transfers. Appropriate adjustments are made to the interest accruals and any imputed transfers to take into account any difference between the projected fixed rate and the actual rate.

(5) *Example.*—The provisions of this paragraph (g) are illustrated by the following example:

Example. (i) On January 1, 2010, Employer *V* and Employee *F* enter into a split-dollar life insurance arrangement under which *F* is named as the policy owner. On January 1, 2010, *V* makes a $100,000 premium payment, repayable in 15 years. The premium payment is a split-dollar term loan. Under the arrangement between the parties, interest is payable on the split-dollar loan each year on January 1, starting January 1, 2011, at a rate equal to the value of 1-year LIBOR as of the payment date. The short-term AFR (based on annual compounding) at the time of the loan is 7 percent. Repayment of both the premium payment and the interest due thereon is nonrecourse to *F*. However, the parties made a representation under paragraph (d)(2) of this section. Assume that the value of 1-year LIBOR on January 1, 2010, is 8 percent, compounded annually.

(ii) The loan is subject to this paragraph (g) because the loan is a variable rate debt instrument that bears interest at a qualified floating rate. Because the interest rate is reset each year, under paragraph (g)(3)(ii) of this section, the short-term AFR (based on annual compounding) is the appropriate test rate used to determine whether the loan provides for sufficient interest. Moreover, under paragraph (g)(3)(ii) of this section, to determine whether the loan provides for sufficient interest, the loan is treated as if it provided for a fixed rate of interest equal to 8 percent, compounded annually. Based on a discount rate of 7 percent, compounded annually (the short-term AFR), the present value of the payments under the loan is $109,107.91. The loan provides for sufficient interest because the loan's imputed loan amount of $109,107.91 (the present value of the payments) is more than the amount loaned of $100,000. Therefore, the loan is not a below-market split-dollar term loan, and interest on the loan is taken into account under paragraph (f) of this section.

(h) *Adjustments for interest paid at less than the stated rate.*—(1) *Application.*—(i) *In general.*—To the extent required by this paragraph (h), if accrued but unpaid interest on a split-dollar loan is subsequently waived, cancelled, or forgiven by the lender, then the waiver, cancellation, or forgiveness is treated as if, on that date, the interest had in fact been paid to the lender and retransferred by the lender to the borrower. The amount deemed transferred and retransferred is determined under paragraph (h)(2) or (3) of this section. Except as provided in paragraph (h)(1)(iv) of this section, the amount treated as retransferred by the lender to the borrower under paragraph (h)(2) or (3) of this section is increased by the deferral charge determined under paragraph (h)(4) of this section. To determine the character of any retransferred amount, see paragraph (e)(1)(i) of this section. See § 1.61-22(b)(6) for the treatment of amounts other than interest on a split-dollar loan that are waived, cancelled, or forgiven by the lender.

(ii) *Certain split-dollar term loans.*—For purposes of this paragraph (h), a split-dollar term loan described in paragraph (e)(5) of this section (for example, a split-dollar term loan payable not later than the death of an individual) is subject to the rules of paragraph (h)(3) of this section.

(iii) *Payments treated as a waiver, cancellation, or forgiveness.*—For purposes of this paragraph (h), if a payment by the lender (or a person related to the lender) to the borrower is, in substance, a waiver, cancellation, or forgiveness of accrued but unpaid interest, the payment by the lender (or person related to the lender) is treated as an amount retransferred to the borrower by the lender under this paragraph (h) and is subject to the deferral charge in paragraph (h)(4) of this section to the extent that the payment is, in substance, a waiver, cancellation, or forgiveness of accrued but unpaid interest.

(iv) *Treatment of certain nonrecourse split-dollar loans.*—For purposes of this paragraph (h), if the parties to a split-dollar life insurance arrangement make the representation described in paragraph (d)(2) of this section and the interest actually paid on the split-dollar loan is less than the interest required to be accrued on the split-dollar loan, the excess of the interest required to be accrued over the interest actually paid is treated as waived, cancelled, or forgiven by the lender under this paragraph (h). However, the amount treated as retransferred under paragraph (h)(1)(i) of this section is not increased by the deferral charge in paragraph (h)(4) of this section.

(2) *Split-dollar term loans.*—In the case of a split-dollar term loan, the amount of interest deemed transferred and retransferred for purposes of paragraph (h)(1) of this section is determined as follows:

(i) If the loan's stated rate is less than or equal to the appropriate AFR (the AFR used to test the loan for sufficient interest under paragraph (e) of this section), the amount of interest deemed transferred and retransferred pursuant to this paragraph (h) is the excess of the amount of interest payable at the stated rate over the interest actually paid.

(ii) If the loan's stated rate is greater than the appropriate AFR (the AFR used to test the loan for sufficient interest under paragraph (e) of this section), the amount of interest deemed transferred and retransferred pursuant to this paragraph (h) is the excess, if any, of the amount of interest payable at the AFR over the interest actually paid.

(3) *Split-dollar demand loans.*—In the case of a split-dollar demand loan, the amount of interest deemed transferred and retransferred for purposes of paragraph (h)(1) of this section is equal to the aggregate of—

(i) For each year that the split-dollar demand loan was outstanding in which the loan was a below-market split-dollar demand loan, the excess of the amount of interest payable at the stated rate over the interest actually paid allocable to that year; plus

(ii) For each year that the split-dollar demand loan was outstanding in which the loan was not a below-market split-dollar demand loan, the excess, if any, of the amount of interest payable at the appropriate rate used for purposes of imputation for that year over the interest actually paid allocable to that year.

(4) *Deferral charge.*—The Commissioner may prescribe the method for determining the deferral charge treated as retransferred by the lender to the borrower under paragraph (h)(1) of this section. Until the Commissioner prescribes otherwise, the deferral charge is determined under paragraph (h)(4)(i) of this section for a split-dollar term loan subject to paragraph (h)(2) of this section and under paragraph (h)(4)(ii) of this section for a split-dollar demand loan subject to paragraph (h)(3) of this section.

(i) *Split-dollar term loan.*—The deferral charge for a split-dollar term loan subject to paragraph (h)(2) of this section is determined by multiplying the hypothetical underpayment by the applicable underpayment rate, compounded daily, for the period from the date the split-dollar loan was made to the date the interest is waived, cancelled, or forgiven. The hypothetical underpayment is equal to the amount determined under paragraph (h)(2) of this section, multiplied by the highest rate of income tax applicable to the borrower (for example, the highest rate in effect under section 1 for individuals) for the taxable year in which the split-dollar term loan was made. The applicable underpayment rate is the average of the quarterly underpayment rates in effect under section 6621(a)(2) for the period from the date the split-dollar loan was made to the date the interest is waived, cancelled, or forgiven.

(ii) *Split-dollar demand loan.*—The deferral charge for a split-dollar demand loan subject to paragraph (h)(3) of this section is the sum of the following amounts determined for each year the loan was outstanding (other than the year in which the waiver, cancellation, or forgiveness occurs): For each year the loan was outstanding, multiply the hypothetical underpayment for the year by the applicable underpayment rate, compounded daily, for the applicable period. The hypothetical underpayment is equal to the amount determined under paragraph (h)(3) of this section for each year, multiplied by the highest rate of income tax applicable to the borrower for that year (for example, the highest rate in effect under section 1 for individuals). The applicable underpayment rate is the average of the quarterly underpayment rates in effect under section 6621(a)(2) for the applicable period. The applicable period for a year is the period of time from the last day of that year until the date the interest is waived, cancelled, or forgiven.

(5) *Examples.*—The provisions of this paragraph (h) are illustrated by the following examples:

Example 1. (i) On January 1, 2009, Employer *Y* and Employee *B* entered into a split-dollar life insurance arrangement under which *B* is named as the policy owner. On January 1, 2009, *Y* made a $100,000 premium payment, repayable on December 31, 2011, with interest of 5 percent, compounded annually. The premium payment is a split-dollar term loan. Assume the short-term AFR (based on annual compounding) at the time the loan was made was 5 percent. Repayment of both the premium payment and the interest due thereon was fully recourse to *B*. On December 31, 2011, *Y* is repaid $100,000 but *Y* waives the remainder due on the loan ($15,762.50). Both *Y* and *B* use the calendar year as their taxable years.

(ii) When the split-dollar term loan was made, the loan was not a below-market loan under paragraph (e)(4)(ii) of this section. Under paragraph (f) of this section, *Y* was required to accrue compound interest of 5 percent each year the loan remained outstanding. *B*, however, was not entitled to any deduction for this interest under paragraph (c) of this section.

(iii) Under paragraph (h)(1) of this section, the waived amount is treated as if, on December 31, 2011, it had in fact been paid to *Y* and was then retransferred by *Y* to *B*. The amount deemed transferred to *Y* and retransferred to *B* equals the excess of the amount of interest payable at the stated rate ($15,762.50) over the interest actually paid ($0), or $15,762.50. In addition, the amount deemed retransferred to *B* is increased by the deferral charge determined under paragraph (h)(4) of this section. Because of the employment relationship between *Y* and *B*, the total retransferred amount is treated as compensation paid by *Y* to *B*.

Example 2. (i) On January 1, 2009, Employer *Y* and Employee *B* entered into a split-dollar life insurance arrangement under which *B* is named as the policy owner. On January 1, 2009, *Y* made a $100,000 premium payment, repayable on the demand of *Y*, with interest of 7 percent, compounded annually. The premium payment is a split-dollar demand loan. Assume the blended annual rate (based on annual compounding) in 2009 was 5 percent and in 2010 was 6 percent. Repayment of both the premium payment and the interest due thereon was fully recourse to *B*. On December 31, 2010, *Y* demands repayment and is repaid its $100,000 premium payment in full; however, *Y* waives all interest due on the loan. Both *Y* and *B* use the calendar year as their taxable years.

(ii) For each year that the split-dollar demand loan was outstanding, the loan was not a below-market loan under paragraph (e)(3)(ii) of this section. Under paragraph (f) of this section, *Y* was required to accrue compound interest of 7 percent each year the loan remained outstanding. *B*, however, was not entitled to any deduction for this interest under paragraph (c) of this section.

(iii) Under paragraph (h)(1) of this section, a portion of the waived interest is treated as if, on December 31, 2010, it had in fact been paid to *Y* and was then retransferred by *Y* to *B*. The amount of interest deemed transferred to *Y* and retransferred to *B* equals the excess, if any, of the amount of interest payable at the blended annual rate for each year the loan is outstanding over the interest actually paid with respect to that year. For 2009, the interest payable at the blended annual rate is $5,000 ($100,000 × 0.05). For 2010, the interest payable at the blended annual rate is $6,000 ($100,000 × 0.06). Therefore, the amount of interest deemed transferred to *Y* and retransferred to *B* equals $11,000. In addition, the amount deemed retransferred to *B* is increased by the deferral charge determined under paragraph (h)(4) of this section. Because of the employment relationship between *Y* and *B*, the total retransferred amount is treated as compensation paid by *Y* to *B*.

(i) [Reserved]

(j) *Split-dollar loans that provide for contingent payments.*—(1) *In general.*—Except as provided in paragraph (j)(2) of this section, this paragraph (j) provides rules for a split-dollar dollar loan that provides for one or more contingent payments. This paragraph (j), rather than § 1.1275-4, applies to split-dollar loans that provide for one or more contingent payments.

(2) *Exceptions.*—(i) *Certain contingencies.*—For purposes of this section, a split-dollar loan does not provide for contingent payments merely because—

(A) The loan provides for options described in paragraph (e)(4)(iii)(B) of this section (for example, certain call options, put options, and options to extend); or

(B) The loan is described in paragraph (e)(5) of this section (relating to certain split-dollar term loans, such as a split-dollar term loan payable not later than the death of an individual).

(ii) *Insolvency and default.*—For purposes of this section, a payment is not contingent merely because of the possibility of impairment by insolvency, default, or similar circumstances. However, if any payment on a split-dollar loan is nonrecourse to the borrower, the payment is a contingent payment for purposes of this paragraph (j) unless the parties to the arrangement make the written representation provided for in paragraph (d)(2) of this section.

(iii) *Remote and incidental contingencies.*—For purposes of this section, a payment is not a contingent payment merely because of a contingency that, as of the date the split-dollar loan is made, is either remote or incidental (within the meaning of § 1.1275-2(h)).

(iv) *Exceptions for certain split-dollar loans.*—This paragraph (j) does not apply to a split-dollar loan described in § 1.1272-1(d) (certain debt instruments that provide for a fixed yield) or a split-dollar loan described in paragraph (g) of this section (relating to split-dollar loans providing for certain variable rates of interest).

(3) *Contingent split-dollar method.*—(i) *In general.*—If a split-dollar loan provides for one or more contingent payments, then the parties account for the loan under the contingent split-dollar method. In general, except as provided in this paragraph (j), this method is the same as the noncontingent bond method described in § 1.1275-4(b).

(ii) *Projected payment schedule.*—(A) *Determination of schedule.*—No comparable yield is required to be determined. The projected payment schedule for the loan includes all noncontingent payments and a projected payment for each contingent payment. The projected payment for a contingent payment is the lowest possible value of the payment. The projected payment schedule, however, must produce a yield that is not less than zero. If the projected payment schedule produces a negative yield, the schedule must be reasonably adjusted to produce a yield of zero.

(B) *Split-dollar term loans payable upon the death of an individual.*—If a split-dollar term loan described in paragraph (e)(5)(ii)(A) or (v)(A)(*1*) of this section provides for one or more contingent payments, the projected payment schedule is determined based on the term of the loan as determined under paragraph (e)(5)(ii)(C) or (v)(B)(*2*) of this section, whichever is applicable.

(C) *Certain split-dollar term loans conditioned on the future performance of substantial services by an individual.*—If a split-dollar term loan described in paragraph (e)(5)(iii)(A)(*1*) or (v)(A)(*2*) of this section provides for one or more contingent payments, the projected payment schedule is determined based on the term of the loan as determined under paragraph (e)(5)(iii)(C) or (v)(B)(*2*) of this section, whichever is applicable.

(D) *Demand loans.*—If a split-dollar demand loan provides for one or more contingent payments, the projected payment schedule is determined based on a reasonable assumption as to when the lender will demand repayment.

(E) *Borrower/lender consistency.*—Contrary to § 1.1275-4(b)(4)(iv), the lender rather than the borrower is required to determine the projected payment schedule and to provide the schedule to the borrower and to any indirect participant as described in paragraph (e)(2) of this section. The lender's projected payment schedule is used by the lender, the borrower, and any indirect participant to compute interest accruals and adjustments.

(iii) *Negative adjustments.*—If the issuer of a split-dollar loan is not allowed to deduct interest or OID (for example, because of section 163(h) or 264), then the issuer is not required to include in income any negative adjustment carryforward determined under § 1.1275-4(b)(6)(iii)(C) on the loan, except to the extent that at maturity the total payments made over the life of the loan are less than the issue price of the loan.

(4) *Application of section 7872.*—(i) *Determination of below-market status.*—The yield based on the projected payment schedule determined under paragraph (j)(3) of this section is used to determine whether the loan is a below-market split-dollar loan under paragraph (e) of this section.

(ii) *Adjustment upon the resolution of a contingent payment.*—To the extent that interest has accrued under section 7872 on a split-dollar loan and the interest would not have accrued under this paragraph (j) in the absence of section 7872, the lender is not required to recognize income under § 1.1275-4(b) for a positive adjustment and the borrower is not treated as having interest expense for a positive adjustment. To the same extent, there is a reversal of the tax consequences imposed under paragraph (e) of this section for the prior imputed transfer from the lender to the borrower. This reversal is taken into account in determining adjusted gross income.

(5) *Examples.*—The following examples illustrate the rules of this paragraph (j). For purposes of this paragraph (j)(5), assume that the contingent payments are neither remote nor incidental. The examples are as follows:

Example 1. (i) On January 1, 2010, Employer *T* and Employee *G* enter into a splitdollar life insurance arrangement under which *G* is named as the policy owner. On January 1, 2010, *T* makes a $100,000 premium payment. On December 31, 2013, *T* will be repaid an amount equal to the premium payment plus an amount based on the increase, if any, in the price of a specified commodity for the period the loan is outstanding. The premium payment is a split-dollar term loan. Repayment of both the premium payment and the interest due thereon is recourse to *G*. Assume that the appropriate AFR for this loan, based on annual compounding, is 7 percent. Both *T* and *G* use the calendar year as their taxable years.

(ii) Under this paragraph (j), the split-dollar term loan between *T* and *G* provides for a contingent payment. Therefore, the loan is subject to the contingent split-dollar method. Under this method, the projected payment schedule for the loan provides for a noncontingent payment of $100,000 and a projected payment of $0 for the contingent payment (because it is the lowest possible value of the payment) on December 31, 2013.

(iii) Based on the projected payment schedule and a discount rate of 7 percent, compounded annually (the appropriate AFR), the present value of the payments under the loan is $76,289.52. Under paragraphs (e)(4) and (j)(4)(i) of this section, the loan does not provide for sufficient interest because the loan's imputed loan amount of $76,289.52 (the present value of the payments) is less than the amount loaned of $100,000. Therefore, the loan is a below-market split-dollar term loan and the loan is recharacterized as consisting of two portions: an imputed loan amount of $76,289.52 and an imputed transfer of $23,710.48 (amount loaned of $100,000 minus the imputed loan amount of $76,289.52).

(iv) In accordance with section 7872(b)(1) and paragraph (e)(4)(iv) of this section, on the date the loan is made, *T* is treated as transferring to *G* $23,710.48 (the imputed transfer) as compensation. In addition, *T* must take into account as OID an amount equal to the imputed transfer. See § 1.1272-1 for the treatment of OID.

Example 2. (i) Assume, in addition to the facts in *Example 1*, that on December 31, 2013, *T* receives $115,000 (its premium payment of $100,000 plus $15,000).

(ii) Under the contingent split-dollar method, when the loan is repaid, there is a $15,000 positive adjustment ($15,000 actual payment minus $0 projected payment). Under paragraph (j)(4) of this section, because *T* accrued imputed interest under section 7872 on this split-dollar loan to *G* and this interest would not have accrued in the absence of section 7872, *T* is not required to include the positive adjustment in income, and *G* is not treated as having interest expense for the positive adjustment. To the same extent, *T* must include in income, and *G* is entitled to deduct, $15,000 to reverse their respective prior tax consequences imposed under paragraph (e) of this section (*T*'s prior deduction for imputed compensation deemed paid to *G* and *G*'s prior inclusion of this amount). *G* takes the reversal into account in determining adjusted gross income. That is, the $15,000 is an "above-the-line" deduction, whether or not *G* itemizes deductions.

Example 3. (i) Assume the same facts as in *Example 2*, except that on December 31, 2013, *T* receives $127,000 (its premium payment of $100,000 plus $27,000).

(ii) Under the contingent split-dollar method, when the loan is repaid, there is a $27,000 positive adjustment ($27,000 actual payment minus $0 projected payment). Under paragraph (j)(4) of this section, because *T* accrued imputed interest of $23,710.48 under section 7872 on this split-dollar loan to *G* and this interest would not have accrued in the absence of section 7872, *T* is not required to include $23,710.48 of the positive adjustment in income, and *G* is not treated as having interest expense for the positive adjustment. To the same extent, in 2013, *T* must include in income, and *G* is entitled to deduct, $23,710.48 to reverse their respective prior tax consequences imposed under paragraph (e) of this section (*T*'s prior deduction for imputed compensation deemed paid to *G* and *G*'s prior inclusion of this amount). *G* and *T* take these reversals into account in determining adjusted gross income. Under the contingent split-dollar method, *T* must include in income $3,289.52 upon resolution of the contingency ($27,000 positive adjustment minus $23,710.48).

(k) *Payment ordering rule.*—For purposes of this section, a payment made by the borrower to or for the benefit of the lender pursuant to a split-dollar life insurance arrangement is applied to all direct and indirect split-dollar loans in the following order—

(1) A payment of interest to the extent of accrued but unpaid interest (including any OID)

See p. 15 for regulations not amended to reflect law changes

on all outstanding split-dollar loans in the order the interest accrued;

(2) A payment of principal on the outstanding split-dollar loans in the order in which the loans were made;

(3) A payment of amounts previously paid by a non-owner pursuant to a split-dollar life insurance arrangement that were not reasonably expected to be repaid by the owner; and

(4) Any other payment with respect to a split-dollar life insurance arrangement, other than a payment taken into account under paragraphs (k)(1), (2), and (3) of this section.

(l) [Reserved]

(m) *Repayments received by a lender.*—Any amount received by a lender under a life insurance contract that is part of a split-dollar life insurance arrangement is treated as though the amount had been paid to the borrower and then paid by the borrower to the lender. Any amount treated as received by the borrower under this paragraph (m) is subject to other provisions of the Internal Revenue Code as applicable (for example, sections 72 and 101(a)). The lender must take the amount into account as a payment received with respect to a split-dollar loan, in accordance with paragraph (k) of this section. No amount received by a lender with respect to a split-dollar loan is treated as an amount received by reason of the death of the insured.

(n) *Effective date.*—(1) *General rule.*—This section applies to any split-dollar life insurance arrangement entered into after September 17, 2003. For purposes of this section, an arrangement is entered into as determined under § 1.61-22(j)(1)(ii).

(2) *Modified arrangements treated as new arrangements.*—If an arrangement entered into on or before September 17, 2003 is materially modified (within the meaning of § 1.61-22(j)(2)) after September 17, 2003, the arrangement is treated as a new arrangement entered into on the date of the modification. [Reg. § 1.7872-15.]

☐ [*T.D.* 9092, 9-11-2003.]

[Reg. § 1.7872-16]

§ 1.7872-16. Loans to an exchange facilitator under § 1.468B-6.—(a) *Exchange facilitator loans.*—This section provides rules in applying section 7872 to an exchange facilitator loan (within the meaning of § 1.468B-6(c)(1)). For purposes of this section, the terms *deferred exchange, exchange agreement, exchange facilitator, exchange funds, qualified intermediary, replacement property,* and *taxpayer* have the same meanings as in § 1.468B-6(b).

(b) *Treatment as demand loans.*—For purposes of section 7872, except as provided in paragraph (d) of this section, an exchange facilitator loan is a demand loan.

(c) *Treatment as compensation-related loans.*—If an exchange facilitator loan is a below-market loan, the loan is a compensation-related loan under section 7872(c)(1)(B).

(d) *Applicable Federal rate (AFR) for exchange facilitator loans.*—For purposes of section 7872, in the case of an exchange facilitator loan, the applicable Federal rate is the lower of the short-term AFR in effect under section 1274(d)(1) (as of the day on which the loan is made), compounded semiannually, or the 91-day rate. For purposes of the preceding sentence, the 91-day rate is equal to the investment rate on a 13-week (generally 91-day) Treasury bill with an issue date that is the same as the date that the exchange facilitator loan is made or, if the two dates are not the same, with an issue date that most closely precedes the date that the exchange facilitator loan is made.

(e) *Use of approximate method permitted.*—The taxpayer and exchange facilitator may use the approximate method to determine the amount of forgone interest on any exchange facilitator loan.

(f) *Exemption for certain below-market exchange facilitator loans.*—If an exchange facilitator loan is a below-market loan, the loan is not eligible for the exemptions from section 7872 listed under § 1.7872-5T. However, the loan may be eligible for the exemption from section 7872 under § 1.7872-5(b)(16) (relating to exchange facilitator loans in which the amount treated as loaned does not exceed $2,000,000).

(g) *Effective/applicability date.*—This section applies to exchange facilitator loans issued on or after October 8, 2008.

(h) *Example.*—The provisions of this section are illustrated by the following example:

Example. (i) T enters into a deferred exchange with QI, a qualified intermediary. The exchange is governed by an exchange agreement. The exchange funds held by QI pursuant to the exchange agreement are treated as loaned to QI under § 1.468B-6(c)(1). The loan between T and QI is an exchange facilitator loan. The exchange agreement between T and QI provides that no earnings will be paid to T. On December 1, 2008, T transfers property to QI, QI transfers the property to a purchaser for $2,100,000, and QI deposits $2,100,000 in a money market account. On March 1, 2009, QI uses $2,100,000 of the funds in the account to purchase replacement property identified by T, and transfers the replacement property to T. The amount loaned for purposes of section 7872 is $2,100,000 and the loan is outstanding for three months. For purposes of section 7872, under paragraph (d) of this section, T uses the 91-day rate, which is 4 percent, compounded semi-annually. T uses the approximate method for purposes of section 7872.

(ii) Under paragraphs (b) and (c) of this section, the loan from T to QI is a compensation-related demand loan. Because there is no interest payable on the loan from T to QI, the loan is a below-market loan under section 7872. The loan is not exempt under § 1.7872-5(b)(16) because the amount treated as loaned exceeds $2,000,000. Under section 7872(e)(2), the amount of forgone interest on the loan for 2008 is $7000 ($2,100,000*.04/2*1/6). Under section 7872(e)(2), the amount of forgone interest for 2009 is $14,000

($2,100,000*.04/2*2/6). The $7000 for 2008 is deemed transferred as compensation by T to QI and retransferred as interest by QI to T on December 31, 2008. The $14,000 for 2009 is deemed transferred as compensation by T to QI and retransferred as interest by QI to T on March 1, 2009. [Reg. § 1.7872-16.]

□ [*T.D.* 9413, 7-9-2008.]

[Reg. § 301.9100-3]

§ 301.9100-3. Other extensions.—(a) *In general.*—Requests for extensions of time for regulatory elections that do not meet the requirements of § 301.9100-2 must be made under the rules of this section. Requests for relief subject to this section will be granted when the taxpayer provides the evidence (including affidavits described in paragraph (e) of this section) to establish to the satisfaction of the Commissioner that the taxpayer acted reasonably and in good faith, and the grant of relief will not prejudice the interests of the Government.

(b) *Reasonable action and good faith.*—(1) *In general.*—Except as provided in paragraphs (b)(3)(i) through (iii) of this section, a taxpayer is deemed to have acted reasonably and in good faith if the taxpayer—

(i) Requests relief under this section before the failure to make the regulatory election is discovered by the Internal Revenue Service (IRS);

(ii) Failed to make the election because of intervening events beyond the taxpayer's control;

(iii) Failed to make the election because, after exercising reasonable diligence (taking into account the taxpayer's experience and the complexity of the return or issue), the taxpayer was unaware of the necessity for the election;

(iv) Reasonably relied on the written advice of the Internal Revenue Service (IRS); or

(v) Reasonably relied on a qualified tax professional, including a tax professional employed by the taxpayer, and the tax professional failed to make, or advise the taxpayer to make, the election.

(2) *Reasonable reliance on a qualified tax professional.*—For purposes of this paragraph (b), a taxpayer will not be considered to have reasonably relied on a qualified tax professional if the taxpayer knew or should have known that the professional was not—

(i) Competent to render advice on the regulatory election; or

(ii) Aware of all relevant facts.

(3) *Taxpayer deemed to have not acted reasonably or in good faith.*—For purposes of this paragraph (b), a taxpayer is deemed to have not acted reasonably and in good faith if the taxpayer—

(i) Seeks to alter a return position for which an accuracy-related penalty has been or could be imposed under section 6662 at the time the taxpayer requests relief (taking into account any qualified amended return filed within the meaning of § 1.6664-2(c)(3) of this chapter) and the new position requires or permits a regulatory election for which relief is requested;

(ii) Was informed in all material respects of the required election and related tax consequences, but chose not to file the election; or

(iii) Uses hindsight in requesting relief. If specific facts have changed since the due date for making the election that make the election advantageous to a taxpayer, the IRS will not ordinarily grant relief. In such a case, the IRS will grant relief only when the taxpayer provides strong proof that the taxpayer's decision to seek relief did not involve hindsight.

(c) *Prejudice to the interests of the Government.*—(1) *In general.*—The Commissioner will grant a reasonable extension of time to make a regulatory election only when the interests of the Government will not be prejudiced by the granting of relief. This paragraph (c) provides the standards the Commissioner will use to determine when the interests of the Government are prejudiced.

(i) *Lower tax liability.*—The interests of the Government are prejudiced if granting relief would result in a taxpayer having a lower tax liability in the aggregate for all taxable years affected by the election than the taxpayer would have had if the election had been timely made (taking into account the time value of money). Similarly, if the tax consequences of more than one taxpayer are affected by the election, the Government's interests are prejudiced if extending the time for making the election may result in the affected taxpayers, in the aggregate, having a lower tax liability than if the election had been timely made.

(ii) *Closed years.*—The interests of the Government are ordinarily prejudiced if the taxable year in which the regulatory election should have been made or any taxable years that would have been affected by the election had it been timely made are closed by the period of limitations on assessment under section 6501(a) before the taxpayer's receipt of a ruling granting relief under this section. The IRS may condition a grant of relief on the taxpayer providing the IRS with a statement from an independent auditor (other than an auditor providing an affidavit pursuant to paragraph (e)(3) of this section) certifying that the interests of the Government are not prejudiced under the standards set forth in paragraph (c)(1)(i) of this section.

(2) *Special rules for accounting method regulatory elections.*—The interests of the Government are deemed to be prejudiced except in unusual and compelling circumstances if the accounting method regulatory election for which relief is requested—

(i) Is subject to the procedure described in § 1.446-1(e)(3)(i) of this chapter (requiring the advance written consent of the Commissioner);

(ii) Requires an adjustment under section 481(a) (or would require an adjustment under section 481(a) if the taxpayer changed to the method of accounting for which relief is requested in a taxable year subsequent to the taxable year the election should have been made);

(iii) Would permit a change from an impermissible method of accounting that is an issue under consideration by examination, an appeals office, or a federal court and the change would provide a more favorable method or more favorable terms and conditions than if the change were made as part of an examination; or

(iv) Provides a more favorable method of accounting or more favorable terms and conditions if the election is made by a certain date or taxable year.

(3) *Special rules for accounting period regulatory elections.*—The interests of the Government are deemed to be prejudiced except in unusual and compelling circumstances if an election is an accounting period regulatory election (other than the election to use other than the required taxable year under section 444) and the request for relief is filed more than 90 days after the due date for filing the Form 1128, Application to Adopt, Change, or Retain a Tax Year (or other required statement).

(d) *Effect of amended returns-.*—(1) *Second examination under section 7605(b).*—Taxpayers requesting and receiving an extension of time under this section waive any objections to a second examination under section 7605(b) for the issue(s) that is the subject of the relief request and any correlative adjustments.

(2) *Suspension of the period of limitations under section 6501(a).*—A request for relief under this section does not suspend the period of limitations on assessment under section 6501(a). Thus, for relief to be granted, the IRS may require the taxpayer to consent under section 6501(c)(4) to an extension of the period of limitations on assessment for the taxable year in which the regulatory election should have been made and any taxable years that would have been affected by the election had it been timely made.

(e) *Procedural requirements.*—(1) *In general.*—Requests for relief under this section must provide evidence that satisfies the requirements in paragraphs (b) and (c) of this section, and must provide additional information as required by this paragraph (e).

(2) *Affidavit and declaration from taxpayer.*—The taxpayer, or the individual who acts on behalf of the taxpayer with respect to tax matters, must submit a detailed affidavit describing the events that led to the failure to make a valid regulatory election and to the discovery of the failure. When the taxpayer relied on a qualified tax professional for advice, the taxpayer's affidavit must describe the engagement and responsibilities of the professional as well as the extent to which the taxpayer relied on the professional. The affidavit must be accompanied by a dated declaration, signed by the taxpayer, which states: "Under penalties of perjury, I declare that I have examined this request, including accompanying documents, and, to the best of my knowledge and belief, the request contains all the relevant facts relating to the request, and such facts are true, correct, and complete." The individual who signs for an entity must have personal knowledge of the facts and circumstances at issue.

(3) *Affidavits and declarations from other parties.*—The taxpayer must submit detailed affidavits from the individuals having knowledge or information about the events that led to the failure to make a valid regulatory election and to the discovery of the failure. These individuals must include the taxpayer's return preparer, any individual (including an employee of the taxpayer) who made a substantial contribution to the preparation of the return, and any accountant or attorney, knowledgeable in tax matters, who advised the taxpayer with regard to the election. An affidavit must describe the engagement and responsibilities of the individual as well as the advice that the individual provided to the taxpayer. Each affidavit must include the name, current address, and taxpayer identification number of the individual, and be accompanied by a dated declaration, signed by the individual, which states: "Under penalties of perjury, I declare that I have examined this request, including accompanying documents, and, to the best of my knowledge and belief, the request contains all the relevant facts relating to the request, and such facts are true, correct, and complete."

(4) *Other information.*—The request for relief filed under this section must also contain the following information—

(i) The taxpayer must state whether the taxpayer's return(s) for the taxable year in which the regulatory election should have been made or any taxable years that would have been affected by the election had it been timely made is being examined by a district director, or is being considered by an appeals office or a federal court. The taxpayer must notify the IRS office considering the request for relief if the IRS starts an examination of any such return while the taxpayer's request for relief is pending;

(ii) The taxpayer must state when the applicable return, form, or statement used to make the election was required to be filed and when it was actually filed;

(iii) The taxpayer must submit a copy of any documents that refer to the election;

(iv) When requested, the taxpayer must submit a copy of the taxpayer's return for any taxable year for which the taxpayer requests an extension of time to make the election and any return affected by the election; and

(v) When applicable, the taxpayer must submit a copy of the returns of other taxpayers affected by the election.

(5) *Filing instructions.*—A request for relief under this section is a request for a letter ruling. Requests for relief should be submitted in accordance with the applicable procedures for requests for a letter ruling and must be accompanied by the applicable user fee.

(f) *Examples.*—The following examples illustrate the provisions of this section:

Example 1. Taxpayer discovers own error. Taxpayer A prepares A's 1997 income tax return. A is unaware that a particular regulatory election is available to report a transaction in a particular manner. A files the 1997 return without making the election and reporting the transaction in a different manner. In 1999, A hires a qualified tax professional to prepare A's 1999 return. The professional discovers that A did not make the election. A promptly files for relief in accordance with this section. Assume paragraphs (b)(3)(i) through (iii) of this section do not apply. Under paragraph (b)(3)(i) of this section, A is deemed to have acted reasonably and in good faith because A requested relief before the failure to make the regulatory election was discovered by the IRS.

Example 2. Reliance on qualified tax professional. Taxpayer B hires a qualified tax professional to advise B on preparing B's 1997 income tax return. The professional was competent to render advice on the election and B provided the professional with all the relevant facts. The professional fails to advise B that a regulatory election is necessary in order for B to report income on B's 1997 return in a particular manner. Nevertheless, B reports this income in a manner that is consistent with having made the election. In 2000, during the examination of the 1997 return by the IRS, the examining agent discovers that the election has not been filed. B promptly files for relief in accordance with this section, including attaching an affidavit from B's professional stating that the professional failed to advise B that the election was necessary. Assume paragraphs (b)(3)(i) through (iii) of this section do not apply. Under paragraph (b)(1)(v) of this section, B is deemed to have acted reasonably and in good faith because B reasonably relied on a qualified tax professional and the tax professional failed to advise B to make the election.

Example 3. Accuracy-related penalty. Taxpayer C reports income on its 1997 income tax return in a manner that is contrary to a regulatory provision. In 2000, during the examination of the 1997 return, the IRS raises an issue regarding the reporting of this income on C's return and asserts the accuracy-related penalty under section 6662. C requests relief under this section to elect an alternative method of reporting the income. Under paragraph (b)(3)(i) of this section, C is deemed to have not acted reasonably and in good faith because C seeks to alter a return position for which an accuracy-related penalty could be imposed under section 6662.

Example 4. Election not requiring adjustment under section 481(a). Taxpayer D prepares D's 1997 income tax return. D is unaware that a particular accounting method regulatory election is available. D files D's 1997 return without making the election and uses another permissible method of accounting. The applicable regulation provides that the election is made on a cut-off basis (without an adjustment under section 481(a)). In 1998, D requests relief under this section to make the election under the regulation. If D were granted an extension of time to make the election, D would pay no less tax than if the election had been timely made. Assume that paragraphs (c)(2)(i), (iii), and (iv) of this section do not apply. Under paragraph (c)(2)(ii) of this section, the interests of the Government are not deemed to be prejudiced because the election does not require an adjustment under section 481(a).

Example 5. Election requiring adjustment under section 481(a). The facts are the same as in *Example 4* of this paragraph (f) except that the applicable regulation provides that the election requires an adjustment under section 481(a). Under paragraph (c)(2)(ii) of this section, the interests of the Government are deemed to be prejudiced except in unusual or compelling circumstances.

Example 6. Under examination by the IRS. A regulation permits an automatic change in method of accounting for an item on a cut-off basis. Taxpayer E reports income on E's 1997 income tax return using an impermissible method of accounting for the item. In 2000, during the examination of the 1997 return by the IRS, the examining agent notifies E in writing that its method of accounting for the item is an issue under consideration. Any change from the impermissible method made as part of an examination is made with an adjustment under section 481(a). E requests relief under this section to make the change pursuant to the regulation for 1997. The change on a cut-off basis under the regulation would be more favorable than if the change were made with an adjustment under section 481(a) as part of an examination. Under paragraph (c)(2)(iii) of this section, the interests of the Government are deemed to be prejudiced except in unusual and compelling circumstances because E seeks to change from an impermissible method of accounting that is an issue under consideration in the examination on a basis that is more favorable than if the change were made as part of an examination.

[Reg. § 301.9100-3.]

☐ [*T.D.* 8742, 12-30-97.]

[Reg. § 301.9100-6T]

§ 301.9100-6T. Time and manner of making certain elections under the Deficit Reduction Act of 1984 (Temporary).—

* * *

(g) *Election by an estatestate or trust to recognize gain or loss on the distribution of property (other than cash) to a beneficiary.*—This paragraph applies to the election made by a trust or estate to recognize gain or loss on the distribution of property (other than cash) to a beneficiary under section 643(d) of the Code as amended by section 81 of the Act. The election is available for distributions made after June 1, 1984, in taxable years ending after such date. The election must be made by the fiduciary who is required to make the return of the estate or trust under section 641 and §1.641(b)-2. The election shall be made by such fiduciary on the tax return of the estate or trust for the taxable year with respect to which the distribution of property was made and must be filed by the due date (including extensions) of such return. Until the Form 1041, U.S. Fiduciary Income Tax Return is revised, the election should be made by including the gain or loss on the Schedule D (or other appropriate schedule, if applicable) of the Form 1041 and attaching the statement described in paragraph (a)(3) of this section to the tax return on which the election is made and including on that statement the name and taxpayer identification number of the distributee. For distributions made after June 1, 1984, and before July 18, 1984, the election must be filed by the later of the due date (including extensions) of the tax return of the estate or trust for the taxable year with respect to which the distribution was made or January 1, 1985. For those distributions, the fiduciary may make the election in the manner described above on a tax return, or amended return, for the year with respect to which the distribution was made. An election under section 643(d) may be revoked only with the consent of the Commissioner. The request for revocation of an election should be made by the fiduciary in the form of a ruling request and must contain the information required by regulations and revenue procedures pertaining thereto.

* * *

(k) *Election of extension of time for payment of estate tax for interests in certain holding companies.*—An election under section 6166(b)(8), as added by section 1021(a) of the Act, or under section 1021(d)(2) of the Act, shall be made by including on the notice of election under section 6166 required by §20.6166-1(b) a statement that an election is being made under section 6166(b)(8) or section 1021(d)(2) of the Act (whichever is applicable) and the facts which formed the basis for the executor's conclusion that the estate qualified for such election. If a taxpayer makes an election described in this paragraph (k), then the special 4-percent interest rate of section 6601(j) and the 5-year deferral of principal payments of section 6166(a)(3) are not available. Thus, the first installment of tax is due on the date prescribed by section 6151(a) and subsequent installments bear interest at the rate determined under section 6621. If the executor makes an election described in this paragraph (k) and the notice of election under section 6166 fails to state the amount of tax to be paid in installments or the number of installments, then the election is presumed to be for the maximum amount so payable and for payment thereof in 10 equal annual installments, beginning on the date prescribed in section 6151(a). The elections described under this paragraph (k) are available for estates of decedents dying after July 18, 1984.

* * *

(q) *No elections for closed year.*—Any election under this section which is allowed to be made by filing an amended return may only be made if the period for making a claim for refund or credit with respect to the taxable year for which such election is to be effective has not expired. This paragraph shall not apply to the election under paragraph (a)(2)(iv) of this section with respect to the election under section 1078 of the Act.

(r) *Additional information required.*—Later regulations or revenue procedures issued under provisions of the Code or Act covered by this section may require the furnishing of information in addition to that which was furnished with the statement of election described herein. In such event the later regulations or revenue procedures will provide guidance with respect to the furnishing of such additional information. [Temporary Reg. §301.9100-6T.]

☐ [*T.D. 7976, 9-5-84. Amended by T.D.* 8062, 11-5-85. *Redesignated by T.D.* 8435, 9-18-92. *Amended by T.D.* 9172, 1-3-2005 *and T.D.* 9911, 10-9-2020.]

[Reg. §301.9100-8]

§301.9100-8. Time and manner of making certain elections under the Technical and Miscellaneous Revenue Act of 1988.—(a) *Miscellaneous elections.*—(1) *Elections to which this paragraph applies.*—This paragraph applies to the elections set forth below provided under the Technical and Miscellaneous Revenue Act of 1988, 102 Stat. 3342 (the Act). General rules regarding the time for making the elections are provided in paragraph (a)(2) of this section. General rules regarding the manner for making the elections are provided in paragraph (a)(3) of this section. Special rules regarding the time and manner for making certain elections are contained in paragraphs (a) through (i) of this section. In this paragraph (a)(1), a cross-reference to a special rule applicable to an election is shown in brackets at the end of the description of the "Availability of Election." Paragraph (j) of this section lists certain elections provided under the Act that are not addressed in this section. Paragraph (k) of this section provides that additional information with respect to elections may be required by future regulations or revenue procedures.

Section of Act	*Section of Code*	*Description of Election*	*Availability of Election*
		* * *	
1014(c) (1)	664(b)	Election by a beneficiary of a trust to which section 664 of the Code applies to obtain certain benefits of section 1403(c)(2) of the 1986 Act, relating to the ratable inclusion of certain income over 4 taxable years.	Available for taxable years beginning after December 31, 1986, provided the trust was required to change its taxable year under section 1403(a) of the 1986 Act. Election is made by attaching a statement to an amended return for the trust beneficiary's first taxable year beginning after December 31, 1986. Amended return must be filed on or before January 22, 1990. If no such election is filed, the benefits of section 1403(c)(2) are waived.
1014(c) (2)	652 662	Election by any trust beneficiary (other than a beneficiary of a trust to which section 664 of the Code applies), to waive the benefits of section 1403(c)(2) of the 1986 Act.	Available for taxable years beginning after December 31, 1986. Election is made by attaching a statement to an amended return for the trust beneficiary's first taxable year beginning after December 31, 1986. Amended return must be filed on or before January 22, 1990.
1014(d) (3)(B); 1014(d) (4)	643(g) (2)	Election to have certain payments of estimated tax made by a trust or estate treated as paid by the beneficiary.	Available for taxable years beginning after December 31, 1986. In the case of an estate, the election is available only for a taxable year reasonably expected to be the estate's last taxable year. Election must be made by the fiduciary of the trust or estate on or before the 65th day after the close of the taxable year for which the election is made. The election must be made by that date by filing Form 1041-T with the Internal Revenue Service Center where the trust's return for such taxable year is required to be filed. The trust's return (or amended return) for that year must include a copy of the Form 1041-T.
		* * *	
5031(a)	7520(a)	Election to use 120 percent of the Applicable Federal Midterm rate for either of the two months preceding a valuation date in valuing certain interests transferred to charity for which an income, estate, or gift tax charitable deduction is allowable.	Available in cases where the valuation date occurs on or after May 1, 1989. The election is made by attaching a statement to the last income, estate, or gift tax return filed before the due date, or if a timely return is not filed, the first return filed after the due date. The statement shall contain the following: (1) a statement that an election under section 7520(a) is being made; (2) the transferor's name and taxpayer identification number as they appear on the return; (3) a description of the interest being valued; (4) the recipients, beneficiaries, or donees of the transferred interest; (5) the date of the transfer; (6) the Applicable Federal Midterm rate that is used to value the transferred interest and the month to which the rate pertains.

Section of Act	*Section of Code*	*Description of Election*	*Availability of Election*
5033(a) (2)	2056A(d)	Election to treat a trust for the benefit of a surviving spouse who is not a U.S. citizen as a Qualified Domestic Trust, transfers to which are deductible under section 2056(a) of the Code.	Available in the case of estates of decedents dying after November 11, 1988. The election is made by the executor on the last Federal estate tax return filed by the executor before the due date of the return, or if a timely return is not filed by the executor, on the first estate tax return filed by the executor after the due date. However, elections made on or after May 5, 1991, may not be made on any return filed more than one year after the time prescribed for filing the return (including extensions).
		* * *	
6152(a) 6152(c) (3)	2056(b) (7)(C) (ii)	Election to treat a survivor annuity payable to a surviving spouse that is otherwise deductible under section 2056(b)(7)(C) of the Code as a nondeductible terminable interest.	Available in the case of estates of decedents dying after December 31, 1981, and in no event will the time for making the election expire before November 11, 1990. [See paragraph (e) of this section.]
6152(b) 6152(c) (3)	2523(f) (6)(B)	Election to treat a joint and survivor annuity in which the donee spouse has a survivorship interest that is otherwise deductible under section 2523(f)(6)(A) of the Code as a nondeductible terminable interest.	Available in the case of transfers made after December 31, 1981, and in no event will the time for making the election expire before November 11, 1990. [See paragraph (f) of this section.]
6152(c) (2)	2056(b) (7)(C) (ii) 2523(f) (6)(B)	Election to treat as deductible for estate or gift tax purposes under sections 2056(b)(7)(C) or 2523(f)(6) of the Code, respectively, a survivor's annuity payable to a surviving spouse reported on an estate or gift tax return filed prior to November 11, 1988, as a nondeductible terminable interest.	Available to estates of decedents dying after December 31, 1981, or to transfers made after December 31, 1981, where: (1) the estate or gift tax return was filed prior to November 11, 1988; (2) the annuity was not deducted on the return as qualified terminable interest property under sections 2056(b)(7) or 2523(f) of the Code; and (3) the executor or donor elects to treat the interest as a deductible terminable interest under sections 2056(b)(7)(C) or 2523(f)(6) prior to November 11, 1990. [See paragraph (g) of this section.]

* * *

(2) *Time for making elections.*—(i) *In general.*—Except as otherwise provided in this section, the elections described in paragraph (a)(1) of this section must be made by the later of—

(A) The due date (taking into account any extensions of time to file obtained-by the taxpayer) of the tax return for the first taxable year for which the election is effective, or

(B) January 22, 1990 (in which case the election generally must be made by amended return).

(ii) *No extension of time for payment.*—Payments of tax due must be made in accordance with chapter 62 of the Code.

(3) *Manner of making elections.*—Except as otherwise provided in this section, the elections described in paragraph (a)(1) of this section must be made by attaching a statement to the tax return for the first taxable year for which the election is to be effective. If such tax return is filed prior to the making of the election, the statement must be attached to an amended tax return of the first taxable year for which the election is to be effective. Except as otherwise provided in the return or in the instructions accompanying the return for the taxable year, the statement must—

(i) Contain the name, address and taxpayer identification number of the electing taxpayer;

(ii) Identify the election;

(iii) Indicate the section of the Code (or, if the provision is not codified, the section of the Act) under which the election is made;

(iv) Specify, as applicable, the period for which the election is being made and the property or other items to which the election is to apply; and

(v) Provide any information required by the relevant statutory provisions and any information requested in applicable forms and instructions, such as the information necessary to show that the taxpayer is entitled to make the election.

Notwithstanding the foregoing, an amended return need not be filed for an election made prior to October 23, 1989 if the taxpayer made the election in a reasonable manner.

(4) *Revocation.*—(i) *Irrevocable elections.*—The elections described in this section that are made under the following sections of the Act are irrevocable: 1002(a)(11)(A) (Code section 168(b)(2)), 1002(a)(23)(B), 1002(l)(1)(A) (Code section 42(b)(2)(A)(ii)), 1002(l)(2)(B) (Code section 42(f)(1)), 1005(c)(11), 1008(c)(4)(A) (Code section 460(b)(3)), 1014(c)(1), 1014(c)(2), 1014(d)(3)(B) and 1014(d)(4) (Code section 643(g)(2)), 2004(m)(5), 4004(a) (Code section 42(j)(5)(B)), 5033(a)(2) (Code section 2056A(d)), 6006(a) (Code section 1(i)(7)), 6026(a) (Code section 263A(h)), 6026(b)(1) (Code section 263A(d)(1)), 6152(a) and 6152(c)(3) (Code section 2056(b)(7)(C)(ii)), 6152(b) and 6152(c)(3) (Code section 2523(f)(6)(B)), 6152(c)(2) (Code sections 2056(b)(7)(C)(ii) and 2523(f)(6)(B)), and 6180(b)(1) (Code section 142(i)(2)).

(ii) *Elections revocable with the consent of the Commissioner.*—The elections described in this section that are made under the following sections of the Act are revocable only with the consent of the Commissioner: 1006(d)(15), 1006(j)(1)(C), 1006(t)(18)(B), 1009(d) (Code section 165(l)), 1010(f)(1) (Code section 831(b)(2)(A)), 1010(f)(2) (Code section 835(a)), 1012(d)(4) (Code section 865(f)), 1012(d)(6) (Code section 865(g)(3)), 1012(d)(8) (Code section 865(h)(2)), 1012(l)(2) (Code section 245(a)(10)), 1012(n)(3), 1012(bb)(4) (Code section 904(g)(10)), 2004(j)(1), 5031(a) (Code section 7520(a)), 6026(c) (Code section 263A(d)(3)(B)), and 6277.

(iii) *Freely revocable elections.*—The election described in this section that is made under section 6011 of the Act is revocable without the consent of the Commissioner. (See section 121(c) of the Code and § 1.121-4 of the regulations.)

* * *

(e) *Election to treat a survivor annuity payable to a surviving spouse as a nondeductible terminable interest.*—Where the time for making the election under section 2056(b)(7)(C)(ii) of the Code to treat the survivor annuity as nondeductible otherwise expires before November 11, 1990, the election may be made before November 11, 1990, by filing with the Service Center where the original return was filed supplemental information under § 20.6081-1(c) of the Estate Tax Regulations containing:

(1) A statement that the election under section 2056(b)(7)(C)(ii) of the Code is being made;

(2) The applicable revised schedules;

(3) A recomputation of the tax due; and

(4) Payment of any additional tax due.

(f) *Election to treat a joint and survivor annuity in which the donee spouse has a survivor interest as a nondeductible terminable interest.*—Where the time for making the election under section 2523(f)(6)(B) of the Code to treat the interest as nondeductible otherwise expires before November 11, 1990, the election may be made before November 11, 1990, by filing with the appropriate Service Center an original return (or an amended return if an original return was filed) containing:

(1) A statement that the election under section 2523(f)(6)(B) is being made;

(2) A recomputation of the tax due; and

(3) Payment of any additional tax due.

(g) *Election to treat survivor's annuity payable to the surviving spouse as qualified terminable interest property deductible under sections 2056(b)(7)(C) or 2523(f)(6) of the Code in the case of a return filed prior to November 11, 1988.*—(1) In the case of an estate tax election under section 2056(b)(7)(C) the election is made by filing with the Service Center where the estate tax return was filed supplemental information under § 20.6081-1(c) of the Estate Tax Regulations (and timely claim for refund under section 6511 of the Code, if applicable) containing:

(i) A statement that the election under section 6152(c)(2) of the Technical and Miscellaneous Revenue Act of 1988 is being made;

(ii) The applicable revised schedules; and

(iii) A recomputation of the estate's tax liability showing the amount of any refund due.

(2) In the case of a gift tax election under section 2523(f)(6) of the Code, the election is made by filing with the Service Center where the original return was filed an amended return (and timely claim for refund under section 6511, if applicable) containing:

(i) A statement that the election under section 6152(c)(2) of the Technical and Miscellaneous Revenue Act of 1988 is being made;

(ii) The applicable revised schedules; and

(iii) A recomputation of the gift tax liability showing the amount of any refund due.

* * *

(k) *Additional information required.*—Later regulations or revenue procedures issued under provisions of the Code or Act covered by this section may require the furnishing of information in addition to that which was furnished with the statement of election described in this section. In that event, the later regulations or revenue procedures will provide guidance with respect to the furnishing of additional information. [Reg. § 301.9100-8.]

☐ [*T.D. 8267, 9-21-89. Redesignated and amended by T.D.* 8435, 9-18-92.]

PROPOSED REGULATIONS

Table of Contents

Text of Proposed Regulations

COMPUTATION OF TAXABLE INCOME

Prizes and Awards

Exclusions: Prizes and Awards: Employee Achievement Awards.—Reproduced below is the text of a proposed amendment of Reg. §1.102-1, relating to prizes and awards and employee achievement awards (published in the Federal Register on January 9, 1989).

☐ Par. 4. Section 1.102-1 is amended as follows:

(a) The last sentence of paragraph (a) is removed.

(b) A new paragraph (f) is added immediately following paragraph (e) to read as follows.

§1.102-1. Gifts and inheritances.

* * *

(f) *Exclusions.*—(1) *In general.*—Section 102 does not apply to prizes and awards (including employee achievement awards) (see section 74); certain de minimis fringe benefits (see section 132); any amount transferred by or for an employer to, or for the benefit of, an employee (see section 102(c)); or to qualified scholarships (see section 117).

(2) *Employer/Employee transfers.*—For purposes of section 102(c), extraordinary transfers to the natural objects of an employer's bounty will not be considered transfers to, or for the benefit of, an employee if the employee can show that the transfer was not made in recognition of the employee's employment. Accordingly, section 102(c) shall not apply to amounts transferred between related parties (*e.g.*, father and son) if the purpose of the transfer can be substantially attributed to the familial relationship of the parties and not to the circumstances of their employment.

EXEMPT ORGANIZATIONS

Qualified State Tuition Programs: Distributions: Reporting Requirements

Qualified State Tuition Programs: Distributions: Reporting Requirements.—Reg. §1.529-5, relating to qualified state tuition programs (QSTPs) and affecting QSTPs established and maintained by a state, or an agency or instrumentality of a state, and individuals receiving distributions from QSTPs, is proposed (published in the Federal Register on August 24, 1998) (REG-106177-97).

§1.529-5. Estate, gift, and generation-skipping transfer tax rules relating to qualified State tuition programs.—(a) *Gift and generation-skipping transfer tax treatment of contributions after August 20, 1996, and before August 6, 1997.*—A contribution on behalf of a designated beneficiary to a QSTP (or to a program that meets the transitional rule requirements under §1.529-6(b)) after August 20, 1996, and before August 6, 1997, is not treated as a taxable gift. The subsequent waiver of qualified higher education expenses of a designated beneficiary by an educational institution (or the subsequent payment of higher education expenses of a designated beneficiary to an educational institution) under a QSTP is treated as a qualified transfer under section 2503(e) and is not treated as a transfer of property by gift for purposes of section 2501. As such, the contribution is not subject to the generation-skipping transfer tax imposed by section 2601.

(b) *Gift and generation-skipping transfer tax treatment of contributions after August 5, 1997.*—(1) *In general.*—A contribution on behalf of a designated beneficiary to a QSTP (or to a program that meets the transitional rule requirements under §1.529-6(b)) after August 5, 1997, is a completed gift of a present interest in property under section 2503(b) from the person making the contribution to the designated beneficiary. As such, the contribution is eligible for the annual gift tax exclusion provided under section 2503(b). The portion of a contribution excludible from taxable gifts under section 2503(b) also satisfies the requirements of section 2642(c)(2) and, therefore, is also excludible for purposes of the generation-skipping transfer tax imposed under section 2601. A contribution to a QSTP after August 5, 1997, is not treated as a qualified transfer within the meaning of section 2503(e).

(2) *Contributions that exceed the annual exclusion amount.*—(i) Under section 529(c)(2)(B) a donor may elect to take certain contributions to a QSTP into account ratably over a five year period in determining the amount of gifts made during the calendar year. The provision is applicable only with respect to contributions not in excess of five times the section 2503(b) exclusion amount available in the calendar year of the contribution. Any excess may not be taken into account ratably and is treated as a taxable gift in the calendar year of the contribution.

(ii) The election under section 529(c)(2)(B) may be made by a donor and his or her spouse with respect to a gift considered to be made one-half by each spouse under section 2513.

(iii) The election is made on Form 709, Federal Gift Tax Return, for the calendar year in which the contribution is made.

(iv) If in any year after the first year of the five year period described in section 529(c)(2)(B), the amount excludible under section 2503(b) is increased as provided in section 2503(b)(2), the donor may make an additional contribution in any one or more of the four remaining years up to the difference between the exclusion amount as increased and the original exclusion amount for the year or years in which the original contribution was made.

(v) *Example.*—The application of this paragraph (b)(2) is illustrated by the following example:

Example. In Year 1, when the annual exclusion under section 2503(b) is $10,000, P makes a contribution of $60,000 to a QSTP for the benefit of P's child, C. P elects under section 529(c)(2)(B) to account for the gift ratably over a five year period beginning with the calendar year of contribution. P is treated as making an excludible gift of $10,000 in each of Years 1 through 5 and a taxable gift of $10,000 in Year 1. In Year 3, when the annual exclusion is increased to $12,000, P makes an additional contribution for the benefit of C in the amount of $8,000. P is treated as making an excludible gift of $2,000 under section 2503(b); the remaining $6,000 is a taxable gift in Year 3.

(3) *Change of designated beneficiary or rollover.*—(i) A transfer which occurs by reason of a change in the designated beneficiary, or a rollover of credits or account balances from the account of one beneficiary to the account of another beneficiary, is not a taxable gift and is not subject to the generation-skipping transfer tax if the new beneficiary is a member of the family of the old beneficiary, as defined in § 1.529-1(c), and is assigned to the same generation as the old beneficiary, as defined in section 2651.

(ii) A transfer which occurs by reason of a change in the designated beneficiary, or a rollover of credits or account balances from the account of one beneficiary to the account of another beneficiary, will be treated as a taxable gift by the old beneficiary to the new beneficiary if the new beneficiary is assigned to a lower generation than the old beneficiary, as defined in section 2651, regardless of whether the new beneficiary is a member of the family of the old beneficiary. The transfer will be subject to the generation-skipping transfer tax if the new beneficiary is assigned to a generation which is two or more levels lower than the generation assignment of the old beneficiary. The five year averaging rule described in paragraph (b)(2) of this section may be applied to the transfer.

(iii) *Example.*—The application of this paragraph (b)(3) is illustrated by the following example:

Example. In Year 1, P makes a contribution to a QSTP on behalf of P's child, C. In Year 4, P directs that a distribution from the account for the benefit of C be made to an account for the benefit of P's grandchild, G. The rollover distribution is treated as a taxable gift by C to G, because, under section 2651, G is assigned to a generation below the generation assignment of C.

(c) *Estate tax treatment for estates of decedents dying after August 20, 1996, and before June 9, 1997.*—The gross estate of a decedent dying after August 20, 1996, and before June 9, 1997, includes the value of any interest in any QSTP which is attributable to contributions made by the decedent to such program on behalf of a designated beneficiary.

(d) *Estate tax treatment for estates of decedents dying after June 8, 1997.*—(1) *In general.*—Except as provided in paragraph (d)(2) of this section, the gross estate of a decedent dying after June 8, 1997, does not include the value of any interest in a QSTP which is attributable to contributions made by the decedent to such program on behalf of any designated beneficiary.

(2) *Excess contributions.*—In the case of a decedent who made the election under section 529(c)(2)(B) and paragraph (b)(3)(i) of this section who dies before the close of the five year period, that portion of the contribution allocable to calendar years beginning after the date of death of the decedent is includible in the decedent's gross estate.

(3) *Designated beneficiary decedents.*—The gross estate of a designated beneficiary of a QSTP includes the value of any interest in the QSTP. [Reg. § 1.529-5.]

ESTATES, TRUSTS, BENEFICIARIES, AND DECEDENTS

Charitable Contributions: Substantiation

Charitable Contributions: Substantiation Requirements.—Amendments to Reg. § 1.642(c)-1, relating to deductions in excess of $5,000 claimed for charitable contributions of property, are proposed (published in the Federal Register on May 5, 1988).

* * *

☐ Par. 2. Paragraph (a)(1) of § 1.642(c)-1 is amended by revising the first sentence to read as set forth below.

§ 1.642(c)-1. Unlimited deduction for amounts paid for charitable purpose.—(a) *In general.*—(1) Any part of the gross income of an estate or trust which, pursuant to the terms of the governing instrument, is paid (or treated under paragraph (b) of this section as paid) during the taxable year for a purpose specified in section 170(c) shall be allowed as a deduction to such estate or trust in lieu of the limited charitable contributions deduction authorized by section 170(a) (provided that the recordkeeping and return requirements for charitable contribution deductions contained in § 1.170A-13 are satisfied). * * *

Charitable Contributions: Substantiation

Charitable Contributions: Substantiation Requirements.—Amendments to Reg. § 1.642(c)-2, relating to deductions in excess of $5,000 claimed for charitable contributions of property, are proposed (published in the Federal Register on May 5, 1988).

☐ Par. 3. Section 1.642(c)-2 is amended by adding a new paragraph (e) immediately after paragraph (d) to read as set forth below.

§ 1.642(c)-2. Unlimited deduction for amounts permanently set aside for a charitable purpose.—

* * *

(e) *Substantiation requirements.*—No deduction shall be allowed under paragraphs (a), (b)(2), or (c) of this section unless the recordkeeping and return requirements for charitable contribution deductions contained in § 1.170A-13 are satisfied.

Annuities: Interests: Valuation: Actuarial Tables

Annuities: Interests: Valuation: Actuarial Tables.—Amendments to Reg. § 1.642(c)-6, relating to the use of actuarial tables in valuing annuities, interests for life or terms of years, and remainder or reversionary interests, are proposed (published in the Federal Register on May 5, 2022) (REG-122770-18) (corrected June 6, 2022).

☐ Par. 4. Section 1.642(c)-6 is amended by:

1. Revising paragraph (d).

2. Redesignating paragraph (e) as paragraph (g) of § 1.642(c)-6A.

3. Adding new paragraph (e) and revising paragraph (f).

The revisions and addition read as follows:

§ 1.642(c)-6. Valuation of a remainder interest in property transferred to a pooled income fund.

* * *

(d) *Valuation.*—The present value of the remainder interest in property transferred to a pooled income fund on or after [applicability date of the Treasury decision adopting these regulations as final regulations], is determined under paragraph (e) of this section. The present value of the remainder interest in property transferred to a pooled income fund for which the valuation date is before [applicability date of the Treasury decision adopting these regulations as final regulations] is determined under the following sections:

Table 6 to paragraph (d)

Valuation Dates		*Applicable Regulations*
After	*Before*	
-	01-01-52	1.642(c)-6A(a)
12-31-51	01-01-71	1.642(c)-6A(b)
12-31-70	12-01-83	1.642(c)-6A(c)
11-30-83	05-01-89	1.642(c)-6A(d)
04-30-89	05-01-99	1.642(c)-6A(e)
04-30-99	05-01-09	1.642(c)-6A(f)
04-30-09	AD	1.642(c)-6A(g)

AD = [applicability date of the Treasury decision adopting these regulations as final regulations].

(e) *Present value of the remainder interest in the case of transfers to pooled income funds for which the valuation date is on or after [applicability date of the Treasury decision adopting these regulations as final regulations].*—(1) *In general.*—In the case of transfers to pooled income funds for which the valuation date is on or after [applicability date of the Treasury decision adopting these regulations as final regulations], the present value of a remainder interest is determined under this section. See, however, § 1.7520-3(b) (relating to exceptions to the use of prescribed tables under certain circumstances). The present value of a remainder interest that is dependent on the termination of the life of one individual is computed by using the formula in § 20.2031-7(d)(2)(ii)(B) of this chapter to derive factors from the appropriate mortality table. For the convenience of taxpayers, actuarial factors have been computed by IRS and appear in Table S. Table S will be available beginning May 5, 2022, at no charge, electronically via the IRS website at *https://www.irs.gov/retirement-plans/actuarial-tables* (or a corresponding URL as may be updated from time to time). Table S is referenced and explained by IRS Publication 1457 "Actuarial Valuations Version 4A," which will be available after [date of publication of the final rule in the **Federal Register**]. For purposes of the computations under this section, the age of an individual is the age at the individual's nearest birthday.

(2) *Transitional rule for valuation of transfers to pooled income funds.*—For purposes of section 170, 2055, 2106, and 2522, or 2624, in the case of transfers to a pooled income fund for which the valuation date is on or after January 1, 2021, and before [applicability date of the Treasury decision adopting these regulations as final regulations], the present value of the remainder interest under this section is determined by using the section 7520 interest rate for the month in which the valuation date occurs (see § § 1.7520-1(b) and 1.7520-2(a)(2)) and the appropriate actuarial factors derived from the selected mortality table, either Table 2010CM in § 20.2031-7(d)(7)(ii) of this chapter or Table 2000CM in § 20.2031-7A(g)(4) of this chapter, at the option of the donor or the decedent's executor, as the case may be. For the convenience of taxpayers, actuarial factors based on Table 2010CM appear in the proposed version of Table S, and actuarial factors based on Table 2000CM appear in the current version of Table S, which will be available beginning May 5, 2022, at no charge, electronically via the IRS website at *https://www.irs.gov/retirement-plans/actuarial-tables* (or a corresponding URL as may be updated from time to time). The donor or decedent's executor must consistently use the same mortality basis with respect to each interest (income, remainder, partial, etc.) in the same property, and with respect to all transfers occurring on the valuation date. For example, gift and income tax charitable deductions with respect to the same transfer must be determined based on factors with the same mortality basis, and all assets includible in the gross estate and/or estate tax deductions claimed must be valued based on factors with the same mortality basis.

(3) *Present value of a remainder interest.*—The present value of a remainder interest in property transferred to a pooled income fund is computed on the basis of—

(i) Life contingencies determined from the values of *lx* that are set forth in Table 2010CM in § 20.2031-7(d)(7)(ii) of this chapter (see § 20.2031-7A of this chapter for certain prior periods); and

(ii) Discount at a rate of interest, compounded annually, equal to the highest yearly rate of return of the pooled income fund for the three taxable years immediately preceding its taxable year in which the transfer of property to the fund is made. For purposes of this paragraph (e), the yearly rate of return of a pooled income fund is determined as provided in paragraph (c) of this section unless the highest rate of return is deemed to be the rate described in paragraph (e)(4) of this section for funds in existence less than 3 taxable years. For purposes of this paragraph (e)(3)(ii), the first taxable year of a pooled income fund is considered a taxable year even though the taxable year consists of less than 12 months. However, appropriate adjustments must be made to annualize the rate of return earned by the fund for that period. Where it appears from the facts and circumstances that the highest yearly rate of return of the fund for the three taxable years immediately preceding the taxable year in which the transfer of property is made has been purposely manipulated to be substantially less than the rate of return that otherwise would be reasonably anticipated with the purpose of obtaining an excessive charitable deduction, that rate of return may not be used. In that case, the highest yearly rate of return of the fund is determined by treating the fund as a pooled income fund that has been in existence for less than three preceding taxable years.

(4) *Pooled income funds in existence less than three taxable years.*—If a pooled income fund has been in existence less than three taxable years immediately preceding the taxable year in which the transfer is made to the fund and the transfer to the fund is made on or after May 1, 1989, the highest rate of return is deemed to be the interest rate (rounded to the nearest two-tenths of one percent) that is one percent less than the highest annual average of the monthly section 7520 rates for the three calendar years immediately preceding the calendar year in which the transfer to the pooled income fund is made. The deemed rate of return for transfers to new pooled income funds is recomputed each calendar year using the monthly section 7520 rates for the three year period immediately preceding the calendar year in which each transfer to the fund is made until the fund has been in existence for three taxable years and can compute its highest rate of return for the three taxable years immediately preceding the taxable year in which the transfer of property to the fund is made in accordance with the rules set forth in the first sentence of paragraph (e)(3)(ii) of this section.

(5) *Computation of value of remainder interest.*—(i) *Factor.*—The factor that is used in determining the present value of a remainder interest that is dependent on the termination of the life of one individual is the factor obtained through use of the formula in § 20.2031-7(d)(2)(ii)(B) of this chapter to derive factors from the appropriate mortality table. For the convenience of taxpayers, actuarial factors have been computed by IRS and appear in Table S. Table S will be available beginning May 5, 2022, at no charge, electronically via the IRS website at *https://www.irs.gov/retirement-plans/actuarial-tables*. Table S is referenced and explained in IRS Publication 1457 "Actuarial Valuations Version 4A," which will be available after [date of publication of the final rule in the **Federal Register**]. In using the section of Table S for the interest rate equal to the appropriate yearly rate of return, the appropriate remainder factor is opposite the number that corresponds to the age of the individual upon whose life the value of the remainder interest is based (See § 1.642(c)-6A for certain prior periods). The tables referenced by IRS Publication 1457 "Actuarial Valuations Version 4A" include factors for yearly rates of return from 0.2 to 20

percent, inclusive, in increments of two-tenths of one percent. For other situations, see paragraph (b) of this section. If the yearly rate of return is a percentage that is between the yearly rates of return for which factors are provided by Table S, an exact method of obtaining the applicable factors (such as through software using the actual rate of return and the actuarial formulas provided in § 20.2031-7(d)(2)(ii)(B) of this chapter) or a linear interpolation must be used, provided whichever method used is applied consistently. The present value of the remainder interest is determined by multiplying the fair market value of the property on the valuation date by the appropriate remainder factor.

(ii) *Sample factors from actuarial Table S.*—For purposes of the example in paragraph (e)(5)(iii) of this section, the following factors from Table S will be used:

Table 7 to paragraph (e)(5)(ii)

Factors from Table S - Based on Table 2010CM			
Interest at 5.4 Percent			
Age	Annuity	Life Estate	Remainder
55	13.2515	0.71558	0.28442
Interest at 5.6 Percent			
Age	Annuity	Life Estate	Remainder
55	12.9710	0.72637	0.27363

(iii) *Example of interpolation.*—After [applicability date of the Treasury decision adopting these regulations as final regulations], A, whose age is 54 years and 8 months, transfers $100,000 to a pooled income fund, and retains a life income interest in the property. The highest yearly rate of return earned by the fund for its 3 preceding taxable years is 5.43 percent. In Table S, the remainder factor opposite 55 years under 5.4 percent is 0.28442 and under 5.6 percent is 0.27363. The present value of the remainder interest is $28,280, computed as illustrated in Figure 1 to this paragraph (e)(5)(iii).

Figure 1 to paragraph (e)(5)(iii) – Illustration of interpolation method

A.	Remainder Factor at 5.4 percent for age 55	0.28442
B.	Less: Remainder Factor at 5.6 percent for age 55	- 0.27363
C.	Difference: A - B	0.01079

D. Interpolation Adjustment:

$$\frac{5.43\% - 5.40\%}{5.60\% - 5.40\%} = \frac{z}{0.01079}$$

E. $$\frac{5.43\% - 5.40\%}{5.60\% - 5.40\%} \cdot 0.01079 = z = 0.00162$$

F.	Remainder Factor at 5.4 percent for age 55	0.28442
G.	Less: Interpolation Adjustment z	- 0.00162
H.	Interpolated Factor: F - G	0.28280
I.	Amount Transferred	$ 100,000
J.	Present Value of Remainder Interest: H x I	$ 28,280

(6) *Actuarial tables.*—In the case of transfers for which the valuation date is on or after [applicability date of the Treasury decision adopting these regulations as final regulations], the present value of a remainder interest dependent on the termination of one life in the case of a transfer to a pooled income fund is determined by using the formula in § 20.2031-7(d)(2)(ii)(B) of this chapter to derive factors from the appropriate mortality table. For the convenience of taxpayers, actuarial factors have been computed by IRS and appear in Table S. Table S will be available beginning May 5, 2022, at no charge, electronically via the IRS website at *https://www.irs.gov/retirement-plans/actuarial-tables*. Table S is referenced and explained in IRS Publication 1457 "Actuarial Valuations Version 4A," which will be available after [date of publication of the final rule in the **Federal Register**].

(f) *Applicability date.*—This section applies on and after [applicability date of the Treasury decision adopting these regulations as final regulations].

Annuities: Interests: Valuation: Actuarial Tables

Annuities: Interests: Valuation: Actuarial Tables.—Amendments to Reg. § 1.642(c)-6A, relating to the use of actuarial tables in valuing annuities, interests for life or terms of years, and remainder or reversionary interests, are proposed (published in the Federal Register on May 5, 2022) (REG-122770-18).

☐ Par. 6. Section 1.642(c)-6A is amended by:

1. Revising the section heading.

2. In newly redesignated paragraph (g):

i. The heading and paragraphs (g)(1) through (5) and (g)(6) introductory text are revised.

ii. Paragraph (g)(7) is added.

The revisions and addition read as follows:

§ 1.642(c)-6A. Valuation of charitable remainder interests for which the valuation date is before [applicability date of the Treasury decision adopting these regulations as final regulations].

* * *

(g) *Present value of the remainder interest in the case of transfers to pooled income funds for which the valuation date is on or after May 1, 2009, and before [applicability date of the Treasury decision adopting these regulations as final regulations].*—(1) *In general.*—In the case of transfers to pooled income funds for which the valuation date is on or after May 1, 2009, and before [applicability date of the Treasury decision adopting these regulations as final regulations], the present value of a remainder interest is determined under this section. See, however, § 1.7520-3(b) (relating to exceptions to the use of prescribed tables under certain circumstances). The present value of a remainder interest that is dependent on the termination of the life of one individual is computed by the use of Table S in paragraph (g)(6) of this section. For purposes of the computations under this section, the age of an individual is the age at the individual's nearest birthday.

(2) *Transitional rules for valuation of transfers to pooled income funds.*—(i) For purposes of section 2055, 2106, or 2624, if on May 1, 2009, the decedent was under a mental disability so that the disposition of the property could not be changed, and the decedent died on or after May 1, 2009, but before [applicability date of the Treasury decision adopting these regulations as final regulations] without having regained the ability to dispose of the decedent's property, or if the decedent died within 90 days of the date that the decedent first regained that ability on or after May 1, 2009, but before [applicability date of the Treasury decision adopting these regulations as final regulations], the present value of a remainder interest is determined as if the valuation date with respect to the decedent's gross estate is either before May 1, 2009, or after April 30, 2009, at the option of the decedent's executor.

(ii) For purposes of section 170, 2055, 2106, 2522, or 2624, in the case of transfers to a pooled income fund for which the valuation date is on or after May 1, 2009, and before July 1, 2009, the present value of the remainder interest under this section is determined by using the section 7520 interest rate for the month in which the valuation date occurs (see §§ 1.7520-1(b) and 1.7520-2(a)(2)) and the appropriate actuarial tables under either paragraph (f)(6) or (g)(6) of this section, at the option of the donor or the decedent's executor, as the case may be.

(iii) For purposes of paragraphs (g)(2)(i) and (ii) of this section, where the donor or decedent's executor is given the option to use the appropriate actuarial tables under either paragraph (f)(6) or (g)(6) of this section, the donor or decedent's executor must consistently use the same mortality basis with respect to each interest (income, remainder, partial, etc.) in the same property, and with respect to all transfers occurring on the valuation date. For example, gift and income tax charitable deductions with respect to the same transfer must be determined based on factors with the same mortality basis, and all assets includible in the gross estate and/or estate tax deductions claimed must be valued based on factors with the same mortality basis.

(3) *Present value of a remainder interest.*—The present value of a remainder interest in property transferred to a pooled income fund is computed on the basis of —

(i) Life contingencies determined from the values of l_x that are set forth in Table 2000CM in § 20.2031-7A(g)(4) of this chapter; and

(ii) Discount at a rate of interest, compounded annually, equal to the highest yearly rate of return of the pooled income fund for the three taxable years immediately preceding its taxable year in which the transfer of property to the fund is made. The provisions of § 1.642(c)-6(c) apply for determining the yearly rate of return. However, where the taxable year is less than 12 months, the provisions of § 1.642(c)-6(e)(3)(ii) apply for the determining the yearly rate of return.

(4) *Pooled income funds in existence less than three taxable years.*—The provisions of § 1.642(c)-6(e)(4) apply for determining the highest yearly rate of return when the pooled income fund has been in existence less than three taxable years.

(5) *Computation of value of remainder interest.*—The factor that is used in determining the present value of a remainder interest that is dependent on the termination of the life of one individual is the factor from Table S in paragraph (g)(6) of this section under the appropriate yearly rate of return opposite the number that corresponds to the age of the individual upon whose life the value of the remainder interest is based. Table S in paragraph (g)(6) of this section includes factors for yearly rates of return from 0.2 to 14 percent, inclusive, in increments of two-tenths of one percent. Actuarial factors that do not appear in paragraph (g)(6) of this section may be computed directly by using the formula in § 20.2031-7(d)(2)(ii)(B) of this chapter to derive factors from the appropriate mortality table. For the convenience of taxpayers, actuarial factors have been computed by IRS and appear in Table S that is referenced and explained by IRS Publication 1457, "Actuarial Valuations Version 3A" (2009). The table is available at no charge, electronically via the IRS website at *https://www.irs.gov/retirement-plans/actuarial-tables* (or a corresponding URL as may be updated from time to time). For other situations, see § 1.642(c)-6(b). If the yearly rate of return is a percentage that is between the yearly rates of return for which factors are provided by Table S, an exact method of obtaining the applicable factors (such as through software using the actual rate of return and actuarial formulas provided in § 20.2031-7(d)(2)(ii)(B) of this chapter) or a linear interpolation must be used, provided whichever method used is applied consistently. The present value of the remainder interest is determined by multiplying the fair market value of the property on the valuation date by the appropriate remainder factor. For an example of a computation of the present value of a remainder interest requiring a linear interpolation adjustment, see § 1.642(c)-6(e)(5).

(6) *Actuarial tables.*—In the case of transfers for which the valuation date is on or after May 1, 2009, and before [applicability date of the Treasury decision adopting these regulations as final regulations], and without regard to the headings in the tables in this paragraph (g)(6) that do not contain this termination date for the applicability of the tables, the present value of a remainder interest dependent on the termination of one life in the case of a transfer to a pooled income fund is determined by using the following tables:

* * *

(7) *Applicability dates.*—Paragraphs (g)(1) through (6) of this section apply on and after May 1, 2009, and before [applicability date of the Treasury decision adopting these regulations as final regulations].

Gross Income of Beneficiary

Gross Income of Beneficiary: Character of Amounts.—Reproduced below is the text of the proposed amendment of Reg. § 1.652(b)-1, relating to the character of amounts included in the gross income of a beneficiary (published in the Federal Register on April 30, 1975).

☐ Section 1.652(b)-1 is amended by deleting "72(n)" and inserting in lieu thereof "402(a)(2)". As amended § 1.652(b)-1 reads as follows:

§ 1.652(b)-1. Character of amounts.—In determining the gross income of a beneficiary, the amounts includible under § 1.652(a)-1 have the same character in the hands of the beneficiary as in the hands of the trust. For example, to the extent that the amounts specified in § 1.652(a)-1 consist of income exempt from tax under section 103, such amounts are not included in the beneficiary's gross income. Similarly, dividends distributed to a beneficiary retain their original character in the beneficiary's hands for purposes of determining the availability to the beneficiary of the dividends received credit under section 34 (for dividends received on or before December 31, 1964) and the dividend exclusion under section 116. Also, to the extent that the amounts specified in § 1.652(a)-1 consist of "earned income" in the hands of the trust under the provisions of section 1348 such amount shall be treated under section 1348 as "earned income" in the hands of the beneficiary. Similarly, to the extent the amounts specified in § 1.652(a)-1 consist of an amount received as a part of a lump sum distribution from a qualified plan and to which the provisions of section 402(a)(2) would apply in the hands of the trust, such amount shall be treated as subject to such section in the hands of the beneficiary except where such amount is deemed under section 666(a) to have been distributed in a preceding taxable year of the trust and the partial tax described in section 668(a)(2) is determined under section 668(b)(1)(B). The tax treatment of amounts determined under § 1.652(a)-1 depends upon the beneficiary's status with respect to them, not upon the status of the trust. Thus, if a beneficiary is deemed to have received foreign income of a foreign trust, the includibility of such income in his gross income depends upon his taxable status with respect to that income.

Estates and Trusts: Charitable Remainder Trusts

Estates and Trusts: Charitable Remainder Trusts.—Reproduced below is the text of a proposed amendment of Reg. § 1.664-1, relating to transfers for public, charitable and religious uses (published in the Federal Register on December 19, 1975).

☐ Paragraph (f) of § 1.664-1 is amended by revising the heading of subparagraph (3) and by adding a new subparagraph (4) at the end thereof. These revised and added provisions read as follows:

§ 1.664-1. Charitable remainder trusts.

* * *

(f) *Effective date.*—* * *

(3) *Amendment of certain trusts created after July 31, 1969.*—* * *

(4) *Certain wills and trusts in existence on September 21, 1974.*—(i) In the case of a will executed before September 21, 1974, or a trust created (within the meaning of applicable local law) after July 31, 1969, and before September 21, 1974, which is amended pursuant to section 2055(e)(3) and § 20.2055-2(g), a charitable remainder trust resulting from such amendment will be treated as a charitable remainder trust from the date it would be deemed created under § 1.664-1(a)(4) and (5), whether or not such date is after September 20, 1974.

(ii) Property transferred to a trust created (within the meaning of applicable local law) before August 1, 1969, whose governing instrument provides that an organization described in section 170(c) receives an irrevocable remainder interest in such trust shall be deemed transferred to a trust created on the date of such transfer, provided that the transfer occurs after July 31, 1969, and prior to October 18, 1971, and pursuant to an amendment provided in § 20.2055-2(g), the transferred property and any undistributed income therefrom is severed and placed in a separate trust as of the date of the amendment.

* * *

Annuities: Interests: Valuation: Actuarial Tables

Annuities: Interests: Valuation: Actuarial Tables.—Amendments to Reg. §§ 1.664-2 and 1.664-4, relating to the use of actuarial tables in valuing annuities, interests for life or terms of years, and remainder or reversionary interests, are proposed (published in the Federal Register on May 5, 2022) (REG-122770-18).

☐ Par. 7. Section 1.664-2 is amended by revising paragraphs (c) and (e) as follows:

§ 1.664-2. Charitable remainder annuity trust.

* * *

(c) *Calculation of the fair market value of the remainder interest of a charitable remainder annuity trust.*—For purposes of sections 170, 2055, 2106, and 2522, the fair market value of the remainder interest of a charitable remainder annuity trust (as described in this section) is the net fair market value (as of the appropriate valuation date) of the property placed in trust less the present value of the annuity. For purposes of this section, valuation date means, in general, the date on which the property is transferred to the trust by the donor regardless of when the trust is created. In the case of transfers to a charitable remainder annuity trust for which the valuation date is after April 30, 1999, if an election is made under section 7520 and § 1.7520-2(b) to compute the present value of the charitable interest by using the interest rate component for either of the 2 months preceding the month in which the transfer is made, the month so elected is the valuation date for purposes of determining the interest rate and mortality tables. For purposes of section 2055 or 2106, the valuation date is the date of death unless the alternate valuation date is elected in accordance with section 2032 in which event, and within the limitations set forth in section 2032 and the regulations in this part under section 2032, the valuation date is the alternate valuation date. If the decedent's estate elects the alternate valuation date under section 2032 and also elects, under section 7520 and § 1.7520-2(b), to use the interest rate component for one of the 2 months preceding the alternate valuation date, the month so elected is the valuation date for purposes of determining the interest rate and mortality tables. The present value of an annuity is computed under § 20.2031-7(d) of this chapter for transfers for which the valuation date is on or after [applicability date of the Treasury decision adopting these regulations as final regulations], or under § 20.2031-7A(a) through (g) of this chapter, whichever is applicable, for transfers for which the valuation date is before [applicability date of the Treasury decision adopting these regulations as final regulations]. See, however, § 1.7520-3(b) (relating to exceptions to the use of prescribed tables under certain circumstances).

* * *

(e) *Applicability date.*—Paragraph (c) of this section applies on and after [applicability date of the Treasury decision adopting these regulations as final regulations].

☐ Par. 8. Section 1.664-4 is amended by:

1. Revising paragraphs (a)(1) and (d).
2. In paragraph (e):

i. Redesignating the paragraph heading as the heading for § 1.664-4A(g) and paragraphs (e)(1), (2), (5), and (7) as § 1.664-4A(g)(1), (2), (5), and (6), respectively.

ii. Adding a new paragraph heading and new paragraphs (e)(1), (2), and (5).

iii. Revising the heading for paragraph (e)(6).

iv. Redesignating the text of paragraph (e)(6) as paragraph (e)(6)(iii).

v. Adding paragraphs (e)(6)(i) and (ii).

vi. Revising the introductory text of newly redesignated paragraph (e)(6)(iii), preceding Table D.

vii. Adding a new paragraph (e)(7).

3. Revising paragraph (f).

The additions and revisions read as follows:

§ 1.664-4. Calculation of the fair market value of the remainder interest in a charitable remainder unitrust.—(a) * * *

(1) Life contingencies determined as to each life involved, from the values of *lx* set forth in Table 2010CM in § 20.2031-7(d)(7)(ii) of this chapter in the case of transfers for which the valuation date is on or after [applicability date of the Treasury decision adopting these regulations as final regulations]; or from Table 2000CM contained in § 20.2031-7A(g)(4) of this chapter in the case of transfers for which the valuation date is on or after May 1, 2009, and before [applicability date of the Treasury decision adopting these regulations as final regulations]. See § 20.2031-7A(a) through (f) of this chapter, whichever is applicable, for transfers for which the valuation date is before May 1, 2009;

* * *

(d) *Valuation.*—The fair market value of a remainder interest in a charitable remainder unitrust (as described in § 1.664-3) for transfers for which the valuation date is on or after [applicability date of the Treasury decision adopting these regulations as final regulations], is its present value determined under paragraph (e) of this section. The fair market value of a remainder interest in a charitable remainder unitrust (as described in § 1.664-3) for transfers for which the valuation date is before [applicability date of the Treasury decision adopting these regulations as final regulations], is its present value determined under the following sections:

Table 1 to paragraph (d)

Valuation Dates		Applicable Regulations
After	*Before*	
-	01-01-52	1.664-4A(a)
12-31-51	01-01-71	1.664-4A(b)
12-31-70	12-01-83	1.664-4A(c)
11-30-83	05-01-89	1.664-4A(d)
04-30-89	05-01-99	1.664-4A(e)
04-30-99	05-01-09	1.664-4A(f)
04-30-09	AD	1.664-4A(g)

AD = [applicability date of the Treasury decision adopting these regulations as final regulations].

(e) *Valuation of charitable remainder unitrusts having certain payout sequences for transfers for which the valuation date is on or after [applicability date of the Treasury decision adopting these regulations as final regulations].*—(1) *In general.*—Except as otherwise provided in paragraph (e)(2) of this section, in the case of transfers for which the valuation date is on or after [applicability date of the Treasury decision adopting these regulations as final regulations], the present value of a remainder interest is determined under paragraphs (e)(3) through (7) of this section, provided that, in a short taxable year, the trustee shall prorate the unitrust amount as provided in § 1.664-3(a)(1)(v). See, however, § 1.7520-3(b) (relating to exceptions to the use of the prescribed tables under certain circumstances).

(2) *Transitional rule for valuation of charitable remainder unitrusts.*—For purposes of section 170, 2055, 2106, and 2522, or 2624, in the case of transfers to a charitable remainder unitrust for which the valuation date is on or after January 1, 2021, and before [applicability date of the Treasury decision adopting these regulations as final regulations], the present value of a remainder interest based on one or more measuring lives is determined under this section by using the section 7520 interest rate for the month in which the valuation date occurs (see §§ 1.7520-1(b) and 1.7520-2(a)(2)) and the appropriate actuarial factors derived from the selected mortality table, either Table 2010CM in § 20.2031-7(d)(7)(ii) of this chapter or Table 2000CM in § 20.2031-7A(g)(4) of this chapter, at the option of the donor or the decedent's executor, as the case may be. For the convenience of taxpayers, actuarial factors based on Table 2010CM appear in the proposed version of Table U(1), and actuarial factors based on Table 2000CM appear in the current version of Table U(1), which will be available beginning May 5, 2022, at no charge, electronically via the IRS website at *https://*

www.irs.gov/retirement-plans/actuarial-tables (or a corresponding URL as may be updated from time to time). The donor or decedent's executor must consistently use the same mortality basis with respect to each interest (income, remainder, partial, etc.) in the same property, and with respect to all transfers occurring on the valuation date. For example, gift and income tax charitable deductions with respect to the same transfer must be determined based on factors with the same mortality basis, and all assets includible in the gross estate and/or estate tax deductions claimed must be valued based on factors with the same mortality basis.

* * *

(5) *Period is the life of one individual.*—(i) *Factor.*—If the period described in § 1.664-3(a)(5) is the life of one individual, the factor that is used in determining the present value of the remainder interest for transfers for which the valuation date is on or after [insert the applicability date of the Treasury decision adopting these regulations as final regulations] is the factor obtained through the use of the formula in Figure 1 to this paragraph (e)(5)(i). The prescribed mortality table is Table 2010CM as set forth in § 20.2031-7(d)(7)(ii) of this chapter, or for periods before [applicability date of the Treasury decision adopting these regulations as final regulations], the appropriate table found in § 20.2031-7A of this chapter. Table 2010CM is referenced by IRS Publication 1458, "Actuarial Values Version 4B." The mortality tables prescribed for periods before [applicability date of the Treasury decision adopting these regulations as final regulations] are referenced by prior versions of IRS Publication 1458. Alternatively, the remainder factors have been determined for the convenience of taxpayers and appear in Table U(1) under the appropriate adjusted payout rate. Table U(1) will be available beginning May 5, 2022, at no charge, electronically via the IRS website at *https://www.irs.gov/retirement-plans/actuarial-tables* (or a corresponding URL as may be updated from time to time). Table U(1) is referenced and explained by IRS Publication 1458 "Actuarial Valuations Version 413," which will be available after [date of publication of the final rule in the **Federal Register**]. For purposes of the computations described in this paragraph (e)(5), the age of an individual is the age of that individual at the individual's nearest birthday. If the adjusted payout rate is an amount that is between adjusted payout rates for which factors are provided in the appropriate table, an exact method of obtaining the applicable factors (such as through software using the actual adjusted payout rate and the actuarial formula in this paragraph (e)(5)) or a linear interpolation must be used, provided whichever method used is applied consistently. The present value of the remainder interest is determined by multiplying the net fair market value (as of the valuation date as determined in § 1.664-4(e)(4)) of the property placed in trust by the factor determined under this paragraph (e)(5). If the adjusted payout rate is from 0.2 to 20.0 percent, inclusive, taxpayers may see the actuarial tables referenced and explained by IRS Publication 1458 "Actuarial Valuations Version 413". Alternatively, the Commissioner may supply a factor upon a request for a ruling. See paragraph (b) of this section.

Figure 1 to paragraph (e)(5)(i) – Formula for determining unitrust remainder factors

$$\left(1+\frac{i}{2}\right)\sum_{t=0}^{\infty} v^{t+1}\left({}_{t+1}q_x - {}_{t}q_x\right)$$

where:

r = the adjusted payout rate;

v = 1 - r;

i = r / (1 – r)

$${}_{t}q_x = 1 - \frac{l_{x+t}}{l_x} \;;$$

x = the age of the measuring life (determined as age at nearest birthday); and

l_x = the number associated with age x as set forth in the prescribed mortality table, representing the number of persons alive at age x.

(ii) *Sample factors from actuarial Table U(1).*—For purposes of the example in paragraph (e)(5)(iii) of this section, the following factors from Table U(1) and Table F(3.2) (see paragraph (e)(6)(ii) of this section) will be used:

Table 2 to paragraph (e)(5)(ii)

Factors from Table U(1) - Based on Table 2010CM			
	Adjusted Payout Rate		
Age	4.8%	5.0%	5.2%
77	0.61491	0.60343	0.59223

Factors from Table F(3.2)			
Factors for Computing Adjusted Payout Rates for Unitrusts			
Interest at 3.2 Percent			
# of Months from Annual Valuation to First Payout		Adjustment Factors for Payments at End of Period	
At Least	But Less Than	Annual	Semiannual
6	7	0.984374	0.976683

(iii) *Example of interpolation.*—After [applicability date of the Treasury decision adopting these regulations as final regulations], A, whose age is 76 years and 11 months, transfers $100,000 to a charitable remainder unitrust on January 1st. The trust instrument requires that the trust pay to A semiannually (on June 30 and December 31) 5 percent of the fair market value of the trust assets as of January 1st during A's life. The section 7520 rate for January is 3.2 percent. Under Table F(3.2), the appropriate adjustment factor is 0.976683 for semiannual payments payable at the end of the semiannual period. The adjusted payout rate is 4.8834% (5% × 0.976683). Based on interpolating between the remainder factors in Table U(1), the present value of the remainder interest is $61,012, computed as illustrated in Figure 2 to this paragraph (e)(5)(iii).

Figure 2 to paragraph (e)(5)(iii) – Illustration of unitrust interpolation method

A.	Table U(1) Factor at 4.8 percent for age 77		0.61491
B.	Less: Table U(1) Factor at 5.0 percent for age 77	-	0.60343
C.	Difference: A - B		0.01148

D. Interpolation Adjustment:

$$\frac{4.8834\% - 4.80\%}{5.0\% - 4.80\%} = \frac{z}{0.01148}$$

E.

$$\frac{4.8834\% - 4.80\%}{5.0\% - 4.80\%} \cdot 0.01148 = z = 0.00479$$

F.	Table U(1) Factor at 4.8 percent for age 77		0.61491
G.	Less: Interpolation Adjustment z	-	0.00479
H.	Interpolated Factor: F - G		0.61012
I.	Amount Transferred	$	100,000
J.	Present Value of Remainder Interest: H x I	$	61,012

(6) *Actuarial Table D and Tables F (0.2) through F(20.0) for transfers for which the valuation date is on or after May 1, 1989.*—(i) *Remainder factors for charitable remainder unitrusts.*—For transfers for which the valuation date is on or after May 1, 1989, the present value of a charitable remainder unitrust interest that is dependent upon a term of years is determined by using the

formula in Figure 3 to this paragraph (e)(6)(i). For the convenience of taxpayers, actuarial factors have been computed by IRS and appear in Table D. Table D can be found on the IRS website at *https://www.irs.gov/retirement-plans/actuarial-tables* (or a corresponding URL as may be updated from time to time). Table D is referenced and explained in IRS Publication 1458 "Actuarial Valuations Version 413," which will be available after [date of publication of the final rule in the **Federal Register**]. The remainder factors from Table D also can be found in paragraph (e)(6)(iii) of this section, but only for adjusted payout rates from 4.2 to 14 percent, inclusive. For transfers for which the valuation date is on or after [applicability date of the Treasury decision adopting these regulations as final regulations], where the present value of a charitable remainder unitrust interest is dependent on the termination of a life interest, see paragraph (e)(5) of this section. See, however, § 1.7520-3(b) (relating to exceptions to the use of prescribed tables under certain circumstances).

Figure 3 to paragraph (e)(6)(i) – Formula for determining term certain unitrust remainder factors

$$(1 - r)^n$$

where:

n = the term in years or fractions of a year; and

r = the adjusted payout rate.

(ii) *Unitrust payout rate adjustment factors*.—For transfers for which the valuation date is on or after May 1, 1989, the unitrust payout rate adjustment factors are determined by using the formula in Figure 4 to this paragraph (e)(6)(ii). For the convenience of taxpayers, actuarial factors have been computed by IRS, for interest rates from 0.2 to 20 percent, inclusive, and appear in Tables F(0.2) through F(20.0). Tables F(0.2) through F(20.0) can be found on the IRS website at *https://www.irs.gov/retirement-plans/actuarial-tables* (or a corresponding URL as may be updated from time to time). Tables F(0.2) through F(20.0) are referenced and explained in IRS Publication 1458 "Actuarial Valuations Version 413," which will be available after [date of publication of the final rule in the **Federal Register**]. The factors from Table F also can be found in paragraph (e)(6)(iii) of this section, but only for interest rates from 4.2 to 14 percent, inclusive.

Figure 4 to paragraph (e)(6)(ii) – Formula for determining unitrust payout rate adjustment factors

$$\frac{(1 + i)^{(1/p)} \cdot i \cdot v^{(d/12)}}{p\,(1 + i)[(1 + i)^{(1/p)} - 1]}$$

where:

p = the number of payments per year;

i = the applicable interest rate under section 7520 of the Internal Revenue Code;

v = 1 / (1 + i) ; and

d = the number of months between the annual valuation date and the regular first payout date of a standard full year of the trust.

(iii) *Table D and Tables F(4.2) through F(14.0)*.—The unitrust remainder factors from Table D, for interest rates from 4.2 to 14 percent, inclusive, and the unitrust payout factors from Tables F(4.2) through F(14.0) are as follows:

* * *

(7) *Actuarial Table U(1) for transfers for which the valuation date is on or after [applicability date of the Treasury decision adopting these regulations as final regulations]*.—The present value of a remainder interest in a charitable remainder unitrust that is dependent on the termination of a life interest is determined by using the section 7520 rate, Tables F(0.2) through (20.0) (see paragraph (e)(6)(ii) of this section), and the formula in paragraph (e)(5)(i) of this section to derive factors from the appropriate mortality table. For the convenience of taxpayers, actuarial factors have been computed by IRS and appear in Table

U(1). For transfers for which the valuation date is on or after [applicability date of the Treasury decision adopting these regulations as final regulations], the actuarial tables will be available beginning May 5, 2022, at no charge, electronically via the IRS website at *https://www.irs.gov/retirement-plans/actuarial-tables*. These actuarial tables are referenced and explained by IRS Publication 1458, "Actuarial Valuations Version 4B" (2022). This publication will be available after [date of publication of the final rule in the **Federal Register**]. See, however, § 1.7520-3(b) (relating to exceptions to the use of prescribed tables under certain circumstances).

(f) *Applicability date.*—This section applies on and after [applicability date of the Treasury decision adopting these regulations as final regulations].

Annuities: Interests: Valuation: Actuarial Tables

Annuities: Interests: Valuation: Actuarial Tables.—Amendments to Reg. § 1.664-4A, relating to the use of actuarial tables in valuing annuities, interests for life or terms of years, and remainder or reversionary interests, are proposed (published in the Federal Register on May 5, 2022) (REG-122770-18).

☐ Par. 10. Section 1.664-4A is amended by:

1. Revising the section heading.

2. In newly redesignated paragraph (g):

i. Revising the heading and paragraphs (g)(1) and (2).

ii. Adding paragraphs (g)(3) and (4).

iii. Revising paragraph (g)(5).

iv. In paragraph (g)(6), revising the introductory text.

v. Adding paragraph (g)(7).

The additions and revisions read as follows:

§ 1.664-4A. Valuation of charitable remainder interests for which the valuation date is before [applicability date of the Treasury decision adopting these regulations as final regulations].

* * *

(g) *Valuation of charitable remainder unitrusts having certain payout sequences for transfers for which the valuation date is on or after May 1, 2009, and before [applicability date of the Treasury decision adopting these regulations as final regulations].*—(1) *In general.*—Except as otherwise provided in paragraph (g)(2) of this section, in the case of transfers for which the valuation date is on or after May 1, 2009, and before [applicability date of the Treasury decision adopting these regulations as final regulations], the present value of a remainder interest is determined under paragraphs (g)(3) through (6) of this section, provided that the amount of the payout as of any payout date during any taxable year of the trust is not larger than the amount that the trust could distribute on such date under § 1.664-3(a)(1)(v) if the taxable year of the trust were to end on such date. See, however, § 1.7520-3(b) (relating to exceptions to the use of the prescribed tables under certain circumstances).

(2) *Transitional rules for valuation of charitable remainder unitrusts.*—(i) For purposes of sections 2055, 2106, or 2624, if on May 1, 2009, the decedent was under a mental disability so that the disposition of the property could not be changed, and the decedent died on or after May 1, 2009, but before [applicability date of the Treasury decision adopting these regulations as final regulations], without having regained the ability to dispose of the decedent's property, or if the decedent died within 90 days of the date that the decedent first regained that ability on or after May 1, 2009, but before [applicability date of the Treasury decision adopting these regulations as final regulations], the present value of a remainder interest under this section is determined as if the valuation date with respect to the decedent's gross estate is either before May 1, 2009, or after April 30, 2009, at the option of the decedent's executor.

(ii) For purposes of sections 170, 2055, 2106, 2522, or 2624, in the case of transfers to a charitable remainder unitrust for which the valuation date is on or after May 1, 2009, and before July 1, 2009, the present value of a remainder interest based on one or more measuring lives is determined under this section by using the section 7520 interest rate for the month in which the valuation date occurs (see §§ 1.7520-1(b) and 1.7520-2(a)(2)) and the appropriate actuarial tables under either paragraph (f)(6) or (g)(6) of this section, at the option of the donor or the decedent's executor, as the case may be.

(iii) For purposes of paragraphs (g)(2)(i) and (ii) of this section, where the donor or decedent's executor is given the option to use the appropriate actuarial tables under either paragraph (f)(6) or (g)(6) of this section, the donor or decedent's executor must consistently use the same mortality basis with respect to each interest (income, remainder, partial, etc.) in the same property, and with respect to all transfers occurring on the valuation date. For example, gift and income tax charitable deductions with respect to the same transfer must be determined based on factors with the same mortality basis, and all assets includible in the gross estate and/or estate tax deductions claimed must be valued based on factors with the same mortality basis.

(3) *Adjusted payout rate.*—The adjusted payout rate is determined by applying the formula in § 1.664-4(e)(6)(ii) for the section 7520 interest rate applicable to the transfer to derive a

factor. For the convenience of taxpayers, actuarial factors have been computed by IRS, for interest rates from 0.2 to 20 percent, inclusive, and appear in Tables F(0.2) through F(20.0). Tables F(0.2) through F(20.0) can be found on the IRS website at *https://www.irs.gov/retirement-plans/actuarial-tables* (or a corresponding URL as may be updated from time to time). Tables F(0.2) through F(20.0) are referenced and explained in IRS Publication 1458 "Actuarial Valuations Version 3B." The payout adjustment factors from Table F can also be found in § 1.664-4(e)(6)(iii), but only for interest rates from 4.2 to 14 percent, inclusive. Alternatively, the Commissioner may supply a factor upon a request for a ruling. See § 1.664-4(b). See § 1.664-4(e) for rules applicable in determining the adjusted payout rate.

(4) *Period is a term of years.*—If the period described in § 1.664-3(a)(5) is a term of years, the factor that is used in determining the present value of the remainder interest is determined by applying the formula in § 1.664-4(e)(6)(i) under the appropriate adjusted payout rate corresponding to the number of years in the term. For the convenience of taxpayers, actuarial factors have been computed by IRS and appear in Table D. Table D can be found on the IRS website at *https://www.irs.gov/retirement-plans/actuarial-tables* (or a corresponding URL as may be updated from time to time). Table D is referenced and explained in IRS Publication 1458 "Actuarial Valuations Version 3B." The remainder factors from Table D also can be found in § 1.664-4(e)(6)(iii), but only for adjusted payout rates from 4.2 to 14 percent, inclusive. If the adjusted payout rate is a percentage that is between the adjusted payout rate for which factors are provided by Table D, an exact method of obtaining the applicable factors (such as through software using the actual rate of return and the actuarial formula provided in § 1.664-4(e)(6)(i)) or a linear interpolation must be used, provided whichever method used is applied consistently. The present value of the remainder interest is determined by multiplying the net fair market value (as of the appropriate valuation date) of the property placed in trust by the factor determined under this paragraph (g)(4). Generally, for purposes of this section, the valuation date is, in the case of an inter vivos transfer, the date on which the property is transferred to the trust by the donor, and, in the case of a testamentary transfer under sections 2055, 2106, or 2624, the valuation date is the date of death. See § 1.664-4(e)(4) for additional rules regarding the valuation date, and for an example that illustrates the application of this paragraph (g)(4).

(5) *Period is the life of one individual.*—If the period described in § 1.664-3(a)(5) is the life of one individual, the factor that is used in determining the present value of the remainder interest for transfers for which the valuation date is on or after May 1, 2009, and before [applicability date of the Treasury decision adopting these regulations as final regulations], may be computed directly by using the formula in § 1.664-4(e)(5)(i) to derive factors from the appropriate mortality table. For the convenience of taxpayers, actuarial factors have been computed by IRS and appear in Table U(1). Table U(1) can be found on the IRS website at *https://www.irs.gov/retirement-plans/actuarial-tables* (or a corresponding URL as may be updated from time to time). Table U(1) is referenced and explained in IRS Publication 1458 "Actuarial Valuations Version 3B." The remainder factors from Table U(1) also can be found in paragraph (g)(6) of this section, but only for adjusted payout rates from 4.2 to 14 percent, inclusive. For purposes of the computations described in this paragraph (g)(5), the age of an individual is the age of that individual at the individual's nearest birthday. If the adjusted payout rate is a percentage that is between the adjusted payout rate for which factors are provided by Table U(1), an exact method of obtaining the applicable factors (such as through software using the actual rate of return and the actuarial formula provided in § 1.664-4(e)(5)(i)) or a linear interpolation must be used, provided whichever method used is applied consistently. The rules provided in § 1.664-4(e)(5) apply for determining the present value of the remainder interest. See § 1.664-4(e)(5) for an example illustrating the application of this paragraph (g)(5) (using current actuarial tables).

(6) *Actuarial Table U(1) for transfers for which the valuation date is on or after May 1, 2009, and before [applicability date of the Treasury decision adopting these regulations as final regulations].*—For transfers for which the valuation date is on or after May 1, 2009, and before [applicability date of the Treasury decision adopting these regulations as final regulations], and without regard to the headings in the tables in this paragraph (g)(6) that do not contain this termination date for the applicability of the tables, the present value of a charitable remainder unitrust interest that is dependent on the termination of a life interest is determined by using the section 7520 rate, Table U(1) in this paragraph (g)(6), and Tables F(4.2) through F(14.0) in § 1.664-4(e)(6)(iii). See, however, § 1.7520-3(b) (relating to exceptions to the use of prescribed tables under certain circumstances). Actuarial factors that do not appear in the following tables may be computed directly by using the formula in § 1.664-4(e)(5)(i) to derive factors from the appropriate mortality table. For the convenience of taxpayers, actuarial factors have been computed by IRS and appear in Table U(1) that is referenced and explained by IRS Publication 1458, "Actuarial Valuations Version 3B" (2009). The table is available at no charge, electronically via the IRS website at *https://www.irs.gov/retirement-plans/actuarial-tables* (or a corresponding URL as may be updated from time to time).

* * *

(7) *Applicability dates.*—Paragraphs (g)(1) through (6) of this section apply on and after May 1, 2009, and before [applicability date of the Treasury decision adopting these regulations as final regulations].

Application of the Grantor Trust Rules to Nonexempt Employees' Trusts

Application of the Grantor Trust Rules to Nonexempt Employees' Trusts.—Amendments to Reg. §§1.671-1 and 1.671-2, relating to the application of the grantor trust rules to nonexempt employees' trusts, are proposed (published in the Federal Register on September 27, 1996) (REG-209826-96).

☐ Par. 2. Section 1.671-1 is amended by adding paragraphs (g) and (h) to read as follows:

§1.671-1. Grantors and others treated as substantial owners; scope.

* * *

(g) *Domestic nonexempt employees' trust.*—(1) *General rule.*—An employer is not treated as an owner of any portion of a nonexempt employees' trust described in section 402(b) that is part of a deferred compensation plan, and that is not a foreign trust within the meaning of section 7701(a)(31), regardless of whether the employer has a power or interest described in sections 673 through 677 over any portion of the trust. See section 402(b)(3) and §1.402(b)-1(b)(6) for rules relating to treatment of a beneficiary of a nonexempt employees' trust as the owner of a portion of the trust.

(2) *Example.*—The following example illustrates the rules of paragraph (g)(1) of this section:

Example. Employer X provides nonqualified deferred compensation through Plan A to certain of its management employees. Employer X has created Trust T to fund the benefits under Plan A. Assets of Trust T may not be used for any purpose other than to satisfy benefits provided under Plan A until all plan liabilities have been satisfied. Trust T is classified as a trust under §301.7701-4 of this chapter, and is not a foreign trust within the meaning of section 7701(a)(31). Under §1.83-3(e), contributions to Trust T are considered transfers of property to participants within the meaning of section 83. On these facts, Trust T is a nonexempt employees' trust described in section 402(b). Because Trust T is a nonexempt employees' trust described in section 402(b) that is part of a deferred compensation plan, and that is not a foreign trust within the meaning of section 7701(a)(31), Employer X is not treated as an owner of any portion of Trust T.

(h) *Foreign employees' trust.*—(1) *General rules.*—Except as provided under section 679 or as provided under this paragraph (h)(1), an employer is not treated as an owner of any portion of a foreign employees' trust (as defined in paragraph (h)(2) of this section), regardless of whether the employer has a power or interest described in sections 673 through 677 over any portion of the trust.

(i) *Plan of CFC employer.*—If a controlled foreign corporation (as defined in section 957) maintains a deferred compensation plan funded through a foreign employees' trust, then, with respect to the controlled foreign corporation, the provisions of subpart E apply to the portion of the trust that is the fractional interest described in paragraph (h)(3) of this section.

(ii) *Plan of U.S. employer.*—If a United States person (as defined in section 7701(a)(30)) maintains a deferred compensation plan that is funded through a foreign employees' trust, then, with respect to the U.S. person, the provisions of subpart E apply to the portion of the trust that is the fractional interest described in paragraph (h)(3) of this section.

(iii) *Plan of U.S.-related foreign partnership employer.*—(A) *General rule.*—If a U.S.-related foreign partnership (as defined in paragraph (h)(1)(iii)(B) of this section) maintains a deferred compensation plan funded through a foreign employees' trust, then, with respect to the U.S.-related foreign partnership, the provisions of subpart E apply to the portion of the trust that is the fractional interest described in paragraph (h)(3) of this section.

(B) *U.S.-related foreign partnership.*—For purposes of this paragraph (h), a U.S.-related foreign partnership is a foreign partnership in which a U.S. person or a controlled foreign corporation owns a partnership interest either directly or indirectly through one or more partnerships.

(iv) *Application of §1.1297-4 to plan of foreign non-CFC employer.*—A foreign employer that is not a controlled foreign corporation may be treated as an owner of a portion of a foreign employees' trust as provided in §1.1297-4.

(v) *Application to employer entity.*—The rules of paragraphs (h)(1)(i) through (h)(1)(iv) of this section apply to the employer whose employees benefit under the deferred compensation plan funded through a foreign employees' trust, or, in the case of a deferred compensation plan covering independent contractors, the recipient of services performed by those independent contractors, regardless of whether the plan is maintained through another entity. Thus, for example, where a deferred compensation plan benefitting employees of a controlled foreign corporation is funded through a foreign employees' trust, the controlled foreign corporation is considered to be the grantor of the foreign employees' trust for purposes of applying paragraph (h)(1)(i) of this section.

(2) *Foreign employees' trust.*—A foreign employees' trust is a nonexempt employees' trust described in section 402(b) that is part of a deferred compensation plan, and that is a foreign trust within the meaning of section 7701(a)(31).

(3) *Fractional interest for paragraph (h)(1).*—(i) *In general.*—The fractional interest for a foreign employees' trust used for purposes of paragraph (h)(1) of this section for a taxable year of the employer is an undivided fractional interest in the trust for which the fraction is equal to the relevant amount for the employer's taxable year divided by the fair market value of trust assets for the employer's taxable year.

(ii) *Relevant amount.*—(A) *In general.*—For purposes of applying paragraph (h)(3)(i) of this section, and except as provided in paragraph (h)(3)(iii) of this section, the relevant amount for the employer's taxable year is the amount, if any, by which the fair market value of trust assets, plus the fair market value of any assets available to pay plan liabilities that are held in the equivalent of a trust within the meaning of section 404A(b)(5)(A), exceed the plan's accrued liability. The following rules apply for this purpose:

(1) The plan's accrued liability is determined using a projected unit credit funding method that satisfies the requirements of § 1.412(c)(3)-1, taking into account only liabilities relating to services performed through the measurement date for the employer or a predecessor employer.

(2) The plan's accrued liability is reduced (but not below zero) by any liabilities that are provided for under annuity contracts held to satisfy plan liabilities.

(3) Any amount held under an annuity contract that exceeds the amount that is needed to satisfy the liabilities provided for under the contract (e.g., the value of a participation right under a participating annuity contract) is added to the fair market value of any assets available to pay plan liabilities that are held in the equivalent of a trust.

(4) If the relevant amount as determined under this paragraph (h)(3)(ii), without regard to this paragraph (h)(3)(ii)(A)(4), is greater than the fair market value of trust assets, then the relevant amount is equal to the fair market value of trust assets.

(B) *Permissible actuarial assumptions for accrued liability.*—For purposes of paragraph (h)(3)(ii)(A) of this section, a plan's accrued liability must be calculated using an interest rate and other actuarial assumptions that the Commissioner determines to be reasonable. It is appropriate in determining this interest rate to look to available information about rates implicit in current prices of annuity contracts, and to look to rates of return on high-quality fixed-income investments currently available and expected to be available during the period prior to maturity of the plan benefits. If the qualified business unit computes its income or earnings and profits in dollars pursuant to the dollar approximate separate transactions method under § 1.985-3, the employer must use an exchange rate that can be demonstrated to clearly reflect income, based on all relevant facts and circumstances, including appropriate rates of inflation and commercial practices.

(iii) *Exception for reasonable funding.*—The relevant amount does not include an amount that the taxpayer demonstrates to the Commissioner is attributable to amounts that were properly contributed to the trust pursuant to a reasonable funding method, applied using actuarial assumptions that the Commissioner determines to be reasonable, or any amount that the taxpayer demonstrates to the Commissioner is attributable to experience that is favorable relative to any actuarial assumptions used that the Commissioner determines to be reasonable. For this paragraph (h)(3)(iii) to apply to a controlled foreign corporation employer described in paragraph (h)(1)(i) of this section, the taxpayer must indicate on a statement attached to a timely filed Form 5471 that the taxpayer is relying on this rule. For purposes of this paragraph (h)(3)(iii), an amount is considered contributed pursuant to a reasonable funding method if the amount is contributed pursuant to a funding method permitted to be used under section 412 (e.g., the entry age normal funding method) that is consistently used to determine plan contributions. In addition, for purposes of this paragraph (h)(3)(iii), if there has been a change to that method from another funding method, an amount is considered contributed pursuant to a reasonable funding method only if the prior funding method is also a funding method described in the preceding sentence that was consistently used to determine plan contributions. For purposes of this paragraph (h)(3)(iii), a funding method is considered reasonable only if the method provides for any initial unfunded liability to be amortized over a period of at least 6 years, and for any net change in accrued liability resulting from a change in funding method to be amortized over a period of at least 6 years.

(iv) *Reduction for transition amount.*—The relevant amount is reduced (but not below zero) by any transition amount described in paragraphs (h)(5), (h)(6), or (h)(7) of this section.

(v) *Fair market value of assets.*—For purposes of paragraphs (h)(3)(i) and (ii) of this section, for a taxable year of the employer, the fair market value of trust assets, and the fair market value of other assets held in the equivalent of a trust within the meaning of section 404A(b)(5)(A), equals the fair market value of those assets, as of the measurement date for the employer's taxable year, adjusted to include contributions made after the measurement date and by the end of the employer's taxable year.

(vi) *Annual valuation.*—For purposes of determining the relevant amount for a taxable year of the employer, the fair market value of plan assets, and the plan's accrued liability as described in paragraphs (h)(3)(ii) and (iii) of this section, and the normal cost as described in paragraph (h)(4) of this section, must be determined as of a consistently used annual measurement date within the employer's taxable year.

(vii) *Special rule for plan funded through multiple trusts.*—In cases in which a plan is funded through more than one foreign employees' trust, the fractional interest determined under paragraph (h)(3)(i) of this section in each trust is determined by treating all of the trusts as if their assets were held in a single trust for which the fraction is determined in accordance with the rules of this paragraph (h)(3).

(4) *De minimis exception.*—If the relevant amount is not greater than the plan's normal cost for the plan year ending with or within the employer's taxable year, computed using a funding method and actuarial assumptions as described in paragraph (h)(3)(ii) of this section or as described in paragraph (h)(3)(iii) of this section if the requirements of that paragraph are met, that are used to determine plan contributions, then the relevant amount is considered to be zero for purposes of applying paragraph (h)(3)(i) of this section.

(5) *General rule for transition amount.*—(i) *General rule.*—If paragraphs (h)(6) and (h)(7) of this section do not apply to the employer, the transition amount for purposes of paragraph (h)(3)(iv) of this section is equal to the preexisting amount multiplied by the applicable percentage for the year in which the employer's taxable year begins.

(ii) *Preexisting amount.*—The preexisting amount is equal to the relevant amount of the trust, determined without regard to paragraphs (h)(3)(iv) and (h)(4) of this section, computed as of the measurement date that immediately precedes September 27, 1996 disregarding contributions to the trust made after the measurement date.

(iii) *Applicable percentage.*—The applicable percentage is equal to 100 percent for the employer's first taxable year ending after this document is published as a final regulation in the Federal Register and prior taxable years of the employer, and is reduced (but not below zero) by 10 percentage points for each subsequent taxable year of the employer.

(6) *Transition amount for new CFCs.*—(i) *General rule.*—In the case of a new controlled foreign corporation employer, the transition amount for purposes of paragraph (h)(3)(iv) is equal to the pre-change amount multiplied by the applicable percentage for the year in which the new controlled foreign corporation employer's taxable year begins.

(ii) *Pre-change amount.*—The pre-change amount for purposes of paragraph (h)(6)(i) is equal to the relevant amount of the trust, determined without regard to paragraphs (h)(3)(iv) and (h)(4) of this section and disregarding contributions to the trust made after the measurement date, for the new controlled foreign corporation employer's last taxable year ending before the corporation becomes a new controlled foreign corporation employer.

(iii) *Applicable percentage.*—(A) *General rule.*—Except as provided in paragraph (h)(6)(iii)(B) of this section, the applicable percentage is equal to 100 percent for a new controlled foreign corporation employer's first taxable year ending after the corporation becomes a controlled foreign corporation. The applicable percentage is reduced (but not below zero) by 10 percentage points for each subsequent taxable year of the new controlled foreign corporation.

(B) *Interim rule.*—For any taxable year of a new controlled foreign corporation employer that ends on or before the date this document is published as a final regulation in the Federal Register, the applicable percentage is equal to 100 percent. The applicable percentage is reduced by 10 percentage points for each subsequent taxable year of the new controlled foreign corporation employer that ends after the date this document is published as a final regulation in the Federal Register.

(iv) *New CFC employer.*—For purposes of paragraph (h)(6) of this section, a new controlled foreign corporation employer is a corporation that first becomes a controlled foreign corporation within the meaning of section 957 after September 27, 1996. A new controlled foreign corporation employer includes a corporation that was a controlled foreign corporation prior to, but not on, September 27, 1996 and that first becomes a controlled foreign corporation again after September 27, 1996.

(v) *Anti-stuffing rule.*—Notwithstanding paragraph (h)(6)(iii) of this section, if, prior to becoming a controlled foreign corporation, a corporation contributes amounts to a foreign employees' trust with a principal purpose of obtaining tax benefits by increasing the pre-change amount, the applicable percentage with respect to those amounts is 0 percent for all taxable years of the new controlled foreign corporation employer.

(7) *Transition amount for new U.S.-related foreign partnerships.*—(i) *General rule.*—In the case of a new U.S.-related foreign partnership employer, the transition amount for purposes of paragraph (h)(3)(iv) of this section is equal to the pre-change amount multiplied by the applicable percentage for the year in which the new U.S.-related foreign partnership employer's taxable year begins.

(ii) *Pre-change amount.*—The pre-change amount for purposes of paragraph (h)(7)(i) of this section is equal to the relevant amount of the trust, determined without regard to paragraphs (h)(3)(iv) and (h)(4) of this section and disregarding contributions to the trust made after the measurement date, for the entity's last taxable year ending before the entity becomes a new U.S.-related foreign partnership employer.

(iii) *Applicable percentage.*—(A) *General rule.*—Except as provided in paragraph (h)(7)(iii)(B) of this section, the applicable percentage is equal to 100 percent for a new U.S.-related foreign partnership employer's first taxable year ending after the entity becomes a new U.S.-related foreign partnership employer. The applicable percentage is reduced (but not below zero) by 10 percentage points for each subsequent taxable year of the new U.S.-related foreign partnership employer.

(B) *Interim rule.*—For any taxable year of a new U.S.-related foreign partnership employer that ends on or before the date this document is published as a final regulation in the Federal Register, the applicable percentage is equal to 100 percent. The applicable percentage is reduced by 10 percentage points for each subsequent taxable year of the new U.S.-related foreign partnership employer that ends after the date this document is published as a final regulation in the Federal Register.

(iv) *New U.S.-related foreign partnership employer.*—For purposes of paragraph (h)(7) of this section, a new U.S.-related foreign partnership employer is an entity that was a foreign corporation other than a controlled foreign corporation, or that was a foreign partnership other than a U.S.-related foreign partnership, and that changes from this status to a U.S.-related foreign partnership after September 27, 1996. A new U.S.-related foreign partnership employer includes a corporation that was a U.S.-related foreign partnership prior to, but not on, September 27, 1996 and that first becomes a U.S.-related foreign partnership again after September 27, 1996.

(v) *Anti-stuffing rule.*—Notwithstanding paragraph (h)(7)(iii) of this section, if, prior to becoming a new U.S.-related foreign partnership employer, an entity contributes amounts to a foreign employees' trust with a principal purpose of obtaining tax benefits by increasing the pre-change amount, the applicable percentage with respect to those amounts is 0 percent for all taxable years of the new U.S.-related foreign partnership employer.

(8) *Examples.*—The following examples illustrate the rules of paragraph (h) of this section. In each example, the employer has a power or interest described in sections 673 through 677 over the foreign employees' trust, and the monetary unit is the applicable functional currency (FC) determined in accordance with section 985(b) and the regulations thereunder.

Example 1. (i) Employer X is a controlled foreign corporation (as defined in section 957). Employer X maintains a defined benefit retirement plan for its employees. Employer X's taxable year is the calendar year. Trust T, a foreign employees' trust, is the sole funding vehicle for the plan. Both the plan year of the plan and the taxable year of Trust T are the calendar year.

(ii) As of December 31, 1997, Trust T's measurement date, the fair market value (as described in paragraph (h)(3)(iv) of this section) of Trust T's assets is FC 1,000,000, and the amount of the plan's accrued liability is FC 800,000, which includes a normal cost for 1997 of FC 50,000. The preexisting amount for Trust T is FC 40,000. Thus, the relevant amount for 1997 is FC 160,000 (which is greater than the plan's normal cost for the year). Employer X's shareholder does not indicate on a statement attached to a timely filed Form 5471 that any of the relevant amount qualifies for the exception described in paragraph (h)(3)(iii) of this section. Therefore, the fractional interest for Employer X's taxable year ending on December 31, 1997, is 16 percent. Employer X is treated as the owner for federal income tax purposes of an undivided 16 percent interest in each of Trust T's assets for the period from January 1, 1997 through December 31, 1997. Employer X must take into account a 16 percent pro rata share of each item of income, deduction or credit of Trust T during this period in computing its federal income tax liability.

Example 2. Assume the same facts as in *Example 1,* except that Employer X's shareholder indicates on a statement attached to a timely filed Form 5471 and can demonstrate to the satisfaction of the Commissioner that, in reliance on paragraph (h)(3)(iii) of this section, FC 100,000 of the fair market value of Trust T's assets is attributable to favorable experience relative to reasonable actuarial assumptions used. Accordingly, the relevant amount for 1997 is FC 60,000. Because the plan's normal cost for 1997 is less than FC 60,000, the de minimis exception of paragraph (h)(4) of this section does not apply. Therefore, the fractional interest for Employer X's taxable year ending on December 31, 1997, is 6 percent. Employer X is treated as the owner for federal income tax purposes of an undivided 6 percent interest in each of Trust T's assets for the period from January 1, 1997, through December 31, 1997. Employer X must take into account a 6 percent pro rata share of each item of income, deduction or credit of Trust T during this period in computing its federal income tax liability.

(9) *Effective date.*—Paragraphs (g) and (h) of this section apply to taxable years of an employer ending after September 27, 1996.

☐ Par. 3. Section 1.671-2 is amended by adding paragraph (f) to read as follows:

§1.671-2. Applicable principles.

* * *

(f) For purposes of subtitle A of the Internal Revenue Code, a person that is treated as the owner of any portion of a trust under subpart E is considered to own the trust assets attributable to that portion of the trust.

GAIN OR LOSS ON DISPOSITiON OF PROPERTY

Annuity Contracts: Exchanges of Property

Annuity Contracts: Exchanges of Property.—Amendments to Reg. §1.1001-1, providing guidance on the taxation of the exchange of property for an annuity contract, are proposed (published in the Federal Register on October 18, 2006) (REG-141901-05).

☐ Par. 3. In §1.1001-1, paragraphs (h), (i) and (j) are added to read as follows:

§1.1001-1. Computation of gain or loss.

* * *

(h) [Reserved.]

(i) [Reserved.]

(j) *Certain annuity contracts received in exchange for property.*—(1) *In general.*—If an annuity contract (other than an annuity contract that either is a debt instrument subject to sections 1271 through 1275, or is received from a charitable organization in a bargain sale governed by §1.1011-2) is received in exchange for property, receipt of the contract shall be treated as a receipt of property in an amount equal to the fair market value of the contract, whether or not the contract is the equivalent of cash. The amount realized attributable to the annuity contract is the fair market value of the annuity contract at the time of the exchange, determined under section 7520. For the timing of the recognition of gain or loss, if any, see §1.451-1(a). In the case of a transfer in part a sale and in part a gift, see paragraph (e) of this section. In the case of an annuity contract that is a debt instrument subject to sections 1271 through 1275, see paragraph (g) of this section. In the case of a bargain sale to a charitable organization, see §1.1011-2.

(2) *Effective date.*—(i) *In general.*—Except as provided in paragraph (j)(2)(ii), this paragraph (j) is effective for exchanges of property for an annuity contract (other than an annuity contract that either is a debt instrument subject to sections 1271 through 1275, or is received from a charitable organization in a bargain sale governed by §1.1011-2) after October 18, 2006.

(ii) This paragraph (j) is effective for exchanges of property for an annuity contract (other than an annuity contract that either is a debt instrument subject to sections 1271 through 1275, or is received from a charitable organization in a bargain sale governed by §1.1011-2) after April 18, 2007, if the following conditions are met—

(A) The issuer of the annuity contract is an individual;

(B) The obligations under the annuity contract are not secured, either directly or indirectly; and

(C) The property transferred in exchange for the annuity contract is not subsequently sold or otherwise disposed of by the transferee during the two-year period beginning on the date of the exchange. For purposes of this provision, a disposition includes without limitation a transfer to a trust (whether a grantor trust, a revocable trust, or any other trust) or to any other entity even if solely owned by the transferor.

Imputed Interest: OID: Safe Haven Rates: Related Party Sales

Imputed Interest: Original Issue Discount: Safe Haven Interest Rates.—Reproduced below is the text of a proposed amendment to Reg. §1.1012-2, relating to (1) the tax treatment of debt instruments issued after July 1, 1982, that contain original issue discount, (2) the imputation of and the accounting for interest with respect to sales and exchanges of property occurring after December 31, 1984, and (3) safe haven interest rates for loans or advances between commonly controlled taxpayers and safe haven leases between such taxpayers (published in the Federal Register on April 8, 1986).

☐ Par. 21. Section 1.1012-2 is revised to read as follows:

§1.1012-2. Certain sales or exchanges between related parties.—(a) *In general.*—In the case of a sale or exchange of property in which the relationship between the seller and the buyer is such that the sale or exchange is not necessarily an arm's-length transaction, the transaction shall be examined to determine whether the value of the consideration provided by the buyer is greater than or less than the value of the property. If the value of the consideration exceeds the value of the property, this excess shall not be treated as relating to the sale or exchange and will be recharacterized according to the relationship between the parties. If the value of the property exceeds the value of the consideration, this excess generally shall be treated as transferred from the seller to the buyer based on the relationship between the parties and not as transferred in exchange for the debt instrument. The preceding sentence shall not apply to any transaction that would be characterized as in part a gift and in part a sale under §1.170A-4(c)(2) and §1.1011-2(b) or under §1.1015-4.

(b) *Value.*—In applying this section to any sale or exchange where all or a part of the consideration furnished by the buyer consists of one or more debt instruments issued by the buyer to the seller, then, for purposes of this section—

(1) The value of any such debt instrument to which section 1274 applies or which has adequate stated interest within the meaning of section 1274(c)(2) or §1.483-2 shall be its issue price;

(2) The value of any such debt instrument issued under a contract to which section 483

applies shall be the amount described in §1.483-3(a)(2)(i); and

(3) In determining whether the value of the consideration furnished by the buyer exceeds the value of the property, the value of the property shall be determined by reference to the price that an unrelated buyer (having the same creditworthiness as the actual buyer) would be willing to pay for the property in an arm's-length transaction if seller financing (taken into account at its issue price) were offered on the same terms as those offered to the actual buyer.

(c) *Examples.*—The provisions of this section may be illustrated by the following examples:

Example (1). (i) On January 1, 1986, Corporation X sells nonpublicly traded property to A, the sole shareholder of X. In consideration for the sale, A makes a down payment of $200,000 and issues a debt instrument calling for a single payment of $1,000,000 due in five years. No interest is provided for in the debt instrument. Because A is the sole shareholder of X, the transaction must be examined to determine whether the value of the property exceeds the value of the consideration furnished by A. For this purpose, the value of the property is its fair market value (determined without regard to any seller financing).

(ii) Assume that the fair market value of the property is $900,000 and that the issue price of the debt instrument under §1.1274-4 is $643,928. Thus, the value of the consideration furnished by A is $843,928 (the sum of $200,000 (the portion of the consideration attributable to the down payment) and $643,928 (the portion of the consideration attributable to the debt instrument)). Since the value of the property ($900,000) exceeds the value of the consideration ($843,928), X Corporation is treated as having made a distribution to shareholder A to which section 301 applies. The amount of the distribution is $56,072 (the difference between $900,000 and $843,928). The basis of the property in the hands of A is $900,000 ($843,928 (consideration actually furnished by A) increased by $56,072 (the amount of the section 301 distribution)).

Example (2). The facts are the same as in Example (1) except that the fair market value of the property is $800,000. X is not treated as having made a section 301 distribution to A and A's basis in the property is $800,000. The transaction need not be examined for excessive consideration since a sale from a corporation to a shareholder ordinarily would not be used to disguise a contribution to capital from the shareholder to the corporation.

Example (3). (i) C sells nonpublicly traded property to his employer D for $300,000 in cash and D's debt instrument having a face amount of $1,000,000, payable in 5 years with interest payable semiannually at a rate of 9 percent. Because D is C's employer, the transaction must be examined to determine if a portion of the amount designated as consideration for the property is in fact disguised compensation.

(ii) Assume that the fair market value of the property (assuming no seller financing), is $1,000,000 and that the issue price of D's debt instrument is $1,000,000. Assume further that a buyer unrelated to D and having the same creditworthiness as C would be willing to pay $1,200,000 for the property if allowed to pay $300,000 in cash and $900,000 in the form of a 5-year debt instrument calling for semiannual payments of interest at a rate of 9 percent. The value of the consideration furnished by D is $1,300,000 (cash of $300,000 plus a debt instrument having an issue price of $1,000,000). Since this amount exceeds the value of the property by $100,000, only $200,000 of the $300,000 transferred from D to C is treated as consideration furnished for the property. The remaining $100,000 is treated as compensation. D's basis in the property is $1,200,000 (cash consideration of $200,000 plus a debt instrument with an issue price of $1,000,000).

Example (4). The facts are the same as in Example (3) except that the property could be sold to the unrelated buyer for $1,400,000 (assuming a down payment of $300,000 and 5-year seller financing at 9 percent for the balance of the purchase price). Because the value of the consideration furnished by D ($1,300,000) does not exceed the value of the property ($1,400,000), D is not treated as having paid compensation to C. D's basis in the property is $1,300,000. The transaction need not be examined for insufficient consideration since employees ordinarily do not make bargain sales to their employers. [Reg. §1.1012-2.]

Estate and Person Acquiring Property from Decedent: Consistent Basis Reporting

Estate and Person Acquiring Property from Decedent: Consistent Basis Reporting.—Reg. §1.1014-10, providing guidance regarding the requirement that a recipient's basis in certain property acquired from a decedent be consistent with the value of the property as finally determined for Federal estate tax purposes, is proposed (published in the Federal Register on March 4, 2016) (REG-127923-15).

☐ Par. 2. Section 1.1014-10 is added to read as follows:

§1.1014-10. Basis of property acquired from a decedent must be consistent with Federal estate tax return.—(a) *Consistent basis requirement.*—(1) *In general.*—The taxpayer's initial basis in property described in paragraph (b) of this section may not exceed the property's final value within the meaning of paragraph (c) of this section. This requirement applies whenever the taxpayer reports a taxable event with respect to the property to the Internal Revenue Service (IRS) (for example depreciation or amortization) and continues to apply until the property is sold, exchanged, or otherwise disposed of in one or more transactions that result in the recognition of gain or loss for Federal income tax purposes, regardless of whether the owner on the date of the sale, exchange, or disposition is the same taxpayer who acquired the property from the decedent or as a result of the decedent's death.

(2) *Subsequent basis adjustments.*—The final value within the meaning of paragraph (c) of this section is the taxpayer's initial basis in the property. In computing at any time after the decedent's date of death the taxpayer's basis in property acquired from the decedent or as a result of the decedent's death, the taxpayer's initial basis in that property may be adjusted due to the operation of other provisions of the Internal Revenue Code (Code) governing basis without violating paragraph (a)(1) of this section. Such adjustments may include, for example, gain recognized by the decedent's estate or trust upon distribution of the property, post-death capital improvements and depreciation, and post-death adjustments to the basis of an interest in a partnership or S corporation. The existence of recourse or non-recourse debt secured by property at the time of the decedent's death does not affect the property's basis, whether the gross value of the property and the outstanding debt are reported separately on the estate tax return or the net value of the property is reported. Therefore, post-death payments on such debt do not result in an adjustment to the property's basis.

(b) *Property subject to consistency requirement.*—(1) *In general.*—Property subject to the consistency requirement in paragraph (a)(1) of this section is any property that is includable in the decedent's gross estate under section 2031,any property subject to tax under section 2106, and any other property the basis of which is determined in whole or in part by reference to the basis of such property (for example as the result of a like-kind exchange or involuntary conversion) that generates a tax liability under chapter 11 of subtitle B of the Code (chapter 11) on the decedent's estate in excess of allowable credits, except the credit for prepayment of tax under chapter 11.

(2) *Exclusions.*—For purposes of paragraph (b)(1) of this section, property that qualifies for an estate tax charitable or marital deduction under section 2055, 2056, or 2056A, respectively, does not generate a tax liability under chapter 11 and therefore is excluded from the property subject to the consistency requirement in paragraph (a)(1) of this section. For purposes of paragraph (b)(1) of this section, tangible personal property for which an appraisal is not required under § 20.2031-6(b) is deemed not to generate a tax liability under chapter 11 and therefore also is excluded from the property subject to the consistency requirement in paragraph (a)(1) of this section.

(3) *Application.*—For purposes of paragraph (b)(1) of this section, if a liability under chapter 11 is payable after the application of all available credits (other than a credit for a prepayment of estate tax), the consistency requirement in paragraph (a)(1) of this section applies to the entire gross estate (other than property excluded under paragraph (b)(2) of this section) because all such property contributes to the liability under chapter 11 and therefore is treated as generating a tax liability under chapter 11. If, however, after the application of all such available credits, no tax under chapter 11 is payable, the entire gross estate is excluded from the application of the consistency requirement.

(c) *Final value.*—(1) *Finality of estate tax value.*—The *final value* of property reported on a return filed pursuant to section 6018 is its value as finally determined for purposes of the tax imposed by chapter 11. That value is —

(i) The value reported on a return filed with the Internal Revenue Service (IRS) pursuant to section 6018 once the period of limitations for assessment of the tax under chapter 11 has expired without that value having been timely adjusted or contested by the IRS,

(ii) If paragraph (c)(1)(i) of this section does not apply, the value determined or specified by the IRS once the periods of limitations for assessment and for claim for refund or credit of the tax under chapter 11 have expired without that value having been timely contested;

(iii) If paragraphs (c)(1)(i) and (ii) of this section do not apply, the value determined in an agreement, once that agreement is final and binding on all parties; or

(iv) If paragraphs (c)(1)(i), (ii), and (iii) of this section do not apply, the value determined by a court, once the court's determination is final.

(2) *No finality of estate tax value.*—Prior to the determination, in accordance with paragraph (c)(1) of this section, of the final value of property described in paragraph (b) of this section, the recipient of that property may not claim an initial basis in that property in excess of the value reported on the statement required to be furnished under section 6035(a). If the final value of the property subsequently is determined under paragraph (c)(1) of this section and that value differs from the value reported on the statement required to be furnished under section 6035(a), then the taxpayer may not rely on the statement initially furnished under section 6035(a) for the value of the property and the taxpayer may have a deficiency and underpayment resulting from this difference.

(3) *After-discovered or omitted property.*—(i) *Return under section 6018 filed.*—In the event property described in paragraph (b)(1) of this section is discovered after the estate tax return under section 6018 has been filed or otherwise is omitted from that return (after-discovered or omitted property), the final value of that property is determined under section (c)(3)(i)(A) or (B) of this section.

(A) *Reporting prior to expiration of period of limitation on assessment.*—The final value of the after-discovered or omitted property is determined in accordance with paragraph (c)(1) or (2) of this section if the executor, prior to the expiration of the period of limitation on assessment of the tax imposed on the estate by chapter 11, files with the IRS an initial or supplemental estate tax return under section 6018 reporting the property.

(B) *No reporting prior to expiration of period of limitation on assessment.*—If the executor does not report the after-discovered or omitted property on an initial or supplemental Federal estate tax return filed prior to the expiration of the period of limitation on assessment of the tax imposed on the estate by chapter 11, the final value of that unreported property is zero. See *Example 3* of paragraph (e) of this section.

(ii) *No return under section 6018 filed.*—If no return described in section 6018 has been filed, and if the inclusion in the decedent's gross estate of the after-discovered or omitted property would have generated or increased the estate's tax liability under chapter 11, the final value, for purposes of section 1014(f), of all property described in paragraph (b) of this section is zero until the final value is determined under paragraph (c)(1) or (2) of this section. Specifically, if the executor files a return pursuant to section 6018(a) or (b) that includes this property or the IRS determines a value for the property, the final value of all property described in paragraph (b) of this section includible in the gross estate then is determined under paragraph (c)(1) or (2) of this section.

(d) *Executor.*—For purposes of this section, *executor* has the same meaning as in section 2203 and includes any other person required under section 6018(b) to file a return.

(e) *Examples.*—The following examples illustrate the application of this section.

Example 1. (i) At D's death, D owned 50% of Partnership P, which owned a rental building with a fair market value of $10 million subject to nonrecourse debt of $2 million. D's sole beneficiary is C, D's child. P is valued at $8 million. D's interest in P is reported on the return required by section 6018(a) at $4 million. The IRS accepts the return as filed and the time for assessing the tax under chapter 11 expires. C sells the interest for $6 million in cash shortly thereafter.

(ii) Under these facts, the final value of D's interest is $4 million under paragraph (c)(1)(i) of this section. Under section 742 and § 1.742-1, C's basis in the interest in P at the time of its sale is $5 million (the final value of D's interest ($4 million) plus 50% of the $2 million nonrecourse debt). Following the sale of the interest, C reports taxable gain of $1 million. C has complied with the consistency requirement of paragraph (a)(1) of this section.

(iii) Assume instead that the IRS adjusts the value of the interest in P to $4.5 million, and that value is not contested before the expiration of the time for assessing the tax under chapter 11. The final value of D's interest in P is $4.5 million under paragraph (c)(1)(ii) of this section. Under section 742 and § 1.742-1, C claims a basis of $5.5 million at the time of sale and reports gain on the sale of $500,000. C has complied with the consistency requirement of paragraph (a)(1) of this section.

Example 2. (i) At D's death, D owned (among other assets) a private residence that was not encumbered. D's sole beneficiary is C. D's executor reports the value of the residence on the return required by section 6018(a) as $600,000 and pays the tax liability under chapter 11. The IRS timely contests the reported value and determines that the value of the residence is $725,000. The parties enter into a settlement agreement that provides that the value of the residence for purposes of the tax imposed by chapter 11 is $650,000. Pursuant to paragraph (c)(1)(iii) of this section, the final value of the residence is $650,000.

(ii) Several years later, C adds a master suite to the residence at a cost of $45,000. Pursuant to section 1016(a), C's basis in the residence is increased by $45,000 to $695,000. Subsequently, C sells the residence to an unrelated third party for $900,000. C claims a basis in the residence of $695,000 and reports a gain of $205,000 ($900,000 – $695,000). C has complied with the consistency requirement of paragraph (a)(1) of this section.

Example 3. (i) The facts are the same as in *Example 2* but, after the expiration of the period for assessing the tax imposed by chapter 11, the executor discovers property that had not been reported on the return required by section 6018(a) but which, if reported, would have generated additional chapter 11 tax on the entire value of the newly discovered property. Pursuant to paragraph (c)(3)(i)(B) of this section, C's basis in the residence of $695,000 does not change, but the final value of the additional unreported property is zero.

(ii) Alternatively, assume that no return was required to be filed under section 6018 before discovering the additional property (and none in fact was filed) but, after the application of the applicable credit amount, D's taxable estate including the unreported property would have been $200,000. Pursuant to paragraph (c)(3)(ii) of this section, the final value of all property included in D's gross estate that is described in paragraph (b) of this section is zero until the executor files an estate tax return with the IRS pursuant to section 6018 or the IRS determines a value for the property. In either of those events, the final value of property described in paragraph (b) of this section reported on the return is determined in accordance with paragraph (c)(1) or (c)(2) of this section.

Example 4. (i) At D's death, D's gross estate includes a residence valued at $300,000 encumbered by nonrecourse debt in the amount of $100,000. Title to the residence is held jointly by D and C (D's daughter) with rights of survivorship. D provided all the consideration for the residence and the entire value of the residence was included in D's gross estate. The executor reports the value of the residence as $200,000 on the return required by section 6018 filed with the IRS for D's estate and claims no other deduction for the debt. The statement required by section 6035 reports the value of the residence as

$300,000. C sells the residence before the final value is determined under paragraph (c)(1) of this section for $375,000 and claims a gain of $75,000 on C's Federal income tax return.

(ii) A court subsequently determines that the value of the residence was $290,000 and the time for contesting this value in any court expires before the expiration of the period for assessing C's income tax for the year of C's sale of the property. The final value of the residence is $290,000 pursuant to paragraphs (c)(1)(iv) and (c)(2) of this section. Because C claimed a basis in the residence that exceeds the final value, C may have a deficiency and underpayment.

(f) *Effective/applicability date*.—Upon the publication of the Treasury Decision adopting these rules as final in the **Federal Register**, this section will apply to property acquired from a decedent or by reason of the death of a decedent whose return required by section 6018 is filed after July 31, 2015. Persons may rely upon these rules before the date of publication of the Treasury Decision adopting these rules as final in the **Federal Register**. [Reg. § 1.1014-10.]

ESTATE TAX

Estate and Gift Taxes: Basic Exclusion Amount

Estate and Gift Taxes: Basic Exclusion Amount.—Amendments of Reg § 20.2010-1, relating to the basic exclusion amount (BEA) applicable to the computation of Federal estate and gift taxes, are proposed (published in the Federal Register on April 27, 2022) (REG-118913-21).

☐ Par. 2. Section 20.2010-1 is amended by:

1. Adding paragraph (c)(3); and

2. Revising the first sentence of paragraph (f)(2) and adding a sentence after the second sentence.

The revision and additions read as follows:

§ 20.2010-1. Unified credit against estate tax; in general.

* * *

(c) * * *

(3) *Exception to the special rule*.—(i) *Transfers to which the special rule does not apply*.—Except as provided in paragraph (c)(3)(ii) of this section, the special rule of paragraph (c) of this section does not apply to transfers includible in the gross estate, or treated as includible in the gross estate for purposes of section 2001(b), including without limitation the following transfers:

(A) Transfers includible in the gross estate pursuant to section 2035, 2036, 2037, 2038, or 2042, regardless of whether all or any part of the transfer was deductible pursuant to section 2522 or 2523;

(B) Transfers made by enforceable promise to the extent they remain unsatisfied as of the date of death;

(C) Transfers described in § 25.2701-5(a)(4) or § 25.2702-6(a)(1) of this chapter; and

(D) Transfers that would have been described in paragraph (c)(3)(i)(A), (B), or (C) of this section but for the transfer, relinquishment, or elimination of an interest, power, or property, effectuated within 18 months of the date of the decedent's death by the decedent alone, by the decedent in conjunction with any other person, or by any other person.

(ii) *Transfers to which the special rule continues to apply*.—Notwithstanding paragraph (c)(3)(i) of this section, the special rule of paragraph (c) of this section applies to the following transfers:

(A) Transfers includible in the gross estate in which the value of the taxable portion of the transfer, determined as of the date of the transfer, was 5 percent or less of the total value of the transfer; and

(B) Transfers, relinquishments, or eliminations described in paragraph (c)(3)(i)(D) of this section effectuated by the termination of the durational period described in the original instrument of transfer by either the mere passage of time or the death of any person.

(iii) *Examples*.—In each example, the basic exclusion amount on the date of the gift was $11.4 million, the basic exclusion amount on the date of death is $6.8 million, and both amounts include hypothetical inflation adjustments. The donor's executor does not elect to use the alternate valuation date and, unless otherwise stated, the donor never married and made no other gifts during life.

(A) *Example 1*.—Individual A made a completed gift of A's promissory note in the amount of $9 million. The note remained unpaid as of the date of A's death. The assets that are to be used to satisfy the note are part of A's gross estate, with the result that the note is treated as includible in the gross estate for purposes of section 2001(b) and is not included in A's adjusted taxable gifts. Because the note is treated as includible in the gross estate and does not qualify for the 5 percent de minimis rule in paragraph (c)(3)(ii)(A) of this section, the exception to the special rule found in paragraph (c)(3) of this section applies to the gift of the note. The credit to be applied for purposes of computing A's estate tax is based on the $6.8 million basic exclusion amount as of A's date of death, subject to the limitation of section 2010(d). The result would be the same if A or a person empowered to act on A's behalf had paid the note within the 18 months prior to the date of A's death.

(B) *Example 2*.—Assume that the facts are the same as in paragraph (c)(3)(iii)(A) of this section (*Example 1*) except that A's promissory note had a value of $2 million and, on the same date that A made the gift of the promissory note, A also made a gift of $9 million in cash. The cash gift was paid immediately, whereas the $2 million note remained unpaid as of the date of A's death. The assets that are to be used to satisfy the note are part of A's gross estate, with the result that the note is treated as includible in the gross estate for purposes of section 2001(b) and is not included in A's adjusted taxable gifts. Because the $2 million note is treated as includible in the gross estate and does not qualify for the 5 percent de minimis rule in paragraph (c)(3)(ii)(A) of this section, the exception to the special rule found in paragraph (c)(3) of this section applies to the gift of the note. On the other hand, the $9 million cash gift was paid immediately, and no portion of that gift is includible or treated as includible in the gross estate. Because the amount allowable as a credit in computing the gift tax payable on A's $9 million cash gift exceeds the credit based on the $6.8 million basic exclusion amount allowable on A's date of death, the special rule of paragraph (c) of this section applies to that gift. The credit to be applied for purposes of computing A's estate tax is based on a basic exclusion amount of $9 million, the amount used to determine the credit allowable in computing the gift tax payable on A's $9 million cash gift.

(C) *Example 3.*—Assume that the facts are the same as in paragraph (c)(3)(iii)(A) of this section (*Example 1*) except that, prior to A's gift of the note, the executor of the estate of A's predeceased spouse elected, pursuant to §20.2010-2, to allow A to take into account the predeceased spouse's $2 million DSUE amount. Assume further that A's promissory note had a value of $2 million on the date of the gift, and that A made a gift of $9 million in cash a few days later. The cash gift was paid immediately, whereas the $2 million note remained unpaid as of the date of A's death. The assets that are to be used to satisfy the note are part of A's gross estate, with the result that the note is treated as includible in the gross estate for purposes of section 2001(b) and is not included in A's adjusted taxable gifts. Because A's DSUE amount was sufficient to shield the gift of the note from gift tax, no basic exclusion amount was applicable to the $2 million gift pursuant to paragraph (c)(1)(ii)(A) of this section and the special rule of paragraph (c) of this section does not apply to that gift. On the other hand, the $9 million cash gift was paid immediately, and no portion of that gift is includible or treated as includible in the gross estate. Because the amount allowable as a credit in computing the gift tax payable on A's $9 million cash gift exceeds the credit based on the $6.8 million basic exclusion amount allowable on A's date of death, the special rule of paragraph (c) of this section applies to that gift. The credit to be applied for purposes of computing A's estate tax is based on A's $11 million applicable exclusion amount, consisting of the $2 million DSUE amount plus the $9 million amount used to determine the credit allowable in computing the gift tax payable on A's $9 million cash gift.

(D) *Example 4.*—Individual B transferred $9 million to a grantor retained annuity trust (GRAT), retaining a qualified annuity interest within the meaning of §25.2702-3(b) of this chapter valued at $8,550,000. The taxable portion of the transfer valued as of the date of the transfer was $450,000. B died during the term of the GRAT. The entire GRAT corpus is includible in the gross estate pursuant to §20.2036-1(c)(2). Because the value of the taxable portion of the transfer was 5 percent or less of the total value of the transfer determined as of the date of the gift, the 5 percent de minimis rule in paragraph (c)(3)(ii)(A) of this section is met and the exception to the special rule found in paragraph (c)(3) of this section does not apply to the gift. However, because the total of the amounts allowable as a credit in computing the gift tax payable on B's post-1976 gift of $450,000 is less than the credit based on the $6.8 million basic exclusion amount allowable on B's date of death, the special rule of paragraph (c) of this section does not apply to the gift. The credit to be applied for purposes of computing B's estate tax is based on the $6.8 million basic exclusion amount as of B's date of death, subject to the limitation of section 2010(d).

(E) *Example 5.*—Assume that the facts are the same as in paragraph (c)(3)(iii)(D) of this section (*Example 4*) except that B's qualified annuity interest is valued at $8 million. The taxable portion of the transfer valued as of the date of the transfer was $1 million. Because the value of the taxable portion of the transfer was more than 5 percent of the total value of the transfer determined as of the date of the gift, the 5 percent de minimis rule in paragraph (c)(3)(ii)(A) of this section is not met and the exception to the special rule found in paragraph (c)(3) of this section applies to the gift. The credit to be applied for purposes of computing B's estate tax is based on the $6.8 million basic exclusion amount as of B's date of death, subject to the limitation of section 2010(d).

(F) *Example 6.*—Assume that the facts are the same as in paragraph (c)(3)(iii)(D) of this section (*Example 4*) except that B's qualified annuity interest is valued at $2 million. The taxable portion of the transfer valued as of the date of the transfer was $7 million. B survived the term of the GRAT. Because B survived the original unaltered term of the GRAT, no part of the value of the assets transferred to the GRAT is includible in B's gross estate, and the exception to the special rule found in paragraph (c)(3) of this section does not apply to the gift. Moreover, because the amount allowable as a credit in computing the gift tax payable on B's $7 million gift exceeds the credit based on the $6.8 million basic exclusion amount allowable on B's date of death, the special rule of paragraph (c) of this section applies to the gift. The credit to be applied for purposes of computing B's estate tax is based on a basic exclusion amount of $7 million, the amount used to determine the credit allowable in computing the gift tax payable on B's transfer to the GRAT.

(G) *Example 7.*—Individual C transferred $9 million to a grantor retained income trust (GRIT), retaining an income interest valued at $0 pursuant to section 2702(a)(2)(A). The taxable portion of the transfer valued as of the date of the transfer was $9 million. C died during the term of the GRIT. The entire GRIT corpus is includible in C's gross estate pursuant to section 2036(a)(1) because C retained the right to receive all of the income of the GRIT. Because the transferred assets are includible in the gross estate and do not qualify for the 5 percent de minimis rule in paragraph (c)(3)(ii)(A) of this section, the exception to the special rule found in paragraph (c)(3) of this section applies to the gift. The credit to be applied for purposes of computing C's estate tax is based on the $6.8 million basic exclusion amount as of C's date of death, subject to the limitation of section 2010(d).

* * *

(f) * * *

(2) *Exceptions.*—Except as specifically provided in this paragraph (f)(2), paragraphs (c) and (e)(3) of this section apply to estates of decedents dying on or after November 26, 2019. * * * Paragraph (c)(3) of this section is applicable to the estates of decedents dying on or after April 27, 2022. * * *

Annuities: Interests: Valuation: Actuarial Tables

Annuities: Interests: Valuation: Actuarial Tables.—Amendments to Reg. § 20.2031-0, relating to the use of actuarial tables in valuing annuities, interests for life or terms of years, and remainder or reversionary interests, are proposed (published in the Federal Register on May 5, 2022) (REG-122770-18).

☐ Par. 13. Section 20.2031-0 is revised to read as follows:

§ 20.2031-0. Table of contents.—This section lists the section headings and undesignated center headings that appear in the regulations under section 2031.

Below-Market Loans

Below-Market Interest Rate Loans: Tax Reform Act of 1984.—Reproduced below is the text of a proposed amendment of Reg. § 20.2031-4, detailing the estate tax treatment of lenders and borrowers with respect to below-market term loans made after June 6, 1984, and below-market demand loans outstanding after such date (published in the Federal Register on August 20, 1985).

☐ Par. 7. Section 20.2031-4 is amended by adding a new sentence at the end to read as follows:

§ 20.2031-4. Valuation of notes.

* * * See § 20.7872-1 for special rules in the case of gift loans (within the meaning of § 1.7872-4(b)) made after June 6, 1984.

* * *

Annuities: Interests: Valuation: Actuarial Tables

Annuities: Interests: Valuation: Actuarial Tables.—Amendments to Reg. § 20.2031-7, relating to the use of actuarial tables in valuing annuities, interests for life or terms of years, and remainder or reversionary interests, are proposed (published in the Federal Register on May 5, 2022) (REG-122770-18).

☐ Par. 14. Section 20.2031-7 is amended by:

1. Revising paragraph (c), the heading of paragraph (d), and paragraphs (d)(1) through (5).
2. Redesignating paragraph (d)(7) as paragraph (g)(4) of § 20.2031-7A.
3. Adding new paragraph (d)(7).
4. Revising paragraph (e).

The revisions and addition read as follows:

§20.2031-7. Valuation of annuities, interests for life or a term of years, and remainder or reversionary interests.

* * *

(c) *Actuarial valuations.*—The present value of annuities, interests for life or a term of years, and remainder or reversionary interests for estates of decedents for which the valuation date of the gross estate is on or after [applicability date of the Treasury decision adopting these regulations as final regulations], is determined under paragraph (d) of this section. The present value of annuities, interests for life or a term of years, and remainder or reversionary interests for estates of decedents for which the valuation date of the gross estate is before [applicability date of the Treasury decision adopting these regulations as final regulations], is determined under the following sections:

Table 1 to paragraph (c)

Valuation Dates		Applicable Regulations
After	*Before*	
-	01-01-52	20.2031-7A(a)
12-31-51	01-01-71	20.2031-7A(b)
12-31-70	12-01-83	20.2031-7A(c)
11-30-83	05-01-89	20.2031-7A(d)
04-30-89	05-01-99	20.2031-7A(e)
04-30-99	05-01-09	20.2031-7A(f)
04-30-09	AD	20.2031-7A(g)

AD = [applicability date of the Treasury decision adopting these regulations as final regulations].

(d) *Actuarial valuations on or after [applicability date of the Treasury decision adopting these regulations as final regulations].*—(1) *In general.*—Except as otherwise provided in paragraph (b) of this section and §20.7520-3(b) (pertaining to certain limitations on the use of prescribed tables), if the valuation date for the gross estate of the decedent is on or after [applicability date of the Treasury decision adopting these regulations as final regulations], the fair market value of annuities, interests for life or a term of years, and remainder or reversionary interests is the present value determined by using standard or special section 7520 actuarial factors. These factors are derived by using the actuarial formulas provided in paragraph (d)(2) of this section, the appropriate section 7520 interest rate, and, if applicable, the mortality component for the valuation date of the interest that is being valued. For purposes of the computations described in this section, the age of an individual is the age of that individual at the individual's nearest birthday. For the convenience of taxpayers, paragraph (d)(2) of this section provides for published tables of factors for specific types of interests. These published tables provide factors for rates from 0.2 to 20 percent, inclusive, at intervals of two-tenths of one percent. In general, appropriate factors instead may be computed directly from the actuarial formulas provided in paragraph (d)(2) of this section. In some cases, specific examples in this part and IRS publications illustrate approximation methods (for example, interpolation) for obtaining factors when the required valuation rate falls between two listed rates (such as in the case of a pooled income fund's rate of return or a unitrust's adjusted payout rate). Exact methods of obtaining the applicable actuarial factors are allowed, such as through software using the actual rate of return and the actuarial formulas provided in paragraph (d)(2) of this section; the approximation method provided in this part must be used if more exact methods are not available. See §§20.7520-1 through 20.7520-4.

(2) *Specific interests.*—(i) *Pooled income funds and charitable remainder trusts.*—The fair market value of a remainder interest in a pooled income fund, as defined in §1.642(c)-5 of this chapter, is its value determined under §1.642(c)-6(e). The fair market value of a remainder interest in a charitable remainder annuity trust, as defined in §1.664-2(a), is the present value determined under §1.664-2(c). The fair market value of a remainder interest in a charitable remainder unitrust, as defined in §1.664-3, is its present value determined under §1.664-4(e). The fair market value of a life interest or an interest for a term of years in a charitable remainder unitrust is the fair market value of the property as of the date of valuation less the fair market value of the remainder interest on that date determined under §1.664-4(e)(4) and (5).

(ii) *Ordinary remainder and reversionary interests.*—(A) *Remainder and reversionary interests for a term of years.*—If the interest to be valued is a remainder or reversionary interest to take effect after a definite number of years, the present value of the interest is computed by multiplying the value of the property by the appropriate remainder factor (that corresponds to the applicable section 7520 interest rate and the stated term). The factor for an ordinary remainder interest following a term certain may be found using the formula in Figure 1 to this paragraph (d)(2)(ii)(A). For the convenience of taxpayers, actuarial factors have been computed by IRS and appear in Table B. Table B can be found on the IRS website at *https://www.irs.gov/retirement-plans/actuarial-tables* (or a corresponding URL as may be updated from time to time). Table B is referenced and explained in IRS Publication 1457 "Actuarial Valuations Version 4A," which will be available after [date of publication of the final rule in the **Federal Register**]. The remainder factors from Table B also can be found in paragraph (d)(6) of this section, but only for interest rates from 4.2 to 14 percent, inclusive. For information about obtaining special factors for other situations, see paragraph (d)(4) of this section.

Figure 1 to paragraph (d)(2)(ii)(A) – Formula for determining term certain remainder factors

$$\left(\frac{1}{1+i}\right)^n$$

where:

n = the term of years; and

i = the interest rate specified under section 7520 of the Internal Revenue Code.

(B) *Remainder and reversionary interests dependent on the life of one individual.*—If the interest to be valued is a remainder or reversionary interest to take effect after the death of one individual, the present value of the interest is computed by multiplying the value of the property by the appropriate remainder factor (that corresponds to the applicable section 7520 interest rate and the age of the measuring life of the life interest that precedes the remainder interest). The factor for an ordinary remainder interest following the death of one individual may be found using the formula in Figure 2 to this paragraph (d)(2)(ii)(B). The prescribed mortality table is Table 2010CM as set forth in paragraph (d)(7)(ii) of this section, or for periods before [applicability date of the Treasury decision adopting these regulations as final regulations], the appropriate table found in § 20.2031-7A. For the convenience of taxpayers, actuarial factors have been computed by IRS and appear in Table S. Table S will be available beginning May 5, 2022, at no charge, electronically via the IRS website at *https://www.irs.gov/retirement-plans/actuarial-tables* (or a corresponding URL as may be updated from time to time). Table S is referenced and explained by IRS Publication 1457 "Actuarial Valuations Version 4A," which will be available after [date of publication of the final rule in the **Federal Register**]. For information about obtaining special factors for other situations, see paragraph (d)(4) of this section.

Figure 2 to paragraph (d)(2)(ii)(B) – Formula for determining single life remainder factors

$$\left(1+\frac{i}{2}\right)\sum_{t=0}^{\infty} v^{t+1}\left({}_{t+1}q_x - {}_{t}q_x\right)$$

where:

i = the applicable interest rate under section 7520 of the Internal Revenue Code;

v = 1 / (1 + i) ;

$${}_{t}q_x = 1 - \frac{l_{x+t}}{l_x} \ ;$$

x = the age of the measuring life (determined as age at nearest birthday); and

l_x = the number associated with age x as set forth in the prescribed mortality table, representing the number of persons alive at age x.

(iii) *Ordinary interests for a term of years and life interests.*—If the interest to be valued is the right of a person to receive the income of certain property, or to the use of certain property, for a term of years or for the life of one individual, the present value of the interest is computed by multiplying the value of the property by the appropriate actuarial factor for an interest for a term of years or for a life interest (that corresponds to the applicable section 7520 interest rate and the durational period). The actuarial factor for an ordinary income interest for a term certain may be found by subtracting from 1.000000 the factor for an ordinary remainder interest following the same term certain that is determined under the formula in paragraph (d)(2)(ii)(A) of this section. For the convenience of taxpayers, actuarial factors have been computed by IRS and appear in the "Income Interest" column of Table B which can be found on the IRS website at *https://www.irs.gov/retirement-plans/actuarial-tables* (or a corresponding URL as may be updated from time to time). The actuarial factor for an ordinary income interest for the life of one individual may be found by subtracting from 1.00000 the factor for an ordinary remainder interest following the life of the same individual that is determined in paragraph (d)(2)(ii)(B) of this section. For the convenience of taxpayers, actuarial factors have been computed by IRS and appear in the "Life Estate" column of Table S. Table S (applicable when the valuation date is on or after [applicability date of the Treasury decision adopting these regulations as final regulations]) can be found on the IRS website at *https://www.irs.gov/retirement-plans/actuarial-tables*. Table B and Table S are referenced and explained by IRS Publication 1457 "Actuarial Valuations Version 4A". See §20.2031-7A or earlier versions of Publication 1457 for valuation of interests before [applicability date of the Treasury decision adopting these regulations as final regulations]. For information about obtaining special factors for other situations, see paragraph (d)(4) of this section.

(iv) *Annuities.*—(A) If the interest to be valued is the right of a person to receive an annuity that is payable at the end of each year for a term of years or for the life of one individual, the present value of the interest is computed by multiplying the aggregate amount payable annually by the appropriate annuity factor (that corresponds to the applicable section 7520 interest rate and annuity period). The appropriate annuity factor for an annuity payable for a term of years is computed by subtracting from 1.000000 the factor for an ordinary remainder interest following the same term certain that is determined under the formula in paragraph (d)(2)(ii)(A) of this section and then dividing the result by the applicable section 7520 interest rate expressed as a number with at least four decimal places. For the convenience of taxpayers, actuarial factors have been computed by IRS and appear in the "Annuity" column of Table B which can be found on the IRS website at *https://www.irs.gov/retirement-plans/actuarial-tables* (or a corresponding URL as may be updated from time to time). The appropriate annuity factor for an annuity payable for the life of one individual is computed by subtracting from 1.00000 the factor for an ordinary remainder interest following the life of the same individual that is determined under the formula in paragraph (d)(2)(ii)(B) of this section and then dividing the result by the applicable section 7520 interest rate expressed as a number with four decimal places. For the convenience of taxpayers, actuarial factors have been computed by IRS and appear in the "Annuity" column of Table S. Table S (applicable when the valuation date is on or after [applicability date of the Treasury decision adopting these regulations as final regulations]) can be found on the IRS website at *https://www.irs.gov/retirement-plans/actuarial-tables*. Table B and Table S are referenced and explained in IRS Publication 1457 "Actuarial Valuations Version 4A". See §20.2031-7A or earlier versions of Publication 1457 for valuation of interests before [applicability date of the Treasury decision adopting these regulations as final regulations]. For information about obtaining special factors for other situations, see paragraph (d)(4) of this section.

(B) If the annuity is payable at the end of semiannual, quarterly, monthly, or weekly periods, the product obtained by multiplying the annuity factor by the aggregate amount payable annually is then multiplied by the applicable adjustment factor at the appropriate interest rate component for payments made at the end of the specified periods. The applicable adjustment factor may be found using the formula in Figure 3 to this paragraph (d)(2)(iv)(B). For the convenience of taxpayers, actuarial factors have been computed by IRS and appear in Table K. Table K, which is referenced and explained by Publication 1457, can be found on the IRS website at *https://www.irs.gov/retirement-plans/actuarial-tables*. The provisions of this paragraph (d)(2)(iv)(B) are illustrated by the example in paragraph (d)(2)(iv)(B)(2) of this section. *Figure 3 to paragraph (d)(2)(iv)(B) – Formula for determining annuity adjustment factor at the end of the specified period*

$$\frac{i}{p\left[(1+i)^{(1/p)}-1\right]}$$

where:

p = the number of payments per year; and

i = the interest rate specified under section 7520 of the Internal Revenue Code.

(1) Sample factors from actuarial Table S and Table K. For purposes of the example in paragraph (d)(2)(iv)(B)(2) of this section, the following factors from Table S and Table K will be used:

Table 2 to paragraph (d)(2)(iv)(B)(1)

Factors from Table S - Based on Table 2010CM			
Interest at 3.2 Percent			
Age	Annuity	Life Estate	Remainder
75	9.4053	0.30097	0.69903

Factors from Table K			
Adjustment Factors for Annuities Payable at the End of Each Interval			
Interest Rate	Semi-Annually	Quarterly	Monthly
3.2%	1.0079	1.0119	1.0146

(2) *Example.* At the time of the decedent's death, the survivor/annuitant, age 75, is entitled to receive an annuity of $15,000 per year for life payable in equal monthly installments at the end of each month. The section 7520 rate for the month in which the decedent died is 3.2 percent. Under Table S, the annuity factor at 3.2 percent for an individual aged 75 is 9.4053. Under Table K, the adjustment factor under the column for payments made at the end of each monthly period at the rate of 3.2 percent is 1.0146. The aggregate annual amount, $15,000, is multiplied by the factor 9.4053 and the product then is multiplied by 1.0146. The present value of the annuity at the date of the decedent's death is, therefore, $143,139.26 ($15,000 × 9.4053 × 1.0146).

(C) If an annuity is payable at the beginning of annual, semiannual, quarterly, monthly, or weekly periods for a term of years, the value of the annuity is computed by multiplying the aggregate amount payable annually by the annuity factor described in paragraph (d)(2)(iv)(A) of this section; and the product so obtained then is multiplied by the applicable adjustment factor at the appropriate interest rate component for payments made at the beginning of specified periods. The applicable adjustment factor may be found using the formula in Figure 4 to this paragraph (d)(2)(iv)(C). For the convenience of taxpayers, actuarial factors have been computed by IRS and appear in Table J. Table J, which is referenced and explained by Publication 1457, can be found on the IRS website at *https://www.irs.gov/retirement-plans/actuarial-tables.* If an annuity is payable at the beginning of annual, semiannual, quarterly, monthly, or weekly periods for one or more lives, the value of the annuity is the sum of the first payment plus the present value of a similar annuity, the first payment of which is not to be made until the end of the payment period, determined as provided in paragraph (d)(2)(iv)(B) of this section.

Figure 4 to paragraph (d)(2)(iv)(C) – Formula for determining annuity adjustment factor at the beginning of the specified period

$$\frac{i}{p\left[(1 - v)^{(1/p)}\right]}$$

where:

p = the number of payments per year;

v = 1 / (1 + i); and

i = the interest rate specified under section 7520 of the Internal Revenue Code.

(v) *Annuity and unitrust interests for a term of years or until the prior death of an individual.*—See § 25.2512-5(d)(2)(v) of this chapter for examples explaining how to compute the present value of an annuity or unitrust interest that is payable until the earlier of the lapse of a specific number of years or the death of an individual.

(3) *Transitional rule.* If a decedent dies on or after January 1, 2021, and before [applicability date of the Treasury decision adopting these regulations as final regulations], the fair market value of annuities, interests for life or a term of years, and remainder or reversionary interests based on one or more measuring lives included in the gross estate of the decedent is their present value determined under this section by using the section 7520 interest rate for the month in which the valuation date occurs (see §§ 20.7520-1(b) and 20.7520-2(a)(2)) and factors derived from the selected mortality table, either Table 2010CM in paragraph (d)(7)(ii) of this section or Table 2000CM in § 20.2031-7A(g)(4), at the option of the donor or the decedent's executor, as the case may be. For the convenience of taxpayers, actuarial factors based on Table 2010CM appear in the proposed version of Table S, and actuarial factors based on Table 2000CM appear in the current version of Table S, which will be available as provided in paragraph (d)(4) of this section. The decedent's executor must consistently use the same mortality basis with respect to each interest (income, remainder, partial, etc.) in the same

property, and with respect to all transfers occurring on the valuation date. For example, gift and income tax charitable deductions with respect to the same transfer must be determined based on factors with the same mortality basis, and all assets includible in the gross estate and/or estate tax deductions claimed must be valued based on factors with the same mortality basis.

(4) *Publications and actuarial computations by the Internal Revenue Service.*—The factor for determining the present value of a remainder interest that is dependent on the termination of the life of one individual may be computed by using the formula in paragraph (d)(2)(ii)(B) of this section to derive factors from the appropriate mortality table. For the convenience of taxpayers, actuarial factors have been computed by IRS and appear in Table S. The factor for determining the present value of a remainder interest following a term certain may be computed by using the formula in paragraph (d)(2)(ii)(A) of this section. For the convenience of taxpayers, actuarial factors have been computed by IRS and appear in Table B. Adjustment factors for term certain annuities payable at the beginning of each interval may be computed by using the formula in paragraph (d)(2)(iv)(C) of this section. For the convenience of taxpayers, actuarial factors have been computed by IRS and appear in Table J. Adjustment factors for annuities payable at the end of each interval may be computed by using the formula in paragraph (d)(2)(iv)(B) of this section. For the convenience of taxpayers, actuarial factors have been computed by IRS and appear in Table K. These tables will be available beginning May 5, 2022, at no charge, electronically via the IRS website at *https://www.irs.gov/retirement-plans/actuarial-tables* (or a corresponding URL as may be updated from time to time). IRS Publication 1457, "Actuarial Valuations Version 4A" (2022), references and explains the factors contained in the actuarial tables and also includes examples that illustrate how to compute many special factors for more unusual situations. This publication will be available after [date the Treasury decision adopting these regulations as final regulations is published in the **Federal Register**]. Table B, Table J, and Table K also can be found in paragraph (d)(6) of this section, but only for interest rates from 4.2 to 14 percent, inclusive. If a special factor is required in the case of an actual decedent, the special factor may be calculated by the executor using the actuarial formulas in paragraph (d)(2) of this section or the executor may request a ruling to obtain the factor from the Internal Revenue Service. The request for a ruling must be accompanied by a recitation of the facts including a statement of the date of birth for each measuring life, the date of the decedent's death, any other applicable dates, and a copy of the will, trust, or other relevant documents. A request for a ruling must comply with the instructions for requesting a ruling published periodically in the Internal Revenue Bulletin (see §§601.201 and 601.601(d)(2)(ii)(*b*) of this chapter) and must include payment of the required user fee.

(5) *Examples.*—The provisions of this section are illustrated by the examples in this paragraph (d)(5). For purposes of these examples, the following factors from Table S, Table B, and Table K will be used:

Table 3 to paragraph (d)(5)

Factors from Table S - Based on Table 2010CM			
Interest at 3.2 Percent			
Age	Annuity	Life Estate	Remainder
31	23.8334	0.76267	0.23733
46	20.0146	0.64047	0.35953
Interest at 4.6 Percent			
Age	Annuity	Life Estate	Remainder
65	11.7691	0.54138	0.45862

Factors from Table B			
Annuity, Income, and Remainder Interests for a Term Certain			
Interest at 2.6 Percent			
Years	Annuity	Income Interest	Remainder
5	4.6325	0.120445	0.879555

Factors from Table K			
Adjustment Factors for Annuities Payable at the End of Each Interval			
Interest Rate	Semi-Annually	Quarterly	Monthly
2.6%	1.0065	1.0097	1.0119
3.2%	1.0079	1.0119	1.0146

(i) *Example 1: Remainder payable at an individual's death.*—The decedent, or the decedent's estate, was entitled to receive certain property worth $50,000 upon the death of A, to whom the income was bequeathed for life. At the time of the decedent's death, A was 65 years and 5 months old. In the month in which the decedent died, the section 7520 rate was 4.6 percent. Under Table S, the remainder factor at 4.6 percent for determining the present value of the remainder interest due at the death of a person aged 65, A's age at A's nearest birthday to the date of the decedent's death, is 0.45862. The present value of the remainder interest at the date of the decedent's death is, therefore, $22,931 ($50,000 times 0.45862).

(ii) *Example 2: Income payable for an individual's life.*—A's parent bequeathed an income interest in property to A for life, with the remainder interest passing to B at A's death. At the time of the parent's death, the value of the property was $50,000 and A was 30 years and 10 months old. The section 7520 rate at the time of the parent's death was 3.2 percent. Under Table S, the factor at 3.2 percent for determining the present value of the life estate given to a person aged 31, A's age at A's nearest birthday to the date of the decedent's death, is 0.76267. The present value of A's income interest at the time of the parent's death is, therefore, $38,133.50 ($50,000.00 × 0.76267).

(iii) *Example 3: Annuity payable for an individual's life.*—A purchased an annuity for the benefit of both A and B. Under the terms of the annuity contract, at A's death, a survivor annuity of $10,000 per year, payable in equal semiannual installments made at the end of each interval is payable to B for life. At A's death, B was 45 years and 7 months old. Also, at A's death, the section 7520 rate was 3.2 percent. Under Table S, the factor at 3.2 percent for determining the present value of an annuity interest payable until the death of a person age 46 (B's age at B's nearest birthday to the date of A's death) is 20.0146. The adjustment factor from Table K at an interest rate of 3.2 percent for semiannual annuity payments made at the end of the period is 1.0079. The present value of the annuity at the date of A's death is, therefore, $201,727.15 ($10,000 × 20.0146 × 1.0079).

(iv) *Example 4: Annuity payable for a term of years.*—The decedent, or the decedent's estate, was entitled to receive an annuity of $10,000 per year payable in equal quarterly installments at the end of each quarter throughout a term certain. At the time of the decedent's death, the section 7520 rate was 2.6 percent. A quarterly payment had been made immediately prior to the decedent's death and payments were to continue for 5 more years. Under Table B for the interest rate of 2.6 percent, the factor for the present value of an annuity with a term of 5 years is 4.6325. The adjustment factor from Table K at an interest rate of 2.6 percent for quarterly annuity payments made at the end of the quarter is 1.0097. The present value of the annuity is, therefore, $46,774.35 ($10,000 × 4.6325 × 1.0097).

* * *

(7) *Actuarial Table S and Table 2010CM where the valuation date is on or after [applicability date of the Treasury decision adopting these regulations as final regulations].*—(i) *Determination of required factors.*—Except as provided in § 20.7520-3(b) (pertaining to certain limitations on the use of prescribed tables), for determination of the present value of a remainder interest that is dependent on the termination of a life interest, where the valuation date is on or after [applicability date of the Treasury decision adopting these regulations as final regulations], actuarial factors computed directly by using the formula in paragraph (d)(2)(ii)(B) of this section, Table 2010CM, and the section 7520 rate are used in the application of the provisions of this section. For the convenience of taxpayers, the actuarial factors, when the section 7520 interest rate component is from 0.2 to 20 percent, inclusive, have been computed by IRS and can be found in Table S. Table S will be available beginning May 5, 2022, at no charge, electronically via the IRS website at ***https://www.irs.gov/retirement-plans/actuarial-tables***. Table S is also referenced and explained by IRS Publication 1457 "Actuarial Valuations Version 4A," which will be available after [date the Treasury decision adopting these regulations as final regulations is published in the **Federal Register**].

(ii) *Table 2010CM.*—

Table 4 to paragraph (d)(7)(ii)

Age x	l_x	Age x	l_x	Age x	l_x
0	100,000.00	**37**	97,193.66	**74**	71,177.55
1	99,382.28	**38**	97,058.84	**75**	69,174.83
2	99,341.16	**39**	96,915.25	**76**	67,044.59
3	99,313.80	**40**	96,761.20	**77**	64,773.93
4	99,292.72	**41**	96,595.51	**78**	62,366.05
5	99,276.45	**42**	96,416.30	**79**	59,795.50
6	99,261.55	**43**	96,220.61	**80**	57,080.84
7	99,248.33	**44**	96,005.41	**81**	54,213.71
8	99,236.50	**45**	95,768.60	**82**	51,205.27
9	99,226.09	**46**	95,509.98	**83**	48,059.88
10	99,217.03	**47**	95,229.06	**84**	44,808.51
11	99,208.80	**48**	94,923.45	**85**	41,399.79
12	99,199.98	**49**	94,589.88	**86**	37,895.25
13	99,188.21	**50**	94,225.50	**87**	34,313.98
14	99,170.64	**51**	93,828.33	**88**	30,700.82
15	99,145.34	**52**	93,398.01	**89**	27,106.68

Age x	l_x	Age x	l_x	Age x	l_x
16	99,111.91	**53**	92,934.52	**90**	23,586.75
17	99,070.69	**54**	92,438.08	**91**	20,198.02
18	99,021.50	**55**	91,907.95	**92**	16,996.17
19	98,964.16	**56**	91,342.02	**93**	14,032.08
20	98,898.61	**57**	90,737.24	**94**	11,348.23
21	98,824.20	**58**	90,090.97	**95**	8,975.661
22	98,741.32	**59**	89,401.06	**96**	6,931.559
23	98,652.16	**60**	88,665.95	**97**	5,218.261
24	98,559.87	**61**	87,883.66	**98**	3,823.642
25	98,466.80	**62**	87,051.88	**99**	2,722.994
26	98,373.71	**63**	86,167.86	**100**	1,882.108
27	98,280.09	**64**	85,226.77	**101**	1,261.083
28	98,185.51	**65**	84,221.59	**102**	818.2641
29	98,089.05	**66**	83,142.34	**103**	513.7236
30	97,989.90	**67**	81,978.28	**104**	311.8784
31	97,887.47	**68**	80,728.83	**105**	183.0200
32	97,781.58	**69**	79,387.95	**106**	103.8046
33	97,672.13	**70**	77,957.53	**107**	56.91106
34	97,559.20	**71**	76,429.84	**108**	30.17214
35	97,442.53	**72**	74,797.63	**109**	15.47804
36	97,321.14	**73**	73,049.33	**110**	0.000000

(e) *Applicability date*.—This section applies on and after [applicability date of the Treasury decision adopting these regulations as final regulations].

Annuities: Interests: Valuation: Actuarial Tables

Annuities: Interests: Valuation: Actuarial Tables.—Amendments to Reg. §20.2031-7A, relating to the use of actuarial tables in valuing annuities, interests for life or terms of years, and remainder or reversionary interests, are proposed (published in the Federal Register on May 5, 2022) (REG-122770-18).

☐ Par. 16. Section 20.2031-7A is amended by:

1. Revising the section heading.
2. Adding paragraphs (g) heading and (g)(1) through (3).
3. In newly redesignated paragraph (g)(4), the heading and introductory text are revised.
4. Adding paragraph (g)(5).

The revisions and additions read as follows:

§20.2031-7A. Valuation of annuities, interests for life or a term of years, and remainder or reversionary interests for estates of decedents for which the valuation date of the gross estate is before [applicability date of the Treasury decision adopting these regulations as final regulations].

* * *

(g) *Valuation of annuities, interests for life or a term of years, and remainder or reversionary interests for estates of decedents for which the valuation date of the gross estate is on or after May 1, 2009, and before [applicability date of the Treasury decision adopting these regulations as final regulations]*.—(1) *In general*.—Except as otherwise provided in §§20.2031-7(b) and 20.7520-3(b) (pertaining to certain limitations on the use of prescribed tables), if the valuation date for the gross estate of the decedent is on or after May 1, 2009, and before [applicability date of the Treasury decision adopting these regulations as final regulations], the fair market value of annuities, interests for life or a term of years, and remainder or reversionary interests is the present value of the interests determined by using standard or special section 7520 actuarial factors and the valuation methodology described in §20.2031-7(d). These factors are derived by using the appropriate section 7520 interest rate and, if applicable, the mortality component for the valuation date of the interest that is being valued. See §§20.7520-1 through 20.7520-4. See paragraph (g)(4) of this section for determination of the appropriate table for use in valuing these interests.

(2) *Transitional rules*.—(i) If a decedent dies on or after May 1, 2009, and if, on May 1, 2009, the decedent was under a mental disability so that the disposition of the decedent's property could not be changed, and the decedent dies before [applicability date of the Treasury decision adopting these regulations as final regulations] either without having regained the ability to dispose of the decedent's property or within 90 days of the date on which the decedent first regains that ability, the fair market value of annuities, interests for life or a term of years, and remainder or reversionary interests included in the gross estate of the decedent is their present value determined either under this section or under the corresponding section applicable at the time the decedent first became subject to the mental disability, at the option of the decedent's executor. For example, see paragraph (d) of this section.

(ii) If a decedent dies on or after May 1, 2009, and before July 1, 2009, the fair market value of annuities, interests for life or a term of years, and remainder or reversionary interests based on one or more measuring lives included in the gross estate of the decedent is their present value determined under this section by using the section 7520 interest rate for the month in which the valuation date occurs (see §§20.7520-1(b) and 20.7520-2(a)(2)) and the appropriate actuarial tables under either paragraph (f)(4) or (g)(4) of this section, at the option of the decedent's executor.

(iii) For purposes of paragraphs (g)(2)(i) and (ii) of this section, where the decedent's executor is given the option to use the appropriate actuarial tables under either paragraph (f)(4) or (g)(4) of this section, the decedent's executor must consistently use the same mortality basis with respect to each interest (income, remainder, partial, etc.) in the same property, and with respect to all transfers occurring on the valuation date. For example, gift and income tax charitable deductions with respect to the same transfer must be determined based on factors with the same mortality basis, and all assets includible in the gross estate and/or estate tax deductions claimed must be valued based on factors with the same mortality basis.

(3) *Publications and actuarial computations by the Internal Revenue Service*.—The factor for determining the present value of a remainder interest that is dependent on the termination of the life of one individual may be computed by using the formula in §20.2031-7(d)(2)(ii)(B) to derive factors from the appropriate mortality table. For the convenience of taxpayers, actuarial factors have been computed by IRS and appear in Table S. The factor for determining the present value of a remainder interest following a term certain may be computed by using the formula in §20.2031-7(d)(2)(ii)(A). For the convenience of taxpayers, actuarial factors have been computed by IRS and appear in Table B. Adjustment factors for term certain annuities payable at the beginning of each interval may be computed by using the formula in §20.2031-7(d)(2)(iv)(C). For the convenience of taxpayers, actuarial factors have been computed by IRS and appear in Table J. Adjustment factors for annuities payable at the end of each interval may be computed by using the formula in §20.2031-7(d)(2)(iv)(B). For the convenience of taxpayers, actuarial factors have been computed by IRS and appear in Table K. These tables are referenced and explained by IRS Publication 1457, "Actuarial Values Version 3A," (2009). Publication 1457 includes examples that illustrate how to compute many special factors for more unusual situations. The actuarial tables are available, at no charge, electronically via the IRS website at *https://www.irs.gov/retirement-plans/actuarial-tables* (or a corresponding URL as may be updated from time to time). Table S also can be found in paragraph (g)(4) of this section, but only for interest rates from 0.2 to 14 percent, inclusive. Table B, Table J, and Table K also can be found in §20.2031-7(d)(6), but only for interest rates from 4.2 to 14 percent, inclusive. If a special factor is required in the case of an actual decedent, the special factor may be calculated by the executor using the actuarial formulas in §20.2031-7(d)(2) or the executor may request a ruling to obtain the factor from the Internal Revenue Service. The request for a ruling must be accompanied by a recitation of the facts including a statement of the date of birth for each measuring life, the date of the decedent's death, any other applicable dates, and a copy of the will, trust, or other relevant documents. A request for a ruling must comply with the instructions for requesting a ruling published periodically in the Internal Revenue Bulletin (see §§601.201 and 601.601(d)(2)(ii)(*b*) of this chapter) and must include payment of the required user fee.

(4) *Actuarial tables*.—Except as provided in §20.7520-3(b) (pertaining to certain limitations on the use of prescribed tables), actuarial factors based on Table 2000CM must be used in the application of the provisions of this section. The factor for determining the present value of a remainder interest that is dependent on the termination of the life of one individual may be computed by using the formula in §20.2031-7(d)(2)(ii)(B) to derive factors from the appropriate mortality table. For the convenience of taxpayers, actuarial factors, when the section 7520 interest rate component is from 0.2 to 20 percent, inclusive, have been computed by IRS and appear in Table S (applicable on and after May 1, 2009, and before [applicability date of the Treasury decision adopting these regulations as final regulations]). These actuarial tables, as referenced and explained by IRS Publication 1457 "Actuarial Valuations Version 3A," are available, at no charge, electronically via the IRS website at *https://www.irs.gov/retirement-plans/actuarial-tables*. Table S (notwithstanding the lack of the applicable termination date in its heading), where the section 7520 interest rate component is from 0.2 to 14 percent, inclusive, and Table 2000CM are as follows: * * * * *

(5) *Applicability dates*.—Paragraphs (g)(1) through (4) of this section apply on and after May 1, 2009, and before [applicability date of the Treasury decision adopting these regulations as final regulations].

Annuities: Interests: Valuation: Actuarial Tables

Annuities: Interests: Valuation: Actuarial Tables.—Amendments to Reg. §20.2032-1, relating to the use of actuarial tables in valuing annuities, interests for life or terms of years, and remainder or reversionary interests, are proposed (published in the Federal Register on May 7, 2009) (REG-107845-08).

☐ Par. 8. Section 20.2032-1 is amended by revising paragraphs (f)(1) and (h) to read as follows:

§20.2032-1. Alternate valuation.

* * *

(f) * * *

(1) [The text of this proposed paragraph (f)(1) is the same as the text of § 20.2032-1T(f)(1) as added by T.D. 9448].

* * *

(h) [The text of this proposed paragraph (h) is the same as the text of § 20.2032-1T(h) as added by T.D. 9448].

Estate Tax: Gross Estate: Alternate Valuation Date: Election

Estate Tax: Gross Estate: Alternate Valuation Date: Election.—Amendments to Reg. § 20.2032-1, providing guidance respecting the election to use the alternate valuation method under Code Sec. 2032, are proposed (published in the Federal Register on November 18, 2011) (REG-112196-07).

☐ Par. 2. For each entry in the table, each paragraph in the "Old Paragraph" column is redesignated as indicated in the "New Paragraph" column:

Old Paragraph	New Paragraph
20.2032-1(c)(1)	20.2032-1(c)(1)(i)
20.2032-1(c)(3)	20.2032-1(c)(3)(i)
20.2032-1(c)(3)(i)	20.2032-1(c)(3)(i)(A)
20.2032-1(c)(3)(ii)	20.2032-1(c)(3)(i)(B)
20.2032-1(c)(3)(iii)	20.2032-1(c)(3)(i)(C)
20.2032-1(c)(3)(iv)	20.2032-1(c)(3)(i)(D)
20.2032-1(c)(3)(v)	20.2032-1(c)(3)(i)(E)
20.2032-1(f)	20.2032-1(f)(2)
20.2032-1(f)(1)	20.2032-1(f)(2)(i)
20.2032-1(f)(2)	20.2032-1(f)(2)(ii)

☐ Par. 3. Section 20.2032-1 is amended by:

1. Revising paragraph (a) introductory text.
2. Revising paragraphs (a)(1) and (a)(2).
3. Revising newly-designated paragraph (c)(1)(i), newly-designated paragraph (c)(3)(i)(C), paragraph (e) introductory text, the introductory text of paragraph (e) *Example 1* preceding the table, the last sentence in newly-designated paragraph (f)(2) introductory text, newly-designated paragraph (f)(2)(i), and the second sentence in newly-designated paragraph (f)(2)(ii).
4. Adding new paragraphs (c)(1)(ii), (c)(1)(iii), (c)(1)(iv), (c)(4), (c)(5), (f)(1), and (f)(3).
5. Adding a paragraph heading and a new second sentence in paragraph (c)(2) introductory text.
6. Adding a paragraph heading to paragraph (c)(3).
7. Designating the undesignated language following newly-designated paragraph (c)(3)(i)(E) as paragraph (c)(3)(ii) and adding a paragraph heading to this paragraph.
8. Designating the table in paragraph (e) as *Example 1* and adding paragraph (e) *Example 2* following the table.
9. Revising the paragraph heading and adding two sentences at the end of paragraph (h).

The additions and revisions read as follows.

§ 20.2032-1. Alternate valuation.—(a) *In general.*—In general, section 2032 provides for the valuation of a decedent's gross estate at a date (alternate valuation date) other than the date of the decedent's death. More specifically, if an executor elects the alternate valuation method under section 2032, the property includible in the decedent's gross estate on the date of death (decedent's interest) is valued as of whichever of the following dates is applicable:

(1) Any property distributed, sold, exchanged, or otherwise disposed of within 6 months (1 year, if the decedent died on or before December 31, 1970) after the decedent's death (alternate valuation period) is valued as of the date on which it is first distributed, sold, exchanged, or otherwise disposed of (transaction date).

(2) Any property not distributed, sold, exchanged, or otherwise disposed of during the alternate valuation period is valued as of the date 6 months (1 year, if the decedent died on or before December 31, 1970) after the date of the decedent's death (6-month date).

* * *

(c) *Meaning of "distributed, sold, exchanged, or otherwise disposed of".*—(1) *In general.*

(i) *Transactions included.*—The phrase "distributed, sold, exchanged, or otherwise disposed of" comprehends all possible ways by which property ceases to form a part of the gross estate. This phrase includes, but is not limited to:

(A) The use of money on hand at the date of the decedent's death to pay funeral or other expenses of the decedent's estate;

(B) The use of money on hand at the date of the decedent's death to invest in other property;

(C) The exercise of employee stock options;

(D) The surrender of stock for corporate assets in partial or complete liquidation of a corporation, and similar transactions involving partnerships or other entities;

(E) The distribution by the estate (or other holder) of included property as defined in paragraph (d) of this section;

(F) The transfer or exchange of property for other property, whether or not gain or loss is currently recognized for income tax purposes;

(G) The contribution of cash or other property to a corporation, partnership, or other entity, whether or not gain or loss is currently recognized for income tax purposes;

(H) The exchange of interests in a corporation, partnership, or other entity (entity) for one or more different interests (for example, a different class of stock) in the same entity or in an acquiring or resulting entity or entities (see, however, paragraph (c)(1)(ii) of this section); and

(I) Any other change in the ownership structure or interests in, or in the assets of, a corporation, partnership, or other entity, an interest in which is includible in the gross estate, such that the included property after the change does not reasonably represent the included property at the decedent's date of death (see, however, paragraph (c)(1)(iii)(A) of this section). Such a change in the ownership structure or interests in or in the assets of an entity includes, without limitation—

(1) The dilution of the decedent's ownership interest in the entity due to the issuance of additional ownership interests in that entity;

(2) An increase in the decedent's ownership interest in the entity due to the entity's redemption of the interest of a different owner;

(3) A reinvestment of the entity's assets; and

(4) A distribution or disbursement of property (other than excluded property as defined in paragraph (d) of this section) by the entity (other than expenses, such as rents and salaries, paid in the ordinary course of the entity's business), with the effect that the fair market value of the entity before the occurrence does not equal the fair market value of the entity immediately thereafter.

(ii) *Exchange of an interest in an existing corporation, partnership, or other entity includible in the gross estate.*—If an interest in a corporation, partnership, or other entity (entity is includible in the gross estate at death and that interest is exchanged as described in paragraph (c)(1)(i)(H) of this section for one or more different interests in the same entity or in an acquiring or resulting entity or entities, the transaction does not result in an exchange or disposition under section 2032(a)(1) and paragraph (c)(1)(i)(H) of this section if, on the date of the exchange, the fair market value of the interest in the entity equals the fair market value of the interest(s) in the same entity or the acquiring or resulting entity or entities. Such transactions may include, without limitation, reorganizations, recapitalizations, mergers, or similar transactions. In determining whether the exchanged properties have the same fair market value, a difference in value equal to or less than 5 percent of the fair market value, as of the transaction date, of the property interest includible in the gross estate on the decedent's date of death is ignored. If the transaction satisfies the requirements of this paragraph, the property to be valued on the 6-month date (or on the transaction date, if any, subsequent to this transaction) is the property received in the exchange, rather than the property includible in the decedent's gross estate at the date of death. This paragraph has no effect on any other provision of the Internal Revenue Code that is applicable to the transaction. For example, even if the transaction does not result in a deemed exchange as a result of satisfying the requirements of this paragraph, the provisions of chapter 14 may be applicable to determine fair market value for Federal estate tax purposes.

(iii) *Distributions from an account or entity in which the decedent held an interest at death.*

(A) *In general.*—If during the alternate valuation period, an estate (or other holder of the decedent's interest) receives a distribution or disbursement (to the extent the distribution or disbursement consists of included property, as defined in paragraph (d) of this section) (payment) from a partnership, corporation, trust (including an IRA, Roth IRA, 403(b), 401(k), Thrift Savings Plan, etc.), bank account or similar asset, or other entity (entity), and an interest in that entity is includible in the gross estate, the payment does not result in a distribution under paragraph (c)(1)(i)(I) of this section. However, this rule applies only if, on the date of the payment, the fair market value of the decedent's interest in the entity before the payment equals the sum of the fair market value of the payment made to the estate (or other holder of the decedent's interest in the entity) and the fair market value of the decedent's interest in the entity, not including any excluded property, after the payment. In this case, the alternate valuation date of the payment is the date of the payment, and the alternate valuation date of the decedent's remaining interest in the entity, if any, is the 6-month date (or the transaction date, if any, subsequent to this payment). If this requirement is not met, the payment is a distribution under paragraph (c)(1)(i) of this section, and the alternate valuation date of the decedent's entire interest in the entity is the date of the payment. For purposes of this section, a distribution or disbursement is deemed to consist first of excluded property, if any, and then of included property, as those terms are defined in paragraph (d) of this section.

(B) *Special rule.*—If the decedent's interest in an entity that is includible in the gross estate consists of the amount needed to produce an annuity, unitrust, remainder, or other such payment valued under section 2036, then assuming the distribution satisfies the general rule set forth in paragraph (c)(1)(iii)(A) of this section, the value of each distribution (to the extent it is deemed to consist of included property) payable (whether or not actually paid) during the alternate valuation period shall be added to the value of the entity on the alternate valuation date. The sum of the fair market value of these distributions when made and the fair market value of the entity on the alternate valuation date shall be used as the fair market value of the entity in computing the amount, valued as of the alternate valuation date, to be included in the decedent's gross estate under section 2036. See *Example* 2 of paragraph (e) of this section.

(iv) *Aggregation.*—For purposes of this section, a special aggregation rule applies in two situations to determine the value to be included in the gross estate pursuant to an alternate valuation election. Those two situations arise when, during the alternate valuation period, less than all of the interest includible in the decedent's gross estate in a particular property is the subject of a transaction described in paragraphs (c)(1)(i), (c)(1)(ii), (c)(1)(iii), or (c)(2) of this section. In one situation, one or more portions of the includible interest are subject to such a transaction and a portion is still held on the 6-month date. In the other situation, the entire interest includible in the gross estate is disposed of in two or more such transactions during the alternate valuation period, so that no part of that interest remains on the 6-month date. In both of these situations, the fair market value of each portion of the interest includible in the gross estate is to be determined as follows. The fair market value of each portion subject to such a transaction, and the portion remaining, if any, on the 6-month date, is the fair market value, as of the transaction date, or the 6-month date for any remaining portion, of the entire interest includible in the gross estate on the decedent's date of death, multiplied by a fraction. The numerator of that fraction is the portion of the interest subject to that transaction, or the portion remaining on the 6-month date, and the denominator is the entire interest includible in the gross estate at the decedent's date of death.

(2) *Property distributed.*—* * * Property is not considered "distributed" merely because property passes directly at death as a result of a beneficiary designation or other contractual arrangement or by operation of law. * * *

(3) *Person able to sell, exchange, or otherwise dispose of property includible in the gross estate.*—(i) * * *

(A) * * *

(B) * * *

(C) An heir, devisee, or other person to whom title to property passes directly on death by reason of a beneficiary designation or other contractual arrangement or by operation of law;

(D) * * *

(E) * * *

(ii) *Binding contracts.*—* * *

(4) *Certain post-death events.*—If the effect of any other provision of the Internal Revenue Code is that a post-death event is deemed to have occurred on the date of death, the post-death event will not be considered a transaction described in paragraph (c)(1)(i) of this section. For example, the grant, during the alternate valuation period, of a qualified conservation easement in accordance with section 2031(c) is not a transaction described in paragraph (c)(1)(i) of this section. Pursuant to section 2031(c), the post-death grant of the easement is effective for Federal estate tax purposes as of the date of the decedent's death. As a result, for purposes of determining both the estate's eligibility to make an election under this section and the value of the property on the alternate valuation date, the fair market value of the property as of the date of death must be compared to the fair market value of that property as of the alternate valuation date, in each case as that value is adjusted by reason of the existence of the section 2031(c) qualified easement.

(5) *Examples.*—The application of paragraph (c) of this section is illustrated in the following examples. In each example, decedent's (D's) estate elects to value D's gross estate under the alternate valuation method, so that the alternate valuation date of the property includible in the gross estate on D's date of death is either the transaction date or the 6-month date. In each example, assume that the only factors affecting value during the alternate valuation period, and the only occurrences described in paragraphs (c)(1)(i) and (c)(2) of this section, are those described in the example.

Example 1. At D's death, D owned property with a fair market value of $100X. Two months after D's death (Date 1), D's executor and D's family members formed a limited partnership. D's executor contributed all of the property to the partnership and received an interest in the partnership in exchange. The investment of the property in the partnership is a transaction described in paragraph (c)(1)(i)(F) and/or (G) of this section. As a result, the alternate valuation date of the property is the date of its contribution and the value to be included in D's gross estate is the fair market value of the property immediately prior to its contribution to the partnership. The result would be the same if D's estate instead had contributed property to a limited partnership formed prior to D's death by D and/or other parties, related or unrelated to D. Further, the result would be the same if D's estate had contributed the property to a corporation, publicly traded or otherwise, or other entity after D's death and prior to the 6-month date.

Example 2. At D's death, D held incentive stock options that were qualified under section 422. D's executor exercised all of the stock options prior to the 6-month date. The exercise of the stock options is a transaction described in paragraph (c)(1)(i)(C) of this section. Thus, the alternate valuation date of the stock options is the date of their exercise and the value to be included in D's gross estate is the fair market value of the stock options immediately prior to their exercise. The result would be the same if the stock options were not qualified under section 422 and were taxable under section 83 upon exercise.

Example 3. D's gross estate includes a controlling interest in Y, a corporation. During the alternate valuation period, Y issued additional shares of stock and awarded them to certain key employees. D's interest in Y was diluted to a non-controlling interest by Y's issuance of the additional stock. Y's issuance of the stock is a transaction described in paragraph (c)(1)(i)(I) of this section. The value to be included in D's gross estate is the fair market value of D's stock immediately prior to Y's issuance of the additional stock. The result would be the same if D's estate included a minority interest in Y on the date of death and that interest became a controlling interest during the alternate valuation period as the result of Y's redemption of the shares of another shareholder.

Example 4. At D's death, D owned stock in Y, a corporation. During the alternate valuation period, the Board of Directors of Y contributed all of Y's assets to a partnership in exchange for interests therein. The contribution is a transaction described in paragraph (c)(1)(i)(I)(*3*) of this section. Therefore, the alternate valuation date of D's stock in Y is the date of the reinvestment of Y's assets and the value to be included in D's gross estate is the fair market value of D's stock in Y immediately prior to the reinvestment. The result would be the same even if the Board of Directors had contributed only a portion of Y's assets to the partnership during the alternate valuation period.

Example 5. (i) At D's death, D owned common stock in Y, a corporation. Two months after D's death (Date 1), there was a reorganization of Y. In the reorganization, D's estate exchanged all of its stock for a new class of stock in X. On the date of the reorganization, the difference between the fair market value of the stock D's estate received and the fair market value on that date of the stock includible in D's gross estate at death was greater than 5% of the fair market value, as of the date of the reorganization, of the stock D held at death. The reorganization is a transaction described in paragraph (c)(1)(i)(H) of this section and does not satisfy the exception described in paragraph (c)(1)(ii) of this section. Thus, the alternate valuation date is the date of the reorganization and the value to be included in D's gross estate is the fair market value of the stock immediately prior to the reorganization. This result is not affected by whether or not the reorganization is a tax-free reorganization for Federal income tax purposes. The result would be the same if the stock had been held, for example, in an IRA with designated beneficiaries. See paragraph (c)(3)(i)(C) of this section.

(ii) If, instead, the difference between the two fair market values as of the date of the reorganization was equal to or less than 5% of the fair market value, as of the date of the reorganization, of the stock D held at death, the reorganization would satisfy the exception provided in paragraph (c)(1)(ii) of this section. Thus, the alternate valuation date would be the 6-month date. The value to be included in D's gross estate would be the fair market value, determined as of the 6-month date, of the new class of stock in Y that D's estate received in the reorganization.

Example 6. (i) At D's death, D owned an interest in Partnership X that is includible in D's gross estate. During the alternate valuation period, X made a cash distribution to each of the partners. The distribution consists entirely of included property as defined in paragraph (d) of this section. The distribution is a transaction described in paragraph (c)(1)(i)(I)(*4*) of this section. On the date of the distribution, the fair market value of D's interest in X before the distribution equaled the sum of the distribution paid to D's estate and the fair market value of D's interest in X immediately after the distribution. Thus, pursuant to paragraph (c)(1)(iii)(A) of this section, the alternate valuation date of the property distributed is the date of the distribution, and the alternate valuation date of D's interest in X is the 6-month date.

(ii) If, instead, the fair market value of D's interest in X before the distribution did not equal the sum of the distribution paid to D's estate and the fair market value of D's interest in X (not including any excluded property) immediately after the distribution, then pursuant to paragraph (c)(1)(i)(I)(*4*) of this section, the alternate valuation date of D's entire interest in X would be the date of the distribution.

Example 7. D died owning 100% of Blackacre. D's will directs that an undivided 70% interest in Blackacre is to pass to Trust A for the benefit of D's surviving spouse, and an undivided 30% interest is to pass to Trust B for the benefit of D's surviving child. Three months after D's death (Date 1), the executor of D's estate distributed a 70% interest in Blackacre to Trust A. Four months after D's death (Date 2), the executor of D's estate distributed a 30% interest in Blackacre to Trust B. The following values are includible in D's gross estate pursuant to paragraphs (c)(1)(i)(E) and (c)(1)(iv): the fair market value of the 70% interest in Blackacre, determined by calculating 70% of the fair market value of all (100%) of Blackacre as of Date 1; and the fair market value of the 30% interest in Blackacre, determined by calculating 30% of the fair market value of all (100%) of Blackacre as of Date 2.

Example 8. At D's death, D owned 100% of the units of a limited liability company (LLC). Two months after D's death (Date 1), D's executor sold 20% of the LLC units to an unrelated third party. Three months after D's death (Date 2), D's executor sold 40% of the LLC units to D's child. On the 6-month date, the estate held the remaining 40% of the units in the LLC. The alternate valuation date of the units sold is their sale date (Date 1 and Date 2, respectively) pursuant to paragraph (a) of this section. The alternate valuation date of the units remaining in the estate is the 6-month date, as these units have not been distributed, sold, exchanged, or otherwise disposed of in a transaction described in paragraphs (c)(1)(i) or (c)(2) of this section prior to this date. Pursuant to paragraph (c)(1)(iv) of this section, the value of the units disposed of on Date 1 and Date 2 is the fair market value of the 20% and 40% interests, determined by calculating 20% and 40% of the fair market value as of Date 1 and Date 2, respectively, of all the units (100%) includible in the gross estate at D's death. Similarly, the value of the units held on the 6-month date to be included in D's gross estate is the fair market value of those units, determined by taking 40% of the fair market value on the 6-month date of all of the units (100%) includible in the gross estate at D's death. As a result, the fact that the partial sales resulted in the creation of three minority interests is not taken into account in valuing under section 2032 any portion of the LLC interests held by D at D's death.

Example 9. Husband died owning an interest in a brokerage account titled in the names of Husband and Wife with rights of survivorship. On Husband's death, the account held marketable securities, corporate bonds, municipal bonds, certificates of deposit, and cash. During the alternate valuation period, Wife's stockbroker advised her that the account could not be held under the social security number of a deceased individual. Accordingly, approximately one month after Husband's death, Wife directed the stockbroker to transfer the account into an account titled in Wife's sole name. Because title to the joint account passes to Wife at the moment of Husband's death by operation of law, the transfer of the joint account into an account in Wife's sole name is not a transaction described in paragraph (c)(1)(i) of this section. Accordingly, the value of the assets held in Wife's solely owned account will be includible in Husband's gross estate at their fair market value on the 6-month date. The result would be the same if the brokerage firm automatically transferred title to the account into Wife's name, or if Wife changed the beneficiary designation for the account. Finally, the result would be the same if, instead of an account with a brokerage firm, the assets were held in Husband's retirement account (IRA or similar trust such as a Roth IRA, 403(b) plan, or 401(k) plan) or Wife's ownership of the account was the result of a contract (a beneficiary designation form) rather than operation of law.

Example 10. Assume the same facts as in *Example 9* except that, during the alternate valuation period, Wife directed the stockbroker to sell a bond in the account. The sale is a transaction described in paragraph (c)(1)(i)(I)(*4*) of this section. Wife is an individual described in paragraph (c)(3)(i)(D) of this section. Thus, the alternate valuation date of the bond is the date of its sale. The values to be included in D's gross estate are the fair market value of the bond on date of its sale, and the fair market value of the balance of the account on the 6-month date. The result would be the same if the bond had matured and was retired during the alternate valuation period. The result also would be the same if the bond was held within a retirement account (IRA or similar trust such as a Roth IRA, 403(b) plan, or 401(k) plan).

Example 11. Assume the same facts as in *Example 9* except that, during the alternate valuation period, Wife withdrew cash from the account or otherwise received income or other disbursements from the account. Each such withdrawal or disbursement from the account (to the extent it consists of included property as defined in paragraph (d) of this section) is a distribution described in paragraph (c)(1)(i)(I)(*4*) of this section. Provided that, on the date of each distribution, the fair market value of the account before the distribution (not including excluded property) equals the sum of the included property distributed and the fair market value of the included property in the account immediately after the distribution in accordance with paragraph (c)(1)(iii)(A) of this section, the alternate valuation date for each distribution is the date of the distribution and the alternate valuation date for the account is the 6-month date. The value to be included in the gross estate is the fair market value of each distribution of included property (determined as of the date of distribution) and the fair market value of the account on the 6-month date. The result would be the same if the assets were held in an IRA or similar trust, such as a Roth IRA, 403(b) plan, or 401(k) plan.

Example 12. Husband died with a retirement account, having named his three children, in specified shares totaling 100%, as the designated beneficiaries of that account. During the alternate valuation period, the account was divided into three separate retirement accounts, each in the name of a different child and funded with that child's designated share. The division of the retirement account is not a transaction described in paragraph (c)(1)(i) of this section by reason of paragraph (c)(2) of this section, so the alternate valuation date for each of the new accounts is the 6-month date.

Example 13. (i) D's gross estate includes real property. During the alternate valuation period, D's executor grants a conservation easement that restricts the property's use under local law but does not satisfy the requirements of section 2031(c). The easement reduces the fair market value of the property. The executor's grant of the conservation easement is a transaction described in paragraph (c)(1)(i)(E) of this section and does not satisfy the exception described in paragraph (c)(4) of this section. Therefore, the alternate valuation date for the property is the date the easement was granted, and the value to be included in D's gross estate is the fair market value of the property immediately prior to the grant.

(ii) Assume, instead, that the easement satisfied the requirements of section 2031(c) and, thus, satisfied the exception described in paragraph (c)(4) of this section. Pursuant to paragraph (c)(4), for purposes of determining both the estate's eligibility to make an election under section 2032 and the value of the property on the 6-month date, the section 2031(c) qualified easement is taken into account in determining both the fair market value of the property on D's date of death and the fair market value of the property on the 6-month date.

* * *

(e) *Examples.*—The application of paragraph (d) of this section regarding "included property" and "excluded property" is illustrated by the following examples.

Example 1. Assume that the decedent (D) died on January 1, 1955:***

Example 2. (i) At death, D held a qualified interest described in section 2702(b) in the form of an annuity in a grantor retained annuity trust (GRAT) D had created and funded with $150,000. The trust agreement provides for an annual annuity payment of $12,000 per year to D or D's estate for a term of 10 years. At the expiration of the 10-year term, the remainder is to be distributed to D's child. D dies prior to the expiration of the 10-year term. On D's date of death, the fair market value of the property in the GRAT is $325,000.

(ii) The only assets in the GRAT are an apartment building and a bank account. Three months after D's date of death, an annuity payment of $12,000 is paid in cash to D's estate. The monthly rents from the apartment building total $500. After the date of death and prior to the payment date, the GRAT received $1,500 in excluded property in the form of rent. Pursuant to paragraph (c)(1)(iii)(A) of this section, $1,500 of the $12,000 distributed is deemed to be excluded property for purposes of section 2032. The distribution is a transaction described in paragraph (c)(1)(i)(I)(4) of this section. On the date of the distribution, the fair market value of D's interest in the GRAT before the distribution equals the sum of the distribution paid to D's estate and the fair market value of D's interest in the GRAT immediately after the distribution. Thus, pursuant to paragraph (c)(1)(iii)(A) of this section, the alternate valuation date for the $10,500 cash distribution, which is included property, is the date of its distribution, and the alternate valuation date of the GRAT is the 6-month date.

(iii) The calculation of the value of D's interest in the GRAT includible in D's gross estate at D's death pursuant to section 2036 must be computed under the special rule of paragraph (c)(1)(iii)(B) of this section as a result of the estate's election to use the alternate valuation method under section 2032. On the 6-month date, the section 7520 interest rate is 6% and the fair market value of the property in the GRAT is $289,500. Pursuant to paragraph (c)(1)(iii)(B) of this section, the fair market value of the GRAT property deemed to be included property is $300,000 ($289,500 plus $10,500). Accordingly, for purposes of determining the fair market value of the corpus includible in D's gross estate under section 2036(a)(1) as of the 6-month date, see § 20.2036-1(c)(2), using a GRAT corpus of $300,000 and, pursuant to paragraph (f)(2)(i) of this section, a section 7520 rate of 6%.

(f) *Post-death factors and occurrences.*—(1) *In general.*—The election to use the alternate valuation method under section 2032 permits property includible in the gross estate on the decedent's date of death to be valued on the 6-month date, rather than on the date of death. Thus, the election permits a valuation for Federal estate tax purposes that reflects the impact of factors such as economic or market conditions, occurrences described in section 2054 (to the extent not compensated by insurance or otherwise, and not deducted under that section), and other factors or occurrences during the alternate valuation period, as set forth in guidance issued by the Secretary. Those factors and occurrences do not include the mere lapse of time described in paragraph (f)(2) of this section, or transactions described in paragraph (c)(1)(i) or (c)(2) of this section that are not excluded under paragraphs (c)(1)(ii), (c)(1)(iii)(A), and (c)(4) of this section. Generally, management decisions made in the ordinary course of operating a business, such as a corporation, a partnership, or other business entity, are taken into account under this section as occurrences related to economic or market conditions. To the extent, however, that these decisions change the ownership or control structure of the business entity, or otherwise are included in paragraph (c)(1)(i) or (c)(2) of this section and are not excluded by paragraphs (c)(1)(ii), (c)(1)(iii)(A), or (c)(4) of this section, they will be treated as described in paragraph (c)(1)(i) of this section.

(2) *Mere lapse of time.*—*** The application of this paragraph is illustrated in paragraphs (f)(2)(i) and (f)(2)(ii) of this section:

(i) *Life estates, remainders, and similar interests.*—(A) The fair market value of a life estate, remainder, term interest or similar interest as of the alternate valuation date is determined by applying the methodology prescribed in § 20.2031-7, subject to the following two sentences. The age of each person whose life expectancy may affect the fair market value of the interest shall be determined as of the date of the decedent's death. The fair market value of the property and the applicable interest rate under section 7520 shall be determined using values applicable on the alternate valuation date.

(B) *Examples.*—The application of paragraph (f)(2)(i)(A) of this section is illustrated in the following examples.

Example 1. Assume that the decedent (D) or D's estate was entitled to receive certain property upon the death of A, who was entitled to the income from the property for life. At the time of D's death after April 30, 2009, the fair market value of the property was $50,000, and A was 47 years and 5 months old. In the month in which D died, the section 7520 rate was 6.2%, but rose to 7.4% on the 6-month date. The fair market value of D's remainder interest as of D's date of death was $9,336.00 ($50,000 × 0.18672, the single life remainder factor from Table S for a 47 year old at a 6.2% interest rate), as illustrated in *Example 1* of § 20.2031-7T(d)(5). If, because of economic conditions, the property declined in value during the alternate valuation period and was worth only $40,000 on the 6-month date, the fair market value of the remainder interest would be $5,827 ($40,000 X 0.14568, the Table S value for a 47 year old at a 7.4% interest rate), even though A would have been 48 years old on the 6-month date.

Example 2. D created an intervivos charitable remainder annuity trust (CRAT) described in section 664(d)(1). The trust instrument directs the trustee to hold, invest, and reinvest the corpus of the trust and to pay to D for D's life, and then to D's child (C) for C's life, an amount each year equal to 6% of the initial fair market value of the trust. At the termination of the trust, the corpus, together with the accumulated income, is to be distributed to N, a charitable organization described in sections 170(c), 2055(a), and 2522(a). D died, survived by C. D's estate is entitled to a charitable deduction under section 2055 for the present value of N's remainder interest in the CRAT. Pursuant to § 1.664-2(c) and § 20.7520-2, in determining the fair market value of the remainder interest as of the alternate valuation date, D's executor may elect to use the section 7520 rate in effect for either of the two months immediately preceding the month in which the alternate valuation date occurs. Regardless of the section 7520 rate selected, however, the factor to be used to value the remainder interest is the appropriate factor for C's age on the date of D's death.

(2)(ii) *Patents.*—* * * Six months after the date of the decedent's death, the patent was sold for its then fair market value that had decreased to $60,000 because of the lapse of time. * **

(3) *Examples.* The following examples illustrate the application of this paragraph (f). In each example, decedent's (D's) estate elects to value D's gross estate under the alternate valuation method, so that the alternate valuation date of the property includible in the gross estate on D's date of death is either the transaction date or the 6-month date. In each example, assume that the only factors affecting value, and the only occurrences described in paragraph (c)(1)(i) or (c)(2) of this section, taking place during the alternate valuation period are those described in the example.

Example 1. At D's death, D's gross estate includes a residence. During the alternate valuation period, the fair market value of the residence (as well as the residential market in the area generally) declines due to a reduction in the availability of credit throughout the United States and, consequently, a decline in the availability of mortgages. The decline in the availability of mortgages is an economic or market condition. Therefore, in valuing the residence on the 6-month date, the effect of this decline on the fair market value of the residence is to be taken into account.

Example 2. (i) At D's death, D is the sole shareholder of corporation Y, a manufacturing company. Four months after D's death, Y's physical plant is destroyed as a result of a natural disaster. The disaster affects a large geographic area and, as a result, the economy of that area is negatively affected. Five months after D's death, Y's Board of Directors votes to liquidate and dissolve Y. The liquidation and dissolution proceeding is not completed as of the 6-month date. The natural disaster is a factor that affects economic and market conditions. Therefore, the disaster, to the extent not compensated by insurance or otherwise, is taken into account in valuing the Y stock on the 6-month date.

(ii) Assume instead that Y's plant is severely damaged due to flooding from the failure of pipes in the facility. The damage is an occurrence described in section 2054. Therefore, the damage, to the extent not compensated by insurance or otherwise, is taken into account in valuing the property on the 6-month date.

Example 3. At D's death, D has an interest in an S corporation, W. During the alternate valuation period, it is discovered that an employee of W has embezzled significant assets from W. W does not reasonably expect to recover the funds or any damages from the employee, and insurance proceeds are not sufficient to cover the loss. The theft is an occurrence described in section 2054. Therefore, the theft, to the extent not compensated by insurance or otherwise, is taken into account in valuing D's interest in W on the 6-month date.

(h) *Effective/applicability date.*—* * * All of paragraph (c)(2) of this section except the second sentence of the introductory text, all of paragraph (c)(3) of this section except paragraph (c)(3)(i)(C) of this section, the chart in *Example 1* of paragraph (e) of this section, all of paragraph (f)(2) of this section except the last sentence, and the first and third sentences in paragraph (f)(2)(ii) of this section are applicable to decedents dying after August 16, 1954. All of paragraphs (a) introductory text, (a)(1), (a)(2), (c)(1)(i), (c)(1)(ii), (c)(1)(iii), (c)(1)(iv), (c)(3)(i)(C), (c)(4), (c)(5), (f)(1), (f)(2)(i), and (f)(3) of this section, the second sentence of the introductory text in paragraph (c)(2) of this section, all of paragraph (e) of this section except the chart in *Example 1*, the last sentence in the introductory text of paragraph (f)(2) of this section, and the second sentence in paragraph (f)(2)(ii) of this section are applicable to estates of decedents dying on or after the date of publication of the Treasury decision adopting these rules as final in the **Federal Register**.

Annuities: Interests: Valuation: Actuarial Tables

Annuities: Interests: Valuation: Actuarial Tables.—Amendments to Reg. § 20.2032-1, relating to the use of actuarial tables in valuing annuities, interests for life or terms of years, and remainder or reversionary interests, are proposed (published in the Federal Register on May 5, 2022) (REG-122770-18).

Par. 17. Section 20.2032-1 is amended by revising paragraphs (f)(1) and (h) to read as follows:

§ 20.2032-1. Alternate valuation.

* * *

(f) * * *

(1) *Life estates, remainders, and similar interests.*—(i) *In general.*—The values of life estates, remainders, and similar interests are to be obtained by applying the methods prescribed in § 20.2031-7, using the age of each person, the duration of whose life may affect the value of the interest, as of the date of the decedent's death, and the value of the property as of the alternate valuation date.

(ii) *Sample factors from actuarial Table S.*—The present value of a remainder interest dependent on the termination of one life is determined by using the formula in § 20.2031-7(d)(2)(ii)(B) to derive factors from the appropriate mortality table. For the convenience of taxpayers, actuarial factors have been computed by IRS and appear in Table S. Table S can be found on the IRS website at *https://www.irs.gov/retirement-plans/actuarial-tables* (or a corresponding URL as may be updated from time to time). For purposes of the example in paragraph (e)(5)(iii) of this section, the following relevant factors from Table S is used:

Table 2 to paragraph (f)(1)(ii)

Table S - Based on Table 2010CM			
Interest at 4.2 Percent			
Age	Annuity	Life Estate	Remainder
65	12.2128	0.51294	0.48706
Interest at 4.6 Percent			
Age	Annuity	Life Estate	Remainder
65	11.7691	0.54138	0.45862

(iii) *Example.*—Assume that the decedent, or the decedent's estate, was entitled to receive certain property worth $50,000 upon the death of A, who was entitled to the income for life. At the time of the decedent's death, A was 65 years and 5 months old, and the section 7520 rate was 4.6 percent. The value of the decedent's remainder interest at the date of the decedent's death would, as illustrated in *Example 1* of § 20.2031-7(d)(5)(i), be $22,931.00 ($50,000 x 0.45862). On the date that is 6 months after the decedent's death, A was 65 years and 11 months old, and the section 7520 rate was 4.2 percent. If, because of economic conditions, the property declined in value and was worth only $40,000 on the date that was 6 months after the date of the decedent's death, and the decedent's executor elected to use the alternate valuation date, the value of the remainder interest would be $19,482.40 ($40,000 X 0.48706). When the alternate valuation date is elected, the age of A, and other aspects of valuation which change by reason of the mere passage of time, is determined as of the date of the decedent's death, while the value of the property and the relevant section 7520 interest rate is determined as of the alternate valuation date. Thus, the computation uses A's age of 65 years old at the date of the decedent's death, even though A would be closest to 66 years old on the alternate valuation date.

* * *

(h) *Applicability date.*—Paragraph (b) of this section is applicable to decedents dying on or after January 4, 2005. However, pursuant to section 7805(b)(7), taxpayers may elect to apply paragraph (b) of this section retroactively if the period of limitations for filing a claim for a credit or refund of Federal estate or generation-skipping transfer tax under section 6511 has not expired. Paragraph (f)(1) of this section applies on and after [applicability date of the Treasury decision adopting these regulations as final regulations].

Annuities: Interests: Valuation: Actuarial Tables

Annuities: Interests: Valuation: Actuarial Tables.—Amendments to Reg. § 20.2032-1T, relating to the use of actuarial tables in valuing annuities, interests for life or terms of years, and remainder or reversionary interests, are proposed (published in the Federal Register on May 5, 2022) (REG-122770-18).

☐ Par. 18. Section 20.2032-1T is removed.

§ 20.2032-1T. Alternate valuation.

Annuities: Interests: Valuation: Actuarial Tables

Annuities: Interests: Valuation: Actuarial Tables.—Amendments to Reg. § 20.2036-1, relating to the use of actuarial tables in valuing annuities, interests for life or terms of years, and remainder or reversionary interests, are proposed (published in the Federal Register on May 5, 2022) (REG-122770-18).

☐ Par. 19. Section 20.2036-1 is amended:

1. In paragraph (c)(2)(iv) by designating *Examples 1* through *8* as paragraphs (c)(2)(iv)(A) through (H), respectively.

2. In newly designated paragraphs (c)(2)(iv)(A), (B), (C), (G), and (H) by further redesignating the paragraphs in the first column as paragraphs in the second column:

Old paragraphs	New paragraphs
(c)(2)(iv)(A)(i) and (ii)	(c)(2)(iv)(A)(*1*) and (*2*)
(c)(2)(iv)(B)(i) and (ii)	(c)(2)(iv)(B)(*1*) and (*2*)
(c)(2)(iv)(C)(i), (ii), and (iii)	(c)(2)(iv)(C)(*1*), (*2*), and (*3*)
(c)(2)(iv)(G)(i), (ii), and (iii)	(c)(2)(iv)(G)(*1*), (*2*), and (*3*)
(c)(2)(iv)(G)(*3*)(A), (B), (C), (D), (E), and (F)	(c)(2)(iv)(G)(*3*)(*i*), (*ii*), (*iii*), (*iv*), (*v*), and (*vi*)
(c)(2)(iv)(G)(iv), (v), and (vi)	(c)(2)(iv)(*G*)(*4*), (*5*), and (*6*)
(c)(2)(iv)(H)(i), (ii), (iii), (iv), (v), (vi), and (vii)	(c)(2)(iv)(*H*)(*1*), (*2*), (*3*), (*4*), (*5*), (*6*), and (*7*)

3. By revising newly designated paragraph (c)(2)(iv)(C).

The revision reads as follows:

§ 20.2036-1. Transfers with retained life estate.

* * *

(c) * * *

(2) * * *

(iv) * * *

(C) *Example 3*.—(*1*) D created a CRUT within the meaning of section 664(d)(2). The trust instrument directs the trustee to hold, invest, and reinvest the corpus of the trust and to pay to D for D's life, and then to D's child (C) for C's life, in equal quarterly installments payable at the end of each calendar quarter, an amount equal to 6 percent of the fair market value of the trust as valued on December 15 of the prior taxable year of the trust. At the termination of the trust, the then-remaining corpus, together with any and all accrued income, is to be distributed to N, a charitable organization described in sections 170(c), 2055(a), and 2522(a). D dies six years later, survived by C, who was then age 55. The value of the trust assets on D's death was $300,000. D's executor does not elect to use the alternate valuation date and D's executor does not choose to use the section 7520 interest rate for either of the two months prior to D's death.

(*2*) The amount of the corpus with respect to which D retained the right to the income, and thus the amount includible in D's gross estate under section 2036(a)(1), is that amount of corpus necessary to yield the unitrust payments as interest on the corpus. In this case, such amount of corpus is determined by dividing the trust's equivalent income interest rate by the section 7520 rate (which was 5.4 percent at the time of D's death). The equivalent income interest rate is determined by dividing the trust's adjusted payout rate by the excess of 1 over the adjusted payout rate. Based on Table F(5.4) in § 1.664-4(e)(6)(iii) of this chapter, the appropriate adjusted payout rate for the trust at D's death is 5.807 percent (6 percent × 0.967769). Thus, the equivalent income interest rate is 6.165 percent (5.807 percent / (1 – 5.807 percent)). The ratio of the equivalent interest rate to the assumed interest rate under section 7520 is 114.17 percent (6.165 percent / 5.4 percent). Because this exceeds 100 percent, D's retained payout interest exceeds a full income interest in the trust, and D effectively retained the income from all the assets transferred to the trust. Accordingly, because D retained for life an interest at least equal to the right to all income from all the property transferred by D to the CRUT, the entire value of the corpus of the CRUT is includible in D's gross estate under section 2036(a)(1). (The result would be the same if D had retained, instead, an interest in the CRUT for a term of years and had died during the term.) Under the facts presented, section 2039 does not apply to include any amount in D's gross estate by reason of D's retained unitrust interest. See § 20.2039-1(e).

(*3*) If, instead, D had retained the right to a unitrust amount having an adjusted payout for which the corresponding equivalent interest rate would have been less than the 5.4 percent assumed interest rate of section 7520, then a correspondingly reduced proportion of the trust corpus would be includible in D's gross estate under section 2036(a)(1). Alternatively, if the interest retained by D was instead only one-half of the 6 percent unitrust interest, then the amount included in D's estate would be the amount needed to produce a 3 percent unitrust interest. All of the results in this paragraph (c)(2)(iv)(C)(*3*) *(Example 3)* would be the same if the trust had been a grantor retained unitrust instead of a CRUT.

* * *

Retention of Stock Voting Rights

Gross Estate: Property in Which Decedent Had Interest: Shares of Stock.—Reproduced below is the text of proposed Reg. § 20.2036-2, relating to the estate tax consequences of a decedent's retention of voting rights in a lifetime transfer of stock (published in the Federal Register on August 3, 1983).

☐ Par. There is added immediately after § 20.2036-1 the following new section:

§ 20.2036-2. Special treatment of retained voting rights.—(a) *In general*.—For purposes of section 2036(a)(1) and § 20.2036-1(a), the retention of the right to vote (directly or indirectly) shares of stock of a controlled corporation is a retention of the enjoyment of the transferred property if:

(1) The transfer was made after June 22, 1976;

(2) The corporation was a controlled corporation at any time after transfer of that stock; and

(3) The corporation was a controlled corporation at any time during the three-year period ending on the decedent's death

The rule of this section does not require inclusion of stock in the gross estate if the transferred stock has no voting rights or if the donor has not retained voting rights in the stock transferred. Thus, for example, if a person owning 100 percent of the voting and nonvoting stock of a corporation transfers the nonvoting stock, that person shall not be treated as having retained the enjoyment of the property transferred merely because of voting rights in the stock retained. Stock carrying voting rights that will vest only when conditions occur, such as preferred stock which gains voting rights only if no dividends are paid, is subject to this section. However, if the decedent's right to vote such stock is only in a fiduciary capacity (*e.g.,* because the decedent is trustee of a trust to which the stock has been transferred), such stock is subject to this section only if, after the transfer by the decedent, the conditions occur that give the decedent the right to vote the stock. Stock that possesses voting rights in only extraordinary matters, such as mergers or liquidations shall be subject to this section unless the decedent's retention of voting rights is only in a fiduciary capacity.

(b) *Relinquishment or cessation of voting rights within three years of death.*—In general, the relinquishment or cessation of retained voting rights shall be treated as a "transfer of property" for purposes of section 2035 (transfer within three years of death) if:

(1) The voting rights were retained in a transfer made after June 22, 1976; and

(2) The corporation was a controlled corporation at some point in time occurring after the transfer, before the relinquishment or cessation of voting rights, and within three years of death.

However, to the extent that a relinquishment of voting rights is in exchange for voting rights in another controlled corporation, the relinquishment shall not be treated as a "transfer of property" for purposes of section 2035. See paragraph (e)(3) of this section for the treatment of voting rights in such other corporation.

(c) *Meaning of right to vote.*—For purposes of this section, the term "right to vote" means the power to vote, whether exercisable alone or in conjunction with other persons. The capacity in which the decedent can exercise voting power is immaterial. Accordingly, a fiduciary power exercisable as trustee, co-trustee, or as officer of a corporation is a right to vote stock within the meaning of this section. For purposes of section 2036(b)(1) and § 20.2036-2(a), the constructive ownership rules of section 318 shall not be used to attribute the retention of voting rights to the decedent. Therefore, the fact that a relative of the decedent is trustee of a trust to which the decedent has transferred stock shall not in itself require a finding that the decedent indirectly retained the right to vote that stock. However, any arrangement to shift formal voting power away from the decedent will not be treated for this purpose as a relinquishment of all voting rights if, in substance, the decedent has retained voting power. Moreover, voting power shall be deemed retained in cases where there is any agreement with the decedent, express or implied, that the shareholder, or other holder of the power to vote stock, either will vote the stock in a specified manner or will not vote the stock. If the decedent has the power to obtain the right to vote, such as where he may appoint himself as a trustee of a trust holding the stock, the decedent has retained the right to vote for purposes of section 2036.

(d) *Meaning of controlled corporation.*—(1) *In general.*—For purposes of this section, the term "controlled corporation" means a corporation in which the decedent, with application of the constructive ownership rules of section 318, is deemed to own or have a right to vote stock possessing at least 20 percent of the total combined voting power of all classes of stock.

(2) *Computations.*—(i) *Total combined voting power of all classes of stock.*—For purposes of this paragraph, the total combined voting power of all classes of stock shall include only stock that currently has voting power. Stock that may vote only on extraordinary matters, such as mergers or liquidations, shall be disregarded. Similarly, treasury stock and stock that is authorized but unissued shall be disregarded.

(ii) *Decedent's percentage of total combined voting power.*—For purposes of this paragraph, in determining whether the voting power possessed by the decedent is at least 20 percent of the total combined voting power of all classes of stock, consideration will be given to all the facts and circumstances. Generally, the percentage of voting power possessed by a person in a corporation may be determined by reference to the power of stock to vote for the election of directors. Instruments that do not have voting rights shall be disregarded. Instruments having no voting rights but which may be converted into voting stock shall be disregarded until such conversion occurs. Instruments carrying voting rights that will vest only when conditions, the occurrence of which is indeterminate, have been met will be disregarded until the conditions have occurred which cause the voting rights to vest. An example of such an instrument is preferred stock which gains voting rights only if no dividends are paid.

(iii) *Example.*—The following example illustrates the application of paragraphs (d)(1) through (d)(2)(ii) of this section.

Example. A corporation has three classes of stock outstanding, consisting of 40 shares of class A voting stock, 50 shares of class B voting stock, and 60 shares of class C preferred stock which is nonvoting except for extraordinary matters or unless the arrearages in dividends exceed a specified amount. Assume for purposes of this example that except for extraordinary business matters, the voting stock's only voting power is the right to vote in the election of directors. The class A stockholders are entitled to elect 7 of the 10 corporate directors, and the class B stockholders are entitled to elect the other 3 of the 10 directors. Thus, the class A stock (as a class) possesses 70 percent of the total combined voting power of all classes of stock, and the class B stock (as a class) possesses 30 percent of such voting power. At the time of *D*' s death, *D* has voting rights in 9 shares of class A stock directly; and with the constructive ownership rules of section 318, *D* is deemed to have voting rights in 3 additional shares of class A stock. *D* has no interest in the class B stock and owns all 60 shares of the class C stock. Thus, *D* is deemed to possess 21 percent ((9 + 3) shares/40 shares × 70 percent) of the total combined voting power of all classes of stock. By reason of such voting power, the corporation is a controlled corporation within the meaning of this section.

(e) *Direct versus indirect retention of voting rights*.—(1) *Direct transfers*.—Subject to the limitations contained in paragraph (a) of this section, if the decedent transfers stock of a controlled corporation (except in case of a bona fide sale for adequate and full consideration in money or money's worth), the retention of voting rights in the stock transferred shall require a portion of the fair market value of the stock to be included in the gross estate. For purposes of this paragraph (e)(1), transfers of stock in exchange for, in whole or in part, either property donated by the decedent or property for which the decedent supplied the purchase consideration, will not be considered a bona fide sale for adequate and full consideration. The amount included in the gross estate under this paragraph (e)(1) shall be an amount, not less than zero, equal to the fair market value at death of the stock transferred less the value of any consideration the decedent received in exchange.

(2) *Indirect transfer*.—Section 2036 applies to indirect as well as direct transfers. The acquisition of voting rights in stock acquired through the exercise of other instruments transferred by the decedent (such as through the exercise of warrants or options, or the conversion rights on convertible nonvoting stock or indebtedness) shall cause the stock to be treated as acquired with consideration furnished by the decedent and an indirect transfer by the decedent. If a third party makes a transfer to the trust and the consideration for the transfer was furnished by the decedent, the transfer by the third party to the trust will be treated as a transfer by the decedent to the trust. In addition, if the decedent makes a transfer by gift to a trust, and the trust subsequently acquires stock in which the decedent has voting rights, then for purposes of section 2036(a), the transaction will be treated as an indirect transfer of stock by the decedent (irrespective of whether the acquisition of the stock can be traced to the gift). The amount included in the gross estate in such a case is equal to the fair market value at death of the portion of the stock acquired with funds provided by the decedent. In the case of a purchase of stock from a third party by a trust, the stock shall be treated as purchased with funds provided by the decedent to the extent there are funds in the trust treated as provided by the decedent. For this purpose, the portion of the funds in the trust treated as provided by the decedent shall be determined after each addition to the trust and is equal to a fraction. The numerator of the fraction is the sum of—

(i) The total value of the trust immediately prior to the latest addition multiplied by the fraction of such value treated as provided by the decedent because of prior additions, and

(ii) The amount of the latest addition to the extent provided by the decedent.

The denominator of the fraction is the total value of the trust immediately after the latest addition.

(3) *Exchange of voting rights*.—For purposes of this section, if a decedent is deemed to have retained the right to vote shares of stock of a controlled corporation in a transfer occurring after June 22, 1976, the subsequent relinquishment of those voting rights, in exchange for voting rights in other stock of a controlled corporation, shall be treated as a retention of voting rights in such other stock. Furthermore, for purposes of section 2036(a), such other stock shall be treated as property transferred by the decedent. For example, if a person transfers stock in ABC Corporation (a controlled corporation) after June 22, 1976, to a trust for which that person is a trustee—thus retaining voting rights in a fiduciary capacity—and the trust later sells the ABC Corporation stock, using the proceeds to purchase stock in XYZ Corporation (a controlled corporation), that person will be treated as having retained the right to vote the shares of XYZ Corporation. In such a transaction, the shares of XYZ Corporation shall be treated as transferred by that person. If the stock in XYZ Corporation is acquired directly from the decedent, the amount included in the gross estate shall be determined under paragraph (e)(1) of this section. If the stock in XYZ Corporation is acquired from someone other than the decedent, the amount included in the decedent's gross estate shall be determined under paragraph (e)(2) of this section.

(4) *Examples*.—The following examples illustrate the application of section 2043 and paragraph (e)(1) and (e)(2) of this section.

Example (1). During 1977, *D* transferred by gift $100,000 cash to a trust. During 1979, *D* transferred to the trust 1000 shares of ABC Corporation voting stock worth $100,000. The 1979 transfer was in exchange for $50,000 cash and *D* retained voting rights in all the stock transferred. Assume that at some time after the stock transfer, ABC Corporation is a controlled corporation within the meaning of this section. *D* dies during 1981, at which time the stock is worth $150,000.

As a result of the stock transfer, the amount included in *D'* s gross estate under section 2036 is $100,000, computed as follows:

Fair market value of instruments at death	$150,000
Less consideration received by *D*	50,000
Amount included in *D*'s gross estate	$100,000

Example (2). The facts are the same as in *example (1)* except that the 1979 transfer to the trust (1000 shares of ABC Corporation) was in exchange for $100,000 cash. As a result of the stock transfer, the amount included in *D'* s gross estate under section 2036 is $50,000, computed as follows:

Fair market value of instruments at death	$150,000
Less consideration received by *D*	100,000
Amount included in *D*'s gross estate	$50,000

The 1979 transfer is not considered a *bona fide* sale for adequate and full consideration in money or money's worth since *D* provided the consideration by virtue of his 1977 transfer to the trust.

Example (3). During 1979, *D* transferred by gift 1000 shares of ABC Corporation voting stock worth $100,000 to his wife *W.* During 1980, *W* made a gift of the same stock to a trust. Assume that *D* becomes trustee of the trust and hence acquires the right to vote the stock in that capacity. Assume further that, at some time after *D'* s transfer, ABC Corporation is a controlled corporation within the meaning of this section. *D* dies during 1981, at which time the stock is worth $150,000. The full $150,000 is included in *D'* s gross estate under section 2036.

Example (4). During 1979, *D* transferred by gift $90,000 to a trust that already had $90,000 of funds, all of which is attributable to contributions by persons other than *D.* During 1980, the trust purchased at full fair market value 1000 shares of ABC Corporation voting stock worth $100,000, at which time, because of appreciation, the value of the trust was $210,000. Assume that *D* acquires the right to vote the stock as trustee of the trust and that at some time after the stock purchase, ABC Corporation is a controlled corporation within the meaning of this section. *D* dies during 1981, at which time the stock is worth $150,000. Pursuant to paragraph (e)(2) of this section, at the time of the stock purchase, $105,000 (50 percent of $210,000) of funds in the trust were funds supplied by *D,* $100,000 of which are treated as used to purchase the stock. Accordingly, the amount included in *D'* s gross estate under section 2036, $150,000, is the value at death of the portion of the stock acquired with funds provided by *D.*

Individual Retirement Plans: Simplified Employee Pensions: Qualified Voluntary Employee Contributions

Individual Retirement Plans: Simplified Employee Pensions: Qualified Voluntary Employee Contributions.—Reproduced below are the texts of proposed amendments of Reg. §§20.2039-2 and 20.2039-4, relating to individual retirement plans, simplified employee pensions and qualified voluntary employee contributions (published in the Federal Register on January 23, 1984).

☐ Par. 10. Section 20.2039-2 is revised by adding a new subdivision (ix) to paragraph (c)(1) to read as follows:

§20.2039-2. Annuities under "qualified plans" and section 403(b) annuity contracts.

* * *

(c) *Amounts excludable from the gross estate.*

(1) * * *

(ix) Any deductible employee contributions (within the meaning of section 72(o)(5)) are considered amounts contributed by the employer.

* * *

☐ Par. 11. Section 20.2039-4 is revised by adding a new paragraph (h) to read as follows:

§20.2039-4. Lump sum distributions from "qualified plans;" decedents dying after December 31, 1978.

* * *

(h) *Accumulated deductible employee contributions.*—For purposes of this section, a lump sum distribution includes an amount attributable to accumulated deductible employee contributions (as defined in section 72(o)(5)(B)) in any qualified plan taken into account for purposes of determining whether any distribution from that qualified plan is a lump sum distribution as determined under paragraph (b) of this section. Thus, amounts attributable to accumulated deductible employee contributions in a qualified plan under which amounts are payable in a lump sum distribution are not excludible from the decedent's gross estate under §20.2039-2, unless the recipient makes the section 402(a)/403(c) taxation election with respect to a lump sum distribution payable from that qualified plan.

* * *

Estate Tax: Deduction for Interest Expense and Other Amounts Paid

Estate Tax: Deduction for Interest Expense and Other Amounts Paid.—Amendments to Reg. §§20.2053-1, 20.2053-3 and 20.2053-4, providing guidance on the proper use of present-value principles in determining the amount deductible by an estate for funeral expenses, administration expenses, and certain claims against the estate, are proposed (published in the Federal Register on June 28, 2022) (REG-130975-08).

☐ Par. 2. Section 20.2053-1 is amended by:

1. Adding paragraph (d)(6).

2. Revising the introductory text of paragraph (d)(7).

3. In paragraph (d)(7), *Examples 1* through *3* are designated as paragraphs (d)(7)(i) through (iii), respectively.

4. In newly designated paragraphs (d)(7)(i) and (ii):

i. Removing *"ascertainable,"* and adding *"ascertainable."* in its place.

ii. Adding a sentence to the end of the paragraphs.

5. In newly designated paragraph (d)(7)(iii):

i. Removing *"deduction,"* and *"Example 2"* and adding *"deduction."* and "paragraph (d)(7)(ii) of this section (*Example 2*)" in their places, respectively.

ii. Revising the last sentence of the paragraph.

6. Adding paragraphs (d)(7)(iv) through (vi).

7. Revising paragraph (f).

The additions and revisions read as follows:

§20.2053-1. Deductions for expenses, indebtedness, and taxes; in general.

* * *

(d) * * *

(6) *Limitation on amount deductible.*—(i) *Claims and expenses paid after the grace period.*—(A) *Definitions.*—The following definitions apply for purposes of this paragraph (d):

(1) Grace period.—The *grace period* is the period beginning on the date of the decedent's death and extending through the third anniversary of that date.

(2) Post-grace-period payment.—A *post-grace-period payment* is the amount of a claim or expense described in paragraph (a) of this section not paid or to be paid before the end of the grace period.

(B) *General rule.*—To the extent that a post-grace-period payment otherwise meets the requirements for deductibility of a claim or expense under section 2053 and the regulations in this part thereunder, the amount deductible under section 2053 is limited to the present value, as of the decedent's date of death, of that amount. The present value of each post-grace-period payment is calculated by discounting it from the payment date or expected date of payment to the decedent's date of death. The applicable discount rate is the applicable Federal rate determined under section 1274(d) for the month in which the decedent's death occurs, compounded annually. The length of time from the decedent's date of death to the date of payment or expected date of payment will determine whether the Federal rate applicable to that payment is the Federal mid-term rate or the Federal long-term rate. The Internal Revenue Service publishes the applicable Federal rates for each month in the Internal Revenue Bulletin (*see* §601.601(d)(2)(ii) of this chapter). Any reasonable assumptions and methodology in regard to time period measurements may be used to calculate, in accordance with paragraph (d)(6)(ii) of this section, the present value of the post-grace-period payment(s).

(ii) *Calculating present value of amounts paid or payable.*—(A) *Single post-grace-period payment.*—The amount deductible under section 2053 for a single post-grace-period payment is computed by calculating the present value of such payment as follows:

Amount of future payment x $[1 \div (1 + i)]^t$

Where:

t is the amount of time (expressed in years and fractions of years) from the day after the decedent's date of death to the payment date or expected date of payment; and i is the applicable discount rate.

(B) *Multiple post-grace-period payments.*—The amount deductible under section 2053 for multiple post-grace-period payments is computed by calculating the present value of each such payment using the formula in paragraph (d)(6)(ii)(A) of this section; the sum of the discounted amounts of the post-grace-period payments is the amount that is deductible for such payments.

(C) *Multiple payment dates occurring during and after the grace period.*—A claim or expense described in paragraph (a) of this section may have at least one payment date or expected date of payment during the grace period and at least one payment date or expected date of payment after the grace period. For such a claim or expense, the amount deductible under section 2053 is computed by calculating the present value of each separate post-grace-period payment using the formula in paragraph (d)(6)(ii)(A) of this section, and adding the total of these discounted amounts to any amount of the claim or expense having a payment date or expected date of payment during the grace period. Any amount having a payment date or expected date of payment during the grace period is not discounted in arriving at the amount deductible.

(iii) *Discounting when actual date of payment is unknown.*—With regard to a post-grace-period payment that may be deducted in advance of payment under paragraph (d)(4) of this section or § 20.2053-4(b) or (c), the amount deductible must be determined by computing the present value of the amount of that post-grace-period payment as if that amount will be paid on the expected date of payment. The expected date of payment in settlement or satisfaction of a claim or expense must be determined using all information reasonably available to the taxpayer to make a fair and reasonable estimate of the expected date or dates of payment. For amounts deductible under § 20.2053-4(b) or (c), the expected date or dates of payment must be identified in a written appraisal document of a person that is qualified by knowledge and experience to appraise the claim being valued. *See* § 20.2053-4(b)(1)(iv) and (c)(1)(iv). However, the computation of present value is subject to adjustment if, within the period described in paragraph (d)(2) of this section, the actual date or dates of payment become known and differ from the estimated date or dates of payment. *See* paragraph (d)(6)(vi) of this section.

(iv) *Statement supporting present value computation required.*—A deduction under section 2053 for a claim or expense that is required to be discounted to present value under paragraph (d)(6)(i) of this section must be supported by a statement to be filed with the Form 706 showing the computation of the present value of that item, including, if applicable, the basis for the determination of the expected date(s) of payment.

(v) *Ordering rule.*—In computing the amount deductible for a claim or expense under paragraph (d) of this section, the amount deductible for a claim or expense (otherwise determined under paragraphs (d)(1) through (4) of this section) is discounted to present value under paragraph (d)(6) of this section before applying the limits in § 20.2053-4(b)(2) and (c).

(vi) *Effect of post-death events.*—If a deduction is claimed for the present value of a post-grace-period payment, the claimed deduction is subject to adjustment to reflect any post-death events affecting the amount of such post-grace-period payment and any change in the expected or actual date of payment. *See* paragraph (d)(2) of this section for the period during which post-death events are taken into account.

(vii) *Exceptions.*—The rule in paragraph (d)(6)(i) of this section does not apply to unpaid principal of mortgages and other indebtedness deductible under § 20.2053-7.

(7) *Examples.*—Assume that the amounts described in section 2053(a) are payable out of property subject to claims and are allowable by the law of the jurisdiction governing the administration of the estate, whether the applicable jurisdiction is within or outside of the United States. Assume that, unless otherwise provided, the claims against the estate are not deductible under § 20.2053-4(b) or (c) and all amounts are paid during the grace period. The following examples illustrate the application of this paragraph (d):

(i) * * * However, any amounts that will not be paid on or before the third anniversary of the date of D's death (that is, are not paid during the grace period) are subject to the present value limitation in paragraph (d)(6) of this section.

(ii) * * * If the amount of the claim will not be paid on or before the third anniversary of the date of D's death (that is, the amount is not paid during the grace period), the amount deductible is subject to the present value limitation in paragraph (d)(6) of this section.

(iii) * * * At that time, a deduction will be allowed for the amount that is either paid or meets the requirements of paragraph (d)(4) of this section for deducting certain ascertainable amounts, subject to the present value limitation in paragraph (d)(6) of this section, if applicable.

(iv) *Example 4: Discounting amount paid more than three years after decedent's date of death.*—The facts are the same as in paragraph (d)(7)(ii) of this section (*Example 2*) except that E files a timely protective claim for refund in accordance with paragraph (d)(5) of this section to preserve the estate's right to claim a refund, a final judgment in the amount of $100x is entered against and paid by the estate precisely five years after D's date of death, and the applicable Federal (mid-term) rate determined under section 1274(d) for the month in which D's date of death occurs, compounded annually, is 2.00%. Within a reasonable period of time after the final judgment is entered, E notifies the Commissioner that the contingency has been resolved. E may claim a deduction for the present value of the amount paid in satisfaction of the claim as of D's date of death. Under the facts in this paragraph (d)(7)(iv), the present value of the amount paid in five years equals $\$100x \,/\, (1 + .0200)^5$ or $100x/1.104081 or $90.57x.

(v) *Example 5: Discounting amount to be paid when actual date of payment not known.*—The facts are the same as in paragraph (d)(7)(ii) of this section (*Example 2*) except that the claim is deductible under § 20.2053-4(c) because all amounts deducted by the estate under that paragraph do not exceed $500,000. E obtains a written appraisal document meeting the requirements of § 20.2053-4(c)(iv) and reasonably determines that the future value of the claim is $300,000 (that is, before discounting the claim to its present value). E determines, after considering all available information and making reasonable assumptions, that the expected date of payment of the claim is Date X, which is reflected in the appraisal. Date X is a date after the third anniversary of D's date of death. E may claim a deduction for the present value of the claim as of D's date of death, determined by discounting $300,000 for the period from the date of death to Date X, using the applicable

Federal rate determined under section 1274(d) for the month in which D's death occurs, compounded annually.

(vi) *Example 6: Discounting amount to be paid for series of payments payable over a period that does not end on or before the third anniversary of the decedent's death.*—Pursuant to the terms of a divorce and separation agreement entered on June 1 of Year 1, Decedent (D) is obligated to make annual payments of $100x to Claimant (C) on September 1 of year 1 and each September 1st thereafter until D has made a total of 10 such payments. D dies on December 1 of Year 5 after having made the first five annual payments required under the agreement. The applicable Federal (mid-term) rate determined under section 1274(d) for the month in which D's death occurs, compounded annually, is 2.00%. The executor of D's estate (E) may claim a deduction with respect to C's claim on D's Form 706 under the special rule contained in paragraph (d)(4) of this section because the deductible amount can be ascertained with reasonable certainty. E computes the discounted deductible amount of the claim by adding the undiscounted amount of the three payments that will be made before the third anniversary of D's death ($300x) to the discounted amounts of the two payments that will be made after the third anniversary of D's death. Accordingly, the amount deductible for the claim equals $483.866x ($300x + $92.843x + $91.023x). The individual calculations for the present values of the payments in the last two years of the payment obligation are shown in table 1 to this paragraph (d)(7)(vi).

Table 1 to paragraph (d)(7)(vi)

	(1) t	(2) 1+i	(3) 1/(1+i)	(4) $[1/(1+i)]^t$	(5) $[1/(1+i)]^t \times 100x$
Year 9	3.75	1.0200	0.980392	0.928430	92.843x
Year 10	4.75	1.0200	0.980392	0.910226	91.023x

* * *

(f) *Applicability date.*—The rules of this section apply to the estates of decedents dying on or after [date of publication of the final rule in the **Federal Register**].

☐ Par. 3. Section 20.2053-3 is amended by:

1. Redesignating paragraphs (d) and (e) as paragraphs (e) and (f), respectively.
2. Adding a new paragraph (d).
3. Revising newly redesignated paragraph (f).

The addition and revision read as follows:

§ 20.2053-3. Deduction for expenses of administering estate.

* * *

(d) *Interest expense incurred in administering the estate.*—(1) *Interest payable under section 6601 on unpaid tax.*—(i) *Section 6166 interest.*—As used in paragraph (d)(1) of this section, the phrase "section 6166 interest" means interest payable under section 6601 on unpaid estate tax deferred under section 6166. This includes interest accruing on an installment or other payment under section 6166 during the period of an extension of time for making that payment under section 6161(a)(2)(B). Section 6166 interest is not deductible pursuant to section 2053(c)(1)(D).

(ii) *Non-section 6166 interest.*—As used in paragraph (d)(1) of this section, the phrase "non-section 6166 interest" means interest payable under section 6601 or under state or local law other than section 6166 interest. Non-section 6166 interest that accrues on or after the decedent's date of death on any unpaid tax or penalties may be deductible to the extent permitted by § 20.2053-1 and this section. For purposes of paragraph (d)(1) of this section, penalties include any unpaid additions to tax, additional taxes, and penalties. When non-section 6166 interest accrues on unpaid estate tax deferred under section 6161 or section 6163, the interest expense is actually and necessarily incurred in the administration of the estate for purposes of paragraph (a) of this section because the extension was based on a demonstrated need to defer payment. When non-section 6166 interest accrues on and after the date of a decedent's death on any unpaid tax or penalties in connection with an underpayment of tax or a deficiency, the interest expense generally is actually and necessarily incurred in the administration of the estate for purposes of paragraph (a) of this section.

(iii) *Exception.*—Notwithstanding paragraph (d)(1)(ii) of this section, non-section 6166 interest accruing on unpaid tax and penalties on and after the decedent's date of death, whether in connection with a deferral, underpayment, or deficiency, is not actually and necessarily incurred in the administration of the estate for purposes of paragraph (a) of this section and is not deductible to the extent the interest expense is attributable to an executor's negligence, disregard of applicable rules or regulations (including careless, reckless, or intentional disregard of rules or regulations) as defined in § 1.6662-3(b)(2) of this chapter, or fraud with intent to evade tax. Interest expense is attributable to an executor's negligence, disregard of applicable rules or regulations, or fraud with intent to evade tax to the extent that the underlying deferral, underpayment, or deficiency, is attributable to such conduct by the executor. Similarly, even when the underlying deferral, underpayment, or deficiency is not attributable to such conduct by the executor, the interest expense is attributable to an executor's negligence, disregard of the rules or regulations, or fraud with intent to evade tax to the extent the subsequent accrual of interest is attributable to such conduct by the executor.

(iv) *Examples.*—The following examples illustrate the application of this paragraph (d)(1). In each example, the decedent (D) dies on October 1, Year 1, and the estate tax return is due July 1 of the following calendar year, Year 2. In each example, except as expressly stated, there is no negligence, disregard of applicable rules or regulations, or fraud on the part of the executor.

(A) *Example 1.*—On July 1, Year 2, the executor of D's estate (E) timely files the estate tax return based on values determined in good faith and pays $500,000, which is the estate tax shown on the return. Upon examination, the Internal Revenue Service (IRS) makes an adjustment to the value of an asset includible in the gross estate, resulting in a $25,000 increase in estate tax due. E initially contests the adjustment, but eventually agrees to the assessment of the deficiency in the amount of $25,000. Interest on the deficiency is payable under section 6601 in the amount of $X. E makes a payment in satisfaction of the assessed deficiency and interest. For purposes of paragraph (a) of this section, the interest expense in the amount of $X is considered actually and necessarily incurred in the administration of D's estate, and its deduction reduces the amount of the deficiency.

(B) *Example 2.*—The executor of D's estate (E) files the estate tax return and pays the estate tax shown on the return ($500,000) on July 1 of Year 3, one year after the due date. On August 1, Year 3, the IRS assesses interest on the unpaid tax under section 6601 in the amount of $X, assesses late filing and late payment penalties in accordance with section 6651 in the amount of $Y, and issues a notice and demand for payment of $X and $Y. On August 1, Year 4, E makes payment to the IRS of $Z, which is the total amount due for $X and $Y, as well as interest that accrued on these amounts from August 1, Year 3, to August 1, Year 4, payable under section 6601. The facts establish that E's failure to timely file the return and timely pay the tax and failure to pay the assessed interest and penalties within the period provided in the notice and demand is a result of E's disregard of the rules for filing the return and paying the tax and any assessed penalties. Under the facts in this paragraph (d)(1)(iv)(B), neither the interest payable under section 6601 that accrued on the unpaid tax before notice and demand nor the interest that accrued on the unpaid tax and penalties after notice and demand is an expense that is actually and necessarily incurred in the administration of D's estate for purposes of paragraph (a) of this section.

(C) *Example 3.*—Prior to D's death, the IRS had assessed an income tax deficiency against D for the 2009 tax period in the amount of $75,000, and penalties in the amount of $X. The assessed tax and penalties remained unpaid on D's date of death. On July 1, Year 2, the executor of D's estate (E) timely files the estate tax return and timely pays the estate tax shown on the return to be due. On the same date, E also pays all claims against and liabilities of the estate, except for the assessed income tax deficiency and penalties for the 2009 tax period. Despite E's awareness that the estate had sufficient liquidity and funds to satisfy all estate liabilities, including the 2009 income tax deficiency and penalties, E does not pay the assessed income tax deficiency, penalties, and accrued interest until July 1, Year 4. E's failure to pay the assessed income tax deficiency and penalties for the 2009 tax period is a result of E's disregard of applicable rules or regulations. Even though the underlying income tax deficiency is not attributable to E's negligence, disregard of applicable rules, or fraud with intent to evade tax, the interest that accrued after July 1, Year 2, on the assessed deficiency and penalties is attributable to E's disregard of applicable rules or regulations. Accordingly, the post-July 1, Year 2, interest is not an expense that is actually and necessarily incurred in the administration of D's estate.

(2) *Interest expense on certain loan obligations of the estate.*—Interest on a loan entered into by the estate to facilitate the payment of the estate's tax and other liabilities or the administration of the estate may be deductible depending on all the facts and circumstances. To be a deductible administration expense, interest expense must arise from an instrument or contractual arrangement that constitutes indebtedness under applicable income tax regulations and general principles of Federal tax law. In addition, the interest expense and the loan to which interest expense relates must satisfy the requirement of § 20.2053-1(b)(2) that they are bona fide in nature based on all the facts and circumstances. Further, both the loan to which the interest expense relates and the loan terms must be actually and necessarily incurred in the administration of the decedent's estate and must be essential to the proper settlement of the decedent's estate. *See* paragraph (a) of this section. If the facts and circumstances establish that the interest expense arises from an instrument or contractual arrangement that constitutes indebtedness under general principles of Federal tax law, factors that collectively may support a finding that the interest expense also satisfies the additional requirements under § 20.2053-1(b)(2) and paragraph (a) of this section include, but are not limited to, the following:

(i) The interest rate on and the terms of the underlying loan (whether between related or unrelated parties), including any prepayment penalty, are reasonable given all the facts and circumstances and comparable to an arms-length loan transaction;

(ii) The underlying loan is entered into by an executor of the decedent's estate acting in the capacity of executor or, if no executor is appointed and acting, the person accountable for satisfying the liabilities of the estate;

(iii) The lender properly includes amounts of paid and/or accrued interest (including original issue discount as determined under sections 1271 through 1275 and the regulations in this part under those sections, such as original issue discount attributable to stated interest that is treated as part of the stated redemption price at maturity because it is not payable at least annually) in gross income for Federal income tax purposes, particularly if the lender is a family member of the decedent, a related entity, or a beneficiary of the decedent's estate or trust (as defined in § 20.2053-1(b)(2)(iii));

(iv) The loan proceeds are used to satisfy estate liabilities that are essential to the proper settlement of the estate, including, but not limited to, the Federal estate tax liability;

(v) The loan term and payment schedule correspond to the estate's anticipated ability to make the payments under, and to satisfy, the loan, and the loan term does not extend beyond what is reasonably necessary;

(vi) The only practical alternatives to the loan are the sale of estate assets at prices that are significantly below-market, the forced liquidation of an entity that conducts an active trade or business, or some similar financially undesirable course of action;

(vii) The underlying loan is entered into when the estate's liquid assets are insufficient to satisfy estate liabilities, the estate does not have control (within the meaning of section 2701(b)(2)) of an entity that has liquid assets sufficient to satisfy estate liabilities, the estate has no power to direct or compel an entity in which it has an interest to sell liquid assets to enable the estate to satisfy its liabilities, and the estate's assets are expected to generate sufficient cash flow or liquidity to make the payments required under the loan;

(viii) The estate's illiquidity does not occur after the decedent's death as a result of the decedent's testamentary estate plan to create illiquidity; similarly, the illiquidity does not occur post-death as a deliberate result of the action or inaction of the executor who then had both knowledge or reason to know of the estate tax liability and a reasonable alternative to that action or inaction that could have avoided or mitigated the illiquidity;

(ix) The lender is not a beneficiary of a substantial portion of the value of the estate, and is not an entity over which such a beneficiary has control (within the meaning of section 2701(b)(2)) or the right to compel or direct the making of the loan;

(x) The lender or lenders are not beneficiaries of the estate whose individual share of liability under the loan is substantially similar to his or her share of the estate; and

(xi) The decedent's estate has no right of recovery of estate tax against, or of contribution from, the person loaning the funds.

* * *

(f) *Applicability date.*—The rules of this section apply to the estates of decedents dying on or after [date of publication of the final rule in the **Federal Register**].

☐ Par. 4. Section 20.2053-4 is amended by:

1. Revising paragraphs (b)(1)(iv), (b)(2), and (c)(1)(iv) and (v), the second sentence of paragraph (c)(3), paragraph (d)(5), and paragraph (d)(7)(iii) introductory text.

2. In paragraph (d)(7)(iii), *Examples 1* through *9* are designated as paragraphs (d)(7)(iii)(A) through (I), respectively.

3. In newly designated paragraph (d)(7)(iii)(A), removing "*decision,*" and "§ 20.2053-3(c) or § 20.2053-3(d)(3)" adding "*decision.*" and "§ 20.2053-3(c) or (d)(3)" in their places, respectively.

4. In newly designated paragraphs (d)(7)(iii)(B) and (C), removing "*payment,*", "*Example 1*", and "§ 20.2053-3(c) or § 20.2053-3(d)(3)" and adding "*payment.*", "paragraph (d)(7)(iii)(A) of this section (*Example 1*)", and "§ 20.2053-3(c) or (d)(3)" in their places, respectively.

5. In newly designated paragraph (d)(7)(iii)(D), removing "*defendants,*", "*Example 1*", and "§ 20.2053-3(c) or § 20.2053-3(d)(3)" and adding "*defendants.*", "paragraph (d)(7)(iii)(A) of this section (*Example 1*)", and "§ 20.2053-3(c) or (d)(3)" in their places, respectively.

6. In newly designated paragraph (d)(7)(iii)(E), removing "*payment,*", "*Example 1*", and "§ 20.2053-3(c) or § 20.2053-3(d)(3)" and adding "*payment.*", "paragraph (d)(7)(iii)(A) of this section (*Example 1*)", and "§ 20.2053-3(c) or (d)(3)" in their places, respectively.

7. In newly designated paragraph (d)(7)(iii)(F), removing "*claims,*" and "§ 20.2053-3(c) or § 20.2053-3(d)(3)" and adding "*claims.*" and "§ 20.2053-3(c) or (d)(3)" in their places, respectively.

8. In newly designated paragraph (d)(7)(iii)(G), removing "*enforceability,*" and adding "*enforceability.*" in its place.

9. In newly designated paragraph (d)(7)(iii)(H), removing "*estate,*" and adding "*estate.*" in its place.

10. In newly designated paragraph (d)(7)(iii)(I), removing "*satisfaction,*" and adding "*satisfaction.*" in its place.

11. Adding paragraph (d)(7)(iii)(J).

12. Revising paragraph (f).

The revisions and addition read as follows:

§ 20.2053-4. Deduction for claims against the estate.

* * *

(b) * * *

(1) * * *

(iv) The value of each such claim against the estate is supported by a written appraisal document to be filed with the Form 706,

United States Estate (and Generation-Skipping Transfer) Tax Return, or successor form, and the written appraisal document—

(A) Adequately reflects post-death events that have occurred prior to the date on which a deduction is claimed on an estate's Form 706;

(B) Reports, considers, and appropriately weighs all relevant facts and elements of value as are known or are reasonably determinable at the time of the appraisal, including the underlying facts of the claim against the estate, potential litigating risks, and the current status of the claim and procedural history;

(C) Takes into account post-death events reasonably anticipated to occur;

(D) Identifies an expected date or dates of payment (for purposes of determining the applicability of the present value limitation in § 20.2053-1(d)(6));

(E) Explains in detail the methods and analysis that support the appraisal's conclusions;

(F) Is prepared, signed under penalties of perjury, and dated by a person who is qualified by knowledge and experience to appraise the claim being valued and is not a family member of the decedent, a related entity, or a beneficiary of the decedent's estate or revocable trust (as those terms are defined in § 20.2053-1(b)(2)(iii)), a family member of a beneficiary or a related entity as to a beneficiary (as those terms would be defined in § 20.2053-1(b)(2)(iii) if references therein to the decedent were replaced with a reference to such beneficiary, and without regard to the limitations in § 20.2053-1(b)(2)(iii) based on the decedent's date of death), or an employee or other owner of any of them; and

(G) Includes a statement providing the basis for the person's qualifications to appraise the claim being valued;

* * *

(2) *Limitation on deduction.*—The deduction under this paragraph (b) is limited to the value of the related claims or particular assets included in decedent's gross estate. *See* § 20.2053-1(d)(6)(v) for the impact of the present value limitation.

* * *

(c) * * *

(1) * * *

(iv) The value of each such claim against the estate is supported by a written appraisal document to be filed with the Form 706, *United States Estate (and Generation-Skipping Transfer) Tax Return*, or successor form, and the written appraisal document—

(A) Adequately reflects post-death events that have occurred prior to the date on which a deduction is claimed on an estate's Form 706;

(B) Reports, considers and appropriately weighs all relevant facts and elements of value as are known or reasonably determinable at the time of the appraisal, including the underlying facts of the claim against the estate, potential litigating risks, and the current status of the claim and procedural history;

(C) Takes into account post-death events reasonably anticipated to occur;

(D) Identifies an expected date or dates of payment (for purposes of determining the applicability of the present value limitation in § 20.2053-1(d)(6));

(E) Explains in detail the methods and analysis that support the appraisal's conclusions;

(F) Is prepared, signed under penalties of perjury, and dated by a person who is qualified by knowledge and experience to appraise the claim being valued, and is not a family member of the decedent, a related entity, or a beneficiary of the decedent's estate or revocable trust (as those terms are defined in § 20.2053-1(b)(2)(iii)), a family member of a beneficiary or a related entity as to a beneficiary (as those terms would be defined in § 20.2053-1(b)(2)(iii) if references therein to the decedent were replaced with a reference to such beneficiary, and without regard to the limitations in § 20.2053-1(b)(2)(iii) based on the decedent's date of death), or an employee or other owner of any of them; and

(G) Includes a statement providing the basis for the person's qualifications to appraise the claim being valued;

(v) The total amount deducted by the estate under paragraph (c) of this section does not exceed $500,000 (*see* § 20.2053-1(d)(6)(v) for the impact of the present value limitation);

* * *

(3) * * * Assume that each claim is paid within three years after the decedent's death, and that the value of each claim is determined from a written appraisal document that meets the requirements of paragraph (c)(1)(iv) of this section. * * *

(d) * * *

(5) *Claims founded upon a promise.*—(i) *In general.*—To be deductible, a claim founded on a promise must represent a personal obligation of the decedent existing at the time of the decedent's death, and the claim must be enforceable against the decedent's estate. In addition, except with regard to pledges or subscriptions (*see* § 20.2053-5), the deduction for a claim founded upon a promise or agreement is limited to the extent that the promise or agreement was bona fide and in exchange for adequate and full consideration in money or money's worth; that is, the promise or agreement must have been bargained for at arm's length and the price must have been an adequate and full equivalent reducible to money value.

(ii) *Decedent's promise to guarantee a debt.*—A deduction for a claim founded upon a decedent's agreement to guarantee a debt of another is a claim founded on a promise and is subject to the limitation in paragraph (d)(5)(i) of this section. For purposes of section 2053, a decedent's agreement to guarantee a debt of an entity in which the decedent had an interest at the time the guarantee was given satisfies the requirement that the agreement be in exchange for adequate and full consideration in money or money's worth if, at the time the guarantee was given, the decedent had control (within the meaning of section 2701(b)(2)) of the entity. Alternatively, this requirement is satisfied to the extent the maximum liability of the decedent under the guarantee did not exceed, at the time the guarantee was given, the fair market value of the decedent's interest in the entity. The bona fide nature of the decedent's agreement to guarantee a debt of a family member, a related entity, or a beneficiary (as defined in § 20.2053-1(b)(2)(iii)) is determined in accordance with § 20.2053-1(b)(2)(ii). For a claim otherwise deductible under this paragraph (d)(5)(ii), the estate's right of contribution or reimbursement will reduce the amount deductible in accordance with § 20.2053-1(d)(3). Payments made pursuant to the decedent's guarantee of a debt are deductible only to the extent that the debt for which the guarantee is given has not been taken into account in computing the value of the gross estate under § 20.2053-7 or otherwise. * * *

(7) * * *

(iii) The claimant (C) is not a family member, related entity, or beneficiary of the estate of decedent (D), unless otherwise provided, and is not the executor (E).

* * *

(J) *Example 10: Guarantee.*—On Date 1, D entered into a guarantee agreement with Bank (C) to secure financing for a closely-held business (LLC) in which D had a controlling interest. LLC was solvent at the time LLC executed a promissory note in the amount of $100x in favor of C. Prior to D's death, LLC became insolvent and stopped making payments on the note. After D's death, C filed a claim against D's estate for payment of the remaining balance due under the note and E paid the full amount due. Although E had a right of contribution against LLC for primary payment of the indebtedness, LLC was insolvent and no part of the debt was collectible at the time E deducted the payment. D's estate may deduct the amount paid to C in satisfaction of D's liability under the guarantee agreement. The guarantee agreement is considered to have been contracted for an adequate and full consideration in money or money's worth. The result would be the same if D did not have control of LLC as long as the fair market value of D's interest in the LLC on Date 1 was at least $100x.

* * *

(f) *Applicability date.*—The rules of this section apply to the estates of decedents dying on or after [date of publication of the final rule in the **Federal Register**].

Charitable Remainder Trusts

Charitable Remainder Trusts: Election: Extended Date.—Reproduced below is the text of a proposed amendment of Reg. § 20.2055-2, relating to the granting of an extension to permit the reformation of charitable remainder trusts (published in the Federal Register on December 19, 1975).

☐ Par. 3. § 20.2055-2 is amended by adding a sentence at the end of paragraph (a) and by adding a new paragraph (g) immediately following § 20.2055-2(f). These added and amended provisions read as follows:

§ 20.2055-2. Transfers not exclusively for charitable purposes.—(a) *Remainders and similar interests.*—* * * See paragraph (g) of this section for special rules relating to certain wills and trusts in existence on September 21, 1974.

* * *

(g) *Special rules applicable in the case of certain wills and trusts in existence on September 21, 1974.*—(1) In general, in the case of a will executed before September 21, 1974, or a trust created (within the meaning of applicable local law) after July 31, 1969, and before September 21, 1974, if—

(i) At the time of the decedent's death a deduction is not allowable solely because of the failure of an interest in property which passes or has passed from the decedent to a person, or for a use, described in section 2055(a) to meet the requirements of section 2055(e)(2)(A), and

(ii) The governing instrument is amended or conformed in accordance with this paragraph so that the interest is in a trust which is a charitable remainder annuity trust or a charitable remainder unitrust (described in section 664) or a pooled income fund (described in section 642(c)(5)), or the governing instrument is treated under paragraph (g)(8) of this section as if it were amended, a deduction shall nevertheless be allowed.

(2) An amendment or conformation pursuant to this paragraph must be made before January 1, 1976, or, if later, on or before the 30th day after the date on which judicial proceedings begun before January 1, 1976 (which are required to amend or conform the governing instrument) become final.

(3) A governing instrument may be amended or conformed under this paragraph only where:

(i) The transfer is not in trust but passes under a will executed before September 21, 1974;

(ii) The transfer is in the form of a testamentary trust created under a will executed before September 21, 1974;

(iii) The transfer was in trust, which was created (within the meaning of applicable local law) after July 31, 1969, and before September 21, 1974, but only if, at the time of the creation of the trust, the governing instrument provides that an organization described in section 170(c) receives an irrevocable remainder interest in such trust;

(iv) Property was transferred inter vivos after July 31, 1969, and before October 18, 1971, to a trust created (within the meaning of applicable local law) before August 1, 1969, which trust provides that an organization described in section 170(c) receives an irrevocable remainder interest in such trust, and the transferred property and any undistributed income therefrom is severed and placed in a separate trust before the applicable date specified in paragraph (g)(2) of this section. An instrument governing a transfer under this subdivision (iv), which is amended pursuant to this paragraph, shall be treated as having made such transfer to a trust deemed created on the date of such transfer;

(v) In the case of a transfer to a pooled income fund made before September 21, 1974 (or a transfer made under a will which was executed before September 21, 1974), the instrument governing the transfer fails to satisfy the requirements of § 1.642(c)-5(b).

However, a governing instrument may not be amended pursuant to this paragraph unless, at the time of the decedent's death, the interest is an irrevocable remainder interest for which a deduction, but for section 2055(e)(2)(A), would be allowable under section 2055(a) and the regulations thereunder. The provisions of section 508(d)(2)(A) (relating to disallowance of certain charitable, etc., deductions) shall not apply to such interest if the governing instrument is amended so as to comply with the requirements of section 508(e) (relating to governing instruments) by the applicable date described in paragraph (g)(2) of this section.

(4) The decree resulting from any judicial proceedings begun to amend a governing instrument pursuant to paragraph (g)(1) of this section must be binding, under local law, on all parties having an interest in the bequest or transfer as well as the fiduciary of the decedent's estate and trustee of the trust to be amended. In the event local law does not require judicial proceedings to amend or conform a governing instrument, a deduction may nevertheless be allowed if the governing instrument is amended or conformed by nonjudicial agreement between all parties having an interest in the bequest or transfer as well as the fiduciary of the decedent's estate and trustee of the trust to be amended, provided that the agreement is binding, under local law, on all such parties. The judicial proceedings or nonjudicial agreement must also account for any distributions made from the deemed date of creation to the date of the amendment in the following manner:

(i) Where the amount of the distributions which would have been made by the trust to a recipient had the amendment pursuant to paragraph (g)(1) of this section been in effect since the creation of the trust exceeds the amount of the distributions made by the trust prior to the amendment, the trust must pay an amount equal to such excess to the recipient;

(ii) Where the amount of the distributions made to the recipient prior to the amendment pursuant to paragraph (g)(1) of this section exceeds the amount of the distributions which would have been made by such trust if the amended provisions of such trust had been in effect from the time of creation of such trust, the recipient must pay an amount equal to such excess to the trust.

See § 1.664-1(d)(4) for rules relating to the year of inclusion in the case of an underpayment to a recipient and the allowance of a deduction in the case of an overpayment to a recipient.

(5) Where a charitable remainder trust (as described in § 1.664-1(a)(1)(iii)(a)) results from an amendment pursuant to this paragraph, the trust will be treated as a charitable remainder trust for all purposes from the date it would be deemed created under § 1.664-1(a)(4) and (5), whether or not such date is after September 20, 1974. Subject to the limitations imposed by section 6511, the estate tax charitable deduction is allowable and the charitable remainder trust is exempt from Federal income taxation. For the application of certain excise taxes pursuant to section 4947(a)(2) see § 53.4947-1(c)(1)(iii) and (c)(6). In amending a governing instrument pursuant to paragraph (g)(1) of this section, the exchange of a noncharitable beneficiary's interest in an unqualified transfer in trust for an interest in a qualified transfer in trust will not be treated as an act of self-dealing (described in section 4941) or a taxable expenditure (described in section 4945).

(6) If, on the due date for filing the estate tax return (including any extensions thereof), proceedings to amend or conform a governing instrument pursuant to paragraph (g)(1) of this section have not become final, such return shall be filed with the tax computed as if no deduction were allowable under this paragraph. When the proceedings to amend or conform such instrument have become final (within the applicable date described in paragraph (g)(2) of this section), a deduction shall be allowed upon the filing of a claim for credit or refund (within the limitations of section 6511). In the case of a credit or refund as a result of an amendment or conformation made pursuant to this paragraph, no interest shall be allowed for the period prior to the expiration of the 180th day after the date on which the claim for credit or refund is filed.

(7) If a governing instrument is amended under this paragraph, then, except as provided in paragraph (g)(8)(ii) of this section, the amount of the deduction allowable under this section shall be the amount that equals the value of the interest which, under the rules of section 2055 (including the rules governing disclaimers) passes to, or for the use of, an organization described in section 2055(a).

(8)(i) In the case of a will executed before September 21, 1974, or a trust created (within the meaning of applicable local law) before such date and after July 31, 1969, that creates an interest for which a deduction would be allowable under section 2055(a) but for section 2055(e)(2)(A), if the date of death of the decedent is prior to January 1, 1976, and if on or before the filing date of the estate tax return (including any extension thereof)—

(A) The interest is in a charitable trust which, if a deduction under section 2055(a) had been allowed, would be in a trust described in section 4947(a)(1), or

(B) Such interest passes directly to a person or for a use described in section 2055(a) (as, for example, by reason of the termination of an intervening interest),

the governing instrument shall be treated as if it were amended or conformed pursuant to paragraph (g)(1) of this section and a deduction shall be allowed. See section 508(d)(2) and § 1.508-2(b) for the disallowance of such a deduction in the case of an interest in a trust described in section 4947(a)(1) if the governing instrument fails to meet the requirements of section 508(e) by the end of the taxable year of the trust in which the filing date of the estate tax return occurs. A governing instrument treated as amended under this subdivision (i) may not thereafter be amended. The provisions of this subparagraph shall not apply if the requirements of subdivision (A) or (B) of this subdivision (ii) are satisfied as a result of an amendment of a dispositive provision of the governing instrument occurring since the date of death of the decedent.

(ii) The amount of the deduction for a transfer which is treated under this paragraph as if it were amended will be determined as if the transfer were a charitable remainder annuity trust which provides an annuity of 6 percent of the initial fair market value payable from the date of death—

(A) In the case of a transfer providing a life estate, for the expected lives of the noncharitable beneficiaries as determined on the date of death of the decedent, or

(B) In the case of a transfer providing a term of years, for the term of years as expressed in the governing instrument, but not to exceed 20 years.

Any distributions made to a recipient from the date of death of the decedent to the date on which the transfer is deemed to be amended (*i.e.,* the date the transfer satisfies the requirements of paragraph (g)(8)(i) of this section) must be taken into account under this subdivision (ii) in determining the amount of the deduction, to the extent that the adjustments in such distributions required by paragraph (g)(4) of this section, determined as if the charitable remainder annuity trust were deemed created at the date of death of the decedent, have not been made on or before the filing date of the estate tax return. [Reg. § 20.2055-2.]

Annuities: Interests: Valuation: Actuarial Tables

Annuities: Interests: Valuation: Actuarial Tables.—Amendments to Reg. § 20.2055-2, relating to the use of actuarial tables in valuing annuities, interests for life or terms of years, and remainder or reversionary interests, are proposed (published in the Federal Register on May 5, 2022) (REG-122770-18).

☐ Par. 20. Section 20.2055-2 is amended by revising paragraphs (e)(3)(iii) and (f)(4) and (6) to read as follows:

§ 20.2055-2. Transfers not exclusively for charitable purposes.

* * *

(e) * * *

(3) * * *

(iii)(A) The rule in paragraphs (e)(2)(vi)(*a*) and (e)(2)(vii)(*a*) of this section that guaranteed annuity interests or unitrust interests, respectively, may be payable for a specified term of years or for the life or lives of only certain individuals generally is effective in the case of transfers pursuant to wills and revocable trusts when the decedent dies on or after April 4, 2000. Two exceptions from the application of the rule in paragraphs (e)(2)(vi)(*a*) and (e)(2)(vii)(*a*) of this section are provided for transfers pursuant to a will or revocable trust executed on or before April 4, 2000. One exception is for a decedent who dies on or before July 5, 2001, without having republished the will (or amended the trust) by codicil or otherwise. The other exception is for a decedent who was, on April 4, 2000, under a mental disability that prevented a change in the disposition of the decedent's property, and who either does not regain competence to dispose of such property before the date of death, or dies prior to the later of 90 days after the date on which the decedent first regains competence, or July 5, 2001, without having republished the will (or amended the trust) by codicil or otherwise. If a guaranteed annuity interest or unitrust interest created pursuant to a will or revocable trust when the decedent dies on or after April 4, 2000, uses an individual other than one permitted in paragraphs (e)(2)(vi)(*a*) and (e)(2)(vii)(*a*) of this section, and the interest does not qualify for this transitional relief, the interest may be reformed into a lead interest payable for a specified term of years. The term of years is determined by taking the factor for valuing the annuity or unitrust interest for the named individual measuring life and identifying the term of years (rounded up to the next whole year) that corresponds to the equivalent term of years factor for an annuity or unitrust interest. A judicial reformation must be commenced prior to the later of July 5, 2001, or the date prescribed by section 2055(e)(3)(C)(iii). Any judicial reformation must be completed within a reasonable time after it is commenced. A non-judicial reformation is permitted if effective under state law, provided it is completed by the date on which a judicial reformation must be commenced. In the alternative, if a court, in a proceeding that is commenced on or before July 5, 2001, declares any transfer made pursuant to a will or revocable trust where the decedent dies on or after April 4, 2000, and on or before March 6, 2001, null and void ab initio, the Internal Revenue Service will treat such transfers in a manner similar to that described in section 2055(e)(3)(J).

(B) The appropriate annuity factor for an annuity payable for a term of years is computed by subtracting from 1.000000 the factor for an ordinary remainder interest following the same term certain that is determined under the formula in § 20.2031-7(d)(2)(ii)(A) and then dividing the result by the applicable section 7520 interest rate expressed as a number with at least four decimal places. For the convenience of taxpayers, actuarial factors have been computed by IRS and appear in the "Annuity" column of Table B. The appropriate annuity factor for an annuity payable for the life of one individual is computed by subtracting from 1.00000 the factor for an ordinary remainder interest following the life of the same individual that is determined under the formula in § 20.2031-7(d)(2)(ii)(B) and then dividing the result by the applicable section 7520 interest rate expressed as a number with four decimal places. For the convenience of taxpayers, actuarial factors have been computed by IRS and appear in the "Annuity" column of Table S. Table B and Table S can be found on the IRS website at *https://www.irs.gov/retirement-plans/actuarial-tables* (or a corresponding URL as may be updated from time to time). For purposes of the example in paragraph (e)(3)(iii)(C) of this section, the following relevant factors from Table B and Table S are used:

Table 1 to paragraph (e)(3)(iii)(B)

Factors from Table B			
Annuity, Income, and Remainder Interests for a Term Certain			
Interest at 3.2 Percent			
Years	Annuity	Income Interest	Remainder
37	21.5068	0.688218	0.311782
38	21.8089	0.697886	0.302114

Factors from Table S - Based on Table 2010CM			
Interest at 3.2 Percent			
Age	Annuity	Life Estate	Remainder
40	21.7045	0.69454	0.30546

(C) The following example illustrates how to determine the term of years for a reformed interest as discussed in paragraph (e)(3)(iii)(A) of this section. Assume an annuity interest payable for the life of an individual age 40 at the time of the transfer on or after [applicability date of the Treasury decision adopting these regulations as final regulations], with an interest rate of 3.2 percent under section 7520. Under Table S, the annuity factor at 3.2 percent for the life of an individual age 40 is 21.7045. Based on Table B at 3.2 percent, the factor 21.7045 corresponds to a term of years between 37 and 38 years. Accordingly, the annuity interest must be reformed into an interest payable for a term of 38 years.

* * *

(f) * * *

(4) *Other decedents.*—The present value of an interest not described in paragraph (f)(2) of this section is to be determined under § 20.2031-7(d) in the case of decedents where the valuation date of the gross estate is on or after [applicability date of the Treasury decision adopting these regulations as final regulations], or under § 20.2031-7A in the case of decedents where the valuation date of the gross estate is before [applicability date of the Treasury decision adopting these regulations as final regulations].

* * *

(6) *Applicability date.*—Paragraphs (e)(3)(iii) and (f)(4) of this section apply on and after [applicability date of the Treasury decision adopting these regulations as final regulations].

Annuities: Interests: Valuation: Actuarial Tables

Annuities: Interests: Valuation: Actuarial Tables.—Amendments to Reg. § 20.2056A-4, relating to the use of actuarial tables in valuing annuities, interests for life or terms of years, and remainder or reversionary interests, are proposed (published in the Federal Register on May 5, 2022) (REG-122770-18).

☐ Par. 21. Section 20.2056A-4 is amended by:

1. Revising paragraph (c)(4)(ii)(B).

2. In paragraph (d), designating *Examples 1* through *5* as paragraphs (d)(1) through (5), respectively.

3. Revising the headings in newly designated paragraphs (d)(1) through (3).

4. Revising newly designated paragraph (d)(4), newly designated paragraph (d)(5) heading, and paragraph (e).

The revisions read as follows:

§ 20.2056A-4. Procedures for conforming marital trusts and nontrust marital transfers to the requirements of a qualified domestic trust.

* * *

(c) * * *

(4) * * *

(ii) * * *

(B) The total present value of the nonassignable annuity or other payment is the present value of the annuity or other payment as of the date of the decedent's death, determined in accordance with the interest rates and mortality table prescribed by section 7520. The expected annuity term is the number of years that would be required for the scheduled payments to exhaust a hypothetical fund equal to the present value of the scheduled payments. This is determined by first dividing the total present value of the payments by the annual payment. From the quotient so obtained, the expected annuity term is derived by identifying the term of years that corresponds to the lowest annuity factor that is equal to or greater than the quotient. The annuity factor is computed by subtracting from 1.000000 the factor for an ordinary remainder interest following the same term certain that is determined under the formula in § 20.2031-7(d)(2)(ii)(A) and then dividing the result by the applicable section 7520 interest rate expressed as a number with at least four decimal places. For the convenience of taxpayers, actuarial factors have been computed by IRS and appear in the "Annuity" column of Table B which can be found on the IRS website at *https://www.irs.gov/retirement-plans/actuarial-tables* (or a corresponding URL as may be updated from time to time). If the quotient obtained falls between two terms, the longer term is used.

* * *

(d) * * *

(1) *Example 1. Transfer and assignment of probate and nonprobate property to QDOT.*—* * *

(2) *Example 2. Formula assignment.*—* * *

(3) *Example 3. Jointly owned property.*—* * *

(4) *Example 4. Computation of corpus portion of annuity payment.*—(i) The appropriate annuity factor for an annuity payable for the life of one individual is computed by subtracting from 1.00000 the factor for an ordinary remainder interest following the life of the same individual that is determined under the formula in § 20.2031-7(d)(2)(ii)(B) and then dividing the result by the applicable section 7520 interest rate expressed as a number with four decimal places. For the convenience of taxpayers, actuarial factors have been computed by IRS and appear in the "Annuity" column of Table S. The appropriate annuity factor for an annuity payable for a term of years is computed by subtracting from 1.000000 the factor for an ordinary remainder interest following the same term certain that is determined under the formula in § 20.2031-7(d)(2)(ii)(A) and then dividing the result by the applicable section 7520 interest rate expressed as a number with at least four decimal places. For the convenience of taxpayers, actuarial factors have been computed by IRS and appear in the "Annuity" column of Table B. The applicable adjustment factor for annuities that are payable at the end of semiannual, quarterly, monthly, or weekly periods is computed by use of the formula in § 20.2031-7(d)(2)(iv)(B). For the convenience of taxpayers, actuarial factors have been computed by IRS and appear in Table K. These actuarial tables can be found on the IRS website at *https://www.irs.gov/retirement-plans/actuarial-tables*. For purposes of the example in this paragraph (d)(4), the relevant factors from Table S, Table B, and Table K are:

Table 2 to paragraph (d)(4)

Factors from Table S - Based on Table 2010CM			
Interest at 3.6 Percent			
Age	Annuity	Life Estate	Remainder
60	14.6908	0.52887	0.47113

Factors from Table B			
Annuity, Income, and Remainder Interests for a Term Certain			
Interest at 3.6 Percent			
Years	Annuity	Income Interest	Remainder
21	14.5605	0.524177	0.475823
22	15.0198	0.540712	0.459288

Factors from Table K			
Adjustment Factors for Annuities Payable at the End of Each Interval			
Interest Rate	Semi-Annually	Quarterly	Monthly
3.6%	1.0089	1.0134	1.0164

(ii) At the time of D's death, on or after [applicability date of the Treasury decision adopting these regulations as final regulations], D is a participant in an employees' pension plan described in section 401(a). On D's death, D's spouse S, a resident of the United States, becomes entitled to receive a survivor's annuity of $72,000 per year, payable monthly, for life. At the time of D's death, S is age 60. Assume that under section 7520, the appropriate discount rate to be used for valuing annuities in the case of this decedent is 3.6 percent. Under Table S, the annuity factor at 3.6 percent for a person age 60 is 14.6908. The adjustment factor at 3.6 percent in Table K for monthly payments is 1.0164. Accordingly, the right to receive $72,000 per year on a monthly basis is equal to the right to receive $73,180.80 ($72,000 x 1.0164) on an annual basis.

(iii) The corpus portion of each annuity payment received by S is determined as follows:

(A) The first step is to determine the present value of S's annuity payments under the plan ($73,180.80 × 14.6908 = $1,075,084.50).

(B) The second step is to determine the number of years that would be required for S's annuity to exhaust a hypothetical fund of $1,075,084.50. The annuity factor of 14.6908 falls between the Table B term certain annuity factors for 21 and 22 years at an interest rate of 3.6 percent. Accordingly, the expected annuity term is 22 years.

(C) The third step is to determine the corpus amount of the annual payment by dividing the expected term of 22 years into the present value of the hypothetical fund ($1,075,084.50 / 22 = $48,867.48).

(D) In the fourth step, the corpus portion of each annuity payment is determined by dividing the corpus amount of each annual payment by the annual annuity payment (adjusted for payments more frequently than annually as in paragraph (d)(4)(i) of this section) ($48,867.48 / 73,180.80 = 0.67).

(iv) Accordingly, 67 percent of each payment to S is deemed to be a distribution of corpus. A marital deduction is allowed for $1,075,084.50, the present value of the annuity as of D's date of death, if either: S agrees to roll over the corpus portion of each payment to a QDOT and the executor files the Information Statement described in paragraph (c)(5) of this section and the Roll Over Agreement described in paragraph (c)(7) of this section; or S agrees to pay the tax due on the corpus portion of each payment and the executor files the Information Statement described in paragraph (c)(5) of this section and the Payment Agreement described in paragraph (c)(6) of this section.

(5) *Example 5. Transfer to QDOT subject to gift tax.*—* * *

* * *

(e) *Applicability date.*—Paragraphs (c)(4)(ii)(B) and (d)(4) of this section are applicable with respect to decedents dying on or after [applicability date of the Treasury decision adopting these regulations as final regulations].

GIFT TAX

Annual Exclusion for Spousal IRA Transfers

Annual Exclusion: Contributions to Spousal Individual Retirement Accounts.—Reproduced below is the text of proposed Reg. § 25.2503-5, providing that contributions by a working spouse to an individual retirement account for the benefit of a nonworking spouse qualify for the annual gift tax exclusion to the extent that they are deductible for income tax purposes (published in the Federal Register on July 14, 1981).

☐ Par. 13. There is added after § 25.2503-4 the following new section:

§ 25.2503-5. Individual retirement plan for spouse.—(a) *In general.*—For purposes of section 2503(b), any payment made by an individual for the benefit of his or her spouse—

(1) To an individual retirement account described in section 408(a),

(2) To an individual retirement subaccount described in § 1.220-1(b)(3),

(3) For an individual retirement annuity described in section 408(b), or

(4) For a retirement bond described in section 409,

shall not be considered a gift of a future interest in property to the extent that such payment is allowable as a deduction under section 220 for the taxable year for which the contribution is made. Thus, for example, if individual A paid $900 to an individual retirement account for 1980 on behalf of A's spouse, B, of which $875 was deductible, $875 would not be a gift of a future interest.

(b) *Effective date.*—Paragraph (a) of this section is effective for transfers made after December 31, 1976.

Annuities: Interests: Valuation: Actuarial Tables

Annuities: Interests: Valuation: Actuarial Tables.—Amendments to Reg. §§ 25.2512-0 and 25.2512-5, relating to the use of actuarial tables in valuing annuities, interests for life or terms of years, and remainder or reversionary interests, are proposed (published in the Federal Register on May 5, 2022) (REG-122770-18).

☐ Par. 24. Section 25.2512-0 is revised to read as follows:

§ 25.2512-0. Table of contents.—This section lists the section headings that appear in the regulations under section 2512.

§ 25.2512-6 Valuation of certain life insurance and annuity contracts; valuation of shares in an open-end investment company.

§ 25.2512-7 Effect of excise tax.

§ 25.2512-8 Transfers for insufficient consideration.

Actuarial Tables Applicable Before [Applicability Date of the Treasury Decision Adopting These Regulations as Final Regulations]

§ 25.2512-5A Valuation of annuities, interests for life or a term of years, and remainder or reversionary interests transferred before [applicability date of the Treasury decision adopting these regulations as final regulations].

Par. 25. Section 25.2512-5 is amended by revising paragraphs (c), (d), and (e) to read as follows:

§ 25.2512-5. Valuation of annuities, interests for life or a term of years, and remainder or reversionary interests.

* * *

(c) *Actuarial valuations.*—The present value of annuities, interests for life or a term of years, and remainder or reversionary interests transferred by gift on or after [applicability date of the Treasury decision adopting these regulations as final regulations], is determined under paragraph (d) of this section. The present value of annuities, interests for life or a term of years, and remainder or reversionary interests transferred by gift before [applicability date of the Treasury decision adopting these regulations as final regulations], is determined under the following sections:

Table 1 to paragraph (c)

Transfers		*Applicable Regulations*
After	*Before*	
-	01-01-52	25.2512-5A(a)
12-31-51	01-01-71	25.2512-5A(b)
12-31-70	12-01-83	25.2512-5A(c)
11-30-83	05-01-89	25.2512-5A(d)
04-30-89	05-01-99	25.2512-5A(e)
04-30-99	05-01-09	25.2512-5A(f)
04-30-09	AD	25.2512-5A(g)

AD = [applicability date of the Treasury decision adopting these regulations as final regulations].

(d) *Actuarial valuations on or after [applicability date of the Treasury decision adopting these regulations as final regulations].*—(1) *In general.*—Except as otherwise provided in paragraph (b) of this section and § 25.7520-3(b) (relating to exceptions to the use of prescribed tables under certain circumstances), the fair market value of annuities, interests for life or a term of years, and remainder or reversionary interests transferred on or after [applicability date of the Treasury decision adopting these regulations as final regulations], is the present value of such interests determined under paragraph (d)(2) of this section and by using standard or special section 7520 actuarial factors. These factors are derived by using the actuarial formulas provided in § 20.2031-7(d)(2) of this chapter, appropriate section 7520 interest rate, and, if applicable, the mortality component for the valuation date of the interest that is being valued. For purposes of the computations described in this section, the age of an individual is the age of that individual at the individual's nearest birthday. For the convenience of taxpayers, paragraph (d)(2) of this section provides for published tables of factors for specific types of interests. These published tables provide factors for rates from 0.2 to 20 percent, inclusive, at intervals of two-tenths of one percent. In general, appropriate factors instead may be computed directly from the actuarial formulas provided in § 20.2031-7(d)(2) of this chapter. In some cases, specific examples in this part and IRS publications illustrate approximation methods (for example, interpolation) for obtaining factors when the required valuation rate falls between two listed rates (such as in the case of a pooled income fund's rate of return or a unitrust's adjusted payout rate). Exact methods of obtaining the applicable actuarial factors are allowed, such as through software using the actual rate of return and the actuarial formulas provided in § 20.2031-7(d)(2) of this chapter; the approximation method provided in this part must be used if more exact methods are not available. See §§ 25.7520-1 through 25.7520-4. The fair market value of a qualified annuity interest described in section 2702(b)(1) and a qualified unitrust interest described in section 2702(b)(2) is the present value of such interests determined under § 25.7520-1(c).

(2) *Specific interests.*—When the donor transfers property in trust or otherwise and retains an interest therein, generally, the value of the gift is the value of the property transferred less the value of the donor's retained interest. However, if the donor transfers property after October 8, 1990, to or for the benefit of a member of the donor's family, the value of the gift is the value of the property transferred less the value of the donor's retained interest as determined under section 2702. If the donor assigns or relin-

quishes an annuity, an interest for life or a term of years, a remainder or reversionary interest that the donor holds by virtue of a transfer previously made by the donor or another, the value of the gift is the value of the interest transferred. However, see section 2519 for a special rule in the case of the assignment of an income interest by a person who received the interest from a spouse.

(i) *Pooled income funds and charitable remainder trusts.*—The fair market value of a remainder interest in a pooled income fund, as defined in § 1.642(c)-5 of this chapter, is its value determined under § 1.642(c)-6(e) of this chapter (see § 1.642(c)-6A of this chapter for certain prior periods). The fair market value of a remainder interest in a charitable remainder annuity trust, as described in § 1.664-2(a) of this chapter, is its present value determined under § 1.664-2(c) of this chapter. The fair market value of a remainder interest in a charitable remainder unitrust, as defined in § 1.664-3 of this chapter, is its present value determined under § 1.664-4(e) of this chapter. The fair market value of a life interest or term for years interest in a charitable remainder unitrust is the fair market value of the property as of the date of transfer less the fair market value of the remainder interest, determined under § 1.664-4(e)(4) and (5) of this chapter.

(ii) *Ordinary remainder and reversionary interests.*—(A) *Remainder and reversionary interests for a term of years.*—If the interest to be valued is a remainder or reversionary interest to take effect after a definite number of years, the present value of the interest is computed by multiplying the value of the property by the appropriate remainder factor (that corresponds to the applicable section 7520 interest rate and the stated term). The factor for an ordinary remainder interest following a term certain may be found using the formula in § 20.2031-7(d)(2)(ii)(A) of this chapter. For the convenience of taxpayers, actuarial factors have been computed by IRS and appear in Table B. Table B can be found on the IRS website at *https://www.irs.gov/retirement-plans/actuarial-tables* (or a corresponding URL as may be updated from time to time). Table B is referenced and explained in IRS Publication 1457 "Actuarial Valuations Version 4A," which will be available after [date the Treasury decision adopting these regulations as final regulations is published in the **Federal Register**]. The remainder factors from Table B also can be found in paragraph (d)(6) of this section, but only for interest rates from 4.2 to 14 percent, inclusive. For information about obtaining special factors for other situations, see paragraph (d)(4) of this section.

(B) *Remainder and reversionary interests dependent on the life of one individual.*—If the interest to be valued is a remainder or reversionary interest to take effect after the death of one individual, the present value of the interest is computed by multiplying the value of the property by the appropriate remainder factor (that corresponds to the applicable section 7520 interest rate and the age of the measuring life of the life interest that precedes the remainder interest). The factor for an ordinary remainder interest following the death of one individual may be found by using the formula in § 20.2031-7(d)(2)(ii)(B) of this chapter to derive factors from the appropriate mortality table. For the convenience of taxpayers, actuarial factors have been computed by IRS and appear in Table S. Table S will be available beginning May 5, 2022, at no charge, electronically via the IRS website at *https://www.irs.gov/retirement-plans/actuarial-tables* (or a corresponding URL as may be updated from time to time). Table S is referenced and explained by IRS Publication 1457 "Actuarial Valuations Version 4A," which will be available after [date of publication of the final rule in the **Federal Register**]. For information about obtaining special factors for other situations, see paragraph (d)(4) of this section.

(iii) *Ordinary interests for a term of years and life interests.*—If the interest to be valued is the right of a person to receive the income of certain property, or to the use of certain property, for a term of years or for the life of one individual, the present value of the interest is computed by multiplying the value of the property by the appropriate actuarial factor for an interest for a term of years or for a life interest (that corresponds to the applicable section 7520 interest rate and the durational period). The actuarial factor for an ordinary income interest for a term certain may be found by subtracting from 1.000000 the factor for an ordinary remainder interest following the same term certain that is determined under the formula in § 20.2031-7(d)(2)(ii)(A) of this chapter. For the convenience of taxpayers, actuarial factors have been computed by IRS and appear in the "Income Interest" column of Table B which can be found on the IRS website at *https://www.irs.gov/retirement-plans/actuarial-tables* (or a corresponding URL as may be updated from time to time). The actuarial factor for an ordinary income interest for the life of one individual may be found by subtracting from 1.00000 the factor for an ordinary remainder interest following the life of the same individual that is determined in § 20.2031-7(d)(2)(ii)(B) of this chapter. For the convenience of taxpayers, actuarial factors have been computed by IRS and appear in the "Life Estate" column of Table S. Table S (applicable when the valuation date is on or after [applicability date of the Treasury decision adopting these regulations as final regulations]) can be found on the IRS website at *https://www.irs.gov/retirement-plans/actuarial-tables*. Table B and Table S are referenced and explained by IRS Publication 1457 "Actuarial Valuations Version 4A". See § 20.2031-7A of this chapter or earlier versions of Publication 1457 for valuation of interests before [applicability date of the Treasury decision adopting these regulations as final regulations]. For information about obtaining special factors for other situations, see paragraph (d)(4) of this section.

(iv) *Annuities.*—(A) If the interest to be valued is the right of a person to receive an annuity that is payable at the end of each year for a term of years or for the life of one individual, the present value of the interest is computed by multiplying the aggregate amount payable annually by the appropriate annuity factor (that corresponds to the applicable section 7520 interest rate and annuity period). The appropriate annuity factor for an annuity payable for a term of years is computed by subtracting from 1.000000 the factor for an ordinary remainder interest following the same term certain that is determined under the formula in § 20.2031-7(d)(2)(ii)(A) of this chapter and then dividing the result by the applicable section 7520 interest rate expressed as a number with at least four decimal places. For the convenience of taxpayers, actuarial factors have been computed by IRS and appear in the "Annuity" column of Table B which can be found on the IRS website at *https://www.irs.gov/retirement-plans/actuarial-tables* (or a corresponding URL as may be updated from time to time). The appropriate annuity factor for an annuity payable for the life of one individual is computed by subtracting from 1.00000 the factor for an ordinary remainder interest following the life of the same individual that is determined in § 20.2031-7(d)(2)(ii)(B) of this chapter and then dividing the result by the applicable section 7520 interest rate expressed as a number with four decimal places. For the convenience of taxpayers, actuarial factors have been computed by IRS and appear in the "Annuity" column of Table S. Table S (applicable when the valuation date is on or after [applicability date of the Treasury decision adopting these regulations as final regulations]) can be found on the IRS website at *https://www.irs.gov/retirement-plans/actuarial-tables*. Table B and Table S are referenced and explained in IRS Publication 1457 "Actuarial Valuations Version 4A". See § 20.2031-7A of this chapter or earlier versions of Publication 1457 for valuation of interests before [applicability date of the Treasury decision adopting these regulations as final regulations]. For information about obtaining special factors for other situations, see paragraph (d)(4) of this section.

(B) If the annuity is payable at the end of semiannual, quarterly, monthly, or weekly periods, the product obtained by multiplying the annuity factor by the aggregate amount payable annually then is multiplied by the applicable adjustment factor at the appropriate interest rate component for payments made at the end of the specified period. The applicable adjustment factor may be found using the formula in § 20.2031-7(d)(2)(iv)(B) of this chapter. For the convenience of taxpayers, actuarial factors have been computed by IRS and appear in Table K. Table K, which is referenced and explained by Publication 1457, can be found on the IRS website at *https://www.irs.gov/retirement-plans/actuarial-tables*. The provisions of this paragraph (d)(2)(iv)(B) are illustrated by the example in paragraph (d)(2)(iv)(B)(2) of this section.

(1) Sample factors from actuarial Table S and Table K. For purposes of the example in paragraph (d)(2)(iv)(B)(2) of this section, the relevant factors from Table S and Table K are:

Table 2 to paragraph (d)(2)(iv)(B)(1)

Factors from Table S - Based on Table 2010CM			
Interest at 3.2 Percent			
Age	Annuity	Life Estate	Remainder
68	12.2552	0.39217	0.60783

Factors from Table K			
Adjustment Factors for Annuities Payable at the End of Each Interval			
Interest Rate	Semi-Annually	Quarterly	Monthly
3.2%	1.0079	1.0119	1.0146

(2) Example. On July 1 of a year after 2021, the donor agrees to pay the annuitant the sum of $10,000 per year, payable in equal semiannual installments at the end of each period. The semiannual installments are to be made on each December 31st and June 30th. The annuity is payable until the annuitant's death. On the date of the agreement, the annuitant is 68 years and 5 months old. The donee annuitant's age is treated as 68 for purposes of computing the present value of the annuity. The section 7520 rate on the date of the agreement is 3.2 percent. Under Table S, the factor at 3.2 percent for determining the present value of an annuity payable until the death of a person aged 68 is 12.2552. The adjustment factor from Table K in the column for payments made at the end of each semiannual period at the rate of 3.2 percent is 1.0079. The aggregate annual amount of the annuity, $10,000, is multiplied by the factor 12.2552 and the product is multiplied by 1.0079. The present value of the donee's annuity is, therefore, $123,520.16 ($10,000 × 12.2552 × 1.0079).

(C) If an annuity is payable at the beginning of annual, semiannual, quarterly, monthly, or weekly periods for a term of years, the value of the annuity is computed by multiplying the aggregate amount payable annually by the annuity factor described in paragraph (d)(2)(iv)(A) of this section; and the product so obtained then is multiplied by the applicable adjustment factor at the appropriate interest rate component for payments made at the beginning of specified periods. The applicable adjustment factor may be found using the formula in

§ 20.2031-7(d)(2)(iv)(C) of this chapter. For the convenience of taxpayers, actuarial factors have been computed by IRS and appear in Table J. Table J, which is referenced and explained by Publication 1457, can be found on the IRS website at *https://www.irs.gov/retirement-plans/actuarial-tables*. If an annuity is payable at the beginning of annual, semiannual, quarterly, monthly, or weekly periods for one or more lives, the value of the annuity is the sum of the first payment and the present value of a similar annuity, the first payment of which is not to be made until the end of the payment period, determined as provided in paragraph (d)(2)(iv)(B) of this section.

(v) *Annuity and unitrust interests for a term of years or until the prior death of an individual.*—(A) *Annuity interests.*—*(1) In general.*—*(i)* The present value of an annuity interest that is payable until the earlier to occur of the lapse of a specific number of years or the death of an individual may be computed with the use of commutation factors and an applicable adjustment factor. The commutation factors are computed directly with the set of formulas in Figure 1 to this paragraph (d)(2)(v)(A)(*1*)(*i*). The prescribed mortality table is Table 2010CM as set forth in § 20.2031-7(d)(7)(ii) of this chapter, or for periods before [applicability date of the Treasury decision adopting these regulations as final regulations], the appropriate table found in § 20.2031-7A of this chapter. For the convenience of taxpayers, actuarial factors have been computed by IRS and appear in Table H. Table H will be available beginning May 5, 2022, at no charge, electronically via the IRS website at *https://www.irs.gov/retirement-plans/actuarial-tables* (or a corresponding URL as may be updated from time to time). Table H is referenced and explained by IRS Publication 1457 "Actuarial Valuations Version 4A," which will be available after May 5, 2022.

Figure 1 to paragraph (d)(2)(v)(A)(1)(i)–Formulas for determining commutation factors

$$D_x = v^x \cdot l_x$$

$$N_{x+1} = \sum_{t=1}^{\infty} D_{x+t}$$

$$M_x = \sum_{t=0}^{\infty} v^{x+t+1} \cdot d_{x+t}$$

$$\mathring{N}_x = N_{x+1} + \frac{1}{2} M_x$$

$$\overline{M}_x = \left(1 + \frac{i}{2}\right) \cdot M_x$$

where:

i = the applicable interest rate under Section 7520 of the Internal Revenue Code;

v = $1 / (1 + i)$;

d_x = $l_x - l_{x+1}$;

x = is the age of the measuring life (determined as age at nearest birthday); and

l_x = the number associated with age x as set forth in the prescribed mortality table, representing the number of persons alive at age x.

(ii) The applicable adjustment factor for annuities that are payable at the end of semiannual, quarterly, monthly, or weekly periods is computed by use of the formula in § 20.2031-7(d)(2)(iv)(B) of this chapter. For the convenience of taxpayers, actuarial factors have been computed by IRS and appear in Table K. Table K can be found on the IRS website at *https://www.irs.gov/retirement-plans/actuarial-tables*. For purposes of the example in paragraph

(d)(2)(v)(A)(2) of this section, the relevant factors from Table H(2.8) and Table K are:

Table 3 to paragraph (d)(2)(v)(A)(1)(ii)

Factors from Table H(2.8)			
Commutation Factors - Based on Table 2010CM			
Interest Rate of 2.8 Percent			
Age (x)	D_x	N_x-factor	Mx-factor
60	16,911.03	271,994.3	9,295.187
70	11,280.80	133,677.8	7,537.826

Factors from Table K			
Adjustment Factors for Annuities Payable at the End of Each Interval			
Interest Rate	Semi-Annually	Quarterly	Monthly
2.8%	1.0070	1.0104	1.0128

(2) *Example.* The donor transfers $100,000 into a trust on January 1, 2022 and retains the right to receive an annuity from the trust in the amount of $10,000 per year, payable in equal semiannual installments at the end of each period. The semiannual installments are to be made on each June 30th and December 31st. The annuity is payable for 10 years or until the donor's prior death. At the time of the transfer, the donor is 59 years and 6 months old. The donor's age is deemed to be 60 for purposes of computing the present value of the retained annuity. If the section 7520 rate for the month in which the transfer occurred is 2.8 percent, the present value of the donor's retained annuity interest for the shorter of life or term would be is $82,363.54, determined in Figure 2 to this paragraph (d)(2)(v)(A)(2).

Figure 2 to paragraph (d)(2)(v)(A)(2) – Illustration of calculation of present value of the donor's retained annuity interest for the shorter of life or term

A.	Initial age	60
B.	Plus: Term of years	10
C.	Sum (Terminal age)	70
D.	$\mathring{N}_x$ factor, Table H(2.8), age 60	271,994.30
E.	Less: $\mathring{N}_x$ factor, Table H(2.8), age 70	133,677.80
F.	Difference	138,316.50
G.	D_x factor, Table H(2.8), age 60	16,911.03
H.	Required Annuity Factor: F / G	8.1791
I.	Table K factor, semiannual payments at 2.8%	1.0070
J.	Annual Annuity Amount	$10,000
K.	Present value of retained interest: H x I x J	$82,363.54

(B) *Unitrust interests.—(1) In general.—(i)* The present value of a unitrust interest that is payable until the earlier to occur of the lapse of a specific number of years or the death of an individual may be computed with the use of an adjusted payout rate factor and a unitrust commutation factor. The adjusted payout rate factor is determined by applying the formula in §1.664-4(e)(6)(ii) of this chapter for the section 7520 interest rate applicable to the transfer. For the convenience of taxpayers, actuarial factors have been computed by IRS, for interest rates from 0.2 to 20 percent, inclusive, and appear in Tables F(0.2) through F(20.0). The unitrust commutation factors are computed directly with the set of formulas in Figure 3 to this paragraph (d)(2)(v)(B)(*1*)(*i*). For the convenience of taxpayers, actuarial factors have been computed by IRS and appear in Table Z. Table F and Table Z can be found on the IRS website at *https://www.irs.gov/retirement-plans/actuarial-tables.*

Figure 3 to paragraph (d)(2)(v)(B)(1)(i) – Formulas for determining unitrust commutation factors

$$^{u}D_x = {}^{u}v^x \cdot l_x$$

$$^{u}N_{x+1} = \sum_{t=1}^{\infty} {}^{u}D_{x+t}$$

$$^{u}M_x = \sum_{t=0}^{\infty} {}^{u}v^{x+t+1} \cdot d_{x+t}$$

$$^{u}\mathring{N}_x = {}^{u}N_{x+1} + \frac{1}{2}\,{}^{u}M_x$$

$$^{u}\overline{M}_x = (1 + \frac{^{u}i}{2}) \cdot {}^{u}M_x$$

where:

r = the adjusted payout rate;

^{u}v = 1 - r;

^{u}i = r / (1 – r);

d_x = $l_x - l_{x+1}$;

x = is the age of the measuring life (determined as age at nearest birthday); and

l_x = the number associated with age x as set forth in the prescribed mortality table, representing the number of persons alive at age x.

(*ii*) For purposes of the example in paragraph (d)(2)(v)(B)(*2*) of this section, the relevant factors from Table F(3.4), Table Z(4.8), and Table Z(5.0) are:

Table 4 to paragraph (d)(2)(v)(B)(1)(ii)

Factors from Table F(3.4)			
Factors for Computing Adjusted Payout Rates for Unitrusts			
Interest at 3.4 Percent			
# of Months from Annual Valuation to First Payout		Adjustment Factors for Payments at End of Period	
At Least	But Less Than	Annual	Semiannual
6	7	0.983422	0.975270

Factors from Table Z(4.8)			
Unitrust Commutation Factors - Based on Table 2010CM			
Adjusted Payout Rate of 4.8 Percent			
Age (x)	$^{U}D_x$	$^{U}N_x$-factor	$^{U}M_x$-factor
60	4,634.189	58,509.09	1,684.151
70	2,491.406	24,541.74	1,254.007

Factors from Table F(3.4)			
Factors for Computing Adjusted Payout Rates for Unitrusts			
Interest at 3.4 Percent			
# of Months from Annual Valuation to First Payout		Adjustment Factors for Payments at End of Period	
At Least	But Less Than	Annual	Semiannual

Factors from Table Z(5.0)			
Unitrust Commutation Factors - Based on Table 2010CM			
Adjusted Payout Rate of 5.0 Percent			
Age (x)	$^{U}D_x$	$^{U}N_x$-factor	$^{U}M_x$-factor
60	4,084.822	50,451.77	1,429.466
70	2,150.356	20,823.44	1,054.386

(2) *Example of interpolation*. The donor who, as of the nearest birthday, is 60 years old, transfers $100,000 to a unitrust on January 1st of a year after 2021. The trust instrument requires that each year the trust pay to the donor, in equal semiannual installments on June 30th and December 31st, 5 percent of the fair market value of the trust assets, valued as of January 1st of that year, for 10 years or until the prior death of the donor. The section 7520 rate for the January in which the transfer occurred is 3.4 percent. Under Table F(3.4), the appropriate adjustment factor is 0.975270 for semiannual payments payable at the end of the semiannual period. The adjusted payout rate is 4.876 percent (5% x 0.975270). The present value of the donor's retained interest is $37,419.00 determined in paragraphs (d)(2)(v)(B)(2)(*i*) through (iii) of this section. Using Table Z, the method required is to prepare two computations, one at a payout rate of 4.8 percent, and one at 5.0 percent, and interpolate between these two in order to get the result at the adjusted payout rate of 4.876 percent. As an alternative to using an interpolation method, it also is acceptable to compute the remainder factor directly from the root actuarial formulas using the actual adjusted payout rate of 4.876%.

(*i*) Determine the terminal age, as illustrated in Figure 4 to this paragraph (d)(2)(v)(B)(2)(*i*).

Figure 4 to paragraph (d)(2)(v)(B)(2)(i)–Illustration of determination of terminal age

A.	Initial age	60
B.	Plus: Term of years	10
C.	Sum (Terminal Age)	70

(*ii*) Determine the Payout Interest Factor at the Table Z payout rates immediately below and above the adjusted payout rate, as illustrated in Figure 5 to this paragraph (d)(2)(v)(B)(2)(*ii*).

Figure 5 to paragraph (d)(2)(v)(B)(2)(ii)–Illustration of determination of payout interest factors

D.	Payout Rate	4.80%	5.00%
E.	Equivalent Interest Rate Factor: D / (1 - D)	0.05042	0.05263
F.	$^{u}\mathring{N}_x$ factor, Table Z, age 60	58,509.09	50,451.77
G.	Less: $^{u}\mathring{N}_x$ factor, TableZ, age 70	24,541.74	20,823.44
H.	Difference	33,967.35	29,628.33
I.	$^{u}D_x$ factor, Table Z, age 60	4,634.189	4,084.822
J.	Intermediate Factor: H / I	7.32973	7.25327
K.	Payout Interest Factor: E x J	0.36956	0.38174

(*iii*) Interpolate between the Payout Interest Factors at 4.8% and 5.0% to determine the Payout Interest Factor at the adjusted rate of 4.876%, as illustrated in Figure 6 to this paragraph (d)(2)(v)(B)(2)(*iii*).

Figure 6 to paragraph (d)(2)(v)(B)(2)(iii)–Illustration of interpolation

L. Payout Interest Factor at 5.00%	0.38174
M. Less: Payout Interest Factor at 4.8%	0.36956
N. Difference: L - M	0.01218
O. Adjusted Payout Rate	4.876%

P. Interpolation Adjustment:

$$\frac{5.00\% - 4.876\%}{5.00\% - 4.80\%} = \frac{z}{0.01218}$$

$$\frac{5.00\% - 4.876\%}{5.00\% - 4.80\%} \cdot 0.01218 = z = 0.00755$$

Q. Payout Interest Factor at 5.00%	0.38174
R. Less: Interpolation Adjustment z	0.00755
S. Interpolated Payout Interest Factor: Q - R	0.37419
T. Amount Transferred	$100,000
U. Present Value of Retained Payout Interest: S x T	$37,419

(3) *Transitional rule.*—If the valuation date of a transfer of property by gift is on or after January 1, 2021, and before [applicability date of the Treasury decision adopting these regulations as final regulations], the fair market value of the interest transferred is determined by using the section 7520 interest rate for the month in which the valuation date occurs (see §§25.7520-1(b) and 25.7520-2(a)(2)) and the appropriate actuarial factors derived from the selected mortality table, either Table 2010CM in §20.2031-7(d)(7)(ii) of this chapter or Table 2000CM in §20.2031-7A(g)(4) of this chapter, at the option of the donor or the decedent's executor, as the case may be. For the convenience of taxpayers, actuarial factors based on Table 2010CM appear in the proposed version of Table S, and actuarial factors based on Table 2000CM appear in the current version of Table S, which will be available as provided in paragraph (d)(4) of this section. With respect to each individual transaction, the donor must consistently use the same mortality basis with respect to each interest (income, remainder, partial, etc.) in the same property, and with respect to all transfers occurring on the valuation date. For example, gift and income tax charitable deductions with respect to the same transfer must be determined based on factors with the same mortality basis, and all assets includible in the gross estate and/or estate tax deductions claimed must be valued based on factors with the same mortality basis.

(4) *Publications and actuarial computations by the Internal Revenue Service.*—The factor for determining the present value of a remainder interest that is dependent on the termination of the life of one individual may be computed by using the formula in §20.2031-7(d)(2)(ii)(B) of this chapter to derive factors from the appropriate mortality table. For the convenience of taxpayers, actuarial factors have been computed by IRS and appear in Table S. The factor for determining the present value of a remainder interest following a term certain may be computed by using the formula in §20.2031-7(d)(2)(ii)(A) of this chapter. For the convenience of taxpayers, actuarial factors have been computed by IRS and appear in Table B. Adjustment factors for term certain annuities payable at the beginning of each interval may be computed by using the formula in §20.2031-7(d)(2)(iv)(C) of this chapter. For the convenience of taxpayers, actuarial factors have been computed by IRS and appear in Table J. Adjustment factors for annuities payable at the end of each interval may be computed by using the formula in §20.2031-7(d)(2)(iv)(B) of this chapter. For the convenience of taxpayers, actuarial factors have been computed by IRS and appear in Table K. These tables will be available

beginning May 5, 2022, at no charge, electronically via the IRS website at *https://www.irs.gov/retirement-plans/actuarial-tables* (or a corresponding URL as may be updated from time to time). IRS Publication 1457, "Actuarial Valuations Version 4A" (2022), references and explains the factors contained in the actuarial tables and also includes examples that illustrate how to compute many special factors for more unusual situations. This publication will be available after [date of publication of the final rule in the **Federal Register**]. Table B, Table J, and Table K also can be found in § 20.2031-7(d)(6) of this chapter, but only for interest rates from 4.2 to 14 percent, inclusive. If a special factor is required, the special factor may be calculated by the taxpayer using the actuarial formula in § 20.2031-7(d)(2) of this chapter or the taxpayer may request a ruling to obtain the factor from the Internal Revenue Service. The request for a ruling must be accompanied by a recitation of the facts including a statement of the date of birth for each measuring life, the date of the gift, any other applicable dates, and a copy of the will, trust, or other relevant documents. A request for a ruling must comply with the instructions for requesting a ruling published periodically in the Internal Revenue Bulletin (see §§ 601.201 and 601.601(d)(2)(ii)(*b*) of this chapter and Rev. Proc. 2021-1, 2021-1 I.R.B. 1, and subsequent updates) and must include payment of the required user fee.

(e) *Applicability date.*—This section applies on and after [applicability date of the Treasury decision adopting these regulations as final regulations].

Imputed Interest: OID: Safe Haven Rates

Imputed Interest: Original Issue Discount: Safe Haven Interest Rates.—Amendments to Reg. § 25.2512-4 and 25.2512-8, relating to (1) the tax treatment of debt instruments issued after July 1, 1982, that contain original issue discount, (2) the imputation of and the accounting for interest with respect to sales and exchanges of property occurring after December 31, 1984, and (3) safe haven interest rates for loans or advances between commonly controlled taxpayers and safe haven leases between such taxpayers, are proposed (published in the Federal Register on August 20, 1985; Reg. § 25.2512-4 was reproposed in the Federal Register on April 8, 1986).

□ Par. 43. Section 25.2512-4 is revised to read as follows:

§ 25.2512-4. Valuation of notes.—The fair market value of notes, secured or unsecured, is presumed to be the amount of unpaid principal, plus accrued interest to the date of the gift, unless the donor establishes a lower value. The fair market value of a debt instrument (as defined in § 1.1275-1(b)) whose issue price is determined under section 1273(b)(1), (2), or (3), or section 1274 is presumed to be its revised issue price (as defined in § 1.1275-1(h)). Unless returned at this value, it must be shown by satisfactory evidence that the note is worth less than the unpaid amount (because of the interest rate, or date of maturity, or other cause), or that the note is uncollectible in part (by reason of the insolvency of the party or parties liable, or for other cause), and that the property, if any, pledged or mortgaged as security is insufficient to satisfy it. See § 25.2512-8 and § 1.1012-2 for special rules relating to certain sales or exchanges of property. See § 25.7872-1 for special rules in the case of gift loans (within the meaning of § 1.7872-4(b)) made after June 6, 1984. [Reg. § 25.2512-4.]

□ Par. 44. Section 25.2512-8 is revised to read as follows:

§ 25.2512-8. Transfers for insufficient or excessive consideration.—Transfers reached by the gift tax are not confined to those only which, being without a valuable consideration, accord with the common law concept of gifts, but embrace as well sales, exchanges, and other dispositions of property for a consideration to the extent that the value of the property transferred by the donor differs from the value in money or money's worth of the consideration given therefor. However, a sale, exchange, or other transfer of property made in the ordinary course of business (a transaction which is bona fide, at arm's length, and free from any donative intent), will be considered as made for consideration in money or money's worth equal to the value of the property transferred. If the buyer issues one or more debt instruments as all or a part of the consideration for the property, then the property and the debt instruments shall be valued in accordance with the rules set forth in § 1.1012-2. A consideration not reducible to a value in money or money's worth, as love and affection, promise of marriage, etc., is to be wholly disregarded, and the entire value of the property transferred contitutes the amount of the gift. Similarly, a relinquishment or promised relinquishment of dower or curtesy, or of a statutory estate created in lieu of dower or curtesy, or of other marital rights in the spouse's property or estate, shall not be considered to any extent a consideration "in money or money's worth." See, however, section 2516 and the regulations thereunder with respect to certain transfers incident to a divorce. [Reg. § 25.2512-8.]

Annuities: Interests: Valuation: Actuarial Tables

Annuities: Interests: Valuation: Actuarial Tables.—Amendments to Reg. § 25.2512-5A, relating to the use of actuarial tables in valuing annuities, interests for life or terms of years, and remainder or reversionary interests, are proposed (published in the Federal Register on May 5, 2022) (REG-122770-18).

☐ Par. 27. Section 25.2512-5A is amended by revising the section heading and adding paragraph (g) to read as follows:

§ 25.2512-5A. Valuation of annuities, interests for life or a term of years, and remainder or reversionary interests transferred before [applicability date of the Treasury decision adopting these regulations as final regulations].

* * *

(g) *Valuation of annuities, interests for life or a term of years, and remainder or reversionary interests transferred on or after May 1, 2009, and before [applicability date of the Treasury decision adopting these regulations as final regulations].*—(1) *In general.*—Except as otherwise provided in § § 25.2512-5(b) and 25.7520-3(b) (pertaining to certain limitations on the use of prescribed tables), if the valuation date of the transferred interest is on or after May 1, 2009, and before [applicability date of the Treasury decision adopting these regulations as final regulations], the fair market value of annuities, interests for life or a term of years, and remainder or reversionary interests transferred by gift is the present value of the interests determined by using standard or special section 7520 actuarial factors and the valuation methodology described in § 25.2512-5(d). Sections 20.2031-7(d)(6) and 20.2031-7A(g)(4) of this chapter and related sections provide tables with standard actuarial factors and examples that illustrate how to use the tables to compute the present value of ordinary annuity, life, term, and remainder interests in property. Sections 20.2031-7(d)(6) and 20.2031-7A(g)(4) also refer to standard and special actuarial factors that may be necessary to compute the present value of similar interests in more unusual fact situations. These factors and examples also generally are applicable for gift tax purposes in computing the values of taxable gifts.

(2) *Transitional rule.*—If the valuation date of a transfer of property by gift is on or after May 1, 2009, and before July 1, 2009, the fair market value of the interest transferred is determined by using the section 7520 interest rate for the month in which the valuation date occurs (see § § 25.7520-1(b) and 25.7520-2(a)(2)) and the appropriate actuarial tables under either § 20.2031-7A(f)(4) or (g)(4) of this chapter, at the option of the donor. However, with respect to each individual transaction and with respect to all transfers occurring on the valuation date, the donor must consistently use the same mortality basis with respect to each interest (income, remainder, partial, etc.) in the same property, and with respect to all transfers occurring on the valuation date. For example, gift and income tax charitable deductions with respect to the same transfer must be determined based on factors with the same mortality basis, and all assets includible in the gross estate and/or estate tax deductions claimed must be valued based on factors with the same mortality basis.

(3) *Publications and actuarial computations by the Internal Revenue Service.*—The factor for determining the present value of a remainder interest that is dependent on the termination of the life of one individual may be computed by using the formula in § 20.2031-7(d)(2)(ii)(B) of this chapter to derive factors from the appropriate mortality table. For the convenience of taxpayers, actuarial factors have been computed by IRS and appear in Table S. The factor for determining the present value of a remainder interest following a term certain may be computed by using the formula in § 20.2031-7(d)(2)(ii)(A) of this chapter. For the convenience of taxpayers, actuarial factors have been computed by IRS and appear in Table B. Adjustment factors for term certain annuities payable at the beginning of each interval may be computed by using the formula in § 20.2031-7(d)(2)(iv)(C) of this chapter. For the convenience of taxpayers, actuarial factors have been computed by IRS and appear in Table J. Adjustment factors for annuities payable at the end of each interval may be computed by using the formula in § 20.2031-7(d)(2)(iv)(B) of this chapter. For the convenience of taxpayers, actuarial factors have been computed by IRS and appear in Table K. These tables are referenced and explained by IRS Publication 1457, "Actuarial Values Version 3A," (2009). Publication 1457 includes examples that illustrate how to compute many special factors for more unusual situations. The actuarial tables are available, at no charge, electronically via the IRS website at *https://www.irs.gov/retirement-plans/actuarial-tables* (or a corresponding URL as may be updated from time to time). Table S also can be found in § 20.2031-7A(g)(4) of this chapter, but only for interest rates from 0.2 to 14 percent, inclusive. Table B, Table J, and Table K also can be found in § 20.2031-7(d)(6) of this chapter, but only for interest rates from 4.2 to 14 percent, inclusive. If a special factor is required in the case of a completed gift, the special factor may be calculated by the donor using the actuarial formulas in § 20.2031-7(d)(2) of this chapter or the donor may request a ruling to obtain the factor from the Internal Revenue Service. The request for a ruling must be accompanied by a recitation of the facts including a statement of the date of birth for each measuring life, the date of the gift, any other applicable dates, and a copy of the will, trust, or other relevant documents. A request for a ruling must comply with the instructions for requesting a ruling published periodically in the Internal Revenue Bulletin (see § § 601.201 and 601.601(d)(2)(ii)(*b*) of this chapter) and must include payment of the required user fee.

(4) *Applicability dates.*—Paragraphs (g)(1) through (3) of this section apply on and after May 1, 2009, and before [applicability date of the Treasury decision adopting these regulations as final regulations].

Annuities: Interests: Valuation: Actuarial Tables

Annuities: Interests: Valuation: Actuarial Tables.—Amendments to Reg. §25.2522(c)-3, relating to the use of actuarial tables in valuing annuities, interests for life or terms of years, and remainder or reversionary interests, are proposed (published in the Federal Register on May 5, 2022) (REG-122770-18).

☐ Par. 28. Section 25.2522(c)-3 is amended by:

1. Designating *Examples 1* through *3* of paragraph (d)(2)(iv) as paragraphs (d)(2)(iv)(A) through (C), respectively.

2. Revising the headings for newly designated paragraphs (d)(2)(iv)(A) and (B), newly designated paragraph (d)(2)(iv)(C), and paragraph (e).

3. Adding paragraph (f).

The revisions and addition read as follows:

§25.2522(c)-3. Transfers not exclusively for charitable, etc., purposes in the case of gifts made after July 31, 1969.

* * *

(d) * * *

(2) * * *

(iv) * * *

(A) *Example 1.*—* * *

(B) *Example 2.*—* * *

(C) *Example 3.*—(*1*) *Factors.* The appropriate annuity factor for an annuity payable for a term of years is computed by subtracting from 1.000000 the factor for an ordinary remainder interest following the same term certain that is determined under the formula in §20.2031-7(d)(2)(ii)(A) of this chapter and then dividing the result by the applicable section 7520 interest rate expressed as a number with at least four decimal places. For the convenience of taxpayers, actuarial factors have been computed by IRS and appear in the "Annuity" column of Table B. The actuarial commutation factors can be computed directly by using the formulas in §25.2512-5(d)(2)(v)(A)(*1*), the section 7520 rate, and Table 2010CM as set forth in §20.2031-7(d)(7)(ii) of this chapter. For the convenience of taxpayers, actuarial factors have been computed by IRS and appear in Table H. Table B and Table H can be found on the IRS website at *https://www.irs.gov/retirement-plans/actuarial-tables* (or a corresponding URL as may be updated from time to time). For purposes of the example in paragraph (d)(2)(iv)(C)(*2*) of this section, the relevant factors from Table B and Table H are:

Table 1 to paragraph (d)(2)(iv)(C)(1)

Factors from Table B			
Annuity, Income, and Remainder Interests for a Term Certain			
Interest at 2.8 Percent			
Years	Annuity	Income Interest	Remainder
10	8.6179	0.241302	0.758698

Factors from Table H(2.8)			
Commutation Factors - Based on Table 2010CM			
Interest Rate of 2.8 Percent			
Age (x)	D_x	N_x-factor	M_x-factor
60	16,911.03	271,994.3	9,295.187
70	11,280.80	133,677.8	7,537.826

(*2*) *Application.* In a year after 2021, D transfers $65,000 in trust with the requirement that a guaranteed annuity interest (as defined in paragraph (c)(2)(vi) of this section) of $5,000 a year, payable annually at the end of each year, be paid to Y Charity for a period of 10 years and that a guaranteed annuity interest (as defined in paragraph (c)(2)(vi) of this section) of $5,000 a year, payable annually at the end of each year, be paid to W, D's wife, aged 60, for 10 years or until her prior death. The annuities are to be paid simultaneously, and the remainder is to be paid to D's children. The section 7520 interest rate for the date of transfer is 2.8 percent, and the taxpayer elects not to use the interest rate from either of the two preceding months. The fair market value of the private annuity is $40,895.50 ($5,000 × 8.1791), as determined pursuant to §25.2512-5(d)(2)(v)(A) and by the use of factors derived from Table H and illustrated in paragraph (d)(2)(iv)(C)(*3*) of this section. The fair market value of the charitable annuity is $43,089.50 ($5,000 × 8.6179), determined using the annuity factor from Table B. It is not evident from the governing instrument of the trust or from local law that the trustee would be required to apportion the trust fund between the wife and charity in the event the fund were insufficient to pay both annuities in a given year. Accordingly, the deduction with respect to the charitable annuity will be limited to $24,104.50 ($65,000 less $40,895.50 [the value of the private annuity]), which is the minimum amount it is evident the charity will receive.

(3) In paragraph (d)(2)(iv)(C)(2) of this section, the actuarial factor for determining the value of the private annuity is derived by the use of factors involving one life and a term of years. The factor is determined as illustrated in Figure 1 to this paragraph (d)(2)(iv)(C)(3).

Figure 1 to paragraph (d)(2)(iv)(C)(3) – Illustration of calculation of annuity factor for shorter of term or life

A.	Initial age	60
B.	Plus: Term of years	10
C.	Sum (Terminal age)	70
D.	$\overset{\circ}{N}_x$ factor, Table H(2.8), age 60	271,994.30
E.	Less: $\overset{\circ}{N}_x$ factor, Table H(2.8), age 70	133,677.80
F.	Difference	138,316.50
G.	D_x factor, Table H(2.8), age 60	16,911.03
H.	Required Annuity Factor: F / G	8.1791

* * *

(e) *Guaranteed annuity and unitrust interests reformed as an interest for a term of years.*—(1) *In general.*—The rule in paragraphs (c)(2)(vi)(*a*) and (c)(2)(vii)(*a*) of this section that guaranteed annuity interests or unitrust interests, respectively, may be payable for a specified term of years or for the life or lives of only certain individuals applies to transfers made on or after April 4, 2000. If a transfer is made on or after April 4, 2000, that uses an individual other than one permitted in paragraphs (c)(2)(vi)(*a*) and (c)(2)(vii)(*a*) of this section, the interest may be reformed into a lead interest payable for a specified term of years. The term of years is determined by taking the factor for valuing the annuity or unitrust interest for the named individual measuring life and identifying the term of years (rounded up to the next whole year) that corresponds to the equivalent term of years factor for an annuity or unitrust interest. See paragraph (e)(4) of this section for an example.

(2) *Judicial and non-judicial reformations.*—A judicial reformation must be commenced prior to October 15th of the year following the year in which the transfer is made and must be completed within a reasonable time after it is commenced. A non-judicial reformation is permitted if effective under state law, provided it is completed by the date on which a judicial reformation must be commenced. In the alternative, if a court, in a proceeding that is commenced on or before July 5, 2001, declares any transfer, made on or after April 4, 2000, and on or before March 6, 2001, null and void ab initio, the Internal Revenue Service will treat such transfers in a manner similar to that described in section 2055(e)(3)(J).

(3) *Sample factors from actuarial Table B and Table S.*—The appropriate annuity factor for an annuity payable for a term of years is computed by subtracting from 1.000000 the factor for an ordinary remainder interest following the same term certain that is determined under the formula in § 20.2031-7(d)(2)(ii)(A) of this chapter and then dividing the result by the applicable section 7520 interest rate expressed as a number with at least four decimal places. For the convenience of taxpayers, actuarial factors have been computed by IRS and appear in the "Annuity" column of Table B. The appropriate annuity factor for an annuity payable for the life of one individual is computed by subtracting from 1.00000 the factor for an ordinary remainder interest following the life of the same individual that is determined under the formula in § 20.2031-7(d)(2)(ii)(B) of this chapter and then dividing the result by the applicable section 7520 interest rate expressed as a number with four decimal places. For the convenience of taxpayers, actuarial factors have been computed by IRS and appear in the "Annuity" column of Table S. Table B and Table S can be found on the IRS website at *https://www.irs.gov/retirement-plans/actuarial-tables*. For purposes of the example in paragraph (e)(4) of this section, the relevant factors from Table B and Table S are:

Table 2 to paragraph (e)(3)

Factors from Table B			
Annuity, Income, and Remainder Interests for a Term Certain			
Interest at 2.4 Percent			
Years	Annuity	Income Interest	Remainder
38	24.7471	0.593929	0.406071
39	25.1436	0.603447	0.396553

Factors from Table S - Based on Table 2010CM			
Interest at 2.4 Percent			
Age	Annuity	Life Estate	Remainder
40	24.9063	0.59775	0.40225

(4) *Example*.—An annuity interest payable for the life of an individual age 40 at the time of the transfer that occurs on or after [applicability date of the Treasury decision adopting these regulations as final regulations] assuming an interest rate of 2.4 percent under section 7520, has an annuity factor reported in Table S of 24.9063. Based on Table B at 2.4 percent, the factor 24.9063 corresponds to a term of years between 38 and 39 years. Accordingly, the annuity interest must be reformed into an interest payable for a term of 39 years. (To determine the value of a charitable remainder interest payable after this annuity interest, the taxpayer then must satisfy the test illustrated in § 25.7520-3(b)(2)(v)(E).)

(f) *Applicability date*.—This section applies only to gifts made after July 31, 1969.

TAX ON GENERATION-SKIPPING TRANSFERS

GST Exemption: Extension of Time

GST Exemption: Extension of Time.—Reg. § 26.2642-7, describing the circumstances and procedures under which an extension of time will be granted under Code Sec. 2642(g)(1), is proposed (published in the Federal Register on April 17, 2008) (REG-147775-06).

☐ Par. 2. Section 26.2642-7 is added to read as follows:

§ 26.2642-7. Relief under section 2642(g)(1).—(a) *In general*.—Under section 2642(g)(1)(A), the Secretary has the authority to issue regulations describing the circumstances in which a transferor, as defined in section 2652(a), or the executor of a transferor's estate, as defined in section 2203, will be granted an extension of time to allocate generation-skipping transfer (GST) exemption as described in sections 2642(b)(1) and (2). The Secretary also has the authority to issue regulations describing the circumstances under which a transferor or the executor of a transferor's estate will be granted an extension of time to make the elections described in section 2632(b)(3) and (c)(5). Section 2632(b)(3) provides that an election may be made by or on behalf of a transferor not to have the transferor's GST exemption automatically allocated under section 2632(b)(1) to a direct skip, as defined in section 2612(c), made by the transferor during life. Section 2632(c)(5)(A)(i) provides that an election may be made by or on behalf of a transferor not to have the transferor's GST exemption automatically allocated under section 2632(c)(1) to an indirect skip, as defined in section 2632(c)(3)(A), or to any or all transfers made by such transferor to a particular trust. Section 2632(c)(5)(A)(ii) provides that an election may be made by or on behalf of a transferor to treat any trust as a GST trust, as defined in section 2632(c)(3)(B), for purposes of section 2632(c) with respect to any or all transfers made by that transferor to the trust. This section generally describes the factors that the Internal Revenue Service (IRS) will consider when an extension of time is sought by or on behalf of a transferor to timely allocate GST exemption and/or to make an election under section 2632(b)(3) or (c)(5). Relief provided under this section will be granted through the IRS letter ruling program. See paragraph (h) of this section.

(b) *Effect of Relief*.—If an extension of time to allocate GST exemption is granted under this section, the allocation of GST exemption will be considered effective as of the date of the transfer, and the value of the property transferred for purposes of chapter 11 or chapter 12 will determine the amount of GST exemption to be allocated. If an extension of time to elect out of the automatic allocation of GST exemption under section 2632(b)(3) or (c)(5) is granted under this section, the election will be considered effective as of the date of the transfer. If an extension of time to elect to treat any trust as a GST trust under section 2632(c)(5)(A)(ii) is granted under this section, the election will be considered effective as of the date of the first (or each) transfer covered by that election.

(c) *Limitation on relief*.—The amount of GST exemption that may be allocated to a transfer as the result of relief granted under this section is limited to the amount of the transferor's unused GST exemption under section 2631(c) as of the date of the transfer. Thus, if, by the time of the making of the allocation or election pursuant to relief granted under this section, the GST exemption amount under section 2631(c) has increased to an amount in excess of the amount in effect for the date of the transfer, no portion of the increased amount may be applied to that earlier transfer by reason of the relief granted under this section.

(d) *Basis for determination.*—(1) *In general.*—Requests for relief under this section will be granted when the transferor or the executor of the transferor's estate provides evidence (including the affidavits described in paragraph (h) of this section) to establish to the satisfaction of the IRS that the transferor or the executor of the transferor's estate acted reasonably and in good faith, and that the grant of relief will not prejudice the interests of the Government. Paragraphs (d)(2) and (d)(3) of this section set forth nonexclusive lists of factors the IRS will consider in determining whether this standard of reasonableness, good faith, and lack of prejudice to the interests of the Government has been met so that such relief will be granted. In making this determination, IRS will consider these factors, as well as all other relevant facts and circumstances. Paragraph (e) of this section sets forth situations in which this standard has not been met and, as a result, in which relief under this section will not be granted.

(2) *Reasonableness and good faith.*—The following is a nonexclusive list of factors that will be considered to determine whether the transferor or the executor of the transferor's estate acted reasonably and in good faith for purposes of this section:

(i) The intent of the transferor to timely allocate GST exemption to a transfer or to timely make an election under section 2632(b)(3) or (c)(5), as evidenced in the trust instrument, the instrument of transfer, or other relevant documents contemporaneous with the transfer, such as Federal gift and estate tax returns and correspondence. This may include evidence of the intended GST tax status of the transfer or the trust (for example, exempt, non-exempt, or partially exempt), or more explicit evidence of intent with regard to the allocation of GST exemption or the election under section 2632(b)(3) or (c)(5).

(ii) Intervening events beyond the control of the transferor or of the executor of the transferor's estate as the cause of the failure to allocate GST exemption to a transfer or the failure to make an election under section 2632(b)(3) or (c)(5).

(iii) Lack of awareness by the transferor or the executor of the transferor's estate of the need to allocate GST exemption to the transfer, despite the exercise of reasonable diligence, taking into account the experience of the transferor or the executor of the transferor's estate and the complexity of the GST issue, as the cause of the failure to allocate GST exemption to a transfer or to make an election under section 2632(b)(3) or (c)(5).

(iv) Consistency by the transferor with regard to the allocation of the transferor's GST exemption (for example, the transferor's consistent allocation of GST exemption to transfers to skip persons or to a particular trust, or the transferor's consistent election not to have the automatic allocation of GST exemption apply to transfers to one or more trusts or skip persons pursuant to section 2632(b)(3) or (c)(5)). Evidence of consistency may be less relevant if there has been a change of circumstances or change of trust beneficiaries that would otherwise explain a deviation from prior GST exemption allocation decisions.

(v) Reasonable reliance by the transferor or the executor of the transferor's estate on the advice of a qualified tax professional retained or employed by one or both of them and, in reliance on or consistent with that advice, the failure of the transferor or the executor to allocate GST exemption to the transfer or to make an election described in section 2632(b)(3) or (c)(5). Reliance on a qualified tax professional will not be considered to have been reasonable if the transferor or the executor of the transferor's estate knew or should have known that the professional either—

(A) Was not competent to render advice on the GST exemption; or

(B) Was not aware of all relevant facts.

(3) *Prejudice to the interests of the Government.*—The following is a nonexclusive list of factors that will be considered to determine whether the interests of the Government would be prejudiced for purposes of this section:

(i) The interests of the Government would be prejudiced to the extent to which the request for relief is an effort to benefit from hindsight. The interests of the Government would be prejudiced if the IRS determines that the requested relief is an attempt to benefit from hindsight rather than to achieve the result the transferor or the executor of the transferor's estate intended at the time when the transfer was made. A factor relevant to this determination is whether the grant of the requested relief would permit an economic advantage or other benefit that would not have been available if the allocation or election had been timely made. Similarly, there would be prejudice if a grant of the requested relief would permit an economic advantage or other benefit that results from the selection of one out of a number of alternatives (other than whether or not to make an allocation or election) that were available at the time the allocation or election could have been timely made, if hindsight makes the selected alternative more beneficial than the other alternatives. Finally, in a situation where the only choices were whether or not to make a timely allocation or election, prejudice would exist if the transferor failed to make the allocation or election in order to wait to see (thus, with the benefit of hindsight) whether or not the making of the allocation of exemption or election would be more beneficial.

(ii) The timing of the request for relief will be considered in determining whether the interests of the Government would be prejudiced by granting relief under this section. The interests of the Government would be prejudiced if the transferor or the executor of the transferor's estate delayed the filing of the request for relief with the intent to deprive the IRS of sufficient time to challenge the claimed identity of the transferor of the transferred property that is the subject of the request for relief, the value of that transferred property for Federal gift or estate tax purposes, or any other aspect of the transfer that is relevant for Federal gift or estate tax purposes. The fact that any period of limitations on the assessment or collection of transfer taxes has expired prior to the filing of a request for relief under this section, however, will not by itself prohibit a grant of relief under this section. Similarly, the combination of the expiration of any such period of limitations with the fact that the asset or interest was valued for transfer tax purposes with the use of a valuation discount will not by itself prohibit a grant of relief under this section.

(iii) The occurrence and effect of an intervening taxable termination or taxable distribution will be considered in determining whether the interests of the Government would be prejudiced by granting relief under this section. The interests of the Government may be prejudiced if a taxable termination or taxable distribution occurred between the time for making a timely allocation of GST exemption or a timely election described in section 2632(b)(3) or (c)(5) and the time at which the request for relief under this section was filed. The impact of a grant of relief on (and the difficulty of adjusting) the GST tax consequences of that intervening termination or distribution will be considered in determining whether the occurrence of a taxable termination or taxable distribution constitutes prejudice.

(e) *Situations in which the standard of reasonableness, good faith, and lack of prejudice to the interests of the Government has not been met.*—Relief under this section will not be granted if the IRS determines that the transferor or the executor of the transferor's estate has not acted reasonably and in good faith, and/or that the grant of relief would prejudice the interests of the Government. The following situations provide illustrations of some circumstances under which the standard of reasonableness, good faith, and lack of prejudice to the interests of the Government has not been met, and as a result, in which relief under this section will not be granted:

(1) *Timely allocations and elections.*—Relief will not be granted under this section to decrease or revoke a timely allocation of GST exemption as described in §26.2632-1(b)(4)(ii)(A)(*1*), or to revoke an election under section 2632(b)(3) or (c)(5) made on a timely filed Federal gift or estate tax return.

(2) *Timing.*—Relief will not be granted if the transferor or executor delayed the filing of the request for relief with the intent to deprive the IRS of sufficient time to challenge the claimed identity of the transferor or the valuation of the transferred property for Federal gift or estate tax purposes. (However, see paragraph (d)(3)(ii) of this section for examples of facts which alone do not constitute prejudice.)

(3) *Failure after being accurately informed.*—Relief will not be granted under this section if the decision made by the transferor or the executor of the transferor's estate (who had been accurately informed in all material respects by a qualified tax professional retained or employed by either (or both) of them with regard to the allocation of GST exemption or an election described in section 2632(b)(3) or (c)(5)) was reflected or implemented by the action or inaction that is the subject of the request for relief.

(4) *Hindsight.*—Relief under this section will not be granted if the IRS determines that the requested relief is an attempt to benefit from hindsight rather than an attempt to achieve the result the transferor or the executor of the transferor's estate intended when the transfer was made. One factor that will be relevant to this determination is whether the grant of relief will give the transferor the benefit of hindsight by providing an economic advantage that may not have been available if the allocation or election had been timely made. Thus, relief will not be granted if that relief will shift GST exemption from one trust to another trust unless the beneficiaries of the two trusts, and their respective interests in those trusts, are the same. Similarly, relief will not be granted if there is evidence that the transferor or executor had not made a timely allocation of the exemption in order to determine which of the various trusts achieved the greatest asset appreciation before selecting the trust that should have a zero inclusion ratio.

(f) *Period of limitations under section 6501.*—A request for relief under this section does not reopen, suspend, or extend the period of limitations on assessment or collection of any estate, gift, or GST tax under section 6501. Thus, the IRS may request that the transferor or the transferor's executor consent, under section 6501(c)(4), to an extension of the period of limitation on assessment or collection of any or all gift and GST taxes for the transfer(s) that are the subject of the requested relief. The transferor or the transferor's executor has the right to refuse to extend the period of limitations, or to limit such extension to particular issues or to a particular period of time. See section 6501(c)(4)(B).

(g) *Refunds.*—The filing of a request for relief under section 2642(g)(1) with the IRS does not constitute a claim for refund or credit of an overpayment and no implied right to refund will arise from the filing of such a request for relief. Similarly, the filing of such a request for relief does not extend the period of limitations under section 6511 for filing a claim for refund or credit of an overpayment. In the event the grant of relief under section 2642(g)(1) results in a potential claim for refund or credit of an overpayment, no such refund or credit will be allowed to the taxpayer or to the taxpayer's estate if the period of limitations under section 6511 for filing a claim for a refund or credit of the Federal gift, estate, or GST tax that was reduced by the granted relief has expired. The period of limitations under section 6511 is generally the later of three years from the time the original return is filed or two years from the time the tax was paid. If the IRS and the taxpayer agree to extend the period for assessment of tax, the period for filing a claim for refund or credit will be extended. Section 6511(c). The taxpayer or the taxpayer's estate is responsible for preserving any potential claim for refund or credit. A taxpayer who seeks and is granted relief under section 2642(g)(1) will not be regarded as having filed a claim for refund or credit by requesting such relief. In order to preserve a right of refund or credit, the taxpayer or the executor of the taxpayer's estate also must file before the expiration of the period of limitations under section 6511 for filing such a claim any required forms for requesting a refund or credit in accordance with the instructions to such forms and applicable regulations.

(h) *Procedural requirements.*—(1) *Letter ruling program.*—The relief described in this section is provided through the IRS's private letter ruling program. See Revenue Procedure 2008-1 (2008-1 IRB 1), or its successor, (which are available at *www.irs.gov*). Requests for relief under this section that do not meet the requirements of § 301.9100-2 of this chapter must be made under the rules of this section.

(2) *Affidavit and declaration of transferor or the executor of the transferor's estate.*—(i) The transferor or the executor of the transferor's estate must submit a detailed affidavit describing the events that led to the failure to timely allocate GST exemption to a transfer or the failure to timely elect under section 2632(b)(3) or (c)(5), and the events that led to the discovery of the failure. If the transferor or the executor of the transferor's estate relied on a tax professional for advice with respect to the allocation or election, the affidavit must describe—

(A) The scope of the engagement;

(B) The responsibilities the transferor or the executor of the transferor's estate believed the professional had assumed, if any; and

(C) The extent to which the transferor or the executor of the transferor's estate relied on the professional.

(ii) Attached to each affidavit must be copies of any writing (including, without limitation, notes and e-mails) and other contemporaneous documents within the possession of the affiant relevant to the transferor's intent with regard to the application of GST tax to the transaction for which relief under this section is being requested.

(iii) The affidavit must be accompanied by a dated declaration, signed by the transferor or the executor of the transferor's estate that states: "Under penalties of perjury, I declare that I have examined this affidavit, including any attachments thereto, and to the best of my knowledge and belief, this affidavit, including any attachments thereto, is true, correct, and complete. In addition, under penalties of perjury, I declare that I have examined all the documents included as part of this request for relief, and, to the best of my knowledge and belief, these documents collectively contain all the relevant facts relating to the request for relief, and such facts are true, correct, and complete."

(3) *Affidavits and declarations from other parties.*—(i) The transferor or the executor of the transferor's estate must submit detailed affidavits from individuals who have knowledge or information about the events that led to the failure to allocate GST exemption or to elect under section 2632(b)(3) or (c)(5), and/or to the discovery of the failure. These individuals may include individuals whose knowledge or information is not within the personal knowledge of the transferor or the executor of the transferor's estate. The individuals described in paragraph (h)(3)(i) of this section must include—

(A) Each agent or legal representative of the transferor who participated in the transaction and/or the preparation of the return for which relief is being requested;

(B) The preparer of the relevant Federal estate and/or gift tax return(s);

(C) Each individual (including an employee of the transferor or the executor of the transferor's estate) who made a substantial contribution to the preparation of the relevant Federal estate and/or gift tax return(s); and

(D) Each tax professional who advised or was consulted by the transferor or the executor of the transferor's estate with regard to any aspect of the transfer, the trust, the allocation of GST exemption, and/or the election under section 2632(b)(3) or (c)(5).

(ii) Each affidavit must describe the scope of the engagement and the responsibilities of the individual as well as the advice or service(s) the individual provided to the transferor or the executor of the transferor's estate.

(iii) Attached to each affidavit must be copies of any writing (including, without limitation, notes and e-mails) and other contemporaneous documents within the possession of the affiant relevant to the transferor's intent with regard to the application of GST tax to the transaction for which relief under this section is being requested.

(iv) Each affidavit also must include the name, and current address of the individual, and be accompanied by a dated declaration, signed by the individual that states: "Under penalties of perjury, I declare that I have personal knowledge of the information set forth in this affidavit, including any attachments thereto. In addition, under penalties of perjury, I declare that I have examined this affidavit, including any attachments thereto, and, to the best of my knowledge and belief, the affidavit contains all the relevant facts of which I am aware relating to the request for relief filed by or on behalf of [transferor or the executor of the transferor's estate], and such facts are true, correct, and complete."

(v) If an individual who would be required to provide an affidavit under paragraph (h)(3)(i) of this section has died or is not competent, the affidavit required under paragraph (h)(2) of this section must include a statement to that effect, as well as a statement describing the relationship between that individual and the transferor or the executor of the transferor's estate and the information or knowledge the transferor or the executor of the transferor's estate believes that individual had about the transfer, the trust, the allocation of exemption, or the election. If an individual who would be required to provide an affidavit under paragraph (h)(3)(i) of this section refuses to provide the transferor or the executor of the transferor's estate with such an affidavit, the affidavit required under paragraph (h)(2) of this section must include a statement that the individual has refused to provide the affidavit, a description of the efforts made to obtain the affidavit from the individual, the information or knowledge the transferor or the executor of the transferor's estate believes the individual had about the transfer, and the relationship between the individual and the transferor or the executor of the transferor's estate.

(i) *Effective/applicability date.*—Section 26.2642-7 applies to requests for relief filed on or after the date of publication of the Treasury decision adopting these proposed rules as final regulations in the **Federal Register**. [Reg. § 26.2642-7.]

GIFTS AND BEQUESTS FROM EXPATRIATES

Gifts and Bequests from Covered Expatriates: Imposition of Tax

Gifts and Bequests from Covered Expatriates: Imposition of Tax.—Reg. §§ 28.2801-0—28.2801-7, relating to a tax on United States citizens and residents who receive gifts or bequests from certain individuals who relinquished United States citizenship or ceased to be lawful permanent residents of the United States on or after June 17, 2008, are proposed (published in the Federal Register on September 10, 2015) (REG-112997-10).

☐ Sections 28.2801-0 to 28.2801-7 are added to read as follows:

§ 28.2801-0. Table of contents.—This section lists the captions in §§ 28.2801-1 through 28.2801-7.

[Reg. §28.2801-0.]

§28.2801-1. Tax on certain gifts and bequests from covered expatriates.—(a) *In general.*—Section 2801 of the Internal Revenue Code (Code) imposes a tax (section 2801 tax) on covered gifts and covered bequests, including distributions from foreign trusts attributable to covered gifts or covered bequests, received by a United States citizen or resident (U.S. citizen or resident) from a covered expatriate during a calendar year. Domestic trusts, as well as foreign trusts electing to be treated as domestic trusts for purposes of section 2801, are subject to tax under section 2801 in the same manner as if the trusts were U.S. citizens. See section 2801(e)(4)(A)(i) and (e)(4)(B)(iii). Accordingly, the section 2801 tax is paid by the U.S. citizen or resident, domestic trust, or foreign trust electing to be treated as a domestic trust for purposes of section 2801 that receives the covered gift or covered bequest. For purposes of this part 28, references to a U.S. citizen or U.S. citizens are considered to include a domestic trust and a foreign trust electing to be treated as a domestic trust for purposes of section 2801.

(b) *Effective/applicability date.*—This section applies on and after the date of publication of a Treasury decision adopting these rules as final regulations in the **Federal Register**. Once these regulations have been published as final regulations in the **Federal Register**, taxpayers may rely upon the final rules of this part for the period beginning June 17, 2008, and ending on the date preceding the date these regulations are published as final regulations in the **Federal Register**. [Reg. §28.2801-1.]

§28.2801-2. Definitions.—(a) *Overview.*—This section provides definitions of terms applicable solely for purposes of section 2801 and the corresponding regulations.

(b) *Citizen or resident of the United States.*—A citizen or resident of the United States (U.S. citizen or resident) is an individual who is a citizen or resident of the United States under the rules applicable for purposes of chapter 11 or 12 of the Code, as the case may be, at the time of receipt of the covered gift or covered bequest. Furthermore, for purposes of this part 28, references to U.S. citizens also include domestic trusts, as well as foreign trusts electing to be treated as a domestic trust under § 28.2801-5(d). See § 28.2801-1(a)(1).

(c) *Domestic trust.*—The term *domestic trust* means a trust defined in section 7701(a)(30)(E). For purposes of this part 28, references to a domestic trust include a foreign trust that elects under § 28.2801-5(d) to be treated as a domestic trust solely for purposes of section 2801.

(d) *Foreign trust.*—(1) *In general.*—The term *foreign trust* means a trust defined in section 7701(a)(31).

(2) *Electing foreign trust.*—The term *electing foreign trust* is a foreign trust that has in effect a valid election to be treated as a domestic trust solely for purposes of section 2801. See § 28.2801-5(d).

(e) *U.S. recipient.*—The term *U.S. recipient* means a citizen or resident of the United States, a domestic trust, and an electing foreign trust that receives a covered gift or covered bequest, whether directly or indirectly, during the calendar year. The term U.S. recipient includes U.S. citizens or residents receiving a distribution from a foreign trust not electing to be treated as a domestic trust for purposes of section 2801 if the distributions are attributable (in whole or in part) to one or more covered gifts or covered bequests received by the foreign trust. This term also includes the U.S. citizen or resident shareholders, partners, members, or other interest-holders, as the case may be (if any), of a domestic entity that receives a covered gift or covered bequest.

(f) *Covered bequest.*—The term *covered bequest* means any property acquired directly or indirectly by reason of the death of a covered expatriate, regardless of its situs and of whether such property was acquired by the covered expatriate before or after expatriation from the United States. The term also includes distributions made by reason of the death of a covered expatriate from a foreign trust that has not elected under § 28.2801-5(d) to be treated as a domestic trust for purposes of section 2801 to the extent the distributions are attributable to covered gifts or covered bequests made to the foreign trust. See § 28.2801-3 for additional rules and exceptions applicable to the term *covered bequest*.

(g) *Covered gift.*—The term *covered gift* means any property acquired by gift directly or indirectly from an individual who is a covered expatriate at the time the property is received by a U.S. citizen or resident, regardless of its situs and of whether such property was acquired by the covered expatriate before or after expatriation from the United States. The term also includes distributions made, other than by reason of the death of a covered expatriate, from a foreign trust that has not elected under § 28.2801-5(d) to be treated as a domestic trust for purposes of section 2801 to the extent the distributions are attributable to covered gifts or covered bequests made to the foreign trust. See § 28.2801-3 for additional rules and exceptions applicable to the term *covered gift*.

(h) *Expatriate and covered expatriate.*—The term *expatriate* has the same meaning for purposes of section 2801 as that term has in section 877A(g)(2). The term *covered expatriate* has the same meaning for purposes of section 2801 as that term has in section 877A(g)(1). The determination of whether an individual is a covered expatriate is made as of the expatriation date as defined in section 877A(g)(3), and if an expatriate meets the definition of a covered expatriate, the expatriate is considered a covered expatriate for purposes of section 2801 at all times after the expatriation date. However, an expatriate (as defined in section 877A(g)(2)) is not treated as a covered expatriate for purposes of section 2801 during any period beginning after the expatriation date during which such individual is subject to United States estate or gift tax (chapter 11 or chapter 12 of subtitle B) as a U.S. citizen or resident. See section 877A(g)(1)(C). An individual's status as a covered expatriate will be determined as of the date of the most recent expatriation, if there has been more than one.

(i) *Indirect acquisition of property.*—An indirect acquisition of property, as referred to in the definitions of a covered gift and covered bequest, includes—

(1) Property acquired as a result of a transfer that is a covered gift or covered bequest to a corporation or other entity other than a trust or estate, to the extent of the respective ownership interest of the recipient U.S. citizen or resident in the corporation or other entity;

(2) Property acquired by or on behalf of a U.S. citizen or resident, either from a covered expatriate or from a foreign trust that received a covered gift or covered bequest, through one or more other foreign trusts, other entities, or a person not subject to the section 2801 tax;

(3) Property paid by a covered expatriate, or distributed from a foreign trust that received a covered gift or covered bequest, in satisfaction of a debt or liability of a U.S. citizen or resident, regardless of the payee of that payment or distribution;

(4) Property acquired by or on behalf of a U.S. citizen or resident pursuant to a non-covered expatriate's power of appointment granted by a covered expatriate over property not in trust, unless the property previously was subjected to section 2801 tax upon the grant of the power or the covered expatriate had no more than a non-general power of appointment over that property; and

(5) Property acquired by or on behalf of a U.S. citizen or resident in other transfers not made directly by the covered expatriate to the U.S. citizen or resident.

(j) *Power of appointment.*—The term *power of appointment* refers to both a general and non-general power of appointment. A general power of appointment is as defined in sections 2041(b) and 2514(c) of the Code and a non-general power of appointment is any power of appointment that is not a general power of appointment.

(k) *Effective/applicability date.*—This section applies on and after the date of publication of a Treasury decision adopting these rules as final regulations in the **Federal Register**. Once these regulations have been published as final regulations in the **Federal Register**, taxpayers may rely upon the final rules of this part for the period beginning June 17, 2008, and ending on the date preceding the date these regulations are published as final regulations in the **Federal Register**. [Reg. § 28.2801-2.]

§ 28.2801-3. Rules and exceptions applicable to covered gifts and covered bequests.— (a) *Covered gift.*—Subject to the provisions of paragraphs (c), (d), and (e) of this section, the term *gift* as used in the definition of covered gift in § 28.2801-2(g) has the same meaning as in chapter 12 of subtitle B, but without regard to the exceptions in section 2501(a)(2), (a)(4), and (a)(5), the per-donee exclusion under section 2503(b) for certain transfers of a present interest, the exclusion under section 2503(e) for certain educational or medical expenses, and the waiver of certain pension rights under section 2503(f).

(b) *Covered bequest.*—Subject to the provisions of paragraphs (c), (d), and (e) of this section, property acquired "by reason of the death of a covered expatriate" as described in the definition of covered bequest in § 28.2801-2(f) includes any property that would have been includible in the gross estate of the covered expatriate under chapter 11 of subtitle B if the covered expatriate had been a U.S. citizen at the time of death. Therefore, in addition to the items described in § 28.2801-2(f), the term *covered bequest* includes, without limitation, property or an interest in property acquired by reason of a covered expatriate's death—

(1) By bequest, devise, trust provision, beneficiary designation or other contractual arrangement, or by operation of law;

(2) That was transferred by the covered expatriate during life, either before or after expatriation, and which would have been includible in the covered expatriate's gross estate under section 2036, section 2037, or section 2038 had the covered expatriate been a U.S. citizen at the time of death;

(3) That was received for the benefit of a covered expatriate from such covered expatriate's spouse, or predeceased spouse, for which a valid qualified terminable interest property (QTIP) election was made on such spouse's, or predeceased spouse's, Form 709, "U.S. Gift (and Generation-Skipping Transfer) Tax Return," Form 706, "United States Estate (and Generation-Skipping Transfer) Tax Return," or Form 706-NA, "United States Estate (and Generation-Skipping Transfer) Tax Return, Estate of nonresident not a citizen of the United States," which would have been included in the covered expatriate's gross estate under section 2044 if the covered expatriate was a U.S. citizen at the time of death; or

(4) That otherwise passed from the covered expatriate by reason of death, such as—

(i) Property held by the covered expatriate and another person as joint tenants with right of survivorship or as tenants by the entirety, but only to the extent such property would have been included in the covered expatriate's gross estate under section 2040 if the covered expatriate had been a U.S. citizen at the time of death;

(ii) Any annuity or other payment that would have been includible in the covered expatriate's gross estate if the covered expatriate had been a U.S. citizen at the time of death;

(iii) Property subject to a general power of appointment held by the covered expatriate at death; or

(iv) Life insurance proceeds payable upon the covered expatriate's death that would have been includible in the covered expatriate's gross estate under section 2042 if the covered expatriate had been a U.S. citizen at the time of death.

(c) *Exceptions to covered gift and covered bequest.*—The following transfers from a covered expatriate are exceptions to the definition of covered gift and covered bequest.

(1) *Reported taxable gifts.*—A transfer of property that is a taxable gift under section 2503(a) and is reported on the donor's timely filed Form 709 is not a covered gift, provided that the donor also timely pays the gift tax, if any, shown as due on that return. A transfer excluded from the definition of a taxable gift, such as a transfer of a present interest not in excess of the annual exclusion amount under section 2503(b), is not excluded from the definition of a covered gift under this paragraph (c)(1) even if reported on the donor's Form 709.

(2) *Property reported as subject to estate tax.*—Property that is included in the gross estate of the covered expatriate and is reported on a timely filed Form 706 or Form 706-NA is not a covered bequest, provided that the estate also timely pays the estate tax, if any, shown as due on that return. For this purpose, estate tax imposed on distributions from or on the remainder of a qualified domestic trust (QDOT) are deemed to be reported on a timely filed Form 706, if the tax due thereon was timely paid. Thus, if the covered expatriate's gross estate is not of sufficient value to require the filing of a Form 706-NA, for example, and no Form 706-NA is timely filed, the property passing from that covered expatriate is not excluded from the definition of a covered bequest under the rule of this paragraph (c)(2). Further, this exclusion does not apply to the property not on such a form, whether or not subject to United States estate tax (that is, non U.S.-situs property that passes to U.S. citizens or residents).

(3) *Transfers to charity.*—A gift to a donee described in section 2522(b) or a bequest to a beneficiary described in section 2055(a) is not a covered gift or covered bequest to the extent a charitable deduction under section 2522 or section 2055 would have been allowed if the cov-

ered expatriate had been a U.S. citizen or resident at the time of the transfer.

(4) *Transfers to spouse.*—A transfer from a covered expatriate to the covered expatriate's spouse is not a covered gift or covered bequest to the extent a marital deduction under section 2523 or section 2056 would have been allowed if the covered expatriate had been a U.S. citizen or resident at the time of the transfer. To the extent that a gift or bequest to a trust (or to a separate share of the trust) would qualify for the marital deduction, the gift or bequest is not a covered gift or covered bequest. For purposes of this paragraph (c)(4), a marital deduction is deemed not to be allowed for qualified terminable interest property (QTIP) or for property in a qualified domestic trust (QDOT) unless a valid QTIP and/or QDOT election is made. The term *covered bequest* also does not include assets in a QDOT funded for the benefit of a covered expatriate by the covered expatriate's predeceased spouse, but only if a valid election was made on the predeceased spouse's Form 706 or Form 706-NA to treat the trust as a QDOT.

(5) *Qualified disclaimers.*—A transfer pursuant to a covered expatriate's qualified disclaimer, as defined in section 2518(b), is not a covered gift or covered bequest from that covered expatriate.

(d) *Covered gifts and covered bequests made in trust.*—For purposes of section 2801, when a covered expatriate transfers property to a trust in a transfer that is a covered gift or covered bequest as determined under this section, the transfer of property is treated as a covered gift or covered bequest to the trust, without regard to the beneficial interests in the trust or whether any person has a general power of appointment or a power of withdrawal over trust property. Accordingly, the rules in section 2801(e)(4) and § 28.2801-4(a) apply to determine liability for payment of the section 2801 tax. The U.S. recipient of a covered gift or a covered bequest to a domestic trust or an electing foreign trust is the domestic or electing foreign trust, and the U.S. recipient of a covered gift or a covered bequest to a non-electing foreign trust is any U.S. citizen or resident receiving a distribution from the non-electing foreign trust. See § 28.2801-2(e) for the definition of a U.S. recipient.

(e) *Powers of appointment.*—(1) *Covered expatriate as holder of power.*—The exercise or release of a general power of appointment held by a covered expatriate over property, whether or not in trust (even if that covered expatriate was a U.S. citizen or resident when the general power of appointment was granted), for the benefit of a U.S. citizen or resident is a covered gift or covered bequest. The lapse of a general power of appointment is treated as a release to the extent provided in sections 2041(b)(2) and 2514(e). Furthermore, the exercise of a power of appointment by a covered expatriate that creates another power of appointment as described in section 2041(a)(3) or section 2514(d) for the benefit of a U.S. citizen or resident is a covered gift or a covered bequest.

(2) *Covered expatriate as grantor of power.*—The grant by a covered expatriate to an individual who is a U.S. citizen or resident of a general power of appointment over property not transferred in trust by the covered expatriate is a covered gift or covered bequest to the powerholder. For the rule applying to the grant by a covered expatriate of a general power of appointment over property in trust, see paragraph (d) of this section.

(f) *Examples.*—The provisions of this section are illustrated by the following examples:

Example 1. Transfer to spouse. In Year 1, CE, a covered expatriate domiciled in Country F, a foreign country with which the United States does not have a gift tax treaty, gives $300,000 cash to his wife, W, a U.S. resident and citizen of Country F. Under paragraph (c)(4) of this section, the $100,000 exemption for a noncitizen spouse, as indexed for inflation in Year 1, is excluded from the definition of a covered gift under section 2801 because only that amount of the transfer would have qualified for the gift tax marital deduction if CE had been a U.S. citizen at the time of the gift. See sections 2801(e)(3) and 2523(i). The remaining amount ($300,000 less the $100,000 exemption for a noncitizen spouse as indexed for inflation), however, is a covered gift from CE to W. W must timely file Form 708, "U.S. Return of Gifts or Bequests from Covered Expatriates," and timely pay the tax. See §§ 28.6011-1(a), 28.6071-1(a), and 28.6151-1(a). W also must report the transfer on Form 3520, "Annual Return to Report Transactions with Foreign Trusts and Receipt of Certain Foreign Gifts," and any other required form. See § 28.2801-6(c)(1).

Example 2. Reporting property as subject to estate tax. (i) CE, a covered expatriate domiciled in Country F, a foreign country with which the United States does not have an estate tax treaty, owns a condominium in the United States with son, S, a U.S. citizen. CE and S each contributed their actuarial share of the purchase price when purchasing the condominium and own it as joint tenants with rights of survivorship. On December 14, Year 1, CE dies. At the time of CE's death, the fair market value of CE's share of the condominium, $250,000, is included in CE's gross estate under sections 2040 and 2103.

(ii) On September 14 of the following calendar year, Year 2, the executor of CE's estate timely files a Form 4768, "Application for Extension of Time to File a Return and/or Pay U.S. Estate (and Generation-Skipping Transfer) Taxes," requesting a 6-month extension of time to file Form 706-NA, and a 1-year extension of time to pay the estate tax. The IRS grants both extensions but CE's executor fails to file the Form 706-NA until after March 14 of the calendar year immediately following Year 2.

(iii) S learns that the executor of CE's estate did not timely file Form 706-NA. Because CE is a covered expatriate, S received a covered bequest as defined under § 28.2801-2(f) and paragraph (b) of this section. S must timely file Form 708 and pay the section 2801 tax. See §§28.6011-1(a), 28.6071-1(a), and 28.6151-1(a). S also must file Form 3520 to report a large gift or bequest from a foreign person, and any other required form. See §28.2801-6(c)(1).

Example 3. Covered gift in trust with grant of general power of appointment over trust property. (i) On October 20, Year 1, CE, a covered expatriate domiciled in Country F, a foreign country with which the United States does not have a gift tax treaty, transfers $500,000 in cash from an account in Country F to an irrevocable foreign trust created on that same date. Under section 2511(a), no gift tax is imposed on the transfer and thus, CE is not required to file a U.S. gift tax return. Under the terms of the foreign trust, A, CE's child and a U.S. resident, and Q, A's child and a U.S. citizen, may receive discretionary distributions of income and principal during life. At A's death, the assets remaining in the foreign trust will be distributed to B, CE's other U.S. resident child, or if B is not living at the time of A's death, then to CE's then-living issue, *per stirpes*. The terms of the foreign trust also allow A to appoint trust principal and/or income to A, A's estate, A's creditors, the creditors of A's estate, or A's issue at any time. On March 5, Year 2, A exercises this power to appoint and causes the trustee to distribute $100,000 to Q.

(ii) On October 20, Year 1, the irrevocable foreign trust receives a covered gift for purposes of section 2801, but no section 2801 tax is imposed at that time. On March 5, Year 2, when Q receives $100,000 from the irrevocable foreign trust pursuant to the exercise of A's power of appointment, Q has received a distribution attributable to a covered gift and section 2801 tax is imposed on Q as of the date of the distribution. *See* §28.2801-4(d). Q must timely file Form 708 to report the covered gift from a foreign person (specifically, from CE). See section 6039F(a) and §§28.6011-1(a), 28.6071-1(a), and 28.6151-1(a). Under section 2501, A makes a taxable gift to Q of $100,000 when A exercises the general power of appointment for Q's benefit. See section 2514(b). Accordingly, A must report A's $100,000 gift to Q on a timely filed Form 709. See section 6019. Because A is considered the transferor of the $100,000 for gift and GST tax purposes, the distribution to Q is not a generation-skipping transfer under chapter 13. See §26.2652-1(a)(1). Furthermore, because the $100,000 is being distributed from a foreign trust, Q must report the gift on a Form 3520 as a distribution from a foreign trust. See §28.2801-6(c)(2).

Example 4. Lapse of power of appointment held by covered expatriate. (i) A, a U.S. citizen, creates an irrevocable domestic trust for the benefit of A's issue, CE, and CE's children. CE is a covered expatriate, but CE's children are U.S. citizens. CE has the right to withdraw $5,000 in each year in which A makes a contribution to the trust, but the withdrawal right lapses 30 days after the date of the contribution. In Year 1, A funds the trust, but CE fails to exercise CE's right to withdraw $5,000 within 30 days of the contribution. The $5,000 lapse is not considered to be a release of the power, so it is neither a gift for U.S. gift tax purposes, nor a covered gift for purposes of section 2801 under paragraph (e)(1) of this section.

(g) *Effective/applicability date.*—This section applies on and after the date of publication of a Treasury decision adopting these rules as final regulations in the **Federal Register**. Once these regulations have been published as final regulations in the **Federal Register**, taxpayers may rely upon the final rules of this part for the period beginning June 17, 2008, and ending on the date preceding the date these regulations are published as final regulations in the **Federal Register**. [Reg. §28.2801-3.]

§28.2801-4. Liability for and payment of tax on covered gifts and covered bequests; computation of tax.—(a) *Liability for tax.*—(1) *U.S. citizen or resident.*—A U.S. citizen or resident who receives a covered gift or covered bequest is liable for payment of the section 2801 tax.

(2) *Domestic trust.*—(i) *In general.*—A domestic trust that receives a covered gift or covered bequest is treated as a U.S. citizen and is liable for payment of the section 2801 tax. See section 2801(e)(4)(A)(i) and §28.2801-2(b).

(ii) *Generation-skipping transfer tax.*—A trust's payment of the section 2801 tax does not result in a taxable distribution under section 2621 to any trust beneficiary for purposes of the generation-skipping transfer tax to the extent that the trust, rather than the beneficiary, is liable for the section 2801 tax.

(iii) *Charitable remainder trust.*—A domestic trust qualifying as a charitable remainder trust (as that term is defined in §1.664-1(a)(1)(iii)(*a*)) is subject to section 2801 when it receives a covered gift or covered bequest. Section 2801(e)(3) excepts from the definition of covered gift and covered bequest property with respect to which a deduction under section 2522 or section 2055, respectively, would have been allowed if the covered expatriate had been a U.S. citizen or resident at the time of the transfer. See §28.2801-3(c)(3). As a result, the charitable remainder interest's share of each transfer to the charitable remainder trust is not a covered gift or covered bequest. To compute the amount of covered gifts and covered bequests taxable to the charitable remainder trust for a calendar year, the charitable remainder trust will (A) calculate, in accordance with the regulations under section 664 and as of the date of the trust's receipt of the contribution, the value of the remainder interest in each contribution received in such calendar year that would have been a covered gift or covered bequest without regard to section 2801(e)(3), (B) subtract the remainder interest in each such contribution from the amount of that contribution to compute the annuity or unitrust (income) interest in that contribution, and (C) add the total of such income interests, each of which is the portion of the contribution that constitutes a covered gift or covered bequest to the trust. The charitable remainder trust then computes its section 2801 tax in accordance with paragraph (b) of this section.

(iv) *Migrated foreign trust.*—A foreign trust (other than one electing to be treated as a domestic trust under § 28.2801-5(d)) that has previously received a covered gift or covered bequest and that subsequently becomes a domestic trust as defined under section 7701(a)(30)(E) (migrated foreign trust), must file a timely Form 708, "U.S. Return of Gifts or Bequests from Covered Expatriates," for the taxable year in which the trust becomes a domestic trust. The section 2801 tax, if any, must be paid by the due date of that Form 708. On that Form 708, the section 2801 tax is calculated in the same manner as if such trust was making an election under § 28.2801-5(d) to be treated as a domestic trust solely for purposes of the section 2801 tax. Accordingly, the trustee must report and pay the section 2801 tax on all covered gifts and covered bequests received by the trust during the year in which the trust becomes a domestic trust, as well as on the portion of the trust's value at the end of the year preceding the year in which the trust becomes a domestic trust that is attributable to all prior covered gifts and covered bequests. Because the migrated foreign trust will be treated solely for purposes of section 2801 as a domestic trust for the entire year during which it became a domestic trust, distributions made to U.S. citizens or residents during that year but before the date on which the trust became a domestic trust will not be subject to section 2801.

(3) *Foreign trust.*—(i) *In general.*—A foreign trust that receives a covered gift or covered bequest is not liable for payment of the section 2801 tax unless the trust makes an election to be treated as a domestic trust solely for purposes of section 2801 as provided in § 28.2801-5(d). Absent such an election, each U.S. recipient is liable for payment of the section 2801 tax on that person's receipt, either directly or indirectly, of a distribution from the foreign trust to the extent that the distribution is attributable to a covered gift or covered bequest made to the foreign trust. See § 28.2801-5(b) and (c) regarding distributions from foreign trusts.

(ii) *Income tax deduction.*—The U.S. recipient of a distribution from a foreign trust is allowed a deduction against income tax under section 164 in the calendar year in which the section 2801 tax is paid or accrued. The amount of the deduction is equal to the portion of the section 2801 tax attributable to such distribution, but only to the extent that portion of the distribution is included in the U.S. recipient's gross income. The amount of the deduction allowed under section 164 is calculated as follows:

(A) First, the U.S. recipient must determine the total amount of distribution(s) from the foreign trust treated as covered gifts and covered bequests received by that U.S. recipient during the calendar year to which the section 2801 tax payment relates.

(B) Second, of the amount determined in paragraph (a)(3)(ii)(A) of this section, the U.S. recipient must determine the amount that also is includable in the U.S. recipient's gross income for that calendar year. For purposes of this paragraph (a)(3)(ii)(B), distributions from foreign trusts includable in the U.S. recipient's gross income are deemed first to consist of the portion of those distributions, if any, that are attributable to covered gifts and covered bequests.

(C) Finally, the U.S. recipient must determine the portion of the section 2801 tax paid for that calendar year that is attributable to the amount determined in paragraph (a)(3)(ii)(B) of this section, the covered gifts and covered bequests received from the foreign trust that are also included in the U.S. recipient's gross income. This amount is the allowable deduction. Thus, for a calendar year taxpayer, the deduction is determined by multiplying the section 2801 tax paid during the calendar year by the ratio of the amount determined in paragraph (a)(3)(ii)(B) of this section to the total covered gifts and covered bequests received by the U.S. recipient during the calendar year to which that tax payment relates (that is, 2801 tax liability x [foreign trust distributions attributable to covered gifts and covered bequests that are also included in gross income / total covered gifts or covered bequests received]).

(b) *Computation of tax.*—(1) *In general.*—The section 2801 tax is computed by multiplying the net covered gifts and covered bequests (as defined in paragraph (b)(2) of this section) received by a U.S. recipient during the calendar year by the greater of—

(i) The highest rate of estate tax under section 2001(c) in effect for that calendar year; or

(ii) The highest rate of gift tax under section 2502(a) in effect for that calendar year. See paragraph (f) of this section, *Example 1.*

(2) *Net covered gifts and covered bequests.*—The net covered gifts and covered bequests received by a U.S. recipient during the calendar year is the total value of all covered gifts and covered bequests received by that U.S. recipient during the calendar year, less the section 2801(c) amount, which is the dollar amount of the perdonee exclusion in effect under section 2503(b) for that calendar year.

(c) *Value of covered gift or covered bequest.*—The value of a covered gift or covered bequest is the fair market value of the property as of the date of its receipt by the U.S. recipient. See paragraph (d) of this section regarding the determination of the date of receipt. As in the case of chapters 11 and 12, the fair market value of a covered gift or covered bequest is the price at which such property would change hands between a willing buyer and a willing seller, neither being under any compulsion to buy or to sell and both having reasonable knowledge of relevant facts. The fair market value of a covered gift is determined in accordance with the federal gift tax valuation principles of section 2512 and chapter 14 and the corresponding regulations. The fair market value of a covered bequest is determined by applying the federal estate tax valuation principles of section 2031 and chapter 14 and the corresponding regulations, but without regard to sections 2032 and 2032A.

(d) *Date of receipt*.—(1) *In general*.—The section 2801 tax is imposed upon the receipt of a covered gift or covered bequest by a U.S. recipient.

(2) *Covered gift*.—The date of receipt of a covered gift is the same as the date of the gift for purposes of chapter 12 as if the covered expatriate had been a U.S. citizen at the time of the transfer. Thus, for a gift of stock, if the covered expatriate delivers a properly endorsed stock certificate to the U.S. recipient, the date of delivery is the date of receipt for purposes of this section. Alternatively, if the covered expatriate delivers the stock certificate to the issuing corporation or its transfer agent in order to transfer title to the U.S. recipient, the date of receipt is the date the stock is transferred on the books of the corporation. For a transfer of assets by a covered expatriate to a domestic revocable trust, the trust receives the transfer on the date the covered expatriate relinquishes the right to revoke the trust. If, before the donor's relinquishment of the right to revoke the trust, the revocable trust distributes property to a U.S. citizen or resident not in discharge of a support or other obligation of the donor, then the U.S. recipient receives a covered gift on the date of that distribution. For an asset subject to a claim of right of another involving a bona fide dispute, the date of receipt is the date on which such claim is extinguished.

(3) *Covered bequest*.—The date of receipt of a covered bequest is the date of distribution from the estate or the decedent's revocable trust rather than the date of death of the covered expatriate. However, the date of receipt is the date of death for property passing on the death of the covered expatriate by operation of law, or by beneficiary designation or other contractual agreement. Notwithstanding the previous sentences, for an asset subject to a claim of right of another involving a bona fide dispute, the date of receipt is the date on which such claim is extinguished.

(4) *Foreign trusts*.—The date of receipt by a U.S. citizen or resident of property from a foreign trust that has not elected to be treated as a domestic trust under § 28.2801-5(d) is the date of its distribution from the foreign trust.

(5) *Powers of appointment*.—(i) *Covered expatriate as holder of power*.—In the case of the exercise, release, or lapse of a power of appointment held by a covered expatriate that is a covered gift pursuant to § 28.2801-3(e)(1), the date of receipt is the date of the exercise, release, or lapse of the power. In the case of the exercise, release, or lapse of a power of appointment held by a covered expatriate that is a covered bequest pursuant to § 28.2801-3(e)(1), the date of receipt is (*A*) the date the property subject to the power is distributed from the decedent's estate or revocable trust when the power of appointment is over property in such estate or trust, or (*B*) the date of the covered expatriate's death when the power of appointment is over property passing on the covered expatriate's death by operation of law, by beneficiary designation, or by other contractual agreement.

(ii) *Covered expatriate as grantor of power*.—The date of receipt of property subject to a general power of appointment granted by a covered expatriate to a U.S. citizen or resident over property not transferred in trust that constitutes a covered gift or covered bequest pursuant to § 28.2801-3(e)(2) is the first date on which both the power is exercisable by the U.S. citizen or resident and the property subject to the general power has been irrevocably transferred by the covered expatriate. The date of receipt of property subject to a general power of appointment over property in a domestic trust or an electing foreign trust is determined in accordance with paragraphs (d)(2) and (d)(3) of this section, and over property in a non-electing foreign trust is determined in accordance with paragraph (d)(4) of this section. See § 28.2801-3(d) for the rule applying to covered gifts and covered bequests made in trust.

(6) *Indirect receipts*.—The date of receipt by a U.S. citizen or resident of a covered gift or covered bequest received indirectly from a covered expatriate is the date of its receipt, as determined under paragraph (d)(2) or (d)(3) of this section, by the U.S. citizen or resident who is the first recipient of that property from the covered expatriate to be subject to section 2801 with regard to that property. For example, the date of receipt of property (i) subject to a non-general power of appointment over property not held in trust given by a covered expatriate to a foreign person (other than another covered expatriate) is the date that property is received by the U.S. citizen or resident in whose favor the power was exercised, and (ii) received through one or more entities not subject to section 2801 is the date of its receipt by the U.S. citizen or resident from a conduit entity.

(e) *Reduction of tax for foreign estate or gift tax paid*.—The section 2801 tax is reduced by the amount of any gift or estate tax paid to a foreign country with respect to the covered gift or covered bequest. For this purpose, the term *foreign country* includes possessions and political subdivisions of foreign states. However, no reduction is allowable for interest and penalties paid in connection with those foreign taxes. To claim the reduction of section 2801 tax, the U.S. recipient must attach to the Form 708 a copy of the foreign estate or gift tax return and a copy of the receipt or cancelled check for payment of the foreign estate or gift tax. The U.S. recipient also must report, on an attachment to the Form 708:

(1) The amount of foreign estate or gift tax paid with respect to each covered gift or covered bequest and the amount and date of each payment thereof;

(2) A description and the value of the property with respect to which such taxes were imposed;

(3) Whether any refund of part or all of the foreign estate or gift tax has been or will be claimed or allowed, and the amount; and

(4) All other information necessary for the verification and computation of the amount of the reduction of section 2801 tax.

(f) *Examples.*—The provisions of this section are illustrated by the following examples.

Example 1. Computation of tax. In Year 1, A, a U.S. citizen, receives a $50,000 covered gift from B and an $80,000 covered bequest from C. Both B and C are covered expatriates. In Year 1, the highest estate and gift tax rate is 40 percent and the section 2801(c) amount is $14,000. A's section 2801 tax for Year 1 is computed by multiplying A's net covered gifts and covered bequests by 40 percent. A's net covered gifts and covered bequests for Year 1 are $116,000, which is determined by reducing A's total covered gifts and covered bequests received during Year 1, $130,000 ($50,000 + $80,000), by the section 2801(c) amount of $14,000. A's section 2801 tax liability is then reduced by any foreign estate or gift tax paid under paragraph (e) of this section. Assuming A, B, and C paid no foreign estate or gift tax on the transfers, A's section 2801 tax liability for Year 1 is $46,400 ($116,000 x 0.4).

Example 2. Deduction of section 2801 tax for income tax purposes. In Year 1, B receives a covered bequest of $25,000. Also in Year 1, B receives an aggregate $500,000 of distributions from a non-electing foreign trust of which $100,000 was attributable to a covered gift. In Year 1, the highest estate and gift tax rate is 40 percent and the section 2801(c) amount is $14,000. Based on information provided by the trustee of the foreign trust, B includes $50,000 of the aggregate distributions from the foreign trust in B's gross income for Year 1. Under paragraph (a)(3)(ii) of this section, B (a cash basis taxpayer) is entitled to an income tax deduction under section 164 for the calendar year in which the section 2801 tax is paid. In Year 2, B timely reports the distributions from the foreign trust and pays $44,400 in section 2801 tax (($125,000 - $14,000) x 0.4). In Year 2, B is entitled to an income tax deduction because B paid the section 2801 tax in Year 2 on the Year 1 covered gift and covered bequest. B's Year 2 income tax deduction is computed as follows:

(i) $100,000 of B's total covered gifts and covered bequests of $125,000 received in Year 1 consisted of the portion of the distributions from the foreign trust attributable to covered gifts and covered bequests received by the trust. See paragraph (a)(3)(ii)(A) of this section.

(ii) $50,000 of the $500,000 of trust distributions were includable in B's gross income for Year 1. This amount is deemed to consist first of distributions subject to the section 2801 tax ($100,000). Thus, the entire amount included in B's gross income ($50,000) also is subject to the section 2801 tax, and is used in the numerator to determine the income tax deduction available to B. See paragraph (a)(3)(ii)(B) of this section.

(iii) The portion of B's section 2801 tax liability attributable to distributions from a foreign trust is $17,760 ($44,400 x ($50,000/$125,000)). Therefore, B's deduction under section 164 is $17,760. See paragraph (a)(3)(ii)(C) of this section.

Example 3. Date of receipt; bona fide claim. On October 10, Year 1, CE, a covered expatriate, died testate as a resident of Country F, a foreign country with which the United States does not have an estate tax treaty. CE designated his son, S, as the beneficiary of CE's retirement account. S is a U.S. citizen. CE's wife, W, who is a citizen and resident of Country F, elects to take her elective share of CE's estate under local law. S contests whether the retirement account is property subject to the elective share. S and W agree to settle their respective claims by dividing CE's assets equally between them. On December 15 of Year 2, Country F's court enters an order accepting the terms of the settlement agreement and dismissing the case. Under paragraph (d)(3) of this section, S received a covered bequest of one-half of CE's retirement account on December 15, Year 2, when W's claim of right was extinguished.

(g) *Effective/applicability date.*—This section applies on and after the date of publication of a Treasury decision adopting these rules as final regulations in the **Federal Register**. Once these regulations have been published as final regulations in the **Federal Register**, taxpayers may rely upon the final rules of this part for the period beginning June 17, 2008, and ending on the date preceding the date these regulations are published as final regulations in the **Federal Register**. [Reg. § 28.2801-4.]

§ 28.2801-5. Foreign trusts.—(a) *In general.*—The section 2801 tax is imposed on a U.S. recipient who receives distributions, whether of income or principal, from a foreign trust to the extent the distributions are attributable to one or more covered gifts or covered bequests made to that foreign trust. See paragraph (d) of this section regarding a foreign trust's election to be treated as a domestic trust for purposes of section 2801.

(b) *Distribution defined.*—For purposes of determining whether a U.S. recipient has received a distribution from a foreign trust, the term *distribution* means any direct, indirect, or constructive transfer from a foreign trust. This determination is made without regard to whether any portion of the trust is treated as owned by the U.S. recipient or any other person under subpart E of part I, subchapter J, chapter 1 of the Code (pertaining to grantors and others treated as substantial owners) and without regard to whether the U.S. recipient of the transfer is designated as a beneficiary by the terms of the trust. For purposes of section 2801, the term distribution also includes each disbursement from a foreign trust pursuant to the exercise, release, or lapse of a power of appointment, whether or not a general power. In addition to the reporting requirements under this section, see section 6048(c) regarding the information reporting requirement for U.S. persons receiving a distribution or deemed distribution from a foreign trust during the year.

(c) *Amount of distribution attributable to covered gift or covered bequest.*—(1) *Section 2801 ratio.*—(i) *In general.*—A foreign trust may have received covered gifts and covered bequests as well as contributions that were not covered gifts or covered bequests. Under such circumstances, the fair market value of the foreign trust at any time consists in part of a portion of the trust attributable to the covered gifts and covered bequests it has received (covered portion) and in part of a portion of the trust attributable to other contributions (non-covered portion). The covered portion of the trust includes the ratable portion of appreciation and income that has accrued on the foreign trust's assets from the date of the contribution of the covered gifts and covered bequests to the foreign trust. For purposes of section 2801, the amount of each distribution from the foreign trust, whether made from the income or principal of the trust, that is considered attributable to the foreign trust's covered gifts and covered bequests is determined on a proportional basis, by reference to the section 2801 ratio (as described in paragraph (c)(1)(ii) of this section), and not by the identification or tracing of particular trust assets. Specifically, this portion of each distribution is determined by multiplying the distributed amount by the percentage of the trust that consists of its covered portion immediately prior to that distribution (section 2801 ratio). Thus, for example, the section 2801 ratio of a foreign trust whose assets are comprised exclusively of covered gifts or covered bequests and the income and appreciation thereon, would be 1 and the full amount of each distribution from that foreign trust to a U.S. citizen or resident would be subject to section 2801.

(ii) *Computation.*—The section 2801 ratio, which must be redetermined after each contribution to the foreign trust, is computed by using the following fraction:

$$\text{Section 2801 ratio} = \frac{(X + Y)}{Z}$$

where,

X = The value of the trust attributable to covered gifts and covered bequests, if any, immediately before the contribution (pre-contribution value); this value is determined by multiplying the fair market value of the trust assets immediately prior to the contribution by the section 2801 ratio in effect immediately prior to the current contribution. This amount will be zero for all years prior to the year in which the foreign trust receives its first covered gift or covered bequest;

Y = The portion, if any, of the fair market value of the current contribution that constitutes a covered gift or covered bequest; and

Z = The fair market value of the trust immediately after the current contribution. See paragraph (e) of this section, *Example 1*, for an illustration of this computation.

(2) *Effect of reported transfer and tax payment.*—Once a section 2801 tax has been timely paid on property that thereafter remains in a foreign trust, that property is no longer considered to be, or to be attributable to, a covered gift or covered bequest to the foreign trust for purposes of the computation described in paragraph (c)(1)(ii) of this section. For purposes of the prior sentence, a section 2801 tax is deemed to have been timely paid on amounts for which no section 2801 tax was due as long as those amounts were reported as a covered gift or covered bequest on a timely filed Form 708, "U.S. Return of Gifts or Bequests from Covered Expatriates."

(3) *Inadequate information to calculate section 2801 ratio.*—If the trustee of the foreign trust does not have sufficient books and records to calculate the section 2801 ratio, or if the U.S. recipient is unable to obtain the necessary information with regard to the foreign trust, the U.S. recipient must proceed upon the assumption that the entire distribution for purposes of section 2801 is attributable to a covered gift or covered bequest.

(d) *Foreign trust treated as domestic trust.*—(1) *Election required.*—To be considered an electing foreign trust, so that the foreign trust is treated as a domestic trust solely for purposes of the section 2801 tax, a valid election is required.

(2) *Effect of election.*—(i) A valid election subjects the electing foreign trust to the section 2801 tax on (A) all covered gifts and covered bequests received by the foreign trust during that calendar year, (B) the portion of the trust attributable to covered gifts and covered bequests received by the trust in prior years, as determined in paragraph (d)(3)(iii) of this section, and (C) all covered gifts and covered bequests received by the foreign trust during calendar years subsequent to the first year in which the election is effective, unless and until the election is terminated. To the extent that covered gifts and covered bequests are subject to the section 2801 tax under the prior sentence, those trust receipts are no longer treated as a covered gift or covered bequest for purposes of determining the portion of the trust attributable to covered gifts and covered bequests. Therefore, upon making a valid election, the foreign trust's section 2801 ratio described in paragraph (c)(1)(ii) of this section will be zero until the effective date of any termination of the election and the subsequent receipt of any covered gift or covered bequest, and a distribution made from the foreign trust while this election is in effect is not taxable under section 2801 to the recipient trust beneficiary.

(ii) This election has no effect on any distribution from the foreign trust that was made to a U.S. recipient in a calendar year prior to the calendar year for which the election is made. Thus, even after a valid election is made, a distribution to a U.S. recipient in a calendar year prior to the calendar year for which the election is made that was attributable to one or more covered gifts or covered bequests continues to be a distribution attributable to one or more covered gifts or covered bequests and the section 2801 ratio in place at the time of the distribution continues to apply to that distribution. Furthermore, an election under this section does not relieve the U.S. recipient from the information reporting requirements of section 6048(c).

(3) *Time and manner of making the election.*—(i) *When to make the election.*—The election is made on a timely filed Form 708 for the calendar year for which the foreign trust seeks to subject itself to the section 2801 tax as described in paragraph (d)(2)(i) of this section. The election may be made for a calendar year whether or not the foreign trust received a covered gift or covered bequest during that calendar year. See §28.6071-1.

(ii) *Requirements for a valid election.*—To make a valid election to be treated as a domestic trust for purposes of section 2801, the electing foreign trust must timely file a Form 708 and must, on such form—

(A) Make the election, timely pay the section 2801 tax, if any, as determined under paragraph (d)(3)(iii) of this section, and include a computation illustrating how the trustee of the electing foreign trust calculated both the section 2801 ratio described in paragraph (c)(1)(ii) of this section and the section 2801 tax;

(B) Designate and authorize a U.S. agent as provided in paragraph (d)(3)(iv) of this section;

(C) Agree to file Form 708 annually;

(D) List the amount and year of all prior distributions attributable to covered gifts and covered bequests made to a U.S. recipient and provide the name, address, and taxpayer identification number of each U.S. recipient; and

(E) Notify each permissible distributee that the trustee is making the election under this paragraph (d) and provide to the IRS a list of the name, address, and taxpayer identification number of each permissible distributee. For this purpose, a permissible distributee is any U.S. citizen or resident who:

(1) Currently may or must receive distributions from the trust, whether of income or principal;

(2) May withdraw income or principal from the trust, regardless of whether the right arises or lapses upon the occurrence of a future event; or

(3) Would have been described in paragraph (d)(3)(ii)(E)*(1)* of this section if either the interests of all persons described in (d)(3)(ii)(E)*(1)* or (E)(2) had just terminated or the trust had just terminated.

(iii) *Section 2801 tax payable with the election.*—To make a valid election to be treated as a domestic trust for purposes of section 2801, the electing foreign trust must timely pay the section 2801 tax on all covered gifts and covered bequests received by the electing foreign trust in the calendar year for which the Form 708 is being filed. In some cases, an electing foreign trust may have received covered gifts or covered bequests in prior calendar years during which no such election was in effect. In those cases, the trustee must also, at the same time, report and pay the tax on the fair market value, determined as of the last day of the calendar year immediately preceding the year for which the Form 708 is being filed, of the portion of the trust attributable to covered gifts and covered bequests received by such trust in prior calendar years (except as provided in paragraph (d)(6)(iii) of this section with regard to an imperfect election). That portion is determined by multiplying the fair market value of the trust, as of the December 31 immediately preceding the year for which the election is made, by the section 2801 ratio in effect on that date, as calculated under paragraph (c)(1)(ii) of this section. If the trustee does not have sufficient books and records to determine what amount of the corpus and undistributed income is attributable to undistributed prior covered gifts and covered bequests, then that amount is deemed to be the entire fair market value of the trust as of that December 31. See paragraph (c)(3) of this section.

(iv) *Designation of U.S. agent.*—(A) *In general.*—The trustee of an electing foreign trust must designate and authorize a U.S. person, as defined in section 7701(a)(30), to act as an agent for the trust solely for purposes of section 2801. By designating a U.S. agent, the trustee of the foreign trust agrees to provide the agent with all information necessary to comply with any information request or summons issued by the Secretary. Such information may include, without limitation, copies of the books and records of the trust, financial statements, and appraisals of trust property.

(B) *Role of designated agent.*—Acting as an agent for the trust for purposes of section 2801 includes serving as the electing foreign trust's agent for purposes of section 7602 ("Examination of books and witnesses"), section 7603 ("Service of summons"), and section 7604 ("Enforcement of summons") with respect to—

(1) Any request by the Secretary to examine records or produce testimony related to the proper identification or treatment of covered gifts or covered bequests contributed to the electing foreign trust and distributions attributable to such contributions; and

(2) Any summons by the Secretary for records or testimony related to the proper identification or treatment of covered gifts or covered bequests contributed to the electing foreign trust and distributions attributable to such contributions.

(C) *Effect of appointment of U.S. agent.*—An electing foreign trust that appoints such an agent is not considered to have an office or a permanent establishment in the United States, or to be engaged in a trade or business in the United States, solely because of the agent's activities as an agent pursuant to this section.

(4) *Annual certification or filing requirement.*—The trustee of an electing foreign trust must file a timely Form 708 annually either to

report and pay the section 2801 tax on all covered gifts and covered bequests received by the trust during the calendar year, or to certify that the electing foreign trust did not receive any covered gifts or covered bequests during the calendar year.

(5) *Duration of status as electing foreign trust.*—(i) *In general.*—A valid election (one that meets all of the requirements of paragraph (d)(3) of this section) is effective as of January 1 of the calendar year for which the Form 708 on which the election is made is filed. The election, once made, applies for all calendar years until the election is terminated as described in paragraph (d)(5)(ii) of this section.

(ii) *Termination.*—An election to be treated as a domestic trust for purposes of section 2801 is terminated either by the failure of the foreign trust to make the annual filing, together with any payment of the section 2801 tax, as required by paragraph (d)(4) of this section, or by the failure of the foreign trust to timely pay any additional amount of section 2801 tax (in accordance with the requirements of paragraph (d)(6)(ii) of this section) with respect to recalculations described in paragraph (d)(6) of this section (a failure that results in an imperfect election). A termination, if any, is effective as of the beginning of the calendar year for which the trustee fails to make the annual filing required by paragraph (d)(4) of this section or for which the trustee fails to pay any of the amounts described in this paragraph (d)(5)(ii). In the case of a terminated election, the trustee should notify promptly each permissible distributee, as defined in paragraph (d)(3)(ii)(E) of this section, that the foreign trust's election was terminated as of January 1 of the applicable year (with the actual year of the termination being set forth in the notice), and that each U.S. recipient of a distribution made from the foreign trust on and after that date is subject to the section 2801 tax on the portion of each such distribution that is attributable to covered gifts and covered bequests. See paragraph (d)(6)(iii)(B) of this section for an additional notification requirement in the case of an imperfect election.

(iii) *Subsequent elections.*—If a foreign trust's election is terminated under paragraph (d)(5)(ii) of this section, the foreign trust is not prohibited from making another election in a future year, subject to the requirements of paragraph (d)(3) of this section.

(6) *Dispute as to amount of section 2801 tax owed by electing foreign trust.*—(i) *Procedure.*—If the Commissioner disputes the value of a covered gift or covered bequest, or otherwise challenges the computation of the section 2801 tax, that is reported on the electing foreign trust's timely filed Form 708 for any calendar year, the Commissioner will issue a letter (but not a notice of deficiency as defined in section 6212) to the trustee of the electing foreign trust and the appointed U.S. agent that details the disputed information and the proper amount of section 2801 tax as recalculated. The foreign trust must pay the additional amount of section 2801 tax including interest and penalties, if any, in accordance with the requirements of paragraph (d)(6)(ii) of this section, on or before the due date specified in the letter to maintain its election.

(ii) *Effect of timely paying the additional section 2801 tax amount.*—If the trustee of the foreign trust timely pays the additional amount(s) specified in the Commissioner's letter, or such other amount as agreed to by the Commissioner, and enters into a closing agreement with the IRS as described in section 7121, then the foreign trust's election to be treated as a domestic trust under paragraph (d) of this section remains in effect. In addition, in the absence of fraud, malfeasance, or misrepresentation of a material fact, that payment, in conjunction with the closing agreement, will be deemed to render any determination of value to which the closing agreement applies as final and binding on both the IRS and the foreign trust. Thus, subsequently, the IRS will not be able to challenge the section 2801 tax due from either the foreign trust or any of its beneficiaries who are U.S. citizens or residents for the year for which that Form 708 was filed by the foreign trust, except with respect to any covered gifts or covered bequests not reported on that return, and neither the foreign trust nor any of its beneficiaries will be able to file a claim for refund with respect to section 2801 tax paid by the foreign trust on the covered gifts and covered bequests reported on that Form 708.

(iii) *Effect of failing to timely pay the additional section 2801 tax amount (imperfect election).*—(A) *In general.*—If the foreign trust fails to timely pay the additional amount of section 2801 tax with interest and penalties, if any, claimed to be due by the IRS in accordance with the requirements of paragraph (d)(6)(ii) of this section, then the foreign trust's valid election is terminated and becomes an imperfect election. The foreign trust's election is terminated, and is converted into an imperfect election, retroactively as of the first day of the calendar year for which was filed the Form 708 with respect to which the additional amount of section 2801 tax is claimed to be due by the IRS. Thus, the value the foreign trust has reported on the Form 708 and on which the trust has paid the section 2801 tax is no longer considered to be attributable to covered gifts or covered bequests when computing the section 2801 ratio described in paragraph (c)(1)(ii) of this section applicable to distributions made by the foreign trust to U.S. recipients during the calendar year for which the Form 708 was filed and thereafter. The U.S. recipients of distributions from the foreign trust, however, should take into consideration the additional value determined by the IRS, on which the foreign trust did not timely pay the section 2801 tax, when computing the section 2801 ratio to be applied to a distribution from the trust. See paragraph (c) of this section. Any disagreement with regard to that additional value will be an issue to be resolved as part of the review of that U.S. recipient's own Form 708 reporting a distribution.

(B) *Notice to permissible beneficiaries.*—If the trustee of the foreign trust fails to remit the additional payment of the section 2801 tax including all interest and penalties, if any, in accordance with the requirements of paragraph (d)(6)(ii) of this section, by the due date stated in the IRS letter, the trustee should notify promptly each permissible distributee, as defined in paragraph (d)(3)(ii)(E) of this section, of the amount of additional value on which the foreign trust did not timely pay the section 2801 tax as determined by the IRS and that:

(*1*) The foreign trust's election was terminated as of January 1 of the applicable year (with the actual year of the termination being set forth in the notice); and

(*2*) Each U.S. recipient of a distribution made from the foreign trust on and after that termination date is subject to the section 2801 tax on the portion of each such distribution attributable to covered gifts and covered bequests.

(C) *Reasonable cause.*—If a U.S. recipient received a distribution from such trust on or after January 1 of the year for which the election was terminated and the election became an imperfect election, provided the U.S. recipient files a Form 708 and pays the section 2801 tax within a reasonable period of time after being notified by the trustee of the foreign trust or otherwise becoming aware that a valid election was not in effect when the distribution was made, the U.S. recipient's failure to timely file and pay are due to reasonable cause and not willful neglect for purposes of section 6651. For this purpose, a reasonable period of time is not more than six months after the U.S. recipient is notified by the trustee or the U.S. recipient otherwise becomes aware that a valid election is not in effect.

(D) *Interim period.*—If a foreign trust's valid election is terminated and becomes an imperfect election, there is a period of time (interim period) after the effective date of the termination of the election during which both the foreign trust and its U.S. beneficiaries are likely to continue to comply with section 2801 as it applies to an electing foreign trust with a valid election in place. The interim period begins on the effective date of the termination of the foreign trust's election that resulted in an imperfect election as described in paragraph (d)(6)(iii)(A) of this section, and ends on December 31 of the calendar year immediately preceding the calendar year in which the additional section 2801 tax claimed by the IRS is due. As under the rule in paragraph (d)(6)(iii)(A) of this section regarding imperfect elections, the covered gifts and covered bequests received by the foreign trust during this interim period, which the foreign trust has reported on its timely filed Form 708 and on which the foreign trust has timely paid the section 2801 tax, are no longer considered to be covered gifts and covered bequests for purposes of computing the section 2801 ratio described in paragraph (c)(1)(ii) of this section as it applies to distributions made by non-electing foreign trusts to their U.S. beneficiaries. In addition, each distribution made by the foreign trust to a U.S. citizen or resident during this interim period must be reported on that U.S. recipient's Form 708 by applying the section 2801 ratio to that distribution. Once the interim period has ended, the foreign trust has no election in place and the rules of section 2801(e)(4)(B)(i) will apply until the foreign trust subsequently (if ever) makes another valid election to be treated as a domestic trust for purposes of section 2801.

(7) *No overpayment caused solely by virtue of defect in election.*—Any remittance of section 2801 tax made by a foreign trust electing to be treated as a domestic trust does not become an overpayment solely by virtue of a defect in the election. Instead, if at some subsequent time the IRS determines that the election was not in fact a valid election, then the election shall be considered valid only with respect to the covered gifts or covered bequests on which the section 2801 tax was timely paid by the foreign trust and each covered gift and covered bequest on which the section 2801 tax has been timely paid is no longer treated as a covered gift or covered bequest for purposes of determining the portion of the foreign trust attributable to covered gifts and covered bequests. See paragraphs (d)(2)(i) and (d)(6)(iii) of this section.

(e) *Examples.*—The provisions of this section are illustrated by the following examples.

Example 1. Computation of section 2801 ratio. A and B each contribute $100,000 to a foreign trust. A (but not B) is a covered expatriate and A's contribution is a covered gift. The section 2801 ratio immediately after these two contributions is 0.50, computed as follows: the pre-contribution value of the trust ($0) times the pre-contribution section 2801 ratio (-0-), plus the current covered gift ($100,000), divided by the post-contribution fair market value of the trust ($200,000). See § 28.2801-5(c). Therefore, 50 percent of each distribution from the trust is subject to the section 2801 tax until the next contribution is made to the trust. If the trustee distributes $40,000 to C, a U.S. citizen, before the trust receives any other contributions, then $20,000 ($40,000 x 0.5) is a covered gift to C.

Example 2. Computation of section 2801 ratio when multiple contributions are made to foreign trust. (i) In 2005, A, a U.S. citizen, established and funded an irrevocable foreign trust with $200,000 and reported the transfer as a completed gift. On January 1 of each of the following three years (2006 through 2008), A contributed an additional $100,000 to the foreign trust. A reported A's contributions to the foreign trust as completed gifts on timely filed Forms 709, for calendar years 2005 through 2008. On August 8, 2008, a date after the effective date of section 2801 (June 17, 2008), A expatriated and became a covered expatriate. On January 1 of a year after 2008 (Year X), A makes an additional $100,000 contribution to the trust. The aggregate $600,000 contributed to the trust by A, both before and after expatriation, are the only contributions to the trust. Each year, the trustee of the foreign trust provides beneficiary B, a U.S. citizen, with an accounting of the trust showing each receipt and disbursement of the trust during that year, including the date and amount of each contribution by A.

(ii) The fair market value of the trust was $610,000 immediately prior to A's contribution to the trust on January 1, Year X. Therefore, upon the Year X contribution of A's first and only covered gift, the portion of the trust attributable to covered gifts and covered bequests (covered portion) changed from zero to 0.14 ([(section 2801 ratio of 0 x $610,000 fair market value pre-contribution) plus the $100,000 covered gift]/ $710,000 fair market value post-contribution). See paragraph (c) of this section.

(iii) In February of Year X, B received a distribution of $225,000 from the foreign trust. Although A contributed a total of $600,000 to the foreign trust, A contributed only $100,000 while A was a covered expatriate. Under paragraph (c) of this section, the portion of the $225,000 distribution from the foreign trust attributable to a covered gift is $31,500 ($225,000 x 0.14 (section 2801 ratio)) because the distribution is made proportionally from the covered and non-covered portions of the trust. See paragraph (c)(1) of this section. Accordingly, B received a covered gift of $31,500.

(iv) Pursuant to the terms of the foreign trust, the trust made a terminating distribution on August 5, Year X, when B turned 35, and B received the balance of the appreciated trust, $505,000. The portion of this distribution attributable to covered gifts and covered bequests is $70,700 ($505,000 x 0.14). Therefore, B has received covered gifts from the foreign trust during Year X in the total amount of $102,200 ($31,500 + $70,700).

Example 3. Termination of foreign trust election. The trustee of a foreign trust that received a covered gift makes a valid election to be treated as a domestic trust under § 28.2801-5(d) for Year 1. However, the trustee fails to file timely the Form 708 for the next year, Year 2. The foreign trust election is terminated as of January 1, Year 2, under paragraph (d)(5)(ii) of this section. Thus, any distributions made to U.S. recipients during Year 1 have a section 2801 ratio of zero and are not subject to the section 2801 tax. However, any such distributions made during Year 2 are subject to the section 2801 tax to the extent the distributions are attributable to a covered gift or covered bequest received by the trust during Year 2. Unless the trustee makes a new election as described in paragraph (d)(5)(iii) of this section, beginning in Year 2, the foreign trust's section 2801 ratio must be recomputed each time the foreign trust receives a contribution.

Example 4. Imperfect election by foreign trust. (i) In Year 1, CE, a covered expatriate, gives a 20 percent limited partnership interest in a closely held business to a foreign trust created for the benefit of CE's child, A, who is a U.S. citizen. The limited partnership interest is a covered gift. The trustee of the foreign trust makes a valid election to have the trust treated as a domestic trust for purposes of section 2801, trustee timely files a Form 708, and timely pays the section 2801 tax on the reported fair market value of the covered gift ($500,000). Later in Year 1, the trust makes a $100,000 distribution to A.

(ii) In Year 2, CE contributes $200,000 in cash to the foreign trust. The cash is a covered gift. The trustee of the foreign trust timely files a Form 708 reporting the transfer and pays the section 2801 tax. The trust does not make a distribution to any beneficiary during Year 2. Late in Year 3, the IRS disputes the reported value of the partnership interest transferred in Year 1 and determines that the proper valuation on the date of the gift was $800,000. In Year 3, the IRS issues a letter to the trustee of the foreign trust detailing its finding of the increased valuation and of the resulting additional section 2801 tax including accrued interest, if any, due on or before a later date in Year 3 specified in the letter. The foreign trust fails to pay the additional section 2801 tax liability on or before that due date.

(iii) Under paragraph (d)(6)(iii) of this section, the foreign trust's election for Year 1 is an imperfect election; although it timely filed its return reporting the transfer and paid the tax, it failed to timely pay the additional section 2801 tax when the IRS notified the trust of an additional amount of section 2801 tax claimed to be due. Accordingly, the foreign trust's election is deemed to have terminated as of January 1 of Year 1. In computing the foreign trust's section 2801 ratio upon the receipt of the covered gift in Year 1, the $500,000 of value on which the section 2801 tax was timely paid is no longer deemed to be a covered gift. See paragraph (d)(6)(iii) of this section. When the trustee advises A of the letter from the IRS, A must file a late Form 708 reporting the portion of the Year 1 distribution attributable to covered gifts and covered bequests. Although A may owe section 2801 tax and interest, A will not owe any penalties under section 6651 as long as A files the Form 708 and pays the tax within a reasonable period of time after A receives notice of the termination of the election from the trustee of the foreign trust or otherwise becomes aware of the termination of the election. See paragraph (d)(6)(iii)(C) of this section.

(iv) When A files the Form 708, the IRS will verify whether A treated the $300,000 undervaluation claimed by the IRS as a covered gift in computing the section 2801 ratio. As with any other item reported on that return, A has the burden to prove the value of the covered gift to the foreign trust, and the IRS may challenge that value. If A treats the $300,000 as a covered gift to the trust, under paragraph (c)(1)(ii) of this section, the section 2801 ratio after the Year 1 contribution is 0.375 ($0 + ($300,000)/$800,000)). Thus, 37.5 percent of all distributions made to A from the foreign trust during Year 1 are subject to the section 2801 tax.

(v) The foreign trust's timely filing of the Form 708 for Year 2 and the timely payment of the section 2801 tax shown on that return is not a valid election under paragraph (d)(5)(iii) of this section because the trust did not timely pay the section 2801 tax on all covered gifts and covered bequests in prior years as required in paragraph (d)(3) of this section; that is, the tax on the additional $300,000 of value of the Year 1 transfer. However, under paragraph (d)(6)(iii)(D) of this section, because the foreign trust timely filed and paid the section 2801 tax on the Year 2 covered gift of $200,000, and the additional unpaid tax was not due until Year 3, the $200,000 amount is no longer considered a covered gift for purposes of computing the section 2801 ratio.

Example 5. Subsequent election after termination of foreign trust election. The facts are the same as in *Example 4*. In Year 3, the foreign trust does not receive a covered gift or covered bequest. However, the trustee decides that making another election to be treated as a domestic trust would be in the best interests of the trust's beneficiaries. Accordingly, by the due date for the Form 708 for Year 3, the trustee timely files the return and pays the section 2801 tax on the portion of the trust attributable to covered gifts and covered bequests. See paragraph (d)(5)(iii) of this section. The trustee calculates the portion of the trust attributable to covered gifts and covered bequests received by the trust in prior calendar years by multiplying the fair market value of the trust on December 31, Year 2, by the section 2801 ratio in effect on that date. See paragraph (d)(3)(iii) of this section. The foreign trust is an electing foreign trust in Year 3.

(f) *Effective/applicability date*.—This section applies on and after the date of publication of a Treasury decision adopting these rules as final regulations in the **Federal Register**. Once these regulations have been published as final regulations in the **Federal Register**, taxpayers may rely upon the final rules of this part for the period beginning June 17, 2008, and ending on the date preceding the date these regulations are published as final regulations in the **Federal Register**. [Reg. § 28.2801-5.]

§ 28.2801-6. Special rules and cross-references.—(a) *Determination of basis*.—For purposes of determining the U.S. recipient's basis in property received as a covered gift or covered bequest, see sections 1015 and 1014, respectively. However, section 1015(d) does not apply to increase the basis in a covered gift to reflect the tax paid under this section. For purposes of determining a U.S. recipient's basis in property received as a covered bequest from a decedent who died during 2010 and whose executor elected under section 301(c) of the Tax Relief, Unemployment Insurance Reauthorization, and Job Creation Act of 2010 not to have the estate tax provisions apply, see section 1022.

(b) *Generation-skipping transfer tax*.—Transfers made by a nonresident not a citizen of the United States (NRA transferor) are subject to generation-skipping transfer (GST) tax only to the extent those transfers are subject to federal estate or gift tax as defined in § 26.2652-1(a)(2). In applying this rule, taxable distributions from a trust and taxable terminations are subject to the GST tax only to the extent the NRA transferor's contributions to the trust were subject to federal estate or gift tax as defined in § 26.2652-1(a)(2). See § 26.2663-2. A transfer is subject to federal estate or gift tax, regardless of whether a federal estate or gift tax return reporting the transfer is timely filed and regardless of whether chapter 15 applies because of a covered expatriate's failure to timely file and pay the section 2801 tax, if applicable.

(c) *Information returns*.—(1) *Gifts and bequests*.—Pursuant to section 6039F and the corresponding regulations, and to the extent provided in Notice 97-34, 1997-1 CB 422, and Form 3520, Part IV, each U.S. person (other than an organization described in section 501(c) and exempt from tax under section 501(a)) who treats an amount received from a foreign person (other than through a foreign trust) as a gift or bequest (including a covered gift or covered bequest) must report such gift or bequest on Part IV of Form 3520 if the value of the total of such gifts and bequests exceeds a certain threshold. A U.S. citizen or resident, as defined in § 28.2801-2(b) but not including a foreign trust that elects to be treated as a domestic trust, is included within the definition of a U.S. person for purposes of section 6039F.

(2) *Foreign trust distributions*.—Pursuant to section 6048(c) and the corresponding regulations, and to the extent provided in Notice 97-34 and Part III of Form 3520, U.S. persons must report each distribution received during the taxable year from a foreign trust on Part III of Form 3520. Under section 6677(a), a penalty of the greater of $10,000 or 35 percent of the gross value of the distribution may be imposed on a U.S. person who fails to timely report the distribution. A U.S. citizen or resident as defined in § 28.2801-2(b), but not including a foreign trust that elects to be treated as a domestic trust, generally is required to report such a distribution under section 6048(c).

(3) *Penalties and use of information*.—The filing of Form 706, Form 706-NA, Form 708, or Form 709 does not relieve a U.S. citizen or resident who is required to file Form 3520 from any penalties imposed under section 6677(a) for failure to comply with section 6048(c), or from any penalties imposed under section 6039F(c) for failure to comply with section 6039F(a). Pursuant to section 6039F(c)(1)(A), the Secretary may determine the tax consequences of the receipt of a purported foreign gift or bequest.

(d) *Application of penalties*.—(1) *Accuracy-related penalties on underpayments*.—The section 6662 accuracy-related penalty may be imposed upon any underpayment of tax attributable to—

(i) A substantial valuation understatement under section 6662(g) of a covered gift or covered bequest; or

(ii) A gross valuation misstatement under section 6662(h) of a covered gift or covered bequest.

(2) *Penalty for substantial and gross valuation misstatements attributable to incorrect appraisals*.—The section 6695A penalty for substantial and gross valuation misstatements attributable to incorrect appraisals may be imposed upon

any person who prepares an appraisal of the value of a covered gift or covered bequest.

(3) *Penalty for failure to file a return and to pay tax*.—See section 6651 for the application of a penalty for the failure to file Form 708, or the failure to pay the section 2801 tax.

(e) *Effective/applicability date*.—This section applies on and after the date of publication of a Treasury decision adopting these rules as final regulations in the **Federal Register**. Once these regulations have been published as final regulations in the **Federal Register**, taxpayers may rely upon the final rules of this part for the period beginning June 17, 2008, and ending on the date preceding the date these regulations are published as final regulations in the **Federal Register**. [Reg. § 28.2801-6.]

§ 28.2801-7. Determining responsibility under section 2801.—(a) *Responsibility of recipients of gifts and bequests from expatriates*.—It is the responsibility of the taxpayer (in this case, the U.S. citizen or resident receiving a gift or bequest from an expatriate or a distribution from a foreign trust funded at least in part by an expatriate) to ascertain the taxpayer's obligations under section 2801, which includes making the determination of whether the transferor is a covered expatriate and whether the transfer is a covered gift or covered bequest.

(b) *Disclosure of return and return information*.—(1) *In general*.—In certain circumstances, the Internal Revenue Service (IRS) may be permitted, upon request of a U.S. citizen or resident in receipt of a gift or bequest from an expatriate, to disclose to the U.S. citizen or resident return or return information of the donor or decedent expatriate that may assist the U S. citizen or resident in determining whether the donor or decedent was a covered expatriate and whether the transfer was a covered gift or covered bequest. The U.S. citizen or resident may not rely upon this information, however, if the U.S. citizen or resident knows, or has reason to know, that the information received from the IRS is incorrect. The circumstances under which such information may be disclosed to a U.S. citizen or resident, and the procedures for requesting such information from the IRS, will be as provided by publication in the Internal Revenue Bulletin (see § 601.601(d)(2)(ii)(b)).

(2) *Rebuttable presumption*.—Unless a living donor expatriate authorizes the disclosure of his or her relevant return or return information to the U.S. citizen or resident receiving the gift, there is a rebuttable presumption that the donor is a covered expatriate and that the gift is a covered gift. A taxpayer who reasonably concludes that a gift or bequest is not subject to section 2801 may file a protective Form 708 in accordance with § 28.6011-1(b) to start the period for the assessment of any section 2801 tax.

(c) *Effective/applicability date*.—This section applies on and after the date of publication of a Treasury decision adopting these rules as final regulations in the **Federal Register**. Once these regulations have been published as final regulations in the **Federal Register**, taxpayers may rely upon the final rules of this part for the period beginning June 17, 2008, and ending on the date preceding the date these regulations are published as final regulations in the **Federal Register**. [Reg. § 28.2801-7.]

INFORMATION AND RETURNS

Gifts and Bequests from Covered Expatriates: Imposition of Tax

Gifts and Bequests from Covered Expatriates: Imposition of Tax.—Reg. § 28.6001-1, relating to a tax on United States citizens and residents who receive gifts or bequests from certain individuals who relinquished United States citizenship or ceased to be lawful permanent residents of the United States on or after June 17, 2008, is proposed (published in the Federal Register on September 10, 2015) (REG-112997-10).

☐ Section 28.6001-1 is added to read as follows:

§ 28.6001-1. Records required to be kept.—(a) *In general*.—Every U.S. recipient as defined in § 28.2801-2(e) subject to taxation under chapter 15 of the Internal Revenue Code must keep, for the purpose of determining the total amount of covered gifts and covered bequests, such permanent books of account or records as are necessary to establish the amount of that person's aggregate covered gifts and covered bequests, and the other information required to be shown on Form 708, "United States Return of Tax for Gifts and Bequests from Covered Expatriates." All documents and vouchers used in preparing the Form 708 must be retained by the person required to file the return so as to be available for inspection whenever required.

(b) *Supplemental information*.—In order that the Internal Revenue Service (IRS) may determine the correct tax, the U.S. recipient as defined in § 28.2801-2(e) must furnish such supplemental information as may be deemed necessary by the IRS. Therefore, the U.S. recipient must furnish, upon request, copies of all documents relating to the covered gift or covered bequest, appraisals of any items included in the aggregate amount of covered gifts and covered bequests, copies of balance sheets and other financial statements obtainable by that person relating to the value of stock or other property constituting the covered gift or covered bequest, and any other information obtainable by that person that may be necessary in the determination of the tax. See section 2801 and the corresponding regulations. For every policy of life insurance listed on the return, the U.S. recipient must procure a statement from the insurance company on Form 712 and file it with the IRS office where the return is filed. If specifically requested by the Commissioner, the insurance company must file this statement directly with the Commissioner. [Reg. § 28.6001-1.]

Gifts and Bequests from Covered Expatriates: Imposition of Tax

Gifts and Bequests from Covered Expatriates: Imposition of Taxs.—Reg. § 28.6011-1, relating to a tax on United States citizens and residents who receive gifts or bequests from certain individuals who relinquished United States citizenship or ceased to be lawful permanent residents of the United States on or after June 17, 2008, is proposed (published in the Federal Register on September 10, 2015) (REG-112997-10).

☐ Section 28.6011-1 is added to read as follows:

§ 28.6011-1. Returns.—(a) *Return required.*—The return of any tax to which this part 28 applies must be made on Form 708, "United States Return of Tax for Gifts and Bequests from Covered Expatriates," according to the instructions applicable to the form. With respect to each covered gift and covered bequest received during the calendar year, the U.S. recipient as defined in § 28.2801-2(e) must include on Form 708 the information set forth in § 25.6019-4. The U.S. recipient must file Form 708 for each calendar year in which a covered gift or covered bequest is received. The U.S. recipient who receives the covered gift or covered bequest during the calendar year is the person required to file the return. A U.S. recipient is not required to file such form, however, for a calendar year in which the total fair market value of all covered gifts and covered bequests received by that person during that calendar year is less than or equal to the section 2801(c) amount, which is the dollar amount of the per-donee exclusion in effect under section 2503(b) for that calendar year.

(b) *Protective return.*—(i) A U.S. citizen or resident (as defined in § 28.2801-2(b)) that receives a gift or bequest from an expatriate and reasonably concludes that the gift or bequest is not a covered gift or a covered bequest from a covered expatriate may file a protective Form 708 in order to start the period for assessment of tax. To be a protective Form 708, it must provide all of the information otherwise required on Form 708, along with an affidavit, signed under penalties of perjury, setting forth the information on which that U.S. citizen or resident has relied in concluding that the donor or decedent, as the case may be, was not a covered expatriate, or that the transfer was not a covered gift or a covered bequest, as well as that person's efforts to obtain other information that might be relevant to these determinations. If that U.S. citizen or resident has obtained information from the Internal Revenue Service (IRS) (as described in § 28.2801-7(b)(1)), it must attach a copy of such information. The U.S. citizen or resident also must attach a copy of a completed Form 3520, Part III, for all trust distributions, or Part IV for all gifts and bequests, if applicable. If the return meets the requirements of this paragraph (b)(i), and if the IRS does not assess a section 2801 tax liability for that tax year within the limitations period for assessment stated in section 6501, the IRS may not later assess a section 2801 tax with regard to any transfer reported on that Form 708.

(ii) A U.S. citizen or resident who receives a gift or bequest from an expatriate and who files a protective Form 708 meeting the requirements of paragraph (b)(i) of this section showing no tax due, absent fraud or other special factors, will not be subject to any additions to tax for late filing under section 6651(a)(1) or for late payment under section 6651(a)(2), even if the gift or bequest is determined to be a covered gift or covered bequest from a covered expatriate within the limitations period for assessment stated in section 6501. Notwithstanding the foregoing, however, if a U.S. citizen or resident knows, or has reason to know, that the information provided by the IRS or any other source is incorrect or incomplete, that U.S. citizen or resident may not rely on that information, and except as provided in the preceding paragraph (b)(i) of this section, may be subject to all of the generally applicable provisions governing assessment of tax, collection of tax, and penalties. See sections 6501, 6502, 6651 and 6662.

(c) *Effective/applicability dates.*—This section applies on and after the date of publication of a Treasury decision adopting these rules as final regulations in the **Federal Register**. [Reg. § 28.6011-1.]

Reportable Transactions: Disclosure: Patented Transactions

Reportable Transactions: Disclosure: Patented Transactions.—Amendments to Reg. § 1.6011-4, providing rules to the disclosure of reportable transactions, including patented transactions, under Code Secs. 6011 and 6111, are proposed (published in the Federal Register on September 26, 2007) (REG-129916-07).

☐ Par. 2. Section 1.6011-4 is amended by:

1. Revising paragraphs (b)(7) and (c)(3)(i)(F).

2. Adding to paragraph (c)(3)(ii) *Examples 4, 5, 6,* and *7*.

3. Revising paragraph (h)(2).

The revisions and additions read as follows:

§ 1.6011-4. Requirement of statement disclosing participation in certain transactions by taxpayers.

* * *

(b) * * *

(7) *Patented transactions.*—(i) *In general.*—A patented transaction is a transaction for which a taxpayer pays (directly or indirectly) a fee in any amount to a patent holder or the patent holder's agent for the legal right to use a tax planning method that the taxpayer knows or has reason to know is the subject of the patent. A patented transaction also is a transaction for which a taxpayer (the patent holder or the patent holder's agent) has the right to payment for another person's use of a tax planning method that is the subject of the patent.

(ii) *Definitions.*—For purposes of this paragraph (b)(7), the following definitions apply:

(A) *Fee.*—The term *fee* means consideration in whatever form paid, whether in cash or in kind, for the right to use a tax planning method that is the subject of a patent. The term *fee* includes any consideration the taxpayer knows or has reason to know will be paid indirectly to the patent holder or patent holder's agent, such as through a referral fee, fee-sharing arrangement, or license. The term *fee* does not include amounts paid in settlement of, or as the award of damages in, a suit for damages for infringement of the patent.

(B) *Patent.*—The term *patent* means a patent granted under the provisions of title 35 of the United States Code, or any foreign patent granting rights generally similar to those under a United States patent. See § 1.1235-2(a). The term *patent* includes patents that have been applied for but not yet granted.

(C) *Patent holder.*—A person is a patent holder if—

(1) The person is a holder as defined in § 1.1235-2(d) and (e);

(2) The person would be a holder as defined in § 1.1235-2(d)(2) if the phrase *S corporation or trust* was substituted for the word *partnership* and the phrase *shareholder or beneficiary* was substituted for the words *member* and *partner;*

(3) The person is an employer of a holder as defined in § 1.1235-2(d) and the holder transferred to the employer all substantial rights to the patent as defined in § 1.1235-2(b); or

(4) The person receives all substantial rights to the patent as defined in § 1.1235-2(b) in exchange (directly or indirectly) for consideration in any form.

(D) *Patent holder's agent.*—The term *patent holder's agent* means any person who has the permission of the patent holder to offer for sale or exchange, to sell or exchange, or to market a tax planning method that is the subject of a patent. The term *patent holder's agent* also means any person who receives (directly or indirectly) for or on behalf of a patent holder a fee in any amount for a tax planning method that is the subject of a patent.

(E) *Payment.*—The term *payment* includes consideration in whatever form paid, whether in cash or in kind, for the right to use a tax planning method that is the subject of a patent. For example, if a patent holder or patent holder's agent receives payment for a patented transaction and a separate payment for another transaction, part or all of the payment for the other transaction may be treated as payment for the patented transaction if the facts and circumstances indicate that the payment for the other transaction is in consideration for the patented transaction. The term *payment* also includes amounts paid in settlement of, or as the award of damages in, a suit for damages for infringement of the patent.

(F) *Tax planning method.*—The term *tax planning method* means any plan, strategy, technique, or structure designed to affect Federal income, estate, gift, generation skipping transfer, employment, or excise taxes. A patent issued solely for tax preparation software or other tools used to perform or model mathematical calculations or to provide mechanical assistance in the preparation of tax or information returns is not a tax planning method.

(iii) *Related parties.*—For purposes of this paragraph (b)(7), persons who bear a relationship to each other as described in section 267(b) or 707(b) will be treated as the same person.

* * *

(c) * * *

(3) * * *

(i) * * *

(F) *Patented transactions.*—A taxpayer has participated in a patented transaction, as defined in paragraph (b)(7) of this section, if the taxpayer's tax return reflects a tax benefit from the transaction (including a deduction for fees paid in any amount to the patent holder or patent holder's agent). A taxpayer also has participated in a patented transaction, as defined in paragraph (b)(7) of this section, if the taxpayer is the patent holder or patent holder's agent and the taxpayer's tax return reflects a tax benefit in relation to obtaining a patent for a tax planning method (including any deduction for amounts paid to the United States Patent and Trademark Office as required by title 35 of the United States Code and attorney's fees) or reflects income from a payment received from another person for the use of the tax planning method that is the subject of the patent.

* * *

(ii) * * *

Example 4. (i) A, an individual, creates a tax planning method and applies for a U.S. patent. A pays attorney fees in relation to obtaining the patent and A pays the fee required under title 35 of the United States Code for the patent application. Subsequently, C pays a fee to A for the legal right to use the tax planning method that C knows or has reason to know is the subject of A's patent. A's tax return reflects both a deduction for an amount paid in relation to obtaining a patent and income from C's payment to A for the legal right to use the tax planning method that is the subject of the patent. C's tax return reflects a deduction for an amount paid to A for the right to use the tax planning method that is the subject of the patent.

(ii) A is a patent holder under paragraph (b)(7)(ii)(C)(*1*) of this section. The transaction is a reportable transaction for A under paragraph (b)(7) of this section because A has the right to payment for another person's use of the tax planning method that is the subject of the patent. The transaction is a reportable transaction for C under paragraph (b)(7) of this section, because C paid a fee to A for the legal right to use a tax planning method that C knew or had reason to know was the subject of a patent. A has participated in the transaction in the year in which A's tax return reflects a tax benefit in relation to obtaining the patent or reflects income from C's payment to A for the legal right to use the tax planning method that is the subject of the patent. C has participated in the transaction in the year in which C's tax return reflects the deduction for any amount paid to A for the legal right to use the tax planning method that is the subject of the patent. C also participates in the transaction for any years for which any other tax benefit from the transaction is reflected on C's tax return.

Example 5. (i) A, an individual, is the employee of B, a corporation. A creates a tax planning method and applies for a U.S. patent but B pays the fee required under title 35 of the United States Code for A's patent application. Pursuant to A's employment contract with B, B holds all substantial rights to the patent. B's tax return reflects a deduction for the amount paid in relation to obtaining the patent.

(ii) A and B are patent holders under paragraph (b)(7)(ii)(C)(*1*) and (3) of this section, respectively. The transaction is not a reportable transaction for A under paragraph (b)(7) of this section because A does not have the right to payment for another person's use of the tax planning method that is the subject of the patent. The transaction is a reportable transaction for B under paragraph (b)(7) of this section because B holds all substantial rights to the patent and has the right to payment for another person's use of the tax planning method that is the subject of the patent. B has participated in the transaction in the year in which B's tax return reflects a tax benefit in relation to obtaining the patent. B also participates in the transaction for any years for which B's tax return reflects income from a payment received from another person for the use of the tax planning method that is the subject of the patent.

Example 6. (i) Assume the facts as in *Example 4*, except that A agrees to license the patent to F, a financial institution. The license agreement between A and F provides that F may offer the tax planning method to its clients and if a client decides to use the tax planning method, F must pay A for each client's use of the tax planning method. F offers the tax planning method to G who uses the tax planning method and knows or has reason to know it is the subject of a patent. F charges G for financial planning services and pays A for G's use of the tax planning method. A's tax return reflects income from the payment received from F. F's tax return reflects income from the payment received from G, and G's tax return reflects a deduction for the fees paid to F.

(ii) F is a patent holder's agent under paragraph (b)(7)(ii)(D) of this section because F has the permission of the patent holder to offer for sale or exchange, to sell or exchange, or to market a tax planning method that is the subject of a patent. F also is a patent holder's agent under paragraph (b)(7)(ii)(D) of this section because F receives (directly or indirectly) a fee in any amount for a tax planning method that is the subject of a patent for or on behalf of a patent holder. The transaction is a reportable transaction for both A and F under paragraph (b)(7) of this section because A and F each have the right to payment for another person's use of the tax planning method that is the subject of the patent. The transaction is a reportable transaction for G under paragraph (b)(7) of this section because G paid a fee (directly or indirectly) to a patent holder or a patent holder's agent for the legal right to use a tax planning method that G knew or had reason to know was the subject of the patent. A has participated in the transaction in the years in which A's tax return reflects income from the payment received from F for G's use of the tax planning method that is the subject of the patent. F has participated in the transaction in the years in which F's tax return reflects income from the payment received from G for use of the tax planning method that is the subject of the patent. G has participated in the transaction in the years in which G's tax return reflects a deduction for the fees paid to F. G also participates in the transaction for any years for which any other tax benefit from the transaction is reflected on G's tax return.

Example 7. Assume the same facts as in *Example 4*. J uses a tax planning method that is the same as the tax planning method that is the subject of A's patent. J does not pay any fees to any patent holder or patent holder's agent with respect to the tax planning method that is the subject of the patent. A sues J for infringement of the patent and J pays A an amount for damages. A's tax return reflects as income the amounts for damages received from J. The transaction is not a reportable transaction for J under paragraph (b)(7) of this section because J did not pay any fees (as defined in paragraph (b)(7)(ii)(A) of this section) (directly or indirectly) to a patent holder or patent holder's agent for the legal right to use a tax planning method that J knew or had reason to know was the subject of the patent. A has participated in a reportable transaction under paragraph (b)(7) of this section in the year in which A's tax return reflects income from a payment (the amount received as an award for damages in a suit for damages for infringement of the patent) received from another person for the use of the tax planning method that is the subject of a patent.

* * *

(h) * * *

(2) *Patented transactions.*—Upon the publication of the Treasury decision adopting these rules as final regulations in the **Federal Register**, paragraphs (b)(7), (c)(3)(i)(F), and (c)(3)(ii) *Examples 4* through *7* of this section will apply to transactions entered into on or after September 26, 2007.

Estate and Person Acquiring Property from Decedent: Consistent Basis Reporting

Estate and Person Acquiring Property from Decedent: Consistent Basis Reporting.—Amendments to Reg. § 1.6035-1, providing guidance regarding the requirement that a recipient's basis in certain property acquired from a decedent be consistent with the value of the property as finally determined for Federal estate tax purposes, are proposed (published in the Federal Register on March 4, 2016) (REG-127923-15). Proposed Reg. § 1.6035-2 has been adopted by T.D. 9797 on December 1, 2016. Proposed Reg. § 1.6035-3 was removed by T.D. 9849 on March 11, 2019.

☐ Par. 3. Section 1.6035-1 is revised to read as follows:

§ 1.6035-1. Basis information to persons acquiring property from decedent.—(a) *Required Information Return and Statement(s).*—(1) *In general.*—An executor (defined in paragraph (g)(1) of this section) required to file a return under section 6018 for an estate must file an Information Return (defined in paragraph (g)(2) of this section) with the Internal Revenue Service (IRS) to report the value of certain property (described in paragraph (b)(1) of this section) included in the decedent's gross estate for purposes of the tax imposed by chapter 11 of subtitle B of the Internal Revenue Code (chapter 11) and other information prescribed by the Information Return and the instructions thereto. The value to be reported is the final value of the property as described in § 1.1014-10(c). This executor also must furnish a Statement (defined in paragraph (g)(3) of this section) to each beneficiary who has (or will) acquire, whether from the decedent or by reason of the death of the decedent, property reported on the Information Return to identify the property the beneficiary is to receive and to report the value of that property and other information prescribed by the Statement and instructions thereto. The Information Return and each Statement are required to be filed and furnished by the date provided in paragraph (d) of this section. If, after the Information Return and Statement are filed and furnished, there are certain changes in the final value and/or the recipient of property as described in paragraph (e) or (f) of this section, the executor must file a supplemental Information Return with the IRS and furnish a supplemental Statement to the beneficiary. Subsequent transfers of all or a portion of property previously reported (or required to be reported) on the Information Return required by paragraph (a) of this section, in transactions in which the transferee acquires the property with the transferor's basis, require additional reporting as described in paragraph (f) of this section.

(2) *Exception.*—Paragraph (a)(1) of this section applies only to the executor of an estate required by section 6018 to file an estate tax return. Accordingly, notwithstanding § 20.2010-2(a)(1), the executor does not have to file or furnish the Information Return or Statement(s) referred to in paragraph (a)(1) of this section if the executor is not required by section 6018 to file an estate tax return for the estate, even if the executor does file such a return for other purposes, e.g., to make a generation-skipping transfer tax exemption allocation or election, to make the portability election under section 2010(c)(5), or to make a protective filing to avoid any penalty if an asset value is later determined to cause a return to be required or otherwise.

(b) *Property for which reporting is required.*—(1) *In general.*—The property to which the reporting requirement under paragraph (a)(1) of this section applies is all property reported or required to be reported on a return under section 6018. This includes, for example, any other property whose basis is determined in whole or in part by reference to that property (for example as the result of a like-kind exchange or involuntary conversion). Of the property of a deceased nonresident non-citizen, this includes only the property that is subject to U.S. estate tax; similarly, this includes only the decedent's one-half of community property. Nevertheless, the following property is excepted from the reporting requirements—

(i) Cash (other than a coin collection or other coins or bills with numismatic value);

(ii) Income in respect of a decedent (as defined in section 691);

(iii) Tangible personal property for which an appraisal is not required under § 20.2031-6(b); and

(iv) Property sold, exchanged, or otherwise disposed of (and therefore not distributed to a beneficiary) by the estate in a transaction in which capital gain or loss is recognized.

(2) *Examples.*—The following examples illustrate the provisions of paragraph (b)(1) of this section.

Example 1. Included in D's gross estate are the contents of his residence. Pursuant to § 20.2031-6(a), the executor attaches to the return required by section 6018 filed for D's estate a room by room itemization of household and personal effects. All articles are named specifically. In each room a number of articles, none of which has a value in excess of $100, are grouped. A value is provided for each named article. Included in the household and personal effects are a painting, a rug, and a clock, each of which has a value in excess of $3,000. Pursuant to § 20.2031-6(b), the executor obtains an appraisal from a disinterested, competent appraiser(s) of recognized standing and ability, or a disinterested dealer(s) in the class of personalty involved for the painting, rug, and clock. The executor attaches these appraisals to the estate tax return for D's estate. Pursuant to paragraph (b)(1)(iii) of this section, the reporting requirements of paragraph (a)(1) of this section apply only to the painting, rug, and clock.

Example 2. Included in D's estate are shares in C, a publicly traded company. Shortly after D's death but prior to the filing of the estate tax return for D's estate, C is acquired by T, also a publicly traded company. For the shares in C includible in D's estate, the estate receives new shares in T and cash in a fully taxable transaction. Pursuant to paragraph (b)(1)(iv) of this section, the reporting requirements of paragraph (a)(1) of this section do not apply to the new shares in T or the cash.

(c) *Beneficiaries.*—(1) *In general.*—As provided in paragraph (a)(1) of this section, the executor must furnish to each beneficiary (including a beneficiary who is also an executor) receiving property that must be reported on the Information Return filed with the IRS, the Statement containing the required information regarding that beneficiary's property. For purposes of this provision, the beneficiary of a life estate is the life tenant, the beneficiary of a remainder interest is the remainderman(men) identified as if the life tenant were to die immediately after the decedent, and the beneficiary of a contingent interest is a beneficiary, unless the contingency has occurred prior to the filing of the Form 8971. If the contingency subsequently negates the inheritance of the beneficiary, the executor must do supplemental reporting in accordance with paragraph (e) of this section to report the change of beneficiary.

(2) *Beneficiary not an individual.*—If the beneficiary is a trust or another estate, the executor must furnish the beneficiary's Statement to the trustee or executor of the trust or estate, rather than to the beneficiaries of that trust or estate. If the beneficiary is a business entity, the executor must furnish the Statement to the entity. However, see paragraph (f) of this section for additional reporting requirements in the event the trust, estate, or entity transfers all or a portion of the property in a transaction in which the transferee acquires the basis of the trust, estate, or entity.

(3) *Beneficiary not determined.*—If, by the due date provided in paragraph (d) of this section, the executor has not determined what property will be used to satisfy the interest of each beneficiary, the executor must report on the Statement for each such beneficiary all of the property that the executor could use to satisfy that beneficiary's interest. Once the exact distribution has been determined, the executor may, but is not required to, file and furnish a supplemental Information Return and Statement as provided in paragraph (e)(3) of this section.

(4) *Beneficiary not located.*—An executor must use reasonable due diligence to identify and locate all beneficiaries. If the executor is unable to locate a beneficiary by the due date of the Information Return provided in paragraph (d) of this section, the executor must so report on that Information Return and explain the efforts the executor has taken to locate the beneficiary and to satisfy the obligation of reasonable due diligence. If the executor subsequently locates the beneficiary, the executor must furnish the beneficiary with that beneficiary's Statement and file a supplemental Information Return with the IRS within 30 days of locating the beneficiary. A copy of the beneficiary's Statement must be attached to the supplemental Information Return. If the executor is unable to locate a beneficiary and distributes the property to a different beneficiary who was not identified in the Information Return as the recipient of that property, the executor must file a supplemental Information Return with the IRS and furnish the substitute beneficiary with that beneficiary's Statement within 30 days after the property is distributed. See paragraph (e)(1) of this section. A copy of the substitute beneficiary's Statement must be attached to the supplemental Information Return.

(d) *Due dates.*—(1) *In general.*—Except as provided in § 1.6035-2T, the executor must file the Information Return with the IRS, and must furnish to each beneficiary the Statement with regard to the property to be received by that beneficiary, on or before the earlier of—

(i) The date that is 30 days after the due date of the estate tax return required by section 6018 (including extensions, if any), or

(ii) The date that is 30 days after the date on which that return is filed with the IRS.

(2) *Transition rule.*—If the due date of an estate tax return required to be filed by section 6018 is on or before July 31, 2015, but the executor does not file the return with the IRS until after July 31, 2015, then the Information Return and Statement(s) are due on or before the date that is 30 days after the date on which the estate tax return is filed, except as provided in § 1.6035-2T.

(e) *Duty to supplement.*—(1) *In general.*—In the event of any adjustment to the information required to be reported on the Information Return or any Statement as described in paragraph (e)(2) of this section, the executor must file a supplemental Information Return with the IRS including all supplemental Statements and furnish a corresponding supplemental Statement to each affected beneficiary by the due date described in paragraph (e)(4) of this section.

(2) *Adjustments requiring supplement.*—Except as provided in paragraph (e)(3) of this section, an adjustment to which the duty to supplement applies is any change to the information required to be reported on the Information Return or Statement that causes the information as reported to be incorrect or incomplete. Such changes include, for example, the discovery of property that should have been (but was not) reported on an estate tax return described in section 6018, a change in the value of property pursuant to an examination or litigation, or a change in the identity of the beneficiary to whom the property is to be distributed (pursuant to a death, disclaimer, bankruptcy, or otherwise). Such changes also include the executor's disposition of property acquired from the decedent or as a result of the death of the decedent in a transaction in which the basis of new property received by the estate is determined in whole or in part by reference to the property acquired from the decedent or as a result of the death of the decedent (for example as the result of a like-kind exchange or involuntary conversion). Changes requiring supplement pursuant to this paragraph (e)(2) are not inconsequential errors or omissions within the meaning of § 301.6722-1(b) of this chapter.

(3) *Adjustments not requiring supplement.*—(i) *In general.*—A supplemental Information Return and Statement may but they are not required to be filed or furnished-

(A) To correct an inconsequential error or omission within the meaning of § 301.6722-1(b) of this chapter, or

(B) To specify the actual distribution of property previously reported as being available to satisfy the interests of multiple beneficiaries in the situation described in paragraph (c)(3) of this section.

(ii) *Example.*—Paragraph (e)(3)(i)(B) of this section is illustrated by the following example.

Example 1. D's Will provided for D's residuary estate to be distributed to D's three children (E, F, and G). D's residuary estate included stock in a publicly traded company (X), a personal residence, and three paintings. On the due date of the Information Return and Statement required by paragraph (a)(1) of this section, D's executor had not yet determined which property each child would receive from D's residuary estate in satisfaction of that child's bequest. In accordance with paragraph (c)(3) of this section, D's executor reported on the Information Return filed with the IRS and on each child's own Statement that E, F, and G each might receive an interest in the stock in X, the personal residence, and the three paintings. Several months later, the executor determined that E would receive the stock in X, F would receive the residence, and G would receive the paintings. Paragraph (e)(3)(i)(B) of this section provides that the executor may but is not required to file a supplemental Information Return with the IRS and furnish supplemental Statements to E, F, and G to accurately report which beneficiary received what property.

Example 2. D's Will provided that D's jewelry and household effects (personalty) are to be distributed among D's three children (E, F, and G) as determined by E, F, and G. In accordance with paragraph (c)(3) of this section, D's executor reports on the Information Return filed with the IRS and on each child's own Statement each item of personalty other than items described in paragraph (b)(1)(iii) of this section. Several months later, E, F, and G determine who is to receive each item of personalty. Paragraph (e)(3)(i)(B) of this section provides that the executor may but is not required to file a supplemental Information Return with the IRS and furnish supplemental Statements to E, F, and G to accurately report which beneficiary received which item(s) of personalty.

(4) *Due date of supplemental reporting.*—(i) *In general.*—Except as provided in paragraph (e)(4)(ii) of this section, the supplemental Information Return must be filed and each supplemental Statement must be furnished on or before 30 days after—

(A) The final value within the meaning of § 1.1014-10(c)(1) is determined;

(B) The executor discovers that the information reported on the Information Return or Statement is otherwise incorrect or incomplete, except to the extent described in paragraph (e)(3)(i) of this section; or

(C) A supplemental estate tax return under section 6018 is filed reporting property not reported on a previously filed estate tax return pursuant to § 1.1014-10(c)(3)(i). In this case, a copy of the supplemental Statement provided to each beneficiary of an interest in this property must be attached to the supplemental Information Return.

(ii) *Probate property or property from decedent's revocable trust.*—With respect to property in the probate estate or held by a revocable trust at the decedent's death, if an event described in paragraph (e)(4)(i)(A), (B), or (C) of this section occurs after the decedent's date of death but before or on the date the property is distributed to the beneficiary, the due date for the supplemental Information Return and corresponding supplemental Statement is the date that is 30 days after the date the property is distributed to the beneficiary. If the executor chooses to furnish to the beneficiary on the Statement information regarding any changes to the basis of the reported property as described in § 1.1014-10(a)(2) that occurred after the date of death but before or on the date of distribution, that basis adjustment information (which is not part of the requirement under section 6035) must be shown separately from the final value required to be reported on that Statement.

(f) *Subsequent transfers.*—If all or any portion of property that previously was reported or is required to be reported on an Information Return (and thus on the recipient's Statement or supplemental Statement) is distributed or transferred (by gift or otherwise) by the recipient in a transaction in which a related transferee determines its basis, in whole or in part, by reference to the recipient/transferor's basis, the recipient/transferor must, no later than 30 days after the date of the distribution or other transfer, file with the IRS a supplemental Statement and furnish a copy of the same supplemental Statement to the transferee. The requirement to file a supplemental Statement and furnish a copy to the transferee similarly applies to the distribution or transfer of any other property the basis of which is determined in whole or in part by reference to that property (for example as the result of a like-kind exchange or involuntary conversion). In the case of a supplemental Statement filed by the recipient/transferor before the recipient/transferor's receipt of the Statement described in paragraph (a) of this section, the supplemental Statement will report the change in the ownership of the property and need not provide the value information that would otherwise be required on the supplemental Statement. In the event the transfer occurs before the final value is determined within the meaning of proposed §1.1014-10(c), the transferor must provide the executor with a copy of the supplemental Statement filed with the IRS and furnished to the transferee in order to notify the executor of the change in ownership of the property. When the executor subsequently files any Return and issues any Statement required by paragraphs (a) or (e) of this section, the executor must provide the Statement (or supplemental Statement) to the new transferee instead of to the transferor. For purposes of this provision, a related transferee means any member of the transferor's family as defined in section 2704(c)(2), any controlled entity (a corporation or any other entity in which the transferor and members of the transferor's family (as defined in section 2704(c)(2)), whether directly or indirectly, have control within the meaning of section 2701(b)(2)(A) or (B)), and any trust of which the transferor is a deemed owner for income tax purposes. If the transferor chooses to include on the supplemental Statement provided to the transferee information regarding any changes to the basis of the reported property as described in §1.1014-10(a)(2) that occurred during the transferor's ownership of the property, that basis adjustment information (which is not part of the requirement under section 6035) must be shown separately from the final value required to be reported on that Statement.

(g) *Definitions.*—For purposes of this section, the following terms are defined as follows—

(1) *Executor* has the same meaning as in section 2203 and includes any other person required under section 6018(b) to file a return.

(2) *Information Return* means the Form 8971, including each beneficiary's Statement as defined in paragraph (g)(3) of this section required to be furnished, or any successor form issued by the IRS for this purpose.

(3) *Statement* means the payee statement described as Schedule A of the Information Return furnished to a beneficiary or any successor form or schedule issued by the IRS for this purpose.

(h) *Penalties.*—(1) *Failure to timely file complete and correct Information Return.*—For provisions relating to the penalty provided for failure to file an Information Return required by section 6035(a)(1) on or before the required filing date, failure to include all of the required information on an Information Return, or the filing of an Information Return that includes incorrect information, see section 6721 and the regulations thereunder. See section 6724 and the regulations thereunder for rules relating to waivers of penalties for certain failures due to reasonable cause.

(2) *Failure to timely furnish correct Statements.*—For provisions relating to the penalty provided for failure to furnish a Statement required by section 6035(a)(2) on or before the prescribed date, failure to include all of the required information on a Statement, or the filing of a Statement that includes incorrect information, see section 6722 and the regulations thereunder. See section 6724 and the regulations thereunder for rules relating to waivers of penalties for certain failures due to reasonable cause.

(i) *Effective/applicability date.*—Upon the publication of the Treasury Decision adopting these rules as final in the **Federal Register**, this section will apply to property acquired from a decedent or by reason of the death of a decedent whose return required by section 6018 is filed after July 31, 2015. Persons may rely upon these rules before the date of publication of the Treasury Decision adopting these rules as final in the **Federal Register**.

Gifts and Bequests from Covered Expatriates: Imposition of Tax

Gifts and Bequests from Covered Expatriates: Imposition of Tax.—Reg. §28.6060-1, relating to a tax on United States citizens and residents who receive gifts or bequests from certain individuals who relinquished United States citizenship or ceased to be lawful permanent residents of the United States on or after June 17, 2008, is proposed (published in the Federal Register on September 10, 2015) (REG-112997-10).

☐ Section 28.6060-1 is added to read as follows:

§28.6060-1. Reporting requirements for tax return preparers.—(a) *In general.*—A person that employs one or more signing tax return preparers to prepare a return or claim for refund of any tax to which this part 28 applies, other than for the person, at any time during a return period, must satisfy the recordkeeping and inspection requirements in the manner stated in §1.6060-1 of this chapter.

(b) *Effective/applicability date.*—This section applies to returns and claims for refund filed on or after the date of publication of a Treasury decision adopting these rules as final regulations in the **Federal Register**. [Reg. § 28.6060-1.]

Gifts and Bequests from Covered Expatriates: Imposition of Tax

Gifts and Bequests from Covered Expatriates: Imposition of Tax.—Reg. § 28.6071-1, relating to a tax on United States citizens and residents who receive gifts or bequests from certain individuals who relinquished United States citizenship or ceased to be lawful permanent residents of the United States on or after June 17, 2008, is proposed (published in the Federal Register on September 10, 2015) (REG-112997-10).

☐ Section 28.6071-1 is added to read as follows:

§ 28.6071-1. Time for filing returns.—(a) *In general.*—(1) A U.S. recipient as defined in § 28.2801-2(e) must file Form 708, "U.S. Return of Gifts or Bequests from Covered Expatriates," on or before the fifteenth day of the eighteenth calendar month following the close of the calendar year in which the covered gift or covered bequest was received. Notwithstanding the preceding sentence, the due date for a Form 708 reporting a covered bequest that is not received on the decedent's date of death under § 28.2801-4(d)(3) is the later of—

(i) The fifteenth day of the eighteenth calendar month following the close of the calendar year in which the covered expatriate died; or

(ii) The fifteenth day of the sixth month of the calendar year following the close of the calendar year in which the covered bequest was received.

(2) If a U.S. recipient receives multiple covered gifts and covered bequests during the same calendar year, the rule in paragraph (a)(1) of this section may result in different due dates and the filing of multiple returns reporting the different transfers received during the same calendar year.

(b) *Migrated foreign trust.*—The due date for a Form 708 for the year in which a foreign trust becomes a domestic trust is the fifteenth day of the sixth month of the calendar year following the close of the calendar year in which the foreign trust becomes a domestic trust.

(c) *Certain returns by foreign trusts.*—(1) *Election under § 28.2801-5(d) for calendar year in which no covered gift or covered bequest received.*—A foreign trust making an election to be treated as a domestic trust for purposes of section 2801 under § 28.2801-5(d) for a calendar year in which the foreign trust received no covered gifts or covered bequests must file a Form 708 on or before the fifteenth day of the sixth month of the calendar year following the close of the calendar year for which the election is made.

(2) *Certification to maintain election under § 28.2801-5(d) for calendar year in which no covered gift or covered bequest received.*—An electing foreign trust filing a Form 708 to certify that the electing foreign trust did not receive any covered gifts or covered bequests during the calendar year must file the Form 708 on or before the fifteenth day of the sixth month of the calendar year following the close of that calendar year. See § 28.2801-5(d)(4).

(d) *Transition period.*—The Form 708 reporting covered gifts or covered bequests received on or after June 17, 2008, and before the date of publication of a Treasury decision adopting these rules as final regulations in the **Federal Register**, will be due within a reasonable period of time after the date of that publication as specified in the final regulations, but in no event before the due date of the first return required under the final regulations for covered gifts or covered bequests received after the final regulations are published.

(e) *Effective/applicability dates.*—This section applies to each Form 708 filed on or after the date on which a Treasury decision is published adopting these rules as final regulations in the **Federal Register**. [Reg. § 28.6071-1.]

Gifts and Bequests from Covered Expatriates: Imposition of Tax

Gifts and Bequests from Covered Expatriates: Imposition of Tax.—Reg. § 28.6081-1, relating to a tax on United States citizens and residents who receive gifts or bequests from certain individuals who relinquished United States citizenship or ceased to be lawful permanent residents of the United States on or after June 17, 2008, is proposed (published in the Federal Register on September 10, 2015) (REG-112997-10).

☐ Section 28.6081-1 is added to read as follows:

§ 28.6081-1. Automatic extension of time for filing returns reporting gifts and bequests from covered expatriates.—(a) *In general.*—A U.S. recipient as defined in § 28.2801-2(e) may request an extension of time to file a Form 708, "U.S. Return of Gifts or Bequests from Covered Expatriates," by filing Form 7004, "Application for Automatic Extension of Time to file Certain Business Income Tax, Information, and Other Returns." A U.S. recipient must include on Form 7004 an estimate of the amount of section 2801 tax liability and must file Form 7004 with the Internal Revenue Service office designated in the Form's instructions (except as provided in § 301.6091-1(b) of this chapter for hand-carried documents).

(b) *Automatic extension.*—A U.S. recipient as defined in § 28.2801-2(e) will be allowed an automatic six-month extension of time beyond the date prescribed in §28.6071-1 to file Form 708 if Form 7004 is filed on or before the due date for filing Form 708 in accordance with the procedures under paragraph (a) of this section.

(c) *No extension of time for the payment of tax.*—An automatic extension of time for filing a return granted under paragraph (b) of this section will not extend the time for payment of any tax due with such return.

(d) *Penalties.*—See section 6651 regarding penalties for failure to file the required tax return or failure to pay the amount shown as tax on the return.

(e) *Effective/applicability dates.*—This section applies to applications for an extension of time to file Form 708 filed on or after the date of publication of a Treasury decision adopting these rules as final regulations in the **Federal Register**. [Reg. §28.6081-1.]

Gifts and Bequests from Covered Expatriates: Imposition of Tax

Gifts and Bequests from Covered Expatriates: Imposition of Tax.—Reg. §28.6091-1, relating to a tax on United States citizens and residents who receive gifts or bequests from certain individuals who relinquished United States citizenship or ceased to be lawful permanent residents of the United States on or after June 17, 2008, is proposed (published in the Federal Register on September 10, 2015) (REG-112997-10).

☐ Section 28.6091-1 is added to read as follows:

§28.6091-1. Place for filing returns.—A U.S. recipient as defined in §28.2801-2(e) must file Form 708, "U.S. Return of Gifts and Bequests from Covered Expatriates," with the Internal Revenue Service office designated in the instructions applicable to the Form. [Reg. §28.6091-1.]

Gifts and Bequests from Covered Expatriates: Imposition of Tax

Gifts and Bequests from Covered Expatriates: Imposition of Tax.—Reg. §28.6101-1, relating to a tax on United States citizens and residents who receive gifts or bequests from certain individuals who relinquished United States citizenship or ceased to be lawful permanent residents of the United States on or after June 17, 2008, is proposed (published in the Federal Register on September 10, 2015) (REG-112997-10).

☐ Section 28.6101-1 is added to read as follows:

§28.6101-1. Period covered by returns.—See §28.6011-1 for the rules relating to the period covered by the return. [Reg. §28.6101-1.]

Gifts and Bequests from Covered Expatriates: Imposition of Tax

Gifts and Bequests from Covered Expatriates: Imposition of Tax.—Reg. §28.6107-1, relating to a tax on United States citizens and residents who receive gifts or bequests from certain individuals who relinquished United States citizenship or ceased to be lawful permanent residents of the United States on or after June 17, 2008, is proposed (published in the Federal Register on September 10, 2015) (REG-112997-10).

☐ Section 28.6107-1 is added to read as follows:

§28.6107-1. Tax return preparer must furnish copy of return or claim for refund to taxpayer and must retain a copy or record.—(a) *In general.*—A person who is a signing tax return preparer of any return or claim for refund of any tax to which this part 28 applies must furnish a completed copy of the return or claim for refund to the taxpayer and retain a completed copy or record in the manner stated in §1.6107-1 of this chapter.

(b) *Effective/applicability dates.*—This section applies to returns and claims for refund filed on or after the date of publication of a Treasury decision adopting these rules as final regulations in the **Federal Register**. [Reg. §28.6107-1.]

Gifts and Bequests from Covered Expatriates: Imposition of Tax

Gifts and Bequests from Covered Expatriates: Imposition of Tax.—Reg. §28.6109-1, relating to a tax on United States citizens and residents who receive gifts or bequests from certain individuals who relinquished United States citizenship or ceased to be lawful permanent residents of the United States on or after June 17, 2008, is proposed (published in the Federal Register on September 10, 2015) (REG-112997-10).

☐ Section 28.6109-1 is added to read as follows:

§28.6109-1. Tax return preparers furnishing identifying numbers for returns or claims for refund.—(a) *In general.*—Each tax return or claim for refund of the tax under chapter 15 of subtitle B of the Internal Revenue Code prepared by one or more signing tax return preparers must include the identifying number of the preparer required by §1.6695-1(b) of this chapter to sign the return or claim for refund in the manner stated in §1.6109-2 of this chapter.

(b) *Effective/applicability date.*—This section applies on and after the date of publication of a Treasury decision adopting these rules as final regulations in the **Federal Register**. [Reg. § 28.6109-1.]

Tax Return Preparer: Furnishing Identifying Number

Tax Return Preparer: Furnishing Identifying Number.—Amendments to Reg. § 1.6109-2, providing guidance on the eligibility of tax return preparers to obtain a preparer tax identification number (PTIN), are proposed (published in the Federal Register on February 15, 2012) (REG-124791-11).

☐ Par. 2. Section 1.6109-2 is amended by adding a new sentence to the end of paragraph (a)(1) and revising paragraphs (d), (f), (h) and (i) to read as follows:

§ 1.6109-2. Tax return preparers furnishing identifying numbers for returns or claims for refund and related requirements.

(a) * * *

(1) * * * For purposes of this section only, the terms *tax return* and *claim for refund of tax* include all tax forms submitted to the Internal Revenue Service unless specifically excluded by the Internal Revenue Service in other appropriate guidance.

* * *

(d)(1) Beginning after December 31, 2010, all tax return preparers must have a preparer tax identification number or other prescribed identifying number that was applied for and received at the time and in the manner, including the payment of a user fee, as may be prescribed by the Internal Revenue Service in forms, instructions, or other appropriate guidance.

(2) Except as provided in paragraph (h) of this section, to obtain a preparer tax identification number or other prescribed identifying number, a tax return preparer must be one of the following:

(i) An attorney;

(ii) A certified public accountant;

(iii) An enrolled agent;

(iv) A registered tax return preparer authorized to practice before the Internal Revenue Service under 31 U.S.C. 330 and the regulations thereunder;

(v) An individual 18 years of age or older who is supervised, in the manner the Internal Revenue Service prescribes in forms, instructions, or other appropriate guidance, as a tax return preparer by an attorney, certified public accountant, enrolled agent, enrolled retirement plan agent, or enrolled actuary authorized to practice before the Internal Revenue Service under 31 U.S.C. 330 and the regulations thereunder; or

(vi) An individual 18 years of age or older who certifies that the individual is a tax return preparer exclusively with respect to tax returns and claims for refund of tax that are not covered, at the time the tax return preparer applies for or renews the number, by a minimum competency examination prescribed by the Internal Revenue Service in forms, instructions, or other appropriate guidance. An individual must comply with any requirements at the time and in the manner that the Internal Revenue Service may prescribe in forms, instructions, or other appropriate guidance.

* * *

(f) As may be prescribed in forms, instructions, or other appropriate guidance, the Internal Revenue Service may conduct a Federal tax compliance check and a suitability check on a tax return preparer who applies for or renews a preparer tax identification number or other prescribed identifying number.

* * *

(h) The Internal Revenue Service, through forms, instructions, or other appropriate guidance, may prescribe exceptions to the requirements of this section, including the requirement that an individual be authorized to practice before the Internal Revenue Service before receiving a preparer tax identification number or other prescribed identifying number, as necessary in the interest of effective tax administration.

(i) *Effective/applicability date.*—Paragraph (a)(1) of this section applies to tax returns and claims for refund filed after December 31, 2008, except the last sentence of paragraph (a)(1), which applies to tax returns and claims for refund filed on or after the date that final regulations are published in the **Federal Register**. Paragraph (a)(2)(i) of this section applies to tax returns and claims for refund filed on or before December 31, 2010. Paragraph (a)(2)(ii) of this section applies to tax returns and claims for refund filed after December 31, 2010. Paragraph (d)(1) of this section applies to tax return preparers after December 31, 2010. Paragraph (d)(2) of this section applies to tax return preparers on or after the date that final regulations are published in the **Federal Register**. Paragraph (e) of this section applies after September 30, 2010. Paragraph (f) of this section applies on or after the date that final regulations are published in the **Federal Register**. Paragraphs (g) and (h) of this section apply after September 30, 2010.

TIME AND PLACE FOR PAYING TAX

Gifts and Bequests from Covered Expatriates: Imposition of Tax

Gifts and Bequests from Covered Expatriates: Imposition of Tax.—Reg. § 28.6151-1, relating to a tax on United States citizens and residents who receive gifts or bequests from certain individuals who relinquished United States citizenship or ceased to be lawful permanent residents of the

United States on or after June 17, 2008, is proposed (published in the Federal Register on September 10, 2015) (REG-112997-10).

☐ Section 28.6151-1 is added to read as follows:

§28.6151-1. Time and place for paying tax shown on returns.—The tax due under this part 28 must be paid at the time prescribed in §28.6071-1 for filing the return, and at the place prescribed in §28.6091-1 for filing the return. [Reg. §28.6151-1.]

User Fees: Enrolled Actuaries

User Fees: Enrolled Actuaries.—Amendments of Reg. §§300.7 and 300.8, relating to imposing user fees for enrolled actuaries, are proposed (published in the Federal Register on October 5, 2022) (REG-100719-21).

☐ Par. 2. Amend §300.7 by revising paragraphs (b) and (d) to read as follows:

§300.7. Enrollment of enrolled actuary fee.

* * *

(b) *Fee.* The fee for initially enrolling as an enrolled actuary with the Joint Board for the Enrollment of Actuaries is $680.00.

* * *

(d) *Applicability date.* This section is applicable beginning [DATE 30 DAYS AFTER DATE OF PUBLICATION OF THE FINAL RULE IN THE FEDERAL REGISTER].

☐ Par. 3. Amend §300.8 by revising paragraphs (b) and (d) to read as follows:

§300.8. Renewal of enrollment of enrolled actuary fee.

* * *

(b) *Fee.* The fee for renewal of enrollment as an enrolled actuary with the Joint Board for the Enrollment of Actuaries is $680.00.

* * *

(d) *Applicability date.* This section is applicable beginning [DATE 30 DAYS AFTER DATE OF PUBLICATION OF THE FINAL RULE IN THE FEDERAL REGISTER].

INTEREST

Modification of Interest Payments for Certain Periods

Modification of Interest Payments for Certain Periods.—Reproduced below is the text of proposed amendments to Reg. §301.6601-1, relating to the accrual of interest on overpayments and underpayments of tax (published in the Federal Register on October 9, 1984).

☐ Paragraph 1. Section 301.6601-1 is amended as follows:

1. Paragraph (d) is revised to read as set forth below.
2. Paragraphs (e)(1) and (e)(3) are revised to read as set forth below.
3. New paragraphs (e)(4) and (e)(5) are added as set forth below.

§301.6601-1. Interest on underpayments.

* * *

(d) *Suspension of interest; waiver of restrictions on assessment.*—In the case of a deficiency determined by a district director (or an assistant regional commissioner, appellate) with respect to any income, estate, gift tax, or excise tax imposed by chapters 41, 42, 43, 44, and 45, if the taxpayer files with such internal revenue officer an agreement waiving the restrictions on assessment of such deficiency, and if notice and demand for payment of such deficiency is not made within 30 days after the filing of such waiver, no interest shall be imposed on the deficiency for the period beginning immediately after such 30th day and ending on the date notice and demand is made. In the case of an agreement with respect to a portion of the deficiency, the rules as set forth in this paragraph are applicable only to that portion of the deficiency to which the agreement relates.

(e) *Income tax reduced by carryback.*—(1)(i) The carryback of a net operating loss, net capital loss, or a credit carryback as defined by §301.6611-1(f)(1) shall not affect the computation of interest on any income tax for the period commencing with the last day prescribed for the payment of such tax and ending with the filing date, as defined in paragraph (e)(4) of this section, for the taxable year in which the loss or credit arises. For example, if the carryback of a net operating loss, a net capital loss, or a credit carryback to a prior taxable period eliminates or reduces a deficiency in income tax for that period, the full amount of the deficiency will bear interest at the annual rate established under section 6621 from the last date prescribed for payment of such tax until the filing date for the taxable year in which the loss or credit arose. Interest will continue to run beyond such filing date on any portion of the deficiency which is not eliminated by the carryback. With respect to any portion of a credit carryback from a taxable year attributable to a net operating loss carryback, a capital loss carryback or other credit carryback from a subsequent taxable year, such credit carryback shall not affect the computation of interest on any income tax for the period commencing with the last day prescribed for the payment of such tax and ending with the filing date for such subsequent taxable year.

(ii) The provisions of paragraph (e)(1)(i) of this section are illustrated by the following examples.

Example (1). Corporation L is a calendar year taxpayer. For taxable years 1980 and 1981, L reported no income tax liability. For 1982, L has an underpayment of income tax of $500. In 1983, L has a net operating loss which L carries back to 1982, reducing the underpayment to $200. For purposes of computing the interest on the underpayment of income tax for 1982, interest will accrue on the $500 beginning on March 15, 1983. Beginning on March 16, 1984, interest on the 1982 income tax underpayment will accrue on only $200.

Example (2). Corporation R is a calendar year taxpayer. For taxable years 1980, 1981 and 1982, R reported no income tax liability. In 1983, R had a net operating loss which could not be carried forward to 1984 because R had reported no income tax liability for 1984. As a result of an audit conducted on R in 1985, a $500 deficiency is assessed on R for taxable year 1982. R applied the 1983 net operating loss to the $500 assessed deficiency, thus reducing the deficiency to $200. Interest begins accruing on the $500 deficiency on March 15, 1983. Beginning on March 16, 1984, interest on the 1982 deficiency will accrue on only $200.

* * *

(3) Where there has been an allowance of an overpayment attributable to a net operating loss carryback, a capital loss carryback or a credit carryback as defined by § 301.6611-1(f)(1) and all or part of such allowance is later determined to be excessive, interest shall be computed on the excessive amount from the filing date for the year in which the net operating loss, net capital loss, or credit arose until the date on which the repayment of such excessive amount is received. Where there has been an allowance of an overpayment with respect to any portion of a credit carryback from a taxable year attributable to a net operating loss carryback or a capital loss carryback from a subsequent taxable year and all or part of such allowance is later determined to be excessive, interest shall be computed on the excessive amount from the filing date for such subsequent taxable year until the date on which the repayment of such excessive amount is received.

(4) For purposes of paragraph (e) of this section, the term "filing date" means the last day fixed by law or regulation for filing the return of income tax for the taxable year (determined without regard to any extension of time).

(5) Section 301.6601-1(e)(1), (3) and (4) apply to interest accruing after October 3, 1982. See 26 CFR 301.6601-1(e) (revised as of April 1, 1982) for rules applicable to interest accruing before October 4, 1982.

ADDITIONS TO TAX, ADDITIONAL AMOUNTS, ASSESSABLE PENALTIES

Estate and Person Acquiring Property from Decedent: Consistent Basis Reporting

Estate and Person Acquiring Property from Decedent: Consistent Basis Reporting.—Reg. § 1.6662-8, providing guidance regarding the requirement that a recipient's basis in certain property acquired from a decedent be consistent with the value of the property as finally determined for Federal estate tax purposes, is proposed (published in the Federal Register on March 4, 2016) (REG-127923-15).

☐ Par. 6. Section 1.6662-8 is added to read as follows:

§ 1.6662-8. Inconsistent estate basis reporting.—(a) *In general.*—Section 6662(a) and (b)(8) impose an accuracy-related penalty on the portion of any underpayment of tax required to be shown on a return that is attributable to an inconsistent estate basis.

(b) *Inconsistent estate basis.*—In accordance with section 6662(k), there is an *inconsistent estate basis* to the extent that a taxpayer claims a basis, without regard to the adjustments described in § 1.1014-10(a)(2), in property described in paragraph (c) of this section that exceeds that property's final value as determined under § 1.1014-10(c).

(c) *Applicable property.*—The property to which this section applies is property described in § 1.1014-10(b) that is reported or required to be reported on a return required by section 6018 filed after July 31, 2015.

(d) *Effective/applicability date.*—Upon the publication of the Treasury Decision adopting these rules as final in the **Federal Register**, this section will apply to property described in § 1.1014-10(b) acquired from a decedent or by reason of the death of a decedent whose return required by section 6018 is filed after July 31, 2015. Persons may rely upon these rules before the date of publication of the Treasury Decision adopting these rules as final in the **Federal Register**. [Reg. § 1.6662-8.]

Gifts and Bequests from Covered Expatriates: Imposition of Tax

Gifts and Bequests from Covered Expatriates: Imposition of Tax.—Reg. §§ 28.6694-1—28.6694-4, relating to a tax on United States citizens and residents who receive gifts or bequests from certain individuals who relinquished United States citizenship or ceased to be lawful

permanent residents of the United States on or after June 17, 2008, is proposed (published in the Federal Register on September 10, 2015) (REG-112997-10).

☐ Sections 28.6694-1 to 28.6694-4 are added to read as follows:

§ 28.6694-1. Section 6694 penalties applicable to return preparer.—(a) *In general.*—For general rules regarding section 6694 penalties applicable to preparers of returns or claims for refund of the tax under chapter 15 of subtitle B of the Internal Revenue Code (Code), see § 1.6694-1 of this chapter.

(b) *Effective/applicability date.*—This section applies to returns and claims for refund filed, and advice provided, on or after the date of publication of a Treasury decision adopting these rules as final regulations in the **Federal Register**. [Reg. § 28.6694-1.]

§ 28.6694-2. Penalties for understatement due to an unreasonable position.—(a) *In general.*—A person who is a tax return preparer of any return or claim for refund of any tax under chapter 15 of subtitle B of the Code is subject to penalties under section 6694(a) in the manner stated in § 1.6694-2 of this chapter.

(b) *Effective/applicability date.*—This section applies to returns and claims for refund filed, and advice provided, on or after the date of publication of a Treasury decision adopting these rules as final regulations in the **Federal Register**. [Reg. § 28.6694-2.]

§ 28.6694-3. Penalties for understatement due to an unreasonable position.—(a) *In general.*—A person who is a tax return preparer of any return or claim for refund of any tax under chapter 15 of subtitle B of the Code is subject to penalties under section 6694(b) in the manner stated in § 1.6694-3 of this chapter.

(b) *Effective/applicability date.*—This section applies to returns and claims for refund filed, and advice provided, on or after the date of publication of a Treasury decision adopting these rules as final regulations in the **Federal Register**. [Reg. § 28.6694-3.]

§ 28.6694-4. Extension of period of collection when tax return preparer pays 15 percent of a penalty for understatement of taxpayer's liability and certain other procedural matters.—(a) *In general.*—For rules relating to the extension of the period of collection when a tax return preparer who prepared a return or claim for refund of tax under chapter 15 of subtitle B of the Code pays 15 percent of a penalty for understatement of taxpayer's liability, and for procedural matters relating to the investigation, assessment, and collection of the penalties under section 6694(a) and (b), the rules under § 1.6694-4 of this chapter apply.

(b) *Effective/applicability date.*—This section applies to returns and claims for refund filed, and advice provided, on or after the date of publication of a Treasury decision adopting these rules as final regulations in the **Federal Register**. [Reg. § 28.6694-4.]

Gifts and Bequests from Covered Expatriates: Imposition of Tax

Gifts and Bequests from Covered Expatriates: Imposition of Tax.—Reg. §§ 28.6695-1 and 28.6696-1, relating to a tax on United States citizens and residents who receive gifts or bequests from certain individuals who relinquished United States citizenship or ceased to be lawful permanent residents of the United States on or after June 17, 2008, is proposed (published in the Federal Register on September 10, 2015) (REG-112997-10).

☐ Section 28.6695-1 is added to read as follows:

§ 28.6695-1. Other assessable penalties with respect to the preparation of tax returns for other persons.—(a) *In general.*—A person who is a tax return preparer of any return or claim for refund of any tax under chapter 15 of subtitle B of the Internal Revenue Code (Code) is subject to penalties for failure to furnish a copy to the taxpayer under section 6695(a) of the Code, failure to sign the return under section 6695(b) of the Code, failure to furnish an identification number under section 6695(c) of the Code, failure to retain a copy or list under section 6695(d) of the Code, failure to file a correct information return under section 6695(e) of the Code, and negotiation of a check under section 6695(f) of the Code, in the manner stated in § 1.6695-1 of this chapter.

(b) *Effective/applicability date.*—This section applies to returns and claims for refund filed on or after the date of publication of a Treasury decision adopting these rules as final regulations in the **Federal Register**.[Reg. § 28.6695-1.]

☐ Section 28.6696-1 is added to read as follows:

§ 28.6696-1. Claims for credit or refund by tax return preparers and appraisers.—(a) *In general.*—For rules regarding claims for credit or refund by a tax return preparer who prepared a return or claim for refund for any tax under chapter 15 of subtitle B of the Internal Revenue Code (Code), or by an appraiser that prepared an appraisal in connection with such a return or claim for refund under section 6695A of the Code, the rules under § 1.6696-1 of this chapter will apply.

(b) *Effective/applicability date.*—This section applies to returns and claims for refund filed, appraisals, and advice provided, on or after the date of publication of a Treasury decision adopting these rules as final regulations in the **Federal Register**. [Reg. § 28.6696-1.]

Estate and Person Acquiring Property from Decedent: Consistent Basis Reporting

Estate and Person Acquiring Property from Decedent: Consistent Basis Reporting.—Amend ments to Reg. §§301.6721-1 and 301.6722-1, providing guidance regarding the requirement that a recipient's basis in certain property acquired from a decedent be consistent with the value of the property as finally determined for Federal estate tax purposes, are proposed (published in the Federal Register on March 4, 2016) (REG-127923-15).

☐ Par. 8. Section 301.6721-1 is amended by removing the word "or" at the end of paragraph (g)(2)(x), removing the period and adding "; or" at the end of paragraph (g)(2)(xi), and adding paragraph (g)(2)(xii).

The addition reads as follows:

§301.6721-1. Failure to file correct information returns.

* * *

(g) * * *

(2) * * *

(xii) Section 6035 (relating to basis of property acquired from decedents).

* * *

☐ Par. 9. Section 301.6722-1 is amended by removing the word "or" at the end of paragraph (d)(2)(xxxiii), removing the period and adding a semi-colon in its place followed by the word "or" at the end of paragraph (d)(2)(xxxiv), and adding paragraph (d)(2)(xxxv).

The addition reads as follows:

§301.6722-1. Failure to furnish correct payee statements.

* * *

(d) * * *

(2) * * *

(xxxv) Section 6035 (relating to basis of property acquired from decedents).

* * *

Correct Payee Statements: Failure to File Correct Information: Penalties

Correct Payee Statements: Failure to File Correct Information: Penalties.—Amendments to Reg. §301.6722-1, relating to penalties for failure to file correct information returns or furnish correct payee statements, are proposed (published in the Federal Register on October 17, 2018) (REG-118826-16).

☐ Par. 6. Section 301.6722-1 is amended by:

1. Revising paragraphs (a)(1), (a)(2)(ii), and (b)(2)(i).
2. In paragraphs (b)(2)(ii) and (iii), removing the comma at the end of each paragraph and adding a semicolon in its place.
3. Revising paragraph (b)(3) introductory text.
4. In paragraph (b)(3), designate *Examples 1* and 2 as paragraphs (b)(3)(i) and (ii).
5. Revising paragraph (c)(1).
6. Redesignating paragraphs (c)(2)(i), (ii), and (iii) as paragraphs (c)(2)(ii), (iii), and (iv).
7. Adding a new paragraph (c)(2)(i).
8. Revising newly redesignated paragraphs (c)(2)(ii) and (iii).
9. Redesignating paragraphs (d) and (e) as paragraphs (e) and (g).
10. Adding a new paragraph (d).
11. Revising newly redesignated paragraphs (e)(1), (e)(2) introductory text, and (e)(2)(xxxiii) and (xxxiv).
12. Adding paragraphs (e)(2)(xxxv), (xxxvi), and (xxxvii), (e)(4), and (f).
13. Revising newly redesignated paragraph (g).

The revisions and additions read as follows:

§301.6722-1. Failure to furnish correct payee statements.—(a) *Imposition of penalty.*—(1) *General rule.*—A penalty of $250 is imposed for each payee statement (as defined in section 6724(d)(2) and paragraph (e)(2) of this section) with respect to which a failure (as defined in section 6722(a) and paragraph (a)(2) of this section) occurs. No more than one penalty will be imposed under this paragraph (a) with respect to a single payee statement even though there may be more than one failure with respect to such statement. However, the penalty shall apply to failures on composite substitute payee statements as though each type of payment and other required information were furnished on separate statements. A "composite substitute payee statement" is a single document created by a filer to reflect several types of payments made to the same payee. The total amount imposed on any person for all failures during any calendar year with respect to all payee statements shall not exceed $3,000,000. See section 6722(e) and paragraph (c) of this section for higher penalties when a failure is due to intentional disregard of the requirement to furnish timely correct payee statements. See paragraph (d) of this section for a safe harbor exception for certain de minimis errors. See paragraph (f) of this section for inflation adjustments to penalty amounts. See § 301.6724-1(a)(1) for a waiver of the penalty for a failure that is due to reasonable cause.

(2) * * *

(ii) A failure to include all of the information required to be shown on a payee statement or the inclusion of incorrect information ("failure to include correct information"). A failure to furnish timely includes a failure to furnish a written statement to the payee in a statement mailing as required under sections 6042(c), 6044(e), 6049(c), and 6050N(b), as well as a failure to furnish the statement on a form acceptable to the Internal Revenue Service. Except as provided in paragraph (b) or (d) of this section, a failure to include correct information encompasses a failure to include the information required by applicable information reporting statutes or by any administrative pronouncements issued thereunder (such as regulations, revenue rulings, revenue procedures, or information reporting forms).

(b) * * *

(2) * * *

(i) A dollar amount, except as provided in paragraph (d) of this section;

* * *

(3) *Examples.*—The provisions of this paragraph (b) may be illustrated by the following examples which do not take into account any possible application of the penalty for intentional disregard under paragraph (c) of this section, the safe harbor exception for certain de minimis errors under paragraph (d) of this section, or the reasonable cause waiver under § 301.6724-1(a):

* * *

(c) *Higher penalty for intentional disregard of requirement to furnish timely correct payee statements.*—(1) *Application of section 6722(e).*—If a failure is due to intentional disregard of the requirement to furnish timely correct payee statements, the amount of the penalty shall be determined under paragraph (c)(2) of this section. Whether a failure is due to intentional disregard of the requirement to furnish timely correct payee statements is based upon the facts and circumstances surrounding the failure. The facts and circumstances considered include those under § 301.6721-1(g)(3), which shall apply in determining whether a failure under this section is due to intentional disregard.

(2) * * *

(i) Paragraph (d) of this section shall not apply;

(ii) The $3,000,000 limitation under paragraph (a) of this section shall not apply and the penalty under this paragraph (c)(2) shall not be taken into account in applying the $3,000,000 limitation to penalties not determined under this paragraph (c)(2);

(iii) The penalty imposed under paragraph (a) of this section shall be $500 or, if greater, the statutory percentage; and

* * *

(d) *Safe harbor exception for certain de minimis errors.*—(1) *In general.*—Except as provided in paragraphs (c) and (d)(3) of this section, the penalty under section 6722(a) and paragraph (a) of this section is not imposed for a failure described in section 6722(a)(2)(B) and paragraph (a)(2)(ii) of this section (failure to include correct information on payee statement) when the failure relates to an incorrect dollar amount and is a de minimis error. When this safe harbor applies to a payee statement and the payee statement was otherwise correct and timely furnished no correction is required and, for purposes of this section, the payee statement is treated as having been furnished with all of the correct required information.

(2) *Definition of de minimis error.*—For purposes of paragraph (d) of this section, an error in a dollar amount is de minimis if the difference between any single amount in error and the correct amount is not more than $100, and, if the difference is with respect to an amount of tax withheld, it is not more than $25. For purposes of this paragraph (d)(2), tax withheld includes any amount required to be shown on an information return or payee statement (as defined in section 6724(d)(1) and (d)(2), respectively) withheld under section 3402, as well as any such amount that is creditable under sections 27, 31, 33, or 1474.

(3) *Election to override the safe harbor exception.*—(i) *In general.*—Except as provided in paragraphs (d)(3)(vi) and (vii) of this section, the safe harbor exception provided for by this paragraph (d) does not apply to any payee statement if the person to whom the statement is required to be furnished (the payee) makes an election that the safe harbor not apply with respect to the statement.

(ii) *Timing of election.*—The payee must elect no later than the later of 30 days after the date on which the payee statement is required to be furnished to the payee, or October 15 of the calendar year, to receive a correct payee statement required to be furnished in that calendar year without having the safe harbor under paragraph (d)(1) of this section apply. The date of an election is the date the election is received by the filer. For purposes of this section, the provisions of section 7502 relating to timely mailing treated as timely delivery apply in determining the date an election is considered to be received by the filer, treating delivery to the filer as if the filer were an agency, officer, or office under such section. The election shall remain in effect for all subsequent years unless revoked under paragraph (d)(3)(vii) of this section.

(iii) *Manner for making the election.*—Except as provided in paragraph (d)(3)(v) of this section, the payee must make the election by delivering the election in writing to the filer. Except as provided in paragraph (d)(3)(v) of this section, the written election must be made in writing on paper. The payee may deliver the election in person, by mail by United States Postal Service, or by a designated delivery service as defined under section 7502(f)(2). If the filer has not otherwise provided an address under paragraph (d)(3)(v) of this section, the payee shall send the written election to the filer's address appearing on the payee statement furnished by the filer to the payee with respect to which the election is being made or as directed by that person upon appropriate inquiry by the payee. The written election must:

(A) Clearly state that the payee is making the election;

(B) Provide the payee's name, address, and taxpayer identification number (TIN) (as defined in section 7701(a)(41) of the Internal Revenue Code) to the filer;

(C) If the payee wants the election to apply only to specific types of statements, identify the type of payee statement(s) and account number(s), if applicable, to which the election applies (for example, Form 1099-DIV, "Dividends and Distributions"); and

(D) Provide any other information required by the Internal Revenue Service in forms, instructions, or publications.

(iv) *Payee statements to which the election applies.*—An election by a payee under paragraph (d)(3)(i) of this section applies to all types of payee statements the filer is required to furnish to the payee, unless the payee specifies otherwise on the election under paragraph (d)(3)(iii)(C) of this section.

(v) *Reasonable alternative manner for making the election in cases of notification by the filer.*—(A) *In general.*—If the filer satisfies the requirements of paragraph (d)(3)(v)(B) of this section, and provides for a reasonable alternative manner as described in paragraph (d)(3)(v)(E) of this section, a payee may decide to make the election under paragraph (d)(3)(i) of this section pursuant to that reasonable alternative manner.

(B) *Notification of payee of reasonable alternative manner for making election.*—The filer may elect to provide notification to the payee of a reasonable alternative manner to make the election under paragraph (d)(3)(i) of this section, as described in paragraph (d)(3)(v)(E) of this section. To provide a valid notification under this paragraph (d)(3)(v)(B), the filer must provide notification to the payee that:

(1) Is in writing (either on paper or in electronic format);

(2) Is timely provided to the payee under paragraph (d)(3)(v)(D) of this section;

(3) Explains to the payee to whom that filer is required to furnish a payee statement of the payee's ability to elect, under paragraph (d)(3)(i) of this section, that the safe harbor exceptions for de minimis errors not apply, and of the payee's ability to choose to make the election using the default method under paragraph (d)(3)(iii) of this section;

(4) Provides an address to which the payee may send an election under paragraphs (d)(3)(i) and (iii) of this section;

(5) Provides any reasonable alternative manner or manners, as described in paragraph (d)(3)(v)(E) of this section, that the filer is making available for the payee to make the election under paragraph (d)(3)(i) of this section; and

(6) Describes the information required for making the election described by paragraphs (d)(3)(iii)(A) through (D) of this section. Solely for purposes of the reasonable alternative manner, the notification may provide that some or all of the information described in paragraph (d)(3)(iii)(B) of this section is not required and may provide that the provision of an account number as referenced in paragraph (d)(3)(iii)(C) of this section is required if the payee decides to use the reasonable alternative manner for the election.

(C) *Notification of revocation procedures.*—A notification under this paragraph (d)(3)(v) may also provide the procedures for making a revocation of an election under paragraph (d)(3)(vii) of this section. Solely for purposes of the reasonable alternative manner, the notification may provide that some or all of the information described in paragraph (d)(3)(vii)(B) of this section is not required and may provide that the provision of an account number as referenced in paragraph (d)(3)(vii)(E) of this section is required if the payee decides to use a reasonable alternative manner for making a revocation.

(D) *Time for providing notification of reasonable alternative manner for making payee election.*—A notification under this paragraph (d)(3)(v) will be timely under paragraph (d)(3)(v)(B)(2) of this section if:

(1) The notification is provided with, or at the time of, the furnishing of the payee statement; or

(2) The filer previously provided a valid notification under paragraph (d)(3)(v) of this section to the payee with, or at the time of, the furnishing of a payee statement associated with a particular account, in which case notification will be considered to have been timely provided with respect to subsequent payee statements associated with that particular account. If the filer wishes to provide for a different reasonable alternative manner than a previous reasonable alternative manner, the filer must provide new notification in compliance with the timeliness rule of paragraph (d)(3)(v)(D)(*1*) of this section, and must accept payee elections under the previous reasonable alternative manner for a period of at least 60 days after the receipt of the new notification by the payee.

(E) *Reasonable alternative manner.*—A reasonable alternative manner described in a notification under paragraph (d)(3)(v)(B) of this section may include that a payee election under paragraph (d)(3)(i) of this section may be made electronically (for example, via e-mail or web site) or telephonically. The reasonable alternative manner may not impose any prerequisite, condition, or time limitation on, or otherwise limit, the payee's ability to make an election under paragraph (d)(3)(iii) of this section, except as described in paragraphs (d)(3)(ii) and (iii) of this section; it may only offer a reasonable alternative manner or manners for making this election under this paragraph (d)(3)(v).

(vi) *Election not available for certain information.*—The election to override the safe harbor exception provided for by paragraph (d)(3)(i) of this section is not available with respect to information that may not be altered under specific information reporting rules. See, for example, § 1.6045-4(i)(5) of this chapter.

(vii) *Revocation of election.*—The payee may revoke a prior election by submitting a revocation to the filer. The effect of a revocation of a prior election is that the safe harbor for certain de minimis errors will apply to the payee statements that the payee identifies and that are furnished or are due to be furnished after the revocation is received. The revocation will remain in effect until the payee makes a valid and timely election under paragraph (d)(3)(i) of this section. The date of a revocation is the date the revocation is received by the filer. For purposes of this section, the provisions of section 7502 relating to timely mailing treated as timely delivery apply in determining the date a revocation is considered to be received by the filer, treating delivery to the filer as if the filer were an agency, officer, or office under such section. The revocation must be made in the same manner or manners described for making the election, that is pursuant to either paragraph (d)(3)(iii) or (v) of this section, as the payee chooses if paragraph (d)(3)(v) of this section is applicable. Except as provided under paragraph (d)(3)(v)(B)(*6*) of this section, the revocation must:

(A) Clearly state that the payee is revoking the payee's prior election;

(B) Provide the payee's name, address, and TIN to the filer;

(C) Provide the name of the filer;

(D) Identify the type of payee statement(s) (for example, Form 1099-DIV) to which the revocation applies;

(E) Identify the account number(s), if applicable, to which the revocation applies; and

(F) Provide any other information required by the Internal Revenue Service in forms, instructions or publications.

(viii) *Reasonable cause.*—See § 301.6724-1(h) for rules relating to waiver of the section 6722 penalty in cases where the safe harbor exception provided for by paragraph (d)(1) of this section does not apply because of an election under paragraph (d)(3)(i) of this section.

(4) *Record retention.*—To facilitate proof of compliance with reporting and other obligations under the internal revenue laws, filers must retain records of any election or revocation by the payee under paragraph (d)(3)(i) or (vii) of this section, respectively, and any notification made under paragraph (d)(3)(v) of this section for as long as the contents of the election, revocation, or notification may be material in the administration of any internal revenue law. For rules regarding record retention, see section 6001 and § 1.6001-1 of this chapter. For additional procedures applicable to record retention in the context of electronic storage, see Rev. Proc. 97-22, 1997-1 C.B. 652, Rev. Proc. 98-25, 1998-1 C.B. 689, and any subsequently published guidance.

(5) *Examples.*—The provisions of paragraphs (d)(1) through (4) of this section may be illustrated by the following examples, which do not address any possible application of the penalty for intentional disregard under paragraph (c) of this section or the reasonable cause waiver under § 301.6724-1(a):

(i) *Example 1.* (A) Filer W is required to file with the IRS by February 28, 2019, and furnish to Payee A by February 15, 2019, Form 1099-B "Proceeds From Broker and Barter Exchange Transactions," because Filer W is a broker who sold stocks on behalf of Payee A resulting in proceeds of $5000 during calendar year 2018. Filer W properly withheld an amount of $1736 under applicable backup withholding rules because Payee A failed to furnish Payee A's TIN to Filer W. On the Form 1099-B, Filer W reports as follows: Box 1d, Proceeds, $4900; and Box 4, Federal income tax withheld, $1761. Filer W otherwise correctly and timely files and furnishes the Form 1099-B. Payee A does not make an election under paragraph (d)(3)(i) of this section.

(B) The safe harbor exception for de minimis errors provided for by paragraph (d)(1) of this section applies, because the differences between each of the amounts reported in error and the correct amounts are not more than the applicable limits. The error in the dollar amount reported in Box 1d, Proceeds, is de minimis because the difference between the amount in error ($4900) and the correct amount ($5000) is not more than $100; it is exactly $100. The error in the dollar amount reported in Box 4, Federal income tax withheld, is de minimis because the $25 difference between the amount in error ($1761) and the correct amount ($1736) is not more than $25, the limit for an error with respect to an amount reported for tax withheld.

(ii) *Example 2.* (A) The facts are the same as in *Example 1* in paragraph (d)(5)(i) of this section, except that Filer W reports $1710 as the amount in Box 4, Federal income tax withheld.

(B) The safe harbor exception for de minimis errors provided for by paragraph (d)(1) of this section does not apply because the Form 1099-B contains a failure that is not a de minimis error. The difference between the amount in error ($1710) and the correct amount ($1736) is $26, which is more than the $25 limit for de minimis errors with respect to an amount reported for tax withheld.

(iii) *Example 3.* (A) In 2019, Filer X provides Payee B with valid notification of a reasonable alternative manner under paragraph (d)(3)(v) of this section for making the payee election under paragraph (d)(3)(i) of this section. Payee B timely elects pursuant to the reasonable alternative manner during 2019. Payee B elects with respect to all payee statements that Filer X is required to furnish to Payee B. In January 2020, Filer X decides to provide for a different, but also valid, reasonable alternative manner; Filer X provides notification of this different reasonable alternative manner to Payee B, and Payee B receives notification of this different reasonable alternative manner, pursuant to paragraph (d)(3)(v)(B) of this section, on January 16, 2020.

(B) Payee B decides to revoke Payee B's prior election, with respect to the Forms 1099-DIV that Filer X is required to furnish to Payee B. Under paragraph (d)(3)(vii) of this section, Payee B may provide the revocation to Filer X in any of three different manners. First, Payee B may provide the revocation to Filer X in the same manner as if Payee B were making an election under the default manner of paragraph (d)(3)(iii) of this section; Payee B may do so at any time. Second, having received notification from Filer X of the different reasonable alternative manner on January 16, 2020, Payee B may provide the revocation to Filer X in the same manner as if Payee B were making an election under the different reasonable alternative manner pursuant to paragraph (d)(3)(v) of this section. Third, because Filer X previously provided notification of a reasonable alternative manner (2019 alternative) before providing notification of a different reasonable alternative manner on January 16, 2020, (2020 alternative), Payee B may provide the revocation to Filer X in the same manner as if Payee B were making an election under the previous reasonable alternative manner (2019 alternative); Payee B may do so for a period of 60 days after January 16, 2020, pursuant to paragraph (d)(3)(v)(D)(2) of this section.

(e) *Definitions.*—(1) *Payee.*—See § 301.6721-1(h)(5) for the definition of "payee."

(2) *Payee statement.*—For purposes of this section the term "payee statement" has the same meaning as payee statement as defined by section 6724(d)(2), including any statement required to be furnished under—

* * *

(xxxiii) Section 6055 (relating to information returns reporting minimum essential coverage);

(xxxiv) Section 6056 (relating to information returns reporting on offers of health insurance coverage by applicable large employer members);

(xxxv) Section 6035, other than a statement described in section 6724(d)(1)(D), (relating to basis information with respect to property acquired from decedents, generally Schedule A of Form 8971, "Information Regarding Beneficiaries Acquiring Property From a Decedent");

(xxxvi) Section 6050Y(a)(2), 6050Y(b)(2), or 6050Y(c)(2) (relating to certain life insurance contract transactions); or

(xxxvii) Section 6226(a)(2) (regarding statements relating to alternative to payment of imputed underpayment by a partnership) or under any other provision of this title which provides for the application of rules similar to section 6226(a)(2).

* * *

(4) *Filer.*—For purposes of this section the term "filer" means a person that is required to furnish a payee statement as defined in paragraphs (e)(2) and (3) of this section under the applicable information reporting section described in paragraphs (e)(2) and (3) of this section.

(f) *Adjustment for inflation.*—Each of the dollar amounts under paragraphs (a), (b), and (c) of this section and paragraphs (a), (b), (d)(1), and (e) of section 6722 shall be adjusted for inflation pursuant to section 6722(f).

(g) *Applicability date.*—This section applies with respect to payee statements required to be furnished on or after January 1 of the calendar year immediately following the date of publication of a Treasury decision adopting these rules as final regulations in the **Federal Register**.

MISCELLANEOUS PROVISIONS

Annuities: Interests: Valuation: Actuarial Tables

Annuities: Interests: Valuation: Actuarial Tables.—Amendments to Reg. § 20.7520-1, relating to the use of actuarial tables in valuing annuities, interests for life or terms of years, and remainder or reversionary interests, are proposed (published in the Federal Register on May 5, 2022) (REG-122770-18).

☐ Par. 22. Section 20.7520-1 is amended by revising paragraphs (a)(1) and (2), (b)(2), (c), and (d) and adding paragraphs (e) and (f) to read as follows:

§ 20.7520-1. Valuation of annuities, interests for life or a term of years, and remainder or reversionary interests.

(a) * * *

(1) Except as otherwise provided in this section and in § 20.7520-3 (relating to exceptions to the use of prescribed tables under certain circumstances), in the case of estates of decedents with valuation dates after April 30, 1989, the fair market value of annuities, interests for life or a term of years (including unitrust interests), and remainder or reversionary interests is their present value determined under this section. See § 20.2031-7(d) (and, for periods prior to

[applicability date of the Treasury decision adopting these regulations as final regulations], § 20.2031-7A) for the computation of the value of annuities, interests for life or a term of years, and remainder or reversionary interests, other than interests described in paragraphs (a)(2) and (3) of this section.

(2) For a transfer to a pooled income fund, see § 1.642(c)-6(e) of this chapter (or, for periods prior to [applicability date of the Treasury decision adopting these regulations as final regulations], § 1.642(c)-6A) with respect to the valuation of the remainder interest.

* * *

(b) * * *

(2) *Mortality component.*—The mortality component reflects the mortality data most recently available from the United States census. As new mortality data becomes available after each decennial census, the mortality component described in this section will be revised and the revised mortality component tables will be published in IRS publications at that time. For decedents' estates with valuation dates on or after [applicability date of the Treasury decision adopting these regulations as final regulations], the mortality component table (Table 2010CM) is in § 20.2031-7(d)(7)(ii) and is referenced by IRS Publication 1457, "Actuarial Valuations Version 4A," and can be found on the IRS website at *https://www.irs.gov/retirement-plans/actuarial-tables* (or a corresponding URL as may be updated from time to time). See § 20.2031-7A for mortality component tables applicable to decedents' estates with valuation dates before [applicability date of the Treasury decision adopting these regulations as final regulations].

(c) *Actuarial factors.*—The present value on the valuation date of an annuity, an interest for life or a term of years, and a remainder or reversionary interest is computed by using the section 7520 interest rate component that is described in paragraph (b)(1) of this section and the mortality component that is described in paragraph (b)(2) of this section. Actuarial factors for determining these present values may be calculated by using the formulas in § 20.2031-7(d)(2). For the convenience of taxpayers, the IRS has computed actuarial factors and displayed them on tables that are referenced and explained by publications of the Internal Revenue Service. If a special factor is required in order to value an interest, the special factor may be calculated by the taxpayer using the actuarial formulas in § 20.2031-7(d)(2) or the taxpayer may request a ruling to obtain the factor from the Internal Revenue Service. The request for a ruling must be accompanied by a recitation of the facts, including the date of birth for each measuring life and copies of relevant instruments. A request for a ruling must comply with the instructions for requesting a ruling published periodically in the Internal Revenue Bulletin (see Rev. Proc. 2021-1, 2021-1 I.R.B. 1, and subsequent updates, and §§ 601.201 and 601.601(d)(2)(ii)(*b*) of this chapter) and must include payment of the required user fee.

(d) *IRS publications referencing and explaining actuarial tables with rates from 0.2 to 20 percent, inclusive, at intervals of two-tenths of one percent, for valuation dates on and after [applicability date of the Treasury decision adopting these regulations as final regulations].*—The publications listed in paragraphs (d)(1) through (3) of this section will be available after [date the Treasury decision adopting these regulations as final regulations is published in the **Federal Register**]. The underlying actuarial tables reference and explained by these publications will be available beginning May 5, 2022, at no charge, electronically via the IRS website at *https://www.irs.gov/retirement-plans/actuarial-tables:*

(1) IRS Publication 1457, "Actuarial Valuations Version 4A" (2022). This publication references tables of valuation factors and provides examples that show how to compute other valuation factors, for determining the present value of annuities, interests for life or a term of years, and remainder or reversionary interests, measured by one or two lives. These factors also may be used in the valuation of interests in a charitable remainder annuity trust as defined in § 1.664-2 of this chapter and a pooled income fund as defined in § 1.642(c)-5 of this chapter. This publication references and explains Table S (single life remainder factors), Table R(2) (two-life last-to-die remainder factors), Table B (actuarial factors used in determining the present value of an interest for a term of years), Table H (commutation factors), Table J (term certain annuity beginning-of-interval adjustment factors), and Table K (annuity end-of-interval adjustment factors). See earlier versions of the publication, § 1.642(c)-6A of this chapter, or § 20.2031-7A for Table S applicable to valuation dates before [applicability date of the Treasury decision adopting these regulations as final regulations]. See earlier versions of the publication for Table R(2) applicable to valuation dates before [applicability date of the Treasury decision adopting these regulations as final regulations]. Earlier versions of the publication also contain earlier versions of Table R(2). Table B, Table J, and Table K also can be found in § 20.2031-7(d)(6), but only for interest rates from 4.2 to 14 percent, inclusive.

(2) IRS Publication 1458, "Actuarial Valuations Version 4B" (2022). This publication references and explains term certain tables and tables of one and two life valuation factors for determining the present value of remainder interests in a charitable remainder unitrust as defined in § 1.664-3 of this chapter. This publication references Table U(1) (unitrust single life remainder factors), Table U(2) (unitrust two-life last-to-die remainder factors), Table D (actuarial factors used in determining the present value of a remainder interest postponed for a term of years), Table F (adjustment payout rate factors), and Table Z (unitrust commutation factors). See earlier versions of the publication or § 1.664-4A of this chapter for Table U(1) applicable to valuation dates before [applicability date of the Treasury decision adopting these regulations as final regulations]. Earlier versions of the publication also contain earlier versions of Table U(2). Table

D also can be found in § 1.664-4(e)(6)(iii) of this chapter, but only for adjusted payout rates from 4.2 to 14 percent, inclusive. Table F also can be found in § 1.664-4(e)(6)(iii) of this chapter, but only for interest rates from 4.2 to 14 percent, inclusive.

(3) IRS Publication 1459, "Actuarial Valuations Version 4C" (2022). This publication references and explains Table C, which provides factors for making adjustments to the standard remainder factor for valuing gifts of depreciable property. See § 1.170A-12 of this chapter.

(4) The publications identified in paragraphs (d)(1) through (3) of this section also reference Table 2010CM, the mortality component table.

(e) *Use of approximation methods for obtaining factors when the required valuation rate falls between two listed rates.*—For certain cases, this part and IRS publications provide approximation methods (for example, interpolation) for obtaining factors when the required valuation rate falls between two listed rates (such as in the case of a pooled income fund's rate of return or a unitrust's adjusted payout rate). In general, exact methods of obtaining the applicable factors are allowed, such as through software using the actual rate of return and the proper actuarial formulas used for the published factors at the listed rates, provided such direct methods are applied consistently. The actuarial formula in § 20.2031-7(d)(2)(ii)(B) is used to determine the remainder factor for pooled income funds and the actuarial formula in § 1.664-4(e)(5)(i) of this chapter is used to determine the remainder factor for unitrusts. The approximation method provided in this part must be used if more exact methods are not available.

(f) *Applicability date.*—This section applies on and after [applicability date of the Treasury decision adopting these regulations as final regulations].

Annuities: Interests: Valuation: Actuarial Tables

Annuities: Interests: Valuation: Actuarial Tables.—Amendments to Reg. §§ 25.7520-1 and 25.7520-3, relating to the use of actuarial tables in valuing annuities, interests for life or terms of years, and remainder or reversionary interests, are proposed (published in the Federal Register on May 5, 2022) (REG-122770-18).

☐ Par. 29. Section 25.7520-1 is amended by revising paragraphs (a)(1) and (2), (b)(2), (c), and (d) and adding paragraphs (e) and (f) to read as follows:

§ 25.7520-1. Valuation of annuities, interests for life or a term of years, and remainder or reversionary interests.

(a) * * *

(1) Except as otherwise provided in this section and in § 25.7520-3(b) (relating to exceptions to the use of prescribed tables under certain circumstances), in the case of certain gifts after April 30, 1989, the fair market value of annuities, interests for life or a term of years (including unitrust interests), and remainder or reversionary interests is their present value determined under this section. See § 20.2031-7(d) of this chapter (and, for periods prior to [applicability date of the Treasury decision adopting these regulations as final regulations], § 20.2031-7A of this chapter) for the computation of the value of annuities, interests for life or a term of years, and remainder or reversionary interests, other than interests described in paragraphs (a)(2) and (3) of this section.

(2) In the case of a gift to a pooled income fund on or after [applicability date of the Treasury decision adopting these regulations as final regulations], see § 1.642(c)-6(e) of this chapter (or, for periods prior to [applicability date of the Treasury decision adopting these regulations as final regulations], § 1.642(c)-6A of this chapter) with respect to the valuation of the remainder interest.

* * *

(b) * * *

(2) *Mortality component.*—The mortality component reflects the mortality data most recently available from the United States census. As new mortality data becomes available after each decennial census, the mortality component described in this section will be revised and the revised mortality component tables will be published in the IRS publications at that time. For gifts with valuation dates on or after [applicability date of the Treasury decision adopting these regulations as final regulations], the mortality component table (Table 2010CM) is in § 20.2031-7(d)(7)(ii) of this chapter, and is referenced by IRS Publication 1457, "Actuarial Valuations Version 4A," and can be found on the IRS website at *https://www.irs.gov/retirement-plans/actuarial-tables* (or a corresponding URL as may be updated from time to time). See § 20.2031-7A of this chapter for mortality component tables applicable to gifts for which the valuation date falls before [applicability date of the Treasury decision adopting these regulations as final regulations].

(c) *Actuarial factors.*—The present value on the valuation date of an annuity, an interest for life or a term of years, and a remainder or reversionary interest is computed by using the section 7520 interest rate component that is described in paragraph (b)(1) of this section and the mortality component that is described in paragraph (b)(2) of this section. Actuarial factors for determining these present values may be calculated using the formulas in § 20.2031-7(d)(2) of this chapter. For the convenience of taxpayers, the IRS has computed actuarial factors and displayed them on tables that are referenced and explained by publications of the Internal Revenue Service. If a special factor is required in order to value an interest, the special factor may be calculated by the taxpayer using the actuarial formulas in § 20.2031-7(d)(2) of this chapter or the taxpayer may request a ruling to obtain the factor from the Internal Revenue Service. The request for a ruling must be accompanied by a recitation of the facts, including the date of birth for each measuring life and copies of relevant instruments. A request for a ruling must comply with the instructions for requesting a ruling published periodically in the Internal Revenue Bulletin (see Rev. Proc. 2021-1, 2021-1 I.R.B. 1, and subsequent updates, and §§ 601.201 and 601.601(d)(2)(ii)(*b*) of this chapter) and must include payment of the required user fee.

(d) *IRS publications referencing and explaining actuarial tables with rates from 0.2 to 20 percent, inclusive, at intervals of two-tenths of one percent, for valuation dates on or after [applicability date of the Treasury decision adopting these regulations as final regulations]*.—The publications listed in paragraphs (d)(1) through (3) of this section will be available after [date of publication of the final rule in the **Federal Register**]. The underlying actuarial tables referenced and explained by these publications will be available beginning May 5, 2022, at no charge, electronically via the IRS website at *https://www.irs.gov/retirement-plans/actuarial-tables:*

(1) IRS Publication 1457, "Actuarial Valuations Version 4A" (2022). This publication references tables of valuation factors and provides examples that show how to compute other valuation factors, for determining the present value of annuities, interests for life or a term of years, and remainder or reversionary interests, measured by one or two lives. These factors may also be used in the valuation of interests in a charitable remainder annuity trust as defined in § 1.664-2 of this chapter and a pooled income fund as defined in § 1.642(c)-5 of this chapter. This publication references and explains Table S (single life remainder factors), Table R(2) (two-life last-to-die remainder factors), Table B (actuarial factors used in determining the present value of an interest for a term of years), Table H (commutation factors), Table J (term certain annuity beginning-of-interval adjustment factors), and Table K (annuity end-of-interval adjustment factors). See earlier versions of the publication, § 1.642(c)-6A of this chapter, or § 20.2031-7A of this chapter for Table S applicable to valuation dates before [applicability date of the Treasury decision adopting these regulations as final regulations]. Earlier versions of the publication also contain earlier versions of Table R(2). Table B, Table J, and Table K also can be found in § 20.2031-7(d)(6) of this chapter, but only for interest rates from 4.2 to 14 percent, inclusive.

(2) IRS Publication 1458, "Actuarial Valuations Version 4B" (2022). This publication references and explains term certain tables and tables of one and two life valuation factors for determining the present value of remainder interests in a charitable remainder unitrust as defined in § 1.664-3 of this chapter. This publication references Table U(1) (unitrust single life remainder factors), Table U(2) (unitrust two-life last-to-die remainder factors), Table D (actuarial factors used in determining the present value of a remainder interest postponed for a term of years), Table F (adjustment payout rate factors), and Table Z (unitrust commutation factors). See earlier versions of the publication or § 1.664-4A of this chapter for Table U(1) applicable to valuation dates before [applicability date of the Treasury decision adopting these regulations as final regulations]. Earlier versions of the publication also contain earlier versions of Table U(2). Table D also can be found in § 1.664-4(e)(6)(iii) of this chapter, but only for adjusted payout rates from 4.2 to 14 percent, inclusive. Table F also can be found in § 1.664-4(e)(6)(iii) of this chapter, but only for interest rates from 4.2 to 14 percent, inclusive.

(3) IRS Publication 1459, "Actuarial Valuations Version 4C" (2022). This publication references and explains Table C, which provides factors for making adjustments to the standard remainder factor for valuing gifts of depreciable property. See § 1.170A-12 of this chapter.

(4) The publications identified in paragraphs (d)(1) through (3) of this section also reference Table 2010CM, the mortality component table.

(e) *Use of approximation methods for obtaining factors when the required valuation rate falls between two listed rates*.—For certain cases, this part and IRS publications provide approximation methods (for example, interpolation) for obtaining factors when the required valuation rate falls between two listed rates (such as in the case of a pooled income fund's rate of return or a unitrust's adjusted payout rate). In general, exact methods of obtaining the applicable factors are allowed, such as through software using the actual rate of return and the proper actuarial formula, provided such direct methods are applied consistently. The actuarial formula in § 20.2031-7(d)(2)(ii)(B) of this chapter is used to determine the remainder factor for pooled income funds and the actuarial formula in § 1.664-4(e)(5)(i) of this chapter is used to determine the remainder factor for unitrusts. The approximation method provided in this part must be used if more exact methods are not available.

(f) *Applicability date*.—This section applies on and after [applicability date of the Treasury decision adopting these regulations as final regulations].

☐ Par. 30. Section 25.7520-3 is amended by:

1. Designating *Examples 1* through 5 of paragraph (b)(2)(v) as paragraphs (b)(2)(v)(A) through (E), respectively.

2. Revising the heading of newly designated paragraphs (b)(2)(v)(A).

3. In newly designated paragraph (b)(2)(v)(B):

i. Revising the heading.

ii. Removing *"Example 1"* and "this paragraph" and adding in their places "paragraph (b)(2)(v)(A) of this section (*Example 1*)" and "this paragraph (b)(2)(v)(B)", respectively.

4. Revising the heading for newly designated paragraph (b)(2)(v)(C).

5. In newly designated paragraph (b)(2)(v)(D):

i. Revising the heading.

ii. Removing *"Example 3"* and adding "paragraph (b)(2)(v)(C) of this section (*Example 3*)" in its place.

6. Revising newly designated paragraph (b)(2)(v)(E) and paragraphs (b)(4) and (c).

The revisions read as follows:

§25.7520-3. Limitation on the application of section 7520.

* * *

(b) * * *

(2) * * *

(v) * * *

(A) *Example 1. Unproductive property.*—* * *

(B) *Example 2. Beneficiary's right to make trust productive.*—* * *

(C) *Example 3. Annuity trust funded with unproductive property.*—* * *

(D) *Example 4. Unitrust funded with unproductive property.*—* * *

(E) *Example 5: Eroding corpus in an annuity payable from a trust or other limited.*—
(*1*) The present value of an annuity interest (and any other interest dependent on the present value of an annuity), when the annuity is paid from an eroding and limited fund, is determined by actuarial factors reflecting the term certain period to the exhaustion of the fund, as shown in Table 1 to this paragraph (b)(2)(v)(E)(*1*). The period to exhaustion is determined using annuity factors. The appropriate annuity factors for an annuity payable for a term of years is computed by subtracting from 1.000000 the factor for an ordinary remainder interest following the same term certain that is determined under the formula in §20.2031-7(d)(2)(ii)(A) of this chapter and then dividing the result by the applicable section 7520 interest rate expressed as a number with at least four decimal places. For the convenience of taxpayers, actuarial factors have been computed by IRS and appear in the "Annuity" column of Table B. If the annuity is for life (or for a period depending in part on life) and the period to exhaustion is shorter than the possible life period, actuarial commutation factors may be used in determining the present value. The actuarial commutation factors can be computed directly by using the formulas in §25.2512-5(d)(2)(v)(A)(*1*), the section 7520 rate, and Table 2010CM as set forth in §20.2031-7(d)(7)(ii) of this chapter. For the convenience of taxpayers, actuarial factors have been computed by IRS and appear in Table H. Table B and Table H can be found on the IRS website at *https://www.irs.gov/retirement-plans/actuarial-tables* (or a corresponding URL as may be updated from time to time). After determining the point of exhaustion of funds, the approximation method for determining the present value of annuity payments so limited by exhaustion in the example in Table 1 to this paragraph (b)(2)(v)(E)(*1*) is to be used if a more exact method (for example, computing the year-by-year present value of each payment until the fund is exhausted) is not used. For purposes of this example, the relevant factors from Table B and Table H(4.4) are:

Table 1 to paragraph (b)(2)(v)(E)(1)

Factors from Table B			
Annuity, Income, and Remainder Interests for a Term Certain			
Interest at 4.4 Percent			
Years	Annuity	Income Interest	Remainder
13	9.7423	0.428661	0.571339
14	10.2896	0.452741	0.547259
50	20.0878	0.883862	0.116138

Factors from Table H(4.4)

Commutation Factors -Based on Table 2010CM

Interest Rate of 4.4 Percent

Factors from Table B			
Annuity, Income, and Remainder Interests for a Term Certain			
Interest at 4.4 Percent			
Years	Annuity	Income Interest	Remainder
Age (x)	D_x	N_x-factor	M_x-factor
60	6,694.636	90,259.34	2,723.225
73	3,151.228	29,432.25	1,856.209
74	2,941.075	26,452.50	1,777.165

(2) The donor, who is age 60 and in normal health, transfers property worth $1,000,000 to a trust on or after [applicability date of the Treasury decision adopting these regulations as final regulations]. The trust will pay a 10 percent ($100,000 per year) annuity to a charitable organization for the life of the donor, payable annually at the end of each period, and the remainder then will be distributed to the donor's child. The section 7520 rate for the month of the transfer is 4.4 percent. First, it is necessary to determine whether the annuity may exhaust the corpus before all annuity payments are made. Because it is assumed under the prescribed mortality component, Table 2010CM, that any measuring life may survive until age 110, any life annuity could require payments until the measuring life reaches age 110. The determination of whether the annuity may exhaust the corpus before the annuity payments terminate is computed with values from Table B as illustrated in Figure 1 to this paragraph (b)(2)(v)(E)(2).

Figure 1 to paragraph (b)(2)(v)(E)(2) – Illustration of determining present value of term certain annuity

A.	Highest age possible under mortality table	110
B.	Less: age of the measuring life at date of transfer	- 60
C.	Difference: number of years annuity obligation may continue	50
D.	Annual annuity payment	$100,000
E.	Table B annuity factor for 50 years at 4.4 percent	20.0878
F.	Present value of term certain annuity: D x E	$2,008,780

(3) Because the present value of an annuity for a term of 50 years exceeds the corpus, the annuity may exhaust the trust before all payments are made. Consequently, the annuity must be valued as an annuity payable for a term of years or until the prior death of the annuitant, with the term of years determined by when the fund will be exhausted by the annuity payments, assuming earnings at the section 7520 rate of 4.4 percent.

(4) If an annuity of $100,000 payable at the end of each year for a period had an annuity factor of 10.0, it would have a present value exactly equal to the principal available to pay the annuity over the term. The annuity factor for 13 years at 4.4 percent in Table B is 9.7423 and the annuity factor for 14 years at 4.4 percent is 10.2896. Thus, it is determined that the $1,000,000 initial transfer will be sufficient to make 13 annual payments of $100,000, but not to make the entire 14th payment. The present value of an annuity of $100,000 payable at the end of each year for 13 years certain is $100,000 times 9.7423 or $974,230. The remaining amount is $25,770. Of the initial transfer amount, $25,770 is not needed to make payments for 13 years, so this amount, as accumulated for 14 years, will be available for the final payment. The 14-year accumulation factor is 1.8273 ($(1 + 0.044)^{14}$ = 1.8273), so the amount available in 14 years is $25,770 times 1.8273 or $47,089.52. Therefore, for purposes of this present value determination, the annuity obligation is treated as being composed of two distinct annuity components. The two annuity components taken together must equal the total annual amount of $100,000. The first annuity component is the exact amount that the trust will have available for the final payment, $47,089.52. The second annuity component then must be $100,000 minus $47,089.52, or $52,910.48. Specifically, the initial corpus will be able to make payments of $52,910.48 per year for 13 years plus payments of $47,089.52 per year for 14 years. The total annuity is valued by adding the present value of the two separate temporary component annuities.

(5) The actuarial factor for determining the value of the annuity of $52,910.48 per year payable for 13 years or until the prior death of a person aged 60 is derived by the use of factors involving one life and a term of years, derived from Table H. The factor is determined as illustrated in Figure 2 to this paragraph (b)(2)(v)(E)(5).

Figure 2 to paragraph (b)(2)(v)(E)(5) – Illustration of determining annuity factor for shorter of life or 13 years

G. Initial age	60
H. Plus: Term of years	+ 13
I. Sum (Terminal age)	73
J. $\mathring{N}_x$ factor, Table H(4.4), age 60	90,259.34
K. Less: $\mathring{N}_x$ factor, Table H(4.4), age 73	- 29,432.25
L. Difference	60,827.09
M. D_x factor, Table H(4.4), age 60	6,694.64
N. Required Annuity Factor: L / M	9.0859

(6) The actuarial factor for determining the value of the annuity $47,089.52 per year payable for 14 years or until the prior death of a person aged 60 is derived by the use of factors involving one life and a term of years, derived from Table H. The factor is determined as illustrated in Figure 3 to this paragraph (b)(2)(v)(E)(6).

Figure 3 to paragraph (b)(2)(v)(E)(6) – Illustration of determining annuity factor for shorter of life or 14 years

O. Initial age	60
P. Plus: Term of years	+ 14
Q. Sum (Terminal age)	74
R. $\mathring{N}_x$ factor, Table H(2.8), age 60	90,259.34
S. Less: $\mathring{N}_x$ factor, Table H(2.8), age 74	- 26,452.50
T. Difference	63,806.84
U. D_x factor, Table H(2.8), age 60	6,694.64
V. Required Annuity Factor: T / U	9.5310

(7) Based on the calculations of paragraph (b)(2)(v)(E)(5) of this section, the present value of an annuity of $52,910.48 per year payable for 13 years or until the prior death of a person aged 60 is $480,739.33 ($52,910.48 × 9.0859). Based on the calculations of paragraph (b)(2)(v)(E)(6) of this section, the present value of an annuity of $47,089.52 per year payable for 14 years or until the prior death of a person aged 60 is $448,810.22 ($47,089.52 × 9.5310). Thus, the present value of the charitable annuity interest is the sum of the two component annuities, $929,549.55 ($480,739.33 + $448,810.22).

* * *

(4) *Example - terminal illness.*—(i) *Sample factors from actuarial Table S.*—The provisions of paragraph (b)(3) of this section are illustrated by the example in paragraph (b)(4)(ii) of this section. The appropriate annuity factor for an annuity payable for the life of one individual is computed by subtracting from 1.00000 the factor for an ordinary remainder interest following the life of the same individual that is determined under the formula in § 20.2031-7(d)(2)(ii)(B) of this chapter and then dividing the result by the applicable section 7520 interest rate expressed as a number with four decimal places. For the convenience of taxpayers, actuarial factors have been computed by IRS and appear in the "Annuity" column of Table S. Table S can be found on the IRS website at *https://www.irs.gov/retirement-plans/actuarial-tables*. For purposes of the example in paragraph (b)(4)(ii) of this section, the relevant factor from Table S is:

Table 2 to paragraph (b)(4)(i)

Factors from Table S - Based on Table 2010CM			
Interest at 4.4 Percent			
Age	Annuity	Life Estate	Remainder
75	8.6473	0.38048	0.61952

(ii) *Example of donor with terminal illness.*—The donor transfers property worth $1,000,000 to a child on or after [applicability date of the Treasury decision adopting these regulations as final regulations], in exchange for the child's promise to pay the donor $80,000 per year for the donor's life, payable annually at the end of each period. The section 7520 interest rate for the month of the transfer is 4.4 percent. The donor is age 75 but has been diagnosed with an incurable illness and has at least a 50 percent probability of dying within 1 year. Under Table S, the annuity factor at 4.4 percent for a person age 75 in normal health is 8.6473. Thus, if the donor were not terminally ill, the present value of the annuity would be $691,784 ($80,000 × 8.6473). Assuming the presumption provided in paragraph (b)(3) of this section does not apply, because there is at least a 50 percent probability that the donor will die within 1 year, the standard section 7520 annuity factor may not be used to determine the present value of the donor's annuity interest. Instead, a special section 7520 annuity factor must be computed that takes into account the projection of the donor's actual life expectancy.

* * *

(c) *Applicability dates.*—Section 25.7520-3(a) is applicable as of May 1, 1989. The provisions of paragraph (b) of this section, except paragraphs (b)(2)(v)(E) and (b)(4) of this section, are applicable to gifts made after December 13, 1995. Paragraphs (b)(2)(v)(E) and (b)(4) of this section are applicable to gifts made on or after [applicability date of the Treasury decision adopting these regulations as final regulations].

DEFINITIONS

Gifts and Bequests from Covered Expatriates: Imposition of Tax

Gifts and Bequests from Covered Expatriates: Imposition of Tax.—Reg. §28.7701-1, relating to a tax on United States citizens and residents who receive gifts or bequests from certain individuals who relinquished United States citizenship or ceased to be lawful permanent residents of the United States on or after June 17, 2008, is proposed (published in the Federal Register on September 10, 2015) (REG-112997-10).

☐ Section 28.7701-1 is added to read as follows:

§28.7701-1. Tax return preparer.—For the definition of the term *tax return preparer,* see §301.7701-15 of this chapter.

GENERAL RULES

Below-Market Loans

Below Market Loans: Interest.—Reproduced below are the texts of proposed Reg. §§1.7872-1—1.7872-14, 20.7872-1 and 25.7872-1, relating to the tax treatment of both lender and borrower in certain below-market interest rate loan transactions (published in the Federal Register on August 20, 1985; proposed Reg. §1.7872-4(e) was reproposed in the Federal Register on April 8, 1986).

☐ New §1.7872-1 is added in the appropriate place. This new section reads as follows:

§1.7872-1. Introduction.—(a) *Statement of purpose.*—Section 7872 generally treats certain loans in which the interest rate charged is less than the applicable Federal rate as economically equivalent to loans bearing interest at the applicable Federal rate, coupled with a payment by the lender to the borrower sufficient to fund all or part of the payment of interest by the borrower. Such loans are referred to as "below-market loans." See §1.7872-3 for detailed definitions of below-market loans and the determination of the applicable Federal rate.

Accordingly, section 7872 recharacterizes a below-market loan as two transactions:

(1) An arm's-length transaction in which the lender makes a loan to the borrower in exchange for a note requiring the payment of interest at the applicable Federal rate; and

(2) A transfer of funds by the lender to the borrower ("imputed transfer").

The timing and the characterization of the amount of the imputed transfer by the lender to the borrower are determined in accordance with the substance of the transaction. The timing and the amount of the imputed interest payment (the excess of the amount of interest required to be paid using the applicable Federal rate, *over* the amount of interest required to be paid according to the loan agreement) by the borrower to the lender depend on the character of the imputed transfer by the lender to the borrower and whether the loan is a term loan or a demand loan. If the imputed transfer by the lender is characterized as a gift, the provisions of chapter 12 of the Internal Revenue Code, relating to gift tax, also apply. All imputed transfers under section 7872 (*e.g.*, interest, compensation, gift) are characterized in accordance with the substance of the transaction, and, except as otherwise provided in the regulations under section 7872, are treated as so characterized for all purposes of the Code. For example, for purposes of section 170, an interest-free loan to a charity referred to in section 170 for which interest is imputed under section 7872, is treated as an interest bearing loan coupled with periodic gifts to the charity in the amount of the imputed transfer, for purposes of section 170. In addition, all applicable information and reporting requirements (*e.g.*, reporting on W-2 and Form 1099) must be satisfied.

(b) *Effective date.*—(1) *In general.*—The provisions of section 7872 generally apply, for periods after June 6, 1984, to demand loans outstanding after that date and to loans other than demand loans made after that date.

(2) *Demand loans repaid before September 17, 1984.*—If a demand loan which was outstanding on June 6, 1984, is repaid before September 17, 1984, section 7872 does not apply to the loan. For purposes of this paragraph (b)(2) only, a loan is treated as repaid if it is repaid, cancelled, forgiven, modified, or otherwise retired. For example, if the loan agreement for an interest-free demand loan, which is outstanding on June 6, 1984, is modified on September 10, 1984, to require the borrower to pay a 5 percent simple rate of interest, then for purposes of this paragraph (b)(2) the original loan is treated as repaid on September 10, 1984, and section 7872 applies to the modified loan beginning on that date.

(3) *Change in loan agreement.*—For purposes of section 7872, any loan which is renegotiated, extended, or revised after June 6, 1984, is treated as a loan made after June 6, 1984. Accordingly, for purposes of the effective date provisions of this paragraph (b) in the case of such a loan, the provisions of section 7872 apply as if the loan were a new loan made on the day the lender and borrower enter into a binding agreement to change the provisions of the loan.

(4) *Other Federal tax consequences.*—Section 7872 does not alter the law applicable to below-market loans for periods prior to the effective date of section 7872. Accordingly, below-market interest rate loans which are not subject to section 7872 by reason of the effective date provisions of this paragraph (b). including loans which are repaid under the rule described in paragraph (b)(2) of this section, may still have Federal tax consequences. See, *e.g.*, *Dickman v. Commissioner*, 465 U.S. — (1984), 104 S. Ct. 1086.

(c) *Key to Code provisions.*—The following key is intended to facilitate research with respect to specific Code provisions. The key identifies the regulations section in which the principal discussion of a particular Code provision appears. As a result of the interrelationship among Code provisions, other regulation sections may also discuss the particular Code provision. Section 1.7872-2 deals with the definition of the term "loan" for purposes of section 7872. The following table identifies the provisions of section 7872 that are dealt with in §§1.7872-2 through 1.7872-14 and lists each provision of Code section 7872 below the regulation section in which it is covered.

§1.7872-2								
(f)	(8)							

§1.7872-3			§1.7872-4			§1.7872-5		
(e)	(1)		(c)	(1)		(g)	(1)	(C)
(f)	(2)		(f)	(3)				
(g)	(1)	(A)						

§1.7872-6			§1.7872-7			§1.7872-8		
(a)			(b)			(c)	(2)	
(d)	(2)		(d)	(2)		(d)	(1)	
			(f)	(1)				
			(f)	(4)				
			(f)	(10)				

§1.7872-9			§1.7872-10			§1.7872-11		
(c)	(3)		(f)	(5)		(f)	(7)	
(f)	(10)		(f)	(6)		(f)	(9)	
						(g)	(1)	(A)
						(g)	(1)	(B)

§1.7872-12			§1.7872-13			§1.7872-14		
(e)	(1)	(A)	(e)	(2)		(e)	(1)	(B)
						(f)	(1)	

See §20.7872-1 for regulations under section 7872(g)(2).

See §25.7872-1 for gift tax regulations.

See §53.4941(d)-2 for interest-free loans between private foundations and disqualified persons. [Reg. §1.7872-1.]

* * *

☐ New § 20.7872-1 is added in the appropriate place to read as follows:

§ 20.7872-1. Certain below-market loans.—For purposes of chapter 11 of the Internal Revenue Code, relating to estate tax, a gift term loan (within the meaning of § 1.7872-4(b)) that is made after June 6, 1984, shall be valued at the lesser of:

(a) the unpaid stated principal, plus accrued interest; or

(b) the sum of the present value of all payments due under the note (including accrual interest), using the applicable Federal rate for loans of a term equal to the remaining term of the loan in effect at the date of death.

No discount is allowed based on evidence that the loan is uncollectible unless the facts concerning collectibility of the loan have changed significantly since the time the loan was made. This section applies with respect to any term loan made with donative intent after June 6, 1984, regardless of the interest rate under the loan agreement, and regardless of whether that interest rate exceeds the applicable Federal rate in effect on the day on which the loan was made.

* * *

☐ New § 25.7872-1 is added in the appropriate place to read as follows:

§ 25.7872-1. Certain below-market loans.—For purposes of Chapter 12 of the Internal Revenue Code, relating to gift tax, if a taxpayer makes a gift loan (within the meaning of § 1.7872-4(b)) that is a term loan (within the meaning of § 1.7872-10(a)(2)) and that is made after June 6, 1984, the excess of the amount loaned over the present value of all payments which are required to be made under the terms of the loan agreement shall be treated as a gift from the lender to the borrower on the date the loan is made. If a taxpayer makes a gift loan that is a demand loan (within the meaning of § 1.7872-10(a)(1)) and that is outstanding during any calendar period after June 6, 1984, and not repaid before September 17, 1984, the amount of foregone interest (within the meaning of section 7872(e)(2)) attributable to that calendar period shall be treated as a gift from the lender to the borrower. The *de minimis* exception described in section 7872(c)(2) applies to the gift tax treatment of a gift loan. In the case of a term gift loan, however, once section 7872 applies to the loan, the *de minimis* exception will not apply to the loan at some later date regardless of whether the aggregate outstanding amount of loans does not continue to exceed the limitation amount. For a detailed analysis of section 7872, see the income tax regulations under section 7872, § 1.7872-1 through § 1.7872-14.

* * *

☐ New §§ 1.7872-2 through 1.7872-14 are added in the appropriate place. These new sections read as follows:

§ 1.7872-2. Definition of loan.—(a) *In general.*—(1) *"Loan" interpreted broadly.*—For purposes of section 7872, the term "loan" includes generally any extension of credit (including, for example, a purchase money mortgage) and any transaction under which the owner of money permits another person to use the money for a period of time after which the money is to be transferred to the owner or applied according to an express or implied agreement with the onwer. The term "loan" is interpreted broadly to implement the anti-abuse intent of the statute. An integrated series of transactions which is the equivalent of a loan is treated as a loan. A payment for property, goods, or services under a contract, however, is not a loan merely because one of the payor's remedies for breach of the contract is recovery of the payment. Similarly, a bona fide prepayment made in a manner consistent with normal commercial practices for services, property, or the use of property, generally, is not a loan; see section 461 and the regulations thereunder for the treatment of certain prepaid expenses and for the special rules of sections 461(h) and (i). However, a taxpayer's characterization of a transaction as a prepayment or as a loan is not conclusive. Transactions will be characterized for tax purposes according to their economic substance, rather than the terms used to describe them. Thus, for example, receipt by a partner from a partnership of money is treated as a loan if it is so characterized under § 1.731-1(c)(2).

(2) *Limitations on applicability of section 7872.*—(i) *In general.*—Section 7872 applies only to certain below-market loans (as defined in section 7872(e)(1)). Section 1.7872-4 lists the categories of below-market loans to which section 7872 generally applies. Certain below-market loans within these categories, however, are exempt from the provisions of section 7872. See § 1.7872-5 for specific exemptions from the rules.

(ii) *Loans to which section 483 or 1274 applies.*—Generally, section 7872 does not apply to any loan which is given in consideration for the sale or exchange of property (within the meaning of section 1274(c)(1)) or paid on account of the sale or exchange of property (within the meaning of section 483(c)(1)), even if the rules of those sections do not apply by reason of exceptions or safe harbor provisions. Any transaction, however, which otherwise is described in section 7872(c)(1)(A), (B), or (C), and is—

(A) a debt instrument that is issued in exchange for property and that is payable on demand.

(B) A debt instrument described in section 1273(b)(3), or

(C) A debt instrument described in section 1275(b), unless the transaction is described in § 1.7872-5(b)(1), not subject to sections 483 and 1274 and is subject to section 7872.

(iii) *Relation to section 482.*—If a below-market loan subject to section 7872 would also be subject to section 482 if the Commissioner chose to apply section 482 to the loan transaction, then section 7872 will be applied first. If the Commissioner chooses to apply section 482, then the loan transaction is subject to section 482 in addition to section 7872.

(3) *Loan proceeds transferred over time.*—In general, each extension of credit or transfer of money by a lender to a borrower is treated as a separate loan. Accordingly, if the loan agreement provides that the lender will transfer the loan proceeds to the borrower in installments, each installment payment is treated as a separate loan. Similarly, in the case of a loan in which the transfer of the loan proceeds to the borrower is subject to a draw-down restriction, each draw-down of loan proceeds is treated as a separate loan.

(b) *Examples of transactions treated as loans.*—(1) *Refundable deposits.*—(i) *In general.*—If an amount is treated for Federal tax purposes as a deposit rather than as a prepayment or an advance payment, the amount is treated as a loan for purposes of section 7872.

(ii) *Partially refundable deposits.*—If an amount is treated for Federal tax purposes as a deposit rather than as a prepayment or an advance payment and the amount is refundable only for a certain period of time or is only partially refundable, then the deposit is treated as a loan only to the extent that it is refundable and only for the period of time that it is refundable.

(iii) *Exception.*—Paragraph (b)(1)(i) does not apply if the deposit is custodial in nature or is held in trust for the benefit of the transferor. The deposit is treated as custodial in nature if the transferee is not entitled to the beneficial enjoyment of the amount deposited including interest thereon (except as security for an obligation of the transferor). Thus, if an amount is placed in escrow to secure a contractual obligation of the transferor, and the escrow agreement provides that all interest earned is paid to the transferor and that the transferee has no rights to or interest in the escrowed amount unless and until the transferor defaults on the obligation, then, in the absence of any facts which indicate that the transaction was entered into for tax avoidance purposes, the deposit is not a loan.

(2) *Permitting agent or intermediary to retain funds.*—An agreement under which an agent or intermediary is permitted to retain possession of money for a period of time before transferring the money to his or her principal is treated as a loan for purposes of section 7872. For example, a taxpayer who enters into an agreement with a broker under which the broker may retain possession of the proceeds from the sale of the taxpayer's property (*e.g.*, securities issued by the taxpayer) for a period of time and uses or invests those funds (other than for the taxpayer's account) is treated as making a loan to the broker for the period of time that the broker retains possession of the proceeds.

(3) *Advances.*—An advance of money to a employee, salesman, or other similar person to defray anticipated expenditures is not treated as a loan for purposes of section 7872 if the amount of money advanced is reasonably calculated not to exceed the anticipated expenditures and if the advance of money is made on a day within a reasonable period of time of the day that the anticipated expenditure will be incurred. An advance or draw of money against a partner's distributive share of income which is treated in the manner described in § 1.731-1(a)(1)(ii) is not a loan for purposes of section 7872. [Reg. § 1.7872-2.]

§ 1.7872-3. Definition of below-market loans.—(a) *In general.*—Section 7872 does not impute interest on loans which require the payment of interest at the applicable Federal rate. This section defines the applicable Federal rate and provides rules for determining whether an interest-bearing loan provides sufficient stated interest to avoid classification as a below-market loan. The term "below-market loan" means any loan if—

(1) In the case of a demand loan, interest is payable at a rate less than the applicable Federal rate; or

(2) In the case of a term loan, the amount loaned exceeds the present value of all payments due under the loan, determined as of the day the loan is made, using a discount rate equal to the applicable Federal rate in effect on the day the loan is made.

Sections 1.7872-13 and 1.7872-14 contain the computations necessary for determining the amount of imputed interest on a below-market loan which is subject to section 7872.

(b) *Applicable Federal rate.*—(1) *In general.*—The applicable Federal rate is an annual stated rate of interest based on semiannual compounding. In addition, the Commissioner may prescribe equivalent rates based on compounding periods other than semiannual compounding (for example, annual compounding, quarterly compounding, and monthly compounding), to facilitate application of this section to loans other than those involving semiannual payments or compounding. Thus, loans providing for annual payments or annual compounding of interest over the entire life of the loan will use the applicable Federal rates based on annual compounding; loans providing for quarterly payments or quarterly compounding over the entire life of the loan will use the applicable Federal rates based on quarterly compounding; and loans providing for monthly payments or monthly compounding over the entire life of the loan will use the applicable Federal rates based on monthly compounding. The shorter of the compounding period or the payment interval determines which rate is appropriate. Loans providing for payments or compounding of interest at other intervals (*e.g.*, daily, weekly, bi-monthly) may use the applicable Federal rates published by the Commissioner based on the shortest compounding period that is longer than the shorter of the compounding period or the payment interval provided for over the entire life of the loan. Thus, loans providing for daily or weekly payments or compounding of interest may use the applicable Federal rate based on monthly compounding; loans providing for bi-monthly payments or compounding of interest will use the applicable Federal rates based on quarterly compounding; etc. Alternatively, taxpayers may compute and use interest rates other than those published by the Commissioner for other interest payment or compounding periods if such rates are equivalent to the applicable Federal rates. Any reference to the applicable Federal rate in the regulations under section 7872 includes the equivalent rates based on different compounding or payment periods.

(2) *Determination of applicable Federal rate.*—(i) *In general.*—The applicable Federal rate for loans described in paragraphs (b)(3), (4), and (5) of this section is defined by reference to Federal statutory rates and alternate Federal rates.

(ii) *Definition of Federal statutory rate.*—The Federal statutory rates are the short-, mid-, and long-term rates in effect under section 1274(d) and their equivalent rates based on different compounding assumptions. These rates are published by the Commissioner for each semiannual period January 1 through June 30 and July 1 through December 31.

(iii) *Definition of alternate Federal rate.*—The alternate Federal rates are the short-, mid-, and long-term rates established by the Commissioner on a monthly basis, and their equivalent rates based on different compounding assumptions. These rates are published by the Commissioner on a monthly basis.

(iv) *Definition of semiannual period.*—For purposes of section 7872 and the regulations thereunder, the first semiannual period means the period in any calendar year beginning on January 1 and ending on June 30, and the second semiannual period means the period in any calendar year beginning on July 1 and ending on December 31.

(3) *Demand loans.*—(i) *In general.*—In the case of a demand loan, the applicable Federal rate for a semiannual period (January 1 through June 30 or July 1 through December 31), is the lower of:

(A) The Federal statutory short-term rate in effect for the semiannual period; or

(B) The special rate for demand loans described in paragraph (b)(3)(ii) of this section.

(ii) *Special rate for demand loans.*—The special rate for demand loans is—

(A) For the semiannual period in which the loan is made, the alternate Federal short-term rate which is in effect on the day the loan is made; and

(B) For each subsequent semiannual period in which the loan is outstanding, the alternate Federal short-term rate which is in effect for the first month of that semiannual period (*i.e.*, January or July).

For a special safe harbor rule for certain variable interest rate demand loans, see paragraph (c)(2) of this section.

(4) *Term loans.*—In the case of a term loan, including a gift term loan or a term loan that is treated as a demand loan as provided in §1.7872-10(a)(5), the applicable Federal rate is the lower of:

(i) The Federal statutory rate for loans of that term in effect on the day the loan is made; or

(ii) The alternate Federal rate for loans of that term in effect on the day the loan is made.

(5) *Loans conditioned on future services.*—In the case of a term loan that is treated as a demand loan as provided in §1.7872-10(a)(5), on the date the condition to perform substantial services is removed or lapses, the demand loan is treated as terminated and a new term loan is created. The applicable Federal rate for the new term loan is the lower of the following:

(i) The applicable Federal rate in effect on the day the original loan was made; or

(ii) The applicable Federal rate in effect on the day the condition lapses or is removed.

(6) *Periods before January 1, 1985.*—For term loans made and demand loans outstanding after June 6, 1984, and before January 1, 1985, the applicable Federal rate under section 7872(f)(2) is as follows:

(i) 10.25 percent, compounded annually;

(ii) 10.00 percent, compounded semiannually;

(iii) 9.88 percent, compounded quarterly; and

(iv) 9.80 percent, compounded monthly.

(c) *Loans having sufficient stated interest.*—(1) *In general.*—Section 7872 does not apply to any loan which has sufficient stated interest. A loan has sufficient stated interest if it provides for interest on the outstanding loan balance at a rate no lower than the applicable Federal rate based on a compounding period appropriate for that loan. See paragraph (b)(1) of this section for a description of appropriate compounding periods. See §1.7872-11(a) for rules relating to waiver of interest.

(2) *Safe harbor for demand loans.*—If the interest rate on a demand loan is changed, either under the terms of the original loan agreement, or subsequently, the loan will be treated as a new loan for purposes of determining the applicable Federal rate for that loan. Thus, the loan will have sufficient stated interest for the remainder of the semiannual period following such change of interest rate if the new interest rate is not less than the lower of the Federal statutory

short-term rate in effect for the semiannual period or the alternate Federal short-term rate in effect on the day the new interest rate takes effect.

(3) *Examples.*—The provisions of this paragraph (c) may be illustrated by the following examples.

Example (1). On December 1, 1984, A makes a $100,000 5-year gift term loan to B, requiring 10 interest payments of $5,000 each, payable on May 31 and November 30 of each year the loan is outstanding. Since the loan requires semiannual interest payments, the appropriate compounding assumption is semiannual compounding. For term loans made during 1984, the applicable Federal rate based on semiannual compounding is 10 percent. The loan is not a below-market loan because it provides for interest at a rate of 10 percent, payable semiannually.

Example (2). Assume the same facts as in Example (1), except the loan requires 5 annual interest payments of $10,000 each, payable on November 30 of each year the loan is outstanding. Since the loan requires annual interest payments, the appropriate compounding assumption is annual compounding. The loan is a below-market loan because, although interest is stated at a rate of 10 percent, a rate that reflects semiannual compounding is not appropriate for a loan with annual payments.

Example (3). Assume the same facts as in Example (2), except that the loan requires 5 annual interest payments of $10,250 each, payable on November 30 of each year that the loan is outstanding. Since the loan requires annual interest payments, the appropriate compounding assumption is annual compounding. For term loans made during 1984, the applicable Federal rate based on annual compounding is 10.25 percent. The loan is not a below-market loan because it provides for interest at a rate of 10.25 percent, compounded annually.

Example (4). Assume the same facts as in Example (1), except that the loan requires 120 monthly interest payments of $816.67 each, payable on the last calendar day of each month that the loan is outstanding. Since the loan requires monthly interest payments, the appropriate compounding assumption is monthly compounding. The loan is not a below-market loan because it requires monthly payments of interest based on a rate of 9.80 percent, the applicable Federal rate of interest on monthly compounding.

Example (5). (i) A makes a demand loan to her son, B, on April 1, 1985. The loan requires quarterly interest payments due at the end of each calendar quarter at a rate of 10 percent. Assume that on April 1, 1985, the Federal statutory short-term rate in effect is 12 percent, compounded quarterly, and that the alternate Federal short-term rate in effect for the month of April is 10 percent, compounded quarterly. The loan is not a below-market loan for the period April 1, 1985, through June 30, 1985.

(ii) Assume that on July 1, 1985, the Federal sttutory short-term rate in effect is 11 percent, compounded quarterly, and the alternate Federal short-term rate in effect for the month of July is 10.20 percent, compounded quarterly. The loan no longer has sufficient stated interest. If A raises the interest rate to at least 10.20 percent, the loan will have sufficient stated interest and will not be a below-market loan for the period of July 1 through December 31, 1985.

(iii) Assume that on July 1, 1985, A increases the interest rate on the loan to 10.20 percent, a rate equal to the alternate Federal short-term rate in effect for July. Further assume that the alternate Federal short-term rate subsequently decreases so that such rate in effect for the month of August decreases to 10 percent. On August 1, 1985, A lowers the interest rate on this loan to 10 percent and does not change that rate for the remainder of the semiannual period. The loan has sufficient stated interest and will not be a below-market loan for the semiannual period beginning on July 1, 1985, even if the alternate Federal rate is greater than 10 percent for any or all of the four remaining months in the semiannual period ending on December 31, 1985.

(d) *Short periods.*—The rules for determining whether a loan has sufficient stated interest also apply to short periods (*e.g.*, a period that is shorter than the interval between interest payments or interest compounding under the loan which may occur at the beginning or end of the loan). For special computational rules and examples relating to short periods, see §1.7872-12.

(e) *Variable rates of interest.*—(1) *In general.*—If a loan requires payments of interest calculated at a rate of interest based in whole or in part on an objective index or combination of indices of market interest rates (*e.g.*, a prime rate, the applicable Federal rate, the average yield on government securities as reflected in the weekly Treasury bill rate, the Treasury constant maturity series, or LIBOR (London interbank offered rate)), the loan will be treated as having sufficient stated interest if—

(i) In the case of a term loan, the rate fixed by the index or indices is no lower than the applicable Federal rate, as determined under paragraph (b)(4) of this section (as modified by paragraph (e)(2) of this section), on the date the loan is made; or

(ii) In the case of a demand loan, the interest rate fixed by the index or indices is no lower than the applicable Federal rate, as determined under paragraph (b)(3) of this section, for each semiannual period that the loan is outstanding. See paragraph (e)(2)(i) of this section for rules relating to variable interest rate demand loans the interest rates of which are tied to the applicable Federal rate.

(2) *Special rules.*—(i) *Demand loans tied to the applicable Federal rate.*—A variable rate demand loan will be treated as having sufficient stated interest if, by the terms of the loan agreement, the interest rate cannot be less than the lower of the Federal statutory short-term rate or the alternate Federal short-term rate in effect at the beginning (or, if the agreement so provides,

at the end) of the payment or compounding period (whichever is shorter).

(ii) *Applicable Federal rate for variable interest rate term loans.*—For purposes of determining the applicable Federal rate, if a term loan requires payments or compounding of interest based on a variable rate (within the meaning of paragraph (e)(1) of this section), the term of the loan shall be treated as being equal to the longest period of time that exists between the dates that, under the loan agreement, the interest rate charged on the loan is required to be recomputed (whether or not the recomputation results in a rate different from the immediately preceding rate). Thus, for example, in the case of a 10 year term loan that charges interest at a variable rate equal to a rate 2 points above the prime rate, and that requires that the interest rate be adjusted every 18 months to reflect any changes in the prime rate, the applicable Federal rate is determined by treating the loan as having a term of 18 months rather than a term of 10 years. Accordingly, the applicable Federal short-term rate rather than the applicable Federal long-term rate shall apply.

(3) The provisions of paragraph (e)(1) of this section may be illustrated by the following examples:

Example (1). On April 1, 1985, A loans $200,000 to B, repayable on demand. The note calls for interest to be paid semiannually on September 30 and March 31 of each year at a rate equal to the alternate Federal short-term rate (based on semiannual compounding) for the month in which the payment is made. The loan has sufficient stated interest.

Example (2). Assume the same facts as in *Example (1)* except that the note calls for interest at a rate equal to the lower of the alternate Federal short-term rate or the statutory Federal short-term rate (in each case, based on semiannual compounding) for the month in which the payment is made. The loan has sufficient stated interest.

Example (3). Assume the same facts as in *Example (1)* except that interest is computed and compounded at the end of each month at a rate equal to the lower of the alternate Federal short-term rate or the statutory Federal short-term rate (in each case, based on monthly compounding) in effect for that month. Accrued interest is payable semiannually on September 30 and March 31 of each year. The loan has sufficient stated interest.

Example (4). Assume the same facts as in *Example (1)* except that interest is payable at the prime rate of a major lending institution at the time each payment is made. The prime rate is not an index which by its terms cannot be less than the lower of the statutory Federal short-term rate or the alternate Federal short-term rate. Therefore, the loan will be tested for sufficient stated interest in each semiannual period under the rules of paragraph (b)(3) of this section.

(f) *Contingent interest.*—[RESERVED] [Reg. § 1.7872-3.]

§ 1.7872-4. Types of below-market loans.—(a) *In general.*—Section 7872 applies only to certain categories of below-market loans. These categories are gift loans, compensation-related loans, corporation-shareholder loans, tax avoidance loans, and certain other loans classified in the regulations under section 7872 as significant tax effect loans (*i.e.*, loans whose interest arrangements have a significant effect on any Federal tax liability of the lender or the borrower).

(b) *Gift loans.*—(1) *In general.*—The term "gift loan" means any below-market loan in which the foregoing of interest is in the nature of a gift within the meaning of Chapter 12 of the Internal Revenue Code (whether or not the lender is a natural person).

(2) *Cross reference.*—See § 1.7872-8 for special rules limiting the application of section 7872 to gift loans. See paragraph (g) of this section for rules with respect to below-market loans which are indirectly gift loans.

(c) *Compensation-related loans.*—(1) *In general.*—A compensation-related loan is a below-market loan that is made in connection with the performance of services, directly or indirectly, between—

(i) An employer and an employee,

(ii) An independent contractor and a person for whom such independent contractor provides services, or

(iii) A partnership and a partner if the loan is made in consideration for services performed by the partner acting other than in his capacity as a member of the partnership.

The imputed transfer (amount of money treated as transferred) by the lender to the borrower is compensation. For purposes of this section, the term "in connection with the performance of services" has the same meaning as the term has for purposes of section 83. A loan from a qualified pension, profit-sharing, or stock bonus plan to a participant of the plan is not, directly or indirectly, a compensation-related loan.

(2) *Loan in part in exchange for services.*—Except as provided in paragraph (d)(2) of this section (relating to a loan from a corporation to an employee who is also a shareholder of the corporation), a loan which is made in part in exchange for services and in part for other reasons is treated as a compensation-related loan for purposes of section 7872(c)(3) only if more than 25 percent of the amount loaned is attributable to the performance of services. If 25 percent or less of the amount loaned is attributable to the performance of services, the loan is not subject to section 7872 by reason of being a compensation-related loan. The loan may, however, be subject to section 7872 by reason of being a below-market loan characterized other than as a compensation-related loan (*e.g.*, corporation-shareholder loan or tax avoidance loan). If—

(i) a loan is characterized as a "compensation-related" loan under this paragraph (c),

(ii) less than 100 percent of the amount loaned is attributable to the performance of services, and

(iii) the portion of the amount loaned that is not attributable to the performance of services is not subject to section 7872,

then the amounts of imputed transfer (as defined in § 1.7872-1(a)(2)) and imputed interest (as defined in § 1.7872-1(a)) are determined only with respect to that part of the loan which is attributable to services. All of the facts and circumstances surrounding the loan agreement and the relationship between the lender and the borrower are taken into account in determining the portion of the loan made in exchange for services.

(3) *Third-party lender as agent.*—A below-market loan by an unrelated third-party lender to an employee is treated as attributable to the performance of services if, taking into account all the facts and circumstances, the transaction is in substance a loan by the employer made with the aid of a third-party lender acting as an agent of the employer. Among the facts and circumstances which indicate whether such a loan has been made is whether the employer bears the risk of default at and immediately after the time the loan is made. The principles of this paragraph (c)(3) also apply with respect to a below-market loan by an unrelated third-party lender to an independent contractor.

(4) *Special rule for continuing care facilities.*—Any loan to a continuing care facility will not be treated, in whole or in part, as a compensation-related loan.

(5) *Cross-references.*—For a special rule in the case of a below-market loan that could be characterized as both a compensation-related loan and a corporation-shareholder loan, see paragraph (d)(2) of this section. See paragraph (g) of this section for rules with respect to below-market loans which are indirectly compensation-related loans.

(d) *Corporation-shareholder loans.*—(1) *In general.*—A below-market loan is a corporation-shareholder loan if the loan is made directly or indirectly between a corporation and any shareholder of the corporation. The amount of money treated as transferred by the lender to the borrower is a distribution of money (characterized according to section 301 or, in the case of an S corporation, section 1368) if the corporation is the lender, or a contribution to capital if the shareholder is the lender.

(2) *Special rule.*—A below-market loan—

(i) from a publicly held corporation to an employee of the corporation who is also a shareholder owning directly or indirectly more than 0.5 percent of the total voting power of all classes of stock entitled to vote or more than 0.5 percent of the total value of shares of all other classes of stock or 0.5 percent of the total value of shares of all other classes of stock or 5 percent of the total value of shares of all classes of stock (including voting stock) of the corporation; or

(ii) from a corporation that is not a publicly held corporation to an employee of the corporation who is also a shareholder owning directly or indirectly more than 5 percent of the total voting power of all classes of stock entitled to vote or more than 5 percent of the total number of shares of all other classes of stock or 5 percent of the total value of shares of all classes of stock (including voting stock) of the corporation;

will be presumed to be a corporation-shareholder loan, in the absence of clear and convincing evidence that the loan is made solely in connection with the performance of services. For purposes of determining the percentage of direct and indirect stock ownership, the constructive ownership rules of section 267(c) apply.

(3) *Cross-reference.*—See paragraph (g) of this section for rules with respect to below-market loans which are indirectly corporation-shareholder loans.

(e) *Tax avoidance loans.*—(1) *In general.*—A tax avoidance loan is any below-market loan one of the principal purposes for the interest arrangements of which is the avoidance of Federal tax with respect to either the borrower or the lender, or both. For purposes of this rule, tax avoidance is a principal purpose of the interest arrangements if a principal factor in the decision to structure the transaction as a below-market loan (rather than, for example, as a market interest rate loan and a payment by the lender to the borrower) is to reduce the Federal tax liability of the borrower or the lender or both. The purpose for entering into the transaction (for example, to make a gift or to pay compensation) is irrelevant in determining whether a principal purpose of the interest arrangements of the loan is the avoidance of Federal tax.

(2) *Certain loans incident to sales or exchanges.*—If, pursuant to a plan that is incident to a sale or exchange of property, a party who is related (within the meaning of section 168(e)(4)(D)) to the seller—

(i) Makes a below-market loan to the buyer of the property, or

(ii) Makes a below-market loan to the seller that is assumed by the buyer in connection with the sale or exchange,

then the loan shall be treated as a tax avoidance loan within the meaning of paragraph (e)(1) of this section. There shall be an irrebuttable presumption that such a plan exists if such a loan is made within one year of the sale or exchange.

(3) *Examples.*—The provisions of paragraph (e) of this section may be illustrated by the following examples:

Example (1). (i) S and T are each wholly-owned subsidiaries of P. S sells property to an individual, A, for cash of $3,000,000. Three months after the sale, T loans to A $2.000,000 for 10 years at an interest rate of 6%, payable semi-annually. On the date the loan is made, the Federal long-term rate is 12%, compounded semiannually.

(ii) The loan from T to A is a tax avoidance loan pursuant to paragraph (e)(2) of this section. The issue price of the debt instrument given in exchange for the loan is $1,311,805, and the total amount of foregone interest is $688,195. On the date the loan is made, A is treated as having received a refund of $688,195 of the purchase price of the property from S, thereby reducing A's basis in the property by this amount. T is treated as having paid a dividend of $688,195 to P, and P is treated as having made a contribution to the capital of S in the same amount.

Example (2). The facts are the same as in example (1), except that T loans the $2,000,000 to S immediately before the sale. A purchases the property for cash of $1,000,000 and assumes S's debt to T. On the date of the sale, the Federal long-term rate is 12%, compounded semiannually. The loan from T to S is a tax-avoidance loan. The issue price of the debt instrument and the amount of foregone interest are the same as in example (1). A's basis in the property is limited to $2,311,805 (see § 1.1274-7(d)). T is treated as having paid a dividend of $688,195 to P, and P is treated as having made a contribution to the capital of S in the same amount.

(f) *Certain below-market loans with significant effect on tax liability ("significant-effect" loans).*—[RESERVED].

(g) *Indirect loans.*—(1) *In general.*—If a below-market loan is made between two persons and, based on all the facts and circumstances, the effect of the loan is to make a gift or a capital contribution or a distribution of money (under section 301 or in the case of an S corporation, section 1368), or to pay compensation to a third person ("indirect participant"), or is otherwise attributable to the relationship of the lender or borrower to the indirect participant, the loan is restructured as two or more successive below-market loans ("deemed loans") for purposes of section 7872, as follows:

(i) A deemed below-market loan made by the named lender to the indirect participant; and

(ii) A deemed below-market loan made by the indirect participant to the borrower.

Section 7872 is applied separately to each deemed loan, and each deemed loan is treated as having the same provisions as the original loan between the lender and the borrower. Thus, for example, if a father makes an interest-free loan to his daughter's corporation, the loan is restructured as a below-market loan from father to daughter (deemed gift loan) and a second below-market loan from daughter to corporation (deemed corporation-shareholder loan). Similarly, if a corporation makes an interest-free loan to another commonly controlled corporation, the loan is restructured as a below-market loan from the lending corporation to the common parent corporation and a second below-market loan from the parent corporation to the borrowing corporation.

(2) *Special rule for intermediaries.*—If a lender and a borrower use another person, such as an individual, a trust, a partnership, or a corporation, as an intermediary or middleman in a loan transaction and a purpose for such use is to avoid the application of section 7872(c)(1)(A), (B), or (C), the intermediary will be ignored and the loan will be treated as made directly between the lender and the borrower. Thus, for example, if a father and a son arrange their below-market loan transaction by having the father make a below-market loan to the father's partnership, followed by a second below-market loan (with substantially identical terms and conditions as the first loan) made by the partnership to the son, the two below-market loans will be restructured as one below-market loan from the father to the son. [Reg. § 1.7872-4.]

§ 1.7872-5. Exempted loans.—(a) *In general.*—(1) *General rule.*—Except as provided in paragraph (a)(2) of this section, notwithstanding any other provision of section 7872 and the regulations thereunder, section 7872 does not apply to the loans listed in paragraph (b) of this section because the interest arrangements do not have a significant effect on the Federal tax liability of the borrower or the lender.

(2) *No exemption for tax avoidance loans.*—If a taxpayer structures a transaction to be a loan described in paragraph (b) of this section and one of the principal purposes of so structuring the transaction is the avoidance of Federal tax, then the transaction will be recharacterized as a tax avoidance loan as defined in section 7872(c)(1)(D).

(b) *List of exemptions.*—Except as provided in paragraph (a) of this section, the following transactions are exempt from section 7872:

(1) Loans which are made available by the lender to the general public on the same terms and conditions and which are consistent with the lender's customary business practices;

(2) Accounts or withdrawable shares with a bank (as defined in section 581), or an institution to which section 591 applies, or a credit union, made in the ordinary course of its business;

(3) Acquisitions of publicly traded debt obligations for an amount equal to the public trading price at the time of acquisition;

(4) Loans made by a life insurance company (as defined in section 816(a)), in the ordinary course of its business, to an insured, under a loan right contained in a life insurance policy and in which the cash surrender values are used as collateral for the loans;

(5) Loans subsidized by the Federal, State (including the District of Columbia), or Municipal government (or any agency or instrumentality thereof), and which are made available under a program of general application to the public;

(6) Employee-relocation loans that meet the requirements of paragraph (c)(1) of this section;

(7) Obligations the interest on which is excluded from gross income under section 103;

(8) Obligations of the United States government;

(9) Loans to a charitable organization (described in section 170(c)), but only if at no time during the taxable year will the aggregate outstanding amount of loans by the lender to all such organizations exceed $10,000;

(10) Loans made to or from a foreign person that meet the requirements of paragraph (c)(2) of this section;

(11) Loans made by a private foundation or other organization described in section 170(c), the primary purpose of which is to accomplish one or more of the purposes described in section 170(c)(2)(B);

(12) Loans made prior to July 1, 1986, to the extent excepted from the application of section 482 for the 6-month (or longer) period referred to in § 1.482-2(a)(3);

(13) For periods prior to July 1, 1986, all money, securities, and property received by a futures commission merchant or by a clearing organization (i) to margin, guarantee or secure contracts for future delivery on or subject to the rules of a qualified board or exchange (as defined in section 1256(g)(7)), or (ii) to purchase, margin, guarantee or secure options contracts traded on or subject to the rules of a qualified board or exchange, and all money accruing to account holders as the result of such futures and options contracts;

(14) Loans where the taxpayer can show that the below market interest arrangements have no significant effect on any Federal tax liability of the lender or the borrower, as described in paragraph (c)(3) of this section; and

(15) Loans, described in revenue rulings or revenue procedures issued under section 7872(g)(1)(C), if the Commissioner finds that the factors justifying an exemption for such loans are sufficiently similar to the factors justifying the exemptions contained in this section.

(c) *Special rules.*—(1) *Employee-relocation loans.*—(i) *Mortgage loans.*—In the case of a compensation-related loan to an employee, where such loan is secured by a mortgage on the new principal residence (within the meaning of section 217 and the regulations thereunder) of the employee, acquired in connection with the transfer of that employee to a new principal place of work (which meets the requirements in section 217(c) and the regulations thereunder), the loan will be exempt from section 7872 if the following conditions are satisfied:

(A) The loan is a demand loan or is a term loan the benefits of the interest arrangements of which are not transferable by the employee and are conditioned on the future performance of substantial services by the employee;

(B) The employee certifies to the employer that the employee reasonably expects to be entitled to and will itemize deductions for each year the loan is outstanding; and

(C) The loan agreement requires that the loan proceeds be used only to purchase the new principal residence of the employee.

(ii) *Bridge loans.*—In the case of a compensation-related loan to an employee which is not described in paragraph (c)(1)(i) of this section, and which is used to purchase a new principal residence (within the meaning of section 217 and the regulations thereunder) of the employee acquired in connection with the transfer of that employee to a new principal place of work (which meets the requirements in section 217(c) and the regulations thereunder), the loan will be exempt from section 7872 if the following conditions are satisfied:

(A) The conditions contained in paragraphs (c)(1)(i)(A), (B), and (C) of this section;

(B) The loan agreement provides that the loan is payable in full within 15 days after the date of the sale of the employee's immediately former principal residence;

(C) The aggregate principal amount of all outstanding loans described in this paragraph (c)(1)(ii) to an employee is no greater than the employer's reasonable estimate of the amount of the equity of the employee and the employee's spouse in the employee's immediately former principal residence, and

(D) The employee's immediately former principal residence is not converted to business or investment use.

(2) *Below-market loans involving foreign persons.*—(i) Section 7872 shall not apply to a below-market loan (other than a compensation-related loan or a corporation-shareholder loan where the borrower is a shareholder that is not a C corporation as defined in section 1361(a)(2)) if the lender is a foreign person and the borrower is a U.S. person, unless the interest income imputed to the foreign lender (without regard to this paragraph) would be effectively connected with the conduct of a U.S. trade or business within the meaning of section 864(c) and the regulations thereunder and not exempt from U.S. income taxation under an applicable income tax treaty.

(ii) Section 7872 shall not apply to a below-market loan where both the lender and the borrower are foreign persons unless the interest income imputed to the lender (without regard to this paragraph) would be effectively connected with the conduct of a U.S. trade or business within the meaning of section 864(c) and the regulations thereunder and not exempt from U.S. income taxation under an applicable income tax treaty.

(iii) For purposes of this section, the term "foreign person" means any person that is not a U.S. person.

(3) *Loans without significant tax effect.*—Whether a loan will be considered to be a loan the interest arrangements of which have a significant effect on any Federal tax liability of the lender or the borrower will be determined ac-

cording to all of the facts and circumstances. Among the factors to be considered are—

(i) whether items of income and deduction generated by the loan offset each other;

(ii) the amount of such items;

(iii) the cost to the taxpayer of complying with the provisions of section 7872 if such section were applied, and

(iv) any non-tax reasons for deciding to structure the transaction as a below-market loan rather than a loan with interest at a rate equal to or greater than the applicable Federal rate and a payment by the lender to the borrower. [Reg. § 1.7872-5.]

§ 1.7872-6. Timing and amount of transfers in connection with gift loans and demand loans.—(a) *In general.*—Section 7872(a) and the provisions of this section govern the timing and the amount of the imputed transfer by the lender to the borrower and the imputed interest payment by the borrower to the lender in the case of a below-market demand loan. Section 7872(a) and this section also govern the timing and the amount of the imputed transfer by the lender to the borrower and the imputed interest payment by the borrower to the lender for income tax purposes in the case of term gift loans. (See section 7872(b), 7872(d)(2), and § 1.7872-7 for rules governing the timing and the amount of the imputed transfer by the lender to the borrower in the case of term gift loans for gift tax purposes.) Section 7872(d)(1) and § 1.7872-8 limit the amount of the imputed interest payment with respect to certain gift loans. See § 1.7872-10(a) for rules for distinguishing demand loans from term loans. See § 1.7872-11(f) for special rules governing loans repayable in foreign currency, which apply notwithstanding any contrary rules set forth in this section.

(b) *Time of transfer.*—(1) *In general.*—Except as otherwise provided in paragraphs (b)(3), (4), and (5) of this section, the foregone interest (as defined in section 7872(e)(2) and paragraph (c) of this section) attributable to periods during any calendar year is treated as transferred by the lender to the borrower (and retransferred by the borrower to the lender) on December 31 of that calendar year and shall be treated for tax purposes in a manner consistent with the taxpayer's method of accounting.

(2) *Example.*—Paragraph (b)(1) of this section may be illustrated by the following example.

Example. On January 1, 1985, E makes a $200,000 interest-free demand loan to F, an employee of E. The loan remains outstanding for the entire 1985 calendar year. E has a taxable year ending September 30. F is a calendar year taxpayer. For 1985, the imputed compensation payment and the imputed interest payment (as computed under paragraph (c) of this section) are treated as made on December 31.

(3) *Gift loans between natural persons.*—In the case of gift loans directly between natural persons within the meaning of § 1.7872-8(a)(2), any imputed transfer and any imputed interest payment to which this section applies during the borrower's taxable year is treated, for both the lender and the borrower, as occurring on the last day of the borrower's taxable year.

(4) *Death, liquidation or termination of borrower.*—If the borrower dies (in the case of a borrower who is a natural person) or is liquidated or otherwise terminated (in the case of a borrower other than a natural person), any imputed transfer and any imputed interest payment arising during the borrower's final taxable year are treated, for both the lender and the borrower, as occurring on the last day of the borrower's final taxable year.

(5) *Repayment of loan.*—If a below-market loan is repaid, any imputed transfer and any imputed interest payment arising during the borrower's taxable year which includes the date of repayment is treated, for both the lender and the borrower, as occurring on the day the loan is repaid.

(c) *Amount of transfer.*—In the case of a below-market loan to which section 7872 applies and which is a demand loan (including a term loan that is treated as a demand loan as provided in § 1.7872-10(a)(5)) or a gift term loan, the foregone interest (as computed under the provisions of § 1.7872-13) with respect to the loan is treated as transferred by the lender to the borrower and retransferred as interest by the borrower to the lender. Generally, for any calendar year the term "foregone interest" means the excess of—

(1) The amount of interest that would have been payable in that year if interest had accrued at the applicable Federal rate (as determined in § 1.7872-13); over

(2) Any interest payable on the loan properly allocable to that year. The amount of foregone interest is computed for each day during the period for which section 7872(a) applies to the loan and is treated as transferred and retransferred on the date specified in paragraph (b) of this section. [Reg. § 1.7872-6.]

§ 1.7872-7. Timing and amount of transfers in connection with below-market term loans.—(a) *In general.*—This section governs the Federal income tax consequences of below-market term loans, other than gift term loans or term loans treated as demand loans under the provisions of § 1.7872-10(a)(5), to which section 7872 applies. It also governs the Federal gift tax consequences of below-market gift term loans. See § 1.7872-11(f) for special rules which govern loans repayable in foreign currency and which apply notwithstanding any contrary rules set forth in this section.

(1) *Timing and amount of transfer from lender to borrower.*—In the case of term loans to which this section applies, the amount of the imputed transfer by the lender to the borrower—

(i) is treated as transferred at the time the loan is made and is treated for tax purposes in a manner consistent with the taxpayer's method of accounting; and

(ii) is equal to the excess of—

(A) The amount loaned (as defined in paragraph (a)(4) of this section); over

(B) The present value (as determined in paragraph (a)(5) of this section and §1.7872-14) of all payments which are required to be made under the terms of the loan agreement, whether express or implied.

(2) *Gift term loans.*—In the case of a gift term loan, the rules of paragraph (a)(1) of this section apply for gift tax purposes only. For rules governing the income tax consequences of gift term loans, see §1.7872-6.

(3) *Treatment of amount equal to imputed transfer as original issue discount.*—(i) *In general.*—Any below-market loan to which paragraph (a)(1) of this section applies shall be treated as having original issue discount in an amount equal to the amount of the imputed transfer determined under paragraph (a)(1) of this section. This imputed original issue discount is in addition to any other original issue discount on the loan (determined without regard to section 7872(b) or this paragraph). For purposes of applying section 1272 to a loan described in this paragraph, the issue price shall be treated as equal to the stated principal reduced by the amount of the imputed transfer and the yield to maturity is the applicable Federal rate.

(ii) *Example.*—The provisions of this paragraph (a)(3) may be illustrated by the following example.

Example. (i) On June 10, 1984, L lends $45,000 to B, a corporation in which L is a shareholder, for five years in exchange for a $50,000 note bearing interest at a below-market rate. Assume that the present value of all payments that B must make to L is $42,000. This loan is a corporation-shareholder term loan under section 7872(c)(1)(C). Accordingly, the amount of the imputed transfer by L to B is determined under the provisions of section 7872(b).

(ii) On June 10, 1984, L is treated as transferring $3,000 (the excess of $45,000 (amount loaned) over $42,000 (present value of all payments)), in accordance with section 7872(b)(1). This imputed transfer is treated as a contribution to B's capital by L. An amount equal to the imputed transfer is treated as original issue discount. This original issue discount is in addition to the $5,000 ($50,000, the state redemption price, less $45,000, the issue price) of original issue discount otherwise determined under section 1273. As a result, the loan is treated as having a total $8,000 of original issue discount.

(4) *Amount loaned.*—The term "amount loaned" means the amount received by the borrower (determined without regard to section 7872). See §1.7872-2(a)(3) for the treatment of the transfer of the loan proceeds to the borrower in installments or subject to draw-down restrictions.

(5) *Present value.*—The present value of all payments which are required to be made under the provisions of the loan agreement is computed as of the date the loan is made (or, if later, as of the day the loan first becomes subject to the provisions of section 7872). The discount rate for the present value computation is the applicable Federal rate as defined in §1.7872-3(b) in effect on the day on which the loan is made. For rules governing the computation of present value, see §1.7872-14. See also *Example (3)* in §1.7872-8(b)(5).

(6) *Basis.*—In the case of a term loan the lender's basis in the note received in exchange for lending money is equal to the present value of all payments which are required to be made under the terms of the loan agreement, whether express or implied, with adjustments as provided for in section 1272(d)(2).

(b) *Special rule for the de minimis provisions.*—(1) *In general.*—If as a result of the application of the *de minimis* provisions of section 7872(c)(2) or (3), a loan becomes subject to section 7872 and this section on a day after the day on which the loan is made, the provisions of this section generally apply to the loan as if the loan were made on that later day. The applicable Federal rate applied to this loan (including for purposes of computing the present value of the loan), however, is the applicable Federal rate (as defined in §1.7872-3(b)) in effect on the day on which the loan is first made. The present value computation described in paragraph (a)(1)(ii)(B) of this section is made as of the day on which section 7872 and this section first apply to the loan. For purposes of making this computation, the term of the loan is equal to the period beginning on the day that section 7872 first applies to the loan and ending on the day on which the loan is to be repaid according to the loan agreement. Any payments payable acording to the loan agreement before the day on which section 7872 and this section first apply to the loans are disregarded.

(2) *Continuing application of section 7872.*—Once section 7872 and this section apply to a term loan, they continue to apply to the loan regardless of whether the *de minimis* provisions of section 7872(c)(2) or (3) apply at some later date. In the case of a gift term loan, this paragraph applies only for gift tax purposes and does not apply for income tax purposes. [Reg. §1.7872-7.]

§1.7872-8. Special rules for gift loans directly between natural persons.—(a) *Special rules for gift loans directly between natural persons.*—(1) *In general.*—Section 7872 (c)(2) and (d) apply special rules to gift loans directly between natural persons if the aggregate outstanding amount of loans (as determined in paragraph (b)(2) of this section) between those natural persons does not exceed specified limitations.

(2) *Loans directly between natural persons.*—(i) For purposes of this section, a loan is made directly between natural persons only if both the lender and borrower are natural persons. For this purpose, a loan by a natural person lender to the guardian (or custodian, in the case of a gift

made pursuant to the Uniform Gift to Minors Act) of a natural person is treated as a loan directly between natural persons. If, however, a parent lends money to a trust of which the child is the sole beneficiary, the loan is not treated as directly between natural persons for purposes of this section.

(ii) A gift loan which results from restructuring an indirect loan as two or more loans (as described in § 1.7872-4(g)) and in which natural persons are deemed to be the lender and the borrower is treated as a loan directly between natural persons. Thus, for example, if an employer makes a below-market loan to an employee's child, the loan is restructured as one loan from the employer to the employee, and a second loan from the employee to his child. The deemed gift loan between the employee and the employee's child is treated as directly between natural persons.

(b) *De minimis exception.*—(1) *In general.*—Except as otherwise provided in paragraph (b)(3) of this section or in § 1.7872-7(a) (with respect to the gift tax consequences of a gift term loan to which the provisions of section 7872 have already been applied), in the case of any gift loan directly between natural persons, the provisions of section 7872 do not apply to any loan outstanding on any day in which the aggregate outstanding amount of loans between the lender and borrower does not exceed $10,000. The *de minimis* rule of this paragraph (b)(1) applies with respect to a gift loan even though that loan could also be characterized as a tax avoidance loan within the meaning of section 7872(c)(1)(D) and § 1.7872-4(e).

(2) *Aggregate outstanding amount of loans.*—The aggregate outstanding amount of loans between natural persons is the sum of the principal amounts of outstanding loans directly between the individuals, regardless of the character of the loans, regardless of the interest rate charged on the loans, and regardless of the date on which the loans were made. For this purpose, the principal amount of a loan which is also subject to section 1272 (without applying the limitation of section 1273(a)(3)) is the "adjusted issue price" as that term is defined in section 1272(a)(4). See § 1.7872-7(a)(3)(i) for the determination of the issue price of a loan which is also subject to section 1272.

(3) *Loans attributable to acquisition or carrying of income-producing assets.*—The *de minimis* exception described in paragraph (b)(1) of this section does not apply to any gift loan directly attributable to the purchase or carrying of the income-producing assets. A gift loan is directly attributable to the purchase or carrying of income-producing assets, for example, if the loan proceeds are directly traceable to the purchase of the income-producing assets, the assets are used as collateral for the loan, or there is direct evidence that the loan was made to avoid disposition of the assets.

(4) *Income-producing assets.*—For purposes of this paragraph (b), the term "income-producing asset" means (i) an asset of a type that generates ordinary income, or, (ii) a market discount bond issued before July 19, 1984. Accordingly, an income-producing asset includes, but is not limited to, a business, a certificate of deposit, a savings account, stock (whether or not dividends are paid), bonds and rental property.

(5) *Examples.*—The provisions of this paragraph (b) may be illustrated by the following examples.

Example (1). (i) As of January 1, 1985, the total aggregate outstanding amount of loans by Parent P, to child, C, is $6,000. None of these loans is a below-market loan. On February 1, 1985, P makes a $3,000 below-market demand loan to C. On March 1, 1985, P makes a $2,000 below-market demand loan to C. On November 1, 1985, C repays $1,500 of principal of the market-rate loans to P; all of the other loans remain outstanding as of December 31, 1985. The below-market loans are gift loans and are the only new loans between P and C for calendar year 1985.

(ii) For the periods January 1, 1985, through February 28, 1985, and November 1, 1985, through December 31, 1985, section 7872 does not apply to the loans between P and C because the outstanding loan balance between P and C does not exceed $10,000 during these periods. For the period beginning on March 1, 1985, and ending on October 31, 1985, however, the aggregate outstanding amount of loans directly between P and C exceeds $10,000. Accordingly, the provisions of section 7872(a) apply to the $3,000 gift loan and $2,000 gift loan during that period.

Example (2). (i) Assume the same facts as in Example (1) except that the $2,000 gift loan made on March 1, 1985, is a term loan for a period of five years. The Federal gift tax and income tax consequences of the $3,000 gift demand loan made on February 1, 1985, are the same as in Example (1).

(ii) With respect to the $2,000 gift term loan, section 7872(b)(1) applies beginning on March 1, 1985, for purposes of computing the amount of the imputed gift by P to C. For the period beginning on March 1, 1985, and ending on October 31, 1985, section 7872(a) applies to the $2,000 gift term loan for purposes of determining the amount and the timing of the imputed interest payment by C to P. For the two-monthly period beginning on November 1, 1985, section 7872(a) does not apply to the $2,000 loan for Federal income tax purposes because the outstanding loan balance between P and C does not exceed $10,000 during this period.

Example (3). (i) Assume the same facts as in Example (1) except that the $3,000 gift loan made on February 1, 1985, is a term loan for a period of five years. The Federal gift tax and income tax consequences of the $2,000 demand gift loan made on March 1, 1985, are identical to those in Example (1).

(ii) On February 1, 1985, section 7872 does not apply to the $3,000 loan because the outstanding loan balance between P and C does not exceed $10,000. On March 1, 1985, however, the aggregate outstanding amount of loans between P and C exceeds $10,000. For Federal gift tax purposes, section 7872(b)(1) applies to the $3,000 loan beginning on March 1, 1985. Under § 1.7872-7(b), the provisions of section 7872 apply to the $3,000 loan for gift and income tax purposes as if the loan had been made on March 1, 1985. See § 1.7872-7(a)(5) for special rules for computing the present value of payments due on the loan. For the eight-month period beginning on March 1, 1985, section 7872(a) applies to the $3,000 loan for purposes of determining the imputed interest payment by C to P. For the two-month period beginning on November 1, 1985, section 7872(a) does not apply to the $3,000 loan for Federal income tax purposes because of the application of the *de minimis* provisions.

Example (4). On June 10, 1984, parent, L, makes an $8,000 interest-free gift term loan to L's child, B. This is the only loan outstanding between L and B during 1984. On June 11, 1984, B invests the $8,000 in corporate stock. The $10,000 *de minimis* provision does not apply to the loan, because the loan proceeds are directly attributable to the purchase of corporate stock, an income-producing asset.

(c) *Limitation on amount of imputed interest payment.*—(1) *In general.*—In the case of a loan between a borrower and a lender both of whom are natural persons (within the meaning of paragraph (a)(2) of this section), for all days during the borrower's taxable year on which the aggregate outstanding amount of loans (within the meaning of paragraph (b)(2) of this section) between the borrower and the lender, is $100,000 or less, the amount of the imputed interest payment by the borrower to the lender with respect to any gift loan is limited to the borrower's net investment income (as determined under paragraph (c)(7) of this section) for the taxable year. This paragraph (c) does not affect the gift tax consequences of any loan under section 7872.

(2) *Tax avoidance loan.*—Paragraph (c)(1) of this section does not apply to any loan which is a tax avoidance loan within the meaning of § 1.7872-4(e).

(3) *No limitation if investment income is manipulated.*—Paragraph (c)(1) of this section does not apply if a borrower can control the timing of the receipt of investment income and actually does manipulate the timing to accelerate or defer the receipt of investment income. For example, if the borrower can, and actually does, control the timing of dividends paid by a closely held corporation, the limitation on the amount of the imputed interest payment does not apply.

(4) *Net investment income of $1,000 or less disregarded.*—If paragraph (c)(1) of this section applies and if the borrower's net investment income (as determined under paragraph (c)(7) of this section) for a taxable year is $1,000 or less, the borrower's net investment income for that year is deemed to be zero for purposes of this paragraph (c).

(5) *No proration of net investment income.*—The entire amount of the borrower's net investment income for a taxable year (as determined under paragraph (c)(7) of this section) is taken into account in determining the maximum imputed interest payment for those days during the year on which the net investment income limitation applies. Accordingly, the amount of net investment income is not allocated among the days of the borrower's taxable year. Further, for a taxable year of a borrower which ends after June 6, 1984, and includes any day or days before June 7, 1984, the entire amount of net investment income for the taxable year is taken into account in determining the maximum imputed interest payment for the days during that year on which the limitation applies.

(6) *Allocation among gift loans.*—In the case of a borrower who has more than one gift loan outstanding during a taxable year, the borrower's net investment income for that year is allocated among the gift loans in proportion to the respective amounts which would be treated as imputed interest payments by the borrower to the lender or lenders with respect to those loans without regard to this paragraph (c). (See Example (2) of paragraph (c)(9) of this section.) No amount of the net investment income is allocable to any gift loan between the lender and the borrower for periods during which the aggregate outstanding amount of loans (within the meaning of paragraph (b)(2) of this section) between the borrower and that lender exceeds $100,000.

(7) *Amounts included in net investment income.*—For purposes of section 7872, net investment income for a taxable year equals the sum of—

(i) Net investment income for that year as determined under section 163(d)(3), excluding any item of income on a deferred payment obligation which is treated under section 7872(d)(1)(E)(iii) and paragraph (c)(7)(ii) of this section as interest received in a prior taxable year ending after June 6, 1984, and

(ii) The amount that is treated under section 7872(d)(1)(E)(iii) as interest received for that year on a deferred payment obligation.

(8) *Deferred payment obligation.*—The term "deferred payment obligation" means a market discount bond issued before July 18, 1984, or an obligation that, if held to maturity, would produce a predictable and regular flow of ordinary income which, under applicable tax rules, is not recognized until a subsequent period. Accordingly, deferred payment obligations include, but are not limited to, those obligations listed in section 7872(d)(1)(E)(iv).

(9) *Examples.*—The provisions of this paragraph (c) may be illustrated by the following examples.

Example (1). On January 1, 1985, parent P makes a $50,000 below-market gift loan to C, P's child, who uses the calendar year as the taxable year. On March 1, 1985, P makes an additional $75,000 market-rate loan to C. On October 1, 1985, C repays $30,000 of the market-rate loan.

Assume that C's net investment income (as determined under paragraph (c)(7) of this section) for 1985 is $2,400. The limitation under section 7872(d)(1) on the amount of imputed interest payment applies to the $50,000 loan for the two-month period beginning on January 1, 1985, and the three-month period beginning on October 1, 1985. Accordingly, the imputed interest payment on the $50,000 loan for 1985 may not exceed $2,400.

Example (2). During 1985, natural person borrower B has three gift loans outstanding, each from a different lender. Each loan is eligible for the entire year for the special limitation on the amount of imputed interest payments under section 7872(d)(1) but none of the loans is eligible for the de minimis exception of paragraph (b) of this section. B's net investment income for 1985 is $6,000. The aggregate imputed interest payments on these loans (determined without regard to section 7872(d)(1)) would be $9,000. The amount of imputed interest payment attributable to each loan after application of section 7872(d)(1) is computed as follows:

Loan	*Imputed interest payments (before application of section 7872(d)(1))*	*Relative share of net investment income (imputed interest payment after application of section 7872(d)(1))*	
1	$3,000	$2,000	$6,000 × $3,000/$9,000)
2	4,000	2,667	(6,000 × 4,000/9,000)
3	2,000	1,333	(6,000 × 2,000/9,000)
Total	$9,000	$6,000	

Consequently, the imputed interest payment to lender 1 cannot exceed $2,000; the imputed interest payment to lender 2 cannot exceed $2,667; and, the imputed interest payment to lender 3 cannot exceed $1,333. [Reg. § 1.7872-8.]

§ 1.7872-9. *De minimis* exception for compensation-related or corporation-shareholder loans.—(a) *In general.*—In the case of any demand loan described in section 7872(c)(1)(B) or (C), the provisions of section 7872 do not apply to any day on which the aggregate outstanding amount of loans between the lender and the borrower does not exceed $10,000. In the case of any term loan described in section 7872(c)(1)(B) or (C) (relating to the *de minimis* rules), the provisions of section 7872 apply to the loan as of the first day on which the aggregate outstanding amount of loans between the lender and the borrower exceeds $10,000. Once section 7872 applies to a term loan, section 7872 continues to apply to the loan regardless of whether the $10,000 limitation applies at some later date.

(b) *Aggregate outstanding amount of loans.*—The aggregate outstanding amount of loans between the lender and the borrower is the sum of the principal amounts of outstanding loans directly between the parties, regardless of the character of the loans, regardless of the interest rate charged on the loans, and regardless of the date on which the loans were made. For this purpose, the principal amount of a loan which is also subject to section 1272 (without applying the limitation of section 1273(a)(3)) is the "adjusted issue price" as that term is defined in section 1272(a)(4). See § 1.7872(a)(3)(i) for the determination of the issue price of a loan which is also subject to section 7872.

(c) *Tax avoidance loan.*—This section does not apply to any loan which is a tax avoidance loan within the meaning of § 1.7872-4(e).

(d) *Example.*—The provisions of this section may be illustrated by the following example:

Example. (i) On January 1, 1985, L made a $4,000 four-year term loan to B, a corporation in which L is a shareholder. On October 15, 1986, L made a $7,000 five-year term loan to B. Both loans are interest-free and are payable on the last day of the loan term. There are no other outstanding loans between L and B. Neither loan is a tax avoidance loan.

(ii) For the period beginning on January 1, 1985 and ending on October 14, 1986, the provisions of section 7872 do not apply to the $4,000 loan because the outstanding loan balance between L and B does not exceed $10,000. On October 15, 1986, however, the aggregate amount of loans between L and B exceeds $10,000. Accordingly, the provisions of section 7872(b) apply to both loans. See § 1.7872-4(d) for the proper Federal tax treatment of the imputed transfer by L to B. For purposes of computing the present value of all payments to be made under the loan agreements, the applicable Federal rate for the $4,000 loan is the applicable Federal rate in effect on January 1, 1985, for loans with a term of 4 years (even though less than three years remain before the loan ends). Under § 1.7872-7(b), the present value of the payment to be made under the $4,000 loan agreement is determined as of October 15, 1986 (the date on which section 7872 first applies to the $4,000 loan) for a loan with a term which begins on October 15, 1986, and ends on January 1, 1989. [Reg. § 1.7872-9.]

§ 1.7872-10. Other definitions.—(a) *"Term" and "demand" loans distinguished.*—For purposes of section 7872—

(1) *Demand loan.*—Any loan which is payable in full at any time on the demand of the lender (or within a reasonable time after the lender's demand), is a "demand loan."

(2) *Term loan.*—A loan is treated as a "term loan" if the loan agreement specifies an ascertainable period of time during which the loan is to be outstanding. For purposes of this rule, a period of time is treated as being ascertainable if the period may be determined actuarially. Thus, a loan agreement which provides that

D loans E $16,000 for E's life will be treated as a term loan because the life expectancy of E may be determined actuarially.

(3) *Acceleration and extension clauses.*—Acceleration clauses and similar provisions that would make a loan due before the time otherwise specified including provisions permitting prepayment of a loan or accelerating the maturity date on disposition of collateral ("due on sale" clauses) are disregarded for purposes of section 7872. Thus, a loan for a term of 15 years is a term loan for 15 years even if it is subject to acceleration upon some action of the borrower. If the loan agreement specifies an ascertainable period of time during which the loan is to be outstanding but contains an extension clause or similar provision that would make the loan due after the time otherwise specified, the loan is a term loan during the ascertainable period and a second demand or term loan thereafter; the classification of the second loan as term or demand depends upon the terms of the extension clause.

(4) *Loans for a period of time not ascertainable.*—[Reserved]

(5) *Certain loans conditioned on future services.*—For all purposes of section 7872 other than determining the applicable Federal rate (see, § 1.7872-3(b)), if the benefits of the interest arrangements of a term loan are not transferable by the individual borrower and are conditioned on the future performance of substantial services by the individual borrower (within the meaning of section 83), the loan is treated as a demand loan. All facts and circumstances must be examined to determine whether the future services to be performed are substantial.

(6) *Revolving credit loans.*—For purposes of section 7872, an extension of credit by reason of the use of a credit card that is available to a broad segment of the general public is treated as a demand loan, and the provisions of section 7872 may apply if the loan is described in one of the categories set forth in § 1.7872-4. The period during which the loan is outstanding begins on the first day on which a finance charge would be assessed if payment of the outstanding balance is not made. For rules governing the computation of foregone interest for demand loans with variable balances, see § 1.7872-13(c).

(b) [Reserved for further definitions as needed.] [Reg. § 1.7872-10.]

§ 1.7872-11. Special rules.—(a) *Waiver, cancellation or forgiveness of interest payments.*—If a loan is made requiring the payment of stated interest and the accrued but unpaid interest is subsequently waived, cancelled, or forgiven by the lender, such waiver, cancellation, or forgiveness is treated as if the interest had in fact been paid to the lender and then retransferred by the lender to the borrower but only if—

(1) the loan initially would have been subject to section 7872 had it been made without interest;

(2) the waiver, cancellation or forgiveness does not include in substantial part the loan principal; and

(3) a principal purpose of the waiver, cancellation, or forgiveness is to confer a benefit on the borrower, such as to pay compensation or make a gift, a capital contribution, a distribution of money under section 301, or a similar payment to the borrower.

The retransferred amount is characterized for Federal tax purposes in accordance with the substance of the transaction. The requisite purpose described in paragraph (a)(iii) of this section is presumed in the case of loans between family members, corporations and shareholders, employers and employees, or an independent contractor and a person for whom such independent contractor provides services unless the taxpayer can show by clear and convincing evidence that the interest obligation was waived, cancelled, or forgiven for a legitimate business purpose of the lender who is acting in the capacity as a creditor seeking to maximize satisfaction of a claim, such as in the case of a borrower's insolvency.

(b) *Disposition of interest or obligation in loan.*—[RESERVED]

(c) *Husband and wife treated as 1 person.*—Section 7872(f)(7) provides that a husband and wife shall be treated as 1 person. Accordingly, all loans to or from the husband will be combined with all loans to or from the wife for purposes of applying section 7872. All loans between a husband and a wife are disregarded for purposes of section 7872.

(d) *Withholding.*—In the case of any loan (term or demand) subject to section 7872, no amount is required to be withheld under chapter 24, relating to the collection of income tax at the source on wages and back-up withholding, with respect to any amount treated as transferred or retransferred under section 7872(a) or (b). Withholding is required where appropriate, however, for purposes of chapter 21, relating to the Federal Insurance Contributions Act, and Chapter 22, relating to the Railroad Retirement Tax Act, on any amount of money treated as transferred and retransferred between the lender and borrower because of the application of section 7872.

(e) *Treatment of renegotiations.*—[RESERVED]

(f) *Loans denominated in foreign currencies.*—(1) *Applicable rate.*—If a loan is denominated in a currency other than the U.S. dollar, then for purposes of section 7872 and the regulations thereunder, a rate that constitutes a market interest rate in the currency in which the loan is denominated shall be substituted for the applicable Federal rate.

(2) *Treatment of imputed transfer as interest.*—(i) *In general.*—If a loan is denominated in a currency other than the U.S. dollar then, notwithstanding section 7872(a)(1)(B), § 1.7872-6, and § 1.7872-7, the amount of imputed interest treated as retransferred by the borrower to the lender shall only be treated as interest to the extent consistent with other principles of tax law

regarding foreign currency lending transactions and to the extent provided in this paragraph (f)(2).

(ii) *Loans denominated in appreciating currencies.*—[Reserved]

(iii) *Loans denominated in depreciating currencies.*—[Reserved]

(3) *Example.*—The provisions of this paragraph (f)(1) may be illustrated by the following example.

Example. A lends her daughter B thse sum of 100,000 foreign currency units, repayable in 5 years with interest payable semiannually at a rate of 12 percent. Assume that the market rate of interest for loans denominated in that foreign currency at the time of the transaction is 30 percent, compounded semiannually, and that the current exchange rate is 5 foreign currency units to the dollar. A has made a below-market gift loan to B. The amount of A's gift to B is the excess of 100,000 foreign currency units (or $20,000) over the present value of all payments to be made under the loan, using a discount rate of 30 percent, which is 54,831 foreign units (or $10,966). Thus, the amount of A's gift is $9,034.

(g) *Reporting requirements.*—(1) *Lender.*—A lender must attach a statement to the lender's income tax return for any taxable year in which the lender either has interest imputed under section 7872 or claims a deduction for an amount deemed to be transferred to a borrower under section 7872. The statement must—

(i) Explain that it relates to an amount includible in income or deductible by reason of section 7872,

(ii) Provide the name, address, and taxpayer identification number of each borrower.

(iii) Specify the amount of imputed interest income and the amount and character of any item deductible by reason of section 7872 attributable to each borrower.

(iv) Specify the mathematical assumptions used (*e.g.*, 360 day calendar year, the exact method or the approximate method for computing interest for a short period (see, § 1.7872-13)) for computing the amounts imputed under section 7872, and

(v) Include any other information required by the return or the instructions thereto.

(2) *Borrower.*—A borrower must attach a statement to the borrower's income tax return for any taxable year in which the borrower either has income from an imputed transfer under section 7872 or claims a deduction for an amount of interest expenst imputed under section 7872. The statement must—

(i) Explain that it relates to an amount includible in income or deductible by reason of section 7872,

(ii) Provide the name, address, and taxpayer identification number of each lender,

(iii) Specify the amount of imputed interest expense and the amount and character of any income imputed under section 7872 attributable to each lender,

(iv) Specify the mathematical assumptions used (*e.g.*, 360 day calendar year, the exact method or the approximate method for computing interest for a short period (see, § 1.7872-13)) for computing the amounts imputed under section 7872, and

(v) Include any other information required by the return or the instructions thereto.

(3) *Special rule for gift loans.*—In the case of a gift loan directly between natural persons, the lender must recognize the entire amount of interest income imputed under section 7872 (determined without regard to section 7872(d)(1)) unless the borrower notifies the lender, in a signed statement, of the amount of the borrower's net investment income properly allocable to the loan according to the provisions of section 7872(d)(1) and § 1.7872-8(c)(6).

(4) *Information and reporting.*—All amounts imputed under section 7872 (*e.g.*, interest, compensation, gift) are characterized in accordance with the substance of the transaction and, except as otherwise provided in the regulations under section 7872, are treated as so characterized for all purposes of the Code. Accordingly, all applicable information and reporting requirements (*e.g.*, reporting on Form W-2 and Form 1099) must be satisfied. [Reg. § 1.7872-11.]

§ 1.7872-12. Computational rules to determine sufficient stated interest for short periods.—(a) *Scope.*—This section provides computational rules only for the purpose of determining whether the interest payable on a loan during a short period is sufficient to prevent characterization of the loan as a below-market loan under § 1.7872-3. For rules for the calculation of the amount of interest to be imputed on a below-market loan, including rules for short periods, see § 1.7872-13 and § 1.7872-14.

(b) *Short period defined.*—(1) *In general.*—A short period (as referred to in § 1.7872-3(d)) for a loan is any period shorter than the regular compounding period or regular payment interval required under the loan agreement. Generally, a short period will arise at the beginning or the end of a loan (or at the time the loan first becomes subject to section 7872 because of the application of the *de minimis* provisions). For example, a loan made on January 17, 1985, and calling for semiannual payments of interest on June 30 and December 31 of each year will have a short period beginning on January 17, 1985, and ending on June 30, 1985.

(2) *Special short periods in the case of demand loans.*—In the case of a demand loan, in addition to any short periods described in paragraph (b)(1) of this section, additional short periods may also arise because of the need to adjust the applicable Federal rate on January 1 and July 1 of each year. These short periods arise in cases when the dates January 1 or July 1 fall within the compounding periods or payment intervals re-

quired under the loan agreement. For example, a below-market demand loan made on April 1, 1985, that is outstanding throughout 1985 and that calls for semiannual interest payments on September 30 and March 31 of each year will have 3 short periods in 1985. The first short period begins on April 1, 1985, and ends on June 30, 1985. The second short period begins on July 1, 1985, and ends on September 30, 1985. The third short period begins on October 1, 1985, and ends on December 31, 1985.

(c) *Interest payable for a short period.*—(1) *Exact method.*—The smallest amount of interest that must be paid for a short period in order to prevent the loan from being a below-market loan is determined by the exact method. The exact method assumes daily compounding of interest.

(2) *Approximate method.*—The approximate method is also provided for the convenience of taxpayers who do not wish to use the exact method. The approximate method assumes simple interest within any compounding period and will always produce an amount of interest for the short period that is slightly higher than that produced under the exact method. Under this method, a sufficient amount of interest for any short period is determined by multiplying the amount that would constitute sufficient stated interest for a full period by a fraction the numerator of which is equal to the length of the short period and the denominator of which is the length of a full period.

(3) *Counting convention.*—In computing the length of a short period, any reasonable convention may be used. Common conventions are "30 days per month/360 days per year", "actual days per month/actual days per year", and "actual days per month/360 days per year". The examples in the regulations under section 7872 all use the "30 days per month/360 days per year" convention.

(d) *Examples.*—This section may be illustrated by the following examples.

Example (1). On February 1, 1986, A makes a $100,000 loan to B for a term of 4 months. The loan is repaid on May 31, 1986. Assume that the applicable Federal rate on February 1, 1986, for a loan of this term is 10 percent, compounded semiannually. Using the exact method, the amount of interest that must be paid on May 31, 1986, if the loan is not to be a below-market loan is $3,306.16, calculated as follows:

$\$100,000 \times [(1 + .10/2)^{4/6} - 1] = \$3,306.16$

Example (2). Assume the same facts as in Example (1). Using the approximate method, a sufficient amount of interest is stated on the loan if $3,333.33 of interest is payable on May 31, 1986, calculated as follows:

$\$100,000 \times [(.10/2) \times (4/6)] = \$3,333.33$

[Reg. § 1.7872-12.]

§ 1.7872-13. Computation of foregone interest.—(a) *Demand loans outstanding for an entire calendar year.*—(1) *In general.*—In the case of a below-market demand loan of a fixed principal amount that remains outstanding for an entire calendar year, the amount of foregone interest (as referred to in § 1.7872-6(c)) shall be the excess of—

(i) The result produced when the "blended annual rate" is multiplied by the principal amount of the loan, over

(ii) The sum of all amounts payable as interest on the loan properly allocable to the calendar year (including all amounts of original issue discount allocated to that year under section 1272).

The "blended annual rate" will be published annually by the Commissioner and is determined generally by blending the applicable Federal rates for demand loans outstanding for the entire year.

(2) *Example.*—Paragraph (a)(1) may be illustrated by the following example.

Example. On January 1, 1985, A makes a $100,000 demand loan to B with stated interest equal to 9 percent. Interest is payable semiannually on June 30, and December 31. The loan remains outstanding for the entire year. On both June 30, and December 31, 1985, B makes a $4,500 payment of interest to A. Assume that the blended annual rate for 1985 is 10.45 percent. The amount of foregone interest is $1,450, computed as follows:

$10,450 = $100,000 × 10.45 percent

$1,450 = $10,450 – $9,000

(b) *Demand loans outstanding for less than an entire calendar year.*—(1) *In general.*—In the case of any below-market demand loan outstanding for less than the calendar year, the amount of foregone interest shall be the excess of—

(i) The amount of interest ("I") which would have been payable on the loan for the year if interest accrued on the loan at the applicable Federal rate and were payable on the date specified in section 7872(a)(2) and § 1.7872-6(b), over

(ii) The sum of all amounts payable as interest on the loan properly allocable to the calendar year (including all amounts of original issue discount allocated to that year under section 1272).

In general, "I" is determined by assuming daily compounding of interest. However, individual taxpayers who are parties to below-market loans in the aggregate of $250,000 or less may choose (see, § 1.7872-11(g)) to compute and report foregone interest under the approximate method set forth in paragraph (b)(2) of this section. If the taxpayer chooses the approximate method but fails to properly compute the amount of foregone interest under that method, the correct amount of foregone interest will be recomputed under the approximate method.

(2) *Approximate method.*—Under the approximate method, "I" is calculated as follows:

(i) *Loan outstanding during one semiannual period only.*—If a loan is outstanding only during one semiannual period of a calendar year, to determine "I", multiply the principal amount of the loan by one-half the applicable

Federal rate based on semiannual compounding in effect for that loan, then multiply the result by a fraction representing the portion of the semiannual period during which the loan was outstanding.

(ii) *Example.*—Paragraph (b)(2)(i) of this section may be illustrated by the following example.

Example. A $200,000 interest-free demand loan is outstanding on January 1, 1986, and is repaid on March 31, 1986. Assume that the applicable Federal rate (based on semiannual compounding) for demand loans made in January 1986 is 10 percent. The amount of interest that would have been payable on the loan for the year if the loan provided for interest at the applicable Federal rate determined under the approximate method is $5,000, computed as follows:

$5,000 = $200,000 × (.10/2) × (3/6)

Because no interest is payable on the loan, this amount is also the amount of foregone interest.

(iii) *Loans outstanding during both semiannual periods.*—If a loan is outstanding for at least part of each semiannual period (but less than the full calendar year), then, under the approximate method, "I" must be calculated in two steps. First, calculate an amount of interest for the first semiannual period by treating the loan as if it were repaid on June 30, using the approach described in paragraph (b)(3)(i) of this section. Second, add this amount of interest to the principal of the loan, and then calculate an amount of interest for the second semiannual period as if the loan of this higher amount were made on July 1, again using the approach described in paragraph (b)(3)(i) of this section. The sum of these two interest amounts is the value for "I" calculated under the approximate method.

(3) *Examples.*—Paragraph (b)(2) of this sectioon may be illustrated by the following examples.

Example (1). On March 1, 1986, A makes a $100,000 interest-free demand loan to B. The loan remains outstanding on December 31, 1986. Assume that the applicable Federal rate for a demand loan made in March 1986, based on semiannual compounding, for the first semiannual period in 1986 is 9.89 percent and that the applicable Federal rate, based on semiannual compounding, for a demand loan outstanding in July 1986 is 10.50 percent. The amount of foregone interest under the exact method is $8,691.76, calculated as follows:

$100,000 × [(1 + .0989/2) $^{4/6}$ (1 + .1050/2) − 1] = $8,691.76

Example (2). (i) Assume the same facts as in Example (1).

The amount of foregone interest under the approximate method is $8,719.92, calculated as follows:

(ii) For the short period March 1 to June 30, 1986, the amount of foregone interest is $3,296.67, calculated as follows:

$3,296.67 = $100,000 × (.0989/2) × (4/6)

(iii) For the second semiannual period in 1986, the amount of foregone interest is computed by first adding the interest for the first semiannual period ($3,296.67) to the original principal amount to obtain a new principal amount of $103,296.67. Foregone interest for the second semiannual period is then $5,423.08, computed as follows:

$5,423.08 = $103,296.67 × (.1050/2)

(iv) Using the approximate method, the amount of foregone interest for 1986 is $8,719.75 ($3,296.67 + $5,423.08).

(c) *Demand loans with fluctuating loan balances.*—If a demand loan does not have a constant outstanding principal amount during a period, the amount of foregone interest shall be computed according to the principles set forth in paragraph (b) of this section, with each increase in the outstanding loan balance being treated as a new loan and each decrease being treated as first a repayment of accrued but unpaid interest (if any), and then a repayment of principal.

(d) *Examples.*—This provisions of paragraph (c) of this section may be illustrated by the following examples.

Example (1). (i) On October 1, 1984, C makes a $50,000 interest-free demand loan to D. On October 1, 1985, C makes an additional interest-free demand loan of $25,000 to D. Assume that section 7872 applies to both loans, that the blended annual rate for 1985 is 10.45 percent, and that the applicable Federal rate based on semiannual compounding for demand loans made in October 1985, is 10.50 percent. The amount of foregone interest for 1985 is calculated as follows:

(ii) $50,000 is outstanding for the entire year. The foregone interest on this amount is ($5,000 × .1045) = $5,225.00

(iii) $25,000 is outstanding for the last three months of 1985. Under the exact method, the amount of foregone interest on this portion of the loan is $647.86, computed as follows:

$25,000 × [(1 + .1050/2) $^{3/6}$ − 1] = $647.86

Under the approximate method, the amount of foregone interest is $656.25, computed as follows:

$25,000 × (.1050/2) × (3/6) = $656.25

(iv) The total amount of foregone interest is $5,872.86 ($5,225.00 + $647.86) under the exact method, and $5,881.25 ($5,225.00 + $656.25) under the approximate method.

Example (2). (i) On September 1, 1985, E makes a $100,000 interest-free demand loan to F. The loan agreement requires F to repay $10,000 of the principal amount of the loan at the end of each month that the loan is outstanding. Assume that section 7872 applies to the loan and that the applicable Federal rate based on semiannual compounding for demand loans made in September 1985, is 10.50 percent. The amount of foregone interest for 1985 is calculated as follows:

(ii) $70,000 is outstanding for four months. Under the exact method, the amount of foregone interest on this portion of the loan is $2,429.05, computed as follows:

$\$70,000 \times [(1 + .1050/2)^{4/6} - 1] = \$2,429.05$

Under the approximate method, the amount of foregone interest on this protion of the loan is $2,450.00, computed as follows:

$\$70,000 \times (.1050/2) \times (4/6) = \$2,450.00$

(iii) $10,000 is outstanding for 3 months. Under the exact method, the amount of foregone interest on this portion of the loan is $259.14, computed as follows:

$\$10,000 \times [(1 + .1050/2)^{3/6} - 1] = \$259.14$

Under the approximate method, the amount of foregone interest on this portion of the loan is $262.50, computed as follows:

$\$10,000 \times (.1050/2) \times (3/6) = \$262.50$

(iv) An additional $10,000 is outstanding 2 months. Under the exact method, the amount of foregone interest on this portion of the loan is $172.02, computed as follows:

$\$10,000 \times [(1 + .1050/2)^{2/6} - 1] = \$172.02$

Under the approximate method, the amount of foregone interest on this portion of the loan is $175.00, computed as follows:

$\$10,000 \times (.1050/2) \times (2/6) = \$175.00$

(v) A final $10,000 is outstanding for 1 month. Under the exact method, the amount of foregone interest on this portion of the loan is $85.65, computed as follows:

$\$10,000 \times [1 + 1050/2)^{1/6} - 1] = \$85.65$

Under the approximate method, the amount of foregone interest on this portion of the loan is $87.50, computed as follows:

$\$10,000 \times (.1050/2) \times (1/6) = \$87.50$

(vi) The total amount of foregone interest is $2,945.86 under the exact method, and $2,975.00 under the approximate method.

(e) *Gift term loans and certain loans conditioned on future services.*—(1) *In general.*—In the case of any gift term loan or any term loan that is treated as a demand loan as provided in §1.7872-10(a)(5), the amount of foregone interest for income tax purposes shall be computed as if the loan were a demand loan, except that:

(i) In applying paragraph (a)(1)(i), use the applicable Federal rate based on annual compounding in effect on the day the loan is made instead of the blended annual rate, and

(ii) In applying paragraph (b), use the applicable Federal rate based on semiannual compounding in effect on the day the loan is made instead of the applicable Federal rate for demand loans in effect during the period for which foregone interest is being computed.

(2) *Example.*—The provisions of this paragraph (e) may be illustrated by the following examples:

Example (1). On January 1, 1986, parent P makes a $200,000 gift term loan to child C. The loan agreement provides that the term of the loan is four years and that 5 percent simple interest is payable annually. Both P and C are calendar year taxpayers, and both are still living on December 31, 1986. Assume that the Federal mid-term rate based on annual compounding in effect on January 1, 1986, is 11.83 percent. The loan is a below-market loan. The amount of foregone interest for each year is $13,660.00, computed as follows:

$(\$200,000) \times .1183 = \$23,660.00$

$\$23,660.00 - \$10,000.00 = \$13,660.00$

For gift tax purposes, an imputed gift is treated as made on January 1, 1986, and is equal to the excess of the amount loaned ($200,000) over the present value of all payments due under the loan, discounted at 11.83 percent compounded annually ($153,360.82), or $41,639.82. For rules for determining the computation of present value, see §1.7872-14.

Example (2). Assume the same facts as in Example (1) except that C repays the loan on September 30, 1987, along with an interest payment of $7,500. For income tax purposes, the imputed payments are treated as transferred on December 31, 1986 and September 30, 1987. The amount of the imputed payments for 1986 are the same as in Example (1). For 1987, under the exact method the amount of foregone interest is $9,994.73, computed as follows:

$\$17,494.73 = \$200,000 \times [(1 + .1183)^{9/12} - 1]$

$\$17,494.73 - \$7,500 = \$9,994.73$

For gift tax purposes, the imputed gift is treated as made January 1, 1986, and is the same as in Example (1).

(f) *Allocation of stated interest.*—If interest that is payable on a demand loan is properly allocable to a period which includes more than one calendar year, the amount of interest to be allocated to each calendar year is determined by using any reasonable method of allocation.

(g) *Counting conventions.*—(1) *Whole periods.*—All whole periods, whether expressed annually, semi-annually, quarterly, or monthly, shall be treated as having equal length. For example, a leap year shall be treated as having the same number of days as a non-leap year; all months shall be treated as having the same number of days.

(2) *Short periods.*—In computing the length of a short period, any reasonable convention may be used. See §1.7872-12(c)(2) for a list of conventions commonly used. [Reg. §1.7872-13.]

§1.7872-14. Determination of present value.—(a) *In general.*—This section provides rules for computing the present value of a payment (as referred to in §1.7872-7(a)(1)) to be made in the future. In general, for purposes of section 7872, the present value of a loan payment to be made in the future is the amount of that payment discounted at the applicable Federal rate from the date in the future that the payment is due to the date on which the computation is made. For this purpose, the computation date is the date the loan first becomes subject to section 7872. To determine the present value of a payment, use the applicable Federal rate in effect on the day the loan is made that reflects the compounding assumption (*i.e.*, annual, semiannual, quarterly, or monthly) that is appropriate for the loan. See § 1.7872-3(b).

(b) *Examples.*—The provisions of this section may be illustrated by the following examples:

Example (1). (i) On July 1, 1984, corporation A makes a $200,000 interest-free three-year term loan to shareholder B. The applicable Federal rate is 10-percent, compounded semiannually.

(ii) The present value of this payment is $149.243.08, determined as follows:

$$\$149{,}243.08 = \frac{\$200{,}000}{[1 + (.10/2)]^{6}}$$

(iii) The excess of the amount loaned over the present value of all payments on the loan ($200,000 – $149,243.08), or $50,756.92, is treated as a distribution of property (characterized according to section 301) paid to B on July 1, 1984. The same amount, $50,756.92, is treated as original issue discount under sections 1272 and 163(e).

Example (2). (i) On July 1, 1984, Employer E makes a $3,000 interest-free three year compensation-related term loan to employee W. On December 1, 1984, E makes an $9,000 interest-free compensation-related demand loan to W. The demand loan remains outstanding throughout December 1984. The two loans are the only loans outstanding between E and W during 1984, and neither is characterized under section 7872(c)(1)(D) as a tax avoidance loan. The applicable Federal rate for all loans for periods before January 1, 1985, is 10 percent, compounded semiannually.

(ii) For the period beginning on July 1, 1984, and ending on November 30, 1984, the provisions of section 7872 do not apply to the $3,000 loan because of the application of the *de minimis* rules of section 7872(c)(3).

(iii) On December 1, 1984, however, the aggregate amount of loans outstanding between E and W exceeds $10,000. As a result, section 7872 applies to both loans for December 1984. Both the imputed transfer and the imputed interest payment with respect to the $9,000 demand loan are determined under section 7872(a). The amount of the imputed transfer by E to W with respect to the $3,000 term loan is determined under section 7872(b)(1). An amount equal to the amount of the imputed transfer with respect to the $3,000 term loan is treated as original issue discount.

(iv) With respect to the $3,000 term loan, the amount of the imputed transfer is equal to the excess of the amount loaned, over the present value of all payments which are required to be made under the $3,000 two-year term loan agreement, determined as of December 1, 1984 (the day section 7872 first applies to the $3,000 loan). The present value of $3,000 payable on June 30, 1987, determined as of December 1, 1984, is $2,331.54, computed as follows:

$$\$2{,}331.54 = \frac{\$3{,}000}{(1 + .10/2)^{5+1/6}}$$

The imputed transfer on the $3,000 loan is $668.46 ($3,000.00 – $2,331.54).

(v) The foregone interest on the $9,000 demand loan is determined as of December 31, 1984, with respect to the one month during 1984 to which section 7872 applies to the loan. The amount of foregone interest for 1984 under the exact method is $73.48, computed as follows:

$$\$73.48 = \$9{,}000 \times [(1 + .10/2)^{1/6} - 1]$$

Example (3). (i) Assume the same facts as in Example (2) except that the provisions of the $3,000 three-year term loan require W to make annual payments of interest at a 5 percent simple rate and except that E makes W the $9,000 loan on November 27, 1985.

(ii) Under the agreement W pays $150 (5 percent of $3,000) on June 30, 1985, June 30, 1986, and June 30, 1987. Since the first of these payments is payable prior to November 27, 1985, only the second and third $150 payments are taken into account. W is treated as paying $150 on June 30, 1986 and $3,150 ($3,000 principal and $150 interest) on June 30, 1987.

(iii) The present value as of November 27, 1984 of the $150 payable on June 30, 1986, is $128.39, computed as follows:

$$\$128.39 = \frac{\$150.00}{(1 + .10/2)^{3+34/180}}$$

(iv) The present value as of November 27, 1984 of the $3,150 payable on June 30, 1987, is $2,445.47, computed as follows:

$$\$2{,}445.47 = \frac{\$3{,}150.00}{(1 + .10/2)^{5+34/180}}$$

The sum of these two present values is $2,573.86 ($128.39 + $2,445.47). Therefore, the amount of the imputed transfer with respect to the $3,000 loan is $426.14 ($3,000.00 – $2,573.86).

(v) The foregone interest on the $9,000 demand loan under the exact method is $83.33 ($9,000 × [(1 + .10/2) $^{34/180}$ – 1]). [Reg. § 1.7872-14.]

ELECTION UNDER ECONOMIC RECOVERY TAX ACT OF 1981

GST Exemption: Extension of Time

GST Exemption: Extension of Time.—Amendments to Reg. § 301.9100-3, describing the circumstances and procedures under which an extension of time will be granted under Code Sec. 2642(g)(1), are proposed (published in the Federal Register on April 17, 2008) (REG-147775-06).

☐ Par. 4. Section 301.9100-3 is amended by adding a newparagraph (g) to read as follows:

§ 301.9100-3. Other extensions.

* * *

(g) *Relief under section 2642(g)(1).*—(1) *Procedures.*—The procedures set forth in this section are not applicable for requests for relief under section 2642(g)(1). For requests for reflief under section 2642(g)(1), see § 26.2642-7.

(2) *Effective/applicability date.*—Paragraph (g) of this section applies to requests for relief under section 2642(g)(1) filed on or after the date of publication of the Treasury decision adopting these rules as final regulations in the **Federal Register.** [§ 301.9100-3.]

RELATED INCOME TAX PROVISIONS INDEX

References are to Code and Regulation sections. C precedes Code section numbers; R precedes Regulation section numbers.

A

B

ESTATE TAX INDEX

References are to Code and Regulation sections. C precedes Code section numbers; R precedes Regulation section numbers.

A

B

C

GIFT TAX INDEX

References are to Code and Regulation sections. C precedes Code section numbers; R precedes Regulation section numbers.

GENERATION-SKIPPING TRANSFER TAX INDEX

References are to Code and Regulation sections. C precedes Code section numbers; R precedes Regulation section numbers.

SPECIAL VALUATION RULES INDEX

References are to Code and Regulation sections. C precedes Code section numbers; R precedes Regulation section numbers.

PROCEDURE AND ADMINISTRATION INDEX

Related Income Tax Provisions

Estate, Gift and Generation-Skipping Transfer Taxes

References are to Code and Regulation sections. C precedes Code section numbers; R precedes Regulation section numbers.

Q

R